BOOKS IN PRINT®

2000–2001

This edition of
BOOKS IN PRINT 2000-2001
was prepared by R.R. Bowker's Database Publishing Group in
collaboration with the Information Technology Department.

Drew Meyer, President & Chief Executive Officer
Michael Cairns, Vice President, Business Development
Dean Hollister, Vice President, Database Production
Randy Mysel, Vice President, Sales & Marketing
Andrew Grabois, Senior Managing Director, Bibliographies
Roy Crego, Managing Director, Books in Print Editorial
Angela D'Agostino, Senior Director, Product Development
Marin Mixon, Director, Marketing

International Standard Book Number/Standard Address Number Agency Publishers Authority Database
Doreen Gravesande, Director
Don Riseborough, Senior Managing Editor
Margot Cronin and Paula Kurdi, Senior Editors
Beverly Palacio and Joy Zichichi, Associate Editors
Kareem Douglas and Janet Weiss, Assistant Editors
Diana Fumando, SAN Senior Editor

Data Acquisition, Bibliographies Group
Joseph Kalina, Managing Editor
Nina Liana, Senior Editor
Gladys Osofisan, Assistant Editor

Quality Assurance & Web Content
Constance Harbison, Director, Quality Assurance
George Krubski, Managing Editor, Web Content, booksinprint.com
Christian Nielsen, Content Specialist Fiction, booksinprint.com
Myriam Nunez, Manager/Data Analysis, QA & Test
Brian Pickton, Senior Editor, Authority Control
Lisa Heft, Senior Editor, Quality Assurance
Jocelyn Kwiatkowski, Thomas Lucas, Michaela Weiland, Lynda Williams and Steve Zaffuto, Assistant Editors

Subject Guide
Paula Entin, Senior Editor
Angela Barrett, Senior Associate Editor
Joseph V. Tondi, Associate Editor
Adrene Broomes, Assistant Editor

Electronic Data Interchange Group
Frank Accurso, Director
Mary Craig Daley, Managing Editor
Kathleen Keiderling, Managing Editor, Data Integration
Christopher Voser, Senior Editor
Brock Brunson, Associate Editor
Ila Joseph-Corley, Assistant Editor

Data Collection & Processing Group
Valerie Harris, Director of Operations, Tampa
Mervaine Ricks, Production Manager
Cheryl Patrick, Lead Project Coordinator
Rhonda McKendrick, Project Coordinator
Lori Burnett, Senior Data Entry Leader

Production
Carlton Dyce, Senior Director
Mitch Letterman, Senior Managing Editor
Melanie Koserowski, Xyvision Administrator/Senior Associate Desktop Publisher
Megan Roxberry, Senior Associate Desktop Publisher
Jeanne Audino, Monalisa Massiah and Maria Pirovano, Associate Desktop Publishers
Clarice D. Isaacs, Assistant Desktop Publisher

Editorial Systems Group
Gary Aiello, Vice President, Information Technology
Mark Heinzelman, Director
Frank Morris, Project Manager
Nana Rizinashvili and Youliang Zhou, Programmers

Computer Operations Group
Keith Moore, Manager, UNIX/Internet Systems
Nick Wikowski, Director, Network/Computer Operations
Jack Murphy, Supervisor

BOOKS IN PRINT®

2000–2001

VOLUME 7

TITLES ◆ L–Q

Bowker™

New Providence, New Jersey

Published by
R.R. Bowker
A division of Reed Elsevier
121 Chanlon Rd., New Providence
New Jersey 07974

Drew Meyer, President and Chief Executive Officer

Telephone: 908-464-6800; Toll-free: 1-888-BOWKER2 (1-888-269-5372); Fax: 908-665-6688
E-mail address: info@bowker.com
URL: http://www.bowker.com

Readers may send any corrections and/or updates to the information in this work to R. R. Bowker through the corrections option on the Bowker Web site at http://www.bowker.com or may send e-mail directly to the address: Corrections@bowker.com. Publishers may update or add to their listings by accessing the Bowker Link Publisher Access System at http://www.bowkerlink.com. Books In Print is also available via subscription on the web at www.booksinprint.com.

International Standard Book Numbers
Set: 0-8352-4291-9
Volume 1: 0-8352-4292-7
Volume 2: 0-8352-4293-5
Volume 3: 0-8352-4294-3
Volume 4: 0-8352-4295-1
Volume 5: 0-8352-4296-X
Volume 6: 0-8352-4297-8
Volume 7: 0-8352-4298-6
Volume 8: 0-8352-4299-4
Volume 9: 0-8352-4300-1

International Standard Serial Number
0068-0214

Library of Congress Control Number
74-643574

Printed in the United States of America

ISBN 0-8352-4291-9
9 780835 242912

Contents of Volume 1

Preface ... *vii*
How To Use Books In Print 2000-2001 ... *ix*
List of Abbreviations ... *xii*
Publishers Weekly Bestsellers Lists ... *xiii*
Authors A - D ... 1

Contents of Volume 2

Authors E - K ... 2999

Contents of Volume 3

Authors L - R ... 6069

Contents of Volume 4

Authors S - Z ... 9267

Contents of Volume 5

Preface ... *vii*
How To Use Books In Print 2000-2001 ... *ix*
List of Abbreviations ... *xii*
Publishers Weekly Bestsellers Lists ... *xiii*
Titles A - D ... 1

Contents of Volume 6

Titles E - K ... 3115

Contents of Volume 7

Titles L - Q ... 6193

Contents of Volume 8

Titles R - Z ... 9209

Contents of Volume 9

Preface ... *vi*
How To Use Books In Print 2000-2001 ... *viii*
Publishers Weekly Bestsellers Lists ... *x*
List of Abbreviations ... *xvi*
Publisher Symbol Index ... 1
Name Index ... 957
Publisher & Distributor Toll-Free & Fax Number Index ... 1859
Wholesaler & Distributor Symbol Index ... 2521
Geographic Index to Wholesalers & Distributors ... 2565
New Publishers Index ... 2587
Inactive & Out-of-Business Publisher Index ... 2627

BOOKS IN PRINT®
2000 - 2001
Volume 7

TITLES
L - Q

L

L

L see Light over the Scaffold & Cell 18: The Prison Letters of Jacques Fesch

"L" The Development of Chicago's Rapid Transit System, 1888-1932. Bruce G. Moffat. LC 94-92465. (Central Electric Railfans' Association Bulletin Ser.: No. 131). (Illus.). 306p. 1995. 55.00 (*0-915348-30-6*) Central Electric.

L. A. Bizzaro! The Insider's Guide to the Obscure, the Absurd & the Perverse in Los Angeles. 5th ed. Matt Maranian & Anthony Lovett. LC 97-919. 1997. pap. 16.95 (*0-312-15562-X*, Buzz Bks) St Martin.

L. A. Breakdown. Lou Mathews. 256p. 1999. 24.95 (*0-947993-80-0*, Pub. by Mlvrn Pubg Co) Brit Bk Co Inc.

L. A. Brethren/Justice, Pt. 1-13D. abr. ed. Eric Fortmeyer. 56p. 1996. pap. 24.00 (*1-928620-04-3*, EFX-699108T0396, Poms Healing) AGI Prods.

L. A. Confidential. James Ellroy. 1990. 19.95 (*0-89296-293-3*); 75.00 (*0-89296-424-3*) Mysterious Pr.

L. A. Confidential. James Ellroy. 1997. pap. text 9.23 (*0-09-925508-1*) Random Hse Value.

L. A. Confidential. James Ellroy. 1991. mass mkt. 5.99 (*0-446-40010-6*, Pub. by Warner Bks) Little.

L. A. Confidential. James Ellroy. 512p. 1997. mass mkt. 12.99 (*0-446-67424-9*, Pub. by Warner Bks) Little.

L. A. Confidential. James Ellroy. 1997. write for info. (*0-446-60605-7*) Warner Bks.

L. A. Confidential: The Screenplay. Brian Helgeland & Curtis Hanson. LC 97-61469. 256p. 1997. mass mkt. 12.99 (*0-446-67427-3*, Pub. by Warner Bks) Little.

L. A. Connects: Westside/Downtown. Carole Cunningham et al. (Illus.). 112p. (Orig.). 1995. pap. 9.95 (*0-9653445-0-9*) L A Connects.

*__L. A. Dead.__ Stuart Woods. (Stone Barrington Ser.). 352p. 2000. 24.95 (*0-399-14664-4*) Putnam Pub Group.

L. A. Discount Shopper's Guide: How to Buy a Car at Fleet Prices, How to Shop & Save for Watches, Furniture, Cameras, etc., Where to Buy Top Quality Merchandise. Richard L. Donner. LC 74-84287. 143 p. 1974. write for info. (*0-8431-0269-1*, Price Stern) Peng Put Young Read.

L. A. Environmental Directory: A Guide to Environmental Groups & Resources in the Greater L. A. Area. Intro. by Eva Kataja. (Illus.). 220p. (Orig.). 1990. pap. 17.00 (*0-9621690-1-3*) UDWC.

L. A. Exiles: A Guide to Los Angeles Writing, 1932-1998. Ed. by Paul Vangelisti & Evan Calbi. LC 99-36747. 330p. 1999. pap. 14.95 (*1-56886-068-4*, Pub. by Marsilio Pubs) SPD-Small Pr Dist.

L. A. Fire, Flood & Mud. Ed. by Victoria Graphics. 1265p. (Orig.). 1996. mass mkt. 3.25 (*0-9655839-0-2*) J D Davis.

L. A. Follies: Design & Other Diversions in a Fractured Metropolis. Sam H. Kaplan. 200p. (Orig.). 1989. pap. 9.95 (*0-9622007-0-0*) Cityscape.

L A Hot & Hip-O's. David Andrusia. 1998. pap. 10.00 (*0-7871-8010-6*, Dove Audio) NewStar Media.

L. A. in Quotes: What We Love & Hate about the City of Angels. Carolyn J. Strickler. 240p. (Orig.). Date not set. pap. 15.00 (*1-888843-61-6*) Bridgeline Pr.

L. A. in the Thirties see Los Angeles in the Thirties, 1931-1941

*__L. A. Justice.__ Christopher A. Darden & Dick Lochte. 448p. 2001. 25.95 (*0-446-52327-5*) Warner Bks.

L. A. Justice. Robert Vernon. LC 92-2426. 254p. 1993. 17.99 (*1-56179-124-5*) Focus Family.

*__L. A. Lost & Found: An Architectural History of Los Angeles.__ unabridged ed. Sam Hall Kaplan. (California Architecture & Architects Ser.: Vol. 21). (Illus.). 224p. 2000. reprint ed. pap. 32.50 (*0-940512-23-8*) Hennessey.

L. A. (Lovers Anonymous) Stephanie Han. LC 95-94335. (Illus.). 88p. (Orig.). 1995. pap. 8.95 (*0-9646433-0-8*) Lala Pr.

L. A. Man. Richard Alleman. 240p. (Orig.). 1990. mass mkt. 12.95 (*0-446-38777-0*, Pub. by Warner Bks) Little.

L. A. Midnight. Rebecca Daniels. (Intimate Moments Ser.: No. 431). 1992. per. 3.39 (*0-373-07431-X*, 5-07431-5) Harlequin Bks.

L. A. Musical History Tour: A Guide to the Rock & Roll Landmarks of Los Angeles. Art Fein. (Illus.). 135p. (Orig.). 1991. pap. 13.95 (*0-571-12932-3*) Faber & Faber.

L. A. My Way: Seventeen Writers Reflect on Los Angeles. Ed. by LaVonne Taylor. LC 90-85129. 224p. 1990. pap. 9.95 (*0-9627735-0-6*) Excllnc Entrps.

L. A. Noir. James Ellroy. LC 98-15470. 848p. 1998. 24.50 (*0-89296-686-6*, Pub. by Mysterious Pr) Little.

L. A. on Foot. David L. Clark. (Illus.). 1985. pap. 4.95 (*0-913290-03-3*) Camaro Pub.

L. A. Pop in the '60s. Anne Ayres et al. LC 89-3256. (Illus.). 144p. 1989. pap. 27.50 (*0-917493-14-1*) Orange Cnty Mus.

L. A. Quake, 1994. Rich Smith. LC 94-9661. (Day of the Disaster Ser.). 32p. 1994. lib. bdg. (*1-56239-320-0*) ABDO Pub Co.

*__L. A. Requiem.__ Robert Crais. LC 99-11176. 391p. 2000. mass mkt. 6.99 (*0-345-43447-1*) Ballantine Pub Grp.

L. A. Requiem. Robert Crais. LC 98-52921. 400p. 1999. 23.95 (*0-385-49583-8*) Broadway BDD.

*__L. A. Requiem.__ large type ed. Robert Crais. LC 00-39858. 2000. write for info. (*1-56895-881-1*) Wheeler Pub.

L. A. Riots: Rage in the City of Angels. Michael D. Cole. LC 98-30263. (American Disasters Ser.). 48p. (YA). (gr. 4-10). 1999. lib. bdg. 18.95 (*0-7660-1219-0*) Enslow Pubs.

L. A. Secret Police. Mike Rothmiller. 1992. mass mkt. 5.99 (*0-671-79657-7*) PB.

L. A. Secret Police. Mike Rothmiller & Ivan G. Goldman. 1992. pap. 5.99 (*0-685-61109-4*) PB.

L. A. Snitch. Marc Berrenson. 256p. (Orig.). 1991. pap. 3.95 (*0-380-76324-9*, Avon Bks) Morrow Avon.

L. A. Stories: The Voices of Cultural Diversity. Carol C. Ottesen. LC 99-14679. 184p. 1999. pap. 24.50 (*0-7618-1402-7*) U Pr of Amer.

L. A. Story & Roxanne: Screenplays. Steve Martin. LC 97-1597. 288p. (Orig.). 1997. pap. 12.00 (*0-8021-3512-9*, Grove) Grove-Atltic.

L. A. Superlatives. Roy Kammerman. 256p. (Orig.). 1987. mass mkt. 3.95 (*0-446-34729-9*, Pub. by Warner Bks) Little.

L. A. T. A Multiple Murder Story. William A. Norman. LC 95-90074. 270p. 1998. 16.95 (*0-533-11459-4*) Vantage.

L. A. Times: A Novel. large type ed. Stuart Woods. LC 93-5160. 518p. 1993. reprint ed. 22.95 (*0-7862-0006-5*) Thorndike Pr.

L. A. Times Encyclopedia of the L. A. Lakers. Steve Springer. (Illus.). 272p. 1998. pap. 29.95 (*1-883792-24-X*) LA Times.

L. A. Unconventional: The Men & Women Who Did L. A. Their Way. Cecilia Rasmusse. (Illus.). 192p. 1998. 29.95 (*1-883792-23-1*) LA Times.

L. A. Unconventional: The Men & Women Who Did L. A. Their Way. Cecilia Rasmussen. (Illus.). 168p. 1998. 29.95 (*1-883792-48-7*) LA Times.

L. A. Woman. Jane E. Lasky. 240p. (Orig.). 1990. mass mkt. 12.95 (*0-446-38779-7*, Pub. by Warner Bks) Little.

L & J Personal Medical & Expense Diary Journal. 24p. 1986. spiral bd. 1.80 (*0-88450-112-4*, 6108) Lawyers & Judges.

*__L. & L. Beancounter's Catalog: Survival Gear for Your Career.__ Larry Bleidner & Peter Scott. 80p. 2000. pap. 9.71 (*1-56751-180-5*, Pub. by Common Courage) LPC InBook.

L & M Maritime Correspondence Course Guide. Lorne & MacLean Marine & Offshore Publications Sta. (C). 1987. 150.00 (*0-7855-4386-4*, Pub. by Lorne & MacLean Marine) St Mut.

L & M Training Resources Manual. Lorne & MacLean Marine & Offshore Publications Sta. (C). 1987. 150.00 (*0-7855-4385-6*, Pub. by Lorne & MacLean Marine) St Mut.

L. Annaei Senecae Dialogorum Libri Duodecim. Lucius Annaeus Seneca. Ed. by Leighton D. Reynolds. (Oxford Classical Texts Ser.). 348p. 1977. text 45.00 (*0-19-814659-0*) OUP.

L. Annaei Senecae Tragoediae. Lucius Annaeus Seneca. Ed. by Otto Zwierlein. (Classical Texts Ser.). 506p. 1986. text 35.00 (*0-19-814657-4*) OUP.

L-Arginine: Biological Aspects & Clinical Application. Oleg Eremin. LC 96-16764. (Medical Intelligence Unit Ser.). 161p. 1997. 99.00 (*1-57059-348-5*) Landes Bioscience.

L. A.'s 99 Best Hole-in-the-Wall Restaurants: A Paul Wallach Guide. P. B. Miller. Ed. by Lynette Ramirez. 1989. 6.95 (*0-9619156-2-5*) P Wallach.

L. C. Armstrong: Making & Unmaking. Kelly Bousman. (Illus.). 28p. (Orig.). 1995. pap. 5.00 (*1-879293-08-0*) Contemp Art Mus.

L. C. Smith Shotguns. William S. Brophy. 35.00 (*0-88227-046-X*) Gun Room.

L-Carnitine. Brian Leibovitz. (Good Health Guides Ser.). 48p. 1999. pap. 3.95 (*0-87983-962-7*, 39627K, Keats Publng) NTC Contemp Pub Co.

*__L-Carnitine: The Supernutrient for Fitness: The Safe & Stress-Free Way to Manage Weight, Increase Physical Performance & Mental.__ Walter Lubeck. (Illus.). 2000. pap. 14.95 (*0-914955-59-4*) Lotus Pr.

L-Carnitine & Its Role in Medicine: From Function to Therapy. Ed. by R. Ferrari et al. (Illus.). 433p. 1992. text 136.00 (*0-12-253940-0*) Acad Pr.

*__L-Carnitine & the Heart.__ Stephen T. Sinatra. (Good Health Guides Ser.). 64p. 2000. pap. 3.95 (*0-658-00412-3*, 004123, Keats Publng) NTC Contemp Pub Co.

*__L. D. Faddeev's Seminar on Mathematical Physics.__ Ed. by M. A. Semenov-Tian-Shansky. (TRANS2 Ser.: Vol. 201). 319p. 2000. 109.00 (*0-8218-2133-4*) Am Math.

L. D. Landau: Low Temperature & Solid State Physics. Haar D. Ter. LC 65-18373. (Men of Physics Ser.). 1965. 92.00 (*0-08-010523-8*, Pub. by Pergamon Repr) Franklin.

L. D. Nimschke: Firearms Engraver. R. L. Wilson. 108p. 1992. 100.00 (*1-884849-02-4*) R&R Bks.

L. D. S. Children's Comments, Vol. 1. Compiled by Arthur Wallace. 60p. 1978. pap. 1.95 (*0-937892-03-3*) LL Co.

L D S Conference Reports: Index. 4.95 (*0-89036-061-8*) Liahona Pub Trust.

L-Dopa & Behavior. fac. ed. Sidney Malitz. LC 75-181306. (Illus.). 144p. pap. 44.70 (*0-7837-7194-0*, 204710500005) Bks Demand.

*__L. E. A. D. - California: Law Enforcement Agency Directory.__ Jim Wylie. Ed. by Cynthia Wylie. 239p. 1999. pap. 24.95 (*1-892704-01-3*) Public Srvc Resrch.

*__L. E. A. D. - Texas: Law Enforcement Agency Directory.__ Jim Wylie. Ed. by Cynthia Wylie. 181p. 1999. pap. 19.95 (*1-892704-00-5*) Public Srvc Resrch.

L. E. A. P. Lifetime Exercise Adherence Plan. Richard L. Brown. (Illus.). 368p. 1999. pap. 13.00 (*0-06-098733-2*) HarpC.

L. E. Phillips: Banker, Oil Man, Civic Leader. Billy M. Jones. (Illus.). 200p. 1981. 10.00 (*0-86546-027-2*) Wichita Ctr Entrep SBM.

L. Emmett Holt: Pioneer of a Children's Century. Robert L. Duffus & L. Emmett Holt, Jr. LC 74-1683. (Children & Youth Ser.: Vol. 25). 310p. 1974. reprint ed. 28.95 (*0-405-05960-4*) Ayer.

L Essn Travaux Pratiques. 3rd ed. Schultz. (FRE.). 192p. 1995. pap. text 29.00 (*0-13-339193-0*) P-H.

L.-F. Celine: The I of the Storm. Charles Krance. LC 91-73322. (French Forum Monographs: No. 75). 185p. (Orig.). 1992. pap. 14.95 (*0-917058-79-8*) French Forum.

L5: Behind the Moon. Stephen Tracy. LC 94-39397. (J). (gr. 5-8). 1994. lib. bdg. 13.95 (*0-382-24761-2*) Silver Burdett Pr.

L5: Behind the Moon. Stephen Tracy. (Illus.). 64p. (J). (gr. 5-8). 1995. pap. 4.95 (*0-382-24707-8*) Silver Burdett Pr.

L-Functions & the Oscillator Representation. S. Rallis. (Lecture Notes in Mathematics Ser.: Vol. 1245). xv, 239p. 1987. 42.95 (*0-387-17694-2*) Spr-Verlag.

L Functions for the Orthogonal Group. D. Ginzburg et al. LC 97-12294. (Memoirs of the American Mathematical Society Ser.: Vol. 128, No. 611). 218p. 1997. pap. 49.00 (*0-8218-0543-6*, MEMO/128/611) Am Math.

L-Functions in Arithmetic. Ed. by J. Coates & M. J. Taylor. (London Mathematical Society Lecture Note Ser.: No. 153). 300p. (C). 1991. pap. text 49.95 (*0-521-38619-5*) Cambridge U Pr.

L. G. Wright Glass Company. James Measell & W. C. Roetteis. LC 98-104831. (Illus.). 1997. 44.95 (*1-57080-031-6*); pap. 34.95 (*1-57080-030-8*) Antique Pubns.

L-Glutamine & Its Uses. 1996. lib. bdg. 250.75 (*0-8490-5893-7*) Gordon Pr.

L. H. Nicolay (1737-1820) & His Contemporaries: Diderot, Rousseau, Voltaire, Gluck, Metastasio, Galiani, d'Escherny, Gessner, Bodmer, Lavater, Wieland, Frederick II, Falconet, W. Robertson, Paul I, Cagliostro, Gellert, & Others. E. Heier. (International Archives of the History of Ideas Ser.: No. 9). 215p. 1965. lib. bdg. 160.50 (*90-247-0185-6*) Kluwer Academic.

L Humour De Jesus see Humor of Jesus

*__L. I. E. A Novel.__ David Hollander. 208p. 2000. 22.95 (*0-375-50443-5*) Villard Books.

L. I. F. E. Life Is War. Nsorowa Mensah. LC 97-90397. 53p. 1998. pap. 8.95 (*0-533-12381-X*) Vantage.

*__L. I. F. E. Living It from Experience.__ Dushawn Moses. (Illus.). 196p. 2000. pap. 19.95 (*0-9676743-0-1*) Allwrite Grp.

L. I. F. E. Blueprint: Spirituality Designed for the Non-Religious. Diana Cornelius. Date not set. write for info. (*0-9702124-0-2*) One Mind.

L-I-T Guide to the Lion, the Witch & the Wardrobe. Charlotte Jaffe & Barbara Roberts. (L-I-T Guides: Literature in Teaching Ser.). 1991. teacher ed. 8.95 (*0-910857-94-6*); teacher ed. 8.95 (*1-56644-006-8*) Educ Impress.

L Is for Lawless. Sue Grafton. 1996. pap. 6.99 (*0-449-45769-9*); mass mkt. 6.99 (*0-449-22149-0*) Fawcett.

L Is for Lawless. Sue Grafton. 1997. pap. 11.00 (*0-449-00067-2*) Fawcett.

L Is for Lawless. Sue Grafton. LC 95-12787. 272p. 1995. 24.00 (*0-8050-1937-5*) H Holt & Co.

L Is for Lawless. large type ed. Sue Grafton. LC 95-23567. 384p. 1996. pap. 24.95 (*0-7838-1383-X*, G K Hall Lrg Type) Mac Lib Ref.

L Is for Lawless. large type ed. Sue Grafton. LC 95-23567. 428p. 1999. 27.95 (*0-7838-1382-1*, G K Hall Lrg Type) Mac Lib Ref.

*__"L" Is for Love.__ Dorothy P. O'Neill. LC 99-90981. 192p. 1999. 18.95 (*0-8034-9386-X*, Avalon Bks) Bouregy.

*__L is for Loving: An ABC for the Way You Feel.__ Ken Wilson-Max. LC 98-54703. (Illus.). 32p. (J). (ps-2). 1999. 14.99 (*0-7868-0527-7*, Pub. by Hyprn Child) Time Warner.

L. J. Henderson on the Social System: Selected Writings. L. J. Henderson. Ed. by Bernard Barber & Morris Janowitz. LC 79-99484. (Heritage of Sociology Ser.). 272p. 1998. lib. bdg. 19.50 (*0-226-32689-6*) U Ch Pr.

L

L. J. Rose of Sunnyslope, 1827-1899: California Pioneer, Fruit Grower, Winemaker, Horse Breeder. L. J. Rose, Jr. (Illus.). 236p. 1993. 19.95 (*0-87328-144-6*) Huntington Lib.

L. L. Bean Canoeing Handbook. Allan A. Swenson. LC 99-41186. (Illus.). 1999. pap. 18.95 (*1-55821-977-3*) Lyons Pr.

*__L. L. Bean Fly-Casting Handbook.__ Macauley Lord. LC 99-51997. (Illus.). 1999. pap. 18.95 (*1-55821-964-1*) Lyons Pr.

L. L. Bean Fly-Fishing for Bass Handbook. Dave Whitlock. (Illus.). 96p. 1988. pap. 10.95 (*0-941130-76-2*) Lyons Pr.

*__L. L. Bean Fly Fishing for Bass Handbook.__ Dave Whitlock. (Illus.). 2000. pap. 18.95 (*1-58574-079-9*) Lyons Pr.

L. L. Bean Fly Fishing for Striped Bass Handbook. Brad Burns. LC 98-16674. (Illus.). 192p. 1998. pap. 19.95 (*1-55821-736-3*) Lyons Pr.

L. L. Bean Fly-Fishing Handbook. rev. ed. Dave Whitlock. LC 96-306. (Illus.). 192p. 1996. pap. 18.95 (*1-55821-437-2*) Lyons Pr.

L. L. Bean Fly-Tying Handbook. Richard W. Talleur & L. L. Bean, Inc. Staff. LC 98-6125. (Illus.). 128p. 1998. pap. 18.95 (*1-55821-708-8*) Lyons Pr.

L. L. Bean Game & Fish Cookbook. Angus Cameron & Judith B. Jones. (Illus.). 475p. 1983. 25.95 (*0-394-51191-3*) Random.

*__L. L. Bean Hiking & Backpacking Handbook.__ Keith McCafferty. LC 99-53860. 1999. pap. 18.95 (*1-55821-940-4*) Lyons Pr.

*__L. L. Bean Outdoor Family Camping Handbook.__ Keith McCafferty. LC 99-25718. (Illus.). 192p. 1999. pap. 18.95 (*1-55821-880-7*) Lyons Pr.

*__L. L. Bean Outdoor Knots Handbook.__ Peter Owen. LC 99-23385. (Illus.). 144p. 1999. pap. 14.95 (*1-55821-871-8*) Lyons Pr.

L. L. Bean Outdoor Photography Handbook. Jim Rowinski & Kate Rowinski. LC 99-17165. (Illus.). 162p. (Orig.). 1999. pap. 18.95 (*1-55821-879-3*) Lyons Pr.

L. L. Bear's Island Adventure. Kate Rowinski. LC 92-71972. (Illus.). 32p. (J). (ps-4). 1992. 4.95 (*0-89272-320-3*) Down East.

L. M. Montgomery. G. Wiggins. (Twayne's United States Authors Ser.). 170p. 1992. 23.95 (*0-8057-3980-7*) Macmillan.

L. M. Montgomery & Canadian Culture. Ed. by Irene Gammel & Elizabeth Epperly. 256p. 1999. text 25.00 (*0-8020-4406-9*) U of Toronto Pr.

L. N. Cottingham (1787-1857) Architect of the Gothic Revival. Janet Myles. (Illus.). 176p. 1995. 35.00 (*0-85331-678-3*, Pub. by Lund Humphries) Antique Collect.

L. N. Tolstoy & D. H. Lawrence: Cross-Currents & Influence. Dorthe G. Engelhardt. Ed. by Horst-Juergen Gerigk & Wilfried Potthoff. LC 96-2975. (Heidelberger Publikationen zur Slavistik, B: Bd. 3). 212p. 1996. 42.95 (*3-631-49804-7*) P Lang Pubng.

L. N. Tolstoy & D. H. Lawrence: Cross-Currents & Influence. Dorthe G. Engelhardt. Ed. by Horst-Juergen Gerigk & Wilfried Potthoff. LC 96-2975. (Heidelberger Publikationen zur Slavistik, B: Bd. 3). 212p. 1996. 42.95 (*0-8204-2977-5*) P Lang Pubng.

*__L-O-V-E.__ Karyn Henley. (Karyn Henley's Playsongs Bks.). (Illus.). (J). 2000. pap. 5.99 (*0-8423-3468-8*) Tyndale Hse.

L. O. V. E. Works: Photojournalism by the Leave Out Violence Kids. Ed. by Brenda Z. Proulx. LC 99-181481. 1999. 19.95 (*0-7737-6008-3*) Genl Dist Srvs.

L1 - Statistical Procedures & Related Topics. Ed. by Yadolah Dodge. LC 97-73621. (Lecture Notes - Monograph Ser.: No. 31). 1997. pap. 69.00 (*0-940600-43-9*) Inst Math.

L-19 Birddog: The Lovable One-Niner. Minard D. Thompson, Jr. (Illus.). 272p. Date not set. 49.95 (*1-56311-236-1*) Turner Pub KY.

L. P. G. A. The Unauthorized Version: A History of the Ladies Professional Golf Association. Liz Kahn. Ed. by Judy Horst. (Illus.). 336p. 1996. 29.95 (*0-88197-126-X*) Group Fore Prods.

L. Ron Hubbard: A Profile. 124p. 1995. pap. 15.00 (*0-88404-995-7*) Bridge Pubns Inc.

L. Ron Hubbard: Messiah or Madman? Bent Corydon. LC 91-39368. 480p. 1992. pap. 12.95 (*0-942637-57-7*) Barricade Bks.

L. Ron Hubbard: Messiah or Madman? Bent Corydon. LC 96-208515. 1994. 24.95 (*1-56980-009-X*) Barricade Bks.

L. Ron Hubbard: Messiah or Madman? Bent Corydon & L. Ron Hubbard. (Illus.). 288p. 1987. 20.00 (*0-8184-0444-2*) Carol Pub Group.

*__L. Ron Hubbard: Three Classic Novels.__ L. Ron Hubbard. 1200p. 2000. 14.98 (*0-7651-1771-1*) Smithmark.

L. Ron Hubbard Presents Writers of the Future, Vol. I. Ed. by Algis Budrys. 1985. pap. 3.95 (*0-88404-170-0*) Bridge Pubns Inc.

L. Ron Hubbard Presents Writers of the Future, Vol. II. Ed. by Algis Budrys. (C). 1986. pap. 3.95 (*0-88404-254-5*) Bridge Pubns Inc.

L. Ron Hubbard Presents Writers of the Future, Vol. III. Ed. by Algis Budrys. (Writers of the Future Ser.). 1987. pap. 4.50 (*0-88404-245-6*) Bridge Pubns Inc.

L. Ron Hubbard Presents Writers of the Future, Vol. IV. Ed. by Algis Budrys. 430p. 1988. mass mkt. 4.95 (*0-88404-314-2*) Bridge Pubns Inc.

L. Ron Hubbard Presents Writers of the Future, Vol. V. Ed. by Algis Budrys. 1989. pap. 4.95 (*0-88404-379-7*) Bridge Pubns Inc.

L. Ron Hubbard Presents Writers of the Future, Vol. VI. Ed. by Algis Budrys. 1990. pap. 4.95 (*0-88404-504-8*) Bridge Pubns Inc.

L. Ron Hubbard Presents Writers of the Future, Vol. VII. Ed. by Algis Budrys. 1991. mass mkt. 5.95 (*0-88404-641-9*) Bridge Pubns Inc.

L. Ron Hubbard Presents Writers of the Future, Vol. VIII. Ed. by Dave Wolverton. 395p. 1992. pap. 5.99 (*0-88404-758-X*) Bridge Pubns Inc.

L. Ron Hubbard Presents Writers of the Future, Vol. IX. Ed. by Dave Wolverton. 1993. mass mkt. 5.99 (*0-88404-823-3*) Bridge Pubns Inc.

L. Ron Hubbard Presents Writers of the Future, Vol. XI. Ed. by Dave Wolverton. 473p. 1995. mass mkt. 6.99 (*0-88404-999-X*) Bridge Pubns Inc.

L. Ron Hubbard Presents Writers of the Future, Vol. XII. Bridge Publications Staff. 496p. 1996. mass mkt. 6.99 (*1-57318-027-0*) Bridge Pubns Inc.

L. Ron Hubbard Presents Writers of the Future, Vol. XIII. Ed. by Dave Wolverton. 1997. pap. 6.99 (*0-614-27310-2*) Bridge PA.

L. Ron Hubbard Presents Writers of the Future No. 14: Anthology. L. Ron Hubbard. Ed. by Dave Wolverton. 1998. mass mkt. 6.99 (*1-57318-154-4*) Bridge Pubns Inc.

L. Ron Hubbard Presents Writers of the Future Vol. X, Vol. X. Ed. by Dave Wolverton. 465p. 1994. mass mkt. 6.99 (*0-88404-900-0*) Bridge Pubns Inc.

L. S. A. T. Study Companion: Logical Reasoning. Jesse W. Nash & Elizabeth T. Nguyen. LC 93-72179. 200p. (Orig.). (C). 1994. pap. 14.95 (*0-9625762-3-9*) Art Review Pr.

*__L. S. Lowery: A Biography.__ Tony Ross. (Illus.). 432p. 1999. 24.95 (*1-902970-01-2*, Pub. by Lowry Pr) Antique Collect.

L. S. Lowry. Michael Leber & Judith Sandling. (Illus.). 144p. (C). 1995. pap. 19.95 (*0-7148-3244-8*, Pub. by Phaidon Press) Phaidon Pr.

L. S. Lowry: A Definitive Study of the Artist's Life & Work. Michael Leber & Judith Sandling. (Illus.). 144p. 1990. text 29.95 (*0-7148-2475-5*) Phaidon Pr.

L. S. Pontryagin: Selected Works, 4 vols., Set. Ed. by R. V. Gamkrelidze. 1776p. 1990. 706.00 (*2-88124-134-4*) Gordon & Breach.

L. S. Pontryagin: Selected Works, Vol. 1. Ed. by R. V. Gamkrelidze & V. A. Steklov. xx, 620p. 1985. text 618.00 (*2-88124-105-0*) Gordon & Breach.

L. S. Pontryagin: Selected Works, 4 Vols., Vol. 4. Ed. by R. V. Gamkrelidze. 1986. text 1368.00 (*2-88124-096-8*) Gordon & Breach.

L. S. Pontryagin, Selected Works Vol. 2: Topological Groups. Ed. by R. V. Gamkrelidze. xxx, 544p. 1986. text 521.00 (*2-88124-133-6*) Gordon & Breach.

L. S. Pontryagin, Selected Works Vol. 3: Algebraic & Differential Topology. Ed. by R. V. Gamkrelidze. xxii, 252p. 1986. text 244.00 (*2-88124-035-6*) Gordon & Breach.

L. S. Pontryagin, Selected Works Vol. 4: The Mathematical Theory of Optimal Processes. Ed. by R. V. Gamkrelidze. LC 84-11707. xxiv, 360p. 1986. text 338.00 (*2-88124-077-1*) Gordon & Breach.

L Squared Moduli Space & a Vanishing Theorem for Donaldson Polynomial Invariants. J. Morgan et al. (Monographs in Geometry & Topology). 232p. (C). 1994. text 42.00 (*1-57146-006-3*) Intl Pr Boston.

L Squared Moduli Spaces on 4-Manifolds with Cylindrical Ends. Clifford H. Taubes. (Monographs in Geometry & Topology). 205p. (C). 1994. text 42.00 (*1-57146-007-1*) Intl Pr Boston.

L. T. Hobhouse: Principles of Sociology, 5 vols., Set. 1240p. (C). (gr. 13 up). 1993. 575.00 (*0-415-09254-X*) Routledge.

L3o Doi the Ky. Thich Nhat Hahn. (VIE.). 434p. 1997. pap. 16.00 (*1-891667-46-7*) La Boi Soc.

L-Ticulation. Mary Zellmer. (Illus.). 4p. 1994. 16.00 (*0-930599-32-2*) Thinking Pubns.

L to the P Harmonic Analysis on SL(2,R) W. Barker. LC 88-22227. (Memoirs Ser.: No. 76/393). 110p. 1988. pap. 17.00 (*0-8218-2456-2*, MEMO/76/393) Am Math.

L-Tryptophan: Current Prospects in Medicine & Drug Safety. Ed. by Walter Kochen & Hans Steinhart. LC 94-16828. x, 458p. (C). 1994. lib. bdg. 306.15 (*3-11-013673-2*) De Gruyter.

L12 Ordered Alloys. Ed. by F. R. Nabarro & M. S. Duesbery. (Part of Disclotions in Solis Ser.: Vol. 10). 632p. 1996. 284.50 (*0-444-82370-0*) Elsevier.

L2-Gain & Passivity Techniques in Nonlinear Control. A. J. Van Der Schaft. LC 96-26597. (Lecture Notes in Control & Information Sciences: Vol. 218). 208p. 1996. pap. 43.00 (*3-540-76074-1*) Spr-Verlag.

L2-Gain & Passivity Techniques in Nonlinear Control. 2nd ed. Arjan Van Der Schaft. LC 99-45693. (Communications & Control Engineering Ser.). xii, 252p. 1999. 99.00 (*1-85233-073-2*) Spr-Verlag.

L-Tyrosine & Its Uses. 1996. lib. bdg. 251.99 (*0-8490-5887-2*) Gordon Pr.

L (U. S. A.) Landia: A De'Cima Ilha. Onesimo T. Almeida. 293p. 1987. pap. 10.00 (*0-318-41700-6*) Gavea-Brown.

L. V. Kantorovich - Selected Works, Vol. 3, Pts. I & II. S. S. Kutateladze. (Classics of Soviet Mathematics Ser.). 1996. text 180.00 (*2-88124-983-3*) Gordon & Breach.

L. V. Kantorovich - Selected Works Pt. I: Descriptive Theory of Sets & Functions, Functional Analysis in Semi-Ordered Spaces, Vol. 3. S. S. Kutateladze & Romanovsky. (Classics of Soviet Mathematics Ser.). 384p. 1996. text 102.00 (*2-88449-012-4*) Gordon & Breach.

L. V. Kantorovich - Selected Works Pt. II: Applied Functional Analysis, Approximation Methods & Computers, Vol. 3. S. S. Kutateladze. (Classics of Soviet Mathematics Ser.). 400p. 1996. text 102.00 (*2-88449-013-2*) Gordon & Breach.

L. V. Prasad: A Monograph. K. N. Sastry. (Orig.). (C). 1993. 12.50 (*81-224-0504-5*) S Asia.

"L" Word. Lynn Mason. (Love Stories Super Edition Ser.: No. 8). (YA). 1998. mass mkt. 4.50 (*0-553-49249-7*) BDD Bks Young Read.

L-Z, May 1968 to May 1973 see Used Book Price Guide: Five Year Edition

LA Annual Report, 1999. 5th ed. Ed. by Jennifer Knight. 1999. pap. 15.00 (*1-928646-03-4*) BenchMark Pubg OR.

*__LA Blue Girl, Vol. 1.__ 3rd ed. Jose Calderon. (Illus.). ii, 150p. 1999. reprint ed. pap. 16.95 (*1-56219-906-4*, CMX 06041) Central Pk Media.

*__LA Blue Girl, Vol. 2.__ 2nd ed. Jose Calderon. (Illus.). ii, 158p. 2000. reprint ed. pap. 16.95 (*1-56219-911-0*, CMX 06042) Central Pk Media.

*__L.A. Confidential.__ Level 5. (C). 2000. 7.00 (*0-582-36473-6*) Addison-Wesley.

*__La Crosse.__ La Crosse County Historical Society Staff. (Images of America Ser.). 1999. pap. 18.99 (*0-7524-1361-9*) Arcadia Publng.

La-Di-Da Hare. J. Patrick Lewis. LC 95-44674. (Illus.). 40p. (J). (gr. 1-4). 1997. 16.00 (*0-689-31925-8*) S&S Childrens.

La-5 in Action. Hans-Heiri Stapfer. (Aircraft in Action Ser.: Vol. 169). (Illus.). 50p. 1998. pap. 9.95 (*0-89747-392-2*, 1169) Squad Sig Pubns.

LA-411, 1998. 19th ed. Media Publishing International Staff. 733p. 1998. spiral bd. 65.00 (*1-879930-06-4*) LA Four-Eleven.

La-Li-Luo Dance Songs of the Chuxiong Yi, Yunnan Province, China. unabridged ed. Alan Thrasher & Alan R. Thrasher. Ed. by Judith C. Tucker. (Illus.). 164p. 1990. pap. write for info. (*0-937203-18-1*) World Music Pr.

L.A. Noir. Steven Gilbar. 1999. 13.95 (*0-9671960-0-0*) S Gilbar Bks.

L.A. Times. Stuart Woods. 400p. 1994. mass mkt. 6.50 (*0-06-109156-1*, Harp PBks) HarpC.

Laa Laa Gets a Guitar. (Teletubbies Coloring Activity Book Ser.: Vol. 3). (Illus.). 32p. (J). 1998. pap. write for info. (*0-7666-0257-5*, Honey Bear Bks) Modern Pub NYC.

Laadi Lexicon (Congo Dialect) Lexique Laadi. Andre Jacquet. (FRE.). 264p. 1982. 75.00 (*0-8288-1619-0*, F37420) Fr & Eur.

Laage (Wilhelm) The Graphic Work: Catalogue Raisonne. Alfred Hagenlocher. (GER., Illus.). 282p. 1969. 125.00 (*1-55660-153-0*) A Wofsy Fine Arts.

Laaketieteellinen Ammattisanasto. 6th ed. A. Hervonen & W. Nienstedt. 315p. 1986. 59.95 (*0-8288-1885-1*, F22390) Fr & Eur.

Laaketieteen Sanakirja. 8th ed. Niilo Pesonen & E. Ponteva. (ENG, FIN, FRE & SWE.). 525p. 1987. 250.00 (*0-8288-1886-X*, M9984) Fr & Eur.

Laam in the Treatment of Opiate Addiction: A Treatment Improvement Protocal. Ed. by Sandra Clunies. 66p. (C). 1999. pap. text 20.00 (*0-7881-7592-0*) DIANE Pub.

La'au Hawaii: Traditional Hawaiian Uses of Plants. Isabella A. Abbott. 162p. 1992. pap. 22.95 (*0-930897-62-5*) Bishop Mus.

*__Lab Activities for the World Wide Web.__ Paula Ladd & Ralph Ruby. 1999. pap. text 14.44 (*1-57676-039-1*) Scott Jones Pubng.

*__Lab Analysis & Scientific Apparatus Services in Mexico: A Strategic Entry Report, 1996.__ Compiled by Icon Group International Staff. (Illus.). 167p. 1999. ring bd. 1670.00 incl. audio compact disk (*0-7418-1288-6*) Icon Grp.

Lab Anatomy of the Mink. 3rd ed. Robert B. Chiasson & William J. Radke. LC 97-70108. 96p. (C). 1997. spiral bd. write for info. (*0-697-04793-8*, WCB McGr Hill) McGrw-H Hghr Educ.

Lab Anatomy of the Vertebrates. Robert B. Chiasson & William J. Radke. 240p. (C). 1992. text. write for info. (*0-697-10160-6*, WCB McGr Hill) McGrw-H Hghr Educ.

Lab Animal Abuse: Vivisection Exposed! Joseph Covino, Jr. LC 87-61519. 533p. (Orig.). 1990. pap. 19.95 (*0-943283-00-0*) New Human Pr.

Lab Assessment of Nutritional Status. Mary Litchford. 119p. 1998. spiral bd. 110.00 (*1-879575-82-5*) Acad Med Sys.

Lab Book: Haitian Creole. Fequiere Vilsaint. (Illus.). 44p. (YA). (gr. 6-12). Date not set. lab manual ed. 12.00 (*1-881839-61-3*) Educa Vision.

Lab Book for "The Context of Chemistry" Simon Bott. (C). 1996. pap. text 18.31 (*1-56870-259-0*) RonJon Pub.

*__Lab Coat Girl: Full of Baloney.__ Margie Palatini. LC 99-41497. 32p. (J). 2000. lib. bdg. 14.49 (*0-7868-2441-7*, Pub. by Hyperion) Little.

*__Lab Coat Girl #3: The Story of a Prima Swanerina.__ Margie Palatini. (Illus.). 96p. (J). 2000. lib. bdg. write for info. (*0-7868-2442-5*) Hyprn Ppbks.

Lab Coat Girl & the Amazing Benjamin Bone. Margie Palatini. LC 98-55226. 32p. 1999. lib. bdg. 13.49 (*0-7868-2440-9*, Pub. by Disney Pr) Little.

Lab Coat Girl & the Amazing Benjamin Bone, Bk. 1. Margie Palatini. LC PZ7.P1755Laf 1999. 32p. (J). (gr. 2-6). 1999. pap. 3.99 (*0-7868-1346-6*, Pub. by Hyprn Ppbks) Little.

*__Lab Coat Girl in Cool Fuel Trudie, Bk. 2.__ Margie Palatini. LC 99-41497. (Illus.). 96p. (J). (gr. 3-7). 2000. pap. 3.99 (*0-7868-1347-4*, Pub. by Hyperion) Time Warner.

Lab Commentary: Matthew. Bruce B. Barton et al. LC 96-15075. 640p. 1996. pap. 14.99 (*0-8423-3034-8*) Tyndale Hse.

Lab Course in Turbo Pascal 3.5. 2nd ed. Nell B. Dale. LC 96-221851. 1997. 16.00 (*0-7637-0333-8*) Jones & Bartlett.

Lab Exer Human Ana & Phys. Morris. (C). 1998. spiral bd., lab manual ed. 32.00 (*0-201-43460-1*) Addison-Wesley.

Lab Exercises for Introductory Biology. Godwin & Gray. 144p. (C). 1992. pap. text 25.80 (*0-536-58297-1*) Pearson Custom.

*__Lab Exercises in Anatomy & Physiology.__ 3rd ed. 160p. (C). 2000. 18.00 (*0-8087-2518-1*) Pearson Custom.

Lab Exercises in Historical Geology. 3rd ed. K. R. Walker et al. 218p. 1991. pap. text 24.95 (*0-88725-148-X*) Hunter Textbks.

Lab Exercises in Microbiology. 3rd ed. Michael Rickard. 152p. (C). 1998. spiral bd. 28.95 (*0-7872-5624-2*, 41562401) Kendall-Hunt.

Lab Exercises in Oceanography. 2nd ed. Bernard W. Pipkin. (C). 1987. pap. text. write for info. (*0-7167-1917-7*) W H Freeman.

Lab Exercises Oceanography: Lab Exercises. 4th ed. Thurman. 304p. (C). 1995. pap. text, lab manual ed. 32.20 (*0-02-420806-X*) P-H.

Lab Exercises Preparatory. 3rd ed. Tyner. 1994. teacher ed. 19.37 (*0-697-24041-X*, WCB McGr Hill) McGrw-H Hghr Educ.

*__Lab Experiences in Anatomy & Physiology.__ 3rd ed. 170p. (C). 2000. 18.00 (*0-8087-2415-0*) Pearson Custom.

*__Lab Experiences in Botany.__ 3rd ed. Wayne C. Rosing. 140p. (C). 2000. spiral bd. 24.95 (*0-7872-7207-8*) Kendall-Hunt.

Lab Experiences in Exercise Science. George. 288p. 1994. pap. text 36.25 (*0-86720-783-3*) Jones & Bartlett.

Lab Experiment Chemistry. 7th annot. ed. Brown. 1996. pap. text, teacher ed. write for info. (*0-13-578352-6*) Allyn.

Lab Experiments. Staves. (C). 1998. pap. text 12.00 (*0-471-32003-X*) Wiley.

Lab Experiments: Action Chemistry. Ruth P. Bolton. 1979. text 26.50 (*0-03-044446-2*) Holt R&W.

Lab Experiments - Chem: Basic Intro. 3rd ed. Miller et al. 1984. pap. text 18.50 (*0-534-02818-7*) Wadsworth Pub.

Lab Experiments for Freshman Chemist at U Alabama. 2nd ed. 296p. (C). 1999. pap. text 7.00 (*0-536-02443-X*) Pearson Custom.

Lab Experiments for Modern Chemistry. 90th ed. Tzimopoulo. 1990. pap. text, teacher ed., lab manual ed. 36.50 (*0-03-014512-0*); pap. text, lab manual ed. 18.25 (*0-03-014513-9*) Holt R&W.

Lab Experiments for Modern Chemistry, 1986. Metcalfe. 1986. pap., student ed. 8.00 (*0-03-001307-0*) H Holt & Co.

Lab Experiments for Modern Physics. 90th ed. Trinklein. 1990. pap. text, lab manual ed. 23.75 (*0-03-014522-8*) Holt R&W.

Lab Experiments for Organic & Biochemistry. 3rd ed. Frederick A. Bettelheim. LC 97-20202. (Golden Sunburst Ser.). 336p. (C). 1997. pap. text, lab manual ed. 45.50 (*0-03-020332-5*) SCP.

Lab Experiments for Organic & Physiological Chemistry. J. E. Hardcastle. (C). 1995. pap. text 24.39 (*1-56870-091-1*) RonJon Pub.

Lab Experiments in Biochemistry. 125p. (C). 1000. per. 34.95 (*0-7872-7224-8*) Kendall-Hunt.

Lab Experiments in General Chemistry. George Lowry et al. 1992. 30.65 (*0-88252-146-2*) Paladin Hse.

*__Lab Experiments in General Chemistry.__ 8th ed. (C). 2000. 20.00 (*0-8087-3460-1*) Pearson Custom.

Lab Experiments to Accompany Kleit's Digital Electronics. Michael Wiesner. 160p. 1987. student ed. 12.20 (*0-317-59588-1*) P-H.

Lab Explorations in Calculus: With Applications to Physics. Joan R. Hundhausen & F. Richard Yeats. LC 92-39764. (C). 1997. pap. 22.20 (*0-06-501719-6*) Addson-Wesley Educ.

Lab Exs In Prin Med Sci. 6th ed. (C). 1990. text 14.80 (*0-8087-7021-7*) S&S Trade.

*__Lab Fever! Living, Loving & Laughing with Labrador Retrievers.__ Bruce Cochran. LC 00-21754. (Illus.). 91p. 2000. pap. 9.95 (*1-57223-262-5*, 2625) Willow Creek Pr.

*__Lab Guide for Human Anatomy, Vol. 201.__ Susan Anderson. 220p. (C). 2000. spiral bd. 35.95 (*0-7872-7244-2*) Kendall-Hunt.

Lab Guide to Plants. Doroothea V. DiCecco. 201p. 1993. pap. text 27.95 (*0-88725-198-6*) Hunter Textbks.

*__Lab Investigations for Biology.__ (C). 2000. write for info. (*0-536-61304-4*) Pearson Custom.

Lab Manual. Abramoff. pap. text, lab manual ed. 16.00 (*0-7167-2634-3*) W H Freeman.

*__Lab Manual: General Chemistry I.__ 200p. 2000. spiral bd. 36.95 (*0-7872-7149-7*) Kendall-Hunt.

Lab Manual & Workbook for Physical Anthropology. 2nd ed. Diane L. France & Arthur D. Horn. Ed. by Clyde Perlee & Simon. 140p. (C). 1992. pap. text, wbk. ed., lab manual ed. 28.75 (*0-314-93445-6*) West Pub.

Lab Manual & Workbook for Physical Anthropology. 8th ed. France. (Anthropology). 2000. pap. text 26.50 (*0-534-51462-6*) Wadsworth Pub.

Lab Manual Arriba: Communicacion y Cultura. Fernandez & Eduardo Zayas-Bazan. 1993. pap. text, lab manual ed. 20.80 (*0-13-044470-7*) P-H.

Lab Manual Automotive Technique. James D. Halderman. 1998. pap. text, lab manual ed. 22.67 (*0-13-760265-0*) S&S Trade.

Lab Manual-Drafting. 2nd ed. Wallach. (Blueprint Reading & Drafting Ser.). 1989. pap., student ed., suppl. ed. 19.95 (*0-02-829850-0*) Thomson Learn.

Lab Manual Experiments to General Chemistry by P. W. Atkins. Pribula. (C). 1995. 4.00 (*0-7167-2042-6*) W H Freeman.

Lab Manual for Bailey & Scott's Diagnostic Microbiology. 9th ed. Beverly P. Gobat & Scott. (Illus.). 224p. (C). (gr. 13). 1998. pap. text, wbk. ed., lab manual ed. 22.00 (*0-8151-5034-2*, 23837) Mosby Inc.

Lab Manual For Biology 1103. 4th ed. Ginn Press. 248p. 1999. pap. text, lab manual ed. 24.00 (*0-536-02024-8*) Pearson Custom.

An Asterisk (*) at the beginning of an entry indicates that the title is appearing for the first time.

Lab Manual for Biology 121. Perry. Date not set. pap., lab manual ed. 20.50 (*0-534-32037-6*) Wadsworth Pub.

Lab Manual for Chem 340/640. Garth Spencer. (Illus.). 90p. 1997. pap., lab manual ed. 9.00 (*1-886855-68-4*) Tavenner Pub.

Lab Manual for Cisco Networking Fundamentals. Cannon. (Networking Ser.). (C). 1999. pap. text 14.00 (*0-619-00091-0*) Course Tech.

Lab Manual for Desktop Publishing: IBM Version for Beginners. Anita O'Brien. 62p. 1992. 24.95 (*1-881950-01-8*) A OBrien.

Lab Manual for Desktop Publishing: IBM Version for Intermediates. Anita O'Brien. 62p. 1992. 22.95 (*1-881950-03-4*) A OBrien.

Lab Manual for Desktop Publishing: Macintosh Version for Beginners. Anita O'Brien. 62p. 1992. 24.95 (*1-881950-00-X*) A OBrien.

Lab Manual for Desktop Publishing: Macintosh Version for Intermediates. Anita O'Brien. 62p. 1992. 22.95 (*1-881950-02-6*) A OBrien.

Lab Manual for General Biology. 3rd ed. C. C. Delgado. 148p. (C). 1999. pap. text, lab manual ed. 19.95 (*0-7872-5684-6*, 41568401) Kendall-Hunt.

Lab Manual for General Biology - Zoology. Richard Pendola. (C). 1993. student ed. 12.54 (*1-56870-069-5*) RonJon Pub.

Lab Manual for General Physics, Pt. I. 3rd ed. Bernard Kern. 242p. (C). 1998. spiral bd., lab manual ed. 26.95 (*0-7872-5467-3*, 41546701) Kendall-Hunt.

Lab Manual for Inorganic Chemistry I. Carol Klein & Donald Carmody. (C). 1993. student ed. 14.67 (*1-56870-086-5*) RonJon Pub.

Lab Manual for Introductory Biology. Carl Lieb et al. 160p. (C). 1995. spiral bd. 16.95 (*0-7872-1696-8*) Kendall-Hunt.

***Lab Manual for Introductory Biology of Bacteria & Viruses.** 2nd ed. Carolyn Bohach. 222p. (C). 1998. spiral bd. 33.95 (*0-7872-5565-3*, 41556501) Kendall-Hunt.

Lab Manual for Ms Windows 2000 Professional. Course Technology Staff. (C). 2000. pap. 15.00 (*0-619-01512-8*) Thomson Learn.

Lab Manual for Physical Science 109L & Extra Materials. 4th ed. Richard Bady. 156p. (C). 1998. spiral bd. 26.95 (*0-7872-4903-3*, 41490301) Kendall-Hunt.

Lab Manual for Physics 211L, General Physics I, Phys 2131. New Mexico State University Staff. 158p. (C). 1998. spiral bd. 18.95 (*0-7872-5135-6*) Kendall-Hunt.

Lab Manual for Physiology. Michael Lisano. 1993. spiral bd. 15.65 (*0-88252-124-1*) Paladin Hse.

***Lab Manual for Principles of Biology 1.** 3rd ed. 102p. (C). 1999. text 24.00 (*0-536-02612-2*) Pearson Custom.

***Lab Manual for Principles of Biology 2.** 3rd ed. 258p. (C). 1999. text 24.00 (*0-536-02613-0*) Pearson Custom.

Lab Manual for Quantitative Analysis Lab: Automated Problem Set for Use with IBM PCs & Lotus-Compatible Spreadsheet Program. Thomas F. George. Ed. by Mary E. George. 24p. (C). 1989. 12.95 (*0-929683-01-3*) Servs by George.

Lab Manual for the Principles of Biology. 2nd ed. John Simpson. 136p. (C). 1999. spiral bd., lab manual ed. 19.95 (*0-7872-5622-6*, 41562201) Kendall-Hunt.

Lab Manual for 12:24. Lon Drake. 1992. 15.35 (*0-88252-090-3*) Paladin Hse.

Lab Manual For Univer Physics. Tony Klarich. 1998. pap. 15.74 (*0-07-233836-9*) McGraw.

Lab Manual in Geosciences. 3rd ed. Charles Tatrum. 158p. (C). 1998. spiral bd., lab manual ed. 23.95 (*0-7872-5595-5*, 41559501) Kendall-Hunt.

***Lab Manual Introduction to Electric Circuits.** Paynter. 1998. pap. text, lab manual ed. 33.40 (*0-02-392501-9*) Macmillan.

Lab Manual Introduction To Programming Using Java 2e. 2nd ed. DECKER HIRSHFIELD. 1999. 15.25 (*0-534-37110-8*) Thomson Learn.

Lab Manual Networking Essentials. Course Technology Staff. (C). 2000. pap. 15.00 (*0-619-01508-X*) Thomson Learn.

Lab Manual of Micro & Small Scale Experiments for the Independent Study of General College Chemistry. 2nd ed. Peter Jeschofnig. (Illus.). 84p. (C). 1998. wbk. ed., lab manual ed. 20.00 (*1-886151-26-1*) Lrning Res Unltd.

Lab Manual of Normal Oral Histology. Holliston L. Riviere. (Illus.). 34.00 (*0-86715-386-5*) Quint Pub Co.

Lab Manual Physics 114. Kong-Thon Tsen. 80p. (C). 1995. spiral bd. 10.95 (*0-7872-1382-9*) Kendall-Hunt.

Lab Manual to Accompany Digital Electronics. 3rd ed. James W. Bignell & Robert L. Donovan. 205p. (C). 1993. pap. text 27.50 (*0-8273-5842-3*) Delmar.

Lab Manual to Accompany Pascal - A Guided Tour: Turbo Pascal Version. Leland L. Beck. 168p. (C). 1994. pap. text 12.95 (*1-884808-02-6*) Comp Educ Pr.

Lab Manual to Accompany Pascal - A Guided Tour: UNIX Version. Leland L. Beck. 168p. 1994. pap. text 12.95 (*1-884808-01-8*) Comp Educ Pr.

Lab Manual to Accompany Programming-Java. 11th ed. Decker. (Miscellaneous/Catalogs Ser.). 1997. pap. 17.95 (*0-534-95597-5*) Wadsworth Pub.

Lab Manual to Accompany the Science of Animal Agriculture. Ray V. Herren & Frank Flanders. 215p. 1993. mass mkt., student ed. 17.00 (*0-8273-5926-8*) Delmar.

Lab Manual Understanding Textiles. Tortora. 464p. 1978. pap. text, lab manual ed. 29.40 (*0-02-420930-9*, Pub. by P-H) S&S Trade.

Lab Manual Windows 2000 Advanced Server. Course Technology Staff. (C). 2000. pap. 15.00 (*0-619-01504-7*) Thomson Learn.

Lab Manual Workbook Golosary, Bk. 2. 2nd ed. Robin & Henry. 1998. pap. text, wbk. ed., lab manual ed. 21.33 (*0-13-895129-2*) P-H.

Lab Materials Physics 151. Bob Erickson. (C). 1993. student ed. 17.64 (*1-56870-087-3*) RonJon Pub.

Lab Mnl General Chem. Judith A. Walmsley & Frank Walmsley. 400p. 1985. pap. text 19.50 (*0-201-08110-5*) Addison-Wesley.

Lab Mnl Custom Bio. Morgan. (C). 1997. spiral bd., lab manual ed. 58.00 (*0-201-30733-2*) Addison-Wesley.

LAB MNL Fundmtl Microbio. 5th ed. I. Edward Alcamo. 320p. (C). 1997. pap. text, lab manual ed. 32.00 (*0-8053-0534-3*) Addison-Wesley.

Lab Mnl Qualitatative Analys Chemistry. Radel. (Chemistry). 1991. lab manual ed. 12.75 (*0-314-90347-X*) Brooks-Cole.

Lab Mnl Ver C Expe Cmput. 4th ed. Glenn Brookshear. (C). 1994. pap. text, lab manual ed. 16.95 (*0-8053-4629-5*) Addison-Wesley.

Lab Notebook. 3rd ed. Oakman. (C). 1998. pap. text 11.50 (*0-471-32404-3*) Wiley.

Lab-on-a-chip: The Revolution in Portable Instrumentation. 2nd ed. John Wiley & Sons. Technical Insights. LC 98-114333. (Illus.). 152p. 1997. pap. write for info. (*0-471-28373-8*) Wiley.

Lab-on-a-chip: The Revolution in Portable Instrumentation. 3rd ed. LC 96-157849. 260p. 1999. spiral bd. 2450.00 (*1-56217-020-1*) Tech Insights.

***Lab Packet for Biology & Society.** Duane P. Hill. (Illus.). 63p. (C). 2000. pap. 20.00 (*0-9674988-3-X*) Archipelago Pubg.

***Lab Packet for 100-Level A&P: Dual Semester Version.** Duane P. Hill. (Illus.). 154p. (C). 1999. pap. 50.00 (*0-9674988-0-5*) Archipelago Pubg.

***Lab Packet for 100-Level A&P: Semester 1 Version.** Duane P. Hill. (Illus.). 73p. (C). 1999. pap. 25.00 (*0-9674988-1-3*) Archipelago Pubg.

***Lab Packet for 100-Level A&P: Semester 2 Version.** Duane P. Hill. (Illus.). 79p. (C). 1999. pap. 25.00 (*0-9674988-2-1*) Archipelago Pubg.

***Lab Pak to Accompany Essentials of Physical Geography.** Gabler. 136p. 1999. 15.00 (*0-03-021054-2*, Pub. by SCP) Harcourt.

***Lab Practicals for the Life Sciences.** Lisa Duvall. 1999. pap. text 16.95 (*1-56870-373-2*) RonJon Pub.

Lab Prep Guide - Biology. 4th ed. Dolphin. 1997. lab manual ed. 11.00 (*0-697-15904-3*, WCB McGr Hill) McGrw-H Hghr Educ.

Lab Rats of Doctor Eclair. John Bianchi. (Illus.). 32p. (J). (gr. k-3). 1997. pap. 6.95 (*0-921285-48-5*) Bungalo Books.

***Lab Reports: How to Write Lab Reports for Science Fairs & Classroom Experiments.** Kimberley Nash. (Illus.). 82p. (YA). (gr. 3-12). 1999. spiral bd., wbk. ed. 14.95 (*0-9653723-3-2*) Resurrection Res.

Lab Research Guide - Microbiology. 2nd ed. Prescott. 1992. lab manual ed. 8.50 (*0-697-14858-0*, WCB McGr Hill) McGrw-H Hghr Educ.

Lab Research in Psychology. David A. Eckerman. 232p. (C). 1995. pap. text, per. 47.95 (*0-7872-1506-6*) Kendall-Hunt.

Lab Resource Guide Study-Animal Div. Hickman, Jr. 1994. 9.74 (*0-697-25985-4*, WCB McGr Hill) McGrw-H Hghr Educ.

***Lab Science Basics.** 4th ed. Linne. 1999. text 26.00 (*0-323-00759-7*) Mosby Inc.

LAB Sections 1-1249, Vol. 123. 104p. 1999. write for info. (*0-327-06972-4*, 57748-12) LEXIS Pub.

LAB Sections 1250-3599, Vol. 124. 105p. 1999. write for info. (*0-327-06973-2*, 57749-12) LEXIS Pub.

LAB Sections 3600-5299, Vol. 125. 143p. 1999. write for info. (*0-327-06974-0*, 57750-12) LEXIS Pub.

LAB Sections 5300-End, Vol. 126. 274p. 1999. write for info. (*0-327-06975-9*, 57751-12) LEXIS Pub.

Lab Separates in Biology. Peter Abramoff. 1971. write for info. (*0-7167-0600-8*) W H Freeman.

Lab Separates in General Chemistry. Robert Franz. 1971. write for info. (*0-7167-0165-0*) W H Freeman.

Lab Sheet Annotations see Miquon Math Lab Series: Complete Home School

***Lab 6.** Peter Lerangis. (Watchers Ser.: No. 6). (J). (gr. 4-7). 1999. pap. 4.50 (*0-590-11501-4*, Apple Classics) Scholastic Inc.

LAB Studies: Character. LC 97-119059. (Bible Studies). 50p. 1996. pap. 5.99 (*0-8423-0161-5*) Tyndale Hse.

LAB Studies: Friendship. (Bible Studies). 54p. 1996. pap. 5.99 (*0-8423-0163-1*) Tyndale Hse.

LAB Studies: Money. (Bible Studies). 52p. 1996. pap. 5.99 (*0-8423-0167-4*) Tyndale Hse.

LAB Studies: Parenting. (Bible Studies). 50p. 1996. pap. 5.99 (*0-8423-0160-7*) Tyndale Hse.

LAB Studies: Priorities. (Bible Studies). 54p. 1996. pap. 5.99 (*0-8423-0162-3*) Tyndale Hse.

LAB Studies: Stress. (Bible Studies). 51p. 1996. pap. 5.99 (*0-8423-0165-8*) Tyndale Hse.

LAB Studies: Worship. (Bible Studies). 53p. 1996. pap. 5.99 (*0-8423-0157-7*) Tyndale Hse.

Lab Studies in Anatomy & Physiology. Dorothy R. Martin & Helen A. Cadwallader. (Illus.). 328p. (C). 1998. pap. text, lab manual ed. 32.95 (*0-88725-277-X*) Hunter Textbks.

Lab Studies in Earth History. 5th ed. James C. Brice et al. 256p. (C). 1992. text. write for info. (*0-697-12176-3*, WCB McGr Hill) McGrw-H Hghr Educ.

***Lab Studies in Physical Geology.** Richard C. Finch. (Illus.). 275p. 2000. pap. text 29.95 (*0-88725-261-3*) Hunter Textbks.

Lab Studies in Physical Geology. 3rd rev. ed. R. C. Finch et al. 268p. 1986. pap. text 23.96 (*0-88725-123-4*) Hunter Textbks.

***Lab Studies of Vertebrates.** 8th abr. ed. Schoenwolf. (Illus.). 384p. 2000. pap. 52.00 (*0-13-857434-0*) P-H.

Lab Tests & Diagnose Procedure. 5th ed. Corbett. LC 99-52568. 800p. 1999. pap. 34.96 (*0-8385-5588-8*, Medical Exam) Appleton & Lange.

Lab Tests for the Assessment of Nutritional Status. 2nd ed. Howerde E. Sauberlich. (Modern Nutrition Ser.). 486p. 1999. boxed set 69.95 (*0-8493-8506-7*) CRC Pr.

Lab Tests of Fired Clay & Metal One-Pot Chimneyless Stoves. Sam Baldwin. 37p. 1988. 8.75 (*0-86619-237-9*) Vols Tech Asst.

Lab Text Anatomy & Phys. The CAT. 6th ed. Anne B. Donnersberger & Anne E. Lesak. (Life Science Ser.). 496p. 1997. spiral bd. 46.25 (*0-7637-0659-0*) Jones & Bartlett.

Lab Text in Anatomy & Physiology. 6th ed. Donersberger. 1996. pap., spiral bd. 42.50 (*0-7637-3985-5*) Jones & Bartlett.

***Lab, the Temple & the Market: Reflections at the Intersection of Science, Religion & Development.** Ed. by Sharon Harper. 300p. 2000. pap. 24.95 (*1-56549-116-5*) Kumarian Pr.

Lab Volt Lab Manual. 2nd ed. Steve Herman. 416p. 1998. pap., lab manual ed. 21.95 (*0-8273-8552-8*) Delmar.

Lab Volt Solutions Manual. 2nd ed. Steve Herman. 32p. 1998. text, teacher ed. 16.95 (*0-8273-8553-6*) Delmar.

***Lab Windows/CVI Programming for Beginners.** Shahid Khalid. 656p. (C). 2000. pap. 55.00 (*0-13-016512-3*) P-H.

Laban Clark: Autobiography about His Early Life from 1778 to 1804. Laban Clark. Ed. by E. Farley Sharp. LC 87-72058. (Illus.). 48p. (Orig.). 1987. pap. 8.95 (*0-914960-66-0*) Academy Bks.

Laban for Actors & Dancers: Putting Laban's Movement Theory into Practice: A Step-by-Step Guide. Jean Newlove. LC 93-40376. 192p. (gr. 13). 1993. pap. 17.99 (*0-87830-044-9*, Thtre Arts Bks) Routledge.

Labanotation: The System of Analyzing & Recording Movement. 3rd rev. ed. Ann Hutchinson. LC 69-11446. 528p. (C). 1987. pap. 25.00 (*0-87830-527-0*, Thtre Arts Bks) Routledge.

Labanotation Quiz Book. Ray Cook. (Illus.). 72p. (Orig.). 1976. pap. text 10.00 (*0-932582-57-5*, Pub. by Dance Notation) Princeton Bk Co.

Labanotation Scores: An International Bibliography, Vol. 1. Mary J. Warner & Frederick E. Warner. LC 84-192250. 392p. (C). 1984. pap. text 37.50 (*0-9621312-0-2*) ICKL.

Labanotation Scores: An International Bibliography, Vol. 2. Mary J. Warner. LC 84-192250. 103p. (C). 1988. pap. text 15.00 (*0-9621312-1-0*) ICKL.

Labanotation Scores Vol. 3: An International Bibliography. Mary J. Warner. LC 84-192250. (Orig.). 1995. pap. text 15.00 (*0-9621312-3-7*) ICKL.

Labanotation Workbook, Vol. II. Allan Miles. 64p. 1970. pap. 12.00 (*0-317-56647-4*) Princeton Bk Co.

Labanotation Workbook, Vol. II. Allan Miles. 64p. (C). 1984. pap. 12.00 (*0-932582-19-2*) Dance Notation.

Labanotation Workbook, Vols. I & II. Alan Miles. 64p. (C). 1995. pap. 12.00 (*0-932582-18-4*, Pub. by Dance Notation) Princeton Bk Co.

Labanotation/IBM Typing Manual. Jo Floyd. (Illus.). 33p. (Orig.). (C). 1974. pap. text 10.00 (*0-932582-14-1*) Dance Notation.

Labat's Regional Anesthesia: Techniques & Clinical Applications. 4th ed. John Adriani. (Modern Concepts of Medicine Ser.). (Illus.). 748p. 1985. 75.00 (*0-87527-187-1*) Green.

Labcoat. Larry D. Soderquist. LC 98-65597. 160p. 1998. 24.95 (*1-57736-088-5*, Hillsboro Pr) Providence Hse.

Label & Package Graphic Design. Robert Demetrician. LC 96-47088. (Illus.). 228p. 1996. 92.00 (*1-885067-02-X*) Jelmar Pub.

Label Design Vol. 4: The Best New U. S. & International Design. Ed. by Rockport Publishers Editorial Staff. (Illus.). 240p. 1994. 49.99 (*1-56496-069-2*, 30600) Rockport Pubs.

Label Designs Vol. 3: The Best New U. S. & International Collection. 256p. 1992. 49.99 (*1-56496-005-6*, 30433) Rockport Pubs.

Label-Free Learning: Supporting Learners with Disabilities. Charlotte H. Keefe. 192p. 1996. pap. text 19.50 (*1-57110-023-7*) Stenhse Pubs.

Label Industry Facts & Guidelines. 2nd ed. 228p. 60.00 (*0-614-25580-5*, 00PO63001) Print Indus Am.

Label Made Me Buy It: From Aunt Jemima to Zonkers - The Best Dressed Boxes, Bottles & Cans from the Past. Ralph Kovel & Terry Kovel. 224p. 1998. 40.00 (*0-609-60168-7*) Crown Pub Group.

Label Me Human: Minority Rights in Stigmatized Canadians. Evellyn Kallen. 275p. 1989. pap. 18.95 (*0-8020-6664-X*); text 37.50 (*0-8020-2696-6*) U of Toronto Pr.

Label Press: Label Printing Software Tamed. Allen Lubow. (Illus.). 188p. (Orig.). 1994. pap. text. write for info. (*1-880773-19-8*) SNX.

Label Printers' Ratios see 1996 PIA Ratios

Label Reader's Pocket Dictionary of Food Additives. Mike Lapchick & Cindy Appleseth. 128p. (Orig.). 1993. pap. 4.95 (*1-56561-027-X*) Wiley.

Label Reader's Pocket Dictionary of Food Additives: A Comprehensive Quick Reference Guide to Mor E Than 250 of Today's Most Common Food Additives. Mike Lapchick. 128p. 1993. pap. 4.95 (*0-471-34744-2*) Wiley.

***Label Sticker Combined Mathpass Envelope.** 1p. (C). 1999. 0.00 (*0-201-64822-9*) HEPC Inc.

Label/A&R/Record Producer Directory. Robert A. Livingston. (Livingston's Complete Music Business Directory Ser.). 290p. 1996. pap. 44.95 (*0-932303-22-6*) GLGLC Music.

Labeled for Life. Julia Anderson. LC 98-67375. 240p. 1998. text 26.95 (*0-7872-5129-1*, 41512901) Kendall-Hunt.

Labeling Facts. 81p. 1994. 225.00 (*0-317-01515-X*) Produce Mktg Assn.

Labeling of Biotechnology Products: Proceedings of a Workshop. 52p. (Orig.). (C). 1994. pap. text 30.00 (*0-7881-1309-7*) DIANE Pub.

Labeling of Home-Use In Vitro Testing Products: Approved Guideline (1996) Contrib. by Rosanne M. Savol. 1996. 75.00 (*1-56238-299-3*, GP14-A) NCCLS.

Labeling Perspective: A Bibliography of Research, No. 779. Ed. by Robert H. Vasoli & John R. Maiolo. 1975. 6.50 (*0-686-20348-8*, Sage Prdcls Pr) Sage.

Labeling Women Deviant. Edwin M. Schur. 288p. (C). 1983. pap. 33.75 (*0-07-554466-0*) McGraw.

LaBelle Cuisine: Recipes to Sing About. Patti LaBelle. LC 98-49145. (Illus.). 240p. 1999. 25.00 (*0-7679-0314-5*) Broadway BDD.

Labelled Compounds & Radiopharmaceuticals Applied in Nuclear Medicine. Alexandru T. Balaban et al. LC 84-5262. 744p. reprint ed. pap. 200.00 (*0-7837-6365-4*, 204607700010) Bks Demand.

***Labelled Deduction.** David Basinger. LC 00-28202. (Applied Logic Ser.). 2000. write for info. (*0-7923-6237-3*) Kluwer Academic.

Labelled Deductive Systems, Vol. 1. Dov M. Gabbay. (Oxford Logic Guides Ser.: No. 33). (Illus.). 510p. 1996. text 120.00 (*0-19-853833-2*) OUP.

***Labelled Non-Classical Logics.** Luca Viganao. LC 99-89297. 2000. write for info. (*0-7923-7749-4*) Kluwer Academic.

Labelling of Deviance: Evaluating a Perspective. 2nd ed. Walter R. Gove. LC 80-50397. 428p. reprint ed. pap. 132.70 (*0-608-05980-3*, 205264600008) Bks Demand.

Labels, Addresses & Signatures of Twentieth Century Italian Violin Makers. Marlin Brinser. 1986. pap. 3.50 (*0-317-39573-4*) Timberwood.

Labels & Tags. David E. Carter. 1998. pap. 35.00 (*0-8230-6623-1*) Watsn-Guptill.

Labels & Tags. Compiled by Rockport Publishers Editors. (Design Library). (Illus.). 80p. 1998. pap. 14.99 (*1-56496-508-2*) Rockport Pubs.

Labels & Tags, Vol. 3. Pie Editorial Staff. 69.95 (*4-89444-074-1*, Pub. by Pie Bks) Bks Nippan.

Labels for Laibel. Dina Rosenfeld. (Illus.). 32p. (J). (ps-1). 1990. 9.95 (*0-922613-35-4*) Hachai Pubng.

Labels of Distiction. Madison Square Press Staff. 1999. pap. 19.95 (*0-688-16225-8*, Wm Morrow) Morrow Avon.

***Labels of Distinction: Microbrewery Label Design.** Spencer Drate & Thomas Olejar. (Illus.). 144p. 1999. pap. 24.95 (*3-927258-64-4*) Gingko Press.

Labels of Distinction: Microbrewery Label Design. Intro. by Charles Finkel. (Illus.). 162p. pap. 34.95 (*0-942604-65-2*) Madison Square.

Laberinto de Fortuna. Juan De Mena. Ed. by Miguel A. Perez Priego. (Nueva Austral Ser.: Vol. 73). (SPA.). 1991. pap. text 12.95 (*84-239-1873-4*) Elliots Bks.

Laberinto de Fortuna O las Trescientas. Juan De Mena. (SPA.). 158p. 1968. 15.95 (*0-8288-7118-3*, S30294) Fr & Eur.

Laberinto de la Afectividad. Enrique Rojas. (Nueva Austral Ser.: Vol. 11). (SPA.). 1991. pap. text 24.95 (*84-239-1811-4*) Elliots Bks.

Laberinto de la Soledad--Postdata-Vuelta. Octavio Paz. 1991. pap. text 13.99 (*968-16-3937-5*) Fondo.

Laberinto de la Soledad y Otras Obras. Octavio Paz. (SPA.). 352p. 1997. pap. 13.95 (*0-14-025883-3*) Viking Penguin.

***Laberinto de la Vida.** Patricio Vaca. 214p. 1999. pap. write for info. (*0-7392-0317-7*, PO3005) Morris Pubng.

Laberinto de Soledad. Octavio Paz. (SPA.). pap. 15.50 (*968-16-0175-0*, Pub. by Fondo) Continental Bk.

Laberinto en la Narrativa Hispanoamericana Contemporanea. Ludmila Kapschutschenko. (Monografias A Ser.: Vol. LXXXV). (SPA.). 115p. (C). 1981. 41.00 (*0-7293-0118-4*, Pub. by Tamesis Bks Ltd) Boydell & Brewer.

Labiatae. Tr. by Israel Program for Scientific Translations Staff from RUS. (Flora of the U. S. S. R. (Flora SSSR) Ser.: Vol. 20). (Illus.). xvii, 389p. 1987. reprint ed. 180.00 (*3-87429-240-1*, 003943, Pub. by Koeltz Sci Bks) Lubrecht & Cramer.

Labiatae: Tribe 3: Stahydeae, Subtribe 3: Lamiineae, Genus 1285 Salvia L./Tribe 5: Meriandreae to Tribe 7: Pogostemoneae/Subfamily VI: Ocimoideae. Tr. by Israel Program for Scientific Translations Staff from RUS. (Flora of the U. S. S. R. (Flora SSSR) Ser.: Vol. 21). (Illus.). xxii, 520p. 1987. reprint ed. 235.00 (*3-87429-241-X*, 003944, Pub. by Koeltz Sci Bks) Lubrecht & Cramer.

La/Biblia de los Oprimidos & Portions of la Hora de la Vida see Bible of the Oppressed

LaBiblia Vida Abundante Abundant Life Bible. Abundant Life Staff. 1993. 16.99 (*0-311-48821-8*) Baptist Spanish.

Labman - Botany. 2nd ed. Moore et al. 1997. pap., lab manual ed. 15.31 (*0-697-28629-0*) McGraw.

Labman Microbiology Appl. Patient. 5th ed. Morello. 1997. 30.00 (*0-07-289071-1*) McGraw.

Labnet: Toward a Community of Practice. Ed. by Richard R. Ruopp et al. (Technology & Education Ser.). 384p. 1993. pap. 45.00 (*0-8058-1294-6*); text 89.95 (*0-8058-1263-6*) L Erlbaum Assocs.

***Labonte Brothers.** Janet Hubbard-Brown. (Race Car Legends Ser.). (Illus.). 64p. 1998. pap. 7.95 (*0-7910-5758-5*) Chelsea Hse.

***Labonte Brothers.** Janet Hubbard-Brown. LC 98-25709. (Race Car Legends Ser.). (Illus.). 64p. (YA). (gr. 3 up). 1999. lib. bdg. 16.95 (*0-7910-5019-X*) Chelsea Hse.

Labor see Rhode Island General Laws, 1998 Cumulative Supplement

Labor see Alaska Administrative Code--Register 150 Supplement (July 1999)

Labor, Vol. 4. Ed. by Lexis Law Publishing Staff. 1998. write for info. (*0-327-06457-9*) LEXIS Pub.

L

Labor: (Selected Articles on Workers & Unions During the Great Depression) Ed. by Melvyn Dubofsky & Stephen Burwood. LC 89-71389. (Great Depression & the New Deal Ser.: Vol. 2). 416p. 1990. text 20.00 (*0-8240-0894-4*) Garland.

Labor Abitration Information System, Vol. 13. Ed. by LRP Publications Staff. 1987. write for info. (*0-934753-27-X*) LRP Pubns.

Labor Abuses in the Global Economy: Women & Children: A Bibliography. Ed. by Joan Nordquist. (Contemporary Social Issues: Vol. 51). 72p. 1998. pap. 20.00 (*1-892068-00-1*) Ref Rsch Serv.

Labor Agreement in Negotiation & Arbitration. 2nd ed. Arnold M. Zack & Richard I. Bloch. 250p. 1996. text 50.00 (*0-87179-870-0*) BNA Books.

Labor Agreement Negotiations. 4th ed. Raymond L. Hilgert. 58p. 1995. 28.95 (*0-87393-383-4*) Dame Pubns.

Labor Agreement Negotiations. 5th ed. Hilgert. LC 97-68557. 1998. pap. 28.95 (*0-87393-721-X*) Dame Pubns.

Labor among Primitive Peoples, Showing the Development of the Obstetric Science of Today. George J. Engelmann. LC 75-23705. (Illus.). reprint ed. 47.50 (*0-404-13257-X*) AMS Pr.

Labor & Administration. John R. Commons. LC 64-17404. (Reprints of Economic Classics Ser.). ix, 431p. 1964. reprint ed. 49.50 (*0-678-00035-2*) Kelley.

Labor & an Integrated Europe. Ed. by Barry J. Eichengreen et al. LC 92-40273. 295p. (C). 1993. 42.95 (*0-8157-8682-4*); pap. 18.95 (*0-8157-8681-6*) Brookings.

Labor & Birth: A Guide for You. Linda Todd. (Illus.). 52p. 1998. 3.00 (*0-934024-03-0*) Intl Childbirth.

Labor & Capital in National Politics. Harwood L. Childs. LC 73-19137. (Politics & People Ser.). (Illus.). 290p. 1974. reprint ed. 23.95 (*0-405-05862-4*) Ayer.

Labor & Community: Mexican Citrus Worker Villages in a Southern California County, 1900-1950. Gilbert G. Gonzalez. LC 93-36584. 280p. (C). 1994. text 39.95 (*0-252-02097-9*); pap. text 14.95 (*0-252-06388-0*) U of Ill Pr.

Labor & Delivery: The Proceedings of the 2nd World Congress on Labor & Delivery, May 1997, Rome Italy. Ed. by Ermelando V. Cosmi. (Illus.). 586p. 1998. 80.00 (*1-85070-973-4*) Prthnon Pub.

Labor & Delivery Policy & Procedure Guideline Manual. Margarete Burns. 400p. 1996. spiral bd. 115.00 (*1-879575-70-1*) Acad Med Sys.

Labor & Democracy in Namibia, 1971-1996. Gretchen Bauer. LC 97-49202. 180p. 1998. text 34.95 (*0-8214-1216-7*); pap. text 17.95 (*0-8214-1217-5*) Ohio U Pr.

Labor & Democracy in the Transition to a Market System. Ed. by Bertram Silverman et al. LC 92-9032. (U. S. - Post-Soviet Dialogues Ser.). 320p. (C). (gr. 13). 1992. text 85.95 (*1-56324-037-8*) M E Sharpe.

Labor & Democracy in the Transition to a Market System. Robert Vogt. Ed. by Bertram Silverman & Murray Yanowitch. LC 92-9032. (U. S. - Post-Soviet Dialogues Ser.). 320p. (gr. 13). 1992. pap. text 38.95 (*1-56324-038-6*) M E Sharpe.

Labor & Desire: Women's Revolutionary Fiction in Depression America. Paula Rabinowitz. LC 91-50259. (Gender & American Culture Ser.). xiv, 212p. (C). 1991. 39.95 (*0-8078-1994-8*); pap. 16.95 (*0-8078-4332-6*) U of NC Pr.

Labor & Economic Growth in 5 Asian Countries: South Korea, Malaysia, Taiwan, Thailand, & the Philippines. Walter Galenson. LC 91-33883. 144p. 1992. 47.95 (*0-275-94200-7*, C4200, Praeger Pubs) Greenwood.

Labor & Economic Reforms in Latin America & the Caribbean. (Regional Perspectives on World Development Report 1995 Ser.). 40p. 1995. pap. 22.00 (*0-8213-3348-8*, 13348) World Bank.

Labor & Employment see Michie's Annotated Code of Maryland, 1998 Supplement

Labor & Employment: Problems, Cases & Materials. 2nd ed. Robert J. Rabi et al. LC 95-3407. (American Casebook Ser.). 946p. (C). 1995. 60.00 (*0-314-05458-8*) West Pub.

Labor & Employment Arbitration, 3 vols. 2nd ed. Bornstein & Gosline. 1988. ring bd. 465.00 (*0-8205-1443-8*, 443) Bender.

Labor & Employment Arbitration in a Nutshell. Dennis R. Nolan. LC 98-10054. (Paralegal). 425p. 1998. pap. text 15.00 (*0-314-21160-8*) West Pub.

Labor & Employment in California: A Guide To Employment Laws, Regulations, & Practices. 2nd ed. Steven B. Eggleston & Bernadette M. O'Brien. 95.00 (*0-327-12402-4*) LEXIS Pub.

Labor & Employment in California: A Guide to Employment Laws, Regulations & Practices. 2nd ed. Steven B. Eggleston et al. LC 98-123299. 1997. write for info. (*1-55834-520-5*) LEXIS Pub.

Labor & Employment in California Issue 3: A Guide to Employment Laws, Regulations & Practice. Bernadette M. O'Brien & Steven B. Eggleston. 200p. 1999. ring bd. write for info. (*0-327-01416-4*, 8022323) LEXIS Pub.

***Labor & Employment in Connecticut, Issue 14.** Jeffrey L. Hirsch. 100p. 1999. ring bd. write for info. (*0-327-01392-3*, 8037719) LEXIS Pub.

Labor & Employment in Connecticut: A Guide to Employment Laws, Regulations, & Practices. Jeffrey L. Hirsch & Alicia B. Davenport. 400p. 1991. ring bd. 89.50 (*0-88063-052-3*, 80376-10, MICHIE) LEXIS Pub.

***Labor & Employment in Florida, Issue 9.** Michael F. Marino & J. David Richeson. 200p. 1999. ring bd. write for info. (*0-327-01385-0*, 8085815) LEXIS Pub.

Labor & Employment in Florida: Law, Policy & Practice, 2 vols., Set. W. Gary Vause. 1000p. (C). 1989. write for info. (*1-877937-00-2*) Stetson U Law.

Labor & Employment in Florida: Law, Policy & Practice, Vol. I. W. Gary Vause. (C). 1989. write for info. (*1-877937-01-0*) Stetson U Law.

Labor & Employment in Florida: Law, Policy & Practice, Vol. II. W. Gary Vause. (C). 1989. write for info. (*1-877937-02-9*) Stetson U Law.

Labor & Employment in Georgia, Issue 6. Hirsch & Quillen. 251p. 1998. ring bd. write for info. (*0-327-00529-7*, 8096516) LEXIS Pub.

Labor & Employment in Georgia: A Guide to Employment Laws, Regulations, & Practices. Jeffrey L. Hirsch & Roger K. Quillen. LC 93-1264. 490p. Date not set. ring bd. 89.50 (*0-409-25718-4*, 80964-10, MICHIE) LEXIS Pub.

Labor & Employment in Georgia: A Guide to Employment Laws, Regulations, & Practices. Jeffrey L. Hirsch & Roger K. Quillen. 1994. suppl. ed. 45.00 (*0-614-03665-8*, MICHIE) LEXIS Pub.

Labor & Employment in Georgia: A Guide to Employment Laws, Regulations & Practices. 1993rd ed. Hirsch & Quillen. 1997. ring bd. 89.50 (*0-327-00974-8*, 80964-10, MICHIE) LEXIS Pub.

Labor & Employment in Illinois, Issue 2. 3rd ed. Maynard G. Sautter. 151p. 1998. ring bd. write for info. (*0-327-00667-6*, 8117113) LEXIS Pub.

Labor & Employment in Illinois, Issue 3. 3rd ed. Maynard G. Sautter. 1999. ring bd. write for info. (*0-327-01133-5*, 8117114) LEXIS Pub.

Labor & Employment in Louisiana. Jonathan L. Alder & Maureen F. Moore. 1994. ring bd., suppl. ed. 45.00 (*0-614-03666-6*, MICHIE) LEXIS Pub.

Labor & Employment in Louisiana. Maureen F. Moore et al. LC 93-19122. 370p. Date not set. ring bd. 95.00 (*0-409-25716-8*, 81356, MICHIE) LEXIS Pub.

Labor & Employment in Louisiana. 2nd rev. ed. Maureen Moore. LC 98-67065. 501p. 1998. ring bd. 105.00 (*0-327-00205-0*) LEXIS Pub.

Labor & Employment in Massachusetts: A Guide to Employment Laws, Regulations & Practices. Jeffrey L. Hirsch. 310p. 1991. ring bd. 89.50 (*0-88063-041-8*, 81528, MICHIE) LEXIS Pub.

Labor & Employment in Massachusetts: A Guide to Employment Laws, Regulations, & Practices. Jeffrey L. Hirsch. 1994. ring bd., suppl. ed. 42.50 (*0-685-73599-0*, MICHIE) LEXIS Pub.

Labor & Employment in Massachusetts: A Guide to Employment Laws, Regulations, & Practices. 2nd rev. ed. John Hirsch. LC 98-67056. 801p. 1998. ring bd. 95.00 (*0-327-00126-7*, 81529-20) LEXIS Pub.

***Labor & Employment in Massachusetts: Employment Laws, Regulations, & Practices.** 2nd ed. Jeffrey L. Hirsch. 1998. ring bd. 115.00 (*0-327-12444-X*, MICHIE) LEXIS Pub.

Labor & Employment in Michigan. Henry Earle. LC 94-79504. 1994. ring bd. 95.00 (*0-250-40710-8*, MICHIE) LEXIS Pub.

Labor & Employment in Nebraska, Issue 6. Jeffrey L. Hirsch & Lisa D. DeBuse. 151p. 1998. ring bd. write for info. (*0-327-00734-6*, 8197116) LEXIS Pub.

Labor & Employment in New Hampshire, Issue 6. Hirsch. 251p. 1998. ring bd. write for info. (*0-327-00737-0*, 8207216) LEXIS Pub.

***Labor & Employment in New Hampshire: A Guide to Employment Laws, Regulations, & Practices.** 2nd ed. Jeffrey L. Hirsch & Andrea K. Johnstone. 600p. 1999. ring bd. 115.00 (*0-327-04979-0*, 8207011) LEXIS Pub.

Labor & Employment in New Hampshire: Guide to Employment Laws, Regulations, & Practices. annuals Jeffrey L. Hirsch et al. 550p. Date not set. ring bd., suppl. ed. 95.00 (*0-409-25664-1*, 81969-10, MICHIE) LEXIS Pub.

Labor & Employment in New Jersey: A Guide to Employment Laws, Regulations, & Practices. Roger B. Jacobs. LC 92-21761. 530p. Date not set. ring bd. 95.00 (*0-409-25670-6*, 82124, MICHIE) LEXIS Pub.

Labor & Employment in New Jersey: A Guide to Employment Laws, Regulations, & Practices. Roger B. Jacobs. 1994. suppl. ed. 42.50 (*0-614-03667-4*, MICHIE) LEXIS Pub.

Labor & Employment in New Mexico. Eric Sirotkin. LC 95-157627. 400p. (Orig.). 1994. pap. 65.00 (*0-409-25715-X*, MICHIE) LEXIS Pub.

Labor & Employment in New York, Issue 1. 2nd ed. Liddle. 151p. 1998. ring bd. write for info. (*0-327-00733-8*, 8218821) LEXIS Pub.

Labor & Employment in New York: Guide to New York Laws, Regulations & Practices. 2nd ed. Jeffrey L. Liddle & Michael F. Marino. 450p. 95.00 (*0-327-12476-8*) LEXIS Pub.

Labor & Employment in Pennsylvania, Issue 6. Marino & Unkovic. 151p. 1998. ring bd. write for info. (*0-327-00585-8*, 8231916) LEXIS Pub.

Labor & Employment in Pennsylvania: A Guide to Employment Laws, Regulations, & Practices. Michael F. Marino & Unkovic. 430p. Date not set. ring bd. 95.00 (*0-409-25674-9*, 82318, MICHIE) LEXIS Pub.

Labor & Employment in Rhode Island: A Guide to Employment Laws, Regulations & Practices. Hirsch & Reuben. 1992. ring bd. 99.00 (*0-327-00942-X*, 82373, MICHIE) LEXIS Pub.

Labor & Employment in Rhode Island: A Guide to Rhode Island Employment Laws, Regulations, & Practices. Jeffrey L. Hirsch & William A. Farrell. LC 92-23848. 1992. suppl. ed. 48.50 (*0-685-74467-1*, MICHIE) LEXIS Pub.

Labor & Employment in Rhode Island: A Guide to Rhode Island Employment Laws, Regulations, & Practices, Issue 4. Stephanie Hirsh et al. LC 92-23848. 280p. 1995. ring bd. 95.00 (*0-409-25663-3*, 82374-14, MICHIE) LEXIS Pub.

Labor & Employment in Vermont: Guide to Employment Laws, Regulations & Practices. Kimberly B. Cheney. 375p. 1994. pap. 65.00 (*0-88063-789-7*, 82712-10, MICHIE) LEXIS Pub.

Labor & Employment in Wisconsin, Issue 2. 3rd ed. Maynard G. Sautter. 151p. 1998. ring bd. write for info. (*0-327-00685-4*, 8283522) LEXIS Pub.

Labor & Employment in Wisconsin, Issue 3. 3rd ed. Maynard G. Sautter. 100p. 1999. ring bd. write for info. (*0-327-01085-1*, 8283523) LEXIS Pub.

Labor & Employment Law. Patrick J. Cihon & James O. Castagnera. (SWC-Business Law). 690p. (C). 1988. mass mkt. 51.75 (*0-534-07842-7*) PWS Pubs.

Labor & Employment Law. 2nd ed. Patrick J. Cihon & James O. Castagnera. 675p. 1992. mass mkt. 79.95 (*0-534-92816-1*) S-W Pub.

Labor & Employment Law. 10th ed. David P. Twomey. LC 97-25884. (LG - Labor Law Ser.). 1997. 85.95 (*0-538-85439-1*) S-W Pub.

***Labor & Employment Law.** 11th ed. Twomey. (SWC-Business Law Ser.). (C). 2000. pap. 85.95 (*0-324-04357-0*) Thomson Learn.

Labor & Employment Law: Compliance & Litigation. Frederick T. Golder. LC 85-26973. 1992. 125.00 (*0-685-12018-X*) West Group.

Labor & Employment Law: Compliance & Litigation. annuals Frederick T. Golder. 1992. suppl. ed. write for info. (*0-318-60193-1*) West Group.

Labor & Employment Law: Problems, Cases & Materials in the Law of Work. Robert J. Rabin et al. (American Casebook Ser.). 1014p. 1988. text 44.50 (*0-314-39695-0*); pap. text, teacher ed. write for info. (*0-314-46970-2*) West Pub.

Labor & Employment Law: Problems, Cases & Materials in the Law of Work 1995 Statutory Supplement. 2nd ed. Robert J. Rabin et al. (American Casebook Ser.). 946p. (C). 1995. pap. 20.00 (*0-314-07069-9*) West Pub.

Labor & Employment Law: Text & Cases. 9th ed. David P. Twomey. (C). 1993. pap. 73.75 (*0-538-82779-3*, LG99IA) S-W Pub.

Labor & Employment Law Desk Book. 2nd ed. Gordon E. Jackson. LC 93-28069. 1200p. (C). 1993. text 79.95 (*0-13-532938-8*) Prntice Hall Bks.

***Labor & Employment Law Desk Book, 2000 Supplement Ed.** Hall Prentice. 1999. pap. text. write for info. (*0-13-012421-4*, Prentice Hall) P-H.

Labor & Employment Law for the Corporate Counselor & General Practitioner. 494p. 1994. pap. 30.00 (*0-614-26703-X*, 1015); pap. 92.00 incl. audio (*0-614-26704-8*, 20154) NYS Bar.

Labor & Employment Law in Connecticut: A Guide to Employment Laws, Regulations, & Practices. Jeffrey L. Hirsch & Alicia B. Davenport. 1991. ring bd. 95.00 (*0-327-01014-2*, 80376, MICHIE) LEXIS Pub.

Labor & Employment Law in the United States. Alvin L. Goldman. LC 96-3203. 1996. 73.00 (*90-411-0981-1*) Kluwer Law Intl.

Labor & Employment Law Newsletter. Scholer Kaye. text 275.00 (*0-8205-2099-3*) Bender.

Labor & Employment Law Problems, Cases & Materials in the Law of Work, Teacher's Manual to Accompany. 2nd ed. Robert J. Rabin et al. (American Casebook Ser.). 96p. 1995. pap. text, teacher ed. write for info. (*0-314-07549-6*) West Pub.

Labor & Employment Policy. John Carmichael, Jr. & Charles Bulmer. (Orig.). (C). 1979. pap. 15.00 (*0-918592-35-6*) Pol Studies.

Labor & Employment Relations. Raymond L. Hogler. LC 94-40806. 464p. (C). 1995. mass mkt. 95.95 (*0-314-04625-9*) West Pub.

Labor & Employment Relations. Marcic. (SWC-Business Law Ser.). 1999. write for info. (*0-314-04594-5*) S-W Pub.

Labor & Farmer Parties in the United States. Nathan Fine. 445p. (Orig.). 1984. reprint ed. pap. 10.50 (*0-916695-02-6*) Ctr Social Hist.

Labor & Immigration in Industrial America. Robert D. Parmet. LC 86-15193. 268p. (C). 1987. reprint ed. pap. text 16.50 (*0-89874-968-9*) Krieger.

Labor & Imperial Democracy in Prewar Japan. Andrew Gordon. (Twentieth-Century Japan: The Emergence of a World Power Ser.: No. 1). (C). 1991. pap. 17.95 (*0-520-08091-2*, Pub. by U CA Pr) Cal Prin Full Svc.

Labor & Industrial Relations Journals & Serials: An Analytical Guide, 14. Ed. by Lucille W. Cameron. LC 89-11887. (Annotated Bibliographies of Serials: A Subject Approach Ser.: No. 14). 248p. 1989. lib. bdg. 65.00 (*0-313-25986-0*, CLR/) Greenwood.

Labor & Internationalism. Lewis L. Lorwin. (Brookings Institution Reprint Ser.). reprint ed. lib. bdg. 32.50 (*0-697-00164-4*) Irvington.

Labor & Laborers Through Mexican History. Ed. by Elsa C. Frost et al. 954p. 1979. pap. 55.00 (*0-8165-0616-7*) U of Ariz Pr.

Labor & Law. Charles Bradlaugh. LC 68-55490. lxiii, 217p. 1972. reprint ed. 37.50 (*0-678-00888-4*) Kelley.

Labor & Liberalization: Trade Unions in the New Russia. Linda J. Cook. LC 97-8847. 129p. (C). 1997. pap. 9.95 (*0-87078-377-7*) Century Foundation.

Labor & Liberty: The La Follette Committee & the New Deal. Jerold S. Auerbach. LC 66-28233. 1966. 29.50 (*0-672-51153-3*); pap. text 12.95 (*0-685-02670-1*) Irvington.

Labor & Lumber. Charlotte Todes. Ed. by Dan C. McCurry & Richard E. Rubenstein. LC 74-30655. (American Farmers & the Rise of Agribusiness Ser.). (Illus.). 1975. reprint ed. 21.95 (*0-405-06830-1*) Ayer.

Labor & Management. Ed. by Richard Morris. LC 76-183137. (Great Contemporary Issues Ser.). (Illus.). 500p. (C). 1973. 30.00 (*0-685-41643-7*) Ayer.

Labor & Management. Ed. by Richard B. Morris. LC 76-183137. (Great Contemporary Issues Ser.). (Illus.). 500p. (C). 1973. 27.95 (*0-405-04163-2*) Ayer.

Labor & Monopoly Capital: The Degradation of Work in the Twentieth Century. Harry Braverman. LC 74-7785. 480p. 1976. pap. 18.00 (*0-85345-370-5*, Pub. by Monthly Rev) NYU Pr.

Labor & Monopoly Capital: The Degradation of Work in the Twentieth Century. 25th ed. Harry Braverman. LC 98-46497. 1998. pap. text 19.00 (*0-85345-940-1*, Pub. by Monthly Rev) NYU Pr.

Labor & Other Capital: The Rights of Each Served & the Wrongs of Both Eradicated. Edward Kellogg. LC 68-27853. (Reprints of Economic Classics Ser.). 298p. 1971. reprint ed. 45.00 (*0-678-00803-5*) Kelley.

Labor & Other Economic Essays. Henry R. Seager. Ed. by Charles A. Gulick, Jr. LC 68-22943. (Essay Index Reprint Ser.). 1977. reprint ed. 23.95 (*0-8369-0859-7*) Ayer.

Labor & Other Questions in South Africa. Indicus. LC 75-77203. 146p. 1969. reprint ed. lib. bdg. 49.50 (*0-8371-1298-2*, INL&) Greenwood.

Labor & Politics. Mollie R. Carroll. LC 74-89723. (American Labor, from Conspiracy to Collective Bargaining Ser., No. 1: No. 1). 1974. reprint ed. 19.95 (*0-405-02110-0*) Ayer.

Labor & Politics in Peru. James L. Payne. LC 65-22335. 1980. reprint ed. 23.95 (*0-915728-05-2*) Lytton Pub.

Labor & Politics in the U. S. Postal Service. V. K. Baxter. (Studies in Work & Industry). (Illus.). 388p. (C). 1994. 45.00 (*0-306-44753-3*, Plenum Trade) Perseus Pubng.

Labor & Property Rights in California Agriculture: An Economic Analysis of the CALRA. Rex L. Cottle et al. LC 82-40318. (Economics Ser.: No. 6). 136p. 1982. 24.95 (*0-89096-132-8*) Tex A&M Univ Pr.

Labor & Safety see Burns Indiana Statutes Annotated 1999 Cumulative Supplement Set: Pocket Part

Labor & the Ambivalent Revolutionaries: Mexico, 1911-1923. Ramon E. Ruiz. LC 75-29087. 162p. reprint ed. pap. 50.30 (*0-608-14764-8*, 202586700046) Bks Demand.

Labor & the American Revolution. Philip S. Foner. LC 76-18034. 256p. 1976. 55.00 (*0-8371-9003-7*, FLA/, Greenwood Pr) Greenwood.

Labor & the Chinese Revolution: Class Strategies & Contradictions of Chinese Communism, 1928-1948. S. Bernard Thomas. LC 83-19045. (Michigan Monographs in Chinese Studies: No. 49). (Illus.). 341p. (C). 1983. text 35.00 (*0-89264-049-9*) Ctr Chinese Studies.

Labor & the Common Welfare. Samuel Gompers. Ed. by Hayes Robbins. LC 70-102240. (Select Bibliographies Reprint Ser.). 1977. 29.95 (*0-8369-5125-5*) Ayer.

Labor & the Common Welfare. Samuel Gompers. LC 79-89735. (American Labor, from Conspiracy to Collective Bargaining Ser., No. 1). 306p. 1974. reprint ed. 19.95 (*0-405-02124-0*) Ayer.

***Labor & the Constitution: Labor & Property, Privacy, Discrimination, & International Relations.** Ed. by David L. Gregory. LC 99-33953. (Controversies in Constitutional Law Ser.: Vol. 2). 392p. 1999. 160.00 (*0-8153-3389-7*) Garland.

Labor & the Course of American Democracy: U. S. History in Latin American Perspective. Charles Bergquist. LC 96-48532. (C). 1996. pap. 22.00 (*1-85984-126-0*, Pub. by Verso) Norton.

Labor & the Economy. 3rd ed. Howard M. Wachtel. 537p. (C). 1993. text 102.50 (*0-03-096544-6*) Dryden Pr.

Labor & the Economy. 4th ed. Howard M. Wachtel. (C). 1996. text. write for info. (*0-03-011307-5*) Harcourt Coll Pubs.

Labor & the Economy: A Guide for Trade Unionists. Labor Center Reporter Editorial Board Staff. (Orig.). 1989. pap. 7.50 (*0-937817-06-6*) CLRE UCAL Berk.

Labor & the Employer. Samuel Gompers. LC 79-156413. (American Labor Ser., No. 2). 1975. reprint ed. 28.95 (*0-405-02921-7*) Ayer.

Labor & the Growth Crisis in Sub-Saharan Africa. (Regional Perspectives on World Development Report 1995 Ser.). 40p. 1995. pap. 22.00 (*0-8213-3343-7*, 13343) World Bank.

Labor & the Legal Process. Harry H. Wellington. LC 68-27769. 422p. reprint ed. pap. 130.90 (*0-8357-9380-X*, 201337900086) Bks Demand.

Labor & the National Economy. rev. ed. Ed. by William G. Bowen & Orley C. Ashenfelter. (Problems of Modern Economy Ser.). (C). 1975. write for info. (*0-393-05456-X*) Norton.

Labor & the Post-Industrial Age. Ed. by Jim Villani. LC 89-62819. (Pig Iron Ser.: No. 16). (Illus.). 128p. 1990. pap. 10.95 (*0-917530-26-8*) Pig Iron Pr.

Labor & the Shut-Down of the Amoskeag Textile Mills: WPA, National Research Report No. L-5. Daniel Creamer & Charles W. Coulter. LC 78-156410. (American Labor Ser., No. 2). (Illus.). 1971. reprint ed. 24.95 (*0-405-02919-5*) Ayer.

Labor & the State in Egypt, 1952-1994: Workers, Unions, & Economic Restructuring. Marsha P. Posusney. LC 97-3929. 384p. 1997. lib. bdg. 52.00 (*0-231-10692-0*) Col U Pr.

Labor & the State in Egypt, 1952-1994: Workers, Unions, & Economic Restructuring. Marsha P. Pripstein. LC 97-3929. 384p. 1997. pap. 18.50 (*0-231-10693-9*) Col U Pr.

Labor & The Wartime State: Labor Relations & Law During World War II. James B. Atleson. LC 97-21069. 312p. 1998. text 49.95 (*0-252-02370-6*) U of Ill Pr.

Labor & the Wartime State: Labor Relations & Law During World War II. James B. Atleson. LC 97-21069. 312p. 1998. text 21.95 (*0-252-06674-X*) U of Ill Pr.

An Asterisk (*) at the beginning of an entry indicates that the title is appearing for the first time.

Labor & Urban Politics: Class Formation & Liberal Reform in Chicago, 1864-97. Richard Schneirov. LC 97-21164. (Working Class in American History Ser.). 400p. 1998. text 49.95 (*0-252-02374-9*); text 21.95 (*0-252-06676-6*) U of Ill Pr.

Labor & Women's Nutrition: A Study of Energy Expenditure, Fertility & Nutritional Status in Ghana. CFNPP Staff et al. (Working Papers). (C). 1993. pap. 7.00 (*1-56401-137-2*) Cornell Food.

Labor & Workforce Development see Alaska Administrative Code--Register 151 Supplement (October 1999)

Labor Arbitration: A Coursebook. Laura J. Cooper & Dennis R. Nolan. (American Casebook Ser.). 557p. (C). 1994. 47.50 (*0-314-04023-4*) West Pub.

Labor Arbitration: A Practical Guide for Advocates. Ed. by ABA, Labor & Employment Law Staff et al. 416p. 1990. trans. 55.00 (*0-87179-635-X*, 0635) BNA Books.

Labor Arbitration: An Annotated Bibliography. Ed. by Charles J. Coleman et al. LC 94-18840. (Cornell Industrial & Labor Relations Bibliography Ser.: No. 17). 352p. 1994. text 37.50 (*0-87546-322-3*, ILR Press) Cornell U Pr.

Labor Arbitration: An Annotated Bibliography, 1991-1996. Ed. by Charles J. Coleman et al. LC 97-30643. (ILR Bibliography Ser.: No. 18). (Illus.). 112p. 1997. text 25.00 (*0-8014-3440-8*) Cornell U Pr.

Labor Arbitration: Cases & Materials for Advocates. William F. Dolson et al. LC 97-2056. 1997. 45.00 (*1-57018-036-9*) BNA Books.

Labor Arbitration: The 1988 National Conference. 1988. audio 185.00 (*1-55917-384-X*) Natl Prac Inst.

Labor Arbitration - What You Need to Know. 3rd rev. ed. Robert Coulson. LC 81-66912. 176p. 1986. pap. 8.00 (*0-943001-05-6*) Am Arbitration.

Labor Arbitration Advocacy: Effective Tactics & Techniques. Jay E. Grenig. 300p. 1993. boxed set 95.00 (*0-614-05878-3*, MICHIE) LEXIS Pub.

Labor Arbitration Advocacy, 1989-92: Effective Tactics & Techniques. Jay E. Grenig & R. Wayne Estes. 300p. 1993. suppl. ed. 45.00 (*1-56257-299-7*, MICHIE) LEXIS Pub.

Labor Arbitration & Dispute Settlements. BNA's Business & Human Resources Services Staff. (Labor Relations Reporter Ser.). 1937. ring bd. 1099.00 (*1-55871-036-1*) BNA.

Labor Arbitration in America: The Profession & Practice. Ed. by Mario F. Bognanno & Charles J. Coleman. LC 92-399. 200p. 1992. 49.95 (*0-275-94375-5*, C4375, Praeger Pubs) Greenwood.

Labor Arbitration in State & Local Government: An Examination of Experience in Eight States & New York City. Richard A. Lester. 1984p. pap. 10.00 (*0-318-20241-7*) PU Indust Rel.

Labor Arbitration Index: 1987 Edition. Ed. by LRP Publications Staff. text. write for info. (*0-934753-29-6*) LRP Pubns.

Labor Arbitration Index, 1990. 1113p. 1990. 135.00 (*0-685-47508-5*, 6010) LRP Pubns.

Labor Arbitration Information System. LRP Publications Staff. text 475.00 (*0-934753-12-1*) LRP Pubns.

Labor Arbitration Information Systems: Indexes-Tables. LRP Publications Staff. write for info. (*0-934753-11-3*) LRP Pubns.

Labor Arbitration Law & Practice in a Nutshell. Dennis R. Nolan. LC 79-4316. (Nutshell Ser.). 358p. (C). 1979. reprint ed. pap. text 15.00 (*0-8299-2032-3*) West Pub.

Labor Arbitration of a Drug-Testing Case. 1987. 15.00 (*1-55917-380-7*, 71112); VHS 250.00 (*1-55917-379-3*) Natl Prac Inst.

Labor Arbitration of a Sexual Harassment Case. Christine Ver Ploeg. 1986. 15.00 (*1-55917-383-1*, 6912); VHS 250.00 (*1-55917-382-3*) Natl Prac Inst.

*__Labor Arbitration (to 1993) An Annotated Bibliography.__ annot. ed. Ed. by Charles J. Coleman & Theodora T. Haynes. 269p. 2000. text 25.00 (*0-7881-9002-4*) DIANE Pub.

Labor Arbitration under Fire. Ed. by James L. Stern & Joyce M. Najita. LC 96-34096. (ILR Press Book). (Illus.). 280p. 1996. text 39.95 (*0-8014-3305-3*) Cornell U Pr.

Labor Argument in the American Protective Tariff Discussion. George B. Mangold. LC 73-156433. (American Labor Ser., No. 2). 1971. reprint ed. 15.95 (*0-405-02931-4*) Ayer.

Labor at the Polls: Union Voting in Presidential Elections, 1952-1976. Jong Oh Ra. LC 77-90729. (Illus.). 192p. 1978. 27.50 (*0-87023-026-3*) U of Mass Pr.

Labor, Autonomy & the State in Latin America. Edward C. Epstein. (Thematic Studies in Latin America). 272p. 1989. text 44.95 (*0-04-445331-0*) Routledge.

*__Labor Camp Socialism: The Gulag in the Soviet Totalitarian System.__ Galina Mikhailovna Ivanova. Ed. by Donald J. Raleigh. Tr. by Carol A. Flath from RUS. LC 99-87794. (New Russian History Ser.). 234p. 2000. pap. text 24.95 (*0-7656-0427-2*) M E Sharpe.

*__Labor Camp Socialism: The Gulag in the Soviet Totalitarian System.__ Galina Mikhailovna Ivanova. Ed. by Donald J. Raleigh. Tr. by Carol A. Flath. LC 99-87794. (New Russian History Ser.). (Illus.). 234p. 2000. text 62.95 (*0-7656-0426-4*) M E Sharpe.

Labor Commitment & Social Change in Developing Areas. Wilbert E. Moore & Arnold S. Feldman. LC 82-6144. 378p. 1982. reprint ed. lib. bdg. 69.50 (*0-313-23572-4*, MOLC, Greenwood Pr) Greenwood.

Labor Composition & U. S. Productivity Growth, 1948-90. (Illus.). 114p. (Orig.). (YA). (gr. 12 up). 1994. pap. text 40.00 (*0-7881-0791-7*) DIANE Pub.

Labor Conditions in Japan. Shuichi Harada. (Columbia University. Studies in the Social Sciences: No. 301). reprint ed. 22.50 (*0-404-51301-8*) AMS Pr.

Labor Cost: 25 Keys to Profitable Success. David V. Pavesic. LC 98-39299. (Restaurant Manager's Pocket Handbook Ser.). 96p. 1999. pap. 12.95 (*0-86730-753-6*, Pub. by Lebhar Friedman) Natl Bk Netwk.

*__Labor Costs & International Trade.__ Stephen S. Golub. 65p. 1999. pap. 9.95 (*0-8447-7129-5*, Pub. by Am Enterprise) Pub Resources Inc.

Labor, Crafts & Commerce in Ancient Israel. Moshe Aberbach. LC 94-213374. xii, 294p. 1994. text 30.00 (*965-223-860-0*, Pub. by Magnes Pr) Eisenbrauns.

*__Labor Day.__ Mir Tamim Ansary. LC 98-13720. (Holiday Histories Ser.). (Illus.). 32p. (J). (ps-3). 1999. lib. bdg. 13.95 (*1-57572-703-X*) Heinemann Lib.

Labor Day. A. R. Gurney. LC 99-475292. 1998. pap. 5.25 (*0-8222-1685-X*) Dramatists Play.

*__Labor Day.__ Floyd Kemske. LC 00-31441. 240p. 2000. 22.00 (*0-945774-48-6*, Pub. by Catbird Pr) IPG Chicago.

Labor Day. Geoffrey Scott. LC 81-15485. (Carolrhoda On My Own Bks.). (Illus.). 48p. (J). (gr. k-3). 1982. lib. bdg. 18.60 (*0-87614-178-5*, Carolrhoda) Lerner Pub.

*__Labor Day: Confessions from the Delivery Room.__ Ed. by Ann-Marie Giglio. 200p. 1999. pap. 8.95 (*0-7611-0242-6*) Workman Pub.

Labor Day at Walden Pond. Edward Morin. 64p. (Orig.). 1997. pap. 15.00 (*1-56439-056-X*); text 25.00 (*1-56439-058-6*) Ridgeway.

Labor Day Murder. Lee Harris. (YA). (gr. 8 up). 1998. mass mkt. 5.99 (*0-449-15017-8*, GM) Fawcett.

Labor Demand. Daniel S. Hamermesh. 464p. 1993. pap. text 23.95 (*0-691-02587-8*, Pub. by Princeton U Pr) Cal Prin Full Svc.

Labor Demand & Equilibrium Wage Formation. Ed. by Jan C. Van Ours et al. LC 92-44910. (Contributions to Economic Analysis Ser.: No. 213). 380p. 1992. 119.25 (*0-444-89590-6*, North Holland) Elsevier.

Labor Disputes & the President of the United States. Edward Berman. LC 75-76691. (Columbia University. Studies in the Social Sciences: No. 249). reprint ed. 27.50 (*0-404-51249-6*) AMS Pr.

Labor Divided: Austerity & Working Class Politics in Contemporary Italy. Miriam Golden. LC 88-47726. 320p. 1988. 42.50 (*0-8014-2200-0*) Cornell U Pr.

Labor Divided: Austerity & Working-Class Politics in Contemporary Italy. Miriam Golden. LC 88-47726. 285p. 1988. reprint ed. pap. 88.40 (*0-608-05317-1*, 206585500001) Bks Demand.

Labor Divided: Race & Ethnicity in United States Labor Struggles, 1835-1960. Ed. by Robert Asher & Charles Stephenson. LC 88-26334. (SUNY Series in American Labor History). 378p. (C). 1989. pap. text 24.95 (*0-88706-972-X*) State U NY Pr.

Labor Divided: Race & Ethnicity in United States Labor Struggles, 1835-1960. Ed. by Robert Asher & Charles Stephenson. LC 88-26334. (SUNY Series in American Labor History). 378p. (C). 1990. text 74.50 (*0-88706-970-3*) State U NY Pr.

Labor Economics. Ashenfelter. 1998. 23.00 (*1-57259-684-8*) Worth.

Labor Economics, 4 vols. Ed. by Orley C. Ashenfelter & Kevin F. Hallock. LC 94-44341. (International Library of Critical Writings in Economics: Vol. 47). 2032p. 1995. 680.00 (*1-85278-207-2*) E Elgar.

Labor Economics. George J. Borjas. LC 95-21464. 656p. (C). 1995. 78.75 (*0-07-006597-7*) McGraw.

Labor Economics. George J. Borjas. (C). 1995. pap., student ed. 24.69 (*0-07-006599-3*) McGraw.

Labor Economics. Solomon Blum. LC 79-89719. (American Labor, from Conspiracy to Collective Bargaining Ser., No. 1). 579p. 1977. reprint ed. 33.95 (*0-405-02105-4*) Ayer.

Labor Economics. 2nd ed. Borjas. LC 99-52902. 544p. 1999. 78.75 (*0-07-231198-3*) McGraw.

Labor Economics. 2nd ed. Borjas. 2000. student ed. 19.25 (*0-07-231193-2*) McGraw.

Labor Economics. 6th ed. Marshall & Vernon M. Briggs. 656p. (C). 1988. text 48.95 (*0-256-07090-3*, Irwn McGrw-H) McGrw-H Hghr Educ.

Labor Economics: Problems in Analyzing Labor Markets. Ed. by William Darity, Jr. LC 92-18985. (Recent Economic Thought Ser.). 320p. (C). 1992. lib. bdg. 152.00 (*0-7923-9260-4*) Kluwer Academic.

Labor Economics & Industrial Relations: Markets & Institutions. Ed. by Clark Kerr & Paul D. Staudohar. LC 94-2377. (Wertheim Publications in Industrial Relations). (Illus.). 768p. 1994. text 36.50 (*0-674-50641-3*) HUP.

Labor Economics & Labor Relations. 11th ed. Lloyd G. Reynolds et al. LC 97-10346. 581p. 1997. 96.00 (*0-13-263310-8*) P-H.

Labor Economy: Selected Publication Policy. Stanley P. Stephenson. 240p. (C). 1999. 32.00 (*0-02-417160-3*, Macmillan Coll) P-H.

Labor Education in the U. S. An Annotated Bibliography. Richard E. Dwyer. LC 77-21572. 292p. 1977. 26.50 (*0-8108-1058-1*) Scarecrow.

Labor, Employment & Agricultural Development in West Asia & North Africa. Dennis Tully. (C). 1990. lib. bdg. 114.50 (*0-7923-0816-6*) Kluwer Academic.

Labor, Employment, & the Law: A Dictionary. Christopher T. Anglim. LC 97-20803. (Contemporary Legal Issues Ser.). 576p. 1997. lib. bdg. 45.00 (*0-87436-825-1*) ABC-CLIO.

Labor Enterprises in Israel: The Institutional Economy, Vol. 2. Abraham Daniel. 232p. 1976. pap. text 24.95 (*0-87855-639-7*) Transaction Pubs.

Labor for Love: Stories. Sandy Huss. 128p. 1992. 19.95 (*0-8262-0816-9*) U of Mo Pr.

Labor for the Wind. Paul Wadden. 64p. 1988. pap. 7.00 (*0-933704-76-3*) Dawn Pr.

Labor Force in Economic Development: A Comparison of International Census Data, 1946-1966. John D. Durand. LC 75-2988. 277p. 1975. reprint ed. pap. 85.90 (*0-7837-9332-4*, 206007300004) Bks Demand.

Labor Force in the United States (1890-1960), Vol. 2. J. B. Durand. (Demographic Monographs). xx, 290p. 1968. text 191.00 (*0-677-01550-X*) Gordon & Breach.

Labor Force in War & Transition: 4 Countries. Clarence D. Long. (Occasional Papers: No. 36). 70p. 1952. reprint ed. 20.00 (*0-87014-351-4*) Natl Bur Econ Res.

Labor Force in Wartime America. Clarence D. Long. (Occasional Papers: No. 14). 76p. 1944. reprint ed. 20.00 (*0-87014-329-8*) Natl Bur Econ Res.

Labor Force Participation of Black & White Youth. Donald R. Williams. LC 87-5868. (Research in Business Economics & Public Policy Ser.: No. 11). 133p. reprint ed. pap. 41.30 (*0-8357-1804-2*, 207042500088) Bks Demand.

Labor Force Participation, Sectoral Choice, & Earnings in Conakry, Guinea. Peter Glick & David E. Sahn. (Working Papers: No. 43). 52p. (C). 1993. pap. 7.00 (*1-56401-143-7*) Cornell Food.

Labor Force Policies for Regional Economic Development: The Role of Employment & Training Programs. Stephen F. Seninger. LC 89-3763. (Illus.). 199p. 1989. 55.00 (*0-275-93325-3*, C3325, Praeger Pubs) Greenwood.

Labor Force under Changing Income & Employment. Clarence D. Long. (General Ser.: No. 65). 464p. 1958. reprint ed. 120.70 (*0-87014-064-7*) Natl Bur Econ Res.

*__Labor Guide Manual 1982-2001.__ Chilton. (C). 2000. pap. 93.75 (*0-8019-9337-7*) NP-Chilton.

Labor Guide, 1981-95. Chilton Automotive Editorial Staff. 2112p. 1994. text 137.00 (*0-8019-8571-4*) Nichols Pub.

Labor Guide, 1980-'94. Chilton Automotive Editorial Staff. 1984p. 1993. text 135.00 (*0-8019-8472-6*) Nichols Pub.

Labor Guide, 1979-'93. Chilton Automotive Editorial Staff. 2240p. 1992. text 135.00 (*0-8019-8292-8*) Nichols Pub.

Labor Guide to Labor Law. 4th ed. (C). 2000. text. write for info. (*0-13-016998-6*) S&S Trade.

*__Labor Guide to Labor Law__ 4th ed. Bruce S. Feldacker. LC 99-26652. 652p. 1999. 84.00 (*0-13-016523-9*) P-H.

Labor Histories: Class, Politics, & the Working Class Experience. Eric Arnesen et al. LC 97-45358. (Working Class in American History Ser.). 400p. 1998. text 49.95 (*0-252-02407-9*); text 19.95 (*0-252-06710-X*) U of Ill Pr.

Labor History Archives in the United States. Ed. by Daniel J. Leab & Philip P. Mason. LC 91-38550. 286p. 1992. pap. 18.95 (*0-8143-2389-8*) Wayne St U Pr.

Labor History Archives in the United States: A Guide for Researching & Teaching. Ed. by Daniel J. Leab & Philip P. Mason. LC 91-38550. 286p. reprint ed. pap. 88.70 (*0-608-10580-5*, 2071201) Bks Demand.

Labor History Reader. Ed. by Daniel J. Leab & Richard B. Morris. (Working Class in American History Ser.). 496p. 1985. text 39.95 (*0-252-01197-X*); pap. text 19.95 (*0-252-01198-8*) U of Ill Pr.

Labor in America: A History. 6th ed. Melvyn Dubofsky & Foster R. Dulles. LC 99-17713. (Illus.). 475p. (C). 1999. pap. text 27.95 (*0-88295-979-4*) Harlan Davidson.

Labor in an International Economy: Implications for Bargaining & Jobs. (Current Issues Ser.: No. 18). 25p. 1993. reprint ed. 6.50 (*0-89215-174-9*) U Cal LA Indus Rel.

Labor in Colonial New York, 1664-1776. Samuel McKee. 193p. 1993. reprint ed. lib. bdg. 69.00 (*0-7812-5250-4*) Rprt Serv.

Labor in Crisis: The Steel Strike of 1919. David Brody. LC 86-30880. 224p. 1987. pap. text 12.95 (*0-252-01373-5*) U of Ill Pr.

Labor in Crisis: The Steel Strike of 1919. David Brody. LC 82-11746. (Critical Periods of History Ser.). 208p. 1982. reprint ed. lib. bdg. 59.50 (*0-313-23499-X*, BROL, Greenwood Pr) Greenwood.

Labor in Europe & America. U. S. Bureau of Labor Statistics Staff. LC 70-88493. (Illus.). 864p. 1971. reprint ed. lib. bdg. 35.00 (*0-8371-4962-2*, USLE, Greenwood Pr) Greenwood.

Labor in Finland. Carl E. Knoellinger. LC 60-7996. (Wertheim Publications in Industrial Relations). (Illus.). 312p. 1960. 20.00 (*0-674-50650-2*) HUP.

Labor in Illinois: The Affluent Years, 1945-80. Milton Derber. LC 88-1339. 472p. 1989. 47.50 (*0-252-01529-0*) U of Ill Pr.

Labor in International Trade Theory: A New Perspective on Japanese-American Issues. Junichi Goto. LC 89-13880. (Illus.). 213p. 1990. reprint ed. pap. 66.10 (*0-608-05973-0*, 206631000008) Bks Demand.

Labor in Its Relations to Law. Frederic J. Stimson. LC 72-2675. (Select Bibliographies Reprint Ser.). 1977. reprint ed. 18.95 (*0-8369-6865-4*) Ayer.

Labor in Latin America: Comparative Essays on Chile, Argentina, Venezuela & Colombia. Charles W. Bergquist. LC 84-51648. (Illus.). 414p. reprint ed. pap. 30.00 (*0-608-20215-0*, 207146900012) Bks Demand.

Labor in Learning: Public School Treatment of the World of Work. Will Scoggins. 110p. 1993. reprint ed. 8.00 (*0-89215-050-5*) U Cal LA Indus Rel.

Labor in Queensland: From the 1880s to 1988. Ross Fitzgerald & Harold Thornton. LC 88-17278. (Illus.). 422p. (Orig.). (C). 1989. pap. text 34.95 (*0-7022-2152-X*, Pub. by Univ Queensland Pr) Intl Spec Bk.

Labor in the Ancient Near East. Ed. by Marvin A. Powell. (American Oriental Ser.: Vol. 68). (Illus.). xiv, 289p. (C). 1987. 32.00 (*0-940490-68-4*, #HD8656: L33) Am Orient Soc.

Labor in the Capitalist World-Economy. Ed. by Charles Bergquist. LC 83-27015. (Political Economy of the World-System Annuals Ser.: No. 7). (Illus.). 312p. reprint ed. pap. 96.80 (*0-8357-8471-1*, 203473900091) Bks Demand.

Labor in the Philippine Economy. Kenneth K. Kurihara. LC 78-161766. reprint ed. 22.50 (*0-404-09027-3*) AMS Pr.

Labor in the Public & Nonprofit Sectors. Ed. by Daniel S. Hamermesh. LC 74-22495. 287p. 1975. reprint ed. pap. 89.00 (*0-608-02907-6*, 206397100008) Bks Demand.

Labor in the Puerto Rican Economy: Postwar Development & Stagnation. Carlos E. Santiago. LC 91-27268. 192p. 1992. 49.95 (*0-275-94135-3*, C4135, Praeger Pubs) Greenwood.

Labor in the Rural Household Economy of the Zairian Basin. Tshikala B. Tshibaka. LC 92-23773. (Research Reports: Vol. 90). 1992. write for info. (*0-89629-093-X*) Intl Food Policy.

Labor in the Russian Revolution: Factory Committees & Trade Unions, 1917-1918. Gennady Shkliarevsky. LC 92-38982. 336p. 1993. text 49.95 (*0-312-09119-2*) St Martin.

Labor in the South. F. Ray Marshall. LC 67-22870. (Wertheim Publications in Industrial Relations). (Illus.). 420p. 1967. 29.95 (*0-674-50700-2*) HUP.

Labor in the Transportation Industry. Robert C. Lieb. LC 73-13343. (Special Studies in U. S. Economic, Social & Political Issues). 1974. 50.50 (*0-275-28791-2*) Irvington.

Labor in the United States. Ronald L. Filippelli. 320p. (C). 1984. pap. text 38.00 (*0-07-554641-8*) McGraw.

Labor in the West. Hugh T. Lovin. (Illus.). 88p. 1986. pap. text 15.00 (*0-89745-090-6*) Sunflower U Pr.

Labor in the World Social Structure. Ed. by Immanuel Wallerstein. LC 82-16964. (Explorations in the World-Economy Ser.: No. 2). 256p. reprint ed. pap. 79.40 (*0-8357-4863-4*, 203779500009) Bks Demand.

Labor Injunction. Felix Frankfurter & Nathan Greene. 1963. 16.50 (*0-8446-1190-5*) Peter Smith.

Labor into Art: The Theme of Work in Nineteenth-Century American Literature. David S. Herreshoff. LC 90-20754. 180p. reprint ed. pap. 55.80 (*0-608-20179-0*, 207143700012) Bks Demand.

Labor Issues of American International Trade & Investment. Daniel J. Mitchell. LC 76-7052. (Policy Studies in Employment & Welfare: Vol. 24). 126p. reprint ed. pap. 39.10 (*0-608-08790-4*, 206942900004) Bks Demand.

Labor Law see Leyes del Trabajo: Basado en el Titulo 29 de L. P. R. A.

Labor Law. Ed. by David L. Gregory. (International Library of Essays in Law & Legal Theory). (C). 1993. lib. bdg. 150.00 (*0-8147-3050-7*) NYU Pr.

Labor Law. Myron Hill, Jr. et al. (Smith's Review Ser.). 263p. 1988. pap. text 14.95 (*1-56542-160-4*) E Pub Corp.

Labor Law. Margaret C. Jasper. LC 98-17917. (Legal Almanac Ser.). 114p. 1998. text 22.50 (*0-379-11248-5*) Oceana.

Labor Law. 1993. reprint ed. lib. bdg. 89.00 (*0-7812-5248-2*) Rprt Serv.

Labor Law. 3rd ed. Leslie. 1248p. 1992. 56.00 (*0-316-52165-5*, Aspen Law & Bus) Aspen Pub.

Labor Law. 12th ed. Archibald Cox et al. LC 96-20608. (Paralegal). 1194p. 1996. text 42.00 (*1-56662-347-2*) Foundation Pr.

Labor Law: Adaptable to Courses Utilizing Harper & Estreicher's Casebook on Labor Law. Casenotes Publishing Co., Inc. Staff. Ed. by Norman S. Goldenberg et al. (Legal Briefs Ser.). 1996. pap. write for info. (*0-87457-098-0*, 1332) Casenotes Pub.

Labor Law: Adaptable to Courses Utilizing Leslie's Casebook on Labor Relations Law. Casenotes Publishing Co., Inc. Staff. Ed. by Norman S. Goldenberg & Peter Tenen. (Legal Briefs Ser.). 1992. pap. write for info. (*0-87457-097-2*, 1333) Casenotes Pub.

Labor Law: Adaptable to Courses Utilizing Materials by Cox. 7th ed. Cox. LC 87-114965. (Legalines Ser.). 248p. 11.50 (*0-685-18531-1*) Harcourt.

Labor Law: Cases & Materials. 4th ed. Michael Harper & Samual Estreicher. LC 95-82172. 1376p. 1996. 62.00 (*0-316-32513-9*, 25139) Aspen Law.

Labor Law: Cases & Materials, 1994 Case Supplement. 11th ed. Robert A. Gorman & Matthew W. Finkin. (University Casebook Ser.). (Illus.). 163p. 1994. pap. text 7.95 (*1-56662-218-2*) Foundation Pr.

Labor Law: Cases, Materials & Problems. 3rd ed. Bernard D. Meltzer & Stanley D. Henderson. LC 84-81751. (C). 1985. 52.00 (*0-316-56647-0*, Aspen Law & Bus) Aspen Pub.

Labor Law: Collective Bargaining in a Free Society. 4th ed. Walter E. Oberer et al. (American Casebook Ser.). 80p. (C). 1995. pap. text, teacher ed. write for info. (*0-314-04826-X*) West Pub.

Labor Law: Selected Statutes, Forms & Agreements. Michael Harper & Samuel Estreicher. 398p. 1998. pap. text, suppl. ed. 18.95 (*0-316-32510-4*, 25104) Aspen Law.

Labor Law & Business Change: Theoretical & Transactional Perspectives. Ed. by Samuel Estreicher & Daniel G. Collins. LC 88-12401. 361p. 1988. 75.00 (*0-89930-199-1*, ELW/, Quorum Bks) Greenwood.

Labor Law & Industrial Relations in Poland. Maria Matey. 178p. 1989. lib. bdg. 52.50 (*90-6544-401-7*) Kluwer Academic.

Labor Law & Industrial Relations in the United States of America. 2nd ed. Alvin L. Goldman. LC 84-951. 375p. reprint ed. pap. 116.30 (*0-7837-4607-5*, 204432600002) Bks Demand.

Labor Law & the Employment Market: Foundations & Applications. Ed. by Richard A. Epstein & Jeffrey Paul. 237p. (C). 1985. pap. 21.95 (*0-88738-623-7*) Transaction Pubs.

Labor Law Basics: Understanding the Impact of Federal Regulations on Employee Benefits. Stewart R. Sheperd & Peter R. Bulmer. (Building Blocks Ser.: Vol. 29). (Illus.). 32p. (Orig.). 1996. pap. 24.95 (*1-57963-030-8*, A0229) Am Compensation.

Labor Law, Cases & Materials On. 11th ed. Archibald S. Cox et al. (University Casebook Ser.). 1249p. 1990. text 44.95 (*0-88277-829-3*) Foundation Pr.

Labor Law Course (LOLL) 26th ed. 1664p. 1987. 48.50 (*0-685-19817-0*, 5797) CCH INC.

Labor Law Developments. 45th ed. Carol Holgren. text 152.00 (*0-8205-4219-9*) Bender.

Labor Law Developments 1996: Annual Institute. annuals Southwestern Legal Foundation Staff. 1967. write for info. (*0-8205-1352-0*) Bender.

Labor Law for the Rank & Filer. Staughton Lynd. 64p. 1994. pap. 10.00 (*0-88286-222-7*) C H Kerr.

Labor Law for the Rank & Filer. rev. ed. Staughton Lynd. LC 77-95429. 1982. pap. 2.95 (*0-917300-04-1*) Singlejack Bks.

Labor Law for the Union Officer. rev. ed. Duane Beeler. 103p. 1979. reprint ed. pap. 3.95 (*0-317-12248-7*) Union Rep.

Labor Law in a Nutshell. 2nd ed. Douglas L. Leslie. (Nutshell Ser.). 388p. (C). 1991. reprint ed. pap. 21.00 (*0-314-92205-9*) West Pub.

***Labor Law in a Nutshell.** 4th ed. Douglas L. Leslie. 2000. pap. text 23.50 (*0-314-23151-X*) West Pub.

Labor Law in America: Historical & Critical Essays. Ed. by Christopher L. Tomlins & Andrew J. King. LC 92-3996. (Symposia in Comparative History Ser.: Vol. 20). 368p. 1992. text 55.00 (*0-8018-4362-6*) Johns Hopkins.

Labor Law in China: Choice & Responsibility. Hilary K. Josephs. 210p. 1990. boxed set 125.00 (*0-88063-265-8*, 81366-10, MICHIE) LEXIS Pub.

Labor Law, Industrial Relations & Employee Choice: The State of the Workplace in the 1990's. Richard N. Block et al. Ed. by Daniel H. Kruger. LC 96-26103. 116p. (C). 1996. text 34.00 (*0-88099-164-X*); pap. text 15.00 (*0-88099-163-1*) W E Upjohn.

Labor Law Journal, 1949-1993, 46 vols. 1995. 2990.00 (*0-8377-9102-2*, Rothman) W S Hein.

Labor Law Journal, 1949-1993, Vols. 1-43. 1949. 57.50 (*0-685-07516-8*) W S Hein.

Labor Law, 1993, Statutory Supplement to Cases & Material On. 11th ed. Archibald S. Cox et al. 130p. (C). 1992. write for info. (*0-318-70006-9*) Foundation Pr.

Labor Law, Second Edition, Cases & Materials On. 2nd ed. Clyde W. Summers et al. LC 82-7305. (University Casebook Ser.). 1411p. 1982. text 44.00 (*0-88277-061-6*); pap. text, suppl. ed. 8.50 (*0-88277-084-5*) Foundation Pr.

Labor Law Source Book: Texts of 21 Federal Labor Laws. Robert M. Schwartz. Date not set. pap. write for info. (*0-945902-07-7*) Work Rights Pr.

Labor Laws & Their Enforcement. Ed. by Susan M. Kingsbury et al. LC 71-156446. (American Labor Ser., No. 2). (Illus.). 1975. reprint ed. 42.95 (*0-405-02930-6*) Ayer.

Labor Laws of Virginia: 1996 Edition. 140p. pap. 15.00 (*0-327-11399-5*) LEXIS Pub.

Labor Lawyer's Guide to the Rights & Responsibilities of Employee Whistleblowers. Stephen M. Kohn & Michael D. Kohn. LC 88-6017. 200p. 1988. 57.95 (*0-89930-207-6*, KLL/, Quorum Bks) Greenwood.

Labor Leaders in America. Ed. by Melvyn Dubofsky & Warren R. Van Tine. LC 86-4368. (Working Class in American History Ser.). 416p. 1987. text 39.95 (*0-252-01327-1*); pap. text 17.95 (*0-252-01343-3*) U of Ill Pr.

Labor Leadership Education: A Union-University Approach. Irvine L. Kerrison & Herbert A. Levine. LC 73-9255. 188p. 1973. reprint ed. lib. bdg. 69.50 (*0-8371-6996-8*, KELE, Greenwood Pr) Greenwood.

Labor Legislation in Czechoslovakia. Esther Bloss. LC 79-76641. (Columbia University. Studies in the Social Sciences: No. 446). reprint ed. 20.00 (*0-404-51446-4*) AMS Pr.

Labor Lurches Left. Green. 1994. 24.95 (*0-02-912821-8*) S&S Trade.

Labor-Managed Economy: Essays. Jaroslav Vanek. LC 76-16682. (Illus.). 288p. 1977. text 42.50 (*0-8014-0955-1*) Cornell U Pr.

Labor, Management, & Social Policy: Essays in the John R. Commons Tradition. Ed. by Gerald G. Somers. LC 63-10533. (Illus.). 317p. reprint ed. pap. 98.30 (*0-8357-6770-1*, 203544500095) Bks Demand.

Labor-Management Committees: Confrontation, Cooptation, or Cooperation? Charlotte Gold. LC 85-28489. (Key Issues Ser.: No. 29). 60p. (Orig.). 1986. pap. text 8.95 (*0-87546-122-0*, ILR Press) Cornell U Pr.

Labor-Management Contracts at Work: Analysis of Awards Reported by the American Arbitration Association. Morris Stone. LC 78-31591. viii, 307p. 1979. reprint ed. lib. bdg. 75.00 (*0-313-20966-9*, STLW, Greenwood Pr) Greenwood.

Labor-Management Cooperation: New Partnerships or Going in Circles? William N. Cooke. LC 90-46159. 192p. 1990. text 35.00 (*0-88099-099-6*); pap. text 17.00 (*0-88099-100-3*) W E Upjohn.

Labor-Management Cooperation: The American Experience. Irving H. Siegel & Edgar Weinberg. LC 82-8487. 316p. 1982. text 24.00 (*0-911558-99-3*); pap. text 14.00 (*0-911558-98-5*) W E Upjohn.

Labor-Management Cooperation for Productivity. Edgar Weinberg. (Studies in Productivity: Highlights of the Literature Ser.: Vol. 30). 61p. 1983. pap. 55.00 (*0-08-029511-8*) Work in Amer.

Labor-Management Cooperation in a Public Service Industry. Kenneth M. Jennings et al. LC 86-552. 144p. 1986. 55.00 (*0-275-92056-9*, C2056, Praeger Pubs) Greenwood.

Labor-Management Cooperation in Schools: An Idea Whose Time Has Come. Michele A. Woods-Houston & Rima Miller. 28p. 1988. pap. 6.95 (*1-56602-026-3*) Research Better.

Labor Management Laws in California Agriculture. 2nd ed. Howard R. Rosenberg et al. LC 90-85383. x, 179p. 1995. pap. 20.00 (*1-879906-29-5*, 21404) ANR Pubns CA.

Labor-Management Practices Adjuster. Jack Rudman. (Career Examination Ser.: C-433). 1994. pap. 39.95 (*0-8373-0433-4*) Nat Learn.

Labor-Management Relations. 5th ed. Daniel Q. Mills. LC 93-21687. (Series in Management). 704p. (C). 1993. 83.75 (*0-07-042512-4*) McGraw.

Labor-Management Relations among Government Employees. Ed. by Harry Kershen. (Public Sector Contemporary Issues Ser.: Vol. 2). 224p. 1983. pap. 28.95 (*0-89503-033-0*) Baywood Pub.

Labor Management Relations Implications of Reduction in Force & Reengineering. Frank L. Milman. 13p. 1996. pap. 3.75 (*0-16-061092-3*) USGPO.

Labor-Management Relations in a Changing Environment. 2nd ed. Michael Ballot. LC 95-35394. 656p. 1995. text 95.95 (*0-471-11185-6*) Wiley.

Labor Market Adjustments to Structural Change & Technological Progress. Eileen Appelbaum & Ronald Schettkat. LC 90-14230. (Illus.). 264p. 1990. 65.00 (*0-275-93376-8*, C3376, Praeger Pubs) Greenwood.

Labor Market Analysis of Engineers & Technical Workers. Glen G. Cain et al. LC 73-8136. (Policy Studies in Employment & Welfare: No. 18). 96p. reprint ed. pap. 30.00 (*0-608-06041-0*, 206637300008) Bks Demand.

Labor Market & Business Cycle Theories. P. Ferri & E. Greenberg. (Lecture Notes in Economics & Mathematical Systems Ser.: Vol. 325). xi, 183p. 1989. pap. 22.30 (*0-387-50866-X*) Spr-Verlag.

Labor Market & Income Consequences of Participation in TAFE. Mike Long et al. pap. 35.00 (*0-86431-225-3*, Pub. by Aust Council Educ Res) Stylus Pub VA.

Labor Market Areas see Progress in Planning

Labor Market Dynamics of Economic Restructuring: The United States & Germany in Transition. Ronald Schettkat. LC 91-23688. 232p. 1992. 62.95 (*0-275-93910-3*, C3910, Praeger Pubs) Greenwood.

***Labor Market Flexibility in 13 Latin American Countries & the United States.** Jose A. Anaya. LC 99-15436. (Latin American & Caribbean Studies). 48p. 1999. pap. 22.00 (*0-8213-4489-7*, 14489) World Bank.

Labor Market in a Socialist Economy. Gyorgy Sziraczki. (C). 1996. pap. text 19.00 (*0-8133-7879-6*) Westview.

***Labor Market in Africa, 1999.** Compiled by Icon Group International. (Illus.). 254p. 1999. ring bd. 2540.00 incl. audio compact disk (*0-7418-1944-9*) Icon Grp.

***Labor Market in Asia & Oceana, 1999.** Compiled by Icon Group International. (Illus.). 175p. 1999. ring bd. 1750.00 incl. audio compact disk (*0-7418-1960-0*) Icon Grp.

***Labor Market in Europe, 1999.** Compiled by Icon Group International. (Illus.). 212p. 1999. ring bd. 2120.00 incl. audio compact disk (*0-7418-1951-1*) Icon Grp.

***Labor Market in Latin America & the Caribbean, 1999.** Compiled by Icon Group International. (Illus.). 161p. 1999. ring bd. 1610.00 incl. audio compact disk (*0-7418-1959-7*) Icon Grp.

***Labor Market in the Middle East, 1999.** Compiled by Icon Group International. (Illus.). 112p. 1999. ring bd. 1120.00 incl. audio compact disk (*0-7418-1974-0*) Icon Grp.

Labor Market Institutions in Europe: A Socioeconomic Evaluation of Performance. Gunther Schmid. LC 93-47020. (Labor & Human Resources Ser.). 304p. (gr. 13). 1994. pap. text 24.95 (*1-56324-412-8*) M E Sharpe.

Labor Market Institutions in Europe: A Socioeconomic Evaluation of Performance. Ed. by Gunther Schmid. LC 93-47020. (Labor & Human Resources Ser.). 304p. (gr. 13). 1994. text 81.95 (*1-56324-411-X*) M E Sharpe.

Labor Market Planning to Serve the Developmentally Disabled: A Literature Review & Bibliography. Robert A. Beauregard & Bernard P. Indik. 1977. 8.00 (*0-686-19116-1*, 1258-1259, Sage Prdcls Pr) Sage.

Labor Market Politics & the Great War: The Department of Labor, the States, & the First U. S. Employment Service, 1907-1933. William J. Breen. LC 96-36067. 1997. 35.00 (*0-87338-559-4*) Kent St U Pr.

Labor Market Reform & Job Creation: The Unfinished Agenda in Latin America. L. Luis Guasch. LC 98-53590. 124p. 1999. 22.00 (*0-8213-4415-3*) World Bank.

Labor Market Segmentation & Its Implications: Inequality, Deprivation & Entitlement. Dahlia Moore. LC 91-23810. (Library of Sociology: Vol. 21). 356p. 1992. text 25.00 (*0-8240-6994-3*, 665) Garland.

Labor Markets & Integrating National Economies. Ronald G. Ehrenberg. LC 94-14187. (Integrating National Economies: Promise & Pitfalls Ser.). 126p. (C). 1994. 34.95 (*0-8157-2256-7*); pap. 14.95 (*0-8157-2257-5*) Brookings.

Labor Markets & Social Policy in Central & Eastern Europe: The Transition & Beyond. Ed. by Nicholas Barr. (World Bank Publication). (Illus.). 406p. 1994. pap. text 24.95 (*0-19-520998-2*, 60998) OUP.

Labor Markets & Social Policy in Central & Eastern Europe: The Transition & Beyond - Summary. Ed. by Nicholas Barr. 48p. 1994. pap. 22.00 (*0-8213-3002-0*, 13002); pap. 22.00 (*0-8213-3003-9*, 13003); pap. 22.00 (*0-8213-3004-7*, 13004); pap. 22.00 (*0-8213-3005-5*, 13005); pap. 22.00 (*0-8213-3006-3*, 13006); pap. 22.00 (*0-8213-3007-1*, 13007); pap. 22.00 (*0-8213-3008-X*, 13008) World Bank.

Labor Markets & Social Security: Wage Costs, Social Security Financing & Labor Market Reforms in Europe. Ed. by John T. Addison & Paul J. Welfens. LC 97-47707. (Illus.). x, 389p. 1998. 99.00 (*3-540-63784-2*) Spr-Verlag.

Labor Markets in a Global Economy: An Introduction. Ingrid H. Rima. LC 95-41943. (Illus.). 416p. (C). (gr. 13). 1996. text 79.95 (*0-87332-737-3*); pap. text 36.95 (*0-87332-738-1*) M E Sharpe.

Labor Markets in Action: Essays in Empirical Economics. Richard B. Freeman. (Illus.). 368p. 1990. 44.50 (*0-674-50675-8*) HUP.

Labor Markets in an Era of Adjustment, 2 vols., 1. Sue Horton et al. LC 93-34978. (EDI Development Studies). 400p. 1994. pap. 24.00 (*0-8213-2680-5*, 12680) World Bank.

Labor Markets in an Era of Adjustment, 2 vols., 2. Sue Horton et al. LC 93-34978. (EDI Development Studies). 640p. 1994. pap. 34.00 (*0-8213-2681-3*, 12681) World Bank.

Labor Markets in Latin America: Combining Social Protection with Market Flexibility. Ed. by Sebastian Edwards & Nora Lustig. LC 97-22909. 334p. 1997. text 49.95 (*0-8157-2106-4*); pap. text 19.95 (*0-8157-2107-2*) Brookings.

Labor Markets in Transition - International Dimensions. Thomas Donley & M. Oppenheimer. (International Review of Comparative Public Policy Ser.: Vol. 10). 320p. 1999. 78.50 (*0-7623-0375-1*) Jai Pr.

Labor Markets in Transition in Central & Eastern Europe 1989-1995. Christine Allison & Dena Ringold. LC 96-37183. (Technical Papers: No. 352). 80p. 1996. pap. 22.00 (*0-8213-3834-X*) World Bank.

Labor Mediation Trainee. Jack Rudman. (Career Examination Ser.: C-2851). 1994. pap. 34.95 (*0-8373-2851-9*) Nat Learn.

Labor Mediator. Jack Rudman. (Career Examination Ser.: C-2850). 1994. pap. 39.95 (*0-8373-2850-0*) Nat Learn.

Labor Migration in the Atlantic Economies: The European & North American Working Classes During the Period of Industrialization, 16. Dirk Hoerder. LC 85-7975. (Contributions in Labor History Ser.: No. 16). (Illus.). 491p. 1985. 79.50 (*0-313-24637-8*, HLM/) Greenwood.

Labor Mobility: Studies of Labor Turnover & Migration in the Swedish Market. Bertil Holmlund. 208p. (Orig.). 1984. pap. text 71.50 (*91-7204-206-0*) Coronet Bks.

Labor Mobility & Economic Opportunity. Pref. by Paul Webbink. LC 86-25763. 125p. 1987. reprint ed. lib. bdg. 55.00 (*0-313-24975-X*, BALM, Greenwood Pr) Greenwood.

Labor Mobility & Population in Agriculture. Iowa State University of Science & Technology, Cen. LC 74-7535. 231p. 1977. reprint ed. lib. bdg. 65.00 (*0-8371-7584-4*, IOLM, Greenwood Pr) Greenwood.

Labor Monopolies, or Freedom. John W. Scoville. LC 71-172229. (Right Wing Individualist Tradition in America Ser.). 1972. reprint ed. 17.95 (*0-405-00437-0*) Ayer.

Labor Movement: Its Conservative Functions & Social Consequences. Frank Tannenbaum. LC 70-89765. (American Labor, from Conspiracy to Collective Bargaining Ser., No. 1: No. 1). 1974. reprint ed. 19.95 (*0-405-02153-4*) Ayer.

Labor Movement: The Problem of Today: The History, Purpose & Possibilities of Labor Organizations in Europe & America. Ed. by George E. McNeill. LC 66-21683. (Library of American Labor History). (Illus.). x, 639p. 1971. reprint ed. 65.00 (*0-678-00713-6*) Kelley.

Labor Movement in a Government Industry: A Study of Employee Organization in the Postal Service. Sterling D. Spero. LC 73-156425. (American Labor Ser., No. 2). 1977. reprint ed. 23.95 (*0-405-02943-8*) Ayer.

Labor Movement in America. Richard T. Ely. LC 74-89731. (American Labor, from Conspiracy to Collective Bargaining Ser., No. 1). 399p. 1974. reprint ed. 21.95 (*0-405-02119-4*) Ayer.

Labor Movement in Fiction & Non-Fiction, 86 vols., Set. write for info. (*0-404-58400-4*) AMS Pr.

Labor Movements & Dictatorships: The Southern Cone in Comparative Perspective. Paul W. Drake. LC 96-790. 240p. 1996. text 47.50 (*0-8018-5326-5*); pap. text 15.95 (*0-8018-5327-3*) Johns Hopkins.

Labor Movements & Labor Thought: Spain, France, Germany & the United States. Sima Lieberman. LC 85-16859. 302p. 1985. 69.50 (*0-275-90214-5*, C0214, Praeger Pubs) Greenwood.

***Labor of Development: Workers & the Transformation of Capitalism in Kerala, India.** Patrick Heller. LC 99-43546. 2000. pap. text 19.95 (*0-8014-8624-6*) Cornell U Pr.

Labor of Dionysus: A Critique of the State-Form. Michael Hardt & Antonio Negri. LC 93-23422. (Theory out of Bounds Ser.: Vol. 4). 1994. pap. 24.95 (*0-8166-2086-5*) U of Minn Pr.

Labor of Love. Marcia Tucker. LC 95-72645. (Illus.). 96p. (Orig.). 1996. pap. 20.00 (*0-915557-79-7*) New Mus Contemp Art.

***Labor of Love: A Baby's Lullabye.** Mary A. Dockstader. (Illus.). 24p. 1999. pap. write for info. (*0-9668751-1-7*) Tadd Instruct.

Labor of Love: Building an Enduring Romance in Your Marriage. Timothy L. Hall. 144p. 1996. pap. 9.99 (*0-8254-2848-3*) Kregel.

Labor of Love: Critical Reflections on the Writings of Marie-Catherine Desjardins (Mme de Villedieu) Roxanne D. Lalande. LC 99-33242. 224p. 2000. 37.50 (*0-8386-3824-4*) Fairleigh Dickinson.

Labor of Love: How to Write a Eulogy. 2nd rev. ed. Garry Schaeffer. 95p. 1998. pap. 9.95 (*0-9645780-1-8*) GMS Pub.

Labor of Love: Mothers Share the Joy of Childbirth. Judith Zimmer. LC 96-35910. 242p. 1997. pap. 14.95 (*0-471-15703-1*) Wiley.

Labor of Love: The Life & Art of Vinnie Ream. Glenn V. Sherwood. LC 96-70938. (Illus.). 456p. 1997. 60.00 (*0-9615743-6-4*) SunShine CO.

Labor of Love: The Perfect Pregnancy Planner. Janet Bartlett & Barbara McHale. 65p. 1993. spiral bd. 7.95 (*0-9629092-0-3*) Heart-Bound Bks.

Labor of Love, Labor of Sorrow. Jacqueline Jones. 1986. pap. 10.95 (*0-394-74414-4*) Vin Bks.

Labor of Love, Labor of Sorrow: Black Women, Work & the Family from Slavery to the Present. Jacqueline Jones. 448p. 1986. pap. 15.00 (*0-394-74536-1*) Vin Bks.

Labor of Women in the Production of Cotton. Ed. by Dan C. McCurry et al. LC 74-30616. (American Farmers & the Rise of Agribusiness Ser.). (Illus.). 1975. reprint ed. 28.95 (*0-405-06761-5*) Ayer.

Labor on the Illinois Central Railroad, 1852-1900: The Evolution of an Industrial Environment. David L. Lightner. Ed. by Stuart Bruchey. LC 76-39834. (Nineteen Seventy-Seven Dissertations Ser.). (Illus.). 1977. lib. bdg. 36.95 (*0-405-09914-2*) Ayer.

Labor on the Land: Collected Writings, 1936-1970. Paul S. Taylor. 1981. 30.95 (*0-405-14208-0*) Ayer.

Labor on the March. Edward Levinson. (Literature of American Labor Ser.). 344p. 1995. pap. text 17.95 (*0-87546-340-1*, ILR Press) Cornell U Pr.

Labor on the March. Edward Levinson. 329p. 1993. reprint ed. lib. bdg. 89.00 (*0-7812-5249-0*) Rprt Serv.

Labor Organization in the United States & Mexico: A History of Their Relations, 13. Harvey A. Levenstein. LC 79-133498. 258p. 1971. 59.95 (*0-8371-5151-1*, LLO/, Greenwood Pr) Greenwood.

***Labor Organizations of the Reich.** deluxe ed. J. R. Angolia & David Littlejohn. (Illus.). 560p. 1999. 54.95 (*0-912138-76-9*) Bender Pub CA.

***Labor Pain: A Natural Approach to Easing Delivery.** Nicky Wesson. LC 99-461974. 160p. 2000. pap. 12.95 (*0-89281-895-6*) Inner Tradit.

Labor Pains & Labor Power: Women & Childbearing in India. Patricia Jeffery et al. LC 88-29346. 192p. (C). 1989. text 25.00 (*0-86232-485-8*) St Martin.

Labor Parties in Postindustrial Societies. Ed. by Francis F. Pixen. (Europe & the International Order Ser.). 304p. (C). 1992. text 56.95 (*0-19-520926-5*); pap. text 23.95 (*0-19-520927-3*) OUP.

Labor Peacemaker: The Life & Works of Father Leo. C. Brown, S. J. Gladys W. Gruenberg. Ed. by George E. Ganss. LC 80-83552. (Original Studies Composed in English III: No. 4). (Illus.). xiv, 162p. 1981. 4.25 (*0-912422-54-8*); pap. 3.00 (*0-912422-52-1*) Inst Jesuit.

Labor Policies of the National Association of Manufacturers. Albion G. Taylor. LC 73-2536. (Big Business; Economic Power in a Free Society Ser.). 1973. reprint ed. 15.95 (*0-405-05114-X*) Ayer.

Labor Policy of the Free Society. Sylvester Petro. LC 57-6822. 352p. reprint ed. 109.20 (*0-8357-9524-1*, 201236800081) Bks Demand.

Labor Policy of the United States Steel Corporation. Charles A. Gulick, Jr. LC 68-57568. (Columbia University. Studies in the Social Sciences: No. 258). reprint ed. 20.00 (*0-404-51258-5*) AMS Pr.

Labor Politics: Collected Pamphlets, 2 vols., Set. Ed. by Leon Stein & Philip Taft. LC 78-156429. (American Labor, Ser. 2). 1971. 72.95 (*0-405-02952-7*) Ayer.

Labor Politics: Collected Pamphlets, 2 vols., Vol. 1. Ed. by Leon Stein & Philip Taft. LC 78-156429. (American Labor, Ser. 2). 1974. 36.95 (*0-405-02953-5*) Ayer.

Labor Politics: Collected Pamphlets, 2 vols., Vol. 2. Ed. by Leon Stein & Philip Taft. LC 78-156429. (American Labor, Ser. 2). 1974. 36.95 (*0-405-02954-3*) Ayer.

Labor Politics American Style: California Federation of Labor. Philip Taft. LC 68-15644. (Wertheim Publications in Industrial Relations). 296p. 1968. 29.95 (*0-674-50800-9*) HUP.

Labor Politics in a Democratic Republic: Moderation, Division, & Disruption in the Presidential Election of 1928. Vaughn D. Bornet. (Illus.). xviii, 376p. 1996. reprint ed. 15.00 (*0-9632366-3-6*) Bornet Bks.

Labor Problem: Plain Questions & Practical Answers. Ed. by William E. Barnes. LC 75-156404. (American Labor Ser., No. 2). 1977. reprint ed. 19.95 (*0-405-02914-4*) Ayer.

Labor Problems: A Book of Materials for Their Study. Edgar S. Furniss & Laurence R. Guild. LC 71-89733. (American Labor, from Conspiracy to Collective Bargaining Ser., No. 1). 621p. 1977. reprint ed. 37.95 (*0-405-02122-4*) Ayer.

Labor Problems in the Pacific Mandates. John A. Decker. LC 75-30053. (Institute of Pacific Relations Ser.). reprint ed. 47.50 (*0-404-59517-0*) AMS Pr.

Labor Productivity. Peter Chinloy. (Illus.). 160p. 1982. text 32.00 (*0-89011-561-3*) Abt Bks.

Labor Productivity Control: New Approaches for Industrial Engineers & Managers. John C. Martin. LC 90-7449. 320p. 1990. 69.50 (*0-275-93663-5*, C3663, Praeger Pubs) Greenwood.

Labor Productivity in Soviet & American Industry. Walter Galenson. LC 76-49596. 273p. 1977. reprint ed. lib. bdg. 35.00 (*0-8371-9370-2*, GALPS, Greenwood Pr) Greenwood.

Labor Program Administrator. (Career Examination Ser.). 1997. pap. 39.95 (*0-8373-3805-0*, C3805) Nat Learn.

An Asterisk (*) at the beginning of an entry indicates that the title is appearing for the first time.

Labor Progress Handbook: Early Interventions to Prevent & Treat Dystocia. Penny Simkin et al. LC 99-25452. (Illus.). 2000. pap. 29.95 (*0-632-05281-3*) Blackwell Sci.

Labor Prosperity in the '90's. Michael Costa & Mark Duffy. 180p. 1991. pap. 28.00 (*1-86287-060-8*, Pub. by Federation Pr) Gaunt.

***Labor Regulation in a Global Economy.** George Tsogas. (Issues in Work & Human Resources Ser.). (Illus.). 216p. 2000. text 64.95 (*0-7656-0557-0*) M E Sharpe.

Labor Relation Law: Cases & Materials, 1993 Cumulative Supplement. Merrifield et al. 1994. write for info. (*1-55834-116-1*, 13122-10, MICHIE) LEXIS Pub.

Labor Relation Law: Cases & Materials, 1997 Cumulative Supplement. Merrifield et al. 136p. 1997. pap. text 11.00 (*1-55834-262-1*, 13122-13, MICHIE) LEXIS Pub.

Labor Relations. John Fossum. (C). 1978. 35.95 (*0-256-02088-4*, Irwn McGrw-H) McGrw-H Hghr Educ.

Labor Relations. Jack Rudman. (ACT Proficiency Examination Program (PEP) Ser.: Vol. 22). 43.95 (*0-8373-5572-9*) Nat Learn.

Labor Relations. Jack Rudman. (ACT Proficiency Examination Program Ser.: PEP-22). 1994. pap. 23.95 (*0-8373-5522-2*) Nat Learn.

Labor Relations. 2nd ed. Robert L. Sauer. 580p. 1992. 70.60 (*0-02-406250-2*, Macmillan Coll) P-H.

Labor Relations. 6th ed. William H. Holley. (C). 1996. pap. text, teacher ed. 49.50 (*0-03-018013-9*) Harcourt Coll Pubs.

Labor Relations. 9th ed. Arthur A. Sloane & Fred Witney. LC 96-13390. 542p. (C). 1996. 91.00 (*0-13-256728-8*) P-H.

Labor Relations: Development, Structure, Process. 6th ed. John A. Fossum. LC 94-34790. 592p. (C). 1994. text 69.95 (*0-256-13610-6*, Irwn McGrw-H) McGrw-H Hghr Educ.

Labor Relations: Development, Structure, Process. 7th ed. John A. Fossum. LC 98-23634. 1999. write for info. (*0-256-23887-1*, Irwn Prfssnl) McGraw-Hill Prof.

Labor Relations: Japanese Business Novel. Kazuo Watanabe. Ed. by Tamae Prindle. 144p. (C). 1994. lib. bdg. 34.50 (*0-8191-9304-6*) U Pr of Amer.

Labor Relations: Law, Practice & Policy. Julius G. Getman & John D. Blackburn. LC 82-21042. 108p. 1988. reprint ed. pap. text, suppl. ed. write for info. (*0-88277-165-5*) Foundation Pr.

Labor Relations: Law, Practice & Policy. 2nd ed. Julius G. Getman & John D. Blackburn. LC 82-21042. 756p. 1989. reprint ed. text 32.95 (*0-88277-102-7*) Foundation Pr.

Labor Relations: Process & Outcomes. Marcus Sandver. (C). 1995. 58.00 (*0-02-405902-1*, Macmillan Coll) P-H.

Labor Relations: The Basic Processes, Law & Practice. Julius G. Getman & Bertrand B. Pogrebin. (University Textbook Ser.). 396p. 1988. text 25.95 (*0-88277-652-5*) Foundation Pr.

Labor Relations Analyst. Jack Rudman. (Career Examination Ser.: C-3457). 1994. pap. 39.95 (*0-8373-3457-8*) Nat Learn.

***Labor Relations & Collective Bargaining.** 6th ed. 2000. teacher ed. write for info. (*0-13-019604-5*) P-H.

Labor Relations & Collective Bargaining: A Bibliographic Guide to Doctoral Research. Milden J. Fox, Jr. & Patsy C. Howard. LC 83-4612. 297p. 1983. 29.00 (*0-8108-1632-6*) Scarecrow.

***Labor Relations & Collective Bargaining: Cases , Practices, & Law.** 6th ed. Michael Carrell & Christina Heavrin. 640p. 2000. 85.33 (*0-13-019474-3*, Prentice Hall) P-H.

Labor Relations & Collective Bargaining: Cases, Practices & Law. 5th ed. Michael Carrell & Christina Heavrin. LC 97-24221. 606p. (C). 1997. 87.00 (*0-13-768607-2*) P-H.

Labor Relations & Political Change in Eastern Europe: A Comparative Perspective. John Thirkell et al. LC 95-8844. (ILR Press Book Ser.: No.28). 224p. 1995. 39.95 (*0-87546-708-3*, ILR Press) Cornell U Pr.

Labor Relations & the Law. M. Ali Raza & A. Janell Anderson. LC 95-52840. 1996. write for info. (*0-614-95869-5*) P-H.

Labor Relations & the Litigation Explosion. Robert J. Flanagan. LC 87-6404. 122p. 1987. 32.95 (*0-8157-2858-1*); pap. 12.95 (*0-8157-2857-3*) Brookings.

Labor Relations Assistant. Jack Rudman. (Career Examination Ser.: C-1338). 1994. pap. 29.95 (*0-8373-1338-4*) Nat Learn.

Labor Relations at the "New York Daily News" Peripheral Bargaining & the 1990 Strike. Kenneth M. Jennings. LC 93-295. 232p. 1993. 57.95 (*0-275-94587-1*, C4587, Praeger Pubs) Greenwood.

Labor Relations in a Changing Environment. Ed. by Alan Gladstone. xiv, 437p. (C). 1991. lib. bdg. 144.65 (*3-11-012604-4*, 269-91) De Gruyter.

Labor Relations in Education: An International Perspective, 54. Ed. by Bruce S. Cooper. LC 91-37121. (Contributions to the Study of Education Ser.: No. 54). 384p. 1992. 65.00 (*0-313-26707-3*, CIH/, Greenwood Pr) Greenwood.

Labor Relations in Europe: A History of Issues & Developments, 29. Hans Slomp. LC 89-23262. (Contributions in Labor Studies: No. 29). 241p. 1990. 55.00 (*0-313-26756-1*, SLQ/, Greenwood Pr) Greenwood.

Labor Relations in Hospitals & Health Care Facilities: Proceedings of a Conference Presented by the American Arbitration Association & the Federal Mediation & Conciliation Service, 1975. Ed. by A. E. Berkeley & Ann Barnes. LC 75-45236. 110p. reprint ed. pap. 34.10 (*0-608-12567-9*, 202397200035) Bks Demand.

Labor Relations in Professional Sports. Robert C. Berry, IV et al. LC 85-26806. 302p. (C). 1986. 57.95 (*0-86569-137-1*, Auburn Hse) Greenwood.

Labor Relations in the Federal Government Service. Murray B. Nesbitt. LC 75-44255. 559p. reprint ed. pap. 173.30 (*0-608-14107-0*, 202430600036) Bks Demand.

Labor Relations in the Lithographic Industry. Fred C. Munson. LC 63-10872. (Wertheim Publications in Industrial Relations). (Illus.). 290p. 1963. 14.95 (*0-674-50850-5*) HUP.

Labor Relations in the Motor Industry. Herbert A. Turner et al. LC 67-83828. 395p. 1967. 45.00 (*0-678-06027-4*) Kelley.

Labor Relations in the Public Sector. 2nd enl. rev. ed. Richard C. Kearney. LC 92-1579. (Public Administration & Public Policy Ser.: Vol. 47). (Illus.). 480p. 1992. text 69.75 (*0-8247-8743-9*) Dekker.

Labor Relations in the Public Sector: Cases - Material Statistics Appendix. Edwards et al. 1984. pap. text 11.00 (*0-87215-892-6*, 11308-10, MICHIE) LEXIS Pub.

Labor Relations Law. 7th ed. Benjamin J. Taylor & Fred Witney. LC 94-48750. 518p. (C). 1995. 60.80 (*0-13-209900-4*) P-H.

Labor Relations Law: Cases & Materials. 175p. 1998. pap. text, suppl. ed. write for info. (*0-327-00275-1*, 13122-14) LEXIS Pub.

Labor Relations Law: Cases & Materials. 9th ed. Leroy S. Merrifield et al. LC 94-75594. (Contemporary Legal Education Ser.). xxii, 1040 p. 1994. write for info. (*1-55834-138-2*) LEXIS Pub.

Labor Relations Law: Cases & Materials. 10th ed. Charles B. Craver et al. LC 99-60689. 1200p. 1999. text 56.00 (*0-327-00929-2*, 1311712) LEXIS Pub.

Labor Relations Law: 92 Cumulative Supplement. 8th ed. Merrifield et al. 107p. 1992. write for info. (*0-87473-668-4*, 13121-10, MICHIE) LEXIS Pub.

Labor Relations Law in State & Local Government. David A. Dilts et al. LC 92-8405. 208p. 1992. 55.00 (*0-89930-414-1*, DSL, Quorum Bks) Greenwood.

Labor Relations Law in the Public Sector. 4th ed. Harry T. Edwards et al. (Contemporary Legal Education Ser.). 1191p. 1991. 48.00 (*0-87473-768-0*, 13114-10, MICHIE) LEXIS Pub.

Labor Relations Law, Selected Federal Statutes & Sample Bargaining Agreement, 1999 Edition: Selected Federal Statutes & Sample Bargaining Agreement. Charles B. Craver et al. LC 99-60690. 150p. (Orig.). 1999. pap. 15.00 (*0-327-00936-5*, 1311812) LEXIS Pub.

Labor Relations Process. 6th ed. William H. Holley & Kenneth M. Jennings. LC 96-83790. 738p. (C). 1996. text 101.50 (*0-03-018009-0*) Dryden Pr.

Labor Relations Representative. Jack Rudman. (Career Examination Ser.: C-3310). 1994. pap. 29.95 (*0-8373-3310-5*) Nat Learn.

Labor Relations Strategic Guidebook: Practical Techniques for Managing Workplace Issues. Stephen Cabot. 1988. pap. 29.95 (*0-88057-868-8*) Exec Ent Pubns.

Labor Relations Technician. Jack Rudman. (Career Examination Ser.: C-3215). 1994. pap. 29.95 (*0-8373-3215-X*) Nat Learn.

Labor Relations, WWII, Before, During & After: The Autobiography of a One Eyed Jack. Jack L. Rugh. LC 92-93266. (Illus.). 256p. (C). 1992. pap. 25.00 (*0-9632479-4-8*) J L Rugh.

Labor Relations Yearbook, 1979. Bureau of National Affairs Staff. LC 66-19726. 558p. pap. 173.00 (*0-608-14105-4*, 202430800037) Bks Demand.

Labor Rights in Haiti. Lance Compa. 52p. 1989. pap. 5.00 (*1-880103-01-X*) Intl Labor Rghts.

***Labor Rules for the Construction Industry 2000.** 27th ed. R. S. Means Company Staff. 326p. 1999. pap. 189.95 (*0-87629-563-4*) R S Means.

Labor Safety Technician. Jack Rudman. (Career Examination Ser.: C-1595). 1994. pap. 29.95 (*0-8373-1595-6*) Nat Learn.

Labor Savings in American Industry, 1899-1939. Solomon Fabricant. (Occasional Papers: No. 23). 56p. 1945. reprint ed. 20.00 (*0-87014-338-7*) Natl Bur Econ Res.

Labor Services Representative. (Career Examination Ser.: C-3773). pap. 29.95 (*0-8373-3773-9*) Nat Learn.

Labor Shortages: Myth or Reality? Malcolm S. Cohen. LC 94-36244. 200p. 1995. text 49.50 (*0-472-10353-9*, 10353) U of Mich Pr.

***Labor, Solidarity & the Common Good.** S. A. Cortright. LC 00-36106. 2000. write for info. (*0-89089-722-0*) Carolina Acad Pr.

***Labor, Solidarity & the Common Good: Essays on the Ethical Foundations of Management.** Ed. by S. A. Cortright. 168p. 2000. write for info. (*0-89089-718-2*) Carolina Acad Pr.

Labor Songs. Diane Raptosh. LC 97-72802. (Essential Poets Ser.: Vol. 78). 80p. 1999. pap. 10.00 (*1-55071-059-1*) Guernica Editions.

Labor Specialist. Jack Rudman. (Career Examination Ser.: C-2146). 1994. reprint ed. pap. 29.95 (*0-8373-2146-8*) Nat Learn.

Labor Standards Investigator. Jack Rudman. (Career Examination Ser.: C-3210). 1994. pap. 27.95 (*0-8373-3210-9*) Nat Learn.

Labor, State & Capital in Nigeria's Oil Industry. Julius O. Ihonvbere. LC 97-51515. 220p. 1998. text 89.95 (*0-7734-9842-7*) E Mellen.

Labor Statistics & Class Struggle. Marc Linder. LC 94-34677. 130p. 1994. pap. 7.50 (*0-7178-0711-8*) Intl Pubs Co.

Labor Statistics Measurement. Haltiwanger. LC 98-22635. Vol. 60. 456p. 1998. 60.00 (*0-226-31458-8*) U Ch Pr.

Labor Strife & the Economy in the 1970's: A Decade of Discord. Michael J. Kapsa. LC 98-39720. (Studies in the History of American Labor). 148p. 1998. 45.00 (*0-8153-3181-9*) Garland.

Labor Struggle in the Post Office: From Selective Lobbying to Collective Bargaining. Garth L. Mangum & John Walsh. LC 91-43910. (Labor & Human Resources). 293p. (C). (gr. 13). 1992. text 70.95 (*1-56324-028-9*) M E Sharpe.

Labor Struggle in the Post Office: From Selective Lobbying to Collective Bargaining. John Walsh & Garth L. Mangum. LC 91-43910. (Labor & Human Resources Ser.). 293p. (gr. 13). 1992. pap. text 40.95 (*1-56324-146-3*) M E Sharpe.

***Labor Struggles in the Deep South & Other Writings.** Covington Hall. Ed. by David R. Roediger. LC 99-54290. (Illus.). 262p. 2000. 24.00 (*0-88286-244-8*, Pub. by C H Kerr); pap. 14.00 (*0-88286-245-6*) C H Kerr.

Labor Support Forms: A Guide to Doula Charting. Cheri B. Grant. Ed. by Dana Blue. 45p. (C). 1994. student ed. 29.95 (*0-9640082-0-3*) M & W Prods.

Labor Technician. Jack Rudman. (Career Examination Ser.: C-1587). 1994. pap. 29.95 (*0-8373-1587-5*) Nat Learn.

Labor Theory of Culture: A Re-Examination of Engels' Theory of Human Origins. Charles Woolfson. 142p. (Orig.). 1982. pap. 15.95 (*0-7100-0997-6*, Routledge Thoemms) Routledge.

Labor Union Elections & Corporate Financial Performance. rev. ed. John W. Moore. LC 94-45049. (Studies on Industrial Productivity). 173p. 1995. text 15.00 (*0-8153-1973-8*) Garland.

Labor Union Theories in America. Mark Perlman. LC 76-8925. 313p. 1976. reprint ed. lib. bdg. 65.00 (*0-8371-8916-0*, PELU, Greenwood Pr) Greenwood.

Labor Unionism in American Agriculture. U. S. Department of Labor, Bureau of Statistics St. Ed. by Dan C. McCurry & Richard E. Rubenstein. LC 74-30656. (American Farmers & the Rise of Agribusiness Ser.). 1975. reprint ed. 46.95 (*0-405-06831-X*) Ayer.

Labor Unionism in American Agriculture: U. S. Department of Labor, Bulletin No. 836. Stuart Jamieson. Ed. by Carlos E. Cortes. LC 76-1285. (Chicano Heritage Ser.). 1977. reprint ed. 39.95 (*0-405-09508-2*) Ayer.

Labor Unions, 1. Gary M. Fink. LC 76-8734. (Encyclopedia of American Institutions Ser.). 520p. 1977. lib. bdg. 50.95 (*0-8371-8938-1*, FLU/, Greenwood Pr) Greenwood.

Labor Unions & the Economic Performance of Firms. Barry T. Hirsch. LC 91-2576. 142p. 1991. text 33.00 (*0-88099-109-7*); pap. text 14.00 (*0-88099-110-0*) W E Upjohn.

Labor Up-Front in the People's Fight Against the Crisis. Gus Hall. LC 79-26569. 119p. reprint ed. pap. 36.90 (*0-608-12015-4*, 202286200030) Bks Demand.

Labor Visions & State Power: Origins of Business Unionism in the U. S. 1806-1896. Victoria C. Hattam. (Studies in American Politics: Historical, International, & Comparative Perspectives). 280p. 1992. pap. text 16.95 (*0-691-00109-X*, Pub. by Princeton U Pr) Cal Prin Full Svc.

Labor Wars in Cordoba, 1955-1976: Ideology, Work, & Labor Politics in an Argentine Industrial City. James P. Brennan. LC 93-46839. (Harvard Historical Studies: No. 116). 448p. (C). 1994. text 59.95 (*0-674-50851-3*, BRELAB) HUP.

Labor Will Rule: Sidney Hillman & the Rise of American Labor. Steven Fraser. 704p. 1993. pap. text 17.95 (*0-8014-8126-0*) Cornell U Pr.

Labor, Worklife & Industrial Relations: Sources of Information. Ed. by Peter B. Allison. LC 84-4539. (Behavioral & Social Sciences Librarian Ser.: Vol. 3, No. 3). 128p. 1984. text 39.95 (*0-86656-317-2*) Haworth Pr.

Laborare Fratres in Unum. Ed. by David Hiley & Janka Szendrei. (Spolia Berolinensia Ser.: Vol. 7). (GER.). xv, 350p. 1995. write for info. (*3-615-00171-0*) G Olms Pubs.

Laboratoire Central. M. Jacob. (FRE.). 1980. pap. 10.95 (*0-8288-3862-3*, F106210) Fr & Eur.

Laboratories. 1992. 36.00 (*0-86022-385-X*, Pub. by Build Servs Info Assn) St Mut.

Laboratories: A Briefing & Design Guide. Walter Hain. (Briefing & Design Guides Ser.). (Illus.). 144p. (Orig.). (C). 1994. pap. 65.00 (*0-419-19480-0*, E & FN Spon) Routledge.

***Laboratories: A Guide to Planning, Programming & Design.** Fernand W. Dahan. (Illus.). 2000. 100.00 (*0-393-73058-1*) Norton.

Laboratories & Research Facilities. Meisei Publications Editorial Staff. (New Concept in Architecture & Design Ser.). (Illus.). 320p. 1997. 85.00 (*4-938812-25-8*, Pub. by Puroto Gyarak) Bks Nippan.

Laboratories for a Second Course in Computer Science: ANSI Pascal Version. Beverly Jamison et al. LC 93-21450. 1993. mass mkt. 28.95 (*0-534-93901-5*) PWS Pubs.

Laboratories for Parallel Programming. Christopher H. Nevison et al. LC 93-46893. (Computer Science: Artificial Intelligence Ser.). 352p. (C). 1994. spiral bd. 45.00 (*0-86720-470-2*) Jones & Bartlett.

Laboratories in Fiction: Science Education & Popular Media. Noel Gough. 139p. 1993. 105.00 (*0-7300-1605-6*, ECS810, Pub. by Deakin Univ) St Mut.

Laboratories in Mathematical Experimentation: A Bridge Course to Higher Mathematics. Harriet S. Pollatsek & Donal O'Shea. LC 96-37621. (TIMS - Texts in Mathematical Science Ser.). (Illus.). 300p. 1997. pap. 34.95 (*0-387-94922-4*) Spr-Verlag.

Laboratories of Democracy: A New Breed of Governor Creates Models for National Growth. David Osborne. 407p. 1988. pap. 16.95 (*0-87584-233-X*) Harvard Busn.

Laboratories of Virtue: Punishment, Revolution, & Authority in Philadelphia, 1760-1835. Michael Meranze. LC 95-45117. (Published for the Institute of Early American History & Culture Ser.). 384p. (C). 1996. text 19.95 (*0-8078-2277-9*) U of NC Pr.

Laboratories Using Mathematica - Calculus. 6th ed. Swokowski & Michael Olinick. (Mathematics Ser.). 1994. mass mkt. 27.75 (*0-534-93641-5*) PWS Pubs.

***Laboratories, Workshops & Sites - Concepts & Practices of Research in Industrial Europe, 1800-1914.** Robert Fox & Anna Guagnini. LC 99-63056. (Berkeley Papers in History of Science: Vol. 18). (Illus.). 200p. 1999. pap. 24.00 (*0-9672617-0-8*) U Cal Hist Sci Tech.

L

***Laboratorio Zoologia, 1.** (C). 2000. write for info. (*0-8087-5136-0*) Pearson Custom.

Laboratoriumsdiagnostik: Normalbereich der Ergebnisse und Interpretation Abnormer Befunde. 3rd ed. Ed. by E. Deutsch et al. (Illus.). x, 1168p. 1991. 71.50 (*3-8055-5487-7*) S Karger.

Laboratoreis, LB 13-85. Ed. by BSRIA Staff. (C). 1985. 85.00 (*0-86022-132-6*, Pub. by Build Servs Info Assn) St Mut.

Laboratory Accreditation & Data Certification: A Guide for Successful Laboratories. Carla H. Dempsey & James D. Petty. 256p. 1991. lib. bdg. 119.00 (*0-87371-291-9*, L291) Lewis Pubs.

Laboratory Acquired Infection. Collins1 & Kennedy. LC 98-32458. 336p. 1999. text 105.00 (*0-7506-4023-5*) Buttrwrth-Heinemann.

Laboratory-Acquired Infections: History, Incidence, Causes, & Prevention. 3rd ed. C. H. Collins. LC 92-45169. (Illus.). 274p. 1993. pap. 70.00 (*0-7506-0642-8*) Buttrwrth-Heinemann.

Laboratory Activities for Life Span Motor Development. 2nd ed. Kathleen M. Haywood. (Illus.). 168p. 1993. spiral bd. 23.00 (*0-87322-489-2*, BHAY0489) Human Kinetics.

Laboratory Activities for Therapeutic Modalities. 2nd ed. Sara D. Brown & Chad Starkey. (Illus.). 171p. 1998. pap. 23.95 (*0-8036-0353-3*) Davis Co.

Laboratory Activities/Human Anatomy. Leigh Callan. 144p. (C). 1995. spiral bd. 17.95 (*0-7872-0607-5*) Kendall-Hunt.

Laboratory Aging of Asphalt-Aggregate Mixtures: Field Validation. C. A. Bell & Alan J. Weider. 204p. (Orig.). (C). 1994. pap. text 15.00 (*0-309-05770-1*, SHRP-A-390) SHRP.

Laboratory Aide. Jack Rudman. (Career Examination Ser.: C-430). 1994. pap. 23.95 (*0-8373-0430-X*) Nat Learn.

Laboratory Anatomy of the Cat. Robert B. Chiasson & William J. Radke. 208p. (C). 1995. text 29.00 (*0-697-24926-3*, WCB McGr Hill) McGrw-H Hghr Educ.

Laboratory Anatomy of the Cat. 8th ed. Robert B. Chiasson & Ernest Booth. 160p. (C). 1988. text. write for info. (*0-697-04934-5*, WCB McGr Hill) McGrw-H Hghr Educ.

Laboratory Anatomy of the Fetal Pig. 9th ed. Theron O. Odlaug & Robert B. Chiasson. 128p. (C). 1992. spiral bd. write for info. (*0-697-11571-2*, WCB McGr Hill) McGrw-H Hghr Educ.

Laboratory Anatomy of the Fetal Pig. 9th ed. Theron O. Odlaug & Robert B. Chiasson. 136p. (C). 1995. text, lab manual ed. write for info. (*0-697-33297-7*, WCB McGr Hill) McGrw-H Hghr Educ.

Laboratory Anatomy of the Fetal Pig. 10th ed. Theron O. Odlaug & Robert B. Chiasson. 160p. (C). 1994. spiral bd. write for info. (*0-697-15984-1*, WCB McGr Hill) McGrw-H Hghr Educ.

Laboratory Anatomy of the Fetal Pig. 11th ed. Theron O. Odlaug & Robert B. Chiasson. LC 96-61077. 160p. (C). 1996. text 31.25 (*0-697-33324-8*, WCB McGr Hill) McGrw-H Hghr Educ.

Laboratory Anatomy of the Frog & Toad. 6th ed. Robert B. Chiasson & Raymond A. Underhill. 80p. (C). 1993. text 23.50 (*0-697-12313-8*, WCB McGr Hill) McGrw-H Hghr Educ.

Laboratory Anatomy of the Human Body. 4th ed. Bernard B. Butterworth. 208p. (C). 1991. text. write for info. (*0-697-05141-2*, WCB McGr Hill) McGrw-H Hghr Educ.

Laboratory Anatomy of the Mink. 2nd ed. David Klingener. (Laboratory Anatomy Ser.). 64p. (C). 1979. spiral bd. write for info. (*0-697-04629-X*, WCB McGr Hill) McGrw-H Hghr Educ.

Laboratory Anatomy of the Perch. 4th ed. Robert B. Chiasson & William J. Radke. 112p. (C). 1991. text. write for info. (*0-697-04939-6*, WCB McGr Hill) McGrw-H Hghr Educ.

Laboratory Anatomy of the Pigeon. 3rd ed. Robert B. Chiasson. (Laboratory Anatomy Ser.). 116p. (C). 1984. text. write for info. (*0-697-04927-2*, WCB McGr Hill) McGrw-H Hghr Educ.

Laboratory Anatomy of the Rabbit. 3rd ed. Charles A. McLaughlin & Robert B. Chiasson. 124p. (C). 1990. text. write for info. (*0-697-04931-0*, WCB McGr Hill) McGrw-H Hghr Educ.

Laboratory Anatomy of the Shark. 5th ed. Laurence M. Ashley & Robert B. Chiasson. 98p. (C). 1988. text. write for info. (*0-697-05121-8*, WCB McGr Hill) McGrw-H Hghr Educ.

Laboratory Anatomy of the Turtle. Laurence M. Ashley. 100p. (C). 1962. text. write for info. (*0-697-04601-X*, WCB McGr Hill) McGrw-H Hghr Educ.

Laboratory Anatomy of the White Rat. 5th ed. Robert B. Chiasson. 144p. (C). 1987. text. write for info. (*0-697-05132-3*, WCB McGr Hill) McGrw-H Hghr Educ.

L

Laboratory & Clinical Dental Materials. 3rd ed. Karl F. Leinfelder & Duane F. Taylor. Ed. by Douglas V. Moor. (Dental Laboratory Technology Manuals Ser.). xiii, 202p. (C). 1982. pap. 34.95 (*0-8078-7906-1*) U of NC Pr.

Laboratory & Diagnostic Procedures with Nursing Diagnoses. 4th ed. Jane Corbett. LC 95-36448. (C). 1995. pap. text 34.95 (*0-8385-5595-0*, A5595-2) Appleton & Lange.

Laboratory & Diagnostic Test Handbook. M.K. Gaedeke. 825p. (C). 1995. pap. text 33.75 (*0-8053-1359-1*) Benjamin-Cummings.

Laboratory & Diagnostic Tests. 5th ed. Joyce L. Kee. LC 98-20408. (C). 1998. pap. text 31.95 (*0-8385-5596-9*) Appleton & Lange.

Laboratory & Diagnostic Tests: A Pocket Guide. Mary E. McMorrow & Louise Malarkey. Ed. by Thomas Eoyang. LC 97-41310. (Illus.). 480p. 1997. pap. text 19.95 (*0-7216-7303-1*, W B Saunders Co) Harcrt Hlth Sci Grp.

Laboratory & Field Exercises in Oceanography. Patricia Deen & Al Trujillo. 1996. spiral bd. 25.00 (*0-88252-204-3*) Paladin Hse.

Laboratory & Field Investigations in Marine Biology. 5th ed. James L. Sumich & Gordon H. Dudley. 208p. (C). 1992. spiral bd. write for info. (*0-697-05107-2*, WCB McGr Hill) McGrw-H Hghr Educ.

Laboratory & Field Investigations in Marine Biology. 6th ed. James L. Sumich & Gordon H. Dudley. 208p. (C). 1995. text. write for info. (*0-697-15999-X*, WCB McGr Hill) McGrw-H Hghr Educ.

Laboratory & Field Manual of Ecology. Richard Brewer & Margaret McCann. 325p. (C). 1982. pap. text 45.00 (*0-03-057879-5*, Pub. by SCP) Harcourt.

Laboratory & Lecture Guide to Human Anatomy. 5th ed. Lillian W. Naumann & Virginia S. Volker. 160p. (C). 1996. spiral bd. 23.04 (*0-7872-2006-X*) Kendall-Hunt.

Laboratory & Radiologic Tests for Primary Eye Care. Gail Burden & Steven A. Bryant. LC 96-18185. 252p. 1996. pap. text 40.00 (*0-7506-9755-5*) Buttrwrth-Heinemann.

Laboratory & Scientific Computing: A Strategic Approach. Joseph G. Liscouski. (Wiley-Interscience Series on Laboratory Automation: Vol. 1). 224p. 1994. 59.95 (*0-471-59422-9*) Wiley.

***Laboratory & Scientific Equipment in Australia: A Strategic Entry Report, 2000.** Compiled by Icon Group International Staff. (Illus.). 131p. 1999. ring bd. 1310.00 incl. audio compact disk (*0-7418-2162-1*) Icon Grp.

***Laboratory & Scientific Equipment in Hong Kong: A Strategic Entry Report, 1996.** Compiled by Icon Group International Staff. (Illus.). 120p. 1999. ring bd. 1200.00 incl. audio compact disk (*0-7418-1289-4*) Icon Grp.

***Laboratory & Scientific Instruments in Mexico: A Strategic Entry Report, 1999.** Compiled by Icon Group International. (Illus.). 157p. 1999. ring bd. 1570.00 incl. audio compact disk (*0-7418-1845-0*) Icon Grp.

Laboratory & Scientific Instruments in Portugal: A Strategic Entry Report, 1997. Compiled by Icon Group International Staff. (Illus.). 102p. 1999. ring bd. 1020.00 incl. audio compact disk (*0-7418-0860-9*) Icon Grp.

***Laboratory & Scientific Instruments in Thailand: A Strategic Entry Report, 1996.** Compiled by Icon Group International Staff. (Illus.). 143p. 1999. ring bd. 1430.00 incl. audio compact disk (*0-7418-1290-8*) Icon Grp.

Laboratory & Space Plasmas. Ed. by Haruhiko Kikuchi. (Illus.). ix, 657p. 1988. 116.95 (*0-387-96839-3*) Spr-Verlag.

***Laboratory & the Poisoned Patient.** John Fenton. 352p. 1998. pap. 49.00 (*1-890883-04-2*, 202025) Am Assn Clinical Chem.

Laboratory Animal Anaesthesia: A Practical Introduction for Research Workers & Technicians. 2nd ed. P. A. Flecknell. (Illus.). 296p. 1996. text 49.95 (*0-12-260361-3*) Acad Pr.

Laboratory Animal Endocrinology: Hormonal Action, Control Mechanisms & Interactions with Drugs. David D. Woodman. LC 97-11248. 576p. 1997. 240.00 (*0-471-97262-2*) Wiley.

Laboratory Animal Houses. 1991. 36.00 (*0-86022-292-6*, Pub. by Build Servs Info Assn) St Mut.

Laboratory Animal Housing: Proceedings of a Symposium Held at Hunt Valley, Maryland, September 22-23, 1976. National Research Council (U. S.) Staff. LC 78-12545. 228p. reprint ed. pap. 70.70 (*0-8357-3450-1*, 203971100013) Bks Demand.

Laboratory Animal Husbandry: Ethology, Welfare, & Experimental Variables. Michael W. Fox. LC 85-9766. 267p. (C). 1986. pap. text 19.95 (*0-88706-138-9*) State U NY Pr.

Laboratory Animal Science: Handbook on the Humane Use & Care of Animals in Research. Ed. by L. F. Van Zutphen et al. LC 93-7467. 404p. 1993. pap. 92.00 (*0-444-81487-6*) Elsevier.

Laboratory Animal Technology. J. K. Inglis. 1988. 153.00 (*0-08-023772-X*, Pub. by Pergamon Repr) Franklin.

Laboratory Animal Welfare: A Guide to Reference Tools, Legal Materials, Organizations & Federal Agencies. Cheryl R. Nyberg et al. LC 95-116433. 391p. 1994. 105.00 (*0-9616293-9-8*) Boast-Nyberg.

Laboratory Animal Welfare Research - Primates. UFAW Staff. (C). 1988. 110.00 (*0-900767-56-1*) St Mut.

Laboratory Animal Welfare Research - Rodents. UFAW Staff. (C). 1989. 90.00 (*0-685-29233-9*) St Mut.

Laboratory Animals: An Introduction for Experiments. 2nd ed. Ed. by A. A. Tuffery. LC 94-48580. 406p. 1995. 175.00 (*0-471-95257-5*) Wiley.

Laboratory Approach to Introductory Calculus. Halpin. (C). 1994. pap. text 16.25 (*0-07-025580-6*) McGraw.

Laboratory Approach to Teaching Calculus. rev. ed. Ed. by L. Carl Leinbach et al. LC 91-62171. (MAA Notes Ser.). 290p. 1991. pap. text 10.00 (*0-88385-074-5*, NTE-20R) Math Assn.

Laboratory Assistant. Jack Rudman. (Career Examination Ser.: C-1879). 1994. reprint ed. pap. 27.95 (*0-8373-1879-3*) Nat Learn.

Laboratory Assistant (Bacteriology) Jack Rudman. (Career Examination Ser.: C-431). 1994. pap. 27.95 (*0-8373-0431-8*) Nat Learn.

Laboratory Assistant (Chemistry) Jack Rudman. (Career Examination Ser.: C-432). 1994. pap. 27.95 (*0-8373-0432-6*) Nat Learn.

Laboratory Astronomy: Experiments & Exercises. Anthony J. Nicastro. 208p. (C). 1989. text. write for info. (*0-697-08475-2*, WCB McGr Hill) McGrw-H Hghr Educ.

Laboratory Astrophysics & Space Research. Ed. by P. Ehrendfreud et al. LC 98-44100. (Astrophysics & Space Science Library: Vol. 236). 685p. 1998. 299.00 (*0-7923-5338-2*, QB461) Kluwer Academic.

Laboratory Atlas of Anatomy & Physiology. 2nd ed. Eder et al. 1997. pap. 18.74 (*0-697-39480-8*, WCB McGr Hill) McGrw-H Hghr Educ.

***Laboratory Atlas of Anatomy & Physiology.** 3rd ed. Douglas J. Eder et al. LC 00-38014. 2001. write for info. (*0-07-290755-X*) McGraw.

Laboratory Automation. David Savage. pap. text. write for info. (*0-471-36372-3*) Wiley.

Laboratory Automation Technologies in Germany: A Strategic Entry Report, 1997. Compiled by Icon Group International Staff. (Illus.). 99p. 1999. ring bd. 990.00 incl. audio compact disk (*0-7418-1043-3*) Icon Grp.

Laboratory Basis for Anesthesiology. G. Dal Santo. 764p. 1993. text 60.00 (*1-57235-009-1*, Pub. by Piccin Nuova) Gordon & Breach.

Laboratory Basis for Anesthesiology. G. Dal Santo. (Illus.). 764p. 1993. text 66.00 (*88-299-1018-X*, Pub. by Piccin Nuova) Gordon & Breach.

Laboratory Biosafety Manual. 2nd ed. (CHI, ENG, FRE & SPA.). xi, 133p. 1993. pap. text 26.00 (*92-4-154450-3*, 1152213) World Health.

Laboratory Book of Computational Organic Chemistry. Warren J. Hehre et al. (Illus.). 322p. (Orig.). 1996. pap. text 25.00 (*0-9643495-5-8*) Wavefunction.

Laboratory Cat. Brent J. Martin. LC 98-198506. (Laboratory Animal Pocket Reference Ser.). 160p. 1997. spiral bd. 44.95 (*0-8493-2567-6*) CRC Pr.

Laboratory Chemical Standards: The Complete OSHA Compliance Manual. LC 90-23143. 1991. 250.00 (*1-55871-182-1*, BSP 188) BNA PLUS.

Laboratory Companion: A Practical Guide to Materials, Equipment & Techniques. rev. ed. Gary S. Coyne. LC 97-16689. 552p. 1997. 64.95 (*0-471-18422-5*) Wiley.

***Laboratory Concepts in Biology.** 4th ed. (C). 2000. 16.00 (*0-536-61268-4*) Pearson Custom.

Laboratory Corrosion Tests & Standards-STP866. Ed. by G. S. Haynes & Robert Baboian. LC 85-7375. 640p. 1985. text 60.00 (*0-8031-0443-X*, STP866) ASTM.

***Laboratory Course in C++** Nell B. Dale. LC 99-33648. 1999. write for info. (*0-7637-1146-2*) Jones & Bartlett.

Laboratory Course in C++ 3.5. Nell B. Dale & David W. Orshalick. LC 96-32748. (Computer Science Ser.). 424p. 1996. pap. 27.50 (*0-7637-0247-1*) Jones & Bartlett.

Laboratory Course in Pascal: With a Tutorial on THINK. Nell B. Dale. 176p. (C). 1991. disk. write for info. (*0-318-70088-3*) HM Trade Div.

Laboratory Course in Pascal: With a Tutorial on THINK. Nell B. Dale. (Computer Science Ser.). 176p. (C). 1991. pap. 28.75 (*0-669-26957-3*) Jones & Bartlett.

Laboratory Culture & Development of Helicoverpa Armigera. N. J. Armes et al. 1992. pap. 25.00 (*0-85954-325-0*, Pub. by Nat Res Inst) St Mut.

Laboratory Culture & Development of the African Armyworm. S. C. Smith. 1998. pap. 60.00 (*0-85954-485-0*, Pub. by Nat Res Inst) St Mut.

Laboratory Culture & Experimental Techniques Using Termites. M. Pearce. 1997. pap. 60.00 (*0-85954-455-9*, Pub. by Nat Res Inst) St Mut.

Laboratory Data & Patient Care. Ed. by P. L. Kerkhof & M. P. Van Dieijen-Visser. LC 87-35820. (Illus.). 190p. 1988. 55.00 (*0-306-42800-8*, Plenum Trade) Perseus Pubng.

Laboratory Decontamination & Destruction of Aflatoxins, B1, B2, G1, G2 in Laboratory Wastes. International Agency for Research on Cancer Staff. Ed. by M. Castegnaro et al. LC 81-181056. (IARC Scientific Publications: No. 37). 70p. reprint ed. pap. 30.00 (*0-608-20034-4*, 207130600010) Bks Demand.

Laboratory Decontamination & Destruction of Carcinogens in Laboratory Wastes: Some Aromatic Amines & 4-Nitrobiphenyl. Ed. by M. Castegnaro et al. (IARC Scientific Publications: No. 64). 100p. 1985. pap. 12.95 (*0-19-723064-4*) OUP.

Laboratory Decontamination & Destruction of Carcinogens in Laboratory Wastes: Some Mycotoxins. Ed. by M. Castegnaro et al. (IARC Scientific Publications: No. 113). (Illus.). 68p. 1992. pap. text 30.00 (*92-832-2113-3*) OUP.

Laboratory Decontamination & Destruction of Carcinogens in Laboratory Wastes: Some Polycyclic Heterocyclic Hydrocarbons. Ed. by M. Castegnaro et al. (IARC Scientific Publications: No. 114). (Illus.). 58p. 1992. pap. text 20.00 (*92-832-2114-1*) OUP.

Laboratory Design: Approved Guideline (1997) 1997. 85.00 (*1-56238-344-2*, GP18-A) NCCLS.

Laboratory Design: Proposed Guideline (1994) Contrib. by Pennell C. Painter. 1994. 85.00 (*1-56238-246-2*, GP18-P) NCCLS.

Laboratory Design: Recommended Practice RP-7. 2nd ed. National Conference of Standards Laboratories Laboratories Standards Committee. (RP Ser.: No. 7). (Illus.). 181p. 1993. reprint ed. 20.00 (*1-58464-015-4*) Natl Conf Stds Labs.

***Laboratory Design, Construction & Renovation: Participants, Process & Product.** National Research Council Staff et al. 170p. 2000. pap. 35.00 (*0-309-06633-6*) Natl Acad Pr.

Laboratory Design Guide: For Clients, Architects & Their Design Team: The Laboratory Design Process from Start to Finish. Brian Griffin. LC 97-43246. 192p. 1998. pap. text 89.95 (*0-7506-3858-3*) Buttrwrth-Heinemann.

***Laboratory Design Guide: For Clients, Architects & Their Design Team: The Laboratory Design Process from Start to Finish.** 2nd ed. Brian Griffin. LC 00-41610. 2000. write for info. (*0-7506-4671-3*, Architectural Pr) Buttrwrth-Heinemann.

Laboratory Design Handbook. E. Crawley Cooper. 256p. 1994. boxed set 99.95 (*0-8493-8996-8*, 8996) CRC Pr.

Laboratory Design Issues: Technical Guide. J. D. Cook et al. (Technical Guide Ser.: No. 10). 123p. (C). 1994. pap. 150.00 (*0-948237-11-2*, Pub. by H&H Sci Cnslts) St Mut.

Laboratory Details: A Guide to Laboratory Operations. 1996. lib. bdg. 249.99 (*0-8490-8321-4*) Gordon Pr.

Laboratory Diagnosis in Chiropractic Care. David J. Wickes. 400p. 1994. write for info. (*0-683-09041-0*) Lppncott W & W.

Laboratory Diagnosis in Neonatal Calf & Pig Diarrhea: Current Topics in Veterinary Medicine & Animal Science, No. 13. Ed. by P. W. De Leeuw & P. A. Guinee. 210p. 1981. text 101.50 (*90-247-2527-5*) Kluwer Academic.

Laboratory Diagnosis in Ophthalmology Zeynel A. Karciofglu. LC 86-18206. xiii, 268 p. 1987. write for info. (*0-02-362830-8*) Macmillan.

Laboratory Diagnosis of Diseases Caused by Toxic Agents. F. William Sunderman. LC 77-96992. (Illus.). 610p. 1970. 32.50 (*0-87527-079-4*) Green.

Laboratory Diagnosis of Endocrine Diseases. F. William Sunderman. LC 72-171949. (Illus.). 712p. 1971. 37.50 (*0-87527-080-8*) Green.

Laboratory Diagnosis of Infectious Diseases. Ed. by A. Balows et al. (Illus.). 1160p. 1988. 423.00 (*0-387-96755-9*) Spr-Verlag.

Laboratory Diagnosis of Infectious Diseases: Principles & Practice, Vol. 2. Ed. by Edwin H. Lennette et al. (Illus.). 825p. 1988. 350.00 (*0-387-96756-7*) Spr-Verlag.

Laboratory Diagnosis of Kidney Diseases. F. William Sunderman. LC 73-76164. (Illus.). 604p. 1970. 29.50 (*0-87527-077-8*) Green.

Laboratory Diagnosis of Livestock Abortion. 3rd ed. Clyde A. Kirkbride. LC 90-9676. (Illus.). 274p. (C). 1990. pap. text 49.95 (*0-8138-1593-2*) Iowa St U Pr.

Laboratory Diagnosis of Selected Inborn Errors of Metabolism, 4. Vicky A. LeGrys. LC 83-22941. (Methods in Laboratory Medicine Ser.: Vol. 4). 154p. 1984. 45.00 (*0-275-91441-0*, C1441, Praeger Pubs) Greenwood.

Laboratory Diagnosis of Viral Infections. 2nd expanded rev. ed. Ed. by Edwin H. Lennette. (Illus.). 800p. 1991. text 215.00 (*0-8247-8585-1*) Dekker.

***Laboratory Diagnosis of Viral Infections** 3rd rev. expanded ed. Edwin H. Lennette & Thomas F. Smith. LC 99-22924. (Illus.). 880p. 1999. text 195.00 (*0-8247-1952-2*) Dekker.

Laboratory Diagnostic Procedures in the Rheumatic Diseases. 3rd rev. ed. Ed. by Alan S. Cohen. (Illus.). 416p. 1985. text 99.00 (*0-8089-1737-4*, 790879, Grune & Strat) Harcrt Hlth Sci Grp.

***Laboratory DNA Science Quickprint.** 100p. (C). 1999. text 12.50 (*0-536-60587-4*) Pearson Custom.

Laboratory Earth: The Planetary Gamble We Can't Afford to Lose. Steven H. Schneider. (Illus.). 176p. 1998. 11.00 (*0-465-07280-1*, Pub. by Basic) HarpC.

Laboratory Environment. Ed. by Rupert Purchase. 270p. 1994. 89.95 (*0-85186-605-0*, R6605); 89.95 (*0-85186-050-8*, R6605) CRC Pr.

Laboratory Equipment Markets: A Detailed Database on a 25 Billion Dollar Market. Market Intelligence Staff. 270p. 1992. 995.00 (*1-56753-082-6*) Frost & Sullivan.

Laboratory Equipment Specialist. Jack Rudman. (Career Examination Ser.: C-2297). 1994. reprint ed. pap. 27.95 (*0-8373-2297-9*) Nat Learn.

Laboratory Equipment, UL 1262. 3rd ed. (C). 1990. pap. text 95.00 (*1-55989-126-2*) Underwrtrs Labs.

Laboratory Evaluation of Hemostasis & Thrombosis. 3rd ed. Marjorie S. Sirridge & Reaner Shannon. LC 85-21692. 241p. reprint ed. pap. 74.80 (*0-7837-2748-8*, 204312800006) Bks Demand.

Laboratory Evaluation of Piles Installed with Vibratory Drives. (National Cooperative Highway Research Program Report Ser.: No. 316). 51p. 1989. 9.00 (*0-309-04613-0*, NR316) Transport Res Bd.

Laboratory Evaluation of Pulmonary Function. Miller et al. 1987. 26.50 (*0-397-58574-8*) Lppncott W & W.

Laboratory EXAFS Facilities, 1980: University of Washington Workshop. Ed. by Edward A. Stern. (AIP Conference Proceedings Ser.: No. 64). 165p. lib. bdg. 18.25 (*0-88318-163-0*) Am Inst Physics.

Laboratory Exercises. 3rd ed. Lansing Prescott & John P. Harley. 496p. (C). 1996. text, suppl. ed. write for info. (*0-697-21869-4*, WCB McGr Hill) McGrw-H Hghr Educ.

Laboratory Exercises & Field Methods in Marine Biology for South Florida & the Caribbean. Kathleen Sullivan. 1995. per. 29.40 (*0-88252-174-8*) Paladin Hse.

Laboratory Exercises & Observation Guide. Holzinger. (C). 1995. pap. text, student ed., lab manual ed. 25.20 (*0-13-644196-3*) P-H.

Laboratory Exercises for & Introduction to Biological Principles. 4th ed. Gil Desha. 200p. (C). 1996. spiral bd. 21.95 (*0-8403-9190-0*) Kendall-Hunt.

Laboratory Exercises for Animal Sciences & Industry. rev. ed. Linda Martin. 160p. (C). 1995. spiral bd. 25.95 (*0-8403-9248-6*) Kendall-Hunt.

Laboratory Exercises for Astronomy 2073. W. R. Graham. 148p. (C). 1996. pap. text, spiral bd. 20.95 (*0-7872-2483-9*, 41248301) Kendall-Hunt.

Laboratory Exercises for Atmospheric Interactions. Walter E. Martin. 156p. (C). 1996. spiral bd. 14.95 (*0-8403-8389-4*) Kendall-Hunt.

Laboratory Exercises for Biology of Organisms. Massasoit Community College Staff. 204p. (C). 1994. spiral bd. 23.95 (*0-8403-7336-8*) Kendall-Hunt.

Laboratory Exercises for Competency in Respiratory Care. Thomas J. Butler et al. LC 97-41975. (Illus.). 577p. 1998. pap. 47.95 (*0-8036-0248-0*) Davis Co.

Laboratory Exercises for Environmental Geography. 3rd ed. Charles E. Bussing et al. 144p. 1996. spiral bd. 24.95 (*0-8403-8276-6*) Kendall-Hunt.

Laboratory Exercises for General Botany. 4th ed. William K. Davis et al. (Illus.). 110p. (C). 1981. pap. text 10.95 (*0-89641-067-6*) American Pr.

Laboratory Exercises for General Chemistry, Vol. 1. 6th ed. John J. Sousa et al. 198p. (YA). (gr. 11 up). 1990. pap. text, student ed. 19.95 (*0-940139-18-9*) Consortium RI.

Laboratory Exercises for General Chemistry, Vol. 2. 6th ed. John J. Sousa et al. 190p. (YA). (gr. 11 up). 1990. pap. text, student ed. 19.95 (*0-940139-19-7*) Consortium RI.

***Laboratory Exercises for General Ecology & Evolution.** 2nd ed. Carl Freeman et al. 220p. (C). 1999. spiral bd. 31.95 (*0-7872-6420-2*, 41642001) Kendall-Hunt.

Laboratory Exercises for General Zoology. 3rd ed. William K. Davis et al. (Illus.). 131p. 1980. pap. text 10.95 (*0-89641-030-7*) American Pr.

Laboratory Exercises for Health Science Chemistry, Vol. 1. 7th ed. Emanuel G. Terezakis. (Illus.). 175p. (YA). (gr. 11 up). 1989. pap. text, student ed. 19.95 (*0-940139-12-X*) Consortium RI.

Laboratory Exercises for Health Science Chemistry, Vol. 2. 6th ed. Emanuel G. Terezakis. (Illus.). 165p. (YA). (gr. 11 up). 1989. pap. text, student ed. 19.95 (*0-940139-13-8*) Consortium RI.

Laboratory Exercises for Human Biology. 4th ed. Ann W Auleb. 112p. (C). 1990. text 22.00 (*0-536-57719-6*) Pearson Custom.

***Laboratory Exercises for Physics 20073.** Douglas Ingram. 118p. (C). 1999. spiral bd. 25.95 (*0-7872-6012-6*, 41601201) Kendall-Hunt.

Laboratory Exercises for Preparatory Chemistry. Kathy L. Tyner. 352p. (C). 1994. text. write for info. (*0-697-14174-8*, WCB McGr Hill) McGrw-H Hghr Educ.

Laboratory Exercises for Psychology 132, No. 132. Ronald Growney. 53p. (C). 1993. student ed. 9.60 (*1-56870-050-4*) RonJon Pub.

***Laboratory Exercises in Anatomy & Physiology with Cat Dissection.** 6th ed. Gerald Tortora & Robert B. Tallitsch. 691p. (C). 1999. pap. text 54.67 (*0-13-920323-0*) P-H.

Laboratory Exercises in Auditory Evoked Potentials. John A. Ferraro. LC 96-52550. 192p. 1997. pap., lab manual ed. 39.95 (*1-56593-698-1*, 1356) Thomson Learn.

Laboratory Exercises in Biology. 3rd ed. Cartwright et al. 200p. (C). 1997. spiral bd. 26.95 (*0-7872-3547-4*) Kendall-Hunt.

Laboratory Exercises in Biology (End Semester) Frank Graves et al. (Illus.). 80p. (C). 1989. pap., student ed. write for info. (*0-944547-01-X*) Herit Hse Litho.

Laboratory Exercises in Biology (First Semester) Frank Graves et al. 74p. (C). 1989. pap., student ed. write for info. (*0-944547-03-6*) Herit Hse Litho.

Laboratory Exercises in Developmental Biology. Yolanda P. Cruz. (Illus.). 241p. 1993. pap. 19.95 (*0-12-198390-0*) Acad Pr.

Laboratory Exercises in Environmental Geology. Harvey Blatt. 192p. (C). 1993. spiral bd. write for info. (*0-697-17071-3*, WCB McGr Hill) McGrw-H Hghr Educ.

Laboratory Exercises in Environmental Geology. 2nd ed. Harvey Blatt. 224p. (C). 1997. text. write for info. (*0-697-28288-0*, WCB McGr Hill) McGrw-H Hghr Educ.

Laboratory Exercises in Human Anatomy with Cat Dissections. 3rd ed. Gerard J. Tortora. (Illus.). 432p. (C). 1993. pap. text, lab manual ed. 54.00 (*0-02-421021-8*, Macmillan Coll) P-H.

Laboratory Exercises in Human Anatomy with Cat Dissections. 4th ed. Gerald J. Tortora. 505p. (C). 1997. pap. text, lab manual ed. 51.00 (*0-13-268251-6*) P-H.

***Laboratory Exercises in Human Physiology.** Brian Tsukimura. 102p. (C). 1999. spiral bd. 34.95 (*0-7872-5789-3*) Kendall-Hunt.

Laboratory Exercises in Immunology. Farone. 82p. (C). 1998. spiral bd. 41.95 (*0-7872-5311-1*, 41531101) Kendall-Hunt.

Laboratory Exercises in Microbiology. Jaime S. Colome et al. (Illus.). 283p. (C). 1986. 32.50 (*0-314-87262-0*) West Pub.

Laboratory Exercises in Microbiology. 2nd ed. (C). 2001. pap. 42.67 (*0-13-010074-9*) P-H.

Laboratory Exercises in Nutrition. 2nd ed. Bernard A. Marcus. Ed. by Charlotte Petersen & Donald R. Ferruzzi. (Illus.). 34p. (Orig.). (C). 1998. pap. text, lab manual ed. 14.95 (*0-9609098-9-3*) Biomat Pub Co.

Laboratory Exercises in Oceanography. 2nd ed. Bernard W. Pipkin et al. (Illus.). (C). 1987. teacher ed. 4.80 (*0-7167-1845-6*) W H Freeman.

Laboratory Exercises in Physical Geology. Allan Ludman. 240p. (C). 1992. text. write for info. (*0-697-14706-1*, WCB McGr Hill) McGrw-H Hghr Educ.

An Asterisk (*) at the beginning of an entry indicates that the title is appearing for the first time.

Laboratory Exercises in Physical Geology. Temple University Geology Department. 80p. (C). 1993. spiral bd. 15.95 (0-8403-8822-5) Kendall-Hunt.

Laboratory Exercises in Physical Geology. 3rd rev. ed. Kula C. Misra. (Illus.). 282p. 1999. pap. text 32.95 (0-88725-239-7) Hunter Textbks.

***Laboratory Exercises in Plant Biology.** 2nd ed. Dwayne A. Wise et al. 76p. (C). 1999. spiral bd. 18.95 (0-7872-6245-5, 41624501) Kendall-Hunt.

Laboratory Exercises in Plant Pathology: An Instructional Kit. Ed. by A. B. Baudoin et al. 1993. 139.00 (0-89054-086-1) Am Phytopathol Soc.

Laboratory Exercises in Plant Pathology: An Instructional Kit - (Student's Exercises) A. B. A. M. Baudoin & American Phytopathological Society Staff. (C). 1990. pap., student ed. 150.00 (81-85046-86-7, Pub. by Scientific Pubs) St Mut.

Laboratory Exercises in Respiratory Care. 3rd ed. Cynthia Shoup & Terrance Gilmore. (Illus.). 622p. (C). (gr. 13). 1988. pap. text 37.95 (0-8016-4328-7, 04328) Mosby Inc.

Laboratory Experiences General Biology 2nd rev. ed. Jerde Charles & Randall A. Kottel. 270p. (C). 1990. text 39.40 (0-536-57841-9) Pearson Custom.

Laboratory Experiences at USI. Robert E. Mays. 60p. (C). 1995. pap. text 7.21 (0-89917-468-X) Tichenor Pub.

Laboratory Experiences in Exercise Physiology. 2nd ed. Edmund J. Burke & Ernest D. Michael. 1990. student ed. 24.95 (0-614-24658-X) Mouvement Pubns.

Laboratory Experiences in General Biology. 3rd ed. Charles Jerde & Randall A. Kottel. 292p. (C). 1994. text 37.00 (0-536-58574-1) Pearson Custom.

Laboratory Experiences in Group Theory. Ellen M. Parker. LC 96-77787. (Classroom Resource Materials Ser.). (Illus.). 112p. (Orig.). 1996. pap. text, suppl. ed. 26.50 (0-88385-705-7, LABE) Math Assn.

Laboratory Experiences in Introductory Psychology. Barbara Basden & Jones Staff. 160p. (C). 1996. pap. text, per. 14.95 (0-7872-2590-8) Kendall-Hunt.

Laboratory Experiences & Activities in Physical Science. Stephen B. Rodecker & Maryanna Quon-Warner. 342p. (YA). (gr. 7 up). 1993. student ed. 39.95 (0-9638008-0-9) Spectrum CA.

Laboratory Experiments for Astronomy. Paul E. Johnson. 233p. (C). 1987. text, student ed. 37.50 (0-03-009677-4) SCP.

Laboratory Experiments for Chemistry. 7th ed. John H. Nelson. 1996. pap. text 49.00 (0-13-578360-7) P-H.

Laboratory Experiments for Chemistry 1040. 4th ed. Santa Fe Community College Chemistry Department St. (Illus.). 150p. (C). 1997. lab manual ed. 11.95 (0-89892-155-4) Contemp Pub Co of Raleigh.

Laboratory Experiments for the Micro-Trainer. 2nd ed. Christopher E. Strangio. (Illus.). 144p. (C). 1990. 18.00 (0-929955-01-3) CAMI Research.

Laboratory Experiments, Human Structure. Banister & Mekjavic. (Applied Science Ser.). 1993. text 27.75 (0-314-02574-X) S-W Pub.

Laboratory Experiments in Biology. John C. George. (Illus.). 146p. (YA). 1986. spiral bd. 13.00 (0-921369-00-X) J C George Ent.

Laboratory Experiments in College Physics. 7th ed. Chirold D. Epp & Cicero H. Bernard. 400p. 1994. pap. 58.95 (0-471-00251-8) Wiley.

Laboratory Experiments in Economics: 6 Points of View. Ed. by Alvin E. Roth. 232p. 1987. text 64.95 (0-521-33392-X) Cambridge U Pr.

Laboratory Experiments in General Chemistry. J. E. Hardcastle. (C). 1995. pap. text 19.47 (1-56870-115-2) RonJon Pub.

Laboratory Experiments in Liquid Chromatography. William V. Willis. (Illus.). 264p. 1991. per. 120.00 (0-8493-0177-7, QL) CRC Pr.

***Laboratory Experiments in Microbiology.** 215p. (C). 2000. 26.00 (0-536-60510-6) Pearson Custom.

Laboratory Experiments in Microbiology. 4th ed. Ted R. Johnson & Christine L. Case. (C). 1995. pap. text 31.95 (0-8053-8509-6) Benjamin-Cummings.

***Laboratory Experiments in Microbiology.** 5th ed. 120p. (C). 2000. 22.00 (0-536-60877-6) Pearson Custom.

Laboratory Experiments in Microbiology. 5th ed. Ted R. Johnson & Christine L. Case. LC 97-26405. 418p. (C). 1997. pap. text 52.00 (0-8053-8452-9) Benjamin-Cummings.

Laboratory Experiments in Physiology: Custom Laboratory Program. Dee Silverthorn. 2000p. 2001. pap. 37.33 (0-13-229055-3) P-H.

Laboratory Experiments to Operational Ampliers with Linear Intergrate. 2nd ed. Nikola Sorak. 160p. (C). 1990. pap. text, lab manual ed. 23.27 (0-675-20661-8, Merrill Coll) P-H.

Laboratory Explorations for Microelectronic Circuits. 4th ed. Kenneth C. Smith. (Illus.). 208p. (C). 1998. pap. text 17.95 (0-19-511772-7) OUP.

***Laboratory Explorations in Microbiology.** (C). 1999. 20.00 (0-536-02243-7) Pearson Custom.

***Laboratory Fish.** Ed. by Gary K. Ostrander. (Handbook of Experimental Animals Ser.). (Illus.). 500p. 2000. 199.95 (0-12-529650-9) Acad Pr.

***Laboratory for Anthropology: Science & Romanticism in the American Southwest.** Don D. Fowler. 2000. 49.95 (0-8263-2036-8) U of NM Pr.

***Laboratory for Organismal Biology.** 5th ed. 250p. (C). 1999. text 24.00 (0-536-02611-4) Pearson Custom.

Laboratory Fume Hoods: A User's Manual. G. Thomas Saunders. LC 92-39024. 144p. 1993. 54.95 (0-471-56935-6) Wiley.

Laboratory Guide for an Introduction to Physical Science, 8 Vols. 8th ed. James T. Shipman & Clyde D. Baker. 394p. (C). 1996. pap. text 25.56 (0-669-41718-1) HM Trade Div.

Laboratory Guide for Conducting Soil Tests & Plant Analysis. J. B. Jones. 350p. 1994. lib. bdg. 39.95 (1-884015-33-6, SL5336) St Lucie Pr.

Laboratory Guide for Human Histology. rev. ed. David B. Meyer. LC 85-15296. 133p. (Orig.). reprint ed. pap. 41.30 (0-608-10582-1, 207120300009) Bks Demand.

Laboratory Guide for In Vitro Studies of DNA Methylation & Protein - DNA Interactions. Jurgen P. Jost & Hans P. Saluz. (Biomethods Ser.: No. 3). 250p. 1990. 109.50 (0-8176-2369-8) Birkhauser.

Laboratory Guide to Biochemistry, Enzymology, & Protein Physical Chemistry: A Study of Aspartate Transcarbamylase. M. Le Maire et al. (Illus.). 182p. (C). 1991. spiral bd. 39.50 (0-306-43639-6, Plenum Trade) Perseus Pubng.

Laboratory Guide to Biotin-Labeling in Biomolecule Analysis. Ed. by T. Meier & F. Fahrenholz. LC 96-11381. 1996. write for info. (0-8176-5206-X) Birkhauser.

Laboratory Guide to Biotin-Labeling in Biomolecule Analysis. Ed. by T. Meier & F. Fahrenholz. LC 96-11381. 240p. 1996. 89.50 (3-7643-5206-X) Birkhauser.

Laboratory Guide to Cellular & Molecular Techniques for Higher Plants. Ed. by I. Negrutiu & G. Gharti-Chhetri. (Biomethods Ser.: Vol. 4). 392p. 1991. 174.50 (0-8176-2542-9) Birkhauser.

Laboratory Guide to Genomic Sequencing. Jurgen P. Jost & Hans P. Saluz. (Biomethods Ser.: No. 1). 128p. 1988. 79.50 (0-8176-1925-9) Birkhauser.

Laboratory Guide to Glycoconjugate Analysis. Ed. by P. Jackson et al. LC 97-3608. (BioMethods Ser.: No. 9). 350p. 1997. text 89.50 (3-7643-5210-8) Spr-Verlag.

Laboratory Guide to Glycoconjugate Analysis. P. Jackson & J. T. Gallagher. LC 97-3608. (Biomethods Ser.). 1997. write for info. (0-8176-5210-8) Birkhauser.

Laboratory Guide to Graphite Furnace Analytical Atomic Spectroscopy. G. Schlemmer. 1998. 79.95 (3-7643-5770-3) Birkhauser.

Laboratory Guide to Graphite Furnace Analytical Atomic Spectroscopy. G. Schlemmer & B. Radziuk. 200p. 1998. 79.95 (0-8176-5770-3) Birkhauser.

Laboratory Guide to Human Biology. 2nd ed. Amitrano & Lowe. 182p. (C). 1997. spiral bd. 40.95 (0-7872-4277-2, 41427701) Kendall-Hunt.

Laboratory Guide to In Vitro Studies of Protein - DNA Interactions. Ed. by Jurgen P. Jost & Hans P. Saluz. (Biomethods Ser.: Vol. 5). 328p. 1991. 137.00 (0-8176-2627-1) Birkhauser.

Laboratory Guide to In Vitro Transcription. Felipe Sierra. (Biomethods Ser.: Vol. 2). 165p. 1990. 87.50 (0-8176-2357-4) Birkhauser.

Laboratory Guide to Insect Pathogens & Parasites. G. O. Poinar, Jr. & G. M. Thomas. LC 84-9875. (Illus.). 408p. (C). 1984. text 110.00 (0-306-41680-8, Kluwer Plenum) Kluwer Academic.

Laboratory Guide to RNA: Isolation, Analysis & Syntehsis. Paul A. Krieg. LC 96-19936. 445p. 1996. pap. 89.95 (0-471-12536-9) Wiley.

Laboratory Guide to the Anatomy of the Rabbit. 2nd ed. Edward H. Craigie. LC 70-358625. 123p. reprint ed. pap. 38.20 (0-608-15657-4, 203191700077) Bks Demand.

Laboratory Guinea Pig. Lizabeth Terril. LC 97-89103. (Laboratory Animal Pocket Reference Ser.). 192p. 1997. spiral bd. 44.95 (0-8493-2564-1) CRC Pr.

Laboratory Guinea Pig. Lizabeth Terril & Donna Clemons. Ed. by Mark A. Suckow. (Laboratory Animal Pocket Reference Ser.). 128p. 1997. 39.95 (0-614-29973-X, 2564H3Y) CRC Pr.

Laboratory Haematology. Ed. by Israel Chanarin. (Illus.). 464p. 1989. text 59.95 (0-443-03343-9) Church.

Laboratory Hamster & Gerbil. Karl Field & Amber L. Sibold. Ed. by Mark A. Suckow. (Laboratory Animal Pocket Reference Ser.). 128p. 1997. 39.95 (0-614-29975-6, 2566H3Y) CRC Pr.

Laboratory Hamster & Gerbil. Karl Field & Amber L. Sibold. LC 99-174413. (Laboratory Animal Pocket Reference Ser.). 168p. 1998. spiral bd. 44.95 (0-8493-2566-8) CRC Pr.

Laboratory Hamsters. Ed. by G. L. Van Hoosier, Jr. & Charles W. McPherson. (American College of Laboratory Animal Medicine Ser.). 456p. 1987. text 146.00 (0-12-714165-0) Acad Pr.

***Laboratory Handbook for Fractionation of Natural Extracts.** Houghton. (Illus.). 208p. 1998. write for info. (0-412-74910-6) Kluwer Academic.

Laboratory Handbook for General Chemistry. Conrad L. Stanitski et al. (Modular Laboratory Program in Chemistry Ser.). 54p. (C). 1996. pap. text 5.95 (0-87540-491-X, HBK491-X) Chem Educ Res.

Laboratory Handbook of Dermatophytes: A Clinical Guide & Laboratory Manual of Dermatophytes & Other Filamentous Fungi from Skin, Hair & Nails. Julius Kane et al. LC 97-23344. (Illus.). 400p. 1997. text, lab manual ed. 129.95 (0-89863-157-2) Star Pub CA.

Laboratory Handbook of Medical Mycology. Michael R. McGinnis. 1980. text 104.00 (0-12-482850-7) Acad Pr.

Laboratory Handbook of Organic Coatings. M. W. Urban. LC 97-71377. (Illus.). 100p. (C). 1997. 69.95 (1-890086-01-0) Global Pr MN.

Laboratory Helper (Men) Jack Rudman. (Career Examination Ser.: C-446). 1994. pap. 23.95 (0-8373-0446-6) Nat Learn.

Laboratory Helper (Women) Jack Rudman. (Career Examination Ser.: C-447). 1994. pap. 23.95 (0-8373-0447-4) Nat Learn.

Laboratory Histopathology. Woods. 1994. text 210.00 (0-443-04912-2, W B Saunders Co) Harcrt Hlth Sci Grp.

Laboratory Immunology & Serology. Zane. 1999. pap. text. write for info. (0-7216-5002-3, W B Saunders Co) Harcrt Hlth Sci Grp.

Laboratory Immunology & Serology. 3rd ed. Neville J. Bryant. 1992. pap. text 47.00 (0-7216-4212-8, W B Saunders Co) Harcrt Hlth Sci Grp.

Laboratory in Clinical Medicine. 2nd ed. Charles H. Halsted & James A. Halsted. (Illus.). 1083p. 1981. text 165.00 (0-7216-4479-1, W B Saunders Co) Harcrt Hlth Sci Grp.

***Laboratory in Cognition & Perception.** 3rd ed. S. E. Ransdell et al. (Illus.). 208p. (C). 1999. pap. 25.00 (1-892919-00-1) Psychology SW Inc.

Laboratory Information Management Systems. Robert Megargle. 350p. 1996. 70.00 (1-56081-662-7, Wiley-VCH) Wiley.

Laboratory Information Management Systems. Robert Megargle. 300p. 1997. write for info. (0-471-18592-2) Wiley.

Laboratory Information Management Systems: Development & Implementation for a Quality Assurance Laboratory. Mary D. Hinton. LC 94-32824. (Illus.). 360p. 1994. text 75.00 (0-8247-9458-3) Dekker.

Laboratory Inquiries into Concepts of Biology. 7th ed. William Andresen et al. 110p. (C). 1996. spiral bd. 24.95 (0-7872-2294-1) Kendall-Hunt.

Laboratory Inspection Manual. O'Connor & Hannan. LC 93-9055. 408p. 1993. ring bd. 102.00 (0-8342-0500-9, S129) Aspen Pub.

Laboratory Instruction for Introductory Medical Microbiology. Leigh Callan. 80p. (C). 1995. spiral bd. 14.95 (0-8403-7846-7) Kendall-Hunt.

Laboratory Instrumentation. Turner. (Illus.). 400p. 1991. 24.95 (0-8016-5530-7) Mosby Inc.

Laboratory Instrumentation. 4th ed. Mary C. Haven et al. (Industrial Health & Safety Ser.). 492p. 1994. 65.95 (0-471-28572-2, VNR) Wiley.

Laboratory Instrumentation, Chemical Microscopy, Engineering & Technology. Ed. by R. Serre. 294p. 1993. 162.50 (0-444-88973-6) Elsevier.

Laboratory Instrumention. 4th ed. Ed. by Mary C. Haven et al. 512p. 1994. pap. 54.95 (0-442-01520-8, VNR) Wiley.

Laboratory Instruments & Data Management Systems: Design of Software User Interfaces & End-User Software Systems Validation, Operation, & Monitoring; Approved Guideline (1994) Contrib. by Emery J. Stephans. 1995. 75.00 (1-56238-284-5, GP19-A) NCCLS.

Laboratory Investigation of Liver Disease. Johnson & I. G. MacFarlane. (Illus.). 320p. 1989. pap. text 54.00 (0-7020-1376-5) Bailliere Tindall.

Laboratory Investigations: A Manual for General Biology. Michael B. Clark & Michael R. Riddle. (Illus.). 350p. (C). 1998. pap. text, spiral bd., wbk. ed. 27.00 (1-885380-57-7) Suspended Animat.

Laboratory Investigations for Biology. Dickey. (C). 1997. spiral bd., lab manual ed. write for info. (0-201-30463-5) Addison-Wesley.

Laboratory Investigations for General Science, Part II. Edmund A. Marek & Melanie Lewis. (Illus.). 101p. (C). 1982. pap. text 8.95 (0-89641-078-1) American Pr.

Laboratory Investigations for General Science, Pt. I. Edmund A. Marek et al. (Illus.). 89p. 1982. pap. text 9.95 (0-89641-111-7) American Pr.

Laboratory Investigations in Biology: Preliminary Edition. Wayne Faircloth. 92p. (C). 1995. pap. text, spiral bd. 18.95 (0-8403-7942-0) Kendall-Hunt.

Laboratory Investigations in Cell & Molecular Biology. 3rd rev. ed. Allyn Bregman. LC 95-54168. 336p. 1996. pap. 55.95 (0-471-14809-1) Wiley.

Laboratory Investigations into Psychic Phenomena. Hereward Carrington. LC 75-7370. (Perspectives in Psychical Research Ser.). (Illus.). 1975. reprint ed. 23.95 (0-405-07021-7) Ayer.

Laboratory Investigations into the World of Plants. Phillip G. Malnassy. 104p. 1996. spiral bd. 18.95 (0-8403-7085-7) Kendall-Hunt.

***Laboratory Investigations of Soils & Rocks for Engineering Analysis & Design Of Nuclear Power Facilities.** T. Holmes. 61p. 2000. pap. 6.00 (0-16-059081-7) USGPO.

Laboratory Life: The Construction of Scientific Facts. Bruno Latour & Steve Woolgar. LC 85-43378. 296p. 1986. pap. text 18.95 (0-691-02832-X, Pub. by Princeton U Pr) Cal Prin Full Svc.

Laboratory Management. LC 65-5192. (Manual of Practice, Systems Management Ser.: No. 1). 56p. 1981. 11.00 (0-318-16842-1, MOP SM-1) Water Environ.

Laboratory Manual: The Challenge of Chemistry. rev. ed. P. Horrigan. (Illus.). (C). 1997. pap. 29.95 (0-941512-00-2) Marshland Pub.

Laboratory Manual - Kinesiology & Neurophysiology. Barbara E. Gench & Hinson. (C). 1993. student ed. 18.22 (1-56870-081-4) RonJon Pub.

Laboratory Manual for Anatomy & Physiology Pt. I: Covers Skeletal Through Nervous & Special Senses, 20 vols. 2nd ed. William C. Kleinelp, Jr. (Illus.). 100p. (C). 1998. pap. 15.95 (0-929941-22-5, 0929941225) Wood River Pubns.

Laboratory Manual for Anatomy & Physiology Pt. II: Endocrine Through Reproductive, 20 vols. 2nd ed. William C. Kleinelp, Jr. (Illus.). 95p. (C). 1998. pap. 15.95 (0-929941-21-7, 0929941217) Wood River Pubns.

Laboratory Manual for Animal Technicians. Victoria B. Solberg. (Illus.). 174p. (Orig.). 1985. pap. text 32.95 (0-8138-1066-3) Iowa St U Pr.

***Laboratory Manual for Biological Science.** 2nd ed. J. D. Wilhide. 216p. (C). 1999. spiral bd. 26.95 (0-7872-6379-6, 41637901) Kendall-Hunt.

Laboratory Manual for Botany. 7th ed. Margaret Balbach & Lawrence C. Bliss. (Illus.). 413p. (C). 1991. pap. text, student ed. 49.00 (0-03-030184-X, Pub. by SCP) Harcourt.

Laboratory Manual for Classification & Morphology of Rumen Ciliate Protozoa. Burk A. Dehority. 128p. 1993. lib. bdg. 59.95 (0-8493-4875-7, QL368) CRC Pr.

Laboratory Manual for College Physics. Paul Liebenauer. 1995. pap. text 17.98 (1-56581-084-8) Tichenor Pub.

Laboratory Manual for Computer Literacy. Hugh L. McHenry. 138p. 1996. spiral bd. 22.95 (0-7872-2081-7) Kendall-Hunt.

Laboratory Manual for Concepts of Physical Activity. 6th ed. Carol Miller. 96p. (C). 1995. pap. text, spiral bd. 14.95 (0-8403-9559-0) Kendall-Hunt.

Laboratory Manual for Concepts of Physical Activity. 7th ed. Miller et al. 106p. (C). 1998. spiral bd. 18.95 (0-7872-5163-1, 41516301) Kendall-Hunt.

Laboratory Manual for Electronics via Waveform Analysis. E. C. Craig. (Illus.). 144p. 1993. 19.95 (0-387-94136-3) Spr-Verlag.

Laboratory Manual for Elementary Geology. 2nd ed. Julian D. Barksdale et al. (Illus.). ii, 93p. (Orig.). (C). 1969. pap. text 8.95 (0-87015-175-4) Pacific Bks.

***Laboratory Manual for First Semester Physics.** Robert Marchini. 96p. (C). 1998. spiral bd., lab manual ed. 18.95 (0-7872-4697-2) Kendall-Hunt.

Laboratory Manual for Food Microbiology & Biotechnology. 3rd rev. ed. Frederick J. Post. (Illus.). 280p. (C). 1997. pap. text 32.95 (0-89863-178-5, 178-5) Star Pub CA.

Laboratory Manual for Fundamentals of Anatomy & Physiology. 4th ed. Roberta M. Meehan. 751p. (C). 1997. pap. text, lab manual ed. 33.33 (0-13-751850-1) P-H.

Laboratory Manual for General & Oral Pathology. Shigeo Eda et al. (Illus.). 257p. 1991. text 96.00 (4-87417-262-8) Quint Pub Co.

***Laboratory Manual for General Biology I.** Albert Burchsted. 320p. (C). 1999. pap. text 36.95 (0-7872-6096-7, 41609601) Kendall-Hunt.

Laboratory Manual for General Chemistry. 2nd ed. Robert Walker, Jr. Ed. by Donald R. Ferruzzi. (Illus.). 132p. 1998. pap. text 28.95 (0-9609098-2-6) Biomat Pub Co.

Laboratory Manual for General Chemistry. 5th ed. Gregory J. Grant & Gail M. Meyer. 163p. (C). 1996. pap. text, lab manual ed. 19.95 (1-879215-33-0) Sheffield WI.

Laboratory Manual for General Chemistry. 9th ed. Emory University Chemistry Department Staff. (Illus.). 204p. 1997. 18.95 (0-89892-189-9) Contemp Pub Co of Raleigh.

Laboratory Manual for General Microbiology. James Urban. 146p. (C). 1996. pap. text 21.95 (0-7872-2241-0) Kendall-Hunt.

Laboratory Manual for General Zoology. 2nd ed. Martha M. Nez & J. Keitz Haburay. 176p. (C). 1995. spiral bd. 19.95 (0-8403-8541-2) Kendall-Hunt.

Laboratory Manual for Geological Sciences 100. Ohio State University Staff. 148p. (C). 1995. per. 14.95 (0-8403-9457-8) Kendall-Hunt.

Laboratory Manual for Health Microbiology. Donald McGarey. 156p. (C). 1996. pap. text, ring bd. 25.95 (0-7872-2450-2, 41245001) Kendall-Hunt.

Laboratory Manual for Human Anatomy for Use With Models & Prosected Cadavers: With Illustrations Prepared Especially for Coloring. 2nd ed. Victor P. Eroschenko & WAMI Medical Program Staff. LC 96-39426. 448p. (C). 1997. pap. text, lab manual ed. 47.00 (0-673-99558-5) Addson-Wesley Educ.

Laboratory Manual for Human Biology. E. E. Wester et al. (Illus.). 78p. (C). 1990. pap. text 9.95 (0-89892-096-5) Contemp Pub Co of Raleigh.

Laboratory Manual for Human Nutrition. T. Dashman. xv, 237p. 1991. pap. text 46.00 (3-7186-0513-9, Harwood Acad Pubs) Gordon & Breach.

Laboratory Manual for Human Nutrition. 2nd ed. Theodore Dashman & Deborah E. Blocker. 288p. 1996. pap. text 21.00 (3-7186-0608-9, Harwood Acad Pubs) Gordon & Breach.

Laboratory Manual for Intro Ichthyology. Ronald H. Kilgen. 80p. (C). 1998. reprint ed. 9.95 (0-89582-120-6) Morton Pub.

Laboratory Manual for Introduction to Psychology, Custom Pub. Norman. (C). 1993. pap. text 7.25 (0-07-047216-5) McGraw.

Laboratory Manual for Introductory Biology. 3rd ed. Emil K. Urban et al. (Illus.). 196p. (C). 1994. pap. text, lab manual ed. 28.95 (0-88725-211-7) Hunter Textbks.

Laboratory Manual for Introductory Soils. 6th ed. Ray R. Weil. 220p. (C). 1998. per., lab manual ed. 26.95 (0-7872-4635-2, 41463501) Kendall-Hunt.

Laboratory Manual for Legionella. Ed. by T. G. Jarrospm & A. G. Taylor. LC 87-35094. 192p. 1988. 295.00 (0-471-91861-X) Wiley.

Laboratory Manual for Life Science I. John F. Lyon & Siu-Lam Lee. 100p. (C). 1996. spiral bd. 20.95 (0-7872-2325-5) Kendall-Hunt.

Laboratory Manual for Meat Science. 7th ed. G. C. Smith et al. (Illus.). 210p. 2000. 37.95 (0-89641-271-7) American Pr.

Laboratory Manual for Medical Microbiology. Laboratory Manual for Medical Microbiology Staff. Ed. by Schools of Medicine & Dentistry, State University. LC QR0046.L30. (Microbiology Ser.: No. 11). (Illus.). 195p. reprint ed. pap. 60.50 (0-7837-0617-0, 204096200019) Bks Demand.

Laboratory Manual for Morphology & Syntax. rev. ed. Ed. by William Merrifield et al. 291p. 1987. pap. text 18.75 (0-88312-785-7) S I L Intl.

L

An Asterisk (*) at the beginning of an entry indicates that the title is appearing for the first time.

Laboratory Manual for Nonlinear Physics with Maple for Scientists & Engineers. Richard H. Enns. LC 96-40498. 136p. 1997. pap. text 26.50 (*0-8176-3841-5*) Birkhauser.

***Laboratory Manual for Organic Chemistry.** Kenneth Cerny & Marietta Schwartz. 202p. (C). 1999. spiral bd. 23.95 (*0-7872-6294-3*, 41629401) Kendall-Hunt.

Laboratory Manual for Organic Chemistry: A Microscale Approach. William R. Moore & Anthony Winston. 350p. (C). 1995. pap. 50.31 (*0-07-043052-7*) McGraw.

Laboratory Manual for Pascal by Example: From Practice to Principle in Computer Science. Barry A. Burd. (Illus.). (C). 1995. pap. text, lab manual ed. 16.95 (*0-15-568164-8*) OUP.

***Laboratory Manual for Physical Geology.** Eric Baer et al. 166p. (C). 1999. spiral bd., lab manual ed. 20.95 (*0-7872-6416-4*) Kendall-Hunt.

Laboratory Manual for Physical Geology. Norris W. Jones. 224p. 1994. spiral bd. 32.95 (*0-8016-6939-1*) Mosby Inc.

Laboratory Manual for Physical Geology. rev. ed. Paul Feiss et al. 160p. (C). 1995. spiral bd. 22.95 (*0-8403-8567-6*) Kendall-Hunt.

Laboratory Manual for Physical Geology. 9th ed. James H. Zumberge. 240p. (C). 1994. text. write for info. (*0-697-13829-1*, WCB McGr Hill) McGrw-H Hghr Educ.

Laboratory Manual for Physical Science. Gillian Gabelmann. (C). 1996. student ed. 12.50 (*1-884680-04-6*) Gabelmann Pr.

Laboratory Manual for Physical Science 109L: And Extra Materials for Physical Science 109 Lecture. Richard J. Bady. 156p. (C). 1996. pap. text, per. 16.95 (*0-7872-2188-0*) Kendall-Hunt.

Laboratory Manual for Principles of Biology. 5th ed. Caroline Adams et al. 100p. 1995. pap. text, lab manual ed. 17.95 (*0-88725-225-7*) Hunter Textbks.

Laboratory Manual for Principles of Biology I. William Burnett. 132p. (C). 1996. spiral bd. 17.95 (*0-7872-2105-8*) Kendall-Hunt.

Laboratory Manual for Principles of Biology I. 2nd ed. William Burnett. 164p. (C). 1998. spiral bd. 29.95 (*0-7872-5120-8*, 41512001) Kendall-Hunt.

***Laboratory Manual for Principles of General Chemistry.** 6th ed. J. A. Beran. LC 99-32790. 480p. 1999. pap. 58.95 (*0-471-31452-8*) Wiley.

***Laboratory Manual for the Quality Assessment of Water & Wastewater.** Mamta Tomar. LC 99-10114. 1999. 59.95 (*1-56670-382-4*) Lewis Pubs.

Laboratory Manual for the TI-81 Graphing Calculator. David Lissner. Ed. by Pullins. 145p. (C). pap. text 18.50 (*0-314-02386-0*) West Pub.

Laboratory Manual in Animal Biology. W. H. Mason et al. (Illus.). 156p. (Orig.). (C). 1986. pap. 9.95 (*0-89892-067-1*) Contemp Pub Co of Raleigh.

Laboratory Manual in Biochemistry. Henry Zeidan & William V. Dashek. 304p. (C). 1996. text 36.50 (*0-697-16735-6*, WCB McGr Hill) McGrw-H Hghr Educ.

Laboratory Manual in Conceptual Physics. 2nd ed. Bill W. Tillery. 320p. (C). 1994. text. write for info. (*0-697-15834-9*, WCB McGr Hill) McGrw-H Hghr Educ.

Laboratory Manual in Physical Geology. 4th ed. (Prentice Hall College Titles Ser.). (C). 1997. text 73.00 (*0-13-270299-1*, Macmillan Coll) P-H.

Laboratory Manual in Physical Geology. 5th ed. (C). 2000. text, lab manual ed. write for info. (*0-13-016289-2*) P-H.

Laboratory Manual of Analytical Methods of Protein Chemistry (Including Polypeptides), Vols. 2-5. Ed. by P. Alexander et al. Incl. Vol. 3. Determination of the Size & Shape of Protein in Molecules. 1961. Vol. 4. Protein Analysis. 1965. write for info. (*0-318-55172-1*, Pub. by Pergamon Repr) Franklin.

Laboratory Manual of General Ecology. 6th ed. George W. Cox. 272p. (C). 1989. text. write for info. (*0-697-05138-2*, WCB McGr Hill) McGrw-H Hghr Educ.

Laboratory Manual of Genetics. 4th ed. A. M. Winchester & Peter J. Wejksnora. 192p. (C). 1995. text 31.00 (*0-697-12287-5*, WCB McGr Hill) McGrw-H Hghr Educ.

Laboratory Manual of Histochemistry. Linda L. Vacca. 596p. 1985. spiral bd. 47.00 (*0-89004-540-2*) Lppncott W & W.

Laboratory Manual of Histology. 2nd ed. George S. Pappas. 176p. (C). 1993. text, lab manual ed. write for info. (*0-697-12244-1*, WCB McGr Hill) McGrw-H Hghr Educ.

Laboratory Manual of Human Anatomy & Physiology, Vol. 2. 4th ed. Donald R. Ferruzzi. (Illus.). 254p. 1990. pap. text 32.95 (*0-9609098-4-2*) Biomat Pub Co.

Laboratory Manual of Micro & Small Scale Experiments for the Independent Study of General College Chemistry. Peter Jeschofnig. 75p. (C). 1994. pap. 18.95 (*1-886151-25-3*) Lrning Res Unltd.

Laboratory Manual of Neuroanatomy. D. T. Yew & M. I. Chuah. 104p. 1986. text 30.00 (*9971-5-0102-3*) World Scientific Pub.

Laboratory Manual of Neutrophil Function. Julia A. Metcalf et al. 206p. 1986. spiral bd. 38.00 (*0-88167-160-6*) Lppncott W & W.

Laboratory Manual of Neutrophil Function. Julia A. Metcalf et al. LC 85-25792. (Illus.). 205p. reprint ed. pap. 63.60 (*0-608-09729-2*, 206990600007) Bks Demand.

Laboratory Manual of Physical. 2nd ed. H. D. Crockford et al. 368p. (C). 1976. pap. 62.95 (*0-471-18844-1*) Wiley.

Laboratory Manual of Plant Cytological Techniques. Kwiton Jong. vi, 96p. 1997. pap. 20.00 (*1-872291-42-2*) Balogh.

Laboratory Manual of Tests, Procedures & Data for Exercise Physiology. R. G. Eston & T. Reilly. (Illus.). 360p. (C). 1995. 75.00 (*0-419-17880-5*, E & FN Spon) Routledge.

Laboratory Manual T-A Therapeutic Modalities. 3rd ed. Quillen. 192p. (C). 1994. text, lab manual ed. 19.95 (*0-8016-7921-4*) Mosby Inc.

***Laboratory Manual to Accompany Anatomy & Physiology.** Kevin T. Patton. (Illus.). 1998. teacher ed. write for info. (*0-323-00196-3*) Mosby Inc.

Laboratory Manual to Accompany Anatomy & Physiology. Gary A. Thibodeau. 304p. 1987. pap. text 17.95 (*0-8016-4982-X*) Mosby Inc.

***Laboratory Manual to Accompany Fundamental Concepts.** 2nd ed. Vernon Thielmann. 144p. (C). 1999. spiral bd. 24.95 (*0-7872-6215-3*, 41621501) Kendall-Hunt.

Laboratory Manual to Accompany Human Anatomy & Physiology. 6th ed. John W. Hole, Jr. 472p. (C). 1992. text. write for info. (*0-697-12276-X*, WCB McGr Hill) McGrw-H Hghr Educ.

Laboratory Manual to Accompany Introductory Chemistry. 5th ed. Uno Kask et al. 376p. (C). 1993. text, student ed. 24.37 (*0-697-12483-5*, WCB McGr Hill) McGrw-H Hghr Educ.

Laboratory Manual to Accompany Introductory Chemistry. 5th ed. Uno Kask et al. 376p. (C). 1993. text. write for info. (*0-697-12482-7*, WCB McGr Hill); student ed. write for info. incl. VHS (*0-697-20556-8*, WCB McGr Hill) McGrw-H Hghr Educ.

Laboratory Manual to Accompany Mastering Electricity. Stuart Asser & Richard Bahrenburg. 254p. 1993. student ed. 28.00 (*0-8273-4603-4*) Delmar.

Laboratory Market Research. Ed. by Shane Moriarity. 222p. 1986. 15.00 (*0-931880-05-X*) U OK Ctr Econ.

Laboratory Material: Physics 121. UCONN Physics Faculty & Staff. 114p. (C). 1994. 12.69 (*1-56870-131-4*) RonJon Pub.

Laboratory Material: Physics 122. UCONN Physics Faculty & Staff. 130p. (C). 1994. 13.90 (*1-56870-132-2*) RonJon Pub.

Laboratory Mathematics: Medical & Biological Applications. 5th ed. Joe B. Campbell & June M. Campbell. (Illus.). 496p. (C). (gr. 13). 1996. pap. text 33.00 (*0-8151-1397-8*, 25633) Mosby Inc.

Laboratory Measurement of Aerodynamic Noise Generated by Control Valves: ISA Standard S75.07. 12p. 1997. pap. text 20.00 (*1-55617-047-5*, RDS7507) ISA.

Laboratory Medical Mycology. Yousef Al-Doory. LC 79-22500. 420p. reprint ed. pap. 130.20 (*0-7837-1478-5*, 205717300023) Bks Demand.

Laboratory Medicine. Fudge. LC 99-18466. (C). 1999. pap. text. write for info. (*0-7216-7679-0*, W B Saunders Co) Harcrt Hlth Sci Grp.

Laboratory Medicine: Essentials of Anatomic & Clinical Pathology. 2nd ed. John H. Dirckx. 396p. 1995. pap. text 31.00 (*0-934385-61-0*) Hlth Prof Inst.

Laboratory Medicine: Test Selection & Interpretation. Ed. by Joan H. Howanitz & Peter J. Howanitz. (Illus.). 966p. 1991. text 95.00 (*0-443-08576-5*) Church.

Laboratory Medicine: The Selection & Interpretation of Clinical Laboratory Studies. Dennis A. Noe & Robert C. Rock. (Illus.). 1012p. 1993. 135.00 (*0-683-06548-3*) Lppncott W & W.

Laboratory Medicine - Urinalysis & Medical Microscopy. 2nd ed. James A. Freeman & Myrton F. Beeler. LC 82-17254. 631p. reprint ed. pap. 195.70 (*0-7837-2705-4*, 204308400006) Bks Demand.

Laboratory Medicine & the Aging Process. Joseph A. Knight. 1996. 45.00 (*0-89189-397-0*) Am Soc Clinical.

Laboratory Medicine Casebook: Introduction to Clinical Reasoning. Jana Raskova & Nagy Mikhail. 334p. (C). 1996. pap. text 37.95 (*0-8385-5574-8*, A5574-7, Apple Lange Med) McGraw.

Laboratory Medicine in Obstetrics & Gynecology. Gerald D. Willett. (Illus.). 328p. 1994. pap. 39.95 (*0-86542-290-7*) Blackwell Sci.

Laboratory Method for Measuring Fume Generation Rates & Total Fume Emission for Welding & Allied Processes (F1.2-92) 9p. 1992. 27.00 (*0-87171-387-X*) Am Welding.

Laboratory Methodology in Biochemistry. Ed. by Carlo Fini et al. (Illus.). 272p. 1989. lib. bdg. 225.00 (*0-8493-4400-X*, QP551) CRC Pr.

Laboratory Methods for Craft Brewers. Ed. by Rena M. Crumplen. LC 97-77521. (Illus.). 168p. 1997. pap. 65.00 (*1-881696-02-2*) Am Brewing Chems.

Laboratory Methods for the Detection of Mutations & Polymorphisms in DNA. Ed. by Graham R. Taylor. LC 96-26579. 320p. 1997. lib. bdg. 89.95 (*0-8493-9233-0*) CRC Pr.

Laboratory Methods for the Diagnosis of Sexually Transmitted Diseases. 2nd ed. Ed. by Berttina B. Wentworth et al. LC 84-20394. 272p. 1991. 40.00 (*0-87553-128-8*) Am Pub Health.

Laboratory Methods Immunology, 2 vols., Vol. 1. Ed. by Heddy Zola. 280p. 1990. boxed set 225.00 (*0-8493-4481-6*, QR183) CRC Pr.

Laboratory Methods Immunology, 2 vols., Vol. 2. Ed. by Heddy Zola. 252p. 1990. boxed set 225.00 (*0-8493-4482-4*, QR183) CRC Pr.

Laboratory Methods in Food Microbiology. 3rd ed. Wilke F. Harrigan. LC 99-161003. (Illus.). 552p. (C). 1998. pap. 59.95 (*0-12-326043-4*) Acad Pr.

Laboratory Microbiology. 4th ed. L. Jack Bradshaw. 343p. (C). 1992. pap. text 51.00 (*0-03-047442-6*, Pub. by SCP) Harcourt.

Laboratory Mouse. Terrie L. Cunliffe-Beamer. (Laboratory Animal Pocket Reference Ser.). 1998. 39.95 (*0-8493-2563-3*) CRC Pr.

Laboratory Non-Human Primates. Jeffrey D. Fortman & B. Taylor Bennett. (Laboratory Animal Pocket Reference Ser.). 128p. 1999. 39.95 (*0-8493-2562-5*) CRC Pr.

***Laboratory Notes for Introductory Physics 750: 205-206.** John Rollino. 56p. (C). 1998. pap. text 23.95 (*0-7872-0719-5*) Kendall-Hunt.

Laboratory Notes for Physics. 13th ed. University of Pennsylvania, Physics Department Sta. 304p. (C). 1995. spiral bd. 18.95 (*0-8403-9262-1*) Kendall-Hunt.

Laboratory Notes for Physics. 16th ed. Beck et al. 242p. (C). 1998. spiral bd. 31.95 (*0-7872-5357-X*, 41535701) Kendall-Hunt.

Laboratory Notes, Forest Hydrology. Mingteh Chang. (Illus.). 203p. 1982. student ed. 10.00 (*0-938361-03-1*) Austin Univ Forestry.

Laboratory of Dreams: The Russian Avant-Garde & Cultural Experiment. John E. Bowlt. 1999. pap. text 19.95 (*0-8047-3652-9*) Stanford U Pr.

Laboratory of Impure Forms: The Plays of Tadeusz Rozewicz, 35. Halina Filipowicz. LC 90-45327. (Contributions in Drama & Theatre Studies: No. 35). 192p. 1991. 55.00 (*0-313-26805-3*, FTB, Greenwood Pr) Greenwood.

Laboratory of the Mind: Thought Experiments in the Natural Sciences. James R. Brown. (Philosophical Issues in Science Ser.). (Illus.). 208p. (C). 1993. pap. 22.99 (*0-415-09579-4*, B0292) Routledge.

Laboratory on the Nile: A History of the Wellcome Tropical Research Laboratories. Patrick F. D'Arcy. LC 99-27047. 282p. 1999. 49.95 (*0-7890-0728-2*, Pharmctl Prods) Haworth Pr.

Laboratory Organization & Automation. Ed. by D. J. Vonderschmitt. (Clinical Biochemistry Ser.: Vol. 4). 650p. (C). 1990. 353.85 (*3-11-010736-8*) De Gruyter.

Laboratory Outline in Physiology. 2nd ed. Toronto University, Dept. of Physiology Staff. Ed. by R. E. Haist & L. W. Organ. LC QP0044.T6. (Illus.). 89p. reprint ed. pap. 30.00 (*0-8357-8200-X*, 203406700088) Bks Demand.

Laboratory Outlines in Biology. Peter Abramoff & Robert G. Thomson. LC 90-3777. (Illus.). (C). 1991. pap. text 21.60 (*0-7167-2142-2*) W H Freeman.

Laboratory Outlines in Biology. Peter Abramoff & Robert G. Thomson. LC 90-3777. (Illus.). (C). 1991. teacher ed. 12.80 (*0-7167-2208-9*) W H Freeman.

Laboratory Outlines in Biology VI. 6th ed. Peter Abramoff & Robert G. Thompson. LC 94-32653. 528p. (C). 1994. pap. text 32.95 (*0-7167-2633-5*) W H Freeman.

Laboratory Performance Tests for Automotive Gear Lubricants Intended for API GL-5 Service: STP 512A. 130p. 1991. pap. 25.00 (*0-8031-0940-7*, STP512) ASTM.

Laboratory Planetology: Proceedings of the B2 Symposium of COSPAR Scientific Commissioin B Which Was Held During the 30th COSPAR Scientific Assembly, Hamburg, Germany, 11-21 July, 1994. Ed. by D. Mohlmann. (Advances in Space Research Ser.: Vol. 15). 87p. 1995. pap. 97.75 (*0-08-042618-2*, Pergamon Pr) Elsevier.

Laboratory Policy & Procedure Guideline Manual. Billy J. Vanderpool. 281p. 1997. spiral bd. 135.00 (*1-879575-81-7*) Acad Med Sys.

Laboratory Practice of Clinical Toxicology. Eleanor Berman. LC 95-48096. (Illus.). 220p. 1996. pap. 38.95 (*0-398-06582-9*); text 56.95 (*0-398-06581-0*) C C Thomas.

Laboratory Procedure in Clinical Microbiology. 2nd ed. Ed. by J. A. Washington, II. (Illus.). xiv, 885p. 1985. 159.00 (*0-387-96087-2*) Spr-Verlag.

Laboratory Procedures for Medical Assistants. Craig A. Stepp & MaryAnn Woods. Ed. by Margaret Biblis. LC 97-6736. (Illus.). 400p. 1997. pap. text 31.95 (*0-7216-5275-1*, W B Saunders Co) Harcrt Hlth Sci Grp.

Laboratory Procedures for the Medical Office. Tom Palko & Hilda Palko. LC 94-22538. (Illus.). 1995. 34.87 (*0-02-800065-X*) Glencoe.

Laboratory Procedures for Vet Technology. Driskill. pap. text. write for info. (*0-7216-4548-8*, W B Saunders Co) Harcrt Hlth Sci Grp.

Laboratory Procedures for Veterinary Technicians. 3rd ed. Paul W. Pratt. LC 96-43451. (Illus.). 672p. (C). (gr. 13). 1996. pap. text 35.00 (*0-8151-7326-1*, 27768) Mosby Inc.

Laboratory Processes. (Medical Ser.). (Illus.). 216p. 1984. pap. text 14.95 (*0-935920-15-3*, Ntl Pubs Blck) P-H.

Laboratory Processes for Medical Assisting. 3rd ed. LC 92-48295. (Regents Readers Ser.). 224p. 1993. pap. 28.40 (*0-13-722877-5*) Prentice ESL.

Laboratory Production of Cattle Embryos. Ed. by I. Gordon. LC 97-181261. (Biotechnology in Agriculture Ser.: No. 11). (Illus.). 672p. 1994. text 185.00 (*0-85198-928-4*) OUP.

Laboratory Profiles of Equine Diseases. Susan C. Eades & Denise I. Bounous. (Illus.). 304p. (C). (gr. 13). 1996. pap. text 72.00 (*0-8151-1731-0*, 26575) Mosby Inc.

Laboratory Profiles of Small Animal Diseases. 2nd ed. Sodikof. 1995. 77.95 (*0-939674-37-8*) Am Vet Pubns.

Laboratory Projects Manual for Solid-State Electronics. Timothy J. Maloney. 83p. 1994. pap. text 9.25 (*0-9639857-7-9*) Dirk Pubng.

Laboratory Protocols for Conditional Gene Targeting. Raul M. Torres & Ralf Kuhn. LC 97-12588. (Illus.). 180p. 1997. text 47.00 (*0-19-963677-X*) OUP.

Laboratory Protocols for Mutation Detection. Ed. by Ulf Landegren. (Illus.). 204p. 1996. spiral bd. 45.00 (*0-19-857795-8*) OUP.

Laboratory Psychology: A Beginner's Guide. Julia Nunn. (Cognitive Psychology Ser.). 1998. 54.95 (*0-86377-710-4*, Pub. by Psychol Pr); pap. 22.95 (*0-86377-711-2*, Pub. by Psychol Pr) Taylor & Francis.

Laboratory Quality Assurance System. 2nd ed. Thomas A. Ratliff. 372p. 1997. 62.95 (*0-442-02511-4*, VNR) Wiley.

Laboratory Quality Assurance System: A Manual of Quality Procedures with Related Forms. 2nd ed. Thomas A. Ratliff. 256p. 1996. pap. 71.95 (*0-471-28828-4*, VNR) Wiley.

Laboratory Quality Management: QC & QA. George S. Cembrowski & R. Neill Carey. LC 89-6729. (Illus.). 264p. 1989. text 45.00 (*0-89189-277-X*) Am Soc Clinical.

Laboratory Rabbit. Mark A. Suckow & Fred A. Douglas. (Laboratory Animal Pocket Reference Ser.). 144p. 1997. 39.95 (*0-614-29971-3*, 2561H3Y) CRC Pr.

Laboratory Rabbit. Mark A. Suckow & Fred A. Douglas. LC 96-25117. (Laboratory Animal Pocket Reference Ser.). 160p. 1997. spiral bd. 44.95 (*0-8493-2561-7*) CRC Pr.

Laboratory Rat. Patrick Sharp. (Laboratory Animal Pocket Reference Ser.). 240p. 1998. spiral bd. 44.95 (*0-8493-2565-X*) CRC Pr.

Laboratory Rat. Patrick Sharp & Marie LaRegina. Ed. by Mark A. Suckow. (Laboratory Animal Pocket Reference Ser.). 128p. 1997. 39.95 (*0-614-29974-8*, 2565H3Y) CRC Pr.

Laboratory Rat, Vol. 2: Research & Applications. Ed. by Henry J. Baker et al. LC 79-51688. (American College of Laboratory Animal Medicine Ser.). 1980. text 146.00 (*0-12-074902-5*) Acad Pr.

Laboratory Reference for Clinical Neurophysiology. Jay A. Liveson & Dong M. Ma. (Illus.). 528p. 1992. text 69.50 (*0-19-512924-5*) OUP.

Laboratory Regulation Manual, 4 vols. H. Robert Halper & Hope S. Foster. LC 76-56666. ring bd. 729.00 (*0-912862-29-7*) Aspen Pub.

***Laboratory Related Measures of Patient Outcomes: An Introduction.** Ed. by Michael G. Bissell. 2000. pap. text 49.00 (*1-890883-26-3*) Am Assn Clinical Chem.

Laboratory Robotics: A Guide to Planning, Programming & Applications. W. J. Hurst & James W. Mortimer. LC 86-32545. 129p. 1987. 30.00 (*0-89573-322-6*, Wiley-VCH) Wiley.

Laboratory Robots. Richard K. Miller & Terri C. Walker. LC 88-81638. (Survey on Technology & Markets Ser.: No. 47). 50p. 1989. pap. text 200.00 (*1-55865-046-6*) Future Tech Surveys.

Laboratory Safety. ring bd. 160.00 (*1-56238-235-7*, SC10-L) NCCLS.

Laboratory Safety: Principles & Practices. 2nd ed. Ed. by Diane O. Fleming et al. LC 94-24372. (Illus.). 500p. 1995. pap. 69.95 (*1-55581-047-0*) ASM Pr.

***Laboratory Safety & Chemical Hygiene Compliance.** 2nd rev. ed. Peter M. Dell. 176p. 2000. ring bd. 199.00 incl. disk (*0-86587-691-6*, 691) Gov Insts.

Laboratory Safety & Infection Control. Peggy P. Luebbert. (NLM Ser.: No. WA485). 1990. 50.00 incl. VHS (*0-89189-303-2*) Am Soc Clinical.

Laboratory Scientific Instruments in Canada: A Strategic Entry Report, 1997. Compiled by Icon Group International. (Country Industry Report). (Illus.). 134p. 1999. ring bd. 1340.00 incl. audio compact disk (*0-7418-0242-2*) Icon Grp.

Laboratory Shear Strength of Soil-STP 740. Ed. by R. N. Yong & Frank C. Townsend. 720p. 1981. 54.25 (*0-8031-0789-7*, STP740) ASTM.

Laboratory Shear Testing of Soils: A Symposium Sponsored by the National Research Council of Canada & the American Society for Testing & Materials, Ottawa, Canada, September 9, 1963. Symposium on Laboratory Shear Testing of Soils Sta. LC 64-14648. (ASTM Special Technical Publication: No. 361). (Illus.). 515p. reprint ed. pap. 159.70 (*0-7837-5350-0*, 204511000005) Bks Demand.

Laboratory Skills for Biology Teachers. Thomas A. Lonergan. (Illus.). 49p. (Orig.). 1993. pap. text, lab manual ed. write for info. (*1-890264-04-0*) Health-Science.

Laboratory Small Ruminant. Gary L. Borkowski & Matthew Allen. (Laboratory Animal Pocket Reference Ser.). 176p. 1999. spiral bd. 44.95 (*0-8493-2568-4*) CRC Pr.

Laboratory Soil Testing for Engineers. Albert Yeung & Bucky Turk. 1994. spiral bd. 11.35 (*0-88252-172-1*) Paladin Hse.

Laboratory Specialist (Biology), Sr. H. S. Jack Rudman. (Teachers License Examination Ser.: T-34). 1994. pap. 27.95 (*0-8373-8034-0*) Nat Learn.

Laboratory Specialist, Jr. H. S. Jack Rudman. (Teachers License Examination Ser.: T-33). 1994. pap. 27.95 (*0-8373-8033-2*) Nat Learn.

Laboratory Specialist (Physical Sciences), Sr. H. S. Jack Rudman. (Teachers License Examination Ser.: T-35). 1994. pap. 27.95 (*0-8373-8035-9*) Nat Learn.

Laboratory Statistics - Standard Deviation: A Report (1995) 1995. 25.00 (*1-56238-277-2*, EP13-R) NCCLS.

Laboratory Studies in Earth History. 6th ed. Harold L. Levin et al. 256p. (C). 1996. text. write for info. (*0-697-25256-6*, WCB McGr Hill) McGrw-H Hghr Educ.

***Laboratory Studies in Earth History.** 7th ed. James Brice et al. 288p. (C). 2000. pap. 41.25 (*0-07-366130-9*) McGrw-H Hghr Educ.

Laboratory Studies in General Biology. 3rd ed. Eileen Walsh. 368p. (C). 1995. spiral bd. 35.95 (*0-8403-7586-7*) Kendall-Hunt.

Laboratory Studies in Integrated Principles of Zoology. 8th ed. Cleveland P. Hickman, Jr. 432p. (C). 1994. spiral bd., lab manual ed. write for info. (*0-697-23522-X*, WCB McGr Hill) McGrw-H Hghr Educ.

Laboratory Studies in Integrated Zoology. 8th ed. Frances M. Hickman. 420p. 1992. spiral bd. 23.95 (*0-8016-6377-6*) Mosby Inc.

Laboratory Studies in Zoology. 4th ed. James F. Payne et al. 220p. 1990. pap. text 24.95 (*0-88725-130-7*) Hunter Textbks.

An Asterisk (*) at the beginning of an entry indicates that the title is appearing for the first time.

***Laboratory Studies in Zoology.** 5th ed. James F. Payne et al. (Illus.). 240p. 2000. pap. text 26.95 (*0-88725-267-2*) Hunter Textbks.

Laboratory Studies of Heterogeneous Catalytic Processes. E. G. Christoffel. (Studies in Surface Science & Catalysis: No. 42). viv,260p. 1989. 246.00 (*0-444-43025-3*) Elsevier.

Laboratory Studies of Vertebrate & Invertebrate Embryos: Guide & Atlas of Descriptive & Experimental Development. 7th abr. ed. Ed. by Alan R. Sadovnik. (Illus.). 336p. (C). 1994. pap. text 52.00 (*0-02-407602-3*, Macmillan Coll) P-H.

Laboratory Supervisor. Jack Rudman. (Career Examination Ser.: C-3198). 1994. pap. 34.95 (*0-8373-3198-6*) Nat Learn.

***Laboratory Swine.** Peter J. A. Bollen et al. LC 99-57595. (Laboratory Animal Pocket References Ser.). 152p. 1999. spiral bd. 44.95 (*0-8493-1035-0*) CRC Pr.

Laboratory Systems & Spectroscopy. Ed. by James S. Mattson et al. LC 75-32388. (Computers in Chemistry & Instrumentation Ser.: No. 5). (Illus.). 300p. reprint ed. pap. 93.00 (*0-7837-0729-0*, 204105300019) Bks Demand.

Laboratory Technician. Jack Rudman. (Career Examination Ser.: C-1734). 1994. pap. 27.95 (*0-8373-1734-7*) Nat Learn.

Laboratory Technician, Secondary Schools. Jack Rudman. (Teachers License Examination Ser.: T-36). 1994. pap. 27.95 (*0-8373-8036-7*) Nat Learn.

Laboratory Technician Trainee. Jack Rudman. (Career Examination Ser.: C-2909). 1994. pap. 23.95 (*0-8373-2909-4*) Nat Learn.

***Laboratory Techniques: Measuring the Volume of Liquids.** Norman E. Griswold. (Modular Laboratory in Chemistry Ser.). 16p. (C). 1999. pap. text 1.50 (*0-87540-511-8*, TECH 511-8) Chem Educ Res.

Laboratory Techniques: Qualitative Inorganic Analysis Techniques. Norman E. Griswold. Ed. by H. Anthony Neidig. (Modular Laboratory Program in Chemistry Ser.). 16p. (C). 1989. pap. text 1.50 (*0-87540-363-8*, TECH 363-8) Chem Educ Res.

Laboratory Techniques: Safety Precautions. Norman E. Griswold. Ed. by H. Anthony Neidig. (Modular Laboratory Program in Chemistry Ser.). 11p. (C). 1993. pap. text 1.50 (*0-87540-430-8*, TECH 430-8) Chem Educ Res.

Laboratory Techniques for the Branemark System. Ross L. Taylor & Gary F. Bergman. (Illus.). 79p. 1990. ring bd. 52.00 (*0-86715-173-0*) Quint Pub Co.

Laboratory Techniques in Biochemistry & Molecular Biology, Vol. 6. Tim Chard. Incl. Pt. 2. Introduction to Radioimmunoassay & Related Techniques. 1983. 72.25 1978. write for info. (*0-318-51833-3*, North Holland) Elsevier.

Laboratory Techniques in Brucellosis. 2nd ed. G. G. Alton & Lois M. Jones. (Monographs: No. 55). (ENG, FRE, RUS & SPA., Illus.). 92p. 1975. pap. text 35.00 (*92-4-140055-2*, 1140055) World Health.

Laboratory Techniques in Electroanalytical Chemistry. 2nd ed. Ed. by Peter T. Kissenger & William Heineman. (Illus.). 1008p. 1996. text 79.75 (*0-8247-9445-1*) Dekker.

Laboratory Techniques in Rabies. 2nd ed. Ed. by F. Meslin et al. LC 96-212237. (FRE.). 476p. (Orig.). (C). 1996. pap. text 115.00 (*92-4-154479-1*, 1150423) World Health.

***Laboratory Techniques in Renal Cell & Molecular Biology.** Ed. by Y. Tomino. (Illus.). viii, 210p. 2000. spiral bd. 128.00 (*3-8055-6998-X*) S Karger.

Laboratory Techniques in Thrombosis: A Manual. 2nd ed. Jergen Jespersen et al. LC 98-31123. 1998. write for info. (*0-7923-5317-X*) Kluwer Academic.

Laboratory Test Handbook. 3rd ed. David S. Jacobs et al. 1500p. 1994. 46.50 (*0-683-58912-1*) Lppncott W & W.

Laboratory Test Handbook. 4th ed. David S. Jacobs et al. (Clinical Reference Library). 1600p. 1996. 54.75 (*0-916589-36-6*); pap. 49.75 (*0-916589-35-8*) Lexi-Comp.

Laboratory Test Handbook: Concise Edition. David S. Jacobs et al. (Clinical Reference Library). 1142p. 1996. pap. 31.75 (*0-916589-29-3*) Lexi-Comp.

Laboratory Testing Data on Telephone Security Devices & Equipment. abr. ed. Ed. by Michael P. Jones. (Illus.). 36p. 1984. pap. text 6.00 (*0-89904-081-0*) Crumb Elbow Pub.

Laboratory Testing for Cancer: Proceedings of Laboratory for Testing Cancer Conference, Feb. 14-15, 1977. Ed. by H. Schoenfeld et al. (Antibiotics & Chemotherapy Ser.: Vol. 22). (Illus.). 1978. 66.25 (*3-8055-2765-9*) S Karger.

Laboratory Testing for Health Care Professionals. (Specialty Collections). ring bd. 250.00 (*1-56238-296-9*, SC19-L) NCCLS.

Laboratory Testing of Soils & Soft Rocks. Atkinson. (Illus.). 448p. 1998. pap. 164.95 (*0-7514-0388-1*) Thomson Learn.

Laboratory Tests: Implications for Nursing Care. Claire J. Byrne et al. 1981. write for info. (*0-201-00088-1*, Health Sci) Addison-Wesley.

Laboratory Tests: Implications for Nursing Care. 2nd ed. Claire J. Byrne et al. 756p. (C). 1986. pap. text 34.69 (*0-201-12670-2*, Health Sci) Addison-Wesley.

Laboratory Tests & Diagnostic Procedures. 2nd ed. Cynthia C. Chernecky & Barbara J. Berger. Ed. by Barbara N. Cullen. LC 96-43069. (Illus.). 1180p. 1996. pap. text 28.00 (*0-7216-6793-7*, W B Saunders Co) Harcrt Hlth Sci Grp.

Laboratory Tests for the Assessment of Nutritional Status. Howerde E. Sauberlich et al. LC 74-77908. (Monotopic Reprint Ser.). 136p. 1974. reprint ed. 35.00 (*0-8493-0121-1*, QP501, CRC Reprint) Franklin.

Laboratory Textbook for Elementary Astronomy. 8th ed. J. Scott Shaw & Mariam Dittmann. (Illus.). 200p. (C). pap. text, lab manual ed. 27.95 (*0-89892-200-3*) Contemp Pub Co of Raleigh.

Laboratory Textbook for Introductory Astronomy. 5th ed. Kermit E. Duckett. (Illus.). 320p. (Orig.). (C). 1998. pap. text, lab manual ed. 35.00 (*0-89892-131-7*) Contemp Pub Co of Raleigh.

Laboratory Textbook of Anatomy & Physiology. 6th ed. Anne B. Donnersberger & Anne E. Lesak. (Life Science Ser.). (C). 1996. pap., teacher ed. 10.00 (*0-669-39881-0*) Jones & Bartlett.

Laboratory Textbook of Anatomy & Physiology. 7th ed. Anne B. Donnersberger & Anne E. Lesak. LC 99-14177. 1999. write for info. (*0-7637-0915-8*) Jones & Bartlett.

Laboratory Topics in Botany: Biology of Plants. 6th ed. Peter Raven. (Illus.). (C). 1998. text, lab manual ed. 24.60 (*1-57259-605-8*) Worth.

Laboratory Training Manual on the Use of Nuclear Techniques in Insect Research & Control. (Technical Reports: No. 336). 183p. 1992. pap. 65.00 (*92-0-101792-8*, STI/DOC/336, Pub. by IAEA) Bernan Associates.

Laboratory Validation of Ozone Sampling with Spill Proof Impingers (LVOS) 50p. 1983. pap. 39.00 (*0-87171-224-5*) Am Welding.

Laboratory Ventilation Workbook. 2nd rev. ed. D. Jeff Burton. 350p. (C). 1994. pap. text, wbk. ed. 59.95 (*1-883992-02-8*) IVE Inc.

Laboratory Waste Management: A Guidebook. American Chemical Society Task Force on Laboratory. LC 93-45546. 250p. 1994. text 36.95 (*0-8412-2735-7*, Pub. by Am Chemical); pap. text 28.00 (*0-8412-2849-3*, Pub. by Am Chemical) OUP.

Laboratory Workbook for Descriptive Geometry & Computer-Aided Design. 2nd ed. Doran F. Wilkes. (Illus.). iv, 100p. (C). 1988. pap. text 6.25 (*0-8425-2363-4*, Friends of the Library) Brigham.

Laboratory Workbook for Multimedia Calculus. Quinney. 136p. 1995. pap. 25.95 (*0-471-02111-3*) Wiley.

Laboratory/Pathology Words & Phrases. 2nd rev. ed. Ed. by Sally C. Pitman. 648p. (Orig.). 1996. pap. 37.00 (*0-934385-66-1*) Hlth Prof Inst.

***Labored Relations: Law, Politics & the NLRB - A Memoir.** William B. Gould, IV. (Illus.). 395p. (C). 2000. 37.95 (*0-262-07205-X*) MIT Pr.

Laborer. Jack Rudman. (Career Examination Ser.: C-434). 1994. pap. 23.95 (*0-8373-0434-2*) Nat Learn.

Laborer: A Remedy for His Wrongs. William Dealtry. LC 76-89729. (American Labor, from Conspiracy to Collective Bargaining Ser., No. 1). 420p. 1974. reprint ed. 25.95 (*0-405-02116-X*) Ayer.

Laborer Foreman. Jack Rudman. (Career Examination Ser.: C-1337). 1994. pap. 29.95 (*0-8373-1337-6*) Nat Learn.

Laborer Is Worthy of His Hire, Vol VII, No. 5. 5th rev. ed. Stephen V. LeLeers. (Illus.). 74p. 1996. pap. 12.00 (*0-9653675-0-9*) NFPC.

***Laborer Is Worthy of His Hire, Vol. 10.** Willaim P. Daly. Ed. by Bernard F. Stratman. 71p. 1999. pap. 17.00 (*1-893060-04-7*) NFPC.

Laborer Supervisor. Jack Rudman. (Career Examination Ser.: C-3458). 1994. pap. 29.95 (*0-8373-3458-6*) Nat Learn.

Laborers for Liberty: American Women, 1865-1890 see **Young Oxford History of Women in the United States**

Laborers for Liberty: American Women 1865-1890, Vol. 6. Harriet Sigerman. (Young Oxford History of Women in the United States Ser.). (Illus.). 144p. (J). 1998. reprint ed. pap. 10.95 (*0-19-512404-9*) OUP.

Labores de Costura Para el Hogar. Singer Sewing Reference Library Staff. (Singer Sewing Reference Library). (SPA., Illus.). 128p. 1994. 17.95 (*0-86573-292-2*) Creat Pub Intl.

Laboring & Dependent Classes in Colonial America, 1607-1783. Marcus W. Jernegan. LC 80-11342. (Illus.). 256p. 1980. reprint ed. lib. bdg. 65.00 (*0-313-22399-8*, JELD, Greenwood Pr) Greenwood.

Laboring Classes. Orestes A. Brownson. LC 78-17952. 144p. 1978. reprint ed. 50.00 (*0-8201-1314-X*) Schol Facsimiles.

Laboring Classes & Dangerous Classes: In Paris During the First Half of the 19th Century. Louis Chevalier. Tr. by Frank Jellinek from FRE. 512p. 2000. reprint ed. pap. 17.95 (*0-86527-425-8*) Fertig.

Laboring Classes & Dangerous Classes in Paris During the First Half of the 19th Century. Louis Chevalier. Tr. by Frank Jellinek from FRE. 544p. 1973. 45.00 (*0-86527-114-3*) Fertig.

Laboring for Freedom: A New Look at the History of Labor in America. Daniel Jacoby. LC 97-31985. 224p. (gr. 13). 1998. text 69.95 (*0-7656-0251-2*); pap. text 27.95 (*0-7656-0252-0*) M E Sharpe.

Laboring for Rights: Unions & Sexual Diversity Across Nations. Ed. by Gerald Hunt. LC 99-14081. (Queer Politics, Queer Theories Ser.). (Illus.). 328p. 1999. 65.50 (*1-56639-717-0*) Temple U Pr.

***Laboring for Rights: Unions & Sexual Diversity Across Nations.** Gerald Hunt. LC 99-14081. (Queer Politics, Queer Theories Ser.). (Illus.). 328p. 1999. pap. 27.95 (*1-56639-718-9*) Temple U Pr.

Laboring in the Fields of the Lord: Spanish Missions & Southeastern Indians. Jerald T. Milanich. (Illus.). 208p. 1999. 26.95 (*1-56098-940-8*) Smithsonian.

Laboring-Life in the Outpost. Jean Nava. LC 98-92088. (More Than Conquerors Ser.: Vol. 2). (Illus.). 490p. (J). (gr. 4 up). 1998. pap. 12.95 (*0-9659952-1-6*) Kingdom Pr.

Labors. Kevin Griffith. Ed. by Shirley Warren. 28p. 1991. pap. 5.00 (*1-877801-14-3*) Still Waters.

Labor's Capital: The Economics & Politics of Private Pensions. Teresa Ghilarducci. (Illus.). 235p. 1992. 37.50 (*0-262-07139-8*) MIT Pr.

Labor's Flaming Youth: Telephone Operators & Worker Militancy, 1878-1923. Stephen H. Norwood. (Working Class in American History Women in American History Ser.). (Illus.). 360p. 1990. text 34.95 (*0-252-01633-5*) U of Ill Pr.

Labor's Flaming Youth: Telephone Operators & Worker Militancy, 1878-1923. Stephen H. Norwood. (Working Class in American History - Women in American History Ser.). (Illus.). 360p. 1991. pap. text 16.95 (*0-252-06225-6*) U of Ill Pr.

Labors from the Heart: Mission & Ministry in a Catholic University. Ed. by Mark L. Poorman. LC 96-31823. 1997. text 25.00 (*0-268-01424-8*); pap. text 15.00 (*0-268-01425-6*) U of Notre Dame Pr.

Labor's Giant Step: The First Twenty Years of the CIO: 1936-55. Art Preis. LC 72-79771. 538p. 1972. reprint ed. pap. 26.95 (*0-87348-263-8*); reprint ed. lib. bdg. 65.00 (*0-87348-371-5*) Pathfinder NY.

Labor's Grass Roots: A Study of the Local Union. Jack Barbash. LC 73-11839. 250p. 1974. reprint ed. lib. bdg. 65.00 (*0-8371-7064-8*, BALG, Greenwood Pr) Greenwood.

Labor's Great War: The Struggle for Industrial Democracy & the Transformation of the American Workplace, 1912-1921. Joseph A. McCartin. LC 97-9364. 328p. (gr. 13). 1998. pap. 19.95 (*0-8078-4679-1*); lib. bdg. 49.95 (*0-8078-2372-4*) U of NC Pr.

Labor's Joke Book. Ed. & Intro. by Paul Buhle. LC 84-82508. (Illus.). 64p. (Orig.). (C). 1985. pap. 3.95 (*0-9614272-0-5*) WD Pr.

Labor's Last Chance? Heath et al. pap. 35.95 (*1-85521-477-6*) Ashgate Pub Co.

Labor's Lot: The Power, History, & Culture of Aboriginal Action. Elizabeth A. Povinelli. LC 93-2511. (Illus.). 344p. 1994. lib. bdg. 64.00 (*0-226-67673-0*) U Ch Pr.

Labors Lot: The Power, History, & Culture of Aboriginal Action. Elizabeth A. Povinelli. LC 93-2511. (Illus.). 344p. 1994. pap. text 19.95 (*0-226-67674-9*) U Ch Pr.

Labor's New Millions. Mary H. Vorse. LC 71-89768. (American Labor, from Conspiracy to Collective Bargaining Ser., No. 1). 312p. 1971. reprint ed. 20.95 (*0-405-02156-9*) Ayer.

Labor's New Voice: Unions & the Mass Media. Sara U. Douglas. Ed. by Melvin J. Voigt. LC 86-3373. (Communication & Information Science Ser.). 320p. 1986. text 78.50 (*0-89391-352-9*) Ablx Pub.

Labors of a Modern Hercules. Dyer. 512p. 1990. 50.00 (*0-07-103231-2*) McGraw.

Labors of Hercules. Agatha Christie. LC 92-8415. 224p. 1993. 24.95 (*0-399-13777-7*, G P Putnam) Peng Put Young Read.

Labors of Hercules. Agatha Christie. 256p. 1984. reprint ed. mass mkt. 5.99 (*0-425-06785-8*) Berkley Pub.

Labors of Love. Judith R. Weissman & Wendy Lavitt. (Illus.). 50.00 (*0-317-66571-5*) Knopf.

Labors of Love: Decorating Ideas, Craft Projects, & Design Inspiration to Enhance Your Home. Text by Ciba Vaughan. LC 96-1700. (Illus.). 208p. 1996. 27.50 (*0-688-14467-5*, Hearst) Hearst Commns.

Labors of Sisyphus: The Economic Development of Communist China. Maria H. Chang. LC 97-19298. 310p. 1997. 39.95 (*1-56000-330-8*) Transaction Pubs.

***Labors of Sisyphus: The Economic Development of Communist China.** Maria H. Chang. 259p. 1999. pap. 24.95 (*0-7658-0661-4*) Transaction Pubs.

Labors of the Months in Antique & Medieval Art to the End of the 12th Century. James C. Webster. LC 75-128988. (Northwestern University. Humanities Ser.: No. 4). reprint ed. 35.00 (*0-404-50704-2*) AMS Pr.

Labor's Power & Industrial Performance: Automobile Production Regimes in the U. S., Germany, & Japan. Stavros P. Gavroglou. LC 98-37453. (Studies on Industrial Productivity). 352p. 1998. 71.00 (*0-8153-3244-0*) Garland.

Labor's Relation to Church & Community: A Series of Addresses. Institute for Religious & Social Studies Staff. Ed. by Liston Pope. LC 78-167368. (Essay Index Reprints - Religion & Civilization Faith Ser.). 1977. reprint ed. 20.95 (*0-8369-2657-9*) Ayer.

Labor's Struggles, 1945-1950: A Participant's View. Irving Richter. (Illus.). 176p. (C). 1994. text 64.95 (*0-521-41412-1*) Cambridge U Pr.

***Labor's Text: The Worker in American Fiction.** Laura Hapke. LC 00-39029. (Illus.). 544p. (C). 2001. text 60.00 (*0-8135-2879-8*); pap. text 30.00 (*0-8135-2880-1*) Rutgers U Pr.

***Labor's Troubadour.** Joe Glazer. LC 00-9136. (Music in American Life Ser.). 2001. write for info. (*0-252-02612-8*) U of Ill Pr.

Labor's Untold Story. Richard Boyer & Herbert Morais. 380p. 1955. 6.95 (*0-916180-01-8*) United Elec R&M.

Labor's Voice in the Cabinet. John Lombardi. LC 68-58604. (Columbia University. Studies in the Social Sciences: No. 496). reprint ed. 32.50 (*0-404-51496-0*) AMS Pr.

Labor's War at Home: The CIO in World War II. Nelson Lichtenstein. LC 82-4349. 332p. 1987. pap. text 20.95 (*0-521-33573-6*) Cambridge U Pr.

Labor's Workshop of Democracy see **Austria from Habsburg to Hitler**

Labortory Procedures for Medical Office Personnel. Craig A. Stepp & Mary Ann Woods. (Illus.). 460p. 1997. pap., teacher ed. write for info. (*0-7216-5309-X*, W B Saunders Co) Harcrt Hlth Sci Grp.

Laboulbeniales No. 1: Laboulbenia. Sergio Santamaria. (Flora Mycologica Iberica Ser.: Vol. 4). (GER.). 188p. 1998. write for info. (*3-443-65009-0*, Pub. by Gebruder Borntraeger) Balogh.

Laboulbeniales (Fungi, Ascomycetes) Isabelle I. Tavares. (Mycologia Memoirs Ser.: No. 9). (Illus.). 700p. 1985. lib. bdg. 120.00 (*3-7682-1389-7*) Lubrecht & Cramer.

Labour Administration: A General Introduction. J. I. Husband. viii, 88p. 1980. pap. 27.00 (*92-2-102349-4*); pap. 18.00 (*92-2-102350-8*) Intl Labour Office.

Labour & Business in Modern Britain. Ed. by Charles Harvey & John Turner. 256p. 1989. text 35.00 (*0-7146-3365-8*, Pub. by F Cass Pubs) Intl Spec Bk.

Labour & Conservative Party Members, 1900-92: Social Characteristics, Political Attitudes, & Activities. Patrick Seyd et al. LC 95-46955. (Illus.). 360p. 1996. 87.95 (*1-85521-536-5*, Pub. by Dartmth Pub) Ashgate Pub Co.

Labour & Gender: Survival in Urban India. U. Kalpagam. LC 93-34795. 264p. (C). 1994. text 33.50 (*0-8039-9147-9*) Sage.

Labour & Gold in Fiji. Atu Emberson-Bain. LC 93-12431. (Illus.). 294p. (C). 1994. text 74.95 (*0-521-36372-1*) Cambridge U Pr.

Labour & Industry in the Asia-Pacific: Lessons from the Newly Industrialized Countries. Barry Wilkinson. LC 93-35002. (International Management, Organization & Policy Analysis Ser.: No. 54). xvi, 236p. (C). 1994. lib. bdg. 79.95 (*3-11-012676-1*) De Gruyter.

Labour & Locality, Vol. 4. 208p. (C). 1992. 120.00 (*1-85346-182-2*, Pub. by David Fulton) St Mut.

Labour & Machinery Use on the Larger Mainly Arable Farm. Ed. by School of Rural Economics & Related Studies Staff. 1981. 45.00 (*0-7855-7283-X*) St Mut.

Labour & Nationalism in Ireland. J. Dunsmore Clarkson. LC 78-12024. (Columbia University. Studies in the Social Sciences: No. 266). reprint ed. 37.50 (*0-404-51266-6*) AMS Pr.

Labour & Parastatal Politics in Sierra Leone: A Study of African Working-Class Ambivalence. David F. Luke. (Dalhousie African Studies). (Illus.). 306p. (Orig.). (C). 1984. pap. text 25.50 (*0-8191-3958-0*) U Pr of Amer.

Labour & Partition: The Belfast Working Class, 1905-1923. Austen Morgan. 280p. (C). 1987. 54.95 (*0-7453-0326-9*, Pub. by Pluto GBR) Stylus Pub VA.

Labour & Politics, 1900-1906: A History of the Labour Representation Committee. Frank W. Bealey & Henry Pelling. LC 82-15828. 313p. (C). 1982. lib. bdg. 75.00 (*0-313-23693-3*, BELAP, Greenwood Pr) Greenwood.

Labour & Population Programme: An Annotated Bibliography. (Bibliography Ser.: No. 11). xiii, 209p. (Orig.). 1991. pap. 24.75 (*92-2-107748-9*) Intl Labour Office.

Labour & Poverty in Kenya, 1900-80. Paul Collier & Deepak Lal. (Illus.). 240p. 1986. 69.00 (*0-19-828505-1*) OUP.

Labour & Poverty in Rural Tanzania: Ujamaa & Rural Development in the United Republic of Tanzania. Paul Collier et al. (Illus.). 160p. 1991. pap. 22.00 (*0-19-828315-6*) OUP.

Labour & Scottish Nationalism: A History from Keir Hardie to the Present Day. Gerry Hassan. 1999. pap. text 22.50 (*0-85315-884-3*, Pub. by Lawrence & Wishart) NYU Pr.

Labour & Socialist Movements in Europe Before 1914. Ed. by Dick Geary. LC 88-21418. 304p. 1989. pap. 16.50 (*0-85496-705-2*, Pub. by Berg Pubs) NYU Pr.

Labour & Society in Britain & America, Vol. 2. Neville Kirk. (Challenge & Accommodation, 1850-1939 Ser.). 256p. 1993. write for info. (*0-7185-1480-7*) St Martin.

Labour & Society in Britain & America Vol. 1: Capitalism, Custom & Protest, 1780-1850. Neville Kirk. 240p. 1993. write for info. (*0-7185-1342-8*) St Martin.

Labour & Society in Britain & the U. S. A. Vol. 1: Capitalism, Custom, & Protest 1780-1850. Neville Kirk. LC 93-47283. (Illus.). 234p. 1994. 26.95 (*1-85928-021-8*, Pub. by Scolar Pr) Ashgate Pub Co.

Labour & Society in Britain & the U. S. A. Vol. 2: Challenge & Accommodation, 1850-1939. Neville Kirk. LC 93-47283. (Illus.). 434p. 1994. 26.95 (*1-85928-022-6*, Pub. by Scolar Pr) Ashgate Pub Co.

Labour & State in Indonesia: State & Labour in New Order Indonesia. Rob Lambert. (Asia Papers: No. 6). pap. write for info. (*1-875560-71-8*, Pub. by Univ of West Aust Pr) Intl Spec Bk.

Labour & the British State. Barry Jones & Michael Keating. 1985. 36.00 (*0-19-876187-2*); pap. 12.95 (*0-19-876186-4*) OUP.

Labour & the Left in the 1930's. Ben Pimlott. (Illus.). 272p. 1986. reprint ed. pap. text 18.95 (*0-04-941016-4*) Routledge.

Labour & the Political Economy in Israel. Michael Shalev. (Library of Political Economy). (Illus.). 414p. 1992. text 75.00 (*0-19-828513-2*) OUP.

Labour & the Poor in England & Wales, 1849-1851, 3 vols., Vol. 1. Ed. by Jules Ginswick. (Illus.). 1983. 35.00 (*0-7146-2907-3*, Pub. by F Cass Pubs); pap. 17.50 (*0-7146-4038-7*, Pub. by F Cass Pubs) Intl Spec Bk.

Labour & the Poor in England & Wales, 1849-1851, 3 vols., Vol. 2. Ed. by Jules Ginswick. (Illus.). 316p. 1983. 35.00 (*0-7146-2960-X*, Pub. by F Cass Pubs) Intl Spec Bk.

Labour & the Poor in England & Wales, 1849-1851 Vol. 1: Lancashire, Cheshire, Yorkshire, Vol. 2. Ed. by Jules Ginswick. (Illus.). 316p. 1983. pap. 17.50 (*0-7146-4039-5*, Pub. by F Cass Pubs) Intl Spec Bk.

Labour & the Poor in England & Wales, 1849-1851 Vol. 2: Northumberland & Durham, Staffordshire, The Midlands, Vol. 3. Ed. by Jules Ginswick. (Illus.). 228p. 1983. 35.00 (*0-7146-2961-8*, Pub. by F Cass Pubs); pap. 17.50 (*0-7146-4040-9*, Pub. by F Cass Pubs) Intl Spec Bk.

Labour & the Poor in England & Wales, 1849-1951 (The Rural Districts) Eastern Counties, South-Eastern Counties, Vol. VIII. Ed. by Jules Ginswick. (Illus.). 224p. 29.50 (*0-7146-3253-8*, Pub. by F Cass Pubs); pap. 17.50 (*0-7146-4045-X*, Pub. by F Cass Pubs) Intl Spec Bk.

L

Labour & the Poor in England & Wales, 1849-1951 (The Rural Districts) Midlands, Northern Counties, Vol. VI. Ed. & Intro. by Jules Ginswick. (Illus.). 224p. 35.00 (*0-7146-3038-1*, Pub. by F Cass Pubs); pap. 17.50 (*0-7146-4043-3*, Pub. by F Cass Pubs) Intl Spec Bk.

Labour & the Poor in England & Wales, 1849-1951, Vol. 4: (The Towns) Liverpool & Birkenhead. Intro. by Jules Ginswick. 224p. 35.00 (*0-7146-3036-5*, Pub. by F Cass Pubs); pap. 17.50 (*0-7146-4041-7*, Pub. by F Cass Pubs) Intl Spec Bk.

Labour & the Poor in England & Wales, 1849-1951, Vol. 5: (The Towns) Birmingham. Ed. by Jules Ginswick. (Illus.). 224p. 35.00 (*0-7146-3037-3*, Pub. by F Cass Pubs); pap. 17.50 (*0-7146-4042-5*, Pub. by F Cass Pubs) Intl Spec Bk.

Labour & the Poor in England & Wales, 1849-1951, Vol. 7: (The Rural Districts) South-Western Counties. Ed. by Jules Ginswick. 224p. 35.00 (*0-7146-3039-X*, Pub. by F Cass Pubs); pap. 17.50 (*0-7146-4044-1*, Pub. by F Cass Pubs) Intl Spec Bk.

Labour & Working Class in Eastern India: Studies in Colonial History. Ranajit D. Gupta. LC 95-900050. (C). 1995. 42.00 (*81-7074-127-0*, Pub. by KP Bagchi) S Asia.

Labour Arbitration Yearbook 1991, 2 vols. Kaplan et al. 656p. 1991. 95.00 (*0-409-89867-8*, MICHIE); text. write for info. (*0-409-89945-3*, MICHIE) LEXIS Pub.

Labour Arbitration Yearbook 1991, 2 vols., Set. Kaplan et al. 656p. 1991. 180.00 (*0-409-90061-3*, MICHIE) LEXIS Pub.

Labour Aristocracy, 1851-1914. Trevor Lummis. LC 94-6771. 1994. 78.95 (*1-85928-049-8*, Pub. by Scolar Pr) Ashgate Pub Co.

***Labour-Based Road Construction.** Paul Larcher. 200p. 1998. pap. 22.95 (*1-85339-416-5*, Pub. by Intermed Tech) Stylus Pub VA.

Labour Co-Operatives: Retrospect & Prospects. Raymond Louis. vi, 162p. 1983. 31.50 (*92-2-103011-3*); pap. 22.50 (*92-2-103012-1*) Intl Labour Office.

Labour Code of the Kazakh SSR. Tr. & Intro. by William E. Butler. LC 99-196147. 168p. 1995. pap. 55.00 (*1-898029-18-0*, Pub. by Simmonds & Hill Pubng) Gaunt.

Labour Code of the Republic Uzbekistan. Ed. & Tr. by William E. Butler from RUS. LC 99-196148. 136p. 1996. pap. 55.00 (*1-898029-26-1*, Pub. by Simmonds & Hill Pubng) Gaunt.

Labour Control & Labour Resistance in the Agro-Industrial Plantations of Cameroon. Piet Konings. (Monographs from the African Studies Centre, Leiden). 1992. 85.00 (*0-7103-0438-2*, A6772) Routledge.

Labour Copartnership. Henry D. Lloyd. (Notable American Authors Ser.). 1999. reprint ed. lib. bdg. 125.00 (*0-7812-3802-1*) Rprt Serv.

Labour Costs, 1992: Principal Results. (Illus.). 289p. 1996. pap. 30.00 (*92-827-6796-5*, CA93-95-023-3AC, Pub. by Comm Europ Commun) Bernan Associates.

Labour Courts in Latin America. (I.L.O. Studies & Reports: Nos. 13-15). 1969. reprint ed. 51.00 (*0-8115-3336-0*) Periodicals Srv.

Labour Defended Against the Claims of Capital: or The Unproductiveness of Capital Proved with Reference to the Present Combinations Amongst Journeymen. Thomas Hodgskin. LC 68-54736. (Reprints of Economic Classics Ser.). 108p. 1969. reprint ed. 27.50 (*0-678-00004-2*) Kelley.

Labour Dispute Resolution. C. Mischke et al. LC 97-197870. 1997. pap. 32.50 (*0-7021-4156-9*, Pub. by Juta & Co) Gaunt.

Labour Disputes in the Early Days of the Industrial Revolution, 1758-1780. LC 72-2530. (British Labour Struggles Before 1850 Ser.). 1974. 20.95 (*0-405-04423-2*) Ayer.

Labour Disputes in the Mines, 1831-1844. LC 72-2531. (British Labour Struggles Before 1850 Ser.). 1974. 20.95 (*0-405-04424-0*) Ayer.

Labour Economics. Frank Fishwick. 1979. 45.95 (*0-905440-14-5*) St Mut.

Labour Employment in Private Forestry in England & Wales till 1976. F. E. Balman & A. G. Dolan. 1983. 60.00 (*0-7855-7180-9*) St Mut.

Labour, Environment & Industrial Change. Ed. by Godfrey J. Linge & G. A. Van Der Knaap. 256p. 1989. 57.50 (*0-415-00928-6*) Routledge.

Labour Force Estimates & Projections, 1950-2000, 6 vols. Incl. Vol. 1. Asia. pap. 8.55 (*92-2-001666-4*, ILO250); Vol. 2. Africa. pap. 8.55 (*92-2-001667-2*, ILO251); Vol. 4. Europe, Northern America, Oceania & U. S. S. R. 1977. pap. 8.55 (*92-2-001669-9*, ILO253); Vol. 5. World Summary. 1977. pap. 7.15 (*92-2-001670-2*, ILO254); Vol. 6. Methodological Supplement. 1977. pap. 10.00 (*92-2-101671-4*, ILO255); 1977. Set pap. 45.75 (*0-685-12993-4*, ILO95) Intl Labour Office.

***Labour Force Statistics: 1978/1998, 1999 Edition.** OECD Staff. 352p. 2000. pap. 72.00 (*92-64-05881-8*, 30 1999 09 3 P, Pub. by Org for Econ) OECD.

Labour Force Statistics Database: User Reference Manual & Diskette. 30.00 (*92-1-128202-0*) UN.

Labour Force Statistics Database Version 3.0: User Reference Manual & Diskette. 88p. 48.00 (*92-1-128176-8*) UN.

Labour Force Statistics, 1976-1996: 1997 Edition. OECD Staff. 592p. 1997. pap. 97.00 (*92-64-05536-3*, 30-97-05-3, Pub. by Org for Econ) OECD.

***Labour Force Statistics 1977/1997: 1998 Edition.** OECD Staff. 588p. 1999. pap. 98.00 (*92-64-05801-X*, 30 98 06 3 P, Pub. by Org for Econ) OECD.

***Labour Force Survey Methods & Definitions, 1998.** 62p. 2000. pap. 15.00 (*92-828-6891-5*, CA19-98-536-EN-C, Pub. by Comm Europ Commun) Bernan Associates.

***Labour Force Survey Results: 1998-99 Results.** Eurostat Staff. 257p. 2000. pap. 60.00 (*92-828-7104-5*, CA-22-99-531-EN-C, Pub. by Comm Europ Commun) Bernan Associates.

Labour Government & British Industry, 1945-1951. Arnold A. Rogow & Peter Shore. LC 73-22508. 196p. (C). 1974. reprint ed. lib. bdg. 79.50 (*0-8371-6374-9*, ROLG, Greenwood Pr) Greenwood.

Labour Government & Private Industry: The Experience of the 1945-51 Governments. Ed. by Helen Mercer et al. 240p. 1993. 68.00 (*0-7486-0339-5*, Pub. by Edinburgh U Pr) Col U Pr.

Labour Government & the End of Empire, 1945-1951: Economics & International Relations. Ed. by Ronald Hyam. (British Documents on the End of Empire Series A: Vol. 2, Pt. 2). xxii, 498p. 1992. 140.00 (*0-11-290522-6*, Pub. by Statnry Office) Balogh.

Labour Government & the End of Empire, 1945-1951: High Policy & Administrative British Documents on the End of Empire. Ed. by Ronald Hyam. (British Documents on the End of Empire Series A: Vol. 2, Pt. 1). lxxxiv, 372p. 1992. 140.00 (*0-11-290521-8*, Pub. by Statnry Office) Balogh.

Labour Government & the End of Empire, 1945-1951: Race Relations & the Commonwealth. Ed. by Ronald Hyman. (British Documents on the End of Empire Series A: Vol. 2, Pt. 4). xviii, 399p. 1992. 140.00 (*0-11-290524-2*, Pub. by Statnry Office) Balogh.

Labour Government & the End of Empire, 1945-1951: Strategy, Politics & Constitutional Change. Ed. by Ronald Hyam. (British Documents on the End of Empire Series A: Vol. 2, Pt. 3). xxii, 419p. 1992. 99.00 (*0-11-290523-4*, Pub. by Statnry Office) Balogh.

Labour Government's Economic Record 1964-1970. Wilfred Beckerman. LC 72-184050. 343p. 1972. write for info. (*0-7156-0608-5*) G Duckworth.

Labour Government's Economic Record 1964-1970. Wilfred Beckerman. LC 76-351014. (Paperduck Ser.). 343p. 1975. write for info. (*0-7156-0890-8*) G Duckworth.

Labour History & the Labour Movement in Britian. Sidney Pollard. LC 98-54452. (Variorum Collected Studies Ser.). (Illus.). 6p. 1999. text 101.95 (*0-86078-793-1*) Ashgate Pub Co.

Labour in British Society: An Interpretive History. Richard Price. 288p. 1986. 49.95 (*0-85664-736-5*, Pub. by C Helm) Routldge.

***Labour in British Society 1830.** Donald M. MacRaild. LC 99-45253. 2000. text 65.00 (*0-312-23313-2*) St Martin.

***Labour in Crisis: The Second Labour Government, 1929-31.** Neil Riddell. 1999. 79.95 (*0-7190-5084-7*, Pub. by Manchester Univ Pr) St Martin.

Labour in Power? A Study of the Labour Government 1974-1979. David Coates. LC 79-42850. 316p. reprint ed. pap. 98.00 (*0-608-13096-6*, 202521800043) Bks Demand.

Labour in Power, 1945-1951. Kenneth O. Morgan. (Illus.). 564p. (C). 1985. pap. 21.00 (*0-19-285150-0*) OUP.

Labour in the Coal-Mining Industry, 1914-1921. G. D. Cole. (Economic & Social History of the World War Ser.). 1923. 100.00 (*0-317-27503-8*) Elliots Bks.

Labour in the Commonwealth: Book for the Younger Generation. George D. Cole. LC 75-157330. (Select Bibliographies Reprint Ser.). 1977. reprint ed. 18.95 (*0-8369-5790-3*) Ayer.

Labour in the Medieval Islamic World. Maya Shatzmiller. LC 93-2403. (Islamic History & Civilization, Studies & Texts Ser.: Vol. 4). 1994. 170.50 (*90-04-09896-8*) Brill Academic Pubs.

Labour in the Tropical Territories of the Commonwealth. Benjamin C. Roberts. LC 64-25334. 444p. reprint ed. 137.70 (*0-8357-9110-6*, 201792500010) Bks Demand.

Labour in Transition: The Labour Process in East Europe & China. Ed. by Chris Smith & Paul Thompson. (Critical Perspectives on Work & Organization Ser.). 224p. 1992. pap. 29.95 (*0-415-08648-5*) Thomson Learn.

Labour in Transition: The Labour Process in East Europe & China. Ed. by Chris Smith & Paul Thompson. LC 92-24745. (Critical Perspectives on Work & Organization Ser.). 224p. (C). (gr. 13). 1992. pap. 64.95 (*0-415-08295-1*, A9712) Thomson Learn.

Labour Information: A Guide to Selected Sources. (International Labour Bibliography Ser.: No. 8). v, 231p. (Orig.). 1991. pap. 24.75 (*92-2-107274-6*) Intl Labour Office.

Labour Inspection: A Workers' Education Manual. ix, 100p. (Orig.). 1986. pap. 15.75 (*92-2-105359-8*) Intl Labour Office.

Labour Institutions & Economic Development: A Study of Nepal. Ajeet N. Mathur. 1997. pap. 25.00 (*0-7855-7429-8*, Pub. by Ratna Pustak Bhandar) St Mut.

Labour Law. E. A. Lichtenstein. 200p. (C). 1991. pap. 85.00 (*1-85352-564-2*, Pub. by HLT Pubns) St Mut.

Labour Law. Gillian S. Morris & Simon Deakin. 1995. pap. text. write for info. (*0-406-01025-0*, UK, MICHIE) LEXIS Pub.

Labour Law. 2nd ed. W. Breen Creighton & Andrew Stewart. 375p. 1994. pap. 49.00 (*1-86287-134-5*, Pub. by Federation Pr) Gaunt.

Labour Law. 2nd ed. Paul Davies & Mark Freedland. (Law in Context Ser.). 1008p. (C). 1994. pap. text, per. 39.95 (*0-297-78090-5*) Northwestern U Pr.

Labour Law. 4th ed. John Bowers & Simon Honeyball. 442p. 1996. pap. 42.00 (*1-85431-446-7*, Pub. by Blackstone Pr) Gaunt.

Labour Law: An Introduction. W. Breen Creighton & Andrew Stewart. xxx, 306p. 1990. pap. 43.00 (*1-86287-031-4*, Pub. by Federation Pr) Gaunt.

***Labour Law: An Introduction.** 3rd ed. Breen Creighton & Andrew Stewart. 500p. 2000. pap. 55.00 (*1-86287-231-7*, 18629, Pub. by Federation Pr) Gaunt.

Labour Law: Text & Materials. 2nd ed. W. B. Creighton et al. 1993. pap. 125.00 (*0-455-21137-X*, Pub. by LawBk Co) Gaunt.

Labour Law: Text & Materials. 2nd ed. W. Breen Creighton et al. 1993. 165.00 (*0-455-21136-1*, Pub. by LawBk Co) Gaunt.

Labour Law: Text & Materials. 2nd ed. Paul Davies & Mark Freedland. (Law in Context Ser.). xlii, 964p. 1984. reprint ed. text 45.00 (*0-297-78089-1*) W S Hein.

Labour Law - Cases & Materials. Patrick Elias et al. 1980. pap. 64.00 (*0-406-57751-X*, MICHIE) LEXIS Pub.

Labour Law & Freedom: Further Essays in Employment Rights. Lord Wedderburn. 256p. (C). 1995. pap. 42.50 (*0-85315-810-X*, Pub. by Lawrence & Wishart) NYU Pr.

Labour Law & Industrial Relations: Building on Kahn-Freund. Lord Wedderburn et al. 1983. 39.95 (*0-19-825393-1*) OUP.

Labour Law & Industrial Relations at the Turn of the Century: Liber Amicorum in Honour of Professor Roger Blanpain. R. Blanpain et al. LC 98-39644. 1998. 216.00 (*90-411-1084-4*) Kluwer Law Intl.

Labour Law & Industrial Relations in Asia. Deery. Date not set. pap. text. write for info. (*0-582-86902-1*, Pub. by Addison-Wesley) Longman.

Labour Law & Industrial Relations in Austria. Rudolf Strasser & Konrad Grillberger. LC 92-27371. 1992. 60.00 (*90-6544-652-4*) Kluwer Law Intl.

Labour Law & Industrial Relations in Canada. 4th ed. H. W. Arthurs et al. LC 93-42426. 1993. 144.00 (*90-6544-777-6*) Kluwer Law Intl.

Labour Law & Industrial Relations in Canada. 4th ed. H. W. Arthurs et al. 340p. 1993. pap. 54.00 (*0-409-91620-X*, MICHIE) LEXIS Pub.

Labour Law & Industrial Relations in Central & Eastern Europe: From Planned to a Market Economy. Roger Blanpain & Lajos Nagy. LC 96-36287. (Bulletin of Comparative Labour Relations Ser.). 1996. pap. 78.50 (*90-411-0298-1*) Kluwer Law Intl.

Labour Law & Industrial Relations in Denmark. Ole Hasselbalch & Per S. Jacobsen. LC 99-22654. 1999. 78.00 (*90-411-1171-9*) Kluwer Law Intl.

Labour Law & Industrial Relations in Finland. Suwranta. LC 97-1388. 1997. 72.00 (*90-411-0378-3*) Kluwer Law Intl.

Labour Law & Industrial Relations in France. M. Despax & J. Rojot. 314p. 1987. pap. 55.00 (*90-6544-343-6*) Kluwer Law Intl.

Labour Law & Industrial Relations in Great Britain. 2nd ed. Bob Hepple & Sandra Fredman. LC 92-27370. 1992. 52.00 (*90-6544-641-9*) Kluwer Law Intl.

Labour Law & Industrial Relations in Greece. Theodore B. Koniaris. 192p. 1990. pap. 55.00 (*90-6544-510-2*) Kluwer Law Intl.

Labour Law & Industrial Relations in Italy Tiziano Treu. LC 98-46522. 228 p. 1998. write for info. (*88-14-07302-3*) Giuffre.

***Labour Law & Industrial Relations in Italy.** Tiziano Treu. LC 98-46522. 1998. pap. 59.00 (*90-411-1114-X*) Kluwer Law Intl.

Labour Law & Industrial Relations in Japan. 2nd rev. ed. T. A. Hanami. 1985. 64.00 (*90-6544-214-6*) Kluwer Law Intl.

Labour Law & Industrial Relations of the European Community: Maastricht & Beyond. 2nd rev. ed. Roger Blanpain & Chris Engels. LC 93-5813. 1993. write for info. (*90-6544-741-5*) Kluwer Law Intl.

Labour Law at the Crossroads: Changing Employment Relationships. Bellace. LC 96-54218. 1997. 98.00 (*90-411-0366-X*) Kluwer Law Intl.

***Labour Law Diary 1999.** 224p. 1998. 31.50 (*0-7021-4842-3*) Juta & Co.

Labour Law in Australia: Individual Aspects. 2nd ed. E. I. Sykes & D. Yerbury. 1980. pap. 74.00 (*0-409-43853-7*, MICHIE) LEXIS Pub.

Labour Law in New Zealand. John Hughes. lxxi, 902p. 1990. pap. 69.00 (*0-455-20552-3*, Pub. by LawBk Co) Gaunt.

Labour Law in the Netherlands. E. P. Jansen. LC 94-38. (Loeff Legal Ser.: Vol. 2). 1994. 36.50 (*90-6544-807-1*) Kluwer Law Intl.

Labour Law in the Post-Industrial Era: Essays in Honour of Hugo Sinzheimer. Ed. by Lord Wedderburn et al. 160p. 1994. text 57.95 (*1-85521-644-2*, Pub. by Dartmth Pub) Ashgate Pub Co.

Labour Law Industrial. Roger Blanpain. 252p. 1998. pap. text 86.00 (*90-411-0527-1*) Kluwer Law Intl.

Labour Law of Off-Shore Oil. Jonathan Kitchen. 256p. 1976. 35.00 (*0-85664-395-5*) W S Hein.

Labour Laws: One Should Know, 1991. N. Nabhi. (C). 1990. 55.00 (*0-89771-309-5*) St Mut.

Labour Laws in U. P. 3rd ed. P. L. Malik. (C). 1985. 330.00 (*0-7855-5518-8*) St Mut.

Labour Leadership. Johnson. (Journal of History & Politics (Revue d'Histoire et de Politique) Ser.: Vol. 5). (ENG & FRE.). write for info. (*0-7734-8946-0*) E Mellen.

Labour Legislation & Public Policy: A Contemporary History. Paul Davies & Mark Freedland. LC 92-43630. (Clarendon Law Ser.). 726p. 1993. text 75.00 (*0-19-876060-4*, Clarendon Pr); pap. text 35.00 (*0-19-876288-7*, Clarendon Pr) OUP.

Labour Legislation Service. Compiled by Butterworths Editorial Staff. write for info. (*0-409-03783-4*, R270,18) Buttrwrth-Heinemann.

Labour, Life & Poverty. Ferdynand Zweig. 1975. reprint ed. 23.00 (*0-8464-0542-3*) Beekman Pubs.

Labour Litigation: Practical Guide to Procedure & Tactics. Frans Rautenbach. 1993. write for info. (*0-7021-2992-5*, Pub. by Juta & Co) Gaunt.

Labour, Love & Prayer: Female Piety in Ulster Religious Literature, 1850-1914. Andrea E. Brozyma. LC 99-492149. 360p. 1998. 65.00 (*0-7735-1757-X*) McG-Queens Univ Pr.

Labour Management - Misconduct Charge Sheets & Enquiries. H. L. Kumar. (C). 1988. 140.00 (*0-7855-3694-9*) St Mut.

Labour Management Cooperation: A Task for Management. Asian Productivity Organization Staff. LC 96-114705. (Illus.). 130p. 1994. pap. text 7.50 (*92-833-2153-7*) Productivity Inc.

Labour-Management Cooperation for Productivity. Edgar Weinberg. (Work in America Institute Studies in Productivity). 1983. 35.00 (*0-685-06119-1*, Pergamon Pr) Elsevier.

Labour Market Adjustment in New Zealand. Richard I. Harris & Bridget M. Dadly. 1994. 58.95 (*1-85628-613-4*, Pub. by Avebry) Ashgate Pub Co.

Labour Market & Economic Performance: Europe, Japan & the U. S. A. Toshiaki Tachibanaki. LC 94-24882. 1994. text 85.00 (*0-312-12273-X*) St Martin.

Labour Market & Older Workers. OECD Staff. LC 96-149704. (Social Policy Studies: No. 17). (ENG & FRE.). 365p. (Orig.). 1996. pap. 64.00 (*92-64-14585-0*, Pub. by Org for Econ) OECD.

Labour Market & Social Policies in the Slovak Republic. OECD Staff. LC 96-231284. 180p. (Orig.). 1996. pap. 40.00 (*92-64-14830-2*, 14-96-10-1, Pub. by Org for Econ) OECD.

Labour Market Contracts & Institutions: A Cross-National Comparison. Ed. by Joop Hartog & Jules Theeuwes. LC 93-16963. (Contributions to Economic Analysis Ser.: Vol. 218). 362p. 1993. 126.00 (*0-444-89927-8*, North Holland) Elsevier.

Labour Market Development & Structural Change: The Experience of ASEAN & Australia. Ed. by Pang E. Fong. 314p. (Orig.). 1987. pap. 37.50 (*9971-69-118-3*, Pub. by Sngapore Univ Pr) Coronet Bks.

Labour Market Dynamics in the Russian Federation. Ed. by Douglas Lippoldt. LC 98-136141. 161p. 1997. pap. 15.00 (*92-64-15979-7*, 14-97-12-1, Pub. by Org for Econ) OECD.

Labour Market Efficiency in the European Union: Employment Protection & Fixed-Term Contracts. Klaus Schomann et al. LC 98-11170. (Research Studies in the European Economy). (Illus.). 224p. (C). 1998. 85.00 (*0-415-15734-X*) Routledge.

Labour Market Implications of European Ageing. Ed. by Paul Johnson & Klaus F. Zimmermann. 312p. (C). 1993. text 64.95 (*0-521-44398-9*) Cambridge U Pr.

***Labour Market Inequalities: Problems & Policies of Low-Wage Employment in International Perspective.** Ed. by Mary Gregory et al. 304p. 2000. text 74.00 (*0-19-924169-4*) OUP.

Labour Market Information for Decision-Making: The Case of Japan. 252p. (Orig.). 1981. pap. text 22.50 (*92-2-102598-5*) Intl Labour Office.

Labour Market Information Through Key Informants. 85p. 1984. 9.00 (*92-2-103082-2*) Intl Labour Office.

Labour Market Policies in Slovenia. OECD Staff. LC 97-224704. 96p. 1997. pap. 19.00 (*92-64-15606-2*, 14-97-09-1, Pub. by Org for Econ) OECD.

Labour Market Policies in Switzerland. 156p. 1996. pap. 44.00 (*92-64-14788-8*) OECD.

Labour Market Policy. Adrett. 1989. pap. text. write for info. (*0-582-00962-6*, Pub. by Addison-Wesley) Longman.

Labour Market Policy: A European Perspective. 2nd ed. N. J. Adnett. LC 95-26702. 304p. (C). 1996. pap. text 30.94 (*0-582-24885-X*, Pub. by Addison-Wesley) Longman.

***Labour Market Policy & Unemployment: Evaluation of Active Measures in France, Germany, The Netherlands, Spain & Sweden.** J. De Koning & Hugh G. Mosley. LC 00-37606. (Labour Markets & Employment Policy Ser.). 2000. write for info. (*1-84064-279-3*) E Elgar.

Labour Market Policy & Unemployment Insurance. Anders T. Bjorklund et al. (FIEF Studies in Labor Markets & Economic Policy: No. 2). (Illus.). 216p. 1991. 55.00 (*0-19-828323-7*) OUP.

Labour Market Programs for the Poor in Europe. Niacais & Bollens Staff. 160p. 1995. 68.95 (*1-85972-181-8*) Ashgate Pub Co.

***Labour Market Reform in China.** Xin Meng. LC 99-29696. (Trade & Development Ser.). (Illus.). 229p. (C). 2000. 74.95 (*0-521-77126-9*) Cambridge U Pr.

Labour Market Theory: Constructive Reassessment. Ben Fine. LC 98-131005. (Frontiers of Political Economy Ser.). 306p. (C). 1998. 85.00 (*0-415-16676-4*) Routledge.

Labour Markets in Europe Issues Harmonisation & Regulation. Addison, pseud. 1998. pap. 20.99 (*1-86152-418-8*) Thomson Learn.

Labour Markets in the Sudan. I. El-Bagir et al. x, 224p. 1984. pap. 24.75 (*92-2-103749-5*) Intl Labour Office.

Labour Migration. James J. Johnson & John Salt. 215p. (C). 1990. 150.00 (*1-85346-120-2*, Pub. by David Fulton) St Mut.

Labour Migration & Rural Transformation in Colonial Asia. Jan Breman. 88p. 1991. pap. 22.95 (*90-6256-873-4*, Pub. by VU Univ Pr) Paul & Co Pubs.

***Labour Migration & the Recent Financial Crisis in Asia.** OECD Staff. 248p. 2000. pap. 48.00 (*92-64-17173-8*, 81 2000 01 1 P, Pub. by Org for Econ) OECD.

Labour Migration in England, 1800-1850. 2nd ed. Arthur Redford. Ed. by William H. Chaloner. LC 68-6093. (Illus.). xx, 209p. 1968. lib. bdg. 37.50 (*0-678-06766-X*) Kelley.

***Labour Mobility, Earnings & Unemployment: Selected Papers.** John Creedy. LC 99-21906. 320p. 1999. 95.00 (*1-84064-137-1*) E Elgar.

Labour Movement & the Internet: The New Internationalism. Eric Lee. 256p. 1996. pap. 19.95 (*0-7453-1114-8*, Pub. by Pluto GBR) Stylus Pub VA.

An Asterisk (*) at the beginning of an entry indicates that the title is appearing for the first time.

Labour Movement & the Internet: The New Internationalism. Eric Lee. LC 96-28838. 256p. 1996. 55.00 (*0-7453-1119-9*, Pub. by Pluto GBR) Stylus Pub VA.

Labour Movement in Tamilnadu, 1918-1933. C. S. Krishna. 1989. 18.00 (*81-7074-049-5*, Pub. by KP Bagchi) S Asia.

Labour Movement in Thatcher's Britain: Conservative Macro- & Microeconomic Strategies & the Associated Labour Relations Legislation: Their Impact on the British Labour Movement During the 1980s. Geoffrey K. Barlow. (European University Studies, Series 31: Vol. 320). (Illus.). xiii, 224p. 1997. pap. 44.95 (*3-631-31370-5*) P Lang Pubng.

Labour Movement in Thatcher's Britain: Conservative Macro- & Microeconomic Strategies & the Associated Labour Relations Legislation: Their Impact on the British Labour Movement During the 1980s. Geoffrey K. Barlow. (European University Studies, Series 31: Vol. 320). (Illus.). XIII, 224p. 1997. pap. 44.95 (*0-8204-3246-6*) P Lang Pubng.

Labour Movements. Willie Thompson. (Socialist History Ser.: Vol. 9). 128p. 1996. pap. 12.99 (*0-7453-0813-9*, Pub. by Pluto GBR) Stylus Pub VA.

Labour Movements & Agrarian Relations. Ani Lukose. (C). 1991. 23.00 (*81-7033-100-5*, Pub. by Rawat Pubns) S Asia.

Labour Movements, Employers & the State: Conflict & Co-Operation in Britain & Sweden. James Fulcher. 384p. 1991. text 75.00 (*0-19-827289-8*) OUP.

***Labour of Loss: Mourning, Memory & Wartime Bereavement in Australia.** Joy Damousi. LC 99-18523. (Studies in the Social & Cultural History of Modern Warfare: No. 7). 256p. (C). 1999. 64.95 (*0-521-66004-1*); pap. 22.95 (*0-521-66974-X*) Cambridge U Pr.

Labour of Love. Tony Booth. (Illus.). 320p. (Orig.). 1997. pap. 9.95 (*1-85782-181-5*, Pub. by Blake Publng) Seven Hills Bk.

Labour of Love. Borchgrevink & Holte Staff. 160p. 1995. 63.95 (*1-85972-043-9*) Ashgate Pub Co.

Labour of Love: The History of the Nurse's Association in Queensland, 1860-1950. Glenda Strachan & Queensland Nurses' Union Staff. LC 96-202912. xiii, 291 p. 1996. write for info. (*1-86448-053-X*) Allen & Unwn AT.

***Labour of Reading: Desire, Alienation & Biblical Interpretation.** Ed. by Fiona C. Black et al. LC 99-44174. (Semeia Studies). 317p. 1999. pap. 30.00 (*0-88414-011-3*) Soc Biblical Lit.

Labour Pains: Women's Work in Crisis. 2nd ed. Pat Armstrong. 250p. reprint ed. pap. 10.95 (*0-88961-091-6*, Pub. by Womens Pr) LPC InBook.

***Labour Party: A Centenary History.** Brian Brivati & Richard Heffernan. LC 00-27833. 2000. write for info. (*0-312-23458-9*) St Martin.

Labour Party: Socialism & Society since 1951. Steven Fielding. LC 96-32159. (Documents in Contemporary History Ser.). 196p. 1997. text 69.95 (*0-7190-4269-0*, Pub. by Manchester Univ Pr); text 24.95 (*0-7190-4270-4*, Pub. by Manchester Univ Pr) St Martin.

Labour Party & Business 1900-1980. Tiratsoo. 72.95 (*1-85928-252-0*) Ashgate Pub Co.

***Labour Party in Wales, 1900-2000.** Ed. by Deian Hopkins et al. 256p. 2000. 65.00 (*0-7083-1586-0*, Pub. by U Wales Pr) Paul & Co Pubs.

Labour Party since 1945. Thompson. (Socialist History Ser.: Vol. 4). 64p. 1994. pap. 9.99 (*0-7453-0808-2*, Pub. by Pluto GBR) Stylus Pub VA.

Labour Party since 1945: Old Labour - New Labour. Eric Shaw. (Making Contemporary Britain Ser.). 320p. (C). 1996. 71.95 (*0-631-19654-4*); pap. 28.95 (*0-631-19655-2*) Blackwell Pubs.

Labour Party's Defence Policy since 1945. Dan Keohane. LC 92-24749. 224p. 1993. 59.00 (*0-7185-1467-X*) St Martin.

Labour Party's Political Thought: A History. 3rd ed. Geoffrey Foote. LC 96-32090. 584p. 1997. pap. 19.95 (*0-312-16529-3*); text 65.00 (*0-312-16528-5*) St Martin.

Labour People: Leaders & Lieutenants: Hardie to Kinnock. 2nd ed. Kenneth O. Morgan. 382p. pap. 15.95 (*0-19-285270-1*) OUP.

Labour Policy & Administration. Balwant Singh. 191p. 1996. pap. 150.00 (*81-85880-93-X*, Pub. by Print Hse) St Mut.

Labour, Poverty, & Development. Ed. by Giorgio B. Navaretti et al. (Queen Elizabeth House Series in Development Studies). (Illus.). 287p. 1999. text 78.00 (*0-19-829353-4*) OUP.

Labour Problems & Remedies. Ed. by H. L. Kumar. (C). 1990. 110.00 (*0-89771-305-2*) St Mut.

Labour Problems Before the Industrial Revolution, 1727-1745. LC 72-2532. (British Labour Struggles Before 1850 Ser.). 1974. 20.95 (*0-405-04425-9*) Ayer.

Labour Process in the Unorganized Industry. Manjit Singh. (C). 1991. 12.00 (*81-85425-62-0*, Pub. by Manohar) S Asia.

Labour Productivity & Flexibility. Edward J. Amadeo & Susan Horton. LC 97-12037. 256p. 1997. text 69.95 (*0-312-17522-1*) St Martin.

Labour, Race & Colonial Rule: The Copperbelt from 1924 to Independence. Elena L. Berger. (Oxford Studies in African Affairs). 1974. text 55.00 (*0-19-821690-4*) OUP.

Labour Reform & Private Participation in Public-Sector Ports. LC 97-228043. (Cuadernos de la CEPAL Ser.: No. 77). 176p. 2000. 20.00 (*92-1-121211-1*) UN.

Labour Regulation & Black Workers' Struggle in South Africa. Jens Haarlev. (Research Report Ser.: No. 68). 80p. 1983. write for info. (*91-7106-213-0*, Pub. by Nordic Africa) Transaction Pubs.

Labour Relations Act of 1995. D. Du Toit et al. LC 97-162573. 1996. pap. write for info. (*0-409-01280-7*, MICHIE) LEXIS Pub.

Labour Relations & the New Unionism in Contemporary Brazil. Ed Kunzman. LC 98-44284. 256p. 1999. text 65.00 (*0-312-21846-X*) St Martin.

Labour Relations Handbook. Andrew Pons. 272p. 1998. ring bd. 86.50 (*0-7021-2301-3*, Pub. by Juta & Co) Gaunt.

Labour Relations in a Developing Country: A Case Study on Zimbabwe. Mark A. Shadur. LC 94-15635. (Making of Modern Africa). 1994. 87.95 (*1-85628-902-8*, Pub. by Avebry) Ashgate Pub Co.

Labour-Relations in Africa: English-Speaking Countries. (Labour-Management Relations Ser.: No. 64). v, 159p. 1985. pap. 18.00 (*92-2-103467-4*) Intl Labour Office.

Labour Relations in Caribbean Countries Proceedings of a Tripartite Caribbean Seminar on Labour Relations (Castries, St. Lucia, 1-4 November 1988) Ed. by Werner Blenk. (Labour-Management Relations Ser.: No. 75). vi, 124p. (Orig.). 1990. pap. 15.75 (*92-2-107279-7*) Intl Labour Office.

Labour Relations in the Caribbean Region. (Labour-Management Relations Ser.: No. 43). 205p. 1974. 13.50 (*92-2-101084-8*) Intl Labour Office.

Labour Relations in the Public Service: Developing Countries. Muneto Ozaki et al. xv, 205p. (Orig.). 1988. pap. 24.75 (*92-2-106394-1*) Intl Labour Office.

Labour Relations in Transition: Wages, Employment & Industrial Conflict in Russia. Ed. by Simon Clarke. LC 95-49536. (Management & Industry in Russia Ser.). 304p. 1996. 90.00 (*1-85898-411-4*) E Elgar.

Labour Relations in Transition in Eastern Europe. Ed. by Gyorgy Szell. (Studies in Organization: No. 33). x, 369p. (C). 1991. lib. bdg. 59.95 (*3-11-012648-6*, 244-91) De Gruyter.

Labour Resistance in Cameroon: Managerial Strategies & Labour Resistance in the Agro-Industrial Plantations of the Cameroon Development Corporation. Piet Konings. LC 93-17274. 203p. (C). 1993. text 55.00 (*0-435-08086-5*, 08086) Heinemann.

Labour Resistance in Cameroon: Managerial Strategies & Labour Resistance in the Agro-Industrial Plantations of the Cameroon Development Corporation. Piet Konings. LC 93-17274. 203p. (C). 1993. pap. 30.00 (*0-435-08087-3*, 08087) Heinemann.

Labour, Science & Technology in the Age of Valois & Bourbon, 1500-1620. Henry Heller. (Studies in Early Modern History). (Illus.). 270p. (C). 1996. text 59.95 (*0-521-55031-9*) Cambridge U Pr.

Labour Shelter & Global Capitalism. Rod Burgess. (Development & Underdevelopment Ser.). 272p. (C). 1998. 65.00 (*0-415-08841-0*); pap. 24.99 (*0-415-08842-9*) Routledge.

Labour Standards & International Competitiveness: A Comparative Analysis of Developing & Industrialized Countries. Andre Raynauld & Jean-Pierre Vidal. LC 98-21275. 128p. 1999. 70.00 (*1-85898-949-3*) E Elgar.

Labour Standards on Merchant Ships. ix, 187p. 1992. pap. 22.50 (*92-2-107109-X*) Intl Labour Office.

Labour Supply & Regulation. Humbert Wolfe. (Economic & Social History of the World War Ser.). 1923. 125.00 (*0-317-27506-2*) Elliots Bks.

Labour under the Apartheid Regime: Practical Problems & Legal Framework of Labour Relations in South Africa. M. Kittner et al. 144p. 1989. pap. 52.00 (*90-6544-428-9*) Kluwer Law Intl.

Labour under the Marshall Plan: The Politics of Productivity & the Marketing of Management Science. Anthony Carew. LC 87-211445. 303p. reprint ed. pap. 94.00 (*0-608-10581-3*, 207120200009) Bks Demand.

***Labour Unions, Public Policy & Economic Growth.** Tapio Palokangas. 256p. (C). 2000. 64.95 (*0-521-66323-7*) Cambridge U Pr.

Labour Women: Women in British Working Class Politics, 1918-1939. Pamela M. Graves. (Illus.). 287p. (C). 1994. text 59.95 (*0-521-41247-1*); pap. text 22.95 (*0-521-45919-2*) Cambridge U Pr.

Labourers' Perception about Their Work Environment. K. Surti. (C). 1988. 14.00 (*81-204-0337-1*, Pub. by Oxford IBH) S Asia.

Laboureur's Graphic Work: Catalogue Raisonne. Sylvain Laboureur. (FRE., Illus.). 828p. 1989. 185.00 (*1-55660-056-9*) A Wofsy Fine Arts.

Laboureur's Illustrated Books. Sylvain Laboureur. (FRE.). 664p. 1990. 185.00 (*1-55660-139-5*) A Wofsy Fine Arts.

Laboureur's Paintings, Watercolors & Couaches. Sylvain Laboureur. (FRE., Illus.). 516p. 1991. 195.00 (*1-55660-260-X*) A Wofsy Fine Arts.

Labouring Children: British Immigrant Apprentices to Canada, 1869-1924. Joy Parr. LC 95-104383. (Reprints in Canadian History Ser.). 224p. 1993. pap. text 19.95 (*0-8020-7443-X*) U of Toronto Pr.

Labouring Classes in Early Industrial England, 1750-1850. John Rule. LC 85-16665. (Themes in British Social History Ser.). 432p. (C). 1989. pap. 98.00 (*0-582-49172-X*, 73511) Longman.

Labouring Lives: Work & Workers in Nineteenth-Century Ontario. Ed. by Paul Craven. (Ontario Historical Studies). (Illus.). 640p. 1995. text 65.00 (*0-8020-0641-8*); pap. text 29.95 (*0-8020-7594-0*) U of Toronto Pr.

***Labouring to Learn: Towards a Political Economy of Plantations, People & Education in Sri Lanka** Angela Little. LC 98-28307. (International Political Economy Ser.). xxiv, 324p. 1999. write for info. (*0-333-71110-6*) St Martin.

Labouring to Learn: Towards a Political Economy of Plantations, People, & Education in Sri Lanka. Angela Little. LC 98-28307. (International Political Economy Ser.). (Illus.). 270p. 1999. text 72.00 (*0-312-21842-7*) St Martin.

Labour's Apprentices: Working-Class Lads in Late Victorian & Edwardian England. Michael J. Childs. 248p. 1992. 65.00 (*0-7735-0915-1*, Pub. by McG-Queens Univ Pr) CUP Services.

Labour's Apprentices: Working-Class Lads in Late Victorian & Edwardian England. Michael J. Childs. 248p. 1994. pap. 19.95 (*0-7735-1289-6*, Pub. by McG-Queens Univ Pr) CUP Services.

Labour's Conscience: The Labour Left, 1945-51. Jonathan Schneer. 256p. (C). 1988. text 45.00 (*0-04-942193-X*) Routledge.

Labour's Dilemma: The Gender Politics of Auto Workers in Canada, 1937-79. Pamela Sugiman. (Illus.). 294p. 1994. text 50.00 (*0-8020-2895-0*); pap. text 19.95 (*0-8020-7403-0*) U of Toronto Pr.

Labour's Doorstep Politics in London. John E. Turner. LC 77-99160. 412p. reprint ed. pap. 127.80 (*0-608-15959-X*, 203324100084) Bks Demand.

***Labour's First Century.** Ed. by Duncan Tanner et al. (Illus.). 420p. (C). 2000. text 49.95 (*0-521-65184-0*) Cambridge U Pr.

Labour's Grassroots: The Politics of Party Membership. Patrick Seyd & Paul Whiteley. (Illus.). 286p. 1992. pap. text 29.95 (*0-19-827358-4*) OUP.

Labour's High Noon: The Government & the Economy, 1945-51. Ed. by Jim Fyrth. 256p. (C). 1994. pap. 29.95 (*0-85315-786-3*, Pub. by Lawrence & Wishart) NYU Pr.

Labour's Landslide. Geddes. LC 98-2902. 1998. pap. 24.95 (*0-7190-5159-2*, Pub. by Manchester Univ Pr) St Martin.

Labour's Last Chance. Ed. by Anthony Heath et al. 336p. 1994. 93.95 (*1-85521-459-8*, Pub. by Dartmth Pub) Ashgate Pub Co.

Labours of Hercules. Gustave Dore. Tr. by Eric Bosch from FRE. (Illus.). 28p. reprint ed. pap. 2.95 (*0-9631135-2-6*) MCE Publ Co.

Labours of Hercules: An Astrological Interpretation. 2nd ed. Alice A. Bailey. 1974. pap. 12.00 (*0-85330-130-1*) Lucis.

Labours of Love: And Other Sweet Things. Donna B. Turrisi et al. LC 97-91024. 256p. 1997. 17.00 (*0-9660357-0-4*) Labours of Love.

Labour's Promised Land? Culture & Society in Labour Britain, 1945-51. Ed. by Jim Fyrth. 256p. (C). 1995. pap. 32.50 (*0-85315-811-8*, Pub. by Lawrence & Wishart) NYU Pr.

Labour's Reward: Real Wages & Economic Change in the 19th & 20th Century Europe. Ed. by Peter Scholliers & Vera Zamagni. 320p. 1995. 100.00 (*1-85278-971-9*) E Elgar.

Labour's War. Stephen Brooke. (Illus.). 384p. 1992. 95.00 (*0-19-820285-7*) OUP.

Labour's Wrongs & Labour's Remedy: or The Age of Might & the Age of Right. John F. Bray. LC 66-21656. (Reprints of Economic Classics Ser.). 216p. 1968. reprint ed. 35.00 (*0-678-00283-5*) Kelley.

Labouryouse Journey & Serche of Johan Leylande for Englandes Antiquitees. John Leland. LC 74-28871. (English Experience Ser.: No. 750). 1975. reprint ed. 25.00 (*90-221-0750-7*) Walter J Johnson.

***Labrador: A Novel.** Kathryn Davis. 240p. 2000. pap. 13.00 (*0-618-07542-9*, Mariner Bks) HM.

***Labrador Address Book.** Illus. by Leslie Evans. 128p. 2000. spiral bd. 15.95 (*1-55670-988-9*) Stewart Tabori & Chang.

Labrador Coast: A Journal of Two Summer Cruises to That Region. Alpheus S. Packard. LC 74-5862. reprint ed. 65.00 (*0-404-11668-X*) AMS Pr.

Labrador Days: Tales of the Sea Toilers. Wilfred T. Grenfell. LC 73-167451. (Short Story Index Reprint Ser.). 1977. reprint ed. 19.95 (*0-8369-3977-8*) Ayer.

Labrador Doctor: My Life with the Grenfell Mission. Anthony Paddon. 279p. 1989. mass mkt. 6.95 (*0-88780-160-9*, Pub. by Formac Publ Co) Formac Dist Ltd.

Labrador Odyssey: The Journal & Photographs of Eliot Curwen on the Second Voyage of Wilfred Grenfell, 1893. Ed. by Ronald Rompkey. pap. 27.95 (*0-7735-1870-3*) McG-Queens Univ Pr.

Labrador Odyssey: The Journal & Photographs of Eliot Curwen on the Second Voyage of Wilfred Grenfell, 1893. Ed. by Ronald Rompkey. LC 96-194042. (Illus.). 208p. 1996. 49.95 (*0-7735-1366-3*, Pub. by McG-Queens Univ Pr) CUP Services.

Labrador Retriever see Learning about Dogs Series

Labrador Retriever. Bruce Fogle. (Dog Breed Handbks.). (Illus.). 80p. 1996. 14.95 (*0-7894-0569-5*) DK Pub Inc.

Labrador Retriever. Bruce Fogle. LC 95-44068. (Dog Breed Handbks.). 80p. 1999. pap. 7.95 (*0-7894-4196-9*) DK Pub Inc.

***Labrador Retriever.** September B. Morn. LC 99-31346. (Training Your Dog Ser.). 176p. 1999. pap. text 11.95 (*0-7641-0992-8*) Barron.

Labrador Retriever. Charlotte Wilcox. (Learning about Dogs Ser.). (Illus.). 48p. (J). (gr. 3-7). 1996. lib. bdg. 19.00 (*0-516-20248-0*) Childrens.

***Labrador Retriever: A Comprehensive Guide to Buying, Owning & Training.** Steve Smith. (Illus.). 112p. 2000. 14.95 (*1-57223-387-7*) Willow Creek Pr.

Labrador Retriever: An Owner's Guide to a Happy, Healthy Pet. Lisa W. Agresta. (Owner's Guide to a Happy, Healthy Pet Ser.). (Illus.). 160p. 1995. 12.95 (*0-87605-378-9*) Howell Bks.

Labrador Retriever: The Dog That Does It All. Lisa Weiss. LC 98-38488. 256p. 1998. 24.95 (*0-87605-044-5*) Howell Bks.

Labrador Retriever: The History & the People. Richard Wolters. LC 81-82485. (Illus.). 200p. 1981. 39.95 (*0-8227-8037-2*) Petersen Pub.

Labrador Retriever Champions, 1989-1994. Jan Linzy. (Illus.). 105p. 1998. pap. 32.95 (*1-55893-050-7*) Camino E E & Bk.

Labrador Retriever Champions, 1952-1988. Camino E. E. & Bk. Co. Staff. (Illus.). 200p. 1993. pap. 36.95 (*0-940808-96-X*) Camino E E & Bk.

***Labrador Retriever Handbook.** Audrey Pavia. (Pet Handbks.). (Illus.). 2000. pap. text 9.95 (*0-7641-1530-8*) Barron.

Labrador Retrievers. Ariel Books Staff. LC 96-83371. 1996. 4.95 (*0-8362-1520-6*, Arie Bks) Andrews & McMeel.

Labrador Retrievers. Browntrout Publishers Staff. (Illus.). 1997. pap. text 7.95 (*1-56313-919-7*) BrownTrout Pubs Inc.

Labrador Retrievers. Stuart A. Kallen. LC 95-1510. (Dogs Ser.). (Illus.). 24p. (J). (ps-4). 1995. lib. bdg. 13.98 (*1-56239-453-3*) ABDO Pub Co.

Labrador Retrievers. Kerry V. Kern. (Barron's Pet Owner's Manuals Ser.). 1995. pap. 6.95 (*0-8120-9018-7*) Barron.

Labrador Retrievers. Diane McCarty. 1998. pap. text 9.95 (*0-7938-2315-3*, KW040S) TFH Pubns.

Labrador Retrievers: An Owner's Companion. Anthony W. Jury. (Illus.). 192p. 1998. 39.95 (*1-85223-956-5*, Pub. by Crolwood) Trafalgar.

***Labrador Retrievers for Dummies.** Joel Walton. (For Dummies (Lifestyles) Ser.). (Illus.). 334p. 2000. pap. 15.99 (*0-7645-5281-3*) IDG Bks.

Labrador Retrievers Today. Carole Coode. (Illus.). 192p. 1993. 27.95 (*0-87605-207-3*) Howell Bks.

Labrador Saga: Snow Shoes & Rabbit Stew. James M. Hanna. LC 95-92029. 223p. 1995. pap. 10.95 (*0-9640458-3-4*) Cherokee Bks DE.

***Labrador Shooting Dog: Training the Labrador Retriever as an All-Around Sporting Dog.** Mike Gould. Ed. by Gary Hubbell. (Illus.). 303p. 2000. pap. 25.00 (*1-893740-01-3*, LSD113, Pub. by Clinetop) IPG Chicago.

Labrador Tales: A Celebration of America's Favorite Dog. 144p. 1998. pap. 12.95 (*1-885214-16-2*) Azul Edits.

Labrador Village. John C. Kennedy. (Illus.). 140p. (C). 1995. pap. text 10.95 (*0-88133-863-X*) Waveland Pr.

Labrador Winter: The Ethnographic Journals of William Duncan Strong, 1927-1928. William D. Strong. Ed. by Eleanor B. Leacock & Nan A. Rothschild. LC 93-34521. (Illus.). 320p. (C). 1994. text 45.00 (*1-56098-345-0*) Smithsonian.

Labrang: A Tibetan Buddhist Monastery at the Crossroads of Four Civilizations. Paul K. Nietupski. LC 98-5347. (Illus.). 123p. 1999. pap. 24.95 (*1-55939-090-5*) Snow Lion Pubns.

Labraunda: Swedish Excavations & Researches - The Greek Inscriptions, Pt. II: 13-133. Jonas Crampa. (Acta Instituti Atheniensis Regni Sueciae Ser.: Vol. V,III:2). (Illus.). 225p. 1972. pap. 79.95 (*91-85086-07-X*, Pub. by P Astroms) Coronet Bks.

Labraunda Vol. 1, Pt. 3: Swedish Excavations & Researchers - The Temple of Zeus. Niki C. Scoufopoulos. (Swedish Research Institute in Istanbul Ser.). (Illus.). 159p. 1982. pap. 72.50 (*91-970338-2-0*, Pub. by P Astroms) Coronet Bks.

Labraunda Vol. 2, Pt. 2: Stamped Amphora Handles. Marie-Louise Saflund. (Swedish Research Institute in Istanbul-Swedish Excavations & Researches Ser.). (Illus.). 30p. (Orig.). 1980. pap. 19.95 (*91-970338-0-4*, Pub. by P Astroms) Coronet Bks.

Labraunda Vol. 2, Pt. 3: Archaic Pottery. J. J. Jully. (Swedish Research Institute in Istanbul-Swedish Excavations & Researches Ser.). (Illus.). 56p. (Orig.). 1981. pap. 32.50 (*91-970338-1-2*, Pub. by P Astroms) Coronet Bks.

Labraunda Vol. 2, Pt. 5: Marble Sculptures. Ann C. Gunter. (Swedish Research Institute in Istanbul-Swedish Excavations & Researches Ser.). (Illus.). 65p. (Orig.). 1995. pap. 47.50 (*91-970338-4-7*, Pub. by P Astroms) Coronet Bks.

Labrava. Elmore Leonard. LC 98-13559. 288p. 1998. pap. 9.95 (*0-688-16097-2*, Wm Morrow) Morrow Avon.

LaBreeska. LaBreeska Hemphill. LC 75-42869. (Illus.). (Orig.). 1976. pap. 2.98 (*0-9600948-1-4*) Hemphills.

L'Abri. rev. ed. Edith Schaeffer. LC 91-47977. 256p. 1992. reprint ed. pap. 14.99 (*0-89107-668-9*) Crossway Bks.

***Labs Afield.** Denver Bryan & E. Donnall Thomas, Jr. (Illus.). 160p. 2000. 29.50 (*1-57223-389-3*) Willow Creek Pr.

***Labs Afield: The Ultimate Tribute to the World's Greatest Retriever.** Ed. by Todd R. Berger. LC 00-36506. (PetLife Library). (Illus.). 160p. 2000. 29.95 (*0-89658-489-5*) Voyageur Pr.

***Labs for Signals & Systems Using MATLAB.** Virginia Stonick & Bradley. (Electrical Engineering Ser.). 2000. pap. 22.95 (*0-534-37472-7*) Brooks-Cole.

Labs for Signals & Systems Using MATLAB. Virginia Stonick & Kevin Bradley. LC 95-187721. 144p. 1995. pap. 25.95 (*0-534-93808-6*) PWS Pubs.

Labs for Vertebrate Zoology: An Evolutionary Approach. Erik W. Gergus & Gordon W. Schuett. LC 97-67927. (Illus.). 246p. (Orig.). 1997. pap. text 28.00 (*1-884125-69-7*) Cooper Pubng.

***Labs for Vertebrate Zoology: An Evolutionary Approach.** 2nd ed. Erik W. A. Gergus & Gordon W. Schuett. (Illus.). 249p. 2000. lab manual ed. 28.00 (*1-884125-78-6*) Cooper Pubng.

LABSIM: Experimental Design & Data Analysis Simulator. Richard E. Edwards. 176p. 1995. pap., teacher ed. write for info. incl. disk (*0-534-33901-8*); pap., student ed. 30.75 incl. disk (*0-534-33899-2*) Brooks-Cole.

Labtrek: Experiments for General Chemistry. 3rd ed. Jay H. Worrell. (Illus.). 435p. (C). 1997. student ed. 40.95 (*0-89892-154-6*) Contemp Pub Co of Raleigh.

LabTutor: A Friendly Guide to Computer Interfacing & LabVIEW Programming. John K. Eaton. (Illus.). 176p. 1995. pap. text 32.95 (*0-19-509162-0*) OUP.

Labtutor: A Friendly Guide to Computer Interfacing & Labview Programming Package: Labtutor Book & Exercise Disk for Windows. John K. Eaton. (Illus.). 176p. 1995. pap. text 59.95 incl. disk (*0-19-510044-1*) OUP.

***Labview: Data Acquisition & Analysis for the Movement Sciences.** Andrew L. McDonough. LC 00-37491. 256p. 2000. spiral bd. 64.00 (*0-13-012847-3*, Brady Emerg Care) P-H.

***LabVIEW Advanced Programming Techniques.** Richard Bitter. (Illus.). 2000. 84.95 (*0-8493-2049-6*) CRC Pr.

Labview Applications & Solutions. Rahman Jamal. LC 98-34131. 464p. 1998. pap. 60.00 (*0-13-096423-9*) P-H.

LabVIEW for Everyone: Graphic Programming Made Even Easier. Lisa Wells et al. LC 96-19491. 624p. (C). 1996. text 60.00 incl. cd-rom (*0-13-268194-3*) P-H.

***LabVIEW for Telecom, Semiconductor, Automotive, Sound & Vibration & General Test & Measure.** Hall T. Martin. 272p. 2000. pap. 39.00 (*0-13-019963-X*) P-H.

LabVIEW Graphical Programming: Practical Applications in Instrumentation & Control. 2nd ed. Gary W. Johnson. LC 97-17180. (Visual Technology Ser.). (Illus.). 665p. 1997. pap. 50.00 (*0-07-032915-X*) McGraw.

***Labview Internet Applications.** Jeffrey Travis. LC 99-88994. (Illus.). 624p. (C). 2000. pap. 55.00 (*0-13-014144-5*) P-H.

LabVIEW Power Programming. Gary W. Johnson. LC 98-18295. (Illus.). 400p. 1998. pap. 55.00 incl. cd-rom (*0-07-913666-4*) McGraw.

LabVIEW Signal Processing. A. Samant. LC 98-14696. 688p. (C). 1998. pap. 59.00 (*0-13-972449-4*) P-H.

***Labview Version 5.0.** National Instruments Staff. 1999. pap. text, student ed. 85.33 (*0-201-36184-1*) Addison-Wesley.

Labworks: Complete Based Exp Chemistry. Joseph R. Crook. (Chemistry Ser.). 1996. pap., teacher ed. 25.00 (*0-7637-0241-2*) Jones & Bartlett.

Labworks: Complete Based Exp Chemistry, Vol. 1. Joseph R. Crook. (Chemistry Ser.). 184p. (C). 1996. pap. 20.75 (*0-7637-0044-4*) Jones & Bartlett.

Labworks Flight Manual: Mac Version. Mike Seymour. LC 98-125013. 96p. 1997. spiral bd. 10.00 (*0-7637-0679-5*) Jones & Bartlett.

Labworks Flight Manual: Windows Version. Dennis Doney & Paul Arnot. LC 98-139878. (Chemistry Ser.). 88p. 1998. spiral bd. 10.00 (*0-7637-0680-9*) Jones & Bartlett.

Labyrinth see Guernica & Other Plays

Labyrinth. Lee Russell. (Illus.). 1977. 4.94 (*0-940244-03-9*) Flying Buffalo.

Labyrinth. Arishima Takeo. 1991. pap. 22.00 (*0-8191-8293-1*) U Pr of Amer.

Labyrinth. Roger Williamson. (Orig.). 1991. pap. 5.95 (*0-9620218-2-2*) Vann Pr.

Labyrinth. Jim Woodring. (Aliens Ser.). (Illus.). 1997. pap. 17.95 (*1-56971-245-X*) Dark Horse Comics.

***Labyrinth: A Search for the Hidden Meaning of Science.** Peter Pesic. LC 99-46389. (Illus.). 160p. 2000. 21.95 (*0-262-16190-7*) MIT Pr.

Labyrinth: An Essay on the Political Psychology of Change. Richard Wilson. LC 88-4525. 230p. (C). (gr. 13). 1988. text 70.95 (*0-87332-485-4*) M E Sharpe.

Labyrinth: Memoirs of Walter Schellenberg, Hitler's Chief of Counterintelligence. Tr. by Louis Hagen. LC 99-42049. 448p. 1999. pap. text 17.00 (*0-306-80927-3*, Pub. by Da Capo) HarpC.

Labyrinth: Studies on an Archetype. Gaetano Cipolla. (Literary Criticism Ser.: Vol. 1). 160p. (Orig.). (C). 1987. pap. 12.00 (*0-921252-00-5*) LEGAS.

Labyrinth: Symbol of Fear, Rebirth & Liberation. Helmut Jaskolski. Tr. by Michael H. Kohn. LC 96-23353. (Illus.). 176p. (Orig.). 1997. pap. 15.00 (*1-57062-195-0*, Pub. by Shambhala Pubns) Random.

Labyrinth: Symbol of Fear, Rebirth, & Liberation. Helmut Jaskolski. 1997. pap. 15.00 (*0-614-27625-X*) Shambhala Pubns.

Labyrinth Bk. 1: The Sea Siren. Bill Coulton. LC 98-87152. 325p. 1998. 25.00 (*0-7388-0077-5*); pap. 15.00 (*0-7388-0078-3*) Xlibris Corp.

Labyrinth Bk. 2: The Minotaur. Bill Coulton. LC 98-87152. 325p. 1998. 25.00 (*0-7388-0075-9*); pap. 15.00 (*0-7388-0076-7*) Xlibris Corp.

Labyrinth Called Planet Earth. Sherry Cornwell. 120p. 1994. pap. 10.95 (*0-9644429-0-6*) Natarr Pr.

Labyrinth Comics-Portfolio. Gordon Spurlock. 44p. 1995. pap. write for info. (*0-9642478-1-X*) Minotaur Comics.

***Labyrinth Comics Portfolio, No. 2.** Gordon Spurlock & Jody Lane. (Illus.). 100p. 1999. pap. 10.00 (*0-9642478-2-8*) Minotaur Comics.

Labyrinth Fish. Chris Andrews. (Illus.). 1988. pap. 3.15 (*3-923880-87-1*, 16846) Tetra Pr.

Labyrinth Fish. Helmut Pinter. (Illus.). 176p. 1986. 18.95 (*0-8120-5635-3*) Barron.

Labyrinth Fish: The Bubble Nest Builders. Horst Linke. (Illus.). 170p. 1991. 21.95 (*3-89356-137-4*, 16071) Tetra Pr.

Labyrinth in Culture & Society: Pathways to Wisdom. Jacques Attali & Joseph H. Rowe. LC 97-42976. (Illus.). 250p. 1999. pap. 16.95 (*1-55643-265-8*) North Atlantic.

Labyrinth Makers. large type ed. Anthony Price. 369p. 1981. 27.99 (*0-7089-0711-3*) Ulverscroft.

Labyrinth of Capital Gains Tax Policy: A Guide for the Perplexed. Leonard E. Burman. LC 99-6203. 1999. 26.95 (*0-8157-1270-7*) Brookings.

Labyrinth of Desire: Invention & Culture in the Work of Sir Philip Sidney. William Craft. LC 93-39886. (C). 1994. 33.50 (*0-87413-522-2*) U Delaware Pr.

Labyrinth of Dreams. Jack L. Chalker. (G. O. D. Inc. Ser.: Bk. 1). 1992. mass mkt. 3.99 (*0-8125-1928-0*, Pub. by Tor Bks) St Martin.

Labyrinth of Exile: A Life of Theodore Herzl. Ernst Pawel. 1989. text 30.00 (*0-374-18256-6*) FS&G.

Labyrinth of Imagery: Ramon Gomez de la Serna's Novelas de la Nebulosa. Miguel Gonzalez-Gerth. 1986. 69.00 (*0-7293-0234-2*, Pub. by Tamesis Bks Ltd) Boydell & Brewer.

Labyrinth of Love. Carla Vendries. 1997. pap. write for info. (*1-57553-591-2*) Watermrk Pr.

Labyrinth of Memory: Ethnographic Journeys. Ed. by Marea C. Teski & Jacob J. Climo. LC 94-39209. 232p. 1995. 59.95 (*0-89789-409-X*, Bergin & Garvey) Greenwood.

Labyrinth of Memory: The Art of Gerardo Suter. Gerardo Suter. 1999. pap. text 29.95 (*1-879128-18-7*) Americas Soc.

Labyrinth of Nationalism, Complexities of Diplomacy: Essays in Honor of Charles & Barbara Jelavich. Ed. by Richard C. Frucht. 377p. (Orig.). 1992. pap. 22.95 (*0-89357-233-0*) Slavica.

Labyrinth of Night. Allen Steele. 352p. (Orig.). 1992. mass mkt. 5.99 (*0-441-46741-5*) Ace Bks.

Labyrinth of Prosperity. Reuven Brenner. LC 94-177. 312p. 1994. pap. text 21.95 (*0-472-06556-4*, 06556) U of Mich Pr.

Labyrinth of Prosperity. Reuven Brenner. LC 94-177. 312p. 1994. text 51.50 (*0-472-09556-0*, 09556) U of Mich Pr.

Labyrinth of Satan. G. Suster. 1997. mass mkt. 15.95 (*0-340-66649-8*, Pub. by Hodder & Stought Ltd) Trafalgar.

Labyrinth of Solitude: The Other Mexico & Return to the Labyrinth of Solitude & The U. S. A. & The Philanthropic Ogre. Octavio Paz. Tr. by Lysander Kemp from SPA. LC 82-47999. 408p. 1989. pap. 13.95 (*0-8021-5042-X*, Grove) Grove-Atltic.

Labyrinth of the Comic: Theory & Practice from Fielding to Freud. Richard K. Simon. LC 85-6069. xii, 272p. 1986. 44.95 (*0-8130-0831-X*) U Press Fla.

***Labyrinth of the Grail.** William Mann. LC 99-33317. (Illus.). 350p. 1999. pap. 24.95 (*0-9659701-8-3*) Laughing Owl.

Labyrinth of the World & the Paradise of the Heart. John A. Comenius. 170p. 1992. reprint ed. pap. 16.95 (*1-56459-293-6*) Kessinger Pub.

Labyrinth of the World & the Paradise of the Heart. John A. Komensky. LC 73-135812. (Eastern Europe Collection). 1971. reprint ed. 24.95 (*0-405-02754-0*) Ayer.

Labyrinth of Thought: A History of Set Theory & Its Role in Modern Mathematics. J. Ferreiros. LC 99-30044. (Science Networks Historical Studies: Vol. 23). (Illus.). 464p. 1999. 130.00 (*3-7643-5749-5*, Pub. by Birkhauser) Spr-Verlag.

Labyrinth Rims: Sixty Accesses to Green River Overlooks. Jack Bickers. LC 88-83436. (Illus.). 80p. (Orig.). (C). 1989. pap. 6.00 (*0-9621507-6-2*) Four WD Trailguide.

Labyrinthe: Journal Mensuel des Lettres et des Arts, No. 1[00ad]23. Ed. by Albert Skira. LC 68-9228. (Contemporary Art Ser.). (FRE., Illus.). 1969. reprint ed. 76.95 (*0-405-00705-1*) Ayer.

Labyrinths: Explorations in the Critical History of Ideas. Richard Wolin. LC 95-16844. (Critical Perspectives on Modern Culture Ser.). 304p. 1995. pap. 17.95 (*0-87023-990-2*) U of Mass Pr.

Labyrinths: Explorations in the Critical History of Ideas. Richard Wolin. LC 95-16844. (Critical Perspectives on Modern Culture Ser.). 304p. (C). 1995. 50.00 (*0-87023-989-9*) U of Mass Pr.

Labyrinths: The Art of Interactive Writing & Design. Domenic Stansberry. LC 97-19342. 239p. (C). 1997. 35.95 (*0-534-51948-2*) Wadsworth Pub.

***Labyrinths: What Are They?** rev. ed. Kay Torrez. 178p. 1999. 23.50 (*0-9649094-3-X*) Labyrinths.

Labyrinths & Number Mazes. Ilkka Heino. 1995. pap. 12.95 (*0-312-13105-4*) St Martin.

Labyrinths & Volcanoes: Windings Through Sicily. Justin Vitiello. LC 98-42691. 1998. 16.00 (*1-881901-16-5*) LEGAS.

***Labyrinths from the Outside in: Walking to Spiritual Insight - A Beginner's Guide.** Donna Schaper & Carole Ann Camp. 2000. pap. 16.95 (*1-893361-18-7*) SkyLight Paths.

Labyrinths Literacy: Reflections on Literacy Past & Present. Harvey J. Graff. LC 95-2687. (Series in Composition, Literacy & Culture Ser.). 347p. 1995. text 22.95 (*0-8229-5562-8*) U of Pittsburgh Pr.

Labyrinths of Democracy: Adaptations, Linkages, Representation, & Policies in Urban Politics. Heinz Eulau & Kenneth Prewitt. LC 72-77129. 1973. 62.50 (*0-672-51155-X*); pap. text 22.95 (*0-89197-821-6*) Irvington.

Labyrinths of Iron: Subways in History, Myth, Art, Technology, & War. Benson Bobrick. LC 93-41460. (Illus.). 352p. 1995. pap. 16.95 (*0-8050-3109-X*) H Holt & Co.

Labyrinths of Language: Symbolic Landscape & Narrative Design in Modern Fiction. Wendy B. Faris. LC 88-3026. 256p. 1988. text 40.00 (*0-8018-3676-X*) Johns Hopkins.

Labyrinths of Light. Terence Munsey. LC 95-94007. (Stoneman Ser.: Bk. 3). 248p. (Orig.). 1995. mass mkt. 4.99 (*0-9697066-2-6*) Munsey Music.

Labyrinths of Literacy: Reflections of Literacy Past & Present. Harvey J. Graff. 275p. 1987. pap. 34.95 (*1-85000-164-2*, Falmer Pr) Taylor & Francis.

Labyrinths of Speculation. Elwin Rogers. LC 97-92733. (Illus.). 68p. 1997. pap. write for info. (*1-57579-096-3*) Pine Hill Pr.

Labyrinths of the Delta. Tanure Ojaide. 1986. 9.95 (*0-912678-67-4*, Greenfld Rev Pr) Greenfld Rev Lit.

Labyrinths of the Mind: The Self in the Postmodern Age. Daniel R. White & Gert Hellerich. LC 97-30049. (SUNY Series in Postmodern Culture). 224p. (C). 1998. text 59.50 (*0-7914-3787-6*); pap. text 19.95 (*0-7914-3788-4*) State U NY Pr.

Labyrinths, Selected Stories & Other Writings. Jorge Luis Borges. Ed. by Donald A. Yates & James E. Irby. LC 64-25440. 1964. reprint ed. pap. 11.95 (*0-8112-0012-4*, NDP186, Pub. by New Directions) Norton.

Labyrinths, What Are They? Prehistory to 21st Century. rev. ed. Kay Torrez. (Illus.). 125p. 1995. pap. 17.50 (*0-9649094-2-1*) Labyrinths.

***L'Abyssin.** Jean-Christophe Rufin. 2000. pap. 17.95 (*2-07-040697-0*) Gallimard Edns.

Lac Aux Requins see Red Sea Sharks

Lac La Belle. Clarence J. Monette. (Copper Country Local History Ser.: Vol. 28). (Illus.). 128p. 1990. 5.00 (*0-942363-37-X*) C J Monette.

Lac Operon: A Short History of a Genetic Paradigm. Benno Muller-Hill. LC 96-20965. ix, 207p. (Orig.). (C). 1996. pap. text 29.95 (*3-11-014830-7*) De Gruyter.

Lac Tung Buoc Chan: Phuong Phap Thuc Tap Hanh Phuc. Thich Nhat Hahn. Tr. by Chan Nguyen. (VIE.). 154p. 1995. pap. 11.00 (*1-891667-34-3*) La Boi Soc.

Lacaille: Astronomer, Traveler: With a New Translation of His Journal. David S. Evans. (History of Astronomy Ser.: Vol. 9). 1992. pap. 36.00 (*0-88126-284-6*) Pachart Pub Hse.

Lacan. Malcolm Bowie. 224p. 1991. 26.95 (*0-674-50852-1*, BOWLAC) HUP.

Lacan. Malcolm Bowie. 256p. (C). 1993. pap. 16.00 (*0-674-50853-X*) HUP.

***Lacan.** Alain Vanier. 2000. pap. 22.00 (*1-892746-50-6*) Other Pr LLC.

Lacan: The Absolute Master. Mikkel Borch-Jacobsen. Tr. by Douglas Brick from FRE. LC 90-43813. 320p. 1991. 42.50 (*0-8047-1556-4*); pap. 16.95 (*0-8047-1728-1*) Stanford U Pr.

Lacan & Language: A Reader's Guide to "Ecrits" John P. Muller & William J. Richardson. 443p. 1994. pap. 29.95 (*0-8236-8129-7*) Intl Univs Pr.

Lacan & Literature: Purloined Pretexts. Ben Stoltzfus. LC 95-405. (SUNY Series in Psychoanalysis & Culture). 227p. (C). 1996. text 74.50 (*0-7914-2931-8*); pap. text 24.95 (*0-7914-2932-6*) State U NY Pr.

Lacan & Love. Ed. by Renata Salecl. (New Formations Ser.: No. 23). 192p. (C). 1994. pap. 19.95 (*0-85315-764-2*, Pub. by Lawrence & Wishart) NYU Pr.

***Lacan & Political.** Yannis Stavrakakis. LC 98-51212. 188p. 1999. pap. 21.99 (*0-415-17187-3*) Routledge.

***Lacan & Political.** Yannis Stavrakakis. (Thinking the Political Ser.). 200p. (C). (gr. 13). 1999. text 65.00 (*0-415-17186-5*) Routledge.

Lacan & the Human Sciences. Ed. by Alexandre Leupin. LC 90-39325. viii, 191p. 1991. text 45.00 (*0-8032-2894-5*) U of Nebr Pr.

***Lacan & the Matter of Origins.** Shuli Barzilai. LC 99-39702. 1999. pap. text 19.95 (*0-8047-3382-1*) Stanford U Pr.

Lacan & the New Wave in American Psychoanalysis: The Subject & the Self. Ed. by Judith F. Garewich et al. LC 99-26605. (Lacanian Clinical Field Ser.). Orig. Title: The Subject & the Self: Lacan & American Psychoanalysis. 266p. 1998. reprint ed. pap. 22.00 (*1-892746-03-4*, 46034) Other Pr LLC.

Lacan & the Subject of Law: Toward a Psychoanalytic Critical Legal Theory. David S. Caudill. LC 96-24792. 200p. (C). 1997. pap. 15.00 (*0-391-04010-3*); text 49.95 (*0-391-04009-X*) Humanities.

Lacan & Theological Discourse. Ed. by Edith Wyschogrod et al. LC 88-37648. (SUNY Series in Philosophy). 179p. (C). 1989. text 19.50 (*0-7914-0110-3*) State U NY Pr.

Lacan, Discourse, & Social Change: A Psychoanalytic Cultural Criticism. Mark Bracher. LC 92-31172. 224p. (C). 1993. text 37.50 (*0-8014-2784-3*); pap. text 14.95 (*0-8014-8063-9*) Cornell U Pr.

Lacan for Beginners. Phillip Hill. (for Beginners Ser.). (Illus.). 176p. 11.00 (*0-86316-227-4*) Writers & Readers.

***Lacan in America.** Jean-Michel Rabatbe. LC 00-35629. 2000. pap. write for info. (*1-892746-63-8*) Other Pr.

Lacan, Politics, Aesthetics. Ed. by Willy Apollon & Richard Feldstein. LC 94-10967. (SUNY Series in Psychoanalysis & Culture). (Illus.). 341p. (C). 1996. text 59.50 (*0-7914-2371-9*); pap. text 19.95 (*0-7914-2372-7*) State U NY Pr.

Lacanian Psychotherapy with Children: The Broken Piano. Catherine Mathelin. LC 98-36956. (Lacanian Clinical Field Ser.). (Illus.). 200p. 1998. pap. 17.95 (*1-892746-01-8*, 46018) Other Pr LLC.

Lacanian Subject: Between Language & Jouissnace. Bruce Fink. 236p. 1995. pap. text 15.95 (*0-691-01589-9*, Pub. by Princeton U Pr) Cal Prin Full Svc.

Lacanian Theory of Discourse: Subject, Structure, & Society. Ed. by Mark Bracher et al. LC 94-14079. 215p. (C). 1994. text 50.00 (*0-8147-1191-X*) NYU Pr.

Lacanian Theory of Discourse: Subject, Structure, & Society. Mark Bracher. 1997. pap. text 20.00 (*0-8147-1299-1*) NYU Pr.

***Lacan's Seminar on Anxiety.** Robert Harari. 2000. pap. 27.00 (*1-892746-36-0*) Other Pr LLC.

Laccoliths: Mechanics of Emplacement & Growth. Charles E. Corry. LC 88-10166. (Geological Society of America Ser.: Vol. 220). (Illus.). 188p. 1988. reprint ed. pap. 58.30 (*0-608-07746-1*, 206783400010) Bks Demand.

Lace. Shirley Conran. Ed. by Julie Rubenstein. 608p. 1990. mass mkt. 5.99 (*0-671-73745-7*) PB.

Lace. Aurelia Loveman. Ed. by Carla Brenner. (Illus.). 24p. (Orig.). 1988. pap. text 4.00 (*0-911886-36-2*) Walters Art.

Lace. large type ed. Shirley Conran. LC 94-40739. 1994. pap. 22.95 (*1-56895-085-3*) Wheeler Pub.

Lace: A Guide to Identification of Old Lace Types & Techniques. Heather Toomer. 1989. 23.75 (*0-7134-5701-5*) Robin & Russ.

Lace: Australian Wildflowers in Point Ground. Elwyn Kenn. 44p. 1990. pap. 12.95 (*0-86417-288-5*) Robin & Russ.

Lace: Poetry from the Poor, the Homeless, the Aged, the Physically & Emotionally Disabled. Ed. by Arthur Dobrin. LC 79-90011. (Illus.). (Orig.). 1979. 15.00 (*0-89304-036-3*, CCC123); pap. 7.95 (*0-89304-037-1*) Cross-Cultrl NY.

Lace: The Poetry of Fashion, with Representative Values. Bella Veksler. LC 98-4606. 1998. 39.95 (*0-7643-0538-7*) Schiffer.

Lace - Classic. 112p. 1991. pap. 29.95 (*88-7070-060-7*) Belvedere USA.

Lace & Lace Making. Marian Powys. (Illus.). 1981. reprint ed. 50.00 (*1-55888-179-4*) Omnigraphics Inc.

Lace & Lacey Weaves. Mary E. Snyder. 1986. pap. 10.00 (*1-56659-014-0*) Robin & Russ.

Lace & Satin. large type ed. Helen Brooks. 288p. 1995. 23.99 (*0-263-14290-6*, Pub. by Mills & Boon) Ulverscroft.

Lace Curtain. Alexis K. Rotella. 20p. 1988. pap. 6.00 (*0-917951-03-4*) Jade Mtn.

Lace Draping Basics. Gloria Woodruff. LC 91-60864. (Illus.). 54p. 1991. pap. text 9.95 (*0-916809-49-8*) Scott Pubns MI.

Lace for Beginners. Nihon Vogue Staff. (Illus.). 82p. 1984. pap. 13.95 (*0-87040-567-5*) Japan Pubns USA.

Lace for Church Use. Marie-Clare Downham. 1989. 24.95 (*0-7134-5836-4*) Robin & Russ.

Lace for Milady. Joan Smith. 1981. mass mkt. 1.95 (*0-449-50179-5*) Ballantine Pub Grp.

Lace from the Attic: A Victorian Notebook of Knitted Lace Patterns. Nancie Wiseman. LC 98-4351. (Illus.). 1998. pap. 17.95 (*1-883010-40-3*) Interweave.

Lace Heritage: A Guide to Nottingham Lace. David Lowe & Jack Richards. (C). 1988. 60.00 (*0-7855-3794-5*, Pub. by Lace Centre) St Mut.

Lace II. Shirley Conran. Ed. by Julie Rubenstein. 336p. (Orig.). 1988. mass mkt. 5.99 (*0-671-66904-4*) PB.

Lace in Fashion from the Sixteenth to the Twentieth Centuries. Pat Earnshaw. (Illus.). 168p. 1991. pap. 32.00 (*0-9513891-3-0*, Pub. by Gorse) Lacis Pubns.

Lace Machines & Machine Laces. Pat Earnshaw. (Illus.). 288p. 1986. 48.00 (*0-7134-4684-6*, Pub. by Gorse) Lacis Pubns.

Lace Ten Years Documented. Nancy Drew et al. Ed. by Karen Moss. (Illus.). 112p. 1988. pap. 15.00 (*0-937335-03-7*) LA Contemp Exhib.

***Lace Them Up.** Lilly Barnes. (Illus.). 64p. (J). (gr. k-3). 1998. pap. 8.95 (*0-921051-64-6*) Somerville Hse.

Lace Them Up. Lilly Barnes & Patricia Quinlan. (Step by Step Ser.). (Illus.). 32p. (J). (ps-2). 1992. 8.95 (*1-56282-282-9*, Pub. by Hyprn Child) Little.

Lace-Vienna. Ed. by Wolfgang Hageney. (ENG, FRE, GER, ITA & SPA., Illus.). 120p. 1985. pap. 22.95 (*88-7070-052-6*) Belvedere USA.

Laced with Love. Sheila Walker. LC 98-41411. (Illus.). 250p. 1998. pap. 14.95 (*1-884540-38-4*) Haleys.

La/Cena de Le Ceneri see Ash Wednesday Supper

La/Ceremonia Delle Cose see Ceremony of Things

Lacey. Michel Fattah. LC 89-62244. 40p. (J). 1990. 12.95 (*0-915677-47-4*) Roundtable Pub.

Lacey. Norah Hess. 432p. (Orig.). 1996. mass mkt. 5.99 (*0-8439-3941-9*) Dorchester Pub Co.

Lacey & His Friends. David Drake. 320p. (Orig.). 1986. mass mkt. 4.99 (*0-671-65593-0*) Baen Bks.

Lacey O'Neal: A Shoelace Book. Arlen Cohn. LC 99-41980. (Books-in-Motion Ser.). (Illus.). 32p. (J). 1998. 15.95 (*0-939251-99-X*) Accord CO.

Lacey's Crush. Created by Francine Pascal. (Sweet Valley Junior High Ser.: No. 6). 160p. (J). (gr. 3-7). 1999. pap. 3.99 (*0-553-48665-9*) Bantam.

Lacey's Way. Madeline Baker. 448p. (Orig.). 1990. pap. text 4.50 (*0-8439-2918-9*) Dorchester Pub Co.

***Lacey's Way, 1.** Madeline Baker. 448p. (Orig.). 1999. reprint ed. mass mkt. 5.99 (*0-8439-4587-7*, Leisure Bks) Dorchester Pub Co.

Lacey's Way. rev. ed. Madeline Baker. 448p. (Orig.). 1996. mass mkt. 5.99 (*0-8439-3956-7*) Dorchester Pub Co.

Lachaise. Sam Hunter. (Illus.). 208p. 1993. 60.00 (*1-55859-562-7*, Cross Riv Pr) Abbeville Pr.

***Lachaise: Sculpture & Drawings.** Text by Hilton Kramer. LC 98-6089. (Illus.). 152p. 1998. 45.00 (*1-58821-044-8*) Salander OReilly.

Lachapelle Land: Photographs by David LaChapelle. Ed. by Sandy Arrowsmith. LC 96-14275. (Illus.). 150p. 1996. 50.00 (*0-684-83302-6*) Callaway Edns.

Lachenalia Handbook. G. Duncan. (Annals of Kirstenbosch Botanic Gardens Ser.: Vol. 17). (Illus.). 71p. 1988. pap. 15.00 (*0-620-11953-5*, Pub. by Natl Botanical Inst) Balogh.

Laches & Charmides. Plato. Tr. & Intro. by Rosamond K. Sprague. LC 92-6207. 112p. (C). 1992. reprint ed. pap. text 6.95 (*0-87220-134-1*); reprint ed. lib. bdg. 24.95 (*0-87220-135-X*) Hackett Pub.

Laches, Protagoras, Meno & Euthydemus, Vol. II. Tr. by W. R. Lamb. (Loeb Classical Library: No. 165). 530p. 1924. reprint ed. 18.95 (*0-674-99183-4*) HUP.

Lachesis Lapponica: A Tour in Lapland, 2 vols., Set. Carl Von Linne. LC 77-87708. reprint ed. 42.50 (*0-404-16510-9*) AMS Pr.

An Asterisk (*) at the beginning of an entry indicates that the title is appearing for the first time.

Lachlan McGillivray, Indian Trader: The Shaping of the Southern Colonial Frontier. Edward J. Cashin. LC 91-12479. 352p. 1992. 45.00 (0-8203-1368-8) U of Ga Pr.

Lachman's Case Studies in Anatomy. 4th ed. Rev. by Donald R. Cahill. (Illus.). 432p. 1996. pap. text 22.95 (0-19-510297-5) OUP.

Lachnocladiaceae & Coniophoraceae of North Europe. N. Hallenberg. (Illus.). 96p. 1985. pap. text 21.95 (0-685-32408-7) Lubrecht & Cramer.

Lachrimae Lachrimarum. Joshua Sylvester. LC 72-234. (English Experience Ser.: No. 185). 32p. 1969. reprint ed. 25.00 (90-221-0185-1) Walter J Johnson.

Lachrymae Catharinae: Five Collections of Funeral Poetry from 1628. Ed. by Annika Strom. (Studia Latina Stockholmiensia: No. 38). 307p. 1994. pap. 49.50 (91-22-01642-2) Coronet Bks.

Lacht am Besten. Peter Fabrizius. Ed. by Clair H. Bell. LC 57-5200. (GER., Illus.). (C). reprint ed. pap. text 7.95 (0-8290-2376-3) Irvington.

Lacing the Moon. Linda Monacelli. (Cleveland Poets Ser.: No. 17). 40p. 1978. pap. 2.50 (0-914946-11-0) Cleveland St Univ Poetry Ctr.

La/Citta del Sol: Dialogo Poetico see City of the Sun: A Poetical Dialogue

La/Ciudad see City

Lack & Transcendence: The Problem of Death & Life in Psychotherapy, Existentialism, & Buddhism. David Loy. LC 95-255. 224p. (C). 1996. text 49.95 (0-391-03860-5) Humanities.

***Lack Brothers.** McKay. 2000. pap. 17.95 (0-593-04204-2, Pub. by Transworld Publishers Ltd) Trafalgar.

***Lack of Money Is the Root of All Evil: Mark Twain's Common Sense Guide to Investing.** Andrew Leckey. 2001. 22.00 (0-7352-0219-2) PH Pr.

Lack of the Irish: A Mystery Set at the University of Notre Dame. Ralph McInerny. LC 98-21119. 224p. 1998. text 21.95 (0-312-19294-0) St Martin.

Lack of the Irish: A Mystery Set at the University of Notre Dame. Ralph McInerny. (Dead Letter Mysteries Ser.). 1999. mass mkt. 5.99 (0-312-96927-9, Minotaur) St Martin.

Lackawanna. Chester Aaron. LC 83-47667. 224p. (YA). (gr. 7 up). 1986. lib. bdg. 11.89 (0-397-32058-2) HarpC Child Bks.

Lackawanna: Steam Locomotives & Trains, 1934-1937. Robert K. Durham. LC 97-91798. (Steam of the Thirties Ser.). (Illus.). 72p. 1997. pap. 21.00 (0-9644480-8-4) Durham Publng.

Lackawanna - Superpower Railroad of the Northeast. Robert A. Le Massena. (Illus.). 112p. 1998. pap. 26.95 (1-883089-32-8) TLC VA.

***Lackawanna County: An Illustrated History.** Aileen Freeman. (History Ser.). (Illus.). 136p. 2000. 44.95 (1-58192-021-0) Community Comm.

Lackawanna Heritage. John Krause. (Illus.). 48p. 1990. pap. 8.95 (0-911868-69-0, C-69) Carstens Pubns.

Lackawanna Jurist, Scranton, Pa., 1888-1998, 99 vols. in 98, Set. 3500.00 (1-57588-318-X, 302890) W S Hein.

Lackawanna Railroad in Color. David R. Sweetland. LC 90-61261. (Illus.). 128p. 1990. 45.00 (0-9619058-8-3) Morning NJ.

***Lackawanna Railroad Trackside with Henry Peterson.** Michael J. Del Vecchio & Henry W. Peterson. LC 98-68500. (Illus.). 128p. 1999. 54.95 (1-58248-015-X) Morning NJ.

Laclau & Mouffe: Radical Democratic Imaginary. LC 97-53303. 256p. (C). (gr. 13). 1998. 75.00 (0-415-10059-3); pap. 24.99 (0-415-10060-7) Routledge.

Laclos et la Tradition: Essai sur les Sources et la Technique des Liaisons Dangereuses. Versini. 43.75 (0-685-34039-2) Fr & Eur.

La/Composition des Espaces Vertes et le Choix des Vegetaux see Landscape Gardening & the Choice of Plants

Laconia. Warren D. Huse. (Images of America Ser.). 1995. pap. 16.99 (0-7524-0092-4) Arcadia Publng.

Laconian Iconography of the Sixth Century BC. Maria Pipili. (Illus.). 124p. 1987. pap. 39.95 (0-947816-12-7, Pub. by Oxford Univ Comm Arch) David Brown.

LaConner Palates: An Illustrated Cookbook. Patricia Flynn & Patricia McClane. (Illus.). 196p. 1998. pap. 21.95 (0-9659303-0-0) Bkends Publ.

Lacoon. Gotthold Ephraim Lessing. Tr. by Edward A. McCormick. 1962. pap. 5.50 (0-672-60260-1, Bobbs) Macmillan.

Lacordaire. Francois Mauriac & Keith Goesch. (FRE.). 148p. 1976. 29.95 (0-8288-9752-2, F100580) Fr & Eur.

LaCosta Prescription for Longer Life. R. Philip Smith & Patrick Quillin. LC 83-63201. (Illus.). 352p. 1984. 16.95 (0-915677-03-2) Roundtable Pub.

Lacota: Geneva Township, Van Buren County, Michigan. Barbara W. Wood. (Illus.). 154p. 1997. 20.00 (1-877703-45-1) Pavilion Pr.

***Lacquer: Technology & Conversation.** Webb. 2000. 130.00 (0-7506-4412-5) Buttrwrth-Heinemann.

Lacquer & Silver: Oriental Elegance for Western Tables. Fumi Kimura. Tr. by Juliet W. Carpenter from JPN. (Illus.). 184p. 1991. 45.00 (4-7700-1577-1) Kodansha.

Lacquer Miniatures from Palekh. Maria Nekrasova. (Illus.). 1984. 50.00 (0-7855-1551-8) St Mut.

Lacquer of Suzuki: Mutsumi & Suzuki Misako. Oliver R. Impey. (Illus.). 48p. 1993. pap. 6.95 (0-907849-73-3, N733, Pub. by Ashmolean Mus) A Schwartz & Co.

Lacquer of the Islamic Lands. Nasser D. Khalili & B. W. Robinson. LC 97-179012. (Nasser D. Khalili Collection of Islamic Art: Vol. XXII, Pt. I). (Illus.). 276p. (C). 1997. text 250.00 (0-19-727619-9) OUP.

Lacquer of the Islamic Lands. Nasser D. Khalili et al. LC 97-179012. (The NasserD. Khalili Collection of Islamic Art: Vol. XXII). (Illus.). 272p. (C). 1998. text 275.00 (0-19-727626-1) OUP.

Lacquer Screen: A Chinese Detective Story. Robert H. Van Gulik. LC 92-18040. (Illus.). x, 180p. 1992. pap. 6.95 (0-226-84867-1) U Ch Pr.

Lacquered Boxes. Detlev Richter. LC 89-84171. (Illus.). 216p. 1989. 69.95 (0-88740-197-X) Schiffer.

Lacret 8th Grade Early Warning Test (EWT) - Math Basic Skills Workbook. Fabian Lacret-Subirat. (Illus.). 186p. (J). (gr. 7-8). 1996. pap., wbk. ed. 12.00 (0-943144-34-5) Lacret Pub.

Lacret 11th Grade High School Proficiency Test (HSPT) - Math Skills Workbook. Fabian Lacret-Subirat. (Illus.). 252p. (YA). (gr. 9-11). 1995. pap., wbk. ed. 12.00 (0-943144-32-9) Lacret Pub.

***Lacret HS-Math Self-Tutoring (Solving Word-Problems)** Fabian Lacret-Subirat. (Illus.). 220p. (YA). (gr. 9-12). 2000. pap. 32.00 (0-943144-45-0) Lacret Pub.

Lacret 11th Grade High School Proficiency Test (HSPT) - Math Skills Solved Problems: Solved Problems. Fabian Lacret-Subirat. (Illus.). 70p. (YA). (gr. 9-11). 1997. pap. 13.33 (0-943144-39-6) Lacret Pub.

Lacrimal Gland, Tear Film & Dry Eye Syndromes: Basic Science & Clinical Relevance, Vol. 1. D. A. Sullivan. (Advances in Experimental Medicine & Biology Ser.: Vol. 350). (Illus.). 752p. (C). 1994. text 155.00 (0-306-44676-6, Kluwer Plenum) Kluwer Academic.

Lacrimal Gland, Tear Film & Dry Eye Syndromes 2: Basic Science & Clinical Relevance. Ed. by David A. Sullivan et al. LC 98-17987. (Advances in Experimental Medicine & Biology Ser.: No. 438). (Illus.). 1076p. (C). 1998. text 195.00 (0-306-45812-8, Kluwer Plenum) Kluwer Academic.

Lacrimal System. Ed. by Jeffrey J. Hurwitz. LC 95-17719. (Illus.). 352p. 1995. text 140.00 (0-7817-0334-4) Lppncott W & W.

Lacrimal System. Ed. by O. P. Van Bijsterveld et al. LC 91-7055. (Illus.). 113p. 1991. pap. text 40.00 (90-6299-073-8, Pub. by Kugler) Kugler Pubns.

Lacrimal System, 1994. Ed. by J. Hurwitz et al. LC 95-31274. 1996. 63.00 (90-6299-131-9) Kugler Pubns.

Lacrosse. Lois Nicholson. LC 98-13891. (Composite Guide Ser.). (Illus.). 64p. (YA). (gr. 3 up). 1999. lib. bdg. 15.95 (0-7910-4719-9) Chelsea Hse.

Lacrosse: Technique & Tradition. Bob Scott. LC 76-17223. (Illus.). 232p. 1976. pap. 16.95 (0-8018-2060-X) Johns Hopkins.

***LaCrosse: The National Game of the Iroquois.** Diane Hoyt-Goldsmith. LC 97-37742. (Illus.). 31p. (J). (gr. 4-7). 1998. lib. bdg. 16.95 (0-8234-1360-8) Holiday.

***Lacrosse Fundamentals.** rev. ed. Jim Hinkson. (Illus.). 2000. pap. 16.95 (1-894020-77-4) Warwick Publ.

Lacrosse Team Fundamentals. Ben Hinkson. (Illus.). 200p. (Orig.). 1993. pap. 15.95 (1-895629-11-X) Warwick Publ.

Lacrosse Team Strategies. Jim Hinkson. (Illus.). 176p. 1996. pap. 16.95 (1-895629-55-1) Warwick Publ.

Lacroze-Miguens-Prati. Oscar R. Ojeda. (Ten Houses Ser.). (Illus.). 108p. 1996. pap. 19.99 (1-56496-326-8) Rockport Pubs.

Lacs Italiens. (FRE.). 1999. 9.95 (2-06-657101-6) Michelin.

Lactam Based Polyamides, Vol. I. V. Kubanek & Puffr. 328p. 1991. boxed set 225.00 (0-8493-4965-6, QD383) CRC Pr.

Lactam Based Polyamides, Vol. II. Rudolf Puffr & V. Kubanek. 368p. 1991. lib. bdg. 225.00 (0-8493-4966-4, QD383) CRC Pr.

Lactancia Materna. 4th ed. Lawrence. (C). 1996. text 73.88 (84-8174-176-0) Mosby Inc.

Lactanti, L. Caeli Firmiani. Ed. by Heck & Wlosok. (LAT.). 1994. 43.50 (3-519-01934-5, T1934, Pub. by B G Teubner); pap. 24.95 (3-519-01933-7, T1953, Pub. by B G Teubner) U of Mich Pr.

Lactantii Placidi. Ed. by Sweeney. (LAT.). 1997. 43.50 (3-8154-1824-0, T1824, Pub. by B G Teubner) U of Mich Pr.

Lactantii Placidi Vol. I: Scholia in Statium. Ed. by Sweeney. (LAT.). 1997. 160.00 (3-8154-1823-2, T1823, Pub. by B G Teubner) U of Mich Pr.

Lactantius: De Mortibus Persecutorm. Lactantius. Ed. by J. L. Creed. (Oxford Early Christian Texts Ser.). 1985. 59.00 (0-19-826813-0) OUP.

Lactantius & Milton. Kathleen Hartwell. LC 74-17014. (Studies in Milton: No. 22). 1974. lib. bdg. 75.00 (0-8383-1743-X) M S G Haskell Hse.

Lactate: Physiologic, Methodologic & Pathologic Approach. Ed. by P. R. Moret et al. (Illus.). 270p. 1980. 42.95 (0-387-09829-1) Spr-Verlag.

Lactate in Acute Conditions: Proceedings of the International Symposium, Basel, March, 1978. Ed. by H. Bossart & C. Perret. (Illus.). 1979. 77.50 (3-8055-2968-6) S Karger.

Lactate Lift-Off: How to Use Lactate Training to Maximize Your Fitness. unabridged ed. Owen Anderson. LC 98-96158. 180p. 1998. pap. 21.95 (0-9663726-0-3) SSS MI.

***Lactating Sow.** M. W. A. Verstegen. 350p. 1998. 93.00 (90-74134-43-2) Wageningen Pers.

Lactation. Ed. by Bruce L. Larson. (Illus.). 276p. (C). 1985. 42.95 (0-8138-1063-9) Iowa St U Pr.

Lactation: Physiology, Nutrition & Breast Feeding. Ed. by Margaret C. Neville & Marianne R. Neifert. LC 83-17652. 482p. 1983. 95.00 (0-306-41311-6, Plenum Trade) Perseus Pubng.

Lactation: Proceedings. Easter School in Agricultural Science (14th 1967,. Ed. by Ian R. Falconer. LC 76-502285. 489p. reprint ed. pap. 151.60 (0-608-14840-7, 202574000046) Bks Demand.

Lactation: The Breast-Feeding Manual for Health Professionals. Ed. by Gary M. Chan. LC 96-38181. 192p. 1996. pap. 40.00 (0-944496-48-2) Precept Pr.

Lactation Consultant's Clinical Practice Manual. Marie Davis. (Illus.). x, 320p. 1998. ring bd. 145.00 (0-9668111-0-0) Bright Future.

Lactation Consultant's Topical Review & Bibliography of the Literature on Breastfeeding. Ed. by Mary-Margaret Coates. LC 90-61943. 188p. (Orig.). 1990. pap. 12.00 (0-912500-39-5) La Leche.

Lactation of the Dairy Cow Colin T. Whittemore. LC 79-40442. (Longman Handbooks in Agriculture Ser.). 94 p. 1980. write for info. (0-582-45079-9) Addison-Wesley.

Lactation of the Dairy Cow. Colin T. Whittemore. LC 79-40442. (Longman Handbooks in Agriculture Ser.). (Illus.). 102p. reprint ed. pap. 31.70 (0-8357-6181-9, 203447400090) Bks Demand.

***Lactation Specialist: Marketing Your Lactation Practice, Vol. 5.** Rebecca Black. (Illus.). 288p. (C). 1999. pap. text 40.00 (0-7637-1037-7) JB Pubns.

Lactation Specialist Self-Study Series. Rebecca F. Black et al. 900p. 1998. pap. 125.00 (0-7637-0664-7) Jones & Bartlett.

Lactic Acid Bacteria. Ed. by E. L. Foo et al. LC 97-179539. 102p. 1993. reprint ed. 84.99 (1-898486-04-2, Pub. by Horizon Sci) Intl Spec Bk.

Lactic Acid Bacteria. 2nd ed. Ed. by Salminen & Von Wright. LC 97-44104. (Illus.). 640p. 1998. text 195.00 (0-8247-0133-X) Dekker.

Lactic Acid Bacteria: Current Advances in Genetics, Metabolism, & Application of Lactic Acid Bacteria. Ed. by T. Faruk Bozoglu & Bibek Ray. LC 96-16948. (NATO ASI Ser.: Series H, Vol. 98). 404p. 1996. 190.00 (3-540-61117-7) Spr-Verlag.

***Lactic Acid Bacteria: Genetics, Metabolism & Applications.** Wilhelmus Nicolaas Konings et al. LC 99-51737. (C). 1999. write for info. (0-7923-5953-4) Kluwer Academic.

Lactic Acid Bacteria: Genetics, Metabolism & Applications. Ed. by G. Venema et al. LC 96-219168. 358p. 1996. text 202.50 (0-7923-4269-0) Kluwer Academic.

Lactic Acid Bacteria in Health & Disease, Vol. 1. B. J. B. Wood. 485p. 1992. 189.00 (0-8342-1312-5) Aspen Pub.

Lactic Acid Metabolism: A Monograph on Carbohydrate Metabolism in the Blood & Brain of the Suckling Rat. Howard S. Mehler. LC 88-90631. (Illus.). 115p. (C). 1988. 69.95 (0-9621181-0-9) Mehler Pub.

Lactic Acidosis & Energy Metabolism. Ed. by M. Ugarte. 200p. (C). 1996. pap. text 87.00 (0-7923-8716-3) Kluwer Academic.

Lactic Dehydrogenase Virus. Brian W. Mahy & K. E. Rowson. LC 74-34231. (Virology Monographs: Vol. 13). (Illus.). iv, 121p. 1975. 47.00 (0-387-81270-9) Spr-Verlag.

Lactilla, Milkwoman of Clifton: The Life & Writings of Ann Yearsley, 1753-1806. Mary Waldron. LC 95-21787. 1996. 50.00 (0-8203-1801-9) U of Ga Pr.

Lactoferrin: Interactions & Biological Functions. Ed. by T. William Hutchens & Bo Lonnderdal. LC 96-52990. (Experimental Biology & Medicine Ser.: Vol. 28). (Illus.). 416p. 1997. 125.00 (0-89603-366-X) Humana.

***Lactoferrin: Natural - Multifunctional - Antimicrobial.** A. S. Naidu. 184p. 2000. per. 69.95 (0-8493-0909-3) CRC Pr.

Lactoferrin: Structure & Function. Ed. by T. W. Hutchens et al. (Advances in Experimental Medicine & Biology Ser.: Vol. 357). (Illus.). 310p. (C). 1995. text 95.00 (0-306-44734-7, Kluwer Plenum) Kluwer Academic.

***Lactoferrin: Structure, Function & Applications: Proceedings of the 4th International Conference on Lactoferrin: Structure, Function & Applications, Held in Hokkaido, Japan, 18-22 May, 1999.** International Conference on Lactoferrin Staff & Kei-ichi Shimazaki. LC 00-28811. 2000. write for info. (0-444-50317-X) Elsevier.

Lactoperoxidase System: Chemistry & Biological Significance. Kenneth Pruitt & Tenovuov. (Immunology Ser.: Vol. 27). (Illus.). 272p. 1985. text 155.00 (0-8247-7298-9) Dekker.

Lactose Digestion: Clinical & Nutritional Implications. Ed. by David M. Paige & Theodore M. Bayless. LC 81-1537. (Illus.). 300p. 1981. reprint ed. pap. 93.00 (0-608-04011-8, 206474700011) Bks Demand.

***Lactose Free: More Than 100 Delicious Recipes Your Family Will Love.** Lucy Knox & Sarah Lowman. LC 00-24510. (Great Healthy Food Ser.). (Illus.). 2000. pap. 18.00 (0-684-87258-7, Fireside) S&S Trade Pap.

Lactose-Free Cookbook. Sheri Updike. LC 97-51214. 416p. 1998. mass mkt. 14.00 (0-446-67393-5, Pub. by Warner Bks) Little.

Lactose-Free Family Cookbook. Jan Main. (Illus.). 218p. (Orig.). 1996. pap. 17.95 (1-896503-24-1, Pub. by R Rose Inc) Firefly Bks Ltd.

Lactose-Free Foods: A Shoppers Guide. Peter H. Mirsky. LC 95-152873. (Illus.). 70p. 1995. write for info. (0-9644787-0-6) Bullseye Info Servs.

Lactose Intolerance. Merri L. Dobler. 1991. pap. 5.50 (0-88091-097-6, 0881) Am Dietetic Assn.

***Lactosphere: Lactic Acid Bacillus Lactobacillus Sporogenes.** Muhammed Majeed & Lakshmi Prakash. (Illus.). 56p. 1998. pap. write for info. (0-9647856-4-1) Nutrisci Pubs.

Lacturidae. John B. Heppner. (Lepidopterorum Catalogus Ser.: Vol. 10: Fasc. 71). (Illus.). 32p. 2000. pap. text 12.50 (0-945417-60-8) Sci Pubs.

Lacunar & Subcortical Infarctions. Ed. by Geoffrey Donnan et al. (Illus.). 294p. 1995. text 98.00 (0-19-262341-9) OUP.

Lacustrine Basin Exploration - Case Studies & Modern Analogs. Ed. by Barry J. Katz. (AAPG Memoir Ser.: No. 50). (Illus.). 340p. 1990. 29.00 (0-89181-328-4, 564) AAPG.

Lacustrine Facies Analysis. P. Anadon et al. (International Association of Sedimentologists Special Publication Ser.: No. 13). (Illus.). 328p. 1991. 95.00 (0-632-03149-2) Blackwell Sci.

Lacustrine Reservoir & Depositional Systems. Ed. by A. J. Lomando et al. LC 95-103472. (Core Workshop Notes Ser.: No. 19). (Illus.). 388p. 1994. pap. 62.00 (1-56576-011-5) SEPM.

Lacy. Diana Palmer. (Orig.). 1996. pap. 2.99 (0-8041-9703-2) Ivy Books.

Lacy Cut-Paper Designs. Margaret Keilstrup. 64p. 1997. pap. 3.95 (0-486-29512-5) Dover.

Lacy Family in England & Normandy, 1066-1194. Wilfred E. Wightman. LC 80-2206. reprint ed. 37.50 (0-404-18794-3) AMS Pr.

Lacy Knitting of Mary Schiffmann. Nancy Nehring. LC 97-53191. 95p. 1998. pap. 17.95 (1-883010-42-X) Interweave.

Lacy Patterns in Dreams, Vol. 1. limited ed. Lois A. Sutton. (Illus.). 32p. (Orig.). (C). 1997. pap. 4.00 (0-932820-02-6) M P Pubs.

Lacy's Dilemma. Barbara Reeves. 224p. (Orig.). 1995. mass mkt. 3.99 (0-380-77673-1, Avon Bks) Morrow Avon.

Lacy's Flying Leap (Includes Toy) XYZ Group Staff. (Pocket Pets Ser.). (Illus.). 24p. (J). (ps-2). 1997. pap. text 6.95 (1-879332-68-X) Futech Interactive.

Lad: A Dog. Albert Pason Terhune. (J). 24.95 (0-8488-1485-1) Amereon Ltd.

Lad: A Dog. large type ed. Albert Pason Terhune. LC 97-36722. (Perennial Ser.). 341p. (J). (gr. 4-7). 1997. lib. bdg. 22.95 (0-7838-8320-X, G K Hall Lrg Type) Mac Lib Ref.

Lad: A Dog. Albert Pason Terhune. 189p. (J). 1981. reprint ed. lib. bdg. 24.95 (0-89967-022-9, Harmony Rain) Buccaneer Bks.

Lad: A Dog. Albert Pason Terhune. (YA). 1981. reprint ed. lib. bdg. 25.95 (0-89966-348-6) Buccaneer Bks.

Lad, a Dog. Albert Pason Terhune. (J). 1993. 10.09 (0-606-05407-3, Pub. by Turtleback) Demco.

Lad, a Dog: Best Dog in the World. Margo Lundell & Albert Pason Terhune. LC 96-20937. (Hello Reader! Ser.). (Illus.). (J). (gr. 4). 1997. write for info. (0-590-92974-7) Scholastic Inc.

Lad, a Dog: Lad & the Bad Puppy. Margo Lundell & Albert Pason Terhune. LC 96-27681. (Hello Reader! Ser.). (Illus.). (J). 1997. 3.99 (0-590-92981-X) Scholastic Inc.

Lad, a Dog: Lad Is Lost. Margo Lundell & Albert Pason Terhune. LC 96-27682. (Hello Reader! Ser.). (Illus.). 48p. (J). (gr. 2-4). 1997. 3.99 (0-590-92978-X) Scholastic Inc.

Lad, a Dog: Lad to the Rescue. Margo Lundell & Albert Pason Terhune. LC 96-20936. (Hello Reader! Ser.). (Illus.). (J). (gr. 4). 1997. pap. 3.99 (0-590-92973-9, Apple Classics) Scholastic Inc.

Lad from Brantford & Other Essays. David Adams Richards. 1994. pap. 9.00 (0-921411-25-1) Genl Dist Srvs.

Lad in a Kilt. Deborah H. Cummings. (Illus.). 32p. (Orig.). (J). (gr. k-2). 1994. pap. 7.95 (0-9641224-0-5) Tartan Pr.

Lad is Lost. Margo Lundell. (Lad a Dog Ser.). (J). 1998. 9.19 (0-606-13560-X, Pub. by Turtleback) Demco.

Lad of Sunnybank. large type ed. Albert Pason Terhune. LC 99-11711. 261p. 1999. 26.95 (0-7838-8552-0, G K Hall & Co) Mac Lib Ref.

Lad of Sunnybank. Albert Pason Terhune. 275p. 1992. reprint ed. lib. bdg. 24.95 (0-89966-749-X) Buccaneer Bks.

Lad Philisides: Being a Selection of Songs, Pastoral Eclogues & Elegies from the Countess of Pembroke's Arcadia. Philip Sidney. 1993. boxed set 130.00 (0-907664-13-X, Pub. by Old Stiles) St Mut.

Lad Philisides: Being a Selection of Songs, Pastoral Eclogues & Elegies from the Countess of Pembroke's Arcadia. limited ed. Philip Sidney. 1993. 500.00 (0-907664-14-8, Pub. by Old Stiles) St Mut.

Lad to the Rescue. Margo Lundell. (Hello, Reader! Ser.). (J). 1997. 9.19 (0-606-11545-5, Pub. by Turtleback) Demco.

Ladakh. P. N. Chopra. 109p. 1980. 14.95 (0-940500-14-0, Pub. by S Chand & Co) Asia Bk Corp.

Ladakh. P. N. Chopra. 120p. 1987. 35.00 (0-7855-1195-4) St Mut.

Ladakh: Crossroads of High Asia. 2nd ed. Janet Rizvi. (Illus.). 265p. 1998. reprint ed. pap. text 14.50 (0-19-564546-4) OUP.

Ladakh: Ecology & Environment. S. S. Sagwal. (Illus.). xvii, 136p. 1991. 13.00 (81-7024-433-1, Pub. by Ashish Pub Hse) Nataraj Bks.

Ladakh: Nubra the Forbidden Valley. H. P. Ahluwalia. 176p. (C). 1988. 495.00 (81-7002-023-9, Pub. by Himalayan Bks) St Mut.

***Ladakh - Culture, History & Development Between Himalaya & Karakoram: Proceedings of the 8th Colloquium of the International Association for Ladakh Studies Held at Moesgaard, Aarhus University, 5-8 June 1997.** Ed. by Martijn van Beek et al. (Recent Research on Ladakh Ser.: Vol. 8). (Illus.). 414p. 1999. 34.95 (87-7288-791-5, Pub. by Aarhus Univ Pr) David Brown.

Ladakh, the Wonder Land. Teg B. Kapur. 175p. (C). 1987. 32.50 (81-7099-011-4, Pub. by Mittal Pubs Dist) S Asia.

Ladakh Through the Ages. Shridhar Kaul. (C). 1992. 45.00 (81-85182-75-2, Pub. by Indus Pub) S Asia.

Ladakh Through the Ages: Towards a New Identity. Shridhar Kaul & H. N. Kaul. 368p. 1992. 35.95 (1-881338-12-6) Nataraj Bks.

Ladakhi Grammar. Samyukta Koshal. 1979. 18.50 (0-89684-052-2, Pub. by Motilal Bnarsidass) S Asia.

Ladakhi Grammar. Sanyukta Koshal. 1992. reprint ed. 35.00 (0-8288-8453-6, F66520) Fr & Eur.

La/Danseuse du Gai-Moulin see Maigret at the Gai-Moulin

L

L

Ladbak, Physical, Statistical & Historical, with Notices of the Surrounding Countries. Alexander Cunningham. LC 98-905008. xii, 485 p. 1998. write for info. (81-206-1296-5) Asian Educ Servs.

Ladd Family: The Descendants of Daniel of Haverhill, Mass., Joseph of Portsmouth, New Hampshire, John of Burlington, New Jersey, John of Charles City County, Virginia. W. Ladd. (Illus.). 425p. reprint ed. pap. 64.00 (0-8328-0744-3); reprint ed. lib. bdg. 72.00 (0-8328-6568-0) Higginson Bk Co.

Ladd 1988 Election Update. Ladd. (Illus.). pap. 0.00 (0-393-99991-2) Norton.

Ladd Report: Startling New Research Shows How an Explosion of Voluntary Groups, Activities & Charitable Donations are Transforming Our Towns & Cities. Everett C. Ladd. LC 98-31380. 256p. 1999. 26.00 (0-684-83735-8) Free Pr.

Ladder see Lestvitsa

Ladder see Ljestvitsa

Ladder. 1975. 40.95 (0-405-18698-3) Ayer.

***Ladder.** Edward Hays. (Illus.). 207p. 1999. pap. 13.95 (0-939516-46-2) Forest Peace.

Ladder, 9 vols. Daughters of Bilitis. LC 75-12330. (Homosexuality Ser.). 1975. reprint ed. 361.95 (0-405-07371-2) Ayer.

***Ladder & the Escalator: Why We Are What We Are.** Joseph Wechsler. LC 00-100377. 276p. 2000. 24.00 (1-892298-18-X) Abique.

Ladder Crystal Filters. John Pivnichny. (Illus.). 136p. 1999. mass mkt. 14.95 (1-891237-20-9, MFJ-3509) MFJ Ent.

***Ladder of Angels.** Brian Thompson. 272p. (Orig.). 1999. pap. 14.95 (1-871033-48-9, Pub. by Slow Dancer) Dufour.

Ladder of Divine Ascent. St. John Climacus. 273p. 1991. 28.00 (0-943405-03-3) Holy Trnsfgn.

Ladder of High Designs: Structure & Interpretation of the French Lyric Sequence. Ed. by Doranne Fenoaltea & David L. Rubin. 205p. 1991. text 32.50 (0-8139-1271-7) U Pr of Va.

Ladder of Life Series: Activity & Song Book. Ed. by Kay Cuzma. 160p. (J). 1998. pap. 9.99 (0-8280-1125-7) Review & Herald.

Ladder of Life Series Nos. 1 & 2: Faith & Virtue Storybooks & Cassette. Ed. by Kay Cuzma. (J). 1998. 14.99 incl. audio (0-8280-1302-0) Review & Herald.

Ladder of Life Series Nos. 3 & 4: Knowledge & Temperance Storybooks & Cassette. (J). 1998. 14.99 incl. audio (0-8280-1303-9) Review & Herald.

Ladder of Life Series Nos. 5 & 6: Patience & Godliness Storybooks & Cassette. Ed. by Kay Cuzma. (J). 1998. 14.99 incl. audio (0-8280-1304-7) Review & Herald.

Ladder of Life Series Nos. 7 & 8: Kindness & Love Storybooks & Cassette. Ed. by Kay Cuzma. (J). 1998. 14.99 incl. audio (0-8280-1305-5) Review & Herald.

Ladder of Lights. William G. Gray. LC 93-45639. (Illus.). 240p. 1981. pap. 14.95 (0-87728-536-5) Weiser.

Ladder of Memory. unabridged ed. David Koenig. LC 93-79443. 122p. 1993. pap. 12.95 (0-9637357-0-5) Harp Song Pr.

Ladder of the Beatitudes. Jim Forest. LC 98-47780. (Illus.). 176p. 1999. pap. 13.00 (1-57075-245-1) Orbis Bks.

Ladder of Years. Anne Tyler. 336p. 1996. pap. 12.00 (0-449-91057-1, Columbine) Fawcett.

Ladder of Years. Anne Tyler. 1997. mass mkt. 6.99 (0-8041-1347-5) Ivy Books.

Ladder of Years, Bk. 5. Anne Tyler. Date not set. pap. write for info. (0-449-91056-3) Fawcett.

Ladder Ranch Research Project: A Report of the First Season. Margaret Nelson et al. (Maxwell Museum Papers: No. 1). (Illus.). 105p. 1984. pap. 10.00 (0-912535-02-4) Max Mus.

***Ladder to the Clouds: Intrigue & Tradition in Chinese Rank.** Beverley Jackson. LC 99-42578. 320p. 2000. 40.00 (1-58008-127-4) Ten Speed Pr.

Ladder to the Moon. Date not set. write for info. (0-8464-4568-9) Beekman Pubs.

Ladder to the Moon. Douglas Smith. 54p. 1988. pap. 9.95 (0-919626-36-X, Pub. by Brick Bks) Genl Dist Srvs.

Ladder to the Moon: Women in Search of Spirituality. Allegra Taylor. (Illus.). 256p. 1999. pap. 29.95 (0-85207-313-5, Pub. by C W Daniel) Natl Bk Netwk.

Ladder to the Next Floor. Ed. by Rupert Loydell. 200p. pap. write for info. (3-7052-0246-4, Pub. by Poetry Salzburg) Intl Spec Bk.

Ladder to the Sky: How the Gift of Healing Came to the Ojibway Nation. Barbara J. Esbensen. (Illus.). (J). (ps-3). 1989. 15.95 (0-316-24952-1) Little.

Ladder to the Top! Sherman Owens. Date not set. 7.99 (1-57778-039-6, SO-001) Albury Pub.

Ladder Up: Life after Retirement. Evelyn A. Thomas. LC 79-92188. (Illus.). 92p. 1980. 5.95 (0-930626-05-2) Psych & Consul Assocs.

Ladder Up: Secret Steps to Jewish Happiness. Robert L. Kremnizer. LC 96-112733. 128p. 1994. 14.00 (1-881400-10-7) S I E.

***Ladders, 4 vols.** 32p. (J). (gr. k-3). 1999. 43.00 (0-7166-7715-6) World Bk.

Ladders. Albert Pope. LC 95-1240. (Architecture at Rice Ser.: Vol. 34). (Illus.). 208p. (Orig.). 1997. pap. 17.95 (1-885232-01-2) Princeton Arch.

Ladders Dream. Chalker. 1987. mass mkt. write for info. (0-8125-3310-0) Tor Bks.

***Ladders Series, 6 vols.** 192p. (J). (gr. k-3). 2000. write for info. (0-7166-7722-9) World Bk.

***Ladders Series, 8 vols.** 256p. (J). (gr. k-3). 2000. write for info. (0-7166-7724-5) World Bk.

Ladders to Fire. rev. ed. Anais Nin. LC 61-66834. (Cities of the Interior Ser.: Vol. 1). 192p. 1995. reprint ed. pap. 9.95 (0-8040-0181-2) Swallow.

Ladders to Literacy: A Kindergarten Activity Book. Rollanda E. O'Connor et al. 272p. (J). (gr. k). 1998. student ed., spiral bd. 44.95 (1-55766-318-1, 3181) P H Brookes.

Ladders to Literacy: A Preschool Activity Book. Angela Notari-Syverson et al. LC 97-37862. 376p. 1998. 49.95 (1-55766-317-3) P H Brookes.

Ladders We Climb to Who We Are. Margaret Cutchins. 116p. 1996. pap. 9.00 (0-9655119-0-1) Holly Creek Pr.

Laddie. Gene Stratton-Porter. reprint ed. lib. bdg. 26.95 (0-89190-933-8) Amereon Ltd.

Laddie: A True Blue Story. Gene Stratton-Porter. LC 87-4009. (Library of Indiana Classics). 416p. 1988. 24.95 (0-253-33113-7); pap. 12.95 (0-253-20458-5, MB-458) Ind U Pr.

Laddie of the Light. Jane Briggs-Bunting. LC 97-93003. (Illus.). 48p. (J). (gr. 3-6). 1997. teacher ed. 17.00 (0-9649083-1-X) Blck Riv Trad.

Laden Choirs: The Fiction of Patrick White. Peter Wolfe. LC 83-6831. 256p. reprint ed. pap. 79.40 (0-7837-5780-8, 204544600006) Bks Demand.

Ladidah. Hugh Walthall. LC 78-11954. 52p. 1978. 3.50 (0-87886-100-9, Greenfld Rev Pr) Greenfld Rev Lit.

Ladie Borlase's Receiptes Booke. Ed. by David E. Schoonover. LC 98-12061. (Iowa Szathmary Culinary Arts Ser.). (Illus.). 180p. 1998. text 32.95 (0-87745-636-4) U of Iowa Pr.

Ladies. Doris Grumbach. 224p. 1993. pap. 8.95 (0-393-31092-2) Norton.

Ladies' A Shining Constellation of Wit & Beauty. Lily A. Beck. LC 71-156612. (Essay Index Reprint Ser.). 1977. reprint ed. 23.95 (0-8369-2269-9) Ayer.

Ladies: Female Patronage of Restoration Drama. David Roberts. (Oxford English Monographs). 198p. 1989. text 65.00 (0-19-811743-4) OUP.

Ladies: Retold Tales of Goddesses & Heroines. Boris Vallejo. LC 99-62526. (Illus.). 192p. (Orig.). 1999. pap. 22.95 (1-56025-216-2, Thunders Mouth) Avalon NY.

Ladies Almanack. Djuna Barnes. (Cutting Edge: Lesbian Life & Literature Ser.). (Illus.). 128p. (C). 1992. pap. text 16.50 (0-8147-1180-4) NYU Pr.

Ladies Almanack. Djuna Barnes. LC 91-14515. (Illus.). 96p. 1992. reprint ed. pap. 9.95 (0-916583-88-0) Dalkey Arch.

Ladies & Gentle Men: Women Sharing with Women about the Art of Relating to Men. Photos by Frank Marshall. (Illus.). 134p. (Orig.). 1992. pap. 14.00 (0-9634341-0-1) Orphan Pr.

Ladies & Gentlemen. Irvin S. Cobb. LC 78-106266. (Short Story Index Reprint Ser.). 1977. 20.95 (0-8369-3303-6) Ayer.

Ladies & Gentlemen. Janet Guthrie. 1999. text 16.95 (0-670-80178-X) Viking Penguin.

Ladies & Gentlemen: A Parcel of Reconsiderations. James Branch Cabell. LC 68-14897. (Essay Index Reprint Ser.). 1977. 20.95 (0-8369-0269-6) Ayer.

Ladies & Gentlemen Always: The Illustrated Story of Holten High School. Richard P. Zollo & Virginia S. Zollo. LC 94-29213. (Illus.). 1994. write for info. (0-89865-927-2) Donning Co.

***Ladies & Gentlemen, Boys & Girls: Gender in Film at the End of the Twentieth Century.** Ed. by Murray Pomerance. (C). 2001. pap. text 18.95 (0-7914-4886-X) State U NY Pr.

***Ladies & Gentlemen, Boys & Girls: Gender in Film at the End of the Twentieth Century.** Ed. by Murray Pomerance. (C). 2001. text 57.50 (0-7914-4885-1) State U NY Pr.

Ladies & Gentlemen of the Jury. Tom Claffey. ix, 138p. (Orig.). 1997. pap. 14.95 (0-9656375-0-6) Coyote Junction.

Ladies & Gentlemen of the Jury: Greatest Closing Arguments in Modern Law. Michael S. Lief et al. LC 97-50267. 400p. 1998. 26.00 (0-684-83661-0) Scribner.

***Ladies & Gentlemen of the Jury: The Greatest Closing Arguments in Modern Law.** Michael S. Lief et al. LC 97-50267. 400p. 2000. per. 15.00 (0-684-85948-3) S&S Trade.

***Ladies & Not So Gentle Women: Elisabeth Marbury, Anne Morgan, Elsie de Wolfe, Anne Vanderbilt & Their Times.** Alfred A. Lewis. LC 99-55217. 688p. 2000. 39.95 (0-670-85810-2, Viking) Viking Penguin.

Ladies & the Cities: Transformation & Apocalyptic Identity in Joseph & Aseneth, 4 Ezra, the Apocalypse & the Shepherd of Hermas. Edith M. Humphrey. LC 96-132089. (Journal for the Study of the Pseudepigrapha Supplement Ser.: No. 17). 192p. 1995. 57.50 (1-85075-535-3, Pub. by Sheffield Acad) CUP Services.

Ladies at Lunch. Carol M. Woods. (Plays for Senior Actors Ser.: Vol. 1). 12p. (Orig.). 1996. pap. 2.50 (1-57514-271-6, 3089) Encore Perform Pub.

Ladies at Poker. Carol M. Woods. (Plays for Senior Actors Ser.). 1996. pap. 2.50 (1-57514-272-4, 3090) Encore Perform Pub.

Ladies at the Alamo. Paul Zindel. 1977. pap. 5.25 (0-8222-0623-4) Dramatists Play.

***Ladies Auxiliary.** Tova Mirvis. 336p. 2000. pap. 14.00 (0-345-44126-5, Ballantine) Ballantine Pub Grp.

Ladies' Auxiliary: A Novel. Tova Mirvis. LC 99-30720. 352p. 1999. text 23.95 (0-393-04814-4) Norton.

Ladies' Bane: A Miss Silver Mystery. Patricia Wentworth. 1976. reprint ed. lib. bdg. 21.95 (0-88411-737-5) Amereon Ltd.

Ladies Beware: This Could Happen to You. Thomas M. Haskell, Sr. (Illus.). 33p. (Orig.). 1995. pap. 6.95 (0-9645541-0-0) BatCat Pub.

Ladies' Choice, 4. Chris Lynch. (He-Man Women Haters Club Ser.). 1997. 9.60 (0-606-11447-5, Pub. by Turtleback) Demco.

Ladies' Choice: A Collection of Humor by Maine Women. Ed. by Mavis Patterson. LC 89-5533. (Illus.). 95p. (Orig.). 1982. pap. 4.95 (0-945980-15-9) Nrth Country Pr.

Ladies' Day see Aristophanes: Four Comedies

Ladies Day: A Woman's Guide to Pro Baseball. Catherine Rondina & Joseph Romain. (Illus.). 160p. (Orig.). 1997. pap. 12.95 (1-895629-80-2) Warwick Publ.

Ladies Elect: Women in English Local Government, 1865-1914. Patricia Hollis. (Illus.). 560p. 1987. text 85.00 (0-19-822699-3) OUP.

Ladies Elect: Women in English Local Government, 1865-1914. Patricia Hollis. (Illus.). 572p. 1989. pap. 32.00 (0-19-822157-6) OUP.

Ladies Errant: Wayward Women & Social Order in Early Modern Italy. Deanna Shemek. LC 97-32552. 1998. pap. 17.95 (0-8223-2167-X) Duke.

Ladies Errant: Wayward Women & Social Order in Early Modern Italy. Deanna Shemek. LC 97-32552. (Illus.). 256p. 1998. 49.95 (0-8223-2155-6) Duke.

Ladies Fair & Frail. Horace Bleackley. (Biographical Reference Works). xiv, 328p. 1985. reprint ed. 49.00 (0-932051-26-X) Rprt Serv.

Ladies' Farm. Viqui Litman. LC 99-13508. 1999. 23.00 (0-609-60380-9) Crown Pub Group.

Ladies First: Fascinating Facts about Our Nation's First Ladies. LC 95-90986. 115p. 1996. pap. 9.95 (0-9673623-2-6, Wrench Enter) Pinnacle Pubng.

Ladies First: Revelations from a Strong Woman. Queen Latifah & Karen Hunter. LC 98-41533. (Illus.). 173p. 1999. 22.00 (0-688-15623-1, Wm Morrow) Morrow Avon.

***Ladies First: Revelations of a Strong Woman.** Queen Latifah. 208p. 2000. pap. 12.00 (0-688-17583-X) Morrow Avon.

Ladies First: Rhymes & Times of the Presidents' Wives & Other Female Fantasies. Mollee Kruger. LC 94-75756. (Illus.). 112p. (Orig.). 1995. pap. 8.95 (0-913184-06-3) Maryben Bks.

Ladies First: Women in Music Videos. Robin Roberts. LC 96-14969. (Studies in Popular Culture). 184p. 1996. text 45.00 incl. Beta (0-87805-933-4); pap. text 22.50 incl. Beta (0-87805-934-2) U Pr of Miss.

Ladies Flower Garden. Wendy Hobson. 1994. 12.98 (0-7858-0084-0) Bk Sales Inc.

Ladies from St. Petersburg: Three Novellas. Nina Berberova. Tr. by Marian Schwartz. LC 98-18968. (RUS.). 192p. 1998. 19.95 (0-8112-1377-3, Pub. by New Directions) Norton.

***Ladies from St. Petersburg: Three Novellas.** Nina Berberova. Tr. by Marian Schwartz from RUS. 2000. pap. 12.95 (0-8112-1436-2, Pub. by New Directions) Norton.

Ladies' Gallery. Irene Vilar. 1998. pap. 13.00 (0-679-74546-7) Vin Bks.

Ladies' Hand Book of Fancy & Ornamental Work: Civil War Era. Florence Hartley. Ed. by R. L. Shep. LC 91-53165. (Illus.). 256p. 1991. pap. 21.95 (0-914046-13-6) R L Shep.

Ladies in Furs, 1940-1990. Anna Municchi. (Twentieth Century-Histories of Fashion Ser.). (Illus.). 143p. 1996. 29.95 (0-89676-207-6, Costume & Fashion Pr) QSMG Ltd.

Ladies in Furs, 1900-1940. Anna Municchi. (Twentieth Century-Histories of Fashion Ser.). (Illus.). 159p. 1996. 29.95 (0-89676-206-8, Costume & Fashion Pr) QSMG Ltd.

Ladies in Retirement. Edward Percy & Reginald Denham. 1943. pap. 5.25 (0-8222-0624-2) Dramatists Play.

Ladies in the Laboratory? American & British Women in Science, 1800-1900: A Survey of Their Contributions to Research. Mary R. Creese. LC 97-1125. (Illus.). 800p. 1998. 98.50 (0-8108-3287-9) Scarecrow.

Ladies Laughing: Wit As Control in Contemporary American Women Writers. Barbara Levy. (Studies in Humor & Gender: Vol. 3). 200p. 1997. text 26.00 (90-5699-542-1); pap. text 17.00 (90-5699-543-X) Gordon & Breach.

Ladies Legal Companion. Karen L. MacNutt. (Illus.). 87p. (Orig.). 1993. pap. 8.95 (0-9622534-1-3) MacNutt Art Trust.

Ladies' Lib: How Rockland Women Got the Vote. Isabelle K. Savelle. LC 79-89375. (Orig.). 1979. pap. 5.00 (0-911183-03-5) Rockland County Hist.

Ladies Lunch. Patricia O'Brien. 1994. 22.00 (0-671-78906-6) S&S Trade.

Ladies Lunch. Patricia O'Brien. 1996. mass mkt. 5.99 (0-312-95789-0, Pub. by Tor Bks) St Martin.

Ladies' Man. Lorraine Heath. 272p. (Orig.). 1995. mass mkt. 4.99 (0-515-11636-X, Jove) Berkley Pub.

Ladies' Man. Elinor Lipman. LC 98-56450. 240p. 1999. 23.95 (0-679-45694-5) Random House.

***Ladies Man.** Elinor Lipman. (Contemporaries Ser.). 272p. 2000. 12.00 (0-375-70731-X) Vin Bks.

Ladies' Man. Richard Price. LC 99-15174. 1999. pap. 12.00 (0-395-97772-X) HM.

Ladies' Man. Richard Price. 272p. 1993. pap. 9.00 (0-380-77475-5, Avon Bks) Morrow Avon.

***Ladies' Man.** large type ed. Elinor Lipman. LC 99-59452. 2000. 25.95 (1-56895-837-4) Wheeler Pub.

Ladies' Night. Elisabeth Bowers. LC 88-19897. (International Women's Crime Ser.). 238p. (Orig.). 1988. pap. 8.95 (0-931188-65-2) Seal Pr WA.

***Ladies' Night at Finbar's Hotel.** Maeve Binchy et al. Ed. by Dermot Bolger. LC 99-56093. 288p. 2000. pap. 14.00 (0-15-600866-1) Harcourt.

***Ladies' Night at Finbars Hotel.** Dermot Bolger. 2000. write for info. (0-15-100608-3) Harcourt.

***Ladies of Covington Send Their Love.** Joan Avna Medlicott. LC 99-89922. 352p. 2000. text 24.95 (0-312-25329-X) St Martin.

Ladies of Cremorne. mass mkt. 6.95 (0-7472-5128-2) Headline Bk Pub.

Ladies of Genesis. Barbara D. Holender. (Illus.). 54p. (Orig.). 1991. pap. 8.00 (1-879742-00-4) Jewish Wom Rsce.

Ladies of Hanover Square. large type ed. Rona Randall. (Charnwood Large Print Ser.). 1994. 27.99 (0-7089-8795-8) Ulverscroft.

Ladies of Labor, Girls of Adventure: Working Women, Popular Culture, & Labor Politics at the Turn of the Century. Nan Enstad. LC 98-8572. (Popular Cultures, Everyday Lives Ser.). 6p. 1999. 49.50 (0-231-11102-9); pap. 17.50 (0-231-11103-7) Col U Pr.

Ladies of Lambton Green. large type ed. Liza Shepherd. (Linford Mystery Library). 316p. 1988. pap. 16.99 (0-7089-6566-0, Linford) Ulverscroft.

Ladies of Literature. Laura L. Hinkley. LC 74-128260. (Essay Index Reprint Ser.). 1977. 23.95 (0-8369-1955-6) Ayer.

Ladies of Mandrigyn. Barbara Hambly. 1997. pap. 12.00 (0-345-42059-4) Ballantine Pub Grp.

Ladies of Missalonghi. Colleen McCullough. 192p. 1988. mass mkt. 5.99 (0-380-70458-7, Avon Bks) Morrow Avon.

Ladies of Readingtown & Beyond. Barbara Godard. LC 98-65121. vii, 63 p. 1998. write for info. (1-883294-65-7) Masthof Pr.

Ladies of Seneca Falls: The Birth of the Woman's Rights Movement. Miriam Gurko. LC 76-9144. (Studies in the Life of Women). (Illus.). 1987. pap. 11.96 (0-8052-0545-4) Schocken.

Ladies of Shalott: A Victorian Masterpiece in Its Contexts. Brown University, Department of Art Staff. LC 84-73113. (Illus.). 184p. (Orig.). 1985. pap. text 20.00 (0-933519-02-8) D W Bell Gallery.

Ladies of the Camellias. Lillian Garrett-Groag. 1996. pap. 5.25 (0-8222-1501-2) Dramatists Play.

Ladies of the Goldfield Stock Exchange. Sybil Downing. LC 97-730. 352p. 1997. text 23.95 (0-312-86331-4) St Martin.

Ladies of the Goldfield Stock Exchange. Sybil Downing. 1998. mass mkt. 5.99 (0-8125-3927-3, Pub. by Tor Bks) St Martin.

Ladies of the Lake: Tales of Transportation, Tragedy, & Triumph on Lake Chelan. Tom R. Hackenmiller. LC 98-96026. (Illus.). 176p. 1998. pap. 17.95 (0-9663560-0-4) Point Publ.

Ladies of the Lakes. James Clary. (Illus.). 191p. 1994. pap. 24.95 (1-882376-07-2) Thunder Bay Pr.

***Ladies of the Lamplight.** 2nd ed. Kay R Blair. LC 00-102174. (Illus.). 112p. 2000. pap. 11.95 (1-890437-41-7) Western Reflections.

Ladies of the Manor: Wives & Daughters in Country-House Society 1830-1918. Pamela Horn. (Illus.). 224p. 1997. pap. 19.95 (0-7509-1431-9, Pub. by Sutton Pub Ltd) Intl Pubs Mktg.

Ladies of the Night. John Westermann. 288p. 1998. 23.00 (0-671-87124-2, Pocket Books) PB.

Ladies of the Night: Short Stories by Althea Trotman. Althea Trotman. 174p. 1994. per. write for info. (0-920813-57-7) Sister Vis Pr.

Ladies of the Press: The Story of Women in Journalism by an Insider. Isabel Ross. LC 74-3972. (Women in America Ser.). (Illus.). 642p. 1974. reprint ed. 46.95 (0-405-06120-X) Ayer.

Ladies of the Rachmaninoff Eyes. Henry Van Dyke. 214p. 1975. reprint ed. 15.00 (0-911860-49-5) Chatham Bkseller.

Ladies of the Rope: Gurdjieff's Special Left Bank Women's Group. William Patrick Patterson. Ed. by Barbara A. Patterson. (Illus.). 302p. 1998. pap. 16.95 (1-879514-41-9) Arete Commns.

Ladies of the Tower. Ruth Perry & Tim Kelly. 1971. 3.50 (0-87129-586-5, L11) Dramatic Pub.

Ladies of the White House. Laura C. Langford. LC 70-171655. (Illus.). reprint ed. 76.50 (0-404-04608-8) AMS Pr.

Ladies of Vallbona. Archer M. Huntington. 1934. 5.00 (0-87535-034-8) Hispanic Soc.

Ladies of Zamora. Peter Linehan. LC 96-41252. (Illus.). 208p. 1997. 35.00 (0-271-01682-5) Pa St U Pr.

Ladies of Zamora. Peter Linehan. (Illus.). 208p. 1999. pap. 18.95 (0-271-01835-6) Pa St U Pr.

Ladies on the Field: Two Civil War Nurses from Maine on the Battlefields of Virginia. Libby MacCashill & David Novak. (Illus.). 100p. 1996. pap. 10.00 (0-9651858-1-8) Signal Tree.

***Ladies on the Lost: Women, Car Sales, & the Pursuit of the American Dream.** Helene M. Lawson. LC 99-57385. 175p. 2000. text 55.00 (0-8476-9862-9) Rowman.

***Ladies on the Lost: Women, Car Sales, & the Pursuit of the American Dream.** Helene M. Lawson. LC 99-57385. 175p. 2000. pap. 15.95 (0-8476-9863-7) Rowman.

Ladies on Vacation. Carol M. Woods. (Plays for Senior Actors Ser.). 1998. pap. 2.50 (1-57514-273-2, 3091) Encore Perform Pub.

Ladies' Own Erotica. Kensington Ladies' Erotica Society Staff. LC 96-76474. (Illus.). 480p. 1996. reprint ed. 8.98 (1-56731-139-3, MJF Bks) Fine Comms.

Ladies' Own Erotica Book. Kensington Ladies' Erotica Society Staff. (Illus.). 235p. 1984. pap. 11.95 (0-89815-127-9) Ten Speed Pr.

Ladies' Paradise. Emile Zola. Tr. & Tr. by Brian Nelson. (Oxford World's Classics Ser.).Tr. of Au Bonheur des Dames. (Illus.). 470p. 1999. pap. 11.95 (0-19-283602-1) OUP.

Ladies' Paradise. Emile Zola. Tr. by Chris Nelson.Tr. of Au Bonheur des Dames. 1992. pap. 15.95 (0-520-07867-5, Pub. by U CA Pr) Cal Prin Full Svc.

An Asterisk (*) at the beginning of an entry indicates that the title is appearing for the first time.

Ladies' Paradise. Emile Zola. Tr. by Brian Nelson from FRE. LC 91-19594.Tr. of Au Bonheur des Dames. (Illus.). 383p. 1992. 55.00 (*0-520-07349-5*, Pub. by U CA Pr) Cal Prin Full Svc.

Ladies, Please Don't Smash These Windows: Feminist Consciousness & Women's Prose, 1918-38. Maroula Joannou. LC 94-34792. 236p. 1995. 49.50 (*0-85496-909-8*); pap. 19.50 (*1-85973-022-1*) Berg Pubs.

Ladies Rejoice. Tom Fettke. 116p. 1985. spiral bd. 7.99 (*0-8341-9165-2*, MB-535) Lillenas.

***Ladies Room Reader: The Ultimate Women's Trivia Book.** Alicia Alvrez. LC 00-9566. 2000. write for info. (*1-57324-557-7*) Conari Press.

Ladies' Self Instructor in Millinery & Mantua Making, Embroidery & Applique (1853) rev. ed. Ed. by R. L. Shep. LC 88-90812. (Illus.). 252p. 1988. pap. 15.95 (*0-914046-08-X*) R L Shep.

Ladies, Start Your Engines! Secrets for Restoring Romance in Your Relationship. Jan B. King. Ed. by Cliff Carle. 168p. 1996. pap. 7.99 (*1-57644-016-8*) CCC Pubns.

Ladies Trial. John Ford. LC 75-25789. (English Experience Ser.: No. 285). 80p. 1971. reprint ed. 25.00 (*90-221-0285-8*) Walter J Johnson.

Ladies Were Not Expected: Abigail Scott Duniway & Women's Rights. Dorothy N. Morrison. (Illus.). 148p. (J). (gr. 4 up). 1996. reprint ed. pap. 8.95 (*0-87595-168-6*) Oregon Hist.

Ladies Who Kill. Tom Kunci. 1989. mass mkt. 3.95 (*1-55817-249-1*, Pinncle Kensgtn) Kensgtn Pub Corp.

Ladies Who Knit for a Living Stories. Anthony E. Stockanes. LC 81-7421. (Illinois Short Fiction Ser.). 140p. 1981. 9.95 (*0-252-00927-4*) U of Ill Pr.

***Ladies Who Sing with the Band.** Betty B. Lowe. LC 99-49460. (Studies in Jazz: Vol. 36). 160p. 2000. 35.00 (*0-8108-3714-5*) Scarecrow.

Ladies, Women, & Wenches: Choice & Constraint in Antebellum Charleston & Boston. Jane H. Pease & William H. Pease. LC 89-21450. (Gender & American Culture Ser.). xvi, 218p. (C). 1990. pap. 17.95 (*0-8078-4289-3*) U of NC Pr.

Ladies' Work Table: Domestic Needlework in 19th-Century America. Margaret Vincent. LC 88-70509. (Illus.). 160p. (Orig.). 1988. pap. 19.95 (*1-882011-41-4*) Allentown.

Ladino Bible of Ferrara (1553) Tr. & Intro. by Moshe Lazar. LC 92-70756. (Sephardic Classical Library). (LAD.). 766p. 1992. 100.00 (*0-911437-56-8*) Labyrinthos.

***Ladino-English, English-Ladino Concise Dictionary.** Elli Kohen. (ENG & LAD.). 602p. 1999. pap. 19.95 (*0-7818-0658-5*) Hippocrene Bks.

Ladino Five Scrolls: Abraham Asa's Versions of the Hebrew & Aramaic Texts. Ed. by Moshe Lazar & Robert Dilligan. LC 92-73523. (Sephardic Classical Library). (HEB & LAD.). 304p. 1992. text 65.00 (*0-911437-58-4*) Labyrinthos.

Ladino (Judeo-Spanish) Collection of the Lubavitcher Rebbes: A Descriptive Bibliography. Aviva Ben-Ur & Agudas Chassidsi Chabad Staff. LC 96-36991. 168p. 1997. 49.50 (*0-7618-0601-6*) U Pr of Amer.

Ladino Mahzor of Ferrara (1553) Ed. by Moshe Lazar & Robert Dilligan. LC 93-77908. (Sephardic Classical Library). (HEB & LAD.). 320p. 1993. text 55.00 (*0-911437-60-6*) Labyrinthos.

Ladino Pentateuch: (Constantinople, 1547) Tr. & Intro. by Moshe Lazar. LC 88-82628. (Sephardic Classical Library). (HEB & LAD., Illus.). 560p. 1988. lib. bdg. 90.00 (*0-911437-46-0*) Labyrinthos.

***Ladle, Leaf & Loaf: Soup, Salad & Bread for Every Season.** Lisa Cowden. (Illus.). 256p. 2000. pap. 16.00 (*0-395-96715-5*) HM.

Ladle Metallurgy. Julian Szekely et al. (Materials Research & Engineering Ser.). (Illus.). 190p. 1989. 124.95 (*0-387-96798-2*) Spr-Verlag.

Ladle Metallurgy Principles & Practices. R. J. Fruehan. LC 85-80089. 155p. 1985. reprint ed. pap. 48.10 (*0-608-01269-6*, 206201900001) Bks Demand.

Ladle Rat Rotten Hut. 6th ed. Illus. by Jon Vlakos. 12p. (J). 1988. reprint ed. pap. 2.00 (*0-934714-05-3*) Swamp Pr.

Ladles & Jellyspoons: Presentations Haiku, Senryu, Tanka. Francine Porad. (Illus.). 48p. (Orig.). 1995. pap. 12.20 (*1-887381-01-5*) Vandina Pr.

Ladner on Conveyancing in Pennsylvania, 2 vols. 4th rev. ed. Harry S. Cherken. LC 79-53058. 1999. ring bd. 195.00 (*1-887024-34-4*) Bisel Co.

Lado. 3rd ed. Robert Lado. (Lado English Ser.: Vol. 2). 192p. (C). 1989. pap. 15.73 (*0-13-522269-9*) P-H.

Lado, Bk. 1. 3rd ed. Robert Lado. 183p. (C). 1989. pap. 15.73 (*0-13-522244-3*) P-H.

Lado, Bk. 4. 3rd ed. Robert Lado. 192p. (C). 1989. pap. 15.73 (*0-13-522301-6*) P-H.

Lado, Bk. 5. 3rd ed. Lucia Lado. (Lado English Ser.: Vol. 5). 1990. pap. text, wbk. ed. 10.40 (*0-13-522483-7*) P-H.

Lado, Bk. 5. 3rd ed. Robert Lado. (English Ser.). 192p. (C). 1990. pap. text 15.73 (*0-13-522327-X*) P-H.

Lado, Bk. 6. 3rd ed. Robert Lado. 192p. (C). 1990. pap. 15.73 (*0-13-522343-1*) P-H.

Lado a Lado: Gramatica Inglesa y Espanola. Edith R. Farrell & C. Frederick Farrell, Jr.Tr. of Side by Side English & Spanish Grammar. 128p. 1998. pap. 8.95 (*0-8442-0799-3*) NTC Contemp Pub Co.

***Lado Bello del Mal (The Beautiful Side of Evil)** Johanna Michaelsen. (SPA & ENG.). 215p. 1999. 9.99 (*0-88113-535-6*) Caribe Betania.

Lado Book 3. 3rd ed. Lado. 192p. 1989. pap. 15.73 (*0-13-522285-0*) P-H.

Lado English Series. 3rd ed. Robert Lado. (C). 1989. pap. text, wbk. ed. 10.40 (*0-13-522418-7*) P-H.

Lado English Series. 3rd ed. Robert Lado. (C). 1990. pap. text, teacher ed. 24.40 (*0-13-522426-8*) P-H.

Lado English Series, Bk. 2. 2nd ed. Robert Lado. 1987. teacher ed. 11.00 (*0-13-522137-4*, 18758); student ed. 4.50 (*0-13-522079-3*, 18752) Prentice ESL.

Lado English Series, Bk. 4. 2nd ed. Robert Lado. 1987. teacher ed. 11.00 (*0-13-522152-8*, 18754) Prentice ESL.

Lado English Series, Bk. 5. 2nd ed. Robert Lado. (Illus.). 198p. (gr. 7-12). 1987. teacher ed. 11.00 (*0-13-522160-9*, 18761) Prentice ESL.

Lado English Series, Bk. 6. 2nd ed. Robert Lado. (Illus.). 1987. teacher ed. 11.00 (*0-13-522178-1*, 18762) Prentice ESL.

Lado Humano de los Seres Humanos see Human Side of Human Beings: Spanish Translation

Lado Picture Dictionary. rev. ed. Robert Lado. LC 92-36959. (Illus.). 128p. (C). 1993. pap. text 13.87 (*0-13-061680-X*) P-H.

Ladon. Bernard Evslin. (Monsters of Mythology Ser.). (Illus.). 104p. 1990. lib. bdg. 19.95 (*1-55546-254-5*) Chelsea Hse.

Ladonna Harris. Michael Schwartz. LC 96-44089. (Contemporary Native Americans Ser.). (Illus.). 48p. (J). 1997. lib. bdg. 24.26 (*0-8172-3995-2*) Raintree Steck-V.

***LaDonna Harris: A Comanche Life.** LaDonna Harris. Ed. by H. Henrietta Stockel. LC 99-38238. (American Indian Lives Ser.). (Illus.). 184p. 2000. 25.00 (*0-8032-2396-X*) U of Nebr Pr.

Ladron de Cuerpos. Anne Rice. 1996. pap. text 13.95 (*950-08-1433-1*, Pub. by Atlantida) Libros Fronteras.

Ladron de La Mente, Vol. 2. Elias M. Miguel. 128p. (C). 1995. pap. 20.00 (*0-07-044312-2*) McGraw.

Ladron (The Thief) Jan Needle. Tr. by Juan J. Ultrilla. (SPA., Illus.). 116p. (YA). 1991. pap. 6.99 (*968-16-3680-5*, Pub. by Fondo) Continental Bk.

Lad's Bag: Level One. Lavaun Linde & Mary Quishenberry. (Bible Stories for Early Readers Ser.: Bk. 4). (Illus.). 32p. (J). (gr. 1). 1986. pap. text 4.99 (*0-945107-03-X*) Bradshaw Pubs.

Lads in Action. Moore. 192p. 1994. pap. 24.95 (*1-85742-204-X*) Ashgate Pub Co.

Lads in Action: Ethnicity, Identity & Social Process Amongst Australian Skinheads. David Moore. (Popular Cultural Studies). 192p. 1994. 59.95 (*1-85742-203-1*, Pub. by Arena) Ashgate Pub Co.

Lad's Love. Sylvia Kantaris. 64p. 1993. pap. 13.95 (*1-85224-194-2*, Pub. by Bloodaxe Bks) Dufour.

L'Adversus Helvidium di san Girolamo nel Contesto Della Letteratura Ascetico-Marina del Secolo IV. Giancarlo Rocca. (Europaische Hochschulschriften Ser.: Riehe 23, Bd. 646). 111p. 1998. 26.95 (*3-906760-89-8*) P Lang.

Lady. Anne McCaffrey. 1988. mass mkt. 5.99 (*0-345-35674-8*, Del Rey) Ballantine Pub Grp.

Lady. Anne McCaffrey. 461p. 1987. 25.00 (*0-89366-214-3*) Ultramarine Pub.

Lady. Conrad Richter. 20.95 (*0-89190-332-1*) Amereon Ltd.

Lady: Boeing B-17 Flying Fortress. Photos by Dan Patterson. (Living History Ser.: No. 1). (Illus.). 67p. 1993. pap. 15.95 (*0-943231-58-2*) Howell Pr VA.

Lady: Boeing B17 Flying Fortress. Paul Perkins. (Living History Ser.). 70p. 1997. pap. 52.00 (*1-86227-077-5*, Pub. by Spellmnt Pubs) St Mut.

Lady: Burma's Daw Aung San Suu Syi. Barbara Victor. LC 97-47042. (Illus.). 296p. 1998. 26.95 (*0-571-19944-5*) Faber & Faber.

Lady: Lisa Lyon. Robert Mapplethorpe. 1991. pap. 24.95 (*0-312-05290-1*) St Martin.

Lady: Lisa Lyon: Miniature Edition. Robert Mapplethorpe. (Illus.). 128p. 1996. 10.95 (*0-8212-2277-5*, Pub. by Bulfinch Pr) Little.

Lady: Studies of Certain Significant Phases of Her History. Emily J. Putnam. LC 70-108990. 1993. pap. 1.95 (*0-226-68564-0*, P362) U Ch Pr.

Lady: The Story of Claudia Alta (Lady Bird) Johnson. Jean Flynn. 144p. (J). (gr. 7-8). 1992. 14.95 (*0-89015-821-5*) Sunbelt Media.

Lady A: A Teenage DJ. Millie Murray. (Livewire Ser.). (YA). (gr. 6-9). pap. 5.95 (*0-7043-4920-5*, Pub. by Womens Press) Trafalgar.

Lady Alice. Jedediah V. Huntington. (Notable American Authors Ser.). 1992. reprint ed. lib. bdg. 75.00 (*0-7812-3287-2*) Rprt Serv.

Lady Ambassador. Vivian Donald. 1978. mass mkt. 1.75 (*0-451-08268-0*, E8268, Sig) NAL.

Lady & Alex Payton. Nikki Benjamin. (Intimate Moments Ser.). 1996. per. 3.99 (*0-373-07729-7*, 1-07729-6) Silhouette.

Lady & Her Doctor. Evelyn Piper. 320p. 1986. reprint ed. pap. 6.00 (*0-89733-194-X*) Academy Chi Pubs.

Lady & Sons Savannah Country Cookbook. Paula H. Deen. LC 97-41561. 208p. 1998. pap. 14.95 (*0-375-75111-4*) Random.

***Lady & Sons, Too! A Whole New Batch of Recipes from Savannah.** Paula H. Deen. LC 00-41744. 2000. write for info. (*0-375-75605-1*) Random.

Lady & the Clarinet. Michael Cristofer. 102p. 1985. pap. 5.25 (*0-8222-0627-7*) Dramatists Play.

Lady & the Commissioner of Airports: Playscript. Margaret H. Rector. LC 93-28279. 1993. pap. 5.00 (*0-88734-325-2*) Players Pr.

Lady & the Cowboy. Christine A. Wenger. LC 96-36727. (Janet Dailey's Love Scenes Ser.). 1997. pap. 3.50 (*1-56853-029-3*, Signal Hill) New Readers.

Lady & the Falconer. Laura O'Donnell. 384p. 1998. pap. 4.99 (*0-8217-5953-1*) Kensgtn Pub Corp.

Lady & the Fly. Lorkral. (I Love to Read Collection). (Illus.). 46p. (J). (ps-3). 1992. lib. bdg. 12.79 (*0-89565-812-7*) Childs World.

Lady & the Highwayman. large type ed. V. M. Rowlands. 320p. 1994. 27.99 (*0-7089-3139-1*) Ulverscroft.

Lady & the Knight. Lois Greiman. (Highland Brides Ser.). 384p. 1997. mass mkt. 5.99 (*0-380-79433-0*, Avon Bks) Morrow Avon.

Lady & the Laird. Maura Seger. (Historical Ser.: No. 727). 1992. mass mkt. 3.99 (*0-373-28727-5*, 1-28727-5) Harlequin Bks.

Lady & the Lumberjack. Jackie Merritt. (Desire Ser.: No. 683). 1991. per. 2.79 (*0-373-05683-4*) Harlequin Bks.

Lady & the Monk: Four Seasons in Kyoto. Pico Iyer. LC 92-50071. (Vintage Departures Ser.). 1992. pap. 13.00 (*0-679-73834-7*) Vin Bks.

Lady & the Mortician: Playscript. Margaret H. Rector. LC 93-28300. 1993. pap. 5.00 (*0-88734-326-0*) Players Pr.

Lady & the Outlaw. Katherine Compton. 352p. (Orig.). 1994. mass mkt. 4.50 (*0-380-77454-2*, Avon Bks) Morrow Avon.

Lady & the Outlaw. Deloras Scott. (Historical Ser.: Bk. 494). 2000. mass mkt. 4.99 (*0-373-29094-2*, 1-29094-9) Harlequin Bks.

Lady & the Sheriff. Sharon De Vita. (Silver Creek County Ser.). 1997. per. 3.99 (*0-373-24103-8*, 1-24103-3) Silhouette.

Lady & the Spider. Faith McNulty. LC 85-5427. (Illus.). 48p. (J). (gr. 1-4). 1986. 15.00 (*0-06-024191-8*) HarpC Child Bks.

Lady & the Spider. Faith McNulty. LC 85-5427. (Trophy Picture Bk.). (Illus.). 48p. (J). (ps-3). 1987. pap. 5.95 (*0-06-443152-5*, HarpTrophy) HarpC Child Bks.

Lady & the Spider. Faith McNulty. (J). 1987. 11.15 (*0-606-03598-2*, Pub. by Turtleback) Demco.

Lady & the Texan. Bobbi Smith. 400p. (Orig.). 1997. mass mkt. 5.99 (*0-8439-4319-X*, Leisure Bks) Dorchester Pub Co.

Lady & the Tomcat. Bethany Campbell. (Romance Ser.). 1993. per. 2.99 (*0-373-03277-3*, 1-03277-0) Harlequin Bks.

Lady & the Tramp. (Classics Ser.). (Illus.). 96p. (J). (ps-4). 1994. 7.98 (*1-57082-138-0*, Pub. by Mouse Works) Time Warner.

Lady & the Tramp. (Disney Read-Alongs Ser.). (J). 7.99 incl. audio (*1-55723-016-1*) W Disney Records.

Lady & the Tramp. Mouse Works Staff. (J). 1997. 7.98 (*1-57082-728-1*, Pub. by Mouse Works) Time Warner.

Lady & the Tramp. Mouseworks Staff. (Spanish Classics Ser.). (Illus.). (J). 1997. 7.98 (*1-57082-871-7*, Pub. by Mouse Works) Little.

Lady & the Tramp: A Trusty Old Pal. Disney Enterprises, Inc. Staff. (Disney's "Storytime Treasures" Library: Vol. 15). (Illus.). 44p. (J). (gr. 1-6). 1997. 3.49 (*1-57973-011-6*) Advance Pubs.

Lady & the Tramp: My Coloring Book. Golden Books Staff. (J). 1997. pap. text 1.09 (*0-307-08714-X*, 08714, Goldn Books) Gldn Bks Pub Co.

Lady & the Tramp: We're All Different. Mouseworks Staff. (Illus.). (J). 1999. 2.99 (*0-7364-0044-3*, Pub. by Mouse Works) Little.

Lady & the Tramp Easy Reader. Mouseworks Staff. 48p. (J). 1998. 3.95 (*0-7364-0039-7*, Pub. by Mouse Works) Time Warner.

Lady & the Unicorn. Gottfried Buttner. Tr. by Roland Everett. (Illus.). 128p. 1995. 34.95 (*1-869890-52-3*, Pub. by Hawthorn Press) Anthroposophic.

Lady & the Unicorn. Alain Erlande-Brandenburg. LC 94-60291. (Illus.). 228p. 1994. 60.00 (*0-500-23692-5*, Pub. by Thames Hudson) Norton.

Lady & the Unicorn. Sutherland Lyall. (Temporis Ser.). (Illus.). 220p. 2000. 55.00 (*1-85995-519-3*) Parkstone Pr.

Lady & the Unicorn. Kathleen M. Price. LC 94-75989. (Illus.). 32p. 1994. 14.95 (*1-880851-16-4*) Greene Bark Pr.

***Lady & the Vampire.** Colin Murray. (Illus.). 48p. 1999. pap. 10.95 (*1-56163-237-6*, Eurotica) NBM.

Lady & the Virgin: Image, Attitude & Experience in Twelfth-Century France. Penny S. Gold. LC 84-23701. (Women in Culture & Society Ser.). (Illus.). 216p. 1987. pap. text 17.00 (*0-226-30088-9*) U Ch Pr.

Lady & the Wolf. Julie Beard. 1998. mass mkt. 5.99 (*0-425-16425-X*) Berkley Pub.

Lady Anna. Anthony Trollope. Ed. & Intro. by Stephen Orgel. (Oxford World's Classics Ser.). 560p. 1999. pap. 10.95 (*0-19-283718-4*) OUP.

Lady Anna, 2 vols. Anthony Trollope. LC 80-1893. (Selected Works of Anthony Trollope). 1982. reprint ed. lib. bdg. 77.95 (*0-405-14160-2*) Ayer.

Lady Anna (trollope 1990) Skilton. 1990. 34.00 (*1-870587-10-3*) Ashgate Pub Co.

Lady Anne. 1987. mass mkt. 3.95 (*0-446-73490-X*, Pub. by Warner Bks) Little.

Lady Anne Clifford. Richard T. Spence. LC 97-156883. (Illus.). 320p. 1997. 36.00 (*0-7509-1311-8*, Pub. by Sutton Pub Ltd) Intl Pubs Mktg.

Lady Anne's Deception. large type ed. Marion Chesney. (Magna Romance Ser.). 220p. 1992. 27.99 (*0-7505-0153-7*) Ulverscroft.

Lady Architects: Howe, Manning & Almy. Doris Cole & Karen C. Taylor. LC 89-63768. (Illus.). 160p. (Orig.). 1990. pap. text 11.50 (*1-877675-01-6*) Midmarch Arts.

Lady As Saint: A Collection of French Hagiographic Romances of the Thirteenth Century. Ed. by Brigitte Cazelles. LC 91-21158. (Middle Ages Ser.). 346p. 1991. pap. 107.30 (*0-608-04819-4*, 206547600004) Bks Demand.

Lady at Home. Timothy S. Arthur. (Works of Timothy Shay Arthur). 1989. reprint ed. lib. bdg. 79.00 (*0-7812-1798-9*) Rprt Serv.

Lady at Liberty. Hudson Talbott. 32p. (Orig.). (J). 1991. pap. 9.95 (*0-380-76427-X*, Avon Bks) Morrow Avon.

Lady Audley's Secret. Mary Elizabeth Braddon. 496p. 1998. pap. 9.95 (*0-19-283520-3*) OUP.

Lady Audley's Secret. Mary Elizabeth Braddon. 512p. 1998. pap. 10.95 (*0-14-043584-0*) Viking Penguin.

Lady Audley's Secret. Mary Elizabeth Braddon. (Illus.). 286p. 1974. reprint ed. pap. 8.95 (*0-486-23011-2*) Dover.

Lady Baltimore. Owen Wister. 23.95 (*0-8488-0329-9*) Amereon Ltd.

Lady Baltimore. Owen Wister. LC 68-20024. (Americans in Fiction Ser.). reprint ed. pap. text 5.95 (*0-89197-822-4*); reprint ed. lib. bdg. 19.50 (*0-8398-2173-5*) Irvington.

Lady Baltimore. Owen Wister. LC 92-89830. (Southern Classics Ser.). 430p. 1992. reprint ed. pap. 14.95 (*1-879941-13-9*) J S Sanders.

Lady Baltimore. Owen Wister. (BCL1-PS American Literature Ser.). 406p. 1992. reprint ed. lib. bdg. 99.00 (*0-7812-6907-5*) Rprt Serv.

Lady Barbarine see Works of Henry James Jr.: Collected Works

Lady Be Good. Dennis E. McClendon. 204p. 20.95 (*0-8488-2612-4*) Amereon Ltd.

Lady Be Good. Susan Elizabeth Phillips. LC 98-93457. 384p. 1999. mass mkt. 6.99 (*0-380-79448-9*, Avon Bks) Morrow Avon.

***Lady Be Good.** Susan Elizabeth Phillips. 2001. write for info. (*0-380-97572-6*) Morrow Avon.

***Lady Be Good.** large type ed. Susan Elizabeth Phillips. LC 99-22159. (Large Print Book Ser.). 1999. write for info. (*1-56895-733-5*) Wheeler Pub.

Lady Be Good: Erotic Love Stories by Naiad Press Authors. Ed. by Barbara Grier & Christine Cassidy. LC 97-10802. 320p. (Orig.). 1997. pap. 14.95 (*1-56280-180-5*) Naiad Pr.

Lady, Be Good! Vocal Selections. Ed. by Carol Cuellar. 36p. (Orig.). (C). 1988. pap. text 9.95 (*0-7692-0706-5*, SF0212) Wrner Bros.

Lady Be Mine. Catherine Spencer. (Romance Ser.). 1995. per. 2.99 (*0-373-03348-6*, 1-03348-9) Harlequin Bks.

Lady Be Mine. large type ed. Catherine Spencer. (Harlequin Ser.). 1994. lib. bdg. 19.95 (*0-263-13770-8*) Thorndike Pr.

Lady Beetles of the Russian Far East. Victor N. Kuznetson. (Memoir Series of the Center for Systematic Entomology: No. 1). (Illus.). xii, 248p. 1998. pap. 58.00 (*1-877743-27-5*) Sandhill Crane.

Lady Behind the Light. Mercia Fiore. (Illus.). 157p. (Orig.). (YA). (gr. 8-12). 1985. pap. text 5.95 (*0-9616687-0-9*) Fiore Ent.

Lady Besieged: Playscript. Jane Archer. LC 90-53080. (Orig.). 1990. pap. 6.00 (*0-88734-221-3*) Players Pr.

Lady Bird: A Biography of Mrs. Johnson. Jan Jarboe Russell. LC 99-27544. (Lisa Drew Book Ser.). 352p. 1999. 25.50 (*0-684-81480-3*) S&S Trade.

***Lady Bird: A Biography of Mrs. Johnson.** large type ed. Jan Jarboe Russell. LC 99-57106. (Biography Ser.). 632p. 2000. 26.95 (*0-7862-2359-6*, MML06500-171537) Thorndike Pr.

Lady Bird Johnson: Making Our Neighborhoods Beautiful. Charnan Simon. LC 96-36148. (Community Builders Ser.). 48p. (J). 1997. lib. bdg. 23.00 (*0-516-20292-8*) Childrens.

Lady Bird Johnson: Making Our Neighborhoods Beautiful. Charnan Simon. Ed. by Sarah DeCapua. (Community Builders Ser.). (Illus.). 48p. (J). 1998. pap. 6.95 (*0-516-26134-7*) Childrens.

Lady Bird Johnson: Our Environmental First Lady. Lewis L. Gould. LC 87-25331. (Illus.). xv, 312p. 1999. 25.00 (*0-7006-0336-0*) U Pr of KS.

***Lady Bird Johnson: Our Environmental First Lady.** Lewis L. Gould. LC 99-32508. (Modern First Ladies Ser.). (Illus.). 176p. 1999. 25.00 (*0-7006-0992-X*) U Pr of KS.

Lady Blows a Horn. 2nd ed. Nancy L. Mohr. (Illus.). 116p. 1997. 36.00 (*0-9660282-0-1*, HCP-97002) Horse Cntry Pr.

Lady Bluebeard: The True Story of Love & Marriage, Death & Flypaper. William C. Anderson. (Illus.). 208p. 1994. 24.95 (*0-9623868-7-1*) F Pruett.

***Lady Boss.** Jackie Collins. 640p. 1998. per. 7.99 (*0-671-02347-0*, Pocket Books) PB.

Lady Boss. Jackie Collins. 1990. 21.95 (*0-671-94826-1*) S&S Trade.

Lady Boss. Jackie Collins. Ed. by Bill Grose. 640p. 1991. reprint ed. mass mkt. 6.99 (*0-671-74418-6*, Pocket Star Bks) PB.

Lady Bountiful Revisted: Women Philanthropy, & Power. Ed. by Kathleen D. McCarthy. LC 90-32549. 250p. (C). 1990. text 40.00 (*0-8135-1598-X*); pap. text 18.00 (*0-8135-1611-0*) Rutgers U Pr.

Lady Boys, Tom Boys, Rent Boys: Male & Female Homosexualities in Contemporary Thailand. Ed. by Peter A. Jackson & Gerard Sullivan. LC 98-55912. 237p. 1999. 49.95 (*0-7890-0656-1*, Harrington Park); pap. 19.95 (*1-56023-119-X*, Harrington Park) Haworth Pr.

***Lady Buckaroo.** 2000. 30.00 (*0-7862-2120-8*) Mac Lib Ref.

Lady Bug, No. 3063. David M. Schwartz. Ed. by Sue Lewis & Elaine Pascoe. (Life Cycles Ser.). 16p. 1999. pap. 2.99 (*1-57471-553-4*) Creat Teach Pr.

Lady Bug's Ball. Heather Lowenberg. LC 97-10830. (J). 1998. lib. bdg. 9.99 (*0-679-98539-5*, Pub. by Random Bks Yng Read) Random.

Lady by Lamplight. large type ed. Clare Kersey. 288p. 1992. pap. 16.99 (*0-7089-7188-1*) Ulverscroft.

Lady Byron Vindicated. Harriet Beecher Stowe. LC 72-130245. (Studies in Byron: No. 5). 1970. reprint ed. lib. bdg. 75.00 (*0-8383-1135-0*) M S G Haskell Hse.

Lady Byron Vindicated. Harriet Beecher Stowe. (Notable American Authors Ser.). 1999. reprint ed. lib. bdg. 125.00 (*0-7812-8967-X*) Rprt Serv.

***Lady Caroline Wrey's Finishing Touches: Inspirational & Practical Ideas for Embellishments for Your Home.** Caroline Wrey. (Illus.). 128p. 1999. 27.95 (*1-85585-722-7*, Pub. by Collins & Br) Sterling.

L

Lady Cat. Joan Overfield. 304p. 1999. mass mkt. 5.99 (*0-8217-6096-3*) Kensgtn Pub Corp.

Lady Catherines Necklace. Aiken. 176p. 2000. text 21.95 (*0-312-24406-1*) St Martin.

Lady Cecelia'a Charade. Jacquelyn Gillis. 224p. 1996. mass mkt. 4.50 (*0-8217-5523-4*, Zebra Kensgtn) Kensgtn Pub Corp.

Lady Chapel. Candace M. Robb. 1995. mass mkt. 5.50 (*0-312-95460-3*) St Martin.

Lady Charlotte Schreiber: Extracts from Her Journal, 1853-1891. Charlotte E. Schreiber. Ed. by Bessborough. LC 74-5926. (Illus.). 212p. 1974. reprint ed. lib. bdg. 35.00 (*0-8371-7524-0*, SCEJ, Greenwood Pr) Greenwood.

Lady Chatterley: The Making of the Novel. Derek Britton. 256p. 1988. 44.95 (*0-04-800075-2*) Routledge.

Lady Chatterley's Lover. D. H. Lawrence. 1976. 20.95 (*0-8488-0559-3*) Amereon Ltd.

Lady Chatterley's Lover. D. H. Lawrence. Ed. by Lawrence Durrell. (Bantam Classics Ser.). 384p. 1983. mass mkt. 4.95 (*0-553-21262-1*) Bantam.

Lady Chatterley's Lover. D. H. Lawrence. LC 92-39247. 384p. 1993. pap. 12.00 (*0-8021-3334-7*, Grove) Grove-Atltic.

Lady Chatterley's Lover. D. H. Lawrence. 1959. mass mkt. 5.50 (*0-451-52498-5*, CE1787, Sig Classics) NAL.

Lady Chatterley's Lover. D. H. Lawrence. LC 93-15337. 544p. 1993. 17.50 (*0-679-60065-5*) Random.

Lady Chatterley's Lover. D. H. Lawrence. 1981. reprint ed. lib. bdg. 23.95 (*0-89966-375-3*) Buccaneer Bks.

Lady Chatterley's Lover, Set. unabridged ed. D. H. Lawrence. Ed. by Marilyn Kay. 1986. pap. 12.95 incl. audio (*1-882071-10-7*, 012) B&B Audio.

Lady Chatterley's Lover: A Propos of "Lady Chatterley's Lover" D. H. Lawrence. Ed. & Intro. by Michael Squires. 400p. 1995. pap. 10.95 (*0-14-018786-3*) Viking Penguin.

Lady Chatterley's Lover: Loss & Hope. William F. Buckley, Jr. LC 93-7658. (Twayne's Masterworks Ser.). 160p. 1993. pap. 18.00 (*0-8057-8599-X*) Macmillan.

Lady Chatterley's Lover: Loss & Hope. William F. Buckley, Jr. LC 93-7658. (Twayne's Masterworks Ser.: Vol. 123). 160p. 1993. 25.95 (*0-8057-9432-8*) Macmillan.

Lady Chatterley's Lover & a Propos of "Lady Chatterley's Lover" D. H. Lawrence. Ed. by Michael Squires. (Cambridge Edition of the Works of D. H. Lawrence). 522p. (C). 1993. text 105.00 (*0-521-22266-4*) Cambridge U Pr.

Lady Chatterly According to Spike Milligan. large type ed. Spike Milligan. 21.95 (*1-85695-379-3*, Pub. by ISIS Lrg Prnt) Transaction Pubs.

Lady Chatterly's Lover. Spike Milligan. 1995. pap. 11.95 (*0-14-024299-6*, Pub. by Pnguin Bks Ltd) Trafalgar.

Lady Clairval's Marriage. large type ed. Paula Marshall. (Mills & Boon Large Print Ser.). 350p. 1997. 23.99 (*0-263-15182-4*, Pub. by Mills & Boon) Ulverscroft.

***Lady Cornaro: Pride & Prodigy of Venice.** Jane H. Guernsey. LC 99-14133. (Illus.). 276p. 1999. 27.95 (*1-883551-44-7*, College Ave Pr) Attic Studio Pub.

***Lady Cottington's Pressed Fairy.** 2000. pap. 10.99 (*0-7407-0960-7*) Andrews & McMeel.

Lady Cottington's Pressed Fairy Journal. Illus. by Brian Froud. 112p. 1999. 14.95 (*1-55670-904-8*) Stewart Tabori & Chang.

***Lady Crymsyn.** P. N. Elrod. LC 99-89927. (Vampire Files Ser.). (Illus.). (J). 2000. write for info. (*0-441-00724-4*) Ace Bks.

***Lady Day: The Many Faces of Billie Holiday.** Robert G. O'Meally. (Illus.). 208p. 2000. pap. text 20.00 (*0-306-80959-1*) Da Capo.

Lady Day's Diary: The Life of Billie Holliday, 1937-1959. Ken Vail. (Illus.). 272p. pap. 19.95 (*1-86074-131-2*, Pub. by Sanctuary Pubng) Music Sales.

***Lady De Lancey's Narrative: A Story of Duty & Devotion.** David Miller. 224p. 2000. 80.00 (*1-86227-082-1*, Pub. by Spellmnt Pubs) St Mut.

Lady Deceiver. large type ed. Helen Dickson. (Mills & Boon Large Print Ser.). 350p. 1997. 23.99 (*0-263-15147-6*, Pub. by Mills & Boon) Ulverscroft.

Lady Deception. Bobbi Smith. 448p. (Orig.). 1996. pap. text, mass mkt. 5.99 (*0-8439-3951-6*) Dorchester Pub Co.

***Lady Deception.** Bobbi Smith. 448p. (Orig.). 1999. reprint ed. mass mkt. 5.99 (*0-8439-4599-0*, Leisure Bks) Dorchester Pub Co.

Lady Decides. Dorothea Donley. 1999. mass mkt. 4.99 (*0-8217-6389-X*, Zebra Kensgtn) Kensgtn Pub Corp.

Lady Defiant. Suzanne Robinson. 320p. 1992. mass mkt. 5.50 (*0-553-29574-8*) Bantam.

***Lady Delafont's Dilemma.** Donna J. Simpson. 2000. mass mkt. 4.99 (*0-8217-6674-0*) Kensgtn Pub Corp.

Lady Diana Spencer: Princess of Wales. Nancy Whitelaw. LC 98-5378. (Illus.). 112p. (YA). (gr. 5 up). 1998. lib. bdg. 20.95 (*1-883846-35-8*) M Reynolds.

***Lady Diana's Darlings.** Kate Huntington. (Regency Romance Ser.). 2000. mass mkt. 4.99 (*0-8217-6655-4*, Zebra Kensgtn) Kensgtn Pub Corp.

Lady Dilke: A Biography. Betty Askwith. LC 72-452970. x, 246p. 1969. write for info. (*0-7011-1519-X*) Chatto & Windus.

Lady Dither's Ghost: Musical Adaptation of a Sherlock Holmes Mystery. DuMont Howard. (Illus.). 36p. (J). (gr. k up). 1986. pap. 4.00 (*0-88680-263-6*) I E Clark.

Lady Divine. Barbara Sherrod. 224p. 1988. mass mkt. 2.95 (*0-446-34769-8*, Pub. by Warner Bks) Little.

Lady Divine. large type ed. Barbara Sherrod. 480p. 1996. 27.99 (*0-7089-3579-6*) Ulverscroft.

Lady Doctor. large type ed. Peggy Gaddis. LC 94-42790. (Nightingale Ser.). 200p. 1995. pap. 16.95 (*0-7838-1196-9*, G K Hall Lrg Type) Mac Lib Ref.

Lady Dudley Challenge Cup. Jervis Foulds. 198p. (C). 1990. pap. 30.00 (*0-85131-294-2*, Pub. by J A Allen) St Mut.

Lady Elizabeth's Christmas. Lane Riosley. 29p. (Orig.). 1995. pap. 2.50 (*1-57514-220-1*, 3017) Encore Perform Pub.

Lady Ellen Grae. Vera Cleaver & Bill Cleaver. LC 68-10981. (Illus.). (J). (gr. 4-6). 1968. lib. bdg. 12.89 (*0-397-31012-9*) HarpC Child Bks.

Lady Evelyn's Needlework Collection. Mary-Dick Digges et al. (Illus.). 198p. 1988. 39.95 (*0-929339-00-2*) Embroidery Research Pr Inc.

Lady F. 2nd ed. 1998. reprint ed. mass mkt. 6.95 (*1-56333-642-1*) Masquerade.

Lady Farrington's Folly. Nina Porter. 224p. 1993. mass mkt. 3.99 (*0-8217-4202-7*, Zebra Kensgtn) Kensgtn Pub Corp.

***Lady Ferry & Other Uncanny People.** Sarah Orne Jewett. Ed. by Jessica Amanda Salmonson. xxiv, 156p. 1998. 38.50 (*1-899562-56-7*) Ash-Tree.

Lady Follows. Holly Newman. LC 98-41785. (Women of the West Ser.). 384p. 1999. 24.95 (*0-312-86871-5*, Pub. by Forge NYC) St Martin.

***Lady Follows.** Holly Newman. (Women of the West Novels Ser.). 384p. 2000. mass mkt. 6.99 (*0-8125-2407-1*, Pub. by Forge NYC) St Martin.

***Lady Fortune.** Anne Stuart. 2000. mass mkt. 5.99 (*0-8217-6470-5*, Zebra Kensgtn) Kensgtn Pub Corp.

Lady Friends: Hawaiian Ways & the Ties That Define. Karen L. Ito. LC 99-17552. 1999. 39.95 (*0-8014-2636-7*) Cornell U Pr.

***Lady Friends: Hawaiian Ways & the Ties That Define.** Karen L. Ito. LC 99-17552. (Anthropology of Contemporary Issues Ser.). 1999. pap. 15.95 (*0-8014-9939-9*) Cornell U Pr.

Lady from Argentina. large type ed. James A. Pattinson. 320p. 1996. 27.99 (*0-7089-3505-2*) Ulverscroft.

Lady from Atlantis. Robert V. Gerard. LC 94-32349. 256p. 1995. pap. 12.95 (*1-880666-21-9*) Oughten Hse.

Lady from Dublin. William Breault. (Illus.). 131p. reprint ed. pap. 17.00 (*0-910845-44-1*, 556) Landmark Ent.

Lady from Dubuque: A Play in Two Acts. Edward Albee. 1980. pap. 5.25 (*0-8222-0628-5*) Dramatists Play.

Lady from Havana. Luis Santeiro. 1992. pap. 5.25 (*0-8222-0629-3*) Dramatists Play.

Lady from St. Louis. large type ed. Joan Hessayon. 1991. 27.99 (*0-7089-2462-X*) Ulverscroft.

Lady from Savannah: The Life of Juliette Low. Daisy Gordon Lawrence & G. D. Schultz. (Illus.). 383p. 1988. reprint ed. pap. 6.50 (*0-88441-147-8*, 19-401) Girl Scouts USA.

Lady from the Sea see Doll's House & Other Plays

Lady from the Sea see Ibsen: Plays Three

Lady from Toledo: An Historical Novel in Santa Fe. abr. ed. Fray A. Chavez. (Illus.). 200p. (Orig.). 1993. reprint ed. pap. 9.95 (*0-941108-03-1*) Friends Palace Pr.

Lady G I: A Woman's War in the South Pacific. large type ed. Irene Brion. 230p. 1998. 22.95 (*0-7838-8409-5*, G K Hall & Co) Mac Lib Ref.

Lady Gallant. Suzanne Robinson. 368p. 1991. mass mkt. 5.99 (*0-553-29430-X*) Bantam.

Lady Gambler: John Slocum. (Slocum Ser.: Vol. 205). 192p. 1996. pap. text 4.50 (*0-515-11827-3*, Jove) Berkley Pub.

Lady GI: A Woman's War in the South Pacific - The Memoir of Irene Brion. Irene Brion. LC 97-25409. (Illus.). 192p. 1997. 18.95 (*0-89141-633-1*) Presidio Pr.

Lady-Girl Talk - Essays & Poetry - The Drama of a Woman's Life. LC 97-71191. 192p. 1998. pap. 12.95 (*0-9657076-2-8*) Ink Pub GA.

Lady God. Lesa Luders. LC 95-19139. 185p. (Orig.). 1995. pap. 9.95 (*0-934678-59-6*) New Victoria Pubs.

***Lady Godiva.** unabridged ed. Judith Prior. Ed. by William-Alan Landes. 52p. 2000. pap. 10.00 (*0-88734-046-6*) Players Pr.

Lady Gold. Angela Amato & Joe Sharkey. LC 98-14528. 354p. (YA). (gr. 10 up). 1998. text 23.95 (*0-312-18541-3*) St Martin.

Lady Gold. Angela Amato & Joe Sharkey. 384p. 1999. mass mkt. 6.99 (*0-312-96765-9*, St Martins Paperbacks) St Martin.

Lady Gregory. Hazard Adams. (Irish Writers Ser.). 106p. 1973. 8.50 (*0-8387-1085-9*); pap. 1.95 (*0-8387-1207-X*) Bucknell U Pr.

Lady Gregory: An Annotated Bibliography of Criticism. Compiled by E. H. Mikhail. LC 81-50702. xii, 258p. (C). 1982. 45.00 (*0-87875-216-1*) Whitston Pub.

Lady Gregory: Fifty Years Later. Ann Saddlemyer & Colin Smythe. (Irish Literary Studies: Vol. # 13). 484p. 1987. 65.00 (*0-86140-112-3*, Pub. by Smyth) Dufour.

Lady Gregory's Diaries, 1892-1902. Isabella Augusta Gregory. Ed. & Intro. by James Pethica. (Colin Smythe Publication). (Illus.). 400p. 1996. 70.00 (*0-19-521245-2*) OUP.

Lady Hawarden: Studies from Life, 1857-1864. Virginia Dodier. LC 98-89096. (Illus.). 128p. 1999. text 45.00 (*0-89381-815-1*) Aperture.

Lady Head Vases: A Collector's Guide with Prices. Mary Zavada. LC 87-63476. (Illus.). 112p. 1995. reprint ed. pap. 16.95 (*0-88740-880-X*) Schiffer.

Lady Hellfire. Suzanne Robinson. 336p. 1992. mass mkt. 5.99 (*0-553-29678-7*) Bantam.

***Lady, Her Lover & Her Lord.** T. D. Jakes. 2000. pap. text 11.95 (*0-425-16872-7*) Berkley Pub.

***Lady, Her Lover & Her Lord.** T. D. Jakes. LC 98-6298. 224p. 1998. 19.95 (*0-399-14414-5*, G P Putnam) Peng Put Young Read.

Lady, Her Lover & Her Lord. large type ed. T. D. Jakes. LC 99-17233. 384p. 1999. reprint ed. 24.95 (*0-8027-2736-0*) Walker & Co.

Lady Ice. Joan Hohl. 250p. 1995. per. 4.99 (*1-55166-027-X*, 1-66027-3, Mira Bks) Harlequin Bks.

Lady in a Boat: Poems. Merle Collins. 1999. pap. text 12.95 (*1-885214-22-7*) Azul Edits.

Lady in an Empty Dress: Poems. Alexander Petrov. Tr. by R. Burns. 38p. 1990. pap. 9.95 (*0-948259-90-6*, Pub. by Forest Bks) Dufour.

Lady in Distress. large type ed. Brittany Young. LC 92-2671. 217p. 1992. reprint ed. 13.95 (*1-56054-384-1*) Thorndike Pr.

***Lady in Gil.** Rebecca Bradley. 2000. mass mkt. 5.99 (*0-441-00709-0*) Ace Bks.

Lady in Gray, 1 vol. Patricia Oliver. (Signet Regency Romance Ser.). 221p. 1999. mass mkt. 4.99 (*0-451-19500-0*) NAL.

Lady in Kicking Horse Reservoir. Richard Hugo. LC 98-74553. (Classic Contemporaries Ser.). 80p. 1999. reprint ed. pap. 12.95 (*0-88748-308-9*, Pub. by Carnegie-Mellon) Cornell U Pr.

Lady in Love. large type ed. Renee Shann. 368p. 1983. 27.99 (*0-7089-0992-2*) Ulverscroft.

Lady in Medieval England 1000-1500. Peter Coss. LC 98-206650. (Illus.). 208p. 1998. 29.95 (*0-8117-0985-X*) Kitch Keepsakes.

Lady in Pink. Judith A. Bosley. (Sundown Fiction Collection). (Illus.). 64p. (J). (gr. 3). 1993. 3.95 (*0-88336-212-0*) New Readers.

***Lady in Pink.** 5th ed. Judith A. Bosley. (Illus.). 64p. 1999. reprint ed. pap. 5.95 (*1-893916-14-6*, 2008) Project Pr.

Lady in Pink: Reading Level 3. Judith A. Bosley. (Sundown Fiction Collection). 64p. 1993. audio 9.95 (*0-88336-259-7*) New Readers.

Lady in Red. Linda Turner. (Intimate Moments Ser.). 1997. per. 3.99 (*0-373-07763-7*, 1-07763-5) Silhouette.

***Lady in Red.** large type ed. Linda Turner. (Silhouette Ser.). 1999. 21.95 (*0-373-59647-2*) Harlequin Bks.

Lady in the Box see Senora de la Caja de Carton

Lady in the Box. Ann McGovern. LC 97-13633. (Illus.). 40p. (YA). (ps up). 1997. 14.95 (*1-890515-01-9*, Pub. by Turtle Bks) Publishers Group.

***Lady in the Box.** Ann McGovern. (Illus.). 40p. (YA). (ps up). 1999. pap. 7.95 (*1-890515-15-9*, Pub. by Turtle Bks) Publishers Group.

Lady in the Car with Glasses & a Gun. Sebastien Japrisot. Tr. by Helen Weaver from FRE. LC 96-39831. 256p. 1997. pap. 10.95 (*0-452-27777-9*, Plume) Dutton Plume.

Lady in the Dark: Vocal Score. Ed. by Michael Lefferts. (Vocal Score Ser.). 136p. (Orig.). (C). 1981. per. 45.00 (*0-88188-030-2*, 00312238) H Leonard.

Lady in the Lake. Raymond Chandler. Date not set. lib. bdg. 20.95 (*0-8488-2136-X*) Amereon Ltd.

Lady in the Lake. Raymond Chandler. 704p. 1991. Not sold separately (*0-614-32017-8*) Random Hse Value.

Lady in the Lake. Raymond Chandler. LC 87-40475. (Crime Ser.). 288p. 1988. pap. 11.00 (*0-394-75825-0*) Vin Bks.

Lady in the Lake. Raymond Chandler. 1992. pap. 10.00 (*0-679-74088-0*) Random.

Lady in the Lake. Raymond Chandler. 288p. 1994. 35.00 (*1-883402-94-8*) S&S Trade.

Lady in the Lake. Raymond Chandler. 1992. pap. 10.00 (*0-394-23909-1*) Vin Bks.

Lady in the Lake. large type ed. Raymond Chandler. 23.95 (*1-85695-362-9*, Pub. by ISIS Lrg Prnt) Transaction Pubs.

Lady in the Lake. large type ed. Raymond Chandler. LC 93-49683. (Cloak & Dagger Ser.). 347p. 1994. lib. bdg. 20.95 (*0-7862-0175-4*) Thorndike Pr.

Lady in the Loch. Elizabeth Ann Scarborough. LC 98-11567. 272p. 1998. 19.95 (*0-441-00582-9*) Ace Bks.

Lady in the Loch. Elizabeth Ann Scarborough. 258p. 1999. reprint ed. mass mkt. 5.99 (*0-441-00666-3*) Ace Bks.

Lady in the Mirror: Bachelor Arms. Judith Arnold. LC 95-22363. 218p. 1995. per. 3.25 (*0-373-25661-2*) Harlequin Bks.

Lady in the Moon. Alethea A. Adams-Wells. LC 96-90285. 247p. 1996. 20.00 (*0-9645787-1-9*) Unole Pub.

Lady in the Morgue. Jonathan Latimer. 192p. 1988. pap. 4.95 (*0-930330-79-X*) Intl Polygonics.

Lady in the Painting. rev. ed. Fred Wang. 1983. 9.95 (*0-88710-043-0*) Yale Far Eastern Pubns.

Lady in the Painting. rev. ed. Fred Wang. 1983. audio 8.95 (*0-88710-044-9*) Yale Far Eastern Pubns.

Lady in the Picture: Chinese Folklore. Frwd. by Zhong Wen. (Illus.). 249p. 1993. pap. 8.95 (*0-8351-2097-X*) China Bks.

Lady in the Twilight. Mervyn Wall. (Lost Play Ser.). 1971. pap. 1.25 (*0-912262-24-9*) Proscenium.

Lady in Waiting. Denise Domning. 1998. mass mkt. 5.99 (*0-451-40771-7*, Topaz) NAL.

***Lady in Waiting.** Denise Domning. LC 98-51097. 1999. 26.95 (*0-7862-1785-5*) Thorndike Pr.

Lady in Waiting: Developing Your Love Relationships. Debby Jones & Jackie Kendall. LC 96-119935. 196p. (Orig.). 1995. pap. 10.99 (*1-56043-848-7*, Treasure Hse) Destiny Image.

Lady in Waiting: Devotional Journal & Study Guide. Debby Jones & Jackie Kendall. 96p. 1997. pap., student ed. 7.99 (*1-56043-298-5*, Treasure Hse) Destiny Image.

Lady in Waiting: Poems in English & Spanish. Mary H. Rojas. Tr. by Ernesto Lombeida from SPA. LC 93-87093. (Illus.). 88p. (Orig.). 1994. pap. 8.95 (*0-9634090-1-8*) Spillway Pubns.

Lady in White. Denise Domning. 1999. mass mkt. 3.99 (*0-451-40772-5*, Sig) NAL.

***Lady into Fox, Set.** unabridged ed. David Garnett. 1999. 20.95 incl. audio (*1-55685-566-4*) Audio Bk Con.

Lady Is a Doctor. Bank Street Staff. 124p. 2000. pap. 8.95 (*0-07-134335-0*) McGraw.

***Lady Jane's Nemesis.** Patricia Oliver. (Regency Romance Ser.). 2000. mass mkt. 4.99 (*0-451-20069-1*, Sig) NAL.

***Lady Jane's Physician.** large type ed. Anne Ashley. 320p. 2000. 25.99 (*0-263-16274-5*, Pub. by Mills & Boon) Ulverscroft.

Lady Kaguya's Secret: A Japanese Tale. Illus. by Jirina Marton. 48p. (YA). (ps up). 1997. 19.95 (*1-55037-441-9*, Pub. by Annick) Firefly Bks Ltd.

Lady Killer: A Tale of Horror & the Erotic. Anthony Malo. LC 96-85490. 205p. (Orig.). 1998. pap. 12.95 (*0-9640963-3-1*) Artemis Creat.

Lady Killer: Heart Disease: Women at Risk. Suzanne Cambre. Ed. by Anna Hollingsworth. LC 35-3309. (Illus.). 24p. 1995. pap. text 5.95 (*0-939838-38-9*) Pritchett & Hull.

Lady Killers. 1999. 29.95 (*0-517-72269-0*) Random.

Lady Killers. J. R. Roberts. (Gunsmith Ser.: Vol. 198). 1998. mass mkt. 4.99 (*0-515-12303-X*, Jove) Berkley Pub.

Lady Knife-Thrower. Daniel Halpern. 1975. pap. 5.00 (*0-685-73187-1*) Bellevue Pr.

***Lady Knightley's Secret.** large type ed. Anne Ashley. 320p. 1999. 25.99 (*0-263-16019-X*, Pub. by Mgna Lrg Print) Ulverscroft.

Lady Knows the Game: A Woman's Guide to Watching, Understanding & Talking Football. Rhonda V. Smith. (Illus.). 204p. (Orig.). 1985. pap. 9.95 (*0-934507-02-3*) Manchester Pr.

Lady L. Romain Gary. (FRE.). 1973. pap. 10.95 (*0-7859-2631-3*, 207036304X) Fr & Eur.

Lady L. Romain Gary. (Folio Ser.: No. 304). (FRE.). 1973. 8.95 (*2-07-036304-X*) Schoenhof.

Lady Las Vegas: The Inside Story Behind America's Neon Oasis. Susan Berman. (Illus.). 224p. 1997. 29.95 (*1-57500-020-2*, Pub. by TV Bks) HarpC.

***Lady Las Vegas: The Inside Story Behind America's Neon Oasis.** Susan Berman. (Illus.). 223p. 2000. reprint ed. text 30.00 (*0-7881-9265-5*) DIANE Pub.

Lady Laureates: Women Who Have Won the Nobel Prize. 2nd ed. Olga S. Opfell. LC 85-19670. 334p. 1986. 36.00 (*0-8108-1851-5*) Scarecrow.

Lady Lawyer. Dorothy Frooks & Cay Dorney. LC 74-8881. (Illus.). 224p. 1975. 12.50 (*0-8315-0141-3*) Speller.

Lady Legend. Deborah Camp. 416p. (Orig.). 1992. mass mkt. 4.50 (*0-380-76735-X*, Avon Bks) Morrow Avon.

Lady-Lessons. Sarah A. Starr. 256p. 2000. 19.95 (*1-929085-17-6*); lib. bdg. 17.95 (*1-929085-18-4*); mass mkt. 4.95 (*1-929085-16-8*) Rgncy Pr.

Lady-Lessons. large type ed. Sarah A. Starr. 356p. 2000. lib. bdg. 23.95 (*1-929085-19-2*); per. 19.95 (*1-929085-20-6*) Rgncy Pr.

"Lady Lex" & the "Blue Ghost" A Pictorial History of the U. S. S. Lexingtons CU-2 & CU-16. Steven Ewing. LC 83-61338. (Illus.). 48p. 1983. pap. 5.95 (*0-933126-35-2*) Pictorial Hist.

Lady Liberty's Light. Barbara Birenbaum. LC 85-32061. (Historical Adventure Ser.: No. 3). (Illus.). 50p. (J). (gr. 3-5). 1986. 12.95 (*0-935343-12-1*); pap. 5.95 (*0-935343-11-3*) Peartree.

Lady Linford's Return. large type ed. Anne Ashley. (Mills & Boon Large Print Ser.). 350p. 1997. 23.99 (*0-263-15338-X*, Pub. by Mills & Boon) Ulverscroft.

Lady Lissa's Liaison. Lindsay Randall. 224p. 1998. pap. 4.99 (*0-8217-5957-4*) Kensgtn Pub Corp.

Lady Lobo. Kristen Garrett. LC 93-17797. 200p. (Orig.). 1993. pap. 9.95 (*0-934678-49-9*) New Victoria Pubs.

Lady Love. Diana Palmer. 248p. 1995. per. 4.99 (*1-55166-031-8*, 1-66031-5, Mira Bks) Harlequin Bks.

***Lady Love.** Diana Palmer. 2000. per. 3.99 (*1-55166-568-9*, Mira Bks) Harlequin Bks.

Lady Lu. Elisabeth Kidd. 224p. 1990. 18.95 (*0-8027-1086-7*) Walker & Co.

Lady Lu. large type ed. Elisabeth Mansfield. LC 90-44228. 302p. 1990. reprint ed. lib. bdg. 18.95 (*1-56054-050-8*) Thorndike Pr.

Lady Luck: The Theory of Probability. Warren Weaver. (Popular Science Ser.). (Illus.). 384p. 1982. reprint ed. pap. 8.95 (*0-486-24342-7*) Dover.

Lady Lucy's Lover. Marion Chesney. 160p. 1992. reprint ed. 18.00 (*0-7278-4356-7*) Severn Hse.

Lady Macbeth au Village, l'Ange Scelle, la Vagabond Enchante. Nicolas Leskov. (FRE.). 1982. pap. 17.95 (*0-7859-4174-6*) Fr & Eur.

Lady Macbeth of Mtsensk Librettos: English Text 1932 Version. Dmitri Shostakovich. 56p. 1986. pap. 4.95 (*0-7935-3690-1*, 50340730) H Leonard.

Lady MacDonald's Scotland: The Best of Scottish Food & Drink. Lady C. MacDonald. (Illus.). 160p. 1996. pap. 16.95 (*0-8212-2309-7*, Pub. by Bulfinch Pr) Little.

Lady Marshalls, 1980-1990: The Decade of Howard Beth. Marshall County Backboard Club Staff. LC 90-71725. 88p. 1990. 24.95 (*1-56311-016-4*) Turner Pub KY.

***Lady Mary Wortley Montagu: Comet of the Enlightenment.** Isobel Grundy. LC 98-48471. (Illus.). 704p. 1999. 45.00 (*0-19-811289-0*) OUP.

Lady Mary Wortley Montagu & the Eighteenth-Century Familiar Letter. Cynthia Lowenthal. LC 92-41757. 264p. 1994. 40.00 (*0-8203-1545-1*) U of Ga Pr.

Lady Mary Wroth: The First Part of the Countess of Montgomery's Urania. Ed. by Josephine A. Roberts. LC 95-2654. (Renaissance English Text Society Series, Medieval & Renaissance Texts & Studies: Vol. 140). 994p. 1995. 60.00 (*0-86698-176-4*, MR140) MRTS.

Lady Maryann's Dilemma. Karla Hocker. 1990. mass mkt. 3.95 (*0-8217-3106-8*, Zebra Kensgtn) Kensgtn Pub Corp.

Lady Mechanic's Total Car Care for the Clueless. Volpe. LC 98-9435. (Illus.). 197p. (YA). 1998. pap. 13.95 (*0-312-18733-5*) St Martin.

Lady Meed - The Art of Piers Plowman. A. G. Mitchell. LC 72-148891. (Select Bibliographies Reprint Ser.). 1977. 15.95 (*0-8369-5679-6*) Ayer.

Lady Megan's Masquerade. Cindy Holbrock. 1989. mass mkt. 2.95 (*0-8217-2692-7*, Zebra Kensgtn) Kensgtn Pub Corp.

An Asterisk (*) at the beginning of an entry indicates that the title is appearing for the first time.

Lady Midnight. Maria Greene. 352p. 1989. pap. 3.95 (*0-380-75563-7*, Avon Bks) Morrow Avon.
Lady Miracle. Susan King. 352p. 1997. mass mkt. 5.99 (*0-451-40766-0*, Onyx) NAL.
Lady Miracle. Susan King. LC 97-52117. 1998. 25.95 (*0-7862-1398-1*) Thorndike Pr.
Lady Miracle. large type ed. Susan King. LC 98-3230. 1998. 22.95 (*1-56895-552-9*, Wheeler) Wheeler Pub.
Lady Miranda's Masquerade. Lynn Collum. 224p. 1999. mass mkt. 4.99 (*0-8217-6208-7*) Kensgtn Pub Corp.
***Lady Mistress.** Anne Laurence. (Zebra Splendor Historical Romances Ser.). 352p. 2000. mass mkt. 4.99 (*0-8217-6621-X*, Zebra Kensgtn) Kensgtn Pub Corp.
Lady Molly of Scotland Yard. Emmuska Orczy. LC 75-32771. (Literature of Mystery & Detection Ser.). 1976. reprint ed. 25.95 (*0-405-07890-0*) Ayer.
Lady Monster Has a Plan. Blance & Cooke. Date not set. pap. text. write for info. (*0-582-19312-5*, Pub. by Addison-Wesley) Longman.
Lady Monster Helps Out. Blance & Cooke. Date not set. pap. text. write for info. (*0-582-19302-8*, Pub. by Addison-Wesley) Longman.
Lady Moonlight. Kate Freiman. (Magical Love Ser.). 352p. (Orig.). 1999. mass mkt. 5.99 (*0-515-12465-6*, Jove) Berkley Pub.
Lady Morgan the Novelist. James Newcomer. LC 89-43054. 104p. 1990. 26.50 (*0-8387-5177-6*) Bucknell U Pr.
Lady Morgan's Memoirs, 2 vols., Set. Sydney O. Morgan. LC 76-37705. (Women of Letters Ser.). reprint ed. 145.00 (*0-404-56793-2*) AMS Pr.
Lady Moses: A Novel. Lucinda Roy. LC 97-33216. 400p. 1998. 24.00 (*0-06-018244-X*) HarpC.
Lady Moses: A Novel. Lucinda Roy. 400p. 1999. pap. 13.00 (*0-06-093084-5*) HarpC.
Lady Muck. William Mayne. LC 95-14009. (Illus.). 32p. (J). (gr. k-4). 1997. 15.95 (*0-395-75281-7*) HM.
Lady Named Jo: A Musical. Ben Finn & Peter J. Stephens. 1997. pap. 5.50 (*1-57514-298-8*, 0030) Encore Perform Pub.
Lady Next Door. Laura Matthews. 1999. pap. 3.99 (*0-451-17732-0*, Sig) NAL.
Lady Nitwit/La Dama Boda. Lope de Vega. Tr. by William I. Oliver from SPA. LC 98-13215. 182p. (Orig.). 1998. pap. 24.00 (*0-927534-74-6*) Biling Rev-Pr.
Lady Ocean: A Love Story for Children. Guy Mount. (Illus.). (J). (gr. k-6). 1986. pap. 3.00 (*0-9604462-2-2*) Sweetlight.
Lady of Andros. Terence. (Loeb Classical Library: No. 22). 15.50 (*0-674-99025-0*) HUP.
Lady of Avalon. Marion Zimmer Bradley. 457p. 1998. mass mkt. 15.95 (*0-451-45652-1*, ROC) NAL.
Lady of Belmont. John G. Ervine. 95p. 1923. 8.95 (*0-910278-17-2*) Boulevard.
Lady of Claremont House: Isabella Elder, Pioneer & Philanthropist. Joan McAlpine. LC 98-146756. 206 p. 1997. write for info. (*1-874640-97-1*) Argyll Pubng.
Lady of Conquest. Teresa Medeiros. 400p. 1998. mass mkt. 5.99 (*0-553-58114-7*) Bantam.
Lady of Deer Park. Seumas O'Kelly. LC 96-60146. 320p. (Orig.). 2000. pap. 14.95 (*1-885983-14-X*) Turtle Point Pr.
Lady of Expectations. large type ed. Stephanie Laurens. 350p. 1996. 23.99 (*0-263-14646-4*, Pub. by Mills & Boon) Ulverscroft.
Lady of Godey's: Sara Josephia Hale. Ruth E. Finley. LC 74-3949. (Women in America Ser.). (Illus.). 378p. 1974. reprint ed. 35.95 (*0-405-06095-5*) Ayer.
Lady of Gold. Paige Brantley. 352p. 1997. mass mkt. 4.99 (*0-8217-5684-2*, Zebra Kensgtn) Kensgtn Pub Corp.
Lady of Guadalupe. Tomie De Paola. LC 79-19610. (Illus.). 48p. (J). (ps-3). 1980. pap. 8.95 (*0-8234-0403-X*); lib. bdg. 16.95 (*0-8234-0373-4*) Holiday.
***Lady of Hay.** Barbara Erskine. 2000. pap. 15.00 (*1-56649-160-6*) Welcome Rain.
***Lady of Horses.** Judith Tarr. LC 00-27653. 400p. 2000. 27.95 (*0-312-86114-1*) Forge NYC.
Lady of Horses. Judith Tarr. pap. 15.95 (*0-312-87572-X*) St Martin.
Lady of Ice & Fire. Colin Alexander. 352p. 1996. reprint ed. mass mkt. 5.50 (*0-8439-4072-7*, Leisure Bks) Dorchester Pub Co.
Lady of Independent Means. large type ed. Sarah Westleigh. 350p. 1995. 23.99 (*0-263-14422-4*, Pub. by Mills & Boon) Ulverscroft.
***Lady of Kynachan.** Robertson, Jr. 2000. pap. 9.95 (*0-552-14298-0*, Pub. by Transworld Publishers Ltd) Trafalgar.
Lady of Launay. Anthony Trollope. Ed. by John K. Shannon. (Harting Grange Library). (Illus.). 1978. pap. 5.95 (*0-932282-02-4*); lib. bdg. 9.95 (*0-932282-03-2*) Caledonia Pr.
Lady of Legend: The Mystery of the Female Stranger of Gadsby's Tavern. 2nd rev. ed. Ellen E. Morrison. LC 87-460803. (Illus.). 16p. 1986. pap. 1.75 (*0-9622537-2-3*) Morielle Pr.
***Lady of Letters.** Andrea Pickens. 2000. mass mkt. 4.99 (*0-451-20170-1*, Sig) NAL.
Lady of Lyon House. large type ed. Jennifer Wilde. 358p. 1993. 27.99 (*0-7505-0138-3*) Ulverscroft.
Lady of Lyon House. Jennifer Wilde. 224p. 1992. reprint ed. 18.00 (*0-7278-4365-6*) Severn Hse.
***Lady of Lyons or Love & Pride (1838)** Edward Bulwer Lytton. 40p. 1999. reprint ed. pap. 7.00 (*0-7661-0804-X*) Kessinger Pub.
***Lady of Lyonsbridge, 1, 520.** Ana Seymour. (Historical Ser.). 2000. mass mkt. 4.99 (*0-373-29120-5*, 1-29120-2) Harlequin Bks.
Lady of Monkton. large type ed. Elizabeth Byrd. 1990. 27.99 (*0-7089-2151-5*) Ulverscroft.
Lady of Pleasure. Charles E. Eaton. LC 92-54398. 168p. 1993. 17.50 (*0-8453-4847-7*, Cornwall Bks) Assoc Univ Prs.
Lady of Quality. Frances Hodgson Burnett. 22.95 (*0-8488-0252-7*) Amereon Ltd.
Lady of Quality. Mona K. Gedney. 288p. 1996. mass mkt. 4.50 (*0-8217-5521-8*, Zebra Kensgtn) Kensgtn Pub Corp.
Lady of Quality. Georgette Heyer. lib. bdg. 22.95 (*0-8488-1984-5*) Amereon Ltd.
Lady of Quality. large type ed. Rachelle Edwards. (Linford Romance Large Print Ser.). 320p. 1998. pap. 17.99 (*0-7089-5240-2*, Linford) Ulverscroft.
Lady of Repute. large type ed. Janice James. 512p. 1995. 27.99 (*0-7089-3374-2*) Ulverscroft.
Lady of Rome. Francis M. Crawford. (Works of Francis Marion Crawford). 1990. reprint ed. lib. bdg. 79.00 (*0-7812-2557-4*) Rprt Serv.
Lady of Sadness: A Play in 3 Acts. Ray Leland Caley. 57p. 1994. pap. text 14.95 (*0-910987-08-4*) Dragons Lair.
Lady of Seven Emeralds. Clara Wimberly. 288p. 1993. mass mkt. 3.99 (*0-8217-4195-0*, Zebra Kensgtn) Kensgtn Pub Corp.
***Lady of Sherwood.** Jennifer Roberson. 384p. 1999. 24.00 (*1-57566-475-5*, Knsington) Kensgtn Pub Corp.
***Lady of Sherwood.** Jennifer Roberson. 384p. 2000. pap. 14.00 (*1-57566-587-5*) Kensgtn Pub Corp.
***Lady of Skye.** Patricia Cabot. 2001. mass mkt. 6.50 (*0-7434-1027-0*, Sonnet Bks) PB.
Lady of Spain. large type ed. Sally Blake. 1995. 27.99 (*0-7505-0646-6*, Pub. by Mgna Lrg Print) Ulverscroft.
Lady of Summer. Emma F. Merritt. 400p. (Orig.). 1995. mass mkt. 5.50 (*0-380-77984-6*, Avon Bks) Morrow Avon.
Lady of the Aroostook. William Dean Howells. LC 70-98770. 326p. 1970. reprint ed. lib. bdg. 55.00 (*0-8371-2801-3*, HOLA, Greenwood Pr) Greenwood.
Lady of the Aroostook. William Dean Howells. (Notable American Authors Ser.). 1992. reprint ed. lib. bdg. 75.00 (*0-7812-3231-7*) Rprt Serv.
Lady of the Barge. William W. Jacobs. LC 75-101815. (Short Story Index Reprint Ser.). 1977. 21.95 (*0-8369-3203-X*) Ayer.
Lady of the Beasts: The Goddess & Her Sacred Animals. Buffie Johnson. LC 94-16765. (Illus.). 400p. 1994. pap. 24.95 (*0-89281-523-X*) Inner Tradit.
Lady of the Camellias. Alexandre Dumas. 1994. 5.50 (*0-87129-449-4*, L81) Dramatic Pub.
Lady of the Dance: A Movement Approach to the Biblical Figures of Wisdom in Worship & Education. Hal Taussig. (Orig.). 1981. pap. 3.00 (*0-941500-24-1*) Sharing Co.
Lady of the Dawn by Alejandro Casona. unabridged ed. Alejandro Casona. Tr. by Donald B. Gibbs from SPA. LC 98-60107. 90p. 1998. pap. 16.00 (*0-938972-29-4*) Spanish Lit Pubns.
Lady of the Fallen Air: Poems from the Chinese. Chris Howell. 30p. 1998. pap. 7.00 (*0-932264-21-2*) Trask Hse Bks.
Lady of the Forest. Jennifer Roberson. 768p. 1993. mass mkt. 5.99 (*0-8217-4284-1*, Zebra Kensgtn) Kensgtn Pub Corp.
Lady of the Forest. Jennifer Roberson. 608p. 1995. pap. 12.00 (*0-8217-4891-2*, Knsington) Kensgtn Pub Corp.
Lady of the Fountain. Jack Hart. 50p. 1985. pap. 4.95 (*0-89697-262-3*) Intl Univ Pr.
Lady of the Glen. Jennifer Roberson. 1997. pap. 14.95 (*1-57566-129-2*) Kensgtn Pub Corp.
Lady of the Glen. Jennifer Roberson. 576p. 1998. mass mkt. 6.99 (*1-57566-289-2*) Kensgtn Pub Corp.
Lady of the Grape Arbor: Three Generations of Strong New England Women. Doloris Holmes. (Orig.). 1993. pap. write for info. (*0-9640231-8-0*) White Mask.
Lady of the Gun. Faye Adams. 1996. mass mkt. 5.99 (*0-671-52723-1*, Pocket Books) PB.
Lady of the Holy Alliance: The Life of Julie De Krudener. Ernest J. Knapton. LC 39-14081. reprint ed. 22.45 (*0-404-03732-1*) AMS Pr.
***Lady of the Keep.** Sharon Schulze. 2000. per. 4.99 (*0-373-29110-8*) Harlequin Bks.
Lady of the Knight. Tori Phillips. (Historical Ser.). 1999. per. 4.99 (*0-373-29076-4*, 1-29076-6) Harlequin Bks.
***Lady of the Lake.** Mavis Amundson. (Illus.). 40p. 2000. pap. 5.95 (*0-961091O-6-1*) Western Gull Pub.
Lady of the Lake. Betty O. Carpenter. LC 98-89881. 365p. 1999. 25.00 (*0-7388-0315-4*); pap. 15.00 (*0-7388-0316-2*) Xlibris Corp.
Lady of the Lake. Jackie Hall. 192p. 1995. 17.95 (*1-56167-188-6*) Noble House.
Lady of the Lake. Elizabeth Mayne. 1997. per. 4.99 (*0-373-28980-4*, 1-28980-0) Harlequin Bks.
Lady of the Lake in Arthurian Legend. Christopher Dean. LC 93-17436. 68p. 1993. text 49.95 (*0-7734-9302-6*) E Mellen.
Lady of the Last Century: Mrs. Elizabeth Montague. 2nd ed. John Doran. LC 75-37690. (Illus.). reprint ed. 47.50 (*0-404-56744-4*) AMS Pr.
Lady of the Limberlost: A Biography. J. P. Meehan. 24.95 (*0-8488-0094-X*) Amereon Ltd.
Lady of the Lotus-Born: The Life & Enlightenment of Yeshe Tsogyal. Gyalwa Changchub & Namkhai Nyingpo. LC 98-6838. 176p. 1998. 29.95 (*1-57062-384-8*, Pub. by Shambhala Pubns) Random.
Lady of the Masque. large type ed. Pamela Bennetts. 336p. 1994. 27.99 (*0-7089-3127-8*) Ulverscroft.
Lady of the Mists. Clara Wimberly. 288p. 1991. mass mkt. 3.95 (*0-8217-3341-9*, Zebra Kensgtn) Kensgtn Pub Corp.
Lady of the Moon. large type ed. Alex Andrews. (Dales Large Print Ser.). 272p. 1997. pap. 18.99 (*1-85389-716-7*, Dales) Ulverscroft.
Lady of the Night. Cordia Byers. 400p. 1998. mass mkt. 5.99 (*0-8439-4404-8*, Leisure Bks) Dorchester Pub Co.
Lady of the Night. Kate Hoffmann. LC 97-10635. 216p. 1994. per. 2.99 (*0-373-25615-9*, 1-25615-5) Harlequin Bks.
Lady of the Night. Pamela Oldfield. LC 99-18843. 1999. 24.95 (*0-7862-1892-4*) Mac Lib Ref.
***Lady of the Night.** large type ed. Pamela Oldfield. LC 99-18843. 444p. 1999. write for info. (*0-7540-2231-5*, Black Dagger) Chivers N Amer.
Lady of the Night: A Handbook of Moon Magick & Rituals. Edain McCoy. LC 95-32399. (Llewellyn's Modern Witchcraft Ser.). (Illus.). 256p. 1999. pap. 14.95 (*1-56718-660-2*) Llewellyn Pubns.
Lady of the Reeds. Pauline Gedge. LC 95-14837. 513p. 1995. 25.00 (*1-56947-043-X*) Soho Press.
Lady of the Reeds. Pauline Gedge. LC 95-14837. (Hera Ser.). 513p. 1997. pap. 15.00 (*1-56947-072-3*) Soho Press.
Lady of the Rock. Patricia Carter. 1993. pap. 5.00 (*0-86025-417-8*, Pub. by I Henry Pubns) Empire Pub Srvs.
Lady of the Shroud. Bram Stoker. reprint ed. lib. bdg. 21.95 (*0-88411-134-2*) Amereon Ltd.
Lady of the Stars - Stevie Nicks. Edward Wincentsen. (Illus.). 122p. 1994. pap. 14.95 (*0-9642808-0-9*) Wynn Pubng.
Lady of the Strawberries. Helen Chetin & Anita Kurz. 89p. (J). (gr. 3-6). 1982. pap. 3.95 (*0-7725-9013-3*) Stoddart Publ.
Lady of the Upper Kingdom. Merline Lovelace. (Historical Ser.). 1996. per. 4.99 (*0-373-28920-0*, 1-28920-6) Harlequin Bks.
Lady of the Vineyards. Yannis Ritsos. Tr. by Apostolos N. Athanassakis from GRE. LC 80-84407. (ENG & GRE.). 77p. 1980. pap. text 7.00 (*0-918618-10-X*) Pella Pub.
Lady of the Water. Bradley H. Olsen-Ecker. (Illus.). 36p. 1985. pap. 6.95 (*0-9671658-1-4*) B Olsen-Ecker.
Lady of the West. Linda Howard. Ed. by Claire Zion. 384p. (Orig.). 1990. mass mkt. 5.99 (*0-671-66080-2*) PB.
Lady of the West. Linda Howard. (Orig.). 1997. pap. 6.99 (*0-671-01973-2*) PB.
Lady of Valor. Tina St. John. 2000. mass mkt. 6.50 (*0-449-00424-4*) Ballantine Pub Grp.
Lady of Vergi. Ed. & Tr. by Leigh A. Arrathoon. 105p. 1984. pap. 7.95 (*0-89304-299-4*) Solaris Pr.
Lady of Vergi. Ed. by Leigh A. Arrathoon. LC 84-17574.Tr. of Fr. & Eng. xxiv, 105p. 1984. 15.00 (*0-89304-298-6*, CCC170); pap. 7.95 (*0-685-44678-6*) Cross-Cultrl NY.
Lady of Winter. Emma F. Merritt. 384p. (Orig.). 1996. mass mkt. 5.99 (*0-380-77985-4*, Avon Bks) Morrow Avon.
***Lady on My Left.** Catherine Cookson. 2000. mass mkt. 17.95 (*0-552-14569-6*, Pub. by Transworld Publishers Ltd) Trafalgar.
Lady on the Move for the Lord. Deborah Thornton. (Illus.). 260p. 1995. pap. 9.98 incl. audio (*0-9636638-3-6*) Inspirat Prayer.
Lady or the Tiger. Frank R. Stockton. (Classic Short Stories on Tape Ser.). (J). (gr. 6-10). 1988. ring bd. 38.00 (*1-878298-22-4*) Balance Pub.
Lady or the Tiger? Frank R. Stockton. (J). 1999. 7.85 (*0-606-12387-3*) Turtleback.
Lady or the Tiger. Frank R. Stockton. (Illus.). (J). (gr. 1-8). reprint ed. pap. 4.95 (*0-934254-11-7*) Claymont Comm.
Lady or the Tiger: And Other Logic Puzzles. Raymond Smullyan. 226p. 1992. pap. 12.00 (*0-8129-2117-8*, Times Bks) Crown Pub Group.
Lady or the Tiger & Other Short Stories. Frank Stockton. lib. bdg. 18.95 (*0-8488-2115-7*) Amereon Ltd.
Lady or the Tiger & Other Short Stories. Frank R. Stockton. 1992. pap. 2.50 (*0-8125-1956-6*, Pub. by Tor Bks) St Martin.
Lady Oracle. Margaret Atwood. 1984. pap. 4.50 (*0-7704-2179-2*) Bantam.
Lady Oracle. Margaret Atwood. 352p. 1984. mass mkt. 8.99 (*0-7704-2299-3*) Bantam.
Lady Oracle. Margaret Atwood. LC 95-36576. 352p. 1995. pap. 10.95 (*0-553-37781-7*) Bantam.
***Lady Oracle.** Margaret Atwood. LC 97-48403. 368p. 1998. pap. 12.95 (*0-385-49108-5*) Doubleday.
Lady Orpheus. Margareta Waterman. (Illus.). 74p. 1993. pap. 9.00 (*1-878888-11-0*) Nine Muses Books.
Lady Persuaders. Helen Woodward. (Illus.). 1960. 10.95 (*0-8392-1058-2*) Astor-Honor.
Lady Pinkerton Gets Her Man. Jerrie Hurd. 1997. per. 6.50 (*0-671-51911-5*) S&S Trade.
Lady Poems. rev. ed. Terry Stokes. 1977. reprint ed. pap. 2.00 (*0-916696-02-2*) Cross Country.
Lady Poets. (Poets Ser.). 146p. 1993. 5.95 (*0-7117-0399-X*, Pub. by JARR UK) Seven Hills Bk.
***Lady Polly.** large type ed. Nicola Cornick. 320p. 2000. 25.99 (*0-263-16325-3*, Pub. by Mills & Boon) Ulverscroft.
Lady Preacher: Can a Submissive Wife & Mother Be an Ordained Minister. Helen Correll. (Illus.). 328p. (Orig.). 1995. pap. 12.95 (*0-9636177-8-8*) Rhymeo Ink.
Lady President. unabridged ed. Xavier J. Carbajal. Ed. by Sherry L. Jodway. LC 97-92604. 340p. 1997. 24.95 (*0-9654507-0-8*) New Future Pub.
Lady, Put a Man in the Kitchen. Joseph Kemph. LC 87-90975. (Illus.). (Orig.). 1987. pap. 12.95 (*0-9619089-0-4*) J Kemph.
Lady Rachel Russell: One of the Best of Women. Lois G. Schwoerer. LC 87-45478. 320p. 1988. text 52.00 (*0-8018-3515-1*) Johns Hopkins.
Lady Rakehell. 1991. pap. 4.50 (*0-8216-5093-9*, Univ Books) Carol Pub Group.
Lady Rancher. Gertrude M. Roger. (Illus.). 182p. 1979. pap. 12.95 (*0-88839-099-8*) Hancock House.
Lady Reckless. Leslie LaFoy. 320p. 1998. mass mkt. 5.50 (*0-553-57747-6*) Bantam.
Lady Rogue. Carole Nelson Douglas. 416p. (Orig.). 1993. mass mkt. 4.99 (*0-8125-2265-6*) Tor Bks.
Lady Rogue. Suzanne Enoch. 384p. (Orig.). 1997. mass mkt. 5.99 (*0-380-78812-8*, Avon Bks) Morrow Avon.
Lady Rose. Stephen Cosgrove. (Serendipity Bks.). (Illus.). 32p. (Orig.). (J). (ps-3). 1996. pap. 4.99 (*0-8431-3921-8*, Price Stern) Peng Put Young Read.
Lady Rose's Daughter. Humphry Ward. 489p. 1977. reprint ed. lib. bdg. 20.10 (*0-89966-195-5*) Buccaneer Bks.
Lady Sarah's Charade. Nancy Richard-Akers. 1992. mass mkt. 3.99 (*0-380-76531-4*, Avon Bks) Morrow Avon.
***Lady Sarah's Son.** Gayle Wilson. (Historical Ser.: No. 483). 1999. per. 4.99 (*0-373-29083-7*, 1-29083-2) Harlequin Bks.
Lady Says No. Rita C. Estrada. (Temptation Ser.: No. 349). 1991. per. 2.95 (*0-373-25449-0*) Harlequin Bks.
Lady Scandal. Marcy Stewart. 256p. 1998. pap. 4.99 (*0-8217-5955-8*) Kensgtn Pub Corp.
***Lady Serena's Surrender.** Jeanne Savery. (Zebra Regency Romance Ser.). 2000. mass mkt. 4.99 (*0-8217-6607-4*, Zebra Kensgtn) Kensgtn Pub Corp.
***Lady Singleton.** Thomas Medwin. LC 99-85755. 2000. write for info. (*0-8201-1529-0*) Schol Facsimiles.
Lady Sings the Blues. 68p. 1985. pap. 10.95 (*0-7935-2445-8*, 00357202) H Leonard.
Lady Sings the Blues. Billie Holiday & William Dufty. 208p. 1984. pap. 12.95 (*0-14-006762-0*, Penguin Bks) Viking Penguin.
Lady Slings the Booze. Spider Robinson. 272p. 1993. mass mkt. 5.99 (*0-441-46929-9*) Ace Bks.
***Lady Slipper.** Paperblank Book Company Staff. (Wildflowers Ser.). 160p. 1999. 14.95 (*1-55156-017-8*) Paperblank.
Lady Stephanie. Jeanne Savery. 1996. mass mkt. 4.50 (*0-8217-5341-X*, Zebra Kensgtn) Kensgtn Pub Corp.
Lady Susan. Jane Austen. (The Jane Austen Library). (C). 1984. text 37.50 (*0-485-10500-4*, Pub. by Athlone Pr) Humanities.
Lady Susan, the Watsons, Sanditon. Jane Austen. Ed. by Margaret Drabble. (English Library). 224p. 1975. pap. 7.95 (*0-14-043102-0*, Penguin Classics) Viking Penguin.
Lady Take Care. large type ed. George Goodchild. (Linford Mystery Library). 512p. 1996. pap. 16.99 (*0-7089-7873-8*, Linford) Ulverscroft.
***Lady Tasting Tea.** Salsburg. 2000. pap. text. write for info. (*0-7167-4106-7*, Pub. by W H Freeman) VHPS.
Lady Tennyson's Journal. Emily S. Tennyson. Ed. & Intro. by James O. Hoge. LC 80-21387. 415p. reprint ed. pap. 128.70 (*0-608-08544-8*, 206906700002) Bks Demand.
Lady, the Melody & the Word: The Inspirational Story of the First Lady of Gospel Music. Shirley Caesar. LC 97-51908. (Illus.). 256p. 1998. 16.99 (*0-7852-7155-4*, J Thoma Bks) Nelson.
Lady Thorn. Catherine Archer. (Historical Ser.). 1997. per. 4.99 (*0-373-28953-7*, 1-28953-7) Harlequin Bks.
Lady Valiant. Suzanne Robinson. 336p. 1993. mass mkt. 5.50 (*0-553-29575-6*) Bantam.
Lady Vanishes. Carol Lea Benjamin. LC 99-25682. (Rachel Alexander & Dash Mystery Ser.). 276p. 1999. 23.95 (*0-8027-3335-2*) Walker & Co.
Lady Vanishes: Subjectivity & Representation in Castiglione & Ariosto. Valeria Finucci. LC 91-44808. 344p. (C). 1992. 39.50 (*0-8047-2045-2*) Stanford U Pr.
Lady Velvet. Claudette Williams. 288p. 1994. mass mkt. 3.99 (*0-8217-4635-9*, Zebra Kensgtn) Kensgtn Pub Corp.
Lady Vixen. Shirlee Busbee. 544p. 1980. mass mkt. 5.50 (*0-380-75382-0*, Avon Bks) Morrow Avon.
Lady Whilton's Wedding. Barbara Metzger. 1995. mass mkt. 4.50 (*0-449-22351-5*, Crest) Fawcett.
Lady Who Drove Me to the Airport. limited ed. Diane Wakoski. (Metacom Limited Edition Ser.: No. 6). 16p. 1982. 25.00 (*0-911381-05-8*) Metacom Pr.
Lady Who Knows the Game: A Woman's Guide to Watching, Understanding & Talking Football. rev. ed. Rhonda V. Smith. (Illus.). 204p. 1986. reprint ed. pap. 9.95 (*0-934507-13-9*) Manchester Pr.
Lady Who Liked Clean Restrooms: The Chronicle of One of the Strangest Stories Ever. J. P. Donleavy. 128p. 1998. pap. 9.95 (*0-312-18734-3*) St Martin.
Lady Who Loved Animals. Michael Twinn & Pam Adams. LC 90-46603. (Illus.). 32p. (J). (ps-2). 1981. 7.99 (*0-85953-121-X*, Pub. by Childs Play) Random House.
Lady Who Never Was. large type ed. Peter Chambers. (Linford Mystery Large Print Ser.). 1995. pap. 16.99 (*0-7089-7809-6*, Linford) Ulverscroft.
Lady Who Put Salt in Her Coffee. Lucretia Hale. (Illus.). 28p. (J). (ps-3). 1989. 13.95 (*0-15-243475-5*) Harcourt.
Lady Who Sold Furniture. John Metcalf. 150p. (C). 1970. 20.00 (*0-920802-09-5*, Pub. by ECW) Genl Dist Srvs.
Lady Who Tamed Pegasus: Story of Pancho Barnes. Grover T. Tate. (Illus.). 140p. 1984. pap. 9.95 (*0-89288-092-9*) Maverick.
Lady Willpower. Pepper Adams. (Romance Ser.). 1994. per. 2.75 (*0-373-08983-X*, 5-08983-4) Silhouette.
***Lady Windemere's Fan, Set.** unabridged ed. Oscar Wilde. 1999. 19.95 incl. audio (*1-55685-572-9*) Audio Bk Con.
Lady Windermere's Fan see Selected Plays
Lady Windermere's Fan. Ian Small. (C). pap. text. write for info. (*0-393-90090-8*) Norton.
Lady Windermere's Fan. Oscar Wilde. LC 97-47146. (Thrift Editions Ser.). 52p. 1998. pap. 1.00 (*0-486-40078-6*) Dover.
Lady Windermere's Fan. Oscar Wilde. Ed. by Ian Small. (New Mermaid Ser.). (C). 1984. pap. text 9.75 (*0-393-90048-7*) Norton.
Lady Windermere's Fan. Oscar Wilde. Ed. & Intro. by William-Alan Landes. LC 94-39029. 56p. 1995. pap. 7.00 (*0-88734-278-7*) Players Pr.
Lady Windermere's Fan, The Importance of Being Earnest see Works of Oscar Wilde

L

Lady Wisdom, Jesus & the Sages: Metaphor & Social Context in Matthew's Gospel. Celia M. Deutsch. LC 96-32904. 240p. (Orig.). 1996. pap. 20.00 (*1-56338-163-X*) TPI PA.

Lady with a Cool Eye. large type ed. Gwen Moffat. (Linford Mystery Large Print Ser.). 384p. 1998. pap. 17.99 (*0-7089-5290-9*, Linford) Ulverscroft.

Lady with a Hump see Hewitt Early Readers: Level II

Lady with a Laptop. D. M. Thomas. LC 97-4445. 256p. 1997. pap. 10.95 (*0-7867-0425-X*) Carroll & Graf.

Lady with a Mead Cup: Ritual, Prophecy & Lordship in the European Warband from La Tene to the Viking Age. Michael Enright. LC 96-121648. 256p. 1995. 45.00 (*1-85182-188-0*, Pub. by Four Cts Pr) Intl Spec Bk.

***Lady with a Past.** Ryanne Corey. (Desire Ser.: Vol. 1319). 2000. mass mkt. 3.99 (*0-373-76319-0*, 1-76319-2) Harlequin Bks.

Lady with Chains. Roch Carrier. Tr. by Sheila Fischman from FRE. 151p. 1991. reprint ed. pap. 12.95 (*0-88784-511-8*, Pub. by Hse of Anansi Pr) Genl Dist Srvs.

Lady with Lapdog & Other Stories. Anton Chekhov. Tr. by David Magarshack. (Classics Ser.). 288p. (Orig.). 1964. pap. 13.99 (*0-14-044143-3*, Penguin Classics) Viking Penguin.

Lady with the Alligator Purse. Ernest Finney. LC 92-32125. 288p. 1992. 19.00 (*0-944439-46-2*) Clark City Pr.

Lady with the Alligator Purse. Nadine B. Westcott. (J). 1988. 10.15 (*0-606-04727-1*, Pub. by Turtleback) Demco.

Lady with the Alligator Purse. Nadine Bernard Westcott. LC 87-21368. (Illus.). 28p. (J). (ps-3). 1990. pap. 4.95 (*0-316-93136-5*) Little.

Lady with the Alligator Purse, 1. Nadine Bernard Wescott. (Illus.). 24p. (J). (ps). 1998. 5.95 (*0-316-93074-1*) Little.

Lady with the Dog & Other Stories. Anton Chekhov. Tr. by Constance Garnett from RUS. LC 84-6121. (Tales of Anton Chekhov Ser.: Vol. 3). 300p. 1984. reprint ed. pap. 13.00 (*0-88001-050-9*) HarpC.

Lady with the Dog & Other Stories: Russian Reader with Explanatory Notes & Cassette. Anton Chekhov. 252p. 1991. pap. text 12.95 (*0-8285-4900-1*) Firebird NY.

Lady with the Hat. Uri Orlev. Tr. by Hillel Halkin. 192p. (YA). (gr. 7). 1995. 14.95 (*0-395-69957-6*) HM.

Lady with the Hat. Uri Orlev. 1997. 10.09 (*0-606-13562-6*, Pub. by Turtleback) Demco.

Lady with the Pen. Elise Waerenskjold. Ed. by Franklyn D. Scott. LC 78-15856. (Scandinavians in America Ser.). (Illus.). xvii, 183p. 1979. reprint ed. lib. bdg. 21.95 (*0-405-11663-2*) Arno Press.

Lady with the Ship on Her Head. Deborah N. Lattimore. LC 89-11218. (Illus.). 32p. (J). (ps-3). 1990. 14.95 (*0-15-243525-5*) Harcourt.

Lady with the Ship on Her Head. Deborah N. Lattimore. LC 89-11218. (Illus.). 32p. (J). (ps-3). 1992. pap. 6.00 (*0-15-243526-3*) Harcourt.

Lady with the Ship on Her Head. Deborah Nourse Lattimore. (Reading Rainbow Bks.). 1990. 11.20 (*0-606-01029-7*, Pub. by Turtleback) Demco.

Lady Without a Latitude. Susan Phelps. LC 97-72391. 204p. (Orig.). 1997. pap. 14.95 (*0-9651171-3-8*, Lady Line) Ashton Prods.

When You Lack Latitude . . . Susan Phelps. LC 96-79355. 160p. 1998. pap. write for info. (*0-9651171-4-6*) Ashton Prods.

Lady Wore Spurs. Carol Grace. (Silhouette Romance Ser.). 1994. per. 2.75 (*0-373-19010-7*, 5-19010-3) Harlequin Bks.

Lady Wore Spurs. Carol Grace. 1997. per. 42.00 (*0-373-91010-X*) Silhouette.

Lady X Lust's Captive. Giovani Degli Esposti. pap. 9.95 (*1-56097-337-4*, Pub. by Fantagraph Bks) Seven Hills Bk.

Lady, You're Killing Me. large type ed. Peter Chambers. (Linford Mystery Library). 304p. 1994. pap. 16.99 (*0-7089-7568-2*) Ulverscroft.

Ladybird. Grace Livingston Hill. (Grace Livingston Hill Ser.: Vol. 55). 1993. pap. 5.99 (*0-8423-2081-4*) Tyndale Hse.

***Ladybird.** large type ed. Grace Livingston Hill. LC 99-28412. 1999. pap. 26.95 (*0-7862-2090-2*) Mac Lib Ref.

Ladybird. Grace Livingston Hill. 294p. 1975. reprint ed. lib. bdg. 23.95 (*0-89190-013-6*) Amereon Ltd.

Ladybird Baby Book. Illus. by Sarah Ross. 28p. 1989. pap. 3.95 (*0-7214-5198-5*, S808-1, Ladybrd) Penguin Putnam.

Ladybird Bible Storybook see Bible Storybook

Ladybird Castles Book & Stamp Kit. Ladybird Staff. (J). (gr. 2-6). 1997. 7.99 (*0-614-29249-2*, Ladybrd) Penguin Putnam.

Ladybird Guide to Presidents of the United States. (J). (gr. 2-7). 1997. pap. 5.99 (*0-614-28832-0*, Ladybrd) Penguin Putnam.

Ladybird Guide to the Centennial Olympic Games: Atlanta '96. (J). (gr. 2-7). 1996. 4.99 (*0-614-15825-7*, Ladybrd) Penguin Putnam.

Ladybird, Ladybird: A Story of Private Enterprise. E. W. Pasold. 1977. 36.00 (*0-7855-2817-2*, Pub. by Textile Inst) St Mut.

***Ladybird Moves Home.** Fowler. (J). 2000. 10.95 (*0-385-40382-8*, Pub. by Transworld Publishers Ltd) Trafalgar.

Ladybird Mystery. Eunice A. Pennington. 1974. 4.50 (*0-685-42423-5*); pap. 2.50 (*0-685-42424-3*) Pennington.

Ladybird Nursery Rhymes Gift Book. (Large Gift Bk.). 96p. (J). 11.95 (*0-614-02679-2*, Ladybrd) Penguin Putnam.

Ladybird Sharks Book & Stamp Kit. Ladybird Staff. (J). (gr. 2-6). 1997. 7.99 (*0-614-29250-6*, Ladybrd) Penguin Putnam.

Ladybird Tables & Other Facts & Figures. Ladybird Series. (Basic Math Ser.: No. 678-5). (Illus.). (gr. 1-3). pap. 3.50 (*0-7214-0663-7*, Ladybrd) Penguin Putnam.

Ladybirds II: The Continuing Story of American Women in Aviation. Henry M. Holden & Lori Griffith. (Illus.). 333p. 1993. 23.95 (*1-879630-12-5*) Black Hawk Pub.

Ladybirds. Illustrated Key to the Coccinellidae of Europe: Illustrated Key to the Coccinellidae of Europe. B. Klausnitzer. (ENG & GER., Illus.). 300p. 1999. 89.00 (*3-8236-1230-1*, Pub. by Margraf Verlag); pap. 60.00 (*3-8236-1231-X*, Pub. by Margraf Verlag) Balogh.

Ladybucks: Why Certain Women Turn Work into Wealth. Valerie Bohigian. 246p. (Orig.). 1987. 24.95 (*0-396-08852-X*) Valian Assocs.

Ladybug. Sabrina Crewe. LC 96-4830. (Life Cycles Bks.). (Illus.). 32p. (J). (gr. 2-5). 1997. lib. bdg. 21.40 (*0-8172-4366-6*) Raintree Steck-V.

Ladybug. Lynda P. Halley. LC 98-129942. (Beasty Bks.). (Illus.). 12p. (J). (ps-k). 1997. 14.95 (*0-7613-0246-8*) Millbrook Pr.

***Ladybug.** Karen Hartley & Chris Marco. LC 98-11616. (Bug Bks.). (Illus.). 32p. (J). (gr. 1-3). 1998. 19.92 (*1-57572-662-9*) Heinemann Lib.

Ladybug. Susan B. Morgan. 1989. 4.95 (*0-945603-01-0*) Dinnerman Bks.

Ladybug. Illus. by Lorella Rizzatti. (Portable Pets Ser.). 12p. (J). 1998. bds. 5.95 (*0-8109-5628-4*, Pub. by Abrams) Time Warner.

Ladybug. Catharine D. Scherer. LC 83-70738. (Illus.). 10p. (J). (gr. 6-11). 1983. 2.95 (*0-9611024-0-3*) Drum Assocs.

Ladybug. Maggie R. Stone. 112p. (Orig.). 1992. pap. 5.95 (*0-9627059-3-4*) M R Stone Minst.

Ladybug. Barrie Watts. (Stopwatch Ser.). (Illus.). 25p. (J). (gr. k-4). 1991. pap. 3.95 (*0-382-09960-5*); lib. bdg. 9.95 (*0-382-09437-9*, Silver Pr NJ) Silver Burdett Pr.

Ladybug, Reading Level 3-4. Therese Pouyanne. (World Animal Library). (Illus.). 28p. (J). (gr. 2-5). 1983. 12.50 (*0-685-58821-1*) Rourke Corp.

Ladybug, Reading Level 3-4. Therese Pouyanne. (World Animal Library). (Illus.). 28p. (J). (gr. 2-5). 1983. lib. bdg. 18.60 (*0-86592-863-0*) Rourke Enter.

Ladybug & Other Insects. Pascale De Bourgoing. LC 91-15294. (First Discovery Book). (Illus.). 24p. (J). (ps-3). 1991. 11.95 (*0-590-45235-5*, Cartwheel) Scholastic Inc.

Ladybug at Orchard Avenue. Kathleen W. Zoehfeld. LC 95-45892. (Smithsonian's Backyard Ser.). (Illus.). 32p. (J). (ps-2). 1996. 15.95 incl. audio (*1-56899-257-2*); 19.95 incl. audio (*1-56899-261-0*, BC5009) Soundprints.

Ladybug at Orchard Avenue, Incl. large toy. Kathleen W. Zoehfeld. LC 95-45892. (Smithsonian's Backyard Ser.). (Illus.). 32p. (J). (ps-2). 1996. 32.95 (*1-56899-259-9*) Soundprints.

Ladybug at Orchard Avenue, Incl. Sm. & Lg. Plush Toy. Kathleen W. Zoehfeld. LC 95-45892. (Smithsonian's Backyard Ser.). (Illus.). 32p. (J). (ps-2). 1996. 43.95 incl. audio (*1-56899-661-6*) Soundprints.

Ladybug at Orchard Avenue, Micro bk. Kathleen W. Zoehfeld. LC 95-45892. (Illus.). 32p. (J). (ps-2). 1996. 4.95 (*1-56899-258-0*) Soundprints.

Ladybug at Orchard Avenue, Micro bk., incl. small toy. Kathleen W. Zoehfeld. LC 95-45892. (Smithsonian's Backyard Ser.). (Illus.). 32p. (J). (ps-2). 1996. 12.95 (*1-56899-260-2*) Soundprints.

Ladybug Boogie. Martha Mier. 4p. 1994. pap. 2.50 (*0-7390-0761-0*, 5498) Alfred Pub.

Ladybug, Ladybug. Ruth Brown. LC 88-14852. (Illus.). 32p. (J). (ps-1). 1992. pap. 5.99 (*0-14-054543-3*, PuffinBks) Peng Put Young Read.

Ladybug, Ladybug. Ruth Brown. (Picture Puffin Ser.). (Illus.). (J). 1992. 10.19 (*0-606-01712-7*, Pub. by Turtleback) Demco.

Ladybug, Ladybug. Annalisa Suid. (Super-Duper Science Ser.). (Illus.). 80p. (Orig.). (J). (ps-k). 1996. pap. 9.95 (*1-878279-86-6*, MM2015) Monday Morning Bks.

Ladybug, Ladybug. Susanna H. McShea. (Hometown Heroes Mystery Ser.). 352p. 1995. reprint ed. mass mkt. 5.50 (*0-380-71981-9*, Avon Bks) Morrow Avon.

Ladybug on the Move. Richard Fowler. LC 92-19740. (Illus.). 20p. (J). (ps-1). 1993. 13.00 (*0-15-200475-0*, Gulliver Bks) Harcourt.

Ladybug Porches & Seagulls in the Sky: Poems of Childhood. Marea Adessa. LC 89-81087. (Illus.). 70p. (Orig.). 1989. pap. 9.95 (*0-9624708-0-5*) Chesterworks Babcock.

Ladybug/Crab/Turtle/Frog. Lorella Rizzatti. (Portable Pets Ser.). (J). 1998. pap. 95.20 (*0-8109-5099-5*) Abrams.

***Ladybugology.** Michael Elsohn Ross. (Backyard Buddies Ser.). (Illus.). 48p. (J). (gr. 1-4). 2000. pap. 6.95 (*1-57505-435-3*, First Ave Edns) Lerner Pub.

Ladybugology. Michael Elsohn Ross. LC 96-37441. (Illus.). (J). 1997. 19.93 (*1-57505-051-X*, Carolrhoda) Lerner Pub.

***Ladybugs.** (Illus.). 144p. (J). 1999. 9.95 (*0-7683-3645-7*) CEDCO Pub.

Ladybugs. Cheryl Coughlan. 1999. 13.25 (*0-516-21830-1*) Capstone Pr.

Ladybugs. Sylvia A. Johnson. LC 83-18777. (Lerner Natural Science Bks.). (Illus.). 48p. (J). (gr. 4 up). 1983. lib. bdg. 22.60 (*0-8225-1481-8*, Lerner Publctns) Lerner Pub.

Ladybugs. Cheryl Peterson. LC 98-43878. (Insects Ser.). 1999. 13.25 (*0-7368-0242-8*) Capstone Pr.

Ladybugs. Dona H. Rice. (Thematic Units Ser.). 80p. (J). (gr. 1-3). 1997. pap. 9.95 (*1-57690-370-2*) Tchr Create Mat.

Ladybugs. James P. Rowan. (Insects Discovery Library). 24p. (J). (gr. k-4). 1991. lib. bdg. 10.95 (*0-86593-291-3*) Rourke Corp.

Ladybugs. rev. ed. Jean C. Echols. Ed. by Lincoln Bergman & Carl Babcock. (Great Explorations in Math & Science Ser.). (Illus.). 96p. (J). (ps-1). 1999. pap., teacher ed. 13.50 (*0-924886-19-6*, GEMS) Lawrence Science.

Ladybugs & Beetles see Looking at Minibeasts

***Ladybugs & Other Beetles.** Steven Otfinoski & World Book, Inc. Staff. LC 00-21637. (Illus.). 64p. (J). (gr. 1-4). 2000. write for info. (*0-7166-1207-0*) World Bk.

Ladybug's Ball. Heather Lowenberg. LC 97-10830. (J). 1998. 7.99 (*0-679-88539-0*, Pub. by Random Bks Yng Read) Random.

Ladybug's Birthday. Steve Metzger. LC 97-48303. (Side-by-Side Ser.). (Illus.). (J). 1997. write for info. (*0-590-10968-5*); pap. 3.50 (*0-590-02599-6*) Scholastic Inc.

Ladybugs for Loretta. Lois Wickstrom. (Illus.). (J). (gr. k-6). 1978. pap. 2.00 (*0-916176-04-5*) Gripper Prods.

Ladybug's Life. John Himmelman. LC 97-9129. (Nature Upclose Ser.). 32p. (J). (ps-4). 1998. 24.00 (*0-516-20819-5*) Childrens.

Ladybug's Life. John Himmelman. Ed. by Melissa Stewart. (Nature Upclose Ser.). (Illus.). 32p. (J). 1998. pap. 6.95 (*0-516-26353-6*) Childrens.

Ladybugs, True Beetles. Arthur Morton. (Illus.). (J). (gr. k-3). 1994. 12.50 (*1-57842-050-4*) Delmas Creat.

Ladyfingers & Nun's Tummies:From Spare Ribs to Humble Pie: A Lighthearted Look at How Foods Got Their Names. Martha Barnette. (Illus.). 213p. 1998. pap. 12.00 (*0-375-70298-9*) Vin Bks.

Ladykiller. Sheryl Lynn Postman. (Intrigue Ser.). 1995. per. 2.99 (*0-373-22306-4*, 1-22306-4) Harlequin Bks.

Ladykillers. Jonathan Goodman. (Illus.). 192p. 1991. 15.95 (*0-8065-1283-0*, Citadel Pr); pap. 8.95 (*0-8065-1290-3*, Citadel Pr) Carol Pub Group.

Ladylight. Victoria Pade. 368p. (Orig.). 1987. pap. 3.95 (*0-380-75320-0*, Avon Bks) Morrow Avon.

Ladylord. Sasha Miller. 1997. mass mkt. 5.99 (*0-8125-4949-X*, Pub. by Tor Bks) St Martin.

Lady's Choice. Jayne Ann Krentz. 256p. 1997. mass mkt. 6.99 (*1-55166-270-1*, 0-66270-0, Mira Bks) Harlequin Bks.

Lady's Choice. Karen Lockwood. 288p. 1996. mass mkt. 5.99 (*0-515-11959-8*, Jove) Berkley Pub.

Lady's Choice: Ethel Waxham. Ed. by Barbara Love & Frances L. Froidevaux. 394p. 1997. pap. 16.95 (*0-8263-1786-3*) U of NM Pr.

Lady's Country Companion. Jane Louden. (Illus.). 448p. 1998. reprint ed. pap. 75.00 (*0-948285-02-8*) St Mut.

Lady's Day Out in Fredericksburg. Paula Ramsey. 200p. 1992. write for info. (*0-9633537-0-5*) Ladys Day Out.

Lady's Economical Assistant: or The Art of Cutting Out & making the Most Useful Articles of Wearing Apparel. Kathleen Kannik. LC 99-193438. (Illus.). 80p. (Orig.). 1998. pap. 20.00 (*0-9640161-3-3*) Kanniks Korner.

Lady's Experiences in the Wild West in 1883. Rose Pender. LC 78-17690. xiii, 136p. 1978. reprint ed. pap. 7.95 (*0-8032-8711-9*, Bison Books) U of Nebr Pr.

Lady's Girl. Eve Bunting. (Eve Bunting Collection). (Illus.). 40p. (J). (gr. 3-8). 1992. lib. bdg. 12.79 (*0-89565-777-5*) Childs World.

Lady's Guide to Plain Sewing: By a Lady. Kathleen Kannik. 32p. 1993. pap. 10.00 (*0-9640161-0-9*) Kanniks Korner.

Lady's Guide to Plain Sewing Bk. II: By a Lady. Kathleen Kannik. LC 98-228019. (Illus.). 32p. 1997. pap. 10.00 (*0-9640161-2-5*) Kanniks Korner.

Lady's Hand. Bobbi Smith. 400p. (Orig.). 1996. mass mkt. 5.99 (*0-8439-4116-2*) Dorchester Pub Co.

***Lady's Hand.** Bobbi Smith. 400p. (Orig.). 1999. reprint ed. mass mkt. 5.99 (*0-8439-4598-2*, Leisure Bks) Dorchester Pub Co.

Lady's Kitchen see Matbakh Sayidata

Lady's Lesson. Jeanne Savery. 256p. 1997. mass mkt. 4.99 (*0-8217-5754-7*, Zebra Kensgtn) Kensgtn Pub Corp.

Lady's Life in the Rocky Mountains. Isabella Lucy Bird. (Cloth Bound Pocket Ser.). 354p. 1999. 7.95 (*3-8290-0881-3*, 520653) Konemann.

Lady's Life in the Rocky Mountains. Isabella Lucy Bird. LC 60-8748. (Western Frontier Library: No. 14). (Illus.). 1960. reprint ed. pap. 7.95 (*0-8061-1328-6*) U of Okla Pr.

Lady's Life in the Rocky Mountains. Isabella L. Bishop. (American Biography Ser.). 252p. 1991. reprint ed. lib. bdg. 69.00 (*0-7812-8021-4*) Rprt Serv.

Lady's Man. Suzanne Simmons. 1999. mass mkt. 5.99 (*0-312-96825-6*) St Martin.

Lady's Man: Those Marrying McBrides! Linda Turner. (Intimate Moments Ser.: No. 931). 1999. per. 4.25 (*0-373-07931-1*, 1-07931-8) Silhouette.

Lady's Men. large type ed. Mario Martinez. (Large Print Ser.). (Illus.). 384p. 1996. 27.99 (*0-7089-3555-9*) Ulverscroft.

Lady's Men: The Story of World War II's Mystery Bomber & Her Crew. Mario Martinez. (Illus.). 208p. 1995. 29.95 (*1-55750-511-X*) Naval Inst Pr.

Lady's Men: The Story of World War II's Mystery Bomber & Her Crew. Mario Martinez. 1999. pap. 15.95 (*1-55750-553-5*) Naval Inst Pr.

***Lady's Monthly Museum, 1798-1806: An Annotated Index of Signatures & Ascriptions.** E. W. Pitcher. LC 99-55512. (Studies in British & American Magazines : Vol. 2). 356p. 2000. 99.95 (*0-7734-7836-1*) E Mellen.

Lady's Mummy. Bess Willingham. 288p. 1997. mass mkt. 4.99 (*0-8217-5545-5*, Zebra Kensgtn) Kensgtn Pub Corp.

Lady's Not for Burning. rev. ed. Christopher Fry. 1994. pap. 5.25 (*0-8222-1431-8*) Dramatists Play.

Lady's Proposal. Jeanne Savery. 256p. 1998. pap. 4.99 (*0-8217-5992-2*) Kensgtn Pub Corp.

Lady's Ride Across Spanish Honduras. fac. ed. Mary Soltera. LC 64-66325. (Latin American Gateway Ser.). (Illus.). 377p. 1964. reprint ed. pap. 116.90 (*0-608-04513-6*, 206525800001) Bks Demand.

Lady's Sissy Maid. G. Christiano Fitzmaurice. 183p. 1990. 45.00 (*0-9629204-2-8*); pap. 25.00 (*0-9629204-0-1*) Constance Ent.

Ladys Tutor, 1. Robin Schone. 384p. 1999. mass mkt. 4.99 (*0-8217-6288-5*) Kensgtn Pub Corp.

***Lady's Tutor.** Robin Schone. (Splendor Historical Romances Ser.). 2000. mass mkt. 5.99 (*0-8217-6982-0*, Zebra Kensgtn) Kensgtn Pub Corp.

***Lady's Tutor.** Robin Schone. 2000. pap. 12.00 (*1-57566-796-7*, Knsington) Kensgtn Pub Corp.

***Lady's Tutor.** Robin Schone. LC 00-21435. 2000. write for info. (*0-7862-2497-5*) Five Star.

***Lady's Tutor.** large type ed. Robin Schone. LC 00-24173. 2000. pap. 22.95 (*1-56895-873-0*) Wheeler Pub.

Lady's Wager. Mary Spencer. 384p. 1998. mass mkt. 5.99 (*0-440-22492-6*) Dell.

Ladyship. Elisabeth Kidd. 192p. 1989. mass mkt. 3.95 (*0-446-35456-2*, Pub. by Warner Bks) Little.

***Ladysmith.** Lewis Childs. 1998. pap. text 16.95 (*0-85052-611-6*, Pub. by Leo Cooper) Trans-Atl Phila.

***Ladysmith: A Novel.** Giles Foden. LC 99-40731. 304p. 2000. 25.00 (*0-375-40920-3*) Knopf.

Ladysmith: The Siege. Lewis Childs. 1999. pap. 16.95 (*0-85052-653-1*, Pub. by Leo Cooper) Combined Pub.

LadyTown. Stephen Wagshel. 4p. (Orig.). 1991. pap. 1.25 (*1-879629-80-1*) Galaxy Pub CO.

LadyTown. Stephen Wagshel. 4p. (Orig.). 1991. pap. 1.00 (*1-879629-01-1*) Galaxy Pub CO.

Laelias of Mexico. Federico Halbinger & Miguel Soto. (Orquidea (Mex.) Ser.: Vol. 15). (Illus.). 160p. 1997. 39.95 (*968-7889-03-9*) Balogh.

Laelius (Sive) De Amicitia Dialogus. Marcus Tullius Cicero. xii, 58p. 1965. reprint ed. 110.00 (*0-318-71095-1*); reprint ed. pap. 51.00 (*0-318-71096-X*) G Olms Pubs.

Laertion Gamble. Robert Sheckley. (Star Trek: Deep Space Nine Ser.: No. 12). 1995. mass mkt. 5.99 (*0-671-88690-8*) PB.

***Laetitia: Gorgeous, Sexy, Up Close & Personal.** Laetitia Casta. (Illus.). 128p. 1999. 30.00 (*0-670-88819-2*) Viking Penguin.

Laetrile Control for Cancer. Glenn D. Kittler. 1963. 14.00 (*0-8392-1059-0*) Astor-Honor.

LAF Docket of Significant Cases & Projects: January 1, 1987-December 31, 1987. 119p. 1987. 15.00 (*0-685-29763-2*, 43,580) NCLS Inc.

***Lafayette.** JoAnn A. Grote. (Revolutionary War Leaders Ser.). 2000. 18.95 (*0-7910-5973-1*) Chelsea Hse.

***Lafayette.** JoAnn A. Grote. (Revolutionary War Leaders Ser.). (Illus.). 2000. pap. 8.95 (*0-7910-6131-0*) Chelsea Hse.

Lafayette: A Historical Perspective. Orpha Valentine. Ed. by Doug Woolfolk. (Illus.). 120p. 1980. 12.50 (*0-86518-014-8*) Moran Pub Corp.

Lafayette: A Pictorial History. Fern Martin & Paula Woods. (Indiana Pictorial History Ser.). (Illus.). 1994. reprint ed. write for info. (*0-943963-09-5*) G Bradley.

Lafayette & Harriet. 121p. 1988. 15.95 (*0-318-36147-7*); pap. 9.95 (*0-930061-25-X*) Interspace Bks.

Lafayette & the Close of the American Revolution. Louis R. Gottschalk. LC CT0275.L13G6. 472p. reprint ed. pap. 146.40 (*0-608-13369-8*, 202409500035) Bks Demand.

Lafayette & the Liberal Ideal, 1814-1824: Politics & Conspiracy in an Age of Reaction. Sylvia Neely. LC 90-25649. (Illus.). 368p. (C). 1991. 41.95 (*0-8093-1733-8*) S Ill U Pr.

Lafayette Clinic Studies on Schizophrenia. Ed. by Garfield Tourney & Jacques S. Gottlieb. LC 70-630344. (Lafayette Clinic Monographs in Psychiatry: No. 4). 533p. reprint ed. pap. 165.30 (*0-608-16507-7*, 202763900055) Bks Demand.

Lafayette College - Then & Now. Photos by Todd Buchanan. (Illus.). 112p. 1993. 39.95 (*1-56469-006-7*) Harmony Hse Pub.

Lafayette, Colorado: Treeless Plain to Thriving City. Arlee Lee. (Illus.). 382p. Date not set. reprint ed. text 60.00 (*0-88107-154-4*) Curtis Media.

Lafayette Comes to America. Louis R. Gottschalk. LC 35-15130. 198p. reprint ed. pap. 61.40 (*0-608-13373-6*, 202409300035) Bks Demand.

Lafayette County. William K. Walker. LC 82-84542. 1984. 15.00 (*0-87212-173-9*) Libra.

Lafayette County, Arkansas Census, 1860. Bobbie J. McLane. 66p. (Orig.). 1985. pap. 12.00 (*0-929604-35-0*) Arkansas Ancestors.

Lafayette County, Arkansas Marriage Records, 1828-1907. Bobbie J. McLane & Capitola Glazner. 266p. (Orig.). 1982. pap. 25.00 (*0-929604-33-4*) Arkansas Ancestors.

Lafayette Escadrille Pilot Biographies. Dennis Gordon. (Illus.). 271p. 1991. pap. 19.50 (*0-942258-01-0*) Gos Inc.

***Lafayette Flying Corps: American Volunteers in the French Air Service In Wwi.** Dennis Gordon. (Illus.). 500p. 2000. 59.95 (*0-7643-1108-5*) Schiffer.

Lafayette, Hero of Two Nations. Keith Brandt. LC 89-33981. (Illus.). 48p. (J). (gr. 4-6). 1997. pap. 3.95 (*0-8167-1772-9*) Troll Communs.

Lafayette, Hero of Two Nations. Keith Brandt. LC 89-33981. (Illus.). 48p. (J). (gr. 4-6). 1997. lib. bdg. 17.25 (*0-8167-1771-0*) Troll Communs.

Lafayette in America Day by Day. James B. Nolan. LC 72-1709. reprint ed. 38.50 (*0-404-52427-3*) AMS Pr.

Lafayette in the Age of the American Revolution, Selected Letters & Papers, 1776-1790, Vol. I: December 7th, 1776-March 30th, 1778. Le Marquis de Lafayette. Ed.

by Stanley J. Idzerda & Roger E. Smith. LC 76-50268. (Lafayette Papers). (Illus.). 535p. 1977. text 62.50 (*0-8014-1031-2*) Cornell U Pr.

Lafayette in the Age of the American Revolution, Selected Letters & Papers, 1776-1790, Vol. II: April 10th, 1778-March 20th, 1780. Le Marquis de Lafayette. Ed. by Stanley J. Idzerda et al. LC 76-50268. (Lafayette Papers). (Illus.). 520p. 1979. text 62.50 (*0-8014-1246-3*) Cornell U Pr.

Lafayette in the Age of the American Revolution, Selected Letters & Papers, 1776-1790, Vol. III: April 27th, 1780-March 29th, 1781. Le Marquis de Lafayette. Ed. by Stanley J. Idzerda et al. LC 76-50268. (Lafayette Papers). (Illus.). 577p. 1980. text 62.50 (*0-8014-1335-4*) Cornell U Pr.

Lafayette in the Age of the American Revolution, Selected Letters & Papers, 1776-1790, Vol. IV: April 1st, 1781-December 23rd, 1781. Le Marquis de Lafayette. Ed. by Stanley J. Idzerda et al. LC 76-50268. (Lafayette Papers). (Illus.). 600p. 1981. text 62.50 (*0-8014-1336-2*) Cornell U Pr.

Lafayette in the Age of the American Revolution, Selected Letters & Papers, 1776-1790, Vol. V: January 4th, 1782-December 29th, 1785. Le Marquis de Lafayette. Ed. by Stanley J. Idzerda & Robert R. Crout. LC 76-50268. (Lafayette Papers). (Illus.). 528p. 1983. text 62.50 (*0-8014-1576-4*) Cornell U Pr.

Lafayette in the French Revolution: From the October Days Through the Federation. Louis Gottschalk & Margaret Maddox. LC 69-12572. (C). 1973. 25.00 (*0-226-30547-3*) U Ch Pr.

Lafayette in Two Worlds: Public Cultures & Personal Identities in an Age of Revolution. Lloyd S. Kramer. LC 95-21113. (Illus.). 368p. 1996. 39.95 (*0-8078-2258-2*) U of NC Pr.

Lafayette in Two Worlds: Public Cultures & Personal Identities in an Age of Revolutions. Lloyd Kramer. LC 98-21113. (Illus.). 368p. 1999. pap. 19.95 (*0-8078-4818-2*) U of NC Pr.

Lafayette Joins the American Army. Louis R. Gottschalk. LC 37-38848. 380p. reprint ed. pap. 117.80 (*0-608-13370-1*, 202409400035) Bks Demand.

***Lafayette Life: Words & Images Since 1928.** Jane Donovan et al. (Illus.). 175p. 1999. 30.00 (*0-9671720-0-4*) Lafayette Home.

Lafayette, Louisiana. San Antonio Cartographers Staff. 1995. 2.95 (*0-671-56286-X*) Macmillan.

Lafayette, Rhode Island. George W. Gardiner. 267p. 1993. reprint ed. lib. bdg. 32.50 (*0-8328-3499-8*) Higginson Bk Co.

***Lafayette Square.** Albert J. Montesi. (Images of America Ser.). 1999. pap. 18.99 (*0-7385-0022-4*) Arcadia Publng.

Lafayette Square: An Urban Renaissance Timothy G. Conley. LC 74-21699. 116 p. 1974. write for info. (*0-9600796-1-0*) Lafayette Square Pr.

Lafayette's: Stories about Those Who Drank There & Those Who Worked There. Gordon Wilson. 64p. 1998. pap. 10.00 (*0-933292-23-6*) Arts End.

LaFayette's Encyclopedia of American Non Traditional Higher Education, 3 vols., Set. 3rd ed. American Council Staff et al. (Illus.). 498p. 1991. 80.00 (*0-685-30550-3*) ACUPAE.

Lafayette's Encyclopedic Dictionary of Higher Education Worldwide. Jean M. De LaFayette. Ed. by Aunele Naffah & Judith Crawford. (Comparative Lexicon of Postsecondary Education in 140 Countries Ser.). (Illus.). 160p. 1991. 30.00 (*0-939877-26-0*) ACUPAE.

Lafayette's Lexington, Kentucky. Thomas House & Lisa Carter. LC 98-86583. (Images of America Ser.). (Illus.). 128p. 1998. pap. 16.99 (*0-7524-0890-9*) Arcadia Publng.

***Lafcadio: El Leon Que Devolvio el Disparo.** Shel Silverstein. (SPA., Illus.). (J). (gr. 4-7). 1998. 11.00 (*84-264-3663-3*, Pub. by Editorial Lumen) Lectorum Pubns.

Lafcadio Hearn: A Catalogue of the Collection at the Howard-Tilton Memorial Library. Compiled by Ann S. Gwyn. 1977. pap. 5.00 (*0-9603212-0-9*) Tulane Univ.

Lafcadio Hearn & the Vision of Japan. Carl Dawson. LC 91-44785. (Parallax Ser.). (Illus.). 213p. 1992. reprint ed. pap. 66.10 (*0-608-06705-9*, 206690200009) Bks Demand.

Lafcadio Hearn's Creole Cookbook. Lafcadio Hearn. LC 89-26575. 288p. 1990. reprint ed. 19.95 (*0-88289-788-8*) Pelican.

Lafcadio Hearn's Japan: An Anthology of His Writings. Donald Richie. LC 96-60931. 1997. pap. text 16.95 (*0-8048-2096-1*) Tuttle Pubng.

Lafcadio, the Lion Who Shot Back. Shel Silverstein. LC 62-13320. (Illus.). 112p. (J). (gr. 2 up). 1963. 15.95 (*0-06-025675-3*); lib. bdg. 15.89 (*0-06-025676-1*) HarpC Child Bks.

Lafcadio's Adventures. Andre Gide. Tr. by Dorothy Bussy from FRE. LC 79-24000. 1980. reprint ed. lib. bdg. 18.00 (*0-8376-0452-4*) Bentley Pubs.

La/Femmes et les Femmes Daus l'Oeuvre de Saint Bernard see Women & St. Bernard of Clairvaux

Laffirmations: 1,001 Ways to Add Humor to Your Life & Work. Joel Goodman. (Illus.). 380p. (Orig.). 1995. pap. 8.95 (*1-55874-346-4*, 3464) Health Comm.

***Laffite's Lady: An Epic Adventure.** fac. ed. Susan Elliston. Ed. by Cindy Sosinski. LC 99-66919. 602p. 1999. 29.95 (*1-929925-00-X*) FirstPublish.

Lafitte: Terror of the Gulf. 2nd ed. Catherine T. Gonzalez. 76p. (J). (gr. 3-7). 1981. reprint ed. pap. 5.95 (*1-57168-019-5*) Sunbelt Media.

Lafitte Case. Ray Peters. 256p. 1997. 22.95 (*1-885173-27-X*) Write Way.

Lafitte the Pirate. Lyle Saxon. LC 89-3899. (Illus.). 352p. (gr. 7 up). 1989. reprint ed. pap. 14.95 (*0-88289-395-5*) Pelican.

Lafitte, the Pirate of the Gulf. J. H. Ingraham. Ed. by Robert Weatherby. (Masterworks of Literature Ser.). 1991. 13.95 (*0-8084-0425-3*) NCUP.

LaFleur World Gambling Abstract, 1993. Terri LaFleur & Bruce Lafleur. 297p. 1992. pap. 175.00 (*1-883567-56-4*) TLF Pubns.

LaFleur's European Lottery Abstract. Terri LaFleur & Bruce LaFleur. 202p. 1992. pap. 100.00 (*1-883567-53-X*) TLF Pubns.

LaFleur's Lottery Interim Report: Fiscal 1992 Sales & Analysis. Terri LaFleur. 54p. 1992. pap. 40.00 (*1-883567-57-2*) TLF Pubns.

LaFleur's Lottery Interim Report Vol. 2: Fiscal 1993 Sales & Analysis. Terri LaFleur & Bruce LaFleur. 55p. 1993. pap. 45.00 (*1-883567-59-9*) TLF Pubns.

LaFleur's 1995 European Lottery Abstract. Ed. by Bruce LaFleur & Terri LaFleur. 208p. 1995. pap. write for info. (*1-883567-71-8*) TLF Pubns.

LaFleur's 1997 World Lottery Almanac. 5th ed. Ed. by Teresa LaFleur & Bruce LaFleur. 425p. pap. text. write for info. (*1-883567-75-0*) TLF Pubns.

LaFleur's Ninety One North American Gambling Abstract. Terri LaFleur. 258p. 1991. pap. 139.00 (*1-883567-55-6*) TLF Pubns.

LaFleur's Principles of Contemporary Lottery Marketing. Terri LaFleur & Bruce LaFleur. 192p. 1992. pap. 100.00 (*1-883567-51-3*) TLF Pubns.

LaFleur's Video Lottery Terminal & Keno Report. Terri LaFleur & Bruce Lafleur. 70p. 1993. pap. 45.00 (*1-883567-58-0*) TLF Pubns.

LaFleur's Video Lottery Terminal Report. Terri LaFleur & Bruce LaFleur. 68p. 1992. pap. 40.00 (*1-883567-54-8*) TLF Pubns.

LaFleur's World Gambling Almanac, 1994. Terri LaFleur & Bruce LaFleur. 325p. 1993. pap. 185.00 (*1-883567-60-2*) TLF Pubns.

LaFollette's Autobiography: A Personal Narrative of Political Experiences. Robert M. La Follette. Ed. by Allan Nevins. 362p. 1960. reprint ed. pap. 15.95 (*0-299-02194-7*) U of Wis Pr.

Laforgue: Poems. Ed. by J. A. Hiddleston. (Bristol French Texts Ser.). (FRE.). 301p. 1975. pap. 16.95 (*0-631-15940-1*) Blackwell Pubs.

Laforgue y Lugones: Dos Poetas de la Luna. Raquel H. Ferguson. (Monagrafias A Ser.: Vol. LXXIX). (SPA.). 128p. (C). 1981. 51.00 (*0-7293-0097-8*, Pub. by Tamesis Bks Ltd) Boydell & Brewer.

Legacy of the Darksword. Margaret Weis. (Darksword Ser.). 400p. 1998. reprint ed. mass mkt. 6.99 (*0-553-57812-X*) Bantam.

Lagarto del Sotano. Robert Keeshan.Tr. of Alligator in the Basement. (SPA., Illus.). 32p. (J). (gr. k-4). 1996. 14.95 (*1-57749-002-9*) Fairview Press.

Lagarto Torpe. (Leelo Tu Ser.). (SPA.). 1995. pap. 2.98 (*1-85854-313-4*) Brimax Bks.

La/Gauche Face a la Crise see Reflation & Austerity: Economic Policy under Mitterand

L'/Agenda de Mere see Mother's Agenda

L'Agenda De Mere see Mother's Agenda, 1971

L'Agenda de Mere 1963 see Mother's Agenda, 1963

L'Agenda De Mere, 1964, Vol. 5 see Mother's Agenda, 1964

LaGG Fighters in Action. Hans-Heiri Stapfer. (Aircraft in Action Ser.: No. 163). (Illus.). 50p. 1996. pap. 9.95 (*0-89747-364-7*, 1163) Squad Sig Pubns.

Laghu-Yoga-Vasistha. Tr. by K. Narayanaswami Aiyer. 1987. 26.95 (*0-8356-7497-5*) Theos Pub Hse.

Laghukaumudi: A Sanskrit Grammar. Varadaraja. 1995. reprint ed. 22.00 (*0-614-25282-2*, Pub. by Motilal Bnarsidass) S Asia.

Laghukaumudi: A Sanskrit Grammar. Varadaraja. Tr. by James R. Ballantyne. (SAN.). (C). 1995. reprint ed. pap. 22.00 (*81-208-0916-5*, Pub. by Motilal Bnarsidass) S Asia.

Lagniappe, a Little Something Extra. Junior League of Beaumont, Inc. Staff. 352p. 1982. 12.95 (*0-9609604-0-6*) Jr League Beau.

Lagniappe Something a Little Extra Special: Louisiana Cooking from the Kitchen of Chef Walter's Blue Bayou Inn. Walter G. Mazur. Ed. by B. J. Hegeman. LC 95-83544. (Illus.). 144p. (Orig.). 1995. write for info. (*0-942495-51-9*); pap. 14.95 (*0-942495-50-0*) Palmer Pubns Inc.

Lago. Nicolas Abreu-Felippe. LC 91-75689. (Coleccion Caniqui). (SPA.). 124p. (Orig.). 1991. pap. 13.00 (*0-89729-619-2*) Ediciones.

Lago de la Luna. Ivan Gantschev. LC 96-21750. (SPA., Illus.). 32p. (J). (gr. k-3). 1996. 18.95 (*1-55858-600-8*, Pub. by North-South Bks NYC) Chronicle Bks.

Lagonda Heritage. Richard Bird. (Color Library). (Illus.). 128p. 1994. pap. 15.95 (*1-85532-363-X*, Pub. by Osprey) Motorbooks Intl.

Lagoon see Creative Short Stories

Lagoon & Other Stories. Joseph Conrad. Ed. by William Atkinson. LC 97-9268. (The World's Classics Ser.). 322p. 1998. pap. 8.95 (*0-19-283222-0*) OUP.

***Lagoon & Other Stories.** Joseph Conrad. 328p. 2000. pap. 8.95 (*0-19-283619-6*) OUP.

Lagoon Is in My Backyard. Sister Goodwin. 90p. (Orig.). 1984. pap. 4.95 (*0-918408-21-0*) Ishmael Reed.

Lagos: The City Is the People. Margaret Peil. (World Cities Ser.). 256p. 1991. 40.00 (*0-8161-7299-4*, Hall Reference) Macmillan.

Lagrange & Finsler Geometry: Applications to Physics & Biology. Ed. by P. L. Antonelli. (Fundamental Theories of Physics Ser.). 292p. (C). 1996. text 144.00 (*0-7923-3873-1*) Kluwer Academic.

***Lagrange & Lagrange County.** Mueller. (Images of America Ser.). 1999. pap. 18.99 (*0-7385-0191-3*) Arcadia Publng.

***Lagrange & Lagrange Park.** Roseanna Mueller & Robert Mueller. (Images of America Ser.). 128p. 1999. pap. 18.99 (*0-7385-0260-X*) Arcadia Publng.

Lagrange & Legendre Characteristic Classes: ASCM, Vol. 3. V. A. Vassilyev. x, 268p. 1988. text 274.00 (*2-88124-661-3*) Gordon & Breach.

LaGrange Pioneers. James Ellis & Esther Ellis. (Illus.). 395p. 1997. reprint ed. lib. bdg. 44.50 (*0-8328-6971-6*) Higginson Bk Co.

Lagrangian & Hamiltonian Formulation of Plasma Problems. George C. Georges. LC 70-141694. 74p. 1969. 17.50 (*0-403-04503-7*) Scholarly.

Lagrangian & Hamiltonian Mechanics. LC 96-203992. 228p. 1996. lib. bdg. 24.00 (*981-02-2672-1*) World Scientific Pub.

Lagrangian & Hamiltonian Mechanics: Solutions to the Exercises. M. G. Calgin. 240p. 1999. 28.00 (*981-02-3782-0*) World Scientific Pub.

Lagrangian Dynamics. Dare A. Wells. (Schaum's Outline Ser.). 368p. (Orig.). (C). 1967. pap. 15.95 (*0-07-069258-0*) McGraw.

Lagrangian Dynamics: An Introduction for Students. Clive W. Kilmister. LC 68-28883. 144p. reprint ed. pap. 44.70 (*0-608-16611-1*, 202630100049) Bks Demand.

Lagrangian Mechanics of Nonconservative Nonholomic Systems. Dominic G. Edelen. (Mechanics: Dynamical Systems Ser.: No. 2). 314p. 1977. text 161.50 (*90-286-0077-9*) Kluwer Academic.

***L'agricoltura Italiana E l'Integrazione Europea.** Giuliana Laschi. xi, 350p. 1999. 33.95 (*3-906762-37-8*) P Lang Pubng.

Lagrimas del Sol, Level 4. Adapted by Jose Maria Merino. (Leer en Espanol Ser.). (SPA.). (C). 1998. pap. 6.95 (*84-294-3490-9*) Santillana.

Lagrimas y Sonrisas: Extrasis en Poesia. Raul Garcia. (SPA.). 80p. 1986. 11.95 (*0-935361-00-6*) Delmar.

Lags in the Effects of Monetary Policy: A Nonparametric Analysis. Gene C. Uselton. LC 73-84817. (Business Economics & Finance Ser.: No. 2). (Illus.). 190p. reprint ed. pap. 58.90 (*0-7837-0925-0*, 204123000019) Bks Demand.

LaGuardia Airport Runway Extension Program. (PCI Journal Reprints Ser.). 6p. 1966. pap. 10.00 (*0-686-39987-0*, JR40) P-PCI.

LaGuardia Comes to Power, 1933. Arthur Mann. 1969. pap. text 1.95 (*0-226-50331-3*, P331) U Ch Pr.

LaGuardia Comes to Power, 1933. Arthur Mann. LC 81-4124. (Illus.). 199p. 1981. reprint ed. lib. bdg. 55.00 (*0-313-22787-X*, MALC, Greenwood Pr) Greenwood.

Laguerre. Ambrose E. Gonzales. LC 71-37594. (Black Heritage Library Collection). 1977. reprint ed. 21.95 (*0-8369-8970-8*) Ayer.

La/Guerre a Deux Voix see War with Two Voices

La/Guerre a Deux Voix see War with Two Voices: Journalism

Laguna Beach: Local Color. Irean Bean. (Illus.). 76p. 1998. pap. 24.95 (*0-9660793-1-0*) Max Co.

Laguna Heat-MTV. T. Jefferson Parker. 1993. mass mkt. 4.99 (*0-312-95205-8*) St Martin.

Laguna, I Love You: The Best of "Our Town" John Weld. LC 95-37388. (Illus.). 288p. (Orig.). 1996. pap. 14.95 (*1-56474-157-5*) Fithian Pr.

Laguna Niguel: The Legacy & the Promise. Donald M. Decker & Mary L. Decker. LC 90-63225. (Illus.). 120p. 1990. pap. 4.95 (*0-918329-19-1*) Royal Lit.

Laguna Sagrada de San Joaquin. 2nd ed. Lydia Cabrera. (Coleccion del Chicherekù). (SPA., Illus.). 105p. 1993. pap. 19.95 (*0-89729-673-7*) Ediciones.

Laguna Woman. 2nd rev. ed. Leslie Marmon Silko. (Illus.). 48p. (C). 1994. pap. text 24.00 (*0-614-01631-2*) Flood Plain.

Laguna y Asociados. Emilio D. Valcarcel. (SPA.). 224p. 1996. pap. 8.95 (*1-56328-104-X*) Edit Plaza Mayor.

Lahaina: Royal Capital of Hawaii. Roy Nickerson. Ed. by Richard Wirtz. LC 77-94277. (Illus.). 1978. pap. 8.95 (*0-930492-03-X*) Hawaiian Serv.

La/Hija de la Panadera Medieval see Medieval Baker's Daughter: A Bilingual Adventure in Medieval Life with Costumes, Banners, Music, Food, & a Mystery Play

Lahore: A Sentimental Journey. Pran Nevile. (C). 1993. 16.00 (*81-7023-253-8*, Pub. by Allied Pubs) S Asia.

Lahore: Past & Present. M. Baqir. (C). 1993. 14.00 (*81-85557-22-5*, Pub. by Low Price) S Asia.

Lahore: The City Within. Samina Quraeshi. (Illus.). 292p. 1989. 75.00 (*0-7103-0335-1*) Routledge.

***Lahore & Its Rulers: A History of the Reigning Family of Lahore & the Rajas of Jammu.** Ed. by G. Carmichael Symth. 1998. reprint ed. 36.00 (*81-87226-02-1*, Pub. by Shubji Pubns) S Asia.

Lahore Colours. Lahore Colours. (Illus.). 130p. 1998. text 85.00 (*0-19-577822-7*) OUP.

***Lahore Declaration & Nuclear Issues.** Prakash Chandra. LC 99-938603. 1999. 52.50 (*81-7169-571-X*, Pub. by Commonwealth) S Asia.

Lahoul: The Mystery Land in the Himalayas. Ram N. Sahni. LC 94-906761. (C). 1995. 34.00 (*81-7387-017-9*, Pub. by Indus Pub) S Asia.

Lai & the Headhunters, Vol. 2. John Vornholt. (Warriors of Virtue Ser.: No. 2). 112p. 1997. mass mkt. 3.99 (*1-57297-284-X*) Blvd Books.

Lai de l'Oiselet: An Old French Poem of the Thirteenth Century. Lenora D. Wolfgang. LC 90-55268. (Transactions Ser.: Vol. 80, Pt. 5). 250p. (C). 1990. pap. 20.00 (*0-87169-805-6*, T805-WOL) Am Philos.

Laid Back in Hollywood: Remembering. Patricia M. Cotten. Ed. by Margaret Burk & Heather Slater. LC 97-77221. (Illus.). 256p. 1998. 24.95 (*0-9649635-1-5*); pap. 16.95 (*0-9649635-2-3*) Belle Pubng CA.

Laid-Back Leadership: How to Be a Top Manager. Eric Gelb & Nancy Loughlin. 224p. (Orig.). pap. 8.50 (*0-9631289-2-2*) Career Advan.

Laid Bare: A Memoir of Wrecked Lives & the Hollywood Death Trip. John Gilmore. 1996. pap. text 16.95 (*1-878923-08-0*) Amok Bks.

Laid Daughter: A True Story. Helen Bonner. Ed. by Jan Huebsch. 256p. 1995. pap. 16.95 (*1-884178-23-5*) Kairos Ctr.

Laid Fillings: For Evenweave Fabrics - 125 Stitch Diagrams. Jean Taggart. Ed. by Pat Timpanaro & Carole Lake. (Illus.). 198p. (Orig.). (C). 1995. pap. 29.95 (*0-9638758-6-8*) Brockton Pubng.

L

Laienlekture und Buchmarkt im Spaten Mittelalter. Ed. by Thomas Kock & Rita Schlusemann. (Gesellschaft, Kultur und Schrift Ser.: Bd. 5). (GER., Illus.). 303p. 1997. 57.95 (*3-631-31470-1*) P Lang Pubng.

LAIL Speaks: Selected Papers from the 7th International Symposium on Latin American Indian Literatures. Ed. by Mary M. Preuss. LC 90-60870. (Illus.). 160p. (Orig.). (C). 1990. pap. 32.00 (*0-911437-44-4*) Labyrinthos.

Laine & Lin. Catherine Bouquerel. (FRE., Illus.). 104p. 1998. 36.00 (*2-84229-048-8*, DE17, Pub. by C Armand) Lacis Pubns.

LAIPE: Parallel Direct Solvers for Linear System Equations. Jenn-Ching Luo. LC 95-92416. (LAIPE-001 Ser.). 364p. (Orig.). (C). 1995. 23.50 (*0-9644361-1-6*) Paral Integ.

Lair of the Cyclops. Allen L. Wold. 288p. (Orig.). 1992. mass mkt. 4.50 (*0-446-36247-6*, Pub. by Warner Bks) Little.

***Lair of the Devil.** Emile C. Vos. LC 00-190784. 208p. (C). 2000. 12.95 (*0-9700594-0-X*) E C Vos.

Lair of the Dragon. large type ed. Catherine George. (Harlequin Romance Ser.). 1994. lib. bdg. 19.95 (*0-263-13872-0*) Thorndike Pr.

Lair of the Jade Tiger: Friendship: Keeping Friends. J. Thomas Morse et al. Ed. by Betty Gouge et al. LC 85-81270. (KidSkills Interpersonal Skill Ser.). (Illus.). 48p. (J). (gr. 2-3). 1986. lib. bdg. 9.95 (*0-934275-07-6*) Fam Skills.

Lair of the Lizard. E. C. Ayres. LC 98-19405. 288p. 1998. text 22.95 (*0-312-19295-9*) St Martin.

Lair of the Sphinx: A Riddle Book. (Illus.). 144p. 1999. pap. 11.95 (*1-928807-00-3*, 50301) Cloud Kingdom.

Lair of the White Worm. Bram Stoker. 1998. pap. write for info. (*1-902058-01-1*, Pub. by Pulp Fictions) Seven Hills Bk.

***Lair of the Wolf.** Jack Summers. 192p. 2000. pap. 11.95 (*1-56315-271-1*, Pub. by SterlingHse) Natl Bk Netwk.

Laird Across the Loch. large type ed. Marjorie Warby. 1991. 27.99 (*0-7089-2491-3*) Ulverscroft.

Laird & the Lady. Joan M. Grant. 1980. 29.95 (*0-405-11783-3*) Ayer.

Laird of Drammochdyle & His Contemporaries: or Random Sketches Done in Outline with a Burnt Stick. William Alexander. Ed. by William Donaldson. 184p. 1987. text 27.00 (*0-08-034520-4*, Pub. by Aberdeen U Pr); pap. text 19.90 (*0-08-034521-2*, Pub. by Aberdeen U Pr) Macmillan.

Laird of Imchay. large type ed. Carol Marsh. (Linford Romance Library). 240p. 1992. pap. 16.99 (*0-7089-7206-3*) Ulverscroft.

Laird of Lochvinnie. large type ed. Lynn Granger. 254p. 1996. pap. 18.99 (*1-85389-594-6*, Dales) Ulverscroft.

Laird of the West, Vol. 1. John W. Chalmers. 289p. 1981. 19.95 (*0-920490-18-2*) Temeron Bks.

Laird of the Wind. Susan King. 354p. 1998. mass mkt. 6.99 (*0-451-40768-7*, Topaz) NAL.

Laird's Casket. large type ed. Angela Petron. (Linford Romance Library). 1991. pap. 16.99 (*0-7089-6985-2*) Ulverscroft.

Laird's Kitchen: Three Hundred Years of Food in Scotland. Olive M. Geddes. (Illus.). x, 110p. 1994. pap. 38.00 (*0-11-495230-2*, Pub. by Statnry Office) Balogh.

Laird's Luck: And Other Fireside Tales. Arthur T. Quiller-Couch. LC 72-10767. (Short Story Index Reprint Ser.). 1977. reprint ed. 29.95 (*0-8369-4223-X*) Ayer.

Laird's Mount. Madelyn Sanders. (Intrigue Ser.: 234). 1993. per. 2.99 (*0-373-22234-3*, 1-22234-8) Harlequin Bks.

Lais de Marie de France. Adapted by Harry F. Williams. (FRE.). 133p. 1991. pap. 11.50 (*0-942566-06-8*) LinguaText.

Lais et Descorts Francais du XIIIe Siecle, Texte et Musique see Melanges de Musicologie Critique

Lais et Descorts Francais du Treizieme Siecle. Alfred Jeanroy et al. LC 73-178540. (FRE.). reprint ed. 55.00 (*0-404-56622-7*) AMS Pr.

Lais et Fabliaux du 13E Siecle. Louis Brandin. 122p. 1932. 13.95 (*0-8288-7427-1*) Fr & Eur.

Lais of Marie de France. Ed. by Robert W. Hanning & Joan M. Ferrante. 248p. 1995. pap. 14.99 (*0-8010-2031-X*, Labyrinth) Baker Bks.

Lais Villon et les Poemes Varies: Commentaire, Vol. 2. Francois Villon. Ed. by Jean Rychner & Albert Henry. (FRE.). 80p. 1977. pap. 36.95 (*0-7859-5507-0*) Fr & Eur.

Lais Villon et les Poemes Varies: Textes, Vol. 1. Francois Villon. Ed. by Jean Rychner & Albert Henry. (FRE.). 80p. 1977. pap. 14.95 (*0-7859-5506-2*) Fr & Eur.

Laish. Aharon Appelfeld. 1999. write for info. (*0-8052-4159-0*); pap. write for info. (*0-8052-1100-4*) Schocken.

Laisse. Francoise Sagan. (FRE.). 1991. pap. 10.95 (*0-7859-3235-6*, 2266037749) Fr & Eur.

***Laisse: A Common Sense Approach to Dominance & Submission.** Soduire. (Illus.). 234p. 1999. pap. 17.50 (*0-9671287-0-6*) La Laisse.

Laisser Courir, Tome 1. Philip Roth. (FRE.). 384p. 1983. pap. 15.95 (*0-7859-4186-X*, 2070374777) Fr & Eur.

Laisser Courir, Tome II. Philip Roth. (FRE.). 1983. pap. 17.95 (*0-7859-4187-8*) Fr & Eur.

Laissez-Faire Banking. Kevin Dowd. 400p. (C). 1996. pap. 29.99 (*0-415-13732-2*) Routledge.

L

Laissez Parler: Freedom in the Electronic Media. David Kelley & Roger Donway. (Studies in Social Philosophy & Policy: No. 1). 49p. 1982. pap. 21.95 (*0-935756-99-X*) Transaction Pubs.

Lait de L'Oranger. Gisele Halimi. (FRE.). 1990. pap. 14.95 (*0-7859-2600-3*, 2070383229) Fr & Eur.

Laity, American & Catholic: Transforming the Church. William V. D'Antonio et al. LC 95-48857. 192p. (Orig.). 1996. pap. 15.95 (*1-55612-823-1*, LL1823) Sheed & Ward WI.

Laity in Community: Holiness of Everyday Life. Foley & Timothy Schmaltz. 32p. 1996. pap. text 2.95 (*1-55612-080-X*, LL1080) Sheed & Ward WI.

Laity in the Church & in the World: Resources for Ecumenical Dialogue. United States Catholic Conference Staff. 128p. 1998. pap. text 9.95 (*1-57455-247-3*) US Catholic.

Laity in the Middle Ages: Religious Beliefs & Devotional Practices. Andre Vauchez. Ed. by Daniel E. Bornstein. Tr. by Margery J. Schneider from FRE. LC 92-53746. (C). 1993. text 42.50 (*0-268-01297-0*) U of Notre Dame Pr.

Laity in the Middle Ages: Religious Beliefs & Devotional Practices. Andre Vauchez. Ed. by Daniel E. Bornstein. Tr. by Margery J. Schneider from FRE. LC 92-53746. (C). 1996. pap. text 18.00 (*0-268-01309-8*) U of Notre Dame Pr.

La/Jeune Nee see Newly Born Woman

***Lajm 1 Mire Per Ju.**Tr. of Good News for You. (ALB.). 25p. 1998. pap. text 1.00 (*1-885504-46-2*) Church Gwth.

La'Justice (SDQ) de Dieu dans la Bible Hebraique et L'Interpretation Juive et Chretienne. Joze Krasovec. (Orbis Biblicus et Orientalis Ser.: Vol. 76). (GER.). 452p. 1988. text 84.00 (*3-7278-0549-8*, Pub. by Presses Univ Fribourg) Eisenbrauns.

Lakanal the Regicide. John C. Dawson. (Select Bibliographies Reprint Ser.). 1977. 21.95 (*0-8369-5520-X*) Ayer.

Lak'aq. large type ed. Sophie Shield & Agnes Kairaiuak. (ESK., Illus.). 12p. (J). (gr. k-3). 1997. pap. text 6.00 (*1-58084-007-8*) Lower Kuskokwim.

Lakatos: An Introduction. Brendan Larvor. LC 97-26569. 144p. (C). 1998. 65.00 (*0-415-14275-X*); pap. 19.99 (*0-415-14276-8*) Routledge.

Lakatos' Philosophy of Mathematics. T. Koetsler. (Studies in the History & Philosophy of Mathematics: Vol. 3). 312p. 1991. 120.50 (*0-444-88944-2*, North Holland) Elsevier.

Lakay. 2nd ed. Oreste Joseph. Ed. by J. Theodat et al. (CRP., Illus.). 13p. (J). 1995. pap. 3.00 (*1-885566-01-8*) Oresjozef.

Lakbay: Journey of the People of the Philippines. Jaime A. Jacinto & Luis M. Syquia. (New Faces of Liberty Background Essays Ser.). 21p. (Orig.). 1995. pap. 5.00 (*0-936434-84-8*, Pub. by Zellerbach Fam Fund) Intl Spec Bk.

Lake. John Peyton Cooke. 224p. 1989. pap. 3.95 (*0-380-75768-0*, Avon Bks) Morrow Avon.

Lake. Yasunari Kawabata. Ed. by Shaw & Tsuizaki. Tr. by Reiko Tsukimura from JPN. LC 73-89699. Orig. Title: Mizuumi. 160p. 1993. pap. 11.00 (*0-87011-365-8*) Kodansha.

Lake. George Moore. 286p. 1980. 30.00 (*0-900675-75-6*, Pub. by Smyth); pap. 14.95 (*0-901072-82-6*, Pub. by Smyth) Dufour.

***Lake.** Gerhard Roth. Tr. & Afterword by Michael Winkler. LC 99-23591. (Studies in Austrian Literature, Culture & Thought). 2000. pap. write for info. (*1-57241-084-1*) Ariadne CA.

***Lake: A Novel.** Daniel Villasenor. LC 99-89895. 240p. 2000. 24.95 (*0-670-89161-4*, Viking) Viking Penguin.

Lake: New & Selected Poems. Daniel Weissbort. LC 93-7528. 138p. (Orig.). 1993. pap. 13.95 (*1-878818-24-4*, Pub. by Sheep Meadow) U Pr of New Eng.

Lake & Draetta: Letters of Intent & Other Precontractual Documents. 2nd ed. Ralph B. Lake & Ugo Draetta. 1995. write for info. (*0-406-05047-3*, LLI2, MICHIE) LEXIS Pub.

Lake & Geauga Street Atlas, 781-AC. 29th ed. 1998. 4.75 (*1-879116-40-5*, 781-AC) Commercial Survey.

Lake & McHenry Counties Atlas. 1995. spiral bd. (*0-8416-9242-4*) Creative Sales.

Lake & Pond. April P. Sayre. (Exploring Earth's Biomes Ser.). (Illus.). 80p. (J). (gr. 5-8). 1995. lib. bdg. 20.40 (*0-8050-4089-7*) TFC Bks NY.

Lake & the Castle. Arthur Guirdham. 432p. pap. 35.95 (*0-8464-4245-0*) Beekman Pubs.

Lake & the Castle. Arthur Guirdham. (Guirdham Trilogy Ser.). 186p. 1992. pap. 23.95 (*0-85207-251-1*, Pub. by C W Daniel) Natl Bk Netwk.

Lake & the Woods: or Nature's Calendar. Mikhail Prishvin. Tr. by W. L. Goodman from RUS. LC 75-27685. (Illus.). 258p. 1975. reprint ed. lib. bdg. 55.00 (*0-8371-8465-7*, PRLW, Greenwood Pr) Greenwood.

Lake Baikal: Evolution & Biodiversity. Ed. by O. M. Kozhova & L. R. Izmest'eva. (Illus.). xlv, 447p. 1998. 156.00 (*90-5782-001-3*, Pub. by Backhuys Pubs) Balogh.

Lake Baikal Region in the Twenty-First Century: A Model of Sustainable Development or Continued Degradation?: A National Program of Land Use Policies for the Russian Portion of the Lake Baikal Watershed. George D. Davis et al. Tr. by Irina Birnbaum. (Comprehensive Land Use Programs Ser.). (ENG & RUS., Illus.). (Orig.). 1993. pap. text. write for info. (*0-9635624-0-1*) Davis NY.

***Lake Basins Through Space & Time.** E. Gierlowski-Kordesch & K. R. Kelts. LC 99-86268. (Studies in Geology). 2000. write for info. (*0-89181-052-8*) AAPG.

Lake Beyond the Wind. Yahya Yakhlif. Tr. by M. Jayyusi & C. Tingley. LC 98-41185. 1998. pap. 12.95 (*1-56656-301-1*) Interlink Pub.

Lake Biwa. S. Horie. (Monographiae Biologicae). 1984. text 450.50 (*90-6193-095-2*) Kluwer Academic.

Lake Boon. Lewis Halprin. LC 98-87326. (Images of America Ser.). (Illus.). 128p. 1998. pap. 16.99 (*0-7524-1292-2*) Arcadia Publng.

Lake Cargo Coal Rate Controversy. Harvey C. Mansfield. LC 73-76629. (Columbia University. Studies in the Social Sciences: No. 373). reprint ed. 32.50 (*0-404-51373-5*) AMS Pr.

Lake Champlain: A Photographic Discovery. Photos by Paul O. Boisvert. LC 95-67532. (Illus.). 88p. (Orig.). 1995. 25.00 (*1-881535-15-0*); pap. text 16.95 (*1-881535-14-2*) New Eng Pr VT.

Lake Champlain: Key to Liberty. 20th anniversary ed. Ralph N. Hill. (Illus.). ix, 320p. 1995. pap. 24.95 (*0-88150-354-1*, Pub. by Countryman) Norton.

Lake Champlain: Mirror on the Mountains. Michael G. DiNunzio. Ed. by John J. Sheehan & Anne Trachtenberg. (Illus.). 32p. 1995. pap. 5.00 (*0-614-13999-6*) Adirondack Council.

Lake Champlain: Reflections on Our Past. Ed. by Jennie G. Versteeg. (Illus.). 300p. (C). 1989. reprint ed. pap. text 17.95 (*0-944277-19-5*, L26) U VT Ctr Rsch VT.

Lake Champlain: Reflections on Our Past - A Bibliography. Compiled & Pref. by Kristin Peterson-Ishaq. 90p. (Orig.). 1989. pap. text 9.00 (*0-944277-18-7*, U55) U VT Ctr Rsch VT.

Lake Champlain & Lake George. Frederic Van de Water. (American Lakes Ser.). lib. bdg. 26.95 (*0-8488-2038-X*) Amereon Ltd.

Lake Champlain As Centuries Pass. Allen P. Beach. 128p. 1994. pap. 9.95 (*0-9641856-0-1*) LCMM.

Lake Champlain Atlas of Navigational Charts. 2nd rev. ed. (Illus.). 40p. 1999. pap. 76.00 (*0-9657640-1-X*) R W Vogel.

Lake Champlain Ferryboats: A Short History of Lake Champlain & the Story of over 200 Years of Lake Champlain Ferryboats. rev. ed. Jerry P. Williams & Ralph N. Hill. (Illus.). 36p. 1990. pap. 6.95 (*0-9623772-0-1*) Lake Champlain.

***Lake Champlain in Transition: From Research Toward Restoration.** Ed. by Thomas O. Manley & Patricia L. Manley. (Water Science & Application Ser.: Vol. 1). 451p. 1999. 55.00 (*0-87590-350-9*) Am Geophysical.

Lake Chilwa. Ed. by M. Kalk et al. (Monographiae Biologicae: No. 35). 1979. text 234.00 (*90-6193-087-1*) Kluwer Academic.

Lake City. Margaret Bates. 1973. pap. 3.95 (*0-936564-08-3*) Little London.

Lake City Hiking. Lyndon J. Lampert. 136p. 1999. pap. 7.50 (*1-928590-00-4*) Golden Stone CO.

Lake City Places. Lyndon J. Lampert. 136p. 1999. pap. 7.50 (*1-928590-01-2*) Golden Stone CO.

Lake Classic Short Stories New Complete Library, 50 bks. 1995. pap. 499.95 (*0-7854-0617-4*, 40115) Am Guidance.

***Lake Como.** Clayton Chou. 1999. pap. write for info. (*1-58235-085-X*) Watermrk Pr.

Lake Country. Kathleen Stocking. LC 93-46406. 245p. 1994. pap. 18.95 (*0-472-06516-5*, 06516) U of Mich Pr.

Lake Country Cooking Book. Bruce Carlson. (Illus.). 238p. 1993. spiral bd. 11.95 (*1-878488-88-0*) Black Iron.

Lake County, 1884: Account of the Semi-Centennial of Lake Co., with Historical Papers & Other Interesting Records. Ed. by T. H. Ball. (Illus.). 488p. 1997. reprint ed. lib. bdg. 49.50 (*0-8328-6657-1*) Higginson Bk Co.

Lake County, Florida: A Pictorial History. Emmett Peter. LC 94-24867. 1994. write for info. (*0-89865-905-1*) Donning Co.

Lake County, Indiana. Ann Weitgenant. (Illus.). 225p. 1990. 57.50 (*0-88107-170-6*) Curtis Media.

Lake County, Ohio: 1940 WPA History Index. Fay Maxwell. 7p. 1975. 8.00 (*1-885463-14-6*) Ohio Genealogy.

Lake County, Tennessee. Turner Publishing Company Staff. LC 92-85251. 160p. 1993. 49.95 (*1-56311-099-7*) Turner Pub KY.

***Lake County, Tennessee, Memories: History in Pictures & Newsprint.** Emily C. Davis. (Illus.). 344p. 1998. 45.00 (*0-9676742-0-4*) E D Bks.

Lake District. LC 99-223860. (Landmark Visitors Guide Ser.). (Illus.). 224p. (Orig.). 1999. pap. 15.95 (*1-901522-38-5*) Hunter NJ.

Lake District. Colin Baxter. (Illus.). 112p. 1998. 32.95 (*1-900455-29-3*, Pub. by Colin Baxter Ltd) Voyageur Pr.

***Lake District.** Berlitz Publishing Staff. (Pocket Guides Ser.). 1999. pap. text 8.95 (*2-8315-7173-1*) Berlitz.

Lake District. Insight Guides Staff. (Insight Guides). 1998. pap. text 7.95 (*0-88729-537-1*) Langenscheidt.

Lake District. John Morrisey. LC 95-72837. (Passport's Regional Guides of Great Britain Ser.). (Illus.). 128p. 1996. pap. 12.95 (*0-8442-4879-7*, 48797, Passprt Bks) NTC Contemp Pub Co.

***Lake District.** Rough Guides Staff. (Travel Ser.). (Illus.). 2000. pap. 14.95 (*1-85828-533-X*, Pub. by Rough Guides) Penguin Putnam.

Lake District Car Tours. Ed. by Jarrold Printing Staff. (Ordnance Survey Travelmaster Guides Ser.). (Illus.). 96p. (Orig.). 1995. pap. 15.95 (*0-7117-0823-1*, Pub. by JARR UK) Seven Hills Bk.

Lake District Exploramap. Jarrold Printing Staff. 1993. pap. text 4.95 (*0-7117-0547-X*, Pub. by JARR UK) Seven Hills Bk.

Lake District Walks. (Ordnance Survey Pathfinder Guides Ser.). (Illus.). 80p. 1993. pap. 14.95 (*0-7117-0463-5*) Seven Hills Bk.

Lake Dreams the Sky: A Love Story. Swain Wolfe. LC 97-48898. 352p. 1999. pap. 13.00 (*0-06-092993-6*, Cliff Street) HarperTrade.

Lake Dwellings of Switzerland. A. F. Harding. 16p. 1980. pap. 3.00 (*0-614-21822-5*) David Brown.

Lake Dwellings of Switzerland & Other Parts of Europe, 2 vols. 2nd ed. Ferdinand Keller. Tr. by John E. Lee. LC 77-86433. reprint ed. 88.00 (*0-404-16660-1*) AMS Pr.

Lake Effect. Leigh Michaels. (Romance Ser.). 1993. per. 2.99 (*0-373-03275-7*, 1-03275-4) Harlequin Bks.

Lake Effect. Les Roberts. LC 94-31315. 352p. 1994. text 21.95 (*0-312-11537-7*) St Martin.

***Lake Effect.** Les Roberts. 2000. pap. 5.99 (*0-312-97823-5*, St Martins Paperbacks) St Martin.

***Lake Effect: A Lake Superior Mystery.** Mike Savage. 312p. 2000. pap. 11.95 (*1-886028-44-3*, Pub. by Savage Pr) Bookmen Inc.

Lake Erie. Ann Armbruster. LC 96-2028. (True Bk.). (Illus.). 48p. (J). 1996. lib. bdg. 21.00 (*0-516-20011-9*) Childrens.

Lake Erie. Ann Armbruster. (True Bks.). 48p. (J). 1997. pap. 6.95 (*0-516-26102-9*) Childrens.

***Lake Erie.** Harry Beckett. LC 99-14508. 32p. (J). (gr. 3-5). 1999. lib. bdg. 17.45 (*0-86593-527-0*) Rourke Corp.

Lake Erie. Harlan Hatcher. (American Lakes Ser.). lib. bdg. 27.95 (*0-8488-1981-0*) Amereon Ltd.

Lake Erie & Lake St. Clair Handbook. Ed. by Stanley J. Bolsenga & Charles E. Herdendorf. LC 93-10208. (Great Lakes Bks.). (Illus.). 484p. 1993. pap. 24.95 (*0-8143-2470-3*) Wayne St U Pr.

Lake Erie Bibliography in Environmental Sciences. Charles E. Herdendorf et al. (Bulletin New Ser.: Vol. 4, No. 5). 1974. pap. text 4.00 (*0-86727-068-3*) Ohio Bio Survey.

Lake Erie Fisherman: Work, Identity & Tradition. Timothy C. Lloyd & Patrick B. Mullen. (Illus.). 216p. 1990. text 19.95 (*0-252-01662-9*) U of Ill Pr.

***Lake Erie Rehabilitated: Controlling Cultural Eutrophication, 1960s-1990s.** William McGucken. LC 99-53826. (Technology & the Environment Ser.). 2000. pap. 29.95 (*1-884836-58-5*) U Akron Pr.

Lake Erie Shore: Images of Nature. Connie S. Girard. LC 95-75945. (Illus.). 96p. (Orig.). 1995. pap. 25.00 (*1-887018-06-9*) March Fourth Pub.

Lake Erie Smallmouth. Mark Hicks. (Illus.). 148p. 1999. lib. bdg. 14.95 (*0-9643309-3-8*) Big River.

Lake Erie Sojourn: An Autumn Tour of the Parks, Public Places & History of the Lake Erie Shore. Jim Mollenkopf. LC 98-67389. (Illus.). 128p. 1998. pap. 10.95 (*0-9665910-0-3*) Lake Cat.

***Lake Erie Vacationland in Ohio: Revisiting a 1941 Travel Guide to the Sandusky Bay Region.** Intro. by Connie Smith Girard. LC 99-74162. (American Guide Ser.). 112p. 1999. pap. 14.00 (*1-887018-41-7*) March Fourth Pub.

Lake Erie Walleye, Vol. 1. Mark Hicks. (Illus.). 128p. (Orig.). 1996. pap., mass mkt. 14.95 (*0-9643309-1-1*) Big River.

Lake Erken - 50 Years of Limnological Research. (Advances in Limnology Ser.: Vol. 51). (GER., Illus.). vi, 272p. 1998. write for info. (*3-510-47053-2*, Pub. by E Schweizerbartsche) Balogh.

Lake Fishing with a Fly. Randall Kaufmann. Ed. by Ron Cordes. (Illus.). 149p. (Orig.). 1984. pap. 26.95 (*0-936608-25-0*) F Amato Pubns.

Lake Fly Fishing Guide. Jim Bradbury & Beverly Miller. LC 95-111066. 146p. 1994. pap. 9.95 (*1-878175-72-6*) F Amato Pubns.

Lake Frome Monster. Arthur W. Upfield. (Napoleon Bonaparte Mysteries Ser.). reprint ed. lib. bdg. 18.95 (*0-89190-557-X*) Amereon Ltd.

Lake Frome Monster. 2nd large type ed. Arthur W. Upfield. 273p. 1993. 21.95 (*1-85695-340-8*, Pub. by ISIS Lrg Prnt) Transaction Pubs.

Lake Front. Ruth Russell. LC 74-22811. (Labor Movement in Fiction & Non-Fiction Ser.). (Illus.). reprint ed. 45.00 (*0-404-58467-5*) AMS Pr.

Lake Garda: English Edition. Casa Bonechi. 128p. pap. text 12.95 (*88-7009-261-5*, Pub. by Bonechi) Eiron.

Lake Geneva, WI. Pamela Vollbracht. (Illus.). 133p. 1994. 35.00 (*0-88107-247-8*) Curtis Media.

***Lake George.** Gale J. Halm & Mary H. Sharp. LC 00-104040. (Images of America Ser.). (Illus.). 128p. 2000. pap. 18.99 (*0-7524-1320-1*) Arcadia Publng.

Lake George. A. S. Hopkins. 22p. 1993. reprint ed. lib. bdg. 69.00 (*0-7812-5255-5*) Rprt Serv.

Lake George Reflections: Island History & Lore. Frank Leonbruno. Ed. by Ginger Henry. LC 98-7370. (Illus.). 236p. 1998. pap. 18.00 (*0-935796-97-5*) Purple Mnt Pr.

Lake Glubokoe. N. N. Smirnov. (Developments in Hydrobiology Ser.). 1987. text 168.00 (*90-6193-618-7*) Kluwer Academic.

Lake Havasu City Cookbook, Vol. 1. Raymond Korv & Peggy Korv. (Illus.). 54p. (Orig.). 1992. pap. 12.00 (*1-56216-061-3*) Systems Co.

Lake Havasu Cookbook. F. L. Bouquet. (Illus.). 120p. (Orig.). 1990. 25.00 (*0-937041-78-5*); pap. 18.00 (*0-937041-79-3*) Systems Co.

Lake Hole Cave: Archaeology in Johnson County, Tennessee. Howard S. Shutt. (Illus.). 64p. (Orig.). 1994. pap. 6.95 (*1-57072-004-5*) Overmountain Pr.

Lake Hollywood. John Guare. Date not set. pap. 5.95 (*0-8222-1737-6*) Dramatists Play.

Lake House & Other Stories (Chapbook) Charles P. Sweetman. 45p. 1993. pap. 5.00 (*0-916092-22-4*) Tex Ctr Writers.

Lake House Cookbook. Trudie Styler & Joseph Sponzo. 224p. 1999. 35.00 (*0-609-60412-0*) Crown.

Lake Huron. Ann Armbruster. LC 96-2026. (True Bk.). (Illus.). 48p. (J). 1996. lib. bdg. 21.00 (*0-516-20012-7*) Childrens.

Lake Huron. Ann Armbruster. (True Bks.). 48p. (J). 1997. pap. 6.95 (*0-516-26103-7*) Childrens.

***Lake Huron.** Contrib. by Harry Beckett. LC 99-13024. (Great Lakes of North America Ser.). 32p. 1999. lib. bdg. write for info. (*0-86593-525-4*) Rourke Corp.

Lake Huron. Fred Landon. (American Lakes Ser.). lib. bdg. 27.95 (*0-8488-1989-6*) Amereon Ltd.

Lake Huron EcoSystem: Ecology, Fisheries & Management. M. Munawar et al. 485p. 1995. 170.00 (*90-5103-117-3*, Pub. by SPB Acad Pub) Balogh.

Lake Huron 1980 Intensive Survey: Summary Report to the Surveillance Work Group. fac. ed. Ed. by David M. Dolan et al. LC QH0541.5.L3L. (Illus.). 149p. 1986. pap. 46.20 (*0-7837-8621-2*, 207523100007) Bks Demand.

Lake Huron Poker: The Gem of Safe Harbors! Karl W. Grube. 75p. (YA). (gr. 7-12). 1995. pap. 24.00 (*0-9627003-4-7*) Games By Grube.

Lake Illustrated Classics Collection 5, 12 bks. 1994. pap. 39.95 (*0-7854-0787-1*, 40530); pap., student ed. 19.50 (*0-7854-0789-8*, 40577) Am Guidance.

Lake Illustrated Classics Collection 5 Classroom Library, 36 bks. 1994. pap. 99.95 (*0-7854-0786-3*, 40535) Am Guidance.

Lake Illustrated Classics Collection 5 Readalong Basic Set. 1994. pap., student ed. 129.95 incl. audio (*0-7854-0788-X*, 40540) Am Guidance.

Lake Illustrated Classics Collection 4, 12 bks. 1994. pap. 39.95 (*0-7854-0759-6*, 40480); pap., student ed. 19.50 (*0-7854-0761-8*, 40527) Am Guidance.

Lake Illustrated Classics Collection 4 Classroom Library, 36 bks. 1994. pap., student ed. 99.95 (*0-7854-0758-8*, 40485) Am Guidance.

Lake Illustrated Classics Collection 4 Readalong Basic Set. 1994. pap., student ed. 129.95 incl. audio (*0-7854-0760-X*, 40490) Am Guidance.

Lake Illustrated Classics Collection 1 Through 5 & Shakespeare Complete Set, 72 bks. 1994. pap. 249.95 (*0-7854-0660-3*, 40300) Am Guidance.

Lake Illustrated Classics Collection 1 Through 5 & Shakespeare Complete Library, 216 bks. 1994. pap. 599.95 (*0-7854-0659-X*, 40305) Am Guidance.

Lake Illustrated Classics Collection 1 Through 5 & Shakespeare Complete Readalong Set. 1994. pap., student ed. 799.95 incl. audio (*0-7854-0661-1*, 40310) Am Guidance.

Lake Illustrated Classics Collection 1 Basic Set, 12 bks. 1994. pap. 39.95 (*0-7854-0700-6*, 40315) Am Guidance.

Lake Illustrated Classics Collection 1 Classroom Library, 36 bks. 1994. pap., student ed. 99.95 (*0-7854-0674-3*, 40320) Am Guidance.

Lake Illustrated Classics Collection 1 Readalong Basic Set. 1994. pap., student ed. 129.95 incl. audio (*0-7854-0701-4*, 40325) Am Guidance.

Lake Illustrated Classics Collection 1 Student Exercise Book. (YA). (gr. 6-12). 1994. pap., student ed. 19.50 (*0-7854-0702-2*, 40367) Am Guidance.

Lake Illustrated Classics Collection 3, 12 bks. 1994. pap. 39.95 (*0-7854-0731-6*, 40430); pap., student ed. 19.50 (*0-7854-0733-2*, 40477) Am Guidance.

Lake Illustrated Classics Collection 3 Classroom Library, 36 bks. 1994. pap. 99.95 (*0-7854-0730-8*, 40435) Am Guidance.

Lake Illustrated Classics Collection 3 Readalong Basic Set. 1994. pap., student ed. 129.95 incl. audio (*0-7854-0732-4*, 40440) Am Guidance.

Lake Illustrated Classics Collection 2. 1994. student ed. 19.50 (*0-7854-0680-8*, 40427); pap. 39.95 (*0-7854-0678-6*, 40370) Am Guidance.

Lake Illustrated Classics Collection 2 Classroom Library, 36 bks. 1994. pap. 99.95 (*0-7854-0677-8*, 40375) Am Guidance.

Lake Illustrated Classics Collection 2 Readalong Basic Set. 1994. pap., student ed. 129.95 incl. audio (*0-7854-0679-4*, 40380) Am Guidance.

Lake Illustrated Classics Shakespeare Collection. 1994. student ed. 19.50 (*0-7854-0818-5*, 40627); pap. 39.95 (*0-7854-0816-9*, 40580) Am Guidance.

Lake Illustrated Classics Shakespeare Collection Classroom Library, 36 bks. 1994. pap. 99.95 (*0-7854-0815-0*, 40585) Am Guidance.

Lake Illustrated Classics Shakespeare Collection Readalong Basic Set. 1994. pap., student ed. 129.95 incl. audio (*0-7854-0817-7*, 40590) Am Guidance.

Lake Joseph, 1860-1910: An Illustrated Notebook. William Gray. (Illus.). 128p. 1994. 40.00 (*1-55046-128-1*, Pub. by Boston Mills) Genl Dist Srvs.

Lake Kariba. E. K. Balon. 1974. text 389.50 (*90-6193-076-6*) Kluwer Academic.

Lake Kinneret: Lake of Tiberias, Sea of Galilee. Colette Serruya. (Monographiae Biologicae: No.32). 1978. text 206.50 (*90-6193-085-5*) Kluwer Academic.

Lake Linden's Disastrous Fire of 1887. (Copper Country Local History Ser.: Vol. 33). (Illus.). 128p. 1988. 3.00 (*0-942363-32-9*) C J Monette.

Lake Linden's Living History - 1985. Clarence J. Monette. (Copper Country Local History Ser.: Vol. 29). (Illus.). 112p. (Orig.). 1987. pap. 2.50 (*0-942363-28-0*) C J Monette.

Lake Linden's Yesterday: A Pictorial History, Vol. I. (Copper Country Local History Ser.: Vol. 10). (Illus.). 87p. 1977. 2.50 (*0-942363-09-4*) C J Monette.

Lake Linden's Yesterday: A Pictorial History, Vol. II. (Copper Country Local History Ser.: Vol. 16). (Illus.). 128p. 1980. 4.00 (*0-942363-15-9*) C J Monette.

Lake Linden's Yesterday: A Pictorial History, Vol. III. (Copper Country Local History Ser.: Vol. 22). (Illus.). 104p. 1983. 2.50 (*0-942363-21-3*) C J Monette.

Lake Log, 1978: An Annual Review of the Great Lakes Shipping Season. Ed. by Gary L. Bailey. (Illus.). 80p. 1979. write for info. (*0-932690-02-5*) Ctr for Arch Collects.

An Asterisk (*) at the beginning of an entry indicates that the title is appearing for the first time.

Lake Louise. (Orchestra Collection: for the Clavinova & Yamaha Disk Ser.). 1995. disk 34.95 (*0-7935-6931-1*) H Leonard.

***Lake Malawi Cichlids.** Mark Smith. (Complete Pet Owner's Manuals Ser.). 2000. pap. text. write for info. (*0-7641-1525-1*, Pub. by Barron) Prodn Assocs.

***Lake Mattamuskeet: New Holland & Hyde County.** Lewis Forrest. (Images of America Ser.). (Illus.). 128p. 1999. pap. 18.99 (*0-7385-0271-5*) Arcadia Publng.

Lake McIlwaine: The Eutrophication & Recovery of a Tropical African Man-Made Lake. J. A. Thorton. 1982. text 171.00 (*90-6193-102-9*) Kluwer Academic.

Lake Mead & Hoover Dam: The Story Behind the Scenery. James C. Maxon. LC 79-87573. (Illus.). 48p. (Orig.). 1980. pap. 7.95 (*0-916122-61-1*) KC Pubns.

Lake Mead & Hoover Dam: The Story Behind the Scenery. James C. Maxon. Tr. by Brigitte Morales. (GER., Illus.). 48p. (Orig.). 1993. pap. 8.95 (*0-88714-734-8*) KC Pubns.

Lake Mead & Hoover Dam: The Story Behind the Scenery. James C. Maxon. Tr. by Frances Y. Lee. (CHI., Illus.). (Orig.). 1993. pap. 8.95 (*0-88714-780-1*) KC Pubns.

Lake Mead & Hoover Dam: The Story Behind the Scenery. James C. Maxon. Tr. by Saori Petzinger. (JPN., Illus.). 48p. (Orig.). 1993. pap. 8.95 (*0-88714-781-X*) KC Pubns.

Lake Mead Boating Guide: Places to Go & Things to See & Do. Geoffrey Schneider & Rose Houk. LC 97-32496. (Illus.). 56p. 1998. pap. 7.95 (*1-877856-78-9*) SW Pks Mnmts.

Lake Mead National Recreation Area. Rose Houk. LC 96-70356. 16p. 1997. pap. 3.95 (*1-877856-65-7*) SW Pks Mnmts.

Lake Mead National Recreation Area, Nevada. rev. ed. Ed. by Trails Illustrated Staff. (Illus.). 1995. 8.99 (*0-925873-04-7*) Trails Illustrated.

Lake Meredith National Recreation Area. Laurence E. Parent. Ed. by Ronald J. Foreman & Sandra Scott. LC 92-62160. (Illus.). 16p. (Orig.). 1993. pap. 3.95 (*1-877856-16-9*) SW Pks Mnmts.

Lake Merritt. Frank Jakubowsky. 60p. (Orig.). (J). 1988. pap. 4.95 (*0-932588-10-7*) Jesus Bks.

Lake Metabolism & Management: Papers Emanating from the Limnological Jubilee Symposium of Uppsala University, 1477-1977. Ed. by W. Rodhe et al. (Advances in Limnology Ser.: Vol. 13). (GER., Illus.). iv, 349p. (Orig.). 1979. 76.00 (*3-510-47011-7*, Pub. by E Schweizerbartsche) Balogh.

Lake Michigan. Ann Armbruster. LC 96-2029. (True Bk.). (Illus.). 48p. (J). 1996. lib. bdg. 21.00 (*0-516-20013-5*) Childrens.

Lake Michigan. Ann Armbruster. (True Bks.). 48p. (J). 1997. pap. 6.95 (*0-516-26104-5*) Childrens.

***Lake Michigan.** Contrib. by Harry Beckett. LC 99-13023. (Great Lakes of North America Ser.). 32p. 1999. lib. bdg. write for info. (*0-86593-524-6*) Rourke Corp.

Lake Michigan. Milo M. Quaife. (American Lakes Ser.). lib. bdg. 26.95 (*0-8488-2014-2*) Amereon Ltd.

***Lake Michigan: A Guide to Small Towns, Rural Areas & Natural Attractions.** Donna Marchetti. 327p. 2000. pap. 16.95 (*1-881139-25-5*) Glovebox Guidebks.

Lake Michigan Islands, 2 vols., Set. Kathleen C. Firestone. (C). 1996. write for info. (*0-9625631-3-7*) MI Islands Rsch.

Lake Michigan Poker: The Gem of Lighthouses! Karl W. Grube. 75p. (YA). (gr. 7-12). 1995. pap. 24.00 (*0-9627003-3-9*) Games By Grube.

Lake Michigan Shipwrecks: South Haven to Grand Haven. Kit Lane. (Saugatuck Maritime Ser.: Vol. 4). (Illus.). 192p. (Orig.). 1997. pap. 15.50 (*1-877703-03-6*) Pavilion Pr.

Lake Michigan's Railroad Car Ferries. Karl Zimmermann. (Illus.). 64p. (Orig.). 1993. pap. 24.95 (*0-944119-11-5*) Andover Junction.

Lake Minchumina Prehistory: An Archeological Analysis. Charles E. Holmes. (Aurora Ser.: Vol. 2). (Illus.). x, 176p. 1986. pap. 15.00 (*1-890396-02-8*) AK Anthropological.

Lake, Mire & River Environment During the Last 150000 Years: Proceedings of the INQUA-IGCP 158 Meetings on the Palaeohydrological Changes During the Last 150000 Years, Bern, June, 1985. Ed. by G. Lang & C. Schluchter. (Illus.). 248p. (C). 1988. text 91.00 (*90-6191-849-9*, Pub. by A A Balkema) Ashgate Pub Co.

Lake Moriman Our Inland Sea. rev. ed. Diana C. Gleasner. (Illus.). 72p. 1986. reprint ed. 15.95 (*0-9651185-2-5*) B & D Gleasner.

Lake, Nanda & Draetta: Breach & Adaption of International Contracts. Ralph B. Lake et al. 1992. write for info. (*0-406-02055-8*, DLNB, MICHIE) LEXIS Pub.

Lake News. Barbara Delinsky. 384p. 1999. 23.50 (*0-684-86432-0*) S&S Trade.

Lake News. large type ed. Barbara Delinsky. LC 99-31498. 1950. 30.00 (*0-7838-8660-8*, G K Hall Lrg Type) Mac Lib Ref.

***Lake News.** large type ed. Barbara Delinsky. LC 99-31498. 581p. 1999. 30.00 (*0-7838-8659-4*, G K Hall Lrg Type) Mac Lib Ref.

***Lake News.** Barbara Delinsky. 544p. 2000. reprint ed. mass mkt. 7.99 (*0-671-03619-X*, Pocket Star Bks) PB.

Lake Norman - Piedmont History. Marvin K. Brotherton. LC 94-78239. 200p. 1995. write for info. (*1-886057-01-X*) Warren Pubg NC.

Lake of Dreams. Sam Enslow. Ed. by Charles G. Gee. 170p. Date not set. pap. 14.95 (*1-889936-14-6*) Skyline Pubs Inc.

Lake of Dreams. Sam Enslow. Ed. by Charles G. Gee. 350p. 1996. 19.95 (*0-9645786-6-2*) VYTIS Pub.

Lake of Dreams. large type ed. Jody McCrae. 244p. 1992. reprint ed. 13.95 (*1-56054-409-0*) Thorndike Pr.

Lake of Fire. unabridged ed. Michael Fowler. LC 98-66502. 177p. 1999. 18.95 (*0-9662139-0-4*) Lakeside MO.

Lake of Fury. large type ed. Bill Knox. (Linford Mystery Library). 368p. 1996. pap. 16.99 (*0-7089-7932-7*) Ulverscroft.

Lake of Lost Love. Mercedes Kelly. (Black Lace Ser.). (Orig.). 1998. mass mkt. 5.95 (*0-352-33220-4*, Pub. by BLA4) London Brdge.

***Lake of Memory Rising: Return of the Five Ancient Truths at the Heart of Religion.** William Fix. LC 99-87106. 288p. 2000. 23.95 (*1-57178-091-2*) Coun Oak Bks.

Lake of the Beginning: A Fable of Salmon & Northern Lights. Ed Gray. LC 98-30023. (Illus.). 126p. 1998. 22.50 (*1-57223-085-1*, 0851) Willow Creek Pr.

Lake of the Big Snake: An African Rain Forest Adventure. Isaac Olaleye. LC 95-80780. (Illus.). 32p. (J). (ps-3). 1998. 15.95 (*1-56397-096-1*) Boyds Mills Pr.

Lake of the Kingfisher. large type ed. Essie Summers. 1991. 27.99 (*0-7089-2454-9*) Ulverscroft.

Lake of the Long Sun. Gene Wolfe. 1995. mass mkt. 5.99 (*0-8125-5068-4*, Pub. by Tor Bks) St Martin.

Lake of the Sky: Lake Tahoe in the High Sierra of California & Nevada. George W. James. (Illus.). 270p. 1992. 39.95 (*0-913814-91-1*); pap. 22.50 (*0-913814-90-3*) Nevada Pubns.

Lake of the Sky: Lake Tahoe in the High Sierras of California & Nevada. George W. James. Ed. by William R. Jones. (Illus.). 96p. 1996. reprint ed. pap. 4.95 (*0-89646-038-X*) Vistabooks.

Lake of the Woods County: A History of People, Places & Events. Ed. by Marlys L. Hirst. (Illus.). 480p. 1996. 29.95 (*0-9654564-0-4*) Lake of the Woods.

Lake of the Woods II. Duane R. Lund. 1984. pap. 8.95 (*0-934860-36-X*) Adventure Pubns.

Lake of the Woods, Yesterday & Today. Duane R. Lund. 112p. 1976. pap. 8.95 (*0-934860-03-3*) Adventure Pubns.

Lake Ontario. Ann Armbruster. LC 96-2081. (True Bk.). (Illus.). 48p. (J). 1996. lib. bdg. 21.00 (*0-516-20014-3*) Childrens.

Lake Ontario. Ann Armbruster. (True Bks.). 48p. (J). 1997. pap. 6.95 (*0-516-26105-3*) Childrens.

***Lake Ontario.** Harry Beckett. LC 99-13175. 32p. 1999. lib. bdg. write for info. (*0-86593-526-2*) Rourke Corp.

Lake Ontario. Arthur Pound. (American Lakes Ser.). lib. bdg. 26.95 (*0-8488-2013-4*) Amereon Ltd.

Lake Peipus 1214. David Nicolle. (Campaign Ser.: No. 47). (Illus.). 96p. 1996. pap. 15.95 (*1-85532-553-5*, Pub. by Ospry) Stackpole.

Lake Petha & the Lost Murals of Chiapas. J. David Wonham. (Pre-Columbian Art Research Institute Monographs: No. 2). (Illus.). 19p. (Orig.). pap. 10.00 (*0-934051-02-X*) Pre-Columbian Art.

Lake Placid Trails. W. D. Mulholland. 22p. 1993. reprint ed. lib. bdg. 69.00 (*0-7812-5261-X*) Rprt Serv.

Lake Poem. Christopher Hollister. LC 92-61231. 55p. 1992. pap. write for info. (*0-9633318-0-9*) White Tail Bks.

Lake Pontchartrain. W. Adolphe Roberts. (American Lakes Ser.). lib. bdg. 26.95 (*0-8488-2021-5*) Amereon Ltd.

Lake Powell: A Different Light. William Smart. LC 94-18654. (Illus.). 96p. 1994. pap. 18.95 (*0-87905-609-6*) Gibbs Smith Pub.

Lake Powell: A Photographic Essay of Glen Canyon National Recreation Area. Gary Ladd. Ed. by Mark A. Schlenz. (Illus.). 96p. 1994. 34.95 (*0-944197-30-2*); pap. 19.95 (*0-944197-29-9*) Companion CA.

Lake Powell - Glen Canyon National Recreation Area. Stewart Aitchison. Ed. by Jeff Nicholas. (Pocket Portfolio Ser.: Vol. 13). (Illus.). 32p. 1999. pap. 5.95 (*1-58071-000-X*, Pub. by Panorama Intl) Falcon Pub Inc.

Lake Powell Monument Valley. Casa Bonechi. 64p. text 10.95 (*88-7009-215-1*, Pub. by Bonechi) Eiron.

***Lake Powell's Map to the Stars.** Rolf J. Kappeli. (Illus.). 5p. 1999. pap. 16.95 (*1-928893-01-5*) Star Gazers.

Lake Prespa, North-Western Greece: A Unique Balkan Wetland. Ed. by Alain J. Crivelli & George Catsadorakis. LC 97-31472. (Developments in Hydrobiology Ser.: No. 122). 196p. 1997. text 154.00 (*0-7923-4795-1*) Kluwer Academic.

Lake Recreation in Southern California for Week Enders. rev. ed. Herschell Whitmer & Scott Whitmer. (Illus.). 187p. 1996. pap. write for info. (*0-9619015-4-3*) H Whitmer Assocs.

Lake Region. Jack Barnes & Diane Barnes. (Images of America Ser.). (Illus.). 128p. 1998. pap. 16.99 (*0-7524-0204-8*) Arcadia Publng.

Lake Region of Central Africa: A Picture of Exploration. Richard F. Burton. LC 77-116278. (Illus.). 572p. 1972. reprint ed. 95.00 (*0-403-00442-X*) Scholarly.

Lake Regions of Central Africa. Richard F. Burton. LC 94-46004. (Illus.). 576p. 1995. pap. text 14.95 (*0-486-28618-5*) Dover.

Lake Restoration by Reduction of Nutrient Loading: Expectations, Experiences, Extrapolations. Ed. by H. Sas. 497p. 1989. lib. bdg. 58.00 (*3-88345-379-X*) Lubrecht & Cramer.

***Lake Ringsjhon.** Eva Bergman & Lars-Anders Hansson. LC 99-43424. (Developments in Hydrobiology Ser.). 1999. write for info. (*0-7923-5955-0*) Kluwer Academic.

Lake, River & Sea: Run Fishes of Canada. 2nd ed. Frederick H. Wooding. 1997. pap. 18.95 (*1-55017-175-5*) Harbour Pub Co.

Lake Sacajawea: Longview's Treasure. Travis Cavens. LC 97-74061. (Illus.). 96p. 1997. pap. 20.00 (*0-9659385-0-6*) Lake Pub.

Lake St. Agnes Site: A Multi-Component Occupation of Avoyelles Parish, La. A. Toth. (Illus.). 52p. 1979. pap. 3.00 (*0-938909-47-9*) Geosci Pubns LSU.

Lake Shore & Michigan Southern Railway. David P. McLellan & Bill Warrick. Ed. by Ginger Riehle. LC 89-20230. (Illus.). 208p. 1989. text 40.00 (*0-933449-09-7*) Transport Trails.

Lake Shore Drive. Patrick Creevy. 384p. 1994. mass mkt. 4.99 (*0-8125-1279-0*) Tor Bks.

***Lake Shore Electric Railway Story.** Herbert H. Harwood & Robert S. Korach. LC 00-39646. (Railroads Past & Present Ser.). (Illus.). 2000. write for info. (*0-253-33797-6*) Ind U Pr.

Lake Shore Project. Mark D. Vance. Ed. by Mary Inbody. (Illus.). 211p. 1998. pap. 12.95 (*1-881116-91-3*) Black Forest Pr.

Lake Sibaya. Ed. by B. R. Allanson. (Monographiae Biologicae: No. 36). 1979. text 211.50 (*90-6193-088-X*) Kluwer Academic.

Lake Simcoe: And Lake Couchiching. Mary Byers. (Illus.). 1999. text 29.95 (*1-55046-269-5*, Pub. by Boston Mills) Genl Dist Srvs.

Lake Smarts: The First Lake Maintenance Handbook. Steve McComas. Ed. by Rachel Reeder. (Illus.). 228p. (Orig.). 1993. pap. 21.95 (*1-880686-11-2*) Terrene Inst.

Lake Stachlin. Ed. by S. Jost Casper. (Monographiae Biologicae). 1985. text 366.50 (*90-6193-512-1*) Kluwer Academic.

Lake Street Extension. Lee Blessing. 1993. pap. 5.25 (*0-8222-1336-2*) Dramatists Play.

Lake Success. Matt Kohn. 68p. 1996. pap. write for info. (*1-887128-16-6*) Soft Skull Pr.

Lake Superior. Ann Armbruster. LC 96-2027. (True Bk.). (Illus.). 48p. (J). 1996. lib. bdg. 21.00 (*0-516-20015-1*) Childrens.

Lake Superior. Ann Armbruster. (True Bks.). 48p. (J). 1997. pap. 6.95 (*0-516-26106-1*) Childrens.

***Lake Superior.** Harry Beckett. LC 98-47525. (Great Lakes of North America Ser.). 32p. (J). (gr. 3-5). 1999. lib. bdg. 17.45 (*0-86593-528-9*) Rourke Corp.

Lake Superior. Grace L. Nute. (American Lakes Ser.). lib. bdg. 26.95 (*0-8488-2009-6*) Amereon Ltd.

***Lake Superior.** Grace Lee Nute. LC 00-20940. (Fesler-Lampert Minnesota Heritage Bks.). (Illus.). 408p. 2000. pap. 15.95 (*0-8166-3581-1*) U of Minn Pr.

Lake Superior. John F. Prevost. LC 98-11983. (Lakes Ser.). (J). 2000. write for info. (*1-57765-104-9*) ABDO Pub Co.

Lake Superior: Its Physical Character: Vegetation, & Animals Compared with Those of Other & Similar Regions. Louis Agassiz. LC 79-125727. (American Environmental Studies). 1972. reprint ed. 24.95 (*0-405-02652-8*) Ayer.

Lake Superior: Story & Spirit. John Mahan & Ann Mahan. LC 96-35972. 1997. write for info. (*1-883755-11-5*) Lost Riv Pr.

Lake Superior Agate. 3rd ed. (C). 1996. write for info. (*0-8087-9569-4*) Pearson Custom.

Lake Superior Agate. 3rd ed. Scott F. Wolter. (Illus.). 103p. 1996. pap. 24.95 (*0-8087-5271-5*) Pearson Custom.

Lake Superior Basin Segment of the Midcontinent Rift System. Ed. by Albert B. Dickas. (IGC Field Trip Guidebooks Ser.). 72p. 1989. 13.00 (*0-87590-557-9*, T344) Am Geophysical.

Lake Superior Checkers: The Gem of English Draughts! Kathryn Grube. 56p. (YA). (gr. 5 up). 1995. pap. 24.00 (*0-9627003-1-2*) Games By Grube.

Lake Superior Country in History & in Story. Guy Burnham. (Illus.). 464p. 1996. reprint ed. pap. 19.50 (*1-889924-00-8*) Paradigm Pr WI.

Lake Superior Cribbage: The Gem of Board Games! Karl W. Grube & Kathryn Grube. (Illus.). 120p. (YA). (gr. 5 up). 1994. pap. text 24.00 (*0-9627003-6-3*) Games By Grube.

Lake Superior Gold: An Amateur's Guide to Prospecting in the Lake Superior Region. Jim Dwyer. LC 92-14659. 1992. pap. 9.95 (*0-87839-067-7*) North Star.

Lake Superior Images. 2nd rev. ed. Craig Blacklock. (Illus.). 192p. 1998. 49.95 (*1-892472-00-7*) Blacklock Nature.

Lake Superior Images. 2nd rev. ed. Craig Blacklock & Adventure Publishing Staff. (Illus.). 192p. 1998. pap. 29.95 (*0-9634991-8-1*) Blacklock Nature.

Lake Superior Journal: Bela Hubbard's Account of the 1840 Houghton Expedition. Ed. by Bernard C. Peters. LC 82-60622. (Illus.). 113p. 1982. 8.95 (*0-918616-11-5*) Northern Mich.

***Lake Superior Journal: Jim Marshall's Views from the Bridge.** James R. Marshall. Ed. by Paul L. Hayden & Konnie LeMay. LC 99-41485. (Illus.). 192p. 1999. pap. 14.95 (*0-942235-40-1*) LSPC Inc.

Lake Superior Magazine Travel Guide, 1999. 12th ed. Ed. by Paul L. Hayden & Hugh E. Bishop. (Illus.). 154p. 1999. pap. 6.95 (*0-942235-35-5*) LSPC Inc.

Lake Superior 96. 15.95 (*0-942235-26-6*) LSPC Inc.

Lake Superior Place Names: From Bawating to the Montreal. Bernard C. Peters. (Illus.). 111p. 1996. 21.95 (*0-918616-16-6*); pap. 11.95 (*0-918616-18-2*) Northern Mich.

Lake Superior Recreation & Weather: A Four-Season Guide. Martha Walter & Richard DeAngelis. 96p. 1994. pap. 3.95 (*1-885756-06-2*, MICHU-SG-94-705) MI Sea Grant.

Lake Superior Shipwreck Coast. 9th ed. Frederick Stonehouse. LC 85-70794. (Illus.). 1990. pap. 13.95 (*0-932212-43-3*) Avery Color.

Lake Superior, Story & Spirit. John Mahan & Ann Mahan. LC 97-92359. (Illus.). 260p. 1998. 56.00 (*0-9659189-0-4*) Sweetwater Vis.

Lake Superior's North Shore: Wild Places. Jay Steinke. 64p. 1993. 18.95 (*0-9635871-0-2*) Tea Table Bks.

Lake Superior's North Shore & Isle Royale. Kate Crowley & Mike Link. LC 89-14782. (Voyageur Wilderness Ser.). (Illus.). 96p. (Orig.). 1996. pap. 14.95 (*0-89658-115-2*) Voyageur Pr.

Lake Tahoe: A Family Guide. Lisa G. Evans. LC 93-16105. (Outdoor Family Guide Ser.). 224p. (Orig.). 1993. pap. 12.95 (*0-89886-325-2*) Mountaineers.

Lake Tahoe: A Photo Essay of the Lake Tahoe Region. Larry Prosor & Leo Popoff. Ed. by Laurel H. Lippert. (Illus.). 150p. (Orig.). (C). 1992. pap. 19.95 (*0-9620148-0-X*) Fineline Productions.

Lake Tahoe: A Photo Essay of the Lake Tahoe Region. 2nd ed. Larry Prosor & Leo Popoff. Ed. by Laurel H. Lippert. (Illus.). 135p. (Orig.). 1993. 34.95 (*0-9620148-2-6*) Fineline Productions.

Lake Tahoe: The Way It Was Then & Now. Phyllis Zauner. (Western Mini-Histories Ser.). 64p. 1982. pap. 8.95 (*0-936914-13-0*) Zanel Pubns.

***Lake Tahoe: Travelin with the Little White Dog.** John Holland. (Lake Tahoe: 1). 22p. 2000. pap. 24.95 (*0-9700070-0-0*) Littl Whte Dog.

Lake Tahoe & High Sierra in a Nutshell. Leslie D. Cole. (In a Nutshell Ser.). (Illus.). 1995. pap. 5.95 (*1-884497-03-9*) Nutshell TourMaps.

Lake Tahoe Weddings: A Destination Wedding Guide for Brides. Tara W. McNamara. Ed. by Kristy Uzcategui-Taylor. LC 96-83130. (Illus.). 184p. (Orig.). 1996. pap. 16.95 (*0-9651887-2-8*) Dreamweaver Pr.

***Lake Tahoe/Reno Entertainment, 2000.** (Illus.). 422p. 1999. pap. 35.00 (*1-58553-032-8*, 003G) Enter Pubns.

Lake Tahoe's Twenty Best Pavement & Dirt Rides. Ray W. Miskimins. Ed. by Reanne Hemingway-Douglass. (Illus.). 48p. (Orig.). 1995. pap. 5.95 (*0-938665-36-7*) Fine Edge Prods.

Lake Tana & the Blue Nile: Abyssinian Quest. R. E. Cheesman. (Illus.). 400p. 1967. reprint ed. 47.50 (*0-7146-1641-9*, BHA-01641, Pub. by F Cass Pubs) Intl Spec Bk.

Lake Tanganyikan Cichlids. Mark Smith. LC 98-18145. (Barron's Complete Pet Owner's Manuals). 64p. 1998. pap. 6.95 (*0-7641-0615-5*) Barron.

Lake Titicaca: A Synthesis of Limnological Knowledge. Ed. by C. Dejoux & A. Iltis. (Monographiae Biologicae). 584p. (C). 1992. text 374.00 (*0-7923-1663-0*) Kluwer Academic.

Lake Veluwe: A Macrophyte-Dominated System under Eutrophication Stress. Ed. by W. Van Vierssen. LC 93-19534. (Geobotany Ser.). 340p. (C). 1994. text 276.00 (*0-7923-2320-3*) Kluwer Academic.

Lake Victoria. Carl Meister. LC 98-7298. (Lakes Ser.). 2002. lib. bdg. 19.92 (*1-57765-105-7*) ABDO Pub Co.

Lake Victoria Wetlands & the Ecology of the Nile Tilapia, Oreochromis Niliticus Linne. John S. Balirwa. LC 99-496402. (IHE Thesis Ser.: Vol. 11). (Illus.). 247p. (C). 1998. text 42.00 (*90-5410-411-2*, Pub. by A A Balkema) Ashgate Pub Co.

Lake Walk Is a Cakewalk. Kathryn Isola. (Illus.). 20p. (J). (ps-6). 1997. pap. 5.95 (*0-9658821-0-1*) Lakewalk Publ.

Lake Water Nutrient Chemistry & Chlorophyll A in Pasqua, Echo, Mission, Katepwa, Crooked & Round Lakes on the Qu'Appelle River, Saskatchewan R. J. Allan & M. Roy. LC 85-117001. (Scientific Ser.). (ENG & FRE.). v, 68 p. 1980. write for info. (*0-662-10916-3*) Can7 Govern Pub.

Lake with Two Dams: Understanding Mental Illness. William H. Hampton & Virginia S. Burnham. LC 92-46255. 160p. (Orig.). 1993. pap. 14.95 (*0-86534-170-2*) Sunstone Pr.

Lake Wobegon Days. Garrison Keillor. 432p. 1990. pap. 12.95 (*0-14-013161-2*, Penguin Bks) Viking Penguin.

Lake Wobegon U. S. A. Fertility. unabridged ed. Garrison Keillor. 1995. pap. 11.00 incl. audio (*1-56511-110-9*, Pub. by HighBridge) Penguin Putnam.

Lake Wobegon U. S. A. Patience. unabridged ed. Garrison Keillor. 1995. pap. 11.00 incl. audio (*1-56511-109-5*, Pub. by HighBridge) Penguin Putnam.

Lake Wobegon U. S. A. Rhubarb. unabridged ed. Garrison Keillor. 1995. pap. 11.00 incl. audio (*1-56511-112-5*, Pub. by HighBridge) Penguin Putnam.

Lake Wobegon U. S. A. Youth. unabridged ed. Garrison Keillor. 1995. pap. 11.00 incl. audio (*1-56511-111-7*, Pub. by HighBridge) Penguin Putnam.

Lake/Flato Architects. Oscar R. Ojeda. (Illus.). 132p. 1995. pap. 19.99 (*1-56496-233-4*) Rockport Pubs.

Lakeland & Iceland, Being a Glossary of Words in the Dialect of Cumberland, Westmoreland...or Norse. T. Ellwood. (English Dialect Society Publications: No. 77). 1969. reprint ed. pap. 25.00 (*0-8115-0495-6*) Periodicals Srv.

***Lakeland Boating Ports 'O Call Vol. II: Lake Huron Cruise Guide.** 2nd rev. ed. O'Meara-Brown Publications Inc. Staff. (Illus.). 1999. spiral bd. 44.95 (*1-890839-06-X*) OMeara-Brown Pubns.

Lakeland Boating Ports O' Call Lake Erie & Lk. St. Claire: Includes the Detroit & St. Claire Rivers. 2nd rev. ed. Walter O'Meara. Ed. by Randall W. Hess. (Lakeland Boating Ports O'Call Ser.). (Illus.). 304p. 1998. spiral bd. 44.95 (*1-890839-05-1*) OMeara-Brown Pubns.

Lakeland Boating Ports O' Call Lake Michigan: Cruising Guide. 2nd ed. Dave Wallace & John Wooldridge. (Lakeland Boating Ports O'Call Ser.: Vol. 1). (Illus.). 304p. 1995. reprint ed. spiral bd. 44.95 (*1-890839-00-0*) OMeara-Brown Pubns.

Lakeland Boating Ports O' Call Lake Ontario, Vol. 1. Dave Wallace & John Wooldridge. (Lakeland Boating Ports O' Call Ser.). 282p. 1997. spiral bd. 44.95 (*1-890839-03-5*) OMeara-Brown Pubns.

Lakeland CC Special Essentials. Long. 148p. 1995. pap. text 5.00 (*0-13-226671-7*) P-H.

Lakeland Fells Almanac. Bill Birksett. 160p. 1997. 15.00 (*1-897784-59-7*, Pub. by N Wilson Pubng) Interlink Pub.

***Lakeland Landscapes.** Rob Talbot & Robin Whiteman. (Illus.). 2000. pap. 24.95 (*0-7538-0511-1*) Phoenix Hse.

L

Lakeland Landscapes. Rob Talbot & Robin Whiteman. LC 99-458598. (Illus.). 160p. 1997. 39.95 (*0-297-82204-7*, Pub. by Weidenfeld & Nicolson) Trafalgar.
Lakeland Nurse. large type ed. Gill Sanderson. (Mills & Boon Large Print Ser.). 288p. 1997. 23.99 (*0-263-15144-1*, Pub. by Mills & Boon) Ulverscroft.
Lakeland Peaks. W. A. Poucher. (Illus.). 430p. 1998. 22.95 (*0-09-477510-9*, Pub. by Constable & Co) Trafalgar.
Lakeland Poets. Jenny Wilson. (Illus.). 112p. 1997. 8.98 (*0-7858-0046-8*) Bk Sales Inc.
Lakeland Terrier Champions, 1934-1990. Camino E. E. & Bk. Co. Staff. (Illus.). 310p. 1991. pap. 36.95 (*1-55893-023-X*) Camino E E & Bk.
Lakeland Terriers. Seymour N. Weiss. (KW Ser.). (Illus.). 192p. 1993. text 9.95 (*0-86622-592-7*, KW-218) TFH Pubns.
Lakeland to Lindisfarne: A Coast to Coast Walk from Ravenglass to Holy Island. John Gillham. (Illus.). 180p. 1996. pap. 17.95 (*1-85223-975-1*, Pub. by Cro1wood) Trafalgar.
Lakelore: A Tale of Medina, WA. Junius Rochester. 1993. pap. 11.00 (*0-9648950-0-5*) Tommie Pr.
Lakeport. Warren D. Huse & Laconia Historical Society Staff. (Images of America Ser.). 1998. pap. 16.99 (*0-7524-0862-3*) Arcadia Publng.
Lakeport: Ghost Town of the South Oregon Coast. Bert Webber & Margie Webber. LC 90-12071. (Illus.). 192p. 1990. pap. 12.95 (*0-936738-45-6*) Webb Research.
Lakers. James Plumptre. LC 90-40598. 88p. 1990. reprint ed. 40.00 (*1-85477-052-7*) Continuum.
Lakers, Vol. I. Eric E. Hirsimaki. LC 87-91264. 1987. pap. 32.50 (*0-929886-00-3*) Mileposts Pub.
Lakers: A Basketball Journey. rev. ed. Roland Lazenby. (Illus.). 320p. 1995. reprint ed. pap. 14.95 (*1-57028-062-2*, 80622H, Mstrs Pr) NTC Contemp Pub Co.
Lakers, 1950-1959. Eric E. Hirsimaki. (Illus.). 224p. 1991. 39.95 (*0-929886-05-4*) Mileposts Pub.
***Lakes.** Catherine Chambers. LC 99-43374. (Mapping Earthforms Ser.). (Illus.). 2000. lib. bdg. write for info. (*1-57572-524-X*) Heinemann Lib.
***Lakes.** Delphine Durieux. (Illus.). 80p. 1999. 29.95 (*3-929078-88-0*, Kehayoff) te Neues.
Lakes. Neil Morris. LC 96-27639. (The World's Top Ten Ser.). (Illus.). 32p. (J). 1997. lib. bdg. 22.83 (*0-8172-4345-3*) Raintree Steck-V.
Lakes. Andy Owen & Miranda Ashwell. LC 97-34417. (Geography Starts Ser.). (J). 1998. (*1-57572-606-8*) Heinemann.
Lakes & Ponds. 2nd ed. LC 92-60667. 118p. 1992. text 43.95 (*0-87420-730-4*, L01) Urban Land.
Lakes & Rivers. Chris Arvetis & Carole Palmer. LC 93-499. (Where Are We? Ser.). (Illus.). (J). 1993. 3.95 (*0-528-83572-6*) Rand McNally.
Lakes & Snails. Environment & Gastropoda in 1500 Norwegian Lakes, Ponds & Rivers: Environment & Gastropoda in 1500 Norwegian Lakes, Ponds & Rivers. J. Okland. (Illus.). 516p. 1990. 120.00 (*90-73348-02-1*, Pub. by Backhuys Pubs) Balogh.
Lakes & Water Management. V. Ilmavirta et al. 1982. text 176.50 (*90-6193-758-2*) Kluwer Academic.
Lakes, Lures & Lodges: An Angler's Guide to Western Canada. Jake MacDonald. 1993. per. 14.95 (*0-88801-176-8*) LPC InBook.
Lakes of New Mexico: A Guide to Recreation. Andy Sandersier. LC 96-9107. (Coyote Bks.). (Illus.). 353p. 1996. pap. 24.95 (*0-8263-1714-6*) U of NM Pr.
Lakes Ontario, Erie, Michigan, Huron, Superior & the St. Lawrence River. (U. S. Coast Pilot Series, 1999: Vol. 6). 1998. 29.95 (*1-57785-046-7*, 83699PCC) ProStar Pubns.
Lakes, Peaks, & Prairies: Discovering the United States-Canadian Border. Thomas O'Neill. Ed. by Donald J. Crump. LC 84-22775. (Special Publications Series 19: No. 3). (Illus.). 200p. 1984. 12.95 (*0-87044-478-6*); lib. bdg. 12.95 (*0-87044-483-2*) Natl Geog.
Lakes Region. Bruce D. Heald. LC 96-228073. (Images of America Ser.). 1996. pap. 16.99 (*0-7524-0455-5*) Arcadia Publng.
Lakes Region Cuisine: A Centennial Celebration, 1893-1993. Lakes Region General Hospital Auxiliary Staff. LC 93-70329. 1993. spiral bd. 12.50 (*0-87197-365-0*) Favorite Recipes.
Lakes Region II. Bruce D. Heald. (Images of America Ser.). 1998. write for info. (*0-7524-1348-1*) Arcadia Publng.
***Lakes Tie In.** K. M. Lock. 256p. 1998. pap. 13.95 (*0-14-026965-7*, Pub. by Pnguin Bks Ltd) Trafalgar.
***Lakescaping for Wildlife.** Carrol Henderson. (Illus.). 180p. 1999. spiral bd. write for info. (*0-9647451-2-7*) MN Bkstore.
***Lakeside & Marblehead Railroad.** Dean K. Fick. (Illus.). 176p. 2000. 39.95 (*0-9658624-1-0*) Montevallo Hist.
Lakeside City: The Dreaming of Joondalup. Tom Stannage. 270p. 1997. 75.00 (*1-875560-94-7*, Pub. by Univ of West Aust Pr) Intl Spec Bk.
Lakeside City: The Dreaming of Joondalup. Tom Stannage. (Illus.). 274p. 1997. pap. 45.00 (*1-875560-88-2*, Pub. by Univ of West Aust Pr) Intl Spec Bk.
***Lakeside Company: Case Studies In Auditing: J. Trussell Lakeside.** 8th ed. John Trussell. 2000. pap. text 54.00 (*0-13-088517-7*) P-H.
Lakeside Hospital. large type ed. Margaret Barker. 288p. 1995. 23.99 (*0-263-14177-2*, Pub. by Mills & Boon) Ulverscroft.
***Lakeside Master's Study of the Pulse: (Pin-hu Mo Hsueh)** Shi-zhen Li. Tr. by Bob Flaws from CHI. LC 98-71824. 130p. 1998. pap. 15.95 (*1-891845-01-2*) Blue Poppy Pr.
Lakeside Recreation: Corps of Engineers, Western United States. William C. Herow. LC 99-70200. (Illus.). 280p. 1999. pap. 14.95 (*1-885464-34-7*, No. 4010) Roundabout.
Lakeside Season. Cleo Chadwick. 384p. 1995. mass mkt. 3.99 (*0-8217-4817-3*, Pinncle Kensgtn) Kensgtn Pub Corp.
Lakeside Zero. large type ed. Douglas Enefer. 320p. pap. 18.99 (*0-7089-5422-7*) Ulverscroft.
Lakesport's Ancient Homes: Recollections of Major John Aldrich . . . And of the Homes of Lakeport in 1844 with Notes of Their Occupants Then & Later. John Aldrich. (Illus.). 86p. 1997. reprint ed. pap. 15.00 (*0-8328-6003-4*) Higginson Bk Co.
Lakeville Lady. large type ed. Jeanne Bowman. 1990. pap. 16.99 (*0-7089-6871-6*) Ulverscroft.
***Lakewood: New Jersey.** LC 00-104060. (Images of America Ser.). (Illus.). 128p. 2000. pap. 18.99 (*0-7385-0458-0*) Arcadia Publng.
Lakewood - Colorado: An Illustrated Biography, Limited 25th Birthday Edition. Ed. by Pat Wilcox. 320p. 1994. pap. text 16.95 (*0-9641751-1-8*) Lkewds Twenty-Fifth Birthday.
Lakhovsky Multi-Wave Oscillator. 1991. lib. bdg. 79.95 (*0-8490-4274-7*) Gordon Pr.
Lakhovsky Multiple Wave Oscillator Handbook. Compiled by Tom Brown. (Illus.). 160p. 1988. student ed. 19.95 (*0-945685-03-3*) Borderland Sciences.
Lakota. Terry P. Wilson. (Native American Wisdom Ser.). (Illus.). 64p. 1994. 9.95 (*0-8118-0450-X*) Chronicle Bks.
Lakota: An Illustrated History. Sergio Macedo. 56p. 1996. pap. 12.95 (*1-887896-02-3*) Treas Chest Bks.
Lakota & Cheyenne: Indian Views of the Great Sioux War, 1876-1877. Ed. by Jerome A. Greene. LC 94-12473. (Illus.). 240p. 1994. 26.95 (*0-8061-2681-7*) U of Okla Pr.
***Lakota & Cheyenne: Indian Views of the Great Sioux War, 1876-1877.** Jerome A. Greene. (Illus.). 192p. 2000. pap. text 13.95 (*0-8061-3245-0*) U of Okla Pr.

Lakota & Dakota Animal Wisdom Stories. Mark W. McGinnis. (Illus.). 24p. (J). 1994. pap. 11.98 (*1-877976-14-8*, 406-0016) Tipi Pr.
LAKOTA & DAKOTA ANIMAL WISDOM STORIES is a compilation of twelve traditional, northern plains Native American stories retold by Dakota storyteller, Pamela Greenhill Kaizen & are accompanied by twelve full-color illustrations by South Dakota artist & educator Mark W. McGinnis. Leonard R. Bruguier, a descendant of the Yankton chiefs, War Eagle & Struck by the Ree, presents the introduction. The stories use animal characters to deal with the themes of compassion, greed, generosity, protection, survival, hard work, laziness, bravery, foolishness, trickery, & others. They range from simple humor as in THE FROG & THE TURTLE BROTHERS, where two close friends decide to jump in the lake rather than catch colds by getting wet in the rain, to the rich & complex story of THE CRANE, which weaves a tale of compassion & caring for one's neighbors. The animal characters give insightful guidance on human morals & ethics, & give a glimpse into the wonderful wit & wisdom of the Lakota & Dakota people. Mark McGinnis' paintings interpret a critical instant from each story, translating the oral moment to a visual expression of color, texture & shapes. This book is well suited to be read to younger children, to be read by older children, or for adults who enjoy new perspectives into Native American culture. Available for $11.98 plus $3.00 S/H from Tipi Press, St. Joseph's Indian School, Chamberlain, SD 57326; 605-734-3300. ***Publisher Paid Annotation.***

Lakota Belief & Ritual. James R. Walker. Ed. by Raymond J. DeMallie & Elaine A. Jahner. LC 91-15037. (Illus.). xli, 369p. 1991. reprint ed. pap. 18.95 (*0-8032-9731-9*, Bison Books) U of Nebr Pr.
***Lakota Culture, World Economy.** Kathleen Ann Pickering. LC 00-23482. (Illus.). 224p. 2000. text 39.95 (*0-8032-3690-5*) U of Nebr Pr.
Lakota Dawn, 1. Janelle Taylor. 1999. 23.00 (*1-57566-410-0*) Kensgtn Pub Corp.
Lakota Dawn. Janelle Taylor. 304p. 1999. mass mkt. 6.99 (*0-8217-6421-7*, Zebra Kensgtn) Kensgtn Pub Corp.

Lakota Grieving: A Pastoral Response. Stephen Huffstetter. 157p. 1998. pap. 7.95 (*1-877976-20-2*) Tipi Pr.
LAKOTA GRIEVING: A PASTORAL RESPONSE explores the grieving practices & rituals of Lakota Catholics on the Cheyenne River Sioux Reservation in South Dakota. The author, a Roman Catholic priest engaged in ministry on the reservation, proposes that Lakota people have taken rituals from both their Lakota & Christian traditions & created a merged culture to meet their grieving needs. Ethnographic interviews with the Lakota provide an overview of current grieving practices on the reservation. While these stories are quite personal, they also speak to the more universal human feelings & reactions in the response to loss. Lakota traditions & cultural resources that facilitate good grieving & the ways Lakota people can get stuck in their grieving are both explored. The interviews & a review of mortality data show that traumatic deaths, conflicted grieving, & multiple loss complicate grieving. The author offers principles to improve the practice of pastoral ministry to people in grief based on recommendations by Lakota people & from his own ministry among them. ***Publisher Paid Annotation.***

Lakota Healer. Marco Ridomi. LC 99-11452. (Illus.). 96p. (Orig.). 1998. pap. 19.95 (*1-886449-66-X*, P966X, Pub. by Barrytown Ltd) Consort Bk Sales.
Lakota Hoop Dancer. Suzanne Haldane & Jacqueline Left Hand Bull. LC 98-21905. 32p. (J). (gr. 3-6). 1999. 15.99 (*0-525-45413-6*) NAL.
Lakota, Introductory. unabridged ed. 102p. 1989. pap. text 185.00 incl. audio (*0-88432-448-6*, AFLK10) Audio-Forum.
Lakota Life. Ron Zeilinger. (Illus.). 74p. (Orig.). 1986. pap. 3.95 (*1-877976-07-5*, 406-0002) Tipi Pr.
Lakota Myth. James R. Walker. Ed. by Elaine A. Jahner. LC 83-3454. 428p. 1983. pap. 16.95 (*0-8032-9706-8*, Bison Books) U of Nebr Pr.
Lakota Noon: The Indian Narrative of Custer's Defeat. Gregory F. Michno. LC 97-13581. 352p. 1996. 36.00 (*0-87842-356-7*); pap. 18.00 (*0-87842-349-4*) Mountain Pr.
Lakota of the Rosebud: A Contemporary Ethnography. Elizabeth S. Grobsmith. 160p. (C). 1981. pap. text 23.50 (*0-03-057438-2*) Harcourt Coll Pubs.
Lakota Princess. Karen Kay. 384p. (Orig.). 1995. mass mkt. 4.99 (*0-380-77996-X*, Avon Bks) Morrow Avon.
Lakota Recollections of the Custer Fight: New Sources of Indian-Military History. Ed. & Compiled by Richard G. Hardorff. LC 96-46297. (Illus.). vii, 211p. 1997. pap. 10.00 (*0-8032-7293-6*, Bison Books) U of Nebr Pr.
Lakota Renegade. Madeline Baker. 448p. (Orig.). 1995. pap. text 5.99 (*0-8439-3832-3*) Dorchester Pub Co.
***Lakota Renegade, 1.** Madeline Baker. 448p. (Orig.). 1999. reprint ed. mass mkt. 5.99 (*0-8439-4588-5*, Leisure Bks) Dorchester Pub Co.
Lakota Ritual of the Sweat Lodge: History & Contemporary Practice. Raymond A. Bucko. LC 97-47504. (Studies in the Anthropology of North American Indians). (Illus.). 340p. 1999. text 40.00 (*0-8032-1272-0*, Bison Books) U of Nebr Pr.
***Lakota Ritual of the Sweat Lodge: History & Contemporary Practice.** Raymond A. Bucko. LC 97-47504. (Studies in the Anthropology of North American Indians). (Illus.). 340p. 1999. pap. 14.95 (*0-8032-6165-9*, Bison Books) U of Nebr Pr.
Lakota Sioux Children & Elders Talk Together. E. Barrie Kavasch. LC 98-33692. (Library of Intergenerational Learning). 24p. (J). (gr. k-4). 1999. 18.00 (*0-8239-5226-6*, PowerKids) Rosen Group.
Lakota Society. James R. Walker. Ed. by Raymond J. DeMallie. LC 81-14676. (Illus.). xvi, 243p. 1982. reprint ed. pap. 13.95 (*0-8032-9737-8*, Bison Books) U of Nebr Pr.
Lakota Songs. Isaac Brave Eagle. 100p. (C). 1996. 17.00 incl. audio (*1-887786-24-4*) Sky & Sage Bks.
Lakota Surrender. Karen Kay. 384p. (Orig.). 1994. mass mkt. 4.50 (*0-380-77721-5*, Avon Bks) Morrow Avon.

Lakota Tales & Texts in Translation, 2 vols., Set. Eugene Buechel & Paul Manhart. 850p. 1998. 39.95 (*1-877976-22-9*) Tipi Pr.
LAKOTA TALES & TEXTS IN TRANSLATION has a remarkable history of its own. The original Lakota manuscript was rescued from destruction during the violent occupation of the village of Wounded Knee, South Dakota, during the late winter of 1973. In 1970, Paul Manhart, a Catholic priest of the Society of Jesus & at the time a pastor in that village, had published Eugene Buechel, S.J.'s monumental Lakota-English Dictionary, with the late Louis & Daisy Whirlwind Horse assisting. Louis had been a tribal interpreter & Daisy was a highly perceptive translator. Father Manhart had an office in the Sacred Heart of Jesus Church overlooking the mass grave of Lakota visitor victims of the 1890 massacre. At the time of occupation, he had borrowed the original manuscript of Buechel's "Lakota Tales & Texts" from the Holy Rosary Mission archives. He was planning soon to publish it. So he kept it on a lower shelf in the far corner of his small library. Early during the occupation, he & two local men, Benjamin White Butterfly & Ruben Mesteth, took a box & went to the office, only to find it in shambles & the room & library shelves stripped of books - all except the Tales & Texts manuscript in the corner, a dingy home-made book in Lakota long-hand, untouched. All else was gone. In June of 1978 then, "Lakota Tales & Texts" was published in St. Louis. Father Manhart prepared this translation to answer many requests from teachers of history, social sciences, & language; & to lay a groundwork for preparing a series of Lakota language texts for systematically teaching the language in a two or four-year high school course. In Louis & Daisy Whirlwind Horse's words: "Our children will lose some real & conscious contact with their roots unless we continues to record & study Lakota." ***Publisher Paid Annotation.***

Lakota Warrior: A Personal Narrative. Joseph W. Bull. Ed. & Tr. by James H. Howard. LC 98-39666. (ENG & NAI., Illus.). 1998. pap. 15.00 (*0-8032-9806-4*, Bison Books) U of Nebr Pr.
***Lakota Winds.** Janelle Taylor. LC 97-74359. 320p. 1998. 23.00 (*1-57566-267-4*, Knsington) Kensgtn Pub Corp.
Lakota Winds. Janelle Taylor. 1999. mass mkt. 6.99 (*0-8217-6199-4*) Kensgtn Pub Corp.
Lakota Woman Tie In. Mary Crow Dog et al. LC 90-55980. (Illus.). 288p. 1994. pap. 13.00 (*0-06-097389-7*) HarperTrade.

Lakshana: Autopsy of a Century. Mark Slade. LC 94-71048. (West & the Wider World Ser.: Vol. 8). (Illus.). 270p. 1994. 39.95 (*0-940121-24-7*, H206, Cross Roads Bks) Cross Cultural Pubns.
This book takes a personal look at the century about to end & traces the profile of innocence & culture that shaped it. The author is an educator & cultural critic who brings into brilliant focus important consequences for the new millennium. A remarkable collection of art photographs illustrates his cogent points. ***Publisher Paid Annotation.***

Lal Bahadur Shastri: India's Prime Minister 1964-1966 - A Life of Truth in Politics. C. P. Srivastava. LC 95-902068. (Illus.). 498p. 1995. 29.95 (*0-19-563499-3*) OUP.
Lala Laipat Rai. Ed. by Verinder Grover. (C). 1993. 52.00 (*81-7100-426-1*, Pub. by Deep & Deep Pubns) S Asia.
Lalannes. Daniel Marchesseau. LC 98-60281. (Illus.). 157p. 1998. 35.00 (*2-08-013652-6*, Pub. by Flammarion) Abbeville Pr.
Lalapalooza Bird: A One-Act Play. Tim Kelly. (Illus.). 24p. (J). (gr. 5-12). 1981. pap. 3.25 (*0-88680-105-2*) I E Clark.
Lala's Story: A Memoir of the Holocaust. Lala Fishman & Steven Weingartner. LC 97-36776. 347p. 1998. 59.95 (*0-8101-1499-2*); pap. 22.95 (*0-8101-1500-X*) Northwestern U Pr.
L'Alchimiste. Annabel Malak.Tr. of Alchemist. (FRE., Illus.). boxed set 14.95 incl. audio (*2-921997-29-0*, Pub. by Coffragants) Penton Overseas.
Laleen, & Other Stories. Myrtle Johnston. LC 78-157781. (Short Story Index Reprint Ser.). 1977. reprint ed. 21.95 (*0-8369-3893-3*) Ayer.
Laletraesarte Books. unabridged ed. 64p. (Orig.). 1997. pap., per. 3.00 (*0-9657348-0-3*) Laletraesarte.
Lalique. Jessica Hodge. LC 99-40293. (Illus.). 128p. 1999. 17.98 (*1-57145-204-4*, Thunder Bay) Advantage Pubs.
Lalique. Marie-Claude Lalique. (FRE.). 640p. 1993. lib. bdg. 295.00 (*0-7859-3655-6*, 2883000018) Fr & Eur.
***Lalique & His Circle: Eight Art Nouveau Jewelers.** Fritz Falk. 128p. 1999. 60.00 (*3-925369-84-8*, Pub. by Arnoldsche Art Pubs) Antique Collect.
Lalique for Collectors. Mike McClintock. 1986. pap. 17.50 (*0-684-14101-9*, Scribners Ref) Mac Lib Ref.
Lalique Glass: The Complete Illustrated Catalogue for 1932. Rene Lalique.Tr. of Catalogue Des Verreries de Rene Lalique. (Illus.). 149p. 1981. reprint ed. pap. 14.95 (*0-486-24122-X*) Dover.
Lalique Glass from the Collection of Charles & Mary Magriel. Beth C. Wees. (Illus.). 8p. (Orig.). 1986. pap. 2.95 (*0-931102-21-9*) S & F Clark Art.
Lalique (Rene) The Complete Work in Glass: Catalogue Raisonne. Felix Marcilhac. (FRE., Illus.). 1100p. 1989. 375.00 (*1-55660-113-1*) A Wofsy Fine Arts.
Lalita Cult. V. R. Dikshitar. (C). 1991. reprint ed. 10.00 (*81-208-0919-X*, Pub. by Motilal Bnarsidass) S Asia.
***Lalita-Sahasranama: A Comprehensive Study of One Thousand Names of Lalita Maha-Tripurasundari.** L. M. Joshi. LC 98-908463. 1998. 38.00 (*81-246-0104-6*, Pub. by D K Printwrld) S Asia.
Lalita-Vistara: Memoirs of the Early Life of Sakya Sinha (CHS.1-15) Rajendralal L. Mitra. LC 98-906098. 279 p. 1998. write for info. (*81-7030-576-4*) Sri Satguru Pubns.
Lalitavajra's Manual of Buddhist Iconography. Sushama Lohia. (C). 1994. text 88.00 (*81-85689-97-0*, Pub. by Popular Prakashan) S Asia.
Lalkot to Lodi Gardens: Delhi of Sultans. (C). 1996. pap. 12.00 (*81-7167-237-X*, Pub. by Rupa) S Asia.
Lalla Rookh. T. Moore. 304p. 1987. 80.00 (*1-85077-148-0*, Pub. by Darf Pubs Ltd) St Mut.
Lalla Rookh, an Oriental Romance. Thomas Moore. (BCL1-PR English Literature Ser.). 179p. 1992. reprint ed. lib. bdg. 69.00 (*0-7812-7605-5*) Rprt Serv.
Lallie. large type ed. Clover Sinclair. 1990. pap. 16.99 (*0-7089-6924-0*) Ulverscroft.
Lalo & the Red-Hot Chile Pepper. Elizabeth Jimenez. (Illus.). 16p. (J). (gr. 3-5). 1995. pap. 3.95 (*1-57089-153-2*) SpanPr.
La/Lucha de los Dioses: la Idolos de la Opresion y la Busqueda del Dios Liberador see Idols of Death & the God of Life: A Theology
Lam & Other Diseases Characterized by Smooth Muscle Proliferation. Ed. by Joel Moss. LC 99-11317. (Lung Biology in Health & Disease Ser.). (Illus.). 640p. 1999. text 225.00 (*0-8247-0214-X*) Dekker.

An Asterisk (*) at the beginning of an entry indicates that the title is appearing for the first time.

L

Lam Bras Snon Groi Khrid Yig Snan Gsum Mdzes Rgyan see Three Levels of Spiritual Perception: An Oral Commentary on the Three Visions (Nang Sum) of Ngorchen Konchong Lhundrub

Lam Son 719. Nguyen Duy Hinh. 179p. 1989. reprint ed. pap. 18.50 (*0-923135-12-X*) Dalley Bk Service.

Lam Son 719: The South Vietnamese Incursion into Laos. J. F. Loye, Jr. et al. 166p. 1993. reprint ed. pap. 20.00 (*0-923135-54-5*) Dalley Bk Service.

***Lam The Nao Lai Xe Duoc An Tuan: Tinh Thuong Va Hanh Phuc.** Phuong Vinh & Mai Vinh.Tr. of Preventing Car Accidents: Tips on How to Drive Safely. (VIE., Illus.). 28p. (YA). (gr. 10-11). 1999. write for info. (*0-9675524-0-0*) P Vinh.

Lam-thob-tsul see Methods of Achieving the Paths: Stages of Philosophical & Ethical Development According to the Madhyamika Svatantrika School of Buddhism

Lama Farms. Lynn M. Stone. LC 99-25303. (Funky Farms Ser.). 24p. 1999. lib. bdg. write for info. (*0-86593-541-6*) Rourke Corp.

Lama Knows: A Tibetan Legend Is Born. Robert B. Ekvall. LC 81-4160. (Illus.). 144p. 1981. pap. 5.95 (*0-88316-541-4*) Chandler & Sharp.

Lamagna Genealogy. Joseph Lamagna. (Illus.). 44p. (Orig.). 1992. pap. write for info. (*0-9610464-2-2*) J Lamagna.

Lamah U'Maduan Heichan U'Kaman (Who What When Where) Yosef Y. Borovksky. (HEB.). 218p. 1996. 12.00 (*0-8266-1302-0*) Kehot Pubn Soc.

La/Maladie de la Mort see Malady of Death

Lamar Alexander's Little Plaid Book. Lamar Alexander. LC 98-18355. 160p. 1998. pap. 6.95 (*1-55853-579-9*) Rutledge Hill Pr.

Lamar Archaeology: Mississippian Chiefdoms in the Deep South. Ed. by Mark Williams & Gary Shapiro. LC 89-4941. (Illus.). 271p. 1990. reprint ed. pap. 84.10 (*0-608-01684-5*, 206234000002) Bks Demand.

Lamar Dodd: A Retrospective Exhibition. Lamar Dodd. LC 71-133620. 138p. 1970. pap. 20.00 (*0-8203-0307-0*) U of Ga Pr.

Lamarck: The Founder of Evolution; His Life & Work; with Translations of His Writings on Organic Evolution. Alpheus S. Packard. Ed. by I. Bernard Cohen. LC 79-7980. (Three Centuries of Science in America Ser.). (Illus.). 1980. reprint ed. lib. bdg. 42.95 (*0-405-12562-3*) Ayer.

Lamarck & Modern Genetics. H. Graham Cannon. LC 75-10211. 152p. 1975. reprint ed. lib. bdg. 55.00 (*0-8371-8173-9*, CALA, Greenwood Pr) Greenwood.

Lamarck the Mythical Precursor: A Study of the Relations Between Science & Ideology. Madeleine Barthelemy-Madaule. Tr. by Michael Shank from FRE. 176p. 1982. 25.00 (*0-262-02179-X*) MIT Pr.

Lamarck to Darwin: Contributions to Evolutionary Biology, 1809-1859. Ed. by H. Lewis McKinney. 124p. 1971. 10.00 (*0-87291-019-9*) Coronado Pr.

***Lamarck's Signature: How Retrogenes Are Changing Darwin's Natural Selection Paradigm.** Edward J. Steele et al. 320p. 1999. pap. text 15.00 (*0-7382-0171-5*, Pub. by Perseus Pubng) HarpC.

Lamartine. Charles M. Lombard. (Twayne's World Authors Ser.). (C). 1973. lib. bdg. 20.95 (*0-8057-2510-5*) Irvington.

Lamartine & Romantic Unanimism. Albert J. George. LC 71-168106. reprint ed. 20.00 (*0-404-02712-1*) AMS Pr.

Lamartine & the Poetics of Landscape. Mary E. Birkett. LC 82-82427. (French Forum Monographs: No. 38). 105p. (Orig.). 1982. pap. 10.95 (*0-917058-37-2*) French Forum.

Lama's SuperAmerican Coloring Book. Donald O. Black. (Illus.). 7p. (J). (gr. 3). 1991. pap. write for info. (*0-9625753-1-3*) SuperAmerican Bks.

Lamato: A Savannah Ecosystem. Ed. by L. Abbadie et al. (Ecological Studies: Vol. TBA). (Illus.). 350p. 1997. 89.00 (*0-387-94844-9*) Spr-Verlag.

***Lamaze Books & Hands-On ELLIE, Set.** Irene D. H. Sasman. (Illus.). (J). 1999. pap. 299.00 (*1-56831-084-6*) Lrning Connect.

Lamaze Ready Reference Guide for Labor & Birth. 2nd rev. ed. Harriet R. Shapiro et al. (Illus.). 59p. 1997. spiral bd. 9.95 (*0-9624335-0-0*) Shapiro Kuba.

Lamb. Deni Bown. LC 97-131148. (Shaped Board Bks.). (Illus.). 10p. (J). 1997. bds. 3.95 (*0-7894-1545-3*) DK Pub Inc.

Lamb. D K Publishing Staff. LC 99-202129. 1999. 3.95 (*0-7894-4312-0*) DK Pub Inc.

Lamb. Bernard MacLaverty. LC 98-35738. 200p. 1999. pap. write for info. (*0-7540-3476-3*) Chivers N Amer.

Lamb. Bernard MacLaverty. 160p. 1997. pap. 11.00 (*0-393-31701-3*) Norton.

Lamb. Sandy Ray. Ed. by Cheryle Sytsma. (Illus.). 15p. (Orig.). (J). 1991. pap. write for info. (*1-879068-10-9*) Ray-Ma Natsal.

Lamb, 1. Lorella Rizzatti. (Portable Pets Ser.). 1999. 5.95 (*0-8109-5641-1*) Abrams.

Lamb. Lorella Rizzatti. (Portable Pets Ser.). (Illus.). 12p. 1999. bds. 5.95 (*0-8109-5640-3*, Pub. by Abrams) Time Warner.

Lamb. large type ed. Bernard MacLaverty. LC 98-35738. 214p. 1999. 30.00 (*0-7862-1609-3*, G K Hall Lrg Type) Mac Lib Ref.

Lamb & Hazlitt. Charles Lamb. LC 76-168954. reprint ed. 30.00 (*0-404-07359-X*) AMS Pr.

Lamb & the Butterfly. Arnold Sundgaard. LC 88-60092. (Illus.). 32p. (J). (ps-1). 1999. 16.95 (*0-531-05779-8*) Orchard Bks Watts.

Lamb & the Butterfly. Arnold Sundgaard. (Illus.). (J). 1996. pap. 5.95 (*0-590-56643-1*) Scholastic Inc.

Lamb & the Butterfly. Arnold Sundgaard. LC 88-60092. 1996. 11.15 (*0-606-09524-1*, Pub. by Turtleback) Demco.

Lamb & the Elephant: Ideal Imitation & the Context of Renaissance Allegory. John M. Steadman. LC 73-93874. 300p. 1974. reprint ed. pap. 93.00 (*0-608-03168-2*, 206362100007) Bks Demand.

Lamb & the Great Escape see Cabrito y el Gran Escape

Lamb & the Wolf: Readers Theatre for Worship. Kevin Stoltz. 1998. pap. 15.99 (*0-8341-9344-2*) Lillenas.

Lamb at the Altar: The Story of a Dance. Deborah Hay. LC 93-21063. (Illus.). 160p. (C). 1994. pap. 16.95 (*0-8223-1439-8*); text 49.95 (*0-8223-1448-7*) Duke.

Lamb Chop & Friends' Rainy Day Color Game. Susan R. Simms. (Interactive Books - Zoundies Ser.). 12p. (J). (ps-2). 1994. write for info. (*1-57234-022-3*) YES Ent.

Lamb Chop's ABC Adventure. Carol A. Hanshaw. (Comes to Life Bks.). 16p. (J). (ps-2). 1994. write for info. (*1-883366-43-7*) YES Ent.

Lamb Chop's Fables: The Lamb Who Could Featuring Aesop's The Tortoise & the Hare. Shari Lewis. Ed. by Robert A. Doyle. LC 93-46420. (Illus.). 32p. (J). 1994. 14.95 (*0-8094-7804-8*) Time-Life.

Lamb Chop's Play-Along. Ed. by Debbie Cavalier. (Illus.). (Orig.). (J). 1996. pap. text 16.95 (*1-57623-354-5*, PF9612) Wrner Bros.

Lamb Chop's Special Chanukah. Ed. by Debbie Cavalier. (Illus.). 80p. (Orig.). (J). 1996. pap. 14.95 (*0-7604-0088-1*, PF9634) Wrner Bros.

Lamb Count - Auto Class: The Complete Story. Peter Dron. (Crowood Autoclassics Ser.). (Illus.). 192p. 1995. pap. 24.95 (*1-85223-914-X*, Pub. by Crolwood) Motorbooks Intl.

Lamb County, Texas. Madema Ogletree & Lamb County History Book Committee. (Illus.). 549p. 1992. 65.00 (*0-88107-195-1*) Curtis Media.

Lamb in Command. Kenneth Maynard. LC 86-198652. 199p. 1986. write for info. (*0-297-78790-X*, Pub. by Weidenfeld & Nicolson) Trafalgar.

Lamb in Family Meals. 1986. lib. bdg. 69.95 (*0-8490-3785-9*) Gordon Pr.

Lamb in His Bosom. Caroline Miller. 1991. lib. bdg. 35.95 (*1-56849-057-7*) Buccaneer Bks.

Lamb in His Bosom. Caroline Miller. LC 92-38286. (Modern Southern Classics Ser.). 368p. 1993. 24.95 (*1-56145-074-X*); pap. 14.95 (*1-56145-075-8*) Peachtree Pubs.

Lamb in Love. Carrie Brown. LC 98-44580. 348p. 1999. 21.95 (*1-56512-203-8*, 72203) Algonquin Bks.

***Lamb in Love.** large type ed. Carrie Brown. LC 99-22156. (Large Print Book Ser.). 1999. write for info. (*1-56895-732-7*) Wheeler Pub.

***Lamb in Love.** Carrie Brown. 336p. 2000. reprint ed. pap. 11.95 (*0-553-38085-0*) Bantam.

***Lamb in the Laundry, 1 vol., Vol. 12.** Ben M. Baglio. (Animal Ark Ser.: No. 12). 160p. (J). (gr. 3-6). 1999. pap. text 3.99 (*0-439-08642-6*) Scholastic Inc.

Lamb Instructor's Guide. Richard Lamb. (Illus.). 500p. (C). 1986. teacher ed. 10.75 (*0-8053-5831-5*) Benjamin-Cummings.

Lamb Is All the Glory (Revelation) Richard Brooks. (Welwyn Commentary Ser.). 1986. pap. 11.99 (*0-85234-229-2*, Pub. by Evangelical Pr) P & R Pubng.

Lamb of God: Sermons by Clarence Macartney. Clarence E. Macartney. Ed. by Richard A. Bodey. LC 94-23031. 144p. 1994. pap. 9.99 (*0-8254-2151-9*) Kregel.

Lamb of God Vol. I: New Testament. Mary Beth Pozdol. (God's Word for Warriors Ser.). 126p. 1991. spiral bd. 19.95 (*1-889723-11-8*) Family Harvest.

Lamb Prayers. Tessa Richardson-Jones. (Paws for Thought Ser.). (Illus.). 5p. (J). (ps). 1999. 4.95 (*1-901881-76-8*, Pub. by Element Child) Penguin Putnam.

Lamb Problems: Detecting, Diagnosing, Treating. rev. ed. Laura Lawson. LC 92-7300. (Illus.). 264p. (Orig.). 1996. pap. 29.95 (*0-9633923-0-1*) LDF Pubns.

***Lamb Site: A Pioneering Clovis Encampment.** Richard M. Gramly. (Persimmon Press Monographs in Archaeology). (Illus.). 112p. 1999. pap. text 15.95 (*1-882903-09-9*) Persimmon NY.

Lamb to the Slaughter. Elizabeth Quinn. 1996. mass mkt. 5.99 (*0-671-52765-7*) PB.

Lamb to the Slaughter. large type ed. Margaret A. Carr. (Linford Romance Library). 320p. 1992. pap. 16.99 (*0-7089-7239-X*) Ulverscroft.

Lamb White Days. Honor Prime. LC 81-453444. 179p. 1980. write for info. (*0-7188-2437-7*) Lutterwrth.

Lamba Folklore. Clement M. Doke. LC 28-18358. (American Folklore Society Memoirs Ser.: Vol. 20). 1969. reprint ed. 70.00 (*0-527-01072-3*) Periodicals Srv.

Lambada: Blood Road. Bene. pap. 12.95 (*1-56097-240-8*, Pub. by Fantagraph Bks) Seven Hills Bk.

Lambada: Striptease. 5th ed. Sebastian Zefiro. pap. 12.95 (*1-56097-336-6*, Pub. by Fantagraph Bks) Seven Hills Bk.

Lambada Bk. 1: Buttfuque U. Barroso & Helga. (Eros Graphic Novel Ser.). 168p. 1996. pap. 14.95 (*1-56097-221-1*) Fantagraph Bks.

Lambada Bk. 2: Venus with a Hot Crotch. Barroso. (Eros Graphic Novel Ser.). 104p. 1996. pap. 12.95 (*1-56097-226-2*) Fantagraph Bks.

Lambda Calculi: A Guide for Computer Scientists. Chris Hankin. (Graduate Texts in Computer Science Ser.: No. 3). 176p. (C). 1995. text 77.95 (*0-19-853841-3*) OUP.

Lambda Calculus: Its Syntax & Semantics. rev. ed. H. P. Barendregt. (Studies in Logic & the Foundations of Mathematics: No. 103). 622p. 1984. pap. 56.75 (*0-444-87508-5*, North Holland) Elsevier.

Lambda Calculus: Its Syntax & Semantics. 2nd rev. ed. H. P. Barendregt. (Studies in Logic & the Foundations of Mathematics: No. 103). xvi,622p. 1984. 104.00 (*0-444-86748-1*, I-127-84, North Holland) Elsevier.

Lambda Gray: A Practical, Emotional & Spiritual Guide for Gays & Lesbians Who Are Growing Older. Karen W. Reyes et al. Ed. by Lorena F. Farrell. 160p. (Orig.). 1993. pap. 12.95 (*0-87877-179-4*) Newcastle Pub.

Lambda II. Ed. by Roger W. Hendrix et al. LC 81-70528. (Cold Spring Harbor Monographs). 716p. reprint ed. pap. 200.00 (*0-7837-1992-2*, 204226600002) Bks Demand.

Lambence: Poems from Hollywood. Mark Dunster. 17p. 1998. pap. 5.00 (*0-89642-406-5*) Linden Pubs.

Lambency Letters: Radiant Thoughts to Warm Your Heart. Shay Platt. (Illus.). 242p. 1997. pap. text 12.95 (*1-884416-26-8*) A Press.

Lambenkurzung. Hans Drexler. vi, 257p. 1969. write for info. (*0-318-71111-7*) G Olms Pubs.

Lambert de Beaulieu, Benedictus Appenzeller, Bercoy, Besancourt, Boyvin, Briault, Pierre Cadeac, Chevalier, Ciron, Severin Cornet, Thomas Crecquillon, Pierre de la Rue, De la Font, Desbordes, Jacques de Buisson, Estienne Du. Ed. by Jane A. Bernstein. LC 94-946. (Sixteenth-Century Chanson Ser.: No. 9). 280p. 1994. reprint ed. text 105.00 (*0-8240-3108-3*) Garland.

Lambert Doomer: Saemtliche Zeichnungen. Wolfgang Schulz. LC 73-93167. (Disegno Studien zur Geschichte der Europaeischen Handzeichnung Ser.: Vol. 2). (Illus.). 112p. (C). 1974. 180.80 (*3-11-004647-4*) De Gruyter.

Lambert Farm: Public Archaeology & Canine Burials along Narragansett Bay. Jordan E. Kerber. LC 96-78058. 144p. (C). 1996. pap. text 23.50 (*0-15-505190-3*) Harcourt Coll Pubs.

Lambert Wickes: Pirate or Patriot? Norman H. Plummer. (Illus.). 1991. pap. 6.00 (*0-922249-03-2*) Ches Bay Mus.

Lambertville & New Hope. Mastrich Kline et al. (Images of America Ser.). 128p. 1996. pap. 16.99 (*0-7524-0285-4*) Arcadia Publng.

Lambeth: A View from the Two Thirds World. Vinay Samuel & Christopher Sugden. LC 89-49674. 160p. (Orig.). 1989. pap. 8.95 (*0-8192-1526-0*) Morehouse Pub.

Lambeth Apocalypse: Collection of the Archbishop of Canterbury in Lambeth Palace Library, Set, MS 209. limited ed. Nigel Morgan. (Illus.). 383p. 1990. text 3500.00 (*1-872501-55-9*) Gordon & Breach.

Lambeth Conferences: The Solution for Pan-Anglican Organization. William R. Curtis. LC 68-58565. (Columbia University. Studies in the Social Sciences: No. 488). reprint ed. 32.50 (*0-404-51488-X*) AMS Pr.

Lambeth Method of Cake Decoration & Practical Pastries. Joseph A. Lambeth. LC 80-65654. (Illus.). 362p. 1980. reprint ed. 75.00 (*0-916096-23-8*) Books Bakers.

***Lambeth Palace: A History of the Archbishops of Canterbury & Their Houses.** Timothy Tatton Brown. 2000. 35.00 (*0-281-05347-2*, Pub. by Society Prom Christ Know) Intl Pubs Mktg.

Lambic. Jean-Xavier Guinard. (Classic Beer Style Ser.). 169p. 1990. pap. 11.95 (*0-937381-22-5*) Brewers Pubns.

Lambley: A Village Study. Christopher Wier. (C). 1982. text 50.00 (*0-7855-3200-5*, Pub. by Univ Nottingham) St Mut.

Lamborghini. Consumer Guide Editors. (Illus.). 256p. 1993. 21.95 (*0-88176-931-2*, 1010400) Pubns Intl Ltd.

Lamborghini. A. T. McKenna. LC 98-6647. (Ultimate Cars Ser.). 2000. lib. bdg. 21.35 (*1-57765-125-1*) ABDO Pub Co.

Lamborghini. Jay Schleifer. LC 92-11980. (Cool Classics Ser.). (Illus.). 48p. (J). (gr. 5). 1993. lib. bdg. 13.95 (*0-89686-698-X*, Crstwood Hse) Silver Burdett Pr.

Lamborghini: The Fastest. Harry Haines & Shirley Haines. (Car Classics Ser.). (J). 1991. lib. bdg. 16.67 (*0-685-59195-6*) Rourke Corp.

Lamborghini: The Fastest. Shirley Haines & Harry Haines. (Car Classics Ser.). 32p. (YA). (gr. 5-12). 1991. lib. bdg. 15.95 (*0-86593-145-3*) Rourke Corp.

***Lamborghini: The Legend.** David Hodges. (Legends Ser.). (Illus.). 80p. 1998. 7.98 (*0-7651-0846-1*) Smithmark.

Lamborghini: The Spirit of the Bull. Paul W. Cockerham. 1998. pap. text 10.95 (*1-57717-006-7*) Todtri Prods.

Lamborghinis see High Performance

Lamborghinis. Michael Green. (High Performance Ser.). (Illus.). 48p. (J). (gr. 3-7). 1996. 19.00 (*0-516-20246-4*) Childrens.

Lambretta. Andrea Sparrow & David Sparrow. (Color Family Album Ser.). (Illus.). 96p. 1997. 19.95 (*1-874105-77-4*, Pub. by Vloce Pub) Motorbooks Intl.

Lambretta: An Illustrated History. Nigel Cox. (Illus.). 96p. 1996. 29.95 (*0-85429-963-7*, Pub. by GT Foulis) Haynes Manuals.

***Lambs.** Ed. by Barron's Educational Staff. (Cuddle Up Bks.). (Illus.). (J). 2000. 4.95 (*0-7641-5299-8*) Barron.

Lamb's Book of Art 1. Barry Stebbing. Ed. & Illus. by Saundra Stebbing. 100p. (J). (gr. 3-8). 1994. 14.95 (*0-9700405-2-0*) How Great Thou Art.

Lamb's Criticism: A Selection from the Literary Criticism of Charles Lamb. Charles Lamb. (BCL1-PR English Literature Ser.). 1992. reprint ed. lib. bdg. 69.00 (*0-7812-7015-4*) Rprt Serv.

Lamb's Gate Trilogy: Life in the Present Within Freedom & Unified. Georgia Christopherson. LC 98-60753. 224p. (C). 1998. pap. 10.99 (*1-57921-120-8*, Pub. by WinePress Pub) BookWorld.

Lamb's High Feast: Melito, Peri Pascha & the Quartodeciman Paschal Liturgy at Sardis. Alistair Stewart-Sykes. LC 98-27580. (Supplements to Vigiliae Christianae Ser.). 1998. 94.50 (*90-04-11236-7*) Brill Academic Pubs.

Lambs in March & Other Essays. Ann Greene. LC 68-8466. (Essay Index Reprint Ser.). 1977. 20.95 (*0-8369-0497-4*) Ayer.

***Lamb's Lessons.** Lucy Daniels. (Animal Ark Pets Ser.: No. 11). (Illus.). 128p. (J). (gr. 3-5). 2000. pap. 3.99 (*0-439-05168-1*) Scholastic Inc.

Lambs of God. Marele Day. 336p. 1999. reprint ed. pap. 12.95 (*1-57322-722-6*, Riverhd Trade) Berkley Pub.

Lambs on the Ledge: Seeing & Avoiding the Dangers in Ministry. Joyce Strong. LC 96-115780. 166p. 1995. pap. 9.99 (*0-87509-650-6*) Chr Pubns.

Lamb's Poetry for Children. Charles Lamb & Mary Lamb. LC 78-108585. (Granger Index Reprint Ser.). 1977. 19.95 (*0-8369-6113-7*) Ayer.

Lamb's Safely Folded. unabridged ed. William Wileman et al. (Children's Heritage Ser.). 142p. (J). (gr. 4-6). 1995. pap. 6.98 (*1-58339-112-6*, D12) Triangle Press.

Lamb's Supper: The Mass as Heaven on Earth. Scott Hahn. LC 99-23679. 192p. 1999. 19.95 (*0-385-49659-1*) Doubleday.

Lamb's Tale: A Christmas Musical for Kids. Martha Bolton & Dennis Allen. Date not set. pap. 9.99 (*0-8341-9653-0*) Lillenas.

Lambs' Tales from Great Operas. Donald Elliott & Clinton Arrowood. LC 80-84719. (Illus.). 96p. 1981. 12.95 (*0-87645-110-5*); pap. 8.95 (*0-87645-120-2*) Harvard Common Pr.

Lambs, Their Lives, Their Friends & Their Correspondence: New Particulars & New Materials. William C. Hazlitt. reprint ed. 35.00 (*0-404-07369-7*) AMS Pr.

Lamb's War: Essays in Honor of Hugh Barbour. Ed. by John W. Newman & Michael L. Birkel. 286p. (Orig.). 1991. pap. write for info. (*0-318-68396-2*) Earlham Pr.

Lamb's War: Quaker Essays to Honor Hugh Barbour. Ed. by Michael L. Birkel & John W. Newman. 305p. (Orig.). 1992. pap. 19.95 (*1-879117-00-2*) Earlham Pr.

Lambshead Before Interwoven: A Texas Range Chronicle, 1848-1878. Frances M. Holden. LC 81-48374. (Illus.). 252p. (C). 1997. text 24.95 (*0-89096-122-0*) Tex A&M Univ Pr.

Lambshead Legacy: The Ranch Diary of Watt R. Matthews. Ed. by Janet M. Neugebauer. LC 96-41415. (Centennial Series of the Association of Former Students: Vol. 66). (Illus.). 304p. (C). 1997. text 24.95 (*0-89096-738-5*) Tex A&M Univ Pr.

***Lamby Lamb.** Chris Raschka. LC 99-51681. (Thingy Things Ser.). (Illus.). 24p. (J). (ps-k). 2000. bds. 3.99 (*0-7868-0640-0*, Pub. by Hyprn Child) Time Warner.

Lamda Guide to English Literature. Lamda. 109p. 1998. pap. 13.95 (*1-84002-011-3*, Pub. by Oberon Bks Ltd) Theatre Comm.

Lame Deer, Seeker of Visions. Richard Erdoes. 352p. 1994. per. 5.99 (*0-671-88802-1*, WSP) PB.

Lame Deer, Seeker of Visions: The/Life of a Sioux Medicine Man. Richard Erdoes & John Lame Deer. 320p. 1973. per. 11.00 (*0-671-21535-3*) S&S Trade Pap.

Lame Duck in Turbulent Waters: The Next Four Years of Nixon. Gus Hall. 64p. 1972. pap. 0.50 (*0-87898-097-0*) New Outlook.

L'/Ame et L'Amour see Sex in Human Relationships

Lame Excuses People Use to Do Things. Laura C. Schlessinger. 1995. 22.00 (*0-614-15011-6*) HarpC.

Lame Horse. James R. Rooney. LC 97-39892. 1997. 29.95 (*0-929346-55-6*) R Meerdink Co Ltd.

Lame Horse. James Rooney. (Illus.). 237p. 1984. reprint ed. text 19.95 (*0-914327-04-6*) Breakthrgh NY.

Lame Horse - Causes, Symptoms & Treatment. James R. Rooney. 1975. pap. 15.00 (*0-87980-308-8*) Wilshire.

Lame, Mathieu Funktionen. Max J. Strutt. LC 66-23757. 13.95 (*0-8284-0203-5*) Chelsea Pub.

L'ame Parfumee Des Jardins. Catherine Laroze. 1999. 65.00 (*2-909838-16-1*) A Gourcuff.

Lame Prince: The Study of Relational Grace. Nicholas E. Harris. 100p. (Orig.). 1996. pap. 7.95 (*1-57502-227-3*) Morris Pubng.

Lame, un Parler Zime du Nord-Cameroun (Langue Tchadique) Phonologie, Grammaire, Dictionnaire Lame-Francais, Lexique Francais-Lame. Michka Sachnini. (FRE.). 557p. 1982. pap. 79.95 (*0-7859-8079-2*, 2852971410) Fr & Eur.

La/Memoire Longue see Enduring Memory: Time & History in a French Village

***Lameness.** Gray. (Allen Veterinary Handbook). 2000. pap. 27.50 (*0-85131-577-1*, Pub. by J A Allen) Trafalgar.

Lameness in Cattle. 2nd ed. P. R. Greenough et al. (Illus.). 496p. 1991. write for info. (*0-85608-030-6*) Blackwell Sci.

Lameness in Cattle. 3rd ed. Paul R. Greenough. Ed. by Sandra Valkoff. 384p. 1996. text 79.00 (*0-7216-5205-0*, W B Saunders Co) Harcrt Hlth Sci Grp.

Lameness of the Equine Foot. Turner. (C). 1994. text. write for info. (*0-7216-3730-2*, W B Saunders Co) Harcrt Hlth Sci Grp.

Lament: A Novel about How the West Was Blown. David Carson. 192p. 1996. mass mkt. 7.95 (*1-56201-078-6*) Blue Moon Bks.

Lament for a Dead Cowboy. Catherine Dain. 208p. (Orig.). 1994. pap. 4.50 (*0-425-14328-7*, Prime Crime) Berkley Pub.

Lament for a Lady Laird. Margot Arnold, pseud. (Penny Spring & Sir Toby Glendower Mystery Ser.). 224p. 1990. reprint ed. pap. 6.95 (*0-88150-159-X*, Foul Play) Norton.

Lament for a Son. Nicholas Wolterstorff. 111p. (Orig.). 1988. pap. 10.00 (*0-8028-0294-X*) Eerdmans.

Lament for an African Pol. Mongo Beti. Tr. by Richard Bjornson from FRE. LC 84-51443.Tr. of La/Ruine Preque Cocasse d'un Polichinelle. 370p. 1985. 14.50 (*0-89410-304-0*, Three Contnts) L Rienner.

Lament for an Ocean: The Collapse of the Atlantic Cod Fishery: A True Crime Story. Michael Harris. LC 98-162330. 444p. 1998. text 24.95 (*0-7710-3958-1*) McCland & Stewart.

***Lament for an Ocean: The Collapse of the Atlantic Cod Fishery: A True Crime Story.** Michael Harris. 400p. 1999. pap. 16.95 (*0-7710-3960-3*) McCland & Stewart.

An Asterisk (*) at the beginning of an entry indicates that the title is appearing for the first time.

Lament for Art O'Leary: A New Translation by Malachi McCormick. Eileen Dubh O'Connell. Ed. & Tr. by Malachi McCormick. (Illus.). 64p. (C). 1994. pap. 24.00 (*0-943984-64-5*) Stone St Pr.

Lament for Christobel. Audrey Peterson. Ed. by Dana Isaacson. 224p. (Orig.). 1991. mass mkt. 4.50 (*0-671-72969-1*) PB.

Lament for Four Brides. Evelyn Berckman. 20.95 (*0-88411-273-X*) Amereon Ltd.

Lament for Rastafari & Other Plays. Edgar White. LC 81-69653. 208p. 1983. pap. 14.50 (*0-7145-2756-4*) M Boyars Pubs.

Lament for the Death of a Bullfighter: And Other Poems. Federico Garcia Lorca. Tr. by A. L. Lloyd. LC 76-29447. (ENG & SPA.). 1977. reprint ed. 20.00 (*0-404-15302-X*) AMS Pr.

Lament for the Death of a Bullfighter & Other Poems in the Original Spanish with English Translation. Federico Garcia Lorca. Tr. by A. L. Lloyd from SPA. LC 76-57930. 60p. 1977. reprint ed. lib. bdg. 45.00 (*0-8371-9322-2*, GALF, Greenwood Pr) Greenwood.

Lament for the Molly Maguires. Arthur H. Lewis. 308p. 1990. reprint ed. lib. bdg. 26.95 (*0-89966-722-8*) Buccaneer Bks.

Lament of Eve. Johanna Manley. 160p. (Orig.). (C). 1993. pap. 6.68 (*0-9622536-2-6*) Monastery Bks.

Lament of the Cracker Cowboy: Rhymes & Reflections from the Florida Cattle Country. Don Looper. LC 98-94085. 168 p. 1998. write for info. (*0-7392-0004-6*) Morris Pubng.

Lament of the Linnet. Anna M. Ortese. Tr. by Patrick Creagh from ITA. LC 98-159990. 325p. 1999. 24.00 (*1-86046-206-5*, Pub. by Harvill Press) FS&G.

Lament of the Nibelungen. Winder McConnell. (Medvl Ser.). xxiii, 220p. 1994. 60.00 (*1-879751-73-9*) Camden Hse.

Lamentable & Pitifull Description of the Wofull Warres in Flaunders. Thomas Churchyard. LC 76-57372. (English Experience Ser.: No. 790). 1977. reprint ed. lib. bdg. 15.00 (*90-221-0790-6*) Walter J Johnson.

***Lamentation: An Immigrant's Dilemma.** Cyril U. Orji. LC 99-93173. 300p. 1999. pap. write for info. (*0-9670657-0-4*) C U Orji.

Lamentation of Souls see Adam Davy's Five Dreams about Edward 2nd

Lamentation of the Dead: With the Lament for Arthur O'Leary. Peter Levi et al. 40p. 1984. pap. 11.95 (*0-85646-140-7*, Pub. by Anvil Press) Dufour.

Lamentation over the Destruction of Sumer & Ur. Piotr Michalowski. LC 88-33386. (Mesopotamian Civilizations Ser.: Vol. 1). (Illus.). xvi, 219p. (C). 1989. text 42.50 (*0-931464-43-9*) Eisenbrauns.

Lamentations. Dan G. Kent. (Bible Study Commentary Ser.). 80p. 1983. pap. 5.99 (*0-310-44011-4*, 12482P) Zondervan.

Lamentations. Iain W. Provan. (New Century Bible Ser.). 142p. 1991. pap. 14.95 (*0-551-02323-6*, Pub. by Sheffield Acad) CUP Services.

Lamentations: A New Translation with Introduction & Commentary, Vol. 7A. 2nd ed. Delbert R. Hillers. 168p. 1972. 28.00 (*0-385-26407-0*) Doubleday.

Lamentations: From the Matins of Holy & Great Saturday. Tr. by Holy Transfiguration Monastery Staff from GRE. LC 81-80222. 65p. (Orig.). 1981. pap. 7.00 (*0-913026-51-4*) St Nectarios.

Lamentations: Issues & Interpretation. Claus Westermann. Tr. by Charles Muenchow. 252p. 1998. pap. 27.95 (*0-567-29226-6*, Pub. by T & T Clark) Bks Intl VA.

Lamentations & Ecstasies of the Soul. Jeannette A. Allred. Ed. by Robert M. Vogt & Mildred Diaz. (Books That Touch). Date not set. pap. 8.95 (*0-9659765-9-9*) Vonet Pub.

Lamentations-Daniel. Joyce Baldwin. (Bible Study Commentaries Ser.). 128p. 1984. pap. 4.95 (*0-87508-162-2*) Chr Lit.

Lamentations of Jeremiah. Charles R. Swindoll. 52p. 1998. pap., student ed. 5.95 (*1-57972-184-2*) Insight Living.

***Lamentations of the Father.** Ian Frazier. (Illus.). 32p. 2000. 10.95 (*0-664-22238-2*) Westminster John Knox.

Laments. Jan Kochanowski. Tr. by Stanislaw Baranczak & Seamus Heaney. LC 95-13156. 48p. 1995. text 17.50 (*0-374-18290-6*) FS&G.

Laments: A Bilingual Edition. Jan Kochanowski. Tr. by Stanislaw Baranczak & Seamus Heaney. 80p. 1996. pap. 9.00 (*0-374-52489-0*, Noonday) FS&G.

La/Messe: Spiritualite, Historie, Pratique see Mass: Spirituality, History, & Practice

Lamet: Hill Peasants in French Indochina. Karl G. Izikowitz. LC 76-44737. 1977. reprint ed. 34.00 (*0-404-15938-9*) AMS Pr.

Lamia. Christopher P. Nichols & Earl Bentley. 1994. 5.60 (*0-87129-404-4*, L80) Dramatic Pub.

Lamia Anemia. Robert Rushing. 280p. 1988. pap. 8.95 (*0-89697-287-9*) Intl Univ Pr.

Lamiel. Stendhal, pseud. (FRE.). 1983. pap. 13.95 (*0-7859-2904-5*) Fr & Eur.

Lamiel. Stendhal, pseud. (Folio Ser.: No. 1462). (FRE.). pap. 10.95 (*2-07-037462-9*) Schoenhof.

Laminar Boundary Layers: An Account of the Development, Structure & Stability of Laminar Boundary Layers in Incompressible Fluids, Together with a Description of the Associated Experimental Techniques. Ed. by L. Rosenhead. (Illus.). 708p. 1988. reprint ed. pap. 18.95 (*0-486-65646-2*) Dover.

***Laminar Composites.** George Staab. LC 98-55574. 700p. 1999. 79.95 (*0-7506-7124-6*) Buttrwrth-Heinemann.

Laminar Flow Analysis. David F. Rogers. (Illus.). 436p. (C). 1992. text 130.00 (*0-521-41152-1*) Cambridge U Pr.

Laminar Flow & Convective Transport Processes: Scaling Principles & Asymptotic Analysis. L. Gary Leal. (Illus.). 592p. 1992. text 120.00 (*0-7506-9117-4*) Buttrwrth-Heinemann.

Laminar Flow Theory. P. A. Lagerstrom. 288p. 1996. pap. text 19.95 (*0-691-02598-3*, Pub. by Princeton U Pr) Cal Prin Full Svc.

Laminar Motion of Multiphase Media in Conduits. Dzharulla Faizullaev. LC 69-12511. 150p. reprint ed. pap. 46.50 (*0-608-30365-8*, 202068000018) Bks Demand.

Laminar Natural Flow & Laminar Flow Control. Ed. by R. W. Barnwell & M. Yousuff Hussaini. (ICASE - NASA LaRC Ser.). (Illus.). vii, 411p. 1991. 98.95 (*0-387-97737-6*) Spr-Verlag.

Laminar-Turbulent Transition. Ed. by Valery V. Kozlov. (International Union of Theoretical & Applied Mechanics Symposia Ser.). (Illus.). xxxviii, 757p. 1985. 158.95 (*0-387-15250-4*) Spr-Verlag.

Laminar-Turbulent Transition: IUTAM Symposium Sendai, 1994. IUTAM Symposia Staff. Ed. by R. Kobayashi. 532p. 1995. 238.00 (*3-540-59297-0*) Spr-Verlag.

Laminar-Turbulent Transition: IUTAM Symposium, Toulouse, France, September 11-15, 1989. Ed. by R. Michel & D. Arnal. (International Union of Theoretical & Applied Mechanics Symposia Ser.). (Illus.). 704p. 1991. 174.95 (*0-387-52196-8*) Spr-Verlag.

Laminar Turbulent Transitions. Ed. by R. Eppler. (International Union of Theoretical & Applied Mechanics Symposia Ser.). (Illus.). 432p. 1980. 69.95 (*0-387-10142-X*) Spr-Verlag.

Laminar Viscous Flow. Virgilu N. Constantinescu. LC 95-16333. (Mechanical Engineering Ser.). (Illus.). 480p. 1995. 69.95 (*0-387-94528-8*) Spr-Verlag.

Laminate & Solid Surface Countertops: Installation Techniques. National Kitchen & Bath Association Staff. (Illus.). 140p. 1998. pap. text 50.00 (*1-887127-40-2*) Natl Kit Bath.

***Laminated Designs in Wood: Techniques * Patterns * Projects.** Clarence Rannefeld. Ed. by Laura D. Doran. LC 97-25656. (Illus.). 144p. 1998. pap. 19.95 (*1-57990-021-6*, Pub. by Lark Books) Random.

Laminated Hardwood Flooring Standard, ANSI-HPMA LHF. 8p. 1987. 10.00 (*0-318-18926-7*) Hardwd Ply.

Laminated Tests Dates Sheet. Kaplan. 1997. write for info. (*0-684-00529-8*, Fireside) S&S Trade Pap.

***Laminated Timber Construction.** Christian Muller. (ENG., Illus.). 200p. 2000. 65.00 (*3-7643-6267-7*, Pub. by Birkhauser) Princeton Arch.

Laminated Wood-Based Composites to Mass Transfer see Encyclopedia of Chemical Technology

Laminated Wood Boatbuilder: A Step-by-Step Guide for the Backyard Builder. Hub Miller. 1993. pap. 24.95 (*0-87742-386-5*) Intl Marine.

Laminating Techniques in Japanese Swords: A Monograph. W. M. Hawley. (Illus.). 17p. 1986. reprint ed. pap. 5.95 (*0-910704-54-6*) Hawley.

***Laminations.** Murray Edmond. 64p. 2000. pap. 14.95 (*1-86940-222-7*, Pub. by Auckland Univ) Paul & Co Pubs.

Laminectomia Lumbar. Oliver D. Grin & Dorothy L. Bouwman. (Patient Education Ser.). (SPA., Illus.). 18p. (Orig.). 1992. pap. text 4.00 (*0-929689-54-2*) Ludann Co.

Laminins. Rupert Timpl. (Cell Adhesion & Communication Ser). 336p. 1996. text 72.00 (*3-7186-5807-0*, Harwood Acad Pubs) Gordon & Breach.

Lamium (Lamiaceae) J. Mennema. (Leiden Botanical Ser.: No. 11). (Illus.). 198p. 1989. pap. 31.00 (*90-04-09109-2*, Pub. by Rijksherbarium) Balogh.

Lammas Alanna. William Martin. 1998. pap. 17.95 (*1-85224-369-4*, Pub. by Bloodaxe Bks) Dufour.

Lammas Night. Ed. by Josepha Sherman. 288p. 1996. mass mkt. 5.99 (*0-671-87713-5*) Baen Bks.

Lammot du Pont & the American Explosives Industry, 1850-1884. Norman B. Wilkinson. LC 83-21813. (Illus.). 346p. reprint ed. pap. 107.30 (*0-8357-3135-9*, 203939800012) Bks Demand.

LaMoine Lumber & Trading Co. Narrow-Gauge Logging on the Shasta-Trinity Divide. William N. Roy & David W. Braun. LC 92-90822. (Timberbeast Special Publications: Nos. 28-29). 1992. pap. 12.50 (*0-9634695-0-9*) Timberbeast.

***Lamorna Wink.** Martha Grimes. LC 99-55923. 2000. 29.95 (*0-7862-2324-3*) Thorndike Pr.

***Lamorna Wink.** Martha Grimes. (Richard Jury Mystery Ser.). 2000. mass mkt. 6.99 (*0-451-40936-1*, Onyx) NAL.

***Lamorna Wink: A Richard Jury Mystery.** Martha Grimes. LC 99-33525. 338p. 1999. 22.95 (*0-670-88870-2*, Viking) Viking Penguin.

Lamotrek Atoll & Interisland Socioeconomic Ties. rev. ed. William A. Alkire. 190p. (C). 1989. reprint ed. pap. text 11.95 (*0-88133-399-9*) Waveland Pr.

***L'Amour: French Glamour Girls: Retro Nudes of the 1950s & 60s.** Makoto Orui. (Illus.). 144p. 2000. pap. 24.95 (*4-7661-1133-8*) Graphic-Sha.

***L'Amour des Lettre.** Peter Long. 189p. 1999. 38.95 (*3-906762-50-5*, Pub. by P Lang) P Lang Pubng.

Lamp. Virginia D. Dawson. (Illus.). 48p. 1981. 28.00 (*0-88014-030-5*) Mosaic Pr OH.

Lamp at Noon & Other Stories. Sinclair Ross. 136p. 1996. pap. text 5.95 (*0-7710-9996-7*) McCland & Stewart.

Lamp for My Feet: The Bible's Light for Daily Living. Elisabeth Elliot. 140p. (Orig.). 1985. pap. 9.99 (*0-89283-352-1*, Vine Bks) Servant.

Lamp for Orchid. Mary Mellows. 126p. 1986. pap. 22.00 (*0-7223-1987-8*, Pub. by A H S Ltd) St Mut.

Lamp for the Lambchops. Jeff Brown. LC 82-48628. (Illus.). 96p. (J). (gr. 2-6). 1983. 11.95 (*0-06-020693-4*) HarpC Child Bks.

Lamp from the Warlock's Tomb. John Bellairs. (Anthony Monday Mystery Ser.). 168p. (J). (gr. 3-7). 1999. pap. 4.99 (*0-14-130077-9*, PuffinBks) Peng Put Young Read.

Lamp in the Desert. Ethel M. Dell. 1976. 25.95 (*0-8488-0261-6*) Amereon Ltd.

Lamp in the Night: Domestic Violence from a Feminist Perspective. Margaret Minkel & Ruth K. Schutz. 100p. 1992. pap. 10.00 (*0-9634517-0-7*) M Minkel.

Lamp in the Night Wind: St. Columba Story. Eona K. MacNicol. 256p. (C). 1988. 50.00 (*0-85335-006-X*, Pub. by Stuart Titles Ltd) St Mut.

***Lamp Is Lit: Leaves from a Journal.** Ruskin Bond. LC 99-932626. xiii, 200 p. 1998. 18.50 (*0-14-027804-4*, Penguin Classics) Viking Penguin.

Lamp of Beauty: Writings on Art. rev. ed. John Ruskin. Ed. & Selected by Joan Evans. (Arts & Letters Ser.). (Illus.). 424p. (C). 1995. pap. 14.95 (*0-7148-3358-4*, Pub. by Phaidon Press) Phaidon Pr.

Lamp of Experience: Whig History & the Intellectual Origins of the American Revolution. 2nd ed. Trevor Colbourn. LC 97-3351. 1998. 12.00 (*0-86597-158-7*); pap. 5.00 (*0-86597-159-5*) Liberty Fund.

Lamp of Fate. Margaret Pedler. 1976. lib. bdg. 15.25 (*0-89968-217-0*, Lghtyr Pr) Buccaneer Bks.

Lamp of God: A Jewish Book of Light. Freema Gottlieb. LC 89-31234. 520p. 1990. 40.00 (*0-87668-898-9*) Aronson.

Lamp of God: A Jewish Book of Light. Freema Gottlieb. LC 89-31234. 520p. 1996. pap. 40.00 (*1-56821-922-9*) Aronson.

Lamp of Liberation. Ed. by Terry Clifford et al. (Illus.). 112p. 1988. 10.00 (*0-9621371-0-3*) Yeshe Melong.

Lamp of Life Renewed: Daily Meditations for the Easter Season. Roger A. Swenson. LC 88-10480. 115p. 1988. pap. 7.95 (*0-8189-0534-4*) Alba.

Lamp of Mahamudra. Tsele N. Rangdrol. LC 88-34344. 128p. (Orig.). 1989. pap. 9.95 (*0-87773-487-9*, Pub. by Shambhala Pubns) Random.

Lamp of Marvels: Aesthetic Meditations. Ramon Del Valle-Inclan. Tr. by Robert Lima from SPA. LC 86-7172. 160p. 1986. pap. 8.95 (*0-940262-14-2*, Lindisfarne) Anthroposophic.

Lamp of Memory: Ruskin, Tradition & Architecture. Ed. by Michael Wheeler & Nigel Whiteley. (Illus.). 220p. 1992. 79.95 (*0-7190-3710-7*, Pub. by Manchester Univ Pr) St Martin.

Lamp of the Goddess: Lives & Teachings of a Priestess. Rae Beth. LC 95-16719. (Illus.). 160p. (Orig.). 1995. pap. text 9.95 (*0-87728-848-8*) Weiser.

Lamp Posts along the Spiritual Journey. Harry L. Shepherd. 108p. 1991. pap. 6.50 (*0-9629013-0-X*) Feather Prodns.

Lamp Posts along the Spiritual Journey. rev. ed. Harry L. Shepherd. 1994. 7.00 (*0-9629013-3-4*) Feather Prodns.

***Lamp Seasoning: LM-54-99.** IESNA Staff. 4p. 1999. pap. 18.00 (*0-87995-159-1*, LM-54-99) Illum Eng.

Lamp Shade Book: 80 Traditional & Innovative Projects to Create Exciting Lighting Effects. Dawn Cusick. (Illus.). 128p. pap. 14.95 (*0-8069-8700-6*) Sterling.

Lamp unto My Feet. Sharyn Harms. 1998. pap. write for info. (*1-57553-750-8*) Watermrk Pr.

Lamp unto Our Faith. Clarice Albritton & Grace Newby. LC 76-24514. 1976. pap. 4.95 (*0-87516-218-5*) DeVorss.

***Lamp with Prisms.** Joyce Stribling Steward. 80p. 1999. pap. 9.95 (*1-880222-34-5*) Red Apple Pub.

Lamparski's Hidden Hollywood: Where the Stars Lived, Loved & Died. Richard Lamparski. 1981. pap. 8.95 (*0-671-41885-8*, Fireside) S&S Trade Pap.

Lampbrush Chromosomes. H. C. Callan. (Molecular Biology, Biochemistry & Biophysics Ser.: Vol. 36). (Illus.). 290p. 1986. 199.95 (*0-387-16430-8*) Spr-Verlag.

Lampedusa. Rafael Argullol. (SPA.). 140p. 1981. pap. 5.50 (*84-85859-09-X*, 2002) Ediciones Norte.

Lampeter Yesterday. Ed. by Euros Davies & Arthur Roderick. 88p. 1994. pap. 20.95 (*0-8464-4706-1*) Beekman Pubs.

LAMPF Users Group Inc. (Lugi) Symposium: 20 Years of Meson Factory Physics: Accomplishments & Prospects Los Alamos, New Mexico 25-26 October, 1996. Ed. by B. F. Gibson et al. 350p. 1997. 78.00 (*981-02-3246-2*) World Scientific Pub.

LAMPF Workshop on Physics. Ed. by B. F. Gibson et al. LC 91-71304. (AIP Conference Proceedings Ser.: No. 224). 296p. 1991. 88.00 (*0-88318-825-2*) Am Inst Physics.

Lampfish of Twill. Janet T. Lisle. LC 91-8279. (Illus.). 176p. (YA). (gr. 5 up). 1991. 16.95 (*0-531-05963-4*) Orchard Bks Watts.

Lampfish of Twill. Janet T. Lisle. (Illus.). 176p. (J). (gr. 4-7). 1993. pap. 3.50 (*0-590-46040-4*, Apple Paperbacks) Scholastic Inc.

Lampfish of Twill. Janet T. Lisle. (J). 1991. 8.60 (*0-606-05409-X*, Pub. by Turtleback) Demco.

Lampholders, Starters, & Starter Holders for Fluorescent Lamps, UL 542. 7th ed. (C). 1994. pap. text 95.00 (*1-55989-683-3*) Underwrtrs Labs.

Lampkin Genealogy: A Genealogcal History of the Ancestors of David P. Lampkin, Vol. 1. Richard H. Lampkin. LC CS0071.. 870p. 1989. reprint ed. pap. 200.00 (*0-8357-6288-2*, AU0038800001) Bks Demand.

Lampkin Genealogy: A Genealogcal History of the Ancestors of David P. Lampkin, Vol. 2. Richard H. Lampkin. LC CS0071.. 868p. 1989. reprint ed. pap. 200.00 (*0-8357-6289-0*, AU0038800002) Bks Demand.

Lamplight on Cottage Loaves: Fireside Stories of Our Country Past. Joan Kent. (Illus.). 160p. 1994. 34.95 (*0-7126-5766-5*, Pub. by CEN3) Trafalgar.

Lamplight on Cottage Loaves: Fireside Stories of Our Country Past. large type ed. Joan Kent. 1995. 27.99 (*0-7505-0724-1*, Pub. by Mgna Lrg Print) Ulverscroft.

Lamplight over the Lake. large type ed. Margaret Wood. (Linford Romance Library). 304p. 1986. pap. 8.95 (*0-7089-6451-6*, Linford) Ulverscroft.

Lamplighter. Ed. by Nina Baym. (American Women Writers Ser.). 480p. (Orig.). (C). 1988. pap. text 17.00 (*0-8135-1333-2*) Rutgers U Pr.

Lamplighter. Maria Cummins. 1981. reprint ed. lib. bdg. 79.00 (*0-686-71927-1*) Scholarly.

Lamplit Answer. Gjertrud Schnackenberg. 83p. 1986. pap. 6.95 (*0-374-51978-1*) FS&G.

Lampmaking Handbook. Joe Porcelli. (Illus.). 1991. 24.95 (*0-9629053-6-4*) Glass Pr.

Lampman Symposium. Lampman Symposium, 1975, University of Ottawa Staf. Ed. & Intro. by Lorraine McMullen. LC 77-367781. (Re-Appraisals, Canadian Writers Ser.). 148p. 1976. reprint ed. pap. 45.90 (*0-608-02201-2*, 206287100004) Bks Demand.

Lamprecht, der Pfaffe, Alexander: Gedicht Des Zwolften Jahrhunderts, 2 vols. Lamprecht. cxxx, 1164p. 1971. reprint ed. write for info. (*0-318-71265-2*); reprint ed. write for info. (*0-318-71266-0*) G Olms Pubs.

Lamprecht, der Pfaffe, Alexander: Gedicht Des Zwolften Jahrhunderts, 2 vols., Set. Lamprecht. cxxx, 1164p. 1971. reprint ed. write for info. (*0-318-71264-4*) G Olms Pubs.

Lamprophyres. N. M. Rock. 288p. (gr. 13). 1991. mass mkt. 161.95 (*0-442-30396-3*) Chapman & Hall.

Lamps & Lighting. 4th ed. Ed. by J. R. Coaton & A. M. Marsden. LC 97-118955. 1997. write for info. (*0-340-64618-7*, Pub. by E A) Routldge.

Lamps & Lighting. 4th ed. Ed. by J. R. Coaton & A. M. Marsden. 546p. 1996. 130.00 (*0-470-23589-6*) Wiley.

Lamps & Shades: Beautiful Ideas to Make & Decorate. Juliet Bawden. LC 97-183698. (Illus.). 128p. 1997. 27.95 (*1-85368-733-2*, Pub. by New5 Holland) Sterling.

Lamps & Shades: Beautiful Ideas to Make & Decorate. Juliet Bawden. LC 97-183698. (Illus.). 128p. 1999. pap. text 17.95 (*1-85368-761-8*) New5 Holland.

***Lamps at High Noon.** Jack S. Balch. (Radical Novel Reconsidered Ser.). 448p. 2000. reprint ed. pap. 19.95 (*0-252-06939-0*) U of Ill Pr.

Lamps from the Athenian Agora. Judith Perlzweig. (Excavations of the Athenian Agora Picture Bks.: No. 9). (Illus.). 32p. 1964. pap. 3.00 (*0-87661-609-0*) Am Sch Athens.

Lamps Hurled at the Stunning Algebra of Ants. Franklin Rosemont. (Illus.). 72p. (Orig.). 1990. pap. 12.00 (*0-941194-22-1*) Black Swan Pr.

Lamps of Fire. Robert A. Herrera. LC 85-8242. 138p. (Orig.). 1986. pap. 10.95 (*0-932506-40-2*) St Bedes Pubns.

Lamps of Fire. Pedro Rubio. Tr. by Graciela P. Prouty from SPA. (Illus.). 115p. (Orig.). pap. 8.95 (*0-9637601-0-6*) Mount Ctr.

Lamps of the '50s & '60s. Jan Lindenberger. LC 97-68210. (Schiffer Book for Collectors Ser.). (Illus.). 144p. 1997. pap. 16.95 (*0-7643-0355-4*) Schiffer.

Lamps of the Roman Period, First to Seventh Century after Christ. Judith Perlzweig, (Athenian Agora Ser.: Vol. 7). (Illus.). xv, 240p. 1971. reprint ed. 35.00 (*0-87661-207-9*) Am Sch Athens.

Lamps of Tiffany. Egon Neustadt. LC 78-142102. (Illus.). 224p. 1970. 195.00 (*0-913158-01-1*) Neustadt.

Lamps of Tiffany Studios. William Feldstein, Jr. et al. (Illus.). 180p. 1983. 150.00 (*0-8109-1281-3*, Pub. by Abrams) Time Warner.

Lamps of Western Mysticism. Arthur E. Waite. 334p. 1992. reprint ed. pap. 27.00 (*0-922802-88-2*) Kessinger Pub.

Lamps on the Brow: (Science Fiction Stories in the Future) Ben Bova et al. Ed. by James Cahill. 200p. 1998. 125.00 (*0-9640454-7-8*) J Cahill Pubng.

***Lamps, Scrolls & Goatskin Bottles: A Handbook of Bible Customs for Kids.** Julia Hans. (Illus.). 144p. 2000. pap. 14.99 (*0-7847-1165-8*) Standard Pub.

Lampshade Kit. Amelia St. George. (Illus.). 98p. 1994. 19.95 (*0-09-178173-6*, Pub. by Arrow Bks) Trafalgar.

Lampshade Kit: With Ten Ready-to-Use Lampshades & 8 Pull-Out Patterns. Amélia Saint-George. (Illus.). 96p. 1994. pap. 19.95 (*0-917817-36-2*, Trafalgar Sq Pub) Trafalgar.

Lampshades. Carole Morin. LC 98-10744. 192p. 1998. 21.95 (*0-87951-857-X*, Pub. by Overlook Pr) Penguin Putnam.

Lamson of the Gettysburg: The Civil War Letters of Lieutenant Roswell H. Lamson, U. S. Navy. Ed. by James M. McPherson & Patricia R. McPherson. LC 97-11129. (Illus.). 272p. 1997. 25.00 (*0-19-511698-4*) OUP.

Lamson of the Gettysburg: The Civil War Letters of Lieutenant Roswell H. Lamson, U. S. Navy. Ed. by James M. McPherson & Patricia R. McPherson. (Illus.). 272p. 1999. pap. 15.95 (*0-19-513093-6*) OUP.

Lamu: History, Society, & Family in an East African Port City. Patricia W. Romero. LC 96-45647. (Illus.). 360p. (C). 1997. text 44.95 (*1-55876-106-3*) Wiener Pubs Inc.

Lamu: History, Society, & Family in an East African Port City. Patricia W. Romero. LC 96-45647. (Illus.). 360p. (C). 1997. pap. text 18.95 (*1-55876-107-1*) Wiener Pubs Inc.

Lamutisches Woerterbuch. Gerhard Doerfer et al. (GER.). 1181p. 1980. 195.00 (*0-8288-1618-2*, F39233) Fr & Eur.

***Lamy's Legion: The Individual Histories of Secular Clergy Serving in the Army.** (Illus.). 146p. 2000. pap. 25.00 (*0-9665859-1-7*) HRM Bks.

LAN & Internetworking Applications Guide: How Network Software Impacts Network Design. BICSI Staff. (Illus.). 250p. 1999. pap. 29.99 (*1-928886-00-0*) B I C S I.

LAN & Internetworking Design Manual. 3rd rev. ed. BICSI Staff. Orig. Title: LAN Design Manual. (Illus.). 1200p. 1999. ring bd. 329.00 (*1-928886-01-9*) B I C S I.

LAN & WAN Connectivity Markets: Routes, Bridges & Gateways: Are They Obsolete? Market Intelligence Staff. 287p. 1993. 1695.00 (*1-56753-430-9*) Frost & Sullivan.

An Asterisk (*) at the beginning of an entry indicates that the title is appearing for the first time.

***LAN Architectures.** rev. ed. Ken Reed. Ed. by Marilee Aust. (Tech Ser.: Vol. 3CS-112). (Illus.). 410p. 1999. write for info. (*1-58676-035-1*) WestNet Learn.

LAN, ATM & LAN Emulation Technologies. Daniel Minoli & Anthony Alles. LC 96-46062. 309p. 1996. 89.00 (*0-89006-916-6*) Artech Hse.

LAN Basics. Roberta Martine & Robert Mercer. 89p. (Orig.). 1992. pap. write for info. (*0-917845-20-X*) Intertec IL.

LAN Blueprints: Engineering It Right. Gerald T. Charles, Jr. LC 96-44414. (Illus.). 224p. 1997. pap., pap. text 44.95 incl. disk (*0-07-011769-1*) McGraw.

LAN Cables & Apparatus - Markets, Technologies & Opportunities: 1992-1996 Analysis. Amadee Bender et al. (Illus.). 100p. 1992. pap. text 2400.00 (*1-878218-30-1*) World Info Tech.

LAN Connectivity Technology. Business Communications Co., Inc. Staff. 179p. 1991. 1950.00 (*0-89336-759-1*, G129) BCC.

LAN Design Manual see LAN & Internetworking Design Manual

LAN Internetworking: Building the Corporate Network for the 90's. Robin Layland. 1996. 39.75 (*0-201-63360-4*) Addison-Wesley.

LAN-MAN Standards Integrated Services Package, 802.9. 220.00 (*1-55937-707-0*, SH94398) IEEE Standards.

LAN Management with SNMP & RMON. Gilbert Held. LC 96-14112. 371p. 1996. pap. 39.95 (*0-471-14736-2*) Wiley.

LAN Manager's Internet Connectivity Guide. Sidnie Feit & Morrow Long. LC 97-24715. (Illus.). 352p. 1997. pap. 39.95 (*0-07-061622-1*) McGraw.

LAN Performance Optimization. Martin A. Nemzow. 1993. pap. text 29.95 (*0-07-852659-0*) McGraw.

LAN Primer: An Introduction to Local Area Networks. 2nd ed. Greg Nunemacher. 300p. (Orig.). 1995. pap. 26.95 (*1-55851-287-X*, M&T Bks) IDG Bks.

LAN Primer: The Best Introduction to Networking Fundamentals. 3rd ed. Greg Nunemacher. (Illus.). 372p. 1999. reprint ed. pap. text 20.00 (*0-7881-6504-6*) DIANE Pub.

LAN Protocol Handbook. Mark A. Miller. (Illus.). 400p. (Orig.). 1995. pap. 34.95 (*1-55851-099-0*, M&T Bks) IDG Bks.

LAN Security Handbook. Ellen Dutton. LC 94-19132. 1994. 39.95 incl. disk (*1-55851-387-6*, M&T Bks) IDG Bks.

LAN Server Engineer Certification Handbook. New Riders Development Group Staff. (Illus.). 1536p. (Orig.). 1995. pap. 89.99 (*1-56205-406-6*) New Riders Pub.

LAN Support Services. Market Intelligence Staff. 1993. 3200.00 (*1-56753-478-3*) Frost & Sullivan.

***LAN Technologies Explained.** Michael Cummins & Philip Miller. (Illus.). 776p. 2000. pap. 49.95 (*1-55558-234-6*, Digital DEC) Buttrwrth-Heinemann.

LAN Technology & Concepts: Ethernet & Token-Ring Systems. Amit Dutta-Roy. 1993. text 39.95 (*0-07-018395-3*) McGraw.

LAN Times Encyclopedia of Networking. Thomas Sheldon. (LAN Times Ser). 1104p. 1994. pap. 39.95 (*0-07-881965-2*) Osborne-McGraw.

LAN Times Guide to Building High-Speed Networks. Tere Parnell. (LAN Times Ser.). 512p. 1996. pap. text 29.95 (*0-07-882200-9*) Osborne-McGraw.

LAN Times Guide to Building Microsoft Networks. Tom Sheldon. (Lan Times Ser.). 504p. 1997. pap. text 29.95 (*0-07-882179-7*) McGraw.

LAN Times Guide to Interoperability Network Interconnectivity Solutions. Ed. by Tom Sheldon. (LAN Times Ser.). 448p. 1994. text 29.95 (*0-07-882043-X*) Osborne-McGraw.

LAN Times Guide to Managing Remote Connectivity. Salvatore Salamone. LC 97-166739. 1997. pap. text 34.99 (*0-07-882267-X*) Osborne-McGraw.

LAN Times Guide to Multimedia Networking. Nancy A. Cox et al. (Lan Times Ser.). 400p. 1995. pap. text 29.95 (*0-07-882114-2*) Osborne-McGraw.

LAN Times Guide to Networking Windows 95. Eric Harper et al. (LAN Times Ser.). 512p. 1995. pap. text 29.95 (*0-07-882086-3*) Osborne-McGraw.

LAN Times Guide to Security & Data Integrity. Marc Farley et al. LC 96-170512. (LAN Times Ser.). 416p. 1996. pap. text 29.95 (*0-07-882166-5*) McGraw.

LAN Times Guide to SQL. James R. Groff & Paul N. Weinberg. (LAN Times Ser.). 752p. 1994. pap. text 29.95 (*0-07-882026-X*) Osborne-McGraw.

LAN Times Guide to Telephony. David D. Bezar. (LAN Times Ser.). 450p. 1995. pap. 34.95 (*0-07-882126-6*) McGraw.

LAN Times Guide to Wide Area Networks. Barry G. Bestpitch & Tere Parnell. 528p. 1996. pap. text 34.95 (*0-07-882228-9*) Osborne-McGraw.

***Lan Times (1996) Guide to Security & Data Integrity.** Marc Farley et al. (Illus.). 316p. 2000. reprint ed. pap. text 20.00 (*0-7881-9193-4*) DIANE Pub.

LAN to WAN Interconnection. John Enck & Mel Breckman. LC 95-10086. 1995. 40.00 (*0-07-019614-1*) McGraw.

***LAN Wiring.** 2nd ed. Truelove. 500p. 2000. 45.00 (*0-07-135776-9*) McGraw-Hill Prof.

LAN Wiring: An Illustrated Guide to Network Cabling. J. E. Trulove. LC 96-51978. (Illus.). 307p. 1996. pap. 32.95 (*0-07-065302-X*) McGraw.

Lana. Lana R. Fishergerlach. 80p. 1992. pap. text, per. 10.00 (*0-8403-7561-1*) Kendall-Hunt.

Lana. Wayne. 1996. mass mkt. write for info. (*0-312-95639-8*) St Martin.

***Lana Araucana: Our Easter Chick.** LC 98-91267. (Illus.). 16p. (J). (gr. k-2). 2000. pap. 5.95 (*0-9646370-1-4*) Redbud Pr MI.

Lana de Andi. Rhonda Cox. Tr. by Alberto Romo. (Books for Young Learners).Tr. of Andi's Wool. (SPA., Illus.). 12p. (J). (gr. k-2). 1999. pap. text 5.00 (*1-57274-296-8*) R Owen Pubs.

Lanahan Cases & Readings in Abnormal Behavior. Kayla F. Bernheim. 379p. (Orig.). (C). 1997. pap. text 26.25 (*0-9652687-0-5*) Lanahan Pubs.

Lanahan Cases in Developmental Psychopathology. Kayla F. Bernheim et al. 195p. (Orig.). (C). 1999. pap. text 18.75 (*0-9652687-5-6*) Lanahan Pubs.

Lanahan Essentials of the British Polity. John Kingdom. (Illus.). 324p. (Orig.). (C). 1999. pap. text 20.00 (*0-9652687-4-8*) Lanahan Pubs.

Lanahan Readings in Civil Rights & Civil Liberties. Ed. by David M. O'Brien. 319p. (Orig.). (C). 1999. pap. text 23.75 (*0-9652687-6-4*) Lanahan Pubs.

Lanahan Readings in the American Polity. Ed. by Ann G. Serow & Everett C. Ladd. 652p. (C). 1997. pap. text 28.75 (*0-9652687-1-3*) Lanahan Pubs.

***Lanahan Readings in the American Polity.** 2nd rev. ed. Ed. by Ann G. Serow & Everett C. Ladd. 670p. (C). 1999. pap. text 28.75 (*0-9652687-7-2*) Lanahan Pubs.

Lanahan Readings in the Psychology of Women. Ed. by Tomi-Ann Roberts. (Illus.). 574p. (Orig.). (C). 1997. pap. text 28.75 (*0-9652687-2-1*) Lanahan Pubs.

Lanark: A Life in Four Books, 4 bks., Set. Alasdair Gray. LC 95-47625. 576p. 1996. pap. 16.00 (*0-15-600361-9*) Harcourt.

Lancashire. John Champness. (Country Guide Ser.: No. 28). (Illus.). 64p. pap. 8.50 (*0-85263-984-8*, Pub. by Shire Pubns) Parkwest Pubns.

Lancashire. David George. (Records of Early English Drama Ser.). 596p. 1992. text 125.00 (*0-8020-2862-4*) U of Toronto Pr.

Lancashire & Cheshire. (Ordnance Survey Pathfinder Guides Ser.). (Illus.). 80p. (Orig.). 1995. pap. 14.95 (*0-7117-0816-9*, Pub. by JARR UK) Seven Hills Bk.

Lancashire & Cheshire from AD 1540. C. B. Phillips & J. H. Smith. LC 92-23399. (Regional History of England Ser.). 1994. pap. text. write for info. (*0-582-49249-1*) Longman.

Lancashire & the New Liberalism. Peter Clarke. (Modern Revivals in History Ser.). 488p. 1993. 79.95 (*0-7512-0213-4*, Pub. by Gregg Revivals) Ashgate Pub Co.

Lancashire & Yorkshire Passenger Stock. R. W. Rush. 96p. (C). 1985. 39.00 (*0-85361-306-0*) St Mut.

Lancashire Cotton Famine, 1861-1865. Henderson. 216p. 1994. 57.95 (*0-7512-0228-2*) Ashgate Pub Co.

***Lancashire Giant: David Shackleton, Labour Leader & Civil Servant.** Ross M. Martin. 320p. 1999. 53.95 (*0-85323-934-7*, Pub. by Liverpool Univ Pr); pap. 24.95 (*0-85323-944-4*, Pub. by Liverpool Univ Pr) Intl Spec Bk.

Lancashire in Decline: A Study in Entrepreneurship, Technology, & International Trade. Lars G. Sandberg. (Modern Revivals in Economic & Social History Ser.). 296p. 1993. 61.95 (*0-7512-0166-9*, Pub. by Gregg Pub) Ashgate Pub Co.

Lancashire on the Scrapheap: The Cotton Industry, 1945-1970. John Singleton. (Pasold Studies in Textile History: No. 8). (Illus.). 270p. 1991. text 95.00 (*0-19-921061-6*) OUP.

***Lancashire Witches.** W. H. Ainsworth. 252p. 2000. pap. 9.95 (*0-594-01483-2*) Eightn Hundrd.

Lancaster. Harold E. Wright. (Images of America Ser.). 1998. pap. 16.99 (*0-7524-0993-X*) Arcadia Publng.

Lancaster: Auro Lancaster B MK1. Raymond L. Rimell. (Aeroguide Ser.: No. 3). 1986. pap. 6.00 (*0-918805-27-9*) Pac Aero Pr.

Lancaster: RAF Heavy Bomber. Dan Patterson. LC 96-75272. (Living History Ser.: No. 4). (Illus.). 64p. 1996. pap. 15.95 (*1-57427-052-4*) Howell Pr VA.

Lancaster & Fairfield County. (Illus.). 221p. 1997. reprint ed. lib. bdg. 29.50 (*0-8328-6335-1*) Higginson Bk Co.

Lancaster Cotton Industry: A Study in Economic Development. Sydney J. Chapman. LC 68-55503. (Reprints of Economic Classics Ser.). vii, 309p. 1973. reprint ed. 45.00 (*0-678-00896-5*) Kelley.

Lancaster County. Ed Klimuska. LC 98-14320. (Illus.). 144p. 1998. 29.95 (*0-89658-392-9*); pap. 19.95 (*0-89658-397-X*) Voyageur Pr.

Lancaster County: A History, 4 vols. in 2. Ed. by H. M. Klein & E. Melvin Williams. (Illus.). 1656p. 1997. reprint ed. lib. bdg. 172.50 (*0-8328-6420-X*) Higginson Bk Co.

Lancaster County: The Best Food, Fun, Lodging, Shopping & Sights. Alonna F. Smith. LC 96-62098. 200p. 1997. pap. 10.95 (*0-9644975-1-4*) Food Compan Pr.

***Lancaster County & the Great War, South Carolina.** John Chandler Griffin. (Voices Ser.). (Illus.). 96p. 1999. pap. 16.99 (*0-7385-0292-8*) Arcadia Publng.

Lancaster County Architecture, 1700-1850. Gerald S. Lextz. (Illus.). 176p. 1992. write for info. (*0-9635153-0-6*) Hist Preserv Trst.

Lancaster County Churches in the Revolutionary War Era. Martin E. Ressler et al. Ed. by Matthew W. Harrison, Jr. LC 76-21210. (Illus.). 96p. 1976. pap. 5.00 (*0-915010-11-9*) Sutter House.

Lancaster County Cookbook. Louise Stoltzfus & Jan Mast. LC 93-30020. (Illus.). 251p. 1993. pap. 13.95 (*1-56148-092-4*) Good Bks PA.

Lancaster County During the American Revolution Series, 7 bks. Ed. by Joseph E. Walker. Incl. Fighting the Battles: Lancaster's Soldiers March off to War. Frederic S. Klein. LC 75-15438. (Illus.). 56p. 1975. pap. 5.00 (*0-915010-06-2*); Loyalists, Pacifists & Prisoners. Rollin C. Steinmetz. LC 76-21212. (Illus.). 96p. 1976. pap. 5.00 (*0-915010-12-7*); Military Market Basket. John W. Loose. LC 76-21211. (Illus.). 64p. 1976. pap. 5.00 (*0-915010-09-7*); Pennsylvania Rifle. Samuel E. Dyke. LC 74-29189. (Illus.). 64p. 1997. pap. 5.00 (*0-915010-05-4*); Perils of Patriotism: John Joseph Henry & the American Attack on Quebec, 1775. J. Samuel Walker. LC 75-15439. (Illus.). 56p. 1975. pap. 5.00 (*0-915010-08-9*); Revolutionary Leadership. G. Terry Madonna. LC 76-8955. (Illus.). 56p. 1976. pap. 5.00 (*0-915010-07-0*); Way of Life. Jim Kinter. LC 74-29188. (Illus.). 64p. 1976. pap. 5.00 (*0-915010-04-6*); 30.00 (*0-915010-14-3*) Sutter House.

Lancaster County Farm Cook Book. (Pennsylvania Dutch Bks.). 1967. 3.00 (*0-911410-15-5*) Applied Arts.

Lancaster County, Pa. Deed Abstracts 1729 to 1770 & Oaths of Allegiance. enl. rev. ed. R. Thomas Mayhill. 277p. 1979. 24.00 (*0-686-27817-8*) Bookmark.

Lancaster County, PA Cemetery Surname Index. Ed. by Mary Closson. 1988. pap. text 10.50 (*1-55856-008-4*, 235) Closson Pr.

Lancaster County, Pennsylvania Divorces, 1786-1832. Throop. 132p. (Orig.). 1996. pap. 17.00 (*0-7884-0393-1*, T367) Heritage Bk.

Lancaster County Postcards: Windows to Our Past. (Illus.). x, 182p. 1998. 30.00 (*0-9664942-0-2*) Lancaster Co.

Lancaster County, Virginia, Marriage Bonds, 1652-1850. Ida J. Lee. 71p. 1997. reprint ed. pap. 10.00 (*0-8063-0500-2*, 3335) Clearfield Co.

Lancaster County, Virginia Records, Vol. 2. Lindsay O. Duvall. (Virginia Colonial Abstracts, Series II). 1979. reprint ed. 17.50 (*0-89308-063-2*) Southern Hist Pr.

***Lancaster Down: The Extraordinary Tale of Seven Young Bomber Crew at War.** Steve Darlow. 2000. 29.95 (*1-902304-48-9*) Grub St.

Lancaster Family: Thomas & Phebe Lancaster of Bucks County, Penn., & Their Descendants, 1711-1902. H. L. Lancaster. (Illus.). 302p. reprint ed. pap. 45.00 (*0-8328-0748-6*); reprint ed. lib. bdg. 53.00 (*0-8328-0747-8*) Higginson Bk Co.

Lancaster Family of Maryland & Kentucky: History of English Ancestry, Emigration to Colony of Maryland, Pioneers of Kentucky. Samuel Lancaster. (Illus.). 200p. 1993. reprint ed. pap. 32.50 (*0-8328-3360-6*); reprint ed. lib. bdg. 42.50 (*0-8328-3359-2*) Higginson Bk Co.

Lancaster House Competition Policy Inquiry. European Community Enterprise Research Centre Staf. 160p. (C). 1988. text 80.00 (*1-85396-034-9*, Pub. by P Chapman) St Mut.

Lancaster House Constitutional Conference on Rhodesia. Stephen J. Stedman. (Pew Case Studies in International Affairs). 50p. (C). 1986. pap. text 3.50 (*1-56927-341-3*) Geo U Inst Dplmcy.

Lancaster in the Revolution. Charles H. Kessler. LC 75-34256. (Illus.). 164p. 1975. 9.95 (*0-915010-10-0*) Sutter House.

Lancaster Men. Janet Dailey. 1994. mass mkt. 4.99 (*0-671-87506-X*) PB.

***Lancaster, Ohio, 1800-2000: Frontier Town to Edge City.** David R. Contosta. Ed. & Ffwd. by Zane L. Miller. LC 99-21549. (Urban Life & Urban Landscape Ser.). (Illus.). 352p. 1999. text 37.50 (*0-8142-0825-8*) Ohio St U Pr.

***Lancaster, Ohio, 1800-2000: Frontier Town to Edge City.** David R. Contosta. (Urban Life & Urban Landscape Ser.). (Illus.). 360p. 2000. pap. 19.95 (*0-8142-5027-0*) Ohio St U Pr.

Lancaster, PA 200 Years. Historical Briefs, Inc. Staff. Ed. by Thomas Antonucci & Michael Antonucci. 200p. 1993. pap. 19.95 (*0-89677-049-4*) Hist Briefs.

Lancaster, PA WW II. Historical Briefs, Inc. Staff. Ed. by Thomas Antonucci & Michael Antonucci. 176p. 1992. pap. 19.95 (*0-89677-041-9*) Hist Briefs.

Lancaster, PA 1950's. Historical Briefs, Inc. Staff. Ed. by Thomas Antonucci & Michael Antonucci. 200p. 1994. pap. 19.95 (*0-89677-058-3*) Hist Briefs.

Lancaster Platt Lupton Vol. 1: The Legacy of a Fur Trader. David W. Lupton & Dorothy R. Lupton. (Road to Delhi). (Illus.). 124p. (Orig.). 1994. pap. 11.50 (*0-9644165-1-4*) S Platte Valley.

Lancaster Residents Look at Their Public Schools. John Immerwahr. 29p. 1997. pap. 5.00 (*1-889483-50-8*) Public Agenda.

Lancasterian System of Instruction in the Schools of New York City. John F. Reigart. LC 72-89220. (American Education: Its Men, Institutions, & Ideas. Series 1: Its Men, Institutions & Ideas, Ser. 1). 1975. reprint ed. 13.95 (*0-405-01459-7*) Ayer.

***Lancaster's Lake.** Mary Lee Tiernan. (Early History of Sunland, California Ser.: Vol. 6). (Illus.). 20p. 1999. write for info. (*0-9702393-5-1*) Snoops Desktop.

***Lancaster/York Entertainment, 2000.** (Illus.). 883p. 1999. pap. 25.00 (*1-58553-033-6*, 0072) Enter Pubns.

Lancastrian Affinity, 1361 to 1399. Simon Walker. 366p. 1991. text 105.00 (*0-19-820174-5*) OUP.

Lancastrian Chemist: The Early Years of Sir Edward Frankland. Colin A. Russell. 192p. 1986. 69.00 (*0-335-15175-2*) OpUniv Pr.

Lancastrian Letters. Anne Sheldon. (Premier Ser.: Vol. 6). (Illus.). 25p. 1997. pap. 5.00 (*0-9654421-5-2*) Mica Press.

***Lancastrians to Tudors: England 1450-1509.** Andrew Pickering. (Perspectives in History Ser.). 160p. (C). 2000. pap. 12.95 (*0-521-55746-1*) Cambridge U Pr.

Lance & the Shield: The Life & Times of Sitting Bull. Robert Marshall Utley. (Illus.). 432p. 1995. 25.00 (*0-8050-1274-5*, J Macrae Bks) H Holt & Co.

Lance & the Shield: The Life & Times of Sitting Bull. Robert Marshall Utley. (Illus.). 448p. 1994. reprint ed. pap. 14.00 (*0-345-38938-7*) Ballantine Pub Grp.

***Lance Armstrong: The Race of His Life.** Kristin Armstrong. (All Aboard Reading Ser.). (Illus.). (J). 2000. 13.89 (*0-448-42415-0*, Planet Dexter) Peng Put Young Read.

***Lance Armstrong: The Race of His Life.** Kristin Armstrong. (All Aboard Reading Ser.). (Illus.). 48p. (J). (gr. 4-7). 2000. pap. 3.99 (*0-448-42407-X*, Planet Dexter) Peng Put Young Read.

***Lance Armstrong Performance Program: Seven Weeks to the Perfect Ride.** Lance Armstrong et al. (Illus.). 256p. 2000. pap. 15.95 (*1-57954-270-0*) Rodale Pr Inc.

***Lance Armstrong's Comeback from Cancer: A Scrapbook of the Tour de France Winner's Dramatic Career.** Samuel Abt. LC 99-75679. (Illus.). 160p. 1999. pap. text 16.95 (*1-892495-25-2*, Pub. by Van der Plas) Seven Hills Bk.

L

***Lance Comfort.** Brian McFarlane. LC 99-42907. (British Film Directors Ser.). 1999. pap. 19.95 (*0-7190-5484-2*); text 79.95 (*0-7190-5483-4*, Pub. by Manchester Univ Pr) St Martin.

Lance for the Devil. large type ed. Robert Charles. (Linford Mystery Library). 352p. 1997. pap. 16.99 (*0-7089-7990-4*, Linford) Ulverscroft.

Lance of Justice: A Semi-Centennial History of the Legal Aid Society, 1876-1926. John M. Maguire. xi, 305p. 1982. reprint ed. 39.00 (*0-8377-0847-8*, Rothman) W S Hein.

Lance-Pierres. Ernst Junger. (FRE.). 440p. 1976. pap. 11.95 (*0-7859-2637-2*, 207036853X) Fr & Eur.

Lancelot. Walker Percy. 256p. 1989. mass mkt. 5.99 (*0-8041-0380-1*) Ivy Books.

Lancelot: A Fortran Package for Large-Scale Nonlinear Optimization (Release A) A. R. Conn et al. (Computational Mechanics Ser.: No. 17). 330p. 1992. 118.95 (*0-387-55470-X*) Spr-Verlag.

***Lancelot: Novel.** Walker Percy. LC 99-16418. 272p. 1999. pap. 14.00 (*0-312-24307-3*) St Martin.

Lancelot: The Knight of the Cart. Chretien. Tr. by Burton Raffel from FRO. LC 97-14424. 208p. 1997. 35.00 (*0-300-07120-5*) Yale U Pr.

Lancelot: The Knight of the Cart. Chretien De Troyes. Tr. by Burton Raffel from FRO. LC 97-14424. 208p. 1997. pap. 16.00 (*0-300-07121-3*) Yale U Pr.

Lancelot & Guinevere. Richard Hovey. (Notable American Authors Ser.). 1992. reprint ed. lib. bdg. 75.00 (*0-7812-3189-2*) Rprt Serv.

Lancelot & Guinevere: A Casebook. Lori J. Walters. Ed. by Norris J. Lacy. LC 96-2536. (Arthurian Characters & Themes Ser.: Vol. 4). (Illus.). 392p. 1996. reprint ed. text 70.00 (*0-8153-0653-9*, H1513) Garland.

Lancelot Andrewes: Selected Writing. Lancelot Andrewes. Ed. by P.E. Hewison. LC 96-138261. 192p. 1996. pap. 18.95 (*1-85754-118-9*, Pub. by Carcanet Pr) Paul & Co Pubs.

Lancelot-Grail: The Old French Arthurian Vulgate & Post-Vulgate in Translation. Ed. by Norris J. Lacy. LC 92-1674. 296p. 1995. text 35.00 (*0-8153-0748-9*, H1896) Garland.

Lancelot-Grail: The Old French Arthurian Vulgate & Post-Vulgate in Translation, Vol. I. Ed. by Norris J. Lacy. LC 92-1674. 456p. 1992. text 35.00 (*0-8240-7733-4*, H941) Garland.

Lancelot-Grail: The Old French Arthurian Vulgate & Post-Vulgate in Translation, Vol. II. Ed. by Norris J. Lacy. LC 92-1674. 342p. 1993. text 35.00 (*0-8153-0746-2*, H1826) Garland.

Lancelot-Grail: The Old French Arthurian Vulgate & Post-Vulgate in Translation, Vol. 3. Ed. by Norris J. Lacy. LC 92-1674. (Garland Reference Library of the Humanities: Vol. 941). 338p. 1995. text 35.00 (*0-8153-0747-0*, H1878) Garland.

Lancelot-Grail: The Old French Arthurian Vulgate & Post-Vulgate in Translation, Vol. 5. Norris J. Lacy & Martha Asher. LC 92-1674. 456p. 1996. text 35.00 (*0-8153-0757-8*, H1964) Garland.

Lancelot-Grail: The Old French Volgate & Post-Vulgate Cycles in Translation, 5 vols., Set. Ed. by Norris J. Lacy. 3500p. 375.00 (*0-8240-0700-X*) Garland.

Lancelot-Grail Cycle: Text & Transformation. William W. Kibler. LC 94-2962. (Illus.). 256p. (C). 1994. text 42.50 (*0-292-74317-3*) U of Tex Pr.

***Lancelot-Grail Reader: Selections from the Medieval French Arthurian Cycle.** Norris J. Lacy. LC 99-39114. (Reference Library of the Humanities). 350p. 2000. 24.95 (*0-8153-3419-2*) Garland.

***Lancelot Hogben: Scientific Humanist: An Unauthorized Autobiography.** Ed. by Adrian Hogben & Anne Hogben. 254p. 1999. 26.95 (*0-85036-470-1*, Pub. by MRLN) Paul & Co Pubs.

Lancelot in English Literature. August J. App. LC 65-21392. (Arthurian Legend & Literature Ser.: No. 1). (C). 1969. reprint ed. lib. bdg. 75.00 (*0-8383-0504-0*) M S G Haskell Hse.

Lancelot of the Laik. Ed. by Walter W. Skeat. (EETS, OS Ser.: Vol. 6). 1969. reprint ed. 30.00 (*0-8115-3342-5*) Periodicals Srv.

Lancelot of the Laik & Sir Tristrem. Ed. by Alan Lupack. (Teams Middle English Text Ser.). 1997. pap. 12.00 (*1-879288-50-8*) Medieval Inst.

Lancelot of the Lake. Corin Corley. (World's Classics Ser.). 470p. 1989. pap. 12.95 (*0-19-281756-6*) OUP.

***Lancelot of the Lake.** Corin Corley. (Oxford World's Classics Ser.). 472p. 1999. pap. 12.95 (*0-19-283793-1*) OUP.

Lancelot: or The Knight of the Cart. Chretien de Troyes. Tr. by Ruth H. Cline from FRE. LC 89-20283. 272p. 1990. pap. 15.00 (*0-8203-1213-4*) U of Ga Pr.

Lances Sing: A Study of the Igor Tale. Robert Mann. 231p. (Orig.). 1990. pap. 21.95 (*0-89357-208-X*) Slavica.

Lancewood. Alan Marshall. 233p. pap. 18.95 (*0-9585805-1-0*) Intl Spec Bk.

***Lanchester Readings: 1914 to Present, Vol. 1.** John Schuler. 1999. pap. text 60.00 (*1-57321-016-1*) Lanchester Pr.

L

Lanchester Strategy: An Introduction. N. Taoka. LC 97-76465. (Lanchester Strategy: Vol. 1). 1997. pap. text 25.00 (*1-57321-009-9*) Lanchester Pr.

*__Lanchester Theory: Science to Win the Competition, Vol. 1.__ T Onoda. 1999. pap. text 55.00 (*1-57321-015-3*) Lanchester Pr.

Lancia: From Alpha to Zeta & Beyond. Brian Long. 2000. 34.95 (*0-7509-2080-7*) Sutton Pub Ltd.

Lancia Beta: Collector's Guide. B. Long. (Illus.). 128p. 1996. 27.95 (*0-947981-62-4*, Pub. by Motor Racing) Motorbooks Intl.

Lanciers. R. Boleslavski. (FRE.). 376p. 1986. pap. 12.95 (*0-7859-2032-3*, 2070377296) Fr & Eur.

Lancome. Universe Publishing Incorporated Staff & Jacqueline Demornex. 80p. 1999. 18.95 (*0-7893-0327-2*, Pub. by Universe) St Martin.

Land see Earth Strikes Back: How We Use & Abuse Our Planet

Land. Mary Beath & Barry Lopez. (Illus.). (Orig.). 1989. pap. 12.95 (*0-685-26564-1*) P P Rindge.

Land. Park Kyong-ni. Tr. by Agnita Tennant from KOR. LC 95-15879.Tr. of Toji. 512p. 1995. 34.00 (*0-7103-0508-7*) Routledge.

Land. Mildred B. Taylor. 1999. pap. 15.89 (*0-8037-1951-5*, Dial Yng Read) Peng Put Young Read.

Land. Mildred B. Taylor. 2001. 15.99 (*0-8037-1950-7*, Dial Yng Read) Peng Put Young Read.

Land. Jacquetta Hawkes. LC 90-25595. (Concord Library). (Illus.). 272p. 1991. reprint ed. pap. 12.00 (*0-8070-8511-1*) Beacon Pr.

Land: A Novel. Robert K. Swisher, Jr. LC 86-22966. 164p. (Orig.). 1987. pap. 12.95 (*0-86534-095-1*) Sunstone Pr.

Land: A Novel from Brazil. Antonio Torres. Tr. by Margaret Neves from POR. (Readers International Ser.). (Illus.). 136p. (C). 1987. 14.95 (*0-930523-24-5*) Readers Intl.

Land: A Novel from Brazil. Antonio Torres. Tr. by Margaret A. Neves from POR. (Readers International Ser.). (Illus.). 136p. (C). 1987. pap. 7.95 (*0-930523-25-3*) Readers Intl.

Land: Landscape Wood Engravings. Garrick Palmer. 1993. 150.00 (*0-907664-34-2*, Pub. by Old Stiles) St Mut.

Land: Place As Gift, Promise & Challenge in Biblical Faith. Walter Brueggemann. Ed. by John R. Donahue. LC 76-15883. (Overtures to Biblical Theology Ser.: No. 1). 224p. 1977. pap. 17.00 (*0-8006-1526-3*, 1-1526, Fortress Pr) Augsburg Fortress.

Land - Something of Value: Proceedings of a Workshop on Rural Land Values, 2 pts., Pt. 1. Ed. by Gene Wunderlich. LC HD1393.W67. (Lincoln Institute Monograph: Nos. 82-10, 82-11). 112p. reprint ed. pap. 34.80 (*0-7837-5717-4*, 204543000001) Bks Demand.

Land - Something of Value: Proceedings of a Workshop on Rural Land Values, 2 pts., Pt. 2. Ed. by Gene Wunderlich. LC HD1393.W67. (Lincoln Institute Monograph: Nos. 82-10, 82-11). 123p. reprint ed. pap. 38.20 (*0-7837-5718-2*, 204543000002) Bks Demand.

Land above the Trees: A Guide to American Alpine Tundra. Ann Zwinger & Beatrice E. Willard. LC 96-11083. (Illus.). 448p. 1996. reprint ed. pap. 19.95 (*1-55566-171-8*) Johnson Bks.

Land Acquisition. Warren W. Kershow. LC 76-359055. (Special Publication: No. 15002). 28p. 1975. reprint ed. pap. 30.00 (*0-7837-1534-X*, 204181500024) Bks Demand.

Land Acquisition. 3rd ed. D. Brown. 186p. 1991. boxed set 126.00 (*0-409-49102-0*, Austral, MICHIE) LEXIS Pub.

Land Acquisition. 4th ed. D. Brown. LC 97-157537. 1996. write for info. (*0-409-31063-8*, MICHIE) LEXIS Pub.

Land Acquisition Act. Justice Malik. (C). 1990. 70.00 (*0-89771-301-X*) St Mut.

Land Acquisition in Developing Countries: Policies & Procedures of the Public Sector, with Surveys & Case Studies from Korea, India, Thailand, & Ecuador. Michael Kitay. LC 85-7225. (Lincoln Institute of Land Policy Bk.). 219p. reprint ed. pap. 67.90 (*0-7837-5765-4*, 204542800006) Bks Demand.

*__Land Administration.__ Peter F. Dale & John D. McLaughlin. LC 99-36961. (Spatial Information Systems Ser.). 184p. 2000. write for info. (*0-19-823390-6*) OUP.

Land Administration & Practice in Hong Kong. Roger Nissim. 188p. 1998. pap. 29.50 (*962-209-459-7*, Pub. by HK Univ Pr) Coronet Bks.

Land Administration Guidelines. LC 97-133942. 104p. 26.00 (*92-1-116644-6*) UN.

Land Afflicted: Scotland & the Covenanter Wars, 1638-1690. R. C. Paterson. LC 99-494961. 230p. 1998. pap. 36.00 (*0-85976-486-9*, Pub. by J Donald) St Mut.

Land Alive: The World of Nature at One Family's Door. Ronald Rood. LC 92-61232. (Illus.). 160p. (Orig.). 1992. pap. 9.95 (*0-933050-89-5*) New Eng Pr VT.

Land, Always the Land. Mel Ellis. Ed. by Ted J. Rulseh. LC 97-69174. (Illus.). 272p. 1997. 23.95 (*0-9653381-2-6*) Cabin Bkshelf.

*__Land America Leaves Wild.__ Diana Wege. (Illus.). 176p. 2000. 65.00 (*0-295-98008-7*) U of Wash Pr.

Land & Agrarian Reform in the Kyrgyz Republic. Ed. by Peter C. Bloch et al. (Research Paper Ser.: Vol. 128). (Illus.). vii, 130p. (C). 1996. pap. 7.00 (*0-934519-41-2*, RP128) U of Wis Land.

*__Land & Allegiance in Revolutionary Georgia.__ Leslie Wilfred Hall. LC 00-41801. 2001. write for info. (*0-8203-2262-8*) U of Ga Pr.

Land & Ancestors: Cultural Dynamics in the Urnfield Period & the Middle Ages in the Southern Netherlands. Ed. by F. Theuws & N. Roymans. LC 99-212463. (Amsterdam Archaeological Studies). (Illus.). 320p. 1998. 59.50 (*90-5356-278-8*, Pub. by Amsterdam U Pr) U of Mich Pr.

*__Land & Archaeology.__ John G. Evans. (Illus.). 1999. 29.99 (*0-7524-1463-1*, Pub. by Tempus Pubng) Arcadia Publng.

Land & Building Taxes: Their Effect on Economic Development. Ed. by Arthur P. Becker. LC 70-84951. (Publications of the Committee on Taxation, Resources & Economic Development: Vol. 4). 324p. 1969. reprint ed. pap. 100.50 (*0-608-01931-3*, 206258600003) Bks Demand.

Land & Caste in South India. Dharma Kumar. (C). 1992. 23.00 (*81-7304-005-2*, Pub. by Manohar) S Asia.

Land & Claims Adjuster. Jack Rudman. (Career Examination Ser.: C-3459). 1994. pap. 29.95 (*0-8373-3459-4*) Nat Learn.

Land & Class in Kenya. Christopher Leo. (Political Economy of World Poverty Ser.: No. 3). 256p. 1984. pap. 13.95 (*0-8020-6547-3*); text 30.00 (*0-8020-2532-3*) U of Toronto Pr.

Land & Community: European Migration to Rural Texas in the 19th Century. W. Phil Hewitt. (Texas History Ser.). (Illus.). 69p. 1982. pap. text 9.95 (*0-89641-101-X*) American Pr.

Land & Community: Geography in Jewish Studies. Ed. by Harold Brodsky. LC 97-46204. (Studies & Texts in Jewish History & Culture: Vol. 3). 1998. 40.00 (*1-883053-30-7*) Univ Pr MD.

Land & Economy in Ancient Palestine. Jack Pastor. LC 96-41705. 304p. (C). 1997. 75.00 (*0-415-15960-1*) Routledge.

Land & Economy in Baroque Italy: The Valpolicella, 1630-1797. Peter Musgrave. LC 92-14244. 1992. 65.00 (*0-7185-1368-1*); text 54.00 (*0-7185-1449-1*) St Martin.

Land & Energy. Ed. by Bob Hall. (Southern Exposure Ser.). (Illus.). 96p. (Orig.). (C). 1973. pap. 2.50 (*0-943810-01-9*) Inst Southern Studies.

Land & Environment: The Survival of the English Countryside. Victor Bonham-Carter. LC 72-3522. (Illus.). 240p. 1973. 34.50 (*0-8386-1195-8*) Fairleigh Dickinson.

Land & Environmental Art. Ed. by Jeffrey Kastner. (Illus.). 304p. 1998. 59.95 (*0-7148-3514-5*) Phaidon Pr.

Land & Estate Management. John Nix et al. 225p. (C). 1981. text 190.00 (*1-85341-038-1*, Pub. by Surrey Beatty & Sons) St Mut.

Land & Freedom: The Origins of Russian Terrorism, 1876-1879, 7. Deborah Hardy. LC 87-7509. (Contributions to the Study of World History Ser.: No. 7). 224p. 1987. 57.95 (*0-313-25596-2*, HLF/, Greenwood Pr) Greenwood.

Land & Freshwater Mammals of the Ungava Peninsula. Francis Harper. (Miscellaneous Publications: No. 27). 178p. 1961. pap. 7.75 (*0-686-32524-9*) U KS Nat Hist Mus.

Land & Heritage in the Virginia Tidewaters: A History of King & Queen County. Barbara Beigum Kaplan. (Illus.). viii, 279p. 1993. 25.00 (*0-9664788-1-9*) King & Queen.

Land & Housing Policies in Europe & North America: A Comparative Analysis. Ed. by Graham Hallett. 288p. 1988. lib. bdg. 55.00 (*0-415-00511-6*) Routledge.

Land & Housing Policies in Europe & the U. S. A. A Comparative Analysis. Ed. by Graham Hallett. LC 89-101817. 224p. reprint ed. pap. 69.50 (*0-608-20345-9*, 207159800002) Bks Demand.

Land & Its Uses-Actual & Potential: An Environmental Appraisal. Ed. by F. T. Last et al. LC 85-28111. (NATO ASI Conference Series I, Ecology: Vol. 10). 610p. 1986. 110.00 (*0-306-42214-X*, Plenum Trade) Perseus Pubng.

Land & Labor in the Greek World. Alison Burford. LC 92-19191. (Ancient Society & History Ser.). 320p. 1993. text 40.00 (*0-8018-4463-0*) Johns Hopkins.

Land & Labor in United States Cotton Production, 1800-1840. Franklee G. Whartenby. Ed. by Stuart Bruchey. LC 76-45124. (Nineteen Seventy-Seven Dissertations Ser.). (Illus.). 1977. lib. bdg. 23.95 (*0-405-09935-5*) Ayer.

Land & Labour in Latin America: Essays on the Development of Agrarian Capitalism in the Nineteenth & Twentieth Centuries. Ed. by Kenneth Duncan et al. LC 76-11076. (Cambridge Latin American Studies: No. 26). 549p. reprint ed. pap. 156.50 (*0-608-12076-6*, 2024573) Bks Demand.

Land & Labour Relations in South-West Bangladesh: Resources, Power & Conflict. Anjan K. Datta & Institute of Social Studies (Netherlands) Staff. LC 98-14874. 304p. 1998. text 69.95 (*0-312-21543-6*) St Martin.

Land & Landscape: Views of America's History & Culture. (Illus.). 1997. student ed., wbk. ed. 85.00 incl. vdisk (*1-56290-179-6*, CP6054) Crystal.

Land & Landscape in the Philadelphia Region, 2025. David Berry & Robert E. Coughlin. (Discussion Papers: No. 95). 1977. pap. 10.00 (*1-55869-065-4*) Regional Sci Res Inst.

Land & Law in California: Essays on Land Policies. Paul W. Gates. LC 90-47271. (Henry A. Wallace Series on Agricultural History & Rural Studies). 386p. 1991. text 49.95 (*0-8138-0911-8*) Iowa St U Pr.

Land & Learning: Two Irish Clubs. R. B. McDowell. 176p. 1993. 31.95 (*1-874675-14-7*) Dufour.

Land & Leasing. Judith Eubank. Ed. by Jodie Leecraft. (Illus.). 287p. (Orig.). (C). 1984. pap. text 21.00 (*0-88698-094-1*, 1.00110) PETEX.

Land & Leisure in England & Wales. J. Allan Patmore. LC 75-164656. 332p. 1971. 39.50 (*0-8386-1024-2*) Fairleigh Dickinson.

Land & Liberty: Anarchist Influences in the Mexican Revolution. Ricardo F. Magon. Ed. by Dave Poole. (Orig.). 1979. pap. 5.50 (*0-932366-04-X*) Black Thorn Bks.

Land & Life Remembered: Americo-Liberian Folk Architecture. Max Belcher. LC 88-20531. (Illus.). 224p. 1988. pap. 19.95 (*0-8203-1086-7*) U of Ga Pr.

Land & Life Remembered: Americo-Liberian Folk Architecture. Max Belcher. LC 88-20531. (Illus.). 224p. 1988. 35.00 (*0-8203-1085-9*) U of Ga Pr.

Land & Literature of England: A Historical Account. Robert M. Adams. (Illus.). 640p. 1986. reprint ed. pap. 19.95 (*0-393-30343-8*) Norton.

Land & Lordship: Structures of Governance in Medieval Austria. Otto Brunner. Tr. by Howard Kaminsky & James V. Melton from GER. LC 91-31649. (Middle Ages Ser.). 498p. (C). 1992. text 55.00 (*0-8122-8183-7*) U of Pa Pr.

Land & Lordship in Early Modern Japan. Mark Ravina. LC 97-51268. 1998. 45.00 (*0-8047-2898-4*) Stanford U Pr.

*__Land & Lumber: A History of Portage County.__ Michael J. Goc. LC 99-52458. (Illus.). 157p. 1999. 40.00 (*0-938627-47-3*) New Past Pr.

Land & Maritime Zones of Peace in International Law. Surya P. Subedi. LC 96-416. (Oxford Monographs in International Law). 318p. (C). 1996. text 85.00 (*0-19-826096-2*, Clarendon Pr) OUP.

Land & People. Salima Ikram. (In Ancient Egypt Ser.). (Illus.). 32p. (Orig.). (J). (gr. 2-8). 1997. pap. 6.95 (*977-5325-61-7*, Pub. by Hoopoe Bks) AMIDEAST.

Land & People see Celtic Scotland: A History of Ancient Alban

Land & People in the Northern Plains Transition Area. Howard W. Ottoson et al. Ed. by Stuart Bruchey. LC 78-56708. (Management of Public Lands in the U. S. Ser.). (Illus.). 1979. reprint ed. lib. bdg. 31.95 (*0-405-11349-8*) Ayer.

Land & People of Afghanistan. Mary L. Clifford. LC 88-21419. (Portraits of the Nations Ser.). (Illus.). 240p. (J). (gr. 6 up). 1989. lib. bdg. 14.89 (*0-397-32339-5*) HarpC Child Bks.

Land & People of Afghanistan. Mary L. Clifford. LC 88-21419. (Portraits of the Nations Ser.). (Illus.). 240p. (YA). (gr. 6 up). 1989. 18.00 (*0-397-32338-7*) HarpC Child Bks.

Land & People of Austria. rev. ed. Raymond A. Wohlrabe & Werner E. Krusch. LC 72-5518. (Portraits of the Nations Ser.). (Illus.). (J). (gr. 5-9). 1972. lib. bdg. 12.89 (*0-397-31395-0*) HarpC Child Bks.

Land & People of Belgium. rev. ed. Dorothy Loder. LC 72-13301. (Portraits of the Nations Ser.). (Illus.). (J). (gr. 5-9). 1973. lib. bdg. 12.89 (*0-397-31462-0*) HarpC Child Bks.

Land & People of Canada. rev. ed. Frances A. Ross. LC 64-21547. (Portraits of the Nations Ser.). (Illus.). (J). (gr. 5-9). 1964. lib. bdg. 12.89 (*0-397-31567-8*) HarpC Child Bks.

Land & People of Ceylon. rev. ed. Donald N. Wilber. LC 72-15668. (Portraits of the Nations Ser.). (Illus.). (J). (gr. 6 up). 1972. 10.78 (*0-397-31399-3*) HarpC Child Bks.

Land & People of China. John S. Major. LC 88-23427. (Portraits of the Nations Ser.). (Illus.). 288p. (J). (gr. 6 up). 1989. 19.00 (*0-397-32336-0*) HarpC Child Bks.

Land & People of Cuba. Victoria Ortiz. LC 72-11878. (Portraits of the Nations Ser.). (J). (gr. 7 up). 1973. lib. bdg. 12.89 (*0-397-31382-9*, Lppncott) Lppncott W & W.

Land & People of Czechoslovakia. rev. ed. Elvajean Hall. LC 79-37762. (Portraits of the Nations Ser.). (Illus.). (J). (gr. 5-9). 1972. lib. bdg. 12.89 (*0-397-31601-1*) HarpC Child Bks.

Land & People of Egypt. rev. ed. Zaki N. Mahmoud. LC 71-37247. (Portraits of the Nations Ser.). (Illus.). (J). (gr. 6 up). 1972. lib. bdg. 12.89 (*0-397-31259-8*, Lppncott) Lppncott W & W.

Land & People of Finland. rev. ed. Erick Berry. LC 78-37246. (Portraits of the Nations Ser.). (Illus.). (J). (gr. 5-9). 1972. lib. bdg. 11.89 (*0-397-31255-5*) HarpC Child Bks.

Land & People of France. Jonathan Harris. LC 88-19211. (Portraits of the Nations Ser.). (Illus.). 256p. (J). (gr. 6 up). 1989. lib. bdg. 17.89 (*0-397-32321-2*) HarpC Child Bks.

Land & People of France. Jonathan Harris. LC 88-19211. (Portraits of the Nations Ser.). (Illus.). 256p. (YA). (gr. 6 up). 1989. 18.00 (*0-397-32320-4*, HarpTrophy) HarpC Child Bks.

Land & People of Holland. rev. ed. A. J. Barnouw & Raymond A. Wohlrabe. LC 79-37249. (Portraits of the Nations Ser.). (Illus.). (YA). (gr. 6 up). 1972. lib. bdg. 10.89 (*0-397-31254-7*) HarpC Child Bks.

Land & People of Hungary. rev. ed. Emil Lengyel. LC 72-37763. (Portraits of the Nations Ser.). (Illus.). (J). (gr. 5-9). 1972. lib. bdg. 12.89 (*0-397-31545-7*) HarpC Child Bks.

Land & People of Iceland. rev. ed. Erick Berry. LC 72-1569. (Portraits of the Nations Ser.). (Illus.). (J). (gr. 5-9). 1972. lib. bdg. 11.89 (*0-397-31401-9*) HarpC Child Bks.

Land & People of Indonesia. rev. ed. Datus C. Smith, Jr. LC 73-37731. (Portraits of the Nations Ser.). (Illus.). (J). (gr. 5-9). 1983. 11.95 (*0-397-32048-5*) HarpC Child Bks.

Land & People of Indonesia. rev. ed. Datus C. Smith, Jr. LC 73-37731. (Portraits of the Nations Ser.). (Illus.). (J). (gr. 5-9). 1983. lib. bdg. 12.89 (*0-397-32049-3*) HarpC Child Bks.

Land & People of Iran. rev. ed. Helen Hinckley. LC 70-37733. (Portraits of the Nations Ser.). (Illus.). (J). (gr. 5-9). 1973. lib. bdg. 12.89 (*0-397-31202-4*) HarpC Child Bks.

Land & People of Ireland. rev. ed. Elinor O'Brien. LC 76-38335. (Portraits of the Nations Ser.). (Illus.). (J). (gr. 5-9). 1972. lib. bdg. 12.89 (*0-397-31299-7*) HarpC Child Bks.

Land & People of Israel. rev. ed. Gail Hoffman. LC 77-37286. (Portraits of the Nations Ser.). (Illus.). (J). (gr. 5-9). 1972. lib. bdg. 12.89 (*0-397-31258-X*) HarpC Child Bks.

Land & People of Jordan. rev. ed. Paul W. Copeland. LC 72-5362. (Portraits of the Nations Ser.). (Illus.). (J). (gr. 6 up). 1972. 11.74 (*0-397-31403-5*) HarpC Child Bks.

Land & People of Kenya. rev. ed. Edna M. Kaula. LC 68-24413. (Portraits of the Nations Ser.). (Illus.). (J). (gr. 5-9). 1973. lib. bdg. 12.89 (*0-397-31482-5*) HarpC Child Bks.

Land & People of Korea. S. E. Solberg. LC 90-5952. (Portraits of the Nations Ser.). (Illus.). 240p. (YA). (gr. 6 up). 1991. 17.95 (*0-06-021648-4*) HarpC Child Bks.

Land & People of Korea. rev. ed. S. E. Solberg. LC 73-602. (Portraits of the Nations Ser.). (Illus.). (J). (gr. 5-9). 1973. lib. bdg. 12.89 (*0-397-31405-1*) HarpC Child Bks.

Land & People of Lebanon. rev. ed. Viola H. Winder. LC 72-13164. (Portraits of the Nations Ser.). (Illus.). (J). (gr. 5-9). 1965. lib. bdg. 12.89 (*0-397-31407-8*) HarpC Child Bks.

Land & People of Mexico. rev. ed. Elsa Larralde. LC 64-23213. (Portraits of the Nations Ser.). (Illus.). (J). (gr. 5-9). 1964. lib. bdg. 12.89 (*0-397-31552-X*) HarpC Child Bks.

Land & People of Mongolia. John S. Major. LC 89-37790. (Portraits of the Nations Ser.). (Illus.). 224p. (J). (gr. 6 up). 1990. 15.95 (*0-397-32386-7*); lib. bdg. 15.89 (*0-397-32387-5*) HarpC Child Bks.

Land & People of New Zealand. rev. ed. Edna M. Kaula. LC 76-37764. (Portraits of the Nations Ser.). (Illus.). (J). (gr. 5-9). 1964. lib. bdg. 12.89 (*0-397-30748-9*) HarpC Child Bks.

Land & People of Nigeria. rev. ed. Brenda Lu Forman & Harrison Forman. LC 77-37925. (Portraits of the Nations Ser.). (Illus.). (J). (gr. 6 up). 1972. lib. bdg. 12.89 (*0-397-31522-8*) HarpC Child Bks.

Land & People of Pakistan. Mark Weston. LC 91-2847. (Portraits of the Nations Ser.). (Illus.). 224p. (YA). (gr. 6 up). 1992. lib. bdg. 17.89 (*0-06-022790-7*) HarpC Child Bks.

Land & People of Pakistan. rev. ed. Robert Lang. LC 74-792. (Portraits of the Nations Ser.). (Illus.). 160p. (J). (gr. 5-9). 1974. lib. bdg. 12.89 (*0-397-31551-1*) HarpC Child Bks.

Land & People of Sierra Leone. Mary L. Clifford. LC 73-20317. (Portraits of the Nations Ser.). (Illus.). 160p. (J). (gr. 5-9). 1974. 11.95 (*0-397-31490-6*) HarpC Child Bks.

Land & People of Spain. Adrian Shubert. LC 91-9971. (Portraits of the Nations Ser.). (Illus.). 256p. (J). (gr. 6 up). 1992. 18.00 (*0-06-020217-3*); lib. bdg. 17.89 (*0-06-020218-1*) HarpC Child Bks.

Land & People of Syria. rev. ed. Paul W. Copeland. LC 77-37732. (Portraits of the Nations Ser.). (Illus.). (J). (gr. 5-9). 1972. lib. bdg. 11.89 (*0-397-31537-6*) HarpC Child Bks.

Land & People of the Balkans. rev. ed. Dragos D. Kostich. LC 73-7709. (Portraits of the Nations Ser.). (Illus.). (J). (gr. 5-9). 1973. 12.50 (*0-397-31397-7*) HarpC Child Bks.

Land & People of the Congo. Louise Crane. LC 79-141447. (Portraits of the Nations Ser.). (Illus.). 144p. (J). (gr. 5-9). 1971. lib. bdg. 11.89 (*0-397-31172-9*) HarpC Child Bks.

Land & People of the Netherlands. Theo Van Stegeren. LC 90-47650. (Portraits of the Nations Ser.). (Illus.). 256p. (YA). (gr. 6 up). 1992. 17.95 (*0-06-022537-8*) HarpC Child Bks.

Land & People of the Philippines. John J. Nance. LC 76-30543. (Portraits of the Nations Ser.). (J). (gr. 5-9). 1977. lib. bdg. 12.89 (*0-397-31656-9*) HarpC Child Bks.

Land & People of the Soviet Union. William G. Andrews. LC 90-5746. (Portraits of the Nations Ser.). (Illus.). 320p. (J). (gr. 6 up). 1991. 17.95 (*0-06-020034-0*) HarpC Child Bks.

Land & People of the Soviet Union. William G. Andrews. LC 90-5746. (Portraits of the Nations Ser.). (Illus.). 320p. (YA). (gr. 6 up). 1991. lib. bdg. 17.89 (*0-06-020035-9*) HarpC Child Bks.

Land & People of Turkey. William Spencer. LC 89-2421. (Portraits of the Nations Ser.). (Illus.). 224p. (J). (gr. 6 up). 1990. 14.95 (*0-397-32363-8*) HarpC Child Bks.

Land & People of Turkey. rev. ed. William Spencer. LC 72-6041. (Portraits of the Nations Ser.). (Illus.). (J). (gr. 5-9). 1972. lib. bdg. 12.89 (*0-397-31328-4*) HarpC Child Bks.

Land & People of Uruguay. rev. ed. Lavinia Dobler. LC 72-3741. (Portraits of the Nations Ser.). (Illus.). (J). (gr. 5-9). 1972. lib. bdg. 11.89 (*0-397-31391-8*) HarpC Child Bks.

Land & People of Zambia. Eliza T. Dresang. LC 74-23108. (Portraits of the Nations Ser.). (J). (gr. 5-9). 1975. lib. bdg. 11.89 (*0-397-31561-9*) HarpC Child Bks.

Land & People of Zimbabwe. Patricia Cheney. LC 89-36244. (Portraits of the Nations Ser.). (Illus.). 256p. (J). (gr. 6 up). 1990. 15.95 (*0-397-32392-1*) HarpC Child Bks.

Land & Permitting II. (Mineral Law Ser.). 1996. wbk. ed. 125.00 (*0-929047-58-3*) Rocky Mtn Mineral Law Found.

Land & Power: Studies in Italian & European Social History. Christopher Wickham. (Illus.). 326p. 1994. 58.50 (*0-904152-25-1*, Pub. by British Schl Rome) David Brown.

Land & Power: The Impact of the Land Use Act in Southwest Nigeria. Gregory W. Myers. (Research Paper Ser.: Vol. 108). (Illus.). xv, 145p. (C). 1991. pap. 7.00 (*0-934519-18-8*, RP108) U of Wis Land.

*__Land & Power: The Zionist Resort to Force, 1881-1948.__ Anita Shapira. 1999. pap. text 24.95 (*0-8047-3776-2*) Stanford U Pr.

Land & Power in Hawaii: The Democratic Years. George Cooper & Gavan Daws. 528p. 1990. reprint ed. pap. 18.95 (*0-8248-1303-0*) UH Pr.

An Asterisk (*) at the beginning of an entry indicates that the title is appearing for the first time.

Land & Power in Latin America: Agrarian Economics & Social Process in the Andes. Ed. by Benjamin S. Orlove & Glynn Custred. LC 79-26598. 258p. 1980. 39.50 (*0-8419-0476-6*) Holmes & Meier.

Land & Property Development: New Directions. Ed. by Richard Grover. (Illus.). 432p. text 89.95 (*0-419-14830-2*, E & FN Spon) Routledge.

Land & Property Research in the United States. E. Wade Hone. LC 96-52214. 517p. 1997. 49.95 (*0-916489-68-X*) Ancestry.

Land & Resource Planning in the National Forests. Charles F. Wilkinson & H. Michael Anderson. LC 87-17053. 389p. (C). 1987. pap. text 25.00 (*0-933280-38-6*) Island Pr.

Land & Revolution in Iran, 1960-1980. Eric J. Hooglund. (Modern Middle East Ser.: No. 7). 213p. (C). 1982. text 19.95 (*0-292-74633-4*) U of Tex Pr.

Land & Revolution in Iran, 1960-1980. Eric J. Hooglund. LC 81-21959. (Modern Middle East Ser.: Vol. 7). (Illus.). 209p. reprint ed. pap. 64.80 (*0-608-08697-5*, 206922000003) Bks Demand.

Land & Revolution in Modern Greece, 1800-1881: The Transition in the Tenure & Exploitation of Land from Ottoman Rule to Independence. William W. McGrew. LC 84-27789. (Illus.). 355p. 1986. 35.00 (*0-87338-316-8*) Kent St U Pr.

Land & Sea. Michael Green. (Illus.). 48p. 191.40 (*0-7368-0130-8*) Capstone Pr.

Land & Sea. unabridged ed. Carl Schmitt. Ed. & Tr. by Simona Draghici from GER. LC 97-28692.Tr. of Land und Meer. 82p. (Orig.). 1997. pap. text 5.95 (*0-943045-12-6*) Plutarch Pr OR.

Land & Sea Series, 8 bks. Michael Green. Incl. Aircraft Carriers. LC 97-7755. (Illus.). 48p. (J). (gr. 3-4). 1998. lib. bdg. 19.00 (*1-56065-553-4*, Cpstone High Low); Amphibious Vehicles. LC 96-24272. (Illus.). 48p. (J). (gr. 3-4). 1997. lib. bdg. 19.00 (*1-56065-460-0*, Cpstone High Low); Battleships. LC 97-5907. (Illus.). 48p. (J). (gr. 3-4). 1998. lib. bdg. 19.00 (*1-56065-554-2*, Cpstone High Low); Cruisers. LC 97-7756. (Illus.). 48p. (J). (gr. 4-7). 1998. lib. bdg. 19.00 (*1-56065-556-9*, Cpstone High Low); Military Dune Buggies. LC 96-44343. (Illus.). 48p. (J). (gr. 3-4). 1997. lib. bdg. 19.00 (*1-56065-461-9*, Cpstone High Low); Military Motorcycles. LC 96-39036. (Illus.). 48p. (J). (gr. 3-4). 1997. lib. bdg. 19.00 (*1-56065-462-7*, Cpstone High Low); Military Trucks. LC 96-39035. (Illus.). 48p. (J). (gr. 3-4). 1997. lib. bdg. 19.00 (*1-56065-463-5*, Cpstone High Low); Submarines. LC 97-5908. (Illus.). 48p. (J). (gr. 4-7). 1998. lib. bdg. 19.00 (*1-56065-555-0*, Cpstone High Low); (J). 152.00 (*1-56065-649-2*, Cpstone High Low) Capstone Pr.

Land & Society in Early Scotland. Robert A. Dodgshon. (Illus.). 1982. 67.00 (*0-19-822660-8*) OUP.

Land & Society in Edwardian Britain. Brian Short. (Cambridge Studies in Historical Geography: No. 25). (Illus.). 398p. (C). 1997. text 69.95 (*0-521-57035-2*) Cambridge U Pr.

Land & Society in England, 1750-1980. G. E. Mingay. LC 94-1130. (Themes in British Social History Ser.). 288p. (C). 1994. pap. text 27.50 (*0-582-49132-0*, 76879, Pub. by Addison-Wesley) Longman.

Land & Society in India: Agrarian Relations in Colonial North Bihar Bindeshwar Ram. LC 98-901711. xii, 274 p. 1997. write for info. (*81-250-0643-5*, Pub. by Orient Longman Ltd) S Asia.

Land & Society in Malabar. Adrian C. Mayer. LC 73-13032. 158p. 1974. reprint ed. lib. bdg. 55.00 (*0-8371-7103-2*, MASM, Greenwood Pr) Greenwood.

Land & Society in the Christian Kingdom of Ethiopia: From the Thirteenth to the Twentieth Century. Donald Crummey. LC 99-6218. 416p. 1999. 60.00 (*0-252-02482-6*) U of Ill Pr.

Land & Soil. Ed. by T. N. Khoshoo & B. L. Deekshatulu. (Indian National Science Academy Ser.). 1993. text 60.00 (*0-7069-5965-5*, Pub. by Vikas) S Asia.

Land & Spirit of Italy: The Texture of Italian Religious Culture. rev. expanded ed. John Navone. LC 96-3613. 1996. 16.00 (*1-881901-12-2*) LEGAS.

Land & Taxation. Ed. by Nicolaus Tideman. LC 95-165983. (Georgist Paradigm Ser.). 182p. 1994. pap. 24.95 (*0-85683-153-0*, Pub. by Shepheard-Walwyn Pubs) Paul & Co Pubs.

Land & the Book. W. M. Thomson. 736p. 1985. 350.00 (*1-85077-054-9*, Pub. by Darf Pubs Ltd) St Mut.

Land & the Book: An Introduction to the World of the Bible. Charles R. Page & Carl Volz. LC 92-43245. 288p. (Orig.). 1993. pap. 16.95 (*0-687-46289-4*) Abingdon.

Land & the City: Patterns & Processes of Urban Change. Philip Kivell. LC 92-19286. (Geography & Environment Ser.). (Illus.). 240p. (C). 1993. pap. 25.99 (*0-415-08782-1*, A9796) Routledge.

Land & the Constitution in India. Herbert C. Merillat. LC 79-127362. (Studies of the South Asian). 337p. reprint ed. 104.50 (*0-8357-9066-5*, 201538900093) Bks Demand.

Land & the Environment Lifetime Careers Wiltshire (London,Engalnd) Staff. LC 98-150560. (Just the Job! Ser.). 112 p. 1997. write for info. (*0-340-68791-6*) Trafalgar.

Land & the Garden. Vita Sackville-West. (Illus.). 190p. 1989. 24.95 (*0-685-30828-6*) Viking Penguin.

Land & the Loom: Peasants & Profit in Northern France, 1680-1800. Liana Vardi. LC 92-23231. 312p. 1993. text 39.95 (*0-8223-1284-0*) Duke.

***Land & the People of Nineteenth-Century Cork: The Rural Economy & the Land Question.** 2nd ed. James S. Donnelly, Jr. 440p. 1999. pap. 24.95 (*1-898256-79-9*, Pub. by Collins Press) Dufour.

Land & the Uses of Tradition among the Mbeere of Kenya. Jack Glazier. LC 85-17891. (Illus.). 348p. 1986. pap. text 28.50 (*0-8191-4950-0*); lib. bdg. 57.00 (*0-8191-4949-7*) U Pr of Amer.

Land & Water Conservation Fund: Hearing Before the Committee on Energy & Natural Resources, United States Senate, 105th Congress, 1st Session, on the Land & Water Conservation Fund State-Side Program, June 11, 1997. USGPO Staff. LC 98-107141. iii, 56 p. 1997. write for info. (*0-16-055547-7*) USGPO.

Land & Water Development for Agriculture in the Asia-Pacific Region. V. V. Murty & K. Takeuchi. (Illus.). 200p. 1996. lib. bdg. 55.00 (*1-886106-60-6*) Science Pubs.

Land & Water Student Activity Book. National Science Resources Center Staff. (Science & Technology for Children Ser.). (Illus.). 87p. (J). (gr. 4). 1997. pap. text, student ed. write for info. (*0-89278-740-6*, 97-2303) Carolina Biological.

Land & Water Teacher's Guide. National Science Resources Center Staff. (Science & Technology for Children Ser.). (Illus.). 232p. 1997. pap. text, teacher ed. write for info. (*0-89278-739-2*, 97-2302) Carolina Biological.

Land Animals. Rick Detorie. (Magic Answer Bks.). (J). 1990. pap. 1.95 (*0-8125-7321-8*, Pub. by Tor Bks) St Martin.

Land Animals. Joan S. Gottlieb. (Wonders of Science Ser.). 1997. pap., teacher ed. 10.55 (*0-8114-7492-5*); pap., student ed. 11.16 (*0-8114-7486-0*) Raintree Steck-V.

Land Application of Biosolids: Process Design Manual. U. S. Environmental Protection Agency Staff. 308p. 1997. pap. 74.95 (*1-56676-527-7*, 764831) Technomic.

Land Application of Residual Materials. 186p. 1977. pap. 3.00 (*0-87262-081-6*) Am Soc Civil Eng.

Land Application of Sewage Sludge. Uta Krogmann. ring bd. 69.95 (*1-56670-412-X*) Lewis Pubs.

***Land Application of Sewage Sludge: A Guide for Land Appliers on the Requirements of the Federal Standards for the Use or Disposal of Sewage Sludge, 40 CFR, Part 503.** Ed. by Barry Leonard. (Illus.). 107p. (C). 2000. pap. text 30.00 (*0-7881-8710-4*) DIANE Pub.

Land Application of Sludge. Ed. by A. L. Page et al. (Illus.). 168p. 1987. 105.00 (*0-87371-083-5*, S657, CRC Reprint) Franklin.

Land Application of Wastewater Sludge. Ed. by T. M. Younos. LC 87-23732. 96p. 1987. 15.00 (*0-87262-622-9*) Am Soc Civil Eng.

Land Application of Water Treatment Sludges: Impact & Management. 112p. 1990. pap. 25.00 (*0-89867-523-5*, 90566) Am Water Wks Assn.

Land Areas of the National Forest System. Ed. by Barry Leonard. (Illus.). 126p. 1998. pap. text 25.00 (*0-7881-1677-0*) DIANE Pub.

Land Army & Rural Development: A Study of Organisational Innovation in Karnataka. B. S. Bhargava & N. Sivanna. (Illus.). vi, 104p. 1994. 12.00 (*81-7024-630-X*, Pub. by Ashish Pub Hse) Nataraj Bks.

Land Art. Gilles A. Tiberghien. LC 94-24962. (Illus.). 312p. 1995. 65.00 (*1-56898-040-X*) Princeton Arch.

Land Assembly in the Indian Metropolis. R. C. Gupta. (C). 1992. text 24.00 (*81-85565-10-4*, Pub. by Uppal Pub Hse) S Asia.

Land Assessment in Scotland: Proceedings of the Royal Scottish Geographical Society Symposium, University of Edinburgh, May, 1979. Royal Scottish Geographical Society Staff. Ed. by M. F. Thomas & J. T. Coppock. (Illus.). 156p. 1980. 27.00 (*0-08-025716-X*, Pergamon Pr) Elsevier.

Land Atlas, McIntosh County, North Dakota, 1911, with Index of Individuals Owning Land. Compiled by Kermit B. Karns. 42p. 1992. pap. 10.00 (*0-913233-24-2*) AFRA.

Land Banking. Joseph Rosenblum. Ed. by Juyne Linger. 8p. (Orig.). 1978. pap. 8.00 (*0-317-04908-9*) Natl Coun Econ Dev.

Land Banking: European Reality, American Prospect. Ann L. Strong. LC 78-11804. (Johns Hopkins Studies in Urban Affairs). (Illus.). 328p. 1979. reprint ed. pap. 101.70 (*0-608-04043-6*, 206477900011) Bks Demand.

Land Banking Revisited: Massachusetts Breaks the Mold. Jean O. Melious. (Land Policy Roundtable Ser.: No. 107). 51p. (Orig.). 1986. pap. text 5.25 (*1-55844-107-7*) Lincoln Inst Land.

Land-Based Air Power in Third World Crises. (Orig.). 1991. lib. bdg. 79.95 (*0-8490-4385-9*) Gordon Pr.

Land-Based Airpower in Third World Crises. David R. Mets. (Illus.). 171p. 1986. pap. 5.00 (*1-58566-000-0*) Air Univ.

Land-Based & Marine Hazards: Scientific & Management Issues. Ed. by M. I. El-Sabh et al. LC 96-17820. (Advances in Natural & Technological Hazards Research Ser.: Vol. 7). 315p. (C). 1996. text 154.50 (*0-7923-4064-7*) Kluwer Academic.

Land-Based Fighters. David Baker. (Military Aircraft Library). (Illus.). 48p. (J). (gr. 3-8). 1987. 13.95 (*0-685-67591-2*) Rourke Corp.

Land-Based Fighters. David Baker. (Military Aircraft Library). (Illus.). 48p. (J). (gr. 3-8). 1987. lib. bdg. 23.93 (*0-86592-351-5*) Rourke Enter.

Land-Based Marine Pollution: International Law Development. Meng Qing-Nan. 276p. 1987. lib. bdg. 107.00 (*0-86010-909-7*) Kluwer Academic.

Land Before Her: Fantasy & Experience of the American Frontiers, 1630-1860. Annette Kolodny. LC 83-10629. xxi, 293p. 1984. pap. 16.95 (*0-8078-4111-0*) U of NC Pr.

Land Before Honor: Palestinian Women in the Occupied Territories. Kitty Warnock. 224p. 1990. 33.00 (*0-85345-809-X*, Pub. by Monthly Rev); pap. 16.00 (*0-85345-810-3*, Pub. by Monthly Rev) NYU Pr.

Land Before Time: How to Draw Dinosaurs. Q. L. Pearce. LC 99-73110. (Illus.). 64p. (YA). (gr. 1 up). 1999. pap. 6.95 (*0-7373-0237-2*, 02372W) NTC Contemp Pub Co.

Land before Time Beginner Book. Mollie Goode. LC 98-40766. 1999. 7.99 (*0-375-80160-X*) Random.

Land Before Time Dinosaur Q & A. Q. L. Pearce. (Roxbury Park Bks.). (Illus.). 64p. (J). 1999. pap. 7.95 (*0-7373-0281-X*, 0281XW, Pub. by Lowell Hse) NTC Contemp Pub Co.

***Land Before Time Kindergarten Adventure (jewel)** 1998. pap. 0.00 (*1-57303-097-X*) Sound Source.

Land Before Us: A Geological History of Alberta. Royal Tyrrell Museum of Palaeontology Staff & Dennis Budgen. Ed. by Andrew Nikiforuk. (Illus.). 96p. (gr. 4-7). 1994. pap. 17.95 (*0-88995-123-3*, Pub. by Red Deer) Genl Dist Srvs.

Land Before Us: The Making of Ancient Alberta. Royal Tyrrell Museum of Palaeontology Staff & Pat Wishart. Ed. by Andrew Nikiforuk. 1994. pap. 17.95 (*1-55105-053-6*) Lone Pine.

Land Behind Baghdad: A History of Settlement on the Diyala Plains. Robert M. Adams. LC 65-17279. 254p. reprint ed. pap. 78.80 (*0-608-16467-4*, 202676000052) Bks Demand.

Land Below: Torg. (Torg Ser.). 15.00 (*0-87431-322-8*, 20562) West End Games.

Land Beneath the Lake: More Factual Folklore. Mabel W. Martin. LC 98-87715. 199 P. ;p. 1998. write for info. (*0-9629142-3-1*) Janze Pubns.

***Land Beneath the Wind.** Ed. by Frank Stewart et al. (Manoa Ser.: Vol. 11:1). (Illus.). 222p. 1999. pap. 16.00 (*0-8248-2200-5*) UH Pr.

***Land Beneath the Wind: New Writing from America, the Pacific, & Asia.** Ed. by Frank Stewart et al. (Manoa Ser.: No. 10:2). (Illus.). 222p. 1999. pap. 16.00 (*0-8248-2143-2*) UH Pr.

Land Beside the Celtic Sea: Aspect of Cornwall's Past. Richard Pearse. (C). 1989. pap. 30.00 (*0-907566-48-0*, Pub. by Dyllansow Truran) St Mut.

Land Between: Northwestern Ontario Resource Development, 1800 to the 1990s. W. Robert Wightman & Nancy M. Wightman. LC 97-169899. 566p. 1997. text 75.00 (*0-8020-0937-9*, HC117) U of Toronto Pr.

***Land Between: Owens Valley, California.** Rebecca Fish Ewan. LC 00-8202. (Center Books on Space, Place & Time). (Illus.). 176p. 2000. pap. 22.50 (*0-8018-6461-5*) Johns Hopkins.

***Land Between: Owens Valley, California.** Rebecca Fish Ewan. LC 00-8202. (Center Books on Space, Place & Time). (Illus.). 176p. 2000. 55.00 (*0-8018-6460-7*) Johns Hopkins.

Land Between the Rivers. John P. Poston. (Illus.). 323p. 1999. pap. 12.99 (*1-889893-30-7*) Emerald House Group Inc.

Land Between the Rivers: The Southern Illinois Country. C. William Horrell et al. LC 71-156777. (Illus.). 207p. 1982. pap. 18.95 (*0-8093-1119-4*) S Ill U Pr.

Land Between Two Niles: Quaternary Geology & Biology of the Central Sudan. Ed. by Martin A. Williams & D. A. Adamson. 256p. (C). 1982. text 123.00 (*90-6191-096-X*, Pub. by A A Balkema) Ashgate Pub Co.

Land Beyond the Forest: Dracula & Swoop. Mac Wellman. (Sun & Moon Classics/American Theater in Literature Ser.: No. 112). 102p. 1995. pap. 12.95 (*1-55713-228-3*) Sun & Moon CA.

Land Beyond the Forest: Facts, Figures & Fancies from Transylvania, 2 vols. Emily Gerard. LC 77-87731. reprint ed. 56.50 (*0-404-16530-3*) AMS Pr.

Land Beyond the Magic Mirror. Gary Gygax. 1983. 5.50 (*0-394-53157-4*) Random.

Land Beyond the Mountains. Ray Crain. (Illus.). 346p. (C). 1994. 35.00 (*0-9641149-0-9*) Main Graphics.

Land Beyond the Mountains. Janice H. Giles. 1976. 24.95 (*0-88411-644-1*) Amereon Ltd.

Land Beyond the Mountains. Janice H. Giles. LC 95-24117. 320p. 1995. 30.00 (*0-8131-1936-7*); pap. 17.00 (*0-8131-0848-9*) U Pr of Ky.

Land Beyond the Mountains. Janice H. Giles. LC 90-45590. 316p. 1990. reprint ed. 34.95 (*0-87797-186-2*) Cherokee.

Land Beyond the Mountains. 2nd ed. Ray Crain. (Illus.). 393p. 1996. reprint ed. 35.00 (*0-9641149-7-6*) Main Graphics.

***Land Beyond Time Adventure in the Amazon: An Al Ranlom Action Adventure Novel.** Alexander Molnar, Jr. LC 00-190489. 286p. 2000. 25.00 (*0-7388-1786-4*); pap. 18.00 (*0-7388-1787-2*) Xlibris Corp.

Land Bird Communities of Grand Bahama Island: The Structure & Dynamics of an Avifauna. John T. Emlen. 129p. 1977. 10.00 (*0-943610-24-9*) Am Ornithologists.

Land Boom! An Amateur's Guide to Professional Wealth or ... Your Inalienable Right to Your Own Eldorado! Gregory Donovan. LC 83-80389. (Illus.). 76p. (Orig.). 1985. pap. 10.00 (*0-9615229-0-9*) Gregg Inc.

Land Boomers: The Complete Illustrated History. Michael Cannon. (Illus.). 420p. 1995. pap. 39.95 (*0-522-84663-7*, Pub. by Melbourne Univ Pr) Paul & Co Pubs.

Land Buying Checklist. 4th ed. Ralph M. Lewis. 60p. 1990. pap. 20.00 (*0-86718-358-6*) Home Builder.

Land Called Deseret. Janet Dailey. 1992. per. 3.59 (*0-373-89894-0*, 1-89894-9) Harlequin Bks.

Land Called Holy: Palestine in Christian History & Thought. Robert L. Wilken. LC 92-15258. (Illus.). 448p. (C). 1992. 42.50 (*0-300-05491-2*) Yale U Pr.

Land Called Holy: Palestine in Christian History & Thought. Robert L. Wilken. (Illus.). 448p. 1994. pap. 18.00 (*0-300-06083-1*) Yale U Pr.

Land Campaigns of the Civil War. Paul Calore. (Illus.). 272p. 2000. lib. bdg. 39.95 (*0-7864-0323-3*) McFarland & Co.

Land Care Manual. Brian Roberts. 1992. pap. 26.95 (*0-86840-053-X*, Pub. by New South Wales Univ Pr) Intl Spec Bk.

***Land Causes, Accomack County, Virginia, 1727-1826.** Stratton Nottingham. LC 98-75214. 183 p. 1999. reprint ed. 28.50 (*0-8063-1588-1*) Genealog Pub.

Land Ceiling & After. L. C. Gupta. (C). 1995. 12.50 (*81-7033-244-3*, Pub. by Rawat Pubns) S Asia.

Land, Center & Diaspora: Jewish Constructs in Late Antiquity. Isaiah M. Gafni. (JSPS Ser.: Vol. 21). 136p. 1997. 46.50 (*1-85075-644-9*, Pub. by Sheffield Acad) CUP Services.

Land Circle: Writings Collected from the Land. Linda M. Hasselstrom. LC 91-55212. 352p. 1991. 19.95 (*1-55591-082-3*) Fulcrum Pub.

Land Circle: Writings Collected from the Land. Linda M. Hasselstrom. LC 91-55212. 370p. 1993. pap. 12.95 (*1-55591-142-0*) Fulcrum Pub.

Land, City & Trade in the Roman Empire. C. S. Whittaker. LC 93-7202. (Collected Studies: No. CS408). 336p. 1993. 110.95 (*0-86078-380-4*, Pub. by Variorum) Ashgate Pub Co.

Land Claims & Native Manpower: Staffing Regional & Village Corporations Under Alaska Native Claims Settlement Act of 1971. Judith Kleinfeld et al. LC 73-620103. (ISER Reports: No. 36). (Illus.). 52p. 1973. pap. 2.00 (*0-88353-009-0*) U Alaska Inst Res.

Land Claims in the Eastern District of the Orleans Territory: Communicated to the House of Representatives, Jan. 9, 1812. Walter Lowrie. 160p. 1985. reprint ed. pap. 27.50 (*0-89308-582-0*) Southern Hist Pr.

Land Claims of Hancock County, Mississippi, Filed April 2nd 1894. Anne S. Anderson & Marianne R. Pitre. 50p. 1985. lib. bdg. 15.00 (*0-318-04436-6*) L W Anderson Genealogical.

Land Classification for Land Uses, Management & Valuation. National Association of Review Appraisers Staff & Marion E. Everhart. LC 82-74565. (Illus.). 220p. 1983. 19.50 (*0-935988-23-8*, 311) Todd Pub.

Land Clearing & Development in the Tropics: Proceedings of a Conference Organized by the International Institute of Tropical Agriculture, Ibadan, Nigeria, November 1982. Ed. by P. A. Sanchez et al. 488p. (C). 1984. text 95.00 (*90-6191-536-8*, Pub. by A A Balkema) Ashgate Pub Co.

Land Columbus Loved: Santo Domingo. Bertita Harding. 1978. lib. bdg. 250.00 (*0-8490-1383-6*) Gordon Pr.

Land Compensation & Valuation Law in Hong Kong. Gordon N. Cruden. 508p. 1986. 151.00 (*0-409-99525-8*, MICHIE) LEXIS Pub.

Land Concentration & Rural Poverty. 2nd ed. Keith B. Griffin. LC 80-13808. 300p. 1981. pap. 22.00 (*0-8419-0526-6*) Holmes & Meier.

Land Conservation Through Public - Private Partnerships. Ed. by Eve Endicott. LC 92-35638. (Illus.). 320p. (C). 1993. text 50.00 (*1-55963-177-5*); pap. text 27.50 (*1-55963-176-7*) Island Pr.

Land Consolidation & Rural. Bullard. 55.95 (*1-84014-937-X*) Ashgate Pub Co.

Land Contamination Guidance for Chartered Surveyors. RICS Staff. 1995. pap. 30.00 (*0-85406-670-5*, Pub. by R-I-C-S Bks) St Mut.

Land Control & Social Structure in Indian History. Ed. by Robert E. Frykenberg. LC 69-16111. 278p. reprint ed. pap. 86.20 (*0-608-15454-7*, 202930600060) Bks Demand.

Land Covenants. Ernest H. Scamell. 800p. 1996. write for info. (*0-406-08151-4*, MICHIE) LEXIS Pub.

Land Cruising & Prospecting. A. F. Wallace. (Illus.). 175p. pap. 4.00 (*0-936622-14-8*) A R Harding Pub.

Land, Custom & Practice in the South Pacific. Ed. by R. Gerard Ward & Elizabeth Kingdon. (Asia-Pacific Studies: No. 1). (Illus.). 304p. (C). 1995. text 64.95 (*0-521-47289-X*) Cambridge U Pr.

Land Deed Genealogy of Bedford County, Tennessee. Helen C. Marsh & Timothy R. Marsh. (Illus.). 484p. 1987. 40.00 (*0-89308-610-X*, TN 105) Southern Hist Pr.

Land Deed Genealogy of Hancock County, Georgia. Helen Crawford Marsh & Timothy Richard Marsh. LC 97-167563. 1997. write for info. (*0-89308-662-2*) Southern Hist Pr.

Land Degradation: Development & Breakdown of Terrestrial Environments. C. J. Barrow. (Illus.). 313p. (C). 1991. text 90.00 (*0-521-35333-5*) Cambridge U Pr.

Land Degradation & Desertification in Asia & Pacific Region: Proceedings of the International Symposium, CAZRI, Jodhpur (Raj.) Ed. by A. K. Sen & Amal Kar. 1995. pap. 150.00 (*81-7233-107-X*, Pub. by Scientifc Pubs) St Mut.

Land Degradation in Mediterranean Environments of the World: Nature & Extent, Causes & Solutions. A. J. Conacher & Maria Sala. LC 97-29313. 520p. 1998. 165.00 (*0-471-96317-8*) Wiley.

Land Degradation in Tanzania: Perception from the Village. Alemneh Dejence et al. LC 97-18344. (Technical Paper Ser.: No. 370). 92p. 1997. pap. 22.00 (*0-8213-3993-1*, 13993) World Bank.

Land Degradation in the Tropics: Environmental & Policy Issues. Ed. by Michael J. Eden & John T. Parry. LC 96-1983. (Global Development & the Environment Ser.). (Illus.). 256p. (C). 1996. text 110.00 (*1-85567-389-4*) Bks Intl VA.

Land Delivery for Low Income Groups in Third World Cities. Robert-Jan Baken & Jan Van Der Linden. 124p. 1992. 82.95 (*1-85628-373-9*, Pub. by Avebry) Ashgate Pub Co.

***Land Development.** 9th ed. D. Linda Kone. LC 99-52273. 354p. 1999. write for info. (*0-86718-500-7*) Home Builder.

Land Development for Civil Engineers. Thomas R. Dion. 664p. 1993. 120.00 (*0-471-54743-3*) Wiley.

An Asterisk (*) at the beginning of an entry indicates that the title is appearing for the first time.

L

Land Development Handbook: Planning, Engineering, & Surveying. S. Davis Dewberry. LC 95-37873. (Illus.). 1000p. 1995. 140.00 (*0-07-016644-7*) McGraw.

Land Development Law in Queensland. Alan Fogg. lii, 784p. 1987. 125.50 (*0-455-20743-7*, Pub. by LawBk Co) Gaunt.

Land Development Law Reporter. Ed. by Stuart M. Bloch & William B. Ingersoll. 395.00 (*0-318-19272-1*) Land Dev Inst.

Land Disposal of Hazardous Waste: Engineering & Environmental Issues. Ed. by J. R. Gronow et al. 320p. 1988. text 109.00 (*0-470-21222-5*) P-H.

Land Disposal of Wastewater: An Annotated Bibliography, No. 837. Ed. by John P. Hartigan & Gene E. Willeke. 1975. 5.00 (*0-686-20362-3*, Sage Prdcls Pr) Sage.

***Land Disposal Restrictions Compliance Guide, 1.** 400p. 1999. pap. 115.00 (*0-444-10036-9*) Elsevier.

Land Disputes & Ecological Degradation in an Irrigation Scheme: A Case Study of State Farm Divestiture in Chokwe, Mozambique. Christopher Tanner et al. (Research Paper Ser.: Vol. 111). xiv, 72p. (C). 1993. pap. 7.00 (*0-934519-22-6*, RP111) U of Wis Land.

Land Diving: New Poems. Robert Morgan. LC 76-28168. viii, 70p. 1977. pap. 6.95 (*0-8071-0274-1*) La State U Pr.

Land Drainage. E. Farr. 1986. pap. text. write for info. (*0-582-45007-1*, Pub. by Addison-Wesley) Longman.

Land Drainage: A Seminar in the EC Programme of Coordination of Research on Land Use & Rural Resources, Cambridge, UK, 27-31 July 1981. Ed. by M. J. Gardiner. 346p. (C). 1982. text 123.00 (*90-6191-245-8*, Pub. by A A Balkema) Ashgate Pub Co.

Land Drainage: Planning & Design of Agricultural Drainage Systems. Lambert K. Smedema & David W. Rycroft. LC 83-45150. (Illus.). 384p. 1983. text 49.95 (*0-8014-1629-9*) Cornell U Pr.

Land Drainage & Flood Defence Responsibilities. 3rd rev. ed. Institution of Civil Engineers Staff. LC 96-177770. 136p. 1996. 38.00 (*0-7277-2508-4*) Am Soc Civil Eng.

***Land Drainage & Irrigation.** Ed. by Salvatore Ciriacono. LC 98-23062. (Studies in the History of Civil Engineering: No. 3). (Illus.). 1998. text 157.95 (*0-86078-752-4*) Ashgate Pub Co.

Land Dyaks of Sarawak: A Report on a Social Economic Survey of the Land Dyaks of Sarawak. William R. Geddes. LC 77-86980. reprint ed. 46.50 (*0-404-16716-0*) AMS Pr.

Land-Ecological Study of Soils, Vegetation, & Plant Diversity in Colombian Amazonia. J. F. Duivenvoorden & J. M. Lips. (Tropenbos Technical Ser.: No. 12). (Illus.). 438p. 1995. pap. 80.00 (*90-5113-024-4*, Pub. by Backhuys Pubs) Balogh.

Land Ecology: An Introduction to Landscape Ecology As a Base for Land Evaluation, Land Management & Conservation. Isaak S. Zonneveld. (Illus.). 199p. 1995. pap. 50.00 (*90-5103-101-7*, Pub. by SPB Acad Pub) Balogh.

Land, Ecology & Resistance in Kenya, 1880-1952. Heinemann Staff. LC 98-135453. (Social History of Africa Ser.). 1995. write for info. (*0-325-00023-9*) Heinemann.

Land, Ecology & Resistance in Kenya, 1880-1952. A. Fiona D. Mackenzie. LC 98-135453. (Social History of Africa Ser.). 286p. 1998. pap. 26.00 (*0-325-00024-7*) Heinemann.

Land Economics. Folke Dovring. (Agriculture Ser.). 1987. pap. 48.95 (*0-8273-3905-4*) Delmar.

Land Economics Research: Papers Presented at a Symposium Held at Lincoln, Nebraska, June 16-23, 1961. Resources for the Future, Inc. Staff & Farm Foundation Staff. Ed. by Marion Clawson et al. LC 77-86388. (Resources for the Future, Inc. Publications). 296p. reprint ed. 55.00 (*0-404-60327-0*) AMS Pr.

Land Economics Research: Papers Presented at a Symposium Held at Lincoln, Nebraska, June 16-23, 1961, under the Joint Sponsorship of Farm Foundation & Resources for the Future, Inc. Symposium on Land Economics Research Staff. Ed. by Joseph Ackerman et al. LC 62-18173. 290p. reprint ed. pap. 89.90 (*0-7837-3146-9*, 204284000006) Bks Demand.

Land Ethic: Meeting Human Needs for the Land & Its Resources. Si Balch & Society of American Foresters Staff. LC 98-39583. (Forestry Forum Ser.). 1998. pap. write for info. (*0-939970-76-7*) Soc Am Foresters.

Land Evaluation & Expert System for Combating Desertification. Longjun Ci. LC 98-190206. 201p. 1997. write for info. (*7-5038-1824-7*) China Forest.

Land Evaluation for Land-Use Planning & Conservation in Sloping Areas. Ed. by W. Siderius. 334p. (C). 1991. text 475.00 (*81-7089-136-1*, Pub. by Intl Bk Distr) St Mut.

Land Evaluation Guidelines for Rainfed Agriculture: Report of an Expert Consultation, Rome, 1979. 122p. 1980. 14.00 (*92-5-100994-5*, F2104, Pub. by FAO) Bernan Associates.

Land Evaluation Studies in Hungary. D. Loczy. (Studies in Geography in Hungary: No. 23). 95p. (C). 1988. 50.00 (*963-05-5231-0*, Pub. by Akade Kiado) St Mut.

***Land Exchange & Boundary Adjustment Bills: Hearing Before the Subcommittee on Forests & Public Land Management of the Committee on Energy & Natural Resources, United States Senate, One Hundred Fifth Congress, Second Session, on S. 890, S. 1109, S. 1468, S. 1469, S. 1510, S. 1683, S. 1719, S. 1752, S. 1807, H.R. 1439, H.R. 1663, March 25, 1998.** USGPO Staff. LC 98-208202. (S. Hrg. Ser.). iii, 82 p. 1998. write for info. (*0-16-057200-2*) USGPO.

Land Fever: Dispossession & the Frontier Myth. James M. Marshall. LC 86-4030. 248p. 1986. 29.95 (*0-8131-1568-X*) U Pr of Ky.

Land Filled with Flies: A Political Economy of the Kalahari. Edwin N. Wilmsen. LC 89-30724. (Illus.). 418p. 1989. pap. text 27.00 (*0-226-90015-0*) U Ch Pr.

Land Filled with Flies: A Political Economy of the Kalahari. Edwin N. Wilmsen. LC 89-30724. (Illus.). 418p. 1996. lib. bdg. 72.00 (*0-226-90014-2*) U Ch Pr.

Land Finance: Adaptable to Courses Utilizing Berger & Johnston's Casebook on Land Transfer & Finance. Casenotes Publishing Co., Inc. Staff. Ed. by Norman S. Goldenberg & Peter Tenen. (Legal Briefs Ser.). 1993. pap. write for info. (*0-87457-100-6*, 1471) Casenotes Pub.

Land Finance: Adaptable to Courses Utilizing Penney, Broude & Cunningham's Casebook on Land Financing. Casenotes Publishing co., Inc. Staff. Ed. by Norman S. Goldenberg & Peter Tenen. (Legal Briefs Ser.). 1985. pap. write for info. (*0-87457-101-4*, 1470) Casenotes Pub.

Land Financing, Cases & Materials On. 3rd ed. Norman Penney et al. LC 84-24645. (University Casebook Ser.). 1052p. 1984. text 40.95 (*0-88277-199-X*) Foundation Pr.

Land for Housing: Developing a Research Agenda. Ed. by Kelley Roark. LC HD0205.R627. (Monograph Ser.: No. 85-3). 81p. reprint ed. pap. 30.00 (*0-7837-2172-2*, 204249700004) Bks Demand.

Land for Industrial Development. D. Adams. (Illus.). 304p. (C). 1994. 80.00 (*0-419-19180-1*, E & FN Spon) Routledge.

Land for People: Land Tenure & the Very Poor. Claire Whittemore. (C). 1981. pap. text 35.00 (*0-85598-046-X*, Pub. by Oxfam Pubns) St Mut.

Land Forms, Hydrology & Sedimentation. Dibakar Sahu. 1990. 78.50 (*81-85109-99-0*, Pub. by Naya Prokash) S Asia.

Land from the Sea: The Geologic Story of South Florida. J. Edward Hoffmeister. LC 73-20120. (Illus.). 128p. 1974. pap. 22.95 (*0-87024-268-7*) U of Miami Pr.

Land Gains Taxation: The Vermont Case. Thomas L. Daniels. (Occasional Papers: No. 10). (Illus.). 58p. (Orig.). 1986. pap. text 5.00 (*0-944277-15-2*, D36) U VT Ctr Rsch VT.

Land Girls. Angela Huth. LC 96-3369. 378p. 1996. text 23.95 (*0-312-14296-X*) St Martin.

Land Girls. Angela Huth. 378p. 1998. pap. 12.95 (*0-312-17195-1*) St Martin.

Land Grab. Jackson Cole. LC 99-19636. 1999. 19.95 (*0-7838-8577-6*, G K Hall & Co) Mac Lib Ref.

Land Grant Frescoes at The Pennsylvania State University by Henry Varnum Poor. Harold E. Dickson. (Illus.). 24p. 1981. pap. 1.00 (*0-911209-22-0*) Palmer Mus Art.

Land Grants & Adults Residing in Fayette County, AL, 1823-1900. Homer T. Jones. LC 99-214228. 180p. 1998. pap. 25.00 (*1-885480-28-8*) Pioneer Pubng.

Land Grants & Lawsuits Northern New Mexico. Malcolm Ebright. LC 93-30863. (New Mexico Land Grant Ser.). 399p. (C). 1994. pap. 27.50 (*0-8263-1461-9*) U of NM Pr.

Land Grants in Alta, California: A Compilation of Spanish & Mexican Private Land Claims in the State of California. Crisostomo N. Perez. 264p. (C). 1996. 55.00 (*0-910845-55-7*) Landmark Ent.

Land Hermit Crabs. Paul J. Nash. (Illus.). 32p. 1976. pap. 1.79 (*0-87666-907-0*, A-325) TFH Pubns.

Land Hermit Crabs. Neal Pronek. (Illus.). 96p. 1989. 9.95 (*0-86622-967-1*, KW-098) TFH Pubns.

Land Ho! Morgan Robertson. LC 76-101290. (Short Story Index Reprint Ser.). 1977. 23.95 (*0-8369-3227-7*) Ayer.

Land Ho! From Columbus to Cabrillo & How They Managed to Make So Many Mistakes & Still End up Being So Famous. Nancy Winslow Parker. LC 99-23006. (Illus.). 32p. (J). (gr. 1-5). 2001. lib. bdg. 15.89 (*0-06-027760-2*) HarpC Child Bks.

***Land Ho! From Columbus to Cabrillo & How They Managed to Make So Many Mistakes & Still End up Being So Famous.** Nancy Winslow Parker. LC 99-23006. (Illus.). 32p. (J). (gr. 1-5). 2001. 15.95 (*0-06-027759-9*) HarpC Child Bks.

Land Ho! The Mythical World of Rodney Alan Greenblat. Intro. by Trinkett Clark. 47p. 1992. pap. 14.00 (*0-940744-64-3*) Chrysler Museum.

Land Ho! - 1620: A Seaman's Story of the Mayflower, Her Construction, Her Navigation & Her First Landfall. Warren S. Nickerson & Delores B. Carpenter. LC 96-51685. (Illus.). 250p. 1997. pap. 18.95 (*0-87013-465-5*) Mich St U Pr.

Land Holding in the Usangu Plain. Knut Pipping. (Research Report Ser.: No. 33). 122p. 1976. write for info. (*91-7106-097-9*, Pub. by Nordic Africa) Transaction Pubs.

Land Hunger: David L. Payne & the Oklahoma Boomers. Carl C. Rister. LC 75-118. (Mid-American Frontier Ser.). (Illus.). 1975. reprint ed. 23.95 (*0-405-06884-0*) Ayer.

Land Husbandry. Norman Hudson. LC 92-52940. (Illus.). 224p. 1992. text 47.50 (*0-8014-2803-3*) Cornell U Pr.

Land Husbandry: A Framework for Soil & Water Conservation. N. W. Hudson et al. LC 89-5889. (Illus.). 64p. 1989. pap. text 12.00 (*0-935734-20-1*) Soil & Water Conserv.

Land Husbandry: Components & Strategy. Food & Agriculture Organization Staff. (Soils Bulletins Ser.: No. 70). 380p. 1997. pap. 48.00 (*92-5-103451-6*, F34516, Pub. by FAO) Bernan Associates.

Land I Lost. Nuynh Q. Nhuong. (J). 1982. 12.95 (*0-06-024592-1*); lib. bdg. 12.89 (*0-06-024593-X*) HarpC Child Bks.

Land I Lost: A Study Guide. Carolyn Hernandez & Beverly Daniel. Ed. by J. Friedland & R. Kessler. (Novel-Ties Ser.). (J). (gr. 4-6). 1998. pap. text, student ed. 15.95 (*0-7675-0308-2*) Lrn Links.

Land I Lost: Adventures of a Boy in Vietnam. Huynh Q. Nhuong. LC 80-8437. (Trophy Bk.). (Illus.). 128p. (J). (gr. 4-7). 1998. pap. 4.95 (*0-06-440183-9*, HarpTrophy) HarpC Child Bks.

Land I Lost: Adventures of a Boy in Vietnam. Huynh Q. Nhuong. (J). (gr. 4-7). 1996. pap. 19.00 (*0-8446-6586-X*) Peter Smith.

Land I Lost: Adventures of a Boy in Vietnam. Huynh Q. Nhuong. (J). 1982. 9.60 (*0-606-03245-2*, Pub. by Turtleback) Demco.

Land I Lost: Adventures of a Boy in Vietnam. Nuynh Q. Nhuong. LC 80-8437. (Illus.). 128p. (J). (gr. 4-7). 1990. lib. bdg. 15.89 (*0-397-32448-0*) HarpC Child Bks.

***Land I'm Bound To: Photographs.** Jack Leigh. (Illus.). 2000. 75.00 (*0-393-04931-0*) Norton.

Land in African Agrarian Systems. Ed. by Thomas J. Bassett & Donald E. Crummey. LC 92-27696. (Illus.). 430p. (Orig.). (C). 1993. 50.00 (*0-299-13610-8*) U of Wis Pr.

Land in African Agrarian Systems. Ed. by Thomas J. Bassett & Donald E. Crummey. LC 92-27696. (Illus.). 430p. (Orig.). 1993. reprint ed. 133.30 (*0-608-07457-8*, 206768400009) Bks Demand.

Land in California: The Story of Mission Lands, Ranchos, Squatters, Mining Claims, Railroad Grants, Land Scrip, Homesteads. William W. Robinson. (Illus.). 1979. pap. 16.95 (*0-520-03875-4*, Pub. by U CA Pr) Cal Prin Full Svc.

Land in California: The Story of Mission Lands, Ranchos, Squatters, Mining Claims, Railroad Grants, Land Scrip, Homesteads. William W. Robinson. Ed. by Stuart Bruchey. LC 78-56665. (Management of Public Lands in the U. S. Ser.). (Illus.). 1979. reprint ed. lib. bdg. 23.95 (*0-405-11352-8*) Ayer.

Land in Common: Illustrated History of Jackson County, Oregon. Ed. by Joy B. Dunn. (Illus.). 192p. 1996. 24.95 (*0-943388-11-2*) South Oregon.

Land in Her Own Name: Women As Homesteaders in North Dakota. H. Elaine Lindgren. LC 96-20628. (Illus.). 320p. 1996. pap. 17.95 (*0-8061-2886-0*) U of Okla Pr.

***Land in Motion: California's San Andreas Fault.** Michael Collier. 128p. 1999. pap. 19.95 (*0-520-21897-3*, Pub. by U CA Pr) Cal Prin Full Svc.

***Land in the American West: Private Claims & the Common Good.** William G. Robbins. (Illus.). 224p. 2000. pap. 17.50 (*0-295-98020-6*) U of Wash Pr.

Land Information Management: An Introduction with Special Reference to Cadastral Problems in Third World Countries. Peter F. Dale & John D. McLaughlin. (Illus.). 300p. 1988. 69.00 (*0-19-858404-0*) OUP.

Land (Intermediate) Robyn F. Spizman & Marianne D. Garber. (Illus.). 48p. (J). (gr. 4-7). 1992. student ed. 6.99 (*0-86653-675-2*, 1409) Good Apple.

Land into Water - Water into Land: A History of Water Management in Florida. Nelson M. Blake. LC 79-21836. (Florida State University Bks.). 352p. reprint ed. pap. 109.20 (*0-8357-6924-0*, 203798300009) Bks Demand.

Land Investment & the Predevelopment Process: A Guide for Finance & Real Estate Professionals. Alan Rabinowitz. LC 87-32594. 239p. 1988. 67.95 (*0-89930-326-9*, RZP/, Quorum Bks) Greenwood.

Land Is Bright. Archie Binns. LC 91-694. (Northwest Reprints Ser.). 376p. 1992. reprint ed. text 24.95 (*0-87071-508-9*) Oreg St U Pr.

Land Is Bright: Manuscript Edition. Edna Ferber & George S. Kaufman. 1946. pap. 13.00 (*0-8222-0631-5*) Dramatists Play.

Land Is Coming Up: The Berunge of Central Tanzania & Their Environments. Wilhelm Ostberg. (Stockholm Studies in Social Anthropology: No. 34). (Illus.). 258p. (Orig.). 1995. pap. 67.50 (*91-7153-404-0*) Coronet Bks.

Land Is Life: Land Reform & Sustainable Agriculture. Ed. by Nigel Dudley et al. 144p. 1992. pap. 15.95 (*1-85339-146-8*, Pub. by Intermed Tech) Stylus Pub VA.

Land Is Mine: Six Biblical Land Ideologies. Norman Habel. LC 93-24243. (Overtures to Biblical Theology Ser.). 160p. 1993. pap. 17.00 (*0-8006-2664-8*, 1-2664, Augsburg) Augsburg Fortress.

Land Is Shrinking: Population Planning in Asia. Gayl D. Ness & Hirofumi Ando. LC 83-48048. (Johns Hopkins Studies in Development). (Illus.). 253p. reprint ed. pap. 78.50 (*0-608-06174-3*, 206650700008) Bks Demand.

Land Is the Cry! Warren Angus Ferris, Pioneer Texas Surveyor & Founder of Dallas County. Susanne Starling. LC 97-31394. (Illus.). 238p. 1997. 29.95 (*0-87611-161-4*) Tex St Hist Assn.

Land Issues in Japan: A Policy Failure? Ed. by John O. Haley & Kozo Yamamura. 246p. (Orig.). (C). 1992. pap. text 5.00 (*1-879098-01-6*) Soc Japanese.

Land, Labor & Capital in Modern Yucatan: Essays in Regional History & Political Economy. Ed. by Jeffrey T. Brannon & Gilbert M. Joseph. LC 90-46746. (Illus.). 336p. 1991. pap. 104.20 (*0-608-05126-8*, 206568500005) Bks Demand.

Land, Labor, & Rural Poverty: Essays in Development Economics. Pranab K. Bardhan. LC 83-10082. 288p. 1984. text 63.00 (*0-231-05388-6*) Col U Pr.

Land, Labor, & Rural Poverty: Essays in Development Economics. Pranab K. Bardhan. LC 83-10082. 288p. 1987. pap. 21.00 (*0-231-05389-4*, W3894) Col U Pr.

Land, Labor & the Origins of the Israeli-Palestinian Conflict, 1882-1914. Gershon Shafir. 288p. (C). 1996. pap. 16.95 (*0-520-20401-8*, Pub. by U CA Pr) Cal Prin Full Svc.

Land, Labour & Agriculture, 1700-1920: Essays for Gordon Mingay. Ed. by W. A. Holderness & M. E. Turner. 288p. 1991. 60.00 (*1-85285-042-6*) Hambledon Press.

Land, Labour Migration & Politics in Southern Africa, Botswana, Lesotho & Swaziland. Donald K. Kowet. 243p. 1978. write for info. (*91-7106-144-4*, Pub. by Nordic Africa) Transaction Pubs.

Land Law. Ed. by Cedric D. Bell. 394p. 1996. pap. 95.00 (*0-7510-0688-2*, Pub. by HLT Pubns) St Mut.

Land Law. Martin Dixon. (Lecture Notes Ser.). 280p. 1994. pap. write for info. (*1-874241-64-3*, Pub. by Cavendish Pubng) Gaunt.

Land Law. Ed. by Gordon Henry. 300p. (C). 1990. pap. 40.00 (*1-85352-775-0*, Pub. by HLT Pubns) St Mut.

Land Law. Gordon Henry. 270p. (C). 1991. 60.00 (*1-85352-699-1*, Pub. by HLT Pubns); pap. 85.00 (*1-85352-861-7*, Pub. by HLT Pubns) St Mut.

Land Law. Ed. by Gordon Henry. 270p. (C). 1991. pap. 60.00 (*1-85352-377-1*, Pub. by HLT Pubns) St Mut.

Land Law. P. L. Tan et al. (Butterworths Tutorial Ser.). 304p. 1995. pap. write for info. (*0-409-30067-5*, MICHIE) LEXIS Pub.

Land Law. 2nd ed. Peter Butt. liii, 668p. 1988. pap. 61.50 (*0-455-20789-5*, Pub. by LawBk Co) Gaunt.

Land Law. 2nd ed. Martin Dixon. (Questions & Answers Ser.). 284p. 1995. 18.00 (*1-85941-265-3*, Pub. by Cavendish Pubng) Gaunt.

Land Law. 2nd ed. Martin Dixon. (Lecture Notes Ser.). 271p. 1996. pap. 30.00 (*1-85941-170-3*, Pub. by Cavendish Pubng) Gaunt.

Land Law. 2nd ed. Roger Sexton. 425p. 1997. pap. 40.00 (*1-85431-693-1*, Pub. by Blackstone Pr) Gaunt.

Land Law. 2nd ed. Gary Watt. 381p. 1997. pap. 42.00 (*1-85431-694-X*, Pub. by Blackstone Pr) Gaunt.

Land Law. 3rd ed. Peter Butt. 790p. 1996. 125.00 (*0-455-21358-5*, Pub. by LawBk Co); pap. 90.00 (*0-455-21359-3*, Pub. by LawBk Co) Gaunt.

Land Law: Themes & Perspectives. Susan Bright. 620p. 1998. pap. text (*0-19-876455-3*) OUP.

Land Law: Themes & Perspectives. Ed. by Susan Bright & John Dewar. LC 98-3193. 620p. 1998. text 90.00 (*0-19-876454-5*) OUP.

Land Law & Custom in the Colonies. 2nd ed. Charles K. Meek. 337p. 1968. reprint ed. 45.00 (*0-7146-1698-2*, Pub. by F Cass Pubs) Intl Spec Bk.

***Land, Law & Environment: Mythical Land, Legal Boundaries.** Allen Abramson & Dimitrios Theodossopoulos. LC 00-9107. (Anthropology, Culture & Society Ser.). (Illus.). 2000. write for info. (*0-7453-1575-5*, Pub. by Pluto GBR) Stylus Pub VA.

Land, Law, & Lordship in Anglo-Norman England. John Hudson. (Oxford Historical Monographs). (Illus.). 330p. 1997. reprint ed. pap. text 32.00 (*0-19-820688-7*) OUP.

Land Law & Registration, Bk. 1. S. Rowton Simpson. 432p. (C). 1976. text 140.00 (*0-85406-256-4*, Pub. by Surveyors Pubns) St Mut.

Land Law Cases. Ed. by Cedric D. Bell. 380p. 1996. pap. 95.00 (*0-7510-0655-6*, Pub. by HLT Pubns) St Mut.

Land Law in Lesotho. Anita Franklin. 224p. 1995. 79.95 (*1-85628-976-1*, Pub. by Avebry) Ashgate Pub Co.

Land Law in Malaysia: Cases & Commentary. 2nd ed. Teo Keang Sood & Khaw Lake Tee. 1995. boxed set 273.00 (*0-614-05483-4*, SI, MICHIE) LEXIS Pub.

Land Law of Palestine. Frederic M. Goadby & Moses J. Doukhan. viii, 458p. 1998. reprint ed. 140.00 (*1-56169-432-0*) Gaunt.

Land Laws. Frederick Pollock. xii, 218p. 1999. reprint ed. 70.00 (*1-56169-520-3*) Gaunt.

Land Laws. Frederick Pollock. x, 233p. 1979. reprint ed. 36.00 (*0-8377-1001-4*, Rothman) W S Hein.

Land, Laws, & Gods: Magistrates & Ceremony in the Regulation of Public Lands in Republican Rome. Daniel J. Gargola. LC 95-3406. (Studies in the History of Greece & Rome). 1995. text 49.95 (*0-8078-2233-7*) U of NC Pr.

Land Leviathan. Michael Moorcock. 19.95 (*0-89190-153-1*) Amereon Ltd.

Land, Liberties, & Lordship in a Late Medieval Countryside: Agrarian Structures & Change in the Duchy of Wroclaw. Richard C. Hoffmann. LC 89-14659. (Middle Ages Ser.). (Illus.). 582p. (C). 1989. text 58.95 (*0-8122-8090-3*) U of Pa Pr.

Land Lies Open. Theodore C. Blegen. LC 74-27727. 246p. 1975. reprint ed. lib. bdg. 35.00 (*0-8371-7912-2*, BLLO, Greenwood Pr) Greenwood.

Land-Locked & Geographically Disadvantaged States in the International Law of the Sea. Stephen C. Vasciannie. (Oxford Monographs in International Law). 260p. 1990. text 75.00 (*0-19-825287-0*) OUP.

Land-Locked Countries of Africa. Zdenek Cervenka. (Seminar Proceedings Ser.: No. 9). 368p. 1973. write for info. (*91-7106-065-0*, Pub. by Nordic Africa) Transaction Pubs.

Land-Locked States & International Law. Almeen Ali. (C). 1989. 16.00 (*81-7003-102-8*, Pub. by S Asia Pubs) S Asia.

Land-Locked States & International Law: With Special Reference to the Role of Nepal. Almeen Ali. 238p. (C). 1989. 150.00 (*0-89771-088-6*, Pub. by Ratna Pustak Bhandar) St Mut.

Land-Locked States of Africa & Asia. Ed. by Dick Hodder et al. LC 97-38217. 240p. 1997. text 42.50 (*0-7146-4829-9*, Pub. by F Cass Pubs); pap. text 24.50 (*0-7146-4371-8*, Pub. by F Cass Pubs) Intl Spec Bk.

Land Lottery 1901: The Diary of Miss Minnie Johnson. Ardeth Elling Denney. LC 98-93736. (Illus.). 340p. 1998. pap. 16.95 (*0-9667576-0-2*) Blue Beaver.

Land Lottery of Georgia & Other Missing Names of Winners in the Georgia Land Lotteries, 1833. Robert S. Davis, Jr. 100p. 1991. pap. 20.00 (*0-89308-338-0*, GA 88) Southern Hist Pr.

***Land Mammals of Oregon.** B. J. Verts & Leslie N. Carraway. LC 97-27039. 800p. 1998. 80.00 (*0-520-21199-5*, Pub. by U CA Pr) Cal Prin Full Svc.

An Asterisk (*) at the beginning of an entry indicates that the title is appearing for the first time.

Land Management: Public Policy, Control & Participation. Gerhard Larsson. (Swedish Council for Building Research Ser.). (Illus.). 232p. 1997. pap. 72.50 (*91-540-5783-3*, Pub. by Almqvist Wiksell) Coronet Bks.

***Land Management Agencies: Revenue Sharing Payments to States & Counties.** Robert B. Arthur. (Illus.). 72p. (C). 1999. pap. text 20.00 (*0-7881-7731-1*) DIANE Pub.

Land Management & Survival. Ed. by Anders Hjort. (Scandinavian Institute of African Studies). 148p. (Orig.). 1985. pap. text 41.00 (*91-7106-244-0*, Pub. by Nordisk Afrikainstitutet) Coronet Bks.

Land Management in the 70's: Concepts & Models. Ed. by W. L. Bathke & W. A. Haney. (Illus.). 1972. 10.00 (*0-911302-19-0*) San Francisco Pr.

Land Management Issues & Development Strategies in Developing Countries, Vol. 2. Lincoln Institute of Land Policy Staff. Ed. by Sein Lin & Wasin Zaman. LC HD0111.L5. 134p. reprint ed. pap. 41.60 (*0-7837-3873-0*, 204371200002) Bks Demand.

Land Management Specialist. Jack Rudman. (Career Examination Ser.: C-2618). 1994. pap. 29.95 (*0-8373-2618-4*) Nat Learn.

Land Market Assessment: A New Tool for Urban Management. David E. Dowall. LC 93-33937. 82p. 1995. pap. 22.00 (*0-8213-2703-8*, 12703) World Bank.

Land Market Distortion & Tenure Reform. Anthony Y. Koo. LC 82-134. (Illus.). 145p. 1982. reprint ed. pap. 41.40 (*0-608-00168-6*, 2060950) Bks Demand.

Land Markets & Land Policy in a Metropolitan Area: A Case Study of Tokyo. Yuzuru Hanayama. LC 85-13867. (Lincoln Institute of Land Policy Bk.). 179p. reprint ed. pap. 55.50 (*0-7837-3265-1*, 204328400007) Bks Demand.

Land Markets & Legal Contradictions in the Peri-Urban Areas of Accra, Ghana: Informant Interviews & Secondary Data Investigations. R. Kasim Kasanga et al. (Research Paper Ser.: Vol. 127). (Illus.). vi, 83p. (C). 1996. pap. 7.00 (*0-934519-40-4*, RP127) U of Wis Land.

Land Markets, Employment, & Resource Use in the Peri-Urban Green Zones of Maputo, Mozambique: A Case Study of Land Market Rigidities & Institutional Constraints to Economic Growth. Michael Roth et al. (Research Paper Ser.: Vol. 123). (Illus.). xxxi, 122p. (C). 1995. pap. 7.00 (*0-934519-36-6*, RP123) U of Wis Land.

Land, Men & Beliefs: Studies in Early-Modern History. J. P. Cooper. 300p. (C). 1983. 55.00 (*0-907628-26-5*) Hambledon Press.

Land Mines. 1991. lib. bdg. 79.95 (*0-8490-4096-5*) Gordon Pr.

***Land Mines: 100 Million Hidden Killers.** Elaine Landau. LC 99-50597. (Issues in Focus Ser.). (Illus.). 128p. (YA). (gr. 6 up). 2000. lib. bdg. 20.95 (*0-7660-1240-9*) Enslow Pubs.

Land Mines in Angola. Ed. by Human Rights Watch Staff. 80p. (Orig.). 1993. pap. 7.00 (*1-56432-091-X*) Hum Rts Watch.

Land Mines in Cambodia: The Coward's War. Ed. by Human Rights Watch Staff. 160p. (Orig.). 1991. pap. 15.00 (*1-56432-001-4*) Hum Rts Watch.

Land-Mobile ICBMs: Verification & Breakout. Paul K. Davis. (CISA Working Papers: No. 18). 31p. (Orig.). 1980. pap. 15.00 (*0-86682-017-5*) Ctr Intl Relations.

Land-Mobile Radio System Engineering. Gary C. Hess. LC 93-12356. 495p. 1993. 93.00 (*0-89006-680-9*) Artech Hse.

Land Mobile Radio Systems. 2nd ed. Edward Singer. 288p. (C). 1994. 72.00 (*0-13-123159-6*) P-H.

Land Mollusca of North America: North of Mexico, Vol. 1, Pts. 1 & 2. Henry A. Pilsbry. (Monograph Ser.: No. 3). (Illus.). 992p. (Orig.). 1939. reprint ed. pap. 70.00 (*0-910006-11-3*) Acad Nat Sci Phila.

Land Mollusca of North America: North of Mexico, Vol. 2, Pts. 1 & 2. Henry A. Pilsbry. (Illus.). (Orig.). write for info. (*0-685-08428-0*) Acad Nat Sci Phila.

Land Mollusca of North America: North of Mexico, Vol. 2, Pts. 1 & 2. Henry A. Pilsbry. (Monograph Ser.: No. 3). (Illus.). 1112p. (Orig.). 1946. reprint ed. pap. 70.00 (*0-910006-12-1*) Acad Nat Sci Phila.

Land Mosaics: The Ecology of Landscapes & Regions. Richard T. Forman. (Illus.). 652p. (C). 1995. pap. text 47.95 (*0-521-47980-0*) Cambridge U Pr.

Land Navigation for Outdoor Enthusiasts. Bob Newman. (Nuts-N-Bolts Guides Ser.). 32p. 1995. pap. 4.95 (*0-89732-178-2*) Menasha Ridge.

Land Navigation Handbook: The Sierra Club Guide to Map & Compass. William S. Kals. LC 82-16917. (Outdoor Activities Guides Ser.). (Illus.). 288p. 1983. pap. 15.00 (*0-87156-331-2*, Pub. by Sierra) Random.

Land O' Lakes Best-Loved Recipes: Celebrating 75 Years of Quality Cooking. Land O'Lakes Staff & Time-Life Books Editors. LC 96-25442. (Illus.). 96p. (gr. 11). 1999. 14.95 (*0-7835-4860-5*) Time-Life.

Land Observation by Remote Sensing: Theory & Applications. Ed. by Henk J. Buiten & Jan G. Clevers. LC 93-25271. (Current Topics in Remote Sensing Ser.: Vol. 3).Tr. of Remote Sensing Theorie en Toepassingen van Landobservatie. xvi, 642p. 1994. text 182.00 (*2-88124-939-6*); pap. text 47.00 (*2-88124-940-X*) Gordon & Breach.

Land O'Burns: A Guide to the Burns Country. James Mackay & HMSO Staff. (Illus.). 52p. 1996. pap. text 18.00 (*0-11-495766-5*, Pub. by Statnry Office) Balogh.

Land of a Million Elephants. Thomas Phetsadasack & James R. Dillman. 150p. 1996. pap. 24.95 (*0-9630593-9-4*) Gt Falls North.

Land of a Million Elephants. 2nd ed. Asa Baber. (Vietnam Generation Ser.). (Illus.). 142p. (Orig.). (C). 1992. reprint ed. pap. 15.00 (*0-9628524-2-2*) Burning Cities Pr.

Land of a Thousand Dances: Chicano Rock 'n' Roll from Southern California. David Reyes & Tom Waldman. LC 97-50573. 178p. 1998. 50.00 (*0-8263-1929-7*) U of NM Pr.

Land of a Thousand Dances: Chicano Rock 'n' Roll from Southern California. David Reyes & Tom Waldman. LC 97-50573. (Illus.). 178p. 1998. pap. 18.95 (*0-8263-1883-5*) U of NM Pr.

Land of a Thousand Dreams. B. J. Hoff. (Emerald Ballad Ser.: Bk. 3). 4p. (Orig.). 1992. pap. 10.99 (*1-55661-112-9*) Bethany Hse.

***Land of a Thousand Hills: My Life in Rwanda.** Rosamond Halsey Carr & Ann Howard Halsey. (Illus.). 256p. 1999. 23.95 (*0-670-88780-3*, Viking) Viking Penguin.

***Land of a Thousand Hills: My Life in Rwanda.** Rosamund Halsey Carr & Ann Howard Halsey. (Illus.). 2000. pap. 13.00 (*0-452-28202-0*) Penguin Books.

***Land of a Thousand Hills: My Life in Rwanda.** large type ed. Rosamond Halsey Carr & Ann Howard Halsey. LC 00-23135. 2000. 25.95 (*1-56895-858-7*, Compass) Wheeler Pub.

Land of Angels. Eleanor H. Tilghman. (Illus.). 10p. (J). 1996. 13.95 incl. audio (*1-888095-01-6*) T E S T.

Land of Another Sun. Sheila K. Welch. LC 94-66241. (Illus.). 138p. (J). (gr. 3-8). 1995. 16.95 (*0-9638819-2-2*); pap. 10.95 (*0-9638819-3-0*) ShadowPlay Pr.

Land of Bears & Honey: A Natural History of East Texas. Joe C. Truett & Daniel W. Lay. LC 83-26000. (Illus.). 198p. 1984. 19.95 (*0-292-74640-7*) U of Tex Pr.

Land of Bears & Honey: A Natural History of East Texas. Joe C. Truett & Daniel W. Lay. (Illus.). 198p. (C). 1994. reprint ed. pap. 12.95 (*0-292-78134-2*) U of Tex Pr.

Land of Black Gold see Tintin en el Pais Del Oro Negro

Land of Black Gold see Tintin au Pays de l'Or Noir

Land of Black Gold. Herge. Orig. Title: Tintin au Pays de l'Or Noir. (Illus.). 62p. (J). 19.95 (*0-8288-5048-8*) Fr & Eur.

Land of Black Gold. Herge. LC 75-7896. (Adventures of Tintin Ser.). Orig. Title: Tintin au Pays de l'Or Noir. (Illus.). 62p. (J). (gr. 2 up). 1975. pap. 9.95 (*0-316-35844-4*, Joy St Bks) Little.

Land of Bliss, the Paradise of the Buddha of Measureless Light: Sanskrit & Chinese Versions of the Sukhavativyuha Sutras. Tr. & Intro. by Luis O. Gomez. LC 95-35867. (Studies in the Buddhist Traditions). 376p. (C). 1996. text 42.00 (*0-8248-1694-3*); pap. text 18.95 (*0-8248-1760-5*) UH Pr.

Land of Bolivar, 2 vols. James M. Spence. LC 78-175995. reprint ed. 115.00 (*0-404-06177-X*) AMS Pr.

Land of Bright Promise: Advertising the Texas Panhandle & South Plains, 1870-1917. Jan Blodgett. LC 87-2531. (M. K. Brown Range Life Ser.: No. 17). (Illus.). 165p. 1988. 17.95 (*0-292-73037-3*) U of Tex Pr.

Land of Broken Rainbows. Margaret A. Kubo. 32p. 1998. pap. 5.95 (*1-57921-057-0*) WinePress Pub.

Land of Canaan. Jack Preble. 114p. 1965. reprint ed. pap. 9.95 (*0-87012-012-3*) McClain.

A collection of intriguing, hilarious & sometimes tragic tales from the mountains of Tucker & Randolph counties. Fifth Printing, 1995. *Publisher Paid Annotation.*

***Land of Carmel.** Elizabeth Ruth O'Bbard. 1999. pap. 12.95 (*0-85244-504-0*) Gra1cewing.

Land of Chamise & Pines: Historical Accounts & Current Status of Northern Baja California's Vegetation. Richard A. Minnich & Vizca Ino Ernesto Franco. LC 98-13127. (Publications in Botany Ser.). 168p. 1998. 32.00 (*0-520-09825-0*, Pub. by U CA Pr) Cal Prin Full Svc.

Land of Charity: A Descriptive Account of Travancore & Its People. Samuel Mateer. (C). 1991. reprint ed. 29.00 (*81-206-0319-2*, Pub. by Asian Educ Servs) S Asia.

***Land of China.** Lynn M. Stone. LC 00-38724. (China Ser.). (Illus.). 2000. write for info. (*1-55916-318-6*) Rourke Bk Co.

Land of Cochise: Southwestern Arizona. Ed. by J. F. Callender et al. (Guidebook Ser.: No. 29). (Illus.). 348p. 1978. 35.00 (*1-58546-059-1*); pap. 17.00 (*1-58546-060-5*) NMex Geol Soc.

Land of Cockaigne & English Made Simple: Two Plays by David Ives. David Ives. LC 97-208564. 1995. pap. 5.25 (*0-8222-1470-9*) Dramatists Play.

Land of Cotton. John T. Morgan. 1988. 13.95 (*0-9620539-0-2*) Morgan Academy.

Land of Cypress & Pine: More Southeast Arkansas History. James W. Leslie. (Illus.). 216p. 1976. 19.95 (*0-914546-09-0*) J W Bell.

Land of Debris & the Home of Alfredo: A Novel. Kenn Amdahl. 1997. pap. 14.00 (*0-9627815-8-4*) Clearwater Pub.

Land of Desire: Merchants, Power & the Rise of a New American Culture. William Leach. (Illus.). 560p. 1994. pap. 18.00 (*0-679-75411-3*) Vin Bks.

Land of Dinosaurs: Learning Center. rev. ed. Irene Handberg. 8p. 1995. teacher ed. 24.95 (*1-56831-412-4*) Lrning Connect.

Land of Dinosaurs: Learning Center, Set. rev. ed. Irene Handberg. (Illus.). 1995. pap. 59.95 (*1-56831-410-8*) Lrning Connect.

Land of Discord Always: Acadia from Its Beginnings to the Expulsion of Its People, 1604-1755. Charles D. Mahaffie, Jr. LC 95-8904. (Illus.). 328p. 1997. pap. 16.95 (*0-89272-375-0*) Down East.

Land of Dreams. Joan Lowery Nixon. (J). 1994. mass mkt. 4.99 (*0-440-91013-7*) BDD Bks Young Read.

Land of Dreams. Joan Lowery Nixon. (Ellis Island Ser.). 1994. 9.09 (*0-606-07160-1*, Pub. by Turtleback) Demco.

Land of Dreams. Cheryl St. John. LC 95-8360. (Historical Ser.). 299p. 1995. per. 4.50 (*0-373-28865-4*, 1-28865-3) Harlequin Bks.

Land of Dreams: An Israeli Childhood: Recalling the Birth of Israel. Mordecai Schreiber. LC 97-65719. 240p. 1998. pap. 19.95 (*1-887563-39-3*) Schreiber Pub.

Land of Dust: Palestine at the Turn of the Century. Saul S. Friedman. LC 81-43466. (Illus.). 256p. (Orig.). 1982. pap. text 27.00 (*0-8191-2404-4*) U Pr of Amer.

Land of Eagles: A History of Albania from Illyrian Times to the Present. Tajar Zavalani. 420p. 1997. 59.95 (*0-86356-991-9*, Pub. by Saqi) Intl Spec Bk.

Land of Eight Million Dreams. Deena McKinney & Jim Moore. (Changeling: The Dreaming Ser.). (Illus.). 1998. pap. 18.00 (*1-56504-722-2*, 7308) White Wolf.

Land of Empty Houses. John L. Moore. LC 98-3838. 272p. 1998. pap. 12.99 (*0-8054-1648-X*) Broadman.

Land of Enchantment. Janet Dailey. (Janet Dailey Americana Ser.: No. 881). 1992. per. 3.59 (*0-373-89881-9*, 1-89881-6) Harlequin Bks.

Land of Enchantment: Memoirs of Marian Russell along the Santa Fe Trail. M. Russell. LC 80-54564. 163p. 1985. reprint ed. pap. 14.95 (*0-8263-0805-8*) U of NM Pr.

Land of Enchantment from Pike's Peak to the Pacific. Lilian Whiting. 432p. 1981. pap. 15.00 (*0-89540-120-7*, SB-120) Sun Pub.

Land of Enchantment, Land of Conflict: New Mexico in English-Language Fiction. David L. Caffey. LC 98-55985. (Tarleton State University Southwestern Studies in the Humanities: Vol. 11). (Illus.). 240p. 1999. 29.95 (*0-89096-891-8*) Tex A&M Univ Pr.

Land of Exile: Contemporary Korean Fiction. Ed. by Marshall R. Pihl et al. Tr. by Ju-Chan Fulton et al from KOR. LC 93-25238. (Illus.). 304p. (gr. 13). 1993. pap. text 24.95 (*1-56324-195-1*, East Gate Bk) M E Sharpe.

Land of Exile: Contemporary Korean Fiction. Ed. by Marshall R. Pihl et al. Tr. by Bruce Fulton et al from KOR. LC 93-25238. (Illus.). 304p. (C). (gr. 13). 1993. text 65.95 (*1-56324-194-3*, East Gate Bk) M E Sharpe.

Land of Extremes: A Collection from the San Francisco Women Writers Workshop. Priscilla Be et al. (Illus.). 72p. (Orig.). 1991. pap. 5.00 (*1-880306-02-6*) SF Women Writs.

Land of Fact. Lawrence C. Powell. LC 92-72094. 60p. 1992. 30.00 (*0-914421-07-7*) Hist Soc So CA.

Land of Fair Play. Geoffrey Parsons. (Illus.). 180p. (YA). (gr. 7-12). 1994. pap. text 8.00 (*1-930092-98-9*, CLP79995) Christian Liberty.

Land of Fair Play: Answer Key. 2nd ed. Geoffrey Parsons. 180p. 1994. 3.00 (*1-930092-99-7*, CLP79995) Christian Liberty.

Land of Fair Promise: Politics & Reform in Los Angeles Schools, 1885-1941. Judith R. Raftery. LC 91-26888. (Illus.). 312p. (C). 1992. 14.95 (*0-8047-1930-6*) Stanford U Pr.

Land of Far Beyond. Enid Blyton. (Religious Stories Ser.). 128p. (J). (gr. 3 up). 1998. 6.95 (*1-901881-22-9*, Pub. by Element MA) Penguin Putnam.

Land of Feast & Famine. Helge Ingstad. Tr. by Eugene Gay-Tifft. (Illus.). 360p. 1991. 65.00 (*0-7735-0911-9*, Pub. by McG-Queens Univ Pr) CUP Services.

Land of Feast & Famine. Helge Ingstad. Tr. by Eugene Gay-Tifft. (Illus.). 360p. 1992. pap. 24.95 (*0-7735-0912-7*, Pub. by McG-Queens Univ Pr) CUP Services.

Land of Footprints. S. E. White. (Illus.). 448p. 1987. reprint ed. 25.00 (*0-935632-52-2*) Wolfe Pub Co.

Land of Genghis Khan: The Rise & Fall of Nation-States in China's Northern Frontiers. David C. Lai. LC 97-107190. (Illus.). 88p. 1995. pap. 9.95 (*0-919838-20-0*) U of Wash Pr.

Land of Giants: Scandinavia & the Beowulf Saga in the Time of King Arthur. Chris Hind et al. Ed. by Liam Routt. (Pendragon Role Playing Game Ser.). (Illus.). 128p. (Orig.). 1996. pap. 19.95 (*1-56882-055-0*, 2718) Chaosium.

Land of Giants: Where No Good Deed Goes Unpunished. Steve Lopez. LC 95-9628. 230p. (Orig.). 1995. pap. 11.95 (*0-940159-30-9*) Camino Bks.

Land of Go. Lynne Barrett. LC 87-71458. (Fiction Ser.). 1988. 11.95 (*0-88748-044-6*) Carnegie-Mellon.

Land of Gold. Gillian Bradshaw. LC 91-31810. 160p. (J). (gr. 4-7). 1992. 14.00 (*0-688-10576-9*, Grenwillow Bks) HarpC Child Bks.

***Land of Golden Dreams: California in the Gold Rush Decade 1848-1858.** Peter J. Blodgett. LC 99-39377. 144p. 1999. pap. 14.95 (*0-87328-182-9*) Huntington Lib.

***Land of Golden Dreams: California in the Gold Rush Decade, 1848-1858.** Peter J. Blodgett. LC 99-39377. (Illus.). 144p. 1999. 20.95 (*0-87328-183-7*) Huntington Lib.

Land of Golden Sunshine. J. Donald Walters. LC 88-155232. (Illus.). 88p. (Orig.). 1988. pap. 7.95 (*0-916124-40-1*, CCP8) Crystal Clarity.

Land of Gray Wolf. Thomas Locker. LC 90-3915. (J). 1996. 11.19 (*0-606-09525-X*, Pub. by Turtleback) Demco.

Land of Green Ginger. Winifred Holtby. LC 77-12075. 311p. 1977. reprint ed. pap. 9.00 (*0-915864-25-8*) Academy Chi Pubs.

Land of Green Plums. Herta Muller. Tr. by Michael Hofmann from GER. LC 98-28184. 256p. 1998. pap. 16.95 (*0-8101-1597-2*, Hydra Bks) Northwestern U Pr.

Land of Green Plums: A Novel. Herta Muller. Tr. by Michael Hofmann. 256p. 1995. 23.00 (*0-8050-4295-4*) H Holt & Co.

Land of Heart's Desire see Three Irish Plays

Land of Heart's Desire. Alexander Cordell. 1994. lib. bdg. 20.00 (*0-7278-4715-5*) Severn Hse.

Land of Heart's Desire. large type ed. Alexander Cordell. 512p. 1996. 27.99 (*0-7089-3610-5*) Ulverscroft.

Land of Hidden Fires: Lynde Eldars Land. Tarjei Vesaas. Tr. by Fritz Konig & Jerry Crisp. LC 72-11951. 167p. reprint ed. pap. 51.80 (*0-7837-3587-1*, 204345100009) Bks Demand.

Land of Hope. Joan Lowery Nixon. (Ellis Island Ser.: No. 1). 176p. (YA). (gr. 7 up). 1993. mass mkt. 4.50 (*0-440-21597-8*) Dell.

Land of Hope. Joan Lowery Nixon. (Ellis Island Ser.). (J). 1992. 9.09 (*0-606-05265-8*, Pub. by Turtleback) Demco.

Land of Hope: Chicago, Black Southerners, & the Great Migration. James R. Grossman. LC 88-39125. (Illus.). 400p. 1990. pap. 17.00 (*0-226-30995-9*) U Ch Pr.

Land of Hope: Chicago, Black Southerners, & the Great Migration. James R. Grossman. (Illus.). 384p. 1993. 29.95 (*0-226-30994-0*) U Ch Pr.

Land of Hope & Glory: A True Account of the Life & Times of General Marcus Northway, Retired, & of the Character of His Eminent Friends. Marshall Terry. LC 95-46719. (Northway Ser.: Vol. 3). 224p. 1996. 24.95 (*1-57441-006-7*) UNTX Pr.

Land of Hunger. Piero Camporesi. Tr. by Tania Croft-Murray et al from ITA. 224p. (C). 1996. text 58.95 (*0-7456-0888-4*, Pub. by Polity Pr) Blackwell Pubs.

***Land of Hungry Armadillos.** Lawrence David. LC 99-54078. (Illus.). 32p. (J). (gr. 1-4). 2000. 15.95 (*0-385-32698-X*) BDD Bks Young Read.

***Land of I Can: An Adventure in Life.** Susan Gilbert. LC 00-190591. (Illus.). 52p. 2000. 12.95 (*0-9700187-0-3*) Unity Prods.

Land of Idols: Political Mythology in America. Michael J. Parenti. 208p. 1993. pap. text 25.95 (*0-312-09497-3*) St Martin.

Land of Immigrants. David M. Reimers. Ed. by Sandra Stotsky. LC 95-13820. (Immigrant Experience Ser.). (Illus.). 120p. (YA). (gr. 5 up). 1995. lib. bdg. 19.95 (*0-7910-3361-9*) Chelsea Hse.

Land of Immigrants. Ed. by Sandra Stotsky. (Immigrant Experience Ser.). 1998. 9.95 (*0-7910-3383-X*) Chelsea Hse.

Land of Intention. Amy Tudor. 28p. 1997. pap. 5.00 (*1-889806-13-7*) Devils Millhopper.

Land of Israel: Jewish Perspectives. Lawrence A. Hoffman. LC 86-40241. (Studies in Judaism & Christianity in Antiquity: Vol. 6). 352p. 1986. text 40.50 (*0-268-01280-6*) U of Notre Dame Pr.

Land of Israel: National Home or Land of Destiny. Eliezer Schweid. Tr. by Deborah Greniman. LC 84-45015. 224p. 1985. 32.50 (*0-8386-3234-3*) Fairleigh Dickinson.

Land of Israel As a Political Concept in Hasmonean Literature: Recourse to History in Second Century B.C. Claims to the Holy Land. Doron Mendels. 200p. 1987. text 63.50 (*3-16-145147-3*, Pub. by JCB Mohr) Coronet Bks.

Land of Jesus. 128p. pap. text 12.95 (*88-7009-729-3*, Pub. by Bonechi) Eiron.

Land of Journeys' Ending. Mary H. Austin. LC 70-86831. (BCL Ser.: No. I). (Illus.). 1969. reprint ed. 84.50 (*0-404-00435-0*) AMS Pr.

Land of Journeys' Ending. Mary H. Austin. LC 83-1217. (Illus.). 489p. reprint ed. pap. 151.60 (*0-8357-3179-0*, 203944400012) Bks Demand.

Land of Journeys' Ending. Mary H. Austin. (BCL1 - United States Local History Ser.). 459p. 1991. reprint ed. lib. bdg. 99.00 (*0-7812-6330-1*) Rprt Serv.

Land of Journey's Ending. Mary H. Austin. (Collected Works of Mary Hunter Austin). 459p. 1998. reprint ed. lib. bdg. 108.00 (*1-58201-520-1*) Classic Bks.

***Land of Laughs.** Jonathan Carroll. 2001. text. write for info. (*0-312-87311-5*) St Martin.

Land of Lava, Ash, & Sand: The Pinacate Region of Northwestern Sonora. Ronald L. Ives. Ed. by James W. Byrkit & Karen J. Dahood. LC 88-3364. (Illus.). xii, 239p. 1989. 24.95 (*0-910037-26-4*, E) AZ Hist Soc.

***Land of Lehi: Further Evidence for the Book of Mormon.** 2nd ed. Paul Hedengren. (Illus.). 180p. 1999. spiral bd. 14.95 (*0-915073-07-2*) Tepran.

***Land of Lettice Sweetapple: An English Countryside Explored.** Peter Fowler & Ian Blackwell. 176p. 1998. 29.99 (*0-7524-1415-1*, Pub. by Tempus Pubng) Arcadia Publng.

Land of Light: The Tarot. Hilton Hotema. 176p. 1996. reprint ed. pap. 18.00 (*0-7873-0420-4*) Hlth Research.

Land of Listening: Listening: Getting & Giving Attention. J. Thomas Morse et al. Ed. by Betty Gouge et al. LC 85-45429. (KidSkills Interpersonal Skill Ser.). (Illus.). 45p. (J). (gr. 2-3). 1985. lib. bdg. 9.95 (*0-934275-00-9*) Fam Skills.

Land of Little Horses. Rebecca Gilman. 76p. 1998. pap. 5.60 (*0-87129-797-3*, L92) Dramatic Pub.

Land of Little Rain. Mary Austin. LC 97-178695. 1997. pap. 10.95 (*0-14-024919-2*) Penguin Putnam.

***Land of Little Rain.** Mary Austin. 116p. 2000. pap. 9.95 (*1-55709-507-8*) Applewood.

Land of Little Rain. Mary H. Austin. 1973. lib. bdg. 250.00 (*0-87968-182-9*) Gordon Pr.

Land of Little Rain. Mary H. Austin. (Collected Works of Mary Hunter Austin). 280p. 1998. reprint ed. lib. bdg. 98.00 (*1-58201-521-X*) Classic Bks.

Land of Little Rain. Mary H. Austin. (BCL1 - United States Local History Ser.). 280p. 1991. reprint ed. lib. bdg. 79.00 (*0-7812-6331-X*) Rprt Serv.

Land of Little Rain. Mary H. Austin. LC 74-84233. (Zia Bks.). (Illus.). 171p. 1974. reprint ed. pap. 11.95 (*0-8263-0358-7*) U of NM Pr.

Land of Little Rain. unabridged ed. Mary Austin. LC 95-49113. (Thrift Editions Ser.). 96p. 1996. reprint ed. pap. text 1.50 (*0-486-29037-9*) Dover.

Land of Little Rivers: A Story in Photos of Catskill Fly Fishing. Austin Francis. (Illus.). 272p. 1999. 100.00 (*0-393-04855-1*) Norton.

L

Land of Little Sticks. limited ed. James Tate. (Metacom Limited Edition Ser.: No. 4). 20p. 1981. 25.00 (*0-911381-03-1*) Metacom Pr.

Land of Living Men. Ralph W. Trine. 302p. 1998. pap. 27.00 (*0-89540-406-0*, SB-406) Sun Pub.

Land of Lo: A Journey Through Mustang. David A. Glen. (Journeys to Elsewhere Ser.). 64p. 1998. pap. 29.00 (*1-887062-06-8*) Visual XS.

Land of Loss. K. A. Applegate. (Everworld Ser.: No. 2). 208p. (YA). (gr. 7-12). 1999. pap. 4.99 (*0-590-87751-8*, Pub. by Scholastic Inc) Penguin Putnam.

Land of Lost Content: Children & Childhood in Nineteenth-Century French Literature. Rosemary Lloyd. (Illus.). 286p. 1992. text 75.00 (*0-19-815173-X*) OUP.

Land of Love, Art & Genius. Rodney Charles & Nandini Badhwar. LC 97-65717. (Illus.). 180p. 1999. 49.00 (*1-887472-26-6*) Sunstar Pubng.

Land of Many Colors & Nanna-Ya: Pays Mele Suivi de Nanna-Ya. Maryse Conde. Tr. by Nicole Ball from FRE. LC 98-39182. 1999. pap. 12.00 (*0-8032-6395-3*) U of Nebr Pr.

Land of Many Colors & Nanna-Ya (Pays Mele Suivi de Nanna-Ya) Pays Mele Suivi de Nanna-Ya. Maryse Conde. Tr. by Nicole Ball from FRE. LC 98-39182. 1999. text 30.00 (*0-8032-1488-X*) U of Nebr Pr.

Land of Many Hands: Women in the American West. Harriet Sigerman. LC 97-30004. (Illus.). 192p. (YA). (gr. 7 up). 1997. 24.95 (*0-19-509942-7*) OUP.

Land of Many Nations: A Multicultural Play. Hilary Weisman. (Illus.). 21p. (Orig.). (J). (gr. 5-9). 1995. pap., wbk. ed. 10.00 (*1-878668-56-0*) Disc Enter Ltd.

Land of Maybe. large type ed. Sandra Field. 1991. reprint ed. lib. bdg. 18.95 (*0-263-12620-X*) Thorndike Pr.

Land of Metaphorical Desires: The Representation of Amazonia in Brazilian Literature. Pedro Maligo. LC 97-32321. (Wor(l)ds of Change Ser.: Vol. 21). IX, 192p. (C). 1998. 44.95 (*0-8204-3005-6*) P Lang Pubng.

Land of Midian, 2 vols., Set. Richard F. Burton. (Arabia Past & Present Ser.: Vols. 14-15). (Illus.). 1979. 90.00 (*0-900891-55-6*) Oleander Pr.

Land of Milk & Honey. Norton Locke. Ed. by Gwen Costa. LC 90-40784. (Illus.). 350p. 1992. 29.95 (*0-87949-343-7*) Ashley Bks.

Land of Milk & Honey: Poems. Sarah Getty. LC 96-25250. (James Dickey Contemporary Poetry Ser.). 1996. pap. 9.95 (*1-57003-159-2*); text 15.95 (*1-57003-158-4*) U of SC Pr.

Land of Milk & Honey: The Story of Traditional Irish Food & Drink. Brid Mahon. LC 99-194148. 160p. (Orig.). 1998. 12.95 (*1-85635-210-2*, Pub. by Mercier Pr) Irish Amer Bk.

Land of Milk & Honey: The Story of Traditional Irish Food & Drink. Brid Mahon. (Illus.). 176p. (Orig.). 1992. pap. 17.95 (*1-85371-142-X*, Pub. by Poolbeg Pr) Dufour.

Land of Mirrors. Alfred Coppel. 320p. 1988. 18.95 (*0-15-147682-9*) Harcourt.

Land of Mists: Revillagigedo & Gravina Islands, Misty Fiords National Monument, Alaska. 3rd ed. Patricia Roppel. 60p. pap. text 35.00 (*1-57833-111-0*) Todd Commns.

Land of My Dreams. large type ed. Kate North. 464p. 31.99 (*0-7089-4027-7*) Ulverscroft.

Land of My Fathers: A Son's Return to the Basque Country. Robert Laxalt. LC 99-34731. (Basque Ser.). (Illus.). 136p. 2000. 21.00 (*0-87417-338-8*) U of Nev Pr.

Land of My Fathers: 2000 Years of Welsh History. Gwynfor Evans. (Illus.). 1993. reprint ed. pap. 14.95 (*0-86243-265-0*, Pub. by Y Lolfa) Intl Spec Bk.

Land of Nakoda: The Story of the Assiniboine Indians. Writers Program, Montana Staff. LC 73-3634. (American Guide Ser.). reprint ed. 45.00 (*0-404-57934-5*) AMS Pr.

Land of Nam: The Vietnam War in American Film. Eben J. Muse. LC 94-34912. 288p. 1995. 37.00 (*0-8108-2952-5*) Scarecrow.

Land of Narnia: Brian Sibley Explores the World of C. S. Lewis. Brian Sibley. LC 90-4192. (World of Narnia Ser.). (Illus.). 96p. (J). 1998. pap. 9.95 (*0-06-446725-2*) HarpC Child Bks.

Land of Narnia: Brian Sibley Explores the World of C. S. Lewis. Brian Sibley & C. S. Lewis. LC 90-4192. (Illus.). 96p. (YA). (gr. 5 up). 1990. 19.95 (*0-06-025625-7*) HarpC Child Bks.

Land of Nightingales. large type ed. Sally Stewart. (Magna Large Print Ser.). 519p. 1996. 27.99 (*0-7505-0973-2*, Pub. by Mgna Lrg Print) Ulverscroft.

Land of Nine Dragons: Vietnam Today. Joseph R. Yogerst. (Illus.). 204p. 1992. 24.98 (*1-55859-221-0*) Abbeville Pr.

Land of No. Jill Anderson. Ed. by Kathy Blackwelder. LC 87-51628. (Illus.). 40p. (J). (gr. 1-4). 1990. lib. bdg. 14.95 (*0-9608284-5-1*) Timberline Pr.

Land of No Hassles. John Heine. LC 99-18883. 96p. 1999. 7.95 (*1-57587-107-6*) Crane Hill AL.

Land of Nod: And Other Stories. Paul Green. LC 75-33880. 159p. reprint ed. pap. 49.30 (*0-7837-5238-5*, 204497200005) Bks Demand.

***Land of Nod Rockabye.** 1999. pap. 13.95 (*1-56971-356-1*, Pub. by Dark Horse Comics) Penguin Putnam.

Land of Norumbega: Maine in the Age of Exploration & Settlement. Compiled by Susan Danforth. (Illus.). 80p. (Orig.). 1988. pap. 15.00 (*0-9621545-0-4*) ME Humanities.

Land of Numm. John Herron. (Illus.). 14p. (J). 1992. pap. 9.95 (*1-881617-07-6*) Teapot Tales.

Land of One-Armed Men. Nick Stump. 82p. 1993. pap. 12.00 (*0-9634142-1-6*) Loose Canons.

Land of Open Doors: Being Letters from Western Canada, 1911-13. John Burgon Bickersteth. LC 76-41611. (Illus.). 394p. reprint ed. pap. 122.20 (*0-8357-3762-4*, 203648800003) Bks Demand.

Land of Open Hands. Michael G. Michaud. (Illus.). 20p. (Orig.). (C). 1991. pap. 25.00 (*0-9620574-4-4*) MGM Pr.

Land of Opportunity? What's Really Happened to the American Dream. Robert Winter. LC 93-31414. 112p. 1993. 19.95 (*1-883897-00-9*); pap. 8.95 (*1-883897-01-7*) River Rock CA.

Land of Oro Oro. Kathleen Shelton. 52p. 1999. pap. 9.95 (*1-893566-00-5*) Kisco Pubns.

Land of Oz. L. Frank Baum. 21.95 (*0-8488-0785-5*) Amereon Ltd.

Land of Oz. L. Frank Baum. (J). 1997. pap. 2.95 (*0-89375-992-9*) NAL.

Land of Oz. L. Frank Baum. (Illus.). 320p. (YA). (gr. 3 up). 1999. reprint ed. 12.95 (*1-56852-226-6*, Konecky & Konecky) W S Konecky Assocs.

Land of Oz No. 2, 2. L. Frank Baum. LC 79-52645. 288p. (J). 1985. mass mkt. 5.99 (*0-345-33568-6*) Ballantine Pub Grp.

Land of Palestine: West Bank Not East Bank. L. Dean Brown. LC 83-107611. (Middle East Problem Paper Ser.: No. 23). 25p. reprint ed. pap. 30.00 (*0-608-12094-4*, 202413000035) Bks Demand.

Land of Paradox. Noriko Fuku & Andy Grundberg. (Illus.). 64p. 1996. pap. text 36.00 (*1-887040-16-1*) SE Mus Photo.

Land of Paradoxes: Interest Politics in Israel. Yael Yishai. LC 90-10193. (SUNY Series in Israeli Studies). (Illus.). 414p. (C). 1991. pap. text 19.95 (*0-7914-0726-8*) State U NY Pr.

Land of Plenty: Oklahomans in the Cotton Fields of Arizona, 1933-1943. Marsha L. Weisiger. LC 94-36880. (Illus.). 238p. 1995. 24.95 (*0-8061-2696-5*) U of Okla Pr.

Land of Prehistory: A Critical History of American Archaeology. Alice B. Kehoe. LC 97-49609. 256p. (C). 1998. 80.00 (*0-415-92054-X*); pap. 22.99 (*0-415-92055-8*) Routledge.

Land of Promise. Joan Lowery Nixon. LC 92-28591. (Ellis Island Ser.). 1993. 9.09 (*0-606-06359-5*, Pub. by Turtleback) Demco.

Land of Promise. Albert B. Simpson. LC 95-70300. 183p. 1996. pap. 10.99 (*0-87509-621-2*) Chr Pubns.

Land of Promise. T. L. Tedrow. (Days of Laura Ingalls Wilder Ser.). (J). 1992. 10.09 (*0-606-12388-1*, Pub. by Turtleback) Demco.

Land of Promises. Wayne D. Overholser. 176p. 1989. pap. 2.75 (*0-380-70679-2*, Avon Bks) Morrow Avon.

Land of Promises: Aborigines & Development in the East Kimberley. H. C. Coombs et al. LC 89-203658. 165 p. 1989. write for info. (*0-85575-200-9*) AIB & TSIS.

Land of Pure Delight: Selections from the Letters of Thomas Johnes of Hafod 1748 - 1816. Ed. & Intro. by Richard J. Moore-Colyer. 314p. (C). 1992. 50.00 (*0-86383-751-4*, Pub. by Gomer Pr) St Mut.

Land of Pure Delight: Selections from the Letters of Thomas Johnes of Hafod, 1748-1816. Ed. by Richard J. Colyer. 314p. 1992. 47.95 (*0-8464-4702-9*) Beekman Pubs.

Land of Quiet Glory. unabridged ed. Austin Simpson. LC 98-90845. 84p. 1998. pap. write for info. (*0-9666562-0-2*) Austin Simpson.

Land of Rainbows. Cindy Sparks. (Illus.). 24p. (J). (gr. k-3). 1994. pap. 1.10 (*0-9641918-0-6*) Imag Plus.

Land of Rivers: American in Word & Image. Ed. by Peter C. Mancall. (Illus.). 224p. 1996. text 35.00 (*0-8014-3105-0*) Cornell U Pr.

Land of Room Enough & Time Enough: The Story of Monument Valley. rev. ed. Richard E. Klinck. (Illus.). 136p. 1995. reprint ed. pap. 16.95 (*0-9646320-0-4*) Parish Pub.

Land of Saddle-Bags: A Study of the Mountain People of Appalachia. James W. Raine. LC 96-49955. (Illus.). 272p. 1997. pap. 21.00 (*0-8131-0929-9*) U Pr of Ky.

Land of Saddle-Bags: A Study of the Mountain People of Appalachia. James W. Raine. 2000. reprint ed. 35.00 (*1-55888-378-9*) Omnigraphics Inc.

Land of Seven Realms. Illus. by Students of Point Arena Schools Staff. (Land of Six Seasons Ser.). 70p. (Orig.). 1989. pap. 9.00 (*0-944676-05-7*) AHA Bks.

***Land of Silence: A History of Arctic & Antarctic Exploration.** Clements Robert Markham. (Illus.). 540p. 1998. reprint ed. 75.00 (*1-57898-097-6*) Martino Pubng.

Land of Sir Spell-a-Lot: A New Approach to Spelling, Writing, & Thinking. Carla Crutsinger & Katy McDaniel. (Illus.). 220p. (Orig.). (J). (gr. 2). 1997. pap., wbk. ed. 39.95 (*0-944662-06-4*) Brainworks Inc.

***Land of Smiles: A Novel.** T. C. Huo. 1999. 23.95 (*0-525-94281-5*, Dutt) Dutton Plume.

***Land of Smiles: A Novel.** T. C. Huo. 2000. pap. 12.95 (*0-452-28185-7*, Plume) Dutton Plume.

Land of Smiles & Royal White Elephants: Let's Travel to Thailand Together. Jeannette P. Windham. (WIndows on the World Ser.). (Illus.). 80p. (J). (gr. 3-10). 1996. pap. 5.95 (*1-887176-09-8*) Globl Age Pub.

Land of Song: For Primary Grades, Bk. 1. Ed. by K. H. Shute. LC 78-57863. (Granger Poetry Library). (Illus.). (J). (gr. 1-3). 1978. reprint ed. 25.00 (*0-89609-101-5*) Roth Pub Inc.

Land of Sport & Glory: Sport & British Society, 1887-1910. Derek Birley. LC 94-26464. 1995. text 79.95 (*0-7190-4494-4*) Manchester Univ Pr.

Land of Stars. large type ed. Elizabeth Clare. 384p. 1988. 27.99 (*0-7089-1894-8*) Ulverscroft.

Land of Stevin & Huygens. Dirk J. Struik. 182p. 1981. lib. bdg. 93.00 (*90-277-1236-0*) Kluwer Academic.

Land of Stone & Thyme: An Anthology of Palestinian Short Stories. Ed. by Nur Elmessiri & Abdel W. Elmessiri. LC 96-218526. 1998. pap. 12.95 (*0-7043-7092-1*, Pub. by Quartet) Interlink Pub.

Land of Strangers. Lillian Budd. 1993. reprint ed. lib. bdg. 21.95 (*1-56849-165-4*) Buccaneer Bks.

Land of Superior Mirages: New & Selected Poems. Adrien Stoutenburg. Ed. by David R. Slavitt. LC 85-45862. 144p. 1986. 16.50 (*0-8018-3335-3*); pap. 9.95 (*0-8018-3336-1*) Johns Hopkins.

Land of Sweet Liberty. Connie S. Girard. (Illus.). 132p. 1999. pap. 30.00 (*1-887018-77-8*) March Fourth Pub.

Land of Tears Is a Secret Place. Patty L. Lucas. 88p. 1992. student ed. 12.95 (*0-9632065-0-8*) Agape Acad Pr.

Land of the Ancient Corinthians. James Wiseman. (Studies in Mediterranean Archaeology: Vol. L). (Illus.). 150p. (Orig.). 1978. pap. 55.00 (*91-85058-78-5*, Pub. by P Astroms) Coronet Bks.

Land of the Animal Spirits: A One Act Play. Michael P. Jones. (Illus.). 132p. (Orig.). (J). 1985. text 15.00 (*0-89904-113-2*); pap. text 9.99 (*0-89904-114-0*) Crumb Elbow Pub.

Land of the Big. Jan Mogensen. LC 92-18302. (Illus.). 32p. (J). (ps-3). 1993. 14.95 (*1-56656-111-6*, Crocodile Bks) Interlink Pub.

Land of the Blue Flower. Frances Hodgson Burnett. LC 93-19968. (Illus.). 48p. (J). (ps-5). 1993. reprint ed. 15.95 (*0-915811-46-4*, Starseed) H J Kramer Inc.

Land of the Blue Poppy. Frank K. Ward. LC 73-81459. (Illus.). 1973. reprint ed. 12.50 (*0-913728-03-9*) Theophrastus.

Land of the Brave & the Free. Michael Phillips. (Corrie Belle Hollister Ser.: Vol. 7). 32p. (Orig.). (J). 1993. pap. 9.99 (*1-55661-308-3*) Bethany Hse.

Land of the Burnt Thigh. Edith E. Kohl. LC 86-12627. xxxiv, 296p. 1986. pap. 8.95 (*0-87351-199-9*, Borealis Book) Minn Hist.

Land of the Canyons. Laurent Martres. (PhotoTripUSA Ser.). (Illus.). 136p. 1998. pap. 14.95 (*0-916189-04-X*) Graphie Intl.

Land of the Canyons. 2nd rev. ed. Laurent Martres. (Phototrip U. S. A. Ser.). (Illus.). Date not set. pap. 14.95 (*0-916189-07-4*, Phototrip USA) Graphie Intl.

Land of the Cliff-Dwellers. Frederick H. Chapin. LC 74-7945. reprint ed. 52.50 (*0-404-11832-1*) AMS Pr.

***Land of the Commonwealth: A Portrait of the Conserved Landscapes of Massachusetts.** Richard Cheek. (Illus.). 2000. 40.00 (*1-55849-265-8*) U of Mass Pr.

Land of the Crooked Tree. Ulysses P. Hedrick. LC 86-15798. (Great Lakes Bks.). (Illus.). 370p. 1986. reprint ed. pap. 15.95 (*0-8143-1834-7*) Wayne St U Pr.

Land of the Cumbrians: A Study in British Provincial Origins, AD 400-1120. Charles Phythian-Adams. (Illus.). 224p. 1996. 78.95 (*1-85928-327-6*, Pub. by Scolar Pr) Ashgate Pub Co.

Land of the Deepest Shade. Photos by John McWilliams. (Illus.). 108p. 1989. 53.00 (*0-89381-392-3*) Aperture.

Land of the Desert Sun: Texas' Big Bend Country. D. Gentry Steele. LC 98-11929. (Louise Lindsey Merrick Natural Environment Ser.: No. 28). (Illus.). 152p. 1998. 29.95 (*0-89096-824-1*) Tex A&M Univ Pr.

Land of the Desert Sun: Texas' Big Bend Country. D. Gentry Steele. LC 98-11929. (Louise Lindsey Merrick Natural Environment Ser.: Vol. 28). (Illus.). 152p. 1999. pap. 19.95 (*0-89096-835-7*) Tex A&M Univ Pr.

Land of the Dingo People. Percy Trezise. 1999. 16.00 (*0-207-19091-7*) HarpC.

Land of the Dollar. George W. Steevens. LC 79-169775. (Select Bibliographies Reprint Ser.). 1977. reprint ed. 23.95 (*0-8369-5995-7*) Ayer.

Land of the Dons. L. Williams. 1976. lib. bdg. 59.95 (*0-8490-2123-5*) Gordon Pr.

Land of the Dragon. Madge Miller. (J). 1946. 6.00 (*0-87602-148-8*) Anchorage.

Land of the Eagle. Harry F. Casey. 400p. 1997. pap. 12.95 (*0-9659184-0-8*) Scribe Pub.

Land of the Eagle: A Natural History of North America. Robert M. Peck. (Illus.). 288p. 1991. 30.00 (*0-671-75596-X*) Summit Bks.

***Land of the Enchanters: Egyptian Short Stories from the Earliest Times to the Present.** rev. ed. Bernard Lewis. Ed. by Stanley M. Burstein. 200p. 2000. 38.95 (*1-55876-249-3*); pap. 18.95 (*1-55876-250-7*) Wiener Pubs Inc.

Land of the Firebird: The Beauty of Old Russia. 13th ed. Suzanne Massie. LC 80-12860. (Illus.). 493p. (C). 1980. reprint ed. pap. text 30.00 (*0-9644184-1-X*) HeartTree Pr.

Land of the Five Suns. Kay McManus. LC 97-11871. (Looking at Myths & Legends Ser.). (Illus.). 48p. 1997. 12.95 (*0-8442-4762-6*, 47626, Natl Textbk Co) NTC Contemp Pub Co.

Land of the Four Quarters. Olivia Diamond. Ed. by Robert Olmsted. LC 94-66927. (Illus.). 104p. (Orig.). 1994. pap. 8.95 (*0-89002-322-0*) Northwoods Pr.

Land of the Four Winds. Veronica F. Ellis. LC 92-72001. (Illus.). 32p. (J). (gr. 1-4). 1993. 14.95 (*0-940975-38-6*); pap. 6.95 (*0-940975-39-4*) Just Us Bks.

Land of the Four Winds: Kpa Nieh Kpau. Veronica Freeman Ellis. 1993. 12.15 (*0-606-08795-8*, Pub. by Turtleback) Demco.

Land of the Fox: Saga of Outagamie County, Wisconsin. Gordon A. Bubolz. (Illus.). 302p. 1994. reprint ed. lib. bdg. 32.50 (*0-8328-3866-7*) Higginson Bk Co.

Land of the Fragile Giants: Landscapes, Environments, & Peoples of the Loess Hills. Ed. by Cornelia F. Mutel & Mary Swander. LC 94-14909. (Bur Oak Original Ser.). (Illus.). 168p. (Orig.). 1994. pap. 24.95 (*0-87745-477-9*) U of Iowa Pr.

Land of the Free. William Moss. (Cyberpunk Ser.). (Illus.). 120p. (Orig.). 1994. pap., boxed set 18.00 (*0-937279-38-2*, CP3231) Talsorian.

Land of the Free. Archibald Macleish. LC 77-9353. (Photography Ser.). (Illus.). 1977. reprint ed. pap. 7.95 (*0-306-80080-2*) Da Capo.

Land of the Free. Charles A. Seltzer. 1976. reprint ed. lib. bdg. 24.95 (*0-88411-112-1*) Amereon Ltd.

Land of the Free: Bjornstjerne Bjornson's America Letters, 1880-1881. Eva L. Haugen. Ed. by Einar Haugen. 330p. 1978. 20.00 (*0-87732-061-6*) Norwegian-Am Hist Assn.

***Land of the Free: What Makes Americans Different.** David Graham. 1999. 35.00 (*0-89381-871-2*) Aperture.

***Land of the Giants: New York's Polo Grounds.** Stew Thornley. (Illus.). 192p. 2000. 32.50 (*1-56639-796-0*) Temple U Pr.

Land of the Golden Clouds, 1. Archie Weller. 1999. pap. 14.95 (*1-86448-338-5*) Allen & Unwin Pty.

Land of the Good Shadows: The Life Story of Anauta, an Eskimo Woman. Heluiz Washburne & Anauta Blackmore. LC 74-5888. reprint ed. 52.50 (*0-404-11697-3*) AMS Pr.

Land of the Great Gray Wolf. Liz Howell. (Illus.). 70p. (Orig.). 1988. pap. text 5.95 (*0-943120-05-5*) Dragonsbreath.

Land of the Great Image. Maurice Collis. LC 85-13438. (New Directions Classics Ser.). (Illus.). 256p. (Orig.). 1985. reprint ed. pap. 9.95 (*0-8112-0972-5*, NDP612, Pub. by New Directions) Norton.

Land of the Gurkhas. William B. Northey. LC 78-179229. (Illus.). reprint ed. 54.00 (*0-404-54856-3*) AMS Pr.

Land of the Hittites. John Garstang. (C). 1988. 135.00 (*1-85077-204-5*, Pub. by Darf Pubs Ltd) St Mut.

Land of the Lakes. Melvyn Bragg. (Illus.). 248p. 1991. pap. 24.95 (*0-340-52372-7*, Pub. by Hodder & Stought Ltd) Trafalgar.

Land of the Lamas: Notes of a Journey Through China, Mongolia & Tibet. William W. Rockhill. (C). 1988. reprint ed. 32.00 (*81-206-0354-0*, Pub. by Asian Educ Servs) S Asia.

Land of the Leal. James Barke. (Canongate Classics Ser.). 614p. 1997. pap. 13.95 (*0-86241-142-4*) Interlink Pub.

Land of the Lion & the Sun: Persia. A. D. Shabaz. 1977. lib. bdg. 59.95 (*0-8490-2125-1*) Gordon Pr.

Land of the Living. James T. O'Connor. 1993. pap. 5.95 (*0-89942-174-1*, 174/04) Catholic Bk Pub.

Land of the Living: The Danish Folk High Schools & Denmark's Non-Violent Path to Modernization. Steven M. Borish. LC 91-12365. (Illus.). 512p. (C). 1991. 27.95 (*0-931892-62-7*) B Dolphin Pub.

Land of the Living Dead: A Narration of the Perilous Sojourn Therein of George Cowper, Mariner, in the Year 1835. Neal Fyne. Ed. by R. Reginald & Douglas Melville. LC 77-84224. (Lost Race & Adult Fantasy Ser.). (Illus.). 1978. reprint ed. lib. bdg. 25.95 (*0-405-10977-6*) Ayer.

Land of the Long White Cloud: Maori Myths, Tales & Legends. Kiri Te Kanawa. (Illus.). 128p. (J). (gr. 3-5). 1997. pap. 16.95 (*1-86205-075-9*, Pub. by Pavilion Bks Ltd) Trafalgar.

Land of the Lost Teddies. Emma Fischel. (Young Puzzle Adventures Ser.). (Illus.). 32p. (J). (ps-2). 1998. pap. 5.95 (*0-7460-2776-1*, Usborne); lib. bdg. 13.95 (*0-88110-968-1*, Usborne) EDC.

Land of the Lost Teddies Kid Kit. Usborne Books Staff. (Illus.). (J). (ps-2). 1999. 12.95 (*1-58086-037-0*) EDC.

Land of the Miamis: Account of the Struggle to Secure Possession of the North West from the End of the Revolution until 1812. Elmore Barce. (Illus.). 422p. 1997. reprint ed. lib. bdg. 45.00 (*0-8328-7090-0*) Higginson Bk Co.

Land of the Millrats. Richard M. Dorson. LC 81-2944. (Illus.). 265p. (C). 1981. 34.50 (*0-674-50855-6*) HUP.

Land of the Minotaurs. Richard A. Knaak. (DragonLance Lost Histories Ser.: Vol. 4). 1996. pap. 5.99 (*0-7869-0472-0*, Pub. by TSR Inc) Random.

Land of the Moors. B. Meakin. 490p. 1986. 350.00 (*1-85077-100-6*, Pub. by Darf Pubs Ltd) St Mut.

Land of the Morning: Treasures of the Philippines. David Baradas. (Orig.). 1995. pap. write for info. (*1-877742-04-X*) SF Craft & Folk.

Land of the Morning Calm: Korea & American Security. A. James Gregor. 142p. 1990. pap. 14.50 (*0-89633-146-6*); lib. bdg. 31.50 (*0-89633-145-8*) Ethics & Public Policy.

Land of the Nunch: Discovery, Bk 1. Douglas Kirk. Ed. by Valerie Matthews. LC 86-60529. (Illus.). 160p. (Orig.). 1986. pap. 3.95 (*0-934279-02-0*) Morton Falls Pub.

Land of the Ocean Mists: The Wild Ocean Coast West of Glacier Bay. Francis E. Caldwell. Ed. by Robert DeArmond. LC 86-3338. (Illus.). 209p. (Orig.). 1996. 7.95 (*0-88240-311-7*) Anchor Pub.

Land of the Pink Pearl: Recollections of Life in the Bahamas. L. D. Powles. Ed. & Intro. by Neil E. Sealey. (Illus.). 192p. 1996. reprint ed. pap. 12.95 (*0-9643786-3-9*) Media Pubng.

Land of the Poets Ireland. David Lyons. (Illus.). 64p. 1998. 7.98 (*1-85648-324-X*, Thunder Bay) Advantage Pubs.

Land of the Poets Lake District. David Lyons. (Land of the Poets Ser.). (Illus.). 64p. 1998. 7.98 (*1-85648-325-8*, Thunder Bay) Advantage Pubs.

Land of the Poets Scotland. David Lyons. (Illus.). 64p. 1998. 7.98 (*1-85648-323-1*, Thunder Bay) Advantage Pubs.

Land of the Poison Wind. Arthur Magida. 2000. 25.00 (*0-465-01419-4*) HarpC.

Land of the Post Rock: Its Origins, History & People. Grace Muilenburg & Ada Swineford. LC 74-23833. (Illus.). xiv, 210p. 1975. pap. 12.95 (*0-7006-0194-5*) U Pr of KS.

Land of the Quinault. Jacqueline Storm et al. Ed. by Pauline Capoeman. LC 86-60965. (Illus.). 315p. (Orig.). 1990. pap. 24.95 (*0-940359-00-6*) Quinault Ind.

Land of the Red Soil. Douglas Baldwin. (Illus.). 90p. 1990. 9.95 (*0-920304-96-6*, Pub. by Gynergy-Ragweed) U of Toronto Pr.

Land of the Shadow. Gilbert Morris. LC 93-13781. (Appomattox Saga Ser.: Vol. 4). 338p. 1993. 10.99 (*0-8423-5742-4*) Tyndale Hse.

An Asterisk (*) at the beginning of an entry indicates that the title is appearing for the first time.

Land of the Sherpas. Ella Mailart. 1998. pap. 42.00 (*0-7855-7425-5*, Pub. by Ratna Pustak Bhandar) St Mut.

Land of the Sleeping Dinosaurs: A Blackfoot Creation Tale of the Rocky Mountains. Geraldine A. Walton. (Illus.). 304p. 1995. 7.95 (*0-614-06311-6*) Spirit Talk Pr.

Land of the Snow Lion. large type ed. Elaine Brook. (Illus.). 448p. 1988. 27.99 (*0-7089-1908-1*) Ulverscroft.

Land of the Spirit. Thomas N. Page. (Notable American Authors Ser.). 1999. reprint ed. lib. bdg. 125.00 (*0-7812-4713-6*) Rprt Serv.

Land of the Spotted Eagle. Luther Standing Bear. LC 77-14062. (Illus.). xxvii, 259p. 1978. reprint ed. pap. 11.95 (*0-8032-5890-9*, Bison Books) U of Nebr Pr.

Land of the Tamilians & Its Missions. E. R. Baierlein. Tr. by J. D. Gribble. (C). 1995. reprint ed. 24.00 (*81-206-1006-7*, Pub. by Asian Educ Servs) S Asia.

Land of the Tiger: A Natural History of the Indian Subcontinent. Valmik Thapar. 285p. 1998. 29.95 (*0-520-21470-6*, Pub. by U CA Pr) Cal Prin Full Svc.

***Land of the Turkey & the Deer: Recent Research in Yucatan - Archaeology-Ethnography.** Ed. by Ruth Gubler. LC 97-76085. (Illus.). 160p. 1999. pap. 40.00 (*0-911437-72-X*) Labyrinthos.

Land of the Umpqua: A History of Douglas County, Oregon. Stephen D. Beckham. (Illus.). 288p. (Orig.). 1986. pap. 15.00 (*0-9616574-1-3*); text 25.00 (*0-9616574-0-5*) Douglas Cty Planning.

Land of the Winged Horseman: Art in Poland, 1572-1764. Jan K. Ostrowski. (Illus.). 380p. 1999. 65.00 (*0-300-07918-4*) Yale U Pr.

Land of the Winged Horseman: Art in Poland, 1572-1764. Jan K. Ostrowski et al. LC 98-37979. 380p. 1999. 60.00 (*0-88397-131-3*) Art Srvc Intl.

Land of This Bride: Poems of New England & Nearby. William Hunter. (American Poetry Ser.). (Illus.). 68p. (Orig.). 1990. pap. 10.95 (*0-9624440-0-6*); pap. text 8.95 (*0-685-33301-9*) Wild Leaf Pr.

Land of Tomorrow. large type ed. Mons Daveson. (Linford Romance Library). 280p. 1984. pap. 16.99 (*0-7089-6031-6*) Ulverscroft.

Land of Trees: Scannings from Quinault Country, the Grays Harbor Region, & Beyond, 1774-1997. Larry J. Workman et al. LC 97-92588. (Illus.). 1997. write for info. (*0-940359-01-4*) Quinault Ind.

Land of Tuppitry: An Adventure in Imagination. Abigail Nunn. (Illus.). 96p. (J). (gr. 2-4). 1989. reprint ed. pap. 4.95 (*0-9620765-3-8*) Victory Press.

Land of Two Peoples. Martin Buber. Ed. & Comment by Paul R. Mendes-Flohr. 1994. 28.50 (*0-8446-6722-6*) Peter Smith.

Land of U. DeeAnn Champlin. (Little Lyrics Short Vowel Collection: Vol. 5). (Illus.). (J). (gr. k-2). 1998. pap. 12.00 (*1-893429-29-6*) Little Lyrics.

Land of Ulro. Czeslaw Milosz. Tr. by Louis Iribarne. 304p. 1984. text 17.95 (*0-374-18323-6*) FS&G.

Land of Ulro. Czeslaw Milosz. Tr. by Louis Iribarne. LC 84-8157. 304p. 2000. pap. 14.00 (*0-374-51937-4*) FS&G.

Land of Unicorns, 1 vol. Nancy Sippel Carpenter. (Nature Sticker Stories Ser.). (ps-1). 1999. pap. text 4.99 (*0-448-41984-X*) Putnam Pub Group.

Land of Upside Down. Ludwig Tieck. Tr. by Oscar Mandel. LC 76-50288. 123p. 1978. 22.50 (*0-8386-2061-2*) Fairleigh Dickinson.

Land of Uz. G. Wyman Bury. 1999. pap. 30.00 (*1-85964-121-0*) Garnet Publishing Ltd.

Land of Volcanic Ash: A Play in Two Parts. rev. ed. Kubo Sakae. Tr. by David G. Goodman. (Cornell East Asia Ser.: No. 40). 250p. 1993. pap. 14.45 (*0-939657-83-X*) Cornell East Asia Pgm.

Land of Walking Trees: Reflections for the Chronically Ill. Michael Hansen. 1993. pap. 10.00 (*1-86371-169-4*) Harper SF.

Land of War: How Arms Trade Compromises Israel's Security. Abraham Gal. Tr. by Judith S. Gordon from HEB. LC 93-77808. (Illus.). 310p. pap. 14.95 (*0-9636437-1-1*) Gilar Pr.

Land of War: How Arms Trade Compromises Israel's Security. Abraham Gal. Tr. by Judith S. Gordon from HEB. LC 93-77808. (Illus.). 310p. 1993. 19.80 (*0-9636437-0-3*) Gilar Pr.

***Land of Waters: The South American Rainforest & Savannah.** Ro McConnell. (Illus.). 328p. 2000. 32.50 (*1-85776-458-7*, Pub. by Book Guild Ltd) Trans-Atl Phila.

Land of Whistlepunks & Wild Things: Forests Yesterday & Today. Maribeth Darby. LC 97-183210. (Illus.). 128p. (J). 1997. 14.95 (*1-57168-112-4*, Eakin Pr) Sunbelt Media.

Land of Wilno: or My First Journey to Poland, Lithuania & Byelorussia. James M. Badura. 250p. 1995. 32.00 (*0-614-02654-7*); pap. 16.00 (*0-614-02655-5*) Szwede Slavic.

Land of Women: Tales of Sex & Gender from Early Ireland. Lisa M. Bitel. LC 95-39296. (Illus.). 296p. 1996. 42.50 (*0-8014-3095-X*) Cornell U Pr.

Land of Women: Tales of Sex & Gender from Early Ireland. Lisa M. Bitel. (Illus.). 336p. 1998. pap. text 16.95 (*0-8014-8544-4*) Cornell U Pr.

Land of Wooden Gods. Jan Fridegard. Tr. & Afterword by Robert E. Bjork. LC 89-5275. (Modern Scandinavian Literature in Translation Ser.: No. 1). 219p. 1989. reprint ed. pap. 67.90 (*0-608-03990-X*, 206472200010) Bks Demand.

Land of Yamme Bk. 1: A Place for Friends. large type ed. Louise Hudson. (Illus.). 24p. (J). (gr. 2-5). 1998. 12.95 (*0-9665435-0-5*) Sis Act Pub.

Land of Yamme Bk. 2: Where I Find God. large type ed. Louise Hudson. (Illus.). 24p. (J). (gr. 2-5). 1998. 12.95 (*0-9665435-1-3*) Sis Act Pub.

Land of Zini. C. H. Stigand. (Illus.). 251p. 1966. reprint ed. 47.50 (*0-7146-1723-7*, BHA-01723, Pub. by F Cass Pubs) Intl Spec Bk.

Land-Office Business: Land & Housing Prices in Rapidly Growing Metropolitan Areas. Gary Sands. LC 81-47782. (Lincoln Institute of Land Policy Bk.). 171p. reprint ed. pap. 53.10 (*0-7837-3273-2*, 204329200007) Bks Demand.

Land O'Lakes Baking. Land O'Lakes Staff. (Land O'Lakes Cooking Traditions Ser.). (Illus.). 132p. 2000. pap. 14.95 (*0-9663558-3-0*, Pub. by Tiger Oak) Natl Bk Netwk.

Land O'Lakes Comfort Foods. Land O'Lakes Staff. (Land O'Lakes Cooking Traditions Ser.: No. I). (Illus.). 1999. pap. 14.95 (*0-9663558-5-7*, Pub. by Tiger Oak) Natl Bk Netwk.

Land O'Lakes Cookies. Land O'Lakes Staff. (Land O'Lakes Cooking Traditions Ser.). (Illus.). 132p. (Orig.). 1999. pap. 14.95 (*0-9663558-2-2*, Pub. by Tiger Oak) Natl Bk Netwk.

Land O'Lakes Desserts. Land O'Lakes Staff. (Land O'Lakes Cooking Traditions Ser.). (Illus.). 132p. 2000. pap. 14.95 (*0-9663558-4-9*, Pub. by Tiger Oak) Natl Bk Netwk.

Land O'Lakes Holiday Cooking. Land O'Lakes Staff. (Land O'Lakes Cooking Traditions Ser.). (Illus.). 132p. (Orig.). 1999. pap. 14.95 (*0-9663558-6-5*, Pub. by Tiger Oak) Natl Bk Netwk.

Land Operculates: Cyclophoridae, Truncatellidae, Assimineidae, Helicinidae, Vol. 3. (Fauna of British India Ser.). xiv, 386p. 30.00 (*0-88065-092-3*) Scholarly Pubns.

Land or Death: The Peasant Struggle in Peru. Hugo Blanco. LC 73-186689. 178p. 1972. reprint ed. pap. 14.95 (*0-87348-266-2*); reprint ed. lib. bdg. 45.00 (*0-87348-265-4*) Pathfinder NY.

Land or Peace: Whither Israel? Yael Yishai. (Publication Ser.: No. 352). 265p. 1987. 12.78 (*0-8179-8521-2*) Hoover Inst Pr.

Land or Religion? The Sardar & Kherwar Movements in Bihar, 1858-1895. John MacDougall. 1986. 27.00 (*0-8364-1591-4*, Pub. by Manohar) S Asia.

Land Out There: A Scottish Land Anthology. Ed. by George Bruce & Frank Rennie. (Illus.). 248p. 1991. pap. 25.90 (*0-08-040907-5*, Pub. by Aberdeen U Pr) Macmillan.

Land Ownership: Information on the Acreage, Management & Use of Federal & Other Lands. (Illus.). 48p. (Orig.). (C). 1996. pap. text 25.00 (*0-7881-2861-2*) DIANE Pub.

Land Ownership: Similarities & Differences in the Management of Selected State & Federal Land Units. Lloyd L. Adams et al. (Illus.). 57p. (C). 1998. pap. text 20.00 (*0-7881-7552-1*) DIANE Pub.

Land Ownership & Use. 3rd ed. Curtis J. Berger. LC 81-86687. 1983. 56.00 (*0-316-09154-5*, Aspen Law & Bus) Aspen Pub.

Land Ownership Patterns in the Tanana River Basin, Alaska, 1984. Willem W. Van Hees. (Illus.). 20p. 1998. reprint ed. pap. 3.00 (*0-89904-520-0*) Crumb Elbow Pub.

Land Ownership under Colonial Rule: Korea's Japanese Experience, 1900-1935. Edwin Gragert. 224p. (C). 1994. text 44.00 (*0-8248-1497-5*) UH Pr.

Land Pacts see Pacts & Treaties Series

Land Parcel Identifiers for Information Systems. D. David Moyer & Kenneth P. Fisher. LC 73-91110. 465p. 1973. 25.00 (*0-910058-59-8*, 304860); pap. 20.00 (*0-910058-58-X*, 304860) W S Hein.

Land, Peace, & Participation: The Development of Post-War Agricultural Policy in El Salvador & the Role of the Ward Bank. Michael Foley & Geoff Thale. Ed. by George Vickers. Tr. by Juan L. Guillen. 32p. (C). 1997. pap. text. write for info. (*0-929513-39-8*) WOLA.

Land, People & Cultural Institutions. Daniel Boamah-Wiafe. (Illus.). 380p. (C). 1993. pap. write for info. (*0-9624567-5-6*) Wisdom NE.

Land, People & Government: Public Lands Policy in the South. Ed. by Peter J. Larmour et al. LC 82-188428. 203p. reprint ed. pap. 63.00 (*0-7837-3945-1*, 204371000011) Bks Demand.

Land, Piety & Peoplehood. Richard K. MacMaster. LC 84-15790. (Mennonite Experience in America Ser.: Vol. 1). 344p. (Orig.). 1985. pap. 19.99 (*0-8361-1261-X*) Herald Pr.

Land Pirates. large type ed. Jackson Cole. 1981. 12.00 (*0-7089-0729-6*) Ulverscroft.

Land Planner's Environmental Handbook. William B. Honachefsky. LC 90-23204. (Illus.). 722p. 1991. 145.00 (*0-8155-1267-8*) Noyes.

Land Planning in National Parks & Forests: A Selective Bibliography, Nos. 1291-1292. Ed. by Julia Johnson & Glenna Dunning. 1977. 7.00 (*0-686-19693-7*, Sage Prdcls Pr) Sage.

Land Plants: Notes for a Short Course. Ed. by T. W. Broadhead. (Studies in Geology). (Illus.). vi, 226p. pap. 12.00 (*0-910249-14-8*) U of Tenn Geo.

Land Policies in Kern County. Paul W. Gates. 35p. 1978. pap. 2.00 (*0-943500-02-8*) Kern Historical.

Land Policy. Ed. by Michael Bernard & Mark Schneider. (Orig.). 1984. pap. 15.00 (*0-918592-70-4*) Pol Studies.

Land Policy: Problems & Alternatives. 1985. 89.95 (*0-566-00672-3*) Ashgate Pub Co.

Land Policy & Agriculture in Eastern & Southern Africa: Selected Papers Presented at a Workshop Held in Gaborone, Botswana, 14-19 February 1982. 150p. 20.00 (*92-808-0604-1*, E.86.III.A.6) UN.

Land Policy & Boom-Bust Real Estate Markets. Ed. by Jonathan D. Cheney. 32p. 1994. pap. 14.00 (*1-55844-126-3*) Lincoln Inst Land.

Land Policy & Speculation in Pennsylvania, 1779-1800. Norman R. Wilkinson. Ed. by Stuart Bruchey. LC 78-56693. (Management of Public Lands in the U. S. Ser.). (Illus.). 1979. lib. bdg. 31.95 (*0-405-11357-9*) Ayer.

Land Policy in Developing Countries. Lincoln Institute of Land Policy Staff. LC HD1131.L34. (Lincoln Institute Monograph Ser.: No. 84-4). 78p. reprint ed. pap. 30.00 (*0-7837-2156-0*, 204245600004) Bks Demand.

Land Policy in Modern Indonesia: A Study of Land Issues in the New Order Period. Colin MacAndrews. LC 86-5144. (Lincoln Institute of Land Policy Bk.). (Illus.). 127p. reprint ed. pap. 39.40 (*0-7837-5764-6*, 204542700006) Bks Demand.

Land Policy Problems in East Asia - Toward New Choices: A Comparative Study of Japan, Korea & Taiwan. Ed. by Bruce Koppel & D. Young Kim. iv, 460p. 1993. text 18.00 (*0-86638-162-7*) EW Ctr HI.

Land, Politics & Nationalism: A Study of the Irish Land Question. Philip Bull. LC 96-28749. 288p. 1996. text 45.00 (*0-312-16442-4*) St Martin.

Land, Politics, & Society in Eighteenth-Century Tipperary. Thomas P. Power. LC 93-22481. (Illus.). 392p. (C). 1993. text 70.00 (*0-19-820316-0*, Clarendon Pr) OUP.

***Land, Power & Market: A Bihar District under Colonial Rule, 1890-1947.** Jacques Pouchepadass. LC 99-46676. 1999. write for info. (*0-7619-9402-5*) Sage.

Land, Power & People: Rural Elite in Transition, 1801 to 1970. Rajendra Singh. 262p. (C). 1989. text 26.00 (*0-8039-9555-5*) Sage.

Land, Power, & Poverty: Agrarian Transformation & Political Change in Central America. Charles D. Brockett. (Thematic Studies in Latin America). 240p. (C). 1990. text 39.95 (*0-04-497027-7*); pap. text 16.95 (*0-04-445754-5*) Routledge.

Land, Power & Poverty: Agrarian Transformation & Political Conflict in Central America. 2nd ed. Charles D. Brockett. LC 98-5451. (Thematic Studies in Latin America). 288p. (C). 1998. pap. 25.00 (*0-8133-8695-0*, Pub. by Westview) HarpC.

Land Predators. John Stidworthy. (Remarkable World Ser.). (Illus.). 48p. (J). (gr. 3-8). 1996. lib. bdg. 24.26 (*1-56847-416-4*) Raintree Steck-V.

Land Predators: From Bobcats to Badgers. Erin P. Swan. LC 98-2705. (Animals in Order Ser.). (J). 1999. 23.00 (*0-531-11451-1*) Watts.

***Land Predators Around the World.** Erin P. Swan. LC 99-59418. (Animals in Order Ser.). (Illus.). (J). 2001. pap. write for info. (*0-531-11627-1*) Watts.

Land Predators of North America. Erin Pembrey. 1999. pap. text 6.95 (*0-531-15945-0*) Watts.

Land (Primary) Ava D. Drutman. (Illus.). 48p. (J). (gr. 1-3). 1992. student ed. 6.99 (*0-86653-599-3*, 1406) Good Apple.

Land Problem in the Developed Economy. Andrew H. Dawson. LC 83-24360. 280p. 1984. 50.00 (*0-389-20456-0*, N8017) B&N Imports.

Land Problems & Policies. V. Webster Johnson & Raleigh Barlowe. Ed. by Stuart Bruchey. LC 78-53549. (Development of Public Land Law in the U. S. Ser.). 1979. reprint ed. lib. bdg. 33.95 (*0-405-11378-1*) Ayer.

Land Problems & Policies. Ed. by John F. Timmons & William G. Murray. LC 72-2870. (Use & Abuse of America's Natural Resources Ser.). 312p. 1972. reprint ed. 23.95 (*0-405-04537-9*) Ayer.

Land, Property & Construction in the People's Republic of China. Anthony Walker. LC HC0427.92.W3. 152p. 1991. reprint ed. pap. 47.20 (*0-608-01388-9*, 206214900002) Bks Demand.

Land Quality Indicators. Christian Pieri et al. LC 95-44781. (Discussion Paper Ser.: Vol. 315). 74p. 1996. pap. 22.00 (*0-8213-3511-1*) World Bank.

Land Quality Indicators & Their Use in Sustainable Agriculture & Rural Development. LC 98-126635. (Land & Water Bulletin Ser.: No. 5). 212p. 1997. pap. 25.00 (*92-5-103975-5*, F39755, Pub. by FAO) Bernan Associates.

Land Question: Property in Land & the Condition of Labor. Henry George. LC 82-18516. 352p. 1982. 18.00 (*0-911312-59-5*) Schalkenbach.

Land Question in Palestine, 1917-1939. Kenneth W. Stein. LC 83-21872. (Illus.). 336p. reprint ed. pap. 104.20 (*0-608-06017-8*, 206634500008) Bks Demand.

Land Readjustment: A Different Approach to Financing Urbanization. Ed. by William A. Doebele. LC 82-47967. 247p. reprint ed. pap. 76.60 (*0-7837-5763-8*, 204542600006) Bks Demand.

Land Readjustment: A Modern Approach to Urbanization. Gerhard Larsson. LC 93-1214. 160p. 1993. 72.95 (*1-85628-507-3*, Pub. by Avebry) Ashgate Pub Co.

Land Readjustment - The Japanese System: A Reconnaissance & a Digest. Ed. by Luciano Minerbi et al. LC 85-31964. (Lincoln Institute of Land Policy Bk.). (Illus.). 284p. reprint ed. pap. 88.10 (*0-7837-5762-X*, 204542500006) Bks Demand.

Land Reclamation: Achieving Sustainable Benefits: Proceedings of the 4th International Conference, Nottingham, UK, 7-11 September, 1998. Ed. by H. R. Fox et al. (Illus.). 560p. 1998. text 87.00 (*90-5809-002-7*, Pub. by A A Balkema) Ashgate Pub Co.

Land Reclamation: Advances in Research & Technology. LC 92-74908. 381p. 1993. pap. 65.75 (*0-929355-37-7*) Am Soc Ag Eng.

Land Reclamation: An End to Dereliction? M. C. Davies. 422p. 1991. mass mkt. 139.95 (*1-85166-658-3*) Elsevier.

Land Reclamation & Biomass Production Using Municipal Wastewater & Sludge. William E. Sopper et al. LC 82-80452. (Illus.). 544p. 1982. 25.00 (*0-271-00314-6*) Pa St U Pr.

Land Reclamation in Italy. Cesare Longobardi. 1976. lib. bdg. 34.95 (*0-8490-2127-8*) Gordon Pr.

Land-Reclamation in Italy: Rural Revival in the Building of a Nation. Cesare Longobardi. LC 78-180410. (Illus.). reprint ed. 45.00 (*0-404-56134-9*) AMS Pr.

Land Records of Sussex County, Delaware, 1722-1731: Deed Book F, No. 6. Johnita P. Malone. viii, 124p. 1997. pap. text 11.50 (*0-7884-0775-9*, MO45) Heritage Bk.

Land Records of the Attakapas Vol. 2, Pt. 1: Conveyance Records of Attakapas Country, 1804-1818. Glenn R. Conrad. LC 90-81684. 430p. 1990. 24.95 (*0-940984-57-1*) Univ LA Lafayette.

***Land Reform: Proposals for Legislation.** Scotland. Scottish Executive & Scotland. Parliament. LC 99-495122. (Illus.). 1999. write for info. (*0-10-888001-X*) Statnry Office.

Land Reform: The Italian Experience. Russell King. LC 74-161094. 257 p. 1973. write for info. (*0-408-70472-1*) Buttrwrth-Heinemann.

Land Reform - Land Settlement & Cooperatives, 1995. FAO Staff. 110p. 1995. pap. 12.00 (*0-614-25699-2*, F99828, Pub. by FAO) Bernan Associates.

Land Reform, American Style. Ed. by Charles C. Geisler & Frank J. Popper. LC 83-13725. 366p. 1984. text 53.00 (*0-86598-016-0*, R3873) Rowman.

Land Reform & Agrarian Change: Study of a Marwar Village from Raj to Swaraj. R. Thomas Rosin. 260p. 1987. 36.00 (*81-7033-033-5*, Pub. by Rawat Pubns) S Asia.

Land Reform & Economic Development in China: A Study of Institutional Change & Development Finance. Victor D. Lippit. LC 74-15391. 194p. reprint ed. pap. 60.20 (*0-8357-2614-2*, 204010500014) Bks Demand.

Land Reform & Farm Restructuring in Moldova: Progress & Prospects. Zvi Lerman et al. LC 98-27897. (Discussion Paper Ser.: No. 398). 121p. 1998. pap. 22.00 (*0-8213-4317-3*, 14317) World Bank.

Land Reform & Farm Restructuring in Ukraine. Zvi Lerman et al. LC 94-43327. (Discussion Paper Ser.: Vol. 270). 125p. 1995. pap. 22.00 (*0-8213-3149-3*, 13149) World Bank.

Land Reform & Farm Restructuring in Ukraine. Zvi Lerman et al. (RUS.). 148p. 1995. pap. 22.00 (*0-8213-3242-2*, 13242) World Bank.

Land Reform & Social Change in Iran. Afsaneh Najmabadi. LC 87-31630. 256p. reprint ed. pap. 79.40 (*0-7837-6870-2*, 204670000003) Bks Demand.

***Land Reform & Suatainable Development.** R. W. Dixon-Gough. 305p. 1999. 78.95 (*0-7546-1052-7*) Ashgate Pub Co.

Land Reform & the Future of Landownership in South Africa. A. J. Van Der Walt. 133p. 1991. pap. 24.00 (*0-7021-2592-X*, Pub. by Juta & Co) Gaunt.

Land Reform & Tourism Development: Policy Making in the Philippines. Linda K. Richter. 240p. 1982. 22.95 (*0-87073-413-X*); pap. 15.95 (*0-87073-414-8*) Schenkman Bks Inc.

Land Reform & Working-Class Experience in Britain & the United States, 1800-1862. Jamie L. Bronstein. LC 98-28068. viii, 372 p. 1999. write for info. (*0-8047-3451-8*) Stanford U Pr.

Land Reform in China & North Vietnam: Consolidating the Revolution at the Village Level. Edwin E. Moise. LC 82-15900. 319p. 1983. reprint ed. pap. 98.90 (*0-608-03564-5*, 205964800009) Bks Demand.

Land Reform in Latin America: The Dominican Case. Carrie A. Meyer. LC 88-39661. 142p. 1989. 49.95 (*0-275-93202-8*, C3202, Praeger Pubs) Greenwood.

***Land Reform in Russia, 1906-1917: Peasant Responses to Stolypin's Project of Rural Transformation.** Judith Pallot. LC 98-33244. (Illus.). 272p. 1999. text 75.00 (*0-19-820656-9*) OUP.

Land Reform in the Former Soviet Union & Eastern Europe. Stephen K. Wegren. LC 97-17428. 296p. (C). 1998. 90.00 (*0-415-17066-4*) Routledge.

Land Reform in Ukraine: The First Five Years. Csaba Csaki & Zvi Lerman. LC 97-28277. (Discussion Paper Ser.: No. 371R). 126p. 1997. pap. 22.00 (*0-8213-4008-5*, 14008) World Bank.

Land Reform in Ukraine: The First Five Years. Csaba Csaki & Zvi Lerman. (Discussion Paper Ser.: No. 371R). (RUS.). 139p. 1998. pap. 22.00 (*0-8213-4302-5*, 14302) World Bank.

Land Reforms & Changing Agrarian Relations. C. B. Damle. (C). 1993. 29.00 (*81-7033-177-3*, Pub. by Rawat Pubns) S Asia.

Land Reforms & Democratic Development. Roy L. Prosterman & Jeffrey M. Riedinger. LC 87-4188. (Johns Hopkins Studies in Development). 328p. reprint ed. pap. 101.70 (*0-608-06187-5*, 206651900008) Bks Demand.

Land Reforms in India. Bikram Sarkar. 1989. 31.00 (*81-7024-260-6*, Pub. by Ashish Pub Hse) S Asia.

Land Reforms in India: A Survey of Policy, Legislation & Implementation. P. S. Appu. 1998. 40.00 (*81-259-0233-3*, Pub. by Vikas) S Asia.

Land Reforms in India: Achievements, Problems & Prospects. Ed. by M. L. Sharma & R. K. Punia. (C). 1989. 49.50 (*81-202-0252-X*, Pub. by Ajanta) S Asia.

Land Reforms in India: Constitutional & Legal Approach. P. K. Agrawal. 272p. (C). 1993. pap. 225.00 (*81-85880-09-3*, Pub. by Print Hse) St Mut.

Land Reforms in India Vol. 1: Bihar-Institutional Constraints. Ed. by B. N. Yugandhar & K. Gopal Iyer. LC 93-7497. (Illus.). 362p. (C). 1993. text 39.95 (*0-8039-9119-3*) Sage.

Land Reforms in India Vol. 3: Andhra Pradesh - People's Pressure & Administrative Innovations. Ed. by B. N. Yugandhar. 396p. 1997. 36.00 (*0-8039-9304-8*) Sage.

An Asterisk (*) at the beginning of an entry indicates that the title is appearing for the first time.

Land Reforms in India Vol. 4: Karnataka: Promises Kept & Missed. Ed. by Abdul Aziz & Sudhir Krishna. 292p. 1997. 38.00 (*0-8039-9384-6*) Sage.

Land Reforms in Karnataka. M. A. Rajan. 178p. 1986. 17.50 (*0-8364-1938-3*, Pub. by Hindustan) S Asia.

Land Reforms in South Asia: A Study of Sri Lanka. Karori Singh. (C). 1989. 17.50 (*81-7003-115-X*, Pub. by S Asia Pubs) S Asia.

Land Reforms Legislation in India: A Comparative Study. N. C. Behuria. LC 97-905787. 1997. 28.00 (*81-259-0428-X*, Pub. by Vikas) S Asia.

Land Registration & Cadastral Systems: Tools for Land Information & Management. G. Larsson. 1991. pap. 48.95 (*0-582-08952-2*, Pub. by Addison-Wesley) Longman.

Land Release & Development in Areas of Restraint: Restraint Policy & Development Interests. Housing in Dacorum & North Hertfordshire. Paul McNamara. (C). 1984. 35.00 (*0-7855-3843-7*, Pub. by Oxford Polytechnic) St Mut.

***Land Remediation in United Kingdom: A Strategic Entry Report, 1996.** Compiled by Icon Group International Staff. (Illus.). 104p. 1999. ring bd. 1040.00 incl. audio compact disk (*0-7418-1395-5*) Icon Grp.

Land Remembered. Patrick D. Smith. LC 84-12098. 404p. 1984. 18.95 (*0-910923-12-4*) Pineapple Pr.

Land Remembered. Patrick D. Smith. LC 84-12098. 403p. 1996. pap. 12.95 (*1-56164-116-2*) Pineapple Pr.

Land Remembers: The Story of a Farm & Its People - 25th Anniversary Edition. anniversary ed. Ben Logan. LC 99-14993. 277p. 1999. pap. 14.95 (*1-55971-718-1*, NorthWord Pr) Creat Pub Intl.

Land Resource Assessment of Northern Belize. R. B. King et al. (Illus.). 513p. 1992. pap. 120.00 (*0-85954-302-1*, Pub. by Nat Res Inst) St Mut.

Land Resource Economics: The Economics of Real Estate. 4th ed. Raleigh Barlowe. (Illus.). 672p. (C). 1985. text 65.20 (*0-13-522541-8*) P-H.

Land Resource Management in Machakos District, Kenya, 1930-1990. John English et al. LC 93-43860. (Environment Papers: No. 5). 96p. 1994. pap. 22.00 (*0-8213-2734-8*, 12734) World Bank.

Land Resources: Now & for the Future. Anthony Young. LC 97-36654. (Illus.). 332p. (C). 1998. text 74.95 (*0-521-59003-5*) Cambridge U Pr.

***Land Resources: Now & for the Future.** Ed. by Anthony Young. (Illus.). 320p. (C). 2000. pap. 29.95 (*0-521-78559-6*) Cambridge U Pr.

Land Resources: On the Edge of the Malthusian Precipice. Ed. by D. J. Greenland et al. LC 97-43095. (A CAB International Publication). (Illus.). 190p. (C). 1998. pap. text 75.00 (*0-85199-235-8*) OUP.

Land Resources & Their Management for Sustainability in Arid Regions: A Training Programme Sponsored by UNESCO Delhi, CAZRI 1993. A. S. Kolarkar et al. 1996. pap. 150.00 (*81-7233-125-8*, Pub. by Scientific Pubs) St Mut.

Land Resources of Alaska: A Conservation Foundation Study. Hugh A. Johnson & Harold T. Jorgenson. LC 63-15719. 551p. 1963. 12.50 (*0-912006-13-7*) U of Alaska Pr.

Land Restoratn Reclamatn, James A. Harris. (C). 1996. pap. text 51.56 (*0-582-24313-0*, Pub. by Addison-Wesley) Longman.

Land Revenue Administration in Nepal. B. Pokharel. (C). 1991. text 75.00 (*0-7855-0147-9*, Pub. by Ratna Pustak Bhandar) St Mut.

Land Revenue Administration under the Mughals. Noman A. Siddiqi. 193p. 1989. reprint ed. 26.50 (*81-215-0477-5*, Pub. by M Manoharial) Coronet Bks.

Land Revenue Law: Cases & Comment. Badruddin. (C). 1991. 30.00 (*81-7024-396-3*, Pub. by Ashish Pub Hse) S Asia.

Land Rights: The 1990s Property Rights Rebellion. Ed. by Bruce Yandle. 320p. (C). 1995. pap. text 22.95 (*0-8476-8029-0*); lib. bdg. 62.50 (*0-8476-8028-2*) Rowman.

Land Rights & Indigenous Peoples: The Role of the Inter-American Commission on Human Rights. Shelton H. Davis. (Cultural Survival Reports: No. 29). 114p. 1988. 19.95 (*0-939521-42-3*); pap. 8.00 (*0-939521-28-8*) Cultural Survival.

Land Rights & Intra-Household Employment & Resource Use in the Peri-Urban Area of Banjul, the Gambia. Michael Roth et al. (Research Papers: No. 126). (Illus.). 110p. 1996. 7.00 (*0-934519-39-0*, RP 126) U of Wis Land.

Land Rights in Cote d'Ivoire: Survey & Prospects for Project Intervention. John R. Heath. LC 93-41302. (Technical Papers: No. 238). 68p. 1994. pap. 22.00 (*0-8213-2708-9*, 12708) World Bank.

Land Rover. Chris Bennett. (Illus.). 128p. 1996. pap. 10.95 (*1-85532-650-7*, Pub. by Ospry) Stackpole.

Land Rover: The Original 4 X 4. John Tipler. (Illus.). 200p. 1996. 35.95 (*1-85223-946-8*, Pub. by Crolwood) Motorbooks Intl.

Land Rover: The Unbeatable 4x4. 4th ed. K. Slavin et al. (Illus.). 360p. 1994. 39.95 (*0-85429-950-5*, Pub. by J H Haynes & Co) Motorbooks Intl.

Land Rover: Workhouse for the World. Martin Hodder. 1999. write for info. (*1-85960-449-8*) J H Haynes & Co.

Land Rover - Simply the Best. Martin Hodder. LC 98-72317. (Illus.). 160p. 1998. 34.95 (*1-85960-437-4*, Pub. by J H Haynes & Co) Motorbooks Intl.

Land Rover Defender 90, 110 1983-95: Step-by-Step Service Guide. (Porter Manuals Ser.). pap. text. write for info. (*1-899238-06-9*, Pub. by Porter Pub) Nichols Pub.

Land Rover Defender Restoration Manual. Lindsay Porter. LC 98-74169. (Illus.). 192p. 1999. 34.95 (*1-85960-600-8*, Pub. by J H Haynes & Co) Motorbooks Intl.

Land Rover Discovery: An Enthusiast's Companion. James Taylor. (Illus.). 112p. 1994. text 24.95 (*0-947981-79-9*, Pub. by Motor Racing) Motorbooks Intl.

Land Rover Discovery & Range Rover "Classic" 1970-1996. Chilton Automotive Editorial Staff. (Porter Manuals Ser.). (C). 1998. pap. text 26.25 (*1-899238-19-0*, Pub. by Porter Pub) Nichols Pub.

***Land Rover Discovery, 1989-1998.** James Taylor. (Illus.). 128p. 2000. pap. 19.95 (*1-899870-40-7*, 129586AE, Pub. by Motor Racing) Motorbooks Intl.

***Land Rover Series I, II & III Restoration Manual.** Lindsay Porter. (Illus.). 287p. 2000. 34.95 (*1-85960-622-9*, 129320AE, Pub. by Haynes Manuals) Motorbooks Intl.

Land Rover Series II, 1959-1970, Pts. 1 & 2. British Leyland Motors. (Illus.). (Orig.). student ed. 100.00 (*0-8376-0529-6*) Bentley Pubs.

Land Rover Series 1 Workshop Manual, 1948-1958: Gasoline & Diesel. British Leyland Motors. (Illus.). 384p. (Orig.). 65.00 (*0-8376-0516-4*) Bentley Pubs.

Land Rover since 1983: Coil Sprung Models. James Taylor. (Collector's Guide Ser.). (Illus.). 128p. 1996. pap. 27.95 (*1-899870-06-7*, Pub. by Motor Racing) Motorbooks Intl.

***Land Rush.** large type ed. Haycox. LC 99-58962. 372p. 2000. 20.00 (*0-7862-1340-X*, G K Hall Lrg Type) Mac Lib Ref.

***Land, Sea & Air.** Gerald Astor. 1999. write for info. (*1-55611-545-8*, Pub. by D I Fine) Penguin Putnam.

Land-Sea Atmosphere Interactions in the North Atlantic, 1400 to 2000 Years Ago: Proceedings of the American Quaternary Association, 10th Biennial Meeting. 170p. 1988. 10.00 (*0-318-32906-9*) Am Quaternary Assn.

Land, Settlement, & Politics on Eighteenth-Century Prince Edward Island. J. M. Bumsted. 256p. 1987. 65.00 (*0-7735-0566-0*, Pub. by McG-Queens Univ Pr) CUP Services.

Land Settlement in Early Tasmania: Creating an Antipodean England. Sharon Morgan. (Studies in Australian History). 224p. (C). 1992. text 59.95 (*0-521-39031-1*) Cambridge U Pr.

Land Settlement Policies & Population Redistribution in Developing Countries: Achievements, Problems & Prospects. Ed. by Amarjit S. Oberai. LC 87-15837. 409p. 1988. 59.95 (*0-275-92799-7*, C2799, Praeger Pubs) Greenwood.

Land, Sky & All That Is Within: Visionary Photography in the Southwest. James Enyeart. LC 98-4202. 1998. pap. 24.95 (*0-89013-365-4*) Museum NM Pr.

Land Sliding: Imaging Space, Presence, & Power in Canadian Writing. W. H. New. LC 97-170132. (Illus.). 278p. 1997. text 45.00 (*0-8020-4119-1*, PR9185) U of Toronto Pr.

Land Snail Genus Carelia. C. M. Cooke, Jr. (BMB Ser.: No. 85). 1969. reprint ed. 25.00 (*0-527-02191-1*) Periodicals Srv.

Land Snails from Hawaii, Christmas Island & Samoa. H. A. Pilsbry et al. (BMB Ser.: Vol. 47). 1969. reprint ed. pap. 25.00 (*0-527-02153-9*) Periodicals Srv.

Land Snails of the British Isles. A. A. Wardhaugh. (Natural History Ser.: No. 45). (Illus.). 24p. 1989. pap. 5.25 (*0-7478-0027-8*, Pub. by Shire Pubns) Parkwest Pubns.

Land So Dedicated: The History of Houston County Georgia. 2nd rev. ed. Bobbe Hickson Nelson. Ed. by Betty S. Poole. LC 98-61001. (Illus.). 328p. 1998. 35.00 (*0-9666269-0-7*) Southern Trellis.

Land So Fair & Bright: The True Story of a Young Man's Adventures Across Depression America. Russ Hofvendahl. (Illus.). 300p. 1991. 22.95 (*0-924486-10-4*) Sheridan.

Land Speculation - New England's Old Problem: An Original Arno Press Anthology. Ed. by Dan C. McCurry & Richard E. Rubenstein. LC 74-30640. (American Farmers & the Rise of Agribusiness Ser.). 1975. 19.95 (*0-405-06808-5*) Ayer.

***Land Speed Racing.** Steve Hedrickson. LC 99-55962. (Motorcycles Ser.). 48p. (YA). (gr. 5 up). 2000. lib. bdg. 21.26 (*0-7368-0476-5*, Capstone Bks) Capstone Pr.

Land Speed Record. David Tremayne. (Album Ser.: No. 263). (Illus.). 32p. 1989. pap. 6.25 (*0-7478-0115-0*, Pub. by Shire Pubns) Parkwest Pubns.

Land, Spirit, Power: First Nations at the National Gallery of Canada. Ed. by Diana Nemiroff. (Illus.). 96p. 1996. pap. 43.95 (*0-88884-650-9*) U Ch Pr.

Land Stacks Up. Preston Newman. LC 85-90788. 95p. 1985. pap. 4.95 (*0-9619636-0-3*) K Newman.

Land Stacks Up. 2nd ed. Preston Newman. Ed. by Katherine Newman. LC 85-90788. (Appalachian Connection Ser.). (Illus.). 128p. 1993. pap. 5.95 (*0-936015-33-0*) Pocahontas Pr.

Land Still Speaks: A Review of Aboriginal & Torres Strait Islander Language Maintenance & Development Needs & Activities. National Board of Employment, Education & Training. 290p. 1996. pap. 24.95 (*0-644-45945-X*, Pub. by Aust Gov Pub) Accents Pubns.

Land, Struggles & Social Differentiation in Southern Mozambique: A Case Study of Chokwe, Limpopo, 1950-1987. Kenneth Hermele. (Research Report Ser.: No. 82). 64p. 1988. 7.95 (*91-7106-282-3*, Pub. by Nordic Africa) Transaction Pubs.

Land Subsidence: Natural Causes, Measuring Techniques, the Groningen Gasfields: Proceedings: International Symposium (5th: 1995: The Hague, Netherlands) Ed. by Frans B. Barends et al. (Illus.). 426p. (C). 1995. text 110.00 (*90-5410-589-5*, TP715, Pub. by A A Balkema) Ashgate Pub Co.

Land Supply & International Specialisation in Agriculture. N. Csaki. (Geography of World Agriculture Ser.: No. 3). 102p. (C). 1974. 25.00 (*963-05-0172-4*, Pub. by Akade Kiado) St Mut.

Land Surface - Atmosphere Interactions for Climate Modeling: Observations, Models & Analysis. Ed. by Eric F. Wood. (C). 1991. text 218.00 (*0-7923-1004-7*) Kluwer Academic.

Land Surface Evaporation: Measurement & Parameterization. Ed. by T. J. Schmugge & J. C. Andre. (Illus.). 384p. 1991. 161.00 (*0-387-97359-1*) Spr-Verlag.

Land Surface Processes in Hydrology: Trials & Tribulations of Modeling & Measuring. Soroosh Sorooshian & Hoshin V. Gupta. LC 96-43298. (NATO ASI Ser.: Vol. 6). (Illus.). 497p. 1996. 239.00 (*3-540-61767-1*) Spr-Verlag.

Land Survey Descriptions. 10th ed. William C. Wattles & Gurdon H. Wattles. LC 74-78750. 144p. 1974. per. 15.00 (*0-9606962-3-7*) Wattles Pubns.

Land Survey Review Manual. 2nd ed. R. B. Buckner. 437p. (Orig.). 1993. pap. 48.00 (*0-910845-49-2*) Landmark Ent.

Land Survey Systems. John G. McEntyre. (Illus.). 537p. 1986. reprint ed. 60.00 (*0-910845-27-1*, 511) Landmark Ent.

Land Surveying Computations. R. B. Buckner. 108p. 1991. pap. 30.00 (*0-910845-56-5*, 571) Landmark Ent.

Land Surveying Law. John E. Keen. 278p. (C). 1995. pap. text 45.00 (*1-56569-001-X*) Land Survey.

Land Surveying with the HP 48SX 1GX: With the SMI Card. John E. Keen. 39p. (C). 1995. pap. text 20.00 (*1-56569-009-5*) Land Survey.

Land Surveyor. Jack Rudman. (Career Examination Ser.: C-3029). 1994. pap. 29.95 (*0-8373-3029-7*) Nat Learn.

Land Surveyor-in-Training Sample Examination. George M. Cole. LC 98-119612. 70p. 1998. pap. 25.95 (*0-912045-66-3*, LSSE) Prof Pubns CA.

***Land Surveyor Reference Manual.** 3rd ed. Andrew L. Harbin. 488p. 2000. 79.95 (*1-888577-50-9*) Prof Pubns CA.

Land Surveyor Trainee. Jack Rudman. (Career Examination Ser.: C-3030). 1994. pap. 27.95 (*0-8373-3030-0*) Nat Learn.

Land Surveyor's Formulas with Applications. John E. Keen. 278p. (C). 1995. pap. text 45.00 (*1-56569-003-6*) Land Survey.

***Land Surveys.** 2nd ed. Mitchell G. Williams. LC 99-40480. 1999. write for info. (*1-57073-742-8*) Amer Bar Assn.

Land Surveys: A Guide for Lawyers. LC 89-83877. 148p. 1989. pap. 34.95 (*0-89707-417-3*, 543-0094-01) Amer Bar Assn.

Land System in Maryland, 1720-1765. Clarence P. Gould. Ed. by Stuart Bruchey. LC 78-53540. (Development of Public Land Law in the U. S. Ser.). 1979. reprint ed. lib. bdg. 15.95 (*0-405-11376-5*) Ayer.

Land System in Northern India: c. AD 400-700. Saroj Dutta. LC 95-910426. 232p. (C). 1995. 31.00 (*81-215-0657-3*, Pub. by M Manoharial) Coronet Bks.

Land System of the New England Colonies. Melville Egleston. LC 78-63767. (Johns Hopkins University. Studies in the Social Sciences. Thirtieth Ser. 1912: 11-12). reprint ed. 37.50 (*0-404-61034-X*) AMS Pr.

Land System of the United States: An Introduction to the History & Practice of Land Use & Land Tenure. Marion Clawson. LC 68-10250. 155p. reprint ed. pap. 48.10 (*0-608-15675-2*, 203199100077) Bks Demand.

Land Systems & Industrial Economy of Ireland, England, & Continental Countries. Thomas E. Leslie. LC 67-18570. (Reprints of Economic Classics Ser.). vi, 379p. 1968. reprint ed. 49.50 (*0-678-00346-7*) Kelley.

Land Systems of British India: Being a Manual of the Land-Tenures & of the Systems of Land-Revenue Administration Prevalent in the Several Provinces, 3 vols., Set. Baden H. Baden-Powell. (C). 1990. reprint ed. 48.00 (*81-85418-30-6*, Pub. by Low Price) S Asia.

Land Systems Technology: Background Papers Prepared for the Lincoln Institute of Land Policy Seminar on Land Systems Technology. Ed. by Alven H. S. Lam & Dennis W. Robinson. LC G 0070.2.L36. (Lincoln Institute of Land Policy Monograph: No. 86-11). (Illus.). 52p. reprint ed. pap. 30.00 (*0-7837-5755-7*, 204541700006) Bks Demand.

Land Tax Assessments, 1690-1950. (C). 1987. 35.00 (*0-7855-2050-3*, Pub. by Birmingham Midland Soc) St Mut.

Land Tax in China. Huang Han Liang. LC 76-76706. (Columbia University. Studies in the Social Sciences: No. 187). reprint ed. 20.00 (*0-404-51187-2*) AMS Pr.

Land Taxation in Imperial China, 1750-1911. Yeh-Chien Wang. LC 73-80024. (East Asian Monographs: No. 73). 192p. 1974. 31.00 (*0-674-50860-2*) HUP.

Land Tenure, Agrarian Structure, & Comparative Land Use Efficiency in Zimbabwe: Options for Land Tenure Reform & Land Redistribution. Michael R. Roth & John W. Bruce. (Research Paper Ser.: Vol. 117). (Illus.). xi, 182p. (C). 1994. pap. 12.00 (*0-934519-28-5*, RP117) U of Wis Land.

Land Tenure among the Amhara of Ethiopia: The Dynamics of Cognatic Descent. Allan Hoben. 1994. lib. bdg. 16.00 (*0-226-34548-3*) U Ch Pr.

Land Tenure & Agricultural Productivity in Malawi. Carol W. Dickerman & Peter C. Bloch. (LTC Paper Ser.: Vol. 143). vii, 56p. (C). 1991. pap. 7.00 (*0-934519-61-7*, LTC143) U of Wis Land.

Land Tenure & Food Security: A Review of Concepts, Evidence, & Methods. Daniel Maxwell & Keith Wiebe. (Research Paper Ser.: Vol. 129). (Illus.). iii, 37p. (C). 1998. pap. 4.00 (*0-934519-77-3*, RP129) U of Wis Land.

Land Tenure & Investment in African Agriculture: Theory & Evidence. Richard Barrows & Michael Roth. (LTC Paper Ser.: Vol. 136). 29p. (C). 1989. pap. 4.00 (*0-934519-52-8*, LTC136) U of Wis Land.

Land Tenure & Land Taxation in America. A. M. Sakolski. 316p. 1957. 4.00 (*0-911312-32-3*) Schalkenbach.

Land Tenure & Land Use in Southern Haiti: Case Studies of the Les Anglais & Grande Ravine du Sud Watersheds. Rebecca J. McLain et al. (Research Paper Ser.: Vol. 95). (Illus.). xi, 252p. (C). 1988. pap. 12.00 (*0-934519-05-6*, RP95) U of Wis Land.

Land Tenure & Management of Land Resources in Trinidad & Tobago: Institutional Roots of Tenure Insecurity, Pt. 2. Ed. by J. David Stanfield et al. (Research Papers: No. 116). xix, 295p. (Orig.). 1993. pap. 12.00 (*0-934519-27-7*, RP 116) U of Wis Land.

Land Tenure & Social Transformation in the Middle East. Tarif Khalidi. (Illus.). 551p. 1984. text 34.95 (*0-8156-6071-5*, Pub. by Am U Beirut) Syracuse U Pr.

Land Tenure & Taxation in Nepal. Mahesh C. Regmi. 1978. 150.00 (*0-7855-0247-5*, Pub. by Ratna Pustak Bhandar); 150.00 (*0-7855-0316-1*, Pub. by Ratna Pustak Bhandar) St Mut.

Land Tenure & Taxation in Nepal: Mahesh Chandra Regmi, 4 vols. enl. rev. ed. Mahesh C. Regmi. 851p. (C). 1989. reprint ed. 350.00 (*0-89771-108-4*, Pub. by Ratna Pustak Bhandar) St Mut.

Land Tenure & the Biblical Jubilee. Jeffrey A. Fager. (Journal for the Study of the Old Testament Supplement Ser.: No. 155). 135p. 1993. 46.50 (*1-85075-398-9*, Pub. by Sheffield Acad) CUP Services.

Land Tenure & the Management of Land Resources in Trinidad & Tobago, Pt. 1. Ed. by J. David Stanfield et al. (LTC Research Papers: No. 115). (Illus.). xxi, 272p. 1993. pap. 12.00 (*0-934519-26-9*, RP 115) U of Wis Land.

Land Tenure & the Rural Exodus in Chile, Colombia, Costa Rica, & Peru. R. Paul Shaw. LC 75-40048. (Latin American Monographs: Series 2, No. 19). 190p. reprint ed. pap. 58.90 (*0-8357-6722-1*, 203536000095) Bks Demand.

Land Tenure & Unemployment. Frank Geary. LC 77-81147. (Reprints of Economic Classics Ser.). 256p. 1969. reprint ed. 39.50 (*0-678-00509-5*) Kelley.

Land Tenure in the Middle Jubba Valley Somalia: Customary Tenure & the Effect of Land Registration. Catherine Besteman. (Research Paper Ser.: Vol. 104). (Illus.). xv, 106p. (C). 1990. pap. 7.00 (*0-934519-14-5*, RP104) U of Wis Land.

Land Tenure in the Ramesside Period. Sally L. Katary. (Studies in Egyptology). 300p. 1989. 99.50 (*0-7103-0298-3*) Routledge.

Land Tenure Issues in Agricultural Development Projects in Latin America. Thomas Scheweigert. (LTC Paper Ser.: Vol. 132). (Illus.). iii, 67p. (C). 1989. pap. 7.00 (*0-934519-48-X*, LTC132) U of Wis Land.

Land Tenure Issues in Project Design & Strategies for Agricultural Development in Sub-Saharan Africa. John W. Bruce et al. (LTC Paper Ser.: Vol. 128). xxvii, 190p. (C). 1986. pap. 12.00 (*0-934519-43-9*, LTC128) U of Wis Land.

Land Tenure Issues in Rural Haiti: Review of the Evidence. Peter C. Bloch et al. (Research Paper Ser.: Vol. 94). (Illus.). 94p. (C). 1988. pap. 7.00 (*0-934519-04-8*, RP94) U of Wis Land.

Land Tenure, Land Markets, & Institutional Transformation in Zambia. Ed. by Michael Roth. (Research Papers: No. 124). xi, 267p. 1995. 12.00 (*0-934519-37-4*, RP 124) U of Wis Land.

Land Tenure Problems in the Santa Fe Railroad Grant Area. Sanford A. Mosk. Ed. by Stuart Bruchey. LC 80-1333. (Railroads Ser.). (Illus.). 1981. reprint ed. lib. bdg. 15.95 (*0-405-13807-5*) Ayer.

Land Tenure Reform in Senegal: An Economic Study from the Peanut Basin. Elise H. Golan. (Research Papers: No. 101). (Illus.). vii, 137p. (C). 1990. pap. 7.00 (*0-934519-11-0*, RP101) U of Wis Land.

An Asterisk (*) at the beginning of an entry indicates that the title is appearing for the first time.

Land Tenure Reform in the People's Republic of China, 1978-1988. John W. Bruce & Paula Harrell. (Research Papers: No. 100). 70p. (Orig.). 1989. pap. 7.00 (0-934519-10-2, RP 100) U of Wis Land.

Land Tenure Security & State Farm Divestiture in Mozambique: Case Studies in Nhamatanda, Manica & Montepuez Districts. Gregory W. Myers & Harry G. West. (Research Paper Ser.: Vol. 110). (Illus.). xvi, 87p. (C). 1993. pap. 7.00 (0-934519-21-8, RP110) U of Wis Land.

***Land Tenure, Technological Change & Resource Use: Transformation Processes in African Agrarian Systems.** Michael Kirk. (Illus.). xx, 484p. 1999. pap. 56.95 (3-631-30037-9) P Lang Pubng.

Land Tenure, Technological Change & Resource Use: Transformation Processes in African Agrarian Systems. Michael Kirk. LC 99-31220. (Illus.). XX, 484p. 1999. pap. 56.95 (0-8204-3171-0) P Lang Pubng.

***Land That Could Be: Environmentalism & Democracy in the 21st Century.** William A. Shutkin. LC 99-56829. (Urban & Industrial Environment Ser.). (Illus.). 340p. 2000. 27.95 (0-262-19435-X) MIT Pr.

Land That Drank the Rain: Novel. William Hoffman. LC 81-18585. viii, 260p. 1982. 16.95 (0-8071-1004-3) La State U Pr.

Land That England Lost: Argentina & Britain, a Special Relationship. Ed. by Alistair Hennessy & John King. 320p. 1992. text 65.00 (1-85043-491-3) I B T.

Land That Feeds Us. John F. Hart. 400p. 1993. pap. 12.95 (0-393-30950-9) Norton.

Land That Is Very Far Off: A Vision of Heaven. Dottie M. Goard. LC 97-38488. 129p. 1998. pap. 11.95 (0-932727-92-1) Hope Pub Hse.

Land That Kept Its Promise: A History of South Lincoln County. Marjorie H. Hays. (Illus.). 157p. (Orig.). 1977. pap. 12.95 (0-911443-03-7) Lincoln Coun Hist.

Land That Slept Late: The Olympic Mountains in Legend & History. Robert L. Wood. (Illus.). 176p. 1995. pap. 14.95 (0-89886-440-2) Mountaineers.

***Land That Time Forgot.** Edgar Rice Burroughs. LC 98-50000. (Illus.). 448p. 1999. pap. 14.95 (0-8032-6154-3, Bison Books) U of Nebr Pr.

Land, the City, & the Human Spirit. Larry P. Fuller. LC 84-81780. (Symposia Ser.). 166p. 1985. pap. 11.00 (0-89940-414-6) LBJ Sch Pub Aff.

Land the Cleves Built. Douglas Manry. Ed. by Stephen Sloan. (Illus.). 32p. (J). (gr. 2-5). 1989. write for info. (0-9622316-0-6) Sloan Manry Pubs.

***Land the Internet/Tech Job of Your Dreams: Industry Experts Reveal the Secrets to Landing the Best Jobs Available Ever.** Ed. by eBrandedBooks.com Staff. (Internet Opportunities Ser.). 224p. 2000. pap. 17.95 (1-58762-004-9) ebrandedbookscom.

Land They Possessed. Mary W. Breneman. 335p. (Orig.). 1991. pap. 9.95 (0-9632157-1-X) SD Human Fnd.

Land Time Forgot: Black Settlement at Nicodemus, KS. Thomas Wellington, II. 38p. (J). 1995. wbk. ed. write for info. (0-9649015-0-1) Nicodemus.

***Land Title in South Africa.** David Carey-Miller. 2000. pap. 91.50 (0-7021-5120-3, Pub. by Juta & Co) Gaunt.

Land Titles Origins. Alfred N. Chandler. Ed. by Stuart Bruchey. LC 78-56712. (Management of Public Lands in the U. S. Ser.). 1979. reprint ed. lib. bdg. 41.95 (0-405-11324-2) Ayer.

Land to Call Home, Vol. 3. Lauraine Snelling. LC 97-4652. (Red River of the North Ser.). 32p. 1997. pap. 9.99 (1-55661-578-7) Bethany Hse.

Land to Die For. Binka Le Breton. (Illus.). 167p. (Orig.). 1997. pap. 12.95 (0-932863-24-8) Clarity Pr.

Land to Die For. large type ed. Tyler Hatch. 256p. pap. 18.99 (0-7089-5417-0) Ulverscroft.

Land to the Tiller: The Political Economy of Agrarian Reform in South Asia. Ronald J. Herring. LC 82-48903. (Illus.). 336p. 1983. 50.00 (0-300-02725-7) Yale U Pr.

Land-to-the-Tiller in the Mekong Delta: Economic, Social & Political Effects of Land Reform in Four Villages of South Vietnam. Charles S. Callison. LC 83-6745. (Monographs: No. 23). (Illus.). 418p. (Orig.). (C). 1983. pap. text 36.00 (0-8191-3253-5); lib. bdg. 63.00 (0-8191-3252-7) U Pr of Amer.

Land Transactions & Finance. 2nd ed. Grant S. Nelson & Dale A. Whitman. (Black Letter Ser.). 466p. (C). 1988. reprint ed. pap., pap. text 24.50 incl. disk (0-314-68969-9) West Pub.

Land Transactions & Finance. 3rd ed. Grant S. Nelson & Dale A. Whitman. LC 97-35491. (Black Letter Ser.). 497p. (C). 1997. pap., suppl. ed. 24.50 incl. disk (0-314-21104-7) West Pub.

Land Transfer & Finance: Cases & Materials. 4th ed. Curtis J. Berger & Quintin Johnstone. 1424p. 1993. boxed set 60.00 (0-7355-0622-1, 06221) Panel Pubs.

Land Transformation. Berger. 1424p. 1993. 57.00 (0-316-09278-9, Aspen Law & Bus) Aspen Pub.

Land Transformation in Agriculture. Ed. by G. Wolman & F. Fournier. LC 86-19006. (Scientific Committee on Problems of the Environment Ser.: No. 32). 552p. 1999. 383.00 (0-471-91288-3) Wiley.

Land Transport Corridors between Central Asia & Europe. 194p. 25.00 (92-1-119844-5) UN.

Land Transport from Central Asia to Sea Ports in the South & the East. 141p. pap. 15.00 (92-1-119707-4) UN.

Land Transport in Europe. Ed. by Alexander Fenton et al. (Studies of Folklife: No. 4). (Illus.). 512p. (C). 1973. pap. 33.00 (87-480-5901-3, Pub. by Aarhus Univ Pr) David Brown.

Land, Trees & Tenure: Proceedings of an International Workshop on Tenure Issues in Agroforestry, Nairobi, May 27-31, 1985. Ed. by John B. Raintree. (Illus.). 435p. 1987. 15.00 (0-934519-01-3) U of Wis Land.

Land Trust As a Conservation Tool. Susan L. Roakes & Marie Zwolinski. LC 95-32068. (CPL Bibliographies Ser.: Vol. 323). 25p. 1995. pap. 10.00 (0-86602-323-2, Sage Prdcls Pr) Sage.

Land und Meer see Land & Sea

Land under England. Joseph O'Neill. LC 80-14273. 312p. 1981. reprint ed. 22.50 (0-87951-117-6, Pub. by Overlook Pr) Penguin Putnam.

Land Use: A Spatial Approach. Ed. by John F. Lounsbury et al. LC 81-81132. (National Council for Geographic Education, Pacesetter Ser.). (Illus.). 236p. 1981. reprint ed. pap. 73.20 (0-7837-9720-6, 206045100005) Bks Demand.

Land Use: Teacher's Manual to Accompany Cases & Materials. 5th ed. Robert R. Wright & Morton Gitelman. (American Casebook Ser.). 190p. 1997. pap. text, teacher ed., suppl. ed. write for info. (0-314-22810-1) West Pub.

Land-Use - Transport Planning in Hong Kong: The End of an Era: A Review of Principles & Practices. Ed. by Harry T. Dimitriou & Alison H. Cook. LC 98-71406. 404p. 1998. text 76.95 (1-84014-171-9, Pub. by Ashgate Pub) Ashgate Pub Co.

Land Use A-Z. David E. Newton. LC 89-78119. (Single Titles Ser.). 128p. (YA). (gr. 6 up). 1991. lib. bdg. 20.95 (0-89490-260-1) Enslow Pubs.

Land Use & Environment Law Review, 1984. Incl. 1978. LC 70-127585. 42.50 (0-87632-119-8); Pesticide Residues in Food, 1977 Evaluations. 42.50 (0-87632-118-X); 1984. LC 70-127585. 42.50 (0-87632-116-3); 1979. 42.50 (0-87632-120-1); 1979. 1980. 45.00 (0-87632-121-X); LC 70-127585. write for info. (0-318-51095-2) West Group.

Land Use & Forest Resources in a Changing Environment: The Urban-Forest Interface. Ed. by Gordon A. Bradley. (George S. Long Publications). 238p. 1984. 40.00 (0-295-96104-X); pap. 20.00 (0-295-96145-7) U of Wash Pr.

Land Use & Housing in the City of Manila. Floyd T. Waterman & Natividad T. Nacianceno. 48p. (Orig.). 1985. pap. 3.50 (1-55719-110-7) U NE CPAR.

Land-Use & Prehistory in South-East Spain. Antonio Gilman & John B. Thornes. (London Research Series in Geography: No. 8). (Illus.). 256p. (C). 1984. text 55.00 (0-04-913022-6) Routledge.

Land Use & Society: Geography, Law & Public Policy. rev. ed. Rutherford H. Platt. LC 95-39226. 425p. 1995. pap. text 32.00 (1-55963-435-9) Island Pr.

Land Use & Taxation: Applying the Insights of Henry George. Ed. by H. James Brown. LC 97-20086. 106p. (Orig.). 1997. pap. 12.00 (1-55844-124-7) Lincoln Inst Land.

Land Use & the Causes of Global Warming. W. Neil Adger & Katrina Brown. LC 94-15145. 282p. 1995. 200.00 (0-471-94885-3) Wiley.

Land Use & the Constitution. Ed. by Brian Blaesser & Alan Weinstein. LC 88-72355. 291p. (Orig.). 1989. pap. 38.95 (0-918286-58-1, Planners Press) Am Plan Assn.

Land Use & the States. 2nd ed. Robert G. Healy & John S. Rosenberg. LC 79-4864. 284p. 1979. pap. 21.95 (0-8018-2285-8) Resources Future.

Land Use & Urban Form: The Consumption Theory of Land Rent. Grant I. Thrall. 200p. 1987. 29.95 (0-416-35540-4) Routledge.

Land Use Anthology. Ed. by Jon W. Bruce. LC 98-142800. 368p. 1997. pap. 29.95 (0-87084-023-1) Anderson Pub Co.

Land Use, Cases & Materials On. 4th ed. Robert R. Wright & Morton Gitelman. (American Casebook Ser.). 1255p. (C). 1991. text 54.50 (0-314-80779-9) West Pub.

Land Use, Cases & Materials On. 5th ed. Robert R. Wright & Morton Gitelman. LC 97-18363. (American Casebook Ser.). 1287p. (C). 1997. 68.50 (0-314-20535-7) West Pub.

Land-Use Change: Proceedings of the Asahikawa-Sapporo International Symposium. Ed. by R. D. Hill. 260p. (C). 1989. pap. text 34.50 (962-209-239-X, Pub. by HK Univ Pr) Coronet Bks.

Land-Use Changes & Their Environmental Impact in Rural Areas in Europe. Ed. by Reinhard Kronert et al. LC 99-13170. (Man & the Biosphere Ser.: Vol. 24). (Illus.). 450p. 2000. 88.00 (1-85070-047-8) Prthnon Pub.

Land Use Changes in Europe: Processes of Change, Environmental Transformations & Future Patterns. Ed. by F. M. Brouwer et al. (C). 1991. text 234.00 (0-7923-1099-3) Kluwer Academic.

Land Use Considerations in Urban Environmental Management. Janis D. Bernstein. LC 93-40298. (Urban Management Program Ser.: No. 12). 110p. 1994. pap. 22.00 (0-8213-2723-2, 12723) World Bank.

Land Use Controls. Robert C. Ellickson & A. Dan Tarlock. 1239p. 1981. 54.00 (0-316-23299-8, Aspen Law & Bus) Aspen Pub.

Land Use Controls: Present Problems & Future Reform. David Listokin. 406p. 1974. boxed set 14.00 (0-87855-103-4) Transaction Pubs.

Land-Use Controls Annual, 1972 see Land-Use Controls Annual, 1971

Land-Use Controls Annual, 1971. Ed. by Frank S. Bangs, Jr. Incl. Land-Use Controls Annual, 1972. 232p. 1973. pap. 5.00 212p. 1972. Set pap. 5.00 (0-318-13017-3) Am Plan Assn.

Land Use Development in Gretna, Nebraska: A Cost Analysis. CAUR Staff. 76p. (Orig.). 1976. pap. 5.00 (1-55719-072-0) U NE CPAR.

Land Use, Ecology & Conservation of Broadland. Martin George. 558p. (C). 1991. text 295.00 (1-85341-047-0, Pub. by Surrey Beatty & Sons) St Mut.

Land Use Environment: The Shaping of Island County, Washington. Rich White. LC 91-33199. 246p. 1991. reprint ed. pap. 18.95 (0-295-97143-6) U of Wash Pr.

Land Use, Environment & Economic Growth in India. Ajit K. Singh. 327p. 1997. pap. 250.00 (81-7533-025-2, Pub. by Print Hse) St Mut.

Land Use in a Nutshell. 3rd ed. Robert R. Wright. LC 93-48714. (Nutshell Ser.). 336p. (C). 1994. pap. 21.00 (0-314-03502-8) West Pub.

Land Use in America. Henry L. Diamond & Patrick F. Noonan. LC 95-47012. 368p. (Orig.). (C). 1996. pap. text 29.95 (1-55963-464-2) Island Pr.

Land Use in Central Boston, 4. Walter I. Firey. LC 68-23288. (Harvard Sociological Studies Ser.: Vol. 4). (Illus.). 367p. 1968. reprint ed. lib. bdg. 79.50 (0-8371-0073-9, FILU, Greenwood Pr) Greenwood.

Land Use in Early New Jersey: A Historical Geography. Peter O. Wacker & Paul G. Clemens. (Illus.). 321p. 1995. pap. 18.95 (0-911020-30-6) NJ Hist Soc.

Land Use in North-Central Arizona: An Archaeological Survey of Navajo Army Depot, Coconino County, Arizona. Donn R. Grenda. (Statistical Research Technical Ser.: No. 43). (Illus.). 148p. (Orig.). 1993. pap. 14.00 (1-879442-04-3) Stats Res.

Land Use Information: A Critical Survey of United States Statistics, Including Possibilities for Greater Uniformity. Marion Clawson & Charles L. Stewart. LC 66-14380. 422p. reprint ed. pap. 130.90 (0-7837-3141-8, 204284600006) Bks Demand.

Land Use Law. 3rd ed. Daniel R. Mandelker. 632p. 1993. 85.00 (1-55834-126-9, MICHIE) LEXIS Pub.

***Land Use Law, 1999 Supplement: Pocketpart.** 4th ed. Mandelker. 80p. 1999. suppl. ed. write for info. (0-327-01759-7, 6458315) LEXIS Pub.

Land Use Law, 1997. 4th ed. Daniel Mandelker. LC 97-75493. 734p. 1997. text 105.00 (1-55834-701-1, 64584-11, MICHIE) LEXIS Pub.

Land Use Litigation. Frank Schnidman. 1984. 125.00 (0-316-77411-1, Aspen Law & Bus) Aspen Pub.

Land Use Litigation. John W. Shonkwiler & Terry Morgan. 629p. 1986. text. write for info. (0-314-22287-1) West Pub.

Land-Use Planning: A Casebook on the Use, Misuse, & Re-Use of Urban Land. Charles M. Haar & Michael A. Wolf. 1200p. 1989. teacher ed. write for info. (0-316-33683-1, 36831) Aspen Law.

Land-Use Planning: A Casebook on the Use, Misuse, & Re-Use of Urban Land. 3rd ed. Charles M. Haar. 1980. suppl. ed. 6.95 (0-316-33681-5, Aspen Law & Bus) Aspen Pub.

Land-Use Planning: A Casebook on the Use, Misuse, & Re-Use of Urban Land: With Teacher's Manual. 4th ed. Charles M. Haar & Michael Allan Wolf. 1200p. 1989. 58.00 (0-316-33677-7, 36777, Aspen Law & Bus) Aspen Pub.

Land-Use Planning: From Global to Local Challenge. Julius Gy. Fabos. 300p. 1985. pap. 19.95 (0-412-25210-4, 5069) Chapman & Hall.

Land Use Planning: The Ballot Box Revolution. Roger W. Caves. (Library of Social Research: Vol. 187). 260p. (C). 1992. text 59.95 (0-8039-3824-1); pap. text 26.00 (0-8039-3825-X) Sage.

Land Use Planning & Control Law. Julian C. Juergensmeyer & Thomas E. Roberts. LC 98-20943. (Hornbook Ser.). 700p. 1998. 41.00 (0-314-21203-5) West Pub.

Land Use Planning & Economic Analysis, 1990. (Transportation Research Record Ser.: No. 1262). 180p. 1990. 28.00 (0-309-05014-6) Transport Res Bd.

Land Use Planning & Oil & Gas Leasing on Onshore Federal Lands. National Research Council Staff. 180p. 1989. pap. text 25.00 (0-309-04144-9) Natl Acad Pr.

Land Use Planning & Remote Sensing. David T. Lindgren. 1984. text 154.50 (90-247-3083-X) Kluwer Academic.

Land Use Planning & Zoning. Peter J. Loughlin. LC 93-11259. (New Hampshire Practice Ser.: Vol. 15). 600p. 1993. 70.00 (1-56257-361-6, MICHIE) LEXIS Pub.

Land Use Planning & Zoning, 2 vols., Set. Peter J. Loughlin. (NH Practice Ser.: Vols. 1 & 1A). 920p. 1991. ring bd. 140.00 (0-88063-703-X, MICHIE) LEXIS Pub.

Land-Use Planning Applications: Proceedings of the FAO Expert Consultation, Rome, 1990. 212p. 1992. 25.00 (92-5-103131-2, F0312, Pub. by FAO) Bernan Associates.

Land Use Planning, Environmental Protection & Growth Management: The Florida Experience. Robert A. Catlin. LC 97-22724. 270p. (C). 1997. ring bd. 54.95 (1-57504-042-5, 042-5) CRC Pr.

Land Use Planning for Earthquake Hazard Mitigation: A Handbook for Planners. P. A. Bolton et al. (Special Publications: No. 14). 123p. (Orig.). (C). 1986. pap. 20.00 (0-685-28095-0) Natural Hazards.

Land Use Planning in Oregon: A No-Nonsense Handbook in Plain English. Mitch Rohse. LC 86-12457. (Illus.). 296p. 1987. text 29.95 (0-87071-349-3) Oreg St U Pr.

Land Use Planning, Techniques & Policies. Ed. by F. P. Miller et al. (Special Publications: No. 12). 123p. 1984. pap. 8.40 (0-89118-772-3) Soil Sci Soc Am.

Land Use Policy & Problems in the United States. Homestead Centennial Symposium Staff. Ed. by Howard W. Ottoson. LC 63-9096. 480p. reprint ed. pap. 148.80 (0-8357-2940-0, 203919600011) Bks Demand.

Land-Use Policy & the Protection of Georgia's Environment. James E. Kundell. 160p. 1988. pap. 14.95 (0-89854-133-6) U of GA Inst Govt.

Land Use Policy Debate in the United States. Ed. by Judith I. De Neufville. LC 81-13859. (Environment, Development, & Public Policy: Public Policy & Social Services Ser.). 282p. 1981. 49.50 (0-306-40718-3, Plenum Trade) Perseus Pubng.

Land Use Practice & Forms: Handling the Land Use Case. 2nd ed. John J. Delaney et al. LC 96-38796. 1996. write for info. (0-8366-1088-1) West Group.

Land Use Regulation. Peter W. Salsich & Timothy J. Tryniecki. LC 97-36457. 1997. write for info. (1-57073-485-2) Amer Bar Assn.

Land Use Regulation: A Handbook for the Eighties. Leslie et al. 171p. 1984. 12.00 (0-318-04412-9) Stanford Enviro.

Land Use Regulation: Cases & Materials. Daniel P. Selmi & James A. Kushner. LC 99-14054. 912p. 1999. teacher ed. 62.00 (0-7355-0012-6) Panel Pubs.

Land Use Regulation: The Impacts of Alternative Land Use Rights. Michael A. Garrett, Jr. LC 87-15637. 165p. 1987. pap. 13.95 (0-275-92848-9, B2848, Praeger Pubs) Greenwood.

Land Use Regulation: The Impacts of Alternative Land Use Rights. Michael A. Garrett, Jr. LC 87-15637. 165p. 1987. 45.00 (0-275-92802-0, C2802, Praeger Pubs) Greenwood.

Land Use, Stewardship & the Planning Process: Building Sustainable Communities, an Environmental Guide for Local Government. 126p. 1993. 40.00 (1-880386-10-0) Ctr Study Law.

Land-Use Sustainability in the Red River Delta of Vietnam: An Intensively Cultivated & Densely Populated Area. Ed. by Aran Patanothai. LC 96-1721. 1996. write for info. (0-86638-180-5) EW Ctr HI.

Land Use, Teacher's Manual to Accompany Cases & Materials On. 4th ed. Robert W. Wright & Morton Gitelman. (American Casebook Ser.). 172p. 1991. pap. text. write for info. (0-314-87476-3) West Pub.

Land Use to Accompany Cases & Materials On. 2nd ed. David L. Callies et al. (American Casebook Ser.). 200p. 1994. pap. text, teacher ed. write for info. (0-314-04263-6) West Pub.

Land Use-Transport System. 2nd ed. W. R. Blunden & J. A. Black. (Urban & Regional Planning Ser.: Vol. 2). (Illus.). 264p. 1984. text 56.00 (0-08-029836-2, Pergamon Pr); pap. text 27.00 (0-08-029841-9, Pergamon Pr) Elsevier.

Land Use, Urban Form & Environmental Quality. Brian J. L. Berry & Andrew J. Bruzewicz. LC 73-87830. (University of Chicago, Department of Geography, Research Paper Ser.: No. 155). 466p. 1974. reprint ed. pap. 144.50 (0-608-02246-2, 206288700004) Bks Demand.

Land Use Without Zoning. Bernard H. Siegan. LC 72-186339. (Illus.). 288p. 1993. reprint ed. pap. 12.50 (0-9638867-9-7) Bartholdi & Lazarus.

***Land Use, Zoning & Private Controls on Real Estate.** 3rd ed. Michael L. Ades et al. 278p. 1998. pap. 48.00 (1-58757-020-3, GM028) Univ of KY.

Land Uses in American Cities. Harold M. Mayer & Charles R. Hayes. LC 82-81036. (Illus.). 200p. (Orig.). (C). 1983. pap. text 9.95 (0-941226-02-6) Park Pr Co.

Land Uses in American Cities. Harland Bartholomew. LC 55-5059. (Harvard City Planning Studies: No. 15). 208p. reprint ed. pap. 64.50 (0-7837-4098-0, 205792100011) Bks Demand.

Land Utilization in American Samoa. J. W. Coulter. (BMB Ser.: Vol. 170). 1969. reprint ed. pap. 25.00 (0-527-02278-0) Periodicals Srv.

Land Utilization in China: An Extremely Detailed Study of 16,786 Farms, 3 vols., Set. John L. Buck. (Illus.). 1986. reprint ed. 290.00 (0-89986-377-9) Oriental Bk Store.

Land Utilization in the Karst Region of Zgornja Pivka, Slovenia. Paul B. Alexander. LC 75-9151. 132p. 1967. 9.00 (0-686-28379-1) Studia Slovenica.

Land Valuation Law. 7th ed. J. P. McVeagh. 1979. boxed set 58.00 (0-409-64584-2, NZ, MICHIE) LEXIS Pub.

***Land Value Taxation: Can It & Will It Work Today?** Dick Netzer. LC 98-49916. 284p. 1998. pap. 25.00 (1-55844-133-6) Lincoln Ingalls Bks.

Land Value Taxation: Impact Analysis on Omaha-Douglas County, Nebraska. Gary Carlson. 72p. (Orig.). 1976. pap. 6.00 (1-55719-043-7) U NE CPAR.

***Land-Value Taxation: The Equitable & Efficient Source of Public Finance.** Ed. & Contrib. by Kenneth C. Wenzer. LC 98-55374. 320p. 1999. text 99.95 (0-7656-0448-5) M E Sharpe.

***Land-Value Taxation: The Equitable & Efficient Source of Public Finance.** Ed. & Contrib. by Kenneth C. Wenzer. 320p. 2000. reprint ed. pap. text 29.95 (0-7656-0449-3) M E Sharpe.

Land Values & Environmental Characteristics in the Rural-Urban Fringe. Robert E. Coughlin & James Fritz. (Discussion Papers: No. 45). 1971. pap. 10.00 (1-55869-066-2) Regional Sci Res Inst.

Land Values in New York in Relation to Transit Facilities. Edwin H. Spengler. LC 68-58624. (Columbia University. Studies in the Social Sciences: No. 333). reprint ed. 24.00 (0-404-51333-6) AMS Pr.

Land War in Ireland. Wilfred S. Blunt. LC 75-28808. (Celtic Ser.). 528p. reprint ed. 57.50 (0-404-13801-2) AMS Pr.

***Land Was Everything: Letters from an American Farmer.** Victor Davis Hanson. LC 99-55317. 258p. 2000. 24.00 (0-684-84501-6) Free Pr.

Land Was Theirs: Jewish Farmers in the Garden State. Gertrude W. Dubrovsky. LC 90-10740. (Judaic Studies). (Illus.). 272p. (C). 1992. pap. text 32.95 (0-8173-0544-0) U of Ala Pr.

Land, Water, & Culture: New Perspectives on Hispanic Land Grants. Ed. by Charles L. Briggs & John R. Van Ness. LC 87-10957. (New Mexico Land Grant Ser.). (Illus.). 432p. reprint ed. pap. 134.00 (0-7837-5860-X, 204557900006) Bks Demand.

Land, Water & Development: River Basin Systems & Their Sustainable Management. Malcolm Newson. LC 91-39206. (Natural Environment: Problems & Management Ser.). (Illus.). 384p. (C). (gr. 13). 1992. text 89.95 (0-415-05711-6, A7502) Routledge.

An Asterisk (*) at the beginning of an entry indicates that the title is appearing for the first time.

L

Land, Water, & Development: Sustainable Management of River Basin Systems. 2nd ed. Malcolm D. Newson. LC 97-7592. (Illus.). 464p. (C). 1997. 110.00 (*0-415-15506-1*); pap. 32.99 (*0-415-15507-X*) Routledge.

Land, Water, & Settlement in Kern County, California, 1850-1890. Ed. by Stuart Bruchey. LC 78-56723. (Management of Public Lands in the U. S. Ser.). 1979. lib. bdg. 31.95 (*0-405-11328-5*) Ayer.

Land We Live On. Jill Wheeler. (J). (gr. 2-6). 1990. lib. bdg. 11.99 (*1-56239-003-1*, 937470) ABDO Pub Co.

Land Where Our Fathers Died. large type ed. Helen S. Nuelle. (Linford Mystery Library). 384p. 1992. pap. 16.99 (*0-7089-7230-6*) Ulverscroft.

Land Where Two Streams Flow: Music in the German-Jewish Community of Israel. Philip V. Bohlman. LC 88-25902. (Illus.). 280p. 1989. text 24.95 (*0-252-01596-7*) U of Ill Pr.

Land Where We Belong Journey. 1990. 19.95 (*0-9626682-4-9*) Herit Pub TX.

Land Window. John Graham. LC 99-187700. No.5. 56p. 1998. pap. 19.95 (*0-7022-3017-0*) Intl Spec Bk.

***Land Without a Country.** Bonnie Jo Hunt & Lawrence J. Hunt. (Lone Wolf Clan Bks.: Vol. V). (Illus.). 254p. 2000. pap. 15.00 (*1-928800-04-1*) Mad Bear Pr.

Land Without Evil. unabridged ed. Matthew J. Pallamary. LC 99-33503. 352p. 2000. 24.95 (*0-912880-09-0*) Charles Pub.

Land-Without-Evil: Tupi-Guarani Prophetism. Helene Clastres. Tr. by Jacqueline G. Brovender. LC 94-32437. 144p. 1995. text 39.95 (*0-252-02055-3*) U of Ill Pr.

Land Without Evil: Tupi-Guarani Prophetism. Helene Clastres & Jonathan D. Hill. Tr. by Jacqueline Grenez Brovender. LC 94-32437. 144p. 1995. pap. text 13.95 (*0-252-06351-1*) U of Ill Pr.

Land Without Evil: Utopian Journeys Across the South American Watershed. Richard Gott. LC 92-29119. 400p. (C). (gr. 13). 1993. 35.00 (*0-86091-398-8*, A9704, Pub. by Verso) Norton.

Land Without Ghosts: Chinese Impressions of America from the Mid-Nineteenth Century to the Present. Ed. by R. David Arkush & Leo O. Lee. 1989. pap. 17.95 (*0-520-08424-1*, Pub. by U CA Pr) Cal Prin Full Svc.

Land Without Law. Brock Thoene. 480p. 1999. 12.99 (*0-88486-253-4*) Galahad Bks.

Landa List: Grammar Guidelines Proofreading Principles & Punctuation Practices. 3rd rev. ed. David Hatcher & Lane Goddard. 48p. 1998. pap. 5.95 (*1-57420-001-1*) Chatelaine.

Landartz und andere Drucke zu Lebzeiten. Franz Kafka. Ed. by Wolfgang Kittler. (GER.). 384p. 1994. pap. 13.50 (*3-596-12441-7*, Pub. by Fischer Tasch) Intl Bk Import.

Landa's Relacion de las Cosas de Yucatan. Diego De Landa. Ed. by Alfred M. Tozzer. LC 83-45906. reprint ed. 48.00 (*0-404-20150-4*) AMS Pr.

Landau: A Great Physicist & Teacher. Anna Livanova. Tr. by J. B. Sykes. 226p. 1980. 77.00 (*0-08-023076-8*, Pergamon Pr) Elsevier.

Landau: The Physicist & the Man: Recollections of L. D. Landau. Ed. by Isaac M. Khalatnikov. Tr. by J. B. Sykes. (Illus.). 342p. 1989. 158.25 (*0-08-036383-0*, Pergamon Pr) Elsevier.

Landau Fermi Liquid Theory: Concepts & Applications. Gordon Baym & Christopher Pethick. LC 91-16606. 216p. 1991. 105.00 (*0-471-82418-6*) Wiley.

Landau Level Spectroscopy, 2 pts., Set. Ed. by G. Landwehr & E. I. Rashba. 1300p. 1990. 617.00 (*0-444-88874-8*, North Holland) Elsevier.

Landau Theory of Phase Transitions. J. C. Toledano & Pierre Toledano. (Lecture Notes in Physics Ser.: Vol. 3). 472p. 1987. text 79.00 (*9971-5-0025-6*); pap. text 43.00 (*9971-5-0026-4*) World Scientific Pub.

***Landbridge: Contemporary Australian Poetry.** Ed. by John Kinsella. 342p. 1999. pap. 19.95 (*1-86368-269-4*, Pub. by Fremantle Arts) Intl Spec Bk.

Landcare. Andrew Campbell. (Illus.). 356p. 1995. pap. 17.95 (*1-86373-555-0*, Pub. by Allen & Unwin Pty) Paul & Co Pubs.

Juta Legislation Service: Magistrates' Courts Act 32 of 1944. Date not set. ring bd. 37.50 (*0-7021-1646-7*, Pub. by Juta & Co) Gaunt.

Landed Estates in the Colonial Philippines. Nicholas P. Cushner. LC 75-27615. (Monographs: No. 20). 146p. 1976. 11.50 (*0-938692-10-0*) Yale U SE Asia.

Landed Estates of the Esterhazy Princes: Hungary During the Reforms of Maria Theresia & Joseph II. Rebecca Gates-Coon. LC 93-50616. (Studies in Historical & Political Science: No. 112). 1994. text 48.50 (*0-8018-4785-0*) Johns Hopkins.

Landed Interest & the Supply of Food. 4th ed. James Caird. LC 67-16346. (Reprints of Economic Classics Ser.). xx, 184p. 1967. reprint ed. 25.00 (*0-678-05034-1*) Kelley.

Landed Interest & the Supply of Food. 5th rev. ed. James Caird. 184p. 1967. 26.00 (*0-7146-1042-9*, Pub. by F Cass Pubs) Intl Spec Bk.

Landed Patiarchy in Fielding's Novels: Fictional Landscapes, Fictional Genders. Gary Gautier. LC 98-12876. (Studies in British Literature: Vol. 35). 360p. 1998. text 99.95 (*0-7734-8509-0*) E Mellen.

Landed Society & the Farming Community of Essex in the Late 18th & Early 19th Centuries. Colin Shrimpton. Ed. by Stuart Bruchey. LC 77-77185. (Dissertations in European Economic History Ser.). 1978. lib. bdg. 42.95 (*0-405-10798-6*) Ayer.

Lander: One-Shot Antelope Hunt. Ruby W. Dahl et al. (Illus.). 129p. 1986. 19.95 (*0-9617178-0-7*) One-Shot Antelope Hunt.

Lander: One-Shot Antelope Hunt. deluxe limited ed. Ruby W. Dahl et al. (Illus.). 129p. 1986. 50.00 (*0-9617178-1-5*) One-Shot Antelope Hunt.

Lander's List of Orchids Hybrids Addendum, 1961-1970. Scientific Publishers Staff. (C). 1988. 185.00 (*0-7855-3268-4*, Pub. by Scientific) St Mut.

Landes et Marines. Andre Suares. Ed. by Yves-Alain Favre. (FRE., Illus.). 160p. 1995. pap. 64.95 (*0-614-14017-X*) Intl Scholars.

Landes und Reisebeschreibungen: Ein Beitrag Zur Bibliographie der Schweizerischen, Reiselitteratur 1479-1900. Alex Waeber. 641p. 1997. reprint ed. 95.00 (*1-57898-042-9*) Martino Pubng.

Landesherrliche Kanzleien im Spatmittelalter. (Munchener Beitrage zur Mediavistik und Renaissance-Forschung Ser.: Band 35). (GER.). xx, 765p. 1983. 178.00 (*3-615-00166-4*, Pub. by Weidmann) Lubrecht & Cramer.

Landeskunde und Literaturdidaktik. M. Bischof & V. Kessling. Ed. by Gerd Neuner. (Fernstudienangebot Ser.). (GER.). 184p. 1996. 11.25 (*3-468-49677-X*) Langenscheidt.

Landfall. Chris Price. 1995. pap. 15.00 (*0-614-07568-8*, Pub. by Univ Otago Pr) Intl Spec Bk.

Landfall. Nevil Shute. 23.95 (*0-8488-0319-1*) Amereon Ltd.

Landfall in Southern Seas: Proceedings of the 8th Australasian Congress on Genealogy & Heraldry Held at Lincoln University, Christchurch, New Zealand, February, 1997 by the New Zealand Society of Genealogists Inc. under the Auspices of the Australasian Federation of Family History Organizations, 2 vols. Australasian Congress on Genealogy & Heraldry Staff et al. LC 97-198440. 1997. write for info. (*0-473-04140-5*) New Leaf Dist.

Landfall Legalese Vol. I: The Pacific. Alan E. Spears. 192p. (Orig.). 1995. 29.95 (*0-939837-19-6*) Paradise Cay Pubns.

Landfall Legalese Vol. II: The Caribbean. Alan E. Spears. 120p. 1995. 24.95 (*0-939837-20-X*) Paradise Cay Pubns.

Landfall, 1947-1997: A New Zealand Half-Century. Peter Simpson & Chris Price. (Illus.). 240p. 1999. pap. 59.95 (*1-877133-38-8*, Pub. by Univ Otago Pr) Intl Spec Bk.

Landfall 193. Ed. by Chris Price. 184p. 1997. pap. 21.95 (*1-877133-28-0*, Pub. by Univ Otago Pr) S Asia.

Landfall Press: 25 Years of Printmaking. Milwaukee Art Museum Staff. LC 96-77356. (Illus.). 300p. 1996. pap. 39.95 (*0-944110-68-1*, 620663) Milwauk Art Mus.

Landfalls of Paradise: Cruising Guide to the Pacific Islands. 4th ed. Earl Hinz. LC 98-33620. (Illus.). x, 369p. 1999. pap. 44.95 (*0-8248-2115-7*) UH Pr.

Landfill. Ed. by P. Baccini. (Lecture Notes in Earth Sciences Ser.: Vol. 20). (Illus.). 439p. 1989. 72.95 (*0-387-50694-2*) Spr-Verlag.

Landfill Bioreactor Design & Operation. Debra R. Reinhart & Timothy G. Townsend. LC 97-22220. 208p. 1997. boxed set 69.95 (*1-56670-259-3*) Lewis Pubs.

Landfill Closures. Robert M. Koerner. x, 258p. 1991. 145.00 (*1-85166-644-3*, Pub. by Elsvr Adv Tech) Elsevier.

Landfill Closures - Environmental Protection & Land Recovery: Proceedings of Sessions Sponsored by the Environmental Geotechnics Committee of the Geotechnical Engineering Division & the Solid Waste Engineering Committee of the Environmental Engineering Division of the American Society of Civil Engineers in Conjunction with the ASCE Convention in San Diego, California, October 23-27, 1995. Ed. by R. Jeffrey Dunn & Udai P. Singh. (Geotechnical Special Publications: Vol. 53). 248p. 1995. 31.00 (*0-7844-0119-5*) Am Soc Civil Eng.

Landfill Design & Construction. Richard K. Miller & Marcia E. Rupnow. LC 90-83887. (Survey on Technology & Markets Ser.: No. 183). 50p. 1991. pap. text 200.00 (*1-55865-207-8*) Future Tech Surveys.

Landfill Design, Construction & Operational Practice. Department of the Environment Staff. (Waste Management Paper Ser.: No. 26B). 299p. 1995. 50.00 (*0-11-753185-5*, Pub. by Statnry Office) Balogh.

Landfill Emission of Gases into the Atmosphere. Ed. by Victor Popov & Henry Power. LC 98-84460. (Advances in Air Pollution Ser.: Vol. 4). (Illus.). 200p. 1999. 120.00 (*1-85312-616-0*, 6160, Pub. by WIT Pr) Computational Mech MA.

Landfill Golf Courses: Suitable Developments for Otherwise Unsuitable Sites. 210p. 1998. pap. 60.00 (*1-57701-119-8*, 99GCP51) Natl Golf.

Landfill Meditation: Crossblood Stories. Gerald R. Vizenor. LC 91-50375. 211p. 1991. pap. 14.95 (*0-8195-6253-X*, Wesleyan Univ Pr) U Pr of New Eng.

Landfill Methane Gas Recovery. Richard K. Miller & Marcia E. Rupnow. LC 90-83892. (Survey on Technology & Markets Ser.: No. 188). 50p. 1991. pap. text 200.00 (*1-55865-212-4*) Future Tech Surveys.

Landfill of Hazardous Industrial Wastes: A Training Manual. (Tecnical Report Ser.: No. 17). 315p. 40.00 (*92-807-1384-1*) UN.

Landfill Privatization. Richard K. Miller & Marcia E. Rupnow. LC 90-83886. (Survey on Technology & Markets Ser.: No. 182). 50p. 1991. pap. text 200.00 (*1-55865-206-X*) Future Tech Surveys.

Landfill Supervisor. (Career Examination Ser.: C-3639). pap. 29.95 (*0-8373-3639-2*) Nat Learn.

Landfill Waste Pollution & Control. Kenneth Westlake. 160p. 1995. 49.95 (*1-898563-08-X*) Paul & Co Pubs.

Landfilling of Waste: Barriers. Ed. by T. H. Christensen et al. LC 94-211287. (Illus.). 656p. (C). 1994. 200.00 (*0-419-15990-8*, E & FN Spon) Routledge.

Landfilling of Waste - Lining & Leachate Collection. Ed. by Thomas H. Christensen et al. LC 92-26269. 1993. write for info. (*1-85166-898-5*) Elsevier.

Landfilling of Waste Biogas. T. H. Christensen. 864p. (C). (gr. 13). 1996. 220.00 (*0-419-19400-2*) Chapman & Hall.

Landfilling of Waste Leachate. Ed. by T. H. Christensen. 656p. (C). (gr. 13). 1992. text 200.00 (*0-419-16140-6*) Chapman & Bkman.

Landfilling of Water Treatment Plant Coagulant Sludges. (Illus.). 154p. 1992. pap. 52.00 (*0-89867-654-1*, 90616) Am Water Wks Assn.

Landform Dynamics: An Exercise Manual. 2nd ed. Michael Lewis. 78p. (C). per. 70.95 (*0-7872-6626-4*) Kendall-Hunt.

Landform Dynamics: An Exercise Manual. Michael Lewis. 60p. (C). 1997. per. 47.50 (*0-7872-4332-9*) Kendall-Hunt.

Landform Monitoring Modelling & Analysis. S. N. Lane et al. LC 97-5546. 466p. 1998. 125.00 (*0-471-96977-X*) Wiley.

Landforms--Heart of the Colorado Plateau: The Story Behind the Scenery. Gary Ladd. LC 95-75094. (Illus.). 48p. 1995. pap. 7.95 (*0-88714-090-4*) KC Pubns.

Landforms--Heart of the Colorado Plateau: The Story Behind the Scenery. Gary Ladd. Tr. by Brigitte Morales. (GER., Illus.). 48p. 1995. pap. 8.95 (*0-88714-804-2*) KC Pubns.

Landforms Activity Book. Charlene Stout. Ed. by Kathy Rogers. (Hands-On Science Ser.). (Illus.). 48p. 1998. pap., wbk. ed. 6.95 (*1-56472-119-1*) Edupress Inc.

Landforms & Landscapes. 3rd ed. Sherwood Tuttle. 184p. (C). 1980. text. write for info. (*0-697-05020-3*, WCB McGr Hill) McGrw-H Hghr Educ.

Landforms of Iowa. Jean C. Prior. LC 91-16136. (Bur Oak Original Ser.). (Illus.). 168p. 1991. pap. 15.95 (*0-87745-347-0*); text 34.95 (*0-87745-350-0*) U of Iowa Pr.

Landforms of the Earth. H. Frater. 1997. pap. 37.95 incl. cd-rom (*3-540-14610-5*) Spr-Verlag.

Landforms Photo Fun Activities. Linda Milliken. Ed. by Kathy Rogers. (Science Photo Fun Activities Ser.). (Illus.). 8p. 1997. 6.95 (*1-56472-083-7*) Edupress Inc.

Landgrafenpsalter. fac. limited ed. Contrib. by F. Heinzer et al. (Codices Selecti A Ser.: Vol. XCIII). (GER.). 384p. 1992. lthr. 3420.00 (*3-201-01558-X*, Pub. by Akademische Druck-und) Balogh.

Landholders of Northeastern New York, 1739-1802. Fred Q. Bowman. LC 83-80308. 228p. 1987. reprint ed. 20.00 (*0-8063-1026-X*) Genealog Pub.

Landholding & Commercial Agriculture in the Middle East. Ed. by Caglar Keyder & Faruk Tabak. LC 90-35231. (SUNY Series in the Social & Economic History of the Middle East). 267p. (C). 1991. pap. text 21.95 (*0-7914-0551-6*) State U NY Pr.

Landing. Warren Woessner. LC 73-91972. 52p. 1973. 5.95 (*0-87886-035-5*, Greenfld Rev Pr); pap. 2.95 (*0-87886-036-3*, Greenfld Rev Pr) Greenfld Rev Lit.

Landing: A Night of Birds. Katherine Scholes. (Illus.). 71p. (J). (gr. 4-7). 1994. 14.95 (*0-85572-165-0*, Pub. by Hill Content Pubng) Seven Hills Bk.

Landing a Job. Patricia Duffy. (Hire Learning, Schooling That Works Ser.). 1997. pap. text, wbk. ed. 6.95 (*1-56370-189-8*) JIST Works.

Landing at Plymouth. Lucille R. Penna. 1996. 13.00 (*0-679-83201-7*) McKay.

Landing Gear Design for Light Aircraft, Vol. 1. Ladislao Pazmany. Ed. by Pazmany Aircraft Corporation Staff. (Illus.). 252p. 1986. pap. 45.00 (*0-9616777-0-8*) Pazmany Aircraft.

Landing in Minneapolis. Rex McGuinn. 64p. (Orig.). Date not set. pap. 8.95 (*1-879934-06-X*) St Andrews NC.

Landing in Minneapolis. Rex McGuinn. 72p. (Orig.). 1993. pap. 8.95 (*1-879934-19-1*) St Andrews NC.

***Landing It: My Life on & Off the Ice.** Scott Hamilton. (Illus.). 480p. 2000. mass mkt. 6.99 (*0-7860-1149-1*, Pinncle Kensgtn) Kensgtn Pub Corp.

***Landing It: My Life on & off the Ice.** Scott Hamilton & Lorenzo Benet. LC 99-71666. (Illus.). 352p. 1999. 25.95 (*1-57566-466-6*, Knsington) Kensgtn Pub Corp.

***Landing It: My Life on & off the Ice.** large type ed. Scott Hamilton. LC 00-23437. (Biography Ser.). 674p. Date not set. 29.95 (*0-7862-2532-7*, MML06500-171972) Thorndike Pr.

Landing of Rochambeau: Poems. Michael Davidson. 80p. 1985. pap. 7.00 (*0-930901-26-6*) Burning Deck.

Landing of the Pilgrims. James H. Daugherty. (Landmark Bks.). (J). 1978. 11.09 (*0-606-02153-1*, Pub. by Turtleback) Demco.

Landing of the Pilgrims. James Daugherty. LC 80-21430. (Landmark Ser.). (Illus.). 160p. (J). (gr. 5-9). 1981. reprint ed. pap. 5.99 (*0-394-84697-4*, Pub. by Random Bks Yng Read) Random.

***Landing on the Wrong Note: Jazz, Dissonance & Critical Practice.** Ajay Heble. 2000. 75.00 (*0-415-92348-4*); pap. 18.99 (*0-415-92349-2*) Routledge.

Landing on Your Feet: An Inspirational Guide to Surviving, Coping, Prospering from Job Loss. Mara Brown. 1995. pap. 14.95 (*0-07-551377-3*) McGraw.

Landing on Your Feet: Your Guide to Survival in Tough Economic Times. James Waldorf. 192p. 1993. pap. 6.95 (*0-9635497-0-7*) J Waldorf Sales.

***Landing Party.** T. J. McFadden. 368p. 1999. mass mkt. 5.50 (*0-8439-4627-X*, Leisure Bks) Dorchester Pub Co.

Landing Ship Medium (LSM-LSMR), Vol. II. Turner Publishing Company. (Illus.). 168p. Date not set. 39.95 (*1-56311-389-9*) Turner Pub KY.

Landing Signals: An Anthology of Sacramento Poets. Ed. by Ann Menebroker et al. (Illus.). 256p. (Orig.). 1986. pap. 10.00 (*0-914485-09-1*); audio 10.00 (*0-914485-11-3*) Trill Pr.

Landing the Job You Want: How to Have the Best Job Interview of Your Life. William C. Byham & Debra Pickett. Ed. by Mary Matzen. (Illus.). 196p. (Orig.). 1997. pap. 19.95 (*0-9623483-4-1*, BPLJYWPB) Dev Dimensions.

Landing the Job You Want: How to Have the Best Job Interview of Your Life. William Byham & Debra Pickett. LC 99-12529. (Illus.). 195p. 1999. pap. 14.00 (*0-609-80408-1*) Random Hse Value.

Landing Zones: Combat Vets from America's Proud, Fighting South Remember Vietnam. James R. Wilson. 368p. 1993. mass mkt. 5.99 (*0-671-79560-0*) PB.

Landing Zones: Southern Veterans Remember Vietnam. James R. Wilson. LC 90-31859. 312p. (C). 1990. text 29.95 (*0-8223-1041-4*) Duke.

Landings in North Africa, 1942. 1994. lib. bdg. 250.00 (*0-8490-5806-6*) Gordon Pr.

Landings Soft. Elizabeth St. Jacques. (Chapbook Ser.). 16p. (Orig.). 1994. pap. 5.00 (*0-936545-21-6*) Amelia.

Landis Engineering & Mfg. Co. (Illus.). 16p. pap. 5.00 (*0-930163-63-X*) Arlington Bk.

Landis German Song. Nadine Holder. (Illus.). 42p. 1998. pap. 4.95 (*1-883294-68-1*) Masthof Pr.

Landis on Mechanics of Patent Claim Drafting. 3rd ed. Robert C. Faber. 548p. 1990. text 135.00 (*0-87224-006-1*, G1-1003) PLI.

Landis on Mechanics of Patent Claim Drafting. 4th ed. Robert C. Faber et al. LC 98-218545. 1997. 235.00 (*0-87224-096-7*) PLI.

Landis. Report of the 31st Reunion of the Landis-Landes Families Held at Perkasie Park, Perkasie, Bucks Co., Pa., 8/19/50. Ed. by Dorothy K. Landis. 65p. 1996. reprint ed. pap. 13.00 (*0-8328-5278-3*); reprint ed. lib. bdg. 23.00 (*0-8328-5277-5*) Higginson Bk Co.

Landkreis Aachen In der NS-Zeit. Ralph J. Jaud. (Illus.). 791p. 1997. 76.95 (*3-631-31911-8*) P Lang Pubng.

Landlady & Tenant: Poems. Helen Wolfert. LC 79-90842. 102p. 1979. pap. 12.95 (*0-935296-07-7*, Pub. by Sheep Meadow); text 11.95 (*0-935296-06-9*, Pub. by Sheep Meadow) U Pr of New Eng.

Landlady in Bangkok. Karen Swenson. LC 94-9843. (National Poetry Ser.). 96p. 1994. pap. 12.00 (*1-55659-067-9*) Copper Canyon.

Landlady's Daughter. Edward K. Burbridge. 210p. (Orig.). Date not set. pap. 25.00 (*0-9631261-1-3*) LA & Chi Riv Undgrd.

Landlay's Guide to Foreign Guests. William Webb. (C). 1988. 40.00 (*0-7223-2312-3*, Pub. by A H S Ltd) St Mut.

Landleaguers, 3 vols. Anthony Trollope. Ed. by N. John Hall. LC 80-1904. (Selected Works of Anthony Trollope). 1981. reprint ed. lib. bdg. 115.95 (*0-405-14198-X*) Ayer.

Landleaguers: (trollope 1995) Delaney. 1995. 38.00 (*1-870587-41-3*) Ashgate Pub Co.

Landler, Polkas & Mazurkas. Joseph Lanner. (Samtliche Werke fur Klavier Ser.: Vol. 6). 1973. reprint ed. pap. 65.00 (*0-8450-1016-6*) Broude.

Landless Peasants & Rural Poverty in Indonesia & the Philippines. Jean G. Rosenberg & David A. Rosenberg. (Special Series on Landlessness & Near-Landlessness: No. 3). 133p. (Orig.). (C). 1980. pap. text 8.65 (*0-86731-070-7*) Cornell CIS RDC.

Landless Peasants & Rural Poverty in Selected Asian Countries. David A. Rosenberg & Jean G. Rosenberg. (Special Series on Landlessness & Near-Landlessness: No. 2). 108p. (Orig.). (C). 1978. pap. text 7.95 (*0-86731-069-3*) Cornell CIS RDC.

Landlessness & Near-Landlessness in Developing Countries. Milton J. Esman. (Special Series on Landlessness & Near-Landlessness: No. 1). 71p. (Orig.). (C). 1978. pap. text 6.75 (*0-86731-068-5*) Cornell CIS RDC.

***Landline & Cellular Infrastructure Equip in Mexico: A Strategic Entry Report, 1996.** Compiled by Icon Group International Staff. (Illus.). 153p. 1999. ring bd. 1530.00 incl. audio compact disk (*0-7418-1467-6*) Icon Grp.

Landlocked: A Novel. Doris Lessing. LC 95-31489. 352p. 1995. pap. 13.00 (*0-06-097665-9*, Perennial) HarperTrade.

Landlooker. 2nd ed. William Steuber. LC 57-9353. Vol. 1. 372p. 1991. pap. 12.95 (*1-879483-04-1*) Prairie Oak Pr.

Landlooker in the Upper Peninsula of Michigan. John M. Longyear. LC 60-53288. 80p. 1983. reprint ed. 8.95 (*0-938746-06-5*) Marquette Cnty.

***Landlord.** Ken Merrell. Ed. by Stevens Anderson. 460p. 2000. pap. 7.99 (*0-9678510-1-7*) Kay Dee.

Landlord. Peter Vansittart. 187p. 1970. 29.95 (*0-7206-0231-9*) Dufour.

Landlord - Tenant: Rights & Obligations. LawPak Staff. (Illus.). 181p. (Orig.). 1996. pap. 16.95 (*1-879421-04-6*) LawPak.

Landlord - Tenant Rights in Florida: What You Need to Know. William D. Clark. (Florida Legal Ser.). 144p. 1993. pap. 12.95 (*0-88908-782-2*) Self-Counsel Pr.

Landlord & Labor in Late Imperial China: Case Studies from Shandong. Endymion P. Wilkinson et al. Tr. by Jing Su. (East Asian Monographs: No. 80). 300p. 1977. 32.50 (*0-674-50866-1*) HUP.

Landlord & Peasant in Colonial Oaxaca. William B. Taylor. LC 70-153819. (Illus.). xvi, 288p. 1972. 42.50 (*0-8047-0796-0*) Stanford U Pr.

Landlord & Peasant in Early Islam. Zia Ul-Haq. 1983. pap. 22.50 (*1-56744-117-3*) Kazi Pubns.

Landlord & Peasant in Persia: A Study of Land Tenure & Land Revenue Administration. Ann K. Lambton. 550p. 1991. text 65.00 (*1-85043-293-7*, Pub. by I B T) St Martin.

Landlord & Tenant. Ed. by Robert Lee. (C). 1991. text 22.00 (*1-85431-137-9*, Pub. by Blackstone Pr) Gaunt.

Landlord & Tenant. John R. Morris. (Lecture Notes...Ser.). 392p. 1995. pap. 34.00 (*1-85941-045-6*, Pub. by Cavendish Pubng) Gaunt.

Landlord & Tenant. 2nd ed. W. E. Cooper. LC 94-197944. 439p. 1994. pap. 47.50 (*0-7021-3079-6*, Pub. by Juta & Co) Gaunt.

Landlord & Tenant, Vol. 3. Irene L. Heng. (Singapore Law Ser.). 415p. 1990. pap. 80.00 (*0-409-99534-7*, MICHIE) LEXIS Pub.

An Asterisk (*) at the beginning of an entry indicates that the title is appearing for the first time.

Landlord & Tenant: The New Regime & Its Pitfalls. Martin Boxer. 1996. pap. 40.00 (*1-85941-283-1*, Pub. by Cavendish Pubng) Gaunt.

Landlord & Tenant Act, 1987. Hugh Rossi. 1987. pap. 110.00 (*0-7219-1070-X*, Pub. by Scientific) St Mut.

Landlord & Tenant & Their Relationship. Jimmy L. Kum & David J. Kum. 218p. 1992. 49.95 (*0-9626817-4-1*) J L Kum.

Landlord & Tenant Guide to Colorado Evictions. Victor M. Grimm. 170p. (Orig.). 1995. pap. 18.50 (*1-883726-03-4*) Bradford Pub.

Landlord & Tenant in Colonial New York: Manorial Society, 1664-1775. Sung B. Kim. LC 77-24423. (Illus.). 478p. 1978. reprint ed. pap. 148.20 (*0-7837-9020-1*, 204977200003) Bks Demand.

Landlord & Tenant in Practice. Richard Colbey et al. 217p. 1998. pap. 48.00 (*1-85431-720-2*, Pub. by Blackstone Pr) Gaunt.

Landlord & Tenant in Practice. 2nd ed. Richard Colbey et al. 219p. 1999. pap. 50.00 (*1-85431-904-3*, Pub. by Blackstone Pr) Gaunt.

***Landlord & Tenant in Practice.** 3rd ed. Richard Colbey et al. (Inns of Court School of Law Ser.). 219p. 2000. pap. 46.00 (*1-84174-007-1*, Pub. by Blackstone Pr) Gaunt.

Landlord & Tenant in Urban Britain, 1938-1918. David Englander. 1983. pap. 57.00 (*0-19-822680-2*) OUP.

Landlord & Tenant Law. (Legal Ser.). 1992. lib. bdg. 250.00 (*0-8490-5317-X*) Gordon Pr.

Landlord & Tenant Law. 2nd ed. Barbara Martin & Folla Christie. 448p. 1994. pap. 39.95 (*0-632-03469-6*) Blackwell Sci.

Landlord & Tenant Law: The Nature of Tenancies. Susan Bright. (Illus.). 844p. 1995. pap. text 41.00 (*0-19-876349-2*) OUP.

Landlord & Tenant Law: The Nature of Tenancies. Susan Bright & Geoffrey Gilbert. (Illus.). 848p. 1995. text 79.00 (*0-19-876348-4*) OUP.

Landlord & Tenant Law in a Nutshell. 3rd ed. David S. Hill. LC 79-11051. (Nutshell Ser.). 310p. (C). 1994. pap. 21.00 (*0-314-04744-1*) West Pub.

Landlord & Tenant on the Cotton Plantation. Thomas J. Woofter, Jr. LC 77-165691. (FDR & the Era of the New Deal Ser.). 1971. reprint ed. lib. bdg. 29.50 (*0-306-70337-8*) Da Capo.

Landlord & Tenant on the Cotton Plantation. Thomas J. Woofter. LC 74-75537. (Illus.). 288p. 1969. reprint ed. lib. bdg. 45.00 (*0-8371-1035-1*, WOL&) Greenwood.

Landlord & Tenant Practice in New York. Daniel Finkelstein & Lucas A. Ferrara. LC 98-131992. (West's New York Practice Ser.). 1997. write for info. (*0-314-23098-X*) West Pub.

Landlord Assistance Kit. Richard Sheppard & Michael Sheppard. (Illus.). 69p. (Orig.). 1996. pap. text 29.95 (*0-9656493-0-X*) Mortgage Specialists.

Landlord at Lion's Head. William Dean Howells. (Notable American Authors Ser.). 1992. reprint ed. lib. bdg. 75.00 (*0-7812-3250-3*) Rprt Serv.

Landlord at Lion's Head: A Novel. William Dean Howells. LC 75-41144. (Illus.). reprint ed. 45.00 (*0-404-14778-X*) AMS Pr.

Landlord Power & Rural Indebtedness in Colonial Sind. David Cheesman. (SOAS London Studies on South Asia: No. 11). 288p. (C). 1996. text 48.00 (*0-7007-0470-1*, Pub. by Curzon Pr Ltd) UH Pr.

Landlord Remedies in Florida. John J. Boyle. Date not set. ring bd. 80.00 (*0-327-00960-8*, 80871, MICHIE) LEXIS Pub.

Landlord-Tenant Law. pap. 5.00 (*0-317-03734-X*, 37,357L) NCLS Inc.

Landlord-Tenant Problems: Texas Edition. Stuart J. Faber. 1978. pap. 7.95 (*0-89074-059-3*) Lega Bks.

Landlord Tenant Relations. 3.50 (*0-317-57490-6*) Inst Dev Indian Law.

Landlord-Tenant Relations. Mike Daniel & Tom Weathered. 49p. pap. 5.00 (*0-685-23166-6*, 41,575L) NCLS Inc.

Landlord-Tenant Rights in Ontario: Canadian Edition. 10th rev. ed. Ron McInnes. (Legal Ser.). 192p. 1994. pap. 9.95 (*0-88908-493-9*) Self-Counsel Pr.

Landlord-Tenant Solutions in California. Steven A. MacDonald. 196p. 1999. 24.95 (*0-9654726-6-3*) Investment Pub.

Landlording: A Handy Manual for Scrupulous Landlords & Landladies Who Do It Themselves. 8th ed. Leigh Robinson. LC 97-77003. (Illus.). 526p. 1997. pap. 24.95 (*0-932956-21-1*) ExPress.

Landlording As a Second Income: The Survival Handbook. Lawrence L. Stevens. 230p. 1994. 19.95 (*0-8128-4024-0*, Scrbrough Hse) Madison Bks UPA.

Landlords & Capitalists: The Dominant Class of Chle. Maurice Zeitlin & Richard E. Ratcliff. LC 87-33010. 313p. 1988. reprint ed. pap. 97.10 (*0-608-07538-8*, 206775400009) Bks Demand.

Landlords & Governments in Uttar Pradesh. Peter Reeves. (Illus.). 384p. 1992. 35.00 (*0-19-562728-8*) OUP.

Landlords & Land Reform: Socio-Economic Impact on Landlords in Taiwan. Wasim A. Zaman et al. LC HD1333.T34. 115p. reprint ed. pap. 35.70 (*0-7837-3872-2*, 204370800010) Bks Demand.

Landlords & Property: Social Relations in the Private Rented Sector. John Allen & Linda McDowell. (Cambridge Human Geography Ser.). 224p. (C). 1989. text 59.95 (*0-521-36028-5*) Cambridge U Pr.

Landlords & Tenants. Jerome G. Rose. LC 72-82194. 288p. 1976. text 39.95 (*0-87855-042-9*); pap. text 24.95 (*0-87855-538-2*) Transaction Pubs.

Landlords' & Tenants' Guide. Judon Fambrough. LC 96-620024. 95p. 1991. 10.00 (*1-56248-002-2*, 866) TX A&M Univ Real Estate Ctr.

Landlords & Tenants in Mid-Victorian Ireland. W. E. Vaughan. (Illus.). 362p. 1994. text 69.00 (*0-19-820356-X*) OUP.

Landlords Are People Too. Suzanne Taylor-Moore. 48p. 1980. pap. 2.50 (*0-938758-06-3*) MTM Pub Co.

Landlord's Book on Evictions. (Legal Ser.). 1992. lib. bdg. 250.00 (*0-8490-5314-5*) Gordon Pr.

Landlord's Handbook: A Complete Guide to Managing Small Residential Properties. 2nd ed. Daniel Goodwin & Richard Rusdorf. LC 97-37313. 250p. 1998. pap. 29.95 incl. 3.5 ld (*0-7931-2732-7*, 4105-0802, Real Estate Ed) Dearborn.

***Landlord's Law Book.** 7th ed. David W. Brown & Ralph E. Warner. LC 99-86063. 2000. write for info. (*0-87337-581-5*) Nolo com.

Landlord's Law Book Vol. 1: Rights & Responsibilities. 6th rev. ed. David Brown & Ralph E. Warner. (Illus.). 336p. 1998. pap. 34.95 (*0-87337-443-6*) Nolo com.

Landlords'-Owners' Liability (1981) Mark L. Levine. 1989. write for info. (*0-317-00909-5*) Prof Pubns & Educ.

Landlord's Primer for Georgia: A Self-Help Guide for Landlords. Mary Farmer. 120p. 1994. 12.95 (*0-9636735-0-5*) Global Interests.

Landlord's Remedies in Florida. John J. Boyle. 1994. ring bd., suppl. ed. 30.00 (*0-685-25719-3*, MICHIE) LEXIS Pub.

Landlord's Remedies in Florida. Trisha Zeller-James & John J. Boyle. 68p. 1997. ring bd. 80.00 (*0-409-26655-8*, 80872-14, MICHIE) LEXIS Pub.

Landlord's Rights & Duties in California. John J. Talamo & Mark Warda. LC 98-15277. (Legal Survival Guides Ser.). 240p. 1998. pap. 19.95 (*1-57071-359-6*) Sourcebks.

***Landlords' Rights & Duties in Florida.** 8th rev. ed. Mark Warda. (Legal Survival Guides Ser.). 240p. 2000. pap. 19.95 (*1-57248-123-4*, Sphinx Pubng) Sourcebks.

Landlords' Rights & Duties in Illinois. Diana B. Summers & Mark Warda. LC 99-13180. (Legal Survival Guides Ser.). 256p. 1999. pap. 19.95 (*1-57248-078-5*, Sphinx Pubng) Sourcebks.

Landlord's Rights & Duties in Massachusetts. 2nd ed. Joseph P. DiBlasi & Mark Warda. LC 99-33638. (Legal Survival Guides Ser.). 224p. 1999. pap. 19.95 (*1-57248-107-2*, Sphinx Pubng) Sourcebks.

Landlords' Rights & Duties in New York. Brette M. Sember & Mark Warda. LC 97-48346. (Legal Survival Guides Ser.). 224p. (Orig.). 1999. pap. 19.95 (*1-57071-186-0*) Sourcebks.

***Landlords' Rights & Duties in North Carolina.** Jacqueline D. Stanley & Mark Warda. LC 99-35772. (Legal Survival Guides Ser.). 240p. 1999. pap. 19.95 (*1-57248-091-2*, Sphinx Pubng) Sourcebks.

Landlords' Rights & Duties in Pennsylvania. Gerald S. Gaetano & Mark Warda. LC 99-30952. (Legal Survival Guides Ser.). 224p. (Orig.). 1999. pap. 19.95 (*1-57071-179-8*) Sourcebks.

Landlords' Rights & Duties in Texas. 2nd ed. William R. Brown & Mark Warda. LC 99-53002. (Legal Survival Guides Ser.). 208p. 2000. pap. 19.95 (*1-57248-110-2*, Sphinx Pubng) Sourcebks.

Landlord's Troubleshooter. 2nd ed. Robert Irwin. LC 99-29568. 288p. 1999. pap. 17.95 (*0-7931-3344-0*, 19132402) Dearborn.

Landlord/Tenant Law. Margaret C. Jasper. LC 98-45130. (Legal Almanac Ser.). 115p. 1998. text 22.50 (*0-379-11249-3*, 4582349) Oceana.

Landlord/tenant rights in Oregon. Vanessa Grant. 224p. (Orig.). 1997. pap. 15.95 (*1-55180-096-9*) Self-Counsel Pr.

Landlord/Tenant Rights in Oregon. 6th ed. Janay Haas. LC 97-910561. (Oregon Legal Ser.). 328p. 1997. pap. 13.95 (*1-55180-095-0*) Self-Counsel Pr.

Landman's Legal Handbook. 4th ed. 336p. 1982. 36.00 (*0-614-06619-0*, LLH) Rocky Mtn Mineral Law Found.

Landmark. James L. Allen. LC 70-110177. (Short Story Index Reprint Ser.). 1977. 18.95 (*0-8369-3328-1*) Ayer.

Landmark. James L. Allen. (Principle Works of James Lane Allen). 1989. reprint ed. lib. bdg. 79.00 (*0-685-44737-5*) Rprt Serv.

Landmark Abortion Cases: Planned Parenthood vs. Casey. 1400p. 195.00 (*0-89093-819-9*) U Pubns Amer.

Landmark Abortion Cases: Roe vs. Wade. 195.00 (*0-685-71086-6*) U Pubns Amer.

Landmark Abortion Cases: Webster vs. Reproductive Health Services. 195.00 (*0-685-71085-8*) U Pubns Amer.

Landmark American Bridges. Ed. by Eric DeLony. LC 92-24530. 160p. 1993. 43.00 (*0-87262-857-4*) Am Soc Civil Eng.

Landmark American Bridges, Vol. 1. Eric Delony. (Illus.). 152p. 1993. 40.00 (*0-8212-2036-5*, Pub. by Bulfinch Pr) Little.

Landmark American Speeches Vol. I: The 17th & 18th Centuries. Ed. by Maureen Harrison & Steve Gilbert. 272p. 2001. pap. 17.95 (*1-880780-16-X*) Excellent Bks.

Landmark American Speeches Vol. II: The 19th Century. Ed. by Maureen Harrison & Steve Gilbert. 272p. 2001. pap. 17.95 (*1-880780-17-8*) Excellent Bks.

Landmark American Speeches Vol. III: The 20th Century. Ed. by Maureen Harrison & Steve Gilbert. 272p. 2001. pap. 17.95 (*1-880780-18-6*) Excellent Bks.

Landmark Architecture: Pittsburgh & Allegheny County (1985) see Pittsburgh's Landmark Architecture: The Historic Buildings of Pittsburgh & Allegheny County

Landmark Briefs & Arguments of the Supreme Court of the United States: Constitutional Law, 7 vols. Ed. by Philip B. Kurland & Gerhard Casper. LC 75-15202. (Term Supplement 1981 Ser.: Vols. 127-133). 7000p. 1983. 875.00 (*0-89093-553-X*) U Pubns Amer.

Landmark Briefs & Arguments of the Supreme Court of the United States: Constitutional Law, 1793-1973, 80 vols. Supreme Court of the United States Staff et al. LC 75-15202. 80000p. 1977. 12770.00 (*0-89093-000-7*) U Pubns Amer.

Landmark Briefs & Arguments of the Supreme Court of the United States: Constitutional Law 1974 Term Supplement, Vol. 81-82. Ed. by Casper & Philip B. Kurland. LC 75-15202. 2000p. 1974. 305.00 (*0-89093-130-5*) U Pubns Amer.

Landmark Briefs & Arguments of the Supreme Court of the United States: Constitutional Law 1975 Term Supplement, Vol. 83-90. Ed. by Casper & Philip B. Kurland. LC 75-15202. 8000p. 1975. 1215.00 (*0-89093-131-3*) U Pubns Amer.

Landmark Briefs & Arguments of the Supreme Court of the United States: Constitutional Law 1976 Term Supplement, Vol. 91-98. Ed. by Casper & Philip B. Kurland. LC 75-15202. 8000p. 1976. 1215.00 (*0-89093-185-2*) U Pubns Amer.

Landmark Briefs & Arguments of the Supreme Court of the United States: Constitutional Law 1977 Term Supplement, 99-105. Ed. by Casper & Philip B. Kurland. LC 75-15202. 1977. 1065.00 (*0-89093-197-6*) U Pubns Amer.

Landmark Briefs & Arguments of the Supreme Court of the United States: Constitutional Law 1977 Term Supplement, Vols. 99-100. Ed. by Casper & Philip B. Kurland. LC 75-15202. 2000p. 1977. 115.00 (*0-685-57793-7*) U Pubns Amer.

Landmark Briefs & Arguments of the Supreme Court of the United States: Constitutional Law 1977 Term Supplement, Vols. 101-105. Ed. by Casper & Philip B. Kurland. LC 75-15202. 5000p. 1977. 290.00 (*0-89093-277-8*) U Pubns Amer.

Landmark Briefs & Arguments of the Supreme Court of the United States: Constitutional Law 1978 Term Supplement, Vol. 106-112. Ed. by Casper & Philip B. Kurland. LC 75-15202. 7000p. 1978. 1065.00 (*0-89093-299-9*) U Pubns Amer.

Landmark Briefs & Arguments of the Supreme Court of the United States: Constitutional Law 1979 Term Supplement, Vol. 113-119. Ed. by Casper & Philip B. Kurland. LC 75-15202. 7000p. 1980. 1065.00 (*0-89093-474-6*) U Pubns Amer.

Landmark Briefs & Arguments of the Supreme Court of the United States: Constitutional Law, 1980. Ed. by Philip B. Kurland & Gerhard Casper. LC 75-15202. (Term Supplement 1980 Ser.: Vols. 120-126). 7000p. 1982. 1065.00 (*0-685-06909-5*) U Pubns Amer.

Landmark Briefs & Arguments of the Supreme Court of the United States: Constitutional Law, 1982, Vols. 134-142. Ed. by Kurland Casper. LC 75-15202. (Term Supplement 1982 Ser.). 1984. 1370.00 (*0-89093-652-8*) U Pubns Amer.

Landmark Briefs & Arguments of the Supreme Court of the United States: Constitutional Law 1983 Term Supplement, 9 vols., Vols. 143-151. Ed. by Philip B. Kurland & Gerhard Casper. LC 75-15202. 1983. 1370.00 (*0-317-30028-8*) U Pubns Amer.

Landmark Briefs & Arguments of the Supreme Court of the United States: Constitutional Law 1984 Term Supplement, Vols. 152-159. Philip B. Kurland & Gerhard Casper. LC 75-15202. 1986p. 1215.00 (*0-89093-898-9*) U Pubns Amer.

Landmark Briefs & Arguments of the Supreme Court of the United States: Constitutional Law 1985 Term Supplement, Set, Vols. 160-167. LC 75-15202. 600p. 1987. 1215.00 (*0-89093-974-8*) U Pubns Amer.

Landmark Briefs Term Supplement, 1986, Vols. 168-175. 1986. 1215.00 (*0-685-72768-8*) U Pubns Amer.

Landmark Briefs Term Supplement, 1987, Vols. 176-182. 1987. 1065.00 (*0-685-72769-6*) U Pubns Amer.

Landmark Briefs Term Supplement, 1988, Vols. 183-190. 1988. 1215.00 (*0-685-72770-X*) U Pubns Amer.

Landmark Briefs Term Supplement, 1989, Vols. 191-199 & Opinions Vol. 1989. 1520.00 (*0-685-72771-8*) U Pubns Amer.

Landmark Briefs Term Supplement, 1990, Vols. 200-107 & Opinions Vol. 1990. 1370.00 (*0-685-72772-6*) U Pubns Amer.

Landmark Briefs Term Supplement, 1991, Vols. 208-216 & Opinions Vol. 1991. 1520.00 (*0-685-72773-4*) U Pubns Amer.

Landmark Briefs Term Supplement, 1992, Vols. 217-225 & Opinions Vol. 1992. 1520.00 (*0-685-72774-2*) U Pubns Amer.

***Landmark Cases in Public International Law.** M. Fitzmaurice. LC 98-43259. 1998. 297.00 (*90-411-9709-5*) Kluwer Law Intl.

Landmark Constitutional Law Decisions: Briefs & Decisions. James V. Young. LC 93-23802. 474p. (Orig.). (C). 1993. pap. text 39.50 (*0-8191-9184-1*); lib. bdg. 69.50 (*0-8191-9183-3*) U Pr of Amer.

Landmark Decisions of the United States Supreme Court I. Ed. by Maureen Harrison & Steve Gilbert. LC 90-84578. (Landmark Decisions Ser.). 237p. (Orig.). 1991. pap. 16.95 (*0-9628014-1-0*) Excellent Bks.

Landmark Decisions of the United States Supreme Court II. Ed. by Maureen Harrison & Steve Gilbert. (Landmark Decisions Ser.). 237p. (Orig.). 1992. pap. 16.95 (*0-9628014-2-9*) Excellent Bks.

Landmark Decisions of the United States Supreme Court III. Ed. by Maureen Harrison & Steve Gilbert. (Landmark Decisions Ser.). 237p. (Orig.). 1992. pap. 16.95 (*0-9628014-3-7*) Excellent Bks.

Landmark Decisions of the United States Supreme Court IV. Ed. by Maureen Harrison & Steve Gilbert. 228p. 1994. pap. 16.95 (*0-9628014-7-X*) Excellent Bks.

Landmark Decisions of the United States Supreme Court V. Ed. by Maureen Harrison & Steve Gilbert. (Landmark Decisions Ser.). 240p. (Orig.). 1995. pap. 16.95 (*0-9628014-8-8*) Excellent Bks.

Landmark Decisions of the United States Supreme Court VI. Ed. by Maureen Harrison & Steve Gilbert. LC 90-84578. (Landmark Decisions Ser.: Vol. VI). 240p. 1999. pap. 16.95 (*1-880780-21-6*) Excellent Bks.

***Landmark Documents on the U. S. Congress.** Raymond W. Smock. LC 98-36908. 700p. (C). 1998. text 125.00 (*1-56802-399-5*) Congr Quarterly.

Landmark Entertaining Vol. 1: Party Traditions & Favorite Recipes from the Junior League of Abileno. Photos by Steve Butman. (Illus.). 224p. 1996. 24.95 (*0-9611620-0-7*) Jr Leag Abilene.

Landmark Essays on Advanced Composition. Ed. by Gary A. Olson & Julie Drew. (Landmark Essays Ser.: Vol. 10). 250p. (Orig.). 1996. pap. 19.95 (*1-880393-25-5*, Hermagoras) L Erlbaum Assocs.

Landmark Essays on American Public Address. Ed. by Martin J. Medhurst. (Landmark Essays Ser.: Vol. 1). 264p. (Orig.). (C). 1993. pap. 21.00 (*1-880393-04-2*, Hermagoras) L Erlbaum Assocs.

Landmark Essays on Aristotelian Rhetoric, Vol. 14. Ed. by Richard L. Enos & Lois P. Agnew. (Landmark Essays Ser.). 272p. 1998. pap. write for info. (*1-880393-32-8*) L Erlbaum Assocs.

Landmark Essays on Bakhtin, Rhetoric, & Writing. Ed. by Frank Farmer. LC 97-38587. 272p. 1997. pap. write for info. (*1-880393-31-X*) L Erlbaum Assocs.

Landmark Essays on Classical Greek Rhetoric. Ed. by Edward Schiappa. (Landmark Essays Ser.: Vol. 3). 264p. (Orig.). (C). 1994. pap. 17.95 (*1-880393-06-9*, Hermagoras) L Erlbaum Assocs.

Landmark Essays on Contemporary Rhetoric, Vol. 15. Ed. by Thomas B. Farrell. LC 98-26841. (Landmark Essays Ser.). 272p. 1998. pap. write for info. (*1-880393-10-7*) L Erlbaum Assocs.

***Landmark Essays on ESL Writing.** Ed. by Tony Silva & Paul Matsudaira. (A Volume in the Landmark Essays Series). 320p. 2000. pap. write for info. (*1-880393-18-2*) L Erlbaum Assocs.

Landmark Essays on Kenneth Burke. Ed. by Barry Brummett. (Landmark Essays Ser.: Vol. 2). 304p. (C). 1993. pap. text 27.50 (*1-880393-05-0*, Hermagoras) L Erlbaum Assocs.

***Landmark Essays on Rhetoric & Literature.** Craig Kallendorf. LC 98-45701. (Landmark Essays Ser.). 1999. pap. write for info. (*1-880393-26-3*) L Erlbaum Assocs.

Landmark Essays on Rhetoric & the Environment. Craig Waddell. LC 97-5851. (Landmark Essays Ser.). 1998. pap. 26.00 (*1-880393-28-X*, Hermagoras) L Erlbaum Assocs.

Landmark Essays on Rhetorical Criticism. Ed. by Thomas W. Benson. (Landmark Essays Ser.: Vol. 5). 264p. (C). 1993. pap. text 22.50 (*1-880393-08-5*, Hermagoras) L Erlbaum Assocs.

Landmark Essays on Rhetorical Invention in Writing. Ed. by Richard E. Young & Yameng Liu. (Landmark Essays Ser.: Vol. 8). 272p. (Orig.). (C). 1994. pap. 24.50 (*1-880393-14-X*, Hermagoras) L Erlbaum Assocs.

Landmark Essays on the Rhetoric of Science: Case Studies. Ed. by Randy A. Harris. (Landmark Essays Ser.: Vol. 11). 296p. (Orig.). 1996. pap. 24.50 (*1-880393-11-5*, Hermagoras) L Erlbaum Assocs.

Landmark Essays on Voice & Writing. Ed. by Peter Elbow. (Landmark Essays Ser.: Vol. 4). 272p. (Orig.). (C). 1994. pap. 22.50 (*1-880393-07-7*, Hermagoras) L Erlbaum Assocs.

Landmark Essays on Writing Across the Curriculum, Vol. 6. Ed. by Charles Bazerman & David R. Russell. (Landmark Essays Ser.). 272p. (C). 1994. pap. text 22.50 (*1-880393-09-3*, Hermagoras) L Erlbaum Assocs.

Landmark Essays on Writing Centers. Ed. by Christina Murphy & Joe Law. (Landmark Essays Ser.: Vol. 9). 272p. (Orig.). (C). 1995. pap. 22.00 (*1-880393-22-0*, Hermagoras) L Erlbaum Assocs.

Landmark Essays on Writing Process. Ed. by Sondra Perl. (Landmark Essays Ser.: Vol. 7). 264p. (Orig.). (C). 1994. pap. 21.00 (*1-880393-13-1*, Hermagoras) L Erlbaum Assocs.

Landmark Experiments in 20th Century Physics. George L. Trigg. LC 94-40184. (Illus.). 320p. 1995. pap. text 8.95 (*0-486-28526-X*) Dover.

Landmark Guide to Provence & Cote d'Azur. (Landmark Visitors Guide Ser.). (Illus.). 256p. (Orig.). 1999. pap. 17.95 (*1-901522-45-8*) Hunter NJ.

Landmark Hawaii: Favorite Postcard Views of the Islands. Douglas Peebles. 112p. 1989. pap. 11.95 (*0-935180-81-8*) Mutual Pub HI.

Landmark History of New York. Albert Ulmann. 1977. lib. bdg. 59.95 (*0-8490-2128-6*) Gordon Pr.

Landmark in Accounting Theory: The Work of Gabriel A. D. Preinreich. Ed. by Richard P. Brief. LC 95-46235. (New Works in Accounting History). 216p. 1996. text 55.00 (*0-8153-2250-X*) Garland.

Landmark Legal Cases in American History. Roy M. Mersky & Gary Hartman. (Library in a Book Ser.). 320p. 1998. 50.00 (*0-8160-2452-9*) Facts on File.

Landmark Method for Teaching Arithmetic. Christopher L. Woodin. LC 95-40596. (J). (gr. 1-12). 1996. pap. text 25.00 (*0-9624119-2-2*) Landmark Found.

Landmark Method for Teaching Writing. Jean G. Tarricone. LC 95-40595. 1996. pap. text 25.00 (*0-9624119-3-0*) Landmark Found.

Landmark Preservation. David Listokin. (Center for Urban Policy Research Bk.). 166p. 1982. pap. 24.00 (*0-88285-077-6*) Cambridge U Pr.

Landmark Series of Medical & Scientific Articles, 13 bks., Set. (Landmark Ser.). 1978. 270.00 (*0-685-51731-4*) Irvington.

An Asterisk (*) at the beginning of an entry indicates that the title is appearing for the first time.

Landmark Study Skills Guide. Joan Sedita. LC 89-27870. (Orig.). (YA). (gr. 4-12). 1989. pap. text 25.00 (*0-9624119-0-6*) Landmark Found.

Landmark Supreme Court Cases: A Reference Guide. Donald E. Lively. LC 98-44220. 384p. 1999. 59.95 (*0-313-30602-8*) Greenwood.

***Landmark Supreme Court Cases Series.** (Illus.). (YA). (gr. 6 up). 2000. lib. bdg. write for info. (*0-89490-572-4*) Enslow Pubs.

Landmark Thucydides: A Comprehensive Guide to the Peloponnesian War. Robert B. Strassler. (Illus.). 752p. 1996. 45.00 (*0-684-82815-4*) Free Pr.

Landmark Yellow Pages: Where to Find All the Names, Addresses, Facts, & Figures You Need. 2nd ed. National Trust for Historic Preservation Staff. Ed. by Pamela Dwight. LC 95-43942. (Illus.). 408p. 1995. pap. 22.95 (*0-471-14398-7*) Wiley.

LandMarked: Stories of Peggy Simson Curry. Peggy S. Curry. 320p. (Orig.). 1992. pap. 12.95 (*0-931271-17-7*) Hi Plains Pr.

Landmarking: City, Church & Jesuit Urban Strategy. Thomas M. Lucas. LC 97-21981. (Illus.). 245p. 1997. 34.95 (*0-8294-0973-4*, Jesuit Way) Loyola Pr.

Landmarks: A Collection of Essays on the Russian Intelligentsia - 1909. Boris Shragin & Albert Todd. 267p. 1977. text 39.95 (*0-918294-00-2*) Transaction Pubs.

Landmarks: An Exploration of Great Rocks. David Craig. (Illus.). 334p. 1996. pap. 19.95 (*0-7126-7320-2*, Pub. by Jonathan Cape) Trafalgar.

Landmarks: Charleston, Huntington & Beyond. William D. Goebel. (Illus.). 104p. 1991. 29.95 (*0-9631272-0-9*) Landmarks.

***Landmarks: Cottages, Castles & Curiosities of Britain in the Care of the Landmark Trust.** 2000. pap. 16.95 (*0-7538-0693-2*) Phoenix Hse.

Landmarks: Cottages, Castles & Curiosities of Britain in the Care of the Landmark Trust. Derry Brabbs. (Illus.). 160p. 1998. 27.50 (*0-297-82299-3*, Pub. by Weidenfeld & Nicolson) Trafalgar.

Landmarks: Reflections on Anthropology. Andrew Strathern. LC 92-32403. 206p. (Orig.). (C). 1993. pap. 14.00 (*0-87338-479-2*) Kent St U Pr.

Landmarks, Bridges & Visions: Aspects of Maori Culture: Essays Sidney M. Mead. LC 97-161634. 266 p. 1997. write for info. (*0-86473-317-8*) Lubrecht & Cramer.

Landmarks in American Civil Engineering. Daniel L. Schodek. LC 86-20162. (Illus.). 401p. 1987. 60.00 (*0-262-19256-X*) MIT Pr.

***Landmarks in Classical Literature.** Philip Gaskell. 2000. pap. 20.00 (*0-7486-1362-5*, Pub. by Edinburgh U Pr) Col U Pr.

Landmarks in Delhi Administration. Ed. by S. C. Vajpevi & S. P. Verma. LC 98-901193. 374p. 1998. 36.00 (*81-212-0568-9*, Pub. by Gyan Publishing Hse) Nataraj Bks.

Landmarks in Developmental Biology: Compilation of Essays from Roux's Archives Development Biology. Klaus Sander. LC 96-35278. 1997. 79.50 (*3-540-61476-1*) Spr-Verlag.

Landmarks in Digital Computing: A Smithsonian Pictorial History. Peggy A. Kidwell & Paul E. Ceruzzi. LC 93-25428. (Illus.). 160p. (Orig.). 1994. pap. 17.95 (*1-56098-311-6*) Smithsonian.

Landmarks in English Literature. Philip Gaskell. 176p. 1998. 17.00 (*0-7486-1060-X*, Pub. by Edinburgh U Pr) Col U Pr.

Landmarks in Gene Regulation. Ed. by David Latchman. (Landmarks in Science & Medicine Ser.: Vol. 1). (Illus.). 320p. (C). 1997. pap. text 34.00 (*1-85578-109-3*, Pub. by Portland Pr Ltd) Ashgate Pub Co.

Landmarks in Indian Anthropology, 74 vols., Set. Prints India Staff. (C). 1988. 5000.00 (*0-7855-0046-4*, Pub. by Print Hse) St Mut.

Landmarks in Indian Legal & Constitutional History. B. M. Gandi. 1995. 45.00 (*0-7855-2843-1*, Pub. by Eastern Book) St Mut.

Landmarks in Indian Legal & Constitutional History. V. D. Kulshreshtha. (C). 1992. 75.00 (*0-89771-771-6*, Pub. by Eastern Book) St Mut.

Landmarks in Indian Legal & Constitutional History. V. D. Kulshreshtha. 491p. 1981. 120.00 (*0-7855-1313-2*) St Mut.

Landmarks in Intracellular Signalling. Ed. by R. D. Burgoyne & O. M. Peterson. (Landmarks in Science & Medicine Ser.: Vol. 2). (Illus.). 280p. (C). 1997. pap. text 34.00 (*1-85578-101-8*, Pub. by Portland Pr Ltd) Ashgate Pub Co.

Landmarks in Karnataka Administration. Indian Institute of Public Administration Staff & S. Ramanathan. LC 99-931265. 543p. 1998. write for info. (*81-85565-98-8*) S Asia.

Landmarks in Liberty. Malloy. (C). 1993. pap. text 20.50 (*0-07-039823-2*) McGraw.

Landmarks in Linguistic Thought: The Arabic Linguistic Tradition. Kees Versteegh. LC 96-36345. (History of Linguistic Thought Ser.). 216p. (C). 1997. 75.00 (*0-415-14062-5*) Routledge.

Landmarks in Linguistic Thought: The Arabic Linguistic Tradition. 2nd ed. Kees Versteegh. LC 96-36345. (History of Linguistic Thought Ser.). 216p. (C). 1997. pap. 25.99 (*0-415-15757-9*) Routledge.

Landmarks in Linguistic Thought: The Western Tradition from Socrates to Saussure. Roy Harris & Talbot J. Taylor. 240p. 1989. 42.50 (*0-415-00290-7*) Routledge.

Landmarks in Linguistic Thought: The Western Tradition from Socrates to Saussure. 2nd ed. Roy Harris & Talbot J. Taylor. LC 96-27323. (History of Linguistic Thought Ser.). 248p. (C). 1997. 75.00 (*0-415-15361-1*) Routledge.

Landmarks In Linguistic Thought: The Western Tradition from Socrates to Saussure. 2nd ed. Roy Harris & Talbot J. Taylor. LC 96-27323. (Routledge History of Linguistic Thought Ser.). 248p. (C). 1997. pap. 21.99 (*0-415-15362-X*) Routledge.

Landmarks in Mechanical Engineering. ASME International History & Heritage Staff. LC 96-31573. (Illus.). 400p. 1996. pap. 24.95 (*1-55753-094-7*) Purdue U Pr.

Landmarks in Medicine. New York Academy of Medicine Staff. LC 74-142676. (Essay Index Reprint Ser.). 1977. 23.95 (*0-8369-2114-3*) Ayer.

***Landmarks in Modern American Business, 3 Vols.** 960p. 2000. 175.00 (*0-89356-135-5*, Magills Choice) Salem Pr.

Landmarks in Nineteenth Century Painting. Clive Bell. LC 67-30197. (Essay Index Reprint Ser.). 1977. 20.95 (*0-8369-0186-X*) Ayer.

Landmarks in Science: Hippocrates to Carson. Robert B. Downs. LC 82-154. 305p. 1982. lib. bdg. 26.00 (*0-87287-295-5*) Libs Unl.

Landmarks in the Development of the Contractual System. L. Vekas. 192p. (C). 1986. 75.00 (*963-05-3666-8*, 139, Pub. by Akade Kiado) St Mut.

Landmarks in the Hundreds: The Number System. Susan J. Russell & Andee Rubin. Ed. by Priscilla C. Samii & Beverly Cory. LC 94-214850. (Investigations in Number, Data, & Space Ser.). (Illus.). 98p. (Orig.). 1994. pap., teacher ed. 22.95 (*0-86651-796-0*, DS21236) Seymour Pubns.

Landmarks in the Landscape: The Historic Architecture in the National Parks of the West. Harvey H. Kaiser. LC 97-851. 1997. 75.00 (*0-8118-1854-3*) Chronicle Bks.

Landmarks in the Law. Lord Denning. 1984. 40.00 (*0-406-17603-5*; UK, MICHIE); pap. 28.00 (*0-406-17614-0*, U.K., MICHIE) LEXIS Pub.

Landmarks in the Thousands: The Number System. Susan J. Russell & Andee Rubin. Ed. by Priscilla C. Samii et al. (Investigations in Number, Data, & Space Ser.). (Illus.). 110p. (Orig.). 1994. pap., teacher ed. 22.95 (*0-86651-812-6*, DS21250) Seymour Pubns.

Landmarks in the Thousands: The Number System. rev. ed. Susan J. Russell & Andee Rubin. Ed. by Catherine Anderson & Beverly Cory. (Investigations in Number, Data, & Space Ser.). (Illus.). 110p. (Orig.). (YA). (gr. 4 up). 1997. pap. text 22.95 (*1-57232-746-4*, 43893) Seymour Pubns.

Landmarks in Western Science: From Prehistory to the Atomic Age. Peter Whitfield. LC 99-24976. 288p. 1999. 35.00 (*0-415-92533-9*) Routledge.

Landmarks Map of Rockland County (Buff Color or White) rev. ed. Claire K. Tholl. 1987. 15.00 (*0-911183-04-3*) Rockland County Hist.

Landmarks of Albany County, New York Pt. I: History. Ed. by Amasa J. Parker. (Illus.). 1992. reprint ed. lib. bdg. 58.50 (*0-8328-2890-4*) Higginson Bk Co.

Landmarks of Albany County, New York Pt. II: Biography. Amasa J. Parker. (Illus.). 1992. reprint ed. lib. bdg. 58.50 (*0-8328-2891-2*) Higginson Bk Co.

Landmarks of American Presidents: A Traveler's Guide 1. Carl Wheeless. (Traveler's Guide Ser.). 809p. 1995. 55.00 (*0-8103-8301-2*, 108545) Gale.

Landmarks of Church History to the Reformation. enl. rev. ed. Henry Cowan. LC 70-144590. reprint ed. 39.50 (*0-404-01787-8*) AMS Pr.

***Landmarks of Classical Literature.** Ed. by Philip Gaskell. 200p. 1999. 45.00 (*1-57958-192-7*) Fitzroy Dearborn.

Landmarks of Contemporary Drama. Joseph Chiari. LC 76-148616. 233p. (C). 1971. reprint ed. 45.00 (*0-87752-144-1*) Gordian.

***Landmarks of Continental European Literature.** Ed. by Philip Gaskell. 200p. 1999. lib. bdg. 45.00 (*1-57958-191-9*) Fitzroy Dearborn.

Landmarks of Early American Music, 1760-1800. Ed. by Richard F. Goldman. LC 72-1631. reprint ed. 37.50 (*0-404-08309-9*) AMS Pr.

***Landmarks of English Literature.** Ed. by Philip Gaskell. 200p. 1999. lib. bdg. 45.00 (*1-57958-190-0*) Fitzroy Dearborn.

Landmarks of English Literature. Henry J. Nicoll. LC 72-3282. (English Literature Ser.: No. 33). (Illus.). 1972. reprint ed. lib. bdg. 75.00 (*0-8383-1500-3*) M S G Haskell Hse.

Landmarks of Freemasonry. Elbert Bede. 56p. 1980. reprint ed. pap. text 3.95 (*0-88053-020-0*, M 069) Macoy Pub.

Landmarks of Freemasonry, Bks. 1 & 2. Silas H. Shepherd. 181p. 1992. reprint ed. pap. 19.95 (*1-56459-040-2*) Kessinger Pub.

Landmarks of French Classical Drama. Corneille et al. Tr. by David Bryer et al from FRE. 393p. (Orig.). (C). 1991. pap. write for info. (*0-413-63100-1*, A0542, Methuen Drama) Methn.

Landmarks of Gay Drama. Ed. by John M. Clum. 1996. text 65.00 (*0-8133-2502-1*) Westview.

Landmarks of Gay Drama. Ed. by John M. Clum. (C). 1996. pap. text 19.95 (*0-8133-2503-X*) Westview.

Landmarks of Liberty. Robert P. St. John. 340p. 1977. 22.95 (*0-8369-2425-8*) Ayer.

Landmarks of Loudon County: Its History Through Architecture. Joe E. Spence & George Kiley. LC 97-9862. 1997. write for info. (*0-9653759-1-9*) Hallmark Publng.

Landmarks of Modern British Drama, 2 vols., Vol. 2. Ed. by Roger Cornish & Violet Ketels. 624p. (C). 1988. 29.95 (*0-413-59090-9*, A0144); pap. 12.95 (*0-413-57270-6*, A0145) Heinemann.

Landmarks of Modern British Drama: The Plays of the Sixties, Vol. 1. Frwd. by Roger Cornish & Violet Ketels. 732p. (Orig.). (C). 1988. pap. 12.95 (*0-413-57260-9*, A0143, Methuen Drama) Methn.

Landmarks of Monroe County, Containing an Historical Sketch of Monroe County & the City of Rochester...Followed by Brief Historical Sketches of the Towns, with Biography & Family History. William F. Peck et al. (Illus.). 831p. 1997. reprint ed. lib. bdg. 85.00 (*0-8328-6178-2*) Higginson Bk Co.

Landmarks of New Orleans. 2nd rev. ed. Leonard V. Huber. LC 91-66717. (Illus.). 163p. 1991. pap. 12.00 (*1-879714-01-9*) SW PF LA Land.

Landmarks of New York, Vol. III. Barbaralee Diamonstein. LC 97-23865. (Illus.). 544p. 1998. 49.50 (*0-8109-3594-5*, Pub. by Abrams) Time Warner.

Landmarks of Orleans County, Illustrated. With Biographical & Family Sketches. Ed. by Isaac S. Signor. (Illus.). 929p. 1997. reprint ed. lib. bdg. 95.00 (*0-8328-6195-2*) Higginson Bk Co.

Landmarks of Oswego County. Ed. by Judith Wellman et al. (New York State Bks.). (Illus.). 356p. 1987. pap. 24.95 (*0-8156-0221-9*) Syracuse U Pr.

Landmarks of Oswego County, N. Y. with Biographies. Ed. by John C. Churchill et al. (Illus.). 1191p. 1995. reprint ed. lib. bdg. 115.00 (*0-8328-4475-6*) Higginson Bk Co.

Landmarks of Prince George's County: Architectural Photographs. Maryland-National Capital Park & Planning Commissi. LC 92-39873. (Illus.). 144p. 1993. 29.95 (*0-8018-4628-5*) Johns Hopkins.

Landmarks of Rensselaer County, New York, (with Biographies & Genealogies) George B. Anderson. (Illus.). 1195p. 1992. reprint ed. lib. bdg. 109.00 (*0-8328-2446-1*) Higginson Bk Co.

Landmarks of Russian Architecture: A Photographic Survey, Vol. 5. William C. Brumfield. (Documenting the Image Ser.). 256p. 1997. text 49.00 (*90-5699-536-7*); pap. text 23.00 (*90-5699-537-5*) Gordon & Breach.

Landmarks of Science: From the Collections of the Library of Congress. Leonard C. Bruno. LC 89-33579. 362p. 1989. reprint ed. pap. 112.30 (*0-608-02856-8*, 206392000007) Bks Demand.

Landmarks of Steuben County. Ed. by Harlo Hakes. (Illus.). 909p. 1997. reprint ed. lib. bdg. 97.50 (*0-8328-6248-7*) Higginson Bk Co.

Landmarks of the American Revolution: People & Places Vital to the Quest for Independence. rev. ed. Mark M. Boatner. LC 91-27501. 608p. 1992. reprint ed. pap. 188.50 (*0-608-00477-4*, 206129600007) Bks Demand.

Landmarks of the Bronx. 2nd ed. Gary D. Hermalyn & Robert Kornfeld. 1991. pap. 15.00 (*0-941980-26-X*) Bronx County.

Landmarks of the Deccan: A Comprehensive Guide to the Archaeological Remains of the City & Suburbs of Hyderabad. Syed A. Bilgrami. (C). 1992. 20.00 (*81-206-0543-8*, Pub. by Asian Educ Servs) S Asia.

Landmarks of the Rocky Mountain Fur Trade: Two One-Day Self-Guided Tours from Jackson, Wyoming. Pierce Olson. LC 97-43163. (Center Bks.: Vol. 3). (Illus.). 132p. 1997. pap. 11.95 (*1-886402-02-7*) Jackson Hole Hist.

Landmarks of the West: A Guide to Historic Sites. Kent Ruth. LC 85-29014. (Illus.). 319p. 1986. reprint ed. pap. 98.90 (*0-608-02677-8*, 206333000004) Bks Demand.

Landmarks of Tomorrow: A Report on the New "Post-Modern" World. Intro. by Peter Drucker. 280p. 1996. pap. text 24.95 (*1-56000-622-6*) Transaction Pubs.

Landmarks of Tompkins County, Including a History of Cornell University (by Prof. W. T. Hewitt), 2 pts. Ed. by John H. Selkreg. (Illus.). 980p. 1997. reprint ed. lib. bdg. 107.50 (*0-8328-6262-2*) Higginson Bk Co.

Landmarks of Twentieth-Century Design: An Illustrated Handbook. Kathryn Hiesinger & George Marcus. (Illus.). 432p. 1995. pap. 39.95 (*0-7892-0008-2*) Abbeville Pr.

Landmarks of Twentieth-Century Design: An Illustrated Handbook. Kathryn Hiesinger & George Marcus. LC 93-180. (Illus.). 432p. (J). 2000. 60.00 (*1-55859-279-2*, Abbeville Kids) Abbeville Pr.

Landmarks of Wayne County: With Biographical & Family Sketches. Ed. by George W. Cowles et al. (Illus.), 821p. 1997. reprint ed. lib. bdg. 92.00 (*0-8328-6273-8*) Higginson Bk Co.

Landmarks of Wayne County & Detroit: With Biographical & Personal Sketches. rev. ed. Robert B. Ross & George B. Catlin. (Illus.). 1192p. 1997. reprint ed. lib. bdg. 114.50 (*0-8328-6792-6*) Higginson Bk Co.

Landmarks of World Civilization. Raj K. Phul. 390p. 1986. 39.95 (*0-318-36971-0*) Asia Bk Corp.

***Landmarks on the Iron Road: Two Centuries of North American Railroad Engineering.** William D. Middleton. LC 98-55475. (Railroads Past & Present Ser.). 1999. 39.95 (*0-253-33559-0*) Ind U Pr.

Landmauer von Konstantinopel Pt. 2: Aufnahme, Beschreibung und Geschichte. Meyer-Plath & A. M. Schneider. (Denkmaeler Antiker Architektur Ser.: Vol. 8). (GER., Illus.). x, 170p. (C). 1978. reprint ed. 229.25 (*3-11-004992-9*) De Gruyter.

Landmauer von Konstantinopel. Bearbeitet im Auftrage der Deutschen Forschungsgemeinschaft 1. Teil: Zeichnerische Wiederherstellung. Mit Begleitendem Text. Fritz Krischen. (Denkmaeler Antiker Architektur Ser.: Vol. 6). (Illus.). viii, 18p. (C). 1974. reprint ed. 144.65 (*3-11-002238-9*) De Gruyter.

***L&MHP: California, 1999 Supplement.** O. Brandt Caudill, Jr. & Kenneth S. Pope. 1999. 24.95 (*1-55798-550-2*) Am Psychol.

***L&MHP: Minnesota, 1999 Supplement.** Eric S. Janus et al. 1999. 24.95 (*1-55798-548-0*) Am Psychol.

***L&MHP: New York, 1999 Supplement.** James S. Wulach & B. J. Cling. 1999. 24.95 (*1-55798-547-2*) Am Psychol.

Landmine Monitor 1999: Toward a Mine-Free World. Human Rights Watch Staff. 1106p. 1999. pap. 45.00 (*1-56432-231-9*) Hum Rts Watch.

Landmines: A Deadly Legacy. Human Rights Watch Arms Project Staff & Physicians for Human Rights Staff. (Illus.). 528p. (Orig.). 1993. pap. 20.00 (*1-56432-113-4*) Hum Rts Watch.

***Landmines: Exploring the Hidden Crisis, 3 vols.** Ed. by Linda Bongiorno. Incl. Landmines: Exploring the Hidden Crisis: A Standards Based Curriculum Unit for the Middle Grades. Jacquelyn S. Johnson. (Illus.). 100p. 1999. pap. (*0-943804-44-2*); Landmines: Exploring the Hidden Crisis: A Standards Based Curriculum Unit for the Secondary Grades (9-12) J. P. Antony Hurt. (Illus.). 120p. 1999. pap. (*0-943804-43-4*); Landmines: Exploring the Hidden Crisis: A Standards Based Curriculum Unit for the Upper Elementary Grades. Elizabeth Duncan. (Illus.). 35p. 1999. pap. (*0-943804-45-0*); (Illus.). 255p. 1999. pap. write for info. (*0-943804-48-5*) U of Denver Teach.

Landmines: Exploring the Hidden Crisis: A Standards Based Curriculum Unit for the Middle Grades see Landmines: Exploring the Hidden Crisis

Landmines: Exploring the Hidden Crisis: A Standards Based Curriculum Unit for the Secondary Grades (9-12) see Landmines: Exploring the Hidden Crisis

Landmines: Exploring the Hidden Crisis: A Standards Based Curriculum Unit for the Upper Elementary Grades see Landmines: Exploring the Hidden Crisis

Landmines: Legacy of Conflict: a Manual for Development Workers. Rae McGrath. (Illus.). 86p. (C). 1998. reprint ed. pap. text 35.00 (*0-7881-3280-6*) DIANE Pub.

Landmines: Legacy of Conflict: A Manual for Development Workers; Practical Handbooks. Rae McGrath. (Practical Handbooks). (Illus.). 96p. (C). 1994. pap. 12.95 (*0-85598-264-0*, Pub. by Oxfam Pub) Stylus Pub VA.

Landmines & Underdevelopment. Jim Monan. (C). 1995. pap. 4.50 (*962-664-001-4*) Humanities.

Landmines & Unexploded Ordnance: A Resource Book. Rae McGrath. LC 99-52952. 300p. 2000. 79.95 (*0-7453-1264-0*, Pub. by Pluto GBR); pap. 27.95 (*0-7453-1259-4*, Pub. by Pluto GBR) Stylus Pub VA.

***L&N's Memphis Line: Bowling Green, Kentucky to Memphis, Tennessee.** LC 99-74179. (Illus.). 335p. 1999. 39.95 (*0-9671997-0-0*) M F S Line Pubg.

Lando. Louis L'Amour. 176p. 1979. mass mkt. 4.50 (*0-553-27676-X*) Bantam.

Lando. large type ed. Louis L'Amour. (Special Ser.). 222p. 1993. 18.95 (*1-56054-652-2*) Thorndike Pr.

Lando Calrissian Adventures: Lando Calrissian & the Mindharp of Sharu; Lando Calrissian & the Flamewind of Oseon; Lando Calrissian & the Starcave of Thonboka. L. Neil Smith. (Star Wars). (YA). (gr. 5 up). 1994. mass mkt. 5.99 (*0-345-39110-1*, Del Rey) Ballantine Pub Grp.

***Land/Ocean Systems in the Siberian Arctic: Dynamics & History.** Ed. by H. Kassens et al. LC 99-23868. (Illus.). 735p. 1999. 219.00 (*3-540-65676-6*) Spr-Verlag.

***Landolt-Bornstein.** (Numerical Data & Functional Relationships in Science & Technology Ser.). viii, 491p. 2000. 3744.00 (*3-540-66255-3*) Spr-Verlag.

***Landolt-Bornstein.** Ed. by K. R. Hall & K. N. Marsh. vi, 413p. 2000. 3119.00 (*3-540-66233-2*) Spr-Verlag.

***Landolt-Bornstein.** W. Martienssen. (Numerical Data & Functional Relationships in Science & Technology Ser.). 465p. 1999. write for info. (*3-540-64734-1*) Spr-Verlag.

***Landolt-Bornstein.** Ed. by W. Martienssen et al. (Numerical Data & Functional Relationships in Science & Technology Ser.). 373p. 1999. write for info. (*3-540-64735-X*) Spr-Verlag.

***Landolt-Bornstein.** Ed. by H. Schopper. (Numerical Data & Functional Relationships in Science & Technology Ser.). viii, 293p. 1999. 2386.00 (*3-540-63646-3*) Spr-Verlag.

***Landolt-Bornstein: Alipathic & Aromatic Hydrocarbons, Steroids, Carbohydrates.** Ed. by W. Martienssen et al. (Numerical Data & Functional Relationships in Science & Technology - New Series: 35). viii, 310p. 2000. (*3-540-66780-6*) Spr-Verlag.

Landolt-Bornstein: Comprehensive Index 1996. Ed. by Otfried Madelung & W. Martienssen. (Numerical Data & Functional Relationships in Science & Technology Ser.). 352p. 1996. 1562.00 incl. cd-rom (*3-540-60804-4*) Spr-Verlag.

Landolt-Bornstein: Magnetic Properties of Non-Metallic Inorganic Compounds Based on Transition Elements, Vol. 27. Ed. by W. Martienssen. (Group III Ser.). 345p. 1996. 1372.00 (*3-540-54627-8*) Spr-Verlag.

Landolt-Bornstein Subvolume A: Optical Constants. C. Wohlfahrt & B. Wohlfahrt. Ed. by W. Martienssen. (Numerical Data & Functional Relationships in Science & Technology: Group III: Solid State Physics). vii, 400p. 1996. 1671.00 incl. cd-rom (*3-540-60539-8*) Spr-Verlag.

Landolt-Bornstein Subvolume B: Refractive Indices. C. Wohlfahrt & B. Wohlfahrt. Ed. by W. Martienssen. (Numerical Data & Functional Relationships in Science & Technology: Group III: Solid State Physics). 430p. 1996. 1935.00 incl. cd-rom (*3-540-60596-7*) Spr-Verlag.

Landolt-Bornstein Subvolume f: Ga-Gd...Hf-Zr: Phase Equilibria, Crystallographic Data & Values of Thermodynamic Properties of Binary Alloys. B. Predel. Ed. by Otfried Madelung. (Numerical Data & Functional Relationships in Science & Technology, Group IV: Physical Chemistry Ser.: Vol. 5). (Illus.). xxvi, 408p. 1996. 1583.00 (*3-540-60344-1*) Spr-Verlag.

Landolt-Bornstein Vol. 8: Thermodynamic Properties of Organic Compounds & Their Mixtures. Ed. by W. Martienssen & K. N. Marsh. (Illus.). 600p. 1995. 2700.95 (*3-540-58854-X*) Spr-Verlag.

An Asterisk (*) at the beginning of an entry indicates that the title is appearing for the first time.

Landolt-Bornstein Vol. 13: Production of Radionuclides at Intermediate Energies. Ed. by W. Martienssen & H. Schopper. (Illus.). 526p. 1995. 2376.95 (*3-540-59049-8*) Spr-Verlag.

Landolt-Bornstein Vol. 18: Radical Reaction Rates in Liquids. J. A. Howard. Ed. by H. Fischer. 395p. 1997. 1552.00 (*0-387-56057-2*) Spr-Verlag.

Landolt-Bornstein Vol. 24: Physics of Solid Surfaces. Ed. by G. F. Chiarotti. xii, 516p. 1996. 2007.00 (*3-540-56750-X*) Spr-Verlag.

***Landolt-Bornstein Vol. 27: Group III: Condensed Matter, Set.** Ed. by W. Martienssen. viii, 388p. 2000. 2933.00 incl. cd-rom (*3-540-65596-4*) Spr-Verlag.

Landolt-Bornstein Vol. 27: Group III: Condensed Matter, Vol. 27. W. Martienssen. (Illus.). 308p. 1997. 1393.00 (*3-540-60877-X*) Spr-Verlag.

Landon Carter: An Inquiry into the Personal Values & Social Imperatives of the Eighteenth-Century Virginia Gentry. Jack P. Greene. LC 64-19201. 1967. reprint ed. pap. text 7.95 (*0-8139-0111-1*) U Pr of Va.

Landon Genealogy, Boardman Genealogy. James O. Landon. 383p. 1993. reprint ed. pap. 59.50 (*0-8328-2987-0*); reprint ed. lib. bdg. 69.50 (*0-8328-2986-2*) Higginson Bk Co.

Landon Lecture Series on Public Issues: The First Twenty Years, 1966-1986. Ed. by Diana P. Carlin & Meredith A. Moore. 888p. (C). 1990. lib. bdg. 92.00 (*0-8191-7963-9*) U Pr of Amer.

Landon Lectures: Perspectives from the First Twenty Years. Ed. by William L. Richter & Charles E. Reagan. LC 87-81227. (Illus.). 361p. 1987. 25.00 (*0-9616658-1-5*) Friends Lib KSU.

Landon of Kansas. Donald R. McCoy. LC 65-16190. (Illus.). 631p. reprint ed. pap. 195.70 (*0-8357-3807-8*, 203653500003) Bks Demand.

Landone Assorted Titles, No. 1. Brown Landone. 40p. 1996. reprint ed. spiral bd. 8.00 (*0-7873-1249-5*) Hlth Research.

Landone Assorted Titles, No. 2. Brown Landone. 35p. 1994. reprint ed. spiral bd. 8.00 (*0-7873-1043-3*) Hlth Research.

Landone Assorted Titles, No. 3. Brown Landone. 64p. 1994. reprint ed. spiral bd. 9.00 (*0-7873-1042-5*) Hlth Research.

Landone Menus for Thirty One Days. Brown Landone. 40p. 1994. reprint ed. spiral bd. 9.00 (*0-7873-1101-4*) Hlth Research.

Landowner, the Land Surveyor & the Neighbor. John E. Keen. 104p. (C). 1997. pap. text 39.00 (*1-56569-056-7*) Land Survey.

Landowners: Marriage, Debt, & the Estates System 1650-1950. John Habakkuk. 804p. 1994. text 125.00 (*0-19-820398-5*) OUP.

Landowners & Tenants in Roman Egypt: The Social Relations of Agriculture in the Oxyrhynchite Nome. Jane Rowlandson. (Oxford Classical Monographs). (Illus.). 398p. (C). 1996. text 80.00 (*0-19-814735-X*, Clarendon Pr) OUP.

Landowners, Capitalists, & Entrepreneurs: Essays for Sir John Habakkuk. Ed. by F. M. Thompson. (Illus.). 330p. 1994. 59.00 (*0-19-828301-6*) OUP.

***Landowner's Guide to Building Forest Access Roads.** Richard L. Wiest. 47p. 1998. pap. 8.00 (*0-16-060836-8*, Agriculture Dept) USGPO.

***Landowners Guide to State-Protected Plants of Forests in New York State.** Dudley J. Raynal & Donald J. Leopold. (Illus.). 1999. pap. text 19.95 (*0-9670681-0-X*, Pub. by State U NY Coll Enviro) Syracuse U Pr.

Landowner's Guide to Western Water Rights. Mary E. Wolfe. (Illus.). 240p. 1996. pap. text 16.95 (*1-57098-093-4*) Roberts Rinehart.

Landowners in Colonial Peru. Keith A. Davies. (Latin American Monographs: No. 61). (Illus.). 247p. 1984. text 22.50 (*0-292-74639-3*) U of Tex Pr.

Landowners in Poland, 1918-1939. Wojchiech Roszkowski. 1991. text 46.50 (*0-88033-196-8*, Pub. by East Eur Monographs) Col U Pr.

Landowners on the 1897 Wall Map of Carroll County, Indiana: Landowners. Ann Burton & Cheryl Burton. (Illus.). 91p. (Orig.). 1994. pap. 9.00 (*0-937505-09-9*) Glyndwr Resc.

***Landownership in Nepal.** M. C. Regmi. 1999. pap. 185.00 (*0-7855-7605-3*) St Mut.

Landownership in Roman Thracia & Moesia (1st-3rd Century) Boris Gerov. Tr. by Vessela Zhelyaskova. 236p. (Orig.). 1988. pap. 76.00 (*90-256-0940-6*, Pub. by AM Hakkert) BookLink Distributors.

Landowska on Music. Wanda Landowska. 434p. reprint ed. lib. bdg. 59.00 (*0-685-14898-X*) Rprt Serv.

***Landpower & Dual Containment: Rethinking America's Policy in the Gulf.** Stephen C. Pelletiere. 36p. 1999. pap. write for info. (*1-58487-010-9*) SSI US Army.

Landprints: Reflections on Place & Landscape. George Seddon. LC 97-27550. (Illus.). 288p. 1997. text 69.95 (*0-521-58501-5*) Cambridge U Pr.

Landprints: Reflections on Place & Landscape. George Seddon. LC 98-25795. (Illus.). 288p. (C). 1998. pap. text 24.95 (*0-521-65999-X*) Cambridge U Pr.

Landrecht Oder Die Eigenthumlichen Burgerlichen Rechte und Sitten. (GER.). 554p. 1990. reprint ed. write for info. (*3-487-09267-0*) G Olms Pubs.

Landrum-Griffin Act: Twenty Years of Federal Protection of Union Members' Rights. Janice R. Bellace & Alan D. Berkowitz. LC 79-2465. (Labor Relations & Public Policy Ser.: No. 19). 383p. reprint ed. pap. 118.80 (*0-8357-3153-7*, 203941600012) Bks Demand.

Landrum-Griffin Act & Union Democracy. Doris B. McLaughlin & Anita L. Schoomaker. LC 78-12592. 296p. reprint ed. pap. 91.80 (*0-7837-4718-7*, 205907000003) Bks Demand.

Landrum's Quincy, Vol. 1. Carl Landrum & Shirley Landrum. (Illus.). 208p. 1995. 25.00 (*1-884177-50-6*) Justice IL.

Landrum's Quincy, Vol. 2. Carl Landrum & Shirley Landrum. (Illus.). 208p. 1996. 25.00 (*1-884177-51-4*) Justice IL.

Landrum's Quincy, Vol. 3. Carl Landrum & Shirley Landrum. (Illus.). 208p. 1996. 25.00 (*1-884177-52-2*) Justice IL.

Landrum's Quincy, Vol. 4. Carl Landrum & Shirley Landrum. Ed. by Robert S. Hunter. (Illus.). 208p. 1997. 25.00 (*1-884177-53-0*) Justice IL.

***Landry: The Legend & the Legacy.** Bob St. John. 368p. 2000. 24.99 (*0-8499-1670-4*) Word Pub.

***Landry News.** 2000. 4.50 (*0-689-82868-3*) Aladdin.

Landry News. Andrew Clements. LC 98-34376. (Illus.). 128p. (J). (gr. 3-7). 1999. lib. bdg. 15.00 (*0-689-81817-3*) S&S Childrens.

Landry's Law: The Landry Brothers. Kelsey Roberts. (Intrigue Ser.: Bk. 545). 1999. per. 3.99 (*0-373-22545-8*, 1-22545-7) Harlequin Bks.

Lands Across the Sea: Trusts, Taxes & Donative Transfers of Land in the Netherlands & the United States. D. H. Gordon & H. L. Van Mens. 76p. 1990. pap. 33.00 (*90-6544-477-7*) Kluwer Law Intl.

Lands & Peoples, 6 vols. Ed. by Grolier Educational Corp. Staff. LC 98-31328. (Illus.). 2650p. (YA). (gr. 4-12). 1999. lib. bdg. 269.00 (*0-7172-8021-7*) Grolier Educ.

Lands & Rivers see Understanding Science & Nature Series

Lands & Rivers. Time-Life Books Editors. LC 92-34976. (Understanding Science & Nature Ser.). 176p. (J). 1993. lib. bdg. 24.60 (*0-8094-9692-5*) Time-Life.

Lands & Tenants in South India: A Study of Nellore District, 1850-1990. M. Atchi Reddy. LC 96-900191. 228p. (C). 1996. 19.95 (*0-19-563660-0*) OUP.

Lands Between the Miamis: A Bicentennial Celebration of the Dayton Area, Vol. 2. Virginia Ronald & Bruce Ronald. Ed. by Alexander Kaye. (Bicentennial Bookshelf Ser.). (Illus.). 438p. 1996. 34.95 (*0-913428-77-9*) Landfall Pr.

Land's End. Frederik Pohl. 1989. mass mkt. 4.95 (*0-8125-0024-5*, Pub. by Tor Bks) St Martin.

Lands End. Mary Stolz. LC 73-7139. 176p. (YA). (gr. 7 up). 1973. 13.95 (*0-06-025916-7*) HarpC Child Bks.

Land's End. William Henry Hudson. reprint ed. 64.50 (*0-404-03404-7*) AMS Pr.

Lands for the People? The Highland Clearances & the Colonisation of New Zealand: A Biography of John McKenzie. Tom Brooking. (Illus.). 300p. 1996. pap. 39.95 (*1-877133-21-3*, Pub. by Univ Otago Pr) Intl Spec Bk.

Lands of Brighter Destiny: The Public Lands of the American West. Elizabeth Darby Junkin. LC 86-4814. (Illus.). 240p. 1986. 13.95 (*1-55591-000-9*) Fulcrum Pub.

Lands of Cazembe: Lacerda's Journey to Cazembe in 1798. Royal Geography Society. Tr. by Richard F. Burton. LC 69-18974. (Illus.). vii, 272p. 1969. reprint ed. 19.75 (*0-8371-0894-2*, BUC&, Greenwood Pr) Greenwood.

Lands of Father Damien: Kalaupapa, Molokai, Hawaii. James H. Brooker. (Illus.). 135p. (Orig.). 1998. 24.95 (*0-9642197-3-5*) Molokai Fish & Dive.

***Lands of Grass** Allan Fowler. LC 99-32313. (Rookie Read-About Science Ser.). (J). 2000. 19.00 (*0-516-21213-3*) Childrens.

Lands of Intrigue. TSR Inc. Staff. 1997. 29.95 (*0-7869-0697-9*, Pub. by TSR Inc) Random.

Lands of Lore: Guardians of Destiny Unauthorized Game Secrets. Edward Carmien. LC 96-70477. 192p. 1997. pap., per. 14.99 (*0-7615-0928-3*) Prima Pub.

***Lands of Lore III: Prima's Official Strategy Guide.** Development Staff. LC 98-68559. 240p. 1999. pap. 19.99 (*0-7615-2015-5*, Prima Games) Prima Pub.

Lands of Lore II: Official Guide. Bill Keith & Nina Barton. (Illus.). 312p. 1997. 19.99 (*1-56686-288-4*) Brady Pub.

Lands of Memory: Wanderings & Wonderments of a Sephardic Jew. Robert Graziani-Levy. LC 91-75726. (Illus.). 320p. 1992. 19.92 (*0-911437-76-2*) Labyrinthos.

Lands of Mission San Miguel: The Towns, the Mission & the People. Wallace V. Ohles. LC 97-21252. 1997. write for info. (*1-884995-13-6*) Word Dancer.

Lands of Nowhere. Shannah Jay. LC 97-221102. (Chronicles of Tenebrak Ser.). 494p. 1995. write for info. (*0-330-35640-2*) Pan.

Lands Partit Poland. P. Wandycz. LC 74-8312. (History of East Central Europe Ser.: Vol. 7). (Illus.). 472p. 1975. pap. 27.50 (*0-295-95358-6*) U of Wash Pr.

Lands of Pleasure: Essays on Lillian H. Smith & the Development of Children's Libraries. Ed. by Adele M. Fasick et al. LC 89-70024. (Illus.). 188p. 1990. 24.00 (*0-8108-2266-0*) Scarecrow.

Lands of St. Peter: The Papal State in the Middle Ages & the Early Renaissance. Peter Partner. LC 73-182793. (Illus.). 495p. reprint ed. pap. 153.50 (*0-608-17985-X*, 202905600058) Bks Demand.

Lands of the Eastern Caliphate. Guy Le Strange. LC 77-180355. (Cambridge Geographical Ser.). reprint ed. 55.00 (*0-404-56287-6*) AMS Pr.

Lands of the Saracen. Bayard Taylor. (Notable American Authors). 1999. reprint ed. lib. bdg. 125.00 (*0-7812-9756-7*) Rprt Serv.

Lands of the Saracen: Pictures of Palestine, Asia Monor, Sicily & Spain. Bayard Taylor. Ed. by Moshe Davis. LC 77-70749. (America & the Holy Land Ser.). 1977. reprint ed. lib. bdg. 39.95 (*0-405-10294-1*) Ayer.

Lands of the Scottish Kings in England: The Honour of Huntington, the Liberty of Tyndale, & the Honour of Penrith. Margaret F. Moore & P. Hume Brown. LC 70-91997. xii, 141p. 1973. reprint ed. lib. bdg. 35.00 (*0-678-00728-4*) Kelley.

Lands of the Thunderbolt: Sikhim, Chumbi & Bhutan. 3rd ed. Zetland Lord of Ronaldshay. LC 87-16628. (Illus.). 352p. 1987. reprint ed. pap. 12.95 (*0-9617066-6-X*) Snow Lion-SLG Bks.

Lands of the Thunderbolt: Sikhim, Chumbi & Bhutsi. 3rd ed. Lord of Ronaldshay. LC 87-16628. (Illus.). 352p. 1987. reprint ed. 19.95 (*0-9617066-7-8*) Snow Lion-SLG Bks.

Lands, Peoples & Cultures Series, 28 bks. Incl. Canada Celebrates Multiculturalism. Bobbie Kalman. LC 93-34136. (Illus.). 32p. (YA). (gr. 4-9). 1993. pap. 7.95 (*0-86505-300-6*); Canada the Culture. Bobbie Kalman. LC 93-34384. (Illus.). 32p. (YA). (gr. 4-9). 1993. pap. 7.95 (*0-86505-299-9*); Canada the Culture. Bobbie Kalman. LC 93-34384. (Illus.). 32p. (YA). (gr. 3-9). 1993. lib. bdg. 20.60 (*0-86505-219-0*); Canada the Land. Bobbie Kalman. LC 93-23516. (Illus.). 32p. (YA). (gr. 4-9). 1993. pap. 7.95 (*0-86505-297-2*); Canada the Land. Bobbie Kalman. LC 93-23516. (Illus.). 32p. (YA). (gr. 4-9). 1993. lib. bdg. 20.60 (*0-86505-217-4*); Canada the People. Bobbie Kalman. LC 93-34328. (Illus.). 32p. (YA). (gr. 4-9). 1993. pap. 7.95 (*0-86505-298-0*); Canada the People. Bobbie Kalman. LC 93-34328. (Illus.). 32p. (YA). (gr. 3-9). 1993. lib. bdg. 20.60 (*0-86505-218-2*); China - The Culture. Bobbie Kalman. LC 93-27370. (Illus.). 32p. (YA). (gr. 4-9). 1989. pap. 7.95 (*0-86505-289-1*); China - The Culture. Bobbie Kalman. LC 93-27370. (Illus.). 32p. (YA). (gr. 3-9). 1989. lib. bdg. 20.60 (*0-86505-209-3*); China - The Land. Bobbie Kalman. LC 93-27374. (Illus.). 32p. (YA). (gr. 4-9). 1991. pap. 7.95 (*0-86505-287-5*); China - The Land. Bobbie Kalman. LC 93-27374. (Illus.). 32p. (YA). (gr. 3-9). 1989. lib. bdg. 20.60 (*0-86505-207-7*); China - The People. Bobbie Kalman. LC 93-30924. (Illus.). 32p. (YA). (gr. 4-9). 1989. pap. 7.95 (*0-86505-288-3*); China - The People. Bobbie Kalman. LC 93-30924. (Illus.). 32p. (YA). (gr. 3-9). 1989. lib. bdg. 20.60 (*0-86505-208-5*); Greece the Culture. Sierra Adare. LC 98-932174. (Illus.). 32p. (J). (gr. 4-9). 1998. lib. bdg. 20.60 (*0-86505-228-X*); Greece the Culture. Sierra Adare. LC 98-38944. (Illus.). 32p. (J). (gr. 4-9). 1998. pap. 7.95 (*0-86505-308-1*); Greece the Land. Sierra Adare. LC 98-4497. (Illus.). 32p. (J). (gr. 4-9). 1998. lib. bdg. 20.60 (*0-86505-226-3*); Greece the Land. Sierra Adare. LC 98-4497. (Illus.). 32p. (J). (gr. 4-9). 1998. pap. 7.95 (*0-86505-306-5*); Greece the People. Sierra Adare. LC 98-40369. (Illus.). 32p. (J). (gr. 4-9). 1998. pap. 7.95 (*0-86505-307-3*); Greece the People. Sierra Adare. LC 98-40369. (Illus.). 32p. (J). (gr. 4-9). 1998. lib. bdg. 20.60 (*0-86505-227-1*); India: The Culture. Bobbie Kalman. (Illus.). 32p. (YA). (gr. 4-9). 1989. lib. bdg. 20.60 (*0-86505-212-3*); India: The Culture. Bobbie Kalman. LC 93-27372. (Illus.). 32p. (YA). (gr. 4-9). 1989. pap. 7.95 (*0-86505-292-1*); India: The Land. Bobbie Kalman. LC 93-6163. (Illus.). 32p. (YA). (gr. 4-9). 1989. pap. 7.95 (*0-86505-290-5*); India: The Land. Bobbie Kalman. (Illus.). 32p. (YA). (gr. 4-9). 1989. lib. bdg. 20.60 (*0-86505-210-7*); India: The People. Bobbie Kalman. LC 93-30923. (Illus.). 32p. (YA). (gr. 3-9). 1989. lib. bdg. 20.60 (*0-86505-211-5*); India: The People. Bobbie Kalman. LC 93-30923. (Illus.). 32p. (YA). (gr. 4-9). 1989. pap. 7.95 (*0-86505-291-3*); Israel: The Culture. Debbie Smith. LC 98-39914. (Illus.). 32p. (J). (gr. 4-9). 1998. pap. 7.95 (*0-86505-311-1*); Israel the Culture. Debbie Smith. LC 98-39914. (Illus.). 32p. (J). (gr. 4-9). 1998. lib. bdg. 20.60 (*0-86505-231-X*); Israel the Land. Debbie Smith. LC 98-39913. (Illus.). 32p. (J). (gr. 4-9). 1998. lib. bdg. 20.60 (*0-86505-229-8*); Israel the Land. Debbie Smith & Bobbie Kalman. LC 98-39913. (Illus.). 32p. (J). (gr. 4-9). 1998. pap. 7.95 (*0-86505-309-X*); Israel the People. Debbie Smith. LC 98-39915. (Illus.). 32p. (J). (gr. 4-9). 1998. lib. bdg. 20.60 (*0-86505-230-1*); Israel the People. Debbie Smith. LC 98-39915. (Illus.). 32p. (J). (gr. 4-9). 1998. pap. 7.95 (*0-86505-310-3*); Japan - The Culture. Bobbie Kalman. LC 93-27373. (Illus.). 32p. (YA). (gr. 4-9). 1989. pap. 7.95 (*0-86505-286-7*); Japan - The Culture. Bobbie Kalman. LC 93-27373. (Illus.). 32p. (YA). (gr. 3-9). 1989. lib. bdg. 20.60 (*0-86505-206-9*); Japan - The Land. Bobbie Kalman. (Illus.). 32p. (YA). (gr. 4-9). 1989. pap. 7.95 (*0-86505-284-0*); Japan - The Land. Bobbie Kalman. LC 93-6162. (Illus.). 32p. (YA). (gr. 3-9). 1989. lib. bdg. 20.60 (*0-86505-204-2*); Japan - The People. Bobbie Kalman. LC 93-30925. (Illus.). 32p. (YA). (gr. 4-9). 1989. pap. 7.95 (*0-86505-285-9*); Japan - The People. Bobbie Kalman. LC 93-30925. (Illus.). 32p. (YA). (gr. 3-9). 1989. lib. bdg. 20.60 (*0-86505-205-0*); Mexico: The Culture. Bobbie Kalman. LC 93-34765. (Illus.). 32p. (YA). (gr. 4-9). 1993. pap. 7.95 (*0-86505-296-4*); Mexico: The Culture. Bobbie Kalman. LC 93-34765. (Illus.). 32p. (YA). (gr. 3-9). 1993. lib. bdg. 20.60 (*0-86505-216-6*); Mexico: The Land. Bobbie Kalman. LC 93-37747. (Illus.). 32p. (YA). (gr. 4-9). 1993. pap. 7.95 (*0-86505-294-8*); Mexico: The Land. Bobbie Kalman. LC 93-37747. (Illus.). 32p. (YA). (gr. 4-9). 1993. lib. bdg. 20.60 (*0-86505-214-X*); Mexico: The People. Bobbie Kalman. LC 93-34764. (Illus.). 32p. (YA). (gr. 4-9). 1993. pap. 7.95 (*0-86505-295-6*); Mexico: The People. Bobbie Kalman. LC 93-34764. (Illus.). 32p. (YA). (gr. 4-9). 1993. lib. bdg. 20.60 (*0-86505-215-8*); Peru - The Land. Bobbie Kalman. LC 94-874. (Illus.). 32p. (YA). (gr. 4-9). 1994. pap. 7.95 (*0-86505-301-4*); Peru - The Land. Bobbie Kalman. LC 94-874. (Illus.). 32p. (YA). (gr. 4-9). 1994. lib. bdg. 20.60 (*0-86505-221-2*); Peru - The People & Culture. Bobbie D. Kalman & Tammy Everts. LC 94-885. (Illus.). 32p. (YA). (gr. 4-9). 1994. pap. 7.95 (*0-86505-302-2*); Peru - The People & Culture. Bobbie Kalman & Tammy Everts. LC 94-885. (Illus.). 32p. (YA). (gr. 3-9). 1994. lib. bdg. 20.60 (*0-86505-222-0*); Tibet. Bobbie Kalman. LC 93-27371. (Illus.). 32p. (YA). (gr. 4-9). 1990. pap. 7.95 (*0-86505-293-X*); Tibet. Bobbie Kalman. (Illus.). 32p. (YA). (gr. 4-9). 1990. lib. bdg. 20.60 (*0-86505-213-1*); Vietnam - The Culture. Bobbie Kalman. LC 95-51995. (Illus.). 32p. (YA). (gr. 4-9). 1996. pap. 7.95 (*0-86505-305-7*); Vietnam - The Culture. Bobbie Kalman. LC 95-51995. (Illus.). 32p. (YA). (gr. 3-9). 1995. lib. bdg. 20.60 (*0-86505-225-5*); Vietnam - The Land. Bobbie Kalman. LC 95-51992. (Illus.). 32p. (YA). (gr. 4-9). 1996. pap. 7.95 (*0-86505-303-0*); Vietnam - The Land. Bobbie Kalman. LC 95-51992. 32p. (YA). (gr. 3-9). 1996. lib. bdg. 20.60 (*0-86505-223-9*); Vietnam - The People. David Schimpky & Bobbie Kalman. LC 95-37609. (Illus.). 32p. (YA). (gr. 4-9). 1996. pap. 7.95 (*0-86505-304-9*); Vietnam - The People. David Schimpky & Bobbie Kalman. LC 95-37609. (Illus.). 32p. (YA). (gr. 4-9). 1996. lib. bdg. 20.60 (*0-86505-224-7*); (Lands, Peoples & Cultures Ser.). (J). pap. write for info. (*0-86505-358-8*); lib. bdg. write for info. (*0-86505-278-6*) Crabtree Pub Co.

L

Landsailing see Action Sports

Landsailing. Scott Hays. (Action Sports Ser.). (Illus.). 48p. (J). (gr. 3-4). 1992. 19.00 (*0-516-35057-9*) Childrens.

Landsat: Space Technology in Natural Resource Planning. Paul A. Tessar et al. 1976. 1.00 (*1-55614-056-8*) U of SD Gov Res Bur.

Landsat-Based Lineament Analysis, East Texas Basin & Sabine Uplift Area. R. W. Baumgardner, Jr. (Reports of Investigations: RI 167). (Illus.). 26p. 1987. 2.50 (*0-318-23676-1*) U of Tex Econ Geology.

Landscape. (New Concepts in Architecture & Design Ser.). (Illus.). 224p. 1995. 85.00 (*4-938812-22-3*, Pub. by Puroto Gyarak) Bks Nippan.

Landscape. John Kelsey. LC 97-74166. (Illus.). 96p. (Orig.). 1998. pap. text 9.95 (*1-890257-02-8*, Hometime) Hometime Vid.

Landscape. Erika Langmuir. LC 97-67663. (National Gallery Pocket Guides Ser.). 80p. 1997. pap. text 10.00 (*0-300-07321-6*) Yale U Pr.

Landscape: A Comprehensive Guide to Drawing & Painting Nature. Richard McDaniel. LC 97-9185. (Illus.). 176p. 1997. 35.00 (*0-8230-2592-6*) Watsn-Guptill.

Landscape: And Western Art. Malcolm Andrews. (Oxford History of Art Ser.). (Illus.). 256p. 2000. 39.95 (*0-19-210046-7*) OUP.

Landscape: Critical Issues & Resources: Proceedings of the 1983 Conference of Educators in Landscape Architecture, August 6-10, 1983, Utah State University, Logan, Utah. Council of Educators in Landscape Architecture Sta. LC SB0469.. 310p. reprint ed. pap. 96.10 (*0-608-14470-3*, 202108100020) Bks Demand.

Landscape: Politics & Perspectives. Ed. by Barbara Bender. LC 92-39620. 352p. 1993. 49.50 (*0-85496-852-0*, Pub. by Berg Pubs); pap. 22.50 (*0-85496-373-1*, Pub. by Berg Pubs) NYU Pr.

Landscape: Strategies for the Construction of the Contemporary International Landscape. Whitney Library of Design Staff. Ed. by Gustavo Gili. (TwoG). (ENG & SPA., Illus.). 144p. 1997. pap. 37.50 (*0-8230-6589-8*, Whitney Lib) Watsn-Guptill.

Landscape: Theory. Ed. by Carol Di Grappa. LC 80-81182. (Illus.). 176p. 1982. 35.00 (*0-912810-27-0*); pap. 19.95 (*0-912810-32-7*) Lustrum Pr.

***Landscape: 9 + 1 Young Dutch Landscape Architects.** Henk Van Blerck. (Illus.). 2000. pap. 35.00 (*90-5662-133-5*) NAi Uitgevers.

Landscape Aesthetics & Environment Planning: A Critique of Underlying Premises. David Berry. (Discussion Papers: No. 85). 1975. pap. 10.00 (*1-55869-067-0*) Regional Sci Res Inst.

Landscape Alphabet. Michael Twyman. (Illus.). 84p. (C). 1989. reprint ed. 79.00 (*0-903696-10-X*, Pub. by Hurtwood Pr Ltd) St Mut.

Landscape & Architecture: Sharing Common Ground, Defining Turf, Charting New Paths: Proceedings. Council of Educators in Landscape Architecture Sta. Ed. by Margaret McAvin. LC 88-71962. (Illus.). 853p. reprint ed. pap. 200.00 (*0-8357-6182-7*, 203461500090) Bks Demand.

Landscape & Community in England. Alan Everitt. 375p. (C). 1985. 65.00 (*0-907628-42-7*) Hambledon Press.

Landscape & Englishness. David Matless. (Picturing History Ser.). (Illus.). 304p. 1998. 45.00 (*1-86189-022-2*, Pub. by Reaktion Bks) Consort Bk Sales.

Landscape & Figure Composition. Sadakichi Hartmann. LC 72-9206. (Literature of Photography Ser.). 1979. reprint ed. 18.95 (*0-405-04915-3*) Ayer.

Landscape & Garden Products Buyer's Guide: Over 4,000 Products from 700 Suppliers. Home Planners Staff. (Illus.). 192p. 1999. pap. text 19.95 (*1-881955-55-9*) Home Planners.

***Landscape & Identity: Geographies of Nation & Class in England.** Wendy Joy Darby. (Materializing Culture Ser.). 224p. 2000. 65.00 (*1-85973-425-1*, Pub. by Berg Pubs); pap. 22.50 (*1-85973-430-8*, Pub. by Berg Pubs) NYU Pr.

Landscape & Ideology: The English Rustic Tradition, 1740-1860. Ann Bermingham. LC 85-24509. (Illus.). 400p. 1986. 60.00 (*0-520-05287-0*, Pub. by U CA Pr) Cal Prin Full Svc.

Landscape & Light: Essays by Neil M. Gunn. Ed. by Alistair McCleery. 264p. 1987. text 30.00 (*0-08-035060-7*, Pub. by Aberdeen U Pr); pap. text 19.95 (*0-08-035061-5*, Pub. by Aberdeen U Pr) Macmillan.

Landscape & Material Life in Franklin County, Massachusetts, 1770-1860. J. Ritchie Garrison. LC 90-48067. (Illus.). 336p. 1991. text 45.00 (*0-87049-680-8*) U of Tenn Pr.

Landscape & Memory. Simon Schama. 1996. pap. 23.00 (*0-679-73512-7*) Knopf.

Landscape & Memory. Simon Schama. 1996. pap. text 23.00 (*0-679-43512-3*) Vin Bks.

L

Landscape & People of the Franchthi Region, Fascicle 2. Tjeerd H. Van Andel & Susan B. Sutton. LC 87-4156. (Excavations at Franchthi Cave, Greece Ser.). (Illus.). 122p. 1988. pap. 30.00 (*0-253-31975-7*) Ind U Pr.

Landscape & Power. Ed. by W. J. Mitchell. LC 93-4907. 264p. 1994. pap. text 13.95 (*0-226-53207-0*) U Ch Pr.

Landscape & Power. Ed. by W. J. Mitchell. LC 93-4907. 248p. 1999. lib. bdg. 42.50 (*0-226-53206-2*) U Ch Pr.

***Landscape & Power in Ancient Meso.** Koontz et al. 352p. 2000. pap. 75.00 (*0-8133-3732-1*, Pub. by Westview) HarpC.

Landscape & Power in Vienna. Robert Rotenberg. LC 94-42624. (Illus.). 416p. 1995. text 42.50 (*0-8018-4961-6*) Johns Hopkins.

Landscape & Seasons. Jose M. Parramon. (Workbooks for Painting). (Illus.). 32p. 1999. pap. 5.95 (*0-7641-1213-9*) Barron.

Landscape & Settlement in Britain A. D., 400-1066. Ed. by Della Hooke. LC 95-233905. (Illus.). 160p. 1995. pap. text 29.95 (*0-85989-386-3*, Pub. by Univ Exeter Pr) Northwestern U Pr.

Landscape & Settlement in Romanov Russia, 1613 to 1917. Judith Pallot & Denis J. Shaw. (Illus.). 336p. 1990. text 75.00 (*0-19-823246-2*) OUP.

Landscape & Society: Prehistoric Central Italy. Graeme Barker. LC 80-41630. (Studies in Archaeology). 288p. 1981. text 115.00 (*0-12-078650-8*) Acad Pr.

Landscape & Society in Medieval Cumbria. A. J. Winchester. 224p. (C). 1996. 75.00 (*0-85976-179-7*, Pub. by J Donald) St Mut.

Landscape & the Looking Glass: Willa Cather's Search for Value. John H. Randall, 3rd. LC 72-6207. (Illus.). 425p. 1973. reprint ed. lib. bdg. 35.00 (*0-8371-6466-4*, RALG, Greenwood Pr) Greenwood.

Landscape & Townscape in the South West. Ed. by Robert Higham. 142p. 1989. pap. text 17.00 (*0-85989-309-X*, Pub. by Univ Exeter Pr) Northwestern U Pr.

Landscape & Vegetation Ecology of the Kakadu Region, Northern Australia. Ed. by C. Max Finlayson & Isabell Von Oertzen. LC 95-39765. (Geobotany Ser.: No. 23). 202p. 1996. text 173.50 (*0-7923-3770-0*) Kluwer Academic.

Landscape & Western Art. Malcolm Andrews. (Oxford History of Art Ser.). (Illus.). 256p. 2000. pap. 17.95 (*0-19-284233-1*) OUP.

Landscape Approach. Bernard Lassus. LC 98-26259. (Penn Studies in Landscape Architecture). (Illus.). 216p. 1998. 39.95 (*0-8122-3450-2*) U of Pa Pr.

Landscape Approaches in Mammalian Ecology & Conservation. Ed. by William Z. Lidicker, Jr. 216p. 1995. 35.95 (*0-8166-2587-5*) U of Minn Pr.

Landscape Archaeology: Reading & Interpreting the American Historical Landscape. Ed. by Rebecca Yamin & Karen B. Metheny. LC 95-32484. (Illus.). 296p. 1996. text 48.00 (*0-87049-920-3*) U of Tenn Pr.

Landscape Architect. Jack Rudman. (Career Examination Ser.: C-2392). 1994. pap. 29.95 (*0-8373-2392-4*) Nat Learn.

***Landscape Architect Registration Examination: A Guide for Professional Development.** Kay Williams et al. Ed. by Virginia L. Russell. 91p. 1999. lib. bdg. 90.00 (*0-941236-34-X*, 634X) Am Landscape Arch.

Landscape Architect's Consultation. Frank W. Bushell, Sr. (Landscape by Owner Ser.: Vol. 1). (Illus.). 382p. 1996. spiral bd. 45.00 (*0-9650695-0-8*) One Leaf.

Landscape Architects Portable. Dines. 2001. 59.95 (*0-07-134422-5*) McGraw.

Landscape Architecture. Boy Scouts of America. (Illus.). 48p. (YA). (gr. 6-12). 1969. pap. 2.90 (*0-8395-3355-1*, 33355) BSA.

Landscape Architecture. Ed. by Stephen Moorhead & Gordan Grice. (Illus.). 208p. 1998. 44.99 (*1-56496-101-X*) Rockport Pubs.

Landscape Architecture. 3rd rev. ed. John O. Simonds. LC 97-16077. (Illus.). 384p. 1997. 74.95 (*0-07-057709-9*) McGraw.

Landscape Architecture: An Illustrated History in Timelines, Site Plans, & Biography. William A. Mann. 480p. (Orig.). 1993. pap. 64.95 (*0-471-59465-2*) Wiley.

Landscape Architecture: Guidelines to Professional Practice. Lane Marshall. 160p. 1981. 28.95 (*0-941236-00-5*, 6005) Am Landscape Arch.

Landscape Architecture & Town Planning in the Netherlands. Thoth Publishers Editorial Staff & Books Nippan Staff. (Illus.). 212p. Date not set. pap. 55.00 (*90-6868-134-6*, Pub. by Thoth Pubs) Bks Nippan.

Landscape Architecture & Town Planning in the Netherlands: 1995-1997. Ed. by Thoth Publishers Editorial Staff. (Illus.). 176p. pap. 44.95 (*90-6868-194-X*, Pub. by U Thoth) Bks Nippan.

Landscape Architecture Book Catalog: A Bibliography of Holdings on the University of Kentucky Campus Through 1977. Antoinette P. Powell. (University of Kentucky Libraries Occasional Papers: No. 3). 335p. 1982. pap. 10.00 (*0-317-27432-5*) U of KY Libs.

Landscape Architecture, Botanical Gardens, & Arboreta. Blythe Camenson. LC 98-18216. (Opportunities in... Ser.). 160p. 1998. 14.95 (*0-8442-6483-0*, 64830); pap. 11.95 (*0-8442-6534-9*, 65349) NTC Contemp Pub Co.

Landscape Architecture Construction. 2nd ed. H. C. Landphair & F. Klatt. 448p. 1987. 48.25 (*0-444-01286-9*) P-H.

Landscape Architecture Construction. 3rd ed. Harlow Landphair & Fred Klatt. LC 98-24744. (Illus.). 432p. (C). 1998. 78.00 (*0-13-254947-6*) P-H.

Landscape Architecture of Thomas Balsley: Urban Parks & Waterfronts. Jane Gillette. 80p. 1999. pap. 29.95 (*1-888931-19-1*) Spacemkr Pr.

Landscape Architecture Sourcebook: A Guide to Resources on the History & Practice of Landscape Architecture. Diana L. Vogelsong. (Design Reference Ser.: Vol. 1). 1996. lib. bdg. 45.00 (*0-7808-0196-2*) Omnigraphics Inc.

Landscape Art. World of Environmental Design Staff. (Illus.). 256p. 1996. 80.00 (*84-8185-001-2*) Watsn-Guptill.

***Landscape Artists.** ARCO Editorial Board Staff. (Illus.). 2000. pap. 29.95 (*84-8185-236-8*) Arco Edit.

Landscape As Photograph. Estelle Jussim & Elizabeth L. Cock. LC 84-40671. (Illus.). 184p. reprint ed. pap. 57.10 (*0-7837-6220-8*, 208028800004) Bks Demand.

Landscape at the End of the Century. Stephen Dunn. 96p. 1992. pap. 9.95 (*0-393-30853-7*) Norton.

Landscape at the End of the Century: Poems. Stephen Dunn. 1991. 17.95 (*0-393-02972-7*) Norton.

***Landscape Being Born: Selected Poems.** Fiama H. De Brandao. 200p. 2000. pap. 10.95 (*1-892295-77-6*) Green Integer.

Landscape below Ground. Ed. by Dan Neely & Gary Watson. 222p. (C). 1994. pap. text 60.00 (*0-685-75083-3*) Int Soc Arboricult.

Landscape below Ground II. Ed. by Dan Neely & Gary Watson. 266p. (C). 1998. pap. 40.00 (*1-881956-06-7*) Int Soc Arboricult.

Landscape Boundaries: Consequences for Biotic Diversity & Ecological Flows. Ed. by A. J. Hansen & F. Di Castri. (Ecological Studies: Vol. 92). (Illus.). xvii, 452p. 1995. 118.00 (*0-387-97631-0*) Spr-Verlag.

Landscape Change Vol. 1: Geomorphic Responses to Climactic Change. William B. Bull. (Illus.). 352p. 1991. text 90.00 (*0-19-505570-5*) OUP.

Landscape Comes & Goes. Elizabeth M. Gunn. LC 85-73496. 158p. 1985. 24.95 (*0-7206-0638-1*, Pub. by P Owen Ltd) Dufour.

Landscape Construction. Sauter. (Agriculture Ser.). (C). 1999. pap. 16.00 (*0-8273-8428-9*) Delmar.

***Landscape Construction.** David Sauter. LC 99-14917. (Agriculture Ser.). 384p. (C). 1999. pap. 58.95 (*0-8273-8427-0*) Delmar.

Landscape Construction Vol. 1: Walls, Fences & Railings. Kate Fortlage & Elizabeth Phillips. 150p. 1992. 83.95 (*0-566-09041-4*, Pub. by Gower) Ashgate Pub Co.

Landscape Construction Vol. 2: Roads, Paving & Drainage, 3 vols. Michael Ash & Irene Ash. 266p. 1996. text 86.95 (*0-566-09042-2*, Pub. by Gower) Ashgate Pub Co.

Landscape Construction & Detailing. Alan Blanc. LC 96-4922. (Illus.). 210p. 1996. 74.95 (*0-07-005957-8*) McGraw.

***Landscape Construction Procedures, Techniques & Design.** 4th ed. Floyd A. Giles. (Illus.). 250p. (C). 1999. text 44.80 (*0-87563-884-8*) Stipes.

Landscape, Culture, & Power in Chinese Society. Wen-Hsin Yeh & Stephen West. LC 97-48842. (China Research Monographs). xv, 152 p. 1998. pap. 15.00 (*1-55729-061-X*) IEAS.

Landscape Degradation & Biodiversity in Mediterranean-Type Ecosystems. Ed. by P. W. Rundel et al. LC 98-8218. (Ecological Studies: Vol. 136). (Illus.). xxvi, 432p. 1998. 169.00 (*3-540-64475-X*) Spr-Verlag.

Landscape Design: A Practical Approach. 4th ed. LeRoy G. Hannebaum. LC 97-6511. 460p. 1997. 97.00 (*0-13-163230-2*) P-H.

Landscape Design: An International Survey. Ed. by Ken Fieldhouse & Sheila Harvey. LC 92-23782. (Illus.). 1993. 75.00 (*0-87951-474-4*, Pub. by Overlook Pr) Penguin Putnam.

Landscape Design & Construction. Cy DeCosse Incorporated Staff. LC 92-34457. (Black & Decker Home Improvement Library). (Illus.). 128p. 1993. 16.95 (*0-86573-726-6*); pap. 14.95 (*0-86573-727-4*) Creat Pub Intl.

Landscape Design & Gardening Procedures for the Not So Rich. Anne Magill. (Illus.). 104p. (Orig.). 1989. pap. 8.95 (*0-9627632-0-9*) Melrose Garden Pr.

Landscape Design for Elderly & Disabled People. Jane Stoneham. LC 96-203885. 176p. 1996. pap. text 49.50 (*1-870673-20-4*, Pub. by Garden Art Pr) Antique Collect.

Landscape Design Guide Vol. I: Soft Landscape. Adrian Linsey & Ken Fieldhouse. Ed. by Jeremy Dodd. 224p. 1990. text 73.95 (*0-566-09017-1*, Pub. by Gower) Ashgate Pub Co.

Landscape Design Guide Vol. II: Hard Landscape: The Design of Paved Spaces, Landscape Enclosure & Landscape Furniture. Adrian Lisney & Ken Fieldhouse. 224p. 1990. text 71.95 (*0-566-09019-8*, Pub. by Gower) Ashgate Pub Co.

Landscape Design Market in Japan: A Strategic Entry Report, 1996. Compiled by Icon Group International Staff. (Country Industry Report). (Illus.). 161p. 1999. ring bd. 1610.00 incl. audio compact disk (*0-7418-0593-6*) Icon Grp.

Landscape Design with Plants. 2nd ed. Brian Clouston. 1990. 84.00 (*0-8493-7148-1*, SB) CRC Pr.

Landscape Design with Plants. 2nd ed. Brian Clouston. (Illus.). 434p. 1994. pap. write for info. (*0-7506-1962-7*) CRC Pr.

Landscape Designer. rev. ed. Stanley Tools Staff. (Stanley Project Planners Ser.). 1989. pap. 15.95 (*0-924648-03-1*) Stanley Tools.

Landscape Detailing: Enclosures, 2 vols., 1. 3rd ed. Michael Littlewood. LC 92-34847. (Illus.). 208p. 1993. pap. text 64.95 (*0-7506-1304-1*) Buttrwrth-Heinemann.

Landscape Detailing: Structures, Vol. III. 3rd ed. Michael Littlewood. (Illus.). 240p. 1997. pap. text 49.95 (*0-7506-2320-9*) Buttrwrth-Heinemann.

Landscape Doctor: Do-It-Yourself Remedies for Home Planting Problems. Sara J. Von Trapp. LC 94-27431. (Illus.). 144p. 1994. pap. 19.95 (*1-881527-39-5*, Chapters Bks) HM.

Landscape Drawing & Painting. Patricia Monahan. LC 97-38972. (Illus.). 144p. 1998. 24.95 (*0-7621-0031-1*, Pub. by RD Assn) Penguin Putnam.

Landscape Drawing Step by Step. unabridged ed. Wendon Blake. LC 98-21529. (Illus.). 80p. 1998. pap. 6.95 (*0-486-40201-0*) Dover.

Landscape Drawings of Five Centuries, 1400-1900: From the Robert Leitman Collection, Metropolitan Museum of Art. Larry Silver et al. LC 87-34829. (Illus.). 200p. (Orig.). 1987. 25.00 (*0-941680-06-1*) M&L Block.

Landscape Ecological Analysis: Issues & Applications. Jeffrey M. Klopatek & R. H. Gardner. LC 98-33561. 376p. 1999. 79.95 (*0-387-98325-2*) Spr-Verlag.

Landscape Ecology. Richard T. Foreman & Michel Godron. LC 85-12306. 640p. 1986. text 90.95 (*0-471-87037-4*) Wiley.

Landscape Ecology. Z. Navch & A. S. Lieberman. (Environmental Management Ser.). (Illus.). xxviii, 356p. 1989. pap. 49.00 (*0-387-97169-6*) Spr-Verlag.

***Landscape Ecology: A Top-Down Approach.** James Sanderson. LC 99-40288. (Landscape Ecology Ser.). 272p. 1999. boxed set 69.95 (*1-56670-368-9*) Lewis Pubs.

Landscape Ecology: In Honor of Prof. Dr. J. Schmithusen. Ed. by P. C. Muller & C. Rathjens. (Biogeographica Ser.: No. 16). 1979. text 155.50 (*90-6193-217-3*) Kluwer Academic.

Landscape Ecology: Theory & Application. Zev Naveh & A. S. Lieberman. (Environmental Management Ser.). (Illus.). 335p. 1983. 59.50 (*0-387-90849-8*) Spr-Verlag.

Landscape Ecology: Theory & Application. 2nd ed. Zev Naveh & A. S. Lieberman. (Illus.). 400p. 1993. pap. write for info. (*3-540-94059-6*) Spr-Verlag.

Landscape Ecology & Agroecosystems. Ed. by R. G. Bunce et al. 256p. 1993. lib. bdg. 99.95 (*0-87371-918-2*, L918) Lewis Pubs.

Landscape Ecology & Geographical Information Systems (GIS) Ed. by Roy H. Young et al. LC 93-16578. (Applications in Geographic Information Systems Ser.). 300p. 1993. 79.00 (*0-7484-0002-8*, Pub. by Tay Francis Ltd) Taylor & Francis.

Landscape Ecology, Function & Management: Principles from Australia's Rangelands. J. Ludwig et al. (Illus.). 162p. 1997. pap. 59.95 (*0-643-05797-8*, Pub. by CSIRO) Accents Pubns.

***Landscape Ecology in Action.** Almo Farina. LC 99-89516. 2000. write for info. (*0-7923-6165-2*) Kluwer Academic.

Landscape Ecology of Small Mammals. Ed. by Gary W. Barrett & John D. Peles. LC 98-37571. (Illus.). 304p. 1999. 74.95 (*0-387-98646-4*) Spr-Verlag.

Landscape Ecology Principles in Landscape Architecture & Land-Use Planning: Seeking a Balance in Western Water Use. Wenche E. Dramstad et al. LC 96-52477. (Illus.). 80p. 1997. pap. text 19.95 (*1-55963-514-2*, Shearwater Bks) Island Pr.

Landscape Essentials. Cowles Creative Publishing Staff. (Black & Decker Quick Steps Ser.). (Illus.). 80p. (Orig.). 1996. pap. 9.95 (*0-86573-654-5*) Creat Pub Intl.

Landscape Estimating see Landscape Estimating Methods

***Landscape Estimating Methods.** 3rd rev. exp. ed. R. S. Means Company Staff & Sylvia H. Fee. LC 99-462613. Orig. Title: Landscape Estimating. 300p. 1998. 62.95 (*0-87629-534-0*, 67295A) R S Means.

Landscape Etchings of Robert C. Minor. Thomas P. Bruhn. (Illus.). 8p. Date not set. 3.00 (*0-614-10425-4*) W Benton Mus.

Landscape Exhibition of the Four Seasons: Autumn see Seasons

Landscape Exhibition of the Four Seasons: Autumn, 4 vols., Set. (Landscape Exhibition of the Four Seasons Ser.). (Illus.). 91p. (Orig.). 1994. pap. 34.50 (*957-562-006-2*) Heian Intl.

Landscape Exhibition of the Four Seasons: Spring see Seasons

Landscape Exhibition of the Four Seasons: Spring, 4 vols., Set. (Landscape Exhibition of the Four Seasons Ser.). (CHI & ENG., Illus.). 64p. (Orig.). 1994. pap. 39.95 (*957-562-163-8*) Heian Intl.

Landscape Exhibitions of the Four Seasons: Winter see Seasons

Landscape Exhibitions of the Four Seasons: Winter. (CHI & ENG., Illus.). 74p. 1994. reprint ed. pap. 22.00 (*0-89346-802-9*) Heian Intl.

Landscape for a Good Woman: A Story of Two Lives. Carolyn K. Steedman. 166p. 1987. pap. text 15.00 (*0-8135-1258-1*) Rutgers U Pr.

Landscape for Modern Sculpture: Storm King Art Center. rev. ed. John Beardsley. (Illus.). 112p. 1996. 39.95 (*0-7892-0246-8*) Abbeville Pr.

Landscape Forestry. Stephen G. Boyce. 239p. 1995. 110.00 (*0-471-00784-6*) Wiley.

Landscape Function & Disturbance in Arctic Tundra. Ed. by James F. Reynolds & John D. Tenhunen. (Ecological Studies: Vol. 120). (Illus.). 429p. 1996. 139.00 (*3-540-59263-6*) Spr-Verlag.

***Landscape-Gardening.** Ossian Cole Simonds. (ASLA Centennial Reprint Ser.). (Illus.). 368p. 2000. 29.95 (*1-55849-258-5*) U of Mass Pr.

Landscape Gardening: A Source Guide. 1991. lib. bdg. 76.00 (*0-8490-4882-6*) Gordon Pr.

Landscape Gardening & the Choice of Plants. Frederique Tanguy & Marc Tanguy. Tr. by Alan Sheridan. LC 85-3344.Tr. of La/Composition des Espaces Vertes et le Choix des Vegetaux. 153p. reprint ed. pap. 47.50 (*0-8357-3128-6*, 203938900012) Bks Demand.

Landscape Gardening in Japan. Josiah Conder. 1990. pap. 14.95 (*0-486-26559-5*) Dover.

Landscape Graphics. Grant W. Reid. (Illus.). 216p. 1987. pap. 19.95 (*0-8230-7331-9*, Whitney Lib) Watsn-Guptill.

Landscape Handbook for the Tropics. William F. Hill. LC 96-137501. (Illus.). 360p. 1995. 79.50 (*1-870673-11-5*) Antique Collect.

Landscape Heterogeneity & Disturbance. Ed. by M. G. Turner. (Ecological Studies: Vol. 64). (Illus.). 310p. 1987. 138.95 (*0-387-96497-5*) Spr-Verlag.

Landscape Illusion: A Spatial Approach to Painting. Daniel Chard. (Illus.). 144p. 1993. pap. 18.95 (*0-8230-2594-2*) Watsn-Guptill.

Landscape, Image & Design: A Survey of Open Space Planners. David Berry & Gene Steiker. (Discussion Papers: No. 77). 1974. pap. 10.00 (*1-55869-068-9*) Regional Sci Res Inst.

Landscape Images: Recent Photographs by Linda Connor, Judy Fiskin & Ruth Thorne-Thomsen. Richard Lorenz. (Illus.). 40p. 1980. pap. 4.50 (*0-934418-08-X*) Mus Contemp Art.

Landscape in America. Ed. by George F. Thompson. LC 94-18049. (Illus.). 288p. 1995. pap. 24.95 (*0-292-78136-9*); text 55.00 (*0-292-78135-0*) U of Tex Pr.

Landscape in History, 2 vols., Set. 2nd ed. Pregillp. (Landscape Architecture Ser.). (C). 1998. pap. 79.95 (*0-442-02613-7*, VNR) Wiley.

Landscape in History: Americas, Vol. 2. 2nd ed. Pregillp. (Landscape Architecture Ser.). (C). 1998. pap. 39.95 (*0-442-02612-9*, VNR) Wiley.

Landscape in History: Europe, Vol. 1. 2nd ed. P Pregill. (Landscape Architecture Ser.). (C). 1998. pap. 39.95 (*0-442-02609-9*, VNR) Wiley.

Landscape in Literature. Christopher Salter & William Lloyd. Ed. by Salvatore J. Natoli. LC 76-29268. (Resource Papers for College Geography). (C). 1977. pap. text 15.00 (*0-89291-118-2*) Assn Am Geographers.

Landscape in Pen & Wash. Fedarb. 1998. pap. 19.95 (*0-7153-0786-X*, Pub. by D & C Pub) Sterling.

Landscape in Pen & Wash. Paulette Fedarb. (Illus.). 128p. 1996. 24.95 (*0-7153-0284-1*, Pub. by D & C Pub) Sterling.

Landscape in Sight: Looking at America. John B. Jackson. Ed. by Helen L. Horowitz. LC 96-48728. (Illus.). 416p. 1997. 40.00 (*0-300-07116-7*) Yale U Pr.

Landscape in Sight: Looking at America. JOHN BRINCKERHOFF JACKSON. Ed. by Helen L. Horowitz. (Illus.). 416p. 1999. pap. 18.00 (*0-300-08074-3*) Yale U Pr.

Landscape in the Works of Marcel Proust. Francis V. Fardwell. LC 76-168004. (Catholic University of America. Studies in Romance Languages & Literatures: No. 35). reprint ed. 37.50 (*0-404-50335-7*) AMS Pr.

Landscape in Twentieth-Century American Art: Selections from the Metropolitan Museum of Art. Robert Rosenblum et al. (Illus.). 174p. 1991. pap. 25.00 (*0-917418-93-X*) Am Fed Arts.

Landscape Inspirations: A Collection of Drawing & Painting Ideas for Artists. Rockport Publishers Editors. (Inspirations Ser.). (Illus.). 96p. 1997. pap. 12.99 (*1-56496-384-5*, Quarry Bks) Rockport Pubs.

Landscape Interpretation. Duncan. text 112.00 (*0-471-98529-5*); pap. text 37.00 (*0-471-98530-9*) Wiley.

Landscape Irrigation: Design & Management. Stephen W. Smith. LC 96-8028. 240p. 1996. 59.95 (*0-471-03824-5*) Wiley.

Landscape Irrigation Design. Eugene W. Rochester. LC 95-75549. (Illus.). 220p. 1995. spiral bd. 44.00 (*0-929355-61-X*, MO695) Am Soc Ag Eng.

Landscape Is Behind the Door: Bilingual Edition. Pierre Martory. Tr. by John Ashbery. LC 94-11242. 127p. 1994. pap. 13.95 (*1-878818-30-9*, Pub. by Sheep Meadow) U Pr of New Eng.

Landscape It Yourself: A Landscape Architect's Guide to Planning & Designing Your Own Exterior & Interior Landscapes. Jamie Gibbs. (Illus.). 224p. 1988. pap. 14.95 (*0-317-67934-1*, PL-6055, Perennial) HarperTrade.

Landscape Lake Dwellings: Lake Dwellings in a Landscape. Ian Morrison. 80p. (Orig.). 1988. pap. 16.50 (*0-85224-472-X*, Pub. by Edinburgh U Pr) Col U Pr.

Landscape-Level Pronghorn Habitat Evaluation Model for Arizona. A. Alexander et al. (Arizona Game & Fish Department Technical Report: No. 19). (Illus.). 50p. (Orig.). 1996. pap. 5.00 (*0-917563-25-5*) AZ Game & Fish.

Landscape, Liberty & Authority: Poetry, Criticism & Politics from Thomson to Wordsworth. Tim Fulford. (Studies in Eighteenth-Century English Literature & Thought: No. 30). 264p. (C). 1996. text 59.95 (*0-521-55455-1*) Cambridge U Pr.

Landscape Library Users Manual: PowerDraw. 2nd ed. Amr Hawas. Ed. by Susan Stanley. (Powercadd Ser.). (Illus.). 92p. 1989. write for info. (*1-878250-04-3*) Eng Soft NC.

Landscape Lighting Book. Janet L. Moyer. LC 91-44393. 304p. 1992. 90.00 (*0-471-52726-2*) Wiley.

Landscape Linkages & Biodiversity. Ed. by Wendy E. Hudson. LC 91-15607. 194p. 1991. text 40.00 (*1-55963-108-2*); pap. text 25.00 (*1-55963-109-0*) Island Pr.

Landscape Magic: Tricks & Techniques for Rejuvenating Old Yards & Gardens. Douglas Green. Ed. by Paul Dunphy. (Illus.). 144p. 1995. pap. 19.95 (*1-881527-85-9*, Chapters Bks) HM.

***Landscape Maintenance Techniques.** Schaedler. (C). 2000. pap. 45.00 (*0-7668-1557-9*) Delmar.

***Landscape Makeover Book: How to Bring New Life to an Old Yard.** Sara Jane Von Trapp. LC 99-53375. (Illus.). 170p. 2000. pap. 21.95 (*1-56158-259-X*) Taunton.

An Asterisk (*) at the beginning of an entry indicates that the title is appearing for the first time.

L

Landscape Management & Maintenance: A Guide to Its Costing & Organization. Hohn Parker & Peter Bryan. (Illus.). 176p. 1989. text 69.95 (*0-566-09018-X*) Ashgate Pub Co.

Landscape Meanings & Values. Ed. by Edmund C. Penning-Roswell & D. Lowenthal. (Illus.). 160p. 1986. text 39.95 (*0-04-710003-6*) Routledge.

***Landscape Modeling.** Stephen Ervin. (Illus.). 2000. 59.95 (*0-07-135745-9*) McGraw.

Landscape Narratives: Design Practices for Telling Stories. Matthew Potteiger & Jamie Purinton. LC 97-40015. 352p. 1998. pap. 49.95 (*0-471-12486-9*) Wiley.

Landscape of Absence: Emily Dickinson's Poetry. Inder N. Kher. LC 73-86904. 368p. reprint ed. pap. 114.10 (*0-8357-8201-8*, 203377900087) Bks Demand.

Landscape of Anglo-Saxon England. Della Hooke. LC 97-17337. 1998. 95.00 (*0-7185-1727-X*); pap. 27.95 (*0-7185-0161-6*) Bks Intl VA.

Landscape of Belief: Encountering the Holy Land in Nineteenth-Century American Art & Culture. John Davis. LC 95-7051. (Series in Nineteenth-Century Art, Culture, & Society). 351p. 1996. text 75.00 (*0-691-04373-6*, Pub. by Princeton U Pr) Cal Prin Full Svc.

Landscape of Belief: Encountering the Holy Land in Nineteenth-Century American Art & Culture. John Davis. 286p. 1996. pap. text 29.95 (*0-691-05845-8*, Pub. by Princeton U Pr) Cal Prin Full Svc.

Landscape of Britain. M. Reed. (Illus.). 408p. (C). 1997. pap. 29.95 (*0-415-15745-5*, D4178) Routledge.

Landscape of Britain: From the Beginnings to 1914. Michael Reed. (Illus.). 368p. (C). 1990. text 83.00 (*0-389-20933-3*) B&N Imports.

Landscape of Civilisation: As Experienced in the Moody Historical Gardens. Geoffrey Jellicoe. (Illus.). 200p. 1989. 49.50 (*1-870673-01-8*) Antique Collect.

Landscape of Community: A History of Communal Forests in New England. Robert McCullough. LC 94-35541. (Illus.). 423p. 1995. text 55.00 (*0-87451-696-X*) U Pr of New Eng.

Landscape of Craft. Ed. by George Fry. 92p. 1990. 24.95 (*0-86492-130-6*, Pub. by Goose Ln Edits) Genl Dist Srvs.

Landscape of Demons: And the Book of Sara. Gabriel D. Kessler. LC 96-80417. 231p. (Orig.). 1997. pap. 8.95 (*0-9656202-0-4*) Millennium MA.

Landscape of Desire: Partial Stories of the Northern Medieval World. Gillian R. Overing & Marijane Osborn. LC 93-32773. 1994. pap. 16.95 (*0-8166-2375-9*); text 42.95 (*0-8166-2374-0*) U of Minn Pr.

***Landscape of Events.** Paul Virilio. Tr. by Julie Rose from FRE. (Writing Architecture Ser.). (Illus.). 130p. 2000. pap. 15.95 (*0-262-72034-5*) MIT Pr.

Landscape of Exile. Jay Griswold. 99p. (Orig.). 1993. pap. 9.95 (*0-931122-71-6*) West End.

Landscape of Fear: Stephen King's American Gothic. Anthony S. Magistrale. LC 87-72642. 139p. (C). 1988. 26.95 (*0-87972-404-8*) Bowling Green Univ Popular Press.

Landscape of Ghosts. Bill Holm. (Illus.). 128p. 1993. 6.95 (*0-89658-198-5*) Voyageur Pr.

Landscape of Jewish Experience: Paintings by Samuel Bak. Ori Z. Soltes. 1997. pap. 10.00 (*1-881456-38-2*) B B K Natl Jew Mus.

Landscape of Leadership Preparation: Reframing the Education of School Administrators. Joseph Murphy et al. LC 92-16959. 240p. 1992. 61.95 (*0-8039-6027-1*, 81147); pap. 27.95 (*0-8039-6028-X*, 81148) Corwin Pr.

Landscape of Love. large type ed. Sylvia E. Kirk. 208p. 1993. 15.95 (*0-7451-1678-7*, G K Hall Lrg Type) Mac Lib Ref.

Landscape of Man. 3rd expanded ed. Geoffrey Jellicoe & Susan Jellicoe. LC 94-61111. (Illus.). 408p. 1995. pap. 24.95 (*0-500-27819-9*, Pub. by Thames Hudson) Norton.

Landscape of Memory. Milton Meltzer. 1999. pap. 4.99 (*0-14-031985-9*) Viking Penguin.

Landscape of Modernity: Essays on New York City, 1900-1940. Ed. by David Ward & Olivier Zunz. LC 91-43456. (Illus.). 320p. 1992. 39.95 (*0-87154-900-X*) Russell Sage.

Landscape of Modernity: Essays on New York City, 1900-1940. Ed. by David Ward & Olivier Zunz. LC 96-47452. (Illus.). 384p. 1997. reprint ed. pap. text 18.95 (*0-8018-5609-4*) Johns Hopkins.

Landscape of My Disability: Poems by Robert Mauro. Robert Mauro. 36p. 1997. pap. 6.00 (*1-891420-05-4*) Lemonade Factory.

Landscape of Nature in Medieval French Manuscript Illumination. Patricia M. Gathercole. LC 97-35970. (Illus.). 164p. 1997. text 79.95 (*0-7734-8539-2*) E Mellen.

Landscape of Qualitative Research: Theories & Issues. Norman K. Denzin & Yvonna S. Lincoln. LC 98-8869. 1998. pap. 28.95 (*0-7619-1433-1*) Sage.

Landscape of Recreation II: Amusement Parks. Francisco Asensio Cerver. (World of Environmental Designs Ser.). (Illus.). 256p. 1998. 80.00 (*84-8185-010-1*) Watsn-Guptill.

Landscape of Recreation I: Sports Facilities. Francisco Asenio Cerver. (World of Environmental Designs Ser.). (Illus.). 256p. 1998. text 80.00 (*84-8185-009-8*) Arco Edit.

Landscape of Roman Britain. Ken Dark & Petra Dark. (Illus.). 192p. 1996. 33.95 (*0-7509-0964-1*, Pub. by Sutton Pub Ltd) Intl Pubs Mktg.

Landscape of Roman Britain. Ken Dark & Petra Dark. (Illus.). 192p. 1998. pap. 19.95 (*0-7509-1874-8*, Pub. by Sutton Pub Ltd) Intl Pubs Mktg.

Landscape of Soria. Antonio Machado. Tr. by Dennis Maloney from SPA. 24p. 1985. pap. 4.00 (*0-934834-57-1*) White Pine.

Landscape of the Body. John Guare. 1978. pap. 5.25 (*0-8222-0632-3*) Dramatists Play.

Landscape of the Heart: Writings on Daughters & Journeys. Stephen J. Lyons. LC 95-26672. 144p. (C). 1996. pap. 12.95 (*0-87422-133-1*) Wash St U Pr.

Landscape of the Mind: Cultural Transformations of the American West. Richard C. Poulsen. LC 92-2950. (American University Studies: American Literature: Ser. XXIV, Vol. 23). 136p. (C). 1992. text 33.95 (*0-8204-1375-5*) P Lang Pubng.

Landscape of Wisdom: A Guided Tour of Western Philosophy. Christopher Biffle. LC 98-39193. 792p. 1998. pap. text 49.95 (*1-55934-724-4*, 724-4) Mayfield Pub.

Landscape Operations. 3rd ed. Hannebaum. LC 98-39966. 324p. 1998. 89.00 (*0-13-856915-0*) P-H.

Landscape over Zero. Bei Dao. Tr. by David Hinton from ENG. LC 96-20814. (CHI.). 112p. 1996. pap. 9.95 (*0-8112-1334-X*, NDP830, Pub. by New Directions) Norton.

Landscape Painter. Henry James. LC 70-142265. (Short Story Index Reprint Ser.). 1977. 18.95 (*0-8369-3749-X*) Ayer.

***Landscape Painting.** Patricia Monahan. 1999. 14.99 (*0-7858-1145-1*) Book Sales.

Landscape Palimpsest. Sophia McAlpine. 79p. 1997. pap. 19.95 (*0-7326-1165-2*, Pub. by Monash Asia Inst) Intl Spec Bk.

Landscape, Peoplescape & Self-Escape. Litt D. Myong-Won Cho. (C). 1989. pap. text 49.00 (*1-85821-032-1*, Pub. by Pentland Pr) St Mut.

Landscape Perspective. David W. Ehrenfeld. LC 94-46714. (Readings from Conservation Biology Ser.). 252p. 1995. pap. 24.95 (*0-86542-453-5*) Blackwell Sci.

Landscape Perspectives: Photographic Studies. LC 86-50078. (Illus.). 40p. 1986. 12.95 (*0-9601616-4-3*) U MO-St Louis.

***Landscape Perspectives of Land Use Changes.** Ed. by U. Mander & R. H. G. Jongman. (Advances in Ecological Sciences Ser.: Vol. 6). 240p. 2000. 126.00 (*1-85312-848-1*, Pub. by WIT Pr) Computational Mech MA.

Landscape Photography: Better Picture Guides. Michael Busselle. (Better Picture Guide Ser.). (Illus.). 128p. 1998. pap. 19.95 (*2-88046-370-X*, Rotovision) Watsn-Guptill.

Landscape Planning. William M. Marsh. LC 82-13889. (Earth Science Ser.). (Illus.). 225p. 1981. pap. text 16.00 (*0-201-04102-2*) Addison-Wesley.

Landscape Planning: Environmental Applications. 3rd ed. William M. Marsh. LC 97-44579. 448p. 1997. pap. 58.95 (*0-471-24207-1*) Wiley.

Landscape Planning: Landscape Architecture 721, No. 1012. Compiled by Charles Yuill. 1976. 7.00 (*0-686-20390-9*, Sage Prdcls Pr) Sage.

Landscape Planning & Ecological Networks. E. A. Cook & Hubert N. Van Lier. LC 95-117329. (Developments in Landscape Management & Urban Planning Ser.: Vol. 6F). 368p. 1994. 215.50 (*0-444-82084-1*) Elsevier.

Landscape Planning & Environmental Impact Design. 2nd ed. Tom Turner. (Natural & Built Environment Ser.: 11). 425p. 1998. 95.00 (*1-85728-321-X*) Taylor & Francis.

Landscape Plans. Ron Lutsko & Robin S. Menigoz. Ed. by Barbara Feller-Roth. (Illus.). 96p. Date not set. 14.95 (*0-89721-360-2*, Ortho Bks) Meredith Bks.

Landscape Plant Problems (Of the Pacific Northwest) A Pictorial Diagnostic Manual. Ralph S. Byther. (Illus.). 151p. 1998. pap. text 50.00 (*0-7881-7333-2*) DIANE Pub.

Landscape Plants: Their Identification, Culture & Use. Ferrell M. Bridwell. LC 93-28665. (C). 1994. mass mkt. 54.00 (*0-8273-6017-7*) Delmar.

***Landscape Plants for Dry Regions: More than 600 Species from Around the World.** Warren Jones & Charles Sacamano. (Illus.). 400p. 2000. 39.95 (*1-55561-190-7*) Fisher Bks.

Landscape Plants for Eastern North America: Exclusive of Florida & the Immediate Gulf Coast. 2nd ed. Harrison L. Flint. LC 96-34306. 864p. 1997. 125.00 (*0-471-59919-0*) Wiley.

Landscape Plants for Subtropical Climates. Bijan Dehgan. LC 98-24892. (Illus.). 640p. 1998. 49.95 (*0-8130-1627-4*); pap. 24.95 (*0-8130-1628-2*) U Press Fla.

Landscape Plants for Western Regions: An Illustrated Guide to Plants for Water Conservation. Bob Perry. (Illus.). 318p. 1994. 62.00 (*0-9605988-3-9*) Land Design.

Landscape Plants of the Southeast. 5th ed. R. Gordon Halfacre & Anne Shawcroft. LC 79-88976. (Illus.). 1989. 52.00 (*0-916822-14-1*) Sparks Pr.

Landscape Professional Practice. Hugh Clamp. 200p. 1988. text 63.95 (*0-291-39721-2*, Pub. by Gower) Ashgate Pub Co.

Landscape Professional Practice: A Guide to Legislation, Conduct, Appointment Practices & Contract Procedures. 2nd ed. Hutch Clamp. LC 98-38680. 200p. 1999. 96.95 (*0-566-08071-0*) Ashgate Pub Co.

Landscape Projects: Planning, Planting & Building for a More Beautiful Yard & Garden. Reader's Digest Editors. LC 97-27810. (Family Handyman Ser.). 191p. 1998. 19.95 (*0-7621-0047-8*, Pub. by RD Assn) Penguin Putnam.

Landscape Reclaimed. Text by Nancy Princenthal & Harry Philbrick. (Illus.). 72p. 1996. pap. 19.95 (*1-888332-03-4*, 620823) Aldrich Mus.

Landscape Rejuvenation: Remodeling the Home Landscape. Bonnie L. Appleton. Ed. by Sarah M. Clarkson. LC 87-42970. (Illus.). 144p. (Orig.). 1988. pap. 10.95 (*0-88266-496-4*, Garden Way Pub) Storey Bks.

Landscape Rejuvenation: Remodeling the Home Landscape. Bonnie L. Appleton. Ed. by Sarah M. Clarkson. LC 87-42970. (Illus.). (Orig.). 1988. 19.95 (*0-88266-495-6*, Garden Way Pub) Storey Bks.

Landscape Restoration Handbook. Donald Harker. 640p. 1993. lib. bdg. 89.95 (*0-87371-952-2*) CRC Pr.

Landscape Restoration Handbook. 2nd ed. U.S. Golf Association Staff & Donald Harker. LC 98-46072. 600p. 1998. 89.95 (*1-56670-175-9*) Lewis Pubs.

Landscape Sensitivity. D. G. Thomas & R. J. Allison. LC 92-26901. (British Geomorphological Research Group Symposia Ser.). 362p. 1993. 235.00 (*0-471-93636-7*) Wiley.

Landscape Technology: Theory & Application. 2nd rev. ed. Zev Naveh & A. S. Lieberman. (Illus.). 472p. 1994. reprint ed. 60.95 (*0-387-94059-6*) Spr-Verlag.

***Landscape Transformation & the Archaeology of Impact: Disruption & State Formation in Southern Africa.** Warren R. Perry. LC 99-37714. 182p. 1999. 62.00 (*0-306-45955-8*, Kluwer Plenum) Kluwer Academic.

***Landscape Transformed: The Industrial Ecology of an Ironmaking District.** Robert B. Gordon. LC 99-41825. 192p. 2000. write for info. (*0-19-512818-4*) OUP.

Landscape Turned Red: The Battle of Antietam. Stephen W. Sears. (Illus.). 464p. 1993. pap. 16.00 (*0-395-65668-0*, Pub. by Ticknor & Fields) HM.

Landscape Turned Sideways. Yvonne Trainer. 102p. 1988. 12.95 (*0-86492-087-3*, Pub. by Goose Ln Edits) Genl Dist Srvs.

***Landscape Wallcovering.** Joanne K. Warner. (Illus.). 112p. 2000. pap. 24.95 (*1-85759-239-5*, Pub. by Scala Books) Antique Collect.

Landscape with Canals: The Second Part of His Autobiography. L. T. C. Rolt. (Illus.). 192p. 1994. pap. 15.95 (*0-86299-141-2*, Pub. by Sutton Pub Ltd) Intl Pubs Mktg.

Landscape with Cracked Sheep. Mary Arrigan. 128p. 1997. pap. 8.95 (*0-947962-97-2*) Dufour.

Landscape with Dragons: The Battle for Your Child's Mind. Michael Obrien. LC 97-76843. 1998. pap. 12.95 (*0-89870-678-5*) Ignatius Pr.

Landscape with Figures: The Final Part of His Autobiography. L. T. C. Rolt. (Illus.). 256p. 1994. pap. 15.95 (*0-7509-0593-X*, Pub. by Sutton Pub Ltd) Intl Pubs Mktg.

Landscape with Machines: The First Part of His Autobiography. L. T. C. Rolt. (Illus.). 240p. 1994. pap. 15.95 (*0-86299-140-4*, Pub. by Sutton Pub Ltd) Intl Pubs Mktg.

Landscape with Rain. Ralph Gustafson. 1980. pap. 11.95 (*0-7710-3710-4*) McCland & Stewart.

Landscape with Ruins: Selected Poetry of Margherita Guidacci. Tr. by Ruth Feldman from ITA. LC 91-30227. 124p. 1992. 19.95 (*0-8143-2352-9*) Wayne St U Pr.

***Landscape with Smokestacks: The Case of Allegedly Plundered Degas.** Howard J. Trienens. 2000. 24.95 (*0-8101-1820-3*) Northwestern U Pr.

Landscape with Violence. large type ed. John Wainwright. 1981. 12.00 (*0-7089-0690-7*) Ulverscroft.

Landscape Within. Bert Isaac. 1993. 790.00 (*0-907664-26-1*, Pub. by Old Stiles) St Mut.

Landscape Within: An Inquiry on the Structure of Morality. J. Russell Hoverman. LC 93-40270. (International Healthcare Ethics Ser.: Vol. 1). (Illus.). 157p. (C). 1994. text 44.95 (*0-8204-2235-5*) P Lang Pubng.

Landscape Without Gravity: A Memoir of Grief. Barbara Lazear Ascher. LC 92-28088. 158p. 1993. 20.00 (*1-883285-10-0*) Delphinium.

Landscape Without Gravity: A Memoir of Grief. Barbara Lazear Ascher. 158p. 1999. reprint ed. pap. text 10.00 (*0-7881-6287-X*) DIANE Pub.

***Landscape Your Garden.** A. G. Simpson. 1998. pap. 18.95 (*0-86417-873-5*, Pub. by Kangaroo Pr) Seven Hills Bk.

***Landscaper.** Melissa Maupin. LC 99-53793. (Career Explorations Ser.). 48p. (YA). (gr. 5 up). 2000. lib. bdg. 21.26 (*0-7368-0490-0*, Capstone Bks) Capstone Pr.

Landscapes see Artists' Workshop Series

Landscapes. (Illus.). 1991. text 44.00 (*1-56290-071-4*, 6001) Crystal.

Landscapes. Barron's Educational Editors. LC 96-85273. (Art Handbooks). (Illus.). 96p. 1996. 9.95 (*0-8120-6616-2*) Barron.

Landscapes. Alwyn Crawshaw. (Learn to Paint Ser.). (Illus.). 1999. pap. 15.95 (*0-00-413342-0*, Pub. by HarpC) Trafalgar.

Landscapes. Claude Delafosse. Tr. by Pamela Nelson. LC 94-49714. (First Discovery Art Bks.).Tr. of Paysages. (ENG & FRE., Illus.). 28p. (J). (ps-2). 1996. 11.95 (*0-590-50216-6*, Cartwheel) Scholastic Inc.

***Landscapes.** Betsy Hosegood. 196p. 1999. pap. 29.95 (*2-88046-419-6*) Watsn-Guptill.

Landscapes. Penny King. LC 95-50840. (Artists' Workshop Ser.). 1996. 14.15 (*0-606-10247-7*, Pub. by Turtleback) Demco.

***Landscapes.** Sue Lacey. (Start with Art Ser.). (Illus.). (J). 2000. 22.90 (*0-7613-1167-X*, Copper Beech Bks); pap. 6.95 (*0-7613-0843-1*, Copper Beech Bks) Millbrook Pr.

***Landscapes.** Ray K. Metzker. (Illus.). 168p. 2000. 50.00 (*0-89381-911-5*) Aperture.

Landscapes. Clinton Palanca. 182p. 1998. pap. text 18.00 (*971-542-130-X*) UH Pr.

Landscapes. Parramon Editorial Team Staff. LC 97-17667. (We Imagine, We Draw Ser.). (Illus.). 48p. (J). (gr. 4). 1997. 12.95 (*0-7641-5041-3*) Barron.

Landscapes. Peggy Roalf. LC 92-52980. (Looking at Paintings Ser.). (Illus.). 48p. (J). (gr. 3-7). 1992. lib. bdg. 14.89 (*1-56282-302-7*, Pub. by Hyprn Child) Little.

***Landscapes.** Margaret Willes. (Illus.). 48p. 1999. pap. 9.95 (*0-7078-0345-4*, Pub. by Natl Trust) Trafalgar.

Landscapes. World Wide Publications Staff. 1998. pap. text 7.95 (*0-89066-303-3*) World Wide Pubns.

Landscapes, Vol. 5. Norma Poulos. 58p. 1991. pap. 9.95 (*1-57377-081-7*) Easl Pubns.

Landscapes, Vol. 6. Norma Poulos. 62p. 1991. pap. 9.95 (*1-57377-082-5*) Easl Pubns.

Landscapes, Vol. 7. Norma Poulos. 68p. 1992. pap. 9.95 (*1-57377-083-3*) Easl Pubns.

Landscapes, Vol. 8. Norma Poulos. (Illus.). 68p. 1992. pap. 9.95 (*1-57377-084-1*, 019884-1150) Easl Pubns.

***Landscapes: Developing Style in Creative Photography.** Terry Hope. LC 00-24876. (Black & White Photography Ser.). (Illus.). 2000. write for info. (*1-883403-68-5*, Silver Pixel Pr) Saunders Photo.

Landscapes: Humid, Icy, Temperate. Linda P. Williams. LC 93-34129. 64p. 1993. pap. 14.95 (*0-7734-0021-4*, Mellen Poetry Pr) E Mellen.

Landscapes: Selected Writings of J. B. Jackson. J. B. Jackson. Ed. by Ervin H. Zube. LC 78-103475. 168p. 1970. 22.50 (*0-87023-054-9*); pap. 15.95 (*0-87023-072-7*) U of Mass Pr.

***Landscapes: Ways of Imagining the World.** Winchester. 1998. pap. text. write for info. (*0-582-28878-9*) Longman.

Landscapes & Cityscapes for Artists & Craftspeople: From 19th-Century Sources. Ed. by Jim Harter. LC 99-10847. (Illus.). 144p. 1999. pap. text 12.95 (*0-486-40463-3*) Dover.

Landscapes & Communities on the Pacific Rim: From Asia to the Pacific Northwest. Karen K. Gaul & Jackie Hiltz. LC 99-50049. (Illus.). 254p. 2000. text 64.95 (*0-7656-0511-2*, East Gate Bk) M E Sharpe.

***Landscapes & Communities on the Pacific Rim: From Asia to the Pacific Northwest.** Karen K. Gaul & Jackie Hiltz. LC 99-50049. (Study of the Maureen & Mike Mansfield Center Ser.). (Illus.). 254p. 2000. pap. text 24.95 (*0-7656-0512-0*, East Gate Bk) M E Sharpe.

Landscapes & Gardens for Historic Buildings. 2nd ed. Rudy J. Favretti & Joy P. Favretti. LC 97-978. (American Association for State & Local History Book Ser.). 1991. pap. 24.95 (*0-7619-8930-7*) AltaMira Pr.

Landscapes & Illusions: Creating Scenic Imagery with Fabric. Joen Wolfrom. Ed. by Nadene M. Hartley. LC 90-62170. (Illus.). 96p. (Orig.). 1995. pap. 18.95 (*0-914881-32-9*, 10044) C & T Pub.

Landscapes & Language: English for American Academic Disourse. Kay L. Cutchin et al. 256p. (C). 1998. pap. text 19.95 (*0-521-65766-0*) Cambridge U Pr.

Landscapes & Language: English for American Academic Disourse: Instructor's Manual. Kay L. Cutchin et al. 256p. (C). 1998. pap., teacher ed. 6.00 (*0-521-65765-2*) Cambridge U Pr.

Landscapes & Other Pictures. Jeff Wall. 1997. 35.00 (*3-89322-855-1*, Pub. by Edition Cantz) Dist Art Pubs.

Landscapes & Seascapes. Robert Wood. (How to Draw & Paint Ser.). (Illus.). 32p. (Orig.). 1989. pap. 6.95 (*0-929261-33-X*, HT66) W Foster Pub.

Landscapes & Seasons. Jose Maria Parramon. (Workbooks for Painting Ser.). 32p. 1999. pap. text 6.95 (*0-7641-1212-0*) Barron.

Landscapes & Seasons of the Medieval World. Derek A. Pearsall & Elizabeth Salter. LC 73-85089. 316p. reprint ed. pap. 98.00 (*0-608-16809-2*, 202640600049) Bks Demand.

Landscapes Angus Macpherson. Angus Macpherson. 1993. pap. write for info. (*0-9637700-0-4*) AM DSG Pr.

***Landscapes at Risk? The Future of Areas of Outstanding Natural Beauty.** Edward Holdaway & Gerald Smart. LC 00-30862. (Illus.). 2000. write for info. (*0-419-24630-4*, E & FN Spon) Routledge.

Landscapes for an Information Society. Ed. by J. Berleur et al. 528p. 1991. 64.95 (*0-387-97453-9*) Spr-Verlag.

Landscapes for Learning: Creating Outdoor Environments for Children & Youth. Sharon Stine. LC 96-2021. 272p. 1996. 69.95 (*0-471-16222-1*) Wiley.

Landscapes for the Homeless. Anthony Hernandez. (Illus.). 1996. 35.00 (*3-89169-095-9*, Pub. by Sprengel Mus) Dist Art Pubs.

Landscapes from the Middle of the World. Frank Gohlke et al. Ed. by David Featherstone. LC 87-83591. (Illus.). 64p. (Orig.). 1988. pap. 15.95 (*0-933286-50-3*) Frnds Photography.

***Landscapes in Early Childhood Education: Cross-National Perspectives on Empowerment - A Guide for the New Millennium.** Ed. by Jacqueline Hayden. LC 99-52000. (Rethinking Childhood Ser.: Vol. 4). 467p. 2000. pap. text 32.95 (*0-8204-3735-2*) P Lang Pubng.

Landscapes in History: Design & Planning in the Western Tradition. Philip Pregill & Nancy Volkman. 784p. 1992. text 72.95 (*0-442-31804-9*, VNR) Wiley.

***Landscapes in History: Designing & Planning in the Eastern & Western Traditions.** 2nd ed. Philip Pregill & Nancy Volkman. LC 98-25814. 864p. 1999. 89.95 (*0-471-29328-8*) Wiley.

Landscapes in Kansas. limited ed. Robert Sudlow. (Illus.). 96p. 1987. 125.00 (*0-7006-0346-8*) U Pr of KS.

Landscapes in My Mind: The Origins & Structure of the Subjective Experience. Vincenzo R. Sanguineti. LC 99-36302 . 181p. 1999. 30.00 (*1-887841-25-3*, 62943, Psychosocial) Intl Univs Pr.

Landscapes in Pastel. Ken Goldman. LC 94-220564. (How to Draw & Paint Ser.). (Illus.). 32p. (Orig.). 1994. pap. 6.95 (*1-56010-141-5*, HT242) W Foster Pub.

Landscapes in Pencil. Gene Franks. (How to Draw & Paint Ser.). (Illus.). 32p. (Orig.). 1990. pap. 6.95 (*1-56010-054-0*, HT225) W Foster Pub.

L

Landscapes in Recent Painting. Springfield Museum of Fine Arts Staff. (Illus.). 30p. 1981. pap. 5.00 (*0-916746-05-4*) Springfield Lib & Mus.

*__Landscapes in Relief: Carving Techniques & Patterns.__ Lora S. Irish. (Illus.). 108p. 2000. pap. 19.95 (*1-56523-127-9*, Pub. by Fox Chapel Pub) IPG Chicago.

Landscapes in Time & Space: Photography & Photo-Montages by Leslie Starobin; Paintings by Burt Hasen. Ori Z. Soltes. 1997. pap. 5.00 (*1-881456-39-0*) B B K Natl Jew Mus.

Landscapes in Watercolor. Kathy Caudill. (How to Draw & Paint Ser.). (Illus.). 32p. (Orig.). 1995. pap. 6.95 (*1-56010-144-X*, HT245) W Foster Pub.

*__Landscapes in Watercolour.__ Ray Campbell Smith. (Step-by-Step Leisure Arts Ser.: Vol. 9). (Illus.). 2000. pap. 10.95 (*0-85532-849-5*) Srch Pr.

Landscapes, 1975-1979. Michael A. Smith. (Illus.). 20p. 1981. pap. 35.00 (*0-9605646-3-2*) Lodima.

Landscapes, 1975 to 1979, 2 vols. Michael A. Smith. (Illus.). 1981. 1250.00 (*0-9605646-0-8*); 1250.00 (*0-9605646-1-6*); 1250.00 (*0-9605646-2-4*) Lodima.

Landscapes of a New Land: Fiction by Latin American Women. Ed. by Marjorie Agosin. 1989. 19.00 (*0-934834-88-1*); pap. 12.00 (*0-934834-96-2*) White Pine.

*__Landscapes of Abuse: Transforming Feminine Spirit from Powerlessness to Purpose.__ Meta Commerse. (Illus.). 128p. 1999. pap. 19.00 (*0-8059-4827-9*) Dorrance.

Landscapes of Alienation: Ideological Subversion in Kafka, Celine, & Onetti. Jack Murray. LC 90-20976. 288p. 1991. 37.50 (*0-8047-1868-7*) Stanford U Pr.

Landscapes of Arizona: The Geological Story. Ed. by Terah L. Smiley et al. (Illus.). 532p. 1984. lib. bdg. 75.50 (*0-8191-4178-X*) U Pr of Amer.

*__Landscapes of Betrayal, Landscapes of Joy: Curtisville in the Lives of its Teenagers.__ Herb Childress. LC 99-87617. (C). 2000. text 49.50 (*0-7914-4577-1*) State U NY Pr.

*__Landscapes of Betrayal, Landscapes of Joy: Curtisville in the Lives of Its Teenagers.__ Herb Childress. LC 99-87617. 2000. pap. 16.95 (*0-7914-4578-X*) State U NY Pr.

*__Landscapes of Canada.__ Photos by Tim Fitzharris. (Illus.). 24p. 1998. pap. 9.95 (*1-55209-304-2*) Firefly Bks Ltd.

Landscapes of Craters of the Moon National Monument: An Evaluation of Environmental Changes. R. Gerald Wright & Stephen C. Bunting. (Northwest Naturalist Bks.). (Illus.). 336p. (C). 1994. pap. 24.95 (*0-89301-169-X*) U of Idaho Pr.

*__Landscapes of Defence.__ 2000. write for info. (*0-582-38234-3*) Pearson Educ.

*__Landscapes of Desire: Anglo Mythologies of Los Angeles__ William A. McClung. LC 99-23426. 316p. 2000. 35.00 (*0-520-21827-2*, Pub. by U CA Pr) Cal Prin Full Svc.

Landscapes of Development: An Anthology of Readings. Berk. LC 98-28398. (Education Ser.). 1998. pap. 38.95 (*0-534-54378-2*) Wadsworth Pub.

Landscapes of Dorset. Ed. by Roger Guttridge. (C). 1989. 45.00 (*1-85455-073-X*, Pub. by Ensign Pubns & Print) St Mut.

Landscapes of Emotion: Lexical Maps & Scenarios of Emotion Terms in Indonesia. Karl G. Heider. (Studies in Emotion & Social Interaction). 350p. (C). 1991. text 54.95 (*0-521-40151-8*) Cambridge U Pr.

Landscapes of Fear. Yi-Fu Tuan. LC 79-1890. 272p. 1981. reprint ed. pap. 14.95 (*0-8166-1021-5*) U of Minn Pr.

Landscapes of Fear: Perception of Nature & the City in the Middle Ages. Vito Fumagalli. Tr. by Shayne Mitchell from ITA. (Illus.). 220p. (C). 1994. text 61.95 (*0-7456-0754-3*) Blackwell Pubs.

*__Landscapes of Globalization: Globalized Development in Philippines.__ Philip F. Kelly. LC 99-36241. 2000. text. write for info. (*0-415-19159-9*) Routledge.

Landscapes of Jewish Experience. Illus. by Samuel Bak. LC 97-19468. (Tauber Institute for the Study of European Jewry Ser.: No. 25). 131p. 1997. 50.00 (*0-9635318-2-4*, Pub. by Pucker Gallery) U Pr of New Eng.

Landscapes of Learning. Maxine Greene. LC 78-6571. 255p. 1978. pap. text 18.95 (*0-8077-2534-X*) Tchrs Coll.

Landscapes of Legend. John Matthews. LC 98-117298. (Illus.). 160p. 1998. 29.95 (*0-7137-2650-4*, Pub. by Blandford Pr) Sterling.

Landscapes of Literacy: An Ethnographic Study of Functional Literacy in Marginal Philippine Communities. Maria L. Canieso Doronila. 206p. 1997. pap. 22.95 (*1-898942-16-1*, Pub. by Luzac Oriental) Weatherhill.

Landscapes of Longing. 224p. 1998. 35.00 (*0-02-862140-9*) Macmillan.

Landscapes of Loss: The National Past in Postwar French Cinema. Naomi Greene. LC 98-35156. 234p. 1999. pap. 18.95 (*0-691-00475-7*, Pub. by Princeton U Pr) Cal Prin Full Svc.

*__Landscapes of Loss: The National Past in Postwar French Cinema.__ Naomi Greene. LC 98-35156. 1999. 55.00 (*0-691-02959-8*, Pub. by Princeton U Pr) Cal Prin Full Svc.

Landscapes of Louis Remy Mignot: A Southern Painter Abroad. Katherine E. Manthorne. (Illus.). 256p. 1996. 55.00 (*1-56098-701-4*) Smithsonian.

Landscapes of Modern Sport. John Bale. LC 94-16005. 1994. 49.00 (*0-7185-1458-0*); pap. 24.00 (*0-7185-1464-5*) St Martin.

*__Landscapes of Neolithic Ireland.__ Gabriel Cooney. LC 99-23710. 272p. (C). 1999. text 85.00 (*0-415-16976-3*) Routledge.

*__Landscapes of Neolithic Ireland.__ Gabriel A Cooney. LC 99-23710. 272p. 1999. pap. 27.99 (*0-415-16977-1*) Routledge.

Landscapes of Power: From Detroit to Disney World. Sharon Zukin. 1993. pap. 16.95 (*0-520-08288-5*, Pub. by U CA Pr) Cal Prin Full Svc.

*__Landscapes of Power, Landscapes of Conflict: State Formation in the South Scandinavian Iron Age.__ Tina L. Thurston. LC 00-37105. (Fundamental Issues in Archaeology Ser.). 2000. pap. write for info. (*0-306-46320-2*, Kluwer Plenum) Kluwer Academic.

Landscapes of Promise: The Oregon Story, 1800-1940. William Robbins. LC 97-16531. (Weyerhaeuser Environmental Bks.). (Illus.). 416p. 1997. 40.00 (*0-295-97632-2*) U of Wash Pr.

*__Landscapes of Promise: The Oregon Story, 1800-1940.__ William G. Robbins. (Illus.). 416p. 1999. pap. text 19.95 (*0-295-97901-1*) U of Wash Pr.

Landscapes of Rembrandt. Boudewijn Bakker et al. (Illus.). 392p. 69.95 (*90-6868-204-0*, Pub. by U Thoth) Bks Nippan.

Landscapes of Resistance: The German Films of Daniele Huillet & Jean-Marie Straub. Barton Byg. LC 95-7214. (Illus.). 324p. 1995. 55.00 (*0-520-08908-1*, Pub. by U CA Pr); pap. 22.50 (*0-520-08910-3*, Pub. by U CA Pr) Cal Prin Full Svc.

*__Landscapes of Retrospection: The Magoon Collection of British Prints & Drawings, 1739-1760.__ Francesca Consagra et al. Ed. by Sheila Schwartz. (Illus.). 150p. 1999. pap. text. write for info. (*0-9644263-3-1*) F L Loeb Art Ctr.

Landscapes of S. Bohemia in the 19th Century. Collet's Holdings, Ltd. Staff. (CZE, ENG, FRE & GER., Illus.). 1987. 50.00 (*0-7855-1554-2*) St Mut.

Landscapes of Settlement: Prehistory to the Present. Brian K. Roberts. LC 95-22435. (Illus.). 200p. (C). 1996. pap. 27.99 (*0-415-11968-5*) Routledge.

Landscapes of Stone. J. B. Whittow. (Illus.). 144p. text 19.95 (*0-905483-50-2*, Pub. by Whittet Bks) Diamond Farm Bk.

Landscapes of Texas: Photographs from Texas Highways Magazine. Intro. by John Graves. LC 79-5274. (Louise Lindsey Merrick Texas Environment Ser.: No. 3). (Illus.). 162p. 1993. 24.95 (*0-89096-088-7*) Tex A&M Univ Pr.

Landscapes of the Heart. Cathy C. Chisholm. Ed. by Beth Basham. LC 98-33953. (Illus.). 116p. 1998. 13.95 (*1-57895-063-5*) Bridge Resources.

Landscapes of the Interior: Re-Explorations of Nature & the Human Spirit. Don Gayton. LC 96-225662. (Illus.). 176p. 1996. pap. 14.95 (*0-86571-344-8*) New Soc Pubs.

Landscapes of the Mind. Salman Tarik Kureshi. LC 97-930692. 1997. write for info. (*0-19-577810-3*) OUP.

Landscapes of the Mind: Worlds of Sense & Metaphor. J. Douglas Porteous. 228p. 1990. text 40.00 (*0-8020-5857-4*) U of Toronto Pr.

Landscapes of the Moscow Region. V. Gippenreiter. (ENG, FRE & GER.). 148p. 1983. 80.00 (*0-7855-7571-5*) St Mut.

Landscapes of the New West: Gender & Geography in Contemporary Women's Writing. Krista Comer. LC 98-47516. (Cultural Studies of the United States). 288p. 1999. pap. 18.95 (*0-8078-4813-1*); lib. bdg. 45.00 (*0-8078-2485-2*) U of NC Pr.

Landscapes of the Soul: A Spirituality of Place. Robert M. Hamma. 159p. 1999. pap. 9.95 (*0-87793-672-2*) Ave Maria.

Landscapes of the Spirit. Photos by William Neill. LC 96-48370. (Illus.). 120p. (gr. 8). 1998. 40.00 (*0-8212-2338-0*) Little.

Landscapes of the Spirit: The Cities of Eretz Yisrael in Jewish Thought. Naiman A. Zvi. 176p. 1996. 16.95 (*1-56871-092-5*, Pub. by Targum Pr) Feldheim.

Landscapes (of Time, Mind, Heart, Place, Space, Things, Beings & of Souls) Roberta Mendel. (Sketchbook Ser.). 54p. (Orig.). 1995. pap. 10.00 (*0-936424-18-4*, 013) Pin Prick.

*__Landscapes of War.__ Juan Goytisolo. Tr. by Peter Bush. 222p. 2000. pap. 15.95 (*0-87286-373-5*, Pub. by City Lights) Subterranean Co.

Landscapes of Western Australia John A. Scott & Richard Woldendorp. LC 87-129543. 56p. 1986. 39.95 (*0-86422-043-X*) Intl Spec Bk.

*__Landscapes of Wisdom: In Search of a Spirituality of Knowing.__ Jonas Vladas Barciauskas. LC 00-30286. 240p. 2000. pap. 29.50 (*0-7618-1732-8*) U Pr of Amer.

*__Landscapes of Wisdom: In Search of Spirituality.__ Jonas Barciauskas. 240p. 2000. 49.00 (*0-7618-1731-X*) U Pr of Amer.

*__Landscapes of Wonder: Discovering Buddhist Dhamma in the World Around Us.__ Bhikkhu Nyanasobhano. LC 98-17767. 208p. 1998. pap. 14.95 (*0-86171-142-4*) Wisdom MA.

*__Landscapes Painting Book.__ Jose M. Parramon. 1999. pap. text 26.00 (*84-95323-11-7*) LEMA.

*__Landscapes Techniques.__ Jose Maria Parramon. (Illus.). 96p. 2000. pap. 16.95 (*84-89730-88-1*) Lema Pubns.

Landscapes Text & Prints. (Illus.). 16p. 1992. pap. text 52.50 (*0-935493-69-7*) Modern Learn Pr.

Landscapes under the Luggage Rack: Great Paintings of Britain. Greg Norden. 1997. 50.00 (*0-9529602-0-6*, Pub. by Aidan Ellis Pub) Antique Collect.

Landscapes Wet-on-Wet. William Alexander. (Wet-on-Wet Ser.). (Illus.). 32p. 1995. pap. 6.95 (*1-56010-151-2*, HT252) W Foster Pub.

Landscapes with Acrylic & Oil. Donna Bell. 78p. 1993. pap. 10.50 (*1-56770-282-1*) S Scheewe Pubns.

Landscapes with Figures. Liam De Paor. 1998. pap. 30.00 (*1-85182-385-9*, Pub. by Four Cts Pr); boxed set 45.00 (*1-85182-384-0*, Pub. by Four Cts Pr) Intl Spec Bk.

Landscapes with Voices: Poems 1980-95. Yann Lovelock. 126p. pap. write for info. (*3-7052-0433-5*, Pub. by Poetry Salzburg) Intl Spec Bk.

Landscapes with Women: Four American Poets. Martha Bosworth et al. 136p. 1999. pap. 12.00 (*1-880286-37-8*) Singular Speech Pr.

Landscaping. (Home Repair & Improvement Ser.). (Illus.). 136p. 1983. lib. bdg. 20.60 (*0-8094-3515-2*) Time-Life.

Landscaping. (Home Repair & Improvement Ser.). (Illus.). 136p. 1983. 14.60 (*0-8094-3514-4*) Time-Life.

Landscaping. Time-Life Books Editors. LC 94-40921. (Home Repair & Improvement Ser.). (Illus.). 128p. (gr. 11). 1999. spiral bd. 14.95 (*0-7835-3879-0*) Time-Life.

Landscaping: A Five-Year Plan. Theodore James, Jr. LC 98-46036. (Illus.). 272p. 1999. reprint ed. pap. 18.95 (*1-58080-026-2*, Pub. by Burford Bks) Natl Bk Netwk.

Landscaping: Principle & Practices. 4th ed. Jack E. Ingels. 1991. text 42.50 (*0-8273-4683-2*) Delmar.

Landscaping: Principle & Practices. 4th ed. Jack E. Ingels. 1991. pap., teacher ed. 15.25 (*0-8273-4684-0*) Delmar.

Landscaping: Principles & Practice. 5th ed. Jack E. Ingels. LC 96-22507. (Agriculture Ser.). 448p. (C). 1997. mass mkt. 82.95 (*0-8273-6735-X*) Delmar.

Landscaping: Principles & Practices. 5th ed. Jack E. Ingels. (Agriculture Ser.). 1997. teacher ed. 13.95 (*0-8273-6736-8*) Delmar.

Landscaping Basics. Time-Life Books Editors. (Time Life How-To Gardening Ser.). 1997. pap. 14.95 (*0-614-27254-8*) Time-Life.

Landscaping Basics, Time, Life, How. Storey Publishing Staff. 1997. pap. 14.95 (*0-676-57223-5*) Random.

Landscaping Decks, Patios & Balconies. LC 93-86236. (Illus.). 96p. (Orig.). 1994. pap. 9.95 (*0-89721-266-5*, UPC 05938, Ortho Bks) Meredith Bks.

*__Landscaping for All Seasons.__ (Essential Gardening Made Easy Ser.: Vol. 5). (Illus.). 128p. 1999. write for info. (*1-892207-18-4*) Intl Masters Pub.

Landscaping for Birds. Irston R. Barnes & Gilbert Gude. Ed. by Shirley A. Briggs. (Illus.). 54p. 1973. 5.00 (*0-318-13602-3*) Audubon Naturalist.

Landscaping for Dummies: A Reference for the Rest of Us! Ed. by National Gardening Association Editors. LC SB473.G56 1999. (For Dummies Ser.). (Illus.). 384p. 1999. pap. 16.99 (*0-7645-5128-0*) IDG Bks.

Landscaping for Florida's Wildlife: Re-Creating Native Ecosystems in Your Yard. Joseph M. Schaefer & George W. Tanner. LC 96-29672. 96p. 1998. pap. 12.95 (*0-8130-1571-5*) U Press Fla.

Landscaping for Florida's Wildlife: Recreating Native Ecosystems in Your Own Backyard. Joseph M. Schaefer & George W. Tanner. LC 96-29672. 1997. pap. write for info. (*0-916287-21-1*) Univ Fla Food.

Landscaping for Privacy. Sunset Books Editors. LC 84-82289. 96p. 1985. pap. 12.95 (*0-376-03475-0*, 203475, Pub. by Sunset Books) Leisure AR.

Landscaping for Small Spaces. Sunset Books Editors. LC 91-66254. 96p. 1992. pap. 12.95 (*0-376-03706-7*, 203706, Pub. by Sunset Books) Leisure AR.

*__Landscaping for Small Spaces.__ Sunset Editors. 2001. pap. 12.95 (*0-376-03477-7*) Sunset Books.

Landscaping for Water Conservation: Xeriscape! City of Aurora. Ed. by Kimberley M. Knox. LC 89-60959. (Illus.). 94p. (Orig.). 1989. pap. write for info. (*0-9622900-1-7*) City Aurora.

Landscaping for Wildlife. (Illus.). 150p. 1994. pap. text 30.00 (*1-57979-215-4*) DIANE Pub.

Landscaping for Wildlife. Carrol Henderson. (Illus.). 149p. (C). 1995. pap. text 30.00 (*0-7881-2318-1*) DIANE Pub.

Landscaping for Wildlife. Carrol Henderson. 150p. 1994. spiral bd. write for info. (*0-9647451-5-1*) MN Bkstore.

Landscaping for Wildlife in the Pacific Northwest. Russell Link. LC 99-14300. (Illus.). 250p. 1999. pap. 29.95 (*0-295-97820-1*) U of Wash Pr.

Landscaping from the Ground Up. Sara J. Von Trapp. LC 97-6978. (Illus.). 160p. 1997. pap. 19.95 (*1-56158-185-2*, 070312) Taunton.

Landscaping Herbs. Barbara Collins & Floyd Giles. (Illus.). 234p. 1998. pap. text 27.80 (*0-87563-796-5*) Stipes.

Landscaping Illustrated. Sunset Books Editors. LC 83-82500. (Illus.). 176p. 1984. pap. 13.95 (*0-376-03459-9*, 203459, Pub. by Sunset Books) Leisure AR.

Landscaping in Florida: A Photo Idea Book. Mac Perry. LC 88-28875. (Illus.). 256p. 1993. pap. 21.95 (*1-56164-057-3*) Pineapple Pr.

Landscaping in New Jersey: An Environmental Approach to Landscaping in the Garden State. Michael Hawkins. LC 97-93300. (Illus.). 328p. (Orig.). 1997. pap. 16.95 (*0-9655972-0-2*) M Hawkins.

*__Landscaping Indoors: Bringing the Outside Inside.__ Ed. by Scott D. Appell. (Twenty-First Century Gardening Ser.: Vol. 165). (Illus.). 112p. 2000. pap. 9.95 (*1-889538-18-3*, Pub. by Bklyn Botanic) IPG Chicago.

Landscaping Makes Cents: A Homeowner's Guide to Adding Value & Beauty to Your Property. Frederick C. Campbell & Richard L. Dube. LC 96-30159. 176p. (Orig.). 1997. pap. 16.95 (*0-88266-948-6*) Storey Bks.

Landscaping New Homes. Phil Hardgrave. LC 92-18620. (Step-by-Step Visual Guide Ser.). (Illus.). 1993. 7.95 (*1-880281-08-2*) NK Lawn & Garden.

Landscaping New Homes. Philip Hardgrave. (NK Lawn & Garden Step-by-Step Visual Guides Ser.). (Illus.). 80p. (Orig.). 1993. pap. 6.95 (*0-380-76803-8*, Avon Bks) Morrow Avon.

Landscaping Projects. Time-Life Books Editors. (Time Life How-To Gardening Ser.). 1997. pap. 14.95 (*0-614-27252-1*) Time-Life.

Landscaping Projects, Time, Life, How. Storey Publishing Staff. 1997. pap. 14.95 (*0-676-57224-3*) Random.

*__Landscaping Revolution: Garden with Mother Nature, Not Against Her.__ Andy Wasowski & Sally Wasowski. LC 99-23152. (Illus.). 176p. 2000. 27.95 (*0-8092-2665-0*, 266500, Contemporary Bks) NTC Contemp Pub Co.

Landscaping That Saves Energy & Money. rev. ed. Ruth S. Foster. LC 93-40916. (Illus.). 240p. 1994. pap. 17.95 (*1-56440-358-0*) Globe Pequot.

Landscaping the American Dream: The Gardens & Film Sets of Florence Yoch, 1890-1972. James J. Yoch. LC 88-13895. (Illus.). 256p. 1989. 45.00 (*0-8109-1273-2*) Sagapr.

Landscaping the Hamptons. David Seeler. 120p. 1994. pap. 20.00 (*0-89831-037-7*) Sagapr.

Landscaping with Annuals. Reilly. (Country Wisdom Bulletins Ser.: Vol. A-108). 1988. pap. 2.95 (*0-88266-539-1*) Storey Bks.

Landscaping with Antique Roses. Liz Druitt & G. Michael Shoup. (Illus.). 240p. (C). 1992. 34.95 (*0-942391-64-0*) Taunton.

Landscaping with Bulbs. Reilly. (Country Wisdom Bulletins Ser.: Vol. A-99). 1988. pap. 2.95 (*0-88266-498-0*) Storey Bks.

Landscaping with Container Plants. Jim Wilson. (Illus.). 288p. 1994. pap. 28.00 (*0-395-70133-3*) HM.

*__Landscaping with Container Plants.__ Jim Wilson. 1999. 32.25 (*0-8446-7011-1*) Peter Smith.

Landscaping with Herbs. James Adams. LC 87-163339. (Illus.). 223p. 1987. 32.95 (*0-88192-073-8*) Timber.

Landscaping with Herbs. Storey Publishing Staff. 1997. pap. 21.95 (*0-676-57073-9*) Random.

Landscaping with Herbs. Jim Wilson. (Illus.). 256p. 1996. pap. 21.95 (*0-395-70941-5*) HM.

*__Landscaping with Herbs: Beautify Your Yard & Garden with Easy-Care Herbs.__ Nancy J. Ondra. LC 99-50813. (Essential Herbal Handbooks Ser.). (Illus.). 160p. 2000. pap. 14.95 (*0-87596-858-9*, Pub. by Rodale Pr Inc) St Martin.

Landscaping with Native Plants in the Middle-Atlantic Region. Elizabeth N. DuPont. Ed. by Wick Williams. LC 78-21194. (Illus.). 1978. 7.95 (*0-940540-02-9*) Brandywine Conserv.

Landscaping with Native Plants of Texas & the Southwest. George Miller, II. LC 90-44298. (Illus.). 128p. (Orig.). 1991. pap. 19.95 (*0-89658-138-1*) Voyageur Pr.

Landscaping with Nature. Eric Clough. Ed. by Mike Smith. (Illus.). 96p. (Orig.). 1998. pap. 9.95 (*0-89721-341-6*, Ortho Bks) Meredith Bks.

Landscaping with Nature: Using Nature's Designs to Plan Your Yard. Jeff Cox. LC 90-45938. 352p. 1991. 26.95 (*0-87857-911-7*, 01-357-0) Rodale Pr Inc.

Landscaping with Nature: Using Nature's Designs to Plan Your Yard. Jeff Cox. 1996. pap. 16.95 (*0-87596-742-6*) Rodale Pr Inc.

Landscaping with Perennials. Elizabeth Stell & C. Colston Burrell. (Rodale's Successful Organic Gardening Ser.). 1995. pap. 14.95 (*0-87596-664-0*); text 24.95 (*0-87596-663-2*) Rodale Pr Inc.

Landscaping with Stone. Sunset Editors. (Illus.). 2000. pap. 12.95 (*0-376-03476-9*) Sunset Books.

Landscaping with Wildflowers: An Environmental Approach to Gardening. Jim Wilson. (Illus.). 256p. 1993. pap. 21.95 (*0-395-66926-X*) HM.

*__Landscaping with Wood: The Practical Guide to Building Outdoors.__ Scott McBride. LC 98-44061. 1999. pap. text 19.95 (*1-56158-194-1*) Taunton.

Landscaping Your Garden Pond. Dennis Kelsey-Wood. (Illus.). 64p. 1998. 12.95 (*0-7938-0346-2*, WW105) TFH Pubns.

Landschaft in der Aeneis. Hans-Dieter Reeker. xii, 192p. 1971. write for info. (*0-318-71211-3*) G Olms Pubs.

Landschaftsdarstellung in der Deutschen Druckgraphik vor Albrecht Durer. Georg Erb. (Europaische Hochschulschriften, Reihe 28: Bd. 282). (GER., Illus.). 341p. 1997. 63.95 (*3-631-30568-0*) P Lang Pubng.

Landsend. Ledo Ivo. Tr. by Kerry S. Keys from POR. 64p. 1998. pap. 10.00 (*0-930502-37-X*) Pine Pr.

Landside Access to U. S. Ports. Landside Access to Ports Study Committee. LC 92-38897. (Special Reports: No. 238). 198p. 1993. 28.00 (*0-309-05407-9*) Transport Res Bd.

Landsknechts. Douglas Miller. (Men-at-Arms Ser.: No. 58). (Illus.). 48p. pap. 11.95 (*0-85045-258-9*, 9010, Pub. by Ospry) Stackpole.

Landslayer's Law. Tom Deitz. 304p. 1997. mass mkt. 5.99 (*0-380-78649-4*, Avon Bks) Morrow Avon.

*__Landslide: A Kid's Guide to the U S Elections 2000.__ Dan Gutman. 160p. (J). (gr. 4-6). 2000. per. 3.99 (*0-689-83591-4*) Aladdin.

Landslide & Subsidence Liability. John H. Sutter & Mervyn L. Hecht. LC 73-620016. 240p. 1973. 65.00 (*0-88124-033-8*, RE-31030) Cont Ed Bar-CA.

*__Landslide & Subsidence Liability: 9/99 Update.__ Michael E. London. Ed. by Donald R. Briggs. LC 73-620016. 282p. 1999. ring bd. 59.00 (*0-7626-0361-5*, RE-31037) Cont Ed Bar-CA.

Landslide Dams: Processes, Risk & Mitigation. Ed. by Robert L Schuster. (Sessions Proceedings, Geotechnical Special Publication Ser.: No. 3). 164p. 1986. 19.00 (*0-87262-524-9*) Am Soc Civil Eng.

Landslide Hazard in the United States: Case Studies in Planning & Policy Development. Robert B. Okshansky. LC 90-43660. (Environment: Problems & Solutions Ser.). 240p. 1990. text 15.00 (*0-8240-0472-8*) Garland.

Landslide Hazards & Their Mitigation in China. Ed. by Li Tianchi & Wang Shumin. 100p. 1996. 29.50 (*7-03-003078-8*, Pub. by Sci Pr) Lubrecht & Cramer.

Landslide Loss Reduction: A Guide for State & Local Government. Robert L. Wold & Candace L. Jochim. (Special Publications: No. 33). (Illus.). 50p. (Orig.). 1989. pap. 3.00 (*1-884216-46-3*) Colo Geol Survey.

Landslide Processes of the Eastern United States & Puerto Rico. Ed. by Arthur P. Schultz & Randall W. Jibson. LC 89-1948. (Geological Society of America Ser.: Vol. 236). (Illus.). 108p. 1989. reprint ed. pap. 33.50 (*0-608-07760-7*, 206784800010) Bks Demand.

An Asterisk (*) at the beginning of an entry indicates that the title is appearing for the first time.

Landslide Recognition: Identification, Movement & Causes. Ed. by Richard Dikau et al. LC 95-52108. (Geomorphology Texts Ser.). 274p. 1996. 150.00 (*0-471-96477-8*) Wiley.

Landslide Risk Assessment: Proceedings of the Workshop on Landslide Risk Assessment, Honolulu, Hawaii, U. S. A., 19-21.02. 1997. Ed. by David Cruden & Robin Fell. (Illus.). 384p. (C). 1997. text 104.00 (*90-5410-914-9*, Pub. by A A Balkema) Ashgate Pub Co.

Landslides. Ed. by Donald R. Coates. LC 79-123343. (Reviews in Engineering Geology Ser.: No. 3). (Illus.). 264p. 1977. reprint ed. pap. 81.90 (*0-608-00226-7*, 206072900006) Bks Demand.

Landslides: Analysis & Control. (Special Reports: No. 176). 234p. 1978. 18.00 (*0-309-28043-5*) Transport Res Bd.

Landslides: Causes, Consequences & Environment. Michael J. Crozier. 272p. 1986. 57.50 (*0-7099-0790-7*, Pub. by C Helm) Routldge.

Landslides: Extent & Economic Significance: Proceedings of the 28th International Geological Congress: Symposium on Landslides, Washington, DC, 17 July 1989. Ed. by E. E. Brabb & B. L. Harrod. 400p. (C). 1989. text 168.00 (*90-6191-876-6*, Pub. by A A Balkema) Ashgate Pub Co.

Landslides: Glissements de Terrain: Proceedings of the Fifth International Symposium, Lausanne, 10-15 July 1988, 3 vols. Ed. by Christophe Bonnard. 1800p. (C). 1988. text 505.00 (*90-6191-837-5*, Pub. by A A Balkema) Ashgate Pub Co.

Landslides: Investigation & Mitigation. Ed. by A. Keith Turner & Robert L. Schuster. LC 95-40780. (Special Report, Transportation Research Board, National Research Council Ser.: Vol. 247). 673p. 1996. pap. 45.00 (*0-309-06208-X*, 70391) Natl Acad Pr.

Landslides: Landslide Mitigation. Ed. by James E. Slosson et al. LC 92-34189. (Reviews in Engineering Geology Ser.). (Illus.). 128p. Date not set. reprint ed. pap. 39.70 (*0-608-20640-7*, 207207600003) Bks Demand.

Landslides: Proceedings of the 8th International Conference & Field Workshop, Granada, Spain, 27-28 September 1996. Ed. by J. Chacon et al. (Illus.). 408p. (C). 1996. 123.00 (*90-5410-832-0*, Pub. by A A Balkema) Ashgate Pub Co.

***Landslides: Proceedings of the 9th International Conference & Field Trip, Bristol, 16 September 1999.** Ed. by J. Griffith et al. (Illus.). 162p. 1999. text 85.00 (*90-5809-078-7*) A A Balkema.

Landslides 5th Edition, Vol. 1. 1988. 181.00 (*90-6191-838-3*) Ashgate Pub Co.

Landslides 5th Edition, Vol. 2. 1988. 181.00 (*90-6191-839-1*) Ashgate Pub Co.

Landslides 5th Edition, Vol. 3. 1990. 181.00 (*90-6191-840-5*) Ashgate Pub Co.

Landslides 6th Edition, Vol. 1. Bell. 1992. 158.00 (*90-5410-033-8*) Ashgate Pub Co.

Landslides 6th Edition, Vol. 2. Bell. 1992. 158.00 (*90-5410-034-6*) Ashgate Pub Co.

Landslides 6th Edition, Vol. 3. Bell. 1993. 78.00 (*90-5410-035-4*) Ashgate Pub Co.

Landslides 7th Intl, Vol. 1. K. Senneset. 590p. 1996. 162.00 (*90-5410-819-3*) Ashgate Pub Co.

Landslides 7th Intl, Vol. 2. K. Senneset. 800p. 1996. 162.00 (*90-5410-820-7*) Ashgate Pub Co.

Landslides 7th Intl, Vol. 3. K. Senneset. 500p. 1996. 162.00 (*90-5410-821-5*) Ashgate Pub Co.

Landslides - Glissements de Terrain: Proceedings of the Sixth International Symposium, Christchurch, 10-14.02.1991, 3 vols. Ed. by D. H. Bell. (Illus.). 1800p. (C). 1992. text 368.00 (*90-5410-032-X*, Pub. by A A Balkema) Ashgate Pub Co.

Landslides - Landslide Mitigation. Ed. by James E. Slosson et al. LC 92-34189. (Reviews in Engineering Geology Ser.: Vol. 9). 1993. 22.50 (*0-8137-4109-2*) Geol Soc.

***Landslides & Avalanches.** Terry Jennings. (Natural Disasters Ser.). (Illus.). 32p. (J). 1999. lib. bdg. 15.95 (*1-929298-44-7*, Pub. by Thameside Pr) Smart Apple.

Landslides & Their Stabilization. C. Veder & F. Hilbert. (Illus.). 247p. 1981. 178.95 (*0-387-81627-5*) Spr-Verlag.

***Landslides & Tsunamis.** Barbara H. Keating et al. LC 00-30371. (Illus.). 2000. write for info. (*0-8176-6300-2*) Birkhauser.

Landslides (Glissements de Terrain) Proceedings of the 7th International Symposium, Trondheim, Norway, 17-21 June 1996, 3 vols., Set. Ed. by K. Senneset. (Illus.). 2046p. (C). 1996. text 479.00 (*90-5410-818-5*, Pub. by A A Balkema) Ashgate Pub Co.

Landslides in Central California, No. T381. Ed. by Brown. (IGC Field Trip Guidebooks Ser.). 104p. 1989. 28.00 (*0-87590-640-0*) Am Geophysical.

Landslides in the Thick Loess Terrain of Northwest China. Ed. by Edward D. Derbyshire et al. LC 99-24962. 352p. 2000. 245.00 (*0-471-97349-1*) Wiley.

Landslides, Slumps & Creep. Peter Goodwin. (First Bks.). 1998. pap. 6.95 (*0-531-15897-7*) Watts.

Landslides, Slumps, & Creep. Peter Goodwin. LC 96-37288. (First Bk.). (J). 1997. lib. bdg. 22.00 (*0-531-20332-8*) Watts.

Landslides under Static & Dynamic Conditions: Analysis, Monitoring, & Mitigation: Proceeding of Sessions - Sponsored by the Geotechnical Engineering Division of the American Society of Civil Engineers in Conjunction with ASCE Convention in San Diego, California, October 23-27, 1995. Ed. by David K. Keefer & Carlton L. Ho. (Geotechnical Special Publications: Vol. 52). 128p. 1995. 22.00 (*0-7844-0118-7*) Am Soc Civil Eng.

Landsliding in Great Britain, 1995. HMSO Staff. (Department of the Environment Ser.). (Illus.). 381p. 1995. pap. 85.00 (*0-11-752556-1*, HM25561, Pub. by Statnry Office) Balogh.

Landstortzer: Gusmann von Al-Farche Oder Picaro Genannt. Aegidius Albertinus. (Barockromane Ser.). 753p. 1975. reprint ed. 150.00 (*3-487-05442-6*) G Olms Pubs.

Landstortzerin Lustina Dietzin Picara Genandt, 2 vols. in 1. Andrea Perez, pseud. (Barockromane Ser.). 1082p. 1975. reprint ed. write for info. (*3-487-05470-1*) G Olms Pubs.

Landuse & Development. Ed. by Phil O'Keefe & Ben Wisner. LC 78-308975. (African Environment: Special Reports: Vol. 5). 242p. reprint ed. pap. 75.10 (*0-8357-3023-9*, 205711000010) Bks Demand.

Landwirtschaft: Agriculture. V. N. Sinjagin. (GER & RUS.). 1982. 95.00 (*0-8288-1179-2*, M15328) Fr & Eur.

Landwirtschaft - Forstwirtschaft - Gartenbau: Englisch - Deutsch. Peter Muhle. 1991. 150.00 (*0-8288-2481-9*) Fr & Eur.

Landwirtschaft - Umwelt - Sozialismus: Das Agrarpolitische Instrument "Bewirtschaftungsvereinbarung" in den Neuen Landern der Bundesrepublik Deutschland. Martin Benninger. (GER., Illus.). 243p. 1996. 44.95 (*3-631-30983-X*) P Lang Pubng.

Landwirtschaft, Forstwirtschaft, Gartenbau see Agriculture-Forestry-Horticulture Dictionary: English-German

***Landwirtschaftliche Groabetriebe im Transformationsprozea: Eine Untersuchung Fur das Neue Bundesland Mecklenburg-Vorpommern.** Hermut Annuss. (Europaische Hochschulschriften Ser.: Bd. 2553). 252p. 1999. 45.95 (*3-631-35840-7*) P Lang Pubng.

Landwirtschaftliches Woerterbuch in Acht Sprachen: Agricultural Dictionary, 2 vols. (BUL, CZE, ENG, GER & HUN.). 1971. 350.00 (*0-8288-6464-0*, M-7532) Fr & Eur.

Lane: Layne - Lain - Lane Genealogy, Being a Compilation of Names & Historical Information of Male Descendants of 16 Branches of the Layne - Lain - Lane Family in the U. S. F. B. Layne. 336p. 1992. reprint ed. pap. 52.00 (*0-8328-2320-1*); reprint ed. lib. bdg. 62.00 (*0-8328-2319-8*) Higginson Bk Co.

Lane . . . And a Cast of Thousands: A History of the Lane Family of Canada & the U. S. from Their Arrival in 1819 to the Present. James K. Raywalt. (Illus.). 751p. 1992. reprint ed. pap. 89.50 (*0-8328-2407-0*); reprint ed. lib. bdg. 99.50 (*0-8328-2406-2*) Higginson Bk Co.

Lane County: An Illustrated History of the Emerald Empire. Dorothy Velasco. LC 85-16864. 168p. 1985. 22.95 (*0-89781-140-2*) Am Historical Pr.

Lane County History, 1885-1917. Ellen M. Stanley. (Illus.). write for info. (*0-9657838-2-0*) E M Stanley.

Lane Genealogy, 3 vols. in 1, Vols. I, II & III. J. Chapman & J. H. Fitts. (Illus.). 1034p. reprint ed. pap. 144.00 (*0-8328-0750-8*); reprint ed. lib. bdg. 152.00 (*0-8328-0749-4*) Higginson Bk Co.

Lane Medical Litigation Guide, 4 vols. Fred Lane & David A. Birnbaum. LC 81-10167. 1981. ring bd. 525.00 (*0-685-09243-7*) West Group.

Lane Rebels: Evangelicalism & Antislavery in Antebellum America. Lawrence T. Lesick. LC 80-24123. (Studies in Evangelicalism: No. 2). 287p. 1980. 29.00 (*0-8108-1372-6*) Scarecrow.

Lane Victory: The Last Victory Ship in War & in Peace. 2nd rev. ed. Walter W. Jaffee. LC 96-78385. Orig. Title: The Last Victory. (Illus.). xxii, 424p. 1997. 9.95 (*0-9637586-9-1*) Glencannon Pr.

Lane with No Name: Memoirs & Poems of a Malaysian-Chinese Girlhood. Hilary Tham. LC 96-12899. (Three Continents Ser.). 212p. 1997. pap. 16.95 (*0-89410-831-X*, Three Contnts) L Rienner.

Lane with No Name: Memoirs & Poems of a Malaysian-Chinese Girlhood. Hilary Tham. LC 96-12899. (Three Continents Ser.). 212p. 1997. 32.00 (*0-89410-830-1*, Three Contnts) L Rienner.

Lane's Arabic-English Lexicon: Madd al Qamus, 8 vols., Set. Edward W. Lane & Madd A. Qamus. (ARA & ENG.). 3064p. 400.00 (*0-86685-087-2*, LDL0872, Pub. by Librairie du Liban) Intl Bk Ctr.

Lane's Commentary on the Australian Constitution. P. H. Lane. 766p. 1986. suppl. ed. 195.00 (*0-455-20701-1*, Pub. by LawBk Co) Gaunt.

Lane's Commentary on the Australian Constitution. 2nd ed. P. H. Lane. 900p. 1999. 185.00 (*0-455-21440-9*, Pub. by LBC Info Servs) Gaunt.

***Lane's Description of Egypt: Notes & Views in Egypt & Nubia.** Edward W. Lane. (Illus.). 800p. 1999. 39.50 (*977-424-525-3*, Pub. by Am Univ Cairo Pr) Col U Pr.

Lane's English As a Second Language, 6 bks. Richard Lane. Incl. Lane's English Pronunciation Guide. 44p. 1995. pap. text, per. 9.25 (*0-935606-04-1*); Bk. 1. 76p. 1995. pap. text 9.25 (*0-935606-01-7*); Bk. 2. 98p. 1995. pap. text 9.25 Bk. 3. 128p. 1997. pap. text 9.25 Bk. 4. 112p. 1997. pap. text 9.25 Bk. 5. 95p. 1987. pap. text 9.95 Bk. 6. 105p. 1987. pap. text 9.25 (Illus.). 120p. 1987. Set pap. text 9.25 (*0-685-07057-3*) Lane Pr.

Lane's English Pronunciation Guide see Lane's English As a Second Language

Lane's Goldstein Trial Technique, 1969-1990, 3 vols. annuals 3rd ed. Irving Goldstein & Fred Lane. suppl. ed. write for info. (*0-318-65002-9*) West Group.

Lane's Goldstein Trial Technique, 1969-1990, 3 vols., Set. 3rd ed. Irving Goldstein & Fred Lane. LC 84-23915. 350.00 (*0-318-42407-X*) West Group.

***Lanes of Limerick.** 2000. pap. 6.95 (*0-634-01385-8*) H Leonard.

Laney's Lost Momma. Diane J. Hamm. Ed. by Judith Mathews. LC 90-26824. (Illus.). 32p. (J). (ps-1). 1991. lib. bdg. 14.95 (*0-8075-4340-3*) A Whitman.

Lanford Wilson. write for info. (*0-8386-3483-4*) Fairleigh Dickinson.

Lanford Wilson. Gene A. Barnett. LC 87-5657. (Twayne's United States Authors Ser.: No. 490). 184p. (C). 1987. 28.95 (*0-8057-7498-X*) Macmillan.

Lanford Wilson. Mark Busby. LC 87-70029. (Western Writers Ser.: No. 81). (Illus.). 52p. (Orig.). 1987. pap. 4.95 (*0-88430-080-3*) Boise St U W Writ Ser.

Lanford Wilson: Collected Plays 1987-1997, Vol. IV. Lanford Wilson. 320p. 1999. pap. 19.95 (*1-57525-163-9*) Smith & Kraus.

Lanford Wilson: The Talley Trilogy. Lanford Wilson. (Contemporary American Playwrights Ser.: Vol. 3). 272p. 35.00 (*1-57525-069-1*) Smith & Kraus.

Lanford Wilson: The Talley Trilogy. Lanford Wilson. (Contemporary American Playwrights Ser.: Vol. 3). 320p. 1998. pap. 19.95 (*1-57525-133-7*) Smith & Kraus.

Lanford Wilson: 21 Short Plays. Lanford Wilson. (Contemporary Playwrights Ser.). 320p. 1993. pap. 19.95 (*1-880399-31-8*) Smith & Kraus.

Lanford Wilson Vol. I: The Early Plays, 1965-1970. Lanford Wilson. (Contemporary American Playwrights Ser.). 320p. 1996. pap. 19.95 (*1-57525-025-X*) Smith & Kraus.

Lanford Wilson Vol. II: Collected Full Length Plays, 1970-1983. Lanford Wilson. 256p. 1998. pap. 19.95 (*1-57525-119-1*) Smith & Kraus.

***Lanford Wilson Vol. II: Collected Plays: 1970-1983.** Lanford Wilson. 256p. 1998. 35.00 (*1-57525-190-6*) Smith & Kraus.

Lanfranc, a Study of His Life, Work & Writing. Allan J. MacDonald. LC 80-2223. reprint ed. 37.50 (*0-404-18768-4*) AMS Pr.

Lanfranc of Bec. Margaret Gibson. 1978. 55.00 (*0-19-822462-1*) OUP.

Lanfrank's Science of Cirurgie. Lanfranco of Milan. Ed. by R. V. Fleischhacker. (EETS, OS Ser.: No. 102). 1969. 63.00 (*0-527-00103-1*) Periodicals Srv.

Lang English for New America. Carol Crown-Pineiro. 1999. 39.95 (*0-609-60469-4*) Liv Lang.

Lang Hua: Photographs by Lang Hua. Hua Lang. Ed. by Haibo Luo. Tr. by Gang Jin from CHI. (Contemporary Chinese Artists Ser.). (Illus.). 110p. 1996. pap. 19.95 (*0-9644818-7-1*) Waymont Intl.

LANG-PAK: An Interactive Language Design System. Lee E. Heindel & Jerry T. Roberto. LC 74-19544. (Elsevier Computer Science Library: Programming Language: Vol. 1). 196p. reprint ed. pap. 60.80 (*0-608-11629-7*, 202242100026) Bks Demand.

Lang Rongrien Rockshelter: A Pleistocene, Early Holocene Archaeological Site from Krabi, Southwestern Thailand. Douglas D. Anderson. LC 90-11175. (University Museum Monographs: No. 71). (Illus.). x, 86p. 1990. text 25.00 (*0-924171-02-2*) U Museum Pubns.

Langage. Louis Hjelmslev. (FRE.). 201p. 1991. pap. 10.95 (*0-7859-2253-9*, 2070326438) Fr & Eur.

Langage. Andre Martinet. (Methodique Ser.). 1544p. 46.95 (*0-686-56443-X*) Fr & Eur.

Langage. deluxe ed. Andre Martinet. (FRE.). 1544p. 1968. 135.00 (*0-7859-4624-1*) Fr & Eur.

Langage, Cet Inconnu. Julia Kristeva. 1981. pap. 18.95 (*0-7859-2683-6*) Fr & Eur.

Langage de Simonide: Etude sur la Tradition Poetique et Son Renouvellement. Orlando Poltera. (Sapheneia Ser.: Bd. 1). (FRE.). 686p. 1997. 70.95 (*3-906757-32-3*, Pub. by P Lang) P Lang Pubng.

Langage des Geographes Termes, Signes, Couleurs des Cartes Anciennes, 1500-1800. F. Dainville. (FRE.). 404p. 1964. pap. 75.00 (*0-8288-6777-1*, M-6100) Fr & Eur.

Langage en Contexte: Etudes Philosophiques et Linguistiques de Pragmatique. Herman Parret et al. (Linguisticae Investigationes Supplementa Ser.: Vol. 3). iv, 790p. 1980. 143.00 (*90-272-3112-5*, 3) J Benjamins Pubng Co.

Langage et Sciences Humaines: Propos Croises: Actes du Colloque "Langues et Langages" en Hommage a Antoine Culioli (Ecole Normale Superieure, Paris, 11 Decembre 1992) Ed. by Stephane Robert. (Sciences pour la Communication Ser.: Vol. 46). (FRE.). x, 166p. 1995. 28.95 (*3-906754-22-7*, Pub. by P Lang) P Lang Pubng.

Langage Integre Et L'Evalua... Whole Language Checklists. Jane Baskwewill.Tr. of Le Langage Integre et l'Evaluation de l'Enfant: Guide Pratique. (FRE.). mass mkt. 7.99 (*0-590-71981-5*) Scholastic Inc.

Langage, Langue, et Discours Economiques: Economic Language & Conversation. Janine Gallais-Hamonno. (FRE.). 308p. 1982. pap. 35.00 (*0-8288-1554-2*, M6260) Fr & Eur.

Langage Proverbial de Voltaire dans Sa Correspondance (1704-1769) Daniel Calvez. (American University Studies: Romance Languages & Literature: Ser. II, Vol. 103). VIII, 312p. (C). 1988. text 20.95 (*0-8204-0868-9*) P Lang Pubng.

Langage, Tangage Ou Ce Que les Mots Me Disent. Michel Leiris. (Gallimard Ser.). (FRE.). 188p. 1985. pap. 25.95 (*2-07-070442-4*) Schoenhof.

Langages de l'Interpritation Personnalisi (The Languages of Live Interpretation) L'Animation dans les Musies (Animation in Museums) Jean-Marc Blais. (Illus.). 199p. 1998. pap. 19.95 (*0-660-50757-9*, Pub. by CN Mus Civilization) U of Wash Pr.

Langan: Writing Series 1998. Langn. 1998. 0.10 (*0-07-427403-1*) McGraw.

Langan Writing Series 1999. Langn. 1999. 0.10 (*0-07-427404-X*) McGraw.

Langdon Gilkey: Theologian for a Culture in Decline. Brian J. Walsh. 323p. (C). 1991. pap. 29.50 (*0-8191-8355-5*); lib. bdg. 54.50 (*0-8191-8354-7*) U Pr of Amer.

Langdon Warner Through His Letters. Ed. by Theodore Bowie. LC 66-63378. 237p. reprint ed. pap. 73.50 (*0-608-11075-2*, 200573500059) Bks Demand.

Lange & Nietzsche. George J. Stack. LC 83-18891. (Monographien und Texte zur Nietzscge-Forschung Ser.: Band 10). viii, 341p. 1983. 126.95 (*3-11-008866-5*) De Gruyter.

Lang(e)land Family Reunion. unabridged ed. Richard B. Risk, Jr. LC 97-78164. (Illus.). 240p. 1997. pap. 30.00 (*0-9662396-0-1*) AMROB Pub.

L

Langenscheidt Croatian Universal Dictionary. (ENG & CRO.). 555p. 1988. vinyl bd. 6.95 (*0-88729-183-X*) Langenscheidt.

Langenscheidt Czech-German, German-Czech Pocket Dictionary: Langenscheidt Taschenwoerterbuch Tschechisch-Deutsch-Tschechisch. 3rd ed. Rolf Ulbrich. (CZE & GER.). 1055p. 1982. 59.95 (*0-8288-1080-X*, M 6838) Fr & Eur.

Langenscheidt Danish-English Lilliput Dictionary. (DAN & ENG.). 615p. 1957. vinyl bd. 3.25 (*0-88729-467-7*) Langenscheidt.

Langenscheidt Dictionary Building, Civil Engineering: German/English/German. Langenscheidt Staff. (ENG & GER.). 348p. 1997. 295.00 (*0-320-00440-6*) Fr & Eur.

Langenscheidt Dutch-English Lilliput Dictionary. (DUT & ENG.). 640p. 1956. vinyl bd. 3.25 (*0-88729-476-6*) Langenscheidt.

Langenscheidt English-Danish Lilliput Dictionary. (DAN & ENG.). 615p. 1959. vinyl bd. 3.25 (*0-88729-466-9*) Langenscheidt.

Langenscheidt English-Dutch Lilliput Dictionary. (DUT & ENG.). 637p. 1986. vinyl bd. 3.25 (*0-88729-477-4*) Langenscheidt.

Langenscheidt English-French Lilliput Dictionary. (ENG & FRE.). 640p. 1961. vinyl bd. 3.25 (*0-88729-408-1*) Langenscheidt.

Langenscheidt English-German Lilliput Dictionary. (ENG & GER.). 575p. 1977. vinyl bd. 3.25 (*0-88729-404-9*) Langenscheidt.

Langenscheidt English-Italian Lilliput Dictionary. (ENG & ITA.). 640p. 1964. vinyl bd. 3.25 (*0-88729-415-4*) Langenscheidt.

Langenscheidt English-Portuguese Lilliput Dictionary. (ENG & POR.). 640p. vinyl bd. 3.25 (*0-88729-463-4*) Langenscheidt.

Langenscheidt English-Russian Lilliput Dictionary. 1993. vinyl bd. 3.25 (*0-88729-452-9*) Langenscheidt.

Langenscheidt English-Spanish Lilliput Dictionary. (ENG & SPA.). 640p. 1961. vinyl bd. 3.25 (*0-88729-423-5*) Langenscheidt.

Langenscheidt English-Turkish Lilliput Dictionary. (ENG & TUR.). 670p. 1966. vinyl bd. 3.25 (*0-88729-532-0*) Langenscheidt.

Langenscheidt French-English Lilliput Dictionary. (ENG & FRE.). 640p. 1961. vinyl bd. 3.25 (*0-88729-407-3*) Langenscheidt.

Langenscheidt French-German Dictionary: Langenscheidt Handwoerterbuch Franzoesisch-Deutsch. 12th ed. Ernst E. Lange-Kowal. (FRE & GER.). 640p. 1982. 59.95 (*0-8288-0341-2*, M6155) Fr & Eur.

Langenscheidt French-German, German-French Pocket Dictionary: Langenscheidt Taschenwoerterbuch Franzoesisch-Deutsch-Franzoesisch. Ernst E. Lange-Kowal. (FRE & GER.). 1216p. 1982. 39.95 (*0-8288-0343-9*, M8010) Fr & Eur.

Langenscheidt French-German Pocket Dictionary: Langenscheidt Taschenwoerterbuch Franzoesisch-Deutsch. Ernst E. Lange-Kowal. (FRE & GER.). 575p. 1982. 24.95 (*0-8288-0344-7*, M8220) Fr & Eur.

Langenscheidt French Pocket Dictionary. Ed. by Langenscheidt Publishers Staff. (Pocket Dictionaries Ser.). 624p. 1983. pap. 11.95 (*0-88729-104-X*) Langenscheidt.

Langenscheidt French Standard Dictionary. enl. ed. (FRE.). 1278p. 1988. 18.95 (*0-88729-055-8*) Langenscheidt.

Langenscheidt French Standard Dictionary, Thumb-Indexed. 1278p. 1988. vinyl bd. 20.95 (*0-88729-056-6*) Langenscheidt.

Langenscheidt French Universal Dictionary. (FRE & ENG.). 464p. 1980. vinyl bd. 5.95 (*0-88729-162-7*) Langenscheidt.

Langenscheidt German & Ancient Greek Pocket Dictionary: Langenscheidt Taschenwoerterbuch Altgriechisch. Hermann Menge. (GER & GRE.). 1027p. 1986. 49.95 (*0-8288-0510-5*, F19902) Fr & Eur.

Langenscheidt German-Arabic Pocket Dictionary: Langenscheidt Taschenwoerterbuch Deutsch-Arabisch. 7th ed. Kamil Schukry. (ARA & GER.). 440p. 1982. 29.95 (*0-8288-0446-X*, F19922) Fr & Eur.

Langenscheidt German-English Lilliput Dictionary. (ENG & GER.). 576p. 1977. 3.25 (*0-88729-403-0*) Langenscheidt.

Langenscheidt German-French, French-German Dictionary: Langenscheidt Handwoerterbuch Franzoesisch-Deutsch-Franzoesisch. 14th ed. Ernst E. Lange-Kowal. (FRE & GER.). 1314p. 1983. 85.00 (*0-8288-0342-0*, M15629) Fr & Eur.

Langenscheidt German-French Pocket Dictionary: Langenscheidt Taschenwoerterbuch Deutsch-Franzoesisch. Eduard Weymuth. (FRE & GER.). 584p. 1982. 24.95 (*0-8288-1444-9*, M15750) Fr & Eur.

Langenscheidt German-Italian Dictionary: Langenscheidt Handwoerterbuch Deutsch-Italienisch. Herbert Frenzel. (GER & ITA.). 656p. 1982. 59.95 (*0-8288-0371-4*, F39630) Fr & Eur.

Langenscheidt German Pocket Dictionary. 768p. 1993. vinyl bd. 11.95 (*0-88729-105-8*) Langenscheidt.

Langenscheidt German-Polish Pocket Dictionary: Langenscheidt Taschenwoerterbuch Deutsch-Polnisch. 2nd ed. Stanislaw Walewski. (GER & POL.). 632p. 1981. 29.95 (*0-8288-0486-9*, F19810) Fr & Eur.

Langenscheidt German-Russian Pocket Dictionary: Langenscheidt Taschenwoerterbuch Deutsch-Russich. 10th ed. Karl Blattner et al. (GER & RUS.). 604p. 1981. 29.95 (*0-8288-1236-5*, F19670) Fr & Eur.

Langenscheidt German-Spanish Dictionary: Langenscheidt Handwoerterbuch Deutsch-Spanisch. Gisela Haberkamp de Anton. (GER & SPA.). 639p. 1985. 59.95 (*0-8288-0349-8*, F19590) Fr & Eur.

Langenscheidt German Standard Dictionary. 1408p. 1993. 18.95 (*0-88729-043-4*) Langenscheidt.

Langenscheidt German-Swedish Dictionary: Langenscheidt Handwoerterbuch Deutsch-Schwedisch. Britta Dancy et al. (GER & SWE.). 736p. 1985. 95.00 (*0-8288-0526-1*, M15821) Fr & Eur.

Langenscheidt German Universal Dictionary. Holger Freese. Ed. by Brigitte Wolters & Helga Kruger. 688p. 1993. vinyl bd. 5.95 (*0-88729-112-0*) Langenscheidt.

Langenscheidt German/Japanese/German Dictionary. 9th ed. W. Lemm. (GER & JPN.). 379p. 1995. 29.95 (*0-320-00540-2*) Fr & Eur.

Langenscheidt Greek (Classical) Pocket Dictionary. 428p. vinyl bd. 11.95 (*0-88729-081-7*) Langenscheidt.

Langenscheidt Greek (Modern) Standard Dictionary. 1990. 20.95 (*0-88729-062-0*) Langenscheidt.

Langenscheidt Greek (Modern) Standard Dictionary, Thumb-Indexed. 1990. 22.95 (*0-88729-063-9*) Langenscheidt.

Langenscheidt Grosswoerterbuch Altgriechisch-Deutsch: Ancient Greek & German. 24th ed. Hermann Menge & O. Guthling. (GER & GRE.). 762p. 1981. 135.00 (*0-8288-0509-1*, F 19904) Fr & Eur.

Langenscheidt Grosswoerterbuch Franzoesisch-Deutsch. 2nd ed. Karl Sachs & Cesaire Vilatte. (FRE & GER.). 1047p. 1980. 185.00 (*0-8288-0346-3*, M6594) Fr & Eur.

Langenscheidt Hand-Dictionary: German/Italian/German, 2 vols. in 1. (GER & ITA.). 2159p. 1997. 175.00 (*0-320-00490-2*) Fr & Eur.

Langenscheidt Handbook of Business English: Handbuch der Englischen Wirtschaftssprache. J. Rudolph. (ENG & GER.). 415p. 1986. 110.00 (*0-8288-0078-2*, M7374) Fr & Eur.

Langenscheidt Handwoerterbuch Schwedisch-Deutsch: Swedish & German. Britta Dancy et al. (GER & SWE.). 640p. 1980. 95.00 (*0-8288-0527-X*, F60990) Fr & Eur.

Langenscheidt Hebrew (Biblical) Pocket Dictionary. 400p. vinyl bd. 11.95 (*0-88729-082-5*) Langenscheidt.

Langenscheidt Hebrew-German Pocket Dictionary of the Old Testament: Langenscheidt Taschenwoerterbuecher: Hebraeisch-Deutsch zum Alten Testament. 20th ed. Karl Feyerabend. (GER & HEB.). 306p. 1981. 29.95 (*0-8288-2313-8*, M15217) Fr & Eur.

Langenscheidt Italian-English Lilliput Dictionary. (ENG & ITA.). 640p. 1964. vinyl bd. 3.25 (*0-88729-416-2*) Langenscheidt.

Langenscheidt Italian-German Dictionary: Langenscheidt Handwoerterbuch Italienisch-Deutsch. 2nd ed. Walter Frenzel. (GER & ITA.). 558p. 1985. 59.95 (*0-8288-0372-2*, F39640) Fr & Eur.

Langenscheidt Italian Standard Dictionary. 736p. 1990. 18.95 (*0-88729-059-0*) Langenscheidt.

Langenscheidt Italian Standard Dictionary, Thumb-Indexed. R. C. Melzi. 1990. 20.95 (*0-88729-060-4*) Langenscheidt.

Langenscheidt Italian Universal Dictionary. 416p. 1983. vinyl bd. 5.95 (*0-88729-163-5*) Langenscheidt.

Langenscheidt Large German-Italian Dictionary: Langenscheidt Grosswoerterbuch Deutsch-Italienisch. 2nd ed. Vladimiro Macchi. (GER & ITA.). 938p. 1984. 135.00 (*0-8288-0373-0*, F41300) Fr & Eur.

Langenscheidt Large German-Latin Dictionary: Langenscheidt Grosswoerterbuch Deutsch-Latein. 13th ed. Hermann Menge & O. Guthling. (GER & LAT.). 740p. 1982. 95.00 (*0-8288-1026-5*, F58000) Fr & Eur.

Langenscheidt Large Latin-German Dictionary: Langenscheidt Grosswoerterbuch Lateinisch-Deutsch. 21st ed. Hermann Menge & O. Guthling. (GER & LAT.). 813p. 1981. 95.00 (*0-8288-1027-3*, F57990) Fr & Eur.

Langenscheidt Latin-German Dictionary: Langenscheidt Handwoerterbuch Lateinisch-Deutsch. Erich Pertsch. (GER & LAT.). 703p. 1983. 59.95 (*0-8288-1029-X*, F58020) Fr & Eur.

Langenscheidt Latin Pocket Dictionary. (LAT & ENG.). 480p. 1966. vinyl bd. 11.95 (*0-88729-107-4*) Langenscheidt.

Langenscheidt Latin Universal Dictionary. Langenscheidt Staff. 454p. 1966. vinyl bd. 5.95 (*0-88729-173-2*) Langenscheidt.

Langenscheidt Lilliput Dictionary Little Webster. rev. ed. Ed. by Langenscheidt Editorial Staff. 640p. 1995. vinyl bd. 3.25 (*0-88729-521-5*) Langenscheidt.

Langenscheidt Modern Greek-German Pocket Dictionary: Langenscheidt Taschenwoerterbuch Neugriechisch-Deutsch. Heinz F. Wendt. (GER & GRE.). 556p. 1985. 29.95 (*0-8288-1651-4*, F19901) Fr & Eur.

Langenscheidt New Muret-Sanders Encyclopedic Dictionary. Muret-Sanders. Incl. Vol. 1, Pt. 1. Muret-Sanders Encyclopedic German Dictionary: A - M. (ENG & GER.). 883p. 1988. 145.00 (*0-88729-001-9*); Vol. 1, Pt. 2. Muret-Sanders Encyclopedic German Dictionary: A - K. (ENG & GER.). 973p. 1988. 145.00 (*0-88729-003-5*); Vol. 2, Pt. 1. Muret-Sanders Encyclopedic German Dictionary: N - Z. (ENG & GER.). 960p. 1988. 145.00 (*0-88729-002-7*); Vol. 2, Pt. 2. Muret-Sanders Encyclopedic German Dictionary. (ENG & GER.). 1048p. 1988. 145.00 (*0-88729-004-3*); write for info. (*0-318-57088-2*) Langenscheidt.

Langenscheidt Picture Dictionary. Langenscheidt Staff. (ENG & GRE.). (J). (gr. 4-7). 1989. 19.95 (*0-88729-862-1*) Langenscheidt.

Langenscheidt Picture Dictionary. Langenscheidt Staff. (ENG & JPN.). 280p. (J). (gr. 4-7). 1990. 24.95 (*0-88729-855-9*); pap. 14.95 (*0-88729-856-7*); pap. 24.95 (*0-88729-861-3*) Langenscheidt.

Langenscheidt Picture Dictionary. Langenscheidt Staff. (ENG & SPA.). 190p. (J). (gr. 4-7). 1990. 19.95 (*0-88729-854-0*); 19.95 (*0-88729-851-6*); 19.95 (*0-88729-850-8*) Langenscheidt.

Langenscheidt Picture Dictionary. Langenscheidt Staff. (ENG & ITA.). 190p. (J). (gr. 4-7). 1993. 19.95 (*0-88729-853-2*); 19.95 (*0-88729-863-X*); 19.95 (*0-88729-864-8*); 19.95 (*0-88729-865-6*); 19.95 (*0-88729-866-4*); 19.95 (*0-88729-867-2*); pap. 14.95 (*0-88729-859-1*) Langenscheidt.

Langenscheidt Picture Dictionary. Pierre Renyi & Langenscheidt Staff. (ENG & GER., Illus.). 190p. (J). (gr. 4-7). 1993. 19.95 (*0-88729-852-4*); pap. 14.95 (*0-88729-858-3*) Langenscheidt.

Langenscheidt Picture Dictionary, Lithuanian. (ENG & LIT.). 1992. 19.95 (*0-88729-871-0*) Langenscheidt.

Langenscheidt Picture Dictionary, Macedonian. (ENG & MAC.). 1990. 19.95 (*0-88729-869-9*) Langenscheidt.

Langenscheidt Picture Dictionary, Ukranian. (ENG & UKR.). 1992. 19.95 (*0-88729-872-9*) Langenscheidt.

Langenscheidt Picture Dictionary, West Armenian. (ARM & ENG.). 1991. 19.95 (*0-88729-873-7*) Langenscheidt.

Langenscheidt Pocket Arabic-German Dictionary: Langenscheidt Taschenwoerterbuch Arabisch-Deutsch. 6th ed. Georg Krotkoff. (ARA & GER.). 624p. 1982. 29.95 (*0-8288-0445-1*, F19951) Fr & Eur.

Langenscheidt Pocket Danish-German, German-Danish Dictionary: Langenscheidt Taschenwoerterbuch Daenisch-Deutsch-Daenisch. 11th ed. Henning Henningsen. (DAN & GER.). 973p. 1980. 59.95 (*0-8288-1683-2*, F35800) Fr & Eur.

Langenscheidt Pocket Dictionary: German/Italian/German. 31st ed. Frenzel & Macchi. (GER & ITA.). 1244p. 1997. 65.00 (*0-320-00487-2*) Fr & Eur.

Langenscheidt Pocket Dictionary Webster English. Langenscheidt Publishing Staff. 903p. 1997. pap. 10.95 (*0-88729-199-6*) Langenscheidt.

Langenscheidt Pocket German & Modern Greek Dictionary: Langenscheidt Taschenwoerterbuch Deutsch-Neugriechisch. 2nd ed. Heinz F. Wendt. (GER & GRE.). 552p. 1986. 29.95 (*0-8288-1650-6*, F19900) Fr & Eur.

Langenscheidt Pocket Latin Dictionary: Langenscheidt Taschenwoerterbuch Lateinisch. 35th ed. Hermann Menge. (GER & LAT.). 1036p. 1983. 45.00 (*0-8288-1028-1*, F58022) Fr & Eur.

Langenscheidt Pocket Spanish-German, German-Spanish Dictionary: Langenscheidt Taschenwoerterbuch Spanisch-Deutsch-Spanisch. 8th ed. T. Schoen & T. Noeli. (GER & SPA.). 1054p. 1986. 49.95 (*0-8288-0353-6*, S39866) Fr & Eur.

Langenscheidt Polish-German Pocket Dictionary: Langenscheidt Taschenwoerterbuch Polnisch-Deutsch. 4th ed. Stanislaw Walewski. 624p. 1982. 29.95 (*0-8288-0487-7*, F19820) Fr & Eur.

Langenscheidt Polish Pocket Dictionary. T. Grzebieniowski. (POL & ENG.). 800p. 1985. vinyl bd. 12.95 (*0-88729-109-0*) Langenscheidt.

Langenscheidt Portuguese-English Lilliput Dictionary. (ENG & POR.). 640p. vinyl bd. 3.25 (*0-88729-462-6*) Langenscheidt.

Langenscheidt Portuguese-German Pocket Dictionary: Langenscheidt Taschenwoerterbuch Portugiesisch. 2nd ed. Friedrich Irmen. (GER & POR.). 1238p. 1982. 59.95 (*0-8288-0498-2*, F19700) Fr & Eur.

Langenscheidt Portuguese Pocket Dictionary. Langenscheidt Staff. 812p. 1989. vinyl bd. 12.95 (*0-88729-110-4*) Langenscheidt.

Langenscheidt Portuguese Universal Dictionary. Langenscheidt Staff. 383p. 1983. vinyl bd. 5.95 (*0-88729-164-3*) Langenscheidt.

Langenscheidt Routledge German Dictionary of Analytical Chemistry: German-English English-German/Langenscheidt Routledge Worterbuch Chemische Analytik Englisch: Deutsch-Englisch Englisch-Deutsch. Joachim Knepper & Technische Universit at Dresden Staff. LC 97-35944. (GER & ENG.). 419p. (C). 1997. 60.00 (*0-415-17133-4*) Routledge.

Langenscheidt Russian-English Lilliput Dictionary. Langenscheidt Staff. 1993. pap. 3.25 (*0-88729-453-7*) Langenscheidt.

Langenscheidt Russian-German Pocket Dictionary: Langenscheidt Taschenwoerterbuch Russisch-Deutsch. 13th ed. Karl Blattner et al. (GER & RUS.). 568p. 1981. 29.95 (*0-8288-1237-3*, F19680) Fr & Eur.

Langenscheidt Russian Pocket Dictionary. 512p. 1969. vinyl bd. 11.95 (*0-88729-108-2*) Langenscheidt.

Langenscheidt Russian Universal Dictionary. 399p. 1993. vinyl bd. 5.95 (*0-88729-165-1*) Langenscheidt.

Langenscheidt Satzlexikon des Englischen Geschaeftsbriefes. H. Burfeindt-Moral & Zacher Burfeindt-Moral. (ENG & GER.). 400p. 1981. 45.00 (*0-8288-0088-X*, M6087) Fr & Eur.

Langenscheidt Satzlexikon des Franzoesischen Geschaeftsbriefes. H. Burfeindt-Moral & Rohrbacher. (FRE & GER.). 399p. 1981. 45.00 (*0-8288-1271-3*, M7165) Fr & Eur.

Langenscheidt Satzlexikon des Spanischen Geschaeftsbriefes. 5th ed. H. Burfeindt-Moral et al. (GER & SPA.). 395p. 1982. 45.00 (*0-8288-0822-8*, S29928) Fr & Eur.

Langenscheidt Spanish-English Lilliput Dictionary. (ENG & SPA.). 640p. 1961. vinyl bd. 3.25 (*0-88729-424-3*) Langenscheidt.

Langenscheidt Spanish-German, German-Spanish Pocket Dictionary: Langenscheidt Handwoerterbuch Spanisch-Deutsch-Spanisch. Heinz Muller. (GER & SPA.). 1400p. 1987. 110.00 (*0-8288-0352-8*, S39871) Fr & Eur.

Langenscheidt Spanish-German Pocket Dictionary: Langenscheidt Handwoerterbuch Spanisch-Deutsch. Heinz Muller & Guenther Haensch. (GER & SPA.). 656p. 1987. 69.95 (*0-8288-0351-X*, F19592) Fr & Eur.

Langenscheidt Spanish Pocket Dictionary. 656p. 1987. vinyl bd. 11.95 (*0-88729-103-1*) Langenscheidt.

Langenscheidt Spanish Standard Dictionary. 1104p. 1988. 18.95 (*0-88729-052-3*) Langenscheidt.

Langenscheidt Spanish Standard Dictionary, Thumb-Indexed. rev. ed. 1104p. 1988. 20.95 (*0-88729-053-1*) Langenscheidt.

Langenscheidt Spanish Universal Dictionary. (SPA & ENG.). 528p. 1992. vinyl bd. 5.95 (*0-88729-166-X*) Langenscheidt.

Langenscheidt Swedish-German, German-Swedish Pocket Dictionary: Langenscheidt Taschenwoerterbuch Schwedisch-Deutsch-Schwedisch. 3rd ed. Hansgeorg Kornitzky. (GER & SWE.). 1006p. 1987. 59.95 (*0-8288-1067-2*, F19640) Fr & Eur.

Langenscheidt Taschenwoerterbuch Tuerkisch: Turkish-German Pocket Dictionary. 16th ed. Karl Steuerwald. (GER & TUR.). 1176p. 1982. 59.95 (*0-8288-0507-5*, F65530) Fr & Eur.

Langenscheidt Turkish-English Lilliput Dictionary. (ENG & TUR.). 608p. 1966. vinyl bd. 3.25 (*0-88729-533-9*) Langenscheidt.

Langenscheidt Turkish Pocket Dictionary. 768p. 1993. vinyl bd. 12.95 (*0-88729-090-6*) Langenscheidt.

Langenscheidt Turkish Standard Dictionary. 1046p. 1986. 20.95 (*0-88729-047-7*) Langenscheidt.

Langenscheidt Turkish Standard Dictionary, Thumb-Indexed. Langenscheidt Staff. (TUR.). 1046p. 1986. 22.95 (*0-88729-048-5*) Langenscheidt.

Langenscheidt Turkish Universal Dictionary. 447p. 1979. vinyl bd. 5.95 (*0-88729-167-8*) Langenscheidt.

Langenscheidt Universal Dictionary Spanish. Langenscheidt Staff. (SPA.). 380p. 1994. vinyl bd. 5.95 (*0-88729-064-7*) Langenscheidt.

Langenscheidt Universal German Dictionary: German-English - English-German. (ENG & GER.). 560p. (C). 1976. pap. 5.95 (*0-8442-2745-5*, X2745-5) NTC Contemp Pub Co.

Langenscheidt Universal German-Serbocroatian, Serbocroatian-German Dictionary: Langenscheidt Serbokroatisch-Deutsch-Serbokroatisch Universal Woerterbuch. 7th ed. Reinhard Lauer. (GER & SER.). 448p. 1981. 14.95 (*0-8288-1051-6*, F19620) Fr & Eur.

Langenscheidt Universal Hungarian-German, German-Hungarian Dictionary: Langenscheidt Universal Woerterbuch Ungarisch-Deutsch-Ungarisch. 6th ed. Gyorgy Darai. (GER & HUN.). 447p. 1981. 14.95 (*0-8288-1661-1*, M14527) Fr & Eur.

Langenscheidt Universal Russian-English/English-Russian Dictionary. (ENG & RUS.). 5.95 (*0-8442-4723-5*, X4723-5) NTC Contemp Pub Co.

Langenscheidt Universal Spanish-German, German-Spanish Dictionary: Langenscheidt Universal Woerterbuch Spanisch-Deutsch-Spanisch. Langenscheidt Staff. (GER & SPA.). 480p. 1983. 14.95 (*0-8288-0350-1*, S39870) Fr & Eur.

Langenscheidt Universal Turkish-German, German-Turkish Dictionary: Langenscheidt Universal Woerterbuch Tuerkisch-Deutsch-Tuerkisch. 7th ed. Hans-Jurgen Kornrumpf. (GER & TUR.). 431p. 1981. 12.95 (*0-8288-1644-1*, M9931) Fr & Eur.

Langenscheidt Webster Universal Dictionary. 416p. 1993. vinyl bd. 5.95 (*0-88729-190-2*) Langenscheidt.

Langenscheidt's Encyclopedic Dictionary of English & German Vol. 1: English-German A-M. Eduard Muret & Daniel Sanders. (ENG & GER.). 883p. 1992. 195.00 (*0-7859-8385-6*, 3468011202) Fr & Eur.

Langenscheidt's Encyclopedic Dictionary of English & German Vol. 2: English-German N-Z. Eduard Muret & Daniel Sanders. (ENG & GER.). 956p. 1992. 195.00 (*0-7859-8386-4*, 3468011229) Fr & Eur.

Langenscheidt's Encyclopedic Dictionary of English & German Vol. 3: German-English A-K. Eduard Muret & Daniel Sanders. (ENG & GER.). 973p. 1992. 195.00 (*0-7859-8387-2*, 3468011245) Fr & Eur.

Langenscheidt's Encyclopedic Dictionary of English & German Vol. 4: German-English L-Z. Eduard Muret & Daniel Sanders. (ENG & GER.). 1046p. 1992. 195.00 (*0-7859-8388-0*, 3468011261) Fr & Eur.

Langenscheidts Euroworterbucher: Danisch. E. Bodenstein. (DAN.). 1997. pap. write for info. (*3-468-12100-8*) Langenscheidt.

Langenscheidts Euroworterbucher: Englisch. H. Willmann & W. Worsch. 1997. pap. write for info. (*3-468-12120-2*) Langenscheidt.

Langenscheidts Euroworterbucher: Franzosisch. W. Loffler & K. Waeterloos. 1997. pap. write for info. (*3-468-12150-4*) Langenscheidt.

Langenscheidts Euroworterbucher: Griechisch. K. Chrisomalli-Henrich & G. S. Henrich. 1997. pap. write for info. (*3-468-12210-1*) Langenscheidt.

Langenscheidts Euroworterbucher: Italienisch. Langenscheidt-Redaktion. (ITA.). 1997. pap. write for info. (*3-468-12180-6*) Langenscheidt.

Langenscheidts Euroworterbucher: Niederlandisch. F. Beersmans. 1997. pap. write for info. (*3-468-12230-6*) Langenscheidt.

Langenscheidts Euroworterbucher: Polnisch. St. Walewski. (POL.). 1997. pap. write for info. (*3-468-12260-8*) Langenscheidt.

Langenscheidts Euroworterbucher: Portugiesisch. Langenscheidt-Redaktion. (POR.). 1997. pap. write for info. (*3-468-12270-5*) Langenscheidt.

Langenscheidts Euroworterbucher: Spanisch. Langenscheidt-Redaktion. (SPA.). 1997. pap. write for info. (*3-468-12340-X*) Langenscheidt.

Langenscheidts Fachwoerterbuch Fernmeldewesen. (GER & SPA.). 769p. 65.00 (*0-686-56628-9*, M-7537) Fr & Eur.

Langenscheidts Grobworterbucher: Deutsch-Englisch. H. Messinger & Langenscheidt-Redaktion. 1296p. 1997. pap. write for info. (*3-468-02125-9*) Langenscheidt.

Langenscheidts Grobworterbucher: Deutsch-Franzosisch. 1997. pap. write for info. (*3-468-02156-9*) Langenscheidt.

Langenscheidts Grobworterbucher: Deutsch-Italienisch. 1997. pap. write for info. (*3-468-02186-0*) Langenscheidt.

Langenscheidts Grobworterbucher: Grobworterbuch Englisch (Der Kleine Muret- Sanders) H. Willmann et al. 1200p. 1997. pap. write for info. (*3-468-02121-6*) Langenscheidt.

Langenscheidts Grobworterbucher: Grobworterbuch Franzosisch (Sachs-Villatte) 1997. pap. write for info. (*3-468-02151-8*) Langenscheidt.

Langenscheidts Grobworterbucher: Grobworterbuch Italienisch (Sansoni/Macchi) 1997. pap. write for info. (*3-468-02181-X*) Langenscheidt.

Langenscheidts Handworterbucher: Arabisch. L. Kropfitsch. (ARA.). 600p. 1997. pap. write for info. (*3-468-04060-1*) Langenscheidt.

Langenscheidts Handworterbucher: Chinesisch. (CHI.). 1997. pap. write for info. (*3-468-05090-9*) Langenscheidt.

Langenscheidts Handworterbucher: Deutsch-Englisch. S. Brough. 736p. 1997. pap. write for info. (*3-468-04128-4*) Langenscheidt.

Langenscheidts Handworterbucher: Deutsch-Franzosisch. 820p. 1997. pap. write for info. (*3-468-04158-6*) Langenscheidt.

Langenscheidts Handworterbucher: Deutsch-Hebraisch. J. Lavy. 1997. pap. write for info. (*3-468-04165-9*) Langenscheidt.

Langenscheidts Handworterbucher: Deutsch-Italienisch. W. Frenzel et al. 1997. pap. write for info. (*3-468-04186-1*) Langenscheidt.

Langenscheidts Handworterbucher: Deutsch-Spanisch. G. Haberkamp De Anton. (SPA.). 640p. 1997. pap. write for info. (*3-468-04346-5*) Langenscheidt.

Langenscheidts Handworterbucher: Englisch. H. Messinger. (DUT & ENG.). 760p. 1997. pap. write for info. (*3-468-04123-3*) Langenscheidt.

Langenscheidts Handworterbucher: Franzosisch. 1997. pap. write for info. (*3-468-04152-7*) Langenscheidt.

Langenscheidts Handworterbucher: Hebraisch. J. Lavy. 639p. 1997. pap. write for info. (*3-468-04160-8*) Langenscheidt.

Langenscheidts Handworterbucher: Italienisch. W. Frenzel. 560p. 1997. pap. write for info. (*3-468-04181-0*) Langenscheidt.

Langenscheidts Handworterbucher: Katalanisch. L. C. Battle. Ed. by G. Haensch. 1997. pap. write for info. (*3-468-04350-3*) Langenscheidt.

Langenscheidts Handworterbucher: Komplettband. 1997. pap. write for info. (*3-468-05125-5*); pap. write for info. (*3-468-05154-9*); pap. write for info. (*3-468-05182-4*); pap. write for info. (*3-468-05342-8*) Langenscheidt.

Langenscheidts Handworterbucher: Spanisch. G. Haensch. (SPA.). 660p. 1997. pap. write for info. (*3-468-04341-4*) Langenscheidt.

***Langenscheidt's Pocket Dictionary: English-Polish - Polish-English.** Tadeusz Grzebieniowski. (ENG & POL.). 816p. 1999. pap. 13.95 (*0-88729-017-5*) Langenscheidt.

Langenscheidts T1 Standard Plus 3.0 Mit Langenscheidts Handworterbuch Englisch. (GER.). 1997. pap. write for info. (*3-468-90812-1*) Langenscheidt.

Langenscheidts T1 Standard 3.0 Mit Langenscheidts Taschenworterbuch Englisch. (GER.). 1997. pap. write for info. (*3-468-90811-3*) Langenscheidt.

Langenscheidts Taschenworterbucher: Arabisch. (GER.). 1997. pap. write for info. (*3-468-11061-8*) Langenscheidt.

Langenscheidts Taschenworterbucher: Danisch Neubearbeitung. (GER.). 1997. pap. write for info. (*3-468-11102-9*) Langenscheidt.

Langenscheidts Taschenworterbucher: Englisch. (GER.). 1997. pap. write for info. (*3-468-10122-8*); pap. write for info. (*3-468-10128-7*); pap. write for info. (*3-468-11124-X*) Langenscheidt.

Langenscheidts Taschenworterbucher: Franzosisch. (GER.). 1997. pap. write for info. (*3-468-10151-1*); pap. write for info. (*3-468-10156-2*); pap. write for info. (*3-468-11151-7*) Langenscheidt.

Langenscheidts Taschenworterbucher: Hebraisch. (GER.). 1997. pap. write for info. (*3-468-11160-6*) Langenscheidt.

Langenscheidts Taschenworterbucher: Italienisch. (GER.). 1997. pap. write for info. (*3-468-11181-9*) Langenscheidt.

Langenscheidts Taschenworterbucher: Kroatisch. (GER.). 1997. pap. write for info. (*3-468-10310-7*) Langenscheidt.

Langenscheidts Taschenworterbucher: Neugriechisch. (GER.). 1997. pap. write for info. (*3-468-11212-2*) Langenscheidt.

Langenscheidts Taschenworterbucher: Niederlandisch. (GER.). 1997. pap. write for info. (*3-468-11232-7*) Langenscheidt.

Langenscheidts Taschenworterbucher: Polnisch. (GER.). 1997. pap. write for info. (*3-468-11260-2*) Langenscheidt.

An Asterisk (*) at the beginning of an entry indicates that the title is appearing for the first time.

Langenscheidts Taschenworterbucher: Portugiesisch. (GER.). 1997. pap. write for info. (3-468-11272-6) Langenscheidt.

Langenscheidts Taschenworterbucher: Russisch. (GER.). 1997. pap. write for info. (3-468-10291-7); pap. write for info. (3-468-10296-8); pap. write for info. (3-468-11291-2) Langenscheidt.

Langenscheidts Taschenworterbucher: Schwedisch. (GER.). 1997. pap. write for info. (3-468-11302-1) Langenscheidt.

Langenscheidts Taschenworterbucher: Spanisch. (GER.). 1997. pap. write for info. (3-468-11342-0) Langenscheidt.

Langenscheidts Taschenworterbucher: Tschechisch. (GER.). 1997. pap. write for info. (3-468-11361-7) Langenscheidt.

Langenscheidts Taschenworterbucher: Turkisch. (GER.). 1997. pap. write for info. (3-468-11372-2) Langenscheidt.

Langenscheidts Universal - Worterbucher: Kroatisch. (KRO.). 1997. pap. write for info. (3-468-18311-9) Langenscheidt.

Langenscheidts Universal - Worterbucher: Latein. (LAT.). 1997. pap. write for info. (3-468-18200-7) Langenscheidt.

Langenscheidts Universal-Worterbucher: Arabisch. (ARA.). 1997. pap. write for info. (3-468-18060-8) Langenscheidt.

Langenscheidts Universal-Worterbucher: Bulgarisch. (BUL.). 1997. pap. write for info. (3-468-18081-0) Langenscheidt.

Langenscheidts Universal-Worterbucher: Danisch. (DAN.). 1997. pap. write for info. (3-468-18102-7) Langenscheidt.

Langenscheidts Universal-Worterbucher: Englisch. 1997. pap. write for info. (3-468-18122-1) Langenscheidt.

Langenscheidts Universal-Worterbucher: Finnisch. (FIN.). 1997. pap. write for info. (3-468-18141-8) Langenscheidt.

Langenscheidts Universal-Worterbucher: Franzosisch. (FRE.). 1997. pap. write for info. (3-468-18151-5) Langenscheidt.

Langenscheidts Universal-Worterbucher: Griechisch. (GRE.). 1997. pap. write for info. (3-468-18211-2) Langenscheidt.

Langenscheidts Universal-Worterbucher: Indonesisch. (IND.). 1997. pap. write for info. (3-468-18160-4) Langenscheidt.

Langenscheidts Universal-Worterbucher: Islandisch. 1997. pap. write for info. (3-468-18171-X) Langenscheidt.

Langenscheidts Universal-Worterbucher: Italienisch. (ITA.). 1997. pap. write for info. (3-468-18182-5) Langenscheidt.

Langenscheidts Universal-Worterbucher: Japanisch. (JPN.). 1997. pap. write for info. (3-468-18190-6) Langenscheidt.

Langenscheidts Universal-Worterbucher: Niederlandisch. 1997. pap. write for info. (3-468-18232-5) Langenscheidt.

Langenscheidts Universal-Worterbucher: Norwegisch. (NOR.). 1997. pap. write for info. (3-468-18241-4) Langenscheidt.

Langenscheidts Universal-Worterbucher: Polnisch. (POL.). 1997. pap. write for info. (3-468-18261-9) Langenscheidt.

Langenscheidts Universal-Worterbucher: Portugiesisch. (POR.). 1997. pap. write for info. (3-468-18272-4) Langenscheidt.

Langenscheidts Universal-Worterbucher: Rumanisch. (RUM.). 1997. pap. write for info. (3-468-18280-5); pap. 14.75 (3-468-18281-3) Langenscheidt.

Langenscheidts Universal-Worterbucher: Russisch. (RUS.). 1997. pap. write for info. (3-468-18291-0) Langenscheidt.

Langenscheidts Universal-Worterbucher: Schwedisch. (SWE.). 1997. pap. write for info. (3-468-18301-1) Langenscheidt.

Langenscheidts Universal-Worterbucher: Slowakisch. 1997. pap. write for info. (3-468-18321-6) Langenscheidt.

Langenscheidts Universal-Worterbucher: Slowenisch. 1997. pap. write for info. (3-468-18330-5); pap. 14.75 (3-468-18331-3) Langenscheidt.

Langenscheidts Universal-Worterbucher: Spanisch. (SPA.). 1997. pap. write for info. (3-468-18343-7) Langenscheidt.

Langenscheidts Universal-Worterbucher: Tschechisch. 1997. pap. write for info. (3-468-18361-5) Langenscheidt.

Langenscheidts Universal-Worterbucher: Turkisch. (TUR.). 1997. pap. write for info. (3-468-18372-0) Langenscheidt.

Langenscheidts Universal-Worterbucher: Ungarisch. 1997. pap. write for info. (3-468-18382-8) Langenscheidt.

Langenscheidts Woerterbuch der Ungangssprache Franzoesisch. Franz-Joseph Meissner. (FRE & GER.). 245p. 1992. 39.95 (0-7859-8389-9, 3468201583) Fr & Eur.

Lange's Handbook of Chemistry. 14th ed. J. Dean. (Illus.). 1466p. 1992. 110.00 (0-07-016194-1) McGraw.

Lange's Handbook of Chemistry. 15th ed. John A. Dean. (Illus.). 1584p. 1998. 120.00 (0-07-016384-7) McGraw-Hill Prof.

Langevin Equation & Its Applications to Stochastic Problems in Physics, Chemistry. W. t. Coffey & Yu P. Kalmykov. (Contemporary Chemical Physics Ser.). 500p. 1996. text 99.00 (981-02-1651-3) World Scientific Pub.

Langford Business Computer Ethics. Duncan Langford. (C). 1999. pap. text. write for info. (0-201-34279-0) Addison-Wesley.

Langhornes of Langhorne Park: Descendants of Thomas Langhorne (1633?-1687) of Co. Westmoreland, England, & Bucks County, Pennsylvania, Father of Sarah Langhorne, Wife of William Biles, Jr., & of Jeremiah Langhorne, Chief Justice of Pennsylvania. D. Brenton Simons. LC 97-9804. 1997. 29.50 (0-88082-062-4) New Eng Hist.

Langland & Allegory. Jill Mann. (Morton W. Bloomfield Lectures on Medieval English Literature Ser.: Vol. II). (C). 1992. pap. 5.00 (1-879288-15-X) Medieval Inst.

Langland & Chaucer. Ikuzo Iijima. LC 75-170059. reprint ed. 37.50 (0-404-03482-9) AMS Pr.

Langland Piers Plowman. Ed. by J. A. Bennett. xiv, 259p. 1985. reprint ed. 39.00 (0-932051-50-2) Rprt Serv.

Langlands Classification & Irreducible Characters for Real Reductive Groups. Ed. by J. Adams et al. (Progress in Mathematics Ser.: Vol. 104). xii, 318p. 1992. 57.50 (0-8176-3634-X) Birkhauser.

Langland's Fictions. J. A. Burrow. LC 92-26820. (Illus.). 144p. 1993. 39.95 (0-19-811293-9, Clarendon Pr) OUP.

Langley: Man of Science & Flight. J. Gordon Vaeth. LC 66-29472. 127p. reprint ed. 39.40 (0-8357-9920-4, 201237100081) Bks Demand.

Langley School: The First Fifty Years. Mary Lou Bohsali. LC 93-24211. 1993. write for info. (0-89865-875-6) Donning Co.

***Langloz Manuscript: Fugal Improvisation Through Figured Bass.** William Renwick. (Early Music Ser.). (Illus.). 208p. 2001. text 72.00 (0-19-816729-6) OUP.

Langman's Medical Embryology. 6th ed. Thomas W. Sadler. (Illus.). 432p. 1990. pap. 33.00 (0-683-07493-8) Lppncott W & W.

Langman's Medical Embryology. 7th ed. Thomas W. Sadler & Sang-Ho Baik. (KOR., Illus.). 480p. 1997. write for info. (962-356-022-2) Lppncott W & W.

Langman's Medical Embryology. 7th ed. Thomas W. Sadler & Ming-Jia Jou. (CHI., Illus.). 480p. 1996. write for info. (962-356-019-2) Lppncott W & W.

Langmuir-Blodgett Films. G. Roberts. LC 89-72111. (Illus.). 434p. (C). 1990. text 115.00 (0-306-43316-8, Kluwer Plenum) Kluwer Academic.

Langmuir-Blodgett Films: An Introduction. Michael C. Petty. (Illus.). 252p. (C). 1996. text 80.00 (0-521-41396-6); pap. text 32.95 (0-521-42450-X) Cambridge U Pr.

Langoliers. Stephen King. (SPA.). 1995. mass mkt. 4.99 (0-451-18656-7) NAL.

Lang's Ballads of Books. Andrew Lang. LC 75-75714. (Granger Index Reprint Ser.). 1977. 18.95 (0-8369-6024-6) Ayer.

Langsame Sterben: Eine Medizinsoziologische Okologiestudie Uber Den Zusammenhang Zwischen Wohnumfeldbelastung und Krankheit. Gerhard Grossmann. (Illus.). XIV, 238p. 1998. pap. 45.95 (3-631-47223-4) P Lang Pubng.

Langsdorff's Narrative of the Rezanov Voyage. Georg Langsdorff. 1988. 29.95 (0-87770-449-X) Ye Galleon.

Langstaff: A Nineteenth-Century Medical Life. Dacalyn Duffin. (Illus.). 400p. 1993. text 60.00 (0-8020-2908-6); pap. text 17.95 (0-8020-7414-6) U of Toronto Pr.

Langston Hughes see Modern Critical Views Series

Langston Hughes see Voices in Poetry

Langston Hughes. Harold Bloom. (Bloom's World Poets Ser.). 112p. (YA). (gr. 8 up). 1999. lib. bdg. 18.95 (0-7910-5110-2) Chelsea Hse.

Langston Hughes. Cooper. 1997. 24.95 (0-8057-4022-8) Macmillan.

Langston Hughes: A Bio-Bibliography, 2. Compiled by Thomas A. Mikolyzk. LC 90-3613. (Bio-Bibliographies in Afro-American & African Studies: No. 2). 312p. 1990. lib. bdg. 45.00 (0-313-26895-9, MLK/, Greenwood Pr) Greenwood.

Langston Hughes: A Biography. Milton Meltzer. LC 68-21952. (YA). (gr. 7 up). 1968. 14.95 (0-690-48525-5) HarpC Child Bks.

Langston Hughes: An Illustrated Edition. Milton Meltzer. LC 97-1403. (Illus.). 240p. (YA). (gr. 5 up). 1997. pap. 16.95 (0-7613-0327-8); lib. bdg. 39.40 (0-7613-0205-0) Millbrook Pr.

Langston Hughes: Before & Beyond Harlem. Faith Berry. 384p. 1992. pap. 15.95 (0-8065-1307-1, Citadel Pr) Carol Pub Group.

Langston Hughes: Critical Perspectives Past & Present. Henry Louis Gates, Jr. & Kwame Anthony Appiah. LC 92-45756. (Literary Ser.). 255p. 1993. 24.95 (1-56743-016-3, Amistad) HarperTrade.

Langston Hughes: Critical Perspectives Past & Present. Henry Louis Gates, Jr. & Kwame Anthony Appiah. LC 92-45756. (Literary Ser.). 272p. 1993. pap. 14.95 (1-56743-029-5, Amistad) HarperTrade.

Langston Hughes: Folk Dramatist in the Protest Tradition, 1921-1943, 181. Joseph McLaren. LC 95-48416. (Contributions in Afro-American & African Studies: Vol. 181). 248p. 1997. 49.95 (0-313-28719-8, Greenwood Pr) Greenwood.

Langston Hughes: Great American Poet. Patricia McKissack & Fredrick McKissack. LC 92-2583. (Great African Americans Ser.). (Illus.). 32p. (J). (gr. 1-4). 1992. lib. bdg. 14.95 (0-89490-315-2) Enslow Pubs.

Langston Hughes: Poet. Joseph Nazel. (Black American Ser.). (Illus.). 192p. (Orig.). (YA). 1994. mass mkt. 3.95 (0-87067-591-5, Melrose Sq) Holloway.

Langston Hughes: Poet. Jack Rummel. Ed. by Nathan I. Huggins. LC 87-10920. (Black Americans of Achievement Ser.). (Illus.). 111p. (YA). (gr. 5 up). 1987. lib. bdg. 19.95 (1-55546-595-1) Chelsea Hse.

Langston Hughes: Poet. Jack Rummel. Ed. by Nathan I. Huggins. LC 87-10920. (Black Americans of Achievement Ser.). (Illus.). 111p. (YA). (gr. 5 up). 1989. pap. 8.95 (0-7910-0201-2) Chelsea Hse.

Langston Hughes: Poet of the Harlem Renaissance. Christine M. Hill. LC 97-10991. (African-American Biographies Ser.). (Illus.). 128p. (YA). (gr. 6 up). 1997. lib. bdg. 20.95 (0-89490-815-4) Enslow Pubs.

Langston Hughes: The Man, His Art, & His Continuing Influence. Arnold Rampersad. Ed. by C. James Trotman. LC 95-15708. (Critical Studies in Black Life & Culture: Vol. 29). (Illus.). 200p. 1995. text 45.00 (0-8153-1763-8, H1872) Garland.

Langston Hughes: The Poet & His Critics. Richard K. Barksdale. LC 77-8599. 167p. reprint ed. pap. 51.80 (0-608-13298-5, 202561000044) Bks Demand.

Langston Hughes, American Poet. rev. ed. Alice Walker. LC 92-28540. (Illus.). 48p. (J). (gr. 3-6). 1998. 15.95 (0-06-021518-6); lib. bdg. 15.89 (0-06-021519-4) HarpC Child Bks.

Langston Hughes & the Blues. Steven C. Tracy. LC 87-28753. 320p. 1988. text 29.95 (0-252-01457-X) U of Ill Pr.

Langston Hughes & the Chicago Defender: Essays on Race, Politics & Culture, 1942-62. Christopher C. De Santis. LC 94-45656. 240p. 1995. 14.95 (0-252-06474-7) U of Ill Pr.

Langston Hughes Reader. Langston Hughes. LC 58-7871. 502p. 1958. 20.95 (0-8076-0057-1) Braziller.

Langston Hughes, Young Black Poet. Montrew Dunham. (Childhood of Famous Americans Ser.). (J). 1995. 10.30 (0-606-07770-7) Turtleback.

Langston Reader. Langston Hughes. 1976. 31.95 (0-8488-0698-0) Amereon Ltd.

Langstone & Chichester Harbours. Imray, Laurie, Norie & Wilson Ltd. Staff. (Illus.). (C). 1990. text 60.00 (0-7855-5781-4, Pub. by Laurie Norie & Wilson Ltd) St Mut.

Langt Zu, 1. Jim Davis. 1999. pap. text 10.95 (3-8105-0716-4) W Kruger.

Langtang Himal: Flora und Vegetation Als Klimazeiger und -Zeugen Im Himalaya (A Prodromus of the Vegetation Ecology of the Himalayas) Georg Miehe. (Dissertationes Botanicae Ser.: Band 158). (ENG & GER.). xxviii, 530p. 1990. 130.00 (3-443-64070-2, Pub. by Gebruder Borntraeger) Balogh.

Language. Leonard Bloomfield. (C). 1994. text 22.00 (81-208-1195-X, Pub. by Motilal Bnarsidass) S Asia.

Language. Leonard Bloomfield. LC 84-8439. x, 580p. 1984. pap. text 29.00 (0-226-06067-5) U Ch Pr.

Language. Ed. by Brynmill Press Ltd. Staff. (C). 1989. 60.00 (0-907839-00-2, Pub. by Brynmill Pr Ltd) St Mut.

Language. Floyd & Beigel. (C). 1994. text, teacher ed. 16.00 (0-7167-8291-X) W H Freeman.

Language. Guy V. Ottewell. 97p. 1987. pap. text 9.00 (0-934546-17-7) Univ Wrkshop.

Language. 6th ed. Eschholz. LC 95-73169. 750p. 1998. pap. 38.95 (0-312-13308-1) St Martin.

Language see Communication As a Second Language

Language: A Science of Human Behavior. Harry R. Warfel. LC 62-9619. 188p. 1962. 35.00 (0-8201-1047-7) Schol Facsimiles.

Language: Acquisition, Application, Appreciation. Ed. by Warren C. Born. 1997. pap. 10.95 (0-915432-77-3) NE Conf Teach Foreign.

Language: An Introduction. Louis Hjelmslev. LC 70-98119. Orig. Title: Sproget. 158p. 1970. reprint ed. pap. 49.00 (0-608-01880-5, 206253200003) Bks Demand.

Language: An Introduction to the Study of Speech. Edward Sapir. LC 21-20134. 252p. 1955. pap. 9.00 (0-15-648233-9, Harvest Bks) Harcourt.

Language: Answer Key. 3rd ed. Finegan. (C). 1998. pap. text 40.00 (0-15-508438-0, Pub. by Harcourt Coll Pubs) Harcourt.

Language: Contexts & Consequences. N. Coupland & Howard Giles. Ed. by Anthony S. Manstead. (Mapping Social Psychology Ser.). 264p. 1991. pap. 28.95 (0-335-09872-X) OpUniv Pr.

Language: Grade 3. Strickland. 1990. teacher ed. 97.25 (0-15-316422-0) Harcourt Schl Pubs.

Language! Instructor's Manual. Jane F. Greene. (Language!). (Illus.). 394p. 1995. teacher ed. 75.00 (1-57035-065-5, 74LANG) Sopris.

Language: Its Power & Its Abuse. 292p. (C). 1993. 38.60 (0-536-58438-9) Pearson Custom.

Language: Its Structure - Answer Key. 2nd ed. Edward Feinegan. (C). 1995. pap. text 40.00 (0-15-501558-3, Pub. by Harcourt Coll Pubs) Harcourt.

Language: Its Structure & Evolution. Marcel Cohen. Tr. by Leonard Muller from FRE. 157p. (C). 1970. pap. 14.95 (0-8464-1156-3) Beekman Pubs.

Language: Its Structure & Use. 2nd ed. Edward Finegan. LC 93-78400. (Illus.). 580p. (C). 1994. pap. text 51.50 (0-15-500122-1) Harcourt.

Language: Its Structure & Use. 3rd ed. Finegan. (C). 1998. pap. 51.50 (0-15-507827-5, Pub. by Harcourt Coll Pubs) Harcourt.

Language: Learning or Acquisition. Joe E. Pierce. 55p. (Orig.). 1987. pap. 6.95 (0-913244-70-8) Hapi Pr.

Language: Structure, Processing & Disorders. David N. Caplan. (Illus.). 400p. 1992. 55.00 (0-262-03189-2) MIT Pr.

Language: Structure, Processing & Disorders. David Caplan. (Issues in the Biology of Language & Cognition). (Illus.). 536p. 1996. reprint ed. pap. text 27.00 (0-262-53138-0, Bradford Bks) MIT Pr.

Language! Student Book A. Jane F. Greene. (Language!). (Illus.). 56p. (J). (gr. 2-9). 1995. pap., student ed., wbk. ed. 5.25 (1-57035-062-0, 74BK) Sopris.

Language! Student Book B. Jane F. Greene. (Language!). (Illus.). 70p. (J). (gr. 2-9). 1995. pap., student ed., wbk. ed. 5.25 (1-57035-063-9, 74BK) Sopris.

Language! Student Book C. Jane F. Greene. (Language!). (Illus.). 64p. (J). (gr. 2-9). 1995. pap., student ed., wbk. ed. 5.25 (1-57035-064-7, 74BK) Sopris.

Language! Student Book D. Jane F. Greene. (Language!). (Illus.). 80p. (J). (gr. 2-9). 1995. pap., student ed., wbk. ed. 5.25 (1-57035-060-4, 74BK) Sopris.

Language! Student Book E. Jane F. Greene. (Language!). (Illus.). 92p. (J). (gr. 2-9). 1995. pap., student ed., wbk. ed. 5.25 (1-57035-059-0, 74BK) Sopris.

Language! Student Book F. Jane F. Greene. (Language!). (Illus.). 96p. (J). (gr. 2-9). 1995. pap., student ed., wbk. ed. 5.25 (1-57035-061-2, 74BK) Sopris.

Language! Student Book G. Jane F. Greene. (Language!). (Illus.). 90p. (J). (gr. 2-9). 1995. pap., student ed., wbk. ed. 5.25 (1-57035-057-4, 74BK) Sopris.

Language! Student Book H. Jane F. Greene. (Language!). (Illus.). 78p. (J). (gr. 2-9). 1995. pap., student ed., wbk. ed. 5.25 (1-57035-056-6, 74BK) Sopris.

Language! Student Book I. Jane F. Greene. (Language!). (Illus.). 90p. (J). (gr. 2-9). 1995. pap., student ed., wbk. ed. 5.25 (1-57035-058-2, 74BK) Sopris.

Language: The Basics. 2nd ed. R. L. Trask. LC 98-31507. 1999. pap. 16.99 (0-415-20089-X) Routledge.

Language: The Unknown: An Initiation into Linguistics. Julia Kristeva. Tr. by Anne M. Menke from FRE. 384p. 1991. pap. text 19.00 (0-231-06107-2) Col U Pr.

***Language - A Right & a Resource: Approaches to Linguistic Human Rights.** Ed. by Miklos Kontra et al. LC 99-51516. 400p. (C). 2000. 49.95 (963-9116-63-7) Ctrl Europ Univ.

Language, a Magical Enterprise, the Body see Paperplay Mini-Books

***Language a Right & a Resource: Approaches to Linguistic Human Rights.** Miklos Kontra. LC 99-51516. 1999. pap. text 23.95 (963-9116-64-5) Ctrl Europ Univ.

Language A to Z, Bk. 2. Crystal. 1991. pap. text. write for info. (0-582-07564-5, Pub. by Addison-Wesley) Longman.

Language Acquisition. Jill G. De Villiers & Peter A. De Villiers. 384p. 1990. 44.00 (0-674-50931-5) HUP.

Language Acquisition: A Linguistic Introduction. Helen Goodluck. 256p. 1991. pap. 28.95 (0-631-17386-2) Blackwell Pubs.

Language Acquisition: Core Readings. Ed. by Paul Bloom. LC 93-27417. 624p. 1993. pap. text 29.50 (0-262-52187-3) MIT Pr.

***Language Acquisition: Knowledge Representation & Processing.** Antonella Sorace et al. LC 98-51947. 300p. 1999. 57.50 (0-08-043370-7, North Holland) Elsevier.

Language Acquisition: The Age Factor. David Singleton. 1989. 99.00 (1-85359-020-7, Pub. by Multilingual Matters); pap. 44.95 (1-85359-019-3, Pub. by Multilingual Matters) Taylor & Francis.

Language Acquisition after Puberty. Judith R. Strozer. LC 94-5106. (Studies in Romance Linguistics). 244p. 1994. 60.00 (0-87840-244-6); pap. 22.95 (0-87840-245-4) Georgetown U Pr.

***Language Acquisition & Conceptual Development.** Ed. by Melissa Bowerman & Stephen C. Levinson. (Language, Culture & Cognition Ser.: No. 3). (Illus.). 420p. (C). 2000. pap. 27.95 (0-521-59659-9); text 74.95 (0-521-59358-1) Cambridge U Pr.

Language Acquisition & Connectionism. Kim Plunkett. 427p. 1998. 54.95 (0-86377-984-0) Taylor & Francis.

Language Acquisition & Development. Susan Beck. (C). 2002. 35.00 (0-13-523515-4, Macmillan Coll) P-H.

Language Acquisition & Language Breakdown: Parallels & Divergencies. Ed. by Alfonso Caramazza & Edgar B. Zurif. LC 77-4789. 351p. reprint ed. pap. 108.90 (0-7837-2184-6, 204252200004) Bks Demand.

Language Acquisition & Syntactic Theory: A Comparative Analysis of French & English Child Grammars. Amy E. Pierce. 184p. (C). 1992. text 125.00 (0-7923-1553-7) Kluwer Academic.

***Language Acquisition & the Form of the Grammar.** David Lebeaux. LC 00-39775. 2000. write for info. (1-55619-858-2) J Benjamins Pubng Co.

Language Acquisition & the Theory of Parameters. Nina M. Hyams. 1986. pap. text 49.50 (90-277-2219-6) Kluwer Academic.

Language Acquisition by Eye. Ed. by Jill P. Morford et al. LC 99-30894. 276p. 1999. 59.95 (0-8058-2937-7) L Erlbaum Assocs.

Language Acquisition in North America. Ed. by Orlando L. Taylor & Laurence Leonard. LC 98-28126. (Illus.). 279p. 1998. pap. 49.95 (1-56593-862-3, 1684) Thomson Learn.

Language Acquisition of a Bilingual Child see Adquisicion del Lenguaje en un Nino Bilingue

Language Acquisition of a Bilingual Child. Alvino E. Fantini. 265p. 1985. 89.00 (0-905028-40-6, MM17, Pub. by Multilingual Matters); pap. 32.00 (0-905028-39-2, Pub. by Multilingual Matters) Taylor & Francis.

Language Acquisition Problems & Reading Disorders: Aspects of Diagnosis & Intervention. Ed. by Hannelore Grimm & Helmut Skowronek. LC 93-27052. (Prevention & Intervention in Childhood & Adolescence Ser.: No. 14). xii, 360p. (C). 1993. lib. bdg. 82.95 (3-11-014120-5) De Gruyter.

Language Acquisition Studies in Generative Grammar: Papers in Honor of Kenneth Wexler from the 1991 GLOW Workshops. Ed. by Teun Hoekstra & Bonnie Schwartz. LC 93-43090. (Language Acquisition & Language Disorders (LALD) Ser.: No. 8). xii, 401p. 1994. 85.00 (1-55619-244-4) J Benjamins Pubng Co.

Language Across the Curriculum When Students Are Deaf or Hard of Hearing. Barbara Luetke-Stahlman. LC 99-213863. 464p. (C). 1999. pap. 44.00 (1-884362-27-3) Butte Pubns.

An Asterisk (*) at the beginning of an entry indicates that the title is appearing for the first time.

L

Language, Action & Context: The Early History of Pragmatics in Europe & America 1780-1930. Brigitte Nerlich & David D. Clarke. LC 96-13678. (Studies in the History of the Language Sciences: Vol. 80). xiv, 497p. 1996. lib. bdg. 115.00 (*1-55619-616-4*) J Benjamins Pubng Co.

Language Alive in the Classroom. Ed. by Rebecca S. Wheeler. LC 98-53391. 240p. 1999. 65.00 (*0-275-96055-2*, Praeger Pubs); pap. 21.95 (*0-275-96056-0*, Praeger Pubs) Greenwood.

Language & Action: A Reassessment of Speech Act Theory. Danilo Marcondes de Souza Filho. LC 84-4055. (Pragmatics & Beyond Ser.: Vol. V:6). x, 165p. 1985. pap. 50.00 (*0-915027-01-1*) J Benjamins Pubng Co.

Language & Area Studies: Central & Southeastern Europe: A Survey. Ed. by Charles Jelavich. LC 72-8122. 1994. lib. bdg. 35.00 (*0-226-39615-0*) U Ch Pr.

Language & Art in the Navajo Universe. Gary Witherspoon. (Illus.). 244p. 1977. pap. text 23.95 (*0-472-08966-8*, 08966) U of Mich Pr.

Language & Behavior. Russell. 1993. pap. 41.25 (*0-8087-6712-7*) Pearson Custom.

Language & Being: An Analytic Phenomenology. Stephen A. Erickson. LC 74-99823. 173p. reprint ed. pap. 53.70 (*0-608-31005-0*, 201678000005) Bks Demand.

Language & Being in Wittgenstein's "Philosophical Investigations" Jeffrey T. Price. 1973. pap. text 26.95 (*90-279-2443-0*) Mouton.

Language & Bilingualism: More Tests of Tests. John W. Oller, Jr. LC 90-55874. 192p. 1991. 32.50 (*0-8387-5210-1*) Bucknell U Pr.

Language & Cinema. Christian Metz. Tr. by Donna J. Umiker-Sebeok. 1974. text 64.65 (*90-279-2682-4*) Mouton.

Language & Cognition: A Developmental Perspective. Ed. by Esther Dromi & Sidney Strauss. (Human Development Ser.). 240p. (C). 1986. text 73.25 (*0-89391-682-X*) Ablx Pub.

Language & Cognition: Essays in Honor of Arthur J. Bronstein. Ed. by Lawrence J. Raphael et al. LC 83-22987. (Cognition & Language Ser.). 306p. 1984. 70.00 (*0-306-41433-3*, Plenum Trade) Perseus Pubng.

Language & Colonial Power: The Appropriation of Swahili in the Former Belgian Congo, 1880-1938. Johannes Fabian. (Illus.). 212p. 1991. reprint ed. pap. 16.95 (*0-520-07625-7*, Pub. by U CA Pr) Cal Prin Full Svc.

Language & Communication: A Cross-Cultural Encyclopedia. Michael Findlay. LC 98-12300. (Encyclopedias of the Human Experience Ser.). (Illus.). 229p. (YA). (gr. 9 up). 1998. lib. bdg. 65.00 (*0-87436-946-0*) ABC-CLIO.

Language & Communication: Comparative Perspectives. Ed. by Herbert L. Roitblat et al. (Comparative Cognition & Neuroscience Ser.). 520p. 1993. pap. 39.95 (*0-8058-0947-3*); text 110.00 (*0-8058-0946-5*) L Erlbaum Assocs.

Language & Communication: Essential Concepts for User Iterface & Documentation Design. Agnes Kukulska-Hulme. LC 97-41640. (Illus.). 176p. 1999. 45.00 (*0-19-510838-8*) OUP.

Language & Communication: Student Booklet. American Psychological Association Staff. (Human Behavior Curriculum Peoject Ser.). 60p. (Orig.). (gr. 9-12). 1981. pap. text 3.95 (*0-8077-2625-7*) Tchrs Coll.

Language & Communication: Teachers Handbook & Duplication Masters. American Psychological Association Staff. (Human Behavior Curriculum Project Ser.). (Orig.). (gr. 9-12). 1981. pap. 9.95 (*0-8077-2626-5*) Tchrs Coll.

Language & Communication Disorders in Children. 4th ed. Deena K. Bernstein & Ellenmorris Tiegerman. LC 96-48262. 544p. 1997. 72.00 (*0-205-19894-5*) Allyn.

Language & Communication in Israel Vol. 9: Studies of Israeli Society. Ed. by Hanna Herzog & Eliezer Ben-Rafael. 732p. 1999. 69.95 (*1-56000-347-2*); pap. 29.95 (*1-56000-998-5*) Transaction Pubs.

Language & Communication in Mental Retardation: Development, Processes, & Intervention. Sheldon Rosenberg & Leonard Abbeduto. (Topics in Applied Psycholinguistics Ser.). 272p. 1993. text 59.95 (*0-8058-0302-5*) L Erlbaum Assocs.

Language & Communication in Mentally Handicapped People. Michael Beveridge et al. 200p. 1989. 67.50 (*0-412-32390-7*) Chapman & Hall.

Language & Communication in Old Age: Multidisciplinary Perspectives. Ed. by Heidi E. Hamilton & Diana K. Harris. LC 98-38853. (Issues in Aging Ser.: Vol. 9). (Illus.). 350p. 1998. 60.00 (*0-8153-2356-5*, SS1104) Garland.

Language & Communication in People with Learning Disabilities. Michael Beveridge & Gina Conti-Ramsden. 320p. (C). 1997. pap. 24.99 (*0-415-15397-2*) Routledge.

Language & Communication in the Mathematics Classroom. Ed. by Heinz Steinbring et al. LC 98-24453. (Illus.). 360p. 1998. pap. text 24.95 (*0-87353-441-7*) NCTM.

Language & Communication Intervention in the Preschool Child. Ellenmorris Tiegerman. 248p. (C). 1994. pap. text 51.00 (*0-02-420821-3*, Macmillan Coll) P-H.

Language & Communication Studies in South Africa. L. W. Lanham & K. Prinsloo. 1978. 15.50 (*0-19-570144-5*) OUP.

Language & Communicative Practices. William F. Hanks. (Critical Essays in Anthropology Ser.). (Illus.). 352p. (C). 1995. pap. 35.00 (*0-8133-1217-5*, Pub. by Westview) HarpC.

***Language & Community in the Nineteenth Century.** Ed. by Geraint H. Jenkins. LC 99-202784. 440p. 1999. pap. 29.95 (*0-7083-1467-8*, Pub. by Univ Wales Pr) Paul & Co Pubs.

Language & Computers: A Practical Introduction to the Computer Analysis of Language. Geoff Barnbrook. (Edinburgh Textbooks in Empirical Linguistics Ser.). 256p. 1996. 70.00 (*0-7486-0848-6*, Pub. by Edinburgh U Pr); pap. 24.50 (*0-7486-0785-4*, Pub. by Edinburgh U Pr) Col U Pr.

Language & Conceptualization. Ed. by Jan Nuyts & Eric Pederson. LC 96-8776. (Language, Culture & Cognition Ser.: No. 1). (Illus.). 289p. (C). 1997. text 59.95 (*0-521-55303-2*) Cambridge U Pr.

***Language & Conceptualization.** Ed. by Jan Nuyts & Eric Pederson. (Language, Culture & Cognition Ser.: No. 1). (Illus.). 290p. (C). 2000. pap. 24.95 (*0-521-77481-0*) Cambridge U Pr.

Language & Conflict: A Neglected Relationship. Paul A. Chilton et al. LC 98-22409. 65p. 1998. 49.00 (*1-85359-422-9*, Pub. by Multilingual Matters) Taylor & Francis.

Language & Content: Discipline- & Content-Based Approaches to Language Study. Ed. by Merle Krueger & Frank Ryan. (Series on Foreign Language Acquisition Research & Instruction: Vol. 3). 320p. (C). 1993. pap. text 35.96 (*0-669-28920-5*) HM Trade Div.

Language & Context: A Functional Linguistic Theory of Register. Helen Leckie-Tarry. Ed. by David Birch. LC 95-3907. 1995. 64.95 (*1-85567-271-5*) St Martin.

Language & Context: A Functional Linguistic Theory of Register. Helen Leckie-Tarry. Ed. by David Birch. LC 95-3907. 1995. pap. 22.95 (*1-85567-272-3*) St Martin.

Language & Control in Children's Literature. Murray Knowles & Kirsten Malmkjaer. LC 95-7336. 296p. (C). 1995. pap. 25.99 (*0-415-08625-6*) Routledge.

Language & Creative Illusion. Walter Nash. LC 97-46988. (English Language Ser). 1998. text 67.07 (*0-582-29163-1*) Addison-Wesley.

Language & Creative Illusion. Walter Nash. LC 97-46988. (English Language Ser.). 1998. pap. text 26.05 (*0-582-29164-X*) Longman.

Language & Creativity: An Interdisciplinary Essay in Chomskyan Humanism. Bernard D. Den Ouden. vi, 107p. (Orig.). (C). 1975. pap. text 23.10 (*3-11-013329-6*) Mouton.

Language & Culture. Eschholz. 2000. pap. write for info. (*0-312-20107-9*) St Martin.

Language & Culture. Ed. by David Graddol et al. (British Studies in Applied Linguistics: No. 7). 152p. 1993. pap. 24.95 (*1-85359-207-2*, Pub. by Multilingual Matters) Taylor & Francis.

***Language & Culture.** Ed. by Oxford University Press Incorporated Staff. LC 99-169749. 144p. 1998. pap. text 11.95 (*0-19-437214-6*) OUP.

Language & Culture. David L. Shaul & N. Louanna Furbee. LC 99-185332. (Illus.). 305p. (C). 1997. pap. text 14.95 (*0-88133-970-9*) Waveland Pr.

Language & Culture: A Transcending Bond: Essays by American Germanists of Austro-Jewish Descent. Ed. by Susan E. Cernyak-Spatz & Charles S. Merrill. LC 92-35303. (Literature & the Sciences of Man Ser.: Vol. 5). X, 156p. (C). 1994. text 43.00 (*0-8204-1993-1*) P Lang Pubng.

Language & Culture in Depth, Level 5. Elaine Kirn. (ETC Program Ser.). 135p. (C). 1988. pap. 17.81 (*0-07-553781-8*); pap., teacher ed. 32.19 (*0-07-553978-0*); pap., teacher ed. 32.19 (*0-07-556990-6*); pap. text 44.69 (*0-07-556991-4*) McGraw.

Language & Culture in Depth, Level 5. Elaine Kirn. (ETC Program Ser.). 215p. (C). 1988. pap. 20.63 (*0-07-556998-1*) McGraw.

Language & Culture in Learning: Teaching Spanish to Native Speakers of Spanish. Ed. by Barbara J. Merino et al. LC 93-26831. 290p. 1994. 89.95 (*0-7507-0230-3*, Falmer Pr); pap. 27.95 (*0-7507-0231-1*, Falmer Pr) Taylor & Francis.

Language & Deafness. 2nd ed. Peter V. Paul & Stephen P. Quigley. LC 94-4478. (Illus.). 112p. (C). 1994. teacher ed. 24.50 (*1-56593-362-1*, 0695) Singular Publishing.

Language & Deafness. 2nd ed. Peter V. Paul & Stephen P. Quigley. LC 94-4478. (Illus.). 394p. (C). 1994. pap. text 45.00 (*1-56593-108-4*, 0411) Thomson Learn.

Language & Deafness. 2nd ed. Peter V. Paul & Stephen P. Quigley. 252p. (C). 1994. pap. text, student ed. 29.95 (*1-56593-363-X*, 0700) Thomson Learn.

***Language & Deafness.** 3rd ed. Paul. 2001. pap. 47.95 (*1-56593-999-9*) Singular Publishing.

Language & Death: The Place of Negativity. Giorgio Agamben. Tr. by Karen E. Pinkus & Michael Hardt from ITA. (Theory & History of Literature Ser.: Vol. 78). xiii, 112p. (C). 1991. pap. 15.95 (*0-8166-1937-9*); text 39.95 (*0-8166-1936-0*) U of Minn Pr.

Language & Decadence in the Victorian Fin de Siecle. Linda C. Dowling. LC 86-15135. 311p. reprint ed. pap. 96.50 (*0-608-06373-8*, 206673400008) Bks Demand.

Language & Desire: Encoding Sex, Romance & Intimacy. Keith Harvey & Celia Shalom. LC 96-37726. 264p. (C). 1997. 85.00 (*0-415-13691-1*); pap. 24.99 (*0-415-13692-X*) Routledge.

Language & Desire in Seneca's Phaedra. Charles Segal. LC 85-43311. 255p. 1986. reprint ed. pap. 79.10 (*0-608-07156-0*, 206738100009) Bks Demand.

Language & Dialect Distance in a Space of N-Dimensions. Joe E. Pierce. 73p. (Orig.). 1983. pap. 5.95 (*0-685-26996-5*) Hapi Pr.

Language & Discourse. Herman Parret. LC 73-170002. (Janua Linguarum, Ser. Minor: No. 119). (Illus.). 292p. (Orig.). 1971. pap. text 49.25 (*90-279-1854-6*) Mouton.

Language & Discourse: Test & Protest. A Festschift for Petr Sgall. Ed. by Jacob L. Mey. LC 86-6882. (Linguistic & Literary Studies in Eastern Europe: Vol. 19). xiii, 611p. 1986. 127.00 (*90-272-1525-1*) J Benjamins Pubng Co.

Language & Earth: Elective Affinities Between the Emerging Sciences of Linguistics & Geology. Ed. by Bernd Naumann et al. LC 91-35106. (Studies in the History of the Language Sciences: No. 66). xvi, 445p. 1992. 118.00 (*1-55619-361-0*) J Benjamins Pubng Co.

Language & Education. Ed. by George M. Blue & Rosamond Mitchell. (British Studies in Applied Linguistics: No. 11). 140p. 1996. pap. 39.95 (*1-85359-370-2*, Pub. by Multilingual Matters) Taylor & Francis.

Language & Education. Andrew Wilkinson. (Oxford Studies in Education Ser.). 192p. (C). 1977. pap. text 6.50 (*0-19-911101-4*) OUP.

Language & Education in Multilingual Settings. Ed. by Bernard J. Spolsky. 200p. (Orig.). 1986. 74.95 (*0-905028-59-7*, MM25, Pub. by Multilingual Matters); pap. 29.95 (*0-905028-58-9*, Pub. by Multilingual Matters) Taylor & Francis.

Language & Ethnic Identity. Ed. by William B. Gudykunst. 200p. 1988. 59.00 (*1-85359-021-5*, Pub. by Multilingual Matters) Taylor & Francis.

Language & Ethnic Relations: Language & Ethnic Interaction Section of the Sociolinguistics Program of the 9th World Congress of Sociology. Howard Giles & Bernard Saint-Jacques. LC 79-40709. (Illus.). 1979. 121.00 (*0-08-023720-7*, Pub. by Pergamon Repr) Franklin.

Language & Ethnicity in Minority Sociolinguistic Perspective. Joshua A. Fishman. 1989. 99.00 (*1-85359-006-1*, Pub. by Multilingual Matters); pap. 44.95 (*1-85359-005-3*, Pub. by Multilingual Matters) Taylor & Francis.

Language & Experience: Evidence from the Blind Child. Barbara Landau & Lila R. Gleitman. (Cognitive Science Ser.: Vol. No. 8). (Illus.). 256p. 1985. reprint ed. pap. 18.95 (*0-674-51026-7*) HUP.

Language & Experience in Seventeenth Century British Philosophy. Lia Formigari. LC 88-18634. (Studies in the History of the Language Sciences: Vol. 48). viii, 169p. 1988. 47.00 (*90-272-4531-2*) J Benjamins Pubng Co.

***Language & Gender.** Angela Goddard & Lindsey M. Patterson. LC 99-43273. (Intertext Ser.). 112p. 2000. pap. 16.99 (*0-415-20177-2*) Routledge.

Language & Gender: A Reader. Ed. by Jennifer Coates. LC 97-18909. (Illus.). 480p. (C). 1997. text 68.95 (*0-631-19594-7*); pap. text 31.95 (*0-631-19595-5*) Blackwell Pubs.

Language & Gender: An Introduction. Mary M. Talbot. LC 98-31710. (Illus.). 257p. 1999. 59.95 (*0-7456-1679-8*); pap. 26.95 (*0-7456-1680-1*) Blackwell Pubs.

Language & Gender: Making the Difference. Cate Poynton. 104p. (C). 1995. pap. 34.00 (*0-7300-0347-7*, ECS806, Pub. by Deakin Univ) St Mut.

Language & Gender in American Fiction: Howells, James, Wharton, & Cather. Elsa Nettels. LC 96-3429. 200p. (C). 1997. text 29.50 (*0-8139-1724-7*) U Pr of Va.

Language & German Idealism: Fichte's Linguistic Philosophy. Jere P. Surber. LC 95-32633. 200p. (C). 1996. text 55.00 (*0-391-03935-0*) Humanities.

***Language & Gesture.** Ed. by David McNeill. (Language, Culture & Cognition Ser.: No. 2). (Illus.). 400p. (C). 2000. 64.95 (*0-521-77166-8*); pap. 24.95 (*0-521-77761-5*) Cambridge U Pr.

Language & Hemispheric Specialization in Man: Cerebral Event-Related Potentials. Ed. by J. E. Desmedt. (Progress in Clinical Neurophysiology Ser.: Vol. 3). (Illus.). 1977. 85.25 (*3-8055-2629-6*) S Karger.

Language & Historical Representation: Getting the Story Crooked. Hans Kellner. LC 88-40437. (Rhetoric of the Human Sciences Ser.). 352p. reprint ed. pap. 109.20 (*0-608-09912-0*, 206925000003) Bks Demand.

Language & History: Contributions to Comparative Altaistics. Andras Rona-Tas. (Studia Uralo-Altaica Ser.: No. 25). iv, 270p. (C). 1986. pap. 78.00 (*0-317-60113-X*) J Benjamins Pubng Co.

Language & History: Theories & Texts. Tony Crowley. LC 95-1855. (Politics of Language Ser.). 224p. (C). 1995. pap. 25.99 (*0-415-07245-X*) Routledge.

***Language & History in Early Britain: A Chronological Survey of the Brittonic Languages, 1st to 12th Century AD.** 2nd ed. Kenneth Jackson. 786p. 2000. reprint ed. text 85.00 (*1-85182-140-6*, Pub. by Four Cts Pr) Intl Spec Bk.

Language & History in Early England. Helmut Gneuss. LC 96-23383. (Collected Studies: No. CS553). 336p. 1996. 108.95 (*0-86078-601-3*, Pub. by Variorum) Ashgate Pub Co.

Language & History in the Early Germanic World. D. H. Green. LC 97-30144. (Illus.). 454p. (C). 1998. text 69.95 (*0-521-47134-6*) Cambridge U Pr.

***Language & History in the Early Germanic World.** D. H. Green. (Illus.). 452p. (C). 2000. pap. text Price not set. (*0-521-79423-4*) Cambridge U Pr.

Language & Human Action: Conceptions of Language in the Essais of Montaigne. Richard A. Watson. LC 93-467. (Studies in the Humanities: Vol. 12). 97p. (C). 1997. 32.95 (*0-8204-1987-7*, PQ1643) P Lang Pubng.

Language & Human Behavior. Derek Bickerton. LC 95-17023. (Jessie & John Danz Lecture Lectures). 208p. 1996. pap. 14.95 (*0-295-97458-3*) U of Wash Pr.

Language & Human Nature: A French-American Philosopher's Dialogue. Ed. by Paul Kurtz. LC 73-108782. 264p. 1971. 17.50 (*0-87527-022-0*) Green.

Language & Identity in the Middle East & North Africa. Ed. by Yasir Suleiman. 220p. 1996. 65.00 (*0-7007-0410-8*, Pub. by Curzon Pr Ltd) Paul & Co Pubs.

Language & Ideology in Children's Fiction. John Stephens. 308p. (C). 1995. pap. text 37.75 (*0-582-07062-7*, 79281) Longman.

Language & Ideology in Children's Fiction: Language in Social Life Series. John Stephens. (C). 1992. text 66.50 (*0-582-07063-5*) Addison-Wesley.

Language & Ideology in the Prose of Quevedo. William Clamurro. 201p. 1992. 18.50 (*0-936388-50-1*) Juan de la Cuesta.

Language & Imagery in the Old Testament. J. C. Gibson. LC 98-45906. 166p. 1998. pap. 12.95 (*1-56563-090-4*) Hendrickson MA.

Language & Imagery of the Bible. G. B. Caird. 308p. 1997. pap. 24.00 (*0-8028-4221-6*) Eerdmans.

Language & Images of Renaissance Italy. Ed. by Alison Brown. (Illus.). 354p. 1995. text 59.00 (*0-19-820318-7*) OUP.

Language & Information. Zellig S. Harris. (Bampton Lectures in America). 120p. 1988. text 38.50 (*0-231-06662-7*) Col U Pr.

Language & Insight. Roy Schafer. LC 77-20940. (Sigmund Freud Memorial Lectures: 1975-1976). 224p. reprint ed. pap. 69.50 (*0-8357-8202-6*, 203388100087) Bks Demand.

Language & Intelligence in Monkeys & Apes: Comparative Developmental Perspectives. Ed. by Sue T. Parker & Kathleen R. Gibson. (Illus.). 608p. (C). 1994. pap. text 27.95 (*0-521-45969-9*) Cambridge U Pr.

Language & Intergroup Relations in Flanders & in the Netherlands. Ed. by Kas Deprez. (Topics in Sociolinguistics Ser.: No. 6). vi, 198p. 1989. pap. 52.35 (*90-6765-391-8*) Mouton.

Language & International Studies. Georgetown University Round Table Meeting on Lingu. Ed. by Kurt R. Jankowsky. LC 58-31607. 252p. reprint ed. pap. 78.20 (*0-7837-6355-7*, 204606700010) Bks Demand.

Language & International Studies: A Richard Lambert Perspective. Ed. by Sarah J. Moore & Christine A. Morfit. 386p. (C). 1993. pap. text 12.00 (*1-880671-02-6*) NFLC Pubns.

Language & Interpretation in Psychoanalysis. Marshall Edelson. LC 84-2547. xvi, 260p. 1984. pap. text 11.00 (*0-226-18433-1*) U Ch Pr.

Language & Its Forms at Work & Play in the U. S. A. - Index of New Information Including Cultures, Science & Psychiatry. Walter P. Dishinger. 160p. 1995. 47.50 (*0-7883-0492-5*); pap. 44.50 (*0-7883-0493-3*) ABBE Pubs Assn.

Language & Its Functions: A Historico-Critical Study of Views Concerning the Functions of Language from the Prehistoric Philology of Orleans to the Rationalistic Philosophy of Bopp. Pieter A. Verburg. Tr. by Paul Salmon. LC 98-35929. (Studies in the History of Language Sciences: Vol. 84). xxxiv, 577p. 1998. 110.00 (*1-55619-621-0*) J Benjamins Pubng Co.

Language & Its Normal Processing. Vivien C. Tartter. LC 97-45474. 568p. 1998. 55.00 (*0-8039-5994-X*); pap. 30.00 (*0-8039-5995-8*) Sage.

Language & Knowledge in the Late Novels of Henry James. Ruth B. Yeazell. LC 75-46538. viii, 144p. 1980. pap. text 9.95 (*0-226-95095-6*) U Ch Pr.

Language & Language Use: Studies in Spanish. Ed. by Terrell A. Morgan et al. (Illus.). 346p. (Orig.). (C). 1988. pap. text 29.50 (*0-8191-6698-7*); lib. bdg. 52.50 (*0-8191-6697-9*) U Pr of Amer.

Language & Laughter: Comic Diction in the Plays of Bernard Shaw. John A. Mills. LC 68-9339. 192p. reprint ed. pap. 59.60 (*0-608-12772-8*, 202431900037) Bks Demand.

Language & Learning: An Interactional Perspective. Ed. by Gordon Wells & John Nicholls. LC 85-6728. (Contemporary Analysis in Education Ser.). 170p. 1985. pap. text 29.95 (*1-85000-028-X*, Falmer Pr) Taylor & Francis.

Language & Learning: Educating Linguistically Diverse Students. Ed. by Beverly McLeod. LC 93-11659. (SUNY Series, the Social Context of Education). 311p. (C). 1994. pap. text 23.95 (*0-7914-1892-8*) State U NY Pr.

Language & Learning: The Debate Between Jean Piaget & Noam Chomsky. Ed. by Massimo Piattelli-Palmarini. 445p. 1984. pap. 18.50 (*0-674-50941-2*) HUP.

Language & Learning: The Importance of Speech in Children's Development. 2nd ed. James N. Britton. LC 93-22156. 330p. 1993. pap. text 25.00 (*0-86709-335-8*, 0335, Pub. by Boynton Cook Pubs) Heinemann.

Language & Learning for Robots. Colleen Crangle & Patrick C. Suppes. LC 93-43516. (CSLI Lecture Notes Ser.: Vol. 41). 1995. 54.95 (*1-881526-20-8*); pap. 21.95 (*1-881526-19-4*) CSLI.

Language & Learning in Renaissance Italy: Selected Articles. John Monfasani. (Collected Studies: NO. CS460). (Illus.). 352p. 1994. 115.95 (*0-86078-403-7*, Pub. by Variorum) Ashgate Pub Co.

Language & Learning in the Cooperative Classroom. Shlomo Sharan & H. Shachar. (Recent Research in Psychology Ser.). (Illus.). xv, 176p. 1991. 59.95 (*0-387-96708-7*) Spr-Verlag.

Language & Learning to Read: What Teachers Should Know about Language. Ed. by Richard E. Hodges & E. Hugh Rodorf. 256p. 1985. reprint ed. pap. text 22.00 (*0-8191-4259-X*) U Pr of Amer.

Language & Lewis Carroll. Robert D. Sutherland. LC 73-101966. (Janua Linguarum, Ser. Major: No. 26). 1970. text 55.40 (*90-279-0719-6*) Mouton.

Language & Liberation: Feminism, Philosophy, & Language. Ed. & Intro. by Christina Hendricks. LC 98-27369. (SUNY Series in Contemporary Continental Philosophy). 402p. (C). 1999. pap. text 23.95 (*0-7914-4052-4*) State U NY Pr.

Language & Liberation: Feminism, Philosophy, & Language. Ed. by Christina Hendricks & Kelly Oliver. LC 98-27369. (SUNY Series in Contemporary Continental Philosophy). 384p. (C). 1999. text 71.50 (*0-7914-4051-6*) State U NY Pr.

An Asterisk (*) at the beginning of an entry indicates that the title is appearing for the first time.

Language & Liberation for RC Translators. Elis Carlstrom et al. 1997. pap. 3.00 (*1-885357-55-9*) Rational Isl.

Language & Limits: Resisting Reform in English Studies. Myron C. Tuman. LC 97-17224. (Series in Literacy, Culture, & Learning). 224p. (C). 1998. text 59.50 (*0-7914-3651-9*); pap. text 19.95 (*0-7914-3652-7*) State U NY Pr.

Language & Linguistic Origins in Bahrain: The Baharnah Dialect of Arabic. Mahdi A. Al-Tajir. (Library of Arabic Linguistics). 188p. 1983. 99.00 (*0-7103-0024-7*) Routledge.

Language & Linguistics. John Lyons. LC 80-42002. (Illus.). 366p. (C). 1981. pap. text 21.95 (*0-521-29775-3*) Cambridge U Pr.

Language & Linguistics, 4 vols., Set. Roy Harris. (Wellesley Ser.: Pt. III). 1600p. (C). (gr. 13). 1995. text, boxed set 655.00 (*0-415-12206-6*, C0440) Routledge.

Language & Linguistics: An Introduction. Andrew Radford et al. LC 98-44358. (Illus.). 368p. (C). 1999. text 59.95 (*0-521-47261-X*); pap. text 22.95 (*0-521-47854-5*) Cambridge U Pr.

Language & Literacy. Robert S. Pehrsson. 228p. (C). 1996. pap. text, per. 28.95 (*0-7872-2740-4*, 41274001) Kendall-Hunt.

Language & Literacy: Studying Discourse in Communities & Classrooms. Eleanor Kutz. LC 96-39569. (Orig.). 1997. pap. text 29.00 (*0-86709-386-2*, 0386, Pub. by Boynton Cook Pubs) Heinemann.

Language & Literacy: The Sociolinguistics of Reading & Writing. Michael Stubbs. (Education Bks.). 1980. pap. 13.95 (*0-7100-0499-0*, Routledge Thoemms) Routledge.

***Language & Literacy Development in Children Who Are Deaf.** 2nd ed. Barbara R. Schirmer. LC 99-49357. 278p. 2000. 57.00 (*0-205-31493-7*) Allyn.

Language & Literacy in Early Childhood Education. Ed. by Benard Spodek & Olivia N. Saracho. (Yearbook in Early Childhood Education Ser.: Vol. 4). 224p. (C). 1993. text 46.00 (*0-8077-3280-X*); pap. text 22.95 (*0-8077-3279-6*) Tchrs Coll.

Language & Literacy in Social Practice. Ed. by Janet Maybin. LC 93-29932. 264p. 1993. 74.95 (*1-85359-216-1*, Pub. by Multilingual Matters); pap. 29.95 (*1-85359-215-3*, Pub. by Multilingual Matters) Taylor & Francis.

Language & Literacy in the Early Years, Second Edition. 2nd ed. Marian R. Whitehead. LC 97-221323. (One-Off Ser.). (Illus.). 208p. 1997. pap., teacher ed. (*1-85396-341-0*) Corwin Pr.

Language & Literacy in Workplace Education. Giselle Mawer & Lee Fletcher. LC 98-35999. (Language in Social Life Ser.). 1999. write for info. (*0-582-25764-6*) Longman.

Language & Literacy in Workplace Education. Giseller Mawer. LC 98-35999. 336p. 1999. pap. text 29.68 (*0-582-25765-4*) Addison-Wesley.

Language & Literacy Learning in the Early Years: An Integrated Approach. Susan B. Neuman & Kathleen A. Roskos. (Illus.). 320p. (C). 1993. pap. text 46.50 (*0-03-076846-2*, Pub. by Harcourt Coll Pubs) Harcourt.

Language & Literary Theory. Ed. by L. Dolezel et al. (Papers in Slavic Philology: No. 5). vii, 643 p. 1984. pap. 15.00 (*0-930042-59-X*) Mich Slavic Pubns.

Language & Literature see Comprehensive Dissertation Index 1861-1972

Language & Literature see Comprehensive Dissertation Index: Ten Year Cumulation, 1973-1982

Language & Literature see Comprehensive Dissertation Index: Five-Year Cumulation, 1983-1987

Language & Literature: A Reader in Stylistics. Ed. by Ronald A. Carter. (Aspects of English Ser.). 256p. (C). 1982. pap. text 16.95 (*0-04-407017-9*) Routledge.

Language & Literature in the African American Imagination, 154. Ed. by Carol Aisha Blackshire-Belay. LC 92-12509. (Contributions in Afro-American & African Studies: No. 154). 224p. 1992. 55.00 (*0-313-27826-1*, BGG/, Greenwood Pr) Greenwood.

Language & Living Things: Uniformities in Folk Classification & Naming. Cecil H. Brown. LC 83-3238. 322p. reprint ed. pap. 99.90 (*0-8357-7942-4*, 205701500002) Bks Demand.

***Language & Logic.** 225p. (C). 1999. per. 61.95 (*0-7872-6243-9*, 41624301) Kendall-Hunt.

Language & Logic: A Speculative & Condition- Theoretic Study. Johan Van der Auwera. LC 84-24201. (Pragmatics & Beyond Companion Ser.: No. 2). xiv, 256p. 1985. 74.00 (*90-272-5002-2*) J Benjamins Pubng Co.

Language & Logic in the Post Medieval Period. E. J. Ashworth. LC 74-76478. (Synthese Historical Library: No. 12). 319p. 1974. text 176.50 (*90-277-0464-3*) Kluwer Academic.

Language & Logic of Educational Policy. 2nd ed. Dent M Rhodes & Rod Riegle. 124p. (C). 1990. pap. 30.60 (*0-536-57695-5*) Pearson Custom.

Language & Logic of Philosophy. Hubert G. Alexander. 372p. (C). 1988. reprint ed. pap. text 31.00 (*0-8191-6966-8*) U Pr of Amer.

Language & Logic of the Bible: The Earlier Middle Ages. G. R. Evans. 219p. (C). 1991. pap. text 19.95 (*0-521-42393-7*) Cambridge U Pr.

Language & Logos in Boswell's Life of Johnson. William C. Dowling. LC 80-8545. 206p. reprint ed. pap. 63.90 (*0-8357-6928-3*, 203798700009) Bks Demand.

Language & Love: Introduction to Augustine's Religious Thought Through the Confessions Story. William Mallard. LC 93-9070. 1994. 40.00 (*0-271-01037-1*); pap. 17.95 (*0-271-01038-X*) Pa St U Pr.

Language & Masculinity. Sally Johnson. 256p. 1996. pap. 26.95 (*0-631-19768-0*) Blackwell Pubs.

Language & Materialism: Developments in Semiology & the Theory of the Subject. Rosalind Coward & John A. Ellis. 1977. pap. 13.95 (*0-7100-8627-X*, Routledge Thoemms) Routledge.

Language & Maturation. Paula Menyuk. 1981. pap. text 12.00 (*0-262-63075-3*) MIT Pr.

Language & Meaning. Robert C. O'Hara. 224p. (C). 1993. per. 31.95 (*0-8403-8600-1*) Kendall-Hunt.

Language & Meaning: Word Study in Montaigne's "Essais" Ed. by Dikka Berven. LC 94-41683. (Montaigne Ser.: Vol. 4). (Illus.). 344p. 1995. 70.00 (*0-8153-1842-1*) Garland.

Language & Meaning in Cognitive Science: Cognitive Issues & Semantic Theory see Artificial Intelligence & Cognitive Science: Conceptual Issues

Language & Meaning in the Renaissance. Richard Waswo. LC 86-22492. 330p. 1987. reprint ed. pap. 102.30 (*0-608-07529-9*, 206774500009) Bks Demand.

Language & Metre: Resolution, Porson's Bridge, & Their Prosodic Basis. Andrew M. Devine & Laurence D. Stephens. LC 84-1395. (American Philological Association, American Classical Studies). 147p. 1984. pap. 15.95 (*0-89130-735-4*, 40 04 12) OUP.

Language & Metre of Chaucer. Bernhard Brink. Tr. by M. Bentinck Smith. LC 69-13838. 280p. 1970. reprint ed. lib. bdg. 65.00 (*0-8371-1927-8*, BRLM, Greenwood Pr) Greenwood.

Language & Metre of Chaucer. Bernhard A. Brink. (BCL1-PR English Literature Ser.). 280p. 1992. reprint ed. lib. bdg. 79.00 (*0-7812-7170-3*) Rprt Serv.

Language & Mind. Stephen Crain & Diane Lillo-Martin. LC 98-34401. (Blackwell Textbooks in Linguistics). 1999. 69.95 (*0-631-19535-1*); pap. 34.95 (*0-631-19536-X*) Blackwell Pubs.

Language & Mind. Steven Pinker. (Science Masters Ser.). 176p. 2000. pap. write for info. (*0-465-07270-4*) Basic.

Language & Mind. enl. ed. Noam Chomsky. 194p. (C). 1972. pap. text 31.00 (*0-15-549257-8*) Harcourt Coll Pubs.

Language & Money in Rabelais. Gerard P. Lavatori. (Renaissance & Baroque Studies & Texts: Vol. 18). 194p. (C). 1996. text 46.95 (*0-8204-2734-9*) P Lang Pubng.

***Language & Motor Speech Disorder in Adults** 2nd ed. Harvey Halpern. LC 99-32912. 1999. write for info. (*0-89079-826-5*) PRO-ED.

Language & Motor Speech Disorders in Adults. Harvey Halpern. LC 86-569. (PRO-ED Studies in Communicative Disorders). (Illus.). 88p. (Orig.). 1986. pap. text 9.00 (*0-89079-089-2*, 1379) PRO-ED.

Language & Myth. Ernst Cassirer. Tr. by Susanne K. Langer. 103p. 1953. pap. 4.95 (*0-486-20051-5*) Dover.

Language & Narration in Celine's Writings: The Challenge of Disorder. Ian Noble. LC 86-7188. 196p. (C). 1987. text 55.00 (*0-391-03402-2*) Humanities.

***Language & National Security for the 21st Century: The Role of Title VI-Fulbright-Hays in Supporting National Language Capacity.** Richard D. Brecht & William P. Rivers. LC 99-462082. (C). 2000. text 30.00 (*1-880671-06-9*) NFLC Pubns.

***Language & Nationalism in Europe.** Ed. by Stephen Barbour & Cathie Carmichael. (Illus.). 400p. 2000. text 70.00 (*0-19-823671-9*) OUP.

Language & Nationhood: The Canadian Experience. Ronald Wardbaugh. 270p. 1983. pap. 14.95 (*0-919573-17-7*, Pub. by New Star Bks) Genl Dist Srvs.

Language & Natural Theology. Bowman L. Clarke. (Janua Linguarum, Ser. Minor: No. 47). (Orig.). 1966. pap. text 34.65 (*90-279-0580-0*) Mouton.

Language & Negation: The Two-Level Structure That Prevents Paradox. Daniel A. Cowan. LC 76-21954. 112p. 1980. pap. 6.00 (*0-915878-03-8*) Joseph Pub Co.

Language & Other Abstract Objects. Jerrold J. Katz. LC 80-19156. 262p. 1981. 50.00 (*0-8476-6912-2*) Rowman.

Language & Peace. Christina Schaffner & Anita Wenden. LC 94-42384. (Illus.). 280p. 1995. text 77.95 (*1-85521-483-0*, Pub. by Dartmth Pub) Ashgate Pub Co.

***Language & Peace.** Ed. by Christina Schffner & Anita L. Wenden. (War & Society Ser.). 258p. 1999. pap. text 24.00 (*90-5702-480-2*, Harwood Acad Pubs) Gordon & Breach.

Language & Perception. George A. Miller & Philip N. Johnson-Laird. 773p. 1987. pap. 17.95 (*0-674-50948-X*) Belknap Pr.

Language & Philosophy. Justus Hartnack. 140p. 1972. pap. text 53.85 (*90-279-2361-2*) Mouton.

Language & Philosophy. Mikel Dufrenne. Tr. by Henry B. Veatch. LC 68-55630. (Illus.). 106p. 1968. reprint ed. lib. bdg. 49.50 (*0-8371-0396-7*, DULP, Greenwood Pr) Greenwood.

Language & Philosophy: Studies in Method. Max Black. LC 81-6206. (Illus.). 264p. 1981. reprint ed. lib. bdg. 45.00 (*0-313-23082-X*, BLLP, Greenwood Pr) Greenwood.

***Language & Piety in Middle English Romance.** Roger Dalrymple. 282p. 2000. 75.00 (*0-85991-598-0*) Boydell & Brewer.

Language & Political Understanding: The Politics of Discursive Practices. Michael J. Shapiro. LC 81-3069. 263p. reprint ed. pap. 81.60 (*0-8357-8203-4*, 203388800087) Bks Demand.

Language & Politics. Noam Chomsky. Ed. by Carlos P. Otero. 779p. 1998. 57.99 (*0-921689-35-7*, Pub. by Black Rose); pap. 28.99 (*0-921689-34-9*, Pub. by Black Rose) Consort Bk Sales.

Language & Politics. Ed. by Michael Shapiro. (Readings in Social & Political Theory Ser.). 304p. (C). 1984. pap. text 18.50 (*0-8147-7839-9*) NYU Pr.

Language & Politics in Pakistan. Tariq Rahman. LC 97-930020. (Illus.). 340p. 1997. text 32.00 (*0-19-577692-5*) OUP.

Language & Politics in the United States & Canada: Myths & Realities. Ed. by Thomas K. Ricento & Barbara Burnaby. LC 97-38464. 256p. 1998. 79.95 (*0-8058-2838-9*); pap. 39.95 (*0-8058-2839-7*) L Erlbaum Assocs.

Language & Politics of Exclusion: Other in Discourse. Ed. by Stephen H. Riggins. LC 97-4595. (Communication & Human Values Ser.). 336p. (C). 1997. 55.00 (*0-7619-0728-9*, 07289); pap. 24.95 (*0-7619-0729-7*, 07297) Sage.

Language & Power Lewis A. Froman, Jr. LC 98-49227. 1998. write for info. (*1-57392-399-0*) Prometheus Bks.

Language & Power. Plvan. 2000. pap. 36.56 (*0-07-235048-2*) McGraw.

Language & Power. Ed. by Cheris Kramarae et al. LC 84-3412. 320p. 1984. reprint ed. pap. 99.20 (*0-608-01163-0*, 205946300001) Bks Demand.

Language & Power, Bks. III, IV & V. Creel Froman. LC 92-23768. 260p. (C). 1993. text 60.00 (*0-391-03764-1*) Humanities.

Language & Power, Bks. VI & VII. Creel Froman. LC 91-23768. 352p. (C). 1996. text 60.00 (*0-391-03929-6*) Humanities.

Language & Power, Set, Bks. VIII & IX. Creel Froman. LC 91-23768. 340p. (C). 1997. pap. 60.00 (*0-391-03949-0*) Humanities.

Language & Power: Exploring Indonesian Political Culture. Benedict R. Anderson. Ed. by David Laitin. LC 90-55126. (Wilder House Series in Politics, History, & Culture). (Illus.). 352p. 1990. 49.95 (*0-8014-2354-6*); pap. text 18.95 (*0-8014-9758-2*) Cornell U Pr.

Language & Power in the Creation of the U. S. S. R., 1917-1953. Michael G. Smith. LC 98-37960. (Contributions to the Sociology of Language Ser.). 1998. 114.85 (*3-11-016197-4*) De Gruyter.

Language & Prehistory. Vitaly Shevoroshkin. 1994. write for info. (*0-8493-8875-9*) CRC Pr.

Language & Problems of Knowledge: The Managua Lectures. Noam Chomsky. 215p. 1987. pap. text 13.50 (*0-262-53070-8*) MIT Pr.

Language & Problems of Knowledge: The Managua Lectures. Noam Chomsky. 215p. 1987. 27.00 (*0-262-03133-7*) MIT Pr.

Language & Production: A Critique of the Paradigms. Gyorgy Markus. 208p. 1986. text 137.50 (*90-277-2169-6*) Kluwer Academic.

Language & Prosody of the Russian Folk Epic. Roy G. Jones. (Slavistic Printings & Reprintings Ser.: No. 275). (Illus.). 105p. 1972. text 32.30 (*90-279-2330-2*) Mouton.

Language & Psychiatry. Harley C. Shands & James D. Meltzer. LC 73-77388. (Janua Linguarum, Ser. Minor: No. 165). 85p. 1973. pap. text 66.95 (*90-279-2483-X*) Mouton.

Language & Psychology: Historical Aspects of Psycholinguistics. Arthur L. Blumenthal. LC 80-12611. 262p. 1980. reprint ed. 69.50 (*0-89874-167-X*) Elliots Bks.

Language & Reading Comprehension. Ed. by Stanley F. Wanat. LC 77-80380. (Linguistics & Reading Ser.: No. 2). 83p. reprint ed. pap. 30.00 (*0-8357-3361-0*, 203959900013) Bks Demand.

Language & Reading Disabilities. Catts & Kamhi. LC 98-34364. 328p. 1998. pap. text 46.00 (*0-205-27088-3*) Allyn.

Language & Reading Success Andrew Biemiller. LC 99-12368. (From Reading Research to Practice Ser.). 1999. 9.95 (*1-57129-068-0*) Brookline Bks.

***Language & Reading Success: Methods & Materials That Work.** unabridged ed. Andrew Biemiller et al. LC 98-21014. (From Reading Research to Practice Ser.). 80p. 1999. pap. 9.95 (*1-57129-069-9*) Brookline Bks.

Language & Reality: An Introduction to Indian Philosophical Studies. Bimal K. Matilal. 450p. 1986. 31.00 (*0-317-53529-3*, Pub. by Motilal Bnarsidass) S Asia.

***Language & Reality: An Introduction to the Philosophy of Language.** 2nd ed. Michael Devitt & Kim Sterelny. LC 98-47178. 1999. 60.00 (*0-262-04173-1*) MIT Pr.

Language & Reality: An Introduction to the Philosophy of Language. 2nd ed. Michael Devitt & Kim Sterelny. LC 98-47178. (Illus.). 325p. 1999. pap. text 30.00 (*0-262-54099-1*, Bradford Bks) MIT Pr.

Language & Reality: The Philosophy of Language & the Principles of Symbolism. Wilbur M. Urban. LC 75-179543. (Select Bibliographies Reprint Ser.). 1980. reprint ed. 37.95 (*0-8369-6672-4*) Ayer.

Language & Reality in Swift's a Tale of a Tub. Frederik N. Smith. LC 79-15355. (Illus.). 182p. reprint ed. pap. 56.50 (*0-608-09885-X*, 206985100006) Bks Demand.

Language & Reason. Bruce B. Wavell. (Approaches to Semiotics Ser.: No. 74). xxii, 353p. 1986. lib. bdg. 134.65 (*0-89925-092-0*) Mouton.

Language & Reason: A Study of Habermas's Pragmatics. Maeve Cooke. (Studies in Contemporary German Social Thought). (Illus.). 232p. 1997. reprint ed. pap. text 15.00 (*0-262-53145-3*) MIT Pr.

Language & Reflection: An Integrated Approach to Teaching English. Anne R. Gere. LC 91-24608. 320p. 1991. pap. text 59.00 (*0-02-341450-2*, Macmillan Coll) P-H.

Language & Relation: That There Is Language. Christopher Fynsk. LC 96-19903. 1996. write for info. (*0-8047-2713-9*); pap. write for info. (*0-8047-2714-7*) Stanford U Pr.

Language & Relationship in Wordsworth's Writing: Elective Affinities (Studies in Eighteenth- & Nineteenth-Century Literature) Michael Baron. LC 94-20478. (Studies in Eighteenth & Nineteenth Century Literature). 296p. (C). 1995. 85.00 (*0-582-06195-4*, 77031) Longman.

Language & Release: Sarvajnatman's Pancaprakriya. Ivan Kocmarek. xiv, 147p. 1986. 24.00 (*81-208-0004-4*, Pub. by Motilal Bnarsidass) S Asia.

Language & Representation in Information Retrieval. D. C. Blair. xiv,336p. 1990. 135.00 (*0-444-88437-8*) Elsevier.

Language & Rules. Jon Wheatley. LC 70-95011. (Janua Linguarum, Ser. Minor: No. 80). (Orig.). 1970. pap. text 10.80 (*3-10-800275-9*) Mouton.

Language & Schizophrenia. Janusz Wrobel. LC 89-38326. (Linguistic & Literary Studies in Eastern Europe: No. 33). viii, 132p. 1989. 38.00 (*90-272-1539-1*) J Benjamins Pubng Co.

Language & Schooling in the United States. 1994. lib. bdg. 250.00 (*0-8490-8585-3*) Gordon Pr.

Language & Scottish Literature: Teaching Scottish Language & Literature. John Corbett. 288p. 1997. pap. 25.00 (*0-7486-0826-5*, Pub. by Edinburgh U Pr) Col U Pr.

Language & Self-Transformation: A Study of the Christian Conversion Narrative. Peter G. Stromberg. LC 92-34071. (Publications of the Society for Psychological Anthropology). 164p. (C). 1993. text 59.95 (*0-521-44077-7*) Cambridge U Pr.

Language & Sentiment of Flowers. James McCabe. 1999. 14.95 (*1-55709-384-9*, Pub. by Applewood) Consort Bk Sales.

Language & Sexual Difference: Feminist Writing in France. Susan Sellers. LC 91-9078. 216p. 1992. pap. 16.95 (*0-312-06162-5*); text 49.95 (*0-312-06161-7*) St Martin.

Language & Silence: Essays on Language, Literature, & the Inhuman. George Steiner. LC 97-32450. 444p. 1998. pap. 18.00 (*0-300-07471-9*) Yale U Pr.

Language & Social Change in Java: Linguistic Reflexes of Modernization in Traditional Royal Polity. J. Joseph Errington. LC 84-19033. (Monographs in International Studies, Southeast Asia Ser.: No. 65). 210p. 1985. pap. text 25.00 (*0-89680-120-9*) Ohio U Pr.

Language & Social Identity. 2nd ed. Ed. by John J. Gumperz. LC 82-4331. (Studies in Interactional Sociolinguistics: No. 2). 288p. 1983. pap. text 21.95 (*0-521-28897-5*) Cambridge U Pr.

Language & Social Interaction at the Century's Turn: A Special Double Issue of Research on Language & Social Interaction. Ed. by Karen Tracy. 216p. 1999. pap. 40.00 (*0-8058-9807-7*) L Erlbaum Assocs.

Language & Social Reality: The Case of Telling the Convict Code. D. L. Wieder. (Current Continental Research Ser.). 236p. 1988. reprint ed. pap. 27.00 (*0-8191-6464-X*) U Pr of Amer.

Language & Social Relationship in Brazilian Portuguese: The Pragmatics of Politeness. Dale A. Koike. LC 91-28319. (Illus.). 188p. (C). 1992. text 32.50 (*0-292-76532-0*) U of Tex Pr.

Language & Social Situations. Joseph P. Forgas. (Social Psychology Ser.). (Illus.). 250p. 1985. 98.95 (*0-387-96090-2*) Spr-Verlag.

Language & Society. Ed. by William C. McCormack & Stephen A. Wurm. (World Anthropology Ser.). 771p. 1979. text 103.85 (*90-279-7800-X*) Mouton.

Language & Society. 2nd rev. ed. William Downes. LC 97-40832. (Approaches to Linguistics Ser.). (Illus.). 350p. (C). 1998. 64.95 (*0-521-45046-2*); pap. 24.95 (*0-521-45663-0*) Cambridge U Pr.

Language & Society: Steps Towards an Integrated Theory. J. K. Lele & R. Singh. LC 88-24107. (Monographs & Theoretical Studies in Sociology & Anthropology in Honour of Nels Anderson: No. 27). xix, 146p. (Orig.). 1989. pap. 49.00 (*90-04-08789-3*) Brill Academic Pubs.

Language & Society in Biblical Times. Ettien Koffi. 254p. 1995. 64.95 (*1-57309-009-3*); pap. 44.95 (*1-57309-008-5*) Intl Scholars.

Language & Society in Early Modern England: Selected Essays, 1982-1994. Vivian Salmon. (Studies in the History of the Language Sciences: Vol. 77). viii, 276p. 1996. lib. bdg. 79.00 (*1-55619-613-X*) J Benjamins Pubng Co.

Language & Society in la Vida de Lazarillo de Tormes. Harry Sieber. LC 78-8425. 128p. reprint ed. pap. 39.70 (*0-608-06144-1*, 206647700008) Bks Demand.

Language & Society in Post-Communist Europe Selected Papers from the Fifth World Congress of Central & East European Studies, Warsaw, 1995. J. Allan Dunn. LC 98-54304. 1999. text 59.95 (*0-312-22232-7*) St Martin.

Language & Society in South Asia. Michael C. Shapiro & Harold F. Schiffman. 1981. 34.00 (*0-8364-0756-3*) S Asia.

Language & Society in the Middle East & North Africa. Ed. by Yasir Suleiman. 288p. 1998. 75.00 (*0-7007-1078-7*, Pub. by Curzon Pr Ltd) Paul & Co Pubs.

Language & Solitude: Wittgenstein, Malinowski, & the Habsburg Dilemma. Ernest Gellner. LC 97-50568. 248p. (C). 1998. 54.95 (*0-521-63002-9*); pap. 17.95 (*0-521-63997-2*) Cambridge U Pr.

Language & Space. Ed. by Paul Bloom et al. LC 95-36427. (Language, Speech & Communication Ser.). (Illus.). 672p. 1996. 55.00 (*0-262-02403-9*, Bradford Bks) MIT Pr.

Language & Space. Paul Bloom et al. (Language, Speech & Communication Ser.). 616p. 1999. reprint ed. pap. 29.50 (*0-262-52266-7*, Bradford Bks) MIT Pr.

***Language & Space: The Poststructuralist Turn in the Philosophy of Culture.** Ewa Rewers. (Literary & Cultural Theory Ser.). 169p. 1999. pap. 35.95 (*3-631-34444-9*) P Lang Pubng.

L

An Asterisk (*) at the beginning of an entry indicates that the title is appearing for the first time.

***Language & Space: The Poststructuralist Turn in the Philosophy of Culture.** Ewa Rewers. LC 99-46407. (Literary & Cultural Theory Ser.). 169p. (C). 1999. pap. 35.95 (*0-8204-4304-2*) P Lang Pubng.

Language & Species. Derek Bickerton. LC 90-35922. (Illus.). 310p. 1990. 29.95 (*0-226-04610-9*) U Ch Pr.

Language & Species. Derek Bickerton. LC 90-35922. (Illus.). 310p. 1992. pap. 17.95 (*0-226-04611-7*) U Ch Pr.

Language & Speech: Proceedings of the Fifth Convention of the Academia Eurasiana Neurochirurgica, Budapest, September 19-12, 1990. Ed. by E. Pasztor et al. (Acta Neurochirugica - Supplementum Ser.: No. 56). (Illus.). 120p. 1993. 119.95 (*0-387-82386-7*) Spr-Verlag.

Language & Stage in Medieval & Renaissance England. Janette Dillon. LC 97-8795. 288p. (C). 1998. text 59.95 (*0-521-59334-4*) Cambridge U Pr.

Language & Strategy: A Synopitcal Analysis of Key Terms in the Strategic Doctrines of the Nuclear Powers. Stephan Kux. (European University Studies: Political Science: Ser. 31, Vol. 164). 592p. 1990. pap. 79.00 (*3-261-04263-X*) P Lang Pubng.

Language & Structure in Beckett's Plays: With a Beckett Synopsis. Clive Hart & C. George Sandulescu. (Princess Grace Irish Library Lecture: Vol. 2). 36p. 1986. pap. 8.95 (*0-86140-263-4*, Pub. by Smyth) Dufour.

Language & Structure in North America. Ed. by Richard Kostelanetz. (Illus.). 1978. reprint ed. pap. 4.00 (*0-932360-19-X*) Archae Edns.

Language & Structure with Workbook. 2nd ed. Finegan. (C). 1994. 62.50 (*0-15-502966-5*) Harcourt.

Language & Study Skills for Learners of English. Marjorie Romanoff. 144p. (C). 1991. pap. text 23.20 (*0-13-847229-7*, 640306) P-H.

Language & Style in "The Inheritors" David L. Hoover. LC 98-39989. 272p. 1998. 41.00 (*0-7618-1263-6*) U Pr of Amer.

Language & Style of the Gospel of Mark: An Edition of C. H. Turner's "Notes on Marcan Usage" Together with Other Comparable Studies. J. K. Elliott. LC 93-35404. (Supplements to Novum Testamentum Ser.: Vol. 71). xix, 254p. 1993. 110.50 (*90-04-09767-8*) Brill Academic Pubs.

Language & Style of the Vedic Rsis. Tatyana J. Elizarenkova. Ed. by Wendy Doniger. LC 92-40318. (SUNY Series in Hindu Studies). 331p. (C). 1994. pap. text 24.95 (*0-7914-1668-2*) State U NY Pr.

Language & Style of the Vedic Rsis. Tatyana J. Elizarenkova. Ed. by Wendy Doniger. LC 92-40318. (SUNY Series in Hindu Studies). 331p. (C). 1994. text 74.50 (*0-7914-1667-4*) State U NY Pr.

Language & Symbolic Power. Pierre Bourdieu. Ed. by John B. Thompson. Tr. by Gino Raymond & Mathew Adamson. 302p. (C). 1991. 39.95 (*0-674-51040-2*) HUP.

Language & Symbolic Power. Pierre Bourdieu. Ed. by John B. Thompson. Tr. by Mathew Adamson. 302p. (C). 1993. pap. 25.50 (*0-674-51041-0*) HUP.

Language & Technique of the Film. Gianfranco Bettetini. (Approaches to Semiotics Ser.: No. 28). 1973. text 43.10 (*90-279-2412-0*) Mouton.

Language & Text. Ed. by R. N. Srivastava et al. (C). 1992. 42.50 (*81-85163-26-X*, Pub. by Manohar) S Asia.

Language & Text: Studies in Honour of Ashok R. Kelkar. Ed. by R. N. Srivastava et al. x, 310p. 1992. 37.00 (*0-685-62649-0*, Pub. by Kalinga) Nataraj Bks.

Language & Texts: The Nature of Linguistic Evidence. Ed. by Herbert H. Paper. LC 75-36885. 204p. 1975. pap. 10.00 (*0-89824-425-0*) Trillium Pr.

Language & the Brain. Loraine Obler & Kris Gjerlow. (Cambridge Approaches to Linguistics Ser.). (Illus.). 224p. (C). 1998. pap. text 17.95 (*0-521-46641-5*) Cambridge U Pr.

Language & the Brain. Loraine Obler & Kris Gjerlow. LC 97-47554. (Cambridge Approaches to Linguistics Ser.). (Illus.). 224p. (C). 1999. text 54.95 (*0-521-46095-6*) Cambridge U Pr.

***Language & the Brain: Representation & Processing.** Yosef Grodzinsky. (Illus.). 386p. 2000. 75.00 (*0-12-304260-7*) Acad Pr.

Language & the Cognitive Construal of the World. Ed. by John R. Taylor & Robert E. MacLaury. (Trends in Linguistics, Studies & Monographs: No. 82). xiii, 407p. (C). 1995. lib. bdg. 136.95 (*3-11-014301-1*) Mouton.

Language & the Comedia: Theory & Practice. Catherine Larson. LC 89-46406. 1991. 35.00 (*0-8387-5180-6*) Bucknell U Pr.

Language & the Construction of Class Identities: Report from the 1989 Conference on Continuity & Discontinuity in the Democratisation Process. Bo Strath. 564p. (Orig.). 1990. pap. 87.50 (*91-971234-1-2*) Coronet Bks.

Language & the Developing Child. Katrina de Hirsch. 1984. pap. write for info. (*0-89214-001-1*) Intl Dyslexia.

Language & the Document Revolution. 2nd ed. Carol M. Baldwin. (Illus.). 172p. 1999. pap. 25.00 (*0-9666358-2-5*) Lamp Lighter.

Language & the Elderly: A Clinical Perspective. Jane Maxim & Karen Bryan. LC 94-185437. (Illus.). 298p. (Orig.). (C). 1994. pap. text 59.95 (*1-56593-254-4*, 0048) Thomson Learn.

Language & the English Curriculum. John Keen. (English, Language & Education Ser.). 160p. 1992. pap. 33.95 (*0-335-09673-5*) OpUniv Pr.

Language & "the Feminine" in Nietzsche & Heidegger. Jean Graybeal. LC 89-46335. 192p. 1990. 26.95 (*0-253-32628-1*) Ind U Pr.

Language & the History of Thought. Ed. by Nancy Steurer. LC 94-8772. (Library ofThe History of Ideas: Vol. XIII). 272p. (C). 1995. 75.00 (*1-878822-29-2*) Univ Rochester Pr.

Language & the Law. Ed. by John Gibbons. LC 93-5621. (Language in Social Life Ser.). 1999. text. write for info. (*0-582-22976-6*, Pub. by Addison-Wesley) Longman.

Language & the Law: The Semantics of Forensic English. Frederick A. Philbrick. LC 93-78310. ix, 254p. 1993. reprint ed. 42.00 (*0-89941-841-4*, 307860) W S Hein.

***Language & the Lexicon.** David Singleton. (An Arnold Publication). 224p. 2000. pap. 19.95 (*0-340-73174-5*, Pub. by E A); text 65.00 (*0-340-73173-7*, Pub. by E A) OUP.

Language & the Modern State: The Reform of Written Japanese. Nanette Twine. (Nissan Institute/Routledge Japanese Studies Ser.). (Illus.). 304p. (C). (gr. 13). 1991. text 69.95 (*0-415-00990-1*, A5137) Routledge.

Language & the Nation: The Language Question in Sub-Saharan Africa. Ayo Bamgbose. 160p. 1992. pap. 27.50 (*0-7486-0306-9*, Pub. by Edinburgh U Pr) Col U Pr.

Language & the Nuclear Arms Debate. Chilton. (C). 1985. text. write for info. (*0-86187-524-9*) St Martin.

Language & the Phenomenological Reductions of E. Husserl. S. Cunningham. (Phaenomenologica Ser.: No. 70). 112p. 1976. pap. text 66.50 (*90-247-1823-6*, Pub. by M Nijhoff) Kluwer Academic.

Language & the Poet: Verbal Artistry in Frost, Stevens, & Moore. Marie Borroff. LC 78-14567. (Illus.). 1979. 18.00 (*0-226-06651-7*) U Ch Pr.

Language & the Sexes. Francine Frank & Frank Anshen. LC 83-24141. 130p. (C). 1985. pap. text 12.95 (*0-87395-882-9*) State U NY Pr.

Language & the Social Construction of Identity in Creole Situations. Ed. & Contrib. by Marcyliena Morgan. (Special Publications: Vol. 8). 148p. (Orig.). (C). 1994. pap. text 15.95 (*0-934934-40-1*) CAAS Pubns.

Language & the State: Revitalization & Revival in Israel & Eire. LC 96-39544. 1997. 59.00 (*1-85359-390-7*, Pub. by Multilingual Matters) Taylor & Francis.

Language & the Study of Language. William D. Whitney. (Notable American Authors Ser.). 1999. reprint ed. lib. bdg. 125.00 (*0-7812-9963-2*) Rprt Serv.

Language & the Study of Language. 6th ed. William D. Whitney. LC 78-137305. reprint ed. 49.50 (*0-404-06942-8*) AMS Pr.

Language & the Study of Language: Twelve Lectures on the Principles of Linguistic Science. William D. Whitney. 496p. reprint ed. lib. bdg. 76.70 (*3-487-04754-3*) G Olms Pubs.

Language & the Unconscious: Jacques Lacan's Hermeneutics of Psychoanalysis. Hermann Lang. Tr. by Thomas Brockelman. LC 96-50099. (Contemporary Philosophy & the Human Sciences Ser.). 224p. (C). 1997. text 49.95 (*0-391-04035-9*) Humanities.

Language & Theme: Essays on African Literature. Ed. by Emmanuel Obiechina. LC 90-34189. 384p. (Orig.). (C). 1990. 26.95 (*0-88258-045-0*); pap. 14.95 (*0-88258-064-7*) Howard U Pr.

Language & Theology. 2nd ed. Gordon H. Clark. Ed. & Intro. by John W. Robbins. 175p. 1993. pap. 9.95 (*0-940931-90-7*) Trinity Found.

Language & Thinking for Young Children. Ruth Beechick & Jeannie Nelson. (J). 1987. pap. 7.99 (*0-88062-152-4*) Mott Media.

Language & Thinking in School: A Whole Language Curriculum. 3rd ed. Kenneth S. Goodman et al. LC 86-28601. 418p. 1987. boxed set 27.95 (*0-913461-81-4*, 14) R Owen Pubs.

Language & Thought. Noam Chomsky. (Anshen Transdisciplinary Lectureships in Art, Science, & the Philosophy of Culture Ser.). 96p. 1995. pap. 9.95 (*1-55921-076-1*) Moyer Bell.

Language & Thought. John L. Pollock. LC 82-414. 312p. 1982. reprint ed. pap. 96.80 (*0-7837-9423-1*, 206016400004) Bks Demand.

***Language & Thought: A Rational Enquiry into Their Nature & Relationship.** Amorey Gethin. 96p. 1999. pap. 17.95 (*1-871516-72-2*, Pub. by Intellect) Cromland.

Language & Thought: Anshen Transdisciplinary Lectureships in Art, Science, & the Philosophy of Culture Monograph Ser., No. 3. Noam Chomsky. LC 93-36148. (Anshen Transdisciplinary Lectureships in Art, Science, & the Philosophy of Culture Ser.). 96p. 1995. 14.95 (*1-55921-074-5*) Moyer Bell.

Language & Thought: German Approaches to Analytical Philosophy in the 19th Centuries. Hermann J. Cloeren. (Foundations of Communication & Cognition Ser.). 267p. (C). 1988. lib. bdg. 95.40 (*3-11-011301-5*) De Gruyter.

Language & Thought: Interdisciplinary Themes. Ed. by Peter Carruthers & Jill Boucher. LC 97-35248. (Illus.). 338p. (C). 1998. text 59.95 (*0-521-63108-4*); pap. text 19.95 (*0-521-63758-9*) Cambridge U Pr.

Language & Thought in Early Greek Philosophy. Ed. by Kevin Robb. LC 97-129140. (Monist Library of Philosophy). 288p. 1983. 29.95 (*0-914417-01-0*); pap. 12.95 (*0-914417-05-3*) Hegeler Inst.

Language & Thought in Humans & Computers: Theory & Research in Psychology, Artificial Intelligence & Neural Science. Morton Wagman. LC 97-32997. 192p. 1998. 59.95 (*0-275-96179-6*, Praeger Pubs) Greenwood.

Language & Thought of the Child see Jean Piaget

Language & Time & Gertrude Stein. Carolyn F. Copeland. LC 75-16491. 191p. reprint ed. pap. 59.30 (*0-8357-8902-0*, 202593900047) Bks Demand.

Language & Traditions. Betty Colonomos & MJ Bienvenu. (Introduction to American Deaf Culture Ser.: Vol. 3). 54p. (C). 1993. pap. text 8.95 (*1-881133-02-8*, 404-W) Sign Media.

Language & Travel Guide to Mexico. Ila Warner. (Language & Travel Ser.). (Illus.). 320p. (Orig.). 1990. pap. 14.95 (*0-87052-622-7*) Hippocrene Bks.

Language & Understanding. Ed. by John Williams et al. (Illus.). 216p. 1994. pap. text 18.95 (*0-19-437191-3*) OUP.

Language & Uses of Rights: A Biopsy of American Jurisprudence in the Twentieth Century. Samuel J. M. Donnelly. LC 93-40757. 174p. (Orig.). (C). 1994. pap. text 24.50 (*0-8191-9405-0*) U Pr of Amer.

Language & Value, 3. Charles L. Todd & Russell T. Blackwell. LC 68-58919. 259p. 1970. 55.00 (*0-8371-1494-2*, TOL/, Greenwood Pr) Greenwood.

Language & World Creation in Poems & Other Texts. LC 96-52564. (Textual Explorations Ser.). 1997. 46.08 (*0-582-30199-8*) Longman.

Language & Writing. Peggy Burns & Julian Rowe. LC 94-45474. (Legacies Ser.). (Illus.). 48p. (J). (gr. 4-6). 1995. lib. bdg. 24.26 (*1-56847-244-7*) Raintree Steck-V.

Language & Writing: Applications of Linguistics to Rhetoric & Composition. Victor Raskin & Irwin H. Weiser. LC 86-17753. 304p. 1987. text 73.25 (*0-89391-405-3*) Ablx Pub.

Language & Writing in Ancient Egypt. David P. Silverman. LC 89-85821. (Illus.). 52p. (Orig.). (C). 1990. pap. text 7.95 (*0-911239-15-4*) Carnegie Mus.

Language Anxiety: From Theory & Research to Classroom Implications. Elaine Horwitz & Dolly J. Young. 224p. (C). 1990. pap. text 17.40 (*0-13-523465-4*) P-H.

Language Application. Ed. by Warren C. Born. 1976. pap. 10.95 (*0-915432-76-5*) NE Conf Teach Foreign.

Language Architectures & Programming Environments. T. Ichikawa & H. Tsubotani. (Series in Computer Science: No. 34). 300p. 1992. text 61.00 (*981-02-1012-4*) World Scientific Pub.

***Language Argument.** 9th ed. 88p. (C). 1998. pap. 12.00 (*0-321-02667-5*) Addison-Wesley.

Language, Art & Reality in D. H. Lawrence's St. Mawr: A Stylistic Study. Paul Poplawski. LC 96-14248. 284p. 1996. text 89.95 (*0-7734-8823-5*) E Mellen.

Language Arts see Ideas for Teaching Gifted Students

***Language Arts.** (Switched on Schoolhouse Ser.). (Illus.). (J). 2000. 61.95 (*0-7403-0224-8*) Alpha AZ.

Language Arts. Date not set. 4.95 (*1-55708-573-0*, MCJ800) McDonald Pub Co.

Language Arts. Sally Bogemnan & Danielle Egeling. 1991. 6.95 (*1-55708-364-9*, MCC904) McDonald Pub Co.

***Language Arts, Vol. 1.** Kathi Hudson. 80p. 1998. pap. text 10.95 (*0-590-00488-3*) Scholastic Inc.

Language Arts. Innovative Learning Staff. (The Rivers Curriculum Ser.). (gr. 9-13). 2000. pap. text 23.95 (*0-201-49371-3*) Addison-Wesley.

Language Arts. Shane Templeton. (C). 1991. pap. text, teacher ed. 2.76 (*0-395-57212-6*) HM.

Language Arts. 3rd ed. Karen D'Angelo Bromley. LC 97-27515. 528p. 1997. 77.00 (*0-205-26812-9*) P-H.

Language Arts. 3rd ed. Farris. 2000. 40.50 (*0-07-232221-7*) McGraw.

Language Arts. 3rd ed. Ed. by Charles Temple. (C). 1996. text. write for info. (*0-673-52213-X*) Addison-Wesley.

Language Arts: Activities. Shirley E. Myers. (Illus.). 144p. (J). 1997. pap., teacher ed. 14.95 (*1-57690-349-4*, TCM2349) Tchr Create Mat.

Language Arts: Content & Teaching Strategies. 4th ed. Gail E. Tompkins. LC 96-53398. 620p. 1997. 72.00 (*0-13-856907-X*, Merrill Coll) P-H.

***Language Arts: Grade 11, 11 vols.** (Illus.). (YA). (gr. 11). 2000. teacher ed., student ed., boxed set 63.90 (*1-58095-706-4*, LAN1115, Lifepac) Alpha AZ.

***Language Arts: Grade 12, 11 vols.** (Illus.). (YA). (gr. 12). 2000. teacher ed., student ed., boxed set 49.90 (*1-58095-709-9*, LAN1215, Lifepac) Alpha AZ.

Language Arts: (K-6) Essential Learning & Study Guide. Cecilia Kabisch. 156p. (C). 1995. pap. text, per. 17.95 (*0-7872-1919-3*) Kendall-Hunt.

Language Arts: Process, Product, & Assessment. 2nd ed. Pamela J. Farris. LC 95-83394. 448p. (C). 1996. text. write for info. (*0-697-24135-1*) Brown & Benchmark.

Language Arts: Teaching & Learning in the Elementary Schools. John M. Kean & Carl R. Personke. LC 75-38020. 450p. 1976. pap. text 18.50 (*0-312-46620-X*) St Martin.

Language Arts: Testbanks, 2 vols. Shane Templeton. (C). 1997. pap., teacher ed. 11.96 (*0-395-79657-1*) HM.

Language Arts Activites for Children. 4th ed. Norton & Norton et al. LC 98-33598. 432p. 1998. pap. text 37.00 (*0-13-913005-5*) P-H.

Language Arts Activities for the Classroom. 2nd ed. Iris M. Tiedt. LC 86-22289. 366p. 1987. 58.00 (*0-205-10478-9*, H04781) Allyn.

***Language Arts Activities for the Classroom.** 3rd ed. Pamela L. Tiedt et al. LC 00-42144. 2001. write for info. (*0-205-30863-5*) Allyn.

***Language Arts Activities Using the World Wide Web: Grade 4-6+** Debby Reum. Ed. by Marilyn Evans. (Teaching & Learning with the Computer Ser.: Vol. 1). 80p. 1999. pap., teacher ed. 16.95 (*1-55799-747-0*, 068) Evan-Moor Edu Pubs.

Language Arts & Environmental Awareness: 100+ Integrated Books & Activities for Children. Ed. by Patricia L. Roberts. LC 97-32638. 295p. 1998. lib. bdg. 35.00 (*0-208-02427-1*, Linnet Bks) Shoe String.

Language Arts & More: Grade 1. ECS Learning Systems Staff. (ECS Home Study Bk.). (Illus.). 64p. (Orig.). (J). 1995. pap., wbk. ed. 4.95 (*1-57022-027-1*) ECS Lrn Systs.

Language Arts & More: Grade 2. ECS Learning Systems Staff. (ECS Home Study Bk.). (Illus.). 64p. (Orig.). (J). 1995. pap., wbk. ed. 4.95 (*1-57022-028-X*) ECS Lrn Systs.

Language Arts & More: Grade 3. ECS Learning Systems Staff. (ECS Home Study Bk.). (Illus.). 64p. (Orig.). (J). 1995. pap., wbk. ed. 4.95 (*1-57022-029-8*) ECS Lrn Systs.

Language Arts & More: Grade 4. ECS Learning Systems Staff. (ECS Home Study Bk.). (Illus.). 64p. (Orig.). (J). 1995. pap., wbk. ed. 4.95 (*1-57022-030-1*) ECS Lrn Systs.

Language Arts & More: Grade 5. ECS Learning Systems Staff. (ECS Home Study Bk.). (Illus.). 64p. (Orig.). (J). 1995. pap., wbk. ed. 4.95 (*1-57022-031-X*) ECS Lrn Systs.

Language Arts & More: Grade 6. ECS Learning Systems Staff. (ECS Home Study Bk.). (Illus.). 64p. (Orig.). (J). 1995. pap., wbk. ed. 4.95 (*1-57022-032-8*) ECS Lrn Systs.

Language Arts & More: Home Study Collection, 6 bks. Lori Mammen. 56p. (J). (gr. 1-6). 1995. 29.70 (*1-57022-185-5*) ECS Lrn Systs.

Language Arts Folder Fun: Activities for Reinforcement & Enrichment. Kathy Blankenhorn & Joanne Richards. Ed. & Intro. by Leslie Britt. (Illus.). 80p. (J). (gr. 2-5). 1995. pap. text 9.95 (*0-86530-316-9*, 1P316-9) Incentive Pubns.

Language Arts for Gifted Middle School Students. Susan J. Davis & Jerry L. Johns. (Teaching Resources in the ERIC Database (TRIED) Ser.). (Illus.). 1990. pap. 14.95 (*0-927516-16-0*) ERIC-REC.

***Language Arts Grade 5.** Ed. by McGraw-Hill Book Company Staff. (Spectrum Ser.). (Illus.). (J). 2000. pap. 7.95 (*1-57768-475-3*) MG-Hill OH.

***Language Arts Grade 4.** Ed. by McGraw-Hill Book Company Staff. (Spectrum Ser.). (Illus.). (J). 2000. pap. 7.95 (*1-57768-474-5*) MG-Hill OH.

***Language Arts Grade 6.** Ed. by McGraw-Hill Book Company Staff. (Spectrum Ser.). (Illus.). (J). 2000. pap. 7.95 (*1-57768-476-1*) MG-Hill OH.

***Language Arts Grade 3.** Ed. by McGraw-Hill Book Company Staff. (Spectrum Ser.). (Illus.). 208p. (J). 2000. pap. 7.95 (*1-57768-473-7*) MG-Hill OH.

***Language Arts Grade 2.** Ed. by McGraw-Hill Book Company Staff. (Spectrum Ser.). (Illus.). (J). 2000. pap. 7.95 (*1-57768-472-9*) MG-Hill OH.

Language Arts in Contemporary Elementary Classrooms. Arne Sippola. 128p. (C). 1997. per. 33.95 (*0-7872-3681-0*, 41368101) Kendall-Hunt.

***Language Arts in Early Education.** Jayne Sowers & Tammy Race-Holmes. LC 99-55619. (Early Childhood Education Ser.). (C). 2000. pap. 44.95 (*0-7668-0465-8*) Delmar.

Language Arts in the Early Childhood Classroom. John W. Stewig & Mary Jett-Simpson. LC 94-33906. 324p. 1995. 75.95 (*0-534-25080-7*) Wadsworth Pub.

Language Arts Learning Centers for the Primary Grades. Carol A. Poppe & Nancy A. Van Matre. 266p. (C). 1991. pap. text 27.95 (*0-87628-505-1*) P-H.

Language Arts Manual: Introductory Unit & Bibliography. Project Success Enrichment Staff. 152p. 1996. pap. text, spiral bd. 50.00 (*0-7872-2643-2*, 41264301) Kendall-Hunt.

Language Arts Manual: Literary Analysis Unit. Project Success Enrichment Staff. 190p. 1996. pap. text, spiral bd. 40.00 (*0-7872-2644-0*) Kendall-Hunt.

Language Arts Manual: Short Story Unit. Project Success Enrichment Staff. 108p. 1996. pap. text, spiral bd. 40.00 (*0-7872-2645-9*) Kendall-Hunt.

Language Arts Motivators: Grades K-3. Avaril Wedemeyer & Joyce Cejka. 1988. pap. 5.95 (*0-89108-190-9*, 8817) Love Pub Co.

Language Arts Puzzles & Games. Barbara Allman. (Gifted & Talented Ser.). (Illus.). 64p. (J). (gr. k-1). 1999. pap. 4.95 (*0-7373-0206-2*, Pub. by Lowell Hse) NTC Contemp Pub Co.

***Language Arts Puzzles & Games: A Workbook for Ages 6-8.** Martha Cheney. (Gifted & Talented Ser.). (Illus.). 64p. (J). (gr. 1-3). 2000. pap., wbk. ed. 4.95 (*0-7373-0372-7*, 03727W, Pub. by Lowell Hse) NTC Contemp Pub Co.

Language Arts Source. Ed. by Scholastic, Inc. Staff. 1993. pap. 69.00 (*0-590-73814-3*) Scholastic Inc.

Language Arts Thinking Motivators. Thomas J. Palumbo. 96p. (J). (gr. 2-7). 1988. student ed. 11.99 (*0-86653-432-6*, GA1050) Good Apple.

***Language Arts 3-4.** School Zone Publishing Staff. (Illus.). (J). 2000. pap. 3.79 (*0-88743-822-9*) Sch Zone Pub Co.

Language Arts Trivial Pursuit: Intermediate Grades 4-6. Kino Learning Center Staff et al. (Illus.). 64p. (J). (gr. 4-6). teacher ed. 12.99 (*0-86653-648-5*, GA1383) Good Apple.

Language Arts Trivial Pursuit: Junior High Grades 7-9. Kino Learning Center Staff & Mary A. McElmurray. (Illus.). 64p. (J). (gr. 7-9). teacher ed. 12.99 (*0-86653-650-7*, GA1384) Good Apple.

Language Arts Trivial Pursuit: Primary Grades 1-3. Kino Learning Center Staff et al. (Illus.). 64p. (J). (gr. 1-3). teacher ed. 12.99 (*0-86653-646-9*, GA1382) Good Apple.

***Language Arts 2.** School Zone Publishing Staff. (Illus.). (J). 2000. pap. 3.79 (*0-88743-821-0*) Sch Zone Pub Co.

Language As a Cognitive Process Vol. 1: Syntax. Terry Winograd. LC 81-14855. (Computer Science Ser.). (Illus.). 608p. (C). 1983. text 51.75 (*0-201-08571-2*) Addison-Wesley.

Language As a Human Problem. Ed. by Einar Haugen & Morton W. Bloomfield. (C). 1975. 14.00 (*0-393-01112-7*) Norton.

Language, As a Music: Six Marginal Pretexts for Composition. Benjamin Boretz. LC 80-80807. (Illus.). 88p. 1980. lib. bdg. 13.95 (*0-939044-20-X*) Lingua Pr.

Language As Articulate Contact: Toward a Post-Semiotic Philosophy of Communication. John Stewart. LC 94-7309. (SUNY Series in Speech Communication). 303p. (C). 1995. pap. text 19.95 (*0-7914-2288-7*) State U NY Pr.

An Asterisk (*) at the beginning of an entry indicates that the title is appearing for the first time.

Language As Articulate Contact: Toward a Post-Semiotic Philosophy of Communication. John Stewart. LC 94-7309. (SUNY Series in Speech Communication). 303p. (C). 1995. text 59.50 (*0-7914-2287-9*) State U NY Pr.

Language As Behaviour, Language As Code: A Study of Academic English. Lynne Young. LC 90-23244. (Pragmatics & Beyond New Ser.: Vol. 8). ix, 304p. 1991. 94.00 (*1-55619-110-3*) J Benjamins Pubng Co.

Language As Being in the Poetry of Yvor Winters. fac. ed. Grosvenor Powell. LC 79-14975. 196p. 1980. reprint ed. pap. 60.80 (*0-7837-7815-5*, 204757100007) Bks Demand.

Language As Calculus vs. Language As Universal Medium: A Study in Husserl, Heidegger & Gadamer. Martin Kusch. (Synthese Library: No. 207). 376p. 1989. lib. bdg. 160.00 (*0-7923-0333-4*, Pub. by Kluwer Academic) Kluwer Academic.

Language As Gesture: Essays in Poetry. Richard P. Blackmur. LC 77-10141. 440p. 1977. reprint ed. lib. bdg. 52.50 (*0-8371-9782-1*, BLLG, Greenwood Pr) Greenwood.

Language As Historical Determinant: The Normans in Sicily (1061-1200) Joseph F. Privitera & Bettina Privitera. LC 95-77606. 136p. 1995. pap. 18.00 (*1-877965-03-0*, PA2001) AIBDC.

Language As Living Form in Nineteenth Century Poetry. Isobel Armstrong. LC 83-2815. 234p. (C). 1982. text 44.00 (*0-389-20293-2*, 07128) B&N Imports.

Language As Object: Emily Dickinson & Contemporary Art. Ed. by Susan Danley. LC 96-21069. (Illus.). 104p. 1997. pap. 19.95 (*1-55849-066-3*) U of Mass Pr.

Language As Symbolic Action: Essays on Life, Literature, & Method. Kenneth Burke. LC 66-27655. 1966. reprint ed. pap. 19.95 (*0-520-00192-3*, Pub. by U CA Pr) Cal Prin Full Svc.

Language As Work & Trade: A Semiotic Homology for Linguistics & Economics. Ferruccio Rossi-Landi. LC 82-4432. 223p. 1983. 55.00 (*0-89789-022-1*, Bergin & Garvey) Greenwood.

Language Aspects of Ethnic Patterns & Processes in the North Caucasus. Ronald Wixman. LC 78-31304. (University of Chicago, Department of Geography, Research Paper Ser.: No. 191). 258p. reprint ed. pap. 80.00 (*0-608-12519-9*, 202497400040) Bks Demand.

Language Assessment in the Early Years. Anne H. Dyson & Celia Genishi. Ed. by Judith Green & Cynthia Wallat. LC 84-3074. (Language & Learning for Human Service Professions Ser.: Vol. 4). 276p. (C). 1984. pap. 39.50 (*0-89391-246-8*) Ablx Pub.

Language Assessment in the Early Years. Celia Genishi & Anne H. Dyson. Ed. by Cynthia Wallat & Judith Green. LC 84-3074. (Language & Learning for Human Service Professions Ser.: Vol. 4). 276p. (C). 1984. text 73.25 (*0-89391-176-3*) Ablx Pub.

Language at Work: Analyzing Communication in the Workplace to Inform Systems Design. Keith J. Devlin & Duska Rosenberg. LC 96-24100. (Lecture Notes Ser.). 224p. 1996. 59.95 (*1-57586-050-3*); pap. 20.95 (*1-57586-051-1*) CSLI.

Language at Work: Papers from the Annual Meeting of the British Association for Applied Linguistics Held at the University of Birmingham, September, 1997. British Association for Applied Linguistics Staff & Susan Hunston. LC 98-24776. (British Studies in Applied Linguistics). 1998. pap. 39.95 (*1-85359-427-X*, Pub. by Multilingual Matters) Taylor & Francis.

Language Attitudes: Current Trends & Prospects. Ed. by Roger W. Shuy & Ralph W. Fasold. LC 72-97143. 207p. reprint ed. pap. 64.20 (*0-7837-6341-7*, 204605300010) Bks Demand.

Language Attitudes among Arabic-French Bilinguals in Morocco. Abdelali Bentahila. 182p. 1983. 53.00 (*0-905028-15-5*, Pub. by Multilingual Matters) Taylor & Francis.

Language Attitudes in Sub-Saharan Africa: A Sociolinguistic Overview. Efurosibina Adegbija. LC 94-5114. (Multilingual Matters Ser.: Vol. 103). 1994. 49.00 (*1-85359-239-0*, Pub. by Multilingual Matters) Taylor & Francis.

Language Attitudes in the Dutch Language Area. Ed. by Roeland Van Hout & Uus Knops. (Topics in Sociolinguistics Ser.). vi, 202p. (Orig.). (C). 1988. pap. 52.35 (*90-6765-386-1*) Mouton.

Language Attrition Downunder: German Speakers in Australia. Margit Waas. (Studien zur Allgemeinen und Romanischen Sprachwissenschaft Ser.: Bd. 3). (Illus.). 212p. 1996. pap. 42.95 (*0-8204-3173-7*) P Lang Pubng.

Language Attrition Downunder: German Speakers in Australia. Margit Waas. LC 96-50244. (Studien zur Allgemeinen und Romanischen Sprachwissenschaft Ser.: Bd. 3). (Illus.). 212p. 1996. 42.95 (*3-631-30086-7*) P Lang Pubng.

Language Attrition in Progress. Ed. by T. J. Van Els et al. (Studies on Language Acquisition). viii, 224p. 1987. pap. 50.00 (*90-6765-322-5*) Mouton.

Language, Authority & Criticism: Readings on the School Textbook. Suzanne DeCastell et al. 380p. 1989. 99.95 (*1-85000-365-3*, Falmer Pr); pap. 44.95 (*1-85000-366-1*, Falmer Pr) Taylor & Francis.

Language, Authority, & Indigenous History in the "Commentarios Reales" de los Incas. Margarita Zamora. (Cambridge Iberian & Latin American Studies). 224p. 1988. text 64.95 (*0-521-35087-5*) Cambridge U Pr.

Language Aware: Writers Reference. Eschholz. 1997. pap. text 39.60 (*0-312-18517-0*) St Martin.

Language Awareness. 3rd ed. Ed. by Paul A. Eschholz et al. LC 81-51837. 332p. (C). 1982. pap. text 9.56 (*0-312-46693-5*) St Martin.

Language Awareness. 7th ed. Paul A. Eschholz. 1996. pap. text 19.00 (*0-312-14920-4*); pap. text 35.95 (*0-312-13747-8*) St Martin.

Language Awareness. 7th ed. Paul A. Eschholz. 1997. pap. text 5.00 (*0-312-14456-3*) St Martin.

Language Awareness. 8th ed. Eschholz. 2000. pap. text 35.95 (*0-312-19768-3*) St Martin.

Language Awareness & Learning to Read. Ed. by J. Downing & R. Valtin. (Language & Communication Ser.: Vol. 17). (Illus.). 385p. 1984. 118.00 (*0-387-90890-0*) Spr-Verlag.

Language Awareness & Reading. Lynn H. Waterhouse et al. Ed. by Frank B. Murray. LC 80-10842. (IRA Series on the Development of the Reading Process). 69p. reprint ed. pap. 30.00 (*0-8357-8658-7*, 203510500092) Bks Demand.

Language Awareness for Teachers. William H. Mittins. (English, Language & Education Ser.). 160p. 1990. pap. 33.95 (*0-335-09559-3*) OpUniv Pr.

Language Awareness in the Classroom: Applied Linguistics & Language Study. Ed. by Carl James & Peter Garrett. (Applied Linguistics & Language Ser.). 356p. (C). 1991. pap. text 27.95 (*0-582-06737-5*, 78869) Longman.

Language Bases . . . Discourse Bases: Some Aspects of Contemporary French-Language Psycholinguistics Research. Ed. by Gilberte Pieraut-Le Bonniec & Marlene Dolitsky. LC 91-6685. (Pragmatics & Beyond New Ser.: No. 17). vi, 342p. 1991. 59.00 (*1-55619-283-5*) J Benjamins Pubng Co.

Language Beat. Deborah Dunleavy. 96p. (C). 1992. pap. text 16.50 (*0-435-08615-4*, 08615) Heinemann.

Language Behavior: A Book of Readings in Communication. Ed. by Johnnye Akin et al. LC 77-110948. (Janua Linguarum, Ser. Major: No. 41). 1970. text 90.80 (*90-279-1244-0*) Mouton.

Language Behaviour: Acquisition & Evolutionary History. Rangaswamy Narasimhan. LC 97-45132. (Language & Development Ser.). 219p. 1998. write for info. (*0-7619-9232-4*) Sage.

Language, Belief, & Metaphysics. Ed. by Howard E. Kiefer & Milton K. Munitz. LC 69-14643. (Contemporary Philosophic Thought Ser.: Vol. 1). 244p. reprint ed. pap. 75.70 (*0-608-10181-8*, 201011300068) Bks Demand.

Language Beyond Postmodernism: Saying & Thinking in Gendlin's Philosophy. Eugene T. Gendlin & David M. Levin. LC 97-19492. (Studies in Phenomenology & Existential Philosophy). 1997. 89.95 (*0-8101-1358-9*); pap. 29.95 (*0-8101-1359-7*) Northwestern U Pr.

Language Book: A Perma-Bound Teach & Use Handbook for the Middle Level. Florence W. Harris. (Illus.). 355p. 1990. lib. bdg. 17.25 (*0-8000-9338-0*, 173474) Perma-Bound.

Language Brain Boosters. Becky Daniel. (Illus.). 64p. (J). (gr. 1-4). 1992. 8.99 (*0-86653-653-1*, GA1348) Good Apple.

Language Builder: An Essay on the Human Signature in Linguistic Morphogenesis. Claude Hagege. LC 92-42077. (Current Issues in Linguistic Theory Ser.: No. 94). xii, 283p. 1993. 76.00 (*1-55619-155-3*); pap. 29.95 (*1-55619-157-X*) J Benjamins Pubng Co.

Language Builder Picture Cards, No.1. Karen F. Patterson & Angela Nelson. (Illus.). 350p. (ps-3). 1997. 150.00 (*0-9668008-0-X*) Stages Learn.

***Language! Categories: Phonetically Controlled Vocabulary to Read, Classify & Spell.** Nancy Chapel Eberhardt & Denise Powers Sorese. (Language Ser.). 258p. 1999. ring bd. 35.00i (*1-57035-209-7*) Sopris.

Language Change. Ed. by Irmengard Rauch & Gerald F. Carr. LC 82-48626. 286p. 1983. reprint ed. pap. 88.70 (*0-7837-6106-6*, 205915200008) Bks Demand.

Language Change. 2nd ed. R. L. Trask. LC 93-36317. (Language Workbooks Ser.). (Illus.). 104p. (C). 1994. pap. 14.99 (*0-415-08563-2*, B4200) Routledge.

Language Change: Advances in Historical Sociolinguistics. Ed. by Ernst H. Jahr. LC 98-39239. (Trends in Linguistics Ser.). 336p. 1998. 124.00 (*3-11-015634-2*) De Gruyter.

Language Change: Contributions to the Study of Its Causes. Ed. by Leiv E. Breivik & Ernst H. Jahr. (Trends in Linguistics, Studies & Monographs: No. 43). viii, 281p. (C). 1989. lib. bdg. 103.10 (*0-89925-564-7*) Mouton.

Language Change: Progress or Decay? 2nd ed. Jean Aitchison. (Approaches to Linguistics Ser.). 270p. (C). 1991. pap. text 18.95 (*0-521-42283-3*) Cambridge U Pr.

Language Change & Functional Explanations. Ed. by Jadranka C. Gvozdanovic. LC 96-46266. (Trends in Linguistics, Studies & Monographs: Vol. 98). x, 307p. 1997. lib. bdg. 136.55 (*3-11-014913-3*) Mouton.

***Language Change & Language Contact in Pidgins & Creoles.** Society for Pidgin & Creole Linguistics Staff. Ed. by John H. McWhorter. LC 99-48486. (Creole Language Library: Vol. 21). vii, 500p. 2000. 145.00 (*1-55619-668-7*) J Benjamins Pubng Co.

Language Change & Language Structure: Older Germanic Languages in a Comparative Perspective. Ed. by Toril Swan et al. LC 93-45817. (Trends in Linguistics, Studies & Monographs: No. 73). xi, 346p. (C). 1994. lib. bdg. 129.25 (*3-11-013538-8*) Mouton.

Language Change & Linguistic Reconstruction. Henry M. Hoenigswald. LC P 0123.H55. (Phoenix Bks.). 176p. reprint ed. pap. 54.60 (*0-608-18226-5*, 205663400078) Bks Demand.

***Language Change & Typological Variation: Language Change & Phonology.** Edgar C. Polome et al. LC 99-216999. (Journal of Indo-European Studies Monographs: Vol. 30). 319p. (C). 1999. pap. text 48.00 (*0-941694-68-2*) Inst Study Man.

***Language Change & Typological Variation Vol. 2: In Honor of Winfred P. Lehmann, Grammatical Universals & Typology.** Carol F. Justus et al. LC 99-216999. (Journal of Indo-European Studies Monograph Ser.: Vol. 31). 322p. (C). 1999. pap. text 48.00 (*0-941694-69-0*) Inst Study Man.

Language Change in Child & Adult Hebrew: A Psycholinguistic Perspective. Dorit D. Ravid. (Oxford Studies in Sociolinguistics). (Illus.). 256p. 1995. pap. text 24.95 (*0-19-509036-5*) OUP.

Language Change in South American Indian Languages. Ed. by Mary R. Key. LC 90-26311. (Illus.). 312p. (C). 1991. text 34.95 (*0-8122-3060-4*) U of Pa Pr.

Language Characteristics & Schooling in the U. S. A Changing Picture, 1979 & 1989. Edith K. McArthur. (Illus.). 67p. (Orig.). (C). 1994. pap. text 25.00 (*0-7881-0696-1*) DIANE Pub.

Language, Charisma, & Creativity: The Ritual Life of a Religious Movement. Thomas J. Csordas. LC 95-50992. (Illus.). 251p. 1997. 45.00 (*0-520-20469-7*, Pub. by U CA Pr) Cal Prin Full Svc.

Language Choice - Identity Choice. Barbara Kannapell. (Dissertation Ser.). 197p. (C). 1993. pap. text 19.95 (*0-932130-15-1*, LP302) Linstok Pr.

Language Choice in Rural Development. Clinton D. Robinson. LC 92-60918. (International Museum of Cultures Ser.: Vol. 26). x, 52p. 1992. pap. 5.00 (*0-88312-180-8*) S I L Intl.

Language Choices: Conditions, Constraints & Consequences. Ed. by Martin Putz. LC 96-6512. (Impact: Studies in Language & Society: Vol. 1). xxi, 430p. 1997. lib. bdg. 127.00 (*1-55619-850-7*) J Benjamins Pubng Co.

Language Classroom. Ed. by William F. Bottiglia. 84p. 1957. pap. 10.95 (*0-915432-57-9*) NE Conf Teach Foreign.

***Language Codes.** R. Neville Johnston. LC 99-89150. (Illus.). 96p. 2000. pap. 9.95 (*1-57863-144-0*) Weiser.

Language, Cognition & Deafness. Michael Rodda & Carl Grove. (Zillman-Bryant: Communication Ser.). 456p. 1987. text 79.95 (*0-89859-877-X*) L Erlbaum Assocs.

Language, Communication, & Culture: Current Directions. Ed. by Stella Ting-Toomey & Felipe Korzenny. (International & Intercultural Communication Ser.: Vol. 13). 272p. (C). 1989. text 59.95 (*0-8039-3449-1*); pap. text 26.00 (*0-8039-3450-5*) Sage.

Language, Communication & Education. Ed. by Barbara Mayor & A. K. Pugh. 480p. (Orig.). (C). 1986. pap. text 16.95 (*0-7099-3590-0*, Pub. by C Helm) Routldge.

Language, Communication, & Social Meaning. Georgetown University Round Table on Languages & L. Ed. by James E. Alatis. LC 58-31607. (Illus.). 517p. 1993. reprint ed. pap. 160.30 (*0-7837-9430-4*, 206017200005) Bks Demand.

Language, Communication, & the Brain. Ed. by Fred Plum. LC 87-20643. (Association for Research in Nervous & Mental Disease Research Publications: Vol. 66). 318p. 1988. reprint ed. pap. 98.60 (*0-608-04713-9*, 206543400004) Bks Demand.

Language Communication & the Brain: A Neuropsychological Study. Mariusz Maruszewski. Tr. by Grace W. Shugar from POL. (Janua Linguarum, Series Major: No. 80). (Illus.). 217p. 1975. text 57.70 (*90-279-3067-8*) Mouton.

Language Competence: Implications for National Security, 119. Kurt E. Muller. LC 85-31240. (Washington Papers: No. 119). 181p. 1986. 55.00 (*0-275-92213-8*, C2213, Praeger Pubs); pap. 13.95 (*0-275-92214-6*, B2214, Praeger Pubs) Greenwood.

Language, Compilers & Run-Time Systems for Scalable Computers: Selected Papers From The 4th International Workshop, Lcr '98, Pittsburgh, Pa, U. S. A., May 1998. David R. O'Hallaron. LC 98-45572. 151. 1998. pap. 67.00 (*3-540-65172-1*) Spr-Verlag.

Language Complexity Game. Eric Sven Ristad. Ed. by Daniel G. Bobrow et al. (Artificial Intelligence Ser.). (Illus.). 168p. 1993. 30.00 (*0-262-18147-9*) MIT Pr.

Language Comprehension: A Biological Perspective. Ed. by Angela D. Friederici. LC 98-3122. (Illus.). 315p. 1998. 99.95 (*3-540-64232-3*) Spr-Verlag.

Language Comprehension: A Biological Perspective. 2nd ed. Ed. by Angela D. Friederici. LC 98-53846. (Illus.). 320p. 1999. 129.00 (*3-540-64874-7*) Spr-Verlag.

Language Comprehension & the Acquisition of Knowledge. Ed. by J. B. Carroll & R. O. Freedle. LC 72-6708. 396p. reprint ed. pap. 122.80 (*0-8357-9147-5*, 205070600082) Bks Demand.

Language Comprehension As Structure Building. Ed. by M. A. Gernsbacher. 304p. (C). 1990. text 79.95 (*0-8058-0676-8*) L Erlbaum Assocs.

Language Comprehension in Ape & Child. E. Sue Savage-Rumbaugh et al. (Monographs of the Society for Research in Child Development: No. 233, Vol. 58, Nos. 3-4). 510p. (C). 1993. pap. text 19.50 (*0-226-73542-7*) U Ch Pr.

Language Computations. Ed. by Eric S. Ristad. LC 94-28045. (DIMACS Series in Discrete Mathematics & Theoretical Computer Science: 17). 198p. 1994. text 60.00 (*0-8218-6608-7*, DIMACS/17) Am Math.

Language Conflict & Language Planning. Ed. by Ernst H. Jahr. LC 93-6305. (Trends in Linguistics, Studies & Monographs: No. 72). viii, 320p. (C). 1993. lib. bdg. 136.95 (*3-11-013539-6*) Mouton.

Language Conflicts & Language Planning: The Case of Modern Norwegian. Einar I. Haugen. LC 66-14443. 409p. reprint ed. pap. 126.80 (*0-608-30829-3*, 200641800059) Bks Demand.

Language Connection. Roy Harris. LC 99-56515. Date not set. pap. write for info. (*1-890318-46-9*) St Augustines Pr.

Language Connection: Philosophy & Linguistics. Roy Harris. (Bristol Introductions Ser.: No. 2). 180p. 1996. pap. 18.00 (*1-85506-498-7*) Bks Intl VA.

Language Connection: Philosophy & Linguistics. Roy Harris. (Bristol Introductions Ser.: No. 2). 180p. 1997. 40.00 (*1-85506-497-9*) Bks Intl VA.

Language Contact: Theoretical & Empirical Studies. Ed. by Ernst H. Jahr. (Trends in Linguistics, Studies & Monographs: No. 60). vii, 234p. (C). 1992. lib. bdg. 98.50 (*3-11-012802-0*, 49-92) Mouton.

Language Contact - Language Conflict. Ed. by Eran Fraenkel & Christina Kramer. LC 93-19003. (Studies in the Balkans & Turkey in Europe: Vol. 1). 196p. (C). 1993. text 48.95 (*0-8204-1652-5*) P Lang Pubng.

Language Contact & Bilingualism. Rene Appel & Pieter Muysken. 224p. 1995. pap. text 24.95 (*0-7131-6491-3*, Pub. by E A) St Martin.

Language Contact & Change: Spanish in Los Angeles. Carmen Silva-Corvalan. (Oxford Studies in Language Contact). (Illus.). 270p. 1996. reprint ed. pap. text 28.00 (*0-19-823644-1*) OUP.

Language Contact & Change in the Austronesian World. Ed. by Tom Dutton & Darrell Tyron. (Trends in Linguistics, Studies & Monographs: No. 77). 693p. (C). 1994. lib. bdg. 213.85 (*3-11-012786-5*, 170-94) Mouton.

Language Contact & Language Conflict. Martin Putz. LC 93-46217. xvii, 256p. 1994. lib. bdg. 59.00 (*1-55619-479-X*) J Benjamins Pubng Co.

Language Contact, Creolization & Genetic Linguistics. Sarah G. Thomason & Terrence Kaufman. (C). 1988. pap. 19.95 (*0-520-07893-4*, Pub. by U CA Pr) Cal Prin Full Svc.

Language Contact in a Plantation Environment: A Sociolinguistic History of Fiji. Jeff Siegel. (Studies in the Social & Cultural Foundations of Language: No. 5). (Illus.). 320p. 1987. text 85.00 (*0-521-32577-3*) Cambridge U Pr.

Language Contact in the American Deaf Community. Ceil Lucas & Clayton Valli. LC 92-4929. (Illus.). 161p. 1992. text 39.95 (*0-12-458040-8*) Acad Pr.

Language Contact in the Arctic: Northern Pidgins & Contact Languages. Ed. by Ernst H. Jahr & Ingvild Broch. (Trends in Linguistics, Studies & Monographs: No. 88). viii, 340p. (C). 1996. lib. bdg. 144.65 (*3-11-014335-6*) Mouton.

Language, Context, & Text: Aspects of Language in a Social Semiotic Perspective. M. A. Halliday & Rugaiya Hasan. 126p. (C). 1995. pap. 34.00 (*0-7300-0307-8*, ECS805, Pub. by Deakin Univ) St Mut.

Language Continuum: From Infancy to Literacy. Ed. by James F. Kavanagh. LC 91-35642. (Communicating by Language Ser.). 199p. 1991. pap. text 25.00 (*0-912752-56-4*) York Pr.

Language, Counter-Memory, Practice: Selected Essays & Interviews. Michel Foucault. Ed. by Donald F. Bouchard. LC 77-4561. 240p. 1980. pap. text 15.95 (*0-8014-9204-1*) Cornell U Pr.

Language Creation & Language Change: Creolization, Diachrony, & Development. Ed. by Michel De Graff. LC 98-35937. (Learning, Development & Conceptual Change Ser.). (Illus.). 586p. 1999. 65.00 (*0-262-04168-5*) MIT Pr.

Language Crimes: The Use & Abuse of Language Evidence in the Court Room. Roger W. Shuy. 1996. pap. 24.95 (*0-631-20153-X*) Blackwell Pubs.

Language Crystal: The Complete Solution to Civilization's Oldest Puzzle. Lawrence W. Lyons. LC 87-80516. (Illus.). 510p. (Orig.). 1988. pap. 14.76 (*0-942121-18-X*) Grammar Pub.

Language, Culture, & Cognition: A Collection of Studies in First & Second Language Acquisition. Ed. by Lilliam Malave & George S. Duquette. (Multilingual Matters Ser.: No. 69). 300p. 1991. 99.00 (*1-85359-103-3*, Pub. by Multilingual Matters); pap. 39.95 (*1-85359-102-5*, Pub. by Multilingual Matters) Taylor & Francis.

***Language, Culture & Communication: The Meaning of Messages.** 3rd ed. Nancy Bonvillain. LC 99-38023. 405p. 1999. pap. text 39.80 (*0-13-010429-9*) P-H.

Language, Culture, & Communication in Contemporary Europe. Ed. by Charlotte Hoffman. LC 96-6226. 165p. 1996. 45.00 (*1-85359-360-5*, Pub. by Multilingual Matters) Taylor & Francis.

Language, Culture, & Education. Ed. by Michael Beveridge & Gordon Reddiford. 200p. 1993. 59.00 (*1-85359-203-X*, Pub. by Multilingual Matters) Taylor & Francis.

Language, Culture & Nation-Building: Challenges of Modernization. Lachman M. Khubchandani. (C). 1991. 11.50 (*81-85425-41-8*, Pub. by Manohar) S Asia.

Language, Culture, & Personality: Essays in Memory of Edward Sapir. Ed. by Leslie Spier et al. LC 83-12965. 298p. (C). 1983. lib. bdg. 45.50 (*0-313-24183-X*, SPLA, Greenwood Pr) Greenwood.

Language, Culture, & Power: Bilingual Families & the Struggle for Quality Education. Lourdes D. Soto. LC 96-34721. (SUNY Series in the Social Context of Education). 170p. (C). 1996. pap. text 16.95 (*0-7914-3142-8*) State U NY Pr.

Language, Culture, & Society: A Book of Readings. 2nd rev. ed. Ed. by Ben G. Blount. LC 96-133955. 608p. (C). 1995. pap. text 23.95 (*0-88133-850-8*) Waveland Pr.

Language, Culture & Society: An Introduction to Linguistic Anthropology. 2nd ed. Zdenek Salzmann. LC 97-53076. (C). 1998. pap. 35.00 (*0-8133-3404-7*, Pub. by Westview) HarpC.

Language Culture & Society in West Africa. C. W. Wigwe. 92p. (C). 1989. 39.00 (*0-7223-2346-8*, Pub. by A H S Ltd) St Mut.

Language Culture & Young Children: Developing English in the Multi-Ethnic Nursery & Infant School. Ed. by Pat Pinsent. 144p. 1992. pap. 24.95 (*1-85346-184-9*, Pub. by David Fulton) Taylor & Francis.

***Language Death.** David Crystal. 208p. 2000. 19.95 (*0-521-65321-5*) Cambridge U Pr.

L

Language Death: Factual & Theoretical Explorations (with Special Reference to East Africa) Ed. by Matthias Brenzinger. (Contributions to the Sociology of Language Ser.: No. 64). (Illus.). viii, 445p. 1992. lib. bdg. 160.00 (*3-11-013404-7*) Mouton.

Language Delays & Disorders: From Research to Practice. Lydia R. Smiley & Peggy A. Goldstein. LC 97-28437. (Illus.). 352p. (Orig.). 1997. pap. text 39.95 (*1-56593-694-9*, 1384) Thomson Learn.

***Language, Democracy & Devolution in Catalonia** Sue Wright. LC 98-52029. 1999. 44.95 (*1-85359-445-8*) Taylor & Francis.

Language Development. Erika Hoff-Ginsberg. (Psychology Ser.). (Illus.). 512p. (C). 1996. mass mkt. 68.95 (*0-534-20292-6*) Brooks-Cole.

Language Development. Erika Hoff-Ginsberg. 1996. mass mkt., teacher ed. write for info. (*0-534-34347-3*) Brooks-Cole.

Language Development. Peter Jordens & Josine A. Lalleman. (AVT Publications). xii, 180p. (Orig.). (C). 1988. pap. 42.30 (*90-6765-401-9*) Mouton.

Language Development. Peter A. Reich. 400p. 1986. 45.00 (*0-13-523069-1*) P-H.

***Language Development.** 2nd ed. Erika Hoff-Ginsberg. (Psychology). 2000. text 49.25 (*0-534-57789-X*) Wadsworth Pub.

***Language Development.** 5th ed. 2000. teacher ed. write for info. (*0-205-32575-0*) Allyn.

***Language Development.** 5th ed. 560p. (C). 2000. pap. text 61.33 (*0-205-31926-2*) Allyn.

Language Development: A Reader for Teachers. Ed. by Brenda M. Power & Ruth S. Hubbard. LC 95-32102. 294p. (C). 1996. pap. text 34.00 (*0-13-191032-9*) P-H.

Language Development: An Introduction. 4th ed. Robert E. Owens. 576p. 1995. pap. 63.00 (*0-02-390191-8*, Macmillan Coll) P-H.

***Language Development: Audio Cd.** 5th ed. 2000. write for info. (*0-205-32576-9*) Allyn.

Language Development: Learning Language, Learning Culture - Meaning & Choice in Languages. Ed. by Ruqaiya Hasan et al. LC 87-33274. (Advances in Discourse Processes Ser.: Vol. 27). 408p. 1989. text 78.50 (*0-89391-443-6*) Ablx Pub.

Language Development: The Essential Readings. Ed. by Elizabeth Bates. (Illus.). 156p. 1999. 59.95 (*0-631-21744-4*); pap. 24.95 (*0-631-21745-2*) Blackwell Pubs.

Language Development Vol. 1: Syntax & Semantics. Ed. by Stan A. Kuczaj, II. (David Palermo Child Psychology Ser.). 528p. 1981. text 99.95 (*0-89859-100-7*) L Erlbaum Assocs.

Language Development & Disorders. Ed. by Michael Rutter & William Yule. LC 65-80542. (Clinics in Developmental Medicine Ser.: No. 101-102). (Illus.). 482p. (C). 1991. text 85.00 (*0-521-41219-6*, Pub. by Mc Keith Pr) Cambridge U Pr.

Language Development & Individual Differences: A Study of Auxiliary Verb Learning. Brian J. Richards. (Illus.). 270p. (C). 1990. text 69.95 (*0-521-36253-9*) Cambridge U Pr.

Language Development & Language Disorders: A Compendium of Lectures. Nancy E. Wood. (SRCD M Ser.: Vol. 25, No. 3). 1960. pap. 25.00 (*0-527-01585-7*) Periodicals Srv.

***Language Development & Social Interaction in Blind Children.** Miguel Perez-Periera. 200p. 1999. 39.95 (*0-86377-795-3*) L Erlbaum Assocs.

***Language Development, Difference & Disorders.** Kathleen R. Fahey & D. Kim Reid. LC 99-27839. 2000. write for info. (*0-89079-822-2*) PRO-ED.

Language Development from Birth to 3. Moshe Anisfeld. LC 83-82493. 306p. (C). 1984. pap. text 37.50 (*0-89859-625-4*) L Erlbaum Assocs.

Language Development, Grammar, & Semantics: The Contribution of Linguistics to Bilingual Education. Arnold M. Zwicky et al. LC 79-57530. (Bilingual Education Ser.: No. 7). 95p. reprint ed. pap. 30.00 (*0-8357-3362-9*, 203960000013) Bks Demand.

***Language Development Guide: An Introduction to Psychology.** 9th ed. Coon. (Psychology Ser.). 2000. 8.00 (*0-534-57675-3*) Wadsworth Pub.

Language Development in Children with Special Needs: Performative Communication. Irene Johansson. Tr. & Adapted by Eva Thomas. LC 94-393.Tr. of Spakvtveckling Hos Handikappade Barn. 1994. pap. 24.95 (*1-85302-241-1*) Taylor & Francis.

Language Development in Exceptional Circumstances. Ed. by Dorothy Bishop & Kay Mogford-Bevan. (Illus.). 324p. 1988. text 56.00 (*0-443-03800-7*) Church.

Language Development in Schools for Children with Severe Learning Difficulties. John Harris. 240p. 1988. lib. bdg. 45.00 (*0-7099-5702-5*, Pub. by C Helm) Routldge.

Language Development Lessons for Early Childhood. Jean G. DeGaetano. 80p. (J). (gr. k-3). 1998. pap. text 26.00 (*1-886143-43-9*) Grt Ideas Tching.

Language Development of Deaf & Hard-of-Hearing Children: Beyond the Great Debate. Christine Yoshinaga-Itano. 350p. 2001. 49.95 (*1-56593-271-4*, 0593) Thomson Learn.

Language Development of the Preschool Child, Vol. 4. Dorothea McCarthy. LC 74-141549. (University of Minnesota Institute of Child Welfare Monographs: No. 4). (Illus.). 174p. 1975. reprint ed. lib. bdg. 45.00 (*0-8371-5896-6*, CWML, Greenwood Pr) Greenwood.

Language Development Through Content: America, after Independence. Anna Rhamot. 112p. 1987. pap. text 13.40 (*0-201-12930-2*) Addison-Wesley.

Language Development Through Content: America the Early Years. Anna Uhl. 112p. 1987. pap. text 13.40 (*0-201-12929-9*) Addison-Wesley.

Language Development Through Content: Our People & Their Stories. Nancy S. Dunetz. 128p. 1987. pap. text 15.00 (*0-201-11205-1*) Addison-Wesley.

Language Discourse. M. J. McCarthy & Ronald A. Carter. LC 92-40126. (Applied Linguistics & Language Ser.). 1993. pap. text 27.95 (*0-582-08424-5*, 79593) Longman.

Language, Discourse & Literature: An Introductory Reader in Discourse Stylistics. Ed. by Ronald A. Carter & Paul Simpson. LC 88-5678. 272p. (C). 1988. pap. text 22.95 (*0-04-445006-0*) Routledge.

Language, Discourse & Translation in the West & Middle East: Selected & Revised Papers from the Language & Translation Conference, Irbid, Jordan, 1992. Ed. by Robert De Beaugrande et al. LC 94-33138. (Benjamins Translation Library: No. 7). xii, 256p. 1994. lib. bdg. 65.00 (*1-55619-685-7*) J Benjamins Pubng Co.

Language Disorders: A Functional Approach to Assessment & Intervention. 3rd ed. Robert E. Owens. LC 98-34366. 596p. 1998. 71.00 (*0-205-28703-4*) P-H.

Language Disorders Across the Lifespan. Betsy P. Vinson. LC 98-34416. 1998. pap. 57.95 (*1-56593-977-8*) Thomson Learn.

Language Disorders & Language Development. Margaret Lahey. LC 87-22059. 550p. (C). 1988. 101.00 (*0-02-367130-0*, Macmillan Coll) P-H.

Language Disorders in Children. Katharine G. Butler. LC 86-15119. (PRO-ED Studies in Communicative Disorders). 72p. (Orig.). 1986. pap. text 9.00 (*0-89079-098-1*, 1387) PRO-ED.

Language Disorders in Children. Frank R. Kleffner. LC 73-3116. (Studies in Communicative Disorders). 60p. (C). 1973. pap. text. write for info. (*0-672-61292-5*, Bobbs) Macmillan.

Language Disorders in Children: An Introductory Clinical Perspective. Barbara A. Johnson. LC 94-36579. 400p. (C). 1995. pap. 55.95 (*0-8273-5533-5*) Delmar.

Language Disorders in Children & Adolescents. Rhea Paul. (Illus.). 624p. (gr. 13). 1995. text 58.00 (*0-8016-7927-3*, 07927) Mosby Inc.

Language Disorders in Children & Adults: Psycholinguistic Approaches to Therapy. Ed. by Shula Chiat et al. 280p. 1997. 65.00 (*1-56593-878-X*, 1720) Singular Publishing.

Language Disorders in Older Students: Preadolescents & Adolescents. Vicki L. Larson & Nancy L. McKinley. LC 94-34928. 1995. pap. 42.00 (*0-930599-29-2*) Thinking Pubns.

Language Distribution in Databases: An Analysis & Evaluation. Gretchen Whitney. LC 90-34219. 385p. 1990. 47.50 (*0-8108-2323-3*) Scarecrow.

Language Distributions Issues in Bilingual Schooling. Ed. by Rodolfo Jacobson & Christian J. Faltis. (Multilingual Matters Ser.: No. 56). 180p. 1990. 79.00 (*1-85359-046-0*, Pub. by Multilingual Matters); pap. 29.95 (*1-85359-045-2*, Pub. by Multilingual Matters) Taylor & Francis.

Language Disturbance & Intellectual Functioning: A Comparison of the Performance of Hemiplegic Patients with Aphasia & Hemiplegic Patients Without Aphasia in Non-Verbal Tasks of Intellectual Functioning. Carl K. Lubin. LC 68-17904. (Janua Linguarum, Series Minor: No. 48). (Orig.). 1969. pap. text 24.65 (*3-10-800093-4*) Mouton.

Language Diversity & Classroom Discourse. Ceil Lucas & Denise G. Borders. LC 93-37619. (Language & Educational Processes Ser.). 1994. pap. 39.50 (*1-56750-076-5*) Ablx Pub.

Language Diversity & Classroom Discourse. Ed. by Ceil Lucas & Denise G. Borders. LC 93-37619. (Language & Educational Processes Ser.). 1994. text 73.25 (*0-89391-969-1*) Ablx Pub.

***Language Diversity & Cognitive Representations.** Ed. by Catherine Fuchs & Stephane Robert. LC 99-40994. (Human Cognitive Processing Ser.: Vol. 3). x, 229p. 1999. 65.00 (*1-55619-203-7*) J Benjamins Pubng.

***Language Diversity & Education.** David Corson. LC 00-20306. 256p. 2000. write for info. (*0-8058-3448-6*); pap. write for info. (*0-8058-3449-4*) L Erlbaum Assocs.

Language Diversity Surveys As Agents of Change. Joe Nicholas. LC 93-50651. (Multilingual Matters Ser.: No. 102). 176p. 1994. 79.00 (*1-85359-233-1*, Pub. by Multilingual Matters); pap. 34.95 (*1-85359-232-3*, Pub. by Multilingual Matters) Taylor & Francis.

***Language, Economy & Society: The Changing Fortunes of the Welsh Language in the Twentieth Century.** John Aitchison & Harold Carter. 192p. 2000. pap. 32.00 (*0-7083-1552-6*, Pub. by U Wales Pr) Paul & Co Pubs.

Language Education. Frances Christie. (C). 1985. pap. 39.00 (*0-7300-0305-1*, ECS805, Pub. by Deakin Univ) St Mut.

Language Education. Frances Christie. (Language Education Ser.). 64p. 1989. pap. text 9.95 (*0-19-437152-2*) OUP.

Language, Education & Culture. Tariq Rahman. LC 99-921800. 336p. 1999. 26.95 (*0-19-579146-0*) OUP.

Language, Education, & Development: Urban & Rural Tok Pisin in Papua New Guinea. Suzanne Romaine. (Oxford Studies in Language Contact). (Illus.). 410p. 1992. text 105.00 (*0-19-823966-1*) OUP.

Language, Education, & Society. Bhadriraju Krishnamurti. LC 98-5362. (Language & Development Ser.). 1998. 39.95 (*0-7619-9241-3*) Sage.

Language, Education & Society in a Changing World. Ed. by Tina Hickey & Jenny Williams. 300p. 1996. 49.00 (*1-85359-315-X*, Pub. by Multilingual Matters) Taylor & Francis.

Language Education for Intercultural Communication, Vol. 96. Ed. by Dennis Ager et al. LC 93-101. 1993. 74.95 (*1-85359-190-4*, Pub. by Multilingual Matters); pap. 29.95 (*1-85359-204-8*, Pub. by Multilingual Matters) Taylor & Francis.

Language Education in the National Curriculum. Ed. by Christopher J. Brumfit & Michael Stubbs. (Language in Education Ser.). 224p. 1995. pap. 28.95 (*0-631-18901-7*) Blackwell Pubs.

Language, Elites & the State: Nationalism in Puerto Rico & Quebec. Amilcar A. Barreto. LC 97-38541. 176p. 1998. 55.00 (*0-275-96183-4*, Praeger Pubs) Greenwood.

***Language Encounters.** Gray & N. Fiering. LC 99-34723. 2000. 49.95 (*1-57181-210-5*) Berghahn Bks.

Language Engineering & Translation: Consequences of Automation. Juan C. Sager. LC 93-34837. (Benjamins Translation Library: No. 1). xx, 345p. 1994. pap. 29.95 (*1-55619-477-3*); lib. bdg. 85.00 (*1-55619-476-5*) J Benjamins Pubng Co.

Language Equations. E. L. Leiss. LC 98-31040. (Monographs in Computer Science). 304p. 1999. 64.95 (*0-387-98626-X*) Spr-Verlag.

Language, Ethics, & Ontology. Ed. by Douglas W. Shrader. 346p. 1998. pap. 17.00 (*1-883058-74-0*) Global Pubns.

Language, Ethnicity & Education: Case Studies on Immigrant Minority Groups. Peter Broeder. LC 98-45024. (Multilingual Matters Ser.). 1998. 44.95 (*1-85359-430-X*) Taylor & Francis.

Language, Ethnicity, & Education in Wales. Bud B. Khleif. (Contributions to the Sociology of Language Ser.: No. 28). 1979. text 90.00 (*90-279-7898-0*) Mouton.

Language, Ethnicity & the Schools: Policy Alternatives for Bilingual-Bicultural Education. Noel Epstein et al. (Policy Paper: No. 4). ix, 104p. 1977. 4.00 (*0-318-14398-4*) Inst Educ Lead.

Language Exercises for Adults, Bk. C. Betty Jones et al. 1997. pap., student ed. 9.96 (*0-8114-7877-7*) Raintree Steck-V.

Language Exercises for Adults, Bk. D. Betty Jones et al. 1997. pap., student ed. 9.96 (*0-8114-7878-5*) Raintree Steck-V.

Language Exercises for Adults, Bk. A. Betty Jones et al. 1997. pap., student ed. 9.96 (*0-8114-7875-0*) Raintree Steck-V.

Language Exercises for Adults, Bk. B. Betty Jones et al. 1997. pap., student ed. 9.96 (*0-8114-7876-9*) Raintree Steck-V.

Language Exercises for Adults, Bk. E. Betty Jones et al. 1997. pap., student ed. 9.96 (*0-8114-7879-3*) Raintree Steck-V.

Language Exercises for Adults, Bk. F. Betty Jones et al. 1997. pap., student ed. 9.96 (*0-8114-7880-7*) Raintree Steck-V.

Language Exercises for Adults, Bk. G. Betty Jones et al. 1997. pap., student ed. 9.96 (*0-8114-7881-5*) Raintree Steck-V.

Language Exercises for Adults, Bk. H. Betty Jones et al. 1997. pap., student ed. 9.96 (*0-8114-7882-3*) Raintree Steck-V.

Language-Experience Approach to Reading: A Handbook for Teachers of Reading. Denise D. Nessel & Margaret B. Jones. LC 80-27822. 280p. (Orig.). 1981. pap. 15.95 (*0-8077-2596-X*) Tchrs Coll.

Language Experience Approach to Reading & Writing. Carol Dixon. (Illus.). 136p. (C). 1990. pap. 14.80 (*0-13-521352-5*) Alemany Pr.

Language Exploration & Awareness: A Resource Book for Teachers. Larry Andrews. 224p. 1996. pap. write for info. (*0-8058-2627-0*) L Erlbaum Assocs.

Language Exploration & Awareness: A Resource Book for Teachers. 2nd ed. Larry Andrews. LC 97-37791. 256p. 1997. pap. write for info. (*0-8058-2367-0*) L Erlbaum Assocs.

Language Expression. Catherine Nichols. Ed. by Jennifer Whitfield. (Thinking Skills Library). (Illus.). 104p. (Orig.). (J). (gr. 2-5). 1997. pap. text, teacher ed. 9.95 (*1-56784-705-6*) Newbridge Educ.

Language Extinction & the Status of North American Indian Languages. Phoebe R. Hunter. (Studies in Technology & Social Change: No. 23). (Illus.). 65p. (Orig.). (C). 1994. pap. 8.00 (*0-945271-35-2*) ISU-CIKARD.

Language Facilitation: A Complete Cognitive Therapy Program. Jacqueline M. Cimorell-Strong. LC 83-1075. 208p. (C). 1983. spiral bd. 34.00 (*0-936104-96-1*, 1246) PRO-ED.

Language Files: An Introduction to Language. 3rd ed. Instructors of Introduction to Language, the Ohio. Ed. by Bissantz & Johnson. 352p. 1985. pap. text 15.95 (*0-89894-032-X*) Advocate Pub Group.

Language Files: Materials for an Introduction to Language & Linguistics. 6th ed. Ohio State University, Department of Linguistics S. 477p. (C). 1994. pap. text 37.50 (*0-8142-0645-X*) Ohio St U Pr.

Language Files: Materials for an Introduction to Language & Linguistics. 7th ed. Ohio State University Staff et al. LC 97-51188. 523p. 1998. pap. text 37.50 (*0-8142-5003-3*) Ohio St U Pr.

Language for a Catholic Church: A Program of Study. 2nd expanded ed. Thomas H. Groome. LC 91-60173. 80p. (Orig.). 1991. pap. 6.95 (*1-55612-408-2*, LL1408) Sheed & Ward WI.

Language for Hearers. Robert Harris. Ed. by G. McGregor. (Language & Communication Library: Vol. 8). 235p. 1986. 94.00 (*0-08-031852-5*, Pub. by Pergamon Repr) Franklin.

Language for Living. C. Gray. Date not set. pap. text. write for info. (*0-582-76632-X*, Pub. by Addison-Wesley) Longman.

Language, Form & Inquiry: Arthur F. Bentley's Philosophy of Social Science. James F. Ward. LC 83-18006. 288p. 1984. 32.50 (*0-87023-425-0*) U of Mass Pr.

Language Form & Language Function. Frederick J. Newmeyer. LC 98-10471. (Language, Speech & Communication Ser.). (Illus.). 442p. 1998. 40.00 (*0-262-14064-0*) MIT Pr.

***Language Form & Language Function.** Frederick J. Newmeyer. (Language, Speech & Communication Ser.). (Illus.). 448p. (C). 2000. pap. 27.00 (*0-262-64044-9*) MIT Pr.

Language Fundamentals. Kelley. (YA - Adult Education Ser.). 1992. pap. 9.95 (*0-538-70441-1*) S-W Pub.

Language Fundamentals. Jo E. Moore. (Illus.). 240p. (J). (gr. 1-3). 1995. pap., teacher ed. 19.95 (*1-55799-378-5*, 394) Evan-Moor Edu Pubs.

Language Fundamentals. Jo Ellen Moore. Ed. by Marilyn Evans. (Partners in Learning). (Illus.). 192p. (J). (gr. 1-3). Date not set. pap., wbk. ed. 19.95 (*1-58610-140-4*) Learn Horizon.

Language Games & Centers. Morgan & Moore. (Illus.). 112p. (J). (ps-1). 1998. pap., teacher ed. 14.95 (*1-55799-661-X*, 736) Evan-Moor Edu Pubs.

Language Games in Italian. Marcel Danesi. 164p. 1985. pap. text 14.95 (*0-8020-6596-1*) U of Toronto Pr.

Language Games to Play with Your Child: Enhancing Communication fromn Infancy Through Late Childhood. A. McCabe. (Illus.). 286p. (C). 1992. 24.95 (*0-306-44320-1*, Plen Insight) Perseus Pubng.

Language Gap. Clifford A. Wilson & Donald W. Mckeon. LC 83-23269. (Christian Free University Curriculum Ser.). 208p. (Orig.). (C). 1984. pap. 8.99 (*0-310-35771-3*, 12657P) Probe Bks.

Language, Gender & Childhood. Ed. by Valerie Walkerdine et al. (History Workshop Ser.). 256p. (Orig.). 1986. pap. 18.95 (*0-7100-9977-0*, Routledge Thoemms) Routledge.

Language, Gender, & Professional Writing: Theoretical Approaches & Guidelines for Nonsexist Usage. Ed. by Francine W. Frank et al. LC 88-38161. viii, 341p. 1989. pap. 18.00 (*0-87352-179-X*, B819P); lib. bdg. 37.50 (*0-87352-178-1*, B819C) Modern Lang.

Language, Gender, & Sex in Comparative Perspective. Ed. by Susan U. Philips et al. (Studies in the Social & Cultural Foundations of Language: No. 4). (Illus.). 350p. 1987. pap. text 24.95 (*0-521-33807-7*) Cambridge U Pr.

Language, Gesture, & Space. Ed. by Karen Emmorey & Judy S. Reilly. 464p. 1995. text 79.95 (*0-8058-1378-0*) L Erlbaum Assocs.

Language Habits in Human Affairs: An Introduction to General Semantics. Irving J. Lee. LC 78-31179. (Illus.). 278p. 1979. reprint ed. lib. bdg. 72.50 (*0-313-20962-6*, LELH, Greenwood Pr) Greenwood.

Language Habits in Human Affairs: An Introduction to General Semantics. 2nd ed. Irving J. Lee. Ed. by Sanford I. Berman. LC 94-36138. 1994. pap. 21.95 (*0-918970-41-5*) Intl Gen Semantics.

Language Handicaps in Adults. William H. Perkins. (Current Therapy of Communication Disorders Ser.: Vol. 3). 1983. 24.00 (*0-86577-406-4*) Thieme Med Pubs.

Language Handicaps in Children: Current Therapy of Communication Disorders, Vol. 7. Ed. by William H. Perkins. 187p. 1984. 24.00 (*0-86577-405-6*) Thieme Med Pubs.

Language Hierarchies & Interfaces. Ed. by F. L. Bauer & K. Samelson. (Lecture Notes in Computer Science Ser.: Vol. 46). 1977. 35.00 (*0-387-07994-7*) Spr-Verlag.

***Language History: An Introduction.** Andrew L. Sihler. LC 99-49417. (Current Issues in Linguistic Theory Ser.: Vol. 191). xvi, 299p. 2000. 70.00 (*1-55619-968-6*) J Benjamins Pubng Co.

***Language History: An introduction.** Andrew L. Sihler. LC 99-49417. (Current Issues in Linguistic Theory Ser.: Vol. 191). xvi, 299p. 2000. pap. 29.95 (*1-55619-969-4*) J Benjamins Pubng Co.

Language, History, & Identity: Ethnolinguistic Studies of the Arizona Tewa. Paul V. Kroskrity. LC 93-7645. 289p. 1993. 53.00 (*0-8165-1427-5*) U of Ariz Pr.

Language History & Linguistic Description in Africa. Ian Maddieson & Thomas J. Hinnebusch. (Trends in African Linguistics Ser.). 316p. 1997. write for info. (*0-86543-631-2*) Africa World.

Language History & Linguistic Description in Africa. Ian Maddieson & Thomas J. Hinnebusch. (Trends in African Linguistics Ser.). 316p. 1997. pap. 29.95 (*0-86543-632-0*) Africa World.

Language History, Language Change, & Language Relationship: An Introduction to Historical & Comparative Linguistics. Hans H. Hock & Brian D. Joseph. LC 96-3251. (Trends in Linguistics Ser.: Vol. 93). (Illus.). xv, 600p. (C). 1996. pap. text 31.95 (*3-11-014784-X*); lib. bdg. 198.50 (*3-11-014785-8*) Mouton.

Language, History, Style: Leo Spitzer & the Critical Tradition. James V. Catano. 216p. 1988. text 25.95 (*0-252-01530-4*) U of Ill Pr.

Language Ideas & American Culture. 336p. (C). 1997. 39.80 (*0-536-00106-5*, Macmillan Coll) P-H.

Language, Identity & Marginality in Indonesia: The Changing Nature of Ritual Speech on the Island of Sumba. Joel C. Kuipers. LC 97-38770. (Studies in the Social & Cultural Foundations of Language: No. 18). (Illus.). 180p. (C). 1998. 59.95 (*0-521-62408-8*); pap. text 19.95 (*0-521-62495-9*) Cambridge U Pr.

***Language-Ideological Debates.** Ed. by Jan Blommaert. LC 99-32848. 1999. pap. 24.95 (*3-11-016349-7*) De Gruyter.

***Language-Ideological Debates.** Ed. by Jan Blommaert. LC 99-32848. (Language, Power & Social Process Ser.: No. 2). 447p. 1999. 93.00 (*3-11-016350-0*) De Gruyter.

Language Ideologies: Critical Perspectives on the Offical English Movement, 2 vols. Ed. by Roseann Dvenas Gonzalez & Ildiko Melis. 320p. pap. 33.95 (*0-8141-2667-7*, 26677) NCTE.

Language Ideologies: Practice & Theory. Ed. by Bambi B. Schieffelin et al. LC 97-23336. (Oxford Studies in Anthropological Linguistics: No. 16). (Illus.). 352p. 1998. pap. 35.00 (*0-19-510562-1*) OUP.

An Asterisk (*) at the beginning of an entry indicates that the title is appearing for the first time.

Language Ideology & Language Change in Early Modern German: A Sociolinguistic Study of the Consonantal System of Nuremburg. Rosina L. Lippi-Green. LC 94-31088. (Current Issues in Linguistic Theory Ser.: No. 119). xiv, 150p. 1994. lib. bdg. 48.00 (*1-55619-573-7*) J Benjamins Pubng Co.

Language, Ideology, & Point of View. Paul Simpson. LC 92-27422. (Interface Ser.). 208p. (C). 1993. pap. 24.99 (*0-415-07107-0*) Routledge.

Language, Ideology & Social Consciousness: Developing a Sociohistorical Approach. Chik Collings. LC 98-74510. 16p. 1999. text 69.95 (*1-84014-842-X*) Ashgate Pub Co.

***Language Imperative: How Learning Languages Can Enrich Your Life & Expand Your Mind.** Suzette H. Elgin. 304p. 1999. text 24.00 (*0-7382-0254-1*, Pub. by Perseus Pubng) HarpC.

Language in a Black Community. Viv Edwards. 164p. (Orig.). 1986. 69.00 (*0-905028-53-8*, MM24, Pub. by Multilingual Matters); pap. 24.95 (*0-905028-52-X*, Pub. by Multilingual Matters) Taylor & Francis.

Language in a Changing Europe. Ed. by David Graddol & Stephen Thomas. 128p. 1995. pap. 24.95 (*1-85359-300-1*, Pub. by Multilingual Matters) Taylor & Francis.

Language in a Plural Society. Ed. by Lachman M. Khubchandani. (C). 1988. 30.00 (*81-208-0460-0*, Pub. by Motilal Bnarsidass) S Asia.

Language in Action: Categories, Lambdas & Dynamic Logic. Johan Van Benthem. 360p. 1995. pap. text 31.50 (*0-262-72024-8*) MIT Pr.

Language in Action: Categories, Lambdas & Dynamic Logic. John Van Benthem. (Studies in Logic & the Foundations of Mathematics: No. 130). 350p. 1991. 101.00 (*0-444-89000-9*) Elsevier.

***Language in Action: New Studies of Language in Society: Essays in Honor of Roger W. Shuy.** Joy K. Peyton & Roger W. Shuy. LC 99-51425. 1999. write for info. (*1-57273-274-1*) Hampton Pr NJ.

Language in Africa: An Introductory Survey. Ed. by E. Gregersen. (Library of Anthropology: Vol. 3). xviii, 237p. 1977. text 134.00 (*0-677-04380-5*) Gordon & Breach.

Language in America: A Report on Our Deteriorating Semantic Environment. Ed. by Neil Postman et al. LC 73-77137. 1969. text 29.50 (*0-672-53552-1*) Irvington.

Language in American Life: Proceedings of the Georgetown University Modern Language Association Conference, October 6-8, 1977, Washington, D. C. Georgetown University Modern Language Association. Ed. by E. Michael Gerli et al. LC 78-14218. 165p. reprint ed. pap. 51.20 (*0-7837-6322-0*, 204603700010) Bks Demand.

Language in Behavior. 2nd ed. Richard W. Howell & Harold J. Vetter. 299p. 1985. 50.95 (*0-89885-215-3*, Kluwer Acad Hman Sci) Kluwer Academic.

Language in Canada. Ed. by John Edwards. LC 98-200452. (Illus.). 502p. (C). 1998. 89.95 (*0-521-56328-3*) Cambridge U Pr.

Language in Centers. Laverne Warner & Kenneth Craycraft. 144p. 1991. 13.99 (*0-86653-616-7*, GA1335) Good Apple.

Language in Cognitive Development: The Emergence of the Mediated Mind. Katherine Nelson. (Illus.). 448p. (C). 1996. text 54.95 (*0-521-55123-4*) Cambridge U Pr.

Language in Cognitive Development: The Emergence of the Mediated Mind. Katherine Nelson. (Illus.). 448p. (C). 1998. reprint ed. pap. text 21.95 (*0-521-62987-X*) Cambridge U Pr.

Language in Colour: Themes for Teaching Children from Five to Nine Years with Poetry as the Starting Point. Moira Andrew. 1995. pap. 15.95 (*0-947882-10-3*) Incentive Pubns.

Language in Daily Living, Vol. 2. Brian Hodegteth. 1985. 4.29 (*0-8114-1190-7*) Raintree Steck-V.

Language in Daily Use. Strickland. 1983. pap., wbk. ed. 13.00 (*0-15-317030-1*); pap., wbk. ed. 13.75 (*0-15-317031-X*); pap., wbk. ed. 14.25 (*0-15-317032-8*); pap., wbk. ed. 14.25 (*0-15-317033-6*); pap., wbk. ed. 15.75 (*0-15-317034-4*); pap., wbk. ed. 15.75 (*0-15-317035-2*) Harcourt Schl Pubs.

Language in Daily Use, Grade 5. Strickland. 1986. student ed. 41.00 (*0-15-316736-X*) Harcourt Schl Pubs.

Language in Daily Use, Grade 8. Strickland. 1986. 126.50 (*0-15-316749-1*) Harcourt Schl Pubs.

Language in Daily Use: Grade 3. Strickland. 1986. 37.50 (*0-01-531673-4*) Harcourt Schl Pubs.

Language in Daily Use: Grade 7. Strickland. 1986. teacher ed. 115.50 (*0-15-316748-3*) Harcourt Schl Pubs.

Language in Early Childhood Education. rev. ed. Ed. by Courtney B. Cazden. LC 81-82158. (Illus.). 170p. 1981. pap. text 6.00 (*0-912674-74-1*, NAEYC #131) Natl Assn Child Ed.

Language in Education: Ethnolinguistic Essays. Dell H. Hymes. LC 80-27439. (Language & Ethnography Ser.: No. 1). 176p. reprint ed. pap. 54.60 (*0-8357-3364-5*, 203960300013) Bks Demand.

Language in Education in Africa: Tanzanian Perspectives. Ed. by Casmir M. Rubagumya. (Multilingual Matters Ser.: No. 57). 154p. 1990. 74.95 (*1-85359-063-0*, Pub. by Multilingual Matters); pap. 29.95 (*1-85359-062-2*, Pub. by Multilingual Matters) Taylor & Francis.

Language in Emergency Medicine: A Gentle Art of Verbal Self-Defense Handbook. Suzette H. Elgin. 43p. (Orig.). 1990. pap. 10.00 (*1-878709-00-3*) Ozark Ctr Lang Studies Pr.

Language in Ethnicity: A View of Basic Ecological Relations. David Haarmann. (Contributions to the Sociology of Language Ser.: No. 44). (Illus.). iv, 291p. 1986. lib. bdg. 103.85 (*0-89925-097-1*) Mouton.

Language in Evidence: Issues Confronting Aboriginal & Multilingual Australia. Ed. by Diana Eades. 1995. pap. 29.95 (*0-86840-119-6*, Pub. by New South Wales Univ Pr) Intl Spec Bk.

Language in Exile: Three Hundred Years of Jamaican Creole. Barbara Lalla & Jean D'Costa. LC 88-34012. 276p. 1990. text 44.95 (*0-8173-0447-9*) U of Ala Pr.

Language in Geographic Context. Ed. by Colin H. Williams. 1988. 99.00 (*1-85359-002-9*, Pub. by Multilingual Matters); pap. 39.95 (*1-85359-001-0*, Pub. by Multilingual Matters) Taylor & Francis.

Language in Global Perspective: Papers in Honor of the Fiftieth Anniversary of the Summer Institute of Linguistics, 1935-1985. Ed. by Benjamin F. Elson. 626p. (Orig.). 1986. pap. 15.00 (*0-88312-662-1*) S I L Intl.

Language in Hong Kong at Century's End. Martha C. Pennington. 449p. 1998. pap. 52.50 (*962-209-418-X*, Pub. by HK Univ Pr) Coronet Bks.

Language in Its Cultural Embedding: Explorations in the Relativity of Signs & Sign Systems. Harold Haarmann. (Studies in Anthropological Linguistics: No. 4). (Illus.). xiv, 276p. (C). 1990. lib. bdg. 113.85 (*3-11-012086-0*) Mouton.

Language in Law Enforcement. Suzette H. Elgin. 50p. (Orig.). 1993. pap. 10.00 (*1-878709-04-6*) Ozark Ctr Lang Studies Pr.

Language in Literature. Roman Jakobson. Ed. by Krystyna Pomorska & Stephen Rudy. 592p. 1988. pap. 24.95 (*0-674-51028-3*) HUP.

Language in Literature. Roman Jakobson. Ed. by Krystyna Pomorska & Stephen Rudy. LC 86-19465. (Illus.). 592p. 1988. 49.95 (*0-674-51027-5*) HUP.

Language in Literature. Michael Toolan. LC 97-17344. 264p. 1998. text 60.00 (*0-340-66213-1*); pap. text 18.95 (*0-340-66214-X*) OUP.

Language in Mathematical Education: Research & Practice. Ed. by Kevin Durkin & Beatrice Shire. 256p. 1991. pap. 41.95 (*0-335-09366-3*) OpUniv Pr.

Language in Mathematics. Ed. by Jennie Bickmore-Brand. LC 92-46790. 128p. (C). 1993. pap. text 17.00 (*0-435-08340-6*, 08340) Heinemann.

Language in Mental Retardation. J. A. Rondal & Susan Edwards. LC 97-118479. xi, 310p. 1997. write for info. (*1-86156-004-4*) Whurr Pub.

Language in Mental Retardation. Jean A. Rondal. 322p. (Orig.). 1996. pap. 45.00 (*1-56593-812-7*, 1590) Singular Publishing.

Language in Mind & Language in Society: Studies in Linguistic Reproduction. Trevor Pateman. 208p. 1987. text 55.00 (*0-19-824213-1*) OUP.

Language in Motion: Exploring the Nature of Sign. Jerome D. Schein & David A. Stewart. LC 95-12553. 240p. 1995. 24.95 (*1-56368-039-4*) Gallaudet Univ Pr.

Language in Nigeria: Essays in Honor of Ayo Bamgbose. Kola Owolabi. 530p. 1998. 89.95 (*0-86543-654-1*); pap. 29.95 (*0-86543-655-X*) Africa World.

Language in Popular Fiction. Walter Nash. (Interface Ser.). 256p. (C). 1990. pap. text 16.95 (*0-415-02944-9*, A4187) Routledge.

Language in Primates: Perspectives & Implications. Ed. by Judith De Luce & H. T. Wilder. (Language & Communication Ser.: Vol. 11). (Illus.). xi, 198p. 1983. 92.95 (*0-387-90798-X*); pap. 36.00 (*0-387-90799-8*) Spr-Verlag.

Language in Psychotherapy: Strategies of Discovery. R. L. Russell. LC 87-2511. (Emotions, Personality, & Psychotherapy Ser.). (Illus.). 368p. (C). 1987. text 80.00 (*0-306-42422-3*, Kluwer Plenum) Kluwer Academic.

Language in Public Life. fac. ed. Georgetown University Roundtable on Languages & Li. Ed. by G. Richard Tucker & James E. Alatis. LC 58-31607. 328p. 1979. reprint ed. pap. 101.70 (*0-7837-7794-9*, 204755000007) Bks Demand.

Language in Relation to a Unified Theory of the Structure of Human Behavior. Kenneth L. Pike. (Janua Linguarum, Ser. Major: No. 24). 1967. text 118.50 (*90-279-1869-4*) Mouton.

Language in Religion. Ed. by Humphrey Tonkin & Allison A. Keef. LC 89-16548. (Papers of the Center for Research & Documentation on World Language Problems: No. 1). 130p. (C). 1989. lib. bdg. 36.00 (*0-8191-7511-0*) U Pr of Amer.

Language in Society: An Introduction to Sociolinguistics. Suzanne Romaine. (Illus.). 250p. 1994. pap. text 11.95 (*0-19-875134-6*) OUP.

***Language in Society: An Introduction to Sociolinguistics.** 2nd ed. Suzanne Romaine. (Illus.). 290p. 2000. pap. 14.95 (*0-19-873192-2*) OUP.

Language in Tanzania. Ed. by Edgar C. Polome & C. P. Hill. (Survey of Language Use & Language Teaching in Eastern Africa Ser.). 1981. 39.00 (*0-19-724205-7*) OUP.

Language in Tanzania. Ed. by Edgar C. Polome & C. P. Hill. LC 81-147648. (Ford Foundation Language Surveys Ser.). 442p. reprint ed. pap. 137.10 (*0-8357-6964-X*, 203902400009) Bks Demand.

Language in the Americas. Joseph H. Greenberg. LC 86-14359. 456p. 1987. 57.50 (*0-8047-1315-4*) Stanford U Pr.

Language in the Judicial Process. J. N. Levi & A. G. Walker. (Law, Society, & Policy Ser.: Vol. 5). (Illus.). 402p. (C). 1990. 65.00 (*0-306-43551-9*, Plenum Trade) Perseus Pubng.

Language in the Mathematics Classroom: Talking, Representing, Recording. Rachel Griffiths & Margaret Clyne. LC 94-35141. 156p. 1994. pap. text 18.00 (*0-435-08366-X*, 08366) Heinemann.

Language in the Modern World. Simeon Potter. LC 83-8248. 205p. 1983. reprint ed. lib. bdg. 55.00 (*0-313-24009-4*, POLA, Greenwood Pr) Greenwood.

Language in the News: Discourse & Ideology in the British Press. Roger Fowler. 272p. (C). 1991. pap. 20.99 (*0-415-01419-0*, A5441) Routledge.

Language in the Philosophy of Aristotle. Miriam T. Larkin. LC 74-165145. (Janua Linguarum, Ser. Minor: No. 87). 113p. 1971. pap. text 34.65 (*90-279-1843-0*) Mouton.

Language in the Philosophy of Hegel. Daniel Cook. (Janua Linguarum, Ser. Minor: No. 135). 198p. (Orig.). 1973. pap. text 36.95 (*90-279-2402-3*) Mouton.

Language in the U. S. A. Ed. by Charles A. Ferguson et al. 650p. 1981. 95.00 (*0-521-23140-X*); pap. text 35.95 (*0-521-29834-2*) Cambridge U Pr.

Language in the World: A Philosophical Enquiry. M. J. Cresswell. (Cambridge Studies in Philosophy). 170p. (C). 1994. text 54.95 (*0-521-44562-0*) Cambridge U Pr.

Language in Thought & Action. 5th ed. Samuel I. Hayakawa & Alan R. Hayakawa. 214p. 1991. pap. 14.00 (*0-15-648240-1*, Harvest Bks) Harcourt.

Language in Thought & Action. 5th ed. Samuel I. Hayakawa & Alan R. Hayakawa. 287p. (C). 1989. pap. text 37.00 (*0-15-550120-8*, Pub. by Harcourt Coll Pubs) Harcourt.

Language in Time: The Rhythm & Tempo of Spoken Interaction. Peter Auer et al. LC 98-20722. (Oxford Studies in Sociolinguistics). (Illus.). 256p. 1999. text 65.00 (*0-19-510928-7*) OUP.

***Language in Time of Revolution.** Benjamin Harshav. 1999. 17.95 (*0-8047-3540-9*) Stanford U Pr.

Language in Time of Revolution. Benjamin Harshav. 248p. 1994. 35.00 (*0-520-07958-2*, Pub. by U CA Pr) Cal Prin Full Svc.

Language in Wycherley's Plays: Seventeenth-Century Language Theory & Drama. James Thompson. LC 83-1242. 163p. 1984. pap. 50.60 (*0-7837-8413-9*, 205922400009) Bks Demand.

Language in Zambia. Ed. by Sirarpi Ohannessian & Mubanga E. Kashoki. LC 78-325190. (Ford Foundation Language Surveys Ser.). 472p. 1978. reprint ed. pap. 146.40 (*0-8357-3022-0*, 205710900010) Bks Demand.

Language Industries Atlas. P. M. Hearn & D. Button. LC 93-80963. 406p. (YA). (gr. 12). 1994. 80.00 (*90-5199-148-7*, Pub. by IOS Pr) IOS Press.

Language Industries Atlas. 2nd ed. Ed. by G. Kingscott & J. Edwards. LC 95-8175. 400p. (YA). (gr. 12). 1996. 100.00 (*90-5199-252-1*, 252-1) IOS Press.

Language Inequality & Distortion in Intercultural Communication: A Critical Theory Approach. Yukio Tsuda. LC 87-15794. (Pragmatics & Beyond Ser.: Vol VII: 7). xi, 97p. (C). 1987. pap. 35.00 (*1-55619-008-5*) J Benjamins Pubng Co.

Language Instinct: How the Mind Creates Language. Steven Pinker. LC 94-39138. 496p. 1995. pap. 15.00 (*0-06-097651-9*, Perennial) HarperTrade.

***Language Instinct: How the Mind Creates Language.** Steven Pinker. 496p. 2000. pap. 15.00 (*0-06-095833-2*, Perennial) HarperTrade.

Language Instruction for Students with Disabilities. 2nd ed. Edward A. Polloway & Tom E. Smith. 1992. teacher ed. 49.95 (*0-89108-221-2*, 9202) Love Pub Co.

Language Instruction for Students with Disabilities. 2nd ed. Edward A. Polloway & Tom E. C. Smith. 496p. (C). 1999. pap. text 49.95 (*0-89108-269-7*) Love Pub Co.

Language, Intelligence, & Thought. Robin Barrow. 144p. 1993. 70.00 (*1-85278-094-0*) E Elgar.

Language, Interaction, & Social Cognition. Ed. by Gun R. Semin & Klaus Fiedler. (Illus.). 272p. (C). 1992. 65.00 (*0-8039-8530-4*) Sage.

Language Interaction in Curriculum & Instruction: What the Classroom Teacher Needs to Know. 2nd ed. Lee Gruenewald & Sara A. Pollack. LC 90-36047. 134p. 1990. pap. text 28.00 (*0-89079-208-9*, 1488) PRO-ED.

Language International World Directory of Sociolinguistic & Language Planning Organizations. Compiled by Francesc Dominguez & Nuria Lopez. LC 95-23742. (Language International World Directory Ser.: No. 1). xx, 530p. 1995. 130.00 (*1-55619-740-3*) J Benjamins Pubng Co.

Language International World Directory of Translation & Interpreting Schools. Compiled by Brian Harris. LC 97-38872. (Language International World Directory Ser.: Vol. 2). xii, 238p. 1997. lib. bdg. 95.00 (*1-55619-741-1*) J Benjamins Pubng Co.

Language Intervention: Beyond the Primary Grades. Ed. by Donald F. Tibbits. LC 94-41708. (For Clinicians by Clinicians Ser.). 528p. (Orig.). (C). 1995. pap. text 36.00 (*0-89079-624-6*, 6958) PRO-ED.

Language Intervention: Preschool Through the Elementary Years. Marc Fey et al. Ed. by Steven F. Warren. LC 94-13214. (Communication & Language Intervention Ser.: Vol. 5). 416p. 1994. boxed set 42.00 (*1-55766-168-5*) P H Brookes.

Language Intervention & Academic Success. Geraldine P. Wallach & Lynda Miller. LC 90-8725. 253p. (Orig.). (C). 1988. text 36.00 (*0-7506-9735-0*, 1569) Buttrwrth-Heinemann.

Language Intervention & Academic Success. Geraldine P. Wallach & Lynda Miller. LC 90-8725. 253p. (Orig.). (C). 1988. pap. text 27.00 (*0-89079-381-6*, 1569) PRO-ED.

Language Intervention Strategies in Adult Aphasia. 3rd ed. Ed. by Roberta Chapey. LC 92-48908. (Illus.). 6481994p. 1993. 58.00 (*0-683-01513-3*) Lppncott W & W.

Language Intervention with School-Aged Children: Conversation Narrative, & Text. Rita C. Naremore. (Illus.). 292p. (Orig.). (C). 1994. pap. text 49.95 (*1-56593-222-6*, 0582) Thomson Learn.

Language Intervention with Young Children. Marc Fey. LC 90-52762. 358p. (C). 1991. 83.00 (*0-205-13570-6*) Allyn.

Language Intro Kit: Four Individual Sets in a Kit. Marion W. Stuart. text. write for info. (*0-943343-82-8*) Lrn Wrap-Ups.

***Language is the Key: Talking & Books & Talking & Play, Vol. I.** Mary Maddox et al. (Illus.). 92p. 1998. student ed. 95.00 (*1-930690-00-2*) Wash Resrch Instit.

Language Issues. Longman Publishing Staff. 1993. pap. text, student ed. write for info. (*0-582-07775-3*, Pub. by Addison-Wesley) Longman.

Language Issues: Readings for Teachers. (C). 1995. write for info. (*0-8013-1462-3*) Longman.

Language Issues in Deaf Education. Barbara Luetke-Stahlman. LC 99-165358. 376p. (Orig.). (C). 1998. pap., per. 44.00 (*1-884362-26-5*) Butte Pubns.

Language Issues in Literacy & Bilingual - Multicultural Education. Ed. by Masahiko Minami & Bruce P. Kennedy. LC 91-75438. (Reprint Ser.: No. 22). 572p. (C). 1991. pap. 35.95 (*0-916690-24-5*) Harvard Educ Rev.

Language Issues in Nepal. S. Toba. (C). 1992. 35.00 (*0-7855-0189-4*, Pub. by Ratna Pustak Bhandar) St Mut.

Language Issues Workbook. Longman Publishing Staff. 1993. pap. text. write for info. (*0-582-07776-1*, Pub. by Addison-Wesley) Longman.

***Language Knowledge for Primary Teachers: A Guide to Textual, Grammatical & Lexical Study.** Angela C. Wilson. (Illus.). 1999. pap. 26.95 (*1-85346-606-9*) David Fulton.

Language Ladder, Bk. I. Phyllis Childs. (Illus.). 76p. (J). (ps). 1985. student ed. 6.50 (*0-931749-01-8*) PJC Lrng Mtrls.

Language Ladder, Bk. 2. Phyllis Childs. 54p. (J). (ps). 1987. pap., student ed. 5.95 (*0-317-60748-0*) PJC Lrng Mtrls.

Language Learnability & L2 Phonology: The Acquisition of Metrical Parameters. John Archibald. LC 93-31917. (Studies in Theoretical Psycholinguistics: Vol. 19). 220p. (C). 1993. text 146.00 (*0-7923-2486-2*) Kluwer Academic.

Language Learnability & Language Development. Steven Pinker. (Cognitive Science Ser.: No. 7). 456p. 1987. pap. 16.95 (*0-674-51055-0*) HUP.

Language Learnability & Language Development. Steven Pinker. 480p. 1996. pap. 20.95 (*0-674-51053-4*) HUP.

Language Learner. Ed. by Donald D. Eddy. 70p. 1959. pap. 10.95 (*0-915432-59-5*) NE Conf Teach Foreign.

Language, Learners & Computers: Human Intelligence & Artificial Unintelligence. J. Higgins. 1988. pap. text 18.95 (*0-582-55263-X*, 78031) Longman.

Language Learning. write for info. (*0-340-62510-4*, Pub. by E A) Routldge.

Language Learning, No. 49, Suppl. I. Ed. by Jonathan Leather. (Best of Language Learning Ser.: Vol. III). 300p. 1999. pap. 32.95 (*0-631-21609-X*) Blackwell Pubs.

Language Learning: Insights of Learning. Andrew D. Cohen. (J). 1990. mass mkt., teacher ed. 27.95 (*0-8384-2676-X*) Heinle & Heinle.

Language Learning: The Intermediate Phase. Ed. by William F. Bottiglia. 85p. 1963. pap. 10.95 (*0-915432-63-3*) NE Conf Teach Foreign.

Language, Learning, & Behavior Disorders: Developmental, Biological, & Clinical Perspectives. Ed. by Joseph H. Beitchman et al. (Illus.). 582p. (C). 1996. text 129.95 (*0-521-47229-6*) Cambridge U Pr.

Language Learning & Concept Acquisition: Foundational Issues. Ed. by William Demopoulos et al. LC 85-13455. (Theoretical Issues in Cognitive Science Ser.: Vol. 1). 224p. (C). 1986. text 78.50 (*0-89391-316-2*) Ablx Pub.

Language Learning & Deafness. Ed. by Michael Strong. (Cambridge Applied Linguistics Ser.). (Illus.). 320p. 1988. text 64.95 (*0-521-34046-2*); pap. text 24.95 (*0-521-33579-5*) Cambridge U Pr.

Language Learning Disabilities in School-Age Children & Adolescents. Ed. by Geraldine P. Wallach & Katherine G. Butler. LC 93-29233. (Illus.). 544p. (C). 1994. 82.00 (*0-675-22153-6*, Merrill Coll) P-H.

Language Learning for European Citizenship - Final Report (1989-96) 1997. 18.00 (*92-871-3237-2*, Pub. by Council of Europe) Manhattan Pub Co.

Language Learning in Europe: The Challenge of Diversity (Final Conference of the Modern Languages Project No. 12, Strasbourg, 1988) Council of Europe Staff. 1989. 21.00 (*92-871-1696-2*, Pub. by Council of Europe) Manhattan Pub Co.

Language Learning in Intercultural Perspective: Approaches Through Drama & Ethnography. Ed. by Michael Byram & Michael Fleming. LC 97-47530. (Cambridge Language Teaching Library). (Illus.). 318p. (C). 1998. text 59.95 (*0-521-62376-6*); pap. text 21.95 (*0-521-62559-9*) Cambridge U Pr.

Language Learning Material. F. M. Hodgson. 41p. 1961. pap. 2.50 (*0-87825-252-5*) Ed Solutions.

Language Learning Motivation: Pathways to the New Century. Ed. by Rebecca L. Oxford. (Technical Report Ser.: No. 11). 232p. 1996. pap. text 20.00 (*0-8248-1849-0*) Sec Lang Tching.

Language Learning Online: Theory & Practice in the ESL & L2 Computer Classroom Janet K. Swaffar. LC 98-84350. 200 p. 1998. write for info. (*1-891430-12-2*, Labyrinth TX) Daedalus Grp.

Language Learning Practices with Deaf Children. 2nd ed. Patricia L. McAnally et al. LC 93-39470. 321p. (C). 1994. text 38.00 (*0-89079-597-5*, 6667) PRO-ED.

Language Learning Strategies. Rebecca L. Oxford. 342p. (J). 1990. mass mkt. 27.95 (*0-8384-2862-2*, Newbury) Heinle & Heinle.

Language Learning Strategies: Conversation Skills Through Oral Histories. Rebecca L. Oxford. (C). 1990. pap. 18.00 (*0-06-632607-9*) Addson-Wesley Educ.

L

An Asterisk (*) at the beginning of an entry indicates that the title is appearing for the first time.

L

Language Learning Strategies Around the World: Cross-Cultural Perspectives. Ed. by Rebecca L. Oxford. (Technical Reports: No. 13). 320p. 1996. pap. text 20.00 (*0-8248-1910-1*) Sec Lang Tching.

Language Learning the Classroom: Aims & Conditions. M. L. Wales. 51p. (C). 1988. 51.00 (*0-7300-0553-4*, Pub. by Deakin Univ) St Mut.

Language Legislation & Linguistic Rights: Selected Proceedings of the Language Legislation & Linguistic Rights Conference, the University of Illinois at Urbana-Champaign, March, 1996. Ed. by Douglas A. Kibbee. LC 98-26118. (IMPACT: No. 2). xvi, 415p. 1998. text 79.00 (*1-55619-851-5*) J Benjamins Pubng Co.

Language Lessons: For When Your Mom Dies. Mary Clare Griffin. 200p. 1999. pap. 14.95 (*0-9668940-1-4*) DayBue Pubg.

Language Lessons K-Five for Teacher Appraisal Success. Amanda C. Gonzales & Dianne Shannon. Ed. by John Gonzales. (Illus.). 101p. (Orig.). 1988. pap. 12.95 (*0-9618511-3-9*) Teachers Two.

Language, Linguistics, & Leadership: Essays in Honor of Carol M. K. Eastman. Joseph H. O'Mealy et al. LC 98-40514. (Literary Studies--East & West). 1998. 28.00 (*0-8248-1971-3*) UH Pr.

Language, Linguistics & Philology: Papers from the Philological Society Anniversary... Nigel Vincent. Date not set. pap. text 36.95 (*0-631-19068-6*) Blackwell Pubs.

Language Literacy: Lively Approach. 112p. (C). 1997. text 24.00 (*0-06-501398-0*) Addison-Wesley.

Language, Literacy, & Culture: Issues of Society & Schooling. Ed. by Judith A. Langer. LC 87-11450. 256p. (C). 1987. text 73.25 (*0-89391-437-1*) Ablx Pub.

Language, Literacy, & Learning in Educational Practice. Ed. by Barry Stierer & Janet Maybin. LC 93-29911. 264p. 1993. 74.95 (*1-85359-218-8*, Pub. by Multilingual Matters); pap. 29.95 (*1-85359-217-X*, Pub. by Multilingual Matters) Taylor & Francis.

Language Literacy & the Child. 2nd ed. Galda. (C). 1997. pap. text, teacher ed. 42.00 (*0-15-504015-4*) Harcourt Coll Pubs.

Language, Literature & Critical Practice: Ways of Analysing Text. David Birch. 256p. (C). 1989. pap. 24.99 (*0-415-02941-4*) Routledge.

Language, Literature & Critical Practice: Ways of Analysing Text. David Birch. 256p. 1989. 39.95 (*0-415-03121-4*) Routledge.

Language, Literature, & History: Philological & Historical Studies Presented to Erica Reiner. Ed. by Francesca Rochberg-Halton. (American Oriental Ser.: Vol. 67). (Illus.). xii, 439p. (C). 1987. 35.00 (*0-940490-67-6*, #PJ3189: L35) Am Orient Soc.

Language, Literature, & Life: Selected Essays by Robert A. Hall, Jr. Robert A. Hall, Jr. LC 79-26478. (Edward Sapir Monographs in Language, Culture & Cognition: No. 5). viii, 295p. (Orig.). (C). 1978. pap. 32.00 (*0-933104-07-3*) Jupiter Pr.

Language, Literature & Meaning I: Problems of Literary Theory. Ed. by John Odmark. (Linguistic & Literary Studies in Eastern Europe: No. 1). x, 467p. 1979. 97.00 (*90-272-1502-2*) J Benjamins Pubng Co.

Language, Literature & Meaning II: Current Trends in Literary Research. Ed. by John Odmark. (Linguistic & Literary Studies in Eastern Europe: No. 2). x, 569p. 1980. 124.00 (*90-272-1503-0*, 2) J Benjamins Pubng Co.

Language, Literature & National Integration. G. K. Ghosh. xvi, 235p. (C). 1995. 25.00 (*81-7024-655-5*, Pub. by APH Pubng) Nataraj Bks.

Language, Literature, & the Negotiation of Identity: Foreign Worker German in the Federal Republic of Germany. Barbara A. Fennell. LC 97-9887. (Studies in the Germanic Languages & Literatures). 192p. (C). (gr. 13). 1998. lib. bdg. 37.50 (*0-8078-8119-8*) U of NC Pr.

Language, Literature, Linguistics: In Honor of Francis J. Whitfield on his Seventieth Birthday, March 25, 1986. Ed. by Michael S. Flier & Simon Karlinsky. (Illus.). xviii, 249p. (Orig.). 1987. pap. 12.00 (*0-933884-58-3*) Berkeley Slavic.

Language, Logic & Causation: Philosophical Writings of Professor Douglas Gasking. Ed. by I. T. Oakely & L. J. O'Neill. 256p. 1997. pap. 24.95 (*0-522-84756-0*, Pub. by Melbourne Univ Pr) Paul & Co Pubs.

Language, Logic & Concepts. Ed. by Ray Jackendoff et al. LC 98-47084. (Illus.). 470p. 1999. 45.00 (*0-262-10078-9*, Bradford Bks) MIT Pr.

Language, Logic, & Genre: Papers from the Poetics & Literary Theory Section, Modern Language Association. Ed. by Wallace Martin. 54p. 1974. 10.00 (*0-8387-1446-3*) Bucknell U Pr.

Language, Logic, & God. Frederick Ferre. LC 81-27305. viii, 184p. (C). 1994. reprint ed. pap. text 10.00 (*0-226-24457-1*, Midway Reprint) U Ch Pr.

Language, Logic & God. Frederick Ferre. LC 80-27305. (Midway Reprint Ser.). 192p. reprint ed. pap. 59.60 (*0-608-09297-5*, 205417100004) Bks Demand.

Language, Logic & Method. Robert S. Cohen & Marx W. Wartofsky. 484p. 1982. text 234.00 (*90-277-0725-1*, D Reidel) Kluwer Academic.

Language, Logic & Philosophy. Ed. by R. Haller & W. Grassl. (Proceedings of the International Wittgenstein Symposia Ser.: No. 4). 550p. 1980. pap. 52.50 (*0-686-27692-2*) Kluwer Academic.

Language, Logic & Reason in the Church Fathers: A Study of Tertullian, Augustine, & Aquinas. Robert H. Ayers. (Altertumswissenschaftliche Texte und Studien: Bd. 6). viii, 146p. 1979. 25.00 (*3-487-06629-7*) G Olms Pubs.

Language, Logic & Science in India: Some Conceptual & Historical Perspectives, No. 4. Debiprasad Chattopadhyaya et al. Ed. by Ravinder Kumar. LC 95-905858. (PHISPC Monographs: Ser. 4). 100p. (C). 1995. 21.00 (*81-215-0689-1*, Pub. by M Manoharial) Coronet Bks.

Language, Lore & Lyrics. Douglas Hyde. Ed. by Brendan O. Conaire. 202p. 35.00 (*0-7165-2372-8*, Pub. by Irish Acad Pr) Intl Spec Bk.

Language Loss & the Crisis of Cognition: Between Socio- & Psycholinguistics. Dallas K. Kenny. LC 96-28694. (Contributions to the Sociology of Language Ser.: Vol. 73). xiv, 306p. (C). 1996. lib. bdg. 117.05 (*3-11-015125-1*) Mouton.

Language Loyalties: A Source Book on the Official English Controversy. James Crawford. LC 91-29445. (Illus.). 532p. 1992. pap. 17.95 (*0-226-12016-3*) U Ch Pr.

Language Loyalties: A Source Book on the Official English Controversy. James Crawford. LC 91-29445. (Illus.). 536p. 1995. lib. bdg. 45.95 (*0-226-12015-5*) U Ch Pr.

Language Loyalty & Linguistic Variation: A Study in Spanish Cantabria. J. Holmquist. (Topics in Sociolinguistics Ser.). vi, 144p. 1988. pap. 46.15 (*90-6765-355-1*) Mouton.

Language Loyalty in the United States. Joshua A. Fishman et al. Ed. by Francesco Cordasco. LC 77-90409. (Bilingual-Bicultural Education in the U. S. Ser.). 1978. reprint ed. lib. bdg. 47.95 (*0-405-11078-2*) Ayer.

Language Machine. Roy Harris. LC 87-47722. 192p. (C). 1987. 39.95 (*0-8014-2105-5*) Cornell U Pr.

Language Machines: Technologies of Literary & Cultural Production. Jeffrey Masten & Peter Stallybrass. LC 97-7321. (English Institute Ser.). (Illus.). 288p. (C). 1997. pap. 19.99 (*0-415-91864-2*) Routledge.

Language Machines: Technologies of Literary & Cultural Production. Ed. by Jeffrey Masten & Peter Stallybrass. LC 97-7321. (English Institute Ser.). (Illus.). 288p. (C). 1997. 75.00 (*0-415-91863-4*) Routledge.

Language, Madness & the Law. Bruce A. Arrigo. 220p. 1993. text 59.50 (*0-911577-26-2*, Criminal Justice) Willow Tree NY.

Language Maintenance & Language Shift. Ed. by Robert C. Williamson & John A. Van Eerde. (International Journal of the Sociology of Language Ser.: No. 25). 124p. 1980. 60.00 (*90-279-3068-6*) Mouton.

Language Maintenance & Language Shift in Canada: New Dimensions in the Use of Census Language Data. Ed. by Paul G. Lamay. LC 78-319608. (Research Monographs in the Social Sciences: Vol. 3). 113p. 1977. reprint ed. pap. 35.10 (*0-608-02184-9*, 206285300003) Bks Demand.

Language, Man & Society, 23 titles in 31 vols., Set. reprint ed. 1137.50 (*0-404-08490-7*) AMS Pr.

Language Manual: Individual Book. Marion W. Stuart. text. write for info. (*0-943343-71-2*) Lrn Wrap-Ups.

Language, Mathematics, & Linguistics. Charles F. Hockett. (Janua Linguarum, Ser. Minor: No. 60). (Illus.). 1967. pap. text 35.40 (*3-10-800067-5*) Mouton.

Language Matters. Capossela. (C). 1995. pap. text 35.00 (*0-15-502004-8*); pap. text, teacher ed. 30.00 (*0-15-502159-1*) Harcourt Coll Pubs.

Language, Meaning, & Culture: The Selected Papers of C. E. Osgood. Ed. by Charles E. Osgood & Oliver C. Tzeng. LC 89-16055. (Centennial Psychology Ser.). 415p. 1990. 79.50 (*0-275-92521-8*, C2521, Praeger Pubs) Greenwood.

Language Meaning & Religion. R. P. Shrivastava. 1990. 28.50 (*81-202-0271-6*, Pub. by Ajanta) S Asia.

Language Medallion: Grade 1. 1993. pap. text, student ed. 16.75 (*0-15-301050-9*) Harcourt Schl Pubs.

Language Medallion: Grade 2. 1993. pap. text, student ed. 19.00 (*0-15-301051-7*); pap. text, student ed. 28.25 (*0-15-301052-5*) Harcourt Schl Pubs.

Language Medallion: Grade 3. 1993. pap. text, student ed. 35.50 (*0-15-301053-3*) Harcourt Schl Pubs.

Language Medallion: Grade 4. 1993. pap. text, student ed. 35.50 (*0-15-301054-1*) Harcourt Schl Pubs.

Language Medallion: Grade 5. 1993. pap. text, student ed. 39.00 (*0-15-301055-X*) Harcourt Schl Pubs.

Language Medallion: Grade 6. 1993. pap. text, student ed. 40.00 (*0-15-301056-8*) Harcourt Schl Pubs.

Language Medallion: Grade 7. 1993. pap. text, student ed. 41.50 (*0-15-301057-6*) Harcourt Schl Pubs.

Language Medallion: Grade 8. 1993. pap. text, student ed. 41.50 (*0-15-301058-4*) Harcourt Schl Pubs.

Language, Memory, & Aging. Ed. by Leah L. Light & Deborah M. Burke. (Illus.). 296p. (C). 1988. text 64.95 (*0-521-32942-6*) Cambridge U Pr.

Language, Memory, & Aging. Ed. by Leah L. Light & Deborah M. Burke. (Illus.). 293p. (C). 1993. pap. text 22.95 (*0-521-44876-X*) Cambridge U Pr.

Language, Memory, & Thought. John R. Anderson. LC 76-21791. 546p. (C). 1976. text 99.95 (*0-89859-107-4*) L Erlbaum Assocs.

Language, Metaphysics & Death: Death & Afterlife, a Metaphysical Reader. 2nd ed. Ed. by John Donnelly. LC 76-18463. viii, 381p. (C). 1994. reprint ed. 27.00 (*0-8232-1581-4*); reprint ed. pap. 19.00 (*0-8232-1582-2*) Fordham.

Language, Mind, & Art: Essays in Appreciation & Analysis in Honor of Paul Ziff. Ed. by Dale Jamieson. LC 94-9708. 224p. (C). 1994. lib. bdg. 136.00 (*0-7923-2810-8*, Pub. by Kluwer Academic) Kluwer Academic.

Language, Mind, & Brain. Ed. by Thomas W. Simon & Robert J. Scholes. (Illus.). 288p. 1982. text 59.95 (*0-89859-153-8*) L Erlbaum Assocs.

Language, Mind, & Epistomology: On Don Davidson's Philosophy. Ed. by Gerhard Preyer et al. LC 94-7208. (Synthese Library). 464p. (C). 1994. lib. bdg. 204.50 (*0-7923-2811-6*, Pub. by Kluwer Academic) Kluwer Academic.

Language, Minorities & Human Rights. Fernand De Varennes. LC 96-521. (International Studies in Human Rights: No. 45). 552p. 1996. 192.50 (*90-411-0206-X*) Kluwer Law Intl.

Language, Minority Education, & Gender: Linking Social Justice & Power. David Corson. LC 93-8605. (Language & Education Library: Vol. 6). 1993. 74.95 (*1-85359-210-2*, Pub. by Multilingual Matters); pap. 29.95 (*1-85359-209-9*, Pub. by Multilingual Matters) Taylor & Francis.

Language Minority Students & Computers. Intro. by Christian J. Faltis & Robert A. DeVillar. LC 90-39637. (Computers in the Schools Ser.: Vol. 7, Nos. 1-2). 283p. 1990. text 49.95 (*1-56024-034-2*) Haworth Pr.

Language Minority Students in the Mainstream Classroom. Angela L. Carrasquillo & Vivian Rodriguez. 208p. 1995. 69.00 (*1-85359-298-6*, Pub. by Multilingual Matters); pap. 24.95 (*1-85359-297-8*, Pub. by Multilingual Matters) Taylor & Francis.

Language Minority Students with Disabilities. Leonard M. Baca & Estella Almanza. (Exceptional Children at Risk Ser.). 56p. 1991. pap. text 9.00 (*0-86586-214-1*, P357) Coun Exc Child.

Language Mixing in Infant Bilingualism: A Sociolinguistic Perspective. Elizabeth Lanza. (Oxford Studies in Language Contact). (Illus.). 412p. 1997. text 90.00 (*0-19-823575-5*) OUP.

Language, Morality, & Society: An Ethical Model of Communication in Fontane & Hofmannsthal. Glenn A. Guidry. (UC Publications in Modern Philology). 1989. 25.00 (*0-520-09733-5*, Pub. by U CA Pr) Cal Prin Full Svc.

Language, Music, & Mind. Diana Raffman. (Illus.). 180p. 1993. 24.50 (*0-262-18150-9*, Bradford Bks) MIT Pr.

Language Mysticism: The Negative Way of Language in Eliot, Beckett, & Celan. Shira Wolosky. LC 94-19470. 318p. 1995. 39.50 (*0-8047-2387-7*) Stanford U Pr.

***Language Myths.** Peter Trudgill. 208p. 1999. pap. 12.95 (*0-14-026023-4*, Penguin Bks) Viking Penguin.

Language, 1990: Story Starter Grade 3. Strickland. 1990. pap. 44.75 (*0-15-316562-6*) Harcourt Schl Pubs.

Language, 1990: Story Starter Grade 4. Strickland. 1990. pap. 44.75 (*0-15-316563-4*) Harcourt Schl Pubs.

Language, 1990: Story Starter Grade 6. Strickland. 1990. pap. 44.75 (*0-15-316565-0*) Harcourt Schl Pubs.

Language, 1990: Story Starter Grade 7. Strickland. 1990. pap. 44.75 (*0-15-316566-9*) Harcourt Schl Pubs.

Language, 1990: Story Starter Grade 8. Strickland. 1990. pap. 44.75 (*0-15-316567-7*) Harcourt Schl Pubs.

Language, 1990: Writer's Notebook Grade 1. Strickland. 1990. pap. 11.75 (*0-15-316464-6*) Harcourt Schl Pubs.

Language, 1990: Writer's Notebook Grade 2. Strickland. 1990. pap. 11.75 (*0-15-316465-4*) Harcourt Schl Pubs.

Language, 1990: Writer's Notebook Grade 3. Strickland. 1990. pap. 14.00 (*0-15-316466-2*) Harcourt Schl Pubs.

Language, 1990: Writer's Notebook Grade 4. Strickland. 1990. pap. 14.00 (*0-15-316467-0*) Harcourt Schl Pubs.

Language, 1990: Writer's Notebook Grade 5. Strickland. 1990. pap. 14.00 (*0-15-316468-9*) Harcourt Schl Pubs.

Language, 1990: Writer's Notebook Grade 6. Strickland. 1990. pap. 14.00 (*0-15-316469-7*) Harcourt Schl Pubs.

Language, 1990: Writer's Notebook Grade 7. Strickland. 1990. pap. 14.00 (*0-15-316470-0*) Harcourt Schl Pubs.

Language, 1990: Writer's Notebook Grade 8. Strickland. 1990. pap. 14.00 (*0-15-316471-9*) Harcourt Schl Pubs.

Language 90: Grade 1. Strickland. 1990. teacher ed. 70.25 (*0-15-316420-4*) Harcourt Schl Pubs.

Language 90: Grade 2. Strickland. 1991. 29.00 (*0-15-316412-3*) Harcourt Schl Pubs.

Language 90: Grade 3. Harcourt Brace Staff. 1990. 112.00 (*0-15-316431-X*) Harcourt Schl Pubs.

Language 90: Grade 4. Strickland. 1990. teacher ed. 97.25 (*0-15-316423-9*) Harcourt Schl Pubs.

Language 90: Grade 4. Strickland. 1991. 37.00 (*0-15-316414-X*) Harcourt Schl Pubs.

Language 90: Grade 5. Harcourt Brace Staff. 1990. teacher ed. 117.75 (*0-15-316434-4*) Harcourt Schl Pubs.

Language 90: Grade 5. Strickland. 1990. teacher ed. 102.75 (*0-15-316424-7*) Harcourt Schl Pubs.

Language 90: Grade 6. Strickland. 1990. student ed. 44.00 (*0-15-316417-4*) Harcourt Schl Pubs.

Language 90: Grade 7. Harcourt Brace Staff. 1990. 37.95 (*0-15-321132-6*) Harcourt Schl Pubs.

Language 90: Grade 7. Strickland. 1990. teacher ed. 113.50 (*0-15-316426-3*); student ed. 44.00 (*0-15-316418-2*) Harcourt Schl Pubs.

Language 90: Grade 8. Strickland. 1990. teacher ed. 81.00 (*0-15-316421-2*) Harcourt Schl Pubs.

Language Nobody Speaks. Eugene Mirabelli. LC 99-60139. 144p. 1999. 20.00 (*0-935891-02-1*) Spring Harbor.

Language Nobody Speaks: A Novel. Eugene Mirabelli. LC 99-60139. 139p. 1999. pap. 13.00 (*0-935891-03-X*) Spring Harbor.

Language Obsolescence & Revitalization: Linguistic Change in Two Sociolinguistically Contrasting Welsh Communities. Mari C. Jones. LC 97-26924. (Oxford Studies in Language Contact). (Illus.). 462p. 1998. text 135.00 (*0-19-823711-1*) OUP.

Language of a Master: Theories of Style & the Late Writing of Henry James. David W. Smit. LC 87-26524. xvi, 164p. (C). 1988. text 21.95 (*0-8093-1399-5*) S Ill U Pr.

***Language of Accountancy.** Rosa. (C). 1999. pap. text. write for info. (*0-03-025236-9*) Harcourt.

Language of Accountancy. Rosa. 528p. (C). 1999. text 29.50 (*0-03-025252-0*) Harcourt Coll Pubs.

Language of Accounting in English. Sandra Costinett. (English for Careers Ser). 104p. (YA). (gr. 10-12). 1994. pap. text 20.40 (*0-13-523226-0*, 18512) Prentice ESL.

Language of Achilles & Other Papers. Adam M. Parry. (Illus.). 352p. 1989. 98.00 (*0-19-814892-5*) OUP.

Language of Adam: On the Limits & Systems of Discourse. Russell A. Fraser. LC 77-3528. 288p. 1977. text 57.50 (*0-231-04256-6*) Col U Pr.

Language of Advertising: Written Texts. Angela Goddard. LC 97-14926. (Intertext Ser.). 144p. (C). 1998. pap. 14.99 (*0-415-14598-8*) Routledge.

Language of Advertising & Merchandising in English. Rein. 1987. pap. 20.40 (*0-13-523291-0*) P-H.

Language of Advocacy: What to Say & How to Say It in the English-Speaking Courts. Keith Evans. 95p. 1998. pap. 28.00 (*1-85431-835-7*, Pub. by Blackstone Pr) Gaunt.

Language of African Literature. Ed. by Edmund L. Epstein & Robert Kole. LC 96-43316. 250p. 1996. 59.95 (*0-86543-534-0*); pap. 18.95 (*0-86543-535-9*) Africa World.

Language of Allegory: Defining the Genre. Maureen Quilligan. LC 78-74216. 312p. 1992. pap. text 16.95 (*0-8014-8051-5*) Cornell U Pr.

Language of American Popular Entertainment: A Glossary of Argot, Slang, & Terminology. Don B. Wilmeth. LC 80-14795. 305p. 1981. lib. bdg. 69.50 (*0-313-22497-8*, WEN/, Greenwood Pr) Greenwood.

Language of Anatomy see Preliminary Announcement

Language of Animals. Stephen Hart & Franz De Waal. LC 95-34585. (Scientific American Focus Bks.). 1995. 22.50 (*0-8050-3839-6*) H Holt & Co.

Language of Architecture: A Contribution to Architectural Theory. Niels Luning Prak. (Illus.). 1968. 44.65 (*90-279-6394-0*) Mouton.

Language of Argument. 7th ed. Daniel L. McDonald. LC 92-23334. 368p. (C). 1997. pap. 39.00 (*0-06-500583-X*) Addson-Wesley Educ.

Language of Argument. 9th ed. Daniel L. McDonald & Larry W. Burton. LC 98-13713. (Illus.). 400p. (C). 1998. pap. text 38.00 (*0-321-01937-7*) Addson-Wesley Educ.

Language of Art. Moshe Barasch. LC 96-45828. (C). 1997. text 67.50 (*0-8147-1255-X*) NYU Pr.

Language of Art from A to Z. rev. ed. N. E. Lahti. LC 97-60020. Orig. Title: Plain Talk about Art. 185p. 1997. pap. text 11.00 (*0-9620147-3-7*) York Bks.

Language of Atomic Energy in English. Eugene J. Hall. (English for Careers Ser). (Illus.). (YA). (gr. 10 up). 1987. pap. text 7.00 (*0-13-523234-1*, 18514) Prentice ESL.

Language of Balinese Shadow Theater. Mary S. Zurbuchen. LC 87-2267. (Illus.). 308p. 1987. reprint ed. pap. 95.50 (*0-608-07543-4*, 206775600009) Bks Demand.

Language of Ballet: A Dictionary. Thalia Mara. LC 78-181477. (Illus.). 120p. 1987. reprint ed. pap. 11.95 (*0-87127-037-4*) Princeton Bk Co.

Language of Banking: Terms & Phrases Used in the Financial Industry. Michael G. Hales. LC 94-3646. 175p. 1994. lib. bdg. 32.50 (*0-89950-919-3*) McFarland & Co.

Language of Biotechnology: A Dictionary of Terms. John M. Walker & Michael Cox. LC 88-26273. (ACS Professional Reference Bk.). (Illus.). viii, 255p. 1988. pap. 29.95 (*0-8412-1490-5*); ring bd. 49.95 (*0-8412-1489-1*) Am Chemical.

Language of Biotechnology: A Dictionary of Terms. 2nd ed. Ed. by Michael Cox et al. LC 94-23812. (Professional Reference Book). (Illus.). 300p. 1995. pap. text 32.00 (*0-8412-2982-1*, Pub. by Am Chemical) OUP.

Language of Biotechnology: A Dictionary of Terms. 2nd ed. Ed. by Michael Cox & John M. Walker. LC 94-23812. (Professional Reference Book). (Illus.). 300p. 1995. text 55.00 (*0-8412-2957-0*, Pub. by Am Chemical) OUP.

Language of Birds. Rafe Martin. LC 98-48917. (J). 2000. 15.99 (*0-399-22925-6*, G P Putnam) Peng Put Young Read.

Language of Birds. Eoin McNamee. 32p. (Orig.). 1994. pap. 9.95 (*1-874597-18-9*, Pub. by New Island Books) Irish Bks Media.

Language of Birds. Kimi Sugioka. 72p. (Orig.). 1994. pap. 7.00 (*0-916397-32-7*) Manic D Pr.

Language of Business. Cheryl Reimold. 168p. (Orig.). 1992. pap. 58.00 (*0-614-10341-X*, 0101R200) TAPPI.

Language of Business. unabridged ed. (English As a Second Language Course Ser.). 254p. pap. text 59.50 incl. audio (*0-88432-189-4*, S32524) Audio-Forum.

Language of Business: A TAPPI Press Anthology of Published Papers 1980-1991. Cheryl Reimold. LC 92-3287. 175p. reprint ed. pap. 54.30 (*0-7837-1978-7*, 204225200002) Bks Demand.

Language of Business: Dictionnaire Commercial et Economique Bilingue: French-English, English-French. Robert Lenoir. (ENG & FRE.). 920p. 1989. pap. 105.00 (*0-7859-7954-9*, 2717817182) Fr & Eur.

Language of Canaan: Metaphor & Symbol in New England from the Puritans to the Transcendentalists. Mason I. Lowance, Jr. LC 79-21179. 345p. 1980. 37.95 (*0-674-50949-8*) HUP.

Language of Canadian Politics: A Guide to Important Terms & Concepts. rev. ed. John McMenemy. xx, 322p. (C). 1995. pap. 29.95 (*0-88920-230-3*) W Laurier U Pr.

Language of Change: Elements of Therapeutic Communication. Paul Watzlawick. 184p. 1993. pap. 12.95 (*0-393-31020-5*) Norton.

Language of Chemical Engineering in English. Regents. 1987. pap. 6.33 (*0-13-523242-2*) P-H.

An Asterisk (*) at the beginning of an entry indicates that the title is appearing for the first time.

Language of Children: Development in Home & School. 2nd ed. Mathilda Holzman. LC 96-26311. (Illus.). 224p. (C). 1997. pap. text 26.95 (*1-55786-517-5*) Blackwell Pubs.

Language of Children: Evolution & Development of Secondary Consciousness & Language. 2nd ed. Mathilda Holzman. LC 96-26311. (Illus.). 224p. (C). 1997. text 60.95 (*1-55786-516-7*) Blackwell Pubs.

Language of Choice Theory. William Glasser. LC 98-44196. 128p. 1999. pap. 12.00 (*0-06-095323-3*) HarpC.

Language of Cinema. Kevin Jackson. LC 97-38644. 288p. 1998. pap. 19.99 (*0-415-92049-3*) Routledge.

*__Language of Clothes.__ Alison Lurie. LC 99-41520. (Illus.). 272p. 2000. pap. 22.50 (*0-8050-6244-0*, Owl) H Holt & Co.

Language of Colloid & Interface Science: A Dictionary of Terms. Laurier L. Schramm. LC 93-25680. (Illus.). 195p. 1993. text 78.00 (*0-8412-2709-8*, Pub. by Am Chemical); pap. text 45.00 (*0-8412-2710-1*, Pub. by Am Chemical) OUP.

Language of Color. Dorothee L. Mella. (Illus.). 128p. (Orig.). 1988. mass mkt. 11.99 (*0-446-38781-9*, Pub. by Warner Bks) Little.

Language of Commodities: A Commodity Glossary. Rosemary Erickson & George Steinbeck. write for info. (*0-318-59697-0*) S&S Trade.

Language of Computer Programming in English. Keegen. 112p. 1987. pap. text 20.40 (*0-13-523119-1*) P-H.

Language of Computer Publishing. 2nd ed. Donald J. Brenner. Ed. by Dawn M. Essman & Robert C. Brenner. 436p. (Orig.). 1994. pap. 24.95 (*0-929535-14-6*) Brenner Info Group.

Language of Confession, Interrogation & Deception. Roger W. Shuy. LC 97-33752. (Empirical Linguistics Ser.). 216p. 1998. 36.00 (*0-7619-1345-9*); pap. 16.99 (*0-7619-1346-7*) Sage.

*__Language of Contemporary Criticism Clarified.__ Williams Innes Homer. (Illus.). 175p. (C). 1999. pap. 15.95 (*0-932087-58-2*) Sound View Pr.

Language of Cooking. Anne Salisbury. (Series 921). (Orig.). 1978. pap., student ed. 7.00 (*0-8064-0393-4*) Bergwall.

Language of Counseling & the Christian Counselor's Workbook. Jay Edward Adams. (Jay Adams Library). 160p. 1986. pap. 9.99 (*0-310-51061-9*, 12118P) Zondervan.

Language of Courage & Inner Strength: A Wonderful Gift of Inspiring Thoughts. Ed. by Douglas Pagels. LC 99-18692. (Language of...Ser.). (Illus.). 48p. 1999. 14.95 (*0-88396-508-9*, L5089) Blue Mtn Art.

Language of Courtesy: Honorific Speech of Japanese. Miyo Okada. 97p. 1954. 8.95 (*0-88710-041-4*) Yale Far Eastern Pubns.

Language of Creativity: Models, Problem-Solving, Discourse. Ed. by Mark Amsler. LC 85-40360. (Studies in Science & Culture: Vol. 2). 208p. 1986. 32.50 (*0-87413-280-0*) U Delaware Pr.

Language of Cricket. John Eddowes. LC 98-135386. 220p. 1997. pap. 18.95 (*1-85754-270-3*, Pub. by Carcanet Pr) Paul & Co Pubs.

Language of Criticism: Linguistic Models & Literary Theory. Jacqueline M. Henkel. LC 96-25037. 208p. 1996. text 35.00 (*0-8014-2656-1*) Cornell U Pr.

Language of Criticism & the Sciences of Man: The Structuralist Controversy. Ed. by Richard Macksey & Eugenio Donato. LC 78-95789. 367p. reprint ed. pap. 113.80 (*0-608-10122-2*, 200419700041) Bks Demand.

Language of Dance. Mary Wigman. Tr. by Walter Sorell. LC 66-18118. (Wesleyan Paperback Ser.). (Illus.). 122p. 1986. reprint ed. pap. 37.90 (*0-7837-8101-6*, 204790500008) Bks Demand.

Language of Dance Teaching Aids Set I: Choreo-Cut-Outs, Vol. 1. Ann H. Guest. (Illus.). 1986. text 18.00 (*0-677-21550-9*) Gordon & Breach.

Language of Dance Teaching Aids Set II: The Magic Circle, Vol. 2. Ann H. Guest. (Illus.). 1986. text 17.00 (*0-677-21540-1*) Gordon & Breach.

*__Language of Deception: A Discourse Analytical Study.__ Dariusz Galasibnski. LC 00-8039. 2000. pap. write for info. (*0-7619-0916-8*) Sage.

Language of Democracy: Political Rhetoric in the United States & Britain, 1790-1900. Andrew W. Robertson. (Illus.). 240p. 1995. text 37.50 (*0-8014-2899-8*) Cornell U Pr.

Language of Directions: A Programmed Workbook. Mary L. Rush. LC 77-87703. 1977. pap. text 14.95 (*0-88200-113-2*, C1321) Alexander Graham.

Language of Displayed Art. Michael O'Toole. 1995. pap. 24.95 (*0-7185-1940-X*) Bks Intl VA.

Language of Displayed Art. Michael O'Toole. (Illus.). 300p. 1994. 38.50 (*0-8386-3604-7*) Fairleigh Dickinson.

Language of Displayed Art. Michael O'Toole. LC 93-41668. (Illus.). 280p. 1994. write for info. (*0-7185-1632-X*) St Martin.

Language of Doves. Rosemary Wells. LC 95-40283. (Illus.). 48p. (J). (gr. k-3). 1996. 14.99 (*0-8037-1471-8*, Dial Yng Read); 14.89 (*0-8037-1472-6*, Dial Yng Read) Peng Put Young Read.

Language of Drama. David Birch. LC 90-9082. (Language of Literature Ser.). 184p. 1991. text 39.95 (*0-312-05269-3*) St Martin.

*__Language of Drama.__ Keith Sanger. LC 00-32307. (Intertext Ser.). 2000. write for info. (*0-415-21423-8*) Routledge.

Language of Dreams. Patricia Telesco. LC 97-11608. (Illus.). 272p. 1997. pap. 16.95 (*0-89594-836-2*) Crossing Pr.

Language of Easter Island: Its Development & Eastern Polynesian Relationships. Robert Langdon & Darrell T. Tryon. (Polynesian Studies: No. 4). 88p. (C). 1983. pap. text 6.95 (*0-939154-32-3*) Inst Polynesian.

Language of Education. Israel Scheffler. 128p. 1978. 26.95 (*0-398-01656-9*) C C Thomas.

Language of Electroacoustic Music. Ed. by Simon Emmerson. viii, 232p. 1986. text 39.00 (*3-7186-0364-0*) Gordon & Breach.

Language of Emotions: Conceptualization, Expression, & Theoretical Foundation. Ed. by Susanne Niemeier & Rene Dirven. LC 97-4952. xviii, 337p. 1997. 94.00 (*1-55619-514-1*) J Benjamins Pubng Co.

Language of English Studies: A Handbook for Advanced Students of English. John Dent-Young. LC 97-195177. 338p. (Orig.). (C). 1997. pap. text 17.95 (*962-201-648-0*, Pub. by Chinese Univ) U of Mich Pr.

Language of Environment: A New Rhetoric. George Myerson & Yvonne Rydin. LC 96-219744. 256p. 1996. 65.00 (*1-85728-330-9*) U of Wash Pr.

Language of Environment: A New Rhetoric. George Myerson & Yvonne Rydin. LC 96-219744. 256p. 1997. pap. 24.95 (*1-85728-331-7*) U of Wash Pr.

Language of Ethnic Conflict. Irving L. Allen. LC 82-9610. 168p. 1983. pap. text 20.00 (*0-231-05557-9*) Col U Pr.

Language of Evaluation: A Sociolinguistic Approach to the Story of Pedro el Cruel in Ballad & Chronicle. Louise Mirrer-Singer. LC 86-9620. (Purdue University Monographs in Romance Languages: No. 20). xi, 130p. (Orig.). 1986. pap. 35.00 (*0-915027-69-0*) J Benjamins Pubng Co.

Language of Exclusion: The Poetry of Emily Dickinson & Christina Rossetti, 83. Sharon Leder & Andrea Abbott. LC 87-7519. (Contributions in Women's Studies: No. 83). (Illus.). 250p. 1987. 59.95 (*0-313-25629-2*, LLE/, Greenwood Pr) Greenwood.

Language of Existence. Osho. Ed. by Ma S. Suvarna. LC 97-208506. (Zen Ser.). (Illus.). 288p. 1989. 12.95 (*3-89338-054-X*, Pub. by Rebel Hse) Oshos.

Language of Family Therapy: A Systemic Vocabulary & Sourcebook. Fritz B. Simon et al. Orig. Title: Die Sprache den Familientherapie-Ein Vokabular. (Orig.). (C). 1985. pap. 18.00 (*0-9615519-0-9*); text 30.00 (*0-9615519-1-7*) Family Process.

Language of Feelings. David Viscott. 1990. pap. 5.50 (*0-671-73336-2*) S&S Trade.

Language of Fertility. Niravi B. Payne. LC 98-23895. 288p. 1998. pap. 14.00 (*0-609-80198-8*) Crown Pub Group.

*__Language of Fertility: A Revolutionary Mind-Body Program for Conscious Conception.__ Niravi B. Payne. 266p. 2000. reprint ed. text 25.00 (*0-7881-6991-2*) DIANE Pub.

Language of Fiction. Keith Sanger. LC 97-20649. (Intertext Ser.). 128p. (C). 1998. pap. 14.99 (*0-415-14599-6*) Routledge.

Language of Fiction in a World of Pain: Reading Politics as Paradox. Barbara J. Eckstein. LC 90-39345. (New Cultural Studies). 218p. (C). 1990. text 35.00 (*0-8122-8254-X*); pap. text 16.95 (*0-8122-1321-1*) U of Pa Pr.

Language of First-Order Logic: Including the Macintosh (TM) Program Tarski's World 4.0. 3rd rev. ed. Jon Barwise & John Etchemendy. LC 93-419. (CSLI Lecture Notes Ser.: No. 23). 322p. 1993. pap. 37.50 incl. disk (*0-937073-99-7*) CSLI.

Language of Flowers. C. R. Gibson Company Staff. 1997. 6.00 (*0-7667-2208-2*) Gibson.

Language of Flowers. Illus. by Kate Greenaway. LC 92-30765. 1992. pap. 4.95 (*0-486-27372-5*) Dover.

*__Language of Flowers.__ Marina Heilmeyer. (Illus.). 96p. 2001. 29.95 (*3-7913-2396-2*) Prestel Pub NY.

Language of Flowers: A Beginner's Guide. Kristyna Arcarti. (Illus.). 96p. 1997. pap. 11.95 (*0-340-69781-4*, Pub. by Headway) Trafalgar.

Language of Flowers: A History. Beverly Seaton. LC 94-29337. (Victorian Literature & Culture Ser.). 256p. (C). 1995. text 29.50 (*0-8139-1556-2*) U Pr of Va.

Language of Flowers: An Anthology of Poetry & Prose. Books Lorenz. (Illus.). 64p. 1997. 9.95 (*1-85967-334-1*, Lorenz Bks) Anness Pub.

Language of Flowers: Flower Dictionary, Poetry & Flowers. Nancy C. Akmon & Roni Akmon. LC 96-134275. (Illus.). 32p. 1995. 8.95 (*1-884807-13-5*) Blushing Rose.

Language of Folk Art Activity, Vol. 1. Mari Haas. 1995. pap. text. write for info. (*0-8013-1403-8*) Longman.

Language of Foreign Affairs. 115p. 1987. pap. text 20.00 (*0-941375-11-0*) DIANE Pub.

Language of Fractures. Robert J. Schultz. LC 75-43698. 408p. 1976. reprint ed. 42.50 (*0-88275-369-X*) Krieger.

Language of Fractures. 2nd ed. Robert J. Schultz. (Illus.). 336p. 1990. 58.00 (*0-683-07612-4*) Lppncott W & W.

Language of Friendship. Ed. by Susan Polis Schutz. LC 98-42695. (Language of...Ser.). (Illus.). 48p. 1999. 14.95 (*0-88396-479-1*, L4791) Blue Mtn Art.

Language of Gender & Class: Transformation in the Victorian Novel. Patricia Ingham. 208p. (C). 1996. pap. 25.99 (*0-415-08222-6*) Routledge.

Language of Genes: Solving the Mysteries of Our Genetic Past, Present, & Future. Steve Jones. 272p. 1995. pap. 14.95 (*0-385-47428-8*) Doubleday.

Language of George Orwell. Roger Fowler. LC 95-3704. 1995. text 55.00 (*0-312-12642-5*) St Martin.

Language of Gesture. Macdonald Critchley. LC 74-122981. (Studies in Language: No. 41). 1970. reprint ed. lib. bdg. 75.00 (*0-8383-1113-X*) M S G Haskell Hse.

Language of Gestures. Wilhelm M. Wundt. Ed. by Thomas A. Sebeok. LC 73-84206. (Approaches to Semiotics Ser.). 149p. 1973. pap. text 32.35 (*90-279-2486-4*) Mouton.

*__Language of Gifts: The Essential Guide to Meaningful Gift Giving.__ Deanna Washington. LC 99-39286. 250p. 2000. pap. 16.95 (*1-57324-190-3*) Conari Press.

Language of Goldfish. Zibby Oneal. Ed. by D. Brodie. (J). 1990. pap. 4.99 (*0-14-034540-X*, PuffinBks) Peng Put Young Read.

Language of Goldfish: A Novel. Zibby O'Neal. (J). 1990. 10.09 (*0-606-04728-X*, Pub. by Turtleback) Demco.

Language of Handwriting. Richard D. Stocker. (Illus.). 269p. 1994. reprint ed. pap. 9.95 (*0-87877-190-5*) Newcastle Pub.

Language of Happiness. Ed. by Susan Polis Schutz. LC 98-42642. (Language of...Ser.). (Illus.). 48p. 1999. 14.95 (*0-88396-480-5*, L4805) Blue Mtn Art.

Language of Health Care Reform. Kathleen O'Connor. (Illus.). 48p. (Orig.). 1994. pap. 9.95 (*0-9641863-0-6*) Understand Busn.

Language of Herbs. Storey Publishing Staff. 1997. 22.95 (*0-676-57226-X*) Random.

Language of Herbs: Scented by Penhaligon's. Sheila Pickles. (Illus.). 96p. 1997. 22.95 (*1-85793-663-9*, Pub. by Pavilion Bks Ltd) Trafalgar.

Language of Hermeneutics: Gadamer & Heidegger in Dialogue. Rodney R. Coltman. LC 97-42842. (Series in Contemporary Continental Philosophy). 160p. (C). 1998. pap. text 19.95 (*0-7914-3900-3*) State U NY Pr.

Language of Hermeneutics: Gadamer & Heidegger in Dialogue. Rodney R. Coltman. LC 97-42842. (Series in Contemporary Continental Philosophy). 187p. (C). 1998. text 59.50 (*0-7914-3899-6*) State U NY Pr.

Language of Heroes: Speech & Performance in the "Iliad" Richard P. Martin. LC 89-42889. (Myth & Poetics Ser.). 288p. 1989. text 42.50 (*0-8014-2353-8*) Cornell U Pr.

Language of Heroes: Speech & Performance in the "Iliad" Richard P. Martin. LC 89-42889. (Myth & Poetics Ser.). 288p. 1993. pap. text 16.95 (*0-8014-8070-1*) Cornell U Pr.

Language of Hotels in English. Eugene J. Hall. (English for Careers Ser). (Illus.). 112p. (YA). (gr. 10 up). 1987. pap. text 20.40 (*0-13-523150-7*, 18509) Prentice ESL.

Language of Humour. Walter Nash. (English Language Ser.). (C). 1985. pap. text 18.95 (*0-582-29127-5*, 71754) Longman.

Language of Humour. Alison Ross. LC 97-24610. (Intertext Ser.). 128p. (C). 1998. pap. 14.99 (*0-415-16912-7*) Routledge.

Language of Images. Ed. by W. J. Mitchell. LC 80-5225. 314p. 1980. pap. text 17.95 (*0-226-53215-1*, P887) U Ch Pr.

Language of Inequality. Ed. by Nessa Wolfson & Joan Manes. (Contributions to the Sociology of Language Ser.: No. 36). xv, 411p. 1985. pap. 34.95 (*0-89925-069-6*); text 115.40 (*3-11-009946-2*) Mouton.

*__Language of Inquiry.__ Lyn Hejinian. LC 00-37776. (Illus.). 391p. 2000. 45.00 (*0-520-21699-7*); pap. 17.95 (*0-520-21700-4*) U CA Pr.

Language of International Finance in English: Money & Banking. Peter K. Oppenheim. (English for Careers Ser). (Illus.). (YA). (gr. 10 up). 1976. pap. text 4.25 (*0-88345-272-3*, 18504) Prentice ESL.

Language of International Trade in English. Mohr. 128p. 1987. pap. text 15.40 (*0-13-523317-8*) P-H.

Language of Interpretation: Patterns of Discourse in Discussions of Literature. James D. Marshall et al. (Research Reports: No. 27). 158p. 1994. pap. 19.95 (*0-8141-2709-6*) NCTE.

Language of Introductory Health Care. 3rd ed. Chapman & Badasch. (C). 1993. pap., wbk. ed. 11.80 (*0-89303-853-9*) P-H.

Language of Jane Austen, Vol. 13. Norman Page. LC 74-190473. (Language & Style Series, Fourteen Ser.). viii, 208p. 1972. write for info. (*0-631-08280-8*) Blackwell Pubs.

Language of Jazz. Neil Powell. LC 98-193584. 160p. 1998. pap. 18.95 (*1-85754-164-2*, Pub. by Carcanet Pr) Paul & Co Pubs.

Language of Jokes: Analyzing Verbal Play. Delia Chiaro. LC 91-33616. (Interface Ser.). 144p. (Orig.). (C). 1992. pap. 22.99 (*0-415-03090-0*, A6777) Routledge.

Language of Jonathan Fisher, 1768-1847. Raoul N. Smith. (Publications of the American Dialect Society: No. 72). 198p. 1985. pap. text 19.80 (*0-8173-0271-9*) U of Ala Pr.

Language of Journalism: A Glossary of Print-Communications Terms. Ruth K. Kent. LC 71-100624. 184p. reprint ed. pap. 57.10 (*0-7837-0289-2*, 204061000018) Bks Demand.

*__Language of Journalism Vol. 1: Newspaper Culture.__ Melvin J. Lasky. (Newspaper Culture Ser.). 453p. 2000. 39.95 (*0-7658-0001-2*) Transaction Pubs.

Language of Judges. Lawrence M. Solan. LC 92-28628. (Language & Legal Discourse Ser.). (Illus.). 230p. (C). 1993. pap. text 18.95 (*0-226-76791-4*) U Ch Pr.

Language of Judges. Lawrence M. Solan. LC 92-28628. (Language & Legal Discourse Ser.). (Illus.). 230p. (C). 1998. lib. bdg. 49.50 (*0-226-76790-6*) U Ch Pr.

Language of Lace. Betty J. Mills. Ed. by Pat Earnshaw. 35p. 1984. pap. 5.50 (*0-911618-09-0*) Mus Texas.

Language of Landscape. Anne Whiston Spirn. LC 98-7487. (Illus.). 320p. 1998. 40.00 (*0-300-07745-9*) Yale U Pr.

*__Language of Landscape.__ Anne Whiston Spirn. (Illus.). 320p. 2000. pap. 17.95 (*0-300-08294-0*) Yale U Pr.

Language of Leadership. 3rd ed. Marlena Caroselli. 253p. 1990. reprint ed. 24.95 (*0-922411-05-0*) CPD NY.

Language of Leadership in Contemporary France. Helen Drake & John Gaffney. (Illus.). 270p. 1996. text 79.95 (*1-85521-355-9*, Pub. by Dartmth Pub) Ashgate Pub Co.

*__Language of Learning.__ 3rd ed. Hopper et al. (Developmental Study/Study Skills Ser.). 2000. pap. 32.00 (*0-534-52903-8*) Wadsworth Pub.

Language of Learning: A Guide to Education Terms. J. Lynn McBrien & Ronald S. Brandt. LC 97-19649. viii, 115 p. (Orig.). 1997. pap. 13.95 (*0-87120-274-3*, 197155) ASCD.

Language of Learning: Vocabulary for College Success. Jane N. Hopper & Jo Ann Carter-Wells. 349p. (C). 1987. pap. 24.95 (*0-534-08940-2*) Wadsworth Pub.

Language of Learning: Vocabulary for College Success. 2nd ed. Jane N. Hopper & Jo Ann Carter-Wells. 401p. (C). 1993. 28.25 (*0-534-21384-7*) Wadsworth Pub.

Language of Learning & the Language of Love: Uncollected Writings, New Interpretations. W. H. Auden. Ed. by Nicholas Jenkins & Katherine Bucknell. (Illus.). 302p. 1995. text 32.00 (*0-19-812257-8*) OUP.

Language of Letting Go see De Lenguaje Del Adios

Language of Letting Go. M. Beattie. (Meditations Ser.). 10.00 incl. audio (*0-89486-681-8*, 5608G) Hazelden.

Language of Letting Go. M. Beattie. LC 97-75444. 400p. 1998. reprint ed. 7.98 (*1-56731-238-1*, MJF Bks) Fine Comms.

Language of Letting Go: Daily Meditations for Codependents. Melody Beattie. 390p. pap. 14.95 (*0-89486-637-0*, 5076A) Hazelden.

Language of Letting Go: 365 Daily Reflections from Melody Beattie. Melody Beatie. 366p. 1999. 9.95 (*1-56838-325-8*) Hazelden.

Language of Liberty, 1660-1832: Political Discourse & Social Dynamics in the Anglo-American World. J. C. Clark. 422p. (C). 1993. pap. text 24.95 (*0-521-44957-X*) Cambridge U Pr.

Language of Life: A Festival of Poets. Bill Moyers. (Illus.). 480p. 1996. pap., mass mkt. 21.95 incl. audio (*0-385-48410-0*) Doubleday.

Language of Life: Christians Facing the Abortion Challenge. Ann Farmer. 156p. 1996. pap. 39.95 (*0-85439-477-X*, Pub. by St Paul Pubns) St Mut.

Language of Life - A Coloring Book: Images Honoring Geometry & Universal Form - For Children of All Ages. Robert Schneider. (Illus.). 44p. (Orig.). (J). 1996. pap., spiral bd. 6.33 (*0-9656767-0-6*) Org Cons Envir Natural.

Language of Light. Ed. by Michael Moos & Patricia W. Francisco. (Illus.). 180p. (Orig.). 1983. pap. 5.00 (*0-927663-08-2*) COMPAS.

Language of Light: Masterworks from the Collection. Ed. by Marianne Fulton. 32p. 1993. pap. 8.50 (*0-935398-20-1*) G Eastman Hse.

Language of Light Ambits. Bruce Renner. 53p. per. 8.00 (*0-934332-48-7*) LEpervier Pr.

Language of Logic: A Self-Instruction Text. 2nd ed. Morton L. Schagrin. 318p. (C). 1978. pap. 30.00 (*0-07-553682-X*) McGraw.

Language of Love see Irresistible Lenguaje del Amor

Language of Love. Beverley Armstrong. 44p. (Orig.). 1996. pap. 7.95 (*0-7880-0671-1*, Fairway Pr) CSS OH.

Language of Love. Kate Emberg. (Love Stories Ser.). 192p. (YA). (gr. 7-12). 1996. mass mkt. 3.99 (*0-553-56667-9*) Bantam.

Language of Love. Ed. by Susan Polis Schutz. LC 98-42641. (Language of...Ser.). (Illus.). 64p. 1999. 14.95 (*0-88396-478-3*, L4783) Blue Mtn Art.

Language of Love. Dan Weiss. (J). 1996. mass mkt. 4.99 (*0-553-54264-8*) BDD Bks Young Read.

Language of Love. Gary Smalley & John Trent. Ed. by Denise Silvestro. 256p. 1992. reprint ed. mass mkt. 6.99 (*0-671-75047-X*) PB.

Language of Love. rev. ed. Gary Smalley & John Trent. 1991. pap., student ed. 11.00 (*1-56179-020-6*) Focus Family.

*__Language of Love: A Romantic Miscellany, Mini Edition.__ Robyn Officer. 2000. 4.95 (*0-7407-0514-8*) Andrews & McMeel.

Language of Love & Guilt: Mother-Daughter Relationships from a Cross-Cultural Persepective. Ruth Wodak & Muriel R. Schulz. LC 85-30674. x, 253p. 1986. pap. 22.95 (*0-915027-44-5*) J Benjamins Pubng Co.

Language of Love, Power & Health: Heal Your Life Through Language. Vann A. Daniels. Ed. by David W. Daniels et al. (Orig.). 1992. pap. write for info. (*0-9633837-0-1*) Ctr Heal Lang.

Language of Machines: An Introduction to Computability & Formal Languages. Robert W. Floyd & Richard Beigel. LC 93-3910. 706p. (C). 1993. pap. text 70.95 (*0-7167-8266-9*, Computer Sci Pr) W H Freeman.

*__Language of Magazines.__ Linda McLoughlin. LC 99-48842. (Intertext Ser.). 112p. 2000. pap. 16.99 (*0-415-21424-6*) Routledge.

Language of Maps. 16th ed. Phil Gersmehl. (Pathways in Geography Ser.: No. 1). (Illus.). 196p. (Orig.). 1996. student ed., spiral bd. 15.00 (*0-9627379-3-3*) NCFGE.

Language of Maps: A Map Skills Program for Grades 4-6. Haig A. Rushdoony. (Makemaster Bk.). (J). (gr. 4-6). 1983. pap. 12.99 (*0-8224-4242-6*) Fearon Teacher Aids.

Language of Marketing in English. Andrew Jenkins-Murphy. (English for Careers Ser). (Illus.). 112p. (C). 1987. pap. text 15.40 (*0-13-523358-5*, 18529) Prentice ESL.

Language of Marriage: A Gift Two Hearts Will Always Share. A Blue Mountain Arts Collection. LC 99-19311. (Language of...Ser.). (Illus.). 48p. 1999. 14.95 (*0-88396-505-4*, L5054) Blue Mtn Art.

*__Language of Mathematics: Making the Invisible Visible.__ Keith Devlin. (Illus.). 352p. 2000. pap. text 14.95 (*0-7167-3967-4*) W H Freeman.

Language of Medicine. Chabner. 1996. 150.00 (*0-7216-6839-9*) Harcourt.

Language of Medicine. 5th ed. Davi-Ellen Chabner. (Illus.). 1996. pap., teacher ed. write for info. (*0-7216-6027-4*, W B Saunders Co) Harcrt Hlth Sci Grp.

Language of Medicine: A General Guide to Medical Care. Byron K. Cole. 365p. (Orig.). 1997. pap. 19.95 (*0-9656764-0-4*) Medical Info Assocs.

Language of Medicine: A Write-in Text Explaining Medical Terms. 5th ed. Davi-Ellen Chabner. Ed. by Margaret Biblis. LC 95-5451. (Illus.). 880p. 1996. pap. text 39.95 (*0-7216-6026-6*, W B Saunders Co) Harcrt Hlth Sci Grp.

L

***Language of Medicine: A Write-In Text Explaining Medical Terms.** 6th ed. Davi-Ellen Chabner. LC 99-89410. (Illus.). 895p. Date not set. pap. text. write for info. (*0-7216-8569-2*, W B Saunders Co) Harcrt Hlth Sci Grp.

Language of Medicine: Exam/Testbank. 5th ed. Bruce A. Chabner. 1996. pap., suppl. ed. 200.00 (*0-7216-3339-0*, W B Saunders Co) Harcrt Hlth Sci Grp.

Language of Medicine: Its Evolution, Structure, Dynamics. 2nd ed. John Dirckx. LC 83-8863. 206p. 1983. 59.95 (*0-275-91388-0*, C1388, Praeger Pubs) Greenwood.

Language of Medicine in English. Ethel Tiersky. 144p. (C). 1992. pap. text 26.27 (*0-13-521444-0*) P-H.

Language of Metaphors. Andrew Goatly. LC 95-52119. 376p. (C). 1997. pap. 27.99 (*0-415-12877-3*) Routledge.

Language of Metaphors. Andrew Goatly. LC 95-52119. (Illus.). 376p. (C). 1997. 100.00 (*0-415-12876-5*) Routledge.

Language of Metre of Chaucer. B. Brink. LC 68-24899. (Studies in Chaucer: No. 6). 1969. reprint ed. lib. bdg. 75.00 (*0-8383-0917-8*) M S G Haskell Hse.

Language of Modern Music. Donald Mitchell. LC 94-6523. 192p. (C). 1994. pap. text 14.95 (*0-8122-1543-5*) U of Pa Pr.

Language of Modernism. Randy Malamud. Ed. by A. Walton Litz. LC 89-20134. (Studies in Modern Literature: No. 108). 208p. reprint ed. pap. 64.50 (*0-8357-2030-6*, 207073800004) Bks Demand.

Language of Money. 3rd ed. Edna Carew. 368p. 1996. pap. 34.95 (*1-86373-966-1*, Pub. by Allen & Unwin Pty) Paul & Co Pubs.

Language of Morals. Richard M. Hare. 208p. 1991. pap. text 22.00 (*0-19-881077-6*, 12258) OUP.

Language of Motivation & Language of Actions. Maria Nowakowska. LC 72-94491. (Janua Linguarum, Ser. Major: No. 67). (Illus.). 272p. 1973. text 67.70 (*90-279-2385-X*) Mouton.

Language of Music. Deryck Cooke. (Illus.). 304p. (Orig.). 1990. pap. text 28.00 (*0-19-816180-8*) OUP.

Language of Music. Klaus Liepmann. LC 52-12521. 384p. reprint ed. pap. 119.10 (*0-608-10886-3*, AU0015100092) Bks Demand.

Language of Names: What We Call Ourselves & Why It Matters. Justin Kaplan & Anne Bernays. LC 96-26439. 256p. 1997. 21.50 (*0-684-80741-6*) S&S Trade.

Language of Names: What We Call Ourselves & Why It Matters. Justin Kaplan & Anne Bernays. 256p. 1999. pap. 12.00 (*0-684-83867-2*, Touchstone) S&S Trade Pap.

Language of Negotiation: A Handbook of Practical Strategies for Improving Communication. Joan Mulholland. 224p. (C). 1991. text 75.00 (*0-415-06040-0*, Pub. by Tavistock) Routldge.

***Language of New Communication Technologies.** Tim Shortis. LC 00-29104. 2000. write for info. (*0-415-22275-3*) Routledge.

***Language of New Labour.** Norman Fairclough. LC 99-46501. 192p. 2000. pap. 27.99 (*0-415-21827-6*) Routledge.

***Language of New Media.** Lev Manovich. (Illus.). 352p. 2000. 34.95 (*0-262-13374-1*, A Leonardo Bk) MIT Pr.

Language of News Media. Allan Bell. 256p. 1991. pap. 28.95 (*0-631-16435-9*) Blackwell Pubs.

Language of Newspapers. Danuta Reah. LC 97-17315. 136p. (C). 1998. pap. 14.99 (*0-415-14600-3*) Routledge.

Language of 1984: Orwell's English & Ours. Whitney F. Bolton. LC 83-21671. 252p. 1984. reprint ed. pap. 78.20 (*0-608-02609-3*, 206326700004) Bks Demand.

Language of Numbers. EDC Staff. LC 93-43914. (Seeing & Thinking Mathematically in the Middle Grades Ser.). 140p. 1994. spiral bd. 39.50 (*0-435-08349-X*, 08349) Heinemann.

Language of Oppression. Haig A. Bosmajian. LC 83-5866. 164p. 1983. 18.25 (*0-8191-3186-5*) U Pr of Amer.

Language of Ordination: Ministry in an Ecumenical Context. L. William Countryman. LC 92-21970. 112p. 1992. pap. 12.00 (*1-56338-046-3*) TPI PA.

Language of Our Own: The Genesis of Michif, the Mixed Cree-French Language of the Canadian Metis. Peter Bakker. LC 97-7301. (Oxford Studies in Anthropological Linguistics: No. 10). (Illus.). 336p. 1997. text 85.00 (*0-19-509711-4*) OUP.

Language of Our Own: The Genesis of Michif, the Mixed Cree-French Language of the Canadian Metis. rev. ed. Peter Bakker. LC 97-7301. (Oxford Studies in Anthropological Linguistics: No. 10). (Illus.). 336p. 1997. pap. 49.95 (*0-19-509712-2*) OUP.

Language of Oysters. Adamson & Gemes. (Illus.). 168p. 1997. text 30.00 (*90-5703-101-9*) Gordon & Breach.

Language of Parable. William L. Worcester. LC 76-6008. 400p. 1976. reprint ed. pap. 5.95 (*0-87785-155-7*) Swedenborg.

***Language of Perversion & the Language of Love.** Sheldon Bach. LC 94-7906. 224p. 1999. pap. 40.00 (*0-7657-0230-4*) Aronson.

Language of Philosophy. Margaret Chatterjee. 152p. 1981. text 94.00 (*90-247-2372-8*) Kluwer Academic.

Language of Philosophy. Morris Lazerowitz. LC 77-23068. (Boston Studies in the Philosophy of Science: No. 55). 224p. 1977. pap. text 70.50 (*90-277-0862-2*, D Reidel); lib. bdg. 82.50 (*90-277-0826-6*, D Reidel) Kluwer Academic.

Language of Phrygians: Description & Analysis. Vladimir E. Orel. LC 97-44326. 504p. 1997. 75.00 (*0-88206-089-9*) Caravan Bks.

Language of Physics: The Calculus & the Development of Theoretical Physics in Europe, 1750-1870. Elizabeth Garber. LC 98-14004. xix, 399 p. 1999. write for info. (*3-7643-4039-8*) Birkhauser.

Language of Physics: The Calculus & the Development of Theoretical Physics in Europe, 1750-1914. Elizabeth Garber. LC 98-14004. 400p. 1998. 64.50 (*0-8176-4039-8*) Birkhauser.

Language of Planning: Essays on the Origins & Ends of American Planning Thought. Albert Z. Guttenberg. LC 92-41286. 288p. 1993. text 42.50 (*0-252-02003-0*); pap. text 16.95 (*0-252-06307-4*) U of Ill Pr.

Language of Poetry. John McRae. LC 97-17316. (Intertext Ser.). 168p. (C). 1998. pap. 16.99 (*0-415-16928-3*) Routledge.

Language of Political Leadership in Contemporary Britain. John Gaffney. LC 90-32848. 248p. 1991. text 49.95 (*0-312-04638-3*) St Martin.

Language of Political Theory in Seventeenth-Century England. Conal Condren. LC 94-5979. 1994. text 65.00 (*0-312-12183-0*) St Martin.

***Language of Politics.** Adrian Beard. LC 99-23246. (Intertext Ser.). 2000. pap. write for info. (*0-415-20178-0*) Routledge.

Language of Politics. Michael L. Geis. LC 86-29726. 200p. 1987. 72.00 (*0-387-96465-7*) Spr-Verlag.

Language of Politics in America: Shaping Political Consciousness from McKinley to Reagan. David Green. LC 91-46982. 292p. reprint ed. pap. 90.60 (*0-608-20895-7*, 207199400003) Bks Demand.

Language of Politics in the Age of Wilkes & Burke. James T. Boulton. LC 64-55133. (Studies in Political History). 296p. reprint ed. pap. 91.80 (*0-608-16231-0*, 202651100050) Bks Demand.

***Language of Positive Thinking.** Ed. by A Blue Mountain Arts Collection. LC 99-47783. 48p. 1999. 14.95 (*0-88396-541-0*) Blue Mtn Art.

Language of Power Vol. 19: Women & Literature, 1945 to the Present. Roberta Rosenberg. (Writing about Women Ser.). XIII, 273p. (C). 1996. pap. text 29.95 (*0-8204-2799-3*) P Lang Pubng.

Language of Power, the Power of Language: The Effects of Ambiguity on Sociopolitical Structures in Shakespeare's Plays. Stephen Cohen. LC 87-72452. (LeBaron Russell Briggs Prize Honors Essays in English Ser.: 1987). 152p. (Orig.). 1988. pap. 6.30 (*0-674-51056-9*) HUP.

***Language of Prayer: A Blue Mountain Arts Collection.** LC 00-29681. (Illus.). 48p. 2000. 14.95 (*1-58786-002-3*, L4791, Blue Mtn Pr Bks) SPS Studios.

Language of Psalms in Worship: American Revisions of Watts's Psalter. Rochelle A. Stackhouse. LC 96-45995. (Drew Studies in Liturgy: No. 8). 208p. 1997. 52.00 (*0-8108-3267-4*) Scarecrow.

Language of Psycards. Berenice Watt. (Illus.). 1999. pap. 22.95 (*1-86163-056-5*) Capall Bann Pubng.

Language of Psycho-Analysis. Jean Laplanche & Jean-Baptiste Pontalis. Tr. by Donald Micholson-Smith from FRE. LC 73-18418. 510p. (C). 1974. 50.00 (*0-393-01105-4*) Norton.

Language of Psychotherapy. Rudolf Ekstein. LC 88-35143. (Foundations of Semiotics Ser.: No. II). xviii, 336p. 1989. 106.00 (*90-272-3281-4*) J Benjamins Pubng Co.

Language of Public Administration: Bureaucracy, Modernity & Postmodernity. David J. Farmer. LC 94-32613. (FRE, GER & LAT.). 328p. (C). 1995. pap. text 29.95 (*0-8173-0784-2*) U of Ala Pr.

Language of Puritan Feeling: An Exploration in Literature, Psychology, & Social History. David Leverenz. LC 79-18579. 357p. reprint ed. pap. 110.70 (*0-8357-7948-3*, 205702300002) Bks Demand.

***Language of Real Estate.** Barbara Cox. 2000. pap. text. write for info. (*0-13-016843-2*) P-H.

Language of Real Estate. 4th ed. John W. Reilly. LC 93-8367. 455p. 1993. pap. 32.95 (*0-7931-0583-8*, 19610104, Real Estate Ed) Dearborn.

***Language of Real Estate.** 5th ed. John W. Reilly. LC 00-44556. 2000. write for info. (*0-7931-3193-6*, Real Estate Ed) Dearborn.

Language of Real Estate Appraisal. Jeffrey Fisher. 290p. 1990. pap. 34.95 (*0-88462-983-X*, 1556-1101, Real Estate Ed) Dearborn.

Language of Reason. G. B. Keene. LC 93-20604. 180p. 1993. text 79.95 (*0-7734-9305-0*) E Mellen.

Language of Reason. Richards. 1978. text 44.00 (*0-08-021846-6*, Pergamon Pr); pap. text 22.00 (*0-08-021845-8*, Pergamon Pr) Elsevier.

***Language of Recovery.** (Illus.). 48p. 2000. 14.95 (*1-58786-001-5*, L4791, Blue Mtn Pr Bks) SPS Studios.

***Language of Recovery... And Living Life One Day at a Time.** (Illus.). 64p. 2000. pap. 8.95 (*1-58786-006-6*, Blue Mtn Pr Bks) SPS Studios.

Language of Research in Criminal Justice: A Reader. Pamela Tontodonato & Frank E. Hagan. LC 97-17050. 322p. (C). 1997. pap. text 36.00 (*0-205-26898-6*) Allyn.

Language of Riddles: New Perspectives. W. J. Pepicello & Thomas A. Green. LC 84-3551. (Illus.). 175p. reprint ed. pap. 54.30 (*0-608-09864-7*, 206982900006) Bks Demand.

Language of Risk: Conflicting Perspectives on Occupational Health. Ed. by Dorothy Nelkin. LC 85-2211. (Sage Focus Edition Ser.: No. 71). 200p. reprint ed. pap. 62.00 (*0-7837-4565-6*, 204409400003) Bks Demand.

Language of Sadomasochism: A Glossary & Linguistic Analysis. Thomas E. Murray & Thomas R. Murrell. LC 88-25099. 208p. 1989. lib. bdg. 69.50 (*0-313-26481-3*, MYD/, Greenwood Pr) Greenwood.

***Language of Sailing.** Richard Mayne. 320p. 2000. pap. 29.95 (*1-85754-168-5*, Pub. by Carcanet Pr) Paul & Co Pubs.

Language of Satirized Characters in Poetaster: A Socio-Stylistic Analysis, 1597-1602. A. H. King. (Lund Studies in English: Vol. 10). 1969. reprint ed. pap. 45.00 (*0-8115-0553-7*) Periodicals Srv.

Language of Science. Orr & Schutte. 1992. 52.95 (*0-409-11165-1*) Buttrwrth-Heinemann.

Language of Science: A Study of the Relationship Between Literature & Science in the Perspective of a Hermeneutical Ontology, with a Case Study of Darwin's "The Origin of Species" Ilse N. Bulhof. LC 92-26529. (Brill's Studies in Intellectual History: Vol. 34). 207p. 1992. 74.50 (*90-04-09644-2*) Brill Academic Pubs.

Language of Sculpture. William Tucker. LC 85-50440. (Illus.). 1985. pap. 16.95 (*0-500-27104-6*, Pub. by Thames Hudson) Norton.

Language of Sex: An A to Z Guide. Michael Carrera. 192p. 1992. 24.95 (*0-8160-2397-2*) Facts on File.

Language of Sex: Five Voices from Northern France Around 1200. John W. Bawdwin. LC 93-6040. (Chicago Series on Sexuality, History, & Society). 360p. 1994. 37.50 (*0-226-03613-8*) U Ch Pr.

Language of Sex: Five Voices from Northern France Around 1200. John W. Baldwin. (Chicago Series on Sexuality, History, & Society). (Illus.). 332p. 1995. reprint ed. pap. text 17.95 (*0-226-03614-6*) U Ch Pr.

Language of Shakespeare. 2nd ed. N. F. Blake. LC 95-106830. 154p. 1994. text 17.95 (*0-333-49778-3*, Pub. by Macmillan) St Martin.

Language of Shakespeare's Plays. B. Ifor Evans. LC 85-14854. 216p. 1985. lib. bdg. 59.50 (*0-313-24987-3*, ELAS, Greenwood Pr) Greenwood.

Language of Shape: Curvature & Structure of Condensed Matter in Chemistry & Biology. S. Hyde et al. LC 96-37291. 396p. 1996. text 231.25 (*0-444-81538-4*) Elsevier.

Language of Silence: On the Unspoken & the Unspeakable in Modern Drama. Leslie Kane. LC 82-49321. 192p. 1985. 32.50 (*0-8386-3187-8*) Fairleigh Dickinson.

Language of Silence: West German Literature & the Holocaust. Ernestine Schlant. LC 98-41108. 288p. 1999. pap. 20.99 (*0-415-92220-8*) Routledge.

Language of Silence: West German Literature & the Holocaust. Ernestine S. Schlant. 18p. 1999. 75.00 (*0-415-92219-4*) Routledge.

***Language of Slovakia's Rusyns.** Jura Vanko. 2000. 35.00 (*0-88033-437-1*, 539, Pub. by East Eur Monographs) Col U Pr.

Language of Sophocles: Communality, Communication & Involvement. Felix Budelmann. LC 99-13645. (Cambridge Classical Studies). 312p. (C). 1999. 64.95 (*0-521-66040-8*) Cambridge U Pr.

Language of Souls. K. T. Frankovich et al. Ed. by Laurie A. Sullivan. 136p. 2000. 24.95 (*1-894368-00-2*) L1ang Souls.

Language of Spanish Dance. Matteo M. Vittucci & Carola Goya. LC 89-48953. (Illus.). 320p. 1993. pap. 29.95 (*0-8061-2532-2*) U of Okla Pr.

Language of Sport. Adrian Beard. LC 97-15837. (Intertext Ser.). 128p. (C). 1998. pap. 14.99 (*0-415-16911-9*) Routledge.

Language of Stephen Crane's Bowery Tales: Developing Mastery of Character Diction. Alan R. Slotkin. LC 93-21823. 176p. 1993. text 10.00 (*0-8153-1263-6*, H1686) Garland.

Language of Success: A Gift for Those Who Follow Their Dreams. A Blue Mountain Arts Collection. LC 99-18691. (Language of...Ser.). (Illus.). 48p. 1999. 14.95 (*0-88396-504-6*, L5046) Blue Mtn Art.

Language of Success: How to Join the Inner Circle. J. Richard Lawson. 256p. (Orig.). 1989. pap. 19.95 (*0-945071-10-8*) Lawco.

Language of Teaching: A Memorable Gift for Those Who Place a High Value on Education. A Blue Mountain Arts Collection. LC 99-19315. (Language of...Ser.). (Illus.). 48p. 1999. 14.95 (*0-88396-509-7*, L5097) Blue Mtn Art.

Language of Technology. Wim A. Velthuizen & Frans W. Van Schaik. 384p. (C). 1992. pap. 38.00 (*82-00-40759-4*, Pub. by Scand Univ Pr) IBD Ltd.

Language of Technology: Dictionary. Wim A. Velthuizen & Frans W. Van Schaik. 56p. (C). 1992. pap. 6.00 (*82-00-40864-7*, Pub. by Scand Univ Pr) IBD Ltd.

***Language of Teenagers: Words to Remember.** (Illus.). 48p. (YA). 2000. 14.95 (*1-58786-000-7*, L4791, Blue Mtn Pr Bks) SPS Studios.

Language of Thackeray. K. C. Phillipps. (C). 1978. text 26.50 (*0-233-96917-9*) Westview.

Language of the Archetype: Explorations of the Unconscious in Movement, Speech, & Development. Vincent L. Perri. LC 97-66789. 160p. 1997. 15.95 (*1-887750-64-9*) Rutledge Bks.

Language of the Blue Books: The Perfect Instrument of Empire. Gwyneth Tyson Roberts. LC 99-170995. 240p. 1999. pap. 29.95 (*0-7083-1423-6*) Paul & Co Pubs.

Language of the Body. Alexander Lowen. 416p. 1971. pap. 6.95 (*0-02-077310-2*) Macmillan.

Language of the Body: Drawings by Pierre-Paul Prud'hon. Illus. by Pierre-Paul Prud'hon. LC 96-10851. 224p. 1996. 75.00 (*0-8109-3585-6*, Pub. by Abrams) Time Warner.

Language of the Book of Songs. W. A. Dobson. LC 68-92657. (Illus.). 351p. reprint ed. pap. 108.90 (*0-608-11066-3*, 202047300018) Bks Demand.

Language of the Civil War. John D. Wright. (Illus.). 304p. 2001. text, boxed set 62.50 (*1-57356-135-5*) Oryx Pr.

Language of the Classical French Organ: A Musical Tradition Before 1800. expanded rev. ed. Fenner Douglass. LC 94-45846. 251p. 1995. pap. 19.00 (*0-300-06426-8*) Yale U Pr.

Language of the Consciousness Soul. Carl Unger. 1983. pap. 17.95 (*0-916786-56-0*, Saint George Pubns) R Steiner Col.

Language of the Constitution: A Sourcebook & Guide to the Ideas, Terms, & Vocabulary Used by the Framers of the United States Constitution. Thurston Greene et al. LC 91-29197. 1074p. 1991. lib. bdg. 115.00 (*0-313-28202-1*, GLO/, Greenwood Pr) Greenwood.

Language of the Cross. Ed. by Aelred Lacomara. 149p. 1977. 5.95 (*0-8199-0617-4*, Frncscn Herld) Franciscan Pr.

Language of the Cutting Room: A Primary Reference Manual for the Assistant Editor of 35mm Film. 9th rev. ed. Bernard Balmuth. LC 81-84920. (Illus.). 97p. (C). 1996. pap. text 13.50 (*0-9607486-0-1*) Rosallen Pubns.

Language of the Devil: Texture & Archetype in Finnegans Wake. C. George Sandulescu. LC 87-15457. 330p. 1988. 59.95 (*0-8023-1284-5*) Dufour.

Language of the Dragon: A Classical Chinese Reader, Vol. 1. Gregory Chiang. 385p. 1998. pap. 28.95 (*0-88727-298-3*) Cheng & Tsui.

***Language of the Dragon Vol. 2: A Classical Chinese Reader.** Gregory Chiang. 400p. 1999. pap. 29.95 (*0-88727-318-1*) Cheng & Tsui.

***Language of the Dragon Vol. 3: A Classical Chinese Reader.** Gregory Chiang. 200p. 1999. pap. 49.95 (*0-88727-319-X*) Cheng & Tsui.

Language of the Earth. Rhodes & Stone. 350p. 1981. pap. 42.00 (*0-08-025980-4*, Pergamon Pr) Elsevier.

Language of the East Midlands & the Development of Standard English: A Study in Diacronic Phonology. Willard J. Rusch. LC 91-31826. (Berkeley Insights in Linguistics & Semiotics Ser.: Vol. 8). 197p. (C). 1992. text 41.95 (*0-8204-1582-0*) P Lang Pubng.

Language of the Feet: What Feet Can Tell You. Chris Stormer. (Illus.). 142p. 1996. mass mkt. 13.95 (*0-340-64345-5*, Pub. by Hodder & Stought Ltd) Trafalgar.

Language of the Field. Michael Brander. LC 98-203750. 220p. 1998. pap. 25.00 (*1-85754-166-9*, Pub. by Carcanet Pr) Paul & Co Pubs.

Language of the Forest. C. Ross McKenney & David L. Kendall. LC 96-1429. (Illus.). 158p. 1996. reprint ed. write for info. (*0-945980-55-8*) Nrth Country Pr.

***Language of the Former Soviet Republics: Their History & Development.** Gary C. Fouse. LC 99-59842. 472p. 2000. 57.50 (*0-7618-1607-0*) U Pr of Amer.

Language of the Freedmen in Petronius' Cena Trimalchionis. Bret Boyce. LC 91-18778. (Mnemosyne Ser.: Supplement 117). vi, 113p. 1991. 53.50 (*90-04-09431-8*) Brill Academic Pubs.

***Language of the Goddess.** 2nd ed. Marija Gimbutas. LC 00-101120. (Illus.). 424p. 2001. reprint ed. pap. 24.95 (*0-500-28249-8*, Pub. by Thames Hudson) Norton.

Language of the Goddess: Unearthing the Hidden Symbols of Western Civilization. Marija Gimbutas. LC 89-45398. (Illus.). 416p. 1995. pap. 24.00 (*0-06-251243-9*, Pub. by Harper SF) HarpC.

Language of the Gods. Judith M. Tyberg. 1976. 8.95 (*0-930736-00-1*) E-W Cultural Ctr.

Language of the Greek New Testament: Classic Essays. Ed. by Stanley E. Porter. (Journal for the Study of the New Testament, Supplement Ser.: No. 60). 238p. (C). 1991. 70.00 (*1-85075-325-3*, Pub. by Sheffield Acad) CUP Services.

Language of the Hand (1920) Henry Firth & Ed H. Allen. 156p. 1998. reprint ed. pap. 17.95 (*0-7661-0588-1*) Kessinger Pub.

Language of the Hand Palmistry. Cheiro. 1999. 7.99 (*0-517-18930-5*) Random Hse Value.

Language of the Harappans: From Akkadian to Sanskrit. Malati J. Shendge. LC 97-905287. (C). 1997. 58.00 (*81-7017-325-6*, Pub. by Abhinav) S Asia.

Language of the Heart, No. 24. Jeanne Anders. (Serenade Serenata Ser.). 1985. pap. 1.49 (*0-310-46922-8*, 15551P) Zondervan.

Language of the Heart: Bill W.'s Grapevine Writings. Bill W, pseud. LC 88-71930. 432p. 1988. 10.00 (*0-933685-16-5*) A A Grapevine.

***Language of the Heart: Celebrating the Beauty of Love.** Ellyn Sanna. 40p. 2000. 1.99 (*1-57748-648-X*) Barbour Pub.

Language of the Heart: Rituals, Stories, & Information about Death. Carolyn Pogue. 160p. 1998. pap. 14.95 (*1-896836-17-8*) NStone Publ.

Language of the Heart: Bill W's Grapevine Writings see Lenguaje del Corazon: Los Escritos de Bill W. Para el Grapevine

Language of the Heart, 1600-1750: New Cultural Studies. Robert A. Erickson. LC 96-53150. (New Cultural Studies). (Illus.). 296p. 1997. text 36.95 (*0-8122-3394-8*) U of Pa Pr.

Language of the Inka since the European Invasion. Bruce Mannheim. (Illus.). 346p. 1991. text 25.00 (*0-292-74663-6*) U of Tex Pr.

Language of the Islenos: Vestigial Spanish in Louisiana. John M. Lipski. LC 89-13508. 144p. 1990. text 25.00 (*0-8071-1534-7*) La State U Pr.

Language of the King James Bible: An Introduction. Gail Riplinger. (Illus.). 179p. 1998. pap. 10.00 (*0-9635845-1-0*) A V Pubns.

***Language of the Land: Living among the Hadzabe in Africa.** James Stephenson. (Illus.). 224p. 2000. 24.95 (*0-312-24107-0*) St Martin.

***Language of the Land: The Library of Congress Book of Literary Maps.** Martha E. Hopkins & Michael Buscher. LC 98-21591. (Illus.). 328p. 1999. 50.00 (*0-8444-0963-4*) Lib Congress.

Language of the Law. David Mellinkoff. 544p. 1963. pap. text 34.00 (*0-316-56627-6*, Aspen Law & Bus) Aspen Pub.

Language of the Lord: New Discoveries of Chiasma in the Doctrine & Covenants. H. Clay Gorton. 352p. 1993. 19.98 (*0-88290-475-2*, 1033) Horizon Utah.

An Asterisk (*) at the beginning of an entry indicates that the title is appearing for the first time.

L

Language of the Mayas: Structure of Maya Speech & Writing. William C. Barker. 200p. 1991. pap. write for info. (*1-880365-00-6*) Prof Pr NC.

Language of the Media. D. C. Perkins. 430p. (C). 1988. 190.00 (*1-85122-026-7*, Pub. by Domino Bks Ltd); pap. 100.00 (*1-85122-023-2*, Pub. by Domino Bks Ltd) St Mut.

Language of the Metaphysical Poets. Frances Austin. LC 91-26389. (Language of Literature Ser.). 180p. 1992. text 39.95 (*0-312-06885-9*) St Martin.

Language of the New Century Hymnal. Ed. & Compiled by Arthur Clyde. 64p. 1995. pap. 5.00 (*0-8298-1156-7*) Pilgrim OH.

Language of the New Testament. Eugene Van Ness Geotchius. 349p. (C). 1966. text 41.20 (*0-02-344530-0*, Macmillan Coll); pap. text, student ed., wbk. ed. 25.00 (*0-02-344540-8*, Macmillan Coll) P-H.

Language of the Night: Essays on Fantasy & Science Fiction. Ursula K. Le Guin. Ed. by Susan Wood. LC 78-24350. 270p. 1979. 25.00 (*0-399-12325-3*) Ultramarine Pub.

Language of the Oldest Runic Inscriptions: A Linguistic & Historical-Philological Analysis. E. A. Makaev. Tr. by John Meredig & Elmer H. Antonsen from RUS. (Filologisk-Filosofiska Ser.: Vol. 21). 137p. (Orig.). 1996. pap. 39.50 (*91-7402-259-8*) Coronet Bks.

Language of the Papago of Arizona. John A. Mason. LC 52-81. (University of Pennsylvania, Museum Monographs). 88p. reprint ed. pap. 30.00 (*0-608-13538-0*, 202238200026) Bks Demand.

Language of the Parker Chronicle Vol. 2: Word Formation & Syntax. C. Sprockel. 297p. 1973. pap. text 85.50 (*90-247-1530-X*, Pub. by M Nijhoff) Kluwer Academic.

Language of the People. Ed. by William Donaldson. (Illus.). 246p. 1989. text 29.90 (*0-08-037730-0*, Pergamon Pr); pap. text 18.00 (*0-08-037731-9*, Pergamon Pr) Elsevier.

Language of the Piano. (Music Instruction Bks.). 1995. pap. 9.95 (*0-8258-0289-X*, 04131) Fischer Inc NY.

Language of the Qur'an. Bakir Al-Hassani. 1990. 20.00 (*0-685-66738-3*, 43) Tahrike Tarsile Quran.

Language of the Quran: A Concise Text of Arabic Grammar with Ample Applications from the Quran & the Hadith. Bakir Al-Hassani. 120p. 1996. pap. 12.95 (*0-614-21058-5*, 1377) Kazi Pubns.

Language of the Railroader. Ramon F. Adams. LC 77-22346. 192p. 1977. reprint ed. pap. 59.60 (*0-608-13296-9*, 205215200044) Bks Demand.

Language of the Robe: American Indian Trade Blankets. Robert W. Kapoun & Charles J. Lohrmann. LC 96-44485. (Illus.). 192p. 1997. reprint ed. pap. 26.95 (*0-87905-811-0*) Gibbs Smith Pub.

Language of the Salinan Indians. fac. ed. J. Alden Mason. (University of California Publications in American Archaeology & Ethnology: Vol. 14: 1). 154p. (C). 1918. reprint ed. pap. text 16.88 (*1-55567-217-5*) Coyote Press.

Language of the Self: Essays on the Perennial Philosophy. rev. ed. Frithjof Schuon. LC 98-40021. 237p. 1999. pap. 17.00 (*0-941532-26-7*) Wrld Wisdom Bks.

Language of the Senses: Sensory-Perceptual Dynamics in Wordsworth, Coleridge, Thoreau, Whitman, & Dickinson. Kerry McSweeney. 218p. 1998. text 60.00 (*0-7735-1740-5*, Pub. by McG-Queens Univ Pr) CUP Services.

Language of the Skies: The Bilingual Air Traffic Control Conflict in Canada. Sandford F. Borins. (Canadian Public Administration Ser.). 303p. 1983. 49.95 (*0-7735-0402-8*, Pub. by McG-Queens Univ Pr); pap. 27.95 (*0-7735-0403-6*, Pub. by McG-Queens Univ Pr) CUP Services.

Language of the Skies: The Bilingual Air Traffic Control Conflict in Canada. Sandford F. Borins. LC 83-214911. (Canadian Public Administration Ser.). (Illus.). 303p. reprint ed. pap. 94.00 (*0-7837-6905-9*, 204673500003) Bks Demand.

Language of the Soul. Robert Crosbie. (Sangam Texts Ser.). 130p. 1986. pap. 12.75 (*0-88695-026-0*) Concord Grove.

Language of the Soul: Applying Universal Principles for Self-Empowerment. Meredith L. Young. (Agartha Workbook Ser.). (Illus.). 156p. 1987. pap., student ed. 12.50 (*0-913299-52-9*) Stillpoint.

Language of the Stars: A Discourse on the Theory of the Light Changes of Eclipsing Variables. Zdenek Kopal. (Astrophysics & Space Science Library: No. 77). 1979. pap. text 80.00 (*90-277-1044-9*) Kluwer Academic.

***Language of the Third Reich: A Philologist's Notebook.** Victor Klemperer. Tr. by Martin Brady. LC 99-52921. 280p. 1999. 90.00 (*0-485-11526-3*) Athlone Pr.

Language of the Unsayable: The Play of Negativity in Literature & Literary Theory. Ed. by Sanford Budick & Wolfgang Iser. (Irvine Studies in the Humanities). (Illus.). 418p. pap. 17.95 (*0-8047-2483-0*) Stanford Univ Committee on Linguistics.

Language of Theatre. Martin Harrison. LC 97-42204. 316p. 1998. pap. 19.99 (*0-87830-087-2*) Routledge.

Language of Thought. Jerry A. Fodor. 224p. 1980. pap. 17.95 (*0-674-51030-5*) HUP.

Language of Threads. Gail Tsukiyama. LC 99-22212. 288p. 1999. text 23.95 (*0-312-20376-4*) St Martin.

***Language of Threads.** Gail Tsukiyama. (Illus.). 288p. 2000. reprint ed. pap. 12.95 (*0-312-26756-8*, St Martin Griffin) St Martin.

Language of Total Quality. Arturo Onnias. 1993. 24.95 (*0-614-30073-8*) Juran Inst.

Language of Tourism: A Sociolinguistic Perspective. Graham M. Dann. LC 96-206040. (CAB International Publication Ser.). 310p. 1996. text 80.00 (*0-85198-999-3*) OUP.

***Language of Trees: An Illustrated Workbook Introducing NLP Communication Skills.** Ed. & Photos by Sarah L. Rush. (Illus.). xxii, 245p. 2000. pap., wbk. ed. 24.95 (*0-9700272-1-4*) Rushs Arts.

Language of Truth: Contemporary Readings of the Sefat Emet. Arthur Green. 1998. 34.95 (*0-8276-0675-3*) JPS Phila.

Language of Twentieth-Century Art: A Conceptual History. Paul Crowther. LC 97-5248. 240p. 1997. 40.00 (*0-300-07241-4*) Yale U Pr.

Language of Twentieth Century Poetry. Lesley Heffries. LC 93-7481. (Language of Literature Ser.). 1993. text 35.00 (*0-312-09662-3*) St Martin.

Language of Virgil: An Introduction to the Poetry of the Aeneid. rev. ed. Daniel H. Garrison. LC 92-39469. (ENG & LAT., Illus.). XII, 141p. (C). 1993. text 24.95 (*0-8204-2169-3*) P Lang Pubng.

Language of Vision. Gyorgy Kepes. (Illus.). 224p. 1995. pap. 14.95 (*0-486-28650-9*) Dover.

Language of Vision: Meditations on Myth & Metaphor. Jamake Highwater. LC 93-38667. 352p. 1995. pap. 12.95 (*0-8021-3346-0*, Grove) Grove-Atltic.

Language of Visual Effects. Micheal J. McAlister. (Illus.). 176p. 1993. 18.95 (*0-943728-47-9*) Lone Eagle Pub.

Language of Winnicott: A Dictionary & Guide to Understanding His Work. Jan Abram & Harry Karnac. LC 96-50065. 400p. 1997. 50.00 (*1-56821-700-5*) Aronson.

***Language of Yes: Poems.** Joan Peternel. 96p. 2001. pap. 12.00 (*1-56474-354-3*) Fithian Pr.

Language of Yes: Poems 1990-1995. Kevin Crossley-Holland. LC 96-216930. 72p. 1996. pap. 16.95 (*1-870612-37-X*, Pub. by Enitha Pr) Dufour.

Language of Youth Subcultures: Social Identity in Action. Sue Widdicomb & Robin Wooffitt. 256p. (C). 1995. pap. text 36.00 (*0-13-343005-7*) P-H.

***Language Older Than Words.** Derrick Jensen. 400p. 2000. pap. 16.00 (*1-893956-03-2*) Context Bks.

Language on Trial: The Plain English Guide to Legal Writing. Plain English Campaign Staff. (Illus.). 90p. 1996. pap. 7.95 (*1-86105-006-2*, Robson-Parkwest) Parkwest Pubns.

Language-Operational-Gestalt Awareness: A Radically Empirical Pragmatical Phenomenology of the Processes & Systems of Library Experience. Eugene E. Graziano. LC 75-6564. 475p. reprint ed. pap. 135.40 (*0-608-18489-6*, AU00360) Bks Demand.

Language Origin: A Multidisciplinary Approach. Ed. by Bernard H. Bichakjian et al. 544p. (C). 1992. lib. bdg. 247.50 (*0-7923-1369-0*, Pub. by Kluwer Academic) Kluwer Academic.

Language Pack. 12th ed. Hodges. 1995. audio compact disk 35.50 (*0-15-502176-1*) Harcourt.

Language, Paradox, Poetics: A Chinese Perspective. James J. Liu. LC 88-6013. 191p. reprint ed. pap. 59.30 (*0-608-06423-8*, 206663600008) Bks Demand.

Language Parallax: Linguistic Relativism & Poetic Indeterminacy. Paul Friedrich. LC 85-15091. (Texas Linguistics Ser.). 206p. 1986. pap. 10.95 (*0-292-74651-2*); text 18.95 (*0-292-74650-4*) U of Tex Pr.

Language Parts Catalog. Melvin D. Levine. Ed. by Jennifer Noon. (Illus.). (YA). (gr. 7-10). 1999. pap., wbk. ed. 9.00 (*0-8388-1980-X*) Ed Pub Serv.

Language Picture Dictionary. Jean G. DeGaetano. 205p. (J). (ps-2). 1989. pap. text 34.95 (*1-886143-18-8*) Grt Ideas Tching.

Language Planning: An Introduction. Carol M. Eastman. Ed. by L. L. Langness & Robert B. Edgerton. LC 83-1991. (Publications in Anthropology & Related Fields). (Illus.). 288p. (Orig.). (C). 1983. pap. text 14.95 (*0-88316-552-X*) Chandler & Sharp.

Language Planning: Current Issues & Research. Ed. by Roger W. Shuy & Joan Rubin. LC 73-76754. 121p. reprint ed. pap. 37.60 (*0-7837-6337-9*, 204604900010) Bks Demand.

Language Planning: From Practice to Theory, Vol. 108. Robert B. Kaplan & Richard B. Baldauf. LC 97-2118. (Multilingual Matters Ser.). 350p. 1997. 95.00 (*1-85359-372-9*, Pub. by Multilingual Matters); pap. 39.95 (*1-85359-371-0*, Pub. by Multilingual Matters) Taylor & Francis.

Language Planning & Education in Australia & the South Pacific. Ed. by Richard B. Baldauf & Allan Luke. 290p. 1990. 99.00 (*1-85359-048-7*, Pub. by Multilingual Matters); pap. 44.95 (*1-85359-047-9*, Pub. by Multilingual Matters) Taylor & Francis.

Language Planning & Identity Planning. Ed. by Paul Lamy. (International Journal of the Sociology of Language Ser.: No. 20). 1979. pap. text 60.00 (*90-279-7768-2*) Mouton.

Language Planning & Language Education. Ed. by Chris Kennedy. (Illus.). 216p. (C). 1983. text 29.95 (*0-04-407019-5*); pap. text 12.95 (*0-04-407020-9*) Routledge.

***Language Planning & Language Use.** Ed. by Delyth Morris & Glyn Williams. 304p. 2000. 55.00 (*0-7083-1579-8*, Pub. by U Wales Pr) Paul & Co Pubs.

Language Planning & National Development: The Uzbeck Experience. William Fierman. LC 91-19848. (Contributions to the Sociology of Language Ser.: No. 60). xii, 358p. (C). 1991. lib. bdg. 121.55 (*3-11-012454-8*) Mouton.

Language Planning & Social Change. Robert L. Cooper. (Illus.). 224p. (C). 1990. text 59.95 (*0-521-33359-8*) Cambridge U Pr.

Language Planning Around the World: Contexts & Systemic Change. Ed. by Richard d. Lambert et al. LC 94-5826. (National Foreign Language Center Monographs). 1994. 10.00 (*1-880671-03-4*) NFLC Pubns.

Language Planning for Modernization: The Case of Indonesian & Malaysian. Takdir S. (Sutan Takdir) Alisjahbana. (Contributions to the Sociology of Language Ser.: No. 14). 1976. pap. text 26.15 (*90-279-7712-7*) Mouton.

***Language Planning in Malawi, Mozambique & the Philippines, 113.** Robert B. Kaplan. LC 98-52028. 10p. 1999. 49.95 (*1-85359-444-X*) Taylor & Francis.

Language Planning in Multilingual Contexts: Policies, Communities, & Schools in Luxemborg. Kathryn Anne Davis. LC 93-45415. (Studies in Bilingualism (SiBiL): No. 8). xix, 220p. 1994. lib. bdg. 45.00 (*1-55619-539-7*) J Benjamins Pubng Co.

***Language Planning in Nepal, Taiwan & Sweden.** Richard B. Baldauf & Robert B. Kaplan. LC 99-54927. 2000. write for info. (*1-85359-483-0*) Taylor & Francis.

Language Planning in the United States. J. Rubin. (International Journal of the Sociology of Language Ser.: No. 11). 1977. 60.00 (*90-279-7694-5*) Mouton.

Language Planning in Yugoslavia. Ed. by Ranko Bugarski & Celia Hawkesworth. 233p. (Orig.). 1992. pap. 18.95 (*0-89357-232-2*) Slavica.

Language Planning Processes. Rubin Jernudd. 1977. 46.15 (*90-279-3337-5*) Mouton.

Language Planning Processes. Ed. by Joan Rubin et al. (Contributions to the Sociology of Language Ser.: No. 21). 1977. text 43.85 (*90-279-7714-3*) Mouton.

***Language Play.** David Crystal. 272p. 1998. pap. 14.95 (*0-14-027385-9*, Pub. by Pnguin Bks Ltd) Trafalgar.

Language Poetry: Writing As Rescue. Linda Reinfeld. LC 91-24848. (Horizons in Theory & American Culture Ser.). 192p. 1992. text 27.50 (*0-8071-1698-X*) La State U Pr.

Language, Poetry & Poetics: The Generation of the 1890's: Jakobson, Trubetzkoy, Majakovskj - Proceeding of the First Roman Jakobson Colloquim. Krystyna Pomorska et al. (Illus.). 364p. 1987. lib. bdg. 119.25 (*0-89925-098-X*) Mouton.

Language Poets Use. 2nd ed. Winifred Nowottny. 225p. (C). 1965. pap. 14.95 (*0-485-12009-7*, Pub. by Athlone Pr) Humanities.

Language Policies in English-Dominant Countries: Six Case Studies. Ed. by Michael Herriman & Barbara Burnaby. LC 95-42291. (Language & Education Library: Vol. 10). 260p. 1996. 99.00 (*1-85359-347-8*, Pub. by Multilingual Matters); pap. 39.95 (*1-85359-346-X*, Pub. by Multilingual Matters) Taylor & Francis.

Language Policy: Dominant English, Pluralist Challenges. Ed. by William Eggington & Helen Wren. LC 96-6513. xxviii, 170p. 1997. pap. 27.95 (*1-55619-517-6*) J Benjamins Pubng Co.

Language Policy Across the Curriculum. David Corson. (Language & Education Library: No. 1). 328p. 1990. 79.00 (*1-85359-069-X*, Pub. by Multilingual Matters); pap. 24.95 (*1-85359-068-1*, Pub. by Multilingual Matters) Taylor & Francis.

***Language Policy & Identity Politics in the United States.** Ronald Schmidt, Sr. LC 99-87484. (Mapping Racisms Ser.). (Illus.). 296p. 2000. 21.95 (*1-56639-755-3*); pap. 65.50 (*1-56639-754-5*) Temple U Pr.

***Language Policy & Language Issues in the Successor States of the Former USSR.** Sue Wright. LC 99-38842. 91p. 1999. write for info. (*1-85359-463-6*) Taylor & Francis.

***Language Policy & Pedagogy: Essays in Honor of A. Ronald Walton.** Ed. by Richard D. Lambert & Elana Shohamy. LC 99-58745. xii, 270p. 2000. 65.00 (*1-55619-763-2*, JB8007) J Benjamins Pubng Co.

Language Policy & Political Development. Ed. by Brian Weinstein & Lee Thayer. LC 90-284. (Communication: The Human Context Ser.). 288p. (C). 1990. text 73.25 (*0-89391-611-0*) Ablx Pub.

Language Policy & Political Issues in Education. Ruth Wodak & David Corson. LC 97-30201. (Encyclopedia of Language & Education Ser.). 1997. lib. bdg. write for info. (*0-7923-4713-7*) Kluwer Academic.

Language Policy & Social Reproduction: Ireland 1893-1993. Padraig O'Riagain. LC 96-39193. (Oxford Studies in Language Contact). (Illus.). 312p. 1997. text 80.00 (*0-19-823518-6*, Clarendon Pr) OUP.

Language Policy for the European Community: Prospects & Quandries. Ed. by Florian Coulmas. LC 91-32522. (Contributions to the Sociology of Language Ser.: No. 61). x, 311p. (C). 1991. lib. bdg. 113.85 (*3-11-012869-1*) Mouton.

Language Policy in Britain & France: The Processes of Policy. Dennis E. Ager. (Open L Ser.). 224p. 1997. text 99.50 (*0-304-33759-5*) Continuum.

Language Policy in Schools: A Resource for Teachers & Administrators. David Corson. LC 98-28702. 264p. 1998. 59.95 (*0-8058-3005-7*) L Erlbaum Assocs.

Language Policy in Schools: A Resource for Teachers & Administrators. David Corson. LC 98-28702. 264p. 1999. pap. 27.50 (*0-8058-3296-3*) L Erlbaum Assocs.

Language Policy in Schools: Concepts, Context & Cahallenges. 2nd ed. Robert L. Heath & Jennings Bryant. LC 98-28702. (A Volume in LEA's Commnication Theory). 368p. 2000. 59.95 (*0-8058-3007-3*) L Erlbaum Assocs.

Language Policy in the Primary School: Content & Management. Eric Ashworth. LC 87-30334. 1987. write for info. (*0-7099-5128-0*, Pub. by C Helm); pap. write for info. (*0-7099-5140-X*, Pub. by C Helm) Routldge.

Language Power. 2nd ed. Terry G. Trilling & Mary V. Crowley. 512p. 1994. per. 40.95 (*0-8403-8903-5*) Kendall-Hunt.

Language Power. 3rd ed. Trilling et al. 304p. (C). 1997. spiral bd. 34.95 (*0-7872-4253-5*, 41425301) Kendall-Hunt.

Language Power & Ideology: Studies in Political Discourse. Ed. by Ruth Wodak. LC 88-7658. (Critical Theory Ser.: Vol. 7). xx, 288p. (C). 1989. 89.00 (*1-55619-037-9*) J Benjamins Pubng Co.

Language, Power, & Ideology in Brunei Darussalam. Geoffrey C. Gunn. LC 96-39917. (Monographs in International Studies, Southeast Asia Ser.: Vol. 99). 334p. (Orig.). (C). 1996. pap. text 24.00 (*0-89680-192-6*) Ohio U Pr.

***Language! Practice Blackline Masters Book A-F.** Judy Fell Woods. (Language! Ser.). (Illus.). 958p. 1999. ring bd. 39.00 (*1-57035-250-X*, 107MSTR) Sopris.

Language! Practice Instructor's Manual. Judy Fell Woods. (Language! Ser.). (Illus.). 236p. (C). 1998. teacher ed., ring bd. 25.00 (*1-57035-140-6*, 107MAN) Sopris.

Language! Practice Student Book A. Judy Fell Woods. (Language!). (Illus.). 106p. (Orig.). (C). 1998. pap. text, student ed. 5.25 (*1-57035-141-4*, 107BOOK) Sopris.

Language! Practice Student Book B. Judy Fell Woods. (Language!). (Illus.). 136p. (Orig.). (C). 1998. pap. text, student ed. 5.25 (*1-57035-142-2*, 107BOOK) Sopris.

Language! Practice Student Book C. Judy Fell Woods. (Language!). (Illus.). 154p. (Orig.). (C). 1998. pap. text, student ed. 5.25 (*1-57035-143-0*, 107BOOK) Sopris.

Language! Practice Student Book D. Judy Fell Woods. (Language!). (Illus.). 246p. (Orig.). (C). 1998. pap. text, student ed. 5.25 (*1-57035-144-9*, 107BOOK) Sopris.

Language! Practice Student Book E. Judy Fell Woods. (Language!). (Illus.). 164p. (Orig.). (C). 1998. pap. text, student ed. 5.25 (*1-57035-145-7*, 107BOOK) Sopris.

Language! Practice Student Book F. Judy Fell Woods. (Language!). (Illus.). 1102p. (Orig.). (C). 1998. pap. text 5.25 (*1-57035-146-5*, 107BOOK) Sopris.

***Language Processing.** Ed. by Simon Garrod & Martin Pickering. 448p. 1999. 59.95 (*0-86377-836-4*, Pub. by Psychol Pr) Taylor & Francis.

Language Processing & Language Acquisition. Ed. by Lyn Frazier. (C). 1990. lib. bdg. 159.00 (*0-7923-0659-7*) Kluwer Academic.

Language Processing & Second Language Development: Processability Theory. Manfred Pienemann. LC 98-23896. (Studies in Bilingualism: Vol. 15). xviii, 367p. 1998. 69.00 (*1-55619-549-4*) J Benjamins Pubng Co.

Language Processing & the Reading of Literature: Toward a Model of Comprehension. George L. Dillon. LC 77-9861. 240p. reprint ed. pap. 74.40 (*0-8357-3964-3*, 205706000004) Bks Demand.

Language Processing Chinese. Ed. by Hsuan Chih Chen & Ovid J. Tzeng. LC 92-15112. (Advances in Psychology Ser.: Vol. 90). xii,394p. 1992. 164.50 (*0-444-89139-0*, North Holland) Elsevier.

Language Processing in Atypical Populations. Vivien C. Tartter. LC 98-9077. 336p. 1998. 34.00 (*0-7619-1468-4*); pap. 15.99 (*0-7619-1469-2*) Sage.

Language Processing in Bilingual Children. Ed. by Ellen Bialystok. 251p. (C). 1991. pap. text 21.95 (*0-521-37918-0*) Cambridge U Pr.

Language Processing in Bilinguals: Psycholinguistic & Neuropsychological Perspectives. Ed. by Jyotsna Vaid. LC 86-11541. (Neuropsychology & Neurolinguistics Ser.). 319p. reprint ed. pap. 98.90 (*0-7837-2425-X*, 204257200005) Bks Demand.

Language Processing in Children & Adults: An Introduction. Margaret Harris & Max Coltheart. (Illus.). 320p. (C). 1986. text 32.50 (*0-7100-9633-X*, Routledge Thoemms); pap. text 22.50 (*0-7102-0801-4*, Routledge Thoemms) Routledge.

Language Processing in Social Context. Ed. by R. Dietrich & Carl F. Graumann. (Linguistic Ser.: No. 54). (Illus.). x,302p. 1989. 195.50 (*0-444-87144-6*, North Holland) Elsevier.

Language Processing in Spanish. Ed. by Manuel Carreiras et al. 384p. 1996. text 79.95 (*0-8058-1721-2*) L Erlbaum Assocs.

Language Production: Development, Writing & Other Language Processes, Vol. 2. B. Butterworth & Martha L. Hutchinson. 1984. text 138.00 (*0-12-147502-6*) Acad Pr.

***Language! Professional Development Course: Syllabus & Advance Organizer.** 2nd ed. Jane F. Greene. 200p. 1999. pap. 4.50 (*1-57035-255-0*, 74TRAIN) Sopris.

Language Proficiency: Defining, Teaching, & Testing. L. A. Arena. (Topics in Language & Linguistics Ser.). (Illus.). 210p. (C). 1990. 65.00 (*0-306-43710-4*, Plenum Trade) Perseus Pubng.

Language Proficiency & Academic Achievement. 80p. 1984. 59.00 (*0-905028-24-4*, Pub. by Multilingual Matters); pap. 19.95 (*0-905028-23-6*, Pub. by Multilingual Matters) Taylor & Francis.

Language Proficiency Test (LPT) Joan E. Gerard & Gloria Weinstock. 1981. 17.00 (*0-87879-283-X*); student ed. 50.00 (*0-87879-284-8*) Acad Therapy.

Language Program Evaluation: Theory & Practice. Brian K. Lynch. (Cambridge Applied Linguistics Ser.). (Illus.). 208p. (C). 1995. text 54.95 (*0-521-48191-0*); pap. text 20.95 (*0-521-48438-3*) Cambridge U Pr.

Language Programs in Primary Schools, Some Australian Experiences. E. L. Bavin & M. L. Wales. 83p. (C). 1988. 65.00 (*0-7300-0552-6*, Pub. by Deakin Univ) St Mut.

Language, Proof & Logic. Jon Barwise & John Etchemendy. LC 99-41113. (Illus.). 530p. (C). 1999. pap. text 43.95 (*1-889119-08-3*) Seven Bridges.

Language Prototyping: An Algebraic Specification Approach. LC 97-112004. (Amast Series in Computing). 376p. 1996. lib. bdg. 48.00 (*981-02-2732-9*) World Scientific Pub.

An Asterisk (*) at the beginning of an entry indicates that the title is appearing for the first time.

Language, Quantum, Music: Selected Contributed Papers of the Tenth International Congress of Logic, Methodology & Philosophy of Science, Florence, August 1995. Roberto Giuntini et al. LC 99-15080. (Synthese Library). 368p. 1999. 171.00 (*0-7923-5727-2*) Kluwer Academic.

***Language, Quantum, Music: Selected Contributed Papers of the 10th International Congress of Logic, Methodology & Philosophy of Science, Florence, August 1995.** Ed. by Maria Luisa Dalla Chiara et al. (Synthese Library). 368p. 1999. 252.00 (*0-7923-5867-8*, Kluwer Acad) Kluwer Academic.

Language, Race & Social Class in Howell's America. Elsa Nettels. LC 87-18895. 328p. 1988. text 29.95 (*0-8131-1629-5*) U Pr of Ky.

Language, Reality & Analysis: Essays on Indian Philosophy. Ganeswar Misra. Ed. by J. N. Mohanty. LC 90-42506. (Indian Thought & Culture Ser.: Vol. 1). iv, 101p. 1990. 56.00 (*90-04-09305-2*) Brill Academic Pubs.

Language Reclamation: French-Creole Language Teaching in the U. K. & the Caribbean. Hubisi Nwenmely. 160p. 1995. 49.00 (*1-85359-299-4*, Pub. by Multilingual Matters) Taylor & Francis.

Language Reform in China: Documents & Commentary. Ed. by Peter J. Seybolt & Gregory K. Chiang. LC 76-4302. 424p. reprint ed. pap. 131.50 (*0-608-14543-2*, 202481100038) Bks Demand.

Language Regained. Bobi Jones. Ed. by Meic Stephens. (Changing Wales Ser.). 44p. 1993. pap. 11.95 (*0-8464-4716-9*) Beekman Pubs.

Language Relations Across Bering Strait: Reappraising the Archaeological & Linguistic Evidence. Michael D. Fortescue. LC 98-15092. (Open Linguistics Ser.). 1998. write for info. (*0-304-70330-3*) Continuum.

Language Relationship Wordsworths Writing. Michael Baron. LC 94-20478. (Studies in Eighteenth & Nineteenth Century Literature). 296p. (C). 1995. pap. 41.40 (*0-582-06194-6*, 77030) Addson-Wesley Educ.

Language, Religion, & Ethnic Assertiveness: The Growth of Sinhalese Nationalism in Sri Lanka. K. N. Dharmadasa. 384p. (C). 1993. text 65.00 (*0-472-10288-5*, 10288) U of Mich Pr.

Language Repertoires & State Construction in Africa. David D. Laitin. (Cambridge Studies in Comparative Politics). (Illus.). 219p. (C). 1992. text 59.95 (*0-521-41343-5*) Cambridge U Pr.

Language Rhetoric: Rhetoric & the Revolution. John Renwick. 160p. 1990. 60.00 (*0-7486-0122-8*, Pub. by Edinburgh U Pr) Col U Pr.

Language, Rhythm, & Sound: Black Popular Culture into the Twenty-First Century. Adrianne R. Andrews. Ed. by Joseph K. Adjaye. LC 96-45890. 324p. 1997. pap. 19.95 (*0-8229-5620-9*); text 45.00 (*0-8229-3967-3*) U of Pittsburgh Pr.

Language Rights in French Canada. 2nd ed. Pierre A. Coulombe. (Francophone Cultures & Literatures Ser.: Vol. 2). VIII, 183p. (C). 1997. reprint ed. pap. text 32.95 (*0-8204-3938-X*) P Lang Pubng.

Language Rights Survey of Legal Periodicals. Juan Cartagena. LC 90-198063. 9p. 1989. 5.00 (*0-88156-098-7*) Comm Serv Soc NY.

Language! Roots. Anne R. Bebko et al. (Language! Ser.). 716p. 1997. ring bd. 65.00 (*1-57035-136-8*, 99ROOT) Sopris.

Language Sample Analysis: The Wisconsin Guide. Barbara J. Leadholm & Jon F. Miller. 187p. (C). 1992. pap. text 21.00 (*1-57337-011-8*) WI Dept Pub Instruct.

Language, Saussure & Wittgenstein. Roy Harris. 200p. 1988. text 37.50 (*0-415-00084-X*) Routledge.

Language, Saussure & Wittgenstein: How to Play Games with Words. Roy Harris. (History of Linguistic Thought Ser.). 152p. (C). (gr. 13). 1990. pap. 22.99 (*0-415-05225-4*, A4945) Routledge.

Language, Schooling, & Cultural Conflict: The Origins of the French-Language Controversy in Ontario. Chad Gaffield. 272p. 1987. 65.00 (*0-7735-0602-0*, Pub. by McG-Queens Univ Pr) CUP Services.

Language, Schooling, & Cultural Conflict: The Origins of the French-Language Controversy in Ontario. Chad Gaffield. 272p. 1988. pap. 27.95 (*0-7735-0680-2*, Pub. by McG-Queens Univ Pr) CUP Services.

Language, Schooling, & Society. Ed. by Stephen N. Tchudi. LC 85-21327. 193p. (Orig.). (C). 1985. pap. text 21.00 (*0-86709-147-9*, 0147, Pub. by Boynton Cook Pubs) Heinemann.

Language, Schools, & Government in Cameroon. Hugh O. Vernon-Jackson. LC 67-21502. 41p. reprint ed. pap. 30.00 (*0-8357-9601-9*, 201695700005) Bks Demand.

Language, Science, & Action: Korzybski's General Semantics--A Study in Comparative Intellectual History, 9. Ross E. Paulson. LC 83-5490. (Contributions in Intercultural & Comparative Studies: No. 9). (Illus.). 163p. 1983. 49.95 (*0-313-23732-8*, PAL/) Greenwood.

Language Seatwork Without Dittos. Amanda C. Gonzales & Dianne V. Shannon. Ed. by John Gonzales. (Illus.). (Orig.). (C). 1987. pap. 9.95 (*0-9618511-2-0*) Teachers Two.

Language Selection & Switching in Strasbourg. Penelope Gardner-Chloros. (Studies in Language Contact). (Illus.). 240p. 1991. text 80.00 (*0-19-824993-4*) OUP.

Language, Sexuality, & Ideology in Ezra Pound's Cantos. Jean M. Rabate. LC 84-23926. 339p. (C). 1986. text 21.50 (*0-88706-036-6*) State U NY Pr.

Language Shift among Migrants to Lima, Peru. Sarah K. Myers. LC 73-78730. (University of Chicago, Department of Geography, Research Paper Ser.: No. 147). 219p. 1973. reprint ed. pap. 67.90 (*0-608-02278-0*, 206291900004) Bks Demand.

Language Shift & Cultural Reproduction: Socialization, Self & Syncretism in a Papua New Guinea Village. Don Kulick. (Studies in the Social & Cultural Foundations of Language: No. 14). (Illus.). 335p. 1997. pap. text 24.95 (*0-521-59926-1*) Cambridge U Pr.

Language Shift in the United States. Calvin Veltman. LC 83-13272. (Contributions to the Sociology of Language Ser.: No. 34). x, 432p. 1983. 142.35 (*90-279-3210-7*); pap. 70.00 (*90-279-3220-4*) Mouton.

***Language Shifts Among the Scheduled Tribes in India: A Geographical Study.** M. Ishtiaq. 183p. 1999. pap. 225.00 (*81-208-1617-X*, Pub. by Motilal Bnarsidass) St Mut.

Language Shock: The Culture of Conversation. Michael Agar. 288p. 1996. reprint ed. pap. 14.00 (*0-688-14949-9*, Wm Morrow) Morrow Avon.

Language, Sign, & Gender in Beowulf. Gillian R. Overing. LC 89-5922. 160p. (C). 1990. 26.50 (*0-8093-1563-7*) S Ill U Pr.

Language Silenced: Hebrew Culture in the Soviet Union. Yehoshuna A. Gilboa. LC 80-70920. 320p. 1982. 38.50 (*0-8386-3072-3*) Fairleigh Dickinson.

Language Skills in Elementary Education. 4th ed. Paul S. Anderson & Diane K. Lapp. 496p. (C). 1987. text 53.25 (*0-02-303170-0*, Macmillan Coll) P-H.

Language Smarts A1: Quick Word Activities. Randy Wiseman. 46p. (Orig.). (J). (gr. 2-5). 1995. pap. 11.95 (*0-89455-634-7*) Crit Think Bks.

Language Smarts B1: Quick Word Activities. Randy Wiseman. 53p. (Orig.). (J). (gr. 4-7). 1995. pap. 11.95 (*0-89455-635-5*) Crit Think Bks.

Language, Society & Education in Singapore: Issues & Trends. Ed. by S. Gopinathan et al. LC 94-941914. 400p. 1994. pap. 27.50 (*981-210-041-5*, Pub. by Times Academic) Intl Spec Bk.

Language, Society & Education in Singapore: Issues & Trends. 2nd ed. Ed. by S. Gopinathan et al. 1998. 39.00 (*981-210-124-1*, Pub. by Times Academic); pap. 29.00 (*981-210-121-7*, Pub. by Times Academic) Intl Spec Bk.

Language, Society & Power Linda Thomas. LC 98-51931. 1999. pap. write for info. (*0-415-18745-1*) Routledge.

***Language, Society & Power.** Linda Thomas. LC 98-51931. 1999. write for info. (*0-415-18744-3*) Routledge.

Language Sound & Structure. Ed. by Mark Aronoff et al. (Illus.). 360p. 1984. 49.50 (*0-262-01074-7*) MIT Pr.

Language, Speech & Mind: Studies in Honour of Victoria A. Fromkin. Ed. by Larry M. Hyman & Charles N. Li. 350p. 1988. lib. bdg. 67.50 (*0-415-00311-3*) Routledge.

Language Spread: Studies in Diffusion & Social Change. Robert L. Cooper. LC 81-47567. 368p. 1982. reprint ed. pap. 114.10 (*0-7837-6098-1*, 205914400008) Bks Demand.

Language Spread & Language Policy: Issues, Implications, & Case Studies. Georgetown University Round Table Meeting on Langu. Ed. by Peter H. Lowenberg. LC 58-31607. 424p. reprint ed. pap. 131.50 (*0-7837-6358-1*, 204607000010) Bks Demand.

Language, Status, & Power in Iran. William O. Beeman. LC 84-48490. (Advances in Semiotics Ser.). (Illus.). 276p. (C). 1986. 15.95 (*0-253-33139-0*) Ind U Pr.

Language Status in the Post-Cold-War Era. Kurt E. Muller. Ed. by Humphrey Tonkin. LC 96-10297. (Papers of the Center for Research & Documentation on World Language Problems: Vol. 4). 166p. 1996. lib. bdg. 34.50 (*0-7618-0299-1*) U Pr of Amer.

Language Stimulation Activities. Jean G. DeGaetano. (Illus.). 90p. (Orig.). (J). (ps-2). 1996. pap. text 23.00 (*1-886143-31-5*, G833) Grt Ideas Tching.

Language Stories & Literacy Lessons. Jerome C. Harste et al. LC 84-14256. 265p. (Orig.). (C). 1984. pap. text 29.00 (*0-435-08211-6*, 08211) Heinemann.

Language Strategies for Children: Keys to Classroom Success. Vicki L. Prouty & Michele Fagan. LC 97-9031. 1997. pap. 39.00 (*1-888222-01-8*) Thinking Pubns.

Language Strategies for Little Ones. Michele Fagan & Vicki L. Prouty. LC 98-35119. 1998. pap. 39.00 (*1-888222-30-1*) Thinking Pubns.

Language, Structure, & Change: Frameworks of Meaning in Psychotherapy. Jay S. Efran et al. 224p. (C). 1990. 29.95 (*0-393-70103-4*) Norton.

Language Structure & Translation: Essays by Eugene A. Nida. Eugene A. Nida. Ed. by Anwar S. Dil. LC 75-183. (Language Science & National Development Ser.). 300p. 1975. 42.50 (*0-8047-0885-1*) Stanford U Pr.

Language Structure, Discourse & the Access to Consciousness. Ed. by Maxim I. Stamenov. LC 97-13919. (Advances in Consciousness Research Ser.: Vol. 12). xii, 364p. 1997. pap. 49.95 (*1-55619-192-8*) J Benjamins Pubng Co.

Language-Structured Auditory Retention Span Test (LARS) rev. ed. Luis A. Carlson. 1989. write for info. (*0-87879-881-1*); 9.00 (*0-87879-882-X*); lp 18.00 (*0-87879-880-3*) Acad Therapy.

Language Student: Poems. Bin Ramke. LC 86-7439. 64p. 1986. reprint ed. pap. 30.00 (*0-608-00870-2*, 206166200010) Bks Demand.

Language Student. Poems. Bin Ramke. LC 86-7439. 58p. 1986. text 15.95 (*0-8071-1344-1*) La State U Pr.

Language-Study Based on Bantu. F. W. Kolbe. LC 78-154081. (Black Heritage Library Collection). 1977. 18.95 (*0-8369-8792-6*) Ayer.

Language Study for the 1980s: Reports of the MLA-ACLS Language Task Forces. Ed. by Richard I. Brod. LC 79-87582. 106p. reprint ed. pap. 32.90 (*0-608-17986-8*, 202912200058) Bks Demand.

Language Study in Middle School, High School & Beyond. Ed. by Johns S. Simmons & Lawrence Baines. LC 97-39591. 245p. 1998. pap. 29.95 (*0-87207-182-0*, 182) Intl Reading.

Language Style & Social Space: Stylistic Choice in Suriname Javanese. Clare Wolfowitz. (Illinois Studies in Anthropology). 276p. 1992. pap. text 29.95 (*0-252-06160-8*) U of Ill Pr.

Language, Subjectivity, & Freedom in Rousseau's Moral Philosophy. Richard Noble. LC 91-10201. (Political Theory & Political Philosophy Ser.). 256p. 1991. text 10.00 (*0-8153-0136-7*) Garland.

Language Suppressed: The Pronunciation of the Scots Language in the 18th Century. Charles Jones. 288p. 1996. pap. 66.00 (*0-85976-427-3*, Pub. by J Donald) St Mut.

Language Survey Reference Guide. Joseph E. Grimes. 88p. 1995. pap. 9.50 (*0-88312-609-5*) S I L Intl.

Language Surveys in Developing Nations: Papers & Reports on Sociolinguistic Surveys. Ed. by Sirarpi Ohannessian et al. LC 75-7584. 234p. reprint ed. pap. 72.60 (*0-8357-3369-6*, 203961000013) Bks Demand.

Language Switching As an Index of Socialization in the Republic of the Sudan. Peter F. McLoughlin. LC 64-64256. (University of California Publications in Social Welfare: Vol. 1). 78p. reprint ed. pap. 30.00 (*0-608-13935-1*, 202141800021) Bks Demand.

Language System & Its Change: On Theory & Testability. Jadranka C. Gvozdanovic. (Trends in Linguistics, Studies & Monographs). x, 221p. 1985. 93.85 (*0-89925-122-6*) Mouton.

Language Teacher. Ed. by Harold L. Levy. 84p. 1958. pap. 10.95 (*0-915432-58-7*) NE Conf Teach Foreign.

Language Teacher: Commitment & Collaboration. Ed. by John M. Darcey. (Reports of the Northeast Conference on the Teaching of Foreign Languages). 138p. 1987. pap. 10.95 (*0-915432-87-0*) NE Conf Teach Foreign.

Language Teacher Education. Jon Roberts. LC 97-25919. (An Arnold Publication). (Illus.). 356p. 1997. reprint ed. pap. text 19.95 (*0-340-64625-X*) OUP.

Language Teacher Education: The Reflective Trainer. Jon Roberts. LC 97-25919. (Illus.). 356p. 1998. text 75.00 (*0-340-64626-8*, Pub. by E A) OUP.

Language Teachers, Politics & Cultures. Michael Byram. LC 98-31863. 1999. 39.95 (*1-85359-441-5*) Taylor & Francis.

Language Teaching: A Scheme for Teacher Education Vocabulary. Michael McCarthy. Ed. by H. G. Widdowson & C. N. Candlin. (Illus.). 184p. 1990. pap. text 14.95 (*0-19-437136-0*) OUP.

Language Teaching: A Scheme for Teacher Education Writing. Chris Tribble. 186p. 1997. pap. text 14.95 (*0-19-437141-7*) OUP.

Language Teaching: Broader Contexts. Ed. by Robert G. Mead, Jr. 104p. 1966. pap. 10.95 (*0-915432-66-8*) NE Conf Teach Foreign.

Language Teaching & Language Technology. Sake Jager et al. LC 98-11756. 1998. 87.00 (*90-265-1514-6*) Swets.

Language Teaching & Skill Learning. Keith Johnson. (Applied Language Studies). (Illus.). 1995. pap. 24.95 (*0-631-16877-X*) Blackwell Pubs.

Language Teaching Awareness: A Guide to Exploring Beliefs & Practices. Richard Burge & Robert Oprandy. LC 98-48366. (Language Education Ser.). 240p. (C). 1999. pap. text 20.95 (*0-521-63954-9*) Cambridge U Pr.

Language Teaching Awareness: A Guide to Exploring Beliefs & Practices. Jerry G. Gebhard & Robert Oprandy. LC 98-48366. (Language Education Ser.). 240p. (C). 1999. 54.95 (*0-521-63039-8*) Cambridge U Pr.

Language Teaching Games & Contests. 2nd ed. William R. Lee. (Illus.). 214p. 1979. pap. text 13.50 (*0-19-432716-7*) OUP.

Language Teaching Matrix: Curriculum, Methodology, & Materials. Jack C. Richards. (Language Teaching Library). (Illus.). 197p. (C). 1990. pap. text 19.95 (*0-521-38794-9*) Cambridge U Pr.

Language Teaching Methodology. Nunan. 301p. (C). 1991. 25.25 (*0-13-521469-6*, Macmillan Coll) P-H.

Language Teaching Techniques. rev. ed. Raymond C. Clark. LC 80-84109. (Language Resource Handbook Ser.: No. 1). (Illus.). 128p. (Orig.). 1987. pap. text 14.00 (*0-86647-023-9*) Pro Lingua.

Language Test Construction & Evaluation. J. Charles Alderson et al. (Cambridge Language Teaching Library). 320p. (C). 1995. text 59.95 (*0-521-47255-5*); pap. text 22.95 (*0-521-47829-4*) Cambridge U Pr.

Language Testing & Assessment. Caroline Clapham & David Corson. LC 97-30205. (Encyclopedia of Language & Education Ser.). 1997. lib. bdg. write for info. (*0-7923-4702-1*) Kluwer Academic.

***Language Testing & Evaluation: An Introductory Course.** Desmond Allison. 265p. 1999. pap. text 35.00 (*9971-69-226-0*, Pub. by Sngapore Univ Pr) Coronet Bks.

Language Testing in Practice: Designing & Developing Useful Language Tests. Lyle Bachman & Adrian Palmer. (Illus.). 384p. 1996. pap. text 23.95 (*0-19-437148-4*) OUP.

Language Tests at School: A Pragmatic Approach. John W. Oller. LC 79-322102. (Applied Linguistics & Language Studies). 512p. 1979. reprint ed. pap. 158.80 (*0-608-03619-6*, 206444500009) Bks Demand.

***Language, Text & Knowledge: Mental Models of Expert Communication.** Lita Lundquist & R. J. Jarvella. LC 00-35163. 2000. write for info. (*3-11-016724-7*) De Gruyter.

Language, Text, Subject: A Critique of Hispanism. Malcolm K. Read. LC 92-15636. 244p. 1992. 49.95 (*1-55753-027-0*) Purdue U Pr.

Language That Keeps Company with the Moon. Peter Fogo. (By-Invitation-Only Ser.). 15p. 1992. pap. 6.00 (*1-882448-02-2*, Machiavellian) Mac-Kinations.

Language That Makes George Eliot's Fiction. Karen B. Mann. LC 83-257. 240p. reprint ed. pap. 74.40 (*0-8357-6621-7*, 203526600094) Bks Demand.

Language, the Learner, & the School. 4th ed. Douglas Barnes et al. LC 89-22228. 166p. (C). 1989. pap. text 18.50 (*0-86709-251-3*, 0251, Pub. by Boynton Cook Pubs) Heinemann.

Language: The Loaded Weapon: The Use & Abuse of Language Today. Dwight Bolinger. (Longman Linguistics Library). (Illus.). 240p. 1989. pap. text 22.55 (*0-582-29108-9*, 71746) Longman.

***Language, the Novelist & National Identity in Post-Franco Catalonia.** Kathryn Crameri. (Legenda Ser.). 200p. (C). 2000. pap. 49.50 (*1-900755-37-8*, Pub. by E H R C) David Brown.

Language, the Social Mirror. 3rd ed. Elaine O. Chaika. LC 93-42854. 376p. (J). 1994. mass mkt. 27.95 (*0-8384-4731-7*) Heinle & Heinle.

Language, the Time Machine. Ed. by Lars-Erik Edlund & Gunnar Persson. (ENG & SWE.). 227p. 1992. pap. 57.50 (*91-7174-683-8*) Coronet Bks.

Language, Theology, & the Bible: Essays in Honor of James Barr. Ed. by John Barton & Samuel F. Balentine. LC 93-32123. 432p. 1994. 68.00 (*0-19-826191-8*, Clarendon Pr) OUP.

Language Theories & Educational Practice. David Piper. LC 92-28795. 472p. 1992. 109.95 (*0-7734-9864-8*) E Mellen.

Language Therapy. Lewis. 300p. 1990. 64.50 (*1-56593-542-X*, 0215) Singular Publishing.

Language They Speak Is Things to Eat: Fourteen Contemporary North Carolina Poets. Ed. by Michael McFee. LC 94-4239. (Illus.). 270p. 1994. 29.95 (*0-8078-2172-1*); pap. 14.95 (*0-8078-4483-7*) U of NC Pr.

Language, Thought & Consciousness: An Essay in Philosophical Psychology. Peter Carruthers. 308p. (C). 1998. reprint ed. pap. text 24.95 (*0-521-63999-9*) Cambridge U Pr.

Language, Thought, & Logic. John M. Ellis. (Rethinking Theory Ser.). 180p. 1993. 19.95 (*0-8101-1095-4*); pap. 14.95 (*0-8101-1135-7*) Northwestern U Pr.

Language, Thought, & Logic: Essays in Honour of Michael Dummett. Ed. by Richard G. Heck. (Illus.). 318p. 1998. text 77.00 (*0-19-823920-3*) OUP.

Language, Thought, & Other Biological Categories: New Foundation for Realism. Ruth G. Millikan. 368p. 1987. reprint ed. pap. text 22.00 (*0-262-63115-6*, Bradford Bks) MIT Pr.

Language, Thought & Perception. Uhlan Von Slagle. LC 72-94506. (Janua Linguarum, Ser. Major: No. 98). 60p. 1974. pap. text 54.65 (*90-279-3023-6*) Mouton.

Language, Thought & Reality: Selected Writings. Ed. by Benjamin L. Whorf & John B. Carroll. 1964. pap. text 17.50 (*0-262-73006-5*) MIT Pr.

***Language, Thought & the Brain.** Ed. by Tatyana B. Glezerman & Victoria Balkoski. LC 99-38463. (Cognition & Language Ser.). 331p. 1999. 79.50 (*0-306-46096-3*, Kluwer Plenum) Kluwer Academic.

Language Through Literature. Reinhartsen & Riherd. 256p. (C). 1997. per. 48.95 (*0-7872-3737-X*, 41373701) Kendall-Hunt.

Language Through Literature: An Introduction. Paul Simpson. LC 96-16141. (Interface Ser.). 240p. (C). 1996. 65.00 (*0-415-14963-0*); pap. 20.99 (*0-415-14964-9*) Routledge.

Language Through Literature: Creative Language Teaching Through Literature (Pilgrims Longman Resource Books) P. Grundy & Susan Bassnett. (Pilgrims Longman Resource Bks.). 136p. 1995. pap. text 22.39 (*0-582-07003-1*, 79850) Longman.

Language Through Pictures: Full Series, 7 vols. Harris Winitz. (Illus.). (gr. 2-12). 1982. pap. 33.00 (*0-939990-38-5*) Intl Linguistics.

Language Through Play. Patricia Denner. LC 72-84851. (Illus.). (J). (ps-1). 1969. reprint ed. pap. 11.95 (*0-405-00118-5*) Ayer.

Language Through the Looking Glass: Exploring Language & Linguistics. Marina Yaguello. Tr. by Trevor A. Harris. LC 98-7376. (Illus.). 182p. 1998. pap. text 16.95 (*0-19-870005-9*) OUP.

Language Through the Looking Glass: Exploring Language & Linguistics. Marina Yaguello. Tr. by Trevor A. Harris. LC 98-7376. (Illus.). 182p. 1999. text 60.00 (*0-19-870006-7*) OUP.

Language Topics: Essays in Honour of Michael Halliday, 2 vols., I. Ed. by Ross Steele & Terry Threadgold. LC 87-20848. 1160p. (C). 1988. write for info. (*1-55619-029-8*) J Benjamins Pubng Co.

Language Topics: Essays in Honour of Michael Halliday, 2 vols., Set. Ed. by Ross Steele & Terry Threadgold. LC 87-20848. 1160p. (C). 1987. 236.00 (*1-55619-028-X*) J Benjamins Pubng Co.

Language Topics: Essays in Honour of Michael Halliday, 2 vols., Vol. 2. Ed. by Ross Steele & Terry Threadgold. LC 87-20848. 1160p. (C). 1988. write for info. (*1-55619-030-1*) J Benjamins Pubng Co.

Language Transfer: Cross-Linguistic Influence in Language Learning. Terence Odlin. (Cambridge Applied Linguistics Ser.). 224p. (C). 1990. pap. text 22.95 (*0-521-37809-5*) Cambridge U Pr.

Language Transfer in Language Learning. rev. ed. Susan M. Gass & Larry Selinker. LC 92-23741. (Language Acquisition & Language Disorders (LALD) Ser.: No. 5). x, 236p. 1992. pap. 24.95 (*1-55619-248-7*) J Benjamins Pubng Co.

Language Transfer in Language Learning. rev. ed. Ed. by Susan M. Gass & Larry Selinker. LC 92-23741. (Language Acquisition & Language Disorders (LALD) Ser.: No. 5). x, 236p. 1992. 56.00 (*1-55619-240-1*) J Benjamins Pubng Co.

Language Translation Using PCCTS & C++ A Referenced Guide. Terence Parr. Date not set. 34.95 (*0-9627488-5-4*) Automata Pub.

An Asterisk (*) at the beginning of an entry indicates that the title is appearing for the first time.

Language Translations: Functional Terms in Occupational Therapy--German. Carla M. Iwata. LC 99-208339. (Language Translation Ser.). 57 p. 1998. write for info. (1-56900-101-4) Am Occup Therapy.

Language Treasure Chest. Cynthia Wycoff. (Illus.). 39p. 12.00 (0-939161-01-X); 375.00 (0-939161-00-1) Treas Chest Ent.

Language Treasure Chest: Early Explorers Edition. Cynthia W. Geraghty. (Illus.). 1989. 390.00 (0-939161-05-2); suppl. ed. 41.95 (0-939161-06-0) Treas Chest Ent.

Language Treasure Chest: Extra Worksheets. Cynthia Wycoff. (Illus.). 133p. (J). (gr. k-6). 1987. student ed. 29.95 (0-939161-02-8) Treas Chest Ent.

Language Treasure Chest: Teacher's Manual. Cynthia Wycoff. Tr. by Ivan Rodriguez. (SPA.). 39p. teacher ed. 15.00 (0-939161-04-4) Treas Chest Ent.

Language, Truth & Logic. Alfred Jules Ayer. 1990. 21.25 (0-8446-1571-4) Peter Smith.

Language, Truth & Logic. 2nd ed. Alfred Jules Ayer. 160p. 1952. pap. 5.95 (0-486-20010-8) Dover.

Language, Truth & Logic in Mathematics. Jaakko Hintikka. LC 97-29299. (Jaakko Hintikka Selected Papers). 260p. 1997. text 120.50 (0-7923-4766-8) Kluwer Academic.

Language, Truth & Ontology. Ed. by Kevin Mulligan. (Philosophical Studies in Philosophy). 224p. (C). 1992. lib. bdg. 146.50 (0-7923-1509-X, Pub. by Kluwer Academic) Kluwer Academic.

Language, Truth & Poetry. Victor M. Hamm. LC 60-9736. (Aquinas Lectures). 1960. 15.00 (0-87462-125-9) Marquette.

Language, Truth & Poetry. D. G. Martin. 353p. 1975. pap. 14.50 (0-85224-268-9, Pub. by Edinburgh U Pr) Col U Pr.

Language Tutor's Legacy. John D. Healy. LC 80-12976. 1987. pap. 13.95 (0-87949-188-4) Ashley Bks.

Language II. Heidi Dulay et al. (Illus.). 316p. 1982. pap. text 16.95 (0-19-502553-9) OUP.

Language Typology: A Historical & Analytical Overview. Joseph Greenberg. LC 73-87532. (Janua Linguarum, Ser. Minor: No. 184). 82p. (Orig.). 1974. pap. text 18.50 (90-279-2709-X) Mouton.

Language Typology & Syntactic Description, Vol. 1: Clause Structure. Ed. by Timothy Shopen. 409p. 1985. pap. text 36.95 (0-521-27659-4) Cambridge U Pr.

Language Typology, 1988: Typological Models in the Service of Reconstruction. Ed. by W. P. Lehmann & H. J. Hewitt. LC 91-12542. (Current Issues in Linguistic Theory Ser.: Vol. 81). vi, 182p. 1991. 50.00 (1-55619-136-7) J Benjamins Pubng Co.

Language Typology, 1985: Papers from the Linguistic Typology Symposium, Moscow, 9-13 Dec. 1985. Ed. by Winfred P. Lehmann. LC 86-26341. (Current Issues in Linguistic Theory Ser.: No. 47). viii, 200p. 1986. 52.00 (90-272-3541-4) J Benjamins Pubng Co.

Language Typology 1987 - Systemic Balance in Language: Papers from the Linguistic Typology Symposium, Berkeley, 1-3, December 1987. Ed. by Winfred P. Lehmann. LC 90-30. (Current Issues in Linguistic Theory Ser.: Vol. 67). x, 212p. 1990. 52.00 (90-272-3564-3) J Benjamins Pubng Co.

Language Unbound: On Experimental Writing by Women. Nancy Gray. 192p. 1992. text 32.50 (0-252-01851-6); pap. text 12.95 (0-252-06221-3) U of Ill Pr.

Language Understanding: Current Issues. 2nd ed. Judith Greene & Mark Coulson. LC 94-24072. (Open Guides to Psychology Ser.). 160p. 1995. pap. 32.95 (0-335-19437-0) OpUniv Pr.

Language Universals: With Special References to Feature Hierarchies. Joseph H. Greenberg. (Janua Linguarum, Series Minor: No. 59). (Orig.). 1966. pap. text 19.25 (3-11-000165-9) Mouton.

Language Universals & Linguistic Typology. Bernard Comrie. LC 81-52478. (Illus.). (C). 1981. pap. text 10.00 (0-226-11436-8); lib. bdg. 25.00 (0-226-11434-1) U Ch Pr.

Language Universals & Linguistic Typology: Syntax & Morphology. 2nd ed. Bernard Comrie. LC 89-40280. xii, 278p. 1989. pap. text 15.95 (0-226-11433-3) U Ch Pr.

Language Universals & Second Language Acquisition. Ed. by William E. Rutherford. LC 84-9387. (Typological Studies in Language: No. 5). ix, 264p. 1984. pap. 34.95 (0-915027-10-0) J Benjamins Pubng Co.

Language Universals, Markedness Theory & Natural Phonetic Processes. Robert K. Herbert. (Trends in Linguistics, Studies & Monographs: No. 25). x, 299p. 1986. 108.50 (0-89925-123-4) Mouton.

Language Unlimited. Ed. by Scholastic, Inc. Staff. 1986. pap. 9.95 (0-590-49030-3, Scholastic Hardcover) Scholastic Inc.

Language Use: A Philosophical Investigation into the Basic Notions of Pragmatics. P. A. Segerdahl. 304p. 1996. text 65.00 (0-312-12864-9) St Martin.

Language Use & Language Change in Brunei Darussalam. Ed. by Peter W. Martin et al. LC 96-31446. (Monographs in International Studies, Southeast Asia Ser.: Vol. 100). 390p. (Orig.). (C). 1996. pap. text 26.00 (0-89680-193-4) Ohio U Pr.

Language Use & Proficiency in a Multilingual Setting: A Sociolinguistic Survey of Agutaynen Speakers in Palawan, Philippines John S. Quakenbush & Linguistic Society of the Philippines Staff. LC 90-197329. (Special Monograph Issue/Linguistic Society of the Philippines Ser.). xvi, 158 p. 1989. write for info. (971-10-5913-4, Pub. by New Day Pub) S Asia.

Language Use & Social Change. Ed. by W. H. Whiteley. (International African Institute Ser.). (Illus.). 1971. 39.00 (0-19-724183-2) OUP.

Language Use & Social Change: Problems of Multilingualism with Special Reference to Eastern Africa: Studies Presented & Discussed at the International African Seminar at University College, 9th, Dar es Salaam, December 1968. International African Seminar Staff. LC 73-21993. 416p. pap. 129.00 (0-8357-3233-9, 205712700010) Bks Demand.

Language Use in Rural Development: An African Perspective. Clinton D. Robinson. LC 95-50533. (Contributions to the Sociology of Language Ser.: Vol. 70). x, 327p. (C). 1996. lib. bdg. 117.05 (3-11-014687-8) Mouton.

Language, Values, & the Slovak Nation. Ed. by Tibor Pichler & Jana Gasparikova. LC 93-11884. (Cultural Heritage & Contemporary Change Series IVA: Vol. 5). 1993. 45.00 (1-56518-036-4); 17.50 (1-56518-037-2) Coun Res Values.

Language Variation & Change in a Modernizing Arab State. Clive Holes. (Library of Arabic Linguistics). 250p. 1987. 95.00 (0-7103-0244-4) Routledge.

Language Variation As Social Practice. Penelope Eckert. LC 99-22433. (Language in Society Ser.). 300p. 1998. 59.95 (0-631-18603-4) Blackwell Pubs.

Language Variation as Social Practice. Penelope Eckert. LC 99-22433. (Language in Society Ser.). 300p. 1998. pap. 26.95 (0-631-18604-2) Blackwell Pubs.

Language Variation in North American English: Research & Teaching. Ed. by Wayne Glowka & Donald M. Lance. LC 93-9451. xvi, 417p. (Orig.). 1993. pap. 19.75 (0-87352-390-3, E301P); lib. bdg. 37.50 (0-87352-389-X, E301C) Modern Lang.

Language Variety & the Art of the Everyday. Valerie Shepherd. 256p. 1990. text 49.00 (0-86187-984-8) St Martin.

Language Variety & the Art of the Everyday. Valerie Shepherd. 220p. 1993. pap. 14.95 (1-85567-168-9) St Martin.

Language Variety in the South: Perspectives in Black & White. Ed. by Michael B. Montgomery & Guy Bailey. LC 84-16396. (Illus.). 441p. reprint ed. pap. 136.80 (0-608-09233-9, 205273700005) Bks Demand.

Language Variety in the South Revisted. Cynthia G. Bernstein et al. LC 96-29636. 328p. 1994. text 49.95 (0-8173-0882-2) U of Ala Pr.

Language Viewed from the Brain. Iwao K. Honjo. LC 98-43213. (Illus.). x, 158p. 1998. pap. 155.00 (3-8055-6789-8) S Karger.

***Language War.** Robin Lakoff. LC 99-55386. 2000. 24.95 (0-520-22296-2) U CA Pr.

***Language War.** Robin T. Lakoff. LC 99-55386. 352p. 2000. 24.95 (0-520-21666-0, Pub. by U CA Pr) Cal Prin Full Svc.

Language Wars: And Other Writings for Homeschoolers. Ruth Beechick. LC 95-78025. 252p. 1995. pap. 12.00 (0-940319-09-8) Mott Media.

Language Wars & Linguistic Politics. Louis-Jean Calvet. Tr. by Michel Petheram. (Illus.). 232p. 1998. text 90.00 (0-19-823598-4); pap. text 29.95 (0-19-870021-0) OUP.

Language Web: The Power & Problem of Words, the 1996 BBC Reith Lectures. Jean Aitchison. (The 1996 BBC Reith Lectures). (Illus.). 152p. (C). 1997. pap. text 16.95 (0-521-57475-7) Cambridge U Pr.

Language Web: The Power & Problem of Words, the 1996 BBC Reith Lectures. Jean Aitchison. LC 96-43929. (1996 BBC Reith Lectures). (Illus.). 152p. (C). 1997. text 49.95 (0-521-57385-8) Cambridge U Pr.

Language Within Language: Immediacy, a Channel in Verbal Communication. Morton Wiener & Albert Mehrabian. LC 68-15231. (Century Psychology Ser.). (C). 1968. 30.50 (0-89197-267-6) Irvington.

Language Without Geography. Rainer Schulte. LC 98-53796. 82p. 1999. pap. text 14.95 (0-7734-3083-0) E Mellen.

Language Workbook. (J). teacher ed. 3.25 (0-917186-15-X); student ed. 2.30 (0-917186-16-8) McQueen.

Language Works. Lubell. (EC - HS Communication/English Ser.). 1991. mass mkt. 11.95 (0-538-60947-8) S-W Pub.

Language, World & God: An Essay in Ontology. Thomas A. Kelly. 316p. 1997. 69.95 (1-85607-211-8); pap. 49.95 (1-85607-181-2) Intl Scholars.

Language World Creation. Elena Semino. LC 96-52564. (Textual Explorations Ser.). 1997. pap. text 24.09 (0-582-30354-0) Longman.

Language, Writing & the Computer. William S. Wang. LC 85-20454. (Scientific American Reader Ser.). 124p. (C). 1986. pap. text 16.95 (0-7167-1772-7) W H Freeman.

Language Yardstick: Understanding & Assessment. Priscilla L. Vail. LC 98-219510. 100p. 1998. pap. 10.95 (1-56762-084-1) Modern Learn Pr.

Language 1990: Activity Workbook Para Casa Grade K. Strickland. (SPA.). 1990. pap., wbk. ed. 9.50 (0-15-316635-5) Harcourt Schl Pubs.

Language 1990: Activity Workbook Para Casa Grade 1. Strickland. (SPA.). 1990. pap., wbk. ed. 9.50 (0-15-316636-3) Harcourt Schl Pubs.

Language 1990: Activity Workbook Para Casa Grade 2. Strickland. (SPA.). 1990. pap., wbk. ed. 9.50 (0-15-316637-1) Harcourt Schl Pubs.

Language 1990: Activity Workbook Para Casa Grade 3. Strickland. (SPA.). 1990. pap., wbk. ed. 9.50 (0-15-316638-X) Harcourt Schl Pubs.

Language 1990: Activity Workbook Para Casa Grade 4. Strickland. (SPA.). 1990. pap., wbk. ed. 9.50 (0-15-316639-8) Harcourt Schl Pubs.

Language 1990: Activity Workbook Para Casa Grade 5. Strickland. (SPA.). 1990. pap., wbk. ed. 9.50 (0-15-316640-1) Harcourt Schl Pubs.

Language 1990: Activity Workbook Para Casa Grade 6. Strickland. (SPA.). 1990. pap., wbk. ed. 12.50 (0-15-316641-X) Harcourt Schl Pubs.

Language 1990: Activity Workbook Para Casa Grade 7. Strickland. (SPA.). 1990. pap., wbk. ed. 12.50 (0-15-316642-8) Harcourt Schl Pubs.

Language 1990: Activity Workbook Para Casa Grade 8. Strickland. (SPA.). 1990. pap., wbk. ed. 12.50 (0-15-316643-6) Harcourt Schl Pubs.

Language 1990: Grade K. Strickland. 1990. pap. 14.50 (0-15-316409-3) Harcourt Schl Pubs.

Language 1990: Grade 1. Strickland. 1990. pap., teacher ed., wbk. ed. 13.00 (0-15-316456-5) Harcourt Schl Pubs.

Language 1990: Grade 2. Strickland. 1990. pap., teacher ed., wbk. ed. 15.50 (0-15-316457-3); pap., wbk. ed. 9.25 (0-15-316448-4) Harcourt Schl Pubs.

Language 1990: Grade 3. Strickland. 1990. pap., teacher ed., wbk. ed. 17.50 (0-15-316458-1); pap., wbk. ed. 11.00 (0-15-316449-2) Harcourt Schl Pubs.

Language 1990: Grade 4. Strickland. 1990. pap., teacher ed., wbk. ed. 17.50 (0-15-316459-X); pap., wbk. ed. 11.00 (0-15-316450-6) Harcourt Schl Pubs.

Language 1990: Grade 5. Strickland. 1990. pap., teacher ed., wbk. ed. 18.00 (0-15-316460-3); pap., wbk. ed. 11.50 (0-15-316451-4) Harcourt Schl Pubs.

Language 1990: Grade 6. Strickland. 1990. pap., teacher ed., wbk. ed. 18.00 (0-15-316461-1); pap., wbk. ed. 11.50 (0-15-316452-2) Harcourt Schl Pubs.

Language 1990: Grade 7. Strickland. 1990. pap., teacher ed., wbk. ed. 18.75 (0-15-316462-X); pap., wbk. ed. 12.75 (0-15-316453-0) Harcourt Schl Pubs.

Language 1990: Grade 8. Strickland. 1990. pap., teacher ed., wbk. ed. 19.25 (0-15-316463-8); pap., wbk. ed. 12.75 (0-15-316454-9) Harcourt Schl Pubs.

Language 1990: Home Activity Workbook Grade K. Strickland. 1990. pap., wbk. ed. 8.25 (0-15-316626-6) Harcourt Schl Pubs.

Language 1990: Home Activity Workbook Grade 1. Strickland. 1990. pap., wbk. ed. 8.25 (0-15-316627-4) Harcourt Schl Pubs.

Language 1990: Home Activity Workbook Grade 2. Strickland. 1990. pap., wbk. ed. 9.25 (0-15-316628-2) Harcourt Schl Pubs.

Language 1990: Home Activity Workbook Grade 3. Strickland. 1990. pap., wbk. ed. 11.25 (0-15-316629-0) Harcourt Schl Pubs.

Language 1990: Home Activity Workbook Grade 4. Strickland. 1990. pap., wbk. ed. 11.25 (0-15-316630-4) Harcourt Schl Pubs.

Language 1990: Home Activity Workbook Grade 5. Strickland. 1990. pap., wbk. ed. 11.75 (0-15-316631-2) Harcourt Schl Pubs.

Language 1990: Home Activity Workbook Grade 6. Strickland. 1990. pap., wbk. ed. 11.75 (0-15-316632-0) Harcourt Schl Pubs.

Language 1990: Home Activity Workbook Grade 7. Strickland. 1990. pap., wbk. ed. 11.75 (0-15-316633-9) Harcourt Schl Pubs.

Language 1990: Home Activity Workbook Grade 8. Strickland. 1990. pap., wbk. ed. 11.75 (0-15-316634-7) Harcourt Schl Pubs.

Language 1990: Story Starter Grade 1. Strickland. 1990. pap. 44.75 (0-15-316560-X) Harcourt Schl Pubs.

Language 1990: Story Starter Grade 2. Strickland. 1990. pap. 44.75 (0-15-316561-8) Harcourt Schl Pubs.

Languagepoembook. Mark Sonnenfeld. 36p. 1995. 3.00 (0-9632820-9-3) M Sonnenfeld.

Languages. Ed. by Ives Goddard. (Handbook of North American Indians Ser.). (Illus.). 957p. 1997. 74.00 (0-87474-197-1) Smithsonian.

Languages & Children: Making the Match. Helena Curtain & Carol A. Pesola. (MFL Second Language Library). (Illus.). 368p. 1988. pap. text 31.44 (0-201-12290-1) Addison-Wesley.

Languages & Children, Making the Match: Foreign Language Instruction for an Early Start Grades K-8. 2nd ed. Helena Curtain & Carol A. Pesola. LC 93-11014. 1994. pap. text 27.84 (0-8013-1140-3) Longman.

Languages & Compilers for Parallel Computing. David Gelernter et al. (Research Monographs in Parallel & Distributed Computing). 560p. 1990. 46.50 (0-262-57080-7) MIT Pr.

Languages & Compilers for Parallel Computing: Proceedings of the 7th International Workshop Held at Ithaca, New York, U. S. A., August 1994. Seventh International Workshop on Languages & Comp et al. LC 94-47370. (Lecture Notes in Computer Science Ser.: Vol. 892). 1995. 69.00 (3-540-58868-X) Spr-Verlag.

Languages & Compilers for Parallel Computing: Proceedings of 8th International Workshop, LCPC 95, Columbus, Ohio, August 1995. Ed. by C. H. Huang et al. LC 95-51352. (Lecture Notes in Computer Science Ser.: Vol. 1033). 599p. 1996. pap. 94.00 (3-540-60765-X) Spr-Verlag.

Languages & Compilers for Parallel Computing: 10th International Workshop, LCPC '97, Minneapolis, Minnesota, U. S. A., August 7-9, 1997. Proceedings. Ed. by Z. Li et al. (Lecture Notes in Computer Science Ser.: Vol. 1366). xii, 428p. 1998. pap. 67.00 (3-540-64472-5) Spr-Verlag.

***Languages & Compilers for Parallel Computing: 11th International Workshop, LCPC'98, Chapel Hill, NC, USA, August 7-9, 1999, Proceedings.** Ed. by S. Chatterjee et al. (Lecture Notes in Computer Science Ser.: Vol. 1656). xi, 384p. 1999. pap. 62.00 (3-540-66426-2) Spr-Verlag.

Languages & Compilers for Parallel Computing: 4th International Workshop, Santa Clara, California, U. S. A., August 7-9, 1991: Proceedings. Uptal Banerjee et al. Ed. by Alexander Nicolau et al. LC 92-13947. (Lecture Notes in Computer Science Ser.: Vol. 589). x, 419p. 1992. 63.95 (0-387-55422-X); pap. 53.00 (3-540-55422-X) Spr-Verlag.

Languages & Compilers for Parallel Computing: 5th International Workshop, New Haven, Connecticut, August 1992. Alexander Nicolau. Ed. by Uptal Banerjee et al. (Lecture Notes in Computer Science Ser.: Vol. 757). xi, 576p. 1993. 78.00 (0-387-57502-2) Spr-Verlag.

Languages & Compilers for Parallel Computing: 6th International Workshop, Portland, Oregon, U. S. A., August 12-14, 1993: Proceedings. Ed. by Uptal Banerjee et al. LC 93-46748. (Lecture Notes in Computer Science Ser.: Vol. 768). 1994. 93.95 (0-387-57659-2) Spr-Verlag.

Languages & Compilers for Parallel Computing: 9th International Workshop, LCPC '96, San Jose, California, U. S. A., August 8-10, 1996, Proceedings. Ed. by D. Sehr et al. (Lecture Notes in Computer Science Ser.: No. 1239). xvi, 612p. 1997. pap. 91.00 (3-540-63091-0) Spr-Verlag.

Languages & Cultures: Studies in Honor of Edgar C. Polome. Ed. by Mohammad A. Jazayery & Werner Winter. (Trends in Linguistics, Studies & Monographs: No. 36). xvi, 792p. (C). 1988. lib. bdg. 350.00 (0-89925-442-X) Mouton.

Languages & Cultures for Business & the Professions: Selected Proceedings of the 10th Annual EMU Conference on Languages & Communication for World Business & the Professions. Ed. by Geoffrey M. Voght & Ray Schaub. 256p. 1992. pap. text 12.00 (0-9632351-0-9) East Mich U Wrld Coll.

Languages & Dialects of Tibeto-Burman. Ed. by James A. Matisoff. (STEDT Monograph Ser.: Vol. 2). 180p. 1996. pap. text 20.00 (0-944613-26-8) UC Berkeley Ctrs SE Asia.

Languages & Jargons: Contributions to a Social History of Language. 2nd rev. ed. Ed. by Peter Burke & Roy Porter. 214p. 1996. 30.95 (0-7456-1279-2, Pub. by Polity Pr) Blackwell Pubs.

Languages & Linguistics: The Interdependence of Theory, Data & Application. Georgetown University Round Table Meeting on Lingu. Ed. by Deborah Tannen & James E. Alatis. LC 58-31607. 368p. reprint ed. pap. 114.10 (0-7837-6356-5, 204606800010) Bks Demand.

Languages & Linguists. E. Peters. 1998. 37.95 (90-6831-948-5, Pub. by Peeters Pub) Bks Intl VA.

Languages & Literatures see Cultural Heritage of India

Languages & Lives: Essays in Honor of Werner Enninger. Ed. by James R. Dow. VI, 325p. (C). 1996. text 69.95 (0-8204-2713-6) P Lang Pubng.

Languages & Machines: An Introduction to the Theory of Computer Science. 2nd ed. Thomas A. Sudkamp. LC 95-51366. 500p. (C). 1996. 76.00 (0-201-82136-2) Addison-Wesley.

Languages & Peoples of Bornu, 2 vols., Vol. 1. 2nd ed. P. A. Benton. 304p. 1968. 65.00 (0-7146-1635-4, Pub. by F Cass Pubs) Intl Spec Bk.

Languages & Peoples of Bornu, 2 vols., Vol. 2. 2nd ed. P. A. Benton. 373p. 1968. 45.00 (0-7146-1626-5, Pub. by F Cass Pubs) Intl Spec Bk.

Languages & Politics. William M. O'Barr & F. Jean. (Contributions to the Sociology of Language Ser.: No. 10). 1977. text 56.95 (90-279-7761-5) Mouton.

Languages & the Theory of Computation. John Martin. 672p. (C). 1990. text 87.00 (0-07-040659-6) McGraw.

Languages & Their Speakers. Ed. by Timothy Shopen. LC 87-6014. (Illus.). 312p. (C). 1987. reprint ed. pap. text 20.95 (0-8122-1250-9) U of Pa Pr.

Languages & Their Status. Ed. by Timothy Shopen. LC 87-6034. (Illus.). 348p. (C). 1987. reprint ed. pap. text 20.95 (0-8122-1249-5) U of Pa Pr.

Languages & Their Territories. J. A. Laponce. Tr. by A. D. Martin-Sperry from FRE. 275p. 1987. pap. 19.95 (0-8020-6631-3); text 37.50 (0-8020-5703-9) U of Toronto Pr.

Languages As Barrier & Bridge. Ed. by Kurt E. Muller. (Papers of the Center for Research & Documentation on World Language Problems). 140p. (Orig.). (C). 1992. lib. bdg. 45.00 (0-8191-8670-8) U Pr of Amer.

Languages, Compilers & Run-Time Systems for Scalable Computers. Ed. by Boleslaw Szymanski & Balaram Sinharoy. LC 95-37540. 355p. 1995. text 135.50 (0-7923-9635-9) Kluwer Academic.

Languages, Compilers, & Tools for Embedded Systems: ACM Sigplan Workshop Lectures '98, Motreal, Canada, June 9-12, 1998: Proceedings, Vol. 147. Frank Mueller & Azer Bestavros. LC 98-41921. (Lecture Notes in Computer Science Ser.). 1998. pap. 49.00 (3-540-65075-X) Spr-Verlag.

Languages for a Multi-Cultural World in Transition. Ed. by Heidi Byrnes. (Reports of the Northeast Conference on the Teaching of Foreign Languages). 204p. 1992. pap. 12.95 (0-915432-92-7) NE Conf Teach Foreign.

Languages for Automation. Ed. by Shi-Kuo Chang. LC 85-17032. (Management & Information Systems Ser.). 532p. 1985. 120.00 (0-306-42031-7, Plenum Trade) Perseus Pubng.

Languages for Continuous System Simulation, 1986 Conference. Cellier. 148p. 1986. pap. 32.00 (0-911801-08-1, MC-86-1) Soc Computer Sim.

Languages for Developing User Interfaces. Ed. by Brad A. Myers. LC 92-3677. (Illus.). 480p. (C). 1992. text 72.00 (0-86720-450-8) AK Peters.

Languages for Parallel Architectures: Design, Semantics, Implementation Models. Ed. by J. W. De Bakker. LC 89-14705. (Illus.). 289p. reprint ed. pap. 89.60 (0-7837-5872-3, 204559200006) Bks Demand.

Languages for Peace: A Tribute to Kenneth L. Pike. Adam Makkai. (Languages for Peace Ser.: No. 1). (Illus.). 32p. (Orig.). 1983. pap. 10.00 (0-933104-14-6) Jupiter Pr.

Languages for Sensor-Based Control in Robotics. Ed. by Ulrich Rembold & K. Horman. (NATO ASI Series H: Vol. 29). x, 625p. 1987. 127.95 (0-387-17665-9) Spr-Verlag.

L

An Asterisk (*) at the beginning of an entry indicates that the title is appearing for the first time.

Languages for Special Purposes: An International Handbook of Special Languages & Terminology Research see Fachsprachen: Ein Internationales Handbuch zur Fachsprachenforschung und Terminologiewissenschaft

Languages for the American Traveler: Brief & Basic Expressions Made Easy. Malik R. Bey. 100p. (Orig.). 1996. pap. 12.95 (*0-9656137-1-2*) M Bey.

Languages for Work & Life: The Council of Europe & Vocationally Oriented Language Learning. 1997. 21.00 (*92-871-3243-7*, Pub. by Council of Europe) Manhattan Pub Co.

Languages in America: A Pluralist View. Susan J. Dicker. LC 96-21874. (Bilingual Education & Bilingualism Ser.). 250p. 1996. 69.00 (*1-85359-337-0*, Pub. by Multilingual Matters); pap. 19.95 (*1-85359-336-2*, Pub. by Multilingual Matters) Taylor & Francis.

Languages in Conflict: Linguistic Acculturation on the Great Plains. Ed. by Paul Schach. LC 80-12710. 198p. reprint ed. pap. 61.40 (*0-8357-3814-0*, 203654100003) Bks Demand.

Languages in Contact. Uriel Weinreich. 1974. pap. text 26.95 (*90-279-2689-1*) Mouton.

Languages in Contact: An Introductory Textbook on Translation - Manual Introductorio a la Traduccion. Carmen Valero-Garces. 336p. (Orig.). 1995. pap. text 29.50 (*0-8191-9876-5*) U Pr of Amer.

Languages in Contact & Conflict: Contrasting Experiences in the Netherlands & Belgium. Ed. by Sue Wright. LC 94-47320. 98p. 1995. 54.00 (*1-85359-278-1*, Pub. by Multilingual Matters) Taylor & Francis.

Languages in Contact & Contrast: Essays in Contact Linguistics. Ed. by Vladimir Ivir & Damir Kalogjera. (Trends in Linguistics, Studies & Monographs: No. 54). (Illus.). xii, 502p. (C). 1991. lib. bdg. 213.85 (*0-89925-714-3*) Mouton.

Languages in Elementary Schools. Ed. by Kurt E. Muller. 232p. 1989. pap. 10.00 (*0-944675-41-7*) Amer Forum.

Languages in School & Society: Policy & Pedagogy. Ed. by Mary E. McGroarty & Christian J. Faltis. (Contributions to the Sociology of Language Ser.: No. 58). x, 570p. (C). 1991. lib. bdg. 175.40 (*0-89925-716-X*) Mouton.

Languages in the International Perspective. Ed. by Nancy Schweda-Nicholson & Robert J. DiPietro. (Delaware Symposia on Language Studies: Vol. 5). 320p. 1986. text 73.25 (*0-89391-268-9*) Ablx Pub.

Languages of a Bilingual Community. J. R. Rayfield. LC 73-106457. (Janua Linguarum, Ser. Practica: No. 77). 1970. pap. text 40.80 (*90-279-0730-7*) Mouton.

***Languages of Addiction.** Jane Lilienfeld. LC 99-22567. 1999. text 45.00 (*0-312-21850-8*) St Martin.

Languages of Africa: Swahili. Foreign Service Institute Staff. (SWA.). 560p. pap. text 275.00 incl. audio (*0-88432-041-3*, AFW426) Audio-Forum.

Languages of Art. 2nd ed. Nelson Goodman. LC 68-31825. (Illus.). 288p. (C). 1976. 37.95 (*0-915144-35-2*); pap. text 16.95 (*0-915144-34-4*) Hackett Pub.

Languages of Australia & Tasmania. Stephen A. Wurm. LC 75-159473. (Janua Linguarum, Ser. Critica: No. 1). (Illus.). 208p. (Orig.). 1972. pap. text 37.35 (*90-279-2184-9*) Mouton.

Languages of Business. Francesca Bargiela-Chiappini & Sandra Harris. LC 98-173145. 264p. 1998. pap. 30.00 (*0-7486-0833-8*, Pub. by Edinburgh U Pr) Col U Pr.

Languages of China. S. Robert Ramsey. (Illus.). 353p. 1986. pap. text 21.95 (*0-691-01468-X*, Pub. by Princeton U Pr) Cal Prin Full Svc.

Languages of Class: Studies in English Working Class History 1832-1982. Gareth Stedman-Jones. LC 83-7721. 268p. 1984. pap. text 22.95 (*0-521-27631-4*) Cambridge U Pr.

***Languages of Community.** Hillel J. Kieval. LC 99-53814. (Illus.). 344p. 2000. 45.00 (*0-520-21410-2*, Pub. by U CA Pr) Cal Prin Full Svc.

Languages of Criticism & the Structure of Poetry. Ronald S. Crane. LC PN1042.C7. (University of Toronto, Alexander Foundation, the Alexander Lectures: 1951-52). 236p. 1964. reprint ed. pap. 73.20 (*0-608-16159-4*, 203671000005) Bks Demand.

Languages of Criticism & the Structure of Poetry. Ronald S. Crane. LC 86-11387. xviii, 234p. (C). 1996. reprint ed. pap. text 19.50 (*0-226-11797-9*) U Ch Pr.

Languages of Dress in the Middle East. Ed. by Nancy Lindisfarne-Tapper & Bruce Ingham. LC 98-121076. 240p. 1997. 65.00 (*0-7007-0670-4*, Pub. by Curzon Pr Ltd); pap. 25.00 (*0-7007-0671-2*, Pub. by Curzon Pr Ltd) Paul & Co Pubs.

Languages of Eastern Asia. Center for Applied Linguistics Staff et al. LC 76-44593. (Survey of Materials for the Study of the Uncommonly Taught Languages Ser.: No. 5). 51p. reprint ed. pap. 30.00 (*0-8357-3366-1*, 203960500013) Bks Demand.

Languages of Eastern Europe & the Soviet Union. Center for Applied Linguistics Staff et al. LC 76-44589. (Survey of Materials for the Study of the Uncommonly Taught Languages Ser.: No. 2). 53p. reprint ed. pap. 30.00 (*0-8357-3367-X*, 203960600013) Bks Demand.

Languages of Edison's Electric Light. Charles Bazerman. LC 98-51881. (Inside Technology Ser.). 400p. 1999. 39.50 (*0-262-02456-X*) MIT Pr.

Languages of Guatemala. Ed. by Marvin K. Mayers. (Janua Linguarum, Ser. Practica: No. 23). (Orig.). 1966. pap. text 67.70 (*90-279-0642-4*) Mouton.

Languages of Indexing & Classification: A Linguistic Study of Structures & Functions. William J. Hutchins. LC 76-351397. (Librarianship & Information Studies). 156p. reprint ed. pap. 48.40 (*0-8357-8933-0*, 203345200086) Bks Demand.

Languages of Instruction: Policy Implications for Education in Africa. LC 98-700274. (ENG & FRE.). xv, 94p. 1997. pap. 17.50 (*0-88936-829-5*, Pub. by IDRC Bks) Stylus Pub VA.

***Languages of Israel: Policy, Ideology & Practice** Bernard Spolsky & Elana Goldberg Shohamy. LC 99-30515. (Bilingual Education & Bilingualism Ser.). 1999. 39.95 (*1-85359-451-2*) Multilingual Matters.

Languages of Italy. Giacomo Devoto. Tr. by V. Louise Katainen. LC 78-3391. (History & Structure of Languages Ser.). 1978. lib. bdg. 30.00 (*0-226-14368-6*) U Ch Pr.

Languages of Japan. Masayoshi Shibatani. (Cambridge Language Surveys Ser.). (Illus.). 427p. (C). 1990. pap. text 29.95 (*0-521-36918-5*) Cambridge U Pr.

Languages of Jerusalem. Bernard J. Spolsky & Robert L. Cooper. (Oxford Studies in Language Contact). (Illus.). 180p. 1991. text 65.00 (*0-19-823908-4*) OUP.

Languages of Joyce: Selected Papers from the 11th International James Joyce Symposium, Venice, 12-18 June 1988. Ed. by Rosa Maria Bosinelli et al. LC 92-31117. xx, 277p. 1992. pap. 27.95 (*1-55619-474-9*) J Benjamins Pubng Co.

Languages of Joyce: Selected Papers from the 11th International James Joyce Symposium, Venice, 1988. Ed. by Rosa Maria Bosinelli et al. LC 92-31117. xx, 277p. 1992. 74.00 (*1-55619-473-0*) J Benjamins Pubng Co.

Languages of Labor & Gender: Female Factory Work in Germany, 1850-1914. Kathleen Canning. LC 96-793. (Illus.). 352p. 1996. text 45.00 (*0-8014-3123-9*) Cornell U Pr.

Languages of Labour. Ed. by John Belchem & Neville Kirk. LC 97-18807. 232p. 1997. text 74.95 (*1-85928-428-0*, Pub. by Scolar Pr) Ashgate Pub Co.

Languages of Landscape. Mark Roskill. LC 95-36306. 1997. 70.00 (*0-271-01553-5*) Pa St U Pr.

Languages of Law: From Logics of Memory to Nomadic Masks. Peter Goodrich. (Law in Context Ser.). 368p. (C). 1994. pap. text 29.95 (*0-297-82024-9*) Northwestern U Pr.

Languages of Law: From Logics of Memory to Nomadic Masks. Peter Goodrich. (Law in Context Ser.). ix, 353p. (C). 1990. 70.00 (*0-297-82009-5*) W S Hein.

Languages of Learning: How Children Talk, Write, Dance, Draw & Sing Their Understanding of the World. Karen Gallas. (Language & Literacy Ser.). 192p. (C). 1994. text 37.00 (*0-8077-3306-7*); pap. text 16.95 (*0-8077-3305-9*) Tchrs Coll.

Languages of Liberation: The Social Text in Contemporary American Poetry. Walter Kalaidjian. 256p. 1989. text 41.00 (*0-231-06836-0*) Col U Pr.

Languages of Literature in Renaissance Italy. Ed. by P. R. Hainsworth et al. (Illus.). 290p. 1988. text 80.00 (*0-19-815832-7*) OUP.

Languages of Logic: An Introduction. Samuel Guttenplan. (Illus.). 344p. 1987. pap. text 26.95 (*0-631-14625-3*) Blackwell Pubs.

***Languages of Native North America.** Marianne Mithun. LC 98-53576. (Cambridge Language Surveys Ser.). (Illus.). 770p. (C). 1999. 80.00 (*0-521-23228-7*) Cambridge U Pr.

Languages of Paradise: Race, Religion, & Philology in the Nineteenth Century. Maurice Olender. Tr. by Arthur Goldhammer from FRE. 208p. (C). 1992. 36.50 (*0-674-51052-6*) HUP.

Languages of Power: A Source Book of Early Constitutional History. Jefferson Powell. LC 90-85342. 352p. 1991. pap. 19.95 (*0-89089-380-2*); lib. bdg. 45.00 (*0-89089-379-9*) Carolina Acad Pr.

Languages of Power in Islamic Spain. Ross Brann. LC 97-3720. (Occasional Publications of the Department of Near Eastern Studies & the Program of Jewish Studies, Cornell University: Vol. 3). (Illus.). xii, 222p. 1997. 35.00 (*1-883053-28-5*) CDL Pr.

Languages of Psyche: Mind & Body in Enlightenment Thought. Ed. by G. S. Rousseau. LC 90-34872. (Publications from the Clark Library Professorship, UCLA: No. 12). (Illus.). 494p. 1991. 58.00 (*0-520-07044-5*, Pub. by U CA Pr); pap. 18.95 (*0-520-07119-0*, Pub. by U CA Pr) Cal Prin Full Svc.

Languages of Psychoanalysis. John E. Gedo. 224p. 1996. 39.95 (*0-88163-186-8*) Analytic Pr.

***Languages of Sentiment: Cultural Constructions of Emotional Substrates.** Ed. by Gary B. Palmer & Debra J. Occhi. LC 99-33999. (Advances in Consciousness Research Ser.: Vol. 18). vi, 272p. 1999. pap. 34.95 (*1-55619-434-X*) J Benjamins Pubng.

Languages of Southeast Asia & the Pacific. Center for Applied Linguistics Staff. LC 76-44595. (Survey of Materials for the Study of the Uncommonly Taught Languages Ser.: No. 7). 73p. reprint ed. pap. 30.00 (*0-8357-3365-3*, 203960400013) Bks Demand.

Languages of Sub-Saharan Africa. Center for Applied Linguistics Staff et al. LC 76-44594. (Survey of Materials for the Study of the Uncommonly Taught Languages Ser.: No. 6). 93p. reprint ed. pap. 30.00 (*0-8357-3368-8*, 203960800013) Bks Demand.

Languages of the Aboriginal Southeast: An Annotated Bibliography. Karen M. Booker. LC 90-28779. (Native American Bibliography Ser.: No. 15). 265p. 1991. 37.50 (*0-8108-2401-9*) Scarecrow.

Languages of the Brain: Experimental Paradoxes & Principles in Neuropsychology. 5th ed. Karl H. Pribram. 432p. 1982. reprint ed. text 35.00 (*0-913412-22-8*) Brandon Hse.

Languages of the Coast of California North of San Francisco. fac. ed. A. L. Kroeber. (University of California Publications in American Archaeology & Ethnology: Vol. 9: 3). 164p. (C). 1911. reprint ed. pap. text 17.50 (*1-55567-186-1*) Coyote Press.

Languages of the Coast of California South of San Francisco. A. L. Kroeber. (University of California Publications American Archaeology & Ethnology: No. 2). 103p. (C). reprint ed. pap. text 11.56 (*1-55567-603-0*) Coyote Press.

Languages of the Eastern Family of the East New Guinea Highland Stock. Ed. by Howard McKaughan. LC 72-13131. (Anthropological Studies in the Eastern Highlands of New Guinea: No. 1). (Illus.). 848p. 1973. 40.00 (*0-295-95132-X*) U of Wash Pr.

***Languages of the Himalayas: An Ethnolinguistic Handbook.** George Van Driem. LC 97-41872. (Illus.). 550p. 2001. 172.00 (*90-04-10390-2*) Brill Academic Pubs.

Languages of the Mind. Ray S. Jackendoff. LC 91-45159. 200p. 1992. 30.00 (*0-262-10047-9*) MIT Pr.

Languages of the Mind: Essays on Mental Representation. Ray S. Jackendoff. (Illus.). 216p. 1995. reprint ed. pap. text 15.00 (*0-262-60024-2*, Bradford Bks) MIT Pr.

Languages of the Stage: Essays in the Semiology of Theatre. Patrice Pavis. (PAJ Bks.). (Illus.). 206p. (C). 1993. pap. text 16.95 (*0-933826-15-X*) Johns Hopkins.

Languages of the Unsayable: The Play of Negativity in Literature & Literary Theory. Ed. by Sanford Budick & Wolfgang Iser. 416p. 1989. text 49.00 (*0-231-06866-2*) Col U Pr.

Languages of the World. 1995. cd-rom, disk 129.95 (*0-8442-9294-X*, Passprt Bks) NTC Contemp Pub Co.

Languages of the World. Kenneth Katzner. 384p. 1986. pap. 13.95 (*0-7102-0861-8*, 08618, Routledge Thoemms) Routledge.

Languages of the World. Kenneth Katzner. 1990. pap. 13.95 (*0-415-04604-1*) Routledge.

Languages of the World. Ed. by Scott Morris. LC 92-22287. (Using & Understanding Maps Ser.). (Illus.). 48p. (YA). (gr. 5 up). 1993. lib. bdg. 17.95 (*0-7910-1811-3*) Chelsea Hse.

Languages of the World. 3rd ed. Kenneth Katzner. LC 94-24228. (Illus.). 400p. (C). (gr. 13). 1995. pap. 17.99 (*0-415-11809-3*, B4896) Routledge.

Languages of the World: Cataloging Issues & Problems. Ed. by Martin D. Joachim. LC 93-38632. (Cataloging & Classification Quarterly Ser.: Vol. 17, Nos. 1-2). (Illus.). 292p. 1994. lib. bdg. 49.95 (*1-56024-520-4*) Haworth Pr.

Languages of the World for Windows. (CHI, DAN, DUT, ENG & FIN.). 16p. 1994. cd-rom, disk 149.95 (*0-8442-9250-8*, NTC Business Bks) NTC Contemp Pub Co.

Languages of Theatre: Problems in the Translation & Transposition of Drama. O. Zuber. LC 79-41711. 178p. 1980. 90.00 (*0-08-025246-X*, Pub. by Pergamon Repr) Franklin.

***Languages of Theatre Shaped by Women.** Lizbeth Goodman & Jane De Gay. 128p. 2000. pap. 24.95 (*1-871516-78-1*, Pub. by Intellect) Intl Spec Bk.

Languages of Tolkien's Middle-Earth, 001. Ruth S. Noel. 224p. 1980. pap. 14.00 (*0-395-29130-5*) HM.

Languages of Visuality: Crossings Between Science, Art, Politics, & Literature. Ed. by Beate Allert. LC 95-45568. (Kritik Ser.). (Illus.). 284p. (C). 1996. 39.95 (*0-8143-2540-8*); pap. 19.95 (*0-8143-2607-2*) Wayne St U Pr.

Languages of West Africa. Frederick W. Migeod. 1977. 34.95 (*0-405-30129-4*); 34.95 (*0-405-30130-8*) Ayer.

Languages of West Africa, 2 vols. Frederick W. Migeod. LC 72-3001. (Black Heritage Library Collection). 1977. reprint ed. 69.95 (*0-8369-9076-5*) Ayer.

Languages of West Africa: With a Supplementary Bibliography. Diedrich Westermann & M. A. Bryan. LC 76-25958. (Handbook of African Languages Ser.: Pt. 2). 291p. reprint ed. pap. 90.30 (*0-8357-3232-0*, 205712600011) Bks Demand.

***Languages of Witchcraft: Narrative, Ideology & Meaning in Early Modern Culture.** Stuart Clark. LC 00-33302. (Illus.). 2000. pap. write for info. (*0-312-23813-4*) St Martin.

***Languages Within Language: An Evoluative Approach.** Ivan Fonagy. (Foundations of Semiotics Ser.: Vol. 13). 2000. write for info. (*1-55619-038-7*) J Benjamins Pubng Co.

Languaging: The Linguistics of Psychotherapy. L. Michael Hall. 40p. Date not set. pap. 25.00 (*1-890001-11-2*) Empowerment Tech.

Langue & Langage. Hamel. (C). 1996. pap. text 32.50 (*0-15-504309-9*) Harcourt Coll Pubs.

Langue & Langage. 5th ed. O. F. Pucciani. LC 86-29439. (FRE.). 655p. (C). 1996. pap. text 67.50 (*0-15-504317-X*) Harcourt Coll Pubs.

Langue & Societe - Language & Society. Ed. by Douglas C. Walker. LC 79-348311. (Conferences Georges P. Vanier Ser.). (ENG & FRE.). 84p. 1977. reprint ed. pap. 30.00 (*0-608-02178-4*, 206284700004) Bks Demand.

Langue Classique dans la Tourmente see Histoire de la Langue Francaise des Origines a nos Jours

Langue Classique, 1660-1715 see Histoire de la Langue Francaise des Origines a nos Jours

***Langue de l'Autre.** Abdelkebir Khatibi. (Maghrer Pluril Ser.). (FRE.). 100p. 1999. pap. text 19.95 (*0-9665360-1-0*) Les Mains Secret.

Langue des Signes Vol. 3: Dictionnaire Billingue Elementaire. William Moody. (FRE.). 224p. 1990. pap. 105.00 (*0-7859-8227-2*, 2904641025) Fr & Eur.

Langue et Langage. 5th ed. Oreste Pucciani. (C). 1987. pap. text, lab manual ed. 27.75 (*0-03-004042-6*) Harcourt.

Langue et Langage. 5th ed. Oreste Pucciani. (C). 1987. pap. text, teacher ed. 25.75 (*0-03-004039-6*) Harcourt Coll Pubs.

Langue et Language: Le Francais par le Francais. 5th ed. Oreste Pucciani & Jacqueline Hamel. 608p. (C). 1987. text 45.25 (*0-03-004037-X*) Harcourt Coll Pubs.

Langue et les Textes en Grec Ancien: Actes du Colloque Pierre Chantraine (Grenoble, 5-8 Septembre 1989) Ed. by F. Letoublon. 377p. 1992. pap. 97.00 (*90-5063-066-9*, Pub. by Gieben) J Benjamins Pubng Co.

Langue et Litterature. 3rd ed. Thomas H. Brown. LC 83-81015. (FRE.). 380p. (C). 1984. text 48.36 (*0-669-06682-6*); teacher ed. 2.66 (*0-669-07406-3*); student ed. 28.76 (*0-669-06683-4*); audio 31.16 (*0-669-06685-0*) HM Trade Div.

Langue et Litterature: A Second Course in French. 2nd ed. Thomas H. Brown. (Illus.). 448p. (C). 1974. text 24.95 (*0-07-008400-9*) McGraw.

Langue Haitienne en Dix Etapes. Roger E. Savain.Tr. of Haitian-Kreol in Ten Steps. (ENG & FRE.). 128p. 1995. pap. 14.95 (*0-87047-106-6*) Schenkman Bks Inc.

Langue, Langage et Strategies Linguistiques Chez Heidegger. Serge Botet. (Contacts Ser.: Series III, Vol. 36). (FRE.). xii, 552p. 1997. 63.95 (*3-906754-63-4*, Pub. by P Lang) P Lang Pubng.

Langue Wakhi Vol. 2: Essai Grammatical et Dictionnaire Wakhi-Francais, Francais-Wakhi. A. L. Grunberg. (FRE.). 376p. 1988. pap. 115.00 (*0-7859-7993-X*, 2735102890) Fr & Eur.

Languedoc & Roussillon. Andrew Sanger. (Regional Guides of France Ser.). 192p. 1994. pap. 16.95 (*0-8442-9937-5*, Passprt Bks) NTC Contemp Pub Co.

Languedoc & Roussillon. 3rd ed. Andrew Sanger. LC 96-70353. (Passport's Regional Guides of France Ser.). (Illus.). 208p. 1997. pap. 17.95 (*0-8442-9082-3*, 90823, Passprt Bks) NTC Contemp Pub Co.

***Languedoc-Gorges du Tarn Cevennes.** Michelin Staff. (FRE.). 1999. pap. text 20.00 (*2-06-033704-6*) Michelin.

Languedoc/Roussillon Map. 1997. 8.95 (*2-06-700240-6*, 240) Michelin.

Language & Learning: The Home & School Years. 2nd ed. Terry Piper. LC 97-29947. 355p. (gr. 1). 1998. pap. text 53.00 (*0-13-863903-5*, Merrill Coll) P-H.

Languid Love Lyrics. Effie Mihopoulos. (Offset Offshoot Ser.: No. 16). 70p. 1993. pap. 8.00 (*0-941240-18-5*) Ommation Pr.

Languna Canyon Was Once a River. Marcia L. Cohee. (Illus.). 81p. (Orig.). 1991. pap. 7.50 (*0-9624205-2-2*) Inevitable Pr.

Langurs of Abu: Female & Male Strategies of Reproduction. Sarah Blaffer Hrdy. (Illus.). 381p. 1977. 37.00 (*0-674-51057-7*) HUP.

Langurs of Abu: Female & Male Strategies of Reproduction. Sarah Blaffer Hrdy. (Illus.). 381p. 1980. pap. 17.00 (*0-674-51058-5*) HUP.

Langvokale im Hochdeutschen see Phonetisch-Phonologische Untersuchungen zur Vokalentwicklung in den deutschen Dialekten

Lanhydrock Days. John Branfield. (Acorn Modern Classics Ser.). 96p. (YA). (gr. 7-10). 1992. pap. 8.95 (*0-575-05081-0*, Pub. by V Gollancz) Trafalgar.

Lankavatara Sutra. 1987. pap. 27.00 (*0-7100-2165-8*, Routledge Thoemms) Routledge.

Lankavatara Sutra. D. T. Suzuki. 320p. 1998. 110.00 (*0-7103-0600-8*, Pub. by Kegan Paul Intl) Col U Pr.

Lankavatara Sutra. D. T. Suzuki. 300p. 1987. reprint ed. 30.00 (*957-638-031-6*) Oriental Bk Store.

***Lankavatara Sutra: A Mahatana Text.** Tr. by Daisetz Teitaro Suzuki. 356p. 1999. 28.50 (*81-215-0925-4*, Pub. by Munshiram) Coronet Bks.

Lann. Frank Thorne. (Eros Graphic Novel Ser.: No. 11). 88p. 1994. pap. 14.95 (*1-56097-209-2*) Fantagraph Bks.

***Lanna: A Girls' Life.** Anthony DiGiacomo. 100p. 2000. pap. 7.95 (*1-58265-020-9*, 00025) Orphan Press.

Lanna Textbook. Kobkan Thangpijaigul. LC 95-71684. 1996. 89.00 (*1-881265-27-7*) Dunwoody Pr.

Lannigan. large type ed. Ed Bedeaux. (Linford Western Library). 256p. 1993. pap. 16.99 (*0-7089-7305-1*) Ulverscroft.

Lanolt-Boernstein Numerical Data & Functional Relationships in Science & Technology: Astronomy, Astrophysics & Space Research; Astronomy & Astrophysics; Methods, Constants, the Solar System, Group VI; Vol. 3; Subvol. A. Ed. by Otfried Madelung & H. H. Voigt. 240p. 1993. 720.95 (*0-387-56079-3*) Spr-Verlag.

Lanolt-Boernstein Numerical Data & Functional Relationships in Science & Technology: Macroscopic Properties of Matter; Phase Equilibria, Crystallographic Data, & Values of Thermodynamic Properties of Binary Alloys; Ca-Cd...Co-Zr, Group IV; Vol. 5; Subvol. C. B. Predel. Ed. by Otfried Madelung & K. Schafer. 480p. 1993. 1441.95 (*0-387-56072-6*) Spr-Verlag.

Lanolt-Boernstein Numerical Data & Functional Relationships in Science & Technology: Solid State Physics; Nuclear Quadrupole Resonance Spectroscopy Data, Group III; Vol. 31; Subvol. B. K. Chihara & Norio Nakamura. Ed. by A. M. Hellwege & K. Hellwege. 360p. 1993. 1072.95 (*0-387-55147-6*) Spr-Verlag.

Lanquage Law. Ed. by John Gibbons. LC 93-5621. (Language in Social Life Ser.). 1995. pap. text 40.25 (*0-582-10145-X*) Addison-Wesley.

LANs: Applications of IEEE-Ansi 802 Standards. Thomas W. Mardon. 320p. 1989. pap. 39.95 (*0-471-62049-1*) Wiley.

LANs Explained: A Guide to Local Area Networks. William S. Currie. 1989. pap. text 34.95 (*0-470-21427-9*) P-H.

LANs! LANs! LANs! 3rd expanded rev. ed. V. C. Marney-Petix. LC 98-20998. (Self-Paced Learning Ser.). (Illus.). 325p. (Orig.). 1998. pap. 45.95 (*1-880548-40-2*) Numidia Pr.

LANs, WANs, & the Internet. 1997. write for info. (*1-884486-26-6*) Wave Tech.

An Asterisk (*) at the beginning of an entry indicates that the title is appearing for the first time.

Lanscape Exhibition of the Four Seasons: Summer see Seasons

Lanscape Exhibition of the Four Seasons: Summer, 4 vols., Set. (Landscape Exhibition of the Four Seasons Ser.). (CHI & ENG., Illus.). 116p. 1994. pap. 39.95 (*957-562-070-4*) Heian Intl.

Lansdowne's Birds of the Forest. J. F. Lansdowne. 1989. 49.98 (*0-88486-027-2*) Arrowood Pr.

LanSell: Desktop Guide for Connectivity Sales Professional. Thomas B. Cross. 1991. pap. 24.95 (*0-923426-94-9*) Smith Micro.

***Lansingburgh.** Don Rittner. (Images of America Ser.). (Illus.). 128p. (Orig.). 1999. pap. 18.99 (*0-7385-0089-5*) Arcadia Publng.

Lansky. Hank Messick. Date not set. lib. bdg. 24.95 (*0-8488-1808-3*) Amereon Ltd.

Lantana Malangii: Kembang Tembelehan Boyhood Impressions. Boyd A. Melger, pseud. (Illus.). 107p. (Orig.). 1991. pap. write for info. (*0-9622463-5-2*) B Melger.

Lantana Malangii: Kembang Tembelehan Jeugd Impressies. Boyd A. Melger, pseud. (DUT., Illus.). 90p. (Orig.). 1991. pap. write for info. (*0-9622463-4-4*) B Melger.

LANtastic: Running a Low-Cost Network. Tony Dennis. LC 94-2117. (Data Communications & Networks Ser.). 256p. 1994. 30.00 (*0-201-63180-6*) Addison-Wesley.

Lantern Advent Book see Mi Pequeno Calendario de Navidad

Lantern & Other Plays for Children. Abbie F. Brown. LC 77-94333. (One-Act Plays in Reprint Ser.). (Illus.). 1978. reprint ed. 20.00 (*0-8486-2033-X*) Roth Pub Inc.

Lantern Bearers. Rosemary Sutcliff. LC 93-43116. 240p. (J). (gr. 7 up). 1994. pap. 5.95 (*0-374-44302-5*) FS&G.

Lantern Bearers. Rosemary Sutcliff. 1995. 19.50 (*0-8446-6837-0*) Peter Smith.

Lantern-Bearers & Other Essays. Robert Louis Stevenson. Ed. by Jeremy Treglown. LC 99-33329. 290p. 2000. pap. 16.95 (*0-8154-1012-3*) Cooper Sq.

Lantern for Lord Rhys. Margot James. 295p. (C). 1987. 50.00 (*0-86383-380-2*, Pub. by Gomer Pr) St Mut.

Lantern in Her Hand. Bess S. Aldrich. LC 93-39763. ix, 307p. 1994. pap. 10.00 (*0-8032-5922-0*, Bison Books) U of Nebr Pr.

Lantern in Her Hand. Bess S. Aldrich. LC 96-34910. 256p. (YA). (gr. 8 up). 1997. pap. 4.99 (*0-14-038428-6*) Viking Penguin.

Lantern in Her Hand. Bess Streeter Aldrich. (J). 1997. 10.09 (*0-606-11546-3*, Pub. by Turtleback) Demco.

Lantern in Her Hand. Bess S. Aldrich. 278p. Date not set. reprint ed. lib. bdg. 21.95 (*0-88411-260-8*) Amereon Ltd.

Lantern in Her Hand: A Study Guide. Barbara Reeves. Ed. by J. Friedland & R. Kessler. (Novel-Ties Ser.). (J). (gr. 6-8). 1992. pap. text, student ed. 15.95 (*0-88122-716-1*) Lrn Links.

Lantern in the Dawn: Selections from the Writings of John E. Zercher. Ed. by E. Morris Sider & Paul Hostetler. 192p. 1980. 6.95 (*0-916035-08-5*) Evangel Indiana.

Lantern in the Tree. Francis G. Yeoman. LC 77-93987. 160p. write for info. (*0-911978-01-1*) McCormick-Armstrong.

Lantern in the Wind: The Life of Mary Ellen Chase. Ed. by Elienne Squire. LC 94-46762. 208p. (Orig.). 1995. pap. 10.95 (*1-56474-132-X*) Fithian Pr.

Lantern Network. Ted Allbeury. 208p. 1989. 17.95 (*0-89296-185-6*, Pub. by Mysterious Pr) Little.

Lantern on Lewes: Where the Past Is Present. Hazel D. Brittingham. Ed. & Illus. by Elaine Ippolito. LC 99-191660. 96p. 1998. pap. 9.95 (*0-9663956-0-3*) Lewestown Pubs.

Lantern Slides. Edna O'Brien. 240p. 1991. reprint ed. pap. 11.95 (*0-452-26628-9*, Plume) Dutton Plume.

Lantern Slides: The Diaries & Letters of Violet Bonham Carter 1904-1914. Ed. by Mark B. Carter & Mark Pottle. (Illus.). 496p. 1997. pap. (*1-85799-860-X*) Phoenix Hse.

Lanterne of Light. Ed. by Lilian M. Swinburn. (EETS, OS Ser.: No. 151). 1969. reprint ed. 45.00 (*0-8115-3958-X*) Periodicals Srv.

Lanterne Sourde see Oeuvres

***Lanterns: A Memoir of Mentors.** Marian Wright Edelman. LC 99-44228. (Illus.). 176p. 1999. 20.00 (*0-8070-7214-1*) Beacon Pr.

***Lanterns: A Memoir of Mentors.** Marian Wright Edelman. (Illus.). 208p. 2000. pap. 14.00 (*0-06-095859-6*, Perennial) HarperTrade.

Lanterns for Home & Garden. Carolyn Kyle & Chuck Berets. (Illus.). 32p. (Orig.). 1996. pap. 14.95 (*0-935133-58-5*, 20133585) CKE Pubns.

Lanterns from Bloomsbury Square. large type ed. Patricia Hemstock. (Linford Romance Library). 320p. 1996. pap. 16.99 (*0-7089-7964-5*, Linford) Ulverscroft.

Lanterns of God. Ron Sarti. (Chronicles of Scar Ser.: Bk. 3). 1998. mass mkt. 5.99 (*0-380-73026-X*, Eos) Morrow Avon.

Lanterns on the Levee: Recollections of a Planter's Son. William A. Percy. LC 73-90687. (Library of Southern Civilization). xxii, 376p. 1974. 29.95 (*0-8071-1184-8*); pap. 16.95 (*0-8071-0072-2*) La State U Pr.

Lanterns on the River: Essays on Life & Culture in Contemporary South Korea. Diane M. Hoffman. LC 99-22710. 208p. 1999. 50.00 (*0-7391-0074-2*) Lxngtn Bks.

Lanterns That Lit Our World: How to Identify, Date & Restore Old Railroad, Marine, Fire, Carriage, Farm & Other Lanterns. Anthony Hobson. LC 88-81427. (Illus.). 232p. 1991. pap. 15.95 (*0-9614876-5-8*, Pub. by Golden Hl Pr NY) Midpt Trade.

Lanterns That Lit Our World, Book Two: Old Railroad, Fire, Marine, Carriage & Other Lanterns. Anthony Hogson. LC 96-80000. (Illus.). 204p. 1997. pap. 14.95 (*1-889029-00-9*) Golden Hl Pr NY.

Lanthanide & Actinide Chemistry & Spectroscopy. Ed. by Norman M. Edelstein. LC 80-17468. (ACS Symposium Ser.: No. 131). (Illus.). 480p. 1980. reprint ed. pap. 148.80 (*0-608-03233-6*, 206375200007) Bks Demand.

Lanthanide Shift Reagents for Stereochemical Analysis. Ed. by Terrence C. Morill. 206p. 1987. pap. 105.00 (*0-471-18650-3*) Wiley.

Lanthanide Shift Reagents in Stereochemical Analysis, Vol. 5. Terence C. Morrill. (Illus.). 193p. 1987. 65.00 (*0-89573-119-3*, Wiley-VCH) Wiley.

Lanthanide/Actinide Chemistry: A Symposium Co-Sponsored by the Division of Inorganic Chemistry & the Division of Nuclear Chemistry & Technology at the 152nd Meeting of the American Chemical Society, New York, NY, Sept. 13-14, 1966. American Chemical Society Staff. LC 67-31656. (Advances in Chemistry Ser.: No. 71). (Illus.). 371p. 1967. reprint ed. pap. 115.10 (*0-608-06803-9*, 206700000009) Bks Demand.

***Lanthanides: Chemistry & Use in Organic Synthesis.** S. Kobayashi. Ed. by J. M. Brown et al. LC 99-18127. (Topics in Organometallic Chemistry Ser.: Vol. 2). (Illus.). 300p. 1999. 119.00 (*3-540-64526-8*) Spr-Verlag.

Lanthanides in Organic Synthesis. Tsuneo Imamoto. (Best Synthetic Methods Ser.). (Illus.). 154p. 1994. text 51.00 (*0-12-370722-6*) Acad Pr.

Lanthanides, Transition Metal Compounds see Comprehensive Inorganic Chemistry

L'/Anti-Peuple see Antipeople

Lantibiotics & Related Peptides. Ralph W. Jack & Hans-Georg Sahl. LC 97-31727. (Biotechnology Intelligence Unit (SV) Ser.). 263p. Date not set. 129.00 (*1-57059-515-1*) Landes Bioscience.

Lantibiotics & Related Peptides. Ralph W. Jack et al. LC 97-31727. (Biotechnology Intelligence Unit (SV) Ser.). (Illus.). 263p. 1998. text 129.00 (*3-540-63600-5*) Spr-Verlag.

***Lanting Jungles.** Taschen America Staff. (Illus.). 2000. pap. 4.99 (*3-8228-6082-4*) Taschen Amer.

***Lanting Penguins.** Taschen America Staff. (Illus.). 2000. pap. text 4.99 (*3-8228-6654-7*) Taschen Amer.

Lantskip. Francis Blessington. LC 87-1116. 67p. (Orig.). 1987. pap. 8.95 (*0-87233-090-7*) Bauhan.

Lantz Welch's Summation in Firestone vs. Crown Center Redevelopment Corp. Kansas City Hyatt Skywalk Case. Intro. by James W. Jeans, Sr. (Classics of the Courtroom: Vol. XV). 27p. 1988. pap. 10.00 (*0-943380-21-9*) PEG MN.

Lanvin Elisabeth Barille. LC 98-160732. (Fashion Memoir Ser.). 79 p. 1997. write for info. (*0-500-01816-2*) Thames Hudson.

LAN/WAN Network Management Software Service & System Markets: Your First Source about Outsourcing. Market Intelligence Staff. 198p. 1992. 1695.00 (*1-56753-663-8*) Frost & Sullivan.

LAN/WAN Optimization Techniques. Harrell J. Van Norman. LC 91-48236. (Artech House Telecommunications Library). 361p. 1992. reprint ed. pap. 112.00 (*0-608-02364-7*, 206300600004) Bks Demand.

Lanyard: Having Fun with Plastic Lace. Camilla Gryski. Orig. Title: Boondoggle. (J). 1995. 12.15 (*0-606-07771-5*) Turtleback.

Lanyard: Having Fun with Plastic Lace. Camilla Gryski. LC 93-35992. Orig. Title: Boondoggle. (Illus.). 32p. (J). 1994. reprint ed. 15.00 (*0-688-13324-X*, Wm Morrow) Morrow Avon.

Lanyard: Having Fun with Plastic Lace. Camilla Gryski. LC 93-35992. Orig. Title: Boondoggle. (Illus.). 32p. (J). 1994. reprint ed. 14.93 (*0-688-13325-8*, Wm Morrow) Morrow Avon.

Lanyard Fun! Cindy G. Harry. LC 95-217000. (Creative Activity Kit Ser.). 48 p. (J). 1995. write for info. (*0-7853-1303-6*) Pubns Intl Ltd.

Lanyer: A Renaissance Woman Poet. Susanne Woods. LC 98-28562. (Illus.). 224p. 1999. text 39.95 (*0-19-512484-7*) OUP.

Lanz Bulldog Tractors, 1942-1955, Vol. II. Kurt Käfner. (Illus.). 176p. 1993. 45.00 (*0-86417-420-9*, Pub. by Kangaroo Pr) Seven Hills Bk.

Lanz Bulldog Tractors, 1928-1942, Vol. I. Kurt Hafner. (Illus.). 176p. 1993. 45.00 (*0-86417-419-5*, Pub. by Kangaroo Pr) Seven Hills Bk.

Lanzadera Espacial. Peter Murray. LC 93-17916. (Libro Vision Ser.). (SPA., Illus.). 32p. (J). (gr. 2-6). 1994. lib. bdg. 22.79 (*1-56766-038-X*) Childs World.

Lanzhou Lectures on Henstork Integration. P. Y. Lee. (Series in Real Analysis: Vol. 2). 192p. (C). 1989. text 61.00 (*9971-5-0891-5*); pap. text 28.00 (*9971-5-0892-3*) World Scientific Pub.

Lao Basic Course. Warren G. Yates. 423p. 1995. pap. 19.95 (*0-7818-0410-8*) Hippocrene Bks.

Lao Crisis of 1959. George F. Lemmer. 61p. 1961. reprint ed. pap. text 9.50 (*0-923135-38-3*) Dalley Bk Service.

Lao-English Dictionary. A. Kerr. (ENG & LAO.). 1220p. 1992. 66.00 (*0-7859-8907-2*) Fr & Eur.

Lao-English Dictionary. A. Kerr. (ENG & LAO.). 1220p. 1992. 90.00 (*974-8495-69-8*) IBD Ltd.

Lao-English Dictionary. Ed. by William L. Patterson. Tr. by Maria Severino. LC 94-68625. 826p. 1995. 89.00 (*1-881265-17-X*) Dunwoody Pr.

Lao-English Dictionary, 2 Vols., 1. Allen D. Kerr & Sing Bourommavong. LC 82-12826. (Publications in the Languages of Asia: Vol. 2). 642p. reprint ed. pap. 199.10 (*0-608-16034-2*, 203313400001) Bks Demand.

Lao-English Dictionary, 2 Vols., 2. Allen D. Kerr & Sing Bourommavong. LC 82-12826. (Publications in the Languages of Asia: Vol. 2). 612p. reprint ed. pap. 189.80 (*0-608-16035-0*, 203313400002) Bks Demand.

Lao for Beginners: An Introduction to the Spoken & Written Language of Laos. Tatsuo Hoshimo. (LAO.). 210p. 1990. pap. 14.95 (*0-8048-1629-8*) Tuttle Pubng.

Lao Handbook of Maternal & Child Health. Aletha Robinson. 1980. pap. 1.95 (*0-9602790-1-6*) Hlth Frontiers.

Lao Issara: The Memoirs of Oun Sananikone. Oun Sananikone. Ed. by David K. Wyatt. LC 76-356253. (Cornell University, Southeast Asia Program, Data Paper Ser.: No. 100). 86p. reprint ed. pap. 30.00 (*0-608-14219-0*, 202185100023) Bks Demand.

Lao Issara: The Memoirs of Oun Sananikone. Oun Sananikone. Ed. by David K. Wyatt. Tr. by John B. Murdoch from LAO. LC 76-356253. 60p. 1988. reprint ed. pap. 10.50 (*0-923135-01-4*) Dalley Bk Service.

Lao Lao of Dragon Mountain. Margaret Bateson-Hill. (Illus.). (J). 1998. 14.95 (*1-84089-035-5*); pap. 7.95 (*1-84089-011-8*) Zero to Ten.

Lao PDR Economy: Experience with Systemic Transformation & Adjustment. Ed. by I. Otani & C. Do Pham. LC 96-167536. (Occasional Papers: No. 137). 1996. pap. 15.00 (*1-55775-560-4*) Intl Monetary.

Lao Phrasebook: A Language Survival Kit. Joe Cummings. (LAO., Illus.). 176p. 1994. pap. 5.95 (*0-86442-276-8*) Lonely Planet.

Lao Proverbs. Ed. by Russell Marcus. Tr. by Novanta Phengsy from LAO. (Illus.). 56p. 1969. pap. 6.00 (*0-916020-00-2*) Books Marcus.

Lao Ren Cha. John Snyder. (Illus.). 60p. 1999. pap. 14.95 (*0-9623335-2-2*) HSP IL.

Lao Roots: Fragments of a Nordic-Lao Family Saga. Fleur B. Asmussen. 266p. 1999. pap. 23.00 (*974-8299-27-9*, Pub. by Weatherhill) Weatherhill.

***Lao She: China's Master Storyteller.** Britt Towery. 2000. pap. 20.00 (*0-87244-118-0*) Texian.

Lao She & the Chinese Revolution. Ranbir Vohra. LC 73-82346. (East Asian Monographs: No. 55). 199p. 1974. 24.00 (*0-674-51075-5*) HUP.

Lao Textiles & Traditions. Mary Connors. (Images of Asia Ser.). (Illus.). 96p. (C). 1997. text 18.95 (*983-56-0001-5*) OUP.

Lao-ts'an Yu Chi see Travels of Lao Ts'an

Lao-Tse. 283p. 1994. 18.50 (*1-898853-00-2*) Grail Fndtn-Amer.

Lao-Tse: Life & Work of the Forerunner in China. 3rd ed. LC BL1930.L357. 288p. 1995. reprint ed. pap. 14.00 (*1-57461-008-2*) Grail Found Pr.

Lao Tsu. (FRE.). 1985. lib. bdg. 95.00 (*0-8288-3571-3*, F119186) Fr & Eur.

Lao-Tze: Te Tao Ching. Tr. & Comment by Robert G. Henricks. 320p. 1992. pap. 10.00 (*0-345-37099-6*) Ballantine Pub Grp.

Lao Tzu: My Words Are Very Easy to Understand. 2nd ed. Cheng Man-ch'ing. Tr. by Tam Gibbs & Juh-Hua Huang. (CHI & ENG.). 256p. 1981. pap. 16.95 (*0-913028-91-6*) North Atlantic.

Lao Tzu: Tao Te Ching, a Book about the Way & the Power of the Way. Ursula K. Le Guin. 1998. pap. 12.00 (*1-57062-395-3*, Pub. by Shambhala Pubns) Random.

Lao-Tzu: Te-Tao Ching: A New Translation Based on the Recently Discovered Ma-Wang-Tui Texts. Tr. & Comment by Robert G. Henricks. LC 93-15015. 336p. 1993. 15.50 (*0-679-60060-4*) Modern Lib NY.

Lao Tzu & Taoism. Max Kaltenmark. Tr. by Roger Greaves. LC 69-13179. 176p. 1969. 29.50 (*0-8047-0688-3*); pap. 10.95 (*0-8047-0689-1*) Stanford U Pr.

Lao-Tzu & the "Tao-te-Ching" Ed. by Livia Kohn & Michael Lafargue. LC 97-7857. 320p. (C). 1998. pap. text 20.95 (*0-7914-3600-4*) State U NY Pr.

Lao-Tzu & the "Tao-te-Ching" Ed. by Livia Kohn & Michael Lafargue. LC 97-7857. 330p. (C). 1998. text 62.50 (*0-7914-3599-7*) State U NY Pr.

Lao Tzu's Tao Te Ching. Ed. by Timothy Freke. (Illus.). 128p. 1997. pap. 12.95 (*0-7499-1468-8*, Pub. by Piatkus Bks) London Brdge.

***Lao Tzu's Tao Te Ching.** Timothy Freke. 128p. 2000. pap. 9.95 (*0-7499-1966-3*, Pub. by Piatkus Bks) London Brdge.

***Lao Tzu's Tao Te Ching: A Translation of the New Documents Found at Guodian.** Robert Henricks. LC BL1900.L26E5 2000. 2000. 21.95 (*0-231-11816-3*) Col U Pr.

Lao-Tzu's Treatise on the Response of the Tao to Human Actions: Tai-Shang Kan-Ying Pien. Li Ying-chang. (Sacred Literature Ser.). 160p. 1994. 29.95 (*0-7619-8997-8*) AltaMira Pr.

Lao-Tzu's Treatise on the Response of the Tao to Human Actions: Tai-Shang Kan-Ying Pien. Li Ying-Chang. Tr. by Eva Wong from ENG. LC 93-49773. 128p. 1994. 20.00 (*0-06-064956-9*) Harper SF.

Laocoon: An Essay on the Limits of Painting & Poetry. Gotthold Ephraim Lessing. Tr. by Edward A. McCormick. LC 83-23880. 259p. 1984. pap. 15.95 (*0-8018-3139-3*) Johns Hopkins.

Laocoon: The Influence of the Group since Its Rediscovery. Margarete Bieber. LC 67-16850. (Illus.). 78p. reprint ed. pap. 30.00 (*0-7837-3826-9*, 204364700010) Bks Demand.

Laodecian Church. 28p. (Orig.). 1982. pap. 0.95 (*0-937408-17-4*) GMI Pubns Inc.

Laodicea: Christ's Urgent Counsel to a Lukewarm Church in the Last Days. Jack Sequeira. LC 94-33495. 1995. pap. 5.97 (*0-8163-1243-5*) Pacific Pr Pub Assn.

***Laodicean.** Thomas Hardy. (Oxford World Classics Ser.). 512p. 2000. pap. 9.95 (*0-19-283703-6*) OUP.

Laodicean: A Story of To-Day. Thomas Hardy. LC 76-365285. (New Wessex Ser.). 461p. (J). 1975. write for info. (*0-333-17759-2*, Pub. by Macmillan) Macmillan.

Laodicean: A Story of Today. Thomas Hardy. Ed. by J. H. Stape. (Everyman Paperback Classics). 432p. 1997. pap. 8.50 (*0-460-87637-6*, Everyman's Classic Lib) Tuttle Pubng.

Laogai: The Chinese Gulag. Hongda H. Wu. Tr. by Ted Slingerland. (Illus.). 247p. 1999. reprint ed. pap. text 21.00 (*0-7881-6348-5*) DIANE Pub.

***Laoism: The Complete Teachings of Lao Zi.** Tao Huang. 2000. pap. 18.95 (*0-89334-325-0*, Humanics Pub) Humanics Ltd.

Laomi Is Not Home. John Culpepper. 200p. (Orig.). (C). 1989. pap. 4.95 (*0-685-29152-9*) Warm Days Retirement.

Laos see Cultures of the World - Group 15

Laos. Helen Cordell. LC 92-146773. (World Bibliographical Ser.). 254p. 1992. lib. bdg. 82.00 (*1-85109-075-4*) ABC-CLIO.

Laos. Dawn Ellis & Tom Butcher. (Pallas Guide Ser.). (Illus.). 394p. 1997. pap. 24.95 (*1-873429-16-9*, XC3708) Cimino Pub Grp.

***Laos.** Insight Guides Staff. (Insight Compact Guide). 1999. pap. 7.95 (*0-88729-374-3*) Langenscheidt.

Laos. Ed. by Frank M. LeBar & Adrienne Suddard. LC 60-7381. (Area & Country Surveys Ser.). 312p. 1967. 15.00 (*0-87536-915-4*) HRAFP.

Laos. Martin Stuart-Fox. (Marxist Regimes Ser.). 224p. 1986. text 49.00 (*0-86187-426-9*); pap. text 17.50 (*0-86187-427-7*) St Martin.

Laos. U. S. Government Staff. (Country Studies). 1996. 21.00 (*0-614-30801-1*, ULAOS) Claitors.

Laos: A Country Study. 3rd ed. Ed. by Andrea M. Savada. LC 95-17235. (Area Handbook Ser.). 366p. 1995. 21.00 (*0-8444-0832-8*) Lib Congress.

***Laos: A Country Study Guide.** Global Investment & Business Center, Inc. Staff. (World Country Study Guides Library: Vol. 93). (Illus.). 350p. 2000. pap. 59.00 (*0-7397-2391-X*) Intl Business Pubns.

Laos: A Portrait. Stephen Mansfield. (Illus.). 200p. Date not set. 45.00 (*962-7787-03-5*, Pub. by O&A Edits) Weatherhill.

***Laos: Culture & Society.** Ed. by Grant Evans. 373p. 2000. pap. 24.95 (*974-87090-4-3*, Pub. by Silk Worm Bks) U of Wash Pr.

Laos: Major World Nations. Ralph Zickgraf. (Major World Nations Ser.). (Illus.). 144p. (YA). (gr. 5 up). 1999. lib. bdg. 19.95 (*0-7910-4743-1*) Chelsea Hse.

Laos: Son Evolution Politique, Sa Place Dans L'Unions Francaise. Katay D. Sasorith. LC 70-179240. reprint ed. 34.50 (*0-404-54866-0*) AMS Pr.

Laos - A Country Study Guide: Basic Information for Research & Pleasure. Global Investment Center, USA Staff. (World Country Study Guide Library: Vol. 93). (Illus.). 350p. 1999. pap. 59.00 (*0-7397-1490-2*) Intl Business Pubns.

Laos & Laotians. Khamchong Luangpraseut. (ENG & LAO., Illus.). 96p. (Orig.). (J). (gr. 2-5). 1995. pap. 14.95 (*1-879600-41-2*) Pac Asia Pr.

Laos & the Super Powers. Perala Ratnam. 167p. 1980. 15.95 (*0-940500-19-1*, Pub. by Tulsi Pub Hse) Asia Bk Corp.

***Laos Business Intelligence Report, 190 vols.** Global Investment & Business Center, Inc. Staff. (World Business Intelligence Library: Vol. 93). (Illus.). 350p. 2000. pap. 99.95 (*0-7397-2591-2*) Intl Business Pubns.

***Laos Business Law Handbook, 190 vols.** Global Investment & Business Center, Inc. Staff. (Global Business Law Handbooks Library: Vol. 93). (Illus.). 350p. 2000. pap. 99.95 (*0-7397-1990-4*) Intl Business Pubns.

***Laos Business Opportunity Yearbook.** Global Investment & Business Center, Inc. Staff. (Global Business Opportunity Yearbooks Library: Vol. 93). (Illus.). 2000. pap. 99.95 (*0-7397-2191-7*) Intl Business Pubns.

***Laos Business Opportunity Yearbook: Export-Import, Investment & Business Opportunities.** International Business Publications, U. S. A. Staff & Global Investment Center, U. S. A. Staff. (Global Business Opportunity Yearbooks Library: Vol. 93). (Illus.). 350p. 1999. pap. 99.95 (*0-7397-1291-8*) Intl Business Pubns.

Laos' Dilemmas & Options, 1990s. Mya Than. LC 96-49102. 335p. 1997. text 55.00 (*0-312-17310-5*) St Martin.

***Laos Foreign Policy & Government Guide.** Global Investment & Business Center, Inc. Staff. (World Foreign Policy & Government Library: Vol. 89). (Illus.). 350p. 1999. pap. 99.00 (*0-7397-3587-X*) Intl Business Pubns.

***Laos Foreign Policy & Government Guide.** Global Investment & Business Center, Inc. Staff. (World Foreign Policy & Government Library: Vol. 89). (Illus.). 350p. 2000. pap. 99.95 (*0-7397-3791-0*) Intl Business Pubns.

Laos Handbook. Joshua Eliot & Jane Bickersteth. LC 96-72528. (Illus.). write for info. (*0-900751-89-4*) Footprint Handbooks Ltd.

Laos Handbook. Joshua Eliot & Jane Bickersteth. LC 96-72528. (Illus.). 336p. 1997. 16.95 (*0-8442-4921-1*) NTC Contemp Pub Co.

***Laos Handbook.** 2nd ed. Joshua Eliot. (Footprint Handbooks Ser.). 336p. 1999. pap. 15.95 (*0-658-00014-4*, 000144, NTC Business Bks) NTC Contemp Pub Co.

Laos in Pictures. Lerner Publications, Department of Geography Staff. LC 95-37182. (Visual Geography Ser.). (Illus.). (J). 1996. lib. bdg. 19.93 (*0-8225-1906-2*, Lerner Publctns) Lerner Pub.

L

An Asterisk (*) at the beginning of an entry indicates that the title is appearing for the first time.

L

***Laos Investment & Business Guide.** Global Investment & Business Center, Inc. Staff. (Global Investment & Business Guide Library: Vol. 93). (Illus.). 2000. pap. 99.95 (0-7397-1791-X) Intl Business Pubns.

***Laos Investment & Business Guide: Export-Import, Investment & Business Opportunities.** International Business Publications, USA Staff & Global Investment Center, USA Staff. (World Investment & Business Guide Library-99: Vol. 93). (Illus.). 350p. 1999. pap. 99.95 (0-7397-0288-2) Intl Business Pubns.

Laos Profiles. Joel M. Halpern. (Laos Project Papers: No. 18). 175p. 1990. pap. 18.50 (0-923135-19-7) Dalley Bk Service.

***Laos, Thailand Bible.** 1999. 20.95 (5-550-00761-4) Nairi.

Laotian - English Mini-Book Set with Audio. Claudia Schwalm. (ENG & LAO., Illus.). (J). (gr. k-6). 1998. pap. 21.95 incl. audio (1-57371-020-2) Cultural Cnnect.

Laotian Fragments. John C. Pratt. (Vietnam Ser.). 240p. 1985. pap. 3.50 (0-380-69841-2, Avon Bks) Morrow Avon.

Laotian-French Dictionary see Dictionnaire Laotien-Francais

Laotian National Liberation Government Organization. Central Intelligence Agency Staff. 72p. 1964. reprint ed. text 15.00 (0-923135-39-1) Dalley Bk Service.

Laour's Visionary: Lord Hirschfield. Godfrey Gideon. (Illus.). 193p. 1998. 50.00 (1-86066-127-0, Pub. by R Cohen Bks) Trafalgar.

Lap Dancing for Mommy. Erika Lopez. LC 97-7304. (Illus.). 192p. (Orig.). 1997. pap. 14.00 (1-878067-96-6) Seal Pr WA.

Lap of Luxury. William Hamilton. LC 88-22617. 300p. 1990. pap. 8.95 (0-87113-342-3, Atlntc Mnthly) Grove-Atltic.

***Lap Quilting Lives.** Georgia Bonesteel. LC 99-44337. (Illus.). 112p. 1999. pap. 26.95 (1-56477-259-4, B376, That Patchwrk Pl) Martingale & Co.

Lap Quilting with Georgia Bonesteel. Georgia Bonesteel. LC 81-83054. (Illus.). 122p. 1982. 24.95 (0-8487-0524-6) Oxmoor Hse.

***Lap Talks: Casual Conversations with God.** Ramona L. Moore. 156p. 1999. pap. 9.95 (0-7392-0230-8, PO3267) Morris Pubng.

Lap Talks with Granny at Christmas: For Children of All Ages. Linda High. (Illus.). 39p. (J). (ps-6). 1997. 12.95 (0-9661186-2-6) Bks Child.

Lap-Time Song & Play Book. Illus. by Margot Tomes. LC 88-752289. 32p. (J). (ps-1). 1989. 15.95 (0-15-243588-3) Harcourt.

***LAPACK Users' Guide.** 3rd rev. ed. E. Anderson et al. LC 99-48954. (Software, Environments & Tools Ser.: No. 9). xxii, 407p. 2000. pap. 39.00 (0-89871-447-8, SE0009) Soc Indus-Appl Math.

Lapakahi, Hawaii: Archaeological Studies. Ed. by H. David Tuggle & P. Bion Griffin. LC 73-620081. (Asian & Pacific Archaeological Studies). 371p. reprint ed. pap. 115.10 (0-7837-1312-6, 204146000020) Bks Demand.

Laparo-Endoscopic Surgery. 2nd ed. Iris Brune. (Illus.). 400p. 1996. 135.00 (0-86542-900-6) Blackwell Sci.

Laparoscopic Abdominal Surgery. Ed. by John N. Graber et al. LC 92-48730. 250p. 1992. 125.00 (0-07-023989-4) McGraw-Hill HPD.

Laparoscopic Appearance of Endometriosis, Vol. I. 2nd ed. D. C. Martin et al. Ed. by Dan C. Martin. LC 90-60383. (Illus.). 57p. 1990. pap. text 14.00 (0-9616747-3-3) Resurge Pr.

Laparoscopic Appearance of Endometriosis: Color Atlas, Vol. III. 2nd ed. D. C. Martin et al. Ed. by Dan C. Martin. LC 90-60393. (Illus.). 69p. 1990. pap. text 38.00 (0-9616747-6-8) Resurge Pr.

Laparoscopic Cholecystectomy. M. Chellappa. 1994. text 38.00 (981-02-1094-9) World Scientific Pub.

Laparoscopic Cholecystectomy. Tehemton E. Udwadia. (Illus.). 104p. 1993. text 65.00 (0-19-562911-6) OUP.

Laparoscopic Cholecystectomy: Difficult Cases & Creative Solutions. Avram M. Cooperman. (Illus.). 192p. 1992. 100.00 (0-942219-28-7) Quality Med Pub.

Laparoscopic Cholecystectomy: Problems & Solutions. David C. Dunn & Christopher J. Watson. (Illus.). 160p. 1992. 70.00 (0-632-03444-0) Blackwell Sci.

Laparoscopic Cholecystectomy: State of the Art - Journal: Digestive Surgery, Vol. 8, No. 2, 1991. Ed. by J. J. Jakimowicz & T. J. Ruers. (Illus.). 72p. 1991. pap. 45.25 (3-8055-5439-7) S Karger.

Laparoscopic Colorectal Surgery. Ed. by M. W. Buchler & L. Krahenbuhl. (Journal Ser.: Vol. 12, No. 5, 1995). (Illus.). 42p. 1996. pap. 50.50 (3-8055-6282-9) S Karger.

Laparoscopic Colorectal Surgery. Jager. 1996. text 180.00 (0-443-07785-1, W B Saunders Co) Harcrt Hlth Sci Grp.

Laparoscopic Colorectal Surgery. Ed. by Rama M. Jager & Steven D. Wexner. LC 95-35115. 333p. 1995. text 132.00 (0-443-08998-1) Church.

Laparoscopic Colorectal Surgery. Jeffrey W. Milsom & Bartholomaus Bohm. LC 95-16248. (Illus.). 304p. 1995. 129.00 (0-387-94470-2) Spr-Verlag.

Laparoscopic Colorectal Surgery. Steven D. Wexner. LC 98-27804. (Protocols in General Surgery Ser.). 563p. 1999. 131.50 (0-471-24030-3) Wiley.

Laparoscopic Digestive Surgery. Ed. by Pierre Testas & Bernard J. Delaitre. LC 94-5562. (Clinical Surgery International Ser.: Vol. 19). (Illus.). 1994. text 114.00 (0-443-04823-1) Church.

Laparoscopic Hernia Repair. Michael S. Kavic. 160p. 1997. text 49.00 (90-5702-538-8, Harwood Acad Pubs) Gordon & Breach.

Laparoscopic Hernia Repair: A New Standard? Ed. by M. W. Buechler et al. (Progress in Surgery Ser.: Vol. 21). (Illus.). viii, 194p. 1995. 139.25 (3-8055-6047-8) S Karger.

Laparoscopic Hernia Repair: Problems & Solutions. David C. Dunn & Donald Menzies. 160p. 1995. 99.95 (0-86542-908-1) Blackwell Sci.

Laparoscopic Hysterectomy & Oopherectomy: A Practical Manual & Colour Atlas. Jeffrey H. Phipps. LC 93-7324. (Illus.). 120p. 1993. text 110.00 (0-443-04929-7) Church.

Laparoscopic Hysterectomy & Pelvic Floor Reconstruction. R. Garry & Harry Reich. (Illus.). 208p. 1993. 110.00 (0-632-03465-3) Blackwell Sci.

Laparoscopic Hysterectomy & Pelvic Floor Reconstruction. Ed. by C. Y. Liu. (Minimally Invasive Gynecology Ser.). (Illus.). 240p. 1995. 125.00 (0-86542-383-0) Blackwell Sci.

Laparoscopic Surgery. Garth H. Ballantyne et al. (Illus.). 736p. 1994. text 230.00 (0-7216-6648-5, W B Saunders Co) Harcrt Hlth Sci Grp.

Laparoscopic Surgery: A Colloquium. Ed. by Ronald C. Merrell & Robert M. Olson, III. LC 98-15837. (Illus.). 328p. 1998. 99.00 (0-387-98396-1) Spr-Verlag.

Laparoscopic Surgery: Principles & Practice. Ed. by Daniel B. Jones et al. LC 96-49577. (Illus.). 489p. 1997. text 82.00 (1-57626-007-0) Quality Med Pub.

Laparoscopic Surgery: Recent Developments in Basic Research & Clinical Update. Ed. by L. Krahenbuhl & M. W. Buchler. (Digestive Surgery Ser.: Vol. 15, No. 2, 1998). (Illus.). 104p. 1998. pap. 70.50 (3-8055-6677-8) S Karger.

Laparoscopic Surgery: The Implications Of Changing Practice, Vol. 8. Ed. by Michael Hobsley et al. (Arnold Publication). 348p. 1997. pap. text 42.95 (0-340-60760-2, Pub. by E A) OUP.

Laparoscopic Surgery in Gynecological Oncology. Dennis Querleu et al. LC 98-36147. (Illus.). 240p. 1999. 110.00 (0-86542-692-9) Blackwell Sci.

Laparoscopic Surgery in Urology. D. P. Griffith et al. (Illus.). 336p. 1996. text 179.00 (0-86577-548-6) Thieme Med Pubs.

***Laparoscopic Techniques & Advanced Endoscopic Suturing.** Stephen Chew et al. (Illus.). 300p. 2000. 152.50 (9971-69-234-1, Pub. by Sngapore Univ Pr) Coronet Bks.

Laparoscopic Urologic Surgery. Ed. by Leonard G. Gomella et al. LC 92-48530. 304p. 1993. text 142.00 (0-7817-0044-2) Lppncott W & W.

Laparoscopic Urologic Surgery. Ed. by Leonard G. Gomella et al. LC 92-48530. (Illus.). 304p. reprint ed. pap. 94.30 (0-608-09722-5, 206988800007) Bks Demand.

Laparoscopic Urology. Ed. by Ralph V. Clayman et al. LC 92-48957. (Illus.). 450p. 1992. pap. 90.00 (0-942219-41-4) Quality Med Pub.

Laparoscopic Urology. Ed. by Sakti Das & E. David Crawford. LC 93-47167. 1994. text 105.00 (0-7216-3766-3, W B Saunders Co) Harcrt Hlth Sci Grp.

Laparoscopic Urology. 2nd ed. Ed. by Ralph V. Clayman & Elspeth M. McDougall. 1997. 90.00 (1-57626-025-9, C2358) Quality Med Pub.

Laparoscopy: A Clinical Companion. Jean N. Saleh. (Illus.). 288p. 1988. text 115.00 (0-7216-2126-0, W B Saunders Co) Harcrt Hlth Sci Grp.

Laparoscopy & Imaging Techniques. G. Dagnini. Tr. by S. Pearcey from ITA. (Illus.). 272p. 1990. 217.00 (0-387-50999-2) Spr-Verlag.

Laparoscopy & You. Theresa Marousek et al. (Illus.). 40p. 1994. pap. 3.60 (0-317-59849-X) Budlong.

Laparoscopy in Urology, Pt. 1. M. J. Coptcoat & M. R. Joyce. LC 93-11903. (Illus.). 192p. 1994. 99.95 (0-632-03664-8) Blackwell Sci.

Laparoscopy in Women's Health: A Guide for Women. Andrew Friedman. Ed. by Edward E. Wallach. (Women's Health Ser.). (Illus.). 32p. 1996. pap. 2.95 (1-885274-16-5) Health InfoNet Inc.

Laparoscopy Systems & Instruments Markets. (Market Research Reports: No. 314). 190p. 1993. 795.00 (0-317-05007-9) Theta Corp.

LAPD: Patrol, Swat, Air Support, K-9, Crash & Homicide. Samuel M. Katz. LC 97-9046. (Power Ser.). (Illus.). 128p. 1997. pap. 16.95 (0-7603-0230-8) MBI Pubg.

LAPD Chiefs: The Famous, the Infamous & the Forgettable. John Babcock. 29.95 (0-9636381-8-1) Whyte Rose Pr.

La/Pensee De Milton see Milton: Man & Thinker

Lapham Family in America: 13,000 Descendants, Including Descendants of John, Devonshire, Eng. to Providence, RI, 1673, & Thomas, Kent, Eng. to Scituate, MA, 1634, Also Genealogical Notes of Other Lapham Families. B. B. Aldridge. 552p. 1991. reprint ed. pap. 85.00 (0-8328-1794-5); reprint ed. lib. bdg. 95.00 (0-8328-1793-7) Higginson Bk Co.

Lapham's Raiders: Guerrillas in the Philippines, 1942-1945. Robert Lapham & Bernard Norling. LC 95-20719. (Illus.). 312p. 1996. 27.50 (0-8131-1949-9) U Pr of Ky.

Lapham's Rules of Influence. Lewis Lapham. LC 98-33212. 224p. 1999. 19.95 (0-679-42605-1) Random.

L'/Aphasie see Living with Aphasia: Psychosocial Issues

***Lapices.** Alma Flor Ada. (SPA., Illus.). 1999. pap. text 5.95 (1-58105-424-6) Santillana.

Lapidaire Chretien: Its Composition, Its Influence, Its Sources. Leon Baisier. LC 71-94163. (Catholic University of America. Studies in Romance Languages & Literatures: No. 14). 1969. reprint ed. 37.50 (0-404-50314-4) AMS Pr.

Lapidary Carving for Creative Jewelry. Henry Hunt. (Illus.). 132p. 1993. pap. 25.00 (0-945005-10-5) Desert Pr.

Lapidary Inscriptions: Renaissance Essays for Donald A. Stone, Jr. Ed. by Barbara C. Bowen & Jerry C. Nash. LC 91-73323. (French Forum Monographs: No. 74). 205p. (Orig.). 1991. pap. 17.95 (0-917058-78-X) French Forum.

Lapidary Journal Index, 1947-1991: Forty-Four Years of Gem & Jewelry Arts, Minerals & Earth Sciences. 1992. 24.95 (1-880383-11-X) Primedia Inc.

Lapidus on Dulcimer. Joellen Lapidus. (Illus.). 228p. (Orig.). 1978. pap. 9.95 (0-89705-007-X) Almo Pubns.

Lapis Lazuli in Archaeological Contexts. Lissie Von Rosen. (Studies in Mediterranean Archaeology & Literature: No. 93). 56p. (Orig.). 1990. pap. 23.50 (91-7081-004-4, Pub. by P Astroms) Coronet Bks.

Lapis Philosophorum. 3rd ed. John R. Stahl. (Illus.). 24p. (C). 1973. 20.00 (0-945303-01-7) Evanescent Pr.

Lapis-Stone Staircase: Blues with Golden Inlay. Kali Sichen. 104p. (Orig.). 1987. pap. text 9.95 (0-916299-03-1) North Scale Co.

Lapita Peoples: Ancestors of the Oceanic World. Patrick V. Kirch. LC 96-8287. (Peoples of Southeast Asia & the Pacific Ser.). (Illus.). 320p. (C). 1996. 77.95 (1-55786-112-9); pap. 30.95 (1-57718-036-4) Blackwell Pubs.

***Laplace Distribution Revisited: New Applications.** S. Kotz et al. (Illus.). 256p. 2000. 64.95 (0-8176-4166-1) Birkhauser.

Laplace Transform. Richard Ernest Bellman & R. S. Roth. (Series in Modern Applied Mathematics: Vol. 3). 176p. 1984. text 33.00 (9971-966-73-5) World Scientific Pub.

Laplace Transform: Theory & Applications. Joel L. Schiff. LC 99-14037. 240p. 1999. 39.95 (0-387-98698-7) Spr-Verlag.

Laplace Transform Calculus for Partial Differential Operators. Thomas Donaldson. LC 74-7370. (Memoirs Ser.: No. 1/143). 166p. 1974. pap. 18.00 (0-8218-1843-0, MEMO/1/143) Am Math.

Laplace Transform Solution of Differential Equations. Robert D. Strum & John R. Ward. (Orig.). (C). 1968. pap. text 23.20 (0-13-522805-0) P-H.

Laplace Transforms. Murray R. Spiegel. 272p. (Orig.). (C). 1965. pap. 15.95 (0-07-060231-X) McGraw.

Laplace Transforms: Theory & Experiments. Theodore F. Bogart. 148p. 1983. pap. text 21.95 (0-471-87509-0) P-H.

Laplace Transforms & Control Systems Theory for Technology: Including Microprocessor Based Control System. Theodore F. Bogart. LC 81-14708. (Electronic Technology Ser.). 541p. 1982. text 47.95 (0-471-09044-1) P-H.

Laplace Transforms & Control Systems Theory for Technology: Including Microprocessor Based Control System. Theodore F. Bogart. LC 81-14708. (Electronic Technology Ser.). 200p. 1983. pap. text 16.00 (0-471-86325-4) P-H.

Laplacian on a Riemannian Manifold. S. Rosenberg. (London Mathematical Society Student Texts Ser.: No. 31). (Illus.). 182p. (C). 1997. text 59.95 (0-521-46300-9); pap. text 21.95 (0-521-46831-0) Cambridge U Pr.

La/Pluie d'Ete see Summer Rain: A Novel

Lapped Furrows: Correspondence, 1933-1967. Patrick Kavanagh. 300p. 1969. 50.00 (0-914612-02-6) Kavanagh.

Lappische Schildereyen? Michael Philipp. (Europaische Hochschulschriften Ser.: Reihe 36, Vol. 178). (Illus.). XII, 402p. 1998. pap. 56.95 (3-631-33337-4) P Lang Pubng.

Lapps, Vol. 17--17. Roberto Bosi. Tr. by James Cadell. LC 75-32455. 220p. 1977. reprint ed. lib. bdg. 38.50 (0-8371-8545-9, BOTL, Greenwood Pr) Greenwood.

Lapps - Reindeer Herders of Lapland, Reading Level 5. Alan James. (Original People Ser.: Set II). (Illus.). 48p. (J). (gr. 4-8). 1989. 12.50 (0-685-58811-4) Rourke Corp.

Lapps - Reindeer Herders of Lapland, Reading Level 5. Alan James. (Original People Ser.: Set II). (Illus.). 48p. (J). (gr. 4-8). 1989. lib. bdg. 16.67 (0-86625-263-0) Rourke Pubns.

Lapps & Scandinavians: Archaeological Finds from Northern Sweden. Inger Zachrisson. (Illus.). 136p. (Orig.). 1976. pap. text 34.00 (91-7402-005-6) Coronet Bks.

***Lapras Makes a Friend.** Kunimi Kawamura. (Pokemon Tales Ser.: No. 12). (Illus.). 18p. 2000. bds. 4.95 (1-56931-443-8, Pub. by Viz Commns Inc) Publishers Group.

La/Pratique de la Presence de Dieu see Kitchen Saint & the Heritage of Islam

Laprensa: Year of Spanish. 124p. (C). 1996. text 23.60 (0-536-59486-4) Pearson Custom.

La/Promesse de L'Aube see Promise at Dawn

Laproscopic Panhysterectomy with Reconstructive Posterior Culdeplasty & Vaginal Vault Suspension. Adam Ostrzenski. (Illus.). 126p. (C). 1994. 78.00 (0-9638210-0-8) Med Sci Pub.

Laps. Michael Blumenthal. LC 84-8601. 64p. 1984. 15.00 (0-87023-459-5); pap. 9.95 (0-87023-460-9) U of Mass Pr.

Lapsed & the Unity of the Church. St. Cyprian of Carthage. 1982. pap. 3.95 (0-89981-038-1) Eastern Orthodox.

Lapsed W. A. S. P. Poems, 1978-89. Victor Coleman. LC 95-102393. 128p. 1994. pap. 12.00 (1-55022-221-X, Pub. by ECW) Genl Dist Srvs.

Lapses. John Crouse. LC 94-80137. 69p. 1995. 9.00 (1-882022-25-4) O Bks.

Lapses from Full Employment. Arthur C. Pigou. LC 76-52488. (Reprints of Economic Classics Ser.). viii, 72p. 1978. reprint ed. lib. bdg. 19.50 (0-678-01226-1) Kelley.

Lapses in Mathematical Reasoning. V. M. Bradis. LC 99-45828. 216p. 1999. pap. text 7.95 (0-486-40918-X) Dover.

***Lapsing into a Comma: A Curmudgeon's Guide to the Many Things That Can Go Wrong in Print -- And How To Avoid Them.** Bill Walsh. LC 99-53468. 256p. 2000. pap. 14.95 (0-8092-2535-2, 253520, Contemporary Bks) NTC Contemp Pub Co.

Lapsing Out: Embodiments of Death & Rebirth in the Last Writings of D. H. Lawrence. Donald Gutierrez. LC 78-75177. 184p. 1970. 28.50 (0-8386-2293-3) Fairleigh Dickinson.

Lapsit Services for the Very Young: A How-to-Do-It Manual. Linda L. Ernst. LC 95-16177. (How-to-Do-It Manuals Ser.: Vol. 48). (Illus.). 136p. (Orig.). 1995. pap. 38.50 (1-55570-185-X) Neal-Schuman.

***Lapsit Services for the Very Young II: A How-to-Do-It Manual.** Linda Ernst. (How-to-Do-It Manuals for Librarians Ser.). 150p. 2000. pap. 38.50 (1-55570-391-7) Neal-Schuman.

Lapsley Saga. Winifred K. Vass. LC 96-72388. (Illus.). 256p. 1996. 24.95 (1-57736-023-0) Providence Hse.

Lapsnatcher. Bruce Coville. LC 96-21611. (Illus.). 32p. (J). 1997. 15.95 (0-8167-4233-2) BrdgeWater.

Lapstrake Boatbuilding. Walter J. Simmons. (Boatbuilding Ser.: Vol. 2). (Illus.). 98p. 1986. pap. 20.00 (0-924947-01-2) Duck Trap Pr.

Lapstrake Boatbuilding. 3rd ed. Walter J. Simmons. (Illus.). 134p. 1993. spiral bd. 24.95 (0-924947-09-8) Duck Trap Pr.

Laptop Code. Ed. by HarperCollins Publishing Staff. 1942. 200.00 (0-06-009995-X) HarperTrade.

Laptop (IUP) Chuaprasert. pap. text 49.99 (0-471-37520-9) Wiley.

Laptop Publishing for the Field Linguists: An Approach Based on Microsoft Word. Ed. by Priscilla M. Kew & Gary F. Simons. (Occasional Publications in Academic Computing). 150p. 1989. pap. 13.00 (0-88312-637-0) S I L Intl.

Laptops & Mobile Computing. DDC Publishing Staff. 1994. spiral bd. 12.00 (1-56243-136-6, LM-18) DDC Pub.

Lapwai Mission Press. Wilfred P. Schoenberg. Ed. by Tom Trusky. LC 94-70091. (Illus.). 88p. (Orig.). 1994. 19.95 (0-932129-18-8); pap. 10.95 (0-932129-19-6) Heming W Studies.

Lapwing. Peter Weaver. (Natural History Ser.: No. 14). (Illus.). 24p. 1989. pap. 5.25 (0-85263-855-8, Pub. by Shire Pubns) Parkwest Pubns.

Lara. Bernardine Evaristo. 1997. pap. 9.95 (1-899860-45-2) A Royal Pub.

Lara & the Field Mice. Peggie C. Mitchell. (Illus.). 51p. (J). 1998. write for info. (0-7541-0251-3, Pub. by Minerva Pr) Unity Dist.

***Lara Croft: The Art of Virtual Seduction.** Prima Staff & Mark Cohen. LC 00-10073. (Official Strategy Guides Ser.). (Illus.). 139p. (YA). 2000. pap. 19.99 (0-7615-2696-X) Prima Pub.

Lara Croft Cybermodel. Ed. by Chris Owen. (Illus.). 96p. 1998. 22.50 (0-7893-0244-6, Pub. by Universe) St Martin.

***Lara Gets Even.** Katherine Applegate. LC 98-94950. (Making Out Ser.: No. 16). (Illus.). 176p. (YA). (gr. 7-12). 1999. mass mkt. 3.99 (0-380-80872-2, Avon Bks) Morrow Avon.

***Lara Gets Lucky.** Katherine Applegate. LC 99-95488. (Making Out Ser.: No. 23). 176p. (YA). (gr. 7-12). 2000. mass mkt. 3.99 (0-380-81527-3, Avon Bks) Morrow Avon.

Lara Rains & Colonial Rites. Howard A. Fergus. LC 98-124573. 88p. 1999. pap. 12.95 (0-948833-95-5, Pub. by Peepal Tree Pr) Paul & Co Pubs.

Larabi's Ox: Stories of Morocco. Tony Ardizzone. LC 92-5306. (Illus.). 250p. 1992. pap. 13.00 (0-915943-72-7) Milkweed Ed.

***Larach.** large type unabridged ed. Alexandra Raife. 2000. 26.95 (0-7531-5940-6, 159406, Pub. by ISIS Lrg Prnt) ISIS Pub.

Laramide Basement Deformation in the Rocky Mountain Foreland of the Western United States. Ed. by C. J. Schmidt et al. (Special Papers: No. 280). 1993. 47.50 (0-8137-2280-2) Geol Soc.

Laramide Folding Associated with Basement Block Faulting in the Western United States. Ed. by Vincent Matthews. LC 78-54346. (Geological Society of America, Memoir Ser.: No. 151). 400p. reprint ed. pap. 124.00 (0-608-13879-7, 202373100033) Bks Demand.

Laramie. Mark Dunster. 83p. (Orig.). 1975. pap. 4.00 (0-89642-024-8) Linden Pubs.

Laramie County, Wyoming. Jean Bastian. (Illus.). 471p. 1987. 60.00 (0-88107-076-9) Curtis Media.

***Laramie Holds the Range.** Frank H. Spearman. (Illus.). 2000. pap. 19.95 (1-889439-10-X) Paper Tiger NJ.

***Laramie Nelson: Lawless Land.** Romer Zane Grey. 192p. 1999. pap. 3.99 (0-8439-4634-2, Leisure Bks) Dorchester Pub Co.

***Laramie Nelson: Other Side of the Canyon.** Romer Zane Grey. 224p. 1999. pap. 4.50 (0-8439-4610-5, Leisure Bks) Dorchester Pub Co.

Laramie Project. Moises Kaufman. Date not set. pap. 5.95 (0-8222-1780-5) Dramatists Play.

***Laramie Wire: Auditing Cases.** 2000. teacher ed. write for info. (0-13-016920-X) P-H.

***Laramie Wire Manufacturing: Auditing Cases.** 2000. 4.00 (0-13-016929-3) P-H.

Lara's Book: Lara Croft & the Tomb Raider Phenomenon. Douglas Coupland & Kip Ward. LC 98-65455. 200p. 1998. per. 19.99 (0-7615-1580-1) Prima Pub.

***Lara's Lover.** Penny Richards. 2001. mass mkt. 4.50 (0-373-24366-9, 1-24366-9) Silhouette.

Larceny & Old Lace. Tamar Myers. 224p. (Orig.). 1996. mass mkt. 5.99 (0-380-78239-1, Avon Bks) Morrow Avon.

Larch: Languages & Tools for Formal Specification. James J. Horning & John V. Guttag. LC 92-44571. (Texts & Monographs in Computer Science). (Illus.). 250p. 1993. 48.95 (*0-387-94006-5*) Spr-Verlag.

Larch Plantation. Angus Martin. (C). 1989. 39.00 (*0-86554-019-5*, Pub. by Saltire Soc) St Mut.

Larch Plantation. Angus Martin. 1993. pap. 21.00 (*0-86334-069-5*, Pub. by Saltire Soc) St Mut.

Larch Plantation. Angus Martin. 1995. pap. 39.95 (*0-7855-2795-8*, Pub. by Saltire Soc) St Mut.

L'arche des Kerguelen: Voyage aux iles de la Desolation see Arch of Kerguelen: Voyage to the Islands of Desolation

L'Architettura del Paesaggio Americano see American Landscape

Larchmont Manor: A Tale of Trees & Houses. Esther Eder. (Illus.). 1984. pap. 40.00 (*0-9614252-0-2*) Eder Pub.

Larchmont, N. Y. People & Places: Pre-History to 1892. Judith D. Spikes. LC 91-71485. (Illus.). 142p. (Orig.). 1991. pap. 19.95 (*0-9628957-1-7*) Fountain Sq.

Larchmont, New York, the Way It Was: Picture Postcards of Old Larchmont. James H. Levi & Constance A. Levi. (Illus.). 52p. 1990. pap. 14.95 (*0-9628437-0-9*) J H Levi.

Lardcake. David McGimpsey. LC 96-178003. 80p. 1996. pap. 12.00 (*1-55022-278-3*, Pub. by ECW) Genl Dist Srvs.

Larder Chef. 3rd ed. M. J. Leto. 1989. pap. 39.95 (*0-7506-0943-5*) Buttrwrth-Heinemann.

Larder Invaded: Reflections on Three Centuries of Philadelphia Food & Drink. Mary A. Hines et al. LC 87-8. (Illus.). 116p. (Orig.). 1987. pap. 10.00 (*0-914076-70-1*) Lib Co Phila.

Laredo. San Antonio Cartographers Staff. 1995. 2.95 (*0-671-56274-6*) Macmillan.

Laredo's Land. large type ed. Jake Douglas. (Linford Western Library Ser.). 256p. 1997. pap. 16.99 (*0-7089-5125-2*, Linford) Ulverscroft.

La/Regle de saint Benoit, VII, Commentaire doctrinal et spirituel see Rule of St. Benedict: A Doctrinal & Spiritual Commentary

La/Revolution Inconnue see Unknown Revolution: 1917-1922

Larga Noche. Kate William. (Sweet Valley High Ser.: No. 5).Tr. of All Night Long. (YA). (gr. 7 up). 1993. 13.05 (*0-606-10467-4*, Pub. by Turtleback) Demco.

Large Air-Cooled Engine Service Manual, Through 1992, Vol. 2. LC 92-75482. (Illus.). 384p. Date not set. pap. 26.95 (*0-87288-523-2*, LES2-1) Intertec Pub.

Large Air-Cooled Engine Service Manual, 1988 & Prior, Vol. 1. 4th ed. Intertec Publishing Staff. LC 89-45328. (Illus.). 344p. (C). 1989. pap. text 26.95 (*0-87288-330-2*, LES1-4) Intertec Pub.

Large Amplitude Motion in Molecules II. Ed. by F. L. Boschke. (Topics in Current Chemistry Ser.: Vol. 82). (Illus.). 1979. 74.95 (*0-387-09311-7*) Spr-Verlag.

Large & Advanced Battery Technology & Markets. Donald Saxman. LC 98-120781. 416p. 1997. 3150.00 (*1-56965-451-4*, GB-197) BCC.

***Large & in Charge.** Robb Armstrong. (Patrick's Pals Ser.: No. 7). (Illus.). 96p. (J). (gr. 2-7). 1999. pap. 3.99 (*0-06-107073-4*) HarpC.

Large & Middle Enterprises Catalogue of Chinese Printing Industry. 225p. 1996. 160.00 (*0-614-11853-0*, Pub. by HUWEI Cnslts) Am Overseas Bk Co.

Large Animal Anesthesia: Principles & Techniques. Thomas W. Riebold et al. LC 81-15609. 162p. reprint ed. pap. 50.30 (*0-7837-2174-9*, 204251200004) Bks Demand.

Large Animal Anesthesia: Principles & Techniques. 2nd ed. Thomas W. Riebold et al. LC 94-24471. (Illus.). 312p. 1995. text 46.95 (*0-8138-0774-3*) Iowa St U Pr.

Large Animal Internal Medicine. Timothy H. Ogilvie. LC 97-33109. (The National Veterinary Medical Series for Independent Study). 600p. 1997. write for info. (*0-683-18033-9*) Lppncott W & W.

Large Animal Internal Medicine: Diseases of Horses, Cattle, Sheep, & Goats. 2nd ed. Ed. by Bradford P. Smith. LC 95-47494. (Illus.). 2112p. (C). (gr. 13). 1996. text 160.00 (*0-8151-7724-0*, 23783) Mosby Inc.

Large Animal Neurology: A Handbook for Veterinary Clinicians. Ian G. Mayhew. LC 88-34037. (Illus.). 380p. 1989. pap. text 58.00 (*0-8121-1183-4*) Lppncott W & W.

Large Animal Urogenital Surgery. 2nd ed. Dwight F. Wolfe & H. David Moll. LC 98-26257. 464p. 1998. 99.00 (*0-683-09230-8*) Lppncott W & W.

Large Animals in Everyday Life: Stories. Wendy Brenner. 168p. 1997. pap. 11.00 (*0-393-31648-3*) Norton.

Large Animals in Everyday Life: Stories. Wendy Brenner. LC 95-21692. 168p. 1996. 22.95 (*0-8203-1794-2*) U of Ga Pr.

Large Area Vegetation Surveys, Baleul, 1994: Red. Ed. by Jean-Marie Gehu. (Colloque Phytosociologiques Ser.: Vol. XXIII). (ENG & FRE., Illus.). xxx, 735p. 1995. 171.00 (*3-443-70012-8*, Pub. by Gebruder Borntraeger) Balogh.

Large Area Wafer Growth & Processing for Electronic & Photonic Devices - State-of-the-Art Program on Compound Semiconductors XX. J. P. Vilcot et al. (Proceedings Ser.: Vol. 94-18). 336p. 1995. pap. 42.00 (*1-56677-075-0*) Electrochem Soc.

Large Bowel Cancer: Clinical & Basic Science Research, 3. Ed. by Anthony J. Mastromarino & Michael G. Brattain. LC 85-515. (Cancer Research Monographs: Vol. 3). 204p. 1985. 55.00 (*0-275-91319-8*, C1319, Praeger Pubs) Greenwood.

Large Bowel Cancer: Policy, Prevention, Research & Treatment. Ed. by P. Rozen et al. (Frontiers of Gastrointestinal Research Ser.: Vol. 18). (Illus.). viii, 302p. 1991. 242.75 (*3-8055-5269-6*) S Karger.

***Large (c=24) Polycyclic Aromatic Hydrocarbons: Chemistry & Analysis.** John F. Fetzer. LC 00-26054. (Chemical Analysis Ser.). (Illus.). 2001. write for info. (*0-471-36354-5*) Wiley.

Large Catechism Pt. 1: Bible Study. Donald J. Pieper. 1998. 37.99 (*0-8100-0811-4*, 22N0886) Northwest Pub.

***Large Catechism Pt. II: Bible Study.** Donald Pieper. 1999. 37.99 (*0-8100-0812-2*) Northwest Pub.

Large Catechism of Martin Luther. Martin Luther. 105p. 1963. text 14.00 (*0-8006-0885-2*, 1-885, Fortress Pr) Augsburg Fortress.

Large Cichlids: American Cichlids 2: A Handbook for Their Identification, Care & Breeding. Horst Linke & Wolfgang Staeck. (Illus.). 200p. 1995. 28.95 (*1-56465-169-X*, 16758) Tetra Pr.

Large Classes in Action. David Cross. Ed. by C. Vaughan James. LC 95-5585. (International English Language Teaching Ser.). (C). 1998. pap. 18.75 (*0-13-186396-7*) P-H.

Large Clusters of Atoms & Molecules: Proceedings of the NATO Advanced Study Institute on Large Clusters of Atoms & Molecules: Erice, Sicily, Italy, June 19-29, 1995. Ed. by T. P. Martin. LC 96-192. (NATO ASI Series E: Applied Sciences: Vol. 313). 548p. (C). 1996. text 276.00 (*0-7923-3937-1*) Kluwer Academic.

Large Commercial Farmers & Land Reform in Africa: The Case of Zimbabwe. Peter Von Blackenburg. 160p. 1995. 77.95 (*1-85972-029-3*, Pub. by Avebry) Ashgate Pub Co.

Large Concrete Buildings. Rangan. 320p. (C). 1996. 99.95 (*0-582-10130-1*) Addison-Wesley.

Large Corporation & Contemporary Classes. Maurice Zeitlin. (Studies in Political Economy Ser.). 300p. (C). 1989. text 42.00 (*0-8135-1475-4*); pap. text 18.00 (*0-8135-1476-2*) Rutgers U Pr.

Large Dairy Herd Management. H. H. Van Horn & C. J. Wilcox. 1993. 60.00 (*0-9634491-0-9*) Am Dairy Sci.

Large Dams: Learning from the Past, Looking to the Future. LC 97-202535. 150p. 1997. pap. 25.00 (*0-8213-4028-X*, 14028) World Bank.

Large Declaration Concerning the Late Tumults in Scotland: By the King. LC 72-181. (English Experience Ser.: No. 149). 1969. reprint ed. 80.00 (*90-221-0149-5*) Walter J Johnson.

Large Deformation of Materials with Complex Rheological Properties at Normal & High Pressure. V. I. Levitas. 323p. 1996. 175.00 (*1-56072-085-9*) Nova Sci Pubs.

Large Deformations of Solids: Physical Basis & Mathematical Modeling: Proceedings of the International Colloquium "Deformation in the World Today", Ecole Polytechnique, Paris, September 30 - October 2, 1985. International Colloquium "Deformation in the World. Ed. by John H. Gittus & J. Zarka. 528p. 1987. 138.75 (*1-85166-016-X*) Elsevier.

Large Deviation Techniques in Decision, Simulation & Estimation. James A. Buckley. LC 89-77144. 270p. 1990. 149.95 (*0-471-61856-X*) Wiley.

***Large Deviations.** Frank den Hollander. LC 99-58913. (FIM Ser.: Vol. 14). 143p. 2000. 49.00 (*0-8218-1989-5*) Am Math.

Large Deviations & Applications. S. R. Varadhan. LC 83-51046. (CBMS-NSF Regional Conference Series in Applied Mathematics: No. 46). v, 75p. 1984. pap. text 22.50 (*0-89871-189-4*) Soc Indus-Appl Math.

Large Deviations & the Malliavin Calculus. Jean-Michel Bismut. (Progress in Mathematics Ser.: Vol. 45). 216p. 1984. 45.00 (*0-8176-3220-4*) Birkhauser.

Large Deviations for Discrete-Time Processes with Averaging. O. V. Gulinsky & A. Yu Veretennikov. 198p. 1992. 130.00 (*90-6764-148-0*) Coronet Bks.

Large Deviations for Performance Analysis: Queues, Communication & Computing. Adam Shwartz & Alan Weiss. LC 94-40138. 560p. (gr. 13). 1995. ring bd. 69.95 (*0-412-06311-5*, Chap & Hall CRC) CRC Pr.

Large Deviations, Free Energy Functional & Quasi-Potential for a Mean Field Model of Interacting Diffusions. D. Dawson & J. Gartner. LC 89-164. (Memoirs Ser.: Vol. 78/398). 94p. 1989. pap. 16.00 (*0-8218-2461-9*, MEMO/78/398) Am Math.

Large Deviations, Free Energy Functional & Quasi-Potential for a Mean Field Model of Interacting Diffusions. Donald A. Dawson. LC 89-164. (American Mathematical Society Ser.: Vol. 398). 100p. reprint ed. pap. 31.00 (*0-608-10512-0*, 205279500009) Bks Demand.

Large Deviations Techniques & Applications. 2nd ed. Amir Dembo & Ofer Zeitouni. Ed. by A. V. Balakrishnan et al. LC 97-45236. (Applications of Mathematics Ser.: Vol. 38). (Illus.). 416p. 1998. text 59.95 (*0-387-98406-2*) Spr-Verlag.

Large Dictionary Dutch to English. 2nd ed. (DUT & ENG.). 1600p. 1997. 125.00 (*0-320-00022-2*) Fr & Eur.

Large Dictionary Dutch to French. 2nd ed. (DUT & FRE.). 1600p. 1997. 125.00 (*0-320-00018-4*) Fr & Eur.

Large Dictionary Dutch to German. 2nd ed. (DUT & GER.). 1600p. 1997. 125.00 (*0-320-00020-6*) Fr & Eur.

Large Dictionary English to Dutch. 2nd ed. (DUT & ENG.). 1600p. 1997. 125.00 (*0-320-00021-4*) Fr & Eur.

Large Dictionary French to Dutch. 2nd ed. (DUT & FRE.). 1600p. 1997. 125.00 (*0-320-00017-6*) Fr & Eur.

Large Dictionary German to Dutch. 2nd ed. (DUT & GER.). 1600p. 1997. 125.00 (*0-320-00019-2*) Fr & Eur.

Large Dictionary of French Citations: Le Grand Dictionaire des Citations Francaises. Jean-Yves Dournon. (FRE.). 906p. 1982. 75.00 (*0-8288-2284-0*, M14146) Fr & Eur.

Large Diesel Engine Service Manual. 192p. 1983. pap. 26.95 (*0-87288-033-8*, LDS-1) Intertec Pub.

Large Drawings & Objects: Objects from the Arkansas Arts Center. Townsend Wolfe et al. (Illus.). 128p. 1996. pap. 35.00 (*1-884240-17-8*) Arkansas Art Ctr.

Large Encyclopedia of Wine: Gran Enciclopedia del Vino. Hugh Johnson. (SPA.). 544p. 1983. 120.00 (*0-8288-0760-4*, S60534) Fr & Eur.

Large English-Arabic (Al-Mughni Al-Akbar) Hasan S. Karmi. (ARA & ENG.). 1728p. 1987. 85.00 (*0-86685-420-7*, LDL4207, Pub. by Librairie du Liban) Intl Bk Ctr.

Large Estate in Egypt in the Third Century B. C. A Study in Economic History. Michael Rostovtzeff. Ed. by Moses Finley. LC 79-5003. (Ancient Economic History Ser.). 1979. reprint ed. lib. bdg. 27.95 (*0-405-12392-2*) Ayer.

Large Estates & Small Holdings in Europe in the Middle Ages & Modern Times. P. Gunst & T. Hoffman. 400p. (C). 1982. 100.00 (*963-05-3160-7*, Pub. by Akade Kiado) St Mut.

Large Facilities in Physics. M. Jacob & H. Schopper. 450p. 1995. text 99.00 (*981-02-2157-6*) World Scientific Pub.

Large Family: A Blessing & a Challenge. Eugene Diamond. LC 95-79946. 167p. (Orig.). 1996. pap. 9.95 (*0-89870-571-1*) Ignatius Pr.

Large Family System. James H. Bossard & Eleanor S. Boll. LC 74-25536. 325p. 1975. reprint ed. lib. bdg. 38.50 (*0-8371-7871-1*, BOLF, Greenwood Pr) Greenwood.

Large Finite Systems. Ed. by Joshua Jortner et al. (C). 1987. text 247.50 (*90-277-2610-8*) Kluwer Academic.

Large Fire Scene Operations. (Training in a Box Ser.). 50p. 1998. ring bd. 49.00 (*1-57927-038-7*) APCO Inst.

Large Forest Fires. J. M. Moreno. (Illus.). viii, 237p. 1998. pap. 69.50 (*90-73348-80-3*) Balogh.

Large-Format Photography. 2nd rev. ed. Eastman Kodak Company Staff. LC 95-71544. (Illus.). 112p. (C). 1998. pap. 19.95 (*0-87985-771-4*, O-18e, Kodak) Saunders Photo.

Large French-Breton Dictionary: Grand Dictionnaire Francais-Breton. Fransez Vallee. (BRE & FRE.). 992p. 1981. pap. 150.00 (*0-8288-1118-0*, M14497) Fr & Eur.

Large French-Hungarian Dictionary: Grand Dictionnaire Francais-Hongrois, 2 vols. 4th rev. ed. S. Eckhardt. (FRE & HUN.). 2126p. 1981. 125.00 (*0-8288-0516-4*, M8560) Fr & Eur.

Large French-Polish Dictionary: Grand Dictionnaire Francais-Polonais. Wiedza Powszechna. (FRE & POL.). 2220p. 1984. 95.00 (*0-8288-0481-8*, F 53100) Fr & Eur.

Large German-Polish Dictionary: Grosswoerterbuch Deutsch-Polnisch, 2 vols. 6th ed. J. Pipprek. (GER & POL.). 2116p. 1984. 150.00 (*0-8288-0484-2*, F33210) Fr & Eur.

***Large Graphics: Design Innovations for Oversized Spaces.** Cheryl Dangel Cullen. (Illus.). 2000. 45.00 (*1-56496-692-5*) Rockport Pubs.

Large Group: Dynamics & Therapy. Ed. by Lionel Kreeger. LC 75-595075. 344p. pap. 106.70 (*0-608-13604-2*, 205126400093) Bks Demand.

Large Group: Dynamics & Therapy. Ed. by Lionel Kreeger. 344p. 1994. pap. text 33.00 (*0-946439-02-8*, Pub. by H Karnac Bks Ltd) Other Pr LLC.

Large Group Guidance Activities: A K-12 Sourcebook. Ed. by Joe Wittmer & Diane W. Thompson. LC 95-60208. (Illus.). 240p. (Orig.). (C). 1995. pap. text 21.95 (*0-932796-70-2*) Ed Media Corp.

Large Group Interventions: Engaging the Whole System for Rapid Change. Barbara B. Bunker & Billie T. Alban. LC 96-26883. (The Jossey-Bass Business & Management Ser.). 1996. 30.95 (*0-7879-0324-8*) Jossey-Bass.

Large Hazon-Garzanti Italian-English, English-Italian Dictionary: Dizionario Hazon Garzanti Italiano-Inglese-Italiano. 26th ed. M. Hazon. (ENG & ITA.). 2112p. 1980. 125.00 (*0-8288-0366-8*, M9186) Fr & Eur.

***Large Horizontal Country Cottage Collection Photo Album.** Rutledge Hill Press Staff. (Montague House Photograph Albums Ser.). (Illus.). 1999. write for info. (*1-55853-634-5*) Rutledge Hill Pr.

***Large Horizontal Floral Victorian Design Photo Album.** (Montague House Photograph Albums Ser.). 1999. 19.99 (*1-55853-509-8*) Rutledge Hill Pr.

Large Hungarian-French Dictionary: Grand Dictionnaire Hongrois-Francais, 2 vols. 3rd ed. S. Eckhardt. (FRE & HUN.). 2558p. 1984. 125.00 (*0-8288-0517-2*, M8561) Fr & Eur.

Large Igneous Provinces: Continental, Oceanic, & Planetary Flood Volcanism, Vol. 100. Ed. by John J. Mahoney & Millard F. Coffin. LC 97-43026. (Geophysical Monograph Ser.). 1997. 65.00 (*0-87590-082-8*) Am Geophysical.

Large Installation System Administration of Windows NT Conference Proceedings. 88p. 1998. pap. 24.00 (*1-880446-96-0*) USENIX Assn.

Large International Firm in Developing Countries. Edith T. Penrose. LC 76-7581. (Illus.). 311p. 1976. reprint ed. lib. bdg. 65.00 (*0-8371-8850-4*, PELI, Greenwood Pr) Greenwood.

Large Intestine: Physiology, Pathophysiology & Disease. Ed. by Sidney F. Phillips et al. LC 91-14685. (Illus.). 923p. reprint ed. pap. 200.00 (*0-608-09726-8*, 206989300007) Bks Demand.

Large Intestine: Physiology, Pathophysiology, & Diseases. Sidney F. Phillips et al. (Illus.). 928p. 1991. text 223.00 (*0-88167-777-9*) Lppncott W & W.

Large Ion Beams: Fundamentals of Generation & Propagation. A. Theodore Forrester. LC 87-24186. 325p. 1988. 178.50 (*0-471-62557-4*) Wiley.

Large Ions: Their Vaporization, Detection & Structural Analysis. Ed. by Tomas Baer et al. LC 96-6758. (Series in Ion Chemistry & Physics). 198p. 1997. 195.00 (*0-471-96239-2*) Wiley.

Large Jack-Up Applications to Reduce Satellite & Marginal Field Development Costs. Ed. by R. Cliver Hinton. (C). 1989. 110.00 (*0-89771-723-6*, Pub. by Lorne & MacLean Marine) St Mut.

Large Jack-Up Applications to Reduce Satellite & Marginal Field Development Costs. R. Oliver Hinton. 1989. 140.00 (*90-6314-543-8*, Pub. by Lorne & MacLean Marine) St Mut.

Large Lakes: Ecological Structure & Function. Ed. by M. M. Tilzer et al. (Contemporary Bioscience Ser.). xviii, 691p. 1990. 247.95 (*0-387-52103-8*) Spr-Verlag.

Large Land Holdings in Ohio & Their Operation. Paul G. Minneman. Ed. by Stuart Bruchey. LC 78-56664. (Management of Public Lands in the U. S. Ser.). 1979. lib. bdg. 18.95 (*0-405-11344-7*) Ayer.

Large Larousse English-Spanish, Spanish-English Dictionary: Gran Diccionario Larousse Espanol-Ingles-Espanol. rev. ed. Pelayo Garcia. (ENG & SPA.). 1612p. 1983. 49.95 (*0-8288-0734-5*, S31547) Fr & Eur.

Large Loop Excision of the Transformation Zone: A Practical Guide to LLETZ. Ed. by Walter Prendiville. LC 92-49021. 1992. write for info. (*0-442-31708-5*) Chapman & Hall.

Large Macaws: Their Care, Breeding & Conservation. Joanne Abramson et al. Ed. by Jorgen B. Thomsen. (Illus.). 552p. 1996. lib. bdg. 170.00 (*0-9635964-0-3*) Raintree Pubns.

Large Magellanic Cloud. Paul W. Hodge & Frances W. Wright. LC 67-61082. (Smithsonian Publication: No. 4699). 114p. reprint ed. pap. 35.40 (*0-608-17753-9*, 205649800069) Bks Demand.

Large Mammals Activity Book. (Illus.). (J). (ps-6). pap. 2.95 (*0-565-01014-X*, Pub. by Natural Hist Mus) Parkwest Pubns.

Large Mammals of the Central Rockies: A Guide to Their Locations & Ecology. Stephen C. Torbit. (Illus.). 72p. (YA). (gr. 12). 1987. pap. 7.95 (*0-9618450-0-7*) Bennet Creek.

Large Mammals of Yellowstone & Grand Teton National Parks. Karen Craighead. LC 79-65734. (Illus.). 31p. 1999. 2.50 (*0-934948-00-3*, 10247) Yellowstone Assn.

***Large Marine Ecosystems of the Indian Ocean: Assessment, Sustainability & Management.** Kenneth Sherman et al. LC 97-43188. (Large Marine Ecosystem Ser.). (Illus.). 394p. 1998. pap. 77.00 (*0-632-04318-0*) Blackwell Sci.

***Large Marine Ecosystems of the Pacific Rim: Assessment, Sustainability & Management.** Qisheng Tang & Kenneth Sherman. LC 98-18549. (Large Marine Ecosystem Ser.). (Illus.). 1999. pap. 77.00 (*0-632-04336-9*) Blackwell Sci.

Large Meteorite Impacts & Planetary Evolution. Ed. by Burkhard O. Dressler et al. LC 94-34436. (Special Papers: 293). 1994. pap. 72.75 (*0-8137-2293-4*) Geol Soc.

Large Mine Permits & Plants in Utah. Roger L. Bon. (Public Information Ser.: 33). (Illus.). 1996. pap. 2.70 (*1-55791-372-2*, PI33) Utah Geological Survey.

Large Motor Play. Jenny C. Rose. Ed. by Gayle Bittinger. (101 Tips for Toddler Teachers Ser.). (Illus.). 24p. (Orig.). 1997. pap. 3.95 (*1-57029-155-1*, 4016) Totline Pubns.

Large N Expansion in Quantum Field Theory & Statistical Physics. E. Brezin & S. R. Wadia. 600p. 1993. text 162.00 (*981-02-0455-8*); pap. text 86.00 (*981-02-0456-6*) World Scientific Pub.

Large Newspaper Printing Presses & Components Thereof, Whether Assembled or Unassembled, from Germany & Japan: An International Trade Investigation. 212p. pap. text 50.00 (*0-7881-4466-9*) DIANE Pub.

Large or Small, Bronze or Wood, Painted or Plain: Problems & Solutions in Sculpture. David W. Steadman. (Illus.). 31p. 1981. pap. 3.00 (*0-940744-33-3*) Chrysler Museum.

Large-Order Behaviour of Perturbation Theory. Ed. by J. C. Le Guillou & J. Zinn-Justin. (Current Physics Sources & Comments Ser.: Vol. 7). 560p. 1990. 145.00 (*0-685-45103-8*, North Holland); pap. 75.50 (*0-444-88597-8*, North Holland) Elsevier.

Large Order Perturbation Theory & Summation Methods in Quantum Mechanics. G. A. Arteca et al. (Lecture Notes in Chemistry Ser.: Vol. 53). (Illus.). xi, 644p. 1990. 94.95 (*0-387-52847-4*) Spr-Verlag.

Large Order Structural Eigenanalysis Techniques: Algorithms for Finite Element Systems. N. S. Sehmi. 1989. text 84.95 (*0-470-21497-X*) P-H.

Large Panel Building System. (PCI Journal Reprints Ser.). 16p. 1969. pap. 12.00 (*0-686-40018-6*, JR75) P-PCI.

***Large Penguins, 6 vols.** Kimberly Joan Williams & Erik Daniel Stoops. (Young Explorer Series II). 32p. (J). (gr. 3-7). 2000. lib. bdg. 18.60 (*1-890475-21-1*) Faulkners Pub.

Large Plastic Deformation of Crystalline Aggregates. Ed. by C. Teodosiu. (CISM International Centre for Mechanical Sciences Ser.: No. 376). viii, 293p. 1997. pap. 72.00 (*3-211-82909-1*) Spr-Verlag.

Large Plastic Deformations: Fundamentals Aspects & Applications to Metal Forming. Ed. by C. Teodosiu. 484p. 1993. 128.00 (*90-5410-317-5*, Pub. by A A Balkema) Ashgate Pub Co.

Large Polish-German Dictionary: Grosswoerterbuch Polnisch-Deutsch, 2 vols. 5th ed. J. Pipprek. (GER & POL.). 2100p. 1984. 125.00 (*0-8288-0485-0*, M9128) Fr & Eur.

Large Power Transformers. K. Karsai et al. Ed. by L. Kiss. (Studies in Electrical & Electronic Engineering: No. 25). 616p. 1987. 323.50 (*0-444-99511-0*) Elsevier.

Large Print Assortment. Random House Staff. 1998. pap. text 26.00 (*0-676-59839-0*) Random.

L

*Large Print Bible. World Bible Publishing Staff. 1184p. 1999. lthr. 39.99 (0-529-11008-3) World Publng.
*Large Print Bible. large type ed. 2000. 85.00 (0-19-528234-5) OUP.
Large Print Book & Its User. Lorna J. Bell. LC 80-147607. (Library Association Research Publication: No. 22). (Illus.). 326p. reprint ed. pap. 101.10 (0-7837-5299-7, 204505300005) Bks Demand.
Large Print Catholic Prayer Book. large type ed. Ruth Hannan. 121p. 1991. lthr. 7.95 (0-87973-483-3, 483) Our Sunday Visitor.
Large Print Computer Dictionary. large type ed. Donald D. Spencer. LC 94-32000. (Illus.). 196p. (Orig.). 1995. pap. text 24.95 (0-89218-242-3) Camelot Pub.
Large Print Crossword Challenge, Vol. 9. large type ed. Ed. by Daniel Stark & Roslyn Stark. 240p. 1999. 12.95 (0-7624-0455-8) Running Pr.
*Large Print Crosswords Challege #11. Daniel Stark. 2000. pap. text 12.95 (0-7624-0691-7) Running Pr.
Large Print Crosswords Challenge, No. 1. large type ed. Ed. by Daniel Stark & Roslyn Stark. (LP Crosswords Ser.). 240p. 1995. spiral bd. 12.95 (1-56138-513-1) Running Pr.
Large Print Crosswords Challenge, No. 3. large type ed. Ed. by Daniel Stark & Roslyn Stark. (LP Crosswords Ser.). 240p. 1996. pap. 12.95 (1-56138-676-6) Running Pr.
Large Print Crosswords Challenge, Vol. 2. large type ed. Ed. by Daniel Stark & Roslyn Stark. (LP Crosswords Ser.: Vol. 2). 240p. 1995. pap. 12.95 (1-56138-609-X) Running Pr.
Large-Print Crosswords Challenge, Vol. 6. Ed. by Daniel Stark & Roslyn Stark. (Crossword Challenge Ser.). 240p. 1997. spiral bd. 12.95 (0-7624-0119-2) Running Pr.
Large Print Crosswords Challenge #7, No. 7. large type ed. Ed. by Daniel Stark & Roslyn Stark. (Crossword Challenge Ser.). 240p. 1998. spiral bd. 12.95 (0-7624-0248-2) Running Pr.
*Large-Print Crosswords Challenge 10. large type ed. Daniel Stark & Roslyn Stark. 1999. pap. 12.95 (0-7624-0533-3) Running Pr.
*Large Print Easy-Reading Bible. large type ed. 2000. pap. text 9.95 (1-58516-004-0) Am Bible.
Large Print Innovative Cookbook. large type ed. Marilyn R. Riddle. (Illus.). 64p. (Orig.). 1984. pap. 10.00 (0-9603748-3-3) Sandpiper OR.
Large Print Mass Service: Large Print Mass Propers for Each Sunday & Holy Day. large type ed. ring bd. 20.00 (0-317-01853-1) Cath Guild Blind.
*Large Print Popular Bible. 3rd ed. 1999. 16.75 (5-550-00738-X) Nairi.
Large Print Prayer Book. enl. large type ed. Jerome Duesman. 1980. pap. 1.00 (0-8189-0344-9) Alba.
Large Print Puzzle Assortment. V. Nichols. 384p. (Orig.). 1993. pap. 3.95 (1-879424-60-6) Nickel Pr.
Large Print Recipes for a Healthy Life: Low Cholesterol, Low Fat, Low Sodium, No Added Sugar. large type ed. Judith Caditz. 283p. 1992. 19.95 (0-9622368-2-9) Ctr Partially.
Large Print Song Book-Music Edition. large type ed. Ulverscroft Editors. 1981. pap. 18.99 (0-7089-0687-7) Ulverscroft.
*Large Print Spanish Study Bible. 3rd ed. 1999. 14.95 (5-550-00739-8) Nairi.
*Large Print Special Reference Bible. large type ed. Broadman & Holman Publishing Staff. 1999. 28.99 (1-55819-834-2) Broadman.
Large Quantity Recipes. 4th ed. Margaret E. Terrell & Dorothea B. Headlund. 528p. 1988. 64.95 (0-471-28854-3, VNR) Wiley.
Large Quantity Recipes. 4th rev. ed. Margaret E. Terrell & Dorothea V. Headlund. (Illus.). 508p. (C). 1989. text 55.95 (0-442-20486-8, VNR) Wiley.
Large Rock Caverns, 3 vols. K. Saari. 1986. pap. 40.00 (0-08-034080-6, Pergamon Pr) Elsevier.
Large Rock Caverns, 3 vols., Vol. 1-3. K. Saari. 1987. 320.00 (0-08-034079-2, Pergamon Pr) Elsevier.
Large Rotating Machine Winding. 1989. 55.00 (0-85083-045-1) St Mut.
Large Sample Methods in Statistics: An Introduction with Applications. Pranab K. Sen & Julio M. Singer. LC 92-46163. (Texts in Statistical Science Ser.). 382p. (gr. 13). 1994. ring bd. 73.95 (0-412-04221-5, Chap & Hall CRC) CRC Pr.
Large Sample Theory. Thomas Ferguson. LC 94-36492. 1995. write for info. (0-412-99321-X) Chapman & Hall.
Large Sansoni Dictionary of the Italian & English Languages: Grandi Dizionario Sansoni Delle Lingua Italiana e Inglese, 2 vols., Set. Sansoni. Ed. by Vladimiro Macchi. (ENG & ITA.). 1991. lib. bdg. 495.00 (0-8288-9345-4) Fr & Eur.
Large Sansoni Dictionary of the Italian & English Languages: Grandi Dizionario Sansoni Delle Lingua Italiana e Inglese, 2 vols., Vol. 1. Sansoni. Ed. by Vladimiro Macchi. (ENG & ITA.). 1522p. 1991. lib. bdg. write for info. (0-8288-3326-5, M14422) Fr & Eur.
Large Sansoni Dictionary of the Italian & English Languages: Grandi Dizionario Sansoni Delle Lingua Italiana e Inglese, 2 vols., Vol. 2. Sansoni. Ed. by Vladimiro Macchi. (ENG & ITA.). 1650p. 1991. lib. bdg. write for info. (0-8288-3325-7, M14423) Fr & Eur.
Large Sansoni Dictionary of the Italian & German Languages: Grandi Dizionario Sansoni Delle Lingua Italiano e Tedesca, Vol. 1: Italian-German, Vol. 1: Italian-German. 3rd ed. Sansoni. (GER & ITA.). 1652p. 1986. lib. bdg. 350.00 (0-8288-3328-1, M6992) Fr & Eur.
Large Sansoni Dictionary of the Italian & German Languages: Grandi Dizionario Sansoni Delle Lingua Italiano e Tedesca, Vol. 1: Italian-German, Vol. 2: German-Italian. 3rd ed. Sansoni. (GER & ITA.). 1534p. 1986. lib. bdg. 350.00 (0-8288-3327-3, M6991) Fr & Eur.
Large-Scale Adsorption & Chromatography, 2 Vols., Set. Phillip C. Wankat. 259p. 1986. 279.90 (0-8493-5599-0, QD79) CRC Pr.
Large-Scale Adsorption & Chromatography, 2 vols., Vol. 1. Phillip C. Wankat. 259p. 1986. write for info. (0-318-61543-6) CRC Pr.
Large-Scale Adsorption & Chromatography, 2 vols., Vol. 2. Phillip C. Wankat. 259p. 1986. write for info. (0-318-61544-4) CRC Pr.
Large Scale C++ Software Design. John Lakos. (Professional Computing Ser.). 896p. (C). 1996. pap. text 43.95 (0-201-63362-0) Addison-Wesley.
Large Scale Cell Culture Technology. Ed. by Bjorn K. Lydersen. 252p. 1993. 110.00 (0-471-03732-X) Wiley.
Large Scale Ceramics. Jim Robison. 1997. 26.00 (1-889250-05-8) Gentle Br.
Large-Scale Ceramics. Jim Robison. (Illus.). 112p. 1997. text. write for info. (90-5703-551-0, Harwood Acad Pubs) Gordon & Breach.
Large Scale Characteristics of the Galaxy. W. Butler Burton. (International Astronomical Union Highlights Ser.: No. 84). 1979. lib. bdg. 182.50 (90-277-1029-5) Kluwer Academic.
Large Scale Coastal Behavior (1993) Ed. by J. H. List. (Illus.). 238p. (Orig.). (C). 1995. pap. text 60.00 (0-7881-2542-7) DIANE Pub.
Large Scale Collective Motion of Atomic Nuclei. 600p. 1997. 89.00 (981-02-3045-1) World Scientific Pub.
Large Scale Computation & Information Processing in Air Traffic Control. Lucio Bianco. Ed. by Amedeo R. Odoni. (Transportation Analysis Ser.). (Illus.). xiv, 240p. 1993. write for info. (3-540-56950-2) Spr-Verlag.
Large Scale Computation & Information Processing in Air Traffic Control. Ed. by Lucio Bianco & Amedeo R. Odoni. LC 93-11819. (Transportation Analysis Ser.). 1993. 95.95 (0-387-56950-2) Spr-Verlag.
Large Scale Computational Physics on Massively Parallel Computers. H. Herrmann. 296p. 1993. text 95.00 (981-02-1643-2) World Scientific Pub.
*Large Scale Computations in Air Pollution Modelling. Zahari Zlatev. LC 99-21367. (NATO Science Ser.). 21p. 1999. write for info. (0-7923-5677-2) Kluwer Academic.
Large-Scale Computations in Fluid Mechanics, 2 pts. Ed. by Bjorn Engquist et al. LC 84-24534. (Lectures in Applied Mathematics: Vol. 22). 779p. 1985. text 149.00 (0-8218-1122-3, LAM/22) Am Math.
Large-Scale Computations in Fluid Mechanics, 2 pts., Pt. 1. Ed. by Bjorn Engquist et al. LC 84-24534. (Lectures in Applied Mathematics: Vol. 22). 370p. 1985. text 90.00 (0-8218-1129-0, LAM/22.1) Am Math.
Large-Scale Computations in Fluid Mechanics, 2 pts., Pt. 2. Ed. by Bjorn Engquist et al. LC 84-24534. (Lectures in Applied Mathematics: Vol. 22). 409p. 1985. text 90.00 (0-8218-1130-4, LAM/22.2) Am Math.
Large-Scale Conservation Assessment for Neotropical Migratory Land Birds in the Interior Columbia River Basin. Victoria A. Saab & Terrell D. Rich. (Illus.). 64p. (C). 1998. reprint ed. 13.50 (0-89904-904-4); reprint ed. pap. 7.50 (0-89904-905-2) Crumb Elbow Pub.
Large-Scale Constructions in Coastal Environments: Conflict Resolution Strategies. Ed. by M. Vollmer et al. LC 98-34468. (Environmental Science Ser.). (Illus.). 250p. 1998. 109.00 (3-540-64647-7) Spr-Verlag.
Large Scale Control Systems: Theories & Techniques. Magdi S. Mahmoud et al. (Electrical Engineering & Electronics Ser.: Vol. 26). (Illus.). 384p. 1985. text 165.00 (0-8247-7289-X) Dekker.
Large-Scale Development: Benefits, Constraints, & State & Local Policy Incentives. William Nicoson et al. LC 77-74659. (Management & Control of Growth Ser.). 141p. reprint ed. pap. 43.80 (0-608-17347-9, 202980400065) Bks Demand.
Large Scale Dynamics of Interacting Particles. H. Spohn. Ed. by W. Beiglbock et al. (Texts & Monographs in Physics). (Illus.). 352p. 1991. 99.95 (0-387-53491-1) Spr-Verlag.
Large-Scale Geologic Structures. Jacques Debelmas & George Mascle. (Illus.). 330p. (C). 1998. text 69.00 (90-5410-776-6, Pub. by A A Balkema) Ashgate Pub Co.
*Large-Scale Indoor Gardening. William Walker. (Illus.). 98p. 2000. pap. 19.00 (0-9702139-0-5) Mercer Pubng.
Large Scale Integration: Devices, Circuits & Systems. Ed. by M. J. Howes & D. V. Morgan. LC 80-42016. (Wiley Series in Solid State Devices & Circuits). (Illus.). 358p. reprint ed. pap. 111.00 (0-608-15582-9, 202964500062) Bks Demand.
*Large Scale Interactive Fuzzy Multiobjective Programming: Decomposition Approaches. M. Sakawa. (Studies in Fuzziness & Soft Computing: Vol. 48). (Illus.). xiv, 217p. (C). 2000. text 72.00 (3-7908-1293-5, Pub. by Physica-Verlag) Spr-Verlag.
Large Scale Linear & Integer Optimization: A Unified Approach. Richard K. Martin. LC 98-46062. xvii, 740 p. 1999. write for info. (0-7923-8202-1) Kluwer Academic.
Large-Scale Mammalian Cell Culture Technology. Anthony S. Lubiniecki. (Bioprocess Technology Ser.: Vol. 10). (Illus.). 656p. 1990. text 235.00 (0-8247-8327-1) Dekker.
Large Scale Mapping Guidelines. U. S. Department of the Interior U. S. Geology Sur. 1986. 10.90 (0-317-60424-4, C165) Am Congrs Survey.
Large-Scale Mapping Guidelines. United States Geological Survey National Mapping D. 46p. 1986. pap. 10.00 (0-614-06092-3, C165) Am Congrs Survey.
Large Scale Matrix Problems. Ed. by Ake Bjorck et al. LC 80-22058. 412p. reprint ed. pap. 127.80 (0-608-16381-3, 202627500049) Bks Demand.
Large-Scale Model Railroading Handbook. Robert Schleicher. LC 91-31607. (Illus.). 224p. 1992. pap. 18.95 (0-8019-8229-4) Krause Pubns.
*Large-Scale Model Railroading Handbook. 2nd rev. ed. Robert Schleicher. LC 91-31607. (Illus.). 224p. 2000. pap. 23.95 (0-87341-866-2, LSMRH2) Krause Pubns.
Large-Scale Modelling & Interactive Decision Analysis. Ed. by A. P. Wierzbicki et al. (Lecture Notes in Economics & Mathematical Systems Ser.: Vol. 273). 373p. 1986. 46.95 (0-387-16785-4) Spr-Verlag.
Large-Scale Models for Policy Evaluation. Peter W. House & John McLeod. LC 76-57255. (Wiley Series on Systems Engineering & Analysis). 352p. reprint ed. pap. 109.20 (0-608-13396-5, 202248900027) Bks Demand.
Large-Scale Molecular Systems: Quantum & Stochastic Aspects - Beyond the Simple Molecular Picture. Ed. by W. Gans et al. (NATO ASI Ser.: Vol. 258). (Illus.). 614p. (C). 1991. text 186.00 (0-306-43914-X, Kluwer Plenum) Kluwer Academic.
Large-Scale Neuronal Theories of the Brain. Ed. by Christof Koch & Joel L. Davis. LC 93-29736. (Computational Neuroscience Ser.). (Illus.). 355p. 1994. 63.00 (0-262-11183-7, Bradford Bks) MIT Pr.
Large Scale Numerical Optimization. Ed. by Thomas F. Coleman & Yuying Li. LC 90-23912. (Proceedings in Applied Mathematics Ser.: No. 46). 255p. 1990. pap. 40.75 (0-89871-268-8) Soc Indus-Appl Math.
Large-Scale Oceanographic Experiments & Satellites. Ed. by Catherine Gautier & Michele Fieux. 1984. text 147.50 (90-277-1786-9) Kluwer Academic.
Large Scale Optimization: Annual Meeting of the American Institute of Chemical Engineers, 1982. Ed. by G. V. Reklaitis. 100p. 1983. write for info. (0-08-030270-X, Pergamon Pr) Elsevier.
Large Scale Optimization: State of the Art. Ed. by W. W. Hager et al. LC 94-7972. 472p. (C). 1994. text 251.00 (0-7923-2798-5) Kluwer Academic.
Large-Scale Optimization with Applications Pt. 1: Optimization in Inverse Problems & Design. Ed. by Lorenz T. Biegler et al. LC 97-22879. (IMA Volumes in Mathematics & Its Applications Ser.: No. 93). (Illus.). 352p. 1997. text 59.95 (0-387-98287-6) Spr-Verlag.
Large-Scale Optimization with Applications Pt. 1: Optimization in Inverse Problems & Design, Pt. I. Ed. by Lorenz T. Biegler et al. LC 97-22879. (IMA Volumes in Mathematics & Its Applications Ser.: No. 92). (Illus.). 230p. 1997. 59.95 (0-387-98286-8) Spr-Verlag.
Large-Scale Optimization with Applications Pt. 1: Optimization in Inverse Problems & Design, Pt. III. Ed. by Lorenz T. Biegler et al. LC 97-22879. (IMA Volumes in Mathematics & Its Applications Ser.: No. 94). (Illus.). 224p. 1997. text 59.95 (0-387-98288-4) Spr-Verlag.
Large-Scale Organizational Change. Allan M. Mohrman, Jr. et al. LC 89-45602. (Management Ser.). 336p. 1989. text 36.95 (1-55542-164-4) Jossey-Bass.
*Large Scale Organizational Change: An Executive's Guide. Norman Bates & Christopher Laszlo. LC 99-40495. 264p. 1999. pap. text 19.95 (0-7506-7230-7) Buttrwrth-Heinemann.
*Large-Scale Parellel Data Mining. Ed. by M. J. Zaki & C. T. Ho. (Lecture Notes in Artificial Intelligence: Vol. 1759). viii, 261p. 2000. pap. 39.00 (3-540-67194-3) Spr-Verlag.
Large-Scale Pile Tests in Clay: Proceedings of the Conference on Recent Large-Scale Fully Instrumented Pile Tests in Clay Held at the Institution of Civil Engineers, London, June 23-24, 1992. Ed. by J. Clarke. 120p. 1993. 134.00 (0-7277-1918-1) Am Soc Civil Eng.
Large Scale Policy Making. Paul R. Schulman. LC 80-13942. 146p. 1981. lib. bdg. 57.50 (0-444-99075-5, SLS/) Greenwood.
Large-Scale Projects: Claes Oldenburg Coosje van Bruggen. Claes Oldenburg & Coosje Van Bruggen. LC 94-76579. (Illus.). 584p. 1994. 95.00 (1-885254-04-0, Pub. by Monacelli Pr) Penguin Putnam.
Large-Scale Regional Water Resources Planning: The North Atlantic Regional Study. David C. Major & Harry E. Schwarz. (C). 1990. text 124.00 (0-7923-0711-9) Kluwer Academic.
*Large Scale Retailing in Poland: A Strategic Entry Report, 1996. Compiled by Icon Group International Staff. (Illus.). 185p. 1999. ring bd. 1850.00 incl. audio compact disk (0-7418-1250-9) Icon Grp.
Large-Scale Scientific Computing. Ed. by Peter Deuflhard & B. Engquist. (Progress in Scientific Computing Ser.: No. 7). 408p. 1987. 115.00 (0-8176-3355-3) Birkhauser.
Large Scale Structure: Tracks & Traces: Proceedings of the 12th Potsdam Cosmology Workshop, Potsdam, Germany 15 - 19 September 1997. Ed. by Volker Muller et al. 400p. 1998. 88.00 (981-02-3499-6) World Scientific Pub.
Large Scale Structure & Motions in the Universe. Ed. by M. Mezzetti et al. (C). 1988. text 237.50 (0-7923-0082-3) Kluwer Academic.
*Large Scale Structure Formation. Riszea Manrseurei & Robert H. Brandenberger. LC 00-33082. (Astrophysics & Space Science Library). 2000. write for info. (0-7923-6411-2) Kluwer Academic.
Large Scale Structure in the Universe: Proceedings of the International Workshop. J. P. Mucket et al. 380p. 1995. text 92.00 (981-02-2342-0) World Scientific Pub.
Large Scale Structure of Space-Time. Stephen W. Hawking & G. F. Ellis. LC 72-93671. (Illus.). 400p. 1975. pap. text 49.95 (0-521-09906-4) Cambridge U Pr.
Large Scale Structure of the Universe. Ed. by Jaan Einasto & Malcolm S. Longair. 1978. pap. text 100.50 (90-277-0896-7); lib. bdg. 146.00 (90-277-0895-9) Kluwer Academic.
Large-Scale Structures & Peculiar Motions in the Universe. Ed. by D. Latham & L. A. De Costa. (ASP Conference Series Proceedings: Vol. 15). 406p. 1991. 34.00 (0-937707-34-1) Astron Soc Pacific.
Large-Scale Structures in Acoustics & Electromagnetics: Proceedings of a Symposium. National Research Council, Board on Mathematical S. (Orig.). 1996. pap. text 29.00 (0-309-05337-4) Natl Acad Pr.
Large Scale Structures in Nonlinear Physics: Proceedings of a Workshop Held in Villefranche Sur Mer, France, 13-18 January 1991. Ed. by J. D. Fournier & Pierre-Louis Sulem. (Lecture Notes in Physics Ser.: Vol. 392). viii, 353p. 1991. 71.95 (0-387-54899-8) Spr-Verlag.
Large-Scale Structures in the Universe. Anthony P. Fairall. LC 96-28788. (Wiley-Praxis Series in Astronomy & Astrophysics). 218p. 1998. 125.00 (0-471-96252-X); pap. 59.95 (0-471-96253-8) Wiley.
Large-Scale Structures in the Universe. Ed. by W. C. Seitter et al. (Lecture Notes in Physics Ser.: Vol. 310). ii, 335p. 1988. 52.95 (0-387-50135-5) Spr-Verlag.
Large Scale Structures of the Universe. Ed. by Jean Adouze et al. (C). 1988. pap. text 99.50 (90-277-2744-9); lib. bdg. 220.50 (90-277-2742-2) Kluwer Academic.
Large Scale Systems: Decentralization, Structure Constraints, & Fixed Modes. L. Trave et al. (Lecture Notes in Control & Information Sciences: Vol. 120). (Illus.). 384p. 1989. 70.95 (0-387-50787-6) Spr-Verlag.
Large Scale Systems: Theory & Applications: Selected Papers from the 6th IFAC-FORS-IMACS Symposium, Beijing, PRC, 23-25 August 1992. Ed. by B. Liu et al. LC 93-33127. (IFAC Symposia Ser.: Vol. 1993, No. 10). 430p. 1993. 142.00 (0-08-041895-3, Pergamon Pr) Elsevier.
Large Scale Systems: Theory & Applications, 1989. Ed. by K. Reinisch & M. Thoma. (IFAC Proceedings Ser.: No. 9009). 580p. 1990. 255.75 (0-08-035731-8, Pergamon Pr) Elsevier.
Large Scale Systems: Theory & Applications, 1995: A Postprint Volume from the 7th IFAC/IFORS/IMACS Symposium, London, U. K., 11-13 July, 1995. Ed. by P. D. Roberts & J. E. Ellis. LC 95-47896. 962p. 1995. pap. write for info. (0-08-042365-5) Elsevier.
Large-Scale Systems Control & Decision Making. Hiroyuki Tamura. Ed. by Tsuneo Yoshikawa. (Electrical Engineering & Electronics Ser.: Vol. 64). (Illus.). 320p. 1990. text 155.00 (0-8247-8241-0) Dekker.
*Large Scale Systems '98: Theory & Applications, 2 vols. Groumpos Koussoulas. LC 99-32005. (IFAC Proceedings Ser.). 1210p. 1999. pap. 241.00 (0-08-043034-1, Pergamon Pr) Elsevier.
Large-Scale Systems Stability under Structural & Singular Perturbations. L. T. Grujic et al. (Lecture Notes in Control & Information Sciences: Vol. 92). (Illus.). xv, 381p. 1987. 68.95 (0-387-18300-0) Spr-Verlag.
Large-Scale Transport Processes in Oceans & Atmosphere. Ed. by Jurgen Willebrand & D. L. Anderson. 1986. text 184.00 (90-277-2353-2) Kluwer Academic.
Large Scale Water Transfers: Emerging Environmental-Social Experiences. G. N. Golubev & A. Biswag. 168p. 1986. pap. text 75.00 (1-85148-006-4, Tycooly Pub) Weidner & Sons.
Large Sea Creatures. Jason Cooper. LC 92-16072. (Discovery Library of the Sea). (J). 1992. 9.50 (0-685-59714-8) Rourke Corp.
Large Sea Creatures. Jason Cooper. LC 92-16072. (Sea Discovery Library). 24p. (J). (gr. k-4). 1992. lib. bdg. 10.95 (0-86593-231-X) Rourke Corp.
Large Sets of Triple Systems & Related Designs. Kang Qingde. Ed. by Du Dingzhu et al. (Descrete Mathematics & Theoretical Computer Science Ser.: Vol. 3). (Illus.). 201p. 1995. 39.95 (1-880132-13-3) Sci Pr NY.
Large Ship's Log Book. Des. by John P. Kaufman. (Illus.). 175p. 1998. spiral bd. 24.95 (1-892216-08-6) Bristol Fash.
Large Size Silver Coins of the World. 3rd ed. Carl Subak et al. LC 91-61306. (Illus.). 192p. 1991. 60.00 (0-87341-166-8, TM03) Krause Pubns.
Large Sky Reaches Down. Ed. by Susan M. Swanson. (Illus.). 176p. (Orig.). 1986. pap. 7.00 (0-927663-05-8) COMPAS.
Large Space Structures: Dynamics & Control. Ed. by S. N. Atluri & A. K. Amos. (Computational Mechanics Ser.). (Illus.). viii, 356p. 1988. 139.95 (0-387-18900-9) Spr-Verlag.
Large Space Structures Formed by Centrifugal Forces. V. M. Melnikov & V. A. Koshelev. (Earth Space Institute Book Ser.: Vol. 4). 164p. 1998. text 39.00 (90-5699-112-4, ECU55, Harwood Acad Pubs) Gordon & Breach.
Large Spiral Bevel & Hypoid Gears. A. H. Candee. (Technical Papers: Vol. P57). (Illus.). 8p. 1929. pap. text 30.00 (1-55589-415-1) AGMA.
Large Sutra on Perfect Wisdom: With the Divisions of the Abhisamayalankara. Ed. & Tr. by Edward Conze. LC 71-189224. (Center for South & Southeast Asia Studies, UC Berkeley: No. 18). 697p. 1974. pap. 24.95 (0-520-05321-4, Pub. by U CA Pr) Cal Prin Full Svc.
Large Synchronous Machines: Design, Manufacture & Operation. Jack H. Walker. LC 80-41455. (Monographs in Electrical & Electronic Engineering: Vol. 14). (Illus.). 274p. reprint ed. pap. 85.00 (0-608-15988-3, 205673900084) Bks Demand.

An Asterisk (*) at the beginning of an entry indicates that the title is appearing for the first time.

Large Target: A Josephine Fuller Mystery. Lynne Murray. mass mkt. write for info. (*0-312-97537-6*) St Martin.

***Large Target: A Josephine Fuller Mystery.** Lynne Murray. LC 99-89839. 272p. 2000. text 23.95 (*0-312-25456-3*, Minotaur) St Martin.

Large, the Small & the Human Mind. Roger Penrose. Ed. by Malcolm S. Longair. LC 96-35837. (Illus.). 203p. (C). 1997. text 20.95 (*0-521-56330-5*) Cambridge U Pr.

***Large, the Small & the Human Mind.** Roger Penrose. Ed. by Malcolm Longair. (Illus.). 128p. (C). 1999. pap. 12.95 (*0-521-65538-2*) Cambridge U Pr.

***Large, the Small & the Human Mind.** Roger Penrose. Ed. by Malcolm Longair. (Canto Book Ser.). (Illus.). 220p. 2000. pap. 13.95 (*0-521-78572-3*) Cambridge U Pr.

Large Time Behavior of Solutions for General Quasilinear Hyperbolic-Parabolic Systems of Conservation Laws. Tai-Ping Liu & Yanni Zeng. LC 96-44759. (Memoirs of the American Mathematical Society Ser.: Vol. 125/599). 120p. 1997. 39.00 (*0-8218-0545-2*, MEMO/125/599) Am Math.

Large-Time Behavior of Solutions of Linear Dispersive Equations, Vol. 166. Daniel B. Dix. Ed. by A. Dold & F. Takens. LC 97-29078. (Lecture Notes in Mathematics Ser.: Vol. 1668). xiv, 203p. 1997. pap. 41.00 (*3-540-63434-7*) Spr-Verlag.

Large Type American Heritage Basic Dictionary. large type rev. ed. LC 93-13116. 384p. 1993. pap. 13.00 (*0-395-67770-X*) HM.

Large Type Outline Maps of the United States & Its Regions, Set. large type ed. 1994. 2.95 (*0-614-08367-2*, 1-01890-00) Am Printing Hse.

Large Type Treasury of Inspiration. 1986. 8.98 (*0-685-16814-X*, 625334) Random Hse Value.

Large UUSI Finnish-English Dictionary: UUSI Suomi-Englanti Suurssanakirja. R. Hurme. (ENG & FIN.). 1446p. 1984. 250.00 (*0-8288-0532-6*, F41330) Fr & Eur.

Large-Vehicle Safety Research (TRR 1407) Ed. by Alison Tobias. (Transportation Research Record Ser.). (Illus.). 57p. 1993. pap. text 20.00 (*0-309-05552-0*) Transport Res Bd.

***Large Vertical Country Cottage Collection Photo Album.** Rutledge Hill Press Staff. (Montague House Photograph Albums Ser.). (Illus.). 1999. write for info. (*1-55853-635-3*) Rutledge Hill Pr.

***Large Vertical Floral Victorian Design Photo Album.** Rutledge Hill Press Staff. (Montague House Photograph Albums Ser.). (Illus.). 1999. write for info. (*1-55853-508-X*) Rutledge Hill Pr.

Large White Butterfly. Ed. by John Feltwell. 1981. text 318.00 (*90-6193-128-2*) Kluwer Academic.

Large Window on a Small World. Maurice Hill. 1972. pap. 5.25 (*0-8222-0633-1*) Dramatists Play.

Largely Lobster. Julie V. Watson. (Illus.). 96p. 1991. pap. 9.95 (*0-921054-15-7*) Nimbus Publ.

Largemouth Bass. 1998. pap. 10.95 (*1-55971-653-3*, NorthWord Pr) Creat Pub Intl.

Largemouth Bass. Don Oster. LC 83-166989. (Hunting & Fishing Library). (Illus.). 160p. 1983. 19.95 (*0-86573-005-9*) Creat Pub Intl.

Largemouth Bass in the 90s. 1992. pap. 11.95 (*0-929384-11-3*) In-Fisherman.

L'argent see Money

Larger - Than - Life Activities: Colossal Crafts That Teach & Serve. Susan Lingo. LC 98-123020. (Illus.). 112p. (J). 1998. per. 12.99 (*0-7847-0782-0*, 03082) Standard Pub.

***Larger Carnivores of the African Savannas.** J. P. Bothma. 2000. 52.00 (*0-627-02411-4*, Pub. by J L Van Schaik) BHB Intl.

Larger Carnivores of the African Savannas. Jacobus du P. Bothma & Clive Walker. LC 99-21370. 1999. write for info. (*3-540-65660-X*) Spr-Verlag.

Larger Catechism for Members of the Christian Methodist Episcopal Church. rev. ed. Marshall Gilmore. LC 95-75186. (Reader Resource Ser.). 192p. 1995. pap. text 8.00 (*1-883667-11-9*) Christian Meth.

Larger Christian Life. rev. ed. Albert B. Simpson. LC 88-70506. 159p. 1988. pap. 9.99 (*0-87509-408-2*) Chr Pubns.

Larger Earth: Descending Notes of a Grounded Astronaut. David Memmott. (Illus.). 104p. (Orig.). 1996. pap. 9.95 (*1-882633-18-0*) Permeable.

Larger English-Persian Dictionary, 2 vols., Vols. 1 & 2. Soleyman Haim. 1350p. 1984. lib. bdg. 65.00 (*0-939214-45-8*) Mazda Pubs.

Larger Faith: A Short History of American Universalism. Charles A. Howe. LC 92-44086. 1994. pap. 16.00 (*1-55896-308-1*, Skinner Hse Bks) Unitarian Univ.

Larger Firmer Breasts Through Self-Hypnosis. D. M. Borsteen. 101p. 1991. pap. 16.95 (*0-9630685-0-4*) Piedras Pr.

Larger Forms of Musical Composition: An Exhaustive Explanation of the Variations, Rondos, & Sonata Designs. Percy Goetschius. 231p. 1990. reprint ed. lib. bdg. 69.00 (*0-7812-9144-5*) Rprt Serv.

Larger History of the United States. Thomas W. Higginson. (Notable American Authors Ser.). 1992. reprint ed. lib. bdg. 75.00 (*0-7812-3114-0*) Rprt Serv.

Larger Hope, Vol. 2. Russell Miller. 1991. pap. 25.00 (*0-933840-25-X*) Unitarian Univ.

Larger Hope: The Universalist Church in America, Vol. 1. Russell Miller. 1991. pap. 25.00 (*0-933840-00-4*) Unitarian Univ.

Larger Meaning of Religion. James I. Wedgwood. 80p. 1981. pap. text 3.15 (*0-918980-10-0*) St Alban Pr.

Larger Memory: A History of Our Diversity, with Voices. Ronald T. Takaki. LC 98-12931. 384p. 1998. pap. 15.00 (*0-316-31162-6*) Little.

Larger Red Worms. George Holwager. (Illus.). 1952. pap. 6.00 (*0-9600102-3-8*) Shields.

Larger Rhetorical Patterns in Anglo-Saxon Poetry. Adeline C. Bartlett. LC 72-159999. reprint ed. 24.50 (*0-404-00667-1*) AMS Pr.

Larger Role for Positive Sanctions in Cases of Compellence. Gitty M. Amini. (New Ser.: Vol. 12). 34p. 1997. pap. 15.00 (*0-86682-128-7*) Ctr Intl Relations.

Larger Than Death. Lynne Murray. LC 97-67282. 300p. 1997. 23.00 (*0-9642949-0-7*) Orloff Pr.

***Larger Than Death: A Josephine Fuller Mystery.** Lynne Murray. 304p. 2000. mass mkt. 5.99 (*0-312-97277-6*, Minotaur) St Martin.

***Larger Than Life.** George J. Butorac. LC 00-40929. 2000. write for info. (*1-885590-83-0*) Golden West Pub.

Larger Than Life. Robert D. San Souci. (Illus.). 2000. write for info. (*0-15-200398-3*) Harcourt.

Larger Than Life. Scholastic, Inc. Staff. (J). (gr. 4-7). 1996. pap. text 3.99 (*0-590-95728-7*) Scholastic Inc.

Larger Than Life: Folk Heroes of the United States. Penny Cameron. LC 93-47027. 176p. (C). 1994. pap. text 19.53 (*0-13-299470-4*) P-H.

Larger Than Life: Robert Rahway Zakanitch's Big Bungalow Suite. Mary MacNaughton. LC 98-119042. (Illus.). 46p. 1998. pap. 14.95 (*0-295-97672-1*) U of Wash Pr.

Larger Than Life: Stories of Small Churches & Remarkable People. Robert B. Horine. (Illus.). 72p. (Orig.). 1994. pap. 2.95 (*0-88028-155-3*, 1281) Forward Movement.

Larger Than Life: The Life & Times of the Lubavitcher Rebbe Rabbi Menachem M. Schneerson, Vol. I. Shaul S. Deutsch. (Illus.). 277p. 1995. 25.00 (*0-9647243-0-8*) Chasidic Hist Prodns.

Larger Than Life Vol. II: The Lubavitcher Rebbe's Years in Riga & Berlin. Shaul S. Deutsch. (Illus.). 1997. 25.00 (*0-9647243-1-6*) Chasidic Hist Prodns.

Larger Vision: Tower-Room Talks. Anne B. McCall. LC 77-156686. (Essay Index Reprint Ser.). 1977. reprint ed. 20.95 (*0-8369-2283-2*) Ayer.

Largesse. Jean Starobinski. Tr. by Jane M. Todd. LC 96-3405. (Illus.). 214p. 1997. pap. text 29.95 (*0-226-77136-9*); lib. bdg. 75.00 (*0-226-77135-0*) U Ch Pr.

Largest Amount of Good: Quaker Relief in Ireland, 1654-1921. Helen E. Hatton. 384p. 1993. 65.00 (*0-7735-0959-3*, Pub. by McG-Queens Univ Pr) CUP Services.

Largest Elizabeth in the World. Stephen Gregg. 1991. pap. 5.50 (*0-87129-122-3*, L70) Dramatic Pub.

Largest Employers in Metro Denver. 78p. 1996. pap. 20.00 (*1-57975-000-1*) Denver Metro Chamber.

Largest Event: A Library of Congress Resource Guide for the Study of World War II. Peter T. Rohrbach. LC 93-16487. 137p. 1993. pap. 15.00 (*0-8444-0782-8*) Lib Congress.

Largest Event: A Library of Congress Resource Guide for the Study of World War 2. Peter T. Rohrbach. 151p. 1994. pap. text 16.00 (*0-16-043133-6*, Library of Cong) USGPO.

Largest Island: Modern Australian Short Stories. Ed. by Belinda Rikard-Bell. 150p. (C). 1990. 39.00 (*0-7316-5222-3*, Pub. by Pascoe Pub) St Mut.

Largest Island Study Guide-Ridgeway et Al Pascoe Publishing Pty. Ltd. Ed. by Pascoe Publ. Pty. Ltd. Staff. 88p. (C). 1990. 33.00 (*0-7855-6620-1*, Pub. by Pascoe Pub) St Mut.

Largest U. S. Oil & Gas Fields. (Illus.). 76p. (Orig.). (C). 1994. pap. text 25.00 (*0-7881-0497-7*) DIANE Pub.

Largo. Bob Dews, Jr. 140p. (Orig.). pap. 5.95 (*0-9618541-0-3*) Goldn Marsh Pubs.

Largo Atardecer. Sandra Brown. 1998. pap. 6.95 (*84-01-50550-X*) Lectorum Pubns.

***Largo Atardecer.** Sandra Brown. (SPA.). 432p. 2000. pap. 9.50 (*0-553-06125-9*) Bantam.

Largo Desolato. Vaclav Havel. LC 86-31932. 64p. 1987. pap. 11.00 (*0-8021-5163-9*, Grove) Grove-Atltic.

***Largo Teal.** Watson-Guptill Publications Staff. (Sketchbks.). 2000. 7.95 (*0-8230-5717-8*); 10.95 (*0-8230-5721-6*) Watsn-Guptill.

Lari Pittman. Text by Howard Fox et al. (Illus.). 88p. 1996. pap. 29.95 (*0-87587-176-3*, 620661) LA Co Art Mus.

Lari Pittman. Howard N. Fox. (Illus.). 90p. (Orig.). 1996. pap. 29.95 (*0-87587-177-1*) LA Co Art Mus.

***Laria.** Greg Anderson. 2000. 23.95 (*1-891400-50-9*) Champion Pr.

Lariat & Athena Pattern. Tom Felt. (Illus.). 52p. 1986. reprint ed. pap. 4.95 (*1-888939-02-8*) Heisey Collectrs.

Laricollaguas: Ecology, Economy & Demography in a Seventeenth-Century Peruvian Village, Vol. 29. David Robinson. LC 91-16672. 400p. (C). 1998. pap. 55.00 (*0-8133-8022-7*) Westview.

Lariega y el Labrador. Rafael Drullinsky. Ed. by Slusa Staff. (SPA.). 72p. (Orig.). 1985. pap. 9.00 (*0-917129-01-6*) SLUSA.

Larimer County, Colorado War Book. Arlene Ahlbrandt. (Illus.). 126p. 1993. 35.00 (*0-88107-229-X*) Curtis Media.

Larimer, McMasters & Allied Families. R. H. Mellon. (Illus.). 196p. 1990. reprint ed. pap. 31.00 (*0-8328-1483-0*); reprint ed. lib. bdg. 39.00 (*0-8328-1482-2*) Higginson Bk Co.

***Larimont.** Will Cade. 240p. 1999. mass mkt. 4.50 (*0-8439-4618-0*, Leisure Bks) Dorchester Pub Co.

Lark see Jean Anouilh: Five Plays

Lark. Jean Anouilh. 1957. pap. 5.25 (*0-8222-0634-X*) Dramatists Play.

Lark. Norah Hess. 400p. 1999. mass mkt. 5.99 (*0-8439-4522-2*, Leisure Bks) Dorchester Pub Co.

Lark. deluxe ed. Guy Davenport. (Illus.). 16p. 1993. 85.00 (*1-891472-05-4*) Dim Gray.

***Lark, Vol. 2.** Ginny Aiken. (Bellamy's Blossoms Ser.). 2000. pap. 9.99 (*0-8423-3560-9*) Tyndale Hse.

Lark & Sky. Margaret S. Decker. 112p. 1972. pap. 3.00 (*0-913976-04-0*) Discovery Bks.

Lark & the Wren. Mercedes Lackey. (Bardic Voices Ser.: Bk. 1). 496p. 1992. mass mkt. 5.99 (*0-671-72099-6*) Baen Bks.

Lark Ascends: Florence Kate Upton, Artist & Illustrator. Norma S. Davis. LC 91-38840. (Illus.). 240p. 1992. 34.50 (*0-8108-2511-2*) Scarecrow.

Lark in the Morning. Nancy Garden. LC 90-56148. 288p. (YA). (gr. 7 up). 1991. 14.95 (*0-374-34338-1*) FS&G.

Lark Rise to Candle: A Triology. Flora Thompson. 1996. pap. 14.95 (*0-14-018850-9*, Viking) Viking Penguin.

Lark Rise to Candleford. Keith Dewhurst. 171p. 1990. pap. 15.95 (*0-7487-0375-6*) Dufour.

Lark Rise to Candleford. Thompson. 1989. pap. 9.95 (*0-14-011756-3*, Penguin Bks) Viking Penguin.

Lark Shall Sing. Elizabeth Cadell. 21.95 (*0-88411-395-7*) Amereon Ltd.

Lark, the Thrush, the Starling: Translations from Issa. deluxe ed. C. K. Williams. (Burning Deck Poetry Ser.). (Illus.). 1983. pap. 20.00 (*0-930901-15-0*) Burning Deck.

Larkin at Work: A Study of Larkin's Mode of Composition As Seen in His Workbooks. A. T. Tolley. 212p. 1998. 65.00 (*0-85958-661-8*, Pub. by Univ of Hull Pr); pap. 25.00 (*0-85958-662-6*, Pub. by Univ of Hull Pr) Paul & Co Pubs.

Larkin Guide: Enjoying the Riches of Retirement. J. Donald Larkin & Sue Larkin. LC 87-73134. 96p. 1988. spiral bd. 7.95 (*0-9619643-0-8*) Damike Pub.

***Larkin's Blues: Jazz, Popular Music & Poetry.** B. J. Leggett. LC 98-43704. 208p. 1999. 45.00 (*0-8071-2342-0*) La State U Pr.

Larkin's Dulcimer Book. Larkin Bryant. LC 82-84550. (Illus.). 103p. 1998. spiral bd. 10.98 (*0-9667520-0-7*) Riverlark Music.

Larks. George Abbe. (YA). (gr. 7 up). 1974. pap. 8.95 (*0-87233-033-8*) Bauhan.

Larks in the Lincolnshire Marsh. Polly Williams. (C). 1989. text 40.00 (*0-902662-37-6*, Pub. by R K Pubns); pap. text 21.00 (*0-902662-38-4*, Pub. by R K Pubns) St Mut.

Lark's Magic. Michael Pastore. LC 89-51204. (Illus.). 113p. (YA). (gr. 4-12). 1990. pap. 10.00 (*0-927379-36-8*, ZP36) Zorba Pr.

Larkspur. Dorothy Garlock. 416p. 1997. reprint ed. mass mkt. 7.50 (*0-446-60253-1*, Pub. by Warner Bks) Little.

Larkspur Conspiracy. large type ed. Judson Philips. (Linford Mystery Library). 320p. 1998. pap. 17.99 (*0-7089-5219-4*, Linford) Ulverscroft.

***Larkswood Legacy.** large type ed. Nicola Cornick. 320p. 1999. 25.99 (*0-263-16117-X*, Pub. by Mills & Boon) Ulverscroft.

LARMAC Index. (Orig.). 1995. pap. 85.00 (*0-614-10372-X*, MICHIE) LEXIS Pub.

LARMAC Index to California Laws. Ed. by Butterworth Staff. 960p. 1994. pap. 85.00 (*0-250-47276-7*, MICHIE) LEXIS Pub.

LARMAC Index to California Laws: 1994 Edition. Ed. by Butterworth Staff. 960p. 1993. pap. 85.00 (*0-250-47211-2*, MICHIE) LEXIS Pub.

LARMAC Index to California Laws, 1996. 960p. 1996. pap. 85.00 (*1-55834-339-3*, 21233-11, MICHIE) LEXIS Pub.

L'Armee Francaise: An Illustrated History of the French Army, 1790-1885. Edouard Detaille. Tr. by Maureen Carlson Reinertsen. 354p. 1997. 160.00 (*1-86227-000-7*, Pub. by Spellmnt Pubs) St Mut.

Larnyx. Marvin P. Fried. 700p. 1988. 120.00 (*0-316-29360-1*, Little Brwn Med Div) Lppncott W & W.

Larousse, 10 vols. Ed. by Larousse Staff. (FRE.). 1994. 1295.00 (*0-7859-9247-2*) Fr & Eur.

Larousse: Dictionnaire de Francais. Jean Dubois et al. (FRE.). 1059p. 1986. 45.00 (*0-8288-1934-3*, F82260) Fr & Eur.

Larousse: Pluridictionnaire. Larousse Staff. 45.00 (*0-317-45660-1*) Fr & Eur.

***Larousse Active dictionary for Beginners Spanish: Pictures, Songs, Activities & Pronunciation.** Maria E. Buria. (Illus.). 64p. (YA). 2000. 15.95 (*2-03-540170-4*, Larousse LKC) LKC.

***Larousse Advanced Dictionary, Grand Dictionnaire French/English.** (Illus.). 2232p. 2000. 43.95 (*2-03-542262-0*) LKC.

Larousse Annuel: Le Livre de l'Annee, 1995. Ed. by Larousse Staff. 576p. 1995. 95.00 (*0-7859-9803-9*) Fr & Eur.

Larousse Apollo French-Italian, Italian-French Dictionary: Dictionnaire Larousse Apollo Francais-Italien-Francais. C. Margueron & G. Folena. (FRE & ITA.). 992p. 1980. 22.95 (*0-8288-0369-2*, M14295) Fr & Eur.

Larousse Apollo French-Spanish, Spanish-French Dictionary: Dictionnaire Larousse Apollo Francais-Espagnol-Francais. Ramon Garcia-Pelayo. (FRE & SPA.). 912p. 1984. 24.95 (*0-8288-0736-1*, S374) Fr & Eur.

Larousse Business Dictionary: English-French, French-English. Collin. (ENG & FRE.). 704p. 1990. pap. 85.00 (*0-7859-7658-2*, 2034040015) Fr & Eur.

Larousse Business Dictionary English-French - Francais-Anglais. Larousse Staff. 336p. 1990. pap. 59.95 (*0-8288-2394-4*, F137232) Fr & Eur.

***Larousse Concise German/English: English/German Dictionary.** (Illus.). 1290p. 2000. 21.95 (*2-03-540014-7*, Larousse LKC) LKC.

Larousse Concise Spanish/English Dictionary. rev. ed. Larousse Staff. LC 98-75570. 1280p. 1999. 21.95 (*2-03-420413-1*) LKC.

Larousse de la Cuisine. Ed. by Larousse Staff. (FRE.). 800p. 1995. 150.00 (*0-7859-9844-6*) Fr & Eur.

Larousse de la Medecine, 3 vols. Andre Domart & Jacques Bourneuf. 480p. 1982. pap. 34.95 (*0-7859-4820-1*) Fr & Eur.

Larousse de Poche. (FRE.). 1999. 18.95 (*2-03-320106-6*) LKC.

Larousse de Poche. (FRE.). 400p. (C). 1988. pap. 14.95 (*0-8442-1739-5*, VF1739-5) NTC Contemp Pub Co.

Larousse de Poche. Larousse Staff. 8.95 (*0-317-45661-X*); 18.95 (*0-8288-7843-9*, M9357) Fr & Eur.

Larousse de Poche: Dictionnaire des Noms Communs & Noms Propres. (FRE.). 1998. pap. 9.95 (*2-03-320205-4*, Larousse LKC) LKC.

Larousse de Poche: Dictionnaire des Noms Communs et des Noms Propres. Larousse Staff. (FRE.). 864p. 1993. pap. 19.95 (*0-7859-7638-8*, 2033201066) Fr & Eur.

Larousse de Poche Francais-Allemand, Allemand-Francais. Ed. by Larousse Stsff. (FRE & GER.). 768p. 1995. 19.95 (*0-7859-9919-1*) Fr & Eur.

Larousse de Poche Francais-Espangol, Espangol-Francais. Ed. by Larousse Staff. (FRE & SPA.). 768p. 1995. 19.95 (*0-7859-9917-5*) Fr & Eur.

Larousse de Poche Francais-Italien, Italien-Francais. Ed. by Larousse Staff. (FRE & ITA.). 832p. 1995. 19.95 (*0-7859-9920-5*) Fr & Eur.

Larousse de Poche French-English, English-French. Ed. by Larousse Staff. (FRE.). 768p. 1995. 19.95 (*0-7859-9918-3*) Fr & Eur.

Larousse des Animaux Familiers Insolites. Pierre Rousselet-Blanc. (FRE.). 1976. 24.95 (*0-8288-5723-7*, M6334) Fr & Eur.

Larousse des Arbres, des Arbustes et des Arbrisseaux de l'Europe Occidentale. Martin Becker et al. (FRE.). 336p. 1982. 75.00 (*0-8288-1242-X*, F12280) Fr & Eur.

Larousse des Citations Francaises et Etrangeres. Pierre Germa. (FRE.). 900p. 1992. 59.95 (*0-7859-4860-0*, M8682) Fr & Eur.

Larousse des Grands Peintres, Vol. 2. Michel Laclotte. (FRE.). 1984. pap. 32.95 (*0-7859-3945-8*) Fr & Eur.

Larousse des Plantes Qui Guerissent: Dictionary of Healing Plants. Gerard Debuigne. (FRE.). 256p. 1974. 95.00 (*0-8288-6059-9*, M-6104) Fr & Eur.

Larousse des Poissons D'Aquarium. Ed. by Pierre Rousselet-Blanc. (FRE.). 120p. 1975. 59.95 (*0-8288-5912-4*, M6336) Fr & Eur.

Larousse des Prenoms et des Saints. Pierre Pierradrd. (FRE.). 256p. 1976. 42.50 (*0-8288-5725-3*, M6454) Fr & Eur.

Larousse des Vins. Ed. by Larousse Staff. (FRE.). 608p. 1994. 150.00 (*0-7859-9845-4*) Fr & Eur.

Larousse Diccionario Basico Escolar. Ramon Garcia-Pelayo. (SPA.). 1987. 10.05 (*0-606-05410-3*, Pub. by Turtleback) Demco.

Larousse Diccionario Economico Comercial y Financiero. Larousse Staff. 1999. pap. text 9.95 (*970-607-450-3*) Larousse Eds.

Larousse Diccionario School Pocket. Larousse Staff. 1999. pap. text 9.95 (*970-607-630-1*) Larousse Eds.

Larousse Dictionary des Rimes Orales et Ecrites. Leon Warnant. (FRE.). 576p. 1992. 29.95 (*0-7859-0546-4*, 20303403114) Fr & Eur.

Larousse Dictionary of Anglicism: Dictionnaire Larousse des Anglicismes. M. Hofler. (ENG & FRE.). 324p. 1982. 45.00 (*0-8288-0777-9*, M14237); pap. 19.95 (*0-8288-1207-1*, M14237) Fr & Eur.

Larousse Dictionary of Beliefs & Religions. Ed. by Rosemary Goring. 624p. 1994. 30.00 (*0-7523-5000-5*, Chambers LKC) LKC.

Larousse Dictionary of Beliefs & Religions. Frank Whaling. Ed. by Rosemary Goring. 624p. 1995. pap. 14.95 (*0-7523-0000-8*, Larousse LKC) LKC.

Larousse Dictionary of Literary Characters. Ed. by Rosemary Goring. LC 94-75740. 832p. 1994. 35.00 (*0-7523-0001-6*) LKC.

Larousse Dictionary of Literary Characters. Ed. by Rosemary Goring. 864p. 1996. pap. 17.95 (*0-7523-0037-7*) LKC.

Larousse Dictionary of Literature: Larousse Dictionnaire des Litteratures, 2 vols., Set. Larousse Staff. (FRE.). 1888p. 1986. 250.00 (*0-8288-1564-X*, F41450) Fr & Eur.

Larousse Dictionary of Modern Arabic see Dictionnaire Arabe Moderne Larousse: Philosophie, Musique, Science, Vol. 1: A-Co

Larousse Dictionary of Music: Larousse de la Musique, 2 vols., Set. Larousse Staff. 1803p. 1982. 295.00 (*0-8288-2169-0*, M14302) Fr & Eur.

Larousse Dictionary of North American History. Ed. by Bruce Lenman. 320p. 1995. pap. 8.95 (*0-7523-0005-9*, Larousse LKC) LKC.

Larousse Dictionary of Precious Stones: Larousse des Pierres Precieuses. Pierre Bariand et al. (FRE.). 262p. 1985. 75.00 (*0-8288-1467-8*, F12290) Fr & Eur.

Larousse Dictionary of Science & Technology. Ed. by Peter Walker & Hazel Muir. LC 94-73123. 1248p. 1995. 45.00 (*0-7523-0010-5*, Larousse LKC) LKC.

Larousse Dictionary of Scientists. Hazel Muir. LC 94-75739. 608p. 1996. pap. 16.95 (*0-7523-0036-9*) LKC.

Larousse Dictionary of Women. Ed. by Melanie Parry. (Illus.). 608p. 1996. 40.00 (*0-7523-0015-6*, Larousse LKC) LKC.

Larousse Dictionary of World Folklore. Alison Jones. (Illus.). 512p. (YA). (gr. 6 up). 1995. 27.50 (*0-7523-0012-1*, Larousse LKC) LKC.

Larousse Dictionary of World Folklore. Alison Jones. (Illus.). 512p. 1996. pap. 14.95 (*0-7523-0043-1*, Larousse LKC) LKC.

Larousse Dictionary of World History. Ed. by Bruce Lenman. 1024p. 1995. pap. 18.95 (*0-7523-5008-0*, Chambers LKC) LKC.

Larousse Dictionary of Writers. Ed. by Rosemary Goring. 1088p. 1996. pap. 18.95 (*0-7523-0039-3*) LKC.

An Asterisk (*) at the beginning of an entry indicates that the title is appearing for the first time.

L

Larousse Dictionnaire Agricole. Larousse Staff. (FRE.). 195.00 (*0-320-00621-2*) Fr & Eur.

Larousse Dictionnaire Analogique. Larousse Staff. 39.95 (*0-317-45643-1*) Fr & Eur.

Larousse Dictionnaire Analogique. George Niobet. (FRE.). 1992. pap. 59.95 (*0-8288-7857-9*) Fr & Eur.

Larousse Dictionnaire Analogique. 11th ed. Charles Maquet. (FRE.). 600p. 1971. 55.00 (*0-7859-7645-0*, 2033402185) Fr & Eur.

Larousse Dictionnaire Compact Francais-Anglais, Anglais-Francais. Larousse Staff. 1000p. 1993. pap. 49.95 (*0-7859-5599-2*, 2034016319) Fr & Eur.

Larousse Dictionnaire Compact Francais-Anglais, Anglias-Francais. Catherine E. Love. (ENG & FRE.). 1184p. 1993. vinyl bd. 49.95 (*0-7859-7123-8*, 2034016319) Fr & Eur.

Larousse Dictionnaire Complet des Mots Croises. Larousse Staff. (FRE.). 55.00 (*0-7859-7643-4*, 2033402010) Fr & Eur.

Larousse Dictionnaire de la Medecine. Ed. by Andre Domart. (FRE.). 690p. 1991. pap. 16.95 (*0-7859-3944-X*, 2035010063) Fr & Eur.

Larousse Dictionnaire de la Mythologie Grecque et Romaine. Joel Schmidt. (FRE.). 221p. 1993. pap. 29.95 (*0-7859-7681-7*, 2037200676) Fr & Eur.

Larousse Dictionnaire de la Peinture Anglaise et Americaine. Jean-Philippe Breuille. (FRE.). 351p. 1991. pap. 79.95 (*0-7859-7695-7*, 2037400659) Fr & Eur.

Larousse Dictionnaire de la Peinture Espagnole et Portugais du Moyen Age a nos Jours. Larousse Staff. (FRE.). 319p. 1989. pap. 69.95 (*0-7859-7692-2*, 2037400160) Fr & Eur.

Larousse Dictionnaire de la Peinture Flamande et Hollandaise du Moyen Age a nos Jours. Larousse Staff. (FRE.). 493p. 1989. pap. 79.95 (*0-7859-7691-4*, 2037400152) Fr & Eur.

Larousse Dictionnaire de la Philosophie. Didier Julia. (FRE.). 301p. 1991. pap. 28.95 (*0-7859-7683-3*, 2037202148) Fr & Eur.

Larousse Dictionnaire de la Prehistoire. Michel Brezillon. (FRE.). 250p. 1969. pap. 16.95 (*0-7859-7636-1*) Fr & Eur.

Larousse Dictionnaire de la Prononciation. Larousse Staff. 37.50 (*0-317-45654-7*) Fr & Eur.

Larousse Dictionnaire de la Psychologie. Norbert Sillamy. (FRE.). 250p. 1971. pap. 16.95 (*0-7859-7635-3*, 2030754099) Fr & Eur.

Larousse Dictionnaire de la Sculpture. Larousse Staff. (FRE.). 624p. 1992. 195.00 (*0-7859-7671-X*, 2035113091) Fr & Eur.

Larousse Dictionnaire de la Sociologie. Raymond Boudon. (FRE.). 1993. pap. 29.95 (*0-7859-8611-1*, 203720227x) Fr & Eur.

Larousse Dictionnaire de la Sociologie. Larousse Staff. (FRE.). 288p. 1993. pap. 29.95 (*0-7859-7728-7*, 2097202276) Fr & Eur.

Larousse Dictionnaire de l'Ancien Francais. Algirdas J. Greimas. (FRE.). 648p. 1992. 79.95 (*0-8288-7844-7*, F133970) Fr & Eur.

Larousse Dictionnaire de l'Ancien Francais. Larousse Staff. 39.95 (*0-317-45644-X*) Fr & Eur.

Larousse Dictionnaire de l'Argot. Jean-Paul Colin. (FRE.). 763p. 1990. 79.95 (*0-7859-7646-9*, 2033403238) Fr & Eur.

Larousse Dictionnaire de l'Astrologie. Jean-Louis Brau. (FRE.). 222p. 1977. pap. 16.95 (*0-7859-7637-X*, 2030754773) Fr & Eur.

Larousse Dictionnaire de l'Espace. Philippe de La Cotardiere. 280p. 1993. 55.00 (*0-7859-5605-0*, 2037490054) Fr & Eur.

Larousse Dictionnaire de Linguistique. Larousse Staff. (FRE.). 37.50 (*0-8288-7846-3*) Fr & Eur.

Larousse Dictionnaire de Linguistique et des Sciences du Langage. J. Dubois. (FRE.). 672p. 1994. 85.00 (*0-7859-7647-7*, 2033403343) Fr & Eur.

Larousse Dictionnaire de Psychanalyse. Roland Chemama. (FRE.). 307p. 1993. pap. 29.95 (*0-7859-7686-8*, 2037202229) Fr & Eur.

Larousse Dictionnaire de Psychiatrie et de Psychopathologie Clinique. Jacques Postel. (FRE.). 630p. 1993. pap. 29.95 (*0-7859-7685-X*, 2037202210) Fr & Eur.

Larousse Dictionnaire de Psychologie. Larousse Staff. (FRE.). 273p. 1991. pap. 28.95 (*0-7859-7684-1*, 2037202164) Fr & Eur.

Larousse Dictionnaire des Affairs: French-English, English-French. Michel Peron. (ENG & FRE.). 512p. 1969. 45.00 (*0-7859-7631-0*, 2030206091) Fr & Eur.

Larousse Dictionnaire des Anglicismes. Larousse Staff. 37.50 (*0-317-45645-8*); write for info. (*0-8288-7847-1*) Fr & Eur.

Larousse Dictionnaire des Courants Picturaux Tendences, Mouvements, Ecoles, Genres, du Moyen Age a nos Jours. Larousse Staff. (FRE.). 448p. 1990. pap. 79.95 (*0-7859-7694-9*, 2037400616) Fr & Eur.

Larousse Dictionnaire des Difficultes de la Langue Francaise. Larousse Staff. 37.50 (*0-317-45646-6*); write for info. (*0-8288-7848-X*) Fr & Eur.

Larousse Dictionnaire des Difficultes de la Langue Francaise. Adolphe V. Thoams. (FRE.). 435p. 1993. pap. 28.95 (*0-7859-7676-0*, 2037102054) Fr & Eur.

Larousse Dictionnaire des Enfants. Agnes Aster. (FRE.). (J). 1991. 59.95 (*0-7859-7674-4*, 2036521401) Fr & Eur.

Larousse Dictionnaire des Examens Medicaux. Didier Sicard. (FRE.). 328p. 1991. 79.95 (*0-7859-7669-8*, 2035101271) Fr & Eur.

Larousse Dictionnaire des Films: 10,000 Films du Monde Entier. Bernard Rapp. (FRE.). 872p. 1995. 125.00 (*0-7859-7672-8*, 2035123151) Fr & Eur.

Larousse Dictionnaire des Locutions Francaises. Larousse Staff. 37.50 (*0-317-45651-2*) Fr & Eur.

Larousse Dictionnaire des Locutions Francaises. Maurice Rat. (FRE.). 464p. 1970. 49.95 (*0-7859-4628-4*) Fr & Eur.

Larousse Dictionnaire des Mots Croises. Larousse Staff. 39.95 (*0-317-45652-0*) Fr & Eur.

Larousse Dictionnaire des Mots Croises. Larousse Staff. (FRE.). 1956p. 1992. 59.95 (*0-8288-2339-1*, F136840) Fr & Eur.

Larousse Dictionnaire des Mots D'Origine Etrangere. Henriette Walter. (FRE.). 350p. 1991. pap. 31.95 (*0-7859-7675-2*, 2037100272) Fr & Eur.

Larousse Dictionnaire des Nationalites et des Minorites de L'Ex-URSS. Roger Caratini. (FRE.). 255p. 1992. pap. 29.95 (*0-7859-7687-6*, 2037202636) Fr & Eur.

Larousse Dictionnaire des Noms de Famille et Prenoms de France. Larousse Staff. 37.50 (*0-317-45653-9*); write for info. (*0-8288-7851-X*) Fr & Eur.

Larousse Dictionnaire des Noms de Familles et Prenoms. 6th ed. Albert Dauzat. (FRE.). 652p. 1970. 45.00 (*0-7859-8603-0*, 203340207x) Fr & Eur.

Larousse Dictionnaire des Plantes Qui Guerissent. Gerard Debuigne. (FRE.). 256p. 1987. pap. 28.95 (*0-7859-7688-4*, 2037300182) Fr & Eur.

Larousse Dictionnaire des Prenoms et des Saints. Pierre Pierrard. (FRE.). 224p. 1987. pap. 19.95 (*0-7859-1254-1*, 2037300174) Fr & Eur.

Larousse Dictionnaire des Proverbes, Sentences et Maximes. Maurice Maloux. (FRE.). 1992. 59.95 (*0-7859-7648-5*, 2033409066) Fr & Eur.

Larousse Dictionnaire des Proverbs, Sentences et Maximes. Larousse Staff. (FRE.). 37.50 (*0-8288-7852-8*) Fr & Eur.

Larousse Dictionnaire des Rimes Orales et Ecrites. Larousse Staff. 37.50 (*0-317-45656-3*) Fr & Eur.

Larousse Dictionnaire des Rimes Orales et Ecrites. Larousse Staff. (FRE.). 576p. 1992. 27.95 (*0-8288-7401-8*, F12341) Fr & Eur.

Larousse Dictionnaire des Rimes Orales et Ecrites. Leon Warnant. (FRE.). 572p. 1992. 59.95 (*0-7859-8604-9*, 203340904x) Fr & Eur.

Larousse Dictionnaire des Verbes Francais. Larousse Staff. (FRE.). 37.50 (*0-8288-7853-6*) Fr & Eur.

Larousse Dictionnaire du Cinema. Jean-Loup Passek. (FRE.). 800p. 1991. 175.00 (*0-8288-9476-0*) Fr & Eur.

Larousse Dictionnaire du Francais Classique. Jean Dubois. (FRE.). 608p. 1971. 45.00 (*0-7859-7644-2*, 2033402150) Fr & Eur.

Larousse Dictionnaire du Francais Classique. Larousse Staff. 39.95 (*0-317-45648-2*) Fr & Eur.

Larousse Dictionnaire du Francais Contemporain Illustre. Larousse Staff. 29.95 (*0-317-45649-0*); write for info. (*0-8288-7855-2*) Fr & Eur.

Larousse Dictionnaire du Moyen Francais: La Renaissance. Algirdas J. Greimas & T. M. Keane. (FRE.). 668p. 1991. 85.00 (*0-7859-1068-9*, 203340322X) Fr & Eur.

Larousse Dictionnaire Etymologique. Larousse Staff. 39.95 (*0-317-45647-4*) Fr & Eur.

Larousse Dictionnaire Etymologique. Larousse Staff & Albert Dauzat. (FRE.). 626p. 1985. pap. 27.95 (*0-7859-4539-3*) Fr & Eur.

Larousse Dictionnaire Francais. Larousse Staff. (FRE.). 767p. 1991. 32.95 (*0-7859-7639-6*, 2033201392) Fr & Eur.

Larousse Dictionnaire Francaise-Espagnol, Espagnol-Francais Saturne. rev. ed. Pelayo Garcia & Ramon G. Gross. (FRE & SPA.). 1632p. 1993. 85.00 (*0-7859-5600-X*) Fr & Eur.

Larousse Dictionnaire General. 1744p. 1995. 40.00 (*2-03-320300-X*) LKC.

Larousse Dictionnaire General. Patrice Mabourguet. (FRE.). 1690p. 1993. 69.95 (*0-7859-7124-6*, 203320300X) Fr & Eur.

Larousse Dictionnaire Historique, Thematique et Technique des Litteratures, 2 vols. Jacques Demougin. (FRE.). 1985. 395.00 (*0-7859-7665-5*, 2035083001) Fr & Eur.

Larousse Dictionnaire Mots Croises. (FRE.). 1998. 69.95 (*0-320-00359-0*) Fr & Eur.

Larousse Dictionnaire Noms Communs, Noms Propres. (FRE.). 1998. 22.95 (*0-320-00401-5*) Fr & Eur.

Larousse du Chevel. Ed. by Pierre Rousselet-Blanc. (FRE.). 1976. 85.00 (*0-8288-5726-1*, F12080) Fr & Eur.

Larousse Enciclopedia Alfabetica, 10 vols. Ed. by Larousse Editorial Staff. (SPA.). 1994. 995.00 (*0-320-03699-5*) Fr & Eur.

Larousse Encyclopaedia Dictionary (Spanish Edition) see Diccionario Enciclopedia Larousse

Larousse Encyclopedia of Wine. Ed. by Christopher Foulkes. (Illus.). 608p. 1994. 40.00 (*2-03-507022-8*) LKC.

Larousse Encyclopedique, 2 vols. Ed. by Larousse Staff. (FRE.). 2200p. 1994. 195.00 (*0-7859-9303-7*) Fr & Eur.

Larousse Encyclopedique Illustre. Larousse Editors. (FRE., Illus.). 1824p. 1997. 195.00 (*0-7859-9552-8*) Fr & Eur.

Larousse English Dictionary. 1280p. 1997. pap. 15.95 (*2-03-420290-2*, Larousse LKC) LKC.

Larousse Francais-Anglais - Anglais-Francais de Poche. Larousse Staff. 8.95 (*0-317-45658-X*); write for info. (*0-8288-7858-7*) Fr & Eur.

Larousse French & English Dictionary of the Environment & Ecology. Peter Collin & Martine Schuwer. (ENG & FRE., Illus.). 386p. 1992. pap. 75.00 (*0-8288-6975-8*, 2034040031) Fr & Eur.

Larousse French-English - English-French Dictionary. (ENG & FRE.). 540p. (C). 1987. pap. 10.95 (*0-8442-1755-7*, VF1755-7) NTC Contemp Pub Co.

Larousse Gastronomique. Larousse Editors. 1215p. 1996. 295.00 (*0-7859-9475-0*) Fr & Eur.

Larousse Gastronomique. Ed. by Larousse Staff. 1152p. 1984. 195.00 (*0-7859-9800-4*) Fr & Eur.

Larousse Gastronomique: The New American Edition of the World's Greatest Culinary Encyclopedia. Ed. by Jennifer H. Lang. LC 88-1178. (Illus.). 1193p. 1988. 60.00 (*0-517-57032-7*, Crown) Crown Pub Group.

Larousse Grammaire du Francais Contemporain. Jean-Claude Chevalier. (FRE.). 494p. 1964. 34.95 (*0-7859-7082-7*, 2038000441) Fr & Eur.

Larousse Grande Dictionnaire Francais-Anglais, Anglais-Francais, Vol. 1. Faye Carney. (ENG & FRE.). 978p. 1993. 65.00 (*0-614-00398-9*, 2034013018) Fr & Eur.

Larousse Grande Dictionnaire Francais-Anglais, Anglais-Francais, 2 vols., Vol. 2. Faye Carney. (ENG & FRE.). 125.00 (*0-7859-7564-0*, 203401300X) Fr & Eur.

Larousse Illustrated International Encyclopedia. Larousse Staff. 1975. text 11.50 (*0-07-036479-6*) McGraw.

Larousse Informatique: English-French. Peter Collin. (ENG & FRE.). 321p. 1991. pap. 79.95 (*0-7859-7659-0*, 2034040023) Fr & Eur.

Larousse "L3", 3 vols. Larousse Staff. 495.00 (*0-317-45659-8*) Fr & Eur.

Larousse L3, 3 vols., Set. Larousse Staff. 595.00 (*0-8288-7842-0*, M6473) Fr & Eur.

*__Larousse Maxi-Debutants.__ Distribooks Inc. Staff. (FRE., Illus.). 1999. 40.00 (*2-03-320159-7*, Larousse LKC) LKC.

Larousse Medical. Ed. by Larousse Staff. 1142p. 1995. 195.00 (*0-7859-9843-8*) Fr & Eur.

Larousse Mercury French-Spanish, Spanish-French Dictionary: Dictionnaire Mercure Francais-Espagnol-Francais. Larousse Staff. (FRE & SPA.). 1981. 35.00 (*0-8288-0739-6*, S34571) Fr & Eur.

Larousse Mini Dictionary French-English. 640p. pap. 4.95 (*2-03-420913-3*, Larousse LKC) LKC.

*__Larousse Mini German/English: English/German Dictionary.__ (Illus.). 1794p. 2000. vinyl bd. 5.95 (*2-03-540026-0*) LKC.

*__Larousse Mini German/English Dictionary.__ Larousse Staff. (GER.). 672p. 1999. pap. 5.95 (*2-03-420912-5*) LKC.

*__Larousse Mini Italian/English Dictionary.__ Larousse Staff. (ITA.). 640p. 1999. pap. 5.95 (*2-03-420911-7*) LKC.

Larousse of Alcohol: Larousse des Alcools. Jacques Salle & Bernard Salle. 240p. 1981. 75.00 (*0-8288-0759-0*, M10623) Fr & Eur.

Larousse of Cocktails: Larousse des Cocktails. Jacques Salle & Bernard Salle. (FRE.). 256p. 1986. pap. 27.95 (*0-7859-4617-9*) Fr & Eur.

Larousse of Minerals: Larousse des Mineraux. H. J. Schubnel. (FRE.). 368p. 1981. 75.00 (*0-8288-1469-4*, F12650) Fr & Eur.

Larousse Pocket Encyclopedia of Wine. Ed. by Christopher Foulkes. (Illus.). 256p. 1995. 11.95 (*2-03-507201-8*) LKC.

*__Larousse Pocket Italian/English Dictionary.__ Larousse Staff. LC 98-75563. (ITA.). 576p. 1999. pap. 5.50 (*2-03-420715-7*) LKC.

Larousse pour Tous. Larousse Staff. 18.95 (*0-317-45662-8*) Fr & Eur.

Larousse Practical English-Spanish Technical-Scientific Vocabulary: Vocabulario Pratico Larousse Tecnico-Cientifico Ingles-Espanol. Larousse Staff. (ENG & SPA.). 670p. 1984. 9.95 (*0-8288-0663-2*, F13910) Fr & Eur.

Larousse Saturne French-English - English-French Dictionary. M. M. Dubois. 1616p. 1988. 49.95 (*0-685-19997-5*) Fr & Eur.

*__Larousse Sinonimos y Antonimos.__ Distribooks Incorporated, Staff. (SPA.). 1999. pap. 8.95 (*970-607-127-X*, Larousse LKC) LKC.

*__Larousse Standard French-English, English-French Dictionary.__ 1968p. 1999. 32.00 (*2-03-420261-9*) LKC.

*__Larousse Standard Spanish-English - English-Spanish Dictionary.__ 1440p. 1999. 32.95 (*2-03-420281-3*) LKC.

Larousse Thesaurus. Ed. by Larousse Staff. (FRE.). 1148p. 1995. 49.95 (*0-7859-9301-0*) Fr & Eur.

Larousse Universal, 2 vols., Level 2. 295.00 (*0-317-45663-6*) Fr & Eur.

Larousse Universel, 2 vols., Level 2. Larousse Staff. (FRE.). 1800p. 1969. 395.00 (*0-8288-6609-0*, F128509); 295.00 (*0-685-62924-4*, F12850) Fr & Eur.

Larousse's French-English Dictionary. Ed. by Larousse Staff. LC 96-163295. 720p. 1996. per. 5.99 (*0-671-53407-6*) PB.

Larousse's French-English, English-French Dictionary. Marguerite-Mari Dubois. (ENG & FRE.). 1971. 11.09 (*0-606-03767-5*, Pub. by Turtleback) Demco.

Larque on the Wing. Nancy Springer. 2000. 20.00 (*0-380-97234-4*, Avon Bks) Morrow Avon.

Larry: A Biography of Lawrence D. Bell. Donald J. Norton. LC 80-27791. (Illus.). 280p. 1981. text 37.95 (*0-88229-615-9*) Burnham Inc.

Larry: The Stooge in the Middle. Morris Fineburg. 1999. pap. 19.95 (*0-86719-308-5*) Last Gasp.

Larry & Streak: Rescue Party. large type ed. Marshall Grover. (Linford Western Library). 256p. 1987. pap. 16.99 (*0-7089-6405-2*) Ulverscroft.

Larry & the Cookie. Becky B. McDaniel. LC 92-37871. (Rookie Readers Ser.). (Illus.). 32p. (J). (ps-2). 1993. lib. bdg. 17.00 (*0-516-02014-5*) Childrens.

Larry Bird. Sean Dolan. LC 94-5776. (Basketball Legends Ser.). (Illus.). 64p. (J). (gr. 3 up). 1994. lib. bdg. 15.95 (*0-7910-2427-X*) Chelsea Hse.

Larry Bird. Bob Italia. Ed. by Rosemary Wallner. LC 92-20131. (Most Valuable Player Ser.). 32p. (J). 1992. lib. bdg. 13.98 (*1-56239-122-4*) ABDO Pub Co.

Larry Bird: An Indiana Legend. Indianapolis Star News Staff. (Illus.). 200p. 1998. 29.95 (*1-58261-008-8*) Sports Pub.

*__Larry Boy & the Fib from Outer Space.__ Lyrick Publishing Staff. (Veggietales Ser.). (Illus.). 30p. (ps-3). 1999. pap. 6.95 (*1-57064-625-2*) Lyrick Pub.

Larry Burkett's Bill Organizer. Larry Burkett. 1997. pap. text 14.99 (*0-8024-7061-0*) Moody.

Larry Burkett's Little Instruction Book on Managing Your Money. Larry Burkett. 160p. 1997. pap. 6.99 (*1-56292-152-5*) Honor Bks OK.

*__Larry Clark.__ (Illus.). 174p. 1999. 75.00 (*90-71691-45-4*, Pub. by Groninger Museum) RAM Publications.

Larry Cohen: The Radical Allegories of an Independent Filmmaker. Tony Williams. LC 97-10731. (Illus.). 463p. 1997. lib. bdg. 52.50 (*0-7864-0350-0*) McFarland & Co.

Larry Conrad of Indiana: A Biography. Raymond H. Scheele & Indiana University-Purdue University Indianapolis. LC 97-9968. 1997. 29.95 (*0-253-33329-6*) Ind U Pr.

Larry Crabb's Gospel. Martin Bobgan & Deidre Bobgan. LC 98-93330. 1998. pap. 12.00 (*0-941717-14-3*) EastGate Pubs.

Larry Eigner: A Bibliography of His Works. Irving P. Leif. LC 88-27017. (Author Bibliographies Ser.: No. 84). (Illus.). 251p. 1989. 32.00 (*0-8108-2210-5*) Scarecrow.

Larry Fink: Fish & Wine, Larry Fink's Photographs of Portugal. George E. Panichas. (Illus.). 24p. 1997. pap. 8.50 (*0-9660322-0-9*) Lafayette Coll.

Larry Flynt Kills JFK Assassination Article: After Flynt Offered $1,000,000 Reward for Proof of Conspiracy. large type ed. Bruce Campbell Adamson. Ed. by Donald Knight. (Illus.). 65p. 1998. 10.00 (*1-892501-14-7*) B C Adamson.

Larry Gatlin Songbook. Composed by Larry Gatlin. 112p. 1996. otabind 16.95 (*0-7935-6076-4*) H Leonard.

Larry Gorman. Edward Ives. 184p. 1993. pap. 14.95 (*0-86492-152-7*, Pub. by Goose Ln Edits) Genl Dist Srvs.

Larry Gorman: The Man Who Made the Songs. Ed. by Edward D. Ives & Edward Dorson. LC 77-70601. (International Folklore Ser.). (Illus.). 1977. reprint ed. lib. bdg. 21.95 (*0-405-10100-7*) Ayer.

*__Larry Guest Lite: Glib Slants on Sports from the Orlando Sentinel's Award-Winning Columnist.__ Larry Guest. 168p. 1999. pap. 14.95 (*0-942627-54-7*) Woodford Pubng.

Larry Hatteberg's Kansas People. Larry Hatteberg. 1991. pap. 15.95 (*0-9631186-0-9*) Jular KS.

Larry Hatteberg's Kansas People: A Collection of Colorful Personalities from the Sunflower State. Ed. by Howard Inglish. 160p. 1993. 28.00 (*0-9631186-1-7*) Jular KS.

Larry Holmes: Against the Odds. Larry Holmes & Phil Berger. LC 98-26973. 288p. 1998. 24.95 (*0-312-18736-X*, Thomas Dunne) St Martin.

Larry Holmes Boxing Tactics & Techniques. Larry Holmes & Nelson. 1996. pap. 8.95 (*0-8092-5325-9*, Contemporary Bks) NTC Contemp Pub Co.

Larry Hunt's Keys to Successful Quick Printing. Larry Hunt. LC 88-91332. 280p. 1988. pap. 48.00 (*0-9621193-0-X*) L Hunt.

Larry Johnson, King of the Court. Bill Gutman. (Millbrook Sports World Ser.). (J). 1995. 11.15 (*0-606-07772-3*) Turtleback.

*__Larry Kane's Philadelphia.__ Larry Kane. (Illus.). 256p. 2000. 24.50 (*1-56639-806-1*) Temple U Pr.

*__Larry Kirkland: Twenty-Five Years.__ Larry Kirkland. Ed. by Elaine Shinamizy. (Illus.). 112p. 1999. pap. write for info. (*0-9674132-0-6*) LightWater.

Larry L. King: A Writer's Life in Letters: or Reflections in a Bloodshot Eye. Larry L. King. Ed. by Richard Holland. LC 99-22568. (Illus.). 404p. 1999. 24.95 (*0-87565-203-4*, Pub. by Tex Christian) Tex A&M Univ Pr.

Larry L. King: A Writer's Life in Letters, or Reflections in a Bloodshot Eye. Larry L. King & Richard Holland. LC 99-22568. 1999. pap. 27.50 (*0-87565-214-X*) Tex Christian.

Larry Larsen on Bass Tactics. Larry Larsen. LC 92-74325. (Larsen on Bass Ser.). (Illus.). 228p. (Orig.). (C). 1992. pap. text 12.95 (*0-936513-27-6*) Larsens Outdoor.

Larry Legend. Mark Shaw. 384p. 1999. pap. 15.95 (*0-8092-2529-8*, 252980, Mstrs Pr) NTC Contemp Pub Co.

*__Larry Legend: From Superstar to Coach of the Year.__ Mark Shaw. LC 98-27767. (Illus.). 352p. 1998. 23.00 (*1-57028-235-8*, 82358H, Mstrs Pr) NTC Contemp Pub Co.

Larry Lion Learns to Fear Not. Susan Tate. (Petal Pals Ser.). (Illus.). 40p. (J). (gr. k-3). 1993. pap. 3.99 (*1-884395-03-1*) Clear Blue Sky.

*__Larry Lion's Rumbly Rhymes.__ Giles Andreae & David Wojtowycz. (Illus.). (J). (ps-1). 2000. bds. 6.95 (*1-888444-68-1*) Little Tiger.

Larry Little's "Learn Bass Guitar Book" Larry Little. (Illus.). 40p. 1996. pap. 9.95 (*1-884208-10-X*, LLB-18800) Larry Little Co.

Larry Little's "Learn Drums Book" Larry Little & Dave Beyer. (Illus.). 40p. 1996. pap. 9.95 (*1-884208-09-6*, LLB-15800) Larry Little Co.

Larry Little's "Learn Guitar Book" Larry Little. LC 99-172152. (Illus.). 36p. 1996. pap. 9.95 (*1-884208-08-8*, LL-17800) Larry Little Co.

Larry Marder's Beanworld. Larry Marder. (Beanworld Ser.: Bk. 1). Orig. Title: Collection of Tales of the Beanworld Issues #8-11. 128p. 1995. pap. 9.95 (*1-887245-00-6*) Beanworld Pr.

Larry Marder's Beanworld. Larry Marder. (Beanworld Ser.: Bk. 2). Orig. Title: Collection of Tales of the Beanworld Issues #8-11. (Illus.). 104p. 1997. pap. 9.95 (*1-887245-01-4*) Beanworld Pr.

Larry Marder's Beanworld, Vol. 3. Larry Marder. Orig. Title: Collection of Tales of the Beanworld Issues #8-11. (Illus.). 128p. 1998. reprint ed. pap. 11.95 (*1-887245-02-2*) Beanworld Pr.

An Asterisk (*) at the beginning of an entry indicates that the title is appearing for the first time.

***Larry McMillan's Option Strategies Course, 3 Video Set.** Larry McMillian. (Illus.). 40p. 1999. 195.00 (*1-883272-32-7*) Traders Lib.

***Larry Mcmurtry: A Critical Companion.** John M. Reilly. LC 99-49695. (Critical Companions to Popular Contemporary Writers Ser.). 216p. 2000. 29.95 (*0-313-30300-2*) Greenwood.

Larry McMurtry & the Victorian Novel. Roger W. Jones. LC 94-15607. (Tarleton State University Southwestern Studies in the Humanities: No. 5). 112p. 1994. 19.50 (*0-89096-621-4*) Tex A&M Univ Pr.

***Larry Mcmurty: A Reader's Checklist & Reference Guide.** CheckerBee Publishing Staff. 1999. pap. text 4.95 (*1-58598-028-5*) CheckerBee.

Larry Moyer's How to Book: On Personal Evangelism. Larry R. Moyer. LC 98-17621. 128p. 1998. pap. text 7.99 (*0-8254-3179-4*) Kregel.

Larry Nichols Story: Damage Control: How to Get Caught with Your Pants down & Still Get Elected President. David M. Bresnahan. LC 98-12618. 228p. 1998. pap. 14.95 (*1-890828-10-6*, 10-6) Camden Ct.

Larry Niven Checklist. Compiled by Chris Drumm. (Booklet Ser.: No. 10). 24p. (Orig.). 1983. pap. 1.00 (*0-936055-07-3*) C Drumm Bks.

Larry North's Slimdown for Life. Larry North. LC 98-67476. (Illus.). 263p. 1999. 24.00 (*1-57566-403-8*) Kensgtn Pub Corp.

***Larry North's Slimdown for Life: The Real Diet for Real People.** Larry North. 2000. pap. 14.00 (*1-57566-497-6*, Knsington) Kensgtn Pub Corp.

Larry Poons; Paintings, 1971-1981. Kenworth W. Moffett. (Illus.). 32p. (Orig.). 1981. pap. 5.95 (*0-87846-206-6*) Mus Fine Arts Boston.

Larry Poons, 1963-1990. Text by Daniel Robbins & John Zinsser. LC 90-60991. (Illus.). 113p. 1990. pap. 40.00 (*1-58821-060-X*) Salander OReilly.

Larry, Red & Blue. Diane J. Jones. LC 96-900988. (Illus.). 32p. (Orig.). (J). (gr. 2 up). 1997. pap. 12.95 (*0-9699407-2-6*) DJ Jones.

Larry Sitsky: A Bio-Bibliography, 65. Robyn Holmes et al. LC 96-45258. (Bio-Bibliographies in Music Ser.: Vol. 65). 232p. 1997. lib. bdg. 62.95 (*0-313-29020-2*, Greenwood Pr) Greenwood.

Larry Stanton: Drawings & Paintings. Ed. by Henry Geldzahler et al. (Illus.). 96p. 1986. 35.00 (*0-942642-29-5*) Twelvetrees Pr.

Larry the Lizard. Joy Vaughan-Brown. Ed. by Eric H. Brown. (Illus.). 32p. (J). (gr. 3-6). 1998. 12.95 (*1-889306-03-7*) Hilton A Vaughan.

Larry the Lobster: Everyday Songs from Everywhere. Lisa A. Parker. Ed. by Michael D. Bennett. 40p. (Orig.). 1993. pap. 10.95 (*0-934017-19-0*) Memphis Musicraft.

Larry Walker, Intro. by Jim Murray. LC 98-54816. (Baseball Legends Ser.). (Illus.). 64p. (YA). (gr. 3 up). 1999. 16.95 (*0-7910-5159-5*) Chelsea Hse.

Larry Walker: Colorado Hit Man! Tony DeMarco. Ed. by Rob Rains. (Super Star Ser.). 96p. (J). 1999. pap. 4.95 (*1-58261-052-5*) Sprts Pubng.

Larry Wilde Treasury of Laughter. Larry Wilde. (Illus.). 256p. 1992. 25.00 (*0-945040-01-6*) Jester Pr CA.

Larry's Favorite Chocolate Cake. Kent R. Brown. 85p. 1997. pap. 5.50 (*0-87129-649-7*, L14) Dramatic Pub.

Larry's Landscape. 2nd ed. Price. (AB - Accounting Principles Ser.). 1995. mass mkt. 21.95 (*0-538-86089-8*) S-W Pub.

***Larry's Lawn Care Practice Set - Accounting.** 20th ed. Warren. (SWC-Accounting Ser.). 2001. pap. 20.25 (*0-324-05288-X*) Sth-Wstrn College.

Larry's Party. Carol Shields. 352p. 1998. pap. 12.95 (*0-14-026677-1*) Viking Penguin.

Larry's Party. large type ed. Carol Shields. LC 98-14664. 1998. 25.95 (*1-56895-537-5*, Wheeler) Wheeler Pub.

Lars: A Pastoral of Norway. Bayard Taylor. (Notable American Authors). 1999. reprint ed. lib. bdg. 125.00 (*0-7812-8991-2*) Rprt Serv.

Lars Gustafsson & Philip Martin. Lars Gustafsson & Philip Martin. (QRL Poetry Bks.: Vol. XXIII). (SWE.). 1982. 20.00 (*0-614-06404-X*) Quarterly Rev.

Lars Hoftrup & Armand Wargny: A Retrospective of Drawings, Paintings & Prints. Intro. by Alexander D. Falck, Jr. (Illus.). 64p. (Orig.). 1978. pap. 3.75 (*1-877885-01-0*) Arnot Art.

Lars Valerian Ahlfors: Collected Papers, 2 Vols., 1. Intro. by Lars V. Ahlfors. 544p. 1983. 122.00 (*0-8176-3075-9*) Birkhauser.

Lars Valerian Ahlfors: Collected Papers, 2 Vols., 2. Intro. by Lars V. Ahlfors. 544p. 1983. 122.00 (*0-8176-3076-7*) Birkhauser.

Lars Valerian Ahlfors: Collected Papers, 2 Vols., Set. Intro. by Lars V. Ahlfors. 544p. 1980. 194.50 (*0-8176-3077-5*) Birkhauser.

Larsa Year Names. Marcel Sigrist. LC 90-82318. (Assyriological Ser.: AS Vol. 3). 96p. (C). 1990. pap. text 29.99 (*0-943872-54-5*) Andrews Univ Pr.

Larsen's Opening. Bill Wall. (Illus.). 57p. (Orig.). 1986. pap. 6.00 (*0-931462-55-X*) Chess Ent.

***Larsen's Opening.** Tim Wall. (Chess Bks.). (Illus.). 1999. pap. text 15.95 (*0-7134-8584-1*) B T B.

Larsen's Shapes, Colors & Numbers. Margie Larsen. (Barney's Beginnings Ser.). (Illus.). (J). (ps-1). 1996. pap. 2.95 (*0-614-15552-5*) BDD Bks Young Read.

Larson's Book of Rock. Bob Larson. 192p. 1987. pap. 7.99 (*0-8423-5687-8*) Tyndale Hse.

Larson's Book of Spiritual Warfare. Bob Larson. LC 98-51360. 504p. 1999. pap. 15.99 (*0-7852-6985-1*) Nelson.

Larsons Creations: Guitars & Mandolins. Robert C. Hartman. 208p. 1996. pap. 39.95 (*0-931759-77-3*) Centerstream Pub.

Larson's New Book of Cults. Bob Larson. 499p. 1989. pap. 12.99 (*0-8423-2860-2*) Tyndale Hse.

Larson's TI-73 Math Activities: Applications for the Real World. Katherine A. Shaffer. (Illus.). 130p. 1999. wbk. ed. 29.95 (*1-58123-072-9*, MC-MTI-101) Meridian Creative.

Larsson. 1996. pap. 5.99 (*3-8228-9580-6*) Taschen Amer.

L'arte dei Rumore see Art of Noises

Lartigue: Jacques-Henri Latigue, Photographer, Vol. 1. Vicki Goldberg. LC TR653.L384 1998. (Illus.). 288p. (gr. 8). 1998. 95.00 (*0-8212-2549-9*) Little.

Lartigue's Riviera. Text by Kenneth E. Silver. (Illus.). 144p. 1997. 35.00 (*2-08-013640-2*, Pub. by Flammarion) Abbeville Pr.

Larue County, Kentucky, 1850 Census. Mary J. Jones. 97p. 1982. pap. 12.00 (*1-889221-24-4*) Ancestral Trails.

Larue County, Kentucky, 1860 Census. annot. ed. Joyce Howell & Shirley Helton. 114p. 1993. pap. 14.00 (*1-889221-25-2*) Ancestral Trails.

Larue D. Carter Memorial Hospital Case-Study: A Behaviorial Approach to Environmental Normalization in Mental Health Settings. Alfredo R. Missair & Bruce F. Meyer. (Illus.). 16p. 1983. pap. 8.00 (*0-912431-03-2*) Ctr Env Des Res.

La/Ruine Preque Cocasse d'un Polichinelle see Lament for an African Pol

Larum for London. LC 74-133695. (Tudor Facsimile Texts. Old English Plays Ser.: No. 100). reprint ed. 49.50 (*0-404-53400-7*) AMS Pr.

LaRune's Rockpecker Notes: "A Mineral Prospector's Primer" unabridged ed. T. D. LaRune. Ed. by M. S. Worth. LC 94-67809. (Illus.). 543p. (C). 1996. lib. bdg. 36.00 (*1-886499-00-4*, Skill Ware) Skill-Quest.

Larva: Midsummer Night's Babel. Julian Rios. Tr. by Richard A. Francis & Suzanne J. Levine from SPA. LC 90-3773. (Illus.). 685p. 1990. 27.50 (*0-916583-66-X*) Dalkey Arch.

Larvae of Curculionoidae (Insecta: Coleoptera) a Systematic Overview see Fauna of New Zealand Series

Larvae of Marine Bivalves & Echinoderms. V. L. Kasyanov et al. Ed. by David L. Pawson. (Illus.). 296p. 1998. text 98.00 (*1-886106-80-0*, 6800) Science Pubs.

Larvae of Temperate Australian Fishes: Laboratory Guide for Larval Fish Identification. Francisco J. Neira et al. (Illus.). 436p. 1998. 125.00 (*1-875560-72-6*, Pub. by Univ of West Aust Pr); pap. 95.00 (*1-876268-17-4*, Pub. by Univ of West Aust Pr) Intl Spec Bk.

Larvae of the Caddisfly Genera Triaenodes & Ylodes (Trichoptera: Leptoceridae) in North America. James B. Glover. LC 95-71128. (Bulletin Ser.: Vol. 11, No. 2). (Illus.). (C). 1996. pap. text 20.00 (*0-86727-119-1*) Ohio Bio Survey.

Larvae of the Caddisfly Genus Oecetis (Trichoptera: Leptoceridae) in North America. Michael A. Floyd. LC 95-69878. (Bulletin New Ser.: Vol. 10, No. 3). 1995. pap. text 20.00 (*0-86727-116-7*) Ohio Bio Survey.

Larvae of the Gall Midges (Diptera & Cecidomyiidae) B. M. Mamaev & N. P. Krivosheina. Ed. by J. C. Roskam. Tr. by J. H. Wieffering. (Illus.). 304p. (C). 1991. text 123.00 (*90-6191-787-5*, Pub. by A A Balkema) Ashgate Pub Co.

Larvae of the North American Caddisfly Genera (Trichoptera) Glenn B. Wiggins. 1977. text 55.00 (*0-8020-5344-0*) U of Toronto Pr.

Larvae of the North American Caddisfly Genera (Trichoptera) 2nd ed. Glenn B. Wiggins. 456p. 1995. text 110.00 (*0-8020-2723-7*) U of Toronto Pr.

Larval & Juvenile Cephalopods: A Manual for Their Identification. Ed. by Michael J. Sweeney et al. LC 91-22098. (Smithsonian Contributions to Zoology Ser.: No. 513). 290p. reprint ed. pap. 89.90 (*0-7837-2018-1*, 204229300002) Bks Demand.

Larval Fish & Shellfish Transport Through Inlets. Ed. by M. P. Weinstein. LC 88-70511. (Symposium Ser.: No. 3). 165p. 1988. pap. 19.00 (*0-913235-46-6*, 540.03) Am Fisheries Soc.

Larval Forms & Other Zoological Verses. Walter Garstang. LC 85-14114. (Illus.). xvi, 98p. 1985. reprint ed. pap. 6.95 (*0-226-28423-9*) U Ch Pr.

Laryngeal Biomechanics. B. Raymond Fink & Robert J. Demarest. LC 77-26937. (Commonwealth Fund Publications). (Illus.). 176p. 1978. 42.50 (*0-674-51085-2*) HUP.

Laryngeal Cancer. Carl E. Silver. (Illus.). 448p. 1991. text 99.00 (*0-86577-395-5*) Thieme Med Pubs.

Laryngeal Cancer: Proceedings World Congress on Laryngeal Cancer (2nd: 1994 Sydney, N. S. W.) Ed. by Robert Smee & G. Patrick Bridger. LC 94-42694. (International Congress Ser.: No. 1063). 780p. 1995. 292.00 (*0-444-81810-3*) Elsevier.

***Laryngeal Electromyography.** Sataloff. 2002. pap. 40.00 (*0-7693-0168-1*, Pub. by Singular Publishing) Thomson Learn.

Laryngeal Function in Phonation & Respiration. Ed. by Katherine Harris et al. (Illus.). 598p. (Orig.). (C). 1991. reprint ed. pap. text 75.00 (*1-879105-22-5*, A004) Singular Publishing.

Laryngeal Mask Airway: A Review & Practical Guide. J. R. Brimacombe et al. (Illus.). 314p. 1997. pap. text 68.00 (*0-7020-2321-3*, Pub. by Harcourt) Saunders.

Laryngectomee Rehabilitation. 3rd ed. Ed. by Robert L. Keith & Frederic L. Darley. LC 93-39466. (Illus.). (C). 1994. text 44.00 (*0-89079-590-8*, 6688) PRO-ED.

Larynx. 2nd ed. Ed. by Harvey M. Tucker. (Illus.). 336p. 1992. text 99.00 (*0-86577-437-4*) Thieme Med Pubs.

Larynx: A Multidisciplinary Approach. 2nd ed. Marvin P. Fried. (Illus.). 672p. (C). (gr. 13). 1995. text 149.00 (*0-8016-8046-8*, 08046) Mosby Inc.

Larysa & Andrijko Series, Set. (ENG & UKR., Illus.). (J). (gr. 3 up). 1991. 11.75 (*1-882406-04-4*) M A K Pubns.

Larzac. Roger Rawlinson. 212p. 1999. pap. 30.00 (*1-85072-177-7*, Pub. by W Sessions) St Mut.

***Las Alas del Espiritu: Liberar la Identidad Espiritual.** Health Communciations Staff. (SPA.). 2000. pap. 12.95 (*1-55874-782-6*) Health Comm.

***Las Alas del Espiritu: Liberar la Identidad Espiritual.** Dadi Janki. (SPA., Illus.). 160p. 2000. pap. 12.95 (*1-55874-790-7*) Health Comm.

Las Antiguas Escuelas de Sabiduria. Ramtha. Ed. by Diane Munoz-Smith. Tr. by Juan M. Castro. Orig. Title: Ancient Schools of Wisdom. (SPA.). 196p. 1997. pap. 17.00 (*0-9632573-6-6*) Sin Limites.

Las Cruces. San Antonio Cartographers Staff. 1995. 2.95 (*0-671-56277-0*) Macmillan.

Las Cruces: An Illustrated History. Linda G. Harris. LC 93-22913. (Illus.). 144p. (J). 1993. 29.95 (*0-9623682-5-3*) Arroyo Pr.

Las Cruces Country. Ed. by W. R. Seager et al. (Guidebook Ser.: No. 26). (Illus.). 376p. 1975. 15.00 (*1-58546-056-7*) NMex Geol Soc.

***Las Cruces County, Vol. II.** Ed. by G. H. Mack et al. (Guidebook Ser.: No. 49). (Illus.). 325p. 1998. pap. 45.00 (*1-58546-084-2*) NMex Geol Soc.

***Las dos Cruces de Todos Santos.** Maud Oakes. (SPA.). 200p. 2000. pap. 12.95 (*1-886502-33-1*) Yax Te Found.

Las Enfants de la Guerre: Seuls Dans la View au Sud du Soudan. (FRE.). 1994. 4.95 (*92-806-3121-7*) U N I C E.

Las Epistolas Generales: Santiago, I y II Pedro, I, II, III Juan, Judeg. Charles Erdman. (SPA.). 194p. 1986. pap. 6.95 (*0-939125-31-5*) CRC Wrld Lit.

***Las Jovenes Que Viven Con la Infeccion del VIH.** 1998. 5.00 (*1-877966-56-8*) Ctr Women Policy.

***Las Necesidades de Vivienda de las Mujeres Con VIH-SIDA.** 1998. pap. 5.00 (*1-877966-49-5*) Ctr Women Policy.

Las Ocurrencias del Increible Mula Nasrudin. Idries Shah. (SPA.). 1992. pap. 15.00 (*84-7509-404-X*) Paidos Iberica.

Las! Ou Vas-Tu Sans Moy, Je Pleure, Je Me Deux see Florilege du Concert Vocal de la Renaissance

Las Piedras del Cielo see Heaven Stones

***Las Posadas: An Hispanic Christmas Celebration.** Diane Hoyt-Goldsmith. (Illus.). (gr. 4-7). 2000. 6.95 (*0-8234-1635-6*) Holiday.

***Las Praderas.** Two Can Publishing Ltd. Staff. (SPA.). 2000. mass mkt. 4.95 (*1-58728-973-3*) Two Can Pub.

***Las Preguntas De La Vida.** Fernando Savater. 1999. pap. 19.95 (*84-344-1185-7*) Planeta.

***Las Tortillas de Magda.** Becky Chavarria-Chairez. Tr. by Julia Mercedes Castilla. (SPA., Illus.). 32p. (ps-3). 2000. 14.95 (*1-55885-286-7*) Arte Publico.

Las Vegas. pap. 6.95 (*0-528-96517-4*) Rand McNally.

Las Vegas. Frances Anderton & John Chase. LC 98-127802. (Architecture in Context Ser.). (ENG, FRE & GER., Illus.). 80p. 1997. pap. 9.95 (*3-89508-288-0*, 810091) Konemann.

Las Vegas. Frances Anderton & John Chase. (Architecture Guides Ser.). (Illus.). 320p. 1998. pap. 5.95 (*3-89508-639-8*, 520204) Konemann.

***Las Vegas.** Isabella Brega. (Illus.). 2000. 9.99 (*0-7858-1240-7*) Bk Sales Inc.

***Las Vegas.** Scott Doggett. (Lonely Planet Travel Guides Ser.). (Illus.). 256p. 2000. pap. 15.95 (*1-86450-086-7*) Lonely Planet.

***Las Vegas.** Rick Garman. 1999. pap. 15.95 (*0-02-863375-X*) Glencoe.

Las Vegas. Mark Gottdiener & Claudia C. Collins. LC 99-22551. 300p. 1999. 59.95 (*1-57718-136-0*); pap. 22.95 (*1-57718-137-9*) Blackwell Pubs.

Las Vegas. Insight Guides Staff. (Insight Guides). 1998. pap. text 7.95 (*0-88729-538-X*) Langenscheidt.

***Las Vegas.** Alain Legault. 2000. pap. 12.95 (*2-89464-269-5*, Pub. by Ulysses Travel) Globe Pequot.

Las Vegas. Shotenkenchiku-Sha Editors. (Illus.). 180p. 1997. 69.95 (*4-7858-0112-3*, Pub. by Shotenkenchiku-Sha) Bks Nippan.

Las Vegas. Santi Visalli. (Illus.). 192p. 1996. pap. 25.00 (*0-7893-0051-6*) St Martin.

Las Vegas. Santi Visalli. (Illus.). 192p. 1996. 40.00 (*0-7893-0074-5*, Pub. by Universe) St Martin.

Las Vegas. 2nd ed. Deke Castleman. Ed. by Barry Parr. LC 93-1244. (Compass American Guides Ser.). (Illus.). 320p. 1998. pap. 18.95 (*1-878867-47-4*, Compass Amrcn) Fodors Travel.

Las Vegas. 4th ed. Access Press Staff. (Illus.). 144p. 1997. pap. 19.00 (*0-06-277224-4*, Access Trvl) HarpInfo.

Las Vegas: A New Dimension . . . a New Destiny. 3rd ed. Robert Macy & Melinda Macy. 78p. 1996. pap. 10.00 (*0-9649096-2-6*) M M Graphics.

Las Vegas: Access Travel Guide. Richard S. Wurman. write for info. (*0-318-59685-7*) S&S Trade.

***Las Vegas: Also Includes Reno, Lake Tahoe & Laughlin 2001.** Corey Sandler. (Econoguides Ser.). (Illus.). 2000. pap. 17.95 (*0-8092-2638-3*, Contemporary Bks) NTC Contemp Pub Co.

***Las Vegas: Insiders' Guide for Cosmopolitan Travelers.** Dan Levine. (Avant-Guide Bks.). (Illus.). 2000. pap. 19.95 (*1-891603-11-6*) Empire Pr.

Las Vegas: One in a Million. David Hofstede & Mike O'Callaghan. (Urban Tapestry Ser.). (Illus.). 176p. 1995. 39.50 (*1-881096-23-8*) Towery Pub.

***Las Vegas: Pocket Guide.** Berlitz Publishing Staff. (Pocket Guides Ser.). (Illus.). 1999. pap. 8.95 (*2-8315-7142-1*) Berlitz.

Las Vegas: The Great American Playground. Robert D. McCracken. (Illus.). 128p. 1996. pap. 10.95 (*0-9639119-8-8*) Marion Street.

Las Vegas: The Great American Playground. 2nd expanded rev. ed. Robert D. McCracken. LC 97-3272. (Illus.). 160p. 1997. pap. 15.95 (*0-87417-301-9*) U of Nev Pr.

Las Vegas: 16 Hotel & Casinos, 5 Theme Restaurants. Shoichi Muto. LC 98-140734. 1997. 69.95 (*4-7858-0250-2*, Pub. by Shotenkenchiku-Sha) Bks Nippan.

Las Vegas - Southern Nevada: Hometown Living Las Vegas Style. Jack Sheehan. Ed. by Myrtle D. Malone & Margaret D. Bott. 200p. 1992. 25.00 (*1-881547-15-9*) Pioneer Pubns.

Las Vegas Advisor Guide to Slot Clubs. Jeffrey Compton. 118p. (Orig.). 1995. pap. 9.95 (*0-929712-75-7*) Huntington Pr.

Las Vegas Advisor Guide to Slot Clubs. 2nd ed. Jeffery Compton. (Illus.). 240p. 1999. pap. 12.95 (*0-929712-76-5*) Huntington Pr.

Las Vegas & Laughlin. Mark Chiaramonte. 147p. 1999. 6.95 (*1-56413-460-1*) Auto Club.

Las Vegas, As It Began, As It Grew. Stanley W. Paher. LC 70-175144. (Illus.). 1971. 29.95 (*0-913814-01-6*); pap. 19.95 (*0-913814-74-1*) Nevada Pubns.

Las Vegas Behind the Tables! Barney Vinson. 256p. 1988. pap. 6.99 (*0-914839-15-2*) Gollehon Pr.

Las Vegas Behind the Tables!, Pt. 2. Barney Vinson. 256p. 1988. pap. 6.99 (*0-914839-25-X*) Gollehon Pr.

Las Vegas Blackjack Diary. 3rd rev. ed. Stuart Perry. LC 96-72324. 214p. 1997. pap. 19.95 (*1-886070-08-3*) ConJelCo.

Las Vegas Casino Employment Guide. Lisa Alper & Michael Krause. (Illus.). 95p. (Orig.). 1994. pap. 12.95 (*0-9641012-0-3*) Jordan Pubng.

Las Vegas Child Care Resource Guide: A-Z Childrens Directory. Natalie Littlefield. 168p. 1998. spiral bd. 10.95 (*0-9669726-0-0*) Child Care Connection.

Las Vegas Children's Coloring Book: A Family Adventure to Remember. Grant V. Diebold. (Illus.). 32p. (J). (gr. 1-5). 1995. 1.95 (*0-9645900-7-7*) Diebold Pubns.

Las Vegas Cooks! Recipes from Popular Restaurants on the Strip, Downtown, & Across the Las Vegas Valley. Linda Lissen. LC 97-73358. (Illus.). 123p. 1997. pap. 10.95 (*0-9658172-0-2*) All She Wrote.

Las Vegas Cuisine 1998, Vol. 2. rev. ed. Kendall Ashcoff. 100p. 1998. pap. 5.95 (*0-9632234-3-7*) R Hart Mktg.

***Las Vegas Entertainment, 2000.** (Illus.). 550p. 1999. pap. 30.00 (*1-880248-36-0*, 00P1) Enter Pubns.

***Las Vegas for Dummies.** Mary Herczog. (For Dummies Ser.). 336p. 2000. pap. 15.99 (*0-7645-6162-6*) IDG Bks.

Las Vegas for Less. Metropolis International Editors. 2000. pap. text 9.95 (*1-901811-56-5*) Metropolis International.

***Las Vegas Guide.** 5th ed. Ed Kranmar et al. (Illus.). 272p. 1999. pap. 14.95 (*1-892975-10-6*) Open Rd Pub.

Las Vegas Hiking Guide. Paula M. Jacoby-Garrett. LC 98-142168. (Illus.). iv, 89p. 1997. pap. 11.95 (*0-9658439-0-4*) Zing Publ.

Las Vegas Illusion. Carolyn S. DeFever. LC 93-83080. 256p. 1993. text 21.95 (*0-9626117-6-X*) Paisley TX.

Las Vegas JobBank. 2nd ed. Ed. by Adams Media Corporation Staff. (JobBank Ser.). 304p. 1998. pap. 16.95 (*1-58062-031-0*) Adams Media.

***Las Vegas JobBank.** 3rd ed. (JobBank Ser.). 304p. 2000. pap. 16.95 (*1-58062-450-2*) Adams Media.

Las Vegas Nightfighters. Paul Blanton. 108p. 1998. pap. 9.95 (*0-9665355-0-2*) P Blanton.

***Las Vegas on the Dime: An Insider's Guide to Great Deals.** Michael Toole. 144p. 2000. pap. 12.95 (*1-881409-27-9*) Jhnstn Assocs.

***Las Vegas Pocket Guide: Spanish ed.** Berlitz Publishing Staff. (Berlitz Pocket Guide Ser.). 1999. pap. 8.95 (*2-8315-7273-8*) Berlitz.

Las Vegas, Reno, Laughlin, Lake Tahoe. Corey Sandler. LC 95-30905. (Contemporary's Econoguide '97 Ser.). (Illus.). 352p. 1995. pap. 12.95 (*0-8092-3323-1*) NTC Contemp Pub Co.

Las Vegas, Reno, Laughlin, Lake Tahoe: 2000 Edition. Corey Sandler. (Econoguide '99 Ser.). (Illus.). 352p. 1998. pap. 15.95 (*0-8092-3091-7*, Contemporary Bks) NTC Contemp Pub Co.

Las Vegas, Reno, Laughlin, Lake Tahoe: 2000 Edition. Corey Sandler. (Econoguides Ser.). (Illus.). 368p. 1999. pap. 15.95 (*0-8092-2648-0*, 264800, Contemporary Bks) NTC Contemp Pub Co.

***Las Vegas, Reno, Tahoe 2000.** Fodors Travel Publications, Inc. Staff. (Illus.). 1999. pap. 15.00 (*0-679-00360-6*) Fodors Travel.

Las Vegas Ride Guide: Fat Tire Explorations. LaMont J. Singley. (Illus.). 86p. (Orig.). 1995. pap. text 8.95 (*0-9644414-0-3*) Desert Quest Pr.

Las Vegas Secrets: A New Traveler's Guide. rev. ed. Milly Singletary. (Illus.). (Orig.). 1988. pap. 3.95 (*0-941244-00-8*) Singletary Pubns.

Las Vegas Single Track Gourmet. Suzanne Shelp. 2p. 1994. pap. 8.95 (*0-934641-94-3*) Falcon Pub Inc.

***Las Vegas, the Best of Glitter City Vol. 1: An Impertinent Insiders' Guide.** 2nd ed. Don W. Martin & Betty W. Martin. LC 97-67633. (Best of...Ser.). (Illus.). 284p. 2000. pap. 15.95 (*0-942053-33-8*) Pine Cone Pr NV.

Las Vegas to Death Valley Road Guide: History, Geology, Etc. Seen on Roads Between Las Vegas & Death Valley National Park. Roger G. Brandt. LC 96-68899. (Illus.). 80p. (Orig.). 1996. pap. 7.95 (*1-889275-04-2*, 11) Pupfish Publns.

***Las Vegas Trivia.** John Gollehon. 192p. 2000. pap. 6.99 (*0-914839-54-3*) Gollehon Pr.

***Las Vegas 2001.** Ed. by Zagat Publishers Staff. (Illus.). 2000. pap. 9.95 (*1-57006-240-4*) Zagat.

Las Vegas Valley Gardening. Cecelia St. Denis. 178p. 1991. pap. text. write for info. (*0-9637992-3-1*) Rose Garden Club.

Las Vegas Weddings: A Guide for Every Bride. Melissa Cook. (Illus.). 150p. 1999. pap. 12.95 (*0-929712-80-3*) Huntington Pr.

L

Las Vegas with Kids: Where to Go, What to Do in America's Hottest Family Destination. Barbara Land. LC 95-2703. (Illus.). 272p. 1995. pap. 12.95 (*0-7615-0014-6*) Prima Pub.

Las Virtudes Peligrosas see Dangerous Virtues

Lasagna. Jack Bishop. 144p. 1994. pap. 9.95 (*0-8092-3699-0*, 369900, Contemporary Bks) NTC Contemp Pub Co.

Lasagna Gardening: A New Layering System for Bountiful Gardens: No Digging, No Tilling, No Weeding, No Kidding! Patricia Lanza. LC 98-25315. (Illus.). 256p. 1998. pap. 15.95 (*0-87596-962-3*) Rodale Pr Inc.

Lasagna, the Man Behind the Mask: Ronald Cross & the Oka Crisis. Helene Sevigny et al. LC 95-105576. 248p. 1994. pap. 15.95 (*0-88922-348-3*, Pub. by Talonbks) Genl Dist Srvs.

Lasagne. Clifford A. Wright. LC 94-3495. 1995. write for info. (*0-316-95604-X*) Little.

Lasalle & the Discovery of the Great Northwest. Francis Parkman. 560p. 1968. reprint ed. 38.95 (*0-87928-004-2*) Corner Hse.

LaSalle & the Discovery of the Great West. Francis Parkman. 1990. pap. 9.50 (*0-679-72615-2*) Vin Bks.

LaSalle & the Discovery of the Great West. Francis Parkman. Ed. by William R. Taylor. LC 86-22763. 377p. 1986. reprint ed. lib. bdg. 89.50 (*0-313-24223-2*, PDGW, Greenwood Pr) Greenwood.

*__LaSalle & the Exploration of the Mississippi.__ Dan Harmon. (Explorers of the New Worlds Ser.). 2000. 17.95 (*0-7910-5952-9*) Chelsea Hse.

*__LaSalle & the Exploration of the Mississippi.__ Dan Harmon. (Explorers of the New Worlds Ser.). (Illus.). 2000. pap. 8.95 (*0-7910-6162-0*) Chelsea Hse.

LaSalle Banks Guide, 1998-99: Major Publicly Held Corporations & Financial Institutions Headquartered in Illinois. 34th rev. ed. Ed. by Garry J. Nokes. LC 86-640098. (Scholl Corporate Guides Ser.). Orig. Title: First Chicago NBD Guide. 352p. 1998. pap. 29.95 (*0-912519-20-7*) Scholl.

LaSalle Banks Guide, 1997-98: Major Publicly Held Corporations & Financial Institutions Headquartered in Illinois. 33rd rev. ed. Ed. by Garry J. Nokes. LC 86-640098. (Corporate Guides Ser.). Orig. Title: First Chicago NBD Guide. 352p. 1997. pap. 29.95 (*0-912519-19-3*) Scholl.

LaSalle County, Colorado. LaSalle History Book Committee Staff. (Illus.). 178p. 1988. 30.00 (*0-88107-108-0*) Curtis Media.

*__Lasar Guide Star Adaptive Optics for Astronomy.__ N. Ageorges & C. Dainty. (Illus.). 364p. 2000. 145.00 (*0-7923-6381-7*) Kluwer Academic.

*__Lasater Philosophy of Cattle Raising.__ rev. ed. Laurence M. Lasater. Ed. by Marcos Gimenez Zapiola. (Illus.). 116-120p. 2000. pap. text 20.00 (*0-9672336-2-3*) Isa Cattle.

Lascaux (Elie) Paintings, 1921-1959. Raymond Queneau. (FRE., Illus.). 52p. 1959. pap. 35.00 (*1-55660-267-7*) A Wofsy Fine Arts.

*__Lascivious Scenes in the Convent.__ Blue Moon Books Staff. 2000. mass mkt. 7.95 (*1-56201-202-9*) Blue Moon Bks.

Lasciviousness: The Result of Neglect. Creflo A. Dollar, Jr. 1994. write for info. (*0-9634781-7-6*) Wrld Chang Minist.

Lasell a History of the First Junior College for Women. Donald J. Winslow. 291p. 1987. 30.00 (*0-9619720-0-9*) Lasell Coll.

Laser. 1997. 51.00 (*3-540-63916-0*) Spr-Verlag.

Laser. Vicente Aboites. (Ciencia para Todos Ser.). (SPA.). pap. 6.99 (*968-16-3578-7*, Pub. by Fondo) Continental Bk.

Laser. Campbell. (Techknowledge Reference Ser.). (J). (gr. k-12). 1998. pap. 18.95 (*0-538-66139-9*) S-W Pub.

Laser: Its Clinical Uses in Eye Diseases. 2nd ed. Ian J. Constable & Arthur S. Lim. (Illus.). 207p. 1990. text 149.00 (*0-443-04450-3*) Church.

Laser: Light of a Million Uses. Jeff Hecht & Dick Teresi. LC 98-4209. 272p. 1998. pap. 8.95 (*0-486-40193-6*) Dover.

Laser: Supertool of the 1980s. Jeff Hecht & Dick Teresi. LC 83-24261. 272p. 1984. pap. 8.95 (*0-89919-286-6*, Pub. by Ticknor & Fields) HM.

Laser - Optoelectronics in Engineering: Laser 89 Optoelektronik. Ed. by W. Waidelich.Tr. of Laser - Optoelektronik in der Technik. 780p. 1990. 158.95 (*0-387-51433-3*) Spr-Verlag.

Laser - Optoelektronik in der Technik see Laser - Optoelectronics in Engineering: Laser 89 Optoelektronik

Laser Ablation: Mechanism & Applications-II. Ed. by John C. Miller & David Geohegan. (AIP Conference Proceedings Ser.: No. 288). (Illus.). 656p. 1993. text 150.00 (*1-56396-226-8*, AIP Pr) Spr-Verlag.

Laser Ablation: Principles & Aplications. Ed. by John C. Miller. LC 94-5045. (Series in Material Science: Vol. 48). 1994. 64.95 (*0-387-57571-5*) Spr-Verlag.

Laser Ablation: Proceedings of Symposium F - Third International Conference on Laser Ablation - COLA '95 of the 1995 E-MRS Spring Conference, Strasbourg, France, May 22-26, 1995. Ed. by E. Forgarassy et al. LC 96-228479. (European Materials Research Society Symposia Proceedings Ser.: Vol. 55). 940p. 1996. text 336.50 (*0-444-82412-X*, North Holland) Elsevier.

Laser Ablation for Materials Synthesis, Vol. 191. Ed. by J. C. Bravman & D. C. Paine. (Symposium Proceedings Ser.: Vol. 1). 241p. 1990. text 30.00 (*1-55899-080-1*) Materials Res.

Laser Ablation, Mechanisms & Applications: Proceedings of a Workshop Held in Oak Ridge, Tennessee, U. S. A., 8-10 April 1991. Ed. by J. C. Miller & R. F. Haglund, Jr. (Lecture Notes in Physics Ser.: Vol. 389). viii, 362p. 1991. 58.00 (*0-387-97731-7*) Spr-Verlag.

Laser Ablation of Electronic Materials: Basic Mechanisms & Applications. Ed. by E. Fogarassy & S. Lazare. LC 92-13148. (European Materials Research Society Monographs: Vol. 4). xii, 394p. 1992. 196.50 (*0-444-89234-6*, North Holland) Elsevier.

Laser Acceleration of Particles. AIP Conference Staff. Ed. by Paul J. Channell. LC 82-73361. (AIP Conference Proceedings Ser.: No. 91). 276p. 1982. lib. bdg. 32.00 (*0-88318-190-8*) Am Inst Physics.

Laser Acceleration of Particles: Malibu, CA, 1985. Ed. by Chan Joshi & Thomas Katsouleas. LC 85-48028. (AIP Conference Proceedings Ser.: No. 130). 628p. 1985. lib. bdg. 53.50 (*0-88318-329-3*) Am Inst Physics.

Laser Acupuncture, an Introductory Textbook for Treatment of Pain, Paralysis, Spasticity & Other Disorders: Clinical & Research Uses of Laser Acupuncture from Around the World. Margaret A. Naeser & Xiu-Bing Wei. (Illus.). 218p. 1994. spiral bd. 44.95 (*0-9625651-2-1*) Boston Chinese Med.

Laser Advances & Applications: Proceedings of the Fourth National Quantum Electronics Conference, Heriot-Watt University, Edinburgh, September, 1979. National Quantum Electronics Conference (4th: 1979. LC 80-40119. (Illus.). 300p. reprint ed. pap. 93.00 (*0-608-17597-8*, 203044500069) Bks Demand.

Laser & Conventional Refractive Surgery. Ed. by Charles Claove. 416p. 1996. text 52.00 (*0-7279-0918-5*, Pub. by BMJ Pub) Login Brothers Bk Co.

Laser & Electron Beam Processing of Electronic Materials: Proceedings of the Symposium. Symposuim on Laser & Electron Beam Processing of E. Ed. by Lawrence Anderson et al. LC 80-65109. (Electrochemical Society Proceedings Ser.: Vol. 80-1). (Illus.). 560p. 1980. pap. 173.60 (*0-7837-8995-5*, 205926000002) Bks Demand.

Laser & Ion Beam Modification of Materials: Proceedings of the Symposium of the 3rd IUMRS International Conference on Advanced Materials, Sunshine City, Ikebukuro, Tokyo, Japan, August 31-September 4, 1993. Isao Yamada. LC 94-33298. (Transactions of the Materials Research Society of Japan Ser., Vol. 17, Advanced Materials Ser.: Vol. 4). 646p. 1994. 353.25 (*0-444-81994-0*) Elsevier.

Laser & Noncoherent Ocular Effects Vol. 2974: Epidemiology, Prevention & Treatment. Ed. by Bruce E. Stuck & Michael Belkin. LC 97-175320. 240p. 1997. 69.00 (*0-8194-2385-8*) SPIE.

Laser & Optoelectronic Engineering. Hrand M. Muncheryan. 336p. 1991. 132.00 (*1-56032-062-1*) Hemisp Pub.

Laser & Particle-Beam Chemical Processing for Microelectronics. Ed. by D. J. Ehrlich et al. (Materials Research Society Symposium Proceedings Ser.: Vol. 101). 1988. text 17.50 (*0-931837-69-3*) Materials Res.

Laser & Particle-Beam Modification of Chemical Processes on Surfaces Vol. 129: Materials Research Society Symposium Proceedings. Ed. by A. W. Johnson et al. 325p. 1989. text 17.50 (*1-55899-002-X*) Materials Res.

Laser & Plasma Technology. Ed. by C. S. Wong et al. 512p. (C). 1990. text 113.00 (*981-02-0168-0*) World Scientific Pub.

Laser & Plasma Technology: Proceedings of the First Tropical College on Applied Physics. Ed. by S. Lee et al. 696p. 1985. text 159.00 (*9971-978-27-X*) World Scientific Pub.

Laser & Plasma Technology: Proceedings of the Second Tropical College on Applied Physics, University of Malaya, 17 March - 5 April 1986. Ed. by S. Lee. 592p. 1989. text 133.00 (*9971-5-0767-6*) World Scientific Pub.

Laser Anemometry. Ed. by J. Turner & S. M. Fraser. 600p. 1988. 168.95 (*0-387-18756-1*) Spr-Verlag.

Laser Anemometry, 1995: Advances & Applications, Symposium on. Ed. by T. T. Huang et al. LC 85-93243. (1995 ASME/JSME Fluids Engineering Conference Ser.: FED-Vol. 229). 512p. 1995. 156.00 (*0-7918-1484-X*, G00979) ASME.

Laser Anemometry, 1994: Advances & Applications - Symposium on Laser Anemometry, 1994, Lake Tahoe, Nevada. Ed. by T. T. Huang & M. V. Otugen. (FED Ser.). 229p. 1994. pap. 45.00 (*0-7918-1374-6*) ASME.

Laser Applications. William V. Smith. LC 71-119912. (Illus.). 211p. reprint ed. pap. 65.50 (*0-8357-4175-3*, 203695300006) Bks Demand.

Laser Applications Engineering (LAE-96), Vol. 3091. Ed. by Vadim P. Veiko. LC 97-175335. 168p. 1997. 59.00 (*0-8194-2506-0*) SPIE.

Laser Applications for Mechanical Industry. Ed. by S. Martellucci et al. LC 93-10592. (NATO Advanced Study Institutes Series E, Applied Sciences: Vol. 238). 448p. (C). 1993. text 254.00 (*0-7923-2303-3*) Kluwer Academic.

Laser Applications in Medicine & Biology. Incl. LC 77-1665. 288p. 1971. 65.00 (*0-306-37161-8*, Kluwer Plenum); LC 77-1665. 404p. 1974. 79.50 (*0-306-37162-6*, Kluwer Plenum); LC 77-1665. 348p. 1977. 75.00 (*0-306-37163-4*, Kluwer Plenum); LC 77-128514. (Illus.). write for info. (*0-318-55327-9*, Plenum Trade) Perseus Pubng.

Laser Applications in Medicine & Biology, Vol. 4. M. L. Wolbarsht. (Illus.). 310p. (C). 1989. text 110.00 (*0-306-43074-6*, Kluwer Plenum) Kluwer Academic.

Laser Applications in Medicine & Biology, Vol. 5. M. L. Wolbarsht. (Illus.). 392p. (C). 1991. text 120.00 (*0-306-43753-8*, Kluwer Plenum) Kluwer Academic.

Laser Applications in Medicine & Dentistry. Ed. by Gregory B. Altshuler et al. (Europto Ser.: Vol. 2922). 472p. 1996. 110.00 (*0-8194-2324-6*) SPIE.

Laser Applications in Microelectronic & Optoelectronic Manufacturing II, Vol. 2991. Ed. by Jan J. Dubowski. LC 97-194518. 240p. 1997. 69.00 (*0-8194-2402-1*) SPIE.

Laser Applications in Microelectronic & Optoelectronic Manufacturing III. Ed. by Jan J. Dubowski & Peter E. Dyer. LC 98-233181. (Proceedings of SPIE Ser.: Vol. 3274). 354p. 1998. 99.00 (*0-8194-2713-6*) SPIE.

*__Laser Applications in Microelectronic & Optoelectronic Manufacturing IV.__ Ed. by Jan J. Dubowski et al. 546p. 1999. pap. text 120.00 (*0-8194-3088-9*) SPIE.

Laser Applications in Oral & Maxillofacial Surgery. Ed. by Guy A. Catone & Charles C. Alling, 3rd. LC 95-45035. 1997. text 99.00 (*0-7216-5020-1*, W B Saunders Co) Harcrt Hlth Sci Grp.

Laser Applications in Physical Chemistry. Evans. (Optical Engineering Ser.: Vol. 20). (Illus.). 448p. 1989. text 170.00 (*0-8247-8062-0*) Dekker.

Laser Applications in Precision Measurement. Ed. by T. Kemeny & K. Havrilla. 267p. (C). 1988. text 195.00 (*0-941743-38-1*) Nova Sci Pubs.

*__Laser Applications in Surface Science & Technology.__ Rubahn Horst-Gunter. 346p. 1999. pap. 65.95 (*0-471-98450-7*) Wiley.

*__Laser Applications in Surface Science & Technology.__ H.G. Rubahn. LC 98-51716. 346p. 1999. 155.00 (*0-471-98449-3*) Wiley.

Laser Applications to Chemical Analysis. LC 91-68083. (Nineteen Ninety-Two Technical Digest Ser.: Vol. 2). 250p. (Orig.). 1992. pap. 75.00 (*1-55752-214-6*); pap. 48.00 (*1-55752-213-8*) Optical Soc.

Laser Applications to Chemical & Environmental Analysis. (Nineteen Ninety-Eight OSA Technical Digest Ser.: Vol. 3). 200p. (C). 1998. pap. 75.00 (*1-55752-534-X*) Optical Soc.

*__Laser Applications to Chemical & Environmental Analysis: March 9-11, 1998, Sheraton World Resort Orlando, Orlando, Florida.__ Optical Society of America Staff & Laser Institute of America Staff. LC 97-81333. xiii, 214 p. 1998. write for info. (*1-55752-533-1*) Optical Soc.

Laser Applications to Chemical, Biological & Environmental Analysis. LC 95-72749. (Nineteen Ninety-Four Technical Digest Ser.: No. 3). 260p. (Orig.). 1996. pap. write for info. (*1-55752-429-7*) Optical Soc.

Laser-Assisted Microtechnology. Simeon M. Metev & Vadim P. Veiko. LC 94-25834. (Series in Material Science: Vol. 19). 1995. 75.95 (*0-387-53925-5*) Spr-Verlag.

Laser-Assisted Microtechnology. 2nd ed. S. M. Metev & V. P. Veiko. Ed. by U. Gonser et al. LC 98-26049. (Series in Materials Science: Vol. 19). (Illus.). 250p. 1998. 69.95 (*3-540-63973-X*) Spr-Verlag.

Laser-Assisted Transurethral Resection of the Prostate. Stacy J. Childs. LC 93-25355. (Illus.). 96p. 1993. 25.00 (*0-683-01540-0*) Lppncott W & W.

Laser-Beam Interactions with Materials. M. V. Allman. (Materials Science Ser.: Vol. 2). (Illus.). 240p. 1987. 58.00 (*0-387-17568-7*) Spr-Verlag.

Laser-Beam Interactions with Materials: Physical Principles & Applications. Martin Von Allmen & Andreas Blatter. 1995. 59.95 (*3-540-59401-9*) Spr-Verlag.

Laser Beam Mode Selection by Computer Generated Holograms. Victor A. Soifer & Mikhail V. Golub. LC 94-5202. 224p. 1994. boxed set 104.95 (*0-8493-2476-9*) CRC Pr.

Laser Beam Propagation in the Atmosphere. Ed. by H. Weichel. 108p. 1990. text 15.00 (*0-8194-0487-X*, VOL. TT03) SPIE.

Laser Beam Propagation Through Random Media. Larry C. Andrews & Ronald L. Phillips. LC 97-43433. xx, 434p. 1998. 80.00 (*0-8194-2787-X*) SPIE.

Laser Beam Scanning: Opto-Mechanical Devices, Systems & Data Storage Optics. G. F. Marshall. (Optical Engineering Ser.: Vol. 8). (Illus.). 448p. 1985. text 165.00 (*0-8247-7418-3*) Dekker.

Laser Burn. Stephen S. Burkhart. LC 94-36631. 1994. 19.95 (*1-880510-26-X*) State House Pr.

Laser Cathode-Ray Tubes: Proceedings of the Lebedev Physics Institute, Vol. 221. Ed. by Yu M. Popov. LC 94-48607. 315p. (C). 1994. lib. bdg. 165.00 (*1-56072-216-9*) Nova Sci Pubs.

Laser Chemistry in France. R. J. Vetter. 200p. 1990. pap. text 312.00 (*3-7186-5089-4*, Harwood Acad Pubs) Gordon & Breach.

Laser Chemistry in Greece. C. Fotakis. 81p. 1994. pap. text 249.00 (*3-7186-5486-5*, Harwood Acad Pubs) Gordon & Breach.

Laser Chemistry in Japan, Vol. 7, Nos. 2-4. Ed. by I. Tanaka. (Laser Chemistry Ser.). 176p. 1987. pap. text 323.00 (*3-7186-0386-1*) Gordon & Breach.

Laser Chemistry in the U. K., Vol. 9, Nos. 4-6. D. Phillips & R. Grice. Ed. by V. S. Letokhov et al. (Laser Chemistry Ser.). 314p. 1988. pap. text 453.00 (*3-7186-4869-5*) Gordon & Breach.

Laser Chemistry of Organometallics. Ed. by J. Chaiken. LC 93-7877. (ACS Symposium Ser.: No. 530). (Illus.). 334p. 1993. text 85.00 (*0-8412-2687-3*, Pub. by Am Chemical) OUP.

Laser Chemisty in Russia. E. A. Ryabov. 86p. 1993. text 237.00 (*3-7186-5373-7*) Gordon & Breach.

*__Laser Compendium of Higher Education.__ 400p. 1998. pap. text 59.95 (*0-7506-4136-3*) Buttrwrth-Heinemann.

*__Laser Compendium of Higher Education.__ Laser. 832p. 2000. pap. text. write for info. (*0-7506-4782-5*) Buttrwrth-Heinemann.

Laser Compendium of Higher Education. MCC Staff. 460p. 1997. pap. 39.95 (*0-7506-3678-5*) Buttrwrth-Heinemann.

Laser Cookbook: 88 Practical Projects. Gordon McComb. 304p. 1988. pap. 24.95 (*0-07-155335-5*) McGraw.

Laser Cookbook: 99 Practical Projects. Gordon McComb. (Illus.). 304p. 1988. 25.95 (*0-8306-9090-5*, 3090); pap. 19.95 (*0-8306-9390-4*, 3090) McGraw-Hill Prof.

Laser Cooling & Trapping. Harold J. Metcalf & P. Van der Straten. Ed. by J. L. Birman et al. LC 98-55408. (Graduate Texts in Contemporary Physics Ser.). (Illus.). 328p. 1999. text 69.95 (*0-387-98747-9*) Spr-Verlag.

Laser Cooling & Trapping. Harold J. Metcalf & P. Van der Straten. Ed. by J. L. Birman et al. LC 98-55408. (Graduate Texts in Contemporary Physics Ser.). (Illus.). 328p. 1999. pap. text 29.95 (*0-387-98728-2*) Spr-Verlag.

Laser Crystals. 2nd ed. Ed. by Alexander A. Kaminskii. (Optical Sciences Ser.: Vol. 14). (Illus.). 480p. 1990. 71.95 (*0-387-52026-0*) Spr-Verlag.

Laser Cutting & Drilling. (Illus.). 352p. 1996. pap. text 55.00 (*0-614-24704-7*, 404) Laser Inst.

*__Laser Design Toolkit.__ Carl Bergquist. LC 98-68718. 223p. 1999. pap. 29.95 (*0-7906-1183-X*) Prompt Publns.

Laser Diagnostics & Modeling of Combustion. Ed. by K. Iinuma et al. xviii, 355p. 1988. 152.95 (*0-387-18659-X*) Spr-Verlag.

Laser Diagnostics for Combustion Temperature & Species. 2nd ed. Alan C. Eckbreth. (Combustion Science & Technology Ser.). 632p. 1996. text 180.00 (*2-88449-225-9*); pap. text 69.00 (*90-5699-532-4*, TJ254) Gordon & Breach.

Laser Diagnostics for Combustion Temperature & Species, Vol. 7. Alan C. Eckbreth. (Energy & Engineering Science Ser., Abacus Bks.). (Illus.). xxiv, 414p. 1988. text 147.00 (*0-85626-344-3*) Gordon & Breach.

Laser Diagnostics in Fluid Mechanics. B. S. Rinkevichius. LC 96-29931. 1997. write for info. (*1-56700-073-8*) Begell Hse.

Laser Diagnostics in Fluid Mechanics. Bronius S. Rinkevichius. LC 96-29931. 1998. 115.00 (*1-56700-109-2*) Begell Hse.

Laser Diode & LED Applications III, Vol. 3000. Ed. by Kurt J. Linden. 226p. 1997. 69.00 (*0-8194-2411-0*) SPIE.

Laser Diode Modulation & Noise. K. Petermann. (C). 1991. pap. text 102.00 (*0-7923-1204-X*) Kluwer Academic.

Laser Diodes & Applications III, Vol. 3415. Ed. by Pierre Galarneau. LC 99-192658. 1998. 69.00 (*0-8194-2869-8*) SPIE.

Laser Disobstruction & Laser-Assisted Balloon Angioplasty: A Color Atlas. Teruo Matsumoto. Ed. by Gregory Hacke. (Illus.). 97p. 1991. 75.00 (*0-912791-66-7*, Ishiyaku EuroAmerica) Med Dent Media.

Laser-Doppler Blood Flowmetry. Ed. by A. P. Shepherd & P. A. Oberg. 416p. 1990. text 215.50 (*0-7923-0508-6*) Kluwer Academic.

Laser-Electro-Optic Devices, Course 7. Center for Occupational Research & Development Staff. (Laser-Electro-Optics Technology Ser.). (Illus.). 336p. (C). 1986. pap. text 35.00 (*1-55502-050-X*) CORD Commns.

Laser-Electro-Optic Measurements, Course 10. Center for Occupational Research & Development Staff. (Laser Electro-Optics Technology Ser.). (Illus.). 160p. (C). 1980. pap. text 22.00 (*1-55502-053-4*) CORD Commns.

Laser-Electro-Optics. Center for Occupational Research & Development Staff. (Technology Ser.). (Illus.). 3771p. (C). 1980. pap. text 250.00 (*1-55502-017-8*) CORD Commns.

Laser-Electro-Optics Curriculum Planning Guide. Center for Occupational Research & Development Staff. (Laser-Electro-Optics Technology Ser.). (Illus.). 130p. 1985. pap. text 20.00 (*1-55502-018-6*) CORD Commns.

Laser Electrochemistry of Intermediates. V. A. Benderskii & A. V. Benderskii. LC 95-14176. 336p. 1995. boxed set 244.95 (*0-8493-2865-9*, 2865) CRC Pr.

Laser Electronics. Joseph T. Verdeyen. (Illus.). 480p. (C). 1981. 45.95 (*0-13-485201-X*) P-H.

Laser Electronics. 3rd ed. Joseph T. Verdeyen. 1994. write for info. (*0-318-70280-0*) P-H.

Laser Electronics. 3rd ed. Joseph T. Verdeyen. LC 93-2184. 704p. (C). 1994. 105.00 (*0-13-706666-X*) P-H.

Laser Engineering. Kuhn. (C). 1997. student ed. write for info. (*0-02-366922-5*, Macmillan Coll) P-H.

Laser Engineering. Kelin J. Kuhn. LC 97-35211. 498p. 1997. 105.00 (*0-02-366921-7*) P-H.

Laser-Enhanced Ionization Spectroscopy. Ed. by John C. Travis & Gregory C. Turk. LC 95-36614. (Chemical Analysis Ser.: Vol. 136). 334p. 1996. 98.95 (*0-471-57684-0*, Wiley-Interscience) Wiley.

Laser Experimenter's Handbook. Frank G. McAleese. (Illus.). 1979. 11.95 (*0-8306-9770-5*); pap. 10.95 (*0-8306-1123-1*, 1123) McGraw-Hill Prof.

Laser Experimenter's Handbook. 2nd ed. Delton T. Horn. (Illus.). 272p. 1988. 21.95 (*0-8306-9115-4*, 3115) McGraw-Hill Prof.

Laser Experiments for Beginners. Richard N. Zare. LC 94-43481. 270p. 1995. pap. text 28.00 (*0-935702-36-9*) Univ Sci Bks.

Laser Eye Surgery. 1992. lib. bdg. 350.95 (*0-8490-5598-9*) Gordon Pr.

Laser Eye Surgery: A Bibliography, 2 vols., Set. 1995. lib. bdg. 625.95 (*0-8490-8359-1*) Gordon Pr.

Laser Fundamentals. William T. Silfvast. (Illus.). 543p. (C). 1996. text 105.00 (*0-521-55424-1*); pap. text 44.95 (*0-521-55617-1*) Cambridge U Pr.

*__Laser Guide.__ (C). 1998. write for info. (*0-321-02381-1*) Addson-Wesley Educ.

Laser Guidebook. 2nd ed. J. Hecht. 1992. pap. text 44.95 (*0-07-027738-9*) McGraw.

An Asterisk (*) at the beginning of an entry indicates that the title is appearing for the first time.

L

Laser Guidebook. 2nd ed. Jeff Hecht. (Illus.). 512p. 1992. pap. 32.95 (*0-8306-4274-9*, 4307) McGraw-Hill Prof.

Laser Gyroscopes: April 86 - April 90. NASA Staff. 1990. 85.00 (*0-614-18520-3*, 135P24) Info Gatekeepers.

Laser Gyroscopes: April 86 - May 89. NASA Staff. 1989. 85.00 (*0-614-18517-3*, 135P13) Info Gatekeepers.

Laser Gyroscopes: January 70 - December 88. USG/NTIS Staff. 1988. 85.00 (*0-614-18518-1*, 135P14) Info Gatekeepers.

Laser Gyroscopes: January 70 - July 89. U. S. Patent Bibliographic Database Staff. 1989. 85.00 (*0-614-18514-9*, 135P10) Info Gatekeepers.

Laser Gyroscopes: January 87 - May 89. Engineering Index Staff. 1989. 85.00 (*0-614-18515-7*, 135P11) Info Gatekeepers.

Laser Gyroscopes: September 70 - January 90. NTIS Staff. 1990. 85.00 (*0-614-18521-1*, 135P25) Info Gatekeepers.

Laser Handbook, Vol. 3. Ed. by M. L. Stitch. x, 878p. 1986. reprint ed. 371.00 (*0-444-85271-9*, North Holland) Elsevier.

Laser Handbook, Vol. 4. Ed. by M. L. Stitch & M. Bass. x, 594p. 1985. 266.25 (*0-444-86927-1*, North Holland) Elsevier.

Laser Handbook, Vol. 5. Ed. by M. Bass & M. L. Stitch. xvi, 692p. 1985. 291.50 (*0-444-86934-4*, North Holland) Elsevier.

Laser Handbook Vol. 6: Free Electron Lasers. W. B. Colson et al. x, 528p. 1990. 231.00 (*0-444-86953-0*, North Holland) Elsevier.

Laser Handbook ,Volumes 1 & 2, Vols. 1 & 2. Ed. by F. T. Arecchi & E. O. Schulz-Dubois. xxxii, 1948p. 1988. reprint ed. 504.50 (*0-7204-0213-1*, North Holland) Elsevier.

Laser Heating of Metals. A. M. Prokhorov et al. (Optics & Optoelectronics Ser.). (Illus.). 260p. 1990. 130.00 (*0-7503-0040-X*) IOP Pub.

Laser Holography in Geophysics. Ed. by Shuzo Takemoto. 1989. text 49.95 (*0-470-21265-9*) P-H.

Laser in America 1950 to 1970. Joan L. Bromberg. (Illus.). 326p. 1991. 38.50 (*0-262-02318-0*) MIT Pr.

Laser in der Medizin - Laser in Medicine: Proceedings of the 11th International Congress. W. Waudelich & R. Waidelich. (Illus.). 525p. 1994. 118.00 (*0-387-57441-7*) Spr-Verlag.

Laser in der Technik - Laser in Engineering: Proceedings of the 11th International Congress. Ed. by W. Waidelich. (Illus.). 960p. 1994. 143.95 (*0-387-57444-1*) Spr-Verlag.

Laser in der Technik, 1991 (Laser in Engineering, 1991) Vortage des 10. Internationalen Kongresses (Proceedings of the 10th International Congress Laser 91) Ed. by W. Waidelich. 775p. 1992. 139.95 (*0-387-55247-2*) Spr-Verlag.

Laser in der Umweltmesstechnik - Laser in Remote Sensing: Proceedings of the 11th International Congress. Ed. by C. Werner & W. Waidelich. 1994. 71.95 (*0-387-57443-3*) Spr-Verlag.

Laser in Urology: International Symposium, Luebeck, November 1985. Ed. by A. Hofstetter. (Journal: European Urology: Vol. 12, Suppl. 1, 1986). vi, 58p. 1986. pap. 24.50 (*3-8055-4362-X*) S Karger.

Laser-Induced Chemical Processes. Ed. by Jeffrey I. Steinfeld. LC 80-20478. 288p. 1981. 75.00 (*0-306-40587-3*, Plenum Trade) Perseus Pubng.

Laser-Induced Chemical Processes. E. Weitz. Ed. by V. S. Letokhov et al. (Laser Chemistry Ser.: Vol. 9, Nos. 1-3). 198p. 1988. pap. text 134.00 (*3-7186-4856-3*) Gordon & Breach.

Laser Induced Damage in Optical Materials. 1990. lib. bdg. 79.00 (*0-8490-4007-8*) Gordon Pr.

Laser-Induced Damage in Optical Materials. 1999. 125.00 (*0-8194-3220-2*) SPIE.

Laser Induced Damage in Optical Materials-STP 689. Incl. Laser Induced Damage in Optical Materials, 1981 - STP 799. 637p. 1983. pap. 15.00 (*0-8031-0708-0*, STP799); 329p. 1979. Set pap. 5.50 (*0-8031-0389-1*, STP689) ASTM.

Laser Induced Damage in Optical Materials, 1976: Proceedings of a Symposium. American Society for Testing & Materials Staff. Ed. by Alexander J. Glass & Arthur H. Guenther. LC 76-600074. (ASTM Special Technical Publication: No. 622). 412p. reprint ed. pap. 127.80 (*0-608-13150-4*, 201551000094) Bks Demand.

Laser Induced Damage in Optical Materials, 1979: Proceedings of a Symposium Sponsored by National Bureau of Standards, 11th, Boulder, Co., Oct. 30-31, 1979. Symposium on Optical Materials for High Power Lase. Ed. by Harold Bennett et al. LC 80-600100. (ASTM Special Technical Publication: 726). 557p. reprint ed. pap. 172.70 (*0-608-15323-0*, 205633300060) Bks Demand.

Laser Induced Damage in Optical Materials, 1981 - STP 799 see Laser Induced Damage in Optical Materials-STP 689

Laser Induced Damage in Optical Materials, 1982: Proceedings of a Symposium. Symposium on Optical Materials for High Power Lase. Ed. by Harold E. Bennett et al. LC 83-600625. (ASTM Special Technical Publication: No. 847). 499p. reprint ed. pap. 154.70 (*0-608-18792-5*, 203030900068) Bks Demand.

Laser Induced Damage in Optical Materials, 1983, Vol. STP 911. Ed. by B. E. Newnam et al. 560p. 1986. pap. 60.00 (*0-8031-0930-X*, STP911) ASTM.

Laser Induced Damage in Optical Materials, 1984, Vol. STP 954. Ed. by B. E. Newnam et al. 444p. 1986. pap. 60.00 (*0-8031-0960-1*, STP954) ASTM.

Laser Induced Damage in Optical Materials, 1988: Proceedings of a Symposium. Symposium on Optical Materials for High Power Lase. Ed. by Harold E. Bennett et al. LC 89-600787. (ASTM Special Technical Publication Ser.: No. 1099). (Illus.). 575p. reprint ed. pap. 178.30 (*0-608-10487-6*, 207111600009) Bks Demand.

Laser Induced Damage in Optical Materials, 1989: Proceedings of the Boulder Damage Symposium, November 1-3, 1989. Symposium on Optical Materials for High Power Lase. Ed. by Harold E. Bennett et al. LC 91-143803. (ASTM Special Technical Publication Ser.: No. 1117). (Illus.). 669p. reprint ed. pap. 200.00 (*0-608-10488-4*, 207111700009) Bks Demand.

Laser-Induced Damage in Optical Materials, 1996, Vol. 2966. Ed. by Harold E. Bennett et al. 686p. 1997. 116.00 (*0-8194-2370-X*) SPIE.

Laser-Induced Damage in Optical Materials, 1997 Vol. 3244. Ed. by Gregory J. Exarhos et al. 720p. 1998. 116.00 (*0-8194-2683-0*) SPIE.

Laser-Induced Damage in Optical Materials, 1998. Ed. by Gregory J. Exarhos et al. 852p. 1999. pap. text 136.00 (*0-8194-3045-5*) SPIE.

Laser-Induced Discharge Phenomena. Iuri P. Raizer. Ed. by George C. Vlases & Z. Adam Pietrzyk. Tr. by Albin Tybulewicz. LC 77-21738. (Studies in Soviet Science). (Illus.). 380p. 1977. reprint ed. pap. 117.80 (*0-608-05496-8*, 206596500006) Bks Demand.

Laser-Induced Dynamic Gratings. H. J. Eichler et al. (Optical Sciences Ser.: Vol. 50). (Illus.). 270p. 1986. 97.00 (*0-387-15875-8*) Spr-Verlag.

Laser-Induced Interstitial Thermotherapy. Ed. by Gerhard J. Muller & Andre Roggan. LC 95-12212. (Institute Ser.: Vol. PM25). 1995. 95.00 (*0-8194-1859-5*) SPIE.

Laser-Induced Raman Spectroscopy in Crystals & Gases. Ed. by P. P. Pashinin. (Proceedings of the Institute of General Physics of the Academy of Sciences of the U. S. S. R. Ser.: Vol. 2). 215p. (C). 1988. text 165.00 (*0-941743-13-6*) Nova Sci Pubs.

Laser Inspected Gear Geometry. W. North et al. (Technical Papers: Vol. P239.15). 10p. 1981. pap. text 30.00 (*1-55589-311-2*) AGMA.

Laser Interaction & Related Plasma Phenomena. Ed. by George H. Miley. (AIP Conference Proceedings Ser.: No. 318). 696p. 1994. text 150.00 (*1-56396-324-8*) Am Inst Physics.

Laser Interaction & Related Plasma Phenomena, Vol. 7. Ed. by Heinrich Hora & George H. Miley. LC 79-135851. 946p. 1986. 155.00 (*0-306-42406-1*, Plenum Trade) Perseus Pubng.

Laser Interaction & Related Plasma Phenomena, Vol. 8. Ed. by Heinrich Hora & George H. Miley. (Illus.). 764p. 1988. 135.00 (*0-306-43007-X*, Plenum Trade) Perseus Pubng.

Laser Interaction & Related Plasma Phenomena, Vol. 9. Ed. by Heinrich Hora & George H. Miley. (Illus.). 670p. (C). 1991. 186.00 (*0-306-43722-8*, Plenum Trade) Perseus Pubng.

Laser Interaction & Related Plasma Phenomena, Vol. 10. Ed. by George H. Miley & Heinrich Hora. (Illus.). 700p. (C). 1993. 186.00 (*0-306-44353-8*, Plenum Trade) Perseus Pubng.

Laser Interaction & Related Plasma Phenomena, Vols. 1-4. Ed. by Helmut J. Schwarz & Heinrich Hora. Incl. LC 77-1665. 524p. 1970. 85.00 (*0-306-37141-3*, Kluwer Plenum); LC 77-1665. 598p. 1972. 85.00 (*0-306-37142-1*, Kluwer Plenum); LC 79-135851. 458p. 1974. 85.00 (*0-306-37143-X*, Kluwer Plenum); LC 79-135851. 562p. 1974. 85.00 (*0-306-37150-2*, Kluwer Plenum); LC 79-135851. 678p. 1977. 95.00 (*0-306-37144-8*, Kluwer Plenum); LC 79-135851. 576p. 1977. 95.00 (*0-306-37154-5*, Kluwer Plenum); LC 79-135851. (Illus.). write for info. (*0-318-55328-7*, Plenum Trade) Perseus Pubng.

Laser Interaction & Related Plasma Phenomena: 12th International Conference, 2 vols. Sadao Nakai & George H. Miley. Incl. Vol. 1. (Illus.). 784p. 1996. Not sold separately (*1-56396-623-9*, AIP Pr); Vol. 2. (Illus.). 672p. 1996. Not sold separately (*1-56396-624-7*, AIP Pr); (AIP Press Conference Proceedings Ser.: No. 369). 150.00 (*1-56396-445-7*, CP 369, AIP Pr) Spr-Verlag.

Laser Interaction & Related Plasma Phenomena: 13th International Conference. Ed. by George H. Miley & E. Michael Campbell. LC 97-76763. (Conference Proceedings Ser.: Vol. 406). (Illus.). liv, 708p. 1997. 185.00 (*1-56396-696-4*) Am Inst Physics.

Laser Interaction with Matter. Ed. by G. Velarde et al. 512p. (C). 1989. text 125.00 (*9971-5-0769-2*) World Scientific Pub.

Laser Interaction with Matter: Proceedings of the 23rd European Conference, St. John's College, Oxford, 19-23 Sept. 1994. Ed. by S. J. Rose. LC 95-17284. (Institute of Physics Conference Ser.: No. 140). (Illus.). 492p. 1995. 273.00 (*0-7503-0193-7*) IOP Pub.

Laser Interactions with Atoms, Solids, & Plasmas. R. M. More. (NATO ASI Series B, Physics: Vol. 327). (Illus.). 486p. (C). 1994. 145.00 (*0-306-44801-7*, Plenum Trade) Perseus Pubng.

Laser Interferometer Space Antenna: 2nd International LISA Symposium on the Detection & Observation. William M. Folkner. LC 98-88783. 254p. 1998. 90.00 (*1-56396-848-7*) Addison-Wesley.

Laser Interferometry VIII Vol. 2861: Applications. Ed. by Ryszard J. Pryputniewicz et al. 310p. 1996. 76.00 (*0-8194-2249-5*) SPIE.

Laser Interferometry IX Vol. 3478: Techniques & Analysis. Ed. by Malgorzata Kujawinska et al. LC 98-233148. (Proceedings of SPIE Ser.: Vol. 3478). 476p. 1998. 99.00 (*0-8194-2933-3*) SPIE.

Laser Interferometry IX Vol. 3479: Applications. Ed. by Ryszard J. Pryputniewicz et al. LC 98-233176. (Proceedings of SPIE Ser.: Vol. 3479). 366p. 1998. 80.00 (*0-8194-2934-1*) SPIE.

Laser Interferometry VIII Vol. 2860: Techniques & Analysis. Ed. by Malgorzata Kujawinska et al. 416p. 1996. 85.00 (*0-8194-2248-7*) SPIE.

Laser Ionization Mass Analysis. Ed. by Akos Vertes et al. LC 92-34983. (Chemical Analysis: A Series of Monographs on Analytical Chemistry & Its Applications). 584p. 1993. 149.00 (*0-471-53673-3*) Wiley.

Laser Isotope Separation Research & Development in the U. S. S. R. George Levin. Ed. by Anne H. Johnson. xi, 120p. (Orig.). 1989. pap. text 75.00 (*1-55831-093-2*) Delphic Associates.

Laser Jet Companion. 3rd ed. Peter G. Randall & Bennett. 1991. pap. 5.00 incl. 3.5 hd (*0-13-524786-1*) Macmillan USA.

Laser Jet Handbook. 2nd ed. Peter G. Randall & Bennett. 1990. pap. 5.00 incl. 3.5 hd (*0-13-523747-5*) Macmillan USA.

Laser Light Pressure on Atoms. V. G. Minogin & V. S. Letokhov. xii, 248p. 1987. text 228.00 (*2-88124-080-1*) Gordon & Breach.

Laser Light Scattering. unabridged ed. Charles S. Johnson, Jr. & Don A. Gabriel. (Illus.). 112p. 1995. pap. text 6.95 (*0-486-68328-1*) Dover.

Laser Light Scattering in Biochemistry, No. 99. S. E. Harding. 1992. 143.00 (*0-85186-486-4*) CRC Pr.

Laser Lines in Atomic Species see Progress in Quantum Electronics

Laser Lithotripsy. Ed. by R. Steiner. (Illus.). 180p. 1988. 75.00 (*0-387-19480-0*) Spr-Verlag.

Laser Locator: Reference Manual & Workbook. Jeff Painter. Ed. by William Blinn. 1992. 50.00 (*1-880933-01-2*) Mgmt Comp Srvs.

Laser Logos. Forgione. Date not set. pap. text. write for info. (*0-314-03928-7*) West Pub.

Laser Logos, Inc. Forgione & Smith. 1994. 17.75 (*0-314-03803-5*, Pub. by West Pub) Thomson Learn.

Laser Logos Inc. An Accounting Simulation. 3rd ed. Jesse T. Barfield et al. 1997. pap. 18.25 (*0-538-88060-0*) S-W Pub.

Laser Machining: Theory & Practice. (Mechanical Engineering Ser.: No. 210). (Illus.). 274p. 1991. 79.95 (*3-540-97498-9*) Laser Inst.

Laser Machining: Theory & Practice. G. Chryssolouris & P. Sheng. Ed. by Frederick F. Ling. (Mechanical Engineering Ser.). (Illus.). 288p. 1993. 69.95 (*0-387-97498-9*) Spr-Verlag.

Laser Machining & Welding. N. Rykalin et al. (Illus.). 1978. 147.00 (*0-08-022724-4*, Pub. by Pergamon Repr) Franklin.

Laser Manipulation of Atoms & Ions: Proceedings of the Intl. School of Physics "Enrico Fermi", Course CXVIII, July 9-19, 1991. Ed. by W. Phillips et al. LC 92-47136. 798p. 1993. 300.00 (*0-444-89993-6*, North Holland) Elsevier.

Laser Market: Optronics Buyers Guide. Ed. by H. Krauel. (Illus.). 309p. 1987. pap. 51.00 (*0-387-91305-X*) Spr-Verlag.

Laser Material. Fuxi Gan. 350p. 1995. text 74.00 (*981-02-1580-0*) World Scientific Pub.

Laser Material Crystal Growth & Nonlinear Materials & Devices. Ed. by Kathleen I. Schaffers & Lawrence E. Myers. 224p. 1999. pap. text 72.00 (*0-8194-3080-3*) SPIE.

Laser Material Processing. 2nd ed. W. M. Steen. LC 97-46601. (Illus.). xiv, 346p. 1998. pap. 39.95 (*3-540-76174-8*) Spr-Verlag.

Laser Material Processing. 2nd ed. W. M. Steen. (Illus.). 340p. 1997. reprint ed. pap. 39.50 (*3-540-19670-6*, 213) Spr-Verlag.

Laser Material Processing. 3rd ed. W. M. Steen. (Illus.). 256p. 1991. reprint ed. pap. text 58.95 (*0-387-19670-6*, 213) Laser Inst.

Laser Materials & Laser Spectroscopy. Ed. by Z. J. Wan & Z. M. Zhang. 432p. (C). 1989. text 125.00 (*9971-5-0739-0*) World Scientific Pub.

Laser Materials Processing. Ed. by G. Bruck. (Illus.). 375p. 1989. 214.95 (*0-387-51537-2*) Spr-Verlag.

Laser Materials Processing. Ed. by Leonard Migliore. (Manufacturing Engineering & Materials Processing Ser.: Vol. 46). (Illus.). 336p. 1996. text 150.00 (*0-8247-9714-0*) Dekker.

Laser Materials Processing No. III: Proceedings of the Third Symposium on Laser Materials Processing, Sponsored by the TMS Physical Metallurgy, Solidification & Electronics Materials Committees, Held at the TMS Fall Meeting, Chicago, Illinois, September 26-28, 1988. Minerals, Metals & Materials Society Staff. Ed. by Jyoti Mazumder & K. N. Mukherjee. LC 89-61039. (Illus.). 263p. 1989. reprint ed. pap. 81.60 (*0-608-01700-0*, 206235500002) Bks Demand.

Laser Materials Processing ICALEO, '93, Vol. 77, No. 577. LC 95-118090. 1032p. 1993. 140.00 (*0-912035-50-1*) Laser Inst.

Laser Methods for Biomedical Applications Vol. 2965: ALT '96 International Symposium. Ed. by Alexander M. Prokhorov & Costas Fotakis. 212p. 1996. 59.00 (*0-8194-2369-6*) SPIE.

Laser Metrology & Inspection. Ed. by Hans J. Tiziani & Pramod K. Rastogi. 306p. 1999. pap. text 84.00 (*0-8194-3309-8*) SPIE.

Laser Metrology & Machine Performance. Ed. by D. M. Blackshaw et al. 1993. 146.00 (*1-85312-241-6*) Computational Mech MA.

Laser Metrology & Machine Performance. Ed. by A. D. Hope et al. LC 93-71029. (LAMDAMAP Ser.: Vol. 1). 368p. 1993. 146.00 (*1-56252-164-0*, 2416) Computational Mech MA.

Laser Metrology & Machine Performance II. Ed. by A. D. Hope et al. 392p. 1995. 167.00 (*1-85312-355-2*) Computational Mech MA.

Laser Metrology & Machine Performance II. Ed. by A. D. Hope et al. LC 95-68881. (Lamdamap Ser.: Vol. 2). 377p. 1995. 167.00 (*1-56252-276-0*, 3552) Computational Mech MA.

Laser Metrology & Machine Performance IV. Ed. by V. Chiles & D. Jenkinson. LC 99-63949. (Lamdamap Ser.: Vol. 4). 500p. 1999. 245.00 (*1-85312-661-6*, 6616, Pub. by WIT Pr) Computational Mech MA.

Laser Metrology & Machine Performance III. Ed. by D. G. Ford & S. R. Postlethwaite. LC 97-68065. 568p. 1997. 265.00 (*1-85312-536-9*, T50) Computational Mech MA.

Laser Microanalysis. Lieselotte Moenke-Blankenburg. LC 88-34686. (Chemical Analysis: A Series of Monographs on Analytical Chemistry & Its Applications). 304p. 1989. 175.00 (*0-471-63707-6*) Wiley.

Laser Microfabrication: Thin Film Processes & Lithography. Ed. by Daniel J. Ehrlich & Jeffrey Y. Tsao. 587p. 1989. text 151.00 (*0-12-233430-2*) Acad Pr.

Laser Microirridiation of Cells Handbook of Laser Science & Technology, Vol. 1. T. Kasuya & M. Tsukakoshi. viii, 80p. 1989. pap. text 85.00 (*3-7186-4853-9*) Gordon & Breach.

Laser Molecule Interaction: Laser Physics & Molecular Nonlinear Optics. J. R. Lalanne et al. Tr. by L. Orrit from FRE. LC 95-24308. 323p. 1996. 84.95 (*0-471-12066-9*) Wiley.

Laser Optics of Condensed Matter. Ed. by J. L. Birman et al. LC 88-2513. (Illus.). 578p. 1988. 135.00 (*0-306-42816-4*, Plenum Trade) Perseus Pubng.

Laser Optics of Condensed Matter Vol. 2: Physics of Optical Phenomena & Their Use As Probes of Matter. Ed. by E. Garmire et al. (Illus.). 464p. (C). 1991. 150.00 (*0-306-43820-8*, Plenum Trade) Perseus Pubng.

Laser Optoacoustic Spectroscopy. V. S. Letokhov & V. P. Zharov. (Optical Sciences Ser.: Vol. 37). (Illus.). 345p. 1986. 118.95 (*0-387-11795-4*) Spr-Verlag.

Laser Optoacoustics. V. Z. Gusev & A. A. Karabutov. 336p. 1992. 89.95 (*1-56396-036-2*) Spr-Verlag.

Laser-Optoelectronics in Medicine, 1989. Ed. by W. Waidelich.Tr. of Laser-Optoelektronik in der Medizin 1989. (Illus.). 500p. 1990. 96.95 (*0-387-51434-1*) Spr-Verlag.

Laser-Optoelektronik in der Medizin 1989 see Laser-Optoelectronics in Medicine, 1989

Laser Physics. Murray Sargent, III et al. 432p. (C). 1974. pap. 65.00 (*0-201-06903-2*) Addison-Wesley.

Laser Physics. Arthur Maitland & M. H. Dunn. LC 76-97205. 425p. reprint ed. pap. 131.80 (*0-608-10150-8*, 205161200097) Bks Demand.

Laser Physics & Laser Instabilities. L. M. Narducci & N. B. Abraham. 320p. (C). 1988. text 71.00 (*9971-5-0062-0*); pap. text 37.00 (*9971-5-0063-9*) World Scientific Pub.

Laser Pioneers. 2nd rev. ed. Jeff Hecht. (Illus.). 298p. 1991. text 59.00 (*0-12-336030-7*) Acad Pr.

Laser Plasma Interactions 5: Inertial Confinement Fusion; Proceedings of the Forty-Fifth... M. B. Hooper. (Illus.). 336p. 1996. 189.00 (*0-7503-0352-2*) IOP Pub.

Laser Plasma Interactions 4. Ed. by M. B. Hooper. (Scottish Universities Summer School in Physics, a NATO Advanced Study Institute Ser.: No. 35). (Illus.). 400p. 1989. 189.00 (*0-905945-18-2*) IOP Pub.

Laser Plasma Interactions 3. Ed. by M. B. Hooper. (Scottish Universities Summer School in Physics, a NATO Advanced Study Institute Ser.: No. 29). (Illus.). 386p. 1986. 189.00 (*0-905945-12-3*) IOP Pub.

Laser Plasma Theory & Simulation. Hector A. Boldis. (Laser Science & Technology Ser.). 121p. 1994. pap. text 61.00 (*3-7186-5489-X*, Harwood Acad Pubs) Gordon & Breach.

Laser Plastic Surgery: Resurfacing & Cutting. G. H. Sasaki. (Illus.). 328p. 1999. 165.00 (*0-387-98394-5*) Spr-Verlag.

Laser Print It! A Desktop Publishing Guide to Reports, Resumes, Newsletters, Directories, Business Forms, & More. James Cavuoto. 208p. 1986. pap. 16.95 (*0-201-11349-X*) Addison-Wesley.

Laser Printer Problem Solver: A User's Guide to Troubleshooting. Don S. Thompson et al. (Illus.). 242p. 1998. pap. 49.95 (*0-9669486-1-0*, TR430) Genl Rib.

Laser Printing, Typesetting, & Design. Douglas A. Smith & Richard Sonnenblick. 1986. pap. 18.95 (*0-89303-631-5*) P-H.

Laser Probes for Combustion Chemistry. Ed. by David R. Crosley. LC 80-17137. (ACS Symposium Ser.: No. 134). 1980. 54.95 (*0-8412-0570-1*) Am Chemical.

Laser Probes for Combustion Chemistry. Ed. by David R. Crosley. LC 80-17137. (ACS Symposium Ser.: No. 134). (Illus.). 507p. 1980. reprint ed. pap. 157.20 (*0-608-03236-0*, 206375500007) Bks Demand.

Laser Process Monitoring & Control. 314p. 1995. pap. text 55.00 (*0-614-24702-0*, 401) Laser Inst.

Laser Processing & Analysis of Materials. Walter W. Duley. LC 82-18611. 476p. 1983. 110.00 (*0-306-41067-2*, Plenum Trade) Perseus Pubng.

Laser Processing & Chemistry. Dieter Bauerle. LC 96-5. (Illus.). 600p. 1996. 99.50 (*3-540-60541-X*) Spr-Verlag.

Laser Processing & Chemistry. 3rd enl. rev. ed. D. Bauerle. (Advanced Texts in Physics Ser.). 800p. 2000. (*3-540-66891-8*) Spr-Verlag.

Laser Processing of Materials & Industrial Applications, Vol. 2888. Ed. by Shu-Sen Deng & S. C. Wang. 438p. 1996. 102.00 (*0-8194-2289-4*) SPIE.

Laser Processing of Materials & Industrial Applications II. Ed. by Shu-Sen Deng & S. C. Wang. (Proceedings of SPIE Ser.: Vol. 3550). 538p. 1998. 124.00 (*0-8194-3011-0*) SPIE.

An Asterisk (*) at the beginning of an entry indicates that the title is appearing for the first time.

Laser Processing of Surfaces & Thin Films: Proceedings of Symposium H on Laser Processing of Surfaces & Thin Films of the 1996 E-MRS Spring Conference, Strasbourg, France, June 4-7, 1996, Vol. 64. T. Szorenyi. LC 98-149275. (European Materials Research Society Symposia Proceedings Ser.). 670p. 1997. 388.00 (*0-444-20505-5*, Excerpta Medica) Elsevier.

Laser Processing of Thin Films & Microstructures. I. W. Boyd. (Materials Science Ser.: Vol. 3). 310p. 1987. 75.95 (*0-387-17951-8*) Spr-Verlag.

Laser Processing, Surface Treatment & Film Deposition: Proceedings of the NATO Advanced Study Institute, Sesimbra, Portugal, July 3-16, 1994. Ed. by Jyoti Mazumder et al. (NATO ASI Series E: Applied Sciences). 960p. (C). 1996. text 423.00 (*0-7923-3901-0*) Kluwer Academic.

Laser Radar. Kamerman. 350p. 1999. write for info. (*0-12-395030-9*) Acad Pr.

Laser Radar Ranging & Atmospheric Lidar Techniques. Ed. by Ulrich Schreiber & Christian Werner. LC 98-145665. (Europto Ser.: Vol. 3218). 210p. 1997. 69.00 (*0-8194-2650-4*) SPIE.

***Laser Radar Ranging & Atmospheric Lidar Techniques II.** Ed. by Ulrich Schreiber & Christian Werner. 1999. pap. text 72.00 (*0-8194-3460-4*) SPIE.

Laser Radar VII: Advanced Technology for Applications. Ed. by Richard J. Becherer. 1992. 20.00 (*0-8194-0779-8*, 1633) SPIE.

Laser Radar Systems. fac. ed. Albert V. Jelalian. LC 91-36803. (Illus.). 307p. 1992. reprint ed. pap. 95.20 (*0-608-00937-7*, 206172900011) Bks Demand.

Laser Radar Systems & Techniques. Christian G. Bachman. LC 78-31528. 207p. reprint ed. pap. 64.20 (*0-608-15016-9*, 205608300047) Bks Demand.

Laser Radar Technology & Applications II. Ed. by Gary W. Kamerman. 50p. 1997. pap. 89.00 (*0-8194-2480-3*) SPIE.

Laser Radar Technology & Applications III. Ed. by Gary W. Kamerman. (Proceedings of SPIE Ser.: Vol. 3380). 386p. 1998. 89.00 (*0-8194-2829-9*) SPIE.

***Laser Radar Technology & Applications IV.** Ed. by Gary W. Kamerman & Christian Werner. 690p. 1999. pap. text 145.00 (*0-8194-3181-8*) SPIE.

Laser Raman Spectrometry: Analytical Applications. Halina Baranska et al. (Analytical Chemistry Ser.). 392p. 1988. text 74.00 (*0-470-20829-5*) P-H.

Laser Raman Spectroscopy. Marvin C. Tobin. LC 80-11511. 184p. 1982. reprint ed. lib. bdg. 27.50 (*0-89874-159-9*) Krieger.

Laser Remote Chemical Analysis. Ed. by Raymond M. Measures. LC 87-13380. (Chemical Analysis Ser.). 560p. 1988. 215.00 (*0-471-81640-X*) Wiley.

Laser Remote Sensing of Natural Waters Vol. 2964: From Theory to Practice: CIS Selected Papers. Ed. by Victor I. Feigels & Yurij I. Kopilevich. 224p. 1996. 59.00 (*0-8194-2368-8*) SPIE.

***Laser Remote Sensing of the Ocean: Methods & Applications.** Konstantin Voliak & Alexey Bunkin. 248p. 2000. 105.00 (*0-471-38927-7*) Wiley.

Laser Resonators. V. P. Bykov & O. O. Silichev. 350p. 1995. pap. 111.00 (*1-898326-28-2*, Pub. by CISP) Balogh.

***Laser Resonators.** Ed. by Alexis V. Krudyashov & Pierre Galarneau. 342p. 1998. 89.00 (*0-8194-2706-3*) SPIE.

Laser Resonators & the Beam Divergence Problem. Y. A. Anan'ev. (Optics & Optoelectronics Ser.). (Illus.). 460p. 1992. 208.00 (*0-7503-0146-5*) IOP Pub.

***Laser Resonators II.** Ed. by Alexis V. Kudryashov. 354p. 1999. pap. text 72.00 (*0-8194-3081-1*) SPIE.

Laser Safety Guide, Pub. 103. 9th ed. 52p. 1993. pap. text 15.00 (*0-912035-06-4*) Laser Inst.

Laser Sailing for the 1990's. Dick Tillman. (Illus.). 192p. 1991. pap. 16.95 (*0-87742-294-X*) Intl Marine.

Laser Sailing for the 1990s. Dick Tillman. 1991. pap. text 16.95 (*0-07-064610-4*) McGraw.

Laser Satellite Communication & the Telecommunications Industry: The Status, the Problem, & the Opportunity. Contrib. by William H. Mott et al. LC 99-27547. 328p. 2000. 69.50 (*1-56720-329-9*, Quorum Bks) Greenwood.

Laser Scanning Notebook. Leo Beiser. 24p. 1992. 18.00 (*0-8194-1157-4*) SPIE.

Laser Science & Technology. Ed. by Arthur N. Chester et al. LC 88-25582. (Ettore Majorana International Science Series, Life Sciences: Vol. 35). (Illus.). 466p. 1988. 125.00 (*0-306-43033-9*, Plenum Trade) Perseus Pubng.

Laser Sensors. Richard K. Miller & Terri C. Walker. LC 88-72189. (Survey on Technology & Markets Ser.: No. 80). 50p. 1989. pap. text 200.00 (*1-55865-097-0*) Future Tech Surveys.

Laser Skin Rejuvenation. Paul J. Carniol. LC 98-21400. 256p. 1998. text 95.00 (*0-7817-1561-X*) Lppncott W & W.

Laser-Solid Interactions & Laser Processing, 1978: Materials Research Society, Boston. Ed. by John M. Poate et al. LC 79-51564. (AIP Conference Proceedings Ser.: No. 50). (Illus.). 1979. lib. bdg. 26.00 (*0-88318-149-5*) Am Inst Physics.

***Laser-Solid Interactions for Materials Processing: Materials Research Society Symposium Proceedings, Vol. 617.** Ed. by D. Kumar et al. 2000. text 77.00 (*1-55899-525-0*) Materials Res.

Laser Sources & Applications. Ed. by Arthur Miller & D. M. Finlayson. (Scottish Universities Summer School in Physics, a NATO Advanced Study Institute Ser.). (Illus.). 491p. Date not set. pap. 62.00 (*0-7503-0444-8*) IOP Pub.

Laser Sources & Applications: Proceedings of the 47th (1995) Scottish Universities Summer School in Physics, St. Andrews, June 1995. Ed. by Arthur Miller & D. M. Finlayson. LC 96-11209. (SUSSP Publications). (Illus.). 491p. 1996. 263.00 (*0-7503-0375-1*) IOP Pub.

Laser Spectroscopy, VI. H. P. Weber & W. Luthy. (Optical Sciences Ser.: Vol. 40). (Illus.). 442p. 1983. 102.95 (*0-387-12957-X*) Spr-Verlag.

Laser Spectroscopy: Basic Concepts & Instrumentation. W. Demtroeder. (Chemical Physics Ser.: Vol. 5). (Illus.). 694p. 1988. 42.00 (*0-387-10343-0*) Spr-Verlag.

Laser Spectroscopy: Basic Concepts & Instrumentation. 2nd rev. ed. Wolfgang Demtroder. LC 94-11901. (Illus.). 941p. 1996. 69.00 (*0-387-57171-X*) Spr-Verlag.

Laser Spectroscopy: Eleventh International Conference. Gallagher. Ed. by Louis Bloomfield. (AIP Conference Proceedings Ser.: No. 290). (Illus.). 1993. text 125.00 (*1-56396-262-4*, AIP Pr) Spr-Verlag.

Laser Spectroscopy: Proceedings of the 15th School on Quantum Optics. Ed. by J. Heldt & R. Lawruszczuk. 484p. (C). 1988. text 125.00 (*9971-5-0491-X*) World Scientific Pub.

Laser Spectroscopy: Selected Reprints. Ed. by R. Gupta. (Illus.). 149p. 1993. pap. 26.00 (*0-917853-49-0*, RB-62) Am Assn Physics.

Laser Spectroscopy: Techniques & Applications. E. Roland Menzel. LC 94-5323. (Practical Spectroscopy Ser.: 18). (Illus.). 320p. 1994. text 165.00 (*0-8247-9265-3*) Dekker.

Laser Spectroscopy & Its Applications. Ed. by Leon J. Radziemski & Richard W. Solarz. (Optical Engineering Ser.: Vol. 11). (Illus.). 712p. 1986. text 215.00 (*0-8247-7525-2*) Dekker.

Laser Spectroscopy & Nonlinear Optics of Solids: Proceedings of the International Workshop Organized by the Institute for Advanced Studies, University of Malaya, & the Malaysian Institute of Physics (Kuala Lumpur, Malaysia) Ed. by S. Radhakrishna & B. C. Tan. 500p. 1991. 64.95 (*0-387-52943-8*) Spr-Verlag.

***Laser Spectroscopy & Optical Diagnostics.** Ed. by Andrey Y. Chikishev et al. 386p. 1999. pap. text 84.00 (*0-8194-3206-7*) SPIE.

Laser Spectroscopy & Photochemistry on Metal Surfaces. H. L. Dai & W. Ho. (Advanced Series in Physical Chemistry). 1995. text 158.00 (*981-02-1748-X*) World Scientific Pub.

Laser Spectroscopy & Photochemistry on Metal Surfaces, 2 Pts. H. L. Dai & W. Ho. 1000p. 1995. text 112.00 (*981-02-2998-4*) World Scientific Pub.

Laser Spectroscopy & Photochemistry on Metal Surfaces, 2 vol. set. H. L. Dai & W. Ho. LC 96-146533. (Advanced Series in Physical Chemistry: Vol. 5). 1000p. 1995. text 112.00 (*981-02-2999-2*) World Scientific Pub.

Laser Spectroscopy & Photochemistry on Metal Surfaces, Vol. 1. Ed. by H. L. Dai & W. Ho. (Advanced Series in Physical Chemistry: Vol. 5). 1000p. 1995. pap. 61.00 (*981-02-2996-8*) World Scientific Pub.

Laser Spectroscopy & Photochemistry on Metal Surfaces, Vol. 2. Ed. by H. L. Dai & W. Ho. (Advanced Series in Physical Chemistry: Vol. 5). 600p. 1995. pap. 61.00 (*981-02-2997-6*) World Scientific Pub.

Laser Spectroscopy VIII. Ed. by Sune Svanberg & W. Persson. (Optical Sciences Ser.: Vol. 55). (Illus.). 450p. 1987. 73.95 (*0-387-18437-6*) Spr-Verlag.

Laser Spectroscopy V: Proceedings. Ed. by A. R. McKellar et al. (Optical Sciences Ser.: Vol. 30). (Illus.). 495p. 1981. 57.95 (*0-387-10914-5*) Spr-Verlag.

Laser Spectroscopy of Highly Vibrationally Excited Molecules. Ed. by V. S. Letokhov. (Illus.). 396p. 1989. 212.00 (*0-85274-217-7*) IOP Pub.

Laser Spectroscopy of Solids. 2nd ed. Ed. by W. M. Yen & P. M. Selzer. (Topics in Applied Physics Ser.: Vol. 49). 350p. 1986. 62.95 (*0-387-16709-9*) Spr-Verlag.

Laser Spectroscopy of Solids, No. II. Ed. by W. M. Yen. (Topics in Applied Physics Ser.: Vol. 65). (Illus.). 290p. 1989. 111.95 (*0-387-50154-1*) Spr-Verlag.

Laser Spectroscopy VII. T. W. Hansch & Y. R. Shen. (Optical Sciences Ser.: Vol. 49). (Illus.). xv, 419p. 1985. 71.95 (*0-387-15894-4*) Spr-Verlag.

Laser Spectroscopy II: Proceedings of the 3rd International Conference, Jackson Lodge Lodge, Wyoming, July 4-8, 1977. (Optical Sciences Ser.: Vol. 7). (Illus.). 1977. 47.95 (*0-387-08543-2*) Spr-Verlag.

Laser Spectroscopy X: Proceedings of the 10th International Conference, Font-Romeu, France, 16-21 June, 1991. Ed. by M. Ducloy et al. 500p. 1992. text 130.00 (*981-02-0837-5*) World Scientific Pub.

Laser Spectroscopy XII: Proceedings of the 12th International Conference on Laser Spectroscopy, Capri, Italy 11 - 16 June 1995. Ed. by M. Inguscio et al. 400p. 1996. text 78.00 (*981-02-2447-8*, PPglodu-P2919) World Scientific Pub.

Laser Streak. David Musser. 49p. 1998. 9.00 (*0-8059-4450-8*) Dorrance.

Laser Surface Treatment of Metals. Ed. by Clifton W. Draper & Paolo Mazzoldi. 1986. text 326.50 (*90-247-3405-3*) Kluwer Academic.

Laser Surgery. Jonathan H. Talamo. 260p. 1996. text 152.00 (*0-316-83175-1*, Little Brwn Med Div) Lppncott W & W.

Laser Surgery: Advanced Characterization, Therapeutics, & Systems III. 1992. 20.00 (*0-8194-0789-5*, 1643) SPIE.

Laser Surgery in Children. H. P. Berlien & P. P. Schmittenbecher. LC 97-18416. 1997. text. write for info. (*3-540-62633-6*) Spr-Verlag.

Laser Surgery in Gynecology: A Clinical Guide. V. Cecil Wright & John C. Fisher. LC 92-15350. (Illus.). 352p. 1993. text 70.00 (*0-7216-4007-9*, W B Saunders Co) Harcrt Hlth Sci Grp.

Laser Surgery in Ophthalmology. Thomas A. Weingeist & Scott R. Sneed. (Illus.). 206p. (C). 1992. pap. text 135.00 (*0-8385-7903-5*, A7903-6, Apple Lange Med) McGraw.

Laser Surgery of the Posterior Segment. 2nd ed. Steven M. Bloom & Alexander J. Brucker. LC 96-47103. 432p. 1996. text 98.00 (*0-397-58423-7*) Lppncott W & W.

Laser Systems for Photobiology & Photomedicine. Ed. by Arthur N. Chester et al. (NATO ASI Ser.: Vol. 252). (Illus.). 320p. (C). 1991. text 132.00 (*0-306-43886-0*, Kluwer Plenum) Kluwer Academic.

Laser Techniques & Applications in Fluid Mechanics: Proceedings of the 6th International Symposium, Lisbon, Portugal, 20-23 July, 1992. Richard H. Adrian et al. Ed. by D. F. Durao et al. (Illus.). 545p. 1993. 211.95 (*0-387-56879-4*) Spr-Verlag.

***Laser Techniques Applied to Fluid Mechanics: Selected Papers from the Tenth International Symposium, Lisbon, Portugal, July 13-16, 2000.** Ed. by R. J. Adrian et al. LC 00-26917. (Illus.). xi, 638p. 2000. 169.00 (*3-540-66738-5*) Spr-Verlag.

Laser Techniques for Condensed-Phase & Biological Systems, Vol. 3273. Ed. by Norbert F. Scherer & Janice M. Hicks. LC 98-233177. 320p. 1998. 80.00 (*0-8194-2712-8*) SPIE.

Laser Techniques for Extreme Ultraviolet Spectroscopy: Boulder, 1982. American Institute of Physics. Ed. by T. J. McIlrath & R. R. Freeman. LC 82-73205. (AIP Conference Proceedings Ser.: No. 90). 497p. 1982. lib. bdg. 37.00 (*0-88318-189-4*) Am Inst Physics.

Laser Techniques for Investigation of Defects in Semiconductors & Dielectrics. Ed. by A. A. Manenkov. (Proceedings of the Institute of General Physics of the Academy of Sciences of the U. S. S. R. Ser.: Vol. 4). 204p. (C). 1988. text 165.00 (*0-941743-15-2*) Nova Sci Pubs.

Laser Techniques for State-Selected & State-to-State Chemistry IV, Vol. 3271. Ed. by John W. Hepburn et al. 298p. 1998. 80.00 (*0-8194-2710-1*) SPIE.

Laser Techniques for Surface Science III, Vol. 3272. Ed. by Hai-Lung Dai & Hans-Joachim Freund. LC 98-233175. 318p. 1998. 80.00 (*0-8194-2711-X*) SPIE.

Laser Techniques in Chemistry. Ed. by Anne B. Myers & Thomas R. Rizzo. (Techniques of Chemistry Ser.: Vol. 23). 448p. 1995. 139.00 (*0-471-59769-4*) Wiley.

Laser Techniques in Luminescence Spectroscopy. Ed. by Tuan Vo-Dinh & DeLyle Eastwood. LC 90-172. (Special Technical Publication Ser.: No. 1066). (Illus.). 175p. 1990. text 49.00 (*0-8031-1455-9*, STP1066) ASTM.

Laser Techniques in the Extreme Ultraviolet (OSA, Boulder, Colorado, 1984) No. 119: AIP Conference Proceedings. Ed. by S. E. Harris et al. LC 84-72128. (Optical Science & Engineering Ser.: No. 5). 527p. 1984. lib. bdg. 46.25 (*0-88318-318-8*) Am Inst Physics.

Laser Technology. James R. Johnson. Ed. by Karl Wojcikiewicz. LC 84-22442. (Illus.). 500p. 1985. ring bd., vinyl bd. 99.95 (*0-87119-103-2*, EE-110) Heathkit-Zenith Ed.

Laser Technology, Course 3. Center for Occupational Research & Development Staff. LC 85-71925. (Laser-Electro-Optics Technology Ser.). (Illus.). 356p. (C). 1985. pap. text 32.00 (*1-55502-021-6*) CORD Commns.

Laser Technology: Applications in Manufacturing. Center for Occupational Research & Development Staff. (Laser Electro-Optics Technology Ser.). 246p. 1991. pap. text 25.00 (*1-55502-454-8*) CORD Commns.

Laser Technology: Applications in Medicine & Surgery. Center for Occupational Research & Development Staff. (Laser Electro-Optics Technology Ser.). 214p. 1991. pap. text 25.00 (*1-55502-456-4*) CORD Commns.

Laser Technology: Applications in Photonics & Telecommunications. Center for Occupational Research & Development Staff. (Laser Electro-Optics Technology Ser.). 226p. 1991. pap. text 25.00 (*1-55502-455-6*) CORD Commns.

Laser Technology Chemistry. 1988. 45.95 (*0-387-50132-0*) Spr-Verlag.

Laser Technology V Vol. 3186: Physics & Research & Development Trends. Ed. by Wieslaw Wolinski & Michal Malinowski. LC 98-220799. 448p. 1997. 89.00 (*0-8194-2602-4*) SPIE.

Laser Technology V Vol. 3187: Applications in Materials Sciences & Engineering. Ed. by Wieslaw Wolinski & Jerzy Kusinski. 166p. 1997. 59.00 (*0-8194-2617-2*) SPIE.

Laser Technology V Vol. 3188: Applications in Medicine & Ecology. Ed. by Wieslaw Wolinski & Alfreda Graczyk. LC 98-196854. 208p. 1997. 59.00 (*0-8194-2618-0*) SPIE.

Laser Technology in Microelectronics. V. M. Koleshko. 500p. (C). 1996. text 86.00 (*981-02-0602-X*) World Scientific Pub.

Laser Theory. H. Haken. (Illus.). xvi, 320p. 1984. pap. 70.00 (*0-387-12188-9*) Spr-Verlag.

Laser Thermochemistry: Fundamentals & Applications. N. V. Karlov et al. 330p. 1995. boxed set 120.00 (*0-614-17589-5*, Pub. by CISP) Whitman Dist Co.

Laser Thermonuclear Targets & Superdurable Microballoons: Proceedings of the Lebedev Physics Institute, Vol. 220. Ed. by A. I. Isakov. 287p. 1996. lib. bdg. 165.00 (*1-56072-198-7*) Nova Sci Pubs.

Laser-Tissue Interaction & Tissue Optics II. Ed. by Hans J. Albrecht et al. (Europto Ser.: Vol. 2923). 212p. 1996. 66.00 (*0-8194-2325-4*) SPIE.

Laser-Tissue Interaction IX, Vol. 3254. Ed. by Steven L. Jacques. 526p. 1998. 107.00 (*0-8194-2693-8*) SPIE.

***Laser-Tissue Interaction X.** Ed. by Steven L. Jacques et al. 508p. 1999. pap. text 111.00 (*0-8194-3071-4*) SPIE.

Laser-Tissue Interaction III. Ed. by S. L. Jacques. 1992. 20.00 (*0-8194-0792-5*, 1646) SPIE.

Laser-Tissue Interaction, Tissue Optics & Laser Welding III. Ed. by Guy P. Delacretaz et al. LC 98-145663. (Europto Ser.: Vol. 3195). 358p. 1998. 80.00 (*0-8194-2627-X*) SPIE.

Laser-Tissue Interaction VIII, Vol. 2975. Ed. by Steven L. Jacques. 472p. 1997. 107.00 (*0-8194-2386-6*) SPIE.

Laser-Tissue Interactions: Fundamentals & Applications. Markolf H. Niemz. LC 96-118. (Illus.). 299p. 1996. text, student ed. 119.00 (*3-540-60363-8*) Spr-Verlag.

Laser Treatment & Photocoagulation of the Eye. Ed. by R. Birngruber & V. P. Gabel. (Documenta Ophthalmologica Proceedings Ser.). 1984. text 225.00 (*90-6193-732-9*) Kluwer Academic.

Laser Treatment for Naevi. Toshio Ohshiro. 292p. 1995. 315.00 (*0-471-95243-5*) Wiley.

Laser Ultrasonics: Techniques & Applications. C. B. Scruby & L. E. Drain. (Illus.). 464p. 1990. 210.00 (*0-7503-0050-7*) IOP Pub.

Laser Video Disc Companion: A Guide to the High End Delivery System for Home Video. 2nd ed. Douglas R. Pratt. LC 91-67114. 472p. 1992. pap. 24.95 (*0-918432-89-8*) Baseline Bks.

Laser Video File: Fall '91 - Winter '92. 316p. 1991. pap. 3.95 (*1-880492-00-8*) NewVisions.

Laser Video File: Spring - Summer 1992. 400p. (Orig.). 1992. pap. 4.95 (*1-880492-01-6*) NewVisions.

Laser Video File: Spring - Summer 1993. 434p. (Orig.). 1993. pap. 6.95 (*1-880492-03-2*) NewVisions.

***Laser Vision Breakthrough: Everything You Need to Consider Before Making the Decision.** Stephen F. Brint et al. LC 99-89458. 336p. 2000. 24.95 (*0-7615-2087-2*) Prima Pub.

Laser Vision Correction: A New Age in Vision. Harold A. Stein et al. (Illus.). 96p. 1998. pap. 24.95 (*0-9666621-0-5*) Ethis Commns.

Laser Welding. (Illus.). 217p. pap. text 55.00 (*0-614-24703-9*, 402) Laser Inst.

Laser Welding. Christopher Dawes. LC 92-19179. 176p. 1993. 50.00 (*0-07-016123-2*) McGraw.

Laser Welding. Walter W. Duley. LC 98-15242. 251p. 1998. 94.95 (*0-471-24679-4*, Wiley-Interscience) Wiley.

Laser Write It. James Cavuoto. 1986. pap. 16.95 (*0-201-11327-9*) Addison-Wesley.

Lasers see Inventors & Inventions - Group 1

Lasers. (Introductions Ser.). 48p. (YA). (gr. 6 up). 1999. lib. bdg. 15.95 (*0-88110-165-6*) EDC.

Lasers. Joseph H. Eberly & Peter W. Milonni. LC 87-26347. 768p. 1988. 125.00 (*0-471-62731-3*) Wiley.

Lasers. Nina Morgan. LC 96-44293. (20th Century Inventions Ser.). (Illus.). 48p. (J). (gr. 4-9). 1997. lib. bdg. 24.26 (*0-8172-4812-9*) Raintree Steck-V.

Lasers. Lynn Myring. (Introductions Ser.). (Illus.). 48p. (YA). (gr. 6-12). 1984. pap. 7.95 (*0-86020-722-6*) EDC.

Lasers. Anthony E. Siegman. LC 81-51269. (Illus.). 1283p. (C). 1986. 92.50 (*0-935702-11-3*) Univ Sci Bks.

Lasers, Vol. 1. Ed. by Albert K. Levine. LC 66-11288. (Illus.). 3771p. reprint ed. pap. 107.50 (*0-608-31014-X*) Bks Demand.

Lasers, Vol. 1. Ed. by Albert K. Levine & Anthony J. DeMaria. LC 66-11288. (Illus.). 377p. reprint ed. pap. 116.90 (*0-608-10669-0*, 205507100001) Bks Demand.

Lasers, Vol. 3. Ed. by Anthony J. DeMaria. LC 66-11288. (Illus.). reprint ed. pap. 109.20 (*0-608-31015-8*) Bks Demand.

Lasers, Vol. 3. Ed. by Albert K. Levine & Anthony J. DeMaria. LC 66-11288. 383p. reprint ed. pap. 109.20 (*0-608-16654-5*, 2027814) Bks Demand.

Lasers, Vol. 3. Ed. by Albert K. Levine & Anthony J. DeMaria. LC 66-11288. (Illus.). 383p. reprint ed. pap. 118.80 (*0-608-10670-4*, 202781400003) Bks Demand.

Lasers, Vol. 4. Ed. by Albert K. Levine & Anthony J. DeMaria. LC 66-11288. 343p. reprint ed. pap. 106.40 (*0-7837-0022-9*, 202781400004) Bks Demand.

***Lasers: Harnessing the Atom's Light.** James P. Harbison & Robert E. Nahory. 2000. pap. 22.95 (*0-7167-6041-X*, Sci Amer Lib Paperbacks) W H Freeman.

Lasers: Invention to Application. National Academy of Engineering Staff. Ed. by John R. Whinnery. 144p. 1987. pap. text 14.95 (*0-309-03776-X*) Natl Acad Pr.

Lasers: Now & into the Future. Steve Parker & Industrial Art Studio Staff. LC 98-17950. (Future Tech Ser.). (J). 1998. 21.00 (*0-382-39953-6*, Dillon Silver Burdett); pap. 12.00 (*0-382-39954-4*, Dillon Silver Burdett) Silver Burdett Pr.

Lasers: Selected Reprints. Ed. by Donald C. O'Shea & Donald C. Peckham. 144p. 1982. per. 15.00 (*0-917853-74-1*, RB-36) Am Assn Physics.

Lasers: The Light Fantastic. 2nd ed. Clayton L. Hallmark & Delton T. Horn. (Illus.). 280p. 1987. 19.95 (*0-8306-0305-0*, 2905); pap. 12.95 (*0-8306-2905-X*) McGraw-Hill Prof.

Lasers: The New Technology of Light. Charlene W. Billings. LC 92-7324. (Science Sourcebooks Ser.). (Illus.). 128p. (YA). (gr. 7-12). 1992. lib. bdg. 19.95 (*0-8160-2630-0*) Facts on File.

Lasers: The Perioperative Challenge. Kay A. Ball. 256p. 1990. 44.95 (*0-685-51072-7*) Laser Inst.

Lasers: The Perioperative Challenge. 2nd ed. Kay Ball. LC 94-47036. (Illus.). 448p. (C). (gr. 13). 1995. pap. text 35.95 (*0-8151-0524-X*, 24568) Mosby Inc.

Lasers: Theory & Applications. K. Thyagarajan & A. K. Ghatak. LC 81-12176. (Optical Physics & Engineering Ser.). 444p. (C). 1981. 105.00 (*0-306-40598-9*, Plenum Trade) Perseus Pubng.

Lasers: Theory & Practice. John Hawkes & Ian Latimer. LC 94-30468. (International Series in Optoelectronics). 520p. 1994. 39.00 (*0-13-521485-8*) P-H.

Lasers--Physics & Applications. Ed. by P. Atanasov. 650p. (C). 1991. text 151.00 (*981-02-0564-3*) World Scientific Pub.

Lasers & Chemical Change. A. Ben-Shaul et al. (Chemical Physics Ser.: Vol. 10). (Illus.). 497p. 1981. 80.95 (*0-387-10379-1*) Spr-Verlag.

Lasers & Electro-Optics: Fundamentals & Engineering. Christopher C. Davis. (Illus.). 741p. (C). 1996. text 139.95 (*0-521-30831-3*); pap. text 49.95 (*0-521-48403-0*) Cambridge U Pr.

Lasers & Holography. V. V. Rampal & P. C. Mehta. 450p. 1993. text 99.00 (*981-02-1214-3*) World Scientific Pub.

Lasers & Holography: An Introduction to Coherent Optics. rev. ed. Winston E. Kock. (Illus.). 160p. 1981. pap. 5.95 (*0-486-24041-X*) Dover.

Lasers & Masers see Handbook of Laser Science & Technology

Lasers & Mass Spectrometry. Ed. by David M. Lubman. (Oxford Series on Optical Sciences). (Illus.). 560p. 1990. text 105.00 (*0-19-505929-8*) OUP.

Lasers & Optical Engineering. P. K. Das. (Illus.). 480p. 1995. 69.95 (*0-387-97108-4*) Spr-Verlag.

Lasers & Optical Fibers in Medicine. Abraham Katzir. LC 93-12744. (Physical Techniques in Biology & Medicine Ser.). (Illus.). 317p. 1993. text 100.00 (*0-12-401940-4*) Acad Pr.

Lasers & Optical Radiation. (Environmental Health Criteria Ser.: No.23). 154p. 1982. pap. text 21.00 (*92-4-154083-4*, 1160023) World Health.

Lasers & Optics for Manufacturing. Ed. by Andrew C. Tam. LC 96-72442. (Trends in Optics & Photonics Ser.: Vol. 9). (Illus.). 177p. 1997. pap. 55.00 (*1-55752-483-1*) Optical Soc.

Lasers & Quantum Optics. Ed. by L. M. Narducci et al. (CIF Ser.: Vol. 13). 420p. (C). 1990. text 138.00 (*9971-5-0952-0*) World Scientific Pub.

Lasers & Their Applications. Ed. by N. G. Basov. Tr. by Albin Tybulewicz from RUS. LC 76-26590. (Proceedings of the P. N. Lebedev Physics Institute Ser.: No. 76). (Illus.). 231p. 1976. reprint ed. pap. 71.70 (*0-608-05535-2*, 206600300006) Bks Demand.

Lasers & Their Applications: A Source Guide. 1991. lib. bdg. 79.95 (*0-8490-4848-6*) Gordon Pr.

Lasers & Their Applications: Proceedings of the Fourth Summer School. Ed. by A. Y. Spasov. 608p. 1987. text 155.00 (*9971-5-0320-4*) World Scientific Pub.

Lasers & Their Applications in Physical Research. Ed. by N. G. Basov. Tr. by Donald H. McNeill from RUS. LC 78-13582. (Proceedings of the P. N. Lebedev Physics Institute Ser.: No. 91). (Illus.). 234p. 1979. reprint ed. pap. 72.60 (*0-608-05549-2*, 206601700006) Bks Demand.

***Lasers & Their Prospects.** N. Sobolev. 248p. 2000. pap. 22.46 (*0-89875-043-1*) U Pr Pacific.

Lasers as Tools for Manufacturing II, Vol. 2993. Ed. by Leonard R. Migliore & Ronald D. Schaeffer. LC 97-200950. 262p. 1997. 69.00 (*0-8194-2404-8*) SPIE.

Lasers from the Ground Up: Lasers in Chemistry. Journal of Chemical Education Staff. LC TA1673.L36. 63p. 1982. reprint ed. pap. 30.00 (*0-608-00805-2*, 206158200010) Bks Demand.

Lasers in a Closed Sparkle Spin. Jim Dewitt. (Libraries-School Libraries). (Illus.). 64p. 1985. pap. 5.00 (*0-915199-14-9*) Pen-Dec.

Lasers in Acoustics. F. V. Bunkin. (Laser Science & Technology Ser.). 177p. 1991. 130.00 (*3-7186-5061-4*, Harwood Acad Pubs) Gordon & Breach.

Lasers in Agriculture. Yuri I. Posudin. 188p. 1998. 57.50 (*1-57808-016-9*) Science Pubs.

Lasers in Analytical Atomic Spectroscopy. Ed. by Joseph Sneddon et al. LC 96-14917. 275p. 1996. 125.00 (*1-56081-907-3*, Wiley-VCH) Wiley.

Lasers in Analytical Atomic Spectroscopy. Ed. by Joseph Sneddon & Terry L. Thiem. LC 96-14917. 288p. 1997. 135.00 (*0-471-18623-6*, Wiley-VCH) Wiley.

Lasers in Analytical Chemistry. M. J. Houle et al. write for info. (*0-318-55175-6*, Pergamon Pr) Elsevier.

Lasers in Atomic, Molecular & Nuclear Physics. Ed. by V. S. Letokhov. 432p. (C). 1989. text 125.00 (*9971-5-0623-8*) World Scientific Pub.

Lasers in Atomic, Molecular & Nuclear Physics: Proceedings of the 3rd International School on Laser Applications in Atomic, Molecular & Nuclear Physics, August 27-September 4, 1984, Vilnius, U. S. S. R. V. S. Letokhov. xii, 610p. 1986. text 403.00 (*3-7186-0348-9*) Gordon & Breach.

Lasers in Cardiovascular Medicine & Surgery: Fundamentals & Techniques. Ed. by George S. Abela. (Developments in Cardiovascular Medicine Ser.). (C). 1990. text 259.50 (*0-7923-0440-3*) Kluwer Academic.

Lasers in Chemical Analysis. Ed. by Gary M. Hieftje et al. LC 80-84082. (Contemporary Instrumentation & Analysis Ser.). (Illus.). 330p. 1981. 120.00 (*0-89603-027-X*) Humana.

Lasers in Chemistry. D. L. Andrews. (Illus.). 160p. 1986. pap. 45.00 (*0-387-16161-9*) Spr-Verlag.

Lasers in Chemistry. 2nd ed. D. L. Andrews. (Illus.). 192p. 1995. 53.95 (*0-387-51777-4*) Spr-Verlag.

Lasers in Chemistry. 3rd ed. David L. Andrews. LC 97-15162. 228p. 1997. text 57.95 (*3-540-61982-8*) Spr-Verlag.

Lasers in Conservation: An Introduction. Martin Cooper & John Larson. LC 98-156459. (Illus.). 112p. 1998. 79.95 (*0-7506-3117-1*, Butterwrth Archit) Buttrwrth-Heinemann.

Lasers in Cutaneous & Cosmetic Surgery. Gary P. Lask & Nicholas J. Lowe. Ed. by Judy Fletcher. LC 98-7037. (Illus.). 285p. 1999. text. write for info. (*0-443-07639-1*, W B Saunders Co) Harcrt Hlth Sci Grp.

Lasers in Dentistry. Ed. by Leo J. Miserendino & Robert M. Pick. LC 94-41152. (Illus.). 341p. 1995. text 98.00 (*0-86715-282-6*) Quint Pub Co.

***Lasers in Dentistry V.** Ed. by John D. Featherstone et al. 252p. 1999. pap. text 84.00 (*0-8194-3063-3*) SPIE.

Lasers in Dentistry III, Vol. 2973. Ed. by Harvey A. Wigdor et al. LC 97-193065. 252p. 1997. 69.00 (*0-8194-2384-X*) SPIE.

Lasers in Dentistry IV, Vol. 3248. Ed. by John D. Featherstone et al. LC 98-233178. 240p. 1998. 69.00 (*0-8194-2687-3*) SPIE.

Lasers in Dermatology: Bio-Optics & Treatment of Human Skin. Compiled by Optical Society of America Staff. LC 97-68772. (Nineteen Ninety-Seven Technical Digest Ser.: Vol. 15). (Illus.). 72p. 1997. pap. 75.00 (*1-55752-513-7*) Optical Soc.

Lasers in Dermatology: Proceedings of the International Symposium, Ulm, September 26, 1989. Ed. by R. Steiner et al. (Illus.). 176p. 1991. 118.00 (*0-387-51863-0*) Spr-Verlag.

Lasers in Facial Aesthetic & Reconstructive Surgery. Brian S. Biesman. LC 98-21399. 182p. 1998. 99.00 (*0-683-30414-3*) Lppncott W & W.

***Lasers in Facial Plastic Surgery.** Ed. by Gregory Keller et al. (Illus.). 408p. 2000. 169.00 (*0-86577-850-7*) Thieme Med Pubs.

Lasers in General Surgery. Stephen N. Joffe. (Illus.). 336p. 1989. 70.00 (*0-683-04460-5*) Lppncott W & W.

Lasers in Gynecology: Possibilities & Limitations. Ed. by G. Bastert & D. Wallwiener. (Illus.). 528p. 1992. 250.00 (*0-387-53409-1*) Spr-Verlag.

Lasers in Manufacturing. Ed. by W. M. Steen. (Illus.). 250p. 1989. 137.95 (*0-387-51241-1*) Spr-Verlag.

Lasers in Materials Processing. Leo Beckmann. LC 98-125173. 98p. 1997. pap. 132.00 (*0-8194-2517-6*) SPIE.

Lasers in Materials Processing. Ed. by Edward A. Metzbower. LC 83-72954. (Conference Proceedings - American Society for Metals Ser.). (Illus.). 276p. reprint ed. pap. 85.60 (*0-8357-6183-5*, 203431900089) Bks Demand.

Lasers in Materials Science. Ed. by R. P. Agarwala. 307p. 1999. 99.00 (*0-87849-826-5*, Pub. by Trans T Pub) Enfield Pubs NH.

Lasers in Maxillofacial Surgery & Dentisty. Lewis Clayman & Paul Kuo. LC 96-36512. (Illus.). 252p. 1997. text 115.00 (*0-86577-566-4*) Thieme Med Pubs.

Lasers in Medicine. Leon Goldman & James R. Rockwell, Jr. LC 77-163181. (Illus.). x, 386p. 1971. text 453.00 (*0-677-02430-4*) Gordon & Breach.

Lasers in Medicine. R. W. Waynant & G. H. Pettit. (Lasers, Photonics, & Electro-Optics Ser.). (Illus.). 468p. (C). 1997. write for info. (*0-306-45549-8*, Plenum Trade) Perseus Pubng.

Lasers in Medicine, Vol. 1. Ed. by Hans K. Koebner. LC 79-40525. (Illus.). 284p. reprint ed. pap. 88.10 (*0-8357-7880-0*, 203629800001) Bks Demand.

Lasers in Medicine & Dentistry: Diagnostics & Treatment. Ed. by Brij M. Khorana et al. (Europto Ser.: Vol. 2887). 246p. 1996. 85.00 (*0-8194-2288-6*) SPIE.

Lasers in Metallurgy: Proceedings of a Symposium. Ed. by Jyoti Mazumder & K. Mukherjee. LC 81-85419. (Conference Proceedings Ser.). (Illus.). 309p. reprint ed. pap. 95.80 (*0-8357-7502-X*, 203260000080) Bks Demand.

Lasers in Metalworking: A Summary & Forecast. 165p. 1983. pap. 80.00 (*0-317-05222-5*) Elsevier.

Lasers in Modern Industry. Ed. by John F. Ready. LC 79-66705. (Illus.). 276p. reprint ed. pap. 85.60 (*0-8357-6489-3*, 203586000097) Bks Demand.

Lasers in Neurosurgery. Ed. by E. F. Downing et al. (Illus.). 130p. 1989. 71.95 (*0-387-82067-1*) Spr-Verlag.

Lasers in Neurosurgery. Ed. by Jon H. Robertson & W. Craig Clark. (Foundations in Neurological Surgery Ser.). (C). 1988. text 150.00 (*0-89838-966-6*) Kluwer Academic.

Lasers in Nuclear Physics: Proceedings of the Conference on Lasers in Nuclear Physics Held In Oak Ridge, Tennessee, April 22-23, 1982, Vol. 3. Ed. by C. E. Bemis & H. K. Carter. (Nuclear Science Research Conference Ser.). xii, 510p. 1982. 179.00 (*3-7186-0142-7*) Gordon & Breach.

Lasers in Ophthalmic Surgery. David B. Karlin. (Illus.). 352p. 1994. 125.00 (*0-86542-260-5*) Blackwell Sci.

Lasers in Ophthalmology IV, Vol. 2930. Ed. by Reginald Birngruber et al. (Europto Ser.). 238p. 1996. 66.00 (*0-8194-2332-7*) SPIE.

Lasers in Optometry. James J. Thimons. 600p. 1995. text 89.50 (*0-397-51478-6*) Lppncott W & W.

Lasers in Otolaryngology. Davis. (Illus.). 224p. 1990. text 135.00 (*0-7216-3124-X*, W B Saunders Co) Harcrt Hlth Sci Grp.

Lasers in Otorhinolaryngology, & in Head & Neck Surgery. Ed. by H. Rudert & J. A. Werner. (Advances in OtoRhinoLaryngology Ser.: Vol. 49). (Illus.). xii, 264p. 1995. 215.75 (*3-8055-6087-7*) S Karger.

Lasers in Plastic Surgery. Michael I. Kulick. LC 96-53897. 1997. write for info. (*0-387-94891-0*) Spr-Verlag.

Lasers in Polymer Science & Technology Vol. I: Applications. Ed. by Jean-Pierre Fouassier & Jan F. Rabek. 320p. 1989. lib. bdg. 225.00 (*0-8493-4844-7*, TP1140) CRC Pr.

Lasers in Polymer Science & Technology Vol. II: Applications. Ed. by Jean-Pierre Fouassier. 288p. 1989. lib. bdg. 216.00 (*0-8493-4845-5*, TP1140) CRC Pr.

Lasers in Polymer Science & Technology Vol. III: Applications. Ed. by Jean-Pierre Fouassier & Jan F. Rabek. 304p. 1989. lib. bdg. 225.00 (*0-8493-4846-3*, TP1140) CRC Pr.

Lasers in Polymer Science & Technology Vol. IV: Applications. Ed. by Jean-Pierre Fouassier & Jan F. Rabek. 288p. 1989. lib. bdg. 225.00 (*0-8493-4847-1*, TP1140) CRC Pr.

Lasers in Skin Disease. Ronald G. Wheeland. Ed. by James Smith. (American Academy of Facial Plastic & Reconstructive Surgery Monograph: Vol. 5). (Illus.). 128p. 1987. text 85.00 (*0-86577-271-1*) Thieme Med Pubs.

***Lasers in Surface Engineering.** Ed. by Narendra B. Dahotre. LC 98-73964. (Surface Engineering Ser.: Vol. 1). 599p. 1998. 118.00 (*0-87170-665-2*) ASM.

***Lasers in Surgery.** Ed. by R. Rox Anderson et al. 520p. 1999. pap. text 120.00 (*0-8194-3060-9*) SPIE.

Lasers in Surgery: Advanced Characterization, Therapeutics & Systems VIII. Ed. by R. Rox Anderson et al. LC 99-192207. (Proceedings of SPIE Ser.: Vol. 3245). 474p. 1998. 116.00 (*0-8194-2684-9*) SPIE.

Lasers in Surgery Vol. 2970: Advanced Characterization, Therapeutics & Systems VII. Ed. by R. Rox Anderson et al. 632p. 1997. 132.00 (*0-8194-2381-5*) SPIE.

Lasers in Surgery & Medicine: Principles & Practice. Ed. by Carmen A. Puliafito. LC 95-36635. 484p. 1996. 129.95 (*0-471-12070-7*, Wiley-Liss) Wiley.

Lasers in Synthesis, Characterization & Processing of Diamond, Vol. 3484. Ed. by Alexander M. Prokhorov. LC 99-192241. 250p. 1998. write for info. (*0-8194-2942-2*) SPIE.

Lasers in Urological Surgery. Ed. by Alfons G. Hofstetter. LC 97-20861. (Illus.). x, 158p. 1997. 65.00 (*3-540-62452-X*) Spr-Verlag.

Lasers in Urology: Principles & Practice. Ed. by Jack Tinker & T. A. McNicholas. (Bloomsbury Series in Clinical Science). (Illus.). xii, 168p. 1990. 143.00 (*0-387-19615-3*) Spr-Verlag.

Lasers-Induced Plasmas & Applications. Leon J. Radziemski & David A. Cremers. (Optical Engineering Ser.: Vol. 21). (Illus.). 464p. 1989. text 175.00 (*0-8247-8078-7*) Dekker.

Lasers, Molecules, & Methods. Ed. by Joseph O. Hirschfelder et al. LC 87-25442. (Advances in Chemical Physics Ser.). 1022p. 1989. 315.00 (*0-471-62457-8*) Wiley.

***Lasers of Dermatology.** Sean Lanigan. LC 00-24606. 2000. write for info. (*1-85233-277-8*) Spr-Verlag.

Lasers-Physics & Applications. Ed. by A. Y. Spasov. 832p. (C). 1989. text 166.00 (*9971-5-0810-9*) World Scientific Pub.

Lasers, Ray Guns, & Light Cannons! Projects from the Wizard's Workbench. Gordon McComb. LC 97-989. (Illus.). 432p. 1997. pap. 21.95 (*0-07-045035-8*) McGraw.

Lasers, Spectroscopy & New Ideas. Ed. by W. M. Yen & Marc D. Levenson. (Optical Sciences Ser.: Vol. 54). (Illus.). 360p. 1987. 57.00 (*0-387-18296-9*) Spr-Verlag.

Lasers Without Inversion. Sher Alam. LC 97-6632. (Tutorial Texts in Optical Engineering Ser.). 1997. pap. write for info. (*0-8194-2514-1*) SPIE.

***Lasers Without Inversion & Electromagnetically Induced Transparency.** Sher Alam. 1998. 80.00 (*0-8194-3040-4*) SPIE.

Lasertown Blues. Charles Ingrid. (Sand Wars Ser.: Bk. 2). 288p. 1988. pap. 3.95 (*0-88677-393-8*, Pub. by DAW Bks) Penguin Putnam.

Laserwrite It! James Cavuoto. write for info. (*0-318-60210-5*) Addison-Wesley.

Laserwriter Reference. Apple Computer, Inc. Staff. 184p. (C). 1988. 19.95 (*0-201-19258-6*) Addison-Wesley.

Lash of Senorita Scorpion: A Western Trio. large type ed. Les Savage, Jr. LC 98-27481. 1998. 18.95 (*1-57490-149-4*, Sagebrush LP West) T T Beeler.

***Lashed into Lust.** 2000. mass mkt. 7.95 (*1-56201-198-7*) Blue Moon Bks.

Lasher. Anne Rice. 628p. 1995. mass mkt. 7.99 (*0-345-39781-9*) Ballantine Pub Grp.

Lasher. Anne Rice. LC 93-12246. 1993. 30.00 (*0-679-41295-6*) Knopf.

Lasher. Anne Rice. LC 93-12246. 592p. 1994. pap. 14.00 (*0-345-37764-8*) Knopf.

Lasher Lineage: With Supplement. Eileen L. Power. 545p. 1994. reprint ed. lib. bdg. 75.00 (*1-56012-131-9*, 129) Kinship Rhinebeck.

***LA/Shorts.** Ed. by Steven Gilbar. 274p. 2000. pap. 14.95 (*1-890771-29-5*, Pub. by Heyday Bks) SPD-Small Pr Dist.

Lasi of Marie de France. Tr. by Glyn S. Burgess & Keith Busby. (Penguin Classics Ser.). 164p. 1986. pap. 10.95 (*0-14-044759-8*, Penguin Bks) Viking Penguin.

Lasik. Ioannis Pallikaris & Dimitrios Siganos. LC 97-37263. (Illus.). 384p. 1997. text 149.00 (*1-55642-323-3*, 63233) SLACK Inc.

***Lasik: Clinical Co-Management.** Milton M. Hom & Loretta B. Szczotka. (Illus.). 192p. 2000. pap. 40.00 (*0-7506-7214-5*) Buttrwrth-Heinemann.

Lasik: Principles & Techniques. Lucio Buratto & Stephen F. Brint. LC 97-31540. (Illus.). 464p. 1997. text 149.00 (*1-55642-371-3*, 63713) SLACK Inc.

***LASIK: Surgical Techniques & Complications.** 2nd ed. Lucio Buratto & Stephen Brint. LC 99-46441. 624p. 1999. 215.00 (*1-55642-432-9*) SLACK Inc.

***LASIK: Surgical Techniques & Complications.** 2nd ed. Lucio Buratto & Stephen Brint. (SPA., Illus.). 624p. 2000. 215.00 (*1-55642-446-9*) SLACK Inc.

LASIK Complications: Prevention & Management. Howard Gimbel & Ellen E. Anderson Penno. LC 98-34613. (Illus.). 256p. 1998. 80.00 (*1-55642-392-6*, 63926) SLACK Inc.

***Lasik Complications: Prevention & Management.** 2nd ed. Howard V. Gimbel & Ellen E. Anderson Penno. 250p. (C). 2000. text 95.00 (*1-55642-473-6*) SLACK Inc.

Laska. 3rd ed. Vladimir Uhri. (SLO.). 90p. 1996. pap. 4.50 (*1-56983-009-6*) New Creat WI.

Laska a Smeti see Love & Garbage

Lasker Awards: Four Decades of Scientific Medical Progress. Lewis Thomas. LC 86-20225. 108p. reprint ed. pap. 33.50 (*0-608-04696-5*, 206541700004) Bks Demand.

Lasker Story. Albert D. Lasker. 128p. 1994. pap. 11.95 (*0-8442-3099-5*, NTC Business Bks) NTC Contemp Pub Co.

Lasker's Combination Vol. 4: The Tacticions Handbook. Victor Charushin. 112p. 1998. pap. 15.95 (*1-886846-13-8*) Pickard & Son.

Lasker's Manual of Chess. Emanuel Lasker. 390p. (YA). (gr. 7-12). 1960. pap. 8.95 (*0-486-20640-8*) Dover.

Lasko Interview. Clay Jacobsen. LC 98-24177. 412p. 1998. pap. 12.99 (*0-8054-1660-9*) Broadman.

Lasko Tangent. Richard North Patterson. 208p. 1985. mass mkt. 6.99 (*0-345-32532-X*) Ballantine Pub Grp.

***Lasko Tangent.** large type ed. Richard North Patterson. LC 99-59458. 2000. 25.95 (*1-56895-830-7*) Wheeler Pub.

Lasok Polish Civil Law. 1979. lib. bdg. 289.00 (*90-286-0555-X*) Kluwer Academic.

***Lasonya: A Vestige of Western Intrusions.** Rahomme Delind. LC 99-91081. 324p. 1999. 25.00 (*0-7388-0598-X*); pap. 18.00 (*0-7388-0599-8*) Xlibris Corp.

***Lassen Island.** Christian Riese Lassen. (Illus.). 88p. 1999. pap. 24.95 (*1-56931-382-2*) Viz Commns Inc.

Lassen Trail: Memoirs of James Eaton. F. D. Calhoon. (Illus.). 178p. (Orig.). 1987. pap. 6.00 (*0-945862-02-4*) F D Calhoon.

Lassen Volcanic: The Story Behind the Scenery. Ellis Richard. LC 88-80120. (Illus.). 48p. (Orig.). 1988. pap. 7.95 (*0-88714-020-3*) KC Pubns.

Lassen Volcanic National Park. 2nd ed. Jeffrey P. Schaffer. LC 85-41054. (Illus.). 224p. 1986. pap. 16.95 (*0-89997-059-1*) Wilderness Pr.

Lasser's Your Income Tax, 1982. Lasser, J. K., Tax Institute Staff. pap. 5.95 (*0-686-91635-2*) S&S Trade.

Lasset Uns Brucken Bauen... Collected Communications to the XVth Congress of the International Organization for the Study of the Old Testament, Cambridge, 1995. Ed. by Klaus-Dietrich Schunck et al. (Beitrage Zur Erforschung des Alten Testaments und Antiken Judentums Ser.: Vol. 42). 319p. 1998. 56.95 (*3-631-31014-5*) P Lang Pubng.

Lasset Uns Brucken Bauen... Collected Communications to the XVth Congress of the International Organization for the Study of the Old Testament, Cambridge, 1995. Ed. by Klaus Dietrich Schunk et al. (Beitrage zur Erforschung des Alten Testaments & Antiken Judentums Ser.: Vol. 42). (ENG & GER.). 319p. (C). 1998. pap. 56.95 (*0-8204-3229-6*) P Lang Pubng.

***Lassie.** Rosemary Wells. (Illus.). 2000. 12.95 (*84-241-3362-5*) Everest SP.

Lassie: A Collie & Her Influence. Susan Taylor Brown et al. LC 93-73130. (Illus.). 36p. (Orig.). 1993. 12.00 (*0-9615072-2-5*) Dog Museum.

Lassie: The Great Escape. Diane Muldrow. (Look-Look Bks.). (Illus.). 24p. (J). 1998. pap. 3.29 (*0-307-12986-1*, 12986, Goldn Books) Gldn Bks Pub Co.

Lassie: To the Rescue. Marian Bray. Ed. by Jeannie Harmon. LC 95-31856. (Lassie Bks.: Vol. 3). (Illus.). 144p. (Orig.). (J). (gr. 4-7). 1995. pap. 5.25 (*0-7814-0264-6*) Chariot Victor.

Lassie: Treasure at Eagle Mountain. Marian Bray. Ed. by Jeannie Harmon. (Lassie Bks.: Vol. 2). (Illus.). 144p. (Orig.). (J). (gr. 3-6). 1995. pap. 5.25 (*0-7814-0263-8*) Chariot Victor.

Lassie: Under the Big Top. Marian Bray. Ed. by Jeannie Harmon. (Lassie Bks.: Vol. 1). (Illus.). 144p. (Orig.). (J). (gr. 3-6). 1995. pap. 5.99 (*0-7814-0262-X*, Lion) Chariot Victor.

Lassie Come Home. Eric M. Knight. 208p. (J). 1992. pap. 4.50 (*0-440-40760-5*) Dell.

Lassie Come Home. Eric M. Knight. (J). 1968. 9.60 (*0-606-02703-3*, Pub. by Turtleback) Demco.

***Lassie Come-Home.** Rosemary Wells & Eric Knight. LC 99-40725. (Illus.). 64p. (J). (gr. 2-5). 2000. 15.95 (*0-8050-6423-0*) H Holt & Co.

Lassie Come Home. large type ed. Eric M. Knight. (Illus.). 239p. (J). 1996. 22.95 (*0-7838-1691-X*, G K Hall Lrg Type) Mac Lib Ref.

Lassie Come Home. Eric M. Knight. 234p. (J). 1981. reprint ed. lib. bdg. 16.95 (*0-89966-346-X*); reprint ed. lib. bdg. 12.95 (*0-89967-020-2*, Harmony Rain) Buccaneer Bks.

Lassie Come Home. Eric M. Knight. LC 78-3570. (Illus.). 256p. (J). (gr. 4-6). 1995. reprint ed. 16.95 (*0-8050-0721-0*, Bks Young Read) H Holt & Co.

Lassie Come-Home. Rosemary Wells. LC 95-6064. (Illus.). 48p. (J). (gr. 2-4). 1995. reprint ed. 16.95 (*0-8050-3794-2*) H Holt & Co.

Lassie Come-Home. Rosemary Wells. (Illus.). 1998. reprint ed. pap. 7.95 (*0-8050-5995-4*, Owlet BYR) H Holt & Co.

Lassie Danger at Echo Cliffs, No. 5. 144p. (J). 1996. mass mkt. 5.99 (*0-7814-0274-3*) Chariot Victor.

Lassie Hayloft Hideout, No. 4. 144p. (J). 1996. mass mkt. 5.99 (*0-7814-0265-4*) Chariot Victor.

Lassie's Guide to a Family's Best Friend: Raising the Family Dog. unabridged ed. Ace Collins. LC 98-14972. (Illus.). 176p. 1998. pap. 11.95 (*0-307-44074-5*, Whitman Coin) St Martin.

Lassiter. large type ed. Loren Z. Grey. (Nightingale Ser.). 307p. 1992. pap. 14.95 (*0-8161-4949-6*, G K Hall Lrg Type) Mac Lib Ref.

Lassiter. large type ed. Jack Slade. 256p. 1985. pap. 16.99 (*0-7089-6076-6*, Linford) Ulverscroft.

Lassiter: Rimfire. large type ed. Jack Slade. (Linford Western Library). 272p. 1992. pap. 16.99 (*0-7089-7259-4*, Linford) Ulverscroft.

Lassiter: The Man form Yuma. large type ed. Jack Slade. (Linford Western Library). 272p. 1992. pap. 16.99 (*0-7089-7248-9*, Linford) Ulverscroft.

Lassiter Gold. large type ed. Loren Z. Grey. (Nightingale Ser.). 296p. (Orig.). 1991. pap. 14.95 (*0-8161-4951-8*, G K Hall Lrg Type) Mac Lib Ref.

Lassitudes of Fire. Will Patton. (Illus.). 42p. 1999. pap. 5.95 (*0-9666328-4-2*) CUZ Ed.

Lasso the Moon. Dennis Covington. (J). 1996. 20.95 (*0-385-30991-0*) BDD Bks Young Read.

L

L

Lasso the Moon. Dennis Covington. LC 94-26073. 1996. 9.60 (*0-606-09526-8*, Pub. by Turtleback) Demco.

Lasso the Wind: Away to the New West. Timothy Egan. LC 97-50556. 288p. 1998. 25.00 (*0-375-40024-9*) Knopf.

***Lassoed!** Martha Shields. (Romance Ser.: Bk. 1461). 2000. mass mkt. 3.50 (*0-373-19461-7*, 1-19461-2) Silhouette.

Last. 1995. 58.95 (*3-7908-0825-3*) Spr-Verlag.

Last Abbot of Glastonbury & Other Essays. Francis A. Gasquet. LC 72-137376. (Select Bibliographies Reprint Ser.). 1977. 23.95 (*0-8369-5577-3*) Ayer.

Last Act. William Gaddis. 1988. write for info. (*0-318-62737-X*) S&S Trade.

Last Act. Christopher Pike, pseud. (YA). (gr. 8 up). 1991. mass mkt. 3.99 (*0-671-73683-3*, Archway) PB.

Last Act. Christopher Pike, pseud. 1988. 9.09 (*0-606-03841-8*, Pub. by Turtleback) Demco.

Last Act in Palmyra. Lindsey Davis. 432p. 1997. reprint ed. mass mkt. 6.50 (*0-446-40474-8*, Pub. by Warner Bks) Little.

Last Act in Urbino (Il Sipario Ducale) Paolo Volponi. Tr. & Intro. by Peter N. Pedroni. LC 88-81096. 320p. (Orig.). 1995. pap. 15.00 (*0-934977-33-X*) Italica Pr.

Last Actor-Managers. Hesketh Pearson. LC 77-148225. (Biography Index Reprint Ser.). (Illus.). 1977. 23.95 (*0-8369-8072-7*) Ayer.

***Last Adventure.** Reader's Digest Association Staff. LC 00-28606. (Eventful 20th Century Ser.). (Illus.). 2001. write for info. (*0-7621-0289-6*) RD Assn.

Last Adventurer: The Life of Talbot Mundy. Peter B. Ellis. 1984. 25.00 (*0-937986-70-4*) D M Grant.

Last Aerie. Brian Lumley. 832p. 1994. mass mkt. 5.99 (*0-8125-2062-9*, Pub. by Tor Bks) St Martin.

Last Age of the Roman Republic, 146-43 B. C. 2nd ed. Ed. by J. A. Crook et al. (Ancient History Ser.: Vol. 9). (Illus.). 947p. 1994. text 150.00 (*0-521-25603-8*) Cambridge U Pr.

Last Album. Weiss. LC 99-47972. 192p. 2000. text 35.00 (*0-393-01670-6*) Norton.

Last Alchemist. Colin Thompson. LC 98-46756. (Illus.). 32p. (J). (gr. 3-5). 1999. 17.00 (*0-375-80156-1*, Pub. by Knopf Bks Yng Read) Random.

Last Algonquin. Theodore L. Kazimiroff. 1982. 18.95 (*0-8027-0698-3*) Walker & Co.

Last Algonquin. Theodore L. Kazimiroff. 197p. 1997. pap. 12.95 (*0-8027-7517-9*) Walker & Co.

***Last Alien.** 2nd rev. ed. 192p. 2000. pap. 16.95 (*0-9677553-0-1*) D A Kish.

Last Alternatives: Allen Tate. R. K. Meiners. LC 72-4614. (American Literature Ser.: No. 49). 1972. reprint ed. lib. bdg. 75.00 (*0-8383-1594-1*) M S G Haskell Hse.

***Last Amateurs: Playing for Glory & Honor in Division I College Basketball.** John Feinstein. (Illus.). 416p. 2000. 24.95 (*0-316-27701-0*) Little.

Last American. Diego De La Cerda. LC 97-69235. 256p. 1998. pap. 16.95 (*1-57197-084-3*) Pentland Pr.

Last American. Steven Burgauer. (Matthews Chronicles Ser.). 410p. (Orig.). 1996. reprint ed. pap. 12.95 (*0-7610-0438-6*) Zero-g Pr.

Last American. John A. Mitchell. LC 75-104529. reprint ed. lib. bdg. 22.75 (*0-8398-1262-0*) Irvington.

Last American Heroes. Charles W. Sasser. 1994. mass mkt. 5.99 (*0-671-78930-9*) PB.

Last American Puritan: The Life of Increase Mather, 1639-1723. Michael G. Hall. LC 87-7367. (Illus.). 456p. 1990. pap. 25.00 (*0-8195-6238-6*, Wesleyan Univ Pr) U Pr of New Eng.

Last American Rainforest: Tongass. Shelley Gill. (Illus.). 32p. (J). (gr. 2-5). 1997. 16.95 (*0-934007-32-2*); pap. 8.95 (*0-934007-33-0*) Paws Four Pub.

Last American Whale-Oil Company: A History of Nye Lubricants, Inc., 1844-1994. Ed. by Art Parr. (Illus.). iii, 99p. 1996. write for info. (*0-9653026-0-1*); pap. write for info. (*0-9653026-1-X*) Nye Lubricants.

Last & First Men & Star Maker. Olaf Stapledon. 438p. 1968. pap. 10.95 (*0-486-21962-3*) Dover.

Last & First Men & Star Maker. Olaf Stapledon. 1996. 24.50 (*0-8446-2995-2*) Peter Smith.

Last & Greatest Art: Some Unpublished Poetical Manuscripts of Alexander Pope. Ed. by Maynard Mack. LC 81-50304. 448p. 1984. 85.00 (*0-87413-183-9*) U Delaware Pr.

Last & Lost Poems. rev. ed. Delmore Schwartz. LC 88-31396. Vol. 673. 192p. 1989. pap. 9.95 (*0-8112-1096-0*, NDP673, Pub. by New Directions) Norton.

Last Angry Man. Gerald Green. 1976. reprint ed. lib. bdg. 31.95 (*0-89190-121-3*) Amereon Ltd.

Last Angry Man. Gerald Green. 1993. reprint ed. lib. bdg. 28.95 (*1-56849-202-2*) Buccaneer Bks.

Last Angry Principal. Howard L. Hurwitz. LC 88-80826. 258p. (Orig.). 1988. pap. 15.95 (*0-89420-255-3*, 110220, Halcyon) Natl Book.

Last Animals at the Zoo: How Mass Extinction Can Be Stopped. Colin Tudge. LC 91-39773. 266p. 1992. text 30.00 (*1-55963-158-9*) Island Pr.

Last Animals at the Zoo: How Mass Extinction Can Be Stopped. Colin Tudge. LC 91-39773. 266p. 1993. pap. 17.95 (*1-55963-157-0*) Island Pr.

Last Ape: Pygmy Chimpanzee Behavior & Ecology. Takayoshi Kano. Tr. by Evelyn O. Vineberg from JPN. LC 91-2147. (Illus.). 280p. (C). 1992. 47.50 (*0-8047-1612-9*) Stanford U Pr.

Last Apocalypse. James Reston. (Illus.). 336p. 1999. pap. 14.95 (*0-385-48336-8*) Doubleday.

***Last Apostle.** Donald J. Baker, Jr. 2000. pap. 12.95 (*1-891929-56-9*) Four Seasons.

Last Apostles on Earth. rev. ed. Roger W. Sapp. 186p. (C). 1995. pap. 9.95 (*0-9662085-3-6*) All Nations Pubs.

Last April Dancers. Jean Thesman. 224p. (YA). (gr. 7 up). 1989. pap. 2.75 (*0-380-70614-8*, Avon Bks) Morrow Avon.

Last Arab Jews: The Communities of Jerba. Lucette Valensi et al. (Social Orders Ser.). xii, 178p. 1984. text 87.00 (*3-7186-0135-4*) Gordon & Breach.

Last Aristocrats. Ai L. Zhang. (CHI.). pap. 9.95 (*7-5391-0830-4*, Pub. by China Intl Bk) Distribks Inc.

Last Arrow. Marsha Canham. 448p. (Orig.). 1997. mass mkt. 5.99 (*0-440-22257-5*) Dell.

Last Arrow. Marsha Canham. (Orig.). 1997. mass mkt. 5.99 (*0-614-27733-7*) Dell.

Last Assault: The Battle of the Bulge Reassessed. Charles Whiting. LC 94-203303. (Illus.). 238p. 1994. 28.95 (*0-85052-380-X*, Pub. by Leo Cooper) Trans-Atl Phila.

Last Assault, 1944: The Battle of the Bulge Reassessed. Charles Whiting. (Illus.). 288p. 1994. 24.95 (*1-885119-00-3*) Sarpedon.

***Last Attachment: The Story of Byron & Teresa Guiccioli.** Iris Origo. 320p. 2000. pap. 16.95 (*1-885586-50-7*, Pub. by Turtle Point Pr) Dist Art Pubs.

***Last Autopsy.** 140p. 2000. pap. 12.00 (*0-9702176-0-9*, 1001) Night Howl.

Last Avant-Garde: The Making of the New York School of Poets. David Lehman. LC 98-16249. 448p. 1998. 27.50 (*0-385-47542-X*) Doubleday.

***Last Avant-Garde: The Making of the New York School of Poets.** David Lehman. 464p. 1999. pap. 16.95 (*0-385-49533-1*, Anchor NY) Doubleday.

Last Avengers Story. Peter David. (Illus.). 96p. 1996. pap. text 12.95 (*0-7851-0218-3*) Marvel Entrprs.

Last Bachelor. Carolyn Andrews. (Temptation Ser.: Vol. 700). 1998. per. 3.75 (*0-373-25800-3*, 1-25800-3) Harlequin Bks.

Last Bachelor. Betina M. Krahn. 528p. 1994. mass mkt. 5.99 (*0-553-56522-2*) Bantam.

Last Bachelor. large type ed. Betina M. Krahn. LC 94-40020. (Large Print Bks.). 1995. 23.95 (*1-56895-170-1*) Wheeler Pub.

Last Badland. John Hafnor. 140p. 1996. pap. write for info. (*0-9648175-1-9*) Lone Pine CO.

Last Ballad. large type ed. Helen Cannam. (Magna Large Print Ser.). 1994. 27.99 (*0-7505-0697-0*, Pub. by Mgna Lrg Print) Ulverscroft.

Last Banner. Peter May. LC 96-35854. 1996. 22.50 (*0-684-80085-3*) S&S Trade.

Last Banner: The Story of the 1985-86 Celtics, the NBA's Greatest Team of All Time. Peter May. LC 97-51731. 304p. 1998. pap. 9.95 (*1-55850-835-X*) Adams Media.

Last Barbarians. Michel Peissel. 1995. pap. 14.95 (*0-8050-4535-X*) H Holt & Co.

Last Barbarians: The Discovery of the Source of the Meking in Tibet. Michel Peissel. LC 97-27534. 320p. 1995. 27.50 (*0-8050-4534-1*) H Holt & Co.

Last Barrier: The Universal Search for Self-Discovery. Reshad Feild. 224p. 1996. pap. 9.95 (*1-85230-852-4*, Pub. by Element MA) Penguin Putnam.

Last Barrier to Freedom: Internment of Jewish Holocaust Survivors on Cyprus 1946-1949. Morris Laub. LC 84-82475. (Illus.). (Orig.). 1985. pap. 8.95 (*0-943376-25-4*) Magnes Mus.

***Last Basselope.** Berkeley Breathed. (J). 2001. pap. 5.95 (*0-316-12664-0*) Little.

Last Basselope: One Ferocious Story. Berkeley Breathed. LC 92-14467. (Illus.). 32p. (J). (gr. k-3). 1992. 14.95 (*0-316-10761-1*) Little.

Last Bastion. Peter C. Wensberg. LC 94-11243. 224p. 1995. 22.00 (*1-877946-58-3*); pap. 16.00 (*1-57962-001-9*) Permanent Pr.

Last Battle. C. S. Lewis. LC 93-14302. (Chronicles of Narnia Ser.: Bk. 7). (Illus.). 224p. (J). (gr. 4-7). 1994. 16.95 (*0-06-023493-8*); pap. 6.95 (*0-06-440503-6*); pap. 4.95 (*0-06-447108-X*, HarpTrophy); lib. bdg. 16.89 (*0-06-023494-6*) HarpC Child Bks.

Last Battle. C. S. Lewis. (Chronicles of Narnia Ser.: Bk. 7). (J). (gr. 4-8). 1950. 30.00 (*0-7862-2237-9*) Mac Lib Ref.

Last Battle. C. S. Lewis. (Chronicles of Narnia Ser.: Bk. 7). 192p. (J). (gr. 4-8). 1970. pap. 3.95 (*0-02-044210-6*) Macmillan.

Last Battle. C. S. Lewis. LC 93-14302. (Chronicles of Narnia Ser.: Bk. 7). (J). (gr. 4-8). 1994. 12.05 (*0-606-06517-2*, Pub. by Turtleback); 10.05 (*0-606-06518-0*, Pub. by Turtleback) Demco.

Last Battle. Christopher Nicole. 352p. 1993. lib. bdg. 20.00 (*0-7278-4454-7*) Severn Hse.

***Last Battle: Full-Color Collector's Edition.** C. S. Lewis. LC 93-14302. (Chronicles of Narnia Ser.: Bk. 7). (Illus.). 224p. (J). (gr. 4-7). 2000. mass mkt. 7.95 (*0-06-440941-4*, HarpTrophy) HarpC Child Bks.

Last Battle: The Classic History of Battle for Berlin. Cornelius Ryan. (Illus.). 576p. 1995. per. 16.00 (*0-684-80329-1*) S&S Trade Pap.

Last Battle for Saint Stephen's Crown. Attila L. Simontsits. LC 78-63576. (Illus.). xvi, 1141p. (C). 1983. 30.00 (*0-920004-09-1*) Simontsits.

Last Battlemage. Irene Radford. (Dragon Nimbus Ser.: No. 2). 352p. 1998. mass mkt. 6.99 (*0-88677-774-7*, Pub. by DAW Bks) Penguin Putnam.

***Last Battleship: The Story of the USS Missouri.** Scott C. Stone. LC 99-34992. 64p. 1999. pap. 10.00 (*1-57864-082-2*) Donning Co.

Last Bear. Dennis P. D'Amelio. (Illus.). 26p. (J). 1998. pap. write for info. (*1-891528-71-8*) Telescopic Pr.

***Last Beautiful Days of Autumn: A Memoir.** John Nichols. LC 00-25731. (Illus.). 220p. 2000. pap. 14.95 (*1-58096-008-1*) Ancient City Pr.

Last Beloved Women. Charles B. Johnson. 129p. (Orig.). (J). (gr. 4 up). 1995. pap. 5.99 (*1-884505-00-7*) Amer Trail Bks.

Last Best Hope. Ed McBain, pseud. 291p. 1999. mass mkt. 7.50 (*0-446-60673-1*, Pub. by Warner Bks) Little.

Last Best Hope. large type ed. Ed McBain, pseud. LC 98-27664. 383p. 1998. pap. 30.00 (*0-7862-1605-0*) Thorndike Pr.

Last Best Hope: How to Start & Grow Your Own Business. Rod McQueen. 288p. 1996. 29.99 (*0-7710-5630-3*) McCland & Stewart.

Last Best Hope: How to Start & Grow Your Own Business. Rod McQueen. 312p. 1997. pap. text 16.95 (*0-7710-5634-6*) McCland & Stewart.

Last Best Hope of Earth: Abraham Lincoln & the Promise of America. Mark E. Neely, Jr. LC 93-22863. (Illus.). 304p. 1993. text 24.95 (*0-674-51125-5*) HUP.

Last Best Hope of Earth: Abraham Lincoln & the Promise of America. Mark E. Neely, Jr. 320p. 1995. pap. 14.95 (*0-674-51126-3*, NEELAX) HUP.

Last Best Hope on Earth: Abraham Lincoln & the Promise of America. John Rhodehamel & Thomas F. Schwartz. (Illus.). 80p. 1993. pap. 9.00 (*0-87328-142-X*, 142X, Pub. by Huntington Lib) A Schwartz & Co.

Last Best Place: A Montana Anthology. William Kittredge. LC 88-23475. (Illus.). 1158p. 1992. 39.95 (*1-56044-155-0*) Falcon Pub Inc.

Last Best Place: A Montana Anthology. William Kittredge. (Illus.). 1182p. 1990. pap. 29.95 (*0-295-96974-1*) U of Wash Pr.

Last Big Gun Naval Battle: The Battle of Surigao Strait. Howard Sauer. LC 99-21242. (Illus.). 224p. 1999. 26.95 (*1-889901-08-3*) Glencannon Pr.

Last Big One: Hurricane Donna Hits Ft. Myers Beach on Sept. 10, 1960. (Illus.). 79p. 1995. pap. 12.95 (*0-9644574-4-X*) Shoeless Pub.

Last Billable Hour. Susan Wolfe. (Northern California Mysteries Ser.). 192p. 1990. mass mkt. 4.99 (*0-8041-0540-5*) Ivy Books.

Last Bit Bear: A Fable. Sandra C. Robinson. (Illus.). 48p. 1991. pap. 4.95 (*0-911797-09-2*) Roberts Rinehart.

***Last Blue.** deluxe limited ed. Gerald Stern. 8p. 1998. pap. 25.00 (*1-891472-15-1*) Dim Gray.

***Last Blue: Poems.** Gerald Stern. LC 99-55508. 112p. 2000. 22.00 (*0-393-04897-7*) Norton.

***Last Blue Plate Special.** Abigail Padgett. 256p. 2001. 23.95 (*0-89296-731-5*) Mysterious Pr.

***Last Blue Promise.** Rita Bryant. 60p. 1998. pap. 6.00 (*0-935931-97-X*, Gray Matter Pubg) Iberian Pub.

***Last Blues Dance.** Ferdinand Dennis. 256p. 1998. mass mkt. 10.95 (*0-00-649783-7*, Pub. by HarpC) Trafalgar.

Last Boat to Camden Town: An Inspector Christy Kennedy Mystery. Paul Charles. 168p. 1998. 34.95 (*1-899344-29-2*, Pub. by Do-Not Pr) Dufour.

Last Boat to Camden Town: An Inspector Christy Kennedy Mystery. Paul Charles. 168p. 1998. pap. 15.95 (*1-899344-30-6*, Pub. by Do-Not Pr) Dufour.

Last Boer War. H. Rider Haggard. 1977. text 17.95 (*0-8369-9222-9*, 9076) Ayer.

Last Bonanza Kings: The Bourns of San Francisco. Ferol Egan. LC 98-10998. (Illus.). 312p. 1998. 37.95 (*0-87417-319-1*) U of Nev Pr.

Last Book. Dallas Lewis & Lisa M. Lewis. (Illus.). 32p. (J). (gr. 1-2). 1992. 16.00 (*0-9634087-0-4*) Silly Billys Bks.

Last Book. Lisa Lewis & Dallas Lewis. 32p. (J). (gr. 2-4). 1997. 13.95 (*0-9634087-4-7*); pap. 6.95 (*0-9634087-5-5*) Silly Billys Bks.

***Last Book in the Universe.** W. R. Philbrick. LC 99-59878. (Illus.). 192p. (YA). (gr. 5-9). 2001. 16.95 (*0-439-08758-9*) Scholastic Inc.

Last Book of Swords: Sheildbreaker's Story. Fred Saberhagen. (Swords Ser.). 256p. 1999. mass mkt. 5.99 (*0-8125-0577-8*, Pub. by Tor Bks) St Martin.

Last Book of Wonder. Edward J. Dunsany. LC 76-101282. (Short Story Index Reprint Ser.). (Illus.). 1977. 18.95 (*0-8369-3219-6*) Ayer.

Last Book You'll Ever Read: And Other Lessons from the Future. Frank Ogden. 224p. 1994. 22.95 (*0-921912-71-4*) MW&R.

Last Bookmaker. Bob Litwin et al. 288p. 24.95 (*1-880325-18-7*, Pub. by Borderlnds NH) Baker & Taylor.

Last Bookman: A Biography of Vincent Starrett. 2nd rev. expanded enl. ed. Peter Ruber. (Vincent Starrett Memorial Library Ser.: Vol. 3). 172p. 1995. text 24.00 (*1-896032-66-4*) Battered Silicon.

Last Bounty. J. R. Roberts. (Gunsmith Ser.: No. 135). 192p. (Orig.). 1993. pap. 3.99 (*0-515-11063-9*, Jove) Berkley Pub.

***Last Bounty.** large type ed. H. H. Cody. 176p. 1999. pap. 18.99 (*0-7089-5568-1*, Linford) Ulverscroft.

***Last Bounty, 1 vol., Vol. 208.** J. R. Roberts. (Gunsmith Ser.). (Orig.). 1999. mass mkt. 4.99 (*0-515-12512-1*, Jove) Berkley Pub.

Last Bread Pudding: A Comedy Nick Warburton. LC 99-213833. 25 p. 1997. write for info. (*0-573-12145-1*) French.

Last Breath. Diane Hoh. (Nightmare Hall Ser.: No. 17). 176p. (YA). (gr. 7-9). 1994. pap. 3.50 (*0-590-48648-9*) Scholastic Inc.

Last Breath: Space Station Rescue. Stephen P. Cammick. (Illus.). 328p. 1999. pap. 12.95 (*0-9671200-0-4*) Palm Coast Pubg.

***Last Bride in Texas.** Judith Stacy. (Historical Ser.). 2000. mass mkt. 4.99 (*0-373-29141-8*, 1291418) Harlequin Bks.

Last Bridesmaid. Leandra Logan. LC 96-434. 249p. 1995. per. 3.50 (*0-373-16601-X*, 1-16601-6) Harlequin Bks.

Last Bridge Home. Iris Johansen. 256p. 1992. mass mkt. 5.99 (*0-553-29871-2*) Bantam.

Last Bridge Home: New & Selected Poems. Dan Gerber. LC 91-61902. (Illus.). 208p. 1992. 23.95 (*0-944439-38-1*); pap. 12.95 (*0-944439-28-4*) Clark City Pr.

Last Bridge to Victory. Lawrence Cortesi. 320p. 1984. mass mkt. 2.50 (*0-685-08594-5*, Zebra Kensgtn) Kensgtn Pub Corp.

Last British Liberals in Africa: Michael Blundell & Garfield Todd. Dickson A. Mungazi. LC 98-39876. 312p. 1999. 69.50 (*0-275-96283-0*, Praeger Pubs) Greenwood.

Last Brother. Joe McGinniss. 1994. pap. 6.99 (*0-671-89452-8*) PB.

Last Buckaroo. 2nd ed. Mackey Hedges. 352p. 1998. reprint ed. pap. 10.95 (*0-87905-667-3*) Gibbs Smith Pub.

Last Buffalo: The Story of Frederick Arthur Verner, Painter of the Northwest. Joan Murray. (Illus.). 192p. 1985. 95.00 (*0-87951-232-6*, Pub. by Overlook Pr) Penguin Putnam.

Last Buffalo: Walter E. Potts, Oldest Documented Buffalo Soldier. E. B. Hogan. LC 97-94727. (Illus.). 150p. 1998. pap. write for info. (*0-9664746-1-9*) Vidor Pubg.

***Last Buffalo: Walter Potts, Oldest Documented Buffalo Soldier.** E. B. Hogan. LC 99-49608. 2000. write for info. (*1-57168-364-X*) Sunbelt Media.

***Last Buffalo Hunter.** Jake Mosher. 2000. 24.95 (*1-56792-146-9*) Godine.

Last Bus. Robert Swindells. (Illus.). 95p. (J). pap. 7.95 (*0-14-037971-1*, Pub. by Pnguin Bks Ltd) Trafalgar.

Last Bus to Albuquerque: A Commemorative Edition Celebrating Lewis Grizzard. Lewis Grizzard et al. LC 94-77579. (Illus.). 208p. 1994. 20.00 (*1-56352-183-0*) Longstreet.

Last Bus to Woodstock. Colin Dexter. 1996. mass mkt. 5.99 (*0-8041-1490-0*) Ivy Books.

Last Cabbage Stomper. Joe Koprivnik. (Illus.). 92p. 1997. pap. 10.00 (*0-87012-588-5*) McClain.

A lighthearted & honest look at life growing up in the Welch, Elbert, Pinch Back areas of McDowell County, West Virginia. 40 photos enhance this 90-page book on a simpler time in history.

Publisher Paid Annotation.

Last Caboose. Norm Ross. 31p. (Orig.). 1994. pap. 4.95 (*1-884226-03-5*) Dark River.

Last Cacique: Leadership & Politics in a Puerto Rican City. Jorge Heine. LC 92-36910. (Latin American Ser.). 328p. (C). 1993. text 49.95 (*0-8229-3741-7*) U of Pittsburgh Pr.

Last Call. Jack T. Chick. (Illus.). 64p. 1963. pap. 3.50 (*0-937958-06-9*) Chick Pubns.

***Last Call.** Bob Colbert. LC 99-65326. 192p. 2000. pap. 11.95 (*1-56315-259-2*, Pub. by SterlingHse) Natl Bk Netwk.

Last Call. Tim Powers. (Illus.). 576p. 1992. 150.00 (*0-927389-05-3*) Charnel Hse.

Last Call. Tim Powers. 544p. 1993. mass mkt. 4.99 (*0-380-71557-0*, Avon Bks) Morrow Avon.

Last Call. Tim Powers. LC 91-34070. 544p. 1996. pap. 13.00 (*0-380-72846-X*, Avon Bks) Morrow Avon.

Last Call. limited ed. Tim Powers. (Illus.). 576p. 1992. teacher ed. 650.00 (*0-927389-04-5*) Charnel Hse.

Last Call: A Legacy of Madness. Ed. by Raindog. 1994. pap. 20.00 (*1-888662-08-5*) Vinegar Hill.

Last Call: Memoirs of an NFL Referee. Jerry Markbreit & Alan Steinberg. (Illus.). 288p. 1999. 24.95 (*1-58382-030-2*, Pub. by Sports Masters) Partners-West.

Last Call: Poems on Alcoholism, Addiction, & Deliverance. Ed. by Sarah Gorham & Jeffrey Skinner. LC 96-7251. 192p. (Orig.). 1997. pap. 14.95 (*0-9641151-8-2*) Sarabande Bks.

Last Call: Selections from the Best of "Down to Cases" Tom Casey. Ed. by Jack Ronald. 180p. 1997. pap. 14.95 (*0-9661729-0-6*) Graphic Printing.

Last Call: The Preparation of the Bride for the Rapture of the Church. Intro. by R. C. Schaffter. LC 94-200565. 264p. (Orig.). 1994. pap. 10.99 (*0-9633026-1-2*) Clar Call WI.

***Last Call: 10 Common Sense Solutions to America's Biggest Problems.** Rob Nelson. 304p. 2000. pap. 12.95 (*0-440-50903-3*) Delacorte.

***Last Call: 10 Commonsense Solutions to America's Biggest Problems.** Rob Nelson. LC 99-55447. 2000. 12.95 (*0-385-33408-7*, Delta Trade) Dell.

Last Call at the 7-Eleven: Fine Dining at 2 a.m., the Search for Spandex People, & Other Reasons to Go on Living. Kevin Cowherd. Ed. by Bruce Bortz. LC 96-163549. 243p. 1995. 19.95 (*0-9635376-3-6*) Bancroft MD.

Last Call for Gold! How to Cash in Big on the Coming Gold Fever. James Digeorgia. Ed. by Martin D. Weiss. 61p. (Orig.). pap. text 72.00 (*0-941739-06-6*) M D Weiss Pub.

***Last Call for Help: Changing North America One Teen at a Time.** Dayle Maloney. 1999. pap. 14.95 (*0-9664118-5-4*) D L Maloney.

***Last Call of the Bugle.** Jack Gallaway. 1999. pap. 19.95 (*0-7022-3106-1*, Pub. by Univ Queensland Pr) Intl Spec Bk.

Last Camel: Stories about Somalia. Jeanne D'Haem. LC 97-8108. 1997. 59.95 (*1-56902-040-X*); pap. 16.95 (*1-56902-041-8*) Red Sea Pr.

Last Camel Died at Noon. large type ed. Elizabeth Peters, pseud. (Amelia Peabody Mystery Ser.). 574p. 1992. lib. bdg. 21.95 (*0-8161-5357-4*, G K Hall Lrg Type) Mac Lib Ref.

Last Camel Died at Noon. large type ed. Elizabeth Peters, pseud. (Amelia Peabody Mystery Ser.). 576p. 1992. pap. 24.95 (*0-8161-5358-2*, G K Hall Lrg Type) Mac Lib Ref.

Last Camel Died at Noon. Elizabeth Peters, pseud. (Amelia Peabody Mystery Ser.). 480p. 1992. reprint ed. mass mkt. 6.99 (*0-446-36338-3*, Pub. by Warner Bks) Little.

***Last Campaign** Rachel Loden. LC 99-198664. 32p. 1998. write for info. (*0-9624178-8-2*) Slapering Hol.

An Asterisk (*) at the beginning of an entry indicates that the title is appearing for the first time.

Last Campaign. large type ed. Tim Champlin. LC 95-40637. (Five Stars Western Ser.). 1996. 16.95 (*0-7862-0566-0*) Five Star.

***Last Campaign: How Harry Truman Won the 1948 Election.** Zachary Karabell. LC 99-28567. (Illus.). 320p. 2000. 27.50 (*0-375-40086-9*) Knopf.

***Last Campfire: The Life Story of Ted Gray, A West Texas Rancher.** 2nd ed. Barney Nelson. (Illus.). 196p. 2000. reprint ed. 29.95 (*0-9657985-1-8*); reprint ed. pap. 14.95 (*0-9657985-2-6*) Iron Mountain.

Last Cannibals: A South American Oral History. Ellen B. Basso. LC 94-25376. (Illus.). 352p. (C). 1995. pap. 19.95 (*0-292-70819-X*); text 40.00 (*0-292-70818-1*) U of Tex Pr.

***Last Cannoli: A Novel: A Sicilian American Family Comes of Age Through the Ancient Power of Storytelling.** Camille Cusumano. 240p. 1999. per. 19.00 (*1-881901-20-3*) LEGAS.

Last Cannon Shot: A Study of French-Canadian Nationalism, 1837-1850. Jacques Monet. LC 70-455781. 432p. reprint ed. pap. 134.00 (*0-608-16319-8*, 202653700050) Bks Demand.

***Last Cantata.** Philippe Delelis. 2000. write for info. (*1-902881-30-3*, Pub. by Toby Pr Ltd); pap. 15.95 (*1-902881-31-1*, Pub. by Toby Pr Ltd) Toby Pr.

Last Capital: Danville, Virginia, & the Final Days of the Confederacy. John H. Brubaker, 3rd. LC 79-109027. (Illus.). 76p. 1996. 19.95 (*0-9651635-0-4*) Danville Mus.

Last Captive. A. C. Greene. (Illus.). 185p. (J). (gr. 6-9). 1972. 29.95 (*0-88426-004-6*) Encino Pr.

***Last Captured.** Gerard J. Pierre. LC 99-93576. 2000. pap. 11.95 (*0-533-13071-9*) Vantage.

Last Carousel. Nelson Algren. LC 96-48583. 448p. 1997. pap. 14.95 (*1-888363-45-2*) Seven Stories.

Last Cast: Fishing Reminiscences. Rafe Mair. (Illus.). 160p. 1995. 12.95 (*0-88839-346-6*) Hancock House.

Last Cast: Fishing Reminiscences. Rafe Mair. 128p. 1996. pap. 12.95 (*0-88839-384-9*) Hancock House.

Last Castrato. John Spencer Hill. (Worldwide Library Mysteries). 1997. per. 4.99 (*0-373-26229-9*, 1-26229-4, Wrldwide Lib) Harlequin Bks.

Last Castrato. John Spencer Hill. LC 95-9859. 224p. 1995. text 20.95 (*0-312-13107-0*) St Martin.

Last Cathedral. Ty Harrington. 1979. write for info. (*0-318-54921-2*) P-H.

Last Catholic in America. John R. Powers. 224p. 1988. mass mkt. 4.95 (*0-446-31252-5*, Pub. by Warner Bks) Little.

Last Catholic in America. John R. Powers. LC 79-24431. 1981. reprint ed. lib. bdg. 18.00 (*0-8376-0439-7*) Bentley Pubs.

Last Cattle Drive. Robert Day. LC 83-16887. 224p. 1983. reprint ed. 25.00 (*0-7006-0243-7*); reprint ed. pap. 9.95 (*0-7006-0344-1*) U Pr of KS.

Last Cavalier. Heather G. Pozzessere. (Shadows Ser.: No. 1). 1993. mass mkt. 3.50 (*0-373-27001-1*) Silhouette.

Last Cavalier: The Life & Times of John A. Lomax, 1867-1948. Nolan Porterfield. LC 95-50212. (Folklore & Society Ser.). (Illus.). 656p. 1996. 34.95 (*0-252-02216-5*) U of Ill Pr.

***Last Cavaliere.** 1999. per. 4.50 (*0-373-65107-4*, Harlequin) Harlequin Bks.

Last Census of Benton Co. Prior to the Civil War. Compiled by Benton Count Historical Society Staff. 132p. (Orig.). 1992. pap. 10.00 (*0-938041-08-8*) Arc Pr AR.

Last Centuries of Byzantium, 1261-1453. 2nd ed. Donald M. Nicol. LC 92-46203. (Illus.). 483p. (C). 1993. text 89.95 (*0-521-43384-3*); pap. text 29.95 (*0-521-43991-4*) Cambridge U Pr.

Last Century: Selected Poems. Laurence Wieder. 140p. 1995. pap. 9.00 (*0-330-27322-1*, WiseAcre) Red Sea NY.

Last Chamorro Revolt, 1683-1687 see History of Micronesia: A Collection of Source Documents

Last Chance. Mike Blakely. 320p. (Orig.). 1995. 4.99 (*0-8125-3027-6*, Pub. by Forge NYC) St Martin.

Last Chance. Jill M. Landis. 416p. (Orig.). 1995. mass mkt. 5.99 (*0-515-11760-9*, Jove) Berkley Pub.

***Last Chance.** Dee Marvine. 320p. 1999. mass mkt. 4.99 (*0-8439-4475-7*, Leisure Bks) Dorchester Pub Co.

Last Chance. R. L. Stine, pseud. (Fear Street Seniors Ser.: No. 5). 176p. (YA). (gr. 7 up). 1998. mass mkt. 3.99 (*0-307-24709-0*, 24709, Goldn Books) Gldn Bks Pub Co.

Last Chance: Fact-Based Fiction. Ira Spector. LC 97-94337. (Illus.). viii, 455p. 1998. pap. 13.50 (*0-9660369-0-5*) Arius Inc.

Last Chance . . . For the Church to Love the Jewish People. Jeffrey Lowenthal. LC 98-60059. 128p. 1998. pap. 9.95 (*1-57921-099-6*, Pub. by WinePress Pub) BookWorld.

Last Chance at Devil's Canyon. large type ed. Barry Cord. LC 98-37552. 1999. 30.00 (*0-7838-0413-X*, G K Hall Lrg Type) Mac Lib Ref.

Last Chance Bride. Jillian Hart. (Historical Ser.). 1998. per. 4.99 (*0-373-29004-7*, 1-29004-8) Harlequin Bks.

Last Chance Cafe, Bk. 36. Curtiss A. Matlock. (Born in the U. S. A. Ser.). 1997. per. 4.50 (*0-373-47186-6*, 1-47186-1) Harlequin Bks.

Last-Chance Children: Growing up with Older Parents. Monica B. Morris. 176p. 1988. 23.00 (*0-231-06694-5*) Col U Pr.

Last Chance Financial Planning Guide: Make up for Lost Time with Strategies. Anthony Spare. LC 96-39642. (Illus.). 240p. 1997. per. 15.00 (*0-7615-0836-8*) Prima Pub.

***Last Chance for Camp.** Larry Burkett. (Illus.). (J). 2000. 7.99 (*0-8024-0985-7*) Moody.

Last Chance for Eden: Selected Art Criticism. Christopher Knight. Ed. by Malin Wilson. (Illus.). 420p. 1995. 29.95 (*0-9637264-2-0*) Fnd Adv Crit.

Last Chance for Eden: Selected Art Criticism. Christopher Knight. Ed. by MaLin Wilson. (Illus.). 448p. 1996. pap. 16.95 (*0-9637264-4-7*, 620482, Art Issues) Fnd Adv Crit.

Last Chance for Freedom: Reading Level 3. Marcie M. Stadelhofen. (Sundown Fiction Collection). 96p. 1993. 3.95 (*0-88336-206-6*) New Readers.

Last Chance for Glory. Stephen Solomita. LC 93-38616. 304p. 1994. write for info. (*1-883402-27-1*) S&S Trade.

Last Chance for Justice. Larry Geller. 1997. write for info. (*1-57074-351-7*) Greyden Pr.

Last Chance for Justice: The Juror's Lonely Quest. Laurence H. Geller & Peter Hemenway. 376p. 1997. 26.95 (*0-9657115-0-1*) NCDS Pr.

Last Chance for Magic. Ruth Chew. (J). (gr. 4-7). 1996. pap. text 2.99 (*0-590-60210-1*) Scholastic Inc.

Last Chance for Marriage. large type ed. Sandra Paul. 239p. 1992. reprint ed. lib. bdg. 13.95 (*1-56054-541-0*) Thorndike Pr.

Last Chance for Our Children: How You Can Help Save Our Schools. Bill Honig. (Illus.). 240p. 1987. pap. 8.61 (*0-201-12648-6*) Addison-Wesley.

Last Chance for Peace. A. Vance. LC 84-18831. 276p. (Orig.). (C). 1985. 12.95 (*0-930705-01-7*); pap. 9.95 (*0-930705-00-9*) M H Macy & Co.

Last Chance for the Tarzan Holler. Thylias Moss. LC 97-24005. 117p. 1998. 24.00 (*0-89255-229-8*) Persea Bks.

Last Chance for the Tarzan Holler: Poems. Thylias Moss. 128p. 1999. reprint ed. pap. 14.00 (*0-89255-243-3*, Pub. by Persea Bks) Norton.

Last Chance Guide to Financial Success. 2nd rev. ed. Ed. by Russell Stewart. 80p. 1994. pap. 15.00 (*0-915665-29-8*) Premier Publishers.

Last Chance High: How Girls & Boys Drop in & Out of Alternative Schools. Deidre M. Kelly. LC 92-41978. 272p. (C). 1993. 42.00 (*0-300-05272-3*) Yale U Pr.

Last Chance in France. Linda Lowery Keep. (Hannah & the Angels Ser.: No. 8). 144p. (J). (gr. 3-7). 1999. pap. 3.99 (*0-375-80113-8*, Pub. by Random Bks Yng Read) Random.

Last Chance in Manchuria: The Diary of Chang Kia-ngau. Ed. by Ramon H. Myers. Tr. by Dolores Zen. (Publication Series: Archival Documentaries: No. 379). 350p. 1989. text 36.95 (*0-8179-8791-6*) Hoover Inst Pr.

Last Chance Marriage: Kids & Kisses. Rosemary Gibson. (Romance Ser.: Vol. 3514). 1998. per. 3.50 (*0-373-03514-4*, 1-03514-6) Harlequin Bks.

Last Chance Marriage: Kids & Kisses. large type ed. Rosemary Gibson. (Larger Print Ser.: Vol. 360). 1998. per. 3.50 (*0-373-15760-6*, 1-15760-1) Harlequin Bks.

Last Chance Ranch. Mark Emmons. LC 96-76495. (Illus.). 208p. 1996. 20.00 (*1-56352-334-5*) Longstreet.

***Last Chance Ranch.** Cynthia Sterling. (Titled Texans Ser.). 2000. mass mkt. 5.50 (*0-8217-6698-8*, Zebra Kensgtn) Kensgtn Pub Corp.

Last Chance Ranch. Ruth Wind. (Special Edition Ser.). 1995. per. 3.75 (*0-373-09977-0*, 1-09977-9) Silhouette.

Last-Chance Range. large type ed. Dean Owen. (Linford Western Library). 1989. pap. 16.99 (*0-7089-6723-X*, Linford) Ulverscroft.

Last Chance School Success Guide see Breakthrough Strategies to Teach & Counsel Troubled Youth Lesson Series

Last Chance to See. Douglas Adams & Mark Carwardine. (Illus.). 240p. 1992. pap. 10.00 (*0-345-37198-4*) Ballantine Pub Grp.

Last Chants. Lia Matera. (A Willa Jansson Mystery Ser.). 1997. per. 5.99 (*0-671-88096-9*, Pocket Books) PB.

Last Chants. Lia Matera. (Willa Jansson Mystery Ser.). 240p. 1996. 21.00 (*0-684-81085-9*) Simon & Schuster.

Last Chapter. A. W. Rasmussen. 288p. 1973. mass mkt. 5.99 (*0-88368-021-1*) Whitaker Hse.

Last Chapter & Worse. Gary Larson. LC 96-83997. (Far Side Collection). (Illus.). 96p. (Orig.). 1996. pap. 9.95 (*0-8362-2131-1*) Andrews & McMeel.

***Last Charge: The 21st Lancers & the Battle of Omdurman.** Terry Brighton. (Illus.). 128p. 2000. 62.00 (*1-86126-189-6*, 129761AE, Pub. by Cro1wood) Motorbooks Intl.

Last Cheater's Waltz: Beauty & Violence in the Desert Southwest. Ellen Meloy. LC 98-30325. 229p. 1999. 23.00 (*0-8050-4065-X*) H Holt & Co.

Last Cherokee Warriors. 2nd ed. Philip Steele. LC 86-25348. (Illus.). 112p. (YA). (gr. 6-12). 1978. pap. 9.95 (*0-88289-203-7*) Pelican.

Last Chief of Kewahatchie. Louise M. Sims. LC 97-67142. (Illus.). 265p. (Orig.). 1997. pap. 19.95 (*1-57197-074-6*) Pentland Pr.

***Last Childhood: A Family Story of Alzheimer's.** Carrie Knowles. LC 99-87346. 208p. 2000. pap. 12.00 (*0-609-80648-3*, FAM005000, Three Riv Pr) Crown Pub Group.

Last Chivaree: The Hicks Family of Beech Mountain. Robert Isbell. LC 95-42499. 192p. (C). 1996. 24.95 (*0-8078-2266-3*) U of NC Pr.

Last Chocolate Cookie. Jamie Rix. LC 97-7303. (Illus.). 32p. (J). (ps-3). 1998. 4.99 (*0-7636-0411-9*) Candlewick Pr.

Last Choice: Preemptive Suicide in Advanced Age. 2nd ed. C. G. Prado. LC 98-11103. 208p. 1998. pap. 19.95 (*0-275-96150-8*, Praeger Pubs) Greenwood.

Last Choice: Preemptive Suicide in Advanced Age, 63. C. G. Prado. LC 98-11103. (Contributions in Philosophy Ser.: Vol. 63). 208p. 1998. 59.95 (*0-313-30584-6*, Greenwood Pr) Greenwood.

Last Christian: Release of the Siberian Seven. Timothy Chmykhalov & Danny Smith. 208p. 1985. pap. 7.70 (*0-310-34021-7*, 12411P) Zondervan.

Last Christmas. John Bibee. LC 90-4870. (Spirit Flyer Ser.: Vol. 5). (Illus.). 204p. (Orig.). (J). (gr. 3-8). 1990. pap. 6.99 (*0-8308-1204-0*, 1204) InterVarsity.

Last Christmas Present. Matt Novak. LC 92-44513. (Illus.). 32p. (J). (ps-1). 1993. 15.95 (*0-531-05495-0*) Orchard Bks Watts.

Last Christmas Tree. James L. Allen. (Principle Works of James Lane Allen). 1989. reprint ed. lib. bdg. 79.00 (*0-7812-1739-3*) Rprt Serv.

Last Christology of the West: Adoptionism in Spain & Gaul, 785-820. John C. Cavadini. LC 93-9444. (Middle Ages Ser.). 248p. (C). 1993. text 39.95 (*0-8122-3186-4*) U of Pa Pr.

Last Chronicle of Barset see Barsetshire Novels

Last Chronicle of Barset. Anthony Trollope. 1995. 24.00 (*0-679-44366-5*) Knopf.

Last Chronicle of Barset. Anthony Trollope. Ed. by Stephen Gill. (World's Classics Ser.). (Illus.). 924p. 1981. pap. 6.95 (*0-19-281544-X*) OUP.

Last Chronicle of Barset. Anthony Trollope. 864p. 1993. pap. 6.95 (*0-460-87234-6*, Everyman's Classic Lib) Tuttle Pubng.

Last Chronicle of Barset. Anthony Trollope. Ed. by Peter Fairclough. (English Library). 872p. 1981. pap. 9.95 (*0-14-043024-5*, Penguin Classics) Viking Penguin.

Last Chronicle of Barset. Anthony Trollope. (Classics Library). 924p. 1998. pap. 3.95 (*1-85326-231-5*, 2315WW, Pub. by Wrdsworth Edits) NTC Contemp Pub Co.

Last Chronicle of Barset. Anthony Trollope. (Oxford World's Classics Ser.). 704p. 2000. pap. 8.95 (*0-19-283534-3*) OUP.

***Last Chronicle of Barset: (trollope 1997)** Skilton. 1999. 56.00 (*1-870587-69-3*) Ashgate Pub Co.

Last Chukker. J. K. Stanford. 9.50 (*0-8159-6102-2*) Devin.

Last CIAMS, Rasegna 52. (Illus.). 110p. 1992. pap. 35.00 (*88-85322-10-7*, Pub. by Birkhauser) Princeton Arch.

Last Cigarette. Jason Waldrop. LC 99-26525. (First Ser.). 193p. 1999. pap. 14.00 (*0-922811-37-7*) Mid-List.

Last Circle. Stephen Vincent Benet. LC 72-10776. (Short Story Index Reprint Ser.). 1977. reprint ed. 23.95 (*0-8369-4217-5*) Ayer.

Last Citadel: Petersburg, Virginia, June 1864-April 1865. Noah A. Trudeau. LC 93-7020. xviii, 514p. (C). 1993. pap. 19.95 (*0-8071-1861-3*) La State U Pr.

Last City. Pablo O. Monasterio. LC 96-188506. 112p. 1995. 45.00 (*0-944092-32-2*) Twin Palms Pub.

***Last City Room.** Al Martinez. LC 00-31738. 272p. 2000. 22.95 (*0-312-20901-0*, Thomas Dunne) St Martin.

Last Class. Edward Shirley. 2001. write for info. (*0-609-60062-1*, Crown) Crown Pub Group.

Last Client of Luis Montez, Vol. 1. Ramos. 1997. mass mkt. write for info. (*0-312-96105-7*) St Martin.

Last Climb: A Novel of Suspense. Thomas H. Cosgrove. LC 98-53467. 320p. 1999. 23.00 (*0-684-83414-6*) S&S Trade.

***Last Climb: The Legendary Everest Expedition of Malloy & Irvine.** David F. Breashears & Audrey Salkeld. LC 99-41046. 240p. 1999. pap. 35.00 (*0-7922-7538-1*) Natl Geog.

Last Closet: The Real Lives of Lesbian & Gay Teachers. Rita Kissen. LC 96-4128. 198p. 1996. pap. 15.95 (*0-435-08147-0*, 08147) Heinemann.

Last Closet: The Real Lives of Lesbian & Gay Teachers. Rita M. Kissen. LC 96-4128. 198p. 1996. 15.95 (*0-435-07005-3*, 07005) Heinemann.

Last Coin. James P. Blaylock. 336p. 1996. mass mkt. 5.99 (*0-614-96140-8*) Ace Bks.

Last Coin. limited ed. James P. Blaylock. 1988. 60.00 (*0-929480-00-7*) Mark Ziesing.

Last Colonies. Robert Aldrich & John Connell. LC 97-39275. (Illus.). 272p. (C). 1998. 59.95 (*0-521-41461-X*) Cambridge U Pr.

Last Comanche Chief: The Life & Times of Quanah Parker. Bill Neeley. LC 94-38101. (Illus.). 276p. 1996. pap. 16.95 (*0-471-16076-8*) Wiley.

Last Comanche Chief: The Life & Times of Quanah Parks. Bill Neeley. LC 94-38101. (Illus.). 276p. 1995. 24.95 (*0-471-11722-6*) Wiley.

***Last Comes the Egg.** Bruce Duffy. (Nonpareil Ser.: Vol. 91). 368p. 2000. pap. 16.95 (*1-56792-124-8*) Godine.

Last Comes the Egg. Bruce Duffy. LC 96-43418. 359p. 1997. 22.50 (*0-684-80883-8*) S&S Trade.

Last Command. Mike Baron. 1999. pap. text 17.95 (*1-56971-378-2*) Dark Horse Comics.

Last Command. Timothy Zahn. LC 92-43876. (Star Wars: No. 3). 496p. (YA). (gr. 5 up). 1994. mass mkt. 5.99 (*0-553-56492-7*, Spectra) Bantam.

Last Command. Timothy Zahn. (Star Wars: No. 3). (YA). (gr. 5 up). 1994. 11.09 (*0-606-08205-0*, Pub. by Turtleback) Demco.

Last Command, Set. abr. ed. Timothy Zahn. (Star Wars: No. 3). (YA). (gr. 5 up). 1993. audio 16.99 (*0-553-47157-0*) BDD Aud Pub.

Last Computer. Tony Paulin. Ed. by Peter Bumpus. 224p. 1999. pap. 14.95 (*0-9670808-1-9*) Spherical Pub Inc.

Last Conceptual Revolution: A Critique of Richard Rorty's Political Philosophy. Eric M. Gander. LC 98-5277. (Series in the Philosophy of the Social Sciences & Series in Speech Communication). 224p. (C). 1998. text 59.50 (*0-7914-4009-5*); pap. text 19.95 (*0-7914-4010-9*) State U NY Pr.

Last Condor. Mark J. Rauzon. (Illus.). 24p. (Orig.). (J). (gr. 5 up). 1986. pap. 3.95 (*0-935181-02-4*) Marine Endeavors.

Last Confederate. Sanders A. Laubenthal. 1967. 9.95 (*0-685-06845-5*); pap. 5.95 (*0-685-06846-3*) Laubenthal Res.

Last Confederate. Gilbert Morris. (House of Winslow Ser.: Vol. 8). 336p. (Orig.). 1990. pap. 9.99 (*1-55661-109-9*) Bethany Hse.

Last Congress, Vol. 1. Irwin M. Ryan. 464p. 1989. 17.95 (*0-9623535-0-7*) Remco Inc.

Last Conquistador: Juan de Onate & the Settling of the Far Southwest. Marc Simmons. LC 90-50697. 224p. 1993. pap. 13.95 (*0-8061-2368-0*) U of Okla Pr.

Last Conquistador: Mansio Serra de Leguizamon & the Conquest of the Incas. Stuart Stirling. 2000. 34.95 (*0-7509-2246-X*, Pub. by Sutton Publng) Intl Pubs Mktg.

Last Conservative. Robinson Jeffers. 1978. pap. 40.00 (*0-918466-06-7*) Quintessence.

Last Continent. Terry Pratchett. LC 98-44160. 304p. 1999. 24.00 (*0-06-105048-2*) HarpC.

Last Continent. Bernard Stonehouse. pap. 23.95 (*962-217-663-1*) China Guides.

***Last Continent: A Novel of Discworld.** Terry Pratchett. 400p. 2000. mass mkt. 6.50 (*0-06-105907-2*, HarperPrism) HarpC.

Last Contrary: The Story of Wesley Whiteman (Black Bear) Warren E. Schwartz. 140p. 1989. pap. 12.95 (*0-931170-42-7*) Ctr Western Studies.

***Last Conversations of St. Therese.** Mother Agnes of Jesus. 152p. 1998. reprint ed. 15.00 (*0-911845-72-0*) Neumann Pr.

Last Convertible. Anton Myrer. 1993. reprint ed. lib. bdg. 37.95 (*1-56849-240-5*) Buccaneer Bks.

Last Cool Days. John Stewart. 192p. 1996. pap. text 12.95 (*0-920661-55-6*, Pub. by TSAR Pubns) LPC InBook.

Last Cop Out. Mickey Spillane, pseud. 21.95 (*0-89190-839-0*) Amereon Ltd.

Last Corporate Secret: Applying Emotional-Social-Behavioral Audit to Augment to Collective EQ & Improve Organizational Effectiveness. Reuven Bar-On & Rich Handley. 208p. 1998. 24.95 (*0-9664546-2-6*) Pro-Philes.

Last Country Houses. Clive Aslet. LC 82-50439. (Illus.). 1982. 55.00 (*0-300-02904-7*) Yale U Pr.

Last Courtly Lover: Yeats & the Idea of Woman. Gloria C. Kline. LC 83-6941. (Studies in Modern Literature: No. 6). (Illus.). 213p. reprint ed. pap. 66.10 (*0-8357-1409-8*, 207055600001) Bks Demand.

Last Covenant: An Easter Worship Service. Lynda Pujado. LC 96-164471. 34p. (Orig.). 1996. pap. 4.95 (*0-7880-0226-0*) CSS OH.

Last Cowboy. Roger Burke. (Orig.). 1989. pap. 10.00 (*0-685-26592-7*) Columbia Rvr Bk Co.

Last Cowboys: Closing the Open Range in Southeastern New Mexico, 1890s-1920s. Connie Brooks. LC 92-33399. (Illus.). 144p. 1993. reprint ed. pap. 44.70 (*0-608-07275-3*, 206750300009) Bks Demand.

Last Coyote. large type ed. Michael Connelly. (Large Print Bks.). 1995. pap. 23.95 (*1-56895-272-4*) Wheeler Pub.

Last Coyote, Vol. 1. 5th ed. Michael Connelly. LC 94-37437. Vol. 1. 416p. 1996. mass mkt. 7.99 (*0-312-95845-5*) St Martin.

Last Cracker Barrel. Ernest Lyons. LC 75-7562. (Florida Classics Ser.). 201p. (Orig.). 1976. pap. 6.95 (*0-912451-02-5*) Florida Classics.

***Last Crusade.** McKnight. 2000. pap. 17.00 (*0-8133-3385-7*, Pub. by Westview) HarpC.

Last Crusade. Thomas W. Petrisko. 72p. 1996. pap. 4.95 (*1-891903-01-2*) St Andrew Prodns.

Last Crusade: A Novel. Peter Menting. LC 92-3346. 148p. (Orig.). 1993. pap. 14.95 (*0-86534-158-3*) Sunstone Pr.

Last Crusade: Martin Luther King Jr., the FBI & the Poor People's Campaign. Martin Luther King, Jr. et al. LC 97-36992. 208p. 1997. 28.00 (*0-8133-3384-9*, Pub. by Westview) HarpC.

Last Cry: Native American Prophecies; Tales of the End Times. Robert Ghostwolf. Ed. by Cindee Delgado. 319p. (Orig.). 1997. pap. 21.95 (*0-9660668-5-5*) Wolf Lodge.

Last Crypto Jews of Portugal. David A. Canelo. 1991. pap. 15.00 (*0-685-40182-0*) Inst Judaic Std.

Last Curve. Margaret Allison. 383p. 1999. mass mkt. 6.50 (*0-671-56326-2*) PB.

Last Dalai Lama. Michael Goodman. 1986. 22.50 (*0-394-55246-6*) Random.

***Last Dance.** 2000. 25.00 (*0-671-78479-X*) S&S Trade.

Last Dance. Carmen A. Deedy. LC 95-16377. (Illus.). 32p. (J). (gr. 2-6). 1995. 16.95 (*1-56145-109-6*) Peachtree Pubs.

***Last Dance.** Joyce Lavene & Jim Lavene. LC 99-90984. 192p. 1999. 18.95 (*0-8034-9389-4*, Avalon Bks) Bouregy.

Last Dance. Miriam A. Moore. 256p. (Orig.). 1997. mass mkt. 5.99 (*0-380-79118-8*, Avon Bks) Morrow Avon.

***Last Dance.** Elizabeth M. Rees. LC 98-52338. (Heart Beats Ser.: Bk. 6). 224p. (J). (gr. 4-8). 1999. pap. text 3.99 (*0-689-81953-6*) S&S Childrens.

***Last Dance.** Ed McBain. 320p. 2000. reprint ed. per. 7.99 (*0-671-02570-8*) PB.

Last Dance: A Novel of the 87th Precinct. Ed McBain, pseud. LC 99-53534. 360p. 2000. 24.95 (*0-684-85513-5*) S&S Trade.

Last Dance: Encountering Death & Dying. 5th ed. Lynne A. Despelder & Albert L. Strickland. LC 98-3326. 672p. 1998. text 51.95 (*0-7674-0217-0*, 0217-0) Mayfield Pub.

***Last Dance: Man of the Month, Freedom Valley.** Cait London. 2000. per. 3.99 (*0-373-76285-2*) Silhouette.

Last Dance at the Hotel Kempinski: Creating a Life in the Shadow of History. Robin Hirsch. LC 94-48725. 312p. 1995. pap. 19.95 (*0-87451-775-3*) U Pr of New Eng.

Last Dandy, Ralph Barton: American Artist, 1891-1931. Bruce Kellner. (Missouri Biography Ser.). (Illus.). 280p. (C). 1991. 34.95 (*0-8262-0774-X*) U of Mo Pr.

Last Dangerous Christmas. Ed. by E. J. Bojar. (Illus.). 48p. 1997. pap. 5.95 (*1-883847-31-1*) MU Press.

Last Date. Diane Hoh. (Nightmare Hall Ser.: No. 11). 176p. (YA). (gr. 7-9). 1994. pap. 3.50 (*0-590-48133-9*) Scholastic Inc.

Last Date. Edmund Plante. 176p. (Orig.). (YA). (gr. 5 up). 1993. pap. 3.50 (*0-380-77154-3*, Avon Bks) Morrow Avon.

An Asterisk (*) at the beginning of an entry indicates that the title is appearing for the first time.

L

Last Day. Glenn Kleier. 624p. 1998. mass mkt. 7.50 (*0-446-60598-0*, Pub. by Warner Bks) Little.

Last Day Delusions: Insights for an Age of Confusion. Allen Walker. 96p. 1991. pap. 6.95 (*0-945460-11-2*) Upward Way.

Last Day Events. Ellen Gould Harmon White. LC 91-42012. (Christian Home Library). 330p. 1992. 12.99 (*0-8163-1073-4*) Pacific Pr Pub Assn.

Last Day in Limbo: A Modesty Blaise Novel. Peter O'Donnell. 1986. 45.00 (*0-89296-104-X*, Pub. by Mysterious Pr) Little.

Last Day of Hitler: The Legends - the Evidence - the Truth. Anton Joachimsthaler. LC 97-129193. (Illus.). 352p. 1997. 34.95 (*1-85409-380-0*, Pub. by Arms & Armour) Sterling.

Last Day of September. large type ed. Rosemary Gill. (Linford Romance Library). 256p. 1994. pap. 16.99 (*0-7089-7512-7*, Linford) Ulverscroft.

Last Day of Summer. Photos by Jock Sturges. (Illus.). 96p. 1992. 68.00 (*0-89381-494-6*) Aperture.

Last Day of Summer. Photos by Jock Sturges. (Illus.). 96p. 1993. pap. 44.95 (*0-89381-538-1*) Aperture.

Last Day of Summer. limited ed. Sturges & Phillip. 1992. (*0-89381-508-X*) Aperture.

Last Day of the Old World. Adrian Ball. LC 77-18896. 278p. 1978. reprint ed. lib. bdg. 65.00 (*0-313-20202-8*, BALD, Greenwood Pr) Greenwood.

Last Day the Dogbushes Bloomed. Lee Smith. LC 68-28226. (Voices of the South Ser.). 192p. 1994. pap. 12.95 (*0-8071-1935-0*) La State U Pr.

Last Days. William F. Dankenbring. LC 77-79265. 1977. 11.95 (*0-917182-05-7*) Triumph Pub.

Last Days. Marsh. Date not set. 24.00 (*0-465-04418-2*, Pub. by Basic) HarpC.

Last Days. Marsh. pap. 14.00 (*0-465-04419-0*, Pub. by Basic) HarpC.

Last Days. Steven Spielberg. 240p. 1999. text 22.95 (*0-312-20462-0*) St Martin.

Last Days. 2nd ed. Raymond Queneau. Tr. by Barbara Wright from FRE. LC 90-3075. 237p. 1996. reprint ed. pap. 11.95 (*1-56478-140-2*) Dalkey Arch.

Last Days: A Final Wake up Call. James Hammer. 64p. (Orig.). 1996. pap. 10.00 (*1-883893-56-9*) WinePress Pub.

Last Days: A World-Famous Climber Challenges the Himalayas' Tawoche & Menlungtse. John Roskelley. LC 91-12872. (Illus.). 272p. 1991. 24.95 (*0-8117-0889-6*) Stackpole.

Last Days? Spiritual Reality & Physical Illusions. Ventris Nukayis. 272p. (Orig.). 1991. pap. 9.95 (*1-56266-149-3*) Anwol.

Last Days: Teachings of the Modern Prophets. Daniel C. Peterson. LC 97-18818. 320p. 1998. 19.95 (*1-56236-062-0*, Pub. by Aspen Bks) Origin Bk Sales.

Last Days: What's Ahead for the Body of Christ, the Apostate Church, & the World. Bill Rudge. LC 98-65516. 120p. 1998. pap. 7.00 (*1-889809-02-0*) Liv Truth.

Last Days According to Jesus. R. C. Sproul. LC 98-30139. 256p. (C). 1998. 16.99 (*0-8010-1171-X*) Baker Bks.

***Last Days according to Jesus.** R. C. Sproul. 256p. 2000. pap. 12.99 (*0-8010-6340-X*) Baker Bks.

Last Days & Death of Dr. & Gen. William Walker. John C. Moran. (Worthies Library: No. 3). (Illus.). 100p. 1988. 10.00 (*0-318-20644-7*) F M Crawford.

Last Days Are Here Again: A History of the End Times. Richard Kyle. LC 98-13574. 256p. (C). 1998. pap. text 14.99 (*0-8010-5809-0*) Baker Bks.

Last Days Awareness Teacher's Study Guide. Vic Emerson & Pam Emerson. Ed. by Foster Bell. (Illus.). 31p. (Orig.). 1996. pap., teacher ed. 4.95 (*1-889505-00-5*) White Wing Pub.

***Last Days Bible: The New Testament, God's New Agreement with Mankind, Prophecy Edition.** Hartline Marketing Publications Staff. 1999. pap. 12.95 (*0-9642470-1-1*) Life Messengers.

Last Days Handbook see Manual de los Postreros Dias

Last Days Handbook. Robert P. Lightner. LC 97-28259. 256p. 1997. pap. 12.99 (*0-7852-1250-7*) Nelson.

Last Days Here. Eric Chock. (Bamboo Ridge Ser.: Nos. 45-46). 88p. 1989. pap. 8.00 (*0-910043-18-3*) Bamboo Ridge Pr.

Last Days in America. Bob Fraley. 289p. 1984. pap. 8.95 (*0-9612999-0-8*) Chr Life Srvs.

Last Days in New Guinea. Charles A. Monckton. LC 75-35142. reprint ed. 25.00 (*0-404-14158-7*) AMS Pr.

***Last Days Madness: Obsession of the Modern Church.** 4th rev. ed. Gary DeMar. 443p. 1999. pap. 19.95 (*0-915815-35-4*) American Vision.

***Last Days Murder List.** Alice Holman. LC 00-100938. 290p. 2000. pap. 19.95 (*0-9678832-6-1*) Highbridge Pr.

Last Days of Alfred Hitchcock. David Freeman. (Illus.). 240p. 1988. pap. 9.95 (*0-87951-318-7*, Pub. by Overlook Pr) Penguin Putnam.

Last Days of Alfred Hitchcock. David Freeman. LC 99-35833. 281p. 1999. pap. 16.95 (*0-87951-728-X*, Pub. by Overlook Pr) Penguin Putnam.

Last Days of Britian: The Final Betrayal. Lindsay Jenkins. 1999. write for info. (*0-9657812-2-4*) Orange State.

Last Days of British Saint Augustine, 1784-1785: A Spanish Census of the English Colony of East Florida. Lawrence H. Feldman. 116p. 1998. pap. 17.50 (*0-8063-4792-9*, 9320) Clearfield Co.

***Last Days of Charles I.** Graham Edwards. LC 99-216566. 1999. 36.00 (*0-7509-2079-3*) A Sutton.

Last Days of Christ the Vampire. 3rd rev. ed. J. G. Eccarius. 192p. (Orig.). 1996. pap. 10.00 (*1-886625-00-X*) III Pub.

Last Days of David & His Contemporaries. Gordon Lindsay. (Old Testament Ser.: Vol. 24). 1966. 1.95 (*0-89985-144-4*) Christ for the Nations.

***Last Days of Disco with Cocktails at Petrossian Afterwards.** Whit Stillman. 256p. 2000. 23.00 (*0-374-18339-2*) FS&G.

Last Days of Dublin Castle: The Mark Sturgis Diaries. Michael Hopkinson. LC 98-49768. 288p. 1999. 52.50 (*0-7165-2626-3*, Pub. by Irish Acad Pr) Intl Spec Bk.

***Last Days of Eugene Meltsner.** Marshal Younger. LC 00-32530. (Adventures in Odyssey Ser.). (Illus.). 2000. pap. write for info. (*0-8423-4048-3*) Tyndale Hse.

Last Days of God's Church: Is True Christianity Being Forgotten? Ed J. MacWilliams. 1995. pap. 12.95 (*0-926557-09-2*) Blueprint Pubns.

Last Days of Hitler. Hugh R. Trevor-Roper. LC 92-19709. 288p. 1992. pap. 14.95 (*0-226-81224-3*) U Ch Pr.

Last Days of Hitler: The Legends - The Evidence - The Truth. Anton Joachimsthaler. (Illus.). 352p. pap. 19.95 (*1-85409-465-3*) Arms & Armour.

Last Days of Il Duce. Domenic Stansberry. LC 97-21536. 168p. 1998. 22.00 (*1-57962-004-3*) Permanent Pr.

***Last Days of Il Duce.** Domenic Stansberry. LC 99-52530. 176p. 2000. pap. 12.95 (*0-312-25463-6*) St Martin.

Last Days of Il Duce. large type ed. Domenic Stansberry. LC 99-34466. 1999. pap. 25.95 (*0-7862-2071-6*) Mac Lib Ref.

***Last Days of Innocence.** Charlotte Hardy. 496p. 2000. 31.99 (*0-7505-1530-9*) Ulverscroft.

Last Days of Innocence: America at War, 1917-1918. Meirion Harries. 1999. pap. 16.00 (*0-679-74376-6*) Vin Bks.

Last Days of Jesus. T. V. Moore. 212p. (Orig.). 1981. pap. 8.99 (*0-85151-321-2*) Banner of Truth.

Last Days of Jesus & Beginning of the Church. (Little Giants Christian Classics Ser.). (J). (ps-3). 1992. pap. 4.99 (*0-529-07195-9*, LG4) World Publng.

Last Days of John Lennon: An Intimate Memoir. Frederic Seaman. (Illus.). 288p. 1991. 19.95 (*1-55972-084-0*, Birch Ln Pr) Carol Pub Group.

***Last Days of Louisiana Red.** Ishmael Reed. LC 00-20974. 179p. 2000. reprint ed. pap. 11.95 (*1-56478-236-0*, Pub. by Dalkey Arch) Chicago Distribution Ctr.

Last Days of Marie Antoinette: An Historical Sketch. Ronald C. Gower. LC 74-168163. reprint ed. 34.50 (*0-404-07129-5*) AMS Pr.

Last Days of Marilyn Monroe. Donald H. Wolfe. LC 98-36510. (Illus.). 416p. 1998. 25.00 (*0-688-16288-6*, Wm Morrow) Morrow Avon.

Last Days of Pompeii. Edward Bulwer Lytton. Date not set. lib. bdg. 27.95 (*0-8488-1959-4*) Amereon Ltd.

Last Days of Pompeii. Edward Bulwer Lytton. 308p. 1983. reprint ed. lib. bdg. 41.95 (*0-89966-309-5*) Buccaneer Bks.

Last Days of Pompeii. Edward Bulwer Lytton. 435p. 1996. reprint ed. pap. 27.95 (*1-56459-590-0*) Kessinger Pub.

***Last Days of President Suharto.** Ed. by Edward Aspinall et al. 2p. 1999. pap. 24.95 (*0-7326-1175-X*, Pub. by Monash Asia Inst) Intl Spec Bk.

***Last Days of Shelley & Byron.** Edward Trelawney. 224p. 2000. pap. 10.95 (*0-7867-0736-4*, Pub. by Carroll & Graf) Publishers Group.

Last Days of Socrates. Plato. Tr. by Hugh Tredennick & Harold Tarrant. 256p. 1993. pap. 11.95 (*0-14-044582-X*, Penguin Classics) Viking Penguin.

Last Days of Steam in Gwynedd. Mike Hitches. (Illus.). 160p. 1991. 22.95 (*0-86299-924-3*, Pub. by Sutton Pub Ltd) Intl Pubs Mktg.

Last Days of Steam on the Southern: London, Brighton & South Coast Lines & the Isle of Wight. Alan Postlethwaite. (Illus.). 160p. 1994. 26.95 (*0-7509-0413-5*, Pub. by Sutton Pub Ltd) Intl Pubs Mktg.

Last Days of Summer. Steve Kluger. LC 98-11225. 368p. 1999. reprint ed. pap. 12.00 (*0-380-79763-1*, Avon Bks) Morrow Avon.

***Last Days of Summer H.** Steve Kluger. LC 98-11225. 348p. 1998. 21.00 (*0-380-97645-5*, Avon Bks) Morrow Avon.

Last Days of T. E. Lawrence: A Leaf in the Wind. Paul Marriot & Yvonne Argent. LC 97-149225. (Illus.). 208p. 1996. 45.00 (*1-898595-16-X*, Pub. by Alpha Pr Ltd) Intl Spec Bk.

Last Days of T. E. Lawrence: A Leaf in the Wind. Paul Marriot & Yvonne Argent. 208p. 1998. pap. 24.95 (*1-898595-22-4*, Pub. by Alpha Pr Ltd) Intl Spec Bk.

Last Days of Team on the Southern: London & South Western. Alan Postlethwaite. (Illus.). 160p. 1996. 30.95 (*0-7509-1205-7*, Pub. by Sutton Pub Ltd) Intl Pubs Mktg.

Last Days of the Buddha: Mahaparinibbana Sutta. Tr. by Sister Vajira & Francis Story from PLI. 120p. (C). 1989. 4.20 (*955-24-0006-6*, Pub. by Buddhist Pub Soc) Vipassana Res Pubns.

Last Days of the Dinosaurs. Gabriele. (J). 1984. pap. 1.50 (*0-911211-06-3*) Penny Lane Pubns.

Last Days of the Dinosaurs: Text Editions. Joseph Gabriele. (Illus.). 32p. (Orig.). (J). (gr. 1-3). 1985. pap. 1.95 (*0-911211-57-8*) Penny Lane Pubns.

Last Days of the Dog-Men: Stories. Brad Watson. LC 95-36127. 146p. 1996. 19.00 (*0-393-03926-9*) Norton.

Last Days of the New Yorker. Gigi Mahon. 1989. pap. 9.95 (*0-317-02698-4*, Plume) Dutton Plume.

Last Days of the Press see Ultimos Dias de La Prensa

Last Days of the Raj. Trevor Royle. (Illus.). 304p. 1998. pap. 22.95 (*0-7195-5686-4*, Pub. by John Murray) Trafalgar.

Last Days of the Republic. W. Pierton Dooner. Ed. by Roger Daniels. LC 78-54814. (Asian Experience in North America Ser.). 1979. reprint ed. lib. bdg. 21.95 (*0-405-11270-X*) Ayer.

Last Days of the Romanovs. Robert Wilton. 1979. lib. bdg. 250.00 (*0-8490-2954-6*) Gordon Pr.

Last Days of the Romanovs: How Tsar Nicholas the Second & Russia's Imperial Family Were Murdered. Robert Wilton. (Illus.). 194p. (C). 1993. reprint ed. pap. text 6.95 (*0-939484-47-1*, 0970, Inst Hist Rev) Legion Survival.

Last Days of the Sicilians. Blumenthal. 1994. per. 4.95 (*0-671-89461-7*) PB.

Last Days of the Sicilians: The FBI's War Against the Mafia. Ralph Blumenthal. 464p. 1989. mass mkt. 5.99 (*0-671-68277-6*) PB.

Last Days of the Sioux Nation. Robert Marshall Utley. LC 63-7950. (Western Americana Ser.: No. 3). (Illus.). 1966. pap. 16.00 (*0-300-00245-9*, YW15) Yale U Pr.

Last Days of the Steam Railway. Ed. by Alan Postlethwaite. LC 98-134098. (Illus.). 144p. 1998. 44.95 (*0-7509-1504-8*, Pub. by Sutton Pub Ltd) Intl Pubs Mktg.

Last Days of the Titanic: Photographs & Mementos of the Tragic Maiden Voyage. E. E. O'Donnell. (Illus.). 120p. 1997. 24.95 (*1-57098-201-5*) Roberts Rinehart.

***Last Days! When?** Michael Penny. 28p. 2000. pap. 3.00 (*1-880573-59-8*) Bible Search Pubns.

***Last Debate.** Jim Lehrer. 2000. pap. 24.00 (*1-58648-004-9*) PublicAffairs NY.

Last Debate. large type ed. Jim Lehrer. (Niagara Large Print Ser.). 485p. 1996. 29.50 (*0-7089-5838-9*) Ulverscroft.

Last Debt at Newton. Shiff Davis. 192p. 1988. mass mkt. 2.95 (*0-8217-2462-2*, Zebra Kensgtn) Kensgtn Pub Corp.

Last Decade. Karl Roeseler. LC 99-19469. 20p. 1999. pap. 7.00 (*0-942996-37-2*, Pub. by Post Apollo Pr) SPD-Small Pr Dist.

Last Decade: Essays & Reviews, 1965-1975. Lionel Trilling. Ed. by Diana Trilling. LC 79-1849. 256p. 1979. 9.95 (*0-15-148421-X*) Harcourt.

Last Decade: Essays & Reviews, 1965-1975. Lionel Trilling. Ed. by Diana Trilling. LC 79-1849. 256p. 1981. pap. 7.95 (*0-15-648892-2*, Harvest Bks) Harcourt.

Last Decade: The Emergence of Art Photography in the 1890s. Janet E. Buerger. (Illus.). 40p. (Orig.). 1984. pap. 10.00 (*0-935398-09-0*) G Eastman Hse.

Last Decade of Undivided Bengal: Parties, Politics, & Personalities. (C). 1994. text 21.00 (*81-85195-60-9*, Pub. by Minerva) S Asia.

Last Decadent: A Study of Brian Jones. Jeremy Reed. (Illus.). 192p. 1999. pap. 17.95 (*1-871592-71-2*, Pub. by Creation Books) Subterranean Co.

Last Deception of Palliser Wentwood. Imogen De La Bere. LC 99-27155. 1999. text 23.95 (*0-312-20329-2*) St Martin.

Last Defender of Camelot. Roger Zelazny. 320p. (Orig.). 1988. pap. 3.50 (*0-380-70316-5*, Avon Bks) Morrow Avon.

Last Defenders of the Laager: Ian D. Smith & F. W. De Klerk. Dickson A. Mungazi. LC 97-39772. 304p. 1998. 65.00 (*0-275-96030-7*, Praeger Pubs) Greenwood.

Last Deglaciation: Absolute & Radiocarbon Chronologies. Ed. by E. Bard & W. S. Broecker. (NATO ASI Series I: Global Environmental Change: Vol. 2). (Illus.). xiv, 344p. 1992. 159.00 (*0-387-53123-8*) Spr-Verlag.

Last Democrat. Ed. & Pref. by R. W. Bradford. (Illus.). xvi, 184p. (Orig.). 1996. pap. 14.95 (*0-9638732-1-0*) Liberty Pubng.

***Last Deposit: Swiss Banks & Holocaust Victims' Accounts.** Itamar Levin. Tr. by Natasha Dornberg from HEB. LC 98-53398. 280p. 1999. 29.95 (*0-275-96520-1*, Praeger Pubs) Greenwood.

Last Descendant of Aeneas: The Hapsburg & the Mythic Image of the Emperor from Antiquity to the Renaissance. Marie Tanner. LC 92-20186. (Illus.). 272p. (C). 1993. 57.00 (*0-300-05488-2*) Yale U Pr.

***Last Detective.** Peter Lovesey. 336p. 2000. pap. 13.00 (*1-56947-209-2*) Soho Press.

Last Diaries. Leo Tolstoy. Ed. by Robert J. Kastenbaum. Tr. by Lydia W. Kesich. LC 78-22222. (Aging & Old Age Ser.). 1979. reprint ed. lib. bdg. 25.95 (*0-405-11835-X*) Ayer.

Last Diary. W. N. Barbellion. 1973. 250.00 (*0-87968-382-1*) Gordon Pr.

Last Diary of Tsaritsa Alexandra. Alexandra. Ed. by Alexandra Raskina & Vladimir M. Khrustalev. Tr. by Vladimir A. Kozlov. LC 97-15675. (Illus.). 256p. 1997. 20.00 (*0-300-07212-0*) Yale U Pr.

Last Diet Book: You'll Ever Need! David Fisch. 96p. 1997. pap. 4.99 (*1-57644-055-9*) CCC Pubns.

Last Dinner on the Titanic: Menus & Recipes from the Great Liner. Rick Archbold & Dana McCauley. LC 96-47057. (Illus.). 128p. 1997. 24.45 (*0-7868-6303-X*, Pub. by Hyperion) Time Warner.

Last Dinosaur. Katherine H. Brooks. 40p. (Orig.). 1996. pap. 4.00 (*1-886467-12-9*) WJM Press.

Last Dinosaur. Sandy Dengler. LC 93-36488. (Mirage Mysteries Ser.). 276p. (Orig.). 1994. pap. 9.99 (*1-56476-235-1*, 6-3235, Victor Bks) Chariot Victor.

Last Dinosaur Book: The Life & Times of a Cultural Icon. W. J. Mitchell. LC 98-16676. 308p. 1998. 35.00 (*0-226-53204-6*) U Ch Pr.

***Last Dinosaur Egg.** Andrew Hegeman. (Illus.). 36p. (J). (ps-3). 1998. 15.95 (*1-890817-04-X*, Pub. by Winslow Pr) Publishers Group.

Last Ditch. Ngaio Marsh. 1976. 23.95 (*0-8488-0578-X*) Amereon Ltd.

***Last Ditch.** Ngaio Marsh. 288p. 2000. mass mkt. 5.99 (*0-312-97286-5*, St Martins Paperbacks) St Martin.

Last Ditch. large type ed. Manda McGrath. (Ulverscroft Large Print Ser.). 448p. 1997. 27.99 (*0-7089-3761-6*) Ulverscroft.

Last Ditch see Ngaio Marsh

Last Ditch: A Leo Waterman Mystery. G. M. Ford. LC 98-39880. 288p. 1999. 22.00 (*0-380-97557-2*, Avon Bks) Morrow Avon.

***Last Ditch: A Leo Waterman Mystery.** G. M. Ford. (Leo Waterman Mystery Ser.). 320p. 2000. mass mkt. 5.99 (*0-380-79369-5*, Avon Bks) Morrow Avon.

***Last Dive: A Father & Son's Fatal Descent into the Ocean's Depths.** Bernie Chowdhury. 304p. 2000. 25.00 (*0-06-019462-6*) HarpC.

Last Domino? A POW Looks Ahead. Joseph C. Plumb. 96p. 1973. text 7.95 (*1-881886-03-4*) J C Plumb.

Last Don. Mario Puzo. 1997. mass mkt. 7.99 (*0-345-41221-4*) Ballantine Pub Grp.

Last Don. Mario Puzo. 1997. mass mkt. 7.99 (*0-345-91220-9*) Ballantine Pub Grp.

Last Door to Aiya: A Selection of the Best New Science Fiction from the Soviet Union. Tr. by Mirra Ginsburg. LC 68-16347. (YA). (gr. 10 up). 1968. 26.95 (*0-87599-135-1*) S G Phillips.

Last Dragon. Ben Z. Grant. LC 96-10307. (Illus.). 24p. (J). 1996. 12.95 (*1-56763-062-6*) Ozark Pub.

Last Dragon. Susan M. Nunes. LC 93-30631. (Illus.). 32p. (J). 1995. 15.00 (*0-395-67020-9*, Clarion Bks) HM.

Last Dragon. Susan M. Nunes. (Illus.). 32p. 1997. pap. 6.95 (*0-395-84517-3*, Clarion Bks) HM.

Last Dragon. Susan Miho Nunes. (J). 1997. 11.15 (*0-606-11548-X*, Pub. by Turtleback) Demco.

Last Dragonlord. J. Bertin. LC 98-21186. 400p. 1998. text 25.95 (*0-312-86429-9*) St Martin.

***Last Dragonlord.** Joanne Bertin. 1999. mass mkt. 5.99 (*0-8125-4541-9*, Pub. by Forge NYC) St Martin.

***Last Dreamers: New & Selected Poems.** Padraig J. Daly. 150p. 2000. 23.95 (*1-901233-46-4*, Pub. by Dedalus); pap. 15.95 (*1-901233-45-6*, Pub. by Dedalus) Dufour.

Last Drop. John Peel. (Tombstones Ser.: No. 2). (J). (gr. 7 up). 1995. mass mkt. 3.99 (*0-671-53530-7*) PB.

Last Drop. John Peel. (Tombstones Ser.). 1995. 9.09 (*0-606-08648-X*, Pub. by Turtleback) Demco.

***Last Duchess of Malfi.** 1998. pap. write for info. (*0-582-33203-6*) Addison-Wesley.

Last Duchess of Wolff's Lair. Jo-Ann Power. 352p. 1993. mass mkt. 3.99 (*0-8217-4266-3*, Zebra Kensgtn) Kensgtn Pub Corp.

Last Duke. Andrea Kane. (Illus.). (J). 1995. mass mkt. 5.99 (*0-671-86508-0*) PB.

Last Dust Storm. Wilma E. McDaniel. LC 95-9865. 104p. 1995. 20.00 (*1-882413-17-2*); pap. 12.00 (*1-882413-16-4*) Hanging Loose.

***Last Dynasty of the Angels.** George Papadopoulos. Tr. by Charles Moore. LC 98-68080. (Illus.). 338p. (Orig.). 1998. pap. 14.95 (*0-9668015-0-4*) OceanTides Pubg.

Last Earls of Barrymore, 1769-1824. John R. Robinson. LC 72-80506. 286p. 1972. reprint ed. 24.95 (*0-405-08895-7*, Pub. by Blom Pubns) Ayer.

Last Earthly Meeting of Lee & Jackson: A Few Days in May 1863. H. Rondel Rumburg. (Illus.). 52p. (Orig.). (C). 1997. pap. 5.00 (*0-9639730-3-7*) Soc Bibl & So Stud.

Last East Indian Voyage. Henry Middleton. LC 74-25700. (English Experience Ser.: No. 307). 1971. reprint ed. 20.00 (*90-221-0307-2*) Walter J Johnson.

Last Eclipse: Planetary Change & Universal Being. Jonathon R. Spinney. 95p. 1996. pap. 11.95 (*0-9651546-3-7*, Pub. by Med Bear) Partners Pubs Grp.

Last Edwardian at No. Ten: An Impression of Harold MacMillan. George Hutchinson. 12.95 (*0-7043-2232-3*, Pub. by Quartet) Charles River Bks.

Last Edwardians: An Illustrated History of Violet Trefusis & Alice Keppel. John Phillips et al. LC 85-71852. (Illus.). 93p. (Orig.). 1985. pap. 10.00 (*0-934552-44-4*) Boston Athenaeum.

Last Eleven. Jack White. (Abbey Theatre Ser.). 1978. pap. 2.50 (*0-912262-46-X*) Proscenium.

Last Emerging Market: From Asian Tigers to African Lions? The Ghana File. Nathaniel Bowditch. LC 99-18011. 224p. 1999. 55.00 (*0-275-96588-0*) Greenwood.

Last Emperor. Arnold C. Brackman. 384p. 1991. pap. 10.95 (*0-88184-700-3*) Carroll & Graf.

Last Emperors: A Social History of Qing Imperial Institutions. Evelyn Sakakida-Rawski. LC 97-38792. 466p. 1998. 45.00 (*0-520-21289-4*, Pub. by U CA Pr) Cal Prin Full Svc.

***Last Emperors of Vietnam: From Tu Duc To Bao Dai, 7.** Oscar M. Chapuis. LC 99-47094. (Contributions in Asian Studies). 200p. 2000. 65.00 (*0-313-31170-6*, Greenwood Pr) Greenwood.

Last Empire: De Beers, Diamonds, & the World. Stefan Kanfer. 416p. 1995. pap. 14.00 (*0-374-52426-2*, Noonday) FS&G.

Last Empire: DeBeers, Diamonds & the World. Stefan Kanfer. (Illus.). 409p. 1999. pap. text 14.00 (*0-7881-6075-3*) DIANE Pub.

Last Empire: Nationality & the Soviet Future. Ed. by Robert Conquest. (Publication Ser.: No. 325). 406p. 1986. lib. bdg. 27.95 (*0-8179-8251-5*) Hoover Inst Pr.

Last Empire: South Africa, Diamonds, & De Beers from Cecil Rhodes to the Oppenheimers. Stefan Kanfer. LC 92-35976. 1993. text 25.00 (*0-374-15207-1*) FS&G.

Last Empress: The Life & Times of Alexander Feodorovna, Empress of Russia. Greg King. (Illus.). 352p. 1996. pap. 16.95 (*0-8065-1761-1*, Citadel Pr) Carol Pub Group.

Last Empress: The Life & Times of Alexandra Feodorovna, Empress of Russia. Greg King. LC 93-45737. 1994. 24.95 (*1-55972-211-8*, Birch Ln Pr) Carol Pub Group.

Last Empress: The Life & Times of Alexandra Feodorovna, Tsarina of Russia. Greg King. (Illus.). 466p. 1999. reprint ed. lib. bdg. 42.95 (*0-7351-0104-3*) Replica Bks.

Last Enchantment. Mary Stewart. LC 96-66688. Vol. 3. 538p. 1996. pap. 12.95 (*0-449-91176-4*) Fawcett.

Last Enchantment. large type ed. Meg Alexander. 350p. 1995. 23.99 (*0-263-14423-2*) Ulverscroft.

An Asterisk (*) at the beginning of an entry indicates that the title is appearing for the first time.

Last Enchantments. Robert Liddell. 221p. 1991. 29.00 (0-7206-0816-3, Pub. by P Owen Ltd) Dufour.
Last Enemy. Richard Hillary. LC 97-47536. 192p. 1998. pap. 14.95 (1-58080-056-4) Burford Bks.
Last Enemy. Richard Hillary. 1988. pap. 3.95 (0-317-65551-5) St Martin.
*Last Enemy. Pauline Baird Jones. LC 99-47793. 374p. 1999. 24.95 (0-7862-2185-2) Mac Lib Ref.
Last Energy War: The Battle over Utility Deregulation, Vol. 16. Harvey Wasserman. LC 99-39622. (Open Media Pamphlet Ser.). 64p. 1999. pap. text 5.95 (1-58322-017-8, Pub. by Seven Stories) Publishers Group.
*Last English King. Julian Rathbone. LC 99-55913. 400p. 1999. text 24.95 (0-312-24213-1) St Martin.
*Last English Plantation. Jan Lo Shinebourne. 182p. 1999. pap. 12.95 (1-900715-33-3, Pub. by Peepal Tree Pr) Paul & Co Pubs.
Last Episodes of the French Revolution. Ernest Belfort Bax. LC 74-159489. (World History Ser.: No. 48). 1971. lib. bdg. 75.00 (0-8383-1282-9) M S G Haskell Hse.
Last Essays. Frederick E. Birkenhead. LC 78-104996. (Essay Index Reprint Ser.). 1977. 28.95 (0-8369-1546-1) Ayer.
Last Essays. Joseph Conrad. LC 75-117777. (Essay Index Reprint Ser.). 1977. 19.95 (0-8369-1795-2) Ayer.
Last Essays. Maurice H. Hewlett. LC 68-54349. (Essay Index Reprint Ser.). 1977. 20.95 (0-8369-0539-3) Ayer.
Last Essays. Georges Bernanos. LC 68-23409. 263p. 1968. reprint ed. lib. bdg. 38.50 (0-8371-0019-4, BELE, Greenwood Pr) Greenwood.
Last Essays. Maurice H. Hewlett. (BCL1-PR English Literature Ser.). 314p. 1992. reprint ed. lib. bdg. 89.00 (0-7812-7559-8) Rprt Serv.
Last Essays. Friedrich M. Mueller. LC 73-18815. (Second Ser.). reprint ed. 55.00 (0-404-11439-3) AMS Pr.
Last Essays. Frederick E. Smith. (Essay Index Reprint Ser.). 440p. 1982. reprint ed. lib. bdg. 32.50 (0-8290-0809-8) Irvington.
Last Essays: Essays on Language, Folklore & Other Subjects. Friedrich M. Mueller. LC 73-18828. (First Ser.). reprint ed. 55.00 (0-404-11438-5) AMS Pr.
Last Evening with Allston, & Other Papers. Elizabeth P. Peabody. LC 72-2953. reprint ed. 47.50 (0-404-10718-4) AMS Pr.
*Last Ever Notes & Queries. Ed. by Joseph Harker. 224p. 1998. pap. 19.95 (1-85702-876-7, Pub. by Fourth Estate) Trafalgar.
Last Exit to Brooklyn. Hubert Selby, Jr. LC 85-45940. 304p. 1988. pap. 12.00 (0-8021-3137-9, Grove) Grove-Atltic.
Last Exodus. Leonard Schroeter. LC 79-4922. 444p. (Orig.). 1979. reprint ed. pap. 10.95 (0-295-95685-2) U of Wash Pr.
Last Exodus: Every Race, People, & Tribe Inherit God's Promised Land. Andrew N. Mealey. (Illus.). 224p. (Orig.). 1997. pap. 14.95 (0-9656384-6-4) NorRem Pub.
Last Explorer: The Autobiography of Michael Terry. Michael Terry. (Illus.). 137p. 1988. 16.00 (0-08-034398-8, Pergamon Pr) Elsevier.
Last Express: The Official Strategy Game. Rick Barba. LC 96-71683. 216p. 1997. per. 19.99 (0-7615-0989-5) Prima Pub.
Last Extinction. 2nd ed. Ed. by Les Kaufman & Kenneth Mallory. LC 93-12575. (Illus.). 242p. 1993. 30.00 (0-262-11179-9); pap. text 15.00 (0-262-61089-2) MIT Pr.
Last Eyewitness: A True Spy Thriller. Robert James. Ed. by Priscilla Reagan & R. David Heileman. 400p. 1995. lib. bdg. 22.00 (0-916067-07-6) Elec Media Pub.
Last Eyewitness: A True Spy Thriller. Robert James. Ed. by R. David Heileman. LC 95-60744. 395p. 1995. pap. 22.00 (0-916067-08-4) Elec Media Pub.
Last Eyewitnesses: Children of the Holocaust Speak. Wiktoria Sliwowska. Tr. by Julian F. Bussgang from POL. LC 97-52099. 432p. 1998. 59.95 (0-8101-1510-7); pap. 24.95 (0-8101-1511-5) Northwestern U Pr.
*Last Face-Off: The Doug Wickenheiser Story. Ted Pepple. (Illus.). 72p. 2000. 20.00 (0-9655980-1-2) T Pepple.
Last Face You'll Ever See. Ivan Solotaroff. 288p. 2001. 25.00 (0-06-017448-X) HarpC.
Last Face You'll See. Ivan Solotaroff. 2002. pap. 13.00 (0-06-093103-5, Perennial) HarperTrade.
Last Family: A Suspense Novel. John R. Miller. 480p. 1997. reprint ed. mass mkt. 6.99 (0-553-57496-5) Bantam.
Last Farmer: An American Memoir. Howard Kohn. 1989. pap. 8.95 (0-685-28400-X, Perennial) HarperTrade.
Last Fay. Honore de Balzac. Tr. & Intro. by Eric H. Du Plessis. LC 95-47380. (Studies in French Literature: Vol. 23). (Illus.). 216p. 1996. text 89.95 (0-7734-8861-8) E Mellen.
Last Ferry to Clover Bay. Wayne E. Haley. Ed. by Susan Givens. 320p. 1999. pap. 19.95 (0-9661247-1-5) Quiveir Pr.
Last Fiddler Crab. limited ed. Ray Staszko. LC 74-25864. (Living Poets' Library). 1975. pap. 2.50 (0-686-10405-6) Dragons Teeth.
Last Finnish War. Waldemar Erfurth. LC 79-88321. 253p. 1979. lib. bdg. 55.00 (0-313-27082-1, U7082, Greenwood Pr) Greenwood.
*Last Fisherman: A Novel of the Last Pope, the Antichrist & the End... Randy England. 200p. 1999. pap. 11.95 (0-9673607-0-6) Convent Hill.
Last Five Feet. Eunice V. Pike. LC 93-87633. 129p. (Orig.). 1994. pap. 8.00 (0-88312-709-1) S I L Intl.
Last Five Minutes. Fred L. Fifer & Cynthia E. Ledbetter. (Do It Now Ser.). 38p. (J). 1991. student ed. 6.95 (1-885568-11-8) SCE Assocs.
Last Five Pounds: How to Lose Them & Leave Them Forever. Jamie Pope. Ed. by Julie Rubenstein. 384p. 1995. 23.00 (0-671-88453-0) PB.
Last Five Pounds: Liberating Guide to Living Thin. Jamie Pope. 480p. 1996. per. 6.99 (0-671-88454-9, PB Trade Paper) PB.
Last Flesh: Life in the Transhuman Era. Christopher Dewdney. LC 98-164826. 188p. 1998. pap. 20.00 (0-00-638472-2) Collins SF.
Last Flight. Amelia Earhart. (American Biography Ser.). 226p. 1991. reprint ed. lib. bdg. 69.00 (0-7812-8119-9) Rprt Serv.
Last Flight of Amelia Earhart. Amelia Earhart. 224p. reprint ed. 9.95 (0-614-13187-1, 21-37163) EAA Aviation.
Last Flight of Ensign C. Markland Kelly, Junior, U. S. N. R. Bowen P. Weisheit. (Illus.). 88p. 1993. pap. 15.95 (0-9658560-1-1) B P Weisheit.
Last Flight of Ensign C. Markland Kelly, Junior, U. S. N. R. 2nd ed. Bowen P. Weisheit. (Illus.). 88p. 1996. 25.95 (0-9658560-2-X) B P Weisheit.
Last Flight of Frederick J. Noonan (& Amelia Earhart) Bowen P. Weisheit. (Illus.). 54p. 1997. pap. 14.95 (0-9658560-0-3) B P Weisheit.
Last Flight of the Greatest Airship Ever Built. Shelley Tanaka. (Time Quest Bks.). (J). (gr. 3-7). 1996. reprint ed. pap. 6.95 (0-614-15767-6) Scholastic Inc.
Last Flight of "The Lady Jeannette" Willis S. Cole, Jr. LC 99-167483. viii, 288p. 1998. 25.00 (0-9662728-0-3) BCWSCMM.
*Last Flight of the Liberators: The Seventh Flag over Texas. Dave Morris. 222p. 2000. pap. 18.00 (0-7388-2077-6) Xlibris Corp.
Last Flight of the Luftwaffe: The Fate of Schulungslehrgang Elbe, 7 April 1945. Adrian Weir. LC 97-178313. (Illus.). 208p. 1997. 29.95 (1-85409-300-2, Pub. by Arms & Armour) Sterling.
*Last Flight of 007. Frank Woodson. (Take Ten Ser.). (Illus.). 46p. (YA). (gr. 4-12). 1999. pap. 3.95 (1-58659-025-1) Artesian.
Last Flight of 007. Frank Woodson. Ed. by Liz Parker. (Take Ten Bks.). 46p. (YA). (gr. 6-12). 1993. pap. text 3.95 (1-56254-075-0) Saddleback Pubns.
Last Flower. James Thurber. 16.95 (0-89190-270-8) Amereon Ltd.
Last Flower: A Parable in Pictures. James Thurber. LC 98-24195. (Illus.). 112p. 1998. reprint ed. 16.95 (1-888683-45-7) Wooster Bk.
Last Flowers: The Romance Poems of Edgar Allan Poe & Sarah Helen Whitman. Ed. by Brett Rutherford. (Illus.). 1987. 10.00 (0-318-64156-9) Poets Pr.
*Last Flowers: The Romance Poems of Edgar Allan Poe & Sarah Helen Whitman. 2nd rev. ed. Edgar Allan Poe & Sarah Helen Whitman. Ed. by Brett Rutherford. (Illus.). 120p. 2000. pap. 12.95 (0-922558-08-6) Poets Pr.
Last Flowers of Manet. Robert Gordon & Andrew Forge. Tr. by Richard Howard. (Illus.). 48p. 12.98 (0-8109-8164-5, Pub. by Abrams) Time Warner.

Last Forest. G. D. McNeill. 166p. 1940. pap. 11.00 (0-87012-635-0) McClain.
THE LAST FOREST will take you back in time to the 1880's, to the unspoiled West Virginia wilderness. G. D. (Douglas) McNeill's collection of stories begins with the forest primeval, before the railroads & loggers disturbed the tranquility of centuries. It ends fifty years later, with the last virgin forest cut over & despoiled. Anyone who loves good writing & a well-told tale will enjoy THE LAST FOREST. Through its pages fishermen, hunters & hikers can imagine the hardwood forests of the Allegheny Mountains a hundred years ago, then retrace the sorry history of their exploitation & destruction. Much of the book's action takes place along the Cranberry & Williams rivers, an area now protected as federally designated wilderness area. THE LAKE FOREST was written in the 1930's & has been out of print for half a century. (Reprinted 1990,1999).
Publisher Paid Annotation.

Last Four Lives of Annie Besant. Arthur H. Nethercot. LC 63-25862. 499p. reprint ed. pap. 154.70 (0-608-13404-X, 202410200035) Bks Demand.
Last Free Range. James A. Ritchie. 224p. 1995. 19.95 (0-8027-4150-9) Walker & Co.
Last Frontier. Patricia Coughlin. (Men Made in America Ser.). 1995. mass mkt. 3.59 (0-373-45190-3, 1-45190-5) Harlequin Bks.
Last Frontier. Howard Fast. LC 96-48628. 320p. (gr. 13). 1997. pap. 18.95 (1-56324-593-0, N Castle) M E Sharpe.
Last Frontier. Zachary T. Sutley. 1977. 21.95 (0-8369-7126-4, 7960) Ayer.
Last Frontier. Melody Webb. LC 85-1022. (Illus.). 430p. reprint ed. pap. 122.60 (0-7837-1636-2, 2041929) Bks Demand.
Last Frontier: History of Hardeman County, Texas. Bill Neal. (Illus.). 296p. 1997. 29.95 (1-57168-157-4) Sunbelt Media.
Last Frontier: Imagining Other Worlds, from the Copernican Revolution to Modern Science Fiction. Karl S. Guthke. Tr. by Helen Atkins from GER. LC 89-46165. 416p. 1993. pap. text 17.95 (0-8014-9727-2) Cornell U Pr.
Last Frontier: The Social Meaning of Growing Old. Andrea Fontana. LC 77-23186. (Sage Library of Social Research: No. 42). 215p. 1977. reprint ed. pap. 66.70 (0-608-01497-4, 205954100001) Bks Demand.
Last Frontier: The White Man's War for Civilization in Africa. E. Alexander Powell. 1976. lib. bdg. 59.95 (0-8490-2129-4) Gordon Pr.
Last Frontier: Women Lawyers As Rainmakers. 36p. 1993. pap. 14.95 (0-89707-813-6, 511-0314) Amer Bar Assn.
Last Frontier Forests: Ecosystems & Economies on the Edge. Dirk Bryant et al. (FRE.). 44p. 1997. pap. 20.00 (1-56973-221-3); pap. 20.00 (1-56973-223-X) World Resources Inst.
Last Frontier Forests: Ecosystems & Economies on the Edge. Dirk Bryant et al. 44p. 1997. pap. 20.00 (1-56973-198-5) World Resources Inst.
*Last Full Measure. Jeff M. Shaara. LC 97-49383. 576p. 1998. 25.95 (0-345-40491-2) Ballantine Pub Grp.
Last Full Measure. Jeff M. Shaara. LC 99-90092. (Ballantine Reader's Circle Ser.). 560p. 1999. pap. 14.00 (0-345-42548-0) Ballantine Pub Grp.
*Last Full Measure. Jeff M. Shaara. 640p. 2000. mass mkt. 7.99 (0-345-43481-1, Ballantine) Ballantine Pub Grp.
Last Full Measure. large type ed. Jeff M. Shaara. LC 97-51830. 1998. pap. 25.00 (0-375-70291-1) Random.
Last Full Measure: Burials in the Soldiers' National Cemetery at Gettysburg. John W. Busey. Ed. by David G. Martin. (Illus.). 277p. (C). 1988. text 20.00 (0-944413-12-9) Longstreet Hse.
Last Full Measure: The Life & Death of the First Minnesota Volunteers. Richard Moe. LC 92-32687. (Illus.). 368p. 1995. 29.95 (0-8050-2309-7) H Holt & Co.
Last Full Measure: The Life & Death of the First Minnesota Volunteers. Richard Moe. 376p. 1994. reprint ed. pap. 15.00 (0-380-72322-0, Avon Bks) Morrow Avon.
Last Gaiter Button: A Study of the Mobilization & Concentration of the French Army in the War of 1870, 73. Thomas J. Adriance. LC 87-25220. (Contributions in Military Studies Ser.: No. 73). 189p. 1987. 49.95 (0-313-25469-9, ALG/, Greenwood Pr) Greenwood.
Last Gambit. large type ed. David Delman. (Lythway Ser.). 236p. 1992. 15.95 (0-7451-1616-7, G K Hall Lrg Type) Mac Lib Ref.
Last Gamble: Betting on the Future in Four Rocky Mountain Mining Towns. Katherine Jensen & Audie L. Blevins. LC 98-8962. 220p. 1998. 45.00 (0-8165-1854-8) U of Ariz Pr.
Last Gamble on Education. Jack Mezirow et al. 206p. 1988. 10.95 (0-318-36404-2, AEA-1) A A A C E.
Last Gamble on Education: Dynamics of Adult Basic Education - New Dimensions in Program Analysis. Jack Mezirow et al. 206p. 1975. 13.00 (0-88379-010-6) A A A C E.
Last Game. Joan Hoffman. (Start to Read! Ser.). (Illus.). 16p. (J). (gr. k-2). 1992. pap. 2.29 (0-88743-268-9, 06035) Sch Zone Pub Co.
Last Game. Joan Hoffman. (Start to Read! Ser.). (Illus.). 32p. (J). (gr. k-2). 1993. pap. 3.99 (0-88743-429-0, 06081) Sch Zone Pub Co.
Last Gas Station & Other Stories. Tom Clark. LC 80-36765. 220p. (Orig.). 1980. 14.00 (0-87685-457-9); pap. 10.00 (0-87685-456-0) Black Sparrow.
Last Gas Station & Other Stories, signed ed. deluxe ed. Tom Clark. LC 80-36765. 220p. (Orig.). 1980. 20.00 (0-87685-458-7) Black Sparrow.
Last Generation. Marty Galotto. 392p. 1999. 25.00 (0-8059-4635-7) Dorrance.
Last Generation. James Morgan. LC 99-24195. 4p. 1999. 24.95 (1-57524-106-4) Krieger.
Last Generation. C. W. Pearson. 37p. (Orig.). (C). 1997. pap. write for info. (0-9649675-2-9) Gospel Gold.
Last Generation: A History of a Chesapeake Shipbuilding Family. Geoffrey M. Footner. LC 91-3667. (Illus.). 194p. 1991. 37.50 (0-941647-10-2) Calvert MM Pr.
Last Generation: Poetry & Prose. Cherrie Moraga. LC 93-703. 197p. 1993. 30.00 (0-89608-467-1); pap. 14.00 (0-89608-466-3) South End Pr.
Last Generation: Poetry & Prose. Cherrie Moraga. (Not a Luxury Poetry Ser.). 250p. pap. 14.95 (0-88961-189-0, Pub. by Womens Pr) LPC InBook.
Last Generation: Work & Life in the Textile Mills of Lowell, Massachusetts, 1910-1960. Mary H. Blewett. LC 89-77124. (Illus.). 352p. (C). 1990. pap. 19.95 (0-87023-713-6) U of Mass Pr.
*Last Generation of English Catholic Clergy: Parish Priests in the Diocese of Coventry & Lichfield in the Early Sixteenth Century. Tim Cooper. LC 99-32793. (Studies in the History of Medieval Religion). 224p. 1999. 81.00 (0-85115-752-1, Suffolk Records Soc) Boydell & Brewer.
Last Generation of the Roman Republic. Erich S. Gruen. 615p. 1995. pap. 24.95 (0-520-20153-1, Pub. by U CA Pr) Cal Prin Full Svc.
Last Generation of Truth. Daniel L. Butler. (Illus.). 128p. (Orig.). 1989. pap. 7.00 (0-932581-58-7) Word Aflame.
Last Gentleman. Walker Percy. LC 66-18861. 409p. 1966. text 22.95 (0-374-18372-4) FS&G.
Last Gentleman. Walker Percy. 336p. 1989. mass mkt. 5.99 (0-8041-0379-8) Ivy Books.
Last Gentleman. Walker Percy. LC 97-15381. 560p. 1998. 18.50 (0-679-60272-0) Modern Lib NY.
*Last Gentleman: Novel. Walker Percy. LC 99-16417. 416p. 1999. pap. 15.00 (0-312-24308-1) St Martin.
Last Gentlemen. Walker Percy. 320p. 1978. mass mkt. 4.50 (0-380-37796-9, Avon Bks) Morrow Avon.
Last Ghost Dance. Eagle Brooke Medicine Staff. 2000. 13.95 (0-345-40031-3) Ball Well.
Last Giants. Francois Place. Tr. by William Rodarmor from FRE. (Illus.). 78p. 1993. 15.95 (0-87923-990-5) Godine.
Last Gift of Time: Life Beyond 60. Carolyn Heilbrun. 240p. 1998. pap. 12.00 (0-345-42295-3) Ballantine Pub Grp.
Last Gift of Time: Life Beyond 60. Carolyn Heilbrun. LC 96-36186. 240p. 1997. 19.95 (0-385-31325-X, Dial Pr) Dell.
Last Girl. Penelope Evans. 1997. mass mkt. 5.99 (0-312-96315-7) St Martin.
*Last Girl. Penelope Evans. 2000. pap. 10.95 (0-552-99602-5, Pub. by Transworld Publishers Ltd) Trafalgar.
Last Girl in the Land of the Butterflies. Laurel A. Bogen. 64p. (Orig.). 1996. pap. 10.00 (1-889504-00-9) Red Wind Bks.
Last Gladiator. Roberta Carlee. LC 79-91303. (Illus.). 291p. 1979. 12.50 (0-935680-00-4) Kentucke Imprints.
Last Glass of Tea & Other Stories Murhammad Biseartei & Denys Johnson-Davies. LC 95-960303. 139 p. 1994. write for info. (977-424-349-8) Col U Pr.
Last Glass of Tea & Other Stories. Mohamed El-Bisatie. Tr. by Denys Johnson-Davies from ARA. LC 95-22229. 142p. (Orig.). 1998. lib. bdg. 24.00 (0-89410-800-X, Three Contnts) L Rienner.
Last Go Round: A Dime Western. Ken Kesey & Ken Babbs. (Illus.). 256p. 1995. pap. 10.95 (0-14-017667-5, Penguin Bks) Viking Penguin.
Last Good-Bye. H. Michael Frase. 368p. 1998. 24.00 (0-7867-0514-0) Carroll & Graf.
Last Good City. 1998. pap. 15.00 (0-9623556-2-3) Columbia Rvr Bk Co.
*Last Good Freudian. Brenda S. Webster. LC 00-20442. 208p. 2000. 24.95 (0-8419-1395-1) Holmes & Meier.
Last Good Kiss. James Crumley. (Contemporaries Ser.). 244p. 1988. pap. 11.00 (0-394-75989-3) Vin Bks.
Last Good Man. Inglath Cooper. (Superromance Ser.). 1997. per. 3.99 (0-373-70728-2, 1-70728-0) Harlequin Bks.
*Last Good Man. Kathleen Eagle. 384p. 2000. 23.00 (0-380-97815-6) Morrow Avon.
Last Good Man. Daniel Lyons. LC 93-3464. 176p. (C). 1993. 22.95 (0-87023-865-5) U of Mass Pr.
Last Good Man. Daniel Lyons. LC 93-3464. (Associated Writing Programs Award for Short Fiction Ser.). 176p. 1995. pap. 15.95 (0-87023-978-3) U of Mass Pr.
Last Good Moment of Lily Baker. Russell Davis. 1991. pap. 5.25 (0-8222-0635-8) Dramatists Play.
Last Good Night. Emily Listfield. 352p. 1998. mass mkt. 5.99 (1-57566-354-6) Kensgtn Pub Corp.
Last Good Night. large type ed. Emily Listfield. LC 97-32935. 1997. 24.95 (1-57490-128-1, Beeler LP Bks) T T Beeler.
Last Goodbye. Malcolm Bell. LC 98-28822. 352p. 1998. 24.95 (0-312-19310-6, Thomas Dunne) St Martin.
*Last Goodbye. Malcolm Bell. 352p. 2000. mass mkt. 6.99 (0-312-95889-7) St Martin.
Last Goodbye I: Bereavement Guide I. Jim Boulden et al. Ed. by Evelyn M. Ward. (Illus.). 32p. (Orig.). (J). (gr. 6-9). 1994. pap. 5.95 (1-878076-32-9) Boulden Pub.
Last Goodbye II: Bereavement Guide. Jim Boulden & Joan Boulden. Ed. by Evelyn M. Ward. (Illus.). 32p. (Orig.). (YA). (gr. 10-12). 1994. pap. 5.95 (1-878076-33-7) Boulden Pub.
*Last Gospel. David Howard. LC 00-102341. 278p. 2000. write for info. (1-58444-115-1); pap. write for info. (1-58444-116-X) DiscUs Bks.
Last Governor: Chris Patten & the Handover of Hong Kong. Jonathan Dimbleby. LC 98-115639. xvi, 461p. 1997. write for info. (0-316-64018-2) Little.
Last Grain Race. Eric Newby. 304p. 1999. pap. 12.95 (0-86442-768-9) Lonely Planet.
Last Grand Passion. Emma Darcy. (Presents Plus Ser.). 1993. mass mkt. 2.99 (0-373-11592-X, 1-11592-2) Harlequin Bks.
Last Grand Passion. large type ed. Emma Darcy. (Magna Large Print Ser.). 292p. 1998. 29.99 (0-7505-1097-8, Pub. by Mgna Lrg Print) Ulverscroft.
Last Grand Roundup. Albert A. McIntyre. LC 89-90976. (Illus.). 104p. 1989. reprint ed. 12.95 (0-9622654-0-3) Chief Rsch.
Last Great Ace: The Life of Major Thomas B. McGuire, Jr. Charles A. Martin. Ed. by Antoinette D. Martin. LC 98-96647. (Illus.). 384p. 1999. pap. 19.95 (0-9667791-0-X) Fruit Cove.
Last Great Adventure: The Inside Story of Richard Branson & Per Lindstrand's Dramatic Non-Stop Round the World Balloon Flight. Rupert Saunders & Anthony Smith. (Illus.). 144p. 1997. 22.95 (1-85227-489-1, Pub. by Virgin Bks) London Brdge.
Last Great American Hobo. Dale Maharidge & Michael Williamson. LC 92-40480. (Illus.). 288p. 1993. 24.95 (1-55958-299-5) Prima Pub.
Last Great Anointing. Morris Cerullo. LC 99-20264. 216p. 1999. 18.99 (0-8307-2473-7) Gospel Lght.
*Last Great Anointing. Morris Cerullo. LC 99-20264. 216p. 1999. pap. 9.99 (0-8307-2472-9, Regal Bks) Gospel Lght.
Last Great Conflict. A. J. Tomlinson. 241p. 1984. reprint ed. 8.95 (0-317-14173-2, 1925) White Wing Pub.
*Last Great Dance on Earth: A Novel. Sandra Gulland. 2000. pap. 14.00 (0-684-85608-5) Scribner.
Last Great Days of Radio. Lynn Wooley. LC 93-38070. 280p. (Orig.). 1993. pap. 12.95 (1-55622-321-8, Rep of TX Pr) Wordware Pub.
Last Great Frenchman: A Life of General de Gaulle. Charles Williams. LC 94-42881. 544p. 1995. 30.00 (0-471-11711-0) Wiley.
Last Great Frenchman: A Life of General de Gaulle. Charles Williams. LC 94-42881. (Illus.). 544p. 1997. pap. 19.95 (0-471-18071-8) Wiley.
*Last Great Miller: The Four Wheel Drive Indy Car. Griff Borgeson. LC 00-36542. (Illus.). 344p. 2000. 39.00 (0-7680-0500-0, R-244) Soc Auto Engineers.

An Asterisk (*) at the beginning of an entry indicates that the title is appearing for the first time.

Last Great Muslim Empires: History of the Muslim World, III. 2nd ed. F. R. Bagley et al. Tr. by R. C. Bagley from GER. 333p. 1996. reprint ed. pap. text 19.95 (*1-55876-112-8*) Wiener Pubs Inc.

Last Great Necessity: Cemetaries in American History. David C. Sloane. (Creating the North American Landscape Ser.). (Illus.). 288p. 1995. pap. 18.95 (*0-8018-5128-9*) Johns Hopkins.

Last Great Necessity: Cemeteries in American History. David C. Sloane. LC 90-41906. (Creating the North American Landscape Ser.). (Illus.). 288p. 1991. 49.95 (*0-8018-4068-6*) Johns Hopkins.

Last Great Nuclear Debate: NATO & Short-Range Nuclear Weapons in the 1980s. Thomas E. Halverson. LC 94-45759. 262p. 1996. text 69.95 (*0-312-12604-2*) St Martin.

Last Great Plague: AIDS & Related Murder Tools. Ceres. (Phoenix Journals). 255p. 1993. pap. 7.95 (*1-56935-004-3*) Phoenix Source.

Last Great Race: The Iditarod. rev. ed. Tim Jones. LC 88-12182. (Illus.). 288p. 1988. pap. 14.95 (*0-8117-2233-3*) Stackpole.

Last Great Revival. Steve Meeks. 1994. 7.00 (*0-9630425-1-3*) Calvary TX.

*__Last Great Revolution: Turmoil & Transformation in Iran.__ Robin B. Wright. LC 99-27798. 352p. 2000. 27.50 (*0-375-40639-5*) Knopf.

Last Great Roller Coaster Ride. 1989. pap. text 12.95 (*0-9624437-0-0*) Tevis Pub.

Last Great Scout. J. R. Roberts. (Gunsmith Ser.: No. 162). 192p. (Orig.). 1995. mass mkt. 3.99 (*0-515-11635-1*, Jove) Berkley Pub.

Last Great Subsistence Crisis in the Western World. John D. Post. LC 76-41239. 256p. 1977. reprint ed. pap. 79.40 (*0-608-03742-7*, 206456700009) Bks Demand.

Last Great Summer. Carol Stanley. 224p. (YA). (gr. 7-9). 1992. pap. 3.25 (*0-590-45705-5*, Point) Scholastic Inc.

Last Great Victory: The End of World War II, July-August 1945. Stanley Weintraub. (Illus.). 752p. 1996. pap. 16.95 (*0-452-27063-4*, Truman Talley) St Martin.

Last Grey Wolf: A Novel of Treasure & Intrigue Surrounding the "Forgotten" Nazi U-Boat in the Gulf. Tom Townsend. 181p. 1982. 9.95 (*0-89896-009-6*); pap. 5.95 (*0-89896-010-X*) Larksdale.

Last Grizzly & Other Southwestern Bear Stories. Ed. by David E. Brown & John A. Murray. LC 88-14819. 184p. 1988. 22.50 (*0-8165-1067-9*) U of Ariz Pr.

Last Groom on Earth. Kristin James. LC 96-7273. (Desire Ser.). 185p. 1996. per. 3.50 (*0-373-05986-8*, 1-05986-4) Silhouette.

Last Groom on Earth. large type ed. Kristin James. (Silhouette Ser.). 1998. 20.95 (*0-373-59864-5*, Harlequin) Harlequin Bks.

Last Guardian. David Gemmell. 1997. mass mkt. 0.05 (*0-345-37900-4*, Del Rey) Ballantine Pub Grp.

*__Last Guardian.__ Charles Grant. (Warcraft Ser.). 288p. 2000. per. 6.99 (*0-671-04151-7*) PB.

*__Last Guardians: The Crisis in the RCMP - And in Canada.__ Paul Palango. 320p. 2000. pap. 19.99 (*0-7710-6908-1*) McCland & Stewart.

Last Guardians: The Crisis in the RCMP. . . And in Canada. Paul Palango. LC 99-172856. 316p. 1999. text 19.99 (*0-7710-6906-5*) McCland & Stewart.

Last Guests of the Season. Sue Gee. 286p. 1995. pap. 11.95 (*0-09-925641-X*, Pub. by Arrow Bks) Trafalgar.

Last Gun. large type ed. Lee Floren. (Linford Western Library). 1990. pap. 16.99 (*0-7089-6806-6*, Linford) Ulverscroft.

Last Half Century: Societal Change & Politics in America. Morris Janowitz. LC 78-17715. (Illus.). 608p. 1978. lib. bdg. 42.00 (*0-226-39306-2*) U Ch Pr.

Last Half Century: Societal Change & Politics in America. Morris Janowitz. LC 78-17715. (Illus.). 600p. 1979. pap. text 19.50 (*0-226-39307-0*) U Ch Pr.

Last Half Century of Chinese Overseas. Ed. by Elizabeth Sinn. LC 98-159753. xiii, 508p. 1998. 52.50 (*962-209-446-5*, Pub. by HK Univ Pr) Coronet Bks.

Last Hanging at Fallstown. large type ed. Amy Sadler. (Dales Large Print Ser.). 204p. 1996. pap. 18.99 (*1-85389-695-0*, Dales) Ulverscroft.

Last Hanging at Paradise Meadow. Stephen A. Bly. LC 92-13085. (Stuart Brannon Western Adventure Ser.: Vol. 3). 192p. 1992. pap. 8.99 (*0-89107-672-7*) Crossway Bks.

Last Happy Men: The Generation of 1922, Fiction, & the Argentine Reality. Christopher Leland. (Illus.). 232p. 1986. text 39.95 (*0-8156-2376-3*) Syracuse U Pr.

Last Happy Occasion. Alan Shapiro. LC 96-14348. 248p. 1996. 22.95 (*0-226-75032-9*) U Ch Pr.

Last Happy Occasion. Alan Shapiro. 230p. 1997. pap. 12.95 (*0-226-75036-1*) U Ch Pr.

Last Harmattan of Alusine Dunbar. Syl Cheney-Coker. (African Writers Ser.). 398p. (Orig.). (C). 1990. pap. 9.95 (*0-435-90572-4*, 90572) Heinemann.

Last Harvest: The Genetic Gamble That Threatens to Destroy American Agriculture. Paul Raeburn. 269p. 1995. 23.50 (*0-684-80365-8*) S&S Trade.

Last Harvest: The Genetic Gamble That Threatens to Destroy American Agriculture. Paul Raeburn. LC 96-24071. ix, 262p. 1996. pap. 12.00 (*0-8032-8962-6*, Bison Books) U of Nebr Pr.

Last Hawaiian Queen, Liliuokalani see Benchmark Biographies - Group 1

Last Hawk. Catherine Asaro. 1998. mass mkt. 6.99 (*0-8125-5110-9*, Pub. by Tor Bks) St Martin.

Last Hayride. John Maginnis. Ed. by Barbara Phillips. LC 84-80875. (Illus.). 354p. (C). 1994. pap. 9.95 (*0-9614138-1-6*) Darkhorse Pr.

*__Last-He: The Last He-Man.__ John Anton. LC 00-190409. 210p. 2000. 25.00 (*0-7388-1657-4*); pap. 18.00 (*0-7388-1658-2*) Xlibris Corp.

*__Last Heat.__ Peter Blair. LC 99-72869. 72p. 2000. pap. 10.00 (*0-915380-44-7*) Word Works.

Last Heiress. large type ed. Tessa Barclay. 1993. 39.95 (*0-7066-1020-2*, Pub. by Remploy Pr) St Mut.

*__Last Hellion.__ Loretta Chase. LC 99-26433. 1999. 26.95 (*0-7862-1989-0*) Five Star.

Last Hellion. Loretta Chase. 304p. 1998. mass mkt. 5.99 (*0-380-77617-0*, Avon Bks) Morrow Avon.

Last Hero. Alyssa Dean. LC 96-652. (Temptation Ser.). 217p. 1995. per. 3.25 (*0-373-25651-5*, 1-25651-0) Harlequin Bks.

Last Hero. Peter Forbath. 1990. mass mkt. 12.95 (*0-446-39179-4*, Pub. by Warner Bks) Little.

Last Hero. Leslie Charteris. LC 88-82345. 312p. 1988. reprint ed. pap. 4.95 (*0-930330-96-X*, Lib Crime Classics) Intl Polygonics.

Last Hero: The Life of Mickey Mantle. David Falkner. (Illus.). 256p. 1995. 24.00 (*0-684-81424-2*) S&S Trade.

Last Hero: Wild Bill Donovan. Anthony C. Brown. 768p. 1982. 24.95 (*0-686-95975-2*, Times Bks) Crown Pub Group.

Last Hero - Bill Tilman: A Biography of the Explorer. Tim Madge. (Illus.). 288p. 1995. 24.95 (*0-89886-452-6*) Mountaineers.

Last Heroes. Alex Baldwin, pseud. (Men at War Ser.: Vol. 1). 1988. mass mkt. 5.99 (*0-671-67822-1*) PB.

Last Heroes. W. E. B. Griffin. (Men at War Ser.: Vol. 1). 384p. 1998. mass mkt. 7.50 (*0-515-12329-3*, Jove) Berkley Pub.

Last Heroes. W. E. B. Griffin. LC 96-39458. (Men at War Ser.: Vol. 1). 352p. 1997. 24.95 (*0-399-14289-4*, G P Putnam) Peng Put Young Read.

*__Last Heroes.__ large type ed. W. E. B. Griffin. LC 98-29243. 1998. 23.95 (*1-56895-654-1*) Wheeler Pub.

Last Hiding Place. T. Heath. 1989. text 16.95 (*0-88982-040-6*, Pub. by Oolichan Bks) Genl Dist Srvs.

Last Hiding Place. Terrence Heath. 1989. pap. text 12.95 (*0-88982-038-4*, Pub. by Oolichan Bks) Genl Dist Srvs.

*__Last Highlander.__ Claire Cross. 1998. mass mkt. 5.99 (*0-515-12337-4*, Jove) Berkley Pub.

*__Last Hollywood Romance.__ Beverly Bloomberg. 240p. 2000. 22.95 (*1-882593-36-7*) Bridge Wrks.

Last Home for the Aged. Sheldon S. Tobin & Morton A. Lieberman. LC 76-11941. (Jossey-Bass Behavioral Science Ser.). 320p. reprint ed. pap. 99.20 (*0-8357-6900-3*, 203795200009) Bks Demand.

Last Home of Poetry Is the Soul. J. Stephen Keller. (Illus.). 44p. 1998. pap. 6.00 (*1-892609-05-3*) Gracie Pub.

Last Honest Man. Leandra Logan. (Temptation Ser.: No. 393). 1992. per. 2.99 (*0-373-25493-8*, 1-25493-7) Harlequin Bks.

Last Honest Man. Nora Roberts. 248p. 1995. per. 4.99 (*1-55166-020-2*, Mira Bks) Harlequin Bks.

Last Honest Woman. Nora Roberts. (O'Hurley's Ser.). 1990. pap. 2.95 (*0-373-48231-0*) Harlequin Bks.

Last Honest Woman. Nora Roberts. 1999. per. 5.99 (*1-55166-507-7*, 1-66507-4) Silhouette.

*__Last Hope.__ Chloe Hall. 2000. pap. 9.95 (*1-893896-28-5*) Ima Jinn.

Last Hope: The Blood Chit Story. R. E. Baldwin & Thomas W. McGarry. LC 96-70415. (Illus.). 224p. 1997. 49.95 (*0-7643-0222-1*) Schiffer.

Last Hope Ranch. large type ed. Charles A. Seltzer. (Linford Western Library). 352p. 1985. pap. 16.99 (*0-7089-6091-X*, Linford) Ulverscroft.

Last Horizon: Playscript. Nellie McCaslin. LC 93-5270. 24p. (J). 1993. pap. 5.00 (*0-88734-431-3*) Players Pr.

Last Horizons: Hunting, Fishing & Shooting on Five Continents. Peter H. Capstick. (Illus.). 288p. 1988. text 23.95 (*0-312-02535-1*) St Martin.

Last Hostage. John J. Nance. LC 97-44861. 384p. 1998. 23.95 (*0-385-49055-0*) Doubleday.

Last Hostage. large type ed. John J. Nance. LC 98-22082. (Compass Press Large Print Book Ser.). 1998. 26.95 (*1-56895-606-1*, Compass) Wheeler Pub.

*__Last Hostage, Vol. 1.__ John J. Nance. 419p. 1998. 6.99 (*0-312-96639-3*, Pub. by Tor Bks) St Martin.

*__Last Hot Time.__ John M. Ford. 2000. text 22.95 (*0-312-85545-1*) Tor Bks.

Last Hotel for Women. Vicki Covington. 304p. 1996. 23.00 (*0-684-81111-1*) S&S Trade.

*__Last Hotel for Women.__ Vicki Covington. LC 99-20121. 304p. 1999. pap. 16.95 (*0-8173-1003-7*) U of Ala Pr.

Last Hour. Kim Young. 1997. pap. text 9.95 (*0-9656749-1-6*) ACW Press.

Last Hours of Ancient Sunlight: Waking up to Personal & Global Transformation. Thomas C. Hartmann. LC 99-30268. 336p. 1999. 24.00 (*0-609-60546-1*, Crown) Crown Pub Group.

*__Last Hours of Ancient Sunlight: Waking Up to Personal & Global Transformation.__ Thom Hartmann. 336p. 2000. reprint ed. pap. 14.00 (*0-609-80529-0*, Three Riv Pr) Crown Pub Group.

Last House. M. F. K. Fisher. 1997. pap. 13.00 (*0-679-77411-4*) Pantheon.

Last House in America. Jack Micheline. 1976. pap. 15.00 (*0-915016-06-0*) Second Coming.

Last House on the Road: Excursions into a Rural Past. Ronald Jager. 288p. 1996. pap. 12.00 (*0-8070-7063-7*) Beacon Pr.

Last Housewife. Jon Katz. 1995. 19.95 (*0-385-47743-0*) Doubleday.

Last Housewife. large type ed. Jon Katz. (Niagara Large Print Ser.). 1995. 29.50 (*0-7089-5817-7*) Ulverscroft.

Last Housewife in America. Donna Balfe. 32p. (Orig.). 1996. pap. 6.00 (*0-9644333-7-0*) CrossplusRds.

Last Hundred. Hamish Brown. (Illus.). 191p. 1995. 34.95 (*1-85158-607-5*, Pub. by Mainstream Pubng) Trafalgar.

Last Hundred Days of the Soviet Union. Boris Pankin. 356p. 1996. 29.95 (*0-614-19282-X*) St Martin.

*__Last Hundred Days of the Soviet Union.__ Boris Pankin. 282p. 1999. reprint ed. text 30.00 (*0-7881-6588-7*) DIANE Pub.

Last Hundred Yards: The NCO's Contribution to Warfare. H. J. Poole. LC 94-67181. (Illus.). 399p. (Orig.). 1997. pap. 19.95 (*0-9638695-2-3*) Posterity Pr.

Last Hunters - First Farmers: New Perspectives on the Prehistory Transition to Agriculture. Ed. by T. Douglas Price & Anne B. Gebauer. (School of American Research - Advanced Seminar Ser.). (Illus.). 354p. 1995. 50.00 (*0-933452-90-X*); pap. 24.95 (*0-933452-91-8*) Schol Am Res.

Last Hurdle. F. K. Brown. LC 87-29761. (Illus.). 202p. (J). (gr. 3-9). 1988. reprint ed. lib. bdg. 18.50 (*0-208-02212-0*, Linnet Bks) Shoe String.

Last Hurrah. Edward O'Connor. 437p. Date not set. 28.95 (*0-8488-2373-7*) Amereon Ltd.

*__Last Hurrah.__ Edwin O'Connor. 1998. pap. 14.00 (*0-316-19092-6*, Back Bay) Little.

Last Hurrah. Edwin O'Connor. 427p. 1985. reprint ed. pap. 14.95 (*0-316-62659-7*) Little.

Last Husband, & Other Stories. William Humphrey. LC 75-132118. (Short Story Index Reprint Ser.). 1977. 19.95 (*0-8369-3675-2*) Ayer.

Last Ice Sheet Dynamics & Deglaciation in the North European Plain: International Symposium Poznan, Berlin, May 1992. Ed. by M. Boese & S. Kozarski. (Zeitschrift fuer Geomorphologie - Annals of Geomorphology Ser.: Supplementband 95). (Illus.). vi, 149p. 1994. pap. 52.00 (*3-443-21095-3*, Pub. by Gebruder Borntraeger) Balogh.

Last Illusion. Diana Hamilton. (Presents Ser.). 1995. per. 2.99 (*0-373-11716-7*, 1-11716-7) Harlequin Bks.

Last Illusion. large type ed. Diana Hamilton. (Harlequin Ser.). 1995. lib. bdg. 18.95 (*0-263-13936-0*) Thorndike Pr.

Last Images: The Lost Images. Elmont King. (Orig.). 1991. pap. 6.66 (*0-913412-54-6*) Brandon Hse.

Last Imam. Ibrahim Tahir. 280p. 1985. 22.50 (*0-7103-0066-2*) Routledge.

Last in Convoy. James Pattinson. 1958. 10.95 (*0-8392-1060-4*) Astor-Honor.

Last in Convoy. large type ed. James Pattinson. (Ulverscroft Large Print Ser.). 432p. 1998. 29.99 (*0-7089-3931-7*) Ulverscroft.

Last Inca-Atahualpa: An Eyewitness Account of the Conquest of Peru. Charles Spaegel & Ruth E. Norman. Ed. by Unarius Group. (Illus.). 308p. (C). 1993. 21.00 (*0-935097-18-X*) Unarius Acad Sci.

Last Inch: A Middle East Odyssey. Claud Morris. (Illus.). 280p. 1996. 59.50 (*0-7103-0552-4*, Pub. by Kegan Paul Intl) Col U Pr.

Last India Overland. Craig Grant. 456p. 1989. mass mkt. 6.95 (*0-919926-95-9*, Pub. by Coteau) Genl Dist Srvs.

Last Innocent Hour. Margot Abbott. 1993. mass mkt. 5.99 (*0-312-92942-0*) St Martin.

*__Last Innocent Man.__ large type ed. Phillip Margolin. 352p. 1999. 31.99 (*0-7089-9071-1*) Ulverscroft.

Last Innocent Man. Phillip Margolin. 352p. 1995. reprint ed. mass mkt. 7.50 (*0-553-56979-1*) Bantam.

Last Innocent Summer. Zinita Fowler. LC 89-20417. (Chaparral Bks.). 144p. (J). (gr. 6-9). 1990. pap. 11.95 (*0-87565-045-7*) Tex Christian.

Last Innocent White Man in America: And Other Writings. John Leonard. 320p. 1997. pap. 13.00 (*1-56584-348-7*, Pub. by New Press NY) Norton.

Last Innocent White Man in America & Other Writings. John Leonard. LC 92-50838. 320p. 1993. 21.95 (*1-56584-072-0*, Pub. by New Press NY) Norton.

*__Last Innocent Year: America in 1964.__ Jon Margolis. LC 98-48015. (Illus.). 416p. 1999. 25.00 (*0-688-15323-2*, Wm Morrow) Morrow Avon.

*__Last Innocent Year: America in 1964.__ Jon Margolis. 432p. 2000. pap. 14.00 (*0-688-17907-X*) Morrow Avon.

Last Instance. Dan Farrell. 61p. 1999. pap. 9.00 (*1-928650-01-5*, Pub. by Krupskaya) SPD-Small Pr Dist.

*__Last-instar Larvae & Pupae of the Simuliidae of Britain & Ireland: A Key with Brief Ecological Notes.__ Jon Bass. LC 99-184282. (Illus.). 1998. write for info. (*0-900386-58-4*) St Mut.

Last Intellectuals: American Culture in the Age of Academe. Russell Jacoby. 304p. 1989. pap. 14.00 (*0-374-52175-1*) FS&G.

*__Last Intellectuals: American Culture in the Age of Academe.__ Russell Jacoby. 2000. pap. 20.00 (*0-465-03625-2*, Pub. by Basic) HarpC.

Last Interglacial-Glacial Transition in North America. Ed. by P. U. Clark & P. D. Lea. (Special Papers: No. 270). (Illus.). 1992. pap. 31.25 (*0-8137-2270-5*) Geol Soc.

Last Investigation: A Former Federal Investigator Tells What Insiders Know About the Assassination of JFK. Gaeton Fonzi. (Illus.). 464p. 1994. pap. 13.95 (*1-56025-079-8*, Thunders Mouth) Avalon NY.

Last Ivory Hunter. Peter H. Capstick. (Illus.). 288p. 1988. text 21.95 (*0-312-00048-0*) St Martin.

*__Last Jew.__ Noah Gordon. 2000. text 24.95 (*0-312-26504-2*) St Martin.

Last Jew from Wengrow: The Memoirs of a Survivor of the Step-by-Step Genocide in Poland. Ed. by Shraga F. Bielawski & Louis W. Liebovich. LC 90-24127. 184p. 1991. 52.95 (*0-275-93896-4*, C3896, Praeger Pubs) Greenwood.

Last Jewish Shortstop in America. Lowell B. Komie. 225p. 1997. pap. 12.95 (*0-9641957-1-2*) Swordfish-Chicago.

*__Last Jews in Berlin.__ Leonard Gross. 352p. 1999. pap. text 13.95 (*0-7867-0687-2*) Carroll & Graf.

Last Journals of Horace Walpole During the Reign of George Third, 2 vols. Horace Walpole. Ed. by A. Frances Steuart. LC 71-177879. reprint ed. 145.00 (*0-404-06815-4*) AMS Pr.

Last Journey: Reflections for the Time of Grieving. John L. Bell. (Illus.). 56p. 1998. 28.95 incl. audio compact disk (*1-57999-040-1*) GIA Pubns.

Last Judgement: A Jonathan Argyll Mystery. Iain Pears. 1999. mass mkt. 6.50 (*0-425-17148-5*, Prime Crime) Berkley Pub.

Last Judgement: A Jonathan Argyll Mystery. Iain Pears. 1995. 21.00 (*1-57283-001-8*) S&S Trade.

Last Judgement: A Jonathan Argyll Mystery. Iain Pears. LC 95-38120. 224p. 1996. 20.50 (*0-684-81459-5*) S&S Trade.

Last Judgement: The Easelback. mass mkt. write for info. (*0-8478-2271-0*, Pub. by Rizzoli Intl) St Martin.

*__Last Judgement & the Restoration: The Plates, 2 vols.__ Vatican Museums Staff. (Illus.). 245p. 1999. 250.00 (*0-8478-2241-9*, Pub. by Rizzoli Intl) St Martin.

Last Judgment. Horace Hastings. pap. 1.49 (*0-87377-041-2*) GAM Pubns.

Last Judgment in Retrospect. Emanuel Swedenborg. Ed. & Tr. by George F. Dole from LAT.Tr. of De Ultimo Judicio et Babylonia Destructa. 128p. (Orig.). 1996. pap. 9.95 (*0-87785-176-X*) Swedenborg.

*__Last Kabbalist in Lisbon.__ Richard Zimler. LC 97-46184. 318p. 2000. pap. 14.95 (*1-58567-022-7*, Pub. by Overlook Pr) Penguin Putnam.

*__Last Kabbalist of Lisbon.__ Richard Zimler. LC 97-46184. 318p. 1998. 24.95 (*0-87951-834-0*, Pub. by Overlook Pr) Penguin Putnam.

Last Kamikaze: The Story of Admiral Matome Ugaki. Edwin P. Hoyt. LC 92-15694. 256p. 1993. 39.95 (*0-275-94067-5*, C4067, Praeger Pubs) Greenwood.

Last Khedive of Egypt: Memoirs of Abbas Hilmi II. Amira El Azhary Sonbol. 352p. 1998. 45.00 (*0-86372-208-3*, Pub. by Garnet-Ithaca) LPC InBook.

Last King of Paradise. Eugene Burns. LC 72-10607. (Select Bibliographies Reprint Ser.). 1977. reprint ed. 21.95 (*0-8369-7102-7*) Ayer.

Last King of Poland & His Contemporaries. R. Nisbet Bain. LC 71-135789. (Eastern Europe Collection). 1979. reprint ed. 26.95 (*0-405-02731-1*) Ayer.

Last King of Scotland. Giles Foden. LC 98-36722. 336p. 1998. 25.00 (*0-375-40360-4*) Knopf.

*__Last King of Scotland.__ Giles Foden. 352p. 1999. pap. 13.00 (*0-375-70331-4*) Knopf.

*__Last King of Texas.__ Rick Riordan. LC 99-46460. 304p. 2000. 23.95 (*0-553-80156-2*) Bantam.

Last Kings of Thule. Jean Malaurie. Tr. by Adrienne Foulke. LC 85-8765. (Illus.). xx, 490p. 1994. pap. 17.50 (*0-226-50284-8*) U Ch Pr.

Last Klick. Robert Flynn. 363p. 1994. 21.00 (*1-880909-21-9*) Baskerville.

*__Last Knight.__ Candice Proctor. 416p. 2000. mass mkt. 6.99 (*0-8041-1930-9*) Ivy Books.

*__Last Knight: An Introduction to Don Quixote.__ Will Eisner. (Illus.). 32p. (J). (gr. 3-5). 2000. 15.95 (*1-56163-251-1*) NBM.

*__Last Knight of Camelot.__ Edward A. Ryan. 220p. 2000. pap. 14.95 (*0-7414-0361-7*) Buy Books.

Last Knight of Flanders: Remy Schrijnen & His SS-Leigon "Flandern"/Sturmbrigade "Langemarck" Comrades on the Eastern Front, 1941-1945. Allen Brandt. LC 98-84260. 272p. 1998. 29.95 (*0-7643-0588-3*) Schiffer.

Last Known Residence of Mickey Acuna. Dagoberto Gilb. LC 94-5090. 224p. 1995. pap. 11.00 (*0-8021-3419-X*, Grove) Grove-Atltic.

Last Lamb: A Journey Home. Carol Watson. LC 97-69521. 120p. (Orig.). 1998. pap. 6.95 (*0-9659894-0-2*) C Watson.

Last Lambada S. K. Das. LC 99-931543. 169 p. 1998. write for info. (*81-207-2117-9*) Sterling.

Last Lambs: Poems from the Vietnam War. Bill Bauer. LC 97-7510. 72p. (Orig.). 1997. pap. 11.95 (*1-886157-12-X*) BkMk.

Last Lamp. Sue Robishaw. LC 96-94137. 256p. 1996. pap. 14.95 (*0-9652036-0-3*) ManyTracks.

Last Lap: A Sequence in Verse on the Theme of Old Age. Fred P. Green. LC 91-76017. 57p. 1991. 6.95 (*0-916642-44-5*) Agape IL.

Last Lap: The Life & Times of NASCAR's Legendary Heroes. Peter Golenbock. 432p. 1999. 14.95 (*0-02-862825-X*, Pub. by Macmillan) S&S Trade.

Last Lap: The/Life & Times of NASCAR's Legendary Heros. Peter Golenbock. 432p. 1998. 24.95 (*0-02-862147-6*) Macmillan.

*__Last Laugh.__ Phil Berger. 2000. 17.95 (*0-8154-1096-4*) Cooper Sq.

Last Laugh. Lawrence Macapagal. 324p. (Orig.). 1996. mass mkt. 5.99 (*0-9655332-0-4*) Bravo Pr CA.

Last Laugh: A New Philosophy of Near-Death Experiences, Apparitions & the Paranormal. Raymond A. Moody, Jr. LC 98-71589. 196p. 1999. reprint ed. pap. 12.95 (*1-57174-106-2*) Hampton Roads Pub Co.

Last Laugh: Fifty Years of Unusual Undertakings. Edward C. Frederick, Sr. LC 98-209859. 247 p. 1997. pap. 9.95 (*0-9660722-1-9*, 97-LAST-01) Wicked Good.

*__Last Laugh: The Final Word from the First Name in Satire.__ S. J. Perelman. 192p. 2000. pap. 16.95 (*1-58574-152-3*) Lyons Pr.

Last Laugh & Other Stories. Hugo Martinez-Serros. LC 88-6359. 198p. (Orig.). 1988. pap. 9.50 (*0-934770-89-1*) Arte Publico.

Last Laugh, Mr. Moto. John P. Marquand. 192p. Date not set. 20.95 (*0-8488-2363-X*) Amereon Ltd.

Last Laughs: Perspectives on Women & Comedy. Regina Barreca. 322, vip. 1988. pap. text 26.00 (*0-677-22030-8*) Gordon & Breach.

Last Laughs: Perspectives on Women & Comedy, Vol. 2. Regina Barreca. vi, 322p. 1988. text 52.00 (*0-677-22020-0*) Gordon & Breach.

An Asterisk (*) at the beginning of an entry indicates that the title is appearing for the first time.

Last Laughs: The 1986 Mystery Writers of America Anthology. Gregory McDonald. (Illus.). 208p. 1986. 16.95 (*0-89296-246-1*, Pub. by Mysterious Pr) Little.
Last Law There Was. Bill Brooks. 288p. 1995. mass mkt. 3.99 (*0-8217-4908-0*, Pinncle Kensgtn) Kensgtn Pub Corp.
Last Lawmen. Jack Cummings. LC 94-8811. 177p. 1994. 19.95 (*0-8027-4143-6*) Walker & Co.
Last Leaf. Vinod D. Deshmukh. (Illus.). 191p. 1993. pap. 7.50 (*0-615-11302-8*) S V Deshmukh.
Last Leaf. O. Henry. Ed. by Walter Pauk & Raymond Harris. (Classics Ser.). (Illus.). 35p. (YA). (gr. 6-12). 1980. pap., teacher ed. 7.32 (*0-89061-197-1*, 415, Jamestwn Pub); pap. text 5.99 (*0-89061-195-5*, 413, Jamestwn Pub); audio 17.96 (*0-89061-196-3*, 414, Jamestwn Pub) NTC Contemp Pub Co.
Last Leaf. Bill Myers. 12.99 (*0-310-23091-8*) Zondervan.
Last Leaf. O'Henry & William Glennon. 56p. 1996. pap. 3.50 (*0-87129-691-8*, L84) Dramatic Pub.
Last Leaf. James K. Hosmer. (Notable American Authors Ser.). 1992. reprint ed. lib. bdg. 75.00 (*0-7812-3186-8*) Rprt Serv.
Last Leaf First Snowflake to Fall. Leo Yerxa. LC 93-5775. (Illus.). 32p. (J). (gr. k-3). 1994. 16.95 (*0-531-06824-2*) Orchard Bks Watts.
Last Leaf First Snowflake to Fall. Leo Yerxa. LC 93-5775. (Illus.). 32p. (J). (ps-3). 1994. lib. bdg. 17.99 (*0-531-08674-7*) Orchard Bks Watts.
Last Leap. Franklin W. Dixon. (Hardy Boys Casefiles Ser.: No. 118). (YA). (gr. 6 up). 1996. pap. 3.99 (*0-671-56118-9*) PB.
Last Leap. Franklin W. Dixon. (Hardy Boys Casefiles Ser.: No. 118). (YA). (gr. 6 up). 1996. 9.09 (*0-606-11432-7*, Pub. by Turtleback) Demco.
Last Leap. large type ed. Douglas Enefer. (Mystery Library). 272p. 1995. pap. 16.99 (*0-7089-7644-1*, Linford) Ulverscroft.
Last Lectures. Wilfrid P. Ward. LC 67-26793. (Essay Index Reprint Ser.). 1977. 24.95 (*0-8369-0976-3*) Ayer.
Last Left Standing. Barbara T. Russell. LC 94-16732. 128p. (J). (gr. 4-6). 1996. 14.95 (*0-395-71037-5*) Ticknor & Flds Bks Yng Read.
Last Left Standing. Barbara T. Russell. 1998. 9.60 (*0-606-13563-4*, Pub. by Turtleback) Demco.
Last Legion. Chris Bunch. Vol. 1. 344p. 1999. mass mkt. 6.99 (*0-451-45686-6*, ROC) NAL.
Last Lemurian: A Westralian Romance. G. Firth Scott. Ed. by R. Reginald & Douglas Melville. LC 77-84266. (Lost Race & Adult Fantasy Ser.). (Illus.). 1978. reprint ed. lib. bdg. 29.95 (*0-405-11007-3*) Ayer.
Last Leopard: A Life of Giuseppe di Lampedusa David Gilmour. LC 89-118118. 223p. 1988. write for info. (*0-7043-2564-0*) Quartet.
Last Lesson of the Afternoon. Christopher Rush. 320p. 1997. pap. 13.95 (*0-86241-649-3*, Pub. by Canongate Books) Interlink Pub.
Last Letter. Vilhelm Moberg. 1984. mass mkt. 3.63 (*0-446-38118-7*, Pub. by Warner Bks) Little.
Last Letter. Margaret Pemberton. LC 99-490220. 192p. 1998. 22.00 (*0-7278-5325-2*) Severn Hse.
Last Letter Home. Vilhelm Moberg. LC 95-15845. (Emigrant Novels Ser.: Bk. 4). xxxii, 230p. 1995. reprint ed. pap. 15.95 (*0-87351-322-3*, Borealis Book) Minn Hist.
Last Letters from Stalingrad. Tr. by Franz Schneider & Charles Gullans. LC 73-16870. (Illus.). 127p. 1974. reprint ed. lib. bdg. 59.50 (*0-8371-7240-3*, SCLL, Greenwood Pr) Greenwood.
Last Letters of Edgar Allan Poe to Sarah Helen Whitman. Sarah H. Whiteman. (Notable American Authors Ser.). 1999. reprint ed. lib. bdg. 125.00 (*0-7812-9943-8*) Rprt Serv.
***Last Letters of Thomas More.** Ed. by Alvaro De Silva. LC 00-23125. 225p. 2000. 20.00 (*0-8028-3886-3*) Eerdmans.
Last Liberty: The Biography of the S. S. Jeremiah O'Brien. Walter W. Jaffee. LC 93-79678. (Illus.). 1994. 29.95 (*0-9637586-0-8*) Glencannon Pr.
Last Liberty Ship. John C. Pine. 32p. (Orig.). 1997. pap. 7.50 (*0-943430-05-4*) Moveable Feast Pr.
Last Licks: A Spaldeen Story. Cari Best. LC 97-43606. (Illus.). 40p. (YA). (gr. 1 up). 1999. text 15.95 (*0-7894-2513-0*, D K Ink) DK Pub Inc.
***Last Licks: A Spaldeen Story.** Carl Best. 40p. (J). 2000. pap. text 5.95 (*0-7894-2656-0*, D K Ink) DK Pub Inc.
Last Lieutenant, John J. Gobbell. 1997. mass mkt. 6.99 (*0-312-95838-2*) St Martin.
***Last Life.** Claire Messud. 480p. 2000. pap. 14.00 (*0-15-601165-4*) Harcourt.
Last Life: A Novel. Claire Messud. LC 99-25612. 368p. 1999. 24.00 (*0-15-100471-4*, Harvest Bks) Harcourt.
Last Light of Day: Landscape of the Delaware River. Photos by Douglas Petersen. (Illus.). 48p. 1997. 50.00 (*0-9655747-0-9*) Deerfield Edtns.
***Last Line of Defense.** Jeff Kaye. LC 99-91866. 2000. 25.00 (*0-7388-1346-X*); pap. 18.00 (*0-7388-1347-8*) Xlibris Corp.
Last Lines: An Index to the Last Lines of Poetry, 2 vols., Set. Victoria Kline. 2880p. 1991. 145.00 (*0-8160-1265-2*) Facts on File.
Last Linotype: The Story of Georgia & Its Newspapers since World War II. Millard B. Grimes. (Illus.). x, 673p. 1985. 24.95 (*0-86554-190-6*, H176) Mercer Univ Pr.
Last Lion. William Manchester. 1996. write for info. (*0-316-54770-0*) Little.
Last Lion: Biography of Winston Churchill, 1932-40. William Manchester. (Illus.). 800p. (gr. 8). 1988. 45.00 (*0-316-54512-0*) Little.
Last Lion: Visions of Glory: Winston Spencer Churchill. William Manchester. 992p. 1984. pap. 19.95 (*0-385-31348-9*, Delta Trade) Dell.
Last Lion: Winston Spencer Churchill Visions of Glory, 1874-1932. William Manchester. LC 82-24972. (Illus.). 973p. (gr. 8). 1983. 45.00 (*0-316-54503-1*) Little.
Last Lion - Winston Spencer Churchill: Alone, 1932-1940. William Manchester. 800p. 1989. pap. 19.95 (*0-385-31331-4*, Delta Trade) Dell.
Last Lion & Other Stories. Vincenti Blasco-Ibanez & Mariano J. Lorente. pap. 5.95 (*0-8283-1444-6*) Branden Bks.
Last Lists of My Mad Mother. Julie Jensen. 58p. (C). Date not set. pap. 5.60 (*1-58342-016-9*, L96) Dramatic Pub.
Last Lobo. Roalnd Smith. LC 98-42656. 224p. (J). (gr. 5-9). 1999. lib. bdg. 16.49 (*0-7868-2378-X*, Pub. by Disney Pr) Little.
Last Lobo. Roland Smith. LC 98-42656. 178p. (YA). (gr. 5-9). 1999. 15.99 (*0-7868-0428-9*, Pub. by Mouse Works) Time Warner.
***Last Log of the Titanic.** David G. Brown. 224p. 2000. 19.95 (*0-07-136447-1*) McGraw.
Last Long Journey. Roger Cleeve. LC 83-18172. (Phoenix Fiction Ser.). 272p. 1984. pap. 9.95 (*0-226-10990-9*) U Ch Pr.
Last Look. Clyde Robert Bulla. (J). 1995. 9.19 (*0-606-07774-X*, Pub. by Turtleback) Demco.
Last Look at the Old Met. Judith Clancy. LC 79-103983. (Illus.). 54p. 1969. bds. 9.95 (*0-912184-10-8*) Synergistic Pr.
Last Looks. Grace McKeaney. 1984. pap. 5.25 (*0-8222-0636-6*) Dramatists Play.
Last Lords of Palenque: The Lacandon Mayas of the Mexican Rain Forest. Victor Perera & Robert D. Bruce. (Illus.). 320p. 1985. pap. 15.95 (*0-520-05309-5*, Pub. by U CA Pr) Cal Prin Full Svc.
Last (Lose & Stay Trim) Program: A Holistic Approach to Weight Loss. Melissa Caron. 87p. 1997. ring bd. 29.00 (*0-9657924-0-4*, 1001) Write Prodns.
***Last Love in Constantinople: A Tarot Novel for Divination.** Milorad Pavic. 1999. pap. 14.95 (*0-8023-1330-2*) Dufour.
Last Love in Constantinople: A Tarot Novel for Divination. Milorad Pavic. 176p. 1997. 29.95 (*0-7206-1035-4*, Pub. by P Owen Ltd) Dufour.
Last Love in Constantinople: A Tarot Novel for Divination. Milorad Pavic & Christina Pribchevich-Zoric. 184p. 1998. 23.95 (*0-8023-1323-X*) Dufour.
Last Lovely City: Stories. Alice Adams. LC 98-14585. 208p. 1999. 22.00 (*0-679-45441-1*) Knopf.
***Last Lovely City: Stories.** Alice Adams. 208p. 2000. reprint ed. per. 12.95 (*0-671-03618-1*, WSP) PB.
***Last Lover.** Laura Van Wormer. 2000. 22.95 (*1-55166-590-5*, 1-66590-0, Mira Bks) Harlequin Bks.
***Last Lovers on Earth: Stories from Dark Times.** Charles Ortleb. LC 99-74518. 150p. 1999. pap. write for info. (*0-9663454-2-8*) Rubicon Media.
Last Lullaby. Talat S. Hallman. Ed. by Stanley H. Barkan. (Review Turkish Writers Chapbook Ser.: No. 4). 48p. 1989. 15.00 (*0-89304-290-0*); pap. 5.00 (*0-89304-291-9*); pap. 5.00 (*0-685-26721-0*) Cross-Cultrl NY.
Last Lullaby: Mini. Talat S. Hallman. Ed. by Stanley H. Barkan. (Review Turkish Writers Chapbook Ser.: No. 4). 48p. 1989. 15.00 (*0-685-26720-2*) Cross-Cultrl NY.
Last Lullaby: Poetry from the Holocaust. Ed. & Tr. by Aaron Kramer. LC 97-21242. 224p. 1997. 29.95 (*0-8156-0478-5*) Syracuse U Pr.
Last Lullaby: Poetry from the Holocaust. Ed. & Tr. by Aaron Kramer. (Illus.). 1999. pap. 19.95 (*0-8156-0579-X*) Syracuse U Pr.
Last Lutanist & Other Poems. Dean B. Lyman. LC 73-144722. (Yale Series of Younger Poets: No. 15). reprint ed. 18.00 (*0-404-53815-0*) AMS Pr.
Last Machine: Early Cinema & the Birth of the Modern World. Ian Christie. (Illus.). 128p. 1995. pap. 9.95 (*0-85170-505-7*) Ind U Pr.
Last Madam: A Life in the New Orleans Underworld. Christine Wiltz. LC 99-43956. (Illus.). 288p. 2000. 20.00 (*0-571-19954-2*) Faber & Faber.
Last Mafioso. Ovid Demaris. 1980. mass mkt. write for info. (*0-394-59540-8*) Random.
Last Magic Summer: A Season with My Son. Peter Gent. 240p. 1998. reprint ed. pap. 13.00 (*0-688-15561-8*, Quil) HarperTrade.
Last Magician. Stephen Corey. LC 87-60412. 61p. (Orig.). 1987. pap. 7.95 (*0-930501-16-0*) Swallows Tale Pr.
Last Magician. Hospital. 1992. pap. 18.99 (*0-7710-4224-8*) McCland & Stewart.
Last Magician. 2nd rev. ed. Stephen Corey. LC 97-60412. (Illus.). 61p. (Orig.). 1987. pap. 7.95 (*0-930501-17-9*) Swallows Tale Pr.
Last Magician in Blue Haven. Mark Roessler. LC 94-75954. (Illus.). 52p. (Orig.). (J). (gr. 4-8). 1994. pap. 10.00 (*0-9638293-0-0*) Hundelrut Studio.
Last Maharani of Gwalior: An Autobiography. Vijaya R. Scindia & Manohar Malgonkar. LC 87-10134. (Illus.). 279p. (C). 1987. pap. text 16.95 (*0-88706-659-3*) State U NY Pr.
Last Makings. Earle Birney. LC 91-167607. 1991. pap. 14.95 (*0-7710-1471-6*) McCland & Stewart.
Last Mammoth. Margaret Allan. 400p. (Orig.). 1995. mass mkt. 4.99 (*0-451-18463-7*, Sig) NAL.
Last Man. Maurice Blanchot. Tr. by Lydia Davis. (Twentieth-Century Continental Fiction Ser.). 1987. text 34.50 (*0-231-06244-3*) Col U Pr.
Last Man. Mary Wollstonecraft Shelley. Ed. by Anne McWhir. 480p. 1996. pap. 13.95 (*1-55111-076-8*) Broadview Pr.
Last Man. Mary Wollstonecraft Shelley. 1999. pap. 4.95 (*0-451-52576-0*, Sig Classics) NAL.
Last Man. Mary Wollstonecraft Shelley. Ed. & Intro. by Morton D. Paley. LC 98-207341. (Oxford World's Classics Ser.). 512p. 1998. pap. 11.95 (*0-19-283865-2*) OUP.
Last Man. Mary Wollstonecraft Shelley. Ed. by Hugh J. Luke, Jr. LC 92-41933. xxx, 342p. 1993. pap. 14.95 (*0-8032-9217-1*, Bison Books) U of Nebr Pr.
Last Man: Or, Omegarus & Syderia, a Romance in Futurity, 2 vols. Jean B. De Grainville. LC 77-84246. (Lost Race & Adult Fantasy Ser.). 1978. reprint ed. lib. bdg. 39.95 (*0-405-10992-X*) Ayer.
Last Man Alive. Gordon D. Shirreffs. 144p. 1989. pap. 2.95 (*0-380-70642-3*, Avon Bks) Morrow Avon.
Last Man In. Richard E. Braun. (Illus.). 1990. 20.00 (*0-912330-71-6*) Jargon Soc.
Last Man in Montana. Kristine Rolofson. 1997. per. 3.50 (*0-373-25717-1*, 1-25717-9) Silhouette.
***Last Man in Texas: The Malloy Men.** Jan Freed. (Superromance Ser.: Bk. 918). 2000. per. 4.50 (*0-373-70918-8*, 1-70918-7) Harlequin Bks.
Last Man in Town. Susan K. Law. 384p. 1999. mass mkt. 5.99 (*0-380-80496-4*, Avon Bks) Morrow Avon.
Last Man Jailed for Blasphemy. Stephen Papa. LC 97-91370. 92p. 1998. pap. 10.00 (*0-9660325-1-9*) Trillium Bks.
***Last Man on Moon.** Cernan. 2000. mass mkt. write for info. (*0-312-97303-9*) St Martin.
Last Man on the Moon. 5th ed. Eugene A. Cernan & Don Davis. LC 98-48206. (Illus.). 356p. 1999. text 24.95 (*0-312-19906-6*) St Martin.
***Last Man on the Moon: Astronaut Eugene Cernan & America's Race in Space.** Eugene Cernan & Don Davis. (Illus.). 368p. 2000. pap. 14.95 (*0-312-26351-1*, St Martin Griffin) St Martin.
Last Man Out. H. Robert Charles. Ed. by Melissa Roberts. (Illus.). 394p. 1988. 16.95 (*0-89015-647-6*) Sunbelt Media.
Last Man Out. James E. Parker, Jr. 240p. 1997. pap. text 14.95 (*1-887269-33-9*) J Culler & Sons.
Last Man Out. large type ed. Donald Honig. 297p. 1995. 29.50 (*0-7089-5804-4*) Ulverscroft.
***Last Man Out: A Personal Account of the Vietnam War.** James E. Parker, Jr. 256p. 2000. mass mkt. 6.99 (*0-8041-1941-4*) Ivy Books.
Last Man Out: A Personal Account of the Vietnam War. James E. Parker, Jr. (Illus.). 240p. 1997. 23.95 (*1-887269-22-3*) J Culler & Sons.
Last Man Out of China. Ben Hansen. LC 90-80535. 331p. (Orig.). 1990. pap. 11.95 (*0-944806-02-3*) Icarus Press.
Last Man Running. Chris Boucher. 1998. pap. 5.95 (*0-563-40594-5*) BBC.
Last Man Standing. George Chambers. 142p. 1990. 16.95 (*0-932511-19-8*); pap. 8.95 (*0-932511-20-1*) Fiction Coll.
Last Man Standing. Jerome Preisler. 1996. mass mkt. 5.99 (*1-57297-185-1*) Blvd Books.
***Last Man Standing: The Tragedy & Triumph of Geronimo Pratt.** Jack Olsen. LC 00-29436. 384p. 2000. 26.95 (*0-385-49367-3*) Doubleday.
Last Manly Man: A Robin Hudson Mystery. Sparkle Hayter. LC 97-40943. 256p. 1998. 22.00 (*0-688-15517-0*, Wm Morrow) Morrow Avon.
***Last Manly Man: A Robin Hudson Mystery.** Sparkle Hayter. 256p. 1999. reprint ed. pap. 9.95 (*0-688-16972-4*, Wm Morrow) Morrow Avon.
Last Man's Reward. David Patneaude. 192p. (J). (gr. 5-8). 1996. lib. bdg. 14.95 (*0-8075-4370-5*) A Whitman.
Last Man's Reward. David Patneaude. 192p. (YA). (gr. 5-8). 1998. pap. 4.95 (*0-8075-4371-3*) A Whitman.
***Last Man's Reward.** David Patneaude. (J). 1998. 10.05 (*0-606-13564-2*, Pub. by Turtleback) Demco.
***Last Marlin: A Father-Son Story.** Fred Waitzkin. LC 99-46887. 246p. 2000. 23.95 (*0-670-88261-5*, Viking) Viking Penguin.
Last Mass of the Knights Templars. Judith Long. LC 98-91410. 1998. pap. 13.95 (*0-533-12656-8*) Vantage.
Last Master. Gordon Rupert Dickson. 320p. (Orig.). 1984. pap. 2.95 (*0-8125-3562-6*, Pub. by Tor Bks) St Martin.
Last Master: Passion & Anger. John Suchet. 624p. 1998. pap. 14.95 (*0-316-88532-0*) Little.
Last Master Vol. 2: Passion & Pain. John Suchet. 624p. 1999. pap. 16.00 (*0-316-68898-3*) Little.
***Last Master Vol. 3: Passion & Glory.** John Suchet. 416p. 1999. pap. 15.95 (*0-316-88255-0*) Little.
***Last Masterpiece: Frederic Church & Olana.** Stuart Murray. (Illus.). 208p. 2001. 25.00 (*1-884592-27-9*) Images from the Past.
***Last Masters of the Kremlin.** Garri Tabachnik. (RUS.). 516p. 2000. pap. 26.95 (*0-595-00077-0*, toExcel) iUniversecom.
***Last Matriarch.** Sharman Apt Russell. LC 99-6657. 198p. 2000. 19.95 (*0-8263-2131-3*) U of NM Pr.
Last Matriarch. Kisma Stepanich. (Illus.). 312p. 1999. pap. 12.95 (*1-56718-693-9*) Llewellyn Pubns.
Last Meeting of the Knights of the White Magnolia. Preston Jones. 1976. pap. 5.25 (*0-8222-0637-4*) Dramatists Play.
Last Meeting's Lost Cause. Estill C. Pennington. LC 88-91008. (Illus.). 67p. (Orig.). 1988. pap. 20.00 (*0-9632836-4-2*) R M Hicklin.
Last Message from a Distant Star. Little Crow. 27p. 1993. spiral bd. 7.00 (*0-9635440-2-0*) One Wrld Pub.
Last Metro: Francois Truffaut, Director. Ed. by Mirella J. Affron & E. Rubinstein. (Films in Print Ser.). (Illus.). 160p. (C). 1985. 35.00 (*0-8135-1065-1*); pap. 17.00 (*0-8135-1066-X*) Rutgers U Pr.
Last Mile. Francis Neilson. 1971. 250.00 (*0-685-26316-9*) Revisionist Pr.
***Last Mile: Broadband & the Next Internet Revolution.** Jason Wolf. (Illus.). 268p. 2000. 24.95 (*0-07-136349-1*) McGraw.
Last Mile to Huesca. Judith Keene. (Illus.). 178p. 1988. pap. 24.95 (*0-86840-338-5*, Pub. by New South Wales Univ Pr) Intl Spec Bk.
***Last Millennium: A Fresh Look at The Remarkable Days Ahead.** Mac Hammond. 1999. pap. text 13.99 (*1-57794-239-6*) Harrison Hse.
Last Million Years: A History of the Pleistocene in North America. Arthur P. Coleman. LC 75-41062. (BCL Ser.: Ii). reprint ed. 49.50 (*0-404-14656-2*) AMS Pr.
***Last-Minute Bridegroom.** Linda Miles. 1999. mass mkt. 3.50 (*0-373-17439-X*) Harlequin Bks.
Last-Minute Christmas Gifts: Crafting Quick & Classy Presents for Everyone on Your List. Carol Taylor. (Illus.). 128p. 1996. pap. 14.95 (*0-8069-3196-5*) Sterling.
***Last Minute College Financing: It's Never Too Late to Prepare for the Future.** Daniel J. Cassidy. 128p. 2000. pap. 10.99 (*1-56414-468-2*) Career Pr Inc.
Last Minute Cover Letters. Brandon Toropov. LC 98-19376. 160p. 1998. pap. 9.99 (*1-56414-353-8*) Career Pr Inc.
Last Minute Estate Planning: It's Never Too Late to Plan for the Future. Stephen Rosenberg. LC 98-46523. (Last Minute Ser.). 160p. 1998. pap. 9.99 (*1-56414-393-7*) Career Pr Inc.
Last Minute Gifts. Eleanor Burns. 9p. 1991. pap. 6.95 (*0-922705-32-1*) Quilt Day.
Last-Minute Interview Tips. Brandon Toropov. 128p. (Orig.). 1996. pap. 7.99 (*1-56414-240-X*) Career Pr Inc.
***Last Minute Lists: If You Had Only 15 Minutes to Evacuate, What Would You Take With You?** Sandrajeanne Bushell. (Illus.). 46p. 1999. 10.00 (*1-58499-006-6*, 190) Full Spectrums.
***Last-Minute Marriage.** Marisa Carroll. (Superromance Ser.: Bk. 942). 2000. mass mkt. 4.50 (*0-373-70942-0*, 1-70942-7) Harlequin Bks.
***Last-Minute Marriage.** Karen Toller Whittenburg. (Harlequin American Romance Ser.: Vol. 822). 249p. 2000. mass mkt. 4.25 (*0-373-16822-5*) Harlequin Bks.
***Last Minute Meetings.** Fern Dickey. 160p. 2000. pap. 11.99 (*1-56414-497-6*) Career Pr Inc.
Last Minute Optics: A Concise Review of Optics, Refraction & Contact Lenses. David G. Hunter & Constance E. West. LC 96-6823. (Illus.). 144p. 1996. pap. 35.00 (*1-55642-317-9*, 63179) SLACK Inc.
Last Minute Resumes. Brandon Toropov. LC 98-19375. 160p. 1998. pap. 9.99 (*1-56414-354-6*) Career Pr Inc.
Last Minute Retirement Planning: It's Never Too Late to Plan for the Future. Stephen Rosenberg. LC 98-34860. (Last Minute Ser.). 160p. 1998. pap. 9.99 (*1-56414-376-7*) Career Pr Inc.
***Last Minute Speeches & Toasts.** Andrew Frothingham. (Last Minute Ser.). 160p. 2000. pap. 11.99 (*1-56414-493-3*) Career Pr Inc.
Last Minute Study Tips. Ron Fry. (Last Minute Ser.). 128p. 1996. pap. 7.99 (*1-56414-238-8*) Career Pr Inc.
***Last Minute Weddings: It's Still Not Too Late to Plan the Celebration of Your Dreams.** Donna Bankhead & Lynette Blas. LC 99-22503. 128p. 1999. pap. 10.99 (*1-56414-415-1*) Career Pr Inc.
Last Mission. Harry Mazer. LC 79-50674. 192p. (YA). (gr. 7 up). 1981. mass mkt. 4.99 (*0-440-94797-9*, LE) Dell.
Last Mission. Harry Mazer. 192p. (YA). (gr. 7 up). pap. 4.99 (*0-8072-1366-7*) Listening Lib.
Last Mission. Harry Mazer. (Laurel-Leaf Historical Fiction Ser.). 1979. 9.60 (*0-606-02154-X*, Pub. by Turtleback) Demco.
Last Mission: Americans in the R. A. F. Clifford E. Santa. (Illus.). x, 308p. (Orig.). 1998. pap. 16.95 (*0-9645173-2-9*) Four Dir Pub.
Last Mission: Americans In The R.A.F., 1. Clifford E. Santa. 1998. pap. text 16.95 (*0-9669872-0-9*) Duluth.
Last Mission: Behind the Iron Curtain. Stevyn Gibson. LC 98-177760. (Military History Ser.). (Illus.). 224p. 1998. 33.95 (*0-7509-1408-4*, Pub. by Sutton Pub Ltd) Intl Pubs Mktg.
Last Mission - An Eye Witness Account by Jim B. Smith: The B-29 Raid That Ended WWII. A. N. T. Publications Staff & Jim B. Smith. (Illus.). 359p. 1995. text 40.00 (*0-9647476-0-X*) J B Smith.
Last Mission Tanker. Walter W. Jaffee. LC 95-79380. (Illus.). 80p. 1995. pap. 9.95 (*0-9637586-5-9*) Glencannon Pr.
***Last Modem Book.** William Flanagan & Robert Abbott. 224p. 1999. pap. 34.95 (*1-57820-039-3*, Pub. by Telecom Bks) Publishers Group.
Last Modernist: The Films of Theo Angelopoulos. Ed. by Andrew Horton. 144p. 1997. pap. 24.95 (*0-275-96119-2*, Praeger Pubs) Greenwood.
Last Modernist: The Films of Theo Angelopoulos, 66. Ed. by Andrew Horton. LC 97-17113. (Contributions to the Study of Popular Culture: 66). 144p. 1997. 62.95 (*0-313-30564-1*, Greenwood Pr) Greenwood.
***Last Mogul.** Thomas E. Mountin. 2001. text 27.50 (*0-8050-6186-X*) St Martin.
***Last Mogul.** Thomas E. Mountin. 2002. text 15.95 (*0-8050-6187-8*) St Martin.
***Last Monarch.** Murphy & Sapir. (Destroyer Ser.: Bk. 120). 352p. 2000. mass mkt. 5.99 (*0-373-63235-5*, 1-63235-5, Wrldwide Lib) Harlequin Bks.
***Last Mongol Prince: The Life & Times of Demchugdongrob, 1902-1966.** Sechin Jagchid. LC 99-51349. (Studies on East Asia: Vol. 21). (Illus.). 500p. (C). 1999. pap. 50.00 (*0-914584-21-9*) WWUCEAS.
Last Monopoly: Privatizing the Postal Service for the Information Age. Edward L. Hudgins. LC 96-30393. 148p. 1996. 19.95 (*1-882577-31-0*); pap. text 9.95 (*1-882577-32-9*) Cato Inst.
Last Months of Chaucer's Earliest Patron. Albert S. Cook. (Connecticut Academy of Arts & Sciences Ser., Trans.: Vol. 21). 1916. pap. 75.00 (*0-685-22843-6*) Elliots Bks.

Last Months of Chaucer's Earliest Patron. Albert S. Cook. LC 72-1000. reprint ed. 29.50 (*0-404-01698-7*) AMS Pr.

***Last Mortal Generation.** Damien Broderick. 272p. 2000. pap. 14.95 (*1-86436-440-8*, Pub. by New Holland) BHB Intl.

Last Mountain. Robert C. Fleet. 304p. (Orig.). 1994. mass mkt. 4.99 (*0-441-00062-2*) Ace Bks.

Last Mountain: A Life in Papua New Guinea. Ian Downs. LC 85-31585. (Illus.). 298p. 1987. text 29.95 (*0-7022-1985-1*, Pub. by Univ Queensland Pr) Intl Spec Bk.

Last Mountain: The Life of Robert Wood. Violet S. Flume. 1983. 25.95 (*0-8283-1829-8*); pap. 14.95 (*0-8283-1878-6*) Branden Bks.

Last Mountain Man. William W. Johnstone. 208p. 1986. mass mkt. 3.50 (*0-8217-4084-9*, Zebra Kensgtn) Kensgtn Pub Corp.

Last Mountain Man. William W. Johnstone. 208p. 1996. mass mkt. 4.99 (*0-8217-5274-X*, Zebra Kensgtn) Kensgtn Pub Corp.

***Last Mountain Man.** William W. Johnstone. 2000. mass mkt. 5.99 (*0-8217-6856-5*, Zebra Kensgtn) Kensgtn Pub Corp.

Last Mountain Man. large type ed. William W. Johnstone. LC 97-43674. 234p. 1998. 22.95 (*0-7838-8391-9*, G K Hall & Co) Mac Lib Ref.

Last Muckraker. Guttenplan. 1999. pap. 15.00 (*0-06-099501-7*) HarpC.

Last Mughal. G. D. Khosla. 1986. 36.00 (*81-7013-040-9*, Pub. by Navarang) S Asia.

Last Narrow Gauge Train Robbery: An Adventure Novel. Robert K. Swisher, Jr. LC 87-6491. 96p. (Orig.). 1987. pap. 8.95 (*0-86534-106-0*) Sunstone Pr.

Last Navigator: A Young Man, an Ancient Mariner, a Secret of the Sea. Stephen D. Thomas. LC 97-20220. (Illus.). 307p. 1997. pap. 15.95 (*0-07-064574-4*) McGraw.

***Last Nazi.** Roger Morse. 440p. 1999. 28.00 (*0-9671046-0-2*) N Bushwick Inc.

Last Neanderthal. Michael Van Walleghen. LC 98-40137. (Poetry Ser.). 1999. write for info. (*0-8229-5691-8*) U of Pittsburgh Pr.

***Last Neanderthal.** Michael Van Walleghen. 1999. write for info. (*0-8229-4092-2*) U of Pittsburgh Pr.

Last Neanderthal. Michael Van Walleghen. (Pitt Poetry Ser.). 88p. 1999. pap. 12.95 (*0-8229-5696-9*) U of Pittsburgh Pr.

Last Neanderthal: The Rise, Success & Mysterious Extinction of Our Closest Human Relatives. Ian Tattersall. LC 99-40327. 208p. 1999. pap. 25.00 (*0-8133-3675-9*, Pub. by Westview) HarpC.

Last Neanderthal: The Rise, Success & Mysterious Extinction of Our Closest Human Relatives. Ian Tattersall. (Illus.). 208p. 1999. reprint ed. text 40.00 (*0-7881-6103-2*) DIANE Pub.

Last New Land: Stories of Alaska, Past & Present. Ed. by Wayne Mergler. LC 96-30733. (Illus.). 816p. 1996. 34.95 (*0-88240-481-4*, Alaska NW Bks); pap. 22.95 (*0-88240-483-0*, Alaska NW Bks) Gr Arts Ctr Pub.

***Last New World: The Conquest of the Amazon Frontier.** Mac Margolis. (Illus.). 367p. 2000. 23.00 (*0-7881-9395-3*) DIANE Pub.

Last Night. Meryl Sawyer. 448p. 1995. mass mkt. 6.50 (*0-440-22050-5*) Dell.

Last Night. Meryl Sawyer. 448p. 1996. 24.00 (*0-7278-4998-0*) Severn Hse.

Last Night: The Letter from an Unknown Lover. Christian Van Devere. 68p. 1997. pap. 8.95 (*1-57502-636-8*, PO 1806) Morris Pubng.

***Last Night a DJ Saved My Life: The History of the Disc Jockey.** Bill Brewster & Frank Broughton. 336p. 2000. pap. 14.00 (*0-8021-3688-5*, Pub. by Grove-Atltic) Publishers Group.

Last Night at Patty's Saloon. Julie Ryan. (Illus.). (Orig.). 1996. pap. 4.50 (*0-942186-05-2*) Paperbacks Plus.

***Last Night I Danced with a Stranger: An Enlightening Guide to Dream Analysis.** Kirsten Hall. (Illus.). 160p. 2000. 7.98 (*1-57912-106-3*, 81106) Blck Dog & Leventhal.

Last Night I Had a Dream. Brenda Hall. LC 94-68460. (Illus.). 12p. (J). (gr. 1-3). 1994. pap. 7.95 (*0-9637515-7-3*) Dageforde Pub.

Last Night I Had the Strangest Dream: A Peace Reader. Michael Eckert. 98p. (C). 1997. per. 37.95 (*0-7872-3961-5*, 41396101) Kendall-Hunt.

***Last Night I Spent with You: A Novel.** Mayra Montero. Tr. by Edith Grossman. LC 99-86223. 128p. 2000. 19.95 (*0-06-095290-3*) HarpC.

Last Night in Paradise. Katie Roiphe. LC 97-12006. 1997. pap. 12.00 (*0-375-70053-6*) Vin Bks.

Last Night in Rio. Janice Kaiser. 1996. per. 5.99 (*1-55166-174-8*, 1-66174-3, Mira Bks) Harlequin Bks.

Last Night of Ballyhoo. Alfred Uhry. LC 98-164896. 1997. pap. 5.25 (*0-8222-1617-5*) Dramatists Play.

Last Night of Ballyhoo. Alfred Uhry. LC 97-40179. 96p. 1997. pap. text 10.95 (*1-55936-140-9*) Theatre Comm.

Last Night of the Earth Poems. Charles Bukowski. LC 91-45022. 405p. 1998. reprint ed. 25.00 (*0-87685-864-7*); reprint ed. pap. 16.00 (*0-87685-863-9*) Black Sparrow.

Last Night While I Lay Dreaming. Tamany Reinhart. 1998. pap. write for info. (*1-58235-024-8*) Watermrk Pr.

Last Nightmare. John Michael. 118p. (Orig.). 1988. pap. 7.95 (*0-945644-00-0*) Intl Pub Inc.

Last Night's Fun: A Book about Irish Traditional Music. Ciaran Carson. 1997. 21.00 (*0-86547-515-6*) N Point Pr.

Last Night's Fun: In & Out of Time with Irish Music. Ciaran Carson. 1998. 12.00 (*0-86547-531-8*) N Point Pr.

***Last Night's Fun: In & Out of Time with Irish Music.** Ciaran Carson. 198p. 2000. reprint ed. text 21.00 (*0-7881-9087-3*) DIANE Pub.

Last Nights of Paris. Philippe Soupault. Tr. by William Carlos Williams from FRE.Tr. of Les/Dernieres Nuits de Paris. 192p. 1992. reprint ed. pap. 13.95 (*1-878972-05-7*) Exact Change.

Last Nine Days of the Bismarck. C. S. Forester. (J). 18.95 (*0-89190-606-1*) Amereon Ltd.

Last Nine Days of the Bismarck. C. S. Forester. (J). 1959. 14.45 (*0-685-03074-1*) Little.

Last Ninety Days of the War in North Carolina. Cornelia P. Spencer. 287p. 1993. 30.00 (*1-56837-049-0*) Broadfoot.

Last Noel. Jean Hager. LC 97-93748. (Iris House B & B Mystery Ser.). 224p. 1997. mass mkt. 5.99 (*0-380-78637-0*, Avon Bks) Morrow Avon.

Last Noo-Noo. Jill Murphy. LC 94-48927. (Illus.). 32p. (J). (ps up). 1995. 15.99 (*1-56402-581-0*) Candlewick Pr.

Last Noo-Noo. Jill Murphy. (Illus.). 32p. (J). 1998. pap. 5.99 (*0-7636-0391-0*) Candlewick Pr.

***Last Nostalgia: Poems, 1982-1990.** Joe Bolton. LC 99-10535. 1999. pap. 24.00 (*1-55728-558-6*) U of Ark Pr.

Last Notes from Home. Frederick Exley. (Vintage Contemporaries Ser.). 1990. pap. 14.00 (*0-679-72456-7*) Vin Bks.

Last Oasis. Daphne Glazer. 186p. 1993. 13.95 (*0-7126-5264-7*, Pub. by CEN3) Trafalgar.

Last Oasis. 2nd ed. Sandra Postel. LC 97-202393. 1997. pap. 12.95 (*0-393-31744-7*) Norton.

Last of a Breed. Errol D. Severe. LC 96-94739. (Illus.). 366p. 1997. 39.95 (*0-9656957-0-0*) Lighthouse Prodns.

Last of American Freemen: Studies in the Political Culture of the Colonial & Revolutionary South. Robert M. Weir. LC 85-28391. xiv, 236p. 1986. text 25.95 (*0-86554-174-4*, MUP-H164) Mercer Univ Pr.

Last of Days. Moris Farhi. 1984. mass mkt. 3.95 (*0-8217-1485-6*, Zebra Kensgtn) Kensgtn Pub Corp.

Last of Deeds. Eoin McNamee. 96p. 1990. 19.95 (*1-85186-053-3*) Dufour.

Last of Deeds & Love in History. Eoin McNamee. 192p. 1997. pap. 11.00 (*0-312-16879-9*) St Martin.

Last of England. Ted Walker. 224p. 1993. pap. 34.95 (*0-224-03211-9*, Pub. by Jonathan Cape) Trafalgar.

Last of Her Lies: A Maggie Garrett Mystery. Jean Taylor. LC 95-50395. 238p. (Orig.). 1996. pap. 10.95 (*1-878067-75-3*) Seal Pr WA.

Last of How It Was: A Novel. T. R. Pearson. 352p. 1995. pap. 15.00 (*0-8050-3757-8*, Owl) H Holt & Co.

Last of Mohicans. James Fenimore Cooper. 1991. mass mkt. 3.95 (*0-425-12674-9*) Berkley Pub.

Last of Mrs. Lincoln. James Prideaux. 1973. pap. 5.25 (*0-8222-0638-2*) Dramatists Play.

Last of Rose Sommer. Ralph Baber. 250p. 1998. pap. 6.95 (*0-9634733-2-8*) Ogden Pr TX.

Last of Steam. Joe G. Collias. LC 60-14067. (Illus.). 269p. 1994. 39.95 (*0-911581-32-4*); pap. 26.95 (*0-911581-34-0*) Heimburger Hse Pub.

Last of the African Kings. Maryse Conde. Tr. by Richard Philcox. LC 97-7661. xiv, 216p. 1997. pap. 12.00 (*0-8032-6384-8*, Bison Books); text 40.00 (*0-8032-1489-8*) U of Nebr Pr.

Last of the Balfrys. large type ed. Mark Carrel. (Linford Western Library). 272p. 1995. pap. 16.99 (*0-7089-7760-X*, Linford) Ulverscroft.

Last of the Bandit Riders . . . Revisited. Matt Warner et al. (Illus.). 252p. Date not set. reprint ed. pap. 24.95 (*0-9656694-1-6*) Big Moon Traders.

Last of the Barons. Brenda Clarke. 224p. 1998. 24.00 (*0-7278-5311-2*) Severn Hse.

***Last of the Barons.** large type ed. Brenda Clarke. 360p. 1999. 31.99 (*0-7089-4143-5*) Ulverscroft.

Last of the Barons, 3 vols., 2 bks., Set. Edward Bulwer Lytton. LC 79-8159. reprint ed. 84.50 (*0-404-62176-7*) AMS Pr.

***Last of the Barons (1843)** Edward Bulwer Lytton. 350p. 1999. reprint ed. pap. 24.95 (*0-7661-0797-3*) Kessinger Pub.

Last of the Bighams. J. A. Zeigler. 230p. 1984. pap. 7.95 (*0-87844-056-9*) Sandlapper Pub Co.

Last of the Black Emperors: The Hollow Comeback of Marion Barry in the New Age Black Leaders. Jonetta R. Barras. 287p. (Orig.). 1998. pap. 24.00 (*0-9631246-6-8*) Bancroft MD.

Last of the Blue Water Hunters. Carlos Eyles. LC 91-179852. (Illus.). 186p. 1995. pap. 14.95 (*0-922769-15-X*, 34062) Aqua Quest.

Last of the Bohemians. Andre Beucler. Tr. by Geoffrey Sainsbury. LC 79-108841. 1971. reprint ed. lib. bdg. 65.00 (*0-8371-3729-2*, BEBO, Greenwood Pr) Greenwood.

Last of the Breed. Louis L'Amour. 384p. 1987. mass mkt. 5.50 (*0-553-28042-2*) Bantam.

Last of the Breed. Louis L'Amour. (J). 1987. 10.60 (*0-606-03599-0*, Pub. by Turtleback) Demco.

Last of the Breed. Alexander Steele. Ed. by Kevin Ryan. LC 98-86181. (Adventures of Wishbone Ser.: No. 16). (Illus.). 163p. (J). (gr. 4-7). 1999. pap. 3.99 (*1-57064-273-7*, Big Red) Lyrick Pub.

***Last of the Breed.** Alexander Steele & James Fenimore Cooper. LC 99-51755. (Illus.). (J). 2000. lib. bdg. write for info. (*0-8368-2594-2*) Gareth Stevens Inc.

Last of the Buffalo. George B. Grinnell. LC 78-125740. (American Environmental Studies). 1977. reprint ed. 13.95 (*0-405-02665-X*) Ayer.

Last of the Bush Pilots: The Incredible Adventures of the Pioneers of Flight in Alaska. Harmon Helmericks. 368p. 1997. pap. 9.95 (*0-89174-061-9*) Comstock Edns.

Last of the California Girls. Pamela Jekel. 1989. mass mkt. 4.50 (*0-8217-2725-7*, Zebra Kensgtn) Kensgtn Pub Corp.

Last of the Cape Horners. Claude L. Woollard. 1987. 50.00 (*0-7855-2000-7*, Pub. by A H S Ltd) St Mut.

Last of the Cape Horners. Claude L. Woollard. 303p. (C). 1989. 150.00 (*0-7223-9990-1*, Pub. by A H S Ltd); pap. 65.00 (*0-7223-2152-X*, Pub. by A H S Ltd) St Mut.

***Last of the Cape Horners: Firsthand Accounts from the Final Days of the Commercial Tall Ships.** Ed. by Spencer Apollonio. 2000. 26.95 (*1-57488-283-X*) Brasseys.

Last of the Cockleshell Heroes: A World War II Memoir. large type ed. William Sparks & Michael Munn. (Illus.). 215p. 1992. 20.95 (*1-85695-125-1*, Pub. by ISIS Lrg Prnt) Transaction Pubs.

***Last of the Cowboy Heroes: The Westerns of Randolph Scott, Joel McCrea & Audie Murphy.** Robert Nott. LC 99-58785. (Illus.). 205p. 2000. 32.50 (*0-7864-0762-X*) McFarland & Co.

Last of the Curlews. Fred Bodsworth. 136p. 1996. pap. text 5.95 (*0-7710-9874-X*) McCland & Stewart.

Last of the Curlews. Fred Bodsworth. 1993. reprint ed. lib. bdg. 18.95 (*1-56849-179-4*) Buccaneer Bks.

Last of the Dinosaurs. Ed. by Robert Long. (Illus.). 1978. pap. 3.95 (*0-88388-054-7*) Bellerophon Bks.

Last of the Dog Team. William W. Johnstone. 1981. mass mkt. 2.75 (*0-89083-736-8*, Zebra Kensgtn) Kensgtn Pub Corp.

Last of the Dog Team. William W. Johnstone. 352p. 1997. mass mkt. 4.99 (*0-7860-0427-4*, Pinncle Kensgtn) Kensgtn Pub Corp.

Last of the Dream People. Alice Anne Parker. LC 97-37454. 228p. 1998. pap. 12.95 (*0-915811-79-0*) H J Kramer Inc.

Last of the Duanes. large type ed. Zane Grey. 230p. 1996. 16.95 (*0-7862-0627-6*) Thorndike Pr.

Last of the Duanes. large type ed. Zane Grey. LC 95-47970. 401p. 1997. 21.95 (*0-7862-0629-2*) Thorndike Pr.

Last of the Duanes. Zane Grey. 320p. 1998. reprint ed. mass mkt. 4.99 (*0-8439-4430-7*, Leisure Bks) Dorchester Pub Co.

Last of the Empire. Sembene Ousmane. Tr. by Adrian Adams from FRE. (African Writers Ser.). Orig. Title: Le Dernier de L'Empire. 238p. (Orig.). (C). 1983. pap. 11.95 (*0-435-90250-4*, 90250) Heinemann.

Last of the Empires: A History of the Soviet Union, 1945-1991. John Keep. (Illus.). 490p. 1997. pap. text 18.95 (*0-19-289237-1*) OUP.

Last of the Fathers: James Madison & the Republican Legacy. Drew R. McCoy. (Illus.). 384p. (C). 1989. 47.95 (*0-521-36407-8*) Cambridge U Pr.

Last of the Fathers: James Madison & the Republican Legacy. Drew R. McCoy. (Illus.). 406p. (C). 1991. pap. text 19.95 (*0-521-40772-9*) Cambridge U Pr.

Last of the Fathers: Saint Bernard of Clairvaux & the Encyclical Letter, Doctor Mellifluus. Thomas Merton. LC 81-4105. 128p. 1981. pap. 8.00 (*0-15-649438-8*, Harvest Bks) Harcourt.

***Last of the Few: Forty-Two Years of Africian Safaris.** Tony Sanchez-Arino. 242p. 2000. 39.95 (*1-57157-168-X*) Safari Pr.

Last of the Flying Clippers: The Boeing B-314 Story. M. Klaas. LC 97-81405. 320p. 1998. 49.95 (*0-7643-0562-X*) Schiffer.

***Last of the Free: A Millennial History of the Highlands & Islands of Scotland.** James Hunter. 1999. 40.00 (*1-84018-029-3*, Pub. by Mainstream Pubng) Trafalgar.

***Last of the Gaderene.** Mark Gatiss. (Doctor Who Ser.). 288p. 2000. mass mkt. 6.95 (*0-563-55587-4*, Pub. by BBC Bks) Genl Dist Srvs.

Last of the Giants. George Otis, Jr. LC 91-21233. 272p. 1991. pap. 12.99 (*0-8007-9192-4*) Chosen Bks.

***Last of the Gold Diggers.** Harry Horse. 112p. 1998. pap. 7.95 (*0-14-037676-3*, Pub. by Pnguin Bks Ltd) Trafalgar.

Last of the Golden Girls. Susan Swan. 1991. lib. bdg. 19.95 (*1-55970-106-4*) Arcade Pub Inc.

Last of the Good Old Days. Josephine F. Collitt. (Illus.). 80p. 1998. pap. 11.95 (*0-9648441-4-1*) J F Collitt.

Last of the Great Expeditions. Andrew L. Christenson. (Illus.). 32p. 1987. 4.95 (*0-89734-060-4*, PL58-4) Mus Northern Ariz.

Last of the Great Scouts. Zane Grey. lib. bdg. 23.95 (*0-8488-1890-3*) Amereon Ltd.

Last of the Great Scouts. Zane Grey. 288p. 1996. mass mkt. 4.99 (*0-8125-6354-9*, Pub. by Forge NYC) St Martin.

Last of the Handmade Dams: The Story of the Ashokan Reservoir. rev. ed. Bob Steuding. LC 89-9381. (Illus.). 128p. 1989. pap. 12.50 (*0-935796-00-2*) Purple Mnt Pr.

Last of the Jews? Myron Berman. LC 98-38466. 1998. write for info. (*0-7618-1247-4*) U Pr of Amer.

Last of the Joeville Lovers. Anne Eames. 1998. per. 3.75 (*0-373-76142-2*, 1-76142-8) Silhouette.

***Last of the Just.** Andre Schwarz-Bart. Tr. by Stephen Becker from FRE. 374p. 2000. pap. 15.95 (*1-58567-016-2*, Pub. by Overlook Pr) Penguin Putnam.

Last of the Just. Andre Schwarz-Bart. Tr. by Stephen Becker from FRE. LC 60-11947. 374p. (C). 1973. reprint ed. pap. 15.95 (*0-689-70365-1*, 202) Atheneum Yung Read.

Last of the Just. Andre Schwarz-Bart. Tr. by Stephen Becker from FRE. LC 79-24071. 1981. reprint ed. lib. bdg. 22.00 (*0-8376-0456-7*) Bentley Pubs.

Last of the Just. Andre Schwarz-Bart. LC 96-76472. (Library of the Holocaust). 374p. 1996. reprint ed. 9.98 (*1-56731-140-7*, MJF Bks) Fine Comms.

Last of the Lairds. John Galt. 192p. 1989. 35.00 (*0-7073-0170-X*, Pub. by Mercat Pr Bks) St Mut.

Last of the Lightnings: Nostalgic Farewell RAF. Ian Black. (Illus.). 160p. 1996. 52.95 (*1-85260-541-3*, Pub. by J H Haynes & Co) Motorbooks Intl.

Last of the Logans. large type ed. Alex Stuart. 400p. 1989. 27.99 (*0-7089-1999-5*) Ulverscroft.

Last of the Lunatics. John Cawte. 272p. 1998. pap. 24.95 (*0-522-84804-4*, Pub. by Melbourne Univ Pr) Paul & Co Pubs.

***Last of the Maasai.** Mohamed Amin et al. (Illus.). 2000. 45.00 (*1-874041-32-6*, Pub. by Camerapix) Interlink Pub.

Last of the Market Hunters. Dale Hamm & David Bakke. LC 96-13329. 136p. (C). 1996. 29.95 (*0-8093-2075-4*) S Ill U Pr.

Last of the Menu Girls. Denise Chavez. LC 84-72304. 192p. (C). 1986. reprint ed. pap. 11.95 (*0-934770-46-8*) Arte Publico.

Last of the Moccasins. Charles Plymell. 1995. 20.00 (*0-9636829-8-9*); pap. 12.00 (*0-9636829-7-0*) Mother Road.

***Last of the Mohicans.** (Pengiun Readers Lv. 2). (C). 2000. 7.00 (*0-582-42177-2*) Pearson Educ.

Last of the Mohicans. James Fenimore Cooper. 432p. (J). (gr. 7). 1962. mass mkt. 4.95 (*0-451-52503-5*, Sig Classics) NAL.

***Last of the Mohicans.** James Fenimore Cooper. (Signet Classics Ser.). (Illus.). 416p. 2000. mass mkt. 4.95 (*0-451-52765-8*, Sig Classics) NAL.

Last of the Mohicans. James Fenimore Cooper. 1980. 10.05 (*0-606-02760-2*, Pub. by Turtleback) Demco.

Last of the Mohicans. James Fenimore Cooper. (Step-Up Classics). (J). 1993. 9.09 (*0-606-02705-X*, Pub. by Turtleback) Demco.

Last of the Mohicans. James Fenimore Cooper. (Classics Illustrated Study Guides Ser.). (Illus.). 1997. mass mkt. 4.99 (*1-57840-053-8*, Pub. by Acclaim Bks) Penguin Putnam.

Last of the Mohicans. James Fenimore Cooper. (Illustrated Classics Collection 3). 64p. 1994. pap. 4.95 (*0-7854-0699-9*, 40459) Am Guidance.

Last of the Mohicans. James Fenimore Cooper. 27.95 (*0-89190-895-1*) Amereon Ltd.

Last of the Mohicans. James Fenimore Cooper. (Bantam Classics Ser.). (Illus.). 377p. 1982. mass mkt. 4.95 (*0-553-21329-6*, Bantam Classics) Bantam.

Last of the Mohicans. James Fenimore Cooper. (J). 1989. 26.95 (*0-89968-254-5*) Buccaneer Bks.

Last of the Mohicans, 3 vols. James Fenimore Cooper. 30.00 (*0-614-30530-6*) NAVH.

Last of the Mohicans. James Fenimore Cooper. Ed. & Intro. by John McWilliams. (Oxford World's Classics Ser.). (Illus.). 458p. 1998. pap. 8.95 (*0-19-283505-X*) OUP.

Last of the Mohicans. James Fenimore Cooper. Ed. by Sally Peters. 432p. 1992. mass mkt. 5.99 (*0-671-75931-0*) PB.

Last of the Mohicans. James Fenimore Cooper. Ed. by Malvina Vogel. (Great Illustrated Classics Ser.: Vol. 24). (Illus.). 240p. (J). (gr. 3-6). 1992. 9.95 (*0-86611-975-2*) Playmore Inc.

Last of the Mohicans. James Fenimore Cooper. LC 92-35775. (Step into Classics Ser.). (Illus.). 96p. (J). (gr. 4-7). 1993. pap. 3.99 (*0-679-84706-5*, Pub. by Random Bks Yng Read) Random.

Last of the Mohicans. James Fenimore Cooper. LC 86-17694. (Illus.). 376p. (J). 1986. 28.00 (*0-684-18711-6*) Scribner.

Last of the Mohicans. James Fenimore Cooper. Ed. & Intro. by James F. Beard. LC 82-21890. (Writings of James Fenimore Cooper). 418p. 1983. text 19.50 (*0-87395-362-2*) State U NY Pr.

Last of the Mohicans. James Fenimore Cooper. Ed. & Intro. by James F. Beard. LC 82-21890. (Writings of James Fenimore Cooper). 418p. (C). 1983. pap. text 19.95 (*0-87395-470-X*) State U NY Pr.

Last of the Mohicans. James Fenimore Cooper. 480p. 1992. mass mkt. 3.99 (*0-8125-2297-4*, Pub. by Tor Bks) St Martin.

Last of the Mohicans. James Fenimore Cooper. Ed. & Intro. by Richard Slotkin. LC 86-2570. (Classics Ser.). (Illus.). 688p. 1986. pap. 13.99 (*0-14-039024-3*, Penguin Classics) Viking Penguin.

Last of the Mohicans. James Fenimore Cooper. (Classics Library). 432p. 1997. pap. 3.95 (*1-85326-049-5*, 0495WW, Pub. by Wrdsworth Edits) NTC Contemp Pub Co.

Last of the Mohicans. abr. ed. James Fenimore Cooper. Ed. by Naunerle C. Farr. (Now Age Illustrated III Ser.). (Illus.). (J). (gr. 4-12). 1977. pap. text 2.95 (*0-88301-267-7*) Pendulum Pr.

Last of the Mohicans. adapted ed. James Fenimore Cooper. (Living Classics Ser.). (Illus.). 32p. (J). (gr. 3-7). 1997. 14.95 (*0-7641-7048-1*) Barron.

Last of the Mohicans. James Fenimore Cooper. (Works of James Fenimore Cooper). 1990. reprint ed. lib. bdg. 79.00 (*0-7812-2374-1*) Rprt Serv.

Last of the Mohicans. rev. ed. James Fenimore Cooper. 432p. 1994. pap. 5.95 (*0-460-87545-0*, Everyman's Classic Lib) Tuttle Pubng.

Last of the Mohicans. 2nd ed. James Fenimore Cooper. (Illustrated Classic Book Ser.). (Illus.). 61p. (J). (gr. 3 up). 1998. reprint ed. pap. text 4.95 (*1-56767-249-3*) Educ Insights.

Last of the Mohicans: Civil Savagery & Savage Civility. John McWilliams. LC 94-14564. (Twayne's Masterwork Studies: No. 143). (Illus.). 128p. 1994. 29.00 (*0-8057-8389-X*, Twyne) Mac Lib Ref.

Last of the Mohicans: Student Activity Book. Marcia Sohl & Gerald Dackerman. (Now Age Illustrated Ser.). (Illus.). (gr. 4-12). 1976. student ed. 1.25 (*0-88301-291-X*) Pendulum Pr.

Last of the Mohicans Notes. Thomas J. Rountree. (Cliffs Notes Ser.). 64p. 1965. pap. 4.95 (*0-8220-0717-7*, Cliff) IDG Bks.

***Last Of The Mohicans Penguin Audio Rdr Lv 2.** (C). 2000. text 10.67 (*0-582-34279-1*) Pearson Custom.

Last of the Mohicans Read-Along. James Fenimore Cooper. (Illustrated Classics Collections 3). 64p. 1994. pap. 14.95 incl. audio (*0-7854-0740-5*, 40461) Am Guidance.

***Last of the Mohicans Sampler.** (C). 2000. write for info. (*0-582-43939-6*) Pearson Educ.

An Asterisk (*) at the beginning of an entry indicates that the title is appearing for the first time.

L

Last of the Mountain Men: The True Story of an Idaho Solitary. Sylvan Hart. 1994. pap. text 11.95 (*0-9603566-6-5*) Backeddy Bks.

Last of the Mwldan. Idris Mathias. 1997. pap. 26.95 (*0-8464-4578-6*) Beekman Pubs.

Last of the Mwldan. Idris Mathias. 1997. pap. 40.00 (*1-85902-428-9*, Pub. by Gomer Pr) St Mut.

Last of the Name. Charles McGlinchey. LC 86-1161. (Illus.). 144p. 1993. reprint ed. pap. 12.95 (*0-85640-361-X*, Pub. by Blackstaff Pr) Dufour.

Last of the Naturalists: The Career of C. Hart Merriam. Keir B. Sterling. LC 73-17847. (Natural Sciences in America Ser.). (Illus.). 500p. 1977. reprint ed. 30.95 (*0-405-05770-9*) Ayer.

Last of the Ofos. Geary Hobson. LC 99-6472. (Sun Tracks Ser.). 120p. 2000. pap. 12.95 (*0-8165-1959-5*) U of Ariz Pr.

***Last of the Ofos.** Geary Hobson. 120p. 2000. 29.95 (*0-8165-1958-7*) U of Ariz Pr.

Last of the Old Guns. large type ed. Elliot Conway. (Dales Large Print Ser.). 1995. pap. 18.99 (*1-85389-545-8*, Dales) Ulverscroft.

Last of the Old Time Cowboys. Patrick Dearen. LC 98-14583. 1998. pap. text 16.95 (*1-55622-613-6*) Wordware Pub.

***Last of the Old-Time Texans.** Macky Murdock. 250p. 2000. pap. 17.95 (*1-55622-784-1*, Rep of TX Pr) Wordware Pub.

Last of the Plainsmen. Zane Grey. 288p. 1994. mass mkt. 4.99 (*0-8125-3537-5*, Pub. by Tor Bks) St Martin.

Last of the Plainsmen. Zane Grey. LC 78-5380. 1976. reprint ed. lib. bdg. 24.95 (*0-89190-753-X*) Amereon Ltd.

Last of the Plainsmen. Zane Grey. 1990. reprint ed. lib. bdg. 20.95 (*0-89968-511-0*) Buccaneer Bks.

Last of the Prince-Bishops: William Van Mildert & the High Church Movement of the Early Nineteenth Century. E. A. Varley. 277p. (C). 1992. text 75.00 (*0-521-39093-1*) Cambridge U Pr.

Last of the Proconsuls. Ed. by Graham F. Thomas. 160p. 1994. text 39.50 (*1-85043-790-4*, Pub. by I B T) St Martin.

Last of the Race: The Growth of a Myth from Milton to Darwin. Fiona J. Stafford. (Illus.). 338p. 1994. text 59.00 (*0-19-811222-X*) OUP.

Last of the Really Great Whangdoodles. Julie Edwards. LC 73-5482. (Trophy Bk.). (Illus.). 288p. (J). (gr. 4-7). 1989. pap. 4.95 (*0-06-440314-9*, HarpTrophy) HarpC Child Bks.

Last of the Really Great Whangdoodles. Julie Edwards. 1989. 9.60 (*0-606-12390-3*, Pub. by Turtleback) Demco.

Last of the Really Great Whangdoodles. 25th anniversary ed. Julie Edwards. LC 73-5482. (Illus.). 224p. (J). (gr. 4-7). 1999. 16.95 (*0-06-021805-3*) HarpC Child Bks.

Last of the Renshai. Mickey Z. Reichert. 640p. (Orig.). 1992. mass mkt. 6.99 (*0-88677-503-5*, Pub. by DAW Bks) Penguin Putnam.

Last of the Rivermen. Ray Fadich. LC 92-93539. (Illus.). 136p. (Orig.). 1993. pap. 16.95 (*0-9635988-0-5*) R Fadich.

Last of the Savages. Jay McInerney. 1997. pap. 12.00 (*0-679-74952-7*) Vin Bks.

Last of the Savages: A Novel. Jay McInerney. 271p. 1996. 24.00 (*0-679-42845-3*) Knopf.

Last of the Secret Agents. I. M. Phlegming. 230p. (Orig.). 1986. pap. 7.95 (*0-9614706-0-7*) Thalia Bks.

Last of the Seris: The Aboriginal Indians of Kino Bay, Sonora, Mexico. Dane Coolidge & Mary R. Coolidge. LC 71-153199. (Beautiful Rio Grande Classics Ser.). (Illus.). 340p. 1973. reprint ed. lib. bdg. 17.50 (*0-87380-078-8*) Popular E Commerce.

Last of the Southern Girls. Willie Morris. LC 94-209598. (Voices of the South Ser.). 304p. 1994. pap. 16.95 (*0-8071-1956-3*) La State U Pr.

Last of the Tearoom Ladies: And Other Minnesota Tales. Peg Meier. (Illus.). 240p. (Orig.). 1990. pap. 9.95 (*0-933387-02-4*) Neighbors Pub.

***Last of the Templars.** William Watson. (Illus.). 1999. pap. 15.00 (*1-86046-411-4*) Harvill Press.

Last of the "The Waltz Across Texas" & Other Stories. Jo Carson. LC 92-75359. 160p. (Orig.). 1993. pap. 13.50 (*0-917788-53-2*) Gnomon Pr.

***Last of the Thorntons.** Horton Foote. (Sewanee Writers Ser.). 2000. pap. 12.95 (*1-58567-048-0*, Pub. by Overlook Pr) Penguin Putnam.

Last of the Untouchables. Oscar Fraley & Paul Robsky. reprint ed. lib. bdg. 21.95 (*0-89190-478-6*) Amereon Ltd.

Last of the Wallendas. Delilah Wallenda & Nan DeVincentis-Hayes. LC 92-60564. (Illus.). 240p. 1993. 22.95 (*0-88282-116-4*) New Horizon NJ.

Last of the Whaling Captains. G. V. Clark. (C). 1987. 120.00 (*0-85174-498-2*) St Mut.

Last of the Whigs: A Political Biography of Lord Hartington, Later Eighth Duke of Devonshire (1833-1908) Patrick Jackson. LC 92-55030. 1994. 47.50 (*0-8386-3514-8*) Fairleigh Dickinson.

Last of the Whitcombes. Rosemary Schafer. (Orig.). 1978. mass mkt. 1.95 (*0-89083-391-5*, Zebra Kensgtn) Kensgtn Pub Corp.

Last of the White Guys. Barclay Bates. LC 98-74017. 240p. 1999. 18.95 (*0-9667039-9-5*, 1) Bloomsbury.

Last of the Whitfields. Elise Sanguinetti. (Library of Alabama Classics). 288p. 1986. pap. 14.95 (*0-8173-0309-X*) U of Ala Pr.

Last of the Wild: Vanished & Vanishing Giants of the Animal World. Robert M. McClung. LC 96-35814. (Illus.). xii, 292p. (YA). (gr. 6 up). 1997. lib. bdg. 27.50 (*0-208-02452-2*, Linnet Bks) Shoe String.

Last of the Wild Horses. Martin Harbury. 1989. 19.98 (*0-88486-026-4*) Arrowood Pr.

Last of the Wild Horses. Martin Harbury. (Illus.). 192p. 1996. pap. 19.95 (*1-55013-642-9*) Firefly Bks Ltd.

***Last of the Wind Ships.** Alan Villiers. 2000. 55.00 (*0-393-05033-5*) Norton.

Last of the Windjammers, Vol. I. Basil Lubbock. (C). 1987. 126.00 (*0-85174-113-4*) St Mut.

Last of the Windjammers, Vol. II. Basil Lubbock. (C). 1987. 126.00 (*0-85174-114-2*) St Mut.

Last of the Wine. Mary Renault. 480p. 1975. pap. 10.00 (*0-394-71653-1*) Vin Bks.

Last of Your Springs. Donald Kennedy. LC 98-24256. 1998. 29.50 (*0-9664249-0-5*) Stnfrd Hist Soc.

Last Offence. large type ed. Frances Keast. (Dales Mystery Ser.). 306p. 1992. pap. 18.99 (*1-85389-322-6*, Dales) Ulverscroft.

Last Old Place: A Search Through Portugal. Datus C. Proper. LC 92-22628. 1993. 22.00 (*0-671-78226-6*) S&S Trade.

Last Olympics. Russel Chandler. 376p. 1996. 22.95 (*0-9646872-2-4*) Wessex House.

***Last on Earth, Bk. 2.** Marilyn Kaye. 1999. 10.34 (*0-606-16367-0*, Pub. by Turtleback) Demco.

***Last on Earth: The Return, Bk. 3.** Marilyn Kaye. (Last on Earth Ser.: No. 3). 192p. (YA). (gr. 7 up). 1999. mass mkt. 4.99 (*0-380-79834-4*, Avon Bks) Morrow Avon.

Last on Earth Bk. 1: The Vanishing. Marilyn Kaye. 176p. 1998. mass mkt. 4.99 (*0-380-79832-8*, Avon Bks) Morrow Avon.

Last One. large type ed. Angus Ross. 248p. 1993. 15.95 (*0-7451-1666-3*, G K Hall Lrg Type) Mac Lib Ref.

Last One: A Bible for Dummies, Vol. I. Ebbie Saith. 100p. Date not set. pap. write for info. (*1-891597-51-5*, SDC Pr) Mleecole.

Last One: A Bible for Dummies, Vol. II. Ebbie Saith. 100p. Date not set. pap. 9.99 (*1-891597-52-3*, SDC Pr) Mleecole.

Last One Home. Annette Appollo. LC 98-42116. 288p. 1999. 24.00 (*0-06-019208-9*) HarpC.

Last One Home. Annette Appollo. 400p. 2000. mass mkt. 6.99 (*0-06-109721-7*) HarpC.

Last One Home. large type ed. Annette Appollo. LC 99-28425. 470p. 1999. pap. 26.95 (*0-7862-2069-4*) Mac Lib Ref.

Last One Home Is a Green Pig. Edith T. Hurd. LC 59-8972. (I Can Read Bks.). (Illus.). 64p. (J). (ps-3). 1959. lib. bdg. 11.89 (*0-06-022716-8*) HarpC Child Bks.

Last One In see Strange Matter

Last One in Is a Rotten Egg. Leonard Kessler. (I Can Read Bks.). (Illus.). 64p. (J). (gr. 1-3). 1969. lib. bdg. 15.89 (*0-06-023158-0*) HarpC Child Bks.

Last One in Is a Rotten Egg. Leonard Kessler. (I Can Read Bks.). (Illus.). 64p. (J). (gr. 1-3). 1989. pap. 3.75 (*0-06-444118-0*, HarpTrophy) HarpC Child Bks.

Last One in Is a Rotten Egg. Leonard Kessler. LC 98-50882. (I Can Read Bks.). (Illus.). 64p. (J). (gr. 1-3). 1999. pap. 3.95 (*0-06-444262-4*) HarpC Child Bks.

Last One in Is a Rotten Egg. Leonard Kessler. (I Can Read Bks.). (J). (gr. 1-3). 1969. 8.95 (*0-606-04263-6*, Pub. by Turtleback) Demco.

Last One In Is a Rotten Egg. Leonard Kessler. LC 98-50882. (I Can Read Bks.). (Illus.). 48p. (J). (gr. k-3). 1999. lib. bdg. 14.89 (*0-06-028485-4*) HarpC Child Bks.

Last One in Is a Rotten Egg. abr. ed. Leonard Kessler. (I Can Read Bks.). (Illus.). 64p. (J). (gr. 1-3). 1969. 8.95 incl. audio (*1-55994-356-4*, 285382) HarperAudio.

Last One in Is a Rotten Egg. rev. ed. Leonard Kessler. LC 98-50882. (I Can Read Bks.). (Illus.). 64p. (J). (ps-3). 1999. 14.95 (*0-06-028484-6*) HarpC Child Bks.

Last One over the Wall: The Massachusetts Experiment in Closing Reform Schools. 2nd ed. Jerome G. Miller. LC 98-8556. 300p. 1998. pap. text 17.95 (*0-8142-0758-8*) Ohio St U Pr.

Last One up the Hill: A Biography of Thomas F. Waldron. Regina W. Murray. (Illus.). 150p. 1993. 19.95 (*0-9636918-0-5*) R W Murray.

***Last Open Road.** rev. ed. Burt Levy. LC 98-12324. 354p. 1998. 25.00 (*0-9642107-2-X*) Think Fast Ink.

Last Operas & Plays. Gertrude Stein. (PAJ Bks.). 480p. 1995. pap. 18.95 (*0-8018-4985-3*) Johns Hopkins.

Last Order of the Lost Cause: The True Story of a Jewish Family in the "Old South" Raphael Jacob Moses, Major, C. S. A. 1812-1893. Ed. & Compiled by Mel Young. LC 95-23904. (Illus.). 376p. (Orig.). (C). 1995. pap. text 25.00 (*0-7618-0081-6*); lib. bdg. 57.50 (*0-7618-0080-8*) U Pr of Amer.

Last Orders. Brian W. Aldiss. 223p. 1990. mass mkt. 3.95 (*0-88184-617-1*) Carroll & Graf.

Last Orders. Graham Swift. LC 96-46858. 1997. pap. 12.00 (*0-679-76662-6*) Random.

Last Orders. Graham Swift. Date not set. 12.00 (*0-679-44606-0*) Vin Bks.

Last Orders. large type ed. Graham Swift. LC 96-44390. 1997. pap. 20.95 (*0-7862-0942-9*) Thorndike Pr.

Last Orders: And Other Stories. James Meek. 184p. (Orig.). 1992. pap. 14.95 (*0-7486-6127-1*, Pub. by Polygon) Subterranean Co.

Last Palmerston Government: Foreign Policy, Domestic Politics, & the Genesis of "Splendid Isolation" David F. Krein. LC 78-61596. (Replica Edition Ser.). 260p. 1978. reprint ed. pap. 80.60 (*0-608-00016-7*, 206078200006) Bks Demand.

Last Panda. George B. Schaller. LC 92-18869. (Illus.). 312p. (C). 1993. 24.95 (*0-226-73628-8*) U Ch Pr.

Last Panda. George B. Schaller. (Illus.). xx, 312p. 1994. pap. 13.95 (*0-226-73629-6*) U Ch Pr.

Last Parade. rev. ed. Hiland B. Doolittle. LC 98-91277. 320p. 1998. 25.00 (*0-9662742-0-2*) Rome Pub.

Last Paradise. James Houston. LC 97-31878. (Literature of the American West Ser.: No. 2). 384p. 1998. 22.95 (*0-8061-3033-4*) U of Okla Pr.

***Last Paradise.** James D. Houston. 384p. 2000. pap. 15.95 (*0-8061-3290-6*) U of Okla Pr.

Last Parallel: A Marine's War Journal. Martin Russ. LC 99-19089. 352p. 1999. pap. 15.00 (*0-88064-237-8*) Fromm Intl Pub.

Last Parallel: A Marine's War Journal. Martin Russ. 1973. write for info. (*0-8371-6770-1*) Greenwood.

Last Part of the Countesse of Pembrokes Arcadia: The Lady of May. Philip Sidney. Ed. by Albert Feuillerat. LC 62-53056. (Prose Works of Sir Philip Sidney: Vol. 2). 248p. reprint ed. pap. 70.70 (*0-608-13410-4*, 2022469) Bks Demand.

Last Partrician. Beran. 1999. pap. 14.95 (*0-312-20659-3*) St Martin.

Last Party: Stories from My Life with Norman Mailer. Adele Mailer. LC 96-47445. (Illus.). 400p. 1997. 25.00 (*1-56980-098-7*) Barricade Bks.

Last Party: Studio 54, Disco & the Culture of the Night. Anthony Geust-Haden. (Illus.). 432p. 1998. reprint ed. pap. 15.00 (*0-688-16098-0*, Quil) HarperTrade.

Last Passage: Recovering a Death of Our Own. Donald Heinz. LC 98-10378. 320p. 1998. 27.50 (*0-19-511643-7*) OUP.

Last Patrician: Bobby Kennedy & the End of the American Aristocracy. Michael Knox Beran. LC 98-10200. (Illus.). 288p. 1998. text 23.95 (*0-312-18625-8*) St Martin.

Last Patrol. Harry Holmes. (Illus.). 212p. 1994. 34.95 (*1-85310-414-0*) Naval Inst Pr.

***Last Paving Stone.** Y. York. 46p. 1999. pap. 5.50 (*0-87129-952-6*, LA1) Dramatic Pub.

Last Payback. James VanOosting. LC 96-41300. 160p. (J). (gr. 4-7). 1997. 14.95 (*0-06-027491-3*) HarpC Child Bks.

Last Payback. James VanOosting. LC 96-41300. 160p. (J). (gr. 4-7). 1998. pap. 4.95 (*0-06-440722-5*, HarpTrophy) HarpC Child Bks.

Last Payback. James Vanoosting. 1998. 10.15 (*0-606-13565-0*, Pub. by Turtleback) Demco.

Last Pendragon. Robert Rice. 340p. 1992. 19.95 (*0-8027-1180-4*) Walker & Co.

Last Pendragon. large type ed. Robert Rice. 368p. 1992. reprint ed. 17.95 (*1-56054-432-5*) Thorndike Pr.

Last Periods of Shakespeare, Racine, Ibsen. Kenneth Muir. LC 60-9132. 126p. reprint ed. pap. 39.10 (*0-7837-3677-0*, 204355100009) Bks Demand.

Last Pew on the Left. Robert Cameron. LC 94-68048. 224p. 1995. pap. 11.99 (*0-933451-28-8*) Prescott Pr.

Last Phase, 1944-7 (Part One) see Mahatma Gandhi

Last Phase of the War of Independence in Western Greece (December 1827-1829) Domna N. Dontas. xi, 187p. 1990. reprint ed. pap. 42.00 (*90-256-0987-2*, Pub. by AM Hakkert) BookLink Distributors.

Last Philosophical Testament, 1947-68. Bertrand Russell et al. LC 96-40868. (Collected Papers of Bertrand Russell). (Illus.). 880p. (C). 1997. 195.00 (*0-415-09409-7*) Routledge.

Last Philosophy. Don Cupitt. 1995. pap. 18.00 (*0-334-02586-9*) TPI PA.

Last Phoenix: A Novel of Betrayal & Revenge, 2 vols. Karl Douglass. LC 96-72473. 984p. (Orig.). 1997. pap., boxed set 29.95 (*1-888125-02-0*) Publ Consult.

Last Phoenix: The End of Freedom. Michael A. Williams. LC 90-82035. 160p. 1990. lib. bdg. write for info. (*1-878527-03-7*) Black Phoenix Pr.

Last Phonological Rule: Reflections on Constraints & Derivations. Ed. by John A. Goldsmith. LC 92-16786. (Studies in Contemporary Linguistics). 216p. (C). 1993. pap. text 21.95 (*0-226-30155-9*); lib. bdg. 55.00 (*0-226-30154-0*) U Ch Pr.

Last Photo. Smith. Date not set. pap. text. write for info. (*0-582-03147-8*, Pub. by Addison-Wesley) Longman.

Last Photo of the Human Soul. Bill Bissett. LC 94-150289. (Illus.). 144p. 1993. pap. 12.95 (*0-88922-322-X*, Pub. by Talonbks) Genl Dist Srvs.

***Last Physician: Walker Percy & the Moral Life of Medicine.** Ed. by Carl Elliott & John D. Lantos. LC 99-14158. 208p. 1999. 45.95 (*0-8223-2336-2*); pap. 15.95 (*0-8223-2369-9*) Duke.

Last Picture Show. Larry McMurtry. 1976. 22.95 (*0-89190-889-7*) Amereon Ltd.

Last Picture Show. Larry McMurtry. LC 99-24699. 1999. 30.00 (*0-7838-8632-2*) Mac Lib Ref.

Last Picture Show. Larry McMurtry. Ed. by Bill Grose. 320p. 1992. per. 6.99 (*0-671-75381-9*) PB.

Last Picture Show. Larry McMurtry. 1999. pap. 11.00 (*0-684-00817-3*); per. 11.00 (*0-684-85386-8*) S&S Trade.

Last Picture Show. Larry McMurtry. 224p. 1992. pap. 10.00 (*0-671-75487-4*, Touchstone) S&S Trade Pap.

Last Pin. Howard Wandrei. 356p. 1996. 29.00 (*1-878252-25-9*) Fedogan & Bremer.

Last Pink Bits: Travels Through the Remnants of the British Empire. Harry Ritchie. 230p. (J). 1999. mass mkt. (*0-340-66683-8*) Hod1der & Stoughton.

Last Pioneer. Gordon L. Giddings. 1986. write for info. (*0-935087-10-9*) Wright Pub Co.

Last Pioneer: John Taylor, a Mormon Prophet. Samuel W. Taylor. LC 98-4090. Orig. Title: The Kingdom or Nothing: The Life of John Taylor, Militant Mormon. 416p. 1999. reprint ed. pap. 16.95 (*1-56085-115-5*) Signature Bks.

Last Piper. Helen Cavanagh. LC 95-44423. (Illus.). 128p. (J). (gr. 3-7). 1996. mass mkt. 16.00 (*0-689-80481-4*) S&S Bks Yung.

Last Piper. Helen Cavanaugh. (J). 15.00 (*0-671-88421-2*) S&S Bks Yung.

Last Place on Earth. Harold T. Hayes. LC 76-15562. (Illus.). 288p. (C). 1982. pap. 8.95 (*0-8128-6087-X*, Scrbrough Hse) Madison Bks UPA.

Last Place on Earth: Scott & Amundsen's Race to the South Pole. rev. ed. Roland Huntford. Ed. by Jon Krakauer. LC 99-41398. (Modern Library Exploration Ser.). 576p. (Orig.). 1999. pap. 14.95 (*0-375-75474-1*) Modern Lib NY.

Last Place Poems of Jeremy Bloom. (J). (gr. 3-7). Date not set. pap. 3.50 (*0-614-19194-7*, Apple Paperbacks) Scholastic Inc.

Last-Place Sports Poems of Jeremy Bloom. Gordon Korman. LC 49-250420. 112p. (J). (gr. 4-7). 1996. pap. text 3.50 (*0-590-25516-9*) Scholastic Inc.

Last-Place Sports Poems of Jeremy Bloom. Gordon Korman. (J). 1996. 9.09 (*0-606-11551-X*, Pub. by Turtleback) Demco.

***Last Places: A Journey in the North.** Lawrence Millman. 2000. pap. 13.00 (*0-618-08248-4*, Mariner Bks) HM.

Last Places: A Journey in the North. Lawrence Millman. 1990. 18.95 (*0-685-45106-2*) HM Soft-Ref Div.

Last Places: A Journey in the North. Lawrence Millman. 1992. 10.00 (*0-685-59153-0*) McKay.

Last Plantagenets. Thomas B. Costain. 1994. reprint ed. lib. bdg. 45.95 (*1-56849-373-8*) Buccaneer Bks.

Last Plantation. Don K. Wright. LC 90-84383. 544p. (C). 1990. 19.95 (*0-9627870-0-0*) Gray Stone Pr.

Last Plantation. Donald K. Wright. 1991. mass mkt. 4.99 (*0-8125-0991-9*, Pub. by Tor Bks) St Martin.

Last Poem. limited ed. Anna Leonessa. (Illus.). 1995. pap. 5.00 (*1-884185-09-6*) O Zone.

Last Poems. Alfred E. Housman. 1976. 22.95 (*0-8488-1374-X*) Amereon Ltd.

Last Poems. D. H. Lawrence. LC 74-6449. (Studies in D. H. Lawrence: No. 20). 1974. lib. bdg. 75.00 (*0-8383-1954-8*) M S G Haskell Hse.

Last Poems. Elder Olson. LC 84-136. 72p. (C). 1996. pap. 8.95 (*0-226-62898-1*) U Ch Pr.

Last Poems. Peter Reading. 45p. 1995. 15.95 (*0-7011-6100-0*, Pub. by Chatto & Windus) Trafalgar.

Last Poems. limited ed. Rainer Maria Rilke. Tr. by Stephen Mitchell. (ENG & GER., Illus.). 75p. 1989. 95.00 (*0-942067-01-0*) Okeanos Pr.

Last Poems. Alfred E. Housman. 1988. reprint ed. lib. bdg. 21.95 (*0-89966-638-8*) Buccaneer Bks.

Last Poems. Alfred E. Housman. (BCL1-PR English Literature Ser.). 79p. 1992. reprint ed. lib. bdg. 59.00 (*0-7812-7566-0*) Rprt Serv.

Last Poems. D. H. Lawrence. Ed. by Richard Aldington & Giuseppe Orioli. 1971. reprint ed. 49.00 (*0-403-01066-7*) Scholarly.

Last Poems. James Russell Lowell. (Notable American Authors Ser.). 1999. reprint ed. lib. bdg. 125.00 (*0-7812-3890-0*) Rprt Serv.

Last Poems, Volume #67. Dan Pagis. Tr. by Keller. (QRL Poetry Bks.: Vol. XXXI). 1992. 20.00 (*0-614-06444-9*) Quarterly Rev.

Last Poems: Manuscript Materials. William Butler Yeats. Ed. by James Pethica. LC 97-17331. (Cornell Yeats Ser.). (Illus.). 471p. 1996. text 85.00 (*0-8014-3324-X*) Cornell U Pr.

***Last Poems, 1821-1850.** William Wordsworth et al. LC 99-30685. (Cornell Wordsworth Ser.). 1999. write for info. (*0-8014-3625-7*) Cornell U Pr.

Last Poems of Elinor Wylie. Elinor H. Wylie. 110p. 1982. reprint ed. pap. 8.00 (*0-89733-011-0*) Academy Chi Pubs.

Last Poems of Miguel de Unamuno. Tr. & Intro. by Edita Mas-Lopez. LC 73-4295. 121p. 1974. 24.50 (*0-8386-1288-1*) Fairleigh Dickinson.

Last Poems of Philip Freneau. Philip Freneau. (BCL1-PS American Literature Ser.). 136p. 1993. reprint ed. lib. bdg. 69.00 (*0-7812-6938-5*) Rprt Serv.

Last Poets: Vibes from the Scribes Selected Poems. J. Nuriddin & S. El Hadi. LC 91-78312. 92p. 1992. reprint ed. 24.95 (*0-86543-316-X*); reprint ed. pap. 9.95 (*0-86543-317-8*) Africa World.

Last Poets on a Mission: Selected Poetry & a History of the Last Poets. Kim Green. LC 96-25676. (Illus.). 256p. (Orig.). 1996. pap. 12.95 (*0-8050-4778-6*, Owl) H Holt & Co.

Last Polar Bears. Harry Horse. (Illus.). 80p. (J). 1996. pap. 7.95 (*0-14-036382-3*, Pub. by Pnguin Bks Ltd) Trafalgar.

Last Pope. John Hogue. (Illus.). 336p. 1998. 24.95 (*1-86204-202-0*, Pub. by Element MA) Penguin Putnam.

Last Pope. Jerry Marcus. LC 96-78943. 256p. 1997. 19.95 (*0-941394-02-6*) Brittany Pubns.

***Last Pope: Prophesies of St. Malachy for the New Millennium.** John Hogue. (Illus.). 2000. pap. 19.95 (*1-86204-732-4*, Pub. by Element MA) Penguin Putnam.

Last Portrait: Selected Poems. Michelina Buonocore. (Living Poets' Library: No. 37). (Illus.). 54p. 1987. pap. 5.95 (*0-934218-38-2*) Dragons Teeth.

Last Post. National Graves Association of Ireland Staff. Ed. by Seamus MacCiarnain & Vincent Conlon. (Illus.). 234p. 1986. 10.00 (*0-9616291-0-X*) Natl Graves Assn.

Last Prairie. Jones Staff. 208p. 2000. 19.95 (*0-07-135347-X*) McGraw.

***Last Precinct.** Patricia Cornwell. 432p. 2000. 26.95 (*0-399-14625-3*) Putnam Pub Group.

***Last Precinct.** large type ed. Patricia Cornwell. LC 00-21645. 688p. 2000. 26.95 (*0-375-43068-7*) Random Hse Lrg Prnt.

***Last Precinct.** limited ed. Patricia Cornwell. 432p. 2000. 150.00 (*0-399-14639-3*) Putnam Pub Group.

***Last Prince.** Daniel Silva. 2001. 25.95 (*0-375-50090-1*) Random.

Last Princess. (J). 2000. 16.00 (*0-689-82560-9*) Atheneum Yung Read.

Last Princess. Fay Stanley. LC 89-71445. (Illus.). 40p. (J). (gr. 1-4). 1994. pap. 5.95 (*0-689-71829-2*) Aladdin.

L

***Last Princess.** Fay Stanley. (J). 2001. 15.95 (0-688-18020-5, Wm Morrow); lib. bdg. 15.89 (0-06-029215-6, Wm Morrow) Morrow Avon.

Last Princess: The Story of Princess Ka'iulani of Hawai'i. Fay Stanley. LC 89-71445. (Illus.). 40p. (J). (gr. 1-4). 1991. lib. bdg. 18.00 (0-02-786785-4, Four Winds Pr) S&S Childrens.

Last Princess: The Story of Princess Ka'iulani of Hawaii. large type ed. Fay Stanley. (Illus.). 1995. 11.50 (0-614-09596-4, L-34818-00) Am Printing Hse.

Last Principality: Politics, Religion & Society in the Bishopric of Durham, 1494-1660. Univ. of Nottingham Staff. (C). 1988. text 90.00 (1-85041-016-X, Pub. by U of Nottingham) St Mut.

Last Prisoner. David Lorne. 288p. (Orig.). 1991. mass mkt. 4.50 (0-380-76287-0, Avon Bks) Morrow Avon.

Last Private Eye. John Birkett. 192p. 1988. pap. 2.95 (0-380-75488-6, Avon Bks) Morrow Avon.

Last Prodigy: A Biography of Erich Wolfgang Korngold. Brendan G. Carroll. LC 97-4963. (Illus.). 420p. 1997. 34.95 (1-57467-029-8, Amadeus Pr) Timber.

Last Promise. Chris Duffy. Ed. by Kevin Abreau. LC 98-89316. 171p. 1999. pap. 9.99 (1-892617-08-0) Conroca Pubg.

Last Prophet. Sally Stokely. 173p. (Orig.). 1996. pap. 12.95 (1-887650-03-2) Factor Pr.

***Last Proud Rider.** large type ed. Ted Harriott. 352p. 1999. pap. 20.99 (1-85389-921-6) Ulverscroft.

Last Prussian: A Biography of Field Marshal Gerd von Rundstedt 1875-1953. Charles Messenger. (Biography of Field Marshal Gerd von Rundstedt Ser.). 400p. 1991. 24.95 (0-08-036707-0, Pub. by Brasseys) Brasseys.

Last Psalm. Julius Charles. Date not set. write for info. (1-930112-50-5) inchanted.

Last Public Execution in America. Perry T. Ryan. LC 92-91052. (Illus.). 272p. (Orig.). 1992. pap. 12.95 (0-9625504-4-2) P T Ryan.

Last Puff. John W. Farquhar & Gene A. Spiller. 256p. 1991. pap. 11.95 (0-393-30803-0) Norton.

Last Puppy. Frank Asch. LC 80-215. (Illus.). 32p. (J). (ps-3). 1989. pap. 4.95 (0-671-66687-8) S&S Bks Yung.

Last Puppy. Frank Asch. (J). 1980. 10.15 (0-606-04264-4, Pub. by Turtleback) Demco.

Last Puppy: A Study Guide. Garrett Christopher. Ed. by J. Friedland & R. Kessler. (Little Novel-Ties Ser.). (J). (gr. k-2). 1993. pap. text, student ed. 14.95 (0-88122-947-4) Lrn Links.

Last Puritan: A Memoir in the Form of a Novel. George Santayana. Ed. by Herman J. Saatkamp, Jr. & William G. Holsberger. (Scholarly Edition of the Complete Works of George Santayana Ser.). (Illus.). 792p. 1994. 55.00 (0-262-19328-0) MIT Pr.

Last Puritan: A Memoir in the Form of a Novel. George Santayana. Ed. by Herman J. Saatkamp, Jr. & William G. Holsberger. 680p. 1995. pap. text 24.50 (0-262-69178-7) MIT Pr.

Last Puritan: A Memoir in the Form of a Novel. George Santayana. 608p. 1981. 60.00 (0-684-16833-2, Scribners Ref) Mac Lib Ref.

***Last Puzzle & Testament.** Parnell Hall. LC 00-20150. 352p. 2000. 23.95 (0-553-80099-X) Bantam.

Last Quad Gypsy. Richard L. Stover. Ed. by Gwen Costa. LC 90-41017. 1991. pap. 13.95 (0-87949-344-5) Ashley Bks.

Last Quarter. Ivan V. Lalic & Francis R. Jones. 30p. 1987. pap. 9.95 (0-85646-191-1, Pub. by Anvil Press) Dufour.

Last Quest of Gilgamesh. Ludmila Zeman. (Epic of Gilgamesh Ser.). (Illus.). 24p. (J). (gr. 3 up). 1998. reprint ed. pap. 8.95 (0-88776-380-4) Tundra Bks.

Last Quest of Gilgamesh, Pt. III. Ludmila Zeman. LC 93-61787. (Illus.). 24p. (J). (gr. 3 up). 1995. 19.95 (0-88776-328-6) Tundra Bks.

Last Race of the 20th Century. Jude Wanniski. LC 98-87724. 1998. pap. write for info. (0-938081-13-6) Polyconomics.

Last Radio Baby: A Memoir. Raymond Andrews. LC 90-41751. (Illus.). 232p. 1990. 15.95 (1-56145-004-9) Peachtree Pubs.

Last Raid of the Daltons: Reliable Recital of the Battle with the Bandits at Coffeyville, Kansas. David S. Elliott. LC 75-165629. (Select Bibliographies Reprint Ser.). 1977. reprint ed. 17.95 (0-8369-5936-1) Ayer.

Last Rail: The Building of the First Transcontinental Railroad. Darice Bailer. LC 96-15036. (Smithsonian Odyssey Ser.). (Illus.). 32p. (J). (gr. 2-5). 1996. 14.95 (1-56899-362-5); pap. 5.95 (1-56899-363-3) Soundprints.

Last Rail: The Building of the First Transcontinental Railroad, Incl. toy. Darice Bailer. (Smithsonian Odyssey Ser.). (Illus.). 32p. (J). (gr. 2-5). 1996. 29.95 (1-56899-364-1); pap. 17.95 (1-56899-365-X) Soundprints.

Last Rail: The Building of the Transcontinental Railroad. Darice Bailer. (Odyssey Ser.). 32p. (J). (gr. 2-5). 1996. 7.95 incl. audio (1-56899-369-2, C6003) Soundprints.

Last Rail: The Building of the Transcontinental Railroad. Darice Bailer. (Odyssey Ser.). (Illus.). 32p. (J). (gr. 2-5). 1996. 19.95 incl. audio (1-56899-366-8, B5009) Soundprints.

Last Rail, the Building of the First Transcontinental Railroad. Darice Bailer. LC 96-15036. (Smithsonian Institution Odyssey Ser.). 1996. 11.15 (0-606-10248-5, Pub. by Turtleback) Demco.

Last Rainbow. Parke Godwin. LC 84-91010. 480p. (Orig.). 1995. mass mkt. 5.99 (0-380-78000-3, Avon Bks) Morrow Avon.

Last Rainmaker. Sherry Garland. (J). (gr. 5-11). 1997. 12.00 (0-614-28817-7); pap. 6.00 (0-614-28818-5) Harcourt.

Last Rainmaker. Sherry Garland. LC 96-33288. 336p. 1997. 12.00 (0-15-200649-4) Harcourt.

Last Rainmaker. Sherry Garland. LC 96-33288. (J). 1997. 11.10 (0-606-11550-1, Pub. by Turtleback) Demco.

Last Rambles Amongst the Indians of the Rocky Mountains & the Andes. George Catlin. (Works of George Catlin). 1990. reprint ed. lib. bdg. 79.00 (0-685-44759-6) Rprt Serv.

Last Rambles Amongst the Indians of the Rocky Mountains & the Andes. George Catlin. (LC History-America-E). 361p. 1999. reprint ed. lib. bdg. 89.00 (0-7812-4245-2) Rprt Serv.

***Last Rampage: The Escape of Gary Tison.** James W. Clarke. LC 99-29166. (Illus.). 336p. 1999. pap. 16.95 (0-8165-1967-6) U of Ariz Pr.

Last Ranch: A Colorado Community & the Coming Desert. Sam Bingham. LC 97-20012. 1997. pap. 14.00 (0-15-600539-5, Harvest Bks) Harcourt.

Last Rattlesnake Throw & Other Stories, No. 28. Ralph J. Salisbury. LC 98-17270. (American Indian Literature & Critical Studies Ser.). 256p. 1998. 24.95 (0-8061-3088-1) U of Okla Pr.

Last Raven. large type ed. Craig Thomas. (General Ser.). 658p. 1991. 23.95 (0-8161-5149-0, G K Hall Lrg Type) Mac Lib Ref.

Last Raven: A Collection of Short Stories by a Mohawk Author. Richard G. Green. 121p. (Orig.). 1994. pap. 12.95 (0-911737-02-2) Ricara Features.

Last Rays of Summer. 1986. write for info. (1-892683-12-1) Kahn Fine Arts.

Last Real Cowboy. Becky Barker. 1995. per. 3.75 (0-373-07684-3, 1-07684-3) Silhouette.

Last Real Man. Rebecca Flanders. (American Romance Ser.). 1993. per. 3.39 (0-373-16477-7, 1-16477-1) Harlequin Bks.

***Last Real People.** Joseph LaPointe. (Illus.). 200p. 2000. pap. 14.95 (0-9632476-8-9, Pub. by Pinto Pr) North Country.

***Last Real Summer.** Warren Graves. 35p. 1998. pap. 10.00 (0-929741-20-X) Playsmith.

Last Rebel. Joseph Altsheler. Date not set. lib. bdg. 25.95 (0-8488-2123-8) Amereon Ltd.

Last Rebel Yell. Ken Brooks. 146p. (Orig.). 1986. pap. 7.95 (0-9616447-0-2) Seneca Pk Pub.

Last Rebel Yell. Michael A. Grissom. 1994. 19.95 (0-9628099-0-X) Rebel Pr OK.

Last Recreations: Hydras, Eggs, & Other Mathematical Mystifications. Martin Gardner. LC 96-51641. (Copernicus Ser.). (Illus.). 392p. 1999. 25.00 (0-387-94929-1) Spr-Verlag.

***Last Recreations: Hydras, Eggs & Other Mathematical Mystifications.** Martin Gardner. (Illus.). 392p. 1999. 15.00 (0-387-98883-1) Spr-Verlag.

Last Redoubt. large type ed. George Goodchild. (Mystery Library). 512p. 1995. pap. 16.99 (0-7089-7653-0, Linford) Ulverscroft.

***Last Reflections on a War: Bernard B. Fall's Last Comments on Vietnam.** Bernard B. Fall. LC 99-88393. (Illus.). 288p. 2000. 24.95 (0-8117-0904-3) Stackpole.

Last Reformation. F. G. Smith. 256p. reprint ed. 3.25 (0-686-29154-9); reprint ed. pap. 3.50 (0-686-29155-7) Faith Pub Hse.

Last Refuge. Henry B. Fuller. (Collected Works of Henry B. Fuller). 1988. reprint ed. lib. bdg. 59.00 (0-7812-1205-7) Rprt Serv.

Last Refuge. James G. Nelson. LC 72-87214. 230p. reprint ed. pap. 71.30 (0-608-13592-5, 202231400026) Bks Demand.

***Last Refuge of Scoundrels.** Paul Lussier. LC 99-86028. 320p. 2001. 26.95 (0-446-52342-9) Warner Bks.

Last Remaining Seats: Movie Palaces of Tinseltown. Robert Berger & Anne Conser. LC 97-7138. (Illus.). 136p. (Orig.). 1997. pap. 32.00 (0-9643119-6-8) Balcony Pr.

Last Rendezvous. Bonnie J. Hunt & Lawrence J. Hunt. LC 99-93133. (Lone Wolf Clan Bks.: No. III). (Illus.). v, 238p. 1999. pap. 15.00 (1-928800-02-5) Mad Bear Pr.

Last Report on Miracles. Louise Erdrich. Date not set. 13.00 (0-06-093122-1) HarpC.

Last Report on the Miracles at Little No Horse: A Novel. Louise Erdrich. 288p. 2000. 26.00 (0-06-018727-1) HarpC.

Last Resort. Jaqueline Girdner. 1991. mass mkt. 5.50 (0-425-14431-3, Prime Crime) Berkley Pub.

Last Resort. Carolyn Keene & Franklin W. Dixon. (Nancy Drew & Hardy Boys Super Mystery Ser.: No. 5). 224p. (YA). (gr. 6 up). 1990. mass mkt. 3.99 (0-671-67461-7, Archway) PB.

Last Resort. Alison Lurie. 336p. 1999. pap. 13.00 (0-8050-6174-6, Pub. by H Holt & Co) VHPS.

Last Resort. Linda Melvern. 1992. write for info. (0-679-41218-2) McKay.

Last Resort. Photos by Martin Parr. (Illus.). 88p. 1998. 45.00 (1-899235-16-7, 810322, Pub. by Dewi Lewis) Dist Art Pubs.

***Last Resort.** Lynn M. Turner. (Gottingen Witch Ser.). 196p. 2000. pap. 16.99 (1-886199-07-8, Deadly Alibi Pr) Madison Pubng.

Last Resort. large type ed. Alison Lurie. LC 98-30791. 1998. 30.00 (0-7862-1642-5, G K Hall Lrg Type) Mac Lib Ref.

Last Resort: A Harriet Hubbley Mystery, Vol. 3. Jackie Manthorne. LC 96-121518. 192p. 1995. per. 10.95 (0-921881-34-7, Pub. by Gynergy-Ragweed) U of Toronto Pr.

Last Resort: A Novel. Alison Lurie. LC 97-42985. 321p. 1998. 22.00 (0-8050-5866-4) H Holt & Co.

Last Resort: A Study of Consumer Bankrupts. Martin Ryan. 320p. 1995. 82.95 (1-85972-010-2, Pub. by Avebry) Ashgate Pub Co.

Last Resort: Psychosurgery & the Limits of Medicine. Jack D. Pressman. LC 97-14074. (Studies in the History of Medicine). (Illus.). 572p. (C). 1998. text 49.95 (0-521-35371-8) Cambridge U Pr.

Last Resort: Success & Failure in Campaigns for Casinos. John Dombrink & William N. Thompson. LC 89-14821. (Wilbur S. Shepperson Series in History & Humanities). (Illus.). 232p. 1990. 29.95 (0-87417-140-7) U of Nev Pr.

Last Resort Dictionary for Technical Translators - German-English - English-German: Letzte Zuflucht Fuer Technische Uebersetzer. Brigitte M. Walker. LC 91-29628. (ENG & GER.). 436p. 1992. pap. 40.00 (1-56087-013-3) Top Mtn Pub.

Last Resorts. Cleveland Amory. 1973. write for info. (0-8371-6644-6) Greenwood.

Last Resorts: The Cost of Tourism in the Caribbean. Polly Pattullo. LC 97-115879. xiii, 220 p. 1996. write for info. (976-8100-81-8) Ian Randle.

Last Resorts: The Cost of Tourism in the Caribbean. Polly Pattullo. (Illus.). 220p. Date not set. pap. 19.00 (0-85345-977-0, Pub. by Lat Am Bur) Monthly Rev.

Last Resting Places, Being a Compendium of Fact Pertaining to the Mortal Remains of the Famous & Infamous. Ed. by E. H. Breisacher & Sandra Lorentzen. LC 79-52704. (Illus.). 400p. 2000. 35.00 (0-87850-032-4) Darwin Pr.

Last Reveille. David Morrell. 272p. 1994. mass mkt. 5.99 (0-446-36442-8, Pub. by Warner Bks) Little.

***Last Revival: The Death of Christian Civilization & the Return of Hope, Martydom & the New Testament Church.** 2000. 12.99 (0-9700117-0-9) Prophetic.

Last Ride. Tom Eidson. 352p. 1995. mass mkt. 5.99 (0-515-11741-2, Jove) Berkley Pub.

Last Ride. large type ed. Thomas Eidson. 528p. 31.50 (0-7089-3663-6) Ulverscroft.

Last Ride. large type ed. Tom Eidson. LC 95-23556. (Large Print Bks.). 1995. 22.95 (1-56895-241-4) Wheeler Pub.

Last Ride. large type ed. John Hunt. (Linford Western Library Ser.). 272p. 1997. pap. 16.99 (0-7089-5128-7, Linford) Ulverscroft.

Last Ride of Wild Bill & 11 Narrative Poems. Sterling A. Brown. 53p. (YA). (gr. 12 up). 1975. pap. 5.00 (0-910296-02-2) Broadside Pr.

Last Ride to Rocky Mesa. Jack Aintry. 224p. 1989. mass mkt. 2.95 (0-8217-2689-7, Zebra Kensgtn) Kensgtn Pub Corp.

Last Rights. Tim Sebastian. 272p. 1995. mass mkt. 5.50 (0-380-71864-2, Avon Bks) Morrow Avon.

Last Rights. Philip Shelby. 1998. pap. 6.99 (0-671-00131-0) PB.

Last Rights. Philip Shelby. LC 96-41579. 336p. 1997. 23.00 (0-684-82939-8) S&S Trade.

Last Rights. large type ed. Gerald Hammond. (Linford Mystery Library). 304p. 1997. pap. 16.99 (0-7089-5097-3, Linford) Ulverscroft.

Last Rights. large type ed. Philip Shelby. LC 96-45378. (Basic Ser.). 574p. 1997. 26.95 (0-7862-0949-6) Thorndike Pr.

Last Rights: A Practical Guide to Respecting the Rights & Dignity of the Sick & Dying. Douglas C. Smith. 1997. pap. 14.95 (0-614-27649-7) Macmillan USA.

Last Rights? Assisted Suicide & Euthanasia Debated. Ed. by Michael M. Uhlmann. LC 97-41104. 668p. 1998. pap. 35.00 (0-8028-4199-6) Eerdmans.

Last Rights: Death & Dying in Ireland. Patrick Hanafin. Ed. by Fintan O'Toole. LC 98-129228. (Undercurrents Ser.). 140p. 1997. pap. 7.95 (1-85918-156-2, Pub. by Cork Univ) Stylus Pub VA.

Last Rights: Death Control & the Elderly in America. Logue. LC 92-39452. (Lexington Book Series on Social Issues). 372p. 1993. 25.95 (0-669-27370-8) Lxngtn Bks.

Last Rights: Poems by Marvin White. Marvin K. White. LC 98-33109. 138p. 1999. pap. 12.95 (1-55583-510-4, Pub. by Alyson Pubns) Consort Bk Sales.

Last Rights: Revisiting Four Theories of the Press. William E. Berry. Ed. by John C. Nerone & Robert W. McChesney. LC 95-3566. (History of Communication Ser.). 200p. (C). 1995. text 29.95 (0-252-02180-0); pap. text 14.95 (0-252-06470-4) U of Ill Pr.

Last Rights: The Struggle over the Right to Die. Sue Woodman. LC 98-28439. (Illus.). 294p. (C). 1998. 26.95 (0-306-45995-7, Plenum Trade) Perseus Pubng.

Last Rising: The Newport Insurrection of 1839. Ed. by David J. Jones. (Illus.). 288p. 1986. pap. 19.95 (0-19-820102-8) OUP.

Last Rising of the Agricultural Labourers: Rural Life & Protest in Nineteenth-Century England. Barry Reay. (Illus.). 248p. 1990. 69.00 (0-19-820187-7) OUP.

Last Rites. Christopher Buckley. LC 80-12937. 92p. 1980. 4.50 (0-87886-109-2, Greenfld Rev Pr) Greenfld Rev Lit.

Last Rites. John Harvey. LC 98-33766. 312p. 1999. 25.00 (0-8050-4150-8) H Holt & Co.

Last Rites. Created by Warren Murphy & Richard Sapir. LC 95-22338. (Destroyer Ser.). 349p. 1995. per. 4.99 (0-373-63215-0, 1-63215-7) Harlequin Bks.

Last Rites: A Novel. John Harvey. LC 99-15811. (Core Ser.). 1999. 26.95 (0-7838-8674-8, G K Hall Lrg Type) Mac Lib Ref.

Last Rites: A Stevie Houston Mystery. Tracey Richardson. LC 96-45488. 1997. pap. 11.95 (1-56280-164-3) Naiad Pr.

Last Rites: Four Present-Day Adventures for Call of Cthulhu. Ian Winterton. (Call of Cthulhu Roleplaying Ser.). 1999. pap. 14.95 (1-56882-137-9) Chaosium.

Last Rites: The Work of the Modern Funeral Director. Glennys Howarth. LC 95-35982. (Death, Value & Meaning Ser.). 222p. 1996. 36.95 (0-89503-134-5) Baywood Pub.

***Last Rites for the Tipu Maya: Genetic Structuring in a Colonial Cemetery.** Keith P. Jacobi. 400p. 2000. pap. text 32.95 (0-8173-1025-8) U of Ala Pr.

Last Rites Never Came: Memoirs of a University Presidency, 1958-1971. David Marion Delo. LC 92-46302. 1993. 19.95 (1-879852-50-0) Univ Tampa.

Last Ritual: The Thanatopsis of Aleister Crowley. Aleister Crowley. (Illus.). 1993. reprint ed. pap. 9.95 (1-55818-254-3) Holmes Pub.

***Last River: The Tragic Race for Shangri-la.** Todd Balf. 288p. 2000. 24.00 (0-609-60625-5, Crown) Crown Pub Group.

Last Rock Eagle: Selected Poems. Blaga Dimitrova. Tr. by B. Walker et al from BUL. LC 92-72166. 81p. 1993. pap. 16.95 (1-85610-009-X, Pub. by Forest Bks) Dufour.

Last Rock Star: or Liz Phair, a Rant. Camden Joy. LC 98-60059. 224p. 1998. pap. 14.95 (1-891241-07-9) Verse Chorus Pr.

Last Rogue. Deborah Simmons. (Historical Ser.: Vol. 427). 1998. per. 4.99 (0-373-29027-6, 1-29027-9) Harlequin Bks.

Last Romantic: A Life of Max Eastman. William L. O'Neill. 350p. (C). 1990. pap. 24.95 (0-88738-859-0) Transaction Pubs.

Last Romantics. Caroline Seebohm. 352p. 1988. mass mkt. 4.50 (0-380-70467-6, Avon Bks) Morrow Avon.

Last Romantics. Graham G. Hough. LC 75-30028. reprint ed. 34.50 (0-404-14032-7) AMS Pr.

Last Romantics: The Romantic Tradition in British Art: Burne-Jones to Stanley Spencer. Ed. by John Christian. (Illus.). 208p. (C). 1995. reprint ed. pap. 39.95 (0-85331-552-3, Pub. by Lund Humphries) Antique Collect.

Last Roundup. Dottie Henneberry. 82p. 1993. pap. 10.00 (1-882825-18-7) Hse of Prayer.

Last Run. Raymond A. Montgomery. (Choose Your Own Adventure Ser.: No. 153). (J). (gr. 4-8). 1994. 8.60 (0-606-07021-4, Pub. by Turtleback) Demco.

Last Run. Leonard B. Scott. (Orig.). 1990. mass mkt. 5.99 (0-345-36563-1) Ballantine Pub Grp.

Last Run. large type ed. Cynthia Harrod-Eagles. (Dales Large Print Ser.). 304p. 1996. pap. 18.99 (1-85389-446-X, Dales) Ulverscroft.

Last Run. Cynthia Harrod-Eagles. 1994. reprint ed. lib. bdg. 18.00 (0-7278-4679-5) Severn Hse.

Last Run: A Novel. Jimmy Breslin. 288p. 1999. write for info. (0-316-11845-1) Little.

Last Running. John Graves. 1999. pap. text 12.95 (1-55821-953-6) Lyons Pr.

Last Running. John Graves. (Illus.). 64p. 1989. reprint ed. 16.95 (1-55821-061-X) Lyons Pr.

Last Safe House: A Story of the Underground Railroad. Barbara Greenwood. (Illus.). 128p. (J). (gr. 3-6). 1998. 22.95 (1-55074-507-7, Pub. by Kids Can Pr); pap. 14.95 (1-55074-509-3, Pub. by Kids Can Pr) Genl Dist Srvs.

Last Safe Place. Richard Peck. (J). 1996. 20.95 (0-385-30995-3); mass mkt. 4.99 (0-440-91152-4) BDD Bks Young Read.

Last Safe Place on Earth. Richard Peck. 176p. (YA). (gr. 5 up). 1996. mass mkt. 4.99 (0-440-22007-6, LLL BDD) BDD Bks Young Read.

Last Safe Place on Earth. Richard Peck. LC 94-446. 1996. 9.09 (0-606-09528-4, Pub. by Turtleback) Demco.

Last Sailorman. Dick Durham. 168p. 1990. 42.00 (0-86138-067-3, Pub. by T Dalton) St Mut.

Last Samurai: An American Poem about Japanese Courage. James Sutton. LC 97-17133. 164p. 1997. pap. 14.95 (0-7734-2828-3, Mellen Poetry Pr) E Mellen.

Last Sanctuary. Craig Holden. 432p. 1998. pap. 11.95 (0-385-33355-2) Delacorte.

Last Sanctuary. abr. ed. Craig Holden. 1996. pap. 16.95 incl. audio (1-55927-383-6) Audio Renaissance.

Last Sands in the Hourglass: Revelation Explored. Marc Carr. Ed. by Majorie M. Stanley. 294p. (Orig.). 1989. pap. text 7.95 (0-936369-14-0) Son-Rise Pubns.

***Last Santini Virgin.** Maureen Child. (Desire Ser.). 2000. mass mkt. 3.99 (0-373-76312-3, 1-76312-7) Silhouette.

Last Scout. large type ed. Will Cook. LC 97-17585. 1997. lib. bdg. 17.95 (1-57490-055-2, Sagebrush LP West) T T Beeler.

Last Scream. R. L. Stine, pseud. (Fear Street: No. 3). (YA). (gr. 7 up). 1996. per. 3.99 (0-671-52957-9) PB.

Last Scream. R. L. Stine, pseud. (Fear Street: No. 3). (YA). (gr. 7 up). 1996. 9.09 (0-606-10809-2, Pub. by Turtleback) Demco.

Last Seal Pup: The Story of Canada's Seal Hunt. Peter Lust. LC 67-21282. 152p. reprint ed. pap. 47.20 (0-608-13593-3, 202230900026) Bks Demand.

***Last Season.** Ronald Florence. 352p. 2000. text 24.95 (0-312-84873-0) Forge NYC.

Last Secret. Michael Brown. LC 97-42592. 1998. pap. text 14.99 (1-56955-023-9) Servant.

Last Secret: Daughters Sexually Abused by Mothers. Bobbie Rosencrans. Ed. by Euan Bear. LC 98-234806. 261p. 1997. pap. 20.00 (1-884444-36-9) Safer Soc.

Last Seduction. Elda Minger. (Temptation Ser.). 1996. per. 3.50 (0-373-25690-6, 1-25690-8) Harlequin Bks.

Last Seen Alive: A Luke Thanet Mystery. Dorothy Simpson. (Luke Thanet Mystery Ser.). 224p. 1985. 13.95 (0-684-18435-4, Scribners Ref) Mac Lib Ref.

Last Seen Alive: The Search for Missing POWs from the Korean War. Laurence Jolidon. LC 95-77958. (Illus.). 346p. (Orig.). 1995. pap. 15.00 (0-9646982-0-X) Ink-Slinger Pr.

Last Seen Breathing. David Williams. 224p. 1994. 14.99 (0-00-232510-1, Pub. by HarpC) HarpC.

Last Seen in London. large type ed. Anna Clarke. 340p. 1992. pap. 14.95 (0-8161-5452-X, G K Hall Lrg Type) Mac Lib Ref.

***Last Seen in Massilia.** Steven Saylor. LC 00-31744. 288p. 2000. 23.95 (0-312-20928-2, Minotaur) St Martin.

Last Seen in Vermont with a Big, White Dog. Cam J. Montgomery. 192p. (Orig.). 1996. pap. write for info. (1-57502-207-9, P0844) Morris Pubng.

Last Seen on Hopper's Lane. Allais Janet Stegeman. (J). 1985. pap. 2.50 (0-590-41817-3) Scholastic Inc.

An Asterisk (*) at the beginning of an entry indicates that the title is appearing for the first time.

L

Last Seen Wearing. large type ed. Veronica Black. (Dales Ser.). 278p. 1994. pap. 18.99 (*1-85389-422-2*, Dales) Ulverscroft.
Last Seen Wearing: An Inspector Morse Mystery. Colin Dexter. 272p. 1988. mass mkt. 5.99 (*0-553-28003-1*) Bantam.
Last Seen Wearing: An Inspector Morse Mystery. Colin Dexter. 1997. mass mkt. 5.99 (*0-8041-1491-9*) Ivy Books.
Last Selection: A Child's Journey Through the Holocaust. Goldie S. Kalib. LC 91-3869. (Illus.). 296p. (C). 1996. pap. 18.95 (*1-55849-018-3*) U of Mass Pr.
Last Sentence. Jonathan Goodman. 224p. 1996. 19.50 (*0-7451-8677-7*, Black Dagger) Chivers N Amer.
***Last September.** Elizabeth Bowen. 224p. 2000. pap. 12.00 (*0-385-72014-9*, Anchor NY) Doubleday.
Last Served? Gendering the HIV Pandemic. Cindy Patton. LC 94-11502. (Social Aspects of AIDS Ser.). 1994. write for info. (*0-7484-0189-X*, Pub. by Tay Francis Ltd) Taylor & Francis.
Last Served? Gendering the HIV Pandemic. Cindy Patton. LC 94-11502. (Social Aspects of AIDS Ser.). 1994. pap. 19.95 (*0-7484-0190-3*) Taylor & Francis.
***Last Session.** 1998. pap. 16.95 (*1-57560-111-7*, Pub. by Cherry Lane) H Leonard.
Last Settlers. Jennifer Brice. LC 97-45310. (Emerging Writers in Creative Nonfiction Ser.). (Illus.). 190p. 1998. 24.95 (*0-8207-0290-0*) Duquesne.
Last Seven Days: The Story of Jesus & Holy Week. Gwynne H. Davies & John E. Morgan-Wynne. LC 99-28534. (Regent's Study Guide Ser.). 224p. 1999. pap. 16.00 (*1-57312-292-0*) Smyth & Helwys.
Last Seven Months of Anne Frank. Willy Lindwer. 256p. 1992. pap. 12.95 (*0-385-42360-8*, Anchor NY) Doubleday.
Last Shall be First. Murray Angus. 96p. (Orig.). 1991. pap. 9.95 (*1-55021-064-5*, Pub. by NC Ltd) U of Toronto Pr.
Last Shall Be First. J. E. Kirk. LC 93-70050. (Illus.). 326p. (Orig.). 1993. pap. 8.95 (*0-9635066-7-6*) Apogee Arts.
Last Shall Be First: A Challenge for Christian Lawyers. Yvonne Vinkemulder. 8p. (Orig.). 1992. pap. text 3.00 (*0-944561-20-9*) Chr Legal.
Last Shall Be First: The Rhetoric of Reversal in Luke. John O. York. (JSNT Supplement Ser.: No. 46). 208p. 1991. 57.50 (*1-85075-278-8*, Pub. by Sheffield Acad) CUP Services.
Last Shaman: Change in an Amazonian Community. Andrew Gray. LC 96-13120. (Arakmbut of Amazonian Peru Ser.: Vol. 2). (Illus.). 320p. 1997. 59.95 (*1-57181-874-X*) Berghahn Bks.
Last Sheaf: Essays. Edward Thomas. LC 73-167427. (Essay Index Reprint Ser.). 1977. reprint ed. 20.95 (*0-8369-2673-0*) Ayer.
Last Sherlock Holmes Story. Michael Dibdin. 192p. 1996. pap. 10.00 (*0-679-76658-8*) Random.
Last Ship. William Brinkley. 1989. pap. 12.95 (*0-345-35982-8*) Ballantine Pub Grp.
Last Shogun: The Life of Tokugawa Yoshinobu. Ryotar O. Shiba & Juliet W. Carpenter. LC 97-38774. 1998. 25.00 (*1-56836-246-3*) Kodansha.
Last Shot. Hugo Hamilton. 192p. 1992. text 20.00 (*0-374-18404-6*) FS&G.
Last Shot. W. M. Raine. 1976. reprint ed. lib. bdg. 20.95 (*0-88411-553-4*) Amereon Ltd.
Last Shot: City Streets, Basketball Dreams. Darcy Frey. 240p. 1996. per. 11.00 (*0-684-81509-5*, Touchstone) S&S Trade Pap.
Last Sibling: A North Dakota Memoir. Eleanor M. Benrud. LC 90-70816. (Illus.). 93p. (Orig.). 1990. pap. 12.95 (*1-878815-00-8*) Reflected Images.
Last Siege of Seringapatam. E. W. Thompson. (C). 1990. reprint ed. text 12.00 (*0-685-53665-3*, Pub. by Asian Educ Servs) S Asia.
Last Silk Dress. Ann Rinaldi. 352p. (YA). 1990. mass mkt. 4.99 (*0-553-28315-4*) Bantam.
Last Silk Dress. Ann Rinaldi. 352p. 1990. mass mkt. 5.50 (*0-440-22861-1*) Bantam Dell.
Last Silk Dress. Ann Rinaldi. (J). 1988. 10.09 (*0-606-04464-7*, Pub. by Turtleback) Demco.
Last Sin Eater. Francine Rivers. 380p. 1999. pap. 12.99 (*0-8423-3571-4*) Tyndale Hse.
Last Sin Eater: A Novel. Francine Rivers. LC 98-19967. 324p. 1998. 16.97 (*0-8423-3570-6*) Tyndale Hse.
Last Six Months. S. M. Shtemenko. (World at War Ser.: No. 7). 1978. mass mkt. 2.50 (*0-89083-377-X*, Zebra Kensgtn) Kensgtn Pub Corp.
Last Sleep: The Battle of Droop Mountain November 6, 1863. Terry Lowry. (Illus.). 320p. (Orig.). 1996. pap. 17.95 (*1-57510-024-X*) Pictorial Hist.
Last Slice of Rainbow: And Other Stories. Joan Aiken. LC 87-45271. (Charlotte Zolotow Bk.). (Illus.). 160p. (J). (gr. 3-7). 1988. 12.95 (*0-06-020042-1*) HarpC Child Bks.
***Last Snake in Ireland.** Sheila MacGill-Callahan. (Illus.). (J). 2000. pap. 6.95 (*0-8234-1555-4*) Holiday.
Last Snake in Ireland: A Story about St. Patrick. Sheila Macgill-Callahan. LC 98-33504. (Illus.). (YA). (gr. k-6). 1999. 16.95 (*0-8234-1425-6*) Holiday.
Last Song Dogs. Sinclair Browning. 288p. 1999. mass mkt. 5.50 (*0-553-57940-1*) Bantam.
Last Songs of Vagabondia (With Bliss Carman) Richard Hovey. (Notable American Authors Ser.). 1992. reprint ed. lib. bdg. 75.00 (*0-7812-3194-9*) Rprt Serv.
Last Sorcerer: The Real Life of Sir Isaac Newton. Michael James Denham White. LC 97-31909. (Illus.). 402p. 1998. 27.00 (*0-201-48301-7*) Addison-Wesley.
Last Soviet Avant-Garde: OBERIU--Fact, Fiction, Metafiction. Graham Roberts. (Cambridge Studies in Russian Literature). 1997. 290p. (C). 1997. text 64.95 (*0-521-48283-6*) Cambridge U Pr.
Last Spring in Paris. Hans Herlin. Tr. by J. Maxwell Brownjohn. 320p. 1988. pap. 3.95 (*0-380-70565-6*, Avon Bks) Morrow Avon.
Last Spy. large type ed. Bob Reiss. LC 93-22359. 563p. 1993. lib. bdg. 21.95 (*1-56054-696-4*) Thorndike Pr.
Last Stage to Gomorrah. large type ed. Barry Cord. (Linford Western Library). 240p. 1985. pap. 16.99 (*0-7089-6075-8*) Ulverscroft.
***Last Stage West.** large type ed. Frank Bonham. 237p. 2000. pap. 20.95 (*0-7838-9013-3*) Mac Lib Ref.
Last Stand. Brad Ferguson. (Star Trek Next Generation Ser.: No. 37). 288p. 1995. per. 5.99 (*0-671-50105-4*) PB.
Last Stand. Created by Keith Laumer. (Bolos Ser.: Vol. 4). 384p. 1997. per. 5.99 (*0-671-87760-7*) Baen Bks.
Last Stand. Christie McLaren. 2002. write for info. (*0-385-25760-0*) Doubleday.
Last Stand! Bryan Perrett. (Cassell Military Classics Ser.). (Illus.). 240p. 1998. pap. 9.95 (*0-304-35055-9*) Sterling.
***Last Stand, Vol. 1.** Larry Jay Martin. 1999. pap. 6.99 (*0-7860-1062-2*, Pinncle Kensgtn) Kensgtn Pub Corp.
Last Stand! Famous Battles Against the Odds. Bryan Perrett. (Illus.). 240p. 1993. pap. 16.95 (*1-85409-188-3*) Sterling.
Last Stand: Protected Areas & the Defense of Tropical Biodiversity. Ed. by Randall Kramer et al. LC 96-22337. (Illus.). 256p. 1997. text 45.00 (*0-19-509554-5*) OUP.
Last Stand: The War Between Wall Street & Main Street over California's Ancient Redwoods. David Harris. 388p. 1995. 25.00 (*0-8129-2577-7*, Times Bks) Crown Pub Group.
Last Stand: The War Between Wall Street & Main Street over California's Ancient Redwoods. David Harris. 373p. 1996. 25.00 (*0-614-12885-4*, Times Bks) Crown Pub Group.
Last Stand: The War Between Wall Street & Main Street over California's Ancient Redwoods. David Harris. 384p. 1997. pap. 15.00 (*0-87156-944-2*, Pub. by Sierra) Random.
Last Stand at Papago Wells. Louis L'Amour. 144p. 1998. mass mkt. 4.50 (*0-553-25807-9*) Bantam.
Last Stand at Perekop. Bert Byfield. (Russalka Trilogy Ser.). 1999. pap. 9.00 (*1-887121-03-X*) Caravela Bks.
Last Stand at Saber River. Elmore Leonard. 1994. reprint ed. lib. bdg. 29.95 (*1-56849-301-0*) Buccaneer Bks.
Last Stand in the Carolinas: The Battle of Betonville. Mark L. Bradley. (Illus.). 608p. 1996. reprint ed. 32.95 (*1-882810-02-3*, 02-3) Savas Pub.
Last Stand of Asian Autonomies, 1750-1900. Reid. LC 96-46165. (Illus.). 344p. 1997. text 75.00 (*0-312-17249-4*) St Martin.
Last Stand of Chinese Conservatism: The T'ung-Chih Restoration, 1862-1874. Mary C. Wright. xii, 426p. 1957. pap. 17.95 (*0-8047-0476-7*) Stanford U Pr.
Last Stand of Chinese Conservatism: The Tung-Chih Restoration, 1862-1874. Mary C. Wright. LC 57-5946. (Stanford Studies in History, Economics, & Political Science). 443p. reprint ed. pap. 30.00 (*0-608-20169-3*, 207143300011) Bks Demand.
***Last Stand of Mr. America.** Jason Flores-Williams. 206p. 1999. pap. (*0-7437-0000-7*) Pubg Portal.
Last Standing Woman: A Novel. Winona LaDuke. LC 97-1886. 304p. 1997. 14.95 (*0-89658-278-7*) Voyageur Pr.
***Last Standing Woman: A Novel.** Winona LaDuke. LC 97-1886. 304p. 1999. pap. 14.95 (*0-89658-452-6*) Voyageur Pr.
***Last Stands: A Journey Through North America's Vanishing Ancient Rainforests.** Larry Pynn. 224p. 2000. pap. 17.95 (*0-87071-027-3*) Oreg St U Pr.
Last Stands: Notes from Memory. Hilary Masters. 1991. 15.00 (*0-941038-04-1*) Coyne & Chenoweth.
***Last Star: A Novel.** William Proctor. 288p. 2000. pap. 14.99 (*0-7852-6810-3*) Nelson.
Last Star: A Study of Marc Almond. Jeremy Reed. (Illus.). 192p. (Orig.). 1996. pap. 15.95 (*1-871592-61-5*) Creation Books.
Last Star: A Study of Marc Almond. 2nd rev. ed. Jeremy Reed. (Illus.). 192p. (Orig.). 1999. pap. 17.95 (*1-84068-006-7*) Creation Books.
***Last Star at Dawn.** Oliver Johnson. LC 99-33538. (Lightbringer Trilogy Ser.: No. 3). 368p. 1999. mass mkt. 16.95 (*0-451-45567-3*, ROC) NAL.
Last Station: A Novel of Tolstoy's Last Year. Jay Parini. 304p. 1998. pap. 14.00 (*0-8050-5823-0*, Owl) H Holt & Co.
***Last Steam Railroad in America.** Photos by O. Winston Link. (Illus.). 144p. 2000. 19.98 (*0-8109-8201-3*, Pub. by Abrams) Time Warner.
Last Steam Railroad in America: From Tidewater to Whitetop. O. Winston Link & Thomas H. Garver. LC 95-7406. (Illus.). 144p. 1995. 49.50 (*0-8109-3575-9*, Pub. by Abrams) Time Warner.
Last Step: The American Ascent of K2. Rick Ridgeway. (Illus.). 304p. 1999. pap. 21.95 (*0-89886-632-4*) Mountaineers.
Last Stop. Ed. by Joseph Bruchac. 1974. per. 3.00 (*0-912678-10-0*, Greenfld Rev Pr) Greenfld Rev Lit.
Last Stop. Peter Lerangis. (Watchers Ser.: No. 1). 176p. (J). (gr. 4-7). 1998. pap. text 3.99 (*0-590-10996-0*) Scholastic Inc.
Last Stop Liberty. large type ed. D. D. Lang. (Linford Western Library Ser.). 1997. pap. 16.99 (*0-7089-5134-1*, Linford) Ulverscroft.
Last Stop Marriage. Emma Darcy. LC 95-22378. (Presents Ser.). 188p. 1996. mass mkt. 3.25 (*0-373-11785-X*, 1-11785-2) Harlequin Bks.
Last Stop on the Trail. large type ed. H. H. Cody. (Linford Western Library Ser.). 176p. 1997. pap. 16.99 (*0-7089-5148-1*) Ulverscroft.
Last Stop West. Martin Kippenberger. (Illus.). 96p. 1999. pap. 14.95 (*3-89322-506-4*) Edition Cantz.
Last Stories of the Old Duck Hunters, Vol. 3. Gordon MacQuarrie. (Illus.). 151p. 1994. 19.50 (*1-57223-005-3*, 1510) Willow Creek Pr.
Last Stories of the Old Duck Hunters Audio, Vol. 3. abr. ed. Gordon MacQuarrie. (Gordon MacQuarrie Trilogy Ser.). 1994. 16.95 incl. audio (*1-57223-016-9*, 0169) Willow Creek Pr.
***Last Story.** Richard E. Cheverton. 272p. 2000. pap. 18.00 (*0-7388-2068-7*) Xlibris Corp.
Last Story. Christopher Pike, pseud. Ed. by Patricia MacDonald. No. 3. 224p. (YA). (gr. 9 up). 1995. mass mkt. 3.99 (*0-671-87267-2*, Archway) PB.
Last Story. Christopher Pike, pseud. (Remember Me Ser.). (J). 1995. 9.09 (*0-606-08069-4*, Pub. by Turtleback) Demco.
Last Story, the First Story. Richard Thompson. (Young Novels Ser.). (Illus.). 128p. (J). (gr. 4-6). 1996. 8.95 (*1-55037-025-1*, Pub. by Annick); pap. 5.95 (*1-55037-024-3*, Pub. by Annick) Firefly Bks Ltd.
Last Straw. Doris M. Disney. 1988. mass mkt. 2.95 (*0-8217-2286-7*, Zebra Kensgtn) Kensgtn Pub Corp.
Last Straw. Lynn Johnston. (Illus.). 128p. (Orig.). 1985. pap. 8.95 (*0-8362-2070-6*) Andrews & McMeel.
Last Straw. Paula Palangi. LC 91-44346. 32p. (J). (ps-3). 1992. pap. 9.99 (*0-7814-0562-9*, Chariot Bks) Chariot Victor.
Last Straw. Frederick Thury. LC 98-37757. (Illus.). 32p. (J). 1999. 15.95 (*0-88106-152-2*, Talewinds) Charlesbridge Pub.
Last Straw. Frederick Thury. (Illus.). 32p. (J). (ps up). 1998. write for info. (*1-55263-022-6*) Key.
Last Straw & Sociability. Charles Dizenzo. 1970. pap. 5.25 (*0-8222-0639-0*) Dramatists Play.
Last Straw in Egypt: A Rhyming Play about Moses & Pharaoh. Lynda Pujado. 32p. 1999. pap. 4.95 (*0-7880-1344-0*) CSS OH.
Last Stronghold: A Story of the Modoc Indian, War, 1872-1873. Harriett M. Luger. LC 94-26615. (Illus.). x, 224p. (YA). (gr. 6-12). 1995. pap. text 16.50 (*0-208-02403-4*, Linnet Bks) Shoe String.
Last Stubborn Buffalo in Nevada, No. 4. Stephen A. Bly. LC 93-8654. (Nathan T. Riggins Western Adventure Ser.: Vol. 4). 128p. (J). (gr. 4-9). 1993. pap. 4.99 (*0-89107-746-4*) Crossway Bks.
Last Stubborn Cowboy: 4 Tots for 4 Texans. Judy Christenberry. 1999. per. 3.99 (*0-373-16785-7*, 1-16785-7) Harlequin Bks.
Last Studebaker. Robin Hemley. LC 92-15059. 256p. 1992. pap. 12.00 (*1-55597-200-4*) Graywolf.
Last Summer. Alice Carr. 324p. 1997. pap. 17.95 (*0-7528-0075-2*, Pub. by Orion Pubng Grp) Trafalgar.
Last Summer. Cullinan. 1994. text 13.90 (*0-15-302431-3*) Harcourt.
***Last Summer.** Mary Jane Staples. 2000. 27.95 (*0-593-04089-9*, Pub. by Transworld Publishers Ltd); pap. 8.95 (*0-552-14513-0*, Pub. by Transworld Publishers Ltd) Trafalgar.
Last Summer: Brian Buckley's Diary. Hugh Fox. xix, 154p. 1995. pap. 13.00 (*1-879378-13-2*) Xenos Riverside.
Last Summer at Bluefish Cove. deluxe limited ed. Jane Chambers. LC 81-86655. (Gay Play Script Ser.). (Illus.). 107p. (Orig.). 1982. 35.00 (*0-935672-04-4*) T n T Class.
Last Summer at Mars Hill. Elizabeth Hand. mass mkt. 5.99 (*0-06-105731-2*, HarperPrism) HarpC.
Last Summer at Mars Hill. Elizabeth Hand. LC 98-6734. 336p. 1998. pap. 13.00 (*0-06-105348-1*, HarperPrism) HarpC.
Last Summer in Chulimsk. Aleksandr Vampilov. (Russian Theatre Archive Ser.). 65p. 1996. pap. text 4.00 (*3-7186-5840-2*, ECU5, Harwood Acad Pubs) Gordon & Breach.
Last Summer in the Hamptons: The Screenplay. Henry Jaglom. 1996. pap. text 13.95 (*1-878965-04-2*) Rainbow Filmbooks.
Last Summer of Innocence. large type ed. Linda Sole. 658p. 1992. reprint ed. lib. bdg. 18.95 (*1-56054-441-4*) Thorndike Pr.
Last Summer of Our Childhood: Imagery & Style Collection. Margueritte A. Brown. Ed. by Dewilda M. Williams. 104p. 1996. pap. 12.00 (*1-886493-08-1*) NBC Study Pub.
Last Summer with Maizon. large type ed. Jacqueline Woodson. 1993. 29.50 (*0-614-09835-1*, L-34131-00) Am Printing Hse.
Last Summer's Girl. Elizabeth Barnes. (Romance Ser.). 1993. per. 2.99 (*0-373-03278-1*, 1-03278-8) Harlequin Bks.
Last Sunrise. Harold Gordon. Ed. by David Gordon. (Illus.). 295p. 1992. 25.95 (*0-9632589-0-7*); pap. 15.95 (*0-9632589-1-5*) H&J Pub.
Last Supper. Howard Barker. 128p. (Orig.). 1989. pap. 9.95 (*0-7145-4149-4*) Riverrun NY.
***Last Supper.** Phaidon Press Staff. 2000. 19.95 (*0-7148-3940-X*) Phaidon Pr.
Last Supper. large type ed. Charles McCarry. 624p. 1986. 11.50 (*0-7089-8322-7*, Charnwood) Ulverscroft.
Last Supper: Leonardo da Vinci's Masterpiece: A Counted Thread Design. Jean D. Crowther. 12p. 1987. 6.98 (*0-88290-293-8*, 2780) Horizon Utah.
***Last Supper According to Martha & Mary.** Tina Beattie. 2001. pap. 14.95 (*0-8245-1859-4*) Crossroad NY.
Last Supper & Lord's Supper. Ed. by I. Howard Marshall. (Biblical & Theological Classics Library: Vol. 17). 191p. 1997. reprint ed. pap. 9.99 (*0-85364-856-5*, Pub. by Paternoster Pub) OM Literature.
***Last Supper Blood & Rite.** Richard E. Dansky. 2000. pap. 17.95 (*1-56504-253-0*) White Wolf.
Last Supper Restoration: A Play Dan O'Brien. LC 98-209024. 66p. 1998. write for info. (*0-573-62623-5*) French.
Last Suppers. Diane Mott Davidson. LC 94-18886. 304p. 1995. mass mkt. 6.50 (*0-553-57258-X*, Crimeline) Bantam.
***Last Suppers.** large type ed. Diane Mott Davidson. LC 99-11187. 1999. 23.95 (*1-56895-640-1*) Wheeler Pub.
Last Suppers: If the World Ended Tomorrow, What Would Be Your Last Meal? James L. Dickerson. LC 98-55744. (Illus.). 208p. 1999. 24.95 (*0-86730-758-7*, Pub. by Lebhar Friedman) Natl Bk Netwk.
***Last Survivor: In Search of Martin Zaidenstadt.** Timothy W. Ryback. 2000. pap. 12.00 (*0-679-75826-7*) Knopf.
Last Survivor: In Search of Martin Zaidenstadt. Timothy W. Ryback. LC 98-52319. 160p. 1999. 21.00 (*0-679-43971-4*) Pantheon.
Last Survivor: Memoirs of George William Watson, a Horse Soldier in the 12th Virginia Cavalry (CSA) Brian S. Kesterson. LC 93-91376. 73p. 1993. pap. 9.95 (*0-9635802-0-5*) Night Hawk.
***Last Suspect.** Susan E. McCloud. LC 98-70865. 236p. 1998. write for info. (*1-57008-419-X*) Bookcraft Inc.
Last Swan in Sacramento. Stephen Bly. LC 99-21425. (Old California Ser.: Vol. 2). 224p. 1999. pap. 10.99 (*1-58134-109-1*) Crossway Bks.
***Last Swan in Sacramento.** Stephen A. Bly. LC 00-33461. (Old California Ser.). 2000. write for info. (*0-7838-9127-X*, G K Hall & Co) Mac Lib Ref.
Last Switcheroo. Faythines. Ed. by Palmer Publications Staff. (Illus.). 152p. 1989. pap. 10.00 (*0-9625019-0-5*) F M Schremp.
Last Sword of Power. David Gemmell. (The Stones of Power Ser.: Bk. 2). 1996. mass mkt. 5.99 (*0-345-37901-2*) Ballantine Pub Grp.
Last Tales. Isak Dinesen. LC 91-50031. (Vintage International Ser.). 352p. 1991. pap. 13.00 (*0-679-73640-9*) Vin Bks.
Last Tales of Uncle Remus. Illus. by Jerry Pinkney. LC 93-7531. (J). (ps-4). 1994. 18.99 (*0-8037-1303-7*, Dial Yng Read) Peng Put Young Read.
***Last Talons of the Eagle: Secret Nazi Technology Which Could Have Changed the Course of World War II.** Gary Hyland & Anton Gill. (Illus.). 373p. 2000. pap. 11.95 (*0-7472-5964-X*, Pub. by Headline Bk Pub) Trafalgar.
Last Tango in Brooklyn. Kirk Douglas. 384p. 1995. mass mkt. 6.50 (*0-446-60201-9*, Pub. by Warner Bks) Little.
Last Tango in Brooklyn. large type ed. Kirk Douglas. LC 94-25461. 392p. 1994. lib. bdg. 24.95 (*0-8161-7465-2*, G K Hall Lrg Type) Mac Lib Ref.
Last Tango in Pango Pango. Eddie Cope & Buster Cearley. (Illus.). 36p. (Orig.). 1988. pap. 4.00 (*0-88680-293-8*) I E Clark.
Last Tango in Paris. David Thompson. LC 98-229714. (Modern Classics Ser.). (Illus.). 96p. 1998. pap. 10.95 (*0-85170-545-6*) Ind U Pr.
Last Tango of Delores Delgado. Marele Day. 192p. 1993. pap. 9.95 (*1-86373-323-X*, Pub. by Allen & Unwin Pty) IPG Chicago.
***Last Tasmanian Tiger: The History & Extinction of the Thylacine.** Robert R. Paddleford. (Illus.). 336p. (C). 2000. text Price not set. (*0-521-78219-8*) Cambridge U Pr.
Last Teenage Suicide. Norman Geller. (Illus.). (Orig.). (J). (gr. 6-12). 1988. pap. 7.95 (*0-915753-13-8*) N Geller Pub.
Last Templar: A Medieval West Country Mystery. Michael Jecks. (Medieval Murder Mysteries Ser.). 384p. 1996. mass mkt. 9.95 (*0-7472-5061-8*, Pub. by Headline Bk Pub) Trafalgar.
Last Temptation of Christ. Nikos Kazantzakis. 506p. 1988. pap. 11.00 (*0-671-67257-6*, Touchstone) S&S Trade Pap.
Last Temptation of Christ. Nikos Kazantzakis. 512p. 1998. per. 12.00 (*0-684-85256-X*) S&S Trade Pap.
Last Temptation of Hollywood. Larry W. Poland. Ed. by Robert M. Holmes, Jr. 208p. (Orig.). 1988. pap. 6.95 (*0-9621692-0-X*) Mastermed Intl.
Last Ten Pounds. Linda Konner. 192p. 1994. mass mkt. 4.50 (*0-380-72048-5*, Avon Bks) Morrow Avon.
Last Tenement: Confronting Community & Urban Renewal in Boston's West End. Ed. by Sean M. Fisher & Carolyn Hughes. LC 92-70097. (Illus.). 112p. (Orig.). 1992. pap. 17.95 (*0-934865-00-0*) Bostonian Soc.
***Last Term at Malory Towers.** Enid Blyton. (J). 1999. mass mkt. 7.50 (*1-84032-061-3*, Pub. by HOD2) Ulverscroft.
Last Testament, Vol. I. Osho. Ed. by K. Prabhu et al. LC 85-63289. (Interview Ser.). (Illus.). 832p. (Orig.). (C). 1986. pap. 14.95 (*0-88050-250-9*) Oshos.
Last Texas Gun. large type ed. Elliot Long. 240p. 1998. pap. 19.99 (*1-85389-846-5*) Ulverscroft.
Last Thane. Douglas Niles. (DragonLance Chaos War Ser.). 1998. pap. 5.99 (*0-7869-1172-7*, Pub. by TSR Inc) Random.
Last Theorem of Pierre Fermat: A Study. 2nd unabridged ed. I. A. Sakmar. LC 93-92810. (Illus.). 188p. (C). 1994. 50.00 (*0-9647224-0-2*) I A Sakmar.
Last Thing. Regis Martin. LC 97-76855. ii, 167p. 1998. pap. text 12.95 (*0-89870-662-9*) Ignatius Pr.
Last Thing He Wanted. Joan Didion. LC 96-17084. 227p. 1996. 23.00 (*0-679-43331-7*) Knopf.
Last Thing He Wanted. Joan Didion. 240p. 1997. pap. 12.00 (*0-679-75285-4*) Vin Bks.
Last Thing We Talk About: Help & Hope for Those Who Grieve. Joseph Bayly. LC 92-12678. 128p. 1992. pap. text 6.99 (*0-7814-0048-1*, LifeJourney) Chariot Victor.
***Last Thing You Get to Know.** Betty Davis Miller. 2000. pap. 9.95 (*1-930454-05-8*) Swan Scythe.
Last Things. Paul Helm. 160p. (Orig.). 1989. pap. 7.99 (*0-85151-544-4*) Banner of Truth.
***Last Things.** Jenny Offill. 272p. 2000. pap. 11.95 (*0-385-33495-8*, Delta Trade) Dell.
***Last Things.** Jenny Offill. LC 99-10758. 272p. 1999. text 23.00 (*0-374-18405-4*) FS&G.

An Asterisk (*) at the beginning of an entry indicates that the title is appearing for the first time.

L

Last Things: A Novel. Madison Jones. LC 89-30173. 214p. reprint ed. pap. 66.40 (*0-608-09821-3*, 20699890007) Bks Demand.

***Last Things: Death & the Apocalypse in the Middle Ages.** Caroline Walker Bynum. LC 99-34223. 1999. pap. text 24.95 (*0-8122-1702-0*) U of Pa Pr.

***Last Things: Heaven, Hell & Judgement.** Peter Bourne. LC 99-52433. 64p. 2000. pap. 4.50 (*0-930887-36-0*) Wenzel Pr.

Last Things: Hope for This World & the Next. Herman Bavinck. Ed. by John Bolt. Tr. by John Vriend from DUT. LC 96-1438. 208p. (C). (gr. 12). 1996. pap. 19.99 (*0-8010-2088-3*, Gereformeerds D) Baker Bks.

Last Things: What Catholics Believe about Death, Judgment, Heaven & Hell. Sean Wales. LC 95-78253. 64p. (Orig.). 1995. pap. 2.95 (*0-89243-861-4*) Liguori Pubns.

Last Things & Last Plays: Shakespearean Eschatology. Cynthia Marshall. LC 90-9883. 176p. (C). 1991. 26.95 (*0-8093-1689-7*) S Ill U Pr.

Last Things in Shakespeare. Harry Morris. LC 85-1453. (Illus.). 360p. 1985. reprint ed. pap. 111.60 (*0-608-04493-8*, 206523800001) Bks Demand.

Last 30 Days: The War Diary of the German Armed Forces High Command from April to May 1945. Joachim Schultz-Naumann. Tr. by D. G. Smith from GER. (Illus.). 250p. 1991. 24.95 (*0-8191-7729-6*) Madison Bks UPA.

Last 30 Seconds. Maria Muia. LC 98-86292. 325p. 1998. 25.00 (*0-7388-0055-4*); pap. 15.00 (*0-7388-0056-2*) Xlibris Corp.

Last Three Minutes: Conjectures about the Ultimate Fate of the Universe. Paul Davies. 176p. 1996. pap. 10.00 (*0-465-03851-4*, Pub. by Basic) HarpC.

Last Thursday in July: A Memoir of Rachel Nickell. Andre Hanscombe. 288p. 1997. 35.00 (*0-7126-7732-1*, Pub. by CEN3) Trafalgar.

Last Time I Saw Her. Robert Trammell. LC PS3570.R3345. (Salt Lick Samplers Ser.). 21p. 1985. reprint ed. pap. 30.00 (*0-7837-9164-X*, 204986500003) Bks Demand.

Last Time I Saw Mother. Arlene J. Chai. 1997. pap. 10.00 (*0-449-91234-5*) Fawcett.

Last Time I Saw Mother. large type ed. Arlene J. Chai. (Ulverscroft Large Print Ser.). 406p. 1997. 27.99 (*0-7089-3751-9*) Ulverscroft.

Last Time I Saw Paris. Elliot Paul. 1993. reprint ed. lib. bdg. 37.95 (*1-56849-157-3*) Buccaneer Bks.

Last Time I Wore a Dress: A Memoir. Daphne Scholinski & Jane M. Adams. 224p. 1998. reprint ed. pap. 13.00 (*1-57322-696-3*, Riverhd Trade) Berkley Pub.

Last to Die. William Herrick. LC 85-51507. 128p. 1987. 22.00 (*0-933256-47-7*); pap. 16.00 (*0-933256-48-5*) Second Chance.

Last to Die. William Herrick. LC 70-156152. 128p. 1971. 12.50 (*0-671-20985-X*) Ultramarine Pub.

Last to Go. Rand R. Cooper. 320p. 1990. pap. 7.95 (*0-380-70862-0*, Avon Bks) Morrow Avon.

Last to Go: A Family Chronicle. Rand R. Cooper. 304p. 1988. 16.95 (*0-15-148430-9*) Harcourt.

***Last to Know.** large type unabridged ed. Candida Crewe. 1999. 25.95 (*0-7531-5973-2*, 159732, Pub. by ISIS Lrg Prnt) ISIS Pub.

***Last Toast to Lutefisk! 102 Toasts, Tidbits & Trifles for Your Next Lutefisk Dinner.** Gary Legwold. LC 99-65890. (Illus.). 72p. 1999. pap. 8.95 (*0-9652027-1-2*) C Henry.

Last Tortilla: And Other Stories. Sergio Troncoso. LC 98-58155. (Camino del Sol Ser.). 240p. 1999. pap. 17.95 (*0-8165-1961-7*) U of Ariz Pr.

Last Tortilla: And Other Stories. Sergio Troncoso. LC 98-58155. (Camino del Sol - A Latino & Latina Ser.). 240p. 1999. 40.00 (*0-8165-1960-9*) U of Ariz Pr.

Last Tosa: Iwasa Katsumochi Matabei, Bridge to Ukiyo-E. Sandy Kita. LC 98-41191. (Illus.). 368p. (C). 1999. text 42.00 (*0-8248-1826-1*) UH Pr.

Last Touch: Preparing for a Parent's Death. Marilyn R. Becker. LC 92-81726. 160p. (Orig.). 1993. pap. 11.95 (*1-879237-34-2*) New Harbinger.

Last Touches, & Other Stories. Lucy Clifford. LC 76-150470. (Short Story Index Reprint Ser.). 1977. reprint ed. 20.95 (*0-8369-3810-0*) Ayer.

***Last Touchy-Feely Drama on the American Stage & Other Plays.** Greg Gamble & Lee Howard. 91p. (YA). (gr. 10 up). 1999. pap. 5.60 (*0-87129-896-1*, L97) Dramatic Pub.

Last Tower: Legacy of Raistlin. W. Connors & S. Weinlein. 1997. 20.00 (*0-7869-0538-7*, Pub. by TSR Inc) Random.

Last Trail. Zane Grey. 288p. 1994. mass mkt. 4.99 (*0-8125-3467-0*, Pub. by Tor Bks) St Martin.

Last Trail. Zane Grey. 1976. reprint ed. lib. bdg. 22.95 (*0-89190-754-8*) Amereon Ltd.

Last Trail. Zane Grey. 1993. reprint ed. lib. bdg. 18.95 (*1-56849-203-0*) Buccaneer Bks.

Last Trail: The Authorized Edition. Zane Grey. LC 95-39312. vii, 300p. 1996. pap. 12.00 (*0-8032-7063-1*, Bison Books) U of Nebr Pr.

Last Train. Bird & Falk. (New Trend Fiction A Ser.). (J). 1993. pap. text. write for info. (*0-582-80032-3*, Pub. by Addison-Wesley) Longman.

Last Train. Kim Lewis. LC 93-32370. 1996. 11.19 (*0-606-10249-3*, Pub. by Turtleback) Demco.

Last Train. Kim Lewis. LC 93-32370. (Illus.). 32p. (J). (ps-2). 1996. reprint ed. pap. 5.99 (*1-56402-969-7*) Candlewick Pr.

Last Train from Berlin. Beorge Blagonidow. 206p. 1995. pap. 9.95 (*0-7818-0368-3*) Hippocrene Bks.

Last Train from Berlin. W. T. Tyler. 384p. 1995. 22.50 (*0-8050-2338-0*) H Holt & Co.

Last Train from Berlin. large type ed. W. T. Tyler. LC 94-7338. 572p. 1994. 24.95 (*0-8161-7435-0*, G K Hall Lrg Type) Mac Lib Ref.

Last Train from Boot Hill/The Border Guidon, 2 vols. in 1. Gordon D. Shirreffs. 336p. 1992. pap. text, mass mkt. 4.50 (*0-8439-3361-5*) Dorchester Pub Co.

Last Train from Gun Hill. Gordon D. Shirreffs. 1984. mass mkt. 2.95 (*0-451-12687-4*, Sig) NAL.

Last Train North. Lionel Rolfe. 1987. pap. 6.95 (*0-915572-95-8*) Panjandrum.

Last Train North. Clifton L. Taulbert. LC 91-77974. (Illus.). 220p. 1995. 17.95 (*0-933031-62-9*) Coun Oak Bks.

Last Train North. Clifton L. Taulbert. LC 95-2422. 208p. 1995. pap. 9.95 (*0-14-024478-6*, Penguin Bks) Viking Penguin.

Last Train of Christmas. Kaye Jacobs Volk. LC 98-116898. 1997. pap. 3.95 (*1-57734-183-X*, 01113216) Covenant Comms.

Last Train South: The Flight of the Confederate Government from Richmond. James C. Clark. LC 84-42610. (Illus.). 192p. 1997. pap. 25.00 (*0-7864-0469-8*) McFarland & Co.

Last Train to Elkmont: A Look Back at Life on Little River in the Great Smoky Mountains. Vic Weals. (Illus.). 160p. 1993. pap. 9.95 (*0-9629156-1-0*) Olden Pr TN.

Last Train to Freedom. Robert Ronald. LC 97-92659. (Illus.). 184p. 1997. lib. bdg. 18.95 (*0-9660677-0-3*) R Ronald.

***Last Train to Memphis: The Rise of Elvis Presley.** Peter Guralnick. (Illus.). 560p. 2000. 25.00 (*0-7881-9347-3*) DIANE Pub.

Last Train to Memphis: The Rise of Elvis Presley. Peter Guralnick. 576p. (gr. 8). 1994. 27.95 (*0-316-33220-8*) Little.

Last Train to Memphis: The Rise of Elvis Presley. Peter Guralnick. (Illus.). 576p. 1995. pap. 17.95 (*0-316-33225-9*) Little.

***Last Train to Memphis: The Rise of Elvis Presley.** Peter Guralnick. 1998. pap. 16.00 (*0-316-19121-3*, Back Bay) Little.

Last Train to Nibroc. Arlene Hutton. Date not set. pap. 5.95 (*0-8222-1753-8*) Dramatists Play.

Last Train to Toronto: A Canadian Rail Odyssey. Terry Pindell. 400p. 1995. pap. 15.95 (*0-8050-2358-5*, Owl) H Holt & Co.

Last Tram to Lime Street. Joan Jonker. 480p. 1996. pap. 10.95 (*0-7472-5131-2*, Pub. by Headline Bk Pub) Trafalgar.

Last Trapper: An American Saga. LC 96-61361. (Illus.). 456p. (Orig.). 1997. pap. 19.95 (*0-9654818-0-8*) Tanglewood Hill.

Last Travels of Ida Pfeiffer: Inclusive of a Visit to Madagascar. Ida R. Pfeiffer. 1977. text 18.95 (*0-8369-9251-2*, 9104) Ayer.

Last Trek: A Study of the Boer People & the Afrikaner Nation. Sheila Patterson. LC 81-13242. 336p. 1982. reprint ed. lib. bdg. 65.00 (*0-313-23244-X*, PALT, Greenwood Pr) Greenwood.

Last Trial: On the Legends & Lore of the Command to Abraham to Offer Isaac As a Sacrifice - The Akedah. enl. ed. Shalom Spiegel. LC 93-1634. 208p. 1993. reprint ed. pap. 17.95 (*1-879045-29-X*) Jewish Lights.

Last Tribes of El Dorado. Patrick Tierney. 1999. pap. 11.95 (*0-14-013403-4*) Viking Penguin.

Last Trick of Funnyman & Other Stories. Bruce Taylor. (Illus.). (Orig.). 1997. pap. 12.99 (*1-890464-00-7*) Ministry of Whimsy.

Last Trip to Vegas. J. V. Adams. LC 93-79463. 288p. (Orig.). 1993. pap. 5.00 (*0-9612454-1-7*) Jackrabbit.

Last Trolley from Beethovenstraat. Grete Weil. Tr. by John Barrett from GER. LC 95-35209. (Verba Mundi Ser.). 176p. 1997. 22.95 (*1-56792-031-4*) Godine.

Last Trophy: Africa Is a Woman. 2nd ed. Brian Marsh. 304p. 1990. text 16.95 (*0-9624807-1-1*); pap. text 12.95 (*0-9624807-0-3*) PHS Pub Div.

Last True Cowboy. Kathleen Eagle. LC 97-44255. 211p. 1998. 20.00 (*0-380-97522-X*, Avon Bks) Morrow Avon.

Last True Cowboy. Kathleen Eagle. LC 97-44255. 400p. 1999. mass mkt. 6.50 (*0-380-78492-0*, Avon Bks) Morrow Avon.

***Last True Cowboy.** Mary L. Schramski. (Bouquet Ser.: Vol. 40). 2000. mass mkt. 3.99 (*0-8217-6534-5*, Zebra Kensgtn) Kensgtn Pub Corp.

Last Trump. Ingemar Linden. (IC-Studies in the Intercultural History of Christianity: Vol. 17). 372p. 1978. pap. 52.00 (*3-261-02370-8*) P Lang Pubng.

Last Trump. H. L. McLean. LC 90-82592. (Illus.). 245p. (Orig.). 1990. pap. 8.95 (*0-9627225-0-2*) Epiphany Pubns.

Last Trumpet: A History of the English Slide Trumpet. Art Brownlow. LC 96-28052. (Bucina Ser.: No. 1). 277p. 1996. 54.00 (*0-945193-81-5*) Pendragon NY.

Last Tsar. Larissa Iermilova. LC 96-209917. (Illus.). 256p. 1996. 55.00 (*1-85995-208-9*) Parkstone Pr.

Last Tsar: The Life & Death of Nicholas II. Edvard Radzinsky. Tr. by Marian Schwartz from RUS. LC 93-16757. 496p. 1993. reprint ed. pap. 16.95 (*0-385-46962-4*, Anchor NY) Doubleday.

Last Tudor King. large type ed. Hester W. Chapman. (Shadows of the Crown Ser.). 558p. 1974. 27.99 (*0-85456-637-6*) Ulverscroft.

Last Twelve Verses of Mark. Dean J. Burgon. 1996. pap. 15.00 (*1-888328-00-2*) D Burgon Soc.

Last Twig on the Bush. Robert E. L. Nesbitt, Jr. Ed. by Ellen M. Nesbitt. LC 97-66583. 224p. 1999. 16.95 (*0-8158-0530-6*) Chris Mass.

***Last Two Bachelors.** Linda Randall Wisdom & Debbie Macomber. 2000. per. 5.99 (*0-373-83436-5*, 1-83436-5) Harlequin Bks.

Last Two Bachelors: Delaney's Grooms. Linda R. Wisdom. (American Romance Ser.: No. 774). 1999. per. 3.99 (*0-373-16774-1*, 1-16774-1) Harlequin Bks.

Last Tycoon. F. Scott Fitzgerald. 21.95 (*0-89190-604-5*) Amereon Ltd.

Last Tycoon. F. Scott Fitzgerald. (Hudson River Editions Ver.). 176p. 1977. 35.00 (*0-684-15311-4*, Scribners Ref) Mac Lib Ref.

Last Tycoon, 3 vols., Set, Pts. I-III. F. Scott Fitzgerald. Ed. by Matthew J. Bruccoli. (F. Scott Fitzgerald Manuscripts: Vol. 5). 1168p. 1990. reprint ed. text 89.00 (*0-8240-5963-8*) Garland.

***Last UFO Vol. 1: First Descent.** Ed. by Marla J. Scott-Park. LC 00-90630. 35p. 2000. pap. 7.00 (*0-9679893-0-2*) B & M Scott.

Last Ugly Person, & Other Stories. Roger B. Thomas. LC 91-76725. 216p. (Orig.). 1992. pap. 9.95 (*0-89870-395-6*) Ignatius Pr.

Last Umbra: A Novel. Michael K. Blanchard. (Illus.). 428p. 2001. pap. 19.95 (*1-883551-52-8*) Attic Studio Pub.

Last Unicorn. Peter S. Beagle. 224p. 1991. mass mkt. 13.95 (*0-451-45052-3*, ROC) NAL.

Last Unicorn. large type ed. Peter S. Beagle. LC 98-41762. 1998. 23.95 (*0-7838-0395-8*, G K Hall Lrg Type) Mac Lib Ref.

Last Valentine. James Michael Pratt. 1999. mass mkt. 6.99 (*0-312-96822-1*) St Martin.

Last Valentine. large type ed. James Michael Pratt. LC 98-10748. 1998. 24.95 (*1-57490-133-8*, Beeler LP Bks) T T Beeler.

Last Valentine: For Fifty Years She Waited for Him to Return Until...the Last Valentine! James Michael Pratt. 268p. 1996. pap. 13.95 (*0-9651163-1-X*) Harkness Pubng.

Last Valkyrie. Steve Olson. Ed. by J. Allen Kirsch. 224p. (Orig.). 1997. pap. 12.95 (*1-878569-49-X*) Badger Bks Inc.

Last Vampire. Christopher Pike, pseud. Ed. by Patricia MacDonald. (YA). (gr. 9 up). 1994. 14.00 (*0-671-87256-7*, Archway); per. 3.99 (*0-671-87264-8*, Archway) PB.

Last Vampire. Christopher Pike, pseud. 1994. 9.09 (*0-606-06522-9*, Pub. by Turtleback) Demco.

Last Vampire: Collector's Edition, Vol. 2. Christopher Pike, pseud. (Last Vampire Ser.: No. 2). (J). (gr. 9 up). 1998. pap. 6.99 (*0-671-02290-3*, Archway) PB.

Last Vampire Collector's Edition. Christopher Pike, pseud. (Last Vampire Ser.: No. 1, Vols. 1-3). (J). (gr. 9 up). 1998. per. 6.99 (*0-671-02060-9*, Archway) PB.

Last Vampire, Four: Phantom. Christopher Pike, pseud. 1996. 9.09 (*0-606-09529-2*, Pub. by Turtleback) Demco.

Last Vampire, Four: The Phantom. Christopher Pike, pseud. LC 95-81220. (YA). (gr. 9 up). 1996. 14.00 (*0-671-55049-7*) PB.

Last Vampire, Two: Black Blood. Christopher Pike, pseud. Ed. by Patricia MacDonald. (Last Vampire Ser.: No. 2). 208p. (YA). (gr. 9 up). 1994. per. 3.99 (*0-671-87266-4*, Archway) PB.

Last Vampire, Two: Black Blood. Christopher Pike, pseud. 1994. 9.09 (*0-606-07022-2*, Pub. by Turtleback) Demco.

***Last Vanities.** Fleur Jaeggy. Tr. by Tim Parks from ITA. LC 97-44496. 96p. 1998. pap. 11.95 (*0-8112-1374-9*, NDP856, Pub. by New Directions) Norton.

Last Victim. Hannah Kuraoka. 144p. (Orig.). (YA). (gr. 6 up). 1994. mass mkt. 3.99 (*0-380-77375-9*, Avon Bks) Morrow Avon.

Last Victim: A True-Life Journey into the Mind of the Serial Killer. Jason Moss & Jeffrey Kottler. LC 98-34908. (Illus.). 288p. 1999. 24.00 (*0-446-52340-2*, Pub. by Warner Bks) Little.

***Last Victim: A True-Life Journey into the Mind of the Serial Killer.** Jason Moss & Jeffrey Kottler. 294p. 2000. mass mkt. 6.99 (*0-446-60827-0*, Pub. by Warner Bks) Little.

Last Victorians. Arthur A. Baumann. LC 70-104991. (Essay Index Reprint Ser.). 1977. 23.95 (*0-8369-1445-7*) Ayer.

Last Victory see Lane Victory: The Last Victory Ship in War & in Peace

***Last Victory in Russia: SS Panzerkorps & Manstein's Kharkov Counter Offensive.** George M Nipe. (Illus.). 300p. 2000. 59.95 (*0-7643-1186-7*) Schiffer.

Last Viking. Sandra Hill. 400p. 1998. mass mkt. 5.99 (*0-505-52255-1*, Love Spell) Dorchester Pub Co.

***Last Voice They Hear.** Ramsey Campbell. 384p. 1999. pap. 6.99 (*0-8125-4194-4*, Pub. by Forge NYC) St Martin.

Last Voice They Hear. Ramsey Campbell. LC 98-10256. 384p. 1998. text 24.95 (*0-312-86611-9*) St Martin.

Last Von Reckenburg. Louise Von Francois. LC 94-30482. (GERM Ser.). xxx, 370p. 1995. reprint ed. 65.00 (*1-879751-96-8*) Camden Hse.

Last Voyage: And Other Stories. James Hanley. 288p. 1998. pap. text 15.00 (*1-86046-316-9*) Harvill Press.

Last Voyage: The Story of Schooner Third Sea. Harold Stephens. LC 96-60117. (Illus.). 350p. (Orig.). 1996. pap. 16.95 (*0-9642521-3-9*) Wolfenden.

Last Voyage Bk. 3: Torch-Bearers. Alfred Noyes. LC 70-167477. (Granger Index Reprint Ser.). 1977. reprint ed. 18.95 (*0-8369-6282-6*) Ayer.

Last Voyage of el Nuevo Constante: Wreck & Recovery of an Eighteenth Century Spanish Ship off the Louisiana Coast. Charles E. Pearson & Paul E. Hoffman. LC 94-27046. (Illus.). 264p. 1994. 29.95 (*0-8071-1918-0*) La State U Pr.

Last Voyage of the Donna Isabel. Randall Parrish. 369p. 26.95 (*0-8488-2658-2*) Amereon Ltd.

Last Voyage of the Jean F. Anderson. Charles H. Turnbull. (Illus.). 104p. 1990. pap. 12.95 (*0-913372-55-2*) Mystic Seaport.

Last Voyage of the Karluk: The Classic Memoir of an Artic Disaster. William Laird McKinlay. LC 99-17672. 1999. pap. 12.95 (*0-312-20655-0*) St Martin.

Last Voyage of the Lusitania. Adolph A. Hoehling & Mary Hoehling. LC 97-155781. 256p. 1996. pap. 16.95 (*1-56833-078-2*) Madison Bks UPA.

Last Voyage of the Misty Day. Jackie F. Koller. LC 91-17482. 160p. (J). (gr. 4-8). 1992. 14.00 (*0-689-31731-X*) Atheneum Yung Read.

Last Voyage of the Scotian. Bill Freeman. (Bains Ser.). (Illus.). 221p. (YA). 1976. bds. 16.95 (*0-88862-113-2*, Pub. by J Lorimer) Formac Dist Ltd.

Last Voyage of Thomas Cavendish, 1591-1592. Thomas Cavendish. Ed. by David B. Quinn. LC 74-11619. (Studies in the History of Discoveries). x, 182p. (C). 1976. lib. bdg. 48.00 (*0-226-09819-2*) U Ch Pr.

Last Voyages: Cavendish, Hudson, Ralegh: The Original Narratives. Ed. by Philip Edwards. (Illus.). 278p. 1989. text 60.00 (*0-19-812894-0*) OUP.

Last Wacks. Collectors' Guide Publishers Staff. 1996. pap. 24.95 (*0-9698080-3-8*) Hot Wacks.

Last Wagon Out. Zev Spektor. 1990. 13.95 (*1-56062-052-8*); pap. 10.95 (*1-56062-053-6*) CIS Comm.

Last Wali of Swat. Told to Fredrik Barth. 225p. 1985. text 55.50 (*0-231-06162-5*) Col U Pr.

Last Wali of Swat: An Autobiography As Told to Fredrik Barth. Fredrik Barth. 199p. 1985. 2.00 (*82-00-07079-4*, Pub. by Scand Univ Pr) IBD Ltd.

Last Waltz. Mary Balogh. (Regency Romance Ser.). 223p. 1998. mass mkt. 4.99 (*0-451-19147-1*, Sig) NAL.

Last Waltz in Goodhue. Jim Franklin. LC 97-91757. 328p. 1997. pap. 18.95 (*0-9634689-1-X*) Popcorn Pr.

Last Wanderers: Nomads & Gypsies of India. T. S. Randhawa. 227p. 1996. 65.00 (*81-85822-16-6*, Pub. by Mapin Pubng) Antique Collect.

***Last War Trail: The Utes & the Settlement of Colorado.** rev. ed. Robert Emmitt. LC 99-88013. (Illus.). 378p. 2000. pap. 24.95 (*0-87081-540-7*, Pub. by Univ Pr Colo) U of Okla Pr.

Last Warhulk. Richard Baker. 1998. 13.95 (*0-7869-1217-0*, Pub. by TSR Inc) Random.

Last Warpath. Will Henry, pseud. 256p. 1997. reprint ed. mass mkt. 4.50 (*0-8439-4314-9*, Leisure Bks) Dorchester Pub Co.

Last Warrior. Suzanne P. Ellison. LC 97-22937. 140p. (J). (gr. 6-8). 1997. pap. 6.95 (*0-87358-679-4*, Rising Moon Bks); lib. bdg. 12.95 (*0-87358-678-6*, Rising Moon Bks) Northland AZ.

Last Warrior. Kristin Kyle. (Fanfare Ser.). 416p. 1999. mass mkt. 5.99 (*0-553-57963-0*) Bantam.

Last Warriors: Warrior's Honor. Michael Kosser. Ed. by Tom Burke. 1999. mass mkt. 5.99 (*0-312-96884-1*) St Martin.

Last Warriors Book, No. 2. Kosser. 1998. 5.99 (*0-312-96626-1*, Pub. by Tor Bks) St Martin.

Last Watch of the Night: Essays Too Personal & Otherwise. Paul Monette. LC 93-47655. 1994. 21.95 (*0-15-100071-9*) Harcourt.

Last Watch of the Night: Essays Too Personal & Otherwise. Paul Monette. 320p. 1995. pap. 12.00 (*0-15-600202-7*) Harcourt.

Last Waterfront: The People of South Street. Barbara Mensch. LC 84-18779. (Illus.). 188p. 1985. 20.00 (*0-88191-012-0*) Freundlich.

Last Wave. 5th ed. Robert W. Czeschin. 216p. 1991. 14.95 (*0-945332-23-8*) Agora Inc MD.

Last Week. Richard Rouse & Susan Rouse. 1985. 1.00 (*0-89536-726-2*, 5810) CSS OH.

Last Week of Jesus. (Truth in Life Adult Study Work Bks.). iii, 50p. 1998. pap., wbk. ed. write for info. (*0-9620615-4-9*) Guardian Truth Found.

Last Welsh Summer. 2nd ed. Catherine Johnson. 114p. (J). (gr. 4). 1997. reprint ed. pap. 11.95 (*0-8464-4813-0*) Beekman Pubs.

Last White Christmas. Ronald W. Monchak. LC 94-12611. (Illus.). 193p. 1994. 16.95 (*1-879094-17-7*, Avnstoke Pr) Momentum Bks.

***Last Wild Edge: One Woman's Journey from the Arctic Circle to the Olympic Rain Forest.** Susan Zwinger. LC 98-52744. 208p. 1999. pap. 15.00 (*1-55566-241-2*) Johnson Bks.

Last Wild Place. Mike Tomkies. (Illus.). 256p. 1997. pap. 19.95 (*0-224-04355-2*, Pub. by Jonathan Cape) Trafalgar.

Last Wild Place. large type ed. Mike Tomkies. (Illus.). 1989. 11.50 (*0-7089-2065-9*) Ulverscroft.

Last Wild Years. large type ed. Mike Tomkies. (Non-Fiction Ser.). (Illus.). 464p. 1993. 27.99 (*0-7089-2996-6*) Ulverscroft.

***Last Wildcat: The Short Record of T. B. Ellis, Sr.** Thomas B. Ellis, Sr. Ed. by Roger Rice Landers. 1998. mass mkt. 5.00 (*0-9669244-0-1*) Gene Soc Hernando.

Last Wilderness. Murray Morgan. LC 76-41. 290p. 1976. pap. 12.95 (*0-295-95319-5*) U of Wash Pr.

Last Wilderness: Images of the Canadian Wild. 2nd ed. Canadian Nature Federation Staff & Freeman Patterson. (Illus.). 180p. 1990. 50.00 (*1-55013-251-2*) Firefly Bks Ltd.

Last Will & Testament: Simple Will. LawPak Staff. (Illus.). 140p. (Orig.). 1999. pap. 13.95 (*1-879421-01-1*) LawPak.

Last Will & Testament According to the Divine Rites of the Drug Cocaine. Scott Shaw. 32p. (Orig.). 1989. pap. 5.95 (*1-877792-00-4*) Buddha Rose.

Last Will & Testament Kit. Arnold S. Goldstein. 35p. 1991. student ed. 18.95 (*1-56382-137-0*) E-Z Legal.

Last Will & Testament Made E-Z. E-Z Legal Staff. (Made E-Z Ser.). 172p. 1999. pap. 17.95 (*1-56382-427-2*) E-Z Legal.

Last Will & Testament of a Lover: A Journey Through Grief. Clifford Ellis. 208p. 1997. pap. 14.95 (*1-896867-06-5*) Moulin Publ.

Last Will & Testament of an Extremely Distinguished Dog. Eugene O'Neill. (Illus.). 48p. 1999. 18.00 (*0-9633560-5-4*) Durand Pr.

***Last Will & Testament of an Extremely Distinguished Dog.** Eugene O'Neill. LC 99-36351. (Illus.). 48p. 1999. 15.00 (*0-8050-6170-3*) H Holt & Co.

An Asterisk (*) at the beginning of an entry indicates that the title is appearing for the first time.

L

Last Will & Testament of George Washington & Schedule of His Property: To Which Is Appended the Last Will & Testament of Martha Washington. Ed. by John C. Fitzpatrick. LC 92-10576. 1992. write for info. (*0-931917-19-0*) Mt Vernon Ladies.

Last Winter in the United States. F. Barham Zincke. LC 76-130569. (Select Bibliographies Reprint Ser.). 1977. 21.95 (*0-8369-5542-0*) Ayer.

Last Wish. Created by Francine Pascal. (Sweet Valley High Super Edition Ser.). 240p. (YA). (gr. 7 up). 1998. mass mkt. 4.99 (*0-553-49235-7*, Sweet Valley) BDD Bks Young Read.

Last Wish. Betty Rollin. LC 98-19185. 272p. 1998. pap. text 12.00 (*1-891620-01-0*, Pub. by PublicAffairs NY) HarpC.

Last Wish. Betty Rollin. 240p. 1986. pap. 8.95 (*0-446-37032-0*) Warner Bks.

Last Wishes: A Handbook to Guide Your Survivors. Lucinda P. Knox & Michael D. Knox. LC 94-61744. 177p. (Orig.). 1995. pap. 14.95 (*1-56975-024-6*) Ulysses Pr.

Last Wishes: A Psychologist's Guide to Living Life Prepared for Death. Kathleen Cairns. 300p. 1998. pap. 14.95 (*1-891409-01-8*) Life Goes On.

Last Wishes: A Workbook for Recording Your Funeral, Memorial, & Other Final Instructions. Lucinda P. Knox & Michael D. Knox. 144p. (Orig.). 1994. pap. 14.95 (*0-9628460-0-7*) Appld Sci FL.

Last Witness: The Child Survivor of the Holocaust. Judith S. Kestenberg & Ira Brenner. 272p. 1996. text 38.50 (*0-88048-662-7*, 8662) Am Psychiatric.

***Last Witnesses: Reflections on the Wartime Internment of Japanes.** Erica Harth. 1999. text. write for info. (*0-312-22199-1*) St Martin.

Last Wizard. Simon Hawke. 240p. (Orig.). 1997. mass mkt. 5.99 (*0-446-36520-3*, Pub. by Warner Bks) Little.

Last Wizard. Tanya Huff. (Novels of Crystal Ser.: Bk. 2). 288p. 1989. pap. 4.50 (*0-88677-331-8*, Pub. by DAW Bks) Penguin Putnam.

Last Wolf: The Legend of Three Toes. Gary Enright. 208p. (Orig.). 1993. pap. 15.95 (*1-882159-65-9*) Insight.

Last Wolf of Ireland. Elona Malterre. 144p. (J). (gr. 4-9). 1990. 15.00 (*0-395-54381-9*, Clarion Bks) HM.

Last Word. Wallace Benn. 1996. 9.99 (*1-85792-079-1*, Pub. by Christian Focus) Spring Arbor Dist.

***Last Word.** Paul Micou. 2000. pap. 9.95 (*0-552-99502-9*, Pub. by Transworld Publishers Ltd) Trafalgar.

Last Word. Thomas Nagel. 160p. 1997. 22.00 (*0-19-510834-5*) OUP.

***Last Word: A Collection of Insults, Epitaphs & Compliments from the Rich & Famous.** Ed. by Gyles Brandreth. 192p. 2000. reprint ed. text 20.00 (*0-7881-6814-2*) DIANE Pub.

Last Word: An Eschatalogical Theology of Preaching. C. Raymond Holmes. LC 86-73256. 128p. 1987. pap. text 13.99 (*0-943872-93-6*) Andrews Univ Pr.

Last Word: An Insomniac Anthology of Canadian Poetry. Ed. by Michael Holmes. LC 95-218719. 168p. 1997. pap. 12.99 (*1-895837-32-4*) Insomniac.

Last Word: And Other Stories. Graham Greene. LC 99-200035. 1999. pap. 11.95 (*0-14-118157-5*) Penguin Putnam.

***Last Word: Insights About The Church & Ministry.** William H. Willimon. LC 00-44168. 2000. write for info. (*0-687-09002-4*) Abingdon.

Last Word: Letters Between Marcia Nardi & William Carlos Williams. William Carlos Williams. Ed. by Elizabeth M. O'Neil. LC 93-20999. (Illus.). 290p. 1994. pap. text 17.95 (*0-87745-461-2*) U of Iowa Pr.

***Last Word: Questions & Answers from the Popular Column on Everyday Science.** Ed. by Mick O'Hare. LC 99-204863. (Illus.). 238p. 1999. pap. 12.95 (*0-19-286199-9*) OUP.

Last Word: The New York Times Book of Obituaries & Farewells: A Celebration of Unusual Lives. New York Times Staff. Ed. by Marvin Siegel. LC 97-11960. 432p. 1997. 25.00 (*0-688-15015-2*, Wm Morrow) Morrow Avon.

Last Word: The New York Times Book Of Obituaries And Farewells:A Celebration Of Unusual Lives. Ed. by Marvin Siegel. 432p. 1999. pap. 12.00 (*0-688-16637-7*, Quil) HarperTrade.

Last Word: Tombstone Wit & Wisdom. Nicola Gillies. LC 98-193997. 64p. 1997. 4.98 (*1-889461-02-4*) DoveTail Bks.

Last Word: Tombstone Wit & Wisdom. Ed. by Nicola Gillies. 64p. 1997. 4.98 (*0-614-29842-3*) DoveTail Bks.

Last Word: Women, Death, & Divination in Inner Mani. C. Nadia Seremetakis. LC 90-40640. (Illus.). 286p. 1991. pap. text 23.00 (*0-226-74876-6*); lib. bdg. 52.00 (*0-226-74875-8*) U Ch Pr.

Last Word & Other Stories. large type ed. Graham Greene. 184p. 1991. 18.95 (*1-85089-488-4*, Pub. by ISIS Lrg Prnt) Transaction Pubs.

Last Word from Paradise. Peter Beard. write for info. (*0-679-40846-0*) Knopf.

Last Word in Make-Up: A Practical Illustrated Handbook: Manuscript Edition. Rudolph Liszt. (Illus.). 1964. pap. 13.00 (*0-8222-0640-4*) Dramatists Play.

Last Word in Medical Technology. Carol S. Rudler-Barnett & Luann M. Suckley. 239p. 1985. pap. 28.95 (*0-316-76094-3*, Little Brwn Med Div) Lppncott W & W.

Last Word on First Names. Linda Rosenkrantz. 1997. mass mkt. 5.99 (*0-312-96106-5*) St Martin.

Last Word on First Names: The Definite Guide to the Best & Worst in Baby Names. 4th ed. Linda Rosenkrantz. 1995. pap. 9.95 (*0-312-11748-5*) St Martin.

Last Word on Lute Lefse. Gary Legwold. 165p. 1991. pap. 9.95 (*0-934860-78-5*) Adventure Pubns.

Last Word on Lutefisk: Heartwarming Stories, Humor, History-Plus the Lutefisk Dinner Directory. Gary Legwold. LC 96-77791. (Illus.). viii, 168p. 1996. pap. 14.95 (*0-9652027-0-4*) C Henry.

Last Word on Making Money. Rolf B. White. 288p. (Orig.). (YA). 1988. pap. 9.95 (*0-8184-0480-9*); text 17.95 (*0-8184-0475-2*) Carol Pub Group.

Last Word on Making Money. Compiled by Rolf B. White. 272p. (Orig.). (YA). 1992. pap. 4.50 (*0-8216-2512-8*, Carol Paperbacks) Carol Pub Group.

Last Word on Management. Rolf White. 1987. 15.00 (*0-8184-0452-3*) Carol Pub Group.

Last Word on Management: A Collection of Quotations That Offer the Ultimate Wisdom. Rolf B. White. 280p. 1988. reprint ed. pap. 8.95 (*0-8184-0454-X*) Carol Pub Group.

Last Word on Power: Reinvention for Executives Who Want to Change Their World. Tracy Goss. Ed. by Betty Sue Flowers. LC 95-21269. 288p. 1995. 29.95 (*0-385-47492-X*) Doubleday.

Last Word on the Middle East. (ENG & IND.). 1992. pap. write for info. (*0-934920-43-5*, B-34IN) Derek Prince.

Last Word on the Middle East. Derek Prince. 1992. pap. 5.95 (*0-934920-40-0*, B-34) Derek Prince.

***Last Word 2: More Questions & Answers On Everyday Science.** (Illus.). 240p. 2001. pap. 14.95 (*0-19-286204-9*) OUP.

Last Words. Guy Bennett. (New American Poetry Ser.). 1998. pap. 9.95 (*1-55713-336-0*) Sun & Moon CA.

Last Words. H. Smith. pap. 4.95 (*0-88172-124-7*) Believers Bkshelf.

Last Words: A Dictionary of Deathbed Quotations. C. Bernard Ruffin. LC 95-3196. 269p. 1995. lib. bdg. 42.50 (*0-7864-0043-9*) McFarland & Co.

Last Words: Parting Thoughts & Last Meals from Death Row. unabridged ed. Richard K. Nongard. (Illus.). 72p. (Orig.). 1997. pap. 9.95 (*0-9655979-2-X*, 02-97) Peachtree Prof.

***Last Words: The Final Journals of William S. Burroughs.** William S. Burroughs. Ed. by James Grauerholz. LC 99-44259. 320p. 2000. 25.00 (*0-8021-1657-4*, Pub. by Grove-Atltic) Publishers Group.

Last Words: Variations on a Theme in Cultural History. Karl S. Guthke. 224p. 1992. text 35.00 (*0-691-05688-9*, Pub. by Princeton U Pr) Cal Prin Full Svc.

Last Words, Last Laughs. Richard Porteus. Ed. by Laura Vervaecke. LC 97-70329. 192p. (Orig.). 1997. pap. 5.99 (*0-914839-38-1*) Gollehon Pr.

Last Words of Christ in the Way of the Cross: A Drama for Lent. Thomas J. Gardiner. (Christian Drama Ser.). 20p. (Orig.). 1994. pap. 3.00 (*1-57514-139-6*, 3026) Encore Perform Pub.

Last Words of Dutch Schultz: Fiction in the Form of a Film Script. William J. Burroughs. (Illus.). 128p. 1993. reprint ed. pap. 10.45 (*1-55970-211-7*, Pub. by Arcade Pub Inc) Time Warner.

Last Words of Saints & Sinners. Herbert Lockyer. LC 78-85429. 240p. 1975. pap. 11.99 (*0-8254-3111-5*) Kregel.

Last Words of the Resurrected Christ. Richard O. Singleton. LC 99-166152. (Illus.). 96p. 1997. pap. 7.95 (*0-88489-368-5*) St Marys.

Last Words on Evolution, 3. Ernst Haeckel. Tr. by Joseph McCabe from GER. LC 77-72191. (Contributions to the History of Psychology Ser.: Vol. 3, Pt. D). 285p. 1977. reprint ed. lib. bdg. 69.50 (*0-313-26947-5*, U6947, Greenwood Pr) Greenwood.

Last Workshop on Grand Unification. Ed. by P. H. Frampton. 376p. (C). 1989. pap. 40.00 (*981-02-0015-3*); text 127.00 (*981-02-0014-5*) World Scientific Pub.

Last World. Christopher Ransmayr. Tr. by John E. Woods from GER. 256p. 1996. reprint ed. pap. 12.00 (*0-8021-3458-0*, Grove) Grove-Atltic.

Last World. Christopher Ransmayr. Ed. by Jane Rosenman. 256p. 1992. reprint ed. per. 10.00 (*0-671-74962-5*, WSP) PB.

Last World War & the End of Time. Emmett J. Culligan. (Illus.). 210p. 1981. reprint ed. pap. 13.50 (*0-89555-034-2*) TAN Bks Pubs.

Last Worthless Evening: Four Novellas & Two Stories. Andre Dubus. LC 85-45530. 288p. 1986. 13.95 (*0-87923-642-6*) Godine.

Last Worthless Evening: Four Novellas & Two Stories. Andre Dubus. LC 86-45530. 288p. 1986. reprint ed. pap. 12.95 (*1-56792-067-5*) Godine.

Last Writings: Nothingness & the Religious Worldview. Nishida Kitaro. Tr. by David A. Dilworth. LC 86-30931. 176p. 1987. pap. text 16.00 (*0-8248-1554-8*) UH Pr.

Last Writings Vol. 1: Preliminary Studies for Part III of Philosophical Investigations. Ludwig Josef Johann Wittgenstein. Ed. by George H. Von Wright & Heikki Nyman. Tr. by C. J. Luckhardt & M. A. Aue. 283p. 1996. pap. text 22.50 (*0-226-90446-6*, Midway Reprint) U Ch Pr.

Last Writings on the Philosophy of Psychology Vol. 1: Preliminary Studies for Part II of Philosophical Investigations. Ludwig Josef Johann Wittgenstein. Ed. by Heikki Nyman & George H. Von Wright. Tr. by C. J. Luckhardt & M. A. Aue. 268p. (C). 1996. reprint ed. pap. text 17.95 (*0-226-90425-3*) U Ch Pr.

Last Yankee: Full Length. Arthur Miller. 1993. pap. 5.25 (*0-8222-1337-0*) Dramatists Play.

Last Yankee: One Act. Arthur Miller. 1991. pap. 3.25 (*0-8222-0641-2*) Dramatists Play.

Last Yankees: Folkways in Eastern Vermont & the Border Country. Scott E. Hastings, Jr. LC 89-24785. (Illus.). 159p. 1990. pap. 19.95 (*0-87451-677-3*); text 35.00 (*0-87451-510-6*) U Pr of New Eng.

Last Year in Hong Kong: A Love Story. Robert S. Elegant. LC 96-49003. 256p. 1997. 23.00 (*0-688-14890-5*, Wm Morrow) Morrow Avon.

Last Year of Malcolm X: The Evolution of a Revolutionary. George Breitman. LC 67-20467. 169p. 1967. reprint ed. pap. 14.95 (*0-87348-004-X*) Pathfinder NY.

***Last Year of the Gang: A Diary from a Girl's School.** Madeline Macdonald. (Illus.). 234p. 2000. 30.00 (*1-85776-437-4*, Pub. by Book Guild Ltd) Trans-Atl Phila.

Last Year of the German Army: May 1944-May 1945. James Lucas. (Illus.). 240p. 1996. pap. 16.95 (*1-85409-334-7*, Pub. by Arms & Armour) Sterling.

Last Year of the Kriegsmarine: May 1944-May 1945. V. E. Tarrant. LC 93-87779. (Illus.). 288p. 1996. pap. 16.95 (*1-85409-362-2*, Pub. by Arms & Armour) Sterling.

Last Year of the Kriegsmarine: May 1944-May 1945. V. E. Tarrant. LC 93-87779. (Illus.). 256p. 1994. 34.95 (*1-55750-510-1*) Naval Inst Pr.

Last Year of Thomas Mann. Erika Mann. Tr. by Richard Graves. LC 72-126323. (Biography Index Reprint Ser.). 1977. 17.95 (*0-8369-8029-8*) Ayer.

Last Years of Austria - Hungary. Ed. by Mark Cornwall. 192p. 1998. pap. text 23.95 (*0-85989-563-7*) Univ Exeter Pr.

Last Years of Austria-Hungary: Essays in Political & Military History, 1908-1918. Ed. by Mark Cornwall. (Illus.). 168p. 1990. pap. text 17.50 (*0-85989-306-5*, Pub. by Univ Exeter Pr) Northwestern U Pr.

Last Years of Henry Timrod. Ed. by Jay B. Hubbell. LC 78-181907. reprint ed. 32.50 (*0-404-03374-1*) AMS Pr.

Last Years of Rodin. Marcelle Tirel. LC 74-16282. (Studies in French Literature: No. 45). 1974. lib. bdg. 75.00 (*0-8383-1945-9*) M S G Haskell Hse.

Last Years of Sitting Bull. Herbert T. Hoover & Robert C. Hollow. (Illus.). 64p. 1984. pap. 6.50 (*1-891419-07-2*) State Hist ND.

Last Years of Soviet Russian Literature: Prose Fiction, 1975-1991. Deming Brown. LC 92-44724. 218p. (C). 1994. pap. text 18.95 (*0-521-40865-2*) Cambridge U Pr.

Last Years of the English Slave Trade, Liverpool, 1705-1807. Averil Mackenzie-Grieve. 331p. 1968. reprint ed. 35.00 (*0-7146-1895-0*, Pub. by F Cass Pubs) Intl Spec Bk.

Last Years of the Monroe Doctrine, 1945-1993. Gaddis Smith. 280p. 1995. 11.00 (*0-8090-1568-4*) Hill & Wang.

Last Years of the Soviet Empire: Snapshots from 1985-1991. Vladimir Shlapentokh. LC 92-38777. (Illus.). 240p. 1993. 59.95 (*0-275-94440-9*, C4440, Praeger Pubs) Greenwood.

***Last Years of the "Wee Donegal" The County Donegal Railways in Colour, 1950-59.** Robert Robotham. LC 99-176252. (Illus.). 290p. 1998. 24.95 (*1-898392-42-0*, Pub. by Colourpoint) Irish Bks Media.

Last Years of Walker Evans. Jerry L. Thompson. LC 97-60243. (Illus.). 128p. 1997. 24.95 (*0-500-54210-4*, Pub. by Thames Hudson) Norton.

Last Year's Poverty. Tim McNulty. 1987. 25.00 (*0-918116-41-4*) Brooding Heron Pr.

Last 100 Days of the Soviet Union. Boris Pankin. 256p. 1996. 29.95 (*1-85043-878-1*, Pub. by I B T) St Martin.

***Lasting: A Novel.** Suzanne Love Harris. LC 99-47901. 209p. 2000. 21.95 (*0-918056-11-X*, Pub. by Ariadne Pr) Seven Hills Bk.

Lasting Aalto Masterwork: The Library at Mount Angel Abbey. Donald Canty. 1992. pap. 19.95 (*0-918941-04-0*) Mt Angel Abbey.

Lasting Attachments: Stories. Annette Sanford. LC 88-39065. (Southwest Life & Letters Ser.). 168p. 1989. 17.95 (*0-87074-284-1*) SMU Press.

Lasting Calm. Ed. by Joy Esterby. 1997. 69.95 (*1-57553-449-5*) Watermrk Pr.

Lasting Change: Building the Shared Values That Make Companies Great. Rob Lebow & William L. Simon. LC 97-208503. (Business Technology Ser.). 320p. 1997. 24.95 (*0-442-02585-8*, VNR) Wiley.

Lasting Change: The Shared Values Process That Makes Companies Great. Lebow. 272p. 1999. pap. 17.95 (*0-471-32847-2*) Wiley.

Lasting Change: The Shared Values Process That Makes Companies Great. Rob Lebow & William L. Simon. 304p. 1997. 24.95 (*0-471-29264-8*, VNR) Wiley.

Lasting Differences: The High Scope Preschool Curriculum Comparison Study Through Age 23. David P. Weikart & Lawrence J. Schweinhart. LC 96-43660. (Monographs of the High/Scope Educational Research Foundation). 120p. 1997. 19.95 (*1-57379-017-6*, R1057) High-Scope.

Lasting Echoes. Joseph Bruchac. LC 97-11884. (Illus.). 176p. (J). (gr. 5). 1997. 16.00 (*0-15-201327-X*) Harcourt.

Lasting Echoes: An Oral History of Native American People. Joseph Bruchac. 176p. 1999. mass mkt. 5.99 (*0-380-73184-3*, Avon Bks) Morrow Avon.

Lasting Effects of Child Sexual Abuse. Ed. by Gail E. Wyatt & Gloria J. Powell. LC 88-4366. (Sage Focus Editions Ser.: No. 100). 288p. 1988. pap. 89.30 (*0-608-05067-9*, 206562200005) Bks Demand.

Lasting Effects of Child Sexual Abuse. Ed. by Gail E. Wyatt & Gloria J. Powell. (Focus Editions Ser.: Vol. 100). 320p. (C). 1988. text 59.95 (*0-8039-3256-1*); pap. text 26.00 (*0-8039-3257-X*) Sage.

Lasting Elements of Individualism. William E. Hocking. LC 75-3186. reprint ed. 27.50 (*0-404-59188-4*) AMS Pr.

Lasting Friend: Friendship: Making Friends. J. Thomas Morse et al. Ed. by Betty Gouge et al. LC 85-45422. (KidSkills Interpersonal Skill Ser.). (Illus.). 45p. (J). (gr. 2-3). 1985. lib. bdg. 9.95 (*0-934275-06-8*) Fam Skills.

Lasting Gift of Heritage: A History of the North Carolina Society for the Preservation of Antiquities, 1939-1974. David L. Brook. LC 98-141858. (Illus.). 205p. 1997. 24.00 (*0-86526-274-8*) NC Archives.

Lasting Images Price Guide to Adult Entertainment & Fantasy Art Pinup Cards. Jeffrey S. Marks. (Illus.). 60p. (Orig.). 1994. 14.95 (*0-9641536-0-2*) Lasting Images.

Lasting Images Price Guide to Adult Entertainment & Fantasy Art Pinup Cards, Vol. II. Jeffrey S. Marks. (Lasting Images Price Guide Ser.: Vol. 2). (Illus.). 80p. (Orig.). 1995. 18.95 (*0-9641536-1-0*) Lasting Images.

Lasting Images Price Guide to Adult Entertainment & Fantasy Art Pinup Cards, Vol. 3. Jeffrey Marks. (Illus.). 32p. 1997. pap. 19.95 (*0-9641536-2-9*) Lasting Images.

Lasting Impression. Scott D. Trostel. Ed. by Cheryl Pearson. 192p. 1995. 16.95 (*0-925436-10-0*) Cam-Tech Pub.

***Lasting Impressions.** Randall Hartsell. 24p. 1999. pap. 5.95 (*0-7390-0396-8*, 18890) Alfred Pub.

Lasting Impressions. Cheryl Henderson. 1999. 7.95 (*1-56245-359-9*) Great Quotations.

***Lasting Impressions: A Guide to Understanding Fossils in the Northeastern United States.** Karen Edelstein. Ed. by Trudie Calvert. (Illus.). 130p. 1999. pap. 20.00 (*1-57753-182-5*, 147LM26) Corn Coop Ext.

Lasting Impressions: A Short History of English Publishing in Quebec. Bruce Whiteman. LC 94-223668. (Illus.). 104p. (Orig.). 1994. pap. 13.95 (*1-55065-051-3*, Pub. by Vehicule Pr) Genl Dist Srvs.

***Lasting Impressions: Contemporary Prints from the Bruce Brown Collection.** Aprile Gallant & Bruce Brown. Ed. by Jessica Skwire. LC 99-76990. (Illus.). 64p. 2000. pap. write for info. (*0-916857-19-0*) Port Mus Art.

Lasting Impressions: French & American Impressionism from New England Museums. Contrib. by Jean Harris et al. (Illus.). 64p. 1988. 6.00 (*0-916746-13-5*) Springfield Lib & Mus.

***Lasting Impressions: Infant Massage.** Carolyn Molloy & Laura Wiedner-Smith. LC 99-90354. (Illus.). 43p. 1999. pap. 16.95 (*0-9669123-0-6*) Lasting Imp.

Lasting Impressions: Lithography As Art. Pat Gilmour. LC 88-1304. (Illus.). 416p. (C). 1988. 59.95 (*0-8122-8126-8*) U of Pa Pr.

Lasting Impressions: Weaving Literature into the Writing Workshop. Shelley Harwayne. LC 92-24369. 354p. (C). 1993. 35.00 (*0-435-08784-3*, 08784); pap. text 25.00 (*0-435-08732-0*, 08732) Heinemann.

Lasting Joy. Ed. by Melisa Mitchell. 1998. 69.95 (*1-57553-616-1*) Watermrk Pr.

Lasting Legacy. Kay Thorpe. (Presents Ser.). 1993. per. 2.89 (*0-373-11534-2*, 1-11534-4) Harlequin Bks.

Lasting Legacy. large type ed. Kay Thorpe. 1992. reprint ed. 18.95 (*0-263-12895-4*) Mac Lib Ref.

Lasting Legacy: Scrapbooks & Photo Albums That Touch the Heart. Souzzann Y. Carroll. LC 99-174069. 1998. pap. 19.95 (*0-9663318-0-X*) Living Vision.

Lasting Legacy to the Carolinas: The Duke Endowment, 1924-1994. Robert F. Durden. LC 97-31427. 1998. 55.95 (*0-8223-2151-3*) Duke.

Lasting Lessons: A Teacher's Guide to Reflecting on Experience. Clifford E. Knapp. LC 92-23943. (Illus.). 117p. (Orig.). (C). 1992. pap. 12.00 (*1-880785-06-4*) ERIC-CRESS.

Lasting Love. Alistair Begg. 1997. 14.99 incl. audio (*0-8024-3402-9*) Moody.

Lasting Love. Patti Weber. (Orig.). 1996. pap. write for info. (*1-57553-309-X*) Watermrk Pr.

Lasting Love: How to Avoid Marital Failure. Alistair Begg. LC 97-207335. 264p. 1997. 14.99 (*0-8024-3401-0*) Moody.

Lasting Love Relationships. Sondra Ray. 142p. 1995. pap. 16.95 incl. audio (*1-879323-23-0*) Sound Horizons AV.

Lasting Marriages: Men & Women Growing Together. Richard A. Mackey & Bernard A. O'Brien. LC 95-3336. 208p. 1995. 59.95 (*0-275-95075-1*, Praeger Pubs); pap. 19.95 (*0-275-95076-X*, Praeger Pubs) Greenwood.

Lasting Memories: A Guide to Writing Your Family History. Dana Alexander & Amy Shea. 142p. (Orig.). 1996. pap., wbk. ed. 16.95 (*0-9653437-0-7*) Generations NC.

Lasting Mirage. Ed. by Caroline Sullivan. 1997. 69.95 (*1-57553-403-7*) Watermrk Pr.

Lasting Moments, Vol. 1. Ed. by Jef Sturm. 300p. 1998. write for info. (*1-888680-25-3*) Poetry Guild.

Lasting of the Mohicans: History of an American Myth. Martin Barker & Roger Sabin. LC 95-29991. (Studies in Popular Culture). (Illus.). 224p. 1996. 45.00 (*0-87805-858-3*); pap. 16.95 (*0-87805-859-1*) U Pr of Miss.

Lasting Peace: Collected Addresses of Daisaku Ikeda, Vol. 1. Daisaku Ikeda. Tr. by Richard L. Gage et al from JPN. (Illus.). 272p. 1981. 29.95 (*0-8348-0166-3*) Weatherhill.

Lasting Peace: Collected Addresses of Daisaku Ikeda, Vol. 2. Daisaku Ikeda. Tr. by Richard L. Gage et al from JPN. (Illus.). 302p. 1981. 29.95 (*0-8348-0220-1*) Weatherhill.

Lasting Prayers of the Quran & the Prophet Muhammad. Ahmad Z. Hammad. (Illus.). xx, 364p. (Orig.). 1996. write for info. (*0-9650746-1-7*) QLI.

Lasting Prayers of the Quran & the Prophet Muhammad. Ahmad Z. Hammad. xx, 364p. (Orig.). 1996. pap. write for info. (*0-9650746-2-5*) QLI.

Lasting Promise: The Christian Guide to Fighting for Your Marriage. Scott Stanley et al. LC 97-45379. (Psychology Ser.). 256p. 1998. mass mkt. 15.00 (*0-7879-3983-8*) Jossey-Bass.

Lasting Purpose: A Mindset for Success. Sid E. Williams. LC 96-23694. 200p. (Orig.). 1996. pap. 10.95 (*1-55874-432-0*, 4320) Health Comm.

An Asterisk (*) at the beginning of an entry indicates that the title is appearing for the first time.

***Lasting Results, a Teacher's Manual: Rediscovering the Promise of Standards Through Assessment-Based Instruction.** Mark Skelding. (Illus.). 174p. 2000. teacher ed., spiral bd. 24.95 (*1-884430-05-8*, Common Roots Pr) Food Works.

Lasting Salute: Civil & Military Funerals, 1921-1969. B. C. Mossman & M. W. Stark. (Illus.). 428p. (Orig.). (C). 1995. pap. text 60.00 (*0-7881-2072-7*) DIANE Pub.

Lasting Spring: Jessie Catherine Kinsley, Daughter of the Oneida Community. Jessie C. Kinsley. Ed. by Jane K. Rich & Nelson M. Blake. LC 82-19200. (York State Book Ser.). (Illus.). 258p. 1983. reprint ed. pap. 80.00 (*0-608-06964-7*, 206717200009) Bks Demand.

Lasting Valor. Vernon Baker. 1997. 24.95 (*1-885478-30-5*) Genesis Press.

Lasting Valor. Vernon J. Baker & Ken Olsen. 1999. 55.00 (*1-885478-51-8*, Pub. by Genesis Press) BookWorld.

Lasting Valor. Vernon J. Baker & Ken Olson. 320p. 1999. reprint ed. mass mkt. 6.50 (*0-553-58062-0*) Bantam.

Lasting Value: Lessons from a Century of Agility at Lincoln Electric. Joseph A. Maciariello. 240p. 1999. 39.95 (*0-471-33025-6*) Wiley.

Lasting Wealth Is a Matter of Timing. John K. Sosnowy & Richard J. Maturi. LC 96-61386. 250p. 1997. 24.95 (*0-9607298-3-6*) Twntyfirst Cent Pubs.

Lastings of the Mohegans: The Story of the Wolf People. 2nd ed. Melissa J. Fawcett. (Illus.). 68p. (Orig.). 1995. reprint ed. pap. 10.00 (*0-9656933-0-9*) Lttle People.

Last's Anatomy: Regional & Applied. 9th ed. Ed. by R. M. H. McMinn. LC 94-5560. (Illus.). 1994. text 66.00 (*0-443-04662-X*) Church.

Laszlo Moholy-Nagy: Biographical Writings. Louis Kaplan. LC 94-40315. (Illus.). 224p. 1995. text 49.95 (*0-8223-1577-7*); pap. text 16.95 (*0-8223-1592-0*) Duke.

Laszlo Moholy-Nagy: From Budapest to Berlin, 1914-1923. Oliver Botar et al. Ed. by Belena S. Chapp. LC 95-61286. 200p. 1995. pap. 30.00 (*1-887421-00-9*) Univ Gall U of DE.

Latacumba Assignment. John H. Newton. 165p. (C). 1989. 60.00 (*0-7223-2300-X*, Pub. by A H S Ltd) St Mut.

Latah in Southeast Asia: The Ethnography & History of a Culture-Bound Syndrome. Robert L. Winzeler. (Publications of the Society for Psychological Anthropology: No. 7). (Illus.). 188p. (C). 1995. text 59.95 (*0-521-47219-9*) Cambridge U Pr.

Latam Liitellghi (Letter Recognition) rev. ed. M. Poage. (ESK., Illus.). 59p. (J). 1983. pap., wbk. ed. 4.50 (*0-933769-89-X*) Alaska Native.

Latch Key Guard. Matt Christopher. (J). 1999. pap. write for info. (*0-316-14208-5*) Little.

Latchkey Children in the Library & Community: Issues, Strategies, & Programs. Frances S. Dowd. LC 91-3580. 232p. 1991. pap. 29.95 (*0-89774-651-1*) Oryx Pr.

***Latchkey Dog: How the Way You Live Shapes the Behavior of the Dog You Love.** Jodi Andersen. 2000. 22.00 (*0-06-270240-8*, HarpRes) HarpInfo.

Latchkey Kids. Susan Terris. LC 85-25392. 167p. (J). (gr. 7 up). 1986. 15.00 (*0-374-34363-2*) FS&G.

Latchkey Kids: Their Safety & Care. Marilyn Dreilinger & Ron Kerner. (Family Forum Library). 16p. 1992. 1.95 (*1-56688-006-8*) Bur For At-Risk.

Latchkey Kids: Unlocking Doors for Children & Their Families. 2nd ed. Suzanne Lamorey & Bryan E. Robinson. LC 98-40064. 224p. 1998. 36.00 (*0-7619-1259-2*); pap. 15.99 (*0-7619-1260-6*) Sage.

Latchpins of the Lost Cove. Malone Young. (Appalachian Ser.). (Illus.). 216p. (Orig.). 1987. pap. 9.98 (*0-9625490-0-2*) Latchpins Pr.

Latchup in Cmos Technology: The Problem & Its Cure. Ronald R. Troutman. 1986. text 102.00 (*0-89838-215-7*) Kluwer Academic.

Late. Michael Hamburger. LC 98-116524. 64p. 1998. pap. 18.95 (*0-85646-294-2*, Pub. by Anvil Press) Dufour.

Late Achievers: Famous People Who Succeeded Late in Life. Mary E. Snodgrass. (Illus.). x, 286p. 1992. lib. bdg. 28.00 (*0-87287-937-2*) Libs Unl.

Late Adolescence. Sherrod. (JRA Ser.: Vol. 3, No. 3). 1993. 20.00 (*0-8058-9990-1*) L Erlbaum Assocs.

Late Adolescence: Psychoanalytic Studies. Ed. by David D. Brockman. LC 84-25181. xxxvi, 367p. 1985. 60.00 (*0-8236-2948-1*, 02948) Intl Univs Pr.

Late Afternoon Woman. Sondra Zeidenstein. LC 91-34562. (Orig.). 1992. pap. 4.95 (*0-9619111-3-1*) Chicory Blue.

Late & Postglacial Oscillations of Glaciers: Glacial & Periglacial Forms: Colloquium, Trier, 15-17 May 1980. Ed. by H. Schroeder-Lanz. 432p. (C). 1983. text 188.00 (*90-6191-517-1*, Pub. by A A Balkema) Ashgate Pub Co.

***Late & Soon.** large type unabridged ed. E. M. Delafield. 2000. 25.95 (*0-7531-6037-4*, 160374, Pub. by ISIS Lrg Prnt) ISIS Pub.

Late Antique & Byzantine Ivory Carving. Anthony Cutler. LC 98-74057. (Variorum Collected Studies Ser.: No. 617). (Illus.). 350p. 1998. text 161.95 (*0-86078-683-8*, Pub. by Ashgate Pub) Ashgate Pub Co.

Late Antique, Early Christian, & Medieval Art. Meyer Schapiro. LC 79-13333. (Selected Papers of Meyer Schapiro: Vol. 3). (Illus.). 414p. 1993. pap. 19.95 (*0-8076-1295-2*) Braziller.

Late Antiquity. Peter Brown. LC 97-42973. 96p. 1998. pap. 10.00 (*0-674-51170-0*) Belknap Pr.

***Late Antiquity: A Guide to the Post-Classical World.** Ed. by G. W. Bowersock et al. LC 99-25639. (Reference Library). (Illus.). 757p. 1999. 49.95 (*0-674-51173-5*) HUP.

***Late Antiquity: Empire & Successors, AD 425-600, Vol. 14.** Ed. by Averil Cameron et al. (The Cambridge Ancient History Ser.). (Illus.). 1152p. (C). 2001. Price not set. (*0-521-32591-9*) Cambridge U Pr.

Late Antiquity, A. D. 267-700. Alison Frantz. LC 88-7525. (Athenian Agora Ser.: Vol. 24). (Illus.). xxii, 156p. 1988. 65.00 (*0-87661-224-9*) Am Sch Athens.

Late Archaic & Early Woodland Adaptation in the Lower St. Joseph River Valley, Berrien County, MI, Vol. 2. Caven P. Clark et al. (Michigan Cultural Resource Investigation Ser.). 507p. (C). 1990. pap. text. write for info. (*0-9623670-1-X*) MI Dept Trans.

Late Archaic & Early Woodland Research in Virginia, a Synthesis, Vol. 23. Ed. by Theodore R. Reinhart & Mary E. Hodges. 275p. 1991. pap. 28.00 (*1-884626-09-2*) Archeolog Soc.

Late Archaic Chinese: A Grammatical Study. W. A. Dobson. LC 59-38059. 282p. reprint ed. pap. 87.50 (*0-608-10792-1*, 205546400022) Bks Demand.

Late Archaic Components at Modoc Rock Shelter, Randolph County, Illinois. Stephen R. Ahler et al. (Reports of Investigations: No. 48). (Illus.). 143p. 1992. pap. 12.00 (*0-89792-138-0*) Ill St Museum.

Late August on the Kenai River. Tom Sexton. (Illus.). 27p. (Orig.). 1991. pap. 12.50 (*0-9630863-1-6*) Limner Pr.

Late August on the Kenai River. deluxe ed. Tom Sexton. (Illus.). 27p. (Orig.). 1991. 37.50 (*0-9630863-0-8*) Limner Pr.

Late Babylonian Astronomical & Related Texts Copied by J. Schaumberger. Theophilus G. Pinches et al. Ed. by A. J. Sachs & J. Schaumberger. LC 56-1209. (Brown University Studies: No. 18). 326p. reprint ed. pap. 101.10 (*0-608-10243-1*, 200466800045) Bks Demand.

Late Babylonian Letters. Tr. by Reginald C. Thompson. LC 73-18856. (Luzac's Semitic Text & Translation Ser.: No. 17). reprint ed. 32.50 (*0-404-11357-5*) AMS Pr.

Late Babylonian Tablets in the Royal Ontario Museum, Two. G. J. McEwan. (Illus.). 128p. pap. 20.00 (*0-88854-282-8*) Brill Academic Pubs.

Late Babylonian Texts in the Ashmolean Museum. Ed. by Gilbert J. McEwan. (OXECT Ser.). (Illus.). 136p. 1985. pap. text 39.95 (*0-19-815459-3*) OUP.

Late Babylonian Texts in the Nies Babylonian Collection. Paul-Alain Beaulieu. Ed. by Ulla Kasten. LC 94-5455. (Catalogue of the Babylonian Collection at Yale: Vol. 1). 103p. (C). 1994. 48.00 (*1-883053-04-8*) CDL Pr.

Late Babylonian Texts of the Oriental Institute Collection. D. Kelly Weisberg. (Bibliotheca Mesopotamica Ser.: Vol. 24). viii, 87p. (C). 1991. text 31.00 (*0-89003-301-3*); pap. text 21.00 (*0-89003-300-5*) Undena Pubns.

Late Bloomer. Leigh Brooks. 1999. mass mkt. 4.99 (*0-8217-5074-7*) NAL.

Late Bloomer. Peg Sutherland. (Superromance Ser.). 1993. mass mkt. 3.50 (*0-373-70553-0*, 1-70553-2) Harlequin Bks.

Late Bloomers. Brendan Gill. LC 95-49923. (Illus.). 168p. 1996. 14.95 (*1-885183-48-8*) Artisan.

Late Bloomers. Brendan Gill. LC 95-49923. (Illus.). 168p. 1998. pap. 12.95 (*1-57965-108-9*, 85108) Artisan.

***Late Bloomer's Guide to Success at Any Age.** Susan Sully. 272p. 2000. pap. 13.00 (*0-380-81092-1*, Quil) HarperTrade.

Late-Breaking Foreign Policy: The News Media's Influence on Peace Operations. Warren P. Strobel. LC 97-9626. 224p. (Orig.). 1997. 29.95 (*1-878379-68-2*); pap. 14.95 (*1-878379-67-4*) US Inst Peace.

Late Bronze Age & Early Iron Ages of Central Jordan: The Baq'ah Valley Project, 1977-1981. Patrick E. McGovern et al. (University Museum Monographs: No. 65). (Illus.). xxxii, 365p. 1987. text 95.00 (*0-685-67660-9*) U Museum Pubns.

***Late Bronze Age Settlement & Early Iron Age Sanctuary.** Catherine A. Morgan. LC 99-48177. (Isthmia Ser.: Vol. 8). (Illus.). 566p. 1999. 100.00 (*0-87661-938-3*) Am Sch Athens.

Late Bronze Egyptian Garrison at Beth Shan: A Study of Levels VII & VIII. Frances W. James & Patrick E. McGovern. LC 93-17765. (University Museum Monographs: Vol. 85). (Illus.). xxvii, 272p. 1994. text 115.00 (*0-924171-27-8*) U Museum Pubns.

Late Bronze Palestinian Pendants: Innovation in a Cosmopolitan Age. P. E. McGovern. (Journal for the Study of the Old Testament Supplement Monographs Ser.: Vol. 1). 184p. 1987. 57.50 (*0-905774-90-6*, Pub. by Sheffield Acad) CUP Services.

Late Byzantine & Slavonic Communion Cycle: Liturgy & Music. Dimitri E. Conomos. LC 84-12176. (Dumbarton Oaks Studies: Vol. 21). (Illus.). 222p. 1985. 35.00 (*0-88402-134-3*) Dumbarton Oaks.

Late Byzantine Army: Arms & Society, 1204-1453. Mark C. Bartusis. (Middle Ages Ser.). 464p. 1997. pap. text 18.50 (*0-8122-1620-2*) U of Pa Pr.

Late Cainozoic Palaeoclimates of the Southern Hemisphere: Proceedings of an International Symposium Held by the South African Society for Quaternary Research in Swaziland, 29 Aug. 2 September 1983. Ed. by J. C. Vogel. 536p. (C). 1984. text 188.00 (*90-6191-554-6*, Pub. by A A Balkema) Ashgate Pub Co.

Late Capitalism. 2nd ed. Ernst Mandel. 640p. 1998. pap. 20.00 (*1-85984-202-X*, Pub. by Verso) Norton.

Late Carthaginian Child Sacrifice & Sacrificial Monuments in Their Mediterranean Context. Shelby Brown. (Journal for the Study of the Old Testament Supplement Monographs Ser.: Vol. 3). 335p. 1991. 85.00 (*1-85075-240-0*, Pub. by Sheffield Acad) CUP Services.

Late Cenozoic Geomorphic History of the Lower Tumas River Basin in the Central Namib Desert. M. Justin Wilkinson. LC 90-11272. (Geography Ser.). (Illus.). 211p. 1991. pap. text 14.50 (*0-89065-138-8*) U Ch Pr.

Late Cenozoic Glacial Ages. Ed. by Karl K. Turekian. LC 70-140540. (Yale University, Mrs. Hepse Ely Silliman Memorial Lectures). 618p. reprint ed. pap. 191.60 (*0-608-14250-6*, 202204500024) Bks Demand.

Late Cenozoic History of the Pacific Northwest. Ed. by Charles J. Smiley. LC 85-72591. (Illus.). 417p. 1985. 28.95 (*0-934394-06-7*) AAASPD.

Late Cenozoic Lava Dams in the Western Grand Canyon. W. Kenneth Hamblin. LC 93-41609. (Memoir Ser.: No. 183). 1994. 63.75 (*0-8137-1183-5*) Geol Soc.

Late Cenozoic Paleohydrogeology of the Western San Joaquin Valley, California, As Related to Structural Movements in the Central Coast Ranges. George H. Davis & Tyler B. Coplen. LC 89-7545. (Geological Society of America Ser.: Vol. 234). (Illus.). 44p. 1989. reprint ed. pap. 30.00 (*0-608-07758-5*, 206784600010) Bks Demand.

Late Cenozoic Xianshuihe-Xiaojiang, Red River, & Dali Fault Systems of Southwestern Sichuan & Central Yunnan, China, Vol. 327. Erchie Wang. LC 98-38073. (Special Paper Ser.). 108p. 1998. write for info. (*0-8137-2327-2*) Geol Soc.

Late Cenzoic Environments & Hominid Evolution: A Tribute to Bill Bishop. Ed. by P. Andrews & P. Banham. LC 99-491045. 276p. 1999. 115.00 (*1-86239-036-3*, Pub. by Geol Soc Pub Hse) AAPG.

Late Child. Larry McMurtry. 480p. 1996. per. 6.99 (*0-671-56818-3*) PB.

Late Child. large type ed. Larry McMurtry. LC 95-31811. 1995. 26.95 (*1-56895-246-5*, Compass) Wheeler Pub.

Late Child: A Novel. Larry McMurtry. LC 95-2419. 461p. 1995. 25.00 (*0-684-80998-2*) S&S Trade.

Late Ch'ing Finance: Hu Kuang-Yung As an Innovator. John C. Stanley. LC 62-1254. (East Asian Monographs: No. 12). 123p. 1961. 20.00 (*0-674-51165-4*) HUP.

Late Chrysanthemum: 21 Stories from the Japanese. Ed. & Tr. by Lane Dunlop from JPN. 180p. 1991. reprint ed. pap. 12.95 (*0-8048-1578-X*) Tuttle Pubng.

Late Climbs the Sun. Gladys Taber. 23.95 (*0-8488-1192-5*) Amereon Ltd.

Late Cretaceous & Cenozoic History of North American Vegetation (North of Mexico) Alan Graham. LC 97-5713. (Illus.). 370p. 1999. text 95.00 (*0-19-511342-X*) OUP.

Late Cretaceous Depositional Environments & Paleogeography, Santa Ana Mountains, Southern California. Ed. by David J. Bottjer et al. (Illus.). 121p. 1982. pap. 5.00 (*1-878861-48-4*) Pac Section SEPM.

Late Cretaceous San Juan Thrust System, San Juan Islands, Washington. Mark T. Brandon et al. LC 88-4003. (Geological Society of America Ser.: Vol. 221). (Illus.). 94p. 1988. reprint ed. pap. 30.00 (*0-608-07747-X*, 206783500010) Bks Demand.

Late Cypriot Terracotta Figurines: A Study in Context. Patrick Begg. (Studies in Mediterranean Archaeology & Literature: No. 101). (Illus.). 108p. (Orig.). 1991. pap. 29.50 (*91-7081-036-2*, Pub. by P Astroms) Coronet Bks.

Late Devonian Mass Extinctions: The Frasnian-Famennian Crisis. George R. McGhee, Jr. LC 95-38419. (Critical Moments in Paleobiology & Earth History Ser.). (Illus.). 378p. (C). 1996. 58.00 (*0-231-07504-9*); pap. 30.50 (*0-231-07505-7*) Col U Pr.

Late Divorce. Abraham B. Yehoshua. 368p. 1993. pap. 14.00 (*0-15-649447-7*) Harcourt.

Late Dramatic Works of Arthur Schnitzler. Brigitte L. Schneider-Haivorson. (American University Studies: Germanic Languages & Literature: Ser. 1, Vol. 10). 174p. 1983. pap. 18.40 (*0-8204-0009-2*) P Lang Pubng.

Late Education: Episodes in a Life. Alan Moorehead. LC 98-31945. 207p. 1999. pap. 11.00 (*1-56947-163-0*) Soho Press.

Late Educational Psychology. Wakefield. (C). Date not set. write for info. (*0-395-77744-5*) HM.

Late Effects of Treatment for Childhood Cancer. Daniel M. Green. (Current Clinical Oncology Ser.). 200p. 1991. pap. 89.95 (*0-471-56166-5*, Wiley-Liss) Wiley.

Late Egyptian & Coptic Art: An Introduction to the Collections in the Brooklyn Museum. John D. Cooney. (Illus.). 1974. reprint ed. 15.00 (*0-913696-23-4*) Bklyn Mus.

Late Eighteenth-Century Cello Sonatas: Continuo Sonatas for Cello. Ed. by Jane Adas. LC 91-751613. (Eighteenth Century Continuo Sonata Ser.: Vol. 8). 336p. 1991. text 50.00 (*0-8153-0181-2*) Garland.

Late Eighteenth Century Masters: Continuo Sonatas for Violin. Ed. by Jane Adas. LC 91-755879. (Eighteenth Century Continuo Sonata Ser.: Vol. 6). 344p. 1992. text 50.00 (*0-8153-0179-0*) Garland.

Late Eighteenth-Century Sonatas for Woodwinds Continuo Sonatas for Woodwinds: Continuo Sonatas for Woodwinds. Ed. by Jane Adas. LC 91-751612. (Eighteenth Century Continuo Sonata Ser.: Vol. 10). 360p. 1992. text 50.00 (*0-8153-0183-9*) Garland.

Late Eighteenth Century Vegetation of Central & Western New York State on the Basis of Original Land Surveys. P. L. Marks et al. (New York State Museum Bulletin Ser.: No. 484). (Illus.). 55p. (Orig.). 1992. pap. 7.50 (*1-55557-225-1*) NYS Museum.

Late Emancipation of Jerry Stover. Andrew Salkey. Date not set. pap. text. write for info. (*0-582-78559-6*, Pub. by Addison-Wesley) Longman.

Late Empire. David Wojahn. (Poetry Ser.). 77p. (Orig.). (C). 1994. pap. 10.95 (*0-8229-5530-X*); text 19.95 (*0-8229-3793-X*) U of Pittsburgh Pr.

Late Eocene & Oligocene Paleosols from Badlands National Park, South Dakota. Gregory J. Retallack. LC 83-5675. (Geological Society of America, Special Paper: No. 193). 90p. reprint ed. pap. 30.00 (*0-7837-2685-6*, 204306200006) Bks Demand.

Late Eocene Zoogeography of the Eastern Gulf Coast Region. Alan H. Cheetham. LC 63-23109. (Geological Society of America, Memoir Ser.: No. 91). 129p. reprint ed. pap. 40.00 (*0-608-15639-6*, 203179500077) Bks Demand.

Late Fire, Late Snow: New & Uncollected Poems. Robert Francis. LC 92-7991. 80p. (C). 1992. pap. 9.95 (*0-87023-814-0*) U of Mass Pr.

Late Flowers see Pozdnie Ztoety

Late for the Sky: The Mentality of the Space Age. David Lavery. LC 91-24128. 272p. (C). 1992. 26.95 (*0-8093-1767-2*) S Ill U Pr.

Late for Work. Barbara L. McCombs & Linda Brannan. (Skills for Job Success Ser.). (Illus.). 32p. (Orig.). 1990. pap., student ed. 5.95 (*1-56119-013-6*) Educ Pr MD.

Late Formative Irrigation Settlement below Monte Alban: Survey & Excavation on the Xoxocotlan Piedmont, Oaxaca, Mexico. Michael J. O'Brien et al. (Institute of Latin American Studies Special Publication). (Illus.). 254p. 1982. text 27.50 (*0-292-74628-8*) U of Tex Pr.

Late Forties - Halcyon Years on the Baltimore News: A Nostalgic Return. William F. Zorzi, Sr. 48p. (Orig.). (C). 1988. pap. 3.95 (*0-9619316-0-4*) Wilgis & Zorzi.

Late Fourth Century Classicism in the Plastic Arts: A Systematic Study of Sculpture, Ivories & Silver Plate. Bente Kiilerich. (Illus.). 385p. (Orig.). 1993. pap. 57.50 (*87-7492-929-1*, Pub. by Odense Universitets Forlag) Coronet Bks.

Late Fourth Partner: Playscript. rev. ed. A. H. Oberholtzer et al. LC 97-7171. 64p. (Orig.). 1997. pap. 6.00 (*0-88734-201-9*) Players Pr.

Late Geometric & Protoattic Pottery, Mid Eighth to Late Seventh Century B.C. Eva T. Brann. LC 75-322663. (Athenian Agora Ser.: Vol. 8). (Illus.). xiv, 135p. 1971. reprint ed. 30.00 (*0-87661-208-7*) Am Sch Athens.

Late George Aplay. John P. Marquand. 358p. Date not set. 25.95 (*0-8488-2361-3*) Amereon Ltd.

Late George Apley. John P. Marquand. 1994. lib. bdg. 24.95 (*1-56849-446-7*) Buccaneer Bks.

Late George Apley: A Novel in the Form of a Memoir. John P. Marquand. (YA). (gr. 7 up). 1937. 18.95 (*0-685-03075-X*) Little.

Late Georgian Costume: The Tailor's Friendly Instructor (1822) & the Art of Tying the Cravat (1828) J. Wyatt & H. Le Blanc. Ed. by R. L. Shep. LC 91-52904. (Illus.). 176p. 1991. pap. 18.95 (*0-914046-12-8*) R L Shep.

Late Glacial & Postglacial Environmental Changes: Quatrnary, Carboniferous-Permian & Proterozoic. Ed. by I. Peter Martini. LC 95-51665. (Illus.). 360p. 1997. text 70.00 (*0-19-508541-8*) OUP.

Late Gothic Art in Bohemia: The Art of the Court Circle from 1471 to 1526. J. Homolka. (CZE, ENG & GER.). 530p. 1978. 110.00 (*0-7855-1556-9*) St Mut.

Late Gothic to Renaissance Paintings, 1. John Canaday. (C). 1969. 22.25 (*0-393-02415-6*) Norton.

Late Graft Loss: Proceedings of the 28th Conference on Transplantation & Clinical Immunology, 3-5 June 1996. Ed. by J. L. Touraine et al. LC 96-48786. (Transplantation & Clinical Immunology 28 Symposium Fondation Merieux Ser.). 256p. (C). 1997. text 100.50 (*0-7923-4315-8*) Kluwer Academic.

Late, Great Johnny Ace & the Transition from R&B to Rock 'n' Roll. James M. Salem. LC 98-25477. (Music in American Life Ser.). (Illus.). 274p. 1999. 29.95 (*0-252-02444-3*) U of Ill Pr.

Late Great Lakes: An Environmental History. William Ashworth. LC 87-6132. (Great Lakes Bks.). 286p. 1987. pap. 19.95 (*0-8143-1887-8*) Wayne St U Pr.

Late Great Me. David Rogers & Sandra Scoppettone. 127p. (YA). 1977. pap. 5.50 (*0-87129-700-0*, L38) Dramatic Pub.

Late Great Me. Sandra Scoppettone. 256p. (YA). 1984. mass mkt. 4.50 (*0-553-25910-5*) Bantam.

Late Great Me. Sandra Scoppettone. 1977. 9.60 (*0-606-00721-0*, Pub. by Turtleback) Demco.

Late Great Mexican Border: Reports from a Disappearing Line. Ed. by Bobby Byrd & Susannah M. Byrd. LC 96-10507. (Illus.). 240p. 1998. pap. 13.95 (*0-938317-24-5*) Cinco Puntos.

Late, Great Pennsylvania Station. 2nd ed. Lorraine B. Diehl. LC 96-21056. (Illus.). 168p. 1996. reprint ed. pap. 16.95 (*1-56858-060-6*) FWEW.

Late Great Planet Earth. Hal Lindsey & C. C. Carlson. 1970. pap. 9.99 (*0-310-27771-X*, 18089P) Zondervan.

***Late Great 20th Century.** Hal Lindsey. 1999. 19.99 (*1-888848-36-7*) Western Front.

Late Han Chinese: A Study of the Archaic-Han Shift. Wach Dobson. LC 65-976. 162p. reprint ed. pap. 50.30 (*0-7837-0536-0*, 204086400019) Bks Demand.

Late Harvest. Nancy Culbertson. (Illus.). 35p. (Orig.). 1996. pap. 9.95 (*0-9655880-0-9*) N Culbertson.

Late Harvest. large type ed. Barbara Masterton. 384p. 1989. 27.99 (*0-7089-2043-8*) Ulverscroft.

Late Harvest. large type ed. Pamela Street. 252p. 1992. reprint ed. lib. bdg. 16.95 (*1-56054-520-8*) Thorndike Pr.

Late Harvest. Norman Douglas. LC 75-41082. reprint ed. 27.50 (*0-404-14717-8*) AMS Pr.

Late Harvest: Essays & Addresses in American Literature & Culture, 49. Robert E. Spiller. LC 80-543. (Contributions to American Studies: No. 49). 280p. 1981. 65.00 (*0-313-22023-9*, SLH/, Greenwood Pr) Greenwood.

Late Harvest: Miscellaneous Papers Written Between Eighty & Ninety. Charles W. Eliot. LC 78-156638. (Essay Index Reprint Ser.). 1977. reprint ed. 23.95 (*0-8369-2353-7*) Ayer.

Late Harvest: Reflections on the Old Testament. William McKane. 1995. 39.95 (*0-567-09727-7*) Bks Intl VA.

Late Harvest: Rural American Writing by Edward Abbey, Wendell Berry, Carolyn Chute, Annie Dillard, William Gass, Garrison Keillor, Bobbie Ann Mason, Wallace Stegner & Others. Ed. by David R. Pichaske. 452p. 1994. pap. 18.95 (*1-56924-867-2*) Marlowe & Co.

Late Harvey Grosbeck. Gilbert Millstein. LC 73-83658. 285p. 1974. write for info. (*0-385-01133-4*) BDD LT Grp.

An Asterisk (*) at the beginning of an entry indicates that the title is appearing for the first time.

Late Have I Loved Thee. Susan Muto. 1996. 14.95 (*0-8245-1545-5*) Crossroad NY.

Late Have I Loved Thee: The Recovery of Intimacy. Susan A. Muto & Adrian Van Kaam. 144p. 1995. pap. 11.95 (*0-8245-1522-6*) Crossroad NY.

Late Helladic I Pottery of the Southwestern Peloponnesos & Its Local Characteristics, 2 vols. Yannos B. Lolos. (Studies in Mediterranean Archaeology & Literature: No. 50). (Illus.). 1085p. (Orig.). 1985. pap. 177.50 (*91-86098-53-5*, Pub. by P Astroms) Coronet Bks.

Late Helladic Pottery from Prosymna. Kim S. Shelton. (Studies in Mediterranean Archaeology & Literature: No. 138). (Illus.). 365p. (Orig.). 1996. pap. 67.50 (*91-7081-114-8*, Pub. by P Astroms) Coronet Bks.

Late Holocene Alluvial Geomorphology of the Virgin River in the Zion National Park Area, Southwest Utah. R. Hereford et al. LC 96-17656. (Special Papers: No. 309). 1996. pap. 25.00 (*0-8137-2310-8*) Geol Soc.

***Late Holocene Landscapes & Prehistoric Land Use in Warner Valley, Oregon.** Dennis C. Young, Jr. (Illus.). 153p. (C). 1998. pap. text 16.88 (*1-55567-839-4*) Coyote Press.

Late Hour. Mark Strand. LC 77-88904. (C). 1979. pap. 6.95 (*0-689-10977-6*) Atheneum Yung Read.

Late I Have Loved Thee: Stories of Religious Conversion & Commitment in Later Life. Richard M. Erikson. LC 95-19348. 208p. (Orig.). 1995. pap. 14.95 (*0-8091-3594-9*) Paulist Pr.

Late Idyll: The Second Symphony of Johannes Brahms. Reinhold Brinkmann. Tr. by Peter Palmer. LC 94-29128. 256p. 1995. text 56.00 (*0-674-51175-1*, BRILAT) HUP.

Late Idyll: The Second Symphony of Johannes Brahms. Reinhold Brinkmann. Tr. by Peter Palmer. LC 94-29128. 256p. 1997. reprint ed. pap. 22.95 (*0-674-51176-X*) HUP.

Late Imperial Chinese Armies, 1520-1840. Chris Peers & Christa Hook. (Men-at-Arms Ser.: Vol. 307). (Illus.). 48p. 1997. pap. 12.95 (*1-85532-655-8*, Pub. by Osprey) Stackpole.

Late Imperial Culture. Roman De La Campa. Ed. by E. Ann Kaplan et al. LC 94-44394. (Postmodern Occasions Ser.). 240p. (C). 1995. pap. 19.00 (*1-85984-050-7*, C0470, Pub. by Verso) Norton.

Late Imperial Romance. John A. McClure. LC 93-42312. (Haymarket Ser.). 300p. (C). 1994. pap. 19.00 (*0-86091-612-X*, Pub. by Verso) Norton.

Late-Imperial Russia: An Interpretation: Three Visions, Two Cultures, One Peasantry. Adrian Jones. 457p. (C). 1997. pap. 60.95 (*0-8204-3409-4*) P Lang Pubng.

***Late Imperial Russia, 1890-1917.** John F. Hutchinson. LC 98-36186. (Seminar Studies in History). 144p. (C). 1999. pap. 14.20 (*0-582-32721-0*) Addison-Wesley.

Late in Season. Felice Picano. 1997. pap. 12.95 (*0-312-15564-6*) St Martin.

Late Intermediate Occupation at Cerro Azul, Peru. Joyce Marcus. (Technical Reports Ser.: No. 20). xvi, 112p. (Orig.). 1987. pap. 8.00 (*0-915703-12-2*) U Mich Mus Anthro.

Late into the Night: The Last Poems of Yannis Ritsos. Yannis Ritsos. Tr. & Intro. by Martin McKinsey. (Field Translation Ser.: No. 21). 121p. 1995. pap. 12.95 (*0-932440-71-1*) Oberlin Coll Pr.

Late Israelite Prophecy: Studies in Deutero-Prophetic Literature & in Chronicles. David L. Petersen. LC 76-26014. (Society of Biblical Literature, Mongraph Ser.: Vol. 23). 112p. reprint ed. pap. 34.80 (*0-608-08678-9*, 206920100003) Bks Demand.

Late Knight Edition. Damon Knight. LC 84-62283. viii, 150p. 1985. 13.00 (*0-915368-28-5*) New Eng SF Assoc.

Late Lady. Susannah Stacey. 1994. mass mkt. 4.99 (*0-671-73895-X*) PB.

Late Lark. Robey. 1999. pap. write for info. (*0-316-75120-0*) Little.

***Late Lark Singing.** Sybil Marshall. 512p. 1998. pap. 13.95 (*0-14-025840-X*, Pub. by Pnguin Bks Ltd) Trafalgar.

Late, Late in the Evening. large type ed. Gladys Mitchell. (Linford Mystery Library). 400p. 1996. pap. 16.99 (*0-7089-7941-6*) Ulverscroft.

Late Latin Vocabulary of the Variae of Cassiodorus. Odo J. Zimmermann. xx, 277p. 1967. reprint ed. write for info. (*0-318-71249-0*) G Olms Pubs.

Late Latin Vocabulary of the Variae of Cassiodorus. Odo J. Zimmermann. xx, 277p. 1967. reprint ed. write for info. (*0-318-72090-6*) G Olms Pubs.

Late Latin Vocabulary of the Variae of Cassiodorus: With Special Advertence to the Technical Terminology of Administration. Odo J. Zimmermann. (Catholic University of America, Studies in Medieval & Renaissance Latin Language & Literature: No. XV). xx, 277p. 1967. reprint ed. 63.70 (*0-685-66532-1*, 05101687) G Olms Pubs.

Late Leisure. Eleanor R. Taylor. LC 98-44081. (Southern Messenger Poets Ser.). 88p. 1999. pap. 12.95 (*0-8071-2356-0*); text 19.95 (*0-8071-2355-2*) La State U Pr.

Late Liveries: The Road, the Difilements. Peter Thompson. LC 98-48978. 64p. 1999. pap. 14.95 (*0-7734-3112-8*, Mellen Poetry Pr) E Mellen.

Late Man. James P. Girard. Ed. by Lee Goerner. 288p. 1993. text 20.00 (*0-689-12183-0*) Atheneum Yung Read.

Late Marque Spitfire Aces, 1942-45 Vol. 5: Aircraft of the Aces. A. Price. (Illus.). 96p. Date not set. pap. 17.95 (*1-85532-575-6*, Pub. by Osprey) Stackpole.

Late Marx & the Russian Road: Marx & the "Peripheries of Capitalism" Ed. by Teodor Shanin. LC 83-13237. 286p. 1984. pap. 15.00 (*0-85345-647-X*, Pub. by Monthly Rev) NYU Pr.

Late Marxism: Adorno, or the Persistence of the Dialectic. rev. ed. Fredric Jameson. (C). 1996. pap. 18.00 (*1-85984-156-2*, Pub. by Verso) Norton.

Late Mattia Pascal. Luigi Pirandello. Tr. by William Weaver from ITA. LC 87-83302. 262p. 1988. reprint ed. pap. 12.00 (*0-941419-09-6*, Eridanos Library) Marsilio Pubs.

Late Mattia Pascal. 2nd ed. Luigi Pirandello. Ed. by Nicobella Simborowski. (Dedalus European Classic Ser.). 251p. 1999. reprint ed. pap. 8.99 (*0-946626-18-9*, Pub. by Dedalus) Hippocrene Bks.

***Late Medieval Age of Crisis & Renewal, 1300-1500: A Biographical Dictionary.** Ed. by Clayton J. Drees. LC 00-22335. (Great Cultural Eras of the Western World Ser.). 520p. 2000. lib. bdg. 89.00 (*0-313-30588-9*, GR0588, Greenwood Pr) Greenwood.

Late Medieval & Renaissance Philosophy Vol. 3: Ockham, Francis Bacon & the Beginning of the Modern World. Frederick J. Copleston. LC 92-34997. 496p. 1993. pap. 16.95 (*0-385-46845-8*, Image Bks) Doubleday.

Late Medieval Balkans: A Critical Survey from the Late Twelfth Century to the Ottoman Conquest. John V. Fine. (Illus.). 704p. (C). 1994. pap. 29.95 (*0-472-08260-4*, 08260) U of Mich Pr.

***Late Medieval England 1399-1509.** 2000. 79.95 (*0-582-03134-6*) P-H.

Late Medieval England, 1377-1485: A Bibliography of Historical Scholarship, 1975-1989. Joel Thomas Rosenthal. LC 94-6595. 1994. boxed set 45.00 (*1-879288-16-8*) Medieval Inst.

Late-Medieval England, 1377-1485. DeLloyd J. Guth. LC 75-23845. (Conference on British Studies, Bibliographical Handbooks). 155p. reprint ed. pap. 44.20 (*0-608-15732-5*, 2031664) Bks Demand.

Late Medieval Epistle: An International Journal of the Late Middle Ages. Ed. by Carol Poster & Richard J. Utz. (Disputatio Ser.). 250p. 1996. text 49.95 (*0-8101-1449-6*) Northwestern U Pr.

***Late Medieval Europe.** 2000. write for info. (*0-582-25831-6*) Pearson Educ.

Late Medieval Monumental Sculpture in the West Highlands. K. A. Steer & J. W. M. Bannerman. (Royal Commission on the Ancient & Historical Monuments of Scotland Ser.). xxvi, 230p. 1977. 80.00 (*0-11-491383-8*, Pub. by Statnry Office) Balogh.

Late Medieval Philosophy. C. Normore. 1999. pap. 60.00 (*0-8133-2461-0*); pap. 24.00 (*0-8133-2462-9*) Westview.

***Late Medieval Pope Prophecies: The "Genus Nequam" Group.** Ed. by Martha H. Fleming. LC 99-39578. (Medieval & Renaissance Texts & Studies: Vol. 204). (Illus.). 1999. 25.00 (*0-86698-246-9*, MR204) MRTS.

Late-Medieval Religious Texts & Their Transmission: Essays in Honour of A. I. Doyle. Ed. by Alastair J. Minnis. (York Manuscripts Conferences: No. 3). (Illus.). 208p. (C). 1994. 75.00 (*0-85991-386-4*) Boydell & Brewer.

Late Merovingian France: History & Hagiography, 640-720. Paul Fouracre & Richard A. Gerberding. LC 95-21908. (Manchester Medieval Sources Ser.). 400p. 1996. text 79.95 (*0-7190-4790-0*); text 27.95 (*0-7190-4791-9*, Pub. by Manchester Univ Pr) St Martin.

Late Middle Ages. James A. Corrick. (World History Ser.). (Illus.). 128p. (J). (gr. 5-9). 1995. lib. bdg. 22.45 (*1-56006-279-7*, 2797) Lucent Bks.

Late Middle Ages & Era of European Expansion: Byzantines, Mamelukes & Maghribians, Vol. 17. Salo W. Baron. LC 52-404. 163p. 1980. text 87.50 (*0-231-08854-X*) Col U Pr.

Late Middle Ages & Era of European Expansion, 1200-1650: Catholic Restoration & Wars of Religion see Social & Religious History of the Jews

Late Middle Ages & Era of European Expansion, 1200-1650: Citizen or Alien Conjurer see Social & Religious History of the Jews

Late Middle Ages & Era of European Expansion, 1200-1650: Economic Catalyst see Social & Religious History of the Jews

Late Middle Ages & Era of European Expansion, 1200-1650: Inquisition, Renaissance & Reformation see Social & Religious History of the Jews

Late Middle Ages & Era of European Expansion, 1200-1650: On the Empire's Periphery see Social & Religious History of the Jews

Late Middle Ages & Era of European Expansion, 1200-1650: Resettlement & Exploration see Social & Religious History of the Jews

Late Middle Ages & Era of European Expansion, 1200-1650: Under Church & Empire see Social & Religious History of the Jews

Late Middle Ages & the Dawn of Humanism Outside Italy. Ed. by G. Vergeke & Jozef Ijsewijn. (Mediaevalia Lovaniensia Ser.: No. 1). 261p. (Orig.). 1972. pap. 36.50 (*0-614-97102-0*, Pub. by Leuven Univ) Coronet Bks.

***Late Middle Classes.** Simon Gray. 1999. pap. 14.95 (*1-85459-433-8*, Pub. by Theatre Comm) Consort Bk Sales.

Late-Ming Poet Chen Tzu-Lung: Crises of Love & Loyalism. Kang-I S. Chang. LC 90-12485. (Illus.). 203p. 1991. reprint ed. pap. 63.00 (*0-608-07883-2*, 205999000010) Bks Demand.

Late Minoan III Period in Crete: A Survey of Sites, Pottery & Their Distribution. A. Kanta. (Studies in Mediterranean Archaeology: Vol. LVIII). (Illus.). 550p. (Orig.). 1980. pap. 125.00 (*91-85058-95-5*, Pub. by P Astroms) Coronet Bks.

Late Minoan III Pottery: Terminology & Chronology, Acts of a Meeting Held at the Danish Institute at Athens, August 12-14, 1994. Ed. by Erik Hallager & Birgitta P. Hallager. LC 98-107165. (Monographs of the Danish Institute at Athens: Vol. 1). (Illus.). 420p. 1997. 40.00 (*87-7288-731-1*, Pub. by Aarhus Univ Pr) David Brown.

Late Minoan III Burials at Khania: The Tombs, Finds & Deceased in Odos Palama. B. P. Hallager & P. J. McGeorge. (Studies in Mediterranean Archaeology: Vol. XCIII). (Illus.). 120p. (Orig.). 1992. pap. 77.50 (*91-7081-026-5*, Pub. by P Astroms) Coronet Bks.

Late Mississippian & Early Pennsylvanian Conodonts, Arkansas & Oklahoma. Harold A. Lane & Joseph J. Straka. LC 73-90838. (Geological Society of America, Special Paper: No. 152). 204p. reprint ed. pap. 63.30 (*0-608-15183-1*, 202737000055) Bks Demand.

Late Mr. Shakespeare. Robert Nye. LC 98-50763. 400p. (YA). 1999. 25.95 (*1-55970-469-1*, Pub. by Arcade Pub Inc) Time Warner.

***Late Mr. Shakespeare.** Robert Nye. 416p. 2000. pap. 13.95 (*0-14-028952-6*) Viking Penguin.

***Late Modernism: Politic, Fiction, & the Arts between the World Wars.** Tyrus Miller. LC 98-27436. 280p. 1999. pap. 19.95 (*0-520-21648-2*, Pub. by U CA Pr) Cal Prin Full Svc.

Late Modernism: Politics, Fiction, & the Arts Between the World Wars. Tyrus Miller. LC 98-27436. 280p. 1999. 45.00 (*0-520-21035-2*, Pub. by U CA Pr) Cal Prin Full Svc.

Late Monasticism & the Reformation. A. G. Dickens. LC 94-1587. 224p. 1994. 55.00 (*1-85285-091-4*) Hambledon Press.

Late Mrs. Fonsell. large type ed. Velda Johnston. LC 91-32565. (General Ser.). 301p. 1992. lib. bdg. 20.95 (*0-8161-5015-X*, G K Hall Lrg Type) Mac Lib Ref.

Late Neogene Epoch Boundaries. Ed. by T. Saito & L. H. Burckle. (Micropaleontology Special Publications: No. 1). 224p. 1975. 20.00 (*0-686-84248-0*) Am Mus Natl Hist.

Late News from Adam's Acres. Cornel Lengyel. (Living Poets' Library). 1983. pap. 3.50 (*0-934218-25-0*) Dragons Teeth.

Late Night ActiveX. Mark Ginsburg & Eric Tall. LC 98-159777. 528p. 1996. pap. text 44.99 incl. audio compact disk (*1-56276-448-9*, Ziff-Davis Pr) Que.

Late Night Advanced Java. Jason Wehling. LC 98-159776. 624p. 1996. 39.99 (*1-56276-407-1*, Ziff-Davis Pr) Que.

Late Night Calls: Prose Poems & Short Fiction. Mark Vinz. LC 91-61263. 155p. (Orig.). 1992. pap. 8.95 (*0-89823-138-8*) New Rivers Pr.

Late Night Extra. A. Brown. Date not set. 8.99 (*1-871676-73-8*, Pub. by Christian Focus) Spring Arbor Dist.

Late Night Grande Hotel & Other Nanci Griffith Classics. Ed. by Carol Cuellar. 80p. (Orig.). (C). 1992. pap. text 14.95 (*0-7692-0768-5*, P0940SMX) Wrner Bros.

Late Night Guide to C++ Nigel Chapman. LC 96-28089. 376p. 1996. pap. 59.99 (*0-471-95071-8*) Wiley.

Late Night Intrabuilder. Barrie Sosinski. 400p. 1997. pap. text 44.99 incl. cd-rom (*1-56276-533-7*, Ziff-Davis Pr) Que.

Late Night Microsoft Visual J++ Marc Johnson et al. 624p. 1996. 49.99 (*1-56276-452-7*, Ziff-Davis Pr) Que.

Late Night Netscape IFC. Jason Beaver. 574p. 1997. pap. text 49.99 (*1-56276-540-X*, Ziff-Davis Pr) Que.

Late Night on Watling Street. Naughton. Date not set. pap. text. write for info. (*0-582-23367-4*, Pub. by Addison-Wesley) Longman.

Late Night Programming Internet Plug-Ins. Ziff-Davis Development Group Staff. 1997. pap. text 39.99 incl. cd-rom (*1-56276-536-1*, Ziff-Davis Pr) Que.

Late Night Radio. John Tranter. LC 98-221708. 96p. 1998. pap. 10.95 (*0-7486-6238-3*, Pub. by Polygon) Subterranean Co.

Late Night Thoughts on Listening to Mahler's 9th Symphony. Lewis Thomas. 176p. 1995. pap. 12.95 (*0-14-024328-3*, Penguin Bks) Viking Penguin.

Late Night Top Ten Lists. David Letterman. 1994. mass mkt. 5.99 (*0-671-51143-2*) PB.

Late Night VRML 2.0 with Java. Bernie Roehl & Justin Couch. LC 98-160275. 710p. 1997. 44.99 (*1-56276-504-3*, Ziff-Davis Pr) Que.

Late Night with David Letterman Book of Top Ten Lists. Late Night with David Letterman Writers Staff & David Letterman. Ed. by Leslie Wells. 160p. (Orig.). 1990. pap. 12.00 (*0-671-72671-4*) PB.

Late Night with JavaBeans Programming. Ziff-Davis Development Group Staff. 500p. 1997. 44.99 (*1-56276-531-0*, Ziff-Davis Pr) Que.

Late Night with Mac Hack: Mac Tools, Toys & Tales. Doug Houseman. LC 94-22310. 250p. 1994. pap. 29.95 incl. cd-rom (*1-55851-395-7*, M&T Bks) IDG Bks.

Late Nineteenth & Early Twentieth-Century British Literary Biographers. Ed. by Steven Serafin. LC 95-3288. (Dictionary of Literary Biography Ser.: Vol. 149). 367p. 1995. text 155.00 (*0-8103-5710-0*) Gale.

Late Nineteenth-Century American Development: A General Equilibrium History. Jeffrey G. Williamson. LC 74-76946. 362p. reprint ed. pap. 103.20 (*0-608-12914-3*, 2024559) Bks Demand.

Late Nineteenth-Century American Diary Literature. Stephen E. Kagle. (United States Authors Ser.: No. 524). 176p. 1988. 32.00 (*0-8057-7504-8*, Twyne) Mac Lib Ref.

Late Nineteenth Century & Early Twentieth Century Decorative Arts: The Sydney & Frances Lewis Collection in the Virginia Museum of Fine Arts. Frederick R. Brandt. Ed. by Monica M. Hamm. LC 85-22499. (Illus.). 285p. 1985. pap. 24.95 (*0-917046-16-1*) Va Mus Arts.

Late Nineteenth Century, c. 1850 to c. 1900 see History of Technology

Late Nineteenth-Century Debate over Depreciation, Capital & Income: An Original Anthology. LC 75-18458. (History of Accounting Ser.). (Illus.). 1977. 18.95 (*0-405-07542-1*) Ayer.

Late Nineteenth Century U. S. Army, 1865-1898: A Research Guide, 3. Joseph G. Dawson, III. LC 90-41839. (Research Guides in Military Studies: No. 3). 272p. 1990. lib. bdg. 65.00 (*0-313-26146-6*, DWA/, Greenwood Pr) Greenwood.

Late Nite Comic: Broadway Selections. Ed. by Carol Cuellar. 36p. (Orig.). (C). 1991. pap. text 10.95 (*0-7692-0711-1*, VF1737) Wrner Bros.

***Late Novels of Eudora Welty.** Ed. by Jan N. Gretlund & Karl-Heinz Westarp. LC 97-33949. 224p. 1998. lib. bdg. 22.95 (*1-57003-231-9*) U of SC Pr.

Late Nubian Settlement at Arminna West. Bruce G. Trigger. (Publications of the Penn-Yale Expedition to Egypt: No. 2). (Illus.). xx, 128p. 1967. text 35.00 (*0-686-17768-1*) U Museum Pubns.

Late Nubian Settlement at Arminna West, Vol 2. Bruce G. Trigger. 1967. 25.00 (*0-686-00129-X*) Penn-Yale Expedit.

Late of This Parish. large type ed. Marjorie Eccles. 380p. 1993. 27.99 (*0-7505-0516-8*, Pub. by Mgna Lrg Print) Ulverscroft.

Late Old Babylonian Documents & Letters. Jacob J. Finkelstein. LC 72-75190. (Yale Oriental Series. Babylonian Texts: No. 13). 282p. pap. 87.50 (*0-608-11035-3*, 201679600005) Bks Demand.

Late Oligocene Creede Flora, Colorado. Daniel I. Axelrod. LC 87-14300. (University of California Publications in Entomology: No. 130). 247p. (Orig.). 1987. pap. 76.60 (*0-7837-7468-0*, 204919000010) Bks Demand.

Late One Night see Set 9

Late Onset Neurometabolic Genetic Disorders: From Clinical to Molecular Aspects of Lysosomal & Peroxisomal Disease - Journal: Developmental Neuroscience, Vol. 13, Nos. 4-5. Ed. by N. Baumann et al. (Illus.). 196p. 1991. pap. 106.25 (*3-8055-5524-5*) S Karger.

Late Onset Schizophrenia. Robert Howard. LC 99-22797. 1999. 87.00 (*1-871816-39-4*) Taylor & Francis.

Late Operas of Antonio Vivaldi, 1727-1738, Vol. 1. Eric Cross. LC 81-77. (Studies in British Musicology). 287p. reprint ed. pap. 89.00 (*0-8357-1185-4*, 207026300001) Bks Demand.

Late Operas of Antonio Vivaldi, 1727-1738, Vol. 2. Eric Cross. LC 81-77. (Studies in British Musicology). 328p. reprint ed. pap. 101.70 (*0-8357-1186-2*, 207026300002) Bks Demand.

Late Ordovician Brachiopods from the South China Plate & Their Palaeographical Significance No. 59: Special Papers in Palaeontology. Ren-Bin Zhan & L. R. Cocks. (Palaeontological Association Ser.). (Illus.). 70p. 1999. pap. 99.95 (*0-901702-66-8*) Blackwell Pubs.

Late Palaeozoic & Early Mesozoic Circum-Pacific Events & Their Global Correlation. Ed. by J. M. Dickins et al. (World & Regional Geology Ser.: No. 10). (Illus.). 255p. (C). 1997. text 115.00 (*0-521-47175-3*) Cambridge U Pr.

***Late Paleocene - Early Eocene Biotic & Climatic Events in the Marine & Terrestrial Records.** Marie-Pierre Aubry. LC 98-20969. (Illus.). 528p. 1998. 100.00 (*0-231-10238-0*) Col U Pr.

Late Paleocene Mammals from the Cypress Hills, Alberta. Leonard Krishtalka. (Special Publications: No. 2). (Illus.). 77p. (Orig.). 1973. pap. 8.00 (*0-89672-027-6*) Tex Tech Univ Pr.

Late Paleozoic Pelecypods: Pectinacea & Mytilacea, State Geological Survey of Kansas, Vol. 10. Norman D. Newell. Ed. by Stephen Jay Gould. LC 79-8337. (History of Paleontology Ser.). (Illus.). 1980. reprint ed. lib. bdg. 26.95 (*0-405-12722-7*) Ayer.

Late Payments. Michael Z. Lewin. (Lt. Leroy Powder Novel Ser.). 216p. 1996. reprint ed. pap. 10.00 (*0-88150-347-9*, Foul Play) Norton.

Late Period Gabrielino Ceremonial Features from the Lemon Tank Site, San Clemente Island, California. Alice E. Hale. (Illus.). 201p. (C). 1995. pap. text 21.25 (*1-55567-834-3*) Coyote Press.

Late Period Hieratic Wisdom Text (P. Brooklyn 47.218.135) Richard Jasnow. LC 92-60742. (Studies in Ancient Oriental Civilization: No. 52). (Illus.). xviii, 240p. 1992. pap. 35.00 (*0-918986-85-0*) Orient Inst.

Late Phase Allergic Reactions. Ed. by Walter Dorsch. 464p. 1990. lib. bdg. 129.00 (*0-8493-6743-3*, QR188) CRC Pr.

Late Phase Melt Progression Experiment: MP-2, Results & Analysis. R. D. Gasser. 280p. 1997. per. 40.00 (*0-16-062844-X*) USGPO.

Late Pleistocene & Early Holocene Paleoecology & Archaeology of the Eastern Great Lakes Region: Proceedings of the Smith Symposium, Held at the Buffalo Museum of Science, October 24-25, 1986. Ed. by Richard S. Laub et al. LC 88-6094. (Bulletin Ser.: Vol. 33). 316p. (C). 1988. pap. 36.00 (*0-944032-52-4*) Buffalo SNS.

Late Pleistocene Herpetofaunas from Puerto Rico. Gregory Pregill. (Miscellaneous Publications: No. 71). 72p. 1981. 4.25 (*0-317-04884-8*) U KS Nat Hist Mus.

Late Pleistocene History of Northeastern New England & Adjacent Quebec. Ed. by Harold W. Borns, Jr. et al. LC 84-25965. (Geological Society of America Ser.: Vol. 197). (Illus.). 170p. 1985. reprint ed. pap. 52.70 (*0-608-07726-7*, 206781400010) Bks Demand.

Late Pleistocene of U. S. Porter. Date not set. pap. text. write for info. (*0-582-30123-8*, Pub. by Addison-Wesley) Longman.

Late Pleistocene Shouldered Point Assemblages in Western Europe. Jan M. Burdukiewicz. (Illus.). ix, 253p. 1986. pap. 94.50 (*90-04-08100-3*) Brill Academic Pubs.

Late Pleistocene Vertebrate Paleoecology of the West. Arthur H. Harris. (Illus.). 303p. 1984. text 25.00 (*0-292-74645-8*) U of Tex Pr.

L

Late Pleistocene Vertebrates of the Western Ozark Highland, Missouri. Jeffrey J. Saunders. (Reports of Investigations: No. 33). (Illus.). 118p. 1977. pap. 3.50 (*0-89792-066-X*) Ill St Museum.

Late Pleistocene (Woodfordian) Vertebrates from the Driftless Area of Southwestern Wisconsin, the Moscow Fissure Local Fauna. Robert L. Foley. (Reports of Investigations: No. 39). (Illus.). x, 50p. (Orig.). 1984. pap. 5.00 (*0-89792-102-X*) Ill St Museum.

Late Poems of Meng Chiao. Tr. by David Hinton from CHI. LC 96-21157. (Lockert Library of Poetry in Translation). 76p. 1997. pap. 9.95 (*0-691-01236-9*, Pub. by Princeton U Pr); text 27.50 (*0-691-01237-7*, Pub. by Princeton U Pr) Cal Prin Full Svc.

Late Potentials of the Auditory System. David L. McPherson. LC 95-34210. (Evoked Potentials Ser.). 170p. 1995. 39.95 (*1-56593-163-7*, 0473) Thomson Learn.

Late Prehistoric Bison Procurement in Southeastern New Mexico: The 1978 Season at the Garnsey Site (LA-18399) John D. Speth & William J. Parry. (Technical Reports Ser.: No. 12). 369p. 1980. pap. 9.00 (*0-932206-85-9*) U Mich Mus Anthro.

Late Prehistoric Development of Alaska's Native People. Ed. by Robert D. Shaw et al. (Aurora Ser.: Vol. 4). (Illus.). ix, 450p. 1988. pap. 28.00 (*1-890396-04-4*) AK Anthropological.

Late Prehistoric Exchange Network Analysis in Carrizo Gorge & the Far Southwest. Michael S. Shackley. (Illus.). x, 181p. (C). 1981. pap. 20.63 (*1-55567-016-4*) Coyote Press.

***Late Prehistoric Exploitation of the Eurasian Steppe.** Ed. by Marsha Levine et al. (Monographs Ser.). (Illus.). 224p. 1999. lib. bdg. 70.00 (*1-902937-03-1*, Pub. by McDonald Inst) David Brown.

Late Prehistory of the Eastern Sahel: The Mesolithic & Neolithic of Shaqadud, Sudan. Ed. by Anthony E. Marks & Abbas Mohammed-Ali. LC 90-52656. (Illus.). 304p. 1991. pap. text 29.95 (*0-87074-310-4*) SMU Press.

Late Prehistory of the Lake Erie Drainage Basin: A 1972 Symposium Revised. Ed. by David S. Brose. (Illus.). 355p. (Orig.). (C). 1976. pap. 5.00 (*1-878600-01-X*) Cleve Mus Nat Hist.

Late Proterozoic & Cambrian Tectonics, Sedimentation, & Record of Metazoan Radiation in the Western United States. Ed. by Christie Blick. (IGC Field Trip Guidebooks Ser.). 88p. 1989. 21.00 (*0-87590-657-5*, T331) Am Geophysical.

Late Quaternary & Present-Day Fluvial Processes in Central Europe. Ed. by Jurgen Hagedorn. (Zeitschrift fuer Geomorphologie - Annals of Geomorphology Ser.: Supplementband 100). (Illus.). iv, 204p. 1995. pap. 73.00 (*3-443-21100-3*, Pub. by Gebruder Borntraeger) Balogh.

Late Quaternary Chronology & Paleoclimates of the Eastern Mediterranean. Ed. by Renee S. Kra. LC 94-6891. (Illus.). 371p. (Orig.). 1994. pap. 30.00 (*0-9638314-1-0*) Radiocarbon.

Late Quaternary Climate, Tectonism, & Sedimentation in Clear Lake, Northern California Coast Ranges. Ed. by John D. Sims. LC 87-37943. (Geological Society of America Ser.: Vol. 214). (Illus.). 272p. 1988. reprint ed. pap. 84.40 (*0-608-07740-2*, 206782800010) Bks Demand.

Late Quaternary Environment. Wright. 1984. pap. text. write for info. (*0-582-30124-6*, Pub. by Addison-Wesley) Longman.

Late Quaternary Environmental Change: Physical & Human Perspectives. M. Bell. 288p. (C). 1996. pap. 77.00 (*0-582-04514-2*) Addison-Wesley.

Late Quaternary Environmental Change in North-West Europe: Excavations at Holywell Coombe, South-East England. R. C. Preece & D. R. Bridgland. LC 98-70919. (ENG & FRE.). xxi, 422 p. 1998. write for info. (*0-412-83230-5*, Chap & Hall NY) Chapman & Hall.

Late Quaternary Environments & Deep History: A Tribute to Paul S. Martin. Ed. by David W. Steadman & Jim I. Mead. 186p. 1995. pap. 15.00 (*0-9624750-4-1*) L Agenbroad.

Late-Quaternary Environments of the United States Vol. 1: The Late Pleistocene. Ed. by Herbert E. Wright. LC 83-5804. 423p. 1983. reprint ed. pap. 131.20 (*0-608-00798-6*, 205934700001) Bks Demand.

Late-Quaternary Environments of the United States Vol. 2: The Holocene. Herbert E. Wright. LC 83-5804. 295p. 1983. reprint ed. pap. 91.50 (*0-608-00799-4*, 205934700002) Bks Demand.

Late Quaternary History of the Lake Michigan Basin. Ed. by A. F. Schneider & G. S. Fraser. (Special Papers: No. 251). (Illus.). 124p. 1990. pap. 15.00 (*0-8137-2251-9*) Geol Soc.

Late Quaternary Mammalian Biogeography & Enviroments of the Great Plains & Prairies. Ed. by Russell W. Graham et al. (Scientific Papers: Vol. XXII). (Illus.). 491p. (Orig.). (C). 1987. pap. 20.00 (*0-89792-112-7*) Ill St Museum.

Late Quaternary Palaeoceanography of the North Atlantic Margins. Ed. by J. T. Andrews et al. (Geological Society Special Publication Ser.: No. 111). (Illus.). viii, 376p. 1996. 98.00 (*1-897799-61-6*, 350, Pub. by Geol Soc Pub Hse) AAPG.

Late-Quaternary Palynology at Lobsigensee: Regional Vegetation History & Local Lake Development. Brigitta Ammann. (Dissertationes Botanicae Ser.: Band 137). (Illus.). xii, 157p. 1989. pap. 77.00 (*3-443-64049-4*, Pub. by Gebruder Borntraeger) Balogh.

Late Quaternary Sea-Level Correlation & Applications. D. Bruce Scott et al. (C). 1988. text 140.50 (*0-7923-0016-5*) Kluwer Academic.

Late Renaissance Music at the Habsburg Court. Carmelo P. Comberiati. (Monographs on Musicology: Vol. 4). xx, 242p. 1987. text 46.00 (*2-88124-192-1*) Gordon & Breach.

Late Republican Villa at Posto, Francolise. M. A. Cotton. (Illus.). 200p. 1979. 30.00 (*0-904152-03-0*, Pub. by British Schl Rome) David Brown.

Late Returns: A Personal Memoir of Ted Berrigan. Tom Clark. 88p. 1985. pap. 7.00 (*0-939180-38-3*) Tombouctou.

Late Returns: A Personal Memoir of Ted Berrigan. deluxe limited ed. Tom Clark. 88p. 1985. 35.00 (*0-939180-35-9*) Tombouctou.

***Late Roman Army.** Pat Southern. 2000. pap. 25.99 (*0-415-22296-6*) Routledge.

Late Roman Army. Pat Southern & Karen R. Dixon. LC 96-60156. (Illus.). 240p. 1996. 32.50 (*0-300-06843-3*) Yale U Pr.

Late Roman Bronze Coinage. Carson et al. 1990. 25.00 (*0-942666-57-7*) S J Durst.

Late Roman Cavalryman, 236-565 AD. Simon MacDowall. (Warrior Ser.). (Illus.). 64p. 1995. pap. 12.95 (*1-85532-567-5*, Pub. by Ospry) Stackpole.

Late Roman Cemetery at Bletsoe. Michael Dawson. (Bedfordshire Archaeological Monograph Ser.: No. 1, 1994). (Illus.). 68p. 1994. pap. 22.00 (*1-85351-174-9*, Pub. by Oxbow Bks) David Brown.

Late Roman Empire. Glanville Downey. LC 76-18145. (Berkshire Studies). 158p. 1976. reprint ed. pap. 11.50 (*0-88275-441-6*) Krieger.

Late Roman Infantry, 236-565 A.D. Simon MacDowall. (Warrior Ser.). (Illus.). 64p. 1994. pap. 12.95 (*1-85532-419-9*, 9608, Pub. by Ospry) Stackpole.

Late Roman West & the Vandals. Frank M. Clover. LC 93-18599. (Collected Studies: No. CS401). 300p. 1993. 101.95 (*0-86078-354-5*, Pub. by Variorum) Ashgate Pub Co.

Late Roman World & Its Historian: Interpreting Ammianus Marcellinus. Jan W. Drijvers & David Hunt. LC 99-18312. 1999. text. write for info. (*0-415-20271-X*) Routledge.

Late Romances. William Shakespeare. Ed. by David Bevington et al. (Classics Ser.). 688p. 1988. mass mkt. 5.95 (*0-553-21288-5*, Bantam Classics) Bantam.

Late Romances: Poems. Eric Pankey. LC 96-36676. 88p. 1997. 2.99 (*0-679-45454-3*) Knopf.

Late Romances: Poems. Eric Pankey. 1999. pap. 13.00 (*0-679-76605-7*) Knopf.

Late Ruskin. O'Gorman. 74.95 (*1-84014-629-X*) Ashgate Pub Co.

Late-Scholastic & Humanist Theories of the Propostion. G. Nuchelmans. (Verhandelingen der Koninklijke Nederlandse Akademie van Wetenschappen, Afd. Letterkunde, Nieuwe Reeks Ser.: No. 103). 238p. pap. 50.00 (*0-7204-8468-5*) Elsevier.

Late Sequelae in Oncology. J. Dunst. 250p. 1995. 145.00 (*0-387-56936-7*) Spr-Verlag.

Late Sequelae in Oncology. Ed. by J. Dunst & R. Sauer. LC 94-45370. (Medical Radiology Ser.). 1995. write for info. (*3-540-56936-7*) Spr-Verlag.

Late Seventeenth-Century Edinburgh: A Demographic Study. Helen M. Dingwall. (Illus.). 336p. 1994. 86.95 (*1-85928-019-6*, Pub. by Scolar Pr) Ashgate Pub Co.

Late Seventeenth-Century Edinburgh: A Demographic Study. Helen M. Dingwall. LC 93-12545. 256p. 1993. write for info. (*0-7185-1460-2*) St Martin.

Late-Seventeenth-Century English Keyboard Music. Henry Purcell et al. Ed. by Candace Bailey et al. (Recent Researches in Music of the Baroque Era Ser.: Vol. RRB81). (Illus.). xv, 104p. 1997. pap. 40.00 (*0-89579-382-2*) A-R Eds.

Late Shadows. Moshe Holczler. (Holocaust Diaries Ser.). (Illus.). 461p. (C). 1989. 19.95 (*1-56062-022-6*) CIS Comm.

Late Shakespeare: A New World of Words. Simon Palfrey. LC 97-10036. (Oxford English Monographs). 310p. (C). 1997. text 85.00 (*0-19-818619-3*) OUP.

***Late Shakespeare: A New World of Words.** Simon Palfrey. (Oxford English Monographs). 312p. 2000. pap. text 21.00 (*0-19-818689-4*) OUP.

Late Shift: Letterman. Bill Carter. 1996. pap. write for info. (*0-7868-8174-7*) Hyperion.

Late Shift: Letterman, Leno & the Network Battle for the Night. Bill Carter. (Illus.). 336p. (J). 1995. pap. 12.45 (*0-7868-8089-9*, Pub. by Hyperion) Time Warner.

Late Shift: Letterman, Leno & the Network Battle for the Night. Bill Carter. (Illus.). 512p. (J). 1996. mass mkt. 5.99 (*0-7868-8907-1*, Pub. by Hyperion) Time Warner.

Late Show: A Practical, Semiwild Survival Guide for Every Woman in Her Prime or Approaching It. Helen Gurley Brown. 400p. 1994. mass mkt. 5.99 (*0-380-77654-5*, Avon Bks) Morrow Avon.

Late Sixteenth-Century Lists of Law Books at Merton College. Ed. by Alain Wijffels. (Title Libri Pertinentes Ser.: Vol. 1). 150p. 1992. pap. text 20.00 (*0-9518811-0-8*, MRLP1, Pub. by Libri Pertinentes) MRTS.

Late Somatic Effects of Ionizing Radiation. AEC Technical Information Center Staff & Charles Van Cleave. LC 68-62106. 315p. 1968. pap. 15.75 (*0-87079-253-9*, TID-24310); fiche 9.00 (*0-87079-254-7*, TID-24310) DOE.

***Late Sonnet Harvest, 1988-2000.** Carl W. Cobb. LC 00-38657. 80p. 2000. pap. text 14.95 (*0-7734-1266-2*) E Mellen.

Late Soviet Culture: From Perestroika to Novostroika. Ed. by Thomas Lahusen & Gene Kuperman. LC 92-28051. (Post-Contemporary Interventions Ser.). 344p. 1993. text 54.95 (*0-8223-1290-5*); pap. text 19.95 (*0-8223-1291-3*) Duke.

Late Sowings: The Poems of Isaac J. Shleien. Isaac J. Shleien. 72p. 1996. 18.00 (*0-917251-06-7*) Scinta.

Late Sparta: The Spartan Revolution, 243-146 B. C. Benjamin Shimron. (Arethusa Monographs: No. 3). xiv, 167p. (C). 1972. pap. 7.00 (*0-930881-01-X*) Dept Classics.

Late-Stage Dementia Care: A Basic Guide. C. R. Kovach. LC 96-35127. 220p. 1996. pap. 29.95 (*1-56032-515-1*); boxed set 69.95 (*1-56032-514-3*) Taylor & Francis.

Late Stages of Stellar Evolution. Ed. by S. Kwok & Stuart R. Pottasch. 1987. text 201.00 (*90-277-2446-6*) Kluwer Academic.

Late Stages of Stellar Evolution: Computational Methods in Astrophysical Hydrodynamics: Proceedings of the Astrophysical School II Organized by the European Astrophysics Doctoral Network at Ponte de Lima, Portugal, 11-23 September 1989. Ed. by B. C. De Loore et al. (Lecture Notes in Physics Ser.: Vol. 373). viii, 390p. 1991. 26.95 (*0-387-53620-5*) Spr-Verlag.

Late Stages of Stellar Evolution: Proceedings of the I. A. U. Symposium, No. 66, Warsaw, Poland, Sept. 10-12, 1973. International Astronomical Union Staff. Ed. by Roger J. Tayler & James E. Hesser. LC 74-77970. (Symposia of the International Astronomical Union Ser.: No. 66). 250p. 1974. lib. bdg. 112.00 (*90-277-0470-8*) Kluwer Academic.

Late Stars. Jeffrey Skinner. LC 84-7495. (Wesleyan New Poets Ser.). 64p. 1985. pap. 12.95 (*0-8195-1121-8*, Wesleyan Univ Pr) U Pr of New Eng.

Late Start. Daniel Green. LC 89-92426. 120p. 1989. write for info. (*0-9624852-0-9*) Daniel Green.

***Late Start Investor: The Better-Late-Than-Never Guide to Realizing Your Retirement Income.** John F. Wasik. LC 98-17435. 320p. (Orig.). 1999. pap. 14.95 (*0-8050-5502-9*, Owl) H Holt & Co.

Late Stone Age Hunters of the British Isles. Christopher Smith. (Illus.). 216p. (C). 1997. pap. 32.99 (*0-415-07202-6*) Routledge.

Late Stone Age Hunters of the British Isles. 3rd ed. Christopher Smith. LC 91-23152. (Illus.). 240p. (C). 1992. 90.00 (*0-415-03161-3*) Routledge.

Late Stories (Chapbook) R. V. Cassill. 50p. 1995. pap. 5.00 (*0-916092-23-2*) Tex Ctr Writers.

Late String Quartets & the Grosse Fugue, Opp. 127, 130-133, 135. Ludwig van Beethoven. (Miniature Scores Ser.). 1998. pap. 4.95 (*0-486-40111-1*) Dover.

Late Summer Break. Ann B. Knox. LC 94-41553. 158p. 1995. 14.00 (*0-918949-65-3*); pap. 9.00 (*0-918949-64-5*) Knox.

Late-Talking Children. Thomas Sowell. 224p. 1998. pap. 14.00 (*0-465-03835-2*, Pub. by Basic) HarpC.

Late Talking Preschool Children: Children Who May Be Diagnosed As PDD. Jill Smith & Howard Diller. (Illus.). 115p. 1998. pap. 24.00 (*0-9630539-6-5*) Apodixis.

***Late Thoughts in March.** John P. Ward. 64p. 1999. pap. (*1-85411-250-3*, Pub. by Seren Bks) Dufour.

Late to the Kitchen. Grim Reaper Books Staff & Emilie Glen. 24p. 1976. write for info. (*0-318-64122-4*) Poets Pr.

Late Triassic (Norian) Footprint Fauna from the Culpeper Basin, Northern Virginia. Robert E. Weems. LC 84-45904. (Transactions Ser.: Vol. 77, Pt. 1). 1987. pap. 15.00 (*0-87169-771-8*, T771-WER) Am Philos.

Late Twentieth Century Art: Selections from the Sydney & Frances Lewis Collection in the Virginia Museum of Fine Arts. Frederick R. Brandt. Ed. by Donald Spanel. LC 85-21708. (Illus.). 216p. 1985. 35.00 (*0-917046-22-6*) Va Mus Arts.

Late-Victorian & Edwardian British Novelists: First Series, Vol. 153. Ed. by George M. Johnson. 420p. 1995. text 155.00 (*0-8103-5714-3*, 007488) Gale.

Late Victorian Army, 1868-1902. Edward M. Spiers. (History of the British Army Ser.). (Illus.). 336p. 1992. 69.95 (*0-7190-2659-8*, Pub. by Manchester Univ Pr) St Martin.

***Late Victorian Costumes Paper Dolls.** Tom Tierney. (Illus.). (J). 1998. pap. 3.95 (*0-486-40371-8*) Dover.

Late Victorian Farce. Jeffery H. Huberman. LC 86-16154. (Theater & Dramatic Studies: No. 40). (Illus.). 176p. reprint ed. pap. 54.60 (*0-8357-1774-7*, 207061600005) Bks Demand.

***Late Victorian Holocausts: El Nino Famines & the Making of the Third World.** Mike Davis. 2000. 27.00 (*1-85984-739-0*, Pub. by Verso) Norton.

***Late Victorian Houses & Cottages: Floor Plans & Illustrations for 40 House Designs.** Century Architectural Co. LC 98-43893. 1999. pap. text 7.95 (*0-486-40490-0*) Dover.

Late Victorian Poetry, 1880-1899: A Biobibliography. Catherine W. Reilly. 416p. 1995. 140.00 (*0-7201-2001-2*) Continuum.

Late Victorian Women's Tailoring: The Direct System of Ladies' Cutting (1897) 3rd enl. ed. T. H. Holding. Ed. by R. L. Shep. LC 96-46774. Orig. Title: The Direct System of Ladies' Tailoring. (Illus.). 192p. (Orig.). 1997. reprint ed. pap. 19.95 (*0-914046-23-3*) R L Shep.

Late Vistulian (Weichselian) & Holocene Acolian Phenomena in Central & Northern Europe. Ed. by S. Kozarski. (Zeitschrift fuer Geomorphologie - Annals of Geomorphology Ser.: Supplementband 90). (Illus.). vi, 207p. 1991. pap. 88.00 (*3-443-21090-2*, Pub. by Gebruder Borntraeger) Balogh.

Late Winter Child. Vincent Buckley. 38p. 1980. pap. 7.00 (*0-85105-358-0*, Pub. by Smyth) Dufour.

Late Wisconsin Spring. John Koethe. LC 84-42574. (Contemporary Poets Ser.). 60p. 1984. pap. 9.95 (*0-691-01414-0*, Pub. by Princeton U Pr) Cal Prin Full Svc.

Late Woodland Cultures of the Middle Atlantic Region. Jay F. Custer. LC 84-40807. (Illus.). 216p. 1986. 36.50 (*0-87413-285-1*) U Delaware Pr.

***Late Woodland Period on the Lower Tombigbee River.** George W. Shorter, Jr. (Archaeological Monograph Ser.: Vol. 6). (Illus.). 1999. pap. 15.00 (*1-893955-06-0*) Univ S AL Ctr Archa.

***Late Woodland Societies: Tradition & Transformation Across the Midcontinent.** Ed. by Thomas E. Emerson et al. LC 99-87393. (Illus.). 672p. 2000. text 50.00 (*0-8032-1821-4*) U of Nebr Pr.

Late Work. Barbara L. McCombs & Linda Brannan. (Skills for Job Success Ser.). (Illus.). 32p. (Orig.). (YA). (gr. 7-12). 1990. teacher ed. 1.95 (*1-56119-014-4*); disk 39.95 (*1-56119-107-8*) Educ Pr MD.

Late Work, Set. Barbara L. McCombs & Linda Brannan. (Skills for Job Success Ser.). (Illus.). 32p. (Orig.). (YA). (gr. 7-12). 1990. teacher ed., student ed. 54.95 (*1-56119-065-9*) Educ Pr MD.

Late Works, Translations, & Revisions. Ed. by Ernest Warburton. LC 92-33289. (Librettos of Mozart's Operas Ser.: Vol. 4). (Illus.). 584p. 1993. text 40.00 (*0-8153-0111-1*) Garland.

Late 19th Century Furniture by Berkey & Gay. Brian L. Witherell. LC 98-85767. 320p. 1998. pap. 29.95 (*0-7643-0656-1*) Schiffer.

Latecomers. Anita Brookner. (Vintage Contemporaries Ser.). 1990. pap. 12.00 (*0-679-72668-3*) Vin Bks.

Latecomers. large type ed. Anita Brookner. (General Ser.). 259p. 1990. lib. bdg. 19.95 (*0-8161-4892-9*, G K Hall Lrg Type) Mac Lib Ref.

Latecomers in the Global Economy. Ed. by Michael Storper & Tavros B. Thomadakis. LC 97-26309. (Industrial Economic Strategies for Europe Ser.). 256p. (C). 1998. 85.00 (*0-415-14867-7*) Routledge.

Lated Mrs. Null. Frank Stockton. (Notable American Authors Ser.). 1999. reprint ed. lib. bdg. 125.00 (*0-7812-8926-2*) Rprt Serv.

Lateinisch-Griechisch Wortschatz in der Medizin. 3rd ed. Ilse Becher. (GER, GRE & LAT.). 255p. 1991. 59.95 (*0-7859-6874-1*, 3333006278) Fr & Eur.

Lateinische Asop des Romulus. Georg Thiele. ccxxxviii, 360p. 1985. reprint ed. write for info. (*3-487-07663-2*) G Olms Pubs.

Lateinische Epigrammatik im Hohen Mittelalter. Wolfgang Maaz. (Spolia Berolinensia Ser.: Bd. 2). (GER.). viii, 306p. 1992. write for info. (*3-615-00075-7*) G Olms Pubs.

Lateinische Hamilton-Psalter im Berliner Kupferstichkabinett. Wolfgang Augustyn. (Spolia Berolinensia Ser.: Bd. 9). (GER.). x, 450p. 1996. 158.00 (*3-615-00179-6*, Pub. by Weidmann) Lubrecht & Cramer.

Lateinische Inschriften. Heinrich Willemsen. vi, 124p. 1965. write for info. (*3-296-16270-4*) G Olms Pubs.

Lateinische Lehrgedicht im Mittelalter: Analyse Einer Gattung. Thomas Haye. (Mittellateinische Studien & Texte: Vol. 22). (GER.). 480p. 1997. 159.50 (*90-04-10668-5*) Brill Academic Pubs.

Lateinische Ordensdramen des XV-XVIII: Jahrhunderts Mit Deutschen Uebersetzungen. Ed. by Fidel Raedle. (Ausgaben Deutscher Literatur des XV bis XVIII Jahrhunderts Ser.). (C). 1979. 484.65 (*3-11-003383-6*) De Gruyter.

Lateinische Sprache. Wallace M. Lindsay. xiii, 747p. 1984. reprint ed. write for info. (*3-487-07484-2*) G Olms Pubs.

Lateinische Sprachmaterial Im Wortschatze der Deutscshen, Franzosischen und Englischen Sprache. Adolf Hemme. pap. write for info. (*0-318-70801-9*) G Olms Pubs.

Lateinische Sprachmaterial Im Wortschatze der Deutscshen, Franzosischen und Englischen Sprache. Adolf Hemme. (Olms Paperbacks Ser.: No. 48). 1236p. 1979. reprint ed. pap. write for info. (*3-487-06865-6*) G Olms Pubs.

Lateinische Volksetymologie und Verwandtes. Otto Keller. x, 387p. 1974. reprint ed. write for info. (*3-487-05172-9*) G Olms Pubs.

Lateinischen Sequenzen des Mittelalters in Musikalischer und Rhythmischer Beziehung. Karl F. Bartsch. 245p. 1967. reprint ed. 65.00 (*0-318-71254-7*) G Olms Pubs.

Lateinisches und Romanisches Aus Den Etymologiae des Isidorus Von Sevilla. Johann Sofer. xii, 190p. 1975. reprint ed. write for info. (*3-487-05412-4*) G Olms Pubs.

Lately I've Been Thinking. Bobby Markels. (Mendocino Malady Ser.). (Illus.). 58p. (Orig.). Date not set. pap. 6.50 (*1-880991-05-5*) Stone Pub.

Lately Tortured Earth: Exoterrestrial Forces & Quantavolutions in the Earth Sciences. Alfred De Grazia. (Quantavolution Ser.). 516p. 1983. 28.00 (*0-940268-06-X*) Metron Pubns.

Latency. Charles A. Sarnoff. LC 75-34707. 416p. 1981. reprint ed. 60.00 (*0-87668-233-6*) Aronson.

Latency by Herpes Simplex Viruses: Journal: Intervirology, 1991, Vol. 32, No. 2. Ed. by Kenneth I. Berns & R. W. Whitley. (Illus.). 52p. 1991. pap. 37.50 (*3-8055-5362-5*) S Karger.

Lateness: A Book of Poems. David Shapiro. LC 76-47073. 96p. 1977. 14.95 (*0-87951-058-7*, Pub. by Overlook Pr) Penguin Putnam.

Lateness: A Book of Poems. David Shapiro. LC 76-47073. 96p. 1980. pap. 8.95 (*0-87951-111-7*, Pub. by Overlook Pr) Penguin Putnam.

Latent Class Analysis. Allan L. McCutcheon. (Quantitative Applications in the Social Sciences Ser.: Vol. 64). 88p. 1987. pap. 10.95 (*0-8039-2752-5*) Sage.

Latent Class & Discrete Latent Trait Models: Similarities & Differences. Ton Heinen. LC 95-41820. (Advanced Quantitative Techniques in the Social Sciences Ser.: Vol. 6). 235p. 1996. 36.00 (*0-8039-7433-7*) Sage.

Latent Class Scaling Analysis. C. Mitchell Dayton. LC 98-43854. (University Papers Ser.). 1999. pap. 13.95 (*0-7619-1323-8*) Sage.

An Asterisk (*) at the beginning of an entry indicates that the title is appearing for the first time.

Latent Damage Act, 1986: Impact on the Professions & the Construction Industry. Phillip Capper. (C). 1987. 285.00 (*0-7855-4107-1*, Pub. by Witherby & Co) St Mut.

Latent Damage Law: The Expert System. Phillip Capper & Richard Susskind. 120p. 1988. boxed set 60.00 (*0-406-02362-X*, UK, MICHIE) LEXIS Pub.

***Latent Destinies: Cultural Paranoia & Contemporary U. S. Narrative.** Patrick O'Donnell. LC 00-26812. (New Americanists Ser.). 208p. 2000. pap. 17.95 (*0-8223-2587-X*) Duke.

***Latent Destinies: Cultural Paranoia & Contemporary U. S. Narrative.** Patrick O'Donnell. LC 00-26812. 208p. 2000. lib. bdg. 49.95 (*0-8223-2558-6*) Duke.

Latent Dyslipoproteinemias & Atherosclerosis. Ed. by J. L. De Gennes et al. LC 83-43038. (Illus.). 334p. 1984. reprint ed. pap. 103.60 (*0-7837-9569-6*, 206031800005) Bks Demand.

Latent Heat Transfer: An Introduction to Fundamentals. G. S. Lock. (Oxford Engineering Science Ser.: No. 43). (Illus.). 310p. 1996. reprint ed. pap. text 49.95 (*0-19-856284-5*) OUP.

Latent Herpes Virus Infections in Veterinary Medicine. Ed. by G. Wittmann et al. (Current Topics in Veterinary Medicine & Animal Science Ser.). 528p. 1984. text 252.50 (*0-89838-622-5*) Kluwer Academic.

Latent Inhibition & Conditioned Attention Theory. R. E. Lubow. (Problems in the Behavioral Sciences Ser.). (Illus.). 336p. (C). 1989. text 69.95 (*0-521-36307-1*) Cambridge U Pr.

Latent Power of Mammon. Gary S. Maxey. pap. 2.99 (*0-88019-159-7*) Schmul Pub Co.

Latent Power of the Soul. Watchman Nee. Tr. by Stephen Kaung. 86p. 1972. pap. 3.50 (*0-935008-25-X*) Christian Fellow Pubs.

Latent Trait & Latent Class Models. R. Langeheine & J. Rost. LC 88-4141. (Illus.). 328p. (C). 1988. 75.00 (*0-306-42727-3*, Plenum Trade) Perseus Pubng.

Latent Variable Analysis: Applications for Developmental Research. Ed. by Alexander Von Eye & Clifford C. Clogg. (Focus Editions Ser.: Vol. 171). 432p. (C). 1994. text 59.95 (*0-8039-5330-5*); pap. text 26.95 (*0-8039-5331-3*) Sage.

Latent Variable Modeling & Applications to Causality. Ed. by Maia Berkane. LC 96-40195. (Lectures Notes in Statistics Ser.: Vol. 120). 281p. 1997. pap. 44.95 (*0-387-94917-8*) Spr-Verlag.

Latent Variable Models: An Introduction to Factor, Path, & Structural Analysis. 2nd ed. John C. Loehlin. 304p. 1992. pap. 27.00 (*0-8058-1084-6*); text 59.95 (*0-8058-1083-8*) L Erlbaum Assocs.

Latent Variable Models: An Introduction to Factor, Path, & Structural Analysis. 3rd ed. John C. Loehlin. LC 97-48378. 325p. 1998. write for info. (*0-8058-2830-3*); pap. write for info. (*0-8058-2831-1*) L Erlbaum Assocs.

Latent Variable Models & Factor Analysis. write for info. (*0-85264-280-6*) Lubrecht & Cramer.

Latent Variable Models & Factor Analysis. 2nd ed. David J. Bartholomew & Martin Knott. LC 99-461933. (Kendall's Library of Statistics: No. 7). (Illus.). 240p. 1999. text 45.00 (*0-340-69243-X*, Pub. by E A) OUP.

***Latent Vision.** Edward Hewitt. 176p. 2000. 18.99 (*0-7089-5768-4*) Ulverscroft.

Latente Adipositas: Ein Vergleich Latent und Manifest Ausgepragter Ebsucht. Regina Pencik. (Psychologie Ser.: Bd. 599). (Illus.). 157p. 1997. 31.95 (*3-631-32117-1*) P Lang Pubng.

Later. Corinne Jacker. 1979. pap. 5.25 (*0-8222-0642-0*) Dramatists Play.

***Later Anglo-Saxon England.** Andrew Reynolds. (Illus.). 208p. 1999. 32.50 (*0-7524-1432-1*, Pub. by Tempus Pubng) Arcadia Publng.

Later Auden. Edward Mendelson. LC 98-27384. 608p. 1999. text 30.00 (*0-374-18408-9*) FS&G.

***Later Auden.** Edward Mendelson. 608p. 2000. pap. 16.00 (*0-374-52699-0*) FS&G.

Later Auden: From New Year Letter to about the House. George W. Bahlke. LC 74-98179. 208p. 1970. 20.00 (*0-8135-0663-8*) Lib Soc Sci.

Later Biblical Researches in Palestine & in Adjacent Regions: Journal of Travels in the Year 1852. Edward Robinson. Ed. by Moshe Davis. LC 77-70739. (America & the Holy Land Ser.). 1977. reprint ed. lib. bdg. 58.95 (*0-405-10285-2*) Ayer.

Later Biblical Researches in Palestine & the Adjacent Regions. Edward Robinson. (Notable American Authors Ser.). 1999. reprint ed. lib. bdg. 125.00 (*0-7812-8792-8*) Rprt Serv.

Later Calvinism: International Perspectives. Ed. by W. Fred Graham. LC 92-20361. (Sixteenth Century Essays & Studies: Vol. 22). 564p. 1993. 50.00 (*0-940474-23-9*, SCJP) Truman St Univ.

***Later Celtic Art in Britain & Ireland.** Lloyd Robert Laing. LC 88-115996. (Archaeology Ser.: No. 48). (Illus.). 56p. 1999. pap. 10.50 (*0-85263-874-4*, Pub. by Shire Pubns) Parkwest Pubns.

Later Ceramics in South-East Asia: Sixteenth to Twentieth Centuries. Barbara Harrisson. (Oxford in Asia Studies in Ceramics). (Illus.). 138p. 1996. text 90.00 (*967-65-3112-X*) OUP.

Later Childhood & Adolescence Vol. 3: Parenthood in a Free Nation. Ethel Kawin. (Illus.). 351p. 1969. pap. 3.00 (*0-931682-07-X*) Purdue U Pubns.

Later China, Korea, Japan & The Modern World, 2. Yoshinori Takeuchi. LC 98-43116. (Buddhist Spirituality Ser.). 1999. 49.50 (*0-8245-1595-1*) Crossroad NY.

Later Chinese Bronzes. Rose Kerr. (Illus.). 116p. 1990. 65.00 (*1-870076-11-7*, Pub. by Bamboo Pub) Antique Collect.

Later Chinese Bronzes. Rose Kerr. (Illus.). 116p. 1990. 49.95 (*0-19-585149-8*) OUP.

Later, Courtney: A Mother Says Goodbye. Susan C. Evans. LC 96-30182. 1996. 4.95 (*1-56123-096-0*) Centering Corp.

Later Critiques. Augustus J. Ralli. LC 68-26469. (Essay Index Reprint Ser.). 1977. reprint ed. 18.95 (*0-8369-0809-0*) Ayer.

Later Crusades, 1189 to 1311 see History of the Crusades

***Later Diaries, 1961-1972.** Ned Rorem. (Illus.). 456p. 2000. pap. 20.00 (*0-306-80964-8*) Da Capo.

Later Dynasties of Egypt, XXth-XXXIst. P. G. Elgood. (Illus.). vii, 154p. (C). 1993. text 15.00 (*0-89005-005-8*) Ares.

Later Elementary/Middle School Home Learning Enabler Manual. unabridged ed. Cynthia C. Shoemaker. LC 98-96517. (Home Learning Enabler Manuals Ser.). (Illus.). 162p. 1994. 29.95 (*1-892905-02-7*, 803) ECEA Inst.

Later Essays, 1917-1920. Austin Dobson. LC 68-22910. (Essay Index Reprint Ser.). 1977. 18.95 (*0-8369-0379-X*) Ayer.

Later, Gator. Laurence Yep. LC 94-11254. (Illus.). 128p. (J). (ps-3). 1995. lib. bdg. 13.89 (*0-7868-2083-7*, Pub. by Hyprn Child) Little.

Later, Gator. Laurence Yep. (J). 1997. pap. 4.50 (*0-7868-1277-X*, Pub. by Hyprn Child) Little.

Later, Gator. Laurence Yep. LC 94-11254. (Illus.). 128p. (J). (gr. 3-7). 1997. pap. 4.50 (*0-7868-1160-9*, Pub. by Hyprn Ppbks) Little.

Later, Gator. Laurence Yep. (J). 1997. 9.60 (*0-606-11001-1*, Pub. by Turtleback) Demco.

Later Ghaznavids: Slendour & Decay: The Dynasty in Afghanistan & Northern India, 1040-1186. C. E. Bosworth. LC 77-7879. (Persian Studies Ser.: Vol. 7). vi, 196p. 1977. text 22.00 (*0-231-04428-3*) Bibliotheca Persica.

Later Ghaznavids: Splendour & Decay: The Dynasty in Afghanistan & Northern India 1040-1186. Clifford E. Bosworth. (C). 1992. reprint ed. text 20.00 (*81-215-0577-1*, Pub. by M Manoharial) Coronet Bks.

Later Gleanings. William E. Gladstone. LC 72-8478. (Essay Index Reprint Ser.). 1977. reprint ed. 26.95 (*0-8369-7314-3*) Ayer.

Later Greek Religion. Ed. by Edwyn R. Bevan. LC 76-179282. (Library of Greek Thought: No. 9). reprint ed. 27.50 (*0-404-07807-9*) AMS Pr.

Later History of Israel Study Guide, Bk. 1. Constance. 102p. 1988. pap., student ed. 12.99 (*1-889015-44-X*) Explrs Bible.

Later History of Israel Study Guide, Bk. 2. Constance. 108p. 1988. pap., student ed. 12.99 (*1-889015-45-8*) Explrs Bible.

Later History of Israel Study Guide, Bk. 3. Constance. 108p. 1988. pap., student ed. 12.99 (*1-889015-46-6*) Explrs Bible.

Later Hymns & Ballads & Fifty Poems. Fred P. Green. LC 89-80720. 220p. 1989. pap. 18.95 (*0-916642-37-2*, 427) Hope Pub.

Later Incarnations of Francis Bacon. E. Francis Udny. 50p. 1996. reprint ed. pap. 9.95 (*1-56459-536-6*) Kessinger Pub.

Later Italian Pictures in the Collection of Her Majesty the Queen. 2nd ed. Michael Levey. (Pictures in the Royal Collections). (Illus.). 490p. (C). 1991. text 159.95 (*0-521-26328-X*) Cambridge U Pr.

Later Jacobean & Caroline Dramatists. Ed. by Terence P. Logan & Denzell S. Smith. LC 77-25265. (Survey & Bibliography of Recent Studies in English Renaissance Drama). 295p. 1984. reprint ed. pap. 91.50 (*0-8357-2912-5*, 203915000011) Bks Demand.

Later Language Development: Ages 9 Through 19. Ed. by Marilyn A. Nippold. LC 90-52764. 271p. (Orig.). 1988. pap. text 29.00 (*0-89079-304-2*, 1756) PRO-ED.

Later Language Development: The School-Age & Adolescent Years. 2nd ed. Marilyn A. Nippold. LC 97-20020. 1998. pap. text 34.00 (*0-89079-725-0*) PRO-ED.

Later Letters of Edward Lear. Edward Lear. Ed. by Lady Strachey. LC 75-175702. (Select Bibliographies Reprint Ser.). 1977. reprint ed. 27.95 (*0-8369-6617-1*) Ayer.

Later Letters of Peter of Blois. Ed. by Elizabeth Revell. (Auctores Britannici Medii Aevi British Academy Ser.: No. XIII). 424p. 1993. text 125.00 (*0-19-726108-6*) OUP.

Later Letters, 1849-1870, 4 vols, Set. John Stuart Mill. Ed. by Francis E. Mineka & Dwight N. Lindley. LC 75-163833. (Collected Works of John Stuart Mill). 1972. text 125.00 (*0-8020-5261-4*) U of Toronto Pr.

Later Life. A. R. Gurney. 1994. pap. 5.25 (*0-8222-1373-7*) Dramatists Play.

Later Life: The Realities of Aging. 4th ed. Harold G. Cox. LC 95-19675. 386p. 1995. 72.00 (*0-13-409707-6*) P-H.

***Later Life: The Realities of Aging.** 5th ed. Harold Cox. LC 00-27203. (Illus.). 432p. 2000. pap. 57.33 (*0-13-013831-2*) P-H.

Later Life: The Social Psychology of Aging. Ed. by Victor W. Marshall. LC 85-19581. (Illus.). 352p. 1986. reprint ed. pap. 109.20 (*0-608-01164-9*, 205946400001) Bks Demand.

Later Life Families. Timothy H. Brubaker. (Family Studies Text Ser.: Vol. 1). 1985. 42.00 (*0-8039-2293-0*); pap. 18.95 (*0-8039-2294-9*) Sage.

***Later Life of Lord Curzon of Kedleston - Aristocrat, Writer, Politician, Statesman: An Experiment in Political Biography.** G. H. Bennett & Marion Gibson. LC 99-58819. (Studies in British History: Vol. 60). 280p. 2000. text 89.95 (*0-7734-7790-X*) E Mellen.

Later Life Transitions: Older Males in Rural America. Edward A. Powers. 1985. lib. bdg. 145.00 (*0-89838-137-1*) Kluwer Academic.

Later Lyrics. Julia W. Howe. (Notable American Authors Ser.). 1992. reprint ed. lib. bdg. 75.00 (*0-7812-3215-5*) Rprt Serv.

Later Medieval English Prose. Ed. by William Matthews. LC 63-9439. (Goldentree Books in English Literature). (Orig.). 1963. pap. text 17.95 (*0-89197-270-6*) Irvington.

***Later Medieval Europe: Light & Emancipation, Vol. 11.** Christopher Tadgell. (History of Architecture Ser.). 1999. pap. text 12.95 (*0-8230-0386-8*) Watsn-Guptill.

Later Medieval Europe From St Louis Luther. 2nd ed. Daniel Waley. LC 84-10087. (Illus.). 276p. (C). 1989. pap. 31.20 (*0-582-49262-9*, 73553) Addison-Wesley.

Later Medieval Philosophy, 1150-1350. John Marenbon. 248p. (C). 1987. lib. bdg. 35.00 (*0-685-19266-0*) Routledge.

Later Medieval Philosophy, 1150-1350: An Introduction. John Marenbon. 248p. (C). 1991. pap. 27.99 (*0-415-06807-X*, A6265) Routledge.

Later Melodrama in America: Monte Cristo (Ca. 1883) fac. ed. Charles Fechter. Ed. by Anne D. McLucas. LC 94-29684. (Nineteenth-Century American Musical Theater Ser.: Vol. 4). (Illus.). 200p. 1995. text 84.00 (*0-8153-1377-2*) Garland.

Later Mercantilists: Josiah Child, 1603-1699 & John Locke, 1632-1704. Ed. by Mark Blaug. (Pioneers in Economics Ser.: Vol. 5). 416p. 1991. text 180.00 (*1-85278-467-9*) E Elgar.

Later Middle Ages. Ed. by Stephen Medcalf. LC 81-6509. (Context of English Literature Ser.). 300p. 1981. pap. 21.50 (*0-8419-0726-9*) Holmes & Meier.

Later Middle Ages. Eric Voegelin. Ed. & Intro. by David Walsh. (History of Political Ideas Ser.: Vol. III). 296p. 1998. 34.95 (*0-8262-1154-2*) U of Mo Pr.

Later Mughals, 2 vols. in 1. Irvine & Sarker Staff. (C). 1995. 22.00 (*81-85557-56-X*, Pub. by Low Price) S Asia.

Later Nineteenth & Early Twentieth Century English & European Novelists, 6 vols. 2846p. (C). 1997. 785.00 (*0-415-15912-1*) Routledge.

Later Nineteenth & Early Twentieth Century English & European Novelists: Arnold Bennett. Ed. by James Hepburn. (Critical Heritage Ser.). 574p. (C). 1997. 160.00 (*0-415-15911-3*) Routledge.

Later Nineteenth & Early Twentieth Century English & European Novelists: Count Lev Nikolaevich Tolstoy. Ed. by A. V. Knowles. (Critical Heritage Ser.). 476p. (C). 1997. 140.00 (*0-415-15906-7*) Routledge.

Later Nineteenth & Early Twentieth Century English & European Novelists: H. G. Wells. Ed. by Patrick Parrinder. (Critical Heritage Ser.). 368p. (C). 1997. 125.00 (*0-415-15910-5*) Routledge.

Later Nineteenth & Early Twentieth Century English & European Novelists: Joseph Conrad see Modern Critical Views Series

Later Nineteenth & Early Twentieth Century English & European Novelists: Joseph Conrad. Ed. by Norman Sherry. (Critical Heritage Ser.). 412p. (C). 1997. 140.00 (*0-415-15907-5*) Routledge.

Later Nineteenth & Early Twentieth Century English & European Novelists: Rudyard Kipling. Ed. by Roger L. Green. (Critical Heritage Ser.). 428p. (C). 1997. 140.00 (*0-415-15909-1*) Routledge.

Later Novels: A Lost Lady; The Professor's House; Death Comes for the Archbishop; Shadows on the Rock; Lucy Gayheart; Sapphira & the Slave Girl. Willa Cather. Ed. by Sharon O'Brien. LC 89-64130. 988p. 1990. 35.00 (*0-940450-52-6*, Pub. by Library of America) Penguin Putnam.

Later Novels & Other Writings: The Lady in the Lake; The Little Sister; The Long Goodbye; Playback; Double Indemnity; Essays & Letters. Raymond Chandler. Ed. by Frank McShane. 1076p. 1995. 35.00 (*1-883011-08-6*, Pub. by Library of America) Penguin Putnam.

Later On. F. T. Prince. Date not set. pap. 14.95 (*0-85646-103-2*, Pub. by Anvil Press) Dufour.

Later Operetta Pt. I: El Capitan (1896), Music by John Philip Sousa, Libretto by Charles Klein. fac. ed. Ed. by Paul E. Bierley. LC 94-2238. (Nineteenth-Century American Musical Theater Ser.: Vol. 14). (Illus.). 336p. 1994. text 110.00 (*0-8153-1378-0*) Garland.

Later Operetta Pt. II: The Highwaymay, 1897, Music by Reginald de Koven, Libretto by Harry B. Smith. Ed. by Orly L. Krasner. LC 94-2238. (Nineteenth-Century American Musical Theater Ser.: No. 15). (Illus.). 330p. 1994. text 105.00 (*0-8153-1379-9*) Garland.

Later Paintings & Drawings of John Constable, 2 vols., Set. Graham Reynolds. LC 84-40186. (Studies in British Art). (Illus.). 880p. 1984. 300.00 (*0-300-03151-3*) Yale U Pr.

Later Papers of Sir Aubrey Lewis. Aubrey Lewis. 1979. text 37.50 (*0-19-712150-0*) OUP.

Later Periods of Quakerism, 2 vols., Set. Rufus M. Jones. LC 74-109758. 1971. reprint ed. lib. bdg. 125.00 (*0-8371-4248-2*, JOQU, Greenwood Pr) Greenwood.

Later Periods of Quakerism, Vol. 1. Rufus M. Jones. 1971. lib. bdg. 75.00 (*0-8371-4408-6*, Greenwood Pr) Greenwood.

Later Periods of Quakerism, Vol. 2. Rufus M. Jones. 1971. lib. bdg. 70.00 (*0-8371-4409-4*, Greenwood Pr) Greenwood.

Later Phases of the Life Cycle: Demographic Aspects. Ed. by Eugene Grebenik et al. (International Studies in Demography). (Illus.). 264p. 1989. text 65.00 (*0-19-828657-0*) OUP.

Later Philosophy of R. G. Collingwood. Alan Donagan. LC 85-16485. xvi, 332p. 1994. pap. text 20.00 (*0-226-15568-4*) U Ch Pr.

Later Philosophy of Schelling: The Influence of Boehme on the Works of 1809-1815. Robert F. Brown. LC 75-10138. 295p. 1976. 38.50 (*0-8387-1755-1*) Bucknell U Pr.

Later Plato & the Academy see History of Greek Philosophy

Later Plays. Eugene O'Neill. Ed. by Travis Bogard. 409p. (C). 1967. pap. 8.44 (*0-07-553664-1*) McGraw.

Later Poems of John Clare, 1837-1864, Set, Vols. I & II. John Clare. Ed. by Eric Robinson et al. (Oxford English Texts Ser.). (Illus.). 1984. 225.00 (*0-19-811874-0*) OUP.

Later Poetic Manuscripts of Gerard Manley Hopkins: From "The Wreck of the Deutschland" to the Final Dublin Sonnets in Facsimile. Gerard Manley Hopkins. Ed. by Norman H. MacKenzie. LC 91-3809. (Gerard Manley Hopkins Ser.). 911031p. 1991. text 140.00 (*0-8240-7444-0*) Garland.

Later Poetry of Charlotte Perkins Gilman. Charlotte Perkins Gilman. Ed. by Denise D. Knight. LC 96-3865. 200p. 1996. 32.50 (*0-87413-586-9*) U Delaware Pr.

Later Poetry of Wallace Stevens: Phenomenological Parallels with Husserl & Heidegger. Thomas J. Hines. LC 74-6773. 298p. 1975. 39.50 (*0-8387-1613-X*) Bucknell U Pr.

Later Pratt Portraits: Sketched in a New England Suburb. Anna Fuller. LC 79-122709. (Short Story Index Reprint Ser.). (Illus.). 1977. 23.95 (*0-8369-3542-X*) Ayer.

Later Prehistoric Pottery in England & Wales. Sheila M. Elsdon. (Archaeology Ser.: No. 58). (Illus.). 68p. 1989. pap. 10.50 (*0-7478-0004-9*, Pub. by Shire Pubns) Parkwest Pubns.

Later Prehistoric Settlement in SE Scotland. Ed. by D. W. Harding. 210p. 1982. pap. 15.00 (*0-614-21825-X*) David Brown.

Later Prehistory of Eastern & Southern Africa. D. W. Phillipson. (Illus.). 323p. 1978. 49.50 (*0-8419-0347-6*, Africana) Holmes & Meier.

Later Quaternary Construction of Cape Cod, Massachusetts: A Reconsideration of the W. M. Davis Model. Ed. by Elazar Uchupi et al. (Special Papers: No. 309). (Illus.). 69p. 1996. pap. 30.00 (*0-8137-2309-4*) Geol Soc.

Later Realism: A Study of Characterization in the British Novel. Walter L. Myers. LC 73-2801. (Select Bibliographies Reprint Ser). 1977. reprint ed. 20.95 (*0-8369-7166-3*) Ayer.

***Later Reformation in England, 1547-1603.** 2nd ed. Diarmaid MacCulloch. LC 00-42056. (British History in Perspective Ser.). (Illus.). 2000. pap. write for info. (*0-312-23737-5*) St Martin.

Later Renaissance in England: Nondramatic Verse & Prose, 1600-1660. Hershel Baker. (Illus.). 962p. 1996. reprint ed. pap. text 39.95 (*0-88133-842-7*) Waveland Pr.

Later Roman Colonate & Freedom. Miroslava C. Mirkovic. LC 97-907. (Transactions Ser.: Vol. 87, Pt.2). 1997. pap. 18.00 (*0-87169-872-2*) Am Philos.

Later Roman Empire. Ammianus Marcellinus. Tr. by Walter Hamilton. 512p. 1986. pap. 15.95 (*0-14-044406-8*, Penguin Classics) Viking Penguin.

***Later Roman Empire.** Richard Reece. (Illus.). 208p. 1999. 32.50 (*0-7524-1449-6*, Pub. by Tempus Pubng) Arcadia Publng.

Later Roman Empire, AD 284-430. Averil Cameron. LC 92-41000. 256p. 1993. 36.50 (*0-674-51193-X*); pap. 16.00 (*0-674-51194-8*) HUP.

Later Roman Empire, 284-602: A Social, Economic, & Administrative Survey, 2 vols. A. H. Jones. LC 85-24077. (Orig.). 1986. reprint ed. pap. 49.95 (*0-8018-3285-3*) Johns Hopkins.

Later Roman Empire, 284-602: A Social, Economic & Administrative Survey. A. H. Jones. LC 85-24077. 1986. reprint ed. 49.50 (*0-8018-3348-5*) Johns Hopkins.

Later Roman Empire, 284-602: A Social, Economic, & Administrative Survey, Vol. 1. A. H. Jones. LC 85-24077. (Orig.). 1986. reprint ed. pap. 27.50 (*0-8018-3353-1*) Johns Hopkins.

Later Roman Empire, 284-602: A Social, Economic, & Administrative Survey, Vol. 1. Arnold H. Jones. LC 64-20762. 779p. reprint ed. pap. 200.00 (*0-608-13518-6*, 201623000001) Bks Demand.

Later Roman Empire, 284-602: A Social, Economic, & Administrative Survey, Vol. 2. A. H. Jones. LC 85-24077. (Orig.). 1986. reprint ed. pap. 27.50 (*0-8018-3354-X*) Johns Hopkins.

Later Roman Empire, 284-602: A Social, Economic, & Administrative Survey, Vol. 2. Arnold H. Jones. LC 64-20762. 771p. reprint ed. pap. 200.00 (*0-608-13519-4*, 201623000002) Bks Demand.

Later Short Stories. Anthony Trollope. Ed. by John Sutherland. (World's Classics Ser.). 628p. 1995. pap. 10.95 (*0-19-282988-2*) OUP.

Later Short Stories: 1888-1903. Anton Chekhov. Ed. by Shelby Foote. Tr. by Constance Garnett. LC 98-20048. 628p. 1999. 21.95 (*0-679-60316-6*) Modern Lib NY.

Later Stages: Essays in Ontario Theatre from the First World War to the 1970s. Ed. by Ann Saddlemyer & Richard Plant. (Ontario Historical Studies). (Illus.). 480p. 1996. text 60.00 (*0-8020-0671-X*) U of Toronto Pr.

Later Stages: Essays in Ontario Theatre from the First World War to the 1970s. Ed. by Ann Saddlemyer & Richard Plant. (Ontario Historical Studies). (Illus.). 480p. 1997. pap. text 24.95 (*0-8020-7624-6*) U of Toronto Pr.

Later Stuart Tracts. George A. Aitken. LC 64-16748. (Arber's an English Garner Ser.). 1964. reprint ed. 65.00 (*0-8154-0003-9*) Cooper Sq.

Later Stuarts, 1660-1714. 2nd ed. George N. Clark. (Oxford History of England Ser.: Vol. 10). (Illus.). 504p. 1956. text 75.00 (*0-19-821702-1*) OUP.

Later Style of Henry James. Seymour B. Chatman. LC 86-15043. (Language & Style Ser.). 135p. 1986. reprint ed. lib. bdg. 55.00 (*0-313-25218-1*, CHLA, Greenwood Pr) Greenwood.

Later Symphonies. Wolfgang Amadeus Mozart. 285p. 1974. pap. 12.95 (*0-486-23052-X*) Dover.

Later Tudors: England 1547-1603. Penry Williams. LC 97-39068. (New Oxford History of England Ser.). (Illus.). 628p. 1998. reprint ed. pap. 17.95 (*0-19-288044-6*) OUP.

Later Tudors England, 1547-1603. Penry Williams. (New Oxford History of England Ser.: No. 7). (Illus.). 628p. 1995. 45.00 (0-19-822820-1) OUP.

Later Victorian Cambridge. D. A. Winstanley. Ed. by Walter P. Metzger. LC 76-55196. (Academic Profession Ser.). 1977. reprint ed. lib. bdg. 31.95 (0-405-10025-6) Ayer.

Later with the Latex: AIDS. Armando B. Rico. 44p. (Orig.). (YA). 1992. pap. 2.95 (1-879219-06-9) Veracruz Pubs.

Later Work of Austin Osman Spare, 1917-1956. William Wallace. 68p. 1989. write for info. (0-904995-14-3, Pub. by Catalpa Pr Ltd) Penguin Books.

Later Works: Black Boy (American Hunger), the Outsider. Richard Wright. Ed. by Arnold Rampersad. 887p. 1991. 35.00 (0-940450-67-4, Pub. by Library of America) Penguin Putnam.

Later Works of John Dewey, 1885-1953 Vol. 17: Miscellaneous Writings. abr. ed. Ed. by Jo A. Boydston. LC 80-27285. (Later Works of John Dewey, 1925-1953). 606p. (C). 1991. pap. 16.95 (0-8093-1683-8) S Ill U Pr.

Later Works of John Dewey, 1925-1953, 17 vols. John Dewey. Ed. by Jo Ann Boydston. Incl. Vol. 2: 1925-1927: Essays, Reviews, Miscellany, & "The Public & Its Problems" Intro. by James Gouinlock. LC 80-27285. 576p. 1984. 52.00 (0-8093-1131-3); Vol. 3: 1927-1928: Essays, Reviews, Miscellany, & "Impressions of Soviet Russia" Intro. by David Sidorsky. LC 80-27285. 584p. 1984. 52.00 (0-8093-1132-1); 1925. Intro. by Sidney Hook. LC 80-27285. 462p. 1981. 52.00 (0-8093-0986-6); 1925. Intro. by Sidney Hook. LC 80-27285. 434p. 1988. pap. 14.95 (0-8093-1490-8); 1925-1927: Essays, Reviews, Miscellany, & "The Public & Its Problems" Intro. by James Gouinlock. LC 80-27285. 488p. 1988. pap. 16.95 (0-8093-1491-6); 1927-1928: Essays, Reviews, Miscellany, & "Impressions of Soviet Russia" Intro. by David Sidorsky. LC 80-27285. 482p. 1988. pap. 16.95 (0-8093-1492-4); 1929: "The Quest for Certainty" Intro. by Stephen Toulmin. LC 80-27285. 296p. 1984. 52.00 (0-8093-1162-3); 1929: "The Quest for Certainty" Intro. by Stephen Toulmin. LC 80-27285. 288p. 1988. pap. 14.95 (0-8093-1493-2); 1929-1930: Essays, "The Sources of a Science of Education," "Individualism," "Old & New," & "Construction of a Criticism" Intro. by Paul Kurtz. LC 80-27285. 558p. 1984. 52.00 (0-8093-1163-1); 1929-1930: Essays, "The Sources of a Science of Education," "Individualism," "Old & New," & "Construction of a Criticism" Intro. by Paul Kurtz. LC 80-27285. 480p. 1988. pap. 16.95 (0-8093-1494-0); 1931-1932: Essays, Reviews, & Miscellany. Intro. by Sidney Ratner. LC 80-27285. 640p. 1985. 52.00 (0-8093-1199-2); 1931-1932: Essays, Reviews, & Miscellany. Intro. by Sidney Ratner. LC 80-27285. 558p. 1989. pap. 16.95 (0-8093-1574-2); 1932: "Ethics" Ed. by Elizabeth Flower. LC 80-27285. 574p. 1985. 52.00 (0-8093-1200-X); 1932: "Ethics" Ed. by Elizabeth Flower. LC 80-27285. 548p. 1989. pap. 16.95 (0-8093-1575-0); 1933: Essays & "How We Think" rev. ed. Intro. by Richard McKay Rorty. LC 80-27285. 435p. 1986. 52.00 (0-8093-1246-8); 1933: Essays & "How We Think" rev. ed. Intro. by Richard McKay Rorty. LC 80-27285. 410p. 1989. pap. 16.95 (0-8093-1576-9); 1933-1934: Essays, Reviews, Miscellany, & "A Common Faith" Intro. by Milton R. Konvitz. LC 80-27285. 460p. 1987. 52.00 (0-8093-1266-2); 1925-1953: Art As Experience. Ed. by JoAnn Boydston & Harriet F. Simon. LC 80-27285. 434p. 1989. pap. 14.95 (0-8093-1578-5); 1935-1937: Essays & "Liberalism & Social Action" Intro. by John J. McDermott. LC 80-27285. 786p. 1987. 52.00 (0-8093-1267-0); 1938. Intro. by Nagel Ernest. LC 80-27285. 788p. 1986. 52.00 (0-8093-1268-9); 1938-1939: "Experience & Education," "Freedom & Culture," "Theory of Valuation," & Essays. Steven M. Cahn. LC 80-27285. 612p. 1988. 52.00 (0-8093-1425-8); 1939-1941. R. W. Sleeper. LC 80-27285. 612p. 1988. 52.00 (0-8093-1426-6); 1942-1948. LC 80-27285. 724p. 1989. 52.00 (0-8093-1535-1); 1949-1952. Intro. by T. Z. Lavine. LC 80-27285. 779p. 1990. 52.00 (0-8093-1537-8); 1985-1953. Intro. by Sydney Hook. LC 80-27285. 820p. 1991. 52.00 (0-8093-1661-7); LC 80-27285. 1988. pap. write for info. (0-318-68540-X) S Ill U Pr.

Later Works of John Dewey, 1925-1953: Essays, Reviews, Miscellany, & a Common Faith, 1933-1934, Vol. 9. Ed. by Jo A. Boydston. 472p. (C). 1989. pap. text 16.95 (0-8093-1577-7) S Ill U Pr.

Later Works of John Dewey, 1935-1937 Vol. 11: Essays & "Liberalism & Social Action" Ed. by Jo A. Boydston. LC 80-27285. (Later Works of John Dewey, 1925-1953). 634p. (C). 1991. pap. 16.95 (0-8093-1677-X) S Ill U Pr.

Later Works of John Dewey, 1938 Vol. 12: Logic: The Theory of Inquiry. abr. ed. Ed. by Jo A. Boydston. LC 80-27285. (Later Works of John Dewey, 1925-1953). 550p. (C). 1991. pap. 16.95 (0-8093-1678-1) S Ill U Pr.

Later Works of John Dewey, 1938-1939 Vol. 13: "Experience & Education," "Freedom & Culture," "Theory of Valuation," & Essays. abr. ed. Ed. by Jo A. Boydston. LC 80-27285. (Later Works of John Dewey, 1925-1953). 430p. (C). 1991. pap. 16.95 (0-8093-1679-X) S Ill U Pr.

Later Works of John Dewey, 1939-1941 Vol. 14: Essays, Reviews, & Miscellany. abr. ed. Ed. by Jo A. Boydston. LC 80-27285. (Later Works of John Dewey, 1925-1953). 532p. (C). 1991. pap. 16.95 (0-8093-1680-3) S Ill U Pr.

Later Works of John Dewey, 1942-1948 Vol. 15: Essays, Reviews, & Miscellany. abr. ed. Ed. by Jo A. Boydston. LC 80-27285. (Later Works of John Dewey, 1925-1953). 538p. (C). 1991. pap. 16.95 (0-8093-1681-1) S Ill U Pr.

Later Works of John Dewey, 1949-1952 Vol. 16: Essays, Typescripts, & "Knowing & the Known" abr. ed. Ed. by Jo A. Boydston. LC 80-27285. (Later Works of John Dewey, 1925-1953). 522p. (C). 1991. pap. text 16.95 (0-8093-1682-X) S Ill U Pr.

***Later Writings by Pilgram Marpeck & His Circle.** Pilgram Marbeck et al. 1999. pap. text 20.00 (0-9683462-6-X) Pandora Pr.

Later Years: Public Relations Insights, 1956-1986. Edward L. Bernays. Ed. by Paul Swift. (C). 1986. 9.95 (0-9617642-0-1) H Penn Hudson.

Later Years of Childbearing. Larry L. Bumpass & Charles F. Westoff. LC 74-120751. 184p. reprint ed. pap. 57.10 (0-7837-1406-8, 204176000023) Bks Demand.

Later Years of the Saturday Club, 1870-1920. Ed. by Mark A. Howe. LC 68-29217. (Essay Index Reprint Ser.). 1977. reprint ed. 28.95 (0-8369-0548-2) Ayer.

Later Years of Thomas Hardy, 1892-1928. Florence E. Hardy. (BCL1-PR English Literature Ser.). 286p. 1992. reprint ed. lib. bdg. 79.00 (0-7812-7553-9) Rprt Serv.

Later Years, 1674-1702 see William of Orange: Personal Portrait

Later 19th Century Novelists: Critical Heritage, 5 vols., Set. Incl. George Gissing. Ed. by Pierre Coustillas. 582p. (C). 1996. 160.00 (0-415-13468-4); George Meredith. Ed. by Ioan Williams. 549p. (C). 1996. 160.00 (0-415-13465-X); Robert Louis Stevenson. Ed. by Paul Maixner. 560p. (C). 1996. 160.00 (0-415-13467-6); Thomas Hardy. Ed. by R. G. Cox. 524p. (C). 1996. 160.00 (0-415-13466-8); Wilkie Collins. Ed. by Norman Page. 304p. (C). 1996. 125.00 (0-415-13464-1); 2519p. (C). 1996. Set text, boxed set 575.00 (0-415-13463-3) Routledge.

Lateral Asymmetries & Hemispheric Specialization: Theoretical Models & Research. Anke Bouma. xiii, 164p. 1990. 38.00 (90-265-1079-9) Swets.

Lateral Electromagnetic Waves: Theory & Applications to Communications, Geophysical Exploration, & Remote Sensing. Tai T. Wu et al. Ed. by M. Owens. (Illus.). 752p. 1992. 89.95 (0-387-97679-5) Spr-Verlag.

***Lateral Force Design: For the ARE.** Frank Talania. (Illus.). 120p. 2000. pap. 31.95 (0-929176-58-8) Burdick & Landreth Co.

Lateral Logic Mazes for the Serious Puzzler. Larry Evans. (Illus.). 64p. 1996. pap. 5.95 (0-8069-6116-3) Sterling.

Lateral Logic Puzzles. Erwin Brecher. LC 94-18776. (Illus.). 96p. 1994. pap. 4.95 (0-8069-0618-9) Sterling.

***Lateral Mindtrap Puzzles.** Detective Shadow. 2000. pap. 6.95 (0-8069-7135-5) Sterling.

Lateral Preferences & Human Behavior. C. Porac & S. Coren. (Illus.). 288p. 1981. 96.95 (0-387-90596-0) Spr-Verlag.

Lateral Thinking. Book Sales Staff. 1998. pap. text 7.99 (0-7858-0956-2) Bk Sales Inc.

Lateral Thinking. Edward De Bono. 1990. pap. 30.00 (0-14-013779-3) Intl Ctr Creat Think.

Lateral Thinking: Creativity Step by Step. Edward De Bono. LC 89-46085. 304p. 1990. pap. 15.00 (0-06-090325-2, CN325, Perennial) HarperTrade.

Lateral Thinking Puzzlers. Paul Sloane. LC 90-49158. (Illus.). 96p. 1992. pap. 5.95 (0-8069-8227-6) Sterling.

Lateral Thinking Puzzles, Vol. 3. Edward J. Harshman. LC 97-25082. (Illus.). 96p. 1997. 4.95 (0-8069-9938-1) Sterling.

***Lateral Venting of Deflagration-to- Detonation Transition in Hydrogen-Air-Steam Mixtures at Various Initial Temperatures.** G. Ciccarelli. 69p. 1998. pap. 6.00 (0-16-062973-X) USGPO.

Lateral View: Essays on Culture & Style in Contemporary Japan. Donald Richie. LC 91-47645. 248p. (Orig.). 1992. reprint ed. pap. 10.95 (0-9628137-4-5) Stone Bridge Pr.

Lateralisation of Language in the Child. Ed. by Y. Lebrun & O. L. Zangwill. (Neurolinguistics Ser.: Vol. 10). 175p. 1982. 37.25 (90-265-0337-7) Swets.

Laterally Loaded Deep Foundations: Analysis & Performance - STP 835. ASTM Committee D-18 on Soil & Rock. Ed. by J. A. Langer et al. LC 83-72942. 250p. 1984. text 34.00 (0-8031-0207-0, STP835) ASTM.

Laterculi Vocum Latinarum, Voces Latinas et a Fronte et a Tergo Ordinandas Curavit, 2 vols. in 1. Otto Gradenwitz. vi, 546p. 1966. reprint ed. write for info. (0-318-71137-0) G Olms Pubs.

"Laterculus Malalianus" & the School of Archbishop Theodore. Ed. by Jane Stevenson. (Cambridge Studies in Anglo-Saxon England: Ser. 14). 268p. (C). 1995. text 69.95 (0-521-37461-8) Cambridge U Pr.

Laterites - Some Aspects of Current Research: Proceedings of the Laterite Workshop, 1st International Geomorphological Conference, 1985. Ed. by M. J. McFarlane. (Annals of Geomorphology Ser.: Suppl. 64). (Illus.). 180p. 1987. pap. text 68.60 (3-443-21064-3, Pub. by Gebruder Borntraeger) Balogh.

Lateritic Bauxites. Gy Bardossy & G. J. Aleva. (Developments in Economic Geology Ser.: No. 27). 624p. 1990. 242.00 (0-444-98811-4) Elsevier.

Lateritisation Processes: Proceedings of the International Seminar, Trivandrum, India, 11-14 December 1979. 458p. (C). 1981. text 181.00 (90-6191-202-4, Pub. by A A Balkema) Ashgate Pub Co.

Laterna Magica. Ingmar Bergman. (FRE.). 380p. 1991. pap. 14.95 (0-7859-2158-3, 2070383385) Fr & Eur.

Laterna Magica. William Heinesen. Tr. by Tiina Nunnally from DAN. LC 86-31993. (European Short Stories Ser.: No. 1). 160p. (Orig.). 1987. 15.95 (0-940242-22-2); pap. 7.95 (0-940242-23-0) Fjord Pr.

Laterna Magika. Ven Begamudre. LC 98-119639. 208p. 1997. pap. 16.95 (0-88982-166-6, Pub. by Oolichan Bks) Genl Dist Srvs.

La/Terre see Earth

Latest Achievements of Diabetes Research. F. Belfiore & Agata M. Rabuazzo. (Frontiers in Diabetes Ser.; Vol. 7). x, 298p. 1986. 216.75 (3-8055-4261-5) S Karger.

Latest Advances in Environmental Conservation - A Publication of Forum for Environmental Protection. Ed. by R. Mathur. 1998. pap. 150.00 (81-7233-175-4, Pub. by Scientifc Pubs) St Mut.

Latest Advances in Power Generating Facilities Design, Operation & Maintenance & Environmental Improvements. Ed. by M. S. Reddy & D. F. Daniel. (PWR Ser.: Vol. 22). 176p. 1993. 37.50 (0-7918-0997-8, H00829) ASME.

Latest American Revolution. Wilcox. 88p. 1995. pap. text 9.95 (0-312-13299-9) St Martin.

Latest & Best of the Educational Software Selector (TESS), 1993 Edition. (Orig.). 1993. pap. 19.95 (0-916087-16-6) EPIE Inst.

Latest & Greatest Read-Alouds. Sharron L. McElmeel. (Illus.). xv, 210p. 1994. pap. text 18.50 (1-56308-140-7) Libs Unl.

***Latest Contributions to Cross-Cultural Psychology: Selected Papers from the Thirteenth International Congress of the International Association for Cross-Cultural Psychology.** Ed. by Jean-Claude Lasry et al. LC 99-13929. (Conference Proceedings of the International Association for Cross-Cultural Psychology Ser.). 376p. 1999. 84.00 (90-265-1547-2) Swets.

Latest Crisis in Bosnia-Herzegovina: Hearing Before the Commission on Security & Cooperation in Europe, 104th Congress, 1st Session, June 8, 1995. USGPO Staff. LC 96-152241. iii, 12 p. 1996. pap. write for info. (0-16-052556-X) USGPO.

Latest Developments in & Application of Industrial Gear Drives. C. B. Connell. (Technical Papers: Vol. P159.01). (Illus.). 30p. 1952. pap. text 30.00 (1-55589-203-5) AGMA.

Latest Developments in Livestock Housing: Proceedings of the Second Technical Section of the CIGR. American Society of Agricultural Engineers. LC 87-71042. 417p. 1987. pap. 51.00 (0-916150-87-9, P0687) Am Soc Ag Eng.

Latest Epistle of Jim. Roy Shepard. LC 96-35042. 192p. (Orig.). 1996. pap. 14.00 (0-922811-26-1) Mid-List.

***Latest Findings on National Air Quality: 1997 Status & Trends.** 24p. 1999. pap. 2.50 (0-16-063394-X) USGPO.

Latest Findings on the Aetiology & Therapy of Depression. Ed. by P. Kielholz & W. Poeldinger. (Journal: Psychopathology: Vol. 19, Suppl. 2, 1986). (Illus.). vi, 270p. 1987. pap. 83.50 (3-8055-4542-8) S Karger.

Latest Herman. Jim Unger. LC 81-65137. (Illus.). 96p. 1981. pap. 6.95 (0-8362-1168-5) Andrews & McMeel.

Latest Illusion. Donald E. Axinn. LC 94-43028. 96p. 1995. pap. 12.45 (1-55970-298-2, Pub. by Arcade Pub Inc) Time Warner.

Latest Intelligence: An International Directory of Codes Used by Government, Law Enforcement, Military & Surveillance Agencies. James E. Tunnell & Helen L. Sanders. 450p. 1990. pap. 16.95 (0-8306-3531-9) McGraw-Hill Prof.

Latest Literary Essays & Addresses. James Russell Lowell. (Essay Index Reprint Ser.). 1977. reprint ed. 19.95 (0-518-10184-3) Ayer.

Latest Literary Essays & Addresses. James Russell Lowell. (Notable American Authors Ser.). 1999. reprint ed. lib. bdg. 125.00 (0-7812-3898-6) Rprt Serv.

Latest on the Best: Essays on Evolution & Optimality. Ed. by John Dupre. LC 86-27226. 359p. 1987. 47.50 (0-262-04090-5) MIT Pr.

Latest Rage the Big Drum: Dada & Surrealist Performance. Annabelle H. Melzer. LC 80-22656. (Studies in the Fine Arts: The Avant-Garde: No. 7). (Illus.). 290p. reprint ed. pap. 89.90 (0-8357-1639-2, 207023100065) Bks Demand.

Latest Sealings from the Palace & Houses at Knossos. Mervyn R. Popham & Margaret Gill. (BSA Studies: Vol. 1). (Illus.). 123p. (Orig.). 1995. pap. 38.00 (0-904887-24-3) Brit Sch Athens.

Latest Studies on Indian Reservations. J. B. Harrington. (Indian Rights Association Ser.). 233p. (C). 1887. pap. text 24.38 (1-55567-847-5) Coyote Press.

Latest Studies on VDTs, 1993. 3rd ed. Robin Y. Woo. 176p. (C). 1993. pap. 10.00 (1-879887-00-2) Ctr Office Tech.

Latest Will. Lenore Marshall. LC 68-56267. (C). 1969. pap. 2.95 (0-393-04178-6) Norton.

Latest Word on the Last Days. C. S. Lovett. (Illus.). (Orig.). 1980. pap. 8.95 (0-938148-00-1) Prsnl Christianity.

Latest Wrinkle: And Other Signs of Aging. Virginia Cornell. (Illus.). 104p. 1996. pap. 9.95 (0-9627896-3-1) Manifest Pubns.

Latex: A Document Preparation System User's Guide & Reference Manual. 2nd ed. Leslie Lamport. (Illus.). 288p. (C). 1994. pap. text 36.95 (0-201-52983-1) Addison-Wesley.

***Latex Companion.** (C). 1998. write for info. (0-201-39748-X) Addison-Wesley.

LATEX Companion. Michel Goossens et al. (Tools & Techniques for Computer Typesetting Ser.). (Illus.). 560p. (C). 1994. pap. text 37.95 (0-201-54199-8) Addison-Wesley.

LATEX Companion. 2nd ed. Michel Goossens. (C). 1999. pap. text Price not set. (0-201-36299-6) Addison-Wesley.

***Latex Design Companion.** Frank Mittelbach. 400p. (C). 1999. pap. text. write for info. (0-201-36300-3) Addison-Wesley.

Latex Eineeinfuhrung, Vol. 1. 3rd ed. Helmut Kopka. (GER.). (C). 1991. text. write for info. (0-201-55969-2) Addison-Wesley.

Latex Erweiterungsmogilhkeiten. 2nd ed. Helmut Kopka. (GER.). (C). 1991. text. write for info. (0-201-55977-3) Addison-Wesley.

LATEX for Everyone: A Reference Guide & Tutorial for Typesetting Documents Using a Computer. Jane Hahn. LC 93-16767. (Illus.). 368p. (C). 1993. pap. 44.00 (0-13-605908-2) P-H.

LATEX for Everyone: A Reference Guide & Tutorial for Typesetting Documents Using a Computer. 2nd rev. ed. Jane Hahn. (Illus.). 346p. (C). 1991. pap. 19.95 (0-9631044-0-3) Person Tex.

Latex for Linux. Bernice S. Lipkin. LC 98-51994. 530p. 1999. pap. 44.95 (0-387-98708-8) Spr-Verlag.

LATEX Line by Line: Tips & Techniques for Document Processing. 2nd ed. Antoni Diller. LC 98-47326. 528p. 1999. pap. 49.99 (0-471-97918-X) Wiley.

LATEX Macro's Yachimata. S. Fujita. (C). 1995. pap. text. write for info. (0-201-53729-X) Addison-Wesley.

LATEX Notes: Practical Tips for Preparing Technical Documents, Version 1.4. Compiled by Kenneth Shultis. 192p. (C). 1994. pap. 30.80 (0-13-120973-6) P-H.

Latex-Vademecum. 1996. 26.00 (3-540-60522-3) Spr-Verlag.

***LaTeX Web Companion.** Michel Goossens. LC 98-48199. 560p. (C). 1999. pap. text 36.95 (0-201-43311-7) Addison-Wesley.

LATEX 3 Style Guide & Reference Manual. Frank Mittelbach. (C). 1998. pap. text. write for info. (0-201-60024-2) Addison-Wesley.

Latham, John: Art after Physics. Text by Ina Conzen-Meiars et al. (Illus.). 128p. 1991. pap. 70.00 (0-905836-75-8, Pub. by Museum Modern Art) St Mut.

Lathe Book. Ernie Conover. (Illus.). 208p. 1993. pap. 25.95 (1-56158-057-0, 70195) Taunton.

Lathe Cutting Explained. Leo Rizzo. LC 79-730988. 1979. student ed. 7.00 (0-8064-0243-1, 513) Bergwall.

Lathe Design-Construction & Operation. O. E. Perrigo. 1984. reprint ed. pap. 24.95 (0-917914-18-X) Lindsay Pubns.

Lathe Explained. Leo Rizzo. LC 72-737347. 1971. student ed. 7.00 (0-8064-0219-9, 501) Bergwall.

Lathe of Heaven. Ursula K. Le Guin. 176p. 1976. mass mkt. 5.50 (0-380-01320-7, Avon Bks) Morrow Avon.

Lathe of Heaven. Ursula K. Le Guin. 176p. 1997. pap. 12.50 (0-380-79185-4, Avon Bks) Morrow Avon.

Lathe of Heaven. Ursula K. Le Guin. LC 81-18093. 192p. 1982. reprint ed. 14.00 (0-8376-0464-8) Bentley Pubs.

Lathe-Turned Objects: An International Exhibition. Ed. by Albert B. Lecoff. 168p. 1988. pap. 29.95 (0-9624385-2-9) Wood Turn Ctr.

Lathe-Turned Objects: An International Exhibition. Albert B. Lecoff. Ed. by Carol Field & Eileen J. Silver. LC 88-20688. (Illus.). 168p. 1988. text 40.00 (0-9624385-1-0); boxed set 40.00 (0-9624385-0-2) Wood Turn Ctr.

Lathrop: Ancestors & Descendants of Francis Lathrop, 1545-1992. Lois R. White. (Illus.). 82p. 1993. reprint ed. pap. 16.50 (0-8328-2990-0); reprint ed. lib. bdg. 26.50 (0-8328-2991-9) Higginson Bk Co.

Latifundium: Moral Economy & Material Life in a European Periphery. Marta Petrusewicz. Tr. by Judith C. Green from ITA. LC 95-52357. 312p. (C). 1996. text 54.50 (0-472-10342-3, 10342) U of Mich Pr.

Latigo, 1979-1980, Bk. 1. Stan Lynde. LC 91-77330. (Illus.). 88p. (Orig.). 1991. pap. 9.95 (0-9626999-3-4, BK20) Cttnwd Pub.

Latigo, 1980-1981, Bk. 2. Stan Lynde. LC 91-77330. (Illus.). 72p. (Orig.). 1992. pap. 9.95 (0-9626999-7-7, BK21) Cttnwd Pub.

Latigo, 1981-1983, Bk. 3. Stan Lynde. LC 94-72092. (Illus.). 168p. (Orig.). 1994. pap. 18.95 (0-9626999-9-3, BK22) Cttnwd Pub.

Latimer: Apostle to the English. Clara Stuart. 320p. 1986. 18.95 (0-310-41370-2, 11592) Zondervan.

Latimer: Apostle to the English. Clara H. Stuart. 348p. 1997. reprint ed. pap. 14.95 (0-916035-76-X) Evangel Indiana.

Latimers. Henry C. McCook. 1993. reprint ed. lib. bdg. 89.00 (0-7812-5486-8) Rprt Serv.

Latin. (College Board SAT II Subject Test Ser.). 1997. pap. 23.95 (0-8373-6309-8, SATII-9) Nat Learn.

Latin. Jack Rudman. (National Teacher Examination Ser.: NT-18). 1994. pap. 23.95 (0-8373-8408-7) Nat Learn.

Latin. Jack Rudman. (Advanced Placement Test (AP) Ser.: Vol. AP-13). 1997. pap. 23.95 (0-8373-6213-X) Nat Learn.

Latin: A Course for Schools & Colleges. rev. ed. John A. Anderson & Frank J. Groten, Jr. LC 71-102077. (Illus.). 357p. (YA). (gr. 7-12). 1988. reprint ed. 20.00 (0-942573-00-5) Hill School.

Latin: A Structural Approach. Sweet. 522p. 1957. text 29.95 (0-472-08803-3, 08803) U of Mich Pr.

Latin: An Intensive Course. Rita M. Fleischer & Flloyd L. Moreland. LC 75-36500. 1975. pap. 27.50 (0-520-03183-0, Pub. by U CA Pr) Cal Prin Full Svc.

Latin: Better Read Than Dead. G. Sharpley. LC 96-124809. 240p. 1994. pap. 20.95 (1-85399-410-3, Pub. by Brist Class Pr) Focus Pub-R Pullins.

Latin: Language. rev. ed. Educational Services Corporation Staff. (LAT.). 1995. pap. 16.95 incl. audio (0-910542-89-9) Educ Svcs DC.

Latin, a Historical & Linguistic Handbook. Mason Hammond. LC 75-33359. 304p. reprint ed. pap. 94.30 (0-7837-2267-2, 205735500004) Bks Demand.

Latin Adjectives with Partitive Meaning in Republican Literature. Alden G. Vaughan. (LD Ser.: No. 36). 1942. pap. 25.00 (0-527-00782-X) Periodicals Srv.

Latin Affair. Sophie Weston. (Romance Ser.: No. 450). 1999. mass mkt. 3.50 (0-373-17450-0, 1-17450-7) Harlequin Bks.

Latin-Albanian Dictionary (Fjalor Latinisht-Shqip) Henrik Lacaj & Filip Fishta. (ALB & LAT.). 556p. 1980. 24.95 (0-8288-1089-3, F89900) Fr & Eur.

Latin Alive & Well: An Introductory Text. 6th ed. P. L. Chambers. (LAT., Illus.). 292p. (C). 1997. reprint ed. 28.95 (0-9628450-0-0) P L Chambers.

An Asterisk (*) at the beginning of an entry indicates that the title is appearing for the first time.

Latin Alive & Well: Teacher Key. 6th ed. 96p. (C). 1997. pap., teacher ed. 9.95 (*0-9628450-1-9*) P L Chambers.

Latin America. (C). 2000. text 32.00 (*0-205-29730-7*, Longwood Div) Allyn.

Latin America. Ed. by Eduardo Archetti et al. (Sociology of "Developing Societies" Ser.). 320p. (Orig.). 1987. 26.00 (*0-85345-685-2*, Pub. by Monthly Rev) NYU Pr.

***Latin America.** Ana Maria Machado. (Exploration Into... Ser.). (Illus.). (J). 2000. 17.95 (*0-7910-6024-1*) Chelsea Hse.

Latin America. David Preston. (C). 1996. pap. 30.53 (*0-582-30148-3*) Addison-Wesley.

Latin America. Swanson. 1998. pap. 24.95 (*0-7190-5361-7*) St Martin.

Latin America. Ed. by Juan J. Linz & Alfred Stepan. LC 78-594. (Breakdown of Democratic Regimes Ser.). (Illus.). 226p. 1978. reprint ed. pap. 70.10 (*0-608-07334-2*, 206756200009) Bks Demand.

Latin America. rev. ed. Frank Hill. (TravelCard Pac Ser.). 1992. 4.00 (*0-88699-019-X*) Travel Sci.

Latin America. 9th ed. Goodwin. 240p. 2000. pap. 18.75 (*0-07-236586-2*) McGraw.

Latin America see World Architecture 1900-2000: A Critical Mosaic

Latin America: A Concise Interpretive History. 6th ed. E. Bradford Burns. LC 92-38300. 372p. (C). 1993. pap. text 47.00 (*0-13-501321-6*) P-H.

***Latin America: A Directory & Sourcebook.** 2nd ed. 350p. 1998. 590.00 (*0-86338-805-1*, GML12498-112647, Pub. by Euromonitor PLC) Gale.

Latin America: A Guide to Illustrations. A. Curtis Wilgus. LC 81-9070. 278p. 1981. 31.50 (*0-8108-1459-5*) Scarecrow.

Latin America: A Political Dictionary. Ed. by Ernest E. Rossi & Jack C. Plano. LC 92-28946. (Clio Dictionaries in Political Science Ser.). 1992. lib. bdg. 60.00 (*0-87436-608-9*) ABC-CLIO.

Latin America: A Political Dictionary. Ed. by Ernest E. Rossi & Jack C. Plano. LC 92-28946. (Clio Dictionaries in Political Science Ser.). 1992. pap. text 29.95 (*0-87436-698-4*) ABC-CLIO.

Latin America: Case Studies. Ed. by Richard G. Boehm & Sent Visser. LC 84-80211. (National Council for Geographic Education, Pacesetter Ser.). (Illus.). 310p. 1984. reprint ed. pap. 96.10 (*0-7837-9722-2*, 206045300005) Bks Demand.

Latin America: Conflict & Creation: A Historical Reader. Ed. by E. Bradford Burns. LC 92-13345. 336p. (C). 1992. pap. text 39.20 (*0-13-526260-7*) P-H.

Latin America: Conflict & Development since 1945. John Ward. LC 97-241. (Making of the Contemporary World Ser.). (Illus.). 144p. (C). 1997. pap. 14.99 (*0-415-14725-5*) Routledge.

Latin America: Dependency or Interdependence? M. Novak & Jackson. 200p. 1985. 34.00 (*0-8447-2258-8*) Am Enterprise.

Latin America: Diplomacy & Reality. Adolf A. Berle. LC 81-3818. (Council on Foreign Relations Ser.). 144p. 1981. reprint ed. lib. bdg. 55.00 (*0-313-22970-8*, BELAM, Greenwood Pr) Greenwood.

Latin America: Economic & Social Transition to the Twenty-First Century. fac. ed. Enrique V. Iglesias. LC HC0125.I3. (Per Jacobsson Lecture Ser.: 1993). (Illus.). 64p. 1993. reprint ed. pap. 30.00 (*0-7837-7905-4*, 204766100008) Bks Demand.

Latin America: Economic & Social Transition to the Twenty-First Century. Enrique V. Iglesias. LC HC0125.I3. (Per Jacobsson Lecture Ser.: Vol. 1993). (Illus.). 66p. reprint ed. pap. 30.00 (*0-608-08754-8*, 206939300004) Bks Demand.

Latin America: Economic Development & Regional Differentiation. Arthur S. Morris. 256p. (C). 1981. text 56.00 (*0-389-20194-4*, N6976) B&N Imports.

Latin America: Economy & Society since 1930. Ed. by Leslie Bethell. 532p. (C). 1998. text 59.95 (*0-521-59393-X*); pap. text 19.95 (*0-521-59571-1*) Cambridge U Pr.

Latin America: Economy & Society, 1870-1930: A Selection of Chapters from Volume V of The Cambridge History of Latin America. Ed. by Leslie Bethell. 432p. (C). 1989. text 20.95 (*0-521-36376-4*); pap. text 20.95 (*0-521-36898-7*) Cambridge U Pr.

Latin America: From Colonization to Globalization. Noam Chomsky. 1999. pap. 12.95 (*1-876175-13-3*) Ocean Pr NJ.

Latin America: Geographical Perspectives. 2nd ed. Ed. by Harold Blakemore & Clifford Smith. LC 82-20877. 600p. (C). 1983. pap. 25.99 (*0-416-32830-X*, NO.3814) Routledge.

***Latin America: History & Culture, 4 vols.** Barbara A. Tenenbaum. LC 99-23057. 1000p. 1999. 350.00 (*0-684-80576-6*) Scribner.

Latin America: History, Politics & U. S. Policy. 2nd rev. ed. James D. Cockcroft. LC 94-40030. Orig. Title: Neighbors in Turmoil. 1996. pap. text 45.95 (*0-8304-1398-7*) Thomson Learn.

Latin America: International Monetary System & External Financing. 405p. 12.00 (*92-1-121138-7*) UN.

Latin America: Its Cities & Ideas. Jose L. Romero. LC 98-53038. 1999. write for info. (*0-8270-3539-X*) OAS.

Latin America: Its Music & Its People. Lifchitz. 2000. 28.00 (*0-02-864747-5*) S&S Trade.

Latin America: Its Place in World Life. rev. ed. Samuel G. Inman. LC 72-5674. (Essay Index Reprint Ser.). 1977. reprint ed. 30.95 (*0-8369-2993-4*) Ayer.

Latin America: Its Rise & Progress. F. Garcia-Calderon. Tr. by B. Miall. 1977. lib. bdg. 59.95 (*0-8490-2131-6*) Gordon Pr.

Latin America: Perspectives on a Region. 2nd expanded rev. ed. Ed. by Jack W. Hopkins. LC 98-6494. (Illus.). 400p. (C). 1998. pap. text 25.95 (*0-8419-1363-3*) Holmes & Meier.

Latin America: Perspectives on a Region. 2nd expanded rev. ed. Ed. by Jack W. Hopkins. (Illus.). 400p. (C). 1999. 54.95 (*0-8419-1362-5*) Holmes & Meier.

Latin America: Politics & Society since 1930. Ed. by Leslie Bethell. LC 97-11735. 500p. (C). 1998. pap. 21.95 (*0-521-59582-7*); text 59.95 (*0-521-59390-5*) Cambridge U Pr.

Latin America: The Crisis of Debt & Growth. Thomas O. Enders & Richard P. Mattione. LC 83-73219. (Studies in International Economics). 66p. 1984. pap. 8.95 (*0-8157-2387-3*) Brookings.

Latin America: The Emerging Information Power: Papers Presented at the State-of-the-Art Institute, November 8-9, 1993, Washington, DC. Special Libraries Association Staff. LC 94-7599. 177p. 1993. reprint ed. pap. 54.90 (*0-608-00800-1*, 205934800011) Bks Demand.

Latin America: The Peoples & Their History. William H. Beezley & Colin M. MacLachlan. LC 98-88398. 336p. (C). 1999. pap. text 41.50 (*0-15-501563-X*) Acad Pr.

Latin America: The Transition of Democracy. Ronaldo Munck. LC 89-36323. 224p. (C). 1997. pap. 19.95 (*0-86232-819-5*, Pub. by St Martin) St Martin.

Latin America: Tradition & Change. Dorothy Hoobler & Thomas Hoobler. (Illus.). 240p. 1991. pap. text 18.32 (*0-8013-0565-9*) Longman.

Latin America: Underdevelopment or Revolution: Essays on the Development of Underdevelopment & the Immediate Enemy. Andre G. Frank. LC 71-81794. 431p. reprint ed. pap. 133.70 (*0-8357-6184-3*, 203434600089) Bks Demand.

Latin America: What Price the Past? Alan Knight. 34p. 1994. pap. text 8.95 (*0-19-952267-7*) OUP.

Latin America: World in Revolution. Carleton Beals. LC 74-9631. (Illus.). 352p. 1974. reprint ed. lib. bdg. 38.50 (*0-8371-7598-4*, BELAW, Greenwood Pr) Greenwood.

Latin America - Mercosur. Peter Coffey. LC 98-15004. (International Handbooks on Economic Integration). 263p. 1998. 150.00 (*0-7923-8152-1*); pap. 59.95 (*0-7923-8153-X*) Kluwer Academic.

Latin America Aflame see Latinoamerica en Llamas

Latin America after Mexico: Quickening the Pace. Shahid Javed Burki & Sebastian Edwards. LC 96-22783. (World Bank Latin American & Caribbean Studies). 40p. 1996. pap. 22.00 (*0-8213-3629-0*, 13629) World Bank.

Latin America after the Cold War. Mark Falcoff. (Essay Ser.: No. 1). 19p. (Orig.). (C). 1990. pap. text 3.00 (*1-878802-00-3*) J M Ashbrook Ctr Pub Affairs.

Latin America after the Cold War: Implications for U. S. Policy. Douglas Payne et al. (Latin American Affairs (Study Groups) Ser.). (Illus.). 96p. (C). 1991. pap. 9.95 (*1-879128-01-2*) Americas Soc.

Latin America & Caribbean Contemporary Record, 1981-1982, Vol. I. Ed. by Jack W. Hopkins. 892p. 1983. 380.00 (*0-8419-0754-4*) Holmes & Meier.

Latin America & Caribbean Contemporary Record, 1982-1983, Vol. II. Ed. by Jack W. Hopkins. (Illus.). 957p. 1984. 380.00 (*0-8419-0961-X*) Holmes & Meier.

Latin America & Caribbean Contemporary Record, 1983-1984, Vol. III. Ed. by Jack W. Hopkins. (Illus.). 1000p. 1985. 380.00 (*0-8419-1015-4*) Holmes & Meier.

Latin America & Caribbean Contemporary Record, 1984-1985, Vol. IV. Ed. by Jack W. Hopkins. (Latin America & Caribbean Contemporary Record Ser.). (Illus.). 1088p. (C). 1987. 380.00 (*0-8419-1041-3*) Holmes & Meier.

Latin America & Caribbean Contemporary Record, 1985-1986, Vol. V. Ed. by Abraham F. Lowenthal. (Latin America & Caribbean Contemporary Record Ser.). (Illus.). 1000p. (C). 1988. 380.00 (*0-8419-1123-1*) Holmes & Meier.

Latin America & Caribbean Contemporary Record, 1986-1987, Vol. VI. Ed. by Abraham F. Lowenthal. (Latin American & Caribbean Contemporary Record Ser.). 1000p. 1989. 380.00 (*0-8419-1170-3*) Holmes & Meier.

Latin America & Caribbean Contemporary Record, 1987-1988, VII. Ed. by James M. Malloy & Eduardo A. Gamarra. 1000p. 1990. 380.00 (*0-8419-1237-8*) Holmes & Meier.

Latin America & Caribbean Contemporary Record, 1988-1989, Vol. VIII. Ed. by James M. Malloy & Eduardo A. Gamarra. x, 1100p. 1996. 390.00 (*0-8419-1290-4*) Holmes & Meier.

Latin America & Latin American Periodicals, 2 vols., Set. Harvard University Library Staff. Incl. Vol. 1. Classification Schedule, Classified Listing by Call Number. LC 67-1722. 675p. 1966. Vol. 2. Alphabetical Listing by Author or Title, Chronological Listing. LC 67-1722. 817p. 1966. text LC 67-1722. (Widener Library Shelflist: No. 5-6). 1990. 70.00 (*0-674-51247-2*) HUP.

Latin America & Policy Studies. Ed. by Paul Rich. (Policy Studies Review: Vol. 15:2/3). 274p. 1998. pap. write for info. (*0-944285-51-1*) Pol Studies.

Latin America & the Caribbean: A Critical Guide to Research Sources, 2. Ed. by Paula H. Covington et al. LC 91-34622. (Bibliographies & Indexes in Latin American & Caribbean Studies: No. 2). 960p. 1992. lib. bdg. 145.00 (*0-313-26403-1*, CVL/, Greenwood Pr) Greenwood.

Latin America & the Caribbean: A Systematic & Regional Survey. 3rd ed. Brian W. Blouet & Olwyn M. Blouet. LC 96-9925. 512p. 1996. pap. 81.95 (*0-471-13570-4*) Wiley.

Latin America & the Caribbean: An Update & Summary of the Summit of the Americas : Hearing Before the Subcommittee on the Western Hemisphere of the Committee on International Relations, House of Representatives, One Hundred Fifth Congress, Second Session, May 6, 1998. LC 98-192405. iii, 59 p. 1998. write for info. (*0-16-057159-6*) USGPO.

Latin America & the Caribbean: Lands & Peoples. David K. Clawson. LC 96-85795. 432p. (C). 1996. text. write for info. (*0-697-12481-9*, WCB McGr Hill) McGrw-H Hghr Educ.

***Latin America & the Caribbean: Lands & Peoples** 2nd ed. David L. Clawson. LC 99-23060. 2000. write for info. (*0-697-38492-6*) McGrw-H Hghr Educ.

Latin America & the Caribbean: Options to Reduces the Debt Burden. (Libros de la CEPAL: No. 26). 110p. pap. 15.00 (*92-1-121156-5*, 90.II.G.7) UN.

Latin America & the Caribbean: Prospects for Democracy. William F. Gutteridge. LC 96-46504. 352p. 1997. text 78.95 (*1-85521-910-7*, Pub. by Dartmth Pub) Ashgate Pub Co.

Latin America & the Caribbean: The Economic Experience of the Last 15 Years. Economic Commission for Latin America & the Caribb. (Libros de la CEPAL: No. 43). 136p. pap. 17.50 (*92-1-121208-1*, HC130) UN.

Latin America & the Caribbean from a Global Perspective: A Resource Guide for Teachers. Pedro R. Bermudez & Barbara C. Cruz. 174p. (C). 1991. teacher ed., ring bd. 21.00 (*1-879862-00-X*) FL Intl U Latin.

Latin America & the Caribbean in the International System. 4th ed. G. Pope Atkins. LC 98-42262. 472p. 1998. pap. text 35.00 (*0-8133-3383-0*, Pub. by Westview) HarpC.

Latin America & the Caribbean in the International System. 4th ed. G. Pope Atkins. LC 98-42262. 472p. 1998. text 85.00 (*0-8133-3382-2*, Pub. by Westview) HarpC.

***Latin America & the Global Economy: New Faces of Protection.** Ronald D. Fischer. LC 00-31127. 2000. write for info. (*0-312-23527-5*) St Martin.

Latin America & the New International Economic Order. Ed. by Jorge A. Lozoya & Jaime Estevez. LC 79-27384. (Policy Studies on the New International Economic Order). 112p. 1980. 44.00 (*0-08-025118-8*, Pergamon Pr) Elsevier.

Latin America & the Second World War, 1939-1942, Vol. 1. Robert A. Humphreys. 232p. (C). 1981. text 42.50 (*0-485-17710-2*, Pub. by Athlone Pr) Humanities.

Latin America & the Second World War, 1942-1945, Vol. 2. Robert A. Humphreys. 296p. (C). 1981. text 42.50 (*0-485-17711-0*, Pub. by Athlone Pr) Humanities.

***Latin America & the United States: A Documentary History.** Ed. by Robert H. Holden & Eric Zolov. LC 99-31523. (Illus.). 384p. (C). 2000. text 49.95 (*0-19-512993-8*); pap. text 24.95 (*0-19-512994-6*) OUP.

Latin America & the World Economy: Dependency & Beyond. Richard J. Salvucci. 185p. (C). 1996. pap. text 18.76 (*0-669-35174-1*) HM Trade Div.

Latin America & the World Economy since 1800. John H. Coatsworth et al. LC 98-40390. 1998. 49.95 (*0-674-51280-4*); pap. 24.95 (*0-674-51281-2*) HUP.

Latin America & World War I. Percy F. Martin. 1976. lib. bdg. 59.95 (*0-8490-2130-8*) Gordon Pr.

Latin America As Its Literature: Selected Papers of the XIVth Congress of ICLA. Contrib. by E. Coutinho et al. (CNL/World Report Ser.: Vol. XIII). 220p. 1995. pap. 4.95 (*0-918680-55-7*) Griffon House.

Latin America at a Crossroads: The Challenge to the Trilateral Countries. George W. Landau et al. (Triangle Papers: Vol. 39). 1990. 6.00 (*0-930503-62-7*) Trilateral Comm.

Latin America at a Glance. (Industrial Development Review Ser.: No. L128). 1994. 195.00 (*0-85058-777-8*) Economist Intell.

Latin America at a Glance: 1996 Edition. 1996. 250.00 (*0-85058-900-2*, L900) Economist Intell.

Latin America Between the Eagle & the Bear. Salvador De Madariaga. LC 75-25494. 192p. 1976. reprint ed. lib. bdg. 55.00 (*0-8371-8423-1*, MALAM, Greenwood Pr) Greenwood.

Latin America Between the Second World War & the Cold War: Crisis & Containment, 1944-1948. Ed. by Leslie Bethell & Ian Roxborough. LC 92-15357. (Cambridge Latin American Studies: No. 73). 364p. (C). 1993. text 74.95 (*0-521-43032-1*) Cambridge U Pr.

Latin America Between the Second World War & the Cold War: Crisis & Containment, 1944-1948. Ed. by Leslie Bethell & Ian Roxborough. 364p. 1997. pap. text 18.95 (*0-521-57425-0*) Cambridge U Pr.

Latin America Bibliography. Juan M. Perez. LC 98-21207. (Scarecrow Area Bibliographies Ser.: No. 16). 544p. 1999. 79.50 (*0-8108-3496-0*) Scarecrow.

Latin America by Bike: A Complete Touring Guide. Walter Sienko. (Illus.). 240p. 1993. pap. 14.95 (*0-89886-365-1*) Mountaineers.

Latin America by Streetcar: A Pictorial Survey of Urban Rail Transport South of the U. S. A. Allen Morrison. LC 96-83892. (Illus.). 200p. 1996. 30.00 (*0-9622348-3-4*) Bonde Pr.

Latin America Communications Directory, 1997. 3rd ed. 320p. 1996. pap. 299.00 (*1-890403-02-4*) Counterpart.

Latin America Faces the Twenty-First Century: Reconstruction with a Social Justice Agenda. Suzanne Jonas & Edward J. McCaughan. (C). 1994. pap. 25.00 (*0-8133-8688-8*, Pub. by Westview) HarpC.

Latin America in Caricature. John J. Johnson. LC 79-19052. (Texas Pan American Ser.). (Illus.). 340p. 1993. pap. 16.95 (*0-292-74031-X*) U of Tex Pr.

***Latin America in Crisis.** Sherman. 240p. 2000. pap. 29.00 (*0-8133-3540-X*, Pub. by Westview) HarpC.

***Latin America in Crisis.** John W. Sherman. 240p. 2000. 87.00 (*0-8133-3539-6*) Westview.

Latin America in English-Language Reference Books: A Selected, Annotated Bibliography. Ann H. Graham & Richard D. Woods. LC 80-28880. 55p. reprint ed. pap. 30.00 (*0-8357-6427-3*, 203579500097) Bks Demand.

Latin America in Fiction: A Bibliography of Books in English for Adults. A. Curtis Wilgus. (Pan-American Union Bibliographic Ser.: No. 26). 35p. 1985. reprint ed. pap. text 4.25 (*0-913129-13-5*) La Tienda.

Latin America in Graphs, 1994-95: Demographic, Economic & Social Trends. Inter-American Development Bank Staff. 200p. 1995. pap. text 8.00 (*0-940602-79-2*) IADB.

Latin America in Its Architecture. Ed. by Roberto Segre & Fernando K. Kusnetzoff. Tr. by Edith Grossman from SPA. LC 79-27695. (Latin America & Its Culture Ser.: Vol. 2). Orig. Title: America Latina En Su Cultura. 216p. 1982. 49.50 (*0-8419-0532-0*) Holmes & Meier.

Latin America in Perspective. Oxford Analytica Staff. (C). 1991. pap. text. write for info. (*0-395-52583-7*) HM Soft Schl Col Div.

Latin America in the Era of the Cuban Revolution. Thomas C. Wright. LC 91-9647. 256p. 1991. 59.95 (*0-275-93583-3*, C3583, Praeger Pubs); pap. 22.95 (*0-275-94099-3*, B4099, Praeger Pubs) Greenwood.

***Latin America in the Era of the Cuban Revolution.** rev. ed. Thomas C. Wright. LC 99-59654. 256p. 2000. pap. 22.50 (*0-275-96706-9*, Praeger Pubs) Greenwood.

***Latin America in the Era of the Cuban Revolution.** 3rd rev. ed. Thomas C. Wright. LC 99-59654. 256p. 2000. 69.95 (*0-275-96705-0*, C6705, Praeger Pubs) Greenwood.

***Latin America in the New International System.** Ed. by Joseph S. Tulchin & Ralph H. Espach. 280p. 2000. 55.00 (*1-55587-940-3*); pap. 22.50 (*1-55587-917-9*) L Rienner.

Latin America in the Post-Import Substitution Era. Werner Baer & Larry A. Samuelson. 1977. pap. 25.00 (*0-08-021822-9*, Pergamon Pr) Elsevier.

Latin America in the Twentieth Century. Peter Calvert & Susan Calvert. LC 90-31061. 256p. 1991. text 49.95 (*0-312-04759-2*) St Martin.

Latin America in the Twentieth Century. 2nd ed. Peter Calvert & Susan Calvert. LC 92-44989. 240p. 1993. pap. 18.95 (*0-312-09103-6*) St Martin.

Latin America in the United Nations, Vol. 8. John A. Houston. LC 78-2805. (Carnegie Endowment for International Peace, United Nations Studies: No. 8). 345p. 1978. reprint ed. lib. bdg. 65.00 (*0-313-20335-0*, HOLU, Greenwood Pr) Greenwood.

Latin America in the World Economy. Ed. by Roberto P. Korzeniewicz & William C. Smith. LC 96-5794. 296p. 1996. pap. 27.95 (*0-275-95423-4*, Praeger Pubs) Greenwood.

Latin America in the World Economy. Diana Tussie. LC 82-47501. 213p. 1983. text 39.95 (*0-312-47333-8*) St Martin.

Latin America in the World Economy, 181. Ed. by Roberto P. Korzeniewicz & William C. Smith. LC 96-5794. (Contributions in Economics & Economic History Ser.: No. 181). 296p. 1996. 69.50 (*0-313-29814-9*, Greenwood Pr) Greenwood.

***Latin America in the World Economy: Mercantile Colonialism to Global Capitalism.** Frederick Stirton Weaver. 208p. 2000. 65.50 (*0-8133-3808-5*); pap. 29.00 (*0-8133-3809-3*) Westview.

Latin America in the Year 2000: Reactivating Growth, Improving Equity, Sustaining Democracy. Ed. by Archibald R. Ritter et al. LC 91-22939. 280p. 1992. 55.00 (*0-275-93747-X*, C3747, Praeger Pubs) Greenwood.

Latin America in the 1940's: War & Postwar Transitions. Ed. by David Rock. LC 93-29798. 285p. 1994. pap. 17.95 (*0-520-08417-9*, Pub. by U CA Pr) Cal Prin Full Svc.

Latin America in World Politics. 1989. 9.25 (*0-08-037589-8*) Macmillan.

Latin America, Its Problems & Its Promise: A Multidisciplinary Introduction. 3rd ed. Ed. by Jan K. Black. LC 97-40415. 672p. (C). 1998. pap. text 37.00 (*0-8133-2757-1*, Pub. by Westview) HarpC.

Latin America, 1983-1987: A Social Science Bibliography, Vol. 14. Compiled by Robert L. Delorme. LC 88-25081. (Bibliographies & Indexes in Sociology Ser.: No. 14). 407p. 1988. lib. bdg. 85.00 (*0-313-26406-6*, DLA/, Greenwood Pr) Greenwood.

Latin America 1998. 32nd ed. Robert T. Buckman. (World Today Ser.). 1998. pap. 11.50 (*1-887985-13-1*) Stryker-Post.

Latin America on Bicycle. Ed. by Zack Lewis. LC 87-62242. 160p. (Orig.). 1987. pap. 12.95 (*0-930016-07-6*) Pass Pr Trvl Line.

Latin America on Bicycle. rev. ed. Ed. by Paul Glassman. 160p. 1998. pap. 12.95 (*0-930016-27-0*) Pass Pr Trvl Line.

Latin America on File. Valerie Tomaselli-Moschovitis. LC 94-44746. (Illus.). 288p. (J). (gr. 4-12). 1995. ring bd. 165.00 (*0-8160-3225-4*) Facts on File.

***Latin America Profiled: Essential Facts on Society, Business & Politics in Latin America.** Barry Turner. LC 99-53353. (Statesman's Yearbook Factbks.). (Illus.). 2000. pap. 17.95 (*0-312-22995-X*) St Martin.

Latin America Studies Program: Activity Manual. rev. ed. John Zola. Ed. by Kathryn J. Books et al. (Illus.). 165p. (YA). (gr. 7). 1987. 125.00 (*0-87746-076-0*) Graphic Learning.

Latin America Studies Program: Teacher's Guide. John Zola. Ed. by Kathryn J. Books et al. (Illus.). 165p. (gr. 7). 1987. teacher ed. 12.50 (*0-87746-077-9*) Graphic Learning.

Latin America, the Hopeful Option. Eduardo Frei Montalva. LC 78-1358. 288p. reprint ed. pap. 89.30 (*0-8357-8934-9*, 203351100086) Bks Demand.

L

An Asterisk (*) at the beginning of an entry indicates that the title is appearing for the first time.

L

Latin America Through Soviet Eyes: The Evolution of Soviet Perceptions During the Brezhnev Era 1964-1982. Ilya Prizel. (Cambridge Russian, Soviet & Post-Soviet Studies: No. 72). 267p. (C). 1990. text 69.95 (*0-521-37303-4*) Cambridge U Pr.

Latin America Today: An Atlas of Reproducible Pages. rev. ed. Ed. by World Eagle Staff. (Today Ser.). (Illus.). 1997. ring bd. 49.95 (*0-930141-61-X*) World Eagle.

Latin America Transformed: Globalization & Modernity. Robert N. Gwynne. LC 98-44841. (Arnold Publication Ser.). (Illus.). 384p. 1999. text 75.00 (*0-340-73191-5*); pap. text 29.95 (*0-340-69165-4*) OUP.

Latin America vs. East Asia: A Comparative Development Perspective. Ching-Yuan Lin. LC 89-4128. 256p. (gr. 13). 1989. text 74.95 (*0-87332-526-5*, East Gate Bk) M E Sharpe.

Latin America, 1845-1914 see British Documents on Foreign Affairs: Series D: Latin America

Latin America, 1914-1939 see British Documents on Foreign Affairs: Series D: Latin America

Latin America, 1940-1945 see British Documents on Foreign Affairs: Series D: Latin America

Latin America, 1978. Ed. by Grace M. Ferrara. LC 73-83047. 192p. reprint ed. pap. 59.60 (*0-608-11999-7*, 202294300030) Bks Demand.

Latin America, 1996. 30th ed. Pierre E. Dostert. 217p. 1996. pap. 11.50 (*0-943448-99-9*) Stryker-Post.

***Latin America, 1999.** 33rd ed. Robert T. Buckman. 1999. pap. 11.50 (*1-887985-20-4*) Stryker-Post.

Latin America 25,000, 1996. Dun & Bradstreet Staff. 1995. pap. 250.00 (*0-614-25654-2*); disk 295.00 (*1-56203-551-7*) Dun & Bradstreet.

Latin American Adjustment: How Much Has Happened? John Williamson. LC 90-33670. 461p. 1990. reprint ed. pap. 143.00 (*0-7837-9166-6*, 204986700003) Bks Demand.

Latin American Advertising, Marketing & Media Data. 1995. 470.00 (*0-86338-544-3*, Pub. by Euromonitor PLC) Gale.

Latin American & Caribbean Development: Obstacles, Requirements & Options. (Cuadernos de la CEPAL Ser.: No. 55). 184p. 1987. pap. 6.00 (*92-1-121134-4*, E.87.II.G.9) UN.

Latin American & Caribbean Notebook, Vol. 1. Kofi Awoonor. LC 92-70644. 94p. 1993. 24.95 (*0-86543-314-3*); pap. 7.95 (*0-86543-315-1*) Africa World.

Latin American & East European Economies in Transition: A Comparative View. Claude Auroi. LC 97-26196. (EADI Book Ser.: No. 21). 180p. (C). 1998. pap. 29.50 (*0-7146-4403-X*, Pub. by F Cass Pubs) Intl Spec Bk.

***Latin American Antitrust Law.** Radoslav Depolo. 600p. 1999. ring bd. 195.00 (*1-57823-067-5*) Juris Pubng.

***Latin American Architecture: Six Voices.** Malcolm Quantrill & Kenneth Frampton. LC 99-30561. (Studies in Architecture & Culture). (Illus.). 256p. 2000. 60.00 (*0-89096-901-9*) Tex A&M Univ Pr.

Latin American Architecture since 1945. Henry-Russell Hitchcock, Jr. LC 71-169304. (Museum of Modern Art Publications in Reprint). (Illus.). 204p. 1972. reprint ed. 25.95 (*0-405-01563-1*) Ayer.

Latin American Art: Ancient to Modern. John F. Scott. LC 98-46535. (Illus.). 488p. 1999. 49.95 (*0-8130-1645-2*) U Press Fla.

***Latin American Art: Ancient to Modern.** John F. Scott. 2000. reprint ed. pap. 29.95 (*0-8130-1826-9*) U Press Fla.

Latin American Art & Music: A Handbook for Teaching. Ed. by Judith P. Horton. (Latin American Culture Studies Project). 174p. 1989. pap. 9.95 (*0-86728-012-3*) U TX Inst Lat Am Stud.

Latin American Art in the Twentieth Century. Ed. by Edward J. Sullivan. (Illus.). 352p. 1996. pap. 69.95 (*0-7148-3210-3*, Pub. by Phaidon Press) Phaidon Pr.

Latin American Art of the Twentieth Century. Edward Lucie-Smith. LC 92-70861. (World of Art Ser.). (Illus.). 216p. 1993. pap. 14.95 (*0-500-20260-5*, Pub. by Thames Hudson) Norton.

Latin American Artists in New York since 1970. Jacqueline Barnitz. Ed. by Florencia B. Nelson & Janis B. Carton. LC 87-70428. (Illus.). 114p. (Orig.). 1987. pap. 24.00 (*0-935213-10-4*) J S Blanton Mus.

Latin American Artists of the Twentieth Century: A Selection from the Exhibition. (Illus.). 64p. (Orig.). 1993. pap. 14.95 (*0-87070-160-6*, 0-8109-6132-6, Pub. by Mus of Modern Art) Abrams.

Latin American Artists' Signatures & Monograms: Colonial Era to 1996. John Castagno. LC 97-12178. 600p. 1997. 145.00 (*0-8108-3293-3*) Scarecrow.

Latin American Belles-Lettres in English Translation. James A. Granier. 1976. lib. bdg. 69.95 (*0-8490-2132-4*) Gordon Pr.

Latin American Book Trade Consultant: A Directory of Publishers, Printers, Bookstores & Libraries. Florencio O. Garcia. 175p. 1993. pap. 17.00 (*0-929928-17-2*) Fog Pubns.

Latin American Brain Drain to the United States: An Original Anthology. Ed. by Carlos E. Cortes. LC 79-6229. (Hispanics in the United States Ser.). (Illus.). 1981. lib. bdg. 19.95 (*0-405-13176-3*) Ayer.

Latin American Broadcasting. Elizabeth Fox. 1997. 40.00 (*1-86020-515-1*, Pub. by U of Luton Pr) Bks Intl VA.

Latin American Capital Flows: Living with Volatility. Study Group Staff. (Report Ser.). 124p. (Orig.). 1994. pap. 20.00 (*1-56708-046-4*) Grp of Thirty.

***Latin American Capital Markets.** Ed. by Joseph C. Hill & Anne Stetson. 1999. ring bd. 225.00 (*1-57823-065-9*) Juris Pubng.

Latin American Christian Democratic Parties. Edward J. Williams. LC 67-13159. 316p. reprint ed. 98.00 (*0-608-16865-3*, 202756700055) Bks Demand.

***Latin American City.** Alan Gilbert. LC 99-158722. 190p. 1998. pap. 19.00 (*1-899365-22-2*, Pub. by Lat Am Bur) Monthly Rev.

Latin American City. Alan Gilbert. 192p. pap. 16.00 (*0-85345-884-7*) Monthly Rev.

Latin American City. Told to Alan Gilbert. LC 99-158722. 1998. pap. text 19.00 (*0-85345-938-X*, Pub. by Monthly Rev) NYU Pr.

Latin American Civilization: History & Society, 1492 to the Present. 6th rev. ed. Ed. by Benjamin Keen. LC 95-8880. 490p. (C). 1995. pap. 32.00 (*0-8133-8689-6*, Pub. by Westview) HarpC.

Latin American Civilization: History & Society, 1492 to the Present. 7th ed. Ed. by Benjamin Keen. LC 99-49416. 520p. 2000. pap. 30.00 (*0-8133-3623-6*) Westview.

Latin American Classical Composers: A Biographical Dictionary. Ed. by Miguel Ficher et al. 1996. 56.00 (*0-8108-3185-6*) Scarecrow.

Latin American Classics. 62p. 1995. pap. 11.95 (*0-89724-948-8*, AF9545) Wrner Bros.

Latin American Coloring Book. Illus. by Peter Hoover. 64p. (YA). (gr. 3-10). 1997. pap. 2.90 (*0-7399-0189-3*, 2941) Rod & Staff.

Latin-American Community of Israel. Donald L. Herman. LC 84-8324. (Illus.). 151p. 1984. 47.95 (*0-275-91188-8*, C1188, Praeger Pubs) Greenwood.

Latin American Conspiracy. John Van Geldern. LC 91-71506. 302p. 1994. 18.95 (*0-9628923-0-0*) Delta-West.

Latin American Cooking Across the U. S. A. Himilce Novas & Rosemary Silva. LC 97-74754. 352p. 1997. 27.50 (*0-679-44408-4*) Knopf.

Latin American Culture Studies: Information & Materials for Teaching about Latin America. rev. ed. Ed. by Gloria Contreras. (Latin American Culture Studies Project). 310p. (J). (gr. k-12). 1987. pap. text 19.95 (*0-86728-020-4*) U TX Inst Lat Am Stud.

Latin-American Dance Book. B. White. (Ballroom Dance Ser.). 1988. lib. bdg. 79.95 (*0-87700-713-6*) Revisionist Pr.

Latin American Debt. Pedro-Pablo Kuczynski. LC 88-1218. 277p. 1988. reprint ed. pap. 85.90 (*0-608-06410-6*, 206662400008) Bks Demand.

Latin American Debt & Adjustment: External Shocks & Macroeconomic Policies. Ed. by Philip L. Brock et al. LC 88-25021. 283p. 1989. 59.95 (*0-275-93123-4*, C3123, Praeger Pubs) Greenwood.

Latin American Debt & the Politics of International Finance. Ernest J. Oliveri. LC 91-30394. 256p. 1992. 55.00 (*0-275-94123-X*, C4123, Praeger Pubs) Greenwood.

Latin American Debt Crisis: Human Costs & Viable Alternatives. Washington Office on Latin America Staff & Congressional Third World Debt Caucus Staff. (Illus.). 31p. (Orig.). (C). 1989. pap. text 5.00 (*0-929513-06-1*) WOLA.

Latin American Debt in the 1990s: Lessons from the Past & Forecasts for the Future. Ed. by Scott B. MacDonald et al. LC 91-2244. 168p. 1991. 52.95 (*0-275-93903-0*, C3903, Praeger Pubs) Greenwood.

Latin American Democracies: Colombia, Costa Rica, Venezuela. John A. Peeler. LC 84-13209. xiii, 193p. (C). 1985. pap. 17.95 (*0-8078-4153-6*) U of NC Pr.

Latin American Development: Geographical Perspectives. 2nd ed. David A. Preston. LC 96-153681. 313p. (C). 1996. pap. 48.00 (*0-582-23695-9*) Longman.

Latin American Diplomatic History: An Introduction. Harold E. Davis et al. LC 76-58901. viii, 302p. 1977. pap. text 18.95 (*0-8071-0286-5*) La State U Pr.

Latin American Economic Issues: Information Needs & Sources. (Papers of the Seminar on the Acquisition of Latin American Library Materials: No. 26). 1984. pap. 45.00 (*0-917617-00-2*) SALALM.

Latin American Economics. David W. Schodt. (C). 1996. text 36.50 (*0-8133-1126-8*); pap. text 14.95 (*0-8133-1127-6*) Westview.

Latin American Education: Comparative Perspectives. Carlos Torres. 375p. 2000. mass mkt. 28.00 (*0-8133-3668-6*) HarpC.

Latin American Experiments in Neoconservative Economics. Alejandro Foxley. LC 82-20252. 1983. pap. 14.95 (*0-520-05134-3*, Pub. by U CA Pr) Cal Prin Full Svc.

Latin American Fiction Today: A Symposium. Carlos Fuentes et al. Ed. by Rose S. Minc. LC 79-90483. (ENG & SPA.). 198p. (Orig.). 1980. 10.00 (*0-935318-04-6*) Edins Hispamerica.

Latin American Films, 1932-1994: A Critical Filmography. Ronald Schwartz. LC 96-37416. (Illus.). 304p. 1997. lib. bdg. 65.00 (*0-7864-0174-5*) McFarland & Co.

Latin American Frontiers, Borderlands, & Hinterlands: Research Needs & Resources. Ed. by Paula Covington. (Papers of the Seminar on the Acquisition of Latin American Library Materials: No. 33). xv, 494p. (Orig.). 1990. pap. 50.00 (*0-917617-24-X*) SALALM.

Latin American Geography: Historical - Geographical Essays, 1941-1998. Robert C. West. LC 98-37742. (Geoscience & Man Ser.: Vol. 35). (Illus.). 202p. (Orig.). (C). 1998. pap. 25.00 (*0-938909-68-1*) Geosci Pubns LSU.

Latin American Gold. J. C. Cooke & E. A. Elevatorski. LC 98-92274. 336p. 1999. 435.00 (*0-942218-35-3*) Minobras.

Latin American Guide - Cuba. 2nd ed. Andrew Coe. (Illus.). 316p. 1997. pap. text 21.95 (*0-8442-4850-9*, 48509, Passprt Bks) NTC Contemp Pub Co.

Latin American Guitar. Rico Stover. 68p. 1995. pap. 19.95 incl. audio compact disk (*0-7866-0507-3*, 95478BCD) Mel Bay.

Latin American Heroes: Liberators & Patriots from 1500 to the Present. Jerome Adams. (Illus.). 368p. 1993. pap. 9.00 (*0-345-38384-2*) One Wrld.

Latin American History: A Guide to the Literature in English. Robert A. Humphreys. LC 77-752. 210p. 1977. reprint ed. lib. bdg. 59.50 (*0-8371-9490-3*, HULA, Greenwood Pr) Greenwood.

Latin American History: A Teaching Atlas. Cathryn Lombardi & John V. Lombardi. LC 83-675775. (Illus.). 136p. 1983. pap. text 17.95 (*0-299-09714-5*) U of Wis Pr.

Latin American History on File. Victoria Chapman & David Lindroth. LC 95-30231. (Illus.). 288p. (YA). (gr. 6-12). 1996. ring bd. 165.00 (*0-8160-3068-5*) Facts on File.

Latin American Horizons: A Symposium at Dumbarton Oaks, 11th & 12th October, 1986. Ed. by Don S. Rice. LC 92-14833. (Illus.). 382p. 1993. 30.00 (*0-88402-207-2*, RIHO, Dumbarton Rsch Lib) Dumbarton Oaks.

Latin American Identity & Constructions of Difference. Ed. by Amaryll Chanady. LC 93-25437. (Hispanic Issues Ser.: Vol. 10). 304p. 1994. pap. 19.95 (*0-8166-2409-7*); text 44.95 (*0-8166-2408-9*) U of Minn Pr.

Latin American Images, 1985, Vol. II. (ENG & SPA., Illus.). 28p. pap. 12.95 (*0-614-02728-4*) J S Blanton Mus.

Latin American Inflation: Theoretical Interpretations & Empirical Results. Julio H. Cole. LC 87-15156. 104p. 1987. 49.95 (*0-275-92809-8*, C2809, Praeger Pubs) Greenwood.

Latin American Insects & Entomology. Charles L. Hogue. (Illus.). 594p. 1994. 95.00 (*0-520-07849-7*, Pub. by U CA Pr) Cal Prin Full Svc.

***Latin American Insolvency Systems: A Comparative Assessment.** Malcolm Rowat & Jose Astigarraga. LC 98-48419. 103p. 1999. pap. 22.00 (*0-8213-4399-8*) World Bank.

Latin American Jazz for Fingerstyle Guitar. John Zaradin. 56p. 1996. pap. 9.95 (*0-7866-0594-4*, 95556); pap. 24.95 incl. audio compact disk (*0-7866-0596-0*, 95556CDP) Mel Bay.

Latin American Jewish Literature. Lockhart. 1998. 22.95 (*0-8057-7803-9*, Twyne) Mac Lib Ref.

Latin American Jewish Studies: An Annotated Guide to the Literature, 4. Judith L. Elkin & Ana L. Sater. LC 90-13963. (Bibliographies & Indexes in Ethnic Studies: No. 4). 264p. 1990. lib. bdg. 75.00 (*0-313-25936-4*, EGL/, Greenwood Pr) Greenwood.

Latin American Journalism. Micheal B. Salwen & Bruce Garrison. (Communication Textbook Ser. (Journalism sub-ser)). 240p. (C). 1991. text 55.00 (*0-8058-0767-5*); pap. text 29.95 (*0-8058-0768-3*) L Erlbaum Assocs.

Latin American Labor Law Handbook. Kilpatrick Stockton. Ed. by Scott Studebaker. 100p. 1998. pap. 185.00 (*1-893323-13-7*) WorldTrade Exec.

Latin American Labor Organizations. Gerald M. Greenfield & Sheldon L. Maram. LC 86-33613. 943p. 1987. lib. bdg. 215.00 (*0-313-22834-5*, MLA/, Greenwood Pr) Greenwood.

Latin American Land Reforms in Theory & Practice: A Retrospective Analysis. Peter Dorner. LC 91-26440. 118p. (Orig.). 1992. pap. 12.95 (*0-299-13164-5*); lib. bdg. 25.00 (*0-299-13160-2*) U of Wis Pr.

Latin American Laws & Institutions. Albert S. Golbert & Yenny N. Gingold. LC 81-12189. 573p. 1982. 75.00 (*0-275-90804-6*, C0804, Praeger Pubs) Greenwood.

Latin American Leaders. Harold E. Davis. LC 68-56189. reprint ed. 57.00 (*0-8154-0271-6*) Cooper Sq.

Latin American Legal Abbreviations: A Comprehensive Spanish-Portuguese Dictionary with English Translations. Ed. by Francisco A. Avalos. LC 89-17169. 615p. 1989. lib. bdg. 115.00 (*0-313-26200-4*, TLN/, Greenwood Pr) Greenwood.

Latin American Literature: Classification Schedule, Classified Listing by Call Number, Authors & Title Listing. Harvard University Library Staff. LC 68-31060. (Widener Library Shelflist: No. 21). 506p. 1969. text 40.00 (*0-674-51251-0*) HUP.

Latin American Literature: Symptoms, Risks, & Strategies of Poststructuralist Criticism. Bernard McGuirk. LC 96-17603. 272p. (C). 1997. 90.00 (*0-415-07755-9*) Routledge.

***Latin American Lives.** 1189p. 1998. 115.00 (*0-02-865060-3*) Macmillan Gen Ref.

Latin American Male Homosexualities. Ed. by Stephen O. Murray. LC 95-4349. 304p. 1995. 45.00 (*0-8263-1646-8*); pap. 24.95 (*0-8263-1658-1*) U of NM Pr.

Latin American Mammalogy: History, Biodiversity, & Conservation. Michael A. Mares & David J. Schmidly. LC 91-10264. (Oklahoma Museum of Natural History Publications). (Illus.). 480p. 1991. 57.50 (*0-8061-2343-5*) U of Okla Pr.

Latin American Markets: A Guide to Company & Industry Information Sources. 2nd ed. 425p. 1995. 335.00 (*1-56365-036-3*) Wash Res.

Latin American Marxism: A Bibliography. Ed. by Harry E. Vanden. LC 90-26224. 892p. 1991. text 40.00 (*0-8240-9193-0*, 137) Garland.

Latin American Masses & Minorities: Their Images & Realities, 2 vols. Ed. by Dan C. Hazen. (Papers of the Seminar on the Acquisition of Latin American Library Materials: No. 30). 719p. (Orig.). 1987. pap. 57.50 (*0-917617-11-8*) SALALM.

Latin American Masterpieces. Ramis Barquet et al. (Illus.). 32p. (Orig.). 1997. pap. write for info. (*0-9658637-1-9*) Galeria Ramis.

Latin American Media Directory. unabridged ed. Ed. by Sandra Marina.Tr. of Guia De Medios Latinoamericanos. 350p. (Orig.). 1997. pap. 77.00 (*0-9656399-0-8*) Fla Internatl Univ.

Latin American Merchant Shipping in the Age of Global Competition, 209. Rene De La Pedraja. LC 98-30493. (Contributions in Economics & Economic History Ser.: Vol. 209). 200p. 1999. 59.95 (*0-313-30840-3*, Greenwood Pr) Greenwood.

Latin American Military History: An Annotated Bibliography. Ed. by David G. LaFrance & Errol D. Jones. LC 92-12606. (Military History Bibliographies Ser.: Vol. 12). 752p. 1992. text 40.00 (*0-8240-4634-X*, H01024) Garland.

Latin American Military Institution. Ed. by Robert Wesson. LC 85-28301. 247p. 1986. 59.95 (*0-275-92084-4*, C2084, Praeger Pubs) Greenwood.

Latin American Music, vol. 1. Contrib. by Kuss. 2001. 100.00 (*0-02-865022-0*) Macmillan.

Latin American Music, vol. 2. 2nd ed. Kuss. 2001. 100.00 (*0-02-865023-9*) Macmillan.

Latin American Music: An Encyclopedic History, 2 vols., 2 vols. Kuss. LC 98-52674. 2000p. 1998. per. 210.00 (*0-02-864971-0*, Schirmer Books) Mac Lib Ref.

***Latin-American Mythology.** Hartley B. Alexander. (LC History-America-E). 379p. 1999. reprint ed. lib. bdg. 89.00 (*0-7812-4292-4*) Rprt Serv.

Latin American Narcotics Trade & U. S. National Security, 240. Ed. by Donald J. Mabry. LC 89-12030. (Contributions in Political Science Ser.: No. 240). 216p. 1989. 59.95 (*0-313-26786-3*, MLJ/, Greenwood Pr) Greenwood.

Latin American Nations in World Politics. 2nd ed. Ed. by Heraldo Munoz & Joseph S. Tulchin. 288p. (C). 1996. pap. 26.00 (*0-8133-0873-9*, Pub. by Westview) HarpC.

Latin American Newspapers in Libraries in the United States. Ed. by A. E. Gropp. 1976. lib. bdg. 59.95 (*0-8490-2133-2*) Gordon Pr.

Latin American Oil Companies & the Politics of Energy. Ed. by John D. Wirth. LC 84-29457. (Latin American Studies). 322p. 1985. reprint ed. pap. 99.90 (*0-608-02047-8*, 206270000003) Bks Demand.

Latin American Painting. Fernando Lozano. (Illus.). 64p. 1991. 32.00 (*1-56721-005-8*) Twnty-Fifth Cent Pr.

Latin American Peasant. Andrew Pearse. (Library of Peasant Studies: No. 1). 299p. 1975. 49.50 (*0-7146-3047-0*, Pub. by F Cass Pubs); pap. 15.00 (*0-7146-4021-2*, Pub. by F Cass Pubs) Intl Spec Bk.

Latin American Percussion. Birger Sulsbruck. (Illus.). 184p. 1986. pap. 39.95 (*0-8464-3396-6*) Beekman Pubs.

Latin American Percussion. rev. ed. Birger Sulsbruck. 1986. pap. 39.95 (*0-685-69087-3*, WH29822); VHS 41.95 (*0-685-69088-1*, VC29822) Shawnee Pr.

Latin American Perspectives: Exploration, Mining, & Processing. Ed. by Osvalde A. Bascur. LC 99-162967. (Illus.). 412p. 1998. pap. 82.00 (*0-87335-155-X*, 155-X) SMM&E Inc.

Latin American Philosophy in the Twentieth Century: Man, Values, & the Search for Philosophical Identity. Ed. by Jorge J. E. Gracia. LC 86-91551. 269p. 1986. pap. 25.95 (*0-87975-333-1*) Prometheus Bks.

Latin-American Philosophy of Law in the Twentieth Century. Josef L. Kunz. viii, 120p. 1981. reprint ed. 37.50 (*0-8377-0736-6*, Rothman) W S Hein.

Latin American Play Index, 1920-1962, Vol. 1. Herbert H. Hoffman. LC 83-8736. 160p. 1984. 21.00 (*0-8108-1671-7*) Scarecrow.

Latin American Play Index, 1962-1980, Vol. 2. Herbert H. Hoffman. LC 83-8736. 135p. 1983. 21.00 (*0-8108-1633-4*) Scarecrow.

Latin-American Plays. Tr. by Sebastian Doggart. (International Collection). 256p. (Orig.). 1996. pap. 25.95 (*1-85459-249-1*, Pub. by N Hern Bks) Theatre Comm.

Latin American Policies of U. S. Allies: Balancing Global Interests & Regional Concerns. Ed. by Williams Perry & Peter Wehner. LC 85-12259. 206p. 1985. 57.95 (*0-275-90220-X*, C0220, Praeger Pubs) Greenwood.

Latin American Policy of Warren G. Harding. Kenneth J. Grieb. LC 74-26229. 237p. 1976. reprint ed. pap. 73.50 (*0-608-00737-4*, 206151300009) Bks Demand.

Latin American Political Economy in the Age of Neoliberal Reform: Theoretical & Comparative Perspectives for the 1990's. Carlos H. Acuna & Eduardo A. Gamarra. Ed. by William C. Smith et al. LC 93-44981. 232p. (C). 1994. pap. 21.95 (*1-56000-731-1*, Pub. by U Miami N-S Ctr) L Rienner.

Latin American Political Guide. 20th ed. James L. Busey. 113p. 1995. 8.50 (*0-912188-08-1*) Juniper Edit.

Latin American Political Thought & Ideology. Miguel Jorrin & John D. Martz. LC 71-109461. 468p. reprint ed. pap. 145.10 (*0-8357-3864-7*, 203659600004) Bks Demand.

Latin American Political Yearbook, 1998. Ed. by Robert G. Breene, Jr. 275p. 1999. 49.95 (*1-56000-386-3*) Transaction Pubs.

Latin American Political Yearbook, 1997. Ed. by Robert G. Breene, Jr. 256p. 1997. text 49.95 (*1-56000-350-2*) Transaction Pubs.

Latin American Politics. Klaren. 50.00 (*0-8133-3682-1*); 27.50 (*0-8133-3683-X*) Westview.

Latin American Politics. Palmer. 2000. pap. text. write for info. (*0-312-17853-0*) St Martin.

Latin American Politics: A New World of Possibility. Howard J. Wiarda. LC 94-18453. 222p. (C). 1994. pap. text 32.50 (*0-534-20988-2*) Harcourt.

Latin American Politics: A Theoretical Framework. Torcuato S. Di Tella. (Translations from Latin America Ser.). 348p. 1989. text 27.50 (*0-292-74661-X*) U of Tex Pr.

Latin American Politics & Development. 4th ed. Howard J. Wiarda. LC 96-16359. (C). 1996. pap. 37.00 (*0-8133-8493-1*, Pub. by Westview) HarpC.

***Latin American Politics & Development.** 5th ed. Wiarda. 592p. 2000. pap. 32.00 (*0-8133-3769-0*, Pub. by Westview) HarpC.

An Asterisk (*) at the beginning of an entry indicates that the title is appearing for the first time.

Latin American Politics in Perspective. Martin C. Needler. 1990. 16.50 (0-8446-2639-2) Peter Smith.

***Latin American Popular Culture: An Introduction.** William H. Beezley & Linda Curcio-Nagy. 286p. 2000. 55.00 (0-8420-2710-6); 21.95 (0-8420-2711-4) Scholarly Res Inc.

Latin American Popular Theatre: The First Five Centuries. Judith A. Weiss et al. LC 92-19063. (Illus.). 279p. reprint ed. pap. 86.50 (0-608-20969-4, 207184100002) Bks Demand.

Latin American Population & Urbanization Analysis: Maps & Statistics, 1950-1982. Richard W. Wilkie. LC 83-620019. (Statistical Abstract of Latin America Supplement Ser.: Vol. 8). 431p. 1985. pap. 27.50 (0-87903-247-2) UCLA Lat Am Ctr.

Latin American Population Studies. Thomas Lynn Smith. LC 61-63016. (University of Florida Monographs: Social Sciences: No. 8). 92p. reprint ed. pap. 30.00 (0-7837-5005-6, 204467200004) Bks Demand.

Latin American Populism in Comparative Perspective. Ed. by Michael L. Conniff. LC 80-54572. 271p. reprint ed. pap. 84.10 (0-8357-4641-0, 203757200008) Bks Demand.

Latin American Product Guide. Ed. by C. DePaula. 450p. 1994. pap. 125.00 (0-915344-42-4) Todd Pubns.

Latin American Prospects for the 1980's: Equity, Democratization & Development. Ed. by Archibald R. Ritter & David H. Pollock. LC 82-18039. 330p. 1983. 65.00 (0-275-91064-4, C1064, Praeger Pubs) Greenwood.

Latin American Psychology: A Guide to Research & Training. Gerardo Marin et al. LC 87-17409. 220p. 1987. pap. 29.95 (0-912704-84-5) Am Psychol.

Latin American Psychology: A Guide to Research & Training. Gerardo Marin et al. LC 87-17409. 223p. 1987. reprint ed. pap. 69.20 (0-608-04560-8, 206529900001) Bks Demand.

Latin American Religion in Motion: Tracking Innovation, Unexpected Change, & Complexity. Christian Smith & Joshua Prokopy. LC 98-28932. 1p. 1999. pap. 18.99 (0-415-92106-6) Routledge.

Latin American Religion in Motion: Tracking Innovation, Unexpected Change & Complexity. Christian Smith & Joshua Prokopy. LC 98-28932. 1999. 65.00 (0-415-92105-8) Routledge.

Latin American Research & Publications at the University of Texas at Austin, 1893-1969. University of Texas at Austin, Institute of Latin. LC 74-185491. (Guides & Bibliographies Ser.: No. 3). 197p. reprint ed. pap. 61.10 (0-608-17214-6, 202732400055) Bks Demand.

Latin American Revolutionaries: Groups, Goals, Methods. Michael Radu & Vladimir Tismaneanu. 386p. 1998. text 50.00 (0-7881-5730-2) DIANE Pub.

Latin American Revolutionaries: Groups, Goals, Methods. R. Radu & W. Vladimir Tismaneanu. 400p. 1989. 60.00 (0-08-037429-8, 3715M) Brasseys.

Latin American Revolutionary Poetry (Poesia Revolucionaria Latinoamericana) A Bilingual Anthology. Ed. by Robert Marquez. LC 73-90079. 503p. 1974. reprint ed. pap. 156.00 (0-7837-3907-9, 204375500010) Bks Demand.

Latin American Revolutions, 1808-1826: Old & New World Origins. Ed. by John Lynch. LC 94-16521. 424p. 1994. 27.95 (0-8061-2661-2) U of Okla Pr.

Latin American Revolutions, 1808-1826: Old & New World Origins. Ed. by John Lynch. LC 94-16521. 1996. pap. 16.95 (0-8061-2663-9) U of Okla Pr.

Latin American Rhythms for Guitar: Intermediate Level. Jorge Morel. 32p. 1997. pap. 17.95 incl. audio compact disk (0-7866-2476-0, 96214BCD) Mel Bay.

Latin American Scholarship since World War II: Trends in History, Political Science, Literature, Geography, & Economics. Ed. by Roberto Esquenazi-Mayo & Michael C. Meyer. LC 73-125101. 347p. reprint ed. pap. 107.60 (0-8357-2941-9, 203919700011) Bks Demand.

Latin-American School of Physics: XXX ELAF. Octavio Castanos et al. (AIP Press Conference Proceedings Ser.: No. 365). (Illus.). 432p. 1996. 145.00 (1-56396-567-4, CP 365, AIP Pr) Spr-Verlag.

Latin-American School of Physics XXXI FLAF: New Perspectives on Quantum Mechanics. Ed. by Shahen Hacyan et al. LC 99-60216. (AIP Conference Proceedings Ser.). (Illus.). 382p. 1999. 100.00 (1-56396-856-8) Am Inst Physics.

Latin American Short Stories. Ed. by Alan Ryan. 1999. 29.95 (0-670-83632-X) Viking Penguin.

Latin American Short Story: A Critical History. Ed. by Margaret Sayers Peden. (Critical History of the Modern Short Story Ser.). 164p. 1983. 23.95 (0-8057-9351-8, Twyne) Mac Lib Ref.

Latin American Short Story: An Annotated Guide to Anthologies & Criticism, 34. Compiled by Daniel Balderston. LC 92-7336. (Bibliographies & Indexes in World Literature Ser.: No. 34). 552p. 1992. lib. bdg. 79.50 (0-313-27360-X, BLJ, Greenwood Pr) Greenwood.

Latin American Societies in Transition. Robert C. Williamson. LC 96-26879. 288p. 1997. 65.00 (0-275-95750-0); pap. 24.95 (0-275-95751-9) Greenwood.

Latin American Society & Legal Culture: A Bibliography, 5. Compiled by Frederick E. Snyder. LC 85-5593. (Bibliographies & Indexes in Law & Political Science Ser.: No. 5). 188p. 1985. lib. bdg. 55.00 (0-313-24858-3, SLM/, Greenwood Pr) Greenwood.

Latin American Soul: Bilingual Poetry. (ENG & SPA.). 80p. 1997. pap. 10.00 (0-9656013-0-7) Grace Pr.

Latin American Sovereign Debt Management: Legal & Regulatory Aspects. Ed. by Ralph Reisner et al. (Illus.). 273p. 1992. pap. text 14.50 (0-940602-33-4) IADB.

Latin American Spanish. DK Publishing Staff. LC 98-51187. (Eyewitness Travel Guide Phrase Bks.). 128p. 1999. pap. text 6.95 (0-7894-4187-X) DK Pub Inc.

***Latin American Spanish.** Kindersley Dorling. 144p. 2000. pap. 9.95 (0-7894-6544-2) DK Pub Inc.

Latin American Spanish. John M. Lipski. LC 93-31346. (Linguistics Library). 1994. write for info. (0-582-08761-9, Pub. by Addison-Wesley) Longman.

Latin American Spanish. John M. Lipski. LC 93-31346. (Linguistics Library). 1995. pap. text 31.31 (0-582-08760-0) Addison-Wesley.

Latin American Spanish. 3rd ed. Ed. by Sally Steward. (Illus.). 320p. 1998. pap. 6.95 (0-86442-558-9) Lonely Planet.

Latin-American Spanish Cassette Pack. rev. ed. (Cassettepack Ser.). 1998. pap. 17.95 incl. audio (2-8315-6333-X) Berlitz.

***Latin American Spanish Dictionary.** 2nd ed. Random House Dictionary Staff. 736p. 1999. pap. 12.95 (0-375-70736-0) Random Ref & Info.

***Latin American Spanish Dictionary.** 2nd ed. Random House Staff. 736p. 1999. 24.95 (0-375-40720-0) Random Ref & Info.

Latin American Spanish in Three Months. Isabel Cisneros. LC 98-48008. (Hugo Three Month Language Courses Ser.). 256p. 1999. pap. text 14.95 (0-7894-4215-9) DK Pub Inc.

Latin American Spanish Phrase Book. 2nd rev. ed. Berlitz Editors. (Berlitz Phrase Book & Dictionary Ser.). (SPA., Illus.). 224p. 1998. pap. 7.95 (2-8315-6242-2) Berlitz.

***Latin-American Spanish Reference Dictionary.** Berlitz Publishing Staff. (Bilingual Reference Dictionaries). (SPA & ENG.). 692p. 2000. pap. text 14.95 (2-8315-7330-0, Pub. by Berlitz) Globe Pequot.

***Latin American Sport: An Annotated Bibliography, 1988-1998, 3.** Compiled by Joseph L. Arbena. LC 99-11260. (Bibliographies & Indexes on Sports History Ser.: Vol. 3). 264p. 1999. lib. bdg. 75.00 (0-313-29611-1) Greenwood.

Latin American States & Political Refugees. Keith W. Yundt. LC 88-15563. 247p. 1988. 59.95 (0-275-92942-6, C2942, Praeger Pubs) Greenwood.

Latin American Studies: A Basic Guide to Sources. 2nd ed. Ed. by Robert A. McNeil & Barbara G. Valk. LC 89-34133. 470p. 1990. 48.00 (0-8108-2236-9) Scarecrow.

Latin American Studies into the Twenty-First Century: New Focus, New Formats, New Challenges. Ed. by Deborah L. Jakubs. xii, 467p. (Orig.). (C). 1994. pap. 52.00 (0-917617-38-X) SALALM.

Latin American Telecommunications Service & Equipment Markets: Emphasis on Service Offers Investment Opportunities to Equipment Manufacturers. Market Intelligence Staff. 375p. 1994. 2695.00 (1-56753-937-8) Frost & Sullivan.

Latin American Television. 3rd ed. 1998. 799.00 (1-58090-002-X) Baskerville Comm.

Latin American Television: A Global View. John Sinclair. LC 98-28580. 200p. 1999. text 65.00 (0-19-815930-7); pap. text 19.95 (0-19-815929-3) OUP.

***Latin American Theatre in Translation: An Anthology of Work from Mexico, the Caribbean & the Southern Cone.** Charles Philip Thomas. LC 00-190399. 540p. 2000. 25.00 (0-7388-1635-3); pap. 18.00 (0-7388-1636-1) Xlibris Corp.

Latin American Theories of Development & Underdevelopment. Cristobal Kay. (Development & Underdevelopment Ser.). 304p. 1989. 49.95 (0-415-01422-0) Routledge.

Latin American Thought: A Historical Perspective. Harold E. Davis. LC 78-181564. 279p. reprint ed. pap. 86.50 (0-608-09815-9, 206998300007) Bks Demand.

***Latin American Tokens.** 2nd ed. Russell Rulau. LC 92-71453. (Illus.). 480p. 2000. pap. 37.95 (0-87341-566-3) Krause Pubns.

Latin American Tokens: A Guide Book & Catalog 1700-1920. Russell Rulau. LC 92-71453. (Illus.). 410p. 1992. pap. 29.95 (0-87341-200-1, TL01) Krause Pubns.

Latin American Trade Agreements. Thomas A. O'Keefe. 500p. 1997. ring bd. 185.00 (1-57105-027-2) Transnatl Pubs.

Latin American Trade & Cooperation for Development. (International Trade Ser.). 132p. 1978. 4.00 (0-8270-2060-0) OAS.

Latin American Trade Misinvoicing As an Instrument of Capital Flight & Duty Evasion. Rudiger Dornbusch. 32p. 1990. pap. text 8.00 (0-940602-32-6) IADB.

Latin American Trade Patterns. Donald W. Baerresen et al. LC 80-479. (Illus.). 329p. 1980. reprint ed. lib. bdg. 79.50 (0-313-22288-6, BALT, Greenwood Pr) Greenwood.

Latin American Trumpet Music. Gabriel Rosati. 120p. 1996. spiral bd. 15.00 incl. audio compact disk (0-7866-0726-2, 95601BCD) Mel Bay.

Latin American Underdevelopment: A History of Perspectives in the United States, 1870-1965. James W. Park. LC 94-37209. (Illus.). 312p. 1995. text 42.50 (0-8071-1969-5) La State U Pr.

Latin American University Students: A Six Nation Study. Arthur Liebman et al. LC 70-180152. (Center for International Affairs Ser.). (Illus.). 322p. 1972. 34.95 (0-674-51275-8) HUP.

Latin American Urban Research, Vol. 1. Ed. by Francine F. Rabinovitz & Felicity M. Trueblood. LC 78-103483. 314p. reprint ed. pap. 97.40 (0-608-14194-1, 202194200026) Bks Demand.

Latin American Urbanization: Historical Profiles of Major Cities. Gerald M. Greenfield. LC 93-13015. 560p. 1994. lib. bdg. 135.00 (0-313-25937-2, GFZ/) Greenwood.

Latin American Vanguards: The Art of Contentious Encounters. Vicky Unruh. LC 93-42216. (C). 1995. 55.00 (0-520-08561-2, Pub. by U CA Pr); pap. 24.95 (0-520-08794-1, Pub. by U CA Pr) Cal Prin Full Svc.

Latin American Views of U. S. Policy: Politics of Latin America. Ed. by Heraldo Munoz. LC 85-19365. (Hoover Institute Ser.). 162p. 1985. 52.95 (0-275-92048-8, C2048, Praeger Pubs) Greenwood.

Latin American Women: Historical Perspectives, 3. Ed. by Asuncion Lavrin. LC 77-94758. (Contributions in Women's Studies: No. 3). 343p. 1978. 67.95 (0-313-20309-1, LLA/, Greenwood Pr) Greenwood.

Latin American Women & the Search for Social Justice. Francesca Miller. LC 91-50371. (Illus.). 342p. 1991. pap. 22.95 (0-87451-558-0) U Pr of New Eng.

Latin American Women Artists, Kahlo & Look Who Else: A Selective, Annotated Bibliography, 21. Cecilia Puerto. LC 96-7150. (Art Reference Collection Ser.). 260p. 1996. lib. bdg. 77.95 (0-313-28934-4, Greenwood Pr) Greenwood.

Latin American Women Artists of the United States: The Works of 33 Twentieth-Century Women. Robert Henkes. LC 98-43600. (Illus.). 259p. 1999. lib. bdg. 40.00 (0-7864-0519-8) McFarland & Co.

Latin American Women Artists, 1915-1995 (Artistas Latinoamericanas, 1915-1995) Geraldine P. Biller et al. Tr. by Liliana H. Rosenthal et al. (SPA., Illus.). 204p. 1995. pap. 34.95 (0-944110-50-9) Milwauk Art Mus.

***Latin American Women Dramatists: Theater, Texts, & Theories.** Ed. by Catherine Larson & Margarita Vargas. LC 98-34127. 320p. 1998. 39.95 (0-253-33461-6); pap. 19.95 (0-253-21240-5) Ind U Pr.

Latin American Women Writers. Myriam Y. Jehenson. (Twayne's World Authors Ser.). 200p. 1995. text 22.95 (0-8057-8299-0, Twyne) Mac Lib Ref.

Latin-American Women Writers: Class, Race, & Gender. Myriam Y. Jehenson. LC 94-33936. (SUNY Series in Feminist Criticism & Theory). 201p. (C). 1995. pap. text 19.95 (0-7914-2560-6) State U NY Pr.

Latin American Women Writers: Yesterday & Today. Ed. by Yvette E. Miller & Charles M. Tatum. Tr. by Robert Lima et al. 202p. 1977. reprint ed. pap. 12.50 (0-935480-56-0) Lat Am Lit Rev Pr.

Latin American Women's Writing: Feminist Readings in Theory & Crisis. Ed. by Anny B. Jones & Catherine Davies. (Oxford Hispanic Studies). 264p. 1996. text 65.00 (0-19-871512-9) OUP.

Latin American Women's Writing: Feminist Readings in Theory & Crisis. Anny B. Jones & Catherine Davies. (Oxford Hispanic Studies). 264p. 1997. pap. text 19.95 (0-19-871513-7) OUP.

Latin American Writers. Ed. by Stanley H. Barkan et al. 1991. boxed set 75.00 (0-89304-940-9); boxed set 50.00 (0-685-49048-3) Cross-Cultrl NY.

Latin American Writers. Lynn M. Shirey. LC 96-18378. (Global Profiles Ser.). (YA). (gr. 5-12). 1996. 19.95 (0-8160-3202-5) Facts on File.

Latin American Writers, 3 vols., Set. Ed. by Carlos A. Sole, Jr. & Maria I. Abreu. LC 88-35481. (Scribner Writers Ser.). 1497p. 1989. 300.00 (0-684-18463-X, Scribners Ref) Mac Lib Ref.

Latin American Writers, Vol. 1. Gary F. Sole. 1989. 100.00 (0-684-18597-0) Mac Lib Ref.

Latin American Writers, Vol. 2. Gary F. Sole. 1989. 100.00 (0-684-18598-9) Mac Lib Ref.

Latin American Writers, Vol. 3. Gary F. Sole. 1989. 100.00 (0-684-18599-7) Mac Lib Ref.

Latin American Writers on Gay & Lesbian Themes: A Bio-Critical Sourcebook. Ed. by David W. Foster. LC 94-2191. 544p. 1994. lib. bdg. 99.50 (0-313-28479-2) Greenwood.

Latin Americana Research in the United States & Canada: A Guide & Directory. Robert P. Haro. LC 72-138653. 123p. reprint ed. pap. 38.20 (0-608-14068-6, 202420700035) Bks Demand.

***Latin Americanism.** Roman De la Campa. LC 98-56167. (Cultural Studies of the Americas). 1999. pap. 18.95 (0-8166-3117-4) U of Minn Pr.

Latin Americans. Hugh O'Shaughnessy. LC 90-60713. (Illus.). 143p. 1990. 18.95 (0-563-21393-0) Parkwest Pubns.

Latin Americans: Their Love-Hate Relationship with the United States. rev. ed. Carlos Rangel. 322p. 1987. pap. 24.95 (0-88738-692-X) Transaction Pubs.

Latin Americans: Understanding Their Legacy. Randall Hansis. LC 96-21487. 336p. (C). 1996. pap. 35.00 (0-07-026081-8) McGraw.

Latin Americans in Texas. Pauline R. Kibbe. LC 73-14205. (Mexican American Ser.). (Illus.). 338p. 1977. reprint ed. 26.95 (0-405-05679-6) Ayer.

Latin America's Christian Democratic Parties: A Political Economy. Edward A. Lynch. LC 92-23069. 224p. 1992. 57.95 (0-275-94464-6, C4464, Praeger Pubs) Greenwood.

Latin America's Economic Development: Confronting Crisis. 2nd rev. ed. Ed. by James L. Dietz. 401p. 1995. pap. 23.95 (1-55587-600-5) L Rienner.

Latin America's Economic Future. Ed. by Graham Bird & Ann Helwege. (Surrey Seminars in Applied Economics Ser.). (Illus.). 339p. 1994. text 79.95 (0-12-099645-6) Acad Pr.

Latin America's Economy: Diversity, Trends & Conflicts. Eliana Cardoso & Ann Helwege. 354p. 1995. pap. text 22.00 (0-262-53125-9) MIT Pr.

Latin America's International Relations & Their Domestic Consequences: War & Peace, Dependency & Autonomy, Integration & Disintegration. Intro. by Jorge I. Dominguez. LC 93-45524. (Essays on Mexico, Central & South America Ser.: Vol. 6). 464p. 1994. text 84.00 (0-8153-1490-6) Garland.

Latin America's Journey to the Market: From Macroeconomic Shocks to Institutional Therapy. Moises Naim. LC 94-42487. (Occasional Papers: No. 62). 1994. pap. 9.95 (1-55815-457-4) ICS Pr.

Latin America's New Historical Novel. Seymour Menton. LC 93-787. (Texas Pan American Ser.). 240p. (C). 1993. text 30.00 (0-292-75157-5) U of Tex Pr.

Latin America's Turnaround: The Paths to Privatization & Foreign Investment. Ed. by Paul H. Boeker. 250p. (Orig.). 1993. pap. 19.95 (1-55815-247-4) ICS Pr.

***Latin American Cultural Criticism: Re-Interpreting a Continent.** Patricia D'Allemand. LC 00-21154. (Studies in Latin American Literature & Culture : 7). 208p. 2000. pap. text 89.95 (0-7734-7811-6) E Mellen.

L

Latin & American Dances. Doris Lavelle. (Ballroom Dance Ser.). 1984. lib. bdg. 79.95 (0-87700-512-5) Revisionist Pr.

Latin & Roman Culture in Joyce. R. J. Schork. LC 96-33050. (Florida James Joyce Ser.). 321p. 1997. 49.95 (0-8130-1472-7) U Press Fla.

Latin & Roman Culture in Joyce: The Wake Lock Picked. R. J. Schork. LC 96-24031. (Florida James Joyce Ser.). 321p. 1997. 49.95 (0-8130-1465-4) U Press Fla.

Latin & the Romance Languages in the Early Middle Ages. Ed. by Roger Wright. LC 95-41360. 272p. 1996. pap. 17.95 (0-271-01569-1) Pa St U Pr.

Latin & Vernacular: Studies in Late-Medieval Texts & Manuscripts. Ed. by Alastair J. Minnis. (University of York: Centre for Medieval Studies Manuscripts Conference Proceedings: No. 1). 163p. (C). 1989. 75.00 (0-85991-286-8) Boydell & Brewer.

Latin & Vernacular Poets of the Middle Ages. Peter Dronko. (Collected Studies: No. CS352). 350p. 1991. text 115.95 (0-86078-303-0, Pub. by Variorum) Ashgate Pub Co.

Latin Aristotle. L. Opuscula Minio-Paluello. xii, 590p. 1972. text 95.00 (0-317-54477-2, Pub. by AM Hakkert) Coronet Bks.

Latin Ballroom Dancing. Earl Atkinson. (Ballroom Dance Ser.). 1983. lib. bdg. 79.95 (0-87700-481-1) Revisionist Pr.

Latin Ballroom Dancing: Including Rumba, Cha Cha Cha, Tango, Samba, Mambo, Merengue & Paso Doble. Earl Atkinson. (Ballroom Dance Ser.). 1986. lib. bdg. 250.00 (0-8490-3626-7) Gordon Pr.

Latin Bicentennial. (ENG & SPA., Illus.). 12p. (Orig.). 1977. pap. text 10.00 (0-941980-04-9) Bronx County.

Latin-Bulgarian Dictionary. M. Voinov. (BUL & LAT.). 840p. 1980. 79.95 (0-8288-1616-6, M9831) Fr & Eur.

Latin by Stave Analysis. H. Schofield. 95p. 1969. 4.95 (0-85225-490-3) Ed Solutions.

Latin-Chinese-English Names of Fishes. Ed. by Cheng Qingtai. (CHI, ENG & LAT.). 296p. 1996. 12.00 (7-03-000454-X, Pub. by Sci Pr) Lubrecht & Cramer.

Latin Church in Cyprus, 1195-1312. Nicholas Coureas. LC 97-23242. 376p. 1997. text 83.95 (1-85928-447-7, Pub. by Ashgate Pub) Ashgate Pub Co.

Latin Church in the Crusader States: The Secular Church. Bernard Hamilton. 402p. (C). 1980. lib. bdg. 109.95 (0-86078-072-4, Pub. by Variorum) Ashgate Pub Co.

Latin Church Music in England, 1460-1575. Hugh Benham. LC 79-25063. (Music Reprint Ser.: 1980). (Illus.). 1980. reprint ed. lib. bdg. 35.00 (0-306-76025-8) Da Capo.

Latin, Classical, Artes Latinae, Pt. III. Waldo E. Sweet. (LAT., Illus.). 404p. 1969. pap. 145.00 incl. audio (1-57970-033-0, S26150) Audio-Forum.

Latin, Classical, Artes Latinae, Pt. IV. Waldo E. Sweet. (LAT., Illus.). 283p. 1969. pap. 145.00 (1-57970-034-9, S26250) Audio-Forum.

Latin Club. 12th ed. Lillian B. Lawler. 73p. (YA). (gr. 9-12). 4.95 (0-939507-08-0, B905) Amer Classical.

***Latin Commentaries on Ovid from the Renaissance.** Ann Moss. LC 98-46745. (Library of Renaissance Humanism). 1998. write for info. (1-893009-02-5) Summertown.

Latin Compositions in the Sixth Fascicle of the Notre-Dame Manuscript Wolfenbuttel 1099, Pt. 1. Gordon A. Anderson. (Wissenschaftliche Abhandlungen-Musicological Studies: Vol. 24). 1981. lib. bdg. 67.00 (0-931902-02-9) Inst Mediaeval Mus.

Latin Compositions in the Sixth Fascicle of the Notre-Dame Manuscript Wolfenbuttel 1099, Pt. 2. Gordon A. Anderson. (Wissenschaftliche Abhandlungen-Musicological Studies: Vol. 24). 1981. lib. bdg. 67.00 (0-931902-03-7) Inst Mediaeval Mus.

Latin Cooking. Lydia Darbyshire. 1999. 12.99 (0-7858-1112-5) Bk Sales Inc.

***Latin Course Part I.** 2nd ed. Maurice Balme & James Morwood. (Oxford Latin Course Ser.). (Illus.). 160p. (C). 1999. text 24.95 (0-19-521550-8) OUP.

***Latin Course Part II.** 2nd ed. Maurice Balme & James Morwood. (Oxford Latin Course Ser.). (Illus.). 176p. (C). 1999. text 24.95 (0-19-521551-6) OUP.

***Latin Course Part III.** 2nd ed. Maurice Balme & James Morwood. (Oxford Latin Course Ser.). (Illus.). 224p. (C). 1999. text 25.95 (0-19-521552-4) OUP.

***Latin Crosswords.** Ed. by Peter Jones & David Dare-Plumpton. 244p. 2000. pap. 10.95 (0-7867-0760-7, Pub. by Carroll & Graf) Publishers Group.

Latin Croswords from Acta Divrna. R. D. Wormald. (C). 1982. pap. text 39.00 (0-900269-23-5, Pub. by Old Vicarage) St Mut.

Latin Culture & Medieval Germanic Europe: Proceedings from the First Germania Latina Conference Held at the University of Groningen, 26 May 1989. Ed. by Richard North & Tette Hofstra. LC 95-103216. (Mediaevalia Groningana Ser.: No. 11). 128p. 1992. pap. 34.00 (90-6980-059-4, Pub. by Egbert Forsten) Hod1der & Stoughton.

An Asterisk (*) at the beginning of an entry indicates that the title is appearing for the first time.

Latin-Dansk Rode Ordboger (Latin-Danish Dictionary) 7th ed. Thure Hastrup. 1983. 49.95 (*0-7859-3728-5*) Fr & Eur.

Latin de Gregoire de Tours. Max Bonnet. viii, 787p. 1968. reprint ed. 160.00 (*0-318-71079-X*) G Olms Pubs.

Latin Deli: Prose & Poetry. Judith O. Cofer. LC 92-44782. 172p. 1993. 22.95 (*0-8203-1556-7*) U of Ga Pr.

Latin Deli: Telling the Lives of Barrio Women. Judith O. Cofer. 182p. 1995. pap. 11.00 (*0-393-31313-1*, Norton Paperbks) Norton.

Latin d'Espagne d'Apres les Inscriptions. Albert J. Carnoy. 293p. 1983. reprint ed. 65.00 (*3-487-03384-4*) G Olms Pubs.

Latin Dictionary. A. Wilson. (ENG & LAT.). 320p. 1995. pap. 9.95 (*0-8442-3812-0*, Teach Yrslf) NTC Contemp Pub Co.

Latin Dictionary: Founded on Andrews Edition of Freund's Latin Dictionary. Charlton T. Lewis & Charles Short. (LAT.). 2,024p. 1956. text 175.00 (*0-19-864201-6*) OUP.

Latin Diminutives in -Ello-a & -Illo-a: A Study in Diminutive Formation. George K. Strodach. (LD Ser.: No. 14). 1933. pap. 25.00 (*0-527-00760-9*) Periodicals Srv.

Latin-English & English-Latin Dictionary. D. A. Kidd. (ENG & LAT.). 43.95 (*0-87557-050-X*) Saphrograph.

Latin-English & English-Latin Dictionary. Ed. by S. C. Woodhouse. (Routledge Pocket Dictionaries Ser.). (ENG & LAT.). 496p. (Orig.). 1982. pap. 13.95 (*0-7100-9267-9*, Routledge Thoemms) Routledge.

Latin-English-Chinese Dictionary of Medical Terms. Commercial Press Staff. (CHI, ENG & LAT.). 761p. 1979. 95.00 (*0-8288-4815-7*, M9564) Fr & Eur.

Latin-English Dictionary. 1115p. 1986. 17.95 (*0-8198-4443-8*) Pauline Bks.

Latin Epigraphy. John E. Sandys. 348p. 1974. pap. 25.00 (*0-89005-062-7*) Ares.

Latin-Estonian-Russian Medical Dictionary, Vol. 1. A. Valdes & J. V. Veski. 640p. (C). 1982. 95.00 (*0-7855-6446-2*, Pub. by Collets) St Mut.

Latin-Estonian-Russian Medical Dictionary, Vol. 2. A. Valdes & J. V. Veski. 768p. (C). 1983. 95.00 (*0-7855-5058-5*, Pub. by Collets) St Mut.

Latin-Estonian-Russian Medical Dictionary, Vol. A-N. A. Vales & J. V. Veski. (EST, LAT & RUS.). 640p. 1982. 80.00 (*0-7855-1759-6*, Pub. by Collets) St Mut.

Latin-Estonian-Russian Medical Dictionary, Vol. O-Z. A. Valdes & J. V. Veski. (EST, LAT & RUS.). 768p. 1983. 80.00 (*0-7855-1758-8*, Pub. by Collets) St Mut.

***Latin Fake Book.** 464p. 1999. spiral bd. 35.00 (*0-634-01103-0*) H Leonard.

Latin Fakebook. 160p. (Orig.). 1993. pap. 24.95 (*0-89724-080-4*, FB1962) Wrner Bros.

***Latin Favorites.** 64p. 1999. pap. 8.95 (*0-7935-9817-6*) H Leonard.

***Latin Favorites for Easy Piano.** 80p. 1999. pap. 9.95 (*0-634-00633-9*) H Leonard.

Latin Fiction: Latin Novel in Context. Heinz Hofmann. LC 98-37100. 1999. text. write for info. (*0-415-14721-2*) Routledge.

***Latin Flavors on the Grill.** Douglas Rodriguez & Andrew DiCataldo. (Illus.). 224p. 2000. 39.95 (*1-58008-055-3*) Ten Speed Pr.

Latin for All Occasions. Henry Beard. (Illus.). 128p. 1990. 12.95 (*0-394-58660-3*) Villard Books.

Latin for Americans, Bk. 1. 8th annot. ed. Ullman et al. 1997. teacher ed. write for info. (*0-02-640915-1*) Glencoe.

Latin for Americans, Bk. 2. 8th annot. ed. Ullman et al. 1997. teacher ed. write for info. (*0-02-640923-2*) Glencoe.

Latin for Americans, Bk. 3. 8th annot. ed. Ullman et al. 1997. teacher ed. write for info. (*0-02-640945-3*) Glencoe.

Latin for Americans: Second Book. Berthold L. Ullman. LC 97-147184. x, 530p. 1997. 44.47 (*0-02-640913-5*) Glencoe.

Latin for Beginners. Dorsey P. Salerno. 121p. (YA). (gr. 6-12). 9.25 (*0-939507-09-X*, B13) Amer Classical.

Latin for Beginners. Illus. by John Schakell & Roger Priddy. (Beginners Ser.). 48p. 1995. 8.95 (*0-8442-8632-X*, 8632X, Passprt Bks) NTC Contemp Pub Co.

Latin for Elementary School Students. Robin R. Brooks. 16p. 1991. pap. text 3.05 (*0-939507-23-4*, B8) Amer Classical.

Latin for Even More Occasions (Lingua Latina Multo Pluribus Occasionibus) Henry Beard. 96p. 1991. 13.00 (*0-679-40674-3*) Villard Books.

Latin for Kids: Of All the Gaul. Carole Marsh. (Of All the Gaul Ser.). (Illus.). (J). (gr. 2-10). 1994. 29.95 (*0-935326-17-0*) Gallopade Intl.

Latin for Lawyers. Lazar Emanuel. (Orig.). 1999. pap. text 15.95 (*1-56542-226-0*) E Pub Corp.

Latin for Lawyers: Containing I. A Course in Latin, with Legal Maxims & Phrases As a Basis of Instruction. II. A Collection of over One Thousand Latin Maxims, with English Translations, Explanatory Notes, & Cross-References. III. A Vocabulary of Latin Words, 1915. E. Hilton Jackson. LC 92-74408. viii, 312p. 1995. reprint ed. 50.00 (*0-9630106-4-6*, 307990) Lawbk Exchange.

Latin for People (Latina Pro Populo) Alexander Humez & Nicholas D. Humez. 206p. 1978. pap. 13.95 (*0-316-38149-7*) Little.

Latin for Pigs. Lisa A. Rogak. 1999. pap. 6.95 (*0-452-27540-7*, Plume) Dutton Plume.

Latin for Reading: A Beginner's Textbook with Exercises. rev. ed. Glenn M. Knudsvig et al. 464p. 1986. pap. text 24.95 (*0-472-08064-4*, 08064) U of Mich Pr.

Latin for Reading: A Beginner's Textbook with Exercises. rev. ed. Glenn M. Knudsvig et al. 464p. 1986. teacher ed. 9.95 (*0-472-08071-7*, 08071) U of Mich Pr.

Latin for the Illiterati: Exorcizing the Ghosts of a Dead Language. Jon R. Stone. LC 95-47985. 216p. (C). 1996. 60.00 (*0-415-91774-3*); pap. 17.99 (*0-415-91775-1*) Routledge.

Latin-French Dictionary see Dictionnaire Latin-Francais

Latin Genius. Anatole France, pseud. Ed. by F. Chapman & J. L. May. Tr. by Wilfrid S. Jackson. LC 78-177957. (Essay Index Reprint Ser.). 1977. reprint ed. 23.95 (*0-8369-2497-5*) Ayer.

Latin Glory: Airline Color Schemes of South America. Michael Magnusson. LC 96-139551. (Illus.). 112p. 1995. pap. 21.95 (*0-7603-0024-0*) MBI Pubg.

***Latin Gold.** 24p. 1999. pap. 5.95 (*0-634-00567-7*); pap. 5.95 (*0-634-00568-5*); pap. 5.95 (*0-634-00569-3*); pap. 5.95 (*0-634-00570-7*); pap. 5.95 (*0-634-00571-5*); pap. 5.95 (*0-634-00572-3*); pap. 5.95 (*0-634-00573-1*); pap. 5.95 (*0-634-00574-X*) H Leonard.

Latin Grammar. William G. Hale & Carl D. Buck. LC 65-19660. (Alabama Linguistic & Philological Ser.: Vol. 8). 400p. 1966. pap. text 19.95 (*0-8173-0350-2*) U of Ala Pr.

Latin Grammar. Robert J. Henle. (Henle Latin Ser.). (LAT.). 270p. 1958. pap., per. 9.50 (*0-8294-0112-1*, HLATG) Loyola Pr.

Latin Grammar. Allyson McGill. 1977. pap. text 4.95 (*0-8120-5056-8*) Barron.

Latin Grammar. James Morwood. 256p. 1999. pap. 12.95 (*0-19-860277-4*) OUP.

Latin Grammar. Charles E. Bennett. 288p. (C). 1995. reprint ed. pap. text 15.95 (*0-89341-753-X*) Hollowbrook.

Latin Grammar. rev. ed. B. Gildersleeve & G. Lodge. (Advanced Language Ser.). 560p. 1997. pap. text 33.95 (*1-85399-521-5*, Pub. by Brist Class Pr) Focus Pub-R Pullins.

Latin Grammar: Answer Key. Douglas Wilson & Karen Craig. (Mars Hill Textbook Ser.). 82p. (J). spiral bd. 8.00 (*1-885767-38-2*) Canon Pr ID.

Latin Grammar: Grammar, Vocabularies, & Exercises in Preparation for the Reading of the Missal & Breviary. Cora C. Scanlon & Charles L. Scanlon. Ed. by Newton Thompson. LC 79-112494. 1991. reprint ed. pap. text 16.50 (*0-89555-002-4*) TAN Bks Pubs.

Latin Grammar: Student Edition. rev. ed. Douglas Wilson & Karen Craig. (Mars Hill Textbook Ser.). (J). (gr. 6). student ed., spiral bd. 20.00 (*1-885767-37-4*) Canon Pr ID.

Latin Grammar for Schools & Colleges. George M. Lane. (Notable American Authors Ser.). 1999. reprint ed. lib. bdg. 125.00 (*0-7812-3698-3*) Rprt Serv.

Latin Grammar for Schools & Colleges. rev. ed. George M. Lane. LC 78-107458. reprint ed. 29.50 (*0-404-00634-5*) AMS Pr.

***Latin Grammar 2: Student Edition.** Karen L. Craig. (Mars Hill Textbook Ser.). 250p. (YA). 1999. pap., student ed. 23.00 (*1-885767-61-7*) Canon Pr ID.

***Latin Grammar 2: Student Edition.** Karen L. Craig. (Mars Hill Textbook Ser.). 250p. (YA). (gr. 7). 1999. student ed., spiral bd. 23.00 (*1-885767-60-9*) Canon Pr ID.

Latin Historical Inscriptions. G. McN. Rushforth. xxxii, 144p. 1980. pap. 25.00 (*0-89005-179-8*) Ares.

Latin Historical Inscriptions. G. McN. Rushforth. LC 70-107831. (Select Bibliographies Reprint Ser.). 1977. 21.95 (*0-8369-5196-4*) Ayer.

***Latin Hits.** (E-Z Play Today Ser.: Vol. #266). 64p. 1998. pap. 6.95 (*0-7935-8941-X*) H Leonard.

Latin-Hungarian Concise Dictionary. 9th ed. A. Gyorkossy. (HUN & LAT.). 616p. 1986. 49.95 (*0-8288-1063-X*, M8574) Fr & Eur.

Latin-Hungarian Pocket Dictionary. I. Tegyey. 392p. (C). 1993. pap. 21.00 (*963-05-6096-8*, Pub. by Akade Kiado) St Mut.

Latin Hymns. Adrian Fortescue. (Illus.). 192p. 1994. text 19.95 (*0-912141-13-1*) Roman Cath Bks.

Latin Hymns. Francis A. March. (Notable American Authors Ser.). 1999. reprint ed. lib. bdg. 125.00 (*0-7812-3943-5*) Rprt Serv.

Latin in Motion. Dorsey P. Salerno. 66p. 1991. 14.00 (*0-939507-03-X*, B14) Amer Classical.

Latin in Our Language. P. Barker. 78p. (C). 1993. pap. text 8.95 (*1-85399-376-X*, Pub. by Brist Class Pr) Focus Pub-R Pullins.

Latin in Three Months. (Hugo's Language Courses Ser.: No. 526). 242p. 1939. pap. 9.00 (*0-8226-0526-0*) Littlefield.

***Latin in Use: Amersterdam Studies in the Pragmatics of Latin.** Rodie Risselada. LC 99-192394. (Amsterdam Studies in Classical Philology Ser.: Vol. 8). viii, 120p. 1999. 45.00 (*90-5063-297-1*, Pub. by Gieben) J Benjamins Pubng Co.

Latin Influence on Jazz. Otto Werner. 96p. (C). 1992. pap. text, per. 17.95 (*0-8403-8176-X*, 40817601) Kendall-Hunt.

Latin-inus, -ina, -inus, & -ineus: From Proto-Indo-European to the Romance Languages. Jonathan L. Butler. LC 73-631070. (U. C. Publ. in Linguistics Ser.: Vol. 68). 154p. reprint ed. pap. 47.80 (*0-8357-9633-7*, 201509900092) Bks Demand.

Latin Jammin' pap. 12.95 incl. audio (*0-7935-3450-X*, 00696550); pap. 14.95 incl. audio compact disk (*0-7935-3451-8*, 00696551) H Leonard.

Latin Journey: Cuban & Mexican Immigrants in the United States. Alejandro Portes & Robert L. Bach. LC 83-9292. 432p. 1985. pap. 16.95 (*0-520-05004-5*, Pub. by U CA Pr) Cal Prin Full Svc.

Latin Kingdom of Jerusalem. Claude R. Conder. LC 78-180331. reprint ed. 72.50 (*0-404-56238-8*) AMS Pr.

***Latin Kings Netas Bloods: Apartheid Prisons, Crime & Gangbangas.** Muhammad Morra Abdul-Wahhab. (Illus.). 82p. 1999. pap. 10.00 (*0-9676612-1-8*) Dar Us Salafyh.

Latin Ladles. Douglas Rodriguez. LC 97-31653. (Illus.). 128p. (Orig.). 1998. pap. text 17.95 (*0-89815-851-6*) Ten Speed Pr.

Latin Language. Leonard R. Palmer. LC 87-40564. 384p. 1988. pap. 21.95 (*0-8061-2136-X*) U of Okla Pr.

Latin Laughs: A Production of Plautus' Poenulus. Ed. by John H. Starks, Jr. et al. Tr. by Matthew Panciera et al. 1997. pap. text, teacher ed. 30.00 (*0-86516-347-2*); pap. text, student ed. 18.00 (*0-86516-323-5*) Bolchazy-Carducci.

Latin Learning in Mediaeval Ireland. Mario Esposito. Ed. by Michael Lapidge. (Collected Studies: No. CS285). 336p. (C). 1988. reprint ed. lib. bdg. 117.95 (*0-86078-233-6*, Pub. by Variorum) Ashgate Pub Co.

Latin Letters in Early Christian Ireland. Michael W. Herren. (Collected Studies: CS527). 336p. 1996. text 115.95 (*0-86078-581-5*, Pub. by Variorum) Ashgate Pub Co.

***Latin Letters of C. S. Lewis.** C. S. Lewis & Don G. Calabria. Ed. & Tr. by Martin Moynihan. LC 98-18477. Orig. Title: Letters: A Study in Friendship. (LAT.). 126p. 1998. 18.00 (*1-890318-34-5*) St Augustines Pr.

Latin Literature. Harvard University Library Staff. (Widener Library Shelflist: No. 59). 610p. 1979. text 55.00 (*0-674-51295-2*) HUP.

Latin Literature: A History. Gian B. Conte. Ed. by Glenn W. Most. Tr. by Joseph B. Solodow. LC 93-20985. (C). 1994. 65.00 (*0-8018-4638-2*) Johns Hopkins.

Latin Literature: A History. Gian Biagio Conte. Tr. by Joseph B. Solodow. 864p. 1999. pap. 29.95 (*0-8018-6253-1*) Johns Hopkins.

Latin Literature from Seneca to Juvenal: A Critical Study. G. O. Hutchinson. LC 92-17935. 382p. 1993. text 75.00 (*0-19-814690-6*, Clarendon Pr) OUP.

Latin Literature of the Christian Epoch. Krishna Chaitanya. (C). 1994. text 18.50 (*81-220-0342-7*, Pub. by Konark Pubs) S Asia.

Latin Liturgical Repertories Before the Octoechos: The Romano-Frankish Daily Office. Jean Claire. (Etudes Gregoriennes Ser.: Vol. XV). (FRE.). 110p. (C). reprint ed. pap. 28.95 (*1-55725-035-9*, 4031, Pub. by Abbey St Peter Solesmes) Paraclete MA.

Latin Lives of the Saints. Edmund Hogan. LC 78-72684. (Royal Irish Academy. Todd Lecture Ser.: Vol. 5). reprint ed. 21.50 (*0-404-60565-6*) AMS Pr.

Latin Love Elegy. Ed. by R. Maltby. 151p. 1980. pap. 16.95 (*0-906515-01-7*, Pub. by Brist Class Pr) Focus Pub-R Pullins.

Latin Love Elegy. Ed. by R. Maltby. vi, 143p. 1991. reprint ed. 14.00 (*0-86516-061-9*) Bolchazy-Carducci.

***Latin Lovers: True Stories of Latin Men in Love.** Erasmo Guerra. LC 99-41478. 200p. 1999. pap. text 15.95 (*1-891305-13-1*) Painted Leaf.

***Latin Lullaby.** Ellipsis Arts Staff. 1998. 15.95 (*1-55961-475-7*, Ellipsis Arts) Relaxtn Co.

Latin Lyric & Elegiac Poetry: An Anthology of New Translations. Ed. by Diane J. Rayor & William W. Batstone. LC 94-37902. 384p. 1995. text 70.00 (*0-8153-0087-5*, H1425); pap. text 26.95 (*0-8153-1540-6*, H1425) Garland.

Latin Made Simple. rev. ed. Rhoda Hendricks. 288p. 1992. pap. 12.95 (*0-385-41339-4*) Doubleday.

Latin Manuscript Books Before 1600: A List of the Printed Catalogues & Unpublished Inventories of Extant Collections. 3rd ed. Paul O. Kristeller. LC 66-3585. 311p. reprint ed. pap. 96.50 (*0-7837-5608-9*, 204551400005) Bks Demand.

Latin Masks of Ezra Pound. Ronald E. Thomas. LC 83-5734. (Studies in Modern Literature: No. 4). (Illus.). 196p. reprint ed. pap. 60.80 (*0-8357-1407-1*, 207044600091) Bks Demand.

Latin Mass Revival. 144p. 1996. pap. 25.95 (*0-912141-45-X*) Roman Cath Bks.

***Latin Metre.** D. S. Raven. (Advanced Language Ser.). 124p. (C). 1998. pap. text 27.95 (*1-85399-564-9*, Pub. by Brist Class Pr) Focus Pub-R Pullins.

Latin Mission for the 21st Century see Misiones Latinas para el Siglo XXI

Latin Monasticism in Norman Sicily. L. T. White, Jr. (Medieval Academy Bks.: No. 31). 1967. reprint ed. 25.00 (*0-910956-12-X*) Medieval Acad.

Latin Moon in Manhattan. Jaime Manrique. LC 92-40802. 1993. pap. 9.95 (*0-312-08835-3*) St Martin.

Latin Motet: Indices to Printed Collections, 1500-1600. Harry B. Lincoln. (Wissenschaftliche Abhandlungen-Musicological Studies: Vol. 59). xii, 835p. 1993. lib. bdg. 220.00 (*0-931902-80-0*) Inst Mediaeval Mus.

Latin Music Collection. Warner Brothers Staff. 1995. pap. 19.95 (*0-89724-750-7*, MF9540) Wrner Bros.

Latin Music Handbook. Andrew A. Aros. LC 78-59987. (Illus.). 1978. pap. 6.50 (*0-932352-00-6*) Applause Pubns.

Latin Music Through the Ages. Cynthia Kaldis. 87p. 1991. pap. 15.00 (*0-86516-242-5*) Bolchazy-Carducci.

Latin Music through the Ages. Perf. by Larayette Chamber Singers. 87p. audio 15.00 (*0-86516-249-2*) Bolchazy-Carducci.

Latin Music Yearbook, 1980. Andrew A. Aros. (Vinyl Gold Ser.: No. 2). (Orig.). 1980. pap. 6.50 (*0-932352-02-2*) Applause Pubns.

Latin Mystique: Les Poetes de l'Antiphonaire et la Symbolique au Moyen Age. Remy De Gourmont. LC 77-10268. 400p. reprint ed. 57.50 (*0-404-16320-3*) AMS Pr.

Latin Names Explained: A Guide to the Scientific Classification of Reptiles, Birds, & Mammals. A. F. Gotch. LC 95-61608. (Illus.). 736p. 1996. 55.00 (*0-8160-3377-3*) Facts on File.

Latin Nights, Bk. 4. Elizabeth M. Rees. (Heart Beats Ser.: Bk. 4). 192p. (J). (gr. 4-8). 1998. mass mkt. 3.99 (*0-689-81951-X*) S&S Childrens.

Latin '98: Theoretical Informatics: Third Latin American Symposium, Campinas, Brazil, April 20-24, 1998. Ed. by C. L. Lucchesi et al. LC 98-3115. (Lecture Notes in Computer Science: Vol. 1380). xi, 391p. 1998. pap. 67.00 (*3-540-64275-7*) Spr-Verlag.

Latin '95: Theoretical Informatics: Proceedings of the Second Latin American Symposium, Valpariso, Chile, April 17-21, 1995. Ed. by Ricardo Baez-Yates et al. LC 95-10547. (Lecture Notes in Computer Science Ser.: Vol. 911). 1995. write for info. (*0-387-59175-3*) Spr-Verlag.

***Latin Odes of Jean Dorat.** Jean Dorat & David R. Slavitt. LC 00-21664. 96p. 2000. 20.00 (*0-914061-80-1*) Orchises Pr.

Latin Palaeography: Antiquity & the Middle Ages. Bernhard Bischoff. 303p. (C). 1990. text 80.00 (*0-521-36473-6*) Cambridge U Pr.

Latin Palaeography: Antiquity & the Middle Ages. Bernhard Bischoff. 303p. (C). 1990. pap. text 27.95 (*0-521-36726-3*) Cambridge U Pr.

Latin Parens, Its Meanings & Uses. Merle M. Odgers. (Language Dissertations Ser.: No. 3). 1928. pap. 25.00 (*0-527-00749-8*) Periodicals Srv.

Latin Passages for Translation & Comprehension. 48p. 1981. pap. text 10.95 (*0-521-28355-8*) Cambridge U Pr.

Latin Percussion in Perspective. Dominick Moio. 64p. 1997. pap. 19.95 incl. audio compact disk (*0-7866-2870-7*, 96682BCD) Mel Bay.

Latin Perfect Endings -ere & -erunt. C. F. Bauer. (LD Ser.: Vol. 13). 1933. pap. 25.00 (*0-527-00759-5*) Periodicals Srv.

Latin Phrase Book. C. Meissner. 347p. (C). 1992. pap. text 25.95 (*0-7156-1470-3*, Pub. by G Duckworth) Focus Pub-R Pullins.

Latin Phrase Book. C. Meissner. Tr. by H. W. Auden from GER. 338p. 1989. reprint ed. pap. text 15.95 (*0-89341-567-7*, Longwood Academic) Hollowbrook.

Latin Phrasebook. C. Messiner. Tr. by H. W. Auden. 338p. 1998. reprint ed. pap. 14.95 (*0-7818-0666-6*) Hippocrene Bks.

Latin Phrases & Quotations. Richard Branyon. LC 96-38585. 180p. 1997. reprint ed. pap. 14.95 (*0-7818-0260-1*) Hippocrene Bks.

Latin Plus. Douglas Lacey. 1986. student ed. 12.50 (*0-89894-020-6*); student ed. 12.50 (*0-685-11183-0*); student ed. 12.95 (*0-89894-021-4*); pap. text 12.50 (*0-89894-018-4*) Advocate Pub Group.

Latin Poems Commonly Attributed to Walter Mapes. Walter Map. Ed. by Thomas Wright. (Camden Society, London. Publications, First Ser.: No. 16). reprint ed. 95.00 (*0-404-50116-8*) AMS Pr.

Latin Poems Commonly Attributed to Walter Mapes. Thomas Wright. 401p. reprint ed. lib. bdg. 63.70 (*0-685-13789-9*, 05101837) G Olms Pubs.

Latin Poems of John Milton. John Milton. (BCL1-PR English Literature Ser.). 382p. 1992. reprint ed. lib. bdg. 89.00 (*0-7812-7377-3*) Rprt Serv.

Latin Poems of Richard Ledrede, OFM, Bishop of Ossory, 1317-1360. Ed. by Edmund Colledge. 164p. text 29.14 (*0-88844-030-8*) Brill Academic Pubs.

Latin Poetic Irony in the Roman de la Rose, v. Marc M. Pelen. LC 87-10242. (Vinaver Studies in French). 1987. write for info. (*0-905205-32-4*) F Cairns Pubns.

Latin Poetry. Richard A. LaFleur. 1987. teacher ed. 28.00 (*0-8013-0140-8*, 75804); pap. text 12.57 (*0-8013-0133-5*, 75797) Longman.

Latin Poetry. VARR. (J). Date not set. pap. 50.24 (*0-669-33266-6*) HM.

Latin Poetry of George Herbert: A Bilingual Edition. George Herbert. Tr. by Mark McCloskey & Paul R. Murphy. LC 64-22888. (ENG & LAT.). 181p. 1965. 32.50 (*0-8290-0018-6*); pap. text 12.95 (*0-8290-0380-0*) Irvington.

Latin Poets & Roman Life. Jasper Griffin. 240p. 1994. pap. 25.95 (*1-85399-430-8*, Pub. by Brist Class Pr) Focus Pub-R Pullins.

Latin Poets & Roman Life. Jasper Griffin. LC 85-16534. ix, 226p. 1986. 39.95 (*0-8078-1682-5*) U of NC Pr.

Latin Poets & Roman Life. Jasper Griffin. LC 85-16534. 240p. 1986. reprint ed. pap. 74.40 (*0-7837-9039-2*, 204979000003) Bks Demand.

Latin Pops Easy Piano Brimhall. 56p. 1996. pap. 10.95 (*1-57623-750-8*, AF9693) Wrner Bros.

***Latin Primer II Teacher's Packet.** Julie M. Garfield. (Latin Primer Ser.). 48p. (J). 2000. spiral bd. 15.00 (*1-930443-07-2*, C227, Pub. by Logos Schl) Canon Pr ID.

Latin Primer I: Student Edition. large type ed. Martha Wilson. (Mars Hill Textbook Ser.). 118p. 1992. student ed., spiral bd. 15.00 (*1-885767-41-2*, N-101) Canon Pr ID.

Latin Primer I: Teacher Edition. large type ed. Martha Wilson. (Mars Hill Textbook Ser.). 122p. 1992. teacher ed., spiral bd. 15.00 (*1-885767-42-0*, N-102) Canon Pr ID.

***Latin Primer I: Teacher's Packet.** Julie Garfield. 104p. (J). (gr. 3-4). 1999. teacher ed., spiral bd. 15.00 (*1-930443-05-6*, C187, Pub. by Logos Schl) Veritas Pr PA.

Latin Primer III: Student Edition. Martha Wilson. (Mars Hill Textbook Ser.). 254p. (J). (gr. 5). student ed., spiral bd. 18.00 (*1-885767-32-3*) Canon Pr ID.

Latin Primer III: Teacher Edition. Martha Wilson. (Mars Hill Textbook Ser.). 254p. teacher ed., spiral bd. 18.00 (*1-885767-33-1*) Canon Pr ID.

Latin Primer II: Student Edition. large type ed. Martha Wilson. (Mars Hill Textbook Ser.). 136p. 1992. student ed., spiral bd. 15.00 (*1-885767-43-9*, N-103) Canon Pr ID.

An Asterisk (*) at the beginning of an entry indicates that the title is appearing for the first time.

Latin Primer II: Teacher Edition. large type ed. Martha Wilson. (Mars Hill Textbook Ser.). 156p. 1992. spiral bd. 15.00 (*1-885767-44-7*, N-104) Canon Pr ID.

Latin Pronunciation. George M. Lane. (Notable American Authors Ser.). 1999. reprint ed. lib. bdg. 125.00 (*0-7812-3697-5*) Rprt Serv.

Latin Pronunciation. Harry T. Peck. (Notable American Authors Ser.). 1999. reprint ed. lib. bdg. 125.00 (*0-7812-8716-2*) Rprt Serv.

Latin Prose Composition. Ed. by North & Hillard. LC 96-137203. (LAT.). 310p. (Orig.). (C). 1988. pap. 20.00 (*0-86516-308-1*) Bolchazy-Carducci.

***Latin Prose Composition.** M. A. North & A. E. Hillard. (Classical Reprints Ser.). 320p. (Orig.). (C). 1999. reprint ed. pap. text 20.95 (*0-941051-91-9*) Focus Pub-R Pullins.

Latin Prose Composition. M. A. North & A. E. Hillard. LC 89-2646. 300p. (Orig.). 1989. reprint ed. pap. text 15.95 (*0-89341-568-5*, Longwood Academic) Hollowbrook.

Latin Prose Rhythm: A New Method of Investigation. H. D. Broadhead. (C). 1995. reprint ed. pap. text 14.95 (*0-89341-755-6*) Hollowbrook.

Latin Punctuation in the Classical Age. E. Otha Wingo. (Janua Linguarum, Ser. Practica: No. 133). 166p. 1972. pap. text 55.40 (*90-279-2323-X*) Mouton.

Latin-Quarter Courtship: And Other Stories. Henry Harland. LC 70-178439. (Short Story Index Reprint Ser.). 1977. reprint ed. 20.95 (*0-8369-4040-7*) Ayer.

Latin Reader for Colleges. Harry L. Levy. LC 62-18119. 1962. pap. text 9.00 (*0-226-47602-2*) U Ch Pr.

Latin Reader for Colleges. Harry L. Levy. LC 62-18119. (Midway Reprint Ser.). xii, 276p. 1989. reprint ed. pap. text 17.95 (*0-226-47601-4*) U Ch Pr.

Latin Readings. Ed. by Gertrude Drake. 112p. 1984. pap. 13.00 (*0-86516-044-9*) Bolchazy-Carducci.

Latin Readings: Teacher's Manual. Ed. by Gertrude Drake. 112p. 1984. pap., teacher ed. 8.00 (*0-86516-043-0*) Bolchazy-Carducci.

Latin Readings in the History of Medicine. Robert J. Smutny. (ENG & LAT.). 456p. (Orig.). (C). 1994. pap. text 39.00 (*0-8191-9766-1*) U Pr of Amer.

***Latin Real Book.** (Orig.). 1999. pap. 40.00 (*0-634-00692-4*); pap. 40.00 (*0-634-00693-2*) H Leonard.

Latin Real Book. 572p. (Orig.). 1997. pap. 40.00 (*1-883217-05-9*, 28) Sher Music.

Latin Roots & Their Modern English Spelling. Raymond E. Laurita. 500p. 2000. pap. 24.95 (*0-914051-41-5*) Leonardo Pr.

Latin Sans Peine. Albert O. Cherel. 24.95 (*0-685-11288-8*); audio 125.00 (*0-685-01739-7*) Fr & Eur.

Latin sans Peine: Latin for French Speakers. Assimil Staff. (FRE & LAT.). 28.95 (*0-8288-4390-2*, F14190) Fr & Eur.

Latin Satins. Terri De la Pena. LC 94-15169. 220p. (Orig.). 1994. pap. 10.95 (*1-878067-52-4*) Seal Pr WA.

Latin Selections (Florilegium Latinum) A Dual-Language Book. Moses Hadas & Thomas Suits. xviii, 284p. 1992. reprint ed. pap. 9.95 (*0-486-27059-9*) Dover.

***Latin Sensations.** Herbon Marquez. LC 00-8876. 2000. pap. write for info. (*0-8225-9695-4*) Lerner Pub.

Latin Sentence & Idiom: A Composition Course. R. Colebourn. 292p. 1987. reprint ed. 25.95 (*0-86292-265-8*, Pub. by Brist Class Pr) Focus Pub-R Pullins.

Latin Sexual Vocabulary. James N. Adams. LC 90-4697. 284p. 1990. reprint ed. pap. text 19.95 (*0-8018-4106-2*) Johns Hopkins.

Latin Siege Warfare in the Twelfth Century. R. Rogers. (Oxford Historicals Monographs). (Illus.). 304p. 1997. pap. text 21.00 (*0-19-820689-5*) OUP.

***Latin Songs.** Hal Leonard Publishing Company Staff. (Paperback Songs Ser.). (LAT.). 256p. 2000. pap. 6.95 (*0-634-01751-9*) H Leonard.

Latin Squares: New Developments in the Theory & Applications. J. Denes & A. D. Keedwell. (Annals of Discrete Mathematics Ser.: No. 46). 454p. 1991. 169.50 (*0-444-88899-3*, North Holland) Elsevier.

Latin, Sr. H. S. Jack Rudman. (Teachers License Examination Ser.: T-37). 1994. pap. 27.95 (*0-8373-8037-5*) Nat Learn.

Latin Studies in Groningen, 1877-1977. Ed. by Heinz Hofmann. x, 145p. (Orig.). 1991. pap. 30.00 (*90-6980-039-X*, Pub. by Egbert Forsten) Hodlder & Stoughton.

Latin Study Aid. Charles W. DaParma et al. (J). 1987. pap. 2.75 (*0-87738-035-X*) Youth Ed.

Latin-Swedish Dictionary (Latinsk-Svensk Ordbok) 4th ed. A. W. Ahlberg & N. Lundquist. (LAT & SWE.). 941p. 1982. 125.00 (*0-8288-1068-0*, M2818) Fr & Eur.

Latin Text of the Ancrene Riwle from Merton College MS 44 & British Museum MS Cotton Vitellius E.vii. Ed. by C. D'Evelyn. (EETS Original Ser.: Vol. 216). 1963. reprint ed. 30.00 (*0-19-722216-1*, Pub. by EETS) Boydell & Brewer.

Latin Texts & Commentaries Series, 30 bks., Set. Ed. by W. R. Connor. (Illus.). 1979. lib. bdg. 940.00 (*0-405-11594-6*) Ayer.

Latin Texts from the Fourth to the Fifteenth Centuries. Ed. by Louis Roberts. (Sources for the History of Cyprus Ser.: Vol. VIII). 300p. 1999. pap. 70.00 (*0-9651704-8-9*) Greece & Cyprus Res.

Latin Textual Criticism. James A. Willis. LC 71-106601. (Illinois Studies in Language & Literature: Vol. 61). 247p. reprint ed. pap. 76.60 (*0-608-13987-4*, 202226900026) Bks Demand.

Latin Textual Criticism in Antiquity. rev. ed. James E. Zetzel. Ed. by W. R. Connor. LC 80-2673. (Monographs in Classical Studies). 1981. lib. bdg. 38.95 (*0-405-14056-8*) Ayer.

Latin, the Language of the Health Sciences. Rudolph Masciantonio. (Illus.). 42p. (J). (gr. 7-12). 1992. spiral bd. 4.05 (*0-939507-43-9*, B313) Amer Classical.

Latin Thematic Genitive Singular. Andrew M. Devine. 136p. (Orig.). 1972. reprint ed. pap. 56.50 (*0-915838-60-5*) Anma Libri.

Latin Tinge: The Impact of Latin American Music on the United States. John S. Roberts. LC 78-26543. (Illus.). 246p. 1985. pap. 12.95 (*0-9614458-1-5*) Original Music.

Latin Tinge: The Impact of Latin American Music on the United States. 2nd ed. John Storm Roberts. LC 98-19580. (Illus.). 304p. 1999. pap. 14.95 (*0-19-512101-5*) OUP.

Latin to Finnish Dictionary. 4th ed. Frederick J. Streng. (FIN & LAT.). 858p. 1992. 90.00 (*0-320-00077-X*) Fr & Eur.

Latin to Greek Wortschatz In der Medizin. 4th ed. Ilse Becher. (GRE & LAT.). 255p. 1995. 69.95 (*0-320-00554-2*) Fr & Eur.

***Latin Treatises on Poetry from Renaissance England.** J. W. Binns et al. LC 99-44198. (Library of Renaissance Humanism: Vol. 6). 1999. lib. bdg. 45.00 (*1-893009-03-3*) Summertown.

***Latin 2000: Theoretical Informatics: Fourth Latin American Symposium Punta del Esk, Uruguay, April 10-14, 2000, Proceedings.** Latin American Symposium on Theoretical Informatics Staff. Ed. by G. H. Gonnet et al. LC 00-35819. (Lecture Notes in Computer Science Ser.: Vol. 1776). xiv, 484p. 2000. pap. 73.00 (*3-540-67306-7*) Spr-Verlag.

Latin Verses in Confessio Amantis: An Annotated Translation. Sian Echard. Tr. by Claire Fanger. (Medieval Texts & Studies: No. 7). 95p. 1991. text 32.00 (*0-937191-19-1*) Mich St U Pr.

Latin Via Ovid: A First Course. 2nd ed. Norman Goldman & Jacob E. Neuhuis. LC 82-72266. (Illus.). 524p. 1997. 19.95 (*0-8143-1732-4*) Wayne St U Pr.

Latin Violin: How to Play Charanga, Salsa & Latin Jazz Violin. Sam Bardfeld. 1999. pap. 25.00 incl. audio compact disk (*0-9628467-7-5*, Pub. by Gerard Sarzin Pub) Music Sales.

***Latin Vulgate Bible.** Latin Vulgate Staff. (LAT.). 2000. 105.98 (*1-58516-085-7*) Am Bible.

Latin Word Lists. John K. Colby. (C). 1978. pap. text 3.95 (*0-88334-097-6*) Longman.

Latin Workbook for Beginning Students. Donna Gerard. (Illus.). 89p. (YA). 1993. spiral bd., wbk. ed. 12.00 (*0-939507-44-7*, B26) Amer Classical.

Latin Writings: A Selection. John Milton. Ed. & Tr. by John K. Hale. LC 98-52891. (Medieval & Renaissance Texts & Studies: No. 191). (ENG & LAT.). 264p. 1998. 26.00 (*0-86698-233-7*, MR191) MRTS.

Latin Writings of John Wyclyf: An Annotated Catalogue. Williell R. Thomson. xxii, 352p. pap. 39.43 (*0-88844-363-3*) Brill Academic Pubs.

Latin Writings of the Italian Humanists. Ed. by Florence A. Gragg. (College Classical Ser.). xxxvi, 434p. (gr. 11-12). 1981. reprint ed. pap. text 20.00 (*0-89241-110-4*); reprint ed. lib. bdg. 35.00 (*0-89241-356-5*) Caratzas.

Latin '92. Ed. by I. Simon et al. (Lecture Notes in Computer Science Ser.: Vol. 583). 545p. 1992. 82.95 (*0-387-55284-7*) Spr-Verlag.

Latin '95: Theoretical Informatics: Second Latin American Symposium, Valparaiso, Chile, April 17-21, 1995. Proceedings. Ed. by Eric Goles et al. (Lecture Notes in Computer Science Ser.: Vol. 911). ix, 525p. 1995. 81.00 (*3-540-59175-3*) Spr-Verlag.

Latina: Women's Voices from the Borderlands. Ed. by Lillian Castillo-Speed. 288p. 1995. per. 13.00 (*0-684-80240-6*) S&S Trade Pap.

Latina Adolescent Childbearing in East Los Angeles. Pamela I. Erickson. LC 97-30037. 216p. (C). 1998. 27.50 (*0-292-72093-9*, ERILAT); pap. 14.95 (*0-292-72094-7*, ERILAP) U of Tex Pr.

Latina & Latino Voices in Literature for Children & Teenagers. Frances A. Day. LC 96-44895. 228p. 1997. pap. text 28.00 (*0-435-07202-1*, 07202) Heinemann.

***Latina Beauty: A Get - Gorgeous Guide For Every Mujer.** Belen Aranda-Alvarad. (Illus.). 224p. 2000. 29.95 (*0-7868-6669-1*, Pub. by Hyperion) Time Warner.

***Latina in the Land of Hollywood & Other Essays on Media Culture.** Angharad N. Valdivia. LC 99-6622. 210p. 2000. 17.95 (*0-8165-1935-8*) U of Ariz Pr.

Latina Issues: Fragments of Historia(elle) (Her story) Ed. by Antoinette S. Lopez. LC 99-29040. (Paperback Ser.). 442p. 1999. reprint ed. pap. 24.95 (*0-8153-3406-0*) Garland.

Latina Issues: Fragments of Historia(elle) (Herstory) Ed. by Antoinette S. Lopez. LC 94-34157. (Latinos in the United States Ser.: Vol. 2). (Illus.). 456p. 1995. text 88.00 (*0-8153-1771-9*) Garland.

Latina Lite Cooking: 200 Delicious Lowfat Recipes from All over the Americas. Maria D. Beatriz. LC 97-27741. 432p. (Orig.). 1998. mass mkt. 9.99 (*0-446-67297-1*, Pub. by Warner Bks) Little.

Latina Performance: Traversing the Stage. Alicia Arrizon. LC 99-11577. (Illus.). 272p. 1999. text 39.95 (*0-253-33508-6*) Ind U Pr.

***Latina Performance: Traversing the Stage.** Alicia Arrizon. LC 99-11577. (Unnatural Acts Ser.). (Illus.). 218p. 1999. pap. 18.95 (*0-253-21285-5*) Ind U Pr.

Latina Politics, Latino Politics: Gender, Culture, & Political Participation in Boston. Carol Hardy-Fanta. LC 92-27093. 288p. 1993. 59.95 (*1-56639-031-1*); pap. 22.95 (*1-56639-032-X*) Temple U Pr.

Latina Realities: Essays on Healing, Migration & Sexuality. Oliva Espin. LC 97-20925. (New Directions in Theory & Psychology Ser.). 224p. 1997. text 69.00 (*0-8133-3233-8*, Pub. by Westview) HarpC.

Latina Realities: Essays on Healing, Migration & Sexuality. Oliva Espin. LC 97-20925. (New Directions in Theory & Psychology Ser.). 224p. (C). 1997. pap. text 22.00 (*0-8133-3234-6*, Pub. by Westview) HarpC.

***Latina Self-Portraits: Interviews with Contemporary Women Writers.** Ed. by Bridget A. Kevane & Juanita Heredia. LC 99-50785. 166p. 2000. 45.00 (*0-8263-1971-8*); pap. 19.95 (*0-8263-1972-6*) U of NM Pr.

Latina Vivit! A Guide to Lively Latin Classes. 2nd ed. Linda R. McCrae. LC 96-135973. (ENG & LAT., Illus.). 149p. (Orig.). 1995. reprint ed. pap. text 20.00 (*0-86516-273-5*) Bolchazy-Carducci.

Latinam Poetry see Antologia de la Poesia Latinoamericana

Latinamericanos: El Mundo de Pablo Neruda & el Mundo Imaginario de Jorge Luis Borges. Reve Tamayo et al. Ed. by Lucinda M. Phillips. (SPA., Illus.). 156p. (Orig.). 1987. pap. 16.50 (*0-9618899-1-8*) R T Enterprises.

***Latinas! Women of Achievement.** Ed. by Diane Telgen & Jim Kamp. (Illus.). 405p. 2000. reprint ed. pap. text 19.00 (*0-7881-9034-2*) DIANE Pub.

Latinas in the United States: Social, Economic, & Political Aspects: A Bibliography. Ed. by Joan Nordquist. LC 96-199935. (Contemporary Social Issues: A Bibliography Ser.: No. 40). 72p. (Orig.). (C). 1995. pap. 20.00 (*0-937855-78-2*) Ref Rsch Serv.

Latine Cantemus. Tr. & Illus. by Franz Schlosser. (LAT.). vii, 135p. (Orig.). 1996. pap. 15.00 (*0-86516-315-4*) Bolchazy-Carducci.

Latine Grammar of P. Ramus. Pierre D. La Ramee. LC 78-26236. (English Experience Ser.: No. 289). 1971. reprint ed. 25.00 (*90-221-0289-0*) Walter J Johnson.

Latinity & Literary Society at Rome. W. Martin Bloomer. LC 96-45632. 336p. 1997. text 39.95 (*0-8122-3390-5*) U of Pa Pr.

Latinization of the U. S. Gonzalez. 1999. write for info. (*0-201-40759-0*) Addison-Wesley.

Latino America: Photographs by Cecilia Arboleda. Alison D. Nordstrom. 12p. 1993. pap. text 12.00 (*1-887040-05-6*) SE Mus Photo.

Latino Art & Culture in the United States. (Illus.). 75p. (YA). (gr. 6 up). 1996. 85.00 incl. VHS, sl. (*1-56290-166-4*, 6053) Crystal.

Latino College Students. Ed. by Michael A. Olivas. LC 86-5697. (Bilingual Education Ser.). 384p. reprint ed. pap. 119.10 (*0-608-08642-8*, 206916500003) Bks Demand.

Latino Communication Patterns. Daniel F. Duran. Ed. by Carlos E. Cortes. LC 79-6203. (Hispanics in the United States Ser.). (Illus.). 1981. lib. bdg. 55.95 (*0-405-13154-2*) Ayer.

Latino Cultural Citizenship: Claiming Identity, Space & Rights. Ed. by William Flores & Rina Benmayor. LC 97-5518. 280p. 1997. 27.50 (*0-8070-4634-5*) Beacon Pr.

Latino Cultural Citizenship: Claiming Identity, Space & Rights. Ed. by William Flores & Rina Benmayor. 1998. pap. 15.00 (*0-8070-4635-3*) Beacon Pr.

Latino Elders & the Twenty-First Century: Issues & Challenges for Culturally Competent Research & Practice. Ed. by Melvin Delgado. LC 98-51288. 251p. 1998. 49.95 (*0-7890-0657-X*) Haworth Pr.

Latino Employment, Labor Organizations, & Immigration. Ed. by Antoinette S. Lopez. LC 94-33597. (Latinos in the United States Ser.: Vol. 4). 416p. 1994. text 88.00 (*0-8153-1773-5*) Garland.

Latino Empowerment: Progress, Problems, & Prospects, 23. Ed. by Roberto E. Villarreal et al. LC 88-15492. (Contributions in Ethnic Studies: No. 23). 176p. 1988. 47.95 (*0-313-26347-7*, VLP/, Greenwood Pr) Greenwood.

Latino Ethnic Consciousness: The Case of Mexican Americans & Puerto Ricans in Chicago. Felix M. Padilla. LC 85-8576. 196p. 1986. pap. 14.00 (*0-268-01275-X*); text 29.00 (*0-268-01274-1*) U of Notre Dame Pr.

Latino Families in Therapy: A Guide to Multicultural Practice. Celia J. Falicov. LC 98-2636. 303p. 1998. lib. bdg. 32.00 (*1-57230-364-6*) Guilford Pubns.

***Latino Families in Therapy: A Guide to Multicultural Practice.** Celia J. Falicov. (Family Therapy Ser.). 303p. 2000. pap. 19.95 (*1-57230-593-2*) Guilford Pubns.

Latino Family & the Politics of Transformation. David T. Abalos. LC 93-19612. (Praeger Series in Transformational Politics & Political Science). 192p. 1993. 55.00 (*0-275-94527-8*, Praeger Pubs) Greenwood.

Latino Family & the Politics of Transformation. David T. Ablos. LC 93-19612. (Series in Transformational Politics & Political Science). 152p. 1993. pap. 19.95 (*0-275-94809-9*, Praeger Pubs) Greenwood.

Latino Fiction & the Modernist Imagination: Literature of the Borderlands. John S. Christie. LC 98-31294. (Latino Communities Ser.). 224p. 1998. 53.00 (*0-8153-3246-7*) Garland.

Latino Folk Illness. L. M. Pachter. 110p. 1993. pap. text 82.00 (*2-88124-636-2*) Gordon & Breach.

Latino Gay Men & HIV: Culture, Sexuality & Risk Behavior. Rafael M. Diaz. LC 97-23167. 208p. (C). 1997. pap. 18.99 (*0-415-91388-8*) Routledge.

Latino Gay Men & HIV: Culture, Sexuality & Risk Behavior. Rafael M. Diaz. LC 97-23167. 208p. (C). 1997. 75.00 (*0-415-91387-X*) Routledge.

Latino Guide to Personal Money Management. Laura Castaneda & Laura Castellanos. LC 99-13522. (Illus.). 311p. 1999. pap. 16.95 (*1-57660-058-0*, Pub. by Bloomberg NJ) Norton.

Latino Health in the U. S. A Growing Challenge. Ed. by Carlos W. Molina & Marilyn Aguirre-Molina. LC 96-147979. 513p. 1994. pap. 42.50 (*0-87553-215-2*) Am Pub Health.

Latino Heretics. Tony Diaz. 213p. 1999. pap. 12.95 (*1-57366-077-9*, Pub. by Fiction Coll) SPD-Small Pr Dist.

Latino Heritage: A Guide to Juvenile Books about Latino People & Cultures. Isabel Schon. LC 95-32165. (Latino Heritage Ser.: No. 5). 210p. 1995. 34.50 (*0-8108-3057-4*) Scarecrow.

Latino High School Graduation: Defying the Odds. Harriet D. Romo & Toni Falbo. LC 95-16645. (Hogg Foundation Ser.). (Illus.). (C). 1996. pap. 17.95 (*0-292-72495-0*); text 37.50 (*0-292-72494-2*) U of Tex Pr.

***Latino Holiday Book: From Cinco de Mayo to Dia de los Muertos - The Celebrations & Traditions of Hispanic-Americans.** Valerie Menard. 240p. 2000. pap. 15.95 (*1-56924-646-7*) Marlowe & Co.

Latino Homicide. Martinex. 2000. 75.00 (*0-8133-6801-4*) HarpC.

Latino Immigrant Youth: Passages from Adolescence to Adulthood. Timothy Ready. LC 91-19038. (Studies in Education & Culture: Vol. 5). 282p. 1991. text 46.00 (*0-8153-0057-3*, SS728) Garland.

Latino Language & Communicative Behavior. Ed. by Richard P. Duran. (Advances in Discourse Processes Ser.: Vol. 6). 384p. 1981. pap. 42.50 (*0-89391-093-7*); text 78.50 (*0-89391-038-4*) Ablx Pub.

Latino Language & Education: Communication & the Dream Deferred. Ed. by Antoinette S. Lopez. LC 94-36776. (Latinos in the United States Ser.: Vol. 5). (Illus.). 440p. 1995. reprint ed. text 88.00 (*0-8153-1774-3*) Garland.

Latino Literacy: The Complete Guide to Hispanic American Culture & History. Frank De Varona. 384p. 1995. 30.00 (*0-8050-3858-2*); pap. 16.95 (*0-8050-3859-0*) H Holt & Co.

Latino Literacy: The Complete Guide to Hispanic American Culture & History. Frank De Varona. (Illus.). 192p. 1996. pap. 22.50 (*0-8050-5031-0*) H Holt & Co.

Latino Looks: Images of Latinas & Latinos in the U. S. Media. Ed. by Clara E. Rodriguez. LC 97-1840. (C). 1997. pap. text 25.00 (*0-8133-2766-0*, Pub. by Westview) HarpC.

Latino Manifesto: A Critique of the Race Debate in U. S. Latino Community. Ed. by Bridget Fenner. 200p. 1998. pap. 19.95 (*0-9671122-0-6*) Cimarron Pubs.

***Latino Metropolis.** Victor M. Valle & Rodolfo D. Torres. LC 00-8646. (Globalization & Community Ser.). 2000. pap. 18.95 (*0-8166-3030-5*) U of Minn Pr.

Latino Periodicals: A Selection Guide. Ciuerena. 1995. 40.00 (*0-8161-7334-6*, G K Hall & Co) Mac Lib Ref.

Latino Periodicals: A Selection Guide. Ed. by Salvador Guerena & Vivian M. Pisano. LC 98-16582. 159p. 1998. pap. 30.00 (*0-7864-0540-6*) McFarland & Co.

Latino Politics in California: Su Voto Es Su Voz. Ed. by Anibal Yanez-Chavez. 139p. 1996. pap. 12.95 (*1-878367-34-X*) UCSD Ctr US-Mex.

Latino Poverty & Economic Development in Massachusetts. Ed. by Edwin Melendez & Miren Uriarte. LC 93-34381. 212p. (Orig.). 1994. pap. 14.95 (*0-87023-894-9*) U of Mass Pr.

***Latino Poverty in the New Century: Inequalities, Challenges & Barriers.** Maria Vidal de Haymes et al. 176p. (C). 2000. 49.95 (*0-7890-1160-3*) Haworth Pr.

***Latino Poverty in the New Century: Inequities, Challenges & Barriers.** Maria V. de Haymes et al. LC 00-38853. (Illus.). 176p. 2000. pap. 24.95 (*0-7890-1161-1*) Haworth Pr.

***Latino Read-Aloud Stories.** Maite Suarez Rivas. LC 00-20007. Vol. 7. (Illus.). 384p. (J). (gr. 4-7). 1999. 12.98 (*1-57912-091-1*) Blck Dog & Leventhal.

Latino Reader: An American Literary Tradition, 1542 to the Present Day. Ed. by Harold Augenbraum & Margarite Fernandez-Olmos. 400p. 1997. pap. 16.00 (*0-395-76528-5*) HM.

Latino Reader: Culture, Politics & Society. Ed. by Antonia Darder & Rodolfo D. Torres. LC 97-14134. 448p. 1998. pap. text 31.95 (*1-55786-987-1*) Blackwell Pubs.

Latino Reader: Culture, Politics & Society. Ed. by Antonio Darder & Rodolfo D. Torres. LC 97-14134. 448p. 1997. text 73.95 (*1-55786-986-3*) Blackwell Pubs.

Latino Social Movements: Historical & Theoretical Perspectives. Rodolfo D. Torres. LC 98-33289. (New Political Science Reader Ser.). 1999. pap. 21.99 (*0-415-92299-2*) Routledge.

Latino Success. Terence Failde. 1997. per. 12.00 (*0-684-83342-5*, Fireside) S&S Trade Pap.

Latino Success: Insights from America's Most Powerful Latino Business Executives. Augusto A. Failde & William S. Doyle. 256p. 1996. 22.00 (*0-684-81312-2*) Simon & Schuster.

Latino Task Force Report on the Year 2000: Health Promotion Objectives & Recommendations for California. 72p. (Orig.). (C). 1993. pap. text 25.00 (*0-7881-0088-2*) DIANE Pub.

Latino Voices. Ed. by Frances R. Aparicio. LC 93-42893. (Writers of America Ser.). (Illus.). 144p. (YA). (gr. 7 up). 1994. lib. bdg. 23.90 (*1-56294-388-X*) Millbrook Pr.

Latino Volunteer & Non-Profit Organizations: A Directory. Ed. by Samuel Mark. 135p. 1989. pap. text 20.00 (*1-883638-11-9*) Rose Inst.

Latino Vote at Mid-Decade. Tombas Rivera Center Staff. LC 98-143027. viii, 28 p. 1996. write for info. (*1-57240-005-6*) T Rivera Ctr.

Latino Women of Color. Darlene Mathis. Date not set. mass mkt. write for info. (*0-345-40692-3*) Ballantine Pub Grp.

Latinoamerica. 2nd ed. Chang-Rodriguez. (C). 1991. mass mkt. 37.95 (*0-8384-3540-8*) Heinle & Heinle.

Latinoamerica: Presente & Pasado. Arturo A. Fox. LC 97-32055. 392p. 1998. pap. text 37.33 (*0-13-016940-4*) P-H.

L

Latinoamerica: Su Civilizacion y Su Cultura. Eugenio C. Rodriquez. 432p. (C). 1983. mass mkt. 18.50 (*0-8384-3541-6*, Newbury) Heinle & Heinle.

Latinoamerica en Dos Mil Conciertos. H. Merchand. (SPA.). 122p. 1974. 5.00 (*0-8288-7063-2*) Fr & Eur.

Latinoamerica en Llamas. Pablo A. Deiros & Carlos Mraida.Tr. of Latin America Aflame. (SPA.). 288p. 1994. 9.99 (*0-89922-457-1*, C085-4571) Caribe Betania.

Latinoamerica: Su Civilizacisn y Su Cultura. 3rd ed. Eugenio Chang-Rodrmguez et al. 466p. pap. 46.95 (*0-8384-0325-5*, Pub. by Heinle & Heinle) Thomson Learn.

Latinola Condition: A Critical Reader. Ed. by Richard Delgado & Jean Stefancic. LC 98-13514. 672p. 1998. text 75.00 (*0-8147-1894-9*); pap. text 25.00 (*0-8147-1895-7*) NYU Pr.

Latinos: A Biography of the People. Earl Shorris. 544p. 1994. pap. 14.00 (*0-380-72190-2*, Avon Bks) Morrow Avon.

Latinos: A Biography of the People. Earl Shorris. 640p. 1992. 25.00 (*0-393-03360-0*) Norton.

Latinos: A Biography of the People. Earl Shorris. 1992. 19.10 (*0-606-06116-9*, Pub. by Turtleback) Demco.

Latinos & Blacks in the Cities: Policies for the 1990's. Harriet D. Romo. (Symposia Ser.). 236p. 1990. pap. 10.50 (*0-89940-423-5*) LBJ Sch Pub Aff.

***Latinos & Economic Development in California.** Elias Lopez et al. 54p. 1999. pap. write for info. (*1-58703-107-8*, CRB-99-008) CA St Libry.

Latinos & Education. Ed. by Andoria Darder. 485p. (C). 1997. 80.00 (*0-415-91181-8*) Routledge.

Latinos & Education. Ed. by Antonia Darder. 485p. (C). 1997. pap. 25.99 (*0-415-91182-6*) Routledge.

Latinos & Political Coalitions: Political Empowerment for the 1990s. Ed. by Roberto E. Villarreal & Norma G. Hernandez. LC 91-4768. (Contributions in Ethnic Studies: No. 27). 248p. 1991. pap. 20.95 (*0-275-94092-6*, B4092, Praeger Pubs) Greenwood.

Latinos & Political Coalitions: Political Empowerment for the 1990s, 27. Ed. by Roberto E. Villarreal & Norma G. Hernandez. LC 91-4768. (Contributions in Ethnic Studies: No. 27). 248p. 1991. 62.95 (*0-313-27834-2*, VLT, Greenwood Pr) Greenwood.

Latinos & Politics: A Selected Research Bibliography. F. Chris Garcia et al. 288p. (C). 1991. text 34.00 (*0-292-74654-7*) U of Tex Pr.

Latinos & Schools. Ciro Sepulveda. 160p. 1998. pap. 14.95 (*1-888867-14-0*) Biblos Pr.

Latinos & the Political System. Ed. by F. Chris Garcia. LC 87-40616. 501p. (C). 1990. pap. text 23.00 (*0-268-01286-5*) U of Notre Dame Pr.

Latinos & the U. S. Political System: Two-Tiered Pluralism. Rodney E. Hero. 256p. (C). 1992. pap. 22.95 (*0-87722-910-4*) Temple U Pr.

Latinos en el Mundo Islamico. Frederico Bertuzzi.Tr. of Latins to the Islamic World. (SPA.). 1990. 4.50 (*1-56063-146-5*, 498495); pap. write for info. (*0-614-27069-3*) Editorial Unilit.

Latinos in a Changing U. S. Economy: Comparative Perspectives on Growing Inequality. Rebecca Morales & Frank Bonilla. (Series on Race & Ethnic Relations: Vol. 7). (Illus.). 316p. (C). 1993. text 52.00 (*0-8039-4923-5*); pap. text 24.00 (*0-8039-4924-3*) Sage.

***Latinos in Art.** James D. Cockcroft & Jane Canning. LC 99-89464. (Book Report Biography Ser.). 2000. 26.00 (*0-531-11312-4*) Orchard Bks Watts.

***Latinos in Baseball: Sammy Sosa; Roberto Alomar; Tino Martinez; Moises Alou; Pedro Martinez; Bobby Bonilla; Alex Rodriguez; Bernie Williams; Manny Ramirez; Vinny Castilla; Ivan Rodriguez; Ramon Martinez, 12 vols.** (Illus.). 768p. (YA). (gr. 5 up). 2000. lib. bdg. 227.40 (*1-58415-053-X*) M Lane Pubs.

Latinos in Beisbol. James D. Cockcroft. LC 96-11876. (Hispanic Experience in the Americas Ser.). 196p. (J). 1996. lib. bdg. 24.00 (*0-531-11284-5*) Watts.

Latinos in Beisbol. James D. Cockcroft. (Hispanic Experience in the Americas Ser.). 208p. (J). 1997. pap. 9.95 (*0-531-15834-9*) Watts.

***Latinos in Ethnic Enclaves: Immigrant Workers & the Competition for Jobs.** Stephanie Bohon. LC 00-39314. (Latino Communities Ser.). 2000. pap. write for info. (*0-8153-3765-5*) Garland.

Latinos in Museums: A Heritage Reclaimed. Ed. by Antonio Rios-Bustamante & Christine Marin. LC 97-26230. (Public History Ser.). (Illus.). 142p. (C). 1998. 19.50 (*0-89464-981-7*) Krieger.

Latinos in New York: Communities in Transition. Ed. by Haslip-Viera et al. 400p. 1997. pap. text 18.00 (*0-268-01315-2*) U of Notre Dame Pr.

Latinos in Texas: A Socio-Demographic Profile. Tomas's Rivera Center Staff. Ed. & Pref. by Rodolfo O. De La Garza. Pref. by Harry Pachon. (Sourcebks.). (Illus.). 117p. (Orig.). 1995. pap. 15.00 (*1-57240-002-1*) T Rivera Ctr.

***Latinos in the Limelight, 8 vols.** Chelsea House Publishing Staff. 2000. 143.60 (*0-7910-6096-9*) Chelsea Hse.

Latinos in the Struggle for Equal Education. James D. Cockcroft. (Hispanic Experience in the Americas Ser.). (Illus.). 176p. (YA). (gr. 9-12). 1995. lib. bdg. 24.00 (*0-531-11226-8*) Watts.

Latinos in the United States: An Original Anthology. Ed. by Carlos E. Cortes. LC 79-6232. (Hispanics in the United States Ser.). (Illus.). 1981. lib. bdg. 73.95 (*0-405-13179-8*) Ayer.

Latinos in the United States: Social Economic & Political Aspects: A Bibliography. Ed. by Joan Nordquist. (Contemporary Social Issues: A Bibliographic Ser.: No. 34). 72p. (C). 1994. pap. 20.00 (*0-937855-66-9*) Ref Rsch Serv.

Latinos in the United States: The Sacred & the Political. David T. Abalos. LC 85-41010. 224p. 1988. pap. text 14.00 (*0-268-01278-4*) U of Notre Dame Pr.

Latinos Unidos. Enrique T. Trueba. (Freire & Macedo, Critical Perspectives Ser.). 216p. 1998. pap. 17.95 (*0-8476-8729-5*) Rowman.

Latinos Unidos: From Cultural Diversity to the Politics of Solidarity. Enrique T. Trueba. (Freire & Macedo, Critical Perspectives Ser.). 216p. 1998. 62.50 (*0-8476-8728-7*) Rowman.

Latinos Unidos: From Cultural Diversity to the Politics of Solidarity. Enrique T. Trueba. LC 98-8617. (Critical Perspectives Ser.: Vol. 110). 216p. 1999. 62.50 (*0-8476-8596-9*); pap. 17.95 (*0-8476-8597-7*) Rowman.

Latins & Greeks in the Eastern Mediterranean after 1204. Ed. by Benjamin Arbel et al. 256p. 1989. text 35.00 (*0-7146-3372-0*, Pub. by F Cass Pubs) Intl Spec Bk.

Latins Anonymous: Plays. Edward J. Olmos et al. LC 96-26649. 103p. 1996. pap. 11.95 (*1-55885-172-0*, Pub. by Arte Publico) Empire Pub Srvs.

Latins in the Levant: A History of Frankish Greece. William Miller. LC 75-41193. reprint ed. 72.50 (*0-404-14689-9*) AMS Pr.

Latins to the Islamic World see Latinos en el Mundo Islamico

Latinsko - Hrvatski Rjecnik. 6th ed. Mirko Divkovic. (CRO & LAT.). 1990. 195.00 (*0-8288-3950-6*, F107540) Fr & Eur.

***Lationo U. S. A. A Cartoon History.** Ilan Savans. (Illus.). 192p. 2000. 19.95 (*0-465-08221-1*, Pub. by Basic) HarpC.

Latitude Hooks & Azimuth Rings: How to Build & Use 18 Traditional Navigational Instruments. Dennis Fisher. 1994. 19.95 (*0-07-021120-5*) Intl Marine.

Latitude Zero. James Axler. (Deathlands Ser.: No. 12). 1991. mass mkt. 4.50 (*0-373-62512-X*) Harlequin Bks.

Latitude Zero. James Axler. (Deathlands Ser.: Bk. 12). 1999. per. 5.99 (*0-373-62550-2*, 1-62550-8, Wrldwide Lib) Harlequin Bks.

Latitudes. Edwin Muir. 322p. 1977. 21.95 (*0-8369-2665-X*) Ayer.

Latitudes: New Writing from the North. Ed. by Susan Johnson & Mary Roberts. LC 86-11329. 223p. 1987. pap. 16.95 (*0-7022-2022-1*) Intl Spec Bk.

Latitudes of Their Going. C. B. Follett. 44p. (Orig.). 1993. pap. 3.00 (*1-880575-15-9*) Hot Pepper.

Latitudinarianism in the Seventeenth-Century Church of England. Martin I. Griffin, Jr. Ed. by Lila Freedman. LC 92-11342. (Brill's Studies in Intellectual History: Vol. 32). x, 216p. 1992. 79.00 (*90-04-09653-1*) Brill Academic Pubs.

Latkes & Applesauce: A Hannukah Story. Fran Manushkin. (Illus.). 32p. (J). (gr. k-3). 1992. pap. 4.99 (*0-590-42265-0*, Blue Ribbon Bks) Scholastic Inc.

Latkes & Applesauce: A Hanukkah Story. Fran Manushkin. (Blue Ribbon Bks.). 1992. 10.15 (*0-606-01890-5*, Pub. by Turtleback) Demco.

Latkes, Latkes, Good to Eat: A Chanukah Story. Naomi Howland. LC 97-50616. (Illus.). 32p. (J). (gr. k-3). 1999. 15.00 (*0-395-89903-6*, Clarion Bks) HM.

Latmoss, a Catalogue of Neotropical Mosses. Claudio M. Delgadillo et al. 191p. 1995. 24.00 (*0-915279-35-5*, MSB-56) Miss Botan.

Lato W Pensylwanii. O. Waclaw & T. Chabrowski. 61p. 1966. pap. 2.50 (*0-940962-12-8*) Polish Inst Art & Sci.

Latogeneia: The Poetry of Athenadorus. Athenadorus. LC 96-86551. 75p. 1996. pap. 14.95 (*1-890000-04-3*, 001-0510-021208) Danaan Pr.

Latrine Building: A Handbook for Implementing the Sanplat System. Bjorn Brandberg. (Illus.). 208p. 1997. pap. 19.50 (*1-85339-306-1*, Pub. by Intermed Tech) Stylus Pub VA.

Latrobe & Rominson, the Engineer As Agent of Technological Transfer: The Engineer As Agent of Technological Transfer. Barbara Benson. (Illus.). 72p. 1975. pap. 1.25 (*0-914650-07-6*) Hagley Museum.

Latrobe's View of America, 1795-1820: Selections from the Watercolors & Sketches. Benjamin H. Latrobe. Ed. by Edward C. Carter et al. LC 84-7580. (Papers of Benjamin Henry Latrobe: No. 3). (Illus.). 420p. 1985. 55.00 (*0-300-02949-7*) Yale U Pr.

Latte Developers Guide. 800p. 1996. 49.99 (*1-57521-100-9*) Sams.

***Latte for One & Loving It!** Tosha Williams & Melanie Dobson. LC 99-39734. 300p. 2000. pap. 11.99 (*1-56476-763-9*) SP Pubns.

Latte Frontrunner. Jeff Duntemann. 400p. 1996. pap. text 29.99 (*1-57610-004-9*) Coriolis Grp.

Latte' Programming Explorer. Jeff Duntemann. 500p. 1996. pap. text 39.99 incl. cd-rom (*1-57610-005-7*) Coriolis Grp.

***Latter-Day Commentary on the Book of Mormon.** K. Douglas Bassett. 1999. 25.95 (*1-57734-534-7*, 01114298) Covenant Comms.

Latter Day Confucian: Reminiscences of William Hung, 1893-1980, Vol. 131. Susan C. Egan. LC 87-20193. (East Asian Monographs). 200p. 1988. 25.00 (*0-674-51297-9*) HUP.

Latter-Day Letters: Christmas. Lori G. Vanus. (Illus.). 32p. (J). (gr. k-6). 1998. pap. 7.95 (*1-892318-01-6*) White Stone Pub.

Latter-Day Letters: The New Testament. Lori G. Vanus. (Illus.). 56p. (J). (gr. k-6). 1998. pap. 9.95 (*1-892318-00-8*) White Stone Pub.

Latter-Day Pamphlets. Ed. by Thomas Carlyle. LC 72-37771. (Essay Index Reprint Ser.). 1977. reprint ed. 23.95 (*0-8369-2584-X*) Ayer.

Latter-Day Phamplets see Works of Thomas Carlyle

***Latter-Day Prophecies.** Jess Walker. 56p. 1998. pap. write for info. (*1-882194-36-5*) TN Valley Pub.

***Latter-Day Prophets.** Emerson R. West. 1999. pap. 15.95 (*1-57734-555-X*, 01114468) Covenant Comms.

Latter Day Saint Beliefs. Steven L. Sheilds. 1986. pap. 11.00 (*0-8309-0522-7*) Herald Pub Hse.

Latter Day Saint Churches: An Annotated Bibliography. Steven L. Shields. LC 87-19835. (Sects & Cults in America Ser.: Vol. 11, No. 337). 304p. 1987. text 25.00 (*0-8240-8582-5*) Garland.

Latter-Day Saint Commentary on the Old Testament. Ellis T. Rasmussen. LC 93-47675. (Illus.). 718p. 1994. 25.95 (*0-87579-712-1*) Deseret Bk.

***Latter-Day Saint Heroes & Heroines: True Stories of Courage & Faith.** Marlene B. Sullivan. LC 99-37731. (Illus.). 176p. 1999. pap. 11.95 (*1-56236-242-9*, Pub. by Aspen Bks) Origin Bk Sales.

Latter-Day Saint Social Life, Vol. 12. Ed. by James T. Duke. LC 97-75396. 1998. 24.95 (*1-57008-396-7*) Bookcraft Inc.

Latter-Day Saints. Edgar P. Kaiser. LC 95-22606. (How to Respond Ser.). 64p. 1995. pap. 3.99 (*0-570-04673-4*, 12-6006) Concordia.

Latter Day Saints: A Study of the Mormons in the Light of Economic Conditions. Ruth Kauffman & Reginald W. Kauffman. LC 94-6260. 392p. 1994. pap. text 17.95 (*0-252-06423-2*) U of Ill Pr.

***Latter Day Saints: A Study of the Mormons in the Light of Economic Conditions.** Ruth Kauffman & Reginald Wright Kauffman. 363p. 2000. reprint ed. pap. 20.00 (*0-7881-9425-9*) DIANE Pub.

Latter Day Saints' Emigrants' Guide. William Clayton. Ed. by Stanley B. Kimball & Gregory M. Franzwa. 1983. pap. 13.95 (*0-935284-27-3*) Patrice Pr.

Latter-Day Saints' Emigrants Guide: Being a Table of Distances Showing All the Springs, Creeks, Hills, Mountains, Camping Places, & All Other Notable Places from Council Bluffs to the Valley of the Great Salt Lake. William Clayton. 24p. 1973. pap. 4.95 (*0-87770-040-0*) Ye Galleon.

***Latter Days: A Guided Tour Through Six Billion Years of Mormonism.** Coke Newell. LC 00-27195. (Illus.). 288p. 2000. text 24.95 (*0-312-24108-9*) St Martin.

Latter Days of the Law: Images of Chinese Buddhism, 850-1850. Ed. by Marsha Weidner. LC 94-10842. (Illus.). 416p. (C). 1994. pap. text 36.00 (*0-8248-1662-5*) UH Pr.

Latter End: A Miss Silver Mystery. Patricia Wentworth. 25.95 (*0-89190-924-9*) Amereon Ltd.

Latter Reign. Raymond Dorrough. 112p. (Orig.). 1993. pap. 8.99 (*1-56043-759-6*, Treasure Hse) Destiny Image.

Lattice. Henry Alley. LC 85-20102. 287p. 1986. 19.95 (*0-918056-03-9*) Ariadne Pr.

Lattice Bracelets Beadwork, Bk. II. C. J. David. 58p. 1997. 11.95 (*0-9655049-1-3*) Am Supply Co.

Lattice Bracelets Beadwork Book I. C. J. David. Ed. by Kristen David. (Illus.). 50p. 1996. spiral bd. 9.95 (*0-9655049-0-5*) Am Supply Co.

Lattice Dynamical Foundations of Continuum Theories. Attila Askar. 208p. 1986. text 40.00 (*9971-978-89-X*) World Scientific Pub.

Lattice Dynamics & Semiconductor Physics: Festchrift for Prof. Kun Huang. Z. Z. Gan et al. 626p. 1989. text 137.00 (*981-02-0059-5*, PC-PB960) World Scientific Pub.

Lattice Dynamics of Molecular Crystals. S. Califano et al. (Lecture Notes in Chemistry Ser.: Vol. 26). 309p. 1981. pap. 36.00 (*0-387-10868-8*) Spr-Verlag.

Lattice Effects in High TC Superconductors: Proceedings of the Workshop, Santa Fe, New Mexico, 13-15 January 1992. Ed. by T. Egami et al. 500p. 1992. text 121.00 (*981-02-0970-3*) World Scientific Pub.

***Lattice Fermions & Structure of the Vacuum.** V. Mitrjushkin & G. Schierholz. LC 00-42086. (NATO Science Ser.). 2000. write for info. (*0-7923-6429-5*) Kluwer Academic.

Lattice Gardener. William C. Mulligan. LC 95-8158. (Illus.). 192p. 1995. pap. 35.00 (*0-02-587885-9*) Macmillan.

Lattice-Gas Cellular Automata: Simple Models of Complex Hydrodynamics. Daniel H. Rothman & Stephane Zaleski. LC 96-51777. (Collection Alea - Saclay: Vol. 5). (Illus.). 304p. (C). 1997. text 74.95 (*0-521-55201-X*) Cambridge U Pr.

***Lattice-Gas Cellular Automata & Lattice Boltzmann Models.** Dieter A. Wolf-Gladrow. Ed. by A. Dold et al. LC 99-87056. (Lecture Notes in Mathematics Ser.: Vol. 1725). ix, 308p. 2000. pap. 59.80 (*3-540-66973-6*) Spr-Verlag.

Lattice Gas Methods: Theory, Applications & Hardware. Gary D. Doolen. LC 91-10010. (Physica D Ser.). (Illus.). 348p. 1991. pap. text 39.00 (*0-262-54063-0*) MIT Pr.

Lattice Gas Methods of Partial Differential Equations. Gary D. Doolen et al. (Santa Fe Institute Ser.). (Illus.). 576p. (C). 1990. 54.95 (*0-201-15679-2*); pap. 34.95 (*0-201-13232-X*) Addison-Wesley.

Lattice Gauge Theories. H. J. Rothe. 396p. (C). 1992. text 86.00 (*981-02-0606-2*); pap. text 46.00 (*981-02-0607-0*) World Scientific Pub.

Lattice Gauge Theories: An Introduction. 2nd ed. 520p. 1997. 29.00 (*981-02-3032-X*) World Scientific Pub.

Lattice Gauge Theories: An Introduction. 2nd ed. Heinz J. Rothe. Vol. 59. 528p. pap. 26.00 (*981-02-3742-1*) World Scientific Pub.

Lattice Gauge Theories & Monte Carlo Simulations. Ed. by C. Rebbi. 658p. 1983. text 89.00 (*9971-950-70-7*); pap. text 46.00 (*9971-950-71-5*) World Scientific Pub.

Lattice Gauge Theory: A Challenge in Large-Scale Computing. Ed. by B. Bunk et al. LC 86-15155. (NATO ASI Series B, Physics: Vol. 140). 342p. 1986. 95.00 (*0-306-42376-6*, Plenum Trade) Perseus Pubng.

Lattice Gauge Theory, Supersymmetry & Grand Unification: Proceedings of the 7th Johns Hopkins Workshop on Current Problems in Particle Theory, Bad Honnef-Bonn, June 21-23, 1983. G. Domokos & S. Kovesi-Domokos. 300p. (C). 1983. 64.00 (*9971-950-63-4*); pap. 33.00 (*9971-950-62-6*) World Scientific Pub.

Lattice Gauge Theory Using Parallel Processors: China Center of Advanced Science & Technology (World Laboratory) Symposium-Workshop, May 21 to June 2, 1987, Vol. 1. Ed. by Xiaoyuan Li et al. xii, 644p. 1987. text 264.00 (*2-88124-234-0*) Gordon & Breach.

Lattice Gauge Theory '86. Ed. by H. Satz et al. LC 87-12276. (NATO ASI Series B, Physical Sciences: Vol. 159). (Illus.). 442p. 1987. 105.00 (*0-306-42607-2*, Plenum Trade) Perseus Pubng.

Lattice Higgs Workshop. Ed. by B. Berg et al. 300p. 1988. text 77.00 (*9971-5-0686-6*) World Scientific Pub.

Lattice Methods for Multiple Integration. I. H. Sloan & Joe S. (Illus.). 250p. 1994. text 75.00 (*0-19-853472-8*) OUP.

Lattice Mismatched Thin Films. Ed. by Eugene A. Fitzgerald. (Illus.). 212p. pap. 55.00 (*0-87339-444-5*) Minerals Metals.

Lattice Models of Polymers. Carlo Vanderzande. LC 97-32153. (Lecture Notes in Physics Ser.: No. 11). (Illus.). 236p. (C). 1998. pap. text 34.95 (*0-521-55993-6*) Cambridge U Pr.

Lattice Models of Protein Folding, Dynamics & Thermodynamics. Andrzej Kolinski & Jeffrey Skolnick. LC 96-24470. (Molecular Biology Intelligence Unit Ser.). 203p. 1996. 99.00 (*1-57059-382-5*) Landes Bioscience.

Lattice of Chapters of Mathematics: Interpretations Between Theorems. Alan S. Stern et al. LC 89-18632. (Memoirs Ser.: Vol. 426). 70p. 1990. pap. 18.00 (*0-8218-2488-0*, MEMO/84/426) Am Math.

Lattice of Interpretability Types of Varieties. O. C. Garcia & W. Taylor. LC 84-10997. (Memoirs of the American Mathematical Society Ser.: Vol. 50/305). 125p. 1984. pap. 19.00 (*0-8218-2308-6*, MEMO/50/305) Am Math.

Lattice-Ordered Groups: Advances & Techniques. Ed. by Alastair M. Glass & W. Charles Holland. (C). 1989. text 191.50 (*0-7923-0116-1*) Kluwer Academic.

Lattice-Ordered Groups: An Introduction. Ed. by Marlow Anderson & Todd Feil. (C). 1988. text 106.00 (*90-277-2643-4*) Kluwer Academic.

Lattice Points. Ekkehard Kratzel. (C). 1989. text 209.50 (*90-277-2733-3*) Kluwer Academic.

Lattice Structures on Banach Spaces. Nigel J. Kalton. LC 93-466. (Memoirs of the American Mathematical Society Ser.: No. 493). 92p. 1993. pap. 29.00 (*0-8218-2557-7*, MEMO/103/493) Am Math.

Lattice Theoretic Background of the Dimension Theory of Operator Algebras. Lynn H. Loomis. LC 52-42839. (Memoirs Ser.: No. 1/18). 36p. 1972. pap. 17.00 (*0-8218-1218-1*, MEMO/1/18) Am Math.

Lattice Theoretic Background of the Dimension Theory of Operator Algebras. Lynn H. Loomis. LC QA0003.A57. (Memoirs of the American Mathematical Society Ser.: No. 18). 42p. reprint ed. pap. 30.00 (*0-7837-5925-8*, 204572400007) Bks Demand.

Lattice Theory. Pure Mathematics Symposium Staff. Ed. by R. P. Dilworth. LC 50-1183. (Proceedings of Symposia in Pure Mathematics Ser.: Vol. 2). 208p. 1961. text 33.00 (*0-8218-1402-8*, PSPUM/2) Am Math.

Lattice Theory. Garrett D. Birkhoff. LC 66-23707. (Colloquium Publications: Vol. 25). 418p. 1940. reprint ed. pap. 34.00 (*0-8218-1025-1*, COLL/25) Am Math.

Lattice Theory of Elastic Constants. Ed. by S. Sengupta. 350p. 1988. text 120.00 (*0-87849-564-9*, Pub. by Trans T Pub) Enfield Pubs NH.

Lattices, Semigroups & Universal Algebra. Ed. by J. Almeida et al. (Illus.). 350p. (C). 1990. text 132.00 (*0-306-43412-1*, Kluwer Plenum) Kluwer Academic.

Lattices with Unique Complements. V. N. Salii. LC 87-35091. (Translations of Mathematical Monographs: No. 69). 113p. 1988. text 63.00 (*0-8218-4522-5*, MMONO/69) Am Math.

***Latticework: The New Investing.** Robert G. Hagstrom. 2000. 27.95 (*1-58799-000-8*) Texere.

Latvia. Ed. by Lerner Geography Department Staff. LC 92-7260. (Then & Now Ser.). (Illus.). 64p. (YA). (gr. 5 up). 1992. lib. bdg. 23.93 (*0-8225-2802-9*, Lerner Publctns) Lerner Pub.

***Latvia, 6 vols. , Set.** Robert Barlas. LC 99-30168. (Cultures of the World Ser.: Vol. 19). 128p. (YA). (gr. 5-9). 2000. lib. bdg. 35.64 (*0-7614-0977-7*, Benchmark NY) Marshall Cavendish.

***Latvia: A Country Study Guide.** Global Investment & Business Center, Inc. Staff. (World Country Study Guides Library: Vol. 94). (Illus.). 350p. 2000. pap. 59.00 (*0-7397-2392-8*) Intl Business Pubns.

Latvia: IMF Economic Review. International Monetary Fund Staff. v, 69p. 1992. pap. 10.00 (*1-55775-253-2*) Intl Monetary.

Latvia: Independence Renewed. Janis J. Penikis. 1997. pap. 17.95 (*0-8133-1838-6*) Westview.

Latvia: Independence Renewed. Janis J. Penikis. (Post-Soviet Republics Ser.). 2000. pap. 49.95 (*0-8133-0013-4*) Westview.

Latvia: The Bradt Travel Guide. 2nd ed. Stephen Baister & Patrick Chris. (Illus.). 320p. 1999. pap. text 17.95 (*1-898323-90-9*) Globe Pequot.

Latvia: The Transition to a Market Economy. LC 93-3018. (Country Study Ser.). 330p. 1993. pap. 22.00 (*0-8213-2324-5*, 12324) World Bank.

Latvia - A Country Study Guide: Basic Information for Research & Pleasure. Global Investment Center, USA Staff. (World Country Study Guide Library: Vol. 94). (Illus.). 350p. 1999. pap. 59.00 (*0-7397-1491-0*) Intl Business Pubns.

Latvia Business & Investment Opportunities Yearbook-98: Business, Investment, Export-Import. Contrib. by Russian Information & Business Center, Inc. Staff. (Business & Investment Opportunity Library-98). (Illus.). 350p. 1998. pap. 99.00 (*1-57751-935-3*) Intl Business Pubns.

An Asterisk (*) at the beginning of an entry indicates that the title is appearing for the first time.

***Latvia Business Intelligence Report, 190 vols.** Global Investment & Business Center, Inc. Staff. (World Business Intelligence Library: Vol. 94). (Illus.). 350p. 2000. pap. 99.95 (*0-7397-2592-0*) Intl Business Pubns.

***Latvia Business Law Handbook, 190 vols.** Global Investment & Business Center, Inc. Staff. (Global Business Law Handbooks Library: Vol. 94). (Illus.). 350p. 2000. pap. 99.95 (*0-7397-1991-2*) Intl Business Pubns.

Latvia Business Law Handbook-98. Russian Information & Business Center Inc. Staff. (World Business Law Library-98). (Illus.). 350p. 1998. pap. 99.00 (*1-57751-805-5*) Intl Business Pubns.

***Latvia Business Opportunity Yearbook.** Global Investment & Business Center, Inc. Staff. (Global Business Opportunity Yearbooks Library: Vol. 94). (Illus.). 2000. pap. 99.95 (*0-7397-2192-5*) Intl Business Pubns.

***Latvia Business Opportunity Yearbook: Export-Import, Investment & Business Opportunities.** International Business Publications, U. S. A. Staff & Global Investment Center, U. S. A. Staff. (Global Business Opportunity Yearbooks Library: Vol. 94). (Illus.). 350p. 1999. pap. 99.95 (*0-7397-1292-6*) Intl Business Pubns.

***Latvia Export-Import & Business Directory: Ultimate Directory for Conducting Export-Import Operations in the Country. Largest Exporters & Importers, Strategic Government & Business Contacts, Selected Export-Import Regulations & More.** International Business Publications, USA Staff & Global Investment Center, USA Staff. (World Export-Import & Business Library: 18). (Illus.). 250p. 2000. pap. 99.95 (*0-7397-3395-8*) Intl Business Pubns.

***Latvia Foreign Policy & Government Guide.** Global Investment & Business Center, Inc. Staff. (World Foreign Policy & Government Library: Vol. 90). (Illus.). 350p. 1999. pap. 99.00 (*0-7397-3588-8*) Intl Business Pubns.

***Latvia Foreign Policy & Government Guide.** Global Investment & Business Center, Inc. Staff. (World Foreign Policy & Government Library: Vol. 90). (Illus.). 350p. 2000. pap. 99.95 (*0-7397-3792-9*) Intl Business Pubns.

***Latvia Government & Business Contacts Handbook: Strategic Governent & business Contacts for Conducting Successful Business, Export-Import & Investment Activity, 110 vols.** International Business Publications, USA Staff & Global Investment Center, USA Staff. (World Export-Import & Business Library: 17). (Illus.). 250p. 2000. pap. 99.95 (*0-7397-6055-6*) Intl Business Pubns.

***Latvia Government & Business Contacts Handbook: Strategic Government & Business Contacts for Conducting Succesful Business, Export-Import & Investment Activity, 110.** International Business Publications, USA Staff & Global Investment Center, USA Staff. (World Export-Import & Business Library: 49). (Illus.). 250p. 2000. pap. 99.95 (*0-7397-6088-2*) Intl Business Pubns.

Latvia in Transition. Juris Dreifelds. LC 97-721. 224p. (C). 1996. text 59.95 (*0-521-47131-1*) Cambridge U Pr.

***Latvia Industrial & Business Directory.** Global Investment & Business Center, Inc. Staff. (NIS Industrial & Business Directories Ser.: Vol. 9). (Illus.). 350p. 1999. pap. 99.00 (*0-7397-0708-6*) Intl Business Pubns.

***Latvia Investment & Business Guide.** Global Investment & Business Center, Inc. Staff. (Global Investment & Business Guide Library: Vol. 94). (Illus.). 2000. pap. 99.95 (*0-7397-1792-8*) Intl Business Pubns.

Latvia Investment & Business Guide: Economy, Export-Import, Business & Investment Climate, Business Contacts. Contrib. by Russian Information & Business Center, Inc. Staff. (Russia, NIS & Emerging Markets Investment & Business Library-98). (Illus.). 350p. 1998. pap. 99.00 (*1-57751-855-1*) Intl Business Pubns.

***Latvia Investment & Business Guide: Export-Import, Investment & Business Opportunities.** International Business Publications, USA Staff & Global Investment Center, USA Staff. (World Investment & Business Guide Library-99: Vol. 94). (Illus.). 350p. 1999. pap. 99.95 (*0-7397-0289-0*) Intl Business Pubns.

Latvian: Easy Way to Latvian. unabridged ed. Liga K. Streips. (LAV.). 283p. audio 185.00 (*0-88432-442-7*, AFLV10) Audio-Forum.

Latvian Business Laws, 1990-91: Economic Legislation of the Republic of Latvia in English. Intro. by Igor I. Kavass. LC 95-25262. x, 246p. 1995. 50.00 (*0-89941-987-9*, 308940) W S Hein.

Latvian Collections: Anglo-Saxon & Later British Coins. Tatjana Berga. (Sylloge of Coins of the British Isles, Vol 45; British Academy Ser.). (Illus.). 88p. 1997. text 80.00 (*0-19-726163-9*) OUP.

Latvian Deportations, 1940-Present. LC 86-50748. 1986. 7.00 (*0-317-60719-7*) World Fed Free Latvians.

Latvian Dissent: Case Histories of the 1983 Soviet Campaign to Silence Political Dissidents in Occupied Latvia. 1983. 4.50 (*0-685-13492-X*) World Fed Free Latvians.

***Latvian Dreams: Knitted Designs from Weaving Patterns.** Joyce Williams. Ed. by Lizbeth Upitis. (Illus.). 192p. 2000. write for info. (*0-942018-19-2*) Schoolhouse WI.

Latvian-English - English-Latvian Practical Dictionary. M. Sosare & I. Birzvalka. (ENG & LAV.). 474p. 1993. pap. 16.95 (*0-7818-0059-5*) Hippocrene Bks.

Latvian-English Dictionary. E. Turkina. 1991. lib. bdg. 39.95 (*0-8288-2628-5*) Fr & Eur.

Latvian-English Dictionary. Phil E. Turkina. (ENG & LAV.). 43.95 (*0-87557-052-6*) Saphrograph.

Latvian-English Dictionary. 4th ed. E. Turkina. (ENG & LAV.). 638p. 1982. 29.95 (*0-8288-1622-0*, F58230) Fr & Eur.

Latvian Gambit. Tony Kosten. 1995. pap. 20.00 (*0-8050-3903-1*, Pub. by Batsford Chess) H Holt & Co.

Latvian Gambit Made Easy. John Elburg. 38p. (Orig.). 1991. pap. 6.00 (*0-945470-16-9*) Chess Ent.

Latvian Impact on the Bolshevik Revolution. Andrew Ezergailis. 1983. text 75.50 (*0-88033-035-X*, 144, Pub. by East Eur Monographs) Col U Pr.

Latvian Language for the Use of Students: Grammar, Vocabulary & Exercises. Antonia Millers. LC 79-89077. (ENG & LAV.). 170p. (C). 1979. 20.00 (*0-912852-26-7*) Echo Pubs.

Latvian Legion: Heroes, Nazis or Victims. Ed. by Andrew Ezergailis. 100p. (Orig.). 1997. pap. write for info. (*1-998601-24-2*) Hist Inst Latvia.

Latvian Mittens. rev. ed. Lizbeth Upitis. (ENG & LAV.). 1997. reprint ed. pap. 25.00 (*0-942018-14-1*) Schoolhouse WI.

Latvian Storyteller: The Repertoire of Janis Plavnieks. Inta G. Carpenter. Ed. by Richard M. Dorson. LC 80-725. (Folklore of the World Ser.). 1981. lib. bdg. 28.95 (*0-405-13306-5*) Ayer.

Latvian Twelve Steps & Twelve Traditions. Alcoholics Anonymous World Services, Inc., Staff. 1993. 8.45 (*0-916856-61-5*) AAWS.

Latvians: A Short History. Andrejs Plakans. (Publication Ser.: No. 422). (Illus.). 257p. (C). 1995. 39.95 (*0-8179-9301-0*); pap. 24.95 (*0-8179-9302-9*) Hoover Inst Pr.

***Latvia's Transition to a Market Economy: Political Determinants of Economic Reform Policy.** Marja Nissinen. LC 98-40719. 300p. 1999. text 65.00 (*0-312-21989-X*) St Martin.

Latviesu Valodas Prasmes Limenis (Threshold Level in Latvian) (LAV.). 1997. 25.00 (*92-871-3266-6*, Pub. by Council of Europe) Manhattan Pub Co.

Lau Islands, Fiji. A. M. Hocart. (BMB Ser.: No. 62). 1969. reprint ed. 35.00 (*0-527-02168-7*) Periodicals Srv.

***Lau vs. Nichols: Bilingual Education in Public Schools.** Stephanie Sammartino McPherson. (Landmark Supreme Court Cases Ser.). (Illus.). 104p. (YA). (gr. 6 up). 2000. lib. bdg. 20.95 (*0-7660-1472-X*) Enslow Pubs.

Laubach Way to English, Wkbk. 1. 1993. 5.60 (*0-88336-371-2*) New Readers.

Laubach Way to English, Wkbk. 2. 1993. 5.60 (*0-88336-372-0*) New Readers.

Laubach Way to English, Wkbk. 3. 1993. 6.60 (*0-88336-397-6*) New Readers.

Laubach Way to English, Wkbk. 4. 1993. 8.00 (*0-88336-374-7*) New Readers.

Laubach Way to English: Leader Guide. (Illus.). (J). (gr. k-4). 1997. teacher ed. 10.95 (*0-88336-690-8*) New Readers.

Laubach Way to English: Tutor Workshop Handbook. (J). (gr. k-4). 1997. 5.00 (*0-88336-695-9*) New Readers.

Laubach Way to English Level 1: Sounds & Names of Letters. 1993. teacher ed. 9.95 (*0-88336-391-7*); 8.95 (*0-88336-355-0*) New Readers.

Laubach Way to English Level 1: Sounds & Names of Letters. (Illus.). 1993. 3.95 (*0-88336-392-5*) New Readers.

Laubach Way to English Level 2: Short Vowel Sounds. 1993. teacher ed. 13.95 (*0-88336-393-3*) New Readers.

Laubach Way to English Level 2: Short Vowel Sounds. (Illus.). 1993. 4.95 (*0-88336-394-1*) New Readers.

Laubach Way to English Level 3: Long Vowel Sounds. 1993. teacher ed. 13.95 (*0-88336-395-X*) New Readers.

Laubach Way to English Level 3: Long Vowel Sounds. (Illus.). 1993. 4.95 (*0-88336-396-8*) New Readers.

Laubach Way to Reading Bks. 1-3: Teacher Materials. 1997. 7.00 (*0-88336-694-0*); teacher ed. 10.95 (*0-88336-689-4*) New Readers.

Laubach Way to Reading Level 2: Short Vowel Sounds. 1993. teacher ed. 5.95 (*0-88336-912-5*); wbk. ed. 6.60 (*0-88336-902-8*); 2.60 (*0-88336-922-2*); 0.75 (*0-88336-932-X*); 0.40 (*0-88336-942-7*); 5.00 (*0-88336-927-3*); audio 12.95 (*0-88336-915-X*); audio 10.95 (*0-88336-938-9*); audio 16.95 (*0-88336-082-9*); disk 39.95 (*0-88336-002-0*); disk 39.95 (*0-88336-007-1*); disk 29.95 (*0-88336-013-6*); disk 29.95 (*0-88336-022-5*) New Readers.

Laubach Way to Reading Level 4: Other Vowel Sounds & Consonant Spellings. 1993. 6.60 (*0-88336-930-3*); 3.40 (*0-88336-924-9*); teacher ed. 9.95 (*0-88336-914-1*); wbk. ed. 8.00 (*0-318-70324-6*); wbk. ed. 9.00 (*0-88336-904-4*); student ed. 1.00 (*0-88336-346-1*); 0.75 (*0-88336-934-6*); 0.40 (*0-88336-944-3*); audio 16.95 (*0-88336-940-0*); audio 16.95 (*0-88336-917-6*); audio 16.95 (*0-88336-084-5*); disk 39.95 (*0-88336-004-7*); disk 39.95 (*0-88336-009-8*); Apple II 29.95 (*0-88336-016-0*); Apple II 29.95 (*0-88336-024-1*) New Readers.

Laubach Way to Reading Level 4: Other Vowel Sounds & Consonant Spellings, Bk. 4. 1993. 2.60 (*0-88336-958-3*) New Readers.

Laubach Way to Reading, Level 1: Sounds & Names of Letters, Bks. 1-4. Incl. 1993. 6.60 (*0-88336-901-X*); 1993. 5.95 (*0-88336-911-7*); 1993. audio 12.95 (*0-88336-910-9*); 1993. 0.75 (*0-88336-931-1*); 1993. 0.40 (*0-88336-941-9*); 1993. 2.60. 1993. disk 29.95 (*0-88336-011-X*); 1993. 39.95 (*0-88336-001-2*); 1993. 39.95 (*0-88336-006-3*); 1993. 39.95 (*0-88336-008-X*); 1993. 29.95 (*0-88336-021-7*); 1993. 4.20 (*0-88336-926-5*); 1993. audio 16.95 (*0-88336-081-0*); 1993. 2.60 (*0-88336-921-4*); 1993. wbk. ed. 5.60. 1993. audio 10.95 (*0-88336-937-0*); 1993. Set disk 185.00 (*0-318-70396-3*) New Readers.

Laubach Way to Reading, Level 3: Long Vowel Sounds. Incl. 1993. 9.00 (*0-88336-903-6*); 1993. 7.95 (*0-88336-913-3*); 1993. audio 16.95 (*0-88336-916-8*); 1993. 0.75 (*0-88336-933-8*); 1993. 0.40 (*0-88336-943-5*); 1993. 2.60 (*0-88336-957-5*); 1993. 39.95 (*0-88336-003-9*); 1993. 3.5 hd 39.95. 1993. 29.95 (*0-88336-014-4*); 1993. 29.95 (*0-88336-023-3*); 1993. 5.32 (*0-88336-909-5*); 1993. 3.95 (*0-88336-919-2*); 1993. 3.40 (*0-88336-923-0*); 1993. audio 10.95 (*0-88336-939-7*); 1993. 5.00 (*0-88336-929-X*); 1993. audio 16.95 (*0-88336-083-7*); 1993. 3.60 (*0-88336-320-8*); 1993. 3.40 (*0-88336-328-3*); 1993. wbk. ed. 6.60 1993. 2.60 (*0-318-70392-0*) New Readers.

Laubmoose Fennoskandias. V. F. Brotherus. (Flora Fennica Ser.: Vol. 1). (GER., Illus.). 635p. 1974. reprint ed. 150.00 (*3-87429-078-6*, 002455, Pub. by Koeltz Sci Bks) Lubrecht & Cramer.

Laubwaldgesellschaften der Frankenalb. Horst Kuenne. (Illus.). 1969. 40.00 (*3-7682-0610-6*) Lubrecht & Cramer.

Laubwerfenden Eichenwaelder Kretas. Ursula Matthas. (Dissertationes Botanicae Ser.: Band 119). (GER., Illus.). 172p. 1988. pap. 53.00 (*3-443-64031-1*, Pub. by Gebruder Borntraeger) Balogh.

Lauch Your Own Magazine: A Guide for Succeeding in Today's Marketplace. Samir Husni. LC 98-85707. (Illus.). 1998. pap. 26.95 (*0-9661049-0-0*) Hamblett Hse.

Laud del Desterrado. Matias Montes-Huidobro. 182p. 1995. pap. 10.95 (*1-55885-082-1*) Arte Publico.

Laud MS Troy Book, Set, Pts. 1 & 2. Ed. by J. E. Wuelfing. (EETS, OS Ser.: Nos. 121-2). 1969. reprint ed. 75.00 (*0-527-00119-8*) Periodicals Srv.

Laudate Pueri (E Major) For Soprano Solo & Orchestra. Johann Sebastian Bach. Ed. by Richard Charteris. (Classical Music Ser.: Vol. 4). iv, 163p. 1998. pap. 54.00 (*1-56571-165-3*, CL004) PRB Prods.

***Laudate Pueri (G Major) For Soprano, Tenor & Orchestra.** Johann Sebastian Bach. Ed. by Richard Charteris. (Classical Music Ser.: Vol. 5). (Illus.). viii, 217p. 1999. pap. 58.00 (*1-56571-170-X*, CL005) PRB Prods.

Laude in the Middle Ages. Tr. by Vincenzo Traversa from ITA. LC 92-10252. (Am. Univ. Studies, II: Vol. 197). XXXVIII, 432p. (C). 1994. text 65.95 (*0-8204-1932-X*) P Lang Pubng.

Lauderdale County, Alabama: Annotated Index to Chancery Court Records, 1827-1830. Teresa B. Campbell et al. viii, 53p. (Orig.). 1985. pap. 7.00 (*0-933253-03-6*) Natchez Trace.

Lauderdale's Notes on Adam Smith's Wealth of Nations. James M. Lauderdale. Ed. by Chuhei Sugiyama. LC 95-11820. 176p. (C). (gr. 13). 1995. 85.00 (*0-415-12284-8*) Routledge.

Lauds: Poems from Hollywood. Mark Dunster. 11p. 1998. pap. 5.00 (*0-89642-559-2*) Linden Pubs.

Laud's Laboratory: The Diocese of Bath & Wells in the Early Seventeenth Century. Margaret F. Stieg. LC 80-70185. (Illus.). 416p. 1982. 60.00 (*0-8387-5019-2*) Bucknell U Pr.

Laugh: Portraits of the Greatest Comedians & the Stories They Tell Each Other. Photos by William Claxton. LC 99-19846. (Illus.). 112p. 1999. 30.00 (*0-688-15891-9*, Wm Morrow) Morrow Avon.

Laugh? I Nearly Went to Miami! A Comedy. Miles Tredinnick. LC 88-179069. 66 p. 1986. write for info. (*0-573-01633-X*) S French Trade.

Laugh a Day Keeps the Doctor Away. Irvin S. Cobb. (Collected Works of Irvin S. Cobb). 246p. 1998. reprint ed. lib. bdg. 88.00 (*1-58201-595-3*) Classic Bks.

***Laugh a Lot! Song-Stretching Activities for Children's Favorite Tunes.** Pamela Ott. (Illus.). 96p. 1999. pap. 14.95 (*0-7619-7546-2*) Corwin Pr.

Laugh, a Smile, a Tear: Fifty Years of Pastoral Memories. rev. ed. Kenneth H. Greves. LC 98-24297. (Illus.). 144p. 1998. pap. 12.95 (*0-9633083-6-X*) Quixote Pubns.

Laugh Again see Sonrie Otra Vez: Experimenta el Gozo Rebosante

Laugh Again. Charles R. Swindoll. 256p. 1992. 19.99 (*0-8499-0957-0*) Word Pub.

Laugh Again. Charles R. Swindoll. 1995. pap. 12.99 (*0-8499-3679-9*) Word Pub.

Laugh Again. large type ed. Charles R. Swindoll. (EasyRead Type Ser.). 322p. 1993. reprint ed. pap. 12.95 (*0-8027-2672-0*) Walker & Co.

Laugh Again: Experience Outrageous Joy, Mini Book. abr. ed. Charles R. Swindoll. LC 93-19144. 1993. 4.99 (*0-8499-5027-9*) Word Pub.

Laugh Again A Study of Philippians: Experience Outrageous Joy. Charles R. Swindoll. 127p. 1998. pap., student ed. 5.95 (*1-57972-183-4*) Insight Living.

Laugh-Along Mystery see Walt Disney's Read & Grow Library

Laugh & Cry Your Way to Freedom: Changed into His Image Through Inner Healing. John R. Chappell. 126p. 1999. pap. 8.99 (*1-884369-97-9*, Serenity Bks) McDougal Pubng.

***Laugh & Grow Rich: How to Profit from Humor in Any Business.** Rick Segel & Darren LaCroix. (Illus.). xviii, 260p. 2000. pap. 19.95 (*0-9674586-0-9*) Specific Hse.

Laugh & Laugh & Laugh. Fay Harbison & Ellen M. Surber. Ed. by Ralph K. Baber. LC 96-35899. 208p. (Orig.). 1996. pap. 11.95 (*0-9634733-1-X*) Ogden Pr TX.

Laugh & Learn. (Captain Kangaroo Fun-to-Learn Activity Bks.: Vol. 4). (J). 1998. pap. write for info. (*0-7666-0218-4*, Honey Bear Bks) Modern Pub NYC.

Laugh & Learn: A Basic Reader. 2nd ed. Mira B. Felder & Anna B. Bromberg. LC 96-48206. 176p. 1997. pap. text 20.21 (*0-201-83414-6*) Addison-Wesley.

Laugh & Live. Douglas Fairbanks, Jr. 1976. 26.95 (*0-8488-0266-7*) Amereon Ltd.

Laugh & Play. (Illus.). 24p. (J). (gr. k-2). 1995. pap. write for info. (*1-56144-367-0*, Honey Bear Bks) Modern Pub NYC.

Laugh & Tickle, Hug & Pray: Active Family Devotions. Julaine Kammrath. LC 97-10414. 1997. 10.99 (*0-570-04991-1*, 12-3340) Concordia.

***Laugh At Any Mortal Thing.** N. J. Irwin. LC 00-190671. 515p. 2000. 25.00 (*0-7388-1918-2*); pap. 18.00 (*0-7388-1919-0*) Xlibris Corp.

***Laugh at the End of the World: Collected Comic Poems, 1969-1999.** Bill Knott. LC 99-85899. (American Poets Continuum Ser.: Vol. 60). 140p. 2000. pap. 15.00 (*1-880238-84-5*) BOA Edns.

Laugh at Your Muscles: A Light Look at Fibromyalgia. Mark J. Pellegrino. (Illus.). 92p. (Orig.). 1995. pap. 5.95 (*0-9646891-4-6*) Anadem Pubng.

Laugh Away Your Tensions. Lorin D. Whittaker. LC 88-91416. 1989. 18.95 (*0-318-40145-2*) Libra.

Laugh Crafters: Comedy Writing in Radio & TV's Golden Age. Jordan R. Young. LC 98-40829. (Illus.). 351p. 1999. pap. 17.95 (*0-940410-37-0*) Past Times.

Laugh, Cry & Remember: The Journal of a GI Lady! Clarice F. Pollard. Ed. by Mary Westheimer. LC 91-90262. (Illus.). 224p. (Orig.). 1992. pap. 17.95 (*0-9629334-0-6*) Tex Tech Univ Pr.

***Laugh-Eteria.** Douglas Florian. LC 00-29088. (Illus.). 160p. (J). (gr. 2-6). 2000. pap. 6.99 (*0-14-130990-3*, PuffinBks) Peng Put Young Read.

Laugh-eteria: Poems & Drawings. Douglas Florian. LC 98-20047. (Illus.). 160p. (J). 1999. 17.00 (*0-15-202084-5*) Harcourt.

***Laugh-Eteria: Poems & Paintings.** Douglas Florian. LC 98-20047. (J). 1999. 10.01 (*0-15-201859-X*) Harcourt.

Laugh Factor: Stress Management for Law Enforcement. Wally Davis. (Illus.). 116p. (Orig.). 1987. pap. 9.95 (*0-938417-01-0*) Copouts Ink.

***Laugh Factory.** Arnold I. Burns. LC 99-90821. 1999. 25.00 (*0-7388-0534-3*); pap. 18.00 (*0-7388-0535-1*) Xlibris Corp.

***Laugh! I Thought I'd Die (if I Didn't)** Anne W. Schaef. 1999. pap. 12.00 (*0-345-91516-X*) Ballantine Pub Grp.

Laugh! I Thought I'd Die (If I Didn't) Meditations on Healing Through Humor. Anne W. Schaef. 1999. pap. 9.00 (*0-345-36097-4*) Ballantine Pub Grp.

Laugh It off & Move On. Lester Glickman. (Illus.). 75p. 1998. pap. 14.95 (*0-9664285-0-1*) L Glickman.

Laugh, Jew, Laugh. Jacob Adler. Tr. by Abraham London. LC 77-116925. (Short Story Index Reprint Ser.). 1977. 19.95 (*0-8369-3427-X*) Ayer.

Laugh Kills Lonesome & Other Poems. Mike Logan. LC 90-84126. (Illus.). 80p. (Orig.). 1990. pap. 9.95 (*1-56044-056-2*) Falcon Pub Inc.

Laugh, Lady: A Woman's Journey. Ellewood. LC 98-90071. (Illus.). 90p. 1998. 9.99 (*1-892074-00-1*) Second Cup Pub.

***Laugh Last: Making Sure Your Heirs Get Theirs** Barbara J. Shotwell. 2001. pap. 14.95 (*0-7868-8494-0*, Pub. by Disney Pr) Time Warner.

Laugh, Lead & Profit: Building Productive Workplaces with Humor. Bob Ross. 125p. (Orig.). (YA). 1989. pap. write for info. (*0-318-65545-4*) Arrowhead Pub.

Laugh, Learn & Live with Mistake. unabridged ed. Patricia T. Kienzle & Kathryn K. Simmons. (Illus.). 60p. (Orig.). 1991. pap. 9.00 (*1-890798-01-0*) P T Kienzle.

Laugh Lines. Ann Berk. 240p. 1990. mass mkt. 4.50 (*0-380-70891-4*, Avon Bks) Morrow Avon.

Laugh Lines. Joan Blank. (Illus.). 96p. (Orig.). 1982. pap. 4.95 (*0-941374-01-7*) Grapetree Prods.

Laugh-Makers: Stand-up Comedy as Art, Business & Life-Style. Robert A. Stebbins. 176p. (C). 1990. 60.00 (*0-7735-0735-3*, Pub. by McG-Queens Univ Pr) CUP Services.

Laugh of Lost Men: An Irish Journey. Brian Lalor. (Illus.). 192p. 1998. 29.95 (*1-85158-858-2*, Pub. by Mainstream Pubng) Trafalgar.

Laugh or Cry It's Your Choice: A Book about Reclaiming Your Lost Self Esteem. Jaswant S. Bagga. (Illus.). 202p. 1989. 10.00 (*0-9624832-0-6*) J S Bagga.

Laugh Quickly. Clyde A. Beakley. 136p. 1992. pap. write for info. (*0-9636782-0-5*) C Beakley.

Laugh to Keep from Crying. Vermadel P. Nienstedt & Lynn Smith. LC 83-91465. (Illus.). 90p. pap. 5.95 (*0-9613010-0-7*) Nienstedt VP & L Smith.

Laugh Twice & Call Me In the Morning: The Best Quotes & Cartoons about Calamities & Cures. Bruce Lansky. LC 98-53471. (Illus.). 112p. (Orig.). 1999. per. 7.00 (*0-671-31656-7*) S&S Trade.

Laugh with Accent, No. 3. 24p. 1996. reprint ed. pap. 3.50 (*0-915708-46-9*) Cheever Pub.

Laugh with Hugh Troy, World's Greatest Practical Joker. Con Troy. (Illus.). 192p. 1984. 13.95 (*0-9610986-0-0*) Trojan Bks.

Laugh with Me/Cry with Me: Inspiration, Pathos, & Humor from Ivan Fitzwater. Ivan W. Fitzwater. LC 89-52014. (Illus.). 131p. (Orig.). 1989. pap. 13.00 (*0-934955-15-8*) Watercress Pr.

Laugh with the Air Force. 1989. pap. 20.00 (*0-907771-31-9*, Pub. by Maritime Bks) St Mut.

Laugh with the Navy. 1989. pap. 20.00 (*0-9506323-5-X*, Pub. by Maritime Bks) St Mut.

Laugh with the Navy Too. Maritime Books Staff. (C). 1986. text 50.00 (*0-907771-01-7*, Pub. by Maritime Bks) St Mut.

***Laugh Your Troubles Away: The Complete History of Riverview Park.** Derek H. Gee & Ralph Lopez. (Illus.). 176p. 2000. pap. 29.95 (*0-9676045-1-6*) Sharpshooters.

Laugh Your Way Across Texas! Special Added Feature: A 'Texas' Dictionary. Joe James. LC 96-155359. (Illus.). 96p. (Orig.). 1996. pap. write for info. (*0-9631584-2-2*) Rocking J Pr.

Laugh Your Way to the Top: The Power of Humor in Meetings & Marketing. Sheila Kessler. LC 90-85526. (Illus.). 112p. (Orig.). 1990. pap. 8.95 (*1-879404-10-9*) Cmpetitive Edge.

Laughable Limericks. Sara W. Brewton & John E. Brewton. LC 65-16179. (Illus.). 160p. (J). (gr. 3-6). 1990. lib. bdg. 12.89 (*0-690-04887-4*) HarpC Child Bks.

Laughable, Loveable, Little Give-Me-As-a-Gift Book, No. 1. Don Cresswell. (Illus.). 24p. (Orig.). 1983. pap. 2.95 (*0-930943-00-7*) Cresswell Ent.

Laughable, Loveable, Little Give-Me-As-a-Gift Book, No. 2. Don Cresswell. (Illus.). 24p. (Orig.). 1984. pap. 2.95 (*0-930943-01-5*) Cresswell Ent.

Laughable Loves. Milan Kundera. LC 99-15600. 304p. 1999. pap. 13.00 (*0-06-099703-6*) HarpC.

Laughable Stories. Bar Hebraeus. Tr. by E. A. Wallis Budge from SYR. LC 73-18852. (Luzac's Semitic Text & Translation Ser.: No. 1). (ENG.). reprint ed. 49.50 (*0-404-11347-8*) AMS Pr.

Laughable Stories Collected by Mar Gregory John Bar-Hebraeus. Ed. by E. A. Wallis Budge. LC 72-173158. 1972. reprint ed. 24.95 (*0-405-08321-1*, Pub. by Blom Pubns) Ayer.

LaughaGraph: Building Self-Esteem Through Humor. David E. Zuccolotto. (Illus.). 181p. reprint ed. student ed. 21.95 (*0-9634378-1-X*) R & Z Pub.

Laugharne. Dylan Thomas & Tryntje V. Seymour. (Illus.). 395.00 (*0-915998-06-8*) Lime Rock Pr.

Laugharne Poems. Thomas R. Crowe. LC 97-183795. 70p. 1997. pap. 10.00 (*0-86381-432-8*) New Native Pr.

***Laughin' Fertility: A Bundle of Observations for the Baby-Making Challenged.** Lisa Safran. LC 99-71448. 157p. 1999. pap. 13.95 (*0-9669858-0-X*) KoKo Pr.

Laughing Africa. Terese Svoboda. LC 89-20520. (Iowa Poetry Prize Ser.). 128p. 1990. pap. 11.95 (*0-87745-272-5*) U of Iowa Pr.

Laughing All over the World: My Life Married to Status Quo. Patti Parfitt. 256p. 1998. pap. 14.95 (*1-85782-198-X*, Pub. by Blake Publng) Seven Hills Bk.

Laughing All the Way. Liz Cashdan. LC 96-140109. 72p. (Orig.). (YA). (gr. 10). 1995. pap. 12.98 (*0-907123-46-5*, Pub. by Five Leaves) AK Pr Dist.

Laughing All the Way. Larry Incollingo. 1989. pap. 9.50 (*0-9619795-1-8*) Reunion Bks.

Laughing & Loving with Autism: A Collection of "Real Life" Warm & Humorous Stories. R. Wayne Gilpin. 127p. 1993. pap. 9.95 (*1-885477-04-X*) Fut Horizons.

Laughing at Ourselves: The Verses of Rufus Lisle. Rufus Lisle. Ed. by Edward T. Houlihan. LC 97-34960. (Illus.). 128p. 1997. 24.80 (*0-87642-015-3*) Henry Clay.

Laughing at the Tao: Debates among Buddhists & Taoists in Medieval China. Livia Kohn. LC 94-20924.Tr. of Hsiao Tao Lun. 264p. 1995. text 49.50 (*0-691-03483-4*, Pub. by Princeton U Pr) Cal Prin Full Svc.

Laughing Bill Hyde. Rex Ellingwood Beach. (Collected Works of Rex Ellingwood Beach). 392p. 1998. reprint ed. lib. bdg. 98.00 (*1-58201-536-8*) Classic Bks.

Laughing Boy. Oliver La Farge. 192p. Date not set. 20.95 (*0-8488-2350-8*) Amereon Ltd.

Laughing Boy. Oliver La Farge. (YA). 1971. mass mkt. 5.95 (*0-451-52467-5*) NAL.

Laughing Boy. Oliver La Farge. 259p. (J). 1981. reprint ed. lib. bdg. 21.95 (*0-89967-041-5*, Harmony Rain) Buccaneer Bks.

Laughing Boy. Oliver LaFarge. 245p. (J). 1981. reprint ed. lib. bdg. 24.95 (*0-89966-367-2*) Buccaneer Bks.

Laughing Buddha: Zen & the Comic Spirit. rev. ed. Conrad Hyers. LC 89-2592. (Illus.). 225p. 1989. pap. 15.95 (*0-89341-560-X*, Longwood Academic) Hollowbrook.

Laughing Cavalier. Emmuska Orczy. 1976. lib. bdg. 18.50 (*0-89968-076-3*, Lghtyr Pr) Buccaneer Bks.

Laughing Classroom: Everyone's Guide to Teaching with Humor & Play. Diane Loomans & Karen J. Kolberg. LC 92-23351. (Illus.). 228p. 1993. pap. 14.95 (*0-915811-44-8*) H J Kramer Inc.

Laughing Corpse. Laurell K. Hamilton. (Anita Blake Vampire Hunter Ser.). 293p. (Orig.). 1994. mass mkt. 6.50 (*0-441-00091-6*) Ace Bks.

Laughing Cry: An African Cock & Bull Story. Henri Lopes. Tr. by Gerald Moore from FRE. (Readers International Ser.). 260p. (C). 1987. 16.95 (*0-930523-32-6*); pap. 8.95 (*0-930523-33-4*) Readers Intl.

Laughing Day. Hope. Ed. by Tim Anders. LC 96-85609. (Life Lessons Ser.). (Illus.). 40p. (J). (gr. k-3). 1998. 15.95 incl. audio (*1-885624-50-6*) Alpine Pubng.

Laughing Day Book. Curt Werner. (Life Lessons Ser.). 1997. pap. 23.95 (*1-885624-52-2*) Alpine Pubng.

Laughing Death: The Untold Story of Kuru. Vincent Zigas. LC 89-24706. (Illus.). 315p. 1990. 29.50 (*0-89603-111-X*) Humana.

Laughing down Lonely Canyons. 3rd ed. James Kavanaugh. LC 90-62965. (Illus.). 96p. 1984. reprint ed. pap. 12.95 (*1-878995-11-1*) S J Nash Pub.

Laughing Eyes. Vicki Quade. (Illus.). (Orig.). 1979. pap. 5.00 (*0-9602604-0-4*) V Quade.

Laughing Eyes: Letters Between Edward & Cole Weston. Ed. by Paulette Weston. (Illus.). 182p. 1999. 39.95 (*1-886312-09-5*) Buying Best.

Laughing Feminism: Subversive Comedy in Frances Burney, Maria Edgeworth, & Jane Austen. Audrey Bilger. LC 98-10828. (Humor in Life & Letters Ser.). 1998. text 39.95 (*0-8143-2722-2*) Wayne St U Pr.

Laughing Gas. P. G. Wodehouse. 22.95 (*0-89190-299-6*) Amereon Ltd.

Laughing Gas. P. G. Wodehouse. 252p. 1984. pap. 12.99 (*0-14-001172-2*, Penguin Bks) Viking Penguin.

Laughing Gas: Nitrous Oxide. 2nd ed. David Wallechinski. Ed. by Michael Shedlin & Saunie Shedlin. (Illus.). 96p. 1992. reprint ed. pap. 12.95 (*0-914171-52-6*) Ronin Pub.

Laughing Gas: Poems New & Selected, 1963-1990. Ruth Whitman. LC 91-13840. 282p. 1991. pap. text 19.95 (*0-8143-2316-2*) Wayne St U Pr.

Laughing Gas: Poems New & Selected, 1963-1990. Ruth Whitman. LC 91-13840. 281p. reprint ed. pap. 87.20 (*0-608-10583-X*, 2071204) Bks Demand.

Laughing Gods, Weeping Virgins: Laughter in the History of Religion. Ingvild S. Gilhus. LC 96-53412. 184p. (C). 1997. pap. write for info. (*0-415-16532-6*) Routledge.

Laughing Gods, Weeping Virgins: Laughter in the History of Religion. Ingvild S. Gilhus. LC 96-53412. 184p. (C). 1997. 75.00 (*0-415-16197-5*) Routledge.

Laughing Hangman. Edward Marston. LC 96-6990. 320p. 1996. text 21.95 (*0-312-14305-2*) St Martin.

Laughing Horse. Barbara Muchnick. 58p. write for info. (*0-318-58342-9*) Just Fun Horse.

Laughing Hysterically. Ed Sikov. Ed. by John Belton. (Film & Culture Ser.). 288p. 1996. pap. 18.50 (*0-231-07983-4*) Col U Pr.

Laughing in the Dark: A Decade of Subversive Comedy. Laurie Stone. LC 96-37636. 304p. 1997. 24.00 (*0-88001-474-1*) HarpC.

Laughing in the Dark: From Colored Girl to Woman of Color - A Journey from Prison to Power. Patrice Gaines. LC 95-8023. 304p. 1995. reprint ed. pap. 14.00 (*0-385-48027-X*, Anchor NY) Doubleday.

Laughing in the Hills. Bill Barich. LC 97-78223. 228p. 1998. reprint ed. pap. 14.00 (*1-886913-20-X*) Ruminator Bks.

Laughing in the Jungle: An Autobiography of an Immigrant in America. Louis Adamic. LC 69-18755. (American Immigration Collection. Series 1). 1969. reprint ed. 43.55 (*0-405-00503-2*) Ayer.

***Laughing in the Kitchen: Short Stories, Poems, Essays, & Memoirs.** Streetfeet Women Staff et al. 226p. 1998. pap. 15.00 (*0-944941-12-5*) Talking Stone Pr.

Laughing into Glory: American Autobiography. Hodge Eagleson. 192p. 1995. lib. bdg. 69.00 (*0-7812-8509-7*) Rprt Serv.

Laughing Kelly & Other Verses. R. A. Lafferty. (Booklet Ser.: No. 11). 16p. (Orig.). 1983. pap. 1.00 (*0-936055-08-1*) C Drumm Bks.

Laughing Ladies. Diane Scharper. 78p. (Orig.). 1993. pap. 9.95 (*0-940475-01-4*) Dolphin-Moon.

***Laughing Lessons: 149 2/3 Ways to Make Teaching & Learning Fun.** Ron Burgess. LC 99-56599. (Illus.). 176p. 2000. pap., teacher ed. 21.95 (*1-57542-075-9*) Free Spirit Pub.

Laughing Lighthouse. Katy Perry. Ed. by Lyons Graphic Design Staff. (Illus.). 16p. (Orig.). (J). (gr. 1-4). 1995. pap. 7.50 (*0-9626825-0-5*) Perry ME.

Laughing Like Dogs. unabridged ed. Carla Perry. LC 96-70940. (Illus.). 76p. (Orig.). 1996. pap. 5.00 (*1-888934-23-9*, Cape Perpetua) Central OR Coast.

Laughing Like Hell: The Harrowing Satires of Jim Thompson. Gay Brewer. LC 95-5337. (Mystery Guides Ser.: No. 17). 144p. 1996. pap. 19.00 (*0-941028-22-4*) Millefleurs.

Laughing Lost in the Mountains: Poems of Wang Wei. Wang Wei. Tr. by Tony Barnstone et al. LC 91-50376. (CHI., Illus.). 244p. 1992. pap. 15.95 (*0-87451-564-5*) U Pr of New Eng.

Laughing Lost in the Mountains: Poems of Wang Wei. Wang Wei. Tr. by Willis Barnstone et al. LC 91-50376. (Illus.). 248p. reprint ed. pap. 76.90 (*0-608-09096-4*, 206973000005) Bks Demand.

Laughing Magician. Jack Vance. LC 97-10172. (Illus.). 486p. 1998. 50.00 (*1-887424-00-8*) Underwood Bks.

Laughing Man. Nancy Van Laan. LC 98-31291. (J). 2000. 17.00 (*0-689-82477-7*) Atheneum Yung Read.

Laughing Matter: An Essay on the Comic. Marcel Gutwirth. LC 92-30520. 224p. 1993. text 29.95 (*0-8014-2783-5*) Cornell U Pr.

Laughing Matters, Vol. 11. Susan Thompsen. 1999. pap. text 6.00 (*1-887369-09-0*, Pub. by Global Cty Pr) Consort Bk Sales.

Laughing Matters: Comic Tradition in India. Lee Siegel. (Illus.). 520p. 1987. 42.00 (*0-226-75691-2*) U Ch Pr.

Laughing Matters: Creative Writing Book. Eleanor Hoomes. (J). Date not set. teacher ed. 9.95 (*1-56644-969-3*, 969-3AP) Educ Impress.

Laughing Matters: On Writing M*A*S*H, Tootsie, Oh, God! & a Few Other Funny Things. large type ed. Larry Gelbart. LC 98-22204. 397p. 1998. write for info. (*0-7838-0294-3*, G K Hall Lrg Type) Mac Lib Ref.

Laughing Matters: Selected Columns by Humorist Pam Robbins. Pam Robbins. LC 98-88047. 90p. (Orig.). 1998. pap. 10.00 (*0-9667357-0-6*) Global Busn Persp.

Laughing Matters: The Paradox of Comedy. Scott C. Shershow. LC 85-16506. 168p. 1986. lib. bdg. 22.50 (*0-87023-509-5*) U of Mass Pr.

Laughing Matters, a Serious Look at Humour. Ed. by John Durant & Jonathan Miller. LC 89-135282. (Illus.). 144p. reprint ed. pap. 44.70 (*0-7837-1594-3*, 204188600024) Bks Demand.

Laughing Monkeys of Gravity. Stephen Bluestone. LC 94-27079. 63p. 1994. pap. 10.95 (*0-86554-452-2*, MUP/P112) Mercer Univ Pr.

Laughing Nine to Five: The Quest for Humor in the Workplace. Clyde H. Fahlman. LC 97-91442. 202p. 1997. pap. 14.95 (*0-9656055-3-1*) Steelhead Pr.

Laughing on Outside John Candy. Martin Knelman. LC 97-16633. (Illus.). 243p. 1997. text 22.95 (*0-312-17179-X*) St Martin.

Laughing on the Outside. Knelman. 272p. 1998. pap. 12.95 (*0-312-19471-4*) St Martin.

Laughing Out Loud: Writing the Comedy-centered Screenplay. Andrew Horton. LC 99-17669. 230p. 2000. pap. 15.95 (*0-520-22015-3*, Pub. by U CA Pr) Cal Prin Full Svc.

Laughing out Loud: Writing the Comedy-Centered Screenplay. Andrew Horton. LC 99-17669. 230p. 2000. 40.00 (*0-520-22014-5*, Pub. by U CA Pr) Cal Prin Full Svc.

Laughing Out Loud & Other Religious Experiences. Thomas Mullen. LC 83-3643. 133p. 1989. pap. 7.50 (*0-944350-11-9*) Friends United.

Laughing Out Loud, I Fly: Poems in English & Spanish. Juan F. Herrera. LC 96-45476. (Illus.). 48p. (J). 1998. 15.95 (*0-06-027604-5*) HarpC.

Laughing Place: A Novel. Pam Durban. Ed. by Barbara Grossman. 352p. 1993. 21.00 (*0-684-19258-6*, Scribners Ref) Mac Lib Ref.

Laughing Place: A Novel. Pam Durban. 352p. 1995. pap. 13.00 (*0-312-13110-0*) St Martin.

Laughing Policeman. Maj Sjowall. LC 92-5000. 1992. pap. 11.00 (*0-679-74223-9*) Vin Bks.

Laughing River: A Folktale for Peace. Elizabeth H. Vega. (Illus.). 32p. (J). 1995. 23.95 incl. audio (*1-877810-37-1*, LAFC) Rayve Prodns.

Laughing River: A Folktale for Peace. Elizabeth H. Vega. LC 94-69051. (Illus.). 32p. (J). (ps-6). 1995. 16.95 (*1-877810-35-5*, LAFB) Rayve Prodns.

Laughing Screaming: Modern Hollywood Horror & Comedy. William Paul. 512p. 1995. pap. 19.50 (*0-231-08465-X*) Col U Pr.

Laughing, Screaming: Modern Hollywood Horror & Comedy. William Paul. LC 93-27388. (Film & Culture Ser.). 510p. (C). 1994. 40.50 (*0-231-08464-1*) Col U Pr.

Laughing Shadows. Drumbeat Publishing Staff. Date not set. pap. text. write for info. (*0-582-78574-X*, Drumbeat) Longman.

***Laughing Sickness.** Kathleen Driskall. LC 99-63909. 68p. (Orig.). 1999. pap. 10.00 (*0-9652520-2-7*) Fleur-de-lis Pr.

***Laughing Stock.** Arnold I. Burns. LC 00-190491. 155p. 2000. 25.00 (*0-7388-1788-0*); pap. 18.00 (*0-7388-1789-9*) Xlibris Corp.

Laughing Stock: A Cow's Guide to Life. Texas B. Bender. LC 93-48165. (Illus.). 112p. 1994. pap. 6.95 (*0-87905-630-4*) Gibbs Smith Pub.

Laughing Stock: Three Short Plays. Romulus Linney. 1984. pap. 5.25 (*0-8222-0643-9*) Dramatists Play.

Laughing Stories of Old Japan. Andrew Dykstra. 120p. 1987. pap. 8.95 (*0-917880-03-X*) Kanji Pr.

Laughing Sutra. Mark Salzman. 1992. pap. 12.00 (*0-679-73546-1*) Vin Bks.

Laughing Terran. Perry A. Chapdelaine, Sr. 176p. 1977. 7.50 (*0-7091-5892-0*) AC Projects.

Laughing Through the Years: A New Treasury of Jewish Humor. large type ed. David C. Gross. 256p. (Orig.). 1992. pap. 13.95 (*0-8027-2657-7*) Walker & Co.

Laughing Time: Collected Nonsense. 2nd ed. William J. Smith. LC 90-55655. (Illus.). 176p. (J). (gr. 4-8). 1990. pap. 3.50 (*0-374-44315-7*) FS&G.

Laughing to Keep from Crying. Langston Hughes. reprint ed. lib. bdg. 21.95 (*0-88411-060-5*) Amereon Ltd.

Laughing to Keep from Crying: Dark Humor in the South. Ke Francis. Ed. by Audrey Hammill. (Illus.). 38p. (Orig.). (C). 1984. pap. 15.00 (*0-944564-04-6*) Alex Mus.

Laughing Together & Other Ironies. Jeffrey Norman. (Illus.). 56p. (Orig.). 1991. pap. write for info. (*0-9628082-0-2*) EyeDea Bks.

Laughing Tomatoes & Other Spring Poems (Jitomates Risuenos y Otros Poemas de Primavera) Francisco X. Alarcon. (ENG & SPA., Illus.). (J). 1997. 21.27 (*0-516-20545-5*) Childrens.

Laughing Tomatoes & Other Spring Poems (Jitomates Risuenos y Otros Poemas de Primavera) Francisco X. Alarcon. LC 96-7459. (ENG & SPA., Illus.). (J). (ps-3). 1997. 15.95 (*0-89239-139-1*) Childrens Book Pr.

Laughing West: Humorous Western Fiction, Past & Present: An Anthology. Ed. by Charles L. Sonnichsen. LC 87-26737. 280p. 1988. 29.95 (*0-8040-0901-5*); pap. 14.95 (*0-8040-0902-3*) Swallow.

Laughing Whitefish. Robert Travor. 222p. Date not set. 21.95 (*0-8488-2615-9*) Amereon Ltd.

Laughing Wild. rev. ed. Christopher Durang. LC 96-158360. 1996. pap. 5.25 (*0-8222-1528-4*) Dramatists Play.

Laughing Wild & Baby with the Bathwater. Christopher Durang. LC 88-13938. 176p. 1989. pap. 10.00 (*0-8021-3130-1*, Grove) Grove-Atltic.

Laughing with God. 2nd rev. ed. Jerry Stocking. Ed. by Charlotte Ward. (Illus.). 140p. 1997. pap. write for info. (*0-9629593-6-7*) Moose Ear Pr.

Laughing with Tears in My Eyes: Tongue in Cheek Jewish Humor. Avram Gabriner. 186p. 1995. 12.95 (*965-229-134-X*, Pub. by Gefen Pub Hse) Gefen Bks.

Laughing Your Way to Good Health. Susan Vass. (Illus.). 72p. (Orig.). 1990. pap. 4.95 (*0-9627545-0-1*) HMR Pubns Grp.

***Laughing Your Way to Passing the Pediatric Boards: The Seriously Funny Study Guide.** (Illus.). 400p. 2000. pap. 99.95 (*0-9700287-0-9*) Medhumor.

Laughs: Funny Stories Selected by Claire Mackay. Ed. by Claire Mackay. LC 96-61148. 208p. (J). (gr. 5-9). 1997. pap. 6.95 (*0-88776-393-6*) Tundra Bks.

Laughs: Lovable, Livable, Laughable Lines. Marcia Kaplan & David Kaplan. (Illus.). 96p. (Orig.). 1995. pap. text 6.95 (*0-9617744-7-9*) Cheers.

Laughs & Landings. Alan M. Hofmeister et al. (Reading for All Learners Ser.). (Illus.). (J). pap. write for info. (*1-56861-205-2*) Swift Lrn Res.

Laughs & Limericks on Aging. Reggie the Retiree, pseud. (Illus.). 96p. 1991. pap. 6.95 (*0-9609960-0-1*) Reggie the Retiree.

Laughs Breed Success, No. 1, No. 1000. Marene P. Fassina. (Illus.). 128p. 1998. pap. 7.95 (*1-892996-04-9*) M Fassina.

Laughs, Luck... & Lucy: How I Came to Create the Most Popular Sitcom of All Time (with Lucy Audio CD) Jess Oppenheimer & Gregg Oppenheimer. LC 96-20756. (Television Ser.). (Illus.). 312p. 1996. 39.95 incl. audio compact disk (*0-8156-0406-8*, OPLL) Syracuse U Pr.

Laughs, Luck...& Lucy: How I Came to Create the Most Popular Sitcom of All Time (with I Love Lucy's Lost Scenes Audio CD) Jess Oppenheimer & Gregg Oppenheimer. (Illus.). 312p. 1999. pap. 19.95 incl. audio compact disk (*0-8156-0584-6*) Syracuse U Pr.

Laughs on Hollywood. Richard Webb & Teet Carle. LC 84-60760. (Illus.). 214p. 1984. 13.95 (*0-915677-09-1*) Roundtable Pub.

Laugh at Your Muscles II: A Second Light Look at Fibromyalgia. Mark J. Pellegrino & Barbara Dawkins. (Illus.). 97p. 1997. pap. 5.95 (*1-890018-15-5*) Anadem Pubng.

Laughter. Henry Bergson. 1996. 26.00 (*0-8446-1666-4*) Peter Smith.

Laughter: A Scientific Investigation. Robert R. Provine. 288p. 1999. 24.00 (*0-316-71102-0*) Little.

***Laughter: A Scientific Investigation.** Robert R. Provine. (Illus.). 256p. 2000. 24.95 (*0-670-89375-7*, Viking) Viking Penguin.

Laughter: A Theological Reflection. Karl-Josef Kuschel. 128p. 1994. 17.95 (*0-8264-0660-2*) Continuum.

Laughter: An Essay on the Meaning of the Comic. Henri Bergson. Tr. by Cloudesley Brereton & Fred Rothwell. (Green Integer Bks.: No. 14). 184p. 1999. reprint ed. pap. 11.95 (*1-892295-02-4*, Pub. by Green Integer) Consort Bk Sales.

Laughter Among Colleagues: A Study of the Social Functions of Humor Among the Staff of a Men. Rose L. Coser. (Reprint Series in Social Sciences). (C). 1993. reprint ed. pap. text 5.00 (*0-8290-3093-X*, S-362) Irvington.

Laughter among the Tears: Living with Alzheimer's. Earline M. Murphy & Deborah M. Clark. (Illus.). 200p. 1998. pap. 13.50 (*0-9665468-0-6*) Fly Away Pr.

Laughter & Tears. George Rarey. Ed. by Damon Rarey. LC 96-61847. (Illus.). 192p. 1996. pap. 49.95 (*1-56550-057-1*) Vis Bks Intl.

Laughter & Tears: The Emotional Life of New Mothers. Elizabeth Bing. LC 96-46089. (Illus.). 272p. (Orig.). 1995. pap. 16.95 (*0-8050-4157-5*, Owl) H Holt & Co.

Laughter at a Wake. Mark A. Johnson. 48p. (Orig.). 1989. pap. 4.00 (*0-944920-04-7*) Bellowing Ark Pr.

Laughter at the Door: A Continued Autobiography Geoffrey Trease. LC 74-195710. 186p. 1974. write for info. (*0-333-16811-9*) Macmillan.

Laughter at the Foot of the Cross. M. A. Screech. 352p. pap. 17.95 (*0-14-012490-X*, Pub. by Pnguin Bks Ltd) Trafalgar.

***Laughter at the Foot of the Cross.** M. A. Screech. LC 99-462571. 352p. 1999. 59.00 (*0-8133-3739-9*, Pub. by Westview) HarpC.

Laughter Beneath the Forest: Poems from Old & Recent Manuscripts. Abraham Sutzkever. Tr. by Barnett Zumoff from YID. LC 96-16445. 1997. 29.50 (*0-88125-555-6*) Ktav.

***Laughter Factor.** Dan Keller. LC 99-91951. 2000. 25.00 (*0-7388-1432-6*); pap. 18.00 (*0-7388-1433-4*) Xlibris Corp.

Laughter for the Devil: The Trials of Gilles de Rais, Companion-in-Arms of Joan of Arc (1440) Gilles De Rais. LC 83-20801. 1984. 29.50 (*0-8386-3190-8*) Fairleigh Dickinson.

Laughter from the Dark: A Life of Gwyn Thomas. Michael Parnell. (Illus.). 242p. 1997. pap. 22.95 (*1-85411-146-9*, Pub. by Seren Bks) Dufour.

Laughter, Grabber & Power: A Prophetic Revelation of the Current & Coming Move of God. Rob Lech. Ed. by Good News Fellowship Min. Staff. 64p. (Orig.). 1997. pap. 4.99 (*1-888081-52-X*) Good News Min.

Laughter in a Genevan Gown: The Works of Frederick Buechner, 1970-1980. Marie-Helene Davies. LC 83-14205. 208p. reprint ed. pap. 64.50 (*0-608-14489-4*, 202531900043) Bks Demand.

Laughter in Appalachia: A Festival of Southern Mountain Humor. Ed. by Billy E. Wheeler & Loyal Jones. LC 86-32263. 160p. 1991. pap. 9.95 (*0-87483-032-X*) August Hse.

Laughter in Hell: The Use of Humor During the Holocaust. Steve Lipman. LC 90-28101. 296p. 1993. pap. 30.00 (*1-56821-112-0*) Aronson.

Laughter in Khaki. Dorothy M. Obe. 138p. (C). 1989. text 50.00 (*0-946270-41-4*, Pub. by Pentland Pr) St Mut.

***Laughter in Quaker Grey.** William H. Sessions. 1999. pap. 21.00 (*0-900657-30-8*, Pub. by W Sessions) St Mut.

Laughter in Quaker Grey. Sessions, William Ltd., Staff. (C). 1989. pap. 21.00 (*0-900657-11-1*, Pub. by W Sessions) St Mut.

Laughter in the Courts of Love: Comedy in Allegory, from Chaucer to Spencer. Frances M. Leonard. LC 81-10676. 184p. 1981. 18.95 (*0-937664-54-5*) Pilgrim Bks OK.

Laughter in the Dark. Vladimir Nabokov. 1989. pap. 8.95 (*0-07-045848-0*) McGraw.

Laughter in the Dark. Vladimir Nabokov. (Vintage International Ser.). 1989. pap. 13.00 (*0-679-72450-8*) Vin Bks.

Laughter in the Dark. Vladimir Nabokov. LC 91-18665. (New Directions Classics Ser.: Vol. 729). 296p. 1991. reprint ed. pap. 11.95 (*0-8112-1186-X*, NDP729, Pub. by New Directions) Penguin Books.

Laughter in the Dark: The Plays of Alan Ayckbourn. Albert E. Kalson. LC 91-58958. 208p. (C). 1993. 33.50 (*0-8386-3479-6*) Fairleigh Dickinson.

Laughter in the Next Room. Osbert Sitwell. 4.95 (*0-7043-3162-4*, Pub. by Quartet) Charles River Bks.

Laughter in the Next Room. Osbert Sitwell. LC 79-152607. 400p. 1972. reprint ed. lib. bdg. 35.00 (*0-8371-6042-1*, SILA, Greenwood Pr) Greenwood.

Laughter in the Shadow of the Trees & Four Other Plays. James Prideaux. 1996. pap. 5.25 (*0-8222-1512-8*) Dramatists Play.

Laughter in the Wilderness: Early American Humor to 1783. W. Kennedy. LC 75-44710. 246p. reprint ed. pap. 76.30 (*0-608-11855-9*, 202320100032) Bks Demand.

Laughter Is the Best Medicine: A Hospital Riddle Book for Kids. Lee Winkler. (Illus.). 64p. (J). (gr. k-4). 1998. pap. 4.95 (*1-888237-18-X*) Baxter Pr.

Laughter Is the Best Meditation: The Best of the Inner Jester. Laren Bright. LC 78-4491. 1979. pap. 5.00 (*0-686-10176-6*) Mandeville LA.

Laughter, Jestbooks & Society in the Spanish Netherlands. Johan Verberckmoes. LC 98-17687. (Early Modern History Ser.). 227p. 1999. text 65.00 (*0-312-21609-2*) St Martin.

Laughter, Joy & Healing. 2nd rev. ed. Donald E. Demaray. (Illus.). 152p. 1995. reprint ed. pap. 9.99 (*0-89367-197-5*) Light & Life Comm.

Laughter Lines: Family Wit & Wisdom. Illus. by Bob Dewar. 88p. (C). 1989. 25.00 (*0-903065-61-4*, Pub. by G Wright Pub) St Mut.

Laughter of Aphrodite: A Novel about Sappho of Lesbos. Peter Green. LC 92-12431. 274p. 1993. 40.00 (*0-520-07966-3*, Pub. by U CA Pr) Cal Prin Full Svc.

Laughter of Aphrodite: A Novel about Sappho of Lesbos. Peter Green. LC 92-12431. 274p. 1995. pap. 15.95 (*0-520-20340-2*, Pub. by U CA Pr) Cal Prin Full Svc.

Laughter of Children. Les Roberts. mass mkt. write for info. (*0-312-97642-9*) St Martin.

***Laughter of Children.** Les Roberts. LC 00-24136. 320p. 2000. text 23.95 (*0-312-25217-X*) St Martin.

Laughter of God. Walter C. Lanyon. 224p. 1983. reprint ed. pap. 10.00 (*1-889870-04-8*) Union Life.

Laughter of Heroes. Jonathan Neale. 128p. 1993. pap. 11.99 (*1-85242-279-3*) Serpents Tail.

Laughter of Love: A Study of Robert Burns. Raymond J. Grant. (Illus.). 207p. (Orig.). 1986. pap. 17.95 (*0-920490-55-7*) Temeron Bks.

***Laughter of Stones.** Bob Carlton. 10p. 1999. pap. 2.00 (*0-9674487-4-3*) Good SAMAR.

Laughter of the Stones. Lee Lozowick. 140p. 1984. pap. 9.95 (*0-934252-00-9*, Pub. by Hohm Pr) SCB Distributors.

Laughter of the Witch: And Other Known Poems. Red J. Arobateau. (Series 1A). 48p. (Orig.). (C). 1995. pap. 15.00 (*0-934172-40-4*) WIM Pubns.

Laughter on a Weekday. Louis Falstein. 1965. 14.95 (*0-8392-1147-3*) Astor-Honor.

Laughter on Record: A Comedy Discography. Warren Debenham. LC 87-35938. (Illus.). 387p. 1988. 37.00 (*0-8108-2094-3*) Scarecrow.

Laughter on the Stairs. Beverley Nichols. LC 98-7155. (Illus.). 260p. 1998. reprint ed. 24.95 (*0-88192-460-1*) Timber.

Laughter over the Left Shoulder. Vladimir Soloukhin. Tr. by D. Martin. 180p. (YA). 1990. 36.00 (*0-7206-0798-1*) Dufour.

Laughter, Pain, & Wonder: Shakespeare's Comedies & the Audience in the Theater. David Richman. LC 89-40413. 200p. 1990. 36.50 (*0-87413-388-2*) U Delaware Pr.

***Laughter Prescription: Inspirational Wit & Cartoons.** Cal Samra & Rose Samra. LC 99-33685. (Holy Humor Ser.). 128p. 1999. pap. 6.95 (*1-57856-286-4*) Waterbrook Pr.

Laughter Ring. Stephen E. Cosgrove. (Song of the Sea Trilogy Ser.: Bk. 2). (Illus.). 72p. 1990. 24.95 (*1-55868-032-2*) Gr Arts Ctr Pub.

Laughter, Silence, & Shouting: An Anthology of Women's Prayers. Kathy Keay. (Illus.). 192p. 1994. pap. 18.00 (*0-551-02889-0*) HarpC.

Laughter Ten Years After: Essays. Jo A. Isaak et al. 64p. 1996. 18.95 (*0-910969-02-7*) Hobart & Wm Smith.

Laughter, the Best Medicine. Robert Holden. 1999. pap. 11.00 (*0-7225-2827-2*) Thorsons PA.

Laughter, the Best Medicine: Jokes, Gags & Laugh Lines from America's Most Popular Magazine. Reader's Digest Editors. LC 97-1844. 1997. pap. 9.95 (*0-89577-977-3*, Pub. by RD Assn) Penguin Putnam.

Laughter Thief. Gary Hill. LC 88-81221. 240p. (Orig.). 1988. pap. 3.95 (*0-930531-01-9*) LOTIC.

Laughter Through Tears: The Yiddish Cinema. Judith Goldberg. LC 80-70900. (Illus.). 176p. 1983. 29.50 (*0-8386-3074-X*) Fairleigh Dickinson.

Laughter Unlimited: Essays on Humor, Satire & the Comic. Ed. by Reinhold Grimm & Jost Hermand. LC 90-50645. (Monatshefte Occasional Volumes Ser.: Vol. 11). 143p. reprint ed. pap. 44.40 (*0-608-20435-8*, 207168800002) Bks Demand.

Laughter, War & Feminism Vol. 11: Elements of Carnival in Three of Jane Austen's Novels. Gabriela Castellanos. LC 93-42550. (Writing about Women Ser.: Vol. 11). XI, 241p. (C). 1995. text 43.95 (*0-8204-2351-3*) P Lang Pubng.

***Laughter Wasn't Rationed: Remembering the War Years in Germany.** Dorothea V. S. Lawson. LC 99-71359. (Illus.). vi, 538p. 1999. pap. 24.95 (*0-9673830-3-X*) Tricor Pr.

Laughter's Gentle Soul: The Life of Robert Benchley. Billy Altman. (Illus.). 384p. (C). 1997. 30.00 (*0-393-03833-5*) Norton.

Laugier: And Eighteenth-Century French Theory. Wolfgang Herrmann. Ed. by John Harris & Alastair Laing. (Studies in Architecture: No. VI). (Illus.). 270p. 1986. pap. 39.95 (*0-302-02752-1*, Pub. by Zwemmer Bks) Intl Spec Bk.

Laukikanyaya Sangraha. Raghunatha V. Udasina. Ed. by Munari L. Nagar & Sasla D. Nagar. (Universal Laws of Interpretation Ser.). (SAN.). xiv, 144p. 1998. pap. 25.00 (*0-943913-29-2*) Intl Lib Ctr.

Laukikanyayanjali: A Handful of Popular Maxims Current in Sanskrit Literature. rev. ed. Ed. by Munari L. Nagar & K. M. Lee. LC 97-51342. (Universal Laws of Interpretation Ser.: Vol. 3). (ENG & SAN.). 361p. 1998. pap. 45.00 (*0-943913-28-4*) Intl Lib Ctr.

Laukikanyayaratnakara: An Ocean of Gem Crystalized As the Maxims of Interpretation, 3 vols. Raghunatha V. Udasina et al. LC 98-45911. (Universal Laws of Interpretation Ser.). 1998. 150.00 (*0-943913-30-6*) Intl Lib Ctr.

Launcelot Granger of Newbury, Mass. & Suffield, Conn. A Genealogical History. J. N. Granger. (Illus.). 587p. 1989. reprint ed. pap. 88.00 (*0-8328-0612-9*); reprint ed. lib. bdg. 96.00 (*0-8328-0611-0*) Higginson Bk Co.

***Launch: A Teacher's Guide to the Code Cards.** Brenda K. Murphy. (Sail Away Ser.). (Illus.). 28p. 1999. pap. text, teacher ed. 8.95 (*1-58504-001-0*) UTW Res Inc.

Launch Day. Peter Campbell. (Illus.). 32p. (J). (gr. 2-4). 1995. pap. 7.95 (*1-56294-190-9*); lib. bdg. 21.40 (*1-56294-611-0*) Millbrook Pr.

Launch Manual: A Young Person's Introduction to the Principles of World Takeover. Jack Dwyer. LC 97-91731. (Illus.). 275p. (YA). (gr. 10 up). 1998. pap. 10.95 (*0-9658366-5-7*) Chairman Pubns.

***Launch Manual: An Introduction to the Principles of World Takeover.** 2nd rev. ed. J. Dwyer. LC 00-90386. 221p. 2000. pap. 10.95 (*0-9658366-6-5*) Chairman Pubns.

Launch Out! Frances J. Roberts. 1964. pap. 3.25 (*0-932814-21-2*) Kings Farspan.

Launch Ramps of Baja California. Michael C. Bales. LC 92-90030. (Illus.). 112p. (Orig.). 1992. pap. 6.95 (*0-9632188-0-8*) Cortez Pubns.

Launched Bridges: Prestressed Concrete Bridges Built On The Ground & Launched Into Their Final Position. abr. ed. Marco Rosignoli. LC 98-4585. 336p. 1998. pap. 79.00 (*0-7844-0314-7*) Am Soc Civil Eng.

Launched from the Castle. Peter R. Doyle. LC 95-2694. (Daring Adventure Ser.: Vol. 7). (J). (gr. 4). 1995. pap. 5.99 (*1-56179-368-X*) Focus Family.

Launching a Baby's Adoption: Practical Strategies for Parents & Professionals. Patricia I. Johnston. LC 96-36909. 256p. 1997. 22.95 (*0-944934-16-1*) Perspect Indiana.

Launching a Baby's Adoption: Practical Strategies for Parents & Professionals. Patricia Irwin Johnston. LC 96-36909. 256p. 1998. pap. 15.00 (*0-944934-20-X*) Perspect Indiana.

Launching a Business on the Web. David Cook & Deborah Sellers. LC 95-69233. (Illus.). 550p. 1995. 39.99 (*0-7897-0188-X*) Que.

Launching a Business on the Web. 3rd ed. David Cook. 1997. 39.99 (*0-7897-1277-6*) Macmillan.

Launching a Great Year. Sharon Rybak. 144p. (J). (ps-2). 1989. 13.99 (*0-86653-507-1*, GA1093) Good Apple.

Launching a Satellite. Peter Mellett. LC 98-52725. (Expert Guide Ser.). 32p. 1999. write for info. (*1-57572-781-1*) Heinemann Lib.

Launching & Operating Satellites: Legal Issues. R. Bender. LC 97-38209. (Utrecht Studies in Air & Space Law: No. 18). 364p. 1997. 115.00 (*90-411-0507-7*) Kluwer Academic.

Launching Democracy in South Africa: The First Open Election, April 1994. Ed. by R. W. Johnson & Lawrence Schlemmer. LC 95-6564. 1996. 37.50 (*0-300-06391-1*) Yale U Pr.

Launching Europe: An Ethnography of European Cooperation in Space Science. Stacia E. Zabusky. LC 94-32074. 280p. 1995. text 49.50 (*0-691-03370-6*, Pub. by Princeton U Pr); pap. text 17.95 (*0-691-02972-5*, Pub. by Princeton U Pr) Cal Prin Full Svc.

Launching New Global Trade Talks Vol. 12: An Action Agenda. Ed. by Jeffrey J. Schott. LC 98-40511. (Special Report Ser.: Vol. 12). 240p. (C). 1998. pap. 20.00 (*0-88132-266-0*) Inst Intl Eco.

The end of the 20th century will mark the beginning of a new era for the world trading system. More than 130 member countries of the World Trade Organization (WTO) will begin negotiations in 1999 on a broad range of subjects, including agriculture, services, intellectual property & trade & environment. The authors in this volume analyze the key issues that should be on the agenda of new WTO negotiations to meet the challenges generated by the Asian financial crisis, concerns about the impact of globalization on firms & workers & the proliferation of regional trading pacts. They present a compelling case for comprehensive trade talks that include new issues such as investment & competition policy, in addition to subjects already part of the WTO's built-in agenda. The overview chapter by Jeffrey J. Schott examines the work of the WTO since its establishment in January 1995 (including its dispute settlement mechanism) & the key challenges facing new trade talks. In addition, Schott proposes a new negotiating strategy to produce concrete results without the lengthy delays of past trade talks. He recommends that governments commit to continuous negotiations in Geneva & use the regularly scheduled meetings of trade ministers to conclude a balanced "round-up" of agreements every two years. An appendix contains statements made with WTO Director General Renato Ruggiero & US Trade Representative Barshefsky on the importance of WTO negotiations & the key US objectives in pursuing those talks. ***Publisher Paid Annotation.***

Launching New Ventures. Allen. 1999. pap. 8.97 (*0-395-91846-4*) HM.

Launching New Ventures: An Entrepreneurial Approach. 2nd ed. Kathleen R. Allen. LC 98-71974. 1998. text 59.96 (*0-395-91845-6*) HM.

Launching of a University. Daniel C. Gilman. 1972. reprint ed. 39.50 (*0-8422-8059-6*) Irvington.

Launching of Duke University, 1924-1949. Robert F. Durden. LC 92-27499. (Illus.). 588p. 1993. text 32.95 (*0-8223-1302-2*) Duke.

Launching of the I. W. W. Paul F. Brissenden. LC 78-169188. (American History & Americana Ser.: No. 47). 1971. reprint ed. lib. bdg. 75.00 (*0-8383-1275-6*) M S G Haskell Hse.

Launching Onto the Web: A Small Business View. William J. Piniarski. (Illus.). 258p. 1998. pap. 19.95 (*1-892614-13-8*) Briarwood VA.

Launching-Points to the Realm of Mind. Tr. by Kenneth Guthrie from GRE. LC 88-22517. 96p. (Orig.). 1988. pap. 11.95 (*0-933999-59-3*) Phanes Pr.

Launching Science & Technology Across the Curriculum Design. Sharon A. Brusic. (Kids & Technology - Mission Twenty-One Ser.). 1993. pap. 9.95 (*0-8273-4950-5*) S-W Pub.

Launching Science & Technology Across the Curriculum Explore. Sharon A. Brusic. (Kids & Technology - Mission Twenty-One Ser.). 1993. pap. 9.95 (*0-8273-4951-3*) S-W Pub.

Launching Science & Technology Across the Curriculum Space. Sharon A. Brusic. (Kids & Technology - Mission Twenty-One Ser.). 1993. pap. 9.95 (*0-8273-4948-3*) S-W Pub.

Launching Science & Technology Across the Curriculum Transportation. Sharon A. Brusic. (Kids & Technology - Mission Twenty-One Ser.). 1993. pap. 9.95 (*0-8273-4949-1*) S-W Pub.

Launching Social Security: A Capture-&-Record Account, 1935-1937. Charles McKinley & Robert W. Frase. LC 70-121771. 543p. reprint ed. pap. 168.40 (*0-8357-6782-5*, 203545900095) Bks Demand.

Launching the Antibiotic Era: Personal Accounts of the Discovery & Use of the First Antibiotics. Edward P. Abraham et al. Ed. by Zanvil A. Cohn & Carol L. Moberg. 112p. 1990. 25.00 (*0-87470-047-7*) Rockefeller.

Launching the "Extended Republic" The Federalist Era. Ed. by Ronald Hoffman & Peter J. Albert. LC 95-46657. (United States Capitol Historical Society Ser.). 327p. (C). 1996. text 37.50 (*0-8139-1624-0*) U Pr of Va.

Launching the Uraguay Round: Clayton Yeutter & the Two-Track Decision. David M. Kennedy. (Pew Case Studies in International Affairs). 50p. (C). 1992. pap. text 3.50 (*1-56927-144-5*) Geo U Inst Dplmcy.

Launching the War on Poverty. Gillette. 1996. 15.95 (*0-8057-9243-0*, Twyne) Mac Lib Ref.

Launching the War on Poverty. Michael L. Gillette. LC 96-18616. (Illus.). 300p. 1996. per. 28.95 (*0-8057-9104-3*, Twyne) Mac Lib Ref.

Launching Your First Small Business: Make the Right Decisions During Your First 90 Days. Joel Handelsman & Small Office/Home Office Editorial Group Staff. (Business Owner's Toolkit Ser.). (Illus.). 192p. 1998. pap. 14.95 (*0-8080-0241-4*, Contin Ed) CCH INC.

Launching Your Home-Based Business: How to Successfully Plan, Finance & Grow Your New Venture. David H. Bangs, Jr. & Andi Axman. LC 97-27091. 272p. 1997. pap. 22.95 (*1-57410-053-X*, 5614-5001) Dearborn.

Launchpad for the 21st Century: Yearbook of the International Space Year. Harvey Meyerson & Danelle K. Simonelli. LC 99-490718. (Advances in the Astronautical Sciences Ser.). (Illus.). 412p. 1995. pap. text, suppl. ed. 50.00 (*0-87703-394-3*, Am Astronaut Soc) Univelt Inc.

Launchpad for the 21st Century: Yearbook of the International Space Year. 2nd ed. Harvey Meyerson & Danelle K. Simonelli. LC 99-490718. (Advances in the Astronautical Sciences Ser.). (Illus.). 412p. 1995. lib. bdg., suppl. ed. 70.00 (*0-87703-393-5*, Am Astronaut Soc) Univelt Inc.

Launderers & Dry Cleaners: London & South. Ed. by ICC Information Group Staff. 1987. 695.00 (*1-85036-928-3*, Pub. by ICC Info Group Ltd) St Mut.

Launderers & Dry Cleaners: Midlands & North. Ed. by ICC Information Group Staff. 1987. 695.00 (*1-85036-923-2*, Pub. by ICC Info Group Ltd) St Mut.

Laundering & Tracing. Ed. by Peter B. H. Birks. 388p. 1996. text 80.00 (*0-19-826101-2*) OUP.

Laundering for Pathfinders: A Basic Youth Enrichment Skill Honor Packet. Lou S. Gattis, III. (Illus.). 20p. (Orig.). (YA). (gr. 5 up). 1988. pap., teacher ed. 5.00 (*0-936241-38-1*) Cheetah Pub.

Laundries - Are They a Good Business to Get Into? Answers to the Most Often-Asked Questions about the Self-Service Laundry Industry. Ben Russell. LC 95-94298. 220p. (Orig.). 1995. pap. 21.95 (*0-9645877-0-X*) Burnside Pub.

Laundromat. Patricia T. Cousin et al. (Visions: African-American Experiences: No. 28). (Illus.). 8p. (Orig.). (J). (gr. k-1). 1996. pap. text 3.00 (*1-57518-027-8*) Arborlake.

Laundromat. unabridged ed. Stephen Cook. Ed. by William-Alan Landes. LC 98-15586. (Illus.). 55p. 1998. pap. 15.00 (*0-88734-205-1*) Players Pr.

Laundromat Blues. Lupe Solis. LC 97-65064. 200p. (Orig.). 1997. pap. 14.95 (*0-89823-177-9*) New Rivers Pr.

***Laundromat-Locomotion: Ein Kunstlerbuch (An Artists' Book)** (Illus.). 168p. 1998. pap. text. write for info. (*90-5705-094-3*, Verlag Kunst) Gordon & Breach.

Laundromatsmell: A Postcard Book of Fifteen Ballpoint Pen Drawings by Michael Scheer. Michael Scheer. (Illus.). 18p. (Orig.). 1997. pap. 9.98 (*0-9649917-0-5*, CSP-1) Cavity Srch.

Laundry & Bourbon. James McLure. 1981. pap. 3.95 (*0-8222-0645-5*) Dramatists Play.

Laundry Bygones. Pamela A. Sambrook. (Album Ser.: No. 107). (Illus.). 32p. 1989. pap. 5.25 (*0-85263-648-2*, Pub. by Shire Pubns) Parkwest Pubns.

Laundry Foreman. Jack Rudman. (Career Examination Ser.: C-2244). 1994. pap. 29.95 (*0-8373-2244-8*) Nat Learn.

Laundry Man. large type ed. Graham Ison. (Linford Mystery Library). 464p. 1997. pap. 16.99 (*0-7089-5110-4*, Linford) Ulverscroft.

Laundry Manager. Jack Rudman. (Career Examination Ser.: C-2427). 1994. pap. 34.95 (*0-8373-2427-0*) Nat Learn.

Laundry Pie. Jeanne Face. LC 97-61046. (Aesop's Fables Running Start Ser.). (Illus.). 32p. (J). (gr. 2-4). 1997. pap. 4.95 (*1-890570-16-8*) Huckleberry CT.

Laundry Room Poems. Bob Hickey. (Illus.). 92p. (Orig.). 1979. pap. 5.95 (*0-9603432-1-0*) STP.

Laundry Staff Training. W. A. Farndale. (C). 1987. pap. 100.00 (*0-7855-3755-4*) St Mut.

Laundry Supervisor. Jack Rudman. (Career Examination Ser.: C-1339). 1994. pap. 29.95 (*0-8373-1339-2*) Nat Learn.

Laundry Washman. Jack Rudman. (Career Examination Ser.: C-1340). 1994. pap. 23.95 (*0-8373-1340-6*) Nat Learn.

Laundry Worker. Jack Rudman. (Career Examination Ser.: C-435). 1994. pap. 23.95 (*0-8373-0435-0*) Nat Learn.

Laundry 101 Where Do I Start? 22p. pap. 1.80 (*0-9615390-7-0*) Aspen West Pub.

Laundrymen: Inside Money Laundering, The World's Third-Largest Business. Jeffrey Robinson. LC 96-8626. 1997. pap. 13.45 (*1-55970-385-7*, Pub. by Arcade Pub Inc) Time Warner.

Laundrymen: Money Laundering: The World's Third-Largest Business. Jeffrey Robinson. 368p. 1996. 25.45 (*1-55970-330-X*, Pub. by Arcade Pub Inc) Time Warner.

Laura see Sunfire Boxed Set, No. 16, Megan

Laura. Vera Caspary. 1955. pap. 5.25 (*0-8222-0646-3*) Dramatists Play.

***Laura.** Vera Caspery. 240p. 2000. per. 14.00 (*0-7434-0010-0*, Pub. by ibooks) S&S Trade.

Laura. Edward Delaunay. LC 99-192598. 224p. 1996. mass mkt. 5.95 (*1-56201-009-3*, 112) Blue Moon Bks.

Laura. Mark Dunster. 19p. 1988. pap. 4.00 (*0-89642-163-5*) Linden Pubs.

Laura. Hilary Norman. 1995. mass mkt. 5.99 (*0-451-18012-7*, Sig) NAL.

Laura. Binette Schroeder. LC 99-18981. (Illus.). 32p. (J). (gr. k-2). 1999. lib. bdg. 15.88 (*0-7358-1171-7*, Pub. by North-South Bks NYC) Chronicle Bks.

***Laura.** Binette Schroeder. LC 99-18981. (Illus.). 32p. (J). (gr. k-2). 1999. 15.95 (*0-7358-1170-9*, Pub. by North-South Bks NYC) Chronicle Bks.

Laura. Alan Shatter. LC 89-82491. 260p. 1990. pap. 10.95 (*1-85371-042-3*, Pub. by Poolbeg Pr) Dufour.

Laura. Larry Watson. LC 99-89060. 336p. 2000. 24.95 (*0-671-56774-8*, Pocket Books) PB.

***Laura.** Larry Watson. 2000. 24.95 (*0-671-56776-4*) PB.

Laura. limited unabridged ed. Arthur Randall. 228p. 1998. 95.00 (*1-881119-04-1*) Pyncheon Hse.

Laura. Vera Caspary. 216p. 1977. reprint ed. lib. bdg. 23.95 (*0-89244-066-X*, Queens House) Amereon Ltd.

Laura. Vera Caspary. 1993. reprint ed. lib. bdg. 29.95 (*1-56849-193-X*) Buccaneer Bks.

Laura. Leonora Sansay. LC 78-64094. reprint ed. 37.50 (*0-404-17168-0*) AMS Pr.

Laura. unabridged ed. Arthur Randall. 228p. 1998. 65.00 (*1-881119-17-3*) Pyncheon Hse.

Laura: A Case Study for the Modularity of Language. Jeni Yamada. (Illus.). 135p. 1990. 30.00 (*0-262-24030-0*) MIT Pr.

Laura: The Life of Laura Ingalls Wilder. Donald Zochert. 1977. 11.09 (*0-606-00902-7*, Pub. by Turtleback) Demco.

Laura: Uncovering Gender & Genre in Wyatt, Donne, & Marvell. Barbara L. Estrin. LC 94-13794. (Post-Contemporary Interventions Ser.). (Illus.). 360p. 1994. text 54.95 (*0-8223-1500-9*); pap. text 18.95 (*0-8223-1499-1*) Duke.

Laura & Jim & What They Taught Me about the Gap Between Educational Theory & Practice. Dona M. Kagan. LC 92-37768. 165p. (C). 1993. text 57.50 (*0-7914-1655-0*); pap. text 18.95 (*0-7914-1656-9*) State U NY Pr.

***Laura & Mr. Edwards.** Illus. by Renee Graef. LC 98-41708. (Little House Chapter Bks.: No. 13). 80p. (J). (gr. 2-5). 1999. lib. bdg. 13.89 (*0-06-027949-4*) HarpC Child Bks.

Laura & Mr. Edwards. Illus. by Renee Graef. LC 98-41708. (Little House Chapter Bks.: No. 13). 80p. (J). (gr. 2-5). 2000. pap. 4.25 (*0-06-442084-1*, HarpTrophy) HarpC Child Bks.

Laura & Nellie. Illus. by Renee Graef. LC 97-11648. (Little House Chapter Bks.: No. 5). 80p. (J). (gr. 2-5). 1998. lib. bdg. 14.89 (*0-06-027496-4*) HarpC.

Laura & Nellie. Illus. by Renee Graef. LC PZ7.L3725 1998. (Little House Chapter Bks.: No. 5). 80p. (J). (gr. k-2). 2000. pap. 4.25 (*0-06-442060-4*, HarpTrophy) HarpC Child Bks.

***Laura & Nellie.** Illus. by Renee Graef. (Little House Chapter Bks.: No. 5). (J). (gr. k-2). 1998. 9.15 (*0-606-12979-0*, Pub. by Turtleback) Demco.

Laura As Novel, Film, & Myth. Eugene McNamara. LC 92-6560. 120p. 1992. 59.95 (*0-7734-9506-1*) E Mellen.

Laura Ashley: Home Decorator. Ebury Press Staff. Date not set. write for info. (*0-609-60432-5*, Crown) Crown Pub Group.

Laura Ashley Color: Using Color to Decorate Your Home. Susan Berry & Laura Ashley (Firm) Staff. LC 98-13022. (Illus.). 208p. 1998. pap. 24.95 (*0-609-80375-1*) C Potter.

Laura Ashley Guide to Country Decorating. Lorrie Mack et al. 208p. (YA). 1993. 34.00 (*1-56282-745-6*, Pub. by Hyperion) Time Warner.

Laura Ashley Guide to Country Decorating. Lorrie Mack et al. (Illus.). 208p. (J). 1994. pap. 17.45 (*0-7868-8086-4*, Pub. by Hyperion) Time Warner.

Laura Ashley's Complete Guide to Home Decorating. Ed. by Charyn Jones. (Illus.). 224p. 1992. pap. 24.00 (*0-517-59077-8*) Harmony Bks.

***Laura Blundy.** Julie Myerson. 272p. 2000. 23.95 (*1-57322-168-6*) Putnam Pub Group.

Laura C. Martin's Southern Gardens: A Gracious History & Traveler's Guide. Laura C. Martin. LC 92-27281. (Illus.). 256p. 1993. 19.98 (*1-55859-323-3*, Artabras) Abbeville Pr.

***Laura Chappell Presents: Packet-Level Protocols: DHCP Workbook.** Laura A. Chappell. (Illus.). 100p. (YA). 2000. wbk. ed. 150.00 (*1-893939-34-0*) podbooks.

***Laura Chappell Presents Vol. 101: Introduction to Network Analysis: Workbook.** Laura A. Chappell. (Illus.). 100p. 2000. wbk. ed. 150.00 (*1-893939-29-4*) podbooks.

***Laura Chappell Presents Vol. 103: Introduction to Cyber Crime Workbook.** Laura A. Chappell. (Illus.). 150p. (YA). 2000. wbk. ed. 150.00 (*1-893939-31-6*) podbooks.

***Laura Chappell Presents Vol. 104: Introduction to Network Design & Data Flows Workbook.** Laura A. Chappell. 100p. (YA). 2000. wbk. ed. 150.00 (*1-893939-32-4*) podbooks.

***Laura Chappell Presents Vol. 201: Packet-Level Protocols: IPv4 Workbook.** Laura A. Chappell. 100p. (YA). 2000. wbk. ed. 150.00 (*1-893939-33-2*) podbooks.

***Laura Chappell Presents Packet-Level Protocols Vol. 203: ICMP Workbook.** Laura A. Chappell. (Illus.). 100p. 2000. wbk. ed. 150.00 (*1-893939-30-8*) podbooks.

Laura Chapter Book Biography. William Anderson. 80p. 13.95 (*0-06-028973-2*) HarpC.

Laura Chapter Book Biography. William Anderson. (Illus.). 80p. (gr. 2-5). mass mkt. 3.95 (*0-06-442133-3*) HarpC.

Laura Chapter Book Biography. William Anderson. (Illus.). 80p. (J). (gr. 2-5). 13.89 (*0-06-028974-0*) HarpC Child Bks.

Laura Charlotte. Kathryn O. Galbraith. LC 88-9898. (Illus.). 32p. (J). (ps-3). 1990. 15.95 (*0-399-21613-8*, Philomel) Peng Put Young Read.

Laura Charlotte. Kathryn O. Galbraith. LC 88-9898. (Illus.). 32p. (J). (ps-3). 1997. pap. 5.99 (*0-698-11437-X*, PapStar) Peng Put Young Read.

Laura Charlotte. Kathryn O. Galbraith. (J). 1997. 11.15 (*0-606-05419-7*, Pub. by Turtleback) Demco.

Laura Dean. Ian A. Montgomery. Ed. by Jacalyn A. Spafford. 150p. (Orig.). (YA). (gr. 9 up). 1997. pap. 9.95 (*1-890538-14-0*) Rhiannon Pubns.

Laura Dennis. Horton Foote. 1996. pap. 5.25 (*0-8222-1484-9*) Dramatists Play.

Laura for Dessert. Jerry Piasecki. (Orig.). (J). 1995. 8.60 (*0-606-07776-6*) Turtleback.

Laura Ingalls Wilder. Fred Erisman. (Western Writers Ser.: No. 112). (Illus.). 55p. 1994. pap. 4.95 (*0-88430-111-7*) Boise St U W Writ Ser.

Laura Ingalls Wilder. Dona H. Rice. (Favorite Authors Ser.). 112p. (J). (gr. 3-5). 1997. pap. 11.95 (*1-55734-452-3*) Tchr Create Mat.

Laura Ingalls Wilder. Janet Spaeth. (Twayne's United States Authors Ser.: No. 517). 120p. (C). 1987. 21.95 (*0-8057-7501-3*, Twyne) Mac Lib Ref.

Laura Ingalls Wilder. Ginger Wadsworth. LC 99-21333. (On My Own Biographies Ser.). 64p. (J). (gr. 1-3). 1999. 19.93 (*1-57505-266-0*, Carolrhoda) Lerner Pub.

***Laura Ingalls Wilder.** Ginger Wadsworth. (J). 2000. pap. text 5.95 (*1-57505-423-X*, Carolrhoda) Lerner Pub.

Laura Ingalls Wilder. Alexandra Wallner. LC 96-52917. (Illus.). 32p. (J). (gr. k-3). 1997. lib. bdg. 16.95 (*0-8234-1314-4*) Holiday.

Laura Ingalls Wilder. Jill Wheeler. Ed. by Rosemary Wallner. LC 92-16568. (Young at Heart Ser.). 1992. pap. 4.95 (*1-56239-374-X*) ABDO Pub Co.

Laura Ingalls Wilder. Jill Wheeler. Ed. by Rosemary Wallner. LC 92-16568. (Young at Heart Ser.). (Illus.). 32p. (J). (gr. 4). 1992. lib. bdg. 14.98 (*1-56239-115-1*) ABDO Pub Co.

***Laura Ingalls Wilder.** Mae Woods. LC 99-88858. (Children's Authors Ser.). 2000. write for info. (*1-57765-113-8*) ABDO Pub Co.

Laura Ingalls Wilder: A Biography. William Anderson. LC 91-33805. (Illus.). 240p. (J). (gr. 4-6). 1992. 16.95 (*0-06-020113-4*) HarpC Child Bks.

Laura Ingalls Wilder: A Biography. William Anderson. LC 91-33805. 256p. (J). (gr. 3-7). 1995. pap. 6.95 (*0-06-446103-3*, HarpTrophy) HarpC Child Bks.

Laura Ingalls Wilder: A Biography. William Anderson. (J). 1995. 11.05 (*0-606-12977-4*, Pub. by Turtleback) Demco.

Laura Ingalls Wilder: Activities Based on Research from the Laura Ingalls Wilder Homes. Laurie E. Rozakis. 1993. pap. 10.95 (*0-590-49271-3*) Scholastic Inc.

Laura Ingalls Wilder: An Annotated Bibliography of Critical, Biographical & Teaching Studies, 24. Jane M. Subramanian. LC 96-33047. (Bibliographies & Indexes in American Literature Ser.). 136p. 1997. lib. bdg. 55.00 (*0-313-29999-4*, Greenwood Pr) Greenwood.

Laura Ingalls Wilder: An Author's Story. Sarah J. Glassock. 1998. pap. 4.95 (*0-8172-7976-8*) Raintree Steck-V.

Laura Ingalls Wilder: Growing up in the Little House. Patricia Reilly Giff. LC 86-28202. (Women of Our Time Ser.). 1988. 10.19 (*0-606-03842-6*, Pub. by Turtleback) Demco.

Laura Ingalls Wilder: Growing up in the Little House. Patricia Reilly Giff. (Women of Our Time Ser.). (Illus.). 64p. (J). (gr. 2-6). 1988. reprint ed. pap. 4.99 (*0-14-032074-1*, PuffinBks) Peng Put Young Read.

Laura Ingalls Wilder: Her Writing, Her Award, Her Libraries, Her Historic Highway. John A. Bass. (Ingalls-Wilder-Lane Signature Ser.: Bk. 15). (Illus.). 100p. 1998. pap. 10.00 (*1-891453-15-7*) Ingalls-Wilder.

Laura Ingalls Wilder: Storyteller of the Prairie. Ginger Wadsworth. LC 96-6273. (J). 1996. lib. bdg. 23.93 (*0-8225-4950-6*, Lerner Publctns) Lerner Pub.

Laura Ingalls Wilder & Rose Wilder Lane, 1937-1939. Ed. by Timothy Walch et al. (Illus.). 49p. (Orig.). 1992. pap. 5.00 (*0-938469-12-6*) Hoover Lib.

Laura Ingalls Wilder Country Cookbook. Laura Ingalls Wilder. 1997. 18.15 (*0-606-12978-2*, Pub. by Turtleback) Demco.

Laura Ingalls Wilder Country Ri. William Anderson. LC 89-46512. (Illus.). 120p. 1996. reprint ed. pap. 22.50 (*0-06-097346-3*, Perennial) HarperTrade.

Laura Ingalls Wilder's: The Iowa Story. William Anderson. (Illus.). 50p. 1989. pap. 4.95 (*0-9610088-9-X*) Anderson Publns.

Laura Ingalls Wilder's Fairy Poems. Laura Ingalls Wilder. LC 97-27878. (Illus.). 48p. (J). 1998. 15.95 (*0-385-32533-9*) BDD Bks Young Read.

Laura Ingalls Wilder's Little Town: Where History & Literature Meet. John E. Miller. (Illus.). 220p. 1995. pap. 14.95 (*0-7006-0713-7*) U Pr of KS.

***Laura Jean the Yards Sale Queen.** (Books to Go Ser.). 1998. pap. write for info. (*0-8136-7874-9*) Modern Curr.

Laura Jensen. Dina Ben-Lev. LC 97-70325. (Western Writers Ser: Vol. 129). (C). 1997. 4.95 (*0-88430-128-1*) Boise St U W Writ Ser.

Laura Keene: A British Actress on the American Stage, 1826-1873. Vernanne Bryan. LC 96-37417. (Illus.). 232p. 1997. lib. bdg. 38.50 (*0-7864-0075-7*) McFarland & Co.

Laura Lemay's Guide to Sizzling Web Site Design. Laura Lemay & Molly Holzschlag. LC 96-70712. 256p. 1997. 45.00 (*1-57521-221-8*) Sams.

Laura Lemay's Web Workshop. Brian Murphy. 1996. 39.99 incl. cd-rom (*0-614-20291-4*, SamsNet Software) MCP SW Interactive.

Laura Lemay's Web Workshop: ActiveX & VBScript. Paul Omax & Roger Cadenhead. LC 96-70390. 450p. 1996. 39.99 (*1-57521-207-2*) Sams.

Laura Lemay's Web Workshop: Advanced Frontpage. 1997. pap. 149.99 (*1-57521-388-5*) Sams.

Laura Lemay's Web Workshop: Advanced Frontpage 97. Denise Tyler. LC 97-65736. 608p. 1997. 39.99 (*1-57521-308-7*) Sams.

Laura Lemay's Web Workshop: Creating Commercial Web Pages. Brian K. Murphey & Edmund T. Smith. LC 96-68246. 528p. 1996. 39.99 (*1-57521-126-2*) Sams.

Laura Lemay's Web Workshop: Creating Webcasting Channels. Paul E. Robichaux. 1997. 39.99 (*1-57521-328-1*) Sams.

Laura Lemay's Web Workshop: Designing with Stylesheets, Tables & Frames. Molly Holzschlag & Laura Lemay. LC 96-71502. 607p. 1997. 39.99 (*1-57521-249-8*) Sams.

Laura Lemay's Web Workshop: Graphics & Web Page Design. Jon Duff & James Mohler. LC 96-68245. 408p. 1996. 55.00 (*1-57521-125-4*) Sams.

Laura Lemay's Web Workshop: Microsoft FrontPage 97. 2nd ed. Laura Lemay & Denise Tyler. 832p. 1997. 39.99 (*1-57521-223-4*) Sams.

Laura Lemay's Web Workshop: Microsoft Frontpage 98. Denise Tyler. LC 97-69585. 864p. 1997. 39.99 (*1-57521-372-9*) Sams.

Laura Lemay's Web Workshop: Netscape Navigator Gold 3. deluxe ed. Ned Snell. LC 96-72267. 400p. 1996. 49.99 (*1-57521-292-7*) Sams.

Laura Lemay's Web Workshop: 3D Graphics & VRML 2.0. Kelly Murdock & Justin Couch. LC 96-68591. 504p. 1996. 39.99 (*1-57521-143-2*) Sams.

Laura Lemay's Web Workshop Net Object Fusion: NetObjects Fusion 2. Kabriel Robichaux & Derrick Woolworth. LC 96-72265. 488p. 1997. 39.99 (*1-57521-278-1*) Sams.

Laura Lemay's Web Workshop Netscape Composer. 2nd ed. Ned Snell. 500p. 1997. pap. text 39.99 incl. cd-rom (*1-57521-300-1*) Sams.

Laura Life of L I Wilder. Donald Zochert. (Illus.). 1977. mass mkt. 5.99 (*0-380-01636-2*, Avon Bks) Morrow Avon.

Laura McKenzie's Travel Guide to Caribbean. Laura McKenzie. 1996. pap. text 14.95 (*1-887161-13-9*) Boru Pubng.

Laura McKenzie's Travel Guide to Ireland. Laura McKenzie. 1996. pap. text 14.95 (*1-887161-14-7*) Boru Pubng.

Laura McKenzie's Travel Guide to Israel. Laura McKenzie. 1996. pap. text 14.95 (*1-887161-15-5*) Boru Pubng.

Laura McKenzie's Travel Guide to London. Laura McKenzie. Ed. by Ann O. Weems. (Laura McKenzie's Travel Guides Ser.). (Illus.). 350p. (Orig.). 1996. pap. text 14.95 (*1-887161-04-X*, Boru Bks) Boru Pubng.

Laura McKenzie's Travel Guide to Mexico. Laura McKenzie. 1996. pap. text 14.95 (*1-887161-16-3*) Boru Pubng.

Laura McKenzie's Travel Guide to Paris. Laura McKenzie. Ed. by Ann O. Weems. (Laura McKenzie's Travel Guides Ser.). (Illus.). 350p. (Orig.). 1996. pap. text 14.95 (*1-887161-03-1*, Boru Bks) Boru Pubng.

Laura McKenzie's Travel Guide to Rome. Laura McKenzie. Ed. by Ann O. Weems. (Laura McKenzie's Travel Guides Ser.). (Illus.). 350p. (Orig.). 1996. pap. text 14.95 (*1-887161-05-8*, Boru Bks) Boru Pubng.

Laura McKenzie's Travel Guide to Spain. Laura McKenzie. 1996. pap. text 14.95 (*1-887161-17-1*) Boru Pubng.

Laura McKenzie's Travel Guide to Virginia. Laura McKenzie. 1996. pap. text 14.95 (*1-887161-18-X*) Boru Pubng.

Laura Poems. Friedrich Schiller. Ed. by Jesse F. Knight. 45p. (Orig.). 1984. pap. 4.95 (*0-930962-07-9*) Villegas Pub.

Laura Ross-Paul: A Decade of Painting, 1981-1990. Paul Sutinen. (Illus.). 1990. pap. 10.00 (*0-914435-19-1*) Marylhurst Art.

***Laura Schildkraut.** 63p. 1998. 12.00 (*0-13-007273-7*) P-H.

Laura the Pet Vet: I'm a Pop-Up Book! Margaret Johnson. (Fisher-Price Pop-Up Playbks.: No. 4). (Illus.). 12p. (J). (gr. k-3). 1998. bds. 4.50 (*1-57584-197-5*, Pub. by Rdrs Digest) Random.

Laura Wilder of Mansfield: Laura Ingalls Wilder Biography. William T. Anderson. (Laura Ingalls Wilder Family Ser.). (Illus.). 36p. 1982. pap. 3.95 (*0-9610088-1-4*) Anderson Publns.

Lauraceae: Nectandra. Jens G. Rohwer. (Flora Neotropica Monographs: No. 60). (Illus.). 333p. 1993. pap. text 43.50 (*0-89327-373-2*) NY Botanical.

Lauraceae Americaneae Monographice Descrips. Carl Mez. 1963. reprint ed. 64.00 (*3-7682-0171-6*) Lubrecht & Cramer.

Lauraceae I (Aniba & Aiouea) Klaus Kubitzki & Susanne S. Renner. LC 82-6290. (Flora Neotropica Monographs: No. 31). (Illus.). 125p. 1982. pap. 22.50 (*0-89327-244-2*) NY Botanical.

Laural/Eda, Chapter 8-19. Shirley P. Schwarzrock & James R. Jensen. 168p. (C). 1987. ring bd. write for info. (*0-697-05838-7*, WCB McGr Hill) McGrw-H Hghr Educ.

Laural/Eda, Chapter 20-30. James R. Jensen & Shirley P. Schwarzrock. 260p. (C). 1987. ring bd. write for info. (*0-697-05839-5*, WCB McGr Hill) McGrw-H Hghr Educ.

Laural/Eda, Chapter 31-39. James R. Jensen & Shirley P. Schwarzrock. 216p. (C). 1987. ring bd. write for info. (*0-697-05840-9*, WCB McGr Hill) McGrw-H Hghr Educ.

Laural/Eda/Prelims-Glossary. James R. Jensen & Shirley P. Schwarzrock. 204p. (C). 1987. ring bd. write for info. (*0-697-05837-9*, WCB McGr Hill) McGrw-H Hghr Educ.

Lauralee. Linda Lael Miller. Ed. by Linda Marrow. 1990. mass mkt. 5.99 (*0-671-70634-9*) PB.

Laural/Ema, Chapter 1-7. Donovan F. Ward & Shirley P. Schwarzrock. 160p. (C). 1987. per. write for info. (*0-697-05833-6*, WCB McGr Hill) McGrw-H Hghr Educ.

Laural/Ema, Chapter 8-25. Donovan F. Ward & Shirley P. Schwarzrock. 213p. (C). 1987. write for info. (*0-697-05834-4*, WCB McGr Hill) McGrw-H Hghr Educ.

Laural/Ema, Chapter 37-45. Donovan F. Ward & Shirley P. Schwarzrock. 88p. (C). 1987. ring bd. write for info. (*0-697-05836-0*, WCB McGr Hill) McGrw-H Hghr Educ.

Laurance S. Rockefeller: Catalyst for Conservation. Robin W. Winks. LC 97-20447. (Illus.). 259p. 1997. text 25.00 (*1-55963-547-9*) Island Pr.

Laura's Album: A Remembrance Scrapbook of Laura Ingalls Wilder. William Anderson. LC 97-49332. (Illus.). 80p. (J). (gr. 3-7). 1998. 21.95 (*0-06-027842-0*) HarpC.

Laura's Baby. Rebecca Winters. (Superromance Ser.: No. 756). 1997. per. 3.99 (*0-373-70756-8*, 1-70756-1) Harlequin Bks.

Laura's Christmas. Laura Ingalls Wilder. (My First Little House Baby Bks.). (Illus.). 16p. (J). (ps). 1998. 6.95 (*0-694-00769-2*) HarpC.

Laura's Christmas Star. Klaus Baumgart. LC 99-27986. (Illus.). 32p. (J). (ps-2). 1999. 16.95 (*1-888444-59-2*, Pub. by Little Tiger) Futech Educ Prods.

Laura's Dream: A Woman's Destiny & Fulfillment. Pearl Hermann & Jeanne B. Ewing. (Illus.). 200p. (Orig.). 1988. pap. 14.95 (*1-884690-07-6*) Owl Press.

Laura's Early Years Collection, Set. Laura Ingalls Wilder. (Little House). (J). (gr. 3-6). 1999. pap. 14.85 (*0-06-449367-9*) HarpC Child Bks.

Laura's Garden. Laura Ingalls Wilder. LC PZ7.L37273 1996. (My First Little House Baby Bks.). (Illus.). 10p. (J). (ps). 1996. 3.95 (*0-694-00778-1*, HarpFestival) HarpC Child Bks.

Laura's Gift. Dee Jacobs. (Illus.). 64p. (J). (gr. 6-12). 1980. pap. 11.95 (*0-938628-01-1*); lib. bdg. 17.95 (*0-938628-00-3*) Oriel Pr.

Laura's Ma. Illus. by Renee Graef. LC 98-23093. (Little House Chapter Bks.: No. 11). 80p. (J). (gr. 2-5). 1999. lib. bdg. 13.89 (*0-06-027897-8*) HarpC Child Bks.

Laura's Ma. Illus. by Renee Graef. LC PZ7.L372735 1999. (Little House Chapter Bks.: No. 11). 80p. (J). (gr. k-2). 2000. pap. 4.25 (*0-06-442083-3*, HarpTrophy) HarpC Child Bks.

Laura's Pa. Illus. by Renee Graef. LC 98-20344. (Little House Chapter Bks.: No. 12). 80p. (J). (gr. 2-5). 1999. lib. bdg. 13.89 (*0-06-027896-X*) HarpC Child Bks.

***Laura's Pa.** Laura Ingalls Wilder. LC PZ7.L37274 1998. (Little House Chapter Bks.: No. 12). (Illus.). 80p. (J). (gr. k-2). 2000. pap. 4.25 (*0-06-442082-5*, HarpTrophy) HarpC Child Bks.

Laura's Rose: The Story of Rose Wilder Lane. William T. Anderson. (Laura Ingalls Wilder Family Ser.). (Illus.). 48p. (Orig.). 1984. pap. text 3.95 (*0-9610088-3-0*) Anderson Publns.

Laura's Skin. J. F. Federspiel. Tr. by Breon Mitchell from GER. LC 90-22487. Orig. Title: Geographie der Lust. 211p. 1993. 18.95 (*0-88064-126-6*); pap. 9.00 (*0-88064-138-X*) Fromm Intl Pub.

Laura's Star. Klaus Baumgart. LC 97-26739. (Illus.). 32p. (J). (ps-2). 1997. 16.95 (*1-888444-24-X*, 21022) Little Tiger.

Laura's Way. large type ed. Beryl Kingston. LC 96-47455. 1997. 23.95 (*0-7862-0940-2*) Thorndike Pr.

Laure: The Collected Writings. E. Laure. Tr. by Jeanine Herman from FRE. 240p. (Orig.). 1995. pap. 13.95 (*0-87286-293-3*) City Lights.

Laure-Ann Toujours. 1993. pap. 4.50 (*0-8216-5097-1*, Univ Books) Carol Pub Group.

Laurea Corona: Studies in Honour of Edward Coleiro. Ed. by Anthony Bonanno. (ENG, FRE, ITA, LAT & SPA.). xxiii, 232p. (Orig.). (C). 1987. pap. 71.00 (*90-6032-300-9*, Pub. by B R Gruner) Humanities.

Laureateship. Edmund K. Broadus. LC 67-22082. (Essay Index Reprint Ser.). 1977. 21.95 (*0-8369-1326-4*) Ayer.

Laurel. Leigh Greenwood. (Seven Brides Ser.). 448p. (Orig.). 1995. pap. text 5.99 (*0-8439-3744-0*) Dorchester Pub Co.

***Laurel.** Cassie Kendall. (Stardust Classics). (J). 1999. boxed set 16.95 (*1-889514-22-5*) Dolls Corp.

Laurel. Isabel Miller. 144p. (Orig.). 1996. pap. 10.95 (*1-56280-146-5*) Naiad Pr.

Laurel. Diane Schwemm. (Year I Turned Sixteen Ser.: No. 3). (YA). (gr. 7 up). 1998. mass mkt. 4.50 (*0-671-00442-5*, Archway) PB.

***Laurel.** 2nd abr. ed. Jane Peart. LC PZ7.P32334Lau 2000. (Orphan Train West Ser.). (Illus.). 160p. (J). (gr. 5-9). 2000. pap. 5.99 (*0-8007-5713-0*) Chosen Bks.

Laurel: Computer as Theatre. Toppan Co. Japan Staff. (C). 1992. pap. text. write for info. (*0-201-55676-6*) Addison-Wesley.

Laurel & Hardy. Annie McGarry. (Illus.). 80p. 1992. 10.98 (*1-55521-792-3*, Chrtwell) Bk Sales Inc.

Laurel & Hardy: A Bio-Bibliography. Wes D. Gehring. LC 89-25708. (Popular Culture Bio-Bibliographies Ser.). 328p. 1990. lib. bdg. 65.00 (*0-313-25172-X*, GLH/, Greenwood Pr) Greenwood.

Laurel & Hardy: From the Forties Forward. Scott MacGillivray. LC 98-16059. (Illus.). 216p. 1998. 40.00 (*1-879511-35-5*, Vestal Pr); pap. 19.95 (*1-879511-41-X*, Vestal Pr) Madison Bks UPA.

Laurel & Hardy: The Magic Behind the Movies. Randy Skretvedt. LC 87-1520. (Vintage Comedy Ser.). (Illus.). 464p. 1987. 21.95 (*0-940410-78-8*, Moonstone Pr) Past Times.

Laurel & Hardy: The Magic Behind the Movies. 2nd rev. ed. Randy Skretvedt. Ed. by Jordan R. Young. (Vintage Comedy Ser.). (Illus.). 496p. 1994. pap. 20.95 (*0-940410-29-X*, Moonstone Pr) Past Times.

Laurel & Hardy in "Big Quizness" Trivia & Film Facts on the Boys. Robert McFerren & Tracie McFerren. Ed. by JoAnn Jones. LC 97-97019. (Illus.). 394p. 1999. pap. 25.00 (*0-9660323-0-6*) Plumtree Pub.

Laurel & Hardy in Hull. Ken Owst. (C). 1989. text 40.00 (*0-948929-34-0*) St Mut.

Laurel & Hardy Theory of Consciousness. Colin Wilson. (Broadside Editions Ser.). 24p. (Orig.). 1986. pap. 3.95 (*0-931191-04-1*) Rob Briggs.

Laurel & Ivy. Robert Kee. 1999. pap. 15.95 (*0-14-023962-6*, Viking) Viking Penguin.

Laurel & the Lawman. Lynn Erickson. 1994. per. 3.50 (*0-373-70614-6*, 1-70614-2) Harlequin Bks.

Laurel & the Lost Treasure. 2nd ed. Cassie Kendall. LC 97-73131. (Stardust Classics). (Illus.). 117p. (J). (gr. 2-6). 1997. 12.95 (*1-889514-09-8*) Dolls Corp.

Laurel & the Lost Treasure. 2nd ed. Cassie Kendall. LC 97-73131. (Stardust Classics). (Illus.). 117p. (J). (gr. 2-6). 1998. pap. 5.95 (*1-889514-10-1*) Dolls Corp.

Laurel & the Sprites' Mischief. Cassie Kendall. LC 99-71561. (Stardust Classics). (Illus.). 122p. (J). (gr. 2-5). 1999. 12.95 (*1-889514-29-2*); pap. 5.95 (*1-889514-30-6*) Dolls Corp.

Laurel & Thorn: The Athlete in American Literature. Robert J. Higgs. LC 80-51014. 208p. reprint ed. pap. 64.50 (*0-7837-2420-9*, 204256600005) Bks Demand.

Laurel County, KY. Carl Keith Greene. (Images of America Ser.). (Illus.). 128p. 1999. pap. 16.99 (*0-7524-0808-9*) Arcadia Publng.

Laurel Culture in Minnesota. James B. Stoltman. LC 73-4190. (Publications of the Minnesota Historical Society: No. 8). (Illus.). 158p. 1973. reprint ed. pap. 49.00 (*0-608-06687-7*, 206688400009) Bks Demand.

***Laurel Highlands - A Hiking Guide.** Monika Vucic et al. (Illus.). iv, 284p. 2000. pap. 11.95 (*0-9700579-0-3*) Allegheny Grp.

Laurel Path. large type ed. Jay Allerton. 1991. 27.99 (*0-7089-2420-4*) Ulverscroft.

Laurel Quarberg: Treading Water. Jannelle M. Riley. (Illus.). 8p. (Orig.). 1994. pap. 8.00 (*1-885163-01-0*) Virginia Beach Ctr.

Laurel Rescues the Pixies. Cassie Kendall. LC 98-65897. (Stardust Classics). (Illus.). 105p. (J). (gr. 2-6). 1998. 12.95 (*1-889514-17-9*); pap. 5.95 (*1-889514-18-7*) Dolls Corp.

Laurel Review: A Literary Periodical. Ed. by William Trowbridge et al. 1999. pap. text 6.00 (*0-317-61673-0*) GreenTower Pr.

Laurel the Woodfairy. 2nd ed. Cassie Kendall. LC 97-73128. (Stardust Classics). (Illus.). 114p. (J). (gr. 2-6). 1998. 12.95 (*1-889514-05-5*); pap. 5.95 (*1-889514-06-3*) Dolls Corp.

Laureles del Cesar. Rene de Goscinny & M. Uderzo. (SPA., Illus.). (J). 24.95 (*0-8288-4976-5*) Fr & Eur.

An Asterisk (*) at the beginning of an entry indicates that the title is appearing for the first time.

L

Laurels: Eight Women Poets. Jean H. Johnson et al. Ed. by Stacy J. Tuthill. LC 97-91288. 185p. 1998. lib. bdg. 20.00 (*0-930526-23-6*, Pub. by SCOP Pubns) Baker & Taylor.

Laurel's Flight. Carol L. Williams. LC 95-25072. (Latter-Day Daughters Ser.). (Illus.). 80p. (J). 1995. pap. 4.95 (*1-56236-502-9*, Pub. by Aspen Bks) Origin Bk Sales.

Laurel's Kitchen Bread Book. Laurel Robertson. 1994. 29.50 (*0-8446-6748-X*) Peter Smith.

Laurel's Kitchen Bread Book. Laurel Robertson. 448p. 1985. pap. 21.95 (*0-394-72434-8*) Random.

Laurel's Kitchen Caring: Whole-Food Recipes for Everyday Home Caregiving. Laurel Robertson. LC 97-22618. (Illus.). 160p. (Orig.). 1997. pap. 12.95 (*0-89815-951-2*) Ten Speed Pr.

Laurel's Kitchen Recipes. Laurel Robertson et al. (Illus.). 352p. 1993. pap. 12.95 (*0-89815-537-1*) Ten Speed Pr.

***Laurelude.** W. N. Herbert. 160p. 1999. pap. (*1-85224-464-X*, Pub. by Bloodaxe Bks) Dufour.

***Lauren: Circle of Friends, No. 879.** Shannon Waverly. (Superromance Ser.: Vol. 879). 1999. mass mkt. 4.25 (*0-373-70879-3*) Harlequin Bks.

Lauren Bacall. Lauren Bacall. 1985. mass mkt. 6.99 (*0-345-33321-7*) Ballantine Pub Grp.

Lauren Bacall: A Bio-Bibliography, 30. Brenda S. Royce. LC 92-12500. (Bio-Bibliographies in the Performing Arts Ser.: No. 30). 312p. 1992. lib. bdg. 55.00 (*0-313-27831-8*, RLL/, Greenwood Pr) Greenwood.

Lauren Bacall: Her Films & Career. Lawrence J. Quirk. (Illus.). 224p. 1986. 19.95 (*0-8065-0935-X*, Citadel Pr) Carol Pub Group.

Lauren Groveman's Kitchen: Nurturing Food for Family & Friends. Illus. by Judith Reed. LC 94-13263. 528p. 1994. 24.95 (*0-8118-0609-X*) Chronicle Bks.

***Lauren Hill.** Meg Greene. LC 99-40740. (Galaxy of Superstars Ser.). (Illus.). 64p. 1999. 17.95 (*0-7910-5495-0*) Chelsea Hse.

***Lauren McGill's Pickle Museum.** Jerdine Nolen & Debbie Tilley. LC 00-9577. (Illus.). (J). 2003. write for info. (*0-15-202279-1*, Pub. by Harcourt) Harcourt.

Lauren Rogers Museum of Art: A Handbook of the Collections. Lauren Rogers Museum of Art Staff. LC 89-5451. (Illus.). 198p. (Orig.). 1989. pap. 19.95 (*0-685-45630-7*) Lauren Rogers.

***Lauren Rottet: The Substance of Style.** Mayer Rus. 144p. 1999. pap. 40.00 (*0-9662230-1-2*, Pub. by Edizioni Pr) Antique Collect.

Laurence Bloomfield in Ireland: A Modern Poem. William Allingham. LC 71-148742. reprint ed. 39.50 (*0-404-00346-X*) AMS Pr.

Laurence Gartel: A Cybernetic Romance. Laurence Gartel & Timothy Binkley. Ed. & Frwd. by Eleanor Flomenhaft. (Illus.). 16p. (Orig.). 1988. pap. 10.00 (*0-933535-03-1*) FA Mus LI.

Laurence Housman. Rodney Engen. (Artist & the Critic Ser.: Vol. 1). 157p. 1983. write for info. (*0-904995-04-6*, Pub. by Catalpa Pr Ltd) Penguin Books.

Laurence Juber Standard Tunings: Techniques & Arrangement/Fingerstyle Guitar, Vol. 1. 1997. VHS 29.95 (*0-7935-7516-8*) H Leonard.

Laurence Olivier & the Art of Film Making. Dale Silviria. LC 83-49017. (Illus.). 312p. 1985. 45.00 (*0-8386-3207-6*) Fairleigh Dickinson.

Laurence Olivier: The Life of an Actor: The Authorized Biography. Derek Granger. 1999. write for info. (*0-316-32429-9*) Little.

Laurence Stallings. Joan T. Brittain. Ed. by Sylvia E. Bowman. LC 74-23831. (Twayne's United States Authors Ser.). 127p. (C). 1975. 17.95 (*0-8057-0686-0*) Irvington.

Laurence Stearne see Early English Novelists: Critical Heritage

Laurence Sterne. Elizabeth Kraft. LC 96-3082. 1996. 32.00 (*0-8057-7058-5*, Twyne) Mac Lib Ref.

Laurence Sterne: The Early & Middle Years. Arthur H. Cash. LC 75-18378. (Illus.). 1975. 85.00 (*0-416-82210-X*, NO. 2126) Routledge.

Laurence Sterne: The Later Years. Arthur H. Cash. 400p. 1986. 60.00 (*0-416-32930-6*, 9922) Routledge.

Laurence Sterne As Satirist: A Reading of Tristram Shandy. Melvyn New. LC 70-79524. 1969. 29.95 (*0-8130-0278-8*) U Press Fla.

Laurens County, South Carolina, Wills, 1784-1840. Colleen Elliott. (Illus.). 336p. 1988. 38.50 (*0-89308-606-1*, SC 85) Southern Hist Pr.

Laurent Series & Their Pade Approximation. Adhemar Bultheel. (Operator Theory Ser.: No. 27). 270p. 1987. 123.00 (*0-8176-1940-2*) Birkhauser.

***Laurentia-Gondwana Connections Before Pangea.** Victor A. Ramos & J. Duncan Keppie. LC 99-47508. (Special Papers). 1999. write for info. (*0-8137-2336-1*) Geol Soc.

Laurentii Vallae Elegatiarum Librorum Concordantiae. Lorenzo Valla et al. (Alpha-Omega Ser.: Reihe B., Bd. X). (GER.). 484p. 1997. write for info. (*3-487-10493-8*) G Olms Pubs.

Laurie & Claire. Kathleen Rowntree. 480p. 1996. pap. 12.95 (*0-552-99608-4*) Bantam.

***Laurie & Claire.** Kathleen Rowntree. 2000. 27.95 (*0-385-40565-0*, Pub. by Transworld Publishers Ltd) Trafalgar.

***Laurie Anderson.** RoseLee Goldberg & Laurie Anderson. LC 99-44944. 204p. 2000. 49.50 (*0-8109-3582-1*, Pub. by Abrams) Time Warner.

Laurie Simmons. Ed. by Rodney Sappington et al. (Explores the Work of Artists in Mid-Career Ser.). (Illus.). 80p. 1994. pap. text 25.00 (*0-923183-13-2*) ART Pr NY.

Laurie Simmons: The Music of Regret. Jan Howard et al. LC 97-72377. (Illus.). 1997. write for info. (*0-912298-69-3*) Baltimore Mus.

Laurie Tells. Linda Lowery. LC 93-9786. (Illus.). (J). (gr. 3-6). 1994. lib. bdg. 19.95 (*0-87614-790-2*, Carolrhoda) Lerner Pub.

Laurie Tells. Linda Lowery. (Illus.). 40p. (J). (gr. 1-4). 1995. pap. 4.95 (*0-87614-961-1*) Lerner Pub.

Laurier, a Study in Canadian Politics. John W. Dafoe. (BCL1 - History - Canada Ser.). 182p. 1991. reprint ed. lib. bdg. 69.00 (*0-7812-6363-8*) Rprt Serv.

Lauriers de Cesar. Rene de Goscinny & M. Uderzo. (FRE., Illus.). (J). 1990. 24.95 (*0-8288-4977-3*) Fr & Eur.

Laurie's Indispensable Babysitter's Guide. Laurie Ramsay. (Illus.). 35p. (YA). (gr. 5 up). 1997. pap. 8.95 (*0-9659146-0-7*) Pascal Inc.

Laurindo Almeida: Contemporary Moods for Classica Guitar. Ed. by Carol Cuellar. 68p. (C). 1979. pap. text 14.95 (*0-7692-0201-2*, TPF0085) Wrner Bros.

Lauris Edmond: A Matter of Timing. 64p. 1996. pap. 12.95 (*1-86940-140-9*, Pub. by Auckland Univ) Paul & Co Pubs.

Lauri's Low-Carb Cookbook. Lauri Knox. 200p. 1999. pap. 12.95 (*0-9667963-0-6*) Avalon Ent.

***Lauri's Low-Carb Cookbook: Rapid Weight Loss with Satisfying Meals!** 2nd ed. Lauri Ann Randolph. 256p. 1999. pap. 19.95 (*0-9667963-1-4*) Avalon Ent.

Laurium, Michigan's Early Days. (Copper Country Local History Ser.: Vol. 27). (Illus.). 112p. 1986. 3.00 (*0-942363-26-4*) C J Monette.

***Lauryn Hill.** Andrews McMeel Publishing Staff. 1999. 4.95 (*0-7407-0420-6*) Andrews & McMeel.

***Lauryn Hill.** Meg Greene. LC 99-40740. (Galaxy of Superstars Ser.). (Illus.). 64p. (YA). (gr. 3). 1999. pap. 9.95 (*0-7910-5496-9*) Chelsea Hse.

***Lauryn Hill.** Cynthia Laslo. (High Interest Bks.). (Illus.). (J). 2000. 19.00 (*0-516-23322-X*) Childrens.

***Lauryn Hill.** Cynthia Laslo. LC 99-44798. (High Interest Bks.). (Illus.). 48p. (J). (gr. 4-7). 2000. pap. 6.95 (*0-516-23522-2*) Childrens.

***Lauryn Hill.** Cynthia Laslo. LC 99-44798. (Celebrity Bios Ser.). 2000. pap. write for info. (*0-531-17610-X*) Watts.

Lauryn Hill: She's Got That Thing. 2nd ed. Chris Nickson. LC 99-204511. (Illus.). 224+8p. 1999. mass mkt. 5.99 (*0-312-97210-5*) St Martin.

***Lau's Laws on Hitting.** Charley Lau, Jr. & Jeff Flanagan. (Illus.). 224p. 2000. pap. 21.95 (*1-886110-95-6*) Addax Pubng.

Lausanne Conference, 1949: A Case Study on Middle Eastern Peacemaking. Neil Caplan. 190p. (C). 1994. pap. text 14.95 (*0-8156-7056-7*, Pub. by Moshe Dayan Ctr) Syracuse U Pr.

Lausiac History. Palladius. (Ancient Christian Writers Ser.: No. 34). 1985. 34.95 (*0-8091-0083-5*) Paulist Pr.

Lausiac History: Palladius. Tr. by E. A. Wallis Budge. 1977. pap. 6.95 (*0-89981-039-X*) Eastern Orthodox.

Lausiac History of Palladius: A Critical Discussion Together with Notes on early Egyptian Monachism, 2 vols. Cuthbert Butler. 575p. reprint ed. lib. bdg. 150.00 (*0-685-13766-X*, 05101497) G Olms Pubs.

Lauter American Literature IV & Moby Dick, 3 vols. 3rd ed. Herman Meville. Ed. by Lauter. (American Heritage Library). (C). Date not set. 51.56 (*0-395-90168-5*) HM.

Lautgeschichte der Tatarischen Dialekte. Arpad Berta. (Studia Uralo-altaica Ser.: Vol. 31). (GER.). 304p. (Orig.). 1989. pap. 83.00 (*0-685-33594-1*, Pub. by Attila Josef Univ) Advent Bks Div.

Lautgesetz-Controversy: A Documentation. (Amsterdam Classics in Linguistics Ser.: No. 9). 587p. 1977. 107.00 (*90-272-0880-8*) J Benjamins Pubng Co.

Lautlehre und Flexionslehre see Schwedische Sprachgeschichte

L'Autobus Magique Se Fait RtTir: Un Livre Sur les Deserts. Tr. by Lucie Duchesne. (Magic School Bus Ser.).Tr. of Magic School Bus All Dried up: A Book about Deserts. (FRE., Illus.). 32p. (J). (gr. k-2). 1996. mass mkt. 5.99 (*0-590-16043-5*) Scholastic Inc.

L'Autre. Jean Baudrillard. LC 99-495143. (Contemporary Artists Ser.). 1999. pap. 29.95 (*0-7148-3842-X*) Phaidon Press.

L'Autre Front, 1914-1918 see French Home Front, 1914-1918

Lautreamont. Gaston Bachelard. Tr. & Contrib. by Robert S. Dupree. Contrib. by James Hillman. LC 86-16866. (Bachelard Translation Ser.). 150p. 1986. 20.00 (*0-911005-08-0*); pap. 16.00 (*0-911005-09-9*) Dallas Inst Pubns.

Lautreamont: Image, Theme & Self-Identity. Robert Pickering. 88p. 1993. 39.00 (*0-85261-289-3*, Pub. by Univ of Glasgow) St Mut.

Lautreamont's Imagery: A Stylistic Approach. Nesselroth. 14.95 (*0-685-34929-2*) Fr & Eur.

Lautrec. Chelsea House Publishing Staff. (World's Greatest Artists Ser.). 1997. 17.95 (*1-85813-948-1*) Chelsea Hse.

Lautrec. Nathaniel Harris. 80p. (YA). (gr. 7 up). 1997. 17.95 (*1-85813-531-1*) Chelsea Hse.

Lautrec: Women. P. Paret. (Rhythem & Color Two Ser.). 1970. 9.95 (*0-8288-9520-1*) Fr & Eur.

Lautrec-Redon. Jere Abbott. LC 74-86435. (Museum of Modern Art Publications in Reprint). (Illus.). 1969. reprint ed. 11.95 (*0-405-01527-5*) Ayer.

Lava. Pamela Ball. LC 97-44194. 192p. 1998. pap. 12.00 (*0-8050-5776-5*, Owl) H Holt & Co.

Lava: A Novel. Pamela Ball. LC 96-31660. 192p. 1997. 21.00 (*0-393-04024-0*) Norton.

Lava: A Saga of Hawaii. Armine Von Tempski. LC 91-27404. 1991. 27.50 (*0-918024-88-9*) Ox Bow.

Lava: A Saga of Hawaii. Armine Von Tempski. LC 91-27404. 1991. reprint ed. pap. 14.95 (*0-918024-89-7*) Ox Bow.

Lava Beds Caves. Charlie Larson & Jo Larson. (Illus.). 56p. (Orig.). (C). 1990. pap. 4.50 (*1-886168-04-0*) ABC Pubng.

Lava Beds National Monument. Susan L. Bean. 48p. 1991. pap. 8.95 (*0-9631392-0-7*) Lava Beds NHA.

Lava Flows & Domes. Ed. by J. Fink. (IAVCEI Proceedings in Volcanology Ser.: Vol. 2). (Illus.). 265p. 1989. 118.95 (*0-387-50684-5*) Spr-Verlag.

Lava of This Land: South African Poetry, 1960-1996. Ed. by Denis Hirson. LC 97-15916. 1997. 49.95 (*0-8101-5068-9*) Northwestern U Pr.

Lava of This Land: South African Poetry, 1970-1996. Ed. by Denis Hirson. LC 97-15916. 1997. pap. text 17.95 (*0-8101-5069-7*) Northwestern U Pr.

Lava River Caves. Charlie Larson & Jo Larson. (Illus.). 24p. (Orig.). (C). 1987. pap. 1.95 (*1-886168-02-4*) ABC Pubng.

Laval City Plan. (Grafocarte Maps Ser.). 1996. 8.95 (*2-7416-0074-0*, 80074) Michelin.

Lavalite World. Philip Jose Farmer. (World of Tiers Ser.: No. 5). 1983. 18.00 (*0-932096-21-2*) Phantasia Pr.

Lavalite World. Philip Jose Farmer. 1993. reprint ed. lib. bdg. 18.95 (*0-89968-401-7*, Lghtyr Pr) Buccaneer Bks.

LaVell: Airing It Out. LaVell Edwards & Lee Benson. LC 95-23342. (Illus.). xxv, 191p. 1995. 14.95 (*1-57345-068-5*, Shadow Mount) Deseret Bk.

Lavelle et le Renouveau de la Metaphysique de l'Etre au XXeme Siecle. Jean Ecole. (Europaea Memoria Ser.: Bd. 4). 305p. 1997. 63.00 (*3-487-10267-6*) G Olms Pubs.

Lavender. Pamela Allardice. (Illus.). 86p. 1994. 18.95 (*0-85572-197-9*, Pub. by Hill Content Pubng) Seven Hills Bk.

Lavender. Karen Hesse. (Illus.). 48p. (J). (gr. 2-4). 1995. 14.95 (*0-8050-2528-6*, Bks Young Read); pap. 4.95 (*0-8050-4257-1*, Redfeather BYR) H Holt & Co.

Lavender. Karen Hesse. LC 93-1439. (Redfeather Bks.). 1995. 10.15 (*0-606-09530-6*, Pub. by Turtleback) Demco.

Lavender: Fragrence of Provence. Hans Silvester. (Illus.). 184p. 1996. 29.95 (*0-8109-3576-7*, Pub. by Abrams) Time Warner.

Lavender: Nature's Way to Relaxation & Health. Philippa Waring. (Illus.). 128p. (Orig.). 1997. pap. 10.95 (*0-285-63370-8*, Pub. by Souvenir Pr Ltd) IPG Chicago.

Lavender: Practical Inspirations for Natural Gifts, Country Crafts & Decorative Displays. Tessa Evelegh. (Illus.). 128p. 1996. 19.95 (*1-85967-206-X*, Lorenz Bks) Anness Pub.

***Lavender: The Grower's Guide.** Virginia McNaughton. (Illus.). 200p. 2000. 29.95 (*0-88192-478-4*) Timber.

Lavender & Lace. Delia Parr. 1996. mass mkt. 5.99 (*0-312-95926-5*) St Martin.

Lavender & Old Lace. Myrtle Reed. 1976. lib. bdg. 13.50 (*0-89968-110-7*, Lghtyr Pr) Buccaneer Bks.

***Lavender Bear of Oz.** Bill Campbell. 160p. (J). 1998. 34.95 (*0-929605-83-7*) Books of Wonder.

Lavender Bear of Oz. Bill Campbell. (Illus.). 160p. (J). 1998. pap. 9.95 (*0-929605-77-2*) Books of Wonder.

Lavender Box: Poems for Children. 2nd rev. ed. Jacqueline Feldman. LC 98-93729. (Illus.). 57p. (J). (gr. k-5). Date not set. 12.95 (*0-9623903-2-1*) Ellicott Pr.

Lavender Culture. Ed. by Allen Young. 540p. (C). 1994. text 55.00 (*0-8147-4216-5*) NYU Pr.

Lavender Culture. Ed. by Allen Young. 540p. (C). 1994. pap. text 19.00 (*0-8147-4217-3*) NYU Pr.

Lavender Flame. Karen Stratford. 384p. (Orig.). 1991. mass mkt. 4.50 (*0-380-76267-6*, Avon Bks) Morrow Avon.

Lavender Garden: Beautiful Varieties to Grow & Gather. Robert Kourik. LC 97-30794. 1998. 18.95 (*0-8118-1570-6*) Chronicle Bks.

Lavender; How to Grow & Use the Fragrant Herb, 1. Ellen Spector Platt. LC 98-41973. 1999. pap. text 19.95 (*0-8117-2849-8*) Kitch Keepsakes.

***Lavender Lies.** Susan Wittig Albert. (China Bayles Mysteries Ser.). 2000. mass mkt. 6.50 (*0-425-17700-9*) Berkley Pub.

Lavender Lies: A China Bayles Mystery. Susan Wittig Albert. LC 99-33252. (China Bayles Mystery Ser.: No. 8). 306p. 1999. 21.95 (*0-425-17032-2*, Prime Crime) Berkley Pub.

Lavender Light: Daily Meditations for Gay Men in Recovery. Adrian Milton. LC 94-32616. 1995. pap. 10.00 (*0-399-51939-4*) Berkley Pub.

Lavender Moon. Troon Harrison. (Illus.). 32p. (J). (ps-2). 1997. pap. 6.95 (*1-55037-454-0*, Pub. by Annick); lib. bdg. 16.95 (*1-55037-455-9*, Pub. by Annick) Firefly Bks Ltd.

Lavender Reflections: Quotations & Affirmations for Gay Men & Lesbians. Eleanor R. Wagner. LC 95-79172. (Illus.). 144p. (Orig.). 1995. pap. 10.95 (*1-886360-02-2*) Alamo Sq Pr.

Lavender Screen: The Gay & Lesbian Films - Their Stars, Directors, Characters & Critics. Boze Hadleigh. LC 97-23433. (Illus.). 288p. 1997. pap. text 19.95 (*0-8065-1896-0*, Citadel Pr) Carol Pub Group.

Lavender Screen: The Gay & Lesbian Films - Their Stars, Makers, Characters & Critics. Boze Hadleigh. (Illus.). 256p. 1992. pap. 17.95 (*0-8065-1341-1*, Citadel Pr) Carol Pub Group.

Lavender Skies. Alison White. Ed. by Lizzy Shamon. 240p. 1998. mass mkt. 5.99 (*0-9667051-0-6*) A White Il.

Lavender, Sweet Lavender. Judyth A. McLeod. (Illus.). 120p. 1994. pap. 14.95 (*0-86417-601-5*, Pub. by Kangaroo Pr) Seven Hills Bk.

***Lavender, Sweet Lavender.** Judyth A. McLeod. 2000. 16.00 (*0-7432-0065-9*) Simon & Schuster.

Lavender Vote: Lesbians, Gay Men, & Bisexuals in American Electoral Politics. Mark Hertzog. (C). 1996. pap. text 19.00 (*0-8147-3530-4*) NYU Pr.

Lavender Vote: Lesbians, Gay Men, & Bisexuals in American Electoral Politics. Mark Hertzog. 264p. (C). 1996. text 50.00 (*0-8147-3529-0*) NYU Pr.

Lavenderblue: A Lesbian Love Story. Rand Hall. Ed. by Nancy E. Valmus. (Pocket Poetry Ser.). 60p. (Orig.). 1989. pap. 4.50 (*0-937025-00-3*) Shadowood Pubns.

Lavender's Blue. Kathleen Lines. (Illus.). 180p. (J). (ps-7). 1990. pap. 15.00 (*0-19-272208-5*) OUP.

Lavender's Blue. Janet Tyers. 208p. mass mkt. 4.99 (*1-55197-058-9*) Picasso Publ.

Lavengro: The Classic Account of Gypsy Life in Nineteenth-Century England. George (Henry) Borrow. (Illus.). 608p. 1991. reprint ed. pap. 12.95 (*0-486-26915-9*) Dover.

Lavenham Industrial Town. Alec Betterton & David Dymond. 144p. 1990. 30.00 (*0-86138-069-X*, Pub. by T Dalton) St Mut.

Lavenham Industrial Town. Alec Betterton & David Dymond. 1994. pap. 35.00 (*0-86138-070-3*, Pub. by T Dalton) St Mut.

Laventhol & Horwath's Small Business Tax Preparation Guide, 1989. Albert B. Ellentuck. 540p. (Orig.). 1988. pap. 14.95 (*0-380-75617-X*, Avon Bks) Morrow Avon.

***L'Aventure: An Introduction to French Language & Francophone Cultures.** Evelyne Charvier-Berman & Anne C. Cummings. 288p. 1998. pap., wbk. ed. 45.95 (*0-471-16586-7*) Wiley.

***L'aventure: A Four Skills Approach to Beginning French Student Text** Cummings. 487p. 1998. text 75.95 incl. audio (*0-471-17723-7*) Wiley.

L'aventure A Four Skills Approach to Beginning French Student Text. Cummings. 487p. 1997. 75.95 incl. audio (*0-471-17720-2*) Wiley.

***Laverda Twins & Triples: The Complete Story.** Mick Walker. (Illus.). 200p. 2000. 34.95 (*1-86126-220-5*, 129766AE, Pub. by Cro1wood) Motorbooks Intl.

La/Verdad Sin Voz see Death of an Anglo

***Lavery Plays, No. 1.** Byrony Lavery. 1998. pap. 14.95 (*0-413-72340-2*) Methn.

Laves: Poems from Hollywood. Mark Dunster. 12p. 1998. pap. 5.00 (*0-89642-489-8*) Linden Pubs.

Lavi ti Moun: Life of a Child. Ed. by Kim Jackson. (Illus.). 50p. 1998. pap. 10.00 (*0-9653234-2-0*) New Missions.

La/Vie Devant Soi see Life Before Us: Madame Rosa

La/Vie Sans Mort see Life Without Death

Lavington Estate Archives. Ed. by Francis W. Steer. 128p. 1964. 45.00 (*0-900801-12-3*) St Mut.

Laviniad: An Epic Poem. Claudio R. Salvucci. 133p. 1994. 20.00 (*0-9644234-0-5*) Evol Pubng & Manuf.

Lavis d'Encadrement see Art of Decorative Matting

Lavish Legacies: Baltimore Album Quilts. Jennifer F. Goldsborough. (Illus.). 140p. (Orig.). 1994. pap. 37.50 (*0-938420-39-9*) MD Hist.

Lavish of Sin. Carlton E. Morse. 224p. 1987. 14.95 (*0-940249-02-2*) Seven Stones Pr.

Lavish Self-Divisions: The Novels of Joyce Carol Oates. Brenda Daly. LC 96-11684. 232p. (C). 1996. 37.50 (*0-87805-885-0*) U Pr of Miss.

Lavision-Christine. Christine De Pisan. Ed. by Mary L. Towner. LC 72-94202. (Catholic University of America. Studies in Romance Languages & Literatures: No. 6). reprint ed. 37.50 (*0-404-50306-3*) AMS Pr.

La/Vita Nuova see New Life

Lavius Egyptus, Vols. 1 & 2. Thomas S. Spivey. 390p. 1998. reprint ed. pap. 24.95 (*0-7661-0340-4*) Kessinger Pub.

Lavoisier: Chemist, Biologist, Economist. Jean-Pierre Poirier. Tr. by Rebecca Balinski. LC 96-35738. (Chemical Sciences in Society Ser.). (Illus.). 544p. 1996. text 49.95 (*0-8122-3365-4*) U of Pa Pr.

Lavoisier: Chemist, Biologist, Economist. rev. ed. Jean-Pierre Poirier. Tr. by Charles C. Gillispie from FRE. (Illus.). 544p. 1998. pap. 19.95 (*0-8122-1649-0*) U of Pa Pr.

Lavoisier - The Crucial Year: The Background & Origin of His First Experiments on Combustion in 1772. Henry Guerlac. (Classics in the History & Philosophy of Science Ser.: Vol. 5). xxii, 240p. 1990. pap. text 48.00 (*2-88124-404-1*) Gordon & Breach.

Lavoisier & the Chemistry of Life: An Exploration of Scientific Creativity. Frederic L. Holmes. LC 84-40152. (Wisconsin Publications in the History of Science & Medicine: No. 4). (Illus.). 592p. 1987. pap. 24.95 (*0-299-09984-9*) U of Wis Pr.

Lavoisier in European Context: Negotiating a New Language for Chemistry. Ed. by Bernadette Bensaude-Vincent & Ferdinando Abbri. LC 95-384. 303p. 1995. 45.95 (*0-88135-189-X*, Sci Hist) Watson Pub Intl.

Lavoisier, 1743-1794. Edouard Grimaux. Ed. by I. Bernard Cohen. LC 80-2124. (Development of Science Ser.). (Illus.). 1981. lib. bdg. 38.95 (*0-405-13963-2*) Ayer.

Lavondyss. Robert Holdstock. 400p. 1991. mass mkt. 4.50 (*0-380-71184-2*, Avon Bks) Morrow Avon.

Lavoroe Lavoratori Nel Mondo Romano & Zur Sozialen und Rechtlichen Bewertung der Freien Arbeit in Rom. Francesco M. Francesco M. De Robertis & Dieter Norr. Ed. by Moses Finley. LC 79-4967. (Ancient Economic History Ser.). (GER & ITA.). 1979. reprint ed. lib. bdg. 42.95 (*0-405-12355-8*) Ayer.

Lavrou & Lopatin: Correspondence, 1870-1883 see Lavrou-Years of Emigration: Letters & Documents

Lavrou-Years of Emigration: Letters & Documents, 2vols. Ed. by Boris Sapir. Incl. Vol. 1. Lavrou & Lopatin: Correspondence, 1870-1883. LC 73-86089. 1975. Vol. 2. Other Correspondence of Lavrou & Varic (Russian Text) LC 73-86089. 1975. LC 73-86089. (Russian Series on Social History: No. 2). 970p. 1975. Set lib. bdg. 278.00 (*90-277-0453-8*) Kluwer Academic.

Lavrsky (Troitsky) Kondakar Vol. 1: The Medieval (Late Twelfth Century) Russian Musical Code. Gregory Myers. (CHU, ENG & GRE., Illus.). 264p. 1998. 249.00 (*954-580-006-2*, Pub. by Heron Pr) Intl Scholars.

L

LaVyrle Spencer: Three Complete Novels. LaVyrle Spencer. 704p. 1991. 10.99 (*0-517-06017-5*) Random Hse Value.

LaVyrle Spencer - Three Complete Novels: Morning Glory; Vows; The Gamble. LaVyrle Spencer. 784p. 1994. pap. 11.98 (*0-399-13923-0*, G P Putnam) Peng Put Young Read.

Law. (Professional Education Ser.). 132p. 1973. 16.95 (*0-318-15860-4*, 107) Natl Ct Report.

Law. Boy Scouts of America. (Illus.). 64p. (YA). (gr. 6-12). 1975. pap. 2.90 (*0-8395-3389-6*, 33389) BSA.

Law. Marjorie Eberts et al. LC 97-43561. (VGM's Career Portraits Ser.). (Illus.). 96p. 1998. 13.95 (*0-8442-4368-X*, 4368X, VGM Career) NTC Contemp Pub Co.

Law. Kathi Mountford & Kim Horsted. 170p. 1990. 160.00 (*0-900239-48-4*, Pub. by Chartered Bank) St Mut.

Law. Roger Vailland. 256p. 1989. pap. 14.95 (*0-907871-11-9*) Hippocrene Bks.

Law. Frederic Bastiat. 78p. 1996. reprint ed. pap. 2.95 (*0-910614-01-6*) Foun Econ Ed.

Law. 2nd ed. Frederic Bastiat. LC 95-83091. 100p. 1996. 12.95 (*1-57246-020-2*) Foun Econ Ed.

Law. 2nd ed. Frederic Bastiat. 1998. 2.95 (*1-57246-074-1*) Foun Econ Ed.

Law. 2nd ed. Frederic Bastiat. LC 98-73568. 1998. 12.95 (*1-57246-073-3*) Foun Econ Ed.

Law. 3rd ed. Summers. Date not set. pap. text, teacher ed. write for info. (*0-314-99990-6*) West Pub.

Law: A Human Process. Donald P. Lay. LC 96-22825. (Paralegal). 200p. 1996. pap. text 14.95 (*0-314-20058-4*) West Pub.

Law: Allegory Roman Civil & Merchant Laws. abr. ed. Intro. by Luanna C. Blagrove. (AMERCE Law Ser.). (Illus.). 250p. 1988. 24.95 (*0-939776-09-X*) Blagrove Pubns.

Law: AMERCE. abr. ed. Intro. by Luanna C. Blagrove. (AMERCE Law Ser.). (Illus.). 250p. 1988. 24.95 (*0-939776-35-9*) Blagrove Pubns.

Law: American AMERCE Emporium. abr. ed. Intro. by Luanna C. Blagrove. (AMERCE Law Ser.). (Illus.). 250p. 1988. 24.95 (*0-939776-37-5*) Blagrove Pubns.

Law: Business or Profession? Julius H. Cohen. 1980. lib. bdg. 79.95 (*0-8490-3133-8*) Gordon Pr.

Law: Its Origin, Growth & Function. James Carter. LC 74-6413. (American Constitutional & Legal History Ser). 1974. reprint ed. lib. bdg. 42.50 (*0-306-70631-8*) Da Capo.

Law: Its Origin Growth & Function: Being a Course of Lectures Prepared for Delivery Before the Law School of Harvard University. James C. Carter. LC 94-75660. viii, 356p. 1994. reprint ed. 110.00 (*1-56169-094-5*) Gaunt.

Law: Lay Urania Deuteronomy Digamma. abr. ed. Intro. by Luanna C. Blagrove. (AMERCE Law Ser.). (Illus.). 250p. 1988. 24.95 (*0-939776-08-1*) Blagrove Pubns.

Law: The Air We Breath: A Look at Law & the Legal System in the Commonwealth Caribbean. Michael Theodore. LC 95-151480. 153p. 1995. pap. 15.00 (*976-8052-05-8*) Gaunt.

Law: The Old Testament of Moses & the Prophets to Israel; the New Testament of Our Lord & Saviour Jesus Christ. (Walk with Jesus Ser.). (Illus.). 170p. (Orig.). 1996. pap. 35.00 (*1-57277-702-8*) Script Rsch.

Law: What I Have Seen, What I Have Heard & What I Have Known. Cyrus Jay. xii, 351p. 1988. reprint ed. 42.50 (*0-8377-2306-X*, Rothman) W S Hein.

Law - Grace Controversy. John G. Reisinger. 1989. pap. 1.49 (*0-87377-092-7*) GAM Pubns.

Law - Latin: A Treatise in Latin with Legal Maxims & Phrases as a Basis of Instruction. 2nd ed. E. Hilton Jackson. xvi, 236p. 1994. reprint ed. 42.00 (*0-8377-2309-4*, Rothman) W S Hein.

Law Abiding Criminals. John Kaplan et al. (S. A. F. Monographs). 72p. 1983. pap. 5.50 (*0-911475-21-4*) Second Amend.

Law above Nations: Supranational Courts & the Legalization of Politics. Ed. by Mary L. Volcansek. LC 97-12134. 168p. 1997. 49.95 (*0-8130-1537-5*) U Press Fla.

Law Accumulation & the Breakdown of the Capitalist System. Henryk Grossman. LC 91-26181. 140p. (C). 1992. 54.95 (*0-7453-0458-3*, Pub. by Pluto GBR); pap. 19.95 (*0-7453-0459-1*, Pub. by Pluto GBR) Stylus Pub VA.

Law Affecting the Valuation of Land in Australia. 2nd ed. Alan A. Hyam. 360p. 1995. pap. 75.00 (*0-455-21318-6*, Pub. by LawBk Co) Gaunt.

Law, Alcohol, & Order: Perspectives on National Prohibition, 110. Eleutherian Mills-Hagley Foundation Staff. Ed. by David E. Kyvig. LC 84-25225. (Contributions in American History Ser.: No. 110). 219p. 1985. 55.00 (*0-313-24755-2*, KLA/) Greenwood.

Law among Nations: An Introduction to Public International Law. 7th ed. Gerhard Von Glahn. LC 95-33138. 848p. (C). 1995. 100.00 (*0-205-18994-6*) Allyn.

Law & Accountancy: Conflict & Cooperation in the 1990s. Ed. by Judith Freedman & Michael Power. 192p. 1992. 75.00 (*1-85396-196-5*, Pub. by P Chapman) Taylor & Francis.

Law & Accounting: Nineteenth-Century American Legal Cases. Ed. by Margo Reid. (Foundations in Accounting Ser.: No. 15). 295p. 1989. reprint ed. text 10.00 (*0-8240-6130-6*) Garland.

Law & Administration. Carol Harlow & Richard Rawlings. (Law in Context Ser.). xxvi, 718p. 1984. text 44.00 (*0-297-78239-8*) W S Hein.

Law & Administration: Nuclear Liability. D. I. Blokhintsev & Jack B. Weinstein. LC 59-8165. (Progress in Nuclear Energy Ser.: Vol. 10). 1962. 221.00 (*0-08-009703-0*, Pub. by Pergamon Repr) Franklin.

Law & Administration of Incorporated Societies. 2nd ed. T. F. Paul. 276p. 1986. pap. 54.00 (*0-409-78744-2*, NZ, MICHIE) LEXIS Pub.

Law & Advertising: Current Legal Issues for Agencies, Advertisers & Attorneys. Dean K. Fueroghne. Ed. by Melissa Davis. LC 95-68129. 505p. (Orig.). (C). 1995. pap. 37.50 (*0-9621415-8-5*, Pub. by Copy Wrkshp) Natl Bk Netwk.

***Law & Advertising, 2000: Current Legal Issues for Agencies, Advertisers & Attorneys.** 2nd rev. ed. Dean Fueroghne. 2000. pap. 60.00 (*1-887229-07-8*) Copy Wrkshp.

Law & Aesthetics. Ed. by Roberta Kevelson. LC 91-37471. (New Studies in Aesthetics: Vol. 11). 469p. (C). 1992. text 70.95 (*0-8204-1816-1*) P Lang Pubng.

Law & Aging: Essentials of Elder Law. Ronald J. Schwartz. 312p. (C). 1997. per. 37.50 (*0-929563-38-7*) Pearson Pubns.

Law & Amateur Sports. Ronald J. Waicukauski. LC 82-47773. 320p. 1983. 17.95 (*0-253-13730-6*) Ind U Pr.

Law & American Health Care. Kenneth R. Wing et al. LC 97-48825. 1998. boxed set 64.00 (*1-56706-646-1*) Aspen Law.

Law & Anarchism. Ed. by Thom Holterman & Henc Van Maarseveen. LC 84-901488. 216p. 1984. reprint ed. pap. 67.00 (*0-608-00452-9*, 206127100007) Bks Demand.

Law & Anthropology. Ed. by Peter Sack & Jonathan Aleck. (International Library of Essays in Law & Legal Theory). 550p. (C). 1992. lib. bdg. 150.00 (*0-8147-7954-9*) NYU Pr.

Law & Anthropology, No. 8. Kuppe. 1996. lib. bdg. 136.50 (*90-411-0194-2*) Kluwer Law Intl.

Law & Anthropology: International Yearbook for Legal Anthropology, Vol. 7. Ed. by Rene Kuppe. 416p. (C). 1994. lib. bdg. 124.00 (*0-7923-3142-7*, Pub. by M Nijhoff) Kluwer Academic.

***Law & Anthropology: International Yearbook for Legal Anthropology, Vol. 10.** Ed. by Rene Kuppe & Richard Potz. 206p. 1999. 129.00 (*90-411-1150-6*) Kluwer Law Intl.

Law & Anthropology: Natural Resource, Environment, & Legal Pluralism, Vol. LAAN 9. Ed. by Rene Kuppe et al. 1997. 215.00 (*90-411-0389-9*) Kluwer Law Intl.

Law & Apocalypse: The Moral Thought of Luis de Leon (1527-1591) Terry A. Kottman. (International Archives of the History of Ideas Ser.: No. 44). 162p. 1972. lib. bdg. 73.50 (*90-247-1183-5*, Pub. by M Nijhoff) Kluwer Academic.

Law & Ardor: An Andrew Broom Mystery. Ralph McInerny. 256p. 1995. 21.00 (*0-684-80462-X*) S&S Trade.

Law & Attitude Change. William K. Muir, Jr. LC 67-28851. 182p. 1985. reprint ed. pap. text 9.00 (*0-226-54628-4*) U Ch Pr.

Law & Authority in a Nigerian Tribe. Charles K. Meek. LC 76-44756. reprint ed. 37.50 (*0-404-15951-6*) AMS Pr.

Law & Banking: Applications. 3rd ed. Craig W. Smith. (Illus.). 280p. (C). 1990. text 57.00 (*0-89982-361-0*) Am Bankers.

Law & Banking: Principles. 3rd ed. James C. Conboy, Jr. 423p. (C). 1990. text 57.00 (*0-89982-362-9*) Am Bankers.

Law & Banking Applications: 1996 Edition. Craig W. Smith. 1996. 60.00 (*0-89982-443-9*) Am Bankers.

Law & Banking Principles. 2nd ed. James C. Conboy, Jr. 425p. (C). 1996. 60.00 (*0-89982-436-6*) Am Bankers.

Law & Body Politics: Regulating the Female Body. Ed. by Jo Bridgeman & Susan Millns. LC 95-102. 328p. 1995. 87.95 (*1-85521-515-2*, Pub. by Dartmth Pub) Ashgate Pub Co.

Law & Bureaucracy: Administrative Discretion & the Limits of Legal Action. Jeffrey L. Jowell. 220p. 1984. text 26.50 (*0-8290-1572-8*) Irvington.

Law & Business. 4th ed. Clark. 1993. teacher ed. 57.81 (*0-07-035165-1*) McGraw.

Law & Business: The Regulatory Environment. 4th ed. Lawrence S. Clark et al. LC 93-24356. (C). 1993. pap., student ed. 28.13 (*0-07-035163-5*) McGraw.

Law & Business: The Regulatory Environment. 4th ed. Lawrence S. Clark et al. LC 93-24356. 1248p. (C). 1994. 92.19 (*0-07-035162-7*) McGraw.

***Law & Business Administration in Canada.** 9th ed. 300p. 2000. teacher ed. write for info. (*0-13-018626-0*) P-H.

***Law & Business Administration in Canada: Study Guide.** 9th ed. Smyth & Soberman. 500p. 2000. pap. 30.60 (*0-13-018629-5*) P-H.

***Law & Business Administration In Canada: Test Item File.** 9th ed. 400p. 2000. text. write for info. (*0-13-018627-9*) S&S Trade.

Law & Business Directory of Bankruptcy Attorneys, 1988. Ed. by Lynn M. LoPucki & Ann T. Reilly. 1988. 125.00 (*0-318-36198-1*) P-H.

Law & Business Directory of Corporate Counsel, 1982-1983. enl. rev. ed. Ed. by Law & Business Inc. Staff. 1496p. 1982. 110.00 (*0-686-89146-5*, H42787) Harcourt.

Law & Business Directory of Corporate Counsel, 1984-1985. rev. ed. Ed. by Law & Business Inc. Staff. 1546p. 1984. 125.00 (*0-15-004278-7*) Harcourt.

Law & Business Directory of Corporate Counsel, 1988-1989, 2 vols. 9th ed. 2400p. 1988. 260.00 (*0-13-526237-2*) P-H.

Law & Business Directory of Major U. S. Law Firms, 2 vols. Ed. by Law & Business Inc. Staff. 1800p. 1984. 200.00 (*0-15-004293-0*) Harcourt.

Law & Business in France: A Guide to French Commercial & Corporate Law. Christopher J. Mesnooh. LC 93-46936. 384p. (C). 1994. lib. bdg. 149.00 (*0-7923-2682-2*) Kluwer Academic.

Law & Business of Computer Software. D. C. Toedt, III. LC 89-71241. (IP Ser.). 1989. ring bd. 140.00 (*0-87632-656-4*) West Group.

Law & Business of International Project Finance: A Resource for Governments, Sponsors, Lenders, Lawyers, & Project Participants. Scott Hoffman. LC 98-4428. 1998. 185.00 (*90-411-0621-9*) Kluwer Law Intl.

Law & Business of Licensing: Licensing in the 1990's, 3 vols. Ed. by Paul B. Bell & Jay Simon. LC 90-1961. (IP Ser.). 1990. ring bd. 375.00 (*0-87632-724-2*) West Group.

***Law & Business of Licensing: Licensing in the 21st Century.** Woody Friedlander & Larry W. Evans. LC 00-31982. 2000. write for info. (*0-8366-1446-1*) West Group.

Law & Business of the Entertainment Industries. 3rd ed. Robert C. Berry et al. LC 95-30662. 800p. 1995. text 59.95 (*0-275-95064-6*, Praeger Pubs) Greenwood.

Law & Business of the Sports Industries: Common Issues in Amateur & Professional Sports. 2nd ed. Robert C. Berry & Glenn M. Wong. LC 92-1745. 864p. 1993. text 59.95 (*0-275-93862-X*, C3862, Praeger Pubs) Greenwood.

Law & Catholic Schools: Approaching the New Millennium. Mary A. Shaughnessy. 106p. (Orig.). 1991. pap. 6.00 (*1-55833-104-2*) Natl Cath Educ.

Law & Changing Society: Administration, Human Rights, Women & Children, Consumer Protection, Education, Commercial Contracts, Narcotic Drugs, Ecological Crisis, Workers Participation, Etc. Ed. by Manju Saxena & Harish Chandra. 1999. 48.00 (*81-7629-184-6*, Pub. by Deep & Deep Pubns) S Asia.

Law & Citizenship in Early Modern France. Charlotte C. Wells. (Studies in Historical & Political Science, 112th Series (1994): No. 3). 240p. 1994. text 37.50 (*0-8018-4918-7*) Johns Hopkins.

Law & Civil War in the Modern World. Ed. by John N. Moore. LC 73-19338. 672p. 1974. reprint ed. pap. 200.00 (*0-608-04013-4*, 206474900011) Bks Demand.

Law & Civilization: The Legal Thought of Roscoe Pound. Edward B. McLean. 342p. (C). 1992. lib. bdg. 55.00 (*0-8191-8698-8*) U Pr of Amer.

Law & Community in Three American Towns. Carol J. Greenhouse et al. 240p. 1994. text 37.50 (*0-8014-2959-5*); pap. text 13.95 (*0-8014-8169-4*) Cornell U Pr.

Law & Competition in Twentieth Century Europe: Protecting Prometheus. David J. Gerber. LC 97-47463. 486p. 1998. text 90.00 (*0-19-826285-X*) OUP.

Law & Contemporary Corrections. Smith. LC 99-13587. (Criminal Justice). 1999. pap. 60.95 (*0-534-56628-6*) Wadsworth Pub.

Law & Contemporary Problems, 1933-1994, 56 vols. mic. film 57.50 (*0-318-57442-X*) W S Hein.

Law & Contemporary Problems, 1933-1994, 59 vols., Set. 1995. 2950.00 (*0-8377-9103-0*, Rothman) W S Hein.

Law & Crisis in the Third World. Ed. by Sammy Adelman & Abdul Paliwala. (African Discourse Ser.: No. 4). 344p. 1993. 65.00 (*0-905450-88-4*, Pub. by H Zell Pubs) Seven Hills Bk.

Law & Development. Ed. by Anthony Carty. (International Library of Essays in Law & Legal Theory). 550p. (C). 1992. lib. bdg. 150.00 (*0-8147-1473-0*) NYU Pr.

***Law & Development: A Record of the Procedures of the Roundtable Meeting of Chief Justices & Ministers Held in Manila, Philippines.** Ed. by Barry Metzger. 71p. (C). 1999. reprint ed. pap. text 20.00 (*0-7881-8243-9*) DIANE Pub.

Law & Development: The Future of Law & Development Research. 91p. 1974. write for info. (*91-7106-090-1*, Pub. by Nordic Africa) Transaction Pubs.

Law & Deviance. Ed. by H. Laurence Ross. LC 81-8905. (Sage Annual Reviews of Studies in Deviance: No. 5). (Illus.). 278p. 1981. reprint ed. pap. 86.20 (*0-608-01165-7*, 205946500001) Bks Demand.

Law & Disagreement: Essays in Jurisprudence 1989-1995. Jeremy Waldron. LC 98-30991. 344p. 1999. text 65.00 (*0-19-826213-2*) OUP.

Law & Disorder. Ed. by Eric R. Bates. (Illus.). 64p. (Orig.). 1990. pap. 5.00 (*0-943810-47-7*) Inst Southern Studies.

Law & Disorder: Criminal Justice in America. Bruce Jackson. LC 84-2574. 336p. 1984. text 24.95 (*0-252-01012-4*) U of Ill Pr.

Law & Disorder: Poems & Pictures. G. B. Fuchs. Tr. by Richard Exner from ENG. LC 77-85670. (German Ser.: Vol. 5). 1979. 17.50 (*0-87775-118-8*); pap. 9.95 (*0-87775-119-6*) Unicorn Pr.

Law & Disorder: The Legitimation of Direct Action As an Instrument of Social Policy. Samuel I. Shuman. LC 78-130426. (Franklin Memorial Lectures Ser.: Vol. 19). 237p. reprint ed. pap. 73.50 (*0-608-16511-5*, 202764000055) Bks Demand.

Law & Disorder in Cyberspace: Abolish the FCC & Let Common Law Rule the Telecosm. Peter W. Huber. LC 97-3345. 288p. 1997. 30.00 (*0-19-511614-3*) OUP.

Law & Disorder in Medieval Ireland: Essays Celebrating the Parliament of 1297. Ed. by James Lydon. 160p. 1997. boxed set 45.00 (*1-85182-257-7*, Pub. by Four Cts Pr) Intl Spec Bk.

Law & Disorder on the Narova River: The Kreenholm Strike of 1872. Reginald E. Zelnik. LC 93-44876. (Centennial Bk.). 1995. 45.00 (*0-520-08481-0*, Pub. by U CA Pr) Cal Prin Full Svc.

Law & Dynamic Administration. Marshall E. Dimock. LC 80-12863. 166p. 1980. 45.00 (*0-275-90470-9*, C0470, Praeger Pubs) Greenwood.

Law & Economic Approach to Criminal Gangs. Liza Vertinsky. 8p. 1999. text 63.95 (*1-84014-898-5*) Ashgate Pub Co.

Law & Economic Development in the Third World. Ed. by P. Ebow Bondzi-Simpson. LC 91-28004. 200p. 1992. 59.95 (*0-275-93925-1*, C3925, Praeger Pubs) Greenwood.

Law & Economic Growth: The Legal History of the Lumber Industry in Wisconsin, 1836-1915. James W. Hurst. LC 83-40287. 980p. reprint ed. pap. 200.00 (*0-608-20442-0*, 207169500002) Bks Demand.

Law & Economic Integration in the European Community. Stephen Weatherill. (Clarendon Law Ser.). 328p. 1996. text 62.00 (*0-19-876311-5*); pap. text 32.00 (*0-19-876312-3*) OUP.

Law & Economic Organization: A Comparative Study of Preindustrial Societies. Katherine Newman. LC 83-7169. 276p. 1983. pap. text 19.95 (*0-521-28966-1*) Cambridge U Pr.

Law & Economic Policy in America: The Evolution of the Sherman Antitrust Act. William Letwin. LC 81-7551. xii, 316p. 1981. pap. text 12.00 (*0-226-47353-8*) U Ch Pr.

Law & Economic Policy in America: The Evolution of the Sherman Antitrust Act. William Letwin. LC 80-21868. 304p. 1980. reprint ed. lib. bdg. 35.00 (*0-313-22651-2*, LELE, Greenwood Pr) Greenwood.

Law & Economic Regulation in Transportation. Paul S. Dempsey & William E. Thoms. LC 85-9593. (Illus.). 360p. 1986. 77.50 (*0-89930-138-X*, DLE/, Quorum Bks) Greenwood.

Law & Economic, Teacher's Manual to Accompany Cases & Materials On. David W. Barnes & Lynn A. Stout. (American Casebook Ser.). 230p. (C). 1992. pap. text. write for info. (*0-314-01042-4*) West Pub.

Law & Economics. 2nd ed. Polinsky. 176p. 1989. pap. text 24.95 (*0-316-71278-7*, Aspen Law & Bus) Aspen Pub.

***Law & Economics.** 3rd ed. Robert Cooter. LC 99-26824. 545p. (C). 1999. 90.00 (*0-321-06482-8*) Addison-Wesley.

Law & Economics, 3 vols., set. Ed. by Richard A. Posner & Francesco Parisi. LC 97-13442. (International Library of Critical Writings in Economics Ser.: No. 81). 2056p. 1997. 645.00 (*1-85278-972-7*) E Elgar.

Law & Economics, Set, Vols. I & II. Ed. by Jules Coleman & Jeffrey Lange. (International Library of Essays in Law & Legal Theory). 1100p. (C). 1992. lib. bdg. 250.00 (*0-8147-1464-1*) NYU Pr.

Law & Economics, Vol. 1. Jules Coleman. (C). 1992. lib. bdg. 125.00 (*0-8147-1462-5*) NYU Pr.

Law & Economics, Vol. 2. Jules Coleman. (C). 1992. lib. bdg. 125.00 (*0-8147-1463-3*) NYU Pr.

Law & Economics: A Comparative Approach to Theory & Practice. Robin P. Malloy. 166p. (C). 1990. pap. text 17.50 (*0-314-72586-5*) West Pub.

Law & Economics: An Institutionalist Perspective. Warren J. Samuels & A. Allan Schmid. 272p. 1980. lib. bdg. 73.50 (*0-89838-049-9*) Kluwer Academic.

Law & Economics: An Introductory Analysis. 2nd ed. Werner Z. Hirsch. 409p. 1988. text 75.00 (*0-12-349481-8*) Acad Pr.

***Law & Economics: An Introductory Analysis.** 3rd ed. Werner Z. Hirsch. LC 98-89452. (Illus.). 358p. 1999. 59.95 (*0-12-349482-6*) Acad Pr.

Law & Economics: New & Critical Perspectives. Ed. by Robin P. Malloy & Christopher K. Braun. (Critic of Institutions Ser.: Vol. 4). 460p. (C). 1995. pap. text 29.95 (*0-8204-2627-X*) P Lang Pubng.

Law & Economics: The Early Journal Literature. Warren J. Samuels. LC 97-51459. 1998. 380.00 (*1-85196-610-2*, Pub. by Pickering & Chatto); 380.00 (*1-85196-611-0*, Pub. by Pickering & Chatto) Ashgate Pub Co.

Law & Economics: The Early Journal Literature. Ed. by Warren J. Samuels. 800p. 1998. 395.00 (*1-85196-612-9*, Pub. by Pickering & Chatto) Ashgate Pub Co.

Law & Economics Anthology: An Anthology. Ed. by Kenneth G. Dau-Schmidt & Thomas S. Ulen. LC 98-228634. 580p. 1998. pap. 29.95 (*0-87084-208-0*) Anderson Pub Co.

Law & Economics Cases & Materials. Charles J. Goetz. LC 83-21787. (American Casebook Ser.). 547p. (C). 1983. 50.50 (*0-314-76541-7*) West Pub.

Law & Economics in a Nutshell. Jeffrey L. Harrison. LC 94-47574. (Nutshell Ser.). 302p. (C). 1995. pap. 21.00 (*0-314-05586-X*) West Pub.

***Law & Economics in Developing Countries.** Edgardo Buscaglia & William E. Ratliff. LC 00-27213. 2001. write for info. (*0-8179-9772-5*) Hoover Inst Pr.

Law & Economics in the Labour Market. Ed. by Roger Van Den Bergh et al. LC 99-26391. (New Horizons in Law & Economics Ser.). 264p. 2000. 95.00 (*1-85898-697-4*) E Elgar.

Law & Economics of Financial Institutions in Australia. J. Stanford & T. Beale. LC 95-231234. 376p. 1995. pap. write for info. (*0-409-30578-2*, MICHIE) LEXIS Pub.

Law & Economics of Transborder Telecommunications: A Symposium. Ernst J. Mestmacker. (Law & Economics of International Telecommunications Ser.). 450p. 1987. 126.00 (*3-7890-1368-4*, Pub. by Nomos Verlags) Intl Bk Import.

Law & Education. Hudgins & Vacca. 656p. 1995. text 50.00 (*1-55834-270-2*, 11760-10, MICHIE) LEXIS Pub.

***Law & Education: Contemporary Issues & Court Decisions.** 5th ed. H. C. Hudgins, Jr. & Richard S. Vacca. 700p. 1999. 54.00 (*0-327-01654-X*, 1176011) LEXIS Pub.

Law & Empire in Late Antiquity. Jill Harries. LC 97-47492. 280p. (C). 1999. text 59.95 (*0-521-41087-8*) Cambridge U Pr.

Law & English Railway Capitalism, 1825-1875. Rande W. Kostal. (Illus.). 432p. 1998. reprint ed. pap. text 42.00 (*0-19-826567-0*) OUP.

An Asterisk (*) at the beginning of an entry indicates that the title is appearing for the first time.

Law & Enlightenment in Britain. Tom D. Campbell. (Enlightenment Rights & Revolution Ser.). 200p. 1990. pap. text 38.00 (0-08-040921-0, Pub. by Aberdeen U Pr) Macmillan.

Law & Environment. P. Leelakrishnan. (C). 1992. 130.00 (0-89771-782-1, Pub. by Eastern Book) St Mut.

***Law & Ethics.** Levy. 440p. 1999. pap. text 24.00 (0-536-02757-9) Pearson Custom.

Law & Ethics: A Guide for the Health Professional. Ed. by Nathan T. Sidley. LC 83-26565. 368p. 1984. 53.95 (0-89885-155-6, Kluwer Acad Hman Sci) Kluwer Academic.

Law & Ethics for Health Occupations. Karen Judson & Sharon Blesie. LC 93-18325. 1993. 20.00 (0-02-800668-2) Glencoe.

Law & Ethics for Medical Careers. 2nd ed. Karen Judson & Sharon Hicks. LC 98-29423. (YA). (gr. 6-12). 1999. student ed. 28.00 (0-02-804755-9) Glencoe.

Law & Ethics in Clinical Laboratory Science. Griffith. (C). 1996. pap. text. write for info. (0-7216-5319-7, W B Saunders Co) Harcrt Hlth Sci Grp.

Law & Ethics in Diagnostic Imaging & Therapeutic Radiology: With Risk Management & Safety Applications. Ed. by Ann M. Obergfell. LC 95-10278. (Illus.). 208p. 1995. text 27.00 (0-7216-5062-7, W B Saunders Co) Harcrt Hlth Sci Grp.

***Law & Ethics in Nursing & Health Care.** Judith C. Hendrick. (Illus.). 240p. 2000. 28.95 (0-7487-3321-3) Standard Pub.

Law & Ethics In The Business Environment. Terry Halbert & Elaine Ingull. Ed. by Fenton & Hill-Whilton. (SWC-Business Law). 382p. (C). 1990. mass mkt. 27.50 (0-314-66804-7) West Pub.

Law & Ethics in the Business Environment. 2nd ed. Terry Halbert. LC 96-183929. 400p. 1996. pap. 39.95 (0-314-20438-5) West Pub.

Law & Ethics of A. I. D. & Embryo Transfer. CIBA Foundation Staff. LC 73-80904. (CIBA Foundation Symposium: New Ser.: No. 17). 118p. reprint ed. pap. 36.60 (0-608-13497-X, 202214800024) Bks Demand.

Law & Ethics of Lawyering. 2nd ed. Geoffrey C. Hazard, Jr. et al. Ed. by Roger C. Cramton. LC 93-36968. (University Casebook Ser.). 1158p. 1993. text. write for info. (1-56662-120-8) Foundation Pr.

Law & Ethics of the Veterinary Profession. James F. Wilson et al. Ed. by Suzanne Neilson. (Illus.). 550p. (C). 1988. 59.95 (0-9621007-0-6) Priority Press.

***Law & Evidence: Criminal Justice, Criminology, Law & Legal Studies.** Charles P. Nemeth. 450p. 2000. 66.67 (0-13-030811-0, Prentice Hall) P-H.

***Law & Evolutionary Biology.** Ed. by Lawrence A. Frolik. 380p. 1999. pap. 29.00 (0-9669673-1-3) Gruter Inst.

Law & Family in Late Antiquity: The Emperor Constantine's Marriage Legislation. Judith E. Grubbs. 400p. 2000. pap. 24.95 (0-19-820822-7) OUP.

Law & Finance of Corporate Acquisitions. 2nd ed. Ronald J. Gilson & Bernard S. Black. LC 93-19904. (University Casebook Ser.). 1603p. 1995. text 52.00 (1-56662-067-8); pap. text. write for info. (0-614-07456-8) Foundation Pr.

Law & Finance of Corporate Acquisitions: 1998 Supplement. 2nd ed. Gilson & Black. 1998. 8.95 (1-56662-601-3) Foundation Pr.

Law & Finance of Corporate Acquisitions, 1993. Ronald J. Gilson & Bernard S. Black. (University Casebook Ser.). 1153p. 1993. pap. text, suppl. ed. 18.95 (1-56662-134-8) Foundation Pr.

Law & Finance of Corporate Insider Trading: Theory & Evidence. Nasser Arshadi. LC 93-19386. 184p. (C). 1993. lib. bdg. 104.50 (0-7923-9360-0) Kluwer Academic.

Law & Force in American Foreign Policy. Edwin C. Hoyt. LC 84-21969. 278p. (Orig.). 1985. pap. text 25.00 (0-8191-4431-2); lib. bdg. 52.00 (0-8191-4430-4) U Pr of Amer.

Law & Forensics: Index of New Information. Herbert A. Muldoon. 150p. 1998. 47.50 (0-7883-2032-7); pap. 44.50 (0-7883-2033-5) ABBE Pubs Assn.

Law & Freedom in the American Family. Hartog. 1995. 24.95 (0-02-914154-0) S&S Trade.

Law & Gender Inequality: The Politics of Women's Rights in India. Agnes. LC 99-938560. (Law in India Ser.). 268p. 1999. text 29.95 (0-19-564587-1) OUP.

Law & Genetics: Regulating a Revolution. Ed. by Roger Brownsword et al. 224p. 1998. pap. 27.00 (1-84113-006-0, Pub. by Hart Pub) Intl Spec Bk.

Law & Ginny Marlow: The Cutlers of the Shady Lady Ranch. Marie Ferrarella. 1999. per. 3.50 (0-373-52083-2, 1-52083-2, Mira Bks) Harlequin Bks.

Law & Gospel: A Study in Integrating Faith & Practice. John W. Montgomery. 52p. 1994. reprint ed. pap. 7.50 (1-896363-00-8) CN Inst for Law.

Law & Gospel: Bad News, Good News. Leroy A. Dobberstein. LC 96-67924. (People's Bible Teachings Ser.). 181 p. 1996. 9.99 (0-8100-0612-X) Northwest Pub.

Law & Gospel: Foundation of Lutheran Ministry. Robert J. Koester. LC 92-61237. 234p. (Orig.). 1993. pap. 10.99 (0-8100-0436-4, 15N0548) Northwest Pub.

Law & Gospel: Philip Melanchthon's Debate with John Agricola of Eisleben over Poentitentia. Timothy J. Wengert. LC 97-38668. (Texts & Studies in Reformation & Post-Reformation Thought Ser.). 240p. (C). 1997. pap. 19.99 (0-8010-2158-8, Labyrinth) Baker Bks.

Law & Government in Colonial Australia. Paul Finn. (Law & Government Ser.). 240p. 1987. 42.00 (0-19-554746-2) OUP.

Law & Government in Mediaeval England & Normandy: Essays in Honour of Sir James Holt. Ed. by George Garnett & John Hudson. LC 93-29054. (Illus.). 405p. (C). 1994. text 69.95 (0-521-43076-3) Cambridge U Pr.

Law & Grace. Alva J. McClain. pap. 3.95 (0-88469-001-6) BMH Bks.

Law & Higher Education: A Casebook, 2 vols., 1. John S. Brubacher. LC 70-150238. 701p. 1975. 45.00 (0-8386-7897-1) Fairleigh Dickinson.

Law & Higher Education: A Casebook, 2 vols., 2. John S. Brubacher. LC 70-150238. 701p. 1975. 45.00 (0-8386-7947-1) Fairleigh Dickinson.

Law & Higher Education: A Casebook, 2 vols., Set. John S. Brubacher. LC 70-150238. 701p. 1975. 60.00 (0-685-02293-5) Fairleigh Dickinson.

Law & Higher Education: Cases & Materials on Colleges in Court. Michael A. Olivas. 1056p. 1993. suppl. ed. 14.95 (0-89089-009-9) Carolina Acad Pr.

Law & Higher Education: Cases & Materials on Colleges in Court. 2nd ed. Michael A. Olivas. LC 96-47275. 1176p. 1997. boxed set 80.00 (0-89089-866-9) Carolina Acad Pr.

Law & History: The Evolution of the American Legal System. Anthony Chase. LC 96-54048. 1997. 25.00 (1-56584-367-3, Pub. by New Press NY) Norton.

Law & History: The Evolution of the American Legal System. Anthony Chase. 219p. 1999. pap. 15.95 (1-56584-516-1, Pub. by New Press NY) Norton.

Law & Identity: Lawyers, Native Americans & Legal Practice. Linda J. Medcalf. LC 78-588. (Sage Library of Social Research: Vol. 62). 148p. reprint ed. pap. 45.90 (0-608-31009-3, 202193100026) Bks Demand.

Law & Ideology in Monarchic Israel. Baruch Halpern & Deborah W. Hobson. (Journal for the Study of the Old Testament Supplement Ser.: No. 124). 235p. (C). 1991. 70.00 (1-85075-323-7, Pub. by Sheffield Acad) CUP Services.

Law & Inflation. Keith S. Rosenn. LC 81-51139. 491p. reprint ed. pap. 152.30 (0-7837-3004-7, 204293700006) Bks Demand.

Law & Insider Trading: In Search of a Level Playing Field. Elizabeth Szockyj. LC 92-34753. 162p. 1993. 42.50 (0-89941-813-9, 307680) W S Hein.

Law & Inter-Corporate Trucking by Conglomerates. W. H. Borghesani, Jr. 1.00 (0-686-31449-2) Private Carrier.

Law & International Law: A Bibliography of Bibliographies. Theodore Besterman. LC 72-178009. 436p. 1971. write for info. (0-87471-051-0) Rowman.

Law & International Order. Kiser Barnes et al. LC 96-227044. 212p. 1996. pap. 17.95 (1-870989-73-2) Bahai.

Law & Interpretation. Ed. by Andrei Marmor. 474p. 1998. reprint ed. pap. text 39.95 (0-19-826487-9) OUP.

Law & Investment in Japan: Cases & Materials. J. Mark Ramseyer et al. (East Asian Legal Studies Project, Harvard Law School). 766p. 1995. text 55.00 (0-674-51375-4, YANLAW) HUP.

Law & Islam in the Contemporary Middle East see Law & Islam in the Middle East

Law & Islam in the Middle East. Ed. by Daisy H. Dwyer. LC 89-18545. Orig. Title: Law & Islam in the Contemporary Middle East. 168p. 1990. 52.95 (0-89789-151-1, H151, Bergin & Garvey) Greenwood.

Law & Its Administration. Harlan F. Stone. LC 33-17836. reprint ed. 29.50 (0-404-06284-9) AMS Pr.

Law & Its Fulfillment: A Pauline Theology of Law. Thomas R. Schreiner. LC 93-3968. 296p. (C). 1998. pap. 19.99 (0-8010-2194-4) Baker Bks.

Law & Its Limitations in the GATT Multilateral Trade System. D. Long. 1985. lib. bdg. 87.50 (90-247-3189-5) Kluwer Academic.

Law & Its Limitations in the GATT Multilateral Trade System. Oliver Long. 172p. (C). 1987. pap. text 64.50 (0-86010-959-3) Kluwer Academic.

Law & Its Presuppositions: Actions, Agents & Rules. S. C. Coval & J. C. Smith. (International Library of Philosophy). 134p. 1986. lib. bdg. 35.00 (0-7102-0446-9, Routledge Thoemms) Routledge.

Law & Jurisdiction in the Middle Ages. Walter Ullmann. (Collected Studies: No. CS283). (ENG & GER.). 350p. (C). 1988. reprint ed. text 120.95 (0-86078-231-X, Pub. by Variorum) Ashgate Pub Co.

Law & Jurisprudence in American History, Cases & Materials: Teacher's Manual to Accompany. 3rd ed. Stephen B. Presser & Jamil S. Zainaldin. (American Casebook Ser.). 125p. 1996. pap. text. write for info. (0-314-20346-X) West Pub.

Law & Jurisprudence of England & America. J. F. Dillon. LC 75-99475. (American Constitutional & Legal History Ser). 1970. reprint ed. lib. bdg. 49.50 (0-306-71854-5) Da Capo.

Law & Justice. Ed. by Stuart Hall & Doreen Massey. (Soundings Ser.). (C). 1996. pap. 19.95 (0-85315-819-3) Humanities.

***Law & Justice.** 5th ed. Abadinsky. (Criminal Justice Ser.). 2001. 35.00 (0-534-53398-1) Wadsworth Pub.

Law & Justice: An Introduction to the American Legal System. 4th rev. ed. Howard Abadinsky. LC 97-12688. (Criminal Justice Ser.). (Illus.). 500p. (C). 1998. pap. text 42.95 (0-8304-1482-7) Thomson Learn.

Law & Justice: Cases & Readings on the American Legal System. Dale A. Nance. LC 94-71947. 744p. (C). 1994. boxed set 60.00 (0-89089-600-3) Carolina Acad Pr.

Law & Justice: Cases & Readings on the American Legal System. 2nd ed. Dale A. Nance. LC 98-89275. xix, 708p. 1999. 75.00 (0-89089-865-0) Carolina Acad Pr.

Law & Justice: Essays in Honor of Robert S. Rankin. Ed. by Carl Beck. LC 74-86476. 370p. reprint ed. pap. 114.70 (0-608-14660-9, 202336700032) Bks Demand.

***Law & Justice in China's New Marketplace.** Ronald C. Keith & Zhiqiu Lin. LC 00-41510. 2000. write for info. (0-333-77090-0, Pub. by Macmillan) St Martin.

Law & Justice in Contemporary Yemen: People's Democratic Republic of Yemen & Yemen Arab Republic. S. H. Amin. 1987. 25.00 (0-946706-36-0, Pub. by Royston Ltd) St Mut.

Law & Justice in the Reagan Administration: The Memoirs of an Attorney General. William F. Smith. (Publication Ser.: No. 409). 260p. 1991. pap. 7.58 (0-8179-9172-7) Hoover Inst Pr.

Law & Justice in Tokugawa Japan, Pt. IV-B. Ed. by John H. Wigmore. 443p. 1986. 77.50 (0-86008-396-9, Pub. by U of Tokyo) Col U Pr.

Law & Justice in Tokugawa Japan: Contract: Commercial Customary Law, Pt. IV-C. Ed. by John H. Wigmore. 443p. 1987. 77.50 (0-86008-404-3, Pub. by U of Tokyo) Col U Pr.

Law & Justice in Tokugawa Japan: Contract, Legal Precedents, Part III-A. Ed. by John H. Wigmore. 1970. 30.00 (0-86008-063-3, Pub. by U of Tokyo) Col U Pr.

Law & Justice in Tokugawa Japan: Contract, Legal Precedents, Part III-B. Ed. by John H. Wigmore. 1976. 32.50 (0-86008-166-4, Pub. by U of Tokyo) Col U Pr.

Law & Justice in Tokugawa Japan: Contract, Legal Precedents, Part III-C. Ed. by John H. Wigmore. 1977. 32.50 (0-86008-186-9, Pub. by U of Tokyo) Col U Pr.

Law & Justice in Tokugawa Japan: Persons, Civil Customary Law, Part VII. Ed. by John H. Wigmore. 275p. 1972. 29.50 (0-86008-065-X, Pub. by U of Tokyo) Col U Pr.

Law & Justice in Tokugawa Japan: Persons, Legal Precedents, Part VIII-A. Ed. by John H. Wigmore. 241p. 1982. 42.50 (0-86008-305-5, Pub. by U of Tokyo) Col U Pr.

Law & Justice in Tokugawa Japan: Persons, Legal Precedents, Part VIII-B. Ed. by John H. Wigmore. (Law & Justice in Tokugawa Japan Ser.). 250p. 1983. 42.50 (0-86008-331-4, Pub. by U of Tokyo) Col U Pr.

Law & Justice in Tokugawa Japan: Property, Civil Customary Law, Part V. Ed. by John H. Wigmore. 1971. 20.00 (0-86008-064-1, Pub. by U of Tokyo) Col U Pr.

Law & Justice in Tokugawa Japan: Property, Legal Precedents, Part VI-A. Ed. by John H. Wigmore. 1977. 32.50 (0-86008-187-7, Pub. by U of Tokyo) Col U Pr.

Law & Justice in Tokugawa Japan: Property, Legal Precedents, Part VI-B. Ed. by John H. Wigmore. 1977. 37.50 (0-86008-232-6, Pub. by U of Tokyo) Col U Pr.

Law & Justice in Tokugawa Japan: Property, Legal Precedents, Part VI-C. Ed. by John H. Wigmore. 1978. 37.50 (0-86008-233-4, Pub. by U of Tokyo) Col U Pr.

Law & Justice in Tokugawa Japan: Property, Legal Precedents, Part VI-D. Ed. by John H. Wigmore. 288p. 1978. 37.50 (0-86008-234-2, Pub. by U of Tokyo) Col U Pr.

Law & Justice in Tokugawa Japan: Property, Legal Precedents, Part VI-E. Ed. by John H. Wigmore. 233p. 1979. 37.50 (0-86008-257-1, Pub. by U of Tokyo) Col U Pr.

Law & Justice in Tokugawa Japan: Property, Legal Precedents, Part VI-G. Ed. by John H. Wigmore. 233p. 1981. 42.50 (0-86008-286-5, Pub. by U of Tokyo) Col U Pr.

Law & Justice Statistics. (Illus.). 85p. (Orig.). (C). 1993. pap. text 20.00 (1-56806-857-3) DIANE Pub.

***Law & Language.** Ed. by Tom Morawetz. LC 99-38742. (International Library of Essays in Law & Legal Theory). 380p. 2000. text 175.95 (1-84014-770-9, Pub. by Ashgate Pub) Ashgate Pub Co.

Law & Language. Ed. by Frederick F. Schauer. LC 92-33362. (International Library of Essays in Law & Legal Theory: Vol. 10). (C). 1993. lib. bdg. 150.00 (0-8147-7952-2) NYU Pr.

Law & Laughter: Illustrated with Portraits of Eminent Members of Bench & Bar. George A. Morton & D. Macleod Malloch. (Illus.). 1989. reprint ed. 38.50 (0-8377-2439-2, Rothman) W S Hein.

Law & Lawyers in Literature. Irving Browne. LC 82-82459. xv, 413p. 1982. reprint ed. 85.00 (0-912004-22-3) Gaunt.

Law & Lawyers in Literature. Irving Browne. xv, 413p. 1982. reprint ed. 42.50 (0-8377-0329-8, Rothman) W S Hein.

Law & Lawyers in the United States: The Common Law under Stress. Erwin N. Griswold. LC 95-81328. viii, 152p. 1996. reprint ed. 42.00 (1-57588-002-4, 309060) W S Hein.

Law & Lawyers of Pickwick. Frank Lockwood. LC 72-1862. (Studies in Dickens: No. 52). 1972. reprint ed. lib. bdg. 75.00 (0-8383-1445-7) M S G Haskell Hse.

Law & Lawyers: or Sketches & Illustrations of Legal History & Biography, 2 vols. Archer Polson. (Illus.). 1982. reprint ed. 85.00 (0-8377-1013-8, Rothman) W S Hein.

Law & Legal Information Directory. 10th ed. 1998. 385.00 (0-7876-1257-X, 00156434) Gale.

Law & Legal System of the Russian Federation. G. M. Danilenko & William Burnham. LC 98-18219. 1998. 105.00 (1-57823-053-5) Juris Pubng.

Law & Legal Theory in Classical & Medieval Islam. Wael B. Hallaq. 224p. 1996. 89.95 (0-614-21200-6, 1449) Kazi Pubns.

Law & Legal Theory in Classical & Medieval Islam. Wael B. Hallaq. (Collected Studies: No. CS474). 344p. 1995. 115.95 (0-86078-456-8, Pub. by Variorum) Ashgate Pub Co.

Law & Legal Theory in England & America. Richard A. Posner. (Claredon Law Lectures). (Illus.). 146p. 1997. text 24.95 (0-19-826471-2) OUP.

Law & Legality in China: The Testament of a China-Watcher. Laszlo Ladany. Ed. by Marie-Luise Nath. 224p. 1992. text 38.00 (0-8248-1473-8) UH Pr.

Law & Legislation in the German Democratic Republic, 1959-1989, 11 vols., Set. Lawyer's Association of G. D. R. Staff. 1982. reprint ed. lib. bdg. 675.00 (0-89941-281-5, 108410) W S Hein.

Law & Letters in American Culture. Robert A. Ferguson. LC 84-8940. (Illus.). 432p. 1984. pap. 17.00 (0-674-51466-1) HUP.

Law & Letters in American Culture. Robert A. Ferguson. (Illus.). 432p. 1984. 42.00 (0-674-51465-3) HUP.

***Law & Liability Pt. 1: Liability Issues.** 1999. pap. write for info. (1-887759-70-0) Am Phys Therapy Assn.

***Law & Liability Pt. 2: Professional Issues.** 1999. pap. write for info. (1-887759-71-9) Am Phys Therapy Assn.

Law & Liberalism in the 1980s. Vincent Blasi. 1991. text 46.00 (0-231-07198-1) Col U Pr.

Law & Liberty in Early New England: Criminal Justice & Due Process, 1620-1692. Edgar J. McManus. LC 92-18719. 296p. 1993. 32.50 (0-87023-824-8) U of Mass Pr.

Law & Life of Rome: 90 B. C. to A. D. 212. J. A. Crook. LC 67-20633. (Aspects of Greek & Roman Life Ser.). 352p. 1984. pap. text 17.95 (0-8014-9273-4) Cornell U Pr.

Law & Liminality in the Bible. Nanette Stahl. LC 96-111135. (Journal for the Study of the Old Testament Supplement Ser.: No. 202). 104p. 1996. 46.50 (1-85075-561-2, Pub. by Sheffield Acad) CUP Services.

Law & Literature. Richard A. Posner. LC 97-28244. 416p. 1999. text 45.00 (0-674-51470-X) HUP.

Law & Literature. Richard A. Posner. LC 97-28244. 416p. 1999. pap. 18.95 (0-674-51471-8) HUP.

Law & Literature: A Misunderstood Relation. Richard A. Posner. LC 88-11210. 384p. 1988. 39.50 (0-674-51468-8) HUP.

***Law & Literature: Current Legal Issues, Vol. 2.** Ed. by Michael Freeman & Andrew D. E. Lewis. LC 99-21442. 796p. 1999. text 115.00 (0-19-829813-7) OUP.

Law & Literature: Possibilities & Perspectives. Ian Ward. xi, 264p. (C). 1995. 59.95 (0-521-47474-4) Cambridge U Pr.

Law & Literature: Text & Theory. Ed. by Lenora Ledwon. LC 95-35321. 520p. 1995. reprint ed. pap. text 26.95 (0-8153-2046-9) Garland.

Law & Literature: Text & Theory. Ed. by Lenora Ledwon. LC 95-35321. (Garland Reference Library of the Humanities: Vol. 1784). xv, 501p. 1995. reprint ed. text 80.00 (0-8153-1472-8, H1784) Garland.

Law & Literature & Other Essays & Addresses. Benjamin N. Cardozo. 190p. 1986. reprint ed. 35.00 (0-8377-2009-5, Rothman) W S Hein.

Law & Literature in Medieval Iceland: 'Ljosvetninga Saga' & 'Valla-Ljots Saga' Theodore M. Andersson & William I. Miller. LC 88-38439. 352p. 1989. 45.00 (0-8047-1532-7) Stanford U Pr.

Law & Literature Perspectives. 2nd ed. Ed. by Bruce Rockwood. (Critic of Institutions Ser.: Vol. 9). 450p. (C). 1998. reprint ed. pap. text 45.95 (0-8204-4044-2) P Lang Pubng.

Law & Liturgy in the Latin Church, 5th-12th Centuries. Roger E. Reynolds. LC 94-4774. (Collected Studies: No. CS457). 1994. 109.95 (0-86078-405-3, Pub. by Variorum) Ashgate Pub Co.

Law & Local Society in Late Imperial China: Northern Taiwan in the Nineteenth Century. Mark A. Allee. LC 94-30283. xii , 348p. 1994. 45.00 (0-8047-2272-2) Stanford U Pr.

Law & Locomotives: The Impact of the Railroad on Wisconsin Law in the Nineteenth Century. Robert S. Hunt. LC 58-3878. (Illus.). 292p. 1958. 10.00 (0-87020-047-X) State Hist Soc Wis.

Law & Logic: A Critical Account of Legal Argument. J. Horovitz. LC 72-76386. (Library of Exact Philosophy: Vol. 8). 240p. 1972. 61.95 (0-387-81066-8) Spr-Verlag.

***Law & Love: The Trials of King Lear.** Paul W. Kahn. LC 99-46345. 192p. 2000. 30.00 (0-300-07828-5) Yale U Pr.

Law & Management of a Counseling Agency or Private Practice. Ronald K. Bullis. Ed. by Theodore P. Remley, Jr. LC 92-20722. (ACA Legal Ser.: Vol. 3). 75p. (C). 1992. pap. text 18.95 (1-55620-101-X, 72303) Am Coun Assn.

Law & Management of Water Resources & Supply. Wisdom & Skeet. 1981. pap. 180.00 (0-7219-0910-8, Pub. by Scientific) St Mut.

***Law & Market Economy: Reinterpreting the Values of Law & Economics.** Robin Paul Malloy. 200p. (C). 2000. text Price not set. (0-521-78214-7); pap. text Price not set. (0-521-78731-9) Cambridge U Pr.

Law & Market Society in Mexico. George M. Armstrong, Jr. LC 88-25934. 173p. 1989. 57.95 (0-275-93117-X, C3117, Praeger Pubs) Greenwood.

Law & Markets in United States History: Different Modes of Bargaining among Interests. James W. Hurst. LC 81-69822. (Curti Lectures: No. 1981). 216p. reprint ed. pap. 67.00 (0-7837-3749-1, 204356500010) Bks Demand.

Law & Martial Arts. Carl Brown. 1999. pap. text 38.95 (1-58133-142-8) Black Belt Mag.

Law & Martial Arts. Carl Brown. LC 97-69903. 1998. pap. 13.95 (0-89750-134-9, 466) Ohara Pubns.

Law & Marxism. Evgeny B. Pashukanis. 196p. (C). pap. 16.95 (0-86104-740-0, Pub. by Pluto GBR) Stylus Pub VA.

Law & Medical Men. R. Vashon Rogers, Jr. xiii, 214p. 1981. reprint ed. 38.00 (0-8377-1032-4, Rothman) W S Hein.

Law & Medicine. Belinda Bennett. LC 97-157544. 191p. 1997. pap. 33.50 (0-455-21456-5, Pub. by LawBk Co) Gaunt.

Law & Medicine: A Special Issue of Law in Context. Ed. by Kerry Petersen. 1994. pap. 19.95 (1-86324-025-X, Pub. by LaTrobe Univ) Intl Spec Bk.

Law & Medicine: Cases & Materials. Walter J. Wadlington et al. LC 80-23725. (University Casebook Ser.). 1039p. 1991. reprint ed. text 38.95 (0-88277-015-2) Foundation Pr.

L

An Asterisk (*) at the beginning of an entry indicates that the title is appearing for the first time.

L

***Law & Medicine: Common Legal Problems in Everyday Practice.** Wai-Ching Leung. 224p. 2000. pap. 44.00 (*0-7506-4190-8*) Buttrwrth-Heinemann.

***Law & Medicine Vol. 3: Current Legal Issues.** Ed. by Michael Freeman & Andrew Lewis. (Current Legal Issues Ser.). 600p. 2000. text 120.00 (*0-19-829918-4*) OUP.

Law & Medicine in Canada. 2nd ed. Gilbert Sharpe. 680p. 1987. boxed set 123.00 (*0-409-86590-7*, MICHIE) LEXIS Pub.

Law & Mental Disability. Michael L. Perlin. 698p. 1994. 50.00 (*1-55834-153-6*, 12695-10, MICHIE) LEXIS Pub.

Law & Mental Disorder. George J. Alexander & Alan W. Scheflin. LC 98-30548. 1224p. 1998. boxed set 85.00 (*0-89089-917-7*) Carolina Acad Pr.

Law & Mental Health: Harmonizing Objectives: A Comparative Survey of Existing Legislation Together with Guidelines for Its Assessment & Alternative Approaches to Improvement. W. Curran & T. Harding. (International Digest of Health Legislation Offprints: Vol. 28, No. 4). 159p. 1977. 25.00 (*92-4-169284-7*) World Health.

Law & Mental Health: International Perspectives, Vol. 2. Ed. by David N. Weisstub. (Law & Mental Health Ser.). 304p. 1986. 96.00 (*0-08-032781-8*, K130, J110, Pergamon Pr) Elsevier.

Law & Mental Health: Research & Policy. Ed. by Saleem A. Shah. LC 85-63002. (Annals of the American Academy of Political & Social Science Ser.: Vol. 484). (Orig.). 1986. text 26.00 (*0-8039-2694-4*); pap. text 17.00 (*0-8039-2695-2*) Sage.

Law & Mental Health Professionals: Alabama. Emily Bentley et al. LC 98-41032. 309p. 1999. 59.95 (*1-55798-512-X*) Am Psychol.

Law & Mental Health Professionals: Arizona. Michael O. Miller & Bruce D. Sales. LC 86-10780. 357p. 1986. 59.95 (*0-912704-50-0*) Am Psychol.

Law & Mental Health Professionals: California. O. Brant Caudill & Kenneth S. Pope. LC 94-40248. 630p. 1995. text 59.95 (*1-55798-276-7*, 431-5100) Am Psychol.

Law & Mental Health Professionals: Connecticut. Sheila Taub. LC 98-8753. 1999. 59.95 (*1-55798-522-7*) Am Psychol.

***Law & Mental Health Professionals: Delaware.** Ann H. Britton & Timothy H. Robs. LC 99-86786. 2000. 59.95 (*1-55798-686-X*) Am Psychol.

Law & Mental Health Professionals: Florida. Randy K. Otto & John Petrila. LC 95-40356. 373p. (C). 1996. text 59.95 (*1-55798-322-4*, 431-5120) Am Psychol.

Law & Mental Health Professionals: Massachusetts. 2nd ed. Jonathan Brant. Ed. by Bruce D. Sales & Michael O. Miller. LC 97-19091. (Law & Mental Health Professionals Ser.). (Illus.). 285p. 1997. 59.95 (*1-55798-446-8*) Am Psychol.

***Law & Mental Health Professionals: Michigan.** Beth K. Clark & Charles R. Clark. 2000. write for info. (*1-55798-715-7*) Am Psychol.

Law & Mental Health Professionals: Minnesota. Eric S. Janus et al. 442p. 1994. text 59.95 (*1-55798-230-9*) Am Psychol.

Law & Mental Health Professionals: Nevada. Krista Johns & Ronald Dillehay. LC 98-6248. 328p. 1998. 59.95 (*1-55798-507-3*) Am Psychol.

Law & Mental Health Professionals: New Jersey. 2nd ed. James S. Wulach. LC 97-30496. 455p. 1997. text 59.95 (*1-55798-371-2*, 431-5041) Am Psychol.

Law & Mental Health Professionals: New York. James S. Wulach. 383p. 1993. text 59.95 (*1-55798-195-7*) Am Psychol.

Law & Mental Health Professionals: Pennsylvania. Donald Bersoff et al. LC 98-25722. 392p. 1998. 59.95 (*1-55798-555-3*) Am Psychol.

Law & Mental Health Professionals: Texas. 2nd ed. Daniel W. Shuman. LC 97-1390. 347p. 1997. 59.95 (*1-55798-405-0*, 431-5025) Am Psychol.

***Law & Mental Health Professionals: Virginia.** Lynne Porfiri & Robert Resnick. LC 99-39617. 344p. 1999. 59.95 (*1-55798-615-0*) Am Psychol.

Law & Mental Health Professionals: Washington. G. Andrew H. Benjamin et al. 144p. 1998. pap., suppl. ed. 24.95 (*1-55798-510-3*) Am Psychol.

Law & Mental Health Professionals: Washington. Ed. by Thomas D. Overcast et al. LC 95-5363. 492p. 1995. text 59.95 (*1-55798-278-3*, 431-5110) Am Psychol.

Law & Mental Health Professionals: Wisconsin. Leonard V. Kaplan & Robert D. Miller. LC 95-40357. (Law & Mental Health Professionals Ser.). 383p. 1995. 59.95 (*1-55798-313-5*, 431-5060) Am Psychol.

Law & Mental Health Professionals: Wyoming. George Blau. LC 97-32112. (Law & Mental Health Professionals Ser.). 541p. 1997. 59.95 (*1-55798-447-6*) Am Psychol.

Law & Mercury-Free Dentistry. Pamela D. Ousley. 260p. (Orig.). 1994. pap. 19.65 (*0-941011-11-9*) Bio-Probe.

Law & Migration. Ed. by Selina Goulbourne. LC 97-31129. (International Library of Studies on Migration: Vol. 6). 488p. 1998. 185.00 (*1-85898-039-9*) E Elgar.

Law & Miss Lamott. Kelly Jamison. 1998. per. 3.50 (*0-373-52080-8*, 1-52080-8) Silhouette.

Law & Modern Society. 2nd ed. P. S. Atiyah. 238p. 1995. pap. text 17.95 (*0-19-289267-3*) OUP.

Law & Modernization in the Church of England: Charles II to the Welfare State. Robert E. Rodes, Jr. LC 91-50567. (Study of the Legal History of Establishment in England Ser.: Vol. 3). (C). 1991. text 40.50 (*0-268-01293-8*) U of Notre Dame Pr.

***Law & Moral Action in World Politics.** Ed. by Cecelia Lynch & Michael Loriaux. LC 99-42360. 272p. 1999. pap. 19.95 (*0-8166-3171-9*, Pub. by U of Minn Pr); lib. bdg. 49.95 (*0-8166-3170-0*, Pub. by U of Minn Pr) Chicago Distribution Ctr.

Law & Morality. Kevin McNamara. 1989. pap. 25.00 (*0-86217-290-X*, Pub. by Veritas Pubns) St Mut.

Law & Morality in Ancient China: The Silk Manuscripts of Huang-Lao. R. P. Peerenboom. (SUNY Series in Chinese Philosophy & Culture). 380p. (C). 1993. text 19.50 (*0-7914-1237-7*) State U NY Pr.

Law & Morals. Roscoe Pound. ix, 144p. 1987. reprint ed. 40.00 (*0-8377-2501-1*, Rothman) W S Hein.

Law & Narrative in the Bible: The Evidence of the Deuteronomic Laws & the Decalogue. Calum M. Carmichael. LC 85-4214. 356p. (C). 1985. 47.50 (*0-8014-1792-9*) Cornell U Pr.

Law & National Security: Access to Strategic Resources. American Bar Association Standing Commission on La. 162p. 1986. pap. 7.00 (*0-318-36441-7*, 355-0014) Amer Bar Assn.

Law & Nursing. John Tingle & Jean V. McHale. LC 97-50289. 256p. 1998. pap. text 35.00 (*0-7506-1594-X*) Buttrwrth-Heinemann.

***Law & Nursing.** 2nd ed. Jean McHale et al. (Illus.). 256p. 2000. pap. text 35.00 (*0-7506-4806-6*) Buttrwrth-Heinemann.

Law & Occupational Injury, Disease, & Death. Warren Freedman. LC 89-10746. 199p. 1990. 65.00 (*0-89930-410-9*, FOP/, Greenwood Pr) Greenwood.

Law & One Man among Many. Arthur E. Sutherland. (Oliver S. Rundell Lectures Ser.). ix, 101p. 1982. reprint ed. 28.00 (*0-8377-1126-6*, Rothman) W S Hein.

Law & Opinion in England in the Twentieth Century. Ed. by Morris Ginsberg. LC 74-7537. 407p. 1974. reprint ed. lib. bdg. 79.50 (*0-8371-7576-3*, GILO, Greenwood Pr) Greenwood.

Law & Order. Pam Adams. LC 90-25106. (Who Cares Ser.). 32p. (J). 1990. pap. 3.99 (*0-85953-354-9*) Childs Play.

Law & Order. Pam Adams. (Who Cares Ser.). (ITA.). (J). 1990. pap. 3.99 (*0-85953-584-3*); pap. 3.99 (*0-85953-839-7*) Childs Play.

Law & Order. James Ciment. LC 94-42471. (Life in America 100 Years Ago Ser.). (Illus.). 100p. (YA). (gr. 5 up). 1995. lib. bdg. 19.95 (*0-7910-2843-7*) Chelsea Hse.

Law & Order. Ed. by W. A. Johnson. 40p. (Orig.). 1983. pap. 7.95 (*0-914981-05-6*) Res Pubns AZ.

Law & Order. Ed. by Cynthia Manson. 272p. 1997. mass mkt. 5.99 (*0-425-15781-4*, Prime Crime) Berkley Pub.

Law & Order. Claude Ollier. Tr. by Ursule Molinaro from FRE. LC 76-133248. (French Ser.). Orig. Title: Le Maintien De L'ordre. 126p. 1971. 4.95 (*0-87376-015-8*) Red Dust.

Law & Order: Modern Criminals. 2nd rev. ed. Ed. by James F. Short, Jr. LC 72-87662. 312p. 1970. pap. text 18.95 (*0-87855-542-0*) Transaction Pubs.

Law & Order: Police Encounters. Ed. by Michael Lipsky. LC 72-91468. 144p. 1970. reprint ed. pap. text 18.95 (*0-87855-563-3*) Transaction Pubs.

Law & Order: The Scales of Justice. rev. ed. Ed. by Abraham S. Blumberg. LC 72-87667. 188p. 1970. pap. text 18.95 (*0-87855-543-9*) Transaction Pubs.

Law & Order: The Story of the Police. John Dumpleton. (Junior Reference Ser.). (Illus.). (J). (gr. 3-7). 1983. reprint ed. 14.95 (*0-7136-1079-4*) Dufour.

Law & Order: The Unofficial Companion. Kevin Courrier & Susan Green. LC 98-7012. (Illus.). 256p. 1998. pap. 16.95 (*1-58063-022-7*) Renaissance.

***Law & Order: The Unofficial Companion.** rev. ed. Kevin Courrier & Susan Green. 1999. pap. 17.95 (*1-58063-108-8*) Renaissance.

Law & Order: Who Cares about Them. Child's Play Staff. (J). 1996. lib. bdg. 11.95 (*0-85953-879-6*) Childs Play.

Law & Order Administration, at District Level with Special Reference to Punjab. K. L. Sharma. 1986. 26.50 (*0-8364-1565-5*) S Asia.

Law & Order in Sung China. Brian E. McKnight. (Studies in Chinese History, Literature & Institutions). (Illus.). 573p. (C). 1992. text 95.00 (*0-521-41121-1*) Cambridge U Pr.

Law & Order in the Capital City: A History of the Washington Police, 1800-1886, Vol. M5. Kenneth G. Alfers. 1976. 5.00 (*1-888028-03-3*) GWU Ctr WAS.

Law & Order in the 20th Century. Amy Leibowitz. 1997. pap. text 9.95 (*0-912517-30-1*) Bluewood Bks.

Law & Order in Upper India: A Study of Oudh. D. B. Trivedi. (C). 1991. text 26.00 (*81-85119-83-X*, Pub. by Northern Bk Ctr) S Asia.

Law & Order LTD: The Rousing Life of Elfego Baca of New Mexico. Kyle S. Crichton. LC 73-14200. (Mexican American Ser.). (Illus.). 258p. 1977. reprint ed. 21.95 (*0-405-05674-5*) Ayer.

Law & Order vs. the Miners: West Virginia, 1906-1933. Richard D. Lunt. 182p. 1992. reprint ed. pap. 12.95 (*0-9627486-2-5*) Applchin Eds.

Law & Organization of International Community Agreements. K. R. Khan. 1982. lib. bdg. 170.00 (*90-247-2554-2*) Kluwer Academic.

Law & Other Things. Hugh P. Macmillan. LC 76-152195. (Essay Index Reprint Ser.). 1977. 18.95 (*0-8369-2196-8*) Ayer.

Law & Other Things. Macmillan. vii, 284p. 1997. reprint ed. 87.50 (*1-56169-299-9*) Gaunt.

Law & Parenthood. Chris Barton & Gillian Douglas. 272p. 1995. pap. text 50.00 (*0-406-04499-6*, MICHIE) LEXIS Pub.

Law & Peace in International Relations - The Oliver Wendell Holmes Lectures, 1940-41. Hans Kelsen. LC 97-80202. xi, 181p. 1997. reprint ed. 65.00 (*1-57588-046-6*, 310000) W S Hein.

Law & People in Colonial America. Peter C. Hoffer. LC 91-26090. 192p. 1992. pap. text 15.95 (*0-8018-4307-3*) Johns Hopkins.

Law & People in Colonial America. 2nd rev. ed. Peter C. Hoffer. LC 97-30937. 179p. 1998. text 38.50 (*0-8018-5822-4*); pap. text 14.95 (*0-8018-5816-X*) Johns Hopkins.

***Law & Philosophy: An Introduction with Readings.** Thomas W. Simon. LC 00-24792. 2000. write for info. (*0-07-027587-4*) McGraw.

Law & Philosophy: The Practice of Theory: Essays in Honor of George Anastaplo, 2 vols., Vols. 1 & 2. Ed. by John A. Murley et al. LC 91-42908. 617p. (C). 1992. 150.00 (*0-8214-1013-X*) Ohio U Pr.

Law & Policy in Public Purchasing: The WTO Agreement on Government Procurement. Ed. by Bernard M. Hoekman & Petros C. Mavroidis. LC 96-52079. (Studies in International Trade Policy). 360p. (C). 1997. text 75.00 (*0-472-10829-8*, 10829) U of Mich Pr.

Law & Policy in the Space Stations' Era. Andrew J. Young. (C). 1989. lib. bdg. 121.50 (*90-247-3722-2*) Kluwer Academic.

Law & Policy of Export Controls: Recent Essays on Key Export Issues. 600p. 1993. pap. 40.00 (*0-89707-906-X*, 521-0089, ABA Intl Law) Amer Bar Assn.

Law & Policy of IMF Conditionality. Erik Denters. LC 96-2484. (Legal Aspects of International Organization Ser.: Vol. 27). 1996. write for info. (*90-411-0211-6*) Kluwer Law Intl.

Law & Policy of International Business: Selected Issues: A Featschrift for William Sprague Barnes. John R. Lacey. 300p. (C). 1991. lib. bdg. 49.00 (*0-8191-8232-X*) U Pr of Amer.

Law & Policy of Producers' Associations. D. E. Pollard. (C). 1984. 59.00 (*0-19-825480-6*) OUP.

Law & Policy of Regional Integration: The NAFTA & Western Hemispheric Integration in the World Trade Organization System. Frederick M. Abbott. LC 94-42026. 1995. lib. bdg. 106.00 (*0-7923-3295-4*) Kluwer Academic.

Law & Policy of Toxic Substances Control: A Case Study of Vinyl Chloride. David D. Doniger. LC 78-24624. 179p. 1979. pap. 15.95 (*0-8018-2235-1*) Resources Future.

Law & Political Science see Comprehensive Dissertation Index 1861-1972

Law & Political Science, Geography & Regional Planning see Comprehensive Dissertation Index: Ten Year Cumulation, 1973-1982

Law & Political Theory. Aquinas, Thomas, Saint. (Summa Theologiae Ser.: Vol. 28). 1966. 10.00 (*0-07-002003-5*) McGraw.

Law & Politics. Felix Frankfurter. Ed. by E. F. Prichard, Jr. & A. Macleish. 1990. 16.50 (*0-8446-0097-0*) Peter Smith.

Law & Politics. Ed. by Holland. (C). 1998. text. write for info. (*0-321-01361-1*) Addson-Wesley Educ.

Law & Politics: A Cross-Cultural Encyclopedia. Daniels Strouthes. LC 95-46014. (Human Experience Ser.). 301p. 1995. lib. bdg. 65.00 (*0-87436-777-8*) ABC-CLIO.

Law & Politics: Readings In Legal & Political Thought, Vol. 1. Ed. by Shadia B. Drury & Rainer Knopff. 270p. (Orig.). (C). 1980. pap. 13.95 (*0-920490-12-3*) Temeron Bks.

Law & Politics: The House of Lords As a Judicial Body, 1800-1976. Robert B. Stevens. LC 78-8500. (Studies in Legal History). 720p. reprint ed. pap. 200.00 (*0-7837-3755-6*, 204357200010) Bks Demand.

Law & Politics: Unanswered Questions. Ed. by David A. Schultz. LC 93-31500. 311p. 1995. pap. 29.95 (*0-8204-2245-2*) P Lang Pubng.

Law & Politics in Aztec Texcoco. Jerome A. Offner. LC 82-4368. (Cambridge Latin American Studies: No. 44). (Illus.). 368p. 1984. text 85.00 (*0-521-23475-1*) Cambridge U Pr.

Law & Politics in China's Foreign Trade. Ed. by Victor H. Li. LC 76-7790. (Asian Law Ser.: No. 4). 488p. 1977. 40.00 (*0-295-95512-0*) U of Wash Pr.

Law & Politics in Eighteenth-Century Germany: The Imperial Aulic Council in the Reign of Charles VI. Michael Hughes. (Royal Historical Society: Studies in History: No. 55). 288p. 1988. 75.00 (*0-86193-212-9*) Boydell & Brewer.

Law & Politics in Jacobean England: The Tracts of Lord Chancellor Ellesmere. Louis A. Knafla. LC 85-82333. (Cambridge Studies in English Legal History). 382p. 1986. reprint ed. 97.00 (*0-912004-57-6*) Gaunt.

Law & Politics in Outer Space: A Bibliography. Irvin L. White et al. LC 78-163011. 184p. reprint ed. pap. 57.10 (*0-608-12766-3*, 202432300037) Bks Demand.

Law & Politics in the International System: Case Studies in Conflict Resolution. Richard B. Finnegan et al. LC 79-66153. (Illus.). 1979. pap. text 19.50 (*0-8191-0793-X*) U Pr of Amer.

Law & Politics of Police Discretion, 4. Gregory H. Williams. LC 83-22741. (Contributions in Criminology & Penology Ser.: No. 4). (Illus.). 218p. 1984. 62.95 (*0-313-24070-1*, WLA/, Greenwood Pr) Greenwood.

Law & Politics of the British Constitution. Woodhouse & Peter J. Madgwick. 304p. (C). 1995. pap. text 41.00 (*0-13-342890-7*) P-H.

Law & Politics of the Supreme Court: Cases & Readings. 2nd ed. Susan Lawrence. 592p. (C). per. write for info. (*0-7872-6732-5*) Kendall-Hunt.

Law & Politics of West-East Technology Transfer. Ed. by Hiroshi Oda. (C). 1991. lib. bdg. 121.50 (*0-7923-0990-1*) Kluwer Academic.

Law & Poverty. S. P. Sharma. (C). 1990. 80.00 (*0-89771-315-X*) St Mut.

***Law & Practice: Companion-Criminal Procedure.** 5th ed. Del Carmen. 2000. pap. 15.00 (*0-534-51474-X*) Thomson Learn.

Law & Practice As to References & the Powers & Duties of Referees. Murray Hoffman. xxvi, 438p. 1997. reprint ed. 125.00 (*1-56169-310-3*) Gaunt.

Law & Practice Concerning Occupational Health in the Member States of the European Community, 5 vols., 1. Commission of the European Communities Staff. (Environmental Resources Limited Ser.). 1985. lib. bdg. 152.50 (*0-86010-626-8*) Kluwer Law Intl.

Law & Practice Concerning Occupational Health in the Member States of the European Community, 5 vols., 2. Commission of the European Communities Staff. (Environmental Resources Limited Ser.). 1985. lib. bdg. 152.50 (*0-86010-627-6*) Kluwer Law Intl.

Law & Practice Concerning Occupational Health in the Member States of the European Community, 5 vols., 3. Commission of the European Communities Staff. (Environmental Resources Limited Ser.). 1985. lib. bdg. 152.50 (*0-86010-628-4*) Kluwer Law Intl.

Law & Practice Concerning Occupational Health in the Member States of the European Community, 5 vols., 4. Commission of the European Communities Staff. (Environmental Resources Limited Ser.). 1985. lib. bdg. 152.50 (*0-86010-794-9*) Kluwer Law Intl.

Law & Practice Concerning Occupational Health in the Member States of the European Community, 5 vols., Set. Commission of the European Communities Staff. (Environmental Resources Limited Ser.). 1987. lib. bdg. 33.00 (*0-86010-921-6*) G & T Inc.

Law & Practice for Mortgage Lenders. Ed. by Phil Broadhurst. 350p. 1990. pap. 125.00 (*0-85297-388-8*, Pub. by Chartered Bank) St Mut.

Law & Practice for Mortgage Lenders. Phil Broadhurst. 1997. pap. 110.00 (*0-85297-424-8*, Pub. by Chartered Bank) St Mut.

Law & Practice for Paraegals. Ed. by Graham Rowley et al. 200p. 1999. pap. (*0-7487-2508-3*) S Thornes Pubs.

Law & Practice Gambling in India: Central & States. S. Sami. (C). 1990. 130.00 (*0-89771-172-6*) St Mut.

Law & Practice in Corporate Control. Chester Rohrlich. LC 34-1197. (Business Enterprises Reprint Ser.). vii, 268p. 1982. reprint ed. lib. bdg. 65.00 (*0-89941-184-3*, 302360) W S Hein.

Law & Practice in Matrimonial Causes. 4th ed. Bernard Passingham & Caroline Harmer. 1985. pap. 60.00 (*0-406-63707-5*, U.K., MICHIE) LEXIS Pub.

Law & Practice in the United Kingdom. 1983. text 78.50 (*0-86010-306-4*) Kluwer Academic.

Law & Practice of Character & Integrity Rolls. A. S. Misra. 348p. 1979. 120.00 (*0-7855-1368-X*) St Mut.

Law & Practice of Commercial Arbitration in North Carolina. C. Allen Foster. 1986. 125.00 (*0-933329-00-8*) Private Adjudication.

Law & Practice of Commissions & Receivers, 1972. V. K. Varadachari. (C). 1972. 17.50 (*0-7855-5409-2*) St Mut.

Law & Practice of Company Accounting. 6th ed. T. R. Johnston et al. 672p. 1982. pap. 44.00 (*0-409-60089-X*, NZ, MICHIE) LEXIS Pub.

Law & Practice of Company Accounting in Australia. 6th ed. T. R. Johnson et al. 1987. pap. 70.00 (*0-409-49185-3*, MICHIE) LEXIS Pub.

Law & Practice of Conveyancing with Precedents. 4th ed. F. M. Brookfield. 593p. 1980. boxed set 108.00 (*0-409-60029-6*, NZ, MICHIE) LEXIS Pub.

Law & Practice of Corporate Receiverships in Malaysia & Singapore. Arthur Andersen. LC 98-474083. 641p. 1997. write for info. (*0-409-99706-4*, MICHIE) LEXIS Pub.

Law & Practice of Diligence. G. Maher & D. J. Cusine. 500p. 1990. boxed set 108.00 (*0-406-11121-9*, U.K., MICHIE) LEXIS Pub.

Law & Practice of Extradition. Henry C. Biron & Kenneth E. Chalmers. xv, 432p. 1981. reprint ed. lib. bdg. 58.00 (*0-8377-0315-8*, Rothman) W S Hein.

Law & Practice of Income Tax, 2 vols., Set. K. Kanga. (C). 1990. 450.00 (*0-89771-269-2*) St Mut.

Law & Practice of Insurance Company Insolvency Revisited. 1162p. 1989. pap. 99.00 (*0-89707-514-5*, 519-0151) Amer Bar Assn.

Law & Practice of Interdicts. Colin Prest. 462p. 1996. 108.00 (*0-7021-3776-6*, Pub. by Juta & Co) Gaunt.

Law & Practice of International Reinsurance Collections & Insolvency. 852p. 1988. 89.95 (*0-89707-374-6*, 519-0080-01) Amer Bar Assn.

Law & Practice of Life Insurance Company Insolvency. LC 93-71490. 448p. 1993. pap. 79.95 (*0-89707-858-6*, 519-0227, ABA Tort) Amer Bar Assn.

Law & Practice of Marine Insurance & Average, 2 vols. Alex L. Parks. LC 87-13667. 1652p. 1987. text 190.00 (*0-87033-368-2*) Cornell Maritime.

Law & Practice of Marine Insurance, Deduced from a Critical Examination of the Adjudged Cases, the Nature & Analogies of the Subject, & the General Usage of Commercial Nations, 2 vols., Set. John Duer. LC 72-37972. (American Law: The Formative Years). 1650p. 1972. reprint ed. 108.95 (*0-405-04010-5*) Ayer.

Law & Practice of Marine Insurance, Deduced from a Critical Examination of the Adjudged Cases, the Nature & Analogies of the Subject, & the General Usage of Commercial Nations, 2 vols., Vol. 1. John Duer. LC 72-37972. (American Law: The Formative Years). 1650p. 1972. reprint ed. 54.95 (*0-405-04011-3*) Ayer.

Law & Practice of Marine Insurance, Deduced from a Critical Examination of the Adjudged Cases, the Nature & Analogies of the Subject, & the General Usage of Commercial Nations, 2 vols., Vol. 2. John Duer. LC 72-37972. (American Law: The Formative Years). 1650p. 1972. reprint ed. 54.95 (*0-405-04012-1*) Ayer.

Law & Practice of Mergers & Take-overs in the UK & USA. Stephen Kenyon-Slade. 700p. 2000. text 105.00 (*0-19-826051-2*) OUP.

Law & Practice of Municipal Home Rule, 1916-1930. Joseph D. McGoldrick. LC 33-22314. reprint ed. 29.50 (*0-404-04128-0*) AMS Pr.

An Asterisk (*) at the beginning of an entry indicates that the title is appearing for the first time.

Law & Practice of Offshore Banking & Finance. Edmund M. Kwaw. LC 95-38765. 256p. 1996. 69.50 (*0-89930-930-5*, Quorum Bks) Greenwood.

Law & Practice of Receivership in Scotland. 2nd ed. J. H. Greene & I. M. Fletcher. 360p. 1992. 130.00 (*0-406-00103-0*, UK, MICHIE) LEXIS Pub.

Law & Practice of Secured Transactions: Working with Article 9. Richard F. Duncan & William H Lyons. LC 87-3695. 450p. 1987. ring bd. 55.00 (*0-318-22530-1*, 00603) Law Journal.

Law & Practice of Secured Transactions: Working with Article 9. Richard F. Duncan & William H. Lyons. 450p. 1987. ring bd. 95.00 (*0-318-23684-2*) NY Law Pub.

Law & Practice of Teacher Negotiations, Incorporating 1973 Supplement. Donald H. Wollett & Robert H. Chanin. LC 70-83777. 1145p. reprint ed. pap. 200.00 (*0-608-12741-8*, 202434400037) Bks Demand.

Law & Practice of the Copyright, Registration & Provisional Registration of Designs: And the Copyright & Registration of Sculpture; with Practical Directions: The Remedies, Pleadings & Evidence in Cases of Piracy; with an Appendix of Tables of Fees, Statutes, & the Rules of the Board of Trade. John P. Norman. LC 96-834. xii, 186p. 1996. reprint ed. 35.00 (*0-8377-2451-1*, Rothman) W S Hein.

Law & Practice of the European Convention on Human Rights & the European Social Charter. Donna Gomien et al. 480p. 1996. pap. 30.00 (*92-871-2956-8*, Pub. by Council of Europe) Manhattan Pub Co.

Law & Practice of the International Court. Shabtai Rosenne. LC 85-2997. 1985. lib. bdg. 304.50 (*90-247-2986-6*) Kluwer Academic.

Law & Practice of the International Court, 1920-1996. Shabtai Rosenne. LC 97-37679. 2068p. 1997. lib. bdg. 617.00 (*90-411-0264-7*, Pub. by M Nijhoff) Kluwer Academic.

Law & Practice of the U. N. Human Rights Committee. Tyag. Date not set. write for info. (*0-7923-2040-9*) Kluwer Law Intl.

Law & Practice of the United Nations. Benedetto Conforti. LC 96-14439. 310p. 1996. 97.00 (*90-411-0233-7*) Kluwer Law Intl.

*__Law & Practice of the United Nations.__ 2nd rev. ed. Benedetto Conforti. LC 00-42028. (Legal Aspects of International Organization Ser.). 2000. write for info. (*90-411-1414-9*) Kluwer Law Intl.

Law & Practice of the World Trade Organization: Commentary, Dispute Resolution & Treaties, 5 vols., Set. Ed. by Joseph F. Dennin. 1995. ring bd. 600.00 (*0-379-21358-3*) Oceana.

Law & Practice of United States Regulation of International Trade, 3 vols. Charles R. Johnston, Jr. 1987. ring bd. 325.00 (*0-379-12099-2*) Oceana.

*__Law & Practice Regulating the Disposition of Surplus Moneys Arising from the Sale of Lands upon Mortgage Foreclosures: With an Appendix of Precedents Including the Practice upon Orders of Reference & the Review Thereof, upon Expections, as Applied to Such Cases.__ John H. Colby. iv, 116p. 1999. reprint ed. 40.00 (*1-56169-555-6*) Gaunt.

Law & Practice Relating Banking. 5th ed. Perry. 1987. pap. write for info. (*0-416-38230-4*) Thomson Learn.

Law & Practice Relating to Appeals from Arbitration Awards. D. Rhidian Thomas. (Lloyd's Commercial Law Library). 640p. 1994. 215.00 (*1-85044-505-2*) LLP.

Law & Practice Relating to Letters Patent for Inventions: With Appendix. Thomas Terrell. xxxii, 378p. 1991. reprint ed. 47.50 (*0-8377-2635-2*, Rothman) W S Hein.

Law & Practice Relating to Pollution Control in the Member States of the European Communities, 10 vols. 2nd ed. Commission of the European Communities. Ed. by Environmental Resources, Ltd. Staff. Incl. Vol. 1. 1986. 35.00 (*0-86010-040-5*); Vol. 2a. 1986. 35.00 (*0-86010-041-3*); Vol. 3. 1986. 35.00 (*0-86010-029-4*); Vol. 4. 1986. 35.00 (*0-86010-033-2*); Vol. 4a. 1986. 35.00 (*0-86010-035-9*); Vol. 5. 1986. 35.00 (*0-86010-032-4*); Vol. 5a. 1986. 35.00 (*0-86010-034-0*); Vol. 6. 1986. 35.00 (*0-86010-031-6*); Vol. 7. 1986. 35.00 (*0-86010-039-1*); Vol. 7a. 1986. 35.00 (*0-86010-042-1*); Vol. 8. 1986. 35.00 (*0-86010-030-8*); Vol. 9. 1986. 35.00 (*0-86010-037-5*); Vol. 11. 1986. 35.00 (*0-86010-038-3*); 1986. Set lib. bdg. 79.50 (*0-86010-806-6*) G & T Inc.

Law & Prediction in the Light of Chaos Research. Gerhard Schurz & Paul A. Weingartner. LC 96-42416. (Lecture Notes in Physics: Vol. 473). x, 291p. 1996. 78.00 (*3-540-61584-9*) Spr-Verlag.

Law & Procedure of Approvals for Tax Concessions. G. Garg. (C). 1990. 155.00 (*0-89771-273-0*) St Mut.

Law & Procedure of Departmental Enquiries (in Private & Public Sectors), 1988, 2 vols. 3rd enl. rev. ed. B. R. Ghaiye. (C). 1990. 220.00 (*0-7855-5265-0*) St Mut.

Law & Procedure of Departmental Enquiries: In Private & Public Sectors, 2 vols., Set. B. R. Ghaiye. (C). 1988. 440.00 (*0-7855-5125-5*) St Mut.

*__Law & Procedure of Departmental Enquiries: In Public & Private Sectors, 2 vols.__ B. R. Ghaiye. 1999. pap. 275.00 (*81-7012-371-2*, Pub. by Eastern Book) St Mut.

Law & Procedure of Departmental Enquiries (in Private & Public Sectors) B. R. Ghaiye. 1747p. (C). 1982. 495.00 (*0-7855-1371-X*) St Mut.

Law & Procedure of Departmental Enquiries (in Private & Public Sectors), 2 vols., Set. 3rd enl. rev. ed. B. R. Ghaiye. (C). 1990. reprint ed. 440.00 (*0-7855-5514-5*) St Mut.

Law & Procedure of Departmental Enquiries (in Public & Private Sectors) B. R. Ghaiye. (C). 1988. 440.00 (*0-7855-6023-8*) St Mut.

Law & Procedure of the International Court of Justice, 2 vols. Gerald Fitzmaurice. 904p. (C). 1986. 370.00 (*0-7855-7009-8*, Pub. by Grotius Pubns Ltd) St Mut.

Law & Procedure of the International Court of Justice, 2 vols., Vol. 1. Gerald Fitzmaurice. 904p. (C). 1986. write for info. (*0-906496-33-0*, Pub. by Grotius Pubns Ltd) St Mut.

Law & Procedure of the International Court of Justice, 2 vols., Vol. 2. Gerald Fitzmaurice. 904p. (C). 1986. write for info. (*0-906496-38-1*, Pub. by Grotius Pubns Ltd) St Mut.

Law & Property-Critical Essays. Baxi Upendra. (C). 1988. 140.00 (*0-7855-3675-2*) St Mut.

Law & Providence in Joseph Bellamy's New England: The Origins of the New Divinity in Revolutionary England. Mark Valeri. (Religion in America Ser.). (Illus.). 224p. 1994. text 52.00 (*0-19-508601-5*) OUP.

Law & Psychiatry: Cold War or Entente Cordiale? Sheldon Glueck. LC 62-19170. (Isaac Ray Award Lectures: 1962). 191p. reprint ed. pap. 59.30 (*0-608-15180-7*, 202581700046) Bks Demand.

Law & Psychiatry III: Selected Papers Presented at the Fourth International Congress on Law & Psychiatry, Pembroke College, Oxford England, 19-22 July 1979. Ed. by David N. Weisstub. 100p. 1981. pap. 18.25 (*0-08-026113-2*, Pergamon Pr) Elsevier.

Law & Psychiatry in the Canadian Context. Ed. by David N. Weisstub. 1981. 150.00 (*0-08-023134-9*, Pergamon Pr) Elsevier.

Law & Psychology. Ed. by Martin L. Levine. LC 95-7995. (International Library of Essays in Law & Legal Theory: No. 16). 500p. (C). 1995. lib. bdg. 150.00 (*0-8147-5064-8*) NYU Pr.

Law & Psychology: The Broadening of the Discipline. Ed. by James R. Ogloff. LC 92-71726. 464p. (C). 1992. boxed set 45.00 (*0-89089-475-2*) Carolina Acad Pr.

Law & Public Affairs. Ed. by Charles Wise & David O'Brien. 168p. 1985. 9.50 (*0-685-25271-X*) Am Soc Pub Admin.

Law & Public Choice: A Critical Introduction. Daniel A. Farber & Philip P. Frickey. 176p. 1991. pap. text 14.95 (*0-226-23803-2*); lib. bdg. 42.00 (*0-226-23802-4*) U Ch Pr.

Law & Public Enterprise in Asia: Colloquim Report & Papers. 421p. 1976. 15.00 (*0-275-23000-7*) Intl Ctr Law.

Law & Reality: Essays on National & International Procedural Law in Honour of Cornelis Carel Albert Voskuil. Ed. by Mathilde Sumampouw et al. LC 92-31348. (T. M. C. Asser Instituut Ser.). 429p. (C). 1992. lib. bdg. 168.00 (*0-7923-1969-9*) Kluwer Academic.

Law & Records in Medieval England: Studies on the Medieval Papacy, Monasteries & Records. Jane E. Sayers. (Collected Studies: No. CS278). 330p. (C). 1988. reprint ed. text 115.95 (*0-86078-226-3*, Pub. by Variorum) Ashgate Pub Co.

Law & Reflexive Politics. Emilios A. Christodoulidis. LC 98-9204. (Law & Philosophy Library). 1998. 119.00 (*0-7923-4954-7*) Kluwer Academic.

Law & Regulation of Common Carriers in the Communications Industry. 2nd ed. Daniel L. Brenner. (C). 1995. text 79.00 (*0-8133-2740-7*, Pub. by Westview) HarpC.

Law & Regulation of International Finance. Ravi C. Tennekoon. 500p. Date not set. text 125.00 (*0-406-10060-8*, 81381-10, MICHIE) LEXIS Pub.

Law & Regulation of International Space Communication. Rita L. White & Harold M. White. LC 87-30744. (Artech House Telecommunications Library). (Illus.). 337p. 1988. reprint ed. pap. 104.50 (*0-608-03154-2*, 206360700007) Bks Demand.

*__Law & Religion.__ Rex J. Ahdar. LC 00-40613. (Issues in Law & Society Ser.). 2000. pap. write for info. (*1-84014-757-1*, Pub. by Scolar Pr) Ashgate Pub Co.

Law & Religion. Feldman. text 65.00 (*0-8147-2678-X*); pap. text 25.00 (*0-8147-2679-8*) NYU Pr.

Law & Religion. Ed. by V. R. Iyer. (C). 1990. 110.00 (*0-89771-152-1*) St Mut.

Law & Religion. Ed. by Wojciech Sadurski. LC 92-4119. (International Library of Essays in Law & Legal Theory). 550p. (C). 1992. lib. bdg. 150.00 (*0-8147-7953-0*) NYU Pr.

Law & Religion. Wake Forest University School of Law Staff. 1985. 10.00 (*0-942225-10-4*) Wake Forest Law.

Law & Religion in Marxist Cuba: A Human Rights Inquiry. Margaret I. Short. LC 92-41035. 182p. (C). 1993. pap. text 18.95 (*1-56000-682-X*) Transaction Pubs.

Law & Responsibility in Warfare: The Vietnam Experience. Ed. by Peter D. Trooboff. LC 74-22431. 304p. reprint ed. pap. 94.30 (*0-8357-3872-8*, 203660400004) Bks Demand.

Law & Revolution: The Formation of the Western Legal Tradition. Harold J. Berman. 672p. 1985. pap. 22.95 (*0-674-51776-8*) HUP.

Law & Rock & Roll. Sciarrino. 1996. pap., wbk. ed. 10.25 (*0-07-057874-5*) McGraw.

Law & School Reform: Six Strategies for Promoting Educational Equity. Ed. by Jay P. Heubert. LC 98-25572. 384p. 1998. 40.00 (*0-300-07595-2*) Yale U Pr.

*__Law & School Reform: Six Strategies for Promoting Educational Equity.__ Jay P. Heubert. 448p. 2000. pap. 18.00 (*0-300-08296-7*) Yale U Pr.

Law & Science, Vol. 1. Ed. by Michael D. Freeman et al. LC 99-168057. (Current Legal Issues Ser.). 336p. 1998. text 69.00 (*0-19-826794-0*) OUP.

Law & Security in Outer Space. American Bar Association, Standing Committee on En. 182p. 1983. pap. 3.00 (*0-685-10018-9*, 355-0003) Amer Bar Assn.

Law & Semiotics, Vol. 1. Ed. by Roberta Kevelson. LC 87-32715. (Illus.). 362p. 1988. 85.00 (*0-306-42803-2*, Plenum Trade) Perseus Pubng.

Law & Semiotics, Vol. 2. Ed. by Roberta Kevelson. (Illus.). 382p. 1989. 85.00 (*0-306-43111-4*, Plenum Trade) Perseus Pubng.

Law & Semiotics, Vol. 3. Ed. by Roberta Kevelson. (Illus.). 410p. (C). 1990. 114.00 (*0-306-43494-6*, Plenum Trade) Perseus Pubng.

Law & Sex Come Together in the '90s: How to Enjoy Inter-Personal Relationship & Stay Out of Court, Too... John V. Esposito. 467p. 1993. write for info. (*1-883898-00-5*) Univ Pubns SC.

Law & Sex Come Together in the '90s: How to Enjoy Inter-Personal Relationships & Stay Out of Court, Too. John V. Esposito. LC 94-90694. 300p. (Orig.). 1996. pap. 24.95 (*0-533-11330-X*) Vantage.

Law & Social Action: Selected Essays of Alexander H. Pekelis. Alexander H. Pekelis. Ed. by Milton R. Konvitz. LC 77-87376. (American Constitutional & Legal History Ser). (Illus.). 1970. reprint ed. lib. bdg. 37.50 (*0-306-71600-3*) Da Capo.

Law & Social Change. Ed. by J. S. Gandhi. (C). 1989. 28.50 (*81-7033-065-3*, Pub. by Rawat Pubns) S Asia.

Law & Social Change. Ed. by John Guy & Hugh Beale. (Royal Historical Society Studies in History: No. 40). 207p. 1984. 75.00 (*0-901050-94-6*) Boydell & Brewer.

Law & Social Change. Ed. by Stuart S. Nagel. LC 73-89941. (Sage Contemporary Social Science Issues Ser.: Vol. 3). 118p. 1974. reprint ed. pap. 36.60 (*0-608-03377-4*, 205964100008) Bks Demand.

Law & Social Change: A Study of Land Reform in Sri Lanka. Martin E. Gold. 272p. 1984. reprint ed. pap. text 14.95 (*0-8290-1576-0*) Irvington.

Law & Social Change: Indo-American Reflection. F. Robert Meagher. (C). 1988. 110.00 (*0-7855-3672-8*) St Mut.

Law & Social Change in Ghana. William B. Harvey. LC 65-17139. 467p. 1966. reprint ed. pap. 144.80 (*0-7837-9348-0*, 206009000004) Bks Demand.

Law & Social Change in Postwar Japan. Frank K. Upham. 288p. 1987. pap. 19.95 (*0-674-51787-3*) HUP.

Law & Social Change Indo-American Reflections. Robert F. Meagher. (C). 1988. 100.00 (*0-89771-287-0*) St Mut.

Law & Social Inquiry: Journal of the American Bar Foundation, 1976-1995, 20 vols. 1976. 1055.00 (*0-8377-9237-1*, Rothman) W S Hein.

*__Law & Social Norms.__ Eric A. Posner. LC 99-88226. 320p. 2000. 39.95 (*0-674-00156-7*) Belknap Pr.

*__Law & Social Order in the United States.__ James Willard Hurst. LC 00-30930. 2000. write for info. (*1-58477-113-5*) Lawbk Exchange.

Law & Social Process in United States History. James W. Hurst. LC 74-173669. (American Constitutional & Legal History Ser). 359p. 1971. reprint ed. lib. bdg. 42.50 (*0-306-70409-9*) Da Capo.

Law & Social Process in United States History. James W. Hurst. LC 87-83583. (Michigan Legal Publications). xvii, 361p. 1987. reprint ed. lib. bdg. 47.50 (*0-89941-627-6*, 305480) W S Hein.

*__Law & Social Status in Classical Athens.__ Ed. by Virginia J. Hunter & Jonathan Edmondson. LC 99-54992. (Illus.). 250p. 2000. text. write for info. (*0-19-924011-6*) OUP.

*__Law & Social Work Practice: A Legal System Approach.__ 2nd ed. Raymond Albert. (Social Work Ser.). (Illus.). 560p. 2000. 59.95 (*0-8261-4891-3*) Springer Pub.

Law & Society. Ed. by Roger Cottrell. LC 94-10239. (International Library of Essays in Law & Theory, Areas Ser.: Vol. 13). 500p. (C). 1994. lib. bdg. 150.00 (*0-8147-1461-7*) NYU Pr.

Law & Society. Ed. by Werner Krawietz. (International Library of Essays in Law & Legal Theory). (C). 1992. text 150.00 (*0-8147-4635-7*) NYU Pr.

Law & Society. Gerald Turkel. LC 95-31347. 320p. 1995. 46.00 (*0-205-13982-5*) Allyn.

*__Law & Society.__ 6th ed. Steven Vago. LC 99-30798. 422p. 1999. 51.00 (*0-13-010420-5*) P-H.

*__Law & Society: An Introduction to Sources for Criminal & Legal History from 1800.__ Michelle Cale. (Readers' Guides Ser.: No. 14). 148p. 1999. pap. text 20.95 (*1-873162-30-8*, Pub. by PRO Pubns) Midpt Trade.

Law & Society: Readings on the Social Study of Law. Stewart Macaulay et al. 700p. (C). 1995. pap. text 41.75 (*0-393-96713-1*) Norton.

Law & Society in Byzantium: Ninth-Twelfth Centuries. Ed. by Angeliki E. Laiou & Dieter Simon. LC 93-29343. (Illus.). 308p. 1994. 35.00 (*0-88402-222-6*) Dumbarton Oaks.

Law & Society in Early Medieval Europe: Studies in Legal History. Katherine F. Drew. (Collected Studies: No. CS271). 302p. (C). 1988. reprint ed. lib. bdg. 106.95 (*0-86078-219-0*, Pub. by Variorum) Ashgate Pub Co.

Law & Society in Modern India. K. D. Gaur. (C). 1989. 425.00 (*0-7855-4765-7*) St Mut.

Law & Society in Modern India. Marc Galanter. 430p. (C). 1993. reprint ed. pap. text 7.95 (*0-19-563205-2*, 11536) OUP.

*__Law & Society in Transition.__ Philippe Nonet et al. 130p. 2000. pap. 24.95 (*0-7658-0642-8*) Transaction Pubs.

Law & Society Reader. Ed. by Richard L. Abel. 450p. (C). 1995. text 55.00 (*0-8147-0617-7*); pap. text 20.00 (*0-8147-0618-5*) NYU Pr.

Law & Sociology: Exploratory Essays. Ed. by William M. Evan. LC 78-23950. 235p. 1979. reprint ed. lib. bdg. 35.00 (*0-313-20729-1*, EVLS, Greenwood Pr) Greenwood.

Law & Space Telecommunications. Francis Lyall. 1989. text 129.95 (*1-85521-039-8*, Pub. by Dartmth Pub) Ashgate Pub Co.

Law & Special Education. Mitchell L. Yell. LC 97-35699. 410p. 1997. pap., teacher ed. 53.67 (*0-02-430872-2*) P-H.

Law & State: The Case of Northern Ireland. Kevin Boyle et al. LC 75-10914. 206p. 1975. lib. bdg. 30.00 (*0-87023-197-9*) U of Mass Pr.

Law & Status among the Kiowa Indians. Jane Richardson. LC 84-45509. (American Ethnological Society Monographs: No. 1). 1988. reprint ed. 23.50 (*0-404-62901-6*) AMS Pr.

Law & Structure of the International Financial System: Regulation in the U. S., EEC, & Japan. John H. Friedland. LC 93-25950. 216p. 1994. 67.95 (*0-89930-837-6*, Quorum Bks) Greenwood.

Law & Structures of Social Action. Kenneth S. Carlston. LC 80-19159. (Library of World Affairs: No. 30). 288p. 1980. reprint ed. lib. bdg. 59.75 (*0-313-20837-9*, CALW, Greenwood Pr) Greenwood.

Law & Taxation, Vol. 1. Ed. by Jill Muehrcke. (Leadership Ser.). 100p. 1990. spiral bd. 20.00 (*0-614-07098-8*) Soc Nonprofit Org.

Law & Taxation, Vol. 2. Ed. by Jill Muehrcke. (Leadership Ser.). 81p. 1993. spiral bd. 20.00 (*0-614-07099-6*) Soc Nonprofit Org.

Law & Terrorism. Friedman. 87.95 (*1-85521-958-1*) Ashgate Pub Co.

Law & the American Future. Ed. by Murray L. Schwartz. 1975. 9.95 (*0-317-00004-7*); pap. 4.95 (*0-317-03136-8*) Am Assembly.

Law & the American Future. Ed. by Murray L. Schwartz. LC 75-34079. 1976. 9.95 (*0-13-526061-2*) Am Assembly.

Law & the American Health Care System. Rand E. Rosenblatt et al. LC 97-200705. (University Casebook Ser.). 1355p. 1997. text 42.00 (*1-56662-481-9*) Foundation Pr.

Law & the American Health Care System. Rand E. Rosenblatt et al. (University Casebook Ser.). 1346p. 1997. pap. text, teacher ed., suppl. ed. write for info. (*1-56662-572-6*) Foundation Pr.

Law & the American Health Care System: 1998 Supplement. Rosenblatt et al. 1998. 12.95 (*1-56662-605-6*) Foundation Pr.

Law & the Arts, 87. Ed. by Susan Tiefenbrun. LC 98-14237. (Contributions in Legal Studies: Vol. 87). 272p. 1999. 59.95 (*0-313-30805-5*, Greenwood Pr) Greenwood.

Law & the Balance of Power: The Automobile Manufacturers & Their Dealers. Stewart Macaulay. LC 66-26503. 224p. 1966. 29.95 (*0-87154-574-8*) Russell Sage.

Law & the Commonwealth. Richard T. Latham. LC 70-104250. 632p. 1970. reprint ed. lib. bdg. 89.50 (*0-8371-3974-0*, LALC, Greenwood Pr) Greenwood.

Law & the Company We Keep. Aviam Soifer. LC 94-46602. 288p. 1995. text 44.50 (*0-674-51298-7*, SOILAW) HUP.

Law & the Conditions of Freedom in the Nineteenth-Century United States. J. Willard Hurst. 150p. 1964. pap. 14.95 (*0-299-01363-4*) U of Wis Pr.

Law & the Conflict of Ideologies: Ninth Round Table on Law & Semiotics. Ed. by Roberta Kevelson. (Semiotics & the Human Sciences Ser.: Vol. 10). 250p. (C). 1996. text 57.95 (*0-8204-3092-7*) P Lang Pubng.

Law & the Countryside. Tim Bonyhady. 290p. 1987. 96.00 (*0-86205-256-4*, U.K., MICHIE); pap. 48.00 (*0-86205-257-2*, U.K., MICHIE) LEXIS Pub.

Law & the Courts. 80p. 1988. pap. 2.50 (*0-89707-331-2*, 235-0006-01) Amer Bar Assn.

Law & the Courts. LC 95-131036. 80p. 1995. pap. 2.50 (*1-57073-049-0*, 235-0027) Amer Bar Assn.

Law & the Disordered: The Consequences of Reform in Mental Health Law. Paul S. Appelbaum. 1994. write for info. (*0-318-72284-4*) OUP.

Law & the Ecological Challenge: Amintaphil, Vol. 2. Ed. by Eugene E. Dais. LC 78-61842. xxiv, 265p. 1979. lib. bdg. 42.00 (*0-930342-66-6*, 300220) W S Hein.

Law & the Elderly in North Carolina. 2nd ed. Michael J. McCann & Mason P. Thomas, Jr. 307p. (C). 1996. pap. text 24.00 (*1-56011-202-6*, 96.10) Institute Government.

Law & the Emergence of Modern Dublin: A Litigation Topography for a Capital City. W. N. Osborough. (Illus.). 256p. 1996. 39.50 (*0-7165-2583-6*, Pub. by Irish Acad Pr) Intl Spec Bk.

*__Law & the Enviroment.__ 2nd ed. Powell. 2000. 23.75 (*0-324-02041-4*) Sth-Wstrn College.

*__Law & the Enviroment.__ 2nd ed. Powell. 2002. pap. 46.00 (*0-324-02040-6*) Thomson Learn.

Law & the Environment. Frona Powell. LC 97-13286. (Miscellaneous/Catalogs Ser.). 600p. 1997. mass mkt. 76.95 (*0-538-87874-6*) West Pub.

Law & the Environment: An Interdisciplinary Reader. Robert V. Percival & Dorothy C. Alevizatos. LC 96-41366. 464p. 1997. 69.95 (*1-56639-523-2*); pap. 29.95 (*1-56639-524-0*) Temple U Pr.

Law & the Family. 2nd ed. John K. Dewar. 546p. 1992. pap. 40.00 (*0-406-00133-2*, UK, MICHIE) LEXIS Pub.

Law & the Family in Africa. Ed. by S. Roberts. 1977. 33.85 (*90-279-7663-5*) Mouton.

Law & the Family in Ireland. Maureen Mullally et al. LC 98-232274. xiv, 1465p. 1998. pap. 20.00 (*1-901657-09-4*, Pub. by Blackhall Pub) Gaunt.

Law & the Family New York, 6 vols. 2nd ed. Henry H. Foster, Jr. et al. 1992. suppl. ed. write for info. (*0-318-61710-2*) West Group.

Law & the Family New York Forms, 6 vols. 2nd ed. Joel R. Brandes et al. LC 95-80415. 3500p. 1995. text 720.00 (*0-7620-0008-2*) West Group.

Law & the Gender Bias. Marcia M. Boumil et al. LC 93-27891. xii, 248p. 1995. pap. 37.50 (*0-8377-0363-8*, Rothman) W S Hein.

Law & the Gorbachev Era: Essays in Honor of Dietrich Andre Loeber. Ed. by Donald D. Barry et al. (C). 1988. lib. bdg. 174.50 (*90-247-3678-1*) Kluwer Academic.

Law & the Gospel. Ernest C. Reisinger. LC 97-197. 232p. (Orig.). 1997. pap. 9.99 (*0-87552-387-0*) P & R Pubng.

Law & the Governance of Renewable Resources. Erling Berge. LC 98-26344. 1998. pap. 29.95 (*1-55815-504-X*) ICS Pr.

L

An Asterisk (*) at the beginning of an entry indicates that the title is appearing for the first time.

Law & the Great Plains: Essays on the Legal History of the Heartland, 82. Ed. by John R. Wunder. LC 95-37979. (Contributions in Legal Studies: No. 82). 208p. 1996. 62.95 (*0-313-29680-4*, Greenwood Pr) Greenwood.

Law & the Heart: A Practical Guide for Successful Lawyer/Client Relationships. 3rd rev. ed. Merit Bennett. LC 96-77235. 168p. 1996. pap. 14.95 (*1-57282-000-4*, D20004) Message NM.

Law & the Human Sciences. Ed. by Roberta Kevelson. LC 91-37475. (Semiotics & the Human Sciences Ser.: Vol. 3). 557p. (C). 1992. text 69.95 (*0-8204-1815-3*) P Lang Pubng.

Law & the Image. Nead. LC 98-50313. 1999. pap. text 19.00 (*0-226-56954-3*) U Ch Pr.

Law & the Image. Nead. LC 98-50313. (Illus.). 288p. 1999. lib. bdg. 47.00 (*0-226-56953-5*) U Ch Pr.

Law & the Indo-China War. John N. Moore. LC 73-166383. 830p. 1972. reprint ed. pap. 200.00 (*0-608-03326-X*, 206403800008) Bks Demand.

Law & the Internal Auditing Profession. James S. Fargason. Ed. by Lee A. Campbell. (Briefing Ser.). 59p. 1992. pap. text 20.00 (*0-89413-265-2*, A837) Inst Inter Aud.

Law & the Internet. Ed. by Lilian Edwards & Charlotte Waelde. LC 98-150239. xix, 264p. 1997. pap. 50.00 (*1-901362-30-2*, Pub. by Hart Pub) Northwestern U Pr.

Law & the Lady. Wilkie Collin. LC 99-236047. 432p. 1999. pap. 10.95 (*0-14-043607-3*, PuffinBks) Peng Put Young Read.

***Law & the Lady.** Wilkie Collins. Ed. & Intro. by Jenny B. Taylor. (Oxford World's Classics Ser.). 462p. 1999. pap. 11.95 (*0-19-283679-X*) OUP.

Law & the Lady: A Novel see Works of Wilkie Collins

Law & the Lawyers. Mohandas Karamchand Gandhi. Ed. by S. B. Kher. 261p. 1982. pap. 9.50 (*0-934676-57-7*) Greenlf Bks.

Law & the Legal System: An Introduction. 2nd ed. Samuel Mermin. LC 81-83102. 496p. (C). 1982. pap. 25.00 (*0-316-56731-0*) Little.

Law & the Liberal Arts. Ed. by Albert Broderick. LC 67-20497. 261p. reprint ed. pap. 81.00 (*0-608-30186-8*, 200521800051) Bks Demand.

Law & the Life Insurance Contract. 7th ed. Muriel L. Crawford. LC 93-29937. (Series in Finance). 720p. (C). 1993. text 67.50 (*0-256-13566-5*, Irwn Prfssnl) McGraw-Hill Prof.

Law & the Life Insurance Contract. 8th ed. Muriel L. Crawford. LC 97-20964. 624p. 1997. 88.44 (*0-256-16699-4*) McGraw.

Law & the Market. Ed. by Megan Richardson & Philip Williams. 235p. 1995. 64.00 (*1-86287-174-4*, Pub. by Federation Pr) Gaunt.

Law & the Media. 3rd ed. Tom Crone. 214p. 1995. pap. 37.95 (*0-7506-2008-0*) Buttrwrth-Heinemann.

Law & the Mental Health Professions: Friction at the Interface. Ed. by Walter E. Barton & Charlotte J. Sanborn. LC 77-90226. xviii, 330p. (Orig.). 1978. 50.00 (*0-8236-2950-3*) Intl Univs Pr.

Law & the Mental Health System: Civil & Criminal Aspects. 2nd ed. Ralph Reisner & Christopher Slobogin. (American Casebook Ser.). 1117p. (C). 1990. text 54.50 (*0-314-73302-7*) West Pub.

Law & the Mental Health System: Civil & Criminal Aspects, Teacher's Manual to Accompany. 2nd ed. Ralph Reisner & Christopher Slobogin. (American Casebook Ser.). 68p. (C). 1992. pap. text. write for info. (*0-314-01378-4*) West Pub.

Law & the Mental Health System: Civil & Criminal Aspects, 1992. 2nd ed. Ralph Reisner & Christopher Slobogin. (American Casebook Ser.). 73p. (C). 1992. pap. text, suppl. ed. 8.00 (*0-314-01301-6*) West Pub.

Law & the Mental Health System: Civil & Criminal Aspects, 1995 Supplement To. 2nd ed. Christopher Slobogin & Ralph Reisner. (American Casebook Ser.). 190p. (C). 1994. pap. text 12.00 (*0-314-05904-0*) West Pub.

Law & the Midwife. Rosemary Jenkins. (Illus.). 224p. 1995. pap. 28.95 (*0-632-03629-X*) Blckwll Scitfc UK.

Law & the Mind: Biological Origins of Human Behavior. Margaret Gruter. (Library of Social Research: Vol. 184). (Illus.). 160p. 1991. 59.95 (*0-8039-4045-9*); pap. 26.00 (*0-8039-4046-7*) Sage.

Law & the Mind: Biological Origins of Human Behavior. Margaret Gruter. LC 90-23412. (Sage Library of Social Research: Vol. 184). 184p. 1991. reprint ed. pap. 57.10 (*0-608-07682-1*, 206777200010) Bks Demand.

Law & the Moral Order: A Study in Ethics & Jurisprudence. W. D. Lamont. 128p. 1981. text 23.90 (*0-08-025742-9*, Pergamon Pr); pap. text 12.95 (*0-08-025746-1*, Pergamon Pr) Elsevier.

Law & the National Labor Policy. Archibald S. Cox. LC 82-20930. 111p. 1983. reprint ed. lib. bdg. 45.00 (*0-313-23794-8*, COLN, Greenwood Pr) Greenwood.

Law & the New Deal: Selected Articles on Legal Issues Surrounding the Depression & Roosevelt's Policies. Ed. by Melvyn Dubofsky & Stephen Burwood. (Articles on the Great Depression Ser.). 344p. 1990. reprint ed. text 20.00 (*0-8240-0899-5*) Garland.

Law & the New Testament: The Question of Continuity. Frank Thielman. LC 99-29119. 1999. pap. 19.95 (*0-8245-1829-2*) Crossroad NY.

Law & the Order of Culture. Ed. by Robert C. Post. LC 90-50927. (Representation Bks.: No. 4). 200p. 1991. 45.00 (*0-520-07500-5*, Pub. by U CA Pr); pap. 14.95 (*0-520-07337-1*, Pub. by U CA Pr) Cal Prin Full Svc.

***Law & the Physician.** 2nd ed. Edward P. Richards & Katharine C. Rathbun. 560p. 1999. 99.00 (*0-8342-1380-X*) Aspen Pub.

Law & the Physician. 2nd ed. Edward P. Richards, III & Katharine C. Rathbun. LC 99-22815. 1999. write for info. (*0-8342-1603-5*) Aspen Pub.

Law & the Poor. Frank J. Parker. LC 72-97696. 230p. reprint ed. pap. 71.30 (*0-8357-8937-3*, 203351200086) Bks Demand.

Law & the Poor: A Socio-Legal Study. M. G. Chitkara. (C). 1991. text 22.50 (*81-7024-391-2*, Pub. by Ashish Pub Hse) S Asia.

Law & the Poor in Canada. Ed. by Irwin Cotler & Herbert Marx. LC 78-305100. 144p. 1977. reprint ed. pap. 44.70 (*0-608-00459-6*, 206127800007) Bks Demand.

Law & the Postmodern Mind: Essays on Psychoanalysis & Jurisprudence. Ed. by David F. Carlson & Peter Goodrich. LC 97-33739. 328p. (C). 1998. text 49.50 (*0-472-10841-7*, 10841) U of Mich Pr.

Law & the Profits. C. Northcote Parkinson. 1993. reprint ed. lib. bdg. 18.95 (*1-56849-101-8*) Buccaneer Bks.

Law & the Promise. Neville. 156p. 1984. reprint ed. pap. 8.95 (*0-87516-532-X*) DeVorss.

Law & the Prophets see Corridors of Time: New Haven & London, 1927-1956

Law & the Public Policy of Race. Robert Johnson. (C). 1998. pap. 30.00 (*1-58073-019-1*) BCP Bks.

***Law & the Public's Health.** 5th ed. Kenneth R. Wing. LC 99-24641. 1999. 56.00 (*1-56793-098-0*) Health Admin Pr.

***Law & the Public's Health: Supplemental Cases.** 5th ed. Kenneth R. Wing. LC 99-11046. 343p. 1999. pap. 56.00 (*1-56793-105-7*) Health Admin Pr.

Law & the Regulators. Tony Prosser. LC 97-12130. 332p. (C). 1997. text 78.00 (*0-19-876391-3*) OUP.

Law & the Rise of Capitalism. M. Tigar. pap. text 18.00 (*1-58367-030-0*) Monthly Rev.

Law & the Rise of Capitalism. Michael E. Tigar. LC 77-70968. 360p. reprint ed. pap. 111.60 (*0-7837-3908-7*, 204375600010) Bks Demand.

Law & the Search for Community. Joel F. Handler. LC 89-29877. (Law in Social Context Ser.). 188p. (C). 1990. text 32.50 (*0-8122-8201-9*) U of Pa Pr.

Law & the Senses: Perception & Regulation. Lionel Bently & Leo Flynn. 272p. 1996. pap. 21.95 (*0-7453-1068-0*, Pub. by Pluto GBR) Stylus Pub VA.

Law & the Senses: Sensational Jurisprudence. Lionel Bently. LC 96-8272. (Law & Social Theory Ser.). 272p. 1996. 64.95 (*0-7453-1069-9*, Pub. by Pluto GBR) Stylus Pub VA.

Law & the Sexes: Explorations in Feminist Jurisprudence. Naffine. 184p. pap. 19.95 (*0-04-442210-5*, Pub. by Allen & Unwin Pty) Paul & Co Pubs.

Law & the Sexual Politics of Interpretation. Beverly Brown. 220p. (C). 1997. 85.00 (*0-485-11475-5*, Pub. by Athlone Pr); pap. 29.95 (*0-485-12114-X*, Pub. by Athlone Pr) Humanities.

Law & the Shaping of Public Education, 1785-1954. David Tyack et al. LC 86-40062. 272p. 1991. pap. text 15.95 (*0-299-10884-8*) U of Wis Pr.

Law & the Shaping of the American Labor Movement. William Forbath. LC 90-49662. 192p. 1991. pap. 17.50 (*0-674-51782-2*, FORLAX) HUP.

Law & the Social Order: Essays in Legal Philosophy. Morris R. Cohen. LC 94-75665. xii, 404p. 1994. reprint ed. 105.00 (*1-56169-093-7*) Gaunt.

Law & the Social Order: Essays in Legal Philosophy. Supplemented by Cohen's "Moral Aspects of Criminal Law" Morris R. Cohen. LC 81-4394. (Social & Moral Thought Ser.). 520p. (Orig.). 1982. pap. 29.95 (*0-87855-876-4*) Transaction Pubs.

Law & the Social Role of Science. Ed. by Harry W. Jones. LC 66-27541. (Illus.). 254p. 1967. 10.00 (*0-87470-007-8*) Rockefeller.

Law & the Social Sciences in the Second Half Century. Julius Stone. LC 65-12433. 128p. reprint ed. pap. 39.70 (*0-608-14142-9*, 205592000039) Bks Demand.

Law & the Song: Hebraic, Christian, & Pagan Revivals in Sixteenth-Century France. Ehsan Ahmed. LC 97-67748. 172p. (C). 1998. lib. bdg. 42.95 (*1-883479-19-3*) Summa Pubns.

***Law & the Spirit of Inquiry: Essays in Honour of Sir Louis Blom-Cooper, QC.** Ed. by Gavin Drewry & Charles Blake. 240p. 1999. text 87.00 (*90-411-9761-3*) Kluwer Law Intl.

Law & the Student Press. George E. Stevens & John B. Webster. LC 73-12276. 148p. reprint ed. pap. 45.90 (*0-608-15238-2*, 202916600059) Bks Demand.

Law & the Team Physician. Elizabeth M. Gallup. LC 93-47607. (Illus.). 192p. 1994. text 24.00 (*0-87322-662-3*, BGAL0662) Human Kinetics.

Law & the Transformation of Aztec Culture, 1500-1700. Susan Kellogg. LC 94-43104. (Illus.). 285p. 1995. 37.95 (*0-8061-2702-3*) U of Okla Pr.

Law & the Treatment of Drug & Alcohol-Dependent Persons: A Comparative Study of Existing Legislation. L. Porter et al. 216p. 1986. pap. text 34.00 (*92-4-156093-2*, 1150243) World Health.

Law & the Unconscious. Tr. by Peter Goodrich et al. LC 97-24051. 1997. text 55.00 (*0-312-21023-X*) St Martin.

Law & the Urban Poor in India. V. R. Iyer. (C). 1988. 17.50 (*81-7018-465-7*) S Asia.

Law & the Weaker Party. Ed. by Steven D. Anderman et al. 1992. write for info. (*0-406-99845-0*, LWPAASET, MICHIE) LEXIS Pub.

Law & the Weaker Party, 5 vols., Set. Steven D. Anderman et al. boxed set 220.00 (*0-614-05550-4*, UK, MICHIE) LEXIS Pub.

Law & the Word. Thomas Troward. 208p. 1993. reprint ed. pap. 10.95 (*0-87516-653-9*) DeVorss.

Law & the Word (1917) Thomas Troward. 208p. 1998. reprint ed. pap. 19.95 (*0-7661-0302-1*) Kessinger Pub.

Law & Theology in Deuteronomy. J. Gordon McConville. (Journal for the Study of the Old Testament Supplement Ser.: Vol. 33). 214p. 1995. 50.00 (*0-905774-78-7*, Pub. by Sheffield Acad); pap. 14.95 (*0-905774-79-5*, Pub. by Sheffield Acad) CUP Services.

Law & Theology in Judaism. David Novak. 1974. 25.00 (*0-87068-245-8*) Ktav.

Law & Theory of Trademarks. George Pickering. 256p. 1998. 70.00 (*1-901362-64-7*, Pub. by Hart Pub) Northwestern U Pr.

Law & Trade Issues of the Japanese Economy: American & Japanese Perspectives. Ed. by Gary R. Saxonhouse & Kozo Yamamura. LC 85-40975. 310p. (C). 1986. 40.00 (*0-295-96343-3*) U of Wash Pr.

Law & Tradition in Judaism. Boaz Cohen. 1959. 17.50 (*0-87068-023-4*) Ktav.

Law & Truth. Dennis Patterson. (Illus.). 200p. 1996. text 49.95 (*0-19-508323-7*) OUP.

Law & Truth. Dennis Patterson. (Illus.). 200p. 1999. pap. 18.95 (*0-19-513247-5*) OUP.

Law & Uncertainty: Risks & Legal Processes. Robert Baldwin & Peter Cane. LC 96-37304. 1997. 146.00 (*90-411-0942-0*) Kluwer Law Intl.

Law & Urban Change in Brazil. Edesio Fernandes. 192p. 1995. 66.95 (*1-85972-125-7*, Pub. by Avebry) Ashgate Pub Co.

Law & Urban Growth: Civil Litigation in the Boston Trial Courts, 1880-1900. Robert A. Silverman. LC 80-7553. (Illus.). 232p. 1981. reprint ed. pap. 72.00 (*0-7837-8597-6*, 204941200011) Bks Demand.

Law & Violence Against Women: Cases & Materials on Systems of Oppression. Beverly Balos & Mary L. Fellows. LC 93-74421. 714p. (C). 1994. boxed set 75.00 (*0-89089-567-8*) Carolina Acad Pr.

Law & Violence Against Women: Cases & Materials on Systems of Oppression. Mary L. Fellows & Beverly Balos. 90p. 1997. teacher ed. 15.00 (*0-89089-159-1*) Carolina Acad Pr.

Law & Vulnerable Elderly People. Sally Greengross. (C). 1989. 45.00 (*0-86242-050-4*, Pub. by Age Concern Eng) St Mut.

***Law & War: An American Story.** Peter H. Maguire. LC 00-31442. (Illus.). 2000. pap. 17.50 (*0-231-12051-6*) Col U Pr.

Law & Wisdom from Ben Sira to Paul: A Traditional Historical Enquiry into the Relation of Law, Wisdom & Ethics. E. J. Schnabel. 400p. (Orig.). 1985. pap. 87.50 (*3-16-144896-0*, Pub. by JCB Mohr) Coronet Bks.

Law & You. Betty Herzog. (Follet Coping Skills Ser.). 64p. 1988. pap. text 5.50 (*0-8428-2339-5*) Cambridge Bk.

Law & You. rev. ed. Elinor P. Swiger. LC 72-88762. 140p. 1980. 9.95 (*0-672-52632-8*, Bobbs) Macmillan.

Law & Your Legal Rights see Law & Your Legal Rights: A Bilingual Guide To Everyday Legal Issues - Un Manual Bilingue Para Asuntos Legal

Law & Your Legal Rights. (SPA & ENG.). (C). 1999. text 26.95 (*0-13-020794-2*) P-H.

Law & Your Legal Rights: A Bilingual Guide To Everyday Legal Issues - Un Manual Bilingue Para Asuntos Legal. Jess J. Araujo. LC 98-21982.Tr. of Law & Your Legal Rights. (SPA & ENG.). 288p. 1998. pap. 16.00 (*0-684-83970-9*) S&S Trade.

Law As a Career. 16p. 1992. pap. 1.50 (*0-89707-731-8*, 235-0020) Amer Bar Assn.

***Law As a Gendering Practice.** Ed. by Dorothy E. Chunn & Dany Lacombe. 320p. 2000. pap. 24.95 (*0-19-541295-8*) OUP.

Law As a Means to an End. Rudolf Von Ihering. (Modern Legal Philosophy Ser.: Vol. 5). lix, 483p. 1998. reprint ed. 163.50 (*1-56169-384-7*) Gaunt.

Law as a Means to an End, 1913. Rudolf von Jhering. Ed. by Joseph H. Drake. Tr. by Isaac Husik from GER. LC 99-23754. 1999. reprint ed. 80.00 (*1-58477-009-0*) Lawbk Exchange.

Law As a System of Signs. R. Kevelson. LC 87-32716. (Topics in Contemporary Semiotics Ser.). (Illus.). 344p. (C). 1988. 65.00 (*0-306-42658-7*, Plenum Trade) Perseus Pubng.

Law As an Instrument of Economic Policy: Comparative & Critical Approaches. Ed. by Terrence Daintith. (European University Institute, Series A (Law): No. 7). 432p. (C). 1987. lib. bdg. 142.35 (*3-11-011430-5*) De Gruyter.

Law As Art. Gary Bagnall. (Applied Legal Philosophy Ser.). (Illus.). 232p. 1996. text 81.95 (*1-85521-758-9*, Pub. by Dartmth Pub) Ashgate Pub Co.

Law As Communication. Ed. by David Nelken. LC 95-46956. (Issues in Law & Society Ser.). (Illus.). 288p. 1996. pap. 32.95 (*1-85521-722-8*, Pub. by Dartmth Pub); text 96.95 (*1-85521-719-8*, Pub. by Dartmth Pub) Ashgate Pub Co.

Law As Culture. Kathy Laster & Veronica Taylor. 264p. 1997. pap. 49.00 (*1-86287-226-0*, Pub. by Federation Pr) Gaunt.

***Law as Culture & Culture as Law: Essays in Honor of John Phillip Reid.** John P. Reid et al. LC 00-26743. 2000. write for info. (*0-945612-99-0*) Madison Hse.

Law As Gospel: Revival & Reform in the Theology of Charles G. Finney. David L. Weddle. LC 85-8303. (Studies in Evangelicalism: No. 6). 293p. 1985. 26.50 (*0-8108-1819-1*) Scarecrow.

Law as Logic & Experience, 1940. Max Radin. LC 99-30670. 2000. reprint ed. 55.00 (*1-58477-008-2*) Lawbk Exchange.

Law As Metaphor: From Islamic Courts to the Palace of Justice. June Starr. LC 90-49066. 243p. (C). 1992. text 21.50 (*0-7914-0781-0*) State U NY Pr.

Law As Politics: Carl Schmitt's Critique of Liberalism. David Dyzenhaus. LC 98-13618. 1998. write for info. (*0-8223-2227-7*); pap. 18.95 (*0-8223-2244-7*) Duke.

Law Assistant. Jack Rudman. (Career Examination Ser.: C-1341). 1994. pap. 27.95 (*0-8373-1341-4*) Nat Learn.

Law Association of Philadelphia: Addresses Delivered March 13, 1902, & Papers Prepared or Republished to Commemorate the Centennial Celebration of the Law Association of Philadelphia, Pennsylvania, 1802-1902. Law Associates of Philadelphia Staff. xii, 462p. 1998. reprint ed. 158.00 (*1-56169-413-4*) Gaunt.

Law at Berkeley: The History of Boalt Hall. Sandra P. Epstein. LC 97-13216. (Illus.). 350p. 1997. pap. 27.95 (*0-87772-375-3*) UCB IGS.

Law at Harvard: A History of Ideas & Men, 1817-1967. Arthur E. Sutherland. LC 67-17320. 448p. reprint ed. pap. 138.90 (*0-7837-2338-5*, 205742600004) Bks Demand.

***Law at the End of Life: The Supreme Court & Assisted Suicide.** Ed. by Carl E. Schneider. (Illus.). 476p. (C). 2000. text 59.50 (*0-472-11157-4*, 11157) U of Mich Pr.

Law at the Margins: Toward Social Participation? Terry Carney. 214p. 1991. text 59.00 (*0-19-553219-8*) OUP.

Law, Authority, & Society: Readings in Ancient & Medieval Social Thought. Ed. by Michael E. Burke & Robert L. Pigeon. LC 95-34404. 1995. text 25.00 (*0-938289-53-5*, 289535) Combined Pub.

Law, Behavior, & Mental Health: Policy & Practice. Steven R. Smith & Robert G. Meyer. 772p. (C). 1987. text 75.00 (*0-8147-7857-7*) NYU Pr.

Law, Behavior, & Mental Health: Policy & Practice. Steven R. Smith & Robert G. Meyer. 772p. (C). 1988. pap. text 27.50 (*0-8147-7887-9*) NYU Pr.

Law Between Two Worlds. Tlali. 1995. pap. text. write for info. (*0-582-28764-2*, Pub. by Addison-Wesley) Longman.

Law, Biology & Culture: The Evolution of Law. Ed. by Margaret Gruter & Paul Bohannon. 226p. 1983. pap. 15.00 (*0-915520-63-X*) Gruter Inst.

Law Book News: A Monthly Review of Current Legal Literature & Journal of Legal Bibliography, 2 vols. viii, 400p. 1989. reprint ed. lib. bdg. 95.00 (*0-8377-0879-6*, Rothman) W S Hein.

***Law Books & Serials in Print, 1999, 3 vols., Set.** Ed. by Bowker Staff. 2000. 695.00 (*0-8352-4073-8*) Bowker.

***Law Books & Serials in Print Supplement 2000: A Multimedia Source Book.** Ed. by Bowker Staff. 740p. 2000. write for info. (*0-8352-4301-X*) Bowker.

***Law Books & Serials in Print 2000: A Multimedia Sourcebook, 3 vols., Set Ed. by Bowker Staff. 3200p. 2000. 725.00 (*0-8352-4286-2*) Bowker.**

A Multimedia Sourcebook "This is a skilled and impressive publication: well thought out, carefully edited, and immaculately produced. -REFERENCE REVIEWS "A well-planned, modern reference tool that will be valuable in all types of law libraries." -TEXAS BAR JOURNAL With over 68,000 titles intended exclusively for legal professionals, this unmatched bibliography lists virtually every available legal resource - books and serials, microfiche, videos and audiocassettes, software, and online databases. Focusing on core legal and related titles, Law Books and Serials in Print 2000 includes descriptive annotations that provide expert guidance on selecting the right sources for every research need. And it now keeps you current with a cumulative supplement at no extra cost. *Publisher Paid Annotation.*

Law Books in Print: Law Books in English Published Throughout the World Through, 1996. 8th ed. LC 97-18317. 1997. 750.00 (*0-87802-177-9*) Glanville.

Law Books in Spanish Translation: A Tentative Bibliography. Phanor J. Eder. LC 66-64733. 193p. reprint ed. pap. 59.90 (*0-8357-6715-9*, 203534900095) Bks Demand.

Law Books Recommended for Libraries: Including 1974, 1975 & 1976 Supplements, 10 vols. Association of American Law Schools Staff. 1967. reprint ed. ring bd. 475.00 (*0-8377-0201-1*, Rothman) W S Hein.

Law Books, Their Purposes & Their Use. Joseph H. Zumbalen. LC 94-76710. Vol. 12. iv, 63p. 1994. reprint ed. 42.00 (*0-89941-890-2*, 308360) W S Hein.

Law Breakers & Other Stories. Robert Grant. (C). 1972. reprint ed. 21.00 (*0-8422-8060-X*) Irvington.

Law Breakers & Other Stories. Robert Grant. (C). 1986. reprint ed. pap. text 6.95 (*0-8290-1871-9*) Irvington.

Law-Bringers. large type ed. Elliot Conway. (Linford Western Large Print Ser.). 240p. 1998. pap. 17.99 (*0-7089-5274-7*, Linford) Ulverscroft.

Law, Bureaucracy & Politics: The Implementation of Title VI of the Civil Rights Act of 1964. Augustus J. Jones, Jr. LC 81-40871. (Illus.). 316p. (Orig.). (C). 1982. pap. text 27.00 (*0-8191-2155-X*) U Pr of Amer.

Law Business: A Tired Monopoly. Joseph W. Bartlett. vii, 198p. 1982. reprint ed. 32.50 (*0-8377-0324-7*, Rothman) W S Hein.

Law Business & Regulation. O'Sullivan & Hunter. 658p. (C). 1998. pap. text 56.75 (*0-536-01523-6*) Pearson Custom.

***Law, Business & Regulation.** 2nd ed. 652p. (C). 1999. 69.00 (*0-536-02685-8*) Pearson Custom.

Law, Business & Society. 4th ed. Tony McAdams et al. LC 94-21204. (Legal Studies in Business). 876p. (C). 1994. text 70.75 (*0-256-14166-5*, Irwn McGrw-H) McGrw-H Hghr Educ.

Law, Business & Society. 5th ed. Tony McAdams et al. LC 97-15193. (C). 1997. text. write for info. (*0-256-23690-9*, Irwn McGrw-H) McGrw-H Hghr Educ.

Law, Business & Society. 6th ed. Tony McAdams. 832p. 2000. 85.63 (*0-07-231401-X*) McGraw.

An Asterisk (*) at the beginning of an entry indicates that the title is appearing for the first time.

Law, Capitalism & Power in Asia: The Rule of Law & Legal Institutions. Kanishka Jayasuriya. LC 99-185718. 2p. 1999. pap. write for info. (*0-415-19743-0*) Routledge.

***Law, Capitalism & Power in Asia: The Rule of Law & Legal Institutions.** Kanishka Jayasuriya. LC 99-185718. 1999. write for info. (*0-415-19742-2*) Routledge.

Law Catalogue, 14 vols., Set. University of Cambridge, Squire Law Library Staff et al. LC 73-17137. 1974. text 700.00 (*0-379-20175-5*) Oceana.

Law Clerk. Jack Rudman. (Career Examination Ser.: C-448). 1994. pap. 27.95 (*0-8373-0448-2*) Nat Learn.

***Law Comes to Texas: The Texas Rangers, 1870-1901.** limited ed. Frederick Wilkins. (Illus.). 416p. 1999. 60.00 (*1-880510-62-6*) State House Pr.

Law Comes to Texas: The Texas Rangers, 1870-1901: The Texas Rangers, 1870-1901. Frederick Wilkins. LC 98-40940. 416p. 1999. pap. 19.95 (*1-880510-61-8*) State House Pr.

***Law Comes to Texas: The Texas Rangers, 1870-1901: The Texas Rangers, 1870-1901.** Frederick Wilkins. LC 98-40940. 416p. 1999. 29.95 (*1-880510-60-X*) State House Pr.

Law Commission (Great Britain) Annual Report, 1996. 31st ed. Stationery Office. 66p. 1997. pap. 25.00 (*0-10-271197-6*, HM11976, Pub. by Statnry Office) Bernan Associates.

Law Commission (Great Britain) Annual Report, 32nd, 1997. annuals (Law Commission (Great Britain) Reports: No. 81022798). 66p. 1998. pap. 25.00 (*0-10-291198-3*, HM 29119, Pub. by Statnry Office) Bernan Associates.

Law Commission of India: Report Prepared by Lotika Sarkar on National Specialized Agencies & Women's Equality. Ed. by Lotika Sarkar. (C). 1988. 80.00 (*0-7855-4776-2*) St Mut.

***Law Commission Seventh Programme of Law Reform: Laid Before Parliament by the Lord High CHancellor Pursuant to Section 3(2) of the Law Commissions Act 1965.** LC 99-229587. 1999. write for info. (*0-10-268199-6*) Statnry Office.

Law Commission Working Papers, 22 vols. 1990. write for info. (*0-406-05617-X*, LCWASET, MICHIE) LEXIS Pub.

Law Courts: The Architecture of George Edmund Street. David B. Brownlee. LC 83-25625. (Architectural History Foundation-MIT Press Ser.: Vol. 8). 432p. 1984. 60.00 (*0-262-02199-4*) MIT Pr.

Law Courts in Papua New Guinea. LC 99-202426. 27p. 1994. pap. write for info. (*9980-85-177-5*, Pub. by Papua New Guinea) UH Pr.

Law Courts, Lawyers & Litigants. Frederick Payler. xiv, 242p. 1980. reprint ed. 38.50 (*0-8377-1006-5*, Rothman) W S Hein.

Law Courts Lawyers & Litigants. Frederick Payler. xiv, 241p. 1997. reprint ed. 76.00 (*1-56169-255-7*) Gaunt.

Law, Crime & Sexuality: Essays in Feminism. Carol Smart. 224p. 1995. text 69.95 (*0-8039-8959-8*); pap. text 25.95 (*0-8039-8960-1*) Sage.

Law, Culture & Regionalism in Early Medieval Spain. Roger Collins. (Collected Studies: No. CS356). 336p. 1992. text 109.95 (*0-86078-308-1*, Pub. by Variorum) Ashgate Pub Co.

Law, Culture, & Values. Ed. by Sava A. Vojcanin. 212p. 1989. 44.95 (*0-88738-305-X*) Transaction Pubs.

Law, Culture, Tradition, & Children's Rights in Eastern & Southern Africa. Welchman Ncube. LC 98-19214. (Issues in Law & Society Ser.). 358p. (C). 1998. text 76.95 (*1-84014-047-X*, KQC145.M55N38, Pub. by Ashgate Pub); pap. text 31.95 (*1-84014-477-7*, KQC145.M44N38, Pub. by Ashgate Pub) Ashgate Pub Co.

Law, Custom, & Social Order: The Colonial Experience in Malawi & Zambia. (African Issues Ser.). 1995. text. write for info. (*0-435-07428-8*) Heinemann.

Law, Custom & Social Order: The Colonial Experience in Malawi & Zambia. Martin Chanock. LC 98-19148. (Social History of Africa Ser.). 1998. pap. 22.50 (*0-325-00016-6*) Heinemann.

Law, Custom, & the Social Fabric in Medieval Europe. Ed. by Bernard S. Bachrach & David Nicholas. LC 89-13759. (Studies in Medieval Culture: No. 28). 1990. pap. 15.95 (*0-918720-31-1*); boxed set 34.95 (*0-918720-30-3*) Medieval Inst.

Law Day Partnerships. 8p. 1986. pap. 3.00 (*0-685-29662-8*, 497-0006-01) Amer Bar Assn.

Law, Decision-Making, & Microcomputers: A Cross-National Perspective. Ed. by Stuart S. Nagel. LC 90-8918. 376p. 1991. 80.00 (*0-89930-503-2*, NLM/, Quorum Bks) Greenwood.

Law Department Investigator. Jack Rudman. (Career Examination Ser.: C-849). 1994. pap. 29.95 (*0-8373-0849-6*) Nat Learn.

Law Department Management, No. A72. 2nd ed. 500p. 1991. ring bd. 125.00 (*0-929576-57-8*) Busn Laws Inc.

Law, Development, & the Ethiopian Revolution. Paul H. Brietzke. LC 80-65574. 600p. 1982. 50.00 (*0-8387-5008-7*) Bucknell U Pr.

Law Dictionary. Ed. by P. H. Collin. (C). 1990. reprint ed. 75.00 (*0-89771-133-5*) St Mut.

Law Dictionary. 4th ed. Steven Gifis. LC 96-1626. (Barron's Legal Guides Ser.). 561p. 1996. mass mkt. 11.95 (*0-8120-3380-9*) Barron.

Law Dictionary. 4th ed. Steven H. Gifis. 640p. 1996. pap. 16.95 (*0-8120-3096-6*) Barron.

Law Dictionary: Adapted to the Constitution & Laws of the United States & the Several States of the American Union; With References to the Civil & Other Systems of Foreign Law, 1839 First Edition, 2 vols. John Bouvier. LC 99-47231. 1187p. 1993. reprint ed. 130.00 (*0-9630106-7-0*) Lawbk Exchange.

Law Dictionary: English to Hindi. K. Chopra. 444p. 1977. 60.00 (*0-7855-1395-7*) St Mut.

Law Dictionary: Explaining the Rise, Progress & Present State of the English Law, Defining & Interpreting the Terms or Words of Art & Comprising Copious Information on the Subjects of Law, Trade & Government, 1811. Thomas E. Tomlins & Giles Jacob. LC 98-49349. 2000. 495.00 (*1-886363-68-4*) Lawbk Exchange.

Law Dictionary: Pocket Edition. Blacks. LC 96-231638. 1996. pap. text 26.00 (*0-314-06690-X*) West Pub.

Law Dictionary: Pronouncing Edition. 7th ed. Amy B. Brann. LC 96-45448. 1996. pap. 19.95 (*0-87084-517-9*) Anderson Pub Co.

Law Dictionary: Technical Dictionary of the Anglo-American Legal Terminology Including Commercial & Political Terms: English-German. 4th ed. Dora V. Beseler & Barbara Jacobs-Wuestefeld. LC 86-4496. 1986. 306.15 (*3-11-010429-6*) De Gruyter.

Law Dictionary & Glossary: Containing Full Definitions of the Principal Terms of the Common & Civil Law, 2 vols., Vol. 2. 2nd ed. Alexander M. Burrill. 658p. 1987. reprint ed. lib. bdg. write for info. (*0-318-62142-8*) W S Hein.

Law Dictionary & Glossary: Containing Full Definitions of the Principal Terms of the Common & Civil Law, Together with Translations & Explanations of the Various Technical Phrases in Different Languages, Occuring in the Ancient & Modern Reports, & Standard Treaties; Embracing, Also, All the Principal Common & Civil Law Maxims. Compiled on the Basis of Spelman's Glossary, & Adapted to the Jurisprudence of the United States;, 2 vols., Vol. 1. 2nd ed. Alexander M. Burrill. xxv, 700p. 1987. reprint ed. 145.00 (*0-8377-1946-1*, Rothman) W S Hein.

Law Dictionary & Glossary: Primarily for the Use of Students but Adapted Also to the Use of the Profession at Large. J. Kendrick Kinney. iv, 706p. 1987. reprint ed. 75.00 (*0-8377-2334-5*, Rothman) W S Hein.

Law Dictionary Containing Definitions of the Terms & Phrases of American & English Jurisprudence, Ancient & Modern, 1910 Second Edition. 2nd ed. Henry C. Black. LC 97-10320. 1314p. 1995. reprint ed. 125.00 (*1-886363-10-2*) Lawbk Exchange.

Law Dictionary (Diccionario de Derecho) 11th ed. R. De Pina. (SPA.). 514p. 1983. 69.95 (*0-8288-1531-3*, S12345) Fr & Eur.

Law Dictionary (English-Arabic) Ibrahim Al-Wahab. 320p. 1972. 29.95 (*0-86685-082-1*, LDL0811, Pub. by Librairie du Liban) Intl Bk Ctr.

Law Dictionary (English to Hindi) K. Chopra. (C). 1992. 140.00 (*0-89771-779-1*, Pub. by Eastern Book) St Mut.

Law Dictionary (English to Hindi) Pocket. K. Chopra. (C). 1991. 110.00 (*0-7855-5593-5*) St Mut.

Law Dictionary (Fachworterbuch der Anglo-Amerikanische Rechtssprache Einschliesslich Wirtschaftlicher und Politischer Begriffe (Deutsch English)) Jacobs-Wustefeld Von Beseler. (GER.). xxiv, 1932p. (C). 1991. lib. bdg. 460.00 (*3-11-010716-3*) De Gruyter.

Law Dictionary for Non-Lawyers. 2nd ed. Daniel Oran. 337p. 1984. pap. text 13.75 (*0-314-85283-2*) West Pub.

Law Dictionary for Non-Lawyers. 3rd ed. Daniel Oran. 303p. 1991. pap. 15.50 (*0-314-87532-8*) West Pub.

Law Dictionary for Non-Lawyers. 3rd ed. Daniel Oran & Mark Tosti. 303p. (C). 1991. mass mkt. 20.00 (*0-314-87535-2*) West Pub.

***Law Dictionary for Non-Lawyers.** 4th ed. Daniel Oran. LC 99-49821. (Illus.). 350p. 1999. pap. 31.95 (*0-7668-1743-1*) Delmar.

Law Dictionary French-Arabic: Dictionnaire Juridique. Najjar. (ARA & FRE.). 1983. 40.00 (*0-86685-303-0*) Intl Bk Ctr.

Law Dictionary Italian-English. 2nd ed. F. De Francis. (ENG & ITA.). 1467p. 1996. 208.00 (*88-14-05001-5*, Pub. by Giuffre) IBD Ltd.

Law Economics. 2nd ed. Robert Cooter & Thomas Ulen. (Illus.). 481p. (C). 1997. text 84.00 (*0-673-46332-X*) Addson-Wesley Educ.

***Law Economics.** 3rd ed. (C). 1999. pap. text 0.00 (*0-321-06894-7*) Addson-Wesley Educ.

Law, Economics, & Philosophy: A Critical Introduction, with Applications to the Law of Torts. Ed. by Mark Kuperberg & Charles Beitz. (Philosophy & Society Ser.). 294p. 1983. pap. 29.50 (*0-8476-7302-2*) Rowman.

Law, Economics & Public Policy. Nicholas Mercuro & Timothy Ryan. Ed. by William Breit & Kenneth G. Elzinga. LC 84-4406. (Political Economy & Public Policy Ser.: Vol. 3). 184p. 1984. 78.50 (*0-89232-396-5*) Jai Pr.

Law Enforcement. Michael Green. 1998. 76.00 (*0-531-19417-5*) Watts.

Law Enforcement. Zachary A. Kelly. LC 99-28689. (Law & Order Ser.). 1999. write for info. (*0-86593-574-2*) Rourke Corp.

Law Enforcement. Zachary A. Kelly. LC 98-6027. (Law & Order Ser.). (J). 1998. write for info. (*0-86625-663-6*) Rourke Pub Grp.

Law Enforcement. 2nd ed. Linda Riekes. Date not set. pap. text, teacher ed. 21.95 (*0-314-91103-0*) West Pub.

Law Enforcement. 2nd ed. Linda Riekes. 1991. mass mkt. 26.75 (*0-314-47362-9*) West Pub.

Law Enforcement: An Introduction. Richard N. Holden. 304p. (C). 1991. text 51.80 (*0-13-524687-3*, 720802) P-H.

Law Enforcement - The Making of a Profession: A Comprehensive Guide for the Police to Achieve & Sustain Professionalism. Neal E. Trautman. 200p. 1988. pap. 29.95 (*0-398-06464-4*) C C Thomas.

Law Enforcement--The Making of a Profession: A Comprehensive Guide for the Police to Achieve & Sustain Professionalism. Neal E. Trautman. 200p. (C). 1988. 45.95 (*0-398-05459-2*) C C Thomas.

Law Enforcement Administrative File System. Barbara J. Birkland et al. (Illus.). 90p. 1987. pap. 19.95 (*0-937935-04-2*) Justice Syst Pr.

Law Enforcement & AIDS: Questions of Justice & Care. Ed. by Gad J. Bensinger & Cyprian Rowe. 58p. 1988. pap. text 7.00 (*0-942854-13-6*) Loyola U Crim.

Law Enforcement & Criminal Justice Associations & Research Centers. Sharon Lyles. 62p. 1996. pap. 5.00 (*0-16-060857-0*) USGPO.

Law Enforcement & Investigation Occupations. Jack Rudman. (Career Examination Ser.: C-3551). 1994. pap. 27.95 (*0-8373-3551-5*) Nat Learn.

Law Enforcement & Police Policy. Ed. by Fred Meyer & Ralph Baker. (C). 1979. pap. 15.00 (*0-918592-31-3*) Pol Studies.

Law Enforcement & Security Functions of State Departments. 75p. (Orig.). (C). 1994. pap. text 25.00 (*1-56806-145-5*) DIANE Pub.

Law Enforcement & the Deaf. rev. ed. Janet L. Duvall. (Illus.). 210p. (C). 1992. pap. text 32.50 (*1-882457-00-5*) Sharp Image.

Law Enforcement & the INS: A Participant Observation Study of Control Agents. George J. Weissinger. 152p. (C). 1996. lib. bdg. 34.50 (*0-7618-0287-8*) U Pr of Amer.

Law Enforcement & the Media: Information Leaks & the Atlanta Olympic Bombing Investigation : Hearing Before the Subcommittee on Terrorism, Technology, & Government Information of the Committee on the Judiciary, United States Senate, One Hundred Fourth Congress, Second Session, on Examining the Law Enforcement Information Leaks During the Atlanta Olympic Bombing Investigation, December 19, 1996. United States Staff. LC 97-215208. (S. Hrg. Ser.). iii, 51 p. 1997. write for info. (*0-16-055190-0*) USGPO.

Law Enforcement & the Youthful Offender: Delinquency & Juvenile Justice. 4th ed. Edward Eldefonso. LC 77-13331. 139p. 1983. pap. text 15.00 (*0-471-87380-2*) P-H.

Law Enforcement Book of Weapons, Ammunition & Training Procedures: Handguns, Rifles & Shotguns. Mason Williams. (Illus.). 544p. 1977. 88.95 (*0-398-03576-8*) C C Thomas.

Law Enforcement Candidate Record. Jack Rudman. (Career Examination Ser.: C-3600). 1994. pap. 29.95 (*0-8373-3600-7*) Nat Learn.

Law Enforcement Career Guide California. LC 96-11263. (Law Enforcement Library). 1996. pap. 20.00 (*1-57685-008-0*) LrningExprss.

Law Enforcement Career Guide Florida. LC 96-11285. (Law Enforcement Library). 1996. pap. 20.00 (*1-57685-016-1*) LrningExprss.

Law Enforcement Career Guide New Jersey. LC 96-4722. (Law Enforcement Library). 1996. pap. 20.00 (*1-57685-024-2*) LrningExprss.

Law Enforcement Career Guide New York. LC 96-4719. (Law Enforcement Library). 1996. pap. 20.00 (*1-57685-007-2*) LrningExprss.

Law Enforcement Career Guide Texas. Learning Express Staff. LC 96-76058. (Law Enforcement Library). 1996. pap. 20.00 (*1-57685-009-9*) LrningExprss.

Law Enforcement Career Planning. Thomas Mahoney. (Illus.). 92p. 1989. 29.95 (*0-398-05589-0*); pap. 20.95 (*0-398-06264-1*) C C Thomas.

Law Enforcement Career Starter. Mary Hesalroad. LC 98-3561. (Career Starters Ser.). 208p. 1998. pap. 14.95 (*1-57685-111-7*) LrningExprss.

Law Enforcement Counterintelligence. Lawrence B. Sulc. LC 96-60178. 200p. (Orig.). 1996. pap. 24.95 (*1-888644-74-5*) Varro Pr.

Law Enforcement Efforts to Combat International Money Laundering Through Black Market Peso Brokering: Hearing Before the Subcommittee on General Oversight & Investigations of the Committee on Banking & Financial Services, House of Representatives, One Hundred Fifth Congress, First Session, October 22, 1997. LC 98-161379. iii, 85p. 1997. write for info. (*0-16-056090-X*) USGPO.

***Law Enforcement Equipment in Australia: A Strategic Entry Report, 1999.** Compiled by Icon Group International. (Illus.). 133p. 1999. ring bd. 1330.00 incl. audio compact disk (*0-7418-1754-3*) Icon Grp.

Law Enforcement Ethics: A Reference Handbook. Joseph P. Hester. LC 97-25964. (Contemporary Ethical Issues Ser.). 250p. 1997. 39.50 (*0-87436-893-6*, FN-1701) ABC-CLIO.

Law Enforcement Exams. 3rd ed. Eve P. Steinberg. 216p. 1998. pap. 12.95 (*0-02-862200-6*, Arc) IDG Bks.

***Law Enforcement Exams.** 4th ed. Arco Editorial Staff. 224p. 2000. pap. 12.95 (*0-7645-6099-9*) IDG Bks.

Law Enforcement Firearms Training. 4th rev. ed. Daniel L. Barber. LC 86-50683. (Illus.). 205p. (Orig.). 1988. reprint ed. pap. text 12.95 (*0-938895-04-4*) D L Barber Ventures.

Law Enforcement Guide to Firearm Silencers. (Criminology Ser.). 1986. lib. bdg. 150.00 (*0-8490-3610-0*) Gordon Pr.

Law Enforcement Handbook. Desmond Rowland & James Bailey. LC 84-18840. 294p. reprint ed. pap. 91.20 (*0-7837-6686-6*, 204630200011) Bks Demand.

Law Enforcement in Colonial New York. Julius L. Goebel & T. Raymond Naughton. LC 71-108239. (Criminology, Law Enforcement, & Social Problems Ser.: No. 122). 1970. reprint ed. 38.00 (*0-87585-122-3*) Patterson Smith.

Law Enforcement in Europe: Building Effective Cooperation. Andre Bossard. LC 93-6574. 100p. 1993. pap. 7.95 (*0-942511-63-8*) OICJ.

Law Enforcement in Los Angeles: Los Angeles Police Department Annual Report, 1924. Los Angeles Police Department Staff. LC 74-3831. (Criminal Justice in America Ser.). 1974. reprint ed. 24.95 (*0-405-06151-X*) Ayer.

Law Enforcement in the Metropolis. Ed. by Donald M. McIntyre. LC 67-31465. (American Bar Foundation Publication Ser.). xvii, 219p. 1967. pap. 20.00 (*1-57588-319-8*, 304870) W S Hein.

Law Enforcement in the Territory of Hawaii. xii, 328p. 1996. reprint ed. 80.00 (*1-56169-222-0*) Gaunt.

***Law Enforcement in the United States.** James A. Conser & Gregory D. Russell. LC 99-45510. 2000. write for info. (*0-8342-1724-4*) Aspen Pub.

Law Enforcement in Tribal Areas. D. K. Ghosh. (C). 1987. 26.50 (*81-7024-100-6*, Pub. by Ashish Pub Hse) S Asia.

Law Enforcement in Washington State: The First 100 Years, 1889-1989. Harriet U. Fish. Ed. by Edward L. Mund. LC 89-50586. (Illus.). 319p. 1989. 25.00 (*0-926635-00-X*) H U Fish.

Law Enforcement Inc. Sidney Becker. 191p. 1973. 25.00 (*0-685-42287-9*) Okpaku Communications.

Law Enforcement Investigations: Observation, Identification, Undercover Operations, Interrogations, Fingerprinting, Polygraph Examinations, Firearms, Ammunition & Crime Scene Processing. 1991. lib. bdg. 79.95 (*0-8490-4235-6*) Gordon Pr.

Law Enforcement Liability Insurance: Current Status. (Illus.). 1991. 32.00 (*0-87326-086-4*) Intl City-Cnty Mgt.

Law Enforcement Management & Administrative Statistics, 1993: Data for Individual State & Local Agencies with 100 or More Officers. Brian A. Reaves & Pheny Z. Smith. (Illus.). 296p. (Orig.). (C). 1995. pap. text 50.00 (*0-7881-2441-2*) DIANE Pub.

***Law Enforcement Management & Administrative Statistics 1997: Data for Individual State & Local Agencies with 100 or More Officers.** Brian A. Reaves & Andrew L. Goldberg. (Illus.). 294p. 1999. pap. text 45.00 (*0-7881-8190-4*) DIANE Pub.

Law Enforcement Manual. Mark Adamson & Daniel DelBagno. 335p. (C). 1994. ring bd. 39.95 (*1-885682-01-8*) Princeton Educ.

Law Enforcement Manual. rev. ed. Mark Adamson et al. 340p. 1997. ring bd. 39.95 (*1-885682-10-7*) Princeton Educ.

Law Enforcement Manual. 3rd rev. ed. Michael A. Petrillo et al. 341p. 1999. ring bd. 39.95 (*1-885682-11-5*) Princeton Educ.

Law Enforcement Memorabilia: Price & Identification Guide. Monty McCord. LC 98-87373. (Illus.). 192p. 1999. per. 19.95 (*0-87341-697-X*) Krause Pubns.

Law Enforcement Officer & AIDS. 1991. lib. bdg. 75.95 (*0-8490-4947-4*) Gordon Pr.

Law Enforcement Officers Killed & Assaulted, 1992. (Illus.). 81p. (Orig.). (C). 1994. pap. text 25.00 (*0-7881-0455-1*) DIANE Pub.

Law Enforcement Officers Killed & Assaulted (1997) Ed. by James V. DeSarno. (Illus.). 93p. 1999. text 25.00 (*0-7881-7912-8*) DIANE Pub.

Law Enforcement Officers Training Manual. 1991. lib. bdg. 79.95 (*0-8490-5163-0*) Gordon Pr.

Law Enforcement on Indian Reservations after Oliphant vs. Suquamish Indian Tribes. 2.00 (*0-944253-07-5*) Inst Dev Indian Law.

Law Enforcement Operations & Management. Ed. by Marilyn D. McShane & Frank P. Williams, 3rd. LC 96-39143. (Criminal Justice Ser.: Vol. 1). 440p. 1997. text 81.00 (*0-8153-2508-8*) Garland.

Law Enforcement Patrol Operations: Police Systems & Practices. 4th ed. Larry D. Nichols. LC 98-67152. (Illus.). 546p. 1998. teacher ed. 45.00 (*0-8211-1311-9*) McCutchan.

Law Enforcement Planning: The Limits of an Economic Analysis, 6. Jeffrey L. Sedgwick. LC 84-4069. (Contributions in Criminology & Penology Ser.: No. 6). (Illus.). 198p. 1984. 52.95 (*0-313-23993-2*, SLE/, Greenwood Pr) Greenwood.

Law Enforcement Planning in South Dakota: A First Report. Donald C. Dahlin. 1970. 1.00 (*1-55614-057-6*) U of SD Gov Res Bur.

***Law Enforcement Policies & Practices Regarding Missing Children & Homeless Youth: Final Report (1993)** James J. Collins. (Illus.). 210p. (C). 1999. reprint ed. pap. text 30.00 (*0-7881-8639-6*) DIANE Pub.

Law Enforcement Policy Analysis: A Sampler. Ed. by Michael J. Bloom. (Illus.). 362p. (Orig.). 1995. pap. write for info. (*0-9648554-1-0*) Prior Plning.

Law Enforcement Report Writing I: Source Book: A Comprehensive Reference-Text. Susan D. Amirie & Abbas Amirie. LC 93-70806. (Illus.). 368p. (Orig.). (C). 1994. pap. 41.95 (*1-883317-00-2*) Acad Pr of Am.

Law Enforcement Report Writing II: Source Workbook: Exercises Accompanying Text. Susan D. Amirie & Abbas Amirie. LC 93-70804. (Illus.). 420p. (Orig.). (C). 1999. pap. 46.95 (*1-883317-01-0*) Acad Pr of Am.

Law Enforcement Report Writing I: Source Book (Reference-Text), 2 vols. 3rd rev. ed. Susan D. Amirie & Abbas Amirie. LC 93-70806. (Illus.). 345p. 1999. pap. text 41.95 (*1-883317-05-3*) Acad Pr of Am.

Law Enforcement Response to Environmental Crime. Joel Epstein et al. (Illus.). 79p. (C). 1995. pap. text 20.00 (*0-7881-2436-6*) DIANE Pub.

***Law Enforcement Street Guide.** Eric Swanson. LC 99-67466. (Illus.). 100p. 2000. 20.00 (*1-885003-33-1*, Pub. by R D Reed Pubs) Midpt Trade.

Law Enforcement Workbook: The Kingion Nonviolence Conflict Reconciliation Program - Strategies for Responding to Conflict & Violence. 2nd ed. David C. Jehnsen & Bernard LaFayette. (Illus.). 85p. 1999. pap. text, wbk. ed. 25.00 (*1-888615-06-0*) Inst Human Rghts.

Law Enforcement Workbook - Kingion Nonviolence Conflict Reconciliation Program: Strategies/or Responding to Conflict & Violence 1-Day Course. David C. Jehnsen & Bernard LaFayette. (Illus.). 17p. 1996. per. 14.50 (*1-888615-02-8*) Inst Human Rghts.

Law, Ethics & Medicine: Studies in Medical Law. P. D. Skegg. 1985. 75.00 (*0-19-825365-6*) OUP.

Law, Ethics & Pathology. Denis Baron. 160p. 1999. pap. 35.00 (*0-7506-0846-3*) Buttrwrth-Heinemann.

Law, Ethics & Reproductive Choice. Marcia M. Boumil. LC 94-15353. xii, 137p. 1994. pap. 35.00 (*0-8377-0365-4*, Rothman) W S Hein.

Law, Ethics & Reproductive Choice: An Anthology of Modern American Legal Humor. Marcia M. Boumil. xix, 165p. 1989. pap. text 27.50 (*0-8377-0356-5*, Rothman) W S Hein.

Law, Ethics, & the Visual Arts. 3rd ed. John H. Merryman & Albert E. Elsen. LC 98-21891. 1998. 270.00 (*90-411-0697-9*) Kluwer Law Intl.

Law, Ethics, & the Visual Arts, 2 vols., Set. 2nd ed. John H. Merryman & Albert E. Elsen. LC 79-65005. (Illus.). 960p. 1987. text 109.95 (*0-8122-8052-0*) U of Pa Pr.

Law Every Nurse Should Know. 5th ed. Helen Creighton. (Illus.). 335p. 1986. pap. text 39.50 (*0-7216-1832-4*, W B Saunders Co) Harcrt Hlth Sci Grp.

Law Extracts of N. Y. S. for the Criminal Justice Services. 205p. 2000. ring bd. 12.95 (*0-930137-07-8*) Looseleaf Law.

Law Extracts of New York City Administrative Code, Health Code & Charter. 130p. 2000. ring bd. 11.95 (*0-930137-15-9*) Looseleaf Law.

Law, Family, & Women: Toward a Legal Anthropology of Renaissance Italy. Thomas Kuehn. xiv, 430p. 1994. pap. text 17.95 (*0-226-45764-8*) U Ch Pr.

Law, Family, & Women: Toward a Legal Anthropology of Renaissance Italy. Thomas Kuehn. (Illus.). 430p. 1997. 46.00 (*0-226-45762-1*) U Ch Pr.

Law-Finders & Law Makers in Medieval England: Collected Studies in Legal & Constitutional History. Helen M. Cam. LC 79-13344. 240p. 1979. reprint ed. lib. bdg. 35.00 (*0-678-08062-3*) Kelley.

Law Firm Accounting. John P. Auinn. 340p. 1986. boxed set 90.00 (*0-318-23680-X*) NY Law Pub.

Law Firm Accounting. John P. Quinn. 340p. 1986. boxed set 65.00 (*0-318-22527-1*, 00602) Law Journal.

Law Firm & the Public Good. Robert A. Katzmann. LC 95-5692. 189p. (C). 1995. 38.95 (*0-8157-4864-7*); pap. 16.95 (*0-8157-4863-9*) Brookings.

Law Firm Breakups: The Law & Ethics of Grabbing & Leaving. Hillman. 1990. 110.00 (*0-316-36379-0*, Aspen Law & Bus) Aspen Pub.

Law Firm Management: A Business Approach. Ed. by Susan S. Samuelson. 480p. 1992. ring bd. 145.00 (*0-316-77002-7*, Aspen Law & Bus) Aspen Pub.

Law Firm Management Guide. Ed. by Robert I. Weil. 208p. 1988. ring bd. 175.00 (*1-888286-00-8*) Altman Weil.

Law Firm Pro Bono Resource Guide. Esther F. Lardent. (Illus.). 450p. 1998. pap. 149.95 (*0-9659548-2-X*) Pro Bono Inst.

Law Firm Set. Hillman. 1990. 110.00 (*0-316-36381-2*, Aspen Law & Bus) Aspen Pub.

Law Firms Managing for Profit. Ashley Balls. 152p. 1998. pap. 39.00 (*1-86287-280-5*, Pub. by Federation Pr) Gaunt.

***Law Firms's Quick Guide to Juris.** David L. Leitner. LC 99-23755. 1999. write for info. (*1-57073-669-3*) Amer Bar Assn.

Law for Accountancy Students. Richard Card & Jennifer James. 655p. 1994. pap. 38.00 (*0-406-02001-9*, UK, MICHIE) LEXIS Pub.

Law for Architects Builders & Engineers (Australia) R. L. Kemelfield. 1985. pap. 43.00 (*0-409-49342-2*, MICHIE) LEXIS Pub.

Law for Business. 5th ed. A. James Barnes et al. LC 93-12225. (Legal Studies in Business). 1080p. (C). 1993. text 68.95 (*0-256-11594-X*, Irwn McGrw-H) McGrw-H Hghr Educ.

Law for Business. 6th ed. A. James Barnes & Terry M. Dworkin. 1080p. (C). 1996. text 68.95 (*0-256-19355-X*, Irwn McGrw-H) McGrw-H Hghr Educ.

Law for Business. 6th rev. ed. Barnes. 1997. 32.50 (*0-256-26897-5*) McGraw.

***Law for Business.** 7th ed. A. James Barnes. LC 99-27985. 1200p. 1999. 86.25 (*0-07-365917-7*) McGraw.

Law for Business. 11th ed. Ashcroft. (LA - Business Law Ser.). (C). 1991. mass mkt. 22.50 (*0-538-81705-4*) S-W Pub.

Law For Business. 11th ed. Ashcroft. (LA - Business Law Ser.). (C). 1992. mass mkt. 24.25 (*0-538-81708-9*) S-W Pub.

Law for Business. 11th ed. John D. Ashcroft & Janet E. Ashcroft. (C). 1991. mass mkt. 40.75 (*0-538-81278-8*, LA92KA) S-W Pub.

Law for Business. 12th ed. John D. Ashcroft & Janet E. Ashcroft. LC 95-13763. (C). 1995. pap. 50.95 (*0-538-84545-7*) S-W Pub.

Law for Business. 12th ed. John D. Ashcroft et al. (LA - Business Law Ser.). (C). 1996. pap., student ed. 19.50 (*0-538-84576-7*); pap., student ed., wbk. ed. 10.50 (*0-538-84577-5*) S-W Pub.

Law for Business. 13th ed. John D. Ashcroft. LC 98-6014. (LA - Business Law Ser.). (C). 1998. pap. 72.95 (*0-538-88095-3*) S-W Pub.

Law for Business. 14th ed. John E. Adamson. (LA - Business Law Ser.). 1992. mass mkt. 49.95 (*0-538-60956-7*) S-W Pub.

Law for Business. 14th ed. Adamson & Norbert J. Mietus. (LA - Business Law Ser.). 1992. mass mkt., wbk. ed. 13.95 (*0-538-60957-5*) S-W Pub.

Law for Business. 14th abr. ed. Adamson & Norbert J. Mietus. (LA - Business Law Ser.). 1992. pap., wbk. ed. 9.95 (*0-538-60959-1*); mass mkt. 44.95 (*0-538-60958-3*) S-W Pub.

Law for Business & Personal Use. 15th ed. John E. Adamson. (LA - Business Law Ser.). (C). 1999. 62.95 (*0-538-68353-8*) S-W Pub.

Law for Business & Personal Use. 15th ed. John E. Adamson. (Business Law). (C). 1999. student ed., wbk. ed. 11.75 (*0-538-68354-6*) S-W Pub.

Law for Business Studies Students. Keith Owens. 536p. 1995. pap. 28.00 (*1-85941-133-9*, Pub. by Cavendish Pubng) Gaunt.

Law for Business Study Guide. 6th ed. James A. Barnes. 280p. (C). 1996. text, student ed. 23.12 (*0-256-25479-6*, Irwn McGrw-H) McGrw-H Hghr Educ.

Law for Cinemas & Videos. Vijay Malik. (C). 1990. 45.00 (*0-7855-5243-X*); text 95.00 (*0-89771-495-4*) St Mut.

***Law for Doctors.** Wai-Ching Leung. LC 00-20659. 224p. 2000. pap. 45.00 (*0-632-05243-0*) Blackwell Sci.

Law for Dummies. John Ventura. LC 96-77268. (For Dummies Ser.). 384p. 1996. pap. 19.99 (*1-56884-860-9*) IDG Bks.

Law for Engineers & Architects. 4th ed. Laurence Simpson & Essel R. Dillavou. LC 58-3219. 530p. reprint ed. pap. 164.30 (*0-608-12017-0*, 202284500030) Bks Demand.

Law for Estate Management Students. 3rd ed. Richard Card et al. 745p. 1990. pap. 44.00 (*0-406-51173-X*, UK, MICHIE) LEXIS Pub.

Law for European Business Studies. Edward S. Pearson. 480p. (Orig.). 1994. pap. 62.50 (*0-273-60474-0*, Pub. by Pitman Pub) Trans-Atl Phila.

Law for Global Business. Eric L. Richards. LC 93-48202. (Legal Studies in Business). (Illus.). 496p. (C). 1994. text 68.95 (*0-256-11372-6*, Irwn McGrw-H) McGrw-H Hghr Educ.

Law for Legal Executives, Pt. 1 Year 1. Timothy Blakemore & Brendan Greene. xxi, 350p. (C). 1991. pap. 60.00 (*1-85431-179-4*, Pub. by Blackstone Pr) Gaunt.

Law for Legal Executives, Pt. 1, Year 2. Timothy Blakemore et al. (C). 1992. 95.00 (*1-85431-194-8*, Pub. by Blackstone Pr) Gaunt.

Law for Legal Executives Pt. 1: Year One. 3rd ed. Timothy Blakemore & Brendan Greene. 1996. write for info. (*1-85431-583-8*, Pub. by Blackstone Pr) Gaunt.

Law for Legal Executives Pt. 1: Year Two. 2nd ed. Graham Rowley et al. 350p. pap. 38.00 (*1-85431-358-4*, Pub. by Blackstone Pr) Gaunt.

Law for Legal Executives Pt. 1: Year Two. 3rd ed. Graham Rowley et al. 400p. 1996. pap. 40.00 (*1-85431-590-0*, Pub. by Blackstone Pr) Gaunt.

Law for Librarians: A Handbook for Librarians in England & Wales. Ian T. McLeod. LC 90-32540. 174p. Date not set. reprint ed. pap. 54.00 (*0-608-20728-4*, 207182600002) Bks Demand.

Law for Living. Howard L. Oleck. 1967. 11.95 (*0-685-92669-9*); pap. 8.00 (*0-685-92670-2*) Prof Bks Serv.

Law for Nurses. Gill Korgaonka & Diana Tribe. 205p. 1995. pap. 32.00 (*1-85941-132-0*, Pub. by Cavendish Pubng) Gaunt.

Law for Personnel Managers: How to Hire the People You Need Without Discriminating. Robert L. Brady. 1982. pap. 24.95 (*1-55645-110-5*) Busn Legal Reports.

Law for Personnel Managers: How to Hire the People You Need Without Discriminating. rev. ed. Robert I. Brady. 1980. per. 25.46 (*1-55645-460-0*, 460) Busn Legal Reports.

Law for Professional Engineers. D. L. Marston. xi, 243p. write for info. (*0-07-548073-5*) McGraw.

***Law for Small Business Owners.** (Complete Idiot's Guide Ser.). 352p. 2000. 18.95 (*0-02-863962-6*) Macmillan Gen Ref.

Law for Social Workers. 3rd ed. Caroline Ball. LC 96-84398. 192p. 1996. 55.95 (*1-85742-326-7*, Pub. by Arena); pap. 29.95 (*1-85742-324-0*, Pub. by Arena) Ashgate Pub Co.

Law for Social Workers. 3rd ed. Hugh Brayne & Gerry Martin. 377p. 1993. 33.00 (*1-85431-288-X*, Pub. by Blackstone Pr) Gaunt.

Law for Social Workers. 4th ed. Hugh Brayne & Gerry Martin. 414p. 1995. pap. 30.00 (*1-85431-442-4*, Pub. by Blackstone Pr) Gaunt.

Law for Social Workers. 5th rev. ed. Hugh Brayne & Gerry Martin. LC 98-178677. 435p. 1997. pap. 36.00 (*1-85431-684-2*, Pub. by Blackstone Pr) Gaunt.

***Law for Social Workers.** 6th ed. Hugh Brayne & Gerry Martin. 479p. 1999. pap. 32.00 (*1-85431-888-8*, Pub. by Blackstone Pr) Gaunt.

Law for the Builder. Stephanie Own. (C). 1987. pap. text. write for info. (*0-582-41619-1*, Pub. by Addison-Wesley) Longman.

Law for the Construction Industry. 2nd ed. Stephanie Owen. xxii, 289p. 1997. pap. 31.00 (*0-582-28708-1*, 15706) Gaunt.

Law for the Elephant: Property & Social Behavior on the Overland Trail. John P. Reid. LC 79-26989. 447p. reprint ed. pap. 138.60 (*0-7837-5287-3*, 204504100005) Bks Demand.

Law for the Elephant: Property & Social Behavior on the Overland Trail. John P. Reid. LC 97-131833. 446p. 1997. reprint ed. pap. 15.00 (*0-87328-164-0*) Huntington Lib.

Law for the Elephant, Law for the Beaver: Essays in the Legal History of the North American West. Ed. by John McLaren et al. 336p. 1992. pap. 19.95 (*0-88977-072-7*) Ninth Judicial CHS.

Law for the Expert Witness. Daniel A. Bronstein. 256p. 1993. boxed set 85.00 (*0-87371-906-9*, L906) Lewis Pubs.

Law for the Expert Witness. 2nd ed. Daniel A. Bronstein. LC 98-49963. 230p. 1999. 49.95 (*0-8493-8135-5*) CRC Pr.

Law for the Horse Breeder. Kenneth A. Wood. 1985. 55.00 (*0-318-03007-1*) Wood Pubns.

Law for the Layman: An Annotated Bibliography of Self-Help Law Books. Frank G. Houdek. LC 91-16613. xiii, 214p. 1991. ring bd. 42.50 (*0-8377-0685-8*, Rothman) W S Hein.

Law for the Layperson: An Annotated Bibliography of Self-Help Law Books. 2nd ed. Jean S. McKnight. LC 96-39509. xvii, 228p. 1997. pap. 47.50 (*0-8377-0869-9*, Rothman) W S Hein.

Law for the Medical Office. (Illus.). xviii, 312p. (Orig.). 1984. pap. text 20.00 (*0-942732-00-6*); student ed. 20.00 (*0-942732-01-4*); 40.00 (*0-685-09161-9*) Am Med Assts.

Law for the Medical Profession. Andrew Dix et al. 336p. 1988. 70.00 (*0-409-49318-X*) Buttrwrth-Heinemann.

Law for the Medical Profession. 2nd ed. Kevin Nicholson & Rob Dixon. LC 96-228827. 350p. 1996. pap. text 67.50 (*0-7506-8929-3*) Buttrwrth-Heinemann.

Law for the Pharmacy Student. William E. Hassan. LC 78-135682. (Illus.). 293p. reprint ed. pap. 90.90 (*0-608-30680-0*, 201455400092) Bks Demand.

Law for the Physician. Carl E. Wasmuth. LC 66-23236. 583p. reprint ed. 180.80 (*0-8357-9409-1*, 201458700094) Bks Demand.

Law for the Small Business Owner. Margaret C. Jasper. (Legal Almanac Ser.). 128p. 1994. text 22.50 (*0-379-11186-1*) Oceana.

Law, Force & Diplomacy at Sea. Ken Booth. 250p. (C). 1985. 39.95 (*0-04-341027-8*); pap. text 18.95 (*0-04-341028-6*) Routledge.

Law, Foreign Policy & the East-West Detente. Ed. by Edward McWhinney. LC 65-899. 131p. reprint ed. pap. 40.70 (*0-608-30687-8*, 201432100089) Bks Demand.

Law from Anarchy to Utopia: An Exposition of the Logical, Epistemological, & Ontological Foundations ofthe Idea of Law, By an Inquiry into the Nature of Legal Propositions & the Basis of Legal Authority. Chhatrapati Singh. LC 85-25997. 322p. 1988. 65.00 (*0-19-561704-5*) OUP.

Law, Gender, & Injustice: A Legal History of U. S. Women. Joan Hoff. 525p. (C). 1991. text 60.00 (*0-8147-3467-7*) NYU Pr.

Law, Gender, & Injustice: A Legal History of U. S. Women. Joan Hoff. (C). 1994. pap. text 22.50 (*0-8147-3509-6*) NYU Pr.

Law Glossary: Being a Selection of the Greek, Latin, Saxon, French, Norman & Italian Sentences, Phrases & Maxims, Found in the Leading English & American Reports & Elementary Works 1856. 4th ed. Thomas Tayler. LC 99-47230. 580p. 1995. reprint ed. 65.00 (*1-886363-12-9*) Lawbk Exchange.

Law Governing Sales of Goods at Common Law & under the Uniform Sales Act. Samuel Williston. LC 98-17403. cix, 1304p. 1998. reprint ed. 175.00 (*0-8377-2793-6*, Rothman) W S Hein.

Law Guide to Teaching. Street. Date not set. pap. text 10.95 (*0-314-40814-2*) West Pub.

Law Handbook for Ohio Law Enforcement Officers. Donald G. Hanna & John R. Kleberg. 1979. pap. text 3.80 (*0-87563-170-3*) Stipes.

Law, Health & Medical Regulation. Shaun McVeigh & Sally Wheeler. (Contemporary Legal Issues Ser.). 250p. 1993. 81.95 (*1-85521-283-8*, Pub. by Dartmth Pub) Ashgate Pub Co.

Law, History, the Low Countries & Europe. R. C. Van Caenegem. LC 94-455. 224p. 1994. 55.00 (*1-85285-088-4*) Hambledon Press.

Law, Ideology & Punishment: Historical Critique of the Liberal Ideal of Criminal Justice. Alan W. Norrie. 244p. (C). 1990. lib. bdg. 108.00 (*0-7923-1013-6*, Pub. by Kluwer Academic) Kluwer Academic.

Law in a Business Context. Bill Cole. 264p. 1990. pap. 29.95 (*0-412-37520-6*) Thomson Learn.

Law in a Business Context. W. Cole et al. (Business in Context Ser.). 300p. 1990. pap. text 29.95 (*0-412-02731-3*, A4469, Chap & Hall NY) Chapman & Hall.

Law in a Changing Society. W. Friedmann. xxvi, 522p. 1988. reprint ed. 62.00 (*0-8377-2134-2*, Rothman) W S Hein.

Law in a Democratic Society. Morton A. Kaplan. LC 92-40244. 237p. (C). 1993. text 24.95 (*0-943852-89-7*) Prof World Peace.

Law in a Digital World. M. Ethan Katsh. (Illus.). 304p. 1995. text 55.00 (*0-19-508017-3*) OUP.

Law in a Therapeutic Key: Developments in Therapeutic Jurisprudence. Ed. by David B. Wexler & Bruce J. Winick. LC 96-85934. 1032p. 1996. pap. 65.00 (*0-89089-988-6*) Carolina Acad Pr.

Law in Action: Ethnomethodological & Conversation Analytic Approaches to Law. Max Travers & John F. Manzo. LC 97-37214. (Socio-Legal Studies). 302p. 1997. 77.95 (*1-84014-078-X*, K380.L388, Pub. by Ashgate Pub) Ashgate Pub Co.

Law in Afghanistan: A Study of the Constitutions, Matrimonial Law & the Judiciary. Mohammad H. Kamali. LC 86-182044. (Social, Economic & Political Studies of the Middle East). viii, 265 p. 1985. write for info. (*90-04-07128-8*) Brill Academic Pubs.

***Law in an Emerging Global Village: A Post-Westphalian Perspective.** Richard Falk. (Innovation in International Law Ser.). 1999. pap. text 22.95 (*1-57105-114-7*) Transnatl Pubs.

Law in an Emerging Global Village: A Post-Westphalian Perspective. Richard A. Falk. LC 98-35606. 1998. 95.00 (*1-57105-066-3*) Transnatl Pubs.

Law in Arkansas Public Schools. Paul E. Peterson. 114p. 1996. pap. text 15.00 (*0-9651331-0-9*) Clearwell Pr.

Law in Arkansas Public Schools. Paul E. Peterson. LC 94-11805. 96p. 1997. pap. 12.95 (*0-944436-21-8*) Pelican.

Law in Arkansas Public Schools. 3rd ed. Paul E. Peterson. 184p. (C). 1998. pap. text 20.00 (*0-9651331-1-7*) Clearwell Pr.

Law in Brief Encounters. W. Michael Reisman. LC 99-13730. 240p. 1999. 27.50 (*0-300-07569-3*) Yale U Pr.

Law in Civil Society. Richard D. Winfield. LC 94-42829. 216p. 1995. 29.95 (*0-7006-0698-X*); pap. 17.95 (*0-7006-0699-8*) U Pr of KS.

Law in Classical Athens. Douglas M. MacDowell. LC 78-54141. (Aspects of Greek & Roman Life Ser.). 280p. 1978. pap. text 16.95 (*0-8014-9365-X*) Cornell U Pr.

Law in Colonial Africa. Kristin Mann & Richard Roberts. LC 90-25784. (Social History of Africa Ser.). 264p. (C). 1991. pap. 22.95 (*0-435-08055-5*, 08055); text 45.00 (*0-435-08053-9*, 08053) Heinemann.

Law in Colonial Massachusetts, 1630 to 1800. Ed. by Daniel R. Coquillette. (Illus.). 608p. 1984. text 40.00 (*0-8139-1052-8*) U Pr of Va.

Law in Context. 2nd ed. Stephen Bottomley & Stephen Parker. 391p. 1997. pap. 54.00 (*1-86287-233-3*, Pub. by Federation Pr) Gaunt.

Law in Context: Enlarging a Discipline. William Twining. LC 97-182417. 372p. 1997. text 75.00 (*0-19-826483-6*) OUP.

Law in Culture & Society. Ed. by Laura Nader. LC 96-34175. 460p. 1997. pap. 19.95 (*0-520-20833-1*, Pub. by U CA Pr) Cal Prin Full Svc.

Law in Daily Life: A Collection of Legal Questions Connected with the Ordinary Events in Everyday Life. R. Von Jhering. xii, 169p. 1985. reprint ed. 35.00 (*0-8377-0743-9*, Rothman) W S Hein.

Law in Environmental Decision-Making: National, European, & International Perspectives. Ed. by TIm Jewell & Jenny Steele. 328p. 1998. text 90.00 (*0-19-826077-6*) OUP.

Law in Everyday Life. Ed. by Austin Sarat & Thomas R. Kearns. LC 93-31233. (Amherst Series in Law, Jurisprudence, & Social Theory). 296p. (Orig.). (C). 1995. pap. text 20.95 (*0-472-08345-7*, 08345) U of Mich Pr.

Law in Film: Resonance & Representation. David A. Black. LC 98-25506. 208p. 1999. 39.95 (*0-252-02459-1*); pap. 17.95 (*0-252-06765-7*) U of Ill Pr.

Law in Galatians. In-Gyu Hong. (Journal for the Study of the New Testament, Supplement Ser.: No. 81). 231p. 1993. 70.00 (*1-85075-391-1*, Pub. by Sheffield Acad) CUP Services.

***Law in Greater Europe: Towards a Common Legal Area: Studies in Honor of Heinrich Klebes.** Heinrich Klebes et al. LC 99-52739. 448p. 1999. 165.00 (*90-411-1306-1*) Kluwer Law Intl.

Law in History, 2 vols., Set. Ed. by David Sugarman. (International Library of Essays in Law & Legal Theory). 500p. (C). 1996. lib. bdg. 250.00 (*0-8147-8025-3*) NYU Pr.

Law in History, Vol. 1. Ed. by David Sugarman. LC 95-52778. (The International Library of Essays in Law & Theory, Areas Ser.: Vol. 17). (C). 1996. lib. bdg. 125.00 (*0-8147-8032-6*) NYU Pr.

Law in History, Vol. 2. Ed. by David Sugarman. LC 95-52778. (The International Library of Essays in Law & Theory, Areas Ser.: Vol. 17). (C). 1996. lib. bdg. 125.00 (*0-8147-8033-4*) NYU Pr.

Law in History, & Other Essays. Edward P. Cheyney. 1977. lib. bdg. 59.95 (*0-8490-2134-0*) Gordon Pr.

***Law in Its Own Right.** Henrik Palmer Olsen & Stuart Toddington. (Legal Theory Today Ser.). 124p. 1999. 35.00 (*1-84113-034-6*, Pub. by Hart Pub); 14.95 (*1-84113-028-1*, Pub. by Hart Pub) Intl Spec Bk.

Law in Japan: The Legal Order in a Changing Society. Arthur T. Von Mehren. LC 62-19226. 744p. reprint ed. pap. 200.00 (*0-7837-2342-3*, 205743000004) Bks Demand.

Law in Literature: An Annotated Bibliography of Law-Related Works. Ed. by Elizabeth V. Gemmette. LC 97-61546. vi, 331p. 1998. 49.50 (*0-87875-498-9*) Whitston Pub.

Law in Literature: Legal Themes in Drama. Ed. by Elizabeth V. Gemmette. x, 554p. 1995. 65.00 (*0-87875-468-7*); pap. 27.50 (*0-87875-471-7*) Whitston Pub.

Law in Literature: Legal Themes in Novellas. Ed. by Elizabeth V. Gemmette. x, 550p. 1996. 65.00 (*0-87875-485-7*); pap. 27.50 (*0-87875-487-3*) Whitston Pub.

Law in Literature: Legal Themes in Short Stories. Elizabeth V. Gemmette. LC 91-44010. 504p. 1992. text 59.95 (*0-275-94097-7*, C4097, Praeger Pubs) Greenwood.

Law in Literature: Legal Themes in Short Stories. Ed. by Elizabeth V. Gemmette. xvi, 448p. 1995. pap. 27.50 (*0-87875-472-5*) Whitston Pub.

Law in Medieval Life & Thought, No. 5. Edward B. King & Susan J. Ridyard. LC 82-50575. 273p. (Orig.). 1990. pap. 25.00 (*0-918769-25-6*) Univ South Pr.

Law in Modern Society. Roberto M. Unger. LC 74-27853. 309p. 1977. pap. 18.95 (*0-02-932880-2*) Free Pr.

Law in Motion: Proceedings of the World Law Conference, Brussels, 1996. Blanpain. LC 97-2852. 1997. 192.00 (*90-411-0386-4*) Kluwer Law Intl.

***Law in Optometric Practice.** Stephen P. Taylor. (Illus.). 192p. 2000. pap. 45.00 (*0-7506-4578-4*) Buttrwrth-Heinemann.

Law in Our Lives: An Introduction. David O. Friedrichs. LC 99-37461. (Illus.). 210p. (C). 2000. pap. text. write for info. (*1-891487-41-8*) Roxbury Pub Co.

Law in Paul's Thought. Hans Hubner. Ed. by John E. Riches. Tr. by James Greig. 186p. 1987. 39.95 (*0-567-09313-1*, Pub. by T & T Clark) Bks Intl VA.

An Asterisk (*) at the beginning of an entry indicates that the title is appearing for the first time.

Law in Philosophical Perspectives: My Philosophy of Law. Luc Wintgens. LC 99-30963. (Law & Philosophy Library). 1999. write for info. (0-7923-5796-5) Kluwer Academic.
Law (in Plain English) for Art & Craft Galleries. Leonard D. DuBoff. Ed. by Linda C. Ligon. 156p. 1993. pap. 14.95 (0-934026-87-4) Interweave.
Law (In Plain English) for Crafts. 5th ed. Leonard D. DuBoff. LC 98-72766. 224p. 1999. pap. 18.95 (1-58115-016-4) Allworth Pr.
Law in Plain English for Craftspeople. 3rd ed. Leonard D. DuBoff. 139p. 1993. reprint ed. pap. 12.95 (0-934026-82-3) Interweave.
Law (In Plain English) for Galleries. 2nd ed. Leonard D. DuBoff. 208p. 1999. pap. text 18.95 (1-58115-026-1) Allworth Pr.
Law (in Plain English) for Health Care Professionals. Leonard D. DuBoff. LC 92-39745. 206p. 1993. 39.95 (0-471-58001-5); pap. 14.95 (0-471-58002-3) Wiley.
Law (in Plain English) for Photographers. Leonard DuBoff. LC 95-75286. 208p. 1995. pap. 18.95 (1-880559-19-6) Allworth Pr.
Law in (Plain English) for Small Businesses. 2nd ed. Leonard D. DuBoff. LC 91-10582. 240p. 1991. 49.95 (0-471-53617-2); pap. 14.95 (0-471-53616-4) Wiley.
Law (in Plain English) for Small Businesses. 3rd rev. ed. Leonard DuBoff. LC 98-70406. 256p. 1998. pap. 19.95 (1-880559-95-1) Allworth Pr.
Law (in Plain English) for Writers. 2nd ed. Leonard D. DuBoff. LC 91-24391. 272p. (Orig.). 1992. pap. 14.95 (0-471-53615-6) Wiley.
Law in Policing: Legal Regulation & Policing Practice. David Dixon. LC 97-226. (Clarendon Studies in Criminology). 384p. 1997. text 78.00 (0-19-826476-3, Clarendon Pr) OUP.
Law in Quest of Itself. Lon L. Fuller. LC 75-41105. reprint ed. 32.50 (0-404-14665-1) AMS Pr.
Law in Quest of Itself, 1966. Lon L. Fuller. LC 99-32863. 1999. reprint ed. 45.00 (1-58477-016-3) Lawbk Exchange.
Law in Radically Different Cultures. John H. Barton et al. LC 82-24802. (American Casebook Ser.). 960p. (C). 1983. 65.00 (0-314-70396-9) West Pub.
Law in Religious Communities in the Roman Period: The Debate over Torah & Nomos in Post-Biblical Judaism & Early Christianity. Ed. by Peter Richardson & Stephen Westerholm. 152p. (C). 1991. pap. 16.95 (0-88920-201-X) W Laurier U Pr.
Law in Russia & the Other Post Soviet Republics No. 4: A Bibliographic Survey of English Language Literature, 1992-1995: Sequel to Soviet Law in English, Gorbachev's Law & Demise of the Soviet Union. annot. ed. Igor I. Kavass. LC 97-13958. Vol. 4. xii, 784p. 1997. 135.00 (1-57588-213-2, 309080) W S Hein.
Law in Shakespeare. 2nd ed. Cushman K. Davis. LC 72-163677. reprint ed. 34.50 (0-404-01988-9) AMS Pr.
Law in Shakespeare, 1883. Cushman K. Davis. LC 98-32333. 1999. 60.00 (1-886363-75-7) Lawbk Exchange.
Law in Social Work Practice. 2nd ed. Andrea Saltzman & David Furman. LC 98-39712. 455p. (C). 1999. pap. text 46.95 (0-8304-1517-3) Thomson Learn.
Law in Sport & Physical Activity. 2nd ed. Annie Clement. 254p. 1998. pap. text 40.00 (0-9658874-1-3) Sport & Law.
Law in the Apocrypha. Ralph Marcus. LC 29-9822. (Columbia University. Oriental Studies: No. 26). reprint ed. 27.50 (0-404-50516-3) AMS Pr.
Law in the Classroom. rev. ed. Mary J. Turner. 342p. 1984. pap. 25.50 (0-89994-297-0) Soc Sci Ed.
Law in the Crisis of Empire 379-455 AD: The Theodosian Dynasty & Its Questors. Tony Honore. (Illus.). 334p. 1998. text 85.00 (0-19-826078-4) OUP.
Law in the Digital Age: The Challenge of Research in Legal Information Centers - An Analytical Justification for Law Libraries. Dan F. Henke & Betty W. Taylor. LC 97-176937. (Law Library Information Reports: No. 19). (Illus.). 251p. 1996. pap. 50.00 (0-87802-108-6) Glanville.
Law in the Domains of Culture. Ed. by Austin Sarat & Thomas R. Kearns. (Illus.). 256p. (C). pap. text 19.95 (0-472-08701-0, 08701) U of Mich Pr.
Law in the Domains of Culture. Ed. by Austin Sarat & Thomas R. Kearns. LC 97-21205. (Amherst Series in Law, Jurisprudence, & Social Thought). 256p. (C). 1998. text 54.50 (0-472-10862-X, 10862) U of Mich Pr.
Law in the Health & Human Services: A Guide for Social Workers, Psychologists, Psychiatrists, & Related Professionals. Donald T. Dickson. LC 94-23670. 1995. 35.00 (0-02-907435-5) Free Pr.
Law in the Middle East Vol. 1: Origin & Development of Islamic Law. Ed. by Majid Khadduri & Herbert J. Liebesny. LC 80-1921. (Growth of Islam Ser.). (Illus.). 416p. (C). 1984. reprint ed. 47.50 (0-404-18974-1) AMS Pr.
Law in the People's Republic of China. Ed. by Ralph H. Folsom & John H. Minan. (C). 1989. lib. bdg. 353.50 (0-7923-0055-6) Kluwer Academic.
Law in the Practice of Psychiatry: A Handbook for Clinicians. Seymour L. Halleck. (Critical Issues in Psychiatry Ser.). 306p. 1980. 55.00 (0-306-40373-0, Plenum Trade) Perseus Pubng.
Law in the Schools. 4th ed. William D. Valente & Christine M. Valente. LC 97-30724. 398p. 1997. 75.00 (0-13-266321-X) P-H.
***Law in the Scriptures: With Explanations of the Law Terms & Legal References in Both the Old & the New Testaments.** fac. ed. Edward J. White. LC 99-59102. 2000. 80.00 (1-58477-076-7) Lawbk Exchange.
Law in the Scriptures: With Explanations of the Law Terms & Legal References in Both the Old & the New Testaments, 2 vols. Edward J. White. LC 90-55182. xxiv, 422p. 1990. reprint ed. 90.00 (0-912004-84-3) Gaunt.
Law in the Scriptures: With Explanations of the Law Terms & Legal References in Both the Old & the New Testaments. Edward J. White. xxiv, 422p. 1990. reprint ed. 95.00 (0-912004-83-5) Gaunt.
Law in the United States. Charles F. Abernathy. 1995. 45.00 (0-935328-76-9) Intl Law Inst.
Law in the United States: A General & Comparative View. Arthur T. Von Mehren. 126p. 1988. pap. 25.00 (90-6544-322-3) Kluwer Law Intl.
Law in the West. Ed. by David J. Langum. (Illus.). 96p. 1985. pap. 15.00 (0-89745-068-X) Sunflower U Pr.
***Law in the Western United States.** Ed. by Gordon Morris Bakken. LC 00-32610. Vol. 6. 448p. 2000. 49.95 (0-8061-3215-9) U of Okla Pr.
Law in the Workplace. American Bar Association, Public Education Staff. 80p. 1987. pap. 2.50 (0-318-36200-7, 235-0015) Amer Bar Assn.
Law in U. S. History: A Teacher Resource Manual. Ed. by Melinda R. Smith & Mary L. Williams. LC 83-10418. 335p. 1983. pap. 23.50 (0-89994-281-4) Soc Sci Ed.
Law, Institution & Legal Politics: Fundamental Problems of Legal Theory & Social Philosophy. Ota Weinberger. 294p. (C). 1991. lib. bdg. 137.50 (0-7923-1143-4, Pub. by Kluwer Academic) Kluwer Academic.
Law, Interpretation & Reality: Essays in Epistemology, Hermeneutics & Jurisprudence. Ed. by Patrick Nerhot. (Law & Philosophy Library). 470p. (C). 1990. lib. bdg. 207.50 (0-7923-0593-0, Pub. by Kluwer Academic) Kluwer Academic.
Law Is a Lady. Nora Roberts. (NR Flowers Ser.: No. 2). 1992. per. 3.59 (0-373-51002-0, 5-51002-9) Harlequin Bks.
Law Is for All: The Authorized Popular Commentary to the Book of the Law. rev. ed. Aleister Crowley. Ed. by Louis U. Wilkinson. LC 96-68645. (Illus.). 304p. 1996. pap. 16.95 (1-56184-090-4) New Falcon Pubns.
Law Is Justice: Notable Opinions of Mr. Justice Cardozo, 1938. Benjamin N. Cardozo. Ed. by A. L. Sainer. LC 99-34154. 1999. reprint ed. 75.00 (1-58477-010-4) Lawbk Exchange.
Law Is No Lady. Helen R. Myers. (Montana Mavericks Ser.). 1995. per. 3.99 (0-373-50172-2, 1-50172-5) Harlequin Bks.
Law Is the Law. unabridged ed. S. Gianinazzi. 1998. pap. 14.95 (1-893336-06-9) B Newton.
Law, Judges & Justice. W. A. Wells. 181p. 1991. pap. 18.00 (0-409-30130-2, Austral, MICHIE) LEXIS Pub.
Law, Justice, & the Individual in Society: Psychological & Legal Issues, 1977. Levine Tapp. 446p. (C). text. write for info. (0-318-69130-2) Harcourt Coll Pubs.
Law, Labor, & Ideology in the Early American Republic. Christopher L. Tomlins. LC 92-17452. 424p. (C). 1993. text 74.95 (0-521-43278-2); pap. text 21.95 (0-521-43857-8) Cambridge U Pr.
Law, Land, & Family: Aristocratic Inheritance in England, 1300 to 1800. Eileen Spring. LC 93-590. 212p. (C). 1997. pap. 18.95 (0-8078-4642-2) U of NC Pr.
Law, Language, & Ethics. William Bishin & Stone. 1972. text 38.00 (0-88277-379-8) Foundation Pr.
Law, Language, & Legal Determinancy. Brian Bix. 232p. (C). 1993. text 49.95 (0-19-825790-2, 8942) OUP.
Law, Language, & Legal Determinancy. Brian Bix. 232p. 1996. pap. text 32.00 (0-19-826050-4) OUP.
Law Law Law on the Internet: The Best Legal Sites & More. Erik J. Heels. LC 98-70596. 1998. pap. 39.95 (1-57073-553-0) Amer Bar Assn.
***Law, Law Reform & the Family.** Stephen Michael Cretney. LC 98-38625. 420p. 1999. 80.00 (0-19-826871-8) OUP.
Law, Lawyers & Lambs. Stillman F. Kneeland. vii, 124p. 1992. reprint ed. 32.50 (0-8377-2341-8, Rothman) W S Hein.
Law Legal Reasoning. Fischer. Date not set. text 54.75 (0-314-33232-4) West Pub.
Law, Legend, & Incest in the Bible: Leviticus 18-20. Calum M. Carmichael. LC 96-52609. 224p. 1996. text 35.00 (0-8014-3388-6) Cornell U Pr.
Law, Legislation & Liberty Vol. 1: Rules & Order. Friedrich A. Hayek. LC 73-82488. 192p. 1978. pap. text 16.00 (0-226-32086-3, P763) U Ch Pr.
Law, Legislation & Liberty Vol. 2: The Mirage of Social Justice. Friedrich A. Hayek. LC 73-82488. 210p. 1978. pap. text 19.00 (0-226-32083-9, P799) U Ch Pr.
Law, Legislation & Liberty Vol. 2: The Mirage of Social Justice. Friedrich A. Hayek. LC 73-82488. 210p. 1999. lib. bdg. 22.00 (0-226-32082-0) U Ch Pr.
Law, Legislation & Liberty Vol. 3: The Political Order of a Free People. Friedrich A. Hayek. 260p. 1981. pap. text 16.95 (0-226-32090-1) U Ch Pr.
Law, Legislative & Municipal Reference Libraries. John B. Kaiser. LC 85-60264. (Legal Bibliographic & Research Reprint Ser.: Vol. 7). 486p. 1985. reprint ed. lib. bdg. 48.50 (0-89941-400-1, 303670) W S Hein.
Law Lesson Plans. Lee P. Arbetman. Date not set. write for info. (0-314-04649-6) West Pub.
Law Lexicon. A. Aiyar. (C). 1990. 165.00 (0-89771-131-9) St Mut.
Law Lexicon: or Dictionary of Jurisprudence: Explaining All the Technical Words & Phrases Employed in the Several Departments of English Law, Including Also the Various Legal Terms Used in Commercial Transactions; Together with an Explanatory As Well As Literal Translation of the Latin Maxims Contained in the Writings of the Ancient & Modern Commentators. J. J. Wharton. vii, 1073p. 1987. reprint ed. 95.00 (0-8377-2740-5, Rothman) W S Hein.
Law, Liability, & Ethics. 3rd ed. Myrtle Flight. LC 97-9100. 336p. (C). 1997. pap. 43.95 (0-8273-8183-2) Delmar.
Law, Liability & Ethics - IML. 3rd ed. Flight. 112p. 1997. teacher ed. 12.00 (0-8273-8184-0) Delmar.
Law, Liability & Ethics for Medical Office Personnel. 2nd ed. Myrtle Flight. LC 92-48661. 258p. 1993. pap. 27.95 (0-8273-3973-9) Delmar.
Law, Liability, & Ethics for Medical Office Personnel: Instructor's Guide. 2nd ed. Myrtle Flight. 58p. 1994. pap. 14.00 (0-8273-3974-7) Delmar.
Law, Liberalism & Free Speech. D. F. Tucker. LC 85-14449. (Philosophy & Society Ser.). 224p. (C). 1986. 62.50 (0-8476-7466-5); pap. text 22.50 (0-8476-7506-8) Rowman.
Law, Liberty & Australian Democracy. B. Gaze & M. Jones. xxxvi, 505p. 1990. pap. 69.00 (0-455-20986-3, Pub. by LawBk Co) Gaunt.
Law, Liberty & Economic Growth. Gerald W. Scully. 20p. 1994. pap. 10.00 (1-56808-053-0, 189) Natl Ctr Pol.
Law, Liberty, & Justice: The Legal Foundations of British Constitutionalism. T. R. Allan. LC 94-36743. 316p. 1995. pap. text 34.00 (0-19-825991-3) OUP.
Law, Liberty & Love. Columbia Cary-Elwes. 256p. 1950. 10.00 (0-8159-6104-9) Devin.
Law, Liberty, & Morality. Herbert L. Hart. LC 62-18743. viii, 88p. 1963. pap. 9.95 (0-8047-0154-7) Stanford U Pr.
Law, Liberty, & Psychiatry: An Inquiry into the Social Uses of Mental Health Practices. Thomas Szasz. LC 63-14187. 296p. 1989. reprint ed. pap. 19.95 (0-8156-0242-1) Syracuse U Pr.
Law Librarianship: A Handbook, 2 vols. Ed. by Heinz P. Mueller et al. No. 19. 1983. write for info. (0-318-57950-2); write for info. (0-318-57951-0) W S Hein.
Law Librarianship: A Handbook, 2 vols., Set. Ed. by Heinz P. Mueller et al. (AALL Publications Ser.: No. 19). 1983. 95.00 (0-8377-0116-3, Rothman) W S Hein.
Law Librarianship: A Handbook for the Electronic Age. Patrick E. Kehoe et al. LC 94-12344. (AALL Publications Ser.: No. 47). xxix, 650p. 1995. 67.50 (0-8377-0147-3, Rothman) W S Hein.
Law Librarianship: Historical Perspectives. American Association of Law Libraries Staff. Ed. by Laura N. Gasaway & Michael G. Chiorazzi. LC 96-9121. (AAAL Publications: No. 52). xxi, 664p. 1996. 75.00 (0-8377-0149-X, Rothman) W S Hein.
Law Library. Peter W. Dixon. 250p. (Orig.). 1988. pap. 4.95 (0-317-91056-6) Lantern Bks.
Law Library - A Living Trust: Proceedings. Institute for Law Librarians, 1963 Staff. (AALL Publications Ser.: No. 7). vi, 58p. 1964. reprint ed. pap. 12.50 (0-8377-0105-8, Rothman) W S Hein.
Law Library Budget & Expenditure Report. Primary Research Staff. 110p. 1993. ring bd. 75.00 (0-9626749-4-X) Primary Research.
Law Library Clerk. Jack Rudman. (Career Examination Ser.: C-2888). 1994. pap. 23.95 (0-8373-2888-8) Nat Learn.
Law Library Journal, 1908-1994, 88 vols., Set. 1996. 3060.00 (0-8377-9105-7, Rothman) W S Hein.
Law Library Management During Fiscal Austerity. Laura N. Gasaway et al. Ed. by Roy M. Mersky. (Law Library Information Reports: Vol. 12). 99p. 1991. pap. 50.00 (0-87802-092-6) Glanville.
Law Library Move: Planning, Preparation & Execution. Miriam A. Murphy et al. LC 97-176940. (Law Library Information Reports: Vol. 18). 1994. pap. 50.00 (0-87802-097-7) Glanville.
Law Library Preservation Issues: An Introduction to Imaging Technology in Law Libraries. C. Taylor Fitchett & Nicholas D. Finke. (Law Library Information Reports: Vol. 17). 1994. pap. 50.00 (0-87802-096-9) Glanville.
Law Library Preservation Issues: Books, Microforms & Electronic Media. Stephen G. Margeton & Willis C. Meredith. (Law Library Information Reports: Vol. 16). 85p. 1994. pap. 50.00 (0-87802-095-0) Glanville.
Law Library Reference Shelf: Annotated Subject Guide. 3rd rev. ed. Elizabeth W. Matthews. LC 95-42097. v, 229p. 1996. 47.50 (0-89941-991-7, 305600) W S Hein.
***Law Library Reference Shelf: Annotated Subject Guide.** 4th rev. ed. Elizabeth W. Matthews. LC 99-21881. vii, 213p. 1999. 48.50 (1-57588-501-8, 323850) W S Hein.
Law Library Staff Organization & Administration. Compiled by Martha J. Dragich & Peter C. Schanck. LC 90-9129. (AALL Publications Ser.: No. 39). xiv, 238p. 1990. 32.50 (0-8377-0137-6, Rothman) W S Hein.
Law Library Systems Directory. Ed. by Carol A. Nicholson et al. LC 93-2893. (American Association of Law Libraries Publications Ser.: No. 44). xix, 332p. 1993. 45.00 (0-8377-0146-5, Rothman) W S Hein.
Law Library Systems Directory. rev. ed. Ed. by Carol A. Nicholson. LC 96-24609. (AALL Publications: No. 53). xxxii, 502p. 1996. ring bd. 67.50 (0-8377-9326-2, Rothman) W S Hein.
Law, Life & Laughter. E. Kahn. 358p. 1992. 40.00 (0-7021-2693-4, Pub. by Juta & Co) Gaunt.
***Law, Life & Laughter Encore: Legal Anecdotes & Portraits from Southern Africa.** Ellison Kahn. LC 99-230528. (Illus.). 320p. 1999. pap. 42.50 (0-7021-4577-7, Pub. by Juta & Co) Gaunt.
Law, Life & Letters, 2 Vols. Frederick E. Birkenhead. LC 71-10997. (Essay Index Reprint Ser.). 1977. reprint ed. 42.95 (0-8369-1450-3) Ayer.
Law Life & Letters, 2 vols., Set. Earl of Birkenhead. 626p. 1996. reprint ed. 145.00 (1-56169-204-2) Gaunt.
Law, Life & Letters, Vol. 1. Frederick E. Smith. (Essay Index Reprint Ser.). 296p. 1982. reprint ed. lib. bdg. 21.50 (0-8290-0810-1) Irvington.
Law, Life & Letters, Vol. 2. Frederick E. Smith. (Essay Index Reprint Ser.). 326p. 1982. reprint ed. lib. bdg. 21.50 (0-8290-0781-4) Irvington.
Law Life & Society. Llewellyn. 1996. 29.95 (0-226-48791-1) U Ch Pr.
Law, Litigants & the Legal Profession. Ed. by E. W. Ives & A. H. Manchester. (Royal Historical Society Studies in History: No. 36). 247p. 1983. 75.00 (0-901050-91-1) Boydell & Brewer.
Law Machine. annuals 4th ed. Marcel Berlins & C. Dyer. 1994. pap. 15.95 (0-14-023478-0, Pub. by Pnguin Bks Ltd) Trafalgar.
Law Made Simple. Barker. 464p. Date not set. pap. text 19.95 (0-7506-2680-1) Buttrwrth-Heinemann.
Law, Magistracy & Crime in Old Regime Paris, 1735-1789 Vol. 1: The System of Criminal Justice. Richard M. Andrews. (Illus.). 630p. (C). 1994. text 80.00 (0-521-36169-9) Cambridge U Pr.
Law-Making & Society in Late Elizabethan England: The Parliament of England, 1584-1601. David Dean. LC 95-47585. (Cambridge Studies in Early Modern British History). 326p. (C). 1996. text 64.95 (0-521-55108-0) Cambridge U Pr.
Law Making in South Dakota. 3rd ed. Thomas C. Geary. 1958. 5.00 (1-55614-058-4) U of SD Gov Res Bur.
Law-Making in the International Civil Aviation Organization, Vol. 7. Thomas Buergenthal. LC 72-80016. (Procedural Aspects of International Law Ser.). xiii, 247p. 1969. 42.00 (0-8156-2139-6, 306520) W S Hein.
Law-Making in the International Community. Gennady M. Danilenko. LC 92-34503. (Developments in International Law Ser.: Vol. 15). 360p. 1993. lib. bdg. 123.50 (0-7923-2039-5) Kluwer Academic.
Law Making, Law Finding & Law Shaping: The Diverse Influences. The Clifford Chance Lectures, Vol. 2. Basil S. Markesinis. (Clifford Chance Lecture Ser.). 236p. (C). 1998. text 70.00 (0-19-826497-6) OUP.
Law-Making Process. 3rd ed. Michael Zander. (Law in Context Ser.). xxiv, 450p. 1989. 40.00 (0-297-79561-9) W S Hein.
Law-Making Process. 4th ed. Michael Zander. LC 95-129154. (Law in Context Ser.). 500p. (C). 1994. pap. text 44.00 (0-406-03502-4) Northwestern U Pr.
***Law-Making Process.** 5th ed. Michael Zander. 496p. 1999. pap. 39.95 (0-406-90409-X, Pub. by Buttrwrth Co Ltd) Northwestern U Pr.
Law, Medicine & Forensic Science. 3rd ed. William J. Curran & E. Donald Shapiro. LC 81-81207. 1181p. (C). 1982. 41.00 (0-316-16510-7, Aspen Law & Bus) Aspen Pub.
Law Medicine Notes: Progress in Medicolegal Relations. William J. Curran. Ed. by Arnold S. Relman. 450p. 1989. 38.50 (0-910133-26-3) Mass Med Pub Div.
Law-Medicine Relation - A Philosophical Exploration: Proceedings of the Eighth Trans-Disciplinary Symposium on Philosophy & Medicine Held at Farmington, Connecticut, November 9-11, 1978. Ed. by Stuart F. Spicker et al. (Philosophy & Medicine Ser.: No. 9). 322p. 1981. text 106.00 (90-277-1217-4) Kluwer Academic.
Law, Mental Health, & Mental Disorder. Ed. by Bruce D. Sales & Daniel W. Shuman. 560p. 1996. mass mkt. 88.95 (0-534-34090-3) Brooks-Cole.
Law Merchant: The Evolution of Commercial Law. Leon E. Trakman. xi, 195p. 1983. 35.00 (0-8377-1207-6, Rothman) W S Hein.
Law Merchant & Negotiable Instruments in Colonial New York, 1664-1730. Herbert A. Johnson. LC 62-20985. (Illus.). 93p. reprint ed. 30.00 (0-8357-9428-8, 201506500098) Bks Demand.
Law Miscellanies. Hugh H. Brackenridge. (Works of Hugh Henry Brackenridge). 1989. reprint ed. lib. bdg. 79.00 (0-7812-2048-3) Rprt Serv.
Law Miscellanies: Containing an Introduction to the Study of the Law. Hugh H. Brackenridge. LC 73-37967. (American Law: The Formative Years). 600p. 1972. reprint ed. 39.95 (0-405-03994-8) Ayer.
Law Modernity Postmodernity. Edgeworth. 78.95 (1-84014-009-7) Ashgate Pub Co.
Law, Morality & Religion: Global Perspectives. Calum Carmichael & David Daube. Ed. by Alan Watson. LC 96-27777. (Studies in Comparative Legal History). 226p. 1996. 40.00 (1-882239-08-3) Robbins Collection.
Law, Morality & Rights. M. A. Stewart. 464p. 1983. text 226.00 (90-277-1519-X, D Reidel) Kluwer Academic.
Law, Morality, & Society: Essays in Honour of H. L. A. Hart. Ed. by P. M. Hacker & Joseph Raz. 1979. pap. 22.50 (0-19-824610-2) OUP.
Law, Morality & Vietnam: The Peace Militants & the Courts. John F. Bannan & Rosemary S. Bannan. LC 73-16522. 253p. reprint ed. pap. 78.50 (0-608-30529-4, 201580900097) Bks Demand.
Law, Morality, & War in the Contemporary World. Richard A. Falk. LC 84-19288. 120p. 1984. reprint ed. lib. bdg. 59.50 (0-313-24682-3, FALM, Greenwood Pr) Greenwood.
Law, Narrative & Reality: An Essay in Intercepting Politics. G. Van Roermund. LC 97-14937. (Law & Philosophy Library). 1997. lib. bdg. 117.50 (0-7923-4621-1) Kluwer Academic.
"Law Never Here" A Social History of African American Responses to Issues of Crime & Justice. Frankie Y. Bailey & Alice P. Green. LC 98-38282. 264p. 1999. 65.00 (0-275-95303-3, Praeger Pubs) Greenwood.
Law Notes for Judges & Lawyers. Joseph W. Kirkpatrick. LC 63-19470. xli, 298p. 1963. lib. bdg. 36.00 (0-89941-602-0, 501890) W S Hein.
Law of Accountancy. Richard F. Fleck & Matthew Patient. 1995. boxed set. write for info. (0-406-02645-9, UK, MICHIE) LEXIS Pub.

L

An Asterisk (*) at the beginning of an entry indicates that the title is appearing for the first time.

L

Law of Adverse Possession. T. K. Murthy & Manatha Ram. (C). 1988. 100.00 (*0-7855-3533-0*) St Mut.

Law of Advertising, 4 vols. George E. Rosden & Peter E. Rosden. 1973. ring bd. 1030.00 (*0-8205-1357-1*) Bender.

Law of Advocates & Solicitors in Singapore & West Malaysia. Tan. 458p. 1991. boxed set 150.00 (*0-409-99593-2*, MICHIE) LEXIS Pub.

Law of Advocates & Solicitors in Singapore & West Malaysia. 2nd ed. Tan Yock Lin. LC 98-223400. cxiv, 1025 p. 1998. write for info. (*0-409-99944-X*) Buttrwrth-Heinemann.

Law of Affirmative Action: Twenty Five Years of Supreme Court Decisions on Race & Remedies. Girardeau A. Spann. LC 99-50402. 2000. text 40.00 (*0-8147-8140-3*) NYU Pr.

Law of Age Discrimination: A Reference Manual. Burton Fretz & Neal Dudovitz. 120p. (Orig.). 1987. pap. text 15.00 (*0-941077-17-9*, 42,450) NCLS Inc.

Law of Agency. V. G. Ramachandran. (C). 1985. 175.00 (*0-7855-5614-1*) St Mut.

Law of Agency. Richard Stone. 196p. 1996. pap. 32.00 (*1-874241-87-2*, Pub. by Cavendish Pubng) Gaunt.

Law of Agency. 2nd ed. Schiff & Leonard Lakin. 192p. (C). 1996. pap. text 28.95 (*0-7872-2318-2*) Kendall-Hunt.

Law of Agency. 3rd ed. A. J. Kerr. 386p. 1991. boxed set 107.00 (*0-409-03731-1*, SA, MICHIE) LEXIS Pub.

Law of Agency & Partnership: Student Edition. 2nd ed. Harold G. Reuschlein & William A. Gregory. (Hornbook Ser.). 683p. (C). 1990. 38.50 (*0-314-56279-6*) West Pub.

Law of Agricultural Tenancies in Scotland. Sir Crispin Agnew of Lochnaw. 250p. 1994. boxed set 88.00 (*0-406-11514-1*, UK, MICHIE) LEXIS Pub.

Law of Allotments. J. F. Garner. 1984. pap. 140.00 (*0-7219-0142-5*, Pub. by Scientific) St Mut.

Law of Apartment Ownership in West Bengal. Sunil K. Mitra. (C). 1989. 180.00 (*0-7855-4745-2*) St Mut.

Law of Arbitration. S. D. Singh. (C). 1991. text 230.00 (*0-89771-511-X*) St Mut.

Law of Arbitration. S. D. Singh. Ed. by G. C. Mathur. 1994. 125.00 (*81-7012-531-6*) St Mut.

Law of Arbitration. 2nd ed. Avtar Singh. (C). 1987. pap. 50.00 (*0-7855-5139-5*) St Mut.

Law of Arbitration. 4th rev. ed. Nathuni Lal. (C). 1983. 85.00 (*0-7855-5647-8*) St Mut.

Law of Arbitration. 9th rev. ed. S. D. Singh. (C). 1988. 200.00 (*0-7855-5645-1*) St Mut.

***Law of Aribration & Conciliation Act 1996.** Avtar Singh. 2000. pap. 45.00 (*81-7012-651-7*, Pub. by Eastern Book) St Mut.

Law of Arrest: Criminal Law & Other Proceedings, 2 vols., Set. Clarence Alexander. cvi, 2260p. 1949. lib. bdg. 78.00 (*0-89941-374-9*, 500210) W S Hein.

Law of Arrest, Bail, Search & Seizure. 2nd ed. R. L. Gupta. (C). 1991. 100.00 (*0-7855-5427-0*) St Mut.

Law of Arrest, Search, Seizure, & Liability Issues: Principles, Cases & Comments. Irving J. Klein. Ed. by Linda Diamond et al. LC 93-74910. (Criminal Justice & Law Ser.). 731p. (C). 1994. text 40.00 (*0-938993-17-8*) Coral Gables Pub.

Law of Arrest, Search, Seizure, & Liability Issues: Supplement. Irving J. Klein. Ed. by Marta Klein et al. 21p. 1995. pap. 7.95 (*0-938993-25-9*) Coral Gables Pub.

Law of Asset Forfeiture. Jimmy Gorole & Sandra Guerra. LC 98-85100. 1998. text 115.00 (*0-327-00119-4*, 60580-10) LEXIS Pub.

***Law of Asset Forfeiture, 1999 Supplement: Pocketpart.** Jimmy Gurule & Sandra Guerra. 80p. 1999. suppl. ed. write for info. (*0-327-01752-X*, 6057910) LEXIS Pub.

Law of Associations: An Operating Legal Manual for Executives & Counsel. 2nd ed. George D. Webster. 1975. ring bd. 255.00 (*0-8205-1364-4*) Bender.

Law of Asylum in the United States. 3rd rev. ed. Deborah Anker. LC 98-66970. 500p. 1998. pap. text 79.00 (*0-9665149-1-2*) Refugee Law Ctr.

Law of Athens, 002. A. R. Harrison. 616p. 1998. 80.00 (*0-87220-415-4*) Hackett Pub.

Law of Athens, 2 vols. A. R. Harrison. Ed. by D. M. MacDowell. Incl. Vol. 1. Law of Athens. LC 98-13464. 372p. (C). 1998. reprint ed. pap. 25.00 (*0-87220-410-3*); Vol. 2. LC 98-13464. 288p. (C). 1998. reprint ed. pap. 25.00 (*0-87220-412-X*); Set pap. 46.00 (*0-87220-414-6*) Hackett Pub.

Law of Athens see Law of Athens

Law of Attachment & Garnishment. Joan F. Garrett. LC 95-211449. (Legal Almanac Ser.). 116p. 1995. text 22.50 (*0-379-11189-6*) Oceana.

Law of Attraction. Penny Jordan. (Presents Ser.). 1994. per. 2.99 (*0-373-11705-1*, 1-11705-0) Harlequin Bks.

***Law of Attraction.** Penny Jordan. 2000. mass mkt. 4.50 (*0-373-63073-5*, 1-63073-0, Harlequin) Harlequin Bks.

Law of Automobile Insurance in South Carolina. Burnet R. Maybank et al. LC 97-150000. 1997. pap. write for info. (*0-943856-43-4*, 535) SC Bar CLE.

***Law of Averages: New & Selected Stories.** Frederick Barthelme. 352p. 2000. 25.00 (*1-58243-115-9*, Pub. by Counterpt DC) HarpC.

***Law of Aviation.** Rowland W. Fixel. LC 99-73234. 150p. 1999. 125.00 (*1-56169-528-9*) Gaunt.

Law of Bails, Forfeiture of Bonds & Habeas Corpus. K. C. Mehrotra. 391p. 1985. 240.00 (*0-7855-1457-0*) St Mut.

Law of Bails, Forfeiture of Bonds & Habeas Corpus. A. N. Saha. (C). 1990. 75.00 (*0-7855-5345-2*) St Mut.

Law of Bails, Forfeiture of Bonds & Habeas Corpus, 1985: With Supplement. 2nd rev. ed. K. C. Mehrotra. (C). 1990. 100.00 (*0-7855-5545-5*) St Mut.

Law of Bails with Model Forms. T. Iyer. (C). 1988. 160.00 (*0-7855-3539-X*) St Mut.

***Law of Balance.** Melford Okilo. 26p. 1999. pap. text 5.00 (*1-879605-61-9*) U Sci & Philos.

Law of Bank Deposits, Collections & Credit Cards. Barkley Clark. 1990. suppl. ed. 145.00 (*0-7913-0484-1*) Warren Gorham & Lamont.

Law of Bank Deposits, Collecfions & Credit Cards. Barkley Clark. 1991. suppl. ed. 48.00 (*0-7913-1050-7*) Warren Gorham & Lamont.

Law of Bankruptcy. Charles J. Tabb. LC 98-148089. (University Casebook Ser.). 1050p. 1997. text 38.25 (*1-56662-475-4*) Foundation Pr.

Law of Bankruptcy in Scotland. David C. Coull. 395p. 1989. boxed set 114.00 (*0-406-10170-1*, U.K., MICHIE) LEXIS Pub.

Law of Baron & Femme, of Parent & Child, Guardian & Ward, Master & Servant & of the Powers of the Courts of Chancery: With an Essay on the Terms Heir, Heirs, Heirs of the Body, 1862. 3rd ed. Tapping Reeve et al. LC 98-36057. 1998. reprint ed. 75.00 (*1-886363-58-7*) Lawbk Exchange.

Law of Baron & Femme, of Parent & Child, of Guardian & Ward, of Master & Servant, & of the Powers of Court of Chancery. Tapping Reeve. Ed. by R H. Helmholz & Bernard D. Reams, Jr. LC 80-84865. (Historical Writings in Law & Jurisprudence Ser.: No. 11, Bk. 14). x, 502p. 1981. reprint ed. lib. bdg. 52.50 (*0-89941-066-9*, 301320) W S Hein.

Law of Becoming. Kate Elliott. (Jaran Ser.: No. 4). 732p. 1994. mass mkt. 5.99 (*0-88677-580-9*, Pub. by DAW Bks) Penguin Putnam.

Law of Being (1920) Helen Boulnois. 112p. 1998. reprint ed. pap. 12.95 (*0-7661-0556-3*) Kessinger Pub.

Law of Benami Transactions. A. Ghosh's. 464p. 1987. 170.00 (*0-7855-2242-5*, Pub. by R Cambray) St Mut.

Law of Betting, Gaming & Lotteries. Ed. by Colin Smith & Stephen Monkcom. 1987. 264.00 (*0-406-29659-6*, U.K., MICHIE) LEXIS Pub.

Law of Bias & Malafides. A. S. Misra. 298p. 1985. 129.00 (*0-7855-7581-2*) St Mut.

Law of Bias & Malafides. 3rd rev. ed. A. S. Misra. (C). 1986. 75.00 (*0-7855-5640-0*) St Mut.

Law of Bills, Notes, & Checks: Illustrated by Leading Cases. 2nd ed. Melville M. Bigelow. LC 96-42490. xliii, 692p. 1996. reprint ed. 75.00 (*0-8377-1983-6*, Rothman) W S Hein.

Law of Blockade. James P. Deane. Ed. by Igor I. Kavass & Adolf Sprudzs. LC 72-76351. (International Military Law & History Ser.: Vol. 5). 218p. 1972. reprint ed. lib. bdg. 39.50 (*0-930342-42-9*, 300230) W S Hein.

Law of Breathing & Chest Development. Robert B. Armitage. 170p. 1996. reprint ed. spiral bd. 13.00 (*0-7873-0040-3*) Hlth Research.

Law of Building & Engineering Contracts & Arbitration. 4th ed. H. S. McKenzie. 349p. 1988. 86.00 (*0-7021-2066-9*, Pub. by Juta & Co) Gaunt.

Law of Business Contracts. Andrew J. Coppola. (Quality Paperback Ser.: No. 230). 190p. (Orig.). 1981. reprint ed. pap. 9.95 (*0-8226-0230-X*) Littlefield.

Law of Business Contracts in the Arab Middle East. Nayla Comair-Obeid. LC 96-17767. (Arab & Islamic Law Ser.). 1996. 175.00 (*90-411-0216-7*) Kluwer Law Intl.

Law of Business Organization. 5th ed. Moye. LC 98-8350. (Paralegal Ser.). 976p. (C). 1998. pap. text 82.95 (*0-314-12806-9*) Delmar.

Law of Business Organization. 5th ed. Moye. 264p. 1998. pap. text, teacher ed. 15.95 (*0-7668-0391-0*) Delmar.

Law Of Business Organization 3. 3rd ed. John E. Moye. Ed. by Tubb. (SWC-Business Law). 692p. (C). 1989. mass mkt. 54.75 (*0-314-47359-9*) West Pub.

Law of Business Organizations. J. S. Covington, Jr. & Susanne W. Evans. LC 91-60808. (Undergraduate & Paralegal Studies). 303p. 1991. pap. 32.40 (*0-916081-22-2*) J Marshall Pub Co.

Law of Business Organizations. 4th ed. John E. Moye. Ed. by Hannan. LC 93-33053. 700p. (C). 1994. mass mkt. 55.25 (*0-314-01219-2*) West Pub.

Law of Business Organizations & Securities. 2nd ed. Robert A. Prentice. LC 93-34759. 879p. (C). 1993. 70.60 (*0-13-530189-0*) P-H.

Law of Buying & Selling. Margaret C. Jasper. LC 96-188004. (Legal Almanac Ser.). 1996. text 22.50 (*0-379-11236-1*) Oceana.

Law of Canadian Corporate Directors. Donaldson & Thorburn. 425p. write for info. (*0-409-80593-9*, MICHIE) LEXIS Pub.

Law of Capital Punishment. Margaret C. Jasper. LC 98-7740. (Legal Almanac Ser.). 110p. 1998. text 22.50 (*0-379-11331-7*) Oceana.

Law of Caribbean Marine Pollution, Vol. IELP. Winston Anderson. LC 97-2541. 1997. 210.00 (*90-411-0662-6*) Kluwer Law Intl.

Law of Carriage (Air, Land & Sea) 3rd ed. Avtar Singh. (C). 1993. 85.00 (*81-7012-494-8*, Pub. by Eastern Book) St Mut.

Law of Carriage of Goods by Land, Sea & Air. Jasper Ridley. Ed. by Geoffrey Whitehead. (C). 1982. pap. 110.00 (*0-7855-2308-1*, Pub. by Scientific) St Mut.

Law of Carriage (Road, Rail, Air & Sea) Avtar Singh. (C). 1988. 90.00 (*0-7855-3326-5*) St Mut.

Law of Causality & Its Limits. Philipp Frank. Ed. & Tr. by Robert S. Cohen from ENG. Tr. by Marie Neurath from ENG. LC 97-8414. (Vienna Circle Collection). 320p. 1998. text 140.50 (*0-7923-4551-7*) Kluwer Academic.

Law of Cause & Effect. Herbert L. Beierle. 1991. pap. 2.00 (*0-940480-23-9*) UNIPress.

Law of Cause & Effect in Ancient Java. J. Fontein. (Verhandelingen der Koninklijke Nederlandse Akademie van Wetenschappen, Afd. Letterkunde, Nieuwe Reeks Ser.: No. 104). 116p. 1989. pap. text 47.00 (*0-444-85670-6*) Elsevier.

Law of Central Sales Tax. 4th rev. ed. S. D. Singh. (C). 1985. 150.00 (*0-7855-5432-7*) St Mut.

Law of Cession. 2nd ed. S. Scott. 311p. 1990. pap. 45.00 (*0-7021-2550-4*, Pub. by Juta & Co) Gaunt.

Law of Chapter 93A: The Massachusetts Consumer & Business Protection Act. Michael C. Gilleran. LC 89-62936. 1989. 110.00 (*0-317-03804-4*) West Group.

Law of Chapter 93A: The Massachusetts Consumer & Business Protection Act. Michael C. Gilleran. LC 89-62936. 1993. suppl. ed. 60.00 (*0-317-06024-4*) West Group.

Law of Charitable Trusts. F. M. Bradshaw. 212p. 1982. boxed set 54.00 (*0-409-49070-9*, AT, MICHIE) LEXIS Pub.

Law of Charities: Cases & Materials - Singapore & Malaysia. K. L. Ter. 380p. 1985. 99.00 (*0-409-99503-7*, MICHIE) LEXIS Pub.

Law of Chattel Mortgages & Conditional Sales & Trust Receipts with Forms. Samuel W. Eager. xxxii, 1104p. 1941. lib. bdg. 38.00 (*0-89941-360-9*, 501870) W S Hein.

Law of Chemical & Pharmaceutical Invention: Patent & Nonpatent Protection. Jerome Rosenstock. 901p. ring bd. 155.00 (*0-316-75788-8*, 57888) Aspen Law.

Law of Chemical & Pharmaceutical Invention: Patent & Nonpatent Protection. Jerome Rosenstock. LC 98-31958. 1998. ring bd. 175.00 (*0-7355-0264-1*) Panel Pubs.

Law of Chemical Regulation & Hazardous Wastes, 3 vols., Set. Donald W. Stever. LC 86-2249. 1986. ring bd. 325.00 (*0-87632-495-2*) West Group.

Law of Child Custody. Margaret C. Jasper. LC 97-12498. (Legal Almanac Ser.). 92p. 1997. text 22.50 (*0-379-11237-X*) Oceana.

Law of Christian Healing. David B. Fitzgerald. 144p. 1977. reprint ed. spiral bd. 16.50 (*0-7873-0325-9*) Hlth Research.

Law of Church & State in America: An Historical Survey & Analysis, 5 vols. Dean M. Kelley. LC 96-41913. 1998. lib. bdg. write for info. (*0-313-29090-3*, Greenwood Pr) Greenwood.

Law of Church & State in America Vol. 1: An Analysis & Sourcebook: The Autonomy of Religious Bodies, Vol. 1. Dean M. Kelley. LC 96-41913. 1998. lib. bdg. write for info. (*0-313-27871-7*, Greenwood Pr) Greenwood.

Law of Church & State in America Vol. 2: An Analysis & Sourcebook: The Outreach Activities of Religious Bodies, Vol. 2. Dean M. Kelley. LC 96-41913. 1998. lib. bdg. write for info. (*0-313-27872-5*, Greenwood Pr) Greenwood.

Law of Church & State in America Vol. 3: An Analysis & Sourcebook: Inculcation of Faith by Religious Bodies, Vol. 3. Dean M. Kelley. LC 96-41913. 1998. lib. bdg. write for info. (*0-313-27873-3*, Greenwood Pr) Greenwood.

Law of Church & State in America Vol. 4: An Analysis & Sourcebook: Freedom for the Practice of Religion, Vol. 4. Dean M. Kelley. LC 96-41913. 1998. lib. bdg. write for info. (*0-313-27874-1*, Greenwood Pr) Greenwood.

Law of Church & State in America Vol. 5: An Analysis & Sourcebook: State Shelters for Religion, Vol. 5. Dean M. Kelley. LC 96-41913. 1998. lib. bdg. write for info. (*0-313-27875-X*, Greenwood Pr) Greenwood.

Law of Cinematograph, Cine Workers & Videos, Etc. B. R. Beotra. (C). 1990. 175.00 (*0-89771-187-4*) St Mut.

Law of Civil RICO. Peter D. Abrams. 1991. 145.00 (*0-316-00479-0*, Aspen Law & Bus) Aspen Pub.

Law of Civil RICO, Set. Douglas E. Abrams. 624p. 1991. boxed set 150.00 (*0-316-00449-9*, 04499, Aspen Law & Bus) Aspen Pub.

Law of Civilization & Decay. Henry (Brooks) Adams. 1975. 250.00 (*0-87968-235-3*) Gordon Pr.

Law of Civilization & Decay. Henry (Brooks) Adams. (Principle Works of Brooks Adams). 1989. reprint ed. lib. bdg. 79.00 (*0-685-27364-4*) Rprt Serv.

Law of Civilization & Decay: An Essay on History. Henry (Brooks) Adams. LC 71-37125. (Essay Index Reprint Ser.). 1977. reprint ed. 23.95 (*0-8369-2478-9*) Ayer.

Law of Co-Operatives. Ian Snaith. 148p. 1984. 49.00 (*0-08-039159-1*, Pergamon Pr) Elsevier.

***Law of Collateral & Direct Inheritance, Legacy, & Succession Taxes: Embracing All American & Many English Decisions with Forms for New York State ...** 2nd ed. Benj. F. Dos Passos. LC 99-73238. 654p. 1999. 170.00 (*1-56169-524-6*) Gaunt.

Law of Commercial Insurance. Mark S. Rhodes. 1992. 138.00 (*0-923240-00-4*) Stndrd Publishing.

Law of Commercial Paper. rev. ed. Andrew J. Coppola. LC 69-14862. (Quality Paperback Ser.: No. 232). (C). 1977. reprint ed. pap. 9.95 (*0-8226-0232-6*) Littlefield.

Law of Commercial Procedure of the United Arab Emirates: Issuing Law: Federal Law No. 18 of 1993. LC 94-15899. (Arab & Islamic Law Ser.). 1994. lib. bdg. 390.50 (*1-85966-080-0*) Kluwer Law Intl.

Law of Commercial Procedure of the United Arab Emirates: Issuing Law: Federal Law No. 18 of 1993. Tr. by Dawoud S. El Alami. (Arab & Islamic Laws Ser.). 214p. (C). 1994. lib. bdg. 330.00 (*1-85333-414-6*, Pub. by Graham & Trotman) Kluwer Academic.

Law of Commercial Transactions & Business Associations: Concepts & Cases. Thomas Bowers et al. LC 94-38814. (Legal Studies in Business). 976p. (C). 1994. text 64.50 (*0-256-17864-X*, Irwn McGrw-H) McGrw-H Hghr Educ.

Law of Commercial Trucking: Damages to Persons & Property. David Nissenberg. LC 94-77560. 1000p. 1994. 105.00 (*1-55834-165-X*, 65200-10, MICHIE) LEXIS Pub.

Law of Commercial Trucking: Damages to Persons & Property, 2 vols. 2nd ed. David N. Nissenberg. LC 98-87770. 1157 p. 1998. 127.00 (*0-327-00350-2*, 6520011) LEXIS Pub.

Law of Commercial Trucking: Damages to Persons & Property, Vol. 1. 2nd ed. David N. Nissenberg. LC 98-87770. 650p. 1998. write for info. (*0-327-00348-0*, 6520510) LEXIS Pub.

Law of Commercial Trucking: Damages to Persons & Property, Vol. 2. 2nd ed. David N. Nissenberg. LC 98-87770. 650p. 1998. write for info. (*0-327-00349-9*, 6520610) LEXIS Pub.

***Law of Commercial Trucking: Damages to Persons & Property, 1999 Supplement: Pocketpart, 2 vols.** 2nd ed. Incl. Vol. 1. 1999. (*0-327-01756-2*); Vol. 2. 1999. (*0-327-01757-0*); 90p. 1999. suppl. ed. write for info. (*0-327-01753-8*, 6520113) LEXIS Pub.

***Law of Company Liquidation.** 4th ed. Ed. by Andrew Keay. 1000p. 1999. 105.00 (*0-455-21647-9*, 18150, Pub. by LBC Info Servs); pap. 87.50 (*0-455-21646-0*, 18150, Pub. by LBC Info Servs) Gaunt.

Law of Company Receiverships in Australia & New Zealand. 2nd ed. Peter Blanchard. LC 95-141464. 1994. 168.00 (*0-409-31098-0*, AT, MICHIE) LEXIS Pub.

Law of Company Takeovers. Peter Little. 569p. 1997. pap. 100.00 (*0-455-21458-1*, Pub. by LawBk Co) Gaunt.

***Law of Comparative Advertising: Directive 97/55/EC in the United Kingdom & Germany.** Ansgar Ohly & Michael Spence. 144p. 1999. 54.00 (*1-84113-117-2*, Pub. by Hart Pub) Intl Spec Bk.

Law of Compulsory - Voluntary Retirement & Registration, Ion Government & Public Sector. A. Arora & M. Malhotra. (C). 1990. 100.00 (*0-89771-294-3*) St Mut.

Law of Compulsory Purchase & Compensation. 4th ed. Keith Davies. 400p. 1984. pap. 48.00 (*0-406-57188-0*, U.K., MICHIE) LEXIS Pub.

Law of Compulsory Purchase & Compensation. 5th ed. Keith Davies. 327p. 1994. 210.00 (*0-85459-922-3*, Pub. by Tolley Pubng) St Mut.

Law of Computer Related Technology Institute. 1984. 100.00 (*0-318-20243-3*, B-5); audio 60.00 (*0-317-01248-7*) Am IPLA.

Law of Computer Technology. 2nd ed. Raymond T. Nimmer. 688p. 1992. 149.50 (*0-7913-1270-4*) Warren Gorham & Lamont.

Law of Condominia & Property Owners' Associations. Warren Freedman & Jonathan B. Alter. LC 91-31949. 344p. 1992. 69.50 (*0-89930-654-3*, FLD/, Quorum Bks) Greenwood.

Law of Condominium Operations, 2 vols. Gary A. Poliakoff. LC 88-8150. (Real Property - Zoning Ser.). 1988. ring bd. 250.00 (*0-685-28164-7*) West Group.

Law of Conduct Rules. M. L. Jand. (C). 1990. 90.00 (*0-89771-290-0*) St Mut.

Law of Confessions. 2nd ed. David Nissman & Ed Hagen. LC 94-67910. 1994. 120.00 (*0-685-59837-3*) West Group.

Law of Conflicts & Foreign Trade. Ferenc Madl & L. Vekas. 379p. (C). 1987. 114.00 (*963-05-4274-9*, Pub. by Akade Kiado) St Mut.

***Law of Conflicts & of International Economic Relations.** Ferenc Madl & Lajos Vekas. 565p. 1998. 110.00 (*963-05-7525-6*, Pub. by Akade Kiado) Intl Spec Bk.

Law of Constructive Contempt: The Shepherd Case Reviewed. John L. Thomas. 270p. 1980. reprint ed. 37.50 (*0-8377-1203-3*, Rothman) W S Hein.

Law of Consumer Protection in India: Justice Within Reach. Gurjeet Singh. LC 98-908482. lvi, 542 p. 1996. write for info. (*81-7100-790-2*, Pub. by Deep & Deep Pubns) S Asia.

Law of Contract. R. H. Christie. LC 95-182395. (Key to Knowledge Ser.). 152p. 1995. pap. write for info. (*0-409-03788-5*, MICHIE) LEXIS Pub.

Law of Contract. D. W. Greig & J. L. Davis. xc, 1542p. 1987. suppl. ed. 155.00 (*0-455-20619-8*, Pub. by LawBk Co); pap., suppl. ed. 100.00 (*0-455-20620-1*, Pub. by LawBk Co); suppl. ed. 38.00 (*0-455-20998-7*, Pub. by LawBk Co); suppl. ed. 52.00 (*0-455-21209-0*, Pub. by LawBk Co) Gaunt.

Law of Contract. Laurence Koffman & Elizabeth MacDonald. 462p. 1992. 75.00 (*1-85190-161-2*, Pub. by Tolley Pubng) St Mut.

***Law of Contract.** Avtar Singh. 2000. pap. 100.00 (*81-7012-671-1*, Pub. by Eastern Book) St Mut.

Law of Contract. Avtar Singh. 1994. 59.00 (*81-7012-529-4*) St Mut.

Law of Contract. 2nd ed. Hugh Collins. LC 95-211352. (Law in Context Ser.). 428p. (C). 1994. pap. text 37.95 (*0-406-03147-9*) Northwestern U Pr.

Law of Contract. 2nd ed. Laurence Koffman & Elizabeth MacDonald. 564p. 1995. pap. 150.00 (*0-85459-999-1*, Pub. by Tolley Pubng) St Mut.

Law of Contract. 3rd ed. Laurence Koffman & Elizabeth Macdonald. 1998. pap. 27.00 (*1-86012-793-2*, LOC3, Pub. by Tolley Pubng) St Mut.

Law of Contract. 5th ed. Avtar Singh. (C). 1989. 90.00 (*0-7855-5137-9*) St Mut.

Law of Contract. 12th ed. Cheshire et al. 768p. 1991. 90.00 (*0-409-90625-5*, MICHIE) LEXIS Pub.

Law of Contract, 3 vols., Set. 2nd ed. V. G. Ramachandran. (C). 1989. suppl. ed. 500.00 (*0-7855-4697-9*) St Mut.

Law of Contract: Blackstone's Law Questions & Answers. 2nd ed. Ian Brown & Adrian Chandler. 307p. 1996. pap. 22.00 (*1-85431-494-7*, Pub. by Blackstone Pr) Gaunt.

Law of Contract During & After War: With Leading Cases, Statutes & Statutory Rules & Orders. 4th ed. William F. Trotter. xli, 727p. 1999. reprint ed. 195.00 (*1-56169-499-1*) Gaunt.

Law of Contract in South Africa. 2nd ed. 816p. 1991. pap. 108.00 (*0-409-01833-3*, SA, MICHIE); boxed set 136.00 (*0-409-01834-1*, SA, MICHIE) LEXIS Pub.

Law of Contract in Three Volumes. V. G. Ramachandran. (C). 1989. 500.00 (*0-89771-776-7*, Pub. by Eastern Book); pap. 300.00 (*0-7855-6805-0*, Pub. by Eastern Book) St Mut.

An Asterisk (*) at the beginning of an entry indicates that the title is appearing for the first time.

L

Law of Contracts. Margaret C. Jasper. LC 95-211447. (Legal Almanac Ser.). 112p. 1995. text 22.50 (*0-379-11192-6*) Oceana.

Law of Contracts. Matthew McKinnon. 464p. 1993. ring bd. 67.00 (*1-879581-08-6*) Lupus Pubns.

Law of Contracts. Pamela R. Tepper. (Paralegal Ser.). 1995. pap., teacher ed. 14.00 (*0-8273-6325-7*) Delmar.

Law of Contracts: A Course of Lectures. John W. Smith. xlvii, 487p. 1992. reprint ed. 57.50 (*0-8377-2649-2*, Rothman) W S Hein.

Law of Contracts & the Uniform Commercial Code. Pamela R. Tepper. LC 94-30039. 448p. (C). 1995. mass mkt. 71.95 (*0-8273-6324-9*) Delmar.

Law of Copyright, 2 vols. Howard B. Abrams. LC 91-4402. (IP Ser.). 1991. ring bd. 240.00 (*0-87632-741-2*) West Group.

Law of Copyright. Terence Prime. 337p. 1992. 110.00 (*1-85190-180-9*, Pub. by Tolley Pubng) St Mut.

*__Law of Copyright.__ 2nd ed. Margaret C. Jasper. LC 99-58626. (Legal Almanac Ser.). 1999. 22.50 (*0-379-11337-6*, 4582497) Oceana.

Law of Copyright, Competition & Industrial Property. Konrad E. Zweigert & Jan Kropholler. Ed. by Gert Kolle & Hans P. Hallstein. (Sources of International Uniform Law Ser.: Vol. III-A First Supplement). 1340p. 1980. lib. bdg. 388.00 (*90-286-0099-X*) Kluwer Academic.

Law of Copyright in Works & Literature & Art & in the Application of Designs: With the Statutes Relating Thereto. Charles P. Phillips. xvi, 261,cxiiip. 1989. reprint ed. 42.50 (*0-8377-1055-3*, Rothman) W S Hein.

Law of Corporate Groups: Problems in Bankruptcy or Reorganization of Parent & Subsidiary Corporations, Including the Law of Corporate Guarantees. Phillip I. Blumberg. LC 84-81755. 1985. 155.00 (*0-316-10033-1*, Aspen Law & Bus) Aspen Pub.

Law of Corporate Groups: Problems in Bankruptcy or Reorganization of Parent & Subsidiary Corporations, Including the Law of Corporate Guaranties. Phillip I. Blumberg. 860p. 1998. boxed set 170.00 (*0-316-10041-2*, Aspen Law & Bus) Aspen Pub.

Law of Corporate Groups: Problems of Parent & Subsidiary Corporations under State Statutory Law. Phillip I. Blumberg. (Law of Corporate Groups Ser.). 878p. 1998. boxed set 170.00 (*0-316-10226-1*, 02261) Aspen Law.

Law of Corporate Groups: Problems of Parent & Subsidiary Corporations under Statutory Law Specifically Applying Enterprise Principles. Phillip I. Blumberg. (Law of Corporate Groups Ser.). 1090p. boxed set 155.00 (*0-316-10139-7*, 01397) Aspen Law.

Law of Corporate Groups: Procedural Problems in the Law of Parent & Subsidiary Corporations. Phillip I. Blumberg. 527p. 1998. boxed set 170.00 (*0-316-10036-6*, Aspen Law & Bus) Aspen Pub.

Law of Corporate Groups: Substantive Law. Phillip I. Blumberg. LC 86-80930. (Law of Substantive Groups Ser.). 687p. 1987. 155.00 (*0-316-10038-2*, Aspen Law & Bus) Aspen Pub.

Law of Corporate Insolvency. (Waterlow Practitioner's Library). 912p. 1990. 140.00 (*0-08-039205-9*, 3003) Macmillan.

Law of Corporate Insolvency in Scotland. 2nd ed. John B. St. Clair & J. E. Young. 525p. 1992. boxed set 175.00 (*0-406-00910-4*, U.K., MICHIE) LEXIS Pub.

Law of Corporate Mortgage Bond Issues. Ralph A. McClelland. Ed. by Bernard D. Reams, Jr. LC 38-7784. (Historical Reprints in Jurisprudence & Classical Legal Literature Ser.). xiii, 1077p. 1983. reprint ed. lib. bdg. 87.50 (*0-89941-251-3*, 303230) W S Hein.

Law of Corporate Officers & Directors: Indemnification & Insurance. Joseph W. Bishop. LC 82-4383. 1990. 130.00 (*0-685-10649-7*) West Group.

Law of Corporate Officers & Directors: Rights, Duties, & Liabilities. Edward Brodsky & M. Patricia Adamski. LC 84-14310. 1990. 130.00 (*0-685-09579-7*) West Group.

Law of Corporations in a Nutshell. 3rd ed. Robert W. Hamilton. (Nutshell Ser.). 518p. 1993. reprint ed. pap. text 17.50 (*0-314-82446-4*) West Pub.

Law of Corporations in a Nutshell. 4th ed. Robert W. Hamilton. LC 96-8960. (Nutshell Ser.). 591p. (C). 1996. pap. 23.50 (*0-314-09874-7*) West Pub.

Law of Corporations, Partnerships, & Sole Proprietorships. Angela Schneeman. LC 92-28841. 1993. text 46.50 (*0-8273-5254-9*) Delmar.

Law of Corporations, Partnerships & Sole Proprietorships. 2nd ed. Angela Schneeman. LC 96-24674. (Paralegal Ser.). (Illus.). 704p. (C). 1996. pap. 84.95 (*0-8273-7568-9*) Delmar.

Law of Corporations, Partnerships & Sole Proprietorships. 2nd ed. Angela Schneeman. (Paralegal Ser.). 1997. teacher ed. 15.95 (*0-8273-7569-7*) Delmar.

Law of Corporations, Partnerships, & Sole Proprietorships Instructor's Guide. Angela Schneeman. 1993. 12.50 (*0-8273-5255-7*) Delmar.

Law of Costs. 2nd ed. 330p. 1984. boxed set 111.00 (*0-409-01909-7*, SA, MICHIE) LEXIS Pub.

Law of Court Fees & Suits Valuation in India. B. Khanna. (C). 1988. 165.00 (*0-7855-3555-1*) St Mut.

Law of Court Fees & Suits Valuation in Uttar Pradesh. 5th rev. ed. S. M. Husain. (C). 1980. 25.00 (*0-7855-5413-0*) St Mut.

Law of Crimes. Ejaz Ahmed. (C). 1988. 410.00 (*0-7855-3545-4*) St Mut.

Law of Crimes. John W. May. xxii, 239p. 1985. reprint ed. 35.00 (*0-8377-0823-0*, Rothman) W S Hein.

Law of Criminal Conspiracies & Agreements. Robert S. Wright. 107p. 1986. reprint ed. 32.50 (*0-8377-2731-6*, Rothman) W S Hein.

Law of Criminal Investigation Study Guide. Davis Publishing Company Staff. 96p. (Orig.). (C). 1989. pap. 28.95 (*1-56325-010-1*) Davis Pub Law.

Law of Criminal Procedure & Evidence Casebook, Vol. 1. A. M. Sorgdrager et al. 264p. 1993. pap. 80.00 (*0-409-05648-0*, SA, MICHIE) LEXIS Pub.

Law of Criminal Procedure & Evidence Casebook, Vol. 2. A. M. Sorgdrager et al. 1993. pap. 58.00 (*0-409-05649-9*, SA, MICHIE) LEXIS Pub.

Law of Culpable Homicide, Murder & Punishment in India. Ed. by S. P. Makkar. (C). 1990. 125.00 (*0-89771-180-7*) St Mut.

Law of Cultural Property & Natural Heritage: Protection, Transfer & Access. Marilyn E. Phelan. 1998. pap. 95.00 (*0-9643080-1-0*) Kalos Kapp.

Law of Damages. J. Visser & J. M. Potgieter. 544p. 1992. pap. write for info. (*0-7021-2803-1*, Pub. by Juta & Co) Gaunt.

Law of Damages in Wisconsin, 3 vols. 2nd ed. 1600p. 1994. ring bd. 145.00 (*0-945574-35-5*) State Bar WI.

Law of Damages Through the Cases. J. Visser & J. M. Potgieter. 450p. 1993. pap. 50.00 (*0-7021-2805-8*, Pub. by Juta & Co) Gaunt.

*__Law of Damages Through the Cases__ 2nd ed. P. J. Visser & J. M. Potgieter. LC 99-186819. xxx, 569p. 1998. write for info. (*0-7021-4528-9*) Juta & Co.

Law of Debt Collection. Margaret C. Jasper. LC 97-16105. (Legal Almanac Ser.). 73p. 1997. text 22.50 (*0-379-11238-8*) Oceana.

Law of Debtor & Creditor: In the United States & Canada. James P. Holcombe. 508p. 1994. reprint ed. 52.50 (*0-8377-2246-2*, Rothman) W S Hein.

Law of Debtors & Creditors. Richard B. Hagedorn et al. (Bankruptcy Law Ser.). 1168p. 1991. suppl. ed. 149.50 (*0-7913-0852-9*) Warren Gorham & Lamont.

Law of Debtors & Creditors. Richard B. Hagedorn et al. (Bankruptcy Law Ser.). 1168p. 1992. suppl. ed. 57.00 (*0-7913-1262-3*) Warren Gorham & Lamont.

Law of Debtors & Creditors: Text, Cases, & Problems. Elizabeth Warren & Jay L. Westbrook. LC 95-81926. 992p. 1996. boxed set 58.00 (*0-316-92361-3*, 23613) Aspen Law.

Law of Debtors & Creditors: Text, Cases, & Problems. Elizabeth Warren & Jay L. Westbrook. 800p. (C). 1986. 38.00 (*0-316-92354-0*, Aspen Law & Bus) Aspen Pub.

Law of Deep Sea-Bed Mining: A Study of the Progressive Development of International Law Concerning the Management of the Polymetallic Nodules of the Deep Sea-Bed. Said Mahmoudi. 362p. 1987. text 121.00 (*91-22-01156-0*) Coronet Bks.

Law of Defamation. Rodney A. Smolla. LC 86-14687. (Entertainment & Communication Law Ser.). 1986. ring bd. 145.00 (*0-87632-512-6*) West Group.

*__Law of Defamation in Canada: A Treatise on the Principles of the Common Law & the Statutes of the Canadian Provinces Concerning Slander & Libel As Civil Wrongs, with the Articles of the Criminal Code of Canada Concerning Libel As an Indictable Offence.__ John King. 1999. reprint ed. 187.50 (*1-56169-562-9*) Gaunt.

Law of Defamation in Commonwealth Africa. Jill Cottrell. LC 97-38535. (Law, Social Change & Development Ser.). 327p. 1998. 82.95 (*1-84014-092-5*, KQC237.L53C68, Pub. by Ashgate Pub) Ashgate Pub Co.

Law of Defamation in Singapore & Malaysia. 2nd ed. Keith R. Evans. 1993. 120.00 (*0-409-99644-0*, MICHIE) LEXIS Pub.

Law of Defamation in South Africa. J. M. Burchell. 392p. 1985. 53.00 (*0-7021-1567-3*, Pub. by Juta & Co); pap. 49.00 (*0-7021-4040-6*, Pub. by Juta & Co) Gaunt.

Law of Defamation, Privacy, Publicity, & Moral Right: Cases & Materials on Protection of Personality Interests. 3rd ed. Sheldon W. Halpern. LC 95-79972. xxviii, 655p. 1995. 55.00 (*0-9637166-1-1*) JPm Bks.

Law of Delhi Development. B. P. Surendra. (C). 1989. 250.00 (*0-7855-4742-8*) St Mut.

Law of Delict. J. M. Thomson. 250p. 1994. pap. 53.00 (*0-406-01024-2*, U.K., MICHIE) LEXIS Pub.

Law of Delict Vol. 1: Aquilian Liability. rev. ed. P. Q. Boberg. 958p. 1989. reprint ed. 90.00 (*0-7021-2315-3*, Pub. by Juta & Co) Gaunt.

Law of Democracy. Samuel Issacharoff & Pamala S. Karlan. LC 97-228473. 733p. 1997. 49.95 (*1-56662-462-2*) Foundation Pr.

Law of Deprivation of Liberty. Fred Cohen. LC 91-73517. 856p. 1991. lib. bdg. 60.00 (*0-89089-463-9*) Carolina Acad Pr.

Law of Desire: Temporary Marriage in Shi'i Iran. Shahla Haeri. LC 89-4343. (Contemporary Issues in the Middle East Ser.). 304p. (Orig.). 1989. pap. text 19.95 (*0-8156-2483-2*) Syracuse U Pr.

Law of Disability Discrimination, 2 vols., set. Colker. 58.95 (*0-87084-242-0*) Anderson Pub Co.

Law of Disability Discrimination. 2nd ed. Ruth Colker & Bonnie P. Tucker. 734p. (C). 1998. 51.95 (*0-87084-240-4*) Anderson Pub Co.

*__Law of Disability Discrimination Handbook: Statutes & Regulatory Guidance.__ 2nd rev. ed. Ruth Colker & Bonnie Poitras Tucker. 488p. 1998. pap. 19.95 (*0-87084-332-X*) Anderson Pub Co.

Law of Dispute Resolution: Arbitration & Alternative Dispute Resolution. Margaret C. Jasper. LC 95-194697. (Legal Almanac Ser.). (Illus.). 124p. 1995. text 22.50 (*0-379-11191-8*) Oceana.

Law of Distressed Real Estate, 4 vols., Set. Baxter Dunaway. LC 85-4161. (Real Property - Zoning Ser.). 1985. ring bd. 495.00 (*0-87632-461-8*) West Group.

Law of Domestic & International Strategic Alliances: A Survey for Corporate Management. Alan S. Gutterman. LC 94-46194. 408p. 1995. 79.50 (*0-89930-549-0*, Quorum Bks) Greenwood.

Law of Domestic Relations in the United States, Vol. 1. Homer H. Clark, Jr. 826p. (C). 1990. reprint ed. text. write for info. (*0-318-67350-9*) West Pub.

Law of Dowry Prohibition, with Rules, State Amendments & Allied Laws. A. Achar & V. Venkanna. (C). 1990. 93.00 (*0-89771-148-3*) St Mut.

Law of Easements. 5th ed. A. Amin & S. Sastris. (C). 1986. suppl. ed. 160.00 (*0-7855-4709-6*) St Mut.

Law of Easements & Licences. L. C. Goyle. (C). 1988. 88.00 (*0-7855-3706-6*) St Mut.

Law of Easements & Licences in Land. John W. Bruce & James W. Ely, Jr. 600p. 1994. suppl. ed. 145.00 (*0-88712-905-6*); suppl. ed. 72.00 (*0-7913-1186-4*) Warren Gorham & Lamont.

Law of Easements, 1984. 5th rev. ed. A. Amin & S. Sastris. (C). 1986. 130.00 (*0-7855-5580-3*) St Mut.

Law of Education. B. W. Boer & V. B. Gleeson. 210p. 1982. 55.00 (*0-409-30923-0*, AT, MICHIE) LEXIS Pub.

Law of Education. Ed. by Peter Liell et al. ring bd. write for info. (*0-406-99895-7*, LE9ASET, MICHIE) LEXIS Pub.

Law of Education, 2 vols., Set. Peter Liell & John Coleman. ring bd. 495.00 (*0-406-02647-5*, UK, MICHIE) LEXIS Pub.

Law of Education in Scotland. David Sillars. 284p. 1993. pap. 61.00 (*0-406-10573-1*, U.K., MICHIE) LEXIS Pub.

Law of Electric Wires in Streets & Highways. E. Quinton Keasbey. Ed. by Bernard D. Reams & R. H. Helmholz. LC 86-62942. (Historical Writings in Law & Jurisprudence Ser.: No. 10). xi, 190p. 1986. reprint ed. lib. bdg. 37.50 (*0-89941-525-3*, 304610) W S Hein.

Law of Electricity in U. P. 3rd ed. Ed. by P. L. Malik. (C). 1991. 110.00 (*0-7855-5577-3*) St Mut.

*__Law of Electronic Banking.__ Melanie L. Fein. LC 99-41882. 1999. ring bd. 175.00 (*0-7355-0372-9*) Panel Pubs.

Law of Electronic Commerce. 3rd ed. Benjamin Wright & Jane K. Winn. LC 98-13936. 1998. ring bd. 175.00 (*1-56706-940-1*) Aspen Law.

Law of Electronic Commerce: EDI, E-Mail, & Internet: Technology, Proof, & Liability. 2nd ed. Benjamin Wright. 462p. ring bd. 145.00 (*0-316-95647-3*, 56465) Aspen Law.

Law of Electronic Commerce: EDI, E-Mail & Internet: Technology, Proof & Liability. 2nd ed. Benjamin Wright. LC 95-78651. 1995. write for info. (*0-316-95620-1*, Aspen Law & Bus) Aspen Pub.

Law of Electronic Fund Transfer Systems. 2nd ed. Donald I. Baker & Roland E. Brandel. 1988. 145.00 (*0-7913-0052-8*); suppl. ed. 61.00 (*0-7913-1247-X*); suppl. ed. 61.00 (*0-685-56110-0*) Warren Gorham & Lamont.

Law of Electronic Funds Transfer. Benjamin Geva. 1992. ring bd. write for info. (*0-8205-1147-1*) Bender.

Law of Electronic Surveillance. 2nd ed. James G. Carr. LC 85-31406. (Criminal Law Ser.). 1986. ring bd. 145.00 (*0-87632-493-6*) West Group.

Law of Eminent Domain in the United States. Carman F. Randolph. cxxv, 462p. 1991. reprint ed. 55.00 (*0-8377-2545-3*, Rothman) W S Hein.

Law of Employment. 3rd ed. G. J. McCarry et al. xxxiv, 618p. 1990. pap. 59.50 (*0-455-20965-0*, Pub. by LawBk Co) Gaunt.

Law of Employment Discrimination: Cases & Commentary. Paul Cox. 720p. 1999. ring bd. 67.00 (*1-879581-67-1*) Lupus Pubns.

Law of Employment Discrimination: Cases & Materials. 4th ed. Joel W. Friedman & George M. Strickler, Jr. LC 97-187879. v, 1346p. 1997. 50.95 (*1-56662-483-5*) Foundation Pr.

Law of Employment Discrimination: Cases & Materials, 1994 Supplement. 3rd ed. Joel W. Friedman & George M. Strickler, Jr. (University Textbook Ser.). 188p. 1994. pap. text 9.95 (*1-56662-194-1*) Foundation Pr.

Law of Employment Discrimination: 1998 Case Supplement. Joel W. Friedman & George M. Strickler, Jr. 1998. write for info. (*1-56662-650-1*) Foundation Pr.

Law of Employment Discrimination, Teacher's Manual for Cases & Materials on The. 3rd ed. Joel W. Friedman & George M. Strickler, Jr. (University Casebook Ser.). 175p. 1993. pap. text. write for info. (*1-56662-119-4*) Foundation Pr.

Law of Employment in North Carolina Public Schools. Robert P. Joyce. 2000. pap. text. write for info. (*1-56011-303-0*, 97.05) Institute Government.

Law of Enclosures. Dale Peck. 320p. 1996. text 23.00 (*0-374-18419-4*) FS&G.

Law of Enclosures. Dale Peck. LC 96-38540. (U Ser.). 1997. per. 12.00 (*0-671-00347-X*, WSP) PB.

Law of Environmental & Toxic Torts: Cases, Materials & Problems. Gerald W. Boston & M. Stuart Madden. LC 93-42310. (American Casebook Ser.). 681p. (C). 1994. 57.50 (*0-314-03354-8*) West Pub.

Law of Environmental Protection, 3 vols. Environmental Law Institute Staff. LC 87-725. (Environmental Law Ser.). 1987. ring bd. 375.00 (*0-87632-541-X*) West Group.

Law of Environmental Protection: Cases, Legislation, Policies. 2nd ed. John E. Bonine & Thomas O. McGarity. (American Casebook Ser.). 1042p. (C). 1991. 62.50 (*0-314-92198-2*) West Pub.

Law of Equal Employment Opportunity. Stephen N. Shulman & John H. Abernathy. 1032p. 1989. boxed set 110.00 (*0-7913-0248-2*) Warren Gorham & Lamont.

*__Law of Equitable Remedies.__ Jeffrey Bruce Berryman. (Essentials of Canadian Law Ser.). 2000. pap. 35.95 (*1-55221-042-1*, Pub. by Irwin Law) Gaunt.

Law of Estates, Trusts, & Gifts. Andersen. 1996. text 50.36 (*0-256-22170-7*) McGraw.

Law of Estoppel - Variation & Waiver. Theresa Villiers & Sean Wilkin. LC 97-34885. 616p. 1998. 133.50 (*0-471-96921-4*) Wiley.

Law of Estoppel in South Africa. P. J. Rabie. 130p. 1992. pap. 49.00 (*0-409-05000-8*, SA, MICHIE); boxed set 85.00 (*0-409-05001-6*, SA, MICHIE) LEXIS Pub.

Law of Evidence. 1999. 84.00 (*1-85431-851-9*, Pub. by Blackstone Pr) Gaunt.

Law of Evidence. Friedthal. Date not set. pap. text, teacher ed. write for info. (*0-88277-268-6*) West Pub.

Law of Evidence. M. Monir. (C). 1990. 175.00 (*0-89771-177-7*) St Mut.

Law of Evidence, 9 cass.; set. Irving Younger. 1979. 795.00 incl. VHS (*1-55917-389-0*, 840); audio 195.00 (*1-55917-387-4*); VHS 795.00 (*1-55917-388-2*) Natl Prac Inst.

*__Law of Evidence.__ 2nd ed. David M. Paciocco & Lee Stuesser. (Essentials of Canadian Law Ser.). xx, 388p. 1999. pap. 31.95 (*1-55221-038-3*, Pub. by Irwin Law) Gaunt.

Law of Evidence. 4th ed. Vepa P. Sarathi. (C). 1989. 75.00 (*0-7855-5565-X*) St Mut.

Law of Evidence: Cases & Statutes = Die Bewysreg: Hofsake En Wetgewing. D. P. Van Der Merwe et al. LC 97-199325. 320p. 1997. write for info. (*0-7021-3902-5*) Juta & Co.

Law of Evidence & Field's Medico Legal Guide. M. Monir. (C). 1988. 175.00 (*0-7855-3535-7*) St Mut.

Law of Evidence & the Medical Record: A Trial Lawyer's Guide. 5th ed. Elliott B. Oppenheim. 120p. 1997. 125.00 (*1-930263-01-5*) Terra Firma NM.

Law of Evidence for Criminal Justice Professionals. 3rd ed. Klein. (Criminal Justice Ser.). 1989. 47.50 (*0-314-48125-7*) Thomson Learn.

Law of Evidence for Criminal Justice Professionals. 4th ed. Irving J. Klein. LC 96-26937. 550p. 1997. 77.95 (*0-314-20077-0*) West Pub.

Law of Evidence in Ancient India. Shraddhakar Supakar. (C). 1990. 150.00 (*0-89771-310-9*) St Mut.

Law of Evidence in Canada. T. L. Bryant et al. 1120p. 1992. pap., student ed. 95.00 (*0-409-90639-5*, MICHIE) LEXIS Pub.

Law of Evidence in India, Pakistan, Bangladesh, Burma & Ceylon. P. G. Sarkar. (C). 1990. 230.00 (*0-89771-150-5*) St Mut.

Law of Evidence in the Sudan. Krishna Vasdev. 1981. pap. 50.00 (*0-406-40610-3*, UK, MICHIE) LEXIS Pub.

Law of Evidence in Victorian England. Christopher Allen. LC 96-49926. (Cambridge Studies in English Legal History). 222p. (C). 1997. text 59.95 (*0-521-58418-3*) Cambridge U Pr.

*__Law of Evidence in Virginia.__ 5th ed. Charles E. Friend. LC 99-63777. 1200p. 1999. 145.00 (*0-327-01482-2*, 6199611) LEXIS Pub.

Law of Evidence in Virginia, 2 vols., Set. 4th ed. Charles E. Friend. 1993. 130.00 (*1-55834-097-1*, 61996-10, MICHIE) LEXIS Pub.

Law of Evidence in Virginia: 1989 Supplement. Charles Friend. 1989. write for info. (*0-87473-515-7*, 61993-10, MICHIE) LEXIS Pub.

Law of Evidence in Virginia, 1998 Cumulative Supplement, 2 vols. 4th ed. Charles E. Friend. 388p. 1998. suppl. ed. write for info. (*0-327-00345-6*, 6199515) LEXIS Pub.

Law of Evidence in Virginia, 1998 Cumulative Supplement, Vol. 1. 4th ed. Charles E. Friend. 388p. 1998. suppl. ed. write for info. (*0-327-00346-4*) LEXIS Pub.

Law of Evidence in Virginia, 1998 Cumulative Supplement, Vol. 2. 4th ed. Charles E. Friend. 388p. 1998. suppl. ed. write for info. (*0-327-00347-2*) LEXIS Pub.

Law of Evidence in Washington. 2nd ed. Robert H. Aronson. LC 93-22768. 560p. 1993. spiral bd. 105.00 (*0-250-40718-3*, MICHIE) LEXIS Pub.

Law of Evidence in Washington. 3rd ed. Robert H. Aronson. 751p. 1998. lib. bdg. 125.00 (*0-327-00901-2*, 8281811) LEXIS Pub.

Law of Evidence with Medico-Legal Guide. M. Monir. (C). 1988. 275.00 (*0-7855-3682-5*) St Mut.

Law of Executory Contracts for the Sale of Real Property. Anson Bingham. xlviii, 862p. 1997. reprint ed. 110.00 (*0-8377-1986-0*, Rothman) W S Hein.

Law of Expert & Opinion Evidence Reduced to Rules: With Illustrations from Adjudged Cases. John D. Lawson. lxxii, 595p. 1982. reprint ed. 55.00 (*0-8377-0813-3*, Rothman) W S Hein.

Law of Expert Testimony. 2nd enl. ed. Henry W. Rogers. xlvii, 542p. 1991. reprint ed. 47.50 (*0-8377-2544-5*, Rothman) W S Hein.

Law of Extradition, International & Inter-State: With an Appendix, Containing Extradition Treaties & Laws of the United States, the Extradition Laws of the States, Several Sections of the English Extradition Act of 1870, & the Opinion of Governor Cullom. 3rd ed. Samuel T. Spear. xiv, 766p. 1983. reprint ed. 95.00 (*0-8377-1131-2*, Rothman) W S Hein.

Law of Extraordinary Legal Remedies. Forrest G. Ferris. LC 72-136387. reprint ed. 55.00 (*0-404-02378-9*) AMS Pr.

Law of Faith. rev. ed. Norman P. Grubb. 242p. 1998. reprint ed. pap. 9.00 (*0-9662957-1-4*) Zerubbabel.

Law of Federal Estate & Gift Taxation, 1978-1990. rev. ed. David Link & Larry D. Soderquist. 100.00 (*0-317-11947-8*) West Group.

Law of Federal Income Taxation, 1994: Pocket Part. 3rd ed. Michael D. Rose. (Hornbook Ser.). 150p. (C). 1994. pap. text. write for info. (*0-314-04332-2*) West Pub.

Law of Federal Mortgage Documents. D. Barlow Burke, Jr. 500p. 1989. 145.00 (*0-316-11701-3*, Aspen Law & Bus) Aspen Pub.

Law of Federal Oil & Gas Leases, 2 vols. Rocky Mountain Mineral Law Staff & Joan A. Reid. 1964. ring bd. 390.00 (*0-8205-1515-9*) Bender.

Law of Federal Taxation. Covins. (Paralegal Ser.). 1995. pap., teacher ed. 10.00 (*0-8273-5989-6*) Delmar.

L

Law of Financial Privacy: A Compliance Guide. 2nd ed. L. Richard Fischer. LC 83-60091. (General Law Ser.). 608p. 1991. 160.00 (*0-7913-0334-9*) Warren Gorham & Lamont.
Law of Financial Services, 8 vols. Harvey L. Pitt et al. 9530p. 1988. ring bd. 695.00 (*0-13-099276-3*) Aspen Law.
Law of Financial Services, 6 vols. Harvey L. Pitt et al. 5000p. 1988. write for info. (*0-318-65468-7*, H44003) P-H.
Law of Financial Success. 104p. 1996. reprint ed. spiral bd. 10.00 (*0-7873-0006-3*) Hlth Research.
Law of Financial Success, 1907. Fiduciary Press Staff. 104p. 1996. reprint ed. pap. 9.95 (*1-56459-742-3*) Kessinger Pub.
Law of Fisheries in the Persian-Arabian Gulf. S. H. Amin. (C). 1983. 39.00 (*0-946706-08-5*, Pub. by Royston Ltd) St Mut.
Law of Fixtures: Common Law & the Uniform Commercial Code. Alphonse M. Squillante. LC 92-15416. (Real Property-Zoning Ser.). 1992. ring bd. 135.00 (*0-87632-858-3*) West Group.
Law of Florida Homeowners' Associations. 3rd rev. ed. Peter M. Dunbar & Charles F. Dudley. LC 98-115009. 1997. pap. 15.95 (*0-937569-18-6*) Suncoast Prof Pub.
Law of Foreign Exchange. Raj Bhala. LC 97-5051. 572p. 1997. 60.00 (*0-89089-682-8*) Carolina Acad Pr.
Law of Fraud & Mistake. 7th ed. William W. Kerr. 794p. 1952. reprint ed. 149.00 (*1-56169-099-6*, Pub. by Sweet & Maxwll) Gaunt.
Law of Fraud & the Procedure Pertaining to the Redress Thereof. Melville M. Bigelow. lix, 696p. 1981. reprint ed. 85.00 (*0-8377-0317-4*, Rothman) W S Hein.
***Law of Fraudulent Conveyances.** Garrard Glenn. xxiv, 774p. 1999. 195.00 (*1-56169-530-0*) Gaunt.
Law of Fraudulent Conveyances. Garrard Glenn. LC 96-78498. xxvi, 774p. 1996. reprint ed. 95.00 (*1-57588-191-8*, 310790) W S Hein.
Law of Fraudulent Transactions, No. 2200. Peter A. Alces. 1989. suppl. ed. 59.00 (*0-7913-1202-X*); boxed set, suppl. ed. 135.00 (*0-7913-0310-1*) Warren Gorham & Lamont.
Law of Fund-Raising. 2nd ed. Bruce R. Hopkins. LC 95-9551. (Nonprofit Law, Finance, & Management Ser.). 762p. 1995. 160.00 (*0-471-12534-2*) Wiley.
Law of Future Interests in California. Richard R. Powell. 91p. 1980. pap. write for info. (*0-318-57529-9*) West Pub.
Law of Game, Salmon & Freshwater Fishing in Scotland. S. Scott Robinson. 336p. 1990. boxed set 124.00 (*0-406-11201-0*, U.K., MICHIE) LEXIS Pub.
Law of General Average. L. Lowndes & R. Rudolf. (C). 1975. 800.00 (*0-7855-4106-3*, Pub. by Witherby & Co) St Mut.
***Law of Giving.** Melford Okilo. 15p. 1999. pap. 5.00 (*1-879605-63-5*) U Sci & Philos.
***Law of God.** B. L. Cocherell et al. 508p. 1999. pap. write for info. (*0-7392-0418-1*, PO3681) Morris Pubng.
Law of God. Bishop Philaret. 86p. Date not set. pap. 5.50 (*1-879038-99-4*, 9014) Synaxis Pr.
Law of God. William S. Plumer. 1995. 34.99 (*0-87377-187-7*) GAM Pubns.
Law of God, for Study at Home & School. Tr. by Susan Price from RUS.Tr. of Zakon Bozhi. (Illus.). 650p. (J). (gr. 1-7). 1993. 50.00 (*0-88465-044-8*) Holy Trinity.
Law of Gravity. Dennis M. Cottrell. Ed. by Charles L. Wyrick, Jr. 329p. 1995. 21.95 (*0-941711-25-0*) Wyrick & Co.
Law of Groups of Companies: An International Bibliography. Ed. by E. Wymeersch & M. Krutithof. 380p. (C). 1992. lib. bdg. 190.50 (*0-7923-1298-8*) Kluwer Academic.
Law of Habeas Corpus. 2nd ed. R. J. Sharpe. 288p. 1990. text 79.00 (*0-19-825404-0*) OUP.
Law of Hazardous Waste: Management, Cleanup, Liability & Litigation, 4 vols. Susan M. Cooke. 1987. ring bd. 760.00 (*0-8205-1307-5*) Bender.
Law of Hazardous Waste Disposal & Remediation: Cases, Legislation, Regulations, Policies (American Casebook Series) Jeffrey G. Miller & Craig N. Johnston. LC 96-8765. (Paralegal). 85p. (C). 1996. text 42.25 (*0-314-06584-9*) West Pub.
Law of Hazardous Wastes & Toxic Substances in a Nutshell. John G. Sprankling & Gregory S. Weber. LC 97-25344. (Paralegal). 507p. (C). 1997. pap. text 16.50 (*0-314-21166-7*) West Pub.
Law of Health Care Organization & Finance: 1995 Supplement. 2nd ed. Barry R. Furrow et al. (American Casebook Ser.). 550p. (C). 1995. pap. text 14.00 (*0-314-06863-5*) West Pub.
Law of Health Records in North Carolina. Anne M. Dellinger & Joan G. Brannon. 86p. (Orig.). (C). 1987. pap. text 12.00 (*1-56011-093-7*, 87.04) Institute Government.
***Law of Her Own: The Reasonable Woman as a Measure of Man.** Caroline Forell. LC 99-6811. 2000. text 38.00 (*0-8147-2676-3*) NYU Pr.
Law of High Technology Innovation. Aryeh S. Friedman. 720p. 1992. ring bd. 115.00 (*0-88063-359-X*, MICHIE) LEXIS Pub.
Law of Higher Education: A Comprehensive Guide to Legal Implications of Administrative Decision Making. 3rd ed. William A. Kaplan & Barbara A. Lee. LC 94-38999. (Higher & Adult Education Ser.). 1056p. 1995. text 75.00 (*0-7879-0052-4*) Jossey-Bass.
Law of Higher Education: Legal Implications of Administrative Decision Making. William A. Kaplin. LC 78-62571. (Jossey-Bass Higher Education Ser.). 538p. reprint ed. pap. 166.80 (*0-608-14797-4*, 202565700045) Bks Demand.
Law of Higher Education, 1980. William A. Kaplin. LC 79-9669. (Jossey-Bass Higher Education Ser.). 208p. reprint ed. pap. 64.50 (*0-608-14796-6*, 202565800045) Bks Demand.
Law of Hindu Religious & Charitable Endowments. V. K. Varadhachari. 1985. 600.00 (*0-7855-1734-0*) St Mut.
Law of Home Schooling. Charles J. Russo et al. 74p. 1994. 26.00 (*1-56534-061-2*) Ed Law Assn.
Law of Homicide in the Sudan. Krishna Vasdev. 1978. pap. 50.00 (*0-406-40609-X*, UK, MICHIE) LEXIS Pub.
Law of Human Rights. Richard Clayton. 700p. 2000. text 175.00 (*0-19-826223-X*) OUP.
Law of Hundis & Negotiable Instruments. 9th ed. C. L. Agarwal. (C). 1989. 80.00 (*0-7855-5463-7*) St Mut.
Law of Hundis & Negotiable Instruments with Supplement, 1979. 9th ed. C. I. Aggarwal. (C). 1979. 75.00 (*0-7855-4710-X*) St Mut.
Law of Illinois: Lincoln's Cases Before the Illinois Supreme Court, from His Entry into the Practice of Law until His Entry into Congress, Vol. 1. John Long. (Illus.). 301p. (Orig.). (C). 1993. pap. text 20.00 (*0-9635192-0-4*) Illinois Co.
Law of Immigration. Margaret C. Jasper. LC 96-183725. (Legal Almanac Ser.). 1996. text 22.50 (*0-379-11198-5*) Oceana.
Law of Income Tax, 3 vols. Shuklendra Acharya. (C). 1990. 195.00 (*0-89771-284-6*) St Mut.
Law of Income Tax. V. K. Sushakumari. 350p. 1982. 110.00 (*0-7855-1722-7*) St Mut.
Law of Income Tax. 3rd ed. Ed. by V. K. Sushakumari. (C). 1982. 40.00 (*0-7855-5532-3*) St Mut.
Law of Income Tax, 2 vols., Set, Vols. 1-2. Sampath Iyengar. (C). 1990. 360.00 (*0-89771-264-1*) St Mut.
Law of Income Tax in India, 6 vols. V. S. Sundaram. (C). 1990. 175.00 (*0-89771-258-7*) St Mut.
Law of Independent Power. Steven Ferrey. LC 89-34161. (Environmental Law Ser.). 1989. ring bd. 145.00 (*0-87632-680-7*) West Group.
Law of Industrial Disputes. O. P. Malhotra. (C). 1985. 650.00 (*0-7855-3528-4*) St Mut.
Law of Infancy & Coverture. 2nd ed. Peregrine Bingham. viii, 396p. 1980. reprint ed. 45.00 (*0-8377-0311-5*, Rothman) W S Hein.
Law of Information Conflict: National Security Law in CyberSpace. Walter G. Sharp, Sr. & Thomas C. Wingfield. LC 99-95501. (Illus.). 200p. 1999. 24.95 (*0-9670326-1-X*) Aegis Res Corp.
Law of Information Technology in Europe, 1992: A Comparison with the U. S. A. Ed. by Alfred P. Meijboom & Corien Prins. (Computer - Law Ser.: Vol. 9). 1991. pap. 67.00 (*90-6544-554-4*) Kluwer Law Intl.
Law of Inhibition & Adjudication. George L. Gretton. 196p. 1987. pap. 56.00 (*0-406-10433-6*, UK, MICHIE) LEXIS Pub.
Law of Injunctions. Arthur D. Wolf & Bruce K. Miller. 1989. write for info. (*0-318-65449-0*, Aspen Law & Bus) Aspen Pub.
Law of Injunctions. 7th ed. L. C. Goyle. (C). 1989. 110.00 (*0-7855-4764-9*) St Mut.
***Law of Insolvency.** Avtar Singh. 2000. pap. 40.00 (*81-7012-663-0*, Pub. by Eastern Book) St Mut.
Law of Insolvency. 2nd ed. Avtar Singh. (C). 1986. 50.00 (*0-685-37447-5*) St Mut.
Law of Insolvency. 3rd ed. Catherine Smith. 491p. 1988. pap. 116.00 (*0-409-05605-7*, SA, MICHIE) LEXIS Pub.
Law of Insolvency: Cumulative Supplement 1993. 2nd ed. 1993. pap. 48.00 (*0-409-79025-7*, NZ, MICHIE) LEXIS Pub.
Law of Insolvency (In Nutshell) 2nd ed. Ed. by Avtar Singh. (C). 1986. 55.00 (*0-7855-5529-3*) St Mut.
Law of Insurance. Poh C. Chai. xxi, 289p. 1986. 54.00 (*9971-70-048-4*, MICHIE) LEXIS Pub.
Law of Insurance. 5th ed. R. Colinvaux. (C). 1984. 600.00 (*0-7855-4105-5*, Pub. by Witherby & Co) St Mut.
Law of Insurance Contract Disputes. 2nd ed. Jeffrey W. Stempel. LC 98-47787. 1998. ring bd. 160.00 (*0-7355-0236-6*) Panel Pubs.
Law of Insurance Contracts. 2nd ed. Malcolm A. Clarke. 827p. 1994. 265.00 (*1-85044-551-6*) LLP.
Law of Intellectual Property in New Zealand. Andrew Brown & Anthony Grant. 716p. 1989. pap. 90.00 (*0-409-78884-8*, NZ, MICHIE) LEXIS Pub.
Law of Intellectual Property in the Middle East. Ed. by A. Amin. 80p. (C). 1991. 150.00 (*0-7855-6801-8*, Pub. by Royston Ltd) St Mut.
Law of Inter-State Commerce: Especially As Applied to the "Act to Regulate Commerce" Approved February 4, 1887; with Notes of Decisions. J. C. Harper. xxi, 225p. 1983. reprint ed. 38.50 (*0-8377-0706-4*, Rothman) W S Hein.
Law of Interdict. 2nd ed. S. Scott Robinson. LC 96-152379. 208p. 1994. boxed set 90.00 (*0-406-01485-X*, UK, MICHIE) LEXIS Pub.
Law of Interim Orders & Receivership. S. M. Ali. (C). 1988. 80.00 (*0-7855-3721-X*) St Mut.
Law of International Business Transactions. Robin Burnett. 296p. 1994. 64.00 (*1-86287-131-0*, Pub. by Federation Pr) Gaunt.
***Law of International Business Transactions.** Dimatteo. 2002. 65.00 (*0-324-04097-0*) Thomson Learn.
***Law of International Business Transactions.** 2nd ed. Robin Burnett. LC 99-205177. 338p. 1999. pap. 59.00 (*1-86287-299-6*, Pub. by Federation Pr) Gaunt.
***Law of International Contracting.** Larry A. DiMatteo. LC 00-42438. 2000. write for info. (*90-411-9592-0*) Kluwer Law Intl.
Law of International Copyright with Special Sections on the Colonies & the United States of America. William Briggs. xx, 850p. 1986. reprint ed. 85.00 (*0-8377-1941-0*, Rothman) W S Hein.
Law of International Organisations. Nigel White. LC 96-16159. (Melland Schill Monographs in International Law). 240p. 1997. text 29.95 (*0-7190-4340-9*, Pub. by Manchester Univ Pr) St Martin.
Law of International Sea Piracy. Barry H. Dubner. (Developments in International Law Ser.: No. 2). 1980. lib. bdg. 70.50 (*90-247-2191-1*) Kluwer Academic.
Law of International Telecommunications in Canada. Nicolas M. Matte & Ram S. Jakhu. (Law & Economics of International Telecommunications Ser.). 131p. 1987. 45.00 (*3-7890-1309-9*, Pub. by Nomos Verlags) Intl Bk Import.
Law of International Telecommunications in India. K. D. Gaur. (Law & Economics of International Telecommunications Ser.). 219p. 1988. 76.00 (*3-7890-1310-2*, Pub. by Nomos Verlags) Intl Bk Import.
Law of International Telecommunications in the Netherlands. A. Wouter Hins & P. Bernd Hugenholtz. (Law & Economics of International Telecommunications Ser.). 231p. 1988. 69.00 (*3-7890-1311-0*, Pub. by Nomos Verlags) Intl Bk Import.
Law of International Telecommunications in the United Kingdom. Verena A. Wiedemann. (Law & Economics of International Telecommunications Ser.). 336p. 1989. 72.00 (*3-7890-1649-7*, Pub. by Nomos Verlags) Intl Bk Import.
Law of International Telecommunications in the United States. Stephen R. Barnett et al. (Law & Economics of International Telecommunications Ser.). 271p. 1988. 89.00 (*3-7890-1308-0*, Pub. by Nomos Verlags) Intl Bk Import.
***Law of International Trade.** Ademuni-Odeke. 413p. 1999. pap. 44.00 (*1-85431-937-X*, 18459, Pub. by Blackstone Pr) Gaunt.
Law of International Trade. Ed. by Pamela Sellman. 374p. 1996. pap. 125.00 (*0-7510-0694-7*, Pub. by HLT Pubns) St Mut.
Law of International Trade Cases. Ed. by Pamela Sellman. 156p. 1996. pap. 125.00 (*0-7510-0660-2*, Pub. by HLT Pubns) St Mut.
Law of International Trade Finance. Norbert Horn. (Studies in Transnational Economic Law). 746p. 1989. 149.00 (*90-6544-395-9*) Kluwer Law Intl.
Law of International Trade in Practice. Delia Coonan & Richard Holt. 259p. 1998. pap. 48.00 (*1-85431-721-0*, Pub. by Blackstone Pr) Gaunt.
Law of International Trade in Practice. 2nd ed. Delia Doonan & Richard Holt. 265p. 1999. pap. 50.00 (*1-85431-905-1*, Pub. by Blackstone Pr) Gaunt.
***Law of International Trade in Practice.** 3rd ed. Delia Coonan & Richard Holt. (Inns of Court School of Law Ser.). 237p. 2000. pap. 46.00 (*1-84174-008-X*, Pub. by Blackstone Pr) Gaunt.
Law of Interstate Commerce & Its Federal Regulation. Frederick N. Judson. xix, 509p. 1981. reprint ed. 49.50 (*0-8377-0735-8*, Rothman) W S Hein.
Law of Interstate Rendition: Erroneously Referred to As Interstate Extradition. James A. Scott. xiv, 534p. 1983. reprint ed. 52.00 (*0-8377-1132-0*, Rothman) W S Hein.
Law of Investment Markets. Robert R. Pennington. 928p. (C). 1990. text 225.00 (*0-632-02372-4*) Blackwell Sci.
Law of Israel. Ed. by Bernard Abramowitz. 29.95 (*0-910218-92-7*) Bennet Pub.
Law of Journalism in Australia. Sally Walker. xlvii, 377p. 1989. pap. 48.50 (*0-455-20908-1*, Pub. by LawBk Co) Gaunt.
Law of Karma. Mirmala Jha. 1985. 19.95 (*81-85157-41-3*) Asia Bk Corp.
Law of Karma. Robert E. Svoboda. (Aghora Ser.: No. II). 322p. 1999. pap. 18.95 (*0-9656208-1-6*, Pub. by Sadhana Pubns) Lotus Pr.
Law of Kidnapping & Sexual Offences. K. K. Singh. (C). 1988. 180.00 (*0-7855-4789-4*) St Mut.
Law of Labor Relations. Ralph A. Newman. LC 53-10762. viii, 310p. 1953. lib. bdg. 37.50 (*0-89941-615-2*, 501940) W S Hein.
Law of Land: Acquisition & Compensation. V. G. Ramachandran. 1995. 120.00 (*81-7012-560-X*, Pub. by Eastern Book) St Mut.
Law of Land Acquisition & Compensation. G. C. Mathur. 1995. 195.00 (*81-7012-571-5*, Pub. by Eastern Book) St Mut.
Law of Land Acquisition & Compensation. 7th ed. V. G. Ramachandran. 1985. 65.00 (*0-7855-1482-1*) St Mut.
Law of Land Acquisition & Compensation, 2 vols., Set. 7th ed. V. G. Ramachandran. (C). 1990. suppl. ed. 425.00 (*0-7855-4714-2*) St Mut.
Law of Land Acquisition & Compensation, with Supplement, 2 vols. 7th ed. V. G. Ramachandran. (C). 1990. text 450.00 (*0-89771-504-7*) St Mut.
Law of Last Resort. Don Pendleton. (Stony Man Ser.: No. 32). 1998. per. 5.50 (*0-373-61916-2*, 1-61916-2, Wrldwide Lib) Harlequin Bks.
Law of Law Firms. Jacob A. Stein. LC 93-74550. 1994. 135.00 (*0-614-07295-6*) West Group.
Law of Lawyering: A Handbook of the Modern Rules of Professional Conduct. Geoffrey C. Hazard, Jr. & W. William Hodes. LC 84-27786. 912p. 1985. suppl. ed. 75.00 (*0-15-004376-7*) Harcourt.
Law of Lawyering: A Handbook on the Model Rules of Professional Conduct. 2nd ed. Geoffrey C. Hazard, Jr. & W. William Hodes. 1868p. 1996. ring bd. 225.00 (*0-13-524232-0*, 43768) Aspen Law.
Law of Lawyering: A Handbook on the Model Rules of Professional Conduct, 2 vols., Set. 2nd ed. Geoffrey C. Hazard, Jr. & W. William Hodes. 1868p. 1990. ring bd. 200.00 (*0-13-108474-7*) Aspen Law.
***Law of Leases.** Clarence M. Lewis. xliii, 674p. 2000. reprint ed. 180.00 (*1-56169-578-5*) Gaunt.
Law of Letters of Credit. John F. Dolan. (Commercial Law Ser.). 616p. 1990. suppl. ed. 145.00 (*0-7913-0658-5*) Warren Gorham & Lamont.
Law of Letters of Credit. John F. Dolan. (Commercial Law Ser.). 616p. 1992. suppl. ed. 51.00 (*0-7913-1243-7*) Warren Gorham & Lamont.
Law of Liability Insurance. Justice Derrington & Ronald S. Ashton. 880p. 1990. boxed set 154.00 (*0-409-49494-1*, Austral, MICHIE) LEXIS Pub.
Law of Liability Insurance, 5 vols., Set. Roland H. Long. 1976. ring bd. 1230.00 (*0-8205-1354-7*) Bender.
Law of Libel & Slander. Margaret C. Jasper. LC 96-183722. (Legal Almanac Ser.). 1996. text 22.50 (*0-379-11197-7*) Oceana.
Law of Libel & Slander in the State of New York, 2 vols., Set. rev. ed. Ernest P. Seelman. LC 64-24239. 1100p. 1968. reprint ed. lib. bdg. 110.00 (*0-89941-364-1*, 500500) W S Hein.
Law of Libel As Affecting Newspapers & Journalists. W. Valentine Ball. (Legal Reprint Ser.). xiii, 165p. 1986. reprint ed. 35.00 (*0-8377-1939-9*, Rothman); reprint ed. 25.00 (*0-421-37560-4*) W S Hein.
Law of Liberty: Victory Through Grace. Adeyemi A. Adedeji. LC 95-77407. 68p. (Orig.). 1995. pap. 5.99 (*0-88270-724-8*) Bridge-Logos.
Law of Liberty in Spiritual Life. Evan H. Hopkins. 186p. (Orig.). 1991. pap. text 6.95 (*0-87508-273-4*) Chr Lit.
Law of Lien. Alfred Silvertown. 192p. 1988. boxed set 88.00 (*0-406-10395-X*, U.K., MICHIE) LEXIS Pub.
Law of Life. Ed. by Jamestown Publishers Staff. 1976. pap. 7.80 (*0-8092-0050-3*, Jamestwn Pub) NTC Contemp Pub Co.
Law of Life. Jack London. Date not set. pap., teacher ed. 7.32 incl. audio (*0-89070-041-9*, Jamestwn Pub) NTC Contemp Pub Co.
Law of Life. Jack London. (Jamestown Classics Ser.). (J). 1995. pap., student ed. 5.99 (*0-89061-040-1*, Jamestwn Pub) NTC Contemp Pub Co.
Law of Life. Melford Okilo. 250p. 1991. text 5.00 (*1-879605-03-1*) U Sci & Philos.
Law of Life & Health Insurance, 5 vols. Bertram Harnett & Irving Lesnick. 1988. ring bd. 550.00 (*0-8205-1569-8*) Bender.
Law of Life & Human Health. G. R. Clements. 313p. 1998. reprint ed. pap. 26.00 (*0-7873-0177-9*) Hlth Research.
Law of Limitation in Three Volumes. V. G. Ramachandran. (C). 1989. 500.00 (*0-89771-788-0*, Pub. by Eastern Book); pap. 300.00 (*0-7855-6804-2*, Pub. by Eastern Book) St Mut.
Law of Limitations. Mew. 382p. 1991. boxed set 77.00 (*0-409-80909-8*, MICHIE) LEXIS Pub.
Law of Limited Partnership. Clement Bates. xxii, 275p. 1996. reprint ed. 42.50 (*0-8377-1982-8*, Rothman) W S Hein.
Law of Loss & Damage & Carrier Liability after the Container Reaches Land or Before It Leaves It. ICHCA Staff. (C). 1975. 40.00 (*0-7855-5080-1*, Pub. by ICHCA) St Mut.
Law of Lotteries, Frauds & Obscenity in the Mails. John L. Thomas. xviii, 358p. 1980. reprint ed. 43.95 (*0-8377-1202-5*, Rothman) W S Hein.
Law of Love. Laura Esquivel.Tr. of Ley del Amor. 1997. pap. 16.00 (*0-609-80127-9*) Random Hse Value.
***Law of Love.** Melford Okilo. 48p. 1999. pap. 5.00 (*1-879605-62-7*) U Sci & Philos.
Law of Love. Martha Schroeder. 512p. 1994. mass mkt. 4.99 (*0-8217-4430-5*, Zebra Kensgtn) Kensgtn Pub Corp.
Law of Love. large type ed. Isobel Neill. (Romance Ser.). 1994. pap. 16.99 (*0-7089-7621-2*, Linford) Ulverscroft.
Law of Love: English Spirituality in the Age of Wyclif. Ed. & Tr. by David L. Jeffrey. LC 87-36582. 414p. reprint ed. pap. 128.40 (*0-7837-3182-5*, 204278600006) Bks Demand.
Law of Love & Love As a Law: Or, Christian Ethics. 3rd ed. Mark Hopkins. LC 75-3196. reprint ed. 42.50 (*0-404-59197-3*) AMS Pr.
Law of Love Enshrined: Selected Essays. John Hatcher & William S. Hatcher. LC 96-109327. 296p. (Orig.). 1996. pap. 21.95 (*0-85398-405-0*) G Ronald Pub.
Law of Maintenance. Ejaz Ahmed. (C). 1988. 85.00 (*0-7855-3560-8*) St Mut.
Law of Mandamus & the Practice Connected with It: With an Appendix of Forms. Halsey H. Moses. iv, 268p. 1981. reprint ed. 43.00 (*0-8377-0838-9*, Rothman) W S Hein.
Law of Marine Collision. Nicholas J. Healy & Joseph C. Sweeney. LC 97-45202. 672p. 1998. text 150.00 (*0-87033-505-7*) Cornell Maritime.
Law of Marine Insurance. Howard N. Bennett. LC 95-47056. 628p. (C). 1996. text 135.00 (*0-19-825844-5*, Clarendon Pr) OUP.
Law of Marine Insurance. Susan Hodges. LC 97-212023. 680p. 1996. pap. 70.00 (*1-85941-227-0*, Pub. by Cavendish Pubng) Gaunt.
Law of Maritime Boundary Delimitation: A Case Study of the Russian Federation. Alex G. Elferink. LC 94-30592. (Publications on Ocean Development: Vol. 24). 464p. (C). 1994. lib. bdg. 149.00 (*0-7923-3082-X*, Pub. by M Nijhoff) Kluwer Academic.
Law of Maritime Delimitation--Reflections. 343p. 1989. text 100.00 (*0-521-46330-0*) Cambridge U Pr.
Law of Maritime Delimitation--Reflections. Prosper Weil. 343p. (C). 1989. 210.00 (*0-949009-40-7*, Pub. by Grotius Pubns Ltd) St Mut.
Law of Maritime Personal Injuries, 2 vols., Set. 4th ed. Martin J. Norris. LC 90-61399. 1990. 215.00 (*0-685-59891-8*) West Group.
Law of Maritime Prize, Pt. IX-C. J. H. Verzijl. Ed. by Wybo P. Heere & J. P. Offerhaus. (International Law in Historical Perspective II Ser.: Vol. XI). 696p. 1992. lib. bdg. 266.00 (*0-7923-0944-8*) Kluwer Academic.

An Asterisk (*) at the beginning of an entry indicates that the title is appearing for the first time.

Law of Marketing. Oswald. (SWC-Business Law Ser.). 2000. pap. 50.00 (*0-324-00902-X*) Thomson Learn.

Law of Marketing in Australia & New Zealand. 2nd ed. John Collinge & Bruce Clarke. 531p. 1989. pap. 65.00 (*0-409-49548-4*, Austral, MICHIE) LEXIS Pub.

Law of Marriage: Based on H. R. Hahlo, the South African Law of Husband & Wife, Vol. 1. June Sinclair & Jacqueline Heaton. 577p. 1996. 107.50 (*0-7021-3601-8*, Pub. by Juta & Co) Gaunt.

Law of Marriage & Divorce. Paras Diwan. (C). 1988. 200.00 (*0-7855-3558-6*) St Mut.

Law of Marriage & Divorce: Giving the Law in All the States & Territories with Approved Forms. Frank Keezer. xvii, 609p. 1991. reprint ed. 58.50 (*0-8377-2339-6*, Rothman) W S Hein.

Law of Marriage & Divorce in India. B. P. Beri. 750p. (C). 1989. 300.00 (*0-7855-1411-2*) St Mut.

Law of Married Women in Massachusetts. 2nd ed. George A. Ernst. xxxvi, 285p. 1993. reprint ed. 42.50 (*0-8377-2106-7*, Rothman) W S Hein.

Law of Mass Communications: Freedom & Control of Print & Broadcast Media. 7th ed. Dwight L. Teeter, Jr. & Don R. Le Duc. LC 92-11005. 1992. text 39.95 (*0-88277-981-8*) Foundation Pr.

Law of Mass Communications: Freedom & Control of Print & Broadcast Media. 8th ed. Dwight L. Teeter, Jr. & Don R. LeDuc. 125p. (C). 1995. pap. text, student ed. write for info. (*1-56662-315-4*) Foundation Pr.

Law of Mass Communications, Freedom & Control of Print & Broadcase Media: Freedom & Control of Print & Broadcast Media. 8th ed. Dwight L. Teeter, Jr. & Don R. Le Duc. 843p. (C). 1995. text 44.95 (*1-56662-245-X*) Foundation Pr.

Law of Mass Communications Freedom & Control of Print & Broadcast Media. 9th ed. Dwight L. Teeter, Jr. et al. LC 98-7518. (University Casebook Ser.). 874p. (C). 1998. text. write for info. (*1-56662-602-1*) Foundation Pr.

Law of Mass Communications, Freedom & Control of Print & Broadcast Media, 1996: Supplement to. 8th ed. Dwight L. Teeter, Jr. & Don R. Le Duc. 146p. (C). 1996. pap. text. write for info. (*1-56662-356-1*) Foundation Pr.

***Law of Master & Servant, 1 vol.** John Macdonnell. xxxiv, 717p. 2000. reprint ed. 188.00 (*1-56169-628-5*) Gaunt.

Law of Medical Liability in a Nutshell. Marcia M. Boumil & Clifford E. Elias. LC 95-35002. (Nutshell Ser.). 266p. (C). 1995. pap. 21.00 (*0-314-06660-8*) West Pub.

Law of Medical Malpractice. Margaret C. Jasper. LC 96-188008. (Legal Almanac Ser.). 1996. text 22.50 (*0-379-11233-7*) Oceana.

Law of Medical Malpractice in Texas: A Primer for the Medical Community. Alan K. Laufman. LC 77-420. (Illus.). 136p. reprint ed. pap. 42.20 (*0-8357-7750-2*, 203610700002) Bks Demand.

Law of Medical Practice in Illinois. Theodore R. LeBlang et al. LC 86-83023. 1986. 125.00 (*0-317-03805-2*) West Group.

Law of Medical Practice in Illinois. Theodore R. LeBlang et al. LC 86-83023. 1993. suppl. ed. 59.95 (*0-317-03806-0*) West Group.

Law of Medical Practice in Ohio. Frank C. Woodside, III et al. LC 89-8553. 1989. 125.00 (*0-317-02930-4*) West Group.

Law of Medical Practice in Ohio. Frank C. Woodside, III et al. LC 89-8553. 1993. suppl. ed. 52.50 (*0-317-05705-7*) West Group.

Law of Medical Practice in Pennsylvania & New Jersey. Barton L. Post et al. LC 83-83245. 1984. 115.00 (*0-318-01198-0*) West Group.

Law of Medical Practice in Pennsylvania & New Jersey. Barton L. Post et al. LC 83-83245. 1992. suppl. ed. 62.50 (*0-317-03240-2*) West Group.

Law of Medicare & Medicaid Fraud & Abuse: 1998 Edition. Timothy Jost & Sharon Davies. LC 97-48611. 1997. pap. 125.00 (*0-314-22936-1*) West Pub.

Law of Mental Health. John Williams. 260p. 1990. 75.00 (*1-85190-083-7*, Pub. by Tolley Pubng) St Mut.

Law of Merchandise & Character Licensing. Charles W. Grimes & Gregory J. Battersby. LC 85-19471. (IP Ser.). 1985. ring bd. 145.00 (*0-87632-477-4*) West Group.

Law of Military Operations: Liber Amicorum Jack Grunawalt. Ed. & Pref. by Michael N. Schmitt. LC 98-16990. (International Law Studies: Vol. 72). 406p. (Orig.). (C). 1998. text. write for info. (*1-884733-10-7*) Naval War Coll.

Law of Mind in Action. Fenwicke L. Holmes. 225p. 1998. pap. 20.00 (*0-89540-414-1*, SB-414) Sun Pub.

***Law of Mines & Mining in the United States, 2 vols.** Daniel Moreau Barringer & John Stokes Adams. 1676p. 2000. reprint ed. 370.00 (*1-56169-587-4*) Gaunt.

Law of Modern Payment Systems & Notes. 2nd ed. Fred H. Miller & Alvin C. Harrell. LC 92-22178. 844p. 1992. pap. 42.95 (*0-87084-562-4*) Anderson Pub Co.

Law of Money & Financial Services in the European Community. J. A. Usher. LC 93-36603. (European Community Law Ser.). 240p. (C). 1994. 75.00 (*0-19-825294-3*, Clarendon Pr) OUP.

***Law of Money & Financial Services in the European Community.** 2nd ed. John Usher. LC 99-56841. (Oxford European Community Law Library Ser.). 320p. 2000. write for info. (*0-19-829877-3*) OUP.

Law of Monopolies: Competition Law & Practice in the U. S. A., E. E. C., Germany & the U. K. David M. Raybould & Alison Firth. 592p. (C). 1991. lib. bdg. 177.00 (*1-85333-624-6*, Pub. by Graham & Trotman) Kluwer Academic.

Law of Monopolies, Restrictive & Unfair Trade Practices. Avtar Singh. 134p. 1984. 60.00 (*0-7855-2999-3*) St Mut.

Law of Monopolies, Restrictive & Unfair Trade Practices. 3rd ed. Avtar Singh. (C). 1993. 42.50 (*81-7012-512-X*, Pub. by Eastern Book) St Mut.

Law of Mortgage Commitments. Charles B. Katzenstein. LC 92-28445. 1992. ring bd. 135.00 (*0-87632-970-9*) West Group.

Law of Mortgages. V. Ghosh. (C). 1988. 250.00 (*0-7855-3549-7*) St Mut.

Law of Motor Vehicles in U. P. P. L. Malik. 820p. 1984. 300.00 (*0-7855-3002-9*) St Mut.

Law of Multi-Bank Financing. Agasha Mugasha. 552p. 1998. text 65.00 (*0-7735-1628-X*, Pub. by McG-Queens Univ Pr) CUP Services.

Law of Municipal Finance. Clayton P. Gillette. write for info. (*0-318-59311-4*, Aspen Law & Bus) Aspen Pub.

Law of Municipal Tort Liability in Georgia. R. Perry Sentell, Jr. 212p. 1988. 24.50 (*0-89854-127-1*) U of GA Inst Govt.

Law of Nations. Emmerich De Vattel. LC 75-31104. 664p. reprint ed. 89.50 (*0-404-13519-6*) AMS Pr.

Law of Nations: An Introduction to the International Law of Peace. 6th ed. James L. Brierly. Ed. by Humphrey Waldock. 460p. 1978. text 54.95 (*0-19-825105-X*) OUP.

Law of Nations Affecting Commerce During War: With a Review of the Jurisdiction, Practice & Proceedings of Prize Courts. Francis H. Upton. xi, 304p. 1988. reprint ed. 42.00 (*0-8377-2704-9*, Rothman) W S Hein.

Law of Nations & the Book of Nature. George H. Williams. Ed. by R. W. Franklin. LC 84-72274. (New Essays in Christian Humanism Ser.: Vol. 1). (Illus.). 60p. (Orig.). 1985. pap. 4.95 (*0-9613867-0-3*) St Johns Univ Christ Hum.

***Law of Nations Considered As Independent Political Communities: On the Right & Duties of Nations in the Time of Peace.** Travers Twiss. xxiii, 378p. 2000. reprint ed. 120.00 (*1-56169-592-0*) Gaunt.

Law of Nations Considered As Independent Political Communities: On the Rights & Duties of Nations in Time of Peace. 2nd ed. Travers Twiss. lvi, 486p. 1985. reprint ed. 55.00 (*0-8377-1208-4*, Rothman) W S Hein.

Law of Nations Considered As Independent Political Communities on the Rights & Duties of Nations in Time of Peace. enl. rev. ed. Travers Twiss. xliii, 486p. 1999. reprint ed. 160.00 (*1-56169-480-0*) Gaunt.

Law of Nations: or The Principles of Natural Law, Vol. 2. Tr. by Joseph H. Drake. LC 95-77192. (Classics in International Law Reprint Ser.: No. 13). 1743p. 1995. reprint ed. 125.00 (*1-57588-257-4*, 310100) W S Hein.

Law of Natural Healing. Charles L. Gilson. 154p. 1996. reprint ed. spiral bd. 17.00 (*0-7873-0349-6*) Hlth Research.

Law of Natural Healing: Developing the Body, Mind & Spirit Through Forces Within. Charles L. Gilson. 1991. lib. bdg. 79.95 (*0-8490-4497-9*) Gordon Pr.

Law of Natural Healing (1905) Charles L. Gilson. 154p. 1996. reprint ed. pap. 15.95 (*1-56459-882-9*) Kessinger Pub.

Law of Naturalization in the United States of America & of Other Countries. Prentiss Webster. xx, 403p. 1981. reprint ed. 48.00 (*0-8377-1309-9*, Rothman) W S Hein.

Law of Naval Warfare. Ed. by Natalino Ronzitti. (C). 1988. lib. bdg. 304.50 (*90-247-3652-8*) Kluwer Academic.

Law of Negligence in Arizona, 1998 Supplement. Jefferson L. Lankford & Douglas A. Blaze. 100p. 1998. pap. write for info. (*0-327-00607-2*, 6421614) LEXIS Pub.

***Law of Negligence in Arizona, 1999 Supplement.** Jefferson L. Lankford & Douglas A. Blaze. 100p. 1999. write for info. (*0-327-01583-7*, 6421615) LEXIS Pub.

***Law of Negotiable Instruments.** 4th ed. James Ogden. xxii, 846p. 1999. reprint ed. 185.00 (*1-56169-549-1*) Gaunt.

Law of Negotiable Instruments (Bills of Exchange) in the Americas: An Analytical Statutory Concordance, 2 vols., Set. rev. ed. Ed. by Hessel E. Yntema. LC 74-7442. (Michigan Legal Publications). (ENG & SPA.). 1974. 84.00 (*1-57588-320-1*, 301930) W S Hein.

Law of Negotiable Instruments in Australia. 2nd ed. M. J. Rajanayagam. Ed. by Brian Conrick. 280p. (C). 1989. 76.00 (*0-409-49527-1*, AT, MICHIE); pap. 56.00 (*0-409-49528-X*, AT, MICHIE) LEXIS Pub.

Law of New Trials, & Other Rehearings, Including Writs of Error, Appeals, Etc. Francis Hilliard. LC 97-70702. lxxvii, 833p. 1997. reprint ed. 95.00 (*1-57588-206-X*, 311160) W S Hein.

Law of No-Fault Insurance. Margaret C. Jasper. LC 96-183723. (Legal Almanac Ser.). 1996. text 22.50 (*0-379-11235-3*) Oceana.

Law of Non-International Armed Conflicts: Protocol II to the 1949 Geneva Conventions. Howard S. Levie. LC 87-1706. 1987. lib. bdg. 217.50 (*90-247-3491-6*) Kluwer Academic.

Law of Non-Navigational Uses of International Watercourses. J. Bruhacs. Tr. by M. Zehery. LC 92-18240. 1993. lib. bdg. 121.00 (*0-7923-1822-6*) Kluwer Academic.

Law of Nuisance. 2nd ed. R. A. Buckley. 242p. 1996. write for info. (*0-406-02675-0*, MICHIE) LEXIS Pub.

Law of Nuisances. Edmund W. Garrett. xxvi, 548p. 1999. reprint ed. 172.50 (*1-56169-511-4*) Gaunt.

Law of Obligations: Essays in Celebration of John Fleming. Peter Cane. LC 98-29125. 474p. 1999. text 90.00 (*0-19-826484-4*) OUP.

Law of Obligations: Roman Foundations of the Civilian Tradition. Reinhard Zimmermann. 1312p. 1990. 180.00 (*0-7021-2347-1*, Pub. by Juta & Co) Gaunt.

Law of Obligations: Roman Foundations of the Civilian Tradition. Reinhard Zimmermann. 1,306p. 1996. reprint ed. pap. text 65.00 (*0-19-876426-X*) OUP.

Law of Obligations & Legal Remedies. Geoffrey Samuel. 376p. 1996. pap. 44.00 (*1-85941-130-4*, Pub. by Cavendish Pubng) Gaunt.

Law of Obligations in the Louisiana Jurisprudence: A Coursebook. 3rd ed. Saul Litvinoff. 928p. 1991. text 50.00 (*0-940448-21-1*) LSU Law Pubns.

Law of Obscenity & Pornography. Margaret C. Jasper. LC 96-213636. (Legal Almanac Ser.). 96p. 1996. text 22.50 (*0-379-11231-0*) Oceana.

Law of Occupational Health & Safety in Ontario. 2nd ed. Grossman. LC 95-149169. (Illus.). 264p. 1992. boxed set 60.00 (*0-409-90414-7*, MICHIE) LEXIS Pub.

Law of Oil & Gas. 3rd ed. Richard W. Hemingway. (Hornbook Ser.). 711p. (C). 1991. 39.00 (*0-314-88941-8*) West Pub.

Law of Oil & Gas. 3rd ed. Richard W. Hemingway. (Practitioner Treatise Ser.). 1063p. 1993. reprint ed. text. write for info. (*0-314-86585-3*) West Pub.

Law of Oil & Gas, 7 vols., Set. rev. ed. Eugene O. Kuntz. 1989. 1100.00 (*0-87084-507-1*) Anderson Pub Co.

Law of Oil & Gas: Teacher's Manual for Cases & Materials on The. 6th ed. Richard C. Maxwell et al. (University Casebook Ser.). 177p. (C). 1992. pap. text. write for info. (*1-56662-030-9*) Foundation Pr.

Law of Oil & Gas Leases, 2 vols. 2nd ed. Earl A. Brown. 1958. ring bd. 250.00 (*0-8205-1160-9*) Bender.

Law of One see ABW (A Better World)

Law of One, Book Five: The Personal Material, No. 5. Don Elkins et al. 208p. (C). 1998. pap. 12.95 (*0-924608-21-8*, Whitford) Schiffer.

Law of One, Book Four Bk. 4: By Ra an Humble Messenger, No. 4. Don Elkins et al. LC 90-72156. 224p. (C). 1982. pap. 12.95 (*0-924608-10-2*, Whitford) Schiffer.

Law of One, Book Three, No. 3. Don Elkins et al. LC 90-72156. 244p. (C). 1982. pap. 14.95 (*0-924608-08-0*, Whitford) Schiffer.

Law of One, Book Two Bk. 2: By Ra an Humble Messenger, No. 2. Don Elkins et al. LC 90-72156. 160p. (C). 1982. pap. 12.95 (*0-924608-09-9*, Whitford) Schiffer.

Law of Ownership of Property & Investigation of Title. 2nd ed. J. C. Verma. (C). 1988. 220.00 (*0-7855-4741-X*) St Mut.

Law of Parental Control, Guardianship & Custody of Minor Children. Paras Diwan. 837p. 1978. 160.00 (*0-7855-1392-2*) St Mut.

Law of Parliamentary Privileges in India. V. G. Ramachandran. 912p. 1972. 135.00 (*0-7855-1329-9*) St Mut.

Law of Partition & Inheritance. Chandeshvara Thakkura. (C). 1990. 70.00 (*0-7855-6555-8*) St Mut.

Law of Partnership. P. N. Chadha. 828p. 1982. 330.00 (*0-7855-1405-8*) St Mut.

Law of Partnership. P. N. Chadha. (C). 1989. 63.00 (*0-7855-5271-5*) St Mut.

Law of Partnership. L. C. Goyle. (C). 1989. 155.00 (*0-7855-4814-9*) St Mut.

Law of Partnership (In a Nutshell) Avtar Singh. 1987. pap. 45.00 (*0-7855-1746-4*) St Mut.

Law of Partnership in India. Ed. by S. T. Desai. (C). 1990. 120.00 (*0-89771-232-3*) St Mut.

Law of Partnership, Including Limited Partnerships. Francis M. Burdick. lii, 422p. 1983. reprint ed. 45.00 (*0-8377-0333-6*, Rothman) W S Hein.

Law of Partnership, Principles, Practices & Taxation. 2nd ed. Avtar Singh. (C). 1993. 150.00 (*81-7012-493-X*, Pub. by Eastern Book) St Mut.

Law of Partnerships & Corporations. Anthony VanDuzer. (Essentials of Canadian Law Ser.). xvii, 394p. 1997. pap. 31.95 (*1-55221-008-1*, Pub. by Irwin Law) Gaunt.

Law of Partnerships in Australia & New Zealand. 6th ed. Keith L. Fletcher. 402p. 1991. 87.00 (*0-455-21056-X*, Pub. by LawBk Co) Gaunt.

***Law of Patents.** 2nd ed. Margaret C. Jasper. LC 99-58008. (Legal Almanac Ser.). 1999. 22.50 (*0-379-11339-2*, 4582519) Oceana.

Law of Patents for Useful Inventions, 3 vols., Set. William C. Robinson. LC 12-38173. 1972. reprint ed. lib. bdg. 130.00 (*0-89941-350-1*, 500480) W S Hein.

Law of Payment Bonds. Kevin L. Lybeck et al. LC 97-47681. 1998. 99.95 (*1-57073-532-8*) Amer Bar Assn.

***Law of Payment Systems & EFT.** Paul S. Turner. LC 99-28241. 1999. ring bd. 175.00 (*0-7355-0371-0*) Panel Pubs.

Law of Pensions & Profit-Sharing. Russell K. Osgood. LC 83-82690. 480p. 1984. suppl. ed. 80.00 (*0-316-66614-9*, Aspen Law & Bus) Aspen Pub.

Law of Peoples. John Rawls. LC 99-34785. 180p. 1999. 22.50 (*0-674-00079-X*) HUP.

Law of Perfect Freedom: Relating to God & Others Through the 10 Commandments. Michael S. Horton. 18.99 (*0-8024-6374-6*, 199) Moody.

Law of Personal Injury. Margaret C. Jasper. LC 96-140884. (Legal Almanac Ser.). 114p. 1996. text 22.50 (*0-379-11225-6*) Oceana.

Law of Persons & the Family. P. Q. Boberg. 820p. 1976. write for info. (*0-7021-0714-X*, Pub. by Juta & Co); pap. 36.00 (*0-7021-0715-8*, Pub. by Juta & Co) Gaunt.

Law of Persons Source Book. 2nd ed. R. A. Jordaan & C. J. Davel. 506p. 1996. pap. 40.00 (*0-7021-3628-X*, Pub. by Juta & Co) Gaunt.

Law of Persons Students' Textbook. C. J. Davel & R. A. Jordaan. 244p. 1994. pap. 26.50 (*0-7021-3273-X*, 15607, Pub. by Juta & Co) Gaunt.

Law of Petroleum & Natural Gas with Forms. George Bryan. xvi, 522p. 1983. reprint ed. 55.00 (*0-8377-0335-2*, Rothman) W S Hein.

Law of Piracy. 2nd rev. ed. Alfred P. Rubin. LC 96-53043. 504p. 1998. 115.00 (*1-57105-035-3*) Transnatl Pubs.

Law of Pleadings. V. Mogha. (C). 1987. 100.00 (*0-7855-3552-7*) St Mut.

Law of Pooling & Utilization: Voluntary, Compulsory, 4 vols. Martin & Bruce M. Kramer. 1957. ring bd. 500.00 (*0-8205-1455-1*) Bender.

Law of Power: Das Gesetz der Macht. Friedrich Von Wieser. Ed. by Warren J. Samuels. Tr. by W. E. Kuhn. LC 83-70450. 1983. 15.00 (*0-318-02061-0*) Bur Busn Res U Nebr.

Law of Preemption. LC 91-70842. 72p. 1991. pap. 20.00 (*0-89707-652-4*, 503-0203, ABA Antitrust) Amer Bar Assn.

Law of Premises Liability. 2nd ed. Joseph A. Page & David A. Elder. 413p. 1988. 78.50 (*0-87084-684-1*) Anderson Pub Co.

Law of Presumptive Evidence: Including Presumptions Both of Law & of Fact & the Burden of Proof Both in Civil & Criminal Cases, Reduced to Rules. John D. Lawson. lxxxix, 648p. 1982. reprint ed. 52.00 (*0-8377-0812-5*, Rothman) W S Hein.

Law of Privacy. annuals rev. ed. David A. Elder. LC 91-60363. (Civil Rights Ser.). 1991. suppl. ed. 125.00 (*0-685-59809-8*) West Group.

Law of Privacy Explained. Robert Ellis Smith. 57p. 1993. pap. 14.50 (*0-930072-10-3*) Privacy Journal.

Law of Private Defence. (C). 1988. 100.00 (*0-7855-3536-5*) St Mut.

Law of Private Limited Companies. Terence Prime & Gary Scanlan. 458p. 1996. write for info. (*0-406-04508-9*, MICHIE) LEXIS Pub.

Law of Privilege. Suzanne B. McNicol. 562p. 1992. 120.00 (*0-455-21149-3*, Pub. by LawBk Co) Gaunt.

Law of Probability. large type ed. Miriam Sharman. (Linford Mystery Library). 1990. pap. 16.99 (*0-7089-6956-9*, Linford) Ulverscroft.

Law of Probation in India. B. D. Khatri. (C). 1988. 150.00 (*0-7855-3318-4*) St Mut.

Law of Probation in India along with Juvenile Justice Act. B. D. Khartri. (C). 1988. 150.00 (*0-7855-4703-7*) St Mut.

Law of Probation in India along with Juvenile Justice Act. B. D. Khatri. (C). 1990. text 160.00 (*0-89771-483-0*) St Mut.

***Law of Process: Study Guide.** John C. Maxwell. (EZ Lesson Plan Ser.). 1999. pap. 7.99 (*0-7852-9672-7*) Tommy Nelson.

Law of Product Liability. Margaret C. Jasper. LC 96-183726. (Legal Almanac Ser.). 1996. text 22.50 (*0-379-11234-5*) Oceana.

Law of Product Warranties, No. 0622. annuals Barkley Clark & Christopher Smith. 1056p. 1984. boxed set, suppl. ed. 155.00 (*0-88712-098-9*) Warren Gorham & Lamont.

Law of Product Warranties, No. 0622. Barkley Clark & Christopher Smith. 1056p. 1992. suppl. ed. 155.00 (*0-7913-0997-5*) Warren Gorham & Lamont.

Law of Products Liability, 2 vols. 3rd ed. Marshall S. Shapo. LC 94-5938. 1994. 185.00 (*0-250-40729-9*, 81376-10, MICHIE) LEXIS Pub.

Law of Products Liability, 1998 Cumulative Supplement. Marshall S. Shapo. 710p. 1998. pap., suppl. ed. write for info. (*0-327-00518-1*, 8137913) LEXIS Pub.

***Law of Products Liability, 1999 Cumulative Supplement.** Marshall S. Shapo. 1000p. 1999. pap. write for info. (*0-327-01666-3*, 8137914) LEXIS Pub.

Law of Products Liability, 1990-1992, 2 vols. 2nd ed. Marshall S. Shapo. 1400p. 1991. boxed set 185.00 (*0-88063-282-8*, MICHIE); suppl. ed. 55.00 (*0-88063-849-4*, MICHIE) LEXIS Pub.

Law of Professional & Amateur Sports, 2 vols. Gary A. Uberstine. LC 88-19744. (Entertainment & Communication Law Ser.). 1988. ring bd. 230.00 (*0-87632-609-2*) West Group.

Law of Professional Responsibility in Ohio. Jack A. Guttenberg & Lloyd B. Snyder. (Ohio Practice Manual Ser.). 569p. (Orig.). 1992. pap. 49.00 (*0-87084-335-4*) Anderson Pub Co.

Law of Property. Frank Webb & Harvey Cohen. 400p. 1996. pap. 30.00 (*1-85941-131-2*, Pub. by Cavendish Pubng) Gaunt.

Law of Property. 2nd ed. Frederick H. Lawson & Bernard Rudden. (Clarendon Law Ser.). (Illus.). 256p. (C). 1982. pap. text 24.95 (*0-19-876129-5*) OUP.

Law of Property. 3rd ed. D. G. Kleyn. 612p. 1992. boxed set 177.00 (*0-409-05315-5*, SA, MICHIE) LEXIS Pub.

Law of Property, an Introductory Survey. 4th ed. Ralph E. Boyer et al. 696p. (C). 1991. 39.50 (*0-314-82936-9*) West Pub.

***Law of Property Casebook for Students.** A. J. Van Der Walt. 342p. 1999. 38.50 (*0-7021-5100-9*, Pub. by Juta & Co) Gaunt.

Law of Property Casebook for Students. 2nd ed. A. J. Van Der Walt. 482p. 1996. pap. 44.00 (*0-7021-3551-8*, Pub. by Juta & Co) Gaunt.

Law of Property Casebook for Students: Sakereg Vonnisbundel Vir Studente. A. J. Van Der Walt. 407p. 1992. pap. write for info. (*0-7021-2927-5*, Pub. by Juta & Co) Gaunt.

Law of Property Casebook for Students (Sakereg Vonnisbundel Vir Studente) 3rd ed. A. J. Van der Walt. (ENG & SPA.). 414p. 1997. pap. 30.50 (*0-7021-4221-2*, Pub. by Juta & Co) Gaunt.

Law of Property in Land. 2nd ed. H. Gibson Rivington. xxiv, 547p. 1999. reprint ed. 172.00 (*1-56169-519-X*) Gaunt.

Law of Property in Shakespeare & the Elizabethan Drama. Paul S. Clarkson & Clyde T. Warren. LC 68-9790. 364p. 1968. reprint ed. 75.00 (*0-87752-022-4*) Gordian.

Law of Property Owners Associations. Robert G. Natelson. 784p. 1989. 125.00 (*0-316-59865-8*, Aspen Law & Bus) Aspen Pub.

Law of Property Rights Protection: Limitations on Governmental Powers. Jan Laitos. LC 98-34101. 1998. boxed set 195.00 (*0-7355-0152-1*) Aspen Law.

L

An Asterisk (*) at the beginning of an entry indicates that the title is appearing for the first time.

Law of Property Students' Handbook. 2nd ed. N. J. Olivier et al. 337p. 1993. pap. 30.00 (*0-7021-2937-2*, Pub. by Juta & Co) Gaunt.

Law of Psychic Phenomena. Thomson J. Hudson. Ed. by Jack Holland. 220p. (Orig.). 1970. reprint ed. pap. 5.00 (*0-87852-000-7*) Inst Human Growth.

Law of Psychic Phenomena: A Working Hypothesis for the Systematic Study of Hypnotism, Spiritism & Mental Therapeutics. Thomas J. Hudson. 412p. 1997. reprint ed. pap. 29.95 (*0-7661-0106-1*) Kessinger Pub.

***Law of Public Communication.** 5th ed. (C). 1999. text. write for info. (*0-321-06334-1*) Addison-Wesley.

***Law of Public Communication.** 5th ed. (C). 2000. cd-rom 67.00 (*0-321-06335-X*) Addison-Wesley.

***Law of Public Communication.** 5th ed. (C). 2000. text. write for info. (*0-321-06336-8*) Addson-Wesley Educ.

Law of Public Communication. 5th ed. Kent Middleton. LC 99-38204. 624p. (C). 1999. pap. text 57.00 (*0-8013-3211-7*) Longman.

Law of Public Communication & 1993 Update Combo Package. 2nd ed. Kent R. Middleton. 1993. 32.95 (*0-8013-1095-4*) Longman.

Law of Public Communication 1993. 2nd ed. (C). 1993. text. write for info. (*0-8013-1136-5*) Longman.

Law of Public Communication 1993. 2nd rev. ed. (C). 1992. text. write for info. (*0-8013-0953-0*); text. write for info. (*0-8013-0954-9*) Longman.

Law of Public Communication 1993. 2nd rev. ed. (C). 1993. text. write for info. (*0-8013-1137-3*) Longman.

Law of Public Education. 4th ed. E. Edmund Reutter, Jr. 1015p. 1994. text 48.00 (*1-56662-154-2*) Foundation Pr.

Law of Puerto Rico, 1998 Index see Leyes de Puerto Rico Anotadas, Indice Edicion, 1998

Law of Purchasing. 1995. 48.00 (*0-929576-07-1*) Busn Laws Inc.

Law of Purchasing, 4 vols., Set, No. 49. 2nd ed. 2100p. 1986. ring bd. 320.00 (*0-929576-06-3*) Busn Laws Inc.

Law of Quasi-Contract. 2nd ed. S. J. Stoljar. xxv, 261p. 1989. 60.00 (*0-455-20808-5*, Pub. by LawBk Co) Gaunt.

Law of Quasi Contracts. Frederic C. Woodward. LC 97-4207. lxi, 498p. 1997. reprint ed. 67.50 (*0-8377-2788-X*, Rothman) W S Hein.

Law of Real Estate Brokers. D. Barlow Burke, Jr. LC 81-81531. 448p. 1983. 95.00 (*0-316-11676-9*, Aspen Law & Bus) Aspen Pub.

Law of Real Estate Brokers: Essential Documents for Representing the Older Client. D. Barlow Burke, Jr. 896p. 1992. 145.00 (*0-316-11700-5*, Aspen Law & Bus) Aspen Pub.

Law of Real Estate Financing. Michael T. Madison & Jeffrey R. Dwyer. LC 80-53430. 916p. 1981. suppl. ed. 160.00 (*0-88262-516-0*) Warren Gorham & Lamont.

Law of Real Property. Michael P. Kearns. LC 92-47071. 460p. (C). 1993. mass mkt. 47.25 (*0-8273-4878-9*) Delmar.

***Law of Real Property.** 2nd ed. Michael P. Kearns. (Paralegal Ser.). (C). 2000. pap. 43.50 (*0-8273-8336-3*) Delmar.

Law of Real Property: Instructor's Guide. Michael P. Kearns. 72p. 1994. pap. 12.50 (*0-8273-4879-7*) Delmar.

Law of Real Property Texas Student Pocket Part. Valerie J. Atkinson. 42p. 1993. 9.95 (*0-8273-6026-6*) Delmar.

Law of Recognition in International Law: Basic Principles. P. K. Menon. LC 94-33966. 1994. write for info. (*0-7734-9109-0*) E Mellen.

Law of Reinsurance, 1 vol. Graydon S. Staring. LC 93-70725. 1993. ring bd. 135.00 (*0-685-68847-X*) West Group.

Law of Reinsurance Claims. 2nd ed. Robert W. Hammesfahr & Scott W. Wright. 435p. 1998. reprint ed. 130.00 (*1-890155-07-1*) Andrews Pubns.

Law of Religious Identity: Models for Post-Communism. Andras Sajo & Shlomo Avineri. LC 98-36798. 1998. 89.00 (*90-411-1077-1*) Kluwer Law Intl.

Law of Religious Institutions. Kashmir Singh. (C). 1989. 160.00 (*0-7855-6132-3*) St Mut.

Law of Remedies, 3 vols. 2nd ed. Dan B. Dobbs. 1992. write for info. (*0-318-69573-1*) West Pub.

***Law of Respect.** John C. Maxwell. 2000. pap. 39.99 (*0-7852-9756-1*) Nelson.

***Law of Respect: Participant's Guide.** John C. Maxwell. 2000. pap. 7.99 (*0-7852-9757-X*) Nelson.

Law of Restitution. Andrew Tettenborn. 195p. 1994. pap. 30.00 (*1-874241-88-0*, Pub. by Cavendish Pubng) Gaunt.

Law of Restitution, 4 vols., Set. George E. Palmer. LC 77-71510. 2768p. 1978. 595.00 (*0-316-69005-8*, Aspen Law & Bus) Aspen Pub.

Law of Restitution in England & Ireland. 2nd ed. Andrew Tettenborn. LC 98-138543. 282p. 1996. pap. 50.00 (*1-85941-201-7*, Pub. by Cavendish Pubng) Gaunt.

Law of Return. Maxine Rodburg. 1999. pap. text 15.95 (*0-88748-313-5*) Carnegie-Mellon.

***Law of Return.** Karen Shenfeld. (Essential Poets Ser.: No. 93). 64p. 1999. pap. 10.00 (*1-55071-092-3*, Pub. by Guernica Editions) SPD-Small Pr Dist.

Law of Revenge. Theresa Collins. 1997. mass mkt. 6.99 (*0-449-22534-8*) Fawcett.

Law of Revenge. Theresa Collins. LC 96-30585. 1997. write for info. (*0-449-91075-X*) Fawcett.

Law of Revenge. large type ed. Theresa Collins. (Niagara Large Print Ser.). 416p. 1997. 29.50 (*0-7089-5888-5*) Ulverscroft.

Law of Reward or Consequences & Christ Our Surety. unabridged ed. Ralph Bouma. 142p. 1997. pap. 5.95 (*1-58339-005-7*, A5) Triangle Press.

Law of Sacrifice. B. P. Wadia. (Sangam Texts Ser.). 135p. 1986. pap. 12.75 (*0-88695-023-6*) Concord Grove.

Law of Sacrifice & What Came from Kirtland M. Russell Ballard. LC 98-72585. (Classic Talk Ser.). 91 p. 1998. write for info. (*1-57345-403-6*) Deseret Bk.

Law of Sale & Lease. A. J. Kerr. 352p. 1984. pap. 107.00 (*0-409-03750-8*, SA, MICHIE) LEXIS Pub.

Law of Sale & Lease. 2nd expanded rev. ed. A. J. Kerr. LC 97-162639. 518p. 1996. pap. write for info. (*0-409-03751-6*, MICHIE) LEXIS Pub.

Law of Sale of Goods & Hire Purchase. 4th ed. Avtar Singh. (C). 1993. 50.00 (*81-7012-513-8*, Pub. by Eastern Book) St Mut.

Law of Sales. Ray D. Henson. LC 85-70932. 350p. 1985. 7.00 (*0-8318-0482-3*, B482) Am Law Inst.

Law of Sales Tax in Uttar Pradesh, 2 vols., Set. 5th ed. S. D. Singh. (C). 1986. 205.00 (*0-7855-5431-9*) St Mut.

Law of Sales Tax in Uttar Pradesh, 2 vols., Set. 5th ed. S. D. Singh. (C). 1991. 95.00 (*0-7855-5430-0*) St Mut.

Law of Sales under the U. C. C. Ann Lousin & Carter H. Klein. write for info. (*0-318-59314-9*, Aspen Law & Bus) Aspen Pub.

Law of Sales under the Uniform Commercial Code. annuals 2nd ed. George I. Wallach. 696p. 1992. suppl. ed. 145.00 (*0-7913-1212-7*) Warren Gorham & Lamont.

Law of Schools, Students & Teachers in a Nutshell. 2nd ed. Kern Alexander & M. David Alexander. LC 94-48764. (Nutshell Ser.). 500p. (C). 1995. pap. 23.50 (*0-314-05882-6*) West Pub.

Law of Seamen, 3 vols., Set. 4th ed. Martin J. Norris. LC 84-52821. 1985. 370.00 (*0-685-59890-X*) West Group.

Law of Secured Transactions under the Uniform Commercial Code. 2nd ed. Barkley Clark. 1988. suppl. ed. 145.00 (*0-7913-0070-6*) Warren Gorham & Lamont.

Law of Secured Transactions under the Uniform Commercial Code, Suppl. 2. 2nd ed. Barkley Clark. 1988. suppl. ed. 66.00 (*0-7913-1195-3*) Warren Gorham & Lamont.

Law of Securities. 5th ed. E. I. Sykes & Sally Walker. 1070p. 1993. 160.00 (*0-455-21178-7*, Pub. by LawBk Co); pap. 110.00 (*0-455-21179-5*, Pub. by LawBk Co) Gaunt.

Law of Securities Regulation: Hornbook Series. Thomas L. Hazen. (Paralegal). 1224p. 1996. 41.00 (*0-314-08587-4*) West Pub.

Law of Self Defense: A Guide for the Armed Citizen. Andrew F. Branca. 238p. 1998. pap. 25.00 (*0-9665119-0-5*) Operon Security.

Law of Self Defense in North Carolina, 1996. John Rubin. LC 96-177889. 215p. (Orig.). (C). 1996. pap. text 18.00 (*1-56011-245-X*, 95.14) Institute Government.

Law of Self-Determination in Law & Practice. Michla Pomerance. 1982. lib. bdg. 90.00 (*90-247-2594-1*) Kluwer Academic.

Law of Selling: Terms & Conditions William A. Hancock. LC 98-204290. 1996. write for info. (*1-56789-026-1*) Busn Laws Inc.

Law of Selling Deskbook. LC 96-106851. 700p. 1995. ring bd. 165.00 (*1-56789-024-5*, 152) Busn Laws Inc.

Law of Sentencing. 2nd ed. Arthur W. Campbell. LC 91-77224. 1991. 120.00 (*0-685-59851-9*) West Group.

Law of Sentencing, Corrections, & Prisoners' Rights, Teacher's Manual to Accompany Cases & Materials on. 4th ed. Sheldon Krantz & Lynn S. Branham. (American Casebook Ser.). 203p. 1991. pap. text. write for info. (*0-314-84990-4*) West Pub.

Law of Sentencing, Probation, & Parole in North Carolina. 2nd ed. Stevens H. Clarke. LC 98-113057. 224p. 1997. text 38.00 (*1-56011-317-0*); pap. text 28.00 (*1-56011-307-3*, 97.06) Institute Government.

Law of Sewers & Drains. J. F. Garner. 1980. 110.00 (*0-7219-0581-1*, Pub. by Scientific) St Mut.

Law Of Sex Discrimination. 2nd ed. J. Ralph Lindgren & Nadine Taub. Ed. by Hannan. LC 93-25946. (Political Science). 550p. (C). 1993. 46.50 (*0-314-02708-4*) West Pub.

Law of Sexual Offences. Ed. by Ram D. Rakesh. (C). 1988. 180.00 (*0-7855-6031-9*) St Mut.

Law of Shipbuilding Contracts. Simon Curtis. (Lloyd's Shipping Law Library). 330p. 1991. 160.00 (*1-85044-334-3*) LLP.

Law of Similars. Christopher A. Bohjalian. LC 98-15807. 275p. 1998. 23.00 (*0-517-70586-9*) Harmony Bks.

***Law of Similars, 1 vol.** Christopher A. Bohjalian. 320p. 2000. pap. 13.00 (*0-679-77147-6*) Vin Bks.

***Law of Similars.** large type ed. Christopher A. Bohjalian. LC 99-30647. (Large Print Book Ser.). 1999. write for info. (*1-56895-723-8*) Wheeler Pub.

Law of Simple Discharge (in Private & Public Sectors) B. R. Ghaiye & Harminde Singh. (C). 1984. 180.00 (*0-7855-5421-1*) St Mut.

Law of Slander, Libel, Scandalum Magnatum, & False Rumors: Including the Rules Which Regulate Intellectual Communications, Affecting the Characters of Individuals & the Interests of the Public; With a Description of the Practice & Pleadings in Personal Actions, Informations, Indictments, Attachments for Contempts & c. Connected with the Subject. Notes by Thomas Huntington. LC 97-1957. xxxv, 456p. 1997. reprint ed. 65.00 (*0-8377-2662-X*, Rothman) W S Hein.

Law of Social Security. 3rd ed. Anthony I. Ogus & E. M. Barendt. 1988. 124.00 (*0-406-63372-X*, MICHIE); pap. 70.00 (*0-406-63370-3*, MICHIE) LEXIS Pub.

Law of Solid Waste, Pollution Prevention, & Recycling. Jeffrey M. Gaba & Donald W. Stever. LC 92-31459. (Environmental Law Ser.). 1992. ring bd. 145.00 (*0-87632-857-5*) West Group.

Law of Speaking Orders. A. S. Misra. 1985. 95.00 (*0-7855-1473-2*) St Mut.

***Law of Special Education.** Margaret C. Jasper. (Legal Almanac Ser.). 188p. 1999. 22.50 (*0-379-11341-4*) Oceana.

Law of Specific Relief. Ed. by P. S. Narayana. (C). 1990. 100.00 (*0-89771-240-4*) St Mut.

Law of Specific Relief. R. Sarkar & G. Singh. (C). 1988. 110.00 (*0-7855-3550-0*) St Mut.

Law of Speech & the First Amendment. Margaret C. Jasper. LC 99-32743. (Legal Almanac Ser.). 148p. 1999. text 22.50 (*0-379-11335-X*) Oceana.

Law of Sports: Includes 1985 Supplement. John C. Weistart & Cym H. Lowell. 1174p. 1985. suppl. ed. 50.00 (*0-672-82337-3*, 64200-10, MICHIE); suppl. ed. 15.00 (*0-87215-888-8*, 64201-10, MICHIE) LEXIS Pub.

Law of Strikes, Lockouts & Labor Organizations. Thomas S. Cogley. xiv, 377p. 1981. reprint ed. 45.00 (*0-8377-0435-9*, Rothman) W S Hein.

***Law of Student Expulsions & Suspensions 1999.** 2nd rev. ed. Lawrence F. Rossow & Jerry Parkinson. 58p. 1999. text 20.00 (*1-56534-071-X*) Ed Law Assn.

Law of Subrogation. Charles Mitchell. 212p. 1995. text 95.00 (*0-19-825938-7*) OUP.

Law of Subrogation. 2nd ed. Henry N. Sheldon. LC 97-77308. vii, 431p. 1998. reprint ed. 135.00 (*1-56169-354-5*) Gaunt.

Law of Success. Napoleon Hill. 1115p. 1996. 44.95 (*1-880369-06-0*) N Hill Found.

Law of Success. Paramahansa Yogananda. 32p. 1980. pap. 0.95 (*0-87612-150-4*) Self Realization.

Law of Success: Using the Power of Spirit to Create Health, Prosperity, & Happiness. Paramahansa Yogananda. 48p. 1998. reprint ed. 8.00 (*0-87612-156-3*) Self Realization.

Law of Succession in New South Wales. 2nd ed. G. L. Certoma. 307p. 1992. 85.00 (*0-455-21082-9*, Pub. by LawBk Co); pap. 65.00 (*0-455-21083-7*, Pub. by LawBk Co) Gaunt.

Law of Succession in Scotland. David Nichols et al. pap. text. write for info. (*0-406-42500-0*, UK, MICHIE) LEXIS Pub.

Law of Succession in South Africa: Includes the 1994 Supplement. M. M. Corbett et al. lvi, 739p. 1980. pap., suppl. ed. 58.50 (*0-7021-1096-5*, 15598, Pub. by Juta & Co) Gaunt.

Law of Succession in South Africa: 1994 Supplement. Ellison Kahn. 216p. 1994. pap. 216.00 (*0-7021-3229-2*, Pub. by Juta & Co) Gaunt.

Law of Succession Students' Handbook. 2nd ed. M. J. De Waal et al. 217p. 1996. pap. 27.50 (*0-7021-3626-3*, 15627, Pub. by Juta & Co) Gaunt.

Law of Suffrage & Elections: Being a Compendium of Cases & Decisions Showing the Origin of the Elective Franchise & Defining Citizenship & Legal Residence, Together with the Clauses of the State Constitutions Prescribing the Qualifications for Suffrage & the Law Governing the Conduct of Elections in the States - With an Appendix Containing the Provisions of the United States Constitution & Revised Statutes Regulation. M. D. Naar. (Illus.). xii, 317p. 1985. reprint ed. 42.00 (*0-8377-0910-5*, Rothman) W S Hein.

Law of Suggestion. rev. ed. Santanelli Publishing Co. Staff. (Illus.). 163p. 1980. reprint ed. pap. 11.00 (*1-878683-04-7*) TAT Found.

***Law of Suretyship.** Edward G. Gallagher & American Bar Association Staff. LC 00-29305. 2000. write for info. (*1-57073-780-0*) Amer Bar Assn.

Law of Suretyship. 5th ed. Arthur A. Stearns. Ed. by James L. Elder. LC 74-170608. 720p. 1973. reprint ed. lib. bdg. 145.00 (*0-8371-6030-8*, STLS, Greenwood Pr) Greenwood.

Law of Suretyship & Guaranty. Peter A. Alces. 320p. 1996. 135.00 (*0-7913-2615-2*) Warren Gorham & Lamont.

Law of Suspension. 3rd rev. ed. M. S. Nila. (C). 1994. 62.50 (*81-7012-523-5*, Pub. by Eastern Book) St Mut.

Law of Tax-Exempt Healthcare Organizations. Thomas K. Hyatt & Bruce R. Hopkins. LC 94-47550. (Nonprofit Law, Finance, & Management Ser.). 704p. 1995. 170.00 (*0-471-30490-5*) Wiley.

***Law of Tax-Exempt Healthcare Organizations.** Thomas K. Hyatt & Bruce R. Hopkins. (Intellectual Property-General, Law, Accounting & Finance, Management, Licensing, Special Topics Ser.). 352p. 2000. pap. text 75.00 (*0-471-36146-1*) Wiley.

Law of Tax-Exempt Organizations. 3rd ed. Bruce R. Hopkins. LC 78-23949. 667p. reprint ed. pap. 200.00 (*0-608-10671-2*, 202242000026) Bks Demand.

Law of Tax-Exempt Organizations. 6th ed. Bruce R. Hopkins. LC 78-23949. 667p. reprint ed. pap. 180.00 (*0-608-30301-1*, 2022420); reprint ed. pap. 180.00 (*0-608-30539-1*, 2022420) Bks Demand.

Law of Tax-Exempt Organizations. 7th ed. Bruce R. Hopkins. LC 97-28975. (Nonprofit Law, Finance, & Management Ser.). 952p. 1998. 165.00 (*0-471-19629-0*) Wiley.

***Law of Tax-exempt Organizations: April 2000 Supplement.** 7th ed. Bruce R. Hopkins. 228p. 2000. pap. 80.00 (*0-471-36144-5*) Wiley.

***Law of Tax-Exempt Organizations. 1999.** 7th ed. Hopkins. (Nonprofit Law, Finance, & Management Ser.). 176p. 1999. pap., suppl. ed. 75.00 (*0-471-29884-0*) Wiley.

Law of Taxation. Francis Hilliard. LC 97-30221. lii, 636p. 1997. reprint ed. 75.00 (*0-8377-2182-2*, Rothman) W S Hein.

Law of Teacher Evaluation, No. 42. Lawrence Rossow & Jerry Parkinson. 81p. (C). 1991. pap. 18.00 (*1-56534-031-0*) Ed Law Assn.

Law of Teacher Evaluation: A Self-Assessment Handbook. Perry A. Zirkel. LC 96-67178. 45p. 1996. pap. 6.00 (*0-87367-488-X*, LTE) Phi Delta Kappa.

Law of Termination of Employment. 5th ed. R. V. Upex & Fiona M. Tolmie. LC 99-159241. lxvii, 511p. 1997. write for info. (*0-421-58940-X*) Sweet & Maxwell.

Law of Territorial Waters of Midocean Archipelagos & Archipelagic States. Barry H. Dubner. 1977. pap. text 51.00 (*90-247-1893-7*) Kluwer Academic.

Law of Texas Medical Malpractice. Jim M. Perdue. LC 85-8205. 660p. 39.50 (*0-913797-08-1*) Houston Law Review.

Law of Textile in India. S. Kumar. (C). 1986. 187.50 (*81-7136-004-1*, Pub. by Periodical Expert) St Mut.

Law of the American Constitution: Its Origin & Development. Charles K. Burdick & Francis M. Burdick. 687p. 1996. reprint ed. 175.00 (*1-56169-217-4*) Gaunt.

Law of the American Constitution: Its Origins & Development. Charles K. Burdick. xviii, 687p. 1987. reprint ed. 65.00 (*0-8377-1948-8*, Rothman) W S Hein.

***Law of the American Constitution: Its Origins & Development.** Francis M. Burdick. xviii, 687p. 1999. reprint ed. 180.00 (*1-56169-487-8*) Gaunt.

Law of the Ancient Romans. Alan Watson. LC 71-128124. 126p. reprint ed. pap. 39.10 (*0-8357-8935-7*, 203343200086) Bks Demand.

Law of the Antitrust. Lawrence A. Sullivan. (Hornbook Ser.). 886p. (C). 1977. reprint ed. 38.00 (*0-314-32432-1*) West Pub.

Law of the Business Enterprise. Ed. by Sally Wheeler. (Oxford Readings in Socio-Legal Studies). 512p. 1995. text 75.00 (*0-19-876346-8*); pap. text 19.95 (*0-19-876347-6*) OUP.

Law of the Car: Everything You Ever Wanted to Know about Buying, Owning, & Selling a Vehicle. Lawrence W. Miles, Jr. 175p. 1993. pap. text. write for info. (*0-9635978-1-7*) Clairidge Pr.

***Law of the Common Agricultural Policy.** James A. McMahon. 194p. 2000. pap. 33.50 (*0-582-30294-3*, Pub. by Pearson Educ) Gaunt.

Law of the Commonwealth & Chief Justice Shaw. Leonard W. Levy. 400p. 1987. text 57.00 (*0-19-504865-2*) OUP.

Law of the Commonwealth & Chief Justice Shaw. Leonard W. Levy. 400p. 1987. pap. text 24.95 (*0-19-504866-0*) OUP.

Law of the Dead. Tess Collins. 1999. mass mkt. 6.99 (*0-8041-1795-0*) Ivy Books.

Law of the Desert Born. Louis L'Amour. 256p. 1984. mass mkt. 4.50 (*0-553-24133-8*) Bantam.

Law of the Desert Born. Louis L'Amour. 192p. 1983. 16.95 (*0-671-06697-8*) Boulevard.

Law of the Desert Born. large type ed. Louis L'Amour. (Special Ser.). 359p. 1993. reprint ed. 18.95 (*1-56054-646-8*) Thorndike Pr.

Law of the Eternal Is Perfect. Tr. by Charles B. Chavel. 128p. 1983. pap. 4.95 (*0-88328-023-X*) Shilo Pub Hse.

***Law of the European Community.** 2nd ed. Christopher Vincenzi. (Foundation Studies in Law). 480p. (Orig.). 1999. pap. 52.50 (*0-273-63846-7*, Pub. by F T P-H) Trans-Atl Phila.

Law of the European Economic Community: A Commentary on the EEC Treaty, 6 vols. Hans Smit & Peter E. Herzog. 1976. ring bd. 1010.00 (*0-8205-1623-6*) Bender.

Law of the European Economic Community: Enterprises, Economic Competition & the Economic Function of the State in the Process of Economic Integration. Ferenc Madl. 329p. (C). 1978. 60.00 (*963-05-1330-7*, Pub. by Akade Kiado) St Mut.

Law of the European Union. 2nd ed. Penelope Kent. 1996. 47.50 (*0-273-63419-4*, Pub. by Pitman Pbg) Trans-Atl Phila.

Law of the European Union Social Chapter. Jeff Kenner. 224p. 1999. 45.00 (*1-901362-69-8*, Pub. by Hart Pub) Intl Spec Bk.

Law of the Father? Patriarchy in the Transition from Feudalism to Capitalism. Mary Murray. LC 94-12147. 176p. (C). 1994. pap. 24.99 (*0-415-04257-7*, B4199) Routledge.

Law of the Fish. Lowell Jaeger. 24p. (Orig.). 1991. pap. 4.50 (*0-9622429-1-8*) Big Mtn.

Law of the Gun. Marshall Trimble. (Arizona Highways Wild West Collection). 192p. 1999. pap. 8.95 (*0-916179-69-9*) Ariz Hwy.

Law of the Harvest: An Inspirational & Instructional Guide to Help Today's Teenagers Take Charge of Their Lives Harold Morris. LC 98-90158. 112p. (YA). 1998. write for info. (*0-9662718-1-5*) Nantucket Publ.

Law of the Heart: Individualism & the Modern Self in American Literature. Sam B. Girgus. LC 78-24340. 192p. reprint ed. pap. 59.60 (*0-8357-7740-5*, 203609700002) Bks Demand.

Law of the Hittites: A Critical Edition. Harry Hoffner. LC 97-21912. (Documenta et Monumenta Orientis Antiqui Ser.). 1997. 147.50 (*90-04-10874-2*) Brill Academic Pubs.

Law of the International Civil Service: International Administrative Tribunals, Vol. 1. 2nd ed. C. F. Amerasinghe. 726p. 1994. text 160.00 (*0-19-825879-8*) OUP.

Law of the International Civil Service: International Administrative Tribunals, Vol. 2. 2nd ed. C. F. Amerasinghe. (Illus.). 582p. 1994. text 210.00 (*0-19-825880-1*) OUP.

Law of the International Criminal Tribunal for the Former Yugoslavia: A Documentary History & Analysis. M. Cherif Bassiouni. LC 95-50417. 1094p. 1996. 135.00 (*1-57105-004-3*) Transnatl Pubs.

Law of the Internet. George B. Delta & Jeffrey H. Matsuura. LC 97-46405. 1997. ring bd. 160.00 (*1-56706-654-2*) Aspen Law.

***Law of the Internet: 1999 Edition.** F. Lawerence Street. 900p. 1999. write for info. (*0-327-10015-X*, 6420512) LEXIS Pub.

Law of the Internet, 1998 Edition. F. Lawrence Street. LC 97-75586. xxxiii, 650 p. 1997. 115.00 (*1-55834-788-7*) LEXIS Pub.

Law of the Internet, 1998. F. Lawrence Street. LC 97-75792. (Law of the Internet Ser.). 830p. 1998. 115.00 (*0-327-00856-3*, 6420511) LEXIS Pub.

***Law of the Jungle.** 2000. per. 14.00 (*0-671-03909-1*) PB.

An Asterisk (*) at the beginning of an entry indicates that the title is appearing for the first time.

Law of the Jungle. Franklin W. Dixon. LC 96-105832. (Hardy Boys Casefiles Ser.: No. 105). (J). (gr. 7 up). 1995. pap. 3.99 (0-671-50428-2) PB.

Law of the Jungle. Franklin W. Dixon. (Hardy Boys Casefiles Ser.: No. 105). (YA). (gr. 6 up). 1995. 9.09 (0-606-08537-8, Pub. by Turtleback) Demco.

Law of the Jungle. Dillon Ingram. LC 94-68203. 325p. 1994. 19.95 (0-9642928-6-6) Palladium Pr.

Law of the Kinsmen. Shaw of Dunfermline. 178p. 1996. reprint ed. 50.00 (1-56169-210-7) Gaunt.

Law of the Land: Two Hundred Years of American Farmland Policy. John Opie. LC 94-28389. (Illus.). xxii, 231p. 1987. reprint ed. pap. text 17.95 (0-8032-8607-4, Bison Books) U of Nebr Pr.

Law of the Lawless. Lee. LC 98-48524. Date not set. 30.00 (0-7838-0442-3, G K Hall Lrg Type) Mac Lib Ref.

***Law of the Lawless** Wayne C. Lee. LC 98-48524. 207 p. 1999. write for info. (0-7540-3653-7) Chivers N Amer.

***Law of the Lifegivers: The Domestication of Desire.** Rene Devisch & Claude Brodeur. 288p. 1999. pap. 27.00 (90-5702-423-3) Gordon & Breach.

***Law of the Lifegivers: The Domestication of Desire.** Rene Devisch & Claude Brodeur. 292p. 1999. text 48.00 (90-5702-422-5, Harwood Acad Pubs) Gordon & Breach.

Law of the Mountain Man. William W. Johnstone. 1995. mass mkt. 4.50 (0-8217-5117-4, Zebra Kensgtn) Kensgtn Pub Corp.

Law of the Mountain Man. William W. Johnstone. 256p. 1998. mass mkt. 4.99 (0-8217-5854-3, Zebra Kensgtn) Kensgtn Pub Corp.

***Law of the Mountain Man, Vol. 1.** large type ed. William W. Johnstone. LC 99-35535. 348p. 1999. 23.95 (0-7838-8730-2, G K Hall Lrg Type) Mac Lib Ref.

Law of the Mountain Man. rev. ed. William W. Johnstone. 256p. 1995. pap. 4.99 (0-8217-5367-3) Kensgtn Pub Corp.

Law of the New Thought. William W. Atkinson. 93p. 1993. pap. 8.00 (0-89540-270-X, SB-270) Sun Pub.

Law of the New Thought. William W. Atkinson. 93p. 1996. reprint ed. spiral bd. 10.00 (0-7873-0057-8) Hlth Research.

Law of the New Thought: A Study of Fundamental Principles & Their Application (1902) William W. Atkinson. 94p. 1996. reprint ed. pap. 7.95 (1-56459-846-2) Kessinger Pub.

Law of the Offerings. Andrew Jukes. LC 68-19198. 220p. 1976. pap. 12.99 (0-8254-2957-9, Kregel Class) Kregel.

Law of the Office & Duties of the Sheriff: With the Writs & Forms Relating to the Office. 2nd ed. Cameron Churchill. lix, 686p. 1999. reprint ed. 187.50 (1-56169-492-4) Gaunt.

Law of the Other: The Mixed Jury & Changing Conceptions of Citizenship, Law, & Knowledge. Marianne Constable. LC 93-28838. (New Practices of Inquiry Ser.). 208p. 1993. pap. text 15.95 (0-226-11498-8) U Ch Pr.

Law of the Other: The Mixed Jury & Changing Conceptions of Citizenship, Law, & Knowledge. Marianne Constable. LC 93-28838. (New Practices of Inquiry Ser.). 208p. 1994. lib. bdg. 38.00 (0-226-11496-1) U Ch Pr.

Law of the Parish Church. 6th ed. William Dale. 210p. 1989. reprint ed. pap. 38.00 (0-406-11400-5, UK, MICHIE) LEXIS Pub.

Law of the Press: A Digest of the Law Specially Affecting Newspapers; with a Chapter on Foreign Press Codes; & an Appendix Containing the Text of All the Leading Statutes. Joseph R. Fisher & James A. Strahan. xxvi, 297p. 1990. reprint ed. 40.00 (0-8377-2136-9, Rothman) W S Hein.

Law of the Psychic Phenomena. Thomson J. Hudson. 410p. 1995. 8.98 (0-7858-0470-6) Bk Sales Inc.

Law of the Range: Portraits of Old-Time Brand Inspectors. Stephen Collector. LC 91-73462. (Illus.). 132p. 1991. 45.00 (0-944439-45-4) Clark City Pr.

Law of the Real Estate Business. 3rd ed. William French & Harold F. Lusk. (C). 1975. 16.60 (0-256-01576-7, Irwn McGrw-H) McGrw-H Hghr Educ.

Law of the Real Estate Business. 4th ed. William French & Harold F. Lusk. (C). 1979. 24.95 (0-256-02167-8, Irwn McGrw-H) McGrw-H Hghr Educ.

Law of the Rhythmic Breath. Ella A. Fletcher. 372p. 1996. reprint ed. spiral bd. 18.50 (0-7873-0326-7) Hlth Research.

Law of the Rhythmic Breath: Teaching the Generation, Conservation, & Control of Vital Force (1908) Ella A. Fletcher. 372p. 1996. reprint ed. pap. 17.95 (1-56459-839-X) Kessinger Pub.

Law of the Road: Or Wrongs & Rights of a Traveller. R. Vashon Rogers, Jr. LC 97-1952. (Legal Recreations Ser.: Vol. IV). viii, 275p. 1997. reprint ed. 41.00 (0-8377-2580-1, Rothman) W S Hein.

Law of the Rope. Jory Sherman. (Gunn Ser.: No. 7). (Orig.). 1981. mass mkt. 2.25 (0-89083-766-X, Zebra Kensgtn) Kensgtn Pub Corp.

***Law of the Sea.** Caminos. 570p. 2000. 180.00 (1-84014-090-9) Ashgate Pub Co.

Law of the Sea. Division for Ocean Affairs & the Law of the Sea Of. (Bulletin Ser.: No. 31). 96p. 1996. pap. 15.00 (0-614-25030-7) UN.

Law of the Sea. 2nd ed. R. R. Churchill & A. V. Lowe. LC 88-10276. (Illus.). 400p. 1988. text 59.95 (0-7190-2634-2, Pub. by Manchester Univ Pr) St Martin.

Law of the Sea: A Manual of the Principles of Admiralty Law for Students, Mariners & Ship Operators. George L. Canfield & George W. Dalzell. xvi, 315p. 1983. reprint ed. 42.50 (0-8377-0442-1, Rothman) W S Hein.

Law of the Sea: A Select Bibliography. 86p. 17.00 (92-1-033077-3) UN.

Law of the Sea: A Select Bibliography. 184p. 1987. 11.50 (92-1-033062-5) UN.

Law of the Sea: A Select Bibliography. 56p. 1989. 11.00 (92-1-033066-8, 90.V.8) UN.

***Law of the Sea: A Select Bibliography.** 1998. Price not set. (92-1-033078-1) UN.

Law of the Sea: Issues in Ocean Resource Management. Ed. by Don Walsh. LC 77-7823. (Praeger Special Studies). 268p. 1977. 59.95 (0-275-90277-3, C0277, Praeger Pubs) Greenwood.

Law of the Sea: Marine Scientific Research. 38p. 1992. 12.00 (92-1-133404-7) UN.

Law of the Sea: Multilateral Treaties : A Reference Guide to Multilateral Treaties & Other International Instruments Related to the United Nations Convention on the Law of the Sea. rev. ed. United Nations Staff. LC 97-217890. xiii, 184p. 1997. write for info. (92-1-133521-3) UN.

Law of the Sea: Neglected Issues, 12th Annual Conference Proceedings. Ed. by J. K. Gamble, Jr. 1979. 8.75 (0-911189-00-9) Law Sea Inst.

Law of the Sea: New Worlds, New Discoveries, 26th Conference Proceedings. Ed. by Edward L. Miles & Tullio Treves. 500p. 58.00 (0-911189-26-2) Law Sea Inst.

Law of the Sea: Ocean Law & Policy. Thomas A. Clingan, Jr. LC 93-3931. 638p. 1994. 95.00 (1-880921-37-5); pap. 75.00 (1-880921-28-6) Austin & Winfield.

Law of the Sea: Oceanic Resources. Erin B. Jones. LC 72-96510. (SMU Law School Study Ser.). 176p. reprint ed. pap. 54.60 (0-8357-8936-5, 203343400086) Bks Demand.

Law of the Sea: Official Text of the United Nations Convention on the Law of the Sea of 10 December 1982 & of the Agreement Relating to the Implementation of Part XI of the United Nations Convention . . . Division for Ocean Affairs & the Law of the Sea Of. LC 97-229152. 294p. 1997. pap. 25.00 (92-1-133522-1, E.97.V.10) UN.

Law of the Sea: Problems from the East Asian Perspective. Ed. by Choon-ho Park & Jae Kyu Park. (Law of the Sea Workshop Ser.: No. 8). 620p. 1987. 42.00 (0-911189-14-9) Law Sea Inst.

Law of the Sea: State Practice in Zones of Special Jurisdiction, 13th Annual Conference Proceedings. Ed. by T. Clingan. 550p. 1982. 14.25 (0-911189-02-5) Law Sea Inst.

***Law of the Sea: The Common Heritage & Emerging Challenges.** Harry N. Scheiber. LC 00-34889. (Publications on Ocean Development). 2000. write for info. (90-411-1401-7) Kluwer Law Intl.

Law of the Sea: U. S. Policy Dilemma. Ed. by Bernard Oxman. LC 83-107880. 184p. (C). 1983. pap. 24.95 (0-917616-53-7); text 44.95 (0-917616-59-6) Transaction Pubs.

Law of the Sea: United Nations Convention on the Law of the Sea. 224p. 1991. 12.95 (0-685-53677-7, E.83.V.5) UN.

Law of the Sea: What Lies Ahead? 20th Annual Conference Proceedings. Ed. by Thomas A. Clingan. 600p. 1988. 45.00 (0-911189-18-1) Law Sea Inst.

***Law of the Sea & Northeast Asia: A Challenge for Cooperation.** Hfui-gwfon Pak. LC 00-42836. (Publications on Ocean Development). 2000. write for info. (90-411-1407-6) Kluwer Law Intl.

Law of the Sea & Ocean Development Issues in the Pacific Basin: 15th Annual Conference Proceeding. Ed. by Edward L. Miles & S. Allen. 638p. 1983. 18.00 (0-911189-06-8) Law Sea Inst.

Law of the Sea Document Yearbook. Nilos. 1900. lib. bdg. write for info. (0-86010-598-9) Kluwer Academic.

Law of the Sea in a Nutshell. Louis B. Sohn & Kristen Gustafson. LC 84-7469. (Nutshell Ser.). 264p. (C). 1984. reprint ed. pap. 21.00 (0-314-82348-4) West Pub.

Law of the Sea in the Asian Pacific Region: Developments & Prospects. Ed. by James Crawford & Donald R. Rothwell. LC 94-4409. (Publications on Ocean Development: Vol. 21). 284p. (C). 1994. lib. bdg. 124.00 (0-7923-2742-X) Kluwer Academic.

Law of the Sea in the 1980's, 14th Annual Conference Proceeding. Ed. by C. H. Park. 636p. 1983. 18.00 (0-911189-05-X) Law Sea Inst.

Law of the Sea in the 1990's: A Framework for Further International Cooperation. Ed. by Tadao Kuribayashi & Edward L. Miles. LC 92-5646. (Proceedings of the 24th Annual Conference of the Law of the Sea Institute Ser.). 550p. 1992. 55.00 (0-911189-23-8) Law Sea Inst.

Law of the Sea, the EU & Its Member States, Vol. POOD 28. Treves & Pineshi. LC 96-49724. (Publications on Ocean Development Ser.). 1996. 192.00 (90-411-0326-0) Kluwer Law Intl.

Law of the Sea Treaty: Some Crucial Questions for the U. K. Simon Webley. (C). 1990. 40.00 (0-907967-03-5, Pub. by Inst Euro Def & Strat) St Mut.

Law of the State of Israel - An Introduction. 2nd ed. Ariel Bin-Nun. 216p. 1992. 34.00 (965-09-0112-4, 73816, Pub. by R Mass Ltd) Lambda Pubs.

Law of the Student Press. 2nd ed. Student Press Law Center Staff. LC 94-68950. 269p. (YA). (gr. 7 up). 1997. pap. 18.00 (0-9643574-0-2) Student Pr Law.

Law of the Sun: The Spiritual Laws & History Governing Past, Present & Future. Ryuho Okawa. 1996. pap. 11.95 (1-85230-807-9, Pub. by Element MA) Penguin Putnam.

Law of the Super Searchers: The Online Secrets of Top Legal Researchers. T R Halvorson. LC 99-37318. 220p. 1999. pap. 24.95 (0-910965-34-X, CyberAge Bks) Info Today Inc.

Law of the Territorial Sea: Evolution & Development. Shekhar Ghosh. (C). 1989. 36.00 (81-85109-69-9, Pub. by Naya Prokash) S Asia.

Law of the Territorial Sea (Evolution & Development) Shekhar Ghosh. (C). 1988. 200.00 (0-7855-3690-6) St Mut.

***Law of the United Nations: A Critical Analysis of Its Fundamental Problems with Supplement.** Hans Kelsen & London Institute of World Affairs Staff. LC 00-25627. 2000. write for info. (1-58477-077-5) Lawbk Exchange.

Law of the Way (1911) Althurian Society Staff. 262p. 1998. reprint ed. pap. 15.95 (0-7661-0674-8) Kessinger Pub.

Law of the Wild. Gwen Hunter. 384p. 1997. 27.00 (0-340-63801-X, Pub. by Hodder & Stought Ltd); pap. 10.95 (0-340-63802-8) Hodder & Stought Ltd.

Law of the Wise. Dennis Burke. 64p. (Orig.). 1995. mass mkt. 5.99 (0-89274-777-3, HH-777) Harrison Hse.

Law of the Workplace: Rights of Employers & Employees. 3rd ed. James W. Hunt & Patricia K. Strongin. LC 93-38145. 200p. 1994. text 45.00 (0-87179-841-7) BNA Books.

***Law of the Year 2000 Problem: Strategies, Claims, & Defenses.** Richard D. Williams & Bruce T. Smyth. LC 98-44819. 1998. ring bd. 160.00 (0-7355-0300-1) Panel Pubs.

Law of the Yukon. Helene Dobrowolsky. LC 96-134759. (Illus.). 192p. 1995. pap. 24.95 (0-9694612-6-7, Pub. by Lost Moose) Genl Dist Srvs.

Law of Theft. 7th ed. J. C. Smith. 1993. pap. 42.00 (0-406-02510-X, MICHIE) LEXIS Pub.

Law of Things & Servitudes. C. G. Van Der Merwe. (Lawsa Student Text Ser.). 305p. 1993. pap. 65.00 (0-409-05938-2, SA, MICHIE) LEXIS Pub.

***Law of Tithes.** 2nd rev. ed. W. Bohun. iv, 472p. 2000. reprint ed. 147.00 (1-56169-608-0) Gaunt.

Law of Title Insurance. D. Barlow Burke, Jr. 592p. 1987. 95.00 (0-316-11707-2, Aspen Law & Bus) Aspen Pub.

Law of Title Insurance. 2nd ed. D. Barlow Burke, Jr. 1052p. 1999. ring bd. 145.00 (0-316-11788-9, 17889) Aspen Law.

***Law of Title Insurance.** 3rd ed. D. Barlow Burke. LC 00-44796. 2000. write for info. (0-7355-1503-4) Panel Pubs.

Law of Tort. B. M. Gandhi. (C). 1990. text 225.00 (0-89771-471-7) St Mut.

Law of Tort. Vivienne Harpwood. (Lecture Notes Ser.). 387p. 1994. pap. write for info. (1-874241-71-6, Pub. by Cavendish Pubng) Gaunt.

Law of Tort. Ed. by P. S. Pillai. (C). 1991. 90.00 (0-89771-797-X, Pub. by Eastern Book) St Mut.

Law of Tort. Ed. by E. D. Pitchford. 490p. 1996. pap. 125.00 (0-7510-0689-0, Pub. by HLT Pubns) St Mut.

Law of Tort. 2nd ed. Vivienne Harpwood. (Lecture Notes Ser.). 422p. 1996. pap. 30.00 (1-85941-171-1, Pub. by Cavendish Pubng) Gaunt.

Law of Tort (A Very Exhaustive Standard Publication) B. M. Gandhi. (C). 1987. 200.00 (0-7855-5407-6) St Mut.

Law of Tort in Hong Kong. D. K. Srivastava & A. D. Tennekone. 488p. 1995. write for info. (0-409-99793-5, MICHIE) LEXIS Pub.

Law of Torts. A. Anand & S. Sastri. (C). 1990. 175.00 (0-89771-256-0) St Mut.

***Law of Torts.** David DeWolf. 660p. (C). 1999. ring bd. 78.00 (1-879581-73-6) Lupus Pubns.

Law of Torts. John G. Flemming. (C). 1988. pap. 240.00 (0-7855-4104-7, Pub. by Witherby & Co) St Mut.

Law of Torts. B. M. Gandhi. 1987. 200.00 (0-7855-2244-1) St Mut.

Law of Torts. Joseph W. Glannon. 512p. 1995. 25.95 (0-316-31599-0, Aspen Law & Bus) Aspen Pub.

***Law of Torts.** Phil Osborne. (Essentials of Canadian Law Ser.). 350p. 2000. pap. 31.95 (1-55221-035-9, Pub. by Irwin Law) Gaunt.

Law of Torts. I. P. Pilla. (C). 1991. 90.00 (0-89771-793-7, Pub. by Eastern Book) St Mut.

Law of Torts. B. S. Sinha. 528p. 1976. 68.00 (0-7855-1701-4) St Mut.

Law of Torts. 2nd ed. David Green. (Questions & Answers Ser.). 262p. 1995. 18.00 (1-85941-266-1, Pub. by Cavendish Pubng) Gaunt.

Law of Torts, 6 vols. 2nd ed. Fowler V. Harper et al. 4160p. 1986. boxed set 695.00 (0-316-32593-7, Aspen Law & Bus) Aspen Pub.

Law of Torts. 7th ed. John G. Fleming. lxix, 706p. 1987. suppl. ed. 99.00 (0-455-20753-4, Pub. by LawBk Co); pap., suppl. ed. 69.00 (0-455-20754-2, Pub. by LawBk Co); suppl. ed. 8.50 (0-455-20959-6, Pub. by LawBk Co) Gaunt.

***Law of Torts.** 7th ed. Melville M. Bigelow. 1999. reprint ed. 145.00 (1-56169-454-1) Gaunt.

Law of Torts. 9th ed. John G. Fleming. LC 98-153670. lxxx, 807p. 1998. write for info. (0-455-21533-2) LawBk Co.

***Law of Torts: A Concise Treatise on the Civil Liability at Common Law & under Modern Statutes for Actionable Wrongs to Person & Property.** Francis M. Burdick. lxxx, 501p. 1999. reprint ed. 146.50 (1-56169-552-1, 18166) Gaunt.

Law of Torts: Blackstone's LLB Cases & Materials. 2nd ed. John Hodgson & John Lewthwaite. 469p. 1998. pap. 42.00 (1-85431-823-3) Gaunt.

Law of Torts: 1995 Cumulative Supplement, No. 1, 6 vols. 2nd ed. Incl. Vol. 1. 2nd ed. 1995. spiral bd., suppl. ed. 27.50 (0-316-32537-6); Vol. 2. 2nd ed. 1995. spiral bd., suppl. ed. 27.50 (0-316-32545-7); Vol. 3. 2nd ed. 1995. spiral bd., suppl. ed. 27.50 (0-316-32546-5); Vol. 4. 2nd ed. 1995. spiral bd., suppl. ed. 27.50 (0-316-32551-1); Vol. 5. 2nd ed. 1995. spiral bd., suppl. ed. 27.50 (0-316-32553-8); Vol. 6. 2nd ed. 1995. spiral bd., suppl. ed. 27.50 (0-316-32558-9); Set suppl. ed. 165.00 (0-316-32751-4, Aspen Law & Bus) Aspen Pub.

Law of Torts: 1995 Cumulative Supplement, No. 2, 6 vols. Gray. Incl. Vol. 3. 1995. 33.00 (0-316-32503-1); Vol. 4. 1995. 33.00 (0-316-32505-8); Vol 5. 1995. 33.00 (0-316-32507-4); Vol. 6. 1995. 33.00 (0-316-32508-2); Vol. 2. 1995. 33.00 (0-316-32502-3); 1995. Set suppl. ed. 165.00 (0-316-32559-7, Aspen Law & Bus) Aspen Pub.

Law of Torts, a Very Exhaustive Standard Publication. Frwd. by D. A. Desai. (C). 1987. 200.00 (0-7855-5113-1) St Mut.

Law of Torts in Australia. 2nd ed. Peter Cane & Francis A. Trindade. 826p. 1993. pap. text 85.00 (0-19-553316-X) OUP.

Law of Torts in Hong Kong. D. K. Srivastava & Aa. D. Tennekone. 300p. pap. write for info. (0-409-99636-X, SI, MICHIE) LEXIS Pub.

Law of Torts in New Zealand. Ed. by S. Todd et al. lxxi, 956p. 1991. 130.00 (0-455-20971-5, Pub. by LawBk Co); pap. 90.00 (0-455-20972-3, Pub. by LawBk Co) Gaunt.

Law of Torts, 1976. 4th ed. B. S. Sinha. (C). 1981. 50.00 (0-7855-5405-X) St Mut.

Law of Town & Country Planning: Including Compulsory Purchase & Compensation. A. J. Lomnicki. 200p. (C). 1991. pap. 75.00 (1-85352-901-X, Pub. by HLT Pubns) St Mut.

Law of Toxic Torts, 3 vols., Set. Michael Dore. LC 86-2249. (Environmental Law Ser.). 1987. ring bd. 375.00 (0-87632-536-3) West Group.

Law of Tracing. Lionel D. Smith. LC 96-29993. 396p. (C). 1997. text 98.00 (0-19-826070-9) OUP.

Law of Trade & Labor Combinations: As Applicable to Boycotts, Strikes, Trade Conspiracies, Monopolies, Pools, Trusts & Kindred Topics. Frederick H. Cooke. xxv, 214p. 1981. reprint ed. 85.00 (0-8377-0430-8, Rothman) W S Hein.

Law of Trade Marks. Nicola Isaacs. 190p. 1996. pap. 53.00 (1-85811-077-7, Pub. by CLT Prof) Gaunt.

Law of Trade Secrets. Robert Dean. l, 629p. 1990. 137.50 (0-455-20806-9, Pub. by LawBk Co) Gaunt.

***Law of Trademarks.** Margaret C. Jasper. LC 99-59098. (Legal Almanac Ser.). 1999. 22.50 (0-379-11342-2, 4582543) Oceana.

Law of Transfer of Property. Vepa P. Sarathi. 1995. pap. 25.00 (81-7012-574-X, Pub. by Eastern Book) St Mut.

Law of Transfer of Property. 3rd ed. Ed. by Vepa P. Sarathi. (C). 1990. text 50.00 (0-89771-506-3) St Mut.

Law of Transnational Business Transactions, 3 vols., Set. Ved P. Nanda. LC 81-2392. (International Business & Law Ser.). 1981. ring bd. 375.00 (0-87632-342-5) West Group.

Law of Treason in England in the Later Middle Ages. J. G. Bellamy. LC 85-81810. (Cambridge Studies in English Legal History). 284p. 1986. reprint ed. 70.00 (0-912004-39-8) Gaunt.

Law of Treason in the United States: Collected Essays, 12. James W. Hurst. LC 70-111264. (Contributions in American History Ser.: No. 12). 291p. 1971. 59.95 (0-8371-4666-6, HLT/, Greenwood Pr) Greenwood.

Law of Treaties. Lord McNair. 800p. 1986. text 175.00 (0-19-825152-1) OUP.

Law of Treaties Between States & International Organizations. P. K. Menon. LC 92-22554. 264p. 1992. text 89.95 (0-7734-9590-8) E Mellen.

Law of Trusts. Eileen E. Gillese. (Essentials of Canadian Law Ser.). xvi, 184p. 1996. pap. 30.95 (1-55221-005-7, Pub. by Irwin Law) Gaunt.

Law of Trusts. I. C. Goyle. (C). 1989. 210.00 (0-7855-4782-7) St Mut.

Law of Trusts. 5th ed. John G. Riddall. 464p. 1996. pap. write for info. (0-406-00905-8, RLT5, MICHIE) LEXIS Pub.

Law of Trusts, No. 1. Fratcher. 1986. 145.00 (0-316-29225-7, Aspen Law & Bus) Aspen Pub.

Law of Trusts, Cases & Text On. 6th ed. George G. Bogert et al. (University Casebook Ser.). 695p. 1991. text 39.95 (0-88277-883-8) Foundation Pr.

Law of Trusts in the West Indies: Cases & Commentary. Gilbert Kodilinye. 165p. 1991. pap. 55.00 (976-629-001-6) Gaunt.

Law of Trusts, Manual for Teachers to Accompany Cases & Text. 6th ed. George G. Bogert et al. (University Casebook Ser.). 90p. (C). 1991. pap. text. write for info. (0-88277-946-X) Foundation Pr.

Law of Tug, Tow & Pilotage. 3rd ed. Alex L. Parks & Edward V. Cattell, Jr. LC 93-49862. 1410p. 1994. text 175.00 (0-87033-448-4) Cornell Maritime.

Law of Unfair Business Competition: Including Chapters on Trade Secrets & Confidential Business Relations; Unfair Interference with Contracts; Libel & Slander of Articles of Merchandise, Trade Names, & Business Credit & Reputation. Harry D. Nims. LC 97-28833. xlvi, 581p. 1997. reprint ed. 125.00 (0-8377-2452-X, Rothman) W S Hein.

Law of Unfair Trade: Including Trade-Marks, Trade Secrets & Good-Will. James L. Hopkins. LC 97-28832. xliv, 437p. 1997. reprint ed. 65.00 (0-8377-2183-0, Rothman) W S Hein.

Law of Unlawful Possession. Alfred V. Crane. xxi, 169p. 1999. reprint ed. 65.00 (1-56169-505-X) Gaunt.

Law of Urban Land Ceiling in India. Narayana Swamy. (C). 1990. 60.00 (0-89771-299-4) St Mut.

Law of Values: An Exposition of the Primary Causes of Stock & Share Fluctuations. Sepharial. 80p. 1995. pap. 7.00 (0-89540-301-3, SB-301) Sun Pub.

***Law of Vendors & Purchasers of Real Property.** Francis Hilliard. LC 99-58130. 2000. 125.00 (1-57588-615-4) W S Hein.

Law of Violence Against Women. Margaret C. Jasper. LC 99-218133. (Legal Almanac Ser.). 145p. 1998. text 22.50 (0-379-11325-2, 4582357) Oceana.

Law of Wages: An Essay in Statistical Economics. Henry L. Moore. LC 65-26371. (Reprints of Economic Classics Ser.). (Illus.). 196p. 1967. reprint ed. 35.00 (0-678-00232-0) Kelley.

L

An Asterisk (*) at the beginning of an entry indicates that the title is appearing for the first time.

Law of Wakfs. Syed A. Habibullah. (C). 1990. 95.00 (*0-89771-245-5*) St Mut.

***Law of War.** Ingrid Detter. LC 99-86452. 384p. (C). 2000. text Price not set. (*0-521-78256-2*); pap. text Price not set. (*0-521-78775-0*) Cambridge U Pr.

Law of War. William Shatner. LC 97-39451. 320p. 1998. 23.95 (*0-399-14360-2*, Ace-Putnam) Putnam Pub Group.

Law of War Between Belligerents: A History & Commentary. Percy Bordwell. xxiv, 374p. 1994. reprint ed. 45.00 (*0-8377-1975-5*, Rothman) W S Hein.

Law of War Crimes: National & International Approaches. Timothy L. McCormack & Gerry J. Simpson. LC 96-22730. 1997. 175.00 (*90-411-0273-6*) Kluwer Law Intl.

Law of Water Rights & Resources. A. Dan Tarlock. LC 88-16645. (Environmental Law Ser.). 1988. ring bd. 145.00 (*0-87632-602-5*) West Group.

***Law of Watercourses.** 7th ed. Joseph K. Angell. (Law Classic Ser.). 424p. 2000. pap. 34.95 (*1-893122-92-1*); pap. 34.95 (*1-893122-93-X*) Beard Bks.

Law of Wetlands Regulation. William L. Want. LC 89-34160. (Environmental Law Ser.). 1989. ring bd. 145.00 (*0-87632-646-7*) West Group.

Law of Wills for Students. Melville M. Bigelow. xxxii, 398p. 1996. reprint ed. 52.50 (*0-8377-1984-4*, Rothman) W S Hein.

Law of Wills in Pennsylvania: Drafting, Interpreting, Contesting with Forms. J. Brooke Aker. LC 83-72488. (Illus.). 567p. 1999. ring bd. 109.50 (*1-887024-35-2*) Bisel Co.

Law of Works Contract & Exemption in Khadi Gram Udyog with U. P. Sales Tax Act. G. Goyal & L. Lal. (C). 1990. 68.00 (*0-89771-272-2*) St Mut.

Law of Writs. 5th rev. ed. V. G. Ramachandran. (C). 1993. 225.00 (*81-7012-504-9*, Pub. by Eastern Book) St Mut.

Law of Zoning in New Jersey, 2 vols. Robert M. Anderson. LC 89-84975. 1612p. 1993. suppl. ed. 65.00 (*0-317-03774-9*) West Group.

Law of Zoning in New Jersey, 2 vols., Set. Robert M. Anderson. LC 89-84975. 1612p. 1989. 200.00 (*0-317-02791-3*) West Group.

Law of Zoning in Pennsylvania, 2 vols. Robert M. Anderson. LC 82-82349. 1993. suppl. ed. 71.50 (*0-317-03158-9*) West Group.

Law of Zoning in Pennsylvania, 2 vols., Set. Robert M. Anderson. LC 82-82349. 1982. 220.00 (*0-317-00349-6*) West Group.

***Law Office Administration & Management.** Wilbur M. Yegge. (C). 2001. pap. 42.00 (*0-7668-1650-8*) Delmar.

Law Office Automation for Paralegals, Administrators & Legal Secretaries. Ashley S. Lipson. 384p. 1989. text 59.95 (*0-13-526583-5*) P-H.

Law Office Computer Literacy. Bernstein. (Paralegal Ser.). (C). 2001. pap. 24.75 (*0-8273-8146-8*) Delmar.

Law Office Dynamics: An Introduction to Legal Administration. Charlotte Smith. 192p. (Orig.). (C). 1992. per. 25.95 (*0-929563-10-7*) Pearson Pubns.

Law Office Economics & Management Manual, 1970-1990, 2 vols., Set. Ed. by Paul Hoffman. LC 72-121883. 200.00 (*0-317-12031-X*) West Group.

Law Office Economics & Management Quarterly, 1990. Ed. by Paul Hoffman. 115.00 (*0-318-42409-6*) West Group.

Law Office Guide to Small Computers. F. D. Rhoads & J. Edwards. (General Publications). (Illus.). 431p. 1984. text 95.00 (*0-07-052091-7*) Shepards.

Law Office Management. Terri M. Lyndall. (Paralegal Ser.). 1992. pap., teacher ed. 9.00 (*0-8273-4866-5*) Delmar.

Law Office Management. Gary A. Munneke. Date not set. pap. text. write for info. (*0-314-06585-7*) West Pub.

Law Office Management. 2nd ed. Jonathan S. Lynton. (C). 1996. text 39.95 (*0-8273-7975-7*) Delmar.

Law Office Management. 2nd rev. ed. Jonathan S. Lynton et al. (Paralegal Ser.). 496p. (C). 1996. mass mkt. 65.95 (*0-8273-7139-X*) Delmar.

Law Office Management - IML. 2nd ed. Lynton, Lyndall & Masinter Staff. (Paralegal Ser.). 48p. 1996. teacher ed. 17.95 (*0-8273-7140-3*) Delmar.

Law Office Management for Paralegals. Jonathan Lynton et al. 1992. pap. 37.95 (*0-8273-4865-7*) Delmar.

Law Office Management, 1989. (Commercial Law & Practice Ser.). 765p. 1989. 17.50 (*0-317-99780-7*, A4-4284) PLI.

Law Office Policy & Procedures Manual. 3rd ed. LC 96-86286. 272p. 1996. pap. 109.95 (*1-57073-359-7*, 511-0375) Amer Bar Assn.

Law Office Procedures. Illa Atwood. 1993. teacher ed. 12.25 (*0-02-800067-6*) Glencoe.

Law Office Procedures. Illa W. Atwood. LC 92-35871. 1993. 33.00 (*0-02-800066-8*) Glencoe.

Law Office Procedures. Long. LC 96-22549. 350p. (C). 1996. mass mkt. 69.95 (*0-314-09238-2*) West Pub.

Law Office Staff Manual: Model Policies & Procedures for Law Office Personnel. 80p. 1992. 89.00 (*0-89707-719-9*, 511-0307); disk 89.00 (*0-89707-070-4*) Amer Bar Assn.

Law Office Staff Manual for Solos & Small Law Firms. LC 95-81074. 112p. 1995. ring bd. 59.95 (*1-57073-249-3*, 511-361) Amer Bar Assn.

Law Office Transcription. Differding. (KK - Legal Secretary Studies). (C). 1991. mass mkt. 21.50 (*0-538-70550-7*) S-W Pub.

Law Office Word Processing with WordPerfect Version 5.1. Robert S. Hunter. (Klear-E-Lex Ser.). 260p. (Orig.). 1993. pap. 19.95 (*1-884177-04-2*) Justice IL.

Law Officer's Pocket Manual. John G. Miles. LC 91-169764. 1999. 15.95 (*0-87179-648-1*) BNA Books.

Law Officer's Pocket Manual, 1999 Edition. John G. Miles. 162p. 1998. spiral bd. 15.95 (*1-57018-059-8*, 1106) BNA Books.

Law on Accidents to Health Service Staff & Volunteers. Ravenswood Publ. Ltd. Staff. (C). 1987. 125.00 (*0-901812-23-4*); pap. 89.00 (*0-901812-24-2*) St Mut.

Law on Medicines, 3 vols., Set. I. H. Harrison. 1987. text 745.50 (*0-85200-820-1*) Kluwer Academic.

Law on Medicines: A Comprehensive Guide. I. H. Harrison. 1986. text 339.00 (*0-85200-897-X*) Kluwer Academic.

Law on Medicines: Distribution & Selling. I. H. Harrison. 1986. lib. bdg. 281.00 (*0-85200-912-7*) Kluwer Academic.

Law on Medicines: Licensing & Manufacture. I. H. Harrison. 1986. text 339.00 (*0-85200-913-5*) Kluwer Academic.

Law on Money Laundering: Statutes & Commentary. Leonard Jason-Lloyd. LC 96-52666. 108p. 1997. 37.50 (*0-7146-4736-5*, Pub. by F Cass Pubs); pap. 22.50 (*0-7146-4284-3*, Pub. by F Cass Pubs) Intl Spec Bk.

Law on Speeding & Radar. 2nd ed. A. Shakoor Manraj & Paul D. Haines. 168p. 1991. boxed set 45.00 (*0-409-90376-0*, MICHIE) LEXIS Pub.

Law on the Electronic Frontier. Ian Lloyd. (Hume Papers on Public Policy 2.4). 96p. 1995. pap. 16.00 (*0-7486-0594-0*, Pub. by Edinburgh U Pr) Col U Pr.

***Law on the Internet.** Cate Banks & Heather Douglas. 128p. 2000. pap. 29.95 (*1-86287-354-2*, Pub. by Federation Pr) Gaunt.

Law on the Midway: The Founding of the University of Chicago Law School. Frank L. Ellsworth. LC 77-78777. 1977. lib. bdg. 8.95 (*0-226-20608-4*) U Ch Pr.

Law on the Net, 2 vols. 2nd rev. ed. James Evans. LC 97-12404. (Illus.). 704p. 1997. 39.95 (*0-87337-384-7*) Nolo com.

Law on Variances. fac. ed. Robert A. Williams. LC KF5698.W5. (Land Policy Roundtable Policy Analysis Ser.: No. 207). 15p. 1980. reprint ed. pap. 30.00 (*0-7837-7826-0*, 204758200007) Bks Demand.

***Law 101: Everything You Need to Know About the American Legal System.** Jay M. Feinman. LC 99-28333. 352p. 2000. 30.00 (*0-19-513265-3*) OUP.

Law, or a Discourse Thereof. Henry Finch. LC 68-57385. xii, 506p. 1969. reprint ed. 22.50 (*0-678-04526-7*) Kelley.

Law, or a Discourse Thereof. Henry Finch. LC 91-77688. x, 520p. 1992. reprint ed. 85.00 (*0-89941-786-8*, 307420) W S Hein.

Law: or A Discourse Thereof: To Which Are Now Added, Notes & References & a Table to the Chapters, 4 bks. Danby Pickering & Henry Finch. (Illus.). 528p. 1969. reprint ed. 22.50 (*0-8377-2125-3*, Rothman) W S Hein.

Law, Order & Government: The Caernarfonshire Justices of the Peace & Gentry, 1559-1640. J. Gwynfor Jones. LC 96-132389. 256p. 1996. 45.00 (*0-7083-1332-9*, Pub. by Univ Wales Pr) Paul & Co Pubs.

Law, Order, & Riots in Mandatory Palestine, 1928-1935. Martin Kolinsky. LC 92-34580. 256p. 1993. text 65.00 (*0-312-09164-8*) St Martin.

Law Out of Context. Alan Watson. LC 99-32393. 256p. 1999. 40.00 (*0-8203-2161-3*) U of Ga Pr.

Law Partnership: Its Rights & Responsibilities. LC 95-80825. 264p. 1996. pap. 69.95 (*1-57073-245-0*, 546-0025) Amer Bar Assn.

Law Partnership: Its Rights & Responsibilities. 2nd ed. George H. Cain & American Bar Association Staff. LC 98-53814. (Illus.). 1999. write for info. (*1-57073-648-0*) Amer Bar Assn.

Law, Personalities, & Politics of the Middle East: Essays in Honor of Majid Khadduri. Ed. by James P. Piscatori & George S. Harris. (Illus.). 270p. (C). 1987. text 60.00 (*0-916808-32-7*) Westview.

***Law, Policy & Development in the Rural Environment.** Ed. by Nicholas Herbert-Young. 176p. 1999. 75.00 (*0-7083-1476-7*, Pub. by Univ Wales Pr) Paul & Co Pubs.

Law, Policy & International Justice: Essays in Honour of Maxwell Cohen. Ed. by William Kaplan & Donald McRae. 520p. 1993. 60.00 (*0-7735-1114-8*, Pub. by McG-Queens Univ Pr) CUP Services.

Law, Policy & Optimizing Analysis. Stuart S. Nagel. LC 86-8140. 347p. 1986. 65.00 (*0-89930-181-9*, NLP/, Quorum Bks) Greenwood.

***Law, Politics & Local Democracy.** Ian Leigh. 300p. 2000. text 85.00 (*0-19-825698-1*) OUP.

***Law, Politics & the Constitution: Essays in Honor of Geoffrey Marshall.** Ed. by David Butler et al. LC 99-21477. (Illus.). 328p. 1999. text 85.00 (*0-19-829585-5*) OUP.

Law, Power, & Justice: Protection of Personal Rights under the Indian Penal Code. 2nd ed. Vasudha Dhagamwar. LC 92-20728. 400p. (C). 1992. text 38.95 (*0-8039-9441-9*) Sage.

Law, Power & Justice in England & Wales. Ed. by Ian K. McKenzie. LC 97-38546. (Law, Power & Justice in Comparative Perspective Ser.). 240p. 1998. 65.00 (*0-275-95881-7*, Praeger Pubs) Greenwood.

***Law, Power & Politics in Niger: Land Struggles & the Rural Code.** Christian Lund. 268p. 1998. pap. 26.95 (*3-8258-3405-0*, Pub. by CE24) Transaction Pubs.

Law, Power, & the Pursuit of Peace. Eugene V. Rostow. LC 67-10669. (Roscoe Pound Lectureship Ser.: 1966). 153p. reprint ed. pap. 47.50 (*0-608-12935-6*, 202468800038) Bks Demand.

Law, Power, & the Sovereign State: The Evolution & Application of the Concept of Sovereignty. Michael R. Fowler & Julie M. Bunck. LC 94-45483. 1995. 28.50 (*0-271-01470-9*); pap. 13.95 (*0-271-00147-X*) Pa St U Pr.

Law Practice. 5th ed. Street. Date not set. text, suppl. ed. 47.25 (*0-314-02753-X*) West Pub.

Law Practice Management: Materials & Cases. Gary A. Munneke. (American Casebook Ser.). 634p. (C). 1991. reprint ed. 57.50 (*0-314-83688-8*) West Pub.

Law Practice Management, Materials & Cases, Teacher's Manual. Gary A. Munneke. (American Casebook Ser.). 123p. (C). 1991. pap. text. write for info. (*0-314-00055-0*) West Pub.

***Law Practice of Abraham Lincoln: Complete Documentary.** Abraham Lincoln. Ed. by Martha L. Brenner et al. 2000. pap. 2000.00 (*0-252-02566-0*) U of Ill Pr.

Law Practice of Alexander Hamilton, Vol. 1. Ed. by Julius L. Goebel, Jr. & Joseph H. Smith. LC 64-13900. 1964. text 150.50 (*0-231-08944-9*) Col U Pr.

Law Practice of Alexander Hamilton, Vol. 2. Ed. by Julius L. Goebel, Jr. & Joseph H. Smith. LC 64-13900. 1969. text 150.50 (*0-231-08945-7*) Col U Pr.

Law Practice of Alexander Hamilton, Vol. 3. Ed. by Julius L. Goebel, Jr. & Joseph H. Smith. LC 64-13900. 1980. text 156.50 (*0-231-08946-5*) Col U Pr.

Law Practice of Alexander Hamilton, Vol. 4. Julius L. Goebel, Jr. 1980. text 156.50 (*0-231-08930-9*) Col U Pr.

Law Practice of Alexander Hamilton, Vol. 5. Ed. by Julius L. Goebel, Jr. & Joseph H. Smith. LC 64-13900. 1981. text 156.50 (*0-231-08929-5*) Col U Pr.

Law Practice Quality Evaluation: An Appraisal of Peer Review & Other Measures to Enhance Professional Performance: The Report on the Williamsburg Peer Review Conference, September 10-12, 1987. Institutional Staff. LC 88-83115. (Illus.). xxxiv, 342p. 1988. pap. text 44.00 (*0-8318-0618-4*, B618) Am Law Inst.

Law, Procedure & Conduct of Meetings. 5th ed. Arthur Lewin. 280p. 1985. pap. 30.00 (*0-7021-1528-2*, Pub. by Juta & Co) Gaunt.

Law, Psychiatry & Morality: Essays & Analysis. Alan A. Stone. LC 84-3000. 277p. 1984. pap. text 6.50 (*0-88048-209-5*, 8209) Am Psychiatric.

Law, Psychiatry & Morality: Essays & Analysis. Alan A. Stone. LC 84-3000. 291p. reprint ed. pap. 90.30 (*0-8357-7806-1*, 203617600002) Bks Demand.

Law, Psychiatry & the Mental Health System. Alexander D. Brooks. 1974. 54.00 (*0-316-10970-3*, Aspen Law & Bus) Aspen Pub.

Law, Psychiatry & the Mental Health System. Alexander D. Brooks. 1980. pap., suppl. ed. 13.00 (*0-316-10971-1*, Aspen Law & Bus) Aspen Pub.

Law Quarterly Review, 1885-1991, 107 vols., Set. 5885.00 (*0-8377-9209-6*, Rothman) W S Hein.

***Law Quickly & Easily on the Internet.** Shane Pollin. (Surf Less Find More! Ser.). 34p. 1999. 9.95 (*1-893957-00-4*) SurfLess.

Law, Records & Information Management: The Court Cases. Donald S. Skupsky & John C. Montana. LC 94-77173. 573p. 1994. 95.00 (*0-929316-32-0*) Info Requirements.

Law Reform & Human Reproduction. Ed. by Sheila A. McLean. (Medico-Legal Issues Ser.). 200p. 1992. 81.95 (*1-85521-026-6*, Pub. by Dartmth Pub) Ashgate Pub Co.

Law Reform & Medical Injury Litigation. Ed. by Sheila A. McLean. (Medico-Legal Issues Ser.). (Illus.). 192p. 1995. text 81.95 (*1-85521-534-9*, Pub. by Dartmth Pub) Ashgate Pub Co.

Law, Reform & Revolution in Afghanistan. A. Amin. 176p. (C). 1991. 150.00 (*0-7855-6802-6*, Pub. by Royston Ltd) St Mut.

Law Reform for All. Ed. by David Bean. 247p. 1996. pap. 34.00 (*1-85431-472-6*, Pub. by Blackstone Pr) Gaunt.

Law-Related Education & Juvenile Justice: Promoting Citizenship among Juvenile Offenders. Ed. by Deborah Williamson et al. LC 97-3473. (Illus.). 284p. 1997. text 59.95 (*0-398-06763-5*); pap. text 44.95 (*0-398-06764-3*) C C Thomas.

Law Relating to Animals. Simon Brooman & Debbie Legge. 462p. 1997. pap. 49.00 (*1-85941-238-6*, Pub. by Cavendish Pubng) Gaunt.

Law Relating to Arms, Ammunition & Explosives, 1985: With Supplement. 4th rev. ed. A. N. Gaur. (C). 1990. 125.00 (*0-7855-5643-5*) St Mut.

Law Relating to Authors & Publishers, No. 1. B. Mackay Cloutman. xvi, 145p. 1999. reprint ed. 50.00 (*1-56169-459-2*) Gaunt.

Law Relating to Banking. Ed. by Sheffield City Poly-CIB Staff. (Bankers Workbook Ser.). (C). 1989. 250.00 (*0-85297-280-6*, Pub. by Chartered Bank) St Mut.

Law Relating to Banking. 5th ed. T. G. Reeday. 1985. pap. 46.00 (*0-406-64769-0*, U.K., MICHIE) LEXIS Pub.

Law Relating to Banking & Financial Institutions. Vijay Malik. (C). 1989. 135.00 (*0-7855-5641-9*) St Mut.

Law Relating to Banking in Hong Kong. 2nd ed. Ed. by Derek Roebuck. 340p. 1996. pap. 47.50 (*962-209-353-1*, Pub. by HK Univ Pr) Coronet Bks.

Law Relating to Banking Services. Paul Cowdell & Jane Cowdell. 484p. 1990. pap. 125.00 (*0-85297-357-8*, Pub. by Chartered Bank) St Mut.

Law Relating to Banking Services. Andrew Laidlaw & G. Roberts. 389p. 1990. pap. 125.00 (*0-85297-320-9*, Pub. by Chartered Bank) St Mut.

Law Relating to Banking Services. L. Laidlaw & Graham Roberts. (C). 1989. 190.00 (*0-85297-277-6*, Pub. by Chartered Bank) St Mut.

Law Relating to Banking Services. 3rd ed. Graham Roberts. 350p. 1998. pap. 105.00 (*0-85297-491-4*, Pub. by Chartered Bank) St Mut.

Law Relating to Building Contracts. M. A. Sujan. (C). 1990. 125.00 (*0-89771-257-9*) St Mut.

Law Relating to Building Societies. John Thorpe. boxed set. write for info. (*0-406-02273-9*, U.K., MICHIE) LEXIS Pub.

Law Relating to Cheque & Its Dishonour. M. Arulselvam. (C). 1990. 70.00 (*0-89771-282-X*) St Mut.

Law Relating to Cohabitation. Anne Barlow. 250p. 1995. pap. 120.00 (*1-86012-047-4*, Pub. by Tolley Pubng) St Mut.

Law Relating to Company Deposits. 277p. 1978. 100.00 (*0-7855-1388-4*) St Mut.

Law Relating to Company Directors & Auditors. S. R. Kapoor. 331p. 1987. reprint ed. 55.00 (*0-7855-1330-2*) St Mut.

Law Relating to Corporate Groups. Ed. by Michael Gillooly. 252p. 1993. 64.00 (*1-86287-110-8*, Pub. by Federation Pr) Gaunt.

Law Relating to Drugs & Cosmetics. Mazhar Husain. (C). 1990. text 200.00 (*0-89771-479-2*) St Mut.

Law Relating to Electricity in India. Shiva Gopal. (C). 1992. 450.00 (*0-7855-0167-3*, Pub. by Eastern Book) St Mut.

Law Relating to Entry, Search & Seizure. David Feldman. 1986. pap. 92.00 (*0-406-19910-8*, UK, MICHIE) LEXIS Pub.

Law Relating to Foreigners, Passports, & Citizenship in India. 6th ed. Mazhar Husain. (C). 1991. 95.00 (*0-7855-5453-X*) St Mut.

Law Relating to Forest & Wild Life Protection. B. L. Babel. (HIN.). (C). 1990. text 80.00 (*0-89771-461-X*) St Mut.

Law Relating to Forest & Wild Life Protection. B. L. Babel. (C). 1990. 75.00 (*0-7855-7550-2*) St Mut.

Law Relating to Forests in Uttar Pradesh. P. L. Malik. 206p. 1984. 110.00 (*0-7855-1446-5*) St Mut.

Law Relating to Health Care Professions. P. F. Bayliss. (C). 1987. 135.00 (*0-901812-63-3*); pap. 100.00 (*0-7855-3753-8*) St Mut.

Law Relating to Highways. M. M. Mittal. (C). 1968. 45.00 (*0-7855-5543-9*) St Mut.

Law Relating to Identification & Expert Opinion. R. L. Gupta. 236p. 1983. 120.00 (*0-7855-2998-5*) St Mut.

Law Relating to Identification & Expert Opinion. 4th ed. R. L. Gupta. (C). 1990. text 125.00 (*0-89771-475-X*) St Mut.

Law Relating to International Banking. Graham Roberts. (Gresham Bks.). 192p. 1997. boxed set 210.00 (*1-85573-330-7*, Pub. by Woodhead Pubng) Am Educ Systs.

Law Relating to International Commercial Disputes. Jonathan Hill. 700p. 1994. 185.00 (*1-85044-596-6*) LLP.

Law Relating to Limitation. M. Arulselvam. (C). 1990. 50.00 (*0-89771-252-8*) St Mut.

Law Relating to Marriage & Divorce. S. C. Jain. 513p. 1979. 20.95 (*0-318-36841-2*) Asia Bk Corp.

Law Relating to Mobile Homes & Caravans. R. J. Gordon. 1985. pap. 125.00 (*0-7219-0811-X*, Pub. by Scientific) St Mut.

Law Relating to Modvat. J. S. Agarwal. (C). 1988. 80.00 (*0-7855-6129-3*) St Mut.

Law Relating to Motor Vehicles. A. P. Mathur. (C). 1990. text 400.00 (*0-89771-498-9*) St Mut.

Law Relating to Motor Vehicles. 9th ed. A. P. Mathur. (C). 1993. 225.00 (*81-7012-416-6*, Pub. by Eastern Book) St Mut.

Law Relating to Private Companies. E. E. Jhirad. (C). 1991. text 250.00 (*0-89771-482-2*) St Mut.

Law Relating to Private Companies. Rev. by Avtar Singh. (C). 1991. 250.00 (*0-89771-699-X*) St Mut.

Law Relating to Receivers in India. T. Woodroffe. (C). 1988. 40.00 (*0-7855-3527-6*) St Mut.

Law Relating to Receivers, Managers, & Administrators. 2nd ed. Hubert A. Picarda. 854p. 1990. boxed set 236.00 (*0-406-10501-4*, U.K., MICHIE) LEXIS Pub.

Law Relating to Religious Liberty & Public Worship. John Jenkins. xxxv, 212p. 1995. reprint ed. 37.50 (*0-8377-2310-8*, Rothman) W S Hein.

Law Relating to Restrictive Trade Practices & Monopolies, Mergers & Take-overs in New Zealand. 2nd ed. John Collinge. 518p. 1982. boxed set 99.00 (*0-409-60125-X*, NZ, MICHIE) LEXIS Pub.

Law Relating to Riots & Unlawful Assemblies: Together with a View of the Duties & Powers of Magistrates, Police Officers, Special Constables, the Military, & Private Individuals, for Their Suppression. 2nd ed. Edward Wise. xii, 131p. 1996. reprint ed. 34.00 (*0-8377-2783-9*, Rothman) W S Hein.

Law Relating to Schools. Neville Harris. 464p. 1995. pap. 175.00 (*0-85459-765-4*, Pub. by Tolley Pubng) St Mut.

Law Relating to Stocks, Bonds & Other Securities in the United States. Francis A. Lewis, Jr. LC 97-28831. xxxiv, 196p. 1997. reprint ed. 42.50 (*0-8377-2418-X*, Rothman) W S Hein.

Law Relating to Suspension of Employees, Officers - Workmen, in Banks. A. Arora & S. Sachdeva. (C). 1990. 55.00 (*0-89771-293-5*) St Mut.

Law Relating to Terrorists. V. K. Dewan. (C). 1990. 120.00 (*0-89771-183-1*) St Mut.

Law Relating to Terrorists. Vijay K. Dewan. 500p. (C). 1990. 120.00 (*0-7855-5240-5*, Pub. by Capital Law Hse) St Mut.

Law Relating to the Mentally Defective. Herbert Davey. (Historical Foundations of Forensic Psychiatry & Psychology Ser.). 568p. 1980. reprint ed. lib. bdg. 55.00 (*0-306-76070-3*) Da Capo.

Law Relating to Theatres, Music-Halls & Other Public Entertainments & to the Performers Therein, Including the Law of Musical & Dramatic Copyright, No. 1. Sidney C. Isaacs. xxxiii, 448p. 1999. reprint ed. 145.00 (*1-56169-460-6*) Gaunt.

Law Relating to Trade Unions & Unfair Labour Practices. K. D. Srivastava. 899p. (C). 1993. 375.00 (*0-7855-0170-3*, Pub. by Eastern Book) St Mut.

Law Relating to Trade Unions & Unfair Labour Practices in India. K. D. Srivastava. (C). 1993. 187.50 (*81-7012-499-9*, Pub. by Eastern Book) St Mut.

***Law Relating to Trading with the Enemy Together with a Consideration of the Civil Rights & Disabilities of Laien Enemies & of the Effect of War on Contracts with Alien Enemies.** Charles H. Huberich. xxxii, 485p. 2000. 130.00 (*1-56169-579-3*) Gaunt.

An Asterisk (*) at the beginning of an entry indicates that the title is appearing for the first time.

Law Relating to Unincorporated Associations. David Lane. 350p. 1996. pap. write for info. (*1-85941-028-6*, Pub. by Cavendish Pubng) Gaunt.

Law Relating to Violent Crime. Barry Mitchell. 380p. 1997. 125.00 (*1-85811-121-8*, Pub. by CLT Prof) Gaunt.

Law Relating to Weights & Measures. P. L. Malik. (C). 1991. 125.00 (*0-89771-794-5*, Pub. by Eastern Book) St Mut.

Law Relating to Weights & Measures. P. L. Malik. 1996. pap. 70.00 (*81-7012-575-8*, Pub. by Eastern Book) St Mut.

*__Law Relating to Weights & Measures.__ P. L. Malik. 2000. pap. 125.00 (*81-7012-660-6*, Pub. by Eastern Book) St Mut.

Law, Religion, Theology: A Selective Annotated Bibliography. F. C. DeCoste & Lillian MacPherson. LC 97-22609. (C). 1997. lib. bdg. 48.00 (*0-933951-75-2*) Locust Hill Pr.

Law Reporting in Britain. Ed. by Chantal Stebbings. 1995. 60.00 (*1-85285-129-5*) Hambledon Press.

Law Reports Citator & Subject Index, 1987-1995. 1995. pap. 70.00 (*1-85044-976-7*) LLP.

Law Reports of Palestine, 1920-1947: Complete Set, 14 vols. LC 94-77703. 1994. reprint ed. 1200.00 (*1-56169-102-X*) Gaunt.

Law Reports of the Bahamas. Ed. by Burton Hall & Charles W. Mackay. 1989. write for info. (*0-406-99868-X*, LRBASET, MICHIE) LEXIS Pub.

Law Reports of Trials of War Criminals: Four Genocide Trials. Ed. by United Nations War Crimes Commission Staff. LC 91-24659. 152p. 1992. reprint ed. lib. bdg. 35.00 (*0-86527-405-3*) Fertig.

Law Reports of Trials of War Criminals: The German High Command Trial. Selected by United Nations War Crimes Commission Staff. LC 92-30079. 135p. 1994. reprint ed. lib. bdg. 35.00 (*0-86527-406-1*) Fertig.

Law Reports of Trials of War Criminals: The I. G. Farben & Krupp Trials. Selected by United Nations War Crimes Commission Staff. LC 92-30707. 1998. 35.00 (*0-86527-410-X*) Fertig.

Law Reports of Trials of War Criminals: The Justice Trial. Selected by United Nations War Crimes Commission Staff. LC 92-29584. 2000. 35.00 (*0-86527-407-X*) Fertig.

Law Reports of Trials of War Criminals: United Nations War Crimes Commission, 15 vols. in 3 bks. Ed. by United Nations War Crimes Commission Staff. LC 97-80284. 1997. reprint ed. 275.00 (*1-57588-403-8*, 311500) W S Hein.

Law, Resistance & the State: The Opposition to Roman Law in Reformation Germany. Gerald Strauss. LC 85-43315. 315p. 1986. reprint ed. pap. 97.70 (*0-608-02948-3*, 206401400008) Bks Demand.

Law Restated: The Roots of the Law. William T. Hughes. LC 89-80600. 291p. 1989. reprint ed. 42.00 (*0-89941-679-9*, 305910) W S Hein.

Law Review Citations, 3 vols., Set. Shepard's Citations, Inc. Staff. 1986. 300.00 (*0-685-23133-X*) Shepards.

Law Review I: A Study of Selected Legal Issues As They Relate to the Park & Recreation Profession. James C. Kozlowski. LC KF5635.K69. 57p. reprint ed. pap. 30.00 (*0-7837-1533-1*, 204181400001) Bks Demand.

Law Review II: A Study of Legal Issues As They Relate to the Park & Recreation Profession. James C. Kozlowski. LC KF5635.K69. 38p. reprint ed. pap. 30.00 (*0-7837-1560-9*, 204185200002) Bks Demand.

Law Rides the Range. large type ed. Walt Coburn. (Linford Western Library). 352p. 1992. pap. 16.99 (*0-7089-7245-4*, Linford) Ulverscroft.

Law School: Global Issues, Local Questions. Ed. by Fiona Cownie. LC 98-47262. 280p. (C). 1999. text 78.95 (*1-85521-856-9*, K100.L39, Pub. by Ashgate Pub) Ashgate Pub Co.

Law School: Legal Education in America from the 1850s to the 1980s. Robert B. Stevens. LC 82-11148. (Studies in Legal History). 350p. 1983. reprint ed. pap. 108.50 (*0-7837-9028-7*, 204977900003) Bks Demand.

Law School Admission Test: Practice Examination Number 1. David M. Tarlow. (Practice Examination Ser.). 30p. 1992. pap. 16.95 (*0-931572-91-6*) Datar Pub.

Law School Admission Test: Practice Examination Number 3. David M Tarlow. (Practice Examination Ser.). 40p. 1992. pap. 16.95 (*0-931572-93-2*) Datar Pub.

Law School Admission Test: Student Guide. David M. Tarlow. (Student Guide Ser.). 120p. 1992. pap. 12.95 (*0-931572-94-0*) Datar Pub.

Law School Admission Test: 1999. Thomas H. Martinson. LC 97-81124. (Illus.). 448p. 1998. pap. text 16.95 (*0-02-862470-X*, Arco) Macmillan Gen Ref.

Law School Admission Test (LSAT) Jack Rudman. (Admission Test Ser.: Vol. 13). 43.95 (*0-8373-5113-8*) Nat Learn.

Law School Admission Test (LSAT) Jack Rudman. (Admission Test Ser.: No. ATS-13). 300p. 1994. pap. 23.95 (*0-8373-5013-1*) Nat Learn.

Law School Admissions. rev. ed. Thomas H. Martinson. (Illus.). 320p. 1998. pap. 20.00 (*0-684-84978-X*) S&S Trade.

Law School Basics. David Hricik. 208p. 1997. pap. 14.95 (*1-889057-06-1*) Nova Pr.

Law School Book Succeeding at Law School. Allan C. Hutchinson & Pam Marshall. xxi, 208p. 1996. pap. 19.95 (*1-55221-001-4*, Pub. by Irwin Law) Gaunt.

Law School Companion. Princeton Review Publishing Staff. (Princeton Review Ser.). 288p. 1995. pap. 15.00 (*0-679-76150-0*) Random.

*__Law School Confidential: A Complete Guide to the Law School Experience.__ Robert H. Miller. LC 00-27851. 352p. 2000. pap. 17.95 (*0-312-24309-X*, St Martin Griffin) St Martin.

Law School News June. Date not set. write for info. (*0-314-07314-0*) West Pub.

Law School News March. Date not set. write for info. (*0-314-06760-4*) West Pub.

Law School Papers of Benjamin F. Butler: New York University School of Law in the 1830's, 39. Benjamin F. Butler. LC 87-11891. (Contributions in Legal Studies: No. 39). 257p. 1987. 65.00 (*0-313-25917-8*, BWL/) Greenwood.

Law School Public Interest Law Support Programs: A Directory. LC 94-73788. 100p. 1995. 25.00 (*1-57073-095-4*, 231-7000) Amer Bar Assn.

Law School Rules: How Not to Sweat the Small Stuff of Law School. T. D. Lewis. Ed. by Jennifer Longden. 190p. 1998. pap. 12.95 (*0-9663893-0-1*) Waterfall NY.

Law School Rules: 115 Survival Strategies to Make the Challenges of Law School Seem Like "Small Stuff" Marion T. D. Lewis. LC 99-30266. 144p. 1999. 14.00 (*0-609-60528-7*) Harmony Bks.

Law School Survival: A Crash Course for Students by Students. Greg Gottesman. LC 98-84552. 256p. 1998. pap. 12.95 (*0-02-862296-0*, Arc) IDG Bks.

Law School Survival Kit. Jeff Adachi. 294p. (C). 1999. pap. text 29.95 (*1-882278-02-X*) Survival Series.

Law School Without Fear: Strategies for Success. Shapo & Shapo Staff. 1998. 15.95 (*1-56662-428-2*) Foundation Pr.

Law Schools Look Ahead: 1959 Conference on Legal Education. Summer Institute on International & Comparative La. (Michigan Legal Publications). xii, 328p. 1986. reprint ed. lib. bdg. 40.00 (*0-89941-498-2*, 304250) W S Hein.

*__Law Schools 2001.__ 3rd ed. Peterson's Guides Staff. 560p. 2000. pap. text 24.95 (*0-7689-0437-4*) Petersons.

*__Law Schools 2000: A Comprehensive Guide to All 181 Accredited U.S. Law Schools.__ 2nd ed. Petersons. 560p. 1999. pap. text 24.95 (*0-7689-0290-8*) Petersons.

Law, Science, & Environment. R. P. Anand et al. 1987. 44.00 (*81-7095-003-1*) S Asia.

Law Science & Medicine. Judith C. Areen et al. (University Casebook Ser.). 276p. 1996. pap. text. write for info. (*1-56662-447-9*) Foundation Pr.

Law, Science & Medicine. Judith C. Areen et al. LC 84-8181. (University Casebook Ser.). 1494p. (C). 1990. reprint ed. text 44.50 (*0-88277-179-5*) Foundation Pr.

Law, Science & Medicine. 2nd ed. Judith C. Areen et al. Ed. by Lawrence Gostin. LC 96-13106. (University Casebook Ser.). 1846p. 1996. text. write for info. (*1-56662-338-3*) Foundation Pr.

Law, Science & Medicine: 1988 Supplement. Judith C. Areen et al. (University Casebook Ser.). 395p. 1990. reprint ed. pap. text 14.50 (*0-88277-702-5*) Foundation Pr.

Law Sections. Lawrence G. Wrenn. 95p. 1994. pap. 8.00 (*0-943616-65-4*) Canon Law Soc.

Law, Sex & Christian Society in Medieval Europe. James A. Brundage. LC 87-10759. xxvi, 646p. 1987. 45.00 (*0-226-07783-7*) U Ch Pr.

Law, Sex & Christian Society in Medieval Europe. James A. Brundage. LC 87-10759. xxvi, 398p. 1990. pap. text 32.50 (*0-226-07784-5*) U Ch Pr.

Law, Sexuality, & Society: The Enforcement of Morals in Classical Athens. David Cohen. 271p. (C). 1994. pap. text 24.95 (*0-521-46642-3*) Cambridge U Pr.

Law, Social, Science & Criminal Theory. Jerome Hall. (N. Y. U. Criminal Law Education & Research Center Publications: Vol. 14). xvi, 333p. 1982. reprint ed. 39.50 (*0-8377-0640-8*, Rothman) W S Hein.

Law, Social Sciences & Public Policy: Towards a Unified Framework. Ed. by Anthony Chin & Alfred Choi. LC 98-942058. 390p. 1998. 49.50 (*9971-69-205-8*, Pub. by Sngapore Univ Pr) Coronet Bks.

Law, Socialism & Democracy. Paul Q. Hirst. 160p. (C). 1986. text 44.95 (*0-04-301253-1*); pap. text 16.95 (*0-04-301254-X*) Routledge.

Law, Society, & Change. Stephen Livingstone & John Morison. 206p. 1990. text 78.95 (*1-85521-105-X*, Pub. by Dartmth Pub) Ashgate Pub Co.

Law, Society, & Economy: Centenary Essays for the London School of Economics & Political Science 1895-1995. Richard Rawlings. LC 96-39194. 396p. 1997. text 85.00 (*0-19-826228-0*) OUP.

Law, Society, & Industrial Justice. Philip Selznick. LC 79-67066. 290p. reprint ed. pap. 89.90 (*0-608-15604-3*, 205659100077) Bks Demand.

Law, Society & the State: Essays in Modern Legal History. Ed. by Louis A. Knafla & Susan W. Binnie. LC 95-198006. 640p. 1995. pap. text 24.95 (*0-8020-6971-1*) U of Toronto Pr.

Law Society of Upper Canada & Ontario's Lawyers, 1797-1997. Christopher Moore. LC 97-127666. (Illus.). 395p. 1997. text 45.00 (*0-8020-4127-2*) U of Toronto Pr.

Law, Soldiers & Combat, 3. Peter Karsten. LC 77-87976. (Contributions in Legal Studies: No. 3). (Illus.). 204p. 1978. 62.95 (*0-313-20042-4*, KSL/, Greenwood Pr) Greenwood.

Law, Space, & the Geographies of Power. Nicholas K. Blomley. LC 94-18264. (Mappings). 259p. 1994. lib. bdg. 35.00 (*0-89862-496-7*, C2496) Guilford Pubns.

*__Law Sports at Gray's Inn (1594) Including Shakespeare's Connection with the Inn's of Court, the Origin of the Capias Utlegatum Re Coke & Bacon, Francis Bacon's Connection with Warwickshire, Together with a Reprint of the Gesta Grayorum.__ fac. ed. Basil Brown. LC 99-49829. 2000. write for info. (*1-58477-056-2*) Lawbk Exchange.

Law, State, & International Legal Order: Essays in Honor of Hans Kelsen. Ed. by Salo Engel. LC 64-16881. 375p. reprint ed. 116.30 (*0-608-16806-8*, 202755700055) Bks Demand.

Law, State & the Working Class in Tanzania. Issa G. Shivji. LC 85-24949. 268p. (Orig.). (C). 1986. pap. text 27.50 (*0-435-08013-X*, 08013) Heinemann.

Law Stenographer. Jack Rudman. (Career Examination Ser.: C-436). 1994. pap. 23.95 (*0-8373-0436-9*) Nat Learn.

Law Stories. Ed. by Gary Bellow & Martha Minow. LC 96-16551. (Law, Meaning, & Violence Ser.). 248p. (C). 1996. text 37.50 (*0-472-10718-6*, 10718) U of Mich Pr.

Law Stories. Ed. by Gary Bellow & Martha Minow. (Law, Meaning, & Violence Ser.). 248p. (C). 1998. pap. text 20.95 (*0-472-08519-0*, 08519) U of Mich Pr.

Law Stories: The Law As Seen from the Outside. Gary Bellow. 1994. 25.00 (*1-56584-091-7*, Pub. by New Press NY) Norton.

Law Students: How to Get a Job When There Aren't Any. William T. Carey. 102p. (Orig.). (C). 1986. lib. bdg. 9.75 (*0-89089-325-X*) Carolina Acad Pr.

Law Student's Companion: A Guide to the Study & Practice of Law. 2nd ed. J. Redgment. 232p. 1988. pap. write for info. (*0-7021-2211-4*, Pub. by Juta & Co) Gaunt.

Law Student's Guide to Scholarships & Grants. Franklin Williams & Mark Fischer. xii, 260p. 1994. pap. 24.95 (*1-879040-95-6*) Scovill Paterson.

Law Summary: A Collection of Legal Tracts on Subjects of General Application in Business. 2nd enl. ed. Benjamin L. Oliver. 391p. 1995. reprint ed. 52.50 (*0-8377-2450-3*, Rothman) W S Hein.

Law Teachers' Manual of the Analysis of Cases & the Use of Law Books. R. A. Daly. (Legal Bibliographic & Research Reprint Ser.: Vol. 11). vi, 226p. 1988. reprint ed. lib. bdg. 40.00 (*0-89941-651-9*, 305640) W S Hein.

Law, the State & Society in China. Ed. & Intro. by Tahirih V. Lee. LC 96-47413. (Chinese Law Ser.). 432p. 1997. text 88.00 (*0-8153-2482-0*) Garland.

Law, the State & the International Community, 2 vols. James B. Scott. LC 70-153354. reprint ed. 75.00 (*0-404-05638-5*) AMS Pr.

Law, the State & the International Community, 2 vols. James B. Scott. LC 77-98796. 1970. reprint ed. lib. bdg. 95.00 (*0-8371-2809-9*, SCLI, Greenwood Pr) Greenwood.

Law Today. Dawson. 1994. pap. text. write for info. (*0-582-05635-7*, Pub. by Addison-Wesley) Longman.

Law Torts, 6 vols., 1. 2nd ed. Gray. 1986. 125.00 (*0-316-32587-2*, Aspen Law & Bus) Aspen Pub.

Law Torts, Vol. 1. 3rd ed. Gray. LC 95-80249. 1995. 155.00 (*0-316-32716-6*, Aspen Law & Bus) Aspen Pub.

Law Torts, 6 vols., Vol. 2. 2nd ed. Gray. 1986. 125.00 (*0-316-32588-0*, Aspen Law & Bus) Aspen Pub.

Law Torts, 6 vols., Vol. 3. 2nd ed. Gray. 1986. 125.00 (*0-316-32589-9*, Aspen Law & Bus) Aspen Pub.

Law Torts, 6 vols., Vol. 4. 2nd ed. Gray. 1986. 125.00 (*0-316-32590-2*, Aspen Law & Bus) Aspen Pub.

Law Torts, 6 vols., Vol. 5. Gray. 1986. 125.00 (*0-316-32591-0*, Aspen Law & Bus) Aspen Pub.

Law Torts, 6 vols., Vol. 6. 2nd ed. Gray. 1986. 125.00 (*0-316-32592-9*, Aspen Law & Bus) Aspen Pub.

Law under Swastika: Studies on Legal History in Nazi Germany. Michael Stolleis. Tr. by Thomas Dunlap. LC 97-36021. 232p. 1997. 29.95 (*0-226-77525-9*) U Ch Pr.

*__Law unto Itself? Essays in the New Louisiana Legal History.__ Ed. by Warren M. Billings & Mark F. Fernandez. 208p. 2000. 34.95 (*0-8071-2583-0*) La State U Pr.

Law Update, 1991. 200p. (C). 1991. pap. 25.00 (*1-85352-899-4*, Pub. by HLT Pubns) St Mut.

Law, Values & Social Practices. Ed. by John Tasioulas. LC 96-35393. (Applied Legal Philosophy Ser.). (Illus.). 256p. 1997. text 78.95 (*1-85521-866-6*, Pub. by Dartmth Pub) Ashgate Pub Co.

Law, Values, & the Environment: A Reader & Selective Bibliography. Ed. by Robert N. Wells, Jr. LC 95-52588. 704p. 1996. 62.00 (*0-8108-3134-1*) Scarecrow.

Law Victims. Okpewho. 1995. pap. text. write for info. (*0-582-26502-9*, Pub. by Addison-Wesley) Longman.

Law, Violence, & Community in Classical Athens. David Cohen. (Key Themes in Ancient History Ser.). 226p. (C). 1995. pap. text 19.95 (*0-521-38837-6*) Cambridge U Pr.

Law vs. Grace. 4th ed. Thomas J. Richburg. (Illus.). 100p. 1996. reprint ed. 14.95 (*1-889466-31-X*, HB001002); reprint ed. pap. 10.95 (*1-889466-32-8*, HB001002) One Way Intl.

Law vs. Justice. V. R. Iyer. (C). 1990. 85.00 (*0-89771-134-3*) St Mut.

Law vs. Life: What Lawyers Are Afraid to Say about the Legal Profession. Walt Bachman. LC 95-60315. 140p. 1995. 17.95 (*0-9627659-8-8*) Four Directions.

Law West of Fort Smith: A History of Frontier Justice in the Indian Territory, 1834-1896. Glenn Shirley. LC 57-6193. (Illus.). xii, 349p. 1968. reprint ed. pap. 14.95 (*0-8032-5183-1*, Bison Books) U of Nebr Pr.

Law West of the Pecos: The Story of Roy Bean. Everett Lloyd. 106p. 1996. reprint ed. 35.00 (*1-56169-195-X*) Gaunt.

Law Without Enforcement: Integrating Mental Health & Justice. Ed. by Nigel Eastman & Jill Peay. 256p. 1998. pap. 36.00 (*1-901362-75-2*, Pub. by Hart Pub) Intl Spec Bk.

*__Law Without Force.__ Gerhart Niemeyer & Michael Henry. 408p. 1999. pap. 29.95 (*0-7658-0640-1*) Transaction Pubs.

Law Without Frontiers: A Comparative Survey of the Rules of Professional Ethics Applicable to the Cross-Border Practice of Law. Ed. by Edwin Godfrey. LC 95-14817. (International Bar Association Ser.). 1995. 128.50 (*90-411-0851-3*) Kluwer Law Intl.

Law Without Lawyers. Goh. 69.95 (*1-84014-744-X*) Ashgate Pub Co.

Law Without Order: Capital Punishment & the Liberals. Bernard L. Cohen. LC 82-45661. reprint ed. 30.00 (*0-404-62410-3*) AMS Pr.

Law, Writing, Meaning: An Essay in Legal Hermeneutics. Patrick Nerhot. (Law & Society Ser.). 224p. (C). 1993. text 65.00 (*0-7486-0391-3*, Pub. by Edinburgh U Pr) Col U Pr.

Lawa'ih - Lawa'ih: A Treatise on Sufism. Nuraud-din'abd-ur-rahman Jami. Tr. by Whinfield. 1978. pap. 10.75 (*0-7229-5136-1*) Theos Pub Hse.

Lawcourts at Athens: Sites, Buildings, Equipment, Procedure, & Testimonia. Alan L. Boegehold. LC 95-18926. (Athenian Agora Ser.: Vol. 28). (Illus.). 1995. 100.00 (*0-87661-228-1*) Am Sch Athens.

Lawd, Judge Dat Preacher, 'Cause It Ain't Nunna Mah Bizness. Ruth L. Frazier. 70p. 1994. pap. 9.95 (*0-9649881-2-7*) Frazier Bks.

Lawd Today! Richard Wright. LC 92-46688. (Northeastern Library of Black Literature). 256p. 1993. reprint ed. pap. text 15.95 (*1-55553-159-8*) NE U Pr.

Lawer Book. 3rd ed. Tim Davison. (C). 1993. text 14.95 (*0-906754-78-X*, Pub. by Fernhurst Bks) St Mut.

Lawes of the Market. LC 74-80198. (English Experience Ser.: No. 676). 22p. 1974. reprint ed. 10.00 (*90-221-0676-4*) Walter J Johnson.

Lawes Resolutions of Women's Rights: or The Lawes Provision for Women. LC 79-84103. (English Experience Ser.: No. 922). 424p. 1979. reprint ed. lib. bdg. 40.00 (*90-221-0922-4*) Walter J Johnson.

Lawful & the Prohibited in Islam. Yusuf Al-Qaradawi. Tr. by Mohammed M. Siddiqui et al from ARA. LC 80-81562. Orig. Title: Al-Halal Wal-Haram Fil Islam. (ENG.). 355p. (Orig.). 1981. pap. 10.00 (*0-89259-016-5*) Am Trust Pubns.

Lawful & the Prohibited in Islam. Yousaf A. Qaradawi. 1982. pap. 15.95 (*1-56744-118-1*) Kazi Pubns.

Lawful Exit: The Limits of Freedom for Help in Dying. Derek Humphry. 168p. (Orig.). 1993. pap. 9.95 (*0-9637280-0-8*) Norris Ln Pr.

Lawful Money Explained. Gertrude Coogan. 1979. lib. bdg. 59.95 (*0-8490-2956-2*) Gordon Pr.

Lawful Occasions. Patrick MacKenzie. 1992. pap. 14.95 (*1-85635-024-X*) Dufour.

Lawful Order: A Case Study of Correctional Crisis & Reform. Leo Carroll. Ed. by Marilyn D. McShane & Frank P. Williams, 3rd. LC 97-39224. (Current Issues in Criminal Justice Ser.: Vol. 23). (Illus.). 384p. 1998. text 70.00 (*0-8153-1617-8*, SS949) Garland.

*__Lawful Orders.__ Jonathan P. Tomes. LC 97-62365. 280p. 1998. 24.95 (*1-880483-00-9*) Veterans Pr.

Lawful Possession. Catherine George. (Romance Ser.). 1994. per. 2.99 (*0-373-03310-9*, 1-03310-9) Harlequin Bks.

Lawful Possession. large type ed. George. 1994. per. 2.99 (*0-373-15556-5*) Harlequin Bks.

Lawful Possession. large type unabridged ed. (Harlequin Ser.). 1994. lib. bdg. 19.95 (*0-263-13585-3*) Mac Lib Ref.

Lawful Pursuit of Gain. Max Radin. LC 75-39268. (Getting & Spending: The Consumer's Dilemma Ser.). 1976. reprint ed. 19.95 (*0-405-08041-7*) Ayer.

Lawful Revolution: Louis Kossuth & the Hungarians, 1848-1849. Istvan Deak. LC 78-22063. Orig. Title: Reluctant Rebels. (Illus.). 415p. 1979. text 29.50 (*0-231-04602-2*) Col U Pr.

Lawful Revolution in Hungary, 1989-1994. Bela K. Kiraly. (Atlantic Studies on Society & Change). 300p. 1996. 42.00 (*0-88033-342-1*, 445, Pub. by East Eur Monographs) Col U Pr.

Lawfully Good Eating. Telephone Pioneers of America, Dixie Chapter No. 2. LC 92-30344. 1992. spiral bd. write for info. (*0-87197-351-0*) Favorite Recipes.

Lawfulness of War for Christians Examined see First American Peace Movement

Lawhorn Site, Vol. 24. John Moselage. Ed. by Robert T. Bray. (Missouri Archaeologist Ser.). (Illus.). 110p. (Orig.). 1962. pap. 3.50 (*0-943414-40-7*) MO Arch Soc.

Lawless. Emily Carmichael. 384p. (Orig.). 1993. mass mkt. 4.99 (*0-446-36409-6*, Pub. by Warner Bks) Little.

*__Lawless.__ Ed Gorman. 272p. 2000. mass mkt. 5.99 (*0-425-17432-8*) Berkley Pub.

Lawless Hideout. large type ed. John Blaze. (Linford Western Library). 256p. 1993. pap. 16.99 (*0-7089-7437-6*, Linford) Ulverscroft.

Lawless Judges. Louis P. Goldberg & Eleanore Levenson. LC 73-138498. (Civil Liberties in American History Ser.). 1970. reprint ed. lib. bdg. 37.50 (*0-306-70070-0*) Da Capo.

*__Lawless Land.__ Dusty Richards. 264p. 2000. mass mkt. 5.99 (*0-312-97410-8*) St Martin.

Lawless Land. large type ed. John Dyson. 1994. pap. 16.99 (*0-7089-7593-3*, Linford) Ulverscroft.

Lawless Land. large type ed. Romer Zane Grey. 1982. 15.95 (*0-7089-0841-1*) Ulverscroft.

Lawless Liberators: Political Banditry & Cuban Independence. Rosalie Schwartz. LC 88-22592. (Illus.). x, 297p. (C). 1989. text 49.95 (*0-8223-0882-7*) Duke.

Lawless Mind. Raziel Abelson. LC 88-12358. 224p. (C). 1988. 32.95 (*0-87722-579-6*) Temple U Pr.

Lawless Range. large type ed. Charles N. Heckelmann. (Linford Western Library). 348p. 1989. pap. 16.99 (*0-7089-6677-2*, Linford) Ulverscroft.

Lawless Range. large type ed. Elliot Long. 184p. 1996. pap. 18.99 (*1-85389-581-4*, Dales) Ulverscroft.

Lawless Roads. Graham Greene. 1992. 23.25 (*0-8446-6539-8*) Peter Smith.

Lawless Roads. Graham Greene. 224p. 1993. pap. 12.95 (*0-14-018580-1*, Penguin Classics) Viking Penguin.

Lawless Roads. large type ed. Graham Greene. 280p. 1991. 21.95 (*1-85089-232-6*, Pub. by ISIS Lrg Prnt) Transaction Pubs.

Lawlessness, Law & Sanction: A Dissertation. Miriam T. Rooney. (Catholic University of America Philosophical Studies: Vol. XXXIV). 176p. 1982. reprint ed. 34.00 (*0-8377-1036-7*, Rothman) W S Hein.

L

L

Lawley - Built: Archives of the Lawley Boat Owners Association. 3rd ed. Ed. by Albert E. Hickey. (Illus.). 194p. 2000. pap. 32.00 (*0-87567-100-4*) Entelek.
Lawlor Ansi C Programming. Date not set. teacher ed. write for info. (*0-314-05415-4*) West Pub.
Lawlor's Radio Values. Michael Lawlor. (Orig.). 1991. pap. 12.50 (*0-9629640-0-X*) Bare Bones.
Lawmakers: Recruitment & Adaptation to Legislative Life, 11. James D. Barber. LC 79-26379. 314p. 1980. reprint ed. lib. bdg. 65.00 (*0-313-22200-2*, BALA, Greenwood Pr) Greenwood.
Lawmaking. 2nd ed. Linda Riekes & Sally M. Ackerly. (Law in Action Ser.). (Illus.). 142p. (J). (gr. 5-9). 1980. pap. text 26.75 (*0-8299-1023-9*); pap. text, teacher ed. 26.75 (*0-8299-1024-7*) West Pub.
Lawmaking & Legislators in Pennsylvania: A Biographical Dictionary, Vol. 2: 1710-1756. Craig W. Horle et al. 1232p. 1997. text 185.00 (*0-8122-3403-0*) U of Pa Pr.
Lawmaking & Legislators in Pennsylvania Vol. I: A Biographical Dictionary, 1682-1709. Craig W. Horle et al. LC 91-13999. (Illus.). 904p. (C). 1991. text 125.00 (*0-8122-3067-1*) U of Pa Pr.
Lawmaking & the Legislative Process: Committees, Connections, & Compromises. National Conference of State Legislatures Staff & Tommy Neal. LC 96-20568. (Illus.). 160p. 1996. pap. 26.50 (*0-89774-944-8*) Oryx Pr.
Lawmaking by Initiative: Issues, Options & Comparisons. Philip L. Dubois & Floyd Feeney. LC 97-27078. (Representation Ser.: Vol. 4). 280p. 1998. text 30.00 (*0-87586-120-2*, 861202) Agathon.
Lawmaking in Illinois: Legislative Politics, People & Processes. Jack R. Van Der Slik & Kent D. Redfield. LC 86-61343. (Illus.). (Orig.). 1989. 19.95 (*0-938943-00-6*) U IL Spgfld Pub Affrs.
Lawmaking in Illinois: Legislative Politics, People & Processes. Jack R. Van Der Slik & Kent D. Redfield. LC 86-61343. (Illus.). 262p. (Orig.). 1989. reprint ed. text 12.50 (*0-938943-01-4*) U IL Spgfld Pub Affrs.
Lawmaking in the European Union. P. P. Craig & Carol Harlow. LC 98-29114. (W. G. Hart Legal Workshop Ser.). 1998. 111.00 (*90-411-9683-8*) Kluwer Law Intl.
Lawman. Laurie Grant. (Historical Ser.: No. 367). 1997. per. 4.99 (*0-373-28967-7*, 1-28967-7) Harlequin Bks.
Lawman. Lisa Plumley. 1999. mass mkt. 4.99 (*0-8217-6386-5*, Zebra Kensgtn) Kensgtn Pub Corp.
Lawman: The Life & Times of Harry Morse, 1835-1912. John E. Boessenecker. LC 97-35009. (Illus.). 384p. 1998. 29.95 (*0-8061-3011-3*) U of Okla Pr.
***Lawman & the Lady.** Pat Warren. (Intimate Moments Ser.). 2000. mass mkt. 4.50 (*0-373-27095-X*, 1-27095--8) Silhouette.
Lawman for Kelly. Myrna Temte. 1997. per. 3.99 (*0-373-24075-9*, 1-24075-3) Silhouette.
Lawman for the Slaughter. Ray Hogan. (Shawn Starbuck Ser.: No. 9). 1980. mass mkt. 1.95 (*0-451-09173-6*, Sig) NAL.
***Lawman Gets Lucky - Beauty & the Bet.** Cathie Linz & Isabel Sharpe. (Duets Ser.: No. 26). 2000. mass mkt. 5.99 (*0-373-44092-8*) Harlequin Bks.
Lawman Lover. Saranne Dawson. (Intrigue Ser.: No. 503). 1999. per. 3.99 (*0-373-22503-2*, 1-22503-6) Harlequin Bks.
***Lawman Meets His Bride.** Meagan McKinney. (Intimate Moments Ser.: Bk. 1037). 2000. mass mkt. 4.50 (*0-373-27107-7*, 1-27107-1) Silhouette.
Lawman (Urban Cowboys) Vicki L. Thompson. LC 95-22366. 217p. 1995. per. 3.25 (*0-373-25663-9*) Harlequin Bks.
Lawman Wore Black. large type ed. Marshall Grover. (Linford Western Library). 1995. pap. 16.99 (*0-7089-7751-0*, Linford) Ulverscroft.
***Lawman's Last Stand.** Vickie Taylor. (Intimate Moments Ser.: Bk. 1014). 2000. per. 4.50 (*0-373-27084-4*, 1-27084-2) Silhouette.
Lawman's Legacy. Phyllis Halldorson. 1997. per. 3.25 (*0-373-19255-X*, 1-19255-8) Silhouette.
***Lawmen.** Charles L. Convis. LC 96-68502. (True Tales of the Old West Ser.: Vol. 14). (Illus.). ii, 62p. 2000. pap. 7.95 (*1-892156-04-0*) Pioneer Pr NV.
Lawmen: Evil Breed. large type ed. J. B. Dancer. (Linford Western Library). 240p. 1989. pap. 16.99 (*0-7089-6713-2*, Linford) Ulverscroft.
Lawmen: Kansas, Bloody Kansas. large type ed. J. B. Dancer. (Linford Western Library). 256p. 1989. pap. 16.99 (*0-7089-6720-5*, Linford) Ulverscroft.
Lawmen: Stories of Men Who Tamed the West. Bryce Milligan. LC 94-70797. (Disney's American Frontier Ser.: Bk. 14). (Illus.). 80p. (J). (gr. 1-4). 1994. pap. 3.50 (*0-7868-4006-4*, Pub. by Disney Pr); lib. bdg. 12.89 (*0-7868-5005-1*, Pub. by Disney Pr) Little.
Lawmen & Desperadoes: A Compendium of Noted, Early California Peace Officers, Badmen & Outlaws 1850-1900. William B. Secrest. LC 91-71133. (Illus.). 344p. 1994. 37.50 (*0-87062-209-9*) A H Clark.
Lawmen in Scarlet: An Annotated Guide to Royal Canadian Mounted Police in Print & Performance. Compiled by Bernard A. Drew. LC 90-8388. (Illus.). 296p. 1990. 31.50 (*0-8108-2330-6*) Scarecrow.
Lawmen of the Old West: The Good Guys. Del Cain. LC 99-46989. 1999. pap. 16.95 (*1-55622-677-2*) Wordware Pub.
Lawn: A Guide to Jefferson's University. Pendleton Hogan. LC 86-23330. (Illus.). 149p. (Orig.). 1987. pap. 7.95 (*0-8139-1109-5*) U Pr of Va.
Lawn: A History of an American Obsession. Virginia S. Jenkins. LC 93-28003. (Illus.). 272p. (Orig.). 1994. pap. 15.95 (*1-56098-406-6*) Smithsonian.
Lawn & Garden. (Fix-It-Yourself Ser.). (Illus.). 144p. 1988. 17.27 (*0-8094-6228-1*); lib. bdg. 23.27 (*0-8094-6229-X*) Time-Life.
Lawn & Garden Owner's Manual: What to Do & When to Do It. Lewis Hill & Nancy Hill. LC 99-47216. (Illus.). 192p. 2000. pap. 21.95 (*1-58017-214-8*, Storey Pub) Storey Bks.
Lawn Art, Kansas. Lu Duerksen & Kathryn Nelson. LC 96-69167. (Illus.). 96p. (Orig.). 1996. pap. 12.95 (*0-9645085-8-3*) Prtnrshp Bk Servs.
Lawn Bowls Straight from the Shoulder. Vic Muir. 140p. (C). 1990. pap. 36.00 (*0-9589209-0-7*, Pub. by Boolarong Pubns) St Mut.
Lawn Care & Gardening: A Down-to-Earth Guide to the Business. Kevin Rossi. LC 93-74400. (Illus.). 240p. (Orig.). 1994. pap. 21.95 (*0-9639371-9-7*) Acton Circle.
Lawn Care for Dummies. National Gardening Association Editors & Lance Walheim. LC 97-81232. (For Dummies Ser.). (Illus.). 376p. 1998. pap. 16.99 (*0-7645-5077-2*) IDG Bks.
Lawn Expert. D. G. Hessayon. (Expert Ser.). (Illus.). 128p. (Orig.). 1991. pap. 12.95 (*0-903505-15-0*, Pub. by Expert Bks) Sterling.
Lawn, Garden & Outdoor Power Equipment Shop Service Set, 12 vols. 1991. ring bd. 219.95 (*0-87288-261-6*, LGSS) Intertec Pub.
Lawn Keeping. Robert W. Schery. 1986. 16.45 (*0-671-60730-8*) S&S Trade.
Lawn Mowers. (Latin American Products Included in the U. S. General System of Preferences Ser.). 1978. pap. text 3.00 (*0-8270-3435-0*) OAS.
Lawn Sprinklers: One-Weekend Design & Installation. Richard L. Austin. (Illus.). 208p. (Orig.). 1989. 23.95 (*0-8306-2093-1*); pap. 12.95 (*0-8306-3193-3*) McGraw-Hill Prof.
Lawn Wars: Lawn Ornaments (A Field Guide) Bryce Muir & Margaret Muir. (Illus.). 32p. (Orig.). 1988. pap. 8.95 (*0-942396-55-3*) Blackberry ME.
Lawnboy. Paul Lisicky. 386p. 1999. pap. 13.95 (*1-885983-40-9*) Turtle Point Pr.
Lawnchair Astronomer. Gerry Descoteaux. LC 94-39694. 144p. 1995. pap. 10.95 (*0-440-50696-4*) Dell.
Lawndale Live! A Retrospective, 1979-1990. Rachel Ranta & Elizabeth Ward. LC 93-80111. (Illus.). 72p. 1993. 15.00 (*1-883754-00-3*) Lawndale Art.
Lawns: Basic Factors, Construction & Maintenance of Fine Turf Areas. 3rd rev. ed. Jonas Vengris. LC 82-82822. (Illus.). 195p. 1982. pap. 15.50 (*0-913702-19-6*) Thomson Pubns.
***Lawns: Quick & Easy Grasses & Groundcovers.** LC 99-86711. (Black & Decker Outdoor Home Ser.). 128p. 2000. pap. text 14.95 (*0-86573-444-5*) Creat Pub Intl.
Lawns & Groundcovers. DK Publishing Staff. 80p. 1999. pap. text 8.95 (*0-7894-4160-8*) DK Pub Inc.
Lawns & Landscaping: One Thousand & One Gardening Questions Answered. Ed. by Garden Way Publishing Editors & Gwen Steege. LC 88-45619. (Illus.). 160p. 1989. 16.95 (*0-88266-535-9*, Garden Way Pub) Storey Bks.
Lawns, Grasses & Groundcovers. Lewis Hill & Nancy Hill. (Rodale's Successful Organic Gardening Ser.). (Illus.). 160p. (Orig.). 1995. pap. 14.95 (*0-87596-666-7*); text 24.95 (*0-87596-665-9*) Rodale Pr Inc.
Lawren Harris. Judith Stoffman. Ed. by Douglas Fetherling. (New Views on Canadian Artists Ser.). (Illus.). 96p. 1996. pap. 18.95 (*1-55082-180-6*, Pub. by Quarry Pr) LPC InBook.
Lawrence. Dengler et al. (Images of America Ser.). 1995. pap. 16.99 (*0-7524-0229-3*) Arcadia Publng.
Lawrence. Walter Armstrong. LC 70-100531. (BCL Ser.: No. 2). (Illus.). reprint ed. 54.50 (*0-404-00385-0*) AMS Pr.
Lawrence, Vol. II. Ken Skulski. (Images of America Ser.). 1999. pap. 16.99 (*0-7524-0561-6*) Arcadia Publng.
Lawrence: History of the Lawrence-Townley & Chase-Townley Estates in England, with Copious Historical & Genealogical Notes of the Lawrence, Chase & Townley Families. James Usher. 110p. 1995. reprint ed. pap. 19.50 (*0-8328-4796-8*); reprint ed. lib. bdg. 29.50 (*0-8328-4795-X*) Higginson Bk Co.
Lawrence: International Personal Tax Planning Encyclopaedia. Ed. by Robert C. Lawrence. 1990. ring bd. write for info. (*0-406-99831-0*, LIPTASET, MICHIE) LEXIS Pub.
Lawrence: "Sons & Lovers" Michael H. Black. (Landmarks of World Literature Ser.). (Illus.). 123p. (C). 1992. pap. text 11.95 (*0-521-36924-X*) Cambridge U Pr.
Lawrence: The Uncrowned King of Arabia. Michael Asher. LC 99-37255. 400p. 1999. text 37.95 (*0-87951-712-3*, Pub. by Overlook Pr) Penguin Putnam.
Lawrence Alma Tadema: Spring. Louise Lippincott. LC 90-49669. (Getty Museum Studies on Art). (Illus.). 100p. 1991. pap. 17.50 (*0-89236-186-7*, Pub. by J P Getty Trust) OUP.
Lawrence among the Women: Wavering Boundaries in Women's Literary Traditions. Carol Siegel. LC 91-6786. (Feminist Issues Ser.). 244p. reprint ed. pap. 75.70 (*0-608-08550-2*, 206907300002) Bks Demand.
Lawrence & Apocalypse. Helen Corke. 130p. (C). 1966. lib. bdg. 75.00 (*0-8383-0655-1*) M S G Haskell Hse.
Lawrence & Comedy. Ed. by Paul Eggert & John Worthen. 230p. (C). 1996. text 54.95 (*0-521-56275-9*) Cambridge U Pr.
Lawrence & His Laboratory: Nuclear Science at Berkeley, 1931-1961. John L. Heilbron et al. LC 81-83681. (Illus.). 106p. (Orig.). 1981. pap. 3.50 (*0-918102-09-X*) U Cal Hist Sci Tech.
Lawrence & His Laboratory Vol. 1: A History of the Lawrence Berkeley Laboratory. John L. Heilbron & Robert W. Seidel. 1989. 48.00 (*0-520-06426-7*, Pub. by U CA Pr) Cal Prin Full Svc.
***Lawrence & Holloman.** M. Ponych. LC 99-174858. 128p. 1999. pap. 11.95 (*0-88922-392-0*) Talonbks.
Lawrence & Mann Overarching: Once Upon the County of Ujamaa; Roll Away der Rock & Other Essays. Don Paul. 360p. 1981. 10.00 (*0-943096-00-6*); pap. 5.00 (*0-943096-01-4*) Harts Spring Wks.
Lawrence & Nietzsche: A Study in Influence. Colin Milton. 264p. 1987. text 37.90 (*0-08-035067-4*, Pub. by Aberdeen U Pr) Macmillan.
Lawrence & the Arab Revolts, 1914-1918. David Nicolle. (Men-at-Arms Ser.: No. 208). (Illus.). 48p. pap. 11.95 (*0-85045-888-9*, 9141, Pub. by Ospry) Stackpole.
Lawrence & the Arabs. Robert Graves. (Illus.). 454p. 1994. pap. 14.95 (*1-56924-989-X*) Marlowe & Co.
Lawrence & the Nature Tradition: A Theme in English Fiction, 1859-1914 Roger Ebbatson. LC 80-155469. xiii, 271p. 1980. write for info. (*0-391-01884-1*) Humanities.
Lawrence at Tregerthen. C. J. Stevens. LC 87-50831. x, 129p. 1988. 35.00 (*0-87875-348-6*) Whitston Pub.
Lawrence California. Date not set. pap. text, teacher ed. write for info. (*0-314-05416-2*) West Pub.
Lawrence Clark Powell. Gerald Haslam. LC 92-52527. (Western Writers Ser.: No. 102). (Illus.). 50p. (Orig.). 1992. pap. 4.95 (*0-88430-101-X*) Boise St U W Writ Ser.
Lawrence County, Arkansas, Loose Probate Papers, 1815-1890. Marion S. Craig. 300p. 1992. reprint ed. pap. 28.00 (*0-941765-81-4*) Arkansas Res.
Lawrence County, Arkansas, Tax Records, 1829-1838. Compiled by Burton R. Knotts. 108p. (Orig.). 1996. pap. 18.00 (*1-56546-095-2*) Arkansas Res.
Lawrence County, Arkansas, Tax Records, 1843-1854. Burton R. Knotts. 188p. 1998. pap. 25.00 (*1-56546-127-4*) Arkansas Res.
Lawrence County, PA Soldiers. Paul W. Myers. 91p. 1988. pap. text 9.00 (*0-933227-86-8*, 314) Closson Pr.
Lawrence County, Tennessee: Pictorial. Turner Publishing Company Staff. LC 94-60851. 228p. 1994. 49.95 (*1-56311-152-7*) Turner Pub KY.
***Lawrence Co., Tennessee, Marriages, 1818-1870.** Silas Emmett Lucas, Jr. 114p. 1999. 25.00 (*0-89308-724-6*) Southern Hist Pr.
Lawrence County the Ozark Region: Its History & Its People, 2 vols. Ed. by A. M. Haswell. (Illus.). 1118p. 1997. reprint ed. lib. bdg. 115.00 (*0-8328-6848-5*) Higginson Bk Co.
Lawrence D. Miles: Recollections. Ed. by James J. O'Brien. (Illus.). 124p. 1988. 17.50 (*0-9619440-0-5*) Value Found.
Lawrence Doyle: The Farmer Poet of Prince Edward Island. Edward D. Ives. 1971. 16.95 (*0-89101-022-X*) U Maine Pr.
Lawrence Durrell. Ed. by Alan W. Friedman. (Critical Essays Ser.). 264p. 1987. 49.00 (*0-8161-8755-X*, Hall Reference) Macmillan.
Lawrence Durrell. rev. ed. John A. Weigel. (Twayne's English Authors Ser.: No. 29). 176p. 1989. 22.95 (*0-8057-6986-2*, 233, Twyne) Mac Lib Ref.
Lawrence Durrell: A Biography. Ian S. MacNiven. (Illus.). 768p. 1998. 36.95 (*0-571-17248-2*) Faber & Faber.
Lawrence Durrell. An Illustrated Checklist. Alan G. Thomas & James A. Brigham. LC 83-6782. (Illus.). 208p. 1983. 17.95 (*0-8093-1021-X*) S Ill U Pr.
Lawrence Durrell: Comprehending the Whole. Ed. by Julius R. Raper et al. 224p. 1994. text 39.95 (*0-8262-0982-3*) U of Mo Pr.
Lawrence Durrell: Conversations. Lawrence Durrell. Ed. by Earl G. Ingersoll. LC 97-25070. 264p. 1998. 41.50 (*0-8386-3723-X*) Fairleigh Dickinson.
Lawrence Durrell's Major Novels: or The Kingdom of the Imagination. Donald P. Kaczvinsky. LC 96-29136. (Illus.). 184p. 1997. 33.50 (*0-945636-99-7*) Susquehanna U Pr.
Lawrence Family Letters of Willow Bank, Flushing, New York, 1846 to 1896. John H. Tennent, IV & Marjorie B. Tennent. LC 97-113693. (Illus.). xliv, 270p. (Orig.). 1996. 35.50 (*0-7884-0530-6*, T155) Heritage Bk.
Lawrence Ferlinghetti: Poet-at-Large. Larry Smith. LC 82-10835. (Illus.). 256p. 1983. pap. 14.95 (*0-8093-1102-X*) S Ill U Pr.
Lawrence Golan Violin Scale System: Intermediate-Advanced Level, Vol. 2. Lawrence Golan. 164p. 1997. spiral bd. 17.95 (*0-7866-2607-0*, 96469) Mel Bay.
Lawrence Halprin. Spacemaker Press Staff. 1998. pap. 29.95 (*0-688-15366-6*, Wm Morrow) Morrow Avon.
Lawrence Hargrave: Aviation Pioneer, Inventor & Explorer. W. Hudson Shaw & Olaf Ruhen. (Illus.). (Orig.). 1989. pap. text 15.95 (*0-7022-2157-0*, Pub. by Univ Queensland Pr) Intl Spec Bk.
Lawrence Homer: Selected Poems. unabridged ed. Lawrence Homer. Ed. by Harvey Lentchner. 32p. reprint ed. per. 6.95 (*0-9615306-1-8*) Poets Playwrights.
Lawrence, Jarry, Zukofsky: A Triptych. Ed. by Dave Oliphant & Gena Dagel. (Manuscript Collections at the Harry Ransom Humanities Research Center). (Illus.). 1986. pap. 20.00 (*0-87959-106-4*) U of Tex H Ransom Ctr.
Lawrence, Kansas. San Antonio Cartographers Staff. 1995. 2.95 (*0-671-56283-5*) Macmillan.
Lawrence Kholberg: Consensus & Controversy. Ed. by Sohan Modgil. LC 86-6361. (International Master Minds Challenged Ser.). 550p. 1986. 138.00 (*1-85000-025-5*, Falmer Pr) Taylor & Francis.
Lawrence Kohlberg's Approach to Moral Education. Clark F. Power et al. 1991. pap. text 22.50 (*0-231-05977-9*) Col U Pr.
Lawrence Kursk. Lawrence. 2000. 35.00 (*0-8133-3673-2*) HarpC.
Lawrence Marr, Loyalist. 108p. (Orig.). 1992. pap. 21.00 (*0-9611702-1-2*) H M Wheeler.
Lawrence of Arabia. Jeremy Wilson. 1999. pap. text 9.95 (*0-7509-1877-2*) A Sutton.
Lawrence of Arabia. B. Liddell Hart. (Quality Paperbacks Ser.). (Illus.). 458p. 1989. reprint ed. pap. text 14.95 (*0-306-80354-2*) Da Capo.
Lawrence of Arabia: A Biographical Inquiry. Richard Aldington. LC 75-36506. (Illus.). 448p. 1976. reprint ed. lib. bdg. 35.00 (*0-8371-8634-X*, ALLA, Greenwood Pr) Greenwood.
Lawrence of Arabia: A Film's Anthropology. Steven C. Caton. LC 98-3621. 1999. 50.00 (*0-520-21082-4*, Pub. by U CA Pr); 19.95 (*0-520-21083-2*, Pub. by U CA Pr) Cal Prin Full Svc.
Lawrence of Arabia & American Culture: The Making of Transatlantic Legend, 47. Joel C. Hodson. LC 95-9873. (Contributions to the Study of Popular Culture Ser.: No. 47). 216p. 1995. 52.95 (*0-313-29617-0*, Greenwood Pr) Greenwood.
Lawrence of Arabia, Strange Man of Letters: The Literary Criticism of T. E. Lawrence. T. E. Lawrence. Ed. by Harold Orlans. LC 92-53456. 1993. 47.50 (*0-8386-3508-3*) Fairleigh Dickinson.
***Lawrence Police Department.** Ronald J. DeSantis. (Images of America Ser.). 1999. pap. 18.99 (*0-7385-0153-0*) Arcadia Publng.
Lawrence Sanders - Three Complete Novels: The Anderson Tapes, the Tenth Commandment, the Fourth Deadly Sin. Lawrence Sanders. LC 96-7270. 752p. 1996. 12.98 (*0-399-14182-0*, G P Putnam) Peng Put Young Read.
Lawrence Sanders - Three Complete Novels: The Sixth Commandment; The Seventh Commandment; The Eighth Commandment. unabridged ed. Lawrence Sanders. LC 94-6726. 784p. 1994. 11.98 (*0-399-13972-9*, G P Putnam) Peng Put Young Read.
Lawrence Taylor. Daniel Hirshberg. LC 97-14225. (Illus.). 96p. (J). (gr. 3 up). 1997. lib. bdg. 15.95 (*0-7910-4429-7*) Chelsea Hse.
Lawrence Tibbett: Singing Actor. Ed. by Andrew Farkas. LC 88-26272. (Opera Biography Ser.: No. 1). (Illus.). 248p. 1989. 29.95 (*0-931340-17-9*, Amadeus Pr) Timber.
Lawrence Township. Kathleen M. Middleton. LC 95-166470. (Images of America Ser.). 1994. pap. 16.99 (*0-7524-0068-1*) Arcadia Publng.
Lawrence W. Little: Recollections of My Years in Carson City: Teaching High School, Testing Highway Materials, Inspecting Heavy Construction, & Playing with Western Nevada Music Groups, 4 vols., Set. Intro. by Mary E. Glass. 1606p. 1981. lib. bdg. 235.00 (*1-56475-207-0*); fiche. write for info. (*1-56475-208-9*) U NV Oral Hist.
Lawrence W. Little: Recollections of My Years in Carson City: Teaching High School, Testing Highway Materials, Inspecting Heavy Construction, & Playing with Western Nevada Music Groups, 4 vols., Vol. I. Intro. by Mary E. Glass. 437p. 1981. lib. bdg. 62.00 (*1-56475-355-7*) U NV Oral Hist.
Lawrence W. Little: Recollections of My Years in Carson City: Teaching High School, Testing Highway Materials, Inspecting Heavy Construction, & Playing with Western Nevada Music Groups, 4 vols., Vol. III. Intro. by Mary E. Glass. 319p. 1981. lib. bdg. 50.00 (*1-56475-357-3*) U NV Oral Hist.
Lawrence W. Little: Recollections of My Years in Carson City: Teaching High School, Testing Highway Materials, Inspecting Heavy Construction, & Playing with Western Nevada Music Groups, 4 vols., Vol. IV. Intro. by Mary E. Glass. 447p. 1981. lib. bdg. 63.00 (*1-56475-358-1*) U NV Oral Hist.
Lawrence W. Little Vol. II: Recollections of My Years in Carson City: Teaching High School, Testing Highway Materials, Inspecting Heave Construction, & Playing with Western Nevada Music Groups. Intro. by Mary E. Glass. 403p. 1981. lib. bdg. 59.00 (*1-56475-356-5*) U NV Oral Hist.
Lawrence Weiner. Contrib. by Alexander Alberro et al. LC 98-230645. (Colour Library). (Illus.). 128p. 1998. pap. 14.95 (*0-7148-3755-5*, Pub. by Phaidon Press) Phaidon Pr.
Lawrence Weiner: Displacement. Lawrence Weiner & Garry Garrels. LC 91-70138. (Illus.). 112p. 1992. 40.00 (*0-944521-22-3*) Dia Ctr Arts.
Lawrence Weiner: Towards a Theatrical Engagement: Ducks on a Pond. (Illus.). 56p. 1983. pap. 52.00 (*90-72191-02-1*, Pub. by Imschoot) Dist Art Pubs.
Lawrence Welk & His Musical Family: A Collective Guide. Karl B. Johnson. (Illus.). 400p. (Orig.). 1999. pap. 45.00 (*0-9644176-3-4*) J Carlson Pr.
Lawrence Welk Show, Then & Now. Ed. & Intro. by Laura Segall. 64p. 1995. pap. write for info. (*0-9645186-0-0*) Welk Music.
Lawrence Welk Songbook, Vol. 225. 128p. 1988. per. 9.95 (*0-7935-1126-7*, 00102080) H Leonard.
Lawrence Welk's Polka Folio: For Piano & Piano Accordion. 64p. 1985. pap. 9.95 (*0-7935-3399-6*, 00123218) H Leonard.
***Lawrence's Dealer Print Prices Annual, 1999.** Ed. by Jodie L. Benson. 1086p. 1999. 145.00 (*0-931036-77-1*) Gordon s Art.
Lawrence's Dealer Print Prices Annual, 1997. annuals Ed. by Jaleen K. Hinz. 1032p. 1997. 125.00 (*0-931036-75-5*) Gordon s Art.
Lawrence's Dealer Print Prices Annual, 1998. annuals Ed. by Jodie L. Benson. 1086p. 1998. 145.00 (*0-931036-76-3*) Gordon s Art.
***Lawrence's Dealer Print Prices, 2000.** Ed. by Lisa Reinhardt. 2000. 145.00 (*0-931036-78-X*) Gordon s Art.
Lawrie Tatum: Indian Agent. Robert Hixon. LC 81-81684. 28p. 1981. pap. 4.00 (*0-87574-238-6*) Pendle Hill.
Lawrie's Meat Science. 6th ed. Lawrie. 352p. 1998. pap. 84.95 (*1-85573-395-1*) Technomic.
***Laws.** Zachary A. Kelly. LC 98-6023. (Law & Order Ser.). 1999. write for info. (*0-86593-573-4*) Rourke Corp.

An Asterisk (*) at the beginning of an entry indicates that the title is appearing for the first time.

Laws. Zachary A. Kelly. LC 98-6023. (Law & Order Ser.). (J). 1998. 16.95 (*0-86625-664-4*) Rourke Pubns.

***Laws.** Plato. Tr. by Benjamin Jowett. LC 99-87820. (Great Books in Philosophy Ser.). 305p. 2000. pap. 9.95 (*1-57392-799-6*) Prometheus Bks.

Laws. Plato. Tr. & Intro. by Trevor J. Saunders. (Classics Ser.). 558p. 1970. pap. 11.95 (*0-14-044222-7*, Penguin Classics) Viking Penguin.

Laws, 2 vols., 1. Tr. by R. G. Bury. (Loeb Classical Library: No. 187, 192). 522p. 1926. text 18.95 (*0-674-99206-7*) HUP.

Laws, 2 vols., 2. Tr. by R. G. Bury. (Loeb Classical Library: No. 187, 192). 590p. 1926. text 18.95 (*0-674-99211-3*) HUP.

Laws: The First Codification see Torah Anthology: Meam Lo'ez

Laws Affecting Children with Special Needs: Selected Federal Statutes & Regulations. Ed. by Sharon T. Walsh & Praticia McKenna. 1990. ring bd. 125.00 (*0-685-38085-8*, 300004) LRP Pubns.

Laws Against Marijuana: The Price We Pay. Arthur D. Hellman. LC 74-34150. 224p. 1975. text 24.95 (*0-252-00438-8*) U of Ill Pr.

Law's Alabama Brigade: In the War Between the Union & the Confederacy. Morris M. Penny & J. Gary Laine. LC 96-44654. (Illus.). 458p. 1997. 37.50 (*1-57249-024-1*) White Mane Pub.

Laws & Customs in Hasidism. Aaron Wertheim. 39.50 (*0-88125-401-0*) Ktav.

Laws & Customs of the Sinhalese or Kandyan Law. Frederic A. Hayley. (C). 1993. reprint ed. text 45.00 (*81-7013-100-6*, Pub. by Navarang) S Asia.

Laws & Explanation in History. William H. Dray. LC 78-25936. 174p. 1979. reprint ed. lib. bdg. 38.50 (*0-313-20790-9*, DRLE, Greenwood Pr) Greenwood.

Laws & Joint Resolutions of the Cherokee Nation: Enacted by the National Council During the Regular & Extra Sessions of 1884-5-6. LC 75-3674. (Constitutions & Laws of the American Indian Tribes Ser. 2: Vol. 7). 1975. reprint ed. 17.00 (*0-8420-1840-9*) Scholarly Res Inc.

Laws & Joint Resolutions of the Cherokee Nation: Enacted During the Regular & Special Sessions of the Years 1881-2-3. LC 75-3673. (Constitutions & Laws of the American Indian Tribes Ser. 2: Vol. 6). 1975. reprint ed. 22.00 (*0-8420-1839-5*) Scholarly Res Inc.

Laws & Joint Resolutions of the Last Session of the Confederate Congress. Confederate States of America, Congress Staff. reprint ed. 39.50 (*0-404-05222-3*) AMS Pr.

Laws & Joint Resolutions of the National Council: Passed & Adopted at the Regular & Extra Sessions of 1870-2. LC 75-3670. (Constitutions & Laws of the American Indian Tribes Ser. 2: Vol. 4). 1975. reprint ed. 15.00 (*0-8420-1837-9*) Scholarly Res Inc.

Laws & Joint Resolutions of the National Council: Passed & Adopted at the Regular Session of 1876. LC 75-3672. (Constitutions & Laws of the American Indian Tribes Ser. 2: Vol. 5). 1975. reprint ed. 12.00 (*0-8420-1838-7*) Scholarly Res Inc.

Laws & Jurisprudence of England & America: Being a Series of Lectures Delivered Before Yale University. John F. Dillon. LC 94-17733. xvi, 431p. 1994. reprint ed. 52.50 (*0-8377-2039-7*, Rothman) W S Hein.

Laws & Legal System of a Free-Market Cuba: A Prospectus for Business. Matias F. Travieso-Diaz. LC 96-9047. 216p. 1996. 67.95 (*1-56720-051-6*, Quorum Bks) Greenwood.

Laws & Liberties of Massachusetts: Reprinted from the Unique Copy of the 1648 Edition in the Henry E. Huntington Library. Contrib. by Richard S. Dunn. LC 98-8646. 1998. 29.95 (*0-87328-173-X*) Huntington Lib.

Laws & Liberties of Massachusetts, 1641-1691, 3 vol., Set. Intro. by John D. Cushing. LC 75-24575. 1976. 125.00 (*0-8420-2074-8*) Scholarly Res Inc.

Laws & Models: Science, Engineering & Technology. Carl W. Hall. LC 99-29327. 560p. 1999. per. 64.95 (*0-8493-2018-6*) CRC Pr.

Laws & Order in Eighteenth-Century Chemistry. Alistair Duncan. LC 96-165706. (Illus.). 262p. 1996. text 90.00 (*0-19-855806-6*) OUP.

Laws & Other Worlds. Fred Wilson. 336p. 1986. text 168.00 (*90-277-2232-3*, D Reidel) Kluwer Academic.

Laws & Policies Affecting Adolescent Health. J. M. Paxman & R. J. Zuckerman. 310p. 1987. pap. text 49.00 (*92-4-156095-9*, 1150263) World Health.

Laws & Regulations of the People's Republic of China Governing Foreign-Related Matters, 1949-1992, 4 vols. Compiled by Bureau of Legislative Affairs of the State Council. (CHI & ENG.). 2684p. 1994. 455.00 (*0-614-11839-5*, Pub. by HUWEI Cnslts) Am Overseas Bk Co.

Laws & Regulations of the State of Maryland Relating to Alcohol Beverages & Tobacco Tax, 1998 Edition. 495p. 1998. 46.00 (*0-327-06444-7*, 2635412, MICHIE) LEXIS Pub.

***Laws & Regulations of the State of Maryland Relating to Alcoholic Beverages & Tobacco Tax 1999 Supplement.** 80p. 1999. Price not set. (*0-327-19700-5*, 2635314) LEXIS Pub.

Laws & Religions 4713 B. C. to 1948 A. D. First Facts in World Order. Fay Maxwell. 23p. 1968. 20.00 (*1-885463-15-4*) Ohio Genealogy.

Laws & Symmetry. Bas C. Van Fraassen. (Illus.). 410p. 1990. pap. text 26.00 (*0-19-824860-1*) OUP.

Laws & Warning Deut., No. 4 see Torah Anthology: Meam Lo'ez

Laws & Writs of Appeal. Ed. & Tr. by Charles T. Gehring from DUT. (New Netherland Documents Ser.). 200p. 1991. text 49.95 (*0-8156-2522-7*) Syracuse U Pr.

Laws Be Their Enemy. large type ed. Frederick E. Smith. 544p. 1996. 27.99 (*0-7089-3509-5*) Ulverscroft.

Law's Community: Legal Theory in Sociological Perspective. Roger Cotterell. (Oxford Socio-Legal Studies). 400p. 1997. pap. text 38.00 (*0-19-826490-9*) OUP.

Laws, Courts & Lawyers: Through the Years in Arizona. James Murphy. LC 79-89656. 261p. reprint ed. pap. 81.00 (*0-608-12770-1*, 202432000037) Bks Demand.

Law's Desire: Sexuality & the Limits of Justice. Carl F. Stychin. LC 95-16087. 200p. (C). 1995. 75.00 (*0-415-11126-9*); pap. 24.99 (*0-415-11127-7*) Routledge.

Law's Empire. Ronald M. Dworkin. LC 85-28566. 486p. 1986. 37.50 (*0-674-51835-7*) Belknap Pr.

Law's Empire. Ronald M. Dworkin. LC 85-28566. 486p. 1990. pap. text 19.95 (*0-674-51836-5*) Belknap Pr.

Laws for Business. 2nd ed. Fisher. Date not set. pap. text, teacher ed. write for info. (*0-314-81930-4*) West Pub.

Laws for the California Surveyor. Ed. by Roy Minnick. 210p. 1996. pap. 40.00 (*0-910845-10-7*, 708) Landmark Ent.

Laws From Heaven for Life on Earth see Studies in Proverbs

***Laws, Gods & Heroes: Thematic Readings in Early Western History.** Hal Drake & Joe Leedom. 301p. (C). 1999. per. 20.95 (*0-7872-6423-7*) Kendall-Hunt.

Laws Governing Executive Branch Agencies: A Guide for Legislators. Mark Shepard. 37p. (C). 1995. pap. text 20.00 (*0-7881-2452-8*) DIANE Pub.

Laws Harsh As Tigers: Chinese Immigrants & the Shaping of Modern Immigration Law. Lucy E. Salyer. LC 94-48276. (Studies in Legal History). 1995. pap. text 19.95 (*0-8078-4530-2*); lib. bdg. 55.00 (*0-8078-2218-3*) U of NC Pr.

Law's Lumber Room. 2nd ed. Francis Watt. LC 72-96203. (First Ser.). 139p. 1973. reprint ed. 40.00 (*0-912004-08-8*); reprint ed. 45.00 (*0-912004-09-6*) Gaunt.

Laws of Angling: A Stringer Full of Fishing's Eternal Verities. Randy Voorhees. LC 98-87736. 1999. 9.95 (*0-8362-7876-3*) Andrews & McMeel.

Laws of Armed Conflicts. rev. ed. D. Scindler & Jiri Toman. 904p. 1981. lib. bdg. 252.50 (*90-286-0199-6*) Kluwer Academic.

Laws of Armed Conflicts: A Collection of Conventions, Resolutions, & Other Documents. 3rd rev. ed. Dietrich Schindler & Jiri Toman. LC 86-2560. (Scientific Collection of the Henry Dunant Institute Ser.). 1988. lib. bdg. 290.00 (*90-247-3306-5*) Kluwer Academic.

Laws of Banking & Finance in the Hong Kong Sar. Berry F. Hsu. 328p. 1998. pap. 42.50 (*962-209-460-0*, Pub. by HK Univ Pr) Coronet Bks.

Laws of Brachos. B. Forst. 1989. 23.99 (*0-89906-220-2*); 19.99 (*0-89906-221-0*) Mesorah Pubns.

Laws of Burgos of 1512 to 1513: Royal Ordinances for the Good Government & Treatment of the Indians. Tr. by Lesley B. Simpson. LC 78-13497. (Illus.). 57p. 1979. reprint ed. lib. bdg. 55.00 (*0-313-21019-5*, CALB) Greenwood.

***Laws of Business for All the States of the Union & the Dominion of Canada: With Forms & Directions for All Transactions & Abstracts of the Laws of All the States on Various Topics.** Theophilus Parsons. LC 99-58129. 822p. 2000. 85.00 (*1-57588-613-8*) W S Hein.

Laws of Chanukah. Aryeh Kaplan. 124p. 1977. pap. 6.00 (*0-940118-48-3*) Moznaim.

Laws of Chaos: Invariant Measures & Dynamical Systems in One Dimension. Abraham Boyarsky & Pawel Gora. LC 97-22134. (Probability & Its Applications). (Illus.). xv, 399p. 1997. write for info. (*3-7643-4003-7*) Birkhauser.

Laws of Chaos: Invariant Measures & Dynamical Systems in One Dimension. Abraham Boyarsky & Pawel Gora. LC 97-22134. (Probability & Its Applications Ser.). (Illus.). 416p. 1997. 59.95 (*0-8176-4003-7*) Birkhauser.

Laws of Choice. Eric Marder. LC 97-7041. 1997. 29.50 (*0-684-83545-2*) S&S Trade.

Laws of City Planning & Zoning. Frank B. Williams. 1982. 46.95 (*0-8434-0067-6*) McGrath NH.

Laws of Consanguinity & Descent of the Iroquois. Lewis Henry Morgan. (Notable American Authors Ser.). 1999. reprint ed. lib. bdg. 125.00 (*0-7812-4586-9*) Rprt Serv.

Laws of Cooking on Sabbath & Festivals. Ehud Rosenberg. 76p. 1986. 8.95 (*1-58330-094-5*) Feldheim.

Laws of Corporations & Other Business Enterprises: 1986 Pocket Part. 3rd ed. Harry G. Henn & John R. Alexander. (Hornbook Ser.). 95p. (C). 1986. reprint ed. pap. text 10.50 (*0-314-24251-1*) West Pub.

Laws of Desire: Questions of Homosexuality in Spanish Writing & Film, 1960-90. Paul J. Smith. LC 92-13021. (Hispanic Studies). (Illus.). 260p. 1992. 75.00 (*0-19-811953-4*, Clarendon Pr); pap. text 22.00 (*0-19-812275-6*, Clarendon Pr) OUP.

Laws of Dharmasastra. B. N. Mani. (C). 1989. 58.00 (*81-7013-025-5*) S Asia.

Laws of Diminishing Returns. R. Faere. (Lecture Notes in Economics & Mathematical Systems Ser.: Vol. 176). (Illus.). 97p. 1980. 27.00 (*0-387-09744-9*) Spr-Verlag.

Laws of Eternity: A Time of New Hope for the World. Ryuho Okawa. 128p. 1998. pap. 9.95 (*1-86204-292-6*, Pub. by Element MA) Penguin Putnam.

Laws of Falling Bodies. Kate Light. LC 97-27243. (Roerich Poetry Prize Winner Ser.). 88p. 1997. pap. text 11.00 (*1-885266-55-3*) Story Line.

Laws of Fesole: Principles of Drawing & Painting from the Tuscan Masters. John Ruskin. LC 95-83004. (Illus.). 208p. 1996. pap. 18.95 (*1-880559-44-7*) Allworth Pr.

***Laws of Fesole: Principles of Drawing & Painting from the Tuscan Masters.** John Ruskin & Bill Beck. (Illus.). 223p. 1999. reprint ed. pap. text 19.00 (*0-7881-6711-1*) DIANE Pub.

Laws of Form. George Spencer-Brown. 184p. 1994. pap. 44.00 (*0-9639899-0-1*) Cognizer.

Laws of Gases. Ed. by I. Bernard Cohen. LC 80-2099. (Development of Science Ser.). (Illus.). 1981. lib. bdg. 38.95 (*0-405-13864-4*) Ayer.

Laws of Harbours & Pilotage. 4th ed. R. P. Douglas & G. K. Green. 344p. 1993. 120.00 (*1-85044-490-0*) LLP.

***Laws of Harm.** Irene Juneal Maran. 630p. 2000. write for info. (*0-940214-00-8*) Acting Off Your Weight.

Laws of History. G. D. Snooks. LC 97-51681. 304p. (C). 1998. 100.00 (*0-415-19050-9*) Routledge.

Laws of Hostility: Politics, Violence, & the Enlightenment. Pierre Saint-Amand. Tr. by Jennifer C. Gage from FRE. LC 96-11840. 176p. (C). 1996. pap. 17.95 (*0-8166-2586-7*); text 44.95 (*0-8166-2585-9*) U of Minn Pr.

Laws of Human Relations & the Rules of Human Actions Derived Therefrom. Hermann H. Gossen. Tr. by Rudolph C. Blitz & Nicholas Georgescu-Roegen from GER. (Illus.). 465p. 1983. 60.00 (*0-262-07090-1*) MIT Pr.

Laws of Illinois Territory, 1809 to 1818. Ed. by Francis S. Philbrick. LC 50-62758. (Illinois Historical Collections: Vol. 25). 1950. 2.50 (*0-912154-11-X*) Ill St Hist Lib.

Laws of Indiana Relating to the Department of Workforce Development, 1998 Edition. 137p. 1998. pap. 12.00 (*0-327-06844-2*, 2425811) LEXIS Pub.

Laws of Indiana Territory, 1801-1809. Francis S. Philbrick. 741p. 1931. 6.25 (*1-885323-45-X*) IN Hist Bureau.

Laws of Indo-European. Ed. by N. E. Collinge. LC 85-9192. (Current Issues in Linguistic Theory Ser.: No. 35). xviii, 273p. 1985. pap. 23.00 (*0-915027-75-5*) J Benjamins Pubng Co.

Laws of Innkeepers: For Hotels, Motels, Restaurants & Clubs. 3rd ed. John E. Sherry. LC 92-30561. 944p. 1993. text 45.00 (*0-8014-2508-5*) Cornell U Pr.

Laws of International Trade, 6 vols., Set, No. 11. 3000p. 1986. ring bd. 490.00 (*0-929576-31-4*) Busn Laws Inc.

Laws of Karma: Deeper Insight to the Esoteric Teachings of Kriya Yoga. Goswami Kriyananda. 1997. pap. text 14.95 (*0-929522-01-X*) Temple Kriya Yoga.

Laws of Kashrvs. B. Forst. 1993. 23.99 (*0-89906-103-6*); 19.99 (*0-89906-104-4*) Mesorah Pubns.

Laws of Land Warfare: A Guide to the U. S. Army Manuals, 132. Donald A. Wells. LC 92-25629. (Contributions in Military Studies Ser.: No. 132). 224p. 1992. 55.00 (*0-313-28639-6*, WRW, Greenwood Pr) Greenwood.

Laws of Life: Applying the Ten Commandments in Today's World. Maralene Wesner & Miles Wesner. 118p. (Orig.). 1990. pap. 7.95 (*0-936715-31-6*) Diversity Okla.

Laws of Life: Nature's Laws to Successful Living. Alfred A. Montapert. 1992. per. 10.00 (*0-614-04219-4*); per. 14.00 (*0-614-24517-6*) Bks of Value.

Laws of Life: With Special Reference to the Physical Education of Girls. rev. ed. Elizabeth Blackwell. Ed. by Elizabeth M. Whatley. (Illus.). 133p. reprint ed. pap. text 8.95 (*0-940151-10-3*) Statesman-Exam.

Laws of Life in Agriculture. Nicolaus Remer. Tr. by K. Castelliz et al from GER. (Illus.). 158p. 1995. pap. 12.95 (*0-938250-40-X*) Bio-Dynamic Farm.

***Laws of Love.** Margaret Pounders. LC 99-66955. 336p. 2000. reprint ed. pap. 12.95 (*0-87159-254-1*, 147) Unity Bks.

Laws of Management Physics: A Handbook for Hands-On Managers. Dick Dadamo. 386p. 1994. pap. 19.95 (*0-929392-35-3*) Annabooks.

Laws of Manu. G. Buhler. 1972. lib. bdg. 250.00 (*0-87968-492-5*) Krishna Pr.

Laws of Manu. Emile Zola. Tr. by Wendy Doniger & Brian K. Smith. 368p. 1992. pap. 13.95 (*0-14-044540-4*, Penguin Classics) Viking Penguin.

Laws of Manu. George Buehler. LC 73-149682. (BCL Ser. II). reprint ed. 34.50 (*0-404-01148-9*) AMS Pr.

Laws of Maryland Relating to Public Libraries, 1998 Edition: MD Public Libraries 98E. 45p. 1998. pap. 9.50 (*0-327-06511-7*, 2632212) LEXIS Pub.

Laws of Meat & Milk: Hebrew Text, English Translation & Commentary Digest. Tr. by Yehoshua Cohen from HEB.Tr. of Chochmas Adam: Hilchos Basur V'Cholov. 288p. 1990. 19.95 (*0-910818-91-6*) Judaica Pr.

Laws of Meat & Milk: Hebrew Text, English Translation & Commentary Digest. Yehoshua Cohen.Tr. of Chochmas Adam: Hilchos Basur V'Cholov. 288p. 1991. pap. 16.95 (*1-880582-42-2*) Judaica Pr.

Laws of Media: The New Science. Marshall McLuhan & Eric McLuhan. 258p. 1988. 30.00 (*0-8020-5782-9*) U of Toronto Pr.

Laws of Media: The New Science. Marshall McLuhan & Eric McLuhan. 262p. 1992. pap. text 18.95 (*0-8020-7715-3*) U of Toronto Pr.

Laws of Migration, Nos. 1 & 2. E. G. Ravenstein. LC 75-38142. (Demography Ser.). (Illus.). 1976. reprint ed. 17.95 (*0-405-07995-8*) Ayer.

Laws of Nature. John W. Carroll. (Studies in Philosophy). (Illus.). 212p. (C). 1994. text 64.95 (*0-521-43334-7*) Cambridge U Pr.

Laws of Nature: An Infallible Justice. A. C. Bhaktivedanta. 121p. 1991. pap. 7.95 (*0-89213-328-7*) Bhaktivedanta.

Laws of Nature: Essays on the Philosophical, Scientific & Historical Dimensions. Ed. by Friedel Weinert. LC 95-13649. (Philosophie & Wissenschaft - Tranzdisziplinaere Studien: Vol. 8). x, 422p. (C). 1995. pap. text 44.60 (*3-11-013918-9*) De Gruyter.

Laws of Nature, Causation, & Supervenience see Analytical Metaphysics

Laws of New Zealand, 20 vols., Set. Ed. by Robin Cooke. 1992. ring bd. 2120.00 (*0-318-72509-6*, MICHIE) LEXIS Pub.

Laws of Night: The Pocket Guide to Mind's Eye Theater. Richard Dansky & Wolf White Wolf Publishing Staff. (Illus.). 144p. (Orig.). 1996. pap. 12.95 (*1-56504-506-8*, 5005) White Wolf.

Laws of North Carolina Relating to Opticians & Rules of the State Board of Opticians, 1998 Edition. 40p. 1999. pap. write for info. (*0-327-07439-6*, 3043611) LEXIS Pub.

Laws of Occultism: Inner Plane Theory & the Fundamentals of Psychic Phenomena. C. C. Zain. LC 94-12550. (Brotherhood of Light Home Study Ser.: Course 1). 175p. 1994. pap. 16.95 (*0-87887-371-6*) Church of Light.

Laws of Our Fathers. Scott Turow. LC 96-16104. 550p. 1996. text 26.95 (*0-374-18423-2*) FS&G.

Laws of Our Fathers. large type ed. Scott Turow. LC 96-42476. 1997. pap. 25.95 (*0-7838-1946-3*, G K Hall Lrg Type) Mac Lib Ref.

Laws of Our Fathers. large type ed. Scott Turow. LC 96-42476. (Core Ser.). 937p. 1996. 27.95 (*0-7838-1945-5*) Thorndike Pr.

Laws of Our Fathers. Scott Turow. 832p. 1997. reprint ed. mass mkt. 7.99 (*0-446-60440-2*, Pub. by Warner Bks) Little.

Laws of Our Fathers: Popular Culture & the U. S. Constitution. Ray B. Browne & Glenn J. Browne. LC 86-70852. 298p. 1986. 25.95 (*0-87972-337-8*); pap. 13.95 (*0-87972-338-6*) Bowling Green Univ Popular Press.

Laws of Pennsylvania, 1982, Vol. 2. Legislative Reference Bureau Staff. 818p. 1983. text 7.70 (*0-8182-0015-4*) Commonweal PA.

Laws of Pennsylvania, 1987. Commonwealth of Pennsylvania Staff. Ed. by Legislative Reference Bureau Staff. 738p. 1988. text 8.70 (*0-8182-0102-9*) Commonweal PA.

Laws of Plato. Plato. Tr. & Notes by Thomas L. Pangle. xiv, 576p. 1988. pap. text 22.50 (*0-226-67110-0*) U Ch Pr.

Laws of Plato, 2 vols. Plato. LC 75-13285. (History of Ideas in Ancient Greece Ser.). 1979. reprint ed. 82.95 (*0-405-07327-5*) Ayer.

Laws of Preventive Detention - Past & Present. Surendra Malik. (C). 1988. 70.00 (*0-7855-3325-7*) St Mut.

Laws of Prosperity. K. Copeland. 1975. pap. 5.95 (*0-8007-0725-7*) K Copeland Pubns.

Laws of Prosperity. Kenneth Copeland. 28p. 1974. pap. 5.95 (*0-88114-952-7*) K Copeland Pubns.

Laws of Puerto Rico Annotated, 41 vols. Michie Editorial Staff. (SPA.). Date not set. 1309.00 (*0-327-01022-3*, 47530, MICHIE) LEXIS Pub.

Laws of Puerto Rico Annotated: 1995-96 Cumulative Supplements. annot. ed. 3650p. 1998. write for info. (*0-327-06347-5*, 4757313) LEXIS Pub.

***Laws of Puerto Rico Annotated: 1997 Cumulative Supplements (English)** 3650p. 1999. pap. write for info. (*0-327-09188-6*, 4757314) LEXIS Pub.

Laws of Puerto Rico Annotated No. 18-19: Replacement Volume. 580p. 1998. 37.50 (*0-327-05862-5*, 47548-11) LEXIS Pub.

Laws of Puerto Rico Annotated No. 20: 1998 Replacement Volume. (Illus.). 550p. 1998. 47.50 (*0-327-05865-X*, 47549-11) LEXIS Pub.

Laws of Puerto Rico Annotated Vol. 4apx: 1998 English Replacement Volume. 615p. 1998. write for info. (*0-327-05978-8*, 47536-11) LEXIS Pub.

Laws of Puerto Rico Annotated Vols. 2-3: 1998 English Replacement Volume. 750p. 1998. write for info. (*0-327-05976-1*, 47532-11) LEXIS Pub.

Laws of Puerto Rico Annotated 1995-96 Cumulative Supplements T 3 (451-880) 65p. Date not set. write for info. (*0-327-07972-X*, 84157-13) LEXIS Pub.

Laws of Puerto Rico Annotated 1995-1996 Cumulative Supplement, Vol. T3. 65p. Date not set. suppl. ed. write for info. (*0-327-06601-6*, 84157-13) LEXIS Pub.

Laws of Puerto Rico Annotated Replacement, Vol. 23. annot. ed. (SPA.). 700p. 1999. write for info. (*0-327-08657-2*, 47481-11) LEXIS Pub.

***Laws of Puerto Rico Annotated T. 1 1999 Replacement Volume.** 600p. 1999. Price not set. (*0-327-09973-9*, 4753111) LEXIS Pub.

***Laws of Puerto Rico Annotated T. 23, S 1-520: 1999 Replacement Volume (English)** 500p. 1999. write for info. (*0-327-09461-3*, 4755211) LEXIS Pub.

***Laws of Puerto Rico Annotated T. 23 SS/n 521-End: 1999 Replacement Volume (English)** 450p. 1999. write for info. (*0-327-09462-1*, 4757511) LEXIS Pub.

***Laws of Puerto Rico Annotated Title 24 Replacement Volume.** annot. ed. (SPA.). 780p. 1999. write for info. (*0-327-08718-8*, 47482-11) LEXIS Pub.

Laws of Puerto Rico Annotated, 1998 Supplement see Leyes de Puerto Rico Anotadas, 1998 Supplement

Laws of Puerto Rico 1995. 3618p. 1999. write for info. (*0-327-07718-2*, 4757916) LEXIS Pub.

Laws of Puerto Rico 1995: English, Vol. 1. 1256p. 1999. write for info. (*0-327-07719-0*, 8465516) LEXIS Pub.

Laws of Puerto Rico 1995: English, Vol. 2. 1203p. 1999. write for info. (*0-327-07720-4*, 8465616) LEXIS Pub.

Laws of Puerto Rico 1995: English, Vol. 3. 1154p. 1999. write for info. (*0-327-07721-2*, 8465916) LEXIS Pub.

Laws of Puerto Rico, 1994, Vol. b. Date not set. write for info. (*0-327-06211-8*, 84656-15) LEXIS Pub.

Laws of Puerto Rico, 1994, Vol. c. Date not set. write for info. (*0-327-06212-6*, 84659-15) LEXIS Pub.

Laws of Puerto Rico, 1994: 1998 Edition, 3 vols. Juan C. Rivera-Rodriguez. 1222p. 1998. pap. write for info. (*0-327-06209-6*, 47579-15) LEXIS Pub.

Laws of Puerto Rico, 1994: 1998 Edition, Vol. 1. Date not set. write for info. (*0-327-06210-X*, 84655-15) LEXIS Pub.

Laws of Puerto Rico, 1993: Acts & Resolutions of Puerto Rico, 1998 Edition, 2 vols. 1310p. 1998. 121.00 (*0-327-05046-2*, 84655-14) LEXIS Pub.

An Asterisk (*) at the beginning of an entry indicates that the title is appearing for the first time.

L

Laws of Puerto Rico, 1997 see Leyes de Puerto Rico, 1997

Laws of Rape. Sue Bessmer. LC 84-18202. (Landmark Dissertations in Women's Studies). 400p. 1985. 65.00 (0-275-90061-4, C0061, Praeger Pubs) Greenwood.

Laws of Ribbis. Yisroel Reisman. 23.99 (0-89906-126-5, LORH); pap. 19.99 (0-89906-127-3, LORP) Mesorah Pubns.

Laws of Russia Tenth to Fifteenth Centuries. Ed. & Tr. by Daniel H. Kaiser. LC 91-48031. (Laws of Russia Ser.: Series I, Volume 1). 384p. (C). 1993. 125.00 (1-884445-04-7) C Schlacks Pub.

Laws of Scientific Hand Reading. William G. Benham. 635p. 1993. reprint ed. pap. 35.00 (0-7873-0090-X) Hlth Research.

Laws of Scientific Hand Reading: A Practical Treatise on the Art Commonly Called Palmistry (1900) William G. Benham. 640p. 1998. reprint ed. pap. 30.00 (0-7661-0504-0) Kessinger Pub.

Laws of Scotland: Stair Memorial Encyclopaedia. Ed. by Robert Black et al. write for info. (0-406-04849-5, LS1SET, MICHIE) LEXIS Pub.

Laws of Small Numbers: Extremes & Rare Events. Michael Falk et al. LC 94-20902. (DMV Seminar Ser.: Bd. 23). 296p. 1994. 59.50 (0-8176-5071-7) Birkhauser.

Laws of Spirit see Lois de l'Esprit

Laws of Spirit: Simple, Powerful Truths for Making Life Work. Dan Millman. Ed. by Nancy Carleton. LC 95-19406. 120p. 1995. 14.00 (0-915811-64-2) H J Kramer Inc.

Laws of Spirit Mediumship. Lena B. Jefts. 40p. 1996. reprint ed. spiral bd. 8.00 (0-7873-0468-9) Hlth Research.

Laws of Tahara. Menachem Moshe Oppen. LC 94-72545. (Pictorial Avodah Ser.: Vol. 5). (Illus.). 170p. 16.95 (1-56062-269-5) CIS Comm.

Laws of the Cherokee Nation: Passed at the Annual Session of the National Council, 1845. LC 75-3668. (Constitutions & Laws of the American Indian Tribes Ser. 2: Vol. 2). 1975. reprint ed. 12.00 (0-8420-1835-2) Scholarly Res Inc.

Laws of the Chickasaw Nation, I. T. Relating to Intermarried & Adopted Citizens & Rights of Freedom. LC 75-3679. (Constitutions & Laws of the American Indian Tribes Ser. 2: Vol. 12). 1975. reprint ed. 11.00 (0-8420-1845-X) Scholarly Res Inc.

Laws of the Choctaw Nation: Passed at the Regular Session of the General Council Convened at Tushka Humma, October 27th, 1889 & Adjourned November 15, 1889. LC 75-3687. (Constitutions & Laws of the American Indian Tribes Ser. 2: Vol. 20). 1975. reprint ed. 12.00 (0-8420-1878-6) Scholarly Res Inc.

Laws of the Choctaw Nation, Passed at the Regular Session of the General Council Convened at Tushka Humma, Oct. 6, 1890, Adjourned Nov. 14, 1890. LC 75-3688. (Constitutions & Laws of the American Indian Tribes Ser. 2: Vol. 21). 1975. reprint ed. 16.00 (0-8420-1879-4) Scholarly Res Inc.

Laws of the Choctaw Nation, Passed at the Regular Session of the General Council Convened at Tushka Humma, Oct. 6, 1890, Adjourned Nov. 14, 1890. LC 75-3689. (Constitutions & Laws of the American Indian Tribes Ser. 2: Vol. 22). 1975. reprint ed. 12.00 (0-8420-1880-8) Scholarly Res Inc.

Laws of the Damascus Document: Sources, Tradition, & Redaction. Charlotte Hempel. LC 98-5513. (Studies on the Texts of the Desert of Judah). 1998. 59.00 (90-04-11150-6) Brill Academic Pubs.

Laws of the Earliest English Kings, Aethelberth First to Aethelstan see Great Britain, Laws, Statutes: England, Laws & Statutes

***Laws of the East.** Peter Woodworth. (Mind's Eye Theatre Ser.). 2000. pap. text 17.95 (1-56504-730-3) White Wolf.

Laws of the Fraternity of the Rosie Crosse (Themis Aurea) Michael Maier. (Illus.). 136p. 1999. 15.50 (0-89314-402-9) Philos Res.

Laws of the Game: How the Principles of Nature Govern Chance. Manfred Eigen & Ruthild Winkler. Tr. by Robert Kimber & Rita Kimber. LC 92-16084. (Science Library). (Illus.). 366p. (C). 1993. pap. 16.95 (0-691-02566-5, Pub. by Princeton U Pr) Cal Prin Full Svc.

LAWs of the Golf Swing: Body-Type Your Swing & Master Your Game. Mike Adams & Tomasi. LC 98-10674. (Illus.). 240p. 1998. 25.00 (0-06-270815-5) HarpC.

Laws of the Heart. 2nd ed. Bill Hybels. 132p. 1993. pap. 9.99 (1-56476-061-8, 6-3061, Victor Bks) Chariot Victor.

Laws of the Higher Life. Annie W. Besant. 1997. pap. 3.25 (0-8356-7103-8) Theos Pub Hse.

Laws of the Hunt. John Wick. (Mind's Eye Theatre Ser.). (Illus.). 1998. pap. 15.00 (1-56504-505-X, 5014) White Wolf.

Laws of the Kingdom: As Presented by the Spirit World Through the Automatic Writings of Frances Bird. Frances Bird. LC 87-22714. (Laws of the Kingdom Ser.: Vol. II). 382p. (Orig.). 1988. pap. 16.95 (1-55768-702-1) LC Pub.

Laws of the Kingdom Volume I: As Presented by the Spirit World, Through the Automatic Writings of Frances Bird. unabridged ed. Frances Bird. LC 87-22714. (Automatic Writings Ser.: Vol. I). 249p. 1988. pap. 44.95 incl. audio (1-55768-701-3) LC Pub.

Laws of the Kings of England from Edmund to Henry First see Great Britain, Laws, Statutes: England, Laws & Statutes

Laws of the Kings of England from Edmund to Henry I. Ed. by A. J. Robertson. LC 80-2210. reprint ed. 57.50 (0-404-18784-6) AMS Pr.

Laws of the Land. 2nd ed. David Baker. Ed. by Orvis C. Burmaster. LC 81-69224. (Ahsahta Press Modern & Contemporary Poets of the West Ser.). 70p. 1981. pap. 6.95 (0-916272-18-4) Ahsahta Pr.

***Laws of the Landscape: How Policies Shape Cities in Europe & America** Pietro S. Nivola. LC 98-58140. 1999. 14.95 (0-8157-6081-7) Brookings.

Laws of the Living Language. John Wolsin. Ed. by David Mitchell. 1999. pap. 7.00 (1-888365-24-2) Assn Waldorf Schls.

Laws of the Markets. Ed. by Michael Callon. (Sociological Review Monographs). 270p. 1998. pap. 33.95 (0-631-20608-6) Blackwell Pubs.

Laws of the Medieval Kingdom of Hungary, 1000-1301. Ed. & Tr. by Janos M. Bak et al. LC 89-10492. (Laws of Hungary Ser.: Series I, Vol. 1). 320p. 1989. 95.00 (1-884445-08-X) C Schlacks Pub.

Laws of the Medieval Kingdom of Hungary, 1301-1457. Ed. & Tr. by Janos M. Bak et al. LC 89-10492. (Laws of Hungary Ser.: Series I, Vol. 2). 500p. (C). 1993. 150.00 (1-884445-09-8) C Schlacks Pub.

Laws of the Medieval Kingdom of Hungary, 1458-1490. Ed. by Janos M. Bak. (Laws of Hungary Ser.: Series I, Vol. 3). xxix, 230p. 1995. 75.00 (1-884445-26-8) C Schlacks Pub.

***Laws of the Night.** limited rev. ed. Jason Carl et al. (Mind's Eye Theatre Ser.). (Illus.). 256p. 1999. 33.95 (1-56504-699-4, 5015) White Wolf.

Laws of the Night. rev. ed. Jason Carl et al. (Mind's Eye Theatre Ser.). (Illus.). 256p. 1999. pap. 19.95 (1-56504-589-0, 5013) White Wolf.

Laws of the People's Republic of China, 1987-1989, Vol. 3. Compiled by Legislative Affairs Commission of the Standing Com. 361p. 1996. 60.00 (7-03-001951-2, Pub. by Sci Pr) Lubrecht & Cramer.

Laws of the People's Republic of China, 1990-1992, Vol. 4. Compiled by Legislative Affairs Commission of the Standing Com. 533p. 1996. 90.00 (7-03-003533-X, Pub. by Sci Pr) Lubrecht & Cramer.

Laws of the People's Republic of China, 1993, Vol. 5. Compiled by Legislative Affairs Commission of the Standing Com. 385p. 1996. 75.00 (7-03-004707-9, Pub. by Sci Pr) Lubrecht & Cramer.

Laws of the Postcolonial. Ed. by Eve Darian-Smith & Peter Fitzpatrick. LC 98-51222. (Law, Meaning & Violence Ser.). 320p. 1999. text 49.50 (0-472-10956-1, 10956) U of Mich Pr.

Laws of the Salian & Ripuarian Franks. Intro. by Theodore J. Rivers. LC 85-48002. (Studies in the Middle Ages: No. 8). 1986. 42.50 (0-404-61438-8) AMS Pr.

Laws of the Salian Franks. Tr. & Intro. by Katherine F. Drew. LC 90-21755. (Middle Ages Ser.). 276p. (C). 1991. text 39.95 (0-8122-8256-6); pap. text 17.95 (0-8122-1322-X) U of Pa Pr.

Laws of the State of Delaware Relating to Financial Institutions, 1997. 376p. suppl. ed. 55.00 (0-327-11323-5) LEXIS Pub.

Laws of the State of Delaware Relating to Financial Institutions, 1998 Supplement. 54p. 1999. write for info. (0-327-07135-4, 2214212) LEXIS Pub.

Laws of the State of New Hampshire Session Laws, 1998. 650p. 1999. write for info. (0-327-08426-X, 45666-14) LEXIS Pub.

Laws of the Sun. Ryuho Okawa. Date not set. write for info. (0-614-17667-0) Penguin Putnam.

Laws of the United States, 2 vols., Set. U. S. House of Representatives Staff. Ed. by Stuart Bruchey. LC 78-53551. (Development of Public Land Law in the U. S. Ser.). 1979. reprint ed. lib. bdg. 98.95 (0-405-11388-9) Ayer.

Laws of the United States Concerning Money, Banking, & Loans, 1778-1909. U. S. National Monetary Commission Staff. LC 78-10669. xxii, 812p. 1978. reprint ed. lib. bdg. 55.00 (0-313-20681-3, LAOU) Greenwood.

Laws of the United States of America, 3 vols., Set. LC 88-45805. 1688p. 1988. reprint ed. 295.00 (0-912004-69-X, 18178) Gaunt.

Laws of the United States of America from the 4th of March, 1789 to the 4th of March, 1815 Including the Constitution of the United States, the Old Act of Confederation, Treaties, & Many Other Valuable Ordinances & Documents with Copious Notes & References, 5 vols., Set. LC 89-45923. 3534p. 1989. reprint ed. 495.00 (0-912004-75-4, 18140) Gaunt.

Laws of the United States Relating to Currency, Finance & Banking from 1789 to 1891. Ed. by Charles F. Dunbar. LC 68-28627. 309p. reprint ed. lib. bdg. 22.50 (0-8371-4585-6, DULU, Greenwood Pr) Greenwood.

Laws of the United States Relating to Currency, Finance & Banking from 1789 to 1896. rev. ed. Compiled by Charles F. Dunbar. LC 69-16856. (Library of Money & Banking History). iv, 310p. 1969. reprint ed. 20.00 (0-678-00476-5) Kelley.

Laws of the United States Relating to the Improvement of Rivers & Harbors from August 11, 1790 to June 29, 1938, 3 vols., Set. Ed. by Office of the Chief of Engineers, U. S. Army Staff. LC 73-5434. reprint ed. 125.00 (0-404-11190-4) AMS Pr.

Laws of the Wild: For Mind's Eye Theatre. Thomas Stratman. (Mind's Eye Theatre Ser.). (Illus.). (Orig.). 1997. pap. 15.00 (1-56504-508-4, 5007) White Wolf.

Laws of the Wild West. Peter Woodworth. (Minds Eye Theatre Ser.). (Illus.). 256p. 1999. pap. 14.95 (1-56504-504-1, 5004) White Wolf.

Laws of Thought. George Boole. 424p. (C). 1958. pap. 10.95 (0-486-60028-9) Dover.

Laws of Thought see Logical Works

Laws of Torts. 1999. 84.00 (1-85431-856-X, Pub. by Blackstone Pr) Gaunt.

Laws of Torts: Blackstone's LLB Leaning Texts. 2nd ed. John Hodgson & John Lewthwaite. 452p. 1998. pap. 42.00 (1-85431-816-0) Gaunt.

Laws of Virginia Related to Financial Institutions: 1998 Edition. LC 98-231099. 515p. 1998. 51.00 (0-327-06294-0, 35502-12) LEXIS Pub.

Laws of Virginia Related to Financial Institutions, 1999 Supplement. 97p. Price not set. (0-327-09716-7, 3550312) LEXIS Pub.

Laws of Virginia Related to Non-Depository Financial Services: 1998 Edition. Ed. by Gail D. Haskins. LC 98-215236. 102p. 1998. 12.50 (0-327-06095-6, 35498-12) LEXIS Pub.

***Laws of Virginia Related to Non-Depository Financial Services, 1999 Supplement.** 15p. 1999. Price not set. (0-327-09720-5, 3549912) LEXIS Pub.

Laws of Virginia Relating to Adult Corrections: 1998 Editions. Lexis Law Publishing Staff. 332p. 1998. pap. 34.00 (0-327-06650-4) LEXIS Pub.

***Laws of Virginia Relating to Adult Corrections 1999 Supplement.** 100p. 1999. Price not set. (0-327-09664-0, 3550112) LEXIS Pub.

Laws of Virginia Relating to the Marine Resources of the Commonwealth: 1998 Edition. 557p. 1998. write for info. (0-327-06341-6, 3551811); 32.00 (0-327-06342-4, 3548212) LEXIS Pub.

***Laws of Virginia Relating to the Marine Resources of the Commonwealth 1999 Supplement.** 48p. 1999. Price not set. (0-327-09747-7, 3440615) LEXIS Pub.

Laws of Virginia Relating to the Virginia Department of Juvenile Justice: 1998 Cumulative Supplement. LC 99-163256. 1998. pap. write for info. (0-327-06208-8, 35548-10) LEXIS Pub.

Laws of Wages, Profits & Rent Investigated. George Tucker. (Notable American Authors). 1999. reprint ed. lib. bdg. 125.00 (0-7812-9834-2) Rprt Serv.

Laws of Wages, Profits & Rents Investigated. George Tucker. LC 63-2335. (Reprints of Economic Classics Ser.). x, 189p. 1964. reprint ed. 37.50 (0-678-00034-4) Kelley.

Laws of War: Constraints on Warfare in the Western World. Ed. by Michael C. Howard et al. (Illus.). 311p. 1997. pap. 19.00 (0-300-07062-4) Yale U Pr.

Laws of War: Constraints on Warfare in the Western World. Ed. by Michael C. Howard et al. LC 94-18818. 310p. 1994. reprint ed. pap. 96.10 (0-608-07892-1, 205999900010) Bks Demand.

Laws of War & the Conduct of the Panama Invasion. Americas Watch Staff. 30p. 1990. 6.00 (0-929692-44-6, Am Watch) Hum Rts Watch.

Laws of War in the Late Middle Ages. Keen. 304p. 1993. 63.95 (0-7512-0189-8) Ashgate Pub Co.

Laws on Credit Transfers & Their Settlement in Member States of the EU Foreward Questionnaire Glossary Comparative Tables Comparative Essays Vol. 1. European Commission. 213p. 1994. pap. 35.00 (92-826-7983-7, C1-28-94-001-EN, Pub. by Comm Europ Commun) Bernan Associates.

Laws on Credit Transfers & Their Settlement in Member States of the EU Member State Reports Vol. 2: Belgium, Denmark, England & Wales. European Commission. 257p. 1994. pap. 40.00 (92-826-7984-5, C1-28-94-002ENC, Pub. by Comm Europ Commun) Bernan Associates.

Laws on Credit Transfers & Their Settlement in Member States of the EU Member States Vol. 4: Italy, Luxembourg, Netherlands, Spain. European Commission. 333p. 1994. pap. 45.00 (92-826-7986-1, Pub. by Comm Europ Commun) Bernan Associates.

Laws on Credit Transfers & Their Settlement in Member States of the EU Member States Reports Vol. 3: Germany, France, Greece & Ireland. European Commission. 311p. 1994. pap. 45.00 (92-826-7985-3, C1-28-94-003-EN, Pub. by Comm Europ Commun) Bernan Associates.

***Law's Order: What Economics Has to Do with Law & Why It Matters.** David D. Friedman. LC 99-58555. 318p. 2000. 29.95 (0-691-01016-1, Pub. by Princeton U Pr) Cal Prin Full Svc.

Laws, Ordinances, Regulations, & Rules Relating to the Judicial Administration of the Republic of China. Republic of China Staff. LC 76-11420. (Studies in Chinese Government & Law). 364p. 1976. reprint ed. lib. bdg. 75.00 (0-313-26957-2, U6957) Greenwood.

Laws, Physics & the Universe: Unit N. Moore. 1998. 13.50 (0-07-043055-1) McGraw.

***Law's Premises & Law's Promise: Jurisprudence after Wittgenstein.** Thomas Morawetz. LC 99-39396. (Collected Essays in Law Ser.). 300p. 1999. text 96.95 (0-7546-2013-1, Pub. by Ashgate Pub) Ashgate Pub Co.

Law's Promise, Law's Expression: Visions of Power in the Politics of Race, Gender, & Religion. Kenneth L. Karst. LC 93-36591. 304p. (C). 1994. 37.50 (0-300-05760-1) Yale U Pr.

Law's Promise, Law's Expression: Visions of Power in the Politics of Race, Gender, & Religion. Kenneth L. Karst. 1995. pap. 18.00 (0-300-06507-8) Yale U Pr.

Laws Regarding Slavery As a Source for Social History of the Period of the Second Temple, the Mishnah & Talmud. E. E. Urbach. Ed. by Moses I. Finley. LC 79-5009. (Ancient Economic History Ser.). 1979. reprint ed. lib. bdg. 15.95 (0-405-12397-3) Ayer.

***Laws, Regulations & Practices Affecting New York Real Estate.** 3rd ed. Michael K. Brady. Ed. by Kenneth Borowiak & Mia Park. (Real Estate Ser.). (Illus.). 300p. 2000. pap. 29.95 (0-9639868-1-3) Natl Appraisal & Cnslt.

Laws Relating to the Department of Public Safety: Reprinted from the Code of Laws of South Carolina 1976. Robin Larner. LC 96-77031. 1300p. 1996. pap. text. write for info. (0-7620-0077-5) West Group.

Laws, Rights & the European Convention on Human Rights: Proceedings at the Colloquy in the Plenary Hall of the Svea Court of Appeals, March 29, 1983, Organized by Institutet for Offentlig Och Internationell Ratt. Ed. by Jacob W. Sundberg. vii, 119p. 1986. pap. 32.00 (0-8377-1142-8, Rothman) W S Hein.

Law's Stories: Narrative & Rhetoric in the Law. Ed. by Peter Brooks & Paul Gewirtz. LC 95-26410. 302p. (C). 1996. 40.00 (0-300-06675-9) Yale U Pr.

Law's Stories: Narrative & Rhetoric in the Law. Ed. by Peter Brooks & Paul Gewirtz. LC 95-26410. 302p. 1998. pap. 16.00 (0-300-07490-5) Yale U Pr.

Laws, Theories & the Principles of Science. Craig Dilworth. (Uppsala Philosophical Studies: No. 44). 108p. (Orig.). 1990. pap. 29.50 (91-506-0787-1) Coronet Bks.

Laws, Theories & Values: Biological Approaches to Understanding. 2nd ed. Jorge A. Quintero. LC 79-50190. (Illus.). 144p. 1980. 10.50 (0-87527-147-2) Green.

Laws to Love By: The Ten Commandments. Phyllis Wezeman. (Illus.). 94p. 1996. pap. 14.95 (1-57438-001-X, 5209) Ed Ministries.

Law's Violence. Ed. by Austin Sarat & Thomas R. Kearns. (Amherst Series in Law, Jurisprudence, & Social Theory). 272p. (C). 1992. text 52.50 (0-472-10390-3, 10390) U of Mich Pr.

Law's Violence. Ed. by Austin Sarat & Thomas R. Kearns. (Illus.). 272p. (C). 1995. pap. text 20.95 (0-472-08317-1, 08317) U of Mich Pr.

Lawson-Chester Genealogy. Compiled by Altshuler General Svc. Staff. 50p. 1994. reprint ed. pap. 10.00 (0-8328-4126-9) Higginson Bk Co.

Lawson Perspective Charts. rev. ed. Philip J. Lawson. 1940. text 39.95 (0-442-13053-8, VNR) Wiley.

Lawson Simlog User. 1993. lab manual ed. 22.50 (0-19-268060-9) OUP.

Lawson Tait: The Rebellious Surgeon, 1845 to 1899. John S. Shepherd. (Illus.). 250p. 1980. 25.00 (0-87291-131-4) Coronado Pr.

Lawson-Westen House: Brentwood, California, 1993: Eric Owen Moss. James Steele. (Architecture in Detail Ser.). (Illus.), 60p. (Orig.). (C). 1995. pap. 29.95 (0-7148-3259-6, Pub. by Phaidon Press) Phaidon Pr.

***Lawson's Fork: Headwaters to Confluence.** David Conrad Taylor & Gary Henderson. (Illus.). 120p. 2000. pap. 14.95 (1-891885-13-8) Hub City Writers.

Lawsuit Defensive Measures: What Your Attorney May Not Tell You. Nahur Greenbird. LC 89-90646. 128p. (Orig.). 1989. pap. 15.95 (0-922958-05-X) H W Parker.

Lawsuit Prevention Techniques for Mental Health Professionals, Chemical Dependency Specialists & Clergy. Barbara E. Calfee. 135p. (Orig.). 1992. pap. 19.95 (0-9633540-1-9) ARC Pub.

Lawsuit Proof: Protecting Your Assets from Lawsuits & Claims. Robert J. Mintz & James J. Rubens. LC 94-79491. (Illus.). (Orig.). 1994. pap. text 19.95 (0-915905-37-X) Lawtech Pub.

Lawsuits. Gideon. 1995. 125.00 (0-316-52506-5, Aspen Law & Bus) Aspen Pub.

Lawsuits & Litigants in Castile, 1500-1700. Richard L. Kagan. LC 80-17565. 298p. 1981. reprint ed. pap. 92.40 (0-608-02059-1, 206271200003) Bks Demand.

Lawsuits of the Rich & Famous. W. Kelsea Wilber & Jeff Trippe. LC 94-67521. 164p. 1994. pap. 10.95 (0-913825-95-6) Galt Pr.

***Lawsuits, Taxes & Asset Protection.** Michael Potter & Kevin Day. 554p. 1999. pap. text 69.95 (1-58275-004-1, Pub. by Black Forest Pr) Epic Bk Promo.

Lawton Girl see Collected Works of Harold Frederic

Lawton Girl. Harold Frederic. (Collected Works of Harold Frederic). 1988. reprint ed. lib. bdg. 59.00 (0-7812-1184-0) Rprt Serv.

LawToons. Jim Keahey. (Illus.), 110p. (Orig.). 1991. pap. 10.45 (0-9631227-0-3) Uxor TX.

Lawyer: A Life of Cases, Counsel & Controversy. Arthur L. Liman. LC 98-27279. 416p. 1998. text 30.00 (1-891620-04-5, Pub. by PublicAffairs NY) HarpC.

Lawyer: Personal & Professional Responsibility. John T. Noonan, Jr. & Richard W. Painter. LC 97-7143. (University Casebook Ser.). 866p. 1997. text. write for info. (1-56662-477-0) Foundation Pr.

Lawyer Advertising. Louise L. Hill. LC 93-6764. 216p. 1993. 55.00 (0-89930-722-1, HLJ/, Quorum Bks) Greenwood.

Lawyer Advertising: Consumer Attitudes, Response Patterns & Motivation Factors. Tom L. Lee. LC 85-11699. 207p. (Orig.). 1985. pap. 325.00 (0-934547-00-9) CRI-Comm Res.

Lawyer Advertising at the Crossroads: Professional Policy Considerations. LC 95-178453. 1995. pap. 15.95 (1-57073-142-X, 406-0015) Amer Bar Assn.

Lawyer & Client: Or, the Trials & Triumphs of the Bar; Illustrated by Scenes in the Court-Room, Etc., Etc. L. B. Proctor. (Illus.). xii, 324p. 1995. reprint ed. 45.00 (0-8377-2553-4, Rothman) W S Hein.

Lawyer & Client: Who's in Charge? Douglas E. Rosenthal. LC 73-83891. 230p. 1974. 29.95 (0-87154-725-2) Russell Sage.

Lawyer & His Community: The Practicing Bar in a Middle-Sized City. Joel F. Handler. LC 67-20759. 238p. reprint ed. pap. 73.80 (0-8357-6185-1, 203427600089) Bks Demand.

Lawyer & His Profession: A Series of Letters to a Solicitor Commencing Business. J. Orton Smith. vi, 135p. 1996. reprint ed. 30.00 (0-8377-2659-X, Rothman) W S Hein.

An Asterisk (*) at the beginning of an entry indicates that the title is appearing for the first time.

Lawyer & Popular Culture: Proceedings of a Conference January 7-8, 1992, Tarlton Law Library, the University of Texas School of Law, Austin, Texas. Ed. by David L. Gunn. LC 93-11349. ix, 202p. 1993. 37.50 (*0-8377-0650-5*, Rothman) W S Hein.

Lawyer & the Libertine. Ian Callinan. 1997. pap. 19.95 (*1-875998-36-5*, Pub. by Central Queensland) Accents Pubns.

***Lawyer as Supervisor, Manager & Motivator.** Mary B. Sheffer & Sophie M. Sparrow. 176p. 2000. pap. 38.00 (*1-55733-021-2*) NALP.

Lawyer (Attorney) Jokes. Linda B. Williams. (Illus.). 72p. 1994. pap. write for info. (*0-9642313-0-1*) Matrix Desgn.

Lawyer Cookbook: Ordering in the Court. Michael L. Ellis, 3rd. (Illus.). (Orig.). 1993. pap. text 3.50 (*0-929178-23-8*) Valley Forge Pub.

Lawyer in History, Literature & Humour. Ed. by William Andrews. 276p. 1982. reprint ed. 35.00 (*0-8377-0211-9*, Rothman) W S Hein.

Lawyer in Literature. John M. Gest. LC 82-81089. xii, 249p. 1982. reprint ed. 59.00 (*0-912004-21-5*) Gaunt.

Lawyer in Literature, 1913. John M. Gest. LC 99-18365. 1999. 60.00 (*1-886363-90-0*) Lawbk Exchange.

Lawyer in the School-Room: Comprising the Laws of All the States on Important Educational Subjects. M. M. Walsh. LC 94-19789. 161p. 1994. reprint ed. 38.00 (*0-8377-2775-8*, Rothman) W S Hein.

Lawyer in the Wilderness. K. H. Digby. LC 81-109957. (Southeast Asia Program, Department of Asian Studies, Cornell University - Data Paper: No. 114). (Illus.). 123p. reprint ed. pap. 38.20 (*0-8357-3116-2*, 203937400012) Bks Demand.

Lawyer Lincoln. Albert A. Woldman. (Illus.). 347p. 1994. pap. 12.95 (*0-7867-0156-0*) Carroll & Graf.

Lawyer Looks at the Constitution. Rex E. Lee. LC 81-1571. (Illus.). xii, 229p. 1981. pap. 12.95 (*0-8425-1904-1*, Friends of the Library) Brigham.

Lawyer Looks at the Gospels. Norman Griffith. LC 97-62532. 800p. 2000. 30.00 (*1-57921-089-9*) WinePress Pub.

Lawyer Manley Vol. 1: First Time Up. Jackie Ranston. 1998. 40.00 (*976-640-049-0*, Pub. by UWI Fac Law); pap. 25.00 (*976-640-050-4*, Pub. by UWI Fac Law) Gaunt.

Lawyer Mobile. Hillman. LC 94-75309. 1994. lib. bdg. 145.00 (*0-316-36431-2*, Aspen Law & Bus) Aspen Pub.

Lawyer Professionalism. Jack L. Sammons. LC 87-73172. 104p. 1988. pap. text 10.75 (*0-89089-324-1*) Carolina Acad Pr.

Lawyer Specialization Bibliography. LC 90-83344. 62p. 1990. pap. 20.00 (*0-89707-592-7*, 481-0010) Amer Bar Assn.

Lawyer Statistical Report. Barbara A. Curran et al. LC 85-72656. 1985. 98.00 (*0-910059-07-1*, 306010); pap., suppl. ed. 30.00 (*0-910059-09-8*, 306010) W S Hein.

Lawyer Statistical Report: The U. S. Legal Profession in the 1990s. Barbara A. Curran & Clara N. Carson. LC 85-72656. 247p. (Orig.). 1994. pap. 30.00 (*0-910059-13-6*) Am Bar Foun.

Lawyer, the Public & Professional Responsibility. Raymond F. Marks et al. LC 70-187314. (American Bar Foundation Publication Ser.). vi, 305p. 1996. pap. 25.00 (*1-57588-321-X*, 304880) W S Hein.

Lawyer Who Blew up His Desk: And Other Tales of Legal Madness. Joseph L. Matthews. LC 97-47373. 242p. 1998. pap. 11.95 (*0-89815-974-1*) Ten Speed Pr.

Lawyer Who Doubled His Bets. Richard E. Dillon. LC 98-90582. 1999. pap. 11.95 (*0-533-12858-7*) Vantage.

Lawyer Within Us All. Albert R. Steward. LC 96-61317. 160p. 1997. 19.95 (*1-881180-03-4*) Trebla Pr.

Lawyering: A Realistic Approach to Legal Practice. James C. Freund. 370p. 1979. boxed set 49.50 (*0-318-21437-7*, 00552); boxed set 70.00 (*0-317-05492-9*, 00552) NY Law Pub.

Lawyering for the Railroad: Business, Law & Power in the New South. William G. Thomas. LC 99-28125. (Illus.). 344p. 1999. pap. text 24.95 (*0-8071-2504-0*) La State U Pr.

Lawyering for the Railroad: Business, Law & Power in the New South. William G. Thomas. LC 99-28125. (Illus.). 344p. 1999. text 47.50 (*0-8071-2367-6*) La State U Pr.

***Lawyering in the International Market.** Ed. by Dennis Campbell & Brian Birkeland. LC 99-42141. (International Business Law Practice Ser.). 450p. 2000. text 125.00 (*1-57105-104-X*) Transnatl Pubs.

Lawyering, Practice & Planning, Teacher's Manual For. Roger S. Haydock et al. (American Casebook Ser.). 142p. (C). 1996. pap. text. write for info. (*0-314-09439-3*) West Pub.

Lawyering Process. Gay Bellow & Moulton. 1978. text 38.00 (*0-88277-448-4*) Foundation Pr.

Lawyering Process: Ethics & Professional Responsibility. Gary Bellow & Bea Moulton. LC 81-67777. (University Casebook Ser.). 460p. 1991. reprint ed. pap. text 18.50 (*0-88277-038-1*) Foundation Pr.

Lawyering Process: Negotiation. Gary Bellow & Bea Moulton. LC 81-67776. (University Casebook Ser.). 297p. (C). 1988. reprint ed. pap. text 15.25 (*0-88277-039-X*) Foundation Pr.

Lawyering Process: Preparing & Presenting the Case. Gary Bellow & Bea Moulton. LC 81-67655. (University Casebook Ser.). 516p. (C). 1981. pap. text 18.95 (*0-88277-040-3*) Foundation Pr.

Lawyering Skills: Depositions & Trials. Peter B. Knapp & Ann Juergens. Ed. by Roger S. Haydock. (American Caseobok Ser.). 120p. 1995. VHS 315.00 (*0-314-08912-8*) West Pub.

Lawyering Skills: Interviewing, Counseling & Negotiation. Peter B. Knapp et al. LC 96-135443. (American Casebook Ser.). 115p. 1995. VHS 315.00 (*0-314-08913-6*) West Pub.

Lawyering Skills: Mediation & Arbitration. Peter B. Knapp et al. LC 98-106318. 120p. 1995. VHS 315.00 (*0-314-08914-4*) West Pub.

Lawyering Through Life: The Origin of Preventive Law. Louis M. Brown. LC 86-10078. xviii, 298p. 1986. reprint ed. 40.00 (*0-8377-0348-4*, Rothman) W S Hein.

Lawyerland. Lawrence Joseph. LC 98-2647. 272p. 1998. pap. 12.95 (*0-452-27993-3*, Plume) Dutton Plume.

Lawyerland: An Unguarded, Street-Level Look at Law & Lawyers Today. Lawrence Joseph. LC 97-905. 192p. 1997. text 22.00 (*0-374-18417-8*) FS&G.

Lawyers. Richard Abel. LC 98-150214. 1997. pap. 24.95 (*1-56584-392-4*, Pub. by New Press NY) Norton.

***Lawyers.** Andrews & McMeel Publishing Staff. 1999. pap. text 5.95 (*0-7407-0407-9*) Andrews & McMeel.

***Lawyers.** Daily. 2000. pap. 9.99 (*0-7407-0809-0*) Andrews & McMeel.

Lawyers: A Client's Manual. Joseph C. McGinn. 1977. 11.95 (*0-13-526814-1*); pap. 5.95 (*0-13-526806-0*) P-H.

Lawyers: A Client's Manual. 3rd ed. Joseph C. McGinn. 1977. audio 215.00 (*0-13-530444-X*) P-H.

Lawyers: A Critical Reader. Ed. by Richard L. Abel. 311p. 1997. 45.00 (*1-56584-324-X*, Pub. by New Press NY) Norton.

***Lawyers: Jokes, Quotes, & Anecdotes.** Andrews & McMeel Publishing Staff. 1999. pap. 5.95 (*0-8362-1543-5*) Andrews & McMeel.

Lawyers: On the Spot. Donna Leigh-Kile. (Illus.). 180p. 1999. pap. 15.95 (*1-883319-80-3*) Frog Ltd CA.

Lawyers Against Labor: From Individual Rights to Corporate Liberalism. Daniel R. Ernst. LC 94-45058. (Illus.). 360p. 1995. text 49.95 (*0-252-02168-1*) U of Ill Pr.

Lawyers Against Labor: From Individual Rights to Corporate Liberalism. Daniel R. Ernst. (Working Class in American History Ser.). (Illus.). 336p. (C). 1995. 18.95 (*0-252-06512-3*) U of Ill Pr.

Lawyer's Alcove: Poems by the Lawyer, for the Lawyer & about the Lawyer. Ed. by Ina R. Warren. LC 89-85975. xii, 317p. 1990. reprint ed. lib. bdg. 65.00 (*0-89941-706-X*, 306070) W S Hein.

Lawyer's Almanac, 1984. Ed. by Law & Business Inc. Staff. 1984. 45.00 (*0-317-12324-6*) Harcourt.

Lawyer's Almanac, 1985: An Encyclopedia of Information about Law, Lawyers, & the Profession. Ed. by Law & Business Inc. Staff. 1018p. 1985. 60.00 (*0-317-29466-0*, #H4383X) Harcourt.

Lawyer's Almanac, 1995. Prentice-Hall Staff. 1300p. 1995. 116.00 (*0-13-126597-0*) Aspen Law.

Lawyers' & Accountants' Guide to Purchase & Sale of a Small Business. Willard D. Horwich. 1989. text 130.00 (*0-685-69597-2*, LAGP) Warren Gorham & Lamont.

Lawyers & Balanced Lives: A Guide to Drafting & Implementing Workplace Policies for Lawyers. LC 90-83772. 90p. 1990. ring bd. 44.95 (*0-89707-584-6*, 492-0001) Amer Bar Assn.

Lawyers & Certified Public Accountants: A Study of Interprofessional Relations. 3rd ed. 19p. 1982. pap. write for info. (*0-318-66159-4*, 447-0001-01) Amer Bar Assn.

Lawyers & Citizens: The Making of a Political Elite in Old Regime France. David A. Bell. (Illus.). 304p. 1994. text 60.00 (*0-19-507670-2*) OUP.

Lawyers & Fundamental Moral Responsibility. Daniel R. Coquillette. LC 94-45186. 344p. (C). 1995. 48.95 (*0-87084-401-6*) Anderson Pub Co.

Lawyers & Judges & Clients at Work & Play: The Truth & Nothing but the Truth. Ron Flanigan. 64p. (Orig.). 1995. pap. 4.95 (*1-886837-00-7*) Blu Wtr Pr.

Lawyers & Law Courts. Honore Daumier. (Illus.). 1967. 12.50 (*0-87505-152-9*) Borden.

Lawyers & Lawmakers of Kentucky. Ed. by H. Levin. (Illus.). 777p. 1982. reprint ed. 40.00 (*0-89308-319-4*) Southern Hist Pr.

Lawyers & Lawsuits a Guide to Litigation: What You Must Know If You Are Being Sued or Are Suing Somebody. Robert A. Izard. 1997. 14.95 (*0-02-861616-2*) Macmillan.

Lawyers & Litigants in Ancient Athens: The Genesis of the Legal Profession. Robert J. Bonner. LC 68-57185. 288p. 1972. reprint ed. 28.95 (*0-405-19013-1*, Pub. by Blom Pubns) Ayer.

Lawyers & Litigants in Ancient Athens: The Genesis of the Legal Profession. Robert J. Bonner. LC 94-75664. xii, 276p. 1994. reprint ed. 75.00 (*1-56169-091-0*, 18183) Gaunt.

Lawyers & Matrimonial Cases: Study of Informal Pressures in Private Professional Practice. Hubert J. O'Gorman. Ed. by Harriet Zuckerman & Robert K. Merton. LC 79-3754. (Dissertations on Sociology Ser.). 1980. lib. bdg. 23.95 (*0-405-12986-6*) Ayer.

Lawyers & Other Reptiles. Jess M. Brallier. (...And Other Reptiles Ser.). 128p. 1992. 12.00 (*0-8092-3919-1*, 391910, Contemporary Bks) NTC Contemp Pub Co.

Lawyers & Politics in the Arab World, 1880-1960. Donald M. Reid. LC 80-71053. (Studies in Middle Eastern History: No. 5). 435p. (C). 1981. 40.00 (*0-88297-028-3*) Bibliotheca.

Lawyers & the Constitution: How Laissez Faire Came to the Supreme Court. Benjamin Twiss. LC 73-10765. 271p. 1974. reprint ed. lib. bdg. 65.00 (*0-8371-7033-8*, TWLC, Greenwood Pr) Greenwood.

Lawyers & the Legal Profession: Cases & Materials, 1994. Schwartz & Simon. 846p. 1994. text 48.00 (*1-55834-208-7*, 13054-11, MICHIE) LEXIS Pub.

Lawyers & the Legal Profession: 1991 Cumulative Supplement. Victor Schwartz. 240p. 1991. pap. text. write for info. (*0-87473-310-3*, 13056-10, MICHIE) LEXIS Pub.

Lawyers & the Legal Profession, 1998 Supplement. 3rd ed. Roy D. Simon, Jr. & Murray L. Schwartz. (Michie Contemporary Legal Education Ser.: No. 98 Cum Su). 250p. (C). 1998. pap., suppl. ed. 15.00 (*0-327-00328-6*, 1305611) LEXIS Pub.

Lawyers & the Making of English Land Law, 1832-1940. J. Stuart Anderson. (Illus.). 376p. 1992. text 79.00 (*0-19-825670-1*) OUP.

***Lawyers & the Media.** Robert L. Rothman. LC 99-53908. 1999. write for info. (*1-57073-763-0*) Amer Bar Assn.

Lawyers & the Promotion of Justice. Esther L. Brown. (Russell Sage Foundation Reprint Ser.). reprint ed. lib. bdg. 39.00 (*0-697-00201-2*) Irvington.

Lawyers & the Rise of Western Political Liberalism: Europe & North America from the Eighteenth to Twentieth Centuries. Ed. by Terence C. Halliday & Lucien Karpik. LC 97-17461. 388p. (Oxford Socio-Legal Studies). 388p. 1998. text 39.95 (*0-19-826288-4*) OUP.

Lawyers & Their Society: A Comparative Study of the Legal Profession in Germany & the United States. Dietrich Rueschemeyer. LC 72-93953. 268p. reprint ed. pap. 83.10 (*0-7837-2327-X*, 205741500004) Bks Demand.

Lawyers As Counsellors: A Client-Centred Approach. David A. Binder et al. (American Casebook Ser.). 427p. (C). 1990. pap. 28.00 (*0-314-77002-X*) West Pub.

Lawyer's Basic Corporate Practice Manual. 3rd ed. Richard E. Deer. LC 84-72759. 320p. 1984. ring bd., suppl. ed. 19.00 (*0-8318-0468-8*, B468/B580) Am Law Inst.

Lawyer's Basic Corporate Practice Manual Supplement. Richard E. Deer. 37p. 1988. pap. text 5.43 (*0-8318-0580-3*, B580) Am Law Inst.

Lawyers Before the Warren Court: Civil Liberties & Civil Rights, 1957-1966. Jonathan D. Casper. LC 74-186342. 231p. reprint ed. pap. 71.70 (*0-608-30523-5*, 201502900092) Bks Demand.

Lawyers Before the Warren Court: Civil Liberties & Civil Rights, 1957-66. Jonathan D. Casper. LC 74-186342. 232p. 1972. text 24.95 (*0-252-00244-X*) U of Ill Pr.

Lawyer's Big Book of Fun. Arnold B. Kanter et al. LC 95-37170. (Illus.). 80p. 1995. pap. 9.95 (*0-8092-3410-6*, 341060, Contemporary Bks) NTC Contemp Pub Co.

Lawyers' Book of Days. Morris L. Cohen. (Illus.). 128p. 1991. 10.95 (*0-88363-291-8*) H L Levin.

***Lawyers' Book of Ethics.** 2000. pap. 4.95 (*0-7407-0887-2*) Andrews & McMeel.

Lawyer's Book of Rules for Effective Legal Writing. Thomas R. Haggard. LC 96-40965. v, 26p. 1997. pap. 6.50 (*0-8377-0686-6*, Rothman) W S Hein.

Lawyer's Calling: Christian Faith & Legal Practice. Joseph G. Allegretti. 192p. 1996. pap. 12.95 (*0-8091-3651-1*, 3651-1) Paulist Pr.

Lawyer's Career Change Handbook: More Than 300 Things You Can Do with a Law Degree. Hindi Greenberg. LC 98-28856. 320p. 1998. pap. 14.00 (*0-380-79572-8*, Avon Bks) Morrow Avon.

Lawyer's Chambers & Other Stories. Lowell B. Komie. 198p. 1994. pap. 12.95 (*0-9641957-0-4*) Swordfish-Chicago.

Lawyers, Clients & Moral Responsibility. Thomas L. Shaffer & Robert F. Cochran. (Miscellaneous Ser.). 138p. (C). 1994. pap. 14.50 (*0-314-03933-3*) West Pub.

Lawyers, Clients & Moral Responsibility: Teacher's Manual to Accompany. Thomas L. Shaffer & Robert F. Cochran, Jr. (American Casebook Ser.). 79p. 1994. pap. text. write for info. (*0-314-04423-X*) West Pub.

***Lawyer's Code of Ethics: A Satire, 1887.** fac. ed. Valmear. LC 99-47484. 2000. write for info. (*1-58477-047-3*) Lawbk Exchange.

Lawyer's Complete Guide to the Perfect Will. Gilbert M. Cantor. 1984. pap. 47.50 (*0-916621-00-6*) Cato Pr.

Lawyers, Courts, & Professionalism: The Agenda for Reform, 50. Rudolph J. Gerber. LC 88-7703. (Contributions in Legal Studies). 170p. 1989. 55.00 (*0-313-26567-4*, GLY, Greenwood Pr) Greenwood.

Lawyers Culture. Pue & Sugarman. 70.95 (*1-84014-766-0*) Ashgate Pub Co.

Lawyer's Desk Book. 8th ed. IBP Research & Editorial Staff. LC 84-19327. 672p. 1984. text 64.50 (*0-87624-325-1*, Inst Busn Plan) P-H.

***Lawyer's Desk Book.** 11th ed. Dana Schilling. LC 99-55711. 800p. (C). 1999. text 96.00 (*0-13-011077-9*) P-H.

Lawyer's Desk Book: 1999 Cumulative Supplement. 10th ed. Prentice-Hall Staff. 288p. (C). 1998. pap. text 39.95 (*0-13-918350-7*) P-H.

Lawyer's Desk Book, 1990-1991 Cumulative Supplement. PH Editorial Staff. 168p. 1990. pap. 40.00 (*0-13-524208-8*) P-H.

Lawyers Desk Guide to Legal Malpractice. 238p. 1992. pap. 85.00 (*0-89707-776-8*, 414-0025) Amer Bar Assn.

Lawyers Desk Reference, 3 vols. 8th ed. Harry M. Philo. (Tort Personal Injury Law Ser.). 1993. 345.00 (*0-685-68852-6*) West Group.

Lawyers Desk Reference, 3 vols., Set. 8th ed. Harry M. Philo. LC 65-12985. 1993. 365.00 (*0-685-59885-3*) West Group.

Lawyers Direct Mail Advertising Handbook. Tom L. Lee. 1989. write for info. (*0-934547-06-8*) CRI-Comm Res.

Lawyers' Ethics. Ed. by Allan Gerson. LC 78-62895. 315p. 1979. 39.95 (*0-87855-293-6*) Transaction Pubs.

Lawyers for Children. 37p. 1990. pap. 16.00 (*0-89707-562-5*, 549-0213) Amer Bar Assn.

Lawyers for Hire: Salaried Professionals at Work. Eve Spangler. LC 85-14339. 251p. reprint ed. pap. 77.90 (*0-7837-6221-6*, 208031200005) Bks Demand.

Lawyer's Guide. Dennis Campbell. 1991. lib. bdg. 153.50 (*90-6544-602-8*) Kluwer Academic.

***Lawyer's Guide to Balancing Life & Work: Taking the Stress Out of Success.** George W. Kaufman. LC 99-72625. ix, 235 p. 1999. 49.95 (*1-57073-700-2*) Amer Bar Assn.

Lawyer's Guide to Cheating, Stealing & Amassing Obscene Wealth. Elliott Egan. (Illus.). 96p. 1992. pap. 7.95 (*0-312-07861-7*) St Martin.

Lawyer's Guide to Doing Business in South Africa. LC 96-200704. 190p. 1996. pap. 40.00 (*1-57073-364-3*, 521-0111, ABA Intl Law) Amer Bar Assn.

Lawyer's Guide to Effective Negotiation & Mediation: CLE Edition. Paul M. Lisnek. 225p. 1992. pap. text. write for info. (*0-314-01679-1*) West Pub.

Lawyers Guide to Estate Planning. LC 95-77231. 288p. 1995. pap. 89.95 (*1-57073-207-8*, 515-0242, ABA Genl Prac) Amer Bar Assn.

Lawyer's Guide to Estate Planning. 2nd ed. L. Rush Hunt. LC 98-30807. xv, 194 p. 1998. 99.95 (*1-57073-615-4*) Amer Bar Assn.

Lawyer's Guide to Financial Planning: Fundamentals for the Legal Practitioner. L. Rush Hunt. LC 97-18484. 1997. pap. write for info. (*1-57073-446-1*) Amer Bar Assn.

Lawyers Guide to Insurance. Ben G. Baldwin & American Bar Association Staff. LC 99-25996. 1999. write for info. (*1-57073-671-5*) Amer Bar Assn.

***Lawyer's Guide to Internet Legal Research.** Kathy Biehl & Tara Calishain. LC 00-41336. 2000. pap. write for info. (*0-8108-3885-0*) Scarecrow.

Lawyer's Guide to Marketing on the Internet. LC 96-85483. 223p. 1996. pap. 64.95 (*1-57073-351-1*, 511-0371) Amer Bar Assn.

Lawyers' Guide to Medical Proof, 7 vols. Marshall Houts. 1967. ring bd. 1010.00 (*0-8205-1353-9*) Bender.

***Lawyers Guide to Mentoring.** Ida O. Abbott. 2000. pap. 38.00 (*1-55733-020-4*) NALP.

Lawyer's Guide to Military Retirement & Benefits in Divorce. Marshal Willick. LC 98-19147. xxii, 370p. 1998. write for info. (*1-57073-572-7*) Amer Bar Assn.

Lawyer's Guide to Public Relations: The Art of Promoting Your Practice. Kimera K. Maxwell & Roger W. Reinsch. LC 89-161995. x, 221 p. 1989. write for info. (*0-941161-64-1*) PES Inc WI.

Lawyer's Guide to Retirement. 3rd ed. David A. Bridewell & Charles Nauts. LC 98-30656. 1998. 74.95 (*1-57073-612-X*) Amer Bar Assn.

Lawyer's Guide to Retirement: Strategies for Attorneys & Their Firms. 2nd ed. LC 93-74995. 336p. 1994. pap. 74.95 (*0-89707-958-2*, 546-0023) Amer Bar Assn.

Lawyer's Guide to the Internet. Frwd. by Roberta C. Ramo. LC 95-75479. 368p. 1995. pap. 29.95 (*1-57073-149-7*) ABA Prof Educ Pubns.

Lawyer's Guide to the Texas Deceptive Trade Practices Act. Richard M. Alderman. 370p. Date not set. ring bd. 120.00 (*0-409-25430-4*, 82587, MICHIE) LEXIS Pub.

Lawyer's Guide to the Texas Deceptive Trade Practices Act, Issue 16. Richard M. Alderman. 201p. 1998. ring bd. write for info. (*0-327-00689-7*, 8258918) LEXIS Pub.

Lawyer's Guide to the Texas Insurance Code, Article 21.21. Christopher Martin. LC 95-44175. Date not set. text 95.00 (*0-250-47249-X*, 64625, MICHIE) LEXIS Pub.

Lawyer's Guide to Writing Well. Tom Goldstein & Jethro K. Lieberman. LC 89-9447. 274p. 1991. pap. 17.95 (*0-520-07321-5*, Pub. by U CA Pr) Cal Prin Full Svc.

Lawyers, Guns & Money. Rebecca Daniels. (Intimate Moments Ser.). 1994. per. 3.50 (*0-373-07563-4*, 5-07563-5) Silhouette.

***Lawyers, Guns & Money: Secrets of the New Inquisition.** Greg Stolze et al. Ed. by John Tynes. (Unknown Armies Ser.). (Illus.). 128p. 1999. pap. 19.95 (*1-887801-78-2*, Atlas Games) Trident MN.

Lawyers, Guns & Money: The Impact of Tort Restriction on Firearms Safety & Gun Control. Kristen Rand. 76p. (Orig.). Date not set. pap. 10.00 (*0-927291-06-1*) Violence Policy Ctr.

Lawyer's Handbook. 3rd ed. LC 92-73390. 675p. 1992. 95.00 (*0-685-65987-9*, 75-003) U MI Law CLE.

Lawyers' Ideals - Lawyers' Practices: Transformations in the American Legal System. Ed. by Robert L. Nelson & David M. Trubek. LC 91-55533. 320p. 1992. text 47.50 (*0-8014-2461-5*); pap. text 18.95 (*0-8014-9710-8*) Cornell U Pr.

Lawyers in a Postmodern World: Translation & Transgression. Ed. by Maureen Cain & Christine B. Harrington. LC 93-35979. (C). 1994. text 50.00 (*0-8147-1504-4*) NYU Pr.

Lawyers in a Postmodern World: Translation & Transgression. Ed. by Maureen Cain & Christine B. Harrington. LC 93-35979. (C). 1994. pap. text 18.50 (*0-8147-1503-6*) NYU Pr.

Lawyers in a Postmodern World: Translation & Transgression. Maureen Cain & Christine B. Harrington. Ed. by Colin Sumner. (New Directions in Criminology Ser.). 336p. 1994. pap. 2.00 (*0-335-09694-8*) OpUniv Pr.

Lawyers in Canada. David A. Stager & Harry W. Arthurs. 352p. 1990. text 60.00 (*0-8020-5874-4*); pap. text 25.00 (*0-8020-6795-6*) U of Toronto Pr.

Lawyers in Early Modern Europe & America. Ed. by Wilfrid Prest. LC 80-22574. 224p. 1981. 39.95 (*0-8419-0679-3*) Holmes & Meier.

Lawyers in God's World: The Love Command as Modern Law. John Porter et al. (Jubilee Ser.: No. 2). 24p. (C). pap. text 1.00 (*0-685-50070-5*) Shiloh Pubns.

Lawyers in Politics: A Study in Professional Convergence. Heinz Eulau & John D. Sprague. LC 84-577. 164p. 1984. reprint ed. lib. bdg. 38.50 (*0-313-24422-7*, EULP, Greenwood Pr) Greenwood.

L

L

Lawyers in Politics: Mid-Nineteenth Century Kentucky As a Case Study. James W. Gordon. LC 90-36931. (Distinguished Studies in American Legal & Constitutional History). 400p. 1990. reprint ed. text 10.00 (*0-8240-0023-4*) Garland.

Lawyers in Society: An Overview. Ed. by Richard L. Abel & Philip S. Lewis. LC 95-36935. 375p. 1995. pap. 19.95 (*0-520-20332-1*, Pub. by U CA Pr) Cal Prin Full Svc.

Lawyers in the Alice: Aboriginals & Whitefella's Law. Jon Faine. 196p. 1993. pap. 34.00 (*1-86287-115-9*, Pub. by Federation Pr) Gaunt.

Lawyers in the Making, 7. Seymour Warkov. LC 79-26229. (National Opinion Research Center Monographs in Social Research Ser.: No. 7). (Illus.). 180p. 1980. reprint ed. lib. bdg. 59.50 (*0-313-22215-0*, WALM, Greenwood Pr) Greenwood.

Lawyers, Judges & Legal Ethics see Jewish Law & Jewish Life

***Lawyer's Law: Procedural, Malpractice & Disciplinary Issues, 1999.** annuals 4th ed. L. Ray Patterson & Pope Brock. 1999. text 42.00 (*0-8205-4055-2*) Bender.

Lawyers' Law Books. 3rd rev. ed. Donald Raistrick. LC 96-47981. 600p. 1996. 125.00 (*1-85739-087-3*) Bowker-Saur.

Lawyers, Law Schools & the Public Service. Esther L. Brown. (Russell Sage Foundation Reprint Ser.). reprint ed. lib. bdg. 37.00 (*0-697-00200-4*) Irvington.

Lawyer's Lawyer: The Life of John W. Davis. William H. Harbaugh. (Illus.). 648p. 1990. reprint ed. pap. text 22.50 (*0-8139-1267-9*) U Pr of Va.

Lawyers! Lawyers! Lawyers! The Country's Funniest Cartoonists Take on the Legal Profession. Ed. by S. Gross. (Illus.). 112p. 1994. 8.95 (*0-8092-3722-9*) NTC Contemp Pub Co.

Lawyers, Legal Education & Development: An Examination of the Process of Reform in Chile. Steven Lowenstein. x, 310p. 1970. pap. 25.00 (*0-8377-0803-6*, Rothman) W S Hein.

Lawyers Legal Search. George N. Foster. LC 85-60263. (Legal Bibliographic & Research Reprint Ser.: Vol. 6). v, 104p. 1985. reprint ed. lib. bdg. 37.00 (*0-89941-399-4*, 303660) W S Hein.

Lawyers, Legislators & Theorists: Developments in English Criminal Jurisprudence, 1800-1957. Keith Smith. LC 98-24188. (Oxford Monographs on Criminal Law & Justice). 424p. 1998. text 85.00 (*0-19-825723-6*) OUP.

Lawyer's Life: Deep in the Heart of Taxes. Edwin S. Cohen. LC 95-108708. 718p. 1994. pap. 34.95 (*0-918255-24-4*) Tax Analysts.

Lawyers, Litigation & English Society, 1450-1900. Christopher W. Brooks. LC 97-45673. 250p. 1997. 55.00 (*1-85285-156-2*) Hambledon Press.

Lawyer's London. Spellmount Ltd. Publishers Staff. (C). 1986. 120.00 (*0-946771-95-2*, Pub. by Spellmnt Pubs) St Mut.

Lawyer's Management Principles: A Course for Assistants, Student Syllabus. Harold W. Adams & Ray Stringham. 1975. pap. text 9.95 (*0-89420-079-8*, 101028) Natl Book.

Lawyer's Management Principles: A Course for Assistants, Student Syllabus. Harold W. Adams & Ray Stringham. (gr. 11-12). 1975. audio 86.90 (*0-89420-200-6*, 101000) Natl Book.

Lawyers Medical Cyclopedia, 11 vols., Vol. 4B. Ed. by Richard Patterson. LC 88-61859. 780p. 1999. write for info. (*0-327-01051-7*, 6204511) LEXIS Pub.

Lawyers Medical Cyclopedia: 1992 Cumulative Supplement & 1991 Index, 10 vols., Set. 3rd ed. Charles J. Frankel & James G. Zimmerly. 1977. 550.00 (*0-87473-005-8*, 62030-10, MICHIE) LEXIS Pub.

Lawyers' Medical Cyclopedia, 1999 Cumulative Supplements. Ed. by Richard Patterson. 744p. 1999. pap. write for info. (*0-327-01324-9*, 6206616) LEXIS Pub.

Lawyer's Medical Cyclopedia of Personal Injuries & Allied Specialties. 4th ed. Ed. by Richard Patterson. LC 96-75647. 630p. 1998. text. write for info. (*0-327-00284-0*, 62044-11) LEXIS Pub.

Lawyer's Medical Cyclopedia of Personal Injuries & Allied Specialties: Winter 1998 General Index. Ed. by Richard Patterson. 446p. 1998. write for info. (*0-327-00296-4*, 62065-18) LEXIS Pub.

***Lawyer's Medical Cyclopedia, Summer 1999 General Index.** Ed. by Richard Patterson. 460p. 1999. write for info. (*0-327-01381-8*, 6206519) LEXIS Pub.

***Lawyers Medical Encyclopedia, Vol. 6A.** 4th ed. Ed. by Richard Patterson. 715p. 1999. write for info. (*0-327-04962-6*, 6205311) LEXIS Pub.

Lawyers' Medical Encyclopedia of Personal Injuries & Allied Specialties, Vols. 3, 4 & 5. 4th ed. Richard Patterson. LC RA1022.U6L38 1996. 1996. 0.00 (*1-55834-638-4*) LEXIS Pub.

Lawyers, Money, & Success: The Consequences of Dollar Obsession. Macklin Fleming. LC 96-54286. 168p. 1997. 55.00 (*1-56720-134-2*, Quorum Bks) Greenwood.

Lawyers Monthly Catalog: Formerly National Legal Bibliography, Set. annuals Peter D. Ward. 1990. pap. 225.00 (*0-89941-698-5*, 304040) W S Hein.

Lawyer's Monthly Catalog Annual, 26 bks., Set. Peter D. Ward & Margaret A. Goldblatt. Orig. Title: National Legal Bibliography Annual. 1986. 1800.00 (*0-89941-476-1*, 355870) W S Hein.

***Lawyers of Dickens & Their Clerks.** Robert D. Neely. LC 00-21520. 2000. write for info. (*1-58477-091-0*) Lawbk Exchange.

Lawyers on Line: Ethical Perspectives in the Use of Telecomputer Communication. LC 85-73715. 143p. 1986. pap. 15.95 (*0-89707-212-X*, 561-0070) Amer Bar Assn.

Lawyers on Psychology & Psychologists on Law. P. J. Van Koppen & D. J. Hessing. viii, 189p. 1989. 27.50 (*90-265-0977-4*) Swets.

Lawyer's Pocketbook 1993. Butterworth Staff. 1993. pap. 45.00 (*0-409-03471-1*, SA, MICHIE) LEXIS Pub.

***Lawyer's Practice & Ideals: A Comparative View.** John J. Barcelbo & Roger C. Cramton. LC 99-33764. 1999. 125.00 (*90-411-9392-8*) Kluwer Law Intl.

Lawyers' Professional Liability. Grant Staff & Rothstein. 168p. 1989. 67.00 (*0-409-80532-7*, MICHIE) LEXIS Pub.

Lawyers' Professional Liability. J. R. Midgley. 208p. 1992. pap. write for info. (*0-7021-2675-6*, Pub. by Juta & Co) Gaunt.

***Lawyers' Professional Negligence & Liability.** John M. Virgo & Brian Watson. 400p. 2000. write for info. (*1-902558-21-9*, Pub. by Palladian Law) Gaunt.

Lawyers' Professional Responsibility in Australia & New Zealand. Gino D. Pont. LC 97-179426. 524p. 1996. pap. 85.00 (*0-455-21441-7*, Pub. by LawBk Co) Gaunt.

Lawyers Publicity Handbook. Tom L. Lee. 145p. 1986. ring bd. 68.00 (*0-934547-02-5*) CRI-Comm Res.

Lawyer's Quest I - Twelve Notions about Lawyers: An Introduction to Discipleship. John D. Robb. (Lawyers' Quest Ser.). 82p. (Orig.). (C). 1986. pap. text 8.00 (*0-944561-09-8*) Chr Legal.

Lawyer's Quick Desk Reference: Pennsylvania Edition. 350p. 1998. student ed., ring bd. 50.00 (*0-933945-10-8*) Legal Coun Elderly.

Lawyer's Quick Guide to E-Mail. Kenneth E. Johnson. LC 98-72942. 1999. pap. 39.95 (*1-57073-594-8*) Amer Bar Assn.

Lawyer's Quick Guide to Microsoft Internet Explorer. G. Burgess Allison. LC 97-74005. 1998. pap. 49.95 (*1-57073-510-7*) Amer Bar Assn.

Lawyer's Quick Guide to Netscape Navigator. G. Burgess Allison. LC 97-71798. 1998. pap. 49.95 (*1-57073-429-1*) Amer Bar Assn.

Lawyer's Quick Guide to Timeslips. Carol L. Schlein. LC 98-72615. 1999. pap. 39.95 (*1-57073-587-5*) Amer Bar Assn.

***Lawyer's Quick Guide to Word 97/2000.** Alan S. Adler & David Greenwald. 1999. pap. 49.95 (*1-57073-733-9*) Amer Bar Assn.

Lawyers Reference Manual of Law Books & Citations. Charles C. Soule. LC 01-7142. x, 497p. 1953. reprint ed. lib. bdg. 58.00 (*0-89941-354-4*, 502160) W S Hein.

Lawyers Register International by Specialties & Fields of Law: Including a Directory of Corporate Counsel. 15th rev. ed. Ed. by Jeannine Dreimiller. 2088p. 1998. 329.00 (*0-936217-50-2*) LR Pub.

Lawyer's Register International by Specialties & Fields of Law: Including a Directory of Corporate Counsel, 3 vols. 16th ed. Ed. by Jeannine Dreimiller. 1978p. 1999. 329.00 (*0-936217-52-9*) LR Pub.

Lawyers Register International by Specialties & Fields of Law Including a Directory of Corporate Counsel. 13th rev. ed. 1996. 229.00 (*0-934607-08-7*) Jury Verdict.

Lawyer's Remembrancer, 1994. 664p. 1994. boxed set 37.00 (*0-406-02689-0*, UK, MICHIE) LEXIS Pub.

Lawyer's Research Companion: A Concise Guide to Sources. Ed. by Gary McCann & Joanne Zich. LC 97-48602. 233p. 1998. pap. 26.95 (*1-57588-442-9*, 310830) W S Hein.

Lawyer's Research Companion: A Concise Guide to Sources. Ed. by Gary McCann & Joanne Zich. LC 97-48602. Bk. 4. xv, 218p. 1998. 39.50 (*1-57588-418-6*, 310830) W S Hein.

Lawyers' Skills: Legal Practice Course Guides. Philip A. Jones. 260p. 1996. pap. 34.00 (*1-85431-421-1*, Pub. by Blackstone Pr) Gaunt.

***Lawyer's Skills: Legal Practice Course Guides, 1999-2000.** 7th ed. Philip A. Jones. 255p. 1999. pap. 38.00 (*1-85431-966-3*, Pub. by Blackstone Pr) Gaunt.

Lawyers' Skills Vol. 1: 1994-95. Philip A. Jones. (Legal Practice Course Guides Ser.). 250p. 1995. pap. 34.00 (*1-85431-371-1*, Pub. by Blackstone Pr) Gaunt.

Lawyers' Skills, 1998-1999. 6th ed. Philip A. Jones et al. 250p. 1998. pap. 40.00 (*1-85431-782-2*, Pub. by Blackstone Pr) Gaunt.

Lawyers' Skills, 1993-1994: Legal Practice Course Guides. Philip A. Jones. 218p. 1993. pap. 34.00 (*1-85431-296-0*, Pub. by Blackstone Pr) Gaunt.

Lawyer's Skills, 1996-1997. 4th ed. Philip A. Jones. (Legal Practice Course Guides Ser.). 250p. 1996. pap. 36.00 (*1-85431-542-0*, Pub. by Blackstone Pr) Gaunt.

Lawyer's Skills 1997-1998. 5th ed. Philip A. Jones. (Legal Practice Course Guides Ser.). 250p. 1997. pap. 38.00 (*1-85431-646-X*, 14621, Pub. by Blackstone Pr) Gaunt.

Lawyers, Social Workers & Families. Stephanie Charlesworth et al. xv, 255p. 1990. pap. 43.00 (*1-86287-030-6*, Pub. by Federation Pr) Gaunt.

Lawyers vs. Educators: Black Colleges & Desegregation in Public Higher Education, 61. Jean L. Preer. LC 81-22567. (Contributions in American Studies: No. 61). 278p. 1982. 55.00 (*0-313-23094-3*, PLE/, Greenwood Pr) Greenwood.

Lawyers Weekly Annual Index Vol. 9: May '89-April '90. 286p. 1990. pap. 60.00 (*0-409-89836-8*, MICHIE) LEXIS Pub.

Lawyers Weekly Bound, Vol. 6. 1987. 124.00 (*0-409-80962-4*, MICHIE) LEXIS Pub.

Lawyers Weekly Bound, Vol. 7. 1988. 143.00 (*0-409-88900-8*, MICHIE) LEXIS Pub.

Lawyers Weekly Bound, Vol. 8. 1989. 188.00 (*0-409-89369-2*, MICHIE) LEXIS Pub.

Lawyers Weekly Bound, Vol. 9. 1208p. 1990. 246.00 (*0-409-89837-6*, MICHIE) LEXIS Pub.

Lawyers Weekly Bound, Vol. 10, 1991. 713p. 1991. pap. 140.00 (*0-409-91132-1*, MICHIE) LEXIS Pub.

Lawyers Will Eat Your Lunch: The Smoking Cockroach Defense. Francis W. Winn. LC 94-79417. (Illus.). 276p. 1994. 24.95 (*1-879234-26-2*) F W Winn.

Lawyer's Wit & Wisdom: Quotations on the Legal Profession, in Brief. Ed. by Bruce Nash & Allan Zullo. LC 94-73880. (Quote Bks.). (Illus.). 224p. 1995. 14.95 (*1-56138-650-2*) Running Pr.

Lawyers' Work: Counseling, Problem Solving, Advocacy & Conduct of Litigation. Jeffrey H. Hartje & Mark E. Wilson. 500p. 1984. pap. 29.50 (*0-88063-001-9*, MICHIE) LEXIS Pub.

Lawyers Work, 1984. Hartje & Wilson. 1995. pap. text 29.50 (*0-409-20422-6*, 81384-10, MICHIE) LEXIS Pub.

***Lawyers You'll Like: Putting Human Rights First.** Michael S. Smith. 140p. 1999. 10.00 (*0-918266-39-4*, Pub. by Intervention Pr) Smyrna.

Lawyers/Accountants Professional & Media/ Communications Liability. Ed. by Diana Kowatch. 60p. 1996. 19.95 (*1-56461-176-0*) Rough Notes.

LAX: Los Angeles International Airport. Freddy Bullock. LC 98-36676. (Airport Ser.). (Illus.). 112p. 1998. pap. 15.95 (*0-7603-0653-2*) MBI Pubg.

Lax: The Los Angeles Experiment: Architecture Design. Mick Mcconnell. 112p. 1994. pap. 25.00 (*0-930829-36-0*) Lumen Inc.

LAX/94: Los Angeles Exhibition Catalogue. Ann Goldstein et al. Ed. by Catherine Gudis & Sherri Schottlaender. (Illus.). 164p. 1994. pap. 22.00 (*1-882299-03-5*) Minic Art Gall.

LAX/92. Gallery at Barnsdall Art Park Directors Staff et al. (Illus.). 126p. (Orig.). pap. 25.00 (*1-882299-01-9*) Minic Art Gall.

Lax '94. (Illus.). 88p. 1995. pap. 22.00 (*0-88229-903-4*) RAM Publications.

Laxatives: A Practical Guide. Francesco Capasso & Timothy S. Gaginella. LC 97-3681. 1997. text. write for info. (*3-540-75037-1*) Spr-Verlag.

Laxdaela Saga. Magnus Magnusson. (Classics Ser.). 272p. (Orig.). 1969. pap. 12.95 (*0-14-044218-9*, Penguin Classics) Viking Penguin.

Laxmi's Vegetarian Kitchen: Simple, Healthful Recipes from India's Great Vegetarian Tradition. Laxmi Hiremath. LC 95-9480. (Illus.). 256p. (Orig.). 1995. pap. 18.95 (*0-9627345-9-4*) Harlow & Ratner.

Laxton's Building Price Book, 1997: Major & Small Works. 169th ed. 1300p. 1997. pap. 194.95 (*0-7506-3272-0*, Pub. by Laxtons) Buttrwrth-Heinemann.

Laxton's General Specification for Major Building & Civil Engineering Projects, 2 vols. Ed. by Schal Property Services Staff. Incl. Vol. 2. Guidance Notes. 1996. pap. Not sold separately 350.00 (*0-7506-3353-0*, Pub. by Laxtons) Buttrwrth-Heinemann.

Laxton's Guide to Budget Estimating. Tweeds. (Laxton's Ser.). 256p. 1997. pap. 95.00 (*0-7506-2967-3*, Pub. by Laxtons) Buttrwrth-Heinemann.

Laxton's Guide to Risk Analysis & Management. Tweeds. (Laxton's Ser.). 250p. 1997. pap. 39.95 (*0-7506-2973-8*, Pub. by Laxtons) Buttrwrth-Heinemann.

Laxton's Guide to Term Maintenance Contracts. Tweeds. (Laxton's Ser.). 192p. 1997. pap. 89.95 (*0-7506-2977-0*, Pub. by Laxtons) Buttrwrth-Heinemann.

Laxton's Measurement Rules for Contractors Quantities. Tweeds. (Laxton's Ser.). 250p. 1997. pap. 95.00 (*0-7506-2976-2*, Pub. by Laxtons) Buttrwrth-Heinemann.

Lay Analysis: Life Inside the Controversy. Robert S. Wallerstein. 520p. 1998. 69.95 (*0-88163-285-6*) Analytic Pr.

Lay Anthony. Joseph Hergesheimer. (Collected Works of Joseph Hergesheimer). 316p. 1998. reprint ed. lib. bdg. 98.00 (*1-58201-653-4*) Classic Bks.

Lay Aside the Weight: Take Control of It Before It Takes Control of You. T. D. Jakes. 184p. 1997. 19.99 (*1-57778-035-3*, Pub. by Albury Pub) Appalach Bk Dist.

Lay Aside the Weight - Workbook & Journal: The Essential Companion to the Bestselling Book. T. D. Jakes. 128p. 1997. wbk. ed. 9.99 (*1-57778-083-3*, Pub. by Albury Pub) Appalach Bk Dist.

Lay Authority & Reformation in the English Church. Robert E. Rodes. LC 82-7038. 319p. 1982. text 34.50 (*0-268-01265-2*) U of Notre Dame Pr.

Lay Bare the Heart: An Autobiography of the Civil Rights Movement. James Farmer. LC 98-21434. 370p. 1998. reprint ed. pap. 14.95 (*0-87565-188-7*) Tex Christian.

Lay Buddhism in Contemporary Japan: Reiyukai Kyodan. Helen Hardacre. LC 83-43075. 294p. reprint ed. pap. 91.20 (*0-7837-1428-9*, 204178300023) Bks Demand.

Lay by Your Needles Ladies, Take the Pen: Writing Women in England, 1500-1700. Ed. by Suzanne Trill et al. LC 97-16333. (An Arnold Publication). 312p. 1997. pap. text 24.95 (*0-340-61450-1*) OUP.

Lay by Your Needles Ladies, Take the Pen: Writing Women in England, 1500-1700. Ed. by Suzanne Trill et al. LC 97-16333. (An Arnold Publication). 312p. (C). 1997. text 60.00 (*0-340-69148-4*) OUP.

***Lay Contemplative: Testimonies, Perspectives, Resources.** Ed. by Virginia Manes & Mary Frohlich. 216p. 2000. pap. text 10.95 (*0-86716-370-4*) St Anthony Mess Pr.

Lay Counseling: Equipping Christians for a Helping Ministry. Siang-Yang Tan. 256p. 1991. pap. 12.99 (*0-310-52931-X*) Zondervan.

Lay Counseling Series, 22 vols., Set. Claude Townsend. Incl. Vol. 1. Counseling Layman. 1985. pap. 3.95 (*0-936709-01-4*); Vol. 2. Counseling & Basic Needs. 1985. pap. 2.95 (*0-936709-02-2*); Vol. 3. How to Know God's Will. 1985. pap. 2.95 (*0-936709-03-0*); Vol. 4. How to Minister to Your Spouse. 1985. pap. 2.95 (*0-936709-04-9*); Vol. 5. How to Be Financially Free. 1985. pap. 2.50 (*0-936709-05-7*); Vol. 6. Brokenness, Discernment & Counseling. 1985. pap. 2.50 (*0-936709-06-5*); Vol. 7. Divine Healing. 1985. pap. 2.95 (*0-936709-07-3*); Vol. 8. Understanding Authority. 1985. pap. 2.50 (*0-936709-08-1*); Vol. 9. Love Transcending in Reaction. 1985. pap. 1.50 (*0-936709-09-X*); Vol. 10. Self-Control & Man's Will. 1985. pap. 1.50 (*0-936709-10-3*); Vol. 11. Basic Principles to Correct Thinking. 1985. pap. 1.50 (*0-936709-11-1*); Vol. 12. Discipline of the Father-Forgiveness. 1985. pap. 1.50 (*0-936709-12-X*); Vol. 13. How to Deal With Anger & Communication. 1985. pap. 1.50 (*0-936709-13-8*); Vol. 14. How to Resist the Devil & Depression. 1985. pap. 1.50 (*0-936709-14-6*); Vol. 15. Conditions for Answered Prayer. 1985. pap. 1.50 (*0-936709-15-4*); Vol. 16. Psychology of Self-Motivation. 1985. pap. 1.50 (*0-936709-16-2*); Vol. 17. Holy Faith. 1985. pap. 1.50 (*0-936709-17-0*); Vol. 18. Child Discipline Made Simple. 1985. pap. 3.95 (*0-936709-18-9*); Vol. 19. Courtship & Marriage. 1985. pap. 1.50 (*0-936709-19-7*); Vol. 20. What Is Salvation of the Soul? 1985. pap. 1.50 (*0-936709-20-0*); Vol. 21. Steps to the Abundant Life. 1985. pap. 1.50 (*0-936709-21-9*); Vol. 22. How to Walk & Talk With God. 1985. pap. 3.95 (*0-936709-22-7*); (Orig.). 1985. Set pap. 50.00 (*0-936709-00-6*) Lay Counsel.

Lay Down My Sword & Shield. James Lee Burke. Date not set. lib. bdg. 24.95 (*0-8488-1779-6*) Amereon Ltd.

Lay Down My Sword & Shield. James Lee Burke. LC 94-33421. 240p. (J). 1995. pap. 10.45 (*0-7868-8039-2*, Pub. by Hyperion) Time Warner.

***Lay Down My Sword & Shield.** James Lee Burke. 389p. 1999. mass mkt. 6.50 (*0-7868-8950-0*, Pub. by Hyperion) Time Warner.

Lay down with Dogs: Hugh Otis Bynum & the Scottsboro First Monday Bombing. Byron Woodfin. LC 96-806. 240p. 1997. 29.95 (*0-8173-0845-8*) U of Ala Pr.

Lay Epistemics & Human Knowledge: Cognitive & Motivational Bases. A. W. Kruglanski. (Perspectives in Social Psychology Ser.). (Illus.). 300p. (C). 1989. 52.50 (*0-306-43078-9*, Plenum Trade) Perseus Pubng.

Lay Folks' Catechism. John Thoresby. Ed. by T. F. Simmons & H. E. Nolloth. (EETS, OS Ser.: No. 118). 1969. reprint ed. 40.00 (*0-527-00116-3*) Periodicals Srv.

Lay Folks' Mass Book. T. F. Simmons. (EETS Original Ser.: Vol. 71). 468p. 1968. reprint ed. 40.00 (*0-19-722071-1*, Pub. by EETS) Boydell & Brewer.

Lay Folks Mass' Book: Four Texts. Ed. by T. F. Simmons. (EETS, OS Ser.: Vol. 71). 1969. reprint ed. 40.00 (*0-8115-3359-X*) Periodicals Srv.

Lay Low & Don't Make the Big. Rich Herschlag & Brian Harris. LC 97-3206. 1997. pap. 9.95 (*0-684-83491-X*, Fireside) S&S Trade Pap.

Lay Man: About Mind see Idiota de Mente

Lay Members of Christ's Faithful People: Christifideles Laici. John Paul, II, pseud. 181p. pap. 5.95 (*0-8198-4459-4*) Pauline Bks.

Lay Minister's Guide to the Book of Common Prayer. rev. ed. Clifford W. Atkinson. LC 88-5147. 96p. 1988. reprint ed. pap. 8.95 (*0-8192-1454-X*) Morehouse Pub.

Lay Ministers, Lay Disciples: Evangelizing Power in the Parish. Frank DeSiano & Susan B. Gerding. LC 99-17006. 224p. 1999. pap. 14.95 (*0-8091-3896-4*) Paulist Pr.

Lay Ministry: A Theological, Spiritual, & Pastoral Handbook. William J. Rademacher. 288p. (C). 1996. pap. 39.95 (*0-85439-378-1*, Pub. by St Paul Pubns) St Mut.

Lay Ministry: Empowering the People of God. Lawrence O. Richards & Gib Martin. 336p. 1988. pap. 17.99 (*0-310-52101-7*, 18218P) Zondervan.

Lay Ministry Revolution: How You Can Join. Eddy Hall & Gary Morsch. LC 95-11012. 128p. 1995. pap. 9.99 (*0-8010-9005-9*) Baker Bks.

Lay Mission Handbook. Ed. by Jeff Bolle. 100p. ring bd. 20.00 (*0-318-21725-2*) Intl Liaison.

Lay My Burden Down: A Folk History of Slavery. Federal Writers' Project Staff. (American Guidebook Ser.). 285p. 1945. reprint ed. 69.00 (*0-403-02212-6*) Somerset Pub.

Lay My Burden Down: A Folk History of Slavery. Federal Writers' Project Staff & Writers Program-WPA Staff. (American Guide Ser.). 1989. reprint ed. lib. bdg. 59.00 (*0-7812-1067-4*, 1067) Rprt Serv.

***Lay My Burden Down: Suicide & the Mental Health Crisis among African Americans.** Alvin F. Poussaint & Amy Alexander. 2000. 25.00 (*0-8070-0960-1*) Beacon Pr.

Lay of Havelok the Dane. 2nd ed. Havelok the Dane. Ed. by Walter W. Skeat & Kenneth Sisam. LC 75-41129. reprint ed. 29.50 (*0-404-14551-5*) AMS Pr.

Lay of Havelok the Dane: Composed in the Reign of Edward I About A. D. 1280. Havelok the Dane. Ed. by Walter W. Skeat. (EETS, ES Ser.: No. 4). 1969. reprint ed. 35.00 (*0-527-00219-4*) Periodicals Srv.

Lay of Marie, 1816. Matilda Betham. LC 93-47134. (Revolution & Romanticism Ser.). 1994. 55.00 (*1-85477-164-7*) Continuum.

Lay of the Land. Brent Olson. (Illus.). 188p. 1998. pap. 11.95 (*0-934904-36-7*, 36-7) J & L Lee.

Lay of the Land: Metaphor As Experience & History in American Life & Letters. Annette Kolodny. LC 74-23950. xiii, 185p. 1984. pap. text 15.95 (*0-8078-4118-8*) U of NC Pr.

Lay of the Land: The Golf Writings of Pat Ward-Thomas. Ed. by Robert MacDonald. (Illus.). 253p. 1990. 28.00 (*0-940889-28-5*) Classics Golf.

Lay of the Last Minstrel. Sir Walter Scott. LC 92-36904. 342p. 1992. reprint ed. 125.00 (*1-85477-112-4*) Continuum.

Lay of the Love. Rainer Maria Rilke. Date not set. reprint ed. pap. write for info. (*0-393-31620-3*) Norton.

An Asterisk (*) at the beginning of an entry indicates that the title is appearing for the first time.

Lay of the Scottish Fiddle: A Tale of Havrede Grace (Verse) James K. Paulding. (Notable American Authors Ser.). 1999. reprint ed. lib. bdg. 125.00 (*0-7812-4739-X*) Rprt Serv.

Lay of Threll: A Fantasy Told in Rhyme. George W. Martin. 130p. (Orig.). 1996. pap. write for info. (*1-57502-162-5*, PO761) Morris Pubng.

Lay on, MacDuff! Charlotte Armstrong. 224p. 1993. mass mkt. 3.99 (*0-8217-4037-7*, Zebra Kensgtn) Kensgtn Pub Corp.

Lay Participation in a Public Local Inquiry. Neil Hutton. 160p. 1986. text 71.95 (*0-566-05192-3*, Pub. by Dartmth Pub) Ashgate Pub Co.

Lay Participation in Criminal Trials: A Case of Croatia. Sanja K. Ivkovich. LC 98-20600. (Illus.). 582p. 1999. 79.95 (*1-57292-130-7*) Austin & Winfield.

Lay Pastor Training Manual. Frank Damazio. 107p. 1997. pap., teacher ed. 21.99 (*1-886849-05-6*); pap., student ed. 14.99 (*1-886849-06-4*) City Bible Pub.

Lay People & Religion in the Early Eighteenth Century. W. M. Jacob. 270p. (C). 1996. text 64.95 (*0-521-57037-9*) Cambridge U Pr.

Lay Preacher. Joseph Dennie. (Notable American Authors Ser.). 1992. reprint ed. lib. bdg. 75.00 (*0-685-49851-4*) Rprt Serv.

Lay Preacher. Joseph Dennie. (BCL1-PS American Literature Ser.). 184p. 1993. reprint ed. lib. bdg. 69.00 (*0-7812-6956-3*) Rprt Serv.

Lay Preacher. Joseph Dennie. LC 43-9749. 196p. 1979. reprint ed. lib. bdg. 50.00 (*0-8201-1204-6*) Schol Facsimiles.

Lay Preaching: State of the Question. Patricia A. Parachini. LC 98-24490. (American Essays in Liturgy Ser.). 68p. 1999. pap. 6.95 (*0-8146-2549-5*) Liturgical Pr.

Lay Presiding: The Art of Leading Prayer. Kathleen Hughes. (American Essays in Liturgy Ser.). 59p. 1988. pap. 4.00 (*0-8146-1933-9*) Liturgical Pr.

Lay Sanctity, Medieval & Modern: A Search for Models. Ed. by Ann W. Astell. LC 99-38114. 256p. 2000. 35.00 (*0-268-01330-6*, Pub. by U of Notre Dame Pr) Chicago Distribution Ctr.

***Lay Sanctity, Medieval & Modern: A Search for Models.** Ed. by Ann W. Astell. LC 99-38114. 264p. 2000. reprint ed. pap. 25.00 (*0-268-01332-2*, Pub. by U of Notre Dame Pr) Chicago Distribution Ctr.

Lay Sermons. James Hogg. Ed. by David Groves. (Collected Works of James Hogg). 220p. 1996. 50.00 (*0-7486-0746-3*, Pub. by Edinburgh U Pr) Col U Pr.

Lay Sermons see Collected Works of Samuel T. Coleridge

Lay Shepherding. Rudolph E. Grantham. 1980. pap. 12.00 (*0-8170-0863-2*) Judson.

Lay Siege to Heaven: A Novel of Saint Catherine of Siena. Louis De Wohl. LC 91-72758. 346p. (YA). (gr. 8 up). 1991. reprint ed. pap. 14.95 (*0-89870-381-6*) Ignatius Pr.

Lay Speakers Grow Spiritually Through Daily Discipline. Anita Fenstermacher. 16p. 1997. pap. 5.95 (*0-88177-198-8*, DR198) Discipleship Res.

Lay Speakers Interpret to Others Our United Methodist Heritage: Advanced Course for the 1997-2000 Quadrennium. Chester E. Custer. 16p. 1997. pap. 5.95 (*0-88177-199-6*, DR199) Discipleship Res.

Lay Speakers Lead in Evangelism. Shirley F. Clement & Roger K. Swanson. 16p. 1997. pap. 5.95 (*0-88177-200-3*, DR200) Discipleship Res.

Lay Speakers Lead in Stewardship: Advanced Course. Herb Mather. 16p. 1997. pap. 5.95 (*0-88177-197-X*, DR197) Discipleship Res.

Lay Speakers Lead in Worship: Advanced Course. Hoyt L. Hickman. 16p. 1998. pap. 5.95 (*0-88177-250-X*, DR250) Discipleship Res.

Lay Speakers Preach: Sharing God's Story in the Pulpit. Barbara Bate. 16p. 1997. pap. 5.95 (*0-88177-196-1*, DR196) Discipleship Res.

Lay Speaking Ministry: Basic Course, 1997-2000. Jack Gilbert & Nan Zoller. 48p. 1997. pap. 9.95 (*0-88177-181-3*, DR181) Discipleship Res.

Lay Speaking Ministry: Guide for Conference & District Committees 1997-2000. James W. Lane. 32p. 1997. pap. 7.95 (*0-88177-203-8*, DR203) Discipleship Res.

***Lay Taxes in England & Wales, 1188-1688.** D. Crook et al. (PRO Handbks.: No. 31). 371p. 1999. pap. text 49.95 (*1-873162-64-2*, Pub. by PRO Pubns) Midpt Trade.

***Lay the Mountains Low.** Johnston. 2001. mass mkt. write for info. (*0-312-97310-1*) St Martin.

Lay the Mountains Low: The Flight of the Nez Perce from Idaho & the Battle of the Big Hole, August 9-10, 1877. Terry C. Johnston. mass mkt. write for info. (*0-312-97547-3*) St Martin.

***Lay the Mountains Low: The Flight of the Nez Perce from Idaho & the Battle of the Big Hole, August 9-10, 1877.** Terry C. Johnston. LC 00-24201. 400p. 2000. text 24.95 (*0-312-26189-6*) St Martin.

Lay Theology. John B. Cobb, Jr. 120p. (Orig.). 1994. pap. 10.99 (*0-8272-2122-3*) Chalice Pr.

***Lay This Body Down: The 1921 Murders of Eleven Plantation Slaves.** Gregory A. Freeman. LC 99-23182. 240p. 1999. 22.00 (*1-55652-357-2*, Pub. by Chicago Review) IPG Chicago.

Lay This Laurel. limited ed. Photos by Richard Benson. LC 73-84997. (Illus.). 80p. 1973. 60.00 (*0-87130-036-2*) Eakins.

Lay Thoughts of a Dean. William R. Inge. LC 71-156663. (Essay Index Reprint Ser.). 1977. reprint ed. 24.95 (*0-8369-2403-7*) Ayer.

Layamon's Arthur: The Arthurian Section of Layamon's Brut. Ed. by W. R. Barron & S. Weinberg. (Illus.). 320p. (Orig.). (C). 1989. pap. text 69.95 (*0-582-03484-1*) Longman.

Layamon's Brut. W. R. Baron. LC 94-48492. 904p. (C). 1995. pap. text 150.00 (*0-582-24651-2*, 77029) Addison-Wesley.

Layamon's "Brut" A History of the Britons. Tr. by Donald G. Bzdyl. (Medieval & Renaissance Texts & Studies: Vol. 65). 304p. 1989. 26.00 (*0-86698-049-0*, MR65) MRTS.

Layamon's Brut: Selections. Layamon. (BCL1-PR English Literature Ser.). 150p. 1992. reprint ed. lib. bdg. 69.00 (*0-7812-7184-3*) Rprt Serv.

Layamon's Brut Vol. II: Text (Lines 8021-End), Vol. II, Text (lines 8021-end) Ed. by G. L. Brook & R. F. Leslie. (EETS Original Ser.: Vol. 277). 1978. 39.50 (*0-19-722279-X*) OUP.

Layamon's "Brut", an Early Arthurian Poem: A Study of Middle English Formulaic Composition. Dennis P. Donahue. LC 91-17743. (Studies in Medieval Literature: Vol. 9). 344p. 1991. lib. bdg. 99.95 (*0-7734-9768-4*) E Mellen.

Layamon's Brut: or Chronicle of Britain, 3 vols. Layamon. Tr. by Frederic Madden. LC 72-137262. reprint ed. 195.00 (*0-404-03910-3*) AMS Pr.

Layayoga: The Definitive Guide to the Chakras & Evoking Kundalini. Shyam Sundar Goswami. LC 99-10266. (Illus.). 368p. 1999. pap. 25.00 (*0-89281-766-6*) Inner Tradit.

Laye: L'Enfant Noir. Ed. by J. Hutchinson. (French Texts Ser.). (FRE.). 1994. pap. 20.95 (*1-85399-408-1*, Pub. by Brist Class Pr) Focus Pub-R Pullins.

Layer Cakes & Sheet Cakes. Lisa Yockelson. LC 96-10485. (American Baking Classics Ser.). 128p. 1996. 15.00 (*0-06-017195-2*) HarpC.

Layer Charge Characteristics of 2:1: Silicate Clay Minerals. Ed. by Ahmed R. Mermut. (CMS Workshop Lectures: Vol. 6). (Illus.). 144p. (C). 1994. pap. text 17.00 (*1-881208-07-9*) Clay Minerals.

Layer 3 Switching: A Guide for IT Professionals. James A. Metzler. LC 99-199263. 280p. 1998. 58.00 (*0-13-919838-5*) P-H.

Layer 3 Switching Network Design Solutions. 400p. 1920. 55.00 (*1-57870-144-9*) Macmillan Tech.

Layered Drink Mixes in Jars. 32p. 1999. pap. 3.95 (*1-885597-28-2*, Kitchen Crfts) Cookbook Cup.

Layered Intrusions. Ed. by R. Grant Cawthorn. LC 96-9423. (Developments in Petrology Ser.: Vol. 15). 542p. 1996. pap. 86.00 (*0-444-82518-5*) Elsevier.

***Layered Learning in Multiagent Systems: A Winning Approach to Robotic Soccer.** Peter Stone. LC 99-49153. (Intelligent Robotics & Autonomous Agents Ser.). 2000. 40.00 (*0-262-19438-4*) MIT Pr.

Layered Materials for Structural Applications. Ed. by J. J. Lewandowski et al. (MRS Symposium Proceedings Ser.: Vol. 434). 314p. 1996. 68.00 (*1-55899-337-1*, 434) Materials Res.

Layered Soup Mixes in Jars. 32p. 1999. pap. 3.95 (*1-885597-27-4*, Kitchen Crfts) Cookbook Cup.

Layered Structure & Reference in a Functional Perspective: Papers from the Functional Grammar Conference in Copenhagen, 1990. Ed. by Michael Fortescue et al. LC 92-3529. (Pragmatics & Beyond New Series (P&BNS): No. 23). xiii, 444p. 1992. 100.00 (*1-55619-291-6*) J Benjamins Pubng Co.

Layered Structures - Heteroepitaxy, Superlattices, Strain & Metastability Vol. 160: Materials Research Society Symposium Proceedings. Ed. by B. W. Dodson et al. 824p. 1990. text 17.50 (*1-55899-048-8*) Materials Res.

Layered Structures & Epitaxy, Vol. 56. Ed. by J. Murray Gibson et al. (Materials Research Society Symposium Proceedings Ser.). 1986. text 17.50 (*0-931837-21-9*) Materials Res.

Layered Structures, Epitaxy, & Interfaces, Vol. 37. Ed. by J. Murray Gibson & L. R. Dawson. LC 85-3077. 1985. text 17.50 (*0-931837-02-2*) Materials Res.

Layered Superconductors: Fabrication, Properties & Applications. Ed. by D. T. Shaw et al. (Materials Research Society Symposium Proceedings Ser.: Vol. 275). 923p. 1992. text 17.50 (*1-55899-170-0*) Materials Res.

Layering an Art of Time & Space. Ed. by Ann L. Hartley. LC 91-60297. (Illus.). 80p. (Orig.). 1991. pap. write for info. (*0-9628851-0-X*) Soc Layerists.

Layering Intrusions. Ed. by R. Grant Cawthorn. LC 96-9423. (Developments in Petrology Ser.: Vol. 15). (Illus.). 542p. 1996. text 184.00 (*0-444-81768-9*) Elsevier.

Layers. Cynthia T. Edwards et al. (Illus.). 114p. (Orig.). 1994. pap. 14.95 (*0-911051-75-9*) Plain View.

Layers & Levels of Representation in Language Theory: A Functional View. Ed. by Jan Nuyts et al. LC 90-33948. (Pragmatics & Beyond New Ser.: No. 13). xii, 348p. 1990. 71.00 (*1-55619-279-7*) J Benjamins Pubng Co.

***Layers in the Determiner Phrase.** Roberto Zamparelli. LC 00-37613. (Outstanding Dissertations in Linguistics Ser.). 2000. pap. write for info. (*0-8153-3769-8*) Garland.

Layers of Flavors. Ray L. Overton. LC 97-76260. (Illus.). 170 p. 1998. 18.95 (*1-56352-464-3*) Longstreet.

Layers of History: The Archaeology of Heritage Square. Johna Hutira et al. (Illus.). 32p. (Orig.). 1995. pap. 6.95 (*1-882572-12-2*) Pueblo Grande Mus.

Layers of Light. Photos by Dag Alveng. (Illus.). 126p. 1995. pap. 65.00 (*82-7384-471-4*) Dist Art Pubs.

***Layers of Time: A History of Ethiopia.** Paul B. Henze. LC 99-33311. 1999. text 35.00 (*0-312-22719-1*) St Martin.

***Laying a Foundation for Tomorrow: Report on the Quality Education for Minorities (QEM) Network Initial Years, July 1, 1990-June 30, 1993.** Shirley McBey. (Illus.). 57p. 1999. reprint ed. pap. text 15.00 (*0-7881-7892-X*) DIANE Pub.

***Laying a Foundation to Introduce Evidence (Preparing & Using Evidence at Trial) Part 1, 2 - Winter 2000 Action Guide, 2 vols.** Donald F. Miles & Charles E. Goff. Ed. by Linda Compton. 112p. 2000. pap. text 58.00i (*0-7626-0394-1*, CP-11236) Cont Ed Bar-CA.

Laying a Foundation with Windows 95. Brian P. Favro. (Illus.). 12p. 1995. teacher ed. 22.00 (*1-887281-26-6*) Labyrinth CA.

Laying a Foundation with Windows 98. Russel Stolins. Ed. by Brian P. Favro. (Illus.). 224p. 1998. pap. text 27.00 (*1-887281-65-7*) Labyrinth CA.

Laying a Foundation with Windows 98: Instructor's Materials. Brian P. Favro. (Illus.). 16p. 1998. teacher ed. 21.00 (*1-887281-66-5*) Labyrinth CA.

Laying a Foundation with Windows 95. Russel Stolins. Ed. by Loralee Winsor & Brian Favro. (Illus.). 150p. (Orig.). (YA). 1996. pap. text 15.95 (*1-887281-10-X*) Labyrinth CA.

Laying a Watercolour Wash. Leslie Worth. (Leisure Arts Ser.: No. 4). (Illus.). 32p. pap. 4.95 (*0-85532-403-1*, 403-1, Pub. by Srch Pr) A Schwartz & Co.

Laying Aside the Weight of Guilt. Linda Culbreth. 23p. (Orig.). 1999. pap. 4.95 (*1-893784-01-0*) Aunt Matilda.

Laying Biblical Foundations. Harold McDougal. LC 99-180276. 162p. 1997. pap. 8.99 (*1-884369-03-0*) McDougal Pubng.

Laying Community Foundations for Your Child with a Disability: How to Establish Relationships That Will Support Your Child after You're Gone. Linda Stengle. LC 96-18172. 218p. (Orig.). (C). 1996. pap. 15.95 (*0-933149-67-0*) Woodbine House.

Laying down the Law. 3rd ed. G. Morris. 352p. 1992. pap. 51.00 (*0-409-30541-3*, Austral, MICHIE) LEXIS Pub.

Laying down the Law. 4th ed. G. Morris et al. LC 97-179793. 424p. 1995. pap. write for info. (*0-409-30952-4*, MICHIE) LEXIS Pub.

***Laying down the Law: A Study of the Theodosian Code.** John F. Matthews. LC 00-35198. (Illus.). 320p. 2000. 40.00 (*0-300-07900-1*) Yale U Pr.

Laying down the Law: Mysticism, Fetishism, & the American Legal Mind. Pierre Schlag. 200p. (C). 1996. text 45.00 (*0-8147-8053-9*) NYU Pr.

Laying down the Law: Mysticism, Fetishism & the American Legal Mind. Pierre Schlag. 195p. 1998. pap. text 16.50 (*0-8147-8054-7*) NYU Pr.

***Laying It on the Line with God: The Risk of Honest Prayer.** Charlie Walton. LC 00-100806. 166p. 2000. pap. 9.95 (*0-89112-437-3*) Abilene Christ U.

Laying of the Noone Walker. large type ed. Rosalind Ashe. 596p. 1988. 27.99 (*0-7089-1844-1*) Ulverscroft.

Laying on of Hands. (ENG & IND.). 1992. pap. write for info. (*0-934920-36-2*, B-14IN) Derek Prince.

Laying on of Hands. Kenneth E. Hagin. 1980. pap. 1.00 (*0-89276-250-0*) Faith Lib Pubns.

Laying on of Hands: A Study of the Elementary Principles of Christ, Bk. 5. Ed. by Joe Oakley. (First Principles Ser.). (Orig.). 1990. pap. 6.00 (*0-318-50021-3*); pap. text, student ed. 5.00 (*0-923968-05-9*) Shady Grove Ch Pubns.

***Laying on of Stones.** D. J. Conway. LC 99-36232. (Illus.). 96p. 2000. pap. 10.95 (*1-58091-029-7*) Crossing Pr.

Laying Out of Gussie Hoot: A Novel. Margot Fraser. LC 90-52659. (Southwest Life & Letters Ser.). 224p. 1990. 17.95 (*0-87074-317-1*) SMU Press.

Laying Out the Body. Lucien Jenkins. 77p. 1993. pap. 15.95 (*1-85411-070-5*, Pub. by Seren Bks) Dufour.

Laying the Foundation: Achieving Christian Maturity. James L. Beall. LC 76-42084. 389p. 1976. pap. 12.99 (*0-88270-198-3*) Bridge-Logos.

Laying the Foundation: The Institutions of Knowledg in Developing Countries. Ed. by Benjamin Alvarez & Hernando Gomez. LC 95-173153. 224p. 1994. pap. 17.50 (*0-88936-684-5*, IDRC6845, Pub. by IDRC Bks) Stylus Pub VA.

Laying the Foundation with Mission & Vision: Creating a Strategic Volunteer Program. (Paragidm Organizational Effectiveness Ser.: Vol. 2). 18p. 1995. pap. write for info. (*1-58534-009-X*) Points of Light.

Laying the Foundations: Human Rights in Kuwait - Obstacles & Opportunities. Ed. by Neil Hicks. (Illus.). 78p. 1993. pap. text 8.00 (*0-934143-62-5*) Lawyers Comm Human.

Laying the Ladder Down: The Emergence of Cultural Holism. Betty J. Craige. LC 92-10934. (Critical Perspectives on Modern Culture Ser.). 176p. 1992. 30.00 (*0-87023-805-1*); pap. 15.95 (*0-87023-806-X*) U of Mass Pr.

***Laying the Roles to Rest.** Charles B. Prewitt. 176p. 1999. pap. 9.95 (*0-9673868-0-2*) C B Prewitt.

Laying up Your Boat. H. Janssen. (Illus.). 128p. 1991. pap. 18.50 (*0-7136-3456-1*) Sheridan.

***Laying Waste.** Duff Wilson. 2001. 25.00 (*0-06-019369-7*) HarpC.

Laying Waste. Duff Wilson. 2002. pap. 14.00 (*0-06-093183-3*, Perennial) HarperTrade.

Laying Ways. Mechthild Cranston. 1990. 26.50 (*0-916379-77-9*) Scripta.

Layla & Majnun. Ganjavi Nizami. Tr. by Colin Turner. 270p. 1997. 15.95 (*1-85782-161-0*, Pub. by Blake Publng) Seven Hills Bk.

Layla Deen & the Case of the Ramadan Rogue. Yahiya Emerick. (Illus.). 47p. (J). (gr. 4-7). 1996. mass mkt. write for info. (*1-889720-01-1*, Pub. by Amirah Pubng) Intl Bks & Tapes.

Laylo Papers: The Complete Guide to Relationships. Tim Downs. (Illus.). 136p. (Orig.). Date not set. pap. 8.99 (*0-9623125-0-9*) T Downs.

Layman Looks at the Lord's Prayer see Meditacoes de Um Leigo

Layman Looks at the Lord's Prayer. W. Phillip Keller. 160p. pap. 9.99 (*0-8024-4644-2*, 200) Moody.

Layman Looks at the Lord's Prayer. large type ed. W. Phillip Keller. LC 99-12645. 208p. 1999. reprint ed. pap. 13.95 (*0-8027-2739-5*) Walker & Co.

Layman Looks at the Love of God. Phillip W. Keller. LC 84-16857. 144p. 1984. pap. 7.99 (*0-87123-898-5*) Bethany Hse.

Layman's Bible Commentary. Incl. Vo. 14. Hosea - Jonah. LC 59-10454. 1964. 6.99 Vol. 10. Proverbs - Song of Solomon. LC 59-10454. 1964. 6.99 Vol. 11. Isaiah. LC 59-10454. 6.99 Vol. 12. Jeremiah, Lamentations. LC 59-10454. 1964. 6.99 Vol. 13. Ezekiel, Daniel. LC 59-10454. 1964. 6.99 Vol. 15. Micah - Malachi. LC 59-10454. 1964. 6.99 Vol. 16. Matthew. LC 59-10454. 1964. 6.99 Vol. 18. Luke. LC 59-10454. 1964. 6.99 Vol. 19. John. LC 59-10454. 6.99 Vol. 20. Acts of the Apostles. LC 59-10454. 1964. 6.99 Vol. 21. Romans - Second Corinthians. LC 59-10454. 1964. 6.99 Vol. 22. Galatians - Colossians. LC 59-10454. 1964. 6.99 Vol. 23. First Thessalonians - Philemon. LC 59-10454. 1964. 6.99 Vol. 24. Hebrews - Second Peter. LC 59-10454. 1964. 6.99 Vol. 25. First John - Revelation. LC 59-10454. 1964. 6.99 LC 59-10454. 1964. 145.00 (*0-8042-3086-2*) Westminster John Knox.

Layman's Bible Commentary: Romans, I Corinthians, Vol. 20. J. W. MacGorman. LC 79-51501. 154p. 1980. 11.99 (*0-8054-1190-9*) Broadman.

Layman's Bible Dictionary. Ed. by George Knight & Rayburn Ray. LC 99-163719. 227p. 1997. 9.97 (*1-57748-163-1*) Barbour Pub.

Layman's Dictionary of Law. G. Macfarlane. 256p. 1984. pap. 10.00 (*0-08-039157-5*, Pergamon Pr) Elsevier.

Layman's Gold Investment Manual: A Book on Picking & Choosing. Michael E. Odell. Ed. by Joe Palmquist. (Illus.). 192p. (Orig.). (C). 1989. pap. 17.95 (*0-924380-00-4*) Veritas Rsch Pub.

Layman's Guide to Acupuncture. Yoshio Manaka et al. LC 72-78590. (Illus.). 144p. 1972. 12.50 (*0-8348-0072-1*); pap. 10.95 (*0-8348-0107-8*) Weatherhill.

Layman's Guide to Applying the Bible. Walter A. Henrichsen. 224p. (Orig.). 1985. pap. 8.95 (*0-310-37691-2*, 11233P) Zondervan.

Layman's Guide to Contracting Your Own Home. David Caldwell. (Illus.). 220p. 1994. pap. 16.95 (*0-9698056-0-8*) Lone Pine.

Laymans Guide to Counseling. Susan Wallace. 1995. pap. 8.99 (*1-56229-408-3*) Pneuma Life Pub.

Layman's Guide to Electronic Eavesdropping: How It's Done & Simple Ways to Prevent It. Ton Larsen. (Illus.). 112p. 1996. pap. 17.00 (*0-87364-879-X*) Paladin Pr.

Layman's Guide to Fasting & Losing Weight: Introduced by Dick Gregory. Phillip E. Partee. Ed. by H. M. Levy, Jr. LC 78-64863. (Illus.). (Orig.). (J). (gr. 10-12). 1979. pap. text 4.95 (*0-685-94383-6*) United Pr.

Layman's Guide to Installing A Small Business Computer. Jack Bender. (Illus.). 128p. 1979. 17.50 (*0-89433-097-7*) Petrocelli.

***Layman's Guide to Interactive Television; Better Understanding How the Internet Is Merging with Television"** Phil Gurian. 120p. 2000. ring bd. 24.95 (*0-9621639-3-7*) Grand Natl Pr.

Layman's Guide to Interpreting the Bible. Walter A. Henrichsen. 112p. (Orig.). 1985. reprint ed. pap. 7.95 (*0-310-37681-5*, 11234P) Zondervan.

***Layman's Guide to Investing: A Young Person's Investment Guide.** Richard Given. (Illus.). 40p. 1999. pap. 14.95 (*0-9671460-1-1*) TRI-S Ltd.

Layman's Guide to Modern Art: Painting for a Scientific Age. Bartlett H. Hayes, Jr. & Mary C. Rathbun. (Illus.). 110p. 1954. write for info. (*1-879886-11-1*) Addison Gallery.

Layman's Guide to New Age & Spiritual Terms. Elaine Murray. LC 92-41892. 208p. (Orig.). 1993. pap. 12.95 (*0-931892-53-8*) B Dolphin Pub.

Layman's Guide to Our Bible see Introduccion a la Biblia

Layman's Guide to Sanctification. H. Ray Dunning. 96p. 1991. pap. 6.99 (*0-8341-1387-2*) Beacon Hill.

Layman's Guide to Scottish Law. Cameron Fyfe. 256p. 1996. pap. 13.95 (*1-85158-718-7*, Pub. by Mainstream Pubng) Trafalgar.

Layman's Guide to Studying the Bible. Walter A. Henrichsen. 144p. (Orig.). 1985. pap. 7.95 (*0-310-37631-9*, 11236P) Zondervan.

Layman's Guide to the Apostles' Creed. H. Ray Dunning. 88p. 1995. pap. 7.99 (*0-8341-1552-2*) Beacon Hill.

Layman's Guide to the FDCPA: Stop Harassing Debt Collection Practices Now! Sean-Paul Sandoval et al. 40p. 1999. pap. 14.95 (*0-9671460-0-3*) TRI-S Ltd.

Layman's Guide to the Fruit of the Spirit. T. David Sustar. LC 90-61210. 1990. pap. 7.99 (*0-87148-033-6*) Pathway Pr.

Layman's Guide to the Great "Reading" Controversy. Arnold Burron. (Issues Paper #11-94 Ser.). 33p. 1994. pap. text 8.00 (*1-57655-139-3*) Independ Inst.

Layman's Guide to the Holy Spirit. Daniel L. Black. LC 88-60360. 1988. pap. 6.99 (*0-87148-529-X*) Pathway Pr.

Layman's Guide to the Lordship Controversy. Richard P. Belcher. 123p. 1990. pap. 7.95 (*0-925703-13-3*) Richbarry Pr.

Layman's Guide to the Sabbath Question. Richard P. Belcher. 161p. 1991. pap. 7.95 (*0-925703-43-5*) Richbarry Pr.

Layman's Guide to Wesleyan Terminology. Marlin Hotle. 72p. (Orig.). 1995. pap. 5.99 (*0-88019-337-9*) Schmul Pub Co.

Layman's Introduction to Robotics. Kelly Derek. (Illus.). 220p. 1986. text 27.95 (*0-89433-265-1*) Petrocelli.

***Layman's Law Guides.** Richard L. Strohm. (Layman's Law Guides Ser.). 1998. 118.65 (*0-7910-4505-6*) Chelsea Hse.

Layman's Look at Light Computers. Edward W. Eckhardt. (Illus.). 85p. (Orig.). 1999. pap. 18.95 (*1-886759-03-0*) IntroTech.

Layman's View of History. Henry O. Taylor. LC 75-41271. reprint ed. 21.00 (*0-404-14616-3*) AMS Pr.

Laymen's View..."What Everyone Should Know about the Holy Bible" unabridged ed. Len Gongola. Ed. by Ed Lacy. 192p. 1999. pap. 9.95 (*0-9671919-0-4*) Son Beam.

L

Layne Genealogy. F. B. Layne. (Illus.). 251p. 1993. reprint ed. pap. 39.00 (*0-8328-2807-6*); reprint ed. lib. bdg. 49.00 (*0-8328-2806-8*) Higginson Bk Co.

Layne Genealogy. F. B. Layne. (Illus.). 251p. 1993. reprint ed. pap. 39.00 (*0-8328-3694-X*); reprint ed. lib. bdg. 49.00 (*0-8328-3693-1*) Higginson Bk Co.

Layoff. Tana Reiff. (That's Life Ser.: Bk. 3). 96p. 1994. pap. 4.95 (*0-7854-1088-0*, 40703); audio 10.95 (*0-7854-1097-X*, 40713) Am Guidance.

Layout. Peter Bonnici. 1999. pap. 35.00 (*2-88046-397-1*, Rotovision) Watsn-Guptill.

Layout. Rockport Publisher Staff. (Graphic Idea Resource Ser.). (Illus.). 96p. 1998. pap. 15.99 (*1-56496-373-X*) Rockport Pubs.

Layout & Design for Calligraphers. Alan Furber. LC 83-18160. (Illus.). 64p. 1984. pap. 9.95 (*0-8008-4573-0*) Taplinger.

Layout & Floor Work. 1996. lib. bdg. 250.75 (*0-8490-8332-X*) Gordon Pr.

Layout & Graphic Design. Raymond A. Ballinger. LC 72-90309. 96 p. 1970. write for info. (*0-289-79634-2*) SVista Bks.

Layout, Design, & Typography: For the Desktop Publisher. 2nd ed. Gerald A. Silver & Myrna L. Silver. (Illus.). 321p. 1997. pap. text 49.00 (*1-880472-12-0*) Edit Enter.

Layout, Design, & Typography for the Desktop Publisher. Gerald A. Silver & Myrna L. Silver. 336p. (C). 1991. spiral bd. write for info. (*0-697-12302-2*) Bus & Educ Tech.

Layout Minimization of CMOS Cells. Robert L. Maziasz & John P. Hayes. (C). 1991. text 106.50 (*0-7923-9182-9*) Kluwer Academic.

Layout of E. H. V. Substations. Robert L. Giles. LC 73-132285. (Institution of Electrical Engineers, IEEE Monograph Ser.: No. 5). 237p. reprint ed. pap. 73.50 (*0-608-30661-4*, 200434500044) Bks Demand.

Layout Source Book. Alan Swann. 9.98 (*1-55521-530-0*) Bk Sales Inc.

Layout Techniques for Landscape Architecture. Gary Austin. (Illus.). 184p. (C). 1995. ring bd. 19.80 (*0-87563-524-5*) Stipes.

***Layout 2.** (Carpentry Lev 4 Ser.). 2000. student ed., ring bd. 12.00 (*0-13-031192-8*) P-H.

***Layout Two.** (Carpentry Lev 4 Ser.). 2000. teacher ed., ring bd. 12.00 (*0-13-031202-9*) P-H.

***Layouts That Really Work.** Robert Harris. (Illus.). 176p. 2000. pap. 24.99 (*1-58180-073-8*, North Lght Bks) F & W Pubns Inc.

Layover. Max Martinez. LC 96-39824. 140p. 1997. 22.95 (*1-55885-199-2*) Arte Publico.

***Layover.** Lisa Zeidner. 288p. 2000. pap. 13.00 (*0-06-095649-6*, Perennial) HarperTrade.

Layperson's Glossary on Functional Electrical Stimulation (FES) Jeanne O. Teeter. 9p. 1992. pap. text 5.00 (*1-888470-01-1*) FES Info Ctr.

Layperson's Guide on Understanding & Interacting with Congress. David S. Germroth & Rebecca J. Hudson. (Illus.). 56p. 1996. pap. 9.95 (*0-9650951-0-X*) R J Hudson Assocs.

Layperson's Guide to Criminal Law. Raneta Lawson Mack. LC 98-53382. 216p. 1999. lib. bdg. 65.00 (*0-313-30556-0*) Greenwood.

Layperson's Guide to Health Insurance Reform. John C. Goodman. 1992. pap. 5.00 (*1-56808-004-2*, BG121) Natl Ctr Pol.

***Layperson's Guide to Historical Archeology in Maryland: Examples from the Lost Towns of Anne Arundel Project.** James G. Gibbs et al. (Illus.). 80p. 1999. pap. 7.95 (*0-9673415-0-7*) Arch Soc MD.

Layperson's Guide to the Forest Codes of Mali Niger & Senegal see Guide Pratique des Codes Forestiers du Mali, du Niger et du Senegal

Layperson's Guide to the Forest Codes of Mali, Niger & Senegal. Kent Elbow & Alain Rochegude. (LTC Paper Ser.: Vol. 139). v, 85p. (C). 1992. pap. 7.00 (*0-934519-56-0*, LTC139) U of Wis Land.

Layperson's Introduction to the New Testament. rev. ed. Carl H. Morgan. 1990. pap. 11.00 (*0-8170-1162-5*) Judson.

Layperson's Introduction to the Old Testament. rev. ed. Robert B. Laurin. 173p. 1990. pap. 12.00 (*0-8170-1163-3*) Judson.

Layperson's Prophecy Handbook for Everyday Use: The Revelation of Jesus Christ & Seventy Weeks of Daniel. Mary E. Lewis. LC 94-77966. (Illus.). 193p. (Orig.). 1994. pap. text 17.95 (*0-9642873-0-7*) Lewis Pubng.

Lays: Poems from Hollywood. Mark Dunster. 13p. 1998. pap. 5.00 (*0-89642-474-X*) Linden Pubs.

Lays of Ancient Rome. Lord Macaulay. LC 97-43667. (Gateway Ser.). 190p. 1997. pap. 12.95 (*0-89526-403-X*, Gateway Editions) Regnery Pub.

Lays of Beleriand. J. R. R. Tolkien. 480p. 1994. reprint ed. mass mkt. 5.99 (*0-345-38818-6*, Del Rey) Ballantine Pub Grp.

Lays of Beleriand Vol. III: In the History of Middle Earth. J. R. R. Tolkien. Ed. by Christopher Tolkien. 400p. 1988. pap. 13.95 (*0-395-48683-1*) HM.

Lays of the Western Gael, & Other Poems. Samuel Ferguson. LC 75-28813. reprint ed. 29.50 (*0-404-13806-3*) AMS Pr.

Laytime & Demurrage. John Schofield. (Lloyd's Shipping Law Library). 402p. 1990. 155.00 (*1-85044-293-2*) LLP.

Layton Looks at Life: Timely Essays on the Past, Present & Future by a Virginia Octogenarian. William W. Layton. 160p. 1995. pap. 9.50 (*0-9649806-3-0*) W W Layton.

***Laywana Pt. 2: The Adventures of Tewa Gar.** Mike Hurley. (Illus.). 374p. 2000. pap. 23.95 (*1-929471-23-8*) Segregansett Pr.

Laywoman's Primer of Breast Cancer. Carl Livingston. (Illus.). 24p. (Orig.). 1980. pap. 2.50 (*0-937816-03-5*) Tech Data.

Lazar Malkin Enters Heaven. Steve Stern. (Library of Modern Jewish Literature). 256p. 1995. pap. 17.95 (*0-8156-0356-8*) Syracuse U Pr.

Lazare Carnot, Republican Patriot. Huntley Dupre. LC 75-29217. (Perspectives in European History Ser.: No. 5). viii, 343p. 1975. reprint ed. lib. bdg. 45.00 (*0-87991-612-5*) Porcupine Pr.

Lazare Carnot Savant: A Monograph Treating Carnot's Scientific Work, with Facsimile Reproduction of His Unpublished Writings on Mechanics & on the Calculus, & an Essay Concerning the Latter by A. P. Youschkevitch. Charles C. Gillispie. LC 78-132238. 371p. 1971. reprint ed. pap. 115.10 (*0-7837-9342-1*, 206008300004) Bks Demand.

Lazarillo de Tormes see Two Spanish Picaresque Novels

Lazarillo de Tormes. (SPA.). 1989. 9.95 (*0-8288-2550-5*) Fr & Eur.

Lazarillo de Tormes. 160p. 1995. 16.95 (*0-7859-9860-8*); 14.95 (*0-7859-9859-4*); 12.95 (*0-7859-9858-6*) Fr & Eur.

Lazarillo de Tormes. (Clasicos Ser.). (SPA.). 78p. 1997. pap. write for info. (*1-881713-04-0*) Pubns Puertorriquenas.

Lazarillo de Tormes. Anonmio. (SPA.). pap. 15.95 (*84-376-0660-8*, Pub. by Ediciones Catedra) Continental Bk.

Lazarillo De Tormes. Ed. by Victor Garcia de la Concha. (Nueva Austral Ser.: No. 12). (SPA.). 1991. pap. text 12.95 (*84-239-1812-2*) Elliots Bks.

Lazarillo de Tormes. unabridged ed. Anonimo. (SPA.). pap. 5.95 (*84-410-0000-X*, Pub. by Bookking Intl) Distribks Inc.

Lazarillo de Tormes. 3rd ed. (SPA.). 136p. 1997. pap. text 4.00 (*1-56328-041-8*) Edit Plaza Mayor.

Lazarillo de Tormes, Level 3. (Leer en Espanol Ser.). (SPA.). (C). 1998. pap. 5.95 (*84-294-3614-6*) Santillana.

Lazarillo de Tormes, No. 156. (SPA.). 336p. 1989. 16.95 (*0-8288-8579-6*) Fr & Eur.

Lazarillo de Tormes: Level B. 8.95 (*0-88436-278-7*) EMC-Paradigm.

***Lazarillo de Tormes: Original Spanish Text with English Translation.** Ed. by Keith Whitlock. Tr. by David Rowland. (Hispanic Classics Ser.). (SPA & ENG., Illus.). 176p. (C). 2000. pap. 22.00 (*0-85668-728-6*, Pub. by Aris & Phillips) David Brown.

***Lazarillo De Torres.** Spain. (SPA.). 1999. 13.00 (*84-481-0623-7*, McGrw-H College) McGrw-H Hghr Educ.

Lazaris Interviews. Lazaris & Jach Pursel. LC 88-70670. 1988. write for info. (*1-55638-072-0*) Concept Synergy.

Lazaro Cardenas: El General Misionero. Enrique Krauze. (Political Biographies of the Mexican Revolution Ser.). (SPA., Illus.). 224p. 1987. pap. 9.99 (*968-16-2293-6*, Pub. by Fondo) Continental Bk.

Lazaro Cardenas: Mexican Democrat. 2nd enl. rev. ed. William C. Townsend & Frank Tannenbaum. (C). 1979. reprint ed. pap. 8.95 (*0-935340-00-9*) Intl Friend.

Lazaro Cardenas: Mini Play. (History of Mexico Ser.). (J). (gr. 5 up). 1977. 5.00 (*0-89550-358-1*) Stevens & Shea.

Lazaro Cardenas y la Revolucion I, II, III. Fernando Benitez. (SPA.). pap. 11.99 (*968-16-0457-1*, Pub. by Fondo) Continental Bk.

Lazaro en el Laberinto. Antonio B. Vallejo. Ed. by Mariano D. Paco. (Nueva Austral Ser.: No. 29). (SPA.). 1991. pap. text 24.95 (*84-239-1829-7*) Elliots Bks.

Lazar's Museum Shop Treasures: The Exclusive Guide to Museum Catalog Shopping. 2nd ed. Elysa Lazar & Eve Miceli. (Illus.). 300p. 1994. pap. 14.95 (*1-881642-05-4*) Lazar Comms.

Lazar's Outlet Shopper's Guide: A Field Guide to Factory Outlet Shopping. 2nd ed. Elysa Lazar & Eve Miceli. 250p. 1994. pap. 12.95 (*1-881642-06-2*) Lazar Comms.

Lazar's Shop by Mail: A Field Guide to Shopping by Mail. 2nd ed. Elysa Lazar & Eve Miceli. (Illus.). 350p. 1993. pap. 14.95 (*1-881642-04-6*) Lazar Comms.

Lazarus. Alain Absire. 256p. 1988. 19.95 (*0-15-149250-6*) Harcourt.

Lazarus & the Fourth Gospel Community. Frederick W. Baltz. LC 95-14581. (Biblical Press Ser.: Vol. 37). 120p. 1996. 59.95 (*0-7734-2428-8*, Mellen Biblical Pr) E Mellen.

***Lazarus & the Hurricane: The Freeing of Rubin "Hurricane" Carter.** Sam Chaiton & Terry Swinton. 384p. 2000. pap. 14.95 (*0-312-25397-4*, St Martin Griffin) St Martin.

Lazarus Child. Robert Mawson. 400p. 1999. mass mkt. 6.50 (*0-553-58005-1*) Bantam.

Lazarus Child. Robert Mawson. 303p. 1998. 32.95 (*0-385-25741-4*) Dov Press.

Lazarus Child. Robert Mawson. LC 98-49018. (Wheeler Large Print Book Ser.). 450 p. 1998. write for info. (*1-56895-696-7*) Wheeler Pub.

Lazarus, Come Forth - Plain Bob (Unbehaved) J. Chester Johnson. 1993. pap. 5.95 (*0-914426-10-9*) Juliet Pr.

Lazarus Generation. Samuel Brassfield. 224p. (Orig.). 1994. pap. 10.99 (*1-56043-795-2*, Treasure Hse) Destiny Image.

Lazarus Heart. aut. limited ed. Poppy Z. Brite. (Illus.). 213p. 1999. 50.00 (*1-887368-19-1*) Gauntlet.

Lazarus Hotel. Jo Bannister. 1999. per. 4.99 (*0-373-26307-4*, 1-26307-8, Wrldwide Lib) Harlequin Bks.

Lazarus Hotel. large type ed. Jo Bannister. (Ulverscroft Large Print Ser.). 432p. 1997. 27.99 (*0-7089-3858-2*) Ulverscroft.

Lazarus Laughs. Christiane Duchesne. 13p. (J). 1977. pap. 5.95 (*0-88862-157-4*, Pub. by J Lorimer) Formac Dist Ltd.

Lazarus Laughs. Christiane Duchesne. Tr. by Rosemary Allison from FRE. (Illus.). 13p. (J). 1977. 10.95 (*0-88862-156-6*, Pub. by J Lorimer) Formac Dist Ltd.

Lazarus Man. Charles L. Calia. 304p. 2001. 24.00 (*0-688-16754-3*, Wm Morrow) Morrow Avon.

Lazarus Method. Kate Hancock. LC 96-2379. (Wick Poetry Chapbook Ser.: No. 12). 38p. 1996. pap. 4.75 (*0-87338-557-8*) Kent St U Pr.

Lazarus New York. Brian Wyant. (Illus.). 128p. 1995. pap. 16.00 (*1-883788-23-4*) Event Horzn.

Lazarus of Bethany. J. W. Haggard. pap. 11.95 (*1-55517-390-X*) CFI Dist.

Lazarus Plot. Franklin W. Dixon. LC 88-21365. (Hardy Boys Casefiles Ser.: No. 4). (YA). (gr. 7 up). 1991. mass mkt. 3.75 (*0-671-73995-6*, Archway) PB.

Lazarus Plot. Franklin W. Dixon. (Hardy Boys Casefiles Ser.: No. 4). (YA). (gr. 6 up). 1987. 8.85 (*0-606-02104-3*, Pub. by Turtleback) Demco.

Lazarus Project. John Bayer. LC 98-49223. 320p. 1999. pap. 12.99 (*0-8054-0172-5*) Broadman.

Lazarus Rising. Anne Stuart. (Here Come the Grooms Ser.: No. 1). 1996. per. 3.99 (*0-373-30101-4*, 1-30101-9) Harlequin Bks.

Lazarus Rumba. Ernesto Mestre. LC 99-21857. 512p. 1999. text 27.50 (*0-312-19907-4*, Picador USA) St Martin.

***Lazarus Rumba.** Ernesto Mestre. 512p. 2000. pap. 15.00 (*0-312-26352-X*) St Martin.

Lazarus Secretarius: The First Hungarian Mapmaker & His Work. L. Stegena. 114p. (C). 1982. 144.00 (*963-05-2683-2*, Pub. by Akade Kiado) St Mut.

Lazarus Syndrome: Burial Alive & Other Horrors of the Undead. Rodney Davies. (Illus.). 224p. 1999. 22.95 (*0-7090-6304-0*, Pub. by R Hale Ltd) Seven Hills Bk.

Lazarus Tree. Robert Richardson. (WWL Mystery Ser.). 1995. per. 3.99 (*0-373-26166-7*, 1-26166-8) Harlequin Bks.

Lazerwarz. Shepherd. 1999. mass mkt. 5.99 (*0-671-57806-5*) S&S Trade.

Laziest Boy in the World. Lensey Namioka. LC 97-9053. (Illus.). (J). (ps-3). 1998. 16.95 (*0-8234-1330-6*) Holiday.

Lazlo Letters. Don Novello. LC 92-7832. (Illus.). 160p. 1992. pap. 7.95 (*1-56305-285-7*, 3285) Workman Pub.

Lazlo's Strike. Theodore V. Olsen. 192p. 1996. reprint ed. mass mkt. 3.99 (*0-8439-4114-6*) Dorchester Pub Co.

***Lazos de Conveniencia.** Sara Orwig. (Deseo Ser.: No. 182).Tr. of Bonds of Convenience. (SPA.). 1999. per. 3.50 (*0-373-35312-X*, 1-35312-7) Harlequin Bks.

***Lazy.** Peter Sotos. 336p. 1999. pap. 19.95 (*1-84068-010-5*, Pub. by Creation Books) Subterranean Co.

Lazy Bear. Brian Wildsmith. (Illus.). 32p. (J). (ps-6). 1987. pap. 9.95 (*0-19-272158-5*) OUP.

Lazy Beaver. Pierre Coran. (Child's World Library). (Illus.). 32p. (J). (gr. k-5). 1992. lib. bdg. 18.50 (*0-89565-743-0*) Childs World.

Lazy Bugs. David A. Carter. (Busy Bug Board Bks.). (J). (ps-k). 1997. bds. 4.99 (*0-614-29109-7*) Litle Simon.

Lazy Cook: Delicious Recipes Take 10 Minutes or Less to Prepare. Catherine O. McManus & Krystyn E. Arnold. Ed. by Kathryn Hall. (Illus.). 208p. 1995. pap. text 12.95 (*1-57090-012-4*) Alexander Dist.

Lazy Cook: From Lobster to Brats - Recipes of the New England, Mid-Atlantic & Great Lakes States Made Easy. Krystyn E. Arnold & Catherine O. McManus. LC 96-45962. 1997. pap. 12.95 (*1-57090-051-5*) Alexander Dist.

Lazy Cook Strikes Again: Recipes That Take 10 Minutes or Less to Prepare & Use Readily Available Ingredients. Catherine O. McManus & Krstyn E. Arnold. LC 98-11601. 1998. write for info. (*1-57090-087-6*) Alexander Dist.

***Lazy Daisy.** David Olsen. LC 00-29558. (Illus.). 32p. (J). (ps-5). 2000. 15.95 (*1-57102-162-0*, Ideals Child) Hambleton-Hill.

Lazy Day Adventure: Water Safety. Jacquie Milligan. (Child Safety Ser.). (Illus.). 48p. 1986. pap. 5.95 (*0-513-01832-8*) Denison.

Lazy Days in the Sun Pt. 1: A Felonious Feline Memoir. 3rd aut. gif. limited ed. Tuxedo Enterprises Editors. Orig. Title: Memories of a Cat: Lazy Days in the Sun. (Illus.). 394p. (Orig.). 1997. pap. 24.95 incl. cd-rom (*0-9657252-3-5*, 3-5) Tuxedo Enter.

Lazy Days Out in Provence. Dana Facaros. (Cadogan Food Lovers Guides Ser.). (Illus.). 192p. 1997. pap. text 9.95 (*1-86011-065-7*, Pub. by Cadgn Bks) Globe Pequot.

Lazy Days Out in Umbria. Dana Facaros. 1997. pap. text 14.95 (*1-86011-051-7*, Pub. by Cadgn Bks) Macmillan.

Lazy Dogs & Snoozing Frogs: Relaxation & Quieting Activities for Children. Darrel Lang & Bill Stinston. 53p. 1988. 10.95 (*0-9611456-4-1*, Coulee Press) Adastra Pub.

Lazy Gardener. Mara Grey. LC 97-38077. 144p. 1999. 12.95 (*0-02-862217-0*) Macmillan.

***Lazy Gourmet.** Susan Mendelson. (Illus.). 224p. 2000. pap. 16.95 (*1-55110-966-2*) Whitecap Bks.

Lazy Gourmet Cookbook. Oxmoor House Staff. LC 97-65857. 240p. 1997. 29.95 (*0-8487-1544-6*) Oxmoor Hse.

Lazy Investor. 224p. 1999. 12.95 (*0-02-862803-9*, Pub. by Macmillan) S&S Trade.

Lazy Jack. Val Biro. (Illus.). 32p. (J). 1995. (*0-19-279956-8*) OUP.

Lazy Jack. Illus. by Bert Dodson. LC 78-18070. 32p. (J). (gr. k-4). 1979. lib. bdg. 15.85 (*0-89375-123-5*) Troll Communs.

Lazy Jack. Illus. by Bert Dodson. LC 78-18070. 32p. (J). (gr. k-4). 1997. pap. 3.95 (*0-89375-101-4*) Troll Communs.

Lazy Jack. Vivian French. LC 94-48930. (Illus.). 40p. (J). (ps up). 1997. reprint ed. pap. 5.99 (*0-7636-0153-5*) Candlewick Pr.

Lazy Jack & the Silent Princess. Mitchell Motomora. (Real Reading Ser.: Level Green). (Illus.). 32p. (J). (gr. 1-4). 1989. pap. 4.95 (*0-8114-6726-0*) Raintree Steck-V.

Lazy Jack & the Silent Princess. Mitchell Motomora. (Real Readers Ser.: Level Green). (Illus.). 32p. (J). (ps-3). 1989. lib. bdg. 21.40 (*0-8172-3529-9*) Raintree Steck-V.

Lazy Learning. LC 97-16416. 1997. text 120.50 (*0-7923-4584-3*) Kluwer Academic.

Lazy Learning: Making the Most of the Brains You Were Born With. D. Beaver. 1994. pap. 12.95 (*1-85230-503-7*, Pub. by Element MA) Penguin Putnam.

***Lazy Lions.** Ladybird Books Staff. 48p. 1999. pap. 4.99 (*0-7214-8035-7*) Ladybird Bks.

Lazy Lions, Lucky Lambs. Patricia Reilly Giff. (Kids of the Polk Street School Ser.: No. 7). (Illus.). 80p. (J). (gr. k-6). 1985. pap. 3.99 (*0-440-44640-6*, YB BDD) BDD Bks Young Read.

Lazy Lions, Lucky Lambs. Patricia Reilly Giff. 73p. (J). (gr. 1-2). pap. 3.50 (*0-8072-1256-3*) Listening Lib.

Lazy Lions, Lucky Lambs. Patricia Reilly Giff. (Kids of the Polk Street School Ser.). 1985. 8.45 (*0-606-00956-6*, Pub. by Turtleback) Demco.

Lazy Little Kitten: Includes Miniature Blanket. Frances Coe. LC 98-44264. (Little Blanket Bks.). (Illus.). 10p. (J). 1999. bds. 3.95 (*0-7641-5178-9*) Barron.

Lazy Man's Guide to Public Speaking. Mary Le Clair & Peter Fortune. 139p. (C). 1986. text 100.00 (*0-9588155-0-X*, Pub. by Peter Fortune) St Mut.

***Lazy Man's Guide to Purchasing a Digital Piano.** Steven L. Cohen. (Illus.). 42p. 1999. pap. 12.95 (*0-9677606-1-5*) S L Cohen.

***Lazy Man's Guide to Purchasing an Acoustic Piano.** Steven L. Cohen. (Illus.). 42p. 1999. pap. 12.95 (*0-9677606-0-7*) S L Cohen.

Lazy Man's Way to Computers. Walter Bell. pap. 24.95 (*1-880071-26-6*) Simple Sftware.

Lazy Man's Way to Riches: DYNA/PSYC Can Give You Everything in the World You Really Want. Joe Karbo. Ed. by Richard G. Nixon. 156p. 1973. 15.00 (*1-884337-00-7*); pap. 10.00 (*1-884337-01-5*) F P Pubng.

Lazy Man's Way to Riches: How to Have Everything in the World You Really Want. rev. ed. Richard G. Nixon & Joe Karbo. LC 93-41887. (Illus.). 318p. 1995. pap. 20.00 (*1-884337-11-2*) F P Pubng.

Lazy Man/The Spring of Youth. Duance Vorhees & Mark Mueller. (Korean Folk Tales for Children Ser.: Vol. 3). (Illus.). 46p. (J). (gr. 2-5). 1991. lib. bdg. 10.95 (*0-930878-73-6*) Hollym Intl.

Lazy Ones. Nellie McCaslin. LC 96-31747. 55p. (Orig.). (YA). (gr. 6-12). 1996. pap. 5.00 (*0-88734-454-2*) Players Pr.

Lazy Person's Guide to Better Nutrition: The Most Digestible Nutrition Book Ever Written! Gordon S. Tessler. (Illus.). 132p. (Orig.). 1984. pap. 9.95 (*1-881924-00-9*) Be Well Pubns.

***Lazy Person's Guide to Fitness.** Charles Swencionis. 384p. 2000. 7.99 (*1-57866-084-X*) Galahad Bks.

Lazy Person's Guide to Fitness. Charles Swencionis & E. Davis Ryan. LC 93-45552. 224p. 1994. pap. 12.00 (*1-56980-004-9*) Barricade Bks.

Lazy South. David Bertelson. LC 80-24033. 284p. 1980. reprint ed. lib. bdg. 65.00 (*0-313-22696-2*, BELS, Greenwood Pr) Greenwood.

Lazy Way to Gaelic. G. Jones. (GAE.). 1994. pap. 9.95 (*0-86243-308-8*) Intl Spec Bk.

Lazy Way to Irish. Ed. by Thomas MacLiam. (IRI., Illus.). 1994. pap. 9.95 (*0-86243-287-1*) Intl Spec Bk.

Lazy Way to Organize Your Stuff. 224p. 1999. 12.95 (*0-02-862801-2*, Pub. by Macmillan) S&S Trade.

Lazy Way to Shed Some Pounds. 224p. 1999. 12.95 (*0-02-862802-0*, Pub. by Macmillan) S&S Trade.

Lazy Way to Wealth, Power, Happiness & Romantic Love. Gary A. Martin. (Illus.). 84p. (Orig.). 1995. pap. 16.95 (*0-9651523-0-8*) Liberty Pubs.

Lazy Way to Welsh. (WEL., Illus.). 1993. pap. 9.95 (*0-86243-240-5*) Intl Spec Bk.

Lazzi: Comic Routines of the Commedia Dell'Arte. Mel Gordon. LC 83-62613. 104p. 1983. pap. 11.95 (*0-933826-69-9*) PAJ Pubns.

LBASIC Reference Manual. 3rd ed. Dar Systems International Staff. Ed. by David A. Partise & Eric A. Seiden. 120p. 1986. pap. 24.95 (*0-916163-98-9*) DAR Syst.

LBEC Contracts. Barnett. 1996. 57.00 (*0-316-08072-1*, Aspen Law & Bus) Aspen Pub.

LBJ: A Biography of Lyndon Baines Johnson. Irwin Unger & Debi Unger. LC 99-22475. (Illus.). 586p. 1999. 30.00 (*0-471-17602-8*) Wiley.

LBJ & Mexican Americans: The Paradox of Power. Julie L. Pycior. LC 96-48458. (Illus.). 392p. 1997. pap. 19.95 (*0-292-76578-9*) U of Tex Pr.

LBJ & Mexican Americans: The Paradox of Power. Julie L. Pycior. LC 96-48458. (Illus.). 392p. 1997. 45.00 (*0-292-76577-0*) U of Tex Pr.

LBJ & the Polls. Bruce E. Altschuler. 160p. 1990. 24.95 (*0-8130-0996-0*) U Press Fla.

LBJ & the Presidential Management of Foreign Relations. Paul Y. Hammond. Ed. by Emmette S. Redford & James E. Anderson. LC 92-13219. (Administrative History of the Johnson Presidency Ser.). 312p. 1992. text 37.50 (*0-292-76536-3*) U of Tex Pr.

LBJ & Vietnam: A Different Kind of War. George C. Herring. Ed. by Emmette S. Redford & James E. Anderson. LC 93-36793. (Administrative History of the Johnson Presidency Ser.). 256p. (C). 1994. 29.95 (*0-292-73085-3*) U of Tex Pr.

LBJ & Vietnam: A Different Kind of War. George C. Herring. LC 93-36793. (Administrative History of the Johnson Presidency Ser.). 244p. 1996. pap. 14.95 (*0-292-73107-8*) U of Tex Pr.

An Asterisk (*) at the beginning of an entry indicates that the title is appearing for the first time.

LC & AACR2: An Album of Cataloging Examples Arranged by Rule Number. Alan M. Greenberg & Carole R. McIver. LC 83-27144. 192p. 1984. 31.00 (*0-8108-1683-0*) Scarecrow.

LC Classification Outline. Library of Congress Staff. 1991. pap. text 5.00 (*0-8444-0684-8*) Lib Congress.

LC-Filters: Design, Testing & Manufacturing. Erich Christian. LC 82-13425. (Wiley Series on Filters). 262p. reprint ed. pap. 81.30 (*0-7837-2833-6*, 205763900006) Bks Demand.

LC-MS: An Introduction. Ardrey. 350p. 1996. 115.00 (*3-527-28633-0*, Wiley-VCH) Wiley.

LC Romanization Tables & Cataloging Policies. Ed. by Linda C. Tseng. 284p. 1990. 34.50 (*0-8108-2353-5*) Scarecrow.

Lca: Life Cycle Assessment. Gunilla Johnson. 1997. 90.00 (*1-85802-128-6*, Pub. by Pira Pub) Bks Intl VA.

LCD Optical Performance: Measuring & Modelling LCDs. M. E. Becker et al. (World Scientific Series on Information Display). 250p. 1997. text 48.00 (*981-02-2296-3*) World Scientific Pub.

LCG: St Statlaw. Blumberg. 1995. 155.00 (*0-316-09990-2*, Aspen Law & Bus) Aspen Pub.

LCI: "Landing Craft Infantry", Vol. I. Turner Publishing Company Staff. (Illus.). 160p. Date not set. 49.95 (*1-56311-123-3*) Turner Pub KY.

LCI: "Landing Craft Infantry", Vol. II. Turner Publishing Company Staff. (Illus.). 160p. Date not set. 49.95 (*1-56311-262-0*) Turner Pub KY.

***LCP Miracle: The Remarkable Nutritional Treatment for ADHD, Dyslexia & Dyspraxia.** Jacqueline Stordy. 2000. pap. 14.00 (*0-345-43872-8*, Ballantine) Ballantine Pub Grp.

LCS (L) Landing Craft Support (Large) Turner Publishing Company Staff. (Illus.). 144p. Date not set. 49.95 (*1-56311-251-5*) Turner Pub KY.

LC's Take: Poetry I. LC Van Savage. LC 98-36371. (Illus.). 128p. 1998. pap. 11.95 (*1-892168-03-0*) Custom Communs.

***LC's Take: Poetry I.** L. C. Van Savage. LC 98-36371. (Illus.). 128p. 2000. pap. 12.95 (*0-9613540-1-1*) Brahms Publishing Co.

LCSH & PRECIS in Library & Information Science: A Comparative Study. Yasar Tonta. (Occasional Papers: No. 194). 1992. pap. 8.00 (*0-685-60650-3*) U of Ill Grad Sch.

***LCSH Century: One Hundred Years with the Library of Congress Subject Headings System.** Alva T. Stone. (A monograph published simultaneously as the Cataloging & Classification Quarterly, Vol. 29, Nos.1/2). 264p. (C). 2000. 69.95 (*0-7890-1168-9*); pap. text 34.95 (*0-7890-1169-7*) Haworth Pr.

LD Child & the ADHD Child: Ways Parents & Professionals Can Help. rev. ed. Suzanne H. Stevens. LC 95-26401. Orig. Title: The Learning-Disabled Child. 1996. pap. 12.95 (*0-89587-142-4*) Blair.

LD Teacher's IEP Companion: Goals, Strategies & Activities for LD Students. Molly Lyle. LC 99-162563. 169 p. 1998. spiral bd. 37.95 (*0-7606-0168-2*) LinguiSystems.

LDAP: Programming Directory-Enabled Applications with Lightweight Directory Access Protocol. Tim Howes & Mark Smith. LC 96-78510. 480p. 1997. 44.99 (*1-57870-000-0*) Macmillan Tech.

***LDAP Programming: Directory Management & Integration.** Clayton Donley. 2000. pap. 44.95 (*1-884777-91-0*) Manning Pubns.

***LDAP Programming with Java.** Rob Weltman & Tony Dahbura. LC 99-54510. 672p. 2000. 49.95 incl. cd-rom (*0-201-65758-9*) Addison-Wesley.

LDC Financial Requirements. Catrinus J. Jepma. 128p. 1992. 82.95 (*1-85628-337-2*, Pub. by Avebry) Ashgate Pub Co.

LDL Online - Laying down the Law Computer-Assisted Legal Research. S. D. Dayal. 184p. 1995. pap. write for info. (*0-409-31165-0*, MICHIE) LEXIS Pub.

LDL Sicilian. Alex Dunne. 1995. pap. 5.00 (*0-938650-42-4*) Thinkers Pr.

LDRC 50-State Survey, 1999: Employment Libel & Privacy Law. Ed. by Libel Defense Staff. 1000p. 1998. pap. 135.00 (*0-913269-18-2*) Libel Defense Resource Ctr.

LDRC 50-State Survey, 1998-99: Media Libel Law. 1000p. 1998. pap. write for info. (*0-913269-15-8*) Libel Defense Resource Ctr.

LDRC 50-State Survey, 1998-99: Media Privacy & Related Law. 1280p. 1998. pap. 135.00 (*0-913269-14-X*) Libel Defense Resource Ctr.

LDRC 50-State Survey, 1999-00 Vol. 5: Media Privacy & Related Law. Libel Defense Staff. 1280p. 1999. pap. 125.00 (*0-913269-16-6*) Libel Defense Resource Ctr.

LDRC 50-State Survey, 1999-00 Vol. 16: Media Libel Law. Libel Defense Staff. 1000p. 1999. pap. 125.00 (*0-913269-17-4*) Libel Defense Resource Ctr.

LDRC 50-State Survey: Current Developments in Media Libel Law. 12th ed. Ed. by Libel Defense Resource Center Staff. xviii, 938p. (C). 1995. pap. text 135.00 (*0-913269-09-3*) Libel Defense Resource Ctr.

LDRC 50-State Survey: Media Privacy & Related Law, Vol. 1. Ed. by Henry R. Kaufman. xxx, 1074p. (Orig.). (C). 1995. pap. text 135.00 (*0-913269-08-5*) Libel Defense Resource Ctr.

LDRC 50-State Survey, 1996-1997 Vol. 2: Media Privacy & Related Law. 2nd rev. ed. 1280p. 1996. pap. 135.00 (*0-913269-10-7*) Libel Defense Resource Ctr.

LDRC 50-State Survey, 1996-1997 Vol. 13: Current Developments in Media Libel Law. 992p. 1996. pap. 135.00 (*0-913269-11-5*) Libel Defense Resource Ctr.

LDRC 50-State Survey, 1997-1998 Vol. 3: Media Privacy & Related Law. 1280p. 1997. pap. 135.00 (*0-913269-12-3*) Libel Defense Resource Ctr.

LDRC 50-State Survey, 1997-1998 Vol. 14: Current Developments in Media Libel Law. 992p. 1997. pap. 135.00 (*0-913269-13-1*) Libel Defense Resource Ctr.

***LDs Grandparents' Idea Book.** Fay A. Klingler. LC 00-20568. 2000. pap. write for info. (*1-57345-646-2*) Bookcraft Inc.

LDS Roots in Egypt. Arthur Wallace. 63p. 1981. pap. 3.95 (*0-937892-08-4*) LL Co.

LDS Teenager's Guide: 365 Awesome Answers for Today's Challenges. Bettyanne Gillette. 128p. (YA). 1996. pap. 6.98 (*0-88290-592-9*, 2071) Horizon Utah.

LDS Women's Treasury: Insight & Inspiration for Today's Woman. LC 96-6504. vii, 497p. 1997. 18.95 (*1-57345-166-5*) Deseret Bk.

Le Baphomet see Baphomet

Le Bateau see Boats

Le Bonheur Obligatoire see Compulsory Happiness

Le Bossu & Voltaire on the Epic: Rene le Bossu, Treatise of the Epic Poem, 1695 & Voltaire, Essay on Epic Poetry, 1727. Ed. by Stuart Curran. LC 73-133363. 374p. 1970. 50.00 (*0-8201-1086-8*) Schol Facsimiles.

Le' Bre' Azza Pades: Erase All Color from the Exterior. Jacquelyn M. P. Powell. 32p. 1999. pap. write for info. (*0-9662848-1-X*) J M P Powell.

Le Chandail de Hockey see Hockey Sweater

Le Chant du Dire-Dire see Song of the Say-Sayer

Le Chateau De Cene see Castle of Communion

Le Chemin de L'Exil see Road to Exile

Le Code: Law in Traditional Vietnam, 3 vols. Tr. by Ngoc H. Nguyen et al. LC 86-8371. 1038p. 1987. text 175.00 (*0-8214-0630-2*) Ohio U Pr.

Le Corbusier. Willi Boesiger. (Illus.). 260p. 1998. pap. 16.95 (*3-7643-5930-7*) Birkhauser.

Le Corbusier. Stephen Gardiner. (Quality Paperbacks Ser.). (Illus.). 140p. 1988. reprint ed. pap. 10.95 (*0-306-80337-2*) Da Capo.

Le Corbusier: An Analysis of Form. 2nd ed. Geoffrey Baker. (Illus.). 336p. (C). (gr. 13). 1991. pap. text 51.95 (*0-7476-0028-7*) Chapman & Hall.

Le Corbusier: An Analysis of Form. 3rd ed. Geoffrey H. Baker. (Illus.). 368p. 1996. pap. 34.95 (*0-442-02432-0*, VNR) Wiley.

Le Corbusier: An Analysis of Form. 3rd ed. Geoffrey H. Baker. 385p. 1996. text 34.95 (*0-471-28813-6*, VNR) Wiley.

Le Corbusier: An Annotated Bibliography. Darlene Brady. LC 82-49267. 320p. 1985. text 81.00 (*0-8240-9134-5*) Garland.

Le Corbusier: Architect, Painter, Poet. Jean Jenger. Tr. by Caroline Beamish. (Discoveries Ser.). (Illus.). 160p. 1996. pap. 12.95 (*0-8109-2880-9*, Pub. by Abrams) Time Warner.

Le Corbusier: Complete Works. Ed. by Birkhauser Staff. 1996. boxed set 500.00 (*3-7643-5515-8*) Birkhauser.

Le Corbusier: Early Works at la Chaux-de-Fonds. Geoffrey H. Baker & Jacques Gubler. (Academy Architecture Ser.). (Illus.). 128p. 1987. 45.00 (*0-312-47582-9*); pap. 30.00 (*0-312-47583-7*) St Martin.

Le Corbusier: Ideas & Forms. rev. ed. William J. Curtis. (Illus.). 240p. (C). 1995. pap. 29.95 (*0-7148-2790-8*, Pub. by Phaidon Press) Phaidon Pr.

Le Corbusier: La Villa Savoye (The Villa Savoye) Jacques Sbriglio. LC 99-17206. 1999. write for info. (*0-8176-5807-6*) Birkhauser.

Le Corbusier: Les Voyages d'Allemagne, Carnets, 5 vols., Set. Guiliano Creleri. LC 95-37459. (Illus.). 500p. 1995. boxed set 250.00 (*1-885254-15-6*, Pub. by Monacelli Pr) Penguin Putnam.

Le Corbusier: The Chapel at Ronchamp. Daniele Pauly. LC 97-35543. (Corbusier Guides Ser.). (GER & ITA., Illus.). 138p. 1997. pap. 16.95 (*3-7643-5759-2*, Pub. by Birkhauser) Princeton Arch.

Le Corbusier: The City of Refuge, Paris 1929-33. Brian B. Taylor. (Illus.). 200p. 1988. 39.00 (*0-226-79134-3*) U Ch Pr.

Le Corbusier: The Creative Search. Geoffrey H. Baker. LC 94-66155. (Architecture Ser.). (Illus.). 320p. 1996. text 64.95 (*0-442-02128-3*, VNR) Wiley.

Le Corbusier: The Quartiers Modernes Fruges. Marylene Ferrand et al. LC 98-38698. (Corbusier Guides Ser.). (ENG & FRE., Illus.). 132p. 1998. pap. 16.95 (*3-7643-5808-4*, Pub. by Birkhauser) Princeton Arch.

Le Corbusier: The Quartiers Modernes Fruges les Quartiers Modernes Fruges. Marylene Ferrand. 1998. write for info. (*0-8176-5808-4*) Birkhauser.

Le Corbusier: The Villa Savoye. Jacques Sbriglio. LC 99-17206. 1998. pap. 16.95 (*3-7643-5807-6*) Birkhauser.

Le Corbusier: The Villas la Roche-Jeanneret. Jacques Sbriglio. LC 96-53005. (Corbusier Guides). (Illus.). 144p. 1996. pap. 16.95 (*3-7643-5433-X*, Pub. by Birkhauser) Princeton Arch.

Le Corbusier Vol. 1: Complete Works, 1910-1929. 14th ed. W. Boesiger. (Illus.). 216p. 1994. 75.00 (*3-7643-5503-4*, Pub. by Birkhauser) Princeton Arch.

Le Corbusier Vol. 2: Complete Works, 1929-1934. Willi Boesiger. (Le Corbusier Ser.). (Illus.). 208p. 1996. 75.00 (*3-7643-5504-2*) Birkhauser.

Le Corbusier Vol. 3: Complete Works, 1934-1938. M. Bill. (Le Corbusier Ser.). 1996. 75.00 (*3-7643-5505-0*) Birkhauser.

Le Corbusier Vol. 4: Complete Works, 1938-1946. Willi Boesiger. (Le Corbusier Ser.). 1996. 75.00 (*3-7643-5506-9*) Birkhauser.

Le Corbusier Vol. 5: Complete Works, 1946-1952. Willi Boesiger. (Le Corbusier Ser.). 1996. 75.00 (*3-7643-5507-7*) Birkhauser.

Le Corbusier Vol. 6: Complete Works, 1957-1965. Willi Boesiger. (Le Corbusier Ser.). 1996. 75.00 (*3-7643-5508-5*) Birkhauser.

Le Corbusier Vol. 7: Complete Works, 1957-1965. Willi Boesiger. (Le Corbusier Ser.). 1996. 75.00 (*3-7643-5509-3*) Birkhauser.

Le Corbusier Vol. 19: Selected Works, 1910-1965. Willi Boesiger. (Illus.). 352p. 1994. 75.00 (*3-7643-5511-5*, Pub. by Birkhauser) Princeton Arch.

Le Corbusier - Complete Works Vol. 8: 1965-1969, Last Works. Willi Boesiger. (Le Corbusier Ser.). 1996. 75.00 (*3-7643-5510-7*, Pub. by Birkhauser) Princeton Arch.

Le Corbusier - Polychromie Architecturale: The "Claviers de Couleurs" from 1931 & 1959, 3 vols. Ed. by Arthur Ruegg. (Illus.). 1997. boxed set 225.00 (*3-7643-5612-X*, Pub. by Birkhauser) Princeton Arch.

Le Corbusier Album. Le Corbusier. LC 96-52593. 1997. 250.00 (*1-885254-58-X*, Pub. by Monacelli Pr) Penguin Putnam.

Le Corbusier & the Mystique of the U. S. S. R. Theories & Projects for Moscow, 1928-1936. Jean-Louis Cohen. (Illus.). 300p. 1991. text 57.50 (*0-691-04076-1*, Pub. by Princeton U Pr) Cal Prin Full Svc.

Le Corbusier & the Mystique of the U. S. S. R. Theories & Projects for Moscow, 1928-1936. Jean-Louis Cohen. Tr. by Kenneth Hylton from RUS. LC 90-25235. (Illus.). 270p. 1992. reprint ed. pap. 83.70 (*0-608-02583-6*, 206322900004) Bks Demand.

Le Corbusier & the Tragic View of Architecture. Charles Jencks. LC 73-84322. (Illus.). 191p. 1974. 28.00 (*0-674-51860-8*); pap. text 14.95 (*0-674-51861-6*) HUP.

Le Corbusier at Work: The Genesis of the Carpenter Center for the Visual Arts. Eduard F. Sekler & William Curtis. LC 77-7315. (Illus.). 490p. 1978. 54.00 (*0-674-52059-9*) HUP.

Le Corbusier for Ever. (Illus.). 192p. 1999. 32.95 (*2-7450-0066-7*) Antique Collect.

Le Corbusier Guide. 2nd rev. ed. Deborah Gans. LC 97-49111. (Illus.). 192p. 1998. pap. 19.95 (*1-56898-119-8*) Princeton Arch.

Le Corbusier 1910-65 - Special Edition. Ed. by W. Boesiger & Barry Price. LC 99-17208. (Illus.). 352p. 1999. pap. 45.00 (*3-7643-6036-4*, Pub. by Birkhauser) Princeton Arch.

***Le Corbusier, Photographed by Rene Burri/Magnum.** Arthur Ruegg & Rene Burri. LC 99-25201. (Illus.). 1999. 80.00 (*3-7643-5999-4*, Pub. by Birkhauser) Princeton Arch.

Le Corbusier Sketchbooks, 1950-1954, Vol. 2. Ed. by Fondation Le Corbusier Staff & Architectural History Foundation Staff. (ENG & FRE., Illus.). 520p. 1981. 200.00 (*0-262-12090-9*) MIT Pr.

Le Corbusier Sketchbooks, 1954-1957, Vol. 3. Ed. by Fondation Le Corbusier Staff & Architectural History Foundation Staff. (ENG & FRE., Illus.). 520p. 1982. 200.00 (*0-262-12092-5*) MIT Pr.

Le Corbusier Sketchbooks, 1957-1964, Vol. 4. Ed. by Fondation Le Corbusier Staff & Architectural History Foundation Staff. (ENG & FRE., Illus.). 520p. 1982. 200.00 (*0-262-12093-3*) MIT Pr.

Le Corbusier Sketchbooks, 1914-1948, Vol. 1. Ed. by Fondation Le Corbusier Staff & Architectural History Foundation Staff. (ENG & FRE., Illus.). 520p. 1981. 200.00 (*0-262-03078-0*) MIT Pr.

Le Corbusier, the Noble Savage: Toward an Archaeology of Modernism. Adolf M. Vogt. Tr. by Radka Donnell. LC 98-4753. (Illus.). 353p. 1998. 50.00 (*0-262-22056-3*) MIT Pr.

Le Corbusier, Varese, the Philips Pavilion: Space Calculated in Seconds. Marc Treib. LC 96-4114. 312p. (C). 1996. text 49.50 (*0-691-02137-6*, Pub. by Princeton U Pr) Cal Prin Full Svc.

Le Corbusier's Formative Years: Charles-Edouard Jeanneret at La Chaux-de-Fonds. H. Allen Brooks. LC 96-22865. 588p. 1997. 65.00 (*0-226-07579-6*) U Ch Pr.

Le Corbusier's Formative Years: Charles-Edouard Jeanneret at La Chaux-de-Fonds. H. Allen Brooks. 1999. pap. text 35.00 (*0-226-07582-6*) U Ch Pr.

Costume en France, 1890. Ari Renan. (Illus.). 274p. pap. 25.00 (*0-87556-185-3*) Saifer.

Le Diable au Corps see Devil in the Flesh

Le dit de Tiamyi see River Below

Le fantome d'Ivan Scapinsky see Battle of the Bunheads

Le Grande Peur sous les Etoiles see Star of Fear, Star of Hope

Le Heros Ordinaire see Ordinary Hero

Le Langage Integre et l'Evaluation de l'Enfant: Guide Pratique see Langage Integre Et L'Evalua...: Whole Language Checklists

Le Libraire see Not for Every Eye

Le Mans 1950 Photo Archive: The Briggs Cunningham Campaign. Ed. by Robert C. Auten. LC 94-77251. (Photo Archive Ser.). (Illus.). 144p. 1994. pap. 29.95 (*1-882256-21-2*) Iconografix.

Le Menagier de Paris see Goodman of Paris

Le Mental Des Cellules see Mind of the Cells

Le Miroir des Id Ees see Mirror of Ideas (Le Miroir des Idees)

Mouvement Religieux a Paris Pendant la Revolution, 1798-1801, 2 vols., Set. Jean F. Robinet. LC 70-174331. (Collection de documents relatifs a l'histoire de Paris pendant la Revolution francaise). reprint ed. 270.00 (*0-404-52567-9*) AMS Pr.

Le Mystere des Cathedrales see Fulcanelli - Master Alchemist: The Mystery of the Cathedrals

Le-N see Milton Encyclopedia

Le ou La? The Gender of French Nouns. Marie Surridge. LC 94-47319. (Modern Languages in Practice Ser.: Vol. 1). 1994. pap. 11.95 (*1-85359-268-4*, Pub. by Multilingual Matters) Taylor & Francis.

Le ou La? The Gender of French Nouns. Marie Surridge. LC 94-47319. (Modern Languages in Practice Ser.: No. 1). 1995. 39.95 (*1-85359-269-2*) Multinational Media.

Le Pagne Noir see Black Cloth: A Collection of African Folk Tales

Le Petit Prince see Principito

Le Pierrot Noir see Another November

Le Pourquoi et le Comment du Langage Integre see Pourquoi et le Comment du Langage Integre

Le Radici Comuni Dell' Europa see Common Roots of Europe

Le Regard et Son Masque see Interface: The Painter & the Mask

Le Sauveur et Son Amour pour Nous see Our Saviour & His Love for Us

Le Sexe du Droit du Travail en Europe see Sex of Labour Law in Europe

Style Louis XVI see Histoire de l'Architecture Classique en France

Style Louis XV see Histoire de l'Architecture Classique en France

Le Tao de l'Amour see Tao of Love: Ancient Chinese Techniques for Increased Sexual Pleasure

Le Tartuffe et Le Bourgeois Gentilhomme see Tartuffe & The Bourgeois Gentleman: A Dual-Language Book

Temps d'Aimer (Les Boussardels, IV) Philippe Heriat. (FRE.). 1973. pap. 11.95 (*0-7859-2321-7*, 2070364607) Fr & Eur.

Le Tombeau des Glaces see Tomb of Ice: Percevan

Le Tout P'tit Serpent see Little Bitty Snake

Turpin Francais, dit le Turpin I: Edition Critique. Ed. by Ronald N. Walpole. (Medieval Texts & Translations Ser.: No. 3). (FRE.). 276p. 1985. text 50.00 (*0-8020-2536-6*) U of Toronto Pr.

Le Vent see Wind

Le Vieux Negre et la Medaille see Old Man & the Medal

Le Voyage du Couronnement see Corontion Voyage

Lea. Regine Desforges. Tr. by Elizabeth Failey-Mueller. 384p. 1987. write for info. (*0-8184-0435-3*) Carol Pub Group.

Lea County, New Mexico: A Pictorial History. Lynn C. Mauldin. LC 97-35685. 1997. write for info. (*1-57864-010-5*) Donning Co.

Lea Dan's Spiritual Reflections: Devotions/Meditations. Lea Dan. Ed. by B. L. Davis. (Value Ser.: Vol. 1). (Orig.). pap. 9.00 (*0-9640982-1-0*) B L Davis.

Lea Muy Rapidamente see Multiplique su Capacidad de Lectura

Leabhar Breac. LC 78-72638. (Celtic Language & Literature Ser.: Goidelic & Brythonic). reprint ed. 145.00 (*0-404-17565-1*) AMS Pr.

Leach Legacy. Marion Whybrow. (Illus.). 192p. 1996. pap. 35.00 (*1-889250-10-4*) Gentle Br.

Leacock: A Biography A. F. Moritz & Theresa A. Moritz. LC 85-169746. 363 p. 1985. write for info. (*0-7737-2027-8*) Stoddart Publ.

Lead. (Metals & Minerals Ser.). 1993. lib. bdg. 250.95 (*0-8490-8967-0*) Gordon Pr.

Lead: A Boot Camp & Intensive Parole Program: An Implementation & Process Evaluation of the First Year at the Fred C. Nells School. Teresa Isorena & Jeff Lara. (Illus.). 91p. (Orig.). (C). 1995. pap. text 25.00 (*0-7881-2438-2*) DIANE Pub.

Lead: A Boot Camp & Intensive Parole Program: The Final Impact Evaluation. Ed. by Francisco J. Alarcon. (Illus.). 155p. (C). 1998. pap. text 30.00 (*0-7881-7172-0*) DIANE Pub.

Lead: Airborne Lead in Perspective. National Research Council (U. S.), Committee on Bi. LC 71-186214. (Its Biologic Effects of Atmospheric Pollutants Ser.). 344p. reprint ed. pap. 106.70 (*0-8357-7700-6*, 203605300002) Bks Demand.

Lead: Environmental Aspects. WHO Staff. (Environmental Health Criteria Ser.: No. 85). 106p. 1989. 21.00 (*92-4-154285-3*) World Health.

Lead a Dead Horse to Water. Michele Scheuring. 198p. mass mkt. 4.99 (*1-55197-210-7*) Picasso Publ.

Lead & Leadmining. Lynn Willies. (Album Ser.: No. 85). (Illus.). 32p. pap. write for info. (*0-85263-596-6*, Pub. by Shire Pubns) Parkwest Pubns.

***Lead & Melody Basics.** Ed. by Scott Nygaard. 64p. 2000. pap. 14.95 (*1-890490-19-9*) String Letter.

Lead & Public Health: Dangers for Children. Erik Millstone. LC 97-22574. 240p. 1997. pap. 24.95 (*1-56032-724-3*); boxed set 75.00 (*1-56032-723-5*) Hemisp Pub.

Lead & Public Health Integrated Risk Assessment. Paul Mushak. (Pharmacology & Toxicology Ser.). 1999. 99.95 (*0-8493-8557-1*, 8557) CRC Pr.

Lead & Reproduction: A Comprehensive Bibliography. Compiled by Ernest L. Abel. LC 84-12846. 118p. 1985. lib. bdg. 59.95 (*0-313-24604-1*, ALR/, Greenwood Pr) Greenwood.

Lead & the Law '97: Regulation, Litigation & Liability. Ed. by Larry Siegelman. 142p. (Orig.). 1997. pap. 200.00 (*0-9633003-9-3*) IAQ Pubns.

Lead & Zinc Statistics, 1960-1988. (Illus.). 250p. 1990. pap. 275.00 (*0-317-05507-0*) Elkay Pub Servs.

***Lead Awareness Week: Teacher's Manual.** Edmund F. Benson & Susan Benson. (Illus.). 1999. pap. text, teacher ed. 25.00 (*1-58614-012-4*) Arise Found.

Lead-Based Paint Abatement. Richard K. Miller et al. (Market Research Survey Ser.: No. 263). 50p. 1996. 200.00 (*1-55865-288-4*) Future Tech Surveys.

Lead-Based Paint Handbook. J. W. Gooch. LC 93-1831. (Topics in Applied Chemistry Ser.). (Illus.). 306p. (C). 1993. text 90.00 (*0-306-44448-8*, Kluwer Plenum) Kluwer Academic.

Lead-Based Paint Hazards: Assessment & Management. ATC Environmental Inc. Staff. Ed. by Vincent M. Coluccio. 320p. 1994. 74.95 (*0-471-28601-X*, VNR) Wiley.

L

An Asterisk (*) at the beginning of an entry indicates that the title is appearing for the first time.

L

Lead-Based Paint Hazards: Assessment & Management. ATC Environmental Inc. Staff. Ed. by Vincent M. Coluccio. (Illus.). 320p. 1994. text 60.95 (*0-442-01715-4*, VNR) Wiley.

Lead Based Paint in Housing. Composed by Diane Publishing Staff. (Illus.). 47p. 1998. pap. text 20.00 (*0-7881-4895-8*) DIANE Pub.

Lead-Based Paint Poisoning: Children Not Fully Protected When Federal Agencies Sell Homes to Public. (Illus.). 48p. (Orig.). (C). 1993. pap. text 30.00 (*0-7881-0079-3*) DIANE Pub.

Lead Blues. Anne-Marie Alonzo. 48p. 1990. pap. 5.00 (*0-920717-43-8*) Guernica Editions.

Lead Blues Licks for Guitar. M. Wolfsohn. 16p. 1991. pap. 6.95 (*0-7935-0985-8*, 006999325) H Leonard.

Lead, Cadmium & Mercury in Food: Assessment of Dietary Intakes & Summary of Heavy Metal Limits of Foodstuffs. 1994. 12.00 (*92-871-2620-8*, Pub. by Council of Europe) Manhattan Pub Co.

Lead Carpenter Handbook: The Complete, Hands-On Guide to Successful Job-Site Management. Timothy Faller. Ed. by Steven Bliss et al. LC 98-74276. 224p. 1998. pap. text 27.95 (*0-9632268-7-8*) Builderburg Grp.

***Lead Carpenter System: A Guide for Remodelers & Their Employees.** Wendy A. Jordan. LC 99-30258. 242p. 1999. pap. write for info. (*0-86718-464-7*) Home Builder.

Lead Compliance Program: A Written Compliance Program. Mark M. Moran. (OSHA Written Compliance Programs Ser.: No. 17). (Illus.). 58p. 1992. ring bd. 169.00 (*1-890966-11-8*) Moran Assocs.

Lead Control Strategies. 384p. 1990. 63.00 (*0-89867-499-9*, 90559) Am Water Wks Assn.

Lead Detection & Abatement Directory, 1993. Intro. by Larry Siegelman. 333p. 1992. pap. 100.00 (*0-9633003-2-6*) IAQ Pubns.

Lead Disclosure & Training: A Strategic & Regulatory Marketplace Review. Ed. by Larry Siegelman. 30p. (Orig.). 1997. pap. 100.00 (*0-9633003-6-9*) IAQ Pubns.

Lead Exposure & Child Development: An International Assessment. Ed. by M. Smith et al. (C). 1989. text 229.00 (*0-7462-0069-2*) Kluwer Academic.

Lead Finishing in Semiconductor Devices: Soldering. A. C. Tan. 268p. 1989. text 61.00 (*9971-5-0679-3*) World Scientific Pub.

Lead, Follow, or Get Out of the Way: How to Be a More Effective Leader in Today's Schools. Robert D. Ramsey. 232p. 1999. 61.95 (*0-8039-6770-5*); pap. 24.95 (*0-8039-6771-3*) Corwin Pr.

***Lead Generation Enigma: Why Salespeople Don't Like Sales Leads & What to Do about It.** Bernie Goldberg. (Illus.). 72p. 1999. pap. 12.95 (*1-879644-11-8*) Direct Mktg.

Lead Generation Handbook. Bernard A. Goldberg. (Illus.). 850p. 1992. text 79.00 (*1-879644-02-9*) Direct Mktg.

Lead Generation Handbook. 2nd deluxe ed. Bernard A. Goldberg. (Illus.). 1999. 79.00 (*1-879644-07-X*) Direct Mktg.

Lead Generation Handbook: How to Generate All the Sales Leads You'll Ever Need-Quickly, Easily & Inexpensively. Robert W. Bly. LC 98-6003. 320p. 1998. 59.95 (*0-8144-0363-8*) AMACOM.

Lead, Guide, & Walk Beside. Ardeth Greene-Kapp. LC 98-35915. 1998. 16.95 (*1-57345-439-7*) Deseret Bk.

Lead Guitar. Gary Turner. (Progressive Ser.). (Illus.). 1997. pap. text 16.95 (*0-9595404-6-6*) Koala Pubns.

Lead Guitar. Harvey Vinson. (Orig.). 1972. pap. 19.95 (*0-8256-4058-X*, AM11198) Music Sales.

Lead Guitar Licks. Brett Duncan. (Progressive Ser.). (Illus.). 1997. pap. 14.95 incl. audio compact disk (*1-875726-00-4*) Koala Pubns.

Lead Guitar Licks. Rikky Rooksby. 64p. 1997. pap. 14.95 incl. cd-rom (*0-7119-4524-1*) Omnibus NY.

Lead Guitar Solos. Brett Duncan. (Progressive Ser.). (Illus.). 1997. pap. text 14.95 incl. cd-rom (*1-875726-37-3*) Koala Pubns.

***Lead Hazard Evaluation & Control in Buildings.** Ed. by William M. Ewing et al. (MNL, Manual Ser.: Vol. 38). (Illus.). 180p. 2000. pap. text 75.00 (*0-8031-2086-9*, MNL38) ASTM.

Lead in Food. 1994. 12.00 (*92-871-2573-2*, Pub. by Council of Europe) Manhattan Pub Co.

Lead in Paint, Soil, & Dust: Health Risks, Exposure Studies, Control Measures, Measurement Methods, & Quality Assurance. Ed. by Michael E. Beard & S. D. Iske. LC 95-17787. 1995. write for info. (*0-8031-1884-8*, STP1226) ASTM.

Lead in the Environment. Ed. by P. Hepple. (Illus.). 82p. 1973. 29.00 (*0-85334-485-X*) Elsevier.

Lead in Your Home Pt. 2: A Parent's Reference Guide. (Illus.). 74p. 1998. pap. 10.00 (*0-16-049580-6*) USGPO.

Lead Is a Silent Hazard. Richard M. Stapleton. LC 94-5320. 160p. 1995. 22.95 (*0-8027-1303-3*); pap. 11.95 (*0-8027-7449-0*) Walker & Co.

Lead, Kindly Light. Desmond L. Morse-Boycott. LC 70-107728. (Essay Index Reprint Ser.). 1977. 18.95 (*0-8369-1529-1*) Ayer.

Lead, Kindly Light. John Henry Newman. Ed. by Hal M. Helms. LC 87-60611. (Living Library). 208p. 1987. pap. 10.95 (*0-941478-78-5*, 930-030, Pub. by Paraclete MA) BookWorld.

Lead, Kindly Light. James Sharp. (Spiritual Life Ser.). 1992. 6.25 (*0-89942-184-9*, 184/09) Catholic Bk Pub.

Lead, Kindly Light: My Journey to Rome. Thomas Howard. LC 96-120363. 80p. 1994. pap. 5.95 (*0-940535-73-4*, UP173) Franciscan U Pr.

Lead Language. large type ed. Gene Tuttle. (Linford Western Large Print Ser.). 368p. 1997. pap. 16.99 (*0-7089-5043-4*) Ulverscroft.

***Lead Me Home: An African American's Guide Through the Grief Journey.** Carleen Brice. LC 99-33771. 192p. 1999. pap. 12.00 (*0-380-79608-2*, Avon Bks) Morrow Avon.

Lead Me On: Frank Goad Clement & Tennessee Politics. Lee S. Greene. LC 81-11459. (Illus.). 574p. reprint ed. pap. 178.00 (*0-7837-7082-0*, 204689400004) Bks Demand.

Lead Me to the Exit. Ellen Moore. LC 77-9949. 1977. 6.95 (*0-918056-01-2*) Ariadne Pr.

Lead Me to the Slaughter. large type ed. Graham Ison. (Mystery Ser.). 416p. 1993. 27.99 (*0-7089-2898-6*) Ulverscroft.

Lead Mining in Britain. Roger Burt. (C). 1989. 110.00 (*0-907566-81-2*, Pub. by Dyllansow Truran) St Mut.

Lead My People. Vincent M. Walsh. 104p. 1980. pap. 4.00 (*0-943374-02-2*) Key of David.

***Lead Now or Step Aside: The Ultimate Handbook for Student Leaders.** Eric Chester. 1999. pap. 16.95 (*0-9651447-4-7*) ChesPress.

***Lead On.** Bert Hagemann & Claudia Newman. (Illus.). 128p. 1999. pap. 12.95 (*1-880505-46-0*, CLC230) Pieces of Lrning.

Lead on, Snoopy. Charles M. Schulz. 1993. mass mkt. 3.99 (*0-449-22023-0*, Crest) Fawcett.

Lead Oxides: Chemistry, Technology, Battery Manufacturing Uses, History. Nels E. Hehner & Everett J. Ritchie. 1974. 15.00 (*0-685-56653-6*) IBMA Pubns.

Lead Paint Abatement. Richard K. Miller & Marcia E. Rupnow. LC 90-83850. (Survey on Technology & Markets Ser.: No. 145). 50p. 1991. pap. text 200.00 (*1-55865-170-5*) Future Tech Surveys.

Lead Paint Poisoning in Urban Children: An Annotated Bibliography, No. 1130. Michael A. Quinn et al. 1976. 6.50 (*0-686-20406-9*, Sage Prdcls Pr) Sage.

Lead Paint Primer: Questions & Answers on Lead Paint Poisoning. John Pesce & Amadeo J. Pesce. (Illus.). 150p. (Orig.). 1991. pap. 9.95 (*0-9628220-1-9*) Star Industries.

Lead Paint Removal: Proceedings of SSPC Symposium Held February 29-March 1, 1988, Arlington, VA. Ed. by Bernard R. Appleman et al. (Illus.). 209p. 1988. pap. text 40.00 (*0-938477-34-X*) SSPC.

Lead Paint Removal from Industrial Structures: Proceedings of the SSPC Lead Paint Removal Conference, Feb. 27-Mar. 1, 1989. Ed. by Janet Rex & Bernard R. Appleman. 114p. 1989. pap. text 40.00 (*0-938477-45-5*, SSPC 89-02) SSPC.

Lead Paint Safety: A Field guide for Painting, Home Maintenance & Renovation Work. 80p. pap. text. write for info. (*0-7881-8845-3*) DIANE Pub.

***Lead Paint Safety: Painting, Home Maintenance & Renovation Work.** 80p. 1999. pap. 6.00 (*0-16-050168-7*) USGPO.

Lead Pencil Miner: Search for Yukon Gold. Jack C. Fisher. (Illus.). 150p. 1998. reprint ed. write for info. (*0-9661772-0-7*) Alamar Bks.

***Lead Pipe Rehabilitation & Replacement Techniques.** Gregory J. Kirmeyer & American Water Works Association Staff. LC 00-24273. 2000. write for info. (*1-58321-061-X*) Am Water Wks Assn.

Lead Poisoning: Exposure, Abatement, Regulation. Ed. by Joseph J. Breen & Cindy R. Stroup. 304p. 1995. lib. bdg. 95.00 (*1-56670-113-9*, L1113) Lewis Pubs.

***Lead Poisoning: Federal Health Care Programs Are Not Effectively Reaching At-Risk Children.** Ed. by Bernice Steinhardt. (Illus.). 105p. (C). 2000. pap. text 25.00 (*0-7567-0016-7*) DIANE Pub.

Lead Poisoning in Childhood. Ed. by Siegfried M. Pueschel et al. LC 95-41441. 1996. 31.95 (*1-55766-232-0*) P H Brookes.

Lead Poisoning of America's School Children: An Action Plan. Dick Amann. 150p. (Orig.). 1991. text 99.50 (*0-917194-21-7*) Prog Studies.

Lead Poisoning Preventing: A Directory of State Contacts, 1994. Doug Farquhar. 141p. 1994. 75.00 (*1-55516-428-5*, 4642) Natl Conf State Legis.

Lead Poisoning Prevention: A Guide for Legislators. National Conference of State Legislatures Staff & Doug Farquhar. 48p. 1996. 65.00 (*1-55516-496-X*, 4638) Natl Conf State Legis.

Lead Poisoning Prevention: Directory of State Contacts, 1995-1996. National Conference of State Legislatures Staff. 193p. 1996. 20.00 (*1-55516-430-7*, 4648) Natl Conf State Legis.

Lead Pollution from Motor Vehicles, 1974-1986: A Select Bibliography. Ed. by P. R. Farmer. 95p. 1987. 54.00 (*1-85166-066-6*) Elsevier.

Lead Regulation Handbook. Edward E. Shea. LC 96-180915. 240p. 1996. pap. text 79.00 (*0-86587-518-9*) Gov Insts.

Lead Rock Licks for Guitar. (Guitar Method Ser.). 16p. 1986. pap. 6.95 (*0-7935-6477-8*) H Leonard.

Lead Rock Method, Vol. 1. 48p. 1981. pap. 6.95 (*0-7935-3219-1*, 00699043) H Leonard.

Lead Seals from Fort Michilimackinac, 1715-1781. Diane L. Adams. (Archaeological Completion Reports: No. 14). (Illus.). 49p. (Orig.). 1989. pap. 8.00 (*0-911872-58-2*) Mackinac St Hist Pks.

Lead Sheet Interpretations. 1995. audio 14.95 (*0-7935-5284-2*) H Leonard.

Lead Sheet Interpretations: Swing & Latin Styles. Howard Burke. (Illus.). 55p. (Orig.). (C). 1993. pap. 8.95 (*1-56516-059-2*) H Leonard.

***Lead Singer's Method.** Blake Neely. (Fast Track Ser.). (Illus.). 2000. pap. 7.95 (*0-634-01426-9*) H Leonard.

***Lead Singers' Songbook 1.** Hal Leonard Publishing Company Staff. (Fast Track Ser.). (Illus.). 2000. pap. 9.95 (*0-634-00954-0*) H Leonard.

Lead, So I Can Follow. Harold Adams. LC 99-55556. (Carl Wilcox Mystery Ser.). 240p. 1999. 22.95 (*0-8027-3336-0*) Walker & Co.

***Lead, So I Can Follow.** Harold Adams. (Carl Wilcox Mystery Ser.). 2000. pap. 8.95 (*0-8027-7596-9*) Walker & Co.

Lead Tech '92 Proceedings: Solutions for a Nation at Risk, 1992-1993. Ed. by Robert Morrow. (Illus.). 650p. 1992. pap. 50.00 (*0-9633003-3-4*) IAQ Pubns.

Lead the Way: Fifty Contemporary Songs. 1993. 1.99 (*0-8341-9077-X*, MB-647A) Lillenas.

Lead Through Strategic Planning. Annabel Beerel. LC 99-208034. (ITBP PROFESSIONAL). 320p. 1998. pap. 19.99 (*1-86152-208-8*) Thomson Learn.

Lead Tin Telluride, Silver Halides & Czochralski Growth. Ed. by William R. Wilcox. LC 81-12584. (Preparation & Properties of Solid State Materials Ser.: No. 6). (Illus.). 279p. reprint ed. pap. 86.50 (*0-7837-4418-8*, 204416200006) Bks Demand.

***Lead to Succeed: 10 Traits of Great Leadership in Business & Life.** Rick Pitino & Bill Reynolds. 288p. 2000. 26.00 (*0-7679-0341-2*) Broadway BDD.

Lead Us Forth from Prison. James Lewisohn. 1977. 3.00 (*0-912678-34-8*, Greenfld Rev Pr) Greenfld Rev Lit.

Lead Us into Temptation. Breandan O'Heithir. 142p. 1991. pap. 10.95 (*1-85371-120-9*) Dufour.

Lead Us into Temptation: The Triumph of American Materialism. James B. Twitchell. LC 98-45385. (Illus.). 336p. 1999. 24.95 (*0-231-11518-0*) Col U Pr.

***Lead us into Temptation: The Triumph of American Materialism.** James B. Twitchell. 2000. reprint ed. pap. 14.95 (*0-231-11519-9*) Col U Pr.

Lead Us Not into Penn Station. Bruce Ducker. LC 93-32742. 224p. 1994. 22.00 (*1-877946-36-2*) Permanent Pr.

Lead Us Not into Temptation. Amy C. Laundrie. (Kayla Montgomery Mystery Ser.: No. 4). 188p. (YA). 1999. pap. 9.99 (*0-88092-454-3*, 4543) Royal Fireworks.

***Lead Us to the Water: Choral Book.** Composed by Tom Kendzia. 128p. 1998. pap. 8.95 (*0-915531-99-2*) OR Catholic.

Lead Versus Health: Sources & Effects of Low Level Lead Exposure. Ed. by Michael Rutter & Robin R. Jones. LC 82-16020. (Wiley-Medical Publication). (Illus.). 395p. reprint ed. pap. 122.50 (*0-8357-8644-7*, 203506800092) Bks Demand.

Lead with Vision: Create a Path for Change. John L. Thompson. LC 99-207569. (ITBP PROFESSIONAL). 180p. 1997. pap. 19.99 (*1-86152-097-2*) Thomson Learn.

Lead Your Staff to Think Like Einstein, Create Like DaVinci, & Invent Like Edison: Powerful Real World Techniques That Work! 2nd ed. Don Blohowiak. LC 94-44810. 125p. 1995. 15.95 (*0-7863-0424-3*, Irwn Prfssnl) McGraw-Hill Prof.

Lead-Zinc Deposits along the Red Sea Coast of Egypt: New Observations & Genetic Models on the Occurences of Um Gheig, Wizr, Essel & Zug El Bohar. Mortada M. El Aref & G. Christian Amstutz. (Monograph Series on Mineral Deposits: No. 21). (Illus.). vii, 103p. 1983. 49.00 (*3-443-12021-0*, Pub. by Gebruder Borntraeger) Balogh.

Lead-Zinc-Tin '80: Proceedings of the World Symposium on Metallurgy & Environmental Control. fac. ed. World Symposium on Metallurgy & Environmental Cont. Ed. by John M. Cigan et al. LC 79-93007. (Illus.). 1059p. 1979. pap. 200.00 (*0-7837-8605-0*, 205253600008) Bks Demand.

Lead Zinc Update. Ed. by Donald O. Rausch et al. LC 77-83619. (Illus.). 422p. 1977. reprint ed. pap. 130.90 (*0-7837-9179-8*, 204987800003) Bks Demand.

Lead-Zinc '90: Proceedings of a World Symposium on Metallurgy & Environmental Control, Sponsored by the TMS Lead, Zinc, & Tin Committee, Held During the 119th TMS Annual Meeting, February 18-21, 1990, in Anaheim, California. Minerals, Metals & Materials Society Staff. Ed. by Thomas S. Mackey & R. David Prengaman. LC 89-61208. (Illus.). 1104p. 1990. reprint ed. pap. 200.00 (*0-608-01702-7*, 206235700002) Bks Demand.

Leadbeater Returns. Robert R. Leichtman. (From Heaven to Earth Ser.). (Illus.). 96p. (Orig.). 1979. pap. 3.50 (*0-89804-055-8*) Ariel GA.

Leadbelly Songbook. Moses Asch & Alan Lomax. (Illus.). 96p. 1962. pap. 12.95 (*0-8256-0042-1*, OK62224, Oak) Music Sales.

Leader see Lider

Leader. H. Herchiel Sims. 67p. 1979. write for info. (*0-9603772-1-2*) H H Sims & Assocs.

Leader: Developing the Skills & Personal Qualities You Need to Lead Effectively. Normand L. Frigon, Sr. & Harry K. Jackson, Jr. Ed. by Adrienne Hickey. LC 96-18401. 176p. (Orig.). 1996. pap. 17.95 (*0-8144-7924-3*) AMACOM.

Leader: Psychohistorical Essays. Ed. by Charles B. Strozier & Daniel Offer. 340p. 1985. 70.00 (*0-306-41784-7*, Plenum Trade) Perseus Pubng.

Leader: The Full Story. Kevin Robertson. (Illus.). 288p. 1996. 39.95 (*0-7509-1003-8*, Pub. by Sutton Pub Ltd) Intl Pubs Mktg.

Leader after God's Own Heart see Lider Conforme al Corazon de Dios

Leader As Coach: Strategies for Coaching & Developing Others. Ed. by David B. Peterson et al. LC 98-125168. (Illus.). 140p. 1996. pap. text 19.95 (*0-938529-14-5*, Pub. by Personnel Decisions) Bookmen Inc.

***Leader as Martial Artist: Techniques & Strategies for Resolving Conflict & Creating Communit.** Arnold Mindell. 2000. pap. text 13.95 (*1-887078-65-7*) Lao Tse Pr.

Leader As Martial Artist: Techniques & Strategies for Resolving Conflict & Creating Community. Arnold Mindell. LC 91-55333. (Illus.). 176p. 1993. pap. 12.00 (*0-06-250640-4*, Pub. by Harper SF) HarpC.

Leader Attitudes & Group Effectiveness. Fred E. Fiedler. LC 81-1151. (Illus.). 69p. 1981. reprint ed. lib. bdg. 45.00 (*0-313-22967-8*, FILA, Greenwood Pr) Greenwood.

Leader Effectiveness Training. Thomas Gordon. 288p. 1980. pap. 15.95 (*0-553-34403-X*) Bantam.

Leader in You. Dale Carnegie. (Illus.). 256p. 1995. per. 7.50 (*0-671-51998-0*) PB.

Leader in You. Dale Carnegie. 240p. 1993. 21.50 (*0-671-79809-X*) S&S Trade.

Leader in You: How to Stop Worrying & Start Living/How to Win Friends & Influence People. Dale Carnegie. 1996. mass mkt. 20.97 (*0-671-85152-7*) PB.

Leader (Lighting) Jack Rudman. (Career Examination Ser.: C-3085). 1994. pap. 27.95 (*0-8373-3085-8*) Nat Learn.

Leader Lore: The Book. Richard Russell & Doug Brewer. (Illus.). 200p. 1993. write for info. (*0-9634786-4-8*) Mass Media Dist.

Leader Makers: 12 Steps Developing People & Getting Lean. Jerry Dunn. (Illus.). 238p. 1998. pap. 39.95 (*1-57502-870-0*, PO2368) Morris Pubng.

Leader Manager. Ed. by John N. Williamson. LC 86-1316. 511p. 1986. 87.95 (*0-471-83693-1*) Wiley.

Leader-Manager: Guidelines for Action. William D. Hitt. LC 87-26973. 356p. 1988. text 24.95 (*0-935470-40-9*) Battelle.

Leader-Manager: Guidelines for Action. William D. Hitt. 280p. 1992. pap. 29.95 (*0-7803-1007-1*, PP3566) Inst Electrical.

Leader of the Band: The Life of Woody Herman. Gene Lees. (Illus.). 432p. 1997. reprint ed. pap. 15.95 (*0-19-511574-0*) OUP.

Leader of the Charge: A Biography of General E. Pickett, C. S. A. Edward G. Longacre. LC 95-40941. 242p. 1998. pap. 14.95 (*1-57249-126-4*) White Mane Pub.

Leader of the Charge: A Biography of George E. Pickett. Ed. by Edward G. Longacre. LC 95-40941. 341p. 1995. 29.95 (*1-57249-006-3*) White Mane Pub.

Leader of the Future. Ed. by Drucker Foundation Staff et al. 352p. 1997. mass mkt. 16.50 (*0-7879-0935-1*) Jossey-Bass.

Leader of the Future: New Essays by World-Class Leaders & Thinkers. Ed. by Drucker Foundation Staff et al. (Management Ser.). 347p. 1996. mass mkt. 24.50 (*0-7879-0180-6*) Jossey-Bass.

Leader of the Pack. Justine Davis. (Intimate Moments Ser.). 1996. per. 3.99 (*0-373-07728-9*, 1-07728-8) Silhouette.

Leader of the Pack. Catherine George. 1992. per. 2.89 (*0-373-03236-6*, 1-03236-6) Harlequin Bks.

Leader of the Pack: How to Take Control of Your Relationship with Your Dog. Nancy Baer & Steve Duno. LC 96-19490. 160p. 1996. mass mkt. 9.99 (*0-06-101019-7*, Harp PBks) HarpC.

Leader of the Resistence. Jules Verne. lib. bdg. 22.95 (*0-8488-2062-2*) Amereon Ltd.

Leader of Volunteers: Frederick Funston & the 20th Kansas in the Philippines. Ed. by Thomas C. Crouch. (Illus.). 249p. 1984. 25.00 (*0-87291-167-5*) Coronado Pr.

Leader of Yourself: Ten Skills of Leadership. Carol C. Wilson. LC 98-90429. 165p. 1998. pap. 13.95 (*0-9661537-0-7*) Ulead Pub.

***Leader Shift: How to Avoid Paradigm Shock.** Doug Murren. (Illus.). 186p. 1999. pap. 9.97 (*1-883906-30-X*) Kingdom Prods.

Leader, the Led & the Psyche: Essays in Psychohistory. Bruce Mazlish. LC 90-35351. 333p. reprint ed. pap. 103.30 (*0-608-09088-3*, 206972200005) Bks Demand.

Leader to Leader: Enduring Insights on Leadership from the Drucker Foundation's Award-Winning Journal. Ed. by Frances Hesselbein & Paul M. Cohen. LC 98-51224. 416p. 1999. text 27.00 (*0-7879-4726-1*) Jossey-Bass.

Leader to Leader: Enduring Lessons on Leadership from the Drucker Foundation's Award-Winning Journal. Ed. by Frances Hesselbein & Paul Cohen. 400p. 1999. 27.00 (*0-7879-4668-0*) Jossey-Bass.

Leader Within: An Empowering Path of Self-Discovery. Howard G. Haas & Robert A. Tamarkin. LC 91-58504. 256p. 1993. 20.00 (*0-88730-561-X*, HarpBusn) HarpInfo.

***Leader Within You: Master 9 Powers to Be the Leader You Always Wanted to Be.** Robert J. Danzig. 192p. 2000. pap. 14.95 (*0-88391-021-7*) F Fell Pubs Inc.

Leader/Activity Guide: A Companion to How to Teach Nutrition to Kids. Connie L. Evers. (Illus.). 64p. 1998. pap., teacher ed. 11.95 (*0-9647970-6-2*) TwentyFour Carrot Pr.

Leaders. Cecilia Fannon. LC 91-11570. (Women Today Ser.). 64p. (J). (gr. 5-7). 1991. 12.95 (*0-685-59201-4*); lib. bdg. 17.95 (*0-86593-118-6*) Rourke Corp.

Leaders. Richard M. Nixon. 1994. lib. bdg. 24.95 (*1-56849-497-1*) Buccaneer Bks.

***Leaders: A Gallery of Biblical Portraits.** Steve Stephens. (Storyteller Ser.). (Illus.). 272p. 2000. pap. 9.99 (*1-57748-679-X*) Barbour Pub.

Leaders: People Who Make a Difference. Gare Thompson. (You Are There Ser.). (Illus.). (J). 1997. lib. bdg. 24.00 (*0-516-20704-0*) Childrens.

Leaders: People Who Make a Difference. Gare Thompson. (You Are There Ser.). (J). (gr. 2-5). 1997. pap. 6.95 (*0-516-26056-1*) Childrens.

Leaders: Strategies for Taking Charge. 2nd ed. Warren G. Bennis & Burt Nana. LC 96-47290. 235p. 1997. pap. 14.00 (*0-88730-839-2*, HarpBusn) HarpInfo.

Leaders: The Strategies for Taking Charge. Warren G. Bennis & Burt Nanus. LC 85-48323. 256p. 1986. reprint ed. pap. 13.00 (*0-06-091336-3*, PL1336, Perennial) HarperTrade.

An Asterisk (*) at the beginning of an entry indicates that the title is appearing for the first time.

Leaders & Followers: A Psychiatric Perspective on Religious Cults Group For The Advancement Of Psychiatry. LC 91-20979. (Reports). ix, 70 p. 1992. write for info. (*0-87318-200-6*) Grp Adv Psych.

Leaders & Followers Vol. 4: Challenges for the Future. Ed. by Trudy Heller et al. LC 86-15369. (Contemporary Studies in Applied Behavioral Science: Vol. 4). 279p. 1988. 73.25 (*0-89232-495-3*) Jai Pr.

***Leaders & Generals (WWII)** William W. Lace. LC 99-33487. (American War Library). (Illus.). 144p. (YA). (gr. 6-9). 2000. lib. bdg. 23.70 (*1-56006-664-4*) Lucent Bks.

Leaders & Lawyers. Irene M. Franck & David M. Brownstone. LC 85-27531. (Work Throughout History Ser.). 200p. 1986. reprint ed. pap. 62.00 (*0-608-02823-1*, 206389000007) Bks Demand.

Leaders & Leadership: An Appraisal of Theory & Research. Mostafa Rejai & Kay Phillips. LC 96-53942. 144p. 1997. 49.95 (*0-275-95880-9*, Praeger Pubs) Greenwood.

Leaders & Leadership in Canada. Ed. by Maureen Mancuso et al. 288p. 1994. pap. text 32.00 (*0-19-540922-1*) OUP.

Leaders & Leadership in Japan. Ed. by Ian Neary. (Japan Library). 224p. (C). 1996. text 45.00 (*1-873410-41-7*, Pub. by Curzon Pr Ltd) UH Pr.

Leaders & Leadership in the School, College & University. Ed. by Peter Ribbins. LC 97-224026. (Management & Leadership in Education Ser.). (Illus.). 240p. 1997. 89.95 (*0-304-33887-7*); pap. 35.00 (*0-304-33888-5*) Continuum.

Leaders & Leading Men of the Indian Territory. H. F. O'Beirne. Ed. by Joe R. Goss & Phillip A. Sperry. (Illus.). 326p. 1994. reprint ed. 49.95 (*1-56869-054-1*) Oldbuck Pr.

Leaders & Masses in the Roman World: Studies in Honor of Zvi Yavetz. Ed. by Zvi Yavetz et al. LC 94-37033. (Mnemosyne, Bibliotheca Classica Batava Ser.: Vol. 139). 1994. 77.50 (*90-04-09917-4*) Brill Academic Pubs.

Leaders & Movements. Hayward Farrar. LC 95-10290. (African American Life Ser.). 48p. (J). (gr. 4-6). 1995. lib. bdg. 23.93 (*1-57103-030-1*) Rourke Pr.

Leaders & Periods of American Finance. Theodore J. Grayson. LC 68-29211. (Essay Index Reprint Ser.). 1977. 39.95 (*0-8369-1240-3*) Ayer.

***Leaders & the Leadership Process: Readings, Self-assesments & Applications.** 2nd ed. Jon L. Pierce & John W. Newstrom. LC 99-34640. 400p. 1999. pap. 53.44 (*0-07-231122-3*) McGraw.

Leaders & the Leadership Process: Readings, Self-Assessments, & Applications. Jon L. Pierce & John W. Newstrom. LC 94-16990. 331p. (C). 1994. text 56.25 (*0-256-16311-1*, Irwn McGrw-H) McGrw-H Hghr Educ.

***Leaders Are Lovers.** Neil Eskelin. 2000. pap. 9.99 (*0-8007-5742-4*) Revell.

Leaders Are Made: A Building Block Approach to Effective Leadership. John Bucciarelli. LC 97-71735. (Illus.). 432p. (C). 1997. 43.00 (*1-878398-17-2*) Blue Note Pubns.

Leader's Change Handbook: An Essential Guide to Setting Direction & Taking Action. Ed. by Jay A. Conger et al. LC 98-40101. (Business & Management Ser.). 442p. 1998. 28.00 (*0-7879-4351-7*) Jossey-Bass.

Leader's Companion: Insights on Leadership Through the Ages. Ed. by J. Thomas Wren. LC 95-2850. 376p. 1995. pap. 16.95 (*0-02-874091-2*) Free Pr.

Leader's Edge: How to Use Communication to Grow Your Business & Yourself. Sandy Linver. 176p. 1994. 19.50 (*0-671-88179-5*) S&S Trade.

Leader's Edge: 5 Skills of Breakthrough Thinking. Guy Hale. 204p. 1995. text 24.95 (*0-7863-0426-X*, Irwn Prfssnl) McGraw-Hill Prof.

Leader's Evangelization Training Guide: Be an Evangelizer? Me? Angeline Bukowiecki. (Evangelizer's Handbook, Evangelistic Series Sisters of the New Convenant). 304p. (C). 1986. text 100.00 (*0-924333-00-6*) Sisters New Covenant.

Leader's Evangelization Training Guide: Evangelii Nuntiandi Weekend. Angeline Bukowiecki & Brigid Meierotto. (Evangelizer's Handbook, Evangelistic Series Sisters of the New Convenant). 77p. (Orig.). (C). 1987. pap. text 25.00 (*0-924333-02-2*) Sisters New Covenant.

Leader's Evangelization Training Guide: Evangelization Outreach. Angeline Bukowiecki & Brigid Meierotto. (Evangelizer's Handbook, Evangelistic Series Sisters of the New Convenant). 48p. (C). 1987. pap. text 10.00 (*0-685-37396-7*) Sisters New Covenant.

Leader's Evangelization Training Guide: Evangelization Outreach. rev. ed. Angeline Bukowiecki & Brigid Meierotto. (Evangelizer's Handbook, Evangelistic Series Sisters of the New Convenant). 64p. (C). 1987. pap. text 10.00 (*0-924333-09-X*) Sisters New Covenant.

Leader's Evangelization Training Guide: Evangelized Anew Weekend. Angeline Bukowiecki & Brigid Meierotto. (Evangelizer's Handbook, Evangelistic Series Sisters of the New Convenant). 73p. (Orig.). (C). 1987. pap. text 25.00 (*0-924333-03-0*) Sisters New Covenant.

Leader's Evangelization Training Guide: Pastoral Leader's Weekend. Angeline Bukowiecki & Brigid Meierotto. (Evangelizer's Handbook, Evangelistic Series Sisters of the New Convenant). 52p. (Orig.). (C). 1987. pap. text 25.00 (*0-924333-05-7*) Sisters New Covenant.

Leader's Evangelization Training Guide: Scripture Handbook. Angeline Bukowiecki & Brigid Meierotto. (Evangelizer's Handbook, Evangelistic Series Sisters of the New Convenant). 173p. (Orig.). (C). 1987. pap. text 35.00 (*0-924333-07-3*) Sisters New Covenant.

Leader's Evanglization Training Guide: Evangelized Anew Weekend. Angeline Bukowiecki & Brigid Meierotto. (Evangelizer's Handbook, Evangelistic Series Sisters of the New Convenant). 73p. (Orig.). (C). 1987. pap. text 25.00 (*0-317-92541-5*) Sisters New Covenant.

Leaders, Fools, & Imposters: Essays on the Psychology of Leadership. Manfred F. Kets de Vries. LC 93-17061. (Management Ser.). 248p. 1993. text 30.95 (*1-55542-562-3*) Jossey-Bass.

Leaders for a New Era: Strategies for Higher Education. Ed. by Madeleine F. Green. LC 96-8913. (ACE-Oryx Series on Higher Education). 272p. (C). 1988. pap. 27.95 (*1-57356-039-1*) Oryx Pr.

Leaders for America's Schools: Perspectives on Educational Administration. Ed. by Daniel E. Griffiths et al. LC 88-60449. 486p. 1988. 43.00 (*0-8211-0616-3*) McCutchan.

Leaders from the 1960s: A Biographical Sourcebook of American Activism. Ed. by David DeLeon. LC 93-31603. 632p. 1994. 75.00 (*0-313-27414-2*, Greenwood Pr) Greenwood.

Leader's Guide. 57p. 1976. write for info. (*0-318-59900-7*) Am Gas Assn.

***Leader's Guide.** Group Publishing Staff. (Homebuilders Couples Ser.). 2000. teacher ed. 6.99 (*0-7644-2249-9*) Group Pub.

Leader's Guide. Navigator Staff. (Design for Discipleship Ser.). 80p. (Orig.). 1980. pap. 5.00 (*0-89109-043-6*) NavPress.

Leader's Guide. rev. ed. Churches Alive Staff. (God in You Ser.). (Illus.). 151p. (Orig.). 1994. pap. 7.00 (*0-89109-098-3*, Diciple Jour) NavPress.

***Leader's Guide: Light for the Journey: A Fresh Focus on Doctrine.** Thelma McDowell. 169p. 1999. pap., teacher ed. 14.95 (*0-911866-47-7*) LifeSprings Res.

Leader's Guide: The Complete Weight Loss Workbook: Proven Techniques for Controlling Weight-Related Health Problems Judith Wylie-Rosett & C. J. Segal-Isaacson. LC 99-26585. 1999. write for info. (*1-58040-025-6*) Am Diabetes.

Leader's Guide: The Recovery Workbook. LeRoy Spaniol et al. 25p. 1994. pap. text, wbk. ed. 4.95 (*1-878512-03-X*) Boston Univ Ctr Psy Rehab.

Leader's Guide: Using the Business Skills Express Series in Career College & School Contract Training Program. Carla Tishler. 64p. 1993. text 10.00 (*0-7863-0226-7*, Irwn Prfssnl) McGraw-Hill Prof.

Leader's Guide: 15 Essential Skills. Randall D. Ponder. LC 98-18539. (Illus.). 221p. 1998. pap. 19.95 (*1-55571-434-X*, LG15P) PSI Resch.

Leaders Guide & Casebook for Simplified S. L. P. Richard Muther. (Supporting Simplified Systematic Layout Planning Ser.). (Illus.). 130p. (C). 1994. ring bd. 236.00 (*0-933684-10-X*) Mgmt & Indus Res Pubns.

***Leader's Guide for Churches: Your Blended Family's Road Map.** Susan D. Archer. (Illus.). 48p. 2000. pap. 12.95 (*0-9668670-2-5*) Together Pubg.

Leader's Guide for Jay E. Adams's Christian Living in the Home: A Teaching Manual for Use in Adult Study Groups. Dorothy P. Anderson. (Orig.). 1977. pap. 3.95 (*0-934688-05-2*) Great Comm Pubns.

Leader's Guide for John W. Sanderson's "The Fruit of the Spirit" A Teaching Manual for Use in Adult Study Groups. Allen D. Curry. (Orig.). 1978. pap. 3.95 (*0-934688-07-9*) Great Comm Pubns.

Leader's Guide for Leadership for Life. Ed. by Joan Weber. 40p. (Orig.). 1997. pap. 19.95 (*1-890516-02-3*) Ctr Minist Dev.

Leader's Guide for T. Norton Sterrett's "How to Understand Your Bible" A Teaching Manual for Use in Adult Study Groups. Joseph A. Pipa. (Orig.). 1977. pap. 3.95 (*0-934688-06-0*) Great Comm Pubns.

Leader's Guide of "Uprooted" Refugees & Forced Migrants. Elizabeth G. Ferris. 32p. 1998. pap., teacher ed. 6.95 (*0-377-00320-4*) Friendship Pr.

Leader's Guide to a Workbook on Biblical Stewardship. Richard E. Rusbuldt. 1994. pap., teacher ed. 6.00 (*0-8028-0830-1*) Eerdmans.

Leader's Guide to Being Your Best: Character Building for Kids 7-10. Barbara A. Lewis. LC 99-46768. 128p. (J). (gr. 2-5). 1999. pap., teacher ed. 18.95 (*1-57542-064-3*) Free Spirit Pub.

Leader's Guide to Change Management: Creating & Sustaining a Dynamic Organization. Lawrence M. Miller & Helene F. Uhlfelder. 160p. 1997. pap. 16.95 (*0-9629679-7-1*) Miller Howard Cnslt.

Leader's Guide to Environmental Liability Management. Thomas M. Missimer. LC 95-53806. 240p. 1996. lib. bdg. 59.95 (*0-87371-994-8*, L994) Lewis Pubs.

Leader's Guide to Europe Study. John O. Gooch. 32p. (Orig.). 1995. teacher ed. 4.95 (*0-377-00291-7*) Friendship Pr.

Leader's Guide to Fighting Invisible Tigers: 12 Sessions on Stress Management & Lifeskills Development. rev. ed. Connie C. Schmitz & Earl Hipp. 136p. 1995. pap., teacher ed. 19.95 (*0-915793-81-4*) Free Spirit Pub.

Leaders Guide to I Like Being Me: Poems for Children about Feeling Special, Appreciating Others & Getting Along. Judy Lalli & Mary M. Whitworth. (Illus.). 80p. 1997. pap. text, teacher ed. 14.95 (*1-57542-026-0*) Free Spirit Pub.

Leader's Guide to I'm Like You, You're Like Me: A Child's Book about Understanding & Celebrating Each Other. Cindy Gainer. (Illus.). 80p. 1998. pap., teacher ed. 16.95 (*1-57542-040-6*) Free Spirit Pub.

Leader's Guide to "Indonesia in Shadow & Light" Karen Campbell-Nelson. (Illus.). 48p. 1998. pap., teacher ed. 6.95 (*0-377-00322-0*) Friendship Pr.

Leader's Guide to Just Because I Am: A Child's Book of Affirmation. Lauren M. Payne. Ed. by Pamela Espeland. (Illus.). 56p. 1994. pap., teacher ed. 13.95 (*0-915793-61-X*) Free Spirit Pub.

Leader's Guide to Keller's Office Safety Handbook. J. J. Keller & Assoc., Inc. Staff. 124p. 1997. spiral bd. 79.00 (*1-57943-392-8*, 5-PSG) J J Keller.

Leader's Guide to Mentor Training. Ed. by Judith W. Little & Linda Nelson. LC 89-80829. viii, 323p. (Orig.). 1990. ring bd. 20.00 (*0-86552-099-2*) U of Oreg ERIC.

Leader's Guide to Safety Committees. LC 96-79889. 220p. 1997. spiral bd. 89.00 (*1-877798-74-6*, 2-PSG) J J Keller.

Leader's Guide to School Restructuring: A Special Report of the NASSP Commission on Restructuring. Ed. by James W. Keefe & J. M. Jenkins. 80p. (Orig.). (C). 1992. pap. 12.00 (*0-88210-257-5*) Natl Assn Principals.

***Leader's Guide to "Stone Soup for the World" Life Changing Stories of Kindness & Courageous Acts of Service.** Marianne Larned. (Illus.). 186p. 1999. pap. text 15.00 (*0-9700364-0-X*) Stone Soup.

Leader's Guide to the Relaxation & Stress Reduction Workbook. 4th rev. ed. Martha Davis. 104p. 1995. pap. 20.95 (*1-57224-036-9*) New Harbinger.

***Leader's Guide to The Struggle to Be Strong: How to Foster Resilience in Teens.** Al Desetta et al. 176p. 2000. pap. 21.95 (*1-57542-080-5*) Free Spirit Pub.

***Leader's Guide to the Study of the Jewish Moral Virtues.** Carol K. Ingall & Eugene B. Borowitz. LC 99-59637. 2000. 7.95 (*0-8276-0696-6*) JPS Phila.

Leader's Guide to We Can Get Along: A Child's Book of Choices. Lauren M. Payne & Claudia Rohling. Ed. by Pamela Espeland. (Illus.). 64p. (Orig.). 1997. pap. 14.95 (*1-57542-014-7*) Free Spirit Pub.

Leader's Guide to What Young Children Need to Succeed: Working Together to Build Assets from Birth to Age 11. Jolene L. Roehlkepartain & Nancy Leffert. 96p. 2000. pap. 14.95 (*1-57542-071-6*) Free Spirit Pub.

***Leader's Handbook.** Jacqueline Barber. (Illus.). (J). 2000. pap. 13.50 (*0-924886-52-8*, GEMS) Lawrence Science.

Leader's Handbook: Making Things Happen, Getting Things Done. Peter Scholtes. LC 97-51902. 415p. 1998. spiral bd. 29.95 (*0-07-058028-6*) McGraw.

Leaders Helping Leaders: A Practical Guide to Administrative Mentoring. John C. Daresh & Marsha A. Playko. LC 93-22401. 1995. 22.95 (*0-590-49219-5*, 17314D7 1993, Scholastic Ref) Scholastic Inc.

***Leader's Imperative: Ethics, Integrity & Responsibility.** Ed. by J. Carl Ficarrotta. LC 00-8224. 340p. 2000. 24.95 (*1-55753-184-6*) Purdue U Pr.

Leaders in American Geography. Ed. by Thomas F. Barton & P. P. Saran. (Illus.). 1993. text 40.00 (*81-85218-73-0*, Pub. by Prestige) Advent Bks Div.

***Leaders in American Geography: Geographic Research, Vol. 2.** P. P. Karan & Cotton Mather. (Illus.). 272p. 2000. 29.95 (*0-9643841-1-6*) NMex Geograp.

Leaders in Education: Their Views on Controversial Issues. Ed. by Glenda F. Roberson & Mary A. Johnson. LC 88-19918. (Illus.). 228p. (Orig.). (C). 1988. pap. text 22.50 (*0-8191-7123-9*) U Pr of Amer.

Leaders in Homoeopathic Therapeutics. E. B. Nash. 1981. 8.95 (*0-685-76565-2*) Formur Intl.

Leaders in Israel: Thumb-Nail Sketches of the Officers of the First Provisional Government. Ed. by Sarah K. Stein. LC 71-179743. (Biography Index Reprint Ser.). 1977. reprint ed. 15.95 (*0-8369-8111-1*) Ayer.

Leaders in Libraries: Styles & Strategies for Success. Brooke E. Sheldon. LC 91-8678. 93p. (C). 1991. pap. text 22.00 (*0-8389-0563-3*, 0563-3) ALA.

Leaders in Medicine see Women in Profile Series

Leaders in Norway, & Other Essays. Agnes M. Wergeland. Ed. by K. Merrill. LC 67-22127. (Essay Index Reprint Ser.). 1977. 19.95 (*0-8369-0981-X*) Ayer.

***Leaders in the Crucible: The Moral Voice of College Presidents.** Stephen James Nelson. LC 00-20485. 250p. 2000. 61.00 (*0-89789-742-0*, H742, Bergin & Garvey) Greenwood.

Leaders in the Making. Phil Stevenson. (Discipleship Ser.). 110p. (Orig.). 1993. pap. 2.75 (*0-89827-123-1*, BKO86) Wesleyan Pub Hse.

Leaders in the Making: A Workbook for Discovering & Developing Church Leaders. Paul N. Benware & Brian Harris. wbk. ed. 12.99 (*0-8024-4928-X*, 201) Moody.

Leaders in the Study of Animal Behavior. Ed. by Donald A. Dewsbury. LC 83-46153. (Illus.). 512p. 1985. 65.00 (*0-8387-5052-4*) Bucknell U Pr.

Leader's Journey to Quality. Dana M. Cound. (Quality & Reliability Ser.: Vol. 31). (Illus.). 208p. 1991. text 65.00 (*0-8247-8574-6*) Dekker.

Leaders Manual: A Structural Guide & Introduction to Kingian Nonviolence (The Philosophy & Methodology) Bernard La Fayette, Jr. & David C. Jehnsen. LC 96-169176. 155p. 1995. pap. text 40.00 (*1-888615-00-1*) Inst Human Rghts.

***Leader's Motivation.** Bob Gordon. (Master Builders Ser.). 1999. pap. text 10.99 (*1-85240-262-8*) SOV5.

Leaders of American Conservation. Ed. by Henry Clepper. LC 75-155206. 365p. reprint ed. 113.20 (*0-8357-9921-2*, 201242900081) Bks Demand.

Leaders of American Impressionism: Mary Cassatt, Childe Hassam, John H. Twachtman & J. Alden Weit. (Brooklyn Museum Publications in Reprint). 12.95 (*0-405-18863-3*, 19595) Ayer.

Leaders of American Impressionism: Mary Cassatt, Childe Hassam, John H. Twachtman & J. Alden Weit. LC 75-128385. (Brooklyn Museum Publications in Reprint). (Illus.). 70p. reprint ed. 6.50 (*0-405-00876-7*) Ayer.

***Leaders of Ancient Greece.** Don Nardo et al. LC 99-18176. (History Makers Ser.). (Illus.). 128p. (YA). (gr. 4-12). 1999. lib. bdg. 23.70 (*1-56006-543-5*) Lucent Bks.

***Leaders of Black Civil Rights.** Marjorie Vernell. LC 99-39569. (History Makers Ser.). (Illus.). 144p. (YA). (gr. 6-9). 2000. lib. bdg. 23.70 (*1-56006-670-9*) Lucent Bks.

Leaders of Freedom. Sister M. Clarita. (Land of Our Lady Ser.: Vol. III). (Illus.). 288p. (YA). (gr. 6-7). 1997. reprint ed. 25.00 (*0-911845-55-0*) Neumann Pr.

Leaders of Leaders Int'l. Mike Phillipps & Marilyn Phillipps. 100p. (Orig.). 1994. pap. text. write for info. (*1-884794-11-4*) Eden Pubng.

Leader's of Leader's USA. Mike Phillipps & Marilyn Phillipps. 100p. 1994. pap. text. write for info. (*1-884794-10-6*) Eden Pubng.

Leaders of Modern India. Sankar Ghose. 454p. 1980. 32.95 (*0-940500-31-0*) Asia Bk Corp.

Leaders of of the North & South. Bill Sell. LC 95-52869. (Civil War Chronicles Ser.: Vol. 2). 128p. 1996. 15.98 (*1-56799-292-7*, MetroBooks) M Friedman Pub Grp Inc.

Leaders of Russia & the Soviet Union Since 1613. John Trayner. 375p. 1999. lib. bdg. 55.00 (*1-57958-132-3*) Fitzroy Dearborn.

Leaders of Socialism: Past & Present. George R. Taylor. LC 68-24857. (Essay Index Reprint Ser.). 1977. 18.95 (*0-8369-0928-3*) Ayer.

Leaders of the Americas Bk. I: Short Biographics & Dialogues. William Pickett. 192p. 1994. pap. text 22.33 (*0-13-102484-1*) P-H.

Leaders of the Civil War: A Biographical & Historiographical Dictionary. Ed. by Charles F. Ritter et al. LC 98-12156. 504p. 1998. lib. bdg. 85.00 (*0-313-29560-3*, Greenwood Pr) Greenwood.

***Leaders of the North & South (Civil War)** Diane Yancey. LC 99-46314. (American War Library). (Illus.). 144p. (YA). (gr. 6-9). 2000. lib. bdg. 23.70 (*1-56006-497-8*) Lucent Bks.

Leaders of the People. Miriam Rinn. LC 98-205440. 64 p. 1999. 8.95 (*0-8167-4929-9*, Troll Medallion) Troll Communs.

Leaders of Thought in the Modern Church. Reuen Thomas. LC 72-8559. (Essay Index Reprint Ser.). 1977. reprint ed. 20.95 (*0-8369-7333-X*) Ayer.

***Leaders of Transition.** Martin Westlake. LC 99-45012. 2000. text 65.00 (*0-312-22867-8*) St Martin.

Leaders of Women's Suffrage. Liza N. Burby. (History Makers Ser.). (Illus.). (YA). (gr. 4-12). 1998. lib. bdg. 22.45 (*1-56006-367-X*) Lucent Bks.

Leaders of World War II. Mike Taylor. LC 97-48570. (World War II Leaders Ser.). (J). 1998. 14.95 (*1-56239-803-2*) ABDO Pub Co.

Leaders on Leadership. Harvard Business Review Staff. 300p. 1992. 34.95 (*0-07-103318-1*) McGraw.

Leaders on Leadership: Interviews with Top Executives. Pref. by Warren G. Bennis. LC 91-40754. (Harvard Business Review Book Ser.). 288p. 1992. 29.95 (*0-87584-307-7*) Harvard Busn.

Leaders on Leadership: The College Presidency. Ed. by James L. Fisher & Martha W. Tack. LC 85-644752. (New Directions for Higher Education Ser.: No. HE 61). 1988. pap. 22.00 (*1-55542-918-1*) Jossey-Bass.

Leaders on Leadership: Wisdom, Advice & Encouragement on the Art of Leading God's People. George Barna. LC 96-52238. 318p. 1997. 14.99 (*0-8307-1862-1*, Regal Bks) Gospel Lght.

***Leaders on Leading: Insights from the Field.** Frwd. by Larry E. Senn. LC 99-91340. 208p. 2000. pap. 14.95 (*0-9648466-6-7*, Pub. by Leadrship Pr) Gulf Pub.

Leader's Reference Material. 593p. 1976. pap. write for info. (*0-318-62028-6*) Am Gas Assn.

Leader's Resource. Navigators Staff. (Life & Ministry of Jesus Christ Ser.). 200p. (Orig.). 1996. pap. 14.00 (*0-89109-972-7*) NavPress.

Leader's Shadow: Exploring & Developing Executive Character William Q. Judge. LC 98-40294. 1999. 29.95 (*0-7619-1539-7*) Sage.

Leader's Shadow Exploring & Developing Executive Character. William Q. Judge. LC 98-40294. 1999. 62.00 (*0-7619-1538-9*) Sage.

***Leader's Vision.** Bob Gordon. (Master Builders Ser.). 1999. pap. 10.99 (*1-85240-263-6*) SOV5.

Leaders Who Changed the Twentieth Century. Jodine Mayberry. LC 92-19032. (Twenty Events Ser.). (Illus.). 48p. (J). (gr. 5-7). 1993. lib. bdg. 24.26 (*0-8114-4926-2*) Raintree Steck-V.

***Leaders Who Make a Difference: Essential Strategies for Meeting the Nonprofit Challenge.** Burt Nanus & Stephen M. Dobbs. LC 99-6757. 304p. 1999. 26.00 (*0-7879-4665-6*) Jossey-Bass.

Leader's Window: Mastering the Four Styles of Leadership to Build High-Perfoming Teams. John D. W. Beck & Neil M. Yeager. 242p. 1994. 90.00 (*0-471-58525-4*); pap. 19.95 (*0-471-02554-2*) Wiley.

***Leader's Window: Mastering the Four Styles of Leadership to Build High-Performing Teams.** John D. Beck & Neil M. Yeager. (Illus.). 242p. 1999. text 30.00 (*0-7881-5982-8*) DIANE Pub.

Leaders with Vision: The Quest for School Renewal. Robert J. Starratt. LC 95-22650. (Illus.). 144p. 1995. 49.95 (*0-8039-6259-2*); pap. 21.95 (*0-8039-6260-6*) Corwin Pr.

Leadershift. Doug Murren. 1994. pap. 16.30 (*0-8307-1691-2*, Regal Bks) Gospel Lght.

Leadership see African Americans: Voices of Triumph

Leadership. (Illus.). 256p. 1994. lib. bdg. write for info. (*0-7835-2255-X*) Time-Life.

Leadership. Bob Avakian. Incl. Anarchism. 1982. 2.25 (*0-89851-068-6*); Bob Avakian Speaks on the Mao Defendants' Railroad & the Historic Battles Ahead. 69p. 1981. 1.50 (*0-89851-047-3*); Communists Are Rebels. 1980. 0.50 If There Is to be Revolution, There Must be a Revolutionary Party. 74p. 1982. 2.00 (*0-89851-056-2*); Important Struggles in Building the RCP. 55p. 1978.

An Asterisk (*) at the beginning of an entry indicates that the title is appearing for the first time.

L

1.00 (*0-89851-018-X*); New Constitution of the RCP, U. S. A. 1981. 0.75 (*0-89851-064-3*); Summing Up the Black Panther Party. 1980. 0.60 (*0-89851-042-2*); 5.00 (*0-89851-059-7*) RCP Pubns.

Leadership. James M. Burns. LC 76-5117. 544p. 1982. pap. 18.00 (*0-06-131975-9*, TB 1975, Torch) HarpC.

Leadership. Daft. LC 98-71914. (C). 1998. text 71.00 (*0-03-022417-9*) Harcourt Coll Pubs.

Leadership. Dubrin. LC 94-76500. (C). 1994. pap. text 54.76 (*0-395-65634-6*) HM.

Leadership. Ginn Press. 1998. pap. text 50.00 (*0-536-02016-7*) Pearson Custom.

Leadership. Portnoy. LC 98-27295. 220p. (C). 1998. pap. text 38.40 (*0-13-921495-X*) P-H.

Leadership. Philip Sadler. 1997. pap. text 19.95 (*0-7494-2124-X*) Kogan Page Ltd.

***Leadership.** Townsend. 254p. 1999. pap. 16.95 (*0-471-32728-X*) Wiley.

Leadership. Cao Van Vien. 201p. 1989. reprint ed. pap. 22.50 (*0-923135-08-1*) Dalley Bk Service.

Leadership. Ed. by A. Dale Timpe. LC 86-24167. (Art & Science of Business Management Ser.: No. 3). (Illus.). 380p. 1987. reprint ed. pap. 117.80 (*0-7837-9918-7*, 206064500006) Bks Demand.

Leadership. 2nd ed. (Complete Idiot's Guide Ser.). 352p. 1900. 18.95 (*0-02-863954-5*) Macmillan Gen Ref.

Leadership, 2 vols. 2nd ed. Dubrin. LC 97-72462. (C). 1997. pap. text 54.76 (*0-395-85664-7*) HM.

Leadership, Vol. 1. Torkom Saraydarian. LC 92-82864. 479p. 1995. 30.00 (*0-929874-24-2*); pap. 25.00 (*0-929874-25-0*) TSG Pub Found.

Leadership, Vol. 2. Torkom Saraydarian. LC 92-82864. 325p. 1996. text 25.00 (*0-929874-50-1*); pap. text 20.00 (*0-929874-51-X*) TSG Pub Found.

Leadership, Vol. 3. Torkom Saraydarian. LC 92-82864. 400p. 1995. 25.00 (*0-929874-55-2*); pap. 20.00 (*0-929874-56-0*) TSG Pub Found.

Leadership, Vol. 4. Torkom Saraydarian. LC 92-82864. 424p. 1997. 30.00 (*0-929874-63-3*); pap. 25.00 (*0-929874-64-1*) TSG Pub Found.

Leadership, Vol. V. Torkom Saraydarian. LC 92-82864. 400p. 1998. 30.00 (*0-929874-65-X*); pap. 25.00 (*0-929874-66-8*) TSG Pub Found.

***Leadership: A Communication Perspective.** Michael Z. Hackman & Craig E. Johnson. 426p. 2000. pap. 24.95 (*1-57766-069-2*) Waveland Pr.

Leadership: A Communication Perspective. 2nd rev. ed. Michael Z. Hackman & Craig E. Johnson. LC 97-205480. (Illus.). 401p. (C). 1996. pap. text 21.95 (*0-88133-886-9*) Waveland Pr.

Leadership: A Compliance Guide to the JACHO Standards. Richard O. Schmidt & Mary Becker. (Illus.). 136p. (Orig.). 1997. pap. text 67.00 (*1-57839-003-6*) Opus Communs.

***Leadership: A Comprehensive Guide to Understanding & Development.** Spencer Campbell. 250p. 2000. pap. 11.95 (*1-885003-56-0*, Pub. by R D Reed Pubs) Midpt Trade.

Leadership: A New Synthesis. James G. Hunt. (Illus.). 357p. 1991. text 52.00 (*0-8039-3767-9*); pap. text 25.00 (*0-8039-3768-7*) Sage.

Leadership: A Relevant & Realistic Role for Principals. Gary M. Crow et al. LC 96-13802. (School Leadership Library). (Illus.). 160p. 1996. 29.95 (*1-883001-24-2*) Eye On Educ.

Leadership: A Skills Training Program, Ages 8-18. Lois F. Roets. 112p. 1997. pap. 20.00 (*0-911943-52-8*) Leadership Pub.

Leadership: A Special Type of Giftedness. Dorothy Sisk & Milda Rosselli. 106p. 1987. pap. 14.99 (*0-89824-197-9*, 1979) Word Aflame.

***Leadership: A Treasury of Great Quotation for Those Who Aspire to Lead.** William Safire. 256p. 2000. 7.99 (*1-57866-104-8*) Galahad Bks.

Leadership: An Exploration. Kevin S. Price. LC 93-85063. 132p. (Orig.). (C). 1993. pap. text 9.95 (*0-9637452-0-4*) Proactive Pubs.

Leadership: ASTD Trainer's Sourcebook. Anne F. Coyle. LC 96-78874. 210p. 1996. pap. 39.95 (*0-07-053439-X*) McGraw.

Leadership: Challenges for Today's Manager. William E. Rosenbach & Robert L. Taylor. 220p. 1989. 29.95 (*0-89397-317-3*) Nichols Pub.

Leadership: Classical, Contemporary & Critical Approaches. Ed. by Keith Grint. (Oxford Management Readers Ser.). (Illus.). 402p. 1997. text 89.00 (*0-19-878182-2*); pap. text 21.00 (*0-19-878181-4*) OUP.

Leadership: Communication Skills for Organizations & Groups. J. Kevin Barge. 304p. 1994. pap. text 24.95 (*0-312-08117-0*) St Martin.

Leadership: Development for Church Growth. Neil B. Wiseman. 144p. 1979. pap. 8.99 (*0-8341-0550-0*) Nazarene.

Leadership: Effective Spiritual Keys for Today's Leaders, 12 pts. Tom Marshall & Tom Muccio. 96p. 1993. audio 40.00 (*0-935779-16-7*); VHS 150.00 (*0-935779-17-5*) Crown Min.

Leadership: Effective Spiritual Keys for Today's Leaders, 12 pts., Set. Tom Marshall & Tom Muccio. 96p. 1993. student ed. 10.00 (*0-935779-15-9*) Crown Min.

Leadership: Enhancing the Lessons of Experience. 2nd ed. Richard L. Hughes et al. 640p. (C). 1995. text 51.95 (*0-256-16212-3*, Irwn McGrw-H) McGrw-H Hghr Educ.

Leadership: Enhancing the Lessons of Experience. 3rd ed. Richard L. Hughes et al. LC 98-36084. 696p. (C). 1998. 71.88 (*0-256-26143-1*) McGraw.

Leadership: Interdisciplinary Reflections. Ed. by R. S. Khare & David Little. LC 84-7222. 146p. (Orig.). 1984. lib. bdg. 41.50 (*0-8191-3969-6*) U Pr of Amer.

***Leadership: Lessons from Bill Snyder.** Robert J. Shoop et al. LC 98-223558. 1999. write for info. (*0-89745-981-4*) Sunflower U Pr.

Leadership: Making Things Happen. Dorothy A. Sisk & Doris J. Shallcross. 139p. (Orig.). 1986. pap. 14.95 (*0-943456-16-9*) Bearly Ltd.

Leadership: Managing in Real Organizations. 2nd ed. Leonard R. Sayles. (C). 1989. text 38.74 (*0-07-055017-4*) McGraw.

Leadership: Multidisciplinary Perspectives. Barbara Kellerman. (Illus.). 320p. (C). 1983. pap. text 41.20 (*0-13-527671-3*) P-H.

Leadership: Passing the Torch, Studies From 1st & 2nd Timothy. Serendipity House Staff. (201 Deeper Bible Study Ser.). 1998. pap. 4.95 (*1-57494-077-5*) Serendipty Hse.

Leadership: Personal Dev & Career Success. Cliff Ricketts. (Agriculture Ser.). 96p. 1996. text, teacher ed. 12.75 (*0-8273-6754-6*) Delmar.

Leadership: Personal Development & Career Success. Cliff Ricketts. LC 95-16642. 576p. 1995. mass mkt. 46.95 (*0-8273-6753-8*) Delmar.

Leadership: Quotations from History's Greatest Motivators. Ed. by Robert A. Fitton. 1997. pap. 18.00 (*0-614-28127-X*) Westview.

Leadership: Quotations from the World's Greatest Motivators. Robert A. Fitton. 352p. (C). 1997. pap. text 30.00 (*0-8133-3288-5*, Pub. by Westview) HarpC.

Leadership: Reflective Human Action. Frances E. Andrews et al. 168p. 1995. ring bd. 75.00 (*1-929083-03-3*) Kappa Omi Nu.

Leadership: Selected Chapters. Richard Hughes et al. (C). 1994. text 25.95 (*0-256-17385-0*, Irwn McGrw-H) McGrw-H Hghr Educ.

Leadership: Strategies for Organizational Effectiveness. James J. Cribbin. LC 81-12722. 304p. reprint ed. pap. 94.30 (*0-7837-4241-X*, 204393000012) Bks Demand.

Leadership: Sustaining Action on Community & Organizational Issues. Janet Ayres et al. Ed. by Julie Stewart. 250p. 1993. student ed., ring bd. 20.00 (*0-936913-08-8*, RRD 164) NCRCRD.

Leadership: The Dynamics of Success. Cyril J. Barber & Gary H. Strauss. 126p. 1982. pap. 4.95 (*0-87921-068-0*) Attic Pr.

Leadership: The Inner Side of Greatness. Peter Koestenbaum. LC 90-50858. (Management Ser.). 389p. 1991. 38.95 (*1-55542-218-7*) Jossey-Bass.

Leadership: The Journey Inward. Delorese Ambrose. 128p. 1995. pap. text, per. 17.95 (*0-7872-0973-2*) Kendall-Hunt.

Leadership: The Key to Professionalization of Nursing. 3rd ed. Bernhard & Michelle Walsh. LC 94-241837. (Illus.). 223p. (C). (gr. 13). 1994. pap. text 35.00 (*0-8151-0526-6*, 24347) Mosby Inc.

***Leadership: The Minister's Responsibility.** Lemuel M. Boyles. 256p. 1999. pap. 10.00 (*1-882449-33-9*, 090112) Messenger Pub.

Leadership: The Multiple-Level Approaches. Fred Dansereau & Francis J. Yammarino. LC 98-11695. (Monographs in Organizational Behavior & Industrial Relations Ser.: Vol. 24A). 1998. 78.50 (*0-7623-0503-7*) Jai Pr.

Leadership: The Multiple-Level Approaches. Fred Dansereau & Francis J. Yammarino. LC 98-11695. (Monographs in Organizational Behavior & Industrial Relations Ser.: Vol. 24B). 1998. 78.50 (*0-7623-0504-5*) Jai Pr.

Leadership: The Multiple Levels Approaches, 2 pts., Set. Fred Danserau & F. Yammarino. (Monographs in Organizational Behavior: Vol. 24). 1998. 157.00 (*0-7623-0469-3*) Jai Pr.

Leadership: Theory & Application. United States Naval Academy. 566p. 1999. pap. text 50.00 (*0-536-01938-X*) Pearson Custom.

***Leadership: Theory & Application.** 2nd ed. 462p. (C). 2000. 50.00 (*0-536-60279-4*) Pearson Custom.

Leadership: Theory & Practice. Peter G. Northouse. LC 96-45796. 274p. 1997. 48.00 (*0-8039-5768-8*) Sage.

Leadership: Theory & Practice. Peter G. Northouse. 256p. (C). 1997. 48.00 (*0-614-25349-7*, 57689); pap. 22.95 (*0-8039-5769-6*, 57696) Sage.

***Leadership: Theory, Application & Skill Developement.** Achua Lussier. 2000. pap. 62.95 (*0-324-04166-7*) Thomson Learn.

Leadership: Understanding the Dynamics of Power & Influence in Organizations. Ed. by Robert P. Vecchio. LC 97-20806. 577p. (C). 1997. pap. 25.00 (*0-268-01316-0*) U of Notre Dame Pr.

Leadership: 10 Steps Every Manager Needs to Know. 3rd ed. Elwood N. Chapman & Sharon Lund O'Neil. LC 99-14824. (Illus.). 180p. (C). 1999. pap. text 28.60 (*0-13-010019-6*) P-H.

Leadership Level Three. Clawson. LC 98-33824. 231p. (C). 1998. pap. text 37.80 (*0-13-010878-2*) P-H.

Leadership . . . Biblically Speaking: The Power of Principle-Based Leadership. David Cottrell. Ed. by Sue Coffman. (Illus.). ix, 210p. 1998. 17.95 (*0-9658788-1-3*) CornerStone Leader.

Leadership - Magic, Myth, or Method? J. W. McLean & William Weitzel. LC 91-34595. 240p. 1992. 22.95 (*0-8144-5054-7*) AMACOM.

Leadership A to Z: A Guide for the Appropriately Ambitious. James O'Toole. LC 99-6416. 352p. 1999. text 22.00 (*0-7879-4658-3*) Jossey-Bass.

Leadership Abroad Begins at Home: U. S. Foreign Economic Policy after the Cold War. Robert L. Paarlberg. (Integrating National Economies Ser.). 144p. (C). 1995. 34.95 (*0-8157-6804-4*); pap. 14.95 (*0-8157-6803-6*) Brookings.

Leadership Aikido: 6 Business Practices that Can Turn Your Life Around. John O'Neil. LC 97-13489. 1997. 25.00 (*0-517-70575-3*) Random.

Leadership Aikido: 6 Business Practices That Can Turn Your Life Around. John O'Neil. 256p. 1999. pap. 14.00 (*0-609-80221-6*) Harmony Bks.

Leadership Alternative: The Ultimate Management Handbook 9-Steps to High Impact Leadership. Jeffrey L. Magee. 1996. pap. text 19.95 (*0-9641240-2-5*) J Magee Intl.

Leadership among Friends. Ron McDonald. 1995. pap. 4.00 (*0-87574-320-X*) Pendle Hill.

***Leadership, an Islamic Perspective.** Rafik I. Beekun & Jamal A. Badawi. LC 99-42025. 1999. write for info. (*0-915957-94-9*) amana pubns.

Leadership & Academic Librarians. Ed. by Terrence F. Mech & Gerard B. McCabe. LC 97-53106. (Greenwood Library Management Collection). 288p. 1998. lib. bdg. 65.00 (*0-313-30271-5*, Greenwood Pr) Greenwood.

Leadership & Administration of Outdoor Pursuits. 2nd ed. Phyllis M. Ford & James Blanchard. LC 92-63339. (Illus.). 429p. (C). 1993. boxed set 33.95 (*0-910251-60-6*) Venture Pub PA.

Leadership & Ambiguity. 2nd ed. Michael D. Cohen & James G. March. 1986. text 27.50 (*0-07-103223-1*) McGraw.

Leadership & Change: Presidential Elections from 1952 to 1976. Warren E. Miller & Teresa E. Levitin. (Illus.). 320p. 1984. reprint ed. pap. text 26.00 (*0-8191-3850-9*) U Pr of Amer.

Leadership & Change in the Western Pacific: Essays Presented to Sir Raymond Firth on the Occasion of His 90th Birthday. Ed. by Richard Feinberg & Karen A. Watson-Gegeo. (Monographs in Social Anthropology). 480p. (C). 1996. 90.00 (*0-485-19566-6*, Pub. by Athlone Pr) Humanities.

Leadership & Church Administration see Liderazgode la Mujer en la Iglesia

Leadership & Command: Aspects of the Anglo-American Military Experience since 1861-1991. Ed. by G. D. Sheffield. LC 96-29792. 1997. 32.95 (*1-85753-117-5*, Pub. by Brasseys) Brasseys.

Leadership & Command in the American Civil War, Vol. 1. Ed. by Steven E. Woodworth. (Campaign Chronicles Ser.). (Illus.). 248p. 1995. 24.95 (*1-882810-00-7*, 107) Savas Pub.

Leadership & Command on the Battlefield: Operations "Just Cause" & "Desert Storm" 55p. (Orig.). (C). 1993. pap. text 30.00 (*0-7881-0143-9*) DIANE Pub.

Leadership & Command on the Battlfield. 1998. lib. bdg. 250.99 (*0-8490-7803-2*) Gordon Pr.

Leadership & Community in Late Ancient Gaul. Raymond Van Dam. (Transformation of the Classical Heritage Ser.: Vol. VIII). (C). 1992. pap. 17.95 (*0-520-07895-0*, Pub. by U CA Pr) Cal Prin Full Svc.

Leadership & Conflict. Speed B. Leas. (Creative Leadership Ser.). 128p. (Orig.). 1982. pap. 12.95 (*0-687-21264-2*) Abingdon.

Leadership & Culture in Indonesian Politics. R. William Liddle. 320p. 1997. pap. 34.95 (*1-86448-196-X*, Pub. by Allen & Unwin Pty) Paul & Co Pubs.

Leadership & Curriculum in the Primary School: The Roles of Senior & Middle Management. Christopher Day et al. LC 93-10937. 1993. write for info. (*1-85396-214-7*) Chapman & Hall.

Leadership & Democracy: The History of the National Union of Public Employees, Vol. 2, 1928-1993. Robert Fryer & Stephen Williams. 256p. (C). 1996. pap. 29.95 (*0-85315-648-4*, Pub. by Lawrence & Wishart) NYU Pr.

Leadership & Development in Arab Society. Ed. by Fuad I. Khuri. 260p. 1982. text 25.95 (*0-8156-6060-X*, Pub. by Am U Beirut) Syracuse U Pr.

Leadership & Diversification: Expanding the Role of Materials Management; 1987 Annual Conference Proceedings. 100p. 1987. 30.00 (*0-318-35034-3*, 142813) AHRMM.

Leadership & Entrepreneurship: Personal & Organizational Development in Entrepreneurial Ventures. Ed. by Raymond W. Smilor & Donald L. Sexton. LC 95-41385. (Entrepreneurship, Principles & Practices Ser.). 200p. 1996. 42.95 (*1-56720-043-5*, Quorum Bks) Greenwood.

Leadership & Futuring: Making Visions Happen. John R. Hoyle. LC 95-14648. (Road Maps to Success Ser.). (Illus.). 80p. 1995. pap. 14.95 (*0-8039-6300-9*) Corwin Pr.

***Leadership & Human Behavior.** United States Naval & Johnson. 376p. 1999. pap. text 39.00 (*0-536-02546-0*) Pearson Custom.

Leadership & Immensity. G. Fredric Bolling. 200p. 1996. 56.95 (*0-566-07763-9*, Pub. by Gower) Ashgate Pub Co.

Leadership & Information Processing: Linking Perceptions & Performance. Robert G. Lord & Karen J. Maher. LC 93-13076. (People & Organizations Ser.). 352p. (C). 1994. reprint ed. pap. 29.99 (*0-415-09901-3*, B2571) Routledge.

Leadership & Innovation: A Biographical Perspective on Entrepreneurs in Government. Ed. by Jameson W. Doig & Erwin C. Hargrove. LC 87-4155. 480p. 1987. text 55.00 (*0-8018-3442-2*) Johns Hopkins.

Leadership & Innovation: Entrepreneurs in Government. Ed. by Jameson W. Doig & Erwin C. Hargrove. LC 89-24685. 300p. reprint ed. pap. 93.00 (*0-608-08805-6*, 206944400004) Bks Demand.

***Leadership & Lifestyle: The Portrait of Paul in the Miletus Speech & 1 Thessalonians.** Steve Walton. (Society for New Testament Studies Monograph Ser.: Vol. 108). 264p. (C). 2000. text Price not set. (*0-521-78006-3*) Cambridge U Pr.

***Leadership & Management.** (C). 2000. 44.00 (*0-536-60804-0*) Pearson Custom.

Leadership & Management in Academic Medicine. Marjorie P. Wilson & Curtis P. McLaughlin. LC 84-48000. (Jossey-Bass Higher Education Ser.). 416p. reprint ed. pap. 129.00 (*0-8357-4962-2*, 203789500009) Bks Demand.

Leadership & Management in Nursing: A New Legacy. (Professional Reference - Nursing Ser.). (C). 2001. pap. 34.95 (*0-8273-7957-9*) Delmar.

Leadership & Management in Universities: Britain & Nigeria. Titus Oshagbemi. (Studies in Organization: No. 14). xx, 249p. (C). 1989. lib. bdg. 64.95 (*3-11-011514-X*) De Gruyter.

***Leadership & Management of Programs for Young Children.** 2nd ed. Cynthia Shoemaker. LC 98-51563. (Illus.). 553p. 2000. 48.00 (*0-13-012940-2*) P-H.

Leadership & Management of Religious Organizations: An Annotated Bibliography. Paul L. Golden. Ed. by Jane E. Gerard. 146p. (Orig.). 1989. pap. 20.00 (*0-9622747-0-4*) De Paul ILRO.

Leadership & Management of Volunteer Programs: A Guide for Volunteer Administrators. James C. Fisher & Kathleen M. Cole. (Nonprofit Sector-Public Administration Ser.). 228p. 1993. text 27.95 (*1-55542-531-3*) Jossey-Bass.

***Leadership & Management Programs for Young Children.** 2nd ed. 1999. text, teacher ed. write for info. (*0-13-013973-4*) P-H.

Leadership & Mangement in Nursing. 2nd ed. Mary Ellen Grohar-Murray & Helen R. Dicroce. LC 96-31743. 312p. (C). 1996. pap. text 34.95 (*0-8385-5646-9*, A5646-3) Appleton & Lange.

Leadership & Negotiation in the Middle East. Ed. by Barbara Kellerman & Jeffrey Z. Rubin. LC 88-10337. 309p. 1988. 59.95 (*0-275-92489-0*, C2489, Praeger Pubs) Greenwood.

Leadership & Nursing Care Management. Ed. by Diane Huber. (Illus.). 683p. 1996. pap., teacher ed. write for info. (*0-7216-6514-4*, W B Saunders Co) Harcrt Hlth Sci Grp.

Leadership & Nursing Care Management. Diane G. Huber. Ed. by Thomas Eoyang. (Illus.). 688p. 1995. pap. text 35.00 (*0-7216-4428-7*, W B Saunders Co) Harcrt Hlth Sci Grp.

Leadership & Nursing Care Management. 2nd ed. Diane Huber. LC 99-54402. (Illus.). 670p. 2000. pap. text. write for info. (*0-7216-7699-5*, W B Saunders Co) Harcrt Hlth Sci Grp.

Leadership & Nursing Care Management. 2nd ed. Diane G. Huber. 1996. pap. text, student ed. 14.95 (*0-7216-6819-4*, W B Saunders Co) Harcrt Hlth Sci Grp.

Leadership & Organization Pt. 2: The Technical. Ed. by John Brion. LC 95-16384. 1996. 86.25 (*1-55938-936-2*) Jai Pr.

Leadership & Organization Pt. 3: Integration. Ed. by John Brion. LC 95-16384. 1996. 86.25 (*1-55938-937-0*) Jai Pr.

***Leadership & Organizational Change: A Special Issue of the European Journal of Work & Organization Psychology.** Ed. by Sandra Schruijer & Leopold Vansina. 160p. 1999. pap. 39.95 (*0-86377-995-6*) L Erlbaum Assocs.

Leadership & Organizational Culture. Peter B. Smith & Mark F. Peterson. 224p. (C). 1988. text 49.95 (*0-8039-8083-3*); pap. text 22.00 (*0-8039-8084-1*) Sage.

Leadership & Organizational Culture: New Perspectives on Administrative Theory & Practice. Ed. by Thomas J. Sergiovanni & John E. Corbally. LC 83-1338. 352p. 1984. pap. text 14.95 (*0-252-01347-6*) U of Ill Pr.

Leadership & Organizations Pt. 1: The Social. Ed. by John M. Brion. LC 95-16384. 1996. 86.25 (*1-55938-935-4*) Jai Pr.

Leadership & Pedagogy. W. John Smyth. 105p. (C). 1986. 48.00 (*0-7300-0416-3*, Pub. by Deakin Univ) St Mut.

Leadership & Performance Beyond Expectations. Bernard M. Bass. LC 84-24724. 224p. 1985. 32.95 (*0-02-901810-2*) Free Pr.

Leadership & Politics: New Perspectives in Political Science. Ed. by Bryan D. Jones. LC 89-33621. (Studies in Government & Public Policy). viii, 304p. 1989. 35.00 (*0-7006-0407-3*); pap. 17.95 (*0-7006-0408-1*) U Pr of KS.

Leadership & Professional Development in Schools: How to Promote Techniques for Effective Professional Learning. John West-Burnham & Fergus O'Sullivan. (School Leadership & Management Ser.). (Illus.). 206p. 1998. pap. 42.50 (*0-273-62409-1*, Pub. by Pitman Pbg) Trans-Atl Phila.

Leadership & Reform: The Secretary-General & the UN Financial Crisis of the Late 1980s. Tapio Kanninen. 1995. lib. bdg. 130.00 (*90-411-0102-0*) Kluwer Academic.

***Leadership & Self-Deception: Getting Out of the Box.** Arbinger Institute Staff. LC 99-86442. 175p. 2000. 22.00 (*1-57675-094-9*, Pub. by Berrett-Koehler) Publishers Group.

Leadership & Shared Vision. Chris Maser. LC 98-216818. (Sustainable Community Development Ser.). 272p. 1998. per. 39.95 (*1-57444-188-4*) St Lucie Pr.

Leadership & Social Cleavages: Political Processes among the Indians in Fiji. L. S. Chauhan. (C). 1988. 26.00 (*81-7033-047-5*, Pub. by Rawat Pubns) S Asia.

***Leadership & Spirit: Breathing New Vitality & Energy into Individuals & Organizations.** Russ S. Moxley. LC 99-6656. 256p. 1999. 30.95 (*0-7879-0949-1*) Jossey-Bass.

Leadership & Succession in the Soviet Union, Eastern Europe & China. Ed. by Martin McCauley & Stephen Carter. LC 85-2370. 270p. (Orig.). (gr. 13). 1986. pap. text 31.95 (*0-87332-347-5*) M E Sharpe.

Leadership & Supervision in Special Services: Promising Ideas & Practices. Ed. by Leonard C. Burrello & David E. Greenburg. LC 87-35266. (Special Services in the Schools Ser.: Vol. 4, Nos. 1 & 2). (Illus.). 136p. 1988. text 39.95 (*0-86656-725-9*) Haworth Pr.

An Asterisk (*) at the beginning of an entry indicates that the title is appearing for the first time.

*Leadership & Team Building: Transforming Congregational Ministry Through Teams. Roger Heuser. 318p. 1999. pap. 12.95 (*1-880562-39-1*) Christ Minist.

Leadership & Teams Education Management. E. Crawford et al. LC 96-42218. (Leadership & Management in Education Ser.). 1997. 108.00 (*0-335-19842-2*); pap. 32.95 (*0-335-19841-4*) OpUniv Pr.

Leadership & Technology: What School Board Members Need to Know. Gerald D. Bailey et al. Ed. by Anne Ward. 194p. (Orig.). 1995. pap. 35.00 (*0-88364-196-8*, 03-135) Natl Sch Boards.

Leadership & the Art of Conversation. Kim H. Krisco. LC 97-15326. (Illus.). 224p. 1997. per. 14.00 (*0-7615-1030-3*) Prima Pub.

Leadership & the Bush Presidency: Prudence or Drift in an Era of Change? Ed. by Ryan J. Barilleaux & Mary E. Stuckey. LC 92-12107. (Praeger Series in Presidential Studies). 256p. 1992. 55.00 (*0-275-94418-2*, C4418, Praeger Pubs) Greenwood.

Leadership & the Computer: Top Executives Reveal How They Personally Use Computers to Communicate, Coach, Convince & Compete. Mary E. Boone. LC 90-49111. (Illus.). 416p. 1991. 24.95 (*1-55958-080-1*) Prima Pub.

Leadership & the Computer: Top Executives Reveal How They Personally Use Computers to Communicate, Coach Convince & Compete. Mary E. Boone. 397p. 1993. 14.95 (*1-892606-08-9*) NDMA Pubng.

Leadership & the Culture of Trust. Gilbert W. Fairholm. LC 93-42804. 256p. 1994. 59.95 (*0-275-94833-1*, Praeger Pubs) Greenwood.

Leadership & the Customer Revolution: The Messy, Unpredictable & Inexplicably Human Challenge of Making the Rhetoric of Change a Reality. Gary M. Heil et al. 290p. 1994. text 26.95 (*0-442-01852-5*, VNR) Wiley.

Leadership & the Customer Revolution: The Messy, Unpredictable & Ones Capably Human Challenge of Making the Rhetoric of Change a Reality. Gary Heil et al. 320p. 1994. 26.95 (*0-471-28631-1*, VNR) Wiley.

Leadership & the Job of the Executive. Jeffrey A. Barach & D. Reed Eckhardt. LC 96-590. 280p. 1996. 59.95 (*0-89930-991-7*, Quorum Bks) Greenwood.

Leadership & the New Science: Discovering Order in a Chaotic World. 2nd rev. ed. Margaret J. Wheatley. LC 99-16514. 200p. 1999. 24.95 (*1-57675-055-8*) Berrett-Koehler.

Leadership & the New Science: Learning about Organization from an Orderly Universe. Margaret J. Wheatley. LC 92-70095. (Illus.). 184p. 1992. 24.95 (*1-881052-01-X*) Berrett-Koehler.

Leadership & the New Science: Learning about Organization from an Orderly Universe. Margaret J. Wheatley. LC 92-70095. (Illus.). 166p. 1994. pap. 15.95 (*1-881052-44-3*) Berrett-Koehler.

Leadership & the One Minute Manager: Increasing Effectiveness Through Situational Leadership. Kenneth Blanchard et al. 112p. 1999. reprint ed. pap. 10.00 (*0-688-16355-6*, Quil) HarperTrade.

Leadership & the One Minute Manager: Increasing Effectiveness Through Situational Leadership. Kenneth Blanchard et al. Ed. by Pat Golbitz. LC 84-62389. (One Minute Manager Ser.). (Illus.). 112p. 1999. 20.00 (*0-688-03969-3*, Wm Morrow) Morrow Avon.

Leadership & the Quest for Integrity. Joseph L. Bacaracco, Jr. & Richard R. Ellsworth. 1989. text 24.95 (*0-07-103207-X*) McGraw.

Leadership & the Quest for Integrity. Joseph L. Badaracco, Jr. & Richard R. Ellsworth. 240p. 1993. pap. 17.50 (*0-87584-408-1*) Harvard Busn.

Leadership & the Quest for Integrity. Harvard Business Review Staff. 240p. 1993. pap. 19.95 (*0-07-103395-5*) McGraw.

Leadership & Urban Regeneration: Cities in North America & Europe. Ed. by Dennis Judd. (Urban Affairs Annual Review Ser.: Vol. 37). 312p. (C). 1990. text 62.00 (*0-8039-3980-9*); pap. text 26.00 (*0-8039-3981-7*) Sage.

Leadership & Urban Regeneration: Cities in North America & Europe. Ed. by Dennis Judd & Michael Parkinson. LC 90-43946. (Urban Affairs Annual Reviews Ser.: No. 37). 311p. 1990. reprint ed. pap. 96.50 (*0-608-04315-X*, 206509400012) Bks Demand.

Leadership & Values: The Organization of Large-Scale Taiwanese Enterprises. Robert H. Silin. (East Asian Monographs: No. 62). 224p. 1976. 30.00 (*0-674-51857-8*) HUP.

Leadership As Legacy: Transformation at the Turn of the Millenium: Proceedings of the 12th Scientific Meeting of the A. K. Rice Institute. Ed. by Leigh S. Estabrook. LC 97-65289. 262p. (Orig.). 1997. pap. text 30.00 (*0-614-29820-2*) Rice Inst.

Leadership, Authority & Powersharing. Henry C. Lindgren. LC 81-18644. 186p. (Orig.). 1982. lib. bdg. 16.50 (*0-89874-251-X*) Krieger.

Leadership Behavior. Ed. by Joseph P. Cangemi et al. LC 97-40212. 196p. (C). 1997. text 49.00 (*0-7618-0940-6*) U Pr of Amer.

Leadership Behavior. Joseph P. Cangemi et al. LC 97-40212. 1997. pap. write for info. (*0-7618-0941-4*) U Pr of Amer.

Leadership Below the Surface Vol. I: If You Are Going to Lead, Lead with Open, Honest Communication & Passion. Russell Helwig. 110p. 1997. per. 14.95 (*0-9660917-0-1*) Ldrship Below.

Business consultants today agree "Old ways of management must change if companies are going to progress." LEADERSHIP BELOW THE SURFACE covers the never before talked about areas that most leaders avoid. It will touch your heart, your spirit & your mind. It is the message for the year 2000. If you are going to lead your market, it is a must read book. Here is what they have said about our book, & our presentations: "Every team, whether in sports or in business, needs good leaders. A must read book. Russ has created some thoughts that will have employees loving their jobs."--Eddie Johnson - 17 year NBA veteran - 6th man Award - Television Announcer. "Your presentation was truly inspiring. You made a HUGE impact on our leaders & employees. Thank you for helping to build our future Intel leaders."--Dale Ham - Intel Corporation, Leadership & Organizational Development. "We have achieved a great deal of positive interaction & problem resolution after reading & discussing your excellent book."--Tom Longust - CEO Longust Distributing. "Russ explores ways to intensify the relationship between leaders & employees. What he shares comes from years of hard work & discipline."--Bob Wade - Former President, Continental Homes. "You brought some great ideas to our television audience. The work place is changing. Your message inspired many viewers."--Jane Werneken - Channel 11 Cox Television, "Let's Get Acquainted With Our Community". "Russ is a managers manager...a true leader, & one of our readers favorites."--Linda Forsythe - Editor in Chief, Thriving Business Strategies Magazine. "Your message is so POWERFUL, it is needed in all areas of life. From the corporate world all the way to the White House."--Bishop David Eddings, Sr. - Pastor First Pentecostal Church. E-Mail Address: lead below@aol.com. www.bookwire.com - Publishing Spotlight. Phone: 623-334-1641. FAX: 623-334-6740.
Publisher Paid Annotation.

*Leadership Bible. Leadership Press Staff. 2000. pap. 18.74 (*0-310-91244-X*) Zondervan.

Leadership Book. rev. ed. Charles J. Keating. LC 77-99300. 144p. 1995. pap. 7.95 (*0-8091-2504-8*) Paulist Pr.

Leadership By Design. Harvard Business Review Staff. 342p. 1998. 27.50 (*0-07-103722-5*) McGraw.

Leadership by Design. Albert A. Vicere & Robert M. Fulmer. LC 97-36910. 352p. 1998. 27.50 (*0-87584-831-1*) Harvard Busn.

Leadership by Design: The Governing Ideals of Effective Leadership. E. Grady Bogue. (Higher & Adult Education Ser.). 185p. 1994. text 30.95 (*0-7879-0034-6*) Jossey-Bass.

Leadership by Encouragement. Don Dinkmeyer-Eckste. 208p. (C). 1993. pap. text 25.95 (*0-8403-8396-7*) Kendall-Hunt.

***Leadership by Encouragement.** S. Dinkmeyer. 1998. pap. 98.00 (*81-86982-02-7*, Pub. by Business Pubns) St Mut.

Leadership by Encouragement. Daniel G. Eckstein & Don Dinkmeyer. 264p. 1995. per. 39.95 (*1-57444-008-X*) St Lucie Pr.

***Leadership by the Book: Tools to Transform Your Workplace.** Kenneth Blanchard et al. 240p. 1999. 20.00 (*1-57856-308-9*); audio 12.00 (*1-57856-313-5*) Waterbrook Pr.

***Leadership By the Book: Walking Your Faith in the Marketplace.** Kenneth Blanchard et al. LC 99-38109. (Illus.). 208p. 1999. 20.00 (*0-688-17239-3*, Wm Morrow) Morrow Avon.

***Leadership Cartoon Treasury, Vol. 3.** Contrib. by Christianity Today Staff. (Illus.). 160p. 1999. pap. 8.99 (*0-8054-1294-8*) Broadman.

***Leadership Cartoon Treasury, Vol. 4.** Contrib. by Christianity Today Staff. (Illus.). 160p. 1999. pap. 8.99 (*0-8054-1295-6*) Broadman.

Leadership Challenge: How to Keep Getting Extraordinary Things Done in Organizations. 2nd rev. ed. James M. Kouzes & Barry Z. Posner. (Management Ser.). 430p. 1995. 28.50 (*0-7879-0110-5*) Jossey-Bass.

Leadership Challenge: How to Keep Getting Things Done in an Organization. 2nd rev. ed. James M. Kouzes & Barry Z. Posner. LC 95-11314. (Illus.). 406p. 1996. mass mkt. 20.00 (*0-7879-0269-1*) Jossey-Bass.

Leadership Challenge of Economic Reforms in Africa. Ed. by Olusegun Obasanjo & Hans D'Orville. 112p. 1991. 65.00 (*0-8448-1680-9*, Crane Russak) Taylor & Francis.

Leadership Challenge Planner: An Action Guide to Achieving Your Personal Best. James M. Kouzes & Barry Z. Posner. 112p. 1999. pap. 12.00 (*0-7879-4568-4*) Jossey-Bass.

Leadership Change in Communist States. Ed. by Raymond C. Taras. 224p. 1989. text 44.95 (*0-04-445277-2*) Routledge.

Leadership Communication. Ernest L. Stech. 216p. 1983. pap. text 25.95 (*0-8304-1305-7*) Burnham Inc.

Leadership Compass: Values & Ethics in Higher Education. John R. Wilcox & Susan L. Ebbs. Ed. by Jonathan D. Fife. LC 92-85441. (ASHE-ERIC Higher Education Reports: No. 92-1). 110p. 1992. 24.00 (*1-878380-14-1*) GWU Grad Schl E&HD.

Leadership, Conflict, & Cooperation in Afro-American Social Thought. John B. Childs. 224p. 1993. pap. 19.95 (*1-56639-085-0*) Temple U Pr.

Leadership Continuum: A Biblical Model for Effective Leading. John Westermann. (Illus.). 270p. (Orig.). 1997. pap. text 17.00 (*0-9656046-2-4*) Lghthse Pub TN.

Leadership Core Competencies. Patricia Guggenheimer & Mary D. Szulc. (Fifty-Minute Ser.). (Illus.). 96p. Date not set. pap. 10.95 (*1-56052-497-9*) Crisp Pubns.

Leadership Counts: Lessons for Public Managers from the Massachusetts Welfare, Training, & Employment Program. Robert D. Behn. (Illus.). 264p. 1994. pap. text 21.00 (*0-674-51853-5*, BEHLEX) HUP.

Leadership Counts: Lessons for Public Managers from the Massachusetts Welfare, Training & Employment Program. Robert D. Behn. 272p. (C). 1992. 32.00 (*0-674-51852-7*) HUP.

Leadership Curriculum. Intro. by Gene P. Carlson. (Illus.). 108p. 1987. ring bd. 150.00 (*0-685-59453-X*) IFSTA.

Leadership Development. American Management Association. 112p. 1998. pap. 250.00 (*0-8144-7975-8*) AMACOM.

Leadership Development. Bruce Goldberg. 1996. 12.00 incl. audio (*1-885577-72-9*) B Goldberg.

Leadership Development. 2nd ed. Glen C. Shinn. 352p. 1986. text 45.95 (*0-07-056913-4*) McGraw.

Leadership Development: A Discipleship Model. Thomas M. Graham. 74p. 1993. pap. text 24.95 (*1-882757-01-7*) Ctr Organ & Minist.

Leadership Development: Building Executive Talent. Robert Fulmer et al. Ed. by Susan Elliott & Craig Henderson. (Illus.). 101p. 1999. spiral bd. 495.00 (*1-928593-07-0*) Am Prodtv Qual.

Leadership Development: Enhancing the Vital Forces in Organizations Bruce J. Avolio. LC 98-51235. (Advanced Topics in Organizational Behavior Ser.). 1999. write for info. (*0-7619-0603-7*) Sage.

Leadership Development: How to Identify Qualities, Use Planning Tools & Choose Models for Good Leadership. Cook Communications Ministries International Staff. (Interlit Imprint Ser.: Vol. 20). (Illus.). 40p. (Orig.). 1996. pap. 6.00 (*1-884752-29-2*, 44420) Cook Min Intl.

Leadership Development: Maturity & Power. Lee Barr & Norma Barr. LC 93-39943. 504p. 1994. pap. 19.95 (*0-89015-945-9*) Sunbelt Media.

Leadership Development for Females Who Went to Catholic Grade School. Patricia Zander & Eric Hummel. Ed. by Franny Van Nevel. 1998. pap. 14.95 (*1-884731-17-1*) Oriel Inc.

Leadership Development for Public Service. Barry A. Passett. LC 70-149755. 149p. reprint ed. pap. 46.20 (*0-608-18159-5*, 203285500081) Bks Demand.

***Leadership Development Program.** Frances A. Karnes & Jane C. Chauvin. LC 99-40485. 2000. 30.00 (*0-910707-33-2*) Gifted Psych Pr.

Leadership Dilemmas - Grid Solutions: An All-New Presentation of the Managerial Grid. 4th ed. Robert R. Blake & Anne E. McCanse. 376p. 1991. 26.95 (*0-87201-488-6*, 1488) Gulf Pub.

Leadership Education: A Source Book of Courses & Programs. Ed. by Mary K. Schwartz et al. 490p. 1998. pap. text 40.00 (*1-882197-41-0*, 339) Ctr Creat Leader.

Leadership Education: Developing Skills for Youth. John F. Feldhusen & William B. Richardson. 1984. pap. 14.99 (*0-89824-166-9*) Trillium Pr.

***Leadership Effectiveness in Community Policing.** Linda Royster Beito. LC 99-67018. 1999. pap. 6.00 (*1-55605-290-1*) Wyndham Hall.

***Leadership Engine: Building Leaders at Every Level.** Price Pritchett et al. 47p. 1998. pap. 5.95 (*0-944002-25-0*) Pritchett Assocs.

Leadership Engine: How Winning Companies Build Leaders at Every Level. Noel M. Tichy & Eli Cohen. 384p. 2001. pap. 16.00 (*0-88730-931-3*, HarpBusn) HarpInfo.

Leadership Engine: How Winning Companies Build Leaders at Every Level. Noel M. Tichy & Eli B. Cohen. LC 97-17807. 384p. 1997. 27.00 (*0-88730-793-0*, ReganBks) HarperTrade.

***Leadership Engine: How Winning Companies Build Leaders at Every Level.** Noel M. Tichy & Eli Cohen. (Illus.). 367p. 2000. reprint ed. text 26.00 (*0-7881-6886-X*) DIANE Pub.

Leadership Engine: How Winning Companies Build Leaders at Every Level, Set. abr. ed. Noel M. Tichy & Eli Cohen. 1997. audio 18.00 (*0-694-51881-6*, NT02R) HarperAudio.

Leadership Equation. Lee Barr & Norma Barr. Ed. by Edwin M. Eakin. 192p. 1989. pap. 14.95 (*0-89015-684-0*) Sunbelt Media.

Leadership, Equity, & School Effectiveness. Ed. by H. Prentice Baptiste, Jr. et al. LC 89-37459. 279p. 1990. pap. 86.50 (*0-608-05604-9*, 206606200006) Bks Demand.

Leadership Every Day. Alan Weiss. 1995. pap. 6.95 (*1-886158-05-3*) Macalester.

Leadership, Factions & Panchayati Raj. Krishna Chakrabortty & Swapan K. Bhattacharyya. (C). 1993. 22.00 (*81-7033-192-7*, Pub. by Rawat Pubns) S Asia.

Leadership Factor. John P. Kotter. 190p. 1988. 32.95 (*0-02-918331-6*) Free Pr.

Leadership for a Changing Church: Charting the Shape of the River. Robert D. Dale. LC 97-40921. 128p. 1998. pap. 14.95 (*0-687-01485-9*) Abingdon.

Leadership for a Culturally Diverse Society. Frances E. Andrews et al. 131p. 1993. ring bd. 35.00 (*1-929083-00-9*) Kappa Omi Nu.

Leadership for a New Century: A Blueprint for a More Participatory Democracy. Marta L. Tellado & Norman Allen. (Illus.). 42p. 1998. pap. text. write for info. (*1-891464-12-4*) J M Burns Academy.

Leadership for Africa: In Honor of Olusegun Obasanjo on His 60th Birthday. Ed. by Hans D'Orville. LC 96-170461. 350p. (Orig.). (C). 1995. 25.00 (*1-885060-03-3*) H dOrville.

***Leadership for Ages 4-8: Identification & Talent Development.** 2nd rev. ed. Lois F. Roets. 2000. teacher ed. 22.00 (*0-911943-70-6*) Leadership Pub.

Leadership for Agricultural Industry. Robert Stewart. Ed. by Max L. Amberson. (Career Preparation for Agriculture-Agribusiness Ser.). (Illus.). (J). (gr. 9-10). 1978. text 17.96 (*0-07-000847-7*) McGraw.

L

***Leadership for America: The Principles of Conservatism.** Ed. by Edwin J. Feulner, Jr. LC 99-55568. (Illus.). xxvi, 318p. 2000. 29.95 (*1-890626-22-8*) Spence Pub.

Leadership for an Age of Higher Consciousness: Administration from a Metaphysical Perspective. Swami Krishnapada. LC 95-81994. 320p. 1998. reprint ed. pap. 14.95 (*1-885414-05-6*) Hari-Nama Pr.

Leadership for an Age of Higher Consciousness: Administration from a Metaphysical Perspective. Swami Krishnapada. LC 95-81994. 320p. (C). 1998. reprint ed. 23.00 (*1-885414-02-1*) Hari-Nama Pr.

Leadership for Change. Charles W. Joiner, Jr. LC 86-25940. 216p. 1987. pap. 28.00 (*0-88730-107-X*, HarpBusn) HarpInfo.

Leadership for Change: An Action Guide for Nurses. 2nd ed. Dorothy A. Brooten et al. LC 64-5153. 192p. 1988. text 19.95 (*0-397-54597-5*, Lippnctt) Lppncott W & W.

Leadership for Change: Human Resource Development in the Federal Government. (Illus.). 52p. 1996. reprint ed. pap. text 30.00 (*0-7881-2628-8*) DIANE Pub.

Leadership for Collaborative Schools. Berry & Stickel. 140p. (C). 1997. per. 23.95 (*0-7872-3941-0*, 41394101) Kendall-Hunt.

***Leadership for Competitive Advantage.** Nick Georgiades & Richard Macdonell. LC 97-31196. 244p. 1998. 67.50 (*0-471-97928-7*) Wiley.

***Leadership for Constructivist Schools.** Arthur Shapiro. 160p. 2000. pap. text 27.95 (*0-8108-3758-7*) Scarecrow.

***Leadership for Constructivist Schools.** Arthur Shapiro. 175p. 2000. 45.00 (*0-8108-3798-6*); pap. 27.95 (*0-8108-3799-4*) Scarecrow.

Leadership for Continuing Development. Ed. by James W. Dodge. (Reports of the Northeast Conference on the Teaching of Foreign Languages). 150p. 1971. pap. 10.95 (*0-685-51936-8*) NE Conf Teach Foreign.

Leadership for Continuous School Improvement. 2nd rev. ed. John H. Hansen & Elaine Liftin. LC 98-61899. 286p. 1999. pap. text 39.95 (*0-9628917-3-8*) Watersun MA.

***Leadership for Dummies.** Marshall Loeb & Stephen Kindel. (For Dummies (Lifestyles) Ser.). 1999. audio 12.00 (*0-694-52221-X*) HarperAudio.

Leadership for Dummies. Marshall Loeb & Stephen Kindel. (For Dummies Ser.). 384p. 1999. pap. 19.99 (*0-7645-5176-0*, Dummies Trade Pr) IDG Bks.

Leadership for Dynamic State Economics. (CED Statement on National Policy Ser.). 104p. 1986. pap. 9.50 (*0-87186-082-1*); lib. bdg. 11.50 (*0-87186-782-6*) Comm Econ Dev.

Leadership for Educational Renewal: Developing a Cadre of Leaders. Ed. by Wilma F. Smith & Gary D. Fenstermacher. LC 98-51242. (Agenda for Education in a Democracy Ser.). 1999. pap. 29.95 (*0-7879-4558-7*) Jossey-Bass.

Leadership for Learning in Music Education. Joseph W. Landon. LC 75-305303. (Contemporary Music Education Ser.). 306p. (Orig.). 1975. reprint ed. pap. 12.95 (*0-943988-02-0*) Music Educ Pubns.

Leadership for Life. Ed. by Joan Weber. 120p. (Orig.). 1997. pap. 12.95 (*1-890516-01-5*) Ctr Minist Dev.

***Leadership for Older Adults: Aging with Purpose & Passion.** Sandra A. Cusack & Wendy J. Thompson. LC 98-28100. 207p. 1998. pap. 29.95 (*0-87630-931-7*) Brunner-Mazel.

Leadership for Primary Health Care: Levels, Functions & Requirements Based on Twelve Case Studies. D. M. Flahault & M. I. Roemer. (Public Health Papers: No. 82). 79p. 1986. pap. text 8.00 (*92-4-130082-5*, 1110082) World Health.

Leadership for Quality: Strategies for Action. Frances Clark. LC 95-37231. 1995. pap. write for info. (*0-07-707828-4*) McGraw.

Leadership for Research Libraries. Ed. by Anne Woodsworth & Barbara Von Wahlde. LC 88-6634. (Illus.). 271p. 1988. 28.00 (*0-8108-2129-X*) Scarecrow.

Leadership for Rural Schools: Lessons for All Educators. Donald M. Chalker. LC 98-87453. xvi, 308p. 1998. 39.95 (*1-56676-695-8*) Scarecrow.

***Leadership for Safe Schools: A Community-Based Approach.** Raymond L. Calabrese. LC 00-44546. 2000. write for info. (*0-8108-3898-2*) Scarecrow.

Leadership for Special Education Administration. Mark B. Goor. LC 94-77141. 256p. (Orig.). (C). 1995. pap. text 52.50 (*0-15-501271-1*, Pub. by Harcourt Coll Pubs) Harcourt.

Leadership for Strategic Change. Christopher Ridgeway & Brian Wallace. 240p. 1996. pap. 76.00 (*0-85292-613-8*, Pub. by IPM Hse) St Mut.

***Leadership for Strategic Change.** Wallace & Ridgeway. 224p. 2000. pap. 59.95 (*0-8464-5101-8*) Beekman Pubs.

Leadership for Students: A Practical Guide for Ages 8-18. Frances A. Karnes & Suzanne M. Bean. 189p. (J). (gr. 3-12). 1995. pap. 17.95 (*1-882664-12-4*) Prufrock Pr.

Leadership for the Common Good: Tackling Public Problems in a Shared-Power World. John M. Bryson & Barbara C. Crosby. LC 92-19032. (Public Administration & Nonprofit Sector Ser.). 464p. 1992. 35.95 (*1-55542-480-5*) Jossey-Bass.

L

Leadership for the Emerging Age. Jerold W. Apps. (Higher & Adult Education Ser.). 272p. 1994. text 32.95 (*0-7879-0036-2*) Jossey-Bass.

Leadership for the Future: Changing Directorial Roles in American History Museums & Historical Societies. Ed. by Bryant F. Tolles, Jr. LC 91-490. (American Association for State & Local History Book Ser.). (Illus.). 208p. 1991. reprint ed. pap. 24.95 (*0-942063-11-2*) AltaMira Pr.

***Leadership for the Schoolhouse: How is It Different? Why is It Important?** Thomas J. Sergiovanni. 2000. pap. 21.95 (*0-7879-5542-6*) Jossey-Bass.

Leadership for the 21st Century: Changing Nations Through the Power of Serving. Ron Boehme. 231p. 1989. pap. 9.99 (*0-9615534-8-0*) YWAM Pub.

Leadership for Tomorrow's Schools. Jerry L. Patterson. LC 93-19133. 1993. pap. 14.95 (*0-87120-209-3*) ASCD.

Leadership for Women & Men: Building an Inclusive Organization. Michael Simmons. 250p. 1996. 61.95 (*0-566-07474-5*, Pub. by Gower) Ashgate Pub Co.

Leadership for Women in the Church see Liderazgo de la Mujer en la Iglesia

Leadership for Women in the Church. Susan Hunt & Peggy Hutcheson. 144p. 1991. pap. 10.99 (*0-310-54021-6*) Zondervan.

Leadership for Youth Ministry. Zeni Fox et al. 165p. 1984. pap. 8.95 (*0-88489-157-7*) St Marys.

***Leadership from the Inside Out: Becoming a Leader for Life.** Kevin Cashman. 224p. 1999. pap. 15.95 (*1-890009-31-8*) Exec Excell.

Leadership from the Inside Out: Becoming a Leader for Life. Kevin Cashman. (Illus.). 224p. 1999. 24.95 (*1-890009-29-6*) Exec Excell.

Leadership from Within. Peter U. Bender & Eric Hellman. LC 97-931931. 240p. 1998. pap. 15.95 (*0-7737-5903-4*) Stoddart Publ.

Leadership Frontiers. Ed. by James G. Hunt & Lars L. Larson. LC 75-17489. (Comparative Administration Research Institute Ser.: No. 11). 228p. reprint ed. pap. 70.70 (*0-608-17130-1*, 202730400055) Bks Demand.

Leadership Games: Experiential Learning for Organizational Development. Stephen S. Kaagan. LC 98-25396. 1998. pap. 29.95 (*0-7619-1721-7*) Sage.

Leadership Gene: Character, Management & Leadership. Cyril Levicki. 1998. 52.50 (*0-273-63557-3*, Pub. by Pitman Pub) Trans-Atl Phila.

Leadership Genius of Jesus: Ancient Wisdom for Modern Business. William Beausay, II. LC 97-38372. 128p. 1998. 14.99 (*0-7852-7165-1*) Nelson.

Leadership, Goals & Power in Higher Education: A Contingency & Open-Systems Approach to Effective Management. Barry M. Richman & Richard N. Farmer. LC 74-9112. (Jossey-Bass Higher Education Ser.). 380p. reprint ed. pap. 117.80 (*0-608-12172-X*, 202387800034) Bks Demand.

Leadership Guide for Board Presidents & Committee Chairpersons. Darla Struck. 92.00 (*0-8342-0404-5*, 04045) Aspen Pub.

Leadership Handbook of Management & Administration. Ed. by James D. Berkley. 544p. 1997. pap. 19.99 (*0-8010-9040-7*) Baker Bks.

Leadership Handbook of Outreach & Care. Ed. by James D. Berkley. 528p. 1997. pap. text 19.99 (*0-8010-9042-3*, Leadership Hand) Baker Bks.

Leadership Handbook of Preaching & Worship. Ed. by James D. Berkley. 544p. 1997. pap. text 19.99 (*0-8010-9041-5*, LEADERSHIP HAND) Baker Bks.

Leadership Handbook Series. Ed. by James D. Berkley. 1616p. 1997. pap. 49.95 (*0-8010-9049-0*) Baker Bks.

Leadership Higher Power 2e. 2nd ed. Andrew Marlatt. 1998. 20.50 (*0-07-228208-8*) McGraw.

***Leadership Images from the New Testament.** David W. Bennett. 192p. 1998. reprint ed. mass mkt. 9.99 (*1-85078-309-8*, Pub. by O M Pubng) OM Literature.

Leadership Imperative. Robert Heller. 1999. pap. 13.95 (*0-452-27543-1*, Plume) Dutton Plume.

Leadership in a Challenging World: A Sacred Journey. Barbara Shipka. 176p. 1997. pap. text 17.95 (*0-7506-9750-4*) Buttrwrth-Heinemann.

Leadership in a Changing World. Ed. by M. David Hoffman & Ruth Wanger. LC 68-8471. (Essay Index Reprint Ser.). 1977. 23.95 (*0-8369-0117-7*) Ayer.

Leadership in a Dynamic Society. Frank E. Kuzmits. (Key Issues Lecture Ser.). 1979. write for info. (*0-672-97329-4*); pap. write for info. (*0-672-97330-8*) Macmillan.

Leadership in a Free Society: Human Relations Based on an Analysis of Present-Day Industrial Civilizations. T. N. Whitehead. Ed. by Leon Stein. LC 77-70548. 1977. reprint ed. lib. bdg. 26.95 (*0-405-10215-1*) Ayer.

Leadership in a Successful Parish. Carol M. Holden & Thomas O. Sweetser. LC 92-20718. 224p. 1992. reprint ed. pap. 12.95 (*1-55612-564-X*, LL1564) Sheed & Ward WI.

Leadership in a Transnational World: The Challenge of Keeping the Peace. Paul D. Miller. LC 93-25820. (National Security Papers: No. 12). 1993. write for info. (*0-89549-098-6*) Inst Foreign Policy Anal.

Leadership in Academic Libraries: Proceedings of the W. Porter Kellam Conference, the University of Georgia, May 7, 1991. Ed. by William G. Potter. LC 92-36461. (Journal of Library Administration: Vol. 17, No.4). 91p. 1993. 39.95 (*1-56024-400-3*) Haworth Pr.

Leadership in Administration: A Sociological Interpretation. Philip Selznick. 162p. (C). 1984. reprint ed. pap. 16.95 (*0-520-04994-2*, Pub. by U CA Pr) Cal Prin Full Svc.

Leadership in America: Consensus, Corruption, & Charisma. Ed. by Peter D. Bathory. LC 77-17714. 1978. pap. text 7.95 (*0-582-28039-7*) Longman.

Leadership in Asia: Persuasive Communication in the Making of Nations, 1850-1950. Robert T. Oliver. 1989. 47.50 (*0-87413-353-X*) U Delaware Pr.

Leadership in Committee: A Comparative Analysis of Leadership Behavior in the U. S. Senate. C. Lawrence Evans. 224p. (C). 1991. text 44.50 (*0-472-10237-0*, 10237) U of Mich Pr.

Leadership in Communist China. John W. Lewis. LC 77-25475. (Illus.). 305p. 1978. reprint ed. lib. bdg. 65.00 (*0-313-20119-6*, LELC, Greenwood Pr) Greenwood.

Leadership in Conflict: The Lessons of History. Steven I. Davis. LC 95-22033. 256p. 1996. text 39.95 (*0-312-12713-8*) St Martin.

***Leadership in Continuing & Distance Education in Higher Education.** Cynthia Shoemaker. LC 97-43211. 288p. (C). 1998. 42.00 (*0-205-26823-4*) Allyn.

Leadership in Dietetics: Achieving a Vision for the Future. Anne M. Barker et al. LC 94-31016. 1994. pap. 28.00 (*0-88091-137-9*) Am Dietetic Assn.

Leadership in Disguise: The Rose of the European Commission in EC Decision-Making on Agriculture in the Uruguay Round. Remco Vahl. LC 97-61061. (Perspectives on Europe Ser.). 328p. 1997. text 78.95 (*1-85972-660-7*, Pub. by Ashgate Pub) Ashgate Pub Co.

Leadership in Early Care & Education. Ed. by Sharon L. Kagan & Barbara T. Bowman. LC 96-72625. 1997. pap. 8.00 (*0-935989-81-1*) Natl Assn Child Ed.

Leadership in Early Childhood: The Pathway to Professionalism. Jillian Rodd. 208p. 1994. pap. 2.00 (*0-335-19303-X*) OpUniv Pr.

Leadership in Early Childhood: The Pathway to Professionalism. Jillian Rodd. LC 93-39282. (Early Childhood Education Ser.). 200p. 1994. pap. text 18.95 (*0-8077-3353-9*) Tchrs Coll.

Leadership in Early Childhood: The Pathway to Professionalism. 2nd ed. Jillian Rodd. 224p. 1998. pap. 29.95 (*1-86448-566-3*, Pub. by Allen & Unwin Pty) Paul & Co Pubs.

Leadership in Early Childhood: The Pathway to Professionalism. 2nd ed. Jillian Rodd. 224p. 1998. pap. write for info. (*0-335-20281-0*) Taylor & Francis.

Leadership in Early Childhood: The Pathway to Professionalism. 2nd ed. Jillian Rodd. 224p. 1998. pap. text 18.95 (*0-8077-3776-3*) Tchrs Coll.

Leadership in Empowered Schools: Themes from Innovative Efforts. Paula M. Short & John T. Greer. LC 95-39286. 201p. (C). 1996. pap. text 37.00 (*0-02-410171-0*, Macmillan Coll) P-H.

Leadership in Europe: A Special Issue of the European Journal of Work & Organizational Psychology. Frank Heller. 1998. pap. 39.95 (*0-86377-982-4*, Pub. by Psychol Pr) Taylor & Francis.

Leadership in Fiji. R. R. Nayacakalou. 1976. 22.00 (*0-19-550462-3*) OUP.

Leadership in Government. Andrew Korac-Kakabadse & Nada Korac-Kakabadse. LC 97-77552. 376p. 1998. text 67.95 (*1-84014-138-7*, Pub. by Ashgate Pub) Ashgate Pub Co.

***Leadership in Healthcare: Values at the Top.** Carson F. Dye. LC 99-47342. (Ache Management Ser.). 145p. 2000. pap. 42.00 (*1-56793-114-6*, LHC-1090) Health Admin Pr.

Leadership in High-Performance Organizational Cultures. Stanley D. Truskie. LC 98-51664. 168p. 1999. 59.95 (*1-56720-236-5*, Quorum Bks) Greenwood.

Leadership in Higher Education: A Handbook for Practicing Administrators. Ed. by Bob W. Miller et al. LC 82-15579. 585p. 1983. lib. bdg. 99.50 (*0-313-22263-0*, MHE/, Greenwood Pr) Greenwood.

Leadership in Instructional Technology. Matthew M. Maurer & George Davidson. LC 96-50444. 333p. 1997. pap. text 52.00 (*0-13-239849-4*) P-H.

Leadership in Isolation: FDR & the Origins of the Second World War. William E. Kinsella, Jr. 282p. 1970. pap. 15.95 (*0-87073-941-7*) Schenkman Bks Inc.

Leadership in Leisure Services: Making a Difference. Debra J. Jordan. LC 96-60762. 524p. (C). 1996. text 39.95 (*0-910251-83-5*, JOR87) Venture Pub PA.

Leadership in Middle Level Education: A National Survey of Middle Level Leaders & Schools. Jerry W. Valentine et al. 160p. (Orig.). (C). 1993. pap. text 12.00 (*0-88210-274-5*) Natl Assn Principals.

***Leadership in Nursing.** Geraldine Cunningham & Kathleen King. (Illus.). 256p. 2000. pap. text 35.00 (*0-7506-3837-0*) Buttrwrth-Heinemann.

Leadership in Nursing Practice. Boyle. 1999. pap. text. write for info. (*0-7216-4915-7*) Harcourt.

Leadership in Organizations. 4th ed. Gary A. Yukl. LC 97-41758. 552p. (C). 1997. 67.00 (*0-13-897521-3*) P-H.

Leadership in Personnel Management in Public Schools. Clarence A. Weber. LC 74-96994. 274p. 1970. 12.50 (*0-87527-084-0*) Green.

***Leadership in Public Fire Safety Education: The Year 2000 & Beyond.** Ed. by Edward M. Wall. (Illus.). 56p. (C). 1999. reprint ed. pap. text 20.00 (*0-7881-8334-6*) DIANE Pub.

Leadership in Recreation. 2nd ed. Russel. 384p. 2000. 52.81 (*0-07-012330-6*) McGraw.

Leadership in Recreation & Leisure Services. 2nd ed. Christopher Edington et al. 1999. 44.95 (*1-57167-131-5*) Sagamore Pub.

Leadership in Safety Management. James R. Thomen. LC 91-16849. 400p. 1991. 110.00 (*0-471-53326-2*) Wiley.

Leadership in Social Administration: Perspectives for the 1980s. Ed. by Felice D. Perlmutter & Simon Slavin. 268p. 1980. pap. 19.95 (*0-87722-201-0*) Temple U Pr.

Leadership in Social Policies. Karl Schweitzer et al. (Journal of History & Politics (Revue d'Histoire et de Politique) Ser.: Vol. 1). (ENG & FRE.). 1980. 49.95 (*0-7734-8954-1*) E Mellen.

Leadership in Space - For Benefits on Earth, 28th Annual AAS Meeting, Oct. 26-29, 1981, San Diego, CA. Ed. by William F. Rector. LC 57-43769. (Advances in the Astronautical Sciences Ser.: Vol. 47). (Illus.). 310p. 1982. 45.00 (*0-87703-168-1*, Am Astronaut Soc) Univelt Inc.

Leadership in Space - For Benefits on Earth, 28th Annual AAS Meeting, Oct. 26-29, 1981, San Diego, CA. Ed. by William F. Rector. LC 57-43769. (Advances in the Astronautical Sciences Ser.: Vol. 47). (Illus.). 310p. 1982. pap. 35.00 (*0-87703-169-X*, Am Astronaut Soc) Univelt Inc.

Leadership in the Classroom. June R. Gilstad. Ed. by Bonnie F. Fisher. 22p. (Orig.). 1985. pap. text 2.00 (*0-939132-11-7*) Hermione Hse.

Leadership in the Fire Service. Robert F. Hamm. Ed. by Everett Hudiburg. LC 88-83431. (Illus.). 132p. (Orig.). 1988. reprint ed. pap. text 16.50 (*0-87939-077-8*) IFSTA.

Leadership in the Global Commons: Building Transnational Citizenship. Barbara C. Crosby. LC 98-40149. 1998. pap. 24.95 (*0-7619-1747-0*) Sage.

***Leadership in the Global Commons: Building Transnational Citizenship.** Barbara C. Crosby. LC 98-40149. 4p. 1998. 52.00 (*0-7619-1746-2*) Sage.

***Leadership in the Habad Movement.** Avrum M. Ehrlich. LC 98-36533. 2000. 40.00 (*0-7657-6055-X*) Aronson.

Leadership in the Interactive Age: A Facilitator's Guide. Barbara Benjamin et al. 17p. 1995. 4.95 (*1-880178-06-0*) Intuitive Discov.

Leadership in the Interactive Age: A Skills Development Workbook. Barbara Benjamin et al. 448p. 1995. 39.95 (*1-880178-05-2*) Intuitive Discov.

Leadership in the Kingdom. Ian Fair. 1996. 22.95 (*0-89112-067-X*) Abilene Christ U.

Leadership in the Modern Presidency. Ed. by Fred I. Greenstein. 440p. 1988. pap. 20.50 (*0-674-51855-1*) HUP.

Leadership in the New Millennium. Sheila Grossman & Theresa M. Valiga. LC 99-42955. (Illus.). 240p. 2000. pap. text 29.95 (*0-8036-0594-3*) Davis Co.

Leadership in the New Testament Church. Earl Johnson. 1995. pap. 7.95 (*1-56229-411-3*) Pneuma Life Pub.

Leadership in the Reagan Presidency: Seven Intimate Perspectives. Ed. by Kenneth W. Thompson. (Portraits of American Presidents Ser.: Vol. 9). 176p. (Orig.). (C). 1992. 24.95 (*0-8191-8473-X*) Madison Bks UPA.

Leadership in the Reagan Presidency, Pt. II: Eleven Intimate Perspectives, Pt. II. Ed. by Kenneth W. Thompson. 262p. (Orig.). (C). 1993. pap. text 27.50 (*0-8191-9052-7*, Pub. by White Miller Center); lib. bdg. 57.00 (*0-8191-9051-9*, Pub. by White Miller Center) U Pr of Amer.

Leadership in the Schoolhouse: How Is It Different? Why Is It Important? Thomas J. Sergiovanni. (Education Ser.). 277p. 1995. text 29.95 (*0-7879-0119-9*) Jossey-Bass.

Leadership in the Soviet National Republics: A Quantitative Study of Recruitment Policy. Grey Hodnett. 432p. 1991. 25.00 (*0-88962-083-0*); pap. 14.95 (*0-88962-084-9*) Mosaic.

Leadership in the Trenches. SHEFFIELD C. LC 99-30645. 368p. 1999. text 75.00 (*0-312-22640-3*) St Martin.

Leadership in the Twenty-First Century. Joseph C. Rost. LC 90-40961. 240p. 1991. 47.95 (*0-275-93670-8*, C3670, Praeger Pubs) Greenwood.

Leadership in the Twenty-First Century. Joseph C. Rost. LC 90-40961. 256p. 1993. pap. 19.95 (*0-275-94610-X*, B4610, Praeger Pubs) Greenwood.

Leadership in the Wesleyan Spirit. Lovett H. Weems, Jr. LC 98-48162. 128p. 1999. pap. 14.95 (*0-687-04692-0*) Abingdon.

Leadership in The Words of Women. 152p. (C). 1999. pap. text 10.95 (*0-536-02285-2*) S&S Trade.

Leadership in Times of Change: A Handbook for Communication & Media Administrators. William G. Christ. LC 98-35455. 1998. pap. 39.95 (*0-8058-2911-3*) L Erlbaum Assocs.

Leadership in Times of Change: A Handbook for Communication & Media Administrators. Ed. by William G. Christ. LC 98-35455. (Communication Ser.). 328p. 1998. write for info. (*0-8058-2698-X*) L Erlbaum Assocs.

Leadership in Urban Government in India. S. L. Kaushik. 256p. 1986. 29.95 (*0-318-36593-6*) Asia Bk Corp.

Leadership in War. Owen S. Connelly, Jr. 0.00 (*0-691-03186-X*) Princeton U Pr.

Leadership in Whitehall. Theakson. LC 98-34979. xi, 266 p. 1999. text 69.95 (*0-312-21965-2*) St Martin.

Leadership in Whole Language: The Principal's Role. Bob Wortman & Myna L. Matlin. LC 95-16692. (Illus.). 160p. (Orig.). (C). 1995. pap. text 17.50 (*1-57110-012-1*) Stenhse Pubs.

Leadership into the 21st Century. large type ed. Richard W. Wetherill. (Orig.). 1992. pap. 9.50 (*1-881074-04-8*) Alpha Pub Hse.

Leadership Investing: Tapping into Your Business Knowledge & Experience to Create a Winning Investment Program. John A. Vann. 1996. 24.95 (*0-614-95728-1*, Irwn Prfssnl) McGraw-Hill Prof.

Leadership Investing: Tapping into Your Business Knowledge & Experience to Create a Winning Investment Program. John A. Vann. 250p. 1996. 24.95 (*0-7863-0469-3*, Irwn Prfssnl) McGraw-Hill Prof.

***Leadership Investment: How the World's Best Organizations Gain Strategic Advantage Through Leadership Development.** Robert M. Fulmer & Marshall Goldsmith. LC 00-33157. 2000. 27.95 (*0-8144-0558-4*) AMACOM.

Leadership IQ: A New Method for Assessing & Improving Your Job Satisfaction & Leadership. Emmett C. Murphy. LC 96-14172. 288p. 1996. 24.95 (*0-471-14712-5*) Wiley.

Leadership IQ: The Groundbreaking Program to Develop & Improve Your Leadership Ability. Emmett C. Murphy. 288p. 1997. pap. 5.99 (*0-471-19327-5*) Wiley.

Leadership Is an Art. Max Depree. 176p. 1990. pap. 14.95 (*0-440-50324-8*, Dell Trade Pbks) Dell.

Leadership Is Common Sense. Herman Cain. LC 98-40000. (Illus.). 196p. 1999. pap. 12.95 (*0-86730-750-1*, Pub. by Lebhar Friedman) Natl Bk Netwk.

Leadership Is Common Sense. Herman Cain. 224p. 1996. 25.95 (*0-471-28796-2*, VNR) Wiley.

Leadership Is Common Sense. Herman Cain. LC 96-31822. (Culinary Arts Ser.). 199p. (C). 1996. 25.95 (*0-442-02368-5*, VNR) Wiley.

Leadership Is Empowering People. Paul R. Britton & John W. Stallings. LC 86-9193. 374p. (Orig.). (C). 1986. pap. text 31.50 (*0-8191-5410-5*) U Pr of Amer.

Leadership Is the Key: Unlocking Your Effectiveness in Ministry. Herb Miller. LC 96-51887. (Leadership Insight Ser.). 176p. 1997. pap. 14.95 (*0-687-01375-5*) Abingdon.

Leadership Jazz: The Art of Conducting Business Through Leadership, Followership, Teamwork, Voice, Touch. Max Depree. 240p. 1993. pap. 13.95 (*0-440-50518-6*, Dell Trade Pbks) Dell.

Leadership, Learning, Change & Commitment: How Managers Can Know When They're Getting Good Advice & When They're Not. Chris Argyris. LC 99-32358. (Illus.). 272p. 2000. 27.50 (*0-19-513286-6*) OUP.

Leadership Legacy. Robert A. Coppenrath. 376p. Date not set. text 24.95 (*1-889534-30-7*) Jay St Pubs.

Leadership, Legitimacy & Conflict in China: From a Charismatic Mao to the Politics of Succession. Frederick C. Teiwes. LC 83-15381. 184p. (C). (gr. 13). 1984. pap. text 34.95 (*0-87332-275-4*) M E Sharpe.

Leadership, Legitimacy & Conflict in China: From a Charismatic Mao to the Politics of Succession. Frederick C. Teiwes. LC 83-15381. 181p. 1984. reprint ed. pap. 56.20 (*0-7837-9927-6*, 206065400006) Bks Demand.

Leadership Lessons: From a Life of Character & Purpose in Public Affairs. Stephen S. Kaagan. LC 96-39380. 198p. 1997. text 39.50 (*0-7618-0642-3*) U Pr of Amer.

***Leadership Lessons for Christian Educators.** Paul G. Kussrow. ix, 161p. 1999. 9.50 (*1-58339-177-0*) Triangle Press.

Leadership Lessons from the Civil War. Tom Wheeler. LC 99-27567. 224p. 1999. 23.95 (*0-385-49518-8*) Doubleday.

Leadership Lessons of Jesus see Jesus el Lider Modelo: Su Ejemplo y Ensenanza para Hoy

Leadership Lessons of Jesus: Timeless Insights for Today's Leaders. Bob Briner & Ray Pritchard. LC 97-13207. 250p. 1997. 14.99 (*0-8054-6356-9*) Broadman.

Leadership Lessons of Robert E Lee. Bill Holton. LC 98-33255. 1999. 6.99 (*0-517-20293-X*) Random Hse Value.

***Leadership Lessons of Ulysses S. Grant: Tips, Tactics & Strategies for Leaders & Managers.** Bil Holton. LC 00-24500. 176p. 2000. 6.99 (*0-517-16180-X*) Random Hse Value.

Leadership Literacy: The Solution to Our Present Crisis. Daniel S. Clemens. (Orig.). 1992. pap. 14.95 (*0-9632640-7-9*) Lead Am.

***Leadership Magic: Practical Tools for Creating Extraordinary Organizations.** Ben Valore-Caplan. (Illus.). 1999. pap. text. write for info. (*0-9671957-0-5*) Wordworks Pr.

Leadership, Management & Career Development for Corporations & Organizations: Facilitator Guide. Fred Leafgren. (Illus.). 113p. 1997. 175.00 (*1-929112-19-X*) Personality Res.

Leadership, Management & Diversity. Brockunier. 1996. 62.50 (*0-07-217797-7*) McGraw.

Leadership Management & the Five Essentials for Success. R. Joyner. 191p. 1991. pap. 9.95 (*1-878327-33-X*) Morning NC.

Leadership: Ministry & Battle see Liderazgo: Ministerio y Batalla

Leadership Moment: Nine True Stories of Triumph & Disaster & Their Lessons for Us All. Michael Useem. LC 98-11282. 320p. 1998. 25.00 (*0-8129-2935-7*, Times Bks) Crown Pub Group.

Leadership Moment: Nine True Stories of Triumph & Disaster & Their Lessons for Us All. Michael Useem. LC 98-11282. (Illus.). 336p. 1999. pap. 14.00 (*0-8129-3230-7*, Times Bks) Crown Pub Group.

***Leadership Now: Achieving Restaurant Management Excellence in 30 Days.** Bill Franz. Ed. by Barbara Freda & Bill Nelson. (Real World Management Ser.). 64p. 2000. pap. 8.95 (*1-879239-21-3*) Pencom.

Leadership Nuts & Bolts. Zweig White & Associates Staff. Ed. by Susan E. Marshall. 152p. 1998. pap. 39.00 (*1-885002-57-2*) Zweig White.

Leadership Odyssey: A Self-Development Guide to New Skills for New Times. Carole S. Napolitano & Lida J. Henderson. LC 97-17810. 288p. 1997. pap. 28.95 (*0-7879-1011-2*) Jossey-Bass.

Leadership of Abraham Lincoln. Don E. Fehrenbacher. LC 77-114013. (Problems in American History Ser.). 204p. reprint ed. pap. 63.30 (*0-608-11517-7*, 202059800018) Bks Demand.

Leadership of & on Behalf of Catholic Schools. Karen M. Ristau & Joseph F. Rogus. (National Congress Catholic Schools for the 21st Century Ser.). 45p. 1991. pap. 2.00 (*1-55833-067-4*) Natl Cath Educ.

An Asterisk (*) at the beginning of an entry indicates that the title is appearing for the first time.

Leadership of Congress. George R. Brown. LC 73-19135. (Politics & People Ser.). 318p. 1974. reprint ed. 23.95 (*0-405-05859-4*) Ayer.

Leadership of Organizations: The Executives Complete Handbook, 3 pts. John M. Brion. LC 95-16384. 1995. 250.00 (*1-55938-934-6*) Jai Pr.

Leadership of Public Bureaucracies Vol. 2: The Administrator As Conservator. Larry D. Terry & Maxine Goodman. (Advances in Public Administration Ser.). (Illus.). 207p. 1995. 49.95 (*0-8039-7146-X*); pap. 21.50 (*0-8039-7147-8*) Sage.

Leadership of Schools: Chief Executives in Education. Angela Thody. (Management & Leadership in Education Ser.). 1997. pap. text 22.50 (*0-304-33360-3*) Continuum.

Leadership of the American Zionist Organization, 1897-1930. Yonathan Shapiro. LC 71-126521. 310p. reprint ed. pap. 96.10 (*0-608-11642-4*, 202226500026) Bks Demand.

Leadership of the Reclamation Movement, 1875-1902. Stanley S. Davison. Ed. by Stuart Bruchey. LC 78-53545. (Development of Public Land Law in the U. S. Ser.). (Illus.). 1979. lib. bdg. 26.95 (*0-405-11365-X*) Ayer.

Leadership on Java: Gentle Hints, Authoritarian Rule. Hans Antlov & Sven Cederroth. (SIAS Monographs: No. 16). 260p. (C). 1996. pap. text 40.00 (*0-7007-0295-4*, Pub. by Curzon Pr Ltd) UH Pr.

***Leadership on the Other Side: No Rules, Just Clues.** William M. Easum. 144p. 2000. pap. 13.00 (*0-687-08588-8*) Abingdon.

Leadership 101: 20 Solid Lessons in Leadership for the New Leader. James Baker. 250p. 1998. pap. 15.95 (*1-878208-74-8*) Guild Pr IN.

Leadership 101. Logos Research Systems Inc. Staff. 1998. pap. write for info. (*1-57799-125-7*) Logos Res Sys.

Leadership 101: Developing Leadership Skills for Resilient Youth, Facilitator's Guide) Mariam G. MacGregor. 135p. 1997. pap., teacher ed. 30.00 (*0-9677981-0-8*) Youthleadership.

Leadership 101: Developing Your Leadership Skills, Student Workbook. Mariam G. MacGregor. 80p. 1997. pap., wbk. ed. 14.00 (*0-9677981-1-6*) Youthleadership.

Leadership Paradox: A Challenge to Servant Leadership in a Power Hungry World. Denny Gunderson. 156p. 1997. pap. 8.99 (*0-927545-87-X*) YWAM Pub.

***Leadership Paradox: Balancing Logic & Artistry in Schools.** Terrence E. Deal. 2000. pap. 21.95 (*0-7879-5541-8*) Jossey-Bass.

Leadership Paradox: Balancing Logic & Artistry in Schools. Terrence E. Deal & Kent D. Peterson. LC 93-48709. (Education-Higher Education Ser.). 154p. 1994. text 29.95 (*1-55542-648-4*) Jossey-Bass.

Leadership, Participation, & Group Behavior. Ed. by Larry L. Cummings & Barry M. Staw. LC 90-4529. 386p. 1990. pap. 25.75 (*1-55938-220-1*) Jai Pr.

Leadership Passion: A Psychology of Ideology. David Loye. LC 76-45481. (Jossey-Bass Behavioral Science Ser.). 269p. reprint ed. pap. 83.40 (*0-608-16953-6*, 202776100056) Bks Demand.

***Leadership Pipeline: How to Build the Leadership Powered Company.** Ram Charan et al. 224p. 2000. 28.50 (*0-7879-5172-2*) Jossey-Bass.

Leadership Plus Administration in School Management. Ulysses V. Spiva. 440p. 1978. 10.95 (*0-317-17268-9*); pap. 7.95 (*0-685-10072-3*) Banner Pr AL.

Leadership Practices Inventory Individual Contributor Observer: With Scoring Sheets. 2nd ed. James M. Kouzes & Barry Z. Posner. 1997. 3.95 (*0-7879-0982-3*, Pfffr & Co) Jossey-Bass.

Leadership Practices Inventory Individual Contributor Participant's Workbook & Self Assessment. 2nd ed. James M. Kouzes & Barry Z. Posner. 1997. pap. text 12.95 (*0-7879-0980-7*, Pfffr & Co) Jossey-Bass.

Leadership Practices Inventory Observer: With Scoring Sheets. 2nd ed. James M. Kouzes & Barry Z. Posner. 1997. 3.95 (*0-7879-0972-6*, Pfffr & Co) Jossey-Bass.

Leadership Practices Inventory Participant's Workbook & Self-Assessment. 2nd ed. James M. Kouzes & Barry Z. Posner. 96p. 1997. pap. text 12.95 (*0-7879-0970-X*, Pfffr & Co) Jossey-Bass.

Leadership Prayers. Richard Kriegbaum. LC 98-19056. 120p. 1998. 9.99 (*0-8423-3689-3*) Tyndale Hse.

Leadership Principles of Jesus: Modern Parables of Achievement & Motivation. Joe D. Batten et al. LC 97-11019. 350p. (Orig.). 1997. pap. 15.99 (*0-89900-782-1*) College Pr Pub.

Leadership Quest. J. Clifton Williams. (Illus.). 304p. (C). 1986. write for info. (*0-941203-00-X*) Ldrship Systs.

Leadership Quest. rev. ed. J. Clifton Williams. 228p. 1996. write for info. (*0-941203-01-8*) Ldrship Systs.

Leadership Realities for Metro Denver. James R. Ellis. (Issue Papers: No. 11-87). 11p. 1987. pap. text 8.00 (*1-57655-018-4*) Independ Inst.

Leadership Report: Key Issues Shaping the Future of Health Care. Alden T. Solovy. LC 99-199466. 277 p. 1999. pap. text 149.00 (*1-55648-241-8*) AHPI.

Leadership Resources: A Guide to Training & Development Tools. Ed. by Mary K. Schwartz et al. 428p. 1998. pap. text 40.00 (*1-882197-42-9*, 340) Ctr Creat Leader.

Leadership Roles & Management Functions in Nursing: Theory & Application. 2nd ed. Bessie L. Marquis & Carol J. Huston. LC 95-36656. 592p. 1995. pap. text 29.95 (*0-397-55236-X*) Lppncott W & W.

***Leadership Roles & Management Functions in Nursing: Theory & Application.** 3rd ed. Bessie L. Marquis & Carol J. Huston. LC 99-14493. 576p. 2000. pap. text 29.95 (*0-7817-1923-2*) Lppncott W & W.

Leadership Secrets. Roberts. 1993. 8.95 (*0-446-77806-0*) Warner Bks.

Leadership Secrets of Attila the Hun. Wess Roberts. LC 88-27739. 110p. 1990. mass mkt. 12.95 (*0-446-39106-9*, Pub. by Warner Bks) Little.

Leadership Secrets of David the King. Bob Yandian. 128p. 1996. pap. 4.99 (*1-880089-31-9*, Pub. by Albury Pub) Appalach Bk Dist.

***Leadership Secrets of Elizabeth I.** Shaun Higgins & Pamela Gilberd. 2000. 20.00 (*0-7382-0390-4*) Perseus Pubng.

Leadership Secrets of Jesus. Mike Murdock. 208p. 1997. 14.99 (*1-56292-163-0*) Honor Bks OK.

Leadership Secrets of the Rogue Warrior: A Commando's Guide to Success. Richard Marcinko. 176p. 1997. per. 14.00 (*0-671-54514-0*, Pocket Books) PB.

Leadership Secrets of the Rogue Warrior: A Commando's Guide to Success. Richard Marcinko & John Weisman. 176p. 1996. 20.00 (*0-671-54515-9*) PB.

***Leadership Secrets of the Rogue Warrior: A Commando's Guide to Success.** ed. Richard Marcinko. 1998. per. 20.00 (*0-671-03675-0*, Pocket Books) PB.

***Leadership Selection in Six Western Democracies.** James W. Davis. 200p. 1999. lib. bdg. 70.00 (*1-57958-111-0*) Fitzroy Dearborn.

Leadership Skills see Career Skills Library

***Leadership Skills.** John Adair. 96p. 2000. pap. 17.95 (*0-8464-5102-6*) Beekman Pubs.

Leadership Skills. Phil Lowe. 120p. 1995. ring bd. 299.00 (*0-7494-1150-3*, Kogan Pg Educ); ring bd. 59.95 (*0-7494-1151-1*, Kogan Pg Educ) Stylus Pub VA.

Leadership Skills: Developing Volunteers for Organizational Success. Emily K. Morrison. LC 94-9333. 240p. (Orig.). 1994. pap. 17.95 (*1-55561-066-8*) Fisher Bks.

Leadership Skills for Jewish Educators: A Casebook. Ed. by Sheila Rosenblum. LC 93-37122. 1994. 35.00 (*0-87441-555-1*) Behrman.

***Leadership Skills for Managers.** Marlene Caroselli. (Briefcase Bks.). 2000. pap. 14.95 (*0-07-136430-7*) McGraw.

Leadership Skills for Managers, Set. pap., wbk. ed. 165.00 incl. audio (*0-7612-0795-3*, 80174NQ1); pap., wbk. ed. 30.00 incl. audio (*0-7612-0798-8*, 80175NQ1) AMACOM.

Leadership Skills for Peer Group Facilitators. Joan Sturkie & Charles Hanson. LC 92-12103. 168p. 1992. pap. text 11.95 (*0-89390-232-2*) Resource Pubns.

Leadership Skills for Performance Improvement: Planning for Quality. Joint Commission on Accreditation of Healthcare Organizations. (Illus.). 169p. 1995. pap. 24.50 (*0-86688-433-5*, PI-300) Joint Comm Hlthcare.

Leadership Skills for Project Managers. Ed. by Jeffrey K. Pinto & Jeffrey W. Trailer. LC 98-12191. (Editor's Choice Ser.: No. 1). (Illus.). 131p. 1998. pap. 32.95 (*1-880410-49-4*) Proj Mgmt Inst.

Leadership Skills for the Nurse Manager: Restructuring the Role of Management in Today's... Kathleen O. Mott. LC 96-7876. 240p. 1996. pap. 32.50 (*0-7863-0860-5*, Irwn Prfssnl) McGraw-Hill Prof.

Leadership Skills for Women: Achieving Impact As a Manager. rev. ed. Marilyn Manning. LC 94-80009. (Fifty-Minutes Ser.). 66p. 1995. pap. 10.95 (*1-56052-325-5*) Crisp Pubns.

Leadership Skills for Women in Medicine. 150p. 1998. pap. 45.00 (*1-58383-009-X*, LEADER9) Robert D Keene.

Leadership Skills for Women in Search of Excellence. 44p. (C). 1998. text 11.95 (*0-536-01121-4*) Pearson Custom.

Leadership Skills Skillbook. Educational Foundation of the National Restaurant. (Management Skills Program Ser.). 40p. (Orig.). 1993. pap. 10.95 (*0-915452-35-9*) Educ Found.

***Leadership Solution.** Jim Shaffer. LC 99-87148. 288p. 2000. 24.95 (*0-07-079063-9*) McGraw.

Leadership Strategies. 2nd ed. John Dolan. 288p. 1994. per., boxed set 32.95 (*0-8403-9423-3*) Kendall-Hunt.

Leadership Strategies, Economic Activity, & Interregional Interaction: Social Complexity in Northeast China. G. Shelach. LC 99-31763. (Fundamental Issues in Archaeology Ser.). (Illus.). 250p. (C). 1999. write for info. (*0-306-46090-4*, Plenum Trade) Perseus Pubng.

***Leadership Strategies for Safe Schools.** 2000. write for info. (*1-57517-279-8*) SkyLght.

***Leadership Strategies for Teachers.** 2000. write for info. (*1-57517-274-7*) SkyLght.

Leadership Strengths Indicator. Julie Ellis. 1990. 25.00 (*0-89824-192-8*); pap. 15.00 (*0-89824-191-X*) Trillium Pr.

Leadership Styles. Anne Lewis. 63p. 1993. pap. 9.95 (*0-87652-178-2*) Am Assn Sch Admin.

Leadership Styles & Soviet Foreign Policy: Stalin, Khrushchev, Brezhnev, Gorbachev. James M. Goldgeier. LC 94-330. (Perspectives on Security Ser.). 1994. text 35.00 (*0-8018-4866-0*) Johns Hopkins.

Leadership Succession. Ed. by Stewart D. Friedman. 160p. 1987. 32.95 (*0-88738-162-6*) Transaction Pubs.

Leadership Succession Systems & Corporate Performance. Stewart D. Friedman. 141p. 1985. pap. 35.00 (*0-317-11516-2*) CU Ctr Career Res.

Leadership That Builds People, Vol. 1. James B. Richards. 143p. (Orig.). 1993. pap. 12.95 (*0-924748-06-0*) Impact Ministries.

Leadership That Builds People, 3 vols., Vol. II. James B. Richards. 165p. (Orig.). 1999. pap. 19.95 (*0-924748-11-7*) Impact Ministries.

Leadership That Works. Leith Anderson. LC 99-6592. 224p. 1999. 16.99 (*1-55661-994-4*) Bethany Hse.

Leadership Theory & Research: Perspectives & Directions. Ed. by Martin M. Chemers & Roya Ayman. (Illus.). 347p. 1992. text 59.95 (*0-12-170609-5*) Acad Pr.

***Leadership 311.** Bethany World Prayer Center Staff. 84p. 1999. pap. text 5.00 (*1-928772-05-6*) Keepsafe.

Leadership Through Church Growth. J. J. Turner. 1976. pap. 6.55 (*0-89137-123-0*) Quality Pubns.

Leadership Through Collaboration: Alternatives to the Hierarchy. Mike Koehler & Jeanne Baxter. LC 96-31390. 220p. 1997. 34.95 (*1-883001-30-7*) Eye On Educ.

Leadership Through Discipleship: Applying the Leadership Principles of the World's Greatest Leader. Dougouglas R. Hartman & Doug Sutherland. 173p. 1990. reprint ed. pap. 7.95 (*1-878008-00-5*) Family Marriage Resc.

Leadership Through Influence. Terry R. Bacon. (Illus.). 148p. 1994. write for info. (*1-57740-001-1*, ILW002) Intl LrningWrk.

Leadership Through the Ages. George F. MacMunn. LC 68-16951. (Essay Index Reprint Ser.). 1977. 19.95 (*0-8369-0657-8*) Ayer.

Leadership to Meet Our Environmental Crisis: Proceedings of the Natural Science Center Conference 1970 - Dayton Ohio. Ed. by Alan R. Mahl. (NCS Conference Proceedings Ser.). (Illus.). (Orig.). 1971. 5.00 (*0-916544-00-1*) Natural Sci Youth.

Leadership Training. Ernest Clevenger. (Illus.). 56p. 1992. pap. 6.00 (*0-88428-058-6*) Parchment Pr.

Leadership Training: A Sourcebook of Activities. Elizabeth M. Christopher & Larry M. Smith. LC 93-34128. 250p. 1993. pap. 49.95 (*0-7494-0988-6*, Kogan Pg Educ) Stylus Pub VA.

Leadership Training for Women in a Community Context: Executive Summary of the Evaluation Report of the Woman's Leadership Development Initiative of the Chicago Foundation for Women. Dimitra Tasiouras. 20p. 1994. write for info. (*0-9643241-0-5*) Chi Fnd Women.

***Leadership Training Manual.** Robert D. Stuart. 66p. 2000. pap. 12.00 (*0-9702562-1-3*) JEB Stuart.

Leadership Trapeze: Strategies for Leadership in Team-Based Organizations. 286p. text 25.00 (*0-7881-9174-8*) DIANE Pub.

Leadership 2000: Success Skills for University Students. Reed Markham. 212p. (C). 1995. text 37.00 (*0-536-59076-1*) Pearson Custom.

Leadership Unit: The Use of Teacher-Scholar Teams to Develop Units for the Gifted. James J. Gallagher. (Illus.). 138p. (C). 1982. pap., teacher ed. 14.99 (*0-89824-036-0*) Trillium Pr.

***Leadership Void: A Reality That's Not Beyond Repair.** Joseph M. Alicea. LC 99-91881. 2000. 25.00 (*0-7388-1364-8*); pap. 18.00 (*0-7388-1365-6*) Xlibris Corp.

Leadership Way: Management for the Nineties. John D. Peyton. 254p. 1991. 24.95 (*0-9628901-5-4*) Davidson Manors.

Leadership When the Heat's On. Danny Cox & John Hoover. 200p. 1992. 24.99 (*0-07-013267-4*) McGraw.

Leadership When the Heat's On. Danny Cox et al. 200p. 1993. pap. 14.95 (*0-07-013312-3*) McGraw.

***Leadership When the Heat's On.** Danny Cox & John Hoover. 200p. 1999. reprint ed. text 25.00 (*0-7881-6826-6*) DIANE Pub.

Leadership Wisdom: A Guide to Producing Extraordinary Results. Larry L. Liberty. LC 94-226132. 272p. (Orig.). 1994. pap. 19.95 (*0-9641669-0-9*) Liberty Cnslting.

***Leadership Wisdom from the Monk Who Sold His Ferrari: The 8 Rituals of Visionary Leaders.** Robin Shilp Sharma. 2000. pap. 18.00 (*0-00-638562-1*) HarpC.

***Leadership Wisdom from the Monk Who Sold His Ferrari: The 8 Rituals of Visionary Leaders: A Fable.** Robin S. Sharma. 240p. 2000. 25.00 (*0-00-255722-3*) HarpC.

Leadership Wisdom of Jesus: Practical Lessons for Today. Charles C. Manz. 188p. 1999. reprint ed. pap. 14.00 (*1-57675-066-3*) Berrett-Koehler.

Leadership Within the School Library & Beyond. Lesley S. Farmer. LC 94-45621. (Professional Growth Ser.). 80p. 1995. pap. 17.95 (*0-938865-40-4*) Linworth Pub.

Leadership Without Easy Answers. Ronald A. Heifetz. LC 94-15184. 368p. 1994. 24.95 (*0-674-51858-6*, HEILEA) Belknap Pr.

Leadership Your Way: Play the Hand You're Dealt & Win. Kim H. Krisco. 149p. (Orig.). 1995. pap. 13.95 (*0-917917-06-5*) Miles River.

Leadership 2000: Preparing Students for Leadership Roles in Today's & Tommorow's Workplace. Dianne Schilling et al. (Illus.). 528p. (Orig.). (YA). (gr. 7-12). 1994. ring bd., wbk. ed. 99.95 (*1-56499-021-4*, IP9021) Innerchoice Pub.

LeaderTalk: Woman to Woman. Michaelene Grassli. 1996. 12.95 (*1-57008-236-7*) Bookcraft Inc.

LeaderTrip: A Lesson in Organizational Transformation. Gene Myers. Ed. by Tim Beauchemin et al. (Illus.). 320p. (Orig.). 1993. text 47.77 (*1-884332-00-5*); pap. text 27.77 (*1-884332-01-3*) Netwrk Pr TX.

Leading. Daryl R. Conner. LC 98-24357. 368p. 1998. 24.95 (*0-471-29557-4*) Wiley.

Leading: The Art of Becoming an Executive. Philip B. Crosby. 214p. 1999. reprint ed. text 20.00 (*0-7881-6189-X*) DIANE Pub.

Leading a Bible Study by Indirect Methods see Como Dirigir un Biblico Estudio por Metodos Indirectos

Leading a Bible Study by Indirect Methods see Huong Dan Mot Lop Hoc Kinh Thanh Bang Phuong Phap Gian Tiep

Leading a Bible Study by Indirect Methods see Conduire une Etude Biblique par des Methodes Indirectes

Leading a Bible Study by Indirect Methods. Charles Brock. 16p. 1975. pap. 1.00 (*1-885504-00-4*) Church Gwth.

Leading a Friends Helping Friends Program. Carol Painter. Ed. by Don L. Sorenson. 160p. (Orig.). (YA). (gr. 9-12). 1989. pap. text 9.95 (*0-932796-29-X*) Ed Media Corp.

Leading a Human Life: Wittgenstein, Intentionality & Romanticism. Richard T. Eldridge. LC 97-7998. 312p. 1997. pap. text 17.95 (*0-226-20313-1*); lib. bdg. 46.00 (*0-226-20312-3*) U Ch Pr.

Leading a Law Practice to Excellence. J. Edwin Dietel. LC 91-76918. 517p. 1992. text 38.00 (*0-8318-0653-2*, B653) Am Law Inst.

Leading a Parent Resource Group see Como Guiar un Grupo de Apoyo

Leading a Parent Resource Group. Patricia Wipfler. (Illus.). 23p. (Orig.). 1990. pap. 3.00 (*1-891670-03-4*) Parents Ldshp.

Leading a Small Group: The Ultimate Road Trip. (Illus.). 167p. (Orig.). (C). 1995. pap., spiral bd. 18.99 (*1-57334-004-9*, 741-HB) WSN Pr.

Leading a Winning Team (for Supervisors) rev. ed. James C. Campbell. (Skill Centered Leadership Ser.). 31p. 1997. pap., wbk. ed. 12.95 incl. audio (*1-891161-66-0*) ClamShell Pub.

***Leading Academic Change: Essential Roles for Department Chairs.** Ann F. Lucas et al. LC 99-6977. (Higher Education Ser.). 320p. 2000. 32.95 (*0-7879-4682-6*, Pfffr & Co) Jossey-Bass.

Leading Academics. Robin Middlehurst. LC 93-14563. 192p. 1994. 123.00 (*0-335-09989-0*); pap. 41.95 (*0-335-09988-2*) OpUniv Pr.

Leading Adult Learners: Handbook for All Christian Groups. Delia Halverson. 112p. (Orig.). 1995. pap. 13.95 (*0-687-00223-0*) Abingdon.

Leading Aerobic Dance-Exercise. Susan K. Wilmoth. LC 85-30237. (Illus.). 254p. reprint ed. pap. 78.80 (*0-608-07052-1*, 206725800009) Bks Demand.

Leading American Essayists: Biographies of Leading Americans. William M. Payne. LC 68-26466. (Essay Index Reprint Ser.). 1977. reprint ed. 28.95 (*0-8369-0778-7*) Ayer.

Leading American Inventors. George Iles. LC 68-8472. (Essay Index Reprint Ser.). 1977. reprint ed. 29.95 (*0-8369-0557-1*) Ayer.

Leading American Novelists. John Erskine. LC 67-22091. (Essay Index Reprint Ser.). 1977. 20.95 (*0-8369-0419-2*) Ayer.

Leading American Treaties. Charles E. Hill. LC 72-94316. reprint ed. 32.50 (*0-404-03267-2*) AMS Pr.

Leading an Elegant Death. Paula Carter. (Mysteries by Design Ser.: Vol. 1). 1999. pap. 5.99 (*0-425-16733-X*, Prime Crime) Berkley Pub.

Leading an Empowered Organization Manual. 4th rev. ed. Ed. by Diane Miller & Donna Wright. 73p. 1997. pap. text 35.00 (*1-886624-07-0*) Creat Hlthcare.

Leading An Inspired Life. E. James Rohn. LC 97-224950. 460p. 1996. 34.95 (*1-55525-459-4*) Nightingale-Conant.

Leading & Being Led. Paul A. Lacey. LC 85-63379. (Orig.). 1985. pap. 4.00 (*0-87574-264-5*) Pendle Hill.

Leading & Leadership. Ed. by Timothy Fuller. (Ethics of Everyday Life Ser.). 312p. 2000. 25.00 (*0-268-01325-X*, Pub. by U of Notre Dame Pr); pap. 15.00 (*0-268-01327-6*, Pub. by U of Notre Dame Pr) Chicago Distribution Ctr.

***Leading & Learning in Schools: Brain-Based Practices.** Henry G. Cram. LC 99-57352. 216p. 2000. pap. 29.95 (*0-8108-3755-2*) Scarecrow.

***Leading & Loving, 6 lessons on 2 cass.; set.** Bruce H. Wilkinson. Ed. by Rick Shaw. (Biblical Manhood Ser.). 1999. wbk. ed. 29.95 incl. VHS (*1-885447-19-1*, 66019) Walk Thru the Bible.

Leading & Managing in Nursing. Patricia S. Yoder Wise. (Illus.). 784p. 1998. teacher ed., suppl. ed. write for info. (*0-8151-9849-3*) Mosby Inc.

***Leading & Managing in Nursing.** 2nd ed. Patricia S. Yoder-Wise. LC 98-11710. (Illus.). 768p. (C). 1998. text. write for info. (*1-55664-401-9*) Mosby Inc.

Leading & Managing in Nursing, Includes Testbank. Patricia S. Yoder-Wise. (Illus.). 1994. teacher ed. write for info. (*1-55664-402-7*) Mosby Inc.

Leading & Managing Your Church. Carl George & Robert Logan. LC 87-28374. 192p. (Orig.). 1988. pap. 11.99 (*0-8007-1575-6*) Revell.

Leading & Managing Your School Guidance Staff: A Manual for School Administrators & Directors of Guidance. Patricia Henderson & Norman C. Gysbers. LC 97-25827. 405p. (Orig.). 1998. pap. text 40.95 (*1-55620-166-4*, 72636) Am Coun Assn.

Leading Antenatal Classes. Judy Priest & Judith Schott. (Illus.). 256p. 1991. pap. text 37.50 (*0-7506-0050-0*) Buttrwrth-Heinemann.

Leading at Mach 2. Steve Sullivan. (Illus.). 209p. 1995. pap. 11.95 (*0-9641053-1-4*) Motivat Resources.

Leading at Mach 2. Steve Sullivan. Ed. by Amy J. Pecora. (Illus.). 209p. 1995. 19.95 (*0-9641053-2-2*) Motivat Resources.

***Leading at the Edge: Leadership Lessons from the Extraordinary Saga of Shackleton's Antarctic Expedition.** Dennis N. T. Perkins et al. LC 99-57868. (Illus.). 256p. 2000. 24.95 (*0-8144-0543-6*) AMACOM.

***Leading Beyond the Walls.** Ed. by Frances Hesselbein et al. LC 99-6508. (Wisdom to Action Ser.). (Illus.). 297p. 1999. 27.00 (*0-7879-4593-5*) Jossey-Bass.

Leading Bible Discussions. rev. ed. James F. Nyquist & Jack Kuhatschek. (LifeGuide Bible Studies). 64p. 1985. pap., wbk. ed. 4.99 (*0-8308-1000-5*, 1000) InterVarsity.

Leading By Design: The Ikea Story. Bertil Torekull. Tr. by Joan Tate. LC 99-30285. (Illus.). 256p. 1999. 26.00 (*0-06-662038-4*) HarpC.

Leading Captivity Captive: The Exile As History & Ideology. Ed. by Lester L. Grabbe. LC 98-213125. (JSOTS Ser.: Vol. 278). 170p. 1998. 57.50 (*1-85075-907-3*, Pub. by Sheffield Acad) CUP Services.

Leading Cases & Materials on the Competition Law of the EEC. 3rd ed. D. J. Gijlstra & F. Murphy. 1984. pap. text 82.00 (*90-6544-111-5*) Kluwer Law Intl.

L

An Asterisk (*) at the beginning of an entry indicates that the title is appearing for the first time.

Leading Cases & Materials on the External Relations Law of the EEC. Edmond L. Volker & J. Steenbergen. 684p. 1986. 176.00 (*90-6544-221-9*); pap. 154.00 (*90-6544-237-5*) Kluwer Law Intl.

Leading Cases in the Bible. David W. Amram. ix, 220p. 1985. reprint ed. 48.50 (*0-8377-0218-6*, Rothman) W S Hein.

Leading Cases in the Common Law. A. W. Simpson. (Illus.). 324p. 1997. reprint ed. pap. text 29.95 (*0-19-826299-X*) OUP.

Leading Cases in the Law of Banking. 5th ed. T. Chorley & T. Smart. 1983. 155.00 (*0-7855-2955-1*, Pub. by Chartered Bank); pap. 60.00 (*0-421-29350-0*, Pub. by Chartered Bank) St Mut.

Leading Cases in the Law of Negligence for 'A' Level. 2nd ed. 1986. pap. 14.00 (*0-406-01682-8*, MICHIE) LEXIS Pub.

Leading Cases of the European Community. 6th ed. Martijn Van Empel. 1994. pap. text 63.00 (*90-6544-827-6*) Kluwer Academic.

Leading Cases of the European Court of Human Rights. annot. ed. Ed. by R. A. Lawson & H. G. Schermers. xv, 788p. 1997. pap. 55.50 (*90-6215-559-6*, Pub. by Maklu Uitgev) Gaunt.

Leading Cases on the Law of the European Communities. 5th ed. Ed. by Edmond L. Volker et al. 755p. 1990. pap. 49.00 (*90-6544-235-9*) Kluwer Law Intl.

Leading Cases Simplified: A Collection of the Leading Cases of the Common Law. John D. Lawson. (Illus.). xxvi, 327p. 1987. reprint ed. 42.00 (*0-8377-2406-6*, Rothman) W S Hein.

Leading Causes of Death by Age, Sex, Race & Hispanic Origin: United States, 1992. Paula Gardner. 98p. 1996. per. 7.50 (*0-16-061441-4*) USGPO.

Leading Causes of Death by Age, Sex, Race, & Hispanic Origins: United States, 1992. Paula Gardner et al. (Illus.). 94p. (C). 1997. pap. text 25.00 (*0-7881-4535-5*) DIANE Pub.

Leading Causes of Death by Age, Sex, Race, & Hispanic Origins: United States, 1992. Paula Gardner et al. LC 96-12601. (Vital & Health Statistics Ser.: Series 20, No. 29). 1996. write for info. (*0-8406-0513-7*) Natl Ctr Health Stats.

Leading Cell Worship. Twyla Brickman. 1997. ring bd. 79.95 incl. Beta (*1-880828-01-4*) Touch Pubns.

Leading Change. (Open Learning for Supervisory Management Ser.). 1986. pap. text 19.50 (*0-08-034162-4*, Pergamon Pr) Elsevier.

Leading Change. (Open Learning for Supervisory Management Ser.). 1986. pap. text 19.50 (*0-08-070013-6*, Pergamon Pr) Elsevier.

Leading Change. John P. Kotter. LC 96-20263. 208p. 1996. 24.95 (*0-87584-747-1*) Harvard Busn.

Leading Change. Nebsm. 96p. pap. text. write for info. (*0-7506-3302-6*) Buttrwrth-Heinemann.

Leading Change. 2nd ed. (Open Learning Super Ser.). 1991. pap. text 26.00 (*0-08-041534-2*, Pergamon Pr) Elsevier.

Leading Change: Overcoming the Ideology of Comfort & the Tyranny of Custom. James O'Toole. LC 94-39421. (Management Ser.). 302p. 1995. mass mkt. 27.00 (*1-55542-608-5*) Jossey-Bass.

Leading Change: The Argument for Values-Based Leadership. James O'Toole. 304p. 1996. pap. 12.50 (*0-345-40254-5*) Ballantine Pub Grp.

Leading Change: The Transportation Electronic Revolution. LC 94-67471. 558p. 1994. pap. 19.00 (*1-56091-548-X*, P283) Soc Auto Engineers.

Leading Change in the Congregation: Spiritual & Organizational Tools for Leaders. Gilbert R. Rendle. LC 97-73984. 1997. pap. 15.75 (*1-56699-187-0*) Alban Inst.

Leading Change, Overcoming Chaos: A Seven Stage Process for Making Change Succeed in Your Organization. Michael L. Heifetz. 224p. 1994. 28.95 (*1-883908-01-9*); pap. 18.95 (*1-883908-02-7*) Threshold Inst.

***Leading Change Through Human Resources: Towards a Globally Competitive India: Papers Presented at the 6th National Conference of the National HRD Network, New Delhi, February 1998** National HRD Network (India). et al. LC 98-904232. xvi, 346 p. 1998. (*0-07-463437-2*) McGraw.

Leading Christians to Christ: Evangelizing the Church. Rob Smith. LC 90-31634. 146p. (Orig.). 1990. pap. 7.95 (*0-8192-1529-5*) Morehouse Pub.

Leading Cities in a Global Economy. 106p. 1995. 25.00 (*1-886152-14-4*, No. 3524) Natl League Cities.

***Leading Congregational Change: A Practical Guide for the Transformational Journey.** Jim Herrington et al. 112p. 2000. pap. 11.95 (*0-7879-4885-3*, Pfffr & Co); text 21.95 (*0-7879-4765-2*, Pfffr & Co) Jossey-Bass.

Leading Congress: New Styles, New Strategies. John J. Kornacki. 187p. 1990. 49.95 (*0-87187-569-1*) Congr Quarterly.

Leading Consciously: A Pilgrimage Toward Self-Mastery. Debashis Chatterjee. LC 98-154520. 256p. 1998. pap. text 18.95 (*0-7506-9864-0*) Buttrwrth-Heinemann.

Leading Constitutional Cases on Criminal Justice, 1994. Lloyd L. Weinreb. 1176p. 1994. pap. text 25.95 (*1-56662-188-7*) Foundation Pr.

Leading Constitutional Cases on Criminal Justice, 1995. Lloyd L. Weinreb. 1200p. 1995. pap. text 26.95 (*1-56662-304-9*) Foundation Pr.

Leading Constitutional Cases on Criminal Justice, 1996. Lloyd L. Weinreb. 1218p. 1996. pap. text. write for info. (*1-56662-396-0*) Foundation Pr.

Leading Constitutional Cases on Criminal Justice, 1998 Edition. Lloyd L. Weinreb. (Pamphlet Ser.). 1081p. 1998. pap. text 27.95 (*1-56662-698-6*) Foundation Pr.

Leading Contemporary Poets: An International Anthology. Ed. by Dasha C. Nisula. (Illus.). (Orig.). 1997. pap. 23.00 (*0-9657851-0-6*) Poetry Intl.

Leading Corporate Transformation: An Executive Briefing. Robert H. Miles. LC 96-51317. (Jossey-Bass Business & Management Ser.). 1997. mass mkt. 25.00 (*0-7879-0327-2*) Jossey-Bass.

***Leading Criminal Justice Ministry: Bringing Shalom.** Compiled by Betty Hassler. 96p. 1998. pap. text 12.95 (*0-7673-9114-4*, LifeWy Press) LifeWay Christian.

Leading Economic Controversies of 1998. Contrib. by Edwin Mansfield. LC 98-125268. (Illus.). (C). 1997. pap. text (*0-393-97225-9*) Norton.

Leading Economic Indicators: New Approaches & Forecasting Records. Ed. by Kajal Lahiri & Geoffrey H. Moore. (Illus.). 480p. (C). 1992. pap. text 30.95 (*0-521-43858-6*) Cambridge U Pr.

Leading Edge: Aerodynamic Design of Ultra-Streamlined Land Vehicles. Goro Tamai. LC 99-29701. (Illus.). 304p. 1999. pap. 44.95 (*0-8376-0860-0*, GRLE) Bentley Pubs.

Leading Edge: Forerunning, Pioneering, & World-Shakers. Marilyn J. Wright. (Illus.). 60p. 1994. pap. 6.00 (*0-9632748-7-2*) Majesty Pubns.

Leading Edge: Innovation & Change in Professional Education. 1986. 5.00 (*0-89333-045-0*) AACTE.

Leading Edge: Leadership Strategies from the New Testament. Robert D. Dale. LC 96-11267. 144p. 1996. pap. 12.95 (*0-687-01506-5*) Abingdon.

Leading Edge Business Planning for Entrepreneurs. James B. Arkebauer. LC 98-52091. 1999. pap. text 22.95 (*1-57410-117-X*) Dearborn.

Leading Edges in Social & Behavioral Science. Ed. by R. Duncan Luce et al. LC 89-24186. 720p. 1990. 59.95 (*0-87154-560-8*) Russell Sage.

Leading European Insurers, 1988-1989. 2nd ed. Witherby & Co. Ltd. Staff. (C). 1988. 1160.00 (*0-7855-4103-9*, Pub. by Witherby & Co) St Mut.

Leading Facts of New Mexican History, 2 vols., Set. Ralph E. Twitchell. (Illus.). 1137p. 1994. reprint ed. lib. bdg. 115.00 (*0-8328-3957-4*) Higginson Bk Co.

Leading Figures in English History: Tudor & Stewart Period. Arthur D. Innes. LC 67-23233. (Essay Index Reprint Ser.). 1977. 23.95 (*0-8369-0559-8*) Ayer.

***Leading for a Change: How to Master the 5 Challenges Faced by Every Leader.** Ralph D. Jacobson. LC 00-24632. 248p. 2000. pap. 19.95 (*0-7506-7279-X*) Buttrwrth-Heinemann.

Leading for Empowerment. Terry R. Bacon. (Illus.). 110p. 1994. write for info. (*1-57740-003-8*, ILW001) Intl LrningWrk.

Leading from the Back of the Line (Leaders Book) Richard Dunn. 80p. (Orig.). 1992. pap. 1.00 (*1-56476-002-2*, 6-3002, Victor Bks) Chariot Victor.

Leading from the Back of the Line (Student Book) Richard Dunn. 48p. (Orig.). (YA). 1992. pap. 0.60 (*1-56476-003-0*, 6-3003, Victor Bks) Chariot Victor.

***Leading from the Center: The Emerging Role of the Chief Academic Officer in Theological Schools.** Jeanne P. McLean. LC 99-17246. (Studies in Theological Education). 301p. 1999. 39.95 (*0-7885-0542-4*, 00 08 10) Duke.

Leading from the Ground Up: The 3rd National Survey of the Community Movement Against Substance Abuse. (Illus.). 40p. (Orig.). (C). 1996. pap. text 20.00 (*0-7881-3081-1*) DIANE Pub.

Leading from the Heart: Choosing Courage over Fear in the Workplace. Kay Gilley. LC 96-26132. 240p. 1996. pap. text 17.95 (*0-7506-9835-7*) Buttrwrth-Heinemann.

***Leading from the Inside Out: The Art of Self-Leadership.** Samuel D. Rima, Sr. 256p. 2000. pap. 14.99 (*0-8010-9104-7*) Baker Bks.

Leading from the Maze: A Personal Pathway to Leadership. Jeff Patnaude. LC 95-45433. 158p. 1996. text 17.95 (*0-89815-745-5*) Ten Speed Pr.

Leading from Within: Developing Personal Direction. Nancy S. Huber. LC 98-13961. (Professional Practices in Adult Education & Human Resource Development Ser.). 126p. (C). 1998. text 21.50 (*1-57524-022-X*) Krieger.

Leading from Within: Martial Arts Skills for Enlightened Business & Management. Robert Pater. LC 99-24435. 224p. 1999. 16.95 (*0-89281-794-1*, Park St Pr) Inner Tradit.

Leading God's People: A Handbook for Elders. Stewart Matthew & Kenneth Scott. 116p. (C). 1989. pap. 35.00 (*0-7855-6818-2*, Pub. by St Andrew) St Mut.

Leading God's People: A Handbook for Elders. Stewart Matthew & Kenneth Scott. 116p. 1993. pap. 40.00 (*0-7152-0696-6*, Pub. by St Andrew) St Mut.

Leading God's People: A Handbook for Elders. Stewart Matthew & Kenneth Scott. 116p. (C). 1988. pap. text 35.00 (*0-7152-0591-9*) St Mut.

Leading Groups to Better Decisions. Erwin Rausch & George Rausch. (Simulation Game Ser.). (GER.). 1971. pap. 35.00 (*0-89401-048-4*) Didactic Syst.

Leading Groups to Better Decisions. Erwin Rausch & George Rausch. (Simulation Game Ser.). 1971. pap. 26.25 (*0-89401-046-8*) Didactic Syst.

Leading Groups to Better Decisions. Erwin Rausch & George Rausch. (Simulation Game Ser.). (FRE.). 1971. pap. 35.00 (*0-89401-047-6*) Didactic Syst.

Leading Head Start Into the Future. 156p. 1997. pap. 14.00 (*0-16-042726-6*) USGPO.

***Leading Health Indicators for Healthy People, 2010: Final Report.** Institute of Medicine Staff. 86p. 1999. pap. 18.00 (*0-309-06539-9*) Natl Acad Pr.

Leading Health Indicators for Healthy People, 2010: First Interim Report. Institute of Medicine Staff. 34p. 1998. pap. text 10.00 (*0-309-06247-0*) Natl Acad Pr.

Leading Health Indicators for Healthy People 2010: Second Interim Report. Institute of Medicine Staff. 82p. 1998. pap. text 15.00 (*0-309-06383-3*) Natl Acad Pr.

Leading Improving Primary Schools: The Work of Heads & Deputies. Geoff Southworth. 162p. 1998. 79.00 (*0-7507-0830-1*, Falmer Pr); pap. 26.95 (*0-7507-0829-8*, Falmer Pr) Taylor & Francis.

Leading in Prayer: A Workbook for Worship. Hughes O. Old. 381p. (Orig.). 1995. pap. 20.00 (*0-8028-0821-2*) Eerdmans.

Leading in the Spirit: A Guidebook for Learning Leaders in the Church. Barbara Bate. 32p. 1997. pap. 12.95 (*0-88177-234-8*, DR234) Discipleship Res.

Leading in Worship: A Sourcebook for Presbyterian Students & Ministers Drawing upon the Biblical & Historic Forms of the Reformed Tradition. Ed. by Terry L. Johnson. LC 96-85225. 191p. 1996. 17.95 (*0-9650367-2-3*) Covenant Fnd.

Leading Initiatives: Leadership, Teamwork & the Bottom Line. Jeremy Tozer. LC 98-154340. 200p. 1998. pap. text 24.95 (*0-7506-8948-X*) Buttrwrth-Heinemann.

Leading into the Twenty-First Century. Fenwick W. English et al. LC 92-5997. 144p. 1992. pap. 19.95 (*0-8039-6023-9*) Corwin Pr.

Leading Issues in African-American Studies. Ed. by Nikongo BaNikongo. LC 97-5379. 1997. pap. 29.95 (*0-89089-669-0*) Carolina Acad Pr.

***Leading Issues in Economic Development.** 7th ed. Gerald M. Meier & James E. Rauch. LC 99-59308. (Illus.). 600p. (C). 2000. pap. text 49.95 (*0-19-511589-9*) OUP.

***Leading Japan: The Role of the Prime Minister.** Tomohito Shinoda. LC 00-22886. 288p. 2000. 65.00 (*0-275-96994-0*, C6994, Praeger Pubs) Greenwood.

***Leading Kids to Books Through Crafts.** Caroline F. Bauer. LC 99-41387. (Mighty Easy Motivator Ser.). 160p. (J). 1999. 30.00 (*0-8389-0769-5*) ALA.

Leading Kids to Books Through MAGIC. Caroline Feller Bauer. LC 95-53049. (Mighty Easy Motivators Ser.). (Illus.). 125p. 1996. 29.00 (*0-8389-0684-2*, 0684-2-2045) ALA.

Leading Kids to Books Through Puppets. Caroline F. Bauer. LC 97-1357. (Mighty Easy Motivators Ser.). (Illus.). 144p. 1997. 22.00 (*0-8389-0706-7*) ALA.

***Leading Labour: Keir Hardie To Tony Blair.** Kevin Jeffreys. 1999. text 39.50 (*1-86064-453-8*) St Martin.

Leading Ladies. Don MacPherson. LC 86-13833. (Illus.). 1986. 25.00 (*0-312-47649-3*) St Martin.

Leading Ladies: A Study of Eight Late Victorian & Edwardian Political Wives. Esther S. Shkolnik. Ed. by William H. McNeill & Peter Stansky. (Modern European History Ser.). 600p. 1987. text 15.00 (*0-8240-7832-2*) Garland.

***Leading Ladies: New Images for Leadership from Biblical & Contemporary Women.** Jeanne Porter. 224p. 2000. pap. 14.95 (*1-880913-45-3*, Pub. by Innisfree Pr) Consort Bk Sales.

***Leading Lady.** Consuelo Vazquez. (Encanto Ser.). 2000. mass mkt. 5.99 (*0-7860-1139-4*) Kensgtn Pub Corp.

Leading Lady: Playscript. Nellie McCaslin. LC 93-14391. 20p. 1993. pap. 5.00 (*0-88734-432-1*) Players Pr.

Leading Lawyer's Case for the Resurrection. Ross Clifford. LC 97-143. 143p. 1996. reprint ed. pap. 12.50 (*1-896363-02-4*) CN Inst for Law.

***Leading-Life at the Battlefront.** Jean Nava. (More Than Conquerors Ser.: Vol. 3). (Illus.). 454p. 1999. pap. 12.95 (*0-9659952-4-0*) Kingdom Pr.

Leading Life-Changing Small Groups: The Willow Creek Guide. William P. Donahue. LC 96-17624. 128p. 1996. pap. 14.99 (*0-310-20595-6*) Zondervan.

Leading Little Ones to God: A Child's Book of Bible Teaching. Marian M. Schoolland. (Illus.). 184p. (J). (ps-5). 1995. pap. 18.00 (*0-8028-5120-7*, Eerdmans Bks) Eerdmans.

Leading Lives: Irish Women in Britain. Rita Wall. (C). 1989. 45.00 (*0-7855-6617-1*) St Mut.

Leading Manufacturing Excellence: A Guide to State-of-the-Art Manufacturing. Patricia E. Moody. LC 96-49899. 398p. 1997. 45.00 (*0-471-16341-4*) Wiley.

***Leading Marines.** Ed. by C. E. Mundy, Jr. (Illus.). 124p. 1999. reprint ed. pap. text 25.00 (*0-7881-8271-4*) DIANE Pub.

***Leading Men to Christ.** Nee Watchman. 1998. pap. 2.00 (*0-7363-0128-3*) Living Stream Ministry.

Leading Minds: An Anatomy of Leadership. Howard Gardner. 416p. 1996. pap. 18.00 (*0-465-08280-7*, Pub. by Basic) HarpC.

Leading Minnesota Companies. Ed. by Duffy Busch. 200p. (Orig.). 1991. pap. 16.00 (*0-932053-13-0*) Prime Pubns.

Leading Motives in the Imagery of Shakespeare's Tragedies. Caroline F. Spurgeon. LC 73-95446. (Studies in Shakespeare: No. 24). (C). 1970. reprint ed. lib. bdg. 75.00 (*0-8383-1203-9*) M S G Haskell Hse.

Leading Organizational Change. Ed. by Jack J. Phillips & Elwood F. Holton. LC 97-74235. (In Action Ser.). 260p. 1997. pap. 50.00 (*1-56286-064-X*) Am Soc Train & Devel.

Leading Organizations: Perspectives for a New Era. Gill R. Hickman. LC 98-25335. 612p. 1998. 65.95 (*0-7619-1422-6*); pap. 32.95 (*0-7619-1423-4*) Sage.

***Leading Organizations Through Transition: Communication & Cultural Change.** Stanley A. Deetz et al. LC 99-50466. 1999. write for info. (*0-7619-2097-8*) Sage.

Leading Out: Mountaineering Stories of Adventurous Women. 2nd ed. Rachel Da Silva. (Illus.). 450p. 1998. pap. 16.95 (*1-58005-010-7*) Seal Pr WA.

Leading Out Loud: The Authentic Speaker, the Credible Leader. Terry Pearce. (Management Ser.). 192p. 1995. mass mkt. 22.50 (*0-7879-0111-3*) Jossey-Bass.

Leading Pennsylvania into the 21st Century: Policy Strategies for the Future. Ed. by Don E. Eberly. LC 90-80890. (Illus.). 408p. (Orig.). 1990. pap. 15.95 (*0-9626032-0-1*) CFPPA.

Leading People. Robert Rosen. 1997. pap. 13.95 (*0-14-024272-4*) Viking Penguin.

Leading People: What School Leaders Can Learn from Military Leadership Development. 2nd ed. William G. Monahan & Edwin R. Smith. LC 94-34930. (Illus.). 216p. 1995. 24.95 (*0-590-49749-9*) Scholastic Inc.

Leading People, Learning from People: Lessons from Education Professionals. Judith Bell & Bernard T. Harrison. LC 98-13869. 177p. 1998. 85.00 (*0-335-20075-3*); pap. 27.95 (*0-335-20074-5*) Taylor & Francis.

Leading Personalities in Statistical Sciences: From the Seventeenth Century to the Present. Norman L. Johnson & Samuel I. Kotz. LC 97-9152. (Probability & Mathematical Ser.). 432p. 1997. pap. 64.95 (*0-471-16381-3*) Wiley.

Leading Primary Schools: The Pleasure, Pain & Principles of Leadership in the Primary School. David Clegg & Shirly Billington. LC 97-19357. 128p. 1998. pap. 25.95 (*0-335-19644-6*) OpUniv Pr.

Leading Product Development: The Senior Manager's Guide to Creating & Shaping the Enterprise. Steven C. Wheelwright & Kim B. Clark. (Illus.). 200p. 1994. 27.00 (*0-02-934465-4*) Free Pr.

Leading Product Innovation: Accelerating Growth in a Product-Based Business. Marvin L. Patterson & John J. Fenoglio, Jr. LC 99-15417. 434p. 1999. 55.00 (*0-471-34517-2*) Wiley.

***Leading Public Organizations.** Rusaw. (C). 1999. pap. text. write for info. (*0-15-508462-3*) Harcourt Coll Pubs.

Leading Questions: A Free Will Baptist Discipleship Manual. Greg McAllister & Jim McAllister. 145p. 1988. ring bd. 12.95 (*0-89265-133-4*) Randall Hse.

Leading Questions: How Hegemony Affects the International Political Economy. Robert Pahre. LC 98-40162. (Studies in International Political Economy). 266p. 1999. text 49.50 (*0-472-10970-7*, 10970) U of Mich Pr.

Leading Reading Assessment. 2nd ed. Shearer. 1997. teacher ed. 22.50 (*0-8058-2917-2*) L Erlbaum Assocs.

***Leading Rule of the Black Working Class: Analysis & Platform Submitted to the NAACP.** Thomas J. Kuna-Jacob. (Illus.). 29p. 1999. 4.14 (*1-878030-37-X*, 019) Assn World Peace.

Leading Schools in a Global Era: A Cultural Perspective. A Special Issue of the Peabody Journal of Education. Ed. by Philip Hallinger & Kenneth Leithwood. 168p. 1998. pap. write for info. (*0-8058-9836-0*) L Erlbaum Assocs.

***Leading Schools in Times of Change.** Christopher Day. LC 99-50029. 2000. pap. write for info. (*0-335-20582-8*) Taylor & Francis.

Leading Sector Fund Trader-Past Issues, January 1987 to December 1988. Ed. by John R. Bathe. 160p. (Orig.). 1989. pap. 50.00 (*0-317-93448-1*) Alphanational.

Leading Sectors & World Powers: The Coevolution of Global Economics & Politics. George Modelski & William R. Thompson. Ed. by Charles W. Kegley & Donald J. Puchala. LC 95-4372. (Studies in International Relations). (Illus.). 300p. 1996. text 49.95 (*1-57003-054-5*) U of SC Pr.

Leading Self-Directed Work Teams: A Guide to Developing New Team Leadership Skills. Kim Fisher. LC 92-28418. 1992. 24.95 (*0-07-021071-3*) McGraw.

***Leading Self-Directed Work Teams: A Guide to Developing New Team Leadership Skills.** 2nd ed. Kimball Fisher. LC 99-45587. 339p. 1999. 24.95 (*0-07-134924-3*) McGraw.

Leading Self-Help Groups: A Guide for Training Facilitators. L. Mallory. LC 83-48659. 72p. 1984. pap. 7.95 (*0-87304-206-9*) Manticore Pubs.

Leading Small Groups: Basic Skills for Church & Community Organizations. Nathan W. Turner. 80p. (Orig.). 1996. pap. 12.00 (*0-8170-1210-9*) Judson.

Leading Social Entrepreneurs. Ashoka: Innovators for the Public Staff. (Illus.). 208p. 1998. pap. 15.00 (*0-9666759-0-8*) Ashoka Innovators.

Leading Spirit in American Art: William Merritt Chase, 1849-1916. Ronald G. Pisano. LC 83-82428. (Illus.). 204p. 1983. 25.00 (*0-935558-14-4*) Henry Art.

Leading Students into Prayer: Ideas & Suggestions from A to Z. Kathleen Glavich. LC 92-62204. (Illus.). 160p. (Orig.). 1993. pap. 14.95 (*0-89622-549-6*) Twenty-Third.

Leading Students into Scripture. 2nd rev. ed. Mary K. Glavich. LC 86-51613. (Illus.). 144p. (Orig.). (J). 1998. pap. 12.95 (*0-89622-328-0*) Twenty-Third.

Leading Systems: Lessons from the Power Lab. Barry Oshry. LC 99-34616. (Illus.). 200p. 1999. pap. text 24.95 (*1-57675-072-8*) Berrett-Koehler.

***Leading Teams.** Rob Yeung. (Essentials Ser.). 64p. 2000. pap. 9.95 (*1-85703-566-6*, Pub. by How To Bks) Midpt Trade.

Leading Teams: Mastering the New Role. John H. Zenger et al. LC 93-12652. 275p. 1993. 35.00 (*1-55623-894-0*, Irwn Prfssnl) McGraw-Hill Prof.

Leading Teams: The Skills for Success. Sam R. Lloyd. LC 95-83968. (How-to Book Ser.). 103p. (Orig.). 1996. pap. 12.95 (*1-884926-51-7*, LEADT) Amer Media.

Leading Teams Effectively in a Diverse Workforce: A Performance Comparison of Asian, Black, Hispanic, & White Men & Women. Vincent W. Kafka. 47p. 1996. pap. 19.95 (*0-913261-35-1*) Effect Learn Sys.

***Leading the Artful Life: From the Pages of Mary Engelbreit's Home Companion/ Interiors Designed with Artistic Intuition.** Mary Engelbreit et al. LC 00-38692. (Illus.). 2000. pap. 27.95 (*0-7407-0997-6*) Andrews & McMeel.

Leading the Assembly in Prayer: A Practical Guide for Lay & Ordained Presiders. Michael J. Begolly. LC 97-5326. 160p. (Orig.). 1997. pap. text 17.95 (*0-89390-398-1*) Resource Pubns.

An Asterisk (*) at the beginning of an entry indicates that the title is appearing for the first time.

Leading the Association: Striking the Right Balance Between Staff & Volunteers. James J. Dunlop. Ed. by Heidi H. Bowers. 148p. 1989. pap. 49.50 (*0-88034-038-X*) Am Soc Assn Execs.

Leading the Charge: Orrin Hatch & 20 Years of America. Lee Roderick. LC 94-2048. 447p. 1994. 22.95 (*1-882723-09-0*) Gold Leaf Pr.

Leading the Cheers. Justin Cartwright. 256p. 1999. 23.95 (*0-7867-0658-9*) Carroll & Graf.

Leading the Church's Song: A Practical Introduction to Leading Congregational Song. Mark P. Bangert. Ed. by Robert Buckley Farley. LC 98-33961. 1999. pap. 20.00 incl. audio compact disk (*0-8066-3591-6*, 3-402, Augsburg) Augsburg Fortress.

Leading the Congregation. Norman Shawchuck & Roger Heuser. 20.00 (*0-687-08420-2*) Abingdon.

Leading the Congregation: Caring for Yourself While Serving the People. Norman Shawchuck & Roger Heuser. LC 93-18258. 272p. (C). 1993. text 24.95 (*0-687-13338-6*) Abingdon.

Leading the Cooperative School. 2nd rev. ed. David W. Johnson & Roger T. Johnson. LC 95-215266. (Illus.). 296p. 1994. pap. text, teacher ed. 20.00 (*0-939603-20-9*) Interaction Bk Co.

Leading the Creative Edge: Gaining Competitive Advantage Through the Power of Creative Problem Solving. Roger L. Firestien. 175p. 1996. 20.00 (*0-89109-975-1*) Pinon Press.

***Leading the Edge of Change: Building Individual & Organizational Capacity for the Evolving Nature of Change.** John L. Bennett. LC 99-68955. 128p. 2000. pap. 11.95 (*0-9678323-0-6*) Paw Print.

Leading the Field: British Native Breeds of Horses & Ponies. Elwyn H. Edwards. (Illus.). 180p. 1993. 39.95 (*0-09-175332-5*, Pub. by S Paul) Trafalgar.

***Leading the Followers by Following the Leader: Radical Look at Radical Leadership.** Dennis L. Gorton & Tom Allen. 256p. 2000. pap. 11.99 (*0-87509-892-4*) Chr Pubns.

Leading the Guidebook Astray. Neale B. Mason. 79p. pap. write for info. (*3-7052-0437-8*, Pub. by Poetry Salzburg) Intl Spec Bk.

Leading the Leader: A Leader's Practical Guide to Dealing with Manipulative Followers. unabridged ed. Nkosiyabo Z. Zvandasara. 152p. 1997. pap. 12.99 (*0-9660442-0-7*) Lesley Bks.

Leading the Learning Organization: Communication & Competencies for Managing Change. Alan T. Belasen. LC 99-11338. (SUNY Series, Human Communication Processes). (Illus.). 480p. (C). 1999. text 71.50 (*0-7914-4367-1*); pap. text 23.95 (*0-7914-4368-X*) State U NY Pr.

Leading the Little Ones to Mary. Sister Mary Lelia. 1959. pap. 3.00 (*0-910984-13-1*) Montfort Pubns.

Leading the Living Organization: Growth Strategies for Management. Lane Tracy. LC 93-41817. 232p. 1994. 55.00 (*0-89930-819-8*, Quorum Bks) Greenwood.

Leading the Next Millennium. 6th ed. Ed. by Graham Strachan. (Illus.). 96p. (C). 1999. pap. text 25.00 (*0-7881-4368-9*) DIANE Pub.

Leading the Organisation to Learn: The 10 Levers for Putting Knowledge & Learning to Work. Mick Cope. (Illus.). 301p. 1998. pap. 45.00 (*0-273-63524-7*, Pub. by F T P-H) Trans-Atl Phila.

Leading the Quality Initiative. Randall R. Willie. Ed. by Susan Annitto. (AT&T Quality Library). (Illus.). 126p. (Orig.). 1990. pap. 19.95 (*0-932764-30-4*, 500-441) AT&T Customer Info.

Leading the Race: The Transformation of the Black Elite in the Nation's Capital, 1880-1920. Jacqueline M. Moore. LC 99-31004. (Illus.). 1999. 37.50 (*0-8139-1903-7*) U Pr of Va.

***Leading the Revolution.** Gary Hamel. 352p. 2000. 29.95 (*1-57851-189-5*, HBS Pr) Harvard Busn.

***Leading the Revolution: Sustaining New Systems & Advancing Performance in Health Care Organizations.** 2nd ed. Cathleen Krueger Wilson & Tim Porter-O'Grady. LC 99-23936. 400p. 1999. 55.00 (*0-8342-1367-2*, 13672) Aspen Pub.

Leading the Sales Team. David Hillier. 152p. 1994. 83.95 (*0-566-07494-X*, Pub. by Gower) Ashgate Pub Co.

Leading the Self-Managing School. Brian J. Caldwell & Jim M. Spinks. (Education Policy Perspectives Ser.). 250p. 1992. 89.95 (*1-85000-656-3*, Falmer Pr); pap. 34.95 (*1-85000-657-1*, Falmer Pr) Taylor & Francis.

***Leading the Sunday School into the 21st Century.** Towns. 2000. 16.99 (*0-8307-1833-8*, Gospel Light) Gospel Lght.

Leading the Team-based Church: How Pastors & Church Staffs Can Grow Together into a Powerful Faith. George Cladis. LC 98-40264. 1999. 21.95 (*0-7879-4119-0*) Jossey-Bass.

Leading the Team Organization: How to Create an Enduring Competitive Advantage. Dean R. Tjosvold & Mary M. Tjosvold. (Illus.). 198p. 1992. 23.95 (*0-669-27972-2*) Lxngtn Bks.

Leading the Transition: Management's Role in Creating a Team-Based Culture. Wilbur L. Pike. LC 94-44928. 116p. 1995. 28.00 (*0-527-76247-4*) Productivity Inc.

Leading the Way: A History of the General Court, 1629-1980. Cornelius Dalton et al. (Illus.). 528p. 1984. write for info. (*0-9613915-0-2*); pap. 4.50 (*0-9613915-1-0*) Mass Sec Commonw.

Leading the Way: Amy Morris Homans & the Beginnings of Professional Education for Women, 64. Betty Spears. LC 85-21872. (Contributions in Women's Studies: No. 64). 193p. 1986. 52.95 (*0-313-25107-X*, SLW/, Greenwood Pr) Greenwood.

Leading the Way: Practical Management Skills for the Long-Term Care Nurse. Karl Pillemer & Philip T. Johnson. Ed. by Martin Schumacher. 50p. 1997. 10.95 (*0-9653629-1-4*) Frontline Pub.

Leading the Way: Principals & Superintendents Look at Math Instruction. Ed. by Marilyn Burns. LC 99-31755. 96p. (Orig.). 1999. pap. 14.95 (*0-941355-21-7*) Math Solns Pubns.

Leading the Way to Competitive Excellence: The Harris Mountaintop Case Study. Ed. by William A. Levinson. LC 97-17504. 346p. 1997. 38.00 (*0-87389-376-X*, H0954) ASQ Qual Pr.

Leading the West: One Hundred Contemporary Painters & Sculptors. Donald J. Hagerty. (Illus.). 224p. 1997. 60.00 (*0-87358-600-X*) Northland AZ.

Leading the West: One Hundred Contemporary Painters & Sculptors. limited ed. Donald J. Hagerty. (Illus.). 224p. 1997. boxed set 250.00 (*0-87358-691-3*) Northland AZ.

***Leading the Wired Organization: The Information Professional's Guide to Managing Technological Change.** Mark Stover. LC 99-28011. 225p. 1999. pap. 49.95 (*1-55570-357-7*) Neal-Schuman.

Leading the World. Johnston. 1997. pap. 15.99 (*1-85792-269-7*, Pub. by Christian Focus) Spring Arbor Dist.

Leading to Change: The Challenge of School Superintendency. Susan M. Johnson. 1996. 29.95 (*0-7879-0214-4*) Jossey-Bass.

Leading Today's Funerals: A Pastoral Guide for Improving Bereavement Ministry. Dan S. Lloyd. LC 96-1639. 128p. (Orig.). 1997. pap. 12.99 (*0-8010-9032-6*) Baker Bks.

***Leading Today's Volunteers: Motivate & Manage Your Team.** Flora MacLeod & Sarah Hogarth. 1999. pap. 13.95 (*1-55180-247-3*) Self-Counsel Pr.

Leading Twin Cities Companies, 1986-87. Ed. by Duffy Busch. (Annual Ser.). 80p. 1987. pap. 10.00 (*0-932053-04-1*) Prime Pubns.

Leading U. S. Supreme Court Tax Cases: Official Syllabi, Notes, & Indices. Walter H. Nagel et al. LC 94-41031. 1994. write for info. (*1-55871-312-3*) Tax Mgmt.

***Leading Volunteers for Results: Building Communities Today.** Jeanne H. Bradner. 128p. 1999. pap. 11.95 (*0-9634395-5-3*) Conversation Pr.

Leading Wesleyan Thinkers. Ed. by Richard S. Taylor. (Great Holiness Classics Ser.: Vol. 3). 436p. 1985. 34.99 (*0-8341-1069-5*) Beacon Hill.

Leading When God Is Moving. Wayne Schmidt. 122p. (Orig.). 1996. pap. 9.95 (*0-89827-166-5*, BK980) Wesleyan Pub Hse.

Leading with Integrity: Competence with Christian Character. Fred Smith. LC 99-6720. (Pastor's Soul Ser.). 176p. 1999. text 16.99 (*1-55661-971-5*) Bethany Hse.

Leading with Knowledge: Winning in the Realm of the Red Queen. Richard C. Huseman & Jon P. Goodman. LC 98-25433. 216p. 1998. 35.00 (*0-7619-1774-8*); pap. 16.99 (*0-7619-1775-6*) Sage.

Leading with Love: How Women & Men Can Transform Their Organizations Through Maternalistic Management. Kathleen D. Sanford. LC 97-91352. (Illus.). v, 250p. 1998. 23.95 (*0-9661753-7-9*) Vashon Pub.

Leading with My Chin. Jay Leno. 304p. 1997. mass mkt. 6.50 (*0-06-109492-7*, Harp PBks) HarpC.

Leading with My Chin. large type ed. Jay Leno. LC 98-52520. (Paperback Ser.). 1999. 22.95 (*0-7838-8524-5*) Thorndike Pr.

Leading with My Heart. Virginia C. Kelley. (Illus.). 288p. 1994. 22.50 (*0-671-88800-5*) S&S Trade.

Leading with My Heart. Virginia C. Kelley & James Morgan. Ed. by Julie Rubenstein. 336p. 1995. pap. 6.50 (*0-671-52295-7*) PB.

Leading with NLP: Essential Leadership Skills for Influencing & Managing People. Joseph O'Connor. (Illus.). 226p. 1999. pap. 16.00 (*0-7225-3767-0*) Thorsons PA.

Leading with Soul: An Uncommon Journey of Spirit. Lee G. Bolman & Terrence E. Deal. LC 94-9277. (The Management Ser.). 206p. 1995. mass mkt. 20.00 (*1-55542-707-3*) Jossey-Bass.

***Leading with the Heart: Coach K's Winning Strategies for Basketball, Business & Life.** Mike Krzyzewski & Donald T. Phillips. LC 99-48672. (Illus.). 304p. 2000. 24.95 (*0-446-52626-6*, Pub. by Warner Bks) Little.

Leading with Vision. Dale Galloway. (Beeson Pastoral Ser.: Vol. 1). 160p. 1999. 19.99 (*0-8341-1724-X*) Beacon Hill.

Leading with Vision. Larry Lashway. LC 97-27661. xii, 148p. 1997. pap. 13.50 (*0-86552-138-7*) U of Oreg ERIC.

Leading Without Power. Max Depree. LC 97-21017. 1997. mass mkt. 19.50 (*0-7879-1063-5*) Jossey-Bass.

Leading Women: How Church Women Can Avoid Leadership Traps & Negotiate the Gender Maze. Carol E. Becker & Norman Shawchuck. 176p. (Orig.). 1995. pap. 14.95 (*0-687-45964-8*) Abingdon.

***Leading Women's Ministries: A Guide to Effectiveness & Excellence in Serving Women.** Pamela Hoover Heim. 151p. 1999. pap. text 15.95 (*0-935797-35-1*) Harvest IL.

Leading World Stock Exchanges: Trading Practices & Organization. Wilford J. Eiteman & David K. Eiteman. LC 65-63678. (Michigan International Business Studies: No. 2). 95p. reprint ed. pap. 30.00 (*0-608-15389-3*, 205636000060) Bks Demand.

Leading Young Children to Music. 6th ed. (C). 2000. write for info. (*0-13-016001-6*) P-H.

***Leading Young Children to Music.** 6th ed. B. Joan Haines & Linda L. Gerber. LC 99-11595. 301p. 2000. pap. text 37.00 (*0-13-976275-2*) S&S Trade.

***Leading Your Business into the Future with the Internet.** Danielle Vallee. 336p. 1999. boxed set 39.95 (*1-57444-252-X*) St Lucie Pr.

Leading Your Church Through Conflict & Reconciliation. Marshall Shelley. 1996. 22.99 (*0-345-39600-6*, Moorings) Ballantine Pub Grp.

Leading Your Church Through Conflict & Reconciliation: 30 Strategies to Transform Your Ministry. Ed. by Marshall Shelley. LC 96-45869. (Library of Leadership Development: No. 1). 32p. 1997. text 19.99 (*1-55661-940-5*) Bethany Hse.

Leading Your Church to Growth see Guiando Su Iglesia al Crecimiento

Leading Your Ministry. Alan E. Nelson. Ed. by Herb Miller. LC 96-12804. (Leadership Insights Ser.). 176p. 1996. pap. 14.95 (*0-687-01964-8*) Abingdon.

Leading Your Positively Outrageous Service Team. T. Scott Gross. 224p. 1994. pap. 12.95 (*1-57101-017-3*) MasterMedia Pub.

Leading Your Sales Team. Jim Pancero. 241p. 1995. 31.50 (*0-85013-200-2*) Dartnell Corp.

Leading Your Students in Worship. Jim Marian. 156p. (Orig.). 1993. pap. 9.99 (*1-56476-086-3*, 6-3086, Victor Bks) Chariot Victor.

Leading Your Team: How to Involve & Inspire Teams. Andrew Leigh & Michael Maynard. (People Skills for Professionals Ser.). (Illus.). 232p. 1996. reprint ed. pap. 19.95 (*1-85788-101-X*) Nicholas Brealey.

Leading Your Team to Excellence: How to Make Quality Decisions. Elaine K. McEwan. LC 95-17300. (Illus.). 192p. 1996. 61.95 (*0-8039-6520-6*); pap. 27.95 (*0-8039-6521-4*) Corwin Pr.

Leadrship & Managment of Programs for Young Children. 2nd ed. (C). 2000. pap. text. write for info. (*0-13-025684-6*) P-H.

Leads & Conclusions. Marshall J. Cook. LC 94-23650. (Elements of Article Writing Ser.). 176p. 1995. 15.99 (*0-89879-661-X*, Wrtrs Digest Bks) F & W Pubns Inc.

Leadville: Colorado's Magic City. Edward Blair. LC 95-13481. (Illus.). 247p. 1996. pap. 25.00 (*0-9623868-9-8*) F Pruett.

Leadville Architecture: Legacy of Silver, 1860-1899. Lawrence Von Bamford. LC 96-86287. (Illus.). 125p. (Orig.). 1996. pap. 10.00 (*0-614-20545-X*) Architect Rsch.

Leadville-Fairplay, CO. rev. ed. Ed. by Trails Illustrated Staff. 1997. 8.99 (*0-925873-31-4*) Trails Illustrated.

Leadville's Ice Palace: A Colossus in the Colorado Rockies. Darlene G. Weir. 464p. 1994. write for info. (*0-9637431-0-4*) Ice Castle.

Leaf. 20p. 1995. pap. 7.95 (*0-7935-5609-0*, 00385005) H Leonard.

Leaf. Evert. 1998. 1.50 (*0-7167-9372-5*) W H Freeman.

***Leaf.** Johnny Ray Moore. (Illus.). 8p. 1999. pap. 3.75 (*1-880612-90-9*) Seedling Pubns.

Leaf & Tendril. John Burroughs. (Works of John Burroughs). 1989. reprint ed. lib. bdg. 79.00 (*0-7812-2195-1*) Rprt Serv.

***Leaf & the Cloud.** Oliver. 64p. 2000. 22.00 (*0-306-80993-1*) Da Capo.

Leaf & the Marble. Iain Crichton Smith. 80p. 1999. pap. 14.95 (*1-85754-400-5*, Pub. by Carcanet Pr) Paul & Co Pubs.

***Leaf Baby.** Barrett. LC 96-75965. (Illus.). 12p. (J). (ps). 1998. pap. 5.95 (*0-15-201057-2*) Harcourt.

Leaf Beetles of Ohio. John A. Wilcox. (Bulletin Ser.: No. 43). 1954. pap. text 5.00 (*0-86727-042-X*) Ohio Bio Survey.

Leaf Book: A Field Guide to Plants of Northern California. Ida Geary & David Cavagnaro. LC 78-188679. (Illus.). 388p. 1976. pap. 6.00 (*0-912908-01-7*) Tamal Land.

Leaf Cell & Hierarchical Compaction Techniques. LC 97-15247. 1997. text 101.00 (*0-7923-9946-3*) Kluwer Academic.

***Leaf Development & Canopy Growth.** Bruce Marshall & J. A. Roberts. LC 00-27795. (Sheffield Biological Sciences Ser.). 2000. write for info. (*0-8493-9769-3*) CRC Pr.

Leaf from Our Table, 2 vols., Set. large type ed. pap. 11.00 (*0-317-01854-X*) Cath Guild Blind.

Leaf from the Great Tree of God: Essays in Honour of Ritamary Bradley, SFCC. Ed. by Margot H. King. (Translation Ser.). 315p. 1994. pap. 25.00 (*0-920669-53-0*, Pub. by Peregrina Pubng) Cistercian Pubns.

***Leaf Fun Sticker Book: Featuring the Art of MaryJo Koch.** MaryJo Koch. (Illus.). 16p. (J). (ps-3). 2000. pap. 3.98 (*0-7651-1690-1*) Smithmark.

Leaf Gnawed to Lace. Pamela M. Perkins-Frederick. (Illus.). 36p. (Orig.). 1992. pap. 5.00 (*0-9625348-4-6*) P Goodrich.

Leaf in the Bitter Wind. Ye Ting-Xing. LC 97-162651. 320p. 1997. 32.95 (*0-385-25603-5*) Doubleday.

Leaf in the Bitter Wind: A Memoir. Ting-xing Ye. (Illus.). 408p. 1998. pap. write for info. (*0-385-25701-5*) Doubleday.

Leaf in the Bitter Wind: A Memoir. Ting-xing Ye. LC 99-71507. 382p. 1999. 23.00 (*1-886913-30-7*, Pub. by Ruminator Bks) Consort Bk Sales.

Leaf in the Wind. large type ed. Margaret Hadley. (Dales Large Print Ser.). 1995. pap. 18.99 (*1-85389-521-0*, Dales) Ulverscroft.

***Leaf in the Wind: I Say, "Yes Lord" Even When I Want to Say, No."** George DeTellis. 150p. 2000. pap. write for info. (*0-9653234-3-9*) New Missions.

***Leaf in Time.** David Walker. Ed. by Fran Balkwill. (Making Sense of Science Ser.). (Illus.). 32p. (J). (gr. 3-7). 1999. pap. 12.00 (*1-85578-097-6*, Pub. by Portland Pr Ltd) Princeton U Pr.

Leaf It to Me Botanical Coloring Book. Anita M. Hamm. 1980. pap. 1.75 (*0-935513-03-5*) Samara Pubns.

Leaf It to Sally Brown. Charles M. Schulz. LC 98-215124. (Illus.). 32p. (ps-3). 1998. 3.50 (*0-694-01030-8*, HarpEntertain) Morrow Avon.

Leaf Men & the Brave Good Bugs. William Joyce. LC 95-40644. (Laura Geringer Bks.). (Illus.). 40p. (J). (ps-3). 1996. 16.95 (*0-06-027237-6*); lib. bdg. 16.89 (*0-06-027238-4*) HarpC Child Bks.

Leaf of Honey: And the Proverbs of the Rainforest. Joseph Shepperd. 319p. 1988. pap. 19.95 (*1-870989-02-3*) Bahai.

Leaf Path. Emily Warn. 63p. (Orig.). 1982. pap. 5.00 (*0-914742-61-2*) Copper Canyon.

Leaf Protein & Its Biproducts in Human & Animal Nutrition. N. W. Pirie. 224p. 1987. text 59.95 (*0-521-33030-0*) Cambridge U Pr.

Leaf Raker. Raewyn Caisley. LC 93-26218. (Voyages Ser.). (Illus.). (J). 1994. 4.25 (*0-383-03756-5*) SRA McGraw.

Leaf Storm. Gabriel Garcia Marquez. Tr. by Gregory Rabassa from SPA. LC 76-138784. Vol. 699. 160p. 1990. pap. 11.00 (*0-06-090699-5*, CN 699, Perennial) HarperTrade.

Leaf Structure: Coastal Vegetation & Mangroves of Venezuela. Ingrid Roth. (Handbuch der Pflanzenanatomie Encyclopedia of Plant Anatomy - Traite d' Anatomie Vegetale Ser.: Vol. 14, Pt. 2). (Illus.). x, 172p. 1992. 80.00 (*3-443-14020-3*, Pub. by Gebruder Borntraeger) Balogh.

Leaf Structure: Montane Regions of Venezuela. Ingrid Roth. LC 96-105750. (Handbuch der Pflanzenanatomie Encyclopedia of Plant Anatomy - Traite d' Anatomie Vegetale Ser.: Vol. 14, Pt. 3). (Illus.). x, 250p. 1995. 111.00 (*3-443-14022-X*, Pub. by Gebruder Borntraeger) Balogh.

Leaf Structure of a Venezuelan Cloud Forest, in Relation to the Microclimate. Ingrid Roth. (Handbuch der Pflanzenanatomie Encyclopedia of Plant Anatomy - Traite d' Anatomie Vegetale Ser.: Vol. 14, Pt. 1). (Illus.). xi, 244p. 1990. 88.00 (*3-443-14018-1*, Pub. by Gebruder Borntraeger) Balogh.

Leaf Threads, Wind Rhymes. Darlene Mathis-Eddy. LC 84-71936. 64p. (Orig.). 1985. pap. 6.95 (*0-935306-31-5*) Barnwood Pr.

Leaf Venation Patterns Vol. 1: Annonaceae. Edward P. Klucking. LC 95-225835. (Handbuch der Pflanzenanatomie Encyclopedia of Plant Anatomy - Traite d' Anatomie Vegetale Ser.). (Illus.). 538p. 1986. 130.00 (*3-443-50001-3*, Pub. by Gebruder Borntraeger) Balogh.

Leaf Venation Patterns Vol. 2: Lauraceae. Edward P. Klucking. (Handbuch der Pflanzenanatomie Encyclopedia of Plant Anatomy - Traite d' Anatomie Vegetale Ser.). (Illus.). 514p. 1987. 142.00 (*3-443-50002-1*, Pub. by Gebruder Borntraeger) Balogh.

Leaf Venation Patterns Vol. 3: Myrtaceae. Edward P. Klucking. (Handbuch der Pflanzenanatomie Encyclopedia of Plant Anatomy - Traite d' Anatomie Vegetale Ser.). (Illus.). 584p. 1988. 153.00 (*3-443-50003-X*, Pub. by Gebruder Borntraeger) Balogh.

Leaf Venation Patterns Vol. 4: Melastomataceae. Edward P. Klucking. (Handbuch der Pflanzenanatomie Encyclopedia of Plant Anatomy - Traite d' Anatomie Vegetale Ser.). (Illus.). 522p. 1989. 153.00 (*3-443-50004-8*, Pub. by Gebruder Borntraeger) Balogh.

Leaf Venation Patterns Vol. 5: Combretaceae. Edward P. Klucking. (Handbuch der Pflanzenanatomie Encyclopedia of Plant Anatomy - Traite d' Anatomie Vegetale Ser.). (Illus.). 436p. 1991. 142.00 (*3-443-50016-1*, Pub. by Gebruder Borntraeger) Balogh.

Leaf Venation Patterns Vol. 6: Flacourtiaceae. Edward P. Klucking. (Handbuch der Pflanzenanatomie Encyclopedia of Plant Anatomy - Traite d' Anatomie Vegetale Ser.). (Illus.). 504p. 1992. 165.00 (*3-443-50017-X*, Pub. by Gebruder Borntraeger) Balogh.

Leaf Venation Patterns Vol. 7: The Classification of Leaf Veneation Patterns. Edward P. Klucking. (Handbuch der Pflanzenanatomie Encyclopedia of Plant Anatomy) - Traite d' Anatomie Vegetale Ser.). 337p. (C). 1995. 159.00 (*3-443-50018-8*, Pub. by Gebruder Borntraeger) Balogh.

Leaf Venation Patterns Vol. 8, Pt. I: Euphorbiaceae, Phyllanthoideae & Oldfieldioideae. Edward P. Klucking. (Handbuch der Pflanzenanatomie Encyclopedia of Plant Anatomy - Traite d' Anatomie Vegetale Ser.). (Illus.). 379p. 1997. 165.00 (*3-443-50021-8*, Pub. by Gebruder Borntraeger) Balogh.

***Leaf Your Weight Behind.** x, 116p. 1999. pap. 15.00 (*0-9671737-0-1*) Nancy Barnes.

Leafhoppers & Planthoppers. Ed. by L. R. Nault & J. G. Rodriguez. LC 85-5383. 500p. 1985. 220.00 (*0-471-80611-0*, Wiley-Interscience) Wiley.

Leafhoppers (Cicadellidae) A Bibliography, Generic Check-List & Index to the World Literature, 1956-1985. P. W. Oman et al. 384p. 1990. text 120.00 (*0-85198-690-0*) OUP.

Leafhoppers of Ohio. Herbert Osborn. (Bulletin Ser.: No. 14). 1928. pap. text 2.00 (*0-86727-013-6*) Ohio Bio Survey.

Leafhoppers of Ohio: Subfamily Typhlocybinae. Dorothy M. Johnson. (Bulletin Ser.: No. 31). 1935. pap. text 4.00 (*0-86727-030-6*) Ohio Bio Survey.

Leafing Page. Roberta Seibert. 24p. (Orig.). 1987. pap. 3.95 (*0-938911-04-X*) Indiv Ed - Poppy Ln.

***Leafing Through Flowers.** 236p. 2000. per. 90.00 (*0-935112-55-3*) Callaway Edns.

***Leafing Through Flowers.** aut. ed. 236p. 2000. per. 150.00 (*0-935112-62-6*) Callaway Edns.

Leafless American. limited ed. Edward Dahlberg. (Illus.). 1967. 32.00 (*0-911796-02-9*) Beacham.

Leafless American & Other Writings. Edward Dahlberg. Ed. & Intro. by Harold Billings. LC 86-18185. (Recovered Classics Ser.). 128p. 1986. reprint ed. 20.00 (*0-914232-83-5*) McPherson & Co.

Leafless American & Other Writings. Edward Dahlberg. Ed. & Intro. by Harold Billings. Intro. by Gerald Burns. LC 86-18185. (Recovered Classics Ser.). 128p. 1986. reprint ed. pap. 10.00 (*0-914232-80-0*) McPherson & Co.

Leaflet Missal Organ Accompaniment. Joseph Cirou et al. 1987. 34.95 (*0-915866-09-9*) Am Cath Pr.

Leaflets from the Danish West Indies: Descriptive of the Social, Political & Commercial Condition of These Islands. Charles E. Taylor. LC 72-100304. (Illus.). 208p. 1970. reprint ed. lib. bdg. 45.00 (*0-8371-2913-3*, TWI&) Greenwood.

Leaflets of the White Rose: A Filmplay. Thomas J. Cox. 119p. (Orig.). (YA). 1991. pap. 14.50 (*1-879710-02-1*) Riverside FL.

***Leafs.** Brian McFarlane. (Original Six Ser.). 208p. (J). (gr. 3-7). 1999. reprint ed. pap. 13.95 (*0-7737-5843-7*, Pub. by Stoddart Publ) Genl Dist Srvs.

Leaf's Boundary. Sheila Zamora. LC 79-20119. 57p. (Orig.). 1980. pap. 4.95 (*0-934332-19-3*) LEpervier Pr.

Leafs vs. the Canadiens: The NHL's Top Teams. James Duplacey. (Hockey Superstars Ser.). (Illus.). 32p. (J). 1996. pap. 6.95 (*1-55074-358-9*) Kids Can Pr.

Leafy Greens. 1995. 5.95 (*0-02-860371-0*) Macmillan.

Leafy Greens. Mark Bittman. LC 95-11777. 288p. 1995. 15.00 (*0-02-860355-9*) Macmillan.

Leafy Hepaticae of Mexico: One Hundred & Twenty-Seven Years After C. M. Gottsche. Margaret Fulford & Aaron J. Sharp. LC 90-48337. (Memoirs Ser.: No. 63). 86p. 1990. pap. text 13.00 (*0-89327-361-9*) NY Botanical.

Leafy Spices. V. Prakash. 144p. 1990. lib. bdg. 149.00 (*0-8493-6723-9*, SB351) CRC Pr.

Leafy Spurge. Ed. by A. K. Watson. 104p. 1985. text 10.00 (*0-911733-03-5*) Weed Sci Soc.

League: A Supplement for the Roleplaying Game Based on Babylon 5. Richard Dakan. 1998. pap. text 25.00 (*1-887990-17-8*) Chameleon Eclectic.

League & Abyssinia see In Savage Times: Leonard Woolf on Peace & War

League Committees & World Order. Harold R. Greaves. LC 76-29430. reprint ed. 39.50 (*0-404-15336-4*) AMS Pr.

League for Industrial Democracy: A Documentary History, 3 vols., Set. Compiled by Bernard K. Johnpoll & Mark R. Yerburgh. LC 80-537. (Documentary Reference Collections). (Illus.). 2587p. 1980. lib. bdg. 395.00 (*0-313-22084-0*, YIN/) Greenwood.

League for Industrial Democracy: A Documentary History, 3 vols., Vol. 1. Compiled by Bernard K. Johnpoll & Mark R. Yerburgh. LC 80-537. (Documentary Reference Collections). (Illus.). xiii, 2587p. 1980. lib. bdg. 175.00 (*0-313-22613-X*, YIN/1) Greenwood.

League for Industrial Democracy: A Documentary History, 3 vols., Vol. 2. Compiled by Bernard K. Johnpoll & Mark R. Yerburgh. LC 80-537. (Documentary Reference Collections). (Illus.). xiii, 2587p. 1980. lib. bdg. 175.00 (*0-313-22614-8*, YIN/2) Greenwood.

League for Industrial Democracy: A Documentary History, 3 vols., Vol. 3. Compiled by Bernard K. Johnpoll & Mark R. Yerburgh. LC 80-537. (Documentary Reference Collections). (Illus.). xiii, 2587p. 1980. lib. bdg. 175.00 (*0-313-22615-6*, YIN/3) Greenwood.

League for Social Reconstruction: Intellectual Origins of the Democratic Left in Canada, 1930-1942. Michiel Horn. 1980. text 32.50 (*0-8020-5487-0*) U of Toronto Pr.

League of Airmen: U. S. Air Power in the Gulf War. James A. Winnefeld et al. LC 93-48872. 361p. 1994. 30.00 (*0-8330-1665-2*, MR-343-AF); pap. text 15.00 (*0-8330-1503-6*, MR-343-AF) Rand Corp.

League of Champions, Bk. 1. Dennis Mallonee. (Illus.). 160p. (Orig.). 1990. pap. 9.95 (*0-929729-01-3*) Heroic Pub CA.

League of Composers' Review see Modern Music

League of Nations & National Minorities: An Experiment. Pablo De Azcarate. (Studies in the Administration of International Law & Organization: No. 5). 1969. reprint ed. 25.00 (*0-527-00883-4*) Periodicals Srv.

League of Nations & the Foreshadowing of the International Monetary Fund. LC 96-51079. (Essays in International Finance). 1996. write for info. (*0-88165-108-7*) Intl Monetary.

League of Nations & the Rule of Law, 1918-1935. Alfred Zimmern. LC 97-77284. xi, 527p. 1998. reprint ed. 160.00 (*1-56169-359-6*) Gaunt.

League of Nations Documents, 1919-1946: A Descriptive Guide & Key to the Microfilm Collection, New Haven, 1973-1975, 3 vols. LC 73-3061. 1215p. 1973. 750.00 (*0-89235-008-3*) Primary Srce Media.

League of Nations from 1919-1929. Gary B. Ostrower. LC 94-8337. (Partners for Peace Ser.: Vol. 1). 192p. pap. 25.00 (*0-89529-636-5*, Avery) Penguin Putnam.

League of Nations from 1929 to 1946. George Gill. LC 94-7634. (Partners for Peace Ser.: Vol. 2). (Illus.). 208p. 1996. pap. 25.00 (*0-89529-637-3*, Avery) Penguin Putnam.

League of Nations in Retrospect: Proceedings of the Symposium Organized by the United Nations Library & the Graduate Institute of International Studies Nov. 1980. LC 83-1421. (United Nations Library, Geneva, Serial Publications: Ser. E: Guides & Studies, No. 3). xii, 427p. 1983. 150.00 (*3-11-008733-2*) De Gruyter.

League of Nations, 1920-46: Organization of Accomplishments - A Retrospective of the First Organization for the Establishment of World Peace. United Nations Library at Geneva Staff. 192p. 22.00 (*92-1-100725-9*, JX1975) UN.

***League of Night & Fog.** David Morrell. 480p. 2000. mass mkt. 6.99 (*0-446-60754-1*, Pub. by Warner Bks) Little.

League of Night & Fog. large type ed. David Morrell. 532p. 1989. 27.99 (*0-7089-1936-7*) Ulverscroft.

League of Terror. Bill Granger. 1991. mass mkt. 5.99 (*0-446-36126-7*, Pub. by Warner Bks) Little.

***League of the Aitolians** John D. Grainger. LC 99-37196. (Mnemosyne, Bibliotheca Classica Batava Ser.). 1999. write for info. (*90-04-10911-0*) Brill Academic Pubs.

League of the Iroquois. L. H. Morgan. (Illus.). 1990. 25.50 (*0-8446-2612-0*) Peter Smith.

League of the Iroquois. Lewis Henry Morgan. 124p. 1995. write for info. (*1-57215-124-2*) World Pubns.

League of the Iroquois. Lewis Henry Morgan. (Illus.). 477p. 1984. reprint ed. pap. 14.95 (*0-8065-0917-1*, Citadel Pr) Carol Pub Group.

League of the Iroquois, 2 vols., Set. Lewis Henry Morgan. 1993. reprint ed. lib. bdg. 150.00 (*0-7812-5160-5*) Rprt Serv.

League of the Scarlet Pimpernel. Emmuska Orczy. 282p. Date not set. 23.95 (*0-8488-2377-X*) Amereon Ltd.

League of the Scarlet Pimpernel. Emmuska Orczy. 238p. 1981. reprint ed. lib. bdg. 35.95 (*0-89966-286-2*) Buccaneer Bks.

League of Their Own. Sarah Gilbert. 224p. (Orig.). 1992. mass mkt. 4.99 (*0-446-36383-9*, Pub. by Warner Bks) Little.

League of Wisconsin Municipalities: A Centennial History. Michael J. Goc & Dave Engel. LC 98-33798. (Illus.). 104p. 1998. 30.00 (*0-938627-43-0*) New Past Pr.

League of Youth see Doll's House & Other Plays

League Park. rev. ed. Peter Jedick. 24p. 1992. reprint ed. pap. 5.95 (*0-9605508-0-1*) Jedick Ent.

League That Failed. David Q. Voigt. LC 97-53304. (American Sports History Ser.). 376p. 1998. 45.00 (*0-8108-3309-3*) Scarecrow.

Leagues Apart. Lawrence S. Ritter. (Illus.). 40p. (J). (ps-3). 1999. mass mkt. 5.95 (*0-688-16693-8*, Wm Morrow) Morrow Avon.

Leagues Apart: The Men & Times of the Negro Baseball Leagues. Lawrence S. Ritter. LC 94-17512. (Illus.). 40p. (J). (gr. 3 up). 1995. lib. bdg. 14.93 (*0-688-13317-7*, Wm Morrow) Morrow Avon.

Leagues Apart: The Men & Times of the Negro Baseball Leagues. Lawrence S. Ritter. LC 94-17512. (Illus.). 40p. (J). (ps up). 1995. 15.00 (*0-688-13316-9*, Wm Morrow) Morrow Avon.

Leah. Lois N. Erickson. (Women of the Bible Ser.). 144p. 1992. pap. 7.99 (*0-8280-0654-7*) Review & Herald.

Leah see People of the Promise Series

Leah, Vol. 1. James R. Shott. LC 99-14889. 1999. 21.95 (*0-7862-1973-4*) Thorndike Pr.

Leah & Leibel's Lighthouse. Michael Muchnik. (Illus.). 48p. (J). 1984. reprint ed. 7.00 (*0-8266-0355-6*, Merkos LInyonei Chinuch) Kehot Pubn Soc.

Leah & the Witches. John T. Richards. (Mandrake Saga Ser.). (Illus.). 203p. 1997. pap. 8.00 (*0-9605980-5-7*) J T Richards.

Leah, New Hampshire: Stories by Thomas Williams. Thomas Williams. LC 91-40940. (Discovery Ser.). 236p. 1993. reprint ed. pap. 12.50 (*1-55597-191-1*) Graywolf.

Leah Schwartz: The Life of a Woman Who Managed to Keep Painting. Leah Schwartz. Ed. by Herman Schwartz. (Illus.). 284p. 1992. 55.00 (*0-685-53646-7*); text 55.00 (*0-912647-07-8*) Strawberry.

***Leah's Dream: Leah.** Florence Joseph Paul. LC 00-190641. 209p. 2000. 25.00 (*0-7388-1887-9*); pap. 18.00 (*0-7388-1886-0*) Xlibris Corp.

Leah's Journey: A Novel. Gloria Goldreich. LC 96-31784. (Library of Modern Jewish Literature). 438p. 1996. reprint ed. pap. 17.95 (*0-8156-0438-6*, GOLJP) Syracuse U Pr.

Leah's Night of Wonder. large type ed. Nan Holcomb. LC 98-26652. (Illus.). 32p. (J). (ps-3). 1998. lib. bdg. 16.95 (*0-944727-35-2*) Jason & Nordic Pubs.

Leah's Pony. Elizabeth Friedrich. LC 95-79657. (Illus.). 32p. (J). (gr. k-3). 1996. 14.95 (*1-56397-189-5*) Boyds Mills Pr.

Leah's Pony. Elizabeth Friedrich. LC 95-79657. (Illus.). 32p. (J). (gr. k-4). 1999. pap. 8.95 (*1-56397-828-8*) Boyds Mills Pr.

Leah's Song. Brenda Imus. 286p. 1997. pap. 12.95 (*0-9648366-8-8*) Crossover Publns.

Leahy's Lads: The Story of the Famous Notre Dame Football Teams of the 1940s. Jack Connor. LC 94-20706. (Illus.). 318p. 1994. 24.95 (*0-912083-75-1*) Diamond Communications.

Leahy's Lads: The Story of the Famous Notre Dame Football Teams of the 1940s. Jack Connor. LC 97-30224. 1997. pap. 16.95 (*0-912083-90-5*) Diamond Communications.

***Leak Detection Evaluations for Underground Storage Tank Systems.** 360p. 1998. ring bd. 31.00 (*0-16-063392-3*) USGPO.

Leak Detection for Underground Storage Tanks. Ed. by Philip B. Durgin & Thomas M. Young. LC 93-14690. (Special Technical Publication Ser.: No. 1161). (Illus.). 240p. 1993. 39.00 (*0-8031-1858-9*, USTANKS) ASTM.

Leak Detection Methods for Plastic Water Distribution Pipes. Osama Hunaidi. LC 99-14006. 1999. write for info. (*0-89867-993-1*) Am Water Wks Assn.

Leak Detectors. Richard K. Miller & Marcia E. Rupnow. (Survey on Technology & Markets Ser.: No. 216). 50p. 1993. pap. text 200.00 (*1-55865-247-7*) Future Tech Surveys.

Leak-Free Pumps & Compressors. LC 96-116438. 412p. 1995. 157.00 (*1-85617-230-9*, R102, Pub. by Elsvr Adv Tech) Elsevier.

Leak in the Heart: Tales from a Woman's Life. Faye Moskowitz. LC 84-48298. 176p. 1987. pap. 12.95 (*0-87923-659-0*) Godine.

Leak in the Landfill: Colorado's Suppressed Report on Solid Waste Policy Finally Seeps Out. Jim McMahon. 96p. 1992. pap. text 8.00 (*1-57655-095-8*) Independ Inst.

Leak Prevention & Corrective Action Technology for Underground Storage Tanks. A. C. Gangadharan et al. LC 87-34745. (Pollution Technology Review Ser.: No. 153). (Illus.). 426p. 1988. 54.00 (*0-8155-1163-9*, 900106) Noyes.

Leak Testing. (Fossil Power Plant Startup Training Ser.: Module 10). 49p. 1984. spiral bd. 17.50 (*0-87683-367-9*) GP Courseware.

Leak Testing: Question & Answer Books H, 4 bks., Set. Incl. Bubble Leak Testing HB. 1994. pap. 31.25 (*0-931403-42-1*, 2033B); Halogen Diode Detector Leak Testing HH. 1995. pap. 31.25 (*0-931403-41-3*, 2033H); 1985. Set pap. 70.00 (*0-685-17519-7*, 2033A) Am Soc Nondestructive.

Leakage: The Bleeding of the American Economy. Treval C. Powers. (Illus.). 350p. (Orig.). 1996. pap. 39.95 (*0-9647121-1-3*) Benchmark CT.

Leakage Rated Dampers for Use in Smoke Control Systems, UL 555S. 3rd ed. (C). 1996. pap. text 95.00 (*1-55989-483-0*) Underwrtrs Labs.

Leakey Family: Leaders in the Search for Human Origins. Delta Willis. LC 92-12522. (Makers of Modern Science Ser.). (Illus.). 144p. (YA). (gr. 7-12). 1992. lib. bdg. 19.95 (*0-8160-2605-X*) Facts on File.

Leakeys. Lisa A. Lambert. LC 92-46046. (Pioneers Ser.). 112p. (J). 1993. lib. bdg. 25.27 (*0-86625-492-7*) Rourke Pubns.

Leakeys: Uncovering the Origins of Humankind. Margaret Poynter. LC 96-40899. (Great Minds of Science Ser.). 128p. (J). (gr. 4-10). 1997. lib. bdg. 20.95 (*0-89490-788-3*) Enslow Pubs.

Leaking: Who Does It? Who Benefits? At What Cost? - A Twentieth Century Fund Paper. Elie Abel. 75p. (C). 1987. text 18.95 (*0-87078-219-3*); pap. text 7.95 (*0-87078-218-5*) Century Foundation.

***Leaking Laffs Between Pampers & Depends.** Barbara Johnson. 176p. 2000. pap. text 12.99 (*0-8499-3705-1*) J Countryman.

Leaking Underground Storage Tank Remediation. Richard K. Miller & Christy H. Gunter. (Market Research Survey Ser.: No. 289). 50p. 1996. 200.00 (*1-55865-313-9*) Future Tech Surveys.

Leaking Underground Storage Tank Trust Fund Amendments Act of 1997: Hearing Before the Subcommittee on Finance & Hazardous Materials of the Committee on Commerce, House of Representatives, 105th Congress, 1st Session, on H.R. 688, March 20, 1997. USGPO Staff. LC 97-186894. iii, 42 p. 1997. write for info. (*0-16-054932-9*) USGPO.

Leaking Underground Storage Tanks: The Slides. Richard L. Johnson. (Illus.). 24p. 1991. pap. 89.95 incl. sl. (*0-9627452-1-9*) Titan Pr OR.

Leaks in Water Distribution Systems. 48p. 1987. pap. 28.00 (*0-89867-379-8*, 20236) Am Water Wks Assn.

Leaky Bodies & Boundaries: Feminism Postmodernism & Bioethics. Margrit Shildrick. LC 97-224464. (Illus.). 264p. (C). 1997. 80.00 (*0-415-14616-X*); pap. 25.99 (*0-415-14617-8*) Routledge.

Leaky Gut Syndrome. Elizabeth Lipski. LC 98-204448. pap. 3.95 (*0-87983-824-8*, 38248K, Keats Publng) NTC Contemp Pub Co.

Leaky Iron Boat: Nursing an Old Barge Through Holland, Belgium, & France. Hart Massey. LC 97-165065. (Illus.). 224p. 1997. pap. 18.95 (*0-7737-5870-4*) Stoddart Publ.

Leale a Su Conejito. Rosemary Wells. (SPA.). (J). 1999. pap. text 6.95 (*0-590-13003-X*) Scholastic Inc.

***Leale a su Conejito.** Rosemary Wells. (SPA., Illus.). 32p. (ps-k). 2000. pap. text 2.99 (*0-439-18314-6*) Scholastic Inc.

***Leale A su Conejito.** Rosemary Wells. (SPA., Illus.). (J). 2000. 8.44 (*0-606-18879-7*) Turtleback.

Lealtad de Sus Clientes. Claudio L. Soriano. (SPA.). 191p. 1994. pap. 15.75 (*84-7978-185-8*, Pub. by Ediciones Diaz) IBD Ltd.

Leamington & Warwick Tramways. S. L. Swingle & K. Turner. (C). 1985. 39.00 (*0-85361-240-4*) St Mut.

Leamos! (Let's Read) Prepare a Sus Hijos a Leer y Escribir (One Hundred One Ideas to Help Your Child Learn to Read & Write) Richard Behm & Mary Behm. Ed. by Warren W. Lewis. Tr. by Joan Hoffman & Angelica Lizarraga. LC 93-781. (ENG & SPA., Illus.). 128p. (Orig.). 1993. pap. 8.95 (*0-927516-36-5*) ERIC-REC.

Leamos! (Let's Read) 101 Ideas Para Ayundar a Sus Hijos a Que Aprendan a Leer y a Escribir - 101 Ideas to Help Your Child Learn to Read & Write. Richard Behm & Mary Behm. Ed. by Warren W. Lewis. Tr. by Joan Hoffman et al. LC 94-21536. (ENG & SPA.). 48p. 1995. pap. 8.95 (*0-927516-60-8*, AG45) ERIC-REC.

Lean Advantage. Clarence Bass. LC 84-71083. (Illus.). 251p. 1984. pap. 14.95 (*0-9609714-2-4*) Clarence Bass.

Lean Advantage 3: Four More Years. Clarence Bass. LC 94-133928. 216p. 1994. pap. 15.95 (*0-9609714-6-7*) Clarence Bass.

Lean Advantage 2: The Second Four Years. Clarence Bass. LC 84-71083. (Illus.). 231p. (Orig.). 1989. pap. 14.95 (*0-9609714-4-0*) Clarence Bass.

Lean Against the Wind: How to Face the Future. James McKarns. LC 93-41498. 150p. (Orig.). 1994. pap. 5.95 (*0-8189-0690-1*) Alba.

Lean & Clean Management: How to Boost Profits & Productivity by Reducing Pollution. Joseph J. Romm. 224p. 1994. 23.00 (*1-56836-037-1*) Kodansha.

Lean & Free Two-Thousand Plus. Dana Thornock. (Illus.). 323p. 1994. pap. 19.95 (*1-56684-034-1*) Evans Bk Dist.

Lean & Lovin' It: Exceptionally Delicious Recipes for Low-Fat Living & Permanent Weight Loss. Don Mauer. Ed. by Rux Martin. (Illus.). 448p. 1996. pap. 16.95 (*1-881527-97-2*, Chapters Bks) HM.

Lean & Luscious. Bobbie Hinman & Millie Snyder. LC 84-91380. (Illus.). 459p. 1985. pap. 12.95 (*0-9613472-0-1*) Hinman-Synder.

Lean & Luscious. rev. ed. Bobbie Hinman & Millie Snyder. (Illus.). 462p. 1986. pap. 15.95 (*0-914629-20-4*) Prima Pub.

Lean & Luscious. 2nd rev. ed. Bobbie Hinman & Millie Snyder. LC 95-3362. (Illus.). 496p. 1995. spiral bd. 16.95 (*0-7615-0015-4*) Prima Pub.

Lean & Luscious & Meatless. Bobbie Hinman & Millie Snyder. 480p. 1998. per. 19.95 (*0-7615-1443-0*) Prima Pub.

Lean & Luscious Favorites: Over 300 Easy-to-Prepare, Delicious Recipes from the Bestselling Series. Bobbie Hinman. LC 97-28462. (Lean & Luscious Ser.). (Illus.). 416p. 1997. spiral bd. 16.00 (*0-7615-0464-6*) Prima Pub.

Lean & Mean: Managing Small Business Growth. Harvard Business Review Staff. 64p. 1991. pap. 19.95 (*0-87584-295-X*) Harvard Busn.

Lean & Mean: Managing Small Business Growth. Harvard Business Review Staff. 100p. 1991. pap. 19.95 (*0-07-103355-6*) McGraw.

Lean & Mean: No Hassle. Morton H. Shaevitz. (J. Hook Ser.). 1994. mass mkt. 5.50 (*0-425-14264-7*) Berkley Pub.

Lean & Mean: Why Large Corporations Will Continue to Dominate the Global Economy. Bennett Harrison. LC 98-100026. (Perspectives on Economic Change Ser.). 363p. 1997. 17.95 (*1-57230-252-6*, C0252) Guilford Pubns.

Lean & Meaningful: A New Culture for Corporate America. Roger E. Herman & Joyce L. Gioia. LC 98-13258. 388p. 1998. 27.95 (*1-886939-07-1*, Pub. by OakHill Pr VA) ACCESS Pubs Network.

Lean Bean Cuisine: Over 100 Meatless Recipes from Around the World. Jay Solomon. LC 94-3862. 256p. 1994. pap. 12.95 (*1-55958-438-6*) Prima Pub.

Lean Body Promise: An Owner's Manual. Vince Quas. LC 89-4162. (Illus.). 288p. (Orig.). 1990. pap. 15.95 (*0-925572-36-5*) Synesis Pr.

Lean Burn Engines. Nick Collings & J. P. Pirault. (Cambridge Engine Technology Ser.). 170p. 1995. write for info. (*0-521-33018-1*) Cambridge U Pr.

Lean But Not Mean: Studies in Organization Structure. James C. Worthy. Ed. by David G. Moore & Ronald G. Greenwood. LC 93-23550. 264p. 1994. text 32.50 (*0-252-02085-5*) U of Ill Pr.

Lean Communications Provider: Managing Profitability in the Global Communications Market. Elizabeth K. Adams & Keith J. Willetts. (Illus.). 252p. 1996. 29.95 (*0-07-070306-X*) McGraw.

Lean Construction. Ed. by L. F. Alarcon. (Illus.). 512p. (C). 1997. text 116.00 (*90-5410-648-4*, Pub. by A A Balkema) Ashgate Pub Co.

Lean for Life. Clarence Bass. (Illus.). 247p. (Orig.). 1992. pap. 15.95 (*0-9609714-5-9*) Clarence Bass.

Lean for Life: How to Lose Weight Rapidly, Safely & Comfortably - & Keep It off for Life. 4th rev. ed. Cynthia S. Graff. 1997. pap. text 18.95 (*1-882180-63-1*) Griffin CA.

Lean Forward, Catch the Echo. Peggy Z. Lynch. 32p. 1998. pap. 5.00 (*1-878149-43-1*) Counterpoint Pub.

Lean into the Wind. Troxey Kemper. 116p. 1997. pap. write for info. (*1-57502-527-2*, PO1562) Morris Pubng.

Lean John, California's Horseback Hero. Randall A. Reinstedt. Ed. by John Bergez. (History & Happenings of California Ser.). (Illus.). 62p. (J). (gr. 3-6). 1996. 13.95 (*0-933818-26-2*); pap. 9.95 (*0-933818-81-5*) Ghost Town.

Lean Logistics: High-Velocity Logistics Infrastructure & the C-5 Galaxy. Timothy Ramey & Project Air Force Staff. LC 98-54431. (Illus.). 135p. 1999. pap. 15.00 (*0-8330-2697-6*, MR-581-AF) Rand Corp.

Lean, Mean & Green... Designing Farm Support Programs in a New Era. Sarah Lynch & Katherine R. Smith. (Policy Study Program Report Ser.: No. 3). (Illus.). 27p. 1994. pap. 7.50 (*1-893182-09-6*) H A Wallace Inst.

Lean, Mean & Lonesome: Man of the Month Anniversary. Annette Broadrick. (Desire Ser.: No. 1237). 1999. mass mkt. 3.75 (*0-373-76237-2*, 1-76237-6) Silhouette.

Lean, Not Mean: Restoring Organizational Trust in a Climate of Downsizing. Jerome M. Rosow et al. (Strategic Partners for High Performance Ser.: Vol. IV). 97p. (Orig.). 1996. pap. 95.00 (*0-89361-053-4*) Work in Amer.

***Lean on Me.** Mike Flanagan. (Rodeo Riders Ser.). 320p. 1999. mass mkt. 6.99 (*0-451-19883-2*) NAL.

Lean on Me. Marion Solomon. 272p. 1996. pap. 12.00 (*1-57566-019-9*) Kensgtn Pub Corp.

Lean on Me. Marion Solomon. 1996. pap. 12.00 (*0-8217-5256-1*) NAL.

Lean on Me. Marion Solomon. 288p. 1994. 22.00 (*0-671-87010-6*) S&S Trade.

Lean on Me. Jack Weyland. LC 96-27284. vii, 279p. (J). 1996. 14.95 (*1-57345-214-9*) Deseret Bk.

Lean on Me: How to Help a Friend with a Problem. Pam Brown. Ed. by Becky Nelson. 32p. (Orig.). (YA). (gr. 7-12). 1993. pap. text 4.95 (*1-56309-068-6*, C936101, Wrld Changers Res) Womans Mission Union.

Lean on Me Gently: Helping the Grieving Child. Doug Manning. 56p. 1998. pap. 5.95 (*1-892785-06-4*) In-Sight Bks Inc.

Lean or Lavish: Two Tempting Versions of Each Dish. Judith Pacht. 1991. pap. 12.95 (*0-446-39221-9*) Warner Bks.

Lean Production. Jansen. 1993. 42.95 (*0-387-56154-4*) Spr-Verlag.
Lean Revolution. L. Kenton. 13.95 (*0-09-178415-8*, Pub. by Random) Trafalgar.
Lean Soil. limited ed. Ronald Pies. 28p. 1985. pap. 7.95 (*0-944754-07-4*) Pudding Hse Pubns.
Lean Star Cuisine. Terry Conlan. Ed. by Trisha Shirey. (Illus.). 304p. (C). 1993. reprint ed. text 19.95 (*0-9619476-1-6*) Lake Austin Resort.
Lean Thinking: Banish Waste & Create Wealth in Your Corporation. James P. Womack & Daniel T. Jones. LC 96-9140. 352p. 1996. 25.50 (*0-684-81035-2*) S&S Trade.
Lean Times in Lankhmar: Swords & Deviltry; Swords Against Death, 2 bks. in 1. Fritz Leiber. (Lankhmar Ser.: Vol. 2). 1997. mass mkt. 5.99 (*1-56504-895-4*, WW 12013, Borealis) White Wolf.
Lean Transformation: How to Change Your Business into a Lean Enterprise. Bruce A. Henderson & Jorge L. Larco. Ed. by Stephen H. Martin. (Illus.). 272p. 1999. 26.95 (*0-9646601-2-1*, Pub. by Oaklea Pr) Bookpeople.
Lean Work: Empowerment & Exploitation in the Global Auto Industry. Ed. by Steve Babson. 382p. (Orig.). 1995. pap. text 27.95 (*0-8143-2535-1*) Wayne St U Pr.
Lean Year & Other Stories. Robert Laxalt. LC 93-33529. (Western Literature Ser.). 208p. 1994. 21.00 (*0-87417-241-1*) U of Nev Pr.
Lean Years, Bk. 1. Erwin A. Thompson. 1994. pap. 8.50 (*5-87550-036-0*) Julia Thompson.
Lean Years, 1934-1951: Diaries of Extraordinary Women of North & South. Wayne L. Wolf & Jack Simmerling. Ed. by Judy Wetherington. 296p. 1998. pap. 30.74 (*0-07-230983-0*) McGraw.
Leander by Walter Hawkesworth: A Variorum Edition with Translation. Ed. by Lawrence M. Caylor. LC 92-37051. (Renaissance Imagination Ser.). 304p. 1993. text 25.00 (*0-8153-0462-5*) Garland.
Leander McNelly: Texas Ranger. Robert Scott. LC 97-51953. (Orig.). 1999. pap. 18.95 (*1-57168-176-0*, Eakin Pr) Sunbelt Media.
Leander Perez: Boss of the Delta. 2nd ed. Glen Jeansonne. LC 95-67724. 480p. 1995. reprint ed. pap. 25.00 (*0-940984-95-4*) Univ LA Lafayette.
Leandro Katz: Two Projects/A Decade. Jorge Castaneda et al. (Illus.). 24p. (Orig.). 1996. pap. 20.00 (*1-882454-04-9*) El Museo Barrio.
Leane Zugsmith: Thunder on the Left. Abe C. Ravitz. LC 92-16381. 130p. 1992. pap. 6.95 (*0-7178-0702-9*) Intl Pubs Co.
Leaner's Dictionary of Polytechnical Terms: Russian-English-French-German. 4th rev. ed. I. Rudakova. (FRE, GER & RUS.). 448p. 1988. 35.00 (*0-7859-7154-8*) Fr & Eur.
Le'Anglais des Sciences. (ENG & FRE., Illus.). (Orig.). 1997. pap. 75.00 incl. audio (*2-7005-1338-X*, Pub. by Assimil) Distribks Inc.
Leaning House Poetry Vol. 1: A Compact Disk Anthology with Readings by the Poets. Ed. by Mark Elliott & Jack Myers. LC 96-75540. 95p. 1996. 23.95 (*0-9651118-0-6*, BP-001) Leaning Hse Pr.
Leaning into the Future: Changing the Way People Change Organizations. George Binney & Colin Williams. LC 95-210676. (Illus.). 192p. 1997. pap. 15.95 (*1-85788-083-8*) Nicholas Brealey.
Leaning Into the Wind. Ed. by Linda Hasselstron et al. 416p. 1998. pap. 14.00 (*0-395-90131-6*) HM.
Leaning into the Wind: The Wilderness of Widowhood. Betty Bryant. LC 75-13031. 96p. reprint ed. pap. 30.00 (*0-608-16807-6*, 202693000053) Bks Demand.
Leaning into the Wind: Women Write from the Heart of the West. Ed. by Linda M. Hasselstrom et al. LC 96-49271. 384p. 1997. 25.00 (*0-395-83738-3*) HM.
Leaning Ivory Tower: Latino Professors in American Universities. Ed. by Raymond V. Padilla & Rudolfo C. Chavez. LC 94-28756. (SUNY Series, United States Hispanic Studies). 224p. (C). 1995. text 54.50 (*0-7914-2427-8*); pap. text 19.95 (*0-7914-2428-6*) State U NY Pr.
Leaning Land: A Gabe Wager Mystery. Rex Burns. LC 97-3581. 246p. 1997. 22.95 (*0-8027-3306-9*) Walker & Co.
***Leaning on the Wind: Under the Spell of the Great Chinook.** Sid Marty. 320p. 2001. reprint ed. pap. 18.95 (*0-7710-5671-0*) McCland & Stewart.
Leaning over the Edge: Poems. Jeanne M. Nichols. 64p. (Orig.). 1993. pap. 8.50 (*1-56474-058-7*) Fithian Pr.
Leaning South. Lyn Lifshin. LC 76-58048. (Contemporary Poets Ser.). 1977. 10.95 (*0-87376-030-1*); pap. 4.95 (*0-87376-031-X*) Red Dust.
Leaning Sycamores: Natural Worlds of the Upper Potomac. Jack Wennerstrom. LC 95-19839. (Illus.). 248p. (C). 1996. 25.95 (*0-8018-5189-0*) Johns Hopkins.
***Leaning the Basics of New Testament Greek.** 1999. pap. text 29.99 (*0-89957-800-4*) AMG Pubs.
Leaning to Hear the Music. Joseph Awad. Ed. by Joseph D. Adams. LC 96-70863. (Illus.). 96p. (Orig.). (C). 1997. pap. 12.00 (*1-880016-24-9*) Road Pubs.
Leaning Towards Infinity: A Novel. Sue Woolfe. 420p. 1998. pap. 14.95 (*0-571-19939-9*) Faber & Faber.
LeAnn Rimes see Galaxy of Superstars
***LeAnn Rimes.** 1999. audio 7.00 (*0-7435-0261-2*) S&S Audio.
***LeAnn Rimes.** 1999. 29.95 (*0-671-31750-4*) S&S Trade.
LeAnn Rimes. Mark Bego. LC 98-23936. (Illus.). 80p. 1998. pap. 9.99 (*0-312-19378-5*) St Martin.
LeAnn Rimes. Paul Joseph. 1999. pap. 5.95 (*1-57765-337-8*) ABDO Pub Co.
LeAnn Rimes. Scott. Date not set. pap. 6.99 (*0-689-82692-3*) S&S Childrens.
LeAnn Rimes. Cathy Alter Zymet. (Galaxy of Superstars Ser.). (Illus.). 64p. (YA). (gr. 3 up). 1999. 16.95 (*0-7910-5152-8*) Chelsea Hse.
LeAnn Rimes: Teen Country Queen. Grace Catalano. 128p. (YA). 1997. mass mkt. 4.99 (*0-440-22737-2*) Dell.
LeAnn Rimes - Blue. Ed. by Jeanette DeLisa. 52p. (Orig.). (YA). 1996. pap. text 16.95 (*1-57623-641-2*, PF9642) Wrner Bros.
Leanna: A Possession of a Woman. Marie Kirahy. 352p. (Orig.). 1996. mass mkt. 5.99 (*0-425-15224-3*) Berkley Pub.
Leanna Builds a Genie Trap. Hazel J. Hutchins. (Illus.). 24p. (J). (ps-3). 1987. pap. 4.95 (*0-920303-55-2*, Pub. by Annick) Firefly Bks Ltd.
Lean's Collecteana, 5 vols., Set. Vincent S. Lean. 1969. reprint ed. 210.00 (*1-55888-181-6*) Omnigraphics Inc.
LEAP: A Description of the LDC Energy Alternatives Planning System. Paul D. Raskin. (Energy, Environment & Development in Africa Ser.: No. 8). 149p. 1986. write for info. (*91-7106-247-5*, Pub. by Nordic Africa) Transaction Pubs.
***Leap: A Memoir of Love & Madness in the Internet Gold Rush.** Tom Ashbrook. 295p. 2000. 26.00 (*0-395-76165-4*) HM.
***Leap: A Memoir of Love & Madness in the Internet Goldrush.** Tom Ashbrook. LC 99-59162. 320p. 2000. 26.00 (*0-395-83934-3*) HM.
Leap: A Traveler in the Garden of Delights. Terry Tempest Williams. LC 99-57914. (Illus.). 352p. 2000. 25.00 (*0-679-43292-2*) Pantheon.
Leap Frog. Mary Buckman. LC 89-63379. (One in a Series of Predictable Readers). (Illus.). (Orig.). (J). (gr. k-2). 1989. pap. text 12.95 (*1-879414-05-8*) Mary Bee Creat.
Leap Frog Series: Zoo Babies; A Morning on the Farm; People in My Neighborhood; Things That Go - Trains & Planes; Kitten's Busy Day; Puppies at the Pet Shop; Teddy Bear & His Friends; Animals of the North; Learn about Dinosaurs; Things That Go - Cars & Trucks; Things That Fly, 12 bks., Set. (Illus.). 16p. (J). 1993. pap. 15.48 (*0-88176-817-0*) Pubns Intl Ltd.
Leap Hops, Pops, & Mops. Suzanne Barchers. (Illus.). 12p. (J). write for info. (*1-58605-017-6*) Knowledge Kids.
Leap in the Dark: A Welsh Airman's Adventures in Occupied Europe, WW II. James A. Davies. (Illus.). 256p. 1994. 29.95 (*0-85052-314-1*, Pub. by Leo Cooper) Trans-Atl Phila.
Leap in the Dark: A Welsh Airman's Adventures in Occupied Europe, WW II. large type ed. James A. Davies. (Illus.). 352p. 1995. 27.99 (*0-7089-3425-0*) Ulverscroft.
Leap in the Dark: AIDS, Art & Contemporary Cultures. Allan Klusacek. Ed. by Ken Morrison. 320p. 1995. pap. 19.95 (*1-55065-020-3*, Pub. by Vehicule Pr) LPC Group.
***Leap into Darkness: Seven Years on the Run in Wartime Europe.** Leo Bretholz & Michael Olesker. LC 99-31373. 288p. 1999. pap. 12.95 (*0-385-49705-9*, Anchor NY) Doubleday.
Leap Into Listening: 83 Reproducible Scenes with Activities for Auditory Memory & Language Expansion. Thomas Webber. (Illus.). 167p. (J). (gr. k-6). 1993. spiral bd., wbk. ed. 26.95 (*1-58650-037-6*, BK-228) Super Duper.
Leap into Literacy Teacher Manual. Ruth Nathan et al. write for info. (*1-58605-016-8*) Knowledge Kids.
Leap into the Enlightened Mind: A Manual for the Advanced Student of A Course in Miracles. Brother John Joseph. LC 99-169966. 83 p. 1992. write for info. (*1-881557-00-6*) Spirit Ranch.
***Leap, Lamb, Leap.** Frances Coe. (Play-Along Puppet Bks.). (Illus.). 4p. (J). (ps-k). 2000. bds. 4.99 (*0-448-42097-X*, G & D) Peng Put Young Read.
Leap Mat Teacher Manual. Janet Fagre & Frederica Breuer. write for info. (*1-58605-015-X*) Knowledge Kids.
Leap of Action: Ideas in the Theology of Abraham Joshua Heschel. Morton C. Fierman. LC 89-37492. (Illus.). 312p. (Orig.). (C). 1990. pap. text 27.00 (*0-8191-7568-4*); lib. bdg. 48.00 (*0-8191-7567-6*) U Pr of Amer.
Leap of Faith. David Y. Cho. LC 84-71457. 120p. 1984. mass mkt. 4.99 (*0-88270-574-1*) Bridge-Logos.
Leap of Faith: An Astronaut's Journey into the Unknown. Gordon Cooper. LC 99-86433. 288p. 2000. 25.00 (*0-06-019416-2*, HarpCollins) HarperTrade.
***Leap of Faith: An Honest-to-Goodness Entrepreneur's Uplifting Journey.** (Illus.). 128p. 1999. 20.00 (*0-9674424-0-0*) Boler Pubng.
***Leap of Faith: Gentle Steps to the Next Timeline.** Robert Shapiro. (Explorer Race Ser.: No. 12). 2000. pap. 14.95 (*1-891824-26-0*, Pub. by Light Tech Pubng) New Leaf Dist.
Leap of Faith: God Must Be a Packer Fan. Steve Rose. (Illus.). 192p. (Orig.). 1996. pap. 12.99 (*0-939995-21-2*) Angel Pr WI.
Leap of Faith: God Must Be a Packer Fan. Steve Rose. (Illus.). 192p. (Orig.). 1996. 25.00 (*0-939995-23-9*) Angel Pr WI.
***Leap of Faith: The Call to Art.** Ellen G. Horovitz. LC 99-37850. (Illus.). 210p. 1999. text 44.95 (*0-398-07001-6*); pap. text 31.95 (*0-398-07002-4*) C C Thomas.
Leap of Faith: True Stories for Young & Old. Peter J. Dyck. LC 90-32837. 120p. (Orig.). 1990. pap. 7.99 (*0-8361-3523-7*) Herald Pr.
Leap of Faith 2: God Loves Packer Fans. Steve Rose. LC 97-37794. (Illus.). 224p. 1997. 27.50 (*1-879483-46-7*) Prairie Oak Pr.
Leap of Faith 2: God Loves Packer Fans. Steve Rose. LC 97-37794. Vol. 2. (Illus.). 224p. 1997. pap. 14.95 (*1-879483-47-5*) Prairie Oak Pr.
***Leap of Strength: A Personal Tour Through the Months Before... & Years after... You Start Your Own Business.** Walt Sutton. 2000. pap. 17.95 (*1-56343-702-3*) Silver Lake.
Leap of the Deer: Memories of a Celtic Childhood. Herbert O'Driscoll. LC 93-41744. 154p. 1994. pap. 10.95 (*1-56101-086-5*) Cowley Pubns.
Leap Over a Wall: Earthy Spirituality for Everyday ChristiansReflections on the Life of David from. Eugene H. Peterson. LC 96-25066. 256p. 1998. pap. 13.00 (*0-06-066522-X*, Pub. by Harper SF) HarpC.
***Leap Second at the Turn of the Millennium.** Donald Platt. 30p. 1999. 25.00 (*0-9621526-1-7*) Ctr Bk Arts.
Leap to Freedom: True Stories of Wildlife Rescue & Rehabilitation. unabridged ed. Marjorie McKenzie Davis. LC 98-91743. (Illus.). viii, 312p. 1998. pap. 12.95 (*0-9667286-0-2*, 98010DAV) Burley Creek Studio.
***Leap to Life: Triumph over Nazi Evil.** Joseph Rebhun. LC 00-29320. 2000. write for info. (*1-893357-05-8*) Ardor Scrib.
Leap to the Sun: Learning Through Dynamic Play. Judith Peck. (Illus.). 158p. 1979. 12.95 (*0-13-527275-0*) P-H.
Leap Tries Again. Justine K. Fontes. (Illus.). 24p. (J). (gr. k-2). write for info. (*1-58605-006-0*) Knowledge Kids.
Leap Year. Peter Cameron. LC 98-10532. 256p. 1998. pap. 12.95 (*0-452-27985-2*, Plume) Dutton Plume.
Leap Year. Steve Erickson. 192p. 1991. pap. 8.95 (*0-380-71369-1*, Avon Bks) Morrow Avon.
Leap Year. Charles North. (Illus.). 7.00 (*0-686-65482-X*); pap. 3.50 (*0-686-65483-8*) Kulchur Foun.
***Leap Year: A Book of Trivia.** Barbara Sutton-Smith. (Illus.). 96p. 1999. pap. 11.95 (*1-55041-598-0*) Fitzhenry & W Ltd.
Leap Year: A Novel. Etienne Van Heerden. LC 98-137616. 369 p. 1997. write for info. (*0-14-026216-4*) Viking Penguin.
Leap Year Day: New & Selected Poems. Maxine Chernoff. 144p. 1998. pap. 9.95 (*1-893032-07-8*) Jensen Daniels.
***Leap Years: Women Reflect on Change, Loss & Love.** 2nd ed. Ed. by Mary Anne Maier & Joan Shaddox Isom. LC 99-27395. 256p. 1999. pap. 16.00 (*0-8070-6515-3*) Beacon Pr.
Leaper - The Amazing Life of the Salmon. Ulco Glimmerveen. (Illus.). (J). 12.95 (*1-86943-042-5*, Pub. by Ashton Scholastic) Scholastic Inc.
Leapfrogging Development. Singh. 1999. text 65.00 (*0-312-21168-6*) St Martin.
Leapfrogging Development? The Political Economy of Telecommunications Restructuring. J. P. Singh. LC 98-43558. (SUNY Series in Global Politics). (Illus.). 300p. (C). 1999. pap. text 22.95 (*0-7914-4294-2*, Suny Pr) State U NY Pr.
Leapfrogging Development? The Political Economy of Telecommunications Restructuring. J. P. Singh. LC 98-43558. (SUNY Series in Global Politics). 320p. (C). 1999. text 68.50 (*0-7914-4293-4*, Suny Pr) State U NY Pr.
Leapfrogging the Competition: Five Giant Steps to Becoming a Market Leader. 2nd rev. ed. Oren Harari. LC 99-15038. 224p. 1999. pap. 16.00 (*0-7615-1973-4*) Prima Pub.
Leapfrogging the Competition: Five Giant Steps to Market Leadership. Oren Harari. 200p. 1997. 24.95 (*0-9657896-0-8*, Am Century Pr) Amer Cntry Pr.
Leapfrogging Through Wetlands. Nancy Field et al. (Illus.). 40p. (Orig.). (J). (gr. 4-6). 1998. pap. 7.95 (*0-941042-18-9*) Dog Eared Pubns.
***Leapin' Lizards & Other Reptiles.** Annalisa McMorrow. (Illus.). (J). 1999. pap. 9.95 (*1-57612-110-0*) Monday Morning Bks.
Leapin' Lizards: And Other Leaps of Faith. Becky Y. Spencer. 138p. 1999. pap. 12.00 (*0-7392-0290-1*, PO3399) Morris Pubng.
Leapin Lizzie. Karl Squier. LC 84-27784. (Illus.). 32p. (J). (gr. k-5). 1985. pap. 7.95 (*0-931905-01-X*); audio 7.95 (*0-931905-02-8*) Lady Lake Learn.
Leapin Lizzie. unabridged ed. Karl Squier. LC 84-27784. (Little People Ser.). (Illus.). 32p. (J). (gr. k-5). 1985. pap. 15.95 incl. audio (*0-931905-00-1*, 05001) Lady Lake Learn.
***Leaping & Creeping the Cobblestones.** 72p. 1999. write for info. (*0-9618774-1-3*) W K Patterson.
Leaping Frogs. Melvin Berger. Ed. by Lisa Trumbauer. (Early Science Big Bks.). (Illus.). 16p. (J). (ps-2). 1995. pap. 16.95 (*1-56784-023-X*) Newbridge Educ.
Leaping Frogs: Mini Book. Melvin Berger et al. Ed. by Lisa Trumbauer. (Early Science Big Bks.). 16p. (J). (ps-2). 1995. pap. 3.95 (*1-56784-048-5*) Newbridge Educ.
Leaping Frogs Theme Pack. Melvin Berger. Ed. by Susan Evento. (Macmillan Early Science Big Bks.). (Illus.). (J). (ps-2). 1995. pap. 49.95 (*1-56784-180-5*) Newbridge Educ.
***Leaping Grasshoppers.** Christine Zuchora-Walske. LC 99-32633. (Pull Ahead Ser.). (Illus.). 32p. (J). (gr. k-2). 2000. pap. 6.95 (*0-8225-3638-2*, First Ave Edns) Lerner Pub.
***Leaping Grasshoppers.** Christine Zuchora-Walski. LC 99-32633. (Pull Ahead Ser.). (Illus.). 32p. (J). (gr. k-2). 2000. 21.27 (*0-8225-3634-X*, Lerner Publctns) Lerner Pub.
Leaping into Literature. Laurie Chapin & Ellen Flegenheimer-Riggle. 144p. (J). (gr. k-3). 1990. 10.99 (*0-86653-561-6*, GA1164) Good Apple.
Leaping into Whole Language: Fifty Nifty Ways to Make a Book. 1993. 16.50 (*0-88076-168-7*) Kaplan Pr.
Leaping Lanny! Wrestling with Rhyme. Lanny Poffo. LC 87-51044. (Illus.). 144p. 6.95 (*0-318-23404-1*) Leilo Pub.
Leaping Lanny! Wrestling with Ryme. Larry Poffo. 1988. pap. 6.95 (*0-9619169-0-7*) Leilo Pub.
Leaping Llama Carpet. Marian Waller. 32p. (J). (gr. 1-5). 1996. 14.95 (*1-86373-958-0*) IPG Chicago.
Leaping Llama Carpet. Marian Waller. (Illus.). 32p. (J). (gr. 1-5). 1996. pap. 5.95 (*1-86373-957-2*) IPG Chicago.
Leaping Man Hill. Carol Emshwiller. LC 99-33522. 208p. 1998. pap. 14.95 (*1-56279-111-7*) Mercury Hse Inc.
Leaping Poetry: An Idea with Poems & Translations. Ed. by Robert Bly. LC 73-6243. 112p. 1978. reprint ed. pap. 12.00 (*0-8070-6393-2*) Beacon Pr.
Leaping Souls: Rabbi Menachem Mendel & the Spirit of Kotzk. Chaim Feinberg. LC 93-25867. 1993. 19.95 (*0-88125-468-1*) Ktav.
Leaping the Abyss: Putting Group Genius to Work. Chris Peterson & Gayle Pergamit. (Illus.). 290p. (Orig.). 1997. pap. 16.95 (*0-9658995-0-0*) Knowhere Pr.
***Leaping the Atlantic Wall: Army Air Forces Campaigns in Western Europe, 1942-1945.** Edward T. Russell. 36p. 1999. pap. 2.00 (*0-16-061384-1*) USGPO.
Leaping up, Sliding Away. Kent Thompson. 92p. 1986. pap. 6.95 (*0-86492-080-6*, Pub. by Goose Ln Edits) Genl Dist Srvs.
***Leaping upon the Mountains: Men Proclaiming Victory over Sexual Child Abuse.** Mike Lew. 320p. 2000. pap. 19.95 (*1-55643-345-X*, Pub. by North Atlantic) Publishers Group.
Leaps: Facing Risks in Offering a Constructive Therapeutic Response When Unusual Measures Are Necessary. Roy M. Mendelsohn. LC 90-22584. 320p. 1992. 55.00 (*0-87668-566-1*) Aronson.
LEAPS - Long-Term Equity Anticipation Securities: What They Are & How to Use Them for Profit & Protection. Harrison Roth. 360p. 1993. text 55.00 (*1-55623-819-3*, Irwn Prfssnl) McGraw-Hill Prof.
Leaps & Boundaries: Psychoanalysis Revisited. Doris Treisman. Ed. by Susan A. Gordon. (Illus.). 110p. (Orig.). (C). 1989. pap. 8.95 (*0-9624424-0-2*) Oceanides Pr.
Leaps & Boundaries: The Prayer Book in the 21st Century. Paul Marshall & Lesley Northrup. LC 97-27226. 224p. 1997. pap. 16.95 (*0-8192-1718-2*) Morehouse Pub.
Leap's Big, Big Bag. Rozanne L. Williams. (Illus.). 12p. (J). (gr. 2). write for info. (*1-58605-012-5*) Knowledge Kids.
Leap's Friends A-Z. Lisa Ann Marsoli. (Illus.). 24p. (J). (gr. k-2). write for info. (*1-58605-008-7*) Knowledge Kids.
Leaps of Faith. Rachel Kranz. LC 99-58517. 576p. 2000. text 25.00 (*0-374-18444-5*) FS&G.
Leaps of Faith: Improvisational Dance in Worship & Education. Cynthia Winton-Henry. Ed. by Doug Adams. 1985. pap. 3.00 (*0-941500-33-0*) Sharing Co.
Leaps of Faith-Science, Miracles & the Search for Supernatural Consolation. Nicholas Humphrey. LC 99-17046. 256p. 1999. 16.00 (*0-387-98720-7*, Copernicus) Spr-Verlag.
Lear. Edward Bond. LC 73-153068. 1972. pap. 10.95 (*0-413-28770-X*) Methn.
Lear. Mark Dunster. 27p. (Orig.). 1995. pap. 4.00 (*0-89642-253-4*) Linden Pubs.
Lear Collection: A Study of Copper Alloy Socket Candlesticks AD 200-1700. Christopher Bangs. LC 94-77257. 398p. 1996. 120.00 (*0-9642224-0-X*) Kings Hill Pubns.
Lear Diaries: The Story of the Royal National Theatre's Productions of Richard III & King Lear. Brian Cox. 224p. 1996. pap. 19.95 (*0-413-69880-7*) Heinemann.
Lear from Study to Stage: Essays in Criticism. Ed. by James Ogden & Arthur H. Scouten. LC 96-50339. (Illus.). 304p. 1997. 46.50 (*0-8386-3690-X*) Fairleigh Dickinson.
Lear-Kritik Im 20. Jahrhundert. Ein Beitrag Zur einer Analyse der Shakespeare-Literatur. Peter Wenzel. (Bochum Studies in English: No. 8). xii, 329p. (Orig.). 1979. pap. write for info. (*90-6032-184-7*) B R Gruner.
Lear Solo. William Shakespeare. 24p. (Orig.). 1996. pap. 3.00 (*1-57514-198-1*, 3087) Encore Perform Pub.
Lear World: A Study of King Lear in Its Dramatic Context. John Reibetanz. LC 76-54829. 154p. reprint ed. pap. 47.80 (*0-8357-4028-5*, 203672000005) Bks Demand.
Learing the Art of Helping. Young. LC 97-30515. 304p. (C). 1997. pap. 41.00 (*0-13-834268-7*) P-H.
***Learing-to-Teach: Cases & Concepts for Novice Teachers & Teacher Educators.** Beynon & Geddis. 2000. pap. 34.60 (*0-13-016655-3*) P-H.
Learing/Using Communication Theories. 6th ed. Littlejohn. (Speech & Theater Ser.). 1998. pap. 15.75 (*0-534-54824-5*) Wadsworth Pub.
Learjets. Geza Szurovy. LC 95-26551. (Enthusiast Color Ser.). (Illus.). 96p. 1996. pap. 13.95 (*0-7603-0049-6*) MBI Pubg.
Learn: When Dinosaurs Learned How to Dance. James E. Abbott. 128p. (C). 1994. pap. 19.95 (*1-885300-00-X*) Quality Mgmt.
Learn Vol. 1: ABC Stories. unabridged ed. Mila Vujovich-LaBarre & Eloise Overlin. (Illus.). 32p. (J). (gr. k-3). 1969. pap. text 4.95 (*1-890753-01-7*) Ganas Co.
Learn a Cuisine: Exploring the Favors of Latin America. Kit. 1999. 34.95 (*1-57990-097-6*, Pub. by Lark Books) Random.
Learn a Cuisine: Exploring the Flavors of India. Kit. 1999. 34.95 (*1-57990-096-8*, Pub. by Lark Books) Random.
Learn a Little Sign Language. Harriet Brown. LC 99-207878. 1999. pap. text 1.95 (*1-56247-736-6*) Pleasant Co.
Learn a New Language: A Creative Guide. Richard D. Davidian. 1988. write for info. (*0-318-63667-0*) Andrews U CIR.
Learn-a-Term: A Course in Medical Terminology. A. Brent Garber & Leroy Sparks. LC 77-82026. 168p. (C). 1977. 49.00 (*0-912862-48-3*) Aspen Pub.
***Learn about ABCs.** (Illus.). 8p. (J). 1998. bds. 4.99 (*1-929174-03-9*) Oshkosh BGosh.
Learn about Alcohol. 16p. 1983. pap. 1.25 (*0-89486-205-7*, 1343B) Hazelden.
Learn about Alcohol & Pregnancy. 16p. 1983. pap. 1.25 (*0-89486-210-3*, 1348B) Hazelden.

L

An Asterisk (*) at the beginning of an entry indicates that the title is appearing for the first time.

Learn about Alcoholism. 16p. 1983. pap. 1.25 (*0-89486-206-5*, 1344B) Hazelden.

***Learn about Animals.** (Illus.). 8p. (J). 1998. bds. 4.99 (*1-929174-04-7*) Oshkosh BGosh.

Learn about Anorexia & Bulimia. (Learn about Ser.). 1985. pap. 1.25 (*0-89486-270-7*) Hazelden.

Learn about Astronomy. Lorenz Books Staff. 64p. (J). 1996. 7.95 (*1-85967-159-4*, Lorenz Bks) Anness Pub.

Learn about Children of Alcoholics. (Learn about Ser.). 15p. (Orig.). 1985. pap. 1.25 (*0-89486-253-7*, 1352B) Hazelden.

Learn about Cocaine & Crack. 16p. 1983. pap. 1.25 (*0-89486-207-3*, 1345B) Hazelden.

Learn about Drinking & Driving. 16p. 1983. pap. 1.25 (*0-89486-209-X*, 1347B) Hazelden.

Learn about English Law see Henry Cecil Reprint Series

Learn about Families & Chemical Dependency. (Learn about Ser.). 16p. (Orig.). 1985. pap. 1.25 (*0-89486-269-3*, 1354B) Hazelden.

Learn about Growing Friendships with Little Bud. Christy Holstead & Pamela Linder. (Illus.). (J). (ps-3). 1992. student ed. 3.98 (*1-881037-00-2*) McGreen Wisdom.

Learn about Insects. Lorenz Books Staff. 1998. 8.95 (*1-85967-644-8*, Lorenz Bks) Anness Pub.

Learn about Marijuana. 16p. 1983. pap. 1.25 (*0-89486-208-1*, 1346B) Hazelden.

Learn about Prescription Drugs. 16p. (Orig.). (C). 1984. pap. 1.25 (*0-89486-240-5*, 1349B) Hazelden.

Learn about Pyramids. Lorenz Books Staff. 1998. 8.95 (*1-85967-643-X*, Lorenz Bks) Anness Pub.

Learn about Shapes. Ron Van Der Meer. LC 99-190565. (Sesame Street Interactive Pop-Ups Ser.). (J). 1998. 11.99 (*0-679-89254-0*, Pub. by Random Bks Yng Read) Random.

Learn about Teaching from Children: An Outstanding Guide for All early Childhood Educators. 5th ed. Barbara Merrill. LC 83-73668. (Illus.). 53p. 1984. 5.00 (*0-9613271-1-1*) RAEYC.

Learn about... Texas Birds. Mark W. Lockwood. Ed. by Georg Zappler. LC 99-165913. (Learn About Ser.). (Illus.). 48p. (J). (gr. 1-6). 1997. pap. 7.95 (*1-885696-17-5*) TX Prks & Wldlife.

Learn about Texas Dinosaurs. Georg Zappler. (Illus.). 44p. (J). (gr. 1-6). 1995. pap. 7.95 (*0-9636765-7-1*) TX Prks & Wldlife.

Learn about Texas Indians. Georg Zappler. (Illus.). 48p. (Orig.). (J). (gr. 1-6). 1996. pap. text 7.95 (*1-885696-02-7*, Pub. by TX Prks & Wldlife) U of Tex Pr.

Learn about Texas Insects. Chris Durden. Ed. by Georg Zappler. (Illus.). 60p. (J). (gr. 1-6). 1999. pap. 7.95 (*1-885696-27-2*, Pub. by TX Prks & Wldlife) U of Tex Pr.

Learn about the Body. Lorenz Books Staff. (Illus.). 64p. (J). 1996. 7.95 (*1-85967-134-9*, Lorenz Bks) Anness Pub.

Learn about the Sea. Robin Kerrod. (Learn about Ser.). (Illus.). 64p. (J). 1998. 7.95 (*1-85967-310-4*, Lorenz Bks) Anness Pub.

Learn about Youth & Drug Addiction. (Learn about Ser.). 15p. (Orig.). 1985. pap. 1.25 (*0-89486-252-9*, 1353B) Hazelden.

***Learn Access 97.** Que Education & Training Staff et al. LC 97-68884. 224p. (C). 1998. pap. text 32.00 (*1-57576-891-7*) Que Educ & Trng.

Learn Access 97 in a Weekend. Diane Tinney. LC 97-75644. 312p. 1998. pap. 19.99 (*0-7615-1379-5*) Prima Pub.

***Learn Access, 2000.** John Preston. LC 98-88901. 342p. 2000. pap. text 37.33 (*1-58076-258-1*) Que Educ & Trng.

Learn ACT 3.0 for Windows 95. Deborah Bean & Neal Berkowitz. LC 97-10867. (Popular Applications Ser.). (Illus.). 250p. (Orig.). (C). 1997. pap. 19.95 (*1-55622-518-0*) Wordware Pub.

***Learn ACT! 2000 for the Advanced User.** Neal Berkowitz & Deborah Bean. (Illus.). 400p. (C). 2000. pap. 39.95 (*1-55622-744-2*) Wordware Pub.

Learn ACT! 3.0 for the Advanced User. Deborah Bean. LC 98-31103. 1998. pap. text 36.95 (*1-55622-588-1*) Wordware Pub.

Learn Activex Development Using Visual Basic 5.0. Nathan Wallace. LC 97-34602. 800p. 1997. pap. text 49.95 (*1-55622-606-3*) Wordware Pub.

Learn Activex Development Using Visual C++ 6.0. Nathan Wallace. LC 99-11679. (Illus.). 370p. 1999. pap. 49.95 (*1-55622-607-1*) Wordware Pub.

Learn Activex Scripting with Microsoft Internet Explorer 4.0. Nathan Wallace. LC 98-13053. 500p. 1998. pap. 44.95 (*1-55622-611-X*) Wordware Pub.

Learn ActiveX Template Library Development with Visual C++ 6.0 With CDROM. Nathan Wallace. (Learn Ser.). (Illus.). 360p. 1999. pap. 52.95 (*1-55622-633-0*) Wordware Pub.

Learn Advanced HTML 4.0. Jose Ramalho. LC 98-26338. 1998. pap. text 39.95 (*1-55622-586-5*) Wordware Pub.

***Learn Advanced JavaScript.** David Bowden. (Illus.). 2000. pap. text 59.95 (*1-55622-728-0*) Wordware Pub.

Learn Advanced JavaScript Programming. Yehuda Shiran & Tomer Shiran. LC 97-26719. 650p. 1997. pap. 49.95 (*1-55622-552-0*) Wordware Pub.

Learn Advanced MFC Programming with Visual C++ 9X. Jim Ross. 1998. pap. text 52.95 (*1-55622-594-6*) Wordware Pub.

Learn Advanced OLE DB Development with Visual C++ 6.0. Nathan Wallace. 1999. pap. 59.95 (*1-55622-658-6*) Wordware.

Learn Albanian - Mesoni Shqip. Gezar Kurti. (ALB & ENG., Illus.). 200p. (Orig.). 1996. pap. text, per. 16.00 (*1-881901-09-2*) LEGAS.

***Learn & Color Set of 4.** Illus. by Miriam Zook. (To Learn & Color Ser.). (J). (gr. 1-3). 1998. 3.90 (*0-7399-0320-9*, 2926) Rod & Staff.

Learn & Do Bible Book. Laura K. Gurvis. (Illus.). 64p. (J). (gr. k-2). pap. 4.95 (*0-87441-530-6*) Behrman.

Learn & Draw Shapes in Outer Space. Illus. by Diana Fisher. (Learn & Draw Kits Ser.). 24p. (J). (ps up). 1998. pap. 12.95 (*1-56010-402-3*, YC1) W Foster Pub.

Learn & Draw with Mickey. Mouseworks Staff. 22p. (J). 1999. 12.99 (*0-7364-0101-6*, Pub. by Mouse Works) Time Warner.

Learn & Draw 1 to 10 under the Sea Learn & Draw One to Ten under the Sea. Illus. by Andrea Tachiera. (Learn & Draw Kits Ser.). 24p. (J). (ps up). 1998. pap. 12.95 (*1-56010-404-X*, YC3) W Foster Pub.

***Learn & Grow.** Sara Miller. (Illus.). 8p. (J). (ps-1). 1999. bds. 15.99 (*1-57584-348-X*, RDYF) Rdrs Digest.

***Learn & Grow Carry Along.** Mouseworks Staff. (J). 1999. 9.99 (*0-7364-0181-4*, Pub. by Mouse Works) Little.

Learn & Grow from A to Z: Learning Centers & Activities for Young Children. Kathy Dunlavy. (Illus.). 160p. (J). (ps-2). 1992. student ed. 14.99 (*0-86653-682-5*, GA1416) Good Apple.

Learn & Live. Lucas, George, Educational Foundation Staff. LC 97-70481. (Illus.). 275p. (Orig.). (J). (gr. k-12). 1997. pap. 20.00 (*0-9656326-0-1*) George Lucas Educ Found.

Learn & Live (Proverbs) Holiness & Wholeness-Welcoming the Saving Reign of God. Ed. by Jack W. Hayford. LC 97-218763. (Spirit-Filled Life Bible Discovery Guide Ser.: No. B10). 160p. pap. 6.99 (*0-7852-1167-5*) Nelson.

Learn & Play. 8p. (J). 1995. 34.99 (*1-888074-05-1*) Pckts Lrning.

Learn & Play in the Garden. Meg Herd. LC 96-86075. (Illus.). 128p. (J). (gr. 1-7). 1997. pap. 9.95 (*0-8120-9780-7*) Barron.

Learn & Play in the Garden Vol. 7: Games, Crafts & Activities for Children. Meg Herd. (Environmental Bks.). (Illus.). 128p. (J). (ps-6). 1999. lib. bdg. 18.95 (*1-56674-242-0*, HTS Bks) Forest Hse.

Learn & Play in the Garden Vol. 7: Games, Crafts & Activities for Children. Meg Herd. (J). 1997. 15.15 (*0-606-11552-8*, Pub. by Turtleback) Demco.

Learn & Play the Recycle Way: Homemade Toys That Teach. Rhoda Redleaf & Audrey Robertson. LC 99-29587. 1999. pap. text 18.95 (*1-884834-40-X*) Redleaf Pr.

Learn & Review, Most Commonly Used Greek Words. (Greek Study Courses Ser.). pap. 4.99 (*0-89957-404-1*) AMG Pubs.

Learn & Review, Vocabulary. (Greek Study Courses Ser.). pap. 39.99 incl. audio (*0-89957-400-9*) AMG Pubs.

Learn & Understand the Magic of Sex Unity: We Are One. Angelie Bliss. (Illus.). 170p. 2000. pap. 21.95 (*0-9651438-1-3*) Air & Water King.

Learn Apple Writer IIe the Easy Way. Katie Layman & Adrienne G. Renner. 1986. 17.95 (*0-13-527060-X*) S&S Trade.

Learn Arabic for English Speakers. (ARA & ENG.). pap. 25.95 (*0-87557-004-6*) Saphrograph.

Learn Arabic Through Words & Simple Phrases. Lily Sayegh. 1987. pap. 7.95 (*0-86685-348-0*) Intl Bk Ctr.

Learn Archiving & File Compression Programming in Visual C++ 9X. Derek Benner. 1998. pap. text 39.95 (*1-55622-599-7*) Wordware Pub.

Learn As You Color Series III: Brachos. M. Liebermann. (J). (ps-2). 1987. 3.25 (*0-914131-88-5*, D720) Torah Umesorah.

Learn at Home, Grade K. American Education. 1999. pap. text 29.95 (*1-56189-508-3*) Amer Educ Pub.

Learn at Home, Grade 1. American Education. 1999. pap. text 29.95 (*1-56189-509-1*) Amer Educ Pub.

Learn at Home, Grade 2. American Education. 1999. pap. text 29.95 (*1-56189-510-5*) Amer Educ Pub.

Learn at Home, Grade 3. American Education. 1999. pap. text 29.95 (*1-56189-511-3*) Amer Educ Pub.

Learn at Home, Grade 4. American Education. 1999. pap. text 29.95 (*1-56189-512-1*) Amer Educ Pub.

Learn at Home, Grade 5. American Education. 1999. pap. text 29.95 (*1-56189-513-X*) Amer Educ Pub.

Learn at Home, Grade 6. American Education. 1999. pap. text 29.95 (*1-56189-514-8*) Amer Educ Pub.

Learn Autocad. Assadipour. Date not set. pap. text, student ed. write for info. (*0-314-03311-4*) West Pub.

Learn AutoCAD LT for Windows in a Day. Ralph Grabowski. LC 94-16806. (Popular Applications Ser.). 160p. 1994. pap. 15.95 incl. disk (*1-55622-426-5*) Wordware Pub.

Learn AutoCAD LT for Windows 95. Ralph Grabowski. LC 96-47403. (Popular Applications Ser.). (Illus.). 250p. 1997. pap. 19.95 incl. disk (*1-55622-538-5*) Wordware Pub.

***Learn AutoCAD LT for Windows 95.** Ralph Grabowski. LC 99-22031. 1999. pap. text 32.95 (*1-55622-690-X*) Wordware Pub.

Learn AutoCAD LT Release 2 for Windows in a Day. Ralph Grabowski. (Popular Applications Ser.). 152p. 1995. pap. 15.95 incl. disk (*1-55622-482-6*) Wordware Pub.

***Learn AutoCAD LT 2000 for Architects.** James Padgett. (Illus.). 400p. (C). 2000. pap. 42.95 (*1-55622-754-X*) Wordware Pub.

***Learn AutoCAD LT 2000 for the Advanced User.** Ralph Grabowski. (Illus.). 400p. (C). 2000. pap. 36.95 (*1-55622-743-4*) Wordware Pub.

***Learn AutoCAD LT 2000.** Ralph Grabowski. (Illus.). 300p. (C). 2000. pap. 32.95 (*1-55622-742-6*) Wordware Pub.

Learn AutoCAD LT 97 for Windows 95 NT. Ralph Grabowski. LC 98-13010. 1998. pap. 24.95 (*1-55622-597-0*) Wordware Pub.

Learn AutoCAD 12 in a Day. Ralph Grabowski. (Popular Applications Ser.). (Illus.). 152p. (Orig.). 1992. pap. 12.95 (*1-55622-241-6*) Wordware Pub.

Learn AutoCAD 12 in a Day. Ralph Grabowski. LC 92-43323. (Popular Applications Ser.). 160p. (Orig.). 1993. pap. 15.95 incl. disk (*1-55622-339-0*) Wordware Pub.

Learn Basic Business Math Using Calculations, Tests. Barbara Muncaster. (KH - Office Machines Ser.). 1985. 1.95 (*0-538-13543-3*) S-W Pub.

Learn Basic Concepts with Cuddles Clown. Sondra Rieck & Lori Stippel. 24p. (J). (ps). 1990. 9.95 (*0-9634082-0-8*) Woodville Pr.

Learn Bengali. 160p. 1992. pap. 7.95 (*0-7818-0224-5*) Hippocrene Bks.

Learn Bengali for English Speakers. (BEN & ENG.). pap. 20.95 (*0-87557-005-4*) Saphrograph.

***Learn Biblical Hebrew.** John H. Dobson. 310p. 1999. pap. text 33.50 (*1-55671-088-7*, Pub. by S I L Intl) Eisenbrauns.

Learn Biochemistry! B. Brown. (Illus.). 304p. 1993. pap. text 25.00 (*0-412-48220-7*) Chapman & Hall.

Learn Blues Harp Effects in 60 Minutes. Pat Conway. 19p. 1998. pap. text 5.95 (*0-7119-5634-0*, AM 936122) Music Sales.

Learn Blues Harp Note Bending in 60 Minutes. Pat Conway. 19p. 1998. pap. text 5.95 (*0-7119-5631-6*, AM 936090) Music Sales.

Learn Bridge in a Weekend. Jonathan Davis. LC 93-722. 1993. 16.00 (*0-679-42752-X*) Knopf.

Learn Bridge in Five Days. Terence Reese. LC 96-24650. 96p. 1996. pap. 7.95 (*0-8069-6166-X*) Sterling.

Learn Burmese for English Speakers. A. Judson. (BUR & ENG.). 1989. pap. 20.95 (*0-87557-121-2*) Saphrograph.

***Learn by Doing: A Hands-on Approach for Physical Anthropology.** Lauren Arenson. 250p. (C). 1999. spiral bd. 43.95 (*0-7872-6291-9*) Kendall-Hunt.

Learn by Doing: A Step-by-Step How-To Guide about Multi-Level Marketing. Gary Molatore. (Illus.). 233p. 1998. pap., wbk. ed. 30.00 (*0-9664144-1-1*) Garys Ideas.

***Learn by Word 2000.** Shelly & Cashman. (Shelly Cashman Ser.). (C). 2000. pap. 38.00 (*0-7895-5992-7*) Course Tech.

Learn C & Save Your Job: C for COBOL Programmers. Kenneth Pugh. 360p. 1993. pap. 29.95 (*0-89435-431-0*) Wiley.

Learn C in Three Days. Sam A. Abolrous. LC 92-11346. (Popular Applications Ser.). (Illus.). 288p. 1992. pap. 19.95 incl. disk (*1-55622-298-X*) Wordware Pub.

Learn C in Two Weeks with Run-C & Cbreeze. Robert J. Traister, Sr. 192p. 1986. 18.50 (*0-13-527078-2*) P-H.

Learn C++ on the Macintosh. Mark Dave. (C). 1996. pap. text. write for info. (*0-201-47945-1*) Addison-Wesley.

Learn C on the Macintosh. 2nd ed. Dave Mark. 496p. 1995. pap. text 34.95 (*0-201-48406-4*) Addison-Wesley.

***Learn C++ in Three Days.** Warren Rachele. 350p. 2000. 29.95 incl. audio compact disk (*1-55622-707-8*) Wordware Pub.

Learn C++ on the PC. Dave Mark. 448p. 1993. pap. 39.95 incl. disk (*0-201-62622-5*) Addison-Wesley.

***Learn Chess.** John Nunn. 2000. pap. 9.95 (*1-901983-30-7*, Pub. by Gambit) BHB Intl.

Learn Chess: A New Way for All, 2 vols., Set. Alexander. 1988. pap. text 19.95 (*0-08-032079-1*, Pergamon Pr) Elsevier.

Learn Chess Vol. 1: A New Way for All. 2nd ed. C. H. Alexander. (Chess Ser.: No. 1). (Illus.). 104p. 1987. 19.90 (*0-08-032067-8*, Pergamon Pr) Elsevier.

Learn Chess from the World Champions. Ed. by David N. Levy. 214p. 1979. pap. text 17.95 (*0-08-021388-X*, Pergamon Pr) Elsevier.

Learn Chess in a Weekend. Kenneth Whyld. LC 92-54793. (Learn in a Weekend Ser.). 1993. 16.00 (*0-679-42229-3*) Knopf.

Learn Chinese for English Speakers. James Summers. (CHI & ENG.). pap. 20.95 (*0-87557-009-7*) Saphrograph.

Learn Chinese the Fast & Fun Way. Lifei Ji. LC 97-73483. (Barron's Fast & Fun Way Ser.). (CHI.). 300p. 1997. pap. text 14.95 (*0-8120-9689-4*) Barron.

Learn Chinese the Fun Way, Vol. 1. Wang Huidi. (CHI & ENG., Illus.). 136p. 1993. pap. 8.95 (*981-01-3038-4*) China Bks.

Learn Chinese the Fun Way, Vol. 2. Wang Huidi. (CHI & ENG., Illus.). 136p. 1993. pap. 8.95 (*981-01-3039-2*) China Bks.

Learn Chinese the Fun Way, Vol. 3. Wang Huidi. (CHI & ENG., Illus.). 136p. 1993. pap. 8.95 (*981-01-3046-5*) China Bks.

Learn Chinese the Fun Way, Vol. 4. Wang Huidi. (CHI & ENG., Illus.). 136p. 1993. pap. 8.95 (*981-01-3061-9*) China Bks.

Learn Chinese the Fun Way, Vol. 5. Wang Huidi. (CHI & ENG., Illus.). 136p. 1993. pap. 8.95 (*981-01-3065-1*) China Bks.

Learn CompuServe for Windows in a Day. Scott Fuller. (Popular Applications Ser.). 160p. (Orig.). 1995. pap. 15.95 (*1-55622-442-7*) Wordware Pub.

***Learn Computer Game Programming with CDX & DirectX 7.0.** Bil Simser. (Illus.). 500p. 2000. pap. 54.95 (*1-55622-756-6*) Wordware Pub.

***Learn Computer Game Programming with DirectX 7.0.** Ian Parberry. (Illus.). 500p. 2000. pap. 49.95 (*1-55622-741-8*) Wordware Pub.

Learn Computers in a Day. Louis Columbus. LC 96-38404. (Popular Applications Ser.). (Illus.). 232p. (Orig.). (C). 1997. pap. 19.95 incl. disk (*1-55622-525-3*) Wordware Pub.

Learn Czech Fast. Radovan Pletka. (Intensive Cassette Ser.). 226p. 1998. spiral bd. 184.00 incl. audio (*1-58214-011-1*) Mltilingl Bks.

Learn Czech for English Speakers. J. Schwarz. (CZE & ENG.). pap. 20.95 (*0-87557-013-5*) Saphrograph.

Learn Danish for English Speakers. (DAN & ENG.). pap. 20.95 (*0-87557-016-X*) Saphrograph.

Learn dBASE Programming in a Day. 2nd ed. Russell A. Stultz. (Popular Applications Ser.). 160p. (Orig.). 1994. pap. 15.95 incl. disk (*1-55622-447-8*) Wordware Pub.

Learn Delphi Today! Jeff Cogswell. 528p. 1996. pap. 34.99 (*1-56884-835-8*) IDG Bks.

***Learn Descriptive Cataloging.** Mary Mortimer. LC 99-46644. (Library Basics Ser.: No. 3). 256p. 2000. reprint ed. pap. 35.00 (*0-8108-3693-9*) Scarecrow.

Learn Desktop Graphics & Design on the Pc. Donald Jenner. 368p. 1994. pap. text 34.95 (*0-201-40788-4*) Addison-Wesley.

***Learn Dewey Decimal Classification.** 21st ed. Mary Mortimer. LC 99-40185. (Library Basics Ser.: No. 2). 145p. 1999. pap. 24.50 (*0-8108-3694-7*) Scarecrow.

Learn Digital Photography in a Weekend. Brad Braun. LC 98-65966. 350p. 1998. per. 19.99 (*0-7615-1532-1*) Prima Pub.

Learn DOS & Windows 95 Without Suffering. 70p. (C). 1996. text 16.80 (*0-536-59927-0*) Pearson Custom.

Learn DOS 6.0 in a Day. Russell A. Stultz. LC 93-46920. (Popular Applications Ser.). 170p. (Orig.). 1994. pap. 12.95 (*1-55622-414-1*) Wordware Pub.

Learn Downhill Skiing in a Weekend. Konrad Bartelski & Robin Neillands. 1992. 16.00 (*0-679-40952-1*) Knopf.

Learn Dutch for English Speakers. (DUT & ENG.). pap. 20.95 (*0-87557-015-1*) Saphrograph.

Learn Encryption Techniques with Visual Basic 9X. Gil Held. LC 98-34653. 1998. pap. text 39.95 (*1-55622-598-9*) Wordware Pub.

Learn English for Hungarian Speakers, 2 vols., Set. Hegedus Lajos. Incl. Advanced Vol. 2. pap. 20.95 (*0-87557-122-0*); Beginners Vol. 1. pap. 20.95 (*0-87557-094-1*); Set pap. 36.00 (*0-87557-095-X*) Saphrograph.

Learn English for Polish Speakers. J. Stanislawski. (ENG & POL.). pap. 20.95 (*0-87557-132-8*) Saphrograph.

Learn English the Fast & Fun Way. D. Arnaldo & Anita Dente. (Barron's Fast & Fun Way Ser.).Tr. of Learn English the Fast & Fun Way for Spanish Speakers. (SPA & ENG.). 304p. 1990. pap. 14.95 (*0-8120-4364-2*) Barron.

***Learn English the Fast & Fun Way for Russian Speakers.** Thomas Beyer, Jr. (Illus.). 128p. 2000. pap. 18.95 (*0-7641-1327-5*) Barron.

Learn English the Fast & Fun Way for Spanish Speakers see Learn English the Fast & Fun Way

Learn English Through Topics about Australia. Cleland. Date not set. pap. text. write for info. (*0-582-66569-8*, Pub. by Addison-Wesley) Longman.

Learn Esperanto for English Speakers. (ENG & ESP.). pap. 20.95 (*0-87557-019-4*, 019-4) Saphrograph.

***Learn Excel 2000.** John Preston et al. 293p. 1999. pap. text 32.00 (*1-58076-261-1*) Que Educ & Trng.

Learn Excel 97. 208p. (C). 1998. pap. text 32.00 (*1-58076-186-0*) Que Educ & Trng.

Learn Finnish for English Speakers. Arthur M. Whitney. (ENG & FIN.). pap. 25.95 (*0-87557-020-8*) Saphrograph.

Learn French. N. Irving. (Learn Languages Ser.). (Illus.). 64p. (YA). (gr. 7 up). 1992. pap. 10.95 (*0-7460-0532-6*, Usborne) EDC.

Learn French. N. Irving. (Learn Languages Ser.). (Illus.). 64p. (YA). (gr. 7-12). 1999. lib. bdg. 18.95 (*0-88110-596-1*, Usborne) EDC.

Learn French. Nicole Irving. (Language Packs Ser.). (FRE & ENG., Illus.). 1993. pap. 21.95 (*0-7460-1439-2*, Usborne) EDC.

Learn French for English Speakers. William R. Patterson. (ENG & FRE.). 230p. pap. 20.95 (*0-87557-023-2*) Saphrograph.

Learn French the Fast & Fun Way. 2nd ed. Elisabeth Leete. (Barron's Fast & Fun Way Ser.). (FRE.). 300p. 1997. pap. text 14.95 (*0-7641-0199-4*) Barron.

Learn French the Fast & Fun Way. 2nd ed. Elisabeth B. Leete & Heywood Wald. LC 97-1365. (Fast & Fun Way Language Bks.). (FRE.). 300p. 1997. 39.95 incl. audio (*0-7641-7027-9*) Barron.

Learn French the Lazy Way. Christopher Desmaison. 240p. 1999. pap. 12.95 (*0-02-863011-4*, Pub. by Macmillan) S&S Trade.

Learn French Together. 1999. 24.95 (*0-609-60574-7*) Liv Lang.

Learn French with Teddy Berlitz. Tony Lang. LC 96-20153. 64p. (J). (ps up). 1996. reprint ed. pap. 12.95 incl. audio (*0-689-81128-4*) Litle Simon.

Learn from the Grandmasters. Ed. by Raymond Keene. 1999. pap. 19.95 (*0-7134-8138-2*) B T B.

Learn from the Legends: Rock Keyboard. Karen A. Krieger & Stephan Foust. 96p. 1999. pap. 9.95 (*0-7390-0078-0*, 18252); pap. 19.95 incl. audio compact disk (*0-7390-0079-9*) Alfred Pub.

Learn from the Masters. Ed. by Frank J. Swetz et al. LC 95-78461. (Classroom Resource Materials Ser.). (Illus.). 312p. 1995. pap. text 31.50 (*0-88385-703-0*, LRM) Math Assn.

Learn from the Masters: Create Your Own Watercolors in the Style of Turner. Peter D. Johnson. (Illus.). 80p. 1992. pap. 16.95 (*0-85532-734-0*, 734-0, Pub. by Srch Pr) A Schwartz & Co.

Learn from the Masters - Cezanne: Create Your Own Watercolors. Peter Johnson. (Illus.). 80p. 1992. pap. 16.95 (*0-85532-735-9*, 735-9, Pub. by Srch Pr) A Schwartz & Co.

Learn Generic CADD 6.0 in a Day. 25th ed. Ralph Grabowski. (Popular Applications Ser.). (Illus.). 144p. (Orig.). 1993. pap. 15.95 incl. disk (*1-55622-304-8*) Wordware Pub.

Learn German. N. Irving. (Learn Languages Ser.). (Illus.). 64p. (YA). (gr. 7 up). 1992. pap. 10.95 (*0-7460-0534-2*) EDC.

An Asterisk (*) at the beginning of an entry indicates that the title is appearing for the first time.

Learn German. N. Irving. (Learn Languages Ser.). (Illus.). 64p. (YA). (gr. 7 up). 1999. lib. bdg. 18.95 (*0-88110-597-X*, Usborne) EDC.

Learn German for English Speakers. P. F. Doring. (ENG & GER.). pap. 20.95 (*0-87557-027-5*) Saphrograph.

Learn German the Fast & Fun Way. 2nd ed. Paul G. Graves. LC 97-8267. (Barron's Fast & Fun Way Ser.). (ENG & GER.). 300p. 1997. 39.95 incl. audio (*0-7641-7024-4*) Barron.

Learn German the Fast & Fun Way Book. 2nd ed. Paul Graves. Ed. by Heywood Wald. LC 97-8267. (GER., Illus.). 252p. 1997. pap. 14.95 (*0-7641-0216-8*) Barron.

Learn German the Lazy Way. Amy Kardel. (Lazy Way Ser.). (GER.). 288p. 1999. pap. 12.95 (*0-02-863165-X*) Free Pr.

Learn Golf in a Weekend. Peter Ballingall. 95p. 1991. 16.00 (*0-394-58747-2*) Knopf.

Learn Golf the Lazy Way. James Y. Bartlett. (Lazy Way Ser.). 288p. 1920. pap. 12.95 (*0-02-863164-1*) Free Pr.

*__Learn Good, Skills at Work: Using Resources, 15 Vols.__ Ait. (Tech Prep Ser.). 1999. pap. 110.00 (*0-538-68964-1*) Sth-Wstrn College.

Learn Graphics File Programming with Delphi 3. Derek A. Benner. LC 97-40626. (Illus.). 400p. 1997. pap. 49.95 (*1-55622-558-X*) Wordware Pub.

Learn Greek for English Speakers. F. Kinchin-Smithma & T. W. Melluish. (ENG & GRE.). pap. 20.95 (*0-87557-031-3*) Saphrograph.

Learn, Grow & Change: Creating Openness to Change & Inclusive Community Involvement. Mary Phillips. (Changing The Paradigm Organizational Effectiveness Ser.: Vol. 5). 30p. 1996. pap. write for info. (*1-58534-014-6*) Points of Light.

*__Learn Guide Anatomy & Physio.__ 9th ed. Tortora. 708p. 1999. pap. 35.95 (*0-471-37467-9*) Wiley.

Learn Guitar Tunings in 60 Minutes. Pat Conway. 19p. 1998. pap. text 5.95 (*0-7119-5633-2*, AM 936111) Music Sales.

Learn Gujarati. Kirit N. Shah. (Illus.). 168p. 1985. pap. text 10.00 (*0-9609614-0-2*) K N Shah.

Learn Gujarati. Kirit N. Shah. Ed. by Terry Strom. LC 91-19422. 1992. 35.00 (*0-9609614-7-X*) K N Shah.

Learn Gujarati. Kirit N. Shah. Ed. by Terry B. Strom. 1992. pap. 20.00 (*0-9609614-8-8*) K N Shah.

Learn Gujarati. enl. ed. Kirit N. Shah. Ed. by Terry B. Strom. LC 91-19422. (GUJ., Illus.). 1992. pap. text 20.00 (*0-9609614-2-9*) K N Shah.

Learn Gujarati, Incl. suppl. 2nd enl. ed. Kirit N. Shah. Ed. by Terry Strom. LC 91-19422. (GUJ., Illus.). 1992. text 30.00 (*0-9609614-3-7*) K N Shah.

*__Learn Hand Reading the Easy Way: Palmistry in Pictures.__ M. Katakkar. 1998. pap. 11.00 (*81-7476-164-0*, Pub. by UBS Pubs) S Asia.

Learn Handwriting. Pen Notes Staff. (J). (gr. 2 up). 1986. spiral bd. 13.00 (*0-939564-00-9*) Pen Notes.

Learn Hawaiian at Home. Kahikahealani Wight. LC 92-73803. (ENG & HAW., Illus.). 192p. 1992. pap. 34.95 incl. audio (*1-880188-21-X*) Bess Pr.

Learn Hawaiian Dancing, Vol. II, Bk. 10. Vicki Corona. (Celebrate the Cultures Ser.). (Illus.). 28p. 1989. pap., student ed. 14.95 (*1-58513-000-1*) Dance Fantasy.

Learn Hebrew: A Comprehensive Course in Modern Hebrew. Isaac Yetiv. 192p. 1973. pap. 11.95 (*0-88328-011-6*) Shilo Pub Hse.

Learn Hebrew for English Speakers, Romanized. Philip Blackman. (ENG & HEB.). pap. 20.95 (*0-87557-032-1*) Saphrograph.

Learn Hebrew Today: Alef-Bet for Adults. Howard I. Bogot & Paul M. Yedwab. (C). 1992. pap. text 7.95 (*0-8074-0483-7*, 101093) UAHC.

Learn Hindi. rev. ed. Kirit N. Shah. Ed. by Raghuveer Chaudhari et al. (HIN., Illus.). 256p. (C). 1997. pap. text 25.00 (*0-9609614-5-3*) K N Shah.

Learn Hindi. 2nd rev. ed. Kirit N. Shah. Ed. by Raghuveer Chaudhari et al. (HIN., Illus.). 256p. (C). 1998. 35.00 (*0-9609614-4-5*) K N Shah.

Learn Hindi: Hindi Sikhiye. Kirit N. Shah. LC 82-99946. (Illus.). 192p. (Orig.). 1983. pap. text 11.00 (*0-9609614-1-0*) K N Shah.

Learn Hindi for English Speakers. (ENG & HIN.). pap. 20.95 (*0-87557-035-6*) Saphrograph.

Learn Hindustani. (ENG & HIN.). pap. 20.95 (*0-87557-037-2*) Saphrograph.

Learn Horseback Riding in a Weekend. Mary G. Watson. (Illus.). 96p. 1998. pap. 10.95 (*0-375-70302-0*) Random.

Learn How to Canoe in One Day: Quickest Way to Start Paddling, Turning, Portaging, & Maintaining. Robert C. Birkby. LC 89-34189. (Illus.). 112p. (Orig.). 1990. pap. 10.95 (*0-8117-2249-X*) Stackpole.

Learn How to Fly Fish in One Day: Quickest Way to Start Tying Flies, Casting Flies, & Catching Fish. Sylvester Nemes. LC 85-20802. (Illus.). 128p. (Orig.). 1986. pap. 11.95 (*0-8117-2185-X*) Stackpole.

Learn How to Learn: Teacher Edition & Planbook. 3rd rev. ed. (Illus.). 114p. 1995. pap. 6.95 (*1-892022-26-5*) Skill Boosters.

Learn How to Learn Study Skills. rev. ed. Herman Ohme. Ed. by Jean Ohme. (Illus.). 256p. 1989. pap. 12.00 (*0-936047-00-3*) CA Educ Plan.

Learn How to Make Balloon Animals & More: Includes Air Pump & Balloons. Terence Gleason. (Illus.). 20p. (J). (gr. 3-6). 1997. pap. 5.99 (*0-9661745-0-X*) Conceptions CA.

Learn How to Save on Installing or Repairing Your Home Driveway Also How to Choose Your Contractor. Alfred Edwards. Ed. by Tom Shean. (Illus.). (Orig.). (C). 1993. pap. write for info. (*1-882253-00-0*) Fam Orig Concepts.

*__Learn How to Share with Josh B'Gosh.__ Illus. by Penny Dann. 10p. 1998. 5.99 (*1-929174-06-3*) Oshkosh BGosh.

Learn How to Study. 2nd ed. Derek Rowntree. (J). 1976. pap. 12.95 (*0-8464-0548-2*) Beekman Pubs.

Learn HTML in a Weekend. Steve Callihan. LC 97-69599. (Computer Bks.). 432p. 1997. per. 24.99 (*0-7615-1293-4*) Prima Pub.

Learn HTML in a Weekend. rev. ed. Steve Callihan. LC 98-67613. (In a Weekend Ser.). 350p. 1998. per. 24.99 (*0-7615-1800-2*) Prima Pub.

Learn HTML on the Macintosh Pages: Everything You Need to Create Your Own World Wide Web Pages. David Lawrence & Dave Mark. 304p. 1996. pap. 29.95 (*0-201-88793-2*) Pearson Custom.

Learn Hungarian for English Speakers. A. H. Whitney. (ENG & HUN.). 264p. pap. 20.95 (*0-87557-044-5*) Saphrograph.

Learn in Brain-Friendly Ways: How to Succeed with Quality Learning Skills. Rudolf E. Klimes. 200p. (C). 1994. pap. text, per. 9.95 (*1-886304-00-9*) LearnWell Pr.

Learn in Your Car: French, Level 1. unabridged ed. Henry N. Raymond. (ENG & FRE.). 1990. pap. 16.95 incl. audio (*1-56015-125-0*) Penton Overseas.

Learn in Your Car: French, Level 1, set. unabridged ed. Henry N. Raymond. (FRE & ENG.). 1990. pap. 34.95 incl. audio compact disk (*1-56015-122-6*) Penton Overseas.

Learn in Your Car: French, Level 2, set. unabridged ed. Henry N. Raymond. LC 84-203565. (FRE & ENG.). 1991. pap. 16.95 incl. audio (*1-56015-129-3*) Penton Overseas.

Learn in Your Car: French, Level 2, set. unabridged ed. Henry N. Raymond. (FRE & ENG.). 1991. pap. 34.95 incl. audio compact disk (*1-56015-119-6*) Penton Overseas.

Learn in Your Car: French, Level 3, set. Henry N. Raymond. LC 84-203565. (FRE & ENG.). 1992. pap. 16.95 incl. audio (*1-56015-133-1*) Penton Overseas.

Learn in Your Car: French, 3 Levels, Set. Henry N. Raymond. (FRE.). 1992. pap. 39.95 incl. audio (*1-56015-138-2*) Penton Overseas.

Learn in Your Car: French, 2 Levels, Set. unabridged ed. Henry N. Raymond. (ENG & FRE.). Date not set. 29.95 incl. audio (*1-56015-121-8*) Penton Overseas.

*__Learn in Your Car: German, Level 1, set.__ Henry N. Raymond. (GER & ENG.). 1999. 34.95 incl. audio compact disk (*1-56015-117-X*) Penton Overseas.

Learn in Your Car: German, Level 1, set. unabridged ed. Henry N. Raymond. (ENG & GER.). (gr. 7). 1990. pap. 16.95 incl. audio (*1-56015-128-5*) Penton Overseas.

Learn in Your Car: German, Level 2, set. unabridged ed. Henry N. Raymond. LC 84-203565. (GER & ENG.). 1991. pap. 16.95 incl. audio (*1-56015-132-3*) Penton Overseas.

Learn in Your Car: German, Level 3, set. Henry N. Raymond. LC 84-203565. (GER & ENG.). 1992. pap. 16.95 incl. audio (*1-56015-136-6*) Penton Overseas.

Learn in Your Car: German, 3 Levels, Set. Henry N. Raymond. (GER.). 1992. pap. 39.95 incl. audio (*1-56015-139-0*) Penton Overseas.

Learn in Your Car: Italian, Level 1, set. unabridged ed. Henry N. Raymond. LC 84-203565. (ITA & ENG.). 1991. pap. 16.95 incl. audio (*1-56015-127-7*) Penton Overseas.

Learn in Your Car: Italian, Level 2, set. unabridged ed. Henry N. Raymond. (ITA.). 1991. pap. 16.95 incl. audio (*1-56015-131-5*) Penton Overseas.

Learn in Your Car: Italian, Level 3, set. Henry N. Raymond. (ITA & ENG.). 1992. pap. 16.95 incl. audio (*1-56015-135-8*) Penton Overseas.

Learn in Your Car: Italian, 3 Levels, Set. unabridged ed. Henry N. Raymond. (ENG & ITA.). 1992. pap. 39.95 incl. audio (*1-56015-140-4*) Penton Overseas.

Learn in Your Car: Japanese, Level 1, set. Henry N. Raymond. (JPN & ENG.). 1992. pap. 16.95 incl. audio (*1-56015-137-4*) Penton Overseas.

Learn in Your Car: Japanese, Level 2, set. unabridged ed. Henry N. Raymond. (JPN & ENG.). 1993. pap. 16.95 incl. audio (*1-56015-143-9*) Penton Overseas.

Learn in Your Car: Japanese, Level 3. Henry N. Raymond. (JPN & ENG.). 1993. pap. 16.95 incl. audio (*1-56015-145-5*) Penton Overseas.

Learn in Your Car: Japanese, 3 Levels, Set. unabridged ed. Henry N. Raymond. (JPN & ENG.). 1993. pap. 39.95 incl. audio (*1-56015-146-3*) Penton Overseas.

Learn in Your Car: Russian, Level 1, set. unabridged ed. Henry N. Raymond. (RUS & ENG.). 1993. pap. 16.95 incl. audio (*1-56015-142-0*) Penton Overseas.

Learn in Your Car: Russian, Level 2, set. Henry N. Raymond. (RUS & ENG.). 1994. pap. 16.95 incl. audio (*1-56015-144-7*) Penton Overseas.

Learn in Your Car: Russian, Level 3. Hank Raymond. (ENG & RUS.). (gr. 7). 1994. pap. 16.95 incl. audio (*1-56015-147-1*) Penton Overseas.

Learn in Your Car: Russian, 3 Levels, Set. Henry N. Raymond. (ENG & RUS.). 1994. pap. 39.95 incl. audio (*1-56015-148-X*) Penton Overseas.

Learn in Your Car: Spanish. Ed. by Denis Girard et al. LC 77-7669. (ENG & FRE.). 1100p. 1977. 24.95 (*0-02-522620-7*, Pub. by Macmillan) S&S Trade.

Learn in Your Car: Spanish, Level 1, set. unabridged ed. Henry N. Raymond. (SPA & ENG.). 1990. pap. 34.95 incl. audio compact disk (*1-56015-149-8*) Penton Overseas.

Learn in Your Car: Spanish, Level 1, set. unabridged ed. Henry N. Raymond. LC 84-203565. (SPA & ENG.). 1990. pap. 16.95 incl. audio (*1-56015-126-9*) Penton Overseas.

Learn in Your Car: Spanish, Level 2, set. unabridged ed. Henry N. Raymond. LC 84-203565. (SPA & ENG.). 1991. pap. 16.95 incl. audio (*1-56015-130-7*) Penton Overseas.

Learn in Your Car: Spanish, Level 2, set. unabridged ed. Henry N. Raymond. (SPA & ENG.). 1991. pap. 34.95 incl. audio compact disk (*1-56015-123-4*) Penton Overseas.

Learn in Your Car: Spanish, Level 3, set. Henry N. Raymond. (SPA & ENG.). 1992. pap. 16.95 incl. audio (*1-56015-134-X*) Penton Overseas.

Learn in Your Car: Spanish, Level 3, set. Henry N. Raymond. (SPA & ENG.). 1992. pap. 34.95 incl. audio compact disk (*1-56015-124-2*) Penton Overseas.

Learn in Your Car: Spanish, 2 Levels, Set. unabridged ed. Henry N. Raymond. (ENG & SPA.). Date not set. pap. 29.95 incl. audio (*1-56015-120-X*) Penton Overseas.

Learn in Your Car: English see Apprendre en Voiture: Anglais

Learn in Your Car: English see Lern Im Auto: Englisch

Learn in Your Car: English see Apprendre en Voiture: Anglais

Learn in Your Car: English see Aprenda en su Auto: Ingles

Learn in Your Car: English see Apprendre en Voiture: Anglais

Learn in Your Car: English see Aprenda en su Auto: Anglais

*__Learn in Your Car Kids: Spanish.__ (SPA & ENG.). (J). 2000. pap. 18.95 incl. audio (*1-56015-107-2*); pap. 21.95 incl. audio (*1-56015-108-0*) Penton Overseas.

Learn Internet Publishing with Microsoft Publisher 97. Russell A. Stultz. LC 96-40198. (Illus.). 300p. 1997. pap. 24.95 incl. disk (*1-55622-551-2*) Wordware Pub.

Learn Internet Publishing with Microsoft Publisher 98. Russell Stultz. LC 98-30915. ix, 333p. 1998. pap. text 29.95 (*1-55622-631-4*) Wordware Pub.

Learn Internet Relay Chat. Kathryn Toyer. LC 96-1798. (Popular Applications Ser.). (Illus.). 300p. (Orig.). (C). 1996. pap. 19.95 (*1-55622-519-9*) Wordware Pub.

Learn Irish for English Speakers. (ENG & GAE.). pap. 20.95 (*0-87557-123-9*) Saphrograph.

Learn Italian for English Speakers. Arthur L. Hayward & C. McFarlane. (ENG & ITA.). 20.95 (*0-87557-046-1*) Saphrograph.

Learn Italian the Fast & Fun Way. 2nd ed. Marcel Danesi & Heywood Wald. LC 97-8788. (ENG & ITA.). 300p. 1997. 39.95 incl. audio (*0-7641-7025-2*) Barron.

Learn Italian the Fast & Fun Way Book. 2nd ed. Marcel Danesi. Ed. by Wald Heywood. LC 97-8788. (Barron's Fast & Fun Way Ser.). (ITA., Illus.). 260p. 1997. pap. 14.95 (*0-7641-0210-9*) Barron.

Learn Italian the Lazy Way. Gabrielle Euvino. 304p. 1999. pap. 12.95 (*0-02-863014-9*, Pub. by Macmillan) S&S Trade.

Learn Italian Together. 1999. 24.95 (*0-609-60576-3*) Liv Lang.

Learn Japanese: New College Text, Vol. 1. John Young & Kimiko Nakajima-Okana. 284p. (C). 1984. pap. text 17.00 (*0-8248-0859-2*) UH Pr.

Learn Japanese: New College Text, Vol. II. John Young & Kimiko Nakajima-Okana. Vol. II. 370p. (C). 1984. pap. text 17.00 (*0-8248-0881-9*) UH Pr.

Learn Japanese: New College Text, Vol. III. John Young & Kimiko Nakajima-Okana. (Learn Japanese: New College Texts Ser.). 336p. 1985. pap. text 18.00 (*0-8248-0896-7*) UH Pr.

Learn Japanese: New College Text, Vol. IV. John Young & Kimiko Nakajima-Okana. LC 83-18060. 370p. 1985. pap. text 19.00 (*0-8248-0951-3*) UH Pr.

Learn Japanese for English Speakers. (ENG & JPN.). pap. 20.95 (*0-87557-049-6*) Saphrograph.

Learn Japanese the Fast & Fun Way. C. Akiyama & N. Akiyama. (Fast & Fun Way Language Bks.). (JPN & ENG.). 256p. 1990. pap. 16.95 (*0-8120-4365-0*) Barron.

Learn Japanese the Fast & Fun Way. 2nd rev. ed. Carol Akiyama & Nobuo Akiyama. LC 98-73386. (ENG & JPN., Illus.). 256p. 1999. pap. 16.95 (*0-7641-0623-6*); pap., boxed set 39.95 incl. audio (*0-7641-7271-9*) Barron.

*__Learn Java by Association with C, Cobol, Fortran, Pascal, Visual Basic: A Practical Dictionary of Programming Languages.__ Dilip Dedhia. 208p. 2000. 33.95 (*0-9679469-0-5*) Engineering Mech.

Learn Java on the Macintosh. Barry Boone & Dave Mark. 496p. 1996. pap. text 34.95 (*0-201-19157-1*) Addison-Wesley.

Learn Lacecraft: More Than 50 Exciting Step-by-Step Projects. Audrey V. Dean. (Illus.), 64p. 1998. text 20.00 (*0-7881-5377-3*) DIANE Pub.

Learn Latin for English Speakers. Patrick S. Casserly. (ENG & LAT.). pap. 20.95 (*0-87557-051-8*) Saphrograph.

*__Learn LC Subject Access.__ Jacki Ganendran. 120p. 1999. pap. 24.50 (*0-8108-3695-5*) Scarecrow.

Learn Letters & Numbers. Illus. by Andrew Geeson. 96p. (J). (ps). 1997. 6.98 (*1-85854-570-6*) Brimax Bks.

*__Learn Library of Congress Classification.__ Helena Dittmann & Jane Hardy. LC 99-42766. (Illus.). 176p. 1999. pap. 29.50 (*0-8108-3696-3*) Scarecrow.

Learn Linux 3-d Graphics Programming. Norman Lin. 2000. pap. text 49.95 (*1-55622-723-X*) Wordware.

Learn Lotus Domino: A Developer's Guide. Rose Kelleher. LC 97-5915. 250p. 1997. pap. 24.95 incl. disk (*1-55622-564-4*) Wordware Pub.

Learn Lotus 1-2-3 Release 5 for Windows in a Day. Jess Schilling. (Popular Applications Ser.). 1995. pap. 15.95 incl. disk (*1-55622-470-2*) Wordware Pub.

Learn Lotus 1-2-3 Release 4 for Windows in a Day. Ed Paulson. LC 93-45769. (Popular Applications Ser.). (Illus.). 136p. 1994. pap. 15.95 incl. disk (*1-55622-408-7*) Wordware Pub.

Learn Lotus 1-2-3 Release 4 in a Day: For Users of Lotus 1-2-3 2.0 Through 4.0 for DOS. Russell A. Stultz. LC 94-30459. 136p. 1994. pap. 15.95 incl. disk (*1-55622-430-3*) Wordware Pub.

Learn Magic. Henry Hay. LC 74-80337. (Illus.). 285p. 1975. reprint ed. 6.95 (*0-486-21238-6*) Dover.

Learn Maori Tribe of New Zealand Dance, Vol. II, Bk. 12. Vicki Corona. (Celebrate the Cultures Ser.). (Illus.). 28p. 1989. pap. 14.95 (*1-58513-002-8*) Dance Fantasy.

Learn Massage in a Weekend. Nitya LaCroix. LC 92-53046. 1992. 16.00 (*0-679-41675-7*) Knopf.

*__Learn Math Quickly: Addition, Subtraction, Multiplication, & Division: Video Plus Workbook A, 5 Videos.__ Janet Scarpone. Incl. Workbook A for Videos A-E: A Basic Math Workbook. 1998. pap. text, wbk. ed. 10.99 (*1-889434-26-4*); Video C. Multiplication Tables. 1998. pap., wbk. ed. 49.99 incl. VHS (*1-889434-36-1*); Video D. Multiplication. 1998. pap., wbk. ed. 49.99 incl. VHS (*1-889434-24-8*); Video A. Addition. 1998. pap., wbk. ed. 49.99 incl. VHS (*1-889434-22-1*); Video B. Subtraction. 1998. pap., wbk. ed. 49.99 incl. VHS (*1-889434-23-X*); Video E. Division. 1998. pap., wbk. ed. 49.99 incl. VHS (*1-889434-25-6*); 1998. Set wbk. ed. 209.00 incl. VHS (*1-889434-42-6*) Learn Quickly.

Learn Math Quickly Series: Videotapes & Workbooks, 16 videos, Janet Scarpone. Incl. Workbook 4 for Videos 13-16. 1998. pap. text, wbk. ed. 10.99 (*1-889434-29-9*); Workbook 1 for Videos 1-5: Provides Practice Lifeskills Problems Plus Pre-Tests & Post-Tests in Fractions & Fraction Word Problems. 62p. 1996. pap. text, wbk. ed. 10.99 (*1-889434-15-9*); Workbook 3 for Videos 9-12: Provides Practice in the Basics of Measurement & Geometry Plus Pre-Test Lifeskills Math Problems & Post Tests. 102p. 1996. pap. text, wbk. ed. 10.99 (*1-889434-17-5*); Workbook 2 for Videos 6-8: Provides Practice in Decimals, Percent, Ratio & Proportion & Includes Pre-Tests & Cumulative Life Skills Word Problem Tests. 55p. 1996. pap. text, wbk. ed. 10.99 (*1-889434-16-7*); Video 1. Fractions 1 - Basics. 1996. pap. text, wbk. ed. 49.99 incl. VHS (*1-889434-01-9*); Video 2. Fractions 2 - More Basics, Addition, Subtraction. 1996. pap. text, wbk. ed. 49.99 incl. VHS (*1-889434-02-7*); Video 3. Fractions 3 - More Subtraction, Multiplication. 1996. pap. text, wbk. ed. 49.99 incl. VHS (*1-889434-03-5*); Video 4. Fractions 4 - More Multiplication, Division. 1996. pap. text, wbk. ed. 49.99 incl. VHS (*1-889434-04-3*); Video 5. Word Problems. 1996. pap. text, wbk. ed. 49.99 incl. VHS (*1-889434-05-1*); Video 6. Decimals. 1996. pap. text, wbk. ed. 49.99 incl. VHS (*1-889434-06-X*); Video 7. Percent. 1996. pap. text, wbk. ed. 49.99 incl. VHS (*1-889434-07-8*); Video 8. Ratio & Proportion. 1996. pap. text, wbk. ed. 49.99 incl. VHS (*1-889434-08-6*); Video 9. Measurement: Area, Perimeter. 1996. pap. text, wbk. ed. 49.99 incl. VHS (*1-889434-09-4*); Video 10. Measurement: Circles, Volume. 1996. pap. text, wbk. ed. 49.99 incl. VHS (*1-889434-10-8*); Video 11. Geometry 1. 1996. pap. text, wbk. ed. 49.99 incl. VHS (*1-889434-11-6*); Video 12. Geometry 2. 1996. pap. text, wbk. ed. 49.99 incl. VHS (*1-889434-12-4*); Video 13. Algebra 1. 1996. pap. text, wbk. ed. 49.99 incl. VHS (*1-889434-13-2*); Video 14. Algebra 2. 1996. pap. text, wbk. ed. 49.99 incl. VHS (*1-889434-14-0*); Video 15. Algebra 3. 1998. pap., wbk. ed. 49.99 incl. VHS (*1-889434-27-2*); Video 16. Algebra 4. 1998. pap., wbk. ed. 49.99 incl. VHS (*1-889434-28-0*); (Learn Math Quickly Ser.). 1996. Set pap., wbk. ed. 669.00 incl. VHS (*1-889434-00-0*) Learn Quickly.

Learn Me Somethin' Michael Schneider. 101p. 1997. pap. 5.50 (*0-87129-774-4*, L89) Dramatic Pub.

Learn Microsoft Access Programming for the Advanced User. Neal Berkowitz. 1998. pap. text 39.95 (*1-55622-589-X*) Wordware Pub.

Learn Microsoft Access 7.0 for Windows 95 in a Day. Russell A. Stultz. (Popular Applications Ser.). 136p. 1996. pap. 15.95 incl. disk (*1-55622-463-X*) Wordware Pub.

Learn Microsoft Access 2.0 in a Day. Russell A. Stultz. LC 94-2523. (Popular Applications Ser.). 144p. 1994. pap. 15.95 incl. disk (*1-55622-417-6*) Wordware Pub.

Learn Microsoft Active Desktop Development with the Internet Client SDK. Nathan Wallace. LC 98-29300. 1998. pap. text 59.95 (*1-55622-628-4*) Wordware Pub.

Learn Microsoft Assembler in a Day. Stephen K. Cunningham. (Popular Applications Ser.). 144p. (Orig.). 1993. pap. 15.95 incl. disk (*1-55622-331-5*) Wordware Pub.

Learn Microsoft Excel 7.0 for Windows 95 in a Day. Russell A. Stultz. (Popular Applications Ser.). 152p. 1995. pap. 15.95 incl. disk (*1-55622-464-8*) Wordware Pub.

Learn Microsoft Exchange Server 5.5 Core Technologies. Ed Paulson. LC 97-44017. 1997. pap. 39.95 (*1-55622-601-2*) Wordware Pub.

Learn Microsoft Front Page, 1997. Kathryn Toyer. LC 97-1894. (Popular Applications Ser.). 300p. (Orig.). (C). 1996. pap. 19.95 incl. disk (*1-55622-520-2*) Wordware Pub.

Learn Microsoft Office 95: Comprehensive Tutorials for Word 7.0, Excel 7.0, Access 7.0, PowerPoint 7.0, Schedule 7.0, Shortcut Bar, Binder & Much More. Russell A. Stultz. LC 96-20770. 550p. 1996. pap. 29.95 incl. disk (*1-55622-499-0*) Wordware Pub.

Learn Microsoft Office 97. Russell A. Stultz. LC 97-1590. (Illus.). 600p. 1997. pap. 29.95 incl. disk (*1-55622-540-7*) Wordware Pub.

Learn! Microsoft Office 97: Getting Organized. Tom Jaffee & Keith White. Date not set. pap. 24.99 (*1-57231-546-6*) Microsoft.

Learn Microsoft Office 2000. Michael Busby. LC 00-28961. 700p. 1999. pap. write for info. (*1-55622-716-7*) Wordware Pub.

Learn Microsoft Power Point 7.0 for Windows 95 in a Day. Russell A. Stultz. (Popular Applications Ser.). 144p. 1996. pap. 15.95 incl. disk (*1-55622-465-6*) Wordware Pub.

L

Learn Microsoft Transaction Server Development. Nathan Wallace. LC 99-26758. 1998. pap. text 54.95 (*1-55622-629-2*) Wordware Pub.
Learn Microsoft Visual Basic 6.0 Now With CDROM. Michael Halvorson. LC 99-21357. (Learn Now Ser.). (Illus.). 536p. 1999. pap. 49.99 (*0-7356-0729-X*) Microsoft.
Learn Microsoft Visual J++ 6.0 Now. Kevin Ingalls & Daniel Jinguji. LC 98-26270. 400p. 39.99 incl. cd-rom (*1-57231-923-2*) Microsoft.
Learn Microsoft Windows NT 4.0 Administration. Louis Columbus. LC QA76. (Illus.). 450p. (Orig.). (C). 1997. pap. 29.95 (*1-55622-513-X*) Wordware Pub.
Learn Microsoft Windows NT 4.0 Networking. 2nd rev. ed. Louis Columbus. 350p. (Orig.). (C). 1997. pap. 39.95 incl. audio compact disk (*1-55622-515-6*) Wordware Pub.
*__Learn Microsoft Windows Script Host 2.0 Now.__ Gunter Born. (DV-DLT Learn Now Ser.). (Illus.). 2000. pap. text 49.99 (*0-7356-0931-4*) Microsoft.
Learn Microsoft Windows 95: Internet Online. Jaffee & White. 1996. text 24.95 (*1-57231-372-2*) Microsoft.
Learn Microsoft Word 7.0 for Windows 95 in a Day. Russell A. Stultz. (Popular Applications Ser.). 159p. 1995. pap. 15.95 incl. disk (*1-55622-466-4*) Wordware Pub.
Learn Microsoft Word 6.0 for Windows in a Day. Russell A. Stultz. LC 94-5036. (Popular Applications Ser.). 144p. 1994. pap. 15.95 incl. disk (*1-55622-423-0*) Wordware Pub.
Learn Microsoft Works in a Day. Jerry Funk. (Popular Applications Ser.). (Illus.). 128p. (Orig.). 1991. pap. 15.95 incl. disk (*1-55622-205-X*) Wordware Pub.
Learn Microsoft Works 3.0 for Windows in a Day. Jerry Funk. LC 93-22182. (Popular Applications Ser.). 136p. (Orig.). 1993. pap. 15.95 (*1-55622-369-2*) Wordware Pub.
Learn Microsoft Works 3.0 for Windows in a Day. Jerry Funk. LC 94-19387. (Popular Applications Ser.). 136p. (Orig.). 1994. pap. 15.95 incl. disk (*1-55622-438-9*) Wordware Pub.
Learn Mishnah. Jacob Neusner. LC 78-5482. (Illus.). (J). (gr. 5-6). 1978. pap. 6.95 (*0-87441-310-9*) Behrman.
Learn Mishnah Notebook. Priscilla Fishman. 128p. (J). (gr. 7-8). 1983. pap. 3.95 (*0-87441-369-9*) Behrman.
Learn More, Smoke Less. Avram Goldstein. 160p. (Orig.). 1990. pap. 12.95 (*0-938013-02-5*) Avva.
Learn MS Excel 2000 VBA Programming. Julitta Korol. LC 99-46575. 445p. 1999. pap. text 39.95 (*1-55622-703-5*) Wordware Pub.
*__Learn MS Publisher 2000 for the Advanced User.__ Russell Stultz. LC 99-39340. 1999. pap. 34.95 (*1-55622-712-4*) Wordware Pub.
Learn Multimedia Programming with Visual Basic 5.0. David L. Cambell. LC 97-20679. (Illus.). 450p. 1997. pap. 39.95 (*1-55622-541-5*) Wordware Pub.
Learn Multimedia with Visual Basic. David L. Campbell. (Illus.). 700p. 1997. 15.00 (*1-57914-029-7*) Campbell-Smith.
Learn Needle Tatting Step-by-Step. 5th rev. ed. Barbara Foster. (Illus.). 28p. 1998. pap. 13.00 (*1-883432-05-7*, T10) Handy Hands.
Learn Networking Essentials. Ed Paulson. 1999. pap. text 29.95 (*1-55622-645-4*) Wordware Pub.
Learn New Testament Greek see Aprenda el Griego del Nuevo Testamento
Learn New Testament Greek. 2nd ed. John H. Dobson. LC 92-45770. 328p. 1993. pap. 14.99 (*0-8010-3019-6*) Baker Bks.
Learn Norwegian: A Practical Course for Foreigners in Spoken & Written Norwegian. 5th ed. S. Klouman. (ENG & NOR.). 1991. pap. 65.00 (*0-7859-8946-3*) Fr & Eur.
Learn Norwegian for English Speakers. C. A. Thimm & T. H. Hanssen. (ENG & NOR.). pap. 20.95 (*0-87557-055-0*) Saphrograph.
Learn Novell Netware Software in a Day: For Versions 3.11-4.0. 3rd ed. Roy Brubaker. (Popular Applications Ser.). (Illus.). 128p. (Orig.). 1993. pap. 15.95 incl. disk (*1-55622-306-4*) Wordware Pub.
*__Learn Object Pascal.__ Warren Rachele. (Illus.). 2000. pap. text 32.95 (*1-55622-719-1*) Wordware Pub.
Learn of Me: A Study of the Teachings of Christ. Maria A. Hirschmann & Betty Pershing. LC 79-90958. (Bible Study & Sharing Ser.: No. 3). 144p. (Orig.). 1980. pap. 4.95 (*0-932878-02-4*, HB-02) Hansi.
*__Learn Office 1997.__ (C). 1999. pap. write for info. (*0-13-016513-1*) P-H.
*__Learn Office 2000 & Cd-rom.__ Preston. 1999. pap. text 42.67 (*0-13-019038-1*, Prentice Hall) P-H.
*__Learn Office 2000 with CD-ROM.__ John Preston et al. 310p. (C). 1999. pap. 50.67 incl. audio compact disk (*1-58076-263-8*) Que Educ & Trng.
*__Learn Office 97 Chap 1-7.__ 1999. write for info. (*0-13-017936-1*) P-H.
Learn OLE DB Development with Visual C++ 6.0. Nathan Wallace. LC 99-34012. 1998. pap. text 54.95 (*1-55622-634-9*) Wordware.
*__Learn on Demand Personal Navigator.__ (C). 1999. write for info. (*0-13-018047-5*) P-H.
*__Learn Oracle 8i.__ Jose A. Ramahlo. (Illus.). 2000. pap. write for info. (*1-55622-731-0*) Wordware Pub.
Learn Oral Communication Quickly Series, 4 videos. Janet Scarpone. Incl. . How to Demonstrate, Introduce, Make a Toast. Perf. by Janet Scarpone. 1998. pap., wbk. ed. 49.99 incl. VHS (*1-889434-32-9*); How to Get over the Fear of Public Speaking & Communication Basics. 1998. pap., wbk. ed. 49.99 incl. VHS (*1-889434-31-0*); How to Persuade, Answer Questions, Accept Awards. 1998. pap., wbk. ed. 49.99 incl. VHS (*1-889434-33-7*); How to Read Aloud. 1998. pap., wbk. ed. 49.99 incl. VHS (*1-889434-34-5*); . Learn Oral Communication Quickly Wookbook. 1998. pap. text, wbk. ed. 9.99 (*1-889434-35-3*); (Learn Oral Communication Quickly Ser.). 1998. Set wbk. ed. 159.00 incl. VHS (*1-889434-30-2*) Learn Quickly.
Learn Oral Communication Quickly Wookbook see Learn Oral Communication Quickly Series
Learn Our Kiswahili see Jifunze Kiswahili Chetu
Learn PageMaker 5.0 in a Day. Kenneth Hughes. LC 93-43429. (Popular Applications Ser.). 136p. (Orig.). 1993. pap. 15.95 incl. disk (*1-55622-374-9*) Wordware Pub.
Learn PAL 4.5 in a Day: Versions 4.0 & 4.5. Timothy Coleman. (Popular Applications Ser.). 192p. 1994. pap. 15.95 incl. disk (*1-55622-368-4*) Wordware Pub.
*__Learn Pascal.__ Sam A. Abolrous. LC 99-88051. (Illus.). 400p. 2000. pap. 39.95 (*1-55622-706-X*) Wordware Pub.
Learn Pascal in Three Days. Sam A. Abolrous. LC 93-12287. (Popular Applications Ser.). 288p. 1993. pap. 19.95 incl. disk (*1-55622-337-4*) Wordware Pub.
Learn Pascal in Three Days. 2nd ed. Sam A. Abolrous. LC 97-14638. 300p. 1997. pap. text 24.95 (*1-55622-567-9*) Wordware Pub.
Learn Patchwork. Lynette-Merlin Syme. 1989. pap. 7.95 (*1-55562-092-2*) Sterling.
Learn Patchwork. Lynette-Merlin Syme. (Illus.). 64p. 1990. pap. 8.95 (*0-8069-7345-5*) Sterling.
*__Learn Peach Tree Accounting: Configuration, Indtallation & Use.__ Deborah Bean. (Illus.). 2000. pap. text 29.95 (*1-55622-710-8*) Wordware Pub.
Learn Persian for English Speakers. (ENG & PER.). pap. 22.95 (*0-87557-059-3*) Saphrograph.
Learn Personal Oracle 8.0 with Power Objects 2.0. Jose Ramalho. LC 98-14500. (Illus.). 433p. 1998. pap. 49.95 (*1-55622-546-6*) Wordware Pub.
Learn Photography in a Weekend. Michael J. Langford. LC 92-53044. 1992. 16.95 (*0-679-41674-9*) Knopf.
*__Learn Piano & Organ Chords in Only One Minute!__ Randy Milano. LC 98-92323. (Illus.). 2000. pap. 21.95 (*0-9679989-0-5*) Empire Pubng Grp.
Learn Polish for English Speakers. (ENG & POL.). pap. 25.95 (*0-87557-061-5*) Saphrograph.
Learn Portuguese for English Speakers. (ENG & POR.). 1974. pap. 20.95 (*0-87557-108-5*) Saphrograph.
*__Learn PowerPoint 2000.__ John M. Preston. (Illus.). 2000. pap. text 32.00 (*1-58076-257-3*) Que Educ & Trng.
Learn PowerPoint 97. Que Education & Training Staff & Dawn Wood. (Illus.). 201p. 1997. teacher ed. 39.99 incl. cd-rom (*1-57576-884-4*) Que Educ & Trng.
Learn PROCOMM Plus 2.0 for Windows in a Day. Richard A. Prendergast. (Popular Applications Ser.). 144p. (Orig.). 1995. pap. 15.95 (*1-55622-443-5*) Wordware Pub.
LEARN Program for Weight Control: Meal Replacement Edition. Kelly D. Brownell. 356p. 1998. pap. 24.95 (*1-878513-17-6*) Am Hlth Pub.
*__LEARN Program for Weight Control: Special Medication Edition.__ rev. ed. Kelly D. Brownell. (Illus.). 356p. 1999. pap. 24.95 (*1-81751-319-2*) Am Hlth Pub.
LEARN Program for Weight Control: Special Medication Edition. rev. ed. Kelly D. Brownell & Thomas A. Wadden. (Illus.). 356p. 1998. pap. text 24.95 (*1-878513-16-8*) Am Hlth Pub.
LEARN Program for Weight Control: Special Medication Edition - Module 1. Kelly D. Brownell & Thomas A. Wadden. (POR., Illus.). 52p. write for info. (*1-81751-325-7*) Am Hlth Pub.
LEARN Program for Weight Control: Special Medication Edition - Module 10. Kelly D. Brownell & Thomas A. Wadden. (POR., Illus.). 16p. pap. write for info. (*1-81751-334-6*) Am Hlth Pub.
LEARN Program for Weight Control: Special Medication Edition - Module 11. Kelly D. Brownell & Thomas A. Wadden. (POR., Illus.). 16p. pap. write for info. (*1-81751-335-4*) Am Hlth Pub.
LEARN Program for Weight Control: Special Medication Edition - Module 12. Kelly D. Brownell & Thomas A. Wadden. (POR., Illus.). 16p. pap. write for info. (*1-81751-336-2*) Am Hlth Pub.
Learn Program for Weight Control: Special Medication Edition - Module 2. Kelly D. Brownell & Thomas A. Wadden. (POR., Illus.). 40p. pap. write for info. (*1-81751-326-5*) Am Hlth Pub.
LEARN Program for Weight Control: Special Medication Edition - Module 3. Kelly D. Brownell & Thomas A. Wadden. (POR.). 44p. pap. write for info. (*1-81751-327-3*) Am Hlth Pub.
Learn Program for Weight Control: Special Medication Edition - Module 4. Kelly D. Brownell & Thomas A. Wadden. (POR., Illus.). 44p. pap. write for info. (*1-81751-328-1*) Am Hlth Pub.
LEARN Program for Weight Control: Special Medication Edition - Module 5. Kelly D. Brownell & Thomas A. Wadden. (POR., Illus.). 16p. pap. write for info. (*1-81751-329-X*) Am Hlth Pub.
LEARN Program for Weight Control: Special Medication Edition - Module 6. Kelly D. Brownell & Thomas A. Wadden. (POR., Illus.). 16p. pap. write for info. (*1-81751-330-3*) Am Hlth Pub.
LEARN Program for Weight Control: Special Medication Edition - Module 7. Kelly D. Brownell & Thomas A. Wadden. (POR., Illus.). 16p. pap. write for info. (*1-81751-331-1*) Am Hlth Pub.
LEARN Program for Weight Control: Special Medication Edition - Module 8. Kelly D. Brownell & Thomas A. Wadden. (POR., Illus.). 16p. pap. write for info. (*1-81751-332-X*) Am Hlth Pub.
LEARN Program for Weight Control: Special Medication Edition - Module 9. Kelly D. Brownell & Thomas A. Wadden. (POR., Illus.). 16p. pap. write for info. (*1-81751-333-8*) Am Hlth Pub.
LEARN Program for Weight Management: Meal Replacement Edition. rev. ed. Kelly D. Brownell. (Illus.). 400p. pap. write for info. (*1-81751-317-6*) Am Hlth Pub.
LEARN Program for Weight Management: Meal Replacement Edition - Module 1. rev. ed. Kelly D. Brownell. (Illus.). 144p. pap. write for info. (*1-81751-321-4*) Am Hlth Pub.
LEARN Program for Weight Management: Meal Replacement Edition - Module 2. rev. ed. Kelly D. Brownell. (Illus.). 128p. pap. write for info. (*1-81751-322-2*) Am Hlth Pub.
LEARN Program for Weight Management: Meal Replacement Edition - Module 3. rev. ed. Kelly D. Brownell. (Illus.). 128p. pap. write for info. (*1-81751-323-0*) Am Hlth Pub.
*__LEARN Program for Weight Management 2000.__ rev. ed. Kelly D. Brownell. (Illus.). 320p. 2000. pap. 27.95 (*1-81751-324-9*) Am Hlth Pub.
Learn Public Speaking (English Only) 25.50 (*0-87557-124-7*) Saphrograph.
Learn Publisher 97 in a Weekend. Nancy Stevenson. LC 97-69043. 336p. 1997. per. 19.99 (*0-7615-1217-9*) Prima Pub.
Learn Quattro Pro 5.0 in a Day. Russell A. Stultz. LC 93-45766. (Popular Applications Ser.). 136p. 1994. pap. 15.95 incl. disk (*1-55622-406-0*) Wordware Pub.
*__Learn Quickbooks 6 in a Weekend.__ Prima Development Staff & Katherine Murray. LC 98-66465. 342p. 1998. per. 19.99 (*0-7615-1384-1*) Prima Pub.
*__Learn Quickbooks Step-by-Step Visually.__ Majo Jacinto. 304p. 1999. 49.00 (*0-9673307-5-0*) Resource Mgmt Inc.
Learn Reading, Writing & Arithmetic: You Cannot Get over If You Think That You Are Slick see Tena, Joshua, & Friends
Learn Red Hat Linux OS Tips. George M. Doss. LC 99-28560. 379p. 1999. pap. 36.95 incl. cd-rom (*1-55622-715-9*) Wordware Pub.
*__Learn Red Hat Linux Server Tips.__ George M. Doss. LC 99-59496. 400p. 2000. 36.95 incl. audio compact disk (*1-55622-714-0*) Wordware Pub.
Learn Rock Climbing in a Weekend. Kevin Walker. (Illus.). 96p. 1998. pap. 10.95 (*0-375-70303-9*) Random.
Learn Rumanian for English Speakers. (ENG & RUM.). pap. 20.95 (*0-87557-065-8*) Saphrograph.
Learn Russian, 2 vols., Set. Nina F. Potapova. 55.00 (*0-87557-137-9*) Saphrograph.
Learn Russian the Fast & Fun Way, 4 cassettes. Thomas R. Beyer, Jr. (Barron's Fast & Fun Way Ser.). (RUS.). 240p. (J). (gr. 6-9). 1993. 39.95 incl. audio (*0-8120-7857-8*) Barron.
Learn Russian the Fast & Fun Way: The Activity Kit That Makes Learning a Language Quick & Easy! Thomas R. Beyer, Jr. LC 92-28052. (JPN & ENG.). 240p. 1993. pap. 16.95 (*0-8120-4846-6*) Barron.
Learn Scuba Diving in a Weekend. Reg Vallintine. (Illus.). 96p. 1998. pap. 10.95 (*0-375-70304-7*) Random.
Learn Serbocroatian for English Speakers. (CRO, ENG & SER.). 1985. 20.95 (*0-87557-075-5*) Saphrograph.
*__Learn Songwriting.__ Caroline Hooper. (Learn to Play Ser.). (Illus.). 48p. (gr. 1-4). 2000. 17.95 (*1-58086-222-5*) EDC.
*__Learn Songwriting.__ Ed. by Caroline Hooper & Nigel M. Hooper. (Learn to Play Ser.). (Illus.). 48p. (J). (gr. 4-7). 2000. pap. 9.95 (*0-7460-3046-0*, Pub. by Usbrne Pbng UK) EDC.
Learn Spanish. 64p. (YA). (gr. 7 up). 21.95 incl. audio (*0-7460-2815-6*, Usborne) EDC.
Learn Spanish. N. Irving. (Learn Languages Ser.). (Illus.). 64p. (YA). (gr. 7-12). 1993. pap. 10.95 (*0-7460-0536-9*, Usborne) EDC.
Learn Spanish. N. Irving. (Learn Languages Ser.). (Illus.). 64p. (YA). (gr. 7 up). 1999. lib. bdg. 18.95 (*0-88110-598-8*, Usborne) EDC.
Learn Spanish: The Lazy Way. Bogumila Michalewicz & Carol Turkington. (Lazy Way Ser.). 352p. 1999. pap. 12.95 (*0-02-862650-8*) Macmillan Gen Ref.
Learn Spanish for English Speakers. rev. ed. William R. Patterson. Ed. by Ronald MacAndrew. (ENG & SPA.). pap. 20.95 (*0-87557-078-X*) Saphrograph.
Learn Spanish the Fast & Fun Way. 2nd ed. Gene M. Hammitt & Heywood Wald. LC 97-5860. (Barron's Fast & Fun Way Ser.). (SPA.). 300p. 1997. 39.95 incl. audio (*0-7641-7026-0*) Barron.
Learn Spanish the Fast & Fun Way Book. 2nd ed. Gene Hammitt. Ed. by Heywood Wald. (SPA., Illus.). 264p. 1997. pap. 14.95 (*0-7641-0205-2*) Barron.
*__Learn Spanish Together.__ Marie-Claire Antonine. (For the Car Ser.). (SPA.). 48p. (ps-3). 2000. 14.95 (*0-609-60650-6*) Liv Lang.
Learn Spanish Together: Educational Activity Set. (Living Language Ser.). 1999. 24.95 incl. audio (*0-609-60575-5*) Liv Lang.
Learn Spanish with Books. Cruisenaire. 1993. pap. 16.95 (*0-201-48268-1*) Addison-Wesley.
Learn SQL. Jose Ramahlo. LC 99-12468. 1999. pap. text 39.95 (*1-55622-639-X*) Wordware Pub.
*__Learn SQL.__ Josbe Antonio Ramalho. LC 99-46367. 1999. pap. 49.95 (*1-55622-661-6*) Wordware Pub.
Learn Squash & Racquetball in a Weekend. Jahangir Khan. LC 93-16704. 1993. 16.00 (*0-679-42753-8*) Knopf.
Learn Successful Investment Techniques. U. L. Prenn. (Illus.). 74p. (Orig.). 1990. pap. 12.00 (*0-937041-94-7*) Systems Co.
Learn Successful Investment Techniques. 2nd ed. U. L. Prenn. (Illus.). 74p. (Orig.). 1992. pap. 15.00 (*1-56216-159-8*) Systems Co.
Learn Swahili for English Speakers. Ernest B. Haddon. (ENG & SWA.). 1989. pap. 25.95 (*0-87557-081-X*) Saphrograph.
Learn Swedish for English Speakers. (ENG & SWE.). pap. 20.95 (*0-87557-084-4*) Saphrograph.
Learn Tahitian Dancing, Vol. II, Bk. 11. Vicki Corona. (Celebrate the Cultures Ser.). (Illus.). 24p. 1989. pap. 14.95 (*1-58513-001-X*) Dance Fantasy.
Learn Talmud. Jacob Neusner. (Illus.). (YA). (gr. 9). 1979. pap. 6.95 (*0-87441-292-7*) Behrman.
Learn Talmud: How to Use The Talmud - The Steinsaltz Edition. Judith Z. Abrams. LC 94-45558. 168p. 1995. pap. 20.00 (*1-56821-463-4*) Aronson.
Learn Thai for English Speakers. (ENG & THA.). pap. 20.95 (*0-87557-125-5*) Saphrograph.
Learn Thai for English Speakers. Saphrograph Corporation Staff. pap. 19.50 (*0-317-02507-4*) P-H.
Learn the Alphabet Activity Book. (Begin to Learn Ser.: No. S812-1). (J). 1989. pap. 1.95 (*0-7214-5109-8*, Ladybrd) Penguin Putnam.
Learn the Alphabet with Noddy. Enid Blyton. (Illus.). 32p. (J). (ps-k). 1999. pap. 3.99 (*0-06-102017-6*, HarpEntertain) Morrow Avon.
*__Learn the Art of Permanent Makeup: A Comprehensive Training Manual.__ Gloria Brandt & Kathryn Lorenzini. 1999. 74.95 (*0-9672362-1-5*) K&G Perm Makeup.
*__Learn the Art of Permanent Makeup: A Comprehensive Training Manual.__ Gloria Brandt & Kathryn Lorenzini. (SPA., Illus.). 68p. 1999. 74.95 (*0-9672362-0-7*) K&G Perm Makeup.
Learn the Internet in a Weekend. William R. Stanek. LC 97-69601. 416p. 1997. per. 19.99 (*0-7615-1295-0*) Prima Pub.
Learn the Kazakh Language in Seventy Steps: Using 200 Sentence Models. (C). 1993. audio 19.00 (*1-881265-14-5*) Dunwoody Pr.
Learn the Kazakh Language in Seventy Steps: Using 200 Sentence Models. Tangat Tangirberdi kyzy Ayapova. 432p. (C). 1993. 54.00 (*1-881265-06-4*) Dunwoody Pr.
Learn the Language of the Holy Qur'an. 4th rev. ed. A. Nadwi. Ed. by Abidullah Ghazi et al. 430p. 1987. 18.00 (*1-56316-009-9*) Iqra Intl Ed Fdtn.
Learn the MFC++ Classes. Shirley Wodtke. LC 96-44177. (Illus.). 700p. (Orig.). (C). 1996. pap. 49.95 incl. disk (*1-55622-512-1*) Wordware Pub.
Learn the MFC++ Classes for Visual C++ 9X. Shirley Wodtke. 1998. pap. text 49.95 (*1-55622-627-6*) Wordware Pub.
*__Learn the Net.__ (Illus.). iii, 200p. 1998. ring bd. 59.95 (*0-914607-56-1*, 1733) Master Tchr.
Learn the Persian Language. C. Elwell-Sutton. (ENG & PER.). 24.50 (*0-87559-120-5*) Shalom.
Learn the Value, 18 bks., Set II, Reading Level 2. Elaine Goley et al. (Illus.). 576p. (J). (gr. 1-4). 1989. 215.10 (*0-685-58776-2*) Rourke Corp.
Learn Think Critically. Martin. (C). 1997. pap. text 14.00 (*0-673-55217-9*) Addison-Wesley.
Learn 3D Design on the Macintosh. Michelle Szabo. LC 96-11467. 351p. 1996. pap., pap. text 34.95 incl. cd-rom (*0-471-14927-6*) Wiley.
Learn 3D Graphics. Richard F. Ferraro. 1056p. 1995. pap. 49.95 incl. cd-rom (*0-201-48332-7*) Addison-Wesley.
Learn to Add & Subtract Activity Book. (Begin to Learn Ser.: No. S812-6). (J). 1989. pap. 1.95 (*0-7214-5114-4*, Ladybrd) Penguin Putnam.
Learn to Attack with Rudolf Spielmann. Eric Schiller. 117p. (Orig.). 1996. pap. 9.95 (*0-945470-82-7*) Chess Ent.
Learn to Be a General Contractor. rev. ed. Carl Heldmann. Ed. by Storey Communications, Inc. Staff. (Illus.). 144p. 1988. reprint ed. pap. text 12.95 (*0-934039-17-8*, SP1131) Hme Dsgn Altntves.
Learn to Be a General Contractor: Build Your Dream House or Do a Renovation. rev. ed. Ed. by Michael Kirchwehm. 132p. 1998. pap. 12.95 (*0-934039-44-5*) Hme Dsgn Altntves.
Learn to Be the Master Student: How to Develop Self-Confidence & Effective Study Skills. Robert Rooney & Anthony Lipuma. LC 92-80281. (Illus.). 248p. (Orig.). (YA). (gr. 9-12). 1992. pap. 14.95 (*0-9632530-8-5*) Maydale Pub.
Learn to Belly Dance, Vol. I, Bk. 10. Vicki Corona. (Celebrate the Cultures Ser.). (Illus.). 34p. 1989. pap. 14.95 (*1-58513-023-0*) Dance Fantasy.
Learn to Carve Faces & Expressions. Harold L. Enlow. LC 80-51871. 56p. 1980. pap. 5,50 (*1-882475-03-8*) Enlow Wood Carv.
Learn to Compose & Notate Music: Beginning Level. Lee Evans & Martha Baker. 24p. 1986. pap. 5.95 (*0-7935-9719-6*) H Leonard.
Learn to Compute: Guide to Apple. Edward J. Coburn. 416p. 1987. pap. 31.95 (*0-8273-2931-8*) Delmar.
Learn to Compute: Guide to Apple. Edward J. Coburn. 416p. 1987. pap., teacher ed. 14.00 (*0-8273-2932-6*) Delmar.
Learn to Cook Without Preservatives: Try Swayam Singh's Gourmet Cooking. Swayam P. Singh. Ed. by B. K. Singh. (Illus.). (Orig.). 1979. pap. 4.99 (*0-686-26610-2*) S Singh.
*__Learn to Count - Funny Bunnies.__ Cyndy Szekeres. (Illus.). 32p. (J). (ps). 2000. bds. 6.99 (*0-439-14994-0*, Cartwheel) Scholastic Inc.
Learn to Count Activity Book. (Begin to Learn Ser.: No. S812-5). (J). 1989. pap. 1.95 (*0-7214-5113-6*, Ladybrd) Penguin Putnam.
Learn to Count & Color with Spot the Cat. Maxine S. Sommers. Ed. by Suzanne Kennedy. (Texas Cool Cat Children's Bks.: Bk. 4). (Illus.). 10p. (Orig.). (J). (gr. k-1). 1993. pap. 2.50 (*0-943991-45-5*) Pound Sterling Pub.
Learn to Count with Noddy. Enid Blyton. (Illus.). 32p. (J). (ps-k). 1999. pap. 3.99 (*0-06-102018-4*, HarpEntertain) Morrow Avon.

An Asterisk (*) at the beginning of an entry indicates that the title is appearing for the first time.

Learn to Country & Western Dance. Larre Bryant. (Illus.). Date not set. pap. text 10.95 (*0-9665370-0-9*) Ruby Moon Pr.

Learn To Dance The SoulSalsa: Seventeen Surprising Steps for Godly Living in the 21st Century. Leonard Sweet. 208p. 2000. pap. 18.99 (*0-310-23014-4*) Zondervan.

Learn to Draw & Paint. Reader's Digest Editors & Eaglemoss Publications Ltd. Staff. LC 96-52461. 288p. 1997. 29.95 (*0-89577-956-0*, Pub. by RD Assn) Penguin Putnam.

Learn to Draw Bugs Bunny & Friends. Ed. by Sydney Sprague. (Looney Tunes Ser.). (Illus.). 37p. (Orig.). (J). (gr. 1 up). 1997. pap. 7.95 (*1-56010-200-4*, LT01) W Foster Pub.

***Learn to Draw Buildings.** David Cook. (Learn to Draw Ser.). (Illus.). 64p. 1999. pap. 14.95 (*0-00-413353-6*, Pub. by HarpC) Trafalgar.

***Learn to Draw Caricatures.** Alex Hughes. (Learn to Draw Ser.). (Illus.). 64p. 1999. pap. 14.95 (*0-00-413328-5*, Pub. by HarpC) Trafalgar.

***Learn to Draw Cartoons.** John Byrne. (Learn to Draw Ser.). (Illus.). 64p. 1999. pap. 14.95 (*0-00-413354-4*, Pub. by HarpC) Trafalgar.

***Learn to Draw Cats.** Darren Bennett. (Learn to Draw Ser.). (Illus.). 64p. 1999. pap. 14.95 (*0-00-413355-2*, Pub. by HarpC) Trafalgar.

***Learn to Draw Countryside.** Bruce Robertson. (Learn to Draw Ser.). (Illus.). 64p. 1999. pap. 14.95 (*0-00-413357-9*, Pub. by HarpC) Trafalgar.

***Learn to Draw Dogs.** David Brown. (Learn to Draw Ser.). (Illus.). 64p. 1999. pap. 14.95 (*0-00-413356-0*, Pub. by HarpC) Trafalgar.

***Learn to Draw Fantasy Art.** Mike Jefferies. (Learn to Draw Ser.). 1999. pap. 14.95 (*0-00-413358-7*, Pub. by HarpC) Trafalgar.

***Learn to Draw Horses.** David Brown. (Learn to Draw Ser.). (Illus.). 64p. 1999. pap. 14.95 (*0-00-413360-9*, Pub. by HarpC) Trafalgar.

Learn to Draw Mickey & Minnie Kit. (Snap Pack Ser.). (Illus.). 28p. (J). (gr. 1 up). 1997. 12.95 (*1-56010-306-X*, DSO1P) W Foster Pub.

Learn to Draw Now! Doug Dubosque. LC 90-27879. (Learn to Draw Ser.). 1991. 13.15 (*0-606-09531-4*, Pub. by Turtleback) Demco.

Learn to Draw Now! Doug C. DuBosque. LC 90-27879. (Illus.). 64p. (Orig.). (J). (gr. 4-7). 1991. pap. 8.95 (*0-939217-16-3*) Peel Prod.

***Learn to Draw People.** Philip Patenall. (Learn to Draw Ser.). (Illus.). 64p. 1999. pap. 14.95 (*0-00-413361-7*, Pub. by HarpC) Trafalgar.

***Learn to Draw Still Life.** Valerie Wiffen. (Learn to Draw Ser.). (Illus.). 64p. 1999. pap. 14.95 (*0-00-413333-1*, Pub. by HarpC) Trafalgar.

Learn to Draw the Muppets. Illus. by Joe Ewers. 40p. (J). (ps up). 1998. pap. 7.95 (*1-56010-398-1*, H01) W Foster Pub.

Learn to Draw the Tasmanian Devil & Friends. Ed. by Sydney Sprague. (Looney Tunes Ser.). (Illus.). 37p. (Orig.). (J). (gr. 1 up). 1997. pap. 7.95 (*1-56010-201-2*, LT02) W Foster Pub.

***Learn to Draw Wildlife.** Peter Partington. (Learn to Draw Ser.). (Illus.). 64p. 1999. pap. 14.95 (*0-00-413362-5*, Pub. by HarpC) Trafalgar.

Learn to Draw Winnie the Pooh Kit. (Snap Pack Ser.). (Illus.). 28p. (J). (gr. 1 up). 1997. 12.95 (*1-56010-307-8*, DSO5P) W Foster Pub.

Learn to Draw 3-D see **Draw 3-D**

Learn to Earn: A Beginner's Guide to the Basics of Investing & Business. Peter Lynch. LC 96-44480. 272p. 1997. 21.95 (*0-471-18003-3*) Wiley.

Learn to Earn: An Introduction to the Basics of Investing & Business. Peter Lynch & John Rothchild. (Illus.). 272p. 1996. per. 13.00 (*0-684-81163-4*) S&S Trade Pap.

Learn to Fish, & You'll Never Be Hungry: The Ultimate Guide to Managing Your Life. Robert Epstein. 202p. 1992. pap. write for info. (*0-9631797-0-5*) Psience Pr.

Learn to Fly RC Helicopters. Dale Hart. (Doug Pratt's Modeling Guides Ser.). (Illus.). 160p. 1991. pap. 12.95 (*0-8306-3619-6*, 3619) McGraw-Hill Prof.

Learn to Grow Old. Paul Tournier. 256p. 1991. reprint ed. pap. 15.95 (*0-664-25190-0*) Westminster John Knox.

Learn to Harmonize & Transpose at the Keyboard. Evans. 16p. 1986. pap. 5.95 (*0-7935-8669-0*) H Leonard.

Learn-to-Knit-Afghan Book. unabridged ed. Barbara G. Walker. 1997. reprint ed. mass mkt. 20.00 (*0-942018-13-3*) Schoolhouse WI.

Learn to Listen, Listen to Learn. Roni S. Lebauer. (Illus.). 256p. (C). 1988. pap. text 33.20 (*0-13-527128-2*) P-H.

***Learn to Listen Listen to Learn.** 2nd ed. Lebauer. LC 99-47758. 2000. pap. text 26.00 (*0-13-919432-0*) P-H.

Learn to Live: The Meaning of the Parables. Ervin Seale. LC 55-7113. 256p. 1992. reprint ed. pap. 10.95 (*0-87516-652-0*) DeVorss.

Learn to Live Fit. 2nd ed. (C). 1996. write for info. (*0-8087-7482-4*) Pearson Custom.

Learn to Love the Haze. Robert Roripaugh. LC 95-44856. 1996. pap. 9.95 (*0-931271-35-5*) Hi Plains Pr.

Learn to Love to Learn. William G. Perry, Jr. 300p. (YA). (gr. 8-12). Date not set. pap. write for info. (*1-887946-01-2*) Comp Age Educ.

Learn to Love Yourself: Instructor's Manual. deluxe ed. Katherine Zimmerman. 72p. 1997. pap., teacher ed. 189.00 (*1-929957-07-6*) TranceTime.

Learn to Make Videos in a Weekend. Roland Lewis. LC 92-54795. 1993. 16.00 (*0-679-42230-7*) Knopf.

Learn to Market Yourself: A Christian Perspective. Ed Cerny. Ed. by Zoe Cerny. (Illus.). 100p. 1999. pap. 12.00 (*0-9661020-1-0*) Coachs Corner.

Learn to Meditate: A Practical Guide to Self-Discovery & Fulfillment. David Fontana. LC 98-39384. (Illus.). 160p. 1999. pap. 14.95 (*0-8118-2250-8*) Chronicle Bks.

Learn to Meditate: Journey Toward Self-Discovery. George McKeever. 161p. (YA). (gr. 8 up). 1998. pap. 9.95 (*1-885479-03-4*) McKeever Pubng.

Learn to Meditate Kit: The Complete Course in Modern Meditation. Patricia Carrington. 128p. 1998. 39.95 (*1-86204-191-1*, Pub. by Element MA) Penguin Putnam.

Learn to Navigate by the Tutorial System Developed at Harvard. Charles A. Whitney & Frances W. Wright. LC 92-10108. (Illus.). 318p. 1992. pap. 24.95 (*0-87033-426-3*) Cornell Maritime.

Learn to Oil Paint with Bill Alexander & Buck Paulson. Shirley Tucker & John Hartman. (Illus.). 24p. 1993. pap. text. write for info. (*1-883576-31-8*, BK-230) Alexander Art.

Learn to Paint Acrylics with Brenda Harris. Shirley Tucker. (Illus.). 24p. 1993. pap. text. write for info. (*1-883576-30-X*, BK-210) Alexander Art.

***Learn to Paint Colour Mixing.** Judy Martin. (Illus.). 1999. pap. text. write for info. (*0-00-413337-4*) HarpC.

Learn to Paint with the Alexander Brush Club. Joyce Fitzrandolph. (Illus.). 24p. (J). (gr. 4-6). pap. text. write for info. (*1-883576-32-6*, KT-220B) Alexander Art.

Learn to Play Acoustic Chord Riffs. Johnny Norris. 48p. 1996. pap. 24.95 incl. cd-rom (*0-7119-3302-2*, AM90239) Music Sales.

Learn to Play All-American Harp, 1 vol. Charlie McCoy. (Learn to Play Ser.). 1998. pap. text 17.95 (*0-7119-5641-3*) Music Sales.

Learn to Play Beethoven. M. Durmin. (Piano Classics Ser.). (Illus.). 64p. (J). (gr. 1 up). 1994. lib. bdg. 17.95 (*0-88110-676-3*, Usborne) EDC.

Learn to Play Beethoven. M. Durmin. (Piano Classics Ser.). (Illus.). 64p. (J). (gr. 4-7). 1994. pap. 9.95 (*0-7460-1026-5*, Usborne) EDC.

Learn to Play Bluegrass Bass. Earl Gately. 44p. 1997. 7.95 (*0-7866-3518-5*, 93638) Mel Bay.

Learn to Play Bluegrass Dobro Guitar. Ken Eidson & Tom Swatzell. 88p. 1997. 17.95 incl. audio compact disk (*0-7866-2768-9*, 93968BCD) Mel Bay.

Learn to Play Bluegrass Mandolin. Bud Orr. 48p. 1980. pap. 7.95 (*0-87166-683-9*, 93720) Mel Bay.

Learn to Play Blues. Anthony Marks & Howard W. Rye. (Learn to Play Ser.). (Illus.). 64p. (J). (gr. 4-7). 1995. lib. bdg. 17.95 (*0-88110-765-4*, Usborne) EDC.

Learn to Play Bottleneck Guitar. Fred Sokolow. 60p. 1991. 17.95 incl. audio compact disk (*0-7866-2746-8*, 94571BCD) Mel Bay.

***Learn to Play Brazillian Jazz Guitar.** David Marshall. 96p. 1999. pap. 19.95 incl. audio compact disk (*0-7866-4159-2*, 97746BCD) Mel Bay.

Learn to Play Bridge the New Way in 4 Short Weeks, Vol. 1. 2nd rev. ed. Gloria Weissman. (Illus.). 37p. (Orig.). 1997. pap. 17.95 (*0-9623884-0-8*) G Weissman.

Learn to Play Country Fiddle. Frank Zucco. 48p. 1977. pap. 7.95 (*0-87166-482-8*, 93418) Mel Bay.

Learn to Play Drums. Ed. by Eileen O'Brien. (Learn to Play Ser.). (Illus.). 48p. (J). (gr. 4-7). 1999. pap. 9.95 (*0-7460-3044-4*, Usborne) EDC.

Learn to Play Electric Guitar. Carolin Hooper. (Learn to Play Ser.). (Illus.). 48p. (Orig.). (J). (gr. 1 up). 1997. pap. 9.95 (*0-7460-2414-2*, Usborne); lib. bdg. 17.95 (*0-88110-932-0*, Usborne) EDC.

Learn to Play Five-String Bass. Mike Hiland. 64p. 1997. 17.95 incl. audio compact disk (*0-7866-2772-7*, 94721BCD) Mel Bay.

Learn to Play Flute Duets. William Eisehauer. 48p. 1975. pap. 7.50 (*0-7390-0869-2*, 860) Alfred Pub.

Learn to Play Go, Vol. IV. Janice Kim & Jeong Soo-Lyuen. (Illus.). 176p. (Orig.). 1997. pap. 14.95 (*0-614-30101-7*) Good Move Pr.

Learn to Play Go, Vol. V. Janice Kim & Jeong Soo-Lyuen. (Illus.). (Orig.). 1997. pap. 14.95 (*0-614-30102-5*) Good Move Pr.

Learn to Play Go Vol. 1: A Master's Guide to the Ultimate Game. 2nd rev. ed. Janice Kim. (Learn to Play Go Ser.: Vol. 1). (Illus.). 172p. (Orig.). (YA). (gr. 5 up). 1997. lib. bdg. 17.95 (*0-9644796-1-3*) Good Move Pr.

Learn to Play Go Vol. 4: Battle Strategies. Janice Kim. (Illus.). 169p. 1997. pap. 14.95 (*0-9644796-4-8*) Good Move Pr.

Learn to Play Guitar. L. Somerville & T. Pells. (Learn to Play Ser.). (Illus.). 64p. (YA). (gr. 6-12). 1988. pap. 9.95 (*0-7460-0193-2*, Usborne); lib. bdg. 17.95 (*0-88110-384-5*, Usborne) EDC.

***Learn to Play Hawaiian Slack Key Guitar.** Mark Nelson & Keola Beamer. 160p. 1999. pap. 24.95 incl. audio compact disk (*0-7866-4109-6*, 96695BCD) Mel Bay.

Learn to Play in the Orchestra, Cello, Bk. 2. Ralph Matesky. 24p. 1973. pap. 6.95 (*0-7390-0730-0*, 856) Alfred Pub.

Learn to Play in the Orchestra, Violin II, Bk. 2. Ralph Matesky. 24p. 1973. pap. 6.95 (*0-7390-0560-X*, 854) Alfred Pub.

Learn to Play Irish Tinwhistle. L. E. McCullough. (Homespun Tapes Ser.). 1996. VHS 19.95 (*0-7935-6867-6*) H Leonard.

Learn to Play Keyboards. Anthony Marks. (Learn to Play Ser.). (Illus.). 48p. (J). (gr. 1 up). 1997. lib. bdg. 17.95 (*0-88110-899-5*, Usborne) EDC.

Learn to Play Keyboards. Anthony Marks. (Learn to Play Ser.). (Illus.). 48p. (J). (gr. 4-7). 1997. pap. 9.95 (*0-7460-2412-6*, Usborne) EDC.

Learn to Play Latin Piano: Authentic Salsa, Mambo, Bosa Nova, Samba & More! Riccardo Scivales. 88p. 1995. spiral bd. 14.95 (*0-943748-71-2*) Cimino Pub Grp.

Learn to Play Mozart. Michael Durnin. (Learn to Play Ser.). (Illus.). 64p. (J). (gr. 4-7). 1993. pap. 9.95 (*0-7460-0964-X*, Usborne) EDC.

Learn to Play on Harmonium. Ram Avtar. (Illus.). 42p. 1980. 12.95 (*0-318-36327-5*) Asia Bk Corp.

Learn to Play on Sitar. Avtar V. Ram. (Illus.). 56p. 1989. 12.95 (*0-940500-41-8*) Asia Bk Corp.

Learn to Play on Tabla No. 2: Advance Course. Ram Avtar. 52p. 1985. 12.95 (*0-318-36328-3*) Asia Bk Corp.

Learn to Play on Veena. Tara Balagopal. (Illus.). 84p. 1982. 12.95 (*0-318-36329-1*) Asia Bk Corp.

Learn to Play Opera Tunes. Caroline Hooper. (Learn to Play Ser.). (Illus.). 48p. (J). (gr. 1 up). 1997. lib. bdg. 17.95 (*0-88110-848-0*, Usborne) EDC.

Learn to Play Opera Tunes. Caroline Hooper. (Learn to Play Ser.). (Illus.). 48p. (J). (gr. 4-7). 1997. pap. 9.95 (*0-7460-2420-7*, Usborne) EDC.

Learn to Play Power Blues Guitar Solos. Alan Warner. 48p. 1997. pap. text 24.95 incl. audio compact disk (*0-7119-3386-3*, AM91062) Music Sales.

Learn to Play Rock Chord Riffs. Alan Warner. 1996. pap. 24.95 incl. cd-rom (*0-7119-3300-6*, AM90237) Music Sales.

Learn to Play Strings/Violin, Bk. 2. Betty Matesky & Ardelle Womack. (Learn to Play Strings Ser.). 32p. 1971. pap. 5.95 (*0-7390-0311-9*, 761) Alfred Pub.

Learn to Play Tennis in a Weekend. John Driscoll & Paul Douglas. 1991. 16.00 (*0-394-58746-4*) Knopf.

Learn to Play the Baritone B. C. Charles F. Gouse. 48p. 1969. pap. 7.50 (*0-7390-0810-2*, 737) Alfred Pub.

Learn to Play the Drum Set, Bk. 1. P. Magadini. 48p. 1980. pap. 5.95 (*0-7935-1199-2*, 06620000) H Leonard.

Learn to Play the Drum Set, Bk. 1. P. Magadini. 48p. 1984. pap. 12.95 (*0-7935-1749-4*, 06620002) H Leonard.

Learn to Play the Drum Set, Bk. 2. P. Magadini. 48p. 1981. pap. 5.95 (*0-7935-1200-X*, 06620001) H Leonard.

Learn to Play the Drum Set, Bk. 2. P. Magadini. 48p. 1988. pap. 12.95 (*0-7935-1750-8*, 06620005) H Leonard.

Learn to Play the Drumset. 6.00 (*0-7935-2138-6*, 06621765) H Leonard.

***Learn to Play the Drumset BK.1: A Professional's Unique Approach to Playing the Drumset.** Peter Magadini. 48p. 1999. pap. 14.95 incl. audio compact disk (*0-634-00524-3*) H Leonard.

***Learn to Play the Drumset BK.2: A Professional's Unique Approach to Playing the Drumset.** Peter Magadini. 48p. 1999. pap. 14.95 incl. audio compact disk (*0-634-00525-1*) H Leonard.

Learn to Play the Harmonica . . . Nashville Style. Charles R. Steelman & Sharon B. Steelman. LC 92-107911. (Illus.). 175p. 1991. pap., spiral bd. 19.95 (*0-9647180-0-6*) Steelman & Assocs.

Learn to Play Trombone, Bk. 1. Charles F. Gouse. 48p. 1969. pap. 6.95 (*0-7390-0552-9*, 736) Alfred Pub.

Learn to Play Tuba, Bk. 2. Charles Gouse. (Learn to Play Ser.). 48p. 1970. pap. 7.50 (*0-7390-0310-0*, 750) Alfred Pub.

Learn to Print Spanish (Aprendiendo a Escribir las Letras) Pen Notes Staff. (J). (ps up). 1989. spiral bd. 12.00 (*0-939564-17-3*) Pen Notes.

Learn to Program with Visual Basic Examples. John Smiley. (Illus.). 485p. 1999. pap. 19.99 (*1-902745-06-X*) Wrox Pr Inc.

Learn to Program with Visual Basic Six. John Smiley. 600p. 1998. pap. 44.95 (*1-902745-00-0*) Wrox Pr Inc.

***Learn to Program with Visual Basic 6 Databases.** John Smiley. 1999. pap. text 29.99 (*1-902745-03-5*) Wrox Pr Inc.

***Learn to Quilt the Lazy Way.** MacMillan Lifestyle Group Staff. (Lazy Way Ser.). 304p. 1999. pap. 12.95 (*0-02-863174-9*) Free Pr.

Learn to Read: For Those That Didn't. Ella Davis. 1999. pap. 59.95 (*1-888185-60-0*) Davis Pubng LA.

Learn to Read Activity Book. (Begin to Learn Ser.: No. S812-4). (J). 1989. pap. 1.95 (*0-7214-5112-8*, Ladybrd) Penguin Putnam.

Learn to Read Arabic. (Illus.). 68p. (J). (ps-5). pap., wbk. ed. 6.95 (*0-86685-769-9*) Intl Bk Ctr.

Learn To Read Arabic. Raja T. Nasr. (ARA.). 45p. pap. 14.95 (*0-86685-194-1*, LDL62027, Pub. by Librairie du Liban) Intl Bk Ctr.

Learn to Read Arabic. Raja T. Nasr. 1977. pap. 5.50 (*0-917062-02-7*); audio 14.95 (*0-86685-631-5*) Intl Bk Ctr.

Learn to Read Arabic: Drills. (Illus.). 68p. (J). (ps-5). pap. 6.95 (*0-86685-770-2*) Intl Bk Ctr.

Learn to Read Arabic: Exercise Book. (ARA & ENG., Illus.). 68p. (J). (ps-5). pap. 7.95 (*0-86685-407-X*) Intl Bk Ctr.

Learn to Read Chinese, Vol. 1. Paul U. Unschuld. 450p. (Orig.). (C). 1995. pap. text 32.00 (*0-912111-46-1*) Paradigm Publns.

Learn to Read Chinese, Vol. 2. Paul U. Unschuld. 450p. (Orig.). (C). 1994. pap. text 32.00 (*0-912111-47-X*) Paradigm Publns.

Learn to Read Hmong, Bk. 1. 104p. 1984. pap. text 2.50 (*0-917003-00-4*) Hmong United.

Learn to Read Music. rev. ed. Howard Shanet. 192p. (Orig.). 1971. per. 11.00 (*0-671-21027-0*) S&S Trade Pap.

Learn to Read New Testament Greek. exp. ed. David A. Black. LC 94-25747. (ENG & GRE.). 224p. 1994. 29.99 (*0-8054-1612-9*) Broadman.

Learn-To-Read Series, 4 bks. Mary S. Shapiro. Incl. Bk. 1. Red, Green, Yellow. Illus. by Debi Hron. 12p. (J). (ps-k). 1984. 3.99 (*0-934361-01-0*); Bk. 2. Play. Photos by Dennis Wisniewski. (Illus.). 14p. (J). (ps-k). 1984. 3.99 (*0-934361-02-9*); Bk. 3. Stop, Start. Illus. by Debi Hron. 14p. (J). (ps-k). 1984. 3.99 (*0-934361-03-7*); Bk. 4. My Play Book, One. Illus. by William D. Hinchberger. 40p. (J). (ps-k). 1984. 3.99 (*0-934361-04-5*); 1984. Set bds. 15.95 (*0-934361-00-2*) Kinder Read.

Learn to Read Spanish in Twenty-Four Hours. Spanish New Learning Center Staff. 1975. pap. 5.95 (*0-89036-083-9*) Liahona Pub Trust.

Learn to Read Teacher's Guide. Alan K. Garinger. (Learn to Read TV Ser.). 60p. 1988. pap. 9.95 (*0-910475-44-X*) KET.

Learn to Read the Need: Identifying Customer Desires. R. Craig Palubiak. Ed. by Jeffrey Kochelek. (Business Person's Handbook Ser.: Vol. 10). 16p. (Orig.). 1998. pap. 8.95 (*1-893308-09-X*) Optim Consult Grp.

Learn-to-Read Treasure Hunts. Steve Cohen. LC 97-185334. (Illus.). 464p. (J). (gr. k-2). 1997. pap. 8.95 (*0-7611-0330-9*, 10338) Workman Pub.

Learn to Read with Phonetic & Non-Phonetic Words. Incl. Nursery Rhymes. (Illus.). 256p. (J). 1992. 14.95 (*0-7935-1769-9*, 00824017); (Illus.). (Orig.). (J). (gr. 1-3). Set pap. (*0-317-11632-0*) LCD.

Learn to Recycle. Annalisa Suid. (Illus.). 48p. (J). (ps-6). 1993. pap. 9.95 (*1-878279-49-1*) Monday Morning Bks.

Learn to Reign. Frances J. Roberts. 1963. pap. 3.25 (*0-932814-22-0*) Kings Farspan.

Learn to Relax. Willis A. Jewell. 1980. pap. 9.95 (*0-930198-01-8*) Jewell-Johnson.

Learn to Relax. C. Eugene Walker. (J Hook Ser.). 1991. pap. 5.99 (*0-425-12996-9*) Berkley Pub.

Learn to Relax: A Fourteen Day Program. John D. Curtis. (Illus.). 112p. (Orig.). 1991. pap. 7.95 (*0-9611456-1-7*, Coulee Press) Adastra Pub.

***Learn to Relax: A Practical Guide to Easing Tension & Conquering Stress.** Mike George. LC 97-33259. (Illus.). 160p. 1998. 14.95 (*0-8118-1908-6*) Chronicle Bks.

***Learn to Relax: Proven Techniques for Reducing Stress, Tension & Anxiety - And Promoting Peak Performance.** 3rd ed. C. Eugene Walker. 208p. 2000. pap. 16.95 (*0-471-37776-7*) Wiley.

Learn to Relax - Really Relax. 4.95 (*0-686-40897-7*, SR2) Transitions.

***Learn to Remember: Practical Techniques & Exercises to Improve Your Memory.** Dominic O'Brien. (Illus.). 160p. 2000. pap. 14.95 (*0-8118-2715-1*) Chronicle Bks.

Learn to Ride Using Sports Psychology. Petra Holzel & Wolfgang Holzel. (Illus.). 176p. 1996. 26.00 (*1-57076-063-2*, Trafalgar Sq Pub) Trafalgar.

Learn to Risk. Bobbie Reed. 1990. pap. 8.99 (*0-310-28711-1*) Zondervan.

Learn to Sail. 2nd ed. Dennis Conner & Michael Levitt. (Illus.). 256p. 1994. text 22.95 (*0-312-11020-0*) St Martin.

Learn to Sail in a Weekend. John P. Driscoll. LC GV811.D68. (Illus.). 96p. 1998. pap. 10.95 (*0-375-70321-7*) Random.

Learn to Sew the Lazy Way. Lydia Wills. (Lazy Way Ser.). (Illus.). 288p. 1999. pap. 12.95 (*0-02-863167-6*) Free Pr.

***Learn to Sing Harmony.** 1998. otabind 34.95 (*0-7935-9951-2*) H Leonard.

Learn to Sing Step by Step. Ronny Lee. 144p. (J). 1984. pap. 14.95 (*0-934401-00-4*) Sunrise Pub NY.

***Learn to Sleep Well: A Practical Guide to Getting a Good Night's Rest.** Christopher Idzikowski. 2000. pap. 14.95 (*0-8118-2894-8*) Chronicle Bks.

Learn to Speak Afrikaans: A Method Based on One Thousand Words. 6th rev. ed. P. W. Groenewald. (C). 1992. reprint ed. pap. 12.75 (*0-86985-278-7*, Pub. by Shuter & Shooter) IBD Ltd.

Learn to Speak Danish. unabridged ed. (Self-Instructional Language Courses Ser.). 200p. 155.00 incl. audio (*0-88432-149-5*, AFDA40) Audio-Forum.

Learn to Speak English & Its Correct Grammar. 219p. (Orig.). 1996. pap. 30.00 (*0-9639359-1-7*) Koegel Ent.

***Learn to Spell 50 Words a Day.** large type ed. Camilia Sadik. 266p. 1998. pap. 21.56 (*0-07-231796-5*) McGraw.

Learn to Surf. James MacLaren. LC 97-1394. (Illus.). 144p. (Orig.). 1997. pap. 12.95 (*1-55821-568-9*) Lyons Pr.

Learn to Surf! A Beginners Guide to the Internet. Barbara Holliday. 10p. 1997. pap. text 9.95 (*1-891727-05-2*) Fun Books.

Learn to Swim: Exploration Journeys. National Safety Council Staff. (Illus.). 176p. (C). 1996. pap. text 10.00 (*0-7637-0221-8*) Jones & Bartlett.

Learn to Swim: Instructor's Manual. National Safety Council Staff & Ellis & Associates Staff. (Emergency Care Ser.). 100p. (C). 1993. pap. text 15.00 (*0-86720-809-0*) Jones & Bartlett.

Learn to Tell Time. Pen Notes Staff. (J). (gr. 1 up). 1995. spiral bd. 13.00 (*0-939564-13-0*) Pen Notes.

Learn to Type Fast: Completely New, Easy Method for Beginners. 4th ed. Barbara Aliaga. (Reference Ser.). 96p. 1988. reprint ed. pap. 12.95 (*0-88908-693-1*) Self-Counsel Pr.

Learn to Use Your Modem in a Day. Richard A. Pendergast. (Popular Applications Ser.). 136p. (Orig.). 1995. pap. 15.95 (*1-55622-445-1*) Wordware Pub.

Learn to Windsurf. Farrel O'Shea. (Illus.). 80p. 1997. pap. 9.95 (*0-7063-7541-6*, Pub. by WrLock) Sterling.

Learn to Write. Sue Kassirer. (J). Date not set. write for info. (*0-679-85297-2*) Random Bks Yng Read.

Learn to Write Activity Book. (Begin to Learn Ser.: No. S812-2). (J). 1989. pap. 1.95 (*0-7214-5110-1*, Ladybrd) Penguin Putnam.

Learn to Write Chinese Characters. Johan A. Bjorksten. LC 93-41542. 123p. 1994. pap. 16.95 (*0-300-05771-7*) Yale U Pr.

Learn to Write Numbers. Pen Notes Staff. (J). (ps up). 1997. spiral bd. 13.00 (*0-939564-19-X*) Pen Notes.

Learn Together! Discovering, Organizing & Designing Cooperative Classrooms. Bev Clevenger. Ed. by Judy Mitchell. (Illus.). 128p. (Orig.). (J). (gr. 3-6). 1995. pap., teacher ed. 12.95 (*1-57310-035-8*) Teachng & Lrning Co.

Learn Torah with . . . 5755 Torah Annual: A Collection of the Year's Best Torah. Ed. by Joel Lurie Grishaver & Stuart Kelman. 420p. 1997. 28.95 (*1-881283-13-5*) Alef Design.

***Learn Torah with 5756 Torah Annual: A Collection of the Years Best Torah.** Ed. by Joel Lurie Grishaver & Stuart Kelman. (Learn Torah with Torah Annuals Ser.: No. 2). 408p. 1999. pap. 21.95 (*1-881283-30-5*) Alef Design.

***Learn Torah with Torah Annual: A Collection of the Years Best Torah,, Vol. 5756.** Joel Lurie Grishaver. 1998. 28.95 (*1-881283-28-3*) Torah Aura.

Learn Turbo Assembler in a Day: Version 3.0. Stephen K. Cunningham. LC 92-24952. (Popular Applications Ser.). (Illus.). 144p. 1992. pap. 15.95 incl. disk (*1-55622-300-5*) Wordware Pub.

Learn Turkish for English Speakers. (ENG & TUR.). 224p. pap. 20.95 (*0-87557-086-0*) Saphrograph.

Learn Urdu for English Speakers. (ENG & URD.). pap. 20.95 (*0-87557-126-3*) Saphrograph.

Learn Vedic Astrology Without Tears. K. N. Rao. (C). 1995. 9.00 (*0-8364-2906-0*, Pub. by Ranjan Pubs) S Asia.

Learn Visio 97: Version 5.0. Ralph Grabowski. LC 97-43820. 1997. pap. text 29.95 (*1-55622-568-7*) Wordware Pub.

***Learn Visio 2000 for the Masters.** Billy Pruchno. (Illus.). 2000. pap. text 39.95 (*1-55622-713-2*) Wordware Pub.

***Learn VISIO 2000 for the Advanced User.** Ralph Grabowski. LC 99-57151. (Illus.). 2000. pap. 34.95 (*1-55622-711-6*) Wordware Pub.

***Learn VISIO 2000 in Three Days.** Ralph Grabowski. 2000. pap. 22.95 (*1-55622-709-4*) Wordware Pub.

Learn Visio 5.0 for the Advanced User. Ralph Grabowski. LC 98-41667. 1998. pap. text 34.95 (*1-55622-595-4*) Wordware Pub.

Learn Visual Basic 5.0 in Three Days. David L. Campell. LC 97-24327. (Illus.). 250p. 1997. pap. 19.95 incl. disk (*1-55622-542-3*) Wordware Pub.

Learn Visual Basic 4.0 in Three Days. Larry W. Smith & David L. Campbell. (Popular Applications Ser.). 176p. 1995. pap. 15.95 incl. disk (*1-55622-458-3*) Wordware Pub.

Learn Visual Basic 5 Now. Microsoft Corporation Staff. 1998. pap. write for info. (*1-57231-445-1*) Microsoft.

Learn Visual C++ Now: Teach Yourself Microsoft Visual C++ the Quick & Easy Way. Chuck Sphar. LC 98-52133. 500p. 1999. 49.99 incl. cd-rom (*1-57231-965-8*) Microsoft.

Learn Visual dBASE 5.5 for Windows in a Day. Antony Moseley. (Popular Applications Ser.). 136p. 1996. pap. 15.95 incl. disk (*1-55622-469-9*) Wordware Pub.

Learn Visual dBASE Programming: A Hands-On Guide to Object-Oriented Database Programming, set. Martin L. Rinehart. 400p. (C). 1995. pap. text 39.95 incl. disk (*0-201-60836-7*) Addison-Wesley.

Learn Watercolor the Edgar Whitney Way. Ron Ranson. (Illus.). 144p. 1997. pap. 22.99 (*0-89134-808-5*, North Lght Bks) F & W Pubns Inc.

Learn Welsh for English Speakers. (ENG & WEL.). 180p. pap. 20.95 (*0-87557-092-5*) Saphrograph.

Learn Western Swing Guitar. Ray Benson. (Homespun Tapes Ser.). 1996. VHS 39.95 (*0-7935-6865-X*) H Leonard.

Learn While You Play. expanded rev. ed. Chava Shapiro. 1997. pap. 4.95 (*0-914131-95-8*, A460) Torah Umesorah.

Learn While You Sleep. James P. Duffy. 224p. (Orig.). 1991. mass mkt. 4.50 (*0-380-76268-4*, Avon Bks) Morrow Avon.

Learn While You Sleep. 2nd ed. David Curtis. LC 60-15692. 1964. 10.00 (*0-87212-007-4*); pap. 5.95 (*0-87212-008-2*) Libra.

Learn Windows in a Day. Brian Dooley. (Popular Applications Ser.). (Illus.). 128p. (Orig.). 1992. pap. 12.95 (*1-55622-263-7*) Wordware Pub.

Learn Windows 98. Stephen Solosky. 149p. (C). 1999. pap. text 32.00 incl. disk (*1-58076-001-5*) Que Educ & Trng.

Learn Windows 98 in a Weekend. Michael Meadbra. LC 97-69602. (Computer Bks.). 225p. 1998. per. 19.99 (*0-7615-1296-9*) Prima Pub.

Learn Windows 95. 2nd annot. ed. Que Education & Training Staff. (Learn Ser.). (Illus.). 192p. 1997. pap., teacher ed. 39.99 incl. cd-rom (*1-57576-970-0*) Que Educ & Trng.

Learn Windows 95 in a Day. Scott Fuller. LC 96-12437. (Popular Applications Ser.). 128p. 1996. pap. 15.95 (*1-55622-493-1*) Wordware Pub.

***Learn Windows NT 4.0 Workstation.** Ken Baldauf. LC 97-68880. (Illus.). 164p. 1999. pap. 32.00 incl. cd-rom (*1-58076-242-5*) Que Educ & Trng.

Learn Windows NT 5.0 Network Security. Amrit Tiwana. 1999. pap. text 49.95 (*1-55622-636-5*) Wordware Pub.

***Learn Windows 95.** 2nd ed. Stephen C. Solosky. LC 98-89905. (Illus.). 165p. (C). 1999. pap. text. write for info. (*1-58076-327-8*) Que Educ & Trng.

Learn Windsurfing in a Weekend. Phil Jones. 1992. 16.00 (*0-679-41277-8*) Knopf.

Learn With Clavinova - Yamaha Disk Orchestra. 1989. pap. 34.95 incl. audio compact disk (*0-7935-6717-3*) H Leonard.

Learn with Dots & Mazes. Stephen R. Covey. (Step Ahead Plus Ser.). (Illus.). 64p. (J). (ps-3). 1995. pap., wbk. ed. 3.49 (*0-307-03648-0*, 03648, Goldn Books) Gldn Bks Pub Co.

Learn with Rap Geography. unabridged ed. Patricia B. Murphy. (Learn with Rap Ser.). (Illus.). 48p. (Orig.). (J). (gr. 2-9). 1995. pap. 19.95 incl. audio (*0-9648725-0-1*) People Are People.

Learn with Rap Geography. 2nd ed. Patricia B. Murphy. (Learn with Rap Ser.). (Illus.). 50p. (Orig.). (J). (gr. 2-9). 1996. pap. text 19.95 incl. audio (*0-9648725-1-X*) People Are People.

Learn with Teddy. (Illus.). 18p. (J). (ps). 1999. bds. write for info. (*1-85854-769-5*) Brimax Bks.

Learn with Teddy ABC. M. Rogers. (Learn with Teddy Ser.). 32p. (J). 1995. 4.98 (*1-85854-150-6*) Brimax Bks.

Learn with Teddy Colors. Kath Mellentin & Tim Wood. (Illus.). 12p. (J). 1997. 11.99 (*1-884628-56-7*, Flyng Frog) Allied Pub MD.

Learn with Teddy Numbers. Kath Mellentin & Tim Wood. (Illus.). 12p. (J). 1997. 11.99 (*1-884628-55-9*, Flyng Frog) Allied Pub MD.

Learn with Thomas. Christopher Awdry. LC 95-74747. (Illus.). (J). (ps-3). 1996. 12.99 (*0-679-87951-X*) McKay.

Learn with Thomas. Christopher Awdry. (Illus.). (J). (ps-2). 1996. 12.99 (*0-614-15712-9*) Random.

Learn Word 97. 2nd ed. Que Education & Training Staff. (Illus.). 237p. 1997. teacher ed. 39.99 incl. cd-rom (*1-57576-882-8*) Que Educ & Trng.

Learn Word 97 in a Weekend. Faithe Wempen. LC 97-69042. 432p. 1997. per. 19.99 (*0-7615-1251-9*) Prima Pub.

***Learn Word 2000 VBA by Example.** Julitta Korol, (Illus.). 500p. 2000. pap. 49.95 (*1-55622-748-5*) Wordware Pub.

***Learn Word 2000 VBA Document Automation.** Scott Driza. (Illus.). 500p. 2000. pap. 54.95 (*1-55622-751-5*) Wordware Pub.

***Learn Word 2000.** John Preston et al. 330p. 1999. pap. text 32.00 (*1-58076-262-X*) Que Educ & Trng.

***Learn Word 97.** 2nd ed. John Preston et al. LC 98-89900. (Illus.). 240p. (C). 1999. pap. text. write for info. (*1-58076-326-X*) Que Educ & Trng.

Learn WordPerfect 5.1, 2 vols. Annette Thomason. (C). 1991. pap. 2.76 (*0-395-56959-1*) HM.

Learn WordPerfect 5.1 Plus in a Day. Elaine E. Pickens. (Popular Applications Ser.). 172p. (Orig.). 1995. pap. 15.95 incl. disk (*1-55622-449-4*) Wordware Pub.

Learn WordPerfect 5.2 for Windows in a Day. John C. Sans. LC 93-7039. (Popular Applications Ser.). 128p. (Orig.). 1993. pap. 15.95 incl. disk (*1-55622-367-6*) Wordware Pub.

Learn WordPerfect Presentations in a Day. Elaine E. Pickens. LC 93-45585. (Popular Applications Ser.). 136p. 1994. pap. 15.95 incl. disk (*1-55622-362-5*) Wordware Pub.

Learn WordPerfect 6.0 for Windows in a Day. Sheila S. Dienes. LC 93-48168. (Popular Applications Ser.). 144p. (Orig.). 1994. pap. 15.95 incl. disk (*1-55622-416-8*) Wordware Pub.

***Learn Writing & Grammar Quickly, 4 videos.** Janet Scarpone. Incl. Grammar Workbook. 1998. pap., wbk. ed. 9.99 (*1-889434-41-8*); How to Write an Essay. (Orig.). 1996. pap. text, wbk. ed. 49.99 incl. VHS (*1-889434-18-3*); More Punctuation. 1998. pap., wbk. ed. 49.99 incl. VHS (*1-889434-40-X*); Parts of Speech. 1998. pap., wbk. ed. 49.99 incl. VHS (*1-889434-38-8*); Punctuation Plus. 1998. pap., wbk. ed. 49.99 incl. VHS (*1-889434-39-6*); Writing Workbook: Provides Pre-Writing Examples, Sample Topics, English Review Sheets, Sample Essays & Critique Sheets. 25p. (Orig.). 1996. pap. text, wbk. ed. 9.99 (*1-889434-20-5*); (Learn Writing & Grammar Quickly Ser.). 1998. Set wbk. ed. 159.00 incl. VHS (*1-889434-43-4*) Learn Quickly.

***Learn XML Tips.** George M. Doss. LC 00-38180. (Illus.). 400p. 2000. pap. write for info. (*1-55622-757-4*) Wordware Pub.

Learn Yoga in a Weekend. Sivananda Yoga Vedanta Center Staff. LC 93-721. 1993. 16.00 (*0-679-42751-1*) Knopf.

Learn Zulu. C. L. Nyembezi. (ENG & ZUL.). 264p. 1990. pap. 15.95 (*0-7859-7521-7*) Fr & Eur.

Learn Zulu. 5th ed. C. L. Nyembezi. (ZUL.). 264p. 1990. reprint ed. pap. 12.75 (*0-7960-0237-1*) IBD Ltd.

Learnability & Cognition: The Acquisition of Argument Structure. Ed. by Steven Pinker & Jacques A. Mehler. (Illus.). 427p. 1991. pap. text 39.95 (*0-262-66073-3*, Bradford Bks) MIT Pr.

Learnability & Linguistic Theory. Ed. by Robert J. Matthews & William Demopoulos. (C). 1989. lib. bdg. 114.50 (*0-7923-0247-8*) Kluwer Academic.

Learnability & Second Languages: A Book of Readings. Ed. by James Pankhurst et al. vi, 208p. 1989. pap. 46.15 (*90-6765-389-6*) Mouton.

Learnability & the Lexicon: Theories & Second Language Acquisition Research. Alan Juffs. LC 96-855. (Language Acquisition & Language Disorders Ser.: No. 12). xi, 277p. 1996. 79.00 (*1-55619-775-6*) J Benjamins Pubng Co.

***Learnability in Optimality Theory.** Bruce Tesar & Paul Smolensky. LC 99-56826. (Illus.). 226p. 1999. 22.50 (*0-262-20126-7*) MIT Pr.

Learnable Classes of Categorial Grammars. Makoto Kanazawa. LC 97-32705. (Studies in Logic, Language & Information). 200p. (C). 1998. text 59.95 (*1-57586-097-X*); pap. text 22.95 (*1-57586-096-1*) CSLI.

Learnables, Bk. 1. 2nd ed. Harris Winitz. (CHI, CZE, ENG, FRE & GER., Illus.). (gr. 2 up). 1976. pap. 45.00 incl. audio (*0-939990-01-6*) Intl Linguistics. THE LEARNABLES is an audio-visual foreign language program which teaches 1,500 basic words & elementary grammatical constructions through the use of pictures. It is used as a first textbook, preparing students for advanced study or may be used as a supplemental textbook or laboratory exercise workbook. Each lesson contains 100 pictures & an audio cassette. Corresponding to each of the pictures is a word, phrase or sentence that the student hears on the cassette. Single word nouns are presented first, followed by phrases & then simple sentences. Individuals quickly understand the foreign language. BASIC STRUCTURES books teach individuals to read the foreign language & are used in association with THE LEARNABLES. All recordings are done by native speakers. THE LEARNABLES are used world-wide & are well accepted by the public. Write for additional information. *Publisher Paid Annotation.*

***Learnables, Bk. 1.** 4th ed. Harris Winitz. (CZE, CHI, ENG, FRE & GER., Illus.). (YA). (gr. 7 up). 1999. pap. 45.00 incl. audio (*1-887371-43-5*) Intl Linguistics.

***Learnables, 6 cassettes, Bk. 2.** 4th ed. Harris Winitz. (CHI, CZE, ENG, FRE & GER., Illus.). 51p. (YA). (gr. 7 up). 1999. pap. 51.00 incl. audio (*1-887371-44-3*) Intl Linguistics.

Learnables, Bk. 3. 2nd ed. Harris Winitz. (CHI, ENG, FRE, GER & RUS., Illus.). 51p. 1999. pap. 45.00 incl. audio (*0-939990-03-2*) Intl Linguistics.

***Learnables, Bk. 4.** Harris Winitz. (CHI, ENG, FRE, GER & RUS., Illus.). 51p. (YA). (gr. 7 up). 1999. pap. 45.00 incl. audio (*1-887371-46-X*) Intl Linguistics.

***Learnables, Bk. 5.** Harris Winitz. (Illus.). 48p. 1999. pap. 45.00 incl. audio (*1-887371-49-4*) Intl Linguistics.

Learnables, Bk. 6. Harris Winitz. (ENG & GER., Illus.). 48p. 1998. pap. 45.00 incl. audio (*0-939990-06-7*) Intl Linguistics.

Learnables, Bk. 7. Harris Winitz. (ENG & GER., Illus.). 48p. 1994. pap. 45.00 incl. audio (*0-939990-07-5*) Intl Linguistics.

Learnables, Bk. 8. Harris Winitz. (ENG & GER., Illus.). 48p. 1998. pap. 45.00 incl. audio (*0-939990-08-3*) Intl Linguistics.

Learnables, Bk. 9. Harris Winitz. (Illus.). 51p. (YA). (gr. 7 up). 1993. pap. text 12.00 (*0-939990-89-X*) Intl Linguistics.

Learnables, Bk. 10. Harris Winitz. (Illus.). 51p. (YA). (gr. 7 up). 1993. pap. text 12.00 (*0-939990-90-3*) Intl Linguistics.

Learned about Flying from That Flying Magazine. 1983. pap. 14.95 (*0-02-579340-3*) Macmillan.

Learned & the Lewed: Studies in Chaucer & Medieval Literature. Ed. by Larry D. Benson. LC 74-78719. (English Studies: No. 5). 448p. 1974. pap. 9.95 (*0-674-51888-8*) HUP.

Learned Blacksmith: The Letters & Journals of Elihu Burritt. Elihu Burritt & Merle E. Curti. 1977. 16.95 (*0-8369-7133-7*) Ayer.

Learned Blacksmith: The Letters & Journals of Elihu Burritt. Elihu Burritt. (BCL1-PS American Literature Ser.). 241p. 1993. reprint ed. lib. bdg. 79.00 (*0-7812-6948-2*) Rprt Serv.

Learned Blacksmith: The Letters & Journals of Elihu Burritt. Merle E. Curti. LC 70-137536. (Peace Movement in America Ser.). ix, 241p. 1972. reprint ed. lib. bdg. 32.95 (*0-89198-063-6*) Ozer.

Learned Dissertation on Dumpling: With a Word upon Pudding: And Pudding & Dumpling Burnt to Pot: or a Compleat Way to the Dissertation on Dumpling. Intro. by Samuel L. Macey. LC 92-22731. (Augustan Reprints Ser.: No. 140). 1970. reprint ed. 14.50 (*0-404-70140-X*, PR3291) AMS Pr.

Learned Doctor William Ames: Dutch Backgrounds of English & American Puritanism. Keith L. Sprunger. LC 77-175172. 305p. reprint ed. pap. 94.60 (*0-608-30360-7*, 202021500016) Bks Demand.

Learned English Language Lessons Vol. 1: An Individualized Tutorial 1999 Platinum Edition. Richard A. Graham. Orig. Title: Learned English Language Lessons: Independent Tutorials. (Illus.). vi, 104p. (YA). (gr. 5 up). 1995. reprint ed. pap. 40.00 (*0-9668516-0-9*) LIIF Soft.

Learned English Language Lessons: Independent Tutorials see Learned English Language Lessons, Vol. 1, An Individualized Tutorial 1999 Platinum Edition

Learned Family (Learned, Larned, Learnard, Lannard & Lerned) Being Descendants of William Learned Who Was of Charlestown, Mass., in 1632. 2nd ed. W. L. Learned & J. G. Learned. (Illus.). 510p. 1989. reprint ed. pap. 75.00 (*0-8328-0760-5*); reprint ed. lib. bdg. 83.00 (*0-8328-0759-1*) Higginson Bk Co.

Learned Hand: The Man & the Judge. Gerald Gunther. (Illus.). 864p. (C). 1995. pap. 19.95 (*0-674-51880-2*) HUP.

Learned Hand on Patent Law. Paul H. Blaustein. LC 82-63003. 350p. 1983. text 50.00 (*0-686-88645-3*); lib. bdg. 50.00 (*0-9610490-0-6*) Pineridge Pub.

Learned Hand's Court. Marvin Schick. LC 78-17390. 371p. 1978. reprint ed. lib. bdg. 59.75 (*0-313-20508-6*, SCLH, Greenwood Pr) Greenwood.

Learned Helplessness: A Theory for the Age of Personal Control. Christopher Peterson et al. (Illus.). 376p. 1995. reprint ed. pap. text 27.50 (*0-19-504467-3*) OUP.

Learned King: The Reign of Alfonso X of Castile. Joseph F. O'Callaghan. LC 93-13417. (Middle Ages Ser.). (Illus.). 408p. (C). 1993. text 51.95 (*0-8122-3226-7*) U of Pa Pr.

Learned Ladies. Moliere. Tr. by Richard Wilbur from FRE. 1977. pap. 5.25 (*0-8222-0648-X*) Dramatists Play.

Learned Ladies. Moliere. Tr. by A. R. Waller. (Drama Classics Ser.). 80p. 1996. pap. 6.95 (*1-85459-375-7*, Pub. by N Hern Bks) Theatre Comm.

Learned Lady. Joan E. Overfield. 192p. (Orig.). 1996. mass mkt. 3.99 (*0-380-78005-4*, Avon Bks) Morrow Avon.

Learned Lady: Letters from Robert Browning to Mrs. Thomas FitzGerald, 1876-1889. Robert Browning. Ed. by E. C. McAleer. LC 66-11358. (Illus.). 244p. 1966. text 31.50 (*0-674-51900-0*) HUP.

Learned Lady in England, 1650-1760. Myra Reynolds. 1976. lib. bdg. 59.95 (*0-8490-2136-7*) Gordon Pr.

Learned Lady in England, 1650-1760. Myra Reynolds. 1990. 16.50 (*0-8446-1382-7*) Peter Smith.

Learned Optimism. Martin E. Seligman. Ed. by Julie Rubenstein. 336p. 1992. reprint ed. pap. 14.00 (*0-671-74158-6*) PB.

Learned Optimism: How to Change Your Mind & Your Life. Martin E. Seligman. 319p. 1998. per. 14.00 (*0-671-01911-2*, PB Trade Paper) PB.

Learned Pigs & Fireproof Women. Ricky Jay. 1987. pap. 12.95 (*0-446-38590-5*) Warner Bks.

Learned Pigs & Fireproof Women: Unique, Eccentric, & Amazing Entertainers: Sonte Eaters, Mind Readers, Poison Resisters, Daredevils, Singing Mice, Etc., Etc., Etc. Ricky Jay. LC 98-73819. (Illus.). 352p. 1998. pap. 16.00 (*0-374-52570-6*) FS&G.

Learned Presidency: Theodore Roosevelt, William Howard Taft, Woodrow Wilson. David H. Burton. LC 86-46327. 224p. 1988. 32.50 (*0-8386-3313-7*) Fairleigh Dickinson.

Learned Societies & English Literary Scholarship in Great Britain & the United States. Harrison R. Steeves. LC 70-112943. 1970. reprint ed. 27.50 (*0-404-06238-5*) AMS Pr.

***Learned Society in a Period of Transition: The Sunni 'Ulama' of Eleventh-Century Baghdad.** Daphna Ephrat. LC 99-54127. (C). 2000. pap. text 16.95 (*0-7914-4646-8*) State U NY Pr.

***Learned Society in a Period of Transition: The Sunni 'Ulama' of Eleventh-Century Baghdad.** Daphna Ephrat. LC 99-54127. (C). 2000. text 49.50 (*0-7914-4645-X*) State U NY Pr.

***Learner Autonomy in Language Learning: Defining the Field & Effecting Change.** Ed. by Sara Cotterall & David Crabbe. (Bayreuth Contributions to Glottodidactics Ser.). x, 184p. 1999. 37.95 (*3-631-34890-8*) P Lang Pubng.

Learner Autonomy in Language Learning: Defining the Field & Effecting Change. Ed. by Sara Cotterall & David Crabbe. LC 99-34316. (Bayreuth Contributions to Glottodidactics Ser.: Vol. 8). (Illus.). x, 184p. 1999. pap. text 37.95 (*0-8204-4337-9*) P Lang Pubng.

Learner Autonomy in Modern Languages. 1997. 18.00 (*92-871-3258-5*, Pub. by Council of Europe) Manhattan Pub Co.

Learner Based Teaching. Colin Campbell & Hanna Kryszewska. Ed. by Alan Maley. (Illus.). 136p. 1992. pap. text 13.95 (*0-19-437163-8*) OUP.

Learner-Centered Classroom & School: Strategies for Increasing Student Motivation & Achievement. Barbara L. McCombs & Jo S. Whisler. LC 96-52661. (Jossey-Bass Education Ser.). 1997. 29.95 (*0-7879-0836-3*) Jossey-Bass.

Learner-Centered Curriculum. David Nunan. (Cambridge Applied Linguistics Ser.). (Illus.). 208p. 1988. pap. text 19.95 (*0-521-35843-4*) Cambridge U Pr.

***Learner-Centered Design: A Cognitive View of Managing Complexity in Product Information & Environmental Design.** Wayne W. Reeves. LC 99-26072. 198p. 1999. 42.00 (*0-7619-0726-2*) Sage.

Learner-Centered Principalship: The Principal as Teacher of Teachers. William G. Webster. LC 94-13734. 280p. 1994. 65.00 (*0-275-94908-7*, Praeger Pubs) Greenwood.

Learner-Centered Reform: Current Issues in Higher Education, 1975. Ed. by Dyckman W. Vermilye. LC 75-24001. (Jossey-Bass Higher Education Ser.). 250p. reprint ed. 77.50 (*0-8357-9330-3*, 201377900087) Bks Demand.

Learner Centredness As Language Education. Ian Tudor. (Cambridge Language Teaching Library). (Illus.). 295p. (C). 1997. text 59.95 (*0-521-48097-3*); pap. text 22.95 (*0-521-48560-6*) Cambridge U Pr.

Learner Characteristics & Adaptive Education. Margaret C. Wang et al. (Handbook of Special Education: Research & Practice Ser.: Vol. 1). (Illus.). 388p. 1987. 133.50 (*0-08-033383-4*, Pergamon Pr) Elsevier.

Learner Controlled Instruction. Frank T. Wydra. Ed. by Danny G. Langdon. LC 79-23017. (Instructional Design Library). 136p. 1980. 27.95 (*0-87778-146-X*) Educ Tech Pubns.

Learner-Directed Assessment in ESL. Ed. by Glayol Ekbatani & Herbert Pierson. LC 99-17875. 192p. 1998. write for info. (*0-8058-3067-7*); pap. write for info. (*0-8058-3068-5*) L Erlbaum Assocs.

Learner English: A Teacher's Guide to Interference & Other Problems. Ed. by Michael Swan & Bernard Smith. (Cambridge Handbooks for Language Teachers Ser.). 284p. 1987. pap. text 20.95 (*0-521-26910-5*) Cambridge U Pr.

Learner English on the Computer. Sylviane Granger. LC 97-36716. (Studies in Language & Linguistics). 1998. pap. text 29.16 (*0-582-29883-0*) Longman.

***Learner Focused Technology Integration.** (C). 2002. pap. text 0.00 (*0-13-016990-0*) HEPC Inc.

Learner in Education for the Professions, As Seen in Education for Social Work. Charlotte Towle. LC 54-11216. 1992. lib. bdg. 12.50 (*0-226-80998-6*) U Ch Pr.

Learner Language & Language Learning. Claus Faerch & Robert Phillipson. 400p. 1984. pap. 29.95 (*0-905028-28-7*, Pub. by Multilingual Matters) Taylor & Francis.

Learner Strategies. Wenden. 301p. (C). 1987. 27.50 (*0-13-527110-X*, Macmillan Coll) P-H.

Learner Strategies for Learner Autonomy. Anita Wenden. 188p. 1991. pap. text 41.00 (*0-13-529603-X*) P-H.

Learner, Text & Context in Foreign Language Acquisition: An Arabic Perspective. Mahdi Alosh. LC 97-35861. (Pathways to Advanced Skills Ser.: Vol. 4). 1997. 26.95 (*0-87415-333-6*, PA04) Foreign Lang.

Learner, the Learning Process, the School. Ed. by William C. Johnson. 241p. 1975. 32.00 (*0-8290-1104-8*) Irvington.

Learner's Arabic-English-Arabic Dictionary, 2 vols., Set. F. Steingass. (ARA & ENG.). 1909p. 1986. 80.00 (*0-8288-0435-4*, M9954) Fr & Eur.

Learner's Chinese-English Dictionary. (CHI & ENG.). 666p. 1987. 19.95 (*9971-940-22-1*) China Bks.

Learners Choice. Aileen Kelly. (C). 1988. 25.00 (*0-7241-6792-7*, Pub. by Univ Nottingham) St Mut.

Learner's Dictionaries of Arabic Idioms: Classical Idioms. Leslie J. McLoughlin. (ARA.). 144p. 1988. pap. 13.95 (*0-86685-467-3*, LDL4673, Pub. by Librairie du Liban) Intl Bk Ctr.

Learner's Dictionaries of Arabic Idioms: Colloquial Idioms. Leslie J. McLoughlin. (ARA.). 144p. 1988. pap. 13.95 (*0-86685-468-1*, LDL4681, Pub. by Librairie du Liban) Intl Bk Ctr.

Learner's Dictionary of English Idioms. Isabel McCaig. 224p. 1986. pap. text 10.50 (*0-19-431254-2*) OUP.

Learner's Dictionary of Haitian Creole. Albert Valdman. LC 97-164567. 1997. text 45.00 (*0-929236-01-7*) IU Creole Inst.

***Learner's Dictionary of Today's Indonesian.** George Quinn. 480p. 2000. 29.95 (*1-86448-543-4*, Pub. by Allen & Unwin Pty) Paul & Co Pubs.

Learner's English-Russian Dictionary. S. Folomkina. (ENG & RUS.). 655p. 1980. 19.95 (*0-8288-1230-6*, M9118) Fr & Eur.

Learner's Guide, Media Matters: Critical Thinking in the Information Age. CNN Staff. (Business Communication Ser.). 1999. mass mkt. 7.95 (*0-538-68776-2*) S-W Pub.

***Learner's Guide, Skills at Work: Applying Technology, Vol. 3.** Ait. (Tech Prep Ser.). 1999. pap., student ed. 8.50 (*0-538-68968-4*) Sth-Wstrn College.

***Learner's Guide, Skills at Work: Developing Interpersonal Skills, Vol. 2.** Ait. (Tech Prep Ser.). 1999. pap. 8.50 (*0-538-68973-0*) Sth-Wstrn College.

***Learner's Guide, Skills at Work: Using Resources.** Ait. (Tech Prep Ser.). 1999. pap. 8.50 (*0-538-68958-7*) Sth-Wstrn College.

***Learner's Guide, Skills at Work Module 4: Understanding Systems.** Ait. (Tech Prep Ser.). 1999. pap. 8.50 (*0-538-69001-1*) Sth-Wstrn College.

***Learner's Guide, Skills at Work Module 5: Acquiring Information.** Ait. (Tech Prep Ser.). 1999. pap. 8.50 (*0-538-69008-9*); pap. 110.00 (*0-538-69013-5*) Sth-Wstrn College.

Learner's Handbook of Modern Chinese Written Expressions. Yu Feng. (Illus.). 170p. (C). pap. text 23.00 (*962-201-868-8*, Pub. by Chinese Univ) U of Mich Pr.

Learner's Hindi-English Dictionary. H. Bahri. (ENG & HIN.). 758p. 1987. 49.95 (*0-8288-1130-X*, M14384) Fr & Eur.

Learners' Hindi-English Dictionary. H. Bahri. xix, 758p. 1994. 14.95 (*1-881338-42-8*) Nataraj Bks.

Learner's Kanji Dictionary. Mark Spahn & Wolfgang Hadamitzky. 928p. 1998. pap. 34.95 (*0-8048-2095-3*) Tuttle Pubng.

***Learner's Pocketbook.** Paul Hayden. 128p. 1999. pap. 8.95 (*1-870471-30-X*, Pub. by Mngmnt Pocketbks) Stylus Pub VA.

Learner's Russian-English Dictionary. B. A. Lapidus & S. V. Shevtsoka. (ENG & RUS.). 550p. 1977. 19.95 (*0-8288-5452-1*, M9117) Fr & Eur.

***Learners to Leaders: Stories about People in Process.** Ed. by David J. Zersen. 120p. 1999. pap. text. write for info. (*1-881848-06-X*) Concordia U Pr.

Learners' Way. Anne Forester & Margaret Reinhard. 320p. (Orig.). 1989. pap. 19.00 (*0-920541-96-8*) Peguis Pubs Ltd.

Learners with Disabilities: A Social Systems Perspective of Special Education. Thomas M. Shea & Anne M. Bauer. 528p. (C). 1993. text. write for info. (*0-697-15370-3*) Brown & Benchmark.

Learners with Disabilities: A Social Systems Perspective of Special Education. Thomas M. Shea & Anne M. Bauer. 528p. (C). 1993. text, student ed. 21.87 (*0-697-21378-1*) Brown & Benchmark.

Learners with Emotional & Behavioral Disorders: An Introduction. Anne M. Bauer. LC 98-16495. 305p. 1998. pap. text 51.00 (*0-13-241373-6*) P-H.

Learners with Mild Disabilities. Raymond. LC 99-48413. 427p. (C). 1999. pap. text 70.00 (*0-205-20064-8*) P-H.

***Learng & Memory.** (C). 1999. pap. text. write for info. (*0-205-31810-X*) Allyn.

***Learng the Art of Helping: Building Blocks & techniques.** 2nd ed. 320p. 2000. pap. 46.00 (*0-13-018396-2*) P-H.

Learng to Succeed: Readgs for College Quikprint. (C). 1997. pap. 19.75 (*0-536-00980-5*) Pearson Custom.

Learnin' the Blues. Joseph Lilore. Ed. by Aaron Stang. 60p. (C). 1987. pap. text 8.95 (*0-7692-1354-5*, GF0303) Wrner Bros.

Learning. Richard F. Luduena. 344p. 1995. pap. 49.95 (*0-471-01887-2*) Wiley.

Learning. 4th ed. A. Charles Catania. LC 97-9015. 462p. 1997. 74.00 (*0-13-235250-8*) P-H.

Learning, Reading Level 2. Elaine Goley. (Learn the Value Ser.: Set II). (Illus.). 32p. (J). (gr. 1-4). 1989. 11.95 (*0-685-58785-1*) Rourke Corp.

Learning: A Survey of Psychological Interpretations. 6th ed. Winfred F. Hill. LC 96-13467. 224p. (C). 1997. pap. text 44.00 (*0-673-99767-7*) Addson-Wesley Educ.

Learning: A Survey of Psychological Interpretations. 7th ed. Winfred F. Hill. (C). 2000. pap. text Price not set. (*0-321-05676-0*) Addson-Wesley Educ.

Learning: Behavior & Cognition. David A. Lieberman. 500p. (C). 1990. mass mkt. 45.50 (*0-534-12318-X*) Brooks-Cole.

Learning: Behavior & Cognition. 2nd ed. David A. Lieberman. (C). 1992. pap. 49.75 (*0-534-17400-0*) Brooks-Cole.

Learning: Behavior & Cognition, Test Items. 2nd ed. David Lieberman. 1992. mass mkt. write for info. (*0-534-17402-7*) Brooks-Cole.

***Learning: Nineteen Scenarios from Everyday Life.** Gerhard Steiner. Tr. by Joseph A. Smith from GER. LC 99-26136. 352p. (C). 1999. 74.95 (*0-521-47220-2*); pap. 29.95 (*0-521-47800-6*) Cambridge U Pr.

Learning: Principles & Applications. 3rd ed. Stephen B. Klein. LC 95-9392. 656p. (C). 1995. 71.56 (*0-07-035158-9*) McGraw.

***Learning: Rule Extraction & Representation.** Angela D. Frederici & Randolf Menzel. LC 98-51761. 1999. 99.95 (*3-11-016133-8*) De Gruyter.

Learning: The Treasure Within - Report to UNESCO of the International Commission Pocket Edition, No. 02000001. 1998. 15.00 (*92-3-103470-7*, U3470, Pub. by UNESCO) Bernan Associates.

***Learning a Field Language.** Robbins Burling. 112p. (C). 2000. pap. 9.95 (*1-57766-123-0*) Waveland Pr.

Learning a Living: A Blueprint for High Performance. (Illus.). 86p. (C). 1993. pap. text 30.00 (*1-56806-709-7*) DIANE Pub.

Learning a Living: A Blueprint for High Performance, 2 vols., Set. 1996. lib. bdg. 605.95 (*0-8490-6902-5*) Gordon Pr.

Learning a Living: A Blueprint for High Performance for America 2000, 2 vols., Set. 1995. lib. bdg. 600.95 (*0-8490-7401-0*) Gordon Pr.

***Learning a Living: A Guide to Planning Your Career & Finding a Job for People with Learning Disabilities, Attention Deficit Disorder & Dyslexia.** Dale S. Brown. LC 99-53658. 256p. 2000. pap. 18.95 (*0-933149-87-5*) Woodbine House.

Learning a Loving Way of Life. Ed. by Virginia S. Halonen & Nancy Mohrbacher. LC 87-81824. (Illus.). 314p. 1987. pap. 5.00 (*0-912500-35-2*) La Leche.

***Learning a Second Language Through Interaction.** Rod Ellis. LC 99-40612. (Studies in Bilingualism: Vol. 17). x, 285p. 1999. 75.00 (*1-55619-736-5*) J Benjamins Pubng Co.

***Learning a Second Language Through Interaction.** Rod Ellis & Sandra Fotos. LC 99-40612. (Studies in Bilingualism: Vol. 17). x, 285p. 1999. pap. 34.95 (*1-55619-737-3*) J Benjamins Pubng Co.

Learning a Second National Language: A Research Report. Ecro J. Laine. LC 95-30855. (Scandinavian University Studies in the Humanities & Social Sciences: Vol. 8). 169p. 1995. 42.95 (*3-631-48813-0*) P Lang Pubng.

Learning a Trade: A Craftsman's Notebooks, 1955-1997. Reynolds Price. LC 98-26692. (Illus.). 640p. 1998. 34.95 (*0-8223-2112-2*) Duke.

***Learning a Trade: A Craftsman's Notebooks, 1955-1997.** Reynolds Price. 624p. 2000. reprint ed. pap. 21.95 (*0-8223-2588-8*) Duke.

Learning Ability Test (LAT) Jack Rudman. (Career Examination Ser.: C-1062). 1994. pap. 23.95 (*0-8373-1062-8*) Nat Learn.

Learning about African Animals. Sy Barlowe. (Learning about Ser.). (Illus.). 16p. 1999. pap. text 1.00 (*0-486-40533-8*) Dover.

Learning about AIDS. Peter Aggleton et al. 1989. pap. text 54.00 (*0-443-04181-4*) Church.

Learning about AIDS: Scientific Social Issues. 2nd ed. Ed. by Peter Aggleton et al. LC 94-16625. 1995. pap. text 63.95 (*0-443-05178-X*) Church.

Learning about AIDS & Other Diseases. 3rd rev. ed. David C. King. (AIDS Awareness Ser.). (Illus.). 25p. (J). (gr. 2-4). 1999. pap. write for info. (*0-8374-3237-5*) Wkly Read Corp.

Learning about AIDS What Teens Need to Know. 9th rev. ed. Illus. by Kathleen White & Sandra F. Maccarone. (AIDS Awareness Ser.). 32p. (YA). (gr. 7-10). 1999. pap. write for info. (*0-8374-3236-7*) Wkly Read Corp.

Learning about AIDS What You Need to Know. 6th rev. ed. Illus. by Kathleen White & Sandra F. Maccarone. (AIDS Awareness Ser.). 32p. (YA). (gr. 4-7). 1999. pap. write for info. (*0-8374-3231-6*) Wkly Read Corp.

Learning about Air. Norris & Evans. (Illus.). 48p. (J). (ps-1). 1995. pap., teacher ed. 5.95 (*1-55799-392-0*, 847) Evan-Moor Edu Pubs.

Learning about Animals. Joy Evans & Jo E. Moore. (Illus.). 48p. (J). (ps-1). 1987. pap. 5.95 (*1-55799-097-2*, EMC807) Evan-Moor Edu Pubs.

***Learning about Assertiveness from the Life of Oprah Winfrey.** Kristin Ward. (Character Building Book Ser.). (Illus.). 24p. (J). (gr. k-4). 1999. 15.93 (*0-8239-5348-3*, PowerKids) Rosen Group.

Learning about Assessment, Learning Through Assessment. National Research Council Staff. Ed. by Mark Driscoll & Deborah Bryant. LC 99-173534. 60p. 1998. pap. text 15.00 (*0-309-06133-4*) Natl Acad Pr.

***Learning about Australian Animals.** R. Soffer. (Learning about Bks.). (Illus.). (J). 2000. pap. 1.00 (*0-486-41010-2*) Dover.

Learning about Backyard Animals. Sy Barlowe. (Learning about Ser.). (Illus.). 16p. 1999. pap. text 1.00 (*0-486-40534-6*) Dover.

Learning about Bees from Mr. Krebs. Alice K. Flanagan. LC 98-44691. (Our Neighborhood Ser.). 32p. (J). (gr. 1-2). 1999. lib. bdg. 19.50 (*0-516-21136-6*) Childrens.

***Learning about Bees from Mr. Krebs.** Alice K. Flanagan. (J). 2000. pap. text 6.95 (*0-516-26539-3*) Childrens.

***Learning about Books & Libraries: A Gold Mine of Games.** Carol K. Lee & Janet Langford. (Illus.). 80p. (J). (gr. k-6). 2000. pap. 15.95 (*1-57950-051-X*, Alleyside) Highsmith Pr.

Learning about Bravery from the Life of Harriet Tubman. Kiki Mosher. (Character Building Bk.: Set 2). (Illus.). 24p. (J). (gr. k-4). 1996. lib. bdg. 15.93 (*0-8239-2424-6*, PowerKids) Rosen Group.

Learning about Building. Norris & Davis. (Illus.). 48p. (J). (ps-1). 1995. pap., teacher ed. 5.95 (*1-55799-395-5*, 850) Evan-Moor Edu Pubs.

Learning about Butterflies. Carolyn Klass & Robert Dirig. (Four-H Ser.). (Illus.). 36p. (YA). (gr. 7-11). 1992. pap. 7.50 (*1-57753-213-9*, 139-M-9) Corn Coop Ext.

Learning about Caring: An Introductory Package for Staff Development in Residential & Day Care. Robin Douglas & Chris Payne. (C). 1988. 115.00 (*0-7855-3734-1*, Pub. by Natl Inst Soc Work); 99.00 (*0-902789-38-4*, Pub. by Natl Inst Soc Work); 188.00 (*0-7855-0088-X*, Pub. by Natl Inst Soc Work) St Mut.

Learning about Cats. Petruccio. (Learning about Bks.). (J). (ps up). 1997. pap. 1.00 (*0-614-28720-0*) Dover.

Learning about Cats. Steven James Petruccio. (Illus.). 16p. (Orig.). 1997. pap. text 1.00 (*0-486-29533-8*) Dover.

Learning about Changes. Norris & Davis. (Illus.). 48p. (J). (ps-1). 1995. pap., teacher ed. 5.95 (*1-55799-397-1*, 852) Evan-Moor Edu Pubs.

***Learning about Charity from the Life of Princess Diana.** Caroline M. Levchuck. LC 98-22111. (Character Building Book 1). (Illus.). 24p. (J). 1999. 17.26 (*0-8239-5344-0*, PowerKids) Rosen Group.

Learning about Chores: Beginning the Process of Learning about Chores. Mary A. Little. (Competent Kids Ser.). 16p. (J). 1995. 19.95 (*1-887514-03-1*) Three Bears.

Learning about Compassion from the Life of Florence Nightingale. Kiki Mosher. LC 96-3511. (Character Building Bk.: Set 2). (Illus.). 24p. (J). (gr. k-4). 1996. lib. bdg. 15.93 (*0-8239-2423-8*, PowerKids) Rosen Group.

***Learning about Courage from the Life of Christopher Reeve.** Jane Kelly Kosek. LC 98-22106. (Character Building Book 1). (Illus.). 24p. (J). 1999. 17.26 (*0-8239-5346-7*, PowerKids) Rosen Group.

***Learning about Creativity from the Life of Steven Spielberg.** Erin M. Hovanec. (Character Building Book Ser.). (Illus.). 24p. (J). (gr. k-4). 1999. 15.93 (*0-8239-5349-1*, PowerKids) Rosen Group.

Learning about Cults. William. 1997. pap. 2.99 (*1-85792-248-4*, Pub. by Christian Focus) Spring Arbor Dist.

Learning About Cultures: Literature, Celebrations, Games & Art Activities. John Gust & J. Meghan McChesney. Ed. by Judy Mitchell. (Illus.). 144p. (Orig.). (J). (gr. 3-6). 1995. pap., teacher ed. 13.95 (*1-57310-012-9*) Teachng & Lrning Co.

Learning about Dance: An Introduction to Dance As an Art Form & Entertainment. 2nd ed. Nora Ambrosio. 274p. (C). per. 24.95 (*0-7872-6421-0*) Kendall-Hunt.

Learning about Dance: An Introduction to Dance As an Art Form & Entertainment. 2nd ed. Nora Ambrosio. LC 97-205459. 192p. 1997. pap. text, per. 27.95 (*0-7872-3422-2*, 41342201) Kendall-Hunt.

Learning about Dedication from the Life of Frederick Douglass. Sam Marlowe. (Character Building Bk.: Set 2). (Illus.). 24p. (J). (gr. k-4). 1996. lib. bdg. 15.93 (*0-8239-2425-4*, PowerKids) Rosen Group.

Learning about Determination from the Life of Gloria Estefan. Jeanne M. Strazzabosco. LC 96-14295. (Character Building Bk.: Set 1). (Illus.). 24p. (J). (gr. k-4). 1996. lib. bdg. 15.93 (*0-8239-2416-5*, PowerKids) Rosen Group.

Learning about Dignity from the Life of Martin Luther King, Jr. Jeanne M. Strazzabosco. LC 96-20210. (Character Building Bk.: Set 1). (Illus.). 24p. (J). (gr. k-4). 1996. 15.93 (*0-8239-2415-7*, PowerKids) Rosen Group.

Learning about Dogs Series, 10 bks. Charlotte Wilcox. Incl. Beagle. LC 97-12208. (Illus.). 48p. (J). (gr. 3-4). 1998. lib. bdg. 19.00 (*1-56065-539-9*, Cpstone High Low); Cocker Spaniel. LC 97-12207. (Illus.). 48p. (J). (gr. 3-4). 1998. lib. bdg. 19.00 (*1-56065-540-2*, Cpstone High Low); Dalmatian. LC 97-8316. (Illus.). 48p. (J). (gr. 3-4). 1998. lib. bdg. 19.00 (*1-56065-541-0*, Cpstone High Low); Doberman Pinscher. LC 97-14023. (Illus.). 48p. (J). (gr. 3-4). 1998. lib. bdg. 19.00 (*1-56065-542-9*, Cpstone High Low); German Shepherd. LC 96-26568. (Illus.). 48p. (J). (gr. 3-4). 1996. lib. bdg. 19.00 (*1-56065-398-1*, Cpstone High Low); Golden Retriever. LC 96-26571. (Illus.). 48p. (J). (gr. 3-4). 1996. lib. bdg. 19.00 (*1-56065-397-3*, Cpstone High Low); Great Dane. LC 97-13113. (Illus.). 48p. (J). (gr. 4-7). 1997. lib. bdg. 19.00 (*1-56065-543-7*, Cpstone High Low); Labrador Retriever. LC 96-26562. (Illus.). 48p. (J). (gr. 3-4). 1996. lib. bdg. 19.00 (*1-56065-396-5*, Cpstone High Low); Rottweiler. LC 96-26563. (Illus.). 48p. (J). (gr. 3-4). 1996. lib. bdg. 19.00 (*1-56065-395-7*, Cpstone High Low); Saint Bernard. LC 97-16363. (Illus.). 48p. (J). (gr. 3-4). 1998. lib. bdg. 19.00 (*1-56065-544-5*, Cpstone High Low); 190.00 (*1-56065-642-5*, Cpstone High Low) Capstone Pr.

Learning about Early Adolescent Development. Sally J. Crosiar. (Illus.). 196p. 1996. teacher ed., ring bd. 31.50 (*1-57753-098-5*, 109LAD) Corn Coop Ext.

Learning about Education. D. Hamilton. 1990. 103.95 (*0-335-09586-0*); pap. 28.95 (*0-335-09585-2*) OpUniv Pr.

Learning about Energy. David J. Rose. LC 85-28218. (Modern Perspectives in Energy Ser.). (Illus.). 528p. (C). 1986. 132.00 (*0-306-42124-0*, Plenum Trade) Perseus Pubng.

Learning about Fairness from the Life of Susan B. Anthony. Kiki Mosher. LC 96-16089. (Character Building Bk.: Set 2). (Illus.). 24p. (J). (gr. k-4). 1996. lib. bdg. 15.93 (*0-8239-2422-X*, PowerKids) Rosen Group.

Learning about Forgiveness from the Life of Nelson Mandela. Jeanne M. Strazzabosco. (Character Building Bk.: Set 1). (Illus.). 24p. (J). (gr. k-4). 1996. lib. bdg. 15.93 (*0-8239-2413-0*, PowerKids) Rosen Group.

Learning about God & Jesus: An Overview of the Gospel in Simple English. Beverly J. Doswald. LC 86-81297. 50p. (Orig.). 1986. pap. 4.25 (*0-938783-00-9*) Helpful Beginnings.

Learning about Honesty from the Life of Abraham Lincoln. Kiki Mosher. LC 96-15666. (Character Building Bk.: Set 2). (Illus.). 24p. (J). (gr. k-4). 1996. lib. bdg. 15.93 (*0-8239-2420-3*, PowerKids) Rosen Group.

Learning about Horses Series, 16 bks. Incl. American Saddlebred Horse. Charlotte Wilcox. (Illus.). 48p. (J). (gr. 3-4). 1996. lib. bdg. 19.00 (*1-56065-364-7*, Cpstone High Low); Appaloosa Horse. Gail B. Stewart. LC 94-29980. (Illus.). 48p. (J). (gr. 3-4). 1994. lib. bdg. 19.00 (*1-56065-243-8*, Cpstone High Low); Arabian Horse. Gail Stewart. LC 94-29981. (Illus.). 48p. (J). (gr. 3-4). 1994. lib. bdg. 19.00 (*1-56065-244-6*, Cpstone High Low); Chincoteague Ponies. Charlotte Wilcox. (Illus.). 48p. (J). (gr. 3-4). 1996. lib. bdg. 19.00 (*1-56065-363-9*, Cpstone High Low); Lipizzaner Horse. Charlotte Wilcox. LC 96-42318. (Illus.). 48p. (J). (gr. 3-4). 1997. lib. bdg. 19.00 (*1-56065-464-3*, Cpstone High Low); Miniature Horses. Charlotte Wilcox. LC 96-42317. (Illus.). 48p. (J). (gr. 3-4). 1997. lib. bdg. 19.00 (*1-56065-465-1*, Cpstone High Low); Morgan Horse. Charlotte Wilcox. (Illus.). 48p. (J). (gr. 3-4). 1996. lib. bdg. 19.00 (*1-56065-362-0*, Cpstone High Low); Mustangs & Wild Horses. Gail B. Stewart. LC 95-11251. (Illus.). 48p. (J). (gr. 3-4). 1996. lib. bdg. 19.00 (*1-56065-301-9*, Cpstone High Low); Palomino Horse. Gail B. Stewart. (Illus.). 48p. (J). (gr. 3-4). 1996. lib. bdg. 19.00 (*1-56065-299-3*, Cpstone High Low); Pinto Horse. Gail B. Stewart. (Illus.). 48p. (J). (gr. 3-4). 1995. lib. bdg. 19.00 (*1-56065-298-5*, Cpstone High Low); Przewalski's Horse. Charlotte Wilcox. LC 96-47696. (Illus.). 48p. (J). (gr. 3-4). 1997. lib. bdg. 19.00 (*1-56065-466-X*, Cpstone High Low); Quarter Horse. Gail B. Stewart. LC 94-26763. (Illus.). 48p. (J). (gr. 3-4). 1994. lib. bdg. 19.00 (*1-56065-242-X*, Cpstone High Low); Shetland Pony. Gail B. Stewart. (Illus.). 48p. (J). (gr. 3-4). 1995. lib. bdg. 19.00 (*1-56065-300-0*, Cpstone High Low); Standardbred Horse. Charlotte Wilcox. LC 96-46930. (Illus.). 48p. (J). (gr. 3-4). 1997. lib. bdg. 19.00 (*1-56065-467-8*, Cpstone High Low); Tennessee Walking Horse. Charlotte Wilcox. LC 95-47770. (Illus.). 48p. (J). (gr. 3-4). 1996. lib. bdg. 19.00 (*1-56065-365-5*, Cpstone High Low); Thoroughbred Horse: Born to Run. Gail B. Stewart. LC 94-22830. (Illus.). 48p. (J). (gr. 3-4). 1994. lib. bdg. 19.00 (*1-56065-245-4*, Cpstone High Low); 304.00 (*1-56065-648-4*, Cpstone High Low) Capstone Pr.

Learning about Immigration Law. Constantinos E. Scaros. (Illus.). 240p. (C). 1997. pap. text. write for info. (*0-9633276-8-2*) Marlen Hill Pub.

***Learning about Integrity from the Life of Eleanor Roosevelt.** Nancy Ellwood. (Character Building Book Ser.). (Illus.). 24p. (J). (gr. k-4). 1999. 15.93 (*0-8239-5345-9*, PowerKids) Rosen Group.

Learning about Islam. Yahiya Emerick. (Illus.). 224p. (J). (gr. 4-6). 1998. pap. text. write for info. (*1-889720-19-4*, Pub. by Amirah Pubng) Intl Bks & Tapes.

Learning about Jesus. 32p. (Orig.). 1995. pap. 1.95 (*0-9620963-5-0*) Inst Rel Rsch.

Learning about Justice from the Life of Cesar Chavez. Jeanne M. Strazzabosco. LC 96-16091. (Character Building Bk.: Set 1). (Illus.). 24p. (J). (gr. k-4). 1996. lib. bdg. 15.93 (*0-8239-2417-3*, PowerKids) Rosen Group.

Learning about Language: Issues for Primary Teachers. Alison J. Sealey. LC 95-23998. (English, Language & Education Ser.). 160p. 1996. pap. 29.95 (*0-335-19203-3*) OpUniv Pr.

Learning about Languages: Upper Elementary Through First Year High School. Elaine D. Lubiner. (SPA.). 91p. (YA). 1992. teacher ed. 22.60 (*0-8442-9371-7*, Natl Textbk Co) NTC Contemp Pub Co.

Learning about Languages: Upper Elementary Through First Year High School. Elaine D. Lubiner. (SPA.). 120p. (YA). 1994. pap. text 11.95 (*0-8442-9370-9*, Natl Textbk Co) NTC Contemp Pub Co.

Learning about Leadership from the Life of George Washington. Kiki Mosher. LC 96-15670. (Character Building Bk.: Set 2). (Illus.). 24p. (J). (gr. k-4). 1996. lib. bdg. 15.93 (*0-8239-2421-1*, PowerKids) Rosen Group.

Learning about Learning. Jacqueline Barber et al. Ed. by Lincoln Bergman et al. (Great Explorations in Math & Science (GEMS) Ser.). (Illus.). 220p. (Orig.). (J). (gr. 6-8). 1996. teacher ed., spiral bd. 25.50 (*0-912511-95-8*, GEMS) Lawrence Science.

***Learning about Learning: Resources for Supporting Effective Learning.** Chris Watkins. LC 00-25184. 2000. pap. write for info. (*0-415-22349-0*) Routledge.

Learning about Learning Disabilities. Ed. by Bernice Y. Wong. (Illus.). 643p. (C). 1991. text 54.95 (*0-12-762530-5*) Acad Pr.

Learning about Learning Disabilities. 2nd ed. Ed. by Bernice Wong. LC 97-80822. (Illus.). 754p. 1998. text 59.95 (*0-12-762532-1*) Morgan Kaufmann.

Learning about Leaves Coloring Book. Ed. by Carol A. Vercz. (Illus.). (J). (gr. k-4). 1997. pap. 4.95 (*0-910119-60-0*) SOCO Pubns.

Learning about Letters. Ed. by Random House Staff. (J). (gr. k up). 1986. pap. 19.95 incl. VHS (*0-394-88319-5*, Pub. by Random Bks Yng Read) Random.

Learning about Liberty: The Cato University Study Guide. Tom G. Palmer & Cato Institute Staff. LC 97-48820. 1997. 10.00 (*1-882577-66-3*) Cato Inst.

Learning about Light & Shadow. Norris & Davis. (Illus.). 48p. (J). (ps-1). 1995. pap., teacher ed. 5.95 (*1-55799-396-3*, 851) Evan-Moor Edu Pubs.

***Learning about Liturgy: Catechesis for Children & Their Families.** Dorothy Kosinski Carola. 192p. 2000. pap. 37.95 (*0-89390-497-X*) Resource Pubns.

Learning about Lupus: A User Friendly Guide. rev. ed. Ed. by Mary E. Moore et al. LC 97-73837. (Illus.). 224p. 1997. pap. text 7.00 (*0-9659530-0-9*) LFDV Inc.

Learning about Lyme Disease. Jo A. Heltzel. (Illus.). 32p. (Orig.). 1992. pap. text 3.75 (*0-9633041-0-0*) Jo Ann Heltzel.

Learning about Machines. Norris & Evans. (Illus.). 48p. (J). (ps-1). 1995. pap., teacher ed. 5.95 (*1-55799-393-9*, 848) Evan-Moor Edu Pubs.

***Learning about Meningitis: Stephen's Story.** Jenny Wilson. 2000. pap. text 2.99 (*1-85792-572-6*) Christian Focus.

Learning about Minerals. Barlowe. (Learning about Ser.). pap. 1.00 (*0-486-40017-4*) Dover.

Learning about Mission: Mission Matters! John Brand. 96p. 1999. pap. text 2.99 (*1-85792-402-9*) Christian Focus.

Learning about Money. Jo E. Moore. (Mathematics Ser.). (Illus.). 32p. (J). (gr. 1-2). 1997. pap., teacher ed. 2.95 (*1-55799-450-1*, 4052) Evan-Moor Edu Pubs.

Learning about Money: Basic Mathematics Skills. Jo Ellen Moore. (Illus.). 32p. (J). (gr. 1-2). 1995. pap., wbk. ed. 2.50 (*1-58610-065-3*, Learn on the Go) Learn Horizon.

Learning about Movement. Norris & Davis. (Illus.). 48p. (J). (ps-1). 1995. pap., teacher ed. 5.95 (*1-55799-394-7*, 849) Evan-Moor Edu Pubs.

Learning about My Body. Joy Evans & Jo E. Moore. (Illus.). 48p. (J). (ps-1). 1987. pap. 5.95 (*1-55799-099-9*, EMC809) Evan-Moor Edu Pubs.

Learning about Myself Handbook for Group Participants. Verna Rickard. LC 97-45067. 64p. 1998. pap. 14.95 (*0-7890-0471-2*, Hawrth Medical) Haworth Pr.

Learning about Myself (LAMS) Program for At-Risk Parents: Learning from the Past--Changing the Future. Verna Rickard. LC 97-45068. (Illus.). 196p. 1998. 39.95 (*0-7890-0107-1*, Maltreatment & Trauma Pr); pap. 24.95 (*0-7890-0474-7*, Maltreatment & Trauma Pr) Haworth Pr.

Learning about Numbers. Ed. by Random House Staff. (J). 1986. pap. 9.95 incl. VHS (*0-394-88315-2*, Pub. by Random Bks Yng Read) Random.

Learning about Our Five Senses. Rosalie Hoover & Barbara Murphy. 64p. (J). (gr. k-3). 1981. 8.99 (*0-86653-013-4*, GA 241) Good Apple.

Learning about Our Speech Helpers: The Speech-Language Pathologist's Complete Guide to Teaching about Our Eyes, Ears, Nose, Mouth, Larynx & Lungs! Sara M. Jackson & Anita K. Robbins. (Illus.). 83p. (J). (gr. k-7). 1990. spiral bd. 23.95 (*1-58650-024-4*, BK-215) Super Duper.

***Learning about Our World & Our Past: Using the Tools & Resources of Geography & U. S. History.** Evelyn Hawkins. (Illus.). 191p. 1999. pap. text 30.00 (*0-7881-8169-6*) DIANE Pub.

***Learning about Our World & Our Past: Using the Tools & Resources of Geography & United States History.** Evelyn Hawkins. LC 98-136267. 198p. 1998. per. 15.00 (*0-16-049432-X*) USGPO.

Learning about Plants. Joy Evans & Jo E. Moore. (Illus.). 48p. (J). (ps-1). 1987. pap. 5.95 (*1-55799-098-0*, EMC808) Evan-Moor Edu Pubs.

Learning about Popular Media. Glen Hudak. 224p. 1996. 75.00 (*0-7507-0340-7*, Falmer Pr); pap. 24.95 (*0-7507-0341-5*, Falmer Pr) Taylor & Francis.

Learning about Punctuation. Ed. by Nigel Hall & Anne Robinson. LC 95-40871. (Language & Education Library: Vol. 9). 200p. 1996. 69.00 (*1-85359-322-2*); pap. 24.95 (*1-85359-321-4*) Heinemann.

Learning about Punctuation. Nigel Hall & Anne Robinson. LC 95-40871. 174p. 1996. pap. text 16.00 (*0-435-07209-9*) Heinemann.

Learning about Rain Forest Animals. Sy Barlowe. (Learning about Ser.). (Illus.). 16p. 1999. pap. text 1.00 (*0-486-40535-4*) Dover.

Learning about Relationships. Ed. by Steve Duck. (Understanding Relationship Processes Ser.: Vol. 2). (Illus.). 224p. (C). 1993. text 39.95 (*0-8039-5157-4*); pap. text 18.95 (*0-8039-5158-2*) Sage.

Learning about Responsiblity from the Life of Colin Powell. Jeanne M. Strazzabosco. (Character Building Bk.: Set 1). (Illus.). 24p. (J). (gr. k-4). 1996. lib. bdg. 15.93 (*0-8239-2414-9*, PowerKids) Rosen Group.

Learning about Rights. John Dunn. 80p. (C). 1993. pap. text 21.00 (*0-900137-37-1*, Pub. by NCCL) St Mut.

Learning about Risk: Consumer & Worker Responses to Hazard Information. W. Kip Viscusi & Wesley A. Magat. 224p. 1987. 43.00 (*0-674-51915-9*) HUP.

Learning about Sex Series, 7 cass.; set. expanded rev. abr. ed. Incl. How to Talk Confidently with Your Children about Sex. Lenore Buth. 160p. 1998. pap. 9.99 incl. VHS (*0-570-03567-8*); How You Are Changing. Jane Graver. LC 98-225633. 64p. (J). (gr. 3-6). 1998. pap. 9.99 (*0-570-03564-3*); Human Sexuality: A Christian Perspective. Roger Sonnenberg. LC 98-19374. 224p. 1998. 16.99 incl. VHS (*0-570-03568-6*); Love, Sex & God. Bill Ameiss. LC 99-192376. 128p. (YA). (gr. 9 up). 1998. pap. 9.99 incl. VHS (*0-570-03566-X*); Sex & the New You. Rich Bimler. 64p. (J). (gr. 6-8). 1998. pap. 9.99 (*0-570-03565-1*); Where Do Babies Come from? Ruth Hummel. LC 98-225645. (Illus.). 32p. (J). (gr. 1-3). 1998. 9.99 (*0-570-03563-5*); Why Boys & Girls Are Different. Carol Greene. LC 98-225651. (Illus.). 32p. (ps-k). 1998. 9.99 (*0-570-03562-7*); (J). (gr. 1-6). 1998. 70.00 incl. VHS (*0-570-03569-4*) Concordia.

Learning about Sexuality: A Practical Beginning. Ed. by Sondra Zeidenstein & Kirsten Moore. 404p. 1996. pap. 20.00 (*0-87834-085-8*) Population Coun.

***Learning about Sharks.** Jan Sovak. (Illus.). (J). 1999. pap. 1.00 (*0-486-40768-3*) Dover.

Learning about Simple Science: Experiments for Young Learners. Joy Evans & Jo E. Moore. (Illus.). 48p. (J). (ps-1). 1987. pap. 5.95 (*1-55799-100-6*, EMC 810) Evan-Moor Edu Pubs.

***Learning about Strength of Character from the Life of Muhammad Ali.** Michele Ingber Drohan. LC 98-26483. (Character Building Book 1). (Illus.). 24p. (J). 1999. 17.26 (*0-8239-5347-5*, PowerKids) Rosen Group.

Learning about the Amish. (Illus.). 30p. (J). (ps up). 1997. pap. 4.00 (*1-890541-35-4*) Americana Souvenirs & Gifts.

Learning about the Civil War: Literature & Other Resources for Young People. Elaine C. Stephens & Jean E. Brown. LC 98-14569. xii, 259p. 1998. pap. text 19.50 (*0-208-02449-2*, Linnet Prof Pubns); lib. bdg. 32.50 (*0-208-02464-6*, Lib Prof Pubns) Shoe String.

Learning about the Earth. Jo E. Moore. (Learning About Science Series for PreK-1: Vol. 2). (Illus.). 48p. 1994. pap. text 5.95 (*1-55799-306-8*, EMC845) Evan-Moor Edu Pubs.

Learning about the Heart. Len Roberts. 28p. 1992. pap. 5.00 (*1-878851-03-9*) Silverfish Rev Pr.

Learning about the Holocaust: Literature & Other Resources for Young People. Elaine C. Stephens et al. LC 95-31545. xv, 198p. (C). 1995. pap. 18.50 (*0-208-02408-5*, Lib Prof Pubns); lib. bdg. 29.50 (*0-208-02398-4*, Lib Prof Pubns) Shoe String.

Learning about the Law, Incl. instr's. manual. Constantinos E. Scaros. 448p. 1997. pap. text, teacher ed. 42.00 (*1-56706-496-5*, 64965) Panel Pubs.

***Learning about the Liturgical Seasons: Catechesis fo Children & Their Families.** Dorothy Kosinski Carola. 80p. 1999. pap. 24.95 (*0-89390-495-3*) Resource Pubns.

***Learning about the Solar System.** B. Lafontaine. (Learning about Bks.). (Illus.). (J). 2000. pap. 1.00 (*0-486-41009-9*) Dover.

Learning about the U. S. Virgin Islands 2nd ed. 36p. (J). (gr. 2). 1996. pap. 2.80 (*0-536-59356-6*) Pearson Custom.

Learning about the U. S. Virgin Island. 36p. (J). (gr. 1). 1994. pap. 3.20 (*0-536-58767-1*) Pearson Custom.

Learning about the U. S. Virgin Islands. 36p. (gr. 2). 1994. pap. 3.20 (*0-536-58768-X*) Pearson Custom.

Learning about the U. S. Virgin Islands. 36p. (J). (gr. 3). 1994. pap. 3.20 (*0-536-58769-8*) S&S Trade.

Learning about the World of Work in the Federal Republic of Germany. FESC. 1986. 40.00 (*0-907659-13-6*) St Mut.

Learning about the World Through Geography. Belinda Antonson. Ed. by Art Cox. (Illus.). 80p. 1997. pap. 8.95 (*1-889931-05-5*) Bayou Printing Inc.

***Learning about True Spirituality: Jesus Our Joy.** Wallace Benn. 2000. pap. text 2.99 (*1-85792-443-6*) Christian Focus.

Learning about U. S. Virgin Islands 2nd ed. 36p. (J). (gr. 1). 1996. pap. 2.80 (*0-536-59355-8*) Pearson Custom.

***Learning about Union with Christ: You Can Live the Life You Should!** Stewart Dinnen. 64p. 2000. pap. text 2.99 (*1-85792-424-X*) Christian Focus.

Learning about Voice: Vocal Hygiene Activities for Children; A Resource Manual. Michael J. Moran & Elizabeth Zylla-Jones. LC 98-10016. (Illus.). 180p. 1998. pap. 49.95 (*1-56593-942-5*, 1866) Thomson Learn.

Learning about Weather. Jo E. Moore. (Learning About Science Series for PreK-1: Vol. 1). (Illus.). 48p. (J). (ps-1). 1994. pap. text 5.95 (*1-55799-305-X*, EMC844) Evan-Moor Edu Pubs.

Learning about Wildflowers. Barlowe. (Learning about Ser.). pap. text 1.00 (*0-486-40016-6*) Dover.

***Learning about Wisconsin: Activities, Historical Documents & Resources Linked to Wisconsin's Model Academic Standards for Social Studies in Grades 4-12.** 250p. 1999. 30.00 (*1-57337-075-4*) WI Dept Pub Instruct.

Learning about Work Ethic from the Life of Cal Ripken, Jr. Jeanne M. Strazzabosco. LC 96-21995. (Character Building Bk.: Set 1). (Illus.). 24p. (J). (gr. k-4). 1996. lib. bdg. 15.93 (*0-8239-2418-1*, PowerKids) Rosen Group.

Learning about Worship. John Wetherwax. 1988. pap., teacher ed. 3.00 (*0-940754-55-X*, 8516); pap., student ed. 6.50 (*0-940754-54-1*, 8515) Ed Ministries.

Learning about Writing: The Early Years. Pam Czerniewska. (Language in Education Ser.). 160p. (C). 1994. pap. 31.95 (*0-631-16963-6*) Blackwell Pubs.

Learning about Your Library: Introducing Books to the TV Generation. 16p. 1993. pap. 3.95 (*0-918734-45-2*) Reymont.

Learning about Your Oral Health, 5 levels. write for info. (*0-318-56834-9*) Am Dental.

Learning about Your Oral Health, 5 levels. (J). (ps). 11.20 (*0-934510-20-2*, W021) Am Dental.

Learning about Your Oral Health, 5 levels, Level I. 11.20 (*0-934510-16-4*, W017) Am Dental.

Learning about Your Oral Health, 5 levels, Level II. 11.20 (*0-934510-17-2*, W018) Am Dental.

Learning about Your Oral Health, 5 levels, Level III. 11.20 (*0-934510-18-0*, W019) Am Dental.

Learning about Your Oral Health, 5 levels, Level IV. 11.20 (*0-934510-19-9*, W020) Am Dental.

Learning Abstract Algebra with ISETL. E. Dubinsky & Uri Leron. 280p. 1993. 49.95 (*0-387-94104-5*) Spr-Verlag.

Learning Abstract Algebra with ISETL. Ed Dubinsky & Uri Leron. 1993. 59.95 (*0-387-94152-5*) Spr-Verlag.

Learning Access 2000. DDC Publishing Staff. 1999. 32.00 (*1-56243-733-X*) DDC Pub.

Learning Access 2000. DDC Publishing Staff. 1999. 31.00 (*1-56243-704-6*) DDC Pub.

Learning Achievements: Proofamatics Instructors Guide Binder. Learning Achievement Corp. Staff. 1983. 40.00 (*0-07-054530-8*) McGraw.

Learning Across Cultures. Ed. by Gary Althen. 200p. 1994. pap. 19.00 (*0-912207-67-1*) NAFSA Washington.

Learning Across the Lifespan: Theories, Research, Policies. Ed. by Albert C. Tuijnman & M. Van der Kamp. LC 92-31196. 277p. 1992. text 84.75 (*0-08-041926-7*, Pergamon Pr) Elsevier.

Learning Action Models: Papers from the 1993 Workshop. Ed. by Wei-Min Shen. (Technical Reports). (Illus.). 70p. (Orig.). 1994. spiral bd. 25.00 (*0-929280-66-0*) AAAI Pr.

Learning Activities. L. Stock. Incl. 1969. pap. 3.85 (*0-87108-174-1*); 1969. pap. write for info. (*0-318-55377-5*) Pruett.

Learning Activities for Business Report Writing. Mary J. Noblitt. 96p. 1986. pap. text 16.50 (*0-471-82931-5*) P-H.

Learning Activities for Fours. 1979. 15.00 (*0-939418-03-7*) Ferguson-Florissant.

Learning Activities for Infants & Toddlers. Stan Wonderley. 1998. pap. 22.95 (*0-933025-68-8*) Blue Bird Pub.

Learning Activities for Kindergarten & Grade One: Language. 1981. 10.00 (*0-939418-11-8*) Ferguson-Florissant.

Learning Activities for Kindergarten & Grade One: Math. 1981. 10.00 (*0-939418-12-6*) Ferguson-Florissant.

Learning Activities for Reading. 4th ed. Selma E. Herr. 220p. (C). 1982. text. write for info. (*0-697-06191-4*) Brown & Benchmark.

Learning Activities for Threes. 1980. 15.00 (*0-939418-04-5*) Ferguson-Florissant.

***Learning Activities Package.** Douglas K. Brumbaugh. 270p. 2000. write for info. (*1-58692-007-3*) Copyright Mgmt.

Learning Activities Series, 4 vols., Set. Kathy Knoblock. (Illus.). 192p. 1998. teacher ed. 23.80 (*1-58232-005-5*, BH 8910254); teacher ed. 47.60 (*1-58232-007-1*, BH 8911058); teacher ed. 53.55 (*1-58232-009-8*, BH 8910159) Bryan Hse.

***Learning Activity & Development.** Ed. by Mariane Hedegaard & Joachim Lompscher. 352p. 1999. 34.95 (*87-7288-815-6*, Pub. by Aarhus Univ Pr) David Brown.

***Learning Adobe Acrobat 4.0: Basic Skills.** Vince E. Yokom. 2000. spiral bd. 30.00 (*1-889231-25-8*) Instrux Ltd.

Learning Adventures in Math. Mega Books Staff. (Learning Adventures Ser.). (Illus.). 80p. (J). (gr. 1-2). 1998. 6.95 (*0-684-84427-3*) S&S Trade.

Learning Adventures in Math. Score Kaplan Staff. (Learning Adventures Ser.). (Illus.). 80p. (J). (gr. 3-4). 1998. 6.95 (*0-684-84432-X*) S&S Trade.

Learning Adventures in Math. Score Kaplan Staff. (Learning Adventures Ser.). (Illus.). 80p. (J). (gr. 5-6). 1998. 6.95 (*0-684-84436-2*) S&S Trade.

Learning Adventures in Reading & Writing. Score Kaplan Staff. (Learning Adventures Ser.). (Illus.). 80p. (J). (gr. 1-2). 1998. 6.95 (*0-684-84429-X*) S&S Trade.

Learning Adventures in Reading & Writing. Score Kaplan Staff. (Learning Adventures Ser.). (Illus.). 80p. (J). (gr. 3-4). 1998. 6.95 (*0-684-84434-6*) S&S Trade.

Learning Adventures in Reading & Writing. Score Kaplan Staff. (Learning Adventures Ser.). (Illus.). 80p. (J). (gr. 5-6). 1998. 6.95 (*0-684-84437-0*) S&S Trade.

***Learning Adventures in Science.** Score Kaplan Staff. (Learning Adventures Ser.). (Illus.). 80p. (J). (gr. 3-4). 1998. 6.95 (*0-684-84431-1*) S&S Trade.

Learning Adventures in Science. Score Kaplan Staff. (Learning Adventures Ser.). (Illus.). 80p. (J). (gr. 5-6). 1998. 6.95 (*0-684-84435-4*) S&S Trade.

Learning Adventures Quiz Me. Kaplan. 80p. (J). (gr. 1-2). 1998. 6.95 (*0-684-84824-4*) S&S Trade.

Learning Adventures Quiz Me. Kaplan Staff. 80p. (J). (gr. 3-4). 1998. 6.95 (*0-684-84825-2*) S&S Trade.

Learning Adventures Quiz Me. Kaplan Staff. 80p. (J). (gr. 5-6). 1998. 6.95 (*0-684-84826-0*) S&S Trade.

Learning after College. R. Nevitt Sanford & Craig Comstock. LC 79-92581. 277p. (Orig.). (C). 1980. 14.95 (*0-917430-04-2*); pap. 11.95 (*0-917430-03-4*) Montaigne.

Learning Age: A Renaissance for a New Britain. LC 98-207492. (Command Papers: Series 81011068, No. 3790). 1998. 25.00 (*0-10-137902-1*, HM79021, Pub. by Statnry Office) Bernan Associates.

Learning Algebra Was Never More Exciting! Algebra Interactive! A. M. Cohen et al. LC 99-40882. 80p. 1999. 39.95 incl. cd-rom (*3-540-65368-6*) Spr-Verlag.

Learning Algebra with Derive. Cheryl Wallgren. (Adaptable Courseware Ser.). 1996. 12.50 (*0-534-49697-0*) Brooks-Cole.

Learning Algorithms: Theory & Applications in Signal Processing. Phil Mars et al. LC 96-26721. 240p. 1996. boxed set 84.95 (*0-8493-7896-6*, 7896) CRC Pr.

Learning Algorithms Theory & Applications. S. Lakshmivarahan. 279p. 1981. 76.95 (*0-387-90640-1*) Spr-Verlag.

Learning All Day: Curriculum for Infants & Toddlers. Donna Couchenour. (Bright Ideas Ser.). 20p. (Orig.). (C). 1994. pap. text 3.00 (*0-942388-14-3*) So Early Chldhood Assn.

Learning All the Time. John Holt. 1990. pap. 12.00 (*0-201-55091-1*) Addison-Wesley.

Learning Alliance: Systems Thinking in Human Resource Development. Robert O. Brinkerhoff & Stephen J. Gill. LC 94-11716. (Management Ser.). 208p. 1994. text 29.95 (*1-55542-711-1*) Jossey-Bass.

***Learning Alliances: Tapping into Talent.** David Clutterbuck. 160p. 2000. pap. 56.95 (*0-8464-5103-4*) Beekman Pubs.

Learning Alternatives in U. S. Education: Where Student & Computer Meet. Beverly Hunter et al. LC 74-31417. 424p. 1975. 49.95 (*0-87778-078-1*) Educ Tech Pubns.

Learning American English. 2nd ed. Grant Taylor. (Saxon Series in English As a Second Language). (C). 1962. pap. text 19.74 (*0-07-062941-2*) McGraw.

Learning American History: Critical Skills for the Survey Course. Michael J. Salevouris & Conal Furay. LC 96-43462. (Illus.). 175p. (C). 1997. pap. text 21.95 (*0-88295-920-4*) Harlan Davidson.

Learning American Sign Language. Humphries. 1992. text 80.60 incl. VHS (*0-13-529801-6*) P-H.

Learning American Sign Language. Tom L. Humphries & Carol A. Padden. 350p. 1992. pap. 51.00 (*0-13-528571-2*) P-H.

Learning & Applying APL. B. Legrand. Tr. by Julian G. Matthews. LC 83-10620. 414p. reprint ed. pap. 128.40 (*0-608-17857-8*, 203265900080) Bks Demand.

Learning & Automated Discovery in AI Systems. Richard K. Miller & Terri C. Walker. LC 88-81889. (Survey on Technology & Markets Ser.: No. 88). 50p. 1989. pap. text 200.00 (*1-55865-087-3*) Future Tech Surveys.

Learning & Awareness. Ference Marton & Shirley Booth. LC 96-46002. (Educational Psychology Ser.). 240p. 1997. 49.95 (*0-8058-2454-5*); pap. 24.95 (*0-8058-2455-3*) L Erlbaum Assocs.

Learning & Behavior. Paul Chance. (C). 1979. mass mkt. 17.75 (*0-534-00700-7*) Brooks-Cole.

Learning & Behavior. 2nd ed. Paul Chance. 330p. (C). 1987. mass mkt. 46.00 (*0-534-08508-3*) Brooks-Cole.

Learning & Behavior. 3rd ed. Paul Chance. LC 93-2435. 1993. pap. 46.50 (*0-534-17394-2*) Brooks-Cole.

Learning & Behavior. 3rd ed. Paul Chance. 1993. pap., teacher ed. write for info. (*0-534-17395-0*) Brooks-Cole.

Learning & Behavior. 3rd ed. Paul Chance. 1995. student ed. write for info. (*0-534-33848-8*) Brooks-Cole.

Learning & Behavior. 4th ed. Paul Chance. LC 98-22400. (Psychology Ser.). 1998. pap. 66.95 (*0-534-34691-X*) Brooks-Cole.

Learning & Behavior. 4th ed. James Mazur. LC 97-12807. 433p. 1997. 73.00 (*0-13-857566-5*) P-H.

Learning & Behavior: Biological, Psychological & Sociocultural Perspectives. 2nd ed. Lewis M. Barker. LC 96-23094. 566p. (C). 1996. 79.00 (*0-13-256975-2*) P-H.

Learning & Behavior Therapy. Ed. by William O'Donohue. LC 97-10769. 568p. (C). 1997. 86.00 (*0-205-18609-2*) Allyn.

Learning & Behaviour. Powell. (Psychology Ser.). 2000. pap. 38.00 (*0-534-36585-X*) Brooks-Cole.

Learning & Categorization in Modular Neural Networks. Jacob Murre. 250p. 1992. pap. 29.95 (*0-8058-1338-1*); text 49.95 (*0-8058-1337-3*) L Erlbaum Assocs.

Learning & Change in the Adult Years: A Developmental Perspective. Mark Tennant & Philip Pogson. LC 94-42160. (Higher & Adult Education Ser.). 238p. 1995. text 32.95 (*0-7879-0082-6*) Jossey-Bass.

Learning & Change, the Problems of Evaulation in Liberal Adult Education. John Wesley Powell. 1960. 2.50 (*0-87060-084-2*, PUC 12) Syracuse U Cont Ed.

Learning & Cognition. 4th ed. Richard J. Harris & Thomas H. Leahey. 526p. (C). 1996. 82.00 (*0-13-235268-0*) P-H.

Learning & Cognition in Autism. Eric Schopler & Gary B. Mesibov. (Critical Issues in Autism Ser.). (Illus.). 368p. (C). 1995. 59.00 (*0-306-44871-8*, Plenum Trade) Perseus Pubng.

Learning & Cognition in Later Life. Ed. by Frank Glendenning. (Studies in Educational Gerontology). 160p. 1996. 55.95 (*1-85742-263-5*, Pub. by Arena) Ashgate Pub Co.

Learning & Cognition in the Mentally Retarded. Ed. by Penelope Brooks et al. LC 84-10289. 576p. 1984. text 115.00 (*0-89859-374-3*) L Erlbaum Assocs.

Learning & Complex Behavior. John W. Donahoe et al. LC 93-22625. 480p. 1993. 88.00 (*0-205-13996-5*) Allyn.

Learning & Comprehension of Text. Ed. by Heinz Mandl et al. LC 83-14050. (Illus.). 470p. reprint ed. pap. 145.70 (*0-8357-4211-3*, 203698800003) Bks Demand.

Learning & Computational Neuroscience: Foundations of Adaptive Networks. Michael Gabriel & John Moore. 650p. 1991. 62.00 (*0-262-07102-9*) MIT Pr.

Learning & Coordination: Enhancing Agent Performance Through Distributed Decision-Making. Steven H. Kim. LC 94-30344. (International Series on Microprocessor-Based & Intelligent Systems Engineering). 1994. text 156.00 (*0-7923-3046-3*) Kluwer Academic.

Learning & Creating with Heartland Cooking. Clara Wiens. 210p. 1995. spiral bd. 13.95 (*1-882420-22-5*) Hearth KS.

Learning & Creative Problem Solving: Principles, Processes & Practices. Rosemary J. Stevenson. Ed. by Cedric Cullingford. (Children, Teachers & Learning Ser.). 192p. 1994. pap. text 33.95 (*0-304-32563-5*) Continuum.

Learning & Culture: American Ethnological Society Proceedings, 1972. Ed. by Solon T. Kimball & Jacquetta H. Burnett. LC 84-45508. 1988. reprint ed. pap. 65.00 (*0-404-62666-1*) AMS Pr.

Learning & Development. Strauss. (Educational Psychology Ser.: Vol. 28, No. 3). 1993. 20.00 (*0-8058-9987-1*) L Erlbaum Assocs.

Learning & Development: A Global Perspective. Ed. by Alan M. Thomas & Edward W. Ploman. LC 86-148508. (Ontario Institute for Studies in Education, Symposium Ser.: No. 15). 248p. reprint ed. pap. 76.90 (*0-7837-2045-9*, 204231600003) Bks Demand.

Learning & Development: Making Connections to Enhance Teaching. Sharon L. Silverman. LC 99-6611. 1999. 32.95 (*0-7879-4463-7*) Jossey-Bass.

An Asterisk (*) at the beginning of an entry indicates that the title is appearing for the first time.

Learning & Development in School: Cultural, Neurological & Psychological Aspects. Elvira S. Lima. Tr. by M. G. Lima. 32p. 1999. pap. 3.25 (*0-9662298-4-3*) Alba Bk Co.

Learning & Education: Psychoanalytic Perspectives. Ed. by Kay H. Field et al. LC 89-35513. (Emotions & Behavior Monographs: No. 6). 1030p. 1990. 90.00 (*0-8236-2954-6*) Intl Univs Pr.

Learning & Emotion: A Biological Synthesis. P. J. Livesey. 328p. (C). 1986. text 59.95 (*0-89859-552-5*) L Erlbaum Assocs.

Learning & Freedom: Policy, Pedagogy, & Paradigms in Indian Education & Schooling. John Shotton. LC 97-32072. 209p. 1998. write for info. (*0-7619-9220-0*); pap. write for info. (*0-7619-9221-9*) Sage.

Learning & Geometry. Ed. by David Kueker & Carl Smith. (Progress in Computer Science & Applied Logic Ser.: Vol. 14). 1995. write for info. (*3-7643-3825-3*) Birkhauser.

Learning & Geometry: Computational Approaches. Ed. by David Kueker & Carl Smith. (Progress in Computer Science & Applied Logic Ser.: Vol. 14). 210p. 1995. 71.00 (*0-8176-3825-3*) Birkhauser.

Learning & Growing Through Tutoring. Bruce Dollar. 130p. 1974. pap. 5.00 (*0-912041-07-2*) Natl Comm Res Youth.

***Learning & Growing Together: Understanding Your Child's Development.** Claire Lerner & Amy Dombro. Ed. by Karen Levine. 56p. 2000. pap. 15.00 (*0-943657-05-9*) ZERO TO THREE.

Learning & Hatred for Meaning. Hugo Kuyper Letiche. 263p. 1984. pap. 33.00 (*90-272-2016-6*) J Benjamins Pubng Co.

Learning & Individual Differences. Phillip L. Ackerman. LC 88-16317. (Psychology Ser.). 343p. (C). 1989. pap. text 27.95 (*0-7167-1985-1*) W H Freeman.

Learning & Individual Differences: Process, Trait, & Content Determinants. Ed. by Phillip L. Ackerman et al. LC 98-31084. 1998. 49.95 (*1-55798-536-7*) Am Psychol.

Learning & Innovation in Economic Development: Selected Essays. Linsu Kim. LC 98-53413. (New Horizons in the Economics of Innovation Ser.). 288p. 1999. 90.00 (*1-84064-026-X*) E Elgar.

Learning & Instruction. Richard Hamilton & Elizabeth Ghatala. LC 93-21680. 448p. (C). 1994. 68.13 (*0-07-023163-X*) McGraw.

Learning & Instruction. Ed. by Merlin C. Wittrock. LC 76-18038. (Readings in Educational Research Ser.). 1977. 46.00 (*0-8211-2255-X*) McCutchan.

Learning & Instruction: A Publication of the European Association of Learning & Instruction. Ed. by Erik De Corte et al. (Illus.). 330p. 1987. 217.00 (*0-08-034769-X*) Franklin.

Learning & Instruction: European Research in an International Context, Vol. 1. Ed. by E. De Corte et al. (Studia Paedagogica: No. 8). 490p. (Orig.). 1987. pap. 57.50 (*90-6186-206-X*, Pub. by Leuven Univ) Coronet Bks.

Learning & Instruction: European Research in an International Context, Vols. 2.1 & 2.2. Ed. by Erik De Corte et al. 712p. 1990. 206.25 (*0-08-040252-6*, Pergamon Pr) Elsevier.

***Learning & Instruction: Theory into Practice.** Margaret E. Gredler. LC 00-36175. 448p. 2000. 68.00 (*0-13-012227-0*, Merrill Coll) P-H.

Learning & Instruction: Theory into Practice. 3rd ed. Margaret E. Gredler. LC 96-8123. 387p. (C). 1996. 71.00 (*0-13-248288-6*) P-H.

Learning & Instruction Vol. 3: European Research in an International Context: Selected Proceedings of the 1989 European Conference for Research on Learning & Instruction. Ed. by Mario Carretero et al. 614p. 1992. text 129.50 (*0-08-041039-1*, Pergamon Pr) Elsevier.

Learning & Instruction: Hyperties. Kearsley. (Education Ser.). 1999. pap., suppl. ed. 24.95 (*0-534-22104-1*) Wadsworth Pub.

Learning & Instruction in Simulation Environments. Douglas M. Towne. LC 94-16154. 350p. 1995. 44.95 (*0-87778-278-4*) Educ Tech Pubns.

Learning & Intelligence: Conversations with Skinner & Wheeler. Maureen Lapan & Raymond Houghton. 142p. 1995. 37.50 (*0-7165-2584-4*, Pub. by Irish Acad Pr) Intl Spec Bk.

***Learning & Knowledge Management in the Firm: From Knowledge Accumulation to Strategic Capabilities.** Gabriela Dutrenit. LC 99-41929. (New Horizons in the Economics of Innovation Ser.). 352p. 2000. 100.00 (*1-84064-204-1*) E Elgar.

***Learning & Libraries in an Information Age: Principles & Practice.** Ed. by Barbara K. Stripling. LC 99-45329. (Principles & Practice Ser.). 375p. 1999. pap. 39.00 (*1-56308-666-2*) Libs Unl.

Learning & Living: Academic Essays. Ephraim Emerton. LC 67-30209. (Essay Index Reprint Ser.). 1977. 20.95 (*0-8369-0416-8*) Ayer.

Learning & Living: How Asset-Building for Youth Can Unify a School's Mission. Eugene C. Roehlkepartain & Donald Draayer. (Everyone's an Asset-Builder Ser.). 16p. 1998. pap. 3.95 (*1-57482-331-0*) Search Inst.

Learning & Living God's Word. Daniel J. Estes. LC 93-42420. 80p. 1993. 4.95 (*0-87227-181-1*, RBP5218) Reg Baptist.

Learning & Loving It: Theme Studies in the Classroom. Ruth Gamberg et al. LC 87-28559. 244p. (Orig.). (C). 1988. pap. text 24.00 (*0-435-08454-2*, 08454) Heinemann.

Learning & Loving, 1790-1960: A Study in the History of the English Adult Education Movement. J. F. Harrison. (Modern Revivals in Economic & Social History Ser.). 440p. (C). 1994. text 75.95 (*0-7512-0285-1*, Pub. by Gregg Revivals) Ashgate Pub Co.

Learning & Loving to Read: The Breakthrough That Ushers Your Child into the Fantastic World of Reading-Through Play! Jill F. Hauser. LC 85-80280. (Illus.). 112p. (Orig.). 1990. pap. 12.95 (*0-934657-03-3*) Learning Excell.

Learning & Memory. Barry Schwartz & Daniel Reisberg. (Illus.). 663p. (C). 1991. text 68.25 (*0-393-95911-2*) Norton.

Learning & Memory. Terry. LC 99-38441. 461p. 1999. 64.00 (*0-205-31408-2*) Allyn.

Learning & Memory. Richard F. Thompson. (Readings from the Encyclopedia of Neuroscience Ser.). 135p. 1989. 38.00 (*0-8176-3393-6*) Birkhauser.

Learning & Memory. 2nd ed. Gordon Staff. (Psychology Ser.). 2000. mass mkt. 38.00 (*0-534-16914-7*) Brooks-Cole.

Learning & Memory: A Biological View. 2nd ed. Ed. by Joe L. Martinez, Jr. & Raymond P. Kesner. (Illus.). 563p. 1991. text 104.00 (*0-12-474992-5*); pap. text 53.00 (*0-12-474993-3*) Acad Pr.

Learning & Memory: An Integrated Approach. John R. Anderson. LC 94-14189. 504p. 1994. text 80.95 (*0-471-58685-4*) Wiley.

***Learning & Memory: An Integrated Approach.** 2nd ed. John R. Anderson. LC 99-32553. 512p. 1999. text 77.95 (*0-471-24925-4*) Wiley.

Learning & Memory: Major Ideas, Principles, Issues & Applications. Robert W. Howard. LC 94-180177. 256p. 1995. 59.95 (*0-275-94641-X*, Praeger Pubs) Greenwood.

Learning & Memory: Mechanisms of Information Storage in the Nervous System. Ed. by H. Matthies. 427p. 1986. 120.00 (*0-08-034186-1*, H222, H223, Pergamon Pr) Elsevier.

Learning & Memory: Test Items. William C. Gordon. 1989. mass mkt. write for info. (*0-534-09499-6*) Brooks-Cole.

Learning & Memory: The Behavioral & Biological Substrates. Ed. by Isidore Gormezano & Edward A. Wasserman. 424p. 1992. text 89.95 (*0-8058-0888-4*) L Erlbaum Assocs.

***Learning & Memory: The Brain in Action.** Marilee Sprenger. LC 99-6551. 113p. 1999. pap. 21.95 (*0-87120-350-2*, 199213) ASCD.

Learning & Memory in Normal Aging. Donald H. Kausler. LC 93-43189. (Illus.). 544p. 1994. text 79.95 (*0-12-402655-9*) Acad Pr.

Learning & Memory of Knowledge & Skills: Durability & Specificity. Ed. by Alice F. Healy & Lyle E. Bourne, Jr. 400p. 1994. 58.00 (*0-8039-5758-0*); pap. 26.95 (*0-8039-5759-9*) Sage.

Learning & Motivation in the Classroom. Ed. by Scott G. Paris et al. LC 83-8962. 347p. reprint ed. pap. 107.60 (*0-7837-2424-1*, 204257100005) Bks Demand.

Learning & Obeying God's Word with Obedience the Bumblebee. Jeryl L. Bratcher. (Illus.). 24p. (Orig.). (J). (ps-4). 1997. pap. write for info. (*1-890192-00-7*) Obedience Ministry.

Learning & Other Essays. John J. Chapman. LC 68-16918. (Essay Index Reprint Ser.). 1977. 19.95 (*0-8369-0290-4*) Ayer.

Learning & Other Things: The History of Education in South Australia. Bob Mossel. 496p. (C). 1989. pap. text 60.00 (*0-89771-025-8*, Pub. by Bob Mossel) St Mut.

Learning & Persuasion in the German Middle Ages: The Call to Judgment. Ernst R. Hintz. Ed. by Chistopher Kleinhenz & Paul Szarmach. LC 97-12532. (Garland Studies in Medieval Literature: No. 15). 216p. 1997. text 50.00 (*0-8153-2182-1*) Garland.

Learning & Physiological Regulation. Barry R. Dworkin. LC 92-564. (John D. & Catherine T. MacArthur Foundation Series on Mental Health & Development). (Illus.). 232p. (C). 1993. 26.50 (*0-226-17600-2*) U Ch Pr.

Learning & Practicing Econometrics. William E. Griffiths et al. LC 92-22788. 896p. (C). 1993. text 92.95 (*0-471-51364-4*) Wiley.

Learning & Practicing Econometrics: S&S Handbook. William E. Griffiths. 408p. 1993. pap. 34.95 incl. disk (*0-471-58553-X*) Wiley.

Learning & Psychosomatic Approach to the Nature & Treatment of Illness: 18th Annual Conference of the Society for Psychosomatic Research. Ed. by Peter G. Mellett. 1977. pap. 53.00 (*0-08-020881-9*, Pergamon Pr) Elsevier.

Learning & Reality: Reflections on Trends in Adult Learning. Robert A. Feilenz & Gary J. Conti. 1989. 5.25 (*0-317-03010-8*, IN336) Ctr Educ Trng Employ.

Learning & Reasoning with Complex Representations: PRICAI '96 Workshops on Reasoning with Incomplete & Changing Information & on Inducing Complex Representations, Cairns, Australia, August 26-30, 1996, Selected Papers. Ed. by G. Antoniou et al. LC 98-18108. (Lecture Notes in Artificial Intelligence Ser.: Vol. 1359). x, 283p. 1998. pap. 49.00 (*3-540-64413-X*) Spr-Verlag.

Learning & Recognition: A Modern Approach. Ed. by K. H. Zhao et al. 304p. (C). 1989. text 129.00 (*9971-5-0787-0*) World Scientific Pub.

***Learning & Remembering: How New & Old Brains Acquire & Recall Information: Recent Discoveries, Practical Applications, Performance Tests, Skill-Building Exercises from Infancy to Old-Age.** Allen D. Bragdon & David Gamon. (Illus.). 128p. 2000. pap. 7.95 (*0-916410-69-2*, Pub. by A D Bragdon) IPG Chicago.

Learning & Remembering from Text: Buttonhole Your Buddy. Donna Litherland. (Illus.). 14p. 1983. pap. text 1.50 (*0-9607888-1-6*) Barney Pr.

Learning & Self-Governing: Questions on the Future of Democracy in America. George Beecher. LC 94-31043. 192p. 1994. 20.00 (*0-912362-12-X*) Adamant Pr.

Learning & Sociological Profiles of Canadian High School Students: An Overview of 15-18 Year Olds & Educational Policy Implications for Dropouts, Exceptional Students, Employed Students, Immigrant Students & Native Youth. Ed. by Paul Anisef. LC 93-32121. 564p. 1993. text 119.95 (*0-7734-9347-6*) E Mellen.

***Learning & Soft Computing: With Support Vector Machines, Neural Networks & Fuzzy Logic Models.** V. Kecman. LC 00-27506. (Complex Adaptive Systems Ser.). 2001. write for info. (*0-262-11255-8*) MIT Pr.

Learning & Strategic Product Innovation: Theory & Evidence for the Semiconductor Industry. Harald Gruber. LC 93-46838. (Studies in Mathematical & Managerial Economics: Vol. 37). 210p. 1994. 113.75 (*0-444-81774-3*, North Holland) Elsevier.

Learning & Study Strategies: Issues in Assessment, Instruction, & Evaluation. Ed. by Claire E. Weinstein et al. (Educational Psychology Ser.). 353p. 1988. text 79.95 (*0-12-742460-1*) Acad Pr.

Learning & Study Strategies Inventory. Claire E. Weinstein & David R. Palmer. 1987. pap. 4.00 (*0-13-031417-X*) Prntice Hall Bks.

Learning & Study Strategies Inventory (LASSI) 2nd ed. Weinstein. (C). 1997. pap. text 4.00 (*0-205-28672-0*) Allyn.

Learning & Studying: Research Perspective. James Hartley. LC 98-167110. (Psychology Focus Ser.). (Illus.). 192p. (C). 1998. 50.00 (*0-415-16851-1*); pap. 16.99 (*0-415-16852-X*) Routledge.

Learning & Talking: A Practical Guide to Oracy Across the Curriculum. Ray Tarleton. LC 88-29874. (Illus.). 173p. reprint ed. pap. 53.70 (*0-608-20389-0*, 207164200002) Bks Demand.

Learning & Teaching: A Programmed Introduction. E. Stones. LC 68-29147. (Illus.). 124p. reprint ed. pap. 38.50 (*0-608-17587-0*, 203042800069) Bks Demand.

Learning & Teaching: Research-Based Methods. 3rd ed. Donald P. Kauchak & Paul D. Eggen. LC 96-53838. 432p. 1997. pap. text 61.00 (*0-205-27089-1*) Allyn.

Learning & Teaching Cognitive Skills. Glen Evans. (C). 1992. pap. 29.95 (*0-86431-094-3*, Pub. by Aust Council Educ Res) Stylus Pub VA.

Learning & Teaching for Continuous Assessment. Michael E. Obinna. LC 97-158430. 88p. 1996. pap. 17.95 (*3-906751-01-5*, Pub. by P Lang) P Lang Pubng.

Learning & Teaching Genre. Ed. by Aviva Freedman & Peter Medway. LC 94-17147. 266p. 1994. pap. text 22.50 (*0-86709-344-7*, 0344, Pub. by Boynton Cook Pubs) Heinemann.

Learning & Teaching in Distance Education: Analyses & Interpretations from an International Perspective. Otto Peters. LC 99-234365. (Illus.). 320p. 65.00 (*0-7494-2855-4*, Kogan Pg Educ) Stylus Pub VA.

Learning & Teaching in Higher: The Experience in Higher Education. M. Prosser. LC 98-23978. 1998. pap. 115.00 (*0-335-19832-5*) OpUniv Pr.

Learning & Teaching in Physical Education. Ed. by Colin C. Hardy & Mick Mawer. LC 99-231297. 232p. 1999. 79.00 (*0-7507-0875-1*, Falmer Pr); pap. text 26.95 (*0-7507-0874-3*, Falmer Pr) Taylor & Francis.

Learning & Teaching in School Sciences: Practical Alternatives. Di Bentley & Mike Watts. 192p. 1989. 110.00 (*0-335-09514-3*); pap. 33.95 (*0-335-09513-5*) OpUniv Pr.

Learning & Teaching in Social Work: Towards Reflective Practice. Ed. by Margaret Yelloly & Mary Henkel. 220p. 1995. pap. 27.00 (*1-85302-237-3*) Taylor & Francis.

Learning & Teaching Mathematics: An International Perspective. Terezinha Nunes & Peter Bryant. LC 97-202039. (Illus.). xiv, 443p. 1997. write for info. (*0-86377-454-7*, Pub. by Psychol Pr) Taylor & Francis.

Learning & Teaching of Foreign Languages. Caleb Gattegno. 45p. 1985. pap. 5.95 (*0-87825-186-3*) Ed Solutions.

Learning & Teaching Style: In Theory & Practice. 2nd ed. Kathleen A. Butler. (Illus.). 318p. (Orig.). 1988. pap. text 32.95 (*0-945852-00-2*, 10) Learners Dimension.

Learning & Teaching the Ways of Knowing. Ed. by Elliot W. Eisner. (National Society for the Study of Education Publication Ser.: No. 84). 320p. 1985. pap. text 12.95 (*0-226-60087-4*) U Ch Pr.

Learning & Teaching the Ways of Knowing: 84th Yearbook, Pt. II. Elliot W. Eisner. LC 84-62254. (National Society for the Study of Education Publication Ser.). 320p. (C). 1985. lib. bdg. 20.00 (*0-226-60140-4*) U Ch Pr.

Learning & Teaching Therapy. Jay Haley. LC 95-50953. (Family Therapy Ser.). 235p. 1996. lib. bdg. 32.00 (*1-57230-035-3*) Guilford Pubns.

Learning & the Marketplace: A Philosophical, Cross-Cultural (And Occasionally Irreverent) Guide for Business & Academe. Alison Kirk. LC 96-13122. 1996. 39.95 (*0-8093-2092-4*); pap. 19.95 (*0-8093-2068-1*) S Ill U Pr.

Learning & the Role of the Trainer. IPM Staff. (Training Delivery Ser.: No. 2). (C). 1994. pap. 93.00 (*0-08-042158-X*, Pub. by IPM Hse) St Mut.

Learning & Thinking Styles: Classroom Interaction. Barbara Z. Presseisen. 160p. 1990. pap. 15.95 (*0-8106-1841-9*) NEA.

Learning & Understanding Personal Computers . . . A Simplified Guide: A Simplified Guide. Terry R. Keiser. 132p. (Orig.). 1994. pap. 24.95 (*0-87218-130-8*) Natl Underwriter.

Learning & Using C++ Gail Anderson. LC 97-27828. 800p. (C). 1997. pap. text 49.95 (*0-13-532748-2*) P-H.

Learning & Using Clarisworks, Including Clarisworks 2.0. Short. (DF - Computer Applications Ser.). 1996. mass mkt. 36.25 (*0-314-04286-5*) West Pub.

Learning & Using Communication Theory. 4th ed. John Little. (Speech & Theater Ser.). 1992. pap., student ed. 12.25 (*0-534-16135-9*) Wadsworth Pub.

Learning & Using Japanese Numbers, 2 cass., Set. Rita L. Lampkin. (JPN.). 96p. 1996. 19.95 incl. audio (*0-8442-8520-X*, Natl Textbk Co) NTC Contemp Pub Co.

Learning & Using Japanese Numbers: Beginning Through Intermediate. Rita Lampkin. LC 96-151824. (JPN.). 96p. (C). pap., student ed. 10.95 (*0-8442-8439-4*, E8439-4) NTC Contemp Pub Co.

Learning & Using Microsoft Works, Microsoft DOS. Short. 1992. mass mkt., student ed. 19.75 (*0-314-01285-0*) West Pub.

Learning & Work: An Exploration in Industrial Ethnography. Charles N. Darrah. LC 95-42416. (Studies in Education & Culture: No. 8). 200p. 1996. text 44.00 (*0-8153-1455-8*, SS1069) Garland.

***Learning & Work in the Risk Society: Lessons for the Labour Market.** Karen Evans. LC 99-88693. 200p. 2000. text 65.00 (*0-312-23160-1*) St Martin.

Learning & Working: Basics for Children. Dorothy Rich. 96p. (Orig.). 1996. pap. 15.95 (*0-8106-2002-2*, 2002-2) NEA.

Learning Annex Guide to Driving Your Woman Wild in Bed. Compiled by Susan Wright. 1992. pap. 8.95 (*0-8065-1331-4*, Citadel Pr) Carol Pub Group.

Learning Annex Guide to Getting Successfully Published: From Typewriter to Royalty Checks: All You Need to Know! Ray Mungo. 256p. 1992. pap. 10.95 (*0-8065-1371-3*, Citadel Pr) Carol Pub Group.

Learning Annex Guide to Starting Your Own Import-Export Business. Compiled by Karen Offitzer. 108p. 1992. pap. 8.95 (*0-8065-1321-7*, Citadel Pr) Carol Pub Group.

Learning Another Language Through Actions. 6th ed. James J. Asher. 278p. 1993. pap. text 15.95 (*1-56018-301-2*) Sky Oaks Prodns.

Learning APOLLO: Basic & Advanced Training. Talula A. Guntner. LC 93-25400. (C). 1993. pap. 41.75 (*0-538-70894-8*) S-W Pub.

Learning APOLLO: Basic & Advanced Training. Talula A. Guntner. 288p. 1994. pap., teacher ed. write for info. (*0-538-70895-6*) S-W Pub.

Learning Approach to Change. Ken Griffiths & Richard Williams. LC 97-26542. 1998. 96.95 (*0-566-07729-9*, Pub. by Gower) Ashgate Pub Co.

Learning Arabic: A Step by Step Approach. Mohi E. Saleh. 1993. pap. 12.00 (*0-89259-129-3*) Am Trust Pubns.

Learning Architectural Drafting. Nicholas Garcia & Diana Pratt-Howe. 192p. 1992. pap. 29.95 (*0-8273-4633-6*) Delmar.

Learning Architectural Drafting & Design Instructors Guide. Nicholas B. Garcia & Susan P. Howe. 1992. pap. 16.00 (*0-8273-4634-4*) Delmar.

Learning Architecture for the 21st Century: The Ecological, Futures & Global Education Field Book. Barbara Barnes. (Illus.). 288p. 1998. pap. text 34.95 (*1-58000-029-0*) Griffin CA.

Learning Arithmetic Using the Graphing Calculator. T. Patrick Burke. (Illus.). vi, 400p. 1997. spiral bd. 45.00 (*0-9657238-0-1*) Calculator Trning.

Learning As a Behavioral Adaptation. Frieman. (Psychology Ser.). 2000. mass mkt. 52.95 (*0-534-34226-4*) Brooks-Cole.

***Learning As a Political Act: Struggles for Learning & Learning from Struggles.** Ed. by Jose A. Segarra & Ricardo Dobles. (Reprint Ser.: Vol. R32). 370p. (C). 1999. pap. 22.95 (*0-916690-35-0*) Harvard Educ Rev.

Learning As a Way of Being: Strategies for Survival in a World of Permanent White Water. Peter B. Vaill. (Business & Management Ser.). 230p. 1996. 23.50 (*0-7879-0246-2*) Jossey-Bass.

Learning As Self-Organization. Ed. by Karl H. Pribram & Joseph King. (INNS Series of Texts, Monographs, & Proceedings). 608p. (C). 1996. pap. 125.00 (*0-8058-2586-X*) L Erlbaum Assocs.

***Learning as Transformation: Critical Perspectives on a Theory in Progress.** Jack Mezirow. LC 00-9158. (Higher & Adult Education Ser.). 2000. 38.95 (*0-7879-4845-4*) Jossey-Bass.

Learning Assessment Journal. 2nd ed. Sarah M. Carroll & Steve W. Beyerlein. Ed. by Eric Wignall. (Illus.). 144p. (C). 1996. pap. text 12.00 (*1-878437-07-0*) Pac Crest Soft.

Learning Assistance & Development Education: A Guide for Effective Practice. Martha E. Casazza & Sharon L. Silverman. LC 95-45303. (Higher & Adult Education Ser.). 256p. 1996. 34.95 (*0-7879-0211-X*) Jossey-Bass.

Learning Asymetrix Toolbook II 6.5: A Self-Paced Guide. John E. Hilbort. Ed. by N. Joy Flasch. (Illus.). 242p. (C). 1998. pap. 39.95 (*1-893485-02-1*) Teletraining Inst.

Learning Asymetrix Toolbook II Assistant 6.5: A Self-Paced Guide. John E. Hilbert. Ed. by N. Joy Flasch. (Illus.). 235p. 1998. pap. 39.95 (*1-893485-01-3*) Teletraining Inst.

Learning at Home: Preschool & Kindergarten. 2nd ed. Ann Ward. 303p. 1988. pap. 49.95 (*0-923463-02-X*) Noble Pub Assocs.

Learning at Home: The Parent, Teacher, Child Alliance. Alex Griffiths & Dorothy Hamilton. 112p. (Orig.). (C). 1990. pap. write for info. (*0-416-97250-0*, AO479, Methuen Drama) Methn.

L

L

Learning at the Back Door: Reflections on Non-Traditional Learning in the Lifespan. Charles A. Wedemeyer. LC 80-52301. 286p. 1981. 24.95 (*0-299-08560-0*) U of Wis Pr.

Learning at the Top. Alan Mumford. LC 95-790. 1995. 19.95 (*0-07-709066-7*) McGraw.

Learning at Work. Sylvia Downs. 130p. 1995. pap. 15.95 (*0-7494-1526-6*, Kogan Pg Educ) Stylus Pub VA.

***Learning at Work: The Learning Organization in Practice.** Brian Blundell et al. 288p. 2000. pap. 37.50 (*0-7494-2788-4*, Pub. by Kogan Page Ltd) Stylus Pub VA.

Learning at Work in a Work-Based Welfare System: Lessons from the School-to-Work Experience. Judith Combes Taylor & Jobs for the Future, Inc. Staff. LC 98-143580. ii, 74 p. 1997. write for info. (*1-887410-86-4*) Jobs for Future.

Learning at Your Fingertips: Brainpackages for Reading, Writing, & Thinking. Steven Hryvniak. (Illus.). 180p. (Orig.). 1997. pap. 14.95 (*1-56072-344-0*, Nova Kroshka Bks) Nova Sci Pubs.

Learning AutoCAD in Twenty Projects. Hossein Assadipour. Ed. by Conty. LC 93-39996. 500p. (C). 1994. pap. text 38.25 (*0-314-02837-4*) West Pub.

Learning Autocad LT for Windows 95: A CADD Desktop Tutor Interactive CD-Rom. Autodesk Press Staff. 21.95 (*0-7668-0269-8*, Pub. by Delmar) Thomson Learn.

Learning Automata: Theory Applications. Kaddour Najim & Alexandr S. Poznyak. LC 94-19346. 238p. 1994. text 107.50 (*0-08-042024-9*, Pergamon Pr) Elsevier.

Learning Automata & Stochastic Optimization, Vol. 225. Alexander S. Poznyak & K. Najim. LC 97-1897. (Lecture Notes in Control & Information Sciences). 1997. pap. 50.00 (*3-540-76154-3*) Spr-Verlag.

Learning Aysemetrix Toolbook II Assistant & Instructor: A Self-Paced Guide to Version 6.0 & 6.1a. John E. Hilbert. Ed. by N. Joy Flasch. (Illus.). 231p. 1998. pap. 39.95 (*1-893485-00-5*) Teletraining Inst.

Learning Banking. Ed. by CIB Staff. (C). 1989. 50.00 (*0-85297-216-4*, Pub. by Chartered Bank) St Mut.

Learning Banking: A Guide to Study, Revision & Examination Techniques. Keith Elliot et al. 1987. 35.00 (*0-85297-154-0*, Pub. by Chartered Bank) St Mut.

Learning Basic Drafting Using Pencil Sketches & AutoCAD. Kirkpatrick. LC 98-38416. 472p. 1998. pap. text 47.00 (*0-13-862095-4*) P-H.

Learning Basic Math & Business Math. 2nd ed. Barbara Muncaster. (MB - Business/Vocational Math Ser.). 1991. mass mkt. 25.95 (*0-538-60815-3*) S-W Pub.

Learning, Behavior & Cognition. 3rd ed. David A. Lieberman. LC 99-36080. (Psychology Ser.). 595p. 1999. mass mkt. 81.95 (*0-534-33925-5*) Brooks-Cole.

Learning Beyond the Classroom. Tom Bentley. LC 98-19892. 208p. (C). (gr. 13). 1998. pap. 24.99 (*0-415-18259-X*, D5920) Routledge.

***Learning Bible.** (Illus.). 2000. 39.95 (*1-58516-017-2*) Am Bible.

***Learning Bible.** American Bible Society Staff. (Illus.). 2000. pap. text 34.95 (*1-58516-025-3*) Am Bible.

Learning Biology with Plant Pathology. Juliet E. Carroll. 1994. 8.00 (*0-941212-16-5*) Natl Assn Bio Tchrs.

Learning Block. Dean E. Grass. 152p. (Orig.). (C). 1981. pap. 6.95 (*0-930298-10-1*) Westwood Pub Co.

Learning Brain. Eric Jensen. LC 94-231770. (Illus.). 368p. 1995. write for info. (*0-9637832-2-X*) Brain Store.

Learning Business Statistics with Microsoft Excel 97. 2nd ed. John L. Neufeld. LC 98-11985. 436p. (C). 1998. pap. text 36.00 (*0-13-923442-X*) P-H.

Learning by All Means: Lessons from the Arts: A Study in the Philosophy of Education. Vernon A. Howard. 158p. 1992. pap. 19.95 (*0-8204-1897-8*) P Lang Pubng.

Learning by All Means: Lessons from the Arts: A Study in the Philosophy of Education. Vernon A. Howard. LC 91-47625. 158p. (C). 1992. text 35.95 (*0-8204-1570-7*) P Lang Pubng.

Learning by Building: Design & Construction in Architectural Education. William Carpenter. LC 96-49073. (Architecture Ser.). (C). 1997. pap. 39.95 (*0-442-02350-2*, VNR) Wiley.

Learning by Building: Design & Construction in Architectural Education. William J. Carpenter. 180p. 1997. pap. 49.95 (*0-471-28793-8*, VNR) Wiley.

Learning by Coloring: Mini-Book Set Linking Beginning Skill with Self-Esteem. (J). (ps-2). 5.98 (*0-89544-315-5*, 315) Silbert Bress.

Learning by Discovery: A Lab Manual for Calculus. Ed. by Anita Solow. LC 92-62279. (Resources for Calculus, Vol. 1; MAA Notes Ser.: Vol. 27). 184p. 1993. pap. text 38.50 (*0-88385-083-4*, NTE-27) Math Assn.

***Learning by Doing.** Jonathan J. Sajiwandani. 250p. 2000. pap. 24.95 (*1-85756-476-6*, Pub. by Janus Pubng) Paul & Co Pubs.

Learning by Doing: Concepts & Models for Service Learning in Accounting, 18 vols. Ed. by Edward Zlotkowski & Dasaratha V. Rama. (Service-Learning in the Disciplines Ser.). 244p. 1998. pap. 28.50 (*1-56377-008-3*, SL01DS) Am Assn Higher Ed.

Learning by Doing: Eighty Activities to Enrich Religion Classes for Young Children. Carole MacClennan. LC 93-60026. (Illus.). 136p. (Orig.). 1993. pap. 14.95 (*0-89622-562-3*) Twenty-Third.

Learning by Doing: How School Districts Are Preparing Students for the New American Workplace. Kristen J. Amundson. (NSBA Best Practices Ser.). 82p. (Orig.). 1994. pap. 15.00 (*0-88364-189-5*, 04-113) Natl Sch Boards.

Learning by Doing: Panasonic Partnerships & Systemic School Reform. Terry Clark & Richard Lacey. (Illus.). 168p. 1997. per. 24.95 (*1-884015-37-9*) St Lucie Pr.

Learning by Doing in Markets, Firms, & Countries. Ed. by Naomi R. Lamoreaux et al. LC 98-8558. 328p. 1999. pap. text 22.50 (*0-226-46834-8*); lib. bdg. 65.00 (*0-226-46832-1*) U Ch Pr.

Learning by Heart. Ronder T. Young. LC 92-46887. 176p. (J). 1993. 14.95 (*0-395-65369-X*) HM.

Learning by Heart. Ronder Thomas Young. (J). 1995. 9.09 (*0-606-07777-4*, Pub. by Turtleback) Demco.

Learning by Heart: AIDS & Schoolchildren in America's Communities. David L. Kirp. 305p. (Orig.). 1990. pap. 14.95 (*0-8135-1609-9*) Rutgers U Pr.

Learning by Heart: Contemporary American Poetry about School. Ed. by Maggie Anderson & David Hassler. LC 98-47405. 246p. 1999. pap. 14.95 (*0-87745-663-1*); text 29.95 (*0-87745-662-3*) U of Iowa Pr.

Learning by Metaphor: A Metaphoric Reading of Two Short Stories by Stephen Crane. Gunnar Backman. (Studia Anglistica Upsaliensia Ser.: No. 75). 203p. (Orig.). 1991. pap. 42.50 (*91-554-2741-3*) Coronet Bks.

Learning by Teaching: Selected Articles on Writing & Teaching. Donald M. Murray. LC 82-20558. 184p. (C). 1982. pap. text 21.50 (*0-86709-025-1*, 0025, Pub. by Boynton Cook Pubs) Heinemann.

Learning by Voting: Sequential Choices in Presidential Primaries & Other Elections. Rebecca B. Morton. (Illus.). 180p. (C). text 44.50 (*0-472-11129-9*, 11129) U of Mich Pr.

Learning C++ Graham. 1991. teacher ed. 79.00 (*0-07-023984-3*) McGraw.

Learning C. Neill Graham. 304p. (C). 1990. pap. 50.94 (*0-07-023983-5*) McGraw.

Learning C. Neill Graham. 304p. (C). 1992. pap. 46.56 (*0-07-023981-9*) McGraw.

Learning C++ A Hands-On Approach. Eric P. Nagler. Ed. by Mixter. LC 93-16017. 650p. (C). 1994. pap. text 41.50 (*0-314-02464-6*) West Pub.

Learning C++ A Hands-On Approach. 2nd ed. Eric P. Nagler. LC 96-20162. 550p. (C). 1999. mass mkt. 55.95 (*0-314-20039-8*) West Pub.

Learning C with Tiny C. Scott B. Guthery. (Illus.). 176p. (Orig.). 1985. pap. 14.95 (*0-8306-1895-3*, 1895P) McGraw-Hill Prof.

Learning C with Tiny C (IBM) Scott B. Guthery. 1991. 24.95 (*0-8306-6620-6*) McGraw-Hill Prof.

Learning CADKey. Richard G. McGinnis. (C). 1991. 28.75 (*0-07-044791-8*) McGraw.

Learning California History: Essential Skills for the Survey Course & Beyond. Gordon Bakken & Brenda Farrington. (Illus.). 186p. (C). 1999. pap. text, wbk. ed. 15.95 (*0-88295-945-X*) Harlan Davidson.

Learning Calligraphy: A Book of Lettering, Design & History. Margaret Shepherd. 128p. 1978. pap. 15.00 (*0-02-015550-6*) Macmillan.

Learning Calligraphy Stroke by Stroke, 3 vols., Set. Arthur Baker. (Illus.). 1987. pap. 11.40 (*0-486-25428-3*) Dover.

Learning Capital: The Economic Idea & Causes of School Quality. Gary Scott. LC 96-3426. 228p. 1996. 48.00 (*0-7618-0489-7*); pap. text 28.50 (*0-7618-0490-0*) U Pr of Amer.

Learning Capitalist Culture: Deep in the Heart of Tejas. Douglas E. Foley. LC 90-34686. (Contemporary Ethnography Ser.). 272p. (C). 1990. text 36.95 (*0-8122-8246-9*); pap. text 16.95 (*0-8122-1314-9*) U of Pa Pr.

Learning Center: Open-Ended Activities. Liz Wilmes & Dick Wilmes. (Illus.). 256p. (Orig.). 1991. pap. 19.95 (*0-943452-13-9*) Building Blocks.

***Learning Center Activities.** Patti Sima & Casey Null. (Illus.). 304p. (J). 1999. pap., teacher ed. 24.95 (*1-57690-508-X*, TCM2508) Tchr Create Mat.

Learning Center Activities: Math. Leonard J. Basile. (Illus.). 80p. (J). (gr. k-2). 1997. pap., teacher ed. 9.95 (*1-57690-071-1*, TCM2071) Tchr Create Mat.

Learning Center Activities: Reading Skills. Leonard J. Basile. (Illus.). 80p. (J). (gr. k-2). 1997. pap., teacher ed. 9.95 (*1-57690-070-3*, TCM2070) Tchr Create Mat.

Learning Center Activities: Science. Deborah Candelora. (Illus.). 80p. (J). (gr. k-2). 1997. pap., teacher ed. 9.95 (*1-57690-072-X*, TCM2072) Tchr Create Mat.

Learning Center Activities for the Full-Day Kindergarten. Abby B. Bergman. 288p. (C). 1990. pap. text 27.95 (*0-87628-512-4*) P-H.

Learning Center Activities for Writing. Kathleen Null. 80p. (J). (gr. k-2). 1997. pap. 9.95 (*1-57690-075-4*) Tchr Create Mat.

Learning Center Activities/Brain Teasers. Carol Monington. 80p. (J). (gr. k-2). 1997. pap. 9.95 (*1-57690-073-8*) Tchr Create Mat.

Learning Center Activities/Holidays. Susie Alexander. 80p. (J). (gr. k-2). 1997. pap. 9.95 (*1-57690-074-6*) Tchr Create Mat.

Learning Center Handbook. (Illus.). 42p. 1986. pap. 5.95 (*0-932967-12-4*) Pacific Shoreline.

Learning Centered Training for Learner Centered Programs. Suzanne Kindervatter. 68p. (Orig.). (C). 1977. pap. 4.00 (*0-932288-40-5*) Ctr Intl Ed U of MA.

Learning Centers. Jodi McClay. LC 96-159854. 1997. pap. text 8.95 (*1-55734-891-X*) Tchr Create Mat.

Learning Centers: Children on Their Own. Association for Childhood Education International Staff. Ed. by Virginia Rapport. LC 71-133244. 84p. reprint ed. pap. 30.00 (*0-608-17255-3*, 202919800059) Bks Demand.

Learning Centers: Development & Operation. Frances Bennie. LC 76-58528. 340p. 1977. 39.95 (*0-87778-097-8*) Educ Tech Pubns.

Learning Centers: Getting Them Started, Keeping Them Going. Michael F. Opitz. LC 94-218729. 96p. 1994. pap. 12.95 (*0-590-49554-2*) Scholastic Inc.

Learning Centers: Second Grade. School Zone Staff. (Illus.). (J). (gr. 2). 1998. pap. 24.95 (*0-88743-237-9*, 14045) Sch Zone Pub Co.

Learning Centers for Child-Centered Classrooms. Janice Pattillo & Elizabeth Vaughan. 112p. 1992. pap. 15.95 (*0-8106-0357-8*) NEA.

Learning Centers for Little Kids. Jeri Carroll. (Illus.). 64p. (J). (ps-2). 1983. student ed. 6.99 (*0-86653-103-3*, GA 458) Good Apple.

Learning Centers for Young Children. 4th rev. ed. Georgia B. Houle. LC 97-176996. (Illus.). 112p. 1997. pap. text 22.95 (*0-940139-43-X*) Consortium RI.

Learning Centers Through the Year. Annette H. Wallace. Ed. by Ina M. Levin. (Illus.). 384p. 1993. student ed. 29.95 (*1-55734-059-5*) Tchr Create Mat.

***Learning Centres.** Amanda Scott. 224p. 1998. pap. 45.00 (*0-7494-2293-9*, Kogan Pg Educ) Stylus Pub VA.

***Learning Centres: A Step-by-Step Guide to Planning, Managing & Evaluating an Organizational Resources.** Amanda Scott. 232p. 1999. pap. 29.95 (*0-7494-3051-6*, Pub. by Kogan Page Ltd) Stylus Pub VA.

Learning Change: One School District Meets Language Across the Curriculum. Nancy B. Lester & Cynthia S. Onore. LC 89-36956. 220p. (C). 1990. pap. text 22.00 (*0-86709-254-8*, 0254, Pub. by Boynton Cook Pubs) Heinemann.

Learning Chest. Virginia M. Smith. (Illus.). 16p. (J). (ps-2). 1997. mass mkt. 24.95 (*0-9662434-0-4*) Achievers Network.

Learning Chinese Measure Words. Ed. by Jiao Fan. (CHI., Illus.). 244p. 1993. 16.95 (*0-8351-2674-9*) China Bks.

Learning Chinese with Fun. Jenny Li. (Illus.). (Orig.). 1967. pap. 3.75 (*0-910286-24-8*) Boxwood.

Learning Christian Leadership. Donald S. Aultman. 1981. 4.95 (*0-87148-501-X*) Pathway Pr.

Learning Circle: A Preschool Teachers Guide to Circle Time. Patty Claycomb. Ed. by Kathleen Charner. (Illus.). 224p. (Orig.). 1988. pap. 14.95 (*0-87659-115-2*) Gryphon Hse.

Learning Circles: Creating Conditions for Professional Development. Michelle Collay et al. LC 98-9058. (1-Off Ser.). (Illus.). 168p. 1998. 51.95 (*0-8039-6675-X*, 82113); pap. 22.95 (*0-8039-6676-8*, 82114) Corwin Pr.

Learning Claris Works 5.0 for School, Home & Office. Irene Smith & Sharon Yoder. Ed. by Joel Southern. LC 99-236308. (Illus.). 344p. 1998. spiral bd. 29.95 (*1-56484-133-2*) Intl Society Tech Educ.

Learning Clinical Reasoning. Jerome P. Kassirer & Richard Kopelman. (Illus.). 350p. 1991. 35.00 (*0-683-04537-7*) Lppncott W & W.

Learning Clock. Illus. by Moira Butterfield & Christine Howe. (J). 4.98 (*1-57717-128-4*) Todtri Prods.

Learning Cognition. 5th ed. (C). Date not set. text. write for info. (*0-13-040199-4*) P-H.

Learning College for the 21st Century. Terry O'Banion. LC 97-8299. (Ace/Oryx Series on Higher Education). 264p. (C). 1997. pap. 27.50 (*1-57356-113-4*) Oryx Pr.

Learning Combination Inventory: Form I. 2nd rev. ed. Christine A. Johnston & Gary R. Dainton. (Illus.). iii, 9p. (J). (gr. k-5). 1998. wbk. ed. 24.99 (*1-892385-00-7*) Let Me Learn.

Learning Combination Inventory: Form II. 2nd rev. ed. Christine A. Johnston & Gary R. Dainton. (Illus.). iii, 9p. (YA). (gr. 6-12). 1998. wbk. ed. 24.99 (*1-892385-01-5*) Let Me Learn.

Learning Combination Inventory: Professional Form. 2nd rev. ed. Christine A. Johnston & Gary R. Dainton. (Illus.). iii, 9p. 1998. pap., wbk. ed. 24.99 (*1-892385-02-3*) Let Me Learn.

Learning Combination Inventory: User's Manual. 2nd rev. ed. Christine A. Johnston & Gary R. Dainton. iii, 21p. 1998. teacher ed. 6.99 (*1-892385-03-1*) Let Me Learn.

Learning Comes to Life: An Active Learning Program for Teenagers. Ellen M. Ilfeld. LC 95-43455. 248p. 1996. 24.95 (*0-929816-90-0*, A2005) High-Scope.

Learning Communication Skills Through Word-Processing. DDC Staff. (DDC Learning Ser.). 1998. 29.00 (*1-56243-627-9*) DDC Pub.

Learning Communities: Creating Connections among Students, Faculty, & Disciplines. Ed. by Faith Gabelnick et al. LC 85-644763. (New Directions for Teaching & Learning Ser.: No. TL 41). 1990. pap. 22.00 (*1-55542-838-X*) Jossey-Bass.

***Learning Communities: New Structures, New Partnerships for Learning.** Ed. by Jodi H. Levine. (Freshman Year Experience Monograph Ser.: No. 26). 120p. 1999. pap. 30.00 (*1-889271-27-6*) Nat Res Ctr.

Learning Communities in Education. John Retallick et al. LC 98-36953. 1999. write for info. (*0-415-19760-0*) Routledge.

***Learning Community: Finding Common Ground in Difference.** Patricia E. Calderwood. LC 00-24926. 2000. pap. write for info. (*0-8077-3952-9*) Tchrs Coll.

Learning Company. James J. Licari. 381p. 1992. 60.00 (*0-07-037715-4*) McGraw.

Learning Company: A Strategy for Sustainable Development. Mike Peddler. 224p. 1994. 24.95 (*0-07-707479-3*) McGraw.

Learning Composite Mathematics, Bk. I. R. S. Lugani et al. 168p. 1997. pap. 50.00 (*81-209-0362-5*, Pub. by Pitambar Pub) St Mut.

Learning Composite Mathematics, Bk. II. R. S. Lugani et al. 168p. 1997. pap. 50.00 (*81-209-0363-3*, Pub. by Pitambar Pub) St Mut.

Learning Composite Mathematics, Bk. III. R. S. Lugani et al. 208p. 1997. pap. 50.00 (*81-209-0364-1*, Pub. by Pitambar Pub) St Mut.

Learning Composite Mathematics, Bk. IV. R. S. Lugani et al. 192p. 1997. pap. 50.00 (*81-209-0365-X*, Pub. by Pitambar Pub) St Mut.

Learning Composite Mathematics, Bk. V. R. S. Lugani et al. 240p. 1997. pap. 60.00 (*81-209-0366-8*, Pub. by Pitambar Pub) St Mut.

Learning Composite Mathematics, Bk. VI. R. S. Lugani et al. 236p. 1997. pap. 60.00 (*81-209-0367-6*, Pub. by Pitambar Pub) St Mut.

Learning Composite Mathematics, Bk. VII. R. S. Lugani et al. 268p. 1997. pap. 60.00 (*81-209-0368-4*, Pub. by Pitambar Pub) St Mut.

Learning Composite Mathematics, Bk. VIII. R. S. Lugani et al. 232p. 1997. pap. 60.00 (*81-209-0369-2*, Pub. by Pitambar Pub) St Mut.

***Learning Computer Applications: Projects & Exercises.** Lisa A. Bucki & Judy Fischer. 446p. 1999. 34.00 (*1-56243-750-X*) DDC Pub.

Learning Computer Graphics: From 3D Models to Animated Movies on Your PC. S. Govil-Pai & R. Pai. LC 98-24060. 200p. 1998. pap. 34.95 incl. cd-rom (*0-387-94898-8*) Spr-Verlag.

Learning Computer Numerical Control. Michael Janke. 1992. pap., teacher ed. 13.50 (*0-8273-4537-2*) Delmar.

Learning Computer Programming: Structured Logic, Algorithms, & Flowcharting. 2nd ed. Gerald A. Silver & Myrna L. Silver. LC 92-70753. (Illus.). 231p. (C). 1992. pap. text 34.00 (*1-880472-07-4*) Edit Enter.

Learning Computers, Bk. I. 1997. pap. 30.00 (*81-209-0752-3*, Pub. by Pitambar Pub) St Mut.

Learning Computers, Bk. II. Chaman Nahal. 1997. pap. 30.00 (*81-209-0753-1*, Pub. by Pitambar Pub) St Mut.

Learning Computers, Bk. III. 1997. pap. 30.00 (*81-209-0754-X*, Pub. by Pitambar Pub); pap., wbk. ed. 20.00 (*81-209-0979-8*, Pub. by Pitambar Pub) St Mut.

Learning Computers, Bk. V. 1997. pap. 33.00 (*81-209-0756-6*, Pub. by Pitambar Pub); pap., wbk. ed. 20.00 (*81-209-0980-1*, Pub. by Pitambar Pub) St Mut.

Learning Computers, Bk. VI. V. B. Aggarwal. 1997. pap. 38.00 (*81-209-0431-1*, Pub. by Pitambar Pub) St Mut.

Learning Computers, Bk. VII. V. B. Aggarwal. 1997. pap. 40.00 (*81-209-0432-X*, Pub. by Pitambar Pub); pap., wbk. ed. 20.00 (*81-209-0749-3*, Pub. by Pitambar Pub) St Mut.

Learning Computers, Bk. VIII. V. B. Aggarwal. 1997. pap. 36.00 (*81-209-0433-8*, Pub. by Pitambar Pub); pap., wbk. ed. 20.00 (*81-209-0662-4*, Pub. by Pitambar Pub) St Mut.

Learning Computers, Bk. IX. V. B. Aggarwal. 1997. pap. 40.00 (*81-209-0434-6*, Pub. by Pitambar Pub); pap., wbk. ed. 22.00 (*81-209-0655-1*, Pub. by Pitambar Pub) St Mut.

Learning Computers, Bk. X. V. B. Aggarwal. 1997. pap. 40.00 (*81-209-0653-5*, Pub. by Pitambar Pub); pap., wbk. ed. 20.00 (*81-209-0440-0*, Pub. by Pitambar Pub) St Mut.

Learning Computers, Speaking English: Comparative Activities for Learning English & Basic Word Processing. Steve Quann & Diana Satin. (Illus.). 150p. (C). write for info. (*0-472-00302-X*) U of Mich Pr.

***Learning Computers, Speaking English: Comparative Activities for Learning English & Basic Word Processing.** Steve Quann & Diana Satin. (Illus.). 208p. (C). 2000. 19.95 (*0-472-08683-9*, 08683); pap. text 16.95 (*0-472-08655-3*, 08655) U of Mich Pr.

Learning Congregation: A New Vision of Leadership. Thomas R. Hawkins. LC 96-36564. 160p. (Orig.). 1997. pap. 15.95 (*0-664-25699-6*) Westminster John Knox.

Learning Connection: Effective Answers to Reading & Learning Difficulties. Steven R. Shapiro. (Illus.). 238p. (Orig.). (C). 1989. pap. text 14.95 (*0-9624688-0-0*) Lrning Cnnect.

Learning Consultation: A Systematic Framework. David Campbell. 176p. 1995. pap. text 30.00 (*1-85575-117-8*, Pub. by H Karnac Bks Ltd) Other Pr LLC.

Learning Contracts. Geoff Anderson et al. 192p. 1996. pap. 29.95 (*0-7494-1847-8*, Kogan Pg Educ) Stylus Pub VA.

Learning, Control & Hybrid Systems: Festschrift in Honor of Bruce Allen Francis & Mathukumalli Vidyasagar on the Occasion of Their 50th Birthdays. Ed. by Y. Yamamoto et al. LC 98-38066. (Lecture Notes in Control & Information Sciences: Vol. 241). (Illus.). xv, 451p. 1998. pap. 105.00 (*1-85233-076-7*) Spr-Verlag.

Learning Conversational Prayer. Rosalind Rinker. 48p. (Orig.). 1992. pap. text 3.95 (*0-8146-2036-1*) Liturgical Pr.

Learning Conversations. Sheila Harri-Augstein & Laurie F. Thomas. 275p. (C). 1991. 85.00 (*0-415-02866-3*, A4774) Routledge.

Learning Cooperative Learning Via Cooperative Learning. George Jacobs et al. (Illus.). 140p. 1997. pap. text 25.00 (*1-879097-42-7*) Kagan Cooperative.

Learning Corel Office 7. Kathy M. Berkemeyer. Ed. by Ayana Gaines. LC 97-190254. (Learning Series Texts). (Illus.). 1997. pap. 27.00 (*1-56243-334-2*, Z-12) DDC Pub.

Learning Corel Web.Graphis Suite. Patricia K. Gibson. Ed. by Vince E. Yokom. (Illus.). 1997. pap. 18.00 (*1-889231-11-8*) Instrux Ltd.

Learning Corel WordPerfect 7. Kathy M. Berkemeyer. Ed. by Ayana Gaines. LC 97-208368. (Learning Series Texts). (Illus.). (Orig.). 1997. pap. text 27.00 (*1-56243-432-2*, Z-16) DDC Pub.

Learning Corel Wordperfect Suite 8. DDC Publishing Staff. LC 99-168703. (Learning Ser.). 1998. pap. text 27.00 (*1-56243-590-6*, Z28) DDC Pub.

***Learning CorelDraw 9: Basic Skills.** Vince E. Yokom. (Illus.). 204p. 1999. spiral bd. 30.00 (*1-889231-21-5*) Instrux Ltd.

Learning CorelWeb.Master.Suite: Basic Skills. Patricia K. Gibson. (Illus.). 277p. 1998. spiral bd. 32.50 (*1-889231-17-7*) Instrux Ltd.

An Asterisk (*) at the beginning of an entry indicates that the title is appearing for the first time.

Learning Counseling & Problem-Solving Skills. Leslie E. Borck & Stephen B. Fawcett. LC 82-2916. 160p. (Orig.). (C). 1982. text 44.95 (0-917724-30-5); pap. text 19.95 (0-917724-35-6) Haworth Pr.

Learning, Creating, & Using Knowledge: Concept Maps As Tools to Understand & Facilitate the Process in Schools & Corporations. Joseph D. Novak. LC 97-33965. 288p. 1998. write for info. (0-8058-2625-4); pap. write for info. (0-8058-2626-2) L Erlbaum Assocs.

Learning Curve: A Management Accounting Tool. Ahmed R. Belkaoui. LC 85-9438. (Illus.). 258p. 1986. 72.95 (0-89930-132-0, BLV/, Quorum Bks) Greenwood.

Learning Curve: Elevating Children's Academic & Social Competence. Judith M. Mishne. LC 95-16867. 256p. 1996. 40.00 (1-56821-568-1) Aronson.

Learning Curve: Lessons on Life, Love & Laundry. Cynthia R. Gregg. Ed. by Margie Adler. 85p. 1998. pap. 11.95 (0-9660006-0-9) Meyer Pub Hse.

Learning Curve Vol. 1: The Guide to Understanding Derivatives. 1999. text 250.00 (0-7863-0513-4, Irwn McGrw-H) McGrw-H Hghr Educ.

Learning Curve Deskbook: A Reference Guide to Theory, Calculations, & Applications. Charles J. Teplitz. LC 90-47589. 312p. 1991. 67.95 (0-89930-522-9, TLC/, Quorum Bks) Greenwood.

***Learning Curves: Hits, Misses & Home Runs.** Retold by Jeff Mortimer. xviii, 416p. 1999. 29.95 (1-879094-65-7) Momentum Bks.

***Learning Curves: Living Your Life in Full & with Style.** Michele Weston. LC 99-46061. (Illus.). 256p. 2000. 24.00 (0-609-60580-1, SEL021000, Crown) Crown Pub Group.

Learning Curves Vol. 1: The Guide to Understanding Derivatives. (Illus.). 180p. 1994. 95.00 (0-9619446-0-9) Institutional Investor.

Learning Curves Vol. 2: The Guide to Understanding Derivatives. (Illus.). 154p. 1995. 95.00 (0-9619446-1-7) Institutional Investor.

Learning Curves Vol. 3: The Guide to Understanding Derivatives. (Illus.). 160p. 1996. 195.00 (0-9619446-2-5) Institutional Investor.

Learning Curves Vol. 4: The Guide to Understanding Derivatives. (Illus.). 193p. 1998. 225.00 (0-9619446-3-3) Institutional Investor.

Learning Cycle: Elementary School Science Teaching & Beyond. Michael F. Marek & Cavallo. LC 96-52276. 1997. pap. text 32.00 (0-435-07133-5, 07133) Heinemann.

Learning Data Analysis with Datadesk. Paul F. Velleman. LC 92-42310. (C). 1993. pap. text 32.95 (0-7167-2201-1) W H Freeman.

Learning Data Analysis with Datadesk Student Version 6.0. Paul Velleman. LC 97-16891. (Illus.). 384p. 1997. cd-rom 66.00 (0-201-25831-5) Addison-Wesley.

Learning Data Analysis with Datadesk Student Version 6.0. Paul F. Velleman. LC 96-22178. (Illus.). 384p. 1996. pap. 47.00 (0-201-57124-2) Addison-Wesley.

Learning dBASE III Plus. Annette Thomason. (C). 1990. write for info. (0-395-35732-2) HM Soft Schl Col Div.

Learning DCOM. Thuan L. Thai. Ed. by Andy Oram. (Illus.). 479p. 1999. pap. 32.95 (1-56592-581-5) OReilly & Assocs.

***Learning Debian GNU/Linux.** Bill McCarty. Ed. by Mark Stone. (Illus.). 400p. 1999. pap. 34.95 incl. cd-rom (1-56592-705-2) OReilly & Assocs.

Learning Decision-Making in the Building Process. Edward T. White. (Illus.). 14p. 1991. pap. 4.00 (1-928643-15-9) Archit Media.

Learning Democracy: Democratic & Economic Values in Unified Germany. Robert Rohrschneider. LC 98-54769. (Comparative Politics Ser.). (Illus.). 326p. 1999. text 72.00 (0-19-829517-0) OUP.

Learning Democracy in Japan: The Social Education of Japanese Adults. J. E. Thomas. 164p. (C). 1986. text 42.75 (0-8039-9729-9) Sage.

Learning Denied. Denny Taylor. LC 90-44977. (Illus.). 112p. (Orig.). (C). 1990. pap. 17.50 (0-435-08545-X, 08545) Heinemann.

Learning Desire: Perspectives on Pedagogy, Culture & the Unsaid. Sharon Todd. LC 97-11238. 288p. (C). 1997. 80.00 (0-415-91766-2); pap. 23.99 (0-415-91767-0) Routledge.

Learning Desktop Publishing Basics with WorkPerfect 5.1. Margaret Brown. 260p. 1991. teacher ed. 5.00 (1-56243-065-3, WDB/TM); spiral bd. 27.00 (1-56243-052-1, WDB); trans. 130.00 (1-56243-067-X, WD-13); trans. 200.00 (1-56243-068-8, WD-26); trans. 200.00 (1-56243-063-0); disk 65.00 (1-56243-062-9, DD-77); disk 12.50 (1-56243-066-1, DD-55) DDC Pub.

Learning Desktop Publishing for Wordperfect 6 for Windows. Iris Blanc. LC 95-127568. 1994. pap. 27.00 (1-56243-191-9, F9) DDC Pub.

Learning Desktop Publishing with WordPerfect 6.1 for Windows. Iris Blanc. LC 95-202883. 1995. pap. 25.00 (1-56243-260-5, Z5) DDC Pub.

Learning Desktop Publishing Word 6.0 for Windows. Mike Singleton. LC 96-135870. 1995. pap. text 27.00 (1-56243-211-7, Z-2) DDC Pub.

Learning, Development, & Culture: Essays in Evolutionary Epistemology. Ed. by Henry C. Plotkin. LC 82-1947. 505p. reprint ed. pap. 156.60 (0-608-16346-5, 202668300051) Bks Demand.

Learning Diabilities Vol. 1: Neuropsychological Correlates & Treatment. Ed. by Dirk J. Bakker. x, 202p. 1989. 55.50 (90-265-0983-9) Swets.

***Learning Differences in the Classroom.** Elizabeth N. Fielding. LC 99-22994. 1999. 3.95 (0-87207-251-7) Intl Reading.

Learning Differences Sourcebook. Nancy S. Boyles & Darlene Contadino. LC 97-37654. 480p. 1998. reprint ed. 30.00 (1-56565-795-0, 07950W, Pub. by Lowell Hse) NTC Contemp Pub Co.

Learning Differences Sourcebook. Nancy S. Boyles & Darlene Contadino. LC 97-37654. 480p. 1998. reprint ed. pap. 19.95 (0-7373-0024-8, 00248W) NTC Contemp Pub Co.

***Learning Difficulties: A Guide for Teachers: Waldorf Insights & Practical Approaches.** 2nd rev. ed. Ed. by Mary Ellen Willby. xiv, 289p. 1999. pap. 19.95 (0-945803-40-0, 00175) R Steiner Col.

Learning Difficulties & Business Administration. Kenneth Lysons. (Special Needs & Business Administration Ser.). 76p. 1993. pap. 27.50 (1-85302-198-9) Taylor & Francis.

Learning Difficulties & Computers: Access to the Curriculum. David Hawkridge & Tom Vincent. 160p. 1992. pap. 22.95 (1-85302-132-6) Taylor & Francis.

Learning Difficulties & Emotional Problems. Ed. by Roy I. Brown & Maurice Chazan. 239p. (Orig.). (C). 1989. pap. text 18.95 (0-920490-89-1) Temeron Bks.

Learning Difficulties in Primary Classrooms: Delivering the Whole Curriculum. Ed. by Kevin Jones & Tony Charlton. 256p. 1992. 67.50 (0-415-08389-3, A9700) Routledge.

Learning Disabilities. (Illus.). 38p. (C). 1995. pap. text 20.00 (0-7881-2031-X) DIANE Pub.

***Learning Disabilities.** Ed. by Laurence L. Greenhill. (Review of Psychiatry Ser.: Vol. 19, No. 5). 196p. 2000. pap. 28.50 (0-88048-383-0) Am Psychiatric.

Learning Disabilities, 6 vols. Lerner. (C). 1992. pap., teacher ed. 3.16 (0-395-64010-5) HM.

Learning Disabilities. Lawrence J. O'Shea et al. LC 97-28717. 480p. 1997. text 62.00 (0-02-389321-4) Macmillan.

Learning Disabilities. Betty B. Osman. 1988. mass mkt. 4.95 (0-446-35554-2, Pub. by Warner Bks) Little.

Learning Disabilities. Margaret Schatzow. 1999. pap. 8.95 (0-14-013322-4) Viking Penguin.

Learning Disabilities. 3rd ed. Karen E. Bender. LC 97-30427. 512p. 1997. 76.00 (0-205-27401-3) P-H.

Learning Disabilities. 3rd ed. Bob Gates. LC 96-49999. 1997. pap. text 42.95 (0-443-05539-4) Church.

Learning Disabilities. 4th ed. Corinne Roth Smith. LC 97-4407. 630p. 1997. 78.00 (0-205-27203-7) P-H.

Learning Disabilities: A Neuropsychological Perspective. Byron P. Rourke & Jerel E. Del Dotto. (Developmental Clinical Psychology & Psychiatry Ser.: Vol. 30). 160p. (C). 1994. text 42.00 (0-8039-5353-4); pap. text 18.95 (0-8039-5354-2) Sage.

Learning Disabilities: A to Z; A Parent's Complete Guide to Learning Disabilities from Preschool to Adulthood. Corinne Smith & Lisa Strick. 416p. 1999. pap. 14.00 (0-684-84468-0) S&S Trade.

Learning Disabilities: An Astrological Approach to Successful Living. Dorothy B. Santangelo. 185p. 1996. pap. text 14.95 (0-9652768-0-5) Rex Art.

Learning Disabilities: Appropriate Practices for a Diverse Population. Barry E. McNamara. LC 97-46378. (SUNY Series, Youth Social Services, Schooling, & Public Policy). 320p. (C). 1998. text 65.50 (0-7914-3883-X); pap. text 21.95 (0-7914-3884-8) State U NY Pr.

Learning Disabilities: Basic Concepts, Assessment Practices, & Instructional Strategies. 4th ed. Patricia I. Myers & Donald D. Hammill. LC 89-29044. (Illus.). 593p. (Orig.). 1990. text 43.00 (0-89079-225-9, 1499) PRO-ED.

Learning Disabilities: Best Practices for Professionals. Ed. by William N. Bender. LC 92-31024. 334p. 1993. 38.00 (1-56372-058-2, 6930) PRO-ED.

***Learning Disabilities: Characteristics, Identification & Teaching Strategies.** 4th ed. William N. Bender. 448p. 2000. 71.00 (0-205-32184-4) Allyn.

Learning Disabilities: Concepts & Characteristics. 3rd ed. Gerald Wallace & James A. McLoughlin. 544p. (C). 1990. 85.00 (0-675-20828-9, Merrill Coll) P-H.

Learning Disabilities: Contemporary Viewpoints. Bryant J. Cratty & Richard L. Goldman. 248p. 1996. pap. text 25.00 (3-7186-0623-2, Harwood Acad Pubs) Gordon & Breach.

Learning Disabilities: Educational Principles & Practices. Doris J. Johnson & Helmer R. Myklebust. LC 66-28287. 336p. (C). 1967. text 36.00 (0-8089-0219-9, 1804) PRO-ED.

Learning Disabilities: Educational Strategies. 5th ed. Bill R. Gearheart. 496p. (C). 1990. 38.20 (0-675-20949-8, Merrill Coll) P-H.

Learning Disabilities: How to Recognize & Manage Learning & Behavioral Problems in Children. Trudy Carlson. LC 95-94110. 144p. (Orig.). 1997. pap. 14.95 (0-9642443-2-2) Benline Pr.

Learning Disabilities: Information & Resources. 2nd ed. Ed. by Landmark Outreach Program Staff. 110p. 1996. pap. 20.00 (0-9624119-4-9) Landmark Found.

Learning Disabilities: Issues & Instructional Interventions. Clayton E. Keller & Daniel P. Hallahan. 32p. 1987. pap. 3.95 (0-8106-1076-0) NEA.

Learning Disabilities: Lifelong Issues. Ed. by Shirley C. Cramer & William Ellis. 352p. (Orig.). 1996. pap. text 36.00 (1-55766-240-1, 2401) P H Brookes.

Learning Disabilities: Nature, Theory & Treatment. Ed. by N. N. Singh et al. (Disorders of Human Learning, Behavior, & Communication Ser.). (Illus.). 600p. 1991. 105.95 (0-387-97590-X) Spr-Verlag.

Learning Disabilities: New Directions for Assessment & Intervention. Ed. by Nancy C. Jordan & Josephine Goldsmith-Phillips. LC 93-22965. 432p. (C). 1993. 68.00 (0-205-14124-2, Longwood Div) Allyn.

Learning Disabilities: The Challenges of Adulthood. Ed. by James R. Patton & Edward A. Polloway. LC 95-14293. 303p. 1996. pap. text 34.00 (0-89079-581-9) PRO-ED.

***Learning Disabilities: The Interaction of Learner, Task, & Setting.** 5th ed. Smith. 2000. 71.00 (0-205-31952-1) Allyn.

Learning Disabilities: The Struggle from Adolescence Toward Adulthood. William M. Cruickshank et al. (Illus.). 304p. (C). 1980. pap. 19.95 (0-8156-2221-X) Syracuse U Pr.

Learning Disabilities: Theoretical & Research Issues. Ed. by H. L. Swanson & Barbara Keogh. 384p. (C). 1990. text 79.95 (0-8058-0392-0) L Erlbaum Assocs.

Learning Disabilities: Theories, Diagnosis, & Teaching Strategies. 4th ed. Janet W. Lerner. LC 84-82413. 640p. (C). 1984. student ed. 14.76 (0-685-10561-X) HM.

Learning Disabilities: Theories, Diagnosis, & Teaching Strategies. 5th ed. Janet W. Lerner. 1988. teacher ed. write for info. (0-318-63320-5); student ed. 13.96 (0-318-36897-8) HM.

Learning Disabilities: What To Do After Diagnosis, Set. Jill Smith & Howard Diller. 1991. pap. text 316.00 (0-9630539-0-6) Apodixis.

Learning Disabilities: What to Do after Diagnosis: A Survival Guide - College & the Workplace, Vol. 4. Jill Smith & Howard Diller. 300p. 1992. pap. text 79.00 (0-9630539-4-9) Apodixis.

Learning Disabilities: What to Do after Diagnosis: A Survival Guide Fourth Through Sixth Grade, Vol. 2. Jill Smith & Howard Diller. 325p. 1991. pap. text 79.00 (0-9630539-2-2) Apodixis.

Learning Disabilities: What to Do after Diagnosis: A Survival Guide Kindergarten Through Third Grade, Vol. 1. Jill Smith & Howard Diller. 375p. 1991. pap. text 79.00 (0-9630539-1-4) Apodixis.

Learning Disabilities: What to Do after Diagnosis: A Survival Guide Seventh Through Twelfth Grade, Vol. 3. Jill Smith & Howard Diller. 325p. 1991. pap. text 79.00 (0-9630539-3-0) Apodixis.

Learning Disabilities Vol. 2: Cognitive, Social, & Remedial Aspects. Ed. by J. J. Dumont. xii, 208p. 1989. 55.50 (90-265-0984-7) Swets.

Learning Disabilities Activity Guide for the Elementary Classroom. Vicki G. La Brie. 50p. (Orig.). 1975. pap. 3.50 (0-89080-029-4) Mercer Hse.

Learning Disabilities & ADHD: A Family Guide to Living & Learning Together. 2nd ed. Betty Osman. LC 97-1211. 228p. 1997. pap. 14.95 (0-471-15510-1) Wiley.

Learning Disabilities & Assistive Technology. 2nd ed. Christopher Lee. (Illus.). 1999. pap. 49.95 (1-928752-13-6) Mc Gowan Pubns.

Learning Disabilities & Brain Function. 2nd ed. William H. Gaddes. (Illus.). 450p. 1992. 40.00 (0-387-96065-1) Spr-Verlag.

Learning Disabilities & Brain Function: A Neuropsychological Approach. 3rd ed. William H. Gaddes & Dorothy Edgell. LC 93-28185. 1993. write for info. (3-540-94041-3) Spr-Verlag.

Learning Disabilities & Brain Function: A Neuropsychological Approach. 3rd ed. William H. Gaddes & Dorothy Edgell. (Illus.). 594p. 1994. 59.95 (0-387-94041-3) Spr-Verlag.

Learning Disabilities & Employment. Ed. by Paul J. Gerber & Dale S. Brown. LC 96-45338. 377p. 1997. pap. text 36.00 (0-89079-717-X, 8334) PRO-ED.

***Learning Disabilities & Life Stories.** LC 99-87271. 304p. (C). 2000. pap. text 30.00 (0-205-32010-4) Allyn.

Learning Disabilities & Psychic Conflict: A Psychoanalytic Casebook. Arden Aibel Rothstein & Jules Glenn. LC 98-51468. 520p. 1999. 78.00 (0-8236-2952-X, 02952) Intl Univs Pr.

Learning Disabilities & Psychosocial Functioning: A Neuropsychological Perspective. Byron P. Rourke & Darren R. Fuerst. LC 91-16388. 198p. 1991. lib. bdg. 32.00 (0-89862-767-2) Guilford Pubns.

Learning Disabilities & Related Disorders: Facts & Current Issues. Ed. by J. Gordon Millicap. LC 77-73607. (Illus.). 189p. reprint ed. pap. 58.60 (0-8357-6186-X, 203426500089) Bks Demand.

Learning Disabilities & Social Activity. Ed. by Gerald S. Coles. 1985. 49.95 (0-915340-15-1) PJD Pubns.

Learning Disabilities & the Law. Peter S. Latham & Patricia H. Latham. 178p. 1993. pap. text 28.00 (1-883560-02-0) JKL Communs.

***Learning Disabilities & the Law.** 2nd ed. Peter S. Latham & Patricia Horan Latham. 2000. pap. 29.00 (1-883560-11-X) JKL Communs.

Learning Disabilities in Adulthood: Persisting Problems & Evolving Issues. Ed. by Paul J. Gerber & Henry B. Reiff. 228p. 1994. 38.00 (1-56372-066-3, 6931) PRO-ED.

***Learning Disabilities in Children.** Peter Burke & Katy Cigno. LC 99-87589. (Working Together for Children, Young People & Their Families Ser.). 2000. pap. write for info. (0-632-05104-3) Blackwell Sci.

Learning Disabilities in the Primary Classroom. Leonora Harding. 208p. (C). 1986. 37.50 (0-7099-3785-7, Pub. by C Helm); pap. 19.95 (0-7099-4764-X, Pub. by C Helm) Routldge.

Learning Disabilities, Literacy, & Adult Education. Ed. by Susan A. Vogel & Stephen M. Reder. LC 98-7641. 377p. 1998. pap. 49.95 (1-55766-347-5, 3475) P H Brookes.

Learning Disabilities 101: A Primer for Parents. Mary Cathryn Haller. LC 98-44036. 1999. 16.95 (1-56825-073-8) Rainbow Books.

Learning Disabilities Sourcebook. Ed. by Linda M. Ross. LC 97-52049. (Health Reference Ser.). 579p. 1998. lib. bdg. 78.00 (0-7808-0210-1) Omnigraphics Inc.

Learning Disabilities Spectrum: ADD, ADHD, & LD. Ed. by Arnold J. Capute et al. LC 93-70191. 265p. 1994. pap. text 32.50 (0-912752-33-5) York Pr.

Learning Disabilities Trap: How to Save Your Child from the Perils of Special Education. Harlow G. Unger. LC 97-37770. 368p. 1997. pap. 14.95 (0-8092-3060-7, 306070, Contemporary Bks) NTC Contemp Pub Co.

Learning Disability. Margaret Schatzow. 1999. pap. 20.00 (0-670-83319-3) Viking Penguin.

Learning Disability: Social Class & the Construction of Inequality in American Education, 18. James G. Carrier. LC 86-400. (Contributions to the Study of Education Ser.: No. 18). 167p. 1986. 47.95 (0-313-25396-X, CLE/, Greenwood Pr) Greenwood.

Learning Disability: The Imaginary Disease. Thomas G. Finlan. LC 93-18136. 208p. 1993. 55.00 (0-89789-345-X, H345, Bergin & Garvey); pap. 17.95 (0-89789-351-4, G351, Bergin & Garvey) Greenwood.

Learning Disability & the Social Context of Caring. Open Learning Foundation Staff. 142p. 1997. pap. write for info. (0-443-05735-4) Church.

Learning Disability in Focus: The Use of Photography in the Care of People with a Learning Disability. Eve. LC 98-45892. 1998. pap. text 24.95 (1-85302-693-X) Taylor & Francis.

Learning Disability Intervention Manual. rev. ed. Stephen B. McCarney & Angela M. Bauer. 217p. 1989. reprint ed. pap. 25.00 (1-878372-07-6) Hawthorne Educ Servs.

Learning Disability Rating Procedure. Gerald J. Spadafore & Sharon J. Spadafore. 32p. (Orig.). 1981. 19.00 (0-685-41947-9); student ed. 48.00 (0-685-53852-4); pap. text 25.00 (0-87879-265-1); 20.00 (0-87879-266-X) Acad Therapy.

Learning Disability Subtyping. S. R. Hooper & W. G. Willis. xiv, 253p. 1988. 94.95 (0-387-96808-3) Spr-Verlag.

Learning Disabled, 7 vols. 7th ed. Lerner. (C). 1996. pap. text, student ed. 21.16 (0-395-79486-2) HM.

Learning Disabled, 7 vols. 7th ed. Janet W. Lerner. LC 96-76924. (C). 1996. text 69.16 (0-395-79685-7) HM.

***Learning Disabled: How You Can Help Them Regain Their Self Confidence.** rev. ed. Janet Buell. 130p. 1999. pap. 19.95 incl. cd-rom (1-929830-01-7) Innovat Pr CA.

Learning Disabled: Testbank, 7 vols. Lerner. (C). Date not set. pap., teacher ed. 11.96 (0-395-79487-0) HM.

Learning-Disabled Child see LD Child & the ADHD Child: Ways Parents & Professionals Can Help

Learning Disabled Child. Sylvia Farnham-Diggory. (Developing Child Ser.). (Illus.). 288p. (C). 1992. 32.50 (0-674-51923-X); pap. text 14.50 (0-674-51924-8) HUP.

Learning Disabled Children Growing Up: A Follow-Up into Adulthood. Otfried Spreen. (Illus.). 176p. 1988. text 39.95 (0-19-520641-X) OUP.

Learning Disablities, 6 vols. Janet W. Lerner. (C). 1992. pap., student ed. 20.36 (0-395-64011-3) HM.

Learning Discrete Mathematics with ISETL. N. Baxter et al. (Illus.). xvii, 416p. 1988. 53.95 (0-387-96898-9) Spr-Verlag.

Learning Disorders. Jacqueline L. Harris. (Bodies in Crisis Ser.). (Illus.). 64p. (J). (gr. 5-8). 1995. lib. bdg. 18.90 (0-8050-2604-5) TFC Bks NY.

***Learning Disorders: A Guide for Parents & Teachers.** William Feldman. (Your Personal Health Ser.). 208p. 2000. pap. 14.95 (1-55209-476-6) Firefly Bks Ltd.

Learning Disorders: An Integration of Neuropsychological & Psychoanalytic Considerations. Arden Rothstein et al. 398p. 1988. 55.00 (0-8236-2956-2) Intl Univs Pr.

***Learning Disorders & Disabilities: A Guide for Parents.** unabridged large type ed. Martin Baren. Ed. by Martin Stein & Dennis Kneel. (Pediatric & Behavioral Health Ser.: No. 1025). (Illus.). 32p. 1999. pap. 2.95 (1-885274-59-9) Health InfoNet Inc.

Learning Disorders in Children. Bernstein. 1998. 28.00 (1-56593-178-5) Thomson Learn.

Learning DOS & Windows. Margaret Brown. 1996. pap. text 27.00 (1-56243-295-8, Z-7) DDC Pub.

Learning DOS Versions 5 & 6: For IBM & Compatibles. Margaret Brown. Ed. by Kathy M. Berkemeyer. (Fast-Teach Learning Ser.). (Illus.). 277p. (Orig.). 1993. spiral bd. 27.00 (1-56243-120-X, D-9) DDC Pub.

Learning Early: Everything Parents Need to Encourage & Develop Their Child's Learning Skills from Birth to Six Years of Age. Dorothy Einon. 240p. 1999. 29.95 (0-8160-4013-3) Facts on File.

Learning Early: Everything Parents Need to Encourage & Develop Their Child's Learning Skills from Birth to Six Years of Age. Dorothy Einon. LC 98-48291. 240p. 1999. pap. 16.95 (0-8160-4014-1, Checkmark) Facts on File.

Learning ECGS, Videotape Series: Instructor's Manual. American Safety Video Publishers Staff. 1993. teacher ed. write for info. (0-8016-8095-6) Mosby Inc.

Learning Echocardiography. 3rd ed. Ed. by Jules Constant. 648p. (C). text 45.00 (0-317-53596-X, Little Brwn Med Div) Lppncott W & W.

Learning Econometrics Using Gaus. George G. Judge et al. 224p. 1989. pap. 43.95 (0-471-51074-2) Wiley.

Learning Economics: A Practical Workbook. Abhau B. Ghiara. 194p. (C). 1997. pap. text, wbk. ed. 29.06 (0-201-32761-9) Addison-Wesley.

Learning Economics: A Practical Workbook. Abhay Ghiara. (C). 1999. pap. text, wbk. ed. write for info. (0-201-34742-3) Addison-Wesley.

Learning Economics: A Practical Workbook-Course Manual in Economics. Rohlf Ghiara. (C). 1997. pap. text 77.00 (0-201-33899-8) Addison-Wesley.

Learning Edge: Advanced Technological Education at Community Colleges. James R. Mahoney. 120p. 2000. pap. 24.00 (0-87117-326-3, 1437) Comm Coll Pr Am Assn Comm Coll.

Learning Edge: How Smart Managers & Smart Companies Stay Ahead. Calhoun W. Wick. (Illus.). 232p. 1996. pap. 14.95 (0-07-070083-4) McGraw.

An Asterisk (*) at the beginning of an entry indicates that the title is appearing for the first time.

Learning Efficiency Test II (Let II) Raymond E. Webster. 1992. teacher ed. 32.00 (*0-87879-941-9*); student ed. 80.00 (*0-87879-940-0*); spiral bd. 20.00 (*0-87879-943-5*); 25.00 (*0-87879-942-7*) Acad Therapy.

Learning Electricity & Electronics with Advanced Educational Technology. Ed. by M. Caillot. (NATO ASI Series F: Computer & Systems Sciences, Special Programme AET: Vol. 115). vii, 329p. 1993. 93.95 (*0-387-56654-6*) Spr-Verlag.

Learning Electronics: Theory & Experiments with Computer-Aided Instruction for the Commodore 64-128. Jesse R. Phagan & William Spaulding. (Illus.). 380p. 1988. 24.95 (*0-8306-7882-4*, 2882); pap. 16.95 (*0-8306-2882-7*) McGraw-Hill Prof.

Learning Electronics: Theory & Experiments with Computer-Aided Instruction for the Commodore 64-128. Jesse R. Phagan & William Spaulding. (Illus.). 370p. 1988. 24.95 (*0-8306-0182-1*, 2982); pap. 16.95 (*0-8306-2982-3*) McGraw-Hill Prof.

Learning Electronics: Theory & Experiments with Computer-Aided Instruction for the Commodore 64-128. Jesse R. Phagan & William Spaulding. (Illus.). 380p. 1989. 24.95 (*0-8306-9082-4*, 3082); pap. 16.95 (*0-8306-9382-3*, 3082) McGraw-Hill Prof.

Learning Electronics - C-64. Jesse R. Phagan & William Spaulding. 1991. 24.95 (*0-8306-6431-9*) McGraw-Hill Prof.

Learning Electronics Theory. Jesse R. Phagan & William Spaulding. 1991. 24.95 (*0-8306-6677-X*) McGraw-Hill Prof.

Learning English: A TV-Video Independent Study Program. Lori Howard et al. Ed. by Michael McLaughlin & Amy Schneider. (Illus.). 240p. (Orig.). (YA). 1992. pap. text 12.50 (*0-937354-76-7*) Delta Systems.

Learning English: Development & Diversity. Joan Swann. Ed. by Neil Mercer. LC 95-46659. (English Language Ser.). (Illus.). 360p. (C). 1996. 80.00 (*0-415-13121-9*); pap. 24.99 (*0-415-13122-7*) Routledge.

Learning English, a Career Investment for Successful Living. Alfred S. Payne. 1995. 14.95 (*0-533-11156-0*) Vantage.

Learning English Basics: The Eight Basic Parts of Speech. 5th ed. Maryhelen H. Hoffman & Lanny L. Hoffman. (English Grammar Comprehensive Workbook Ser.: Vol. 1). 100p. 1991. pap. 49.95 (*1-928592-11-2*) MHP Commns.

Learning English Made Simple. Shelia Henderson. 192p. 1991. pap. 12.95 (*0-385-26794-0*) Doubleday.

Learning English Series, 3 vols., Set. Kathy Knoblock. (Illus.). 144p. 1998. teacher ed. 17.85 (*1-58232-006-3*, BH 8959153); teacher ed. 29.75 (*1-58232-008-X*, BH 8960155) Bryan Hse.

Learning English Skills Through Word-Processing. DDC Staff. (Learning Series Texts). 1998. pap. 27.00 (*1-56243-624-4*) DDC Pub.

Learning English Through Arabic. S. N. Rizvi. 384p. 1992. lib. bdg. 60.00 (*81-209-0505-9*, Pub. by Pitambar Pub) St Mut.

Learning English Through Science. Francis X. Sutman et al. 48p. (Orig.). (C). 1986. pap. text 4.00 (*0-87355-061-7*) Natl Sci Tchrs.

Learning English Thru Topics about Asia. Cleland & Evans. Date not set. pap. text. write for info. (*0-582-87284-7*, Pub. by Addison-Wesley) Longman.

Learning English with the Bible, 3 vols. Louise M. Ebner. 1998. pap. 17.99 (*0-89957-562-5*) AMG Pubs.

Learning English with the Bible: Answer Guide . . . A Systematic Approach to Bible-Based English Grammar. Louise M. Ebner. Orig. Title: Exploring Truths. 47p. 1983. reprint ed. text, student ed. 4.99 (*0-89957-604-4*) AMG Pubs.

Learning English with the Bible: Textbook . . . A Systematic Approach to Bible-Based English Grammar. Louise M. Ebner. Orig. Title: Exploring Truths. 163p. 1983. reprint ed. student ed. 7.99 (*0-89957-565-X*) AMG Pubs.

Learning English with the Bible: Using Punctuation & Capitalization. Louise M. Ebner. 1998. pap. 7.99 (*0-89957-804-7*) AMG Pubs.

Learning English with the Bible Vol. 3: Diagramming Guide...English Grammar Diagrams Based on the Book of Joshua. Louise M. Ebner. Orig. Title: Exploring Truths Through Diagramming. 55p. 1983. pap., student ed. 6.99 (*0-89957-602-8*) AMG Pubs.

Learning English with Writing Composition, Vol. 5. Louise M. Ebner. (Learning English with the Bible Ser.). 1999. pap. text 7.99 (*0-89957-805-5*) AMG Pubs.

Learning Enrichments: A Parent's & Teacher's Handbook. Henry Littlejohn. LC 96-70431. (Illus.). 192p. (Orig.). 1996. pap. 21.95 (*1-56167-337-4*) Noble Hse MD.

Learning Enterprise. Anthony P. Carnevale & Andleila J. Gainer. (Illus.). 54p. (Orig.). (C). 1993. pap. text 30.00 (*1-56806-382-2*) DIANE Pub.

Learning Enterprise: Adult Learning, Human Capital & Economic Development. Lewis J. Perelman. 62p. 1984. 10.00 (*0-934842-44-2*) CSPA.

Learning Environment: An Instructional Strategy. Catherine E. Loughlin & Joseph H. Suina. LC 81-23353. (Illus.). 249p. (C). 1982. pap. text 18.95 (*0-8077-2714-8*) Tchrs Coll.

Learning Environments. Ed. by J. M. Pieters et al. (Recent Research in Psychology Ser.). ix, 364p. 1990. pap. 41.00 (*0-387-52903-9*) Spr-Verlag.

Learning Environments for Young Children. rev. ed. Henry Sanoff & Joan Sanoff. LC 81-81659. 104p. (Orig.). (J). (ps-3). 1981. pap. 15.95 (*0-89334-065-0*) Humanics Ltd.

Learning Environments for Young Children: A Developmental Approach to Shaping Activity Areas. Henry Sanoff & Joan Sanoff. LC 81-81659. (Illus.). 104p. (Orig.). (J). (ps-3). 1981. reprint ed. lib. bdg. 25.95 (*0-89334-225-4*, 2254X16) Humanics Ltd.

Learning Environments for Young Children: Rethinking Library Spaces & Services. Sandra Feinberg et al. LC 98-15275. xvi, 196 p. 1998. 35.00 (*0-8389-0736-9*) ALA.

***Learning Equation: Elementary & Intermediate Algebra Text.** (Mathematics Ser.). 2000. 60.00 (*0-534-36954-5*) Brooks-Cole.

Learning Essay Writing. Marvin Eicher. 48p. (YA). (gr. 7). 1986. pap. 1.90 (*0-7399-0244-X*, 2428) Rod & Staff.

Learning Exam Skills. Harry McVea & Peter Cumper. 122p. 1996. pap. 22.00 (*1-85431-451-3*, Pub. by Blackstone Pr) Gaunt.

Learning Excel 5. DDC Publishing Staff. (Fast-Teach Learning Ser.). 1993. spiral bd. 27.00 (*1-56243-124-2*, E-9) DDC Pub.

Learning Excel 7 for Windows 95. Cathy Vento. 1996. pap. text 27.00 (*1-56243-318-0*, Z-11) DDC Pub.

Learning Excel 7 for Windows 95. Cathy Vento. LC 97-139654. 1996. 31.00 (*1-56243-320-2*, Z-11HC) DDC Pub.

Learning Excel 2000. DDC Publishing Staff. 1999. 32.00 (*1-56243-734-8*) DDC Pub.

***Learning Excel 2000.** DDC Publishing Staff. (Illus.). 382p. 1999. 31.00 (*1-56243-705-4*) DDC Pub.

Learning Experience. Mary Bailey. LC 89-63521. 1990. pap. 13.00 (*0-85330-139-5*) Lucis.

Learning Experience Guide, Nursing. Anne K. Roe. (Nursing Education Ser.). 1989. 15.95 (*0-8273-4348-5*) Delmar.

Learning Experience Guides for Nursing Students: Instructor's Guide. 5th ed. Anne K. Roe et al. 65p. 1994. 15.95 (*0-8273-6172-6*) Delmar.

Learning Experiences in School Renewal: An Exploration of Five Successful Programs. Ed. by Bruce R. Joyce & Emily F. Calhoun. LC 96-22596. viii, 208p. 1996. pap. 14.50 (*0-86552-133-6*) U of Oreg ERIC.

Learning Experiences in Sociology of Sport. Susan L. Greendorfer & Cynthia A. Hasbrook. LC 90-35946. (Illus.). 152p. (C). 1990. spiral bd. 22.00 (*0-87322-298-9*, BGRE0298) Human Kinetics.

Learning Experiences in Sport Psychology. 2nd rev. ed. Glyn Roberts et al. LC 98-30815. 200p. (C). 1998. pap. text, student ed. 25.00 (*0-88011-932-2*, BROB0932) Human Kinetics.

Learning Experiences of Overseas Students. Ed. by Margaret Kinnell. 160p. 1990. 123.00 (*0-335-09589-5*) Taylor & Francis.

Learning Factors in Substance Abuse. 1991. lib. bdg. 69.95 (*0-8490-4371-9*) Gordon Pr.

Learning Factory. Edward R. Alef & Daniel Berg. LC 96-28703. 114p. 1996. pap. text 14.50 (*0-7618-0465-X*) U Pr of Amer.

***Learning Fear.** B. A. Chepaitis. 2000. mass mkt. 5.99 (*0-441-00696-5*) Ace Bks.

Learning for a Lifetime: The Report of the NASBE Study Group on State Board Linkages with Higher Education. 2nd ed. NASBE Study Group on State Board Linkages with Higher Education Staff. 32p. 1994. pap. 7.50 (*1-58434-024-X*) NASBE.

Learning for All. Lawrence W. Lezotte. 92p. 1997. pap. text 24.95 (*1-883247-08-X*) Effect Schls.

Learning for Change: Developing Staff & Practice in Social Work Teams. Gerald G. Smale & Graham Tucson. (C). 1988. 35.00 (*0-7855-0079-0*, Pub. by Natl Inst Soc Work) St Mut.

Learning for Change: Developing Staff & Practice in Social Work Teams. Gerald G. Smale & Graham Tuson. (C). 1988. 35.00 (*0-902789-57-0*, Pub. by Natl Inst Soc Work) St Mut.

***Learning for Earning.** Parsloe & Allen. 96p. 2000. pap. 17.95 (*0-8464-5104-2*) Beekman Pubs.

Learning for Earning: Your Route to Success. 3rd ed. John A. Wanat et al. LC 97-44783. 1998. 42.64 (*1-56637-459-6*) Goodheart.

Learning for Everyone - Welsh Office Green Paper. (Command Papers: No. 3924). 1998. 25.00 (*0-10-139242-7*, HM92427, Pub. by Statnry Office) Bernan Associates.

***Learning for Leadership: Interpersonal & Intergroup.** A .K. Rice. 212p. 1999. pap. 38.00 (*1-85575-233-6*, Pub. by H Karnac Bks Ltd) Other Pr LLC.

Learning for Life: Creating Classrooms for Self-Directed Learning. Ronald J. Areglado et al. (Illus.). 184p. 1996. 55.95 (*0-8039-6385-8*); pap. 24.95 (*0-8039-6386-6*) Corwin Pr.

Learning for Life: Education for an Economically Competitive & Socially Responsible North America. Ed. by Rod Dobell & Michael Neufeld. 134p. 1992. pap. text 10.95 (*0-88982-123-2*, Pub. by Oolichan Bks) Genl Dist Srvs.

Learning for Life: Fifth Grade. Boy Scouts of America Staff. (Illus.). 265p. (J). (gr. 5). 1996. pap. 5.00 (*0-8395-2110-3*, 32110) BSA.

Learning for Life: Moral Education Theory & Practice. Ed. by Andrew Garrod. LC 91-46756. 296p. 1992. 57.95 (*0-275-94045-4*, C4045, Praeger Pubs) Greenwood.

Learning for Life: Politics & Progress in Recurrent Education. Ed. by Frank Molyneaux et al. 336p. 1987. lib. bdg. 59.00 (*0-317-64375-4*, Pub. by C Helm) Routldge.

Learning for Life: Unite 3. Harriet Cabell. 80p. (C). 1995. pap. text, per. 16.95 (*0-7872-0333-5*) Kendall-Hunt.

Learning for Living: Higher Education in East London, 1890-1992. Tyrell Burgess et al. LC 94-46791. (Illus.). 185p. (C). 1995. pap. 19.95 (*0-485-12092-5*, Pub. by Athlone Pr); text 49.95 (*0-485-11434-8*, Pub. by Athlone Pr) Humanities.

Learning for Living - A Catholic Contribution to the Culture of Learning & Teaching in South Africa. Catholic Institute of Education Staff. 64p. 1999. pap. 14.95 (*0-7021-4630-7*, Pub. by Juta & Co) Intl Spec Bk.

Learning for One's Self: Essays on the Individual in Neo-Confucian Thought. William T. De Bary. 1991. text 64.50 (*0-231-07426-3*) Col U Pr.

Learning for Personal Development. Ed. by Lorraine A. Cavaliere & Angela Sgroi. LC 85-644750. (New Directions for Adult & Continuing Education Ser.: No. ACE 53). 130p. 1992. pap., student ed. 22.00 (*1-55542-747-2*) Jossey-Bass.

Learning for Professional Practice: Partnerships for Practice. I. Taylor. LC 97-12125. 192p. 1997. pap. 34.95 (*0-335-19497-4*) OpUniv Pr.

Learning for Success! 1995. pap. 24.95 incl. audio (*1-56052-367-0*) Crisp Pubns.

Learning for Success! 86p. 1995. pap. 149.00 incl. audio, VHS (*1-56052-366-2*) Crisp Pubns.

Learning for Text Categorization: Papers from the AAAI Workshop. Ed. by Mehran Sahami. (Technical Reports: Vol. WS-98-05). (Illus.). 102p. 1998. spiral bd. 25.00 (*1-57735-058-8*) AAAI Pr.

Learning for the Common Good: Liberal Education, Civic Education, & Teaching about Philanthropy. Thomas Jeavons. xiii, 82p. (Orig.). 1991. pap. text 10.00 (*0-911696-52-0*) Assn Am Coll.

Learning for the 21st Century. 5th ed. Osher & Ward. 344p. (C). 1998. per. 32.95 (*0-7872-4742-1*, 41474201) Kendall-Hunt.

Learning Foreign & Second Languages: Perspectives in Research & Scholarship. Ed. by Heidi Byrnes. LC 98-39497. (Teaching Languages, Literatures, & Cultures Ser.: No. 1). 300p. 1998. pap. 19.75 (*0-87352-801-8*, TL01P); lib. bdg. 37.50 (*0-87352-800-X*, TL01C) Modern Lang.

Learning Foundations of Behavior Therapy. Frederick H. Kanfer et al. LC 71-111354. (Series in Psychology). (Illus.). 656p. reprint ed. pap. 200.00 (*0-608-10325-X*, 201235700081) Bks Demand.

Learning French Through the Law. Vivian G. Curran. 300p. 1995. text 60.00 (*0-9650295-0-6*) Juris Pubng.

Learning French with Enza B. Bk. 1: An Introduction to Nouns & Gender. Margaret Harris. (Learning Language with Enza B. Ser.). (Illus.). 95p. (J). (gr. 3-8). 1994. student ed. 15.95 (*1-886332-01-0*) Forlang Foreign.

Learning French with Enza B Bk. 2: Regular Verbs & the Present Tense. (FRE.). Date not set. write for info. (*1-886332-04-5*) Forlang Foreign.

***Learning from Accidents.** Trevor Kletz. (Illus.). 300p. 2001. 85.95 (*0-7506-4883-X*) Buttrwrth-Heinemann.

Learning from Accidents. 2nd rev. ed. Trevor A. Kletz. LC 93-50876. (Illus.). 240p. 1994. text 52.95 (*0-7506-1952-X*) Buttrwrth-Heinemann.

Learning from Adversity: Policy Responses to 2 Oil Shocks. Stanley W. Black. LC 85-23726. (Essays in International Finance Ser.: No. 160). 24p. 1985. pap. text 10.00 (*0-88165-067-6*) Princeton U Int Finan Econ.

Learning from America: Policy Transfer & the Development of the British Workfare State. David P. Dolowitz. LC 97-26461. 224p. 1997. 69.95 (*1-898723-73-7*, Pub. by Sussex Acad Pr) Intl Spec Bk.

Learning from Asian Philosophy. Joel J. Kupperman. LC 98-32349. 224p. 1999. 45.00 (*0-19-512831-1*) OUP.

***Learning from Asian Philosophy.** Joel J. Kupperman. LC 98-32349. 224p. 1999. pap. 19.95 (*0-19-512832-X*) OUP.

***Learning from Assessment - Tools for Examining Assessment Through Standards: A Middle School Mathematics Professional Development Resource.** Tania J. Madfes & Ann Muench. viii, 99p. 1999. 25.00 (*0-914409-11-5*) WestEd.

Learning from Baltimore. Roberto Brambilla & Cranni Longo. 147p. (Orig.). 1979. pap. 21.95 (*0-87855-832-2*) Transaction Pubs.

Learning from Baltimore. Roberto Brambilla & Gianni Longo. LC 79-90201. (Learning from the U. S. A.: What Makes Cities Livable Ser.). (Illus.). 150p. (Orig.). 1979. pap. 6.95 (*0-936020-02-4*) Urban Initiat.

Learning from Capitalists: A Study of Soviet Assimilation of Western Technology. Mikael Sandberg. 264p. (Orig.). 1989. pap. 47.50 (*91-22-01319-9*, Pub. by Umea U Bibl) Coronet Bks.

Learning from Case Studies. G. Easton. 203p. (C). 1982. 160.00 (*0-7855-5655-9*, Pub. by Inst Pur & Supply) St Mut.

Learning from Cast Studies. Geoff Easton. 203p. (C). 1988. 105.00 (*0-7855-3780-5*, Pub. by Inst Pur & Supply) St Mut.

***Learning from Change: Issues & Experiences in Participatory Monitoring & Evaluation.** Marisol Estrella et al. 272p. 2000. pap. 16.95 (*0-88936-895-3*) IDRC Bks.

***Learning from Change: Landmarks in Teaching & Learning in Higher Education from Change Magazine, 1969-1999.** Ed. by Deborah DeZure. 256p. 2000. 49.95 (*1-57922-001-0*); pap. 27.50 (*1-57922-002-9*) Stylus Pub VA.

***Learning from Children.** Jan Lokan & Brian Doig. 162p. 1998. pap. 29.95 (*0-86431-255-5*, Pub. by Aust Council Educ Res) Stylus Pub VA.

Learning from Children: New Beginnings for Teaching Numerical Thinking. Ed Labinowicz. LC 84-234917. 1985. text 26.95 (*0-201-20321-9*) Addison-Wesley.

Learning from Children Who Read at an Early Age. Rhona Stainthorp. 1999. 75.00 (*0-415-17494-5*); pap. 24.99 (*0-415-17495-3*) Routledge.

Learning from China? Development & Environment in Third World Countries. Ed. by Bernhard Glaeser. (Illus.). 256p. 1987. text 55.00 (*0-04-333027-4*) Routledge.

Learning from Computers - Mathematics Education & Technology: Proceedings of the NATO Advanced Research Workshop on Mathematics Education & Technology, Held in Villard-de-Lans, Grenoble, France, May 6-11, 1993. NATO Advanced Research Workshop on Mathematics Education. Ed. by Christine Keitel & Kenneth Ruthven. LC 93-34948. (NATO ASI Series F: Computer & Systems Sciences, Special Programme AET: Vol. 121). 1993. 93.95 (*0-387-57277-5*) Spr-Verlag.

Learning from Conflict: A Handbook for Trainers & Group Leaders. L. B. Hart. 1981. write for info. (*0-201-03144-2*) Addison-Wesley.

Learning from Conflict: A Handbook for Trainers & Group Leaders. 2nd ed. Lois B. Hart. 210p. 1991. ring bd. 59.95 (*0-87425-159-1*) HRD Press.

Learning from Conflict: Studies in Counterinsurgency & Low Intensity Warfare. Richard D. Downie. LC 97-34728. 312p. 1998. 65.00 (*0-275-96010-2*, Praeger Pubs) Greenwood.

Learning from Cooking Experiences: A Teacher's Guide to Accompany Cook & Learn. Thelma Harms. (Illus.). 1981. text, teacher ed. 5.00 (*0-201-09425-8*) Addison-Wesley.

Learning from Data: An Introduction to Statistical Reasoning. 2nd ed. Arthur M. Glenberg. 176p. 1996. pap., teacher ed. write for info. (*0-8058-1785-9*); text 55.00 (*0-8058-1784-0*) L Erlbaum Assocs.

Learning from Data: Artificial Intelligence & Statistics V. Ed. by Doug Fisher & H. J. Lenz. (Lecture Notes in Statistics Ser.: Vol. 112). 464p. 1996. pap. 49.95 (*0-387-94736-1*) Spr-Verlag.

Learning from Data: Concepts, Theory & Methods. Vladimier S. Cherkassky & Filip Mulier. LC 97-43019. (Adaptive & Learning Systems for Signal Processing, Communications & Control Ser.). 464p. 1998. 79.95 (*0-471-15493-8*, Wiley-Interscience) Wiley.

Learning from Data Comp. Glenberg. 1996. write for info. (*0-8058-2298-4*) L Erlbaum Assocs.

***Learning from Difference: Teaching Morrison, Twain, Ellison, & Eliot.** Richard C. Moreland. LC 99-18510. 192p. 1999. text 40.00 (*0-8142-0823-1*) Ohio St U Pr.

Learning from Difference: Teaching Morrison, Twain, Ellison & Eliot. Richard C. Moreland. LC 99-18510. 192p. 1999. pap. text 17.00 (*0-8142-5025-4*) Ohio St U Pr.

Learning from Disaster: Risk Management after Bhopal. Ed. by Sheila Jasanoff. LC 93-48100. (Law in Social Context Ser.). (Illus.). 336p. (Orig.). (C). 1994. text 45.00 (*0-8122-3250-X*); pap. text 19.95 (*0-8122-1532-X*) U of Pa Pr.

Learning from Disruption: Making Better Placements. Sheila Smith. 1994. pap. 35.00 (*1-873868-15-4*) BAAF.

Learning from Experience: A Cross Case Comparison of School to Work Transition Reform Initiatives. Anne M. Rogers et al. (Cross Case Report & Case Studies). 110p. 1995. text, teacher ed. 20.00 (*0-614-24526-5*); pap. text, teacher ed. 10.00 (*0-614-24527-3*) Natl Inst Work.

Learning from Experience: Memory & the Teacher's Account of Teaching. Miriam Ben-Peretz. LC 94-17215. (SUNY Series, Teacher Preparation & Development). 176p. (C). 1995. text 49.50 (*0-7914-2303-4*); pap. text 16.95 (*0-7914-2304-2*) State U NY Pr.

Learning from Failure: The Systems Approach. Joyce Fortune & Geoff Peters. LC 95-8787. 274p. 1995. pap. 118.95 (*0-471-94420-3*) Wiley.

Learning from Gal Oya: Possibilities for Participatory Development. Norman Uphoff. 464p. 1996. pap. 19.95 (*1-85339-351-7*, Pub. by Intermed Tech) Stylus Pub VA.

Learning from Gal Oya: Possibilities for Participatory Development & Post-Newtonian Social Science. Norman T. Uphoff. LC 91-55563. (Illus.). 464p. 1992. text 42.50 (*0-8014-2589-1*) Cornell U Pr.

Learning from Galveston. R. Brambilla et al. LC 81-51442. (Illus.). 112p. (Orig.). 1983. pap. 6.95 (*0-685-05566-3*) Urban Initiat.

Learning from God's Birds. Ruth J. Jay. (Learning From...Ser.). (Illus.). 34p. (J). (ps-4). 1981. pap. 2.99 (*0-934998-05-1*) Evangel Indiana.

Learning from Good & Bad Data. Philip D. Laird. (C). 1988. text 91.00 (*0-89838-263-7*) Kluwer Academic.

Learning from Hannah: Secrets for a Life Worth Living. William H. Thomas. LC 98-54732. (Illus.). 240p. 1999. 21.95 (*1-889242-09-8*) VanderWyk & Burnham.

Learning from Hebrews. Charles W. Ford. LC 80-67467. (Radiant Life Ser.). 127p. 1980. pap. 3.95 (*0-88243-915-4*, 02-0915) Gospel Pub.

***Learning from History: A Black Christian's Perspective on the Holocaust, 63.** Hubert G. Locke. LC 00-22304. (Contributions to the Study of Religion Ser.: Vol. 63). 150p. 2000. 58.00 (*0-313-31569-8*, GM1569, Greenwood Pr) Greenwood.

Learning from Hollywood: Architektur und Film/Architecture & Film. Hans Dieter Schaal. (ENG & GER., Illus.). 128p. 1997. 58.00 (*3-930698-70-6*) Edition A Menges.

Learning from Kohut: Progress in Self Psychology, Vol. 4. Ed. by Arnold Goldberg. (Progress in Self Psychology Ser.). 256p. 1988. text 45.00 (*0-88163-081-0*) Analytic Pr.

Learning from La Jolla: Robert Venturi Remakes a Museum in the Precinct of Irving Gill. Hugh M. Davies & Anne Farrell. LC 96-79507. (Illus.). 1997. 45.00 (*0-934418-48-9*); pap. 22.95 (*0-934418-47-0*) Mus Contemp Art.

Learning from Las Vegas. rev. ed. Robert Venturi et al. (Illus.). 192p. 1977. pap. text 14.95 (*0-262-72006-X*) MIT Pr.

An Asterisk (*) at the beginning of an entry indicates that the title is appearing for the first time.

Learning from Leaders: Corporate Resource Directory. 175p. Date not set. 35.00 (1-58534-039-1) Points of Light.

Learning from Leaders: Welfare Reform Policies & Policy in Five Midwestern States. Ed. by Carol S. Weissert. 225p. 1999. 38.95 (0-914341-67-7, Pub. by Nelson Rockefeller Inst Govt) Brookings.

Learning from Leaders: Welfare Reform Policies & Policy in Five Midwestern States. Ed. by Carol S. Weissert. LC 99-86401. 225p. 2000. pap. 16.95 (0-914341-68-5, Pub. by Nelson Rockefeller Inst Govt) Brookings.

Learning from Leaders Resource Directory. 1997. pap. write for info. (1-58534-024-3) Points of Light.

Learning from "Learning by Doing" Lessons for Economic Growth. Robert M. Solow. LC 96-31847. (Kenneth J. Arrow Lectures). 1997. write for info. (0-8047-2840-2); pap. 14.95 (0-8047-2841-0) Stanford U Pr.

***Learning from Life.** Ed. by Surrey Beatty Staff. 126p. 1999. pap. 60.00 (0-949324-01-9, Pub. by Surrey Beatty & Sons) St Mut.

Learning from Local Authority Budgeting. Howard Elcock & Grant Jordan. 268p. 1987. text 87.95 (0-566-05384-5, Pub. by Avebry) Ashgate Pub Co.

Learning from Maps. Kataoka. 1996. pap. 40.94 (0-07-034369-1) McGraw.

Learning from Mt. Hua: A Chinese Physician's Illustrated Travel Record & Painting Theory. Kathlyn M. Liscomb. LC 96-32050. (RES Monographs on Anthropology & Aesthetics). (Illus.). 245p. (C). 1993. text 95.00 (0-521-41112-2) Cambridge U Pr.

***Learning from Museums: Visitor Experiences & the Making of Meaning.** John H. Falk & Lynn D. Dierking. (American Association for State & Local History Book Ser.). 250p. 2000. 59.00 (0-7425-0294-5); pap. 24.95 (0-7425-0295-3) AltaMira Pr.

***Learning from North-South Links in Microfinance.** Ben Rogaly & Chris Roche. 1998. pap. 11.95 (0-85598-408-2, Pub. by Oxfam Pub) Stylus Pub VA.

Learning from Other Countries: The Cross-National Dimension in Urban Policy Making. Ed. by Masser & Williams. (Illus.). 220p. (C). 1986. 80.00 (0-86094-210-4) Chapman & Hall.

Learning from Other Women: How to Benefit from the Knowledge, Wisdom & Experience of Female Mentors. Carolyn S. Duff. LC 99-28081. 208p. 1999. 22.95 (0-8144-0455-3) AMACOM.

Learning from Other Worlds: Estrangement, Cognition & the Politics of Science Fiction & Utopia. Ed. by Patrick Parrinder. (Liverpool Science Fiction Texts & Studies: 17). 288p. 1999. 49.95 (0-85323-574-0, Pub. by Liverpool Univ Pr); pap. 24.95 (0-85323-534-1, Pub. by Liverpool Univ Pr) U of Pa Pr.

Learning from Others: Good Programs & Successful Campaigns. Chrissie Bamber et al. LC 96-84978. 358p. 1996. pap. text 50.00 (0-912585-11-0) Ctr Law & Ed.

***Learning from Others: International Comparisons in Education.** Diane Shorrocks-Taylor et al. LC 00-30186. (Science & Technology Education Library). 2000. write for info. (0-7923-6343-4) Kluwer Academic.

Learning from Others in Groups: Experimental Learning Approaches. Cary L. Cooper. LC 78-26987. (Illus.). 304p. 1979. 55.00 (0-313-20922-7, COL/, Greenwood Pr) Greenwood.

***Learning from Our Lives: Using Educational Biographies with Adults.** Pierre Dominice. LC 99-50636. 208p. 2000. 27.95 (0-7879-1031-7) Jossey-Bass.

Learning from Our Lives: Women, Research, & Biography in Education. Ed. by Anna Neumann & Penelope L. Peterson. 288p. (C). 1997. text 46.00 (0-8077-3594-9); pap. text 21.95 (0-8077-3593-0) Tchrs Coll.

Learning from Our Mistakes: A Reinterpretation of Twentieth-Century Educational Theory, 14. Henry J. Perkinson. LC 83-26670. (Contributions to the Study of Education Ser.: No. 14). (Illus.). 224p. 1984. 59.95 (0-313-24239-9, PEM/) Greenwood.

Learning from Our Mistakes: Difficulties & Failures in Feminist Therapy. Ed. by Marcia Hill & Esther D. Rothblum. LC 98-35594. 126p. 1998. 29.95 (0-7890-0653-7) Haworth Pr.

Learning from Our Mistakes: Difficulties & Failures in Feminist Therapy. Ed. by Marcia Hill & Esther D. Rothblum. LC 98-35594. 126p. 1998. pap. 14.95 (0-7890-0670-7) Haworth Pr.

Learning from Practice: A Professional Development Text for Legal Externs. J. P. Ogilver et al. LC 92-207844. 346p. 1998. pap. 25.50 (0-314-22873-X) West Pub.

Learning from Practice: Democratic Deliberation & the Promise of Planning Practice. John Forester. 106p. (Orig.). (C). 1997. pap. text 15.00 (0-913749-23-0) U MD Urban Stud.

Learning from Public Library Literacy Programs. Andrew J. Seager. (Illus.). 122p. (Orig.). (C). 1994. pap. text 25.00 (0-7881-0891-3) DIANE Pub.

Learning from Robben Island: Govan Mbeki's Prison Writings. Govan Mbeki. LC 91-3198. 232p. 1991. pap. 15.95 (0-8214-1007-5); text 24.95 (0-8214-1006-7) Ohio U Pr.

Learning from Samuel Wilson, Jr. A Collection of Oral Histories, 1980-1989. Abbye A. Gorin. LC 92-81697. 110p. (Orig.). 1992. pap. 12.00 (1-879714-03-5) SW PF LA Land.

Learning from Seattle. Roberto Brambilla & Gianni Longo. (Learning from the U. S. A.: What Makes Cities Livable Ser.). 150p. 1980. reprint ed. pap. 21.95 (0-87855-833-0) Transaction Pubs.

Learning from Somalia: The Lessons of Armed Humanitarian Intervention. Walter Clarke. LC 96-48453. (C). 1997. pap. 79.00 (0-8133-2793-8, Pub. by Westview) HarpC.

Learning from Somalia: The Lessons of Armed Humanitarian Intervention. Ed. by Walter Clarke & Jeffrey Herbst. LC 96-48453. 288p. (C). 1997. pap. text 28.00 (0-8133-2794-6, Pub. by Westview) HarpC.

Learning from Strangers: The Art & Method of Qualitative Interview Studies. Weiss. 1995. 15.00 (0-02-874128-5) Free Pr.

Learning from Strangers: The Art & Method of Qualitative Interview Studies. Robert S. Weiss. LC 93-24464. 1993. 27.95 (0-02-934625-8) Free Pr.

Learning from Strangers: The Art & Method of Qualitative Interview Studies. Robert S. Weiss. 256p. 1995. pap. 15.00 (0-684-82312-8) Free Pr.

Learning from Success: Campus Case Studies in International Program Development. Ann Kelleher. (Worcester Polytechnic Institute Studies in Science, Technology & Culture: Vol. 15). VII, 444p. (Orig.). (C). 1996. pap. text 38.95 (0-8204-2407-2) P Lang Pubng.

Learning from Success: Health Agency Effort to Improve Community Involvement in Communities Affected by Hazardous Waste Sites. Henry S. Cole & Mark A. Stevens. (Illus.). 219p. (C). 1998. pap. text 40.00 (0-7881-4850-8) DIANE Pub.

Learning from Text Across Conceptual Domains. Ed. by Cynthia R. Hynd. LC 97-43514. 350p. 1998. write for info. (0-8058-2183-X); pap. write for info. (0-8058-2184-8) L Erlbaum Assocs.

Learning from Textbooks: Theory & Practice. Ed. by Bruce K. Britton et al. 208p. 1993. text 49.95 (0-8058-0677-6) L Erlbaum Assocs.

Learning from the Angel. Gunilla Norris. LC 85-80140. 62p. (Orig.). 1985. per. 5.00 (0-916418-59-6) Lotus.

Learning from the Book of Nature. Wiliam Child. (Illus.). 200p. 1996. pap. 6.85 (0-7399-0147-8, 2307) Rod & Staff.

Learning from the Field: A Guide from Experience. William F. Whyte. LC 84-15942. 295p. 1984. 38.95 (0-8039-2161-6); pap. 24.00 (0-8039-3318-5) Sage.

Learning from the Future: Competitive Foresight Scenarios. Liam Fahey & Robert Randall. LC 97-20109. 464p. 1997. 37.95 (0-471-30352-6) Wiley.

Learning from the Greeks: An Exhibition Commemorating the Five-Hundredth Anniversary of the Founding of the Aldine Press. Robert G. Babcock & Mark L. Sosower. LC 94-12098. (Illus.). 85p. (Orig.). 1994. pap. 15.00 (0-8457-3128-9) Yale U Lib.

Learning from the Histories of Rhetoric: Essays in Honor of Winifred Bryan Horner. Ed. by Theresa Enos. LC 92-19715. 200p. (C). 1993. 31.95 (0-8093-1784-2); pap. 17.95 (0-8093-1800-8) S Ill U Pr.

Learning from the Japanese: Japan's Pre-War Development & the Third World. E. Wayne Nafziger. LC 94-27010. (Japan in the Modern World Ser.). 238p. (C). (gr. 13). 1994. text 70.95 (1-56324-485-3, East Gate Bk); pap. text 34.95 (1-56324-486-1, East Gate Bk) M E Sharpe.

Learning from the Japanese City: West Meets East in Urban Design. Barrie Shelton. LC 98-48053. (Studies in History, Planning & the Environment). 1999. 70.00 (0-419-22350-9) Routledge.

Learning from the Land: Teaching Ecology Through Stories & Activities. Brian F. Ellis. LC 97-10995. (Illus.). 150p. 1997. lib. bdg. 23.00 (1-56308-563-1) Teacher Ideas Pr.

Learning from the Land: Wisconsin Land Use. Bobbie Malone. (New Badger History Ser.). (Illus.). 80p. (Orig.). 1998. pap. text 7.95 (0-87020-294-4) U of Wis Pr.

Learning from the Land: Wisconsin Land Use. Bobbie Malone. (New Badger History Ser.). (Illus.). 62p. (Orig.). (J). (gr. 1-12). 1998. pap. text, teacher ed., student ed. 20.00 (0-87020-295-2) U of Wis Pr.

Learning from the Lives of Amazing People. Janice Gudeman. 144p. (J). (gr. 4 up). 1988. student ed. 10.99 (0-86653-446-6, GA1055) Good Apple.

***Learning from the Lizard: Bible Animal Object Lessons.** Samuel J. Hahn. (ps-3). 2000. pap. 8.75 (0-7880-1593-1) CSS OH.

Learning from the Past: What History Teaches Us about School Reform. Ed. by Diane Ravitch & Maris A. Vinovskis. LC 94-27015. 440p. 1995. text 48.50 (0-8018-4920-9); pap. text 18.95 (0-8018-4921-7) Johns Hopkins.

Learning from the Patient. Patrick J. Casement. LC 90-14120. (Psychoanalysis Ser.). 384p. 1990. lib. bdg. 45.00 (0-89862-559-9) Guilford Pubns.

Learning from the Patient. Patrick J. Casement. LC 90-14120. (Psychoanalysis Ser.). 384p. 1992. reprint ed. pap. text 25.00 (0-89862-157-7) Guilford Pubns.

Learning from the Patient: Fundamental Principles see Invatand de la Pacient, Vol. 1, Principii Fundamentale

Learning from the Sages: Selected Studies on the Book of Proverbs. Ed. by Roy B. Zuck. LC 94-9653. 448p. 1995. pap. 24.99 (0-8010-9941-2) Baker Bks.

Learning from the World's Best Central Bankers: Principles & Policies for Subduing Inflation. George M. Von Furstenberg & Michael K. Ulan. LC 98-37470. 7p. 1998. write for info. (0-7923-8303-6) Kluwer Academic.

Learning from the World's Best Central Bankers: Principles & Policies For Subduing Inflation. George M. Von Furstenberg & Michael K. Ulan. LC 98-37470. 1998. 50.00 (0-7923-8304-4) Kluwer Academic.

Learning from Things: Method & Theory of Material Culture Studies. Ed. by W. David Kingery. LC 95-11673. (Illus.). 288p. 1996. text 39.00 (1-56098-607-7) Smithsonian.

Learning from Things: Methods & Theory of Material Culture Studies. Ed. by W. David Kingery. 288p. 1998. pap. text 14.95 (1-56098-883-5) Smithsonian.

Learning from TIMSS: Results of the Third International Mathematics & Science Study, Summary of a Symposium. National Research Council Staff. Ed. by Alexandra Beatty. LC 98-121443. 56p. (C). 1997. pap. text 15.00 (0-309-05975-5) Natl Acad Pr.

Learning from Working: Getting the Most from Your Cooperative Education/Internship Program. 2nd rev. ed. William A. Stull et al. 220p. 1997. pap. text 12.95 (0-9659543-0-7) Career Prods.

Learning from Your Experience with People. 3rd rev. ed. Ron Short. 100p. 1995. pap. 16.95 (0-614-08534-9) Lrng in Action.

Learning Fun. Hermes House Staff. (Point & Say Ser.). (J). 1998. 9.98 (1-84038-156-6) Hermes Hse.

***Learning Fun: A First Word & Picture Book.** Ed. by Lorenz Books Staff. (Point & Say Bks.). (Illus.). (J). 2000. 9.95 (1-85967-802-5, Lorenz Bks) Anness Pub.

Learning Fun at the Treasure House. (Captain Kangaroo Coloring & Activity Bks.: Vol. 1). (Illus.). 32p. (J). 1998. pap. write for info. (0-7666-0223-0, Honey Bear Bks) Modern Pub NYC.

Learning Functional Words & Phrases for Every Day Living. David J. Somers. 1981. 3.75 (0-88323-135-2) Pendergrass Pub.

Learning Functional Words & Phrases for Everyday Living. David J. Somers. (Illus.). 1996. reprint ed. pap. 6.95 (0-88323-250-2, 220) Pendergrass Pub.

Learning Fund: Income Generation Through NFE. A. Iskandar et al. (Technical Notes Ser.: No. 22). 24p. (Orig.). (C). 1982. pap. 2.00 (0-932288-68-5) Ctr Intl Ed U of MA.

Learning Futurebasic: Macintosh Basic Power. L. Frank Turovich. (Learning Library: No. 1). (Illus.). 352p. 1995. pap. 30.00 (0-9639552-0-9) Sentient Fruit.

Learning Futurebasic II: The Toolbox. L. Frank Turovich. (Learning Library: No. 2). (Illus.). 240p. (Orig.). 1996. pap. 30.00 (0-9639552-1-7) Sentient Fruit.

Learning Game. M. Barber. 1997. pap. text 19.95 (0-575-40100-1, Pub. by V Gollancz) Trafalgar.

Learning Game: Arguments for an Education Revolution. Michael Barber. 320p. 1998. pap. 24.95 (0-575-06364-5, Pub. by Indigo) Trafalgar.

Learning Games Without Losers. Sarah Liu & Mary L. Vittitow. (Illus.). 96p. (J). (gr. k-6). 1985. pap. text, student ed. 10.95 (0-86530-039-9, IP 39-9) Incentive Pubns.

Learning Gap. Harold W. Stevenson & James W. Stigler. 240p. 1994. per. 11.00 (0-671-88076-4, Touchstone) S&S Trade Pap.

Learning Geography: An Annotated Bibliography of Research Paths. Alfred S. Forsyth, Jr. (Pathways Ser.: No. 11). 80p. (C). 1995. pap. text 10.00 (1-884136-04-4) NCFGE.

Learning Geography by Stages, Bk. I. J. Fuste & V. N. Nigam. 72p. 1997. pap. 27.00 (81-209-0602-0, Pub. by Pitambar Pub) St Mut.

Learning Geography by Stages, Bk. II. J. Fuste & V. N. Nigam. 80p. 1997. pap. 30.00 (81-209-0603-9, Pub. by Pitambar Pub) St Mut.

Learning Geography by Stages, Bk. III. J. Fuste & V. N. Nigam. 104p. 1997. pap. 35.00 (81-209-0604-7, Pub. by Pitambar Pub) St Mut.

Learning Geography by Stages, Bk. IV. J. Fuste & V. N. Nigam. 168p. 1997. pap. 50.00 (81-209-0605-5, Pub. by Pitambar Pub) St Mut.

Learning Geography by Stages, Bk. V. J. Fuste & V. N. Nigam. 112p. 1997. pap. 40.00 (81-209-0606-3, Pub. by Pitambar Pub) St Mut.

Learning Geography by Stages, Bk. VI. Alexander S. Job & B. N. Ahuja. 100p. 1997. pap. 35.00 (81-209-0607-1, Pub. by Pitambar Pub) St Mut.

Learning Geography by Stages, Bk. VII. Alexander S. Job & B. N. Ahuja. 168p. 1997. pap. 50.00 (81-209-0608-X, Pub. by Pitambar Pub) St Mut.

Learning Geography by Stages, Bk. VIII. Alexander S. Job & B. N. Ahuja. 148p. 1997. pap. 50.00 (81-209-0609-8, Pub. by Pitambar Pub) St Mut.

Learning GNU Emacs. 2nd rev. ed. Eric Raymond et al. 533p. (Orig.). 1996. pap. 29.95 (1-56592-152-6) Thomson Learn.

***Learning Group Leadership: An Experimental Approach.** Jeffrey A. Kottler. 320p. 2000. pap. 49.00 (0-205-32151-8) Allyn.

***Learning Guide- Skills at Work Module 3: Applying Technology, 15 Vos.** Ait. (Tech Prep Ser.). 1999. pap. 110.00 (0-538-68999-4) Sth-Wstrn College.

Learning Guide Marketing. 4th ed. Paczkowski. 1996. pap. text 27.20 (0-13-271768-9) St Martin.

Learning Guide Prin Anat&Phys. 9th ed. Gerard Tortora. (C). 1999. pap. text 22.50 (0-321-05341-9) Addson-Wesley Educ.

***Learning Guide, Skills at Work Module 2: Developing Interpersonal Skills, 15 Vols.** Ait. (Tech Prep Ser.). 1999. pap. 110.00 (0-538-68979-X) Sth-Wstrn College.

***Learning Guide, Skills at Work Module 4: Understanding Systems.** Ait. 1999. pap. 110.00 (0-538-69006-2) Sth-Wstrn College.

Learning Guide the Infinite Geometric Progression Puzzles. Ron Brown & Ginger Brown. (Illus.). 135p. (Orig.). 1994. pap. 16.00 (0-9646339-0-6) With You in Mind.

Learning Guide to Marketing. 3rd ed. Thomas Paczkowski. (C). 1993. pap. text 25.20 (0-13-562778-8) P-H.

Learning Guide to Research on the Internet. Maria Garrido. 304p. 1997. pap., teacher ed. 24.99 (0-7821-1964-6) Sybex.

Learning Gym. Erich Ballinger. (Illus.). 29p. 1996. pap. 9.95 (0-942143-09-4) Edu-Kinesthetics.

Learning Helpers: A Guide to Training & Reflection. rev. ed. National Helpers Network Staff. (Illus.). x, 70p. 1998. ring bd. 55.00 (1-891455-01-X) Natl Helpers.

Learning Helping Skills. (C). 2000. text 33.33 (0-205-29802-8, Longwood Div) Allyn.

Learning Higher Mathematics. Lev S. Pontryagin. (Soviet Mathematics Ser.). (Illus.). 320p. 1984. 82.95 (0-387-12351-2) Spr-Verlag.

Learning Highway: Smart Students & the Net. 2nd rev. ed. Trevor Owen et al. (Illus.). 210p. (YA). (gr. 9 up). 1997. pap. 16.95 (1-55013-878-2) Firefly Bks Ltd.

Learning History in America: Schools, Cultures, & Politics. Ed. by Lloyd Kramer et al. LC 93-25489. 1994. text 44.95 (0-8166-2363-5) U of Minn Pr.

Learning History in America: Schools, Cultures, & Politics. Ed. by Lloyd S. Kramer et al. LC 93-25489. 1994. pap. 17.95 (0-8166-2364-3) U of Minn Pr.

Learning How: BMX Riding. Sue Boulais. Ed. by Jody James. (Learning How Sports Ser.). (Illus.). 48p. (J). (gr. 4-7). 1992. pap. 5.95 (0-944280-41-2); lib. bdg. 14.95 (0-944280-36-6) Bancroft-Sage.

Learning How: Football. Sue Boulais. Ed. by Jody James. (Learning How Sports Ser.). (Illus.). 48p. (J). (gr. 4-7). 1992. pap. 5.95 (0-944280-43-9); lib. bdg. 14.95 (0-944280-37-4) Bancroft-Sage.

Learning How: Gymnastics. Jane M. Leder. Ed. by Jody James. (Learning How Sports Ser.). (Illus.). 48p. (J). (gr. 4-7). 1992. pap. 5.95 (0-944280-40-4); lib. bdg. 14.95 (0-944280-35-8) Bancroft-Sage.

Learning How: Karate. Jane M. Leder. Ed. by Jody James. (Learning How Sports Ser.). (Illus.). 48p. (J). (gr. 4-7). 1992. pap. 5.95 (0-944280-39-0); lib. bdg. 14.95 (0-944280-34-X) Bancroft-Sage.

Learning How: Skateboarding. Jane M. Leder. Ed. by Jody James. (Learning How Sports Ser.). (Illus.). 48p. (J). (gr. 4-7). 1992. pap. 5.95 (0-944280-42-0); lib. bdg. 14.95 (0-944280-33-1) Bancroft-Sage.

Learning How: Soccer. Jane M. Leder. Ed. by Jody James. (Learning How Sports Ser.). (Illus.). 48p. (J). (gr. 4-7). 1992. pap. 5.95 (0-944280-38-2); lib. bdg. 14.95 (0-944280-32-3) Bancroft-Sage.

Learning How the Heart Beats: The Making of a Pediatrician. Claire McCarthy. 256p. 1997. pap. 12.95 (0-14-023156-0) Viking Penguin.

***Learning How to Appreciate Differences.** Susan Kent. LC 00-27184. (Violence Prevention Library). (Illus.). (J). 2000. pap. write for info. (0-8239-5617-2, PowerKids) Rosen Group.

Learning How to Ask: A Sociolinguistic Appraisal of the Role of the Interview in Social Science Research. Charles L. Briggs. (Studies in the Social & Cultural Foundations of Language: No. 1). (Illus.). 175p. 1986. pap. text 17.95 (0-521-31113-6) Cambridge U Pr.

***Learning How to Ask Someone for Help.** Susan Kent. LC 99-44836. (Violence Prevention Library). 2000. lib. bdg. 17.26 (0-8239-5612-1, PowerKids) Rosen Group.

Learning How to Behave: A Historical Study of American Etiquette Books. Arthur Meier Schlesinger, Jr. LC 68-28296. 95p. 1968. reprint ed. lib. bdg. 46.00 (0-8154-0201-5) Cooper Sq.

Learning How to Compete: Workforce Skills & State Development Policies. Dan Pilcher. LC 95-623346. (Investing in People Ser.). 40p. 15.00 (1-55516-349-1, 3126) Natl Conf State Legis.

Learning How to Learn. L. Ron Hubbard. (Illus.). 208p. (J). (gr. 3-7). 43.75 (0-88404-771-7) Bridge Pubns Inc.

Learning How to Learn. Joseph D. Novak & D. Bob Gowin. (Illus.). 150p. 1984. pap. text 16.95 (0-521-31926-9) Cambridge U Pr.

Learning How to Learn. Idries Shah. 302p. 1978. 26.00 (0-900860-59-6, Pub. by Octagon Pr) ISHK.

Learning How to Learn. Robert M. Smith. 200p. 1984. pap. 33.95 (0-335-10585-8) OpUniv Pr.

***Learning How to Learn: A Guide for Getting into College with a Learning Disability, Staying in & Staying Sane.** Joyanne Cobb. LC 99-45582. 2000. 14.95 (0-87868-776-9, CWLA Pr) Child Welfare.

***Learning How to Learn: A Total Breakthrough in Learning Techniques.** Jerry Lucas. LC 00-104326. (Illus.). 384p. 2000. 27.95 (1-930853-02-5) Lucas Ed Systm.

Learning How to Learn: Pathfinder Learning Skills Program, 2 cass.; set. Ralph Eltoft. 100p. 1992. pap. 149.95 incl. VHS (0-9625343-6-6) Creation Enter Intl.

Learning How to Learn: Psychology & Spirituality in the Sufi Way. Idries Shah. 304p. 1996. pap. 14.95 (0-14-019513-0, Penguin Bks) Viking Penguin.

Learning How to Learn 92+ Benzon. 1992. pap., student ed. 18.50 (0-03-054932-9) H Holt & Co.

***Learning How to Make a Difference: A Practical Guide for the Professional Development of Literacy Teachers.** Carol A. Lyons & Gay Su Pinnell. 2001. pap. text. write for info. (0-325-00282-7) Heinemann.

Learning How to Pray for Your Children. 1979. 4.50 (0-918403-05-7) Agape Ministries.

Learning How to Read New Testament Greek: With People Just Like You. Randall D. McGirr. 420p. (Orig.). 1992. pap. 24.95 (0-9631877-0-8) Context Script.

***Learning How to Stay Safe at School.** Susan Kent. LC 00-23839. 2001. write for info. (0-8239-5616-4, PowerKids) Rosen Group.

Learning How to Use New Testament Reference Books: With People Just Like You. Randall D. McGirr. (Illus.). 290p. 1993. pap. 19.95 (0-9631877-1-6) Context Script.

***Learning Human.** Les A. Murray. LC 99-42758. 400p. 2000. 35.00 (0-374-26073-7) FS&G.

***Learning Human: Selected Poems.** Les Murray. 240p. 2001. pap. 13.00 (0-374-52723-7) FS&G.

Learning Human Anatomy. 2nd ed. Julia F. Guy. 384p. (C). 1997. spiral bd. 36.00 (0-8385-5657-4, A-5657-0) Appleton & Lange.

***Learning Human Anatomy Using Anatomical Models.** (C). 2000. 28.00 (0-536-61339-7) Pearson Custom.

L

Learning Human Skills: An Experiential & Reflective Guide for Nurses. 3rd ed. Philip Burnard. LC 95-30494. (Illus.). 288p. 1995. pap. text 37.50 (*0-7506-2441-8*) Buttrwrth-Heinemann.
Learning IBM BASIC for the Personal Computer. rev. ed. David A. Lien. LC 82-73471. (CompuSoft Learning Ser.). (Illus.). 494p. (Orig.). (gr. 7 up). 1984. pap. 19.95 (*0-932760-13-9*) CompuSoft.
Learning IDL. Research Systems Staff. 1997. pap. write for info. (*1-891044-01-X*) Res Sys Inc.
Learning Imperative: Managing People for Continuous Innovation. Intro. by Robert Howard. LC 93-9876. (Harvard Business Review Book Ser.). 352p. 1993. 29.95 (*0-87584-432-4*) Harvard Busn.
Learning Imperative: Managing People for Continuous Innovation. Robert Howard. 304p. 1993. 32.50 (*0-07-103424-2*) McGraw.
***Learning in Action: A Guide to Putting the Learning Organization to Work.** David A. Garvin. LC 99-48911. 2000. 29.95 (*1-57851-251-4*, Pub. by Harvard Busn) Random.
Learning in Adulthood. 2nd ed. Sharan B. Merriam & Rosemary S. Caffarella. LC 98-25498. (Education Ser.). 480p. 1998. 34.95 (*0-7879-1043-0*) Jossey-Bass.
Learning in an Electronic World. Downes & Fatouros. 154p. 1996. pap. text 22.00 (*0-435-07220-X*) Heinemann.
Learning in & Through Art: A Guide to Discipline-Based Art Education. Stephen M. Dobbs. LC 97-31849. 160p. 1998. pap. 20.00 (*0-89236-494-7*, Pub. by J P Getty Trust) OUP.
Learning in Automated Manufacturing: A Local Search Approach. Ed. by E. Pesch et al. (Production & Logistics Ser.). 257p. 1994. 61.95 (*3-7908-0792-3*) Spr-Verlag.
Learning in Chaos. James A. Hite, Jr. LC 99-36243. (Improving Human Performance Ser.). 300p. 1999. 34.95 (*0-88415-427-0*, 5427) Gulf Pub.
Learning in Children: Organization & Development of Cooperation Actions. V. V. Rubstov. 250p. 1991. pap. text 110.00 (*1-56072-005-0*) Nova Sci Pubs.
Learning in Children: Progress in Cognitive Development Research. Ed. by J. Bisanz et al. (Cognitive Development Ser.). (Illus.). 201p. 1983. 84.95 (*0-387-90802-1*) Spr-Verlag.
***Learning in Christ's School.** Ralph Venning. 284p. 1999. reprint ed. pap. 6.99 (*0-85151-764-1*) Banner of Truth.
Learning in College: I Can Relate. Mary K. Bixby. LC 99-15638. (Illus.). 216p. 1999. pap. text 30.00 (*0-13-011465-0*) P-H.
Learning in Dogs: The Principles of Canine Behavior & Learning Implications for Training. Delta Society Working Group Staff. 1995. pap. 9.00 (*0-9627802-3-5*) Delta Soc.
Learning in Embedded Systems. Leslie P. Kaelbling. LC 92-24672. (Cognitive Science - AI - Adaptive Behavior Ser.). (Illus.). 195p. (C). 1993. 35.00 (*0-262-11174-8*, Bradford Bks) MIT Pr.
Learning in Europe: The Erasmus Experience: A Survey of the 1988-89 Erasmus Students. Friedhelm Maiworm et al. (Higher Education Policy Ser.). 160p. 1991. 45.00 (*1-85302-527-5*) Taylor & Francis.
Learning in Graphical Models. Michael I. Jordan. LC 98-38260. (Adaptive Computation & Machine Learning Ser.). 1999. pap. text 50.00 (*0-262-60032-3*) MIT Pr.
Learning in Graphical Models. Michael I. Jordan & North Atlantic Treaty Organization Staff. LC 98-2941. (Nato ASI Ser.). 630p. 1998. write for info. (*0-7923-5017-0*) Kluwer Academic.
Learning in Groups. David Jaques. LC 84-45288. 256p. 1992. 24.95 (*0-88415-070-4*, 5070) Gulf Pub.
***Learning in Groups: A Handbook for Improving Group Learning.** 3rd ed. David Jaques. 224p. 2000. pap. 29.95 (*0-7494-3091-5*, Pub. by Kogan Page Ltd) Stylus Pub VA.
Learning in Humans & Machines. Ed. by Peter Reimann & Hans Spada. LC 95-25493. (Illus.). 324p. 1995. 74.75 (*0-08-042569-0*, Pergamon Pr) Elsevier.
Learning in Infants & Young Children. Michael Howe. LC 75-44902. 216p. 1976. reprint ed. pap. 10.95 (*0-8047-0973-4*) Stanford U Pr.
Learning in Ireland in the Fifth Century & the Transmission of Letters. Kuno Meyer. 1998. pap. 7.50 (*0-89979-104-2*) British Am Bks.
Learning in Language & Literature. Incl. Developing Imagination. Northrop Frye. LC 63-13811. 1963. Insistent Tasks in Language Learning. A. R. MacKinnon. LC 63-13811. 1963. LC 63-13811. 62p. 1990. 6.95 (*0-674-52000-9*) HUP.
Learning in Likely Places: Varieties of Apprenticeship in Japan. Ed. by John Singleton. LC 97-25904. (Learning in Doing Ser.). (Illus.). 400p. (C). 1998. text 64.95 (*0-521-48012-4*) Cambridge U Pr.
Learning in Living Color: Using Literature to Incorporate Multicultural Education Into the Primary Curriculum. Valdez. LC 98-30374. 239p. 1998. pap. text 27.00 (*0-205-27445-5*) P-H.
Learning in Man-Computer Interaction. Thomas Bosser. (Research Reports ESPRIT, Project 385, HUFIT: Vol. 1). xi, 218p. 1987. 29.00 (*0-387-18391-4*) Spr-Verlag.
Learning in Medicine. Ed. by Colin Coles & Hans A. Holm. (Illus.). 212p. (C). 1994. 25.00 (*82-00-21811-2*) Scandnvan Univ Pr.
Learning in Natural & Connectionist Systems: Experiments & a Model. R. Hans Phaf. LC 93-47517. 312p. (C). 1994. text 166.50 (*0-7923-2685-7*) Kluwer Academic.
Learning in Overdrive: Designing Curriculum, Instruction, & Assessment from Standards: A Manual for Teachers. Ruth Mitchell et al. LC 95-40972. (Illus.). 160p. (Orig.). 1995. pap., teacher ed. 17.95 (*1-55591-933-2*) Fulcrum Pub.
Learning in Science: The Implications of Children's Science. Roger Osborne & Peter Freyberg. LC 84-27915. 198p. (Orig.). (C). (gr. 5). 1985. pap. text 22.00 (*0-435-57260-1*, 57260) Heinemann.
Learning in Small Moments: Life in an Urban Classroom. Daniel Meier. (Practitioners Inquiry Ser.: Vol. 3). 176p. (C). 1997. text 44.00 (*0-8077-3627-9*); pap. text 18.95 (*0-8077-3626-0*) Tchrs Coll.
Learning in Social Action. Foley. 192p. 1999. pap. 19.95 (*1-85649-684-8*) St Martin.
Learning in Social Action: A Contribution to Understanding Education & Training. Foley. 192p. 1999. text 55.00 (*1-85649-683-X*) St Martin.
Learning in Social Context: Workers & Adult Education in Nineteenth Century Chicago. Fred M. Schied. LC 93-949. (Illus.). 222p. 1993. pap. 15.95 (*1-879528-04-5*) Ed Studies Pr.
Learning in Spite of Labels. Joyce Herzog. 206p. (YA). (gr. 6 up). 1994. pap. 9.95 (*1-882514-13-0*) Greenleaf TN.
Learning in the Field: An Introduction to Qualitative Research. Gretchen B. Rossman & Sharon F. Rallis. LC 97-33901. 1998. 58.00 (*0-7619-0352-6*); pap. 27.95 (*0-7619-0353-4*) Sage.
Learning in the Mile High City: A Guide to Public & Private Schools in Metro Denver. Cynthia Benegar & Heidi McClain. LC 86-60687. 160p. (Orig.). 1986. pap. 9.95 (*0-9608012-4-3*) Metrosource Pubns.
Learning in the Museum. George E. Hein. LC 97-26899. (Museum Meanings Ser.). (Illus.). 216p. (C). 1998. 85.00 (*0-415-09775-4*); pap. 25.99 (*0-415-09776-2*) Routledge.
Learning in the Natural Laboratory: An Introductory Geology Lab Manual University of North Carolina. Roberson et al. 146p. (C). 1998. spiral bd., lab manual ed. 38.95 (*0-7872-5631-5*, 41563102) Kendall-Hunt.
Learning in the Workplace. Ed. by Victoria J. Marsick. 288p. 1987. lib. bdg. 30.00 (*0-7099-4659-7*, Pub. by C Helm) Routldge.
Learning in Two Languages: From Conflict to Consensus in the Reorganization of Schools. Ed. by Gary Imhoff. 192p. (C). 1990. 34.95 (*0-88738-319-X*) Transaction Pubs.
Learning in Two Worlds. 2nd ed. Bertha Perez & Maria E. Torres-Guzman. LC 95-4930. 232p. (C). 1995. pap. 52.00 (*0-8013-1572-7*) Longman.
Learning In Two Worlds: An Integrated Spanish/English Biliteracy Approach. 3rd ed. Perez. (C). 2000. pap. text. write for info. (*0-8013-3077-7*) Addison-Wesley.
Learning Incorporated Dictionary of Learning Handicaps. 3rd ed. Edward R. Welles. 1970. 1.00 (*0-913692-01-8*) Learning Inc.
Learning Industry: Education for Adult Workers. Nell P. Eurich. LC 90-48700. 298p. (Orig.). 1991. 25.00 (*0-931050-41-3*) Carnegie Fnd Advan Teach.
***Learning, Innovation & Urban Evolution.** David F. Batten. LC 00-40546. 2000. write for info. (*0-7923-8577-2*) Kluwer Academic.
Learning Institutionalized: Teaching in the Medieval University. Ed. by John Van Engen. LC 99-37710. (Notre Dame Conferences in Medieval Studies: No. IX). 288p. 2000. 40.00 (*0-268-01328-4*, Pub. by U of Notre Dame Pr) Chicago Distribution Ctr.
Learning Irish. Michael O. Siadhail. 1995. pap. 25.00 (*0-300-06462-4*) Yale U Pr.
***Learning Irish.** Micheal O Siadhail. (IRI.). 300p. 2000. 39.95 (*0-300-08416-1*) Yale U Pr.
Learning Irish. unabridged ed. Michael O. Siadhail. (Self-Instructional Language Courses). 336p. pap. text 89.95 incl. audio (*0-88432-205-X*, AFIR10) Audio-Forum.
***Learning Is a Verb: The Psychology of Teaching & Learning.** Sherrie Reynolds. LC 99-59722. 160p. (C). 1999. pap. 18.95 (*1-890871-24-9*) Holcomb Hath.
Learning Is Change. Martha M. Leypoldt. LC 70-144082. (Illus.). 159p. 1971. reprint ed. pap. 49.30 (*0-608-00215-1*, 206100800006) Bks Demand.
Learning Is Fun. (Key Words Readers Ser.: C Series, No. 641-10c). (Illus.). (J). (ps-5). pap. 3.50 (*0-7214-0628-9*, Ladybrd) Penguin Putnam.
Learning Is Fun Grades K-1 Workbook. (Illus.). 144p. 1991. pap. 4.95 (*1-56144-059-0*) Modern Pub NYC.
Learning Is Fun Preschool Workbook. (Illus.). 144p. 1991. pap. 4.95 (*1-56144-058-2*) Modern Pub NYC.
Learning Is Fun with Mrs. Perez. Alice Flanagan & Linda Cornwell. LC 97-14089. (Our Neighborhood Ser.). (Illus.). 32p. (J). (gr. 1-2). 1998. 19.50 (*0-516-20774-1*) Childrens.
Learning Is Fun with Mrs. Perez. Alice K. Flanagan. Ed. by Dana Rau. (Our Neighborhood Ser.). (Illus.). 32p. (J). 1998. pap. 6.95 (*0-516-26295-5*) Childrens.
Learning Issues for Intelligent Tutoring Systems. Ed. by Heinz Mandl & Alan M. Lesgold. (Cognitive Science Ser.). (Illus.). 225p. 1988. 58.95 (*0-387-96616-1*) Spr-Verlag.
Learning Italian with Enza B. Bk. 1: An Introduction to Nouns & Gender. Margaret Harris. (Learning Language with Enza B. Ser.). (Illus.). 95p. (J). (gr. 3-8). 1994. student ed. 15.95 (*1-886332-02-9*) Forlang Foreign.
Learning Italian with Enza B Bk. 2: Regular Verbs & the Present Tense. (ITA.). Date not set. write for info. (*1-886332-05-3*) Forlang Foreign.
***Learning Java.** Patrick Niemeyer & Jonathan Knudsen. Ed. by John Posner & Mike Loukides. (Illus.). 650p. 2000. pap. 34.95 incl. cd-rom (*1-56592-718-4*) OReilly & Assocs.
***Learning Journals: A Handbook for Teachers, Lecturers & Journal Writers.** Jenny A. Moon. 160p. 2000. pap. 25.00 (*0-7494-3045-1*, Pub. by Kogan Page Ltd) Stylus Pub VA.
Learning Journals in the K-8 Classroom: Exploring Ideas & Information in the Content Areas. Marcia Popp. LC 97-9830. 248p. 1997. pap. 23.50 (*0-8058-2430-8*) L Erlbaum Assocs.
Learning Journey. Malcolm Jeffreys & Robert Gall. (Illus.). 200p. (Orig.). 1996. pap. text. write for info. (*1-55059-122-3*) Detselig Ents.
Learning Journey on the Red Road. Floyd Looks for Buffalo Hand. Ed. by Marc A. Huminilowycz. 112p. 1998. pap. 14.95 (*0-9663957-0-0*) Looks for Buffalo.
***Learning Journeys: Top Management Experts Share Hard-Earned Lessons on Becoming Great Mentors & Leaders.** Ed. by Ken Shelton et al. 256p. 2000. 24.95 (*0-89106-147-9*, Davies-Black Pub) Consulting Psychol.
Learning, Keeping & Using Language: Selected Papers from the Eighth World Congress of Applied Linguistics, Sydney, 16-21 August 1987, 2 vols., Set. Ed. by M. A. K. Halliday et al. LC 90-335. 1990. 210.00 (*1-55619-100-6*) J Benjamins Pubng Co.
Learning, Keeping & Using Language: Selected Papers from the Eighth World Congress of Applied Linguistics, Sydney, 16-21 August 1987, 2 vols., Vol. 1. Ed. by M. A. K. Halliday et al. LC 90-335. xx, 508p. 1990. 118.00 (*1-55619-104-9*) J Benjamins Pubng Co.
Learning, Keeping & Using Language: Selected Papers from the Eighth World Congress of Applied Linguistics, Sydney, 16-21 August 1987, 2 vols., Vol. 2. Ed. by M. A. K. Halliday et al. LC 90-335. xvi, 488p. 1990. 112.00 (*1-55619-105-7*) J Benjamins Pubng Co.
Learning Keyboarding & Word Processing with Word 97. Iris Blanc. 1997. 29.00 (*1-56243-358-X*, Z-24HC) DDC Pub.
***Learning, Knowledge & Cultural Context.** Linda King. 140p. 1999. pap. 48.00 (*0-7923-6141-5*) Kluwer Academic.
***Learning Lab: Grades 1 & 2 Spring 2000.** (Hands-On Bible Curriculum Ser.). 2000. 39.99 (*0-7644-0182-3*) Group Pub.
***Learning Lab: Grades 1 & 2 Summer 2000.** (Hands-On Bible Curriculum Ser.). 2000. 39.99 (*0-7644-0195-5*) Group Pub.
***Learning Lab: Grades 3 & 4 Spring 2000.** (Hands-On Bible Curriculum Ser.). 2000. 39.99 (*0-7644-0181-5*) Group Pub.
***Learning Lab: Grades 3 & 4 Summer 2000.** (Hands-On Bible Curriculum Ser.). 2000. 39.99 (*0-7644-0194-7*) Group Pub.
***Learning Lab: Grades 5 & 6 Spring 2000.** (Hands-On Bible Curriculum Ser.). 2000. 39.99 (*0-7644-0180-7*) Group Pub.
***Learning Lab: Grades 5 & 6 Summer 2000.** (Hands-On Bible Curriculum Ser.). 2000. 39.99 (*0-7644-0193-9*) Group Pub.
***Learning Lab: Pre-K & K Summer 2000.** (Hands-On Bible Curriculum Ser.). 2000. 49.99 (*0-7644-0197-1*) Group Pub.
***Learning Lab: PreK & K Spring 2000.** (Hands-On Bible Curriculum Ser.). 2000. 49.99 (*0-7644-0184-X*) Group Pub.
***Learning Lab: Preschool Spring 2000.** (Hands-On Bible Curriculum Ser.). 2000. 49.99 (*0-7644-0183-1*) Group Pub.
***Learning Lab: Preschool Summer 2000.** (Hands-On Bible Curriculum Ser.). 2000. 49.99 (*0-7644-0196-3*) Group Pub.
***Learning Lab: Toddlers & 2s Spring 2000.** (Hands-On Bible Curriculum Ser.). 2000. 49.99 (*0-7644-0185-8*) Group Pub.
***Learning Lab: Toddlers & 2s Summer 2000.** (Hands-On Bible Curriculum Ser.). 2000. 49.99 (*0-7644-0198-X*) Group Pub.
Learning Language Addiction Counseling. Miller. LC 98-29190. 243p. 1998. pap. text 46.00 (*0-205-26318-6*) P-H.
Learning, Language, & Invention: Essays Presented to Francis Maddison. A. J. Turner. Ed. by W. D. Hackman. LC 94-27295. 352p. 1994. 96.95 (*0-86078-467-3*, Pub. by Variorum) Ashgate Pub Co.
Learning Language Arts Through Literature: The Blue Book - 1st Grade the Common Sense Reading Program, Set. Debbie Strayer & Susan S. Simpson. 187p. 1992. spiral bd. 80.00 (*1-880892-29-4*) Com Sense FL.
Learning Language Arts Through Literature: The Gold Book - High School. Greg Strayer. 96p. 1992. spiral bd. 18.00 (*1-880892-37-5*) Com Sense FL.
Learning Language Arts Through Literature: The Gray Book - 8th-9th Grade. Diane Welch & Susan S. Simpson. 93p. 1991. spiral bd. 18.00 (*1-880892-35-9*) Com Sense FL.
Learning Language Arts Through Literature: The Green Book - 7th Grade. Diane Welch & Susan S. Simpson. 103p. 1992. spiral bd. 18.00 (*1-880892-34-0*) Com Sense FL.
Learning Language Arts Through Literature: The Orange Book - 4th Grade. Debbie Strayer & Susan S. Simpson. 117p. 1992. spiral bd. 20.00 (*1-880892-32-4*) Com Sense FL.
Learning Language Arts Through Literature: The Purple Book - 5th Grade. Debbie Strayer & Susan S. Simpson. 191p. (J). (gr. 5). 1994. spiral bd. 20.00 (*1-880892-36-7*) Com Sense FL.
Learning Language Arts Through Literature: The Red Book - 2nd Grade. Debbie Strayer & Susan S. Simpson. 124p. 1991. spiral bd. 20.00 (*1-880892-30-8*) Com Sense FL.
Learning Language Arts Through Literature: The Tan Book - 6th Grade. Diane Welch & Susan S. Simpson. 96p. 1990. spiral bd. 18.00 (*1-880892-33-2*) Com Sense FL.
Learning Language Arts Through Literature: The Yellow Book - 3rd Grade. Debbie Strayer & Susan S. Simpson. 118p. 1991. spiral bd. 20.00 (*1-880892-31-6*) Com Sense FL.
Learning Language Arts Through Literature - Orange Student Activity Book. Debbie Strayer & Susan S. Simpson. (Learning Language Arts Through Literature Ser.). 102p. 1992. 16.00 (*1-880892-27-8*) Com Sense FL.
Learning Language Arts Through Literature - Purple Student Activity Book. Debbie Strayer & Susan S. Simpson. (Learning Language Arts Through Literature Ser.). 1994. 16.00 (*1-880892-38-3*) Com Sense FL.
Learning Language Arts Through Literature - Red Student Activity Book. Debbie Strayer & Susan S. Simpson. (Learning Language Arts Through Literature Ser.). 159p. 1992. 16.00 (*1-880892-25-1*) Com Sense FL.
Learning Language Arts Through Literature - Tan Student Activity Book. Diane Welch & Susan S. Simpson. (Learning Language Arts Through Literature Ser.). 171p. 1992. 16.00 (*1-880892-28-6*) Com Sense FL.
Learning Language Arts Through Literature - Yellow Student Activity Book. Debbie Strayer & Susan S. Simpson. (Learning Language Arts Through Literature Ser.). 196p. 1992. 16.00 (*1-880892-26-X*) Com Sense FL.
Learning Language Through Literature: A Sourcebook for Teachers of English in Hong Kong. Ed. by Peter Falveey & Peter Kennedy. LC 98-106748. (Illus.). 216p. (Orig.). 1997. pap. 39.50 (*962-209-434-1*, Pub. by HK Univ Pr) Coronet Bks.
***Learning Language Through Literature in Secondary Schools: A Resource Book for Teachers of English.** Peter Kennedy & Peter Falvey. 138p. 1999. pap. (*962-209-495-3*) HK Univ Pr.
Learning LATEX. David F. Griffiths & Desmond J. Higham. LC 96-43340. (Miscellaneous Bks.: Vol. 55). (Illus.). x, 84p. 1996. pap. 17.00 (*0-89871-383-8*, OT55) Soc Indus-Appl Math.
Learning Latin Through Mythology. Jayne Hanlin & Beverly Lichtenstein. (Illus.). 64p. (C). 1991. pap. text 11.95 (*0-521-39779-0*) Cambridge U Pr.
Learning Law: The Mastery of Legal Logic. Sheldon Margulies & Kenneth Lasson. LC 92-71953. 138p. (C). 1992. pap. text 12.50 (*0-89089-494-9*) Carolina Acad Pr.
Learning, Law & Religion. William P. Griffith. LC 96-124626. 250p. 1996. 60.00 (*0-7083-1314-0*, Pub. by Univ Wales Pr) Paul & Co Pubs.
Learning Leadership. Abraham Zaleznik. 540p. 1992. pap. 19.95 (*0-929387-71-6*) Bonus Books.
Learning Leadership: A Curriculum Guide for a New Generation, Grades K-12. Ed. by Kathy P. Kretman. 146p. 1996. pap. text 15.00 (*1-891464-10-8*) J M Burns Academy.
Learning Legal Reasoning: Briefing, Analysis & Theory. John Delaney. (Delaney Ser.). Orig. Title: How to Brief a Case, An Introduction to Jurisprudence. (Illus.). (C). 1987. pap. text 13.95 (*0-9608514-4-5*) J Delaney Pubns.
Learning Legal Research Skills. Ed. by P. Clinch. (C). 1991. 34.00 (*1-85431-191-3*, Pub. by Blackstone Pr) Gaunt.
Learning Legal Rules. James A. Holland & Julian S. Webb. 241p. (C). 1991. text 27.00 (*1-85431-109-3*, Pub. by Blackstone Pr) Gaunt.
Learning Legal Rules. 2nd ed. James A. Holland & Julian S. Webb. LC 97-100686. 324p. 1993. 36.00 (*1-85431-263-4*, Pub. by Blackstone Pr) Gaunt.
Learning Legal Rules. 3rd ed. James A. Holland & Julian S. Webb. 318p. 1996. pap. 30.00 (*1-85431-535-8*, Pub. by Blackstone Pr) Gaunt.
***Learning Legal Rules.** 4th ed. James A. Holland & Julian S. Webb. 338p. 1999. pap. 23.50 (*1-85431-889-6*, Pub. by Blackstone Pr) Gaunt.
Learning Legal Skills. Simon Lee & Marie Fox. 224p. (C). 1991. text 24.00 (*1-85431-112-3*, Pub. by Blackstone Pr) Gaunt.
***Learning Legal Skills.** 3rd ed. Marie Fox & Christine Bell. 412p. 1999. pap. 29.00 (*1-85431-766-0*, Pub. by Blackstone Pr) Gaunt.
Learning Lessons: Social Organization in the Classroom. Hugh Mehan. LC 78-24298. (Illus.). 247p. reprint ed. pap. 76.60 (*0-8357-8205-0*, 203393700087) Bks Demand.
Learning Letters Through All Five Senses: A Language Development Activity Book. Lois McCue. (Illus.). 76p. (Orig.). 1983. pap. 12.95 (*0-87659-106-3*) Gryphon Hse.
Learning-Life in the Castle: An Allegory of the Christian Way. Jean Nava. LC 97-94200. (More Than Conquerors Ser.: Vol. 1). (Illus.). 1997. pap. 11.95 (*0-9659952-0-8*) Kingdom Pr.
Learning Life Skills: A Curriculum for Group Leaders Helping with the Move Toward Interdependent Living. Martha J. Holden & Jack C. Holden. 124p. 1990. pap. text 28.50 (*1-878848-02-X*) Natl Res Ctr.
Learning Life's Lessons: A Personalized Unit Study Approach. Barbara Wagner. (Illus.). 29p. 1991. pap. text 5.95 (*0-913717-21-5*, 1025) Hewitt Res Fnd.
Learning Limits: College Women, Drugs & Relationships. Kimberly M. Williams. LC 97-31520. 224p. 1998. 55.00 (*0-89789-556-8*, Bergin & Garvey) Greenwood.
***Learning Limits: College Women, Drugs & Relationships.** Kimberly M. Williams. LC 97-31520. 224p. 2000. pap. 24.95 (*0-89789-741-2*, Bergin & Garvey) Greenwood.
Learning Lingo: The Art & Science of Programming with Macromedia Directories. Michael Callery. 352p. 1995. pap. text 34.95 (*0-201-87043-6*) Addison-Wesley.

An Asterisk (*) at the beginning of an entry indicates that the title is appearing for the first time.

Learning, Linking & Critical Thinking: Information Strategies for the K-12 Library Media Curriculum. Hilda K. Weisburg & Ruth Toor. 210p. (Orig.). 1994. pap. 31.50 (*0-931315-08-5*) Lib Learn Res.

Learning Links. Margaret Seagraves et al. 252p. 1992. pap. text 28.95 (*0-88725-168-4*) Hunter Textbks.

Learning Links for Language Arts. Bonnie Mertzlufft et al. (Illus.). 128p. (Orig.). (J). (gr. 1-3). 1997. pap. 14.95 (*1-57612-005-8*, MM2034) Monday Morning Bks.

Learning Links for Math. Bonnie Mertzlufft et al. (Illus.). 128p. (Orig.). (J). (gr. 1-3). 1997. pap. 14.95 (*1-57612-006-6*) Monday Morning Bks.

***Learning Literature in an Era of Change: Innovations in Teaching.** Dona J. Hickey & Donna Reiss. 256p. 2000. 49.95 (*1-57922-017-7*); pap. 22.50 (*1-57922-018-5*) Stylus Pub VA.

Learning LOGO on the TRS-80 Color Computer. Tony Adams et al. (Illus.). 174p. 1984. pap. 24.95 (*0-13-527961-5*) P-H.

Learning Lotus 1-2-3 (DOS) Iris Blanc. 1992. teacher ed. 10.00 (*1-56243-078-5*, L6-TM); pap. 27.00 (*1-56243-077-7*, L-9); trans. 250.00 (*1-56243-079-3*, L-68) DDC Pub.

Learning Machine: A Hard Look at Toronto Schools. Loren J. Lind. 228p. (Orig.). 1974. pap. 9.95 (*0-88784-646-7*, Pub. by Hse of Anansi Pr) Genl Dist Srvs.

Learning Management: Emerging Directions for Learning to Learn in the Workplace. Ed. by Mark E. Cheren. 57p. 1987. 6.00 (*0-318-35270-2*, IN 320) Ctr Educ Trng Employ.

Learning Manual for How the Brain Learns: Instructional Kit (Learning Manual & Sousa Text) abr. ed. David A. Sousa. (Illus.). 159p. 1998. pap. 39.95 (*0-8039-6760-8*) Corwin Pr.

Learning Manual for How the Brain Learns: Manual Only. David A. Sousa. (Illus.). 88p. 1998. pap. 32.95 (*0-8039-6753-5*) Corwin Pr.

Learning Maps & Memory Skills. Ingemar Svantesson. 130p. 1998. pap. 14.99 (*0-7494-2455-9*) Kogan Page Ltd.

Learning Martial Arts see New Action Sports

Learning Martial Arts. Steve Potts. (New Action Sports Ser.). (Illus.). 48p. (J). (gr. 3-7). 1996. lib. bdg. 19.00 (*0-516-20102-6*) Childrens.

Learning Materials in Anatomy. David J. Gerrick. 1978. pap. text 10.00 (*0-685-01375-8*) Dayton Labs.

Learning Materials Workshop Blocks: An Educational Guide. George E. Forman & Karen Hewitt. 73p. (Orig.). (C). 1990. pap., teacher ed. 13.50 (*0-9633806-0-5*) Lrn Materials.

Learning Math with Bible Heroes. Linda Marks. (Illus.). (J). 1997. pap. text 2.29 (*0-7647-0092-8*) Schaffer Pubns.

Learning Math with God's Sea Creatures. Dee Andrews. (Illus.). (J). 1997. pap. text 2.29 (*0-7647-0089-8*) Schaffer Pubns.

Learning Math with Joseph. Dee Andrews. (Illus.). (J). 1997. pap. text 2.29 (*0-7647-0091-X*) Schaffer Pubns.

Learning Math with Noah. Dee Andrews. (Illus.). (J). 1997. pap. text 2.29 (*0-7647-0090-1*) Schaffer Pubns.

Learning Mathematics. 2nd ed. Anthony Orton. 192p. 1992. text 100.00 (*0-304-32553-8*); pap. text 35.95 (*0-304-32555-4*) Continuum.

Learning Mathematics: A Program for Classroom Teachers. Ross McKeown. LC 89-19961. (Illus.). 139p. (Orig.). (C). (gr. k). 1990. pap. text 17.50 (*0-435-08304-X*, 08304) Heinemann.

Learning Mathematics: Constructivist & Interactionist Theories of Mathematical Development. Ed. by Paul Cobb. 196p. (C). 1994. lib. bdg. 85.50 (*0-7923-2823-X*) Kluwer Academic.

Learning Mathematics: The Cognitive Science Approach to Mathematics Education. Robert Davis. LC 84-2853. 400p. 1984. text 73.25 (*0-89391-245-X*) Ablx Pub.

Learning Mathematics & Cooperative Learning: Lesson Plans for Teachers. David W. Johnson & Roger T. Johnson. (Illus.). 173p. (Orig.). 1991. pap. text, teacher ed. 20.00 (*0-939603-13-6*) Interaction Bk Co.

Learning Mathematics & Logo. Ed. by Celia Hoyles & Richard Noss. (Explorations in Logo Ser.). (Illus.). 350p. 1992. 55.00 (*0-262-08207-1*) MIT Pr.

***Learning Mathematics for a New Century: 2000 Yearbook, National Council of Teachers of Mathematics.** Maurice R. Burke. (Illus.). 2000. 29.95 (*0-87353-479-4*) NCTM.

***Learning Mathematics in Elementary & Middle Schools.** 1999. write for info. (*0-13-013967-X*) P-H.

***Learning Mathematics in Elementary & Middle Schools.** George Cathcart et al. LC 99-33271. (Illus.). 417p. (C). 1999. pap. text 63.00 (*0-13-011681-5*) P-H.

Learning Mathematics Through Inquiry. Raffaella Borasi. LC 91-25704. 234p. (C). (gr. 9). 1991. pap. text 29.50 (*0-435-08324-4*, 08324) Heinemann.

Learning Mathematics with Micros. Adrian J. Oldknow & D. V. Smith. LC 83-12642. (Mathematics & Its Applications Ser.). 268p. 1983. text 64.95 (*0-470-27488-3*); pap. text 31.95 (*0-470-27487-5*) P-H.

***Learning MATLAB.** (C). 1999. pap. text 35.00 (*0-9672195-1-5*) MathWorks.

***Learning Mechanical Desktop R4: A Process-Based Approach.** Thomas Short & Anthony Dudek. LC 99-88046. 2000. pap. text. write for info. (*1-56637-722-6*) Goodheart.

Learning Mechanisms in Food Selection. Ed. by Lewis M. Barker et al. LC 77-76779. 632p. 1977. 40.00 (*0-918954-19-3*) Baylor Univ Pr.

Learning Media Assessment of Students with Visual Impairments: A Resource Guide for Teachers. 2nd ed. Alan J. Koenig & M. Cay Holbrook. LC 95-49858. 1995. pap. 25.00 (*1-880366-19-3*) TSBVI.

Learning Media Design. Arizona State University Staff. 1997. pap. text 85.00 (*1-57576-278-1*) Que Educ & Trng.

***Learning Medical Terminology.** 9th ed. Miriam G. Austrin & Harvey R. Austrin. 1998. teacher ed. write for info. (*0-323-00282-X*) Mosby Inc.

***Learning Medical Terminology: A Work Text.** Miriam G. Austrin & Harvey R. Austrin. 1998. text. write for info. incl. audio (*0-8151-0340-9*) Mosby Inc.

***Learning Medical Terminology: A Work Text.** 8th ed. Miriam G. Austrin & Harvey R. Austrin. 1998. teacher ed. write for info. (*0-8151-7898-0*) Mosby Inc.

***Learning Medical Terminology: A Worktext, 9th Ed.** 9th ed. Miriam G. Austrin. LC R123.Y6 1999. 1999. 32.00 (*0-323-00279-X*) Mosby Consmer Hlth.

***Learning Medicine.** 15th ed. Ed. by Peter Richards & Simon Stockill. 141p. 2000. 35.95 (*0-7279-1462-6*) BMJ Pub.

Learning Medicine, 1994. 12th ed. Peter Richards. 120p. 1995. pap. text 12.00 (*0-7279-0999-1*, Pub. by BMJ Pub) Login Brothers Bk Co.

Learning Medicine, 1993. Peter Richards. (Illus.). 108p. 1992. pap. text 12.00 (*0-7279-0820-0*, Pub. by BMJ Pub) Login Brothers Bk Co.

Learning Micro-PROLOG: A Problem-Solving Approach. Tom Conlon. 39.95 (*0-685-43058-8*) Addison-Wesley.

Learning Microsoft BASIC for the Macintosh: New Microsoft 2.X Version. David A. Lien. LC 85-71339. (Illus.). 457p. (Orig.). 1985. pap. 19.95 (*0-932760-34-1*) CompuSoft.

Learning Microsoft Excel 97. Iris Blanc & Cathy Vento. (Fast-Teach Learning Ser.). pap., spiral bd. 25.00 (*1-56243-441-1*, Z-21) DDC Pub.

Learning Microsoft Office for Windows 95. Iris Blanc. 1996. pap. text 27.00 (*1-56243-294-X*, Z-6) DDC Pub.

Learning Microsoft Office 97. Iris Blanc & Cathy Vento. (Fast-Teach Learning Ser.). 29.00 incl. cd-rom (*1-56243-461-6*, Z-19HC) DDC Pub.

Learning Microsoft Office 97. Iris Blanc & Cathy Vento. LC 97-222711. (Fast-Teach Learning Ser.). (Illus.). 494p. 1997. pap. 27.00 (*1-56243-439-X*, Z-19) DDC Pub.

Learning Microsoft Office' Professional Version. Iris Blanc. 1996. 31.00 (*1-56243-300-8*, M-9HC); pap. text 27.00 (*1-56243-261-3*, M-9) DDC Pub.

Learning Microsoft Office 97: Online. Digitalcre. (C). 1998. pap. text 74.00 (*0-03-023591-X*, Pub. by Harcourt Coll Pubs) Harcourt.

Learning Microsoft Powerpoint 97. D D C Publishing Staff. (Learning Ser.). 1997. pap. text 27.00 (*1-56243-442-X*, Z22) DDC Pub.

Learning Microsoft Windows 95. Margaret Brown. LC 96-158357. 1995. spiral bd. 27.00 (*1-56243-233-8*, Z-3) DDC Pub.

Learning Microsoft Windows 95. Margaret Brown. 1996. 29.00 (*1-56243-303-2*, Z-3HC) DDC Pub.

***Learning Microsoft Windows 2000.** DDC Publishing Staff. 1999. pap. 29.00 (*1-56243-748-8*) DDC Pub.

Learning Microsoft Word 97. Iris Blanc. (Fast-Teach Learning Ser.). spiral bd. 29.00 incl. cd-rom (*1-56243-462-4*, Z-20HC) DDC Pub.

***Learning Microsoft Word 97.** Iris Blanc. LC 98-151845. (Fast-Teach Learning Ser.). 1998. pap., spiral bd. 27.00 (*1-56243-440-3*, Z-20) DDC Pub.

Learning Microsoft Works for Windows through Fun Projects: Version 4.0 for Windows 95. Connie Acton. (Illus.). 165p. (YA). 1996. pap. text 16.95 (*1-887281-08-8*) Labyrinth CA.

Learning MicroStation in 20 Projects. Hossein Assadipour. LC 95-31197. 475p. (C). 1996. pap. text 46.95 (*0-314-05539-8*) West Pub.

Learning Modelling with Derive. M. Stewart Townend & David C. Pountney. LC 95-10781. 1995. pap. 19.84 (*0-13-190521-X*) P-H.

Learning Modern Languages at School in the European Union. European Commission Staff. LC 98-197423. (Education, Training, Youth Studies). 147p. 1997. write for info. (*92-828-0081-4*, Pub. by Comm Europ Commun) Bernan Associates.

Learning Modules for the Basic Course in English, Vol. 1. Ed. by Providencia C. Monte. LC 79-22332. 304p. 1980. pap. 7.00 (*0-8477-3324-6*) U of PR Pr.

Learning More about Being a Dad: Beginning the Process of Learning about Being a Dad. Mary A. Little. (Competent Kids Ser.). 16p. (J). 1995. 19.95 (*1-887514-06-6*) Three Bears.

Learning More about Chores: Continuing the Process of Learning about Chores. Mary A. Little. (Competent Kids Ser.). 16p. (J). 1995. 19.95 (*1-887514-04-X*) Three Bears.

Learning More about Community Social Work. Paul Henderson & Tony Scott. 1984. 45.00 (*0-7855-0833-3*, Pub. by Natl Inst Soc Work) St Mut.

Learning More about Community Social Work. Paul Henderson & Tony Scott. (C). 1984. 90.00 (*0-7855-3749-X*, Pub. by Natl Inst Soc Work) St Mut.

Learning More & Teaching Less: A Decade of Innovation in Self-Instruction & Small Group Learning. Ilma M. Brewer. 176p. 1985. 38.00 (*1-85059-003-6*) OpUniv Pr.

Learning More Biochemistry: 100 Case-Oriented Problems. Richard F. Luduena. LC 96-46129. 303p. 1997. pap. 49.95 (*0-471-17054-2*) Wiley.

Learning, Motivation, & Cognition: The Functional Behaviorism of Robert C. Bolles. Ed. by Mark E. Bouton & Michael S. Fanselow. LC 97-25299. (Illus.). 451p. 1997. text 49.95 (*1-55798-436-0*, 431-6910) Am Psychol.

Learning Music Through Rhythm: Music Book Index. Marguerite V. Hood. 180p. 1993. reprint ed. lib. bdg. 69.00 (*0-7812-9673-0*) Rprt Serv.

***Learning My 1, 2, 3s.** (Tele-Skills Ser.). (SPA & ENG.). Illus.). (J). (ps-1). 2000. pap. 8.95 incl. audio (*1-886972-88-5*, Pub. by Emaginit) Penton Overseas.

Learning My Prayers, 8 bks. Piera Paltro. Tr. by Daughters of St. Paul Staff. Incl. Angel of God. (Illus.). 16p. (J). (gr. k-3). 1981. pap. 2.95 (*0-8198-0739-7*, CH0031P); Eternal Rest: A Prayer for People Who Have Died. (Illus.). 15p. (Orig.). (J). (gr. k-3). 1992. pap. 2.50 (*0-8198-2332-5*); Glory to the Father. (Illus.). 21p. (Orig.). (J). (ps up). 1987. pap. 2.50 (*0-8198-3043-7*, CH0227); Hail, Holy Queen. (Illus.). 15p. (Orig.). (J). (gr. k-3). 1992. pap. 2.50 (*0-8198-3365-7*); Hail Mary. (Illus.). 22p. (J). (gr. k-3). 1992. pap. 2.50 (*0-8198-3316-9*); I Believe: The Profession of Faith or Creed. (Illus.). 29p. (Orig.). (J). (gr. k-3). 1992. pap. 2.50 (*0-8198-3664-8*); My Mass. (Illus.). 32p. (J). (gr. k-3). 1992. pap. 2.50 (*0-8198-4765-8*); Our Father. (Illus.). 23p. (Orig.). (J). (ps-1). 1991. pap. 2.95 (*0-8198-5416-6*, CH0416P); Set pap. 18.80 (*0-8198-4483-7*) Pauline Bks.

Learning Navaho, 4 vols. in two, Set. Berard Haile. 35.00 (*0-686-32652-0*) St Michaels.

Learning Navaho, 4 vols. in two, Vols. 1 & 2. Berard Haile. 20.00 (*0-686-32650-4*) St Michaels.

Learning Navaho, 4 vols. in two, Vols. 3 & 4. Berard Haile. 20.00 (*0-686-32651-2*) St Michaels.

Learning Networks: A Field Guide to Teaching & Learning Online. Linda M. Harasim et al. LC 94-46599. (Illus.). 339p. 1995. 40.00 (*0-262-08236-5*) MIT Pr.

Learning, Networks & Statistics. Ed. by G. Della Riccia et al. (CISM International Centre for Mechanical Sciences Ser.: No. 382). (Illus.). viii, 230p. 1997. pap. 64.00 (*3-211-82910-5*) Spr-Verlag.

Learning New Job Skills: How & Where to Obtain the Right Training to Help You Get on at Work. Laurel Alexander. (Jobs & Careers Ser.). 127p. 1997. pap. 19.95 (*1-85703-375-2*, Pub. by How To Bks) Trans-Atl Phila.

Learning New Roles. Christie Costanzo. LC 91-11572. (Women Today Ser.). 64p. (J). (gr. 6-12). 1991. 12.95 (*0-685-59202-2*) Rourke Corp.

Learning New Roles. Christie Costanzo. LC 91-11572. (Women Today Ser.). 64p. (YA). (gr. 6-12). 1991. lib. bdg. 17.95 (*0-86593-117-8*) Rourke Corp.

Learning New Words: Reading & Writing Skills. Phyllis Edwards. Ed. by Jo Ellen Moore. (Illus.). 32p. (J). (gr. 3-4). 1995. pap., wbk. ed. 2.50 (*1-58610-034-3*, Learn on the Go) Learn Horizon.

Learning Numerical Control. Michael Janke. 1992. mass mkt. 39.00 (*0-8273-4536-4*) Delmar.

Learning Objectives for Grades Kindergarten Through Eight. 3rd ed. 71p. 1995. pap. 10.95 (*0-913717-95-9*, 1026) Hewitt Res Fnd.

Learning of God. Amy Carmichael et al. 1986. pap. 8.99 (*0-87508-086-3*) Chr Lit.

Learning of Liberty: The Educational Ideas of the American Founders. Lorraine S. Pangle & Thomas L. Pangle. LC 92-29956. (American Political Thought Ser.). 370p. (Orig.). (C). 1995. pap. 19.95 (*0-7006-0746-3*) U Pr of KS.

***Learning of Love: A Journey Toward Servant Leadership.** William B. Turner. LC 99-45014. 192p. 2000. 20.00 (*1-57312-311-0*) Smyth & Helwys.

Learning of Mathematics: Its Theory & Practice. National Council of Teachers of Mathematics Staff. LC QA0001.N3. (National Council of Teachers of Mathematics Yearbook Ser.: 21st). 365p. reprint ed. pap. 113.20 (*0-608-16588-3*, 202705200053) Bks Demand.

Learning of Mathematics - Its Theory & Practice: Twenty-First Yearbook. NCTM Staff. Ed. by Howard F. Fehr. 353p. 1995. reprint ed. pap. 17.95 (*0-87353-404-2*) NCTM.

Learning of Paul O'Neill. Graeme Woolaston. 220p. (Orig.). 1993. pap. 14.95 (*1-873741-12-X*, Pub. by Millvres Bks) LPC InBook.

***Learning Office 2000.** DDC Publishing Staff. 1999. 32.00 (*1-56243-736-4*) DDC Pub.

Learning Office 2000. DDC Publishing Staff. 1999. 32.00 (*1-56243-638-4*) DDC Pub.

***Learning on Silicon: Adaptive VLSI Neural Systems.** Gert Cauwenberghs & Magdy A. Bayoumi. LC 99-30265. (International Series In Engineering & Computer Science). 1999. write for info. (*0-7923-8555-1*) Kluwer Academic.

Learning on Your Own: Mathematics Projects. Phil Schlemmer. 192p. 1987. pap. text 21.95 (*0-87628-507-8*) Ctr Appl Res.

Learning on Your Own: Research Skills Projects. Phil Schlemmer. 152p. 1986. pap. text 21.95 (*0-87628-508-6*) Ctr Appl Res.

Learning on Your Own: Science Projects. Phil Schlemmer. 232p. 1987. pap. text 21.95 (*0-87628-509-4*) Ctr Appl Res.

Learning on Your Own: Social Studies Projects. Phil Schlemmer. 224p. 1987. pap. text 21.95 (*0-87628-510-8*) Ctr Appl Res.

Learning on Your Own: Writing Projects. Phil Schlemmer. 192p. 1986. pap. text 21.95 (*0-87628-511-6*) Ctr Appl Res.

Learning Online: An Educator's Easy Guide to the Internet. Amy Wolgemuth. LC 95-81133. (Illus.). 156p. (Orig.). 1996. pap. 27.95 (*1-57517-009-4*, 1420) SkyLght.

Learning Opportunities Beyond the School. 2nd rev. ed. Association for Childhood Education International Staff. Ed. by Barbara Hatcher & Shirley Beck. LC 97-20453. (Illus.). 80p. (C). 1997. pap. text. write for info. (*0-87173-138-X*) ACEI.

Learning Oracle Database Programming: A Tutorial for Application Developers. Frances Edelstein. (Learning Oracle Ser.: Vol. 3). 250p. (Orig.). 1997. pap. text 29.95 (*0-9647233-2-8*) Relational Busn Systs.

Learning Oracle Forms 4.5: A Tutorial for Forms Designers. Stephen Edelstein. (Learning Oracle Ser.: Vol. 1). (Illus.). 250p. 1995. pap. text 29.95 (*0-9647233-0-1*) Relational Busn Systs.

Learning Oracle Report Builder 3.0: A Tutorial for Report Designers. (Illus.). 250p. 1999. pap. text 29.95 (*0-9647233-4-4*) Relational Busn Systs.

Learning Oracle Reports 2.5: A Tutorial for Report Designers. Stephen Edelstein. (Learning Oracle Ser.: Vol. 2). (Illus.). 250p. 1996. pap. text 29.95 (*0-9647233-1-X*) Relational Busn Systs.

Learning Organiser. Mike Tilling. 250p. 1999. ring bd. 262.95 (*0-566-08156-3*, Pub. by Ashgate Pub) Ashgate Pub Co.

Learning Organization. Garratt. 1987. 61.95 (*0-566-02743-7*) Ashgate Pub Co.

Learning Organization: Managing Knowledge for Business Success. 1996. 395.00 (*0-85058-855-3*, I855) Economist Intell.

Learning Organization in the Public Services. Jamice A. Cook et al. LC 96-52107. 264p. 1997. text 78.95 (*0-566-07773-6*, Pub. by Gower) Ashgate Pub Co.

Learning Organizations: Developing Cultures for Tomorrow's Workplace. Ed. by Sarita Chawla & John Renesch. (Illus.). 575p. 1995. 35.00 (*1-56327-110-9*) Productivity Inc.

Learning Organizations in Practice. Michael Pearn et al. LC 95-5588. 1995. write for info. (*0-07-707744-X*) McGraw.

Learning Our Letters. Rosene Burkholder. (Jewel Book Ser.: Set 5). (Illus.). 32p. (J). (ps-2). 1994. pap. 2.55 (*0-7399-0050-1*, 2580) Rod & Staff.

***Learning Outside the Lines: Two Ivy League Students with ADHD & Learning Disabilities Show You How to Gain the Academic Edge.** Jonathan Mooney & David Cole. (Illus.). 256p. 2000. pap. 13.00 (*0-684-86598-X*, Fireside) S&S Trade Pap.

Learning Packages in American Education. Ed. by Philip G. Kapfer & Miriam B. Kapfer. LC 72-11507. 248p. 1973. pap. 27.95 (*0-87778-047-1*) Educ Tech Pubns.

Learning PageMaker: A Hands-On Workbook for the Beginner - Macintosh Version. Richard P. Komorowski. (Illus.). 194p. (C). 1989. pap. text 29.95 incl. disk (*0-9624791-0-1*) Lasertyper.

***Learning Partners: A Guide to Educational Activities for Families.** 32p. 2000. pap. 3.25 (*0-16-050208-X*) USGPO.

Learning Partners: Guide to Educational Activities for Families. (Education Department Publication Ser.: Vol. 97-6518R). (Illus.). 32p. 1998. pap. 3.00 (*0-16-049683-7*) USGPO.

Learning Partnerships: How Leading American Companies Implement Organizational Learning. Robert P. Mai & Jerry L. McAdams. LC 95-21265. 240p. 1995. 29.95 (*0-7863-0388-3*, Irwn Prfssnl) McGraw-Hill Prof.

Learning Patterns among Women Professionals: Theory Grounded in the Lives of Nurses. Ed. by Edwin L. Simpson. LC 91-12429. 72p. (Orig.). 1991. lib. bdg. 10.95 (*1-879528-01-0*) Ed Studies Pr.

Learning Patterns & Temperament Styles: A Systematic Guide to Maximizing Student Achievement. Keith J. Golay. LC 82-62144. 109p. (Orig.). 1982. pap. text 12.00 (*0-9610076-0-5*) Manas-Sys.

Learning Peace: The Promise of Ecological & Cooperative Education. Ed. by Betty A. Reardon & Eva Nordland. LC 93-731. (SUNY Series, Global Conflict & Peace Education). 234p. (C). 1994. text 57.50 (*0-7914-1755-7*); pap. text 18.95 (*0-7914-1756-5*) State U NY Pr.

Learning Performance of Retarded & Normal Children, No. 5--5. G. Orville Johnson & Kathryn A. Blake. LC 77-22852. (Syracuse University Special Education & Rehabilitation Monograph Ser.: No. 5). (Illus.). 216p. 1977. reprint ed. lib. bdg. 59.50 (*0-8371-9725-2*, JOLE) Greenwood.

Learning Perl. Randal L. Schwartz. Ed. by Andy Oram. (Computer Science). (Illus.). 274p. 1993. pap. 29.95 (*1-56592-042-2*) Thomson Learn.

Learning Perl. 2nd rev. ed. Randal L. Schwartz & Tom Christiansen. Ed. by Steve Talbott. LC 97-208359. (Illus.). 271p. 1997. pap. 29.95 (*1-56592-284-0*) Thomson Learn.

Learning Perl on Win32 Systems. Randal L. Schwartz et al. Ed. by Andy Oram. LC 98-111595. (Orig.). 1997. pap. 29.95 (*1-56592-324-3*) OReilly & Assocs.

Learning Perl/TK. Nancy Walsh. Ed. by Linda Mui. (Illus.). 376p. 1999. pap. 34.95 (*1-56592-314-6*) OReilly & Assocs.

Learning Pharmacology Through MCQ. 2nd ed. B. J. Large & I. E. Hughes. LC 89-21548. 258p. 1990. pap. 78.50 (*0-471-92708-2*) Wiley.

Learning Phonics & Spelling in a Whole Language Classroom. Scholastic, Inc. Staff. LC 94-199877. 168p. (J). (gr. k-4). 1993. pap. 16.95 (*0-590-49148-2*) Scholastic Inc.

Learning Phonics Through Literature Program, Set. Lakeshore Learning Materials Staff. 1997. pap. write for info. (*1-929255-00-4*, LK600X) Lkeshore Learn Mats.

Learning Pieces. Howard Stein. (Illus.). 80p. 1999. pap. 9.00 (*0-8059-4786-8*) Dorrance.

Learning Poems for Children. Lois Carson. (Illus.). 32p. (J). (gr. k-6). 1999. pap. 7.00 (*0-8059-4667-5*) Dorrance.

Learning Policy. Ainley. LC 99-18546. 236p. 1999. text 69.95 (*0-312-22230-0*) St Martin.

Learning Portuguese Without a Teacher. G. Parisotto. 60p. 1991. write for info. incl. audio (*0-9629515-9-5*); pap. write for info. (*0-9629515-3-6*) Sunrising Pub.

L

An Asterisk (*) at the beginning of an entry indicates that the title is appearing for the first time.

Learning Potential Assessment: Theoretical Methodological & Practical Issues. 2nd ed. J. H. Hamers et al. 384p. 1996. 80.00 (*90-265-1238-4*) Swets.

Learning Power. Kaplan Staff. LC 98-13155. 192p. 1998. pap. 12.00 (*0-684-84939-9*) S&S Trade.

Learning Power: A Student's Guide to Success. Jerry Lafferty. Ed. by Melissa Moore. LC 92-72769. (Illus.). 138p. (Orig.). (YA). (gr. 7-12). 1993. 34.95 incl. audio (*1-881843-29-7*) Alpha Educ Inst.

Learning PowerPoint 2000. DDC Publishing Staff. 1999. 32.00 (*1-56243-735-6*) DDC Pub.

Learning PowerPoint 2000. DDC Publishing Staff. 1999. 31.00 (*1-56243-706-2*) DDC Pub.

Learning Practical Tibetan. rev. ed. Andrew Bloomfield. Tr. by Yanki Tsering. LC 98-9465. Orig. Title: The Tibetan Phrasebook. 186p. 1998. pap. 16.95 (*1-55939-098-0*) Snow Lion Pubns.

***Learning Practices: Assessment & Action for Organizational Improvement.** Anthony Dibella. 250p. 2000. pap. 42.67 (*0-13-017380-0*, Prentice Hall) P-H.

Learning, Practicing & Living the New Careering: A 21st Century Approach. Anna Miller-Tiedeman. LC 98-54392. 275p. 1999. pap. 33.95 (*1-56032-740-5*) Hemisp Pub.

Learning Pre Algebra Step by Step. (C). 1991. write for info. (*0-8087-7228-7*) Pearson Custom.

***Learning Preference Inventory: User's Manual.** Harvey F. Silver et al. 142p. 2000. pap. text 19.95 (*1-58284-027-X*) Silver Strong.

Learning Preference Skills. Lee Owens & Jenny Barnes. (C). 1992. 90.00 (*0-86431-113-3*, Pub. by Aust Council Educ Res) St Mut.

Learning Problems & Learning Disabilities: Moving Forward. Howard Adelman & Linda Taylor. LC 92-9363. 480p. (C). 1992. 43.00 (*0-534-18756-0*) Brooks-Cole.

Learning Process: Educational Theory Implied in Theory of Knowledge. Jesse H. Coursault. LC 76-176674. (Columbia University. Teachers College. Contributions to Education Ser.: No. 16). reprint ed. 37.50 (*0-404-55016-9*) AMS Pr.

Learning Process: Theory & Practice. Rosella Linskie. LC 83-16882. 320p. 1983. reprint ed. pap. text 25.00 (*0-8191-3591-7*) U Pr of Amer.

Learning Process in Psychoanalytic Supervision. Paul A. Dewald. 1987. 72.50 (*0-8236-2965-1*, BN#02965) Intl Univs Pr.

Learning Process Skills. Stanley R. Riley. 128p. (Orig.). 1991. pap. text 15.00 (*0-87879-946-X*) Acad Therapy.

Learning Processes with a Deadly Outcome. Alexander Kluge. Tr. by Christopher Pavsek. LC 95-53160. (Illus.). 152p. 1996. pap. 13.95 (*0-8223-1744-3*); text 36.95 (*0-8223-1735-4*) Duke.

Learning Programs. Peterson's Guides Staff. (The Summer Fun Ser.). 256p. pap. 9.95 (*0-7689-0188-X*) Petersons.

Learning Psychiatry Through MCQ: A Comprehensive Text. fac. ed. Ed. by Tom Sensky. LC 88-223. (Wiley Medical Publication). 269p. 1988. reprint ed. pap. 83.40 (*0-608-00991-1*, 206184700012) Bks Demand.

***Learning Psychotherapy: A Time-Efficient, Research-Based, & Outcome-Measured Training Program.** Bernard D. Beitman & Dongmei Yue. LC 98-50157. (Illus.). 350p. 1999. pap. 40.00 (*0-393-70296-0*) Norton.

Learning Psychotherapy: A Time-Efficient, Research-Based, & Outcome-Measured Training Program. Bernard D. Beitman & Dongmei Yue. 88p. 1999. pap. 30.00 (*0-393-70305-3*) Norton.

Learning Psychotherapy: Rationale & Ground Rules. Hilde Bruch. LC 74-83848. 166p. 1980. pap. 15.95 (*0-674-52026-2*) HUP.

***Learning Python.** Mark Lutz & David Ascher. Ed. by Frank Willison. (Illus.). 312p. 1999. pap. 29.95 (*1-56592-464-9*) OReilly & Assocs.

Learning Re-Abled: The Learning Disability Controversy & Composition Studies. Patricia Dunn. LC 95-9316. 232p. 1995. pap. text 24.50 (*0-86709-360-9*, 0360, Pub. by Boynton Cook Pubs) Heinemann.

Learning Read: Theory & Research. Brian Thompson & Tom Nicholson. LC 98-30943. (Language & Literacy Ser.). 288p. 1999. text 51.00 (*0-8077-3792-5*); pap. text 23.95 (*0-8077-3791-7*) Tchrs Coll.

***Learning Red Hat Linux.** Bill McCarty. Ed. by Mark Stone. (Illus.). 400p. 1999. pap. 32.95 incl. cd-rom (*1-56592-627-7*) OReilly & Assocs.

***Learning Related Outcomes of Computer Technology in K-12 Education.** Kenneth W. Umbach. 27p. 1998. pap. write for info. (*1-58703-089-6*, CRB-98-010) CA St Libry.

Learning Relationships in the Classroom. Dorothy Faulkner et al. LC 98-13944. (Illus.). 320p. (C). 1998. pap. 22.99 (*0-415-17373-6*) Routledge.

Learning, Remembering, Believing: Enhancing Human Performance. National Research Council Staff. Ed. by Daniel Druckman & Robert A. Bjork. 416p. (C). 1994. 39.95 (*0-309-04993-8*) Natl Acad Pr.

Learning Resources Programs That Make a Difference. 112p. 1987. 19.95 (*0-89240-046-3*) Assn Ed Comm Tech.

***Learning Revolution.** 2nd ed. Gordon Dryden. 1999. 30.00 (*1-929284-00-4*) Learning Web.

Learning Revolution: The Challenge of Information Technology in the Academy. Ed. by Diana G. Oblinger & Sean C. Rush. 264p. (C). 1997. text 35.95 (*1-882982-17-7*) Anker Pub.

Learning Robots: 6th European Workshop, EWLR '96, Brighton, U. K., Proceedings. Ed. by Andreas Birk et al. LC 98-55093. (Lecture Notes in Computer Science Ser.: Vol. 1545). ix, 188p. 1999. pap. 37.00 (*3-540-65480-1*) Spr-Verlag.

***Learning Rock Lead Guitar.** Austin Sicard, Jr. 52p. 1998. pap. 14.95 (*0-7866-3453-7*, 94365BCD) Mel Bay.

***Learning Rock Rhythm Guitar.** Austin Sicard, Jr. 48p. 1998. pap. 14.95 (*0-7866-3457-X*, 94532BCD) Mel Bay.

Learning Russian, 4 vols. Nina F. Potapova. Incl. Vol. 1. (ENG & RUS.). 1985. pap. 20.95 (*0-87557-127-1*); Vol. 2. (ENG & RUS.). 1985. pap. 20.95 (*0-87557-128-X*); Vol. 3. (ENG & RUS.). 1985. pap. 20.95 (*0-87557-129-8*); Vol. 4. (ENG & RUS.). 1985. pap. 20.95 (*0-87557-130-1*); 69.50 (*0-87557-073-9*) Saphrograph.

Learning... Sanskrit Alphabet. Thomas Egenes. 188p. (C). 1993. pap. text 16.00 (*0-923569-09-X*, D-02) Maharishi U Mgmt Pr.

Learning SAS in the Computer Lab. Elliott. 1994. teacher ed. 14.25 (*0-534-23443-7*) Brooks-Cole.

Learning SAS in the Computer Lab. 2nd ed. Rebecca J. Elliott. LC 99-41150. (Statistics Ser.). 236p. 1999. pap. text 24.95 (*0-534-35925-6*) Brooks-Cole.

Learning SAS in the Computer Lab. 2nd ed. Rebecca J. Elliott. 2000. pap. text, student ed. write for info. (*0-534-36177-3*) Brooks-Cole.

Learning School: A Guide to Vision-Based Leadership. Richard C. Wallace, Jr. et al. LC 97-4831. (Illus.). 216p. 1997. 61.95 (*0-8039-6408-0*); pap. 27.95 (*0-8039-6409-9*) Corwin Pr.

***Learning School, Learning Systems.** Paul Clarke. 2000. 74.95 (*0-304-70772-4*); pap. 24.95 (*0-304-70773-2*) Continuum.

Learning Science in the Schools: Research Reforming Practice. Ed. by Shawn M. Glynn & Reinders Duit. 392p. 1995. pap. 45.00 (*0-8058-1808-1*); text 99.95 (*0-8058-1807-3*) L Erlbaum Assocs.

Learning Science Process Skills. 3rd ed. Richard Rezba. 288p. 1996. pap., per. 24.95 (*0-8403-8430-0*) Kendall-Hunt.

Learning Science with Science Fiction Films. Terrence Cavanaugh & Catherine Cavanaugh. 238p. 1996. spiral bd. 29.95 (*0-7872-2463-4*, 41246301) Kendall-Hunt.

Learning Search Control Knowledge: An Explanation-Based Approach. Steven Minton. (C). 1988. text 100.50 (*0-89838-294-7*) Kluwer Academic.

Learning Series Book for Lotus 1-2-3 Release 5 for Windows. Kathy Vento. LC 95-175918. (Fast-Teach Learning Ser.). 1995. pap. text 25.00 (*1-56243-142-0*, B-9) DDC Pub.

***Learning Shapes.** Random House Staff. (Star Wars). 16p. (J). (ps-2). 1999. pap. 4.99 (*0-375-80004-2*, Pub. by Random Bks Yng Read) Random.

***Learning Shapes & Colors.** (Tele-Skills Ser.). (SPA & ENG., Illus.). (J). (ps-1). 2000. pap. 8.95 incl. audio (*1-886972-86-9*, Pub. by Emaginit) Penton Overseas.

***Learning Sight Words Is Easy!** Mary Rosenberg. (Illus.). 96p. (J). 2000. pap. 10.95 (*0-439-14113-3*) Scholastic Inc.

***Learning Signs.** Cathy Beylon. 2000. pap. 4.50 (*0-486-40816-7*) Dover.

***Learning Simulink.** 1999. pap. text 35.00 (*0-9672195-2-3*) MathWorks.

Learning Sites: Social & Technological Resources for Learning. Joan Bliss et al. LC 99-24854. (Advances in Learning & Instruction Ser.). 352p. 1999. 82.00 (*0-08-043350-2*, Pergamon Pr) Elsevier.

Learning Skills & Organizer Guide: Learn How to Learn - Primary Edition, 5 vols. (Illus.). 50p. (J). (gr. 1-3). 1997. pap. write for info. (*1-892022-04-4*) Skill Boosters.

Learning Skills & Organizer Guide: Learn How to Learn - Secondary Edition. LC TX-3-990-941. (Illus.). 120p. (J). (gr. 5-7). 1995. pap. write for info. (*1-892022-00-1*) Skill Boosters.

Learning Skills & Organizer Guide: Secondary Teacher Edition. 3rd rev. ed. (Illus.). 157p. 1995. pap. write for info. (*1-892022-02-8*) Skill Boosters.

Learning Skills & Organizer Guide (Elementary) Learn How to Learn - Elementary Edition & Teacher Edition. 2nd rev. ed. (Illus.). 157p. Date not set. pap. write for info. (*1-892022-03-6*) Skill Boosters.

Learning Skills for College & Career. Paul Hettich. LC 91-44480. 337p. (C). 1992. mass mkt. 28.00 (*0-534-17292-X*) Brooks-Cole.

Learning Skills for College & Career. 2nd ed. Paul I. Hettich. LC 97-17468. (Counseling Ser.). 399p. 1997. mass mkt. 41.95 (*0-534-34878-5*) Brooks-Cole.

***Learning Skills for Managers.** Samuel Malone. 180p. 2000. pap. 16.95 (*1-86076-170-4*, Pub. by Oak Tr) Midpt Trade.

Learning Skills for the Science Student. Stefan Bosworth & Marion Brisk. Ed. by Katherine Savige. (Illus.). 75p. 1986. pap. text 5.95 (*0-943202-21-3*) H & H Pubs.

Learning Social Studies & History Through Poetry-Middle & High School Levels: Critical Thinking through Poetry. Ken Siegelman. 70p. 1997. spiral bd. 16.00 (*0-910609-33-0*) Gifted Educ Pr.

***Learning Society: International Perspectives on Core Skills in Higher Education.** Elisabeth Dunne. LC 99-491044. 228p. 1999. 65.00 (*0-7494-2895-3*, Kogan Pg Educ) Stylus Pub VA.

Learning Society Vol. 2: Challenges & Trends. Ed. by Peter Raggatt et al. LC 95-443. (Open University Set Bks.). (Illus.). 312p. (C). 1995. pap. 22.99 (*0-415-13615-6*) Routledge.

Learning Spanish. 2nd ed. Gail Stein. (Complete Idiot's Guide Ser.). (Illus.). 458p. 1999. pap. 17.95 (*0-02-862743-1*) Macmillan.

Learning Spanish with Enza B. Bk. 1: An Introduction to Nouns & Gender. Margaret Harris. (Learning Language with Enza B. Ser.). (Illus.). 95p. (J). (gr. 3-8). 1994. student ed. 15.95 (*1-886332-00-2*) Forlang Foreign.

Learning Spanish with Enza B Bk. 2: Regular Verbs & the Present Tense. Illus. by Patricia DeCroce. (Learning Language with Enza B. Ser.). (SPA.). 60p. (YA). (gr. 6-8). 1993. write for info. (*1-886332-03-7*) Forlang Foreign.

Learning, Speech, & the Complex Effects of Punishment: Essays Honoring George J. Wischner. Ed. by Donald K. Routh. LC 82-18075. 248p. 1982. 49.50 (*0-306-40960-7*, Plenum Trade) Perseus Pubng.

Learning Spirit: Lessons from South Africa. Ana K. Gobledale. LC 94-32058. 144p. (Orig.). 1995. pap. 14.99 (*0-8272-2124-X*) Chalice Pr.

Learning Standard Arabic: Root & Pattern Reference. Don Y. Lee. LC 86-82210. (C). 1988. 69.00 (*0-939758-15-6*) Eastern Pr.

Learning Statistics Through Playing Cards. Thomas R. Knapp. LC 95-41790. (Illus.). 112p. 1996. 39.95 (*0-7619-0108-6*) Sage.

Learning Strategies. John Nisbet & Janet Shucksmith. (Education Bks.). 144p. (C). 1986. text 37.50 (*0-7102-0569-4*, Routledge Thoemms) Routledge.

Learning Strategies & Learning Styles. R. R. Schmeck. LC 88-12586. (Perspectives on Individual Differences Ser.). (Illus.). 390p. (C). 1988. 65.00 (*0-306-42860-1*, Plenum Trade) Perseus Pubng.

Learning Strategies for Allied Health Students. Marilyn Melzer. LC 95-901. (Illus.). 368p. 1995. pap. text 26.95 (*0-7216-5603-X*, W B Saunders Co) Harcrt Hlth Sci Grp.

Learning Strategies for Second Language Users: An Analytical Appraisal with Case Studies. Manfred Prokop. LC 88-39605. (Studies in Education: Vol. 2). 250p. 1989. lib. bdg. 89.95 (*0-88946-937-7*) E Mellen.

***Learning Strategies Handbook Sample Section.** (C). 1999. pap. 0.00 (*0-201-65528-4*) HEPC Inc.

Learning Strategies Hdbk. Anna U. Chamot. LC 99-13597. 1999. 36.00 (*0-201-38548-1*) Addison-Wesley.

Learning Strategies in Nursing: Reading, Study, & Test-Taking. 2nd ed. Marilyn Meltzer & Susan M. Palau. Ed. by Thomas Eoyang. LC 96-20650. (Illus.). 400p. 1997. pap. text 26.00 (*0-7216-6342-7*, W B Saunders Co) Harcrt Hlth Sci Grp.

Learning Strategies in Second Language Acquisition. J. Michael O'Malley & Anna U. Chamot. (Cambridge Applied Linguistics Ser.). (Illus.). 272p. (C). 1990. pap. text 22.95 (*0-521-35837-X*) Cambridge U Pr.

Learning Stress Management Skills: Companion Workbook to Teaching Stress Management Skills. Frances K. Wiggins & Suni Petersen. (Illus.). 59p. (Orig.). (C). 1986. student ed. 5.95 (*0-942937-02-3*) Rivijon Pr.

Learning Structures. 216p. (C). 1995. pap. text 18.95 (*0-9647437-1-X*) RFT Pubng.

Learning Style Perspectives: Impact in the Classroom. Lynne C. Sarasin. LC 99-27754. 110p. 1999. pap. text 21.95 (*1-891859-22-6*) Atwood Pub LLC.

Learning Style Profile Examiner's Manual. rev. ed. James W. Keefe & John S. Monk. 32p. (C). 1990. pap. 4.00 (*0-88210-241-9*) Natl Assn Principals.

Learning Style Profile Technical Manual. James W. Keefe & John S. Monk. (Orig.). 1988. pap. text 20.00 (*0-88210-213-3*) Natl Assn Principals.

Learning Style Theory & Practice. James W. Keefe & Scott D. Thomson. 72p. (Orig.). 1987. pap. text 9.00 (*0-88210-201-X*) Natl Assn Principals.

Learning Styles. Judith Reiff. (What Research Says to the Teacher Ser.). 40p. 1992. pap. 3.95 (*0-8106-1092-2*) NEA.

Learning Styles: Applications in Vocational Education. William C. Knaak. 62p. 1983. 5.75 (*0-318-22141-1*, IN254) Ctr Educ Trng Employ.

Learning Styles: Food for Thought & 130 Practical Tips. Priscilla Vail. (Illus.). 132p. (Orig.). 1992. pap. 10.95 (*1-56762-005-1*) Modern Learn Pr.

Learning Styles: Implications for Improving Educational Practices. Charles S. Claxton & Patricia H. Murrell. Ed. by Jonathan D. Fife. LC 88-70151. (ASHE-ERIC Higher Education Reports: No. 87-4). 120p. (C). 1988. pap. 24.00 (*0-913317-39-X*) GWU Grad Schl E&HD.

Learning Styles: Personal Exploration & Practical Applications. 2nd rev. ed. Kathleen A. Butler. (Illus.). 118p. (YA). (gr. 7-12). 1995. pap. text, student ed. 16.95 (*0-945852-07-X*) Learners Dimension.

Learning Styles: Quiet Revolution in American Secondary Schools. Rita Dunn & Shirley A. Griggs. 88p. 1988. 9.00 (*0-88210-209-5*) Natl Assn Principals.

Learning Styles & Performance Assessment: A Model Teaching Guide. Bobby W. Prewitt & Kathleen A. Butler. 208p. (Orig.). 1993. pap. text 24.95 (*0-945852-04-5*) Learners Dimension.

Learning Styles & Strategies. 2nd ed. Harvey F. Silver & J. Robert Hanson. (Unity in Diversity Ser.: Vol. 1). (Illus.). viii, 208p. 1996. pap. text 29.95 (*1-58284-001-6*, Thoughtful Educ) Silver Strong.

Learning Styles & the Nursing Profession. Rita S. Dunn & Shirley A. Griggs. LC 97-49117. 1998. write for info. (*0-88737-771-8*) Natl League Nurse.

Learning Styles in the ESL/EFL. Joy M. Reid. 240p. (J). 1995. mass mkt. 33.95 (*0-8384-6158-1*) Heinle & Heinle.

Learning Styles Inventory: A Measure of Student Preference for Instructional Techniques. Joseph S. Renzulli & Linda H. Smith. 40p. 1978. pap. 8.95 (*0-936386-14-2*) Creative Learning.

Learning Success. 2nd ed. Wahlstrom. LC 98-33220. (Freshman Orientation/College Success Ser.). 1999. pap. 24.95 (*0-534-53424-4*) Wadsworth Pub.

Learning Success: Being Your Best at College & Life. Carl Wahlstrom & Brian K. Williams. (Illus.). 379p. (C). 1996. pap. 24.25 (*0-534-51346-8*) Wadsworth Pub.

Learning Success: Being Your Best at College & Life. Wahlstrom & Williams. 400p. 1996. pap. text 31.95 (*0-534-51350-6*) Wadsworth Pub.

Learning Success Kit. Mary Nolan. 272p. 1995. ring bd. 49.95 (*0-7872-0577-X*) Kendall-Hunt.

Learning Support for Young People in Transition: Leaving School for Further Education & Work. Jean McGinty & John Fish. 112p. 1992. 123.00 (*0-335-09766-9*); pap. 34.95 (*0-335-09765-0*) OpUniv Pr.

Learning Systems. Eduard Avedyan. 136p. 1995. 49.00 (*3-540-19996-9*) Spr-Verlag.

Learning Systems: Proceedings of the Joint Automatic Control Conference, Ohio State University, Colulmbus, Ohio, 1973. Joint Automatic Control Conference Staff. LC 73-83553. 83p. reprint ed. pap. 30.00 (*0-608-11760-9*, 201691500005) Bks Demand.

Learning Systems & Pattern Recognition in Industrial Control: Proceedings of the 9th Annual Advenced Control Conference. Ed. by Edward J. Kompass & Theodore J. Williams. 91p. 1983. 27.50 (*0-914331-08-6*, Control Engrng) Cahners Busn Des Plaines.

Learning Tabla with Alla Rakha. Jeffrey M. Feldman & Alla Rakha. 102p. 1984. spiral bd. Price not set. incl. audio (*0-9643694-0-9*) Digitala.

Learning Tabla with Alla Rakha: A Manual of Drumming & Recitation. Jeffrey M. Feldman & Alla Rakha. 1984. pap. 16.95 (*0-9643694-3-5*) Digitala.

Learning Tabla with Alla Rakha (Book & Videotape Edition) A Manual of Drumming & Recitation. abr. ed. Ed. & Photos by Jeffrey M. Feldman. 1998. spiral bd. 52.95 incl. VHS (*0-9643694-2-7*) Digitala.

Learning Tactics Inventory: Facilitator's Guide. Center for Creative Leadership Staff. 48p. 1999. pap. text 24.95 (*0-7879-4841-1*) Jossey-Bass.

Learning Tactics Inventory: Participant's Workbook. Center for Creative Leadership Staff. 48p. 1999. pap. text 12.95 (*0-7879-4842-X*) Jossey-Bass.

Learning Talmud: A Guide to Talmud Terminology & Rashi Commentary. Scot A. Berman. LC 96-39697. 1997. pap. 25.00 (*0-7657-5958-6*) Aronson.

Learning Targets: Number Key State 2. Bunson Margaret. 192p. 1998. pap. 45.00 (*0-7487-3597-6*) St Mut.

Learning Targets: Phonics & Spelling Key Stage 2. Bunson Margaret. 160p. 1998. pap. 45.00 (*0-7487-3598-4*) St Mut.

Learning, Teaching & Communication in the Foreign Language Classroom. Ed. by Gabriele Kasper. 224p. (C). 1986. pap. 27.00 (*87-7288-005-8*, Pub. by Aarhus Univ Pr) David Brown.

Learning, Teaching & Researching on the Internet: A Practical Guide for Social Scientists. S. D. Stein. LC 98-8739. 1998. write for info. (*0-582-31935-8*) Longman.

Learning Technology in the European Communities. Ed. by Stefano A. Cerri & John Whiting. 760p. 1991. lib. bdg. 283.50 (*0-7923-1473-5*) Kluwer Academic.

Learning That Lasts: Integrating Learning, Development & Performance in College & Beyond. Marcia Mentkowski. LC 99-50759. 576p. 2000. 38.95 (*0-7879-4482-3*) Jossey-Bass.

Learning That Works: Policy Report, No. 2. Suzanne Knell et al. (Basic Skills Programs in Illinois Corporations Ser.). 51p. 1993. pap. text 25.00 (*1-885095-55-4*) IL Lit Res Dev.

Learning That Works: Programs & Structures Report, No. 1. Barbara Geissler et al. (Basic Skills Programs in Illinois Corporations Ser.). 115p. 1993. pap. text 35.00 (*1-885095-54-6*) IL Lit Res Dev.

Learning the Art of Mathematical Modelling. M. Cross & A. O. Moscardini. LC 84-29770. (Mathematics & Its Applications Ser.). 1985. pap. text 23.95 (*0-470-20169-X*) P-H.

Learning the Bash Shell. Cameron Newham. 310p. (Orig.). 1995. pap. 27.95 (*1-56592-147-X*) Thomson Learn.

Learning the Bash Shell. 2nd ed. Cameron Newham & Bill Rosenblatt. LC 98-132271. 318p. (Orig.). 1998. pap. 29.95 (*1-56592-347-2*) OReilly & Assocs.

Learning the Basics of Microcomputing: An Introductory Computer Software Workbook. 6th ed. Marilyn G. Kletke. (C). 1994. pap. text, wbk. ed. write for info. (*0-07-035148-1*) McGraw.

***Learning the Basics of New Testament Greek Workbook.** rev. ed. George Hodjiantoniole. Ed. by James H. Gee. 160p. (C). 1999. pap. 16.99 (*0-89957-802-0*) AMG Pubs.

Learning the Body. deluxe ed. Futech Interactive Products Staff. (Look, Listen & Learn Ser.). 1999. 14.95 (*1-58224-006-X*) Futech Interactive.

***Learning the Calendar.** (Tele-Skills Ser.). (SPA & ENG., Illus.). (J). (ps-1). 2000. pap. 8.95 incl. audio (*1-886972-87-7*, Pub. by Emaginit) Penton Overseas.

Learning the Classic Guitar, Pt. 1. Aaron Shearer. 136p. 1990. spiral bd. 14.95 (*0-87166-854-8*, 94361) Mel Bay.

Learning the Classic Guitar, Pt. 2. Aaron Shearer. 224p. 1990. spiral bd. 17.95 (*0-87166-855-6*, 94362) Mel Bay.

Learning the Classic Guitar, Pt. 3. Aaron Shearer. 88p. 1997. spiral bd. 19.95 incl. audio compact disk (*0-7866-3209-7*, 94363BCD) Mel Bay.

Learning the Continents. Randy L. Womack & James L. Shoemaker. (Illus.). 96p. (gr. 4 up). 1995. student ed. 10.95 (*1-56500-018-8*) Gldn Educ.

Learning the Continuum: AUPHA Modules for Management Education. (Orig.). (C). 1990. pap. text 140.00 (*0-910591-15-6*) AUPHA Pr.

Learning the Difference: Common Errors Made by Spanish Speakers Learning English. rev. ed. Beatrice Kreppel & David Blot. 78p. (C). 1984. pap. text 5.00 (*0-317-93600-X*) D Blot Pubns.

Learning the Folk Guitar: A Step by Step Method. Phil Johnson. (Illus.). 120p. 1997. pap. 22.95 (*0-9657323-1-2*) Euphoria Falls.

Learning the Hardware: Complete Hardware Description for the PC. Barbara Holliday. (Mr. CPU Ser.: No. 4). 9p. 1997. pap. text 9.95 (*1-891727-03-6*) Fun Books.

An Asterisk (*) at the beginning of an entry indicates that the title is appearing for the first time.

Learning the HP-UX Operating System. Marty Poniatowski. LC 96-18464. 336p. 1996. pap. text 34.99 (*0-13-258534-0*) P-H.

Learning the Internet. DDC Publishing Staff. 1996. 29.00 (*1-56243-346-6*, Z-15HC); pap. text 27.00 (*1-56243-345-8*, Z-15) DDC Pub.

Learning the Internet. 2nd ed. DDC Publishing Staff. LC 99-168428. (Learning Ser.). 1998. pap. text 27.00 (*1-56243-593-0*, Z30) DDC Pub.

Learning the Internet: A Workbook for Beginners. John Burke. 138p. (Orig.). 1996. pap., wbk. ed. 49.95 incl. disk (*1-55570-303-8*) Neal-Schuman.

Learning the Internet: A Workbook for Beginners. John Burke. (Illus.). 138p. (Orig.). 1996. pap., wbk. ed. 32.95 (*1-55570-248-1*) Neal-Schuman.

Learning the Internet for Business. DDC Publishing Staff. (Learning Ser.). 1998. pap. text 27.00 (*1-56243-587-6*, Z27) DDC Pub.

Learning the Korn Shell. Bill Rosenblatt. Ed. by Mike Loukides. (Computer Science). (Illus.). 363p. 1993. pap. 29.95 (*1-56592-054-6*) Thomson Learn.

Learning the Landscape: Inquiry-Based Activities for Comprehending & Composing. Fran Claggett et al. LC 96-20849. 176p. 1996. pap. text 19.50 (*0-86709-395-1*, 0395, Pub. by Boynton Cook Pubs) Heinemann.

Learning the Language. Jay Udall. 76p. (Orig.). 1997. pap. 11.00 (*0-944920-24-1*) Bellowing Ark Pr.

***Learning the Language of Patterns: A Teacher's Guided Tour.** Peter R. Bergethon. (Illus.). 149p. 1999. spiral bd. write for info. (*1-58447-029-1*) Symmetry Lrng.

***Learning the Language of Patterns: Student Science Journal.** Peter R. Bergethon. (Illus.). 74p. (YA). (gr. 4-9). 1999. pap. text. write for info. (*1-58447-030-5*) Symmetry Lrng.

***Learning the Language of Patterns: Teacher Manual.** Peter R. Bergethon. (Illus.). xvi, 74p. 1999. teacher ed., spiral bd. write for info. (*1-58447-031-3*) Symmetry Lrng.

***Learning the Language of Patterns: The Overview.** Peter R. Bergethon. (Illus.). 19p. 1999. pap. text. write for info. (*1-58447-028-3*) Symmetry Lrng.

Learning the Language of Prayer. Joyce Huggett. LC 97-68079. (Illus.). 160p. 1997. 14.95 (*0-8245-1687-7*) Crossroad NY.

Learning the Law. 11th ed. Glanville & Williams. (C). 1982. 200.00 (*0-7855-4102-0*, Pub. by Witherby & Co) St Mut.

Learning the Law: How to Succeed in Law School & Beyond. Steven J. Frank. (Illus.). 226p. 1999. reprint ed. 34.95 (*0-7351-0082-9*) Replica Bks.

Learning the Law: Success in Law School & Beyond. Steven J. Frank. 224p. 1992. pap. 14.95 (*0-8065-1357-8*, Citadel Pr) Carol Pub Group.

Learning the Law: Success in Law School & Beyond. Steven J. Frank. LC 96-50115. 224p. 1997. pap. 16.95 (*0-8065-1871-5*, Citadel Pr) Carol Pub Group.

Learning the Law: Teaching & the Transmission of Law in England, 1150-1900. Jonathan Bush & Alain A. Wijffels. LC 99-32558. 1999. 65.00 (*1-85285-184-8*) Hambledon Press.

Learning the Lessons. Oxfam Staff. 1995. pap. 15.95 (*0-614-11370-9*, Pub. by Oxfam Pub) Stylus Pub VA.

Learning the Lord's Prayer. Phyllis Wezeman. (Illus.). 136p. (J). 1998. pap. 14.95 (*1-57438-016-8*) Ed Ministries.

Learning the Mother Tongue. Clare Painter. 93p. (C). 1995. pap. 34.00 (*0-7300-1249-2*, ECS805, Pub. by Deakin Univ) St Mut.

Learning the New Food Labels: An Educator's Slide Kit. Constance J. Geiger & Patricia H. Harper. 81p. 1994. ring bd. 90.00 incl. sl. (*0-88091-131-X*) Am Dietetic Assn.

Learning the Nighttime Routine: Beginning the Process of Learning the Nighttime Routine. Mary A. Little. (Competent Kids Ser.). 16p. (J). 1995. 19.95 (*1-887514-02-3*) Three Bears.

***Learning the Ropes.** Random House Staff. (J). 2001. mass mkt. 3.99 (*0-375-81160-5*) Random Bks Yng Read.

Learning the Ropes: A Basic Guide to Safe & Fun S-M Lovemaking. Race Bannon. LC 92-73484. 159p. (Orig.). 1993. pap. 12.95 (*1-881943-07-0*) Daedalus Pub.

Learning the Ropes: A Creative Autobiography. Bill Ransom. LC 95-4342. 1995. pap. 5.00 (*0-87421-190-5*) Utah St U Pr.

***Learning the Ropes: An Apprentice to the Last of the Windjammers.** Eric Newby. (Illus.). 144p. 1999. 35.00 (*0-8129-3252-8*, Times Bks) Crown Pub Group.

Learning the Ropes Skills see Career Skills Library

Learning the Rules: The Anatomy of Children's Relationships. Brian J. Bigelow et al. LC 96-15609. (Series on Personal Relationships). 255p. 1996. lib. bdg. 36.00 (*1-57230-084-1*) Guilford Pubns.

Learning the Skills of Peacemaking: A K-6 Activity Guide to Resolving Conflicts, Communicating, & Cooperating. 2nd rev. ed. Naomi Drew. Ed. by Susan Remkus. 272p. 1995. pap. 29.95 (*1-880396-42-4*, JP9642-4) Jalmar Pr.

Learning the Tarot: A Tarot Book for Beginners. Joan Bunning. LC 98-23461. (Illus.). 320p. 1998. pap. 14.95 (*1-57863-048-7*) Weiser.

Learning the 21 Irrefutable Laws of Leadership. John C. Maxwell. 1999. pap., student ed. 7.99 (*0-7852-9436-8*) W1CL.

Learning the UNIX Operating System. 3rd ed. Grace Todino et al. Ed. by Tim O'Reilly. (Illus.). 108p. 1993. pap. 9.95 (*1-56592-060-0*) Thomson Learn.

Learning the UNIX Operating System. 4th ed. Jerry Peek et al. Ed. by Gigi Estabrook. (Illus.). 92p. 1997. reprint ed. pap. 12.95 (*1-56592-390-1*) OReilly & Assocs.

Learning the Value of Virtues Through Journal Writing: Intermediate. Frank Schaffer Publications Staff. 1997. pap. text 3.95 (*0-7647-0201-7*) Schaffer Pubns.

Learning the Value of Virtues Through Journal Writing: Primary. Frank Schaffer Publications Staff. 1997. pap. text 3.95 (*0-7647-0105-3*) Schaffer Pubns.

Learning the VI Editor. 5th rev. ed. Linda Lamb. (Computer Science). 192p. 1990. reprint ed. pap. 24.95 (*0-937175-67-6*) Thomson Learn.

Learning the vi Editor. 6th ed. Linda Lamb & Arnold Robbins. (Illus.). 348p. 1998. pap. 24.95 (*1-56592-426-6*) OReilly & Assocs.

Learning the Virtues That Lead You to God. Romano Guardini. LC 97-48647. Orig. Title: Tugenden: Meditationen Uber Gestalten Sittlichen Lebens. 214p. 1998. reprint ed. pap. 14.95 (*0-918477-64-6*) Sophia Inst Pr.

Learning the Ways of the Holy Spirit see Aprendido las Carateristicas del Espiritu Santo

Learning the Ways of the Holy Spirit. Pat Harrison. 160p. 1998. pap. 7.99 (*0-89274-564-9*, HH-564) Harrison Hse.

Learning the Words of Color. Katherine Oana. Ed. by Tate Baird. LC 86-50866. (Illus.). 32p. (Orig.). (J). (ps-1). 1986. pap. 2.95 (*0-914127-79-9*) Univ Class.

***Learning Theodicy: The Problem of Evil & the Praxis of Religious Education.** Paul Vermeer. LC 99-55712. (Empirical Studies in Theology). 208p. 1999. 60.00 (*90-04-11650-8*) Brill Academic Pubs.

Learning Theories. 3rd ed. Dale H. Schunk. LC 99-34088. (Illus.). 522p. 1999. 68.00 (*0-13-010850-2*) P-H.

Learning Theories for Teachers. 6th ed. Morris L. Bigge & S. Samuel Shermis. LC 98-19891. 384p. (C). 1998. pap. 53.00 (*0-321-02343-9*) Addson-Wesley Educ.

Learning Theories in Educational Practice: An Integration of Psychological Theory & Educational Philosophy. Owen E. Pittenger & C. Thomas Gooding. LC 79-140553. 228p. (C). reprint ed. 70.70 (*0-8357-9922-0*, 205174700005) Bks Demand.

Learning Theory & Its Application to Classroom Teaching. Herbert A. Thelen. 1956. 2.50 (*0-87060-088-5*, PUC 3) Syracuse U Cont Ed.

Learning Theory Approaches to Psychiatry. Ed. by John C. Boulougouris. LC 81-16514. 284p. reprint ed. pap. 88.10 (*0-608-18414-4*, 203044300069) Bks Demand.

Learning Theory in the Practice of Management Development: Evolution & Applications. Sidney A. Mailick et al. LC 97-32993. 184p. 1998. 55.00 (*1-56720-052-4*, Quorum Bks) Greenwood.

Learning Theory, Instructional Theory, & Psychoeducational Design. Glenn E. Snelbecker. 544p. 1985. reprint ed. pap. text 34.00 (*0-8191-4836-9*) U Pr of Amer.

Learning Things: Games That Make Learning Fun for Children 3-8 Years Old. Ellen C. Church. LC 81-82033. (J). (ps-3). 1982. pap. 15.99 (*0-8224-4268-X*) Fearon Teacher Aids.

Learning 3D Studio R4: A Tutorial Approach. Sham Tickoo & David McLees. LC 98-49862. (Illus.). 384p. (YA). (gr. 9-12). 1999. pap. text 37.00 incl. audio compact disk (*1-56637-500-2*) Goodheart.

***Learning 3D Studio VIZ 3.0: A Tutorial Approach.** Sham Tickoo & David McLees. (Illus.). 300p. 2000. pap. text 39.96 (*1-56637-545-2*) Goodheart.

Learning Through Art. Faith R. Tadman. (Illus.). 200p. 1999. pap. 18.95 (*0-89334-300-5*) Humanics Ltd.

Learning Through Art: The Guggenheim Museum Collection. Natalie K. Lieberman & Marilyn J. Goodman. (Guggenheim Museum Publication Ser.). (Illus.). 64p. 1998. pap. 19.95 (*0-8109-6910-6*, Pub. by Abrams) Time Warner.

Learning Through Art & Drama. Robert G. Davidson. 20p. (Orig.). 1987. pap. 5.50 (*0-940754-47-9*) Ed Ministries.

Learning Through Assessment: A Resource Guide for Higher Education. Ed. by Lion F. Gardiner et al. 124p. 1997. pap. 27.00 (*1-56377-004-0*) Am Assn Higher Ed.

Learning Through Child Observation. Mary Fawcett. 127p. 1996. pap. 19.95 (*1-85302-288-8*, Pub. by Jessica Kingsley) Taylor & Francis.

Learning Through Children's Eyes: Social Constructivism & the Desire to Learn. Penny Oldfather et al. LC 99-12929. (Division 15 Ser.: Vol. 12). 120p. 1999. pap. text 17.95 (*1-55798-587-1*, 431619A) Am Psychol.

Learning Through Construction. S. Mainwaring & C. Shouse. 43p. (J). (gr. k-3). 1983. pap. 8.95 (*1-57379-063-X*, E1007) High-Scope.

Learning Through Discussion. Jerome Rabow et al. LC 93-40761. (C). 1994. text 26.00 (*0-8039-5411-5*) Sage.

Learning Through Discussion. 3rd ed. Jerome Rabow et al. LC 93-40761. (C). 1994. pap. text 10.50 (*0-8039-5412-3*) Sage.

Learning Through Drama: Schools Council Drama Teaching Project. Lynn McGregor et al. 224p. 1977. pap. text 15.00 (*0-435-18565-9*, 18565) Heinemann.

Learning Through Experience in Agricultural Industry. Max L. Amberson & B. H. Anderson. 1978. text 16.96 (*0-07-000851-5*) McGraw.

Learning Through Field: A Developmental Approach. Susan F. Cochrane & Marla M. Hanley. LC 98-18643. 189p. 1998. pap. text 35.00 (*0-205-26809-9*) Allyn.

***Learning Through Fun & Games.** Elyssebeth Leigh. (Illus.). 176p. (J). 1999. pap. 29.95 (*0-07-470768-X*) McGraw.

Learning Through Geography. rev. ed. Frances Slater. (Pathways in Geography Ser.: No. 7). (Illus.). 227p. 1993. pap. text 15.00 (*0-9627379-7-6*) NCFGE.

Learning Through Interaction: Technology & Children with Multiple Disabilities. Nick Bozic & Heather Murdoch. LC 96-206652. 192p. 1996. pap. text 29.95 (*1-85346-377-9*, Pub. by David Fulton) Taylor & Francis.

***Learning Through Knowledge Management.** Pervaiz Ahmed. 288p. 2000. pap. 37.95 (*0-7506-4710-8*) Buttrwrth-Heinemann.

Learning Through Language in Early Childhood. Clare Painter. LC 98-2895. (Open Linguistics Ser.). 1998. 82.95 (*0-304-70056-8*) Continuum.

Learning Through Laughter. Robyn Flipse. LC 90-1026. 88p. 1990. reprint ed. pap. 30.00 (*0-608-03028-7*, 206347900006) Bks Demand.

Learning Through Listening. 2nd ed. Karen D. Gans. LC 94-211581. 224p. 1993. per. 37.95 (*0-8403-8728-8*) Kendall-Hunt.

Learning Through Literature: Ecology. Roth & Vaugh. (Illus.). 144p. (J). (gr. 3-5). 1996. pap., wbk. ed. 14.95 (*1-55734-475-2*) Tchr Create Mat.

Learning Through Literature: Native Americans. Liz Rothlein & Sharon Vaughn. (Learning Through Literature Ser.). (Illus.). 144p. (J). (gr. 3-5). 1997. pap., wbk. ed. 14.95 (*1-55734-476-0*) Tchr Create Mat.

Learning Through Literature: Projects & Activities for Linking Literature & Writing. (J). (gr. 4-6). 12.95 (*0-8167-3877-7*) Troll Communs.

Learning Through Literature: U. S. History. Concetta D. Ryan & Teacher Created Materials Staff. (Learning Through Literature Ser.). 144p. (J). (gr. 3-5). 1997. pap. 14.95 (*1-55734-472-8*) Tchr Create Mat.

***Learning Through Movement: Alphabet & Numbers.** Barbara Cracchiolo. 112p. 2000. pap. 12.95 (*1-57690-646-9*) ISI Books.

***Learning Through Movement: Children's Literature.** Christine Shahan. (Illus.). 112p. 2000. pap. 12.95 (*1-57690-001-0*) Tchr Create Mat.

***Learning Through Movement: Monthly Activities.** Barbara Cracchiolo. 112p. 2000. pap. 12.95 (*1-57690-647-7*) Tchr Create Mat.

Learning Through Music. Herbert Levin & Gail Levin. LC 99-163021. (Illus.). 150p. 1998. pap. text 28.00 (*1-891278-00-2*) Barcelona Pubs.

Learning Through Music for Special Children & Their Teachers. Jean H. Tomat & Carmel D. Krutzky. LC 75-25031. 82p. 1975. write for info. (*0-914562-02-9*) Merriam-Eddy.

Learning Through Play. 175p. 1996. pap. text. write for info. (*1-889544-05-1*) Chldrns Res.

Learning Through Play. Paul Chance. (Pediatric Round Table Ser.: No. 3). 60p. (Orig.). 1979. pap. 10.00 (*0-931562-02-3*) J & J Consumer Prods.

Learning through Play. Jan Natanson. LC 98-128644. (Illus.). 128p. 1998. pap. 19.95 (*0-7063-7623-4*) Sterling.

Learning Through Play: Curriculum & Activities for the Inclusive Classroom. Kathleen J. Dolinar et al. LC 93-25976. (C). 1994. mass mkt. 33.25 (*0-8273-5653-6*) Delmar.

Learning Through Play: Curriculum & Activities for the Inclusive Classroom. Kathleen Dolinar et al. LC 93-25976. 113p. 1994. teacher ed. 14.95 (*0-8273-5654-4*) Delmar.

Learning Through Problem Solving. Ed. by Daniel K. Apple et al. (Illus.). 394p. (C). 1992. pap. text 40.00 (*1-878437-20-8*) Pac Crest Soft.

Learning Through Problem Solving: A Special Double Issue of "The Journal of the Learning Sciences" Ed. by Cindy Hmelo & Susan Williams. 180p. 1998. pap. 40.00 (*0-8058-9823-9*) L Erlbaum Assocs.

Learning Through Problems: Number Sense & Computational Stategies. Paul R. Trafton & Diane Theissen. LC 99-23286. 128p. 1999. pap. text 14.00 (*0-325-00126-X*) Heinemann.

Learning Through Real-World Problem Solving: The Power of Integrative Teaching. Nancy G. Nagel. LC 95-35442. (Illus.). 184p. 1996. 55.95 (*0-8039-6359-9*); pap. 24.95 (*0-8039-6360-2*) Corwin Pr.

Learning Through Research. Shirley Cook. Ed. by Catherine Aldy & Jan Keeling. (Illus.). 128p. (Orig.). (J). (gr. 1-6). 1995. pap. text 12.95 (*0-86530-334-7*, IP 334-7) Incentive Pubns.

Learning Through Sewing & Pattern Design. S. Mainwaring. 35p. (J). (gr. k-3). 1976. pap. 8.95 (*1-57379-064-8*, E1006) High-Scope.

Learning Through Simulations: A Guide to the Design & Use of Simulations in Business & Education. John Fripp. LC 92-43603. (Training Ser.). 192p. 1992. pap. 24.95 (*0-07-707588-9*) McGraw.

Learning Through Songs. Herbert Levin & Gail Levin. 80p. 1997. pap. text 16.00 (*1-891278-01-0*) Barcelona Pubs.

Learning Through Supervision & Mentorship to Support the Development of Infants, Toddlers & Their Families: A Sourcebook. Ed. by Emily Fenichel. 175p. (Orig.). 1992. pap. 18.95 (*0-943657-19-9*) ZERO TO THREE.

***Learning Through Symbolism & Celebrations.** Mary A. Love. LC 97-92797. (Illus.). x, 150p. (J). 1998. pap. 18.00 (*1-929548-00-1*) Loves Creat Res.

Learning Through Theatre. Ed. by Anthony Jackson. LC 93-18375. 256p. (C). 1993. pap. 25.99 (*0-415-08610-8*) Routledge.

Learning Through Theatre. Ed. by Anthony Jackson. LC 93-18375. (Illus.). 256p. (C). (gr. 13). 1993. 90.00 (*0-415-08609-4*) Routledge.

Learning Through Work! Designing & Implementing Quality Worksite Learning for High School Students. Richard Kazis et al. 93p. 1994. pap. 24.00 (*1-887410-55-4*) Jobs for Future.

Learning Thru Discussion: Guide for Leaders & Members of Discussion Groups. 2nd rev. ed. William F. Hill. LC 78-87064. 64p. 1969. reprint ed. pap. 30.00 (*0-7837-9902-0*, 206062800006) Bks Demand.

***Learning to Add.** (Tele-Skills Ser.). (SPA & ENG., Illus.). (J). (ps-1). 2000. pap. 8.95 incl. audio (*1-886972-89-3*, Pub. by Emaginit) Penton Overseas.

Learning to Add. National Education Association Staff. 1983. pap. 1.95 (*0-380-82719-0*, Avon Bks) Morrow Avon.

Learning to Argue. Richard Andrews. LC 94-41443. (Education Ser.). (Illus.). 192p. 1995. 95.00 (*0-304-33279-8*); pap. 31.95 (*0-304-33281-X*) Continuum.

***Learning to Argue in Higher Education.** Ed. by Richard Andrews & Sally Mitchell. 237p. 2000. pap. text 27.00 (*0-86709-498-2*, Pub. by Boynton Cook Pubs) Heinemann.

***Learning to Be a Doll Artist.** Martha Armstrong-Hand. LC 99-66913. 138p. 1999. 19.95 (*1-893625-04-4*, MAHD) Scott Pubns MI.

Learning to Be a Family. Ken Smith & Floy Smith. 1985. pap. text 4.95 (*0-934688-16-8*) Great Comm Pubns.

Learning to Be a Family: Leader's Guide. Ken Smith & Floy Smith. (Orig.). 1985. pap. 3.95 (*0-934688-17-6*) Great Comm Pubns.

Learning to Be a More Nurturing Parent: Beginning the Process of Learning to Become a Nurturing Parent. Mary A. Little. (Competent Kids Ser.). 16p. (J). 1995. 19.95 (*1-887514-05-8*) Three Bears.

Learning to Be a Sage: Selections from the "Conversations of Master Chu, Arranged Topically" Tr. by Daniel K. Gardner. 1990. pap. 15.95 (*0-520-06525-5*, Pub. by U CA Pr) Cal Prin Full Svc.

Learning to Be Deaf. Donald A. Evans & William W. Falk. (Contributions to the Sociology of Language Ser.: No. 43). xxi, 252p. 1986. lib. bdg. 90.70 (*0-89925-161-7*) Mouton.

Learning to Be Happy. Jeremiah Burroughs. 1988. pap. 4.99 (*0-946462-16-X*, Pub. by Evangelical Pr) P & R Pubng.

Learning to Be Human. Leston L. Havens. LC 93-43261. 1994. 15.00 (*0-201-62474-5*) Addison-Wesley.

Learning to Be Human in A Push-Button World. Thomas R. Bennett. LC 70-146631. 96p. 1971. write for info. (*0-377-91101-1*) Friendship Pr.

Learning to Be Literate. 2nd ed. Alison E. Garton & Chris Pratt. LC 97-42243. 272p. 1998. pap. 29.95 (*0-631-19317-0*) Blackwell Pubs.

Learning to Be Loyal: Primary Schooling As Nation Building in Alsace & Lorraine, 1850-1940. Stephen L. Harp. LC 97-27645. 1998. 36.00 (*0-87580-234-6*) N Ill U Pr.

Learning to Be Modern: Pound, Eliot & the American University. Gail McDonald. 256p. 1993. text 55.00 (*0-19-811980-1*) OUP.

Learning to Be Partners: An Introductory Training Program for Family Support Staff. Lynn E. Pooley et al. LC 97-37872. 1997. write for info. (*1-885429-16-9*) Family Resource.

Learning to Be Rotuman: Enculturation in the South Pacific. Alan Howard. LC 77-122746. (Anthropology & Education Ser.). 206p. reprint ed. pap. 63.90 (*0-608-13866-5*, 202032300017) Bks Demand.

Learning to Be White: Money, Race & God in America. Thandeka. LC 94-3737. 156p. (C). 1997. 22.95 (*0-8264-1054-5*) Continuum.

Learning to Be You: It's an Inside Job. abr. ed. Brenda Ehrler. 1999. audio 15.95 (*0-9668219-1-2*) Just Be Pubg.

Learning to Be You: It's an Inside Job: Recovery for the Loved Ones of the Substance Addicted. Brenda Ehrler. 126p. 1999. pap. 13.95 (*0-9668219-0-4*) Just Be Pubg.

***Learning to Be You; Day by Day: A Progressive Weekly Guide to Inner Healing.** Brenda Ehrler. 106p. 1999. spiral bd. 8.95 (*0-9668219-3-9*) Just Be Pubg.

***Learning to Be You, It's an Inside Job: Recovery & Healing for the Loved Ones of the Substance-Addicted,** 2nd rev. ed. Brenda Ehrler. LC 98-94072. (Illus.). 160p. 2000. pap. 13.95 (*0-9668219-2-0*) Just Be Pubg.

Learning to Become Rational: The Case of Self-Referential Autoregressive & Non-Stationary Models, Vol. 439. Markus Zenner. (Lecture Notes in Economics & Mathematical Systems Ser.). 201p. 1996. pap. 59.00 (*3-540-61279-3*) Spr-Verlag.

Learning to Behave: A Guide to American Conduct Books Before 1900, 28. Sarah E. Newton. LC 94-2849. 248p. 1994. lib. bdg. 65.00 (*0-313-26752-9*, Greenwood Pr) Greenwood.

Learning to Behave: Curriculum & Whole School Management Approaches to Discipline. Ed. by Neville Jones & Eileen Baglin Jones. (Books for Teachers). 160p. 1992. pap. 25.00 (*0-7494-0821-9*, Kogan Pg Educ) Stylus Pub VA.

Learning to Bow: Inside the Heart of Japan. Bruce S. Feiler. (Illus.). 320p. 1992. pap. 13.00 (*0-395-64726-6*, Pub. by Ticknor & Fields) HM.

Learning to Build & Comprehend Complex Information Structures: Prolog as a Case Study. Ed. by Paul Brna et al. LC 98-43570. (Contemporary Studies in Cognitive Science & Technology: Vol. 3). 430p. 1999. 73.25 (*1-56750-434-5*); pap. 39.50 (*1-56750-435-3*) Ablx Pub.

Learning to Care. Slightly Off Center Writers Group Staff. (Orig.). 1995. pap. 10.95 (*1-56721-096-1*) Twnty-Fifth Cent Pr.

Learning to Care: Effective Goal Setting. write for info. (*0-340-43009-5*, Pub. by E A) Routldge.

Learning to Care: Elementary Kindness in an Age of Indifference. Robert Wuthnow. 304p. 1995. 27.50 (*0-19-509881-1*) OUP.

Learning to Care for Elderly People. write for info. (*0-340-37063-7*, Pub. by E A) Routldge.

Learning to Care in Community Psychiatric Nursing. write for info. (*0-340-39918-X*, Pub. by E A) Routldge.

Learning to Care in Midwifery. write for info. (*0-340-41176-7*, Pub. by E A) Routldge.

Learning to Care in the A & E Department. write for info. (*0-340-39414-5*, Pub. by E A) Routldge.

Learning to Care in the Community. 2nd ed. write for info. (*0-340-55785-0*, Pub. by E A) Routldge.

Learning to Care in the Operating Department. 2nd ed. Kate Nightingale et al. 78p. 1995. pap. 18.95 (*0-340-59492-6*, Pub. by E A) Routldge.

L

Learning to Care in the Operating Department. 2nd ed. Kate Nightingale et al. 112p. 1994. pap. text 18.95 (*1-56593-394-X*, 0816) Singular Publishing.
Learning to Care on the Genito-Urinary Ward. write for info. (*0-340-41308-5*, Pub. by E A) Routldge.
Learning to Care on the Medical Ward. write for info. (*0-340-37062-9*, Pub. by E A) Routldge.
Learning to Care on the Orthopaedic Ward. write for info. (*0-340-37061-0*, Pub. by E A) Routldge.
Learning to Care on the Paediatric Ward. write for info. (*0-340-41175-9*, Pub. by E A) Routldge.
Learning to Care on the Psychiatric Ward. write for info. (*0-340-38498-0*, Pub. by E A) Routldge.
Learning to Change: A Resource for Trainers, Managers & Learners Based on Self Organised Learning. Sheila Harri-Augstein & Ian M. Cameron-Webb. LC 95-791. 1995. 22.95 (*0-07-707896-9*) McGraw.
*__Learning to Change: Lessons from Successful Classroom Change Agents.__ Andy Hargreaves. 2000. 28.95 (*0-7879-5027-0*) Jossey-Bass.
Learning to Change: Opportunities to Improve the Performance of Smaller Manufacturers. National Research Council, Commission on Engineeri. 152p. (C). 1993. pap. text 26.00 (*0-309-04982-2*) Natl Acad Pr.
Learning to Change & Changing to Learn: Managing for the 21st Century. Peter B. Scott-Morgan & Arun Maira. (Illus.). 306p. 1996. 24.95 (*0-07-057720-X*) McGraw.
Learning to Color with Rhymes: A Workbook. Burdys Page. (Illus.). 32p. (Orig.). (J). 1990. pap. 6.95 (*0-86534-146-X*) Sunstone Pr.
Learning to Communicate. Michael Carotta. Ed. by Thomas Zanzig. (Discovering Program Ser.). (Illus.). 46p. 1989. teacher ed. 6.00 (*0-88489-199-2*); pap. 3.00 (*0-88489-198-4*) St Marys.
Learning to Compute 1. Braithwait. 1991. pap. text, student ed. 15.00 (*0-03-047507-4*) Holt R&W.
Learning to Compute 1 & 2: Answer Key. Braithwait. 1991. pap. text 6.00 (*0-03-047512-0*) Holt R&W.
Learning to Compute 2. Braithwait. 1991. pap. text 15.00 (*0-03-047508-2*) Holt R&W.
Learning to Conduct & Rehearse. Daniel L. Kohut & Joe W. Grant. 256p. (C). 1990. text 48.80 (*0-13-526716-1*) P-H.
*__Learning to Control Your Anger: With the Stop, Think & Go Bears.__ Lawrence E. Shapiro. (Illus.). 80p. (J). (gr. k-5). 1999. pap. 19.95 (*1-882732-80-4*, 63802) Childswork.
Learning to Cook with Marion Cunningham. Marion Cunningham & Christopher Hirsheimer. LC 98-31102. (Illus.). 303p. 1999. 29.95 (*0-375-40118-0*) Knopf.
Learning to Cooperate, Cooperating to Learn. R. Slavin et al. LC 84-24832. (Illus.). 486p. (C). 1985. 80.00 (*0-306-41772-3*, Plenum Trade) Perseus Pubng.
*__Learning to Cope: Developing As a Person in Complex Societies.__ Ed. by Erica Frydenberg. (Illus.). 304p. 1999. text 75.00 (*0-19-850318-0*) OUP.
Learning to Cope: Love & Empowerment. Jeanne B. Ewing & Jack London. 300p. (Orig.). 1992. pap. 50.00 (*1-884690-04-1*) Owl Press.
Learning to Count: Student Lesson Folder. Ruth Schoening. 4p. 1987. 1.50 (*0-913191-34-5*) AGEI Pub.
*__Learning to Count 1 2 3 Coloring Book.__ Laveame Phillips. 12p. (J). (ps-1). 1999. pap. 3.00 (*1-930058-02-0*) Lave Phillips.
Learning to Count with Benjamin the Bear: Wipe & Clean Book. Sterling Publishing Staff. (Illus.). 14p. (J). (gr. k-1). 1998. pap. 5.95 (*0-8069-9063-X*) Sterling.
Learning to Curse: Essays in Early Modern Culture. Stephen Greenblatt. 188p. (C). (gr. 13). 1992. pap. 16.95 (*0-415-90352-1*, Pub. by Tavistock) Routldge.
Learning to Dance. Porter. 208p. (J). (gr. 3-7). 15.95 (*0-06-028182-0*) HarpC.
Learning to Dance. T. Porter. 208p. (J). (gr. 3-7). Date not set. mass mkt. 5.95 (*0-06-440751-9*) HarpC.
*__Learning to Dance.__ Tracey Porter. (J). 2001. lib. bdg. 15.89 (*0-06-029239-3*) HarpC Child Bks.
Learning to Dance & Other Stories. Sharon O. Warner. 170p. 1992. pap. 7.95 (*0-89823-132-9*) New Rivers Pr.
Learning to Dance Inside. George Fowler. LC 97-18846. 1997. pap. 10.00 (*0-15-600524-7*, Harcourt Child Bks) Harcourt.
Learning to Deny Self. Book Store Staff. (Truth in Life Adult Study Work Bks.). 52p. 1998. pap., wbk. ed. write for info. (*0-9620615-3-0*) Guardian Truth Found.
Learning to Design, Designing to Learn: Using Technology to Transform the Curriculum. Ed. by Diane P. Balestri et al. 225p. 1992. 75.00 (*0-8448-1706-6*) Taylor & Francis.
Learning to Die. Patricia Henley. LC 78-59940. (Three Rivers Poetry Ser.). 1979. pap. 2.75 (*0-915606-03-8*) Three Rivers Pr.
Learning to Die, Learning to Live. Robert M. Herhold. LC 76-7861. 96p. reprint ed. pap. 30.00 (*0-608-16798-3*, 202692700053) Bks Demand.
Learning to Divide the World: Education at Empire's End. John Willinsky. LC 97-43232. 1998. 22.95 (*0-8166-3076-3*) U of Minn Pr.
Learning to Divide the World: Education at Empire's End. John Willinsky. LC 97-43232. 320p. 1999. pap. 19.95 (*0-8166-3077-1*) U of Minn Pr.
*__Learning to Do What Jesus Did: How to Pray for Physical, Emotional & Spiritual Healing.__ Wholeness Ministries Staff. 1999. 39.99 incl. audio (*1-57472-232-8*) Archer-Ellison.
Learning to Draw. Robert Kaupelis. (Illus.). 144p. 1989. pap. 14.95 (*0-8230-2676-0*) Watsn-Guptill.
Learning to Draw. Parramon's Editorial Team. LC 97-42798. (Learn to Paint Ser.). (Illus.). 64p. 1998. pap. 13.95 (*0-7641-0550-7*) Barron.
*__Learning to Draw: Studies in the Cultural History of a Polite & Useful Art.__ Ann Bermingham. LC 99-59794. (Illus.). 304p. 2000. 75.00 (*0-300-08039-5*) Yale U Pr.
Learning to Dream Again: From Grief to Gratitude. Charles Bugg. 96p. 1993. pap. 8.00 (*1-880837-44-7*) Smyth & Helwys.
*__Learning to Drive.__ William Norwich. 224p. 1998. pap. 12.95 (*0-7472-5584-9*, Pub. by Headline Bk Pub) Trafalgar.
Learning to Earn: School, Work & Vocational Reform in California, 1880-1930. Harvey A. Kantor. LC 87-40363. 256p. reprint ed. pap. 79.40 (*0-608-09911-2*, 206924900003) Bks Demand.
*__Learning to Experience the Etheric World: Empathy, the After-Image & a New Social Ethic.__ Baruch Urieli & Hans Muller Wiedemann. Tr. by Simon Blaxland de Lange. 112p. 2000. pap. 16.95 (*1-902636-00-7*, Pub. by Temple Lodge) Anthroposophic.
Learning to Fall: A Guide for the Spiritually Clumsy. Timothy Merrill. LC 97-50224. 144p. 1998. pap. 12.99 (*0-8272-2126-6*) Chalice Pr.
Learning to Fellowship with God. Larry Kreiger. (Biblical Foundation Ser.: Vol. 7). (Illus.). 48p. 1997. pap. 2.95 (*1-886973-06-7*) Dove Chr Fel.
Learning to Flow with the Spirit of God. Kenneth E. Hagin. 1986. pap. 1.00 (*0-89276-270-5*) Faith Lib Pubns.
Learning to Fly: A Shared Journey. Adrian Plass. (Illus.). 59p. 1996. reprint ed. 25.00 (*1-900507-14-5*, Pub. by Solway) OM Literature.
*__Learning to Fly: Reflections on Fear, Trust & the Joy of Letting Go.__ Sam Keen. 256p. 2000. pap. 14.00 (*0-7679-0177-0*) Broadway BDD.
Learning to Fly: Trapeze-Reflections on Fear, Trust & the Joy of Letting Go. Sam Keen. LC 98-50646. (Illus.). 256p. 1999. 23.00 (*0-7679-0176-2*) Broadway BDD.
Learning to Fly As a Nightingale. Diana Nightingale. 150p. 1997. 25.00 (*0-9655760-0-0*) Keys Pbg FL.
Learning to Fly Gliders: A Flight-Training Handbook & Syllabus. 2nd ed. Robert Wander. 100p. 1993. ring bd. 20.00 (*0-9636227-0-6*) Soaring Bks.
Learning to Fly Helicopters. R. Randall Padfield. 368p. 1992. pap. 24.95 (*0-07-157724-6*) McGraw.
Learning to Fly Helicopters. R. Randall Padfield. 368p. 1992. 29.95 (*0-8306-2113-X*) McGraw-Hill Prof.
Learning to Fly Helicopters. R. Randall Padfield. (Illus.). 354p. 1992. pap. 19.95 (*0-8306-2092-3*) McGraw-Hill Prof.
Learning to Forget. Kenneth E. Hagin. 1985. pap. 1.00 (*0-89276-266-7*) Faith Lib Pubns.
Learning to Forget - A Movie-Docudrama: The Consequences of Undiagnosed Alzheimer's Disease. Ricardo A. Scott. (Ras Cardo Speaks on Life's Conditions & Maladies Ser.: Vol. 41996). (Illus.). 55p. (YA). 1995. pap. 25.95 (*1-883427-81-9*) Crnerstone GA.
Learning to Forgive. Doris Donnelly. (Festival Bks.). 144p. 1986. reprint ed. pap. 8.95 (*0-687-21324-X*) Abingdon.
Learning to Foxtrot. Barbara Unger. 49p. (Orig.). 1989. pap. 14.95 (*0-933466-06-4*) Bellevue Pr.
Learning to Get Dressed: Beginning the Process of Learning to Get Dressed. Mary A. Little. (Competent Kids Ser.). 16p. (J). 1995. 19.95 (*1-887514-00-7*) Three Bears.
*__Learning to Glow: A Nuclear Reader.__ Ed. by John Bradley. LC 99-6961. 330p. 2000. pap. 22.95 (*0-8165-1956-0*) U of Ariz Pr.
Learning to Go to School in Japan: The Transition from Home to Preschool Life. Lois Peak. LC 91-13628. (Illus.). 224p. 1991. pap. 15.95 (*0-520-08387-3*, Pub. by U CA Pr) Cal Prin Full Svc.
Learning to Go to Sleep Alone: Beginning the Process of Learning to Go to Sleep Alone. Mary A. Little. (Competent Kids Ser.). 16p. (J). 1995. 19.95 (*1-887514-01-5*) Three Bears.
Learning to Grieve: Life Skills for Coping with Losses. Geoffrey T. Glassrock & Louise Rowling. 1994. spiral bd. 14.95 (*0-85574-896-6*, Pub. by E J Dwyer) Morehouse Pub.
*__Learning to Grow: A Nuclear Reader.__ Ed. by John Bradley. LC 99-6961. 332p. 2000. lib. bdg. 45.00 (*0-8165-1955-2*) U of Ariz Pr.
Learning to Heal: The Development of American Medical Education. Kenneth M. Ludmerer. 359p. 1996. reprint ed. pap. text 16.95 (*0-8018-5258-7*) Johns Hopkins.
Learning to Heal: The Medical Profession in Colonial Mexico, 1767-1831. Luz M. Hernandez Saenz. LC 96-7585. (Ameican University Studies XXI: No. 17). X, 301p. (C). 1997. text 48.95 (*0-8204-3328-4*) P Lang Pubng.
Learning to Invest: A Beginner's Guide to Building Personal Wealth. 2nd ed. Beatson Wallace. LC 95-37286. (Illus.). 192p. 1995. pap. 11.95 (*1-56440-739-X*) Globe Pequot.
Learning to Keyboard. Dostal. 1992. mass mkt. 35.00 (*0-314-00070-4*) West Pub.
Learning to Keyboard. Dostal. (TA - Typing/Keyboarding Ser.). (C). 1992. mass mkt. 35.00 (*0-314-00072-0*) West Pub.
Learning to Know God: And to Love His Friends. Neva Coyle. 16p. 1993. pap. 8.99 (*1-55661-339-3*) Bethany Hse.
Learning to Labor: How Working Class Kids Get Working Class Jobs. Paul Willis. LC 81-7652. (Morningside Bk.). 226p. 1981. reprint ed. pap. text 20.50 (*0-231-05357-6*) Col U Pr.
Learning to Laugh at Work: The Power of Humor in the Workplace. Robert McGraw. Ed. by Kelly Scanlon & Jane D. Guthrie. LC 95-70451. (Illus.). 70p. 1995. pap. 12.95 (*1-878542-40-0*, 12-0014) SkillPath Pubns.
Learning to Lead. Robert Heller. LC 99-15780. (Essential Managers Handbks.). 72p. 1999. pap. 6.95 (*0-7894-4862-9*) DK Pub Inc.
*__Learning to Lead: A Primer on Economic Development Strategies.__ Maury Forman & James Mooney. 176p. 1999. per. 29.95 (*0-7872-6304-4*) Kendall-Hunt.
Learning to Lead: A Workbook on Becoming a Leader. Warren G. Bennis & Joan Goldsmith. LC 94-2182. 1994. pap. 19.95 (*0-201-56310-X*) Addison-Wesley.
Learning to Lead: A Workbook on Becoming a Leader. 2nd ed. Warren Bennis & Joan Goldsmith. LC 97-17568. 208p. 1997. pap. 15.00 (*0-201-31140-2*) Addison-Wesley.
Learning to Lead: An Action Plan for Success. Elwood N. Chapman & Pat Heim. Ed. by Michael G. Crisp. LC 90-80571. (Fifty-Minute Ser.). (Illus.). 74p. (Orig.). 1990. pap. 10.95 (*1-56052-043-4*) Crisp Pubns.
Learning to Lead: The Art of Transforming Managers into Leaders. Jay A. Conger. LC 92-16934. (Management Ser.). 254p. 1992. text 32.95 (*1-55542-474-0*) Jossey-Bass.
Learning to Lead: The Dynamics of the High School Principalship, 45. Gordon A. Donaldson. LC 90-23094. (Contributions to the Study of Education Ser.: No. 45). 248p. 1991. 65.00 (*0-313-27743-5*, DSH, Greenwood Pr) Greenwood.
Learning to Lead from Your Spiritual Center. Patricia D. Brown. 144p. (Orig.). 1996. pap. 9.95 (*0-687-00612-0*) Abingdon.
Learning to Lead in Higher Education. Paul Ramsden. LC 97-24258. 288p. (C). 1998. pap. 24.99 (*0-415-15200-3*) Routledge.
Learning to Lead in Higher Education. Paul Ramsden. LC 97-24258. 304p. (C). 1998. 75.00 (*0-415-15199-6*) Routledge.
Learning to Learn. Carl Haag et al. Ed. by Donald E. P. Smith. 143p. (Orig.). (C). 1961. pap. text 25.50 (*0-15-550412-6*, Pub. by Harcourt Coll Pubs) Harcourt.
Learning to Learn. Pat Heaton & Gina Mitchell. (C). 1988. 65.00 (*0-904700-49-6*, Pub. by Bath Educ Pubs) St Mut.
Learning to Learn. Kenneth H. Kiewra & Nelson F. Dubois. LC 97-37766. 399p. 1997. pap. text 32.40 (*0-205-26319-4*) P-H.
Learning to Learn. Carolyn Olivier & Rosemary Bowler. LC 96-18548. 288p. 1996. per. 12.00 (*0-684-80990-7*) S&S Trade.
Learning to Learn. Ingrid Pramling. (Recent Research in Psychology Ser.). 144p. 1989. 52.95 (*0-387-97122-X*) Spr-Verlag.
Learning to Learn. Ed. by Sebastian Thrun & Lorien Pratt. LC 97-38183. 368p. 1997. text 126.50 (*0-7923-8047-9*, D Reidel) Kluwer Academic.
Learning to Learn: Making the Transition from Student to Life-Long Learner. Kenneth H. Kiewra & Nelson F. DuBois. (C). 1997. pap. text, teacher ed. write for info. (*0-205-26320-8*, T6320-0) Allyn.
Learning to Learn: Maximizing Your Performance Potential. D. Trinidad Hunt. Ed. by Michelle M. Jerin. 216p. 1992. pap. 10.95 (*1-881904-00-8*) Elan Pr HI.
Learning to Learn: Strengthening Study Skills & Brain Power. Gloria Frender. (Illus.). 240p. (Orig.). (J). (gr. 4-12). 1990. pap. text, teacher ed. 16.95 (*0-86530-141-7*, 190-5) Incentive Pubns.
Learning to Learn: Thinking Skills for the 21st Century. 7th ed. Marcen Heimen & Joshua Slomianko. Orig. Title: Success in College & Beyond. (C). 1998. text 23.00 (*0-9662774-5-7*) Lrning to Learn.
Learning to Learn: Toward a Philosophy of Education. Jerry H. Gill. LC 92-13967. 252p. (C). 1995. pap. 17.50 (*0-391-03889-3*) Humanities.
Learning to Learn Across the Life Span. Robert M. Smith et al. LC 90-40145. (Higher & Adult Education Ser.). 402p. 1990. text 40.95 (*1-55542-279-9*) Jossey-Bass.
Learning to Learn English: A Course in Learner Training. Gail Ellis & Barbara Sinclair. (Illus.). 128p. (C). 1989. pap. text, student ed. 16.95 (*0-521-33816-6*) Cambridge U Pr.
Learning to Learn from Experience. Edward Cell. LC 83-9283. 245p. (C). 1984. text 49.50 (*0-87395-832-2*); pap. text 16.95 (*0-87395-833-0*) State U NY Pr.
Learning to Learn from Text. 2nd ed. Albert Morris. (C). 1993. pap. text. write for info. (*0-201-53933-0*) Addison-Wesley.
Learning to Learn in a Second Language. Pauline Gibbons. LC 92-40291. 128p. (C). 1993. pap. text 18.00 (*0-435-08785-1*, 08785) Heinemann.
*__Learning to Learn Mathematics.__ 3rd ed. 125p. (C). 2000. spiral bd. 21.95 (*0-7872-7223-X*) Kendall-Hunt.
Learning to Leave. rev. ed. Lynette Triere & Richard Peacock. 384p. (Orig.). 1993. mass mkt. 14.99 (*0-446-39483-1*, Pub. by Warner Bks) Little.
Learning to Leave: A Woman's Guide. Lynette Triere & Richard Peacock. 400p. 1988. mass mkt. 12.95 (*0-446-38638-3*, Pub. by Warner Bks) Little.
Learning to Legislate. Richard F. Fenno, Jr. 300p. 1991. 34.95 (*0-87187-628-0*) Congr Quarterly.
Learning to Let Go: When to Say Goodbye to Your Children. Carol Kuykendall. 160p. (Orig.). 1985. pap. 9.99 (*0-310-33621-X*, 12763P) Zondervan.
Learning to Light: Easy & Affordable Techniques for the Photographer. Roger Hicks & Frances Schultz. LC 98-25060. (Illus.). 160p. 1998. pap. 24.95 (*0-8174-4179-4*) Watsn-Guptill.
Learning to Like the Kid in the Mirror see Breakthrough Strategies to Teach & Counsel Troubled Youth Lesson Series
Learning to Listen. Wendy Miller. 1993. 9.95 (*0-687-60633-0*) Abingdon.
Learning to Listen: A Field Guide to Methods of Adult Nonformal Education. Jane K. Vella. 58p. (Orig.). 1980. pap. 4.50 (*0-932288-57-X*) Ctr Intl Ed U of MA.
Learning to Listen: A Guide for Spiritual Friends. Wendy Miller. LC 92-61441. 128p. 1993. pap. 10.00 (*0-8358-0677-4*) Upper Room Bks.
Learning to Listen: A Handbook for Music. Grosvenor Cooper. LC 57-8579. 176p. 1962. pap. text 15.00 (*0-226-11519-4*, P79) U Ch Pr.
Learning to Listen: Positive Approaches & People Who Are Difficult to Serve. Herbert Lovett. 224p. 1996. pap. 29.95 (*1-85302-374-4*) Taylor & Francis.
Learning to Listen: Positive Approaches & People with Difficult Behavior. Herbert Lovett. 224p. 1996. pap. 27.00 (*1-55766-164-2*) P H Brookes.
Learning to Listen - Listening to Learn. Virginia Fulk. LC 98-75489. (Illus.). 80p. (J). (ps-3). 1999. pap. 9.95 (*0-86530-413-0*, IP 413-0) Incentive Pubns.
Learning to Listen in English. Virginia Nelson. 144p. 1991. pap. 39.95 incl. audio (*0-8442-0689-X*, 0689X, Natl Textbk Co) NTC Contemp Pub Co.
Learning to Listen in English: Content-Area Information & Skill-Building Activities on a Variety of Subjects. Virginia Nelson. 1997. pap., teacher ed. 19.95 (*0-8442-0526-5*); pap., student ed., wbk. ed. 14.60 (*0-8442-0525-7*) NTC Contemp Pub Co.
Learning to Listen in English: Content-Area Information & Skill-Building Activities on a Variety of Subjects. Ed. by Virginia Nelson. 1997. pap., student ed. 5.25 (*0-8442-0527-3*) NTC Contemp Pub Co.
Learning to Listen, Learning to Teach: The Power of Dialogue in Educating Adults. Jane Vella. LC 93-43176. 202p. 1997. pap. 18.95 (*0-7879-3963-3*) Jossey-Bass.
Learning to Listen to the Land. Ed. by Bill Willers. LC 91-21890. 280p. 1991. text 30.00 (*1-55963-121-X*) Island Pr.
Learning to Listen to the Land. Ed. by Bill Willers. LC 91-21890. 280p. 1991. pap. 17.95 (*1-55963-120-1*) Island Pr.
Learning to Live. Keith M. Bailey. (Orig.). 1997. mass mkt. 3.99 (*0-87509-709-X*) Chr Pubns.
*__Learning to Live - Living to Learn.__ Carnel Baker. LC 99-97546. xii, 154p. 1999. 10.95 (*1-929943-01-6*) United Pubs.
*__Learning to Live - Living to Learn II.__ Carnel Baker. xiv, 222p. 2000. 13.95 (*1-929943-02-4*) United Pubs.
Learning to Live Again: A Guide for Recovery from Chemical Dependency. rev. ed. Merlene Miller et al. 1992. pap. text 12.50 (*0-8309-0619-3*) Herald Pub Hse.
Learning to Live Again: A Guide for the Recovering Addict. Jill S & Brian S. (Illus.). 168p. 1991. pap. 8.95 (*0-8306-3743-5*, 3743) McGraw-Hill Prof.
Learning to Live Drug Free: A Curriculum Model for Prevention. Kathleen A. McCormick & Charles H. Flatter. (Illus.). 182p. (Orig.). (C). 1994. pap. text 30.00 (*0-7881-0450-0*) DIANE Pub.
Learning to Live in the Country. Kathy Jones. 1978. 45.00 (*0-7045-0253-4*) St Mut.
Learning to Live in the World: Earth Poems. abr. ed. William Stafford. Ed. by Laura Apol. LC 94-9900. 80p. (YA). (gr. 7 up). 1994. 15.95 (*0-15-200208-1*) Harcourt.
Learning to Live, Learning to Love: A Book about You, a Book about Everyone. Joanne Haynes-Klassen. LC 83-80076. (Creative Parenting & Adventures of Squib Ser.). (Illus.). 160p. 1984. pap. 7.95 (*0-915190-38-9*, JP9038-9) Jalmar Pr.
Learning to Live Together at Home & in the World. Jacqueline Haessly. LC 88-31639. 96p. (C). 1988. reprint ed. pap. 6.95 (*0-89390-121-0*) Resource Pubns.
Learning to Live with Depression. E. Brown. 1997. pap. 2.99 (*1-85792-186-0*, Pub. by Christian Focus) Spring Arbor Dist.
Learning to Live with Downsizing: Seven Powerful Lessons for Building a Bridge to Tomorrow. Deborah A. King. LC 96-61798. 164p. (Orig.). 1997. pap. 17.95 (*0-9654932-0-2*) EMI Pubng.
Learning to Live with Evil. Theodore Plantinga. LC 81-22041. 163p. reprint ed. pap. 50.60 (*0-608-14508-4*, 202533900043) Bks Demand.
Learning to Live with the Love of Your Life . . . And Loving It. Neil C. Warren. 1998. pap. 12.99 (*1-56179-651-4*) Tyndale Hse.
Learning to Live Without Violence see Apprender a Vivir Sin Violencia: Manual Para Hombres
Learning to Live Without Violence. rev. ed. Daniel J. Sonkin & Michael Durphy. LC 88-33926. (Family Violence Prevention Ser.). 119p. 1989. pap. 15.95 (*1-884244-16-5*) Volcano Pr.
Learning to Look: A Handbook for the Visual Arts. 2nd ed. Joshua C. Taylor. LC 80-26251. 186p. 1981. pap. 10.00 (*0-226-79154-8*); lib. bdg. 15.00 (*0-226-79152-1*) U Ch Pr.
*__Learning to Look: A Visual Response to Mavis Gallant's Fiction.__ Lesley D. Clement. 304p. 2000. 65.00 (*0-7735-2041-4*, Pub. by McG-Queens Univ Pr) CUP Services.
Learning to Look at Paintings. Mary Acton. LC 97-160203. (Illus.). 272p. (C). 1997. 65.00 (*0-415-14889-8*); pap. 18.99 (*0-415-14890-1*) Routledge.
*__Learning to Love.__ Dana Confair. LC 99-64078. 192p. 1999. pap. 12.95 (*1-56167-519-9*) Am Literary Pr.
*__Learning to Love.__ Gretchen Wolff Pritchard. LC 99-86141. (Journeybook Ser.). 2000. pap. write for info. (*0-89869-322-5*) Church Pub Inc.
Learning to Love. Willard Tate. 1988. pap. 6.99 (*0-89225-321-5*) Gospel Advocate.
Learning to Love. E. Willis. 1982. 5.00 (*0-89858-040-4*) Fill the Gap.
*__Learning to Love__ John Wilson. LC 99-40399. 2000. pap. 19.95 (*0-312-22857-0*) St Martin.
*__Learning to Love.__ John Wilson. LC 99-40399. 2000. text 69.95 (*0-312-22856-2*) St Martin.
Learning to Love. large type unabridged ed. (Harlequin Ser.). 1993. lib. bdg. 18.95 (*0-263-13454-7*) Mac Lib Ref.
Learning to Love: Exploring Solitude & Freedom, 1966-1967. Thomas Merton & Christine M. Bochen. LC 97-19840. (Journals of Thomas Merton: Vol. 6). 416p. 1998. pap. 15.00 (*0-06-065485-6*, Pub. by Harper SF) HarpC.

An Asterisk (*) at the beginning of an entry indicates that the title is appearing for the first time.

Learning to Love Aga. Mel Krantzler. LC 77-6347. 256p. 1987. pap. 13.00 (*0-06-097100-2*, PL 7100, Perennial) HarperTrade.

Learning to Love God. Richard Peace. (Learning to Love Ser.). 96p. (Orig.). 1994. pap. 7.00 (*0-89109-841-0*) NavPress.

Learning to Love My Cancer: How a "Silent Killer" Became a Prescription for Living. Kay Bevan & John V. Bevan. LC 99-93839. 225p. 1999. pap. 12.95 (*0-9671327-0-3*) Charhill Voice.

Learning to Love Others. Richard Peace. (Learning to Love Ser.). 96p. (Orig.). 1994. pap. 7.00 (*0-89109-840-2*) NavPress.

Learning to Love Ourselves. Richard Peace. (Learning to Love Ser.). 96p. (Orig.). 1994. pap. 7.00 (*0-89109-842-9*) NavPress.

Learning to Love People You Don't Like: How to Develop Love & Unity in Every Relationship. Floyd McClung. 120p. 1992. pap. 7.99 (*0-927545-19-5*) YWAM Pub.

Learning to Love Yourself. C. Gaylord Hendricks. 140p. 1982. pap. 10.00 (*0-671-76393-8*, Fireside) S&S Trade Pap.

Learning to Love Yourself: Finding Your Self-Worth. Sharon Wegscheider-Cruse. 125p. (Orig.). 1987. pap. 7.95 (*0-932194-39-7*) Health Comm.

Learning to Love Yourself Workbook. C. Gaylord Hendricks. 204p. 1990. per. 10.00 (*0-671-76392-X*) S&S Trade Pap.

Learning to Make Oboe Reeds. David Shaffer. 1986. 6.00 (*0-933251-07-6*) Mill Creek Pubns.

Learning to Manage: A Good Practice Guide for Tenant Management Organizations. HMSO Staff. (Right to Manage Ser.). 146p. 1994. pap. 60.00 (*0-11-752938-9*, HM29389, Pub. by Statnry Office) Bernan Associates.

***Learning to Manage Conflict: Getting People to Work Together Productively.** Dean R. Tjosvold. 192p. 2000. reprint ed. pap. 26.95 (*0-7391-0133-1*) Lxngtn Bks.

***Learning to Manage Global Environmental Risks.** Social Learning Group Staff. LC 00-38665. (Politics, Science & the Environment Ser.). 2001. pap. write for info. (*0-262-69238-4*) MIT Pr.

Learning to Master Your Chronic Pain. Robert N. Jamison. LC 96-15431. (Illus.). 240p. (Orig.). 1996. pap. 26.95 (*1-56887-019-1*, MCPWBP, Prof Resc Pr) Pro Resource.

Learning to Meditate: A Thirty-Day Introduction to the Practice of Meditation. Thomas Zanzig. 72p. (YA). (gr. 9-12). 1990. pap., student ed. 3.25 (*0-88489-226-3*) St Marys.

Learning to Meditate: A Thirty-Day Introduction to the Practice of Meditation. Thomas Zanzig. (Illus.). 36p. (YA). (gr. 9-12). 1990. teacher ed. 4.50 (*0-88489-227-1*) St Marys.

Learning to Move. Barbara Moraff. 32p. (Orig.). 1982. pap. 5.50 (*0-937013-11-0*) Potes Poets.

Learning to Paint in Oil. Parramon's Editorial Team Staff. LC 97-9415. (Art Guides Ser.). (Illus.). 64p. 1997. pap. text 13.95 (*0-7641-0239-7*) Barron.

Learning to Paint in Pastel. Parramon's Editorial Team Staff. LC 97-9414. (Art Guides Ser.). (Illus.). 64p. 1997. pap. text 13.95 (*0-7641-0241-9*) Barron.

Learning to Paint in Watercolor. Parramon's Editorial Team Staff. LC 97-9413. (Art Guides Ser.). (Illus.). 64p. 1997. pap. text 13.95 (*0-7641-0240-0*) Barron.

***Learning to Parent.** Harriet Smith. 1999. 28.00 (*0-226-76422-2*) U Ch Pr.

Learning to Pedal: Student Lesson Folder. Ruth Schoening. 4p. 1987. 1.50 (*0-913191-35-3*) AGEI Pub.

***Learning to Philosophize.** Kiernan-Lewis. LC 98-53732. (Philosophy Ser.). 1999. pap. 17.95 (*0-534-50589-9*) Wadsworth Pub.

Learning to Plan - & Planning to Learn. 2nd ed. Donald N. Michael. LC HN17.5.M5. 416p. 1997. 44.95 (*0-917917-10-3*); pap. 29.95 (*0-917917-08-1*) Miles River.

Learning to Play by Ear. Lisel Mueller. (W.N.J. Ser.: No. 26). (Illus.). 80p. (Orig.). 1990. pap. 12.00 (*1-55780-138-X*) Juniper Pr ME.

Learning to Play for Young Pianists, Bk. 1. 32p. 1986. pap. 4.95 (*0-7935-5177-3*, 50452750) H Leonard.

Learning to Play for Young Pianists, Bk. 2. 32p. 1986. pap. 5.95 (*0-7935-5267-2*, 50452760) H Leonard.

Learning to Play God. Robert Marion. 1993. mass mkt. 5.99 (*0-449-22192-X*) Fawcett.

Learning to Play Piano, Bk. 2. rev. ed. Denes Agay. (Illus.). 72p. 1992. pap. 8.95 (*0-8256-8070-0*, YK20493, Yorktown Mus) Music Sales.

Learning to Play Piano, Bk. 3. rev. ed. Denes Agay. (Illus.). 72p. 1992. pap. 8.95 (*0-8256-8071-9*, YK20501, Yorktown Mus) Music Sales.

Learning to Play Piano, Bk. 4. rev. ed. Denes Agay. (Illus.). 72p. 1993. pap. 8.95 (*0-8256-8072-7*, YK20519, Yorktown Mus) Music Sales.

Learning to Play Piano Bk. 1: Primer. rev. ed. Denes Agay. (Illus.). 72p. 1991. pap. 8.95 (*0-8256-8069-7*, YK20485, Yorktown Mus) Music Sales.

Learning to Play, Playing to Learn: Games & Activities to Teach Sharing, Caring, & Compromise. Charlie Steffens & Spencer Gorin. LC 97-38131. 256p. 1998. reprint ed. 26.00 (*1-56565-798-5*, 07985W, Pub. by Lowell Hse) NTC Contemp Pub Co.

Learning to Play, Playing to Learn: Games & Activities to Teach Sharing, Caring & Compromise. Charlie Steffens & Spencer Gorin. LC 97-38131. (Illus.). 256p. 1998. reprint ed. pap. 16.00 (*0-7373-0026-4*, 00264W) NTC Contemp Pub Co.

Learning to Pray. Carolyn S. Self & Bill Self. 127p. 1978. pap. 5.95 (*1-57847-055-2*) Genl Conf Svnth-day.

Learning to Print. Pen Notes Staff. (J). (ps up). 1984. spiral bd. 13.00 (*0-939564-01-7*) Pen Notes.

Learning to Program: A Phenomenographic Perspective. Shirley Booth. (Coteborg Studies in Educational Sciences: 89). 308p. (Orig.). 1992. pap. 42.50 (*91-7346-256-X*) Coronet Bks.

Learning to Program: A Problem Solving Approach Israel Urieli & Andy Noori. LC 87-406017. 192p. 1987. write for info. (*0-8403-4256-X*) Kendall-Hunt.

Learning to Program in C. 2nd ed. Thomas Plum. 320p. (Orig.). 1989. pap. text 39.95 (*0-911537-08-2*) Plum Hall.

Learning to Program in Structured COBOL, Part 2. Timothy R. Lister & Edward Yourdon. LC 77-99232. 224p. (C). 1977. pap. 29.00 (*0-685-05484-5*, Yourdon) P-H.

Learning to Program in Structured COBOL, Pt. 1. 2nd ed. Edward Yourdon et al. LC 78-63350. 280p. (C). 1978. pap. 29.00 (*0-685-05485-3*, Yourdon) P-H.

Learning to Program with Visual Basic. Patrick McKeown. LC 98-17343. 512p. 1998. pap. 61.95 (*0-471-19814-5*) Wiley.

***Learning to Protect Your Back: Where Are Your Feet?** Deborah C. Tayloe. Ed. by Lorraine Robinson. (Illus.). 52p. 1999. pap. 19.95 (*0-9672054-9-2*) Creek House Pubns.

Learning to Question. Dantonio. 224p. (C). 2000. pap. 33.27 (*0-205-28036-6*, Macmillan Coll) P-H.

Learning to Quilt the Traditional Way. Annlee Landman. (Illus.). 128p. 1996. pap. 14.95 (*0-8069-0630-8*) Sterling.

Learning to Read: A Cognitive Approach to Reading & Poor Reading. John Beech. 160p. 1985. 22.50 (*1-56593-518-7*, 0008) Singular Publishing.

***Learning to Read: An Integrated View from Research & Practice.** Ed. by Terezinha Nunes. (Neuropsychology & Cognition Ser.). 404p. 1999. pap. 60.00 (*0-7923-5992-5*, Kluwer Acad) Kluwer Academic.

***Learning to Read: An Integrated View from Research & Practice.** Terezinha Nunes. LC 99-41411. (Neuropsychology & Cognition Ser.). 404p. 1999. 215.00 (*0-7923-5513-X*) Kluwer Academic.

Learning to Read: Basic Research & Its Implications. Laurence Rieben & Charles A. Perfetti. 224p. (C). 1991. text 49.95 (*0-8058-0564-8*) L Erlbaum Assocs.

Learning to Read: Psychology in the Classroom. Ed. by Elaine Funnell & Morag Stuart. (Illus.). 208p. 1995. 61.95 (*0-631-19132-1*) Blackwell Pubs.

Learning to Read: The Great Debate. 2nd ed. Jeanne S. Chall. (C). 1995. text 38.50 (*0-15-503080-9*, Pub. by Harcourt Coll Pubs) Harcourt.

Learning to Read: The Quest for Meaning. Malcolm P. Douglass. 176p. 1989. text 26.00 (*0-8077-2970-1*) Tchrs Coll.

Learning to Read: Theory & Research. G. Brian Thompson & Tom Nicholson. LC 97-7445. (Language & Education Library). 1997. write for info. (*1-85359-393-1*, Pub. by Multilingual Matters); pap. write for info. (*1-85359-392-3*, Pub. by Multilingual Matters) Taylor & Francis.

Learning to Read Again. Tom Montag. 1976. 1.00 (*0-916866-01-7*) Cats Pajamas.

Learning to Read & Make Mechanical Drawings. Roy A. Bartholomew & John Orr. (gr. 7-9). 1982. pap. text 7.96 (*0-02-664820-2*); 2.00 (*0-02-664830-X*) Glencoe.

Learning to Read & Make Mechanical Drawings. 6th ed. Bartholomew Orr. 112p. 1988. text 12.72 (*0-02-676350-8*) Glencoe.

Learning to Read & Spell: The Child's Knowledge of Words. Edmund H. Henderson. LC 81-14117. 165p. (C). 1981. 32.00 (*0-87580-078-5*); pap. 16.00 (*0-87580-526-4*) N Ill U Pr.

Learning to Read & Think, Bk. H. Ed. by Jamestown Publishers Staff. 1990. pap., teacher ed. 5.27 (*0-8092-0061-9*, Jamestwn Pub) NTC Contemp Pub Co.

Learning to Read & Write: A Cross-Linguistic Perspective. Ed. by Margaret Harris & Giyoo Hatano. LC 98-36594. (Studies in Cognitive & Perceptual Development: No. 2). (Illus.). 260p. (C). 1999. text 59.95 (*0-521-62184-4*) Cambridge U Pr.

***Learning to Read & Write: Developmentally Appropriate Practices for Young Children.** Susan B. Neuman et al. LC 99-67613. (Illus.). 144p. 1999. pap. text 10.00 (*0-935989-87-0*, NAEYC161) Natl Assn Child Ed.

Learning to Read & Write in One Elementary School. Connie Juel. LC 93-3254. (Illus.). 152p. 1993. 58.95 (*0-387-94038-3*) Spr-Verlag.

Learning to Read & Write Through Classroom Talk. Bridie Rabin-Bisby & Peter Geekie. 96p. 1993. pap. 9.00 (*0-948080-82-5*, Trentham Bks) Stylus Pub VA.

Learning to Read in American Schools: Basic Readers & Content Texts. Ed. by R. C. Anderson et al. LC 83-20701. 320p. (C). 1984. text 59.95 (*0-89859-219-4*) L Erlbaum Assocs.

***Learning to Read in China: Sociolinguistic Perspectives on the Acquisition of Literacy.** John E. Ingulsrud & Kate Allen. LC 99-30316. 192p. 1999. text 79.95 (*0-7734-7961-9*) E Mellen.

Learning to Read in Different Languages. Ed. by Sarah Hudelson. LC 80-36878. (Linguistics & Literacy Ser.: No. 1). 146p. reprint ed. pap. 45.30 (*0-8357-3370-X*, 203961100013) Bks Demand.

Learning to Read in the Computer Age. Anne Meyer & David Rose. (Illus.). 110p. 1999. pap. 9.95 (*1-57129-070-2*) Brookline Bks.

Learning to Read Music. unabridged ed. Incentive Learning Systems. pap. text 14.95 incl. audio (*0-88432-239-4*, S17065) Audio-Forum.

***Learning to Read Music: How to Make Sense of Those Mysterious Symbols.** Peter Nickol. 112p. 2000. pap. 14.95 (*1-85703-390-6*, Pub. by How To Bks) Midpt Trade.

Learning to Read Study Guide. Deakin University Press Staff. 103p. (C). 1986. 45.00 (*0-7300-0390-6*, Pub. by Deakin Univ) St Mut.

Learning to Read the Signs: Reclaiming Pragmatism in Business. F. Byron Nahser. LC 96-39571. 224p. 1997. pap. text 17.95 (*0-7506-9901-9*) Buttrwrth-Heinemann.

Learning to Read Through Music, Games & Reading. Ursula O. Ronnholm. Ed. by Paul F. Ronnholm. Tr. by Miguel Montero. (Illus.). 60p. (Orig.). 1985. pap. text 20.00 (*0-941911-00-4*); audio. write for info. (*0-318-61899-0*) Two Way Bilingual.

Learning to Reason: An Introduction to Logic, Sets & Relations. Nancy Rodgers. 384p. 2000. 74.95 (*0-471-37122-X*) Wiley.

Learning to Resist Temptation: In an Immoral Society. Colin N. Peckham. 1999. pap. text 2.99 (*1-85792-247-6*) Christian Focus.

Learning to Ride. Susan McMaster. (Illus.). 72p. 1994. pap. 12.95 (*1-55082-104-0*, Pub. by Quarry Pr) LPC InBook.

Learning to Ride Horses & Ponies see Complete Guides to Horses & Ponies

Learning to Rock Climb. Michael Loughman. LC 80-28639. (Outdoor Activities Guides Ser.). (Illus.). 192p. 1982. pap. 14.00 (*0-87156-281-2*, Pub. by Sierra) Random.

Learning to Sail. H. A. Calahan. LC 99-50132. 370p. 2000. text 9.95 (*0-486-40728-4*) Dover.

Learning to Sail. B. Fisher. 80p. 1996. 12.98 (*0-7858-0600-8*) Bk Sales Inc.

Learning to Sail. Toghill, Jeff, Sailing School Staff. 1986. pap. 6.95 (*0-393-30298-9*) Norton.

Learning to Sail: The Annapolis Sailing School Guide for Young Sailors. Di Goodman & Ian Brodie. (Illus.). 128p. 1994. pap. 12.95 (*0-07-024014-0*) Intl Marine.

Learning to Say Good-Bye: When a Child's Parent Dies. Eda LeShan. 128p. 1978. pap. 8.00 (*0-380-40105-3*, Avon Bks) Morrow Avon.

Learning to Say No. rev. ed. Roberts Liardon. 64p. (Orig.). 1988. pap. 4.00 (*1-879993-05-8*) Albury Pub.

Learning to Say No: Establishing Healthy Boundaries. Carla Wills-Brandon. 204p. 1990. pap. 8.95 (*1-55874-087-2*) Health Comm.

Learning to Say No: Without Feeling Guilty. Roberts Liardon. 64p. (Orig.). 1996. pap. 5.99 (*1-880089-69-6*, AP-969, Pub. by Albury Pub) Appalach Bk Dist.

Learning to See: Assessment Through Observation. Mary J. Drummond. LC 94-3581. (Illus.). 208p. (C). 1994. pap. text 18.00 (*1-57110-004-0*) Stenhse Pubs.

Learning to See: Historical Perspectives on Modern Popular/Commercial Arts. Alan Gowans. LC 81-80213. 1981. 30.95 (*0-87972-182-0*) Bowling Green Univ Popular Press.

Learning to See: Teaching American Sign Language As a Second Language. 2nd ed. Phyllis P. Wilcox & Sherman E. Wilcox. LC 96-30658. (Illus.). 160p. 1997. 19.95 (*1-56368-059-9*) Gallaudet Univ Pr.

Learning to See Creatively. Bryan F. Peterson. (Illus.). 144p. 1988. pap. 18.95 (*0-8174-4177-8*, Amphoto) Watsn-Guptill.

Learning to See Creatively: How to Compose Great Photographs. Bryan Peterson & DiAMAR Staff. (Illus.). 144p. 1995. pap. 79.95 incl. cd-rom (*1-886393-02-8*, Amphoto) Watsn-Guptill.

Learning to Share My Faith. Chuck Kelley. 96p. 1994. pap. text 1.95 (*0-8054-9864-8*, LifeWay Press) LifeWay Christian.

Learning to Sight Read Jazz, Rock, Latin, & Classical Styles. Bob Montgomery & Willie Hill. (Illus.). 202p. (C). 1994. pap. text 29.95 (*1-880157-16-0*) Ardsley.

Learning to Sign in My Neighborhood. Diane Schmidt & Karen Cameron. 1988. pap. 3.50 (*0-932666-36-1*) T J Pubs.

Learning to Sit in the Silence: A Journal of Caretaking. Elaine M. Starkman. LC 93-28204. 176p. 1993. 14.00 (*0-918949-44-0*); pap. 9.00 (*0-918949-43-2*) Elder Bks.

Learning to Slow down & Pay Attention: A Book for Kids about ADD. 2nd ed. Kathleen G. Nadeau & Ellen B. Dixon. (Illus.). 80p. (J). (gr. 1-5). Date not set. pap. 10.95 (*1-55798-456-5*) Am Psychol.

Learning to SOAR! A Guide for People Who Want to Create Their Own Recovery Programs. Jennifer Wixson. Ed. by Glenn McKee. LC 93-60391. (Illus.). 232p. (Orig.). 1993. pap. 10.95 (*0-9636689-0-0*) White Wave ME.

Learning to Solve Problems by Searching for Macro-Operators. Richard E. Korf. (Research Notes in Artificial Intelligence Ser.). 160p. (C). 1998. pap. text 30.95 (*0-273-08690-1*) Morgan Kaufmann.

***Learning to Speak.** Victor D. Infante. (Pale Ale Poets Ser.). 50p. 1999. pap. 4.95 (*1-929250-11-8*) FarStarFire Pr.

Learning to Speak: The Church's Voice in Public Affairs. Keith Clements. 256p. 1994. pap. 29.95 (*0-567-29266-5*, Pub. by T & T Clark) Bks Intl VA.

Learning to Speak Dog. Harris. 1996. pap. 20.00 (*0-87605-684-2*) Howell Bks.

Learning to Spell. Ed. by Charles A. Perfetti et al. LC 96-51911. 352p. 1997. 79.95 (*0-8058-2160-0*); pap. 45.00 (*0-8058-2161-9*) L Erlbaum Assocs.

Learning to Spell: Administrator's Guide, Bk. 2. Mildred L. Middleton & Eddie Tsang. 64p. 1984. per. 24.90 (*0-8403-3194-0*) Kendall-Hunt.

Learning to Spell: Student Edition, Bk. 2. Mildred L. Middleton. 112p. (YA). (gr. 8 up). 1984. per. 9.90 (*0-8403-3199-1*) Kendall-Hunt.

Learning to Spell: Training Orthographic Problem-Solving with Poor Spellers: A Strategy Instructional Approach. Ivar Braten. 183p. 1991. 18.00 (*82-00-03910-2*) Scandnvan Univ Pr.

Learning to Study. Dostal. 1992. mass mkt. 22.50 (*0-314-01096-3*) West Pub.

Learning to Study, Bk. D. Ed. by Jamestown Publishers Staff. 1994. pap., teacher ed. 5.27 (*0-8092-0063-5*, Jamestwn Pub) NTC Contemp Pub Co.

Learning to Study, Bk. F. Ed. by Jamestown Publishers Staff. 1994. pap. 10.67 (*0-8092-0062-7*, Jamestwn Pub) NTC Contemp Pub Co.

Learning to Study Through Critical Thinking. Jonelle A. Beatrice. LC 94-15557. 304p. (C). 1994. text 15.10 (*0-256-15449-X*, Irwn Prfssnl) McGraw-Hill Prof.

Learning to Study Through Critical Thinking. Jonelle A. Beatrice. 1995. teacher ed. 17.70 (*0-256-15450-3*, Irwn McGrw-H) McGrw-H Hghr Educ.

Learning to Subtract. National Education Association Staff. 1983. pap. 1.95 (*0-380-82735-2*, Avon Bks) Morrow Avon.

Learning to Survive: Black Youth Look for Education & Hope. Atron A. Gentry & Carol C. Peele. LC 93-49637. 192p. 1994. 57.95 (*0-86569-207-6*, Auburn Hse) Greenwood.

Learning to Survive: Black Youth Look for Education & Hope. Atron A. Gentry & Carolyn C. Peele. LC 93-49637. 192p. 1995. pap. 19.95 (*0-86569-261-0*, Auburn Hse) Greenwood.

Learning to Swim. Graham Swift. 1992. write for info. (*0-679-74034-1*) McKay.

***Learning to Swim.** Ann Warren Turner. LC 99-50396. (Illus.). 128p. (YA). (gr. 7 up). 2000. 14.95 (*0-439-15309-3*) Scholastic Inc.

Learning to Swim & Other Stories. Graham Swift. 1992. pap. 10.00 (*0-679-73978-5*) Vin Bks.

Learning to Swim in Swaziland: A Child's Eye-View of a Southern African Country. Nila K. Leigh. LC 92-13223. (Illus.). 48p. (J). (gr. k-3). 1993. 15.95 (*0-590-45938-4*) Scholastic Inc.

Learning to Swim in the Quantum Soup. large type ed. Ted Farrell & Lorrie Mackenzie. (Illus.). 200p. 1998. pap. 12.95 (*0-9667002-0-1*) Loridad.

Learning to Talk. Robin S. Chapman. 69p. (Orig.). 1991. pap. 7.50 (*1-878660-12-8*) Fireweed WL

Learning to Talk. Richard Burns. 79p. 1980. reprint ed. pap. 7.95 (*0-905289-71-4*, Pub. by Enitha Pr) Dufour.

Learning to Talk. Richard Burns. 79p. 1982. reprint ed. 11.95 (*0-905289-76-5*, Pub. by Enitha Pr) Dufour.

***Learning to Talk about Space: The Acquisition of Dutch as a Second Language by Moroccan & Turk.** Saskia Schenning. 1998. pap. 22.00 (*90-361-9988-3*) Tilburg Univ Pr.

Learning to Talk Bear: So Bears Can Listen. Roland Cheek. LC 96-71778. (Illus.). 304p. (Orig.). 1997. pap. 19.95 (*0-918981-02-6*) Skyline Pub.

Learning to Talk, Talking to Learn. Linda Clarke. 1998. pap. text 11.95 (*0-207-19100-X*) HarpC.

Learning to Talk Word Processing. Dianne Galloway. (Modern Office Ser.). (Illus.). 128p. 1984. pap. text 25.95 (*0-13-595919-5*) P-H.

Learning to Teach. Neville S. Bennett & Clive Carre. LC 92-37257. 256p. (C). 1993. pap. 22.99 (*0-415-08310-9*, B0733) Routledge.

Learning to Teach. Ed. by Scholastic, Inc. Staff. 1993. pap. 21.95 (*0-590-49037-0*) Scholastic Inc.

***Learning to Teach.** Serra. LC 99-49272. 223p. 1999. pap. text 28.00 (*0-13-920125-4*) P-H.

Learning to Teach. 3rd ed. Richard I. Arends. LC 93-11851. (C). 1993. text 70.50 (*0-07-002599-1*) McGraw.

Learning to Teach. 4th ed. Richard Arends. LC 97-36997. 576p. 1997. pap. 63.75 (*0-07-006282-X*) McGraw.

Learning to Teach. 5th ed. Richard I. Arends. 2000. 47.00 (*0-07-232164-4*) McGraw.

Learning to Teach: A Critical Approach to the Field Experiences. Christine Shea et al. LC 97-28273. 224p. 1997. pap. write for info. (*0-8058-2446-4*) L Erlbaum Assocs.

Learning to Teach: A Guide for School-Based Initial & In-Service Training. Julian Stern. (Quality in Secondary Schools & Colleges Ser.). 160p. 1995. 21.95 (*1-85346-371-X*, Pub. by David Fulton) Taylor & Francis.

***Learning to Teach: A Handbook for Primary & Secondary School Teachers.** Gill Nicholls. 224p. 1999. pap. 32.50 (*0-7494-2865-1*, Pub. by Kogan Page Ltd) Stylus Pub VA.

***Learning to Teach: Cases & Concepts for Novice Teachers & Educators.** 100p. 2000. teacher ed. write for info. (*0-13-031058-1*) P-H.

Learning to Teach: Training of Trainers for Community Development. Jane K. Vella. LC 89-16200. (Illus.). 76p. (Orig.). 1989. pap. 12.50 (*0-912917-19-9*) UNIFEM.

Learning to Teach: Workshops on Instruction. Learning to Teach Task Force. 86p. 1992. pap. 25.00 (*0-8389-7627-1*) Assn Coll & Res Libs.

Learning to Teach - Not Just for Beginners. rev. ed. Linda Shalaway. LC 98-207467. 304p. 1998. pap. 24.95 (*0-590-25105-8*) Scholastic Inc.

***Learning to Teach Art & Design in the Secondary School.** Nicholas Addison & Lesley Burgess. LC 99-41054. (Learning to Teach Subjects in the Secondary School Ser.). 248p. 2000. pap. write for info. (*0-415-16881-3*) Routledge.

Learning to Teach by Learning to Read: A Primer for Teaching Teachers to Read. 6th ed. Ellis Richardson. (Linguistic Pattern Ser.). (Illus.). 16p. 1997. pap. text. write for info. (*1-56775-078-8*) ISM Teach Systs.

***Learning to Teach Design & Technology in the Secondary School: A Companion to School Experience.** Gwyneth Owen-Jackson. LC 99-87308. (Learning to Teach Subjects in the Secondary School Ser.). 2000. pap. write for info. (*0-415-21693-1*) Routledge.

***Learning to Teach Drama: A Case Narrative Approach.** Joel Norris & Laura McCammon. LC 99-87989. 186p. 2000. pap. text 22.00 (*0-325-00228-2*, Pub. by Boynton Cook Pubs) Heinemann.

L

Learning to Teach English in the Secondary School. Jon Davison & Jane Dowson. LC 97-15889. (Learning to Teach Subjects in the Secondary School Ser.). 352p. (C). 1997. pap. 24.99 (*0-415-15677-7*) Routledge.

Learning to Teach from the Master Teacher (1913) John A. Marquis. 90p. 1998. reprint ed. pap. 9.95 (*0-7661-0509-1*) Kessinger Pub.

Learning to Teach Geography in the Secondary School. David Lambert & David Balderstone. LC 98-56529. 208p. (C). 1999. pap. write for info. (*0-415-15676-9*) Routledge.

Learning to Teach History in the Secondary School. Terry Haydn et al. LC 97-11771. (Learning to Teach Subjects in the Secondary School Ser.). 320p. (C). 1997. pap. 24.99 (*0-415-15453-7*) Routledge.

Learning to Teach in Higher Education. Paul Ramsden. LC 91-20971. 288p. (Orig.). (C). 1991. pap. 24.99 (*0-415-06415-5*, A6590) Routledge.

***Learning to Teach in Secondary School: A Companion to School Experience.** 2nd ed. Susan Anne Capel. LC 98-51546. 482p. 1999. pap. 25.99 (*0-415-19937-9*) Routledge.

Learning to Teach in the Primary Classroom. Anne Proctor et al. LC 94-25720. (Illus.). 208p. (C). 1995. pap. 20.99 (*0-415-11065-3*, B4208) Routledge.

Learning to Teach in Two Cultures: Japan & the United States. Nobuo K. Shimahara & Akira Sakai. LC 94-13184. (Reference Books in International Education: Vol. 27). 280p. 1995. text 52.00 (*0-8153-1081-1*, SS870) Garland.

Learning to Teach in Two Cultures: Japan & the United States. Nobuo K. Shimahara & Akira Sakai. Ed. by Edward R. Beauchamp. LC 94-36321. (Reference Books in International Education: Vol. 27). 280p. 1995. pap. text 23.95 (*0-8153-1924-X*) Garland.

Learning to Teach Mathematics. Maria Goulding. LC 97-202443. 160p. 1997. pap. 25.95 (*1-85346-459-7*, Pub. by David Fulton) Taylor & Francis.

Learning to Teach Mathematics. 2nd ed. Randall J. Souviney. LC 93-16830. (Illus.). 544p. (C). 1993. pap. text 64.60 (*0-02-413841-X*, Macmillan Coll) P-H.

Learning to Teach Mathematics in Secondary School: Companion to School Experience. Sue Johnston-Wilder. LC 98-31035. 1999. pap. write for info. (*0-415-16280-7*) Routledge.

Learning to Teach Modern Foreign Languages in the Secondary School: A Companion for the Student Modern Foreign Languages Teacher. Norbert Pachler & Kit Field. LC 97-18728. (Learning to Teach Subjects in the Secondary School Ser.). 416p. (C). 1997. pap. 25.99 (*0-415-16281-5*) Routledge.

Learning to Teach Number: A Handbook for Students & Teachers in the Primary School. Len Frobisher et al. (Stanley Thornes Teaching Primary Maths Ser.). (Illus.). 304p. 1999. pap. 39.50 (*0-7487-3515-1*, Pub. by S Thornes Pubs) Trans-Atl Phila.

***Learning to Teach Religious Education in the Secondary School: A Companion to School Experience.** Andrew Wright & Ann-Marie Brandom. LC 99-42364. (Learning to Teach Subjects in the Secondary School Ser.). 288p. 2000. pap. write for info. (*0-415-19436-9*) Routledge.

Learning to Teach Russian: Effective Classroom Techniques see Prakticheskaia Metodika Prepodavaniia Russkogo Iazyka Dlia Nachinaiushchikh Prepodavatelei

Learning to Teach Science: A Model for the 21st Century. Ebenezer et al. LC 97-30102. 389p. 1997. 72.00 (*0-02-331334-X*) P-H.

Learning to Teach Science: Activities for Student Teachers & Mentors. Ed. by Martin Monk & Justin Dillon. LC 94-39748. 224p. 1995. 89.95 (*0-7507-0385-7*, Falmer Pr); pap. 29.95 (*0-7507-0386-5*, Falmer Pr) Taylor & Francis.

Learning to Teach Science in Secondary Schools. Tony Turner & Wendy Dimarco. LC 97-29077. (Learning to Teach Subjects in the Secondary School Ser.). 352p. (C). 1998. pap. 25.99 (*0-415-15302-6*) Routledge.

Learning to Teach, Teaching to Learn: Stories of Collaboration in Teacher Education. Ed. by Jean D. Clandinin et al. LC 92-35077. 256p. (C). 1993. text 39.00 (*0-8077-3224-9*); pap. text 19.95 (*0-8077-3223-0*) Tchrs Coll.

Learning to Teach Through Playing: A Brass Method. Herbert C. Mueller. (Illus.). 163p. 1991. pap. 27.50 (*1-56516-005-3*) H Leonard.

Learning to Teach Through Playing a Brass Method. 168p. 1995. spiral bd. 34.00 (*0-7935-7443-9*) H Leonard.

***Learning to Teach Using ICT in Secondary School.** Marilyn Leask & Norbert Pachler. LC 98-48881. (Learning to Teach Subjects in the Secondary School Ser.). 264p. (C). 1999. pap. write for info. (*0-415-19432-6*) Routledge.

Learning to Teach Writing: Does Teacher Education Make a Difference? Mary M. Kennedy. LC 98-10553. 1998. 36.00 (*0-8077-3733-X*) Tchrs Coll.

Learning to Tell Myself the Truth: A 12-Week Guide to Freedom from Anger, Anxiety, Depression. William Backus. LC 93-43432. 224p. 1994. pap. 13.99 (*1-55661-290-7*) Bethany Hse.

***Learning to Tell Time.** (Tele-Skills Ser.). (SPA & ENG., Illus.). (J). (ps-1). 2000. pap. 8.95 incl. audio (*1-886972-85-0*, Pub. by Emaginit) Penton Overseas.

Learning to Think. Eric R. Emmet. LC 85-8157. 172p. 1985. reprint ed. pap. 6.95 (*0-8008-4596-X*) Taplinger.

Learning to Think Environmentally: While There Is Still Time. Lester W. Milbrath. LC 95-34640. (Illus.). 136p. (C). 1996. text 32.50 (*0-7914-2953-9*); pap. text 9.95 (*0-7914-2954-7*) State U NY Pr.

Learning to Think, Thinking to Learn: Proceedings of the 1989 OECD Conference Organized by the Centre for Educational Research & Innovation. Ed. by Stuart Maclure & Peter Davies. (Illus.). 266p. 1991. 87.75 (*0-08-040646-7*, Pergamon Pr); pap. 38.50 (*0-08-040657-2*, Pergamon Pr) Elsevier.

Learning to Trust: Growing Your Faith in God. Bill Jones & Terry Powell. (Daring Disciples Ser.). Date not set. pap. 6.99 (*0-87509-895-9*) Chr Pubns.

***Learning to Trust Again: A Young Woman's Journey to Healing from Sexual Abuse.** Christa Sands. LC 99-41523. 224p. 1999. pap. 12.99 (*1-57293-055-1*) Discovery Hse Pubs.

Learning to Trust God's Faithfulness. Jeanne Caldwell. LC 96-145987. 160p. (Orig.). pap. 7.99 (*0-89274-929-6*, HH-929) Harrison Hse.

Learning to Trust Leader's Guide: Growing Your Faith in God. Bill Jones & Terry Powell. (Daring Disciples Ser.). Date not set. pap. 5.99 (*0-87509-899-1*) Chr Pubns.

Learning to Type with Microsoft Word 97. Shirley Dembo & Cynthia Belis. LC 98-194783. xv, 493p. 1997. 27.00 (*1-56243-551-5*, Z-24) DDC Pub.

Learning to Use Appleworks Version 2. Gary B. Shelly & T. Cashman. (DC - Introduction to Computing Ser.). 1989. mass mkt. 31.95 (*0-538-60864-1*) S-W Pub.

***Learning to Use Computers with Windows 98.** Pamela W. Adams. Ed. by Jenell L. Davis & Sara R. Pressley. (Windows 98 Ser.). (Illus.). 152p. 1999. pap. text 31.83 (*1-58163-088-3*) CPI Train.

***Learning to Use Computers with Windows 95.** Pamela W. Adams. Ed. by Jenell L. Davis & Sara R. Pressley. (Windows 95 Ser.). (Illus.). 147p. 1999. pap. text 31.83 (*1-58163-087-5*) CPI Train.

Learning to Use dBASE IV. Gary B. Shelly et al. 304p. (C). 1990. pap. text. write for info. (*0-538-91215-4*, BF4824) S-W Pub.

Learning to Use dBASE III PLUS. Gary B. Shelly & Thomas J. Cashman. (C). 1989. pap. text. write for info. (*0-318-65189-0*, BF3445) S-W Pub.

Learning to Use Extrasensory Perception. Charles T. Tart. LC 75-43233. 1993. pap. text 3.95 (*0-226-78992-6*) U Ch Pr.

Learning to Use IBM Linkway. Sandra L. Barefield. (Illus.). 165p. (YA). (gr. 9-12). 1993. lib. bdg. 24.95 (*0-9637412-0-9*) Clicker Pub.

Learning to Use Lotus 1-2-3. Gary B. Shelly & Thomas J. Cashman. (C). 1989. pap. text. write for info. (*0-538-91128-X*, BF3585) S-W Pub.

Learning to Use Maps. Roger E. Kranich & Jerry L. Messec. (Illus.). 80p. 1988. text 4.50 (*0-88323-243-X*, 236); 4.50 (*0-88323-150-6*) Pendergrass Pub.

Learning to Use Microcomputer Applications: DOS 6 & Microsoft Windows 3.1 Introductory Concepts & Techniques. Gary B. Shelly et al. (Shelly Cashman Ser.). (C). 1994. mass mkt., teacher ed. write for info. (*0-87709-613-9*) Course Tech.

Learning to Use Microcomputer Applications: WordPerfect 6.0 for DOS. Gary B. Shelly et al. LC 94-26110. (Shelly Cashman Ser.). (C). 1994. pap. 38.95 (*0-87709-584-1*) Course Tech.

Learning to Use Microsoft Excel 5. Gary B. Shelly. 432p. (C). 1994. pap. 38.95 (*0-87709-600-7*) Course Tech.

Learning to Use Microsoft Works IBM. abr. ed. Gloria A. Waggoner. (DC - Introduction to Computing Ser.). 1990. mass mkt. 31.95 (*0-538-60865-X*) S-W Pub.

***Learning to Use My Bible.** 96p. 1999. pap., teacher ed. 19.95 (*0-687-08505-5*) Abingdon.

Learning to Use My Bible: Class Pak. (Illus.). 13.00 (*0-687-08506-3*) Abingdon.

Learning to Use Our Environment: Proceedings of the Institute of Environmental Sciences Technical Meeting, 25th Annual, Seattle, Washington, April 1979. Institute of Environmental Sciences Staff. (Illus.). 625p. 1979. pap. text 75.00 (*0-915414-19-8*) IEST.

***Learning to Use Statistical Tools in Psychology.** 2nd ed. Judith Greene & Manuela D'Oliveira. LC 99-13094. (Open Guides to Psychology Ser.). 240p. 1999. pap. 28.95 (*0-335-20377-9*) Taylor & Francis.

Learning to Use the SPSS Batch System. Elaine C. Nocks & Gilles O. Einstein. (Illus.). 112p. (C). 1986. pap. text 19.00 (*0-13-528019-2*) P-H.

Learning to Use the SPSSx. Gilles O. Einstein & Elaine C. Nocks. (Illus.). 176p. (C). 1987. pap. text 20.20 (*0-13-528050-8*) P-H.

Learning to Use the WWW: Netscape 4. Ernest Ackermann. 1997. text 20.95 (*1-887902-28-7*) Franklin Beedle.

Learning to Use What You Already Know. Stephen A. Stumpf & Joel M. DeLuca. LC 94-16997. (Illus.). 172p. 1994. 19.95 (*1-881052-55-9*) Berrett-Koehler.

Learning to Use Windows Applications: Lotus 1-2-3 Release 4 for Windows. Gary Shelly et al. (Shelly Cashman Ser.). 432p. (C). 1994. pap. 38.95 (*0-87709-443-8*) Course Tech.

Learning to Use Windows Applications: Lotus 1-2-3 Release 4 for Windows. Gary Shelly et al. (Shelly Cashman Ser.). 432p. (C). 1994. mass mkt., teacher ed. write for info. (*0-87709-759-3*) Course Tech.

Learning to Use Windows Applications: Lotus 1-2-3 Release 5 for Windows. Gary B. Shelly et al. (Shelly Cashman Ser.). 448p. (C). 1995. pap. 33.95 (*0-87709-991-X*) Course Tech.

Learning to Use Windows Applications: Lotus 1-2-3 Release 5 for Windows. Gary Shelly et al. (Shelly Cashman Ser.). (C). 1995. mass mkt., teacher ed. 18.50 (*0-87709-992-8*) Course Tech.

Learning to Use Windows Applications: Microsoft Access 2 for Windows. Gary B. Shelly et al. (Shelly Cashman Ser.). (C). 1994. mass mkt., teacher ed. 18.50 (*0-87709-595-7*) Course Tech.

Learning to Use Windows Applications: Microsoft Windows 3.1 Complete Concepts & Techniques. Gary B. Shelly. LC 94-16998. (Shelly Cashman Ser.). 368p. (C). 1994. mass mkt. 38.95 (*0-87709-214-1*) Course Tech.

Learning to Use Windows Applications: Microsoft Windows 3.1 Essentials. Gary B. Shelly et al. LC 93-20655. (Shelly Cashman Ser.). 112p. (C). 1994. mass mkt. 14.65 (*0-87709-408-X*, BF408X) S-W Pub.

Learning to Use Windows Applications: Microsoft Word 6.0 for Windows. Gary B. Shelly et al. LC 94-29288. (Shelly Cashman Ser.). 1994. write for info. (*0-08-770959-7*) Course Tech.

Learning to Use Windows Applications: Microsoft Word 6.0 for Windows. Gary B. Shelly et al. LC 94-29288. (Shelly Cashman Ser.). 352p. (C). 1994. mass mkt. 38.95 (*0-87709-597-3*); mass mkt. 80.95 (*0-87709-765-8*) Course Tech.

Learning to Use Windows Applications: Microsoft Works 3.0 for Windows. Gary B. Shelly et al. LC 94-29401. (Shelly Cashman Ser.). 800p. (C). 1994. pap. text 60.95 (*0-87709-574-4*) Course Tech.

Learning to Use Windows Applications: WordPerfect 5.0 for Windows. Gary B. Shelly & Thomas J. Cashman. LC 93-20656. (Shelly Cashman Ser.). (C). 1994. mass mkt. 33.95 (*0-87709-170-6*, BF1706) S-W Pub.

Learning to Use Windows Applications: Wordperfect 6.1 for Windows. Gary B. Shelly et al. LC 95-35305. (Shelly Cashman Ser.). 368p. 1995. mass mkt. 38.95 (*0-7895-0336-0*) Course Tech.

Learning to Use Windows Applications: WordPerfect 6.1 for Windows. annot. ed. Gary B. Shelly et al. (Shelly Cashman Ser.). 1995. mass mkt., teacher ed. write for info. (*0-7895-0340-9*) Course Tech.

Learning to Use WordPerfect Lotus 1-2-3, & dBASE III Plus. Gary B. Shelly & Thomas J. Cashman. (C). 1989. pap. text. write for info. (*0-538-91124-7*, BF3577) S-W Pub.

Learning to Use Written Language. Iris Tiedt. (J). (gr. 1-3). 1987. pap. 8.99 (*0-8224-4267-1*) Fearon Teacher Aids.

Learning to Walk. Sangharakshita. 192p. (Orig.). 1996. pap. 11.95 (*0-904766-45-4*) Windhorse Pubns.

Learning to Walk: Poems by Joy Kraus. Joy N. Kraus. LC 96-78753. (Illus.). 100p. 1996. pap. 10.00 (*0-9655181-0-8*) Hilltown Pr.

***Learning to Walk by Grace: A Study of Romans 6-11.** Charles R. Swindoll. 121p. 1998. pap., student ed. 5.95 (*1-57972-187-7*) Insight Living.

Learning to Walk with God. Charlie Riggs. 208p. (Orig.). 1990. pap. 7.95 (*0-89066-082-4*) World Wide Pubs.

Learning to Walk with God: A Testimony of Faith & Joy. Dwight Hall. 1997. 29.95 incl. audio (*1-883012-69-4*, RP-3100) Remnant Pubns.

Learning to Warp. Deborah Chandler. (Illus.). 56p. 1995. pap. 7.00 (*1-883010-04-7*) Interweave.

Learning to Weave. rev. ed. Deborah Chandler. LC 94-22905. (Illus.). 232p. 1995. spiral bd. 21.95 (*1-883010-03-9*) Interweave.

Learning to Work. Ed. by Thomas R. Bailey. LC 95-77616. 105p. (C). 1995. pap. 12.95 (*0-8157-0773-8*) Brookings.

Learning to Work: Implications for Career Development & Educational Reform. Kenneth B. Hoyt & Juliette N. Lester. LC 94-46594. (NCDA 1993 Gallup Survey Ser.). 1995. write for info. (*1-885333-01-3*) Nat Career Dev.

Learning to Work: Making the Transition from School to Work. 1997. lib. bdg. 250.99 (*0-8490-7673-0*) Gordon Pr.

Learning to Work: Making the Transition from School to Work. Government Printing Office Staff. 114p. 1995. per. 7.50 (*0-16-048314-X*, Congress) USGPO.

Learning to Work: The Case for Reintegrating Job Training & Education. W. Norton Grubb. 144p. (C). 1996. text 29.95 (*0-87154-367-2*) Russell Sage.

Learning to Work in Groups: A Practical Guide for Members & Trainers. 2nd ed. Matthew B. Miles. LC 98-70680. (Illus.). 360p. (C). 1998. pap. text 32.95 (*0-9658339-8-4*) Educ Intl Pr.

Learning to Work in Groups: A Practical Guide for Members & Trainers. 2nd ed. Matthew B. Miles. LC 80-18150. 357p. 1981. reprint ed. pap. 110.70 (*0-608-02750-2*, 205255800007) Bks Demand.

Learning to Worship with All Your Heart: A Study in the Biblical Foundations of Christian Worship. Robert E. Webber. 104p. 1996. pap. 7.95 (*1-56563-250-8*) Hendrickson MA.

Learning to Write. 2nd ed. Bill Brunskill. 180p. (C). 1991. pap. text 23.22 (*1-56226-059-6*) CAT Pub.

Learning to Write: First Language/Second Language. Aviva Freedman et al. (Applied Linguistics & Language Ser.). 304p. (C). 1983. pap. text 27.95 (*0-582-55371-7*, 74389) Longman.

Learning to Write & Writing to Learn. Ed. by Richard Kretschmer. 192p. (Orig.). 1985. pap. text 7.95 (*0-318-18453-2*) Intl Parents.

Learning to Write Differently: Beginning Writers & Word Processing. Marilyn Cochran-Smith et al. Ed. by Judith Green. (Language & Educational Processes Ser.: Vol. 5). 336p. (C). 1991. pap. 39.50 (*0-89391-762-1*); text 73.25 (*0-89391-761-3*) Ablx Pub.

Learning to Write Fiction from the Masters. Barnaby Conrad. 1996. pap. 14.95 (*0-452-27657-8*, Plume) Dutton Plume.

Learning-to-Write Process in Elementary Classrooms. Suzanne Bratcher. LC 97-8623. 1997. write for info. (*0-8058-2255-0*) L Erlbaum Assocs.

Learning to Write Russian: A Manual of Handwriting. E. N. Sokolova. 44p. 1993. pap. text 4.95 (*0-8285-4924-9*) Firebird NY.

Learning to Write with Benjamin the Bear: Wipe & Clean Book. Sterling Publishing Staff. (Balloon Bks.). (Illus.). 14p. (J). 1998. pap. text 5.95 (*0-8069-3824-2*) Sterling.

Learning to Write/Learning to Learn. John S. Mayher et al. LC 83-15154. 152p. (Orig.). (C). 1983. pap. text 20.00 (*0-86709-073-1*, 0073, Pub. by Boynton Cook Pubs) Heinemann.

Learning Together: A History of Coeducation in American Public Schools. David Tyack & Elisabeth Hansot. LC 92-12983. (Illus.). 384p. 1992. pap. 14.95 (*0-87154-888-7*) Russell Sage.

Learning Together: A Manual for Multiage Grouping. Nancy Bacharach et al. (Illus.). 96p. 1995. pap. 16.95 (*0-8039-6267-3*) Corwin Pr.

Learning Together: A Manual for Multiage Grouping. Nancy Bacharach et al. (Illus.). 96p. 1995. 39.95 (*0-8039-6266-5*) Corwin Pr.

Learning Together: A Source Book on Jewish Family Education. Ed. by Janice P. Alper. LC 87-70964. 477p. 1987. pap. text 22.50 (*0-86705-020-9*) A R E Pub.

Learning Together: A Whole Year in a Primary Classroom. Linda Picciotto. pap. 12.00 (*0-590-74712-6*) Scholastic Inc.

Learning Together: Collaboration for Active Learning in the Elementary Language Arts. Elizabeth A. McAllister. LC 94-12655. (TRIED (Teaching Resources in the ERIC Database) Ser.). (Illus.). 140p. (Orig.). (C). 1995. pap. 16.95 (*1-883790-12-3*, EDINFO Pr) Grayson Bernard Pubs.

Learning Together: Collaborative Activities for Elementary Language Arts Students. Elizabeth A. McAllister. LC 94-12655. (Teaching Resources in the ERIC Database, TRIED Ser.). 1994. 14.95 (*0-927516-42-X*) ERIC-REC.

Learning Together: Educational Ministry Through Small Groups. Pat T. Ellison & David Stark. (People Together the Next Generation of Small Group Ministries Ser.). (Illus.). 64p. 1998. pap. text, wbk. ed. 12.95 (*1-890676-12-8*) Beavers Pond.

Learning Together: One School Reports. Betty M. Young. 107p. 1969. pap. 2.75 (*0-85225-537-3*) Ed Solutions.

Learning Together & Alone. 5th ed. Johnson. LC 98-25026. 260p. 1998. pap. 42.00 (*0-205-28771-9*) Allyn.

Learning Together in the Multicultural Classroom. Elizabeth Coehlo. (Illus.). 108p. 1994. pap. text 16.50 (*0-88751-064-7*, 00771) Heinemann.

Learning Together Through Inquiry: From Columbus to Integrated Curriculum. Kathy G. Short et al. (Illus.). 224p. (C). 1996. pap. text 19.50 (*1-57110-033-4*) Stenhse Pubs.

Learning Together to Work Together for Health: Report on a WHO Study Group. WHO Staff. (Technical Report Ser.: No. 769). 72p. 1998. 9.00 (*92-4-120769-8*) World Health.

Learning Together with Children. 2nd ed. Jeanette Kroese Thomson. 1997. pap. 15.50 (*0-9693410-9-1*) HOH.

Learning Tomorrows: Commentaries on the Future of Education. Ed. by Peter H. Wagschal. LC 78-19763. (Praeger Special Studies). 172p. 1979. 57.95 (*0-275-90433-4*, C0433, Praeger Pubs) Greenwood.

Learning Torah: A Self-Guided Journey Through the Layers of Jewish Learning. Joel Lurie Grishaver. (Illus.). (YA). (gr. 7-9). 1991. pap. text 10.00 (*0-8074-0322-9*, 141000) UAHC.

Learning Translation--Learning the Impossible? A Course of Translation from English into Polish Maria Piotrowska. LC 97-193576. (ENG & POL.). 125p. 1997. write for info. (*83-7052-965-8*, Pub. by Universitas) IBD Ltd.

Learning Tree. 1994. mass mkt. 5.99 (*0-449-45324-3*) Ballantine Pub Grp.

Learning Tree. Gordon Parks, Jr. 1987. mass mkt. 5.99 (*0-449-21504-0*, Crest) Fawcett.

Learning Tree. Gordon Parks, Jr. 1983. 11.09 (*0-606-00946-9*, Pub. by Turtleback) Demco.

Learning Tree: A Unit Plan. Mary B. Collins. 98p. 1992. teacher ed., ring bd. 16.95 (*1-58337-071-4*) Teachers Pet Pubns.

***Learning Tree: Reproducible Teaching Unit.** James Scott. 72p. (Orig.). (YA). (gr. 7-12). 2000. pap. 29.50i (*1-58049-227-4*, TU140) Prestwick Hse.

Learning Tree Series, 5 booklets. (Orig.). 1995. pap. 24.75 (*0-929377-08-7*) Burke-Srour Pubns Inc.

Learning True Love: How I Learned & Practiced Social Change in Vietnam. Frwd. by Maxine H. Kingston. LC 93-31442. 258p. 1993. pap. 16.00 (*0-938077-50-3*) Parallax Pr.

Learning under Stress: Children of Single Parents & the Schools. Margaret B. Hargreaves. LC 90-36579. (Illus.). 130p. 1991. 21.00 (*0-8108-2287-3*) Scarecrow.

Learning, Understanding & Using Spreadsheets. Theodore J. Tepsich. Ed. by Ruby F. Tepsich. LC 90-60729. (Illus.). 225p. (Orig.). (C). 1990. pap. text 24.95 (*0-9618335-5-6*) St George Pub.

Learning University: Towards a New Paradigm? Chris Duke. (Cutting Edge Ser.). 160p. 1992. pap. 34.95 (*0-335-15653-3*) OpUniv Pr.

Learning UNIX. 2nd ed. James Gardner. 646p. 1993. 39.95 (*0-672-30457-0*) Sams.

Learning Unlimited: Practical Strategies & Techniques for Transforming Learning in the Workplace. Alastair Rylatt. 295p. (Orig.). 1999. pap. text 29.95 (*1-875680-11-X*) Woodslane.

Learning Unlimited: Using Homework to Engage Your Child's Natural Style of Intelligence. Dawna Markova & Anne R. Powell. LC 98-16484. 300p. 1998. pap. 13.95 (*1-57324-116-4*) Conari Press.

Learning Unlimited Basic Bass Guitar. Leonard, Hal, Corporation Staff. 40p. 1970. pap. 10.95 incl. audio (*0-7935-1900-4*) H Leonard.

Learning Unlimited Guitar, Level One. Ed. by Will Schmid & Gary Wolk. (Guitar Ser.). (Illus.). 40p. 1970. pap. 4.50 (*0-88188-399-9*, HL00695001) H Leonard.

Learning Unlimited Guitar, Level One. Ed. by Will Schmid & Gary Wolk. (Guitar Ser.). (Illus.). 41p. 1985. audio 10.95 (*0-685-10797-3*, HL 00695000) H Leonard.

Learning VB Script. Paul Lomax. Ed. by Ronald Petrusha. (Illus.). 598p. (Orig.). 1997. pap. 39.95 (*1-56592-247-6*) Thomson Learn.

An Asterisk (*) at the beginning of an entry indicates that the title is appearing for the first time.

Learning Veterinary Terminology. Douglas F. McBride. LC 95-48284. (Illus.). 560p. (C). (gr. 13). 1996. pap. text 30.00 (0-8151-5960-9, 25550) Mosby Inc.
Learning VHDL with WARP2. Cypress Semiconductor Staff. 600p. (C). 1996. 80.00 (0-201-89573-0) Addison-Wesley.
Learning Via Telecommunications. 80p. 1978. 8.95 (0-685-00548-8); pap. 10.95 (0-89240-028-5) Assn Ed Comm Tech.
Learning Victories: Conquering Dyslexic, Attention Deficit & Learning Challenges. Joan M. Smith. (Illus.). 232p. 1998. pap. 19.95 (0-9628758-2-1) Learning Time.
Learning Visio Professional 5.0: Basic Skills. Vince Yokom. (Illus.). 186p. 1998. spiral bd. 28.00 (1-889231-16-9) Instrux Ltd.
***Learning Visio 2000 Professional: Basic Skills.** Vince E. Yokom. 210p. 2000. spiral bd. 28.00 (1-889231-23-1) Instrux Ltd.
***Learning Visio 2000 Standard: Basic Skills.** Vince E. Yokom. (Illus.). 226p. 1999. spiral bd. 28.00 (1-889231-22-3) Instrux Ltd.
Learning Ware for Microsoft Access 7, Instructor's Materials Level 1: QuicKnowledge. (Learning Ware Ser.). (Illus.). 694p. 1997. pap. text 59.95 (0-9653847-9-9, 1QKS045M) Millenum Three.
Learning Ware for Microsoft Access 7 Level 1: QuicKnowledge. (Learning Ware Ser.). (Illus.). 330p. 1997. pap. text 29.95 (0-9653847-8-0, 1QKS045); spiral bd. 29.95 (1-891580-14-0, 1QKS045) Millenum Three.
Learning Ware for Microsoft Excel 7, Instructor's Materials Level 1: QuicKnowledge. (Learning Ware Ser.). (Illus.). 692p. 1997. pap. text 59.95 (0-9653847-5-6, 1QKS043M) Millenum Three.
Learning Ware for Microsoft Powerpoint 7 Level 1: QuicKnowledge. (Learning Ware Ser.). (Illus.). 282p. 1997. pap. text 29.95 (0-9653847-6-4, 1QKS044); spiral bd. 29.95 (1-891580-12-4, 1QKS044) Millenum Three.
Learning Ware for Microsoft Powerpoint 7, Instructor's Materials Level 1: QuicKnowledge. (Learning Ware Ser.). (Illus.). 584p. 1997. pap. text 59.95 (0-9653847-7-2, 1QKS044M) Millenum Three.
Learning Ware for Microsoft Word 7: Quicknowledge, Level One. David J. Glavach. (Learning Ware Ser.). (Illus.). 276p. 1997. pap. 29.95 (0-9653847-2-1, 1QKS042) Millenum Three.
Learning Ware for Microsoft Word 7, Instructor's Materials Level 1: QuicKnowledge. (Learning Ware Ser.). (Illus.). 666p. 1997. pap. text 59.95 (0-9653847-3-X, 1QKS042M) Millenum Three.
Learning Ware for Windows 95: Quicknowledge - Introductory Series - Level 1. David J. Glavach. LC 96-77326. (Illus.). 224p. (Orig.). (C). 1997. pap. 29.95 (0-9653847-0-5); pap., teacher ed. 44.95 (0-9653847-1-3) Millenum Three.
Learning Wheel: Ideas & Activities for Multicultural & Holistic Lesson Planning. rev. ed. Annabelle Nelson. LC 98-27890. (Illus.). 1998. pap. 30.00 (0-9656732-1-9) WHEEL Council.
Learning Windows 98. D D C Publishing Staff. (Learning Ser.). pap. text 29.00 (1-56243-569-8, Z26HC) DDC Pub.
Learning Windows 98. D D C Publishing Staff. LC 99-168123. (Learning Ser.). 1998. pap. text 27.00 (1-56243-487-X, Z26) DDC Pub.
Learning Windows NT Server 4. Allen L. Wyatt. LC 96-69171. (Illus.). 676p. (Orig.). (C). 1996. pap. text 84.00 (1-57576-476-8) Que Educ & Trng.
Learning, Wit, & Wisdom of Shakespeare's Renaissance Women. John W. Crawford. LC 96-51541. (Studies in Renaissance Literature: Vol. 14). 392p. 1997. text 99.95 (0-7734-8737-9) E Mellen.
Learning with Angels. rev. ed. Eugenia Schuler. (Illus.). 24p. 1997. pap. 2.00 (0-934502-03-X) Thursday Pubs.
Learning with Artificial Worlds: Computer Based Modelling in the Curriculum. Ed. by Harvey Mellar et al. LC 94-11536. 218p. 1994. 85.00 (0-7507-0312-1, Falmer Pr); pap. 29.95 (0-7507-0313-X, Falmer Pr) Taylor & Francis.
Learning with Atari LOGO. Daniel Watt. (Illus.). 320p. 1986. pap. text 16.95 (0-07-068579-7, BYTE Bks) McGraw.
Learning with Breadth & Depth. Eleanor Duckworth. 1979. pap. 2.50 (0-918374-09-X) City Coll Wk.
Learning with Computers: Analysing Productive Interactions. Karen Littleton & Paul Light. LC 98-17805. (Illus.). 216p. (C). 1998. 85.00 (0-415-14285-7); pap. 25.99 (0-415-14286-5) Routledge.
Learning with Cuisenaire Rods Booklet. Cuisenaire. 1995. 9.95 (0-201-48270-3) Addison-Wesley.
Learning with Hypercard. Joseph F. Hofmeister. (DF - Computer Applications Ser.). 1991. mass mkt. 25.95 (0-538-61161-8) S-W Pub.
Learning with Labview. Robert Bishop. LC 98-27202. 450p. (C). 1999. pap. 54.00 (0-201-36166-3, Prentice Hall) P-H.
Learning with Leonard & Friends: From A to Z. large type ed. Charles Dunn. Ed. by Sheila Ovange & Scott Groller. LC 98-90168. (Illus.). 64p. (J). (ps-1). 1998. text 17.95 (0-9663240-3-X) C C Dunn.
Learning with Letter Tiles: A Guide to Hands-On Phonics. Joan Westley. 80p. (J). (gr. k-3). 1999. pap. 14.95 (1-893791-01-7) Primry Concpts.
Learning with LinkWay. Abramson. (DF - Computer Applications Ser.). 1994. mass mkt., wbk. ed. 25.95 (0-538-63668-8) S-W Pub.
Learning with Magnetic Card Activities. Esther J. Hasler. (Illus.). 44p. 1989. teacher ed. 4.95 (0-9624519-0-8) Jean-Bert.
Learning with Microcomputers: Readings from Instructional Innovator-5. Intro. by Richard G. Nibeck. 80p. 1983. pap. 10.95 (0-89240-042-0) Assn Ed Comm Tech.
Learning with Molly: In Living with Young Children the Opportunities for Spiritual Reawakening & Discovery Are Without Limit. Karen J. Zurheide. LC 98-128032. (Illus.). 125p. 1997. pap. 8.95 (0-930753-22-4) Spect Ln Pr.
Learning with Movements see Aprendiendo con Movimientos: Metodo TPR Espanol (for Beginners)
Learning with Movements: Total Physical Response English (for Beginners) 3rd ed. Nancy Marquez. 50p. 1996. pap. 9.95 (1-56018-483-3) Sky Oaks Prodns.
Learning with Multiple Representations. Ed. by M. W. Van Someren et al. LC 98-8794. (Advances in Learning & Instruction Ser.). 375p. 1998. write for info. (0-08-043343-X, Pergamon Pr) Elsevier.
Learning with Nested Generalized Exemplars. Steven L. Salzberg. (C). 1990. text 95.50 (0-7923-9110-1) Kluwer Academic.
Learning with Nursery Rhymes. Norris. (Illus.). 112p. (J). (ps-1). 1998. pap., teacher ed. 14.95 (1-55799-666-0, 741) Evan-Moor Edu Pubs.
Learning with Personal Computers. Helga A. Rowe. (C). 1992. 90.00 (0-86431-129-X, Pub. by Aust Council Educ Res) St Mut.
Learning with Puppets: A Guide to Making & Using Puppets in the Classroom. Hans J. Schmidt & Karl J. Schmidt. 85p. 1977. pap. text 6.95 (0-941764-00-1) Puppet Masters.
Learning with Raffi: More Singable Songs : the Famous Raffi Songs, Learning Activities, Patterns, Props & Creative-Play Ideas. Sherril B. Flora. LC 99-178731. 79 p. 1997. write for info. (1-56822-571-7) Instruct Fair.
Learning with Raffi: Singable Songs : the Famous Raffi Songs, Learning Activities, Patterns, Props & Creative-Play Ideas. Sherril B. Flora. LC 99-178724. 80p. 1997. write for info. (1-56822-570-9) Instruct Fair.
Learning with Readers Theatre. Neill Dixon et al. Ed. by Annalee Greenberg. (Building Connections Ser.). (Illus.). 154p. 1996. pap., teacher ed. 19.00 (1-895411-80-7) Peguis Pubs Ltd.
***Learning with Recurrent Neural Networks.** Barbara Hammer. LC 00-34424. (Lecture Notes in Control & Information Sciences). 2000. write for info. (1-85233-343-X) Spr-Verlag.
Learning with Technology: A Constructivist Perspective. Jonassen et al. LC 98-8508. 234p. 1998. pap. text 31.00 (0-13-271891-X) P-H.
Learning with Technology: ASCD Yearbook, 1998. Robert Kosma et al. Ed. by Chris Dede. 226p. 1998. pap. 18.95 (0-87120-298-0, 198000) ASCD.
Learning with Teddy Bears. Elizabeth Graham. 64p. (J). (gr. k-4). pap. 12.50 (1-871098-27-0, Pub. by Claire Pubns) Parkwest Pubns.
Learning with the Community: Concepts & Models for Service-Learning in Teacher Education. Ed. by Joseph A. Erickson et al. (Service Learning in the Disciplines Ser.). 272p. 1998. pap. 28.50 (1-56377-011-3, SL17DS) Am Assn Higher Ed.
***Learning with the Sunday Gospels: Take Home Sheets II: Trinity Sunday to Christ the King.** Leslie J. Francis. 2000. pap. 41.95 (0-264-67498-7) A R Mowbray.
Learning with the Sunday Gospels Pt. 1: Advent to Pentecost. Diane Daryson & Leslie J. Francis. (Illus.). 1998. pap. 27.95 (0-264-67445-6, Pub. by A R Mowbray) Cassell & Continuum.
Learning with Wordsearch. Grace Rohde. 67p. 1998. pap. text 7.95 (1-891559-02-8) R & R.
Learning with Zachar. Lester Laminack. (J). 1995. pap. 10.95 (0-590-73823-2) Scholastic Inc.
Learning Without Boundaries: Technology to Support Distance/Distributed Learning. R. J. Seidel & P. R. Chatelier. LC 95-832. (Defense Research Ser.: Vol. 5). (Illus.). 210p. (C). 1995. 85.00 (0-306-44896-3, Plenum Trade) Perseus Pubng.
Learning Word for Windows/Version 6: Version 6. Michael Singleton. 1996. 31.00 (1-56243-326-1, 1-WDW6HC); pap. 27.00 (1-56243-157-9, 1-WDW6) DDC Pub.
Learning Word-Processing & Typing with Word 97 for Kids. DDC Staff. (Learning Series Texts). (J). 1998. pap. 27.00 (1-56243-623-6) DDC Pub.
***Learning Word Sounds: Kindergarten.** Illus. by Jesus Redondo. (Star Wars). 16p. (J). (ps-2). 1999. pap., wbk. ed. 4.99 (0-375-80005-0, Pub. by Random Bks Yng Read) Random.
Learning Word 2000. DDC Publishing Staff. 1999. 32.00 (1-56243-732-1) DDC Pub.
Learning Word 2000. DDC Publishing Staff. 1999. 31.00 (1-56243-703-8) DDC Pub.
Learning Word 7 for Windows 95. Iris Blanc. 1996. 31.00 (1-56243-317-2, Z-10HC) DDC Pub.
Learning Word 7 for Windows 95. Iris Blanc. 1996. pap. text 27.00 (1-56243-316-4, Z-10) DDC Pub.
Learning WordPerfect 5.0 & 5.1: Through Step-by-Step Exercises & Applications. Iris Blanc. (YA). (gr. 9-12). 1991. teacher ed. 10.00 (1-56243-047-5, W-106); teacher ed. 7.50 incl. disk (1-56243-048-3, SW-25); trans. 250.00 (1-56243-049-1, PW-1) DDC Pub.
Learning WordPerfect 5.0 & 5.1: Through Step-by-Step Exercises & Applications. Iris Blanc. (Fast-Teach Learning Ser.). 1991. spiral bd. 27.00 (1-56243-046-7, W-9) DDC Pub.
Learning WordPerfect 5.0 & 5.1: Through Step-by-Step Exercises & Applications. large type ed. Iris Blanc. 1992. 86.50 (0-614-09875-0, L-18281-00) Am Printing Hse.
Learning WordPerfect 5.1, 2 vols. 2nd ed. Annette Thomason. (C). 1991. write for info. (0-395-56956-7) HM Soft Schl Col Div.
Learning WordPerfect 6 (DOS) Iris Blanc. 1993. pap. 27.00 (1-56243-097-1, P-9) DDC Pub.
Learning WordPerfect 6.0 for Windows. DDC Publishing Staff. (Fast-Teach Learning Ser.). 1993. spiral bd. 27.00 (1-56243-125-0, Z-9) DDC Pub.
Learning WordPerfect 6.0 for Windows. Annette J. Thomason. 600p. (C). 1994. pap. text 32.15 (0-9640751-0-5) Sftware Support.
Learning WordPerfect 6.1 for Windows. Iris Blanc. 1995. pap. 27.00 (1-56243-256-7, H9) DDC Pub.
Learning WordPerfect 6.1 for Windows. Iris Blanc. 1996. 29.00 (1-56243-302-4, H-9HC) DDC Pub.
Learning WordPerfect 6.1 for Windows. Annette J. Thomason. (Illus.). 650p. (C). 1995. write for info. (0-9640751-1-3) Sftware Support.
Learning Wordstar. Annette Thomason. (C). 1991. pap. 32.36 (0-395-46123-5) HM.
Learning Work: A Critical Pedagogy of Work Education. Roger I. Simon et al. LC 90-49196. 216p. 1991. 55.00 (0-89789-237-2, H237, Bergin & Garvey); pap. 21.95 (0-89789-240-2, G240, Bergin & Garvey) Greenwood.
Learning Workplace Writing. Judith R. Rice. LC 93-15880. 336p. 1994. pap. text 52.00 (0-13-337437-8) P-H.
Learning Works 4 for Windows 95. Cynthia Belis. 1996. 27.00 (1-56243-298-2, Z-8) DDC Pub.
Learning Works 3.0 for Windows. Iris Blanc. (Fast-Teach Learning Ser.). 1995. spiral bd. 27.00 (1-56243-180-3, 1-WKW3) DDC Pub.
***Learning XML.** Eric Ray & Chris Maden. Ed. by John Posner. (Illus.). 250p. 2000. 32.95 (0-596-00046-4) OReilly & Assocs.
Learning Your ABCs of Nutrition. Caroline A. Glyman. LC 92-7862. (Cooking Books for Children). (Illus.). 32p. (J). (gr. k-3). 1992. lib. bdg. 14.95 (1-878363-75-1) Forest Hse.
Learning Your Way Through College. Robert N. Leamnson. LC 94-24778. 121p. 1994. 29.95 (0-534-24504-8) Wadsworth Pub.
Learning.Now: Skills for the Information Economy. Stuart Rosenfeld. 250p. 2000. pap. 33.00 (0-87117-325-5) Comm Coll Pr Am Assn Comm Coll.
Learnings from Little Ones: Tales from a Grandfather's Heart. 88p. 1999. mass mkt. write for info. (0-9669875-0-0) Papaco.
***LearningWare for Core1DRAW: Quicknowledge.** 592p. 2000. pap., teacher ed. 59.95 (1-891580-86-8) Millenum Three.
***LearningWare for Core1DRAW: Quicknowledge.** (Illus.). 332p. 2000. spiral bd. 29.95 (1-891580-29-9, 1QKS048) Millenum Three.
***LearningWare for Core1DRAW: Quicknowledge, Level 1.** (Learningware Ser.). (Illus.). 332p. 2000. pap. 29.95 (1-891580-28-0, 1QKS048) Millenum Three.
***LearningWare for Microsoft Excel 7: Quicknowledge, Level 2.** (Learningware Ser.). (Illus.). 566p. 2000. teacher ed. 59.95 (1-891580-87-6, 2QKS012MB); pap. 29.95 (1-891580-08-6, 2QKS012); spiral bd. 29.95 (1-891580-09-4) Millenum Three.
Learning Ware for Microsoft Excel 7 Level 1: QuicKnowledge. (Illus.). 292p. 1997. spiral bd. 29.95 (1-891580-06-X) Millenum Three.
Learning Ware for Microsoft Excel 7 Level 1: QuicKnowledge. David J. Glavach. (Illus.). 292p. 1997. pap. text 29.95 (0-9653847-4-8, 1QKS043) Millenum Three.
***LearningWare for Microsoft, Project 4: Quicknowledge, Level 1.** (Learning Ware Ser.). (Illus.). 524p. 2000. teacher ed. 59.95 (1-891580-89-2); pap. 29.95 (1-891580-16-7, 1QKS049); spiral bd. 29.95 (1-891580-17-5) Millenum Three.
***LearningWare for Microsoft Word 7: Quicknowledge, Level 2.** (Learningware Ser.). (Illus.). 358p. 2000. pap. 29.95 (1-891580-02-7); spiral bd. 29.95 (1-891580-03-5, 2QKS011) Millenum Three.
***Learningware for Microsoft Word 7 Level 1: Quicknowledge.** (Learningware Ser.). (Illus.). 276p. 2000. 29.95 (1-891580-00-0, 1QKS043) Millenum Three.
***LearningWare for PageMaker Level 2: Quicknowledge.** (Learningware Ser.). 458p. 2000. pap., teacher ed. 59.95 (1-891580-87-6, 2QKS047MB) Millenum Three.
***LearningWare for PageMaker 6: Quicknowledge, Level 1.** (Learningware Ser.). (Illus.). 248p. 2000. 29.95 (1-891580-20-5, 1QKS046); pap., teacher ed. 59.95 (1-891580-88-4, 1QKS046MB); spiral bd. 29.95 (1-891580-21-3, 1QKS46) Millenum Three.
***LearningWare for PageMaker 6: Quicknowledge, Level 2.** (Learningware Ser.). 246p. 2000. spiral bd. 29.95 (1-891580-25-6) Millenum Three.
***LearningWare for PageMaker 6: Quicknowledge, Level 2.** (Learningware Ser.). (Illus.). 246p. 2000. pap. 29.95 (1-891580-24-8, 2QKS047) Millenum Three.
Learn2 Guide: Burp a Baby, Carve a Turkey & 108 Other Things. Ed. by Jason Roberts. LC 98-24550. 448p. 1999. pap. 17.95 (0-375-75255-2) Villard Books.
***LearnWare for Microsoft Word 7: Quicknowledge, Level 2.** (Learningware Ser.). (Illus.). 774p. 2000. pap. text, teacher ed. 59.95 (1-891580-93-0, 2QKS011MB) Millenum Three.
***Lear's Daughters: The Studies of the Moscow Art Theatre 1905-1927.** Rebecca B. Gauss. LC 98-33449. (American University Studies XXVI: Vol. 29). (Illus.). 147p. (C). 1999. text 38.95 (0-8204-4155-4) P Lang Pubng.
Leartyeayanabsrautaseutram = Leartyeayana-bsrauta-seutra, 3 Vol. Leartyeayana et al. LC 98-915308. (Kaleameulabseastra-granthamealea Ser.). xxxiii, 1266 p. 1998. write for info. (81-208-1565-3, Pub. by Motilal Bnarsidass) S Asia.
Leary: A Portrait of an Alcoholic. Howard B. LC 95-35824. 144p. (Orig.). 1996. pap. 10.95 (1-56474-152-4) Fithian Pr.
Leary-Evans, Ohio's Free People of Color. Robert E. Greene. LC 79-66917. (Illus.). 88p. (Orig.). 1997. reprint ed. pap. text 5.95 (0-9603320-0-6) R E Greene.
***Lea's Book of Rules for the World.** Lea Delaria & Maggie Cassella. 304p. 2000. pap. 12.95 (0-440-50854-1, Dell Trade Pbks) Dell.
Lea's Chemistry of Cement & Concrete. 4th ed. Ed. by Peter C. Hewlett. (Illus.). 1053p. 1998. text 175.00 (0-470-24416-X) Halsted Pr.
Lea's Chemistry of Cement & Concrete. 4th ed. F. M. Lea & P. C. Hewlett. LC 98-126331. xxi, 1053 p. 1998. write for info. (0-340-56589-6) Arnld Pub.
Lease Agreement Kit, Do It Yourself. Timothy J. Smith. 1991. 9.95 (0-9625456-9-4) SJT Enterprises.
Lease & Finance Evaluation: Applications for Successful Financing Alternatives. Alastair Day. 105p. 1996. pap. 225.00 (1-85564-535-1, Pub. by Euromoney) Am Educ Systs.
Lease Audits: The Essential Guide. Theodore H. Hellmuth. xvii, 350p. 1994. 89.95 (0-934055-03-3, 308450); pap. 59.95 (0-934055-04-1, 308450) Statelaw Guides.
Lease Cars: How to Get One. 3rd ed. Darrell Parrish. (Illus.). 250p. 1997. reprint ed. pap. 9.95 (1-890308-00-5) Bk Express.
Lease Escalators & Other Pass-Through Clauses, 1991. rev. ed. 35p. 1991. pap. 18.95 (0-944298-60-5) Inst Real Estate.
Lease Financing. Ed. by Law & Business Inc. Staff & Legal Times Seminars Staff. LC 82-9507. (Seminar Course Handbks.). 1983. pap. 30.00 (0-686-89371-9, C01074) Harcourt.
Lease or Buy? Principles for Sound Corporate Decision Making. Harvard Business Review Staff. 188p. 1994. 35.00 (0-07-103603-2) McGraw.
Lease or Buy? Principles for Sound Decision Making. James S. Schallheim. LC 94-10236. (Financial Management Association Survey & Synthesis Ser.). 1994. 35.00 (0-87584-558-4) Harvard Busn.
Lease or Purchase: Theory & Practice. Arthur C. Herst. 1984. lib. bdg. 140.50 (0-89838-126-6) Kluwer Academic.
Lease-Purchase America! Acquiring Real Estate in the '90s & Beyond. John Ross. LC 92-81393. 192p. 1993. pap. 12.95 (0-914984-45-4) Starburst.
Lease-Purchase Decision. William L. Ferrara et al. 126p. 1980. pap. 20.00 (0-86641-011-2, 80117) Inst Mgmt Account.
Lease Securitization: Securitizing Lease Receivables in the 1990s. Sudhir Amembal. Ed. by Shawn D. Halladay. LC 93-71547. (Illus.). 200p. (Orig.). pap. 45.00 (0-945988-07-9) Amembal & Halladay.
Lease Your Car for Less: A Consumer's Guide to Vehicle Leasing. 4th ed. Richard L. Kaye. 76p. (Orig.). 1994. pap. 7.95 (0-9623644-5-2) TeleTravel Network.
Leaseholders & Service Charge in Former Local Authority Flats. H. M. S. O. Staff. 102p. 1995. pap. 55.00 (0-11-753087-5, HM30875, Pub. by Statnry Office) Bernan Associates.
Leases & Lease Purchase Agreements, Some Basic Considerations. Sidney D. Hemsley. No. 2. 1985. write for info. (0-318-60755-7) Tenn Muni League.
Leases & Rental Agreements. Marcia Stewart. LC 96-44888. (Quick & Legal Ser.). 160p. 1997. pap. 18.95 (0-87337-355-3) Nolo com.
Leases & Rental Agreements. 2nd ed. Marcia Stewart & Ralph E. Warner. LC 97-34979. 1998. pap. 18.95 (0-87337-452-5) Nolo com.
Leases, Policies & Applications for Not-for-Profit Incubators. 177p. 1990. pap. 42.00 (1-887183-13-2) NBIA.
Leasewriter. Marcia Stewart et al. LC 98-16691. 1998. 129.95 (0-87337-413-4) Nolo com.
Leash Law. Ruth Hayes. (Illus.). 104p. (Orig.). 1989. pap. 4.95 (0-941104-44-3) Real Comet.
Leash on Love: A Book for All Ages. Greta B. Lipson. LC 93-176359. (Illus.). 32p. (J). 1992. 9.95 (0-9630637-0-7) Barclay Bks.
Leashold Reform - The New Law: A Guide to the Housing & Urban Development Act 1993. James Driscoll. 300p. 1993. 96.00 (0-85459-820-0, Pub. by Tolley Pubng) St Mut.
***Leasing.** Glenlake Publishing Company Staff. (The Glenlake Risk Management Ser.). 154p. 2000. 45.00 (1-888998-89-X, 98-89-X) Glenlake Pub.
***Leasing.** Alastair Graham. (Risk Management Ser.). 2000. 45.00 (0-8144-0607-6) AMACOM.
Leasing. D. Wainman. (Waterlow Publications). 250p. 1991. pap. 49.90 (0-08-040865-6) Macmillan.
***Leasing: Corporate Finance.** 1999. pap. 120.00 (0-85297-462-0, Pub. by Chartered Bank) St Mut.
Leasing Agent. Jack Rudman. (Career Examination Ser.: C-1992). 1994. pap. 29.95 (0-8373-1992-7) Nat Learn.
***Leasing & Marketing for Property Managers.** Doug Rossi. Ed. by Christine Ambrose. (Illus.). 420p. 1999. teacher ed., ring bd. 100.00 (1-928594-12-3); student ed., ring bd. 100.00 (1-928594-11-5) BOMI Inst.
Leasing Applications Handbook for the HP-12C. Sudhir P. Amembal et al. (Illus.). 300p. 1991. student ed. 49.95 (0-945988-02-8) Amembal & Halladay.
Leasing Applications Handbook for the HP-17B. Sudhir P. Amembal et al. (Illus.). 335p. 1991. text, student ed. 49.95 (0-945988-01-X) Amembal & Halladay.
Leasing Finance. 3rd ed. Ed. by C. Boobyer. 1997. pap. 200.00 (1-85564-553-X, Pub. by Euromoney) Am Educ Systs.
Leasing Handbook: Everything Purchasing Managers Need to Know - Complete with Facts, Figures, Forms & Checklists. Kalman I. Perlman. 350p. 1991. text 45.00 (1-55738-242-5, Irwn Prfssnl) McGraw-Hill Prof.

Leasing in Emerging Markets, 1977-1995. Laurence Carter. LC 96-28074. (IFC Lessons of Experience Ser.: No. 3). 76p. 1996. pap. 22.00 (*0-8213-3675-4*, 13675) World Bank.

Leasing Law in the European Union (EU) 2nd ed. Howard Rosen. 250p. 1994. pap. 170.00 (*1-85564-208-5*, Pub. by Euromoney) Am Educ Systs.

Leasing Lessons for Smart Shoppers. Mark Eskeldson. LC 97-90048. 144p. (Orig.). 1997. pap. 8.95 (*0-9640560-4-6*) Technews.

***Leasing Market in Poland: A Strategic Entry Report, 1996.** Compiled by Icon Group International Staff. (Illus.). 182p. 1999. ring bd. 1820.00 incl. audio compact disk (*0-7418-1294-0*) Icon Grp.

Leasing of Consumer Goods see Installment Credit Series

Leasing of Federal Lands for Fossil Fuels Production. Stephen L. McDonald. LC 78-23437. 184p. 1979. 21.95 (*0-8018-2194-0*) Resources Future.

Leasing Office & Commercial Space. rev. ed. (Journal Reprint Ser.). pap. 9.95 (*0-944298-05-2*, 867) Inst Real Estate.

Leasing Office Space You Can Afford: Everything Companies Need to Know - from Finding Great Space & Negotiating the Lease to Moving In. Robert J. Cook. 350p. 1992. per. 29.95 (*1-55738-457-6*, 457, Irwn Prfssnl) McGraw-Hill Prof.

Leasing Retail Space. Intro. by A. Alexander Bul. LC 89-83354. (Illus.). 300p. (C). 1990. text 62.95 (*0-944298-41-9*) Inst Real Estate.

Leasing Services in Russia: A Strategic Entry Report, 1997. Compiled by Icon Group International Staff. (Illus.). 149p. 1999. ring bd. 1490.00 incl. audio compact disk (*0-7418-1045-X*) Icon Grp.

Leasing Small Shopping Centers. International Council of Shopping Centers. LC 97-132291. (Illus.). 1997. write for info. (*0-927547-72-4*) Intl Coun Shop.

Leasing Smart. Craig A. Melby & Jane Utzman. LC 96-36097. 100p. (Orig.). 1997. pap. text 14.95 (*0-945456-43-3*) PT Pubns.

Leasing Sourcebook, 1989: A Directory of the U. S. Capital Equipment Leasing Industry. 271p. 1989. pap. 125.00 (*0-936857-02-1*) Bibliotec Systems & Pub.

Leasing Sourcebook, 1987-1988: A Directory of the U. S. Capital Equipment Leasing Industry. 200p. 1987. pap. 110.00 (*0-936857-01-3*) Bibliotec Systems & Pub.

Leasing Sourcebook, 1986: A Directory of the U. S. Capital Equipment Leasing Industry. 136p. (Orig.). 1986. pap. 95.00 (*0-936857-00-5*) Bibliotec Systems & Pub.

Leasing Sourcebook, 1994: The Directory of the U. S. Capital Equipment Leasing Industry, No. 1045-2508. Contrib. by Barbara B. Low. 352p. 1994. pap. 135.00 (*0-936857-05-6*) Bibliotec Systems & Pub.

Leasing Sourcebook, 1997-1998: The Directory of the U. S. Capital Equipment Leasing Industry. Ed. by Barbara B. Low. 360p. (Orig.). 1997. pap. 135.00 (*0-936857-07-2*) Bibliotec Systems & Pub.

Leasing Sourcebook, 1990-1991: A Directory of the U. S. Capital Equipment Leasing Industry. 316p. 1990. pap. 125.00 (*0-936857-03-X*) Bibliotec Systems & Pub.

Leasing Sourcebook, 1992-1993: The Directory of the U. S. Capital Equipment Leasing Industry. Intro. by Barbara B. Low. 340p. 1992. pap. text 135.00 (*0-936857-04-8*) Bibliotec Systems & Pub.

***Leasing Space for Your Small Business.** Fred Steingold & Janet Portman. LC 99-86801. 2000. 34.95 (*0-87337-572-6*) Nolo com.

Leasing the Ivory Tower: The Corporate Takeover of Academia. Lawrence C. Soley. LC 94-39872. 204p. 1995. 30.00 (*0-89608-504-X*) South End Pr.

Leasing the Ivory Tower: The Corporate Takeover of Academia. Lawrence C. Soley. LC 94-39872. 204p. 1995. pap. 13.00 (*0-89608-503-1*) South End Pr.

Leasing Training Self-Study Workbook. Amembal, Deane & Associates Staff. 1995. 295.00 (*1-85564-379-0*, Pub. by Euromoney) Am Educ Systs.

Least-Cost Electric Utility Planning. Harry G. Stoll. LC 88-21980. 800p. 1989. 185.00 (*0-471-63614-2*) Wiley.

Least-Cost Insurance Against Climate Risks: The Cost of Carbon Reductions in Western Europe. Florentin Krause et al. (Energy Policy in the Greenhouse Ser.: Vol. 2). 125p. (Orig.). 1993. pap. 50.00 (*1-883774-02-0*) IPSEP.

Least Cost Utility Planning Handbook, Vol. 1. 61p. 1988. 9.00 (*0-317-05946-7*) NARUC.

Least-Cost Utility Planning Handbook, Vol. II. 83p. 1988. 10.00 (*0-318-50048-5*) NARUC.

Least Dangerous Branch: The Supreme Court at the Bar of Politics. 2nd ed. Alexander M. Bickel. LC 85-52084. 328p. (C). 1986. pap. 20.00 (*0-300-03299-4*, Y-585) Yale U Pr.

Least Detrimental Alternative: A Systematic Guide to Case Planning & Decision Making for Children in Care. Paul D. Steinhauer. 523p. 1991. text 70.00 (*0-8020-2786-5*); pap. text 24.95 (*0-8020-6836-7*) U of Toronto Pr.

Least Developed Countries. 225p. 55.00 (*92-1-112370-4*, E.95.II.D.2); 55.00 (*92-1-112396-8*) UN.

Least Developed Countries. 250p. 1989. 60.00 (*92-1-112289-9*, 90.II.D.4) UN.

Least Developed Countries: A Statistical Profile. LC 97-113023. 60p. pap. 17.00 (*92-1-112387-9*) UN.

Least Developed Countries, 1997 Report. United Nations Conference on Trade & Development Staff. 192p. 1997. pap. 55.00 (*92-1-112410-7*) UN.

Least Developed Countries 1998 Report. United Nations Conference on Trade & Development Staff. 210p. 1998. 40.00 (*92-1-112434-4*) UN.

Least Developed Countries Report, 1992. 1993. pap. text 55.00 (*92-1-112327-5*) UN.

Least Developed Countries Report, 1990. 469p. 1991. 62.00 (*92-1-112225-2*, E.91.II.D.3) UN.

Least Developed Countries Report, 1988. 321p. 60.00 (*92-1-112268-6*) UN.

Least Imperfect Path: A Global Journal for the Future. John D. Ivanko. LC 96-70198. 224p. 1996. pap. 11.99 (*0-9654449-1-0*) Paradigm Pr MI.

***Least Likely Bride.** Jane Feather. LC 99-53477. 320p. 2000. 15.95 (*0-553-80157-0*) Bantam.

***Least Likely Bride.** large type ed. Jane Feather. LC 00-26762. 2000. 26.95 (*1-56895-877-3*) Wheeler Pub.

Least Loved Beasts of the Really Wild West: A Tribute. Ed. by Terril L. Shorb & Yvette A. Schnoeker-Shorb. LC 96-269432. (Illus.). 160p. (Orig.). 1997. pap. 8.95 (*0-9653849-0-X*) Native West Pr.

Least of All. Carol Purdy. LC 86-12613. (Illus.). 32p. (J). (gr. 1-4). 1987. lib. bdg. 12.95 (*0-689-50404-7*) McElderry Bks.

Least of These. Hannah Shively. (Illus.). 32p. 1997. pap. 9.95 (*0-9660304-0-0*) Illus Word.

Least of These: A Christian Social Action Bible Study. R. Adam DeBaugh. 20p. 1994. pap. 2.00 (*1-888493-10-0*) Chi Rho Pr.

Least of These: Religion, Race, & Law in America. Andrew Cook. LC 96-48799. 264p. (C). 1997. pap. 20.99 (*0-415-91647-X*) Routledge.

Least of These: Religion, Race, & Law in America. Anthony Cook. LC 96-48799. 264p. (C). 1997. 75.00 (*0-415-91646-1*) Routledge.

Least of These: Stories of Schoolchildren. Mary Van Cleave. 248p. 1994. pap. 27.95 (*0-8039-6201-0*) Corwin Pr.

Least of These: Stories of Schoolchildren. Mary Van Cleave. LC 94-31984. 248p. 1994. 61.95 (*0-8039-6200-2*) Corwin Pr.

Least of These My Brethren. Daniel J. Baxter. LC 98-4555. 272p. (C). 1998. pap. 13.00 (*0-15-600588-3*) Harcourt.

Least One. Borden Deal. LC 92-13437. (Library of Alabama Classics). 368p. (YA). 1992. pap. 15.95 (*0-8173-0673-0*) U of Ala Pr.

Least One. Maureen H. Read & Patricia M. St. John. LC 88-31445. (Illus.). 192p. (Orig.). 1989. pap. 7.99 (*0-8361-3491-5*) Herald Pr.

Least Restrictive Alternative: Principles & Practices. D. Biklin et al. Ed. by H. Rutherford Turnbull, III. 80p. (Orig.). 1981. pap. 6.00 (*0-940898-06-3*) Am Assn Mental.

Least Restrictive Environment: Its Origins & Interpretations in Special Education. Jean B. Crockett & James M. Kauffman. LC 99-12804. (A Volume in the Special Education & Disability Series). 248p. 1999. 49.95 (*0-8058-3101-0*); pap. 22.50 (*0-8058-3102-9*) L Erlbaum Assocs.

Least Restrictive Environment: The Paradox of Inclusion. Lawrence M. Siegel. 265p. (Orig.). 1994. pap. 27.50 (*0-934753-79-2*) LRP Pubns.

Least Shadow. R. Peter Burnham. (Juniper Bks.: Vol. 63). 84p. (Orig.). 1996. pap. 12.00 (*1-55780-149-5*) Juniper Pr ME.

Least Squares Computations Using Orthogonalization Methods. James W. Longley. LC 84-14939. (Lecture Notes in Pure & Applied Mathematics Ser.). xi, 308p. 1984. write for info. (*0-8247-7232-6*) Dekker.

Least Squares Computations Using Orthogonalization Methods. James W. Longley. LC 84-14939. (Lecture Notes in Pure & Applied Mathematics Ser.: No. 93). 328p. reprint ed. pap. 101.70 (*0-8357-2529-4*, 205240800014) Bks Demand.

Least-Squares Finite Element Method: Theory & Applications in Comutational Fluid Dynamics & Electromagnetics. Bo N. Jiang. Ed. by J. J. Chattot et al. LC 97-51980. (Scientific Computation Ser.). (Illus.). xvi, 422p. 1998. 94.00 (*3-540-63934-9*) Spr-Verlag.

Least-Squares Finite Element Method - Theory & Applications in Computational Fluid Dynamics. B. N. Jiang. 600p. 1997. text 97.00 (*981-02-2228-9*) World Scientific Pub.

Least Squares in Engineering. Edwin F. Coddington & Oscar J. Marshall. LC QA0275.C64. 67p. reprint ed. pap. 30.00 (*0-608-10059-5*, 201416800096) Bks Demand.

Least-Squares Means in the Fixed-Effects General Linear Models. (Technical Report Ser.: No. R-103). 9p. 1997. pap. 3.00 (*1-55544-969-7*, BR5982) SAS Publ.

Least Squares Tutorial. (American Crystallographic Association Lecture Notes Ser.: No. 1). 1974. pap. 15.00 (*0-686-47221-7*) Polycrystal Bk Serv.

Least Toxic Home Pest Control. 2nd rev. ed. Dan Stein. LC 94-4709. (Illus.). 112p. (C). 1994. pap. text 8.95 (*0-913990-07-8*) Book Pub Co.

Least Toxic Home Pest Control: Dan's Practical Guide. Dan Stein. LC 91-12305. (Illus.). 98p. (Orig.). 1991. pap. 8.95 (*0-938493-15-9*) Hulogosi Inc.

Least Worst Death: Essays in Bioethics on the End of Life. Margaret P. Battin. (Illus.). 320p. (C). 1994. pap. text 26.95 (*0-19-508265-6*) OUP.

Least You Need to Know: Stories. Lee Martin. LC 95-35647. 192p. 1996. 21.95 (*0-9641151-2-3*); pap. 13.95 (*0-9641151-3-1*) Sarabande Bks.

Least You Need to Know about Windows 3.1. Steve Eckols. LC 93-28014. (Illus.). 337p. 1993. pap. 20.00 (*0-911625-74-7*) M Murach & Assoc.

Least You Should Know: Form A. 7th ed. Glazier. (C). 1999. pap. text 37.50 (*0-15-508031-8*) Harcourt Coll Pubs.

Least You Should Know about English. 5th ed. Teresa Ferster Glazier. (C). 1996. pap. text 35.50 (*0-15-501631-8*) Harcourt Coll Pubs.

Least You Should Know about English. 7th ed. Teresa Ferster Glazier. (C). 1999. pap. 44.50 (*0-15-507447-4*) Harcourt Coll Pubs.

Least You Should Know about English, Form C. 4th ed. Teresa F. Glazier. 320p. (C). 1989. pap. text 40.50 (*0-03-028664-6*, Pub. by Harcourt Coll Pubs) Harcourt.

Least You Should Know about English, Form C. 4th ed. Teresa F. Glazier. 320p. (C). 1990. pap. text 15.00 (*0-685-59223-5*); 16.00 (*0-685-59224-3*); disk. write for info. (*0-318-69143-4*) Harcourt Coll Pubs.

Least You Should Know about English: Writing Skills. 6th ed. Teresa F. Glazier. LC 97-70645. 272p. (C). 1997. pap. text 35.50 (*0-03-017497-X*, Pub. by Harcourt Coll Pubs) Harcourt.

Least You Should Know About English Writing Skills: Form B. 5th ed. Teresa F. Glazier. LC 93-77652. 300p. (C). 1994. pap. text 35.50 (*0-03-079097-2*) Harcourt Coll Pubs.

Least You Should Know about Vocabulary Building: Word roots. 4th ed. Teresa F. Glazier. 160p. (C). 1993. pap. text 21.50 (*0-15-500220-1*, Pub. by Harcourt Coll Pubs) Harcourt.

Leather. Ed. by ICC Information Group Staff. 1987. 695.00 (*1-85036-933-X*, Pub. by ICC Info Group Ltd) St Mut.

Leather: Preparation & Tanning by Traditional Methods. Lotta Rahme & Dag Hartman. Ed. by Jack C. Thompson. Tr. by David Greenebaum from SWE. LC 95-71505. (Illus.). 100p. (C). 1996. text 24.95 (*1-887719-00-8*) Caber Pr.

Leather Ad - M. Larry Townsend. 1996. reprint ed. mass mkt. 5.95 (*1-56333-380-5*, Badboy) Masquerade.

Leather Ad - S. Larry Townsend. 1996. reprint ed. mass mkt. 5.95 (*1-56333-407-0*, Badboy) Masquerade.

Leather & Fur in Hong Kong: A Strategic Entry Report, 1997. Compiled by Icon Group International Staff. (Illus.). 124p. 1999. ring bd. 1240.00 incl. audio compact disk (*0-7418-0861-7*) Icon Grp.

Leather & Lace No. 2: The Trembling Heart. Dorothy Dixon. (Orig.). 1982. mass mkt. 2.50 (*0-686-97467-0*, Zebra Kensgtn) Kensgtn Pub Corp.

Leather & Lace No. 6: Honeysuckle Love. Carolyn T. Armstrong. 1983. mass mkt. 2.50 (*0-686-82614-0*, Zebra Kensgtn) Kensgtn Pub Corp.

Leather & Latex Care: How to Keep Your Leather & Latex Looking Great. Kelly J. Thibault. LC 95-80430. 63p. (Orig.). 1996. pap. 10.95 (*1-881943-00-3*) Daedalus Pub.

Leather & Soul: A Civil War Odyssey. Waldron M. McLellon. LC 93-74230. 513p. (Orig.). 1994. pap. 16.95 (*1-884489-00-1*) Butternut.

Leather Apparel Design. Francesca Sterlacci. LC 96-17224. (Fashion Merchandising Ser.). (Illus.). 256p. (C). 1997. pap. 49.95 (*0-8273-7772-X*) Delmar.

Leather Apparel Design. Francesca Sterlacci. (Fashion Merchandising Ser.). 1997. teacher ed. 13.95 (*0-8273-7773-8*) Delmar.

Leather Blues. Jack Fritscher. 91p. 1984. pap. 9.95 (*1-890834-27-0*, 2003) Palm Drive.

Leather Braiding. Bruce Grant. LC 60-7746. (Illus.). 191p. 1950. pap. 7.95 (*0-87033-039-X*) Cornell Maritime.

Leather Christian Planner 1999: Pocket Edition. J. Countryman. 1998. lthr. 9.99 (*0-8499-5395-2*) Word Pub.

Leather Contest Guide: A Handbook for Promoters, Contestants, Judges & Titleholders. Guy Baldwin. LC 93-70456. 144p. (Orig.). 1993. pap. 12.95 (*1-881943-08-9*) Daedalus Pub.

Leather Craft & Patterns. D. M. Campana. (Illus.). 1997. 4.50 (*0-939608-49-9*) Campana Art.

Leather Daddy & the Femme. Carol Queen. LC 98-6197. 180p. 1998. pap. 14.00 (*1-57344-037-X*) Cleis Pr.

Leather Duke. large type ed. Frank Gruber. 304p. 1996. 27.99 (*0-7089-3485-4*) Ulverscroft.

Leather Goods Manufacture: Methods & Processes. G. C. Moseley. 340p. 1986. reprint ed. pap. text 25.00 (*0-87556-389-9*) Saifer.

Leather Jacket. Don L. Taylor. (Illus.). 325p. 1989. 19.00 (*0-9639286-1-9*) Prairieville Pr.

Leather Machzor: Yom Kippur. Ash. 49.99 (*0-89906-687-9*, MAYL-A); 49.99 (*0-89906-690-9*, MSYL-A) Mesorah Pubns.

Leather Makin' A Manual of Primitive & Modern Leather Skills. Larry J. Wells. LC 85-80211. (Illus.). 126p. 1985. 14.98 (*0-88290-304-7*) Horizon Utah.

Leather Tooling & Carving. Chris H. Groneman. LC 74-75258. (Illus.). 111p. 1974. reprint ed. pap. 7.95 (*0-486-23061-9*) Dover.

Leather Trisagion from Egypt: (P. Mich 799) David Martinez. (Illus.). 100p. (C). text 25.95 (*3-519-07669-1*) B G Teubner.

Leatherbreeches: Hero of Chancellorsville. Carl A. Keyser. Ed. by Dorothy M. Keyser. (Illus.). 214p. (Orig.). 1989. pap. 10.00 (*0-9626058-1-6*) Amherst NH.

Leatherbreeches' Legacy. Carl A. Keyser. Ed. by Dorothy M. Keyser. (Illus.). 203p. (Orig.). 1990. pap. 10.00 (*0-9626058-0-8*) Amherst NH.

Leathercraft for Pathfinders: A Basic Youth Enrichment Skill Honor Packet. Lou S. Gattis, III. (Illus.). 20p. (Orig.). (YA). (gr. 5 up). 1987. pap., teacher ed. 5.00 (*0-936241-09-8*) Cheetah Pub.

Leathercraft for Pathfinders: An Advanced Youth Enrichment Skill Honor Packet. Lou S. Gattis, III. (Illus.). 20p. (Orig.). (YA). (gr. 5 up). 1987. pap., teacher ed. 5.00 (*0-936241-10-1*) Cheetah Pub.

Leathercrafting: Procedures & Projects. Raymond Cherry. LC 79-83885. (Illus.). 1979. pap. 15.18 (*0-02-672700-5*) Glencoe.

Leatherfolk: Radical Sex, People, Politics, & Practice. Ed. by Mark Thompson. (Illus.). 328p. 1992. reprint ed. pap. 12.95 (*1-55583-187-7*) Alyson Pubns.

***Leatherman's Handbook: Silver Jubilee Edition.** Larry Townsend. 284p. 2000. pap. 15.95 (*1-881684-19-9*) L T Pubns CA.

Leatherman's Handbook: Silver Jubilee Edition. rev. ed. Larry Townsend. LC 98-219688. 1997. pap. 12.95 (*1-56333-559-X*, R Kasak Bks) Masquerade.

Leathermans Handbook II. 1997. pap. 7.99 (*0-503-09999-6*) Carlyle Communications Ltd.

Leathermen Speak Out: An Anthology on Leathersex, Vol. 1. Ed. by Jack Ricardo. 192p. (Orig.). 1991. pap. 14.95 (*0-943595-33-9*) Leyland Pubns.

Leathermen Speak Out: An Anthology on Leathersex, Vol. 2. Ed. by Jack Ricardo. 192p. (Orig.). 1993. pap. 14.95 (*0-943595-40-1*) Leyland Pubns.

Leatherneck Boys: A PFC at the Battle for Guadalcanal. Arthur C. Farrington. (Illus.). 183p. 1994. pap. text 15.95 (*0-89745-180-5*) Sunflower U Pr.

Leatherneck Laffs. Marine Corps Association Staff. 96p. 1980. reprint ed. 1.50 (*0-686-32444-7*) Marine Corps.

Leathersex. Max Exander. (Orig.). 1994. mass mkt. 4.95 (*1-56333-210-8*, Badboy) Masquerade.

Leathersex: A Guide for the Curious Outsider & the Serious Player. Joseph W. Bean. LC 94-71570. 236p. 1994. pap. 14.95 (*1-881943-05-4*) Daedalus Pub.

Leathersex Q & A: Questions about Leathersex & the Leather Lifestyles Answered. Joseph W. Bean. LC 96-85421. 230p. (Orig.). 1996. pap. 16.95 (*1-881943-01-1*) Daedalus Pub.

Leatherstocking, 5 vols., Set. Cooper. 1993. pap. 21.00 (*0-19-521063-8*) OUP.

Leatherstocking Saga. James Fenimore Cooper. (J). (gr. 5-6). 44.95 (*0-8488-0059-1*) Amereon Ltd.

Leatherstocking Tales: The Pathfinder; The Deerslayer. James Fenimore Cooper. Ed. by Blake Navius. LC 84-25060. (Library of America Ser.: Vol. 2). 1051p. 1985. 35.00 (*0-940450-21-6*, C12048, Pub. by Library of America) Penguin Putnam.

Leatherstocking Tales Vol. 1: The Pioneers; The Last of the Mohicans; The Prairie. James Fenimore Cooper. Ed. by Blake Nevius. LC 84-25060. (Library of America Ser.). 1347p. 1985. 40.00 (*0-940450-20-8*, C10461, Pub. by Library of America) Penguin Putnam.

Leatherwoman III: The Clash of the Cultures. Ed. by Laura Antoniov. 1998. mass mkt. 6.95 (*1-56333-619-7*, Rosebud) Masquerade.

Leatherwomen. Ed. by Laura Antoniou. (Orig.). 1998. mass mkt. 6.95 (*1-56333-598-0*, Rosebud) Masquerade.

Leatherwood God. William Dean Howells & Eugene Pattison. LC 74-189640. (Selected Edition of W. D. Howells Ser.). 288p. 1976. 31.95 (*0-253-33285-0*) Ind U Pr.

Leatherwood God. William Dean Howells. LC 76-120773. (Illus.). reprint ed. 28.50 (*0-404-03368-7*) AMS Pr.

Leatherwood God. William Dean Howells. (Notable American Authors Ser.). 1992. reprint ed. lib. bdg. 75.00 (*0-7812-3262-7*) Rprt Serv.

Leatherwood God. William Dean Howells. 1993. reprint ed. lib. bdg. 89.00 (*0-7812-5379-9*) Rprt Serv.

Leatherwood God. William Dean Howells. LC 78-131754. (Illus.). 1970. reprint ed. 14.00 (*0-403-00641-4*) Scholarly.

Leatherwork. Boy Scouts of America. (Illus.). 56p. (YA). (gr. 6-12). 1983. pap. 2.90 (*0-8395-3310-1*, 33310) BSA.

Leatherwork: A Manual of Techniques. Geoffrey West. (Illus.). 160p. 1998. 29.95 (*1-86126-108-X*) Crolwood.

Leatherworker in Eighteenth-Century Williamsburg. Colonial Williamsburg Foundation Staff. (Historic Trades Ser.). (Illus.). 36p. (Orig.). 1967. pap. 2.95 (*0-910412-18-9*) Colonial Williamsburg.

Leatherworking Handbook: A Practical Illustrated Sourcebook of Techniques & Projects. Valerie Michael. (Illus.). 128p. 1995. pap. 19.95 (*0-304-34511-3*, Pub. by Cassell) Sterling.

Leave a Light on for Me: A Novel. 2nd ed. Jean Swallow. LC 99-25340. 304p. 1999. reprint ed. pap. 10.00 (*1-55583-513-9*, Pub. by Alyson Pubns) Consort Bk Sales.

Leave a Message for Willie. Marcia Muller. 214p. 1990. mass mkt. 6.50 (*0-445-40900-2*, Pub. by Warner Bks) Little.

Leave Before You Go Emily Perkins. LC 99-19031. 1999. write for info. (*0-88001-690-6*, Ecco Press) HarperTrade.

***Leave Before You Go.** Emily Perkins. LC 99-19031. 304p. 2000. 23.00 (*0-06-019661-0*, Ecco Press) HarperTrade.

Leave Dreams Be. Nathan Pollack. 55p. 1988. pap. 7.00 (*0-912549-13-0*) Bread & Butter.

Leave Her Alone. Megan McKenna. LC 99-31689. 240p. 1999. pap. 14.00 (*1-57075-269-9*) Orbis Bks.

Leave Her to Heaven. Ben A. Williams. 436p. Date not set. 28.95 (*0-8488-2506-3*) Amereon Ltd.

Leave Her to Heaven. Ben A. Williams. 429p. 1981. reprint ed. lib. bdg. 27.95 (*0-89966-257-9*) Buccaneer Bks.

Leave Herbert Alone. Alma M. Whitney. LC 72-1526. (Illus.). 32p. (J). (ps-3). 1972. reprint ed. 12.95 (*0-201-08623-9*) HarpC Child Bks.

Leave It in the Hands of a Specialist. Jesse Duplantis. (Mini-Bks.). 16p. 1993. pap. 1.00 (*0-89274-646-7*, HH-646) Harrison Hse.

***Leave It Like You Found It.** Bobby Goldsboro. (J). 1998. pap. 6.99 (*1-58083-206-7*) Animazing Ent.

***Leave It Like You Found It.** Bobby Goldsboro. (Illus.). (J). (ps-3). 1998. pap. 3.50 (*1-58083-202-4*) Animazing Ent.

***Leave It to Beany!** Lenora Mattingly Weber. (Beany Malone Ser.). 266p. (J). 1999. reprint ed. pap. 12.95 (*0-9639607-5-X*) Image Cascade.

Leave It to Beaver. Beverly Cleary. 18.95 (*0-88411-248-9*) Amereon Ltd.

Leave It to Beaver. Beverly Cleary. 1993. reprint ed. lib. bdg. 15.95 (*1-56849-194-8*) Buccaneer Bks.

Leave It to Chance: Monster Madness. James Robinson. 104p. Date not set. pap. text 12.95 (*1-56389-536-6*) DC Comics.

Leave It to Chance: Shaman's Rain. Robinson. 104p. pap. 9.95 (*1-56389-586-2*, Pub. by DC Comics) Time Warner.

Leave It to Chance No. II: Trick or Treat & Other Stories. James Robinson. 104p. pap. 12.95 (*1-56389-559-5*) DC Comics.

An Asterisk (*) at the beginning of an entry indicates that the title is appearing for the first time.

Leave It to Chance No. II: Trick or Treat & Other Stories. James Robinson. (Illus.). 104p. 1998. pap. 12.95 (*1-58240-041-5*) Image Comics.

Leave It to God. Christian D. Larson. 1940. pap. 4.50 (*0-87516-191-X*) DeVorss.

Leave It to Me. Bharati Mukherjee. 1998. pap. 12.95 (*0-449-00396-5*) Fawcett.

Leave It to Me. Bharati Mukherjee. LC 97-5833. 1997. 23.00 (*0-679-43427-5*) Knopf.

Leave It to Me. Katherine S. Rorimer. LC 97-91250. 1998. 16.95 (*0-533-12606-1*) Vantage.

Leave It to Psmith. P. G. Wodehouse. 21.95 (*0-89190-297-X*) Amereon Ltd.

Leave It to Psmith. P. G. Wodehouse. 1975. pap. 10.00 (*0-394-72026-1*) Vin Bks.

Leave It to Psmith. P. G. Wodehouse. 1994. reprint ed. lib. bdg. 32.95 (*1-56849-361-4*) Buccaneer Bks.

Leave It to the Hangman. large type ed. Bill Knox. 1990. 27.99 (*0-7089-2322-4*) Ulverscroft.

Leave It to the Molesons! Burny Bos. Tr. by J. Alison James. LC 95-12311. (Illus.). 48p. (J). (gr. 2-4). 1995. lib. bdg. 13.88 (*1-55858-432-3*, Pub. by North-South Bks NYC) Chronicle Bks.

Leave It to the Molesons! Burny Bos. LC 95-12311. (Illus.). 48p. (J). (gr. 1-4). 1998. pap. 5.95 (*1-55858-993-7*, Pub. by North-South Bks NYC) Chronicle Bks.

Leave Love Alone. Lindsay Armstrong. (Presents Ser.). 1992. per. 2.89 (*0-373-11487-7*, 1-11487-5) Harlequin Bks.

Leave Me My Spirit: An American's Story of Fourteen Years in Castro's Prisons. Frwd. by Lawrence K. Lunt. (Illus.). 288p. 1990. 19.95 (*0-918080-58-4*) Affil Writers America.

Leave No Trace: Minimum Impact Outdoor Recreation. Will Harmon. LC 97-15974. (Illus.). 128p. 1997. pap. 6.95 (*1-56044-581-5*) Falcon Pub Inc.

Leave None to Tell the Story: Genocide in Rwanda. Human Rights Watch Africa. LC 99-61313. 807p. 1999. pap. 35.00 (*1-56432-171-1*) Hum Rts Watch.

Leave Only Footprints. A. C. Snow. LC 94-68872. 212p. 1994. 19.95 (*0-935400-19-2*) News & Observer.

Leave, Retard, Leave! Towana J. Brown. (Illus.). 127p. (Orig.). (YA). (gr. 8-12). 1988. pap. 3.50 (*0-9622060-0-8*) T J Brown.

Leave That Cricket Be, Alan Lee. Barbara A. Porte. LC 92-29401. (Illus.). 32p. (J). (gr. k up). 1993. 14.00 (*0-688-11793-7*, Grenwillow Bks) HarpC Child Bks.

***Leave the Crowd Behind.** Les Bowling. 2000. pap. 9.99 (*1-930027-00-1*) Insght Pub.

Leave the Grave Green. Deborah Crombie. 304p. 1996. mass mkt. 5.99 (*0-425-15308-8*) Berkley Pub.

***Leave the Grave Green.** large type ed. Deborah Crombie. LC 00-22864. 2000. pap. 22.95 (*1-56895-846-3*) Wheeler Pub.

***Leave the Mud & Learning to Soar: Workbook for Women Who Want to Get Unstuck in Their Relationships.** Elaine Martens Hamilton. 2000. pap. 15.99 (*1-57293-062-4*) Discovery Hse Pubs.

Leave the Temple: Indian Paths to Human Liberation. Felix Wilfred. LC 92-20801. (Faith Meets Faith Ser.). 208p. reprint ed. pap. 64.50 (*0-608-20254-1*, 207151300012) Bks Demand.

Leave Train: New & Selected Poems. Phoebe Hesketh. 157p. 1995. pap. 17.95 (*1-870612-54-X*, Pub. by Enitha Pr) Dufour.

Leave Your Life Alone. Hubert Van Zeller. LC 72-78934. 128p. 1972. 12.95 (*0-87243-043-X*) Templegate.

Leave Your Nets. Goldsmit. 1978. pap. 7.95 (*0-8065-0627-X*, Citadel Pr) Carol Pub Group.

Leave Your Nets. Joel S. Goldsmith & Lorraine Sinkler. LC 97-52176. 1998. pap. 11.95 (*1-889051-29-2*, I Lvl) Acrpls Bks CO.

Leave Your Nets. Joel S. Goldsmith. LC 97-52176. 150p. 1998. reprint ed. 17.95 (*1-889051-26-8*) Acrpls Bks CO.

Leave Yourself Alone. Eugenia Price. 128p. 1982. pap. 6.70 (*0-310-31431-3*, 16240P) Zondervan.

Leavell & Thorup's Fundamentals of Clinical Hematology. 5th ed. Oscar A. Thorup, Jr. (Illus.). 1040p. 1987. text 135.00 (*0-7216-5679-X*, W B Saunders Co) Harcrt Hlth Sci Grp.

Leaven: A Black & White Story. Douglas Blackburn. (Illus.). 224p. 1991. pap. 24.95 (*0-86980-803-6*, Pub. by Univ Natal Pr) Intl Spec Bk.

Leaven: Canticle for a Changing Parish. Harvey Egan. LC 90-36348. 120p. 1990. pap. 9.95 (*0-87839-058-8*) North Star.

Leaven: 150 Women in Scripture Whose Lives Lift Ours. Jerrie Hurd. LC 95-6361. 172p. 1995. pap. 10.95 (*1-56236-220-8*, Pub. by Aspen Bks) Origin Bk Sales.

Leaven for Doughfaces: Parables Touching Slavery. Darius Lyman, Jr. LC 78-146266. (Black Heritage Library Collection). 1977. 28.95 (*0-8369-8741-1*) Ayer.

***Leaven in the World: Growing in Community Life.** Leaven in the World Editorial Team. LC 00-8663. 2000. write for info. (*0-88489-447-9*) St Marys.

Leaven of Ladies: A History of the Calgary Local Council of Women. Marjorie Norris. LC 95-224737. (Illus.). 288p. (Orig.). 1995. pap. write for info. (*1-55059-123-1*) Detselig Ents.

Leaven of Love. Izette De Forest. (Psychoanalysis: Examined & Re-Examined Ser.). 220p. 1983. reprint ed. lib. bdg. 27.50 (*0-306-76234-X*) Da Capo.

Leaven of Love: A Development of the Psychoanalytic Theory & Technique of Sandor Ferenczi. Izette De Forest. LC 65-14585. 224p. reprint ed. pap. 69.50 (*0-608-11147-3*, 201021300068) Bks Demand.

Leaven of Malice. Robertson Davies. 272p. 1980. pap. 11.95 (*0-14-016789-7*, Penguin Bks) Viking Penguin.

Leaven of the Ancients: Suhrawardi & the Heritage of the Greeks. John Walbridge. LC 98-54756. (SUNY Series in Islam). 320p. (C). 1999. text 78.50 (*0-7914-4359-0*); pap. text 26.95 (*0-7914-4360-4*) State U NY Pr.

Leavenworth Case. Anna K. Green. 1976. lib. bdg. 12.95 (*0-89968-171-9*, Lghtyr Pr) Buccaneer Bks.

Leavenworth Case: A Lawyer's Story. Anna K. Green. LC 79-104467. 481p. 1986. reprint ed. pap. 3.95 (*0-8290-1679-1*); reprint ed. lib. bdg. 14.25 (*0-8398-0666-3*) Irvington.

***Leavenworth Legacy: An Intriguing Story of Two Ex-Convicts from Opposite Sides of the Track.** Ed A. McLaughlin. 216p. 1998. 17.00 (*0-8059-4378-1*) Dorrance.

Leavenworth Schools & the Old Army: Education, Professionalism, & the Officer Corps of the United States Army, 1881-1918., 15. Timothy K. Nenninger. LC 77-91105. (Contributions in Military History Ser.: No. 15). 173p. 1978. 49.95 (*0-313-20047-5*, NFL/) Greenwood.

Leaves see PowerKids Readers Set 2: Nature Books

Leaves. Ed. by Applewood Books Staff. (Wonderlings Ser.). (Illus.). 32p. (Orig.). (J). (ps up). 1996. pap. 1.50 (*1-55709-381-4*) Applewood.

Leaves. Sy Barlowe. (Learning about Ser.). 16p. (J). pap. 1.00 (*0-486-29762-4*) Dover.

Leaves. John Green. (Little Activity Bks.). (J). 1994. pap. 1.00 (*0-486-28094-2*) Dover.

Leaves. Gail Saunders. (Growing Flowers Ser.). 24p. (J). 1998. 13.25 (*0-516-21323-7*) Childrens.

Leaves. Gail Saunders-Smith. LC 98-5046. (Growing Flowers Ser.). (Illus.). (J). 1998. 13.25 (*1-56065-770-7*, Pebble Bks) Capstone Pr.

Leaves. Jean Warren. Ed. by Kathleen Cubley. (Sticker Book Ser.). (Illus.). 32p. (J). (ps). 1998. pap. 3.95 (*1-57029-221-3*, 3711) Totline Pubns.

Leaves: An Address Book. Alice T. Vitale. (Illus.). 128p. 1999. 15.95 (*1-55670-912-9*) Stewart Tabori & Chang.

Leaves: In Magic, Myth & Medicine. Alice T. Vitale. 1997. 29.95 (*0-614-28266-7*) Stewart Tabori & Chang.

Leaves: In Magic, Myth & Medicine. Alice T. Vitole. LC 96-43280. (Illus.). 352p. 1997. 29.95 (*1-55670-554-9*) Stewart Tabori & Chang.

Leaves: Poetry. Peter Jacoby. LC 97-91769. 89p. 1997. pap. 7.95 (*1-883368-01-4*) Ramsey Pr.

Leaves Series B: Bridging School to Home. large type ed. Karen Hoenecke. (Illus.). 8p. (J). (gr. k-2). 1998. pap. 4.25 (*1-879835-39-8*, Kaeden) Kaeden Corp.

Leaves & Fruit. Edmund W. Gosse. LC 70-105017. (Essay Index Reprint Ser.). 1977. 23.95 (*0-8369-1505-4*) Ayer.

Leaves & Stems from Fossil Forests. rev. ed. Raymond E. Janssen. (Popular Science Ser.: Vol. I). (Illus.). 190p. 1979. pap. 4.00 (*0-89792-077-5*) Ill St Museum.

Leaves & Wind Chimes: Haiku for Autumn. Patricia Neubauer. LC 86-90529. (Illus.). 50p. (Orig.). 1986. write for info. (*0-9617265-0-4*); pap. 15.00 (*0-9617265-1-2*) Neubauer Pr.

Leaves from a Child's Garden of Verses. Robert Louis Stevenson. (Illus.). 80p. (J). 1992. 11.98 (*0-8317-5697-7*) Smithmark.

Leaves from a Child's Garden of Verses. Robert Louis Stevenson. (Illus.). 80p. (J). (ps-3). 1993. 14.95 (*1-883746-11-6*) Vermilion.

Leaves from a Child's Garden of Verses. deluxe ed. Robert Louis Stevenson. (Illus.). 80p. (J). (ps-3). 1993. 18.95 (*1-883746-00-0*) Vermilion.

Leaves from a Diary. Syama P. Mookerjee. (Illus.). 260p. 1993. text 26.00 (*0-19-563119-6*) OUP.

Leaves from a Grass House. Don Blanding. pap. 3.95 (*0-681-26819-0*) Booklines Hawaii.

Leaves from a Grass House. Don Blanding. 1972. reprint ed. pap. 3.95 (*0-912180-17-X*) Petroglyph.

Leaves from Gerard's Herball. Ed. by Marcus Woodward. (Illus.). 1990. 12.50 (*0-8446-0971-4*) Peter Smith.

Leaves from Gerard's Herball. Marcus Woodward. (Illus.). 1969. reprint ed. pap. 7.95 (*0-486-22343-4*) Dover.

Leaves from Many Seasons: Selected Papers. O. Hobart Mowrer. LC 82-18977. 353p. 1983. 59.95 (*0-275-91047-4*, C1047, Praeger Pubs) Greenwood.

Leaves from Margaret Smith's Journal. John Greenleaf Whittier. LC 75-104596. 224p. reprint ed. lib. bdg. 22.50 (*0-8398-2167-0*) Irvington.

Leaves from Margaret Smith's Journal. John Greenleaf Whittier. (Notable American Authors Ser.). 1999. reprint ed. lib. bdg. 125.00 (*0-7812-9972-1*) Rprt Serv.

Leaves from My Library. Lord Denning. 1986. 40.00 (*0-406-17615-9*, U.K., MICHIE) LEXIS Pub.

Leaves from the Bodhi Tree: The Art of Pala India (8th-12th Centuries) & Its International Legacy. Susan L. Huntington et al. Ed. by Miranda E. Shaw. (Illus.). 280p. (Orig.). 1989. pap. text 25.00 (*0-937809-09-8*) Dayton Art.

Leaves from the Diary of a Dreamer. Henry T. Tuckerman. (Notable American Authors). 1999. reprint ed. lib. bdg. 125.00 (*0-7812-9848-2*) Rprt Serv.

Leaves from the Family Tree. Penelope J. Allen. 372p. 1982. 45.00 (*0-89308-227-9*) Southern Hist Pr.

Leaves from the Garden: Two Centuries of Garden Writing. Ed. by Clare Best & Caroline Boisset. (Illus.). 412p. 1987. 22.50 (*0-393-02451-2*) Norton.

Leaves from the Inn of the Last Home. Margaret Weis & Tracy Hickman. LC 86-51592. (DragonLance Ser.). (Illus.). 256p. (Orig.). 1987. reprint ed. pap. 18.95 (*0-88038-465-4*) TSR Inc.

Leaves from the Journals of Sir George Smart. George Smart. Ed. by Bertram Cox & C. L. Cox. LC 72-154696. (Music Ser.). 1971. reprint ed. lib. bdg. 47.50 (*0-306-70164-2*) Da Capo.

Leaves from the Jungle. Verrier Elwin. (Illus.). 248p. 1992. 28.00 (*0-19-562852-7*) OUP.

Leaves from the Notebook of a Tamed Cynic. Reinhold Niebuhr. (American Biography Ser.). 198p. 1991. reprint ed. lib. bdg. 59.00 (*0-7812-8299-3*) Rprt Serv.

Leaves from the Notebook of a Tamed Cynic. Reinhold Niebuhr. 152p. 1990. reprint ed. pap. 16.95 (*0-664-25164-1*) Westminster John Knox.

Leaves from the Tree of Life: Vegetarian Whole Foods Cookery & Health Seminar. Lee Heathman & Mildred A. Tillotson. 80p. 1995. teacher ed., ring bd. 10.00 (*0-9638656-4-1*) Gateways Hlth.

Leaves from the Tree of Life: Vegetarian Whole Foods Cookery & Health Seminar. rev. ed. Lee Heathman & Mildred A. Tillotson. (Illus.). 160p. 1996. student ed., ring bd. 25.00 (*0-9638656-1-7*) Gateways Hlth.

Leaves from the Valley. Caroline Harvey. 1997. mass mkt. 8.99 (*0-552-14529-7*) Bantam.

Leaves from the Valley. abr. ed. Joanna Trollope. 1995. mass mkt. 16.95 (*1-85998-165-8*) Trafalgar.

Leaves from the Walnut Tree: Recipes of a Lifetime. Ann Taruschio & Franco Taruschio. (Illus.). 192p. 1998. pap. 24.95 (*1-85793-570-5*, Pub. by Pavilion Bks Ltd) Trafalgar.

***Leaves Have Lost Their Trees.** Dorothy Marie Darke. 115p. 1999. pap. 45.00 (*1-85072-226-9*, Pub. by W Sessions) St Mut.

***Leaves in Bloom.** Patricia Burkard. 1999. pap. write for info. (*1-58235-218-6*) Watermrk Pr.

Leaves in Her Shoes, No. 44. J. L. Jacobs. (Lost Roads Ser.: Vol. 44). 64p. 1997. pap. 12.00 (*0-918786-49-5*) Lost Roads.

Leaves in October. Karen Ackerman. LC 90-550. 128p. (J). (gr. 3-7). 1991. 13.95 (*0-689-31583-X*) Atheneum Yung Read.

Leaves in October. Karen Ackerman. (J). 1991. 9.09 (*0-606-05420-0*, Pub. by Turtleback) Demco.

Leaves in the Wind. LaDonna K. Meinders. LC 89-81374. (Illus.). 152p. (J). 1989. 15.95 (*0-934188-31-9*) Evans Pubns.

Leaves of Autumn. Cal McDonald. 143p. 1998. pap. 7.95 (*0-9662740-0-8*) Peace Arch Bks.

Leaves of Gold: An Inspirational Classic. Clyde F. Lytle. 198p. 1983. 16.99 (*0-915720-74-4*) Brownlow Pub Co.

Leaves of Gold: An Inspirational Classic. deluxe ed. Ed. by Clyde F. Lytle. 198p. 1983. 19.99 (*0-915720-84-1*) Brownlow Pub Co.

Leaves of Gold: An Inspirational Classic for Our Time. Paul C. Brownlow. (Cherished Moments Ser.). (Illus.). 120p. 1996. 12.99 (*1-57051-128-4*) Brownlow Pub Co.

Leaves of Grass. Walt Whitman. 24.95 (*0-8488-0703-0*) Amereon Ltd.

Leaves of Grass. Walt Whitman. (Bantam Classics Ser.). 496p. 1983. mass mkt. 5.95 (*0-553-21116-1*) Bantam.

Leaves of Grass. Walt Whitman. 768p. 1992. pap. 17.50 (*0-679-72514-8*) Fodors Travel.

Leaves of Grass. Walt Whitman. LC 93-11039. 728p. 1993. 19.50 (*0-679-60076-0*) Modern Lib NY.

Leaves of Grass. Walt Whitman. 1954. mass mkt. 5.95 (*0-451-52485-3*, CE1702, Sig Classics) NAL.

***Leaves of Grass.** Walt Whitman. (Classic Ser.). 2000. mass mkt. 5.95 (*0-451-52758-5*, Sig Classics) NAL.

Leaves of Grass. Walt Whitman. Ed. by E. Sculley Bradley & Harold W. Blodgett. (Critical Editions Ser.). 500p. (C). 1973. pap. text 20.25 (*0-393-09388-3*) Norton.

Leaves of Grass. Walt Whitman. Ed. & Intro. by Jerome Loving. (Oxford World's Classics Ser.). 508p. 1998. pap. 6.95 (*0-19-283409-6*) OUP.

Leaves of Grass. Walt Whitman. LC 95-9645. (Literary Classics Ser.). 426p. 1995. pap. text 9.95 (*1-57392-040-1*) Prometheus Bks.

Leaves of Grass. Walt Whitman. LC 98-9348. 450p. 1998. text 27.95 (*1-56000-513-0*) Transaction Pubs.

Leaves of Grass. Walt Whitman. 1986. 13.05 (*0-606-03345-9*, Pub. by Turtleback) Demco.

Leaves of Grass. Walt Whitman. 1999. audio 16.95 (*0-14-086321-4*) Viking Penguin.

Leaves of Grass. fac. ed. Walt Whitman. (Library of American Poets). 95p. 1994. reprint ed. 50.00 (*1-56515-000-7*) Collect Reprints.

***Leaves Of Grass.** large type ed. Walt Whitman. 816p. 2000. 22.00 (*0-06-095697-6*, HarpCollins) HarperTrade.

Leaves of Grass. Walt Whitman. reprint ed. pap. 49.95 (*3-487-00110-1*) Adlers Foreign Bks.

Leaves of Grass. Walt Whitman. 350p. 1983. reprint ed. lib. bdg. 19.95 (*0-89966-472-5*) Buccaneer Bks.

***Leaves of Grass.** 2nd ed. Walt Whitman. 1999. pap. 27.75 (*0-393-97496-0*, Norton Paperbks) Norton.

Leaves of Grass, Vol. 2. Walt Whitman. LC 98-9348. 500p. 1998. text 27.95 (*1-56000-514-9*) Transaction Pubs.

Leaves of Grass: A Legal High of Humorous & Serious Poetry. John Bryant. 91p. (Orig.). 1996. pap. 8.95 (*1-886739-35-8*) Socratic Pr.

Leaves of Grass: America's Lyric-Epic of Self & Democracy. James E. Miller, Jr. (Masterwork Studies). 160p. 1992. 29.00 (*0-8057-8089-0*, Twyne); pap. 14.95 (*0-8057-8565-5*, Twyne) Mac Lib Ref.

Leaves of Grass Authoritative Texts, Prefaces, Whitman on His Art, Criticism. Walt Whitman et al. LC 72-5156. (Norton Critical Editions Ser.). lx, 1008p. 1973. write for info. (*0-393-04354-1*) Norton.

Leaves of Grass: The Original 1855 Edition. Walt Whitman. LC 90-85557. (Humanist Classics Ser.: No. 9). 117p. 1992. pap. text 8.00 (*0-942208-08-0*) Bandanna Bks.

Leaves of Grass & Democratic Vistas. Walt Whitman. 608p. 1994. 5.95 (*0-460-87475-6*, Everyman's Classic Lib) Tuttle Pubng.

Leaves of Grass & Selected Prose. Walt Whitman. 763p. (C). 1981. pap. 7.50 (*0-07-554263-3*) McGraw.

Leaves of Grass & Selected Prose. Walt Whitman. Ed. by Lawrence Buell. 1981. pap. 4.25 (*0-685-03397-X*, T40) Modern Lib NY.

Leaves of Grass & Selected Prose. Walt Whitman. Ed. by Lawrence Buell. 763p. (C). 1981. pap. text. write for info. (*0-318-55436-4*) Random.

Leaves of Grass Notes. V. A. Shahane. (Cliffs Notes Ser.). 80p. 1972. pap. 4.95 (*0-8220-0723-1*, Cliff) IDG Bks.

Leaves of Grass One Hundred Years After. Ed. by Milton Hindus. 149p. 1955. pap. 11.95 (*0-8047-0465-1*) Stanford U Pr.

Leaves of Life. Jayavant D. Dalvi & P. A. Lad. LC 98-915451. 196p. 1998. write for info. (*81-250-1591-4*, Pub. by Orient Longman Ltd) S Asia.

Leaves of Life: Fifty Drawings from the Model. Lawrence Ferlinghetti. 1983. pap. 10.95 (*0-87286-154-6*) City Lights.

Leaves of Life & How to Change Your Mind about Growth, Love, Life, & Living. Jack M. Lorenzo. 90p. 1993. pap. write for info. (*0-9636299-0-5*) INCOM Pub Div.

Leaves of Love. Dorothy P. Ashby. 1997. pap. write for info. (*1-57553-695-1*) Watermrk Pr.

Leaves of Morya's Garden Vol. I: The Call. 3rd ed. Incl. Leaves of Morya's Garden Vol. II: Illumination. 1979. reprint ed. pap. 12.00 (*0-933574-01-0*); (Agni Yoga Ser.). 1978. reprint ed. Set pap. 12.00 (*0-933574-00-2*) Agni Yoga Soc.

Leaves of Morya's Garden, Vol. II, Illumination see Leaves of Morya's Garden, Vol. I, The Call

Leaves of Mourning: Holderlin's Late Work - With an Essay on Keats & Melancholy. Anselm Haverkamp. Tr. by Vernon Chadwick. LC 95-11833. (SUNY Series, Intersections). 163p. (C). 1996. text 44.50 (*0-7914-2739-0*); pap. text 14.95 (*0-7914-2740-4*) State U NY Pr.

***Leaves of Sand, 1.** G. Raymond Humphries. 350p. (Orig.). 2000. pap. 7.50 (*1-892614-27-8*) Briarwood VA.

Leaves of the Banyan Tree. Albert Wendt. LC 83-136664. 416p. 1979. write for info. (*0-582-71770-1*) P Lngmn NZ.

Leaves of the Banyan Tree. Albert Wendt. LC 93-41685. (Talanoa Ser.). 424p. 1994. pap. 16.95 (*0-8248-1584-X*) UH Pr.

Leaves of the Heaven Tree: The Great Compassion of the Buddha. Padma-Chos-Phel & K. Semendra. Tr. by Deborah Black from TIB. LC 97-416. (Tibetan Translation Ser.). 1997. 40.00 (*0-89800-283-4*); pap. 25.00 (*0-89800-285-0*) Dharma Pub.

Leaves of the Past: A Pioneer Register, Including an Overview of the History & Events of Early Tehama County. Ruth H. Hitchcock. (ANCRR Occasional Publications: No. 10). 1980. 35.00 (*0-686-38936-0*) Assn NC Records.

Leaves of Water: New & Selected Poems. Ralph Wright. 96p. 1998. pap. 12.95 (*0-9662104-0-9*) St Louis Abbey.

Leaves Only. Jo A. Mills. 1988. pap. 6.95 (*0-89137-447-7*) Quality Pubns.

***Leaves Postcard Book.** Alice Thoms Vitale. (Illus.). 1999. pap. 10.95 (*1-55670-952-8*) Stewart Tabori & Chang.

Leaves, Roots & Branches: The John Allgaier Family of Kankakee, Illinois. Wayne Allgaier & April L. Allgaier. 198p. 1992. 35.00 (*0-9635551-0-3*) Robin Pr MA.

Leaves the People. Benjamin Saltman. 1974. pap. 2.50 (*0-88031-015-4*) Invisible-Red Hill.

Leavetaking. Mortimer R. Feinberg et al. (C). 1989. pap. text 12.20 (*0-536-05283-2*) Pearson Custom.

Leavetaking. large type ed. George Milner. (Linford Mystery Library). 276p. 1989. pap. 16.99 (*0-7089-6635-7*, Linford) Ulverscroft.

***Leavin Trunk Blues: A Nick Travers Mystery.** Ace Atkins. LC 00-29691. 256p. 2000. text 22.95 (*0-312-24212-3*) St Martin.

***Leaving.** Illus. by Bettye Stroud & Cedric Lucas. LC 99-41352. 2000. write for info. (*0-7614-5067-X*) Marshall Cavendish.

Leaving. Budge Wilson. 208p. (J). (gr. 7-9). 1993. pap. 3.50 (*0-590-46933-9*, Point) Scholastic Inc.

Leaving: Three Stories. Steven Hopkins. LC 78-70051. 56p. 1978. pap. 3.00 (*0-930012-09-7*) J Mudfoot.

Leaving a Doll's House: A Memoir. Claire Bloom. (Illus.). 288p. 1998. pap. 13.95 (*0-316-09383-1*) Little.

Leaving a Godly Legacy. Charles Stanley. (In Touch Study Ser.). 120p. 1999. pap. 7.99 (*0-7852-7289-5*) Nelson.

***Leaving a Legacy: An Inspirational Guide to Taking Action & Making a Difference.** Jim Paluch. LC 98-83119. 1999. pap. text 11.95 (*0-937539-32-5*) Executive Bks.

Leaving a Shadow. Heather Allen. 75p. 1996. pap. 12.00 (*1-55659-113-6*) Copper Canyon.

Leaving a Trace: On Keeping a Journal. Alexandra Johnson. 288p. 2001. 24.95 (*0-316-12020-0*) Little.

Leaving Abusive Partners: From the Scars of Survival to the Wisdom for Change. Cathy Kirkwood. 224p. (C). 1993. text 65.00 (*0-8039-8685-8*); pap. text 21.95 (*0-8039-8686-6*) Sage.

Leaving Alva. Victoria Lipman. LC 97-23021. 1998. 21.50 (*0-684-83415-4*) S&S Trade.

Leaving Anabaptism: From Evangelical Mennonite Brethren to Fellowship of Evangelical Bible Churches. Calvin W. Redekop. LC 98-28701. 268p. 1998. 19.99 (*0-9665021-0-8*) Pandora PA.

Leaving & Coming Back. Jane Flanders. (QRL Poetry Bks.: Vol. XXI). (Illus.). 1980. 20.00 (*0-614-06376-0*) Quarterly Rev.

Leaving, & Other Stories. Budge Wilson. (J). 1990. 8.60 (*0-606-05421-9*, Pub. by Turtleback) Demco.

Leaving & Returning: On America's Contributions to a World Ethic. Stephen C. Rowe. LC 88-47944. 168p. 1989. 32.50 (*0-8387-5163-6*) Bucknell U Pr.

***Leaving Birmingham: Notes of a Native Son.** Paul Hemphill. LC 99-29875. 2000. 19.95 (*0-8173-1022-3*) U of Ala Pr.

Leaving by the Closet Door. Stephen Shrader. 82p. 1970. 2.95 (*0-87886-001-0*, Greenfld Rev Pr) Greenfld Rev Lit.

***Leaving Care in Partnership: Family Involvement with Care Leavers** Peter Marsh. LC 99-201657. (Studies in Evaluating the Children Act 1989). xi, 124p. 1999. write for info. (*0-11-322250-5*, Pub. by Statnry Office) Gale.

L

An Asterisk (*) at the beginning of an entry indicates that the title is appearing for the first time.

L

Leaving Cheyenne. Bill Brooks. 1999. mass mkt. 5.99 (*0-440-22652-X*) Dell.

Leaving Cheyenne. Larry McMurtry. 1976. 22.95 (*0-8488-0373-6*) Amereon Ltd.

***Leaving Cheyenne.** Larry McMurtry. 304p. 2001. per. 12.00 (*0-684-85387-6*) S&S Trade.

Leaving Cheyenne. Larry McMurtry. 256p. 1992. pap. 11.00 (*0-671-75490-4*, Touchstone) S&S Trade Pap.

Leaving Cheyenne. Larry McMurtry. Ed. by Bill Grose. 320p. 1992. reprint ed. pap. 7.50 (*0-671-75380-0*) PB.

Leaving Cloistered Safety. Ken Stone. 24p. 1985. pap. 2.50 (*0-9613465-1-5*) Great Elm.

Leaving Cold Sassy: The Unfinished Sequel to Cold Sassy Tree. Olive Ann Burns. 320p. 1994. pap. 12.95 (*0-385-31220-2*, Delta Trade) Dell.

Leaving Cold Sassy: The Unfinished Sequel to Cold Sassy Tree. Olive Ann Burns. LC 92-5561. 1992. 17.05 (*0-606-06523-7*, Pub. by Turtleback) Demco.

Leaving Cold Sassy: The Unfinished Sequel to Cold Sassy Tree. large type ed. Olive Ann Burns. LC 92-40634. (General Ser.). 336p. 1994. lib. bdg. 22.95 (*0-8161-5702-2*, G K Hall Lrg Type) Mac Lib Ref.

Leaving College: Rethinking the Causes & Cures of Student Attrition. Vincent Tinto. LC 86-11379. x, 256p. (C). 1997. 23.95 (*0-226-80446-1*) U Ch Pr.

Leaving College: Rethinking the Causes & Cures of Student Attrition. 2nd ed. Vincent Tinto. (Illus.). 312p. 1994. 25.00 (*0-226-80449-6*) U Ch Pr.

***Leaving Deep Water: Asian American Women at the Crossroads of Two Cultures.** Claire S. Chow. 302p. 1999. pap. 13.95 (*0-452-28049-4*, Plume) Dutton Plume.

Leaving Early. Barbara L. McCombs & Linda Brannan. (Skills for Job Success Ser.). (Illus.). 32p. (Orig.). (YA). (gr. 7-12). 1990. teacher ed. 1.95 (*1-56119-040-3*); disk 39.95 (*1-56119-120-5*) Educ Pr MD.

Leaving Early. Barbara L. McCombs & Linda Brannan. (Skills for Job Success Ser.). (Illus.). 32p. (Orig.). 1990. pap., student ed. 5.95 (*1-56119-039-X*) Educ Pr MD.

Leaving Early, Set. Barbara L. McCombs & Linda Brannan. (Skills for Job Success Ser.). (Illus.). 32p. (Orig.). (YA). (gr. 7-12). 1990. teacher ed. 54.95 (*1-56119-078-0*) Educ Pr MD.

Leaving Early: Perspectives & Problems in Current Retirement Practice & Policy. Jeanne P. Gordus. LC 80-39653. 88p. (Orig.). 1980. pap. text 4.00 (*0-911558-78-0*) W E Upjohn.

Leaving Earth. Helen Humphreys. LC 98-13088. 224p. 1998. 23.00 (*0-8050-5957-1*) H Holt & Co.

Leaving Earth. Helen Humphreys. 256p. 2000. pap. 12.00 (*0-8050-5958-X*, Owl) H Holt & Co.

***Leaving Earth.** Helen Humphreys. LC 99-87753. 256p. 2000. pap. 13.00 (*0-312-25500-4*, Picador USA) St Martin.

***Leaving Eden.** Ann Chamberlin. 240p. 2000. pap. 13.95 (*0-312-87511-8*) Forge NYC.

Leaving Eden. Ann Chamberlin. LC 99-22072. 240p. 1999. text 23.95 (*0-312-86550-3*) Forge Pr.

***Leaving Eden.** Ann Chamberlin. 2000. mass mkt. 6.99 (*0-8125-9001-5*) Tor Bks.

Leaving Eden: Poems. Nadya Aisenberg. LC 95-60233. 96p. 1996. pap. 14.95 (*1-85610-039-1*, Pub. by Forest Bks) Dufour.

Leaving Eden: To Protect & Manage the Earth. Evan G. Nisbet. (Illus.). 378p. (C). 1991. pap. text 21.95 (*0-521-42579-4*) Cambridge U Pr.

Leaving Egypt. Gene Zeiger. 96p. (Orig.). 1995. pap. 12.00 (*1-877727-50-4*) White Pine.

Leaving Eldorado. Joann Mazzio. LC 92-13853. 176p. (J). (gr. 5-9). 1993. 16.00 (*0-395-64381-3*) HM.

Leaving Emma. Nancy Steele Brokaw. LC 98-22688. 144p. (J). (gr. 4-7). 1999. 15.00 (*0-395-90699-7*, Clarion Bks) HM.

Leaving England: Essays on British Emigration in the Nineteenth Century. Charlotte Erickson. (Illus.). 296p. 1994. text 42.50 (*0-8014-2820-3*) Cornell U Pr.

Leaving Everything Behind: The Songs & Memories of a Cheyenne Woman. Bertha L. Coyote & Virginia Giglio. LC 97-11270. (Illus.). xix, 166p. 1997. 29.95 (*0-8061-2984-0*); 40.00 incl. disk (*0-8061-2987-5*) U of Okla Pr.

Leaving Family Credit. A. Bryson & A. Marsh. (DSS Research Report Ser.). 1996. write for info. (*0-11-762411-X*, Pub. by Statnry Office) Bernan Associates.

Leaving Fishers. Margaret P. Haddix. LC 96-47857. 256p. (YA). (gr. 7 up). 1999. per. 4.99 (*0-689-82461-0*, 076714004504) S&S Childrens.

Leaving Fishers. Margaret Peterson Haddix. 262p. (YA). pap. 4.50 (*0-8072-1541-4*) Listening Lib.

Leaving Fishers. Margaret Peterson Haddix. LC 96-47857. 192p. (J). (gr. 7 up). 1997. 17.00 (*0-689-81125-X*) S&S Childrens.

Leaving Flat Iron Creek. John S. Lloyd. LC 98-96779. (Illus.). 300p. 1998. pap. 18.95 (*0-9668164-3-9*, 001-98) Spalding & Wallace.

Leaving Food Behind: An Inspiring Personal Story of Recovery from Bulimia, Starving, Overeating. Sheila Mather. 144p. 1999. pap. 12.95 (*0-9681812-0-1*) ACCESS Pubs Network.

Leaving for America. Roslyn Bresnick-Perry. LC 92-8450. (Illus.). 32p. (YA). (ps-3). 1992. 14.95 (*0-89239-105-7*) Childrens Book Pr.

Leaving for Good. Alex Holland. (Illus.). 17p. (J). (gr. k-4). 1998. pap. 12.95 (*1-56606-051-6*) Bradley Mann.

Leaving for Townsville. Bronwyn Tate. 304p. 1997. pap. 24.95 (*1-877133-15-9*, Pub. by Univ Otago Pr) Intl Spec Bk.

Leaving Gary. John Sheehan. LC 97-61749. 64p. (Orig.). 1997. pap. 10.95 (*1-882688-16-3*) Tia Chucha Pr.

***Leaving Giant Footprints... Without Stepping on Your Kids.** Jim Wilcox. LC 99-48415. 2000. pap. 3.49 (*0-8341-1874-2*) Beacon Hill.

***Leaving Giant Footprints Without Stepping on Your Kids, 20 bks.** Jim Wilcox. 2000. pap. 69.80 (*0-8341-1796-7*) Beacon Hill.

Leaving Home. 1984. pap. 12.95 (*0-9630404-1-3*) BCJ Pubns.

Leaving Home. Herbert Anderson & Kenneth R. Mitchell. LC 92-33115. (Family Living in Pastoral Perspective Ser.). 1993. pap. 14.00 (*0-664-25127-7*) Westminster John Knox.

Leaving Home. Linda Bosch. (Open Door Bks.). (Illus.). 70p. (Orig.). 1992. pap. text 3.95 (*1-56212-015-8*, 1740-2110) CRC Pubns.

***Leaving Home.** Stephanie Doyon. LC 98-44736. (On the Road Ser.: 1). 224p. (YA). (gr. 7 up). 1999. pap. 3.99 (*0-689-82107-7*, 076714004504) Aladdin.

Leaving Home. Gill Jones. LC 94-41292. 192p. 1995. pap. 31.95 (*0-335-19284-X*) OpUniv Pr.

Leaving Home. Gill Jones. LC 94-41292. 192p. 1995. 109.95 (*0-335-19285-8*) Taylor & Francis.

Leaving Home. Garrison Keillor. LC 99-174801. xxiii, 258 p. 1990. pap. 12.95 (*0-14-013160-4*, Penguin Bks) Viking Penguin.

Leaving Home. J. O'Neill. 1997. mass mkt. 13.95 (*0-340-69496-3*, Pub. by Hodder & Stought Ltd) Trafalgar.

Leaving Home. Pinger. 48p. 1998. spiral bd. 7.81 (*0-07-292781-X*) McGraw.

Leaving Home. Elizabeth Janeway. LC 87-13551. 336p. 1987. reprint ed. pap. 8.95 (*0-935312-73-0*) Feminist Pr.

Leaving Home: A Collection of Lake Wobegon Stories. Garrison Keillor. 1989. 4.98 (*0-670-82011-3*) Grossman.

Leaving Home: A Memoir. large type ed. Art Buchwald. LC 93-44664. 350p. 1994. lib. bdg. 24.95 (*0-7862-0158-4*) Thorndike Pr.

***Leaving Home: Stories.** Hazel Rochman. LC 96-28979. (Illus.). 240p. (J). (gr. 12 up). 1998. pap. 11.00 (*0-06-440706-3*) HarpC.

Leaving Home: Stories. Hazel Rochman & Darlene Z. McCampbell. LC 96-28979. 240p. (YA). (gr. 7 up). 1997. lib. bdg. 16.89 (*0-06-024874-2*) HarpC Child Bks.

Leaving Home: Stories. Ed. by Hazel Rochman & Darlene Z. McCampbell. LC 96-28979. 240p. (YA). (gr. 12 up). 1997. 16.95 (*0-06-024873-4*) HarpC Child Bks.

Leaving Home: The Therapy of Disturbed Young People. 2nd rev. ed. Jay Haley. LC 96-50983. 336p. (YA). 1997. 39.95 (*0-87630-845-0*) Brunner-Mazel.

Leaving Home Before Marriage: Ethnicity, Familism, & Generational Relationships. Frances K. Goldscheider & Calvin Goldscheider. LC 92-56926. 260p. 1996. pap. 14.95 (*0-299-13804-6*) U of Wis Pr.

***Leaving Home But Not Christ.** John Yates & Chris Yates. LC 00-27893. 224p. (YA). 2000. pap. 11.99 (*0-8010-6336-1*) Baker Bks.

Leaving Ireland. Francis Gallagher. Ed. by Martha Asbury. (Illus.). 200p. (Orig.). 1995. pap. 11.95 (*0-9647147-0-1*) Plimsoll Press.

***Leaving Japan: Observations of the Dysfunctional U. S.-Japan Relationship.** Mike Millard. LC 00-41290. (Illus.). 2000. write for info. (*0-7656-0660-7*) M E Sharpe.

***Leaving Japan: Observations on a Dysfunctional U.S.-Japan Relationship.** Mike Millard. 200p. 2000. text 37.95 (*0-7656-0659-3*, East Gate Bk) M E Sharpe.

Leaving Las Vegas. Mike Figgis. (Illus.). 100p. (Orig.). 1996. pap. 12.95 (*0-571-17969-X*) Faber & Faber.

Leaving Las Vegas. John O'Brien. 206p. 1991. 19.50 (*0-922820-12-0*) Watermark Pr.

Leaving Las Vegas. John O'Brien. LC 95-81572. 200p. 1996. reprint ed. pap. 11.00 (*0-8021-3445-9*, Grove) Grove-Atltic.

***Leaving Lines of Gender: A Feminist Genealogy of Language Writing.** Ann Vickery. LC 00-9338. (C). 2000. write for info. (*0-8195-6432-X*, Wesleyan Univ Pr) U Pr of New Eng.

***Leaving Liverpool.** Andrews. 2000. pap. 6.95 (*0-552-13933-5*, Pub. by Transworld Publishers Ltd) Trafalgar.

Leaving Losapas. Roland Merullo. 304p. 1992. pap. 10.00 (*0-380-71750-6*, Avon Bks) Morrow Avon.

Leaving Missouri. Ellen Recknor. 368p. 1997. mass mkt. 5.99 (*0-425-15575-7*) Berkley Pub.

Leaving Money Wisely: A Guide for Middle- & Upper-Income Americans for the 1990s. David W. Belin. 320p. 1991. 21.00 (*0-684-19227-6*, Scribners Ref) Mac Lib Ref.

Leaving Money Wisely: Creative Estate Planning for Middle- & Upper- Income Americans for the 1990s. David W. Belin. 320p. 1993. reprint ed. pap. 12.00 (*0-02-008092-1*) Macmillan.

Leaving Morning. Angela Johnson. LC 91-21123. (Illus.). 32p. (J). (ps-2). 1996. pap. 5.95 (*0-531-07072-7*) Orchard Bks Watts.

Leaving Morning. Angela Johnson. LC 91-21123. 1996. 11.15 (*0-606-09532-2*, Pub. by Turtleback) Demco.

Leaving My Father's House: A Journey to Conscious Femininity. Marion Woodman. LC 90-53600. 352p. 1993. pap. 24.95 (*0-87773-896-3*, Pub. by Shambhala Pubns) Random.

Leaving No Stone Unturned: Pathways in Organometallic Chemistry. F. Gordon Stone. LC 93-28909. (Profiles, Pathways, & Dreams Ser.). (Illus.). 240p. 1993. text 36.00 (*0-8412-1826-9*, Pub. by Am Chemical) OUP.

Leaving No Stone Unturned: Pathways in Organometallic Chemistry. F. Gordon Stone. LC 93-28909. (Profiles, Pathways, & Dreams Ser.). (Illus.). 240p. 1993. pap. write for info. (*0-8412-1827-7*) Am Chemical.

***Leaving No Track: A View of T'ai Chi Ch'uan.** Colin Berg. (Illus.). 112p. 1999. pap. 19.95 (*0-9676465-1-0*) Tadpole Bks.

Leaving Nothing to Chance: Achieving Board Accountability Through Risk Management. Melanie Herman & Leslie White. 32p. 1998. pap. text 16.00 (*0-925299-90-1*) Natl Ctr Nonprofit.

***Leaving Patrick.** large type ed. Prue Leith. LC 99-87701. (General Ser.). 2000. pap. 23.95 (*0-7862-2419-3*) Thorndike Pr.

***Leaving Pico.** Frank X. Gaspar. LC 99-19857. (Hardscrabble Bks.). 224p. 1999. 24.95 (*0-87451-921-7*) U Pr of New Eng.

Leaving Pipe Shop. Deborah E. McDowell. LC 96-48173. 1997. 22.50 (*0-684-81449-8*) S&S Trade.

Leaving Pipe Shop: Memories of Kin. Deborah E. McDowell. 288p. 1998. pap. 13.00 (*0-393-31843-5*) Norton.

Leaving Room for the Angels: Eurythmy & the Art of Teaching. Reg Down. Ed. & Illus. by David Mitchell. 176p. 1996. pap. 18.00 (*1-888365-00-5*) Assn Waldorf Schls.

Leaving Scotland. McLeod. (Scottish Life, Past & Present Ser.). (Illus.). 88p. (Orig.). Date not set. pap. 6.95 (*0-948636-83-1*, 6831, Pub. by Natl Mus Scotland) A Schwartz & Co.

Leaving Siam. Kristi Hart. 16p. 1984. pap. 1.25 (*1-880649-13-6*) Writ Ctr Pr.

Leaving Small's Hotel. Eric Kraft. LC 98-5725. 336p. 1998. text 23.00 (*0-312-18689-4*) St Martin.

Leaving Small's Hotel. Eric Kraft. 352p. 1999. pap. 14.00 (*0-312-20660-7*, Picador USA) St Martin.

Leaving Summer. Donal Harding. LC 95-17566. 192p. (YA). (gr. 5 up). 1996. 15.00 (*0-688-13893-4*, Wm Morrow) Morrow Avon.

***Leaving Summer.** Donal Harding. 1998. 9.09 (*0-606-13566-9*, Pub. by Turtleback) Demco.

***Leaving Summer.** Donald Harding. 192p. (J). (gr. 3-7). 1998. pap. 3.99 (*0-380-72466-9*, Avon Bks) Morrow Avon.

Leaving the Adventist Ministry. Peter H. Ballis. LC 98-33607. (Religion in the Age of Transformation Ser.). 256p. 1999. 59.95 (*0-275-96229-6*, Praeger Pubs) Greenwood.

Leaving the Bench: Supreme Court Justices at the End. David N. Atkinson. LC 98-54752. (Illus.). 264p. 1999. 29.95 (*0-7006-0946-6*) U Pr of KS.

***Leaving the Bench: Supreme Court Justices at the End.** David N. Atkinson. 2000. pap. 16.95 (*0-7006-1058-8*) U Pr of KS.

Leaving the Body. D. Scott Rogo. 204p. 1983. per. 10.00 (*0-671-76394-6*) S&S Trade Pap.

Leaving the Cave: Evolutionary Naturalism in Social-Scientific Thought. Pat D. Hutcheon. xvi, 504p. (C). 1996. pap. 29.95 (*0-88920-279-6*) W Laurier U Pr.

Leaving the Comfort Zone. Terry Crist. 47p. 1991. pap. 5.99 (*0-88368-221-4*) Whitaker Hse.

Leaving the Comfort Zone: A Call to Cutting Edge Christianity. Terry M. Crist, Jr. Ed. by Jimmy Peacock. (Illus.). 150p. (Orig.). (C). 1990. pap. 5.95 (*0-9623768-4-1*) SpiritBuilder.

Leaving the Cradle: Human Exploration of Space in the 21st Century, 28th Goddard Memorial Symposium, Mar. 14-16, 1990, Washington, D.C. Ed. by Thomas O. Paine. LC 57-43769. (Science & Technology Ser.: Vol. 78). (Illus.). 348p. 1991. 70.00 (*0-87703-336-6*, Am Astronaut Soc); pap. 55.00 (*0-87703-337-4*, Am Astronaut Soc) Univelt Inc.

Leaving the Door Open: Poems. David Ignatow. LC 83-20237. 89p. (Orig.). 1984. pap. 12.95 (*0-935296-51-4*, Pub. by Sheep Meadow) U Pr of New Eng.

Leaving the Enchanted Forest: The Path from Relationship Addiction. Stephanie Covington. LC 88-45130. 208p. 1988. pap. 14.00 (*0-06-250163-1*, Perennial) HarperTrade.

Leaving the Fold: A Guide for Former Fundamentalists & Others Leaving Their Religion. Marlene Winell. LC 93-84713. 312p. 1994. pap. 13.95 (*1-879237-51-2*) New Harbinger.

***Leaving the Fold: Candid Conversations with Inactive Mormons.** James W. Ure. LC 99-36057. 268p. 1999. pap. 19.95 (*1-56085-134-1*) Signature Bks.

Leaving the Fold: Testimonies of Former Fundamentalists. Edward T. Babinski. LC 94-26945. (Illus.). 462p. (C). 1995. 33.95 (*0-87975-907-0*) Prometheus Bks.

Leaving the Folks Home. Phil Richards. Date not set. pap. 13.00 (*0-06-093039-X*) HarpC.

Leaving the House. Gray Burr. (Juniper Bks.: No. 57). 26p. (Orig.). 1993. pap. 8.00 (*1-55780-120-7*) Juniper Pr ME.

Leaving the Land. Douglas Unger. LC 95-10945. v, 277p. (C). 1995. pap. 12.00 (*0-8032-9560-X*, Bison Books) U of Nebr Pr.

Leaving the Land Behind: Struggles for Land Reform in U.S. Federal Policy, 1933-1965. Jess Gilbert & Alice O'Connor. (LTC Paper Ser.: Vol. 156). iii, 17p. (C). 1996. pap. 4.00 (*0-934519-74-9*, LTC156) U of Wis Land.

Leaving the Life. Ann E. Menasche. 1997. pap. 17.99 (*0-906500-53-2*, Pub. by Onlywomen Pr) LPC InBook.

Leaving the Light On see **Remedios Caseros**

Leaving the Light On: Building the Memories That Will Draw Kids Home. Gary Smalley & John Trent. 196p. 1994. pap. 12.99 (*0-88070-840-9*, Multnomah Bks) Multnomah Pubs.

Leaving the Military & Landing on Your Feet. Steven L. Cornelius. LC 93-28085. (Illus.). 144p. 1993. pap. 14.95 (*0-942963-38-5*) Distinctive Pub.

Leaving the Twentieth Century: Ideas & Visions of New Musics. Ed. by Frank Denyer & Leigh Landy. (Contemporary Music Review Ser.). 165p. 1997. pap. text 28.00 (*90-5702-104-8*, Harwood Acad Pubs) Gordon & Breach.

Leaving Tracks. Paul B. McCoy. 128p. 1998. pap. 7.95 (*1-56167-466-4*) Am Literary Pr.

Leaving Vietnam: The Journey of Tuan Ngo, a Boat Boy. Sarah S. Kilborne. LC 97-15061. (Illus.). 48p. (J). (gr. 4-6). 1999. pr. 3.99 (*0-689-80797-X*) Aladdin.

Leaving Vietnam: The Journey of Tuan Ngo, a Boat Boy. Sarah S. Kilborne. LC 97-15061. (Illus.). 48p. (J). (gr. 1-4). 1999. 15.00 (*0-689-80798-8*) S&S Childrens.

Leaving Word. David Emmons. Ed. by Vi Gale. LC 78-54881. (First Bk.). (Illus.). 1978. pap. 5.00 (*0-915986-12-4*) Prescott St Pr.

Leaving Word. limited ed. David Emmons. Ed. by Vi Gale. LC 78-54881. (First Bk.). (Illus.). 1978. 20.00 (*0-915986-11-6*) Prescott St Pr.

Leaving Xaia. D. Nurkse. LC 98-75586. 77p. 2000. pap. 13.95 (*1-884800-26-2*, Pub. by Four Way Bks) SPD-Small Pr Dist.

Leaving Yesterday Behind. B. Hines. 1997. pap. 9.99 (*1-85792-313-8*, Pub. by Christian Focus) Spring Arbor Dist.

Leaving Your Mark. 2nd ed. Franklin H. Ernst, Jr. 1973. pap. 4.95 (*0-916944-05-0*) Addressoset.

Leaving Yuba City: New & Selected Poems. Chitra Banerjee Divakaruni. LC 97-6308. 128p. 1997. pap. 13.95 (*0-385-48854-8*, Anchor NY) Doubleday.

Leaving Yuba City: Poems. Chitra Banerjee Divakaruni. 1997. pap. 12.95 (*0-614-27477-X*, Anchor NY) Doubleday.

Leavings. P. D. Cacek. LC 97-68713. 270p. 1997. mass mkt. 5.99 (*1-889120-10-3*) StarsEnd Creations.

Leavings. Edmund Miller. (C). 1995. pap. text 5.00 (*1-878173-41-3*) Birnham Wood.

Leavings: Poems from Hollywood. Mark Dunster. 11p. 1998. pap. 5.00 (*0-89642-520-7*) Linden Pubs.

Leavitt Site: A Parkhill Phase Paleo-Indian Occupation in Central Michigan. Michael J. Shott. LC 92-42187. (Memoirs Ser.: No. 25). xii, 144p. (Orig.). 1993. pap. 20.00 (*0-915703-32-7*) U Mich Mus Anthro.

Lebanese & the World: A Century of Emigration. Ed. by Albert H. Hourani & Nadim Shehadi. 300p. 1993. text 79.50 (*1-85043-303-8*, Pub. by I B T) St Martin.

Lebanese Conflict: Looking Inward. Latif Abul-Husn. LC 97-36617. (Canberra Studies on Peace). 174p. 1997. 42.00 (*1-55587-665-X*) L Rienner.

Lebanese Cookery: An Easy Way. Isabelle David. LC 77-539. (Illus.). 160p. 1982. 8.95 (*0-9607824-0-0*) GaryDavid Prods.

Lebanese Cooking. (Illus.). 64p. 1999. pap. 1.95 (*3-8290-1611-5*) Konemann.

Lebanese Cooking. Wendy Veale. 128p. 1992. 12.98 (*1-55521-779-6*) Bk Sales Inc.

Lebanese Cuisine see **Al Lobnani**

Lebanese Cuisine. Helou. LC 98-13135. 1998. pap. 14.95 (*0-312-18735-1*) St Martin.

Lebanese Cuisine. 12th rev. ed. Madelain Farah. (Illus.). 160p. Date not set. pap. 10.95 (*0-9603050-2-5*); spiral bd. 12.95 (*0-9603050-1-7*) Farahs Lebanese Cuisine.

Lebanese Cuisine: Meals in Minutes. 12th ed. Madelain Farah. (Illus.). 160p. Date not set. spiral bd. 8.95 (*0-9603050-3-3*) Farahs Lebanese Cuisine.

Lebanese Legal System, 2 vols. Ed. by Antoine E. El-Gemayel. 886p. 1986. 115.00 (*90-411-0990-0*) Kluwer Law Intl.

Lebanese Legal System, 2 vols. Ed. by Antoine Elias El-Gemayel. LC 84-81785. 886p. 1985. 241.50 (*0-935328-28-9*) Intl Law Inst.

Lebanese Mountain Cookery. 2nd ed. Mary L. Hamady. (Illus.). 288p. 1987. pap. 19.95 (*1-56792-020-9*) Godine.

Lebanese Prophets of New York. Nadeem N. Naimy. 112p. 1986. text 19.95 (*0-8156-6073-1*, Pub. by Am U Beirut) Syracuse U Pr.

Lebanese Traders in Sierra Leone. H. L. Van Der Laan. (Change & Continuity in Africa Ser.). (Illus.). 386p. (Orig.). 1975. pap. text 42.35 (*90-279-7881-6*) Mouton.

Lebanese Village: An Old Culture in a New Era. George G. Murr. (Illus.). 276p. 1987. 24.95 (*0-86685-419-3*, LDL4193, Pub. by Librairie du Liban) Intl Bk Ctr.

Lebanon see **Fiesta 2!**

Lebanon. Carole Cadwallader & Anna Sutton. (Travellers Survival Kit Ser.). 256p. 1999. pap. 18.95 (*1-85458-217-8*, Pub. by Vac Wrk Pubns) Seven Hills Bk.

Lebanon. Charles Winslow. (Illus.). 360p. (C). 1996. 90.00 (*0-415-14403-5*) Routledge.

Lebanon. 2nd rev. ed. C. H. Bleaney. LC 92-190447. (World Bibliographical Ser.). 264p. 1992. lib. bdg. 84.00 (*1-85109-150-5*) ABC-CLIO.

Lebanon see **Cultures of the World - Group 13**

Lebanon: A Country Study. 3rd ed. Ed. by Thomas Collelo. LC 88-600488. (Area Handbook Ser.). (Illus.). 308p. 1989. text 20.00 (*0-16-001731-9*, S/N 008-020-011) USGPO.

***Lebanon: A Country Study Guide.** Global Investment & Business Center, Inc. Staff. (World Country Study Guides Library: Vol. 95). (Illus.). 350p. 2000. pap. 59.00 (*0-7397-2393-6*) Intl Business Pubns.

Lebanon: A History of Conflict & Consensus. Ed. by Nadim Shehadi & Dana Haffar-Mills. 352p. 1993. text 69.50 (*1-85043-119-1*, Pub. by I B T) St Martin.

Lebanon: A Journey of Beauty. Photos by Samer Al-Jamal. (Illus.). 188p. 1994. 49.95 (*0-9642784-0-5*) Cedar Creative.

Lebanon: A New Era. P. Moore. 1997. 170.00 (*1-85564-547-5*, Pub. by Euromoney) Am Educ Systs.

Lebanon: A State of Siege, 1975-1984. 2nd ed. Antoine J. Abraham. LC 85-51483. 69p. (C). 1989. pap. text 16.00 (*0-932269-21-4*) Wyndham Hall.

Lebanon: Bridge Between East & West. Doris M. Abood. LC 73-84565. (Illus.). 40p. (J). (gr. 5-10). 1973. 3.50 (*0-913228-07-9*) Dillon-Liederbach.

An Asterisk (*) at the beginning of an entry indicates that the title is appearing for the first time.

Lebanon: Major World Nations. Mary Jane Cahill. LC 98-4315. (Major World Nations Ser.). (Illus.). 144p. (YA). (gr. 5 up). 1999. lib. bdg. 19.95 (*0-7910-4981-7*) Chelsea Hse.

Lebanon: New Light in an Ancient Land. Elsa Marston. LC 93-5402. (Illus.). 128p. (YA). (gr. 5 up). 1994. lib. bdg. 14.95 (*0-87518-584-3*, Dillon Silver Burdett) Silver Burdett Pr.

***Lebanon: The Challenge of Independence.** Eyal Zisser. 2000. text 59.50 (*1-86064-537-2*, Pub. by I B T) St Martin.

Lebanon: The Politics of Revolving Doors, 114. Wedi D. Haddad. (Washington Papers: Vol. XIII, No. 114). 172p. 1985. 49.95 (*0-275-90112-2*, C0112, Praeger Pubs) Greenwood.

Lebanon: Three Centuries in a Connecticut Hilltop Town. George M. Milne. (Illus.). 287p. 1996. reprint ed. lib. bdg. 39.00 (*0-8328-4984-7*) Higginson Bk Co.

Lebanon - A Country Study Guide: Basic Information for Research & Pleasure. Global Investment Center, USA Staff. (World Country Study Guide Library: Vol. 95). (Illus.). 350p. 1999. pap. 59.00 (*0-7397-1492-9*) Intl Business Pubns.

Lebanon & Arabism. Raghid El-Solh. 316p. 1999. text. write for info. (*1-86064-051-6*) St Martin.

Lebanon & Israel: Role Play Peacegames. David W. Felder. (Illus.). 48p. 1996. pap. text 8.95 (*0-910959-52-8*, B&G 10C) Wellington Pr.

Lebanon & Phoenicia - Ancient Texts Illustrating Their Physical Geography & Native Industries Vol. 1: The Physical Setting & the Forest. John P. Brown. 1969. pap. 29.95 (*0-8156-6090-1*, Pub. by Am U Beirut) Syracuse U Pr.

Lebanon Business & Investment Opportunities Yearbook, 1998: Business, Investment, Export-Import. Russian Information & Business Center, Inc. Staff. (Business & Investment Opportunities Library, '98). (Illus.). 1998. pap. 99.00 (*1-57751-993-0*) Intl Business Pubns.

***Lebanon Business Intelligence Report, 190 vols.** Global Investment & Business Center, Inc. Staff. (World Business Intelligence Library: Vol. 95). (Illus.). 350p. 2000. pap. 99.95 (*0-7397-2593-9*) Intl Business Pubns.

***Lebanon Business Law Handbook, 190 vols.** Global Investment & Business Center, Inc. Staff. (Global Business Law Handbooks Library: Vol. 95). (Illus.). 350p. 2000. pap. 99.95 (*0-7397-1992-0*) Intl Business Pubns.

***Lebanon Business Opportunity Yearbook.** Global Investment & Business Center, Inc. Staff. (Global Business Opportunity Yearbooks Library: Vol. 95). (Illus.). 2000. pap. 99.95 (*0-7397-2193-3*) Intl Business Pubns.

***Lebanon Business Opportunity Yearbook: Export-Import, Investment & Business Opportunities.** International Business Publications, U. S. A. Staff & Global Investment Center, U. S. A. Staff. (Global Business Opportunity Yearbooks Library: Vol. 95). (Illus.). 350p. 1999. pap. 99.95 (*0-7397-1293-4*) Intl Business Pubns.

***Lebanon Foreign Policy & Government Guide.** Global Investment & Business Center, Inc. Staff. (World Foreign Policy & Government Library: Vol. 91). (Illus.). 350p. 1999. pap. 99.00 (*0-7397-3589-6*) Intl Business Pubns.

***Lebanon Foreign Policy & Government Guide.** Global Investment & Business Center, Inc. Staff. (World Foreign Policy & Government Library: Vol. 91). (Illus.). 350p. 2000. pap. 99.95 (*0-7397-3793-7*) Intl Business Pubns.

***Lebanon Government & Business Contacts Handbook: Strategic Government & Business Contacts for Conducting succesful Business, Export-Import & Investment Activity, 110.** International Business Publications, USA Staff & Global Investment Center, USA Staff. (World Export-Import & Business Library: 50). (Illus.). 250p. 2000. pap. 99.95 (*0-7397-6089-0*) Intl Business Pubns.

Lebanon, Improbable Nation: A Study in Political Development. Leila Meo. LC 75-46621. 246p. 1976. reprint ed. lib. bdg. 65.00 (*0-8371-8727-3*, MELE, Greenwood Pr) Greenwood.

Lebanon in Crisis: Participants & Issues. Ed. by P. Edward Haley & Lewis W. Snider. (C). 1979. text 17.95 (*0-8156-2210-4*) Syracuse U Pr.

Lebanon in Pictures. rev. ed. Ed. by Lerner Publications, Department of Geography Staff. (Visual Geography Ser.). (Illus.). 64p. (YA). (gr. 5 up). 1992. lib. bdg. 19.93 (*0-8225-1832-5*, Lerner Publctns) Lerner Pub.

Lebanon in Strife: Student Preludes to the Civil War. Halim I. Barakat. LC 76-50046. (Modern Middle East Ser.: No. 2). 256p. reprint ed. pap. 79.40 (*0-8357-7724-3*, 203608100002) Bks Demand.

Lebanon in Turmoil: Syria & the Powers in 1860. Abkariyus Iskandar. Tr. by J. F. Scheltema. LC 78-63551. (Yale Oriental Series: Researches: No. 7). 1979. reprint ed. 30.00 (*0-404-60277-0*) AMS Pr.

***Lebanon Investment & Business Guide.** Global Investment & Business Center, Inc. Staff. (Global Investment & Business Guide Library: Vol. 95). (Illus.). 2000. pap. 99.95 (*0-7397-1793-6*) Intl Business Pubns.

Lebanon Investment & Business Guide: Economy, Export-Import, Business & Investment Climate, Business Contacts. Contrib. by Russian Information & Business Center, Inc. Staff. (Russia, NIS & Emerging Markets Investment & Business Library-98). (Illus.). 350p. 1998. pap. 99.00 (*1-57751-915-9*) Intl Business Pubns.

***Lebanon Investment & Business Guide: Export-Import, Investment & Business Opportunities.** International Business Publications, USA Staff & Global Investment Center, USA Staff. (World Investment & Business Guide Library-99: Vol. 95). (Illus.). 350p. 1999. pap. 99.95 (*0-7397-0290-4*) Intl Business Pubns.

Lebanon, New Hampshire in Pictures, Vol. 1. Robert H. Leavitt. LC 97-61675. (Illus.). x, 899p. 1997. write for info. (*0-9660069-0-9*) Whitman Communs.

Lebanon on Hold. Rosemary Hollis & Nadim Shehadi. LC 97-115494. xii, 94 p. 1996. write for info. (*1-86203-020-0*) Brookings.

Lebanon, 1761-1994: The Evolution of a Resilient New Hampshire City. Roger Carroll. LC 94-24652. (Illus.). 320p. 1994. 38.00 (*0-914659-71-5*) Phoenix Pub.

Lebanon, the Land & the Lady. Henri Jalabert. LC 66-6108. 404p. reprint ed. pap. 125.30 (*0-608-16162-4*, 201461700096) Bks Demand.

Lebanon Travellers Survival Kit. (Travellers Survival Kit Guides Ser.). 256p. (Orig.). 1997. pap. 17.95 (*1-85458-147-3*, Pub. by Vac Wrk Pubns) Seven Hills Bk.

Lebanon Vital Records, to the Year 1892: Volume I, Births; Volume III, Deaths. Ed. by George W. Chamberlain. (Illus.). 317p. 1997. reprint ed. pap. 39.00 (*0-8328-5865-X*) Higginson Bk Co.

Lebanon War. A. J. Abraham. LC 95-30698. 216p. 1996. 57.95 (*0-275-95389-0*, Praeger Pubs) Greenwood.

Lebanon's Predicament. Samir Khalaf. LC 86-17175. (Illus.). 328p. 1988. text 61.50 (*0-231-06378-4*) Col U Pr.

***Lebanons Quest: The Search for a National Identity 1926-39.** Meir Zamir. 2000. pap. 22.50 (*1-86064-553-4*) I B T.

Lebanons Quest, the Road to Statehood 1929-1939. Zamir. LC 97-169698. 288p. 1998. text 65.00 (*1-86064-107-5*, Pub. by I B T) St Martin.

Lebanta le Matheba: The Adventure of the Speckled Bank in Sotho. Arthur Conan Doyle. Tr. by Trilby Kent.Tr. of Adventure of the Speckled Band. 32p. 1997. 8.00 (*1-55246-018-5*) Battered Silicon.

Lebbeus Woods. 1992. 45.00 (*0-312-08110-3*) St Martin.

Lebbeus Woods. Lebbeus Woods et al. (Architectural Monographs). (Illus.). 144p. 1992. pap. 38.00 (*1-85490-149-4*) Academy Ed UK.

Lebbeus Woods. Lebbeus Woods et al. (Architectural Monographs). (Illus.). 144p. 1992. 55.00 (*1-85490-148-6*, Pub. by Wiley) Wiley.

Leben- und Sterbenkonnen: Gedanken zur Sterbebegleitung und zur Selbstbestimmung der Person. 2nd ed. R. Harri Wettstein. (GER.). 875p. 1997. 72.95 (*3-906757-25-0*, Pub. by P Lang) P Lang Pubng.

Leben Aus Dem Wort: Beitrage Zum Alten Walter Dietrich. Martin A. Klopfenstein. (Beitrage zur Erforschung des Alten Testaments & Antiken Judentums Ser.: Bd. 40). (GER.). 354p. 1996. 47.95 (*3-906756-65-3*, Pub. by P Lang) P Lang Pubng.

Leben Aus der Schrift Verstehen. Johannes Rutsche. 480p. 1999. 61.95 (*3-906761-83-5*) P Lang.

Leben der Frau von Wallenrodt in Briefen An Einen Freund, 2 vols. Johanna I. Von Wallenrodt. (Fruhe Frauenliteratur in Deutschland Ser.: Bd. 12, 1 u. 12, 2). (GER.). 1278p. 1992. reprint ed. write for info. (*3-487-09605-6*) G Olms Pubs.

Leben der Wolga: Zugleich eine Einfuhrung in die Flussbiologie. Arvid Behning. (Binnengewaesser Ser.: Band V). (GER., Illus.). vi, 162p. 1928. 25.00 (*3-510-40705-9*, Pub. by E Schweizerbartsche) Balogh.

Leben des Galilei. 2nd ed. Bertolt Brecht. Ed. by H. F. Brookes & C. E. Fraenkel. 204p. (Orig.). (C). 1995. pap. text 13.00 (*0-435-38123-7*, 38123) Heinemann.

Leben im Wassertropfen (Life in a Waterdrop) Mikroflora und Mikrofauna des Suesswassers - Ein Bestimmungsbuch (Microscopic Freshwater Flora & Fauna - An Identification Book) H. Streble & D. Krauter. (Kosmos Naturfuehrer (Nature Guides) Ser.). (GER., Illus.). 399p. 1988. 47.00 (*3-440-05909-X*, Pub. by Franckh-Kosmos) Balogh.

Leben im Wassertropfen. Mikroflora und Mikrofauna des Suesswassers: Ein Bestimmungsbuch. Heinz Streble & Dieter Krauter. (GER., Illus.). 336p. 1987. text 35.00 (*3-440-05535-3*) Lubrecht & Cramer.

Leben Jesu Nach Judischen Quellen. Samuel Krauss. (GER.). 310p. 1994. reprint ed. write for info. (*3-487-06237-2*) G Olms Pubs.

Leben, Leib & Liturgie: Die Praktische Theologie Wilhelm Staehlins. Michael Meyer-Blanck. (Arbeiten zur Praktischen Theologie Ser.: Vol. 6). (GER.). xiv, 465p. (C). 1994. lib. bdg. 152.35 (*3-11-014364-X*) De Gruyter.

Leben mit Pferden: Ein Beitrag zur Geschichte der Pferdezucht. Siegfried Lehndorff. (GER., Illus.). 439p. 1956. write for info. (*3-487-08126-1*) G Olms Pubs.

Leben Schleiermachers, 2 vols. Incl. Vol. 2. Schleiermacher's System als Philosophie und Theologie., **2 vols. in 1** Ed. by Martin Redeker. lxxx, 811p. 1966. 143.00 (*3-11-001266-9*); Vol. 1, Pt. 1. 1768-1802. 3rd ed. Ed. by Martin Redeker. xlvi, 567p. 1970. 92.00 (*3-11-006348-4*); Vol. 1, Pt. 2. 1803-1807. Ed. by H. Mulert. xxiv, 251p. 1970. 45.35 (*3-11-006437-5*); (GER.). (C). write for info. (*0-318-51628-4*) De Gruyter.

Leben, Schriften und Philosophie des Plutarch Von Chaeronea. Richard Volkmann. 637p. 1980. reprint ed. write for info. (*3-487-07011-1*) G Olms Pubs.

Leben und die Lehre des Mohammed, 3 vols. Alois Sprenger. ccvi, 1734p. reprint ed. write for info. (*0-318-71567-8*) G Olms Pubs.

Leben und Schicksale des Unbekannten Philosophen Saint-Martin, 3 vols. in 1, Vol. 2. 750p. reprint ed. write for info. (*0-318-71430-2*) G Olms Pubs.

Leben und Werke der Troubadours. Friedrich C. Diez. xvi, 506p. 1965. reprint ed. write for info. (*0-318-71453-1*) G Olms Pubs.

Lebendige Literatur, 3 vols. 3rd ed. Frank G. Ryder & E. Allen McCormick. LC 85-81205. 448p. (C). 1985. pap. 41.56 (*0-395-35959-7*) HM.

Lebendige Literatur: Deutsches Lesebuch Fur Anfanger: Advanced. 3rd ed. pap. write for info. (*0-318-69206-6*, 3-49212) HM Soft Schl Col Div.

***Lebendige Uberlieferung: George - Holderlin - Goethe.** Momme Mommsen. Ed. by Katharina Mommsen. (Germanic Studies in America: Bd. 69). x, 406 p. 1999. 56.95 (*3-906760-67-7*, Pub. by P Lang) P Lang Pubng.

Lebendige Zahlen - Fuenf Exkhursionen. W. Borho et al. (Mathematical Miniatures Ser.: Vol. 1). 116p. (C). 1980. 35.50 (*0-8176-1203-3*) Birkhauser.

Lebens-Ansichten des Katers Murr. unabridged ed. E. T. A. Hoffmann. (World Classic Literature Ser.). (GER.). pap. 7.95 (*3-89507-027-0*, Pub. by Bookking Intl) Distribks Inc.

Lebens-Beschreibung. Gotz V. Berlichingen. xvi, 334p. 1977. reprint ed. 80.00 (*3-487-06112-0*) G Olms Pubs.

***Lebensfuhrung: Annaherungen an Einen Ethischen Grundbegriff.** Thomas Laubach. (Forum Interdisziplinare Ethik Ser.). 288p. 1999. 45.95 (*3-631-35504-1*) P Lang Pubng.

Lebensgeschichte und Religiose Sozialisation: Aspekte der Subjektivitat in Arbeiterautobiographien Aus der Zeit der Industrialisierung Bis 1914. Klaus Reuter. (Erfahrung und Theologie Ser.: Bd. 19). (GER.). 230p. 1991. 46.80 (*3-631-43475-8*) P Lang Pubng.

Lebensmut Im Wartesaal: Die Juedischen DP's im Nachkriegsdeutschland. Angelika Koenigseder & Juliane Wetzel. (GER.). 288p. 1994. pap. 17.25 (*3-596-10761-X*, Pub. by Fischer Tasch) Intl Bk Import.

Lebensohl Convention Complete in Contract Bridge. Ron Andersen. 105p. (Orig.). 1987. pap. 6.95 (*0-87643-048-5*) Barclay Bridge.

Lebenswelt der "Neuen Christlichen Kultur" Christsein Nach Dorothee Solle. Christiane Geisthardt. (Europaische Hochschulschriften Ser.: Reihe 23, Bd. 449). (GER.). VI, 268p. 1992. 48.80 (*3-631-44754-X*) P Lang Pubng.

Lebenswelt und Glaube: Kritik der Lebensweltheorie und Ihre Ubertragung Auf Den Gemeindeaufbau. Harald Wagner. (Erfahrung und Theologie Ser.: Bd. 26). (GER.). 251p. 1996. 51.95 (*3-631-49851-9*) P Lang Pubng.

Lebenswelt und Soziale Probleme. Joachim Matthes. (GER.). 561p. 1982. 49.50 (*3-593-32695-7*) Irvington.

Lebenswelt Von Landwirten Vor Dem Hintergrund des Moglichen Einsatzes Von Rekombinanten Wachstumshormonen Rbst Und Rpst in der Eigenen Tierhaltung: Eine Empirische Untersuchung in Sudniedersachsen. Christof Morawitz. (Illus.). 374p. 1998. 56.95 (*3-631-33444-3*) P Lang Pubng.

Lebenuad Wirken Von James Marion Sims. Ingeborg Dittmer. (De Medicinae Rebus Ser.: Vol. 2). (GER.). 120p. 1983. 17.00 (*0-931902-36-3*) Inst Mediaeval Mus.

Leber des Menschen, the Human Liver: Rasterelektonenmikroskopischer Atlas: A Scanning Electron Microscopic Atlas. F. J. Vonnahme. (Illus.). x, 100p. 1993. 71.50 (*3-8055-5585-7*) S Karger.

Leberchirurgie. B. Ringe. 92p. 42.75 (*3-8055-6670-0*) S Karger.

Lebererkrankungen: Praevention, Progressionshemmung, Rehabilitation. Ed. by R. Nilius & K. J. Paquet. (Illus.). viii, 232p. 1995. 143.50 (*3-8055-6171-7*) S Karger.

Lebermoose Europas. 3rd ed. Karl Mueller. Ed. by T. Herzog. (Rabenhorst's Kryptogamenflora Ser.: No. 6/1). (GER., Illus.). 1365p. 1990. reprint ed. text 299.00 (*81-211-0049-6*, Pub. by Mahendra Pal Singh) Lubrecht & Cramer.

Leberschau, Sundenbock, Asasel in Ugarit und Israel: Leberschau und Jahwestatue in Psalm 27, Psalm 74. Oswald Loretz. (Ugaritisch-Biblische Literatur Ser.: Vol. 3). 138p. 1985. pap. text 34.00 (*3-88733-061-7*, Pub. by UGARIT) Eisenbrauns.

Lebesgue Integral. Zoltan Magyar. LC 97-202930. 106p. 1997. pap. 75.00 (*963-05-7346-6*, Pub. by Akade Kiado) St Mut.

Lebesgue Integral. John C. Burkill. (Cambridge Tracts in Mathematics & Mathematical Physics: No. 40). 95p. reprint ed. pap. 27.10 (*0-608-15697-3*, 2031624) Bks Demand.

Lebesgue Integration on Euclidean Space. Frank Jones. (Computer Science-Math Ser.). 608p. (C). 1993. 57.50 (*0-86720-203-3*) Jones & Bartlett.

Lebesgue Measure & Integration: An Introduction. Frank Burk. LC 97-6510. 312p. 1997. 89.95 (*0-471-17978-7*) Wiley.

Lebesgue-Nikodym Theorem for Vector Valued Radon Measures. Erik Thomas. LC 73-22198. (Memoirs Ser.: No. 1/139). 101p. 1974. pap. 17.00 (*0-8218-1839-2*, MEMO/1/139) Am Math.

Lebesgue Theory in the Bidual of C(X) Samuel Kaplan. LC 96-2232. (Memoirs of the American Mathematical Society Ser.: No. 579). 127p. 1996. pap. 37.00 (*0-8218-0463-4*, MEMO/121/579) Am Math.

Lebesgue's Theory of Integration: Its Origins & Development. 3rd ed. Thomas Hawkins. LC 74-8402. xv, 227p. 1975. text 19.95 (*0-8284-0282-5*) Chelsea Pub.

Lebesque Integration. 2nd ed. Soo-Bong Chae. LC 94-27962. 1994. 43.95 (*0-387-94357-9*) Spr-Verlag.

***Lebesque-Stieltjes Integral.** M. Carter & B. Van Brunt. LC 00-20065. (Undergraduate Texts in Mathematics Ser.). (Illus.). 232p. 2000. 44.95 (*0-387-95012-5*) Spr-Verlag.

***Lebialem Issues & Challenges at Century End.** Ed. by Fuankem Achankeng & John Fonjia Nkemnji. 101p. 1999. pap. text 10.00 (*0-9663613-6-9*) Nkemnji Global.

***Lebialem Story.** M. N. F. Ashu. 135p. 1999. pap. text 20.00 (*0-9663613-1-8*) Nkemnji Global.

Le/Bleu du Ciel see Blue of Noon

LeBoeuf's Home Health Care Handbook: All You Need to Become a Caregiver in Your Home. Gene LeBoeuf. (Illus.). 1996. pap. 24.95 (*0-9648852-0-4*) LeBoeuf & Assocs.

Le/Bouc Emissaire see Scapegoat

LEC Rat: A New Model for Hepatitis & Liver Cancer. Ed. by M. Mori et al. (Illus.). 360p. 1992. 212.00 (*0-387-70079-X*) Spr-Verlag.

Leccionario Edicion Hispanoamerica: Domingos y Solemnidades. (SPA.). 784p. 1994. 98.00 (*0-8146-2347-6*) Liturgical Pr.

Leccionario Edicion Hispanoamerica: Ferial. (SPA.). 632p. 1994. 98.00 (*0-8146-2348-4*) Liturgical Pr.

Leccionario Edicion Hispanoamerica: Santos y Votivas. (SPA.). 736p. 1995. 98.00 (*0-8146-2349-2*) Liturgical Pr.

Lecciones Acerca de la Verdad. H. Emilie Cady. 195p. 1986. pap. 6.95 (*0-87159-081-6*) Unity Bks.

***Lecciones Biblicas Creativas para Jovenes Sobre Juan: Encuentros Con Jesus.** Janice Ashcraft. (SPA.). 2000. pap. 10.99 (*0-8297-2888-0*) Vida Pubs.

***Lecciones Biblicas Creativas para Jovenes Sobre Romanos: Fe al Rojo Vivo!** Chap Clark. (SPA.). 2000. pap. 10.99 (*0-8297-2887-2*) Vida Pubs.

Lecciones Biblicas Especiales para la Escuela Dominical. Contrib. by Lois Keffer. Orig. Title: Selections from Sunday School Specials & Sunday School Specials 2. (SPA.). (J). (ps-6). 1996. pap. 10.99 incl. VHS (*1-55945-669-8*) Group Pub.

Lecciones de Derecho de Familia. Emilio Menendez. LC 76-961. (SPA.). 393p. (Orig.). (C). 1981. 9.60 (*0-8477-3018-2*); pap. 7.50 (*0-8477-3007-7*) U of PR Pr.

Lecciones de la Verdad, Nivel Uno, 1. Witness Lee.Tr. of Truth Lessons, Level One, Volume 3. (SPA.). 184p. 1986. per. 7.25 (*0-87083-242-5*, 15-032-002) Living Stream Ministry.

Lecciones de la Verdad, Nivel Uno, 2. Witness Lee.Tr. of Truth Lessons, Level One, Volume 3. (SPA.). 215p. 1987. per. 8.00 (*0-87083-281-6*, 15033002) Living Stream Ministry.

Lecciones de la Verdad, Nivel Uno, 3. Witness Lee.Tr. of Truth Lessons, Level One, Volume 3. (SPA.). 140p. 1988. per. 6.50 (*0-87083-297-2*, 15-034-002) Living Stream Ministry.

Lecciones de la verdad, nivel uno, Vol. 2. Witness Lee.Tr. of Truth Lessons, Level One, Volume 2. (SPA.). 215p. 1987. per. 8.50 (*0-87083-280-8*) Living Stream Ministry.

Lecciones de Teoria General del Derecho. Emilio Menendez. LC 79-16559. (SPA.). 262p. 1980. pap. text 7.20 (*0-8477-3017-4*) U of PR Pr.

Lecciones de Vida, 2. Witness Lee.Tr. of Life Lessons. (SPA.). 111p. 1987. per. 5.75 (*0-87083-294-8*, 15-011-002) Living Stream Ministry.

Lecciones de Vida, 3. Witness Lee.Tr. of Life Lessons. (SPA.). 95p. 1987. per. 5.50 (*0-87083-295-6*, 15-012-002) Living Stream Ministry.

Lecciones de Vida, 4. Witness Lee.Tr. of Life Lessons. (SPA.). 91p. 1987. per. 5.50 (*0-87083-296-4*, 15-013-002) Living Stream Ministry.

Lecciones de Vida, Vol. 1. Witness Lee.Tr. of Life Lessons. (SPA.). 85p. 1987. per. 5.25 (*0-87083-285-9*, 15-010-002) Living Stream Ministry.

Lecciones para Nuevo Creyentes: Edicion Juvenil. Carlos G. Sanchez & Anthony Echeverry.Tr. of Lessons for New Believers. (SPA.). 64p. 1997. pap. text 2.99 (*0-311-13856-X*) Casa Bautista.

Lecciones Practicas Para el Canto: Practical Lessons in Singing. James C. McKinney. Ed. by Annette H. Herrington. Tr. by Bruce Muskrat from ENG. (SPA., Illus.). 96p. (Orig.). 1991. pap. 6.50 (*0-311-32405-3*) Casa Bautista.

Lecciones Solemnes a las Obras de Don Luis de Gongora y Argote. Jose P. De Salas y Tovara. (Textos y Estudios Clasicos De las Literaturas Hispanicas Ser.). 488p. 1971. reprint ed. write for info. (*3-487-04168-5*) G Olms Pubs.

Lech Lecha-Vayeira see Bereishes-Genesis

Lech Walesa. Tony Kaye. (World Leaders Past & Present Ser.). (Illus.). 120p. (YA). (gr. 5 up). 1989. pap. 8.95 (*0-7910-0689-1*) Chelsea Hse.

Lech Walesa. Caroline E. Lazo. LC 92-39959. (Peacemakers Ser.). (Illus.). 64p. (J). (gr. 4 up). 1993. lib. bdg. 13.95 (*0-87518-525-8*, Dillon Silver Burdett) Silver Burdett Pr.

Lechate Collection & Treatment Systems. Richard K. Miller & Marcia E. Rupnow. LC 90-83891. (Survey on Technology & Markets Ser.: No. 187). 50p. 1991. pap. text 200.00 (*1-55865-211-6*) Future Tech Surveys.

Leche: De la Vaca Al Envase (Milk: From Cow to Carton) Aliki.Tr. of Milk: From Cow to Carton. 1996. 9.95 (*84-261-2757-6*) Lectorum Pubns.

La Leche League: At the Crossroads of Medicine, Feminism & Religion. Jule DeJager Ward. LC 99-12921. (Illus.). 272p. 2000. pap. 15.95 (*0-8078-4791-7*) U of NC Pr.

Leche League: At the Crossroads of Medicine, Feminism, & Religion. Jule DeJager Ward. LC 99-12921. (Illus.). 272p. 2000. lib. bdg. 39.95 (*0-8078-2509-3*) U of NC Pr.

***Leche-Vitrines.** Peter Loewy. (Illus.). 96p. 2000. 25.00 (*3-934296-08-4*) G Kehayoff.

Le/Chemin de France see Flight to France

Le/Chemin du Labyrinthe see Way to the Labyrinth: Memories of East & West

Lechera y Su Cubeta. Dorothy S. Bishop et al.Tr. of Milkmaid & Her Pail. (SPA., Illus.). 64p. 6.95 (*0-8442-7250-7*, 72507) NTC Contemp Pub Co.

Lechera y Su Cubeta (The Milkmaid & Her Pail) Eugenia De Hoogh. (Fabulas Bilingues Ser.). (ENG & SPA.). (J). 1987. 10.15 (*0-606-01305-9*, Pub. by Turtleback) Demco.

Lecherous Professor: Sexual Harassment on Campus. 2nd ed. Billie W. Dziech & Linda Weiner. 288p. 1990. pap. text 15.95 (*0-252-06118-7*) U of Ill Pr.

Lechmere: Hanley Castle & the House of Lechmere. (Illus.). 79p. 1993. reprint ed. pap. 16.00 (*0-8328-3696-6*); reprint ed. lib. bdg. 26.00 (*0-8328-3695-8*) Higginson Bk Co.

L

Lechner's Comprehensive 4 Language Dictionary: Paper - Plastics - Aluminum Foil - Converting Terms. Ed. by Benjamin Lechner. (FRE, GER & SPA.). 240p. 1994. 49.95 (*1-56676-265-0*, 762650) Technomic.
Lechucitas: Owl Babies. Martin Waddell. (SPA., Illus.). 14p. (J). (ps-3). 1995. 13.95 (*0-88272-137-2*) Santillana.
Lechuzas. Lynn M. Stone. (Aves Ser.).Tr. of Owls. 24p. (J). (gr. k-4). 1994. lib. bdg. 10.95 (*0-86593-198-4*) Rourke Corp.
Lecideicole Ascomyceten - Eine Revision der Obligat Lichenicolen Ascomyceten Auf Lecideoiden Flechten. Dagmar Triebel. Ed. by Volkmar Wirth et al. (Bibliotheca Lichenologica: Vol. 35). (GER., Illus.). 278p. 1989. 53.00 (*3-443-58014-9*, Pub. by Gebruder Borntraeger) Balogh.
Lecithin: Technological, Biological, & Therapeutic Aspects. Ed. by Israel Hanin & G. B. Ansell. LC 87-32811. (Advances in Behavioral Biology Ser.: Vol. 33). (Illus.). 206p. 1988. 65.00 (*0-306-42786-9*, Plenum Trade) Perseus Pubng.
Lecithin & Health: Featuring Phosphatidylcholine & Serine. Frank Outhoefer. LC 99-212483. (Illus.). 84p. 1998. pap. 8.95 (*1-890612-03-0*, 58604) Vital Health.
Lecithin Book. Carlson Wade. LC 80-82319. 128p. (Orig.). 1980. pap. 3.95 (*0-87983-226-6*, 32266K, Keats Publng) NTC Contemp Pub Co.
Lecithins. Ed. by B. F. Szuhaj & Gary R. List. 394p. 1985. 40.00 (*0-935315-09-8*) Am Oil Chemists.
Lecithins: Sources, Manufacture, Uses. Ed. by B. F. Szuhaj. 294p. 1989. 80.00 (*0-935315-27-6*) Am Oil Chemists.
L'Ecole Normale Superieure & the Third Republic. Robert J. Smith. LC 81-8810. 201p. (C). 1981. pap. text 24.95 (*0-87395-541-2*) State U NY Pr.
Lecompton's Well Kept Secret. Florence B. Smith. 145p. 1998. pap. 6.00 (*1-893463-05-2*) F B Smith.
Lecon. write for info. Fr & Eur.
Lecon. Roland Barthes. (FRE.). 1989. pap. 10.95 (*0-7859-2713-1*) Fr & Eur.
Lecon. Eugene Ionesco. (FRE.). 39p. 1954. 9.95 (*0-7859-9260-X*) Fr & Eur.
Lecon de Morale. Paul Eluard. (FRE.). 1981. pap. 10.95 (*0-8288-3855-0*, F100070) Fr & Eur.
Lecon de Morale. Paul Eluard. (Poesie Ser.). (FRE.). 184p. 1949. 9.95 (*2-07-032210-6*) Schoenhof.
Lecon de Sainte-Victoire. Peter Handke. (FRE.). 195p. 1991. pap. 14.95 (*0-7859-2621-6*, 2070384381) Fr & Eur.
Lecons de Clavecin et Principes d'Harmonie. fac. ed. Anton Bemetzrieder. (Monuments of Music & Music Literature in Facsimile, II Ser.: Vol. 18). 1966. lib. bdg. 40.00 (*0-8450-2218-0*) Broude.
Lecons sur l'Histoire de la Philosophie, Vol. 2. Georg Wilhelm Friedrich Hegel. (FRE.). 216p. 1991. pap. 10.95 (*0-7859-3382-4*) Fr & Eur.
Lecons sur l'Histoire de Philosophy, Vol. 1. Georg Wilhelm Friedrich Hegel. (FRE.). 254p. 1990. pap. 10.95 (*0-7859-2247-4*, 2070325814) Fr & Eur.
Lecons sur l'Integration et la Recherche des Fonctions Primitives. 3rd ed. Henri Lebesgue. LC 73-921. (FRE.). 340p. (gr. 12 up). 1973. text 24.95 (*0-8284-0267-1*) Chelsea Pub.
Leconte de Lisle: A Hundred & Twenty Years of Criticism, 1850-1970. Dorothy M. DiOrio. (Romance Monographs: No. 1). 1972. pap. 24.00 (*84-400-5555-2*) Romance.
LeConte History & Genealogy, with Particular Reference to Guillaume LeConte of New Rochelle & New York, & His Descendants. Richard L. Anderson. 1350p. 1992. reprint ed. pap. 159.00 (*0-8328-2433-X*); reprint ed. lib. bdg. 169.00 (*0-685-59664-8*) Higginson Bk Co.
Le/Corps Taoiste see Taoist Body
Lecretius No. IV: De Rerum Natura. Lucretius. Ed. by J. Godwin. (Classical Texts Ser.). 1987. pap. 22.00 (*0-85668-309-4*, Pub. by Aris & Phillips) David Brown.
Lecretius No. VI: De Rerum Natura. Lucretius. Ed. by Godwin. 1991. 59.99 (*0-85668-499-6*, Pub. by Aris & Phillips) David Brown.
Lecretus No. IV: De Rerum Natura. Lucretius. Ed. by J. Godwin. (Classical Texts Ser.). 1987. 59.99 (*0-85668-308-6*, Pub. by Aris & Phillips) David Brown.
Le/Cri de l'homme Africain see African Cry
L'Ecriture et le Reste: The Pensees of Pascal in the Exegetical Tradition of Port-Royal. David Wetsel. LC 81-9610. 256p. reprint ed. pap. 79.40 (*0-608-09896-5*, 206986200006) Bks Demand.
LeCross' How to Play & Win at Blackjack. Herman LeCross. 50p. (Orig.). 1996. 20.00 (*0-937408-75-1*) GMI Pubns Inc.
Lectact ENV-ENV News Yr in Revised. Sauncoenv. (C). 1995. teacher ed. 276.50 (*0-03-013883-3*) Harcourt Coll Pubs.
Lectern Bible with Appocrapha. 1464p. 1997. 500.00 (*0-19-107013-0*) OUP.
Lectero Materialiste de L'evangele de Marc see Materialist Reading of the Gospel of Mark
Lectin Methods & Protocols. Ed. by Jonathan M. Rhodes & Jeremy D. Milton. LC 97-28305. (Methods in Molecular Medicine Ser.: Vol. 9). 650p. 1997. 99.50 (*0-89603-396-1*) Humana.
Lectin-Microorganism Interactions. Ed. by R. J. Doyle & Malcolm Slifkin. (Illus.). 416p. 1994. text 195.00 (*0-8247-9113-4*) Dekker.
Lectins. Nathan Sharon & Halina Lis. 176p. 1989. 42.50 (*0-412-27380-2*) Chapman & Hall.
Lectins: Biomedical Perspectives. Ed. by Arpad Pusztai & Susan Bardocz. 368p. 1994. 99.50 (*0-7484-0177-6*, Pub. by Tay Francis Ltd) Taylor & Francis.
Lectins & Blycobiology. Ed. by H. J. Gabius & S. Gabius. (Illus.). 550p. 1993. 147.95 (*0-387-56211-7*) Spr-Verlag.
Lectins & Cancer. Ed. by H. J. Gabius & S. Gabius. (Illus.). x, 329p. 1991. 111.95 (*0-387-54224-8*) Spr-Verlag.
***Lectins & Pathology.** Ed. by Michel Caron & Annie-Pierre Seve. 216p. 2000. text 95.00 (*90-5702-491-8*, Harwood Acad Pubs) Gordon & Breach.
Lectio Divina: An Ancient Prayer That Is Ever New. Mario Massini. Tr. by Edmund C. Lane from ITA. Orig. Title: Lectio Divina: Preghiera Antica e Nuova. 104p. 1998. mass mkt. 5.95 (*0-8189-0813-0*) Alba.
Lectio Divina: And the Practice of Tersian Prayer. Sam Anthony Morello. LC 94-28368. (Pamphlet on American Writers Ser.). 32p. 1995. pap. 3.50 (*0-935216-24-3*) ICS Pubns.
Lectio Divina: Renewing the Ancient Practice of Praying with the Scriptures. M. Basil Pennington. LC 97-45159. 112p. 1998. pap. 13.95 (*0-8245-1736-9*, Crsrd) Crossroad NY.
Lectio Divina: Preghiera Antica e Nuova see Lectio Divina: An Ancient Prayer That Is Ever New
Lectionary, 3 vols. Geoffrey Chapman. 3500p. 1985. write for info. (*0-318-59520-6*) Harper SF.
Lectionary: Hermeneutics & Homiletics. Fritz West. 150p. (Orig.). Date not set. pap. text 11.95 (*0-8146-2121-X*) Liturgical Pr.
Lectionary Vol. 1: Chapel Edition - Sundays. 1998. 49.95 (*0-8146-2532-0*) Liturgical Pr.
Lectionary-Based Catechesis for Children: A Catechist's Guide. Sylvia DeVillers. LC 94-21261. 176p. 1994. pap. 10.95 (*0-8091-3505-1*) Paulist Pr.
Lectionary-Based Gospel Dramas for Advent, Christmas & Epiphany. Sheila O'Connell-Roussell & Terri Vorndran Nichols. (Illus.). 104p. 1997. pap. 23.95 (*0-88489-485-1*) St Marys.
***Lectionary-Based Gospel Dramas for Lent & the Easter Triduum.** Sheila O'Connell-Roussell et al. 128p. 1999. spiral bd. 29.95 (*0-88489-627-7*) St Marys.
Lectionary for Mass: Ceremonial Edition, Vol. 1. 2000. 98.00 (*0-8146-6177-7*) Liturgical Pr.
Lectionary for Mass: Ceremonial Edition: Sundays - Cycle A. 1998. 98.00 (*0-8146-6175-0*) Liturgical Pr.
Lectionary for Mass: Ceremonial Editor. Standard Order Staff. 1999. 98.00 (*0-8146-6179-3*) Liturgical Pr.
Lectionary for Mass: Classic Edition. Standard Order Staff. 1999. 59.95 (*0-8146-2547-9*) Liturgical Pr.
Lectionary for Mass: Classic Edition: Sundays. 1998. 59.95 (*0-8146-2531-2*) Liturgical Pr.
***Lectionary for Mass: Study Edition.** 592p. 1999. pap. 19.95 (*1-56854-335-2*) Liturgy Tr Pubns.
Lectionary for Mass Vol. I: Ceremonial Edition, Cycle B. 1998. 98.00 (*0-8146-6176-9*) Liturgical Pr.
Lectionary for Mass Vol. II: Chapel. Liturgical Press Staff. 1999. 49.95 (*0-8146-2565-7*) Liturgical Pr.
Lectionary for Mass Vol. II: Classic. abr. ed. Liturgical Press Staff. 1999. 59.95 (*0-8146-2564-9*) Liturgical Pr.
Lectionary for Mass for Sundays, Cycle A. 430p. 1994. 39.95 (*0-8146-6001-0*) Liturgical Pr.
Lectionary for Mass for Sundays, Cycle B. Ed. by Stephen J. Hartdegen. 439p. 1993. 39.95 (*0-8146-6002-9*, M Glazier) Liturgical Pr.
Lectionary for Mass (Sundays) Vol. 1: Study Edition. STUDY Staff. 1328p. 1999. pap. 29.95 (*0-8146-2588-6*) Liturgical Pr.
Lectionary for Masses with Children. 1994. 52.00 (*0-89942-065-6*, 65/02) Catholic Bk Pub.
Lectionary for Masses with Children, 3 vols. Incl. Cycle A, Sundays & Weekdays. 688p. 1994. 34.95 (*0-8146-2261-5*); Cycle B, Sundays & Weekdays. 672p. 1993. 34.95 (*0-8146-2262-3*); Cycle C, Sundays & Weekdays. 672p. 1994. 34.95 (*0-8146-2263-1*); 1994. 99.95 (*0-8146-2279-8*); pap. 95.00 (*0-8146-6141-6*) Liturgical Pr.
Lectionary for Masses with Children, Cycle C. Sean McEntee. 192p. (Orig.). (J). (gr. 2-8). 1988. pap. text 19.95 (*0-89622-385-X*) Twenty-Third.
Lectionary for Masses with Children: Sundays, Year C. Ed. by Elizabeth Hoffman. Tr. by American Bible Society Staff. (Illus.). 1994. 35.00 (*0-929650-74-3*, LEC/CC); pap. 10.00 (*1-56854-003-5*, CLC/SE) Liturgy Tr Pubns.
Lectionary for Masses with Children: Sundays, Year A. Ed. by David A. Lysik. Tr. by American Bible Society Staff. (Illus.). 1995. 35.00 (*0-929650-71-9*, LEC/CA); pap. text 10.00 (*1-56854-000-0*, CLA/SE) Liturgy Tr Pubns.
Lectionary for Masses with Children: Sundays, Year B. Ed. by Elizabeth Hoffman. Tr. by American Bible Society Staff. (Illus.). 291p. 1993. 35.00 (*0-929650-73-5*, LEC/CB); pap. 10.00 (*1-56854-002-7*, CLB/SE) Liturgy Tr Pubns.
Lectionary for Masses with Children: Weekdays. 416p. 1994. 29.95 (*0-8146-6139-4*) Liturgical Pr.
Lectionary for Masses with Children: Weekdays. 416p. 1996. pap., student ed. 11.95 (*0-8146-6147-5*, Pueblo Bks) Liturgical Pr.
Lectionary for Masses with Children: Weekdays. Ed. by Elizabeth Hoffman. Tr. by American Bible Society Staff. (Illus.). 503p. 1993. 40.00 (*0-929650-72-7*, LECCWK) Liturgy Tr Pubns.
Lectionary for Masses with Children: Weekdays. Ed. by Elizabeth Hoffman. Tr. by American Bible Society Staff. (Illus.). 503p. 1993. pap. 10.00 (*1-56854-001-9*, CLWKSE) Liturgy Tr Pubns.
Lectionary for Masses with Children 4 vols. Study Edition. 1994. pap. 37.50 (*0-8146-6148-3*, M Glazier) Liturgical Pr.
Lectionary for Masses with Children Cycle C: Sunday. 288p. 1994. 24.95 (*0-8146-6138-6*, Pueblo Bks) Liturgical Pr.
Lectionary for Masses with Children Cycle C: Sunday. 288p. 1996. pap., student ed. 9.95 (*0-8146-6146-7*, Pueblo Bks) Liturgical Pr.
Lectionary for Masses with Children Cycle A: Sundays. 304p. 1996. pap., student ed. 9.95 (*0-8146-6144-0*, Pueblo Bks) Liturgical Pr.
Lectionary for Masses with Children Cycle A: Sundays. Ed. by Stephen J. Hartdegen. 304p. 1994. 24.95 (*0-8146-6136-X*, Pueblo Bks) Liturgical Pr.
Lectionary for Masses with Children Cycle B: Sunday. 288p. 1993. 24.95 (*0-8146-6137-8*, Pueblo Bks) Liturgical Pr.
Lectionary for Masses with Children Cycle B: Sunday. 288p. 1994. pap., student ed. 9.95 (*0-8146-6145-9*, Pueblo Bks) Liturgical Pr.
Lectionary for Sunday Mass: Chapel Edition. rev. ed. (Illus.). 600p. 1998. 38.00 (*0-89942-031-1*, 35/22) Catholic Bk Pub.
Lectionary for Sunday Mass: Pulpit Size Edition. rev. ed. (Illus.). 600p. 1998. 59.00 (*0-89942-090-7*, 90/22); lthr. 87.00 (*0-89942-091-5*, 90/13) Catholic Bk Pub.
***Lectionary for Sunday Mass Cycle C: Precessional Edition.** Processional Edition Staff. 2000. 59.00 (*0-89942-072-9*) Catholic Bk Pub.
Lectionary for Sunday Mass Processional Edition. 1998. 59.00 (*0-89942-070-2*, 70/22) Catholic Bk Pub.
Lectionary for Sunday Mass-Processional Edition (B) Cycle B: Processional Edition. (Illus.). 682p. 1999. 59.00 (*0-89942-071-0*, 71-22) Catholic Bk Pub.
Lectionary for the Christian People, Cycle B. Ed. by Gordon Lathrop & Gail Ramshaw. 273p. 1992. pap. 17.95 (*0-8146-6081-9*, Pueblo Bks) Liturgical Pr.
Lectionary for Worship: Revised Common Lectionary-Year A. 1995. 19.95 (*0-8066-0194-9*, 3-381) Augsburg Fortress.
Lectionary for Worship: Revised Common Lectionary-Year B. 1996. 19.95 (*0-8066-0195-7*, 3-382) Augsburg Fortress.
Lectionary for Worship: Revised Common Lectionary-Year C. 1997. 19.95 (*0-8066-0196-5*, 3-383) Augsburg Fortress.
Lectionary Index for the Catechism of the Catholic Church. Philip J. McBride. 80p. (Orig.). 1994. pap. 15.00 (*0-89390-325-6*) Resource Pubns.
Lectionary Preaching Workbook. Russell F. Anderson. LC 96-12704. (Series V). 1996. pap., wbk. ed. 34.50 (*0-7880-0821-8*) CSS OH.
Lectionary Preaching Workbook. Russell F. Anderson. LC 96-30030. (Series V, Cycle C: Vol. 3). 362p. 1997. pap. 34.50 (*0-7880-1041-7*) CSS OH.
***Lectionary Preaching Workbook.** Russell F. Anderson. 1998. cd-rom 34.50 (*0-7880-0521-9*); mac hd 34.50 (*0-7880-0523-5*) CSS OH.
Lectionary Preaching Workbook. E. Carver McGriff. 1998. pap., wbk. ed. 42.95 incl. disk (*0-7880-1216-9*) CSS OH.
Lectionary Preaching Workbook. E. Carver McGriff. LC 98-6062. (Series VI). (Illus.). 292p. 1998. pap., wbk. ed. 42.95 (*0-7880-1213-4*) CSS OH.
***Lectionary Preaching Workbook.** E. Carver McGriff. LC 98-6062. (Series VI). 336p. 1999. pap., wbk. ed. 46.50 (*0-7880-1367-X*) CSS OH.
Lectionary Preaching Workbook, Cycle B. John Brokhoff. 1984. pap. 28.75 (*0-89536-645-2*) CSS OH.
Lectionary Preaching Workbook, Series V, Cycle A. Russell F. Anderson. LC 95-13959. 1995. pap., wbk. ed. 34.50 (*0-7880-0520-0*) CSS OH.
Lectionary Preaching Workbook, Vol. III, Pt. A. George M. Bass. 1989. pap., wbk. ed. 39.50 (*1-55673-135-3*, 9860) CSS OH.
Lectionary Preaching Workbook: Revised for Use with Revised Common, Episcopal, Luterhan, & Roman Catholic Lectionaries, Small Version, Series IV, Cycle B. John R. Brokhoff. LC 93-5725. 1993. wbk. ed. 23.95 (*1-55673-624-X*, 9349) CSS OH.
***Lectionary Preaching Workbook: Series VI, Cycle C.** E. Carver McGriff. LC 98-6062. 364p. 2000. pap. 55.50 (*0-7880-1701-2*); disk 55.50 (*0-7880-1702-0*) CSS OH.
Lectionary Preaching Workbook: Small Version, Vol. I. George M. Bass. 1996. wbk. ed. 23.95 (*1-55673-243-0*) CSS OH.
Lectionary Preaching Workbook, II, C, Vol. II, Pt. C. Perry H. Biddle, Jr. (Orig.). 1988. pap., wbk. ed. 39.50 (*1-55673-064-0*, 8861) CSS OH.
Lectionary Psalms. Michel Guimont. 208p. 1998. spiral bd. 29.50 (*1-57999-041-X*, G-4986) GIA Pubns.
***Lectionary Psalms.** Michel Guimont. 1999. 29.50 (*5-550-71966-5*); 15.95 (*5-550-71961-4*); pap. 10.95 (*5-550-71964-9*) Nairi.
Lectionary Scenes: 52 Vignettes in Cycle C. Robert F. Crowley. LC 96-46497. 312p. (Orig.). 1997. pap. 34.50 (*0-7880-1060-3*) CSS OH.
Lectionary Scenes: 57 Vignettes. Robert F. Crowley. (Lectionary Ser.). 1998. pap. 25.95 incl. disk (*0-7880-1276-2*) CSS OH.
Lectionary Scenes: 57 Vignettes. Robert F. Crowley. LC 96-46497. (Lectionary Ser.). 340p. 1998. pap. 25.95 (*0-7880-1273-8*) CSS OH.
***Lectionary Scenes: 58 Vignettes.** Robert Crowley. LC 96-46497. (Lectionary Ser.). 314p. 1999. pap. 25.85 (*0-7880-1373-4*) CSS OH.
Lectionary Series from the Common Lectionary, Series B (RSV) Ed. by Michael L. Sherer. (Orig.). 1987. 19.95 (*0-89536-884-6*, 7870) CSS OH.
Lectionary Series from the Revised Common Lectionary: Cycle C, NRSV. rev. ed. (Orig.). 1994. pap. 22.95 (*0-7880-0091-8*) CSS OH.
Lectionary Series from the Revised Common Lectionary Cycle B. rev. ed. (Lectionary Ser.: Vol. B). 1996. 18.95 (*1-55673-650-9*) CSS OH.
***Lectionary Tales for the Pulpit.** Constance Berg. LC 98-9783. (Series II). 148p. 1999. pap. 13.50 (*0-7880-1370-X*) CSS OH.
Lectionary Tales for the Pulpit. Timothy J. Smith. 1998. pap. 10.95 incl. disk (*0-7880-1220-7*) CSS OH.
Lectionary Tales for the Pulpit. Timothy J. Smith. LC 98-9783. (Series II). 128p. 1998. pap. 10.95 (*0-7880-1217-7*) CSS OH.
Lectionary Tales for the Pulpit. John R. Steward. LC 96-52621. (Series II, Cycle C). 88p. (Orig.). 1997. pap. 11.50 (*0-7880-1056-5*) CSS OH.
Lectionary Tales for the Pulpit, Cycle A. Merle G. Franke. LC 95-14053. 120p. 1995. pap. 14.50 (*0-7880-0527-8*) CSS OH.
Lectionary Tales for the Pulpit: Based upon the Revised Common Lectionary, Cycle C. Richard A. Jensen. 1994. pap. 14.50 (*0-7880-0081-0*) CSS OH.
***Lectionary Tales for the Pulpit: Series III, Cycle C.** Constance Berg. 154p. 2000. pap. 13.95 (*0-7880-1707-1*); disk 13.95 (*0-7880-1708-X*) CSS OH.
Lectionary Tales for the Pulpit: 52 Stories. John Sumwalt & Jo Perry-Sumwalt. LC 96-10535. (Lectionary Ser.). 240p. 1996. pap. 16.95 (*0-7880-0817-X*) CSS OH.
Lectionary Texts, Year C: From the Common Lectionary RSV. Episcopal Church Staff. LC 96-160777. 1978. write for info. (*0-89869-091-9*) Church Pub Inc.
Lectionary Worship Aids. Dallas A. Brauninger. 1998. pap. 16.95 incl. disk (*0-7880-1212-6*) CSS OH.
Lectionary Worship Aids. James R. Wilson. LC 95-14052. (Series IV). 1995. pap. 17.95 (*0-7880-0548-0*) CSS OH.
Lectionary Worship Aids. James R. Wilson. LC 95-14052. (Series IV). 1996. pap. text 17.95 (*0-7880-0813-7*) CSS OH.
Lectionary Worship Aids. James R. Wilson. (Series IV). 1997. pap. text 17.75 (*0-7880-0816-1*) CSS OH.
Lectionary Worship Aids. James R. Wilson. LC 95-14052. (Series IV). 214p. 1997. pap. 18.50 (*0-7880-1024-7*) CSS OH.
Lectionary Worship Aids, Series III, Cycle B. B. David Hostetter. LC 92-29803. 1996. 12.95 (*1-55673-622-3*) CSS OH.
Lectionary Worship Aids: For Use with the Revised Common Lectionary. James R. Wilson. (Series IV). 1997. 18.50 (*0-7880-1025-5*); disk 18.50 (*0-7880-1026-3*) CSS OH.
Lectionary Worship Aids: For Use with the Revised Common Lectionary, Sermon. James R. Wilson. (Series IV). 1997. pap. text 18.50 (*0-7880-1083-2*) CSS OH.
***Lectionary Worship Aids: Series V, Cycle B.** Dallas Brauninger. LC 98-2527. 222p. 1999. pap. 18.50 (*0-7880-1364-5*) CSS OH.
***Lectionary Worship Aids: Series V, Cycle C.** Dallas Brauninger. LC 98-2527. 222p. 2000. pap. 20.50 (*0-7880-1598-2*); disk 20.50 (*0-7880-1599-0*) CSS OH.
Lectionary Worship Aids Series III, Cycle A, Vol. III, Pt. A. B. David Hostetter. 1992. pap. 11.95 (*1-55673-555-3*, 9254) CSS OH.
Lectionary Worship Aids Series III, Cycle A, Vol. 4, Cycle C. B. David Hostetter. LC 92-29803. 1994. pap. 14.50 (*0-7880-0076-4*) CSS OH.
Lectionary Worship Aids Series V, Cycle A. Dallas A. Brauninger. LC 98-2527. 232p. 1998. pap. 16.95 (*0-7880-1209-6*) CSS OH.
Lectionary Worship Workbook. Wayne H. Keller. 1998. pap., wbk. ed. 23.75 (*0-7880-1208-8*) CSS OH.
***Lectionary Worship Workbook: Series II, Cycle B.** Wayne H. Keller. LC 98-6061. 220p. 1999. pap., wbk. ed. 36.50 (*0-7880-1361-0*) CSS OH.
***Lectionary Worship Workbook: Series II, Cycle C.** Wayne H. Keller. LC 98-6061. 238p. 2000. pap. 37.95 (*0-7880-1704-7*); disk 37.95 (*0-7880-1705-5*) CSS OH.
Lectionary Worship Workbook Series II, Cycle A. Wayne H. Keller. LC 98-6061. 1998. pap., wbk. ed. 33.75 (*0-7880-1205-3*) CSS OH.
Lectiones Geometricae. Isaac Barrow. 149p. 1976. reprint ed. 65.00 (*3-487-06089-2*) G Olms Pubs.
Lector's Guide to Biblical Pronunciations. Joseph M. Staudacher. LC 75-14609. 72p. 1975. pap. 5.95 (*0-87973-773-5*) Our Sunday Visitor.
Lector's Guide to the Episcopal Eucharistic Lectionary. Frank Mulligan. (Orig.). 1987. pap. 16.00 (*0-9618112-0-X*) St Marks Pr.
Lector's Ministry: Your Guide to Proclaiming the Word. Nancy Benvenga. (RVC Liturgical Ser.). 48p. (Orig.). 1990. pap. 3.95 (*0-9623410-8-8*, Resurrection Pr) Catholic Bk Pub.
***Lector's Pronunciation Guide.** Charles E. Hugenberger. 22p. 1999. pap. 3.95 (*1-885057-14-8*) C E Hugenberger.
Lector's Pronunciation Guide. 2nd ed. Charles E. Hugenberger. 30p. 1998. pap. 3.95 (*1-885057-10-5*) C E Hugenberger.
Lectors' Pronunciation Guide: All of the Proper Nouns & Selected Difficult Words to the Vatican Two Missal Scripture Readings. Charles E. Hugenberger. 28p. 1992. pap. 3.95 (*1-885057-02-4*) C E Hugenberger.
Lectura, Arte del Lenguaje. 5th ed. Antonio Saez. 411p. (C). 1987. pap. 8.00 (*0-8477-2718-1*) U of PR Pr.
Lectura Cosmica del Suroeste-para los Jovenes. Ruben D. Salaz. Tr. by Rita Minkin from ENG. (SPA., Illus.). (YA). (gr. 7 up). 1978. pap. 6.95 (*0-932492-01-0*) Cosmic Hse NM.
Lectura Dantis: Inferno. Allen Mandelbaum. LC 98-34223. 490p. 1998. 45.00 (*0-520-21249-5*, Pub. by U CA Pr); pap. 19.95 (*0-520-21270-3*, Pub. by U CA Pr) Cal Prin Full Svc.
Lectura Dantis Americana: Inferno I. Anthony K. Cassell. Tr. by Robert Hollander & Patrick Creagh. LC 89-4751. (Lectura Dantis Americana Ser.). 280p. (C). 1989. text 39.95 (*0-8122-8176-4*) U of Pa Pr.
Lectura Dantis Americana: Inferno II. Rachel Jacoff & William A. Stephany. LC 89-5558. (Lectura Dantis Americana Ser.). 168p. (C). 1989. text 32.50 (*0-8122-8177-2*) U of Pa Pr.
Lectura Dantis Americana: Inferno III. Maria P. Simonelli. Tr. by Patrick Creagh & Robert Hollander from ITA. LC 93-13922. (ENG & ITA.). 144p. (C). 1993. text 34.50 (*0-8122-3229-1*) U of Pa Pr.

An Asterisk (*) at the beginning of an entry indicates that the title is appearing for the first time.

L

Lectura Eficaz de la Biblia. Gordon D. Fee.Tr. of How to Read Your Bible for All It's Worth. (SPA.). 224p. 1985. pap. 9.99 (*0-8297-1010-8*) Vida Pubs.

Lectura I 39 see Contingency & Freedom: John Duns Scotus Lectura 139

Lectura, 1987, Level 4. Barrera. 1987. 52.50 (*0-15-331024-3*) Harcourt Schl Pubs.

Lectura, 1987, Level 5. Barrera. 1987. 30.25 (*0-15-331025-1*) Harcourt Schl Pubs.

Lectura, 1987, Level 6. Barrera. 1987. 32.25 (*0-15-331027-8*) Harcourt Schl Pubs.

Lectura, 1987, Level 7. Barrera. 1987. 32.25 (*0-15-331028-6*) Harcourt Schl Pubs.

Lectura Secunda I Sent. Distinctiones 2-7 see Lectura Secunda in Librum Primum Sententiarum

Lectura Secunda I Sent. Distinctiones 8-26 see Lectura Secunda in Librum Primum Sententiarum

Lectura Secunda I Sent. Prologus & Distinctio Prima see Lectura Secunda in Librum Primum Sententiarum

Lectura Secunda in Librum Primum Sententiarum, 3 vols. Adam De Wodeham. Incl. Vol. I. Lectura Secunda I Sent. Prologus & Distinctio Prima. 354p. 1991. 75.00 (*1-57659-105-0*); Vol. II. Lectura Secunda I Sent. Distinctiones 2-7. 374p. 1991. 75.00 (*1-57659-106-9*); Vol. III. Lectura Secunda I Sent. Distinctiones 8-26. 491p. 1991. 75.00 (*1-57659-107-7*); 125.00 (*1-57659-104-2*) Franciscan Inst.

Lectura y Representacion: Analisis Cultural de las Novelas Ejemplares de Cervantes. Francisco J. Sanchez. LC 93-385. (Sociocriticism Ser.). 210p. (C). 1993. text 45.95 (*0-8204-2163-4*) P Lang Pubng.

Lecturas Basicas 3/E PB. 3rd ed. Joaquin Valdes. 144p. (C). 1985. pap. text 33.50 (*0-03-000039-4*) Harcourt Coll Pubs.

Lecturas de Aprendizaje y Ensananzas. Angel P. Gomez. (SPA.). pap. 20.99 (*968-16-4896-X*, Pub. by Fondo) Continental Bk.

Lecturas del Taller. Ivonne Sanavitis et al. 118p. 1991. pap. 8.95 (*0-8477-3653-9*) U of PR Pr.

Lecturas (Del Temprano Renacimiento a Valle Inclan) Juan B. Avalle-Arce. 139p. 1990. 28.50 (*0-916379-43-4*) Scripta.

Lecturas desde el fragmento: Escritura Contemporanea e imaginario cultural en Puerto Rico. Myrna Garcia-Calderon. 225p. 1998. pap. 17.00 (*0-9640795-6-9*) Latinoam Edit.

Lecturas Espanolas, No. 36. Azorin, pseud. (SPA.). 146p. 1976. write for info. (*0-8288-8554-0*) Fr & Eur.

Lecturas Italianas, 3 bks., Set. Incl. Bk. 1. Apprendere Leggendo. Philip Cordaro. pap. 1.25 (*0-8477-3302-5*); Bk. 1. Apprendere Leggendo. Philip Cordaro. pap. 1.50 (*0-8477-3303-3*); Bk. 2. Raccontini Divertenti. Philip Cordaro. pap. 1.00 (*0-8477-3304-1*); Bk. 3. Cosi e (se vi pare) Luigi Pirandello. pap. 3.00 (*0-8477-3305-X*); (C). pap. write for info. (*0-8477-3301-7*) U of PR Pr.

Lecturas Periodisticas. 4th ed. Milton M. Azevedo. LC 89-80718. (SPA.). 290p. (C). 1990. pap. text 30.76 (*0-669-17401-7*) HM Trade Div.

Lecturas Periodisticas. 5th ed. Milton M. Azevedo. (SPA.). 285p. (C). 1996. pap. text 30.76 (*0-669-35494-5*) HM Trade Div.

Lecturas Puertorriquenas - Prosa. Margot Arce De Vazquez et al. 1966. 14.95 (*0-87751-011-3*) E Torres & Sons.

Lecture d'Erec: Traces Epiques et Troubadouresques dan le Conte de Chretien de Troyes. Claudia Seebass-Linggi. (Publications Universitaires Europeennes Ser.: Series 13, Vol. 211). (FRE.). 295p. 1996. 52.95 (*3-906756-09-2*, Pub. by P Lang) P Lang Pubng.

Lecture Guide & Student Notes for Calculus, Vol. 2. Ostebee. 1996. teacher ed. 17.00 (*0-03-017408-2*, Pub. by Harcourt Coll Pubs) Harcourt.

Lecture Lab: Image & Text Management Made Easy. Picture Primal. 1998. 89.95 (*0-7484-0855-X*) Taylor & Francis.

Lecture Manual for Soil Science. (C). 1996. write for info. (*0-8087-5668-0*) Pearson Custom.

Lecture Method of Instruction. Martin M. Broadwell. Ed. by Danny G. Langdon. LC 79-23528. (Instructional Design Library). 116p. 1980. 27.95 (*0-87778-147-8*) Educ Tech Pubns.

Lecture Notes. Madden. 108p. (C). 1998. pap. text 10.75 (*0-536-01485-X*) Pearson Custom.

Lecture Notes for Fireworks Display Practice: Mongraphic Series. Kenneth L. Kosanke & Bonnie J. Kosanke. (Pyrotechnic Reference Ser.: Vol. 3). (Illus.). 400p. (Orig.). 1995. pap. 90.00 (*1-889526-03-7*) Jrnl of Pyrotechnics.

Lecture Notes for Human Anatomy & Physiology. Findley & Ouchley. 170p. (C). 1998. 15.95 (*0-7872-5464-9*) Kendall-Hunt.

Lecture Notes for Human Anatomy & Physiology. 2nd ed. Ann Findley & Amy Ouchley. 170p. (C). pap. text 15.95 (*0-7872-6586-1*) Kendall-Hunt.

Lecture Notes for Pyrotechnic Chemistry. 2nd rev. ed. K. L. Kosanke et al. Ed. by B. Sturman et al. (Pyrotechnic Reference Ser.: Vol. 2). (Illus.). 400p. 1997. pap. 90.00 (*1-889526-09-6*) Jrnl of Pyrotechnics.

Lecture Notes for Slides, Understanding Earth. Frank Press & Raymond Siever. 1994. 1.60 (*0-7167-2555-X*) W H Freeman.

Lecture Notes for Structures, Properties & Processing of Materials. Adams. (C). 1996. text. write for info. (*0-06-501217-8*) Addison-Wesley.

***Lecture Notes for Teachers of Psychology, Psychology & You.** 3rd ed. McMahon & Romano. 1999. pap. 24.00 (*0-538-42901-1*) Thomson Learn.

Lecture Notes in Emergency Medicine. 2nd ed. David W. Yates et al. LC 98-36149. (Lecture Notes Ser.). (Illus.). 416p. 1999. pap. text 39.95 (*0-632-02766-5*) Blackwell Sci.

Lecture Notes in Medical Microbiology. 3rd ed. Ed. by T. S. Elliott et al. LC 96-2259. (Lecture Notes Ser.). (Illus.). 352p. 1997. pap. 32.95 (*0-632-02446-1*) Blackwell Sci.

Lecture Notes in Obstetrics. 7th ed. Geoffrey V.P Chamberlain. (Illus.). 296p. (Orig.). 1996. pap. text 29.95 (*0-86542-681-3*) Blackwell Sci.

Lecture Notes in Ophthalmology. 8th ed. Anthony J. Bron et al. LC 96-20972. (Illus.). 224p. 1997. pap. text 29.95 (*0-86542-723-2*) Blackwell Sci.

Lecture Notes in Quantum Chemistry: European Summer School in Quantum Chemistry. Ed. by European Summer School in Quantum Chemistry Staff & B. O. Roos. LC 92-9393. (Lecture Notes in Chemistry Ser.: Vol. 58). vii, 421p. 1997. 98.95 (*0-387-55371-1*) Spr-Verlag.

Lecture Notes in Quantum Chemistry II. Third European Summer School in Quantum Chemistry. Ed. by B. O. Roos. LC 94-38826. (Lecture Notes in Chemistry Ser.: Vol.64). 1994. 65.00 (*0-387-58620-2*) Spr-Verlag.

Lecture Notes in Quantum Chemistry II. Third European Summer School in Quantum Chemistry. Ed. by B. O. Roos. (Lecture Notes in Chemistry Ser.: Vol. 64). 1997. text 72.95 (*3-540-58620-2*) Spr-Verlag.

Lecture Notes on Bucket Algorithms. Luc Devroye. (Progress in Computer Science Ser.: Vol. 6). 1986. 48.50 (*0-8176-3328-6*) Birkhauser.

Lecture Notes on Cardiology. 4th ed. Keith D. Dawkins et al. (Illus.). 288p. 1997. pap. text 29.95 (*0-86542-864-6*) Blackwell Sci.

Lecture Notes on Clinical Anaesthesia. Carol L. Gwinnutt. LC 96-39563. (Illus.). 360p. 1997. pap. text 38.95 (*0-86542-656-2*) Blackwell Sci.

Lecture Notes on Clinical Biochemistry. 5th ed. Lionel Whitby & A. F. Smith. LC 92-48270. (Illus.). 452p. 1993. pap. 29.95 (*0-632-03687-7*) Blackwell Sci.

Lecture Notes on Clinical Biochemistry. 6th ed. A. F. Smith et al. LC 97-43308. (Lecture Notes Ser.). (Illus.). 1998. pap. 33.95 (*0-632-04834-4*) Blackwell Sci.

Lecture Notes on Clinical Medicine. 5th ed. David Rubenstein et al. LC 97-10914. (Lecture Notes Ser.). (Illus.). 320p. (C). 1997. pap. text 32.95 (*0-86542-925-1*) Blackwell Sci.

Lecture Notes on Clinical Pharmacology. 5th ed. John L. Reid et al. LC 96-859. 1996. pap. 29.95 (*0-08-654665-1*) Blackwell Sci.

Lecture Notes on Clinical Skills. 3rd ed. Robert C. Turner & Roger A. Blackwood. LC 96-13667. (Lecture Notes Ser.). (Illus.). 288p. 1997. pap. text 34.95 (*0-86542-971-5*) Blackwell Sci.

Lecture Notes on Dermatology. 7th ed. Bobin A. Graham-Brown & Anthony Burns. (Illus.). 288p. 1996. pap. text 29.95 (*0-86542-635-X*) Blackwell Sci.

Lecture Notes on Diseases of the Ear, Nose & Throat. 8th ed. Peter D. Bull. (Illus.). 113p. 1996. pap. 29.95 (*0-86542-634-1*) Blackwell Sci.

Lecture Notes on Electron Correlation & Magnetism. P. Fazekas. LC 98-51617. (Series on Modern Condensed Matter Physics: Vol. 5). 777p. 1998. text 38.00 (*981-02-2474-5*, Pc-B2945) World Scientific Pub.

Lecture Notes on Elementary Topology & Geometry. I. M. Singer & J. A. Thorpe. LC 76-26137. (Undergraduate Texts in Mathematics Ser.). 1996. 39.95 (*0-387-90202-3*) Spr-Verlag.

Lecture Notes on Epidemiology & Public Health. 4th ed. Richard Farmer et al. LC 95-26229. (Illus.). 288p. 1996. pap. text 29.95 (*0-86542-611-2*) Blackwell Sci.

Lecture Notes on Fullerene Chemistry. Roger Taylor. 1998. 48.00 (*1-86094-104-4*); pap. 22.00 (*1-86094-109-5*) World Scientific Pub.

Lecture Notes on General Surgery. 9th ed. H. Ellis et al. LC 97-42474. (Lecture Notes Ser.). (Illus.). 386p. 1998. pap. 32.95 (*0-86542-768-2*) Blackwell Sci.

Lecture Notes on Geriatrics. 5th ed. Nicholas Coni & Stephen Webster. LC 97-22533. (Lecture Notes Ser.). (Illus.). 1998. pap. 34.95 (*0-86542-750-X*) Blackwell Sci.

Lecture Notes on Gynaecology. 7th rev. ed. Geoffrey V.P. Chamberlain et al. (Lecture Notes Ser.). (Illus.). 275p. 1996. pap. 29.95 (*0-632-03111-5*) Blackwell Sci.

Lecture Notes on Hematology. 6th ed. Nevin C. Hughes-Jones et al. (Illus.). 288p. 1996. pap. 29.95 (*0-632-04039-4*) Blackwell Sci.

Lecture Notes on History Taking & Examination. 2nd ed. Robert C. Turner & R. Blackwood. (Lecture Notes Ser.). (Illus.). 208p. 1991. pap. 21.50 (*0-632-02885-8*) Blackwell Sci.

Lecture Notes on Human Biochemistry. Simon W. Walker et al. (Illus.). 300p. (Orig.). 1998. pap. text 26.95 (*0-86542-622-8*) Blackwell Sci.

Lecture Notes on Human Physiology. 3rd ed. J. Bray et al. (The Lecture Notes Ser.). (Illus.). 736p. 1994. 29.95 (*0-632-03644-3*, Pub. by Blckwll Scitfc UK) Blackwell Sci.

Lecture Notes on Human Physiology. 4th ed. John J. Bray. LC 98-28849. 1999. write for info. (*0-86542-776-3*) Blackwell Sci.

***Lecture Notes on Human Physiology.** 4th ed. John J. Bray et al. LC 98-28849. (Lecture Notes Ser.). (Illus.). 1999. pap. text 34.95 (*0-86542-775-5*) Blackwell Sci.

***Lecture Notes on Immunology.** Gordon Reeves & Ian Todd. (Lecture Notes Ser.). (Illus.). 280p. (C). 2000. pap. 29.95 (*0-632-05636-3*) Blackwell Sci.

Lecture Notes on Immunology. 3rd ed. Gordon Reeves et al. LC 95-39681. (Lecture Notes Ser.). (Illus.). 226p. 1996. pap. 28.95 (*0-632-03812-8*) Blackwell Sci.

Lecture Notes on Introductory Theoretical Astrophysics. R. E. Williams et al. (Astronomy & Astrophysics Ser.: Vol. 3). (Illus.). 1976. 15.00 (*0-912918-14-4*) Pachart Pub Hse.

Lecture Notes on Mixed Type Partial Differential Equations. J. M. Rassia. 152p. (C). 1990. text 43.00 (*981-02-0275-X*); pap. text 23.00 (*981-02-0406-X*) World Scientific Pub.

Lecture Notes on Neurology. 7th ed. Lionel Ginsberg & Ivan T. Draper. LC 98-48820. (Lecture Notes Ser.). (Illus.). 1999. pap. 24.95 (*0-632-04827-1*) Blackwell Sci.

Lecture Notes on Nil-Theta Functions. L. Auslander. LC 77-16471. (CBMS Regional Conference Series in Mathematics: No. 34). 96p. 1978. reprint ed. pap. 19.00 (*0-8218-1684-5*, CBMS/34) Am Math.

Lecture Notes on Nilpotent Groups. Gilbert Baumslag. LC 78-145636. (CBMS Regional Conference Series in Mathematics: No. 2). 73p. 1971. pap. 17.00 (*0-8218-1651-9*, CBMS/2) Am Math.

Lecture Notes on Nilpotent Groups. Gilbert Baumslag. LC 78-145636. (Regional Conference Series in Mathematics: No. 2). 80p. 1971. pap. 30.00 (*0-608-05175-6*, 205259600001) Bks Demand.

Lecture Notes on Obstetrics & Gynacology. Ajoy K. Ghosh. 1985. 95.00 (*0-7855-0741-8*, Pub. by Current Dist) St Mut.

Lecture Notes on Obstetrics & Gynaecology. Geoffrey Chamberlain & Diana Hamilton-Fairly. LC 98-39642. 1999. pap. 29.95 (*0-632-04957-X*) Blackwell Sci.

Lecture Notes on Ophthalmology. 7th ed. P. D. Trevor-Roper. (Lecture Notes Ser.). (Illus.). 138p. 1986. pap. 32.95 (*0-632-01585-3*) Blackwell Sci.

Lecture Notes on Orthopaedics. 3rd ed. T. Duckworth. (Lecture Notes Ser.). (Illus.). 400p. 1992. pap. 24.95 (*0-632-02781-9*) Blackwell Sci.

Lecture Notes on Paediatrics. 5th ed. Meadow. 1986. 17.95 (*0-8016-3372-9*) Mosby Inc.

Lecture Notes on Particles & Fields: Proceedings of the 2nd Mexican School. A. Zepeda. Ed. by J. L. Lucio. 516p. (C). 1987. text 117.00 (*9971-5-0434-0*) World Scientific Pub.

Lecture Notes on Pathology. 4th ed. R. E. Cotton. (Lecture Notes Ser.). (Illus.). 448p. 1992. pap. 34.95 (*0-632-03355-X*) Blackwell Sci.

***Lecture Notes on Psychiatry.** 8th ed. M. Sharpe et al. LC 97-42431. (Lecture Notes Ser.). (Illus.). 224p. 1998. pap. 32.95 (*0-632-03677-X*) Blackwell Sci.

Lecture Notes on Quantum Mechanics. Samuel D. Lindenbaum. 350p. 1999. 46.00 (*981-02-3839-8*) World Scientific Pub.

***Lecture Notes on Radiographic Equipment, Exposure & Radiation Protection.** 3rd ed. Jeffrey Papp. (Illus.). 286p. (C). 1999. pap. text 20.40 (*0-87563-857-0*) Stipes.

Lecture Notes on Radiology. P. R. Patel. LC 97-10069. (Lecture Notes Ser.). (Illus.). 1997. pap. 32.95 (*0-632-04758-5*) Blackwell Sci.

Lecture Notes on Random Evolution. Mark A. Pinsky. 150p. (C). 1991. text 36.00 (*981-02-0559-7*) World Scientific Pub.

Lecture Notes on Respiratory Disease. 5th ed. S. J. Bourke & R. A. L. Brewis. LC 98-3473. (Lecture Notes Ser.). (Illus.). 1998. pap. 34.95 (*0-632-04968-5*) Blackwell Sci.

Lecture Notes on Seiberg-Witten Invariants, Vol. 162. John D. Moore. LC 96-36335. (Lecture Notes in Mathematics Ser.). 105p. 1996. pap. 29.00 (*3-540-61455-9*) Spr-Verlag.

Lecture Notes on 16 & 32 Bit Microprocssors. 2nd ed. Syed J. Mahmud. 340p. (C). 1995. text 42.00 (*0-536-59023-0*) Pearson Custom.

Lecture Notes on Solution Chemistry. Viktor Gutmann & Gerhard Resch. LC 95-24203. 300p. 1995. 38.00 (*981-02-2258-0*) World Scientific Pub.

Lecture Notes on the Free Electron Laser Theory & Related Topics. G. Dattoli et al. 400p. (C). 1993. text 86.00 (*981-02-0565-1*); pap. text 48.00 (*981-02-0566-X*) World Scientific Pub.

***Lecture Notes on the Mathematical Theory of Generalized Boltzmann Models.** N. Bellomo & Mauro L. Schiavo. LC 99-40190. (Series on Advances in Mathematics for Applied Sciences). 1999. pap. write for info. (*981-02-4078-3*) World Scientific Pub.

Lecture Notes on the Mathematical Theory of the Boltzmann Equation. Ed. by N. Bellomo. LC 95-10544. (Series on Advances in Mathematics for Applied Sciences). 250p. 1995. text 71.00 (*981-02-2166-5*) World Scientific Pub.

Lecture Notes on Theoretical Chemistry. W. A. Lester, Jr. et al. 436p. (C). 1994. text 74.00 (*981-02-0321-7*); pap. text 36.00 (*981-02-0322-5*) World Scientific Pub.

Lecture Notes on Topoi & Quasitopol. Oswald Wyler. 304p. (C). 1991. text 40.00 (*981-02-0153-2*) World Scientific Pub.

Lecture Notes on Tropical Medicine. 4th ed. D. Bell et al. (Lecture Notes Ser.). 320p. 1995. pap. 29.95 (*0-632-03839-X*) Blackwell Sci.

Lecture Notes on Turbulence. Ed. by J. Herring & J. McWilliams. 384p. (C). 1989. text 85.00 (*9971-5-0805-2*); pap. text 40.00 (*9971-5-0827-3*) World Scientific Pub.

Lecture Notes on Urology. 5th ed. John P. Blandy. LC 97-23639. (Lecture Notes Ser.). (Illus.). 288p. 1998. pap. 34.95 (*0-632-04202-8*) Blackwell Sci.

Lecture Notes to McMurry & Fay Chemistry. 186p. (C). 1996. text 30.40 (*0-536-59745-6*) Pearson Custom.

Lecture on Bookbinding as a Fine Art, Vol. 8. Robert Hoe. (History of Bookbinding & Design Ser.). (Illus.). 350p. 1990. text 30.00 (*0-8240-4021-X*) Garland.

Lecture on Conscious Dying. Bruce Goldberg. 1994. 12.00 incl. audio (*1-885577-32-X*) B Goldberg.

Lecture on Criminal Procedure. 2nd ed. Ed. by R. V. Kelkar. (C). 1990. 70.00 (*0-7855-5604-4*) St Mut.

Lecture on Eurythmy. Rudolf Steiner. pap. 5.95 (*0-85440-189-X*, 51, Pub. by R Steiner Pr) Anthroposophic.

Lecture on Human Happiness. John Gray. LC 66-21675. (Reprints of Economic Classics Ser.). 83p. 1971. reprint ed. lib. bdg. 29.50 (*0-678-00293-2*) Kelley.

Lecture on Lectures. Arthur T. Quiller-Couch. LC 74-7042. (English Literature Ser.: No. 33). 1974. lib. bdg. 75.00 (*0-8383-1994-7*) M S G Haskell Hse.

Lecture on Masonic Symbolism & a Second Lecture on Symbolism on the Omkara & Other Ineffable Words. Albert Pike. 500p. 1992. reprint ed. pap. 45.00 (*1-56459-162-X*) Kessinger Pub.

Lecture on the Native in the Larger Towns, 1918 & Notes on Natal, 1917. J. S. Marwick & S. G. Rich. (Colin Webb Natal & Zululand Ser.: No. 4). 56p. 1993. pap. 24.95 (*0-86980-902-4*, Pub. by Univ Natal Pr) Intl Spec Bk.

Lecture on the Pedal Organ. Thomas Casson. 1988. reprint ed. lib. bdg. 49.00 (*0-7812-0145-4*) Rprt Serv.

***Lecture Outline Gen Org Bio Chem&prac Exams.** 312p. (C). 1998. 25.75 (*0-536-01377-2*) Pearson Custom.

Lecture Outline to Accompany General Chemistry. 6th ed. Whitten. 504p. (C). 1999. pap. text 28.00 (*0-03-021223-5*, Pub. by SCP) Harcourt.

Lecture Profiles. Elizabeth Warner. 144p. (C). 1996. pap. text, per. 20.95 (*0-7872-2015-9*) Kendall-Hunt.

Lecture Syllabus for Human Biology. 2nd ed. (C). 1993. write for info. (*0-8087-9434-5*) Pearson Custom.

Lecture to Young Men. Sylvester Graham. LC 73-20625. (Sex, Marriage & Society Ser.). 84p. 1974. reprint ed. 17.95 (*0-405-05801-2*) Ayer.

Lecture... Vertebrate Anatomy. 2nd ed. Earl Zimmerman. 104p. (C). 1998. spiral bd. 21.95 (*0-7872-5683-8*, 41568301) Kendall-Hunt.

Lectureactive Nutrition-Nut. Saundersco. (C). 1994. 288.00 (*0-03-013414-5*) Harcourt Coll Pubs.

Lectureactive Users Guide. Archipelag. (C). 1995. pap. text 33.50 (*0-03-018073-2*) Harcourt Coll Pubs.

Lecturer Practitioners. Judith Lamthean. LC 97-24976. 192p. 1995. pap. text 28.95 (*0-7506-2449-3*) Buttrwrth-Heinemann.

Lecturers to Young People. William B. Sprague. 1992. pap. 19.99 (*0-87377-947-9*) GAM Pubns.

Lecturer's Toolkit: A Practical Guide to Teaching, Learning & Assessment. Phil Race & Sally Brown. 224p. 1998. ring bd. 125.00 (*0-7494-2496-6*, Kogan Pg Educ) Stylus Pub VA.

Lectures Against Sociolinguistics. Rajendra Singh. LC 95-49572. XIX, 180p. (C). 1997. pap. 31.95 (*0-8204-3097-8*) P Lang Pubng.

Lectures & Addresses. Rabindranath Tagore. 160p. 1988. 5.50 (*0-333-90349-8*) Asia Bk Corp.

Lectures & Articles on Christian Science. Edward A. Kimball. (Illus.). 1976. 15.00 (*0-911588-01-9*); pap. 10.00 (*0-685-03473-9*) N S Wait.

Lectures & Articles on Christian Science. Edward A. Kimball. 1998. reprint ed. pap. 15.00 (*0-933062-34-6*) R H Sommer.

***Lectures & Articles on Christian Science.** Edward A. Kimball. 1998. reprint ed. 20.00 (*0-933062-35-4*) R H Sommer.

Lectures & Discourses of Earthquakes & Subterraneous Eruptions. Robert Hooke. Ed. by Claude C. Albritton, Jr. LC 77-6521. (History of Geology Ser.). 1978. reprint ed. lib. bdg. 23.95 (*0-405-10443-X*) Ayer.

Lectures & Essays. Jacob Klein. Ed. by Robert B. Williamson & Elliott Zuckerman. 393p. 1986. 22.50 (*0-9603690-2-3*) SJC Annapolis.

Lectures & Essays, Second Series. Henry Nettleship. Ed. by F. Haverfield. LC 72-336. (Essay Index Reprint Ser.). 1977. reprint ed. 23.95 (*0-8369-2812-1*) Ayer.

Lectures & Essays, 2 vols., Set. Alfred Ainger. LC 76-158235. reprint ed. 67.50 (*0-404-00360-5*) AMS Pr.

Lectures & Miscellanies. Henry James, Sr. LC 72-923. (Selected Works of Henry James, Sr.: Vol. 3). 1983. reprint ed. 57.50 (*0-404-10083-X*) AMS Pr.

Lectures & Notes on Shakespeare & Other English Poets: Now First Collected by T. Ashe. Samuel Taylor Coleridge. LC 70-38347. (Select Bibliographies Reprint Ser.). 1977. reprint ed. 27.95 (*0-8369-6764-X*) Ayer.

Lectures & Orations. Henry W. Beecher. Ed. by Newell D. Hillis. LC 72-126662. (BCL Ser. II). 1970. reprint ed. 47.50 (*0-404-00699-X*) AMS Pr.

Lectures & Orations. Henry W. Beecher. (BCL1-PS American Literature Ser.). 330p. 1992. reprint ed. lib. bdg. 79.00 (*0-7812-6674-2*) Rprt Serv.

Lectures & Symposia of the 14th International Cancer Congress Vol. 1: Cancer Research & Treatment Today: Results, Trends & Frontiers. K. Lapis & S. Eckhardt. 266p. (C). 1987. 150.00 (*963-05-4523-3*, Pub. by Akade Kiado) St Mut.

Lectures & Symposia of the 14th International Cancer Congress Vol. 2: Molecular Biology & Differentiation of Cancer Cells, Oncogenes, Growth Factors, Receptors. K. Lapis & S. Eckhardt. 361p. (C). 1987. 190.00 (*963-05-4524-1*, Pub. by Akade Kiado) St Mut.

Lectures & Symposia of the 14th International Cancer Congress Vol. 3: Cytology, Pathology & Cancer Prognosis. K. Lapis & S. Eckhardt. 219p. (C). 1987. 130.00 (*963-05-4525-X*, Pub. by Akade Kiado) St Mut.

Lectures & Symposia of the 14th International Cancer Congress Vol. 4: Carcinogenesis & Tumour Progression. Ed. by K. Lapis & S. Eckhardt. 334p. (C). 1987. 168.00 (*963-05-4526-8*, Pub. by Akade Kiado) St Mut.

Lectures & Symposia of the 14th International Cancer Congress Vol. 5: Novel Approaches in Cancer Therapy. K. Lapis & S. Eckhardt. 387p. (C). 1987. 174.00 (*963-05-4527-6*, Pub. by Akade Kiado) St Mut.

Lectures & Symposia of the 14th International Cancer Congress Vol. 6: Epidemiology, Prevention, Diagnosis. K. Lapis & S. Eckhardt. 365p. (C). 1987. 174.00 (*963-05-4528-4*, Pub. by Akade Kiado) St Mut.

L

Lectures & Symposia of the 14th International Cancer Congress Vol. 7: Oncological Surgery. K. Lapis & S. Eckhardt. 223p. (C). 1987. 130.00 (*963-05-4529-2*, Pub. by Akade Kiado) St Mut.

Lectures & Symposia of the 14th International Cancer Congress Vol. 8: Radiotherapy, Paediatric Oncology, Neurooncology. K. Lapis & S. Eckhardt. 352p. (C). 1987. 180.00 (*963-05-4530-6*, Pub. by Akade Kiado) St Mut.

Lectures & Symposia of the 14th International Cancer Congress Vol. 9: Anticancer Drug Research. Ed. by K. Lapis & S. Eckhardt. 256p. 1987. 132.00 (*963-05-4531-4*, Pub. by Akade Kiado) St Mut.

Lectures & Symposia of the 14th International Cancer Congress Vol. 10: Biological Response Modifiers, Leukaemias & Lymphomas. K. Lapis & S. Eckhardt. 133p. (C). 1987. 75.00 (*963-05-4532-2*, Pub. by Akade Kiado) St Mut.

Lectures & Symposia of the 14th International Cancer Congress Vol. 11: Medical Oncology. K. Lapis & S. Eckhardt. 339p. (C). 1987. 168.00 (*963-05-4533-0*, Pub. by Akade Kiado) St Mut.

Lectures & Symposia of the 14th International Cancer Congress Vol. 12: Endocrine Aspects of Malignancies. Ed. by K. Lapis & S. Eckhardt. 293p. (C). 1987. 168.00 (*963-05-4534-9*) St Mut.

Lectures & Symposia of the 14th International Cancer Congress Vol. 13: Education, Nursing, Organization. K. Lapis & S. Eckhardt. 336p. (C). 1987. 168.00 (*963-05-4535-7*, Pub. by Akade Kiado) St Mut.

Lectures & Symposia of the 14th International Cancer Congress, 13 vols., Set. K. Lapis & S. Eckhardt. (C). 1987. 1875.00 (*963-05-4522-5*) St Mut.

Lectures & Writings see Complete Works of Sister Nivedita

Lectures at Knots '96. 300p. 1997. text 40.00 (*981-02-3094-X*) World Scientific Pub.

Lectures Classiques. Jules Brody. (FRE.). 368p. 1996. lib. bdg. 49.95 (*1-886365-01-6*) Rookwood Pr.

Lectures Complete. Robert G. Ingersoll. (Notable American Authors Ser.). 1992. reprint ed. lib. bdg. 75.00 (*0-7812-3332-1*) Rprt Serv.

Lectures de La Fontaine. LC 94-68512. xxi, 125p. (C). 1994. lib. bdg. 27.95 (*0-9634355-0-7*) Rookwood Pr.

Lectures de la Fontaine. LC 94-68512. (EMF Monographs). xxi, 125p. (Orig.). (C). 1994. pap. 19.95 (*0-9634355-4-X*) Rookwood Pr.

Lectures de Montaigne. Jules Brody. LC 82-82428. (French Forum Monographs: No. 39). 181p. (Orig.). 1982. pap. 14.95 (*0-917058-38-0*) French Forum.

Lectures Delivered at the 20th Anniversary of Clark University. 1974. 18.95 (*0-405-05144-1*) Ayer.

***Lectures 1818-1819 on the History of Philosophy, 2 vols.** Samuel Taylor Coleridge & J. R. Jackson. LC 99-30471. (Collected Works of Samuel Taylor Colerid Ser.: Vol. 8). (Illus.). 1328p. 1999. text 150.00 (*0-691-09875-1*, Pub. by Princeton U Pr) Cal Prin Full Svc.

Lectures, Elementary & Familiar, on English Law. James Francillon. (Second Ser.). viii, 238p. 1987. reprint ed. 37.50 (*0-8377-2132-6*, Rothman) W S Hein.

Lectures, Essays, Sermons. Samuel Johnson. Ed. by S. Longfellow. (Notable American Authors Ser.). 1992. reprint ed. lib. bdg. 75.00 (*0-7812-3499-9*) Rprt Serv.

Lectures et Conversations. Ed. by Karl C. Sandberg. (FRE.). (C). 1970. pap. text 7.95 (*0-89197-272-2*) Irvington.

Lectures et Fantaisies. 2nd ed. Ed. by Marie E. Galanti. (FRE.). 190p. (C). 1992. pap. text 31.56 (*0-669-24452-X*) HM Trade Div.

Lectures for Bankers & Business Executives. Ed. by William McKee. LC 76-107724. (Essay Index Reprint Ser.). 1977. 39.95 (*0-8369-1580-1*) Ayer.

Lectures for Inventors, Delivered at the Public Library, December 1981-June 1982. 1983. pap. 7.50 (*0-89073-072-5*, 291) Boston Public Lib.

Lectures for Young Men. William Allen. (Works of William Allen). 1989. lib. bdg. 79.00 (*0-7812-1769-5*) Rprt Serv.

Lectures from Colombo to Almora. Swami Vivekananda. 1962. pap. 6.50 (*81-7505-081-0*, Pub. by Advaita Ashrama) Vedanta Pr.

Lectures from Markov Processes to Brownian Motion. Kai L. Chung. (Grundlehren der Mathematischen Wissenschaften Ser.). (Illus.). 256p. 1982. 95.95 (*0-387-90618-5*) Spr-Verlag.

Lectures in Abstract Algebra: Basic Concepts, Vol. 1. N. Jacobson. (Graduate Texts in Mathematics Ser.: Vol. 30). 1997. reprint ed. 43.95 (*0-387-90181-7*) Spr-Verlag.

Lectures in Applied Mathematics: Proceedings. University of Colorado, Summer Seminar on Applied. LC 60-12712. (Illus.). 331p. reprint ed. pap. 102.70 (*0-7837-4230-4*, 204391800012) Bks Demand.

Lectures in Black Studies. Ira Lunan-Ferguson. LC 72-83316. (C). 1972. text 10.95 (*0-911724-12-5*) Lunan-Ferguson.

Lectures in Complex Systems, 1989. Ed. by Erica Jen. (Santa Fe Institute Ser.). (Illus.). 896p. (C). 1990. 49.95 (*0-201-50936-9*, 130J90) Addison-Wesley.

Lectures in Corporate Finance. 392p. (C). 1997. text 33.00 (*0-536-00823-X*) Pearson Custom.

Lectures in Differentiable Dynamics. rev. ed. Lawrence Markus. LC 80-16847. (CBMS Regional Conference Series in Mathematics: No. 3). 77p. 1971. pap. 16.00 (*0-8218-1695-0*, CBMS/3) Am Math.

Lectures in Differential & Integral Equations. Kosaku Yoshida. LC 60-53007. (Pure & Applied Mathematics Ser.: Vol. 10). 230p. reprint ed. pap. 71.30 (*0-608-30866-8*, 200707700060) Bks Demand.

Lectures in Functional Analysis & Operator Theory. S. K. Berberian. (Graduate Texts in Mathematics Ser.: Vol. 15). 370p. 1988. 60.95 (*0-387-90080-2*) Spr-Verlag.

Lectures in Fundamentals of Biology: A Foundation in the Essential Concepts of Modern Biology. David Williams. 264p. (C). 1995. pap. text, spiral bd. 19.95 (*0-7872-1541-4*) Kendall-Hunt.

Lectures in Hair Structure & Chemistry for Cosmetology Teachers. A. H. Powitt. (Illus.). 1991. pap. 28.95 (*0-87350-354-6*) Milady Pub.

Lectures in Homological Algebra. P. Hilton. LC 70-152504. (CBMS Regional Conference Series in Mathematics: No. 8). 74p. 1971. reprint ed. pap. 17.00 (*0-8218-1657-8*, CBMS/8) Am Math.

Lectures in Logic. Immanuel Kant. Ed. by J. Michael Young. (Cambridge Edition of the Works of Immanuel Kant). (Illus.). 727p. (C). 1992. text 115.00 (*0-521-36013-7*) Cambridge U Pr.

Lectures in Mathematical Physics, Vol. 1. Robert Hermann. (Math Lecture Notes Ser.: No. 45). 475p. (C). 1970. pap. text 12.50 (*0-8053-3947-7*) Addison-Wesley.

Lectures in Medical Psychology: An Introduction to the Care of Patients. Grete L. Bibring & Ralph J. Kahana. LC 68-57279. 289p. 1969. 42.50 (*0-8236-2970-8*) Intl Univs Pr.

Lectures in Naturopathic Hydrotherapy. Wade Boyle & Andre Saine. (Illus.). 235p. (Orig.). 1988. pap. text 22.50 (*0-9623518-1-4*) Eclectic Med.

Lectures in Parallel Computation. Ed. by Alan Gibbons & Paul G. Spirakis. (International Series on Parallel Computation: No. 4). (Illus.). 447p. (C). 1993. text 59.95 (*0-521-41556-X*) Cambridge U Pr.

Lectures in Particle Physics. Dan Green. LC 95-104201. 484p. 1994. text 109.00 (*981-02-1682-3*); pap. text 61.00 (*981-02-1683-1*) World Scientific Pub.

***Lectures in Philosophy: A Beginner's Guide to the Logic of Discourse & Disputation.** Ira Altman. 102p. 2000. pap. text 11.00i (*1-891877-07-0*) Sheron Ent.

Lectures in Probability & Statistics. Ed. by G. Del Pino & R. Rebolledo. (Lecture Notes in Mathematics Ser.: Vol. 1215). (ENG & FRE.). v, 491p. 1986. 58.30 (*0-387-16822-2*) Spr-Verlag.

Lectures in Probability Theory & Statistics. M. T. Barlow & D. Nualart. Ed. by B. Pierre et al. (Lecture Notes in Mathematics Ser.: Vol. 1690). viii, 237p. 1998. pap. 41.00 (*3-540-64620-5*) Spr-Verlag.

Lectures in Psychiatry: The Functional Psychoses, Vol. 1. Ken Reed. (Illus.). 304p. 1985. 37.50 (*0-87527-339-4*) Green.

Lectures in Real Geometry. Ed. by Fabrizio Broglia. LC 96-31731. (Expositions in Mathematics Ser.: Vol. 23). xiv, 268p. (C). 1996. lib. bdg. 98.95 (*3-11-015095-6*) De Gruyter.

Lectures in Relativity & Gravitation: A Modern Look. A. A. Logunov. Tr. by Alexander Repyev. (Illus.). 256p. 1991. 92.00 (*0-08-037939-7*, Pergamon Pr) Elsevier.

Lectures in Rings & Modules. 3rd ed. Joachim Lambek. LC 75-41494. viii, 184p. 1986. 16.95 (*0-8284-2283-4*) Chelsea Pub.

Lectures in Scattering Theory. A. G. Sitenko. Ed. & Tr. by P. J. Shepherd. 280p. 1971. 123.00 (*0-08-016574-5*, Pub. by Pergamon Repr) Franklin.

Lectures in Statistical Mechanics. George Uhlenbeck et al. LC 62-21480. (Lectures in Applied Mathematics: Vol. 1). 181p. 1963. pap. 45.00 (*0-8218-1101-0*, LAM/1) Am Math.

Lectures in Statistical Mechanics: With an Appendix on Quantum Statistics of Interacting Particles. George E. Uhlenbeck. LC 62-21480. (Lectures in Applied Mathematics: No. 1). (Illus.). 193p. 1963. reprint ed. pap. 59.90 (*0-608-03975-6*, 205256700012) Bks Demand.

Lectures in Synergetics. V. I. Sugakov. LC 98-26350. (Nonlinear Science Ser.). 200p. 1998. 38.00 (*981-02-3495-3*) World Scientific Pub.

Lectures in Systematic Theology. rev. ed. Henry C. Thiessen. 1989. 32.00 (*0-8028-3529-5*) Eerdmans.

Lectures in the History of Mathematics. Henk J. Bos. LC 93-28299. (History of Mathematics Ser.: No. 7). 197p. 1993. pap. 39.00 (*0-8218-0920-2*) Am Math.

Lectures in the History of Mathematics. Henk J. Bos. LC 93-28299. (History of Mathematics Ser.: No. 7). 197p. 1993. 86.00 (*0-8218-9001-8*, HMATH/7) Am Math.

Lectures in the Physics of Highly Correlated Electron Systems. Ed. by Ferdinando Mancini. LC 98-71903. (Conference Proceedings Ser.: Vol. 438). (Illus.). 208p. 1998. 62.00 (*1-56396-789-8*) Spr-Verlag.

Lectures in the Sciences of Complexity. Ed. by Daniel L. Stein. (Santa Fe Institute Ser.). (Illus.). 896p. (C). 1989. 49.95 (*0-201-51015-4*) Addison-Wesley.

***Lectures in the Structure of English.** Robert Carlisle. 210p. (C). 1999. per. 26.95 (*0-7872-6443-1*, 41644301) Kendall-Hunt.

Lectures, 1991: Witte de With. (Happy Day Bks.). (Illus.). 112p. (Orig.). 1991. pap. 24.50 (*90-73362-19-9*, Pub. by Witte De With CFCA) Dist Art Pubs.

Lectures Notes on Geometrical Aspects of Partial Differential Equations. V. V. Zharinov. (Series on Soviet & East European Mathematics: Vol. 8). 372p. (C). 1992. text 61.00 (*981-02-0753-0*) World Scientific Pub.

Lectures of a Chapter, Senate & Council: According to the Forms of the Ancient & Primitive Rite, but Embracing All Systems of Masonry. John Yarker. 104p. 1998. reprint ed. pap. 15.95 (*1-56459-343-6*) Kessinger Pub.

Lectures of Fiber Science in Paper. Alfred H. Nissan. LC TS1120.N5. (Pulp & Paper Technology Ser.: No. 4). (Illus.). 163p. reprint ed. pap. 50.60 (*0-8357-8206-9*, 203395400087) Bks Demand.

Lectures of Professor T. G. Masaryk at the University of Chicago, Summer 1902. Draga Shillinglaw. LC 77-68. 172p. 1978. 28.50 (*0-8387-2094-3*) Bucknell U Pr.

Lectures of the Arya. Albert Pike. 340p. 1992. reprint ed. pap. 45.00 (*1-56459-182-4*) Kessinger Pub.

Lectures on a Method in the Theory of Exponential Sums. M. I. Jutila. viii, 138p. 1988. 30.95 (*0-387-18366-3*) Spr-Verlag.

Lectures on Administrative Law. C. K. Takwani. (C). 1991. 60.00 (*0-89771-774-0*, Pub. by Eastern Book) St Mut.

Lectures on Administrative Law. C. K. Takwani. 366p. 1980. 75.00 (*0-7855-1725-1*) St Mut.

Lectures on Administrative Law. 2nd ed. C. K. Takwani. (C). 1994. 40.00 (*81-7012-524-3*, Pub. by Eastern Book) St Mut.

Lectures on Advanced Numerical Analysis. F. John. (Notes on Mathematics & Its Applications Ser.). xiv, 180p. 1967. text 142.00 (*0-677-00315-3*) Gordon & Breach.

Lectures on Air Pollution & Environmental Impact Analyses. Ed. by Duane A. Haugen. (Illus.). 296p. 1982. 35.00 (*0-933876-42-4*) Am Meteorological.

Lectures on Air Pollution Modeling. Ed. by Akula Venkatram & John C. Wyngaard. (Illus.). 390p. 1988. 50.00 (*0-933876-67-X*) Am Meteorological.

Lectures on Algebraic Topology. A. Dold. LC 79-79062. (Grundlehren der Mathematischen Wissenschaften Ser.: Vol. 200). (Illus.). 377p. 1980. 79.00 (*0-387-10369-4*) Spr-Verlag.

Lectures on Algebraic Topology. 2nd ed. A. Dold. LC 94-39729. (Classics in Mathematics Ser.). 376p. 1995. 35.00 (*3-540-58660-1*) Spr-Verlag.

Lectures on Analytical Mechanics. 2nd ed. Felix R. Gantmacher. write for info. (*0-318-51343-9*) Chelsea Pub.

Lectures on Ancient Philosophy. Manly P. Hall. LC 84-25365. 512p. 1999. pap. 24.95 (*0-89314-820-2*) Philos Res.

Lectures on Applications-Oriented Mathematics. Bernard Friedman. LC 91-216. 257p. 1991. pap. 84.95 (*0-471-54290-3*) Wiley.

***Lectures on Applied Mathematics: Proceedings of the Symposium Organized by the Sonderforschungsbereich 438 "Mathematical Modeling, Simulation & Intelligent Systems" on the Occasion of Karl-Heinz Hoffmann's 60th Birthday, Munich, June 30-July 1, 1999.** Ed. by H. J. Bungartz et al. ix, 329p. 2000. 84.00 (*3-540-66734-2*) Spr-Verlag.

Lectures on Arakelov Geometry. C. Soule et al. (Studies in Advanced Mathematics: No. 33). 185p. (C). 1995. pap. text 25.95 (*0-521-47709-3*) Cambridge U Pr.

Lectures on Architecture. James Elmes. LC 71-174408. 440p. 1979. reprint ed. 30.95 (*0-405-08486-2*, Pub. by Blom Pubns) Ayer.

Lectures on Architecture, 2 vols., I. Eugene E. Viollet-Le-Duc. (Illus.). 1120p. 1987. reprint ed. pap. 13.95 (*0-486-25520-4*) Dover.

Lectures on Architecture, 2 vols., Vol. II. Eugene E. Viollet-Le-Duc. (Illus.). 1120p. 1987. reprint ed. pap. 13.95 (*0-486-25521-2*) Dover.

Lectures on Architecture & Painting see Complete Works of John Ruskin

Lectures on Art. John Ruskin. LC 96-84638. (Illus.). 224p. (Orig.). 1997. pap. 18.95 (*1-880559-54-4*) Allworth Pr.

Lectures on Art. Reginald L. Poole. LC 77-39677. (Essay Index Reprint Ser.). 1977. reprint ed. 16.95 (*0-8369-2781-8*) Ayer.

Lectures on Art, 2 vols. Hippolyte A. Taine. LC 75-137295. (Illus.). reprint ed. 115.00 (*0-404-06333-0*) AMS Pr.

Lectures on Art, & Poems, 1850, & Monaldi, 1841. Washington Allston. LC 67-10124. 646p. 1967. 75.00 (*0-8201-1001-9*) Schol Facsimiles.

Lectures on Art, Artra Pentelici see Complete Works of John Ruskin

Lectures on Art-Poems. Washington Allston. LC 75-171379. (Library of American Art). 1972. reprint ed. lib. bdg. 49.50 (*0-306-70414-5*) Da Capo.

Lectures on Artinian Rings. A. Kertesz & Richard Wiegandt. 427p. (C). 1987. 144.00 (*963-05-4309-5*, Pub. by Akade Kiado) St Mut.

Lectures on Artinian Rings. Andor Kertesz. 428p. (C). 1987. 338.00 (*0-569-09064-4*, Pub. by Collets) St Mut.

Lectures on Atomic & Molecular Physics. LC 97-108901. 320p. 1996. lib. bdg. 34.00 (*981-02-2811-2*) World Scientific Pub.

Lectures on Atomic Energy Industrial & Legal Problems. Summer Institute on International & Comparative La. (Michigan Legal Publications). vi, 280p. 1986. reprint ed. lib. bdg. 40.00 (*0-89941-492-3*, 304190) W S Hein.

Lectures on Bible Prophecy. James A. Borland. 123p. (Orig.). (C). 1991. pap. text 9.95 (*0-936461-03-9*) Univ Book Hse.

Lectures on Bifurcation, Dynamics & Symmetry. Michael Field. (Pitman Research Notes in Mathematics Ser.). 1996. pap. 47.95 (*0-582-30346-X*, Pub. by Addison-Wesley) Longman.

Lectures on Block Theory. 114p. 1991. pap. text 29.95 (*0-521-40565-3*) Cambridge U Pr.

Lectures on Bochner-Riesz Means. K. M. Davis & Y. C. Chang. (London Mathematical Society Lecture Note Ser.: No. 114). 160p. 1987. pap. text 42.95 (*0-521-31277-9*) Cambridge U Pr.

Lectures on C. H. Spurgeon. Eric W. Hayden & Philip Hayden. 1995. pap. 5.00 (*1-56186-250-9*) Pilgrim Pubns.

Lectures on Calvinism. Abraham Kuyper. 199p. 1943. pap. 13.00 (*0-8028-1607-X*) Eerdmans.

Lectures on Celestial Mechanics. rev. ed. Carl L. Siegel & Juergen K. Moser. Tr. by C. I. Kalme from GER. LC 71-155595. (Grundlehren der Mathematischen Wissenschaften Ser.: Vol. 187). 1971. 89.00 (*0-387-05419-7*) Spr-Verlag.

Lectures on Celestial Mechanics. 2nd ed. C. L. Siegel & Juergen K. Moser. Tr. by C. I. Kalme from GER. LC 94-39114. (Classics in Mathematics Ser.).Tr. of Vorlesungen uber Himmelsmechanik. 290p. 1995. 35.00 (*3-540-58656-3*) Spr-Verlag.

Lectures on Church Co-Operation & Orphan Homes. Thomas B. Warren. 1958. pap. 7.00 (*0-934916-48-9*) Natl Christian Pr.

Lectures on Classical Differential Geometry. 2nd ed. Dirk J. Struik. (Illus.). 240p. 1988. reprint ed. pap. 8.95 (*0-486-65609-8*) Dover.

Lectures on Closed Geodesics. Klingenberg. LC 77-13147. (Grundlehren der Mathematischen Wissenschaften Ser.: Vol. 230). 1978. 81.95 (*0-387-08393-6*) Spr-Verlag.

Lectures on Colonization & Colonies Delivered Before the University of Oxford in 1839, 1840, & 1841. 2nd ed. Herman Merivale. LC 67-25954. (Reprints of Economic Classics Ser.). xix, 685p. 1967. reprint ed. 57.50 (*0-678-00273-8*) Kelley.

Lectures on Communications Media Legal & Policy Problems. Summer Institute on International & Comparative La. (Michigan Legal Publications). v, 234p. 1986. reprint ed. lib. bdg. 40.00 (*0-89941-494-X*, 304210) W S Hein.

Lectures on Complex Analysis: Proceedings of the Symposium. Chi-Tai Chuang. 420p. 1988. text 99.00 (*9971-5-0707-2*) World Scientific Pub.

Lectures on Complex Analytic Varieties: Finite Analytic Mappings. Robert C. Gunning. LC 74-2969. (Mathematical Notes Ser.: Vol. 14). 168p. 1974. reprint ed. pap. 52.10 (*0-608-03356-1*, 206406800008) Bks Demand.

Lectures on Complex Approximation. Dieter Gaier. 180p. 1987. 64.00 (*0-8176-3147-X*) Birkhauser.

Lectures on Computational Fluid Dynamics, Mathematical Physics & Linear Algebra. K. Gustafson. LC 98-135825. 180p. 1997. pap. text 28.00 (*981-02-3213-6*) World Scientific Pub.

Lectures on Constructive Mathematical Analysis. B. Kushner. Tr. by E. Mendelson. LC 84-18459. (Translations of Mathematical Monographs: Vol. 60). 346p. 1985. text 129.00 (*0-8218-4513-6*, MMONO/60) Am Math.

***Lectures on Contemporary Probability** Gregory F. Lawler & Lester N. Coyle. LC 99-23838. (Student Mathematical Library). 1999. pap. write for info. (*0-8218-2029-X*) Am Math.

Lectures on Contemporary Syntactic Theories. Peter Sells. LC 87-10243. (CSLI Lecture Notes Ser.: No. 3). 225p. 1986. 59.95 (*0-937073-13-X*); pap. 18.95 (*0-937073-14-8*) CSLI.

Lectures on Cooperative Phenomena in Condensed Matter. Ed. by D. N. Uzunov. 230p. 1997. 89.95 (*954-580-017-8*, Pub. by Heron Pr) Intl Scholars.

Lectures on Cosmology & Action at a Distance Electrodynamics. Fred Hoyle & Jayant V. Narlikar. (Astronomy & Astrophysics Ser.: Vol. 2). 148p. 1996. 38.00 (*981-02-2558-X*); pap. 16.00 (*981-02-2573-3*) World Scientific Pub.

Lectures on Counseling. Jay Edward Adams. (Jay Adams Library). 288p. 1986. pap. 8.95 (*0-310-51121-6*, 12124P) Zondervan.

Lectures on Counterexamples in Several Complex Variables. John E. Fornaess & Berit Stensones. LC 87-2350. (Mathematical Notes Ser.: Vol. 33). (Illus.). 256p. reprint ed. pap. 79.40 (*0-608-09101-4*, 206973500005) Bks Demand.

Lectures on Criminal Procedure. R. V. Kelkar. 403p. 1980. 75.00 (*0-7855-1323-X*) St Mut.

Lectures on Criminal Procedure. 2nd ed. R. V. Kelkar. (C). 1990. 40.00 (*0-7855-5148-4*) St Mut.

Lectures on Curves on Rational & Unirational Surfaces. Masayoshi Miyanishi. (Tata Institute Lecture Notes Ser.). 1979. 38.95 (*0-387-08943-8*) Spr-Verlag.

Lectures on Data Security: Modern Cryptology in Theory & Practice. I. B. Damgard. LC 99-21384. (Lecture Notes in Computer Science Ser.: Vol. 1561). 250p. 1999. 39.00 (*3-540-65757-6*) Spr-Verlag.

Lectures on Deixis. Charles J. Fillmore. LC 96-35248. (CSLI Lecture Notes Ser.). 145p. (C). 1997. 54.95 (*1-57586-007-4*); pap. 17.95 (*1-57586-006-6*) CSLI.

Lectures on Differential & Integral Equations. Kosaku Yosida. 220p. 1991. pap. 8.95 (*0-486-66679-4*) Dover.

Lectures on Differential Equations. Solomon Lefschetz. LC 46-5010. (Annals of Mathematics Studies: No. 14). 216p. reprint ed. pap. 67.00 (*0-608-06640-0*, 206683700009) Bks Demand.

Lectures on Differential Galois Theory. Andy R. Magid. LC 94-10431. (University Lectures: Vol. 7). 105p. 1994. pap. 19.00 (*0-8218-7004-1*, ULECT/7) Am Math.

Lectures on Differential Geometry. Su Buchin. 149p. 1981. text 24.00 (*9971-83-003-5*); pap. text 17.00 (*9971-83-004-3*) World Scientific Pub.

Lectures on Differential Geometry. S. S. Chern et al. LC 98-22031. 250p. 1998. 38.00 (*981-02-3494-5*) World Scientific Pub.

Lectures on Differential Geometry. R. Schoen & S. T. Yau. (Monographs in Geometry & Topology). 414p. 1995. 42.00 (*1-57146-012-8*) Intl Pr Boston.

Lectures on Differential Geometry. 2nd ed. Shlomo Sternberg. LC 81-71141. xvii, 438p. (C). 1983. text 29.50 (*0-8284-0316-3*, 316) Chelsea Pub.

Lectures on Discrete Time Filtering. Richard S. Bucy. LC 93-43310. (Signal Processing & Digital Filtering Ser.). (Illus.). 176p. 1994. 54.95 (*0-387-94198-3*) Spr-Verlag.

Lectures on Divine Humanity. rev. ed. Vladimir Solovyov. Tr. by Peter Zouboff. 189p. 1995. pap. 18.95 (*0-940262-67-3*, Lindisfarne) Anthroposophic.

Lectures on Division Algebras. D. J. Saltman. LC 99-25461. (Regional Conference Series in Mathematics). vii, 120p. 1999. write for info. (*0-8218-0979-2*) Am Math.

Lectures on Dynamical Systems, Structural Stability & Their Application. Ed. by K. K. Lee. 420p. (C). 1992. text 74.00 (*9971-5-0965-2*) World Scientific Pub.

Lectures on Early English History. William Stubbs. vi, 391p. 1980. reprint ed. 45.00 (*0-8377-1109-6*, Rothman) W S Hein.

An Asterisk (*) at the beginning of an entry indicates that the title is appearing for the first time.

Lectures on Economic Development: Japan's Experience & Its Relevance. Kazushi Ohkawa & Hirohisa Kohama. 380p. 1989. 57.50 (*0-86008-438-8*, Pub. by U of Tokyo) Col U Pr.

Lectures on Education. Horace Mann. LC 70-89197. (American Education: Its Men, Institutions, & Ideas. Series 1). 1978. reprint ed. 19.95 (*0-405-01437-6*) Ayer.

Lectures on Education. Horace Mann. (Notable American Authors Ser.). 1999. reprint ed. lib. bdg. 125.00 (*0-7812-3934-6*) Rprt Serv.

Lectures on Electrochemical Corrosion. 3rd expanded ed. Marcel Pourbaix. LC 95-68977. (Illus.). 342p. (C). 1995. reprint ed. pap. text 97.00 (*1-877914-91-6*, 37555) NACE Intl.

Lectures on Elementary Number Theory. Hans Rademacher. LC 76-30495. 156p. 1977. reprint ed. lib. bdg. 18.50 (*0-88275-499-8*) Krieger.

Lectures on Elliptic & Parabolic Equations in Holder Spaces. N. V. Krylov. LC 96-19426. (Graduate Studies in Mathematics). 164p. 1996. text 29.00 (*0-8218-0569-X*, GSM/12) Am Math.

Lectures on Elliptic Curves. J. W. Cassels. (London Mathematical Society Student Texts Ser.: No. 24). (Illus.). 143p. (C). 1991. pap. text 27.95 (*0-521-42530-1*) Cambridge U Pr.

Lectures on Embedded Systems: European Educational Forum School on Embedded Systems, Veldhoven, the Netherlands, November 25-29, 1996. European Educational Forum School on Embedded Systems et al. LC 98-46725. (Lecture Notes in Computer Science Ser.). viii, 421 p. 1998. 49.95 (*3-540-65193-4*) Spr-Verlag.

Lectures on English History & Tragic Poetry. Henry Reed. LC 72-174305. reprint ed. 36.50 (*0-404-05234-7*) AMS Pr.

Lectures on English Poets. James Russell Lowell. (Notable American Authors Ser.). 1999. reprint ed. lib. bdg. 125.00 (*0-7812-3901-X*) Rprt Serv.

Lectures on Entire Functions. B. Y. Levin et al. LC 96-318. (Translations of Mathematical Monographs: Vol. 150). 265p. 1996. text 99.00 (*0-8218-0282-8*, MMONO/150) Am Math.

Lectures on Equations Defining Space Curves. L. Szpiro. (Tata Institute Lectures on Mathematics). (Illus.). 81p. 1980. 35.95 (*0-387-09544-6*) Spr-Verlag.

Lectures on Ergodic Theory & Pesin Theory on Compact Manifolds. Mark Pollicott. (London Mathematical Society Lecture Note Ser.: No. 180). (Illus.). 170p. (C). 1993. pap. text 44.95 (*0-521-43593-5*) Cambridge U Pr.

***Lectures on Ethics.** Immanuel Kant. Ed. by Peter Heath & J. B. Schneewind. (The Cambridge Edition of the Works of Immanuel Kant). 537p. (Orig.). (C). 2000. pap. text Price not set. (*0-521-78804-8*) Cambridge U Pr.

Lectures on Ethics. Immanuel Kant. Tr. by Louis Infield from GER. LC 80-22092. (HPC Classics Ser.). 272p. (Orig.). (C). 1980. reprint ed. pap. text 8.95 (*0-915144-26-3*) Hackett Pub.

Lectures on Ethics, 1900-1901. John Dewey. Ed. by Donald F. Koch. LC 90-36858. 608p. (C). 1991. 57.00 (*0-8093-1663-3*) S Ill U Pr.

Lectures on Exceptional Lie Groups. J. F. Adams. Ed. by Zafer Mahmud & Mamoru Mimura. (Chicago Lectures in Mathematics). (Illus.). 128p. 1996. pap. text 19.95 (*0-226-00527-5*); lib. bdg. 45.00 (*0-226-00526-7*) U Ch Pr.

Lectures on Faith. N. B. Lundwall. pap. 5.95 (*0-88494-442-5*) Bookcraft Inc.

Lectures on Faith. Joseph Smith. LC 84-73495. 88p. 1985. 9.95 (*0-87747-897-X*) Deseret Bk.

Lectures on Faith. Joseph Smith. pap. 5.95 (*1-57734-637-8*) Covenant Comms.

Lectures on Faith in Historical Perspective. Ed. by Dahl & Charles D. Tate. (Monograph Ser.: Vol. 15). 1990. 11.95 (*0-88494-725-4*) Bookcraft Inc.

Lectures on Federal Antitrust Laws. Summer Institute on International & Comparative La. LC 54-1519. (Michigan Legal Publications). xiii, 321p. 1984. reprint ed. lib. bdg. 40.00 (*0-89941-323-4*, 303150) W S Hein.

Lectures on Finite Precision Computations. Francoise C. Chatelin & Valerie Fraysse. LC 95-45140. (Software, Environments & Tools Ser.: No. 1). xvi, 235p. 1996. pap. 47.50 (*0-89871-358-7*, SE01) Soc Indus-Appl Math.

Lectures on Fluid Mechanics. M. Shinbrot. (Notes on Mathematics & Its Applications Ser.). xiv, 222p. (C). 1973. text 220.00 (*0-677-01710-3*) Gordon & Breach.

Lectures on Fluid Mechanics. Sidney Goldstein. LC 60-12712. (Lectures in Applied Mathematics: Vol. 2A). 311p. 1982. reprint ed. pap. 58.00 (*0-8218-0048-5*, LAM 2.1) Am Math.

Lectures on Formally Real Fields. A. Prestel. (Lecture Notes in Mathematics Ser.: Vol. 1093). xi, 125p. 1984. reprint ed. 29.95 (*0-387-13885-4*) Spr-Verlag.

Lectures on Fourier Integrals: With an Author's Supplement on Monotonic Functions, Stieltjes Integrals, & Harmonic Analysis. Salomon Bochner. Tr. by Morris Tenenbaum & Harry Pollard. LC 59-5589. (Annals of Mathematics Studies: No. 42). 343p. reprint ed. pap. 106.40 (*0-608-06637-0*, 206683400009) Bks Demand.

Lectures on Freshman Calculus. Allan Cruse & Millianne Granberg. 1971. pap. 25.95 (*0-201-01301-0*) Addison-Wesley.

Lectures on Functional Analysis & Applications. V. S. Pugachev. LC 99-26757. 1999. pap. text 38.00 (*981-02-3723-5*) World Scientific Pub.

Lectures on Functions of a Complex Variable. Ed. by Wilfred Kaplan. LC 55-7150. 446p. reprint ed. pap. 138.30 (*0-608-30480-8*, 205105000074) Bks Demand.

Lectures on Galen's de Sectis. Agnellus of Ravenna. (Arethusa Monographs: No. 8). xviii, 181p. (C). 1981. pap. 10.00 (*0-930881-05-2*) Dept Classics.

Lectures on Gas Chromatography, 1966. Ed. by Leonard R. Mattick & Herman A. Szymanski. LC 67-9658. (Illus.). 235p. 1967. reprint ed. pap. 72.90 (*0-608-05760-6*, 205972400007) Bks Demand.

Lectures on Gas Chromatography, 1962: Based on Lectures Presented at the Advanced Session of the 4th Annual Gas Chromatography Institute Held at Canisius College, Buffalo, New York, April 23-26, 1962. Ed. by Herman A. Syzmanski. LC 61-15520. (Illus.). 288p. reprint ed. pap. 89.30 (*0-608-11580-0*, 201939100011) Bks Demand.

Lectures on Gas Theory. Ludwig Boltzmann. Tr. by Stephen G. Brush. LC 94-41221. (Illus.). 512p. 1995. pap. text 12.95 (*0-486-68455-5*) Dover.

Lectures on General Relativity. A. Papapetrou. LC 74-81943. 203p. 1974. pap. text 88.00 (*90-277-0540-2*); lib. bdg. 104.50 (*90-277-0514-3*) Kluwer Academic.

Lectures on Geology. John Walker. Ed. by Harold W. Scott. LC 65-24986. 330p. reprint ed. 102.30 (*0-8357-9647-7*, 201576400003) Bks Demand.

Lectures on Geometric Methods in Mathematical Physics. Jerrold E. Marsden. LC 80-54307. (CBMS-NSF Regional Conference Ser.: No. 37). v, 97p. 1981. pap. text 27.00 (*0-89871-170-3*) Soc Indus-Appl Math.

Lectures on Geometric Variational Problems. Ed. by S. Nishikawa & R. Schoen. 154p. 1996. pap. 39.00 (*4-431-70152-4*) Spr-Verlag.

Lectures on Geophysical Fluid Dynamics. Rick Salmon. LC 97-1811. (Illus.). 400p. 1998. text 75.00 (*0-19-510808-6*) OUP.

Lectures on Government & Binding: The Pisa Lectures. 7th ed. Noam Chomsky. (Studies in Generative Grammar: No. 9). x, 371p. 1993. pap. text 24.95 (*3-11-014131-0*) Mouton.

Lectures on Greek Poetry. J. W. Mackail. LC 66-23520. 1910. 28.00 (*0-8196-0180-2*) Biblo.

Lectures on Group Theory & Particle Theory. Henri Bacry. LC 72-78879. (Documents on Modern Physics Ser.). (Illus.). xviii, 580p. (C). 1977. text 531.00 (*0-677-30190-1*) Gordon & Breach.

Lectures on Groups & Vector Spaces for Physicists. Ed. by C. J. Isham. (Lecture Notes in Physics Ser.: Vol. 31). 228p. (C). 1989. text 53.00 (*9971-5-0954-7*); pap. text 28.00 (*9971-5-0955-5*) World Scientific Pub.

Lectures on Hamiltonian Systems. Walter T. Kyner & Jurgen Moser. LC 52-42839. (American Mathematical Society Ser.: No. 81). (Illus.). 31p. reprint ed. pap. 30.00 (*0-608-09203-7*, 205270700003) Bks Demand.

Lectures on Hamiltonian Systems, & Rigorous & Formal Stability of Orbits about an Oblate Planet. Jurgen Moser & Walter T. Kyner. LC 52-42839. (Memoirs Ser.: No. 1/81). 87p. 1989. reprint ed. pap. 19.00 (*0-8218-1281-5*, MEMO/1/81) Am Math.

Lectures on Harmonic Maps. R. Schoen & S. T. Yau. LC 99-162554. (Monographs in Geometry & Topology). 394p. (C). 1997. text. write for info. (*1-57146-002-0*) Intl Pr Boston.

Lectures on Hermite & Laguerre Expansions. Sundaram Thangavelu. LC 93-16643. (Mathematical Notes Ser.: No. 42). 214p. 1993. pap. text 29.95 (*0-691-00048-4*, Pub. by Princeton U Pr) Cal Prin Full Svc.

Lectures on Hermitian-Einstein Metrics for Stable Bundles & Kahler-Einstein Metrics. Yum-Tong Siu. (DMV Seminar Ser.: No. 8). 172p. 1989. 54.00 (*0-8176-1931-3*) Birkhauser.

Lectures on Hilbert Cube Manifolds. T. A. Chapman. LC 76-48316. (CBMS Regional Conference Series in Mathematics: No. 28). 131p. 1977. reprint ed. pap. 19.00 (*0-8218-1678-0*, CBMS/28) Am Math.

***Lectures on Hilbert Schemes of Points on Surfaces.** Hiraku Nakajima. LC 99-39163. (University Lecture Ser.). 132p. 1999. 21.00 (*0-8218-1956-9*) Am Math.

Lectures on Homeopathic Philosophy. James T. Kent. 244p. 1979. reprint ed. pap. 14.95 (*0-913028-61-4*) North Atlantic.

Lectures on Human & Animal Psychology. Wilhelm M. Wundt. 470p. 120.00 (*1-85506-680-7*) Thoemmes Pr.

Lectures on Human & Animal Psychology, 1. Wilhelm M. Wundt. Tr. by J. Creighton from GER. LC 77-72191. (Contributions to the History of Psychology Ser.: Pt. D, Vol. I, Comparative Psychology). 454p. 1977. reprint ed. lib. bdg. 79.50 (*0-313-26945-9*, U6945) Greenwood.

Lectures on Hyperbolic Geometry. R. Benedetti & C. Petronio. LC 92-20163. (Universitext Ser.). (Illus.). 352p. 1996. 39.00 (*0-387-55534-X*) Spr-Verlag.

Lectures on Hyponormal Operators. M. Martin & M. Putinar. (Operator Theory Ser.: No. 39). 304p. 1989. 132.00 (*0-8176-2329-9*) Birkhauser.

Lectures on Ideology & Utopia. Paul Ricoeur. Ed. by George Taylor. LC 86-6813. 384p. 1986. text 68.00 (*0-231-06048-3*) Col U Pr.

Lectures on Inflationary Universe Models & Cosmic Strings. R. Brandenberger. 250p. (C). 1992. text 53.00 (*9971-5-0266-6*); pap. text 30.00 (*9971-5-0267-4*) World Scientific Pub.

Lectures on Integrable Systems. Ed. by Jens Hoope et al. LC 92-18024. (Lecture Notes in Physics, New Series, Monographs: Vol. 10). vii, 111p. 1992. 50.95 (*0-387-55700-8*) Spr-Verlag.

Lectures on Integrable Systems: Proceedings of the Cimpa School in Memory of Jean-Louis Verdier. O. Babelon et al. 368p. 1994. text 68.00 (*981-02-1757-9*) World Scientific Pub.

Lectures on Integrable Systems - In Memory of Jean-Louis Verdier: Proceedings of the Cimpa School. O. Babelon et al. 1994. text 86.00 (*981-02-1713-7*) World Scientific Pub.

Lectures on Integral Transforms. N. I. Akhiezer. LC 88-19393. (Translations of Mathematical Monographs: No. 70). 108p. 1988. text 57.00 (*0-8218-4524-1*, MMONO/70) Am Math.

Lectures on International Law: Delivered in the Middle Temple Hall to the Students of the Inns of Court. Sheldon Amos. xii, 136p. 1983. reprint ed. 30.00 (*0-8377-0215-1*, Rothman) W S Hein.

Lectures on International Law & the United Nations. Summer Institute on International & Comparative La. (Michigan Legal Publications). (12) & 566p. 1986. reprint ed. lib. bdg. 52.00 (*0-89941-495-8*, 304220) W S Hein.

Lectures on International Trade. Jagdish N. Bhagwati & T. N. Srinivasan. LC 82-18030. (Illus.). 464p. 1983. 49.50 (*0-262-02185-4*) MIT Pr.

Lectures on International Trade. 2nd ed. Jagdish N. Bhagwati et al. LC 98-10303. (Illus.). 675p. 1998. 55.00 (*0-262-02443-8*) MIT Pr.

Lectures on International Trade. 2nd ed. Arvind Panagariya & Jagdish N. Bhagwati. 1998. pap. text 22.50 (*0-262-52247-0*) MIT Pr.

Lectures on Jung's Typology. Marie-Louise Von Franz & James Hillman. LC 86-17912. (Seminar Ser.: No. 4). 182p. (Orig.). (C). 1971. pap. 17.00 (*0-88214-104-X*) Spring Pubns.

Lectures on Jurisprudence. Adam Smith. Ed. by R. L. Meek & D. D. Raphael. (Glasgow Edition of the Works & Correspondence of Adam Smith). 654p. 1978. text 110.00 (*0-19-828188-9*) OUP.

Lectures on Jurisprudence. John Austin. 1988. reprint ed. lib. bdg. 75.00 (*0-7812-0393-7*) Rprt Serv.

Lectures on Jurisprudence: Glasgow Edition. Adam Smith. LC 81-23689. 618p. (C). 1982. reprint ed. pap. 7.50 (*0-86597-011-4*) Liberty Fund.

Lectures on Jurisprudence: or the Philosophy of Positive Law. John Austin. 1976. 79.00 (*0-403-06116-4*, Regency) Scholarly.

Lectures on Jurisprudence: or The Philosophy of Positive Law, 2 vols. 4th rev. ed. John Austin. Ed. by Robert Campbell. xxiii, 1169p. 1998. reprint ed. 298.00 (*1-56169-360-X*) Gaunt.

Lectures on Kant's Political Philosophy. Hannah Arendt. Ed. by Ronald S. Beiner. LC 82-4817. 192p. 1982. 17.50 (*0-226-02594-2*) U Ch Pr.

Lectures on Kant's Political Philosophy. Hannah Arendt. Ed. by Ronald S. Beiner. LC 82-4817. 184p. 1989. pap. text 13.00 (*0-226-02595-0*) U Ch Pr.

Lectures on Language Performance. C. E. Osgood. (Language & Communication Ser.: Vol. 7). (Illus.). 368p. 1980. 90.95 (*0-387-09901-8*) Spr-Verlag.

Lectures on Law: Prepared Principally from Kent, by a Lawyer, for the Use of His Sons. John Fine. 320p. 1995. reprint ed. 40.00 (*0-8377-2417-1*, Rothman) W S Hein.

Lectures on Legal History. James B. Ames. Ed. by R. H. Helmholz & Bernard D. Reams, Jr. LC 86-62934. (Historical Writings in Law & Jurisprudence Ser.: No. 3). viii, 553p. 1986. reprint ed. lib. bdg. 47.50 (*0-89941-517-2*, 304530) W S Hein.

Lectures on Legal History. 2nd rev. ed. W. J. Windeyer. xxiv, 335p. 1957. pap. 47.00 (*0-455-14240-8*, Pub. by LawBk Co) Gaunt.

Lectures on Legal History & Miscellaneous Legal Essays. James B. Ames. 1976. lib. bdg. 59.95 (*0-8490-2137-5*) Gordon Pr.

Lectures on Lie Groups. Frank J. Adams. LC 82-51014. (Midway Reprint Ser.). 192p. (C). 1983. pap. text 25.00 (*0-226-00530-5*) U Ch Pr.

Lectures on Lie Groups. Wu Yi Hsiang. LC 98-22021. 1998. 52.00 (*981-02-3522-4*) World Scientific Pub.

Lectures on Lie Groups. Wu-Yi Hsiang. (University Mathematics Ser.: Vol. 2). 200p. 1998. pap. text 26.00 (*981-02-3529-1*) World Scientific Pub.

Lectures on Lie Groups & Lie Algebras. Roger Carter et al. (London Mathematical Society Student Texts Ser.: No. 32). (Illus.). 198p. (C). 1995. text 69.95 (*0-521-49579-2*); pap. text 25.95 (*0-521-49922-4*) Cambridge U Pr.

Lectures on Light: Delivered in the United States in Eighteen Seventy-Two to Eighteen Seventy-Three. John Tyndall. Ed. by I. Bernard Cohen. LC 79-8003. (Three Centuries of Science in America Ser.). (Illus.). 1980. reprint ed. lib. bdg. 18.95 (*0-405-12592-5*) Ayer.

Lectures on Linear Algebra. I. M. Gelfand. 185p. 1989. pap. 7.95 (*0-486-66082-6*) Dover.

Lectures on Linear Algebra. Jin H. Kwak & Sungpyo Hong. LC 97-9062. 380p. 1997. 29.50 (*0-8176-3999-3*) Birkhauser.

Lectures on Linear Algebra. Jin H. Kwak & Sungpyo Hong. LC 97-9062. 380p. 1997. write for info. (*3-7643-3999-3*) Birkhauser.

Lectures on Linear Groups. O. Timothy O'Meara. LC 74-8773. (CBMS Regional Conference Series in Mathematics: No. 22). 87p. 1974. reprint ed. pap. 19.00 (*0-8218-1672-1*, CBMS/22) Am Math.

Lectures on Linear Logic. A. S. Troelstra. LC 91-38902. (Center for the Study of Language & Information-Lecture Notes Ser.). 200p. (C). 1992. 54.95 (*0-937073-78-4*); pap. 19.95 (*0-937073-77-6*) CSLI.

Lectures on Linear Partial Differential Equations. L. Nirenberg. LC 73-4400. (Regional Conference Series in Mathematics: No. 17). 66p. 1973. reprint ed. pap. 30.00 (*0-608-07824-7*, 205266900011) Bks Demand.

Lectures on Linear Partial Differential Equations. Louis Nirenberg. LC 73-4400. (CBMS Regional Conference Series in Mathematics: No. 17). 58p. 1973. reprint ed. pap. 16.00 (*0-8218-1667-5*, CBMS/17) Am Math.

Lectures on Literature. Columbia University Staff. LC 67-22059. (Essay Index Reprint Ser.). 1977. 23.95 (*0-8369-0329-3*) Ayer.

Lectures on Literature. Vladimir Nabokov. LC 79-3690. 416p. 1982. pap. 15.00 (*0-15-649589-9*, Harvest Bks) Harcourt.

Lectures on Literature: British, French & German Writers. Vladimir Nabokov. Ed. by Fredson Bowers. LC 79-3690. 416p. 1980. 19.95 (*0-15-149597-1*) Harcourt.

Lectures on Location Theory. M. J. Beckman. LC 99-25888. (Illus.). xiv, 195p. 1999. 69.95 (*3-540-65736-3*) Spr-Verlag.

Lectures on Longitudinal Analysis. James J. Heckman et al. (Underground Classics in Economics Ser.). 200p. (C). 1999. pap. 25.00 (*0-8133-8889-9*) Westview.

Lectures on Macroeconomics. Oliver J. Blanchard & Stanley Fischer. (Illus.). 656p. 1989. 50.00 (*0-262-02283-4*) MIT Pr.

Lectures on Magnetoionic Theory. K. G. Budden. (Documents on Modern Physics Ser.). xiv, 82p. 1964. text 176.00 (*0-677-00100-2*) Gordon & Breach.

Lectures on Mathematical Combustion. John D. Buckmaster & G. S. Ludford. LC 83-61375. (CBMS-NSF Regional Conference Series in Applied Mathematics: No. 43). viii, 126p. 1983. pap. text 28.50 (*0-89871-186-X*) Soc Indus-Appl Math.

Lectures on Mathematical Physics: Proceedings of the 1st Winter School on Mathematical Physics. Y. M. Cho. 236p. 1989. text 74.00 (*981-02-0065-X*) World Scientific Pub.

Lectures on Mechanics. Jerrold E. Marsden. (London Mathematical Society Lecture Note Ser.: No. 174). (Illus.). 266p. (C). 1992. pap. text 39.95 (*0-521-42844-0*) Cambridge U Pr.

Lectures on Metaphysics & Logic, 4 Vols. William Hamilton. reprint ed. 1500.00 (*3-7728-0170-6*) Adlers Foreign Bks.

Lectures on Microeconomic Theory. rev. ed. Edmond Malinvaud. Tr. by A. Silvey. (Advanced Textbooks in Economics Ser.: Vol. 2). 386p. 1985. 79.50 (*0-444-87650-2*, North Holland) Elsevier.

Lectures on Modern History: Delivered in Oxford, 1859-61. Goldwin A. Smith. LC 78-37865. (Essay Index Reprint Ser.). 1977. reprint ed. 20.95 (*0-8369-2627-7*) Ayer.

Lectures on Modern Magnetism. Beinard Barbara et al. (Illus.). 240p. 1988. 86.95 (*0-387-17558-X*) Spr-Verlag.

Lectures on Modern Novelists. Arthur T. Broes. Ed. by Carnegie Institute of Technology, Department of En. LC 72-1312. (Essay Index Reprint Ser.). 1977. reprint ed. 18.95 (*0-8369-2835-0*) Ayer.

Lectures on Modular Forms. Robert C. Gunning. (Annals of Mathematics Studies: No. 48). 96p. (Orig.). 1963. pap. text 29.95 (*0-691-07995-1*, Pub. by Princeton U Pr) Cal Prin Full Svc.

Lectures on Modular Forms. Robert C. Gunning. LC 62-7403. (Annals of Mathematics Studies: No. 48). (Illus.). 90p. (Orig.). 1962. reprint ed. pap. 30.00 (*0-608-02543-7*, 206318700004) Bks Demand.

Lectures on Moral Philosophy. John Witherspoon. Ed. by Varnum L. Collins. LC 75-3424. reprint ed. 27.50 (*0-404-59420-4*) AMS Pr.

Lectures on Moral Science. Mark Hopkins. LC 75-3197. reprint ed. 37.50 (*0-404-59198-1*) AMS Pr.

Lectures on Mysticism & Nature Worship. Carl H. Bjerregaard. (Second Ser.). 132p. 1996. reprint ed. spiral bd. 14.00 (*0-7873-0112-4*) Hlth Research.

Lectures on Mysticism & Nature Worship, 1897. Carl H. Bjerregaard. 132p. 1996. reprint ed. pap. 12.95 (*1-56459-753-9*) Kessinger Pub.

Lectures on N-Dimensional Quasiconformal Mappings. J. Vaeisaelae. LC 71-177355. (Lecture Notes in Mathematics Ser.: Vol. 229). 144p. 1971. 34.95 (*0-387-05648-3*) Spr-Verlag.

Lectures on Natural Right & Political Science Vol. 4: Heidelberg, 1817-1818, with Additions from the Lectures of 1818-1819. Georg Wilhelm Friedrich Hegel. Tr. by J. Michael Stewart & Peter C. Hodgson from GER. LC 95-31238. (Hegel Lectures: Vol. 4). 275p. 1996. 55.00 (*0-520-20104-3*, Pub. by U CA Pr) Cal Prin Full Svc.

Lectures on Negotiation Analysis. Howard Raiffa. LC 97-1106. 160p. (Orig.). (C). 1996. pap. 10.00 (*1-880711-09-5*) Prog Negot HLS.

Lectures on Nielsen Fixed Point Theory. Boju Jiang. LC 82-20756. (Contemporary Mathematics Ser.: Vol. 14). 110p. 1982. pap. 25.00 (*0-8218-5014-8*, CONM/14) Am Math.

Lectures on Nielsen Fixed Point Theory. Boju Jiang. LC 82-20756. (Contemporary Mathematics Ser.: No. 14). (Illus.). 119p. reprint ed. pap. 36.90 (*0-608-09200-2*, 205270400003) Bks Demand.

Lectures on Non-Linear Plasma Kinetics. V. N. Tsytovich. Ed. by G. Ecker et al. LC 95-32284. (Series on Atoms & Plasmas: Vol. 17). (Illus.). xii, 376p. 1995. 119.00 (*0-387-57844-7*) Spr-Verlag.

Lectures on Non-Perturbative Canonical Gravity. A. Ashtekar. 356p. (C). 1991. text 74.00 (*981-02-0573-2*); pap. text 40.00 (*981-02-0574-0*) World Scientific Pub.

Lectures on Nonlinear Hyperbolic Differential Equations. L. Hormander. (Mathematiques & Applications Ser.: Vol. 26). viii, 289p. (C). 1997. pap. text 32.95 (*3-540-62921-1*) Spr-Verlag.

Lectures on Nonlinear Plasma Kinetics. V. N. Tsytovich. Ed. by D. Ter Haar. LC 95-32284. (Springer Series on Atoms - Plasmas: Vol. 17). 1995. write for info. (*3-540-57844-7*) Spr-Verlag.

Lectures on Nonlinear Wave Equations Vol. II: Monographs in Analysis. Christopher D. Sogge. 159p. 1995. 42.00 (*1-57146-032-2*) Intl Pr Boston.

Lectures on Nonlinear Waves & Shocks. Cathleen S. Morawetz. (Tata Institute Lectures on Mathematics). 137p. 1982. 31.95 (*0-387-10830-0*) Spr-Verlag.

Lectures on Nuclear Theory. 2nd ed. Iakov A. Smorodinskii & L. D. Landau. LC 92-47392.Tr. of Lektsii Po Teorii Atomnogo Iadra. (ENG & RUS., Illus.). vii, 108p. 1993. reprint ed. pap. 5.95 (*0-486-67513-0*) Dover.

An Asterisk (*) at the beginning of an entry indicates that the title is appearing for the first time.

Lectures on Number Theory. A. Hurwitz & Haralambos N. Kritikos. Tr. by W. C. Schulz from GER. 290p. 1985. 47.95 (*0-387-96236-0*) Spr-Verlag.

***Lectures on Number Theory.** Peter G. Lejeune-Dirichlet & Richard Dedekind. LC 99-35565. (History of Mathematics Source Ser.). 1999. write for info. (*0-8218-2017-6*) Am Math.

Lectures on Numerical Mathematics. Heinz Rutishauser. 568p. 1990. 60.50 (*0-8176-3491-6*) Birkhauser.

***Lectures on Operator Theory.** Ed. by B. V. Rajarama Bhat et al. LC 99-52254. (Fields Institute Monographs: Vol. 13). 323p. 2000. 69.00 (*0-8218-0821-4*) Am Math.

Lectures on Operator Theory & Its Applications. Albrecht Bottcher et al. Ed. by Peter Lancaster. LC 95-43465. (Fields Institute Monographs: No. 3). 339p. 1995. 99.00 (*0-8218-0457-X*, FIM/3) Am Math.

Lectures on Organic Chemistry. LC 97-19476. 400p. 1997. text 40.00 (*1-86094-053-6*); lib. bdg. 40.00 (*981-02-2886-4*) World Scientific Pub.

Lectures on P-Adic Differential Equations. Bernard Dwork. (Grundlehren der Mathematischen Wissenschaften Ser.: Vol. 253). (Illus.). 304p. 1982. 149.95 (*0-387-90714-9*) Spr-Verlag.

Lectures on P-adic L-functions. Kenkichi Iwasawa. LC 78-39058. (Annals of Mathematics Studies: No. 74). 114p. reprint ed. pap. 35.40 (*0-608-06426-2*, 206663900008) Bks Demand.

Lectures on P-Divisible Groups. M. Demazure. LC 72-94595. (Lecture Notes in Mathematics Ser.: Vol. 302). 98p. 1986. 31.95 (*0-387-06092-8*) Spr-Verlag.

Lectures on Partial Differential Equations. I. G. Petrovsky. (Illus.). x, 245p. 1992. reprint ed. pap. 9.95 (*0-486-66902-5*) Dover.

***Lectures on Partial Evaluation. Practice & Theory: DIKU 1998 International Summer School, Copenhagen, Denmark, July 1998.** DIKU International Summer School on Partial Evaluation Staff. Ed. by John Hatcliff et al. LC 99-52990. (Lecture Notes in Computer Science Ser.: Vol. 1706). ix, 433p. 1999. 49.95 (*3-540-66710-5*) Spr-Verlag.

Lectures on Petri Nets: Advances in Petri Nets, Vol. 149. Wolfgang Reising. LC 98-47976. 1998. pap. 69.00 (*3-540-65307-4*) Spr-Verlag.

Lectures on Petri Nets: Advances in Petri Nets, Vol. 149. Wolfgang Rising. LC 98-47976. 1998. pap. 95.00 (*3-540-65306-6*) Spr-Verlag.

***Lectures on Phase & Transformations in Nuclear Matter A Practictioner's Guide.** Jorge A. Lopez. 2000. 55.00 (*981-02-4007-4*) World Scientific Pub.

Lectures on Phase Transitions. V. I. Yukalov & A. S. Shumovsky. 248p. (C). 1990. text 86.00 (*9971-5-0492-8*); pap. text 40.00 (*9971-5-0474-X*) World Scientific Pub.

Lectures on Phase Transitions & the Renormalization Group. Nigel Goldenfeld. LC 92-17055. (C). 1992. pap. 45.00 (*0-201-55409-7*) Addison-Wesley.

Lectures on Philosophical Theology. Immanuel Kant. Tr. by Allen W. Wood & Gertrude M. Clark from GER. LC 78-58034. 176p. 1978. text 35.00 (*0-8014-1199-8*); pap. text 13.95 (*0-8014-9379-X*) Cornell U Pr.

Lectures on Philosophy. Simone Weil. Tr. by H. Price from FRE. LC 77-26735. 240p. 1978. pap. text 23.95 (*0-521-29333-2*) Cambridge U Pr.

***Lectures on Physics.** Joseph M. Brown. (Illus.). 1999. pap. text 19.95 (*0-9626768-2-9*) Basic Res Pr.

Lectures on Poetry. John W. Mackail. LC 67-23242. (Essay Index Reprint Ser.). 1977. 22.95 (*0-8369-0650-0*) Ayer.

Lectures on Poetry: Read in the Schools of Natural Philosophy at Oxford. Joseph Trapp. Tr. by William Bowyer & William Clarke. (Anglistica & Americana Ser.: No. 45). v, 358p. 1969. reprint ed. 63.70 (*0-685-66524-0*, 05102515) G Olms Pubs.

Lectures on Political Economy, 2 vols., Set. Knut Wicksell. Ed. by Lionel Robbins. Tr. by E. Classen from SWE. Incl. Lectures on Political Economy Vol. 2: Money. LC 67-28341. 246p. 1967. reprint ed. 37.50 (*0-678-06533-0*); LC 67-28341. (Reprints of Economic Classics Ser.). 1967. reprint ed. 65.00 (*0-678-06520-9*) Kelley.

Lectures on Political Economy: London School of Economics. Mountford Longfield. (LSE Scarce Tracts in Economics Ser.). 280p. (C). 1997. 90.00 (*0-415-14385-3*) Routledge.

Lectures on Political Economy, Vol. 2, Money see Lectures on Political Economy

Lectures on Polytopes. Gunter M. Ziegler. LC 94-21784. (Graduate Texts in Mathematics Ser.: Vol. 152). 392p. 1994. 69.95 (*0-387-94329-3*) Spr-Verlag.

Lectures on Polytopes. Gunter M. Ziegler. LC 94-21784. (Graduate Texts in Mathematics Ser.: 152). (Illus.). 392p. 1997. 32.95 (*0-387-94365-X*) Spr-Verlag.

Lectures on Probability & Second Order Random Fields. Diego B. Hernandez. LC 94-30544. (Series on Advances in Mathematics for Applied Sciences). 250p. 1995. text 48.00 (*981-02-1908-3*) World Scientific Pub.

Lectures on Probability Theory. D. Bakry et al. (Lecture Notes in Mathematics Ser.). 411p. 1994. 79.95 (*0-387-58208-8*) Spr-Verlag.

Lectures on Probability Theory: Ecole d'Ete de Probabilites de Saint-Flour XXIII - 1993. P. Biane et al. Ed. by A. Dold et al. (Lecture Notes in Mathematics Ser.: Vol. 1608). 210p. 1995. pap. 44.95 (*3-540-60015-9*) Spr-Verlag.

Lectures on Probability Theory & Statistics: Ecole d'Ete de Probabilites de Saint-Flour XXVI, 1996. E. Gine et al. Ed. by P. Bernard. (Lecture Notes in Mathematics Ser.: Vol. 1665). x, 424p. pap. 73.00 (*3-540-63190-9*) Spr-Verlag.

***Lectures on Probability Theory & Statistics: Ecole d'Ete de Probabilities de Saint-Flour XXVII - 1997.** J. Bertoin et al. Ed. by P. Bernard. (Lecture Notes in Mathematics Ser.: Vol. 1717). ix, 289p. 2000. pap. 52.80 (*3-540-66593-5*) Spr-Verlag.

Lectures on Probability Theory & Statistics: Ecole d'Ete de Probabilities de St. Flour XXIV - 1994, Vol. VII. R. Dobrushin et al. (Lecture Notes in Mathematics Ser.: Vol. 1648). 300p. 1997. pap. 59.00 (*3-540-62055-9*) Spr-Verlag.

Lectures on Projected Geometry. Dirk Struick. (C). 1998. write for info. (*0-201-56954-X*) Addison-Wesley.

Lectures on Proof Verification & Approximation Algorithms, Vol. 136. Ed. by E. Mayr et al. LC 98-14448. (Lecture Notes in Computer Science Ser.: Vol. 1367). 470p. 1998. pap. 69.00 (*3-540-64201-3*) Spr-Verlag.

***Lectures on Psychology Women.** 2nd ed. Chrisler. LC 99-29468. 1999. 25.25 (*0-07-234860-7*, McGraw-H College) McGraw-H Hghr Educ.

Lectures on QCD, Vol. 481. F. Lenz et al. LC 97-11040. (Lecture Notes in Physics Ser.). 1997. write for info. (*3-540-62543-7*) Spr-Verlag.

Lectures on QCD: Applications. Ed. by F. Lenz et al. LC 97-37132. (Lecture Notes in Physics Ser.: Vol. 496). vii, 483p. 1997. text 110.00 (*3-540-63442-8*) Spr-Verlag.

Lectures on Quantum Electronics. N. V. Karlov. Tr. by Eugene Yankovsky from RUS. (Advances in Science & Technology in the U. S. S. R. Ser.).Tr. of Lektsii Po Kvantovoi Elektronike. 464p. 1992. 154.00 (*0-8493-7538-X*, QC689) CRC Pr.

Lectures on Quantum Groups. Jens C. Jantzen. LC 95-25393. (Graduate Studies in Mathematics: No. 6). 266p. 1995. text 44.00 (*0-8218-0478-2*, GSM/6) Am Math.

Lectures on Quantum Optics. Werner Vogel & Dirk-Gunner Welsch. LC 94-6620. 1994. text 73.45 (*3-05-501387-5*, Pub. by Akademie Verlag) Wiley.

Lectures on Quantum Statistics, 2 vols., Vol. 2. N. N. Bogoliubov. viii, 232p. 1970. text 249.00 (*0-677-20570-8*) Gordon & Breach.

Lectures on Quantum Theory: Mathematical & Structural Foundations. C. J. Isham. 250p. 1995. pap. text 24.00 (*1-86094-001-3*) World Scientific Pub.

Lectures on Quantum Theory: Mathematical & Structural Foundations. Chris J. Isham. 262p. 1995. text 48.00 (*1-86094-000-5*) World Scientific Pub.

Lectures on Quarks, Mesons & Nuclei, 2 vols., Set. Ed. by Ernest M. Henley & Hwang W. Pauchy. 708p. (C). 1989. text 169.00 (*9971-5-0804-4*) World Scientific Pub.

Lectures on Random Voronoi Tesselations. Jesper Moller. LC 94-248. (Lecture Notes in Statistics Ser.: Vol. 87). (Illus.). 144p. 1994. 39.95 (*0-387-94264-5*) Spr-Verlag.

***Lectures on Real Analysis.** J. J. Yeh. 400p. 1999. 68.00 (*981-02-3936-X*) World Scientific Pub.

Lectures on Real Analysis. James Yeh. 400p. 1999. pap. text 38.00 (*981-02-3941-6*) World Scientific Pub.

Lectures on Reimann Surfaces. O. Forster. Ed. by J. H. Ewing et al. Tr. by B. Gilligan from GER. (Graduate Texts in Mathematics Ser.: Vol. 81). (Illus.). viii, 254p. 1993. reprint ed. 54.95 (*0-387-90617-7*) Spr-Verlag.

Lectures on Representation Theory. Jing-Song Huang. 1999. pap. text 29.00 (*981-02-3725-1*) World Scientific Pub.

Lectures on Representation Theory Jing-Song Huang. LC 98-51615. 1999. write for info. (*981-02-3724-3*) World Scientific Pub.

Lectures on Representation Theory & Knizhnik-Zamolodchikov Equations. Pavel I. Etingof et al. LC 98-2948. (Mathematical Surveys & Monographs). 198p. 1998. 49.00 (*0-8218-0496-0*, SURV-ETINGOF) Am Math.

Lectures on Results on Bezout's Theorem. W. Vogel. (Tata Institute Lectures on Mathematics). viii, 136p. 1984. 49.95 (*0-387-12679-1*) Spr-Verlag.

Lectures on Revival. rev. ed. Charles G. Finney. LC 88-32755. 288p. 1989. pap. 11.99 (*1-55661-062-9*) Bethany Hse.

Lectures on Rhetoric & Belles Lettres. Hugh Blair. LC 93-22920. 528p. 1993. 75.00 (*0-8201-1467-7*) Schol Facsimiles.

Lectures on Rhetoric & Belles Lettres. Adam Smith. Ed. by J. C. Bryce. (Glasgow Edition of the Works & Correspondence of Adam Smith). 282p. 1983. text 45.00 (*0-19-828186-2*) OUP.

Lectures on Rhetoric & Belles Lettres (Glasgow Ed.) Adam Smith. LC 85-6884. 291p. 1985. pap. 7.50 (*0-86597-052-1*) Liberty Fund.

Lectures on Rhetoric & Oratory, 1810. John Q. Adams. LC 97-15685. (Scholars' Facsimiles & Reprints Ser.). 850p. 1997. 90.00 (*0-8201-1507-X*) Schol Facsimiles.

Lectures on Riemann Surfaces. Robert C. Gunning. LC 67-11032. (Princeton Mathematical Notes Ser.). 260p. 1966. reprint ed. pap. 80.60 (*0-608-07802-6*, 205986900010) Bks Demand.

Lectures on Rings & Modules. T. Y. Lam. LC 98-18389. (Graduate Tests in Mathematics Ser.: Vol. 189). 420p. 1998. 54.95 (*0-387-98428-3*) Spr-Verlag.

Lectures on Russian Literature. Vladimir Nabokov. Ed. by Fredson Bowers. LC 81-47315. (Illus.). 352p. 1982. pap. 14.00 (*0-15-649591-0*, Harvest Bks) Harcourt.

Lectures on School-Keeping. Samuel R. Hall. LC 76-89185. (American Education: Its Men, Institutions & Ideas, Ser. 1). 1978. reprint ed. 19.95 (*0-405-01420-1*) Ayer.

Lectures on Set Theoretic Topology. M. E. Rudin. LC 74-31124. (CBMS Regional Conference Series in Mathematics: No. 23). 76p. 1975. reprint ed. pap. 16.00 (*0-8218-1673-X*, CBMS/23) Am Math.

***Lectures on Shakespeare.** W. H. Auden. Ed. by Arthur Kirsch. LC 00-28479. (W. H. Auden--Critical Editions Ser.). 452p. 2001. 29.95 (*0-691-05730-3*) Princeton U Pr.

Lectures on Shakespeare, 2 vols. Henry N. Hudson. LC 79-169452. reprint ed. write for info. (*0-404-03375-X*) AMS Pr.

Lectures on Singular Integral Operators. M. Christ. LC 90-20270. (CBMS Regional Conference Series in Mathematics: No. 77). 132p. 1990. pap. 28.00 (*0-8218-0728-5*, CBMS/77) Am Math.

Lectures on Slavery & Its Remedy. Amos A. Phelps. LC 70-92438. 1970. reprint ed. 39.00 (*0-403-00182-X*) Scholarly.

Lectures on Solar & Planetary Dynamos. Ed. by M. R. Proctor & A. D. Gilbert. (Publications of the Newton Institute: No. 2). (Illus.). 389p. (C). 1995. text 85.00 (*0-521-46142-1*); pap. text 31.95 (*0-521-46704-7*) Cambridge U Pr.

Lectures on Solid Surfaces & Interfaces: Proceedings of the International School on Surface Physics, Beijing, 20-30 Mar. 90. Ed. by D. S. Wang & D. H. Shen. 300p. (C). 1990. pap. 44.00 (*981-02-0519-8*); text 118.00 (*981-02-0297-0*) World Scientific Pub.

Lectures on Spaces of Nonpositive Curvature. Werner Ballmann. LC 95-38397. (DMV Seminar Ser.: Vol. 25). 112p. 1995. pap. 32.00 (*3-7643-5242-6*) Birkhauser.

Lectures on Spaces of Nonpositive Curvature. Werner Ballmann. (DMV Seminar Ser.: Vol. 25). 1995. 32.00 (*0-8176-5242-6*) Birkhauser.

Lectures on Statistical Mechanics. Efstratios Manousakes. 1999. write for info. (*0-201-32827-5*) Addison-Wesley.

Lectures on Stochastic Flows & Applications. Hiroshi Kunita. (Tata Institute Lectures on Mathematics). v, 121p. 1987. 28.95 (*0-387-17775-2*) Spr-Verlag.

Lectures on String Theory. D. Lust & S. Theisen. (Lecture Notes in Physics Ser.: Vol. 346). vii, 346p. 1989. 17.95 (*0-387-51882-7*) Spr-Verlag.

Lectures on Surface Science. Ed. by G. R. Castro & M. Cardona. (Illus.). 240p. 1987. 73.95 (*0-387-17318-8*) Spr-Verlag.

Lectures on Symplectic Manifolds. Alan Weinstein. LC 77-3399. (CBMS Regional Conference Series in Mathematics: No. 29). 48p. 1977. pap. 15.00 (*0-8218-1679-9*, CBMS/29) Am Math.

***Lectures on Systems, Control & Information: Lectures at the Morningside Center of Mathematics.** Lei Guo & Stephen Shing-Toung Yau. LC 00-44146. (AMS/IP Studies in Advanced Mathematics Ser.). 2000. write for info. (*0-8218-2009-5*) Am Math.

Lectures on Technology & Social Change in Foreign Cultures. Nils C. Westermark. (Reports on Technology & Social Change). 183p. 1973. 12.00 (*0-945271-20-4*) ISU-CIKARD.

Lectures on the American Civil War. James F. Rhodes. LC 73-160990. (Select Bibliographies Reprint Ser.). 1977. reprint ed. 21.95 (*0-8369-5858-6*) Ayer.

Lectures on the Apocalypse. R. H. Charles. (British Academy, London, Schweich Lectures on Biblical Archaeology Series, 1930). 1969. reprint ed. pap. 25.00 (*0-8115-1261-4*) Periodicals Srv.

Lectures on the Arithmetic Riemann-Roch Theorem. Gerd Faltings. (Annals of Mathematics Studies: No. 127). 123p. 1992. pap. text 19.95 (*0-691-02544-4*, Pub. by Princeton U Pr) Cal Prin Full Svc.

Lectures on the Arthur-Selberg Trace Formula. Stephen S. Gelbart. LC 96-26215. (University Lectures: Vol. 9). 99p. 1996. pap. 19.00 (*0-8218-0571-1*, ULECT/9) Am Math.

Lectures on the Asymptotic Theory of Ideals. D. Rees. (London Mathematical Society Lecture Note Ser.: No. 113). 222p. 1989. pap. text 42.95 (*0-521-31127-6*) Cambridge U Pr.

Lectures on the Bases of Religious Belief. 2nd ed. Charles B. Upton. LC 77-27161. (Hibbert Lectures: 1893). reprint ed. 52.00 (*0-404-60411-0*) AMS Pr.

Lectures on the Calculus of Variations. Gilbert A. Bliss. LC 46-5369. (Phoenix Bks.). 304p. reprint ed. pap. 94.30 (*0-608-16521-2*, 202676400052) Bks Demand.

Lectures on the Calculus of Variations. 3rd ed. Oskar Bolza. LC 73-16324. 14.95 (*0-8284-0145-4*) Chelsea Pub.

***Lectures on the Calculus of Variations & Optimal Control Theory.** L. C. Young. (CHEL Ser.: Vol. 304.H). 337p. 2000. 34.00 (*0-8218-2690-5*) Am Math.

Lectures on the Calculus of Variations & Optimal Control Theory. 2nd ed. Laurence C. Young. LC 79-57387. 1980. 19.95 (*0-8284-0304-X*) Chelsea Pub.

Lectures on the Church of God. W. Kelly. 7.95 (*0-88172-092-5*) Believers Bkshelf.

Lectures on the Complexity of Bilinear Problems. H. F. De Groote. (Lecture Notes in Computer Science Ser.: Vol. 245). (Illus.). v, 135p. 1987. 26.00 (*0-387-17205-X*) Spr-Verlag.

Lectures on the Conflict of Laws & International Contracts. Summer Institute on International & Comparative La. LC 51-62311. (Michigan Legal Publications). xiv, 200p. 1982. reprint ed. lib. bdg. 38.50 (*0-89941-177-0*, 302410) W S Hein.

Lectures on the Constitution of the United States. Samuel F. Miller. xxi, 765p. 1981. reprint ed. 52.00 (*0-8377-0836-2*, Rothman) W S Hein.

Lectures on the Constitution of the United States: Before the Law Class of Mercer University. Emory Speer. 153, xip. 1988. reprint ed. 32.00 (*0-8377-2621-2*, Rothman) W S Hein.

Lectures on the Coupling Method. Torgny Lindvall. LC 92-12811. (Probability & Mathematical Statistics Ser.). 272p. 1992. 115.00 (*0-471-54025-0*) Wiley.

Lectures on the Early History of Institutions. Henry S. Maine. ix, 412p. 1998. reprint ed. 127.50 (*1-56169-438-X*) Gaunt.

Lectures on the Early History of Institutions. 4th ed. Henry S. Maine. ix, 412p. 1998. reprint ed. 127.50 (*1-56169-428-2*) Gaunt.

***Lectures on the Early History of Institutions.** 5th ed. Henry S. Maine. viii, 412p. 1999. reprint ed. 127.50 (*1-56169-473-8*) Gaunt.

***Lectures on the Early History of Institutions.** 6th ed. Henry S. Maine. viii, 812p. 1999. reprint ed. 125.00 (*1-56169-474-6*) Gaunt.

Lectures on the Early History of Institutions: A Sequel to Ancient Law. Henry S. Maine. LC 87-81276. 1987. reprint ed. lib. bdg. 52.00 (*0-89941-562-8*, 305200) W S Hein.

Lectures on the Economic Theory of Taxation: Economic Reform, Socially Optimal Piecemeal Consumption Taxation Structures, & Information. Alan Martina. LC 92-15323. (Lecture Notes in Economics & Mathematical Systems Ser.: Vol. 384). xii, 313p. 1992. 79.95 (*0-387-55538-2*) Spr-Verlag.

Lectures on the Edge-of-the-Wedge Theorem. Walter Rudin. LC 73-145640. (CBMS Regional Conference Series in Mathematics: No. 6). 30p. 1971. pap. 16.00 (*0-8218-1655-1*, CBMS/6) Am Math.

Lectures on the Elementary Psychology of Feeling & Attention. Edward B. Titchener. LC 73-2994. (Classics in Psychology Ser.). 1978. reprint ed. 25.95 (*0-405-05166-2*) Ayer.

Lectures on the Elements of Political Economy. 2nd ed. Thomas Cooper. LC 66-21666. (Reprints of Economic Classics Ser.). 360p. 1971. reprint ed. lib. bdg. 49.50 (*0-678-00776-4*) Kelley.

Lectures on the English Poets. William C. Hazlitt. (BCL1-PR English Literature Ser.). 256p. 1992. reprint ed. lib. bdg. 79.00 (*0-7812-7065-0*) Rprt Serv.

Lectures on the Epistle of Jude. W. Kelly. 6.95 (*0-88172-101-8*) Believers Bkshelf.

Lectures on the Experimental Psychology of the Thought-Processes. Edward B. Titchener. LC 73-2995. (Classics in Psychology Ser.). 1978. reprint ed. 25.95 (*0-405-05167-0*) Ayer.

***Lectures on the Foundations of Quantum Chromodynamics.** A. Smilga. 150p. 2001. 18.00 (*981-02-4331-6*) World Scientific Pub.

Lectures on the Fourteenth Article of Amendment to the Constitution of the United States. W. D. Guthrie. LC 74-118030. (American Constitutional & Legal History Ser). 1970. reprint ed. lib. bdg. 35.00 (*0-306-71941-X*) Da Capo.

***Lectures on the French Revolution.** John E. Acton. LC 99-46818. 2000. 19.00 (*0-86597-280-X*); pap. 11.00 (*0-86597-281-8*) Liberty Fund.

Lectures on the French Revolution. John E. Acton. Ed. by John N. Figgis & Reginald V. Laurence. LC 78-108814. (BCL Ser.: No. II). reprint ed. 62.50 (*0-404-00284-6*) AMS Pr.

Lectures on the Geometry of Manifolds. Liviu I. Nicolaescu. LC 96-28020. 450p. 1996. write for info. (*981-02-2836-8*) World Scientific Pub.

Lectures on the Geometry of Numbers. Carl L. Siegel. (Illus.). x, 160p. 1989. 79.95 (*0-387-50629-2*) Spr-Verlag.

Lectures on the Geometry of Poisson Manifolds. Izu Vaisman. LC 94-1419. (Progress in Mathematics Ser.: Vol. 18). vii, 205p. 1994. 59.00 (*0-8176-5016-4*) Birkhauser.

Lectures on the Geometry of Quantization. Sean Bates & Alan Weinstein. (Berkeley Mathematical Lecture Notes Ser.: Vol. 8). 137p. 1997. pap. 25.00 (*0-8218-0798-6*) Am Math.

Lectures on the Historians of Bohemia. Franz Lutzow. LC 72-173174. 128p. 1972. reprint ed. 18.95 (*0-405-08756-X*, Pub. by Blom Pubns) Ayer.

Lectures on the History & Art of Music: The Louis Charles Elson Memorial Lectures at the Library of Congress 1946-1965. Pref. by Irving Lowens. LC 68-55319. (Music Ser.). 1968. reprint ed. lib. bdg. 32.50 (*0-306-71193-1*) Da Capo.

***Lectures on the History of Moral Philosophy.** John Rawls. (Illus.). 416p. 2000. 45.00 (*0-674-00296-2*); pap. 19.95 (*0-674-00442-6*) HUP.

Lectures on the History of Philosophy Vol. 1: Greek Philosophy to Plato, Vol. 1. Georg Wilhelm Friedrich Hegel. Tr. by E. S. Haldane. LC 95-5478. xlvi, 487p. 1995. pap. 15.00 (*0-8032-7271-5*, Bison Books) U of Nebr Pr.

Lectures on the History of Philosophy Vol. 2: Plato & the Platonists, Vol. 2. Georg Wilhelm Friedrich Hegel. Tr. by Frances H. Simson & E. S. Haldane. LC 95-5478. vi, 453p. 1995. pap. 15.00 (*0-8032-7272-3*, Bison Books) U of Nebr Pr.

Lectures on the History of Philosophy Vol. 3: Medieval & Modern Philosophy, Vol. 3. Georg Wilhelm Friedrich Hegel. Tr. by E. S. Haldane & Frances H. Simson. LC 95-5478. viii, 571p. 1995. pap. 15.00 (*0-8032-7273-1*, Bison Books) U of Nebr Pr.

Lectures on the History of Philosophy Vol. 3: The Lectures of 1825-26 Medieval & Modern Philosophy. Georg Wilhelm Friedrich Hegel. Ed. by Robert F. Brown. 1990. 65.00 (*0-520-06812-2*, Pub. by U CA Pr) Cal Prin Full Svc.

Lectures on the History of Psychiatry. Ed. by R. M. Murray & T. H. Turner. (Squibb Ser.). 223p. 1990. pap. text 25.00 (*0-88048-601-5*, 8601, Pub. by Royal Coll Psych) Parkwest Pubns.

Lectures on the History of Psychiatry. Ed. by R. M. Murray & T. H. Turner. LC 91-46193. (Squibb Ser.). 235p. reprint ed. pap. 72.90 (*0-7837-4059-X*, 204400900011) Bks Demand.

Lectures on the History of Religions. V. Herder. 280p. 1986. 130.00 (*0-7855-1818-5*, Pub. by Archives Pubs) St Mut.

Lectures on the History of Russian Philology see Lektsii Po Istorii Russkoi Slovjesnosti

An Asterisk (*) at the beginning of an entry indicates that the title is appearing for the first time.

Lectures on the History of the French Revolution, 2 vols., Set. W. Smyth. LC 71-175988. reprint ed. 115.00 (0-404-06145-1) AMS Pr.

Lectures on the Hyperreals: An Introduction to Nonstandard Analysis. R. Goldblatt. LC 98-18388. (Graduate Texts in Mathematics Ser.: Vol. 188). 300p. 1998. 49.95 (0-387-98464-X) Spr-Verlag.

Lectures on the I Ching: Constancy & Change. Richard Wilhelm. Ed. by Irene Eber. LC 79-84027. (Bollingen Ser.: Vol. 19, No. 2). 216p. 1979. pap. 10.95 (0-691-01872-3, Pub. by Princeton U Pr) Cal Prin Full Svc.

Lectures on the Influence of the Apostle Paul on the Development of Christianity. Otto Pfleiderer. Tr. by J. Frederick Smith. LC 77-27166. (Hibbert Lectures: 1885). reprint ed. 37.50 (0-404-60406-4) AMS Pr.

Lectures on the Influence of the Institutions, Thought & Culture of Rome, on Christianity & the Development of the Catholic Church. Ernest Renan. Tr. by Charles Austin Beard. LC 77-27170. (Hibbert Lectures: 1880). reprint ed. 32.00 (0-404-60402-1) AMS Pr.

Lectures on the Law & Labor Management Relations. Summer Institute on International & Comparative La. (Michigan Legal Publications). xviii, 502p. 1986. reprint ed. lib. bdg. 52.50 (0-89941-491-5, 304180) W S Hein.

Lectures on the Logic of Computer Programming. Zohar Manna. LC 79-93153. (CBMS-NSF Regional Conference Ser.: No. 31). iv, 49p. 1980. pap. text 19.00 (0-89871-164-9) Soc Indus-Appl Math.

Lectures on the Manuscript Materials of Ancient Irish History. Eugene O'Curry. 750p. 1995. 75.00 (1-85182-183-X, Pub. by Four Cts Pr) Intl Spec Bk.

Lectures on the Mathematics of Finance. Ioannis Karatzas. LC 96-27511. (CRM Monographs: Vol. 8). 148p. 1996. pap. 39.00 (0-8218-0909-1) Am Math.

Lectures on the Mathematics of Finance. Ioannis Karatzas. LC 96-27511. (CRM Monograph Ser.: Vol. 8). 148p. 1996. 39.00 (0-8218-0637-8, CRMN/8) Am Math.

Lectures on the Mean-Value & Omega Theorems for the Riemann Zeta-Function: Tata Institute Lectures on Mathematics & Physics. K. Ramachandra. 180p. 1996. pap. 35.00 (3-540-58437-4) Spr-Verlag.

Lectures on the Measurement & Evaluation of the Performance of Computing Systems. Saul Rosen. (CBMS-NSF Regional Conference Ser.: No. 23). vii, 138p. 1976. reprint ed. pap. text 26.00 (0-89871-020-0) Soc Indus-Appl Math.

Lectures on the Nature & Use of Money. John Gray. LC 68-55724. (Library of Money & Banking History). xvi, 344p. 1972. reprint ed. lib. bdg. 49.50 (0-678-00828-0) Kelley.

Lectures on the Origin & Growth of Religion As Illustrated by Celtic Heathendom. John Rhys. LC 77-27165. (Hibbert Lectures: 1886). reprint ed. 67.50 (0-404-60407-2) AMS Pr.

Lectures on the Origin & Growth of Religion As Illustrated by the Native Religions of Mexico & Peru. Albert D. Reville. LC 77-27167. (Hibbert Lectures: 1884). 45.00 (0-614-07017-1) AMS Pr.

Lectures on the Origin & Growth of Religion As Illustrated by the Native Religions of Mexico & Peru. Albert D. Reville. 1977. lib. bdg. 59.95 (0-8490-2140-5) Gordon Pr.

Lectures on the Origin & Growth of Religion As Illustrated by the Religion of Ancient Egypt. 2nd ed. Peter L. Renouf. LC 77-27171. (Hibbert Lectures: 1879). reprint ed. 39.00 (0-404-60401-3) AMS Pr.

Lectures on the Origin & Growth of Religion As Illustrated by the Religion of the Ancient Babylonians. 2nd ed. Archibald H. Sayce. LC 77-27164. (Hibbert Lectures: 1887). reprint ed. 57.50 (0-404-60408-0) AMS Pr.

Lectures on the Origin & Growth of Religion As Illustrated by the Religion of the Ancient Hebrews. 3rd ed. Claude J. Montefiore. LC 77-27162. (Hibbert Lectures: 1892). reprint ed. 59.50 (0-404-60410-2) AMS Pr.

Lectures on the Origin & Growth of Religion As Illustrated by the Religions of India. Friedrich M. Mueller. LC 73-18816. reprint ed. 45.00 (0-404-11440-7) AMS Pr.

Lectures on the Origin & Growth of the Conception of God as Illustrated by Anthropology & History. Eugene F. Goblet D'Alviella. Tr. by Philip H. Wicksteed. LC 77-27163. (Hibbert Lectures: 1887). reprint ed. 45.00 (0-404-60409-9) AMS Pr.

***Lectures on the Paradigms of Legal Thinking.** Csaba Varga. 120p. 1999. 65.00 (963-05-7662-7, Pub. by Akade Kiado) Intl Spec Bk.

Lectures on the Philosophy & Practice of Slavery, As Exhibited in the Institution of Domestic Slavery in the U. S. With the Duties of Masters to Slaves. William A. Smith. Ed. by Thomas O. Summers. LC 75-83879. (Black Heritage Library Collection). 1977. 19.95 (0-8369-8653-9) Ayer.

Lectures on the Philosophy of History. Georg Wilhelm Friedrich Hegel. Tr. by J. Sibree. 457p. 1956. pap. text 9.95 (0-486-20112-0) Dover.

Lectures on the Philosophy of Law: Designed Mainly As an Introduction to the Study of International Law. William G. Miller. xv, 432p. 1979. reprint ed. 45.00 (0-8377-0834-6, Rothman) W S Hein.

Lectures on the Philosophy of Leibniz. Horace W. Joseph. LC 73-9264. 190p. 1974. reprint ed. lib. bdg. 35.00 (0-8371-7002-8, JOPL, Greenwood Pr) Greenwood.

Lectures on the Philosophy of Religion: One-Volume Edition. The Lectures of 1827. Georg Wilhelm Friedrich Hegel. Ed. by Peter C. Hodgson. 1988. pap. 19.95 (0-520-06020-2, Pub. by U CA Pr) Cal Prin Full Svc.

Lectures on the Philosophy of Religion Vol. 1: Introduction & the Concept of Religion. Georg Wilhelm Friedrich Hegel. Ed. by Peter C. Hodgson. 494p. 1995. pap. 22.50 (0-520-20371-2, Pub. by U CA Pr) Cal Prin Full Svc.

Lectures on the Philosophy of Religion Vol. 2: Determinate Religion. Georg Wilhelm Friedrich Hegel. Ed. by Peter C. Hodgson. 825p. 1995. pap. 27.50 (0-520-20372-0, Pub. by U CA Pr) Cal Prin Full Svc.

Lectures on the Philosophy of Spinoza. Yosef Ben Shlomo. 124p. 1992. pap. 12.00 (965-05-0665-9, Pub. by Israel Ministry Def) Gefen Bks.

Lectures on the Philosophy of World History: Reason in History. Georg Wilhelm Friedrich Hegel. Ed. by D. Forbes & H. B. Nisbet. (Cambridge Studies in the History & Theory of Politics). (GER.). 252p. 1981. pap. text 19.95 (0-521-28145-8) Cambridge U Pr.

Lectures on the Physical Forces (1860) Michael Faraday. 200p. 1998. reprint ed. pap. 24.95 (0-7661-0365-X) Kessinger Pub.

***Lectures on the Physics of Highly Correlated Electron Systems: Fourth Training Course in the Physics of Correlated Electron Systems.** Ed. by Ferdinando Mancini. LC 00-104877. (AIP Conference Proceedings Ser.: Vol. 527). (Illus.). vii, 381p. 2000. 125.00 (1-56396-950-5) Am Inst Physics.

***Lectures on the Present Position of Catholics in England.** John Henry Newman. Ed. by Andrew Nash. (Works of Cardinal Newman: Vol. 1). 592p. 2000. 40.00 (0-268-01323-3, Pub. by U of Notre Dame Pr) Chicago Distribution Ctr.

Lectures on the Psychology of Women. Ed. by Joan C. Chrisler et al. LC 95-40755. 384p. (C). 1995. pap. 34.38 (0-07-011111-1) McGraw.

Lectures on the Relation Between Law & Public Opinion in England: During the Nineteenth Century. Albert V. Dicey & Richard A. Cosgrove. LC 81-2391. (Social Science Classics Ser.). 506p. 1981. pap. 24.95 (0-87855-869-1) Transaction Pubs.

Lectures on the Relation Between Law & Public Opinion in England: During the Nineteenth Century. A. V. Dicey. 524p. 1996. reprint ed. 125.00 (1-56169-227-1) Gaunt.

Lectures on the Relation Between Law & Public Opinion in England: During the Nineteenth Century. 2nd ed. Albert V. Dicey. LC 75-41074. reprint ed. 49.50 (0-404-14532-9) AMS Pr.

***Lectures on the Relation Between Law & Public Opinion in England: During the Nineteenth Century.** 2nd ed. Albert V. Dicey. xciv, 506p. 1999. reprint ed. 180.00 (1-56169-488-6) Gaunt.

Lectures on the Religion of the Semites. William Robertson Smith. Ed. by John Day. (Journal for the Study of the Old Testament Supplement Ser.: Vol. 183). 148p. 1995. 52.50 (1-85075-500-0, Pub. by Sheffield Acad) CUP Services.

Lectures on the Restrictive System. Thomas R. Dew. LC 68-55701. (Reprints of Economic Classics Ser.). viii, 195p. 1969. reprint ed. 35.00 (0-678-00441-2) Kelley.

Lectures on the Revival of Religion by Ministers of the Church of Scotland. Ed. by William M. Hetherington. (Revival Library). xxvi, 444p. 1980. reprint ed. lib. bdg. 17.50 (0-940033-15-1) R O Roberts.

Lectures on the Sacred Poetry of the Hebrews, 2 vols., Set. Robert Lowth. Tr. by G. Gregory from LAT. (Anglistica & Americana Ser.: No. 43). 935p. 1969. reprint ed. 180.70 (0-685-25147-0, 05102488) G Olms Pubs.

Lectures on the Science of Human Life. Sylvester Graham. 700p. 1998. reprint ed. pap. 50.00 (0-7873-0352-6) Hlth Research.

Lectures on the Spectrum of L2 (Gama) G. Floyd L. Williams. LC 90-45313. (Pitman Research Notes in Mathematics Ser.: Vol. 242). 368p. reprint ed. pap. 114.10 (0-608-08054-3, 206901900002) Bks Demand.

Lectures on the Study & Practice of the Law: Delivered in the Law School of Harvard University. Emory Washburn. xii, 318p. 1982. reprint ed. 38.50 (0-8377-2729-4, Rothman) W S Hein.

Lectures on the Theory of Few-Body Systems. V. B. Belyaev. (Nuclear & Particle Physics Ser.). (Illus.). 136p. 1990. 49.95 (0-387-18587-9) Spr-Verlag.

Lectures on the Theory of Integration. Ralph Henstock. 220p. (C). 1988. text 67.00 (9971-5-0450-2); pap. text 36.00 (9971-5-0451-0) World Scientific Pub.

Lectures on the Theory of Stochastic Processes. A. V. Skorokhod. 190p. 1996. 79.50 (90-6764-206-1, Pub. by VSP) Coronet Bks.

Lectures on the Theory of the Nucleus. Ed. by A. G. Sitenko & V. K. Tartakovskii. LC 74-10827. (International Series on Nuclear Energy: Vol. 74). 312p. 1975. 81.00 (0-08-017876-6, Pergamon Pr) Elsevier.

***Lectures on the Topology of 3-Manifolds.** Nikolai Saveliev. LC 99-40959. (Textbook Ser.). 199p. 1999. pap. 34.95 (3-11-016271-7) De Gruyter.

Lectures on Thermodynamics & Statistical Mechanics. Ed. by A. E. Gonzalez et al. 236p. (C). 1989. text 104.00 (981-02-0016-1) World Scientific Pub.

Lectures on Thermodynamics & Statistical Mechanics: Nineteenth Winter Meeting on Statistical Physics. MiLopez De Haro & C. Varea. 228p. 1990. text 92.00 (981-02-0243-1) World Scientific Pub.

Lectures on Thermodynamics & Statistical Mechanics: Proceedings of the XX Winter Meeting on Statistical Physics, Mexico, 8-11 January 1991. M. L. De Haro et al. 300p. (C). 1991. text 74.00 (981-02-0736-0) World Scientific Pub.

Lectures on Thermodynamics & Statistical Mechanics: Proceedings of the XXIII Winter Meeting on Statistical Physics. R. Rodriquez & M. Costas. 292p. 1994. text 71.00 (981-02-1915-6) World Scientific Pub.

Lectures on Three-Dimensional Elasticity. P. G. Ciarlet. (Tata Institute Lectures on Mathematics). 160p. 1984. 26.95 (0-387-12331-8) Spr-Verlag.

Lectures on Three-Manifold Topology. William H. Jaco. LC 79-28488. (CBMS Regional Conference Series in Mathematics: No. 43). 251p. 1982. reprint ed. pap. 16.00 (0-8218-1693-4, CBMS/43) Am Math.

Lectures on Topics in Finite Element Solution of Elliptic Problems. B. Mercier. (Tata Institute Lectures on Mathematics). (Illus.). 191p. 1980. 31.95 (0-387-09543-8) Spr-Verlag.

Lectures on Ulysses: A Facsimile of the Manuscript. limited ed. Vladimir Nabokov. 1980. 85.00 (0-89723-027-2) Bruccoli.

Lectures on Vanishing Theorems. Helene Esnault & Eckart Viehweg. LC 92-36584. (DMV Seminar Ser.: Bd. 20). vii, 164p. 1994. 42.00 (0-8176-2822-3) Birkhauser.

Lectures on Vector Bundles. J. Le Potier. (Studies in Advanced Mathematics: No. 54). (Illus.). 259p. (C). 1997. text 64.95 (0-521-48182-1) Cambridge U Pr.

Lectures on Viscoelasticity Theory. 2nd ed. A. C. Pipkin. (Applied Mathematical Sciences Ser.: Vol. 7). (Illus.). viii, 188p. 1986. 65.95 (0-387-96345-6) Spr-Verlag.

***Lectures on Wastewater Analysis & Interpretation.** Roy-Keith Smith. (Illus.). x, 482p. 1999. pap. write for info. (1-890911-10-0) Genium Pub.

Lectures on Wiener & Kalman Filtering. Thomas Kailath. (CISM International Centre for Mechanical Sciences Ser.: Vol. 140). 187p. 1988. 41.95 (0-387-81664-X) Spr-Verlag.

Lectures on Yoga see Royal Path: Practical Lessons on Yoga

Lectures Poetiques: La Representation Poetique du Discours Theorique Chez Jean-Jacques Rousseau. Guillemette Johnston. LC 95-71125. (FRE.). 234p. 1996. lib. bdg. 39.95 (1-883479-09-6) Summa Pubns.

Lectures Quebecoises et Independance. Paul-Emile Roy. 1998. write for info. (2-89415-238-8) Edits Meridien.

Lectures Read to the Seniors in Harvard College. Edward T. Channing & Charlotte Downey. LC 96-53859. (Scholars' Facsimiles & Reprints Ser.). 336p. 1997. 60.00 (0-8201-1502-9) Schol Facsimiles.

Lectures Spectrum. Williams. 1991. pap. 59.00 (0-582-06863-0, Pub. by Addison-Wesley) Longman.

Lectures to Living Authors. E. H. Lacon Watson. LC 68-54354. (Essay Index Reprint Ser.). 1977. 19.95 (0-8369-0603-9) Ayer.

Lectures to My Students see Discursos a Mis Estudiantes

***Lectures to My Students.** C. H. Spurgeon. 2000. 29.99 (1-85792-417-7) Christian Focus.

Lectures to My Students. 2nd ed. Charles H. Spurgeon. 446p. (Orig.). 1979. pap. 19.99 (0-310-32911-6, 10845P) Zondervan.

Lectures to My Students: Series I, Series II Art of Illustration, Commenting & Commentaries, 4 vols. in 1. Charles H. Spurgeon. 1990. 40.00 (1-56186-100-6) Pilgrim Pubns.

Lectures to the Chinese on American Society. Alfred De Grazia. 268p. 1993. pap. 12.00 (0-385-04773-8) Metron Pubns.

Lectureview for Pathophysiology: Biological & Behavioral Perspectives. 2nd ed. Jacquelyn L. Banasik. Date not set. text. write for info. (0-7216-7180-2, W B Saunders Co) Harcrt Hlth Sci Grp.

Lecturing & Explaining. George Brown. 1978. pap. 15.95 (0-416-70920-6, NO. 2009) Routledge.

Lecturing at Your Best. W. G. Lender & L. Leader. 92p. (C). 1990. pap. 125.00 (0-85297-214-8, Pub. by Chartered Bank) St Mut.

Lecturing to Large Groups. Len Powell. (C). 1979. pap. 30.00 (0-85171-017-4, Pub. by IPM Hse) St Mut.

L'Ecume des Jours. Boris Vian. text 8.95 (0-8219-0858-8) EMC-Paradigm.

Lecuona Ernesto Piano Music. 192p. 1996. per. 16.95 (0-7935-6982-6) H Leonard.

Lecuona's Best Made Easier for You. E. Lecuona. 32p. 1984. pap. 5.95 (0-7935-2401-6, 00009281) H Leonard.

Lecythidaceae Pt. 1: The Actinomorphic-Flowered New World Lecythidaceae Asteranthos, Gustavia, Allantoma & Carinana. Ghillean T. Prance & Scott A. Mori. LC 79-4659. (Flora Neotropica Monographs: No. 21). (Illus.). 270p. 1979. pap. 21.00 (0-89327-193-4) NY Botanical.

Lecythidaceae Pt. 2: The Zygomorphic-Flowered New World Genera (Couroupita, Corythophora, Bertholletia, Couratari, Eschweilera & Lecythis) Ghillean T. Prance & Scott A. Mori. LC 85-647083. (Flora Neotropica Monographs: No. 21). (Illus.). 384p. 1990. pap. text 51.75 (0-89327-345-7) NY Botanical.

Lecythidaceae of a Central Amazonian Moist Forest. Scott A. Mori & Nadja Lepsch-Cunha. LC 95-37040. (Memoirs Ser.: Vol. 75). (Illus.). 55p. (Orig.). 1995. pap. text 12.50 (0-89327-396-1) NY Botanical.

Lecythidaceae of a Lowland Neotropical Forest: La Fumee Mountain French Guiana. Scott A. Mori. LC 87-11182. (Memoirs Ser.: Vol. 44). (Illus.). 190p. 1987. pap. 27.75 (0-89327-315-5) NY Botanical.

Led Astray. Sandra Brown. 1995. per. 4.99 (1-55166-041-5, 1-66041-4, Mira Bks) Harlequin Bks.

Led Astray. Sandra Brown. 1999. mass mkt. 6.99 (1-55166-427-5, 0-66427-6, Mira Bks) Harlequin Bks.

Led Astray. Artemis OakGrove. LC 94-8012. 280p. (Orig.). 1994. pap. 9.95 (1-885084-00-5) Tickerwick.

Led by a Child. Earline R. Cole. 1990. pap. 10.95 (0-938645-34-X) In His Steps.

Led by Love. Maria Do Carmo Bogo. 64p. 1996. pap. 39.95 (0-85439-329-3, Pub. by St Paul Pubns) St Mut.

Led by Love: Worship Resources for Year B. Lavon Bayler. LC 95-51672. 344p. (Orig.). 1996. pap. 16.95 (0-8298-1124-9) Pilgrim OH.

***Led by the Carpenter.** James Kennedy. LC 99-37814. 192p. 1999. 18.99 (0-7852-7039-6) Nelson.

***Led by the Holy Spirit.** Mary Anne Adams. (Illus.). 1999. 5.95 (1-929486-01-4) SonRises Bk Pubg.

***Led by the Master's Hand: Missionary Journeys of Signs, Wonders & Miracles.** Charles W. Doss. 144p. 2000. pap. 9.99 (1-884369-48-0) McDougal Pubng.

Led by the Spirit: Biography of Mother Boniface Keasey. Mary Tonra. 1984. 19.95 (0-89876-095-X) Gardner Pr.

Led by the Spirit: How God Guides & Provides. Billy J. Daugherty. LC 93-74611. 1994. pap. 9.99 (0-88419-364-0) Creation House.

Led by the Spirit: Toward a Practical Theology of Pentecostal Discernment & Decision Making. Stephen E. Parker. LC 96-159687. (JPT Supplement Ser.: No. 7). 227p. 1996. pap. 21.95 (1-85075-746-1, Pub. by Sheffield Acad) CUP Services.

Led-Horse Claim. Mary H. Foote. LC 68-20012. (Americans in Fiction Ser.). 1979. reprint ed. pap. text 8.95 (0-8290-0135-2); reprint ed. lib. bdg. 22.50 (0-8398-0559-4) Irvington.

Led on by Compulsion. Leila James. (Black Lace Ser.). 1995. mass mkt. 5.95 (0-352-33032-5, Pub. by Virgin Bks) London Brdge.

Led On! Step by Step: Scenes from Clerical, Military, Educational & Plantation Life in the South. A. Toomer Porter. LC 75-89383. (Black Heritage Library Collection). 1977. 21.95 (0-8369-8643-1) Ayer.

Led Zeppelin. Ed. by Jeannette Delisa. (Drum Superstar Ser.). 36p. (Orig.). (C). 1989. pap. text 12.95 (0-7692-0696-4, DF0028) Wrner Bros.

Led Zeppelin. Tony Horkins. LC 99-162481. 1998. text 9.95 (0-312-17938-3) St Martin.

Led Zeppelin. Dave Lewis. (Complete Guides to the Music Of...Ser.). (Illus.). 104p. (Orig.). pap. 8.95 (0-7119-3528-9, OP 47350, Pub. by Omnibus Press) Omnibus NY.

Led Zeppelin: A Celebration. Dave Lewis. (Illus.). 128p. pap. 24.95 (0-7119-2416-3, OP 46135) Omnibus NY.

Led Zeppelin: A Visual Documentary. Paul Kendall. (Illus.). 96p. (Orig.). pap. 19.95 (0-7119-0094-9, OP 41896) Omnibus NY.

Led Zeppelin: Classic IV Auth. Guitar. 192p. 1992. pap. 26.95 (0-89724-268-8, GF0488) Wrner Bros.

Led Zeppelin: Good Times, Bad Times. Eddy McSquare. (Illus.). 64p. 1991. pap. 12.95 (0-8256-1312-4, BO10138) Music Sales.

Led Zeppelin: In Their Own Words. Compiled by Paul Kendall. LC 95-207409. (In Their Own Words Ser.). (Illus.). 128p. 1981. pap. 15.95 (0-7119-4866-6, OP 41284) Omnibus NY.

Led Zeppelin: The Concert File. Dave Lewis & Simon Pallett. (Illus.). 176p. 1997. pap. 24.95 (0-7119-5307-4, OP47805) Omnibus NY.

Led Zeppelin: The Press Reports. Robert Godwin. (Illus.). 1997. pap. 23.95 (1-896522-41-6) CN06.

Led Zeppelin - Complete II. Ed. by Carol Cuellar. 260p. (Orig.). (C). 1993. pap. text 29.95 (0-7692-0708-1, VF1940) Wrner Bros.

Led Zeppelin - Live Dreams: A Photographer's Visual History of the Led Zeppelin Live Experience. 2nd ed. Laurance Ratner. Ed. by Eric Wynne. (Illus.). 208p. Date not set. 74.95 (0-9637721-0-4) Margaux Pub.

Led Zeppelin - My Night As the 'Right Fifth Member' Rob Wesley. Ed. by Linda J. Schellhaas. (Illus.). 80p. 1999. pap. 12.95 (0-9659676-0-3) Creat Alter WV.

Led Zeppelin Acoustic Class, Vol. I. Warner. 1995. pap. 19.95 (0-89724-589-X, PG9503) Wrner Bros.

Led Zeppelin Biography. Ritchie Yorke. (Orig.). 1976. pap. 8.95 (0-416-00411-3) Routledge.

Led Zeppelin Blues Classics: Guitar Personality Book. 172p. (Orig.). 1996. pap. 19.95 (1-57623-346-4, PG9611) Wrner Bros.

Led Zeppelin Classic V - Houses of the Holy: Guitar Personality Book. 140p. (Orig.). 1993. pap. 24.95 (0-7692-0564-X, GF0524) Wrner Bros.

Led Zeppelin Complete. Ed. by Carol Cuellar. 232p. (Orig.). (C). 1973. pap. text 19.95 (0-7692-0705-7, VF0266) Wrner Bros.

Led Zeppelin Complete: Guitar Edition. 152p. (Orig.). 1994. pap. 18.95 (0-89724-183-5, GF0056) Wrner Bros.

Led Zeppelin Dazed & Confused: The Stories Behind Every Song. Chris Welch. LC 99-162491. (Illus.). 160p. 1998. pap. 22.95 (1-56025-188-3, Thunders Mouth) Avalon NY.

Led Zeppelin/Classic 1 Auth Guitar. 132p. (Orig.). 1990. pap. 22.95 (0-7692-0559-3, GF0417) Wrner Bros.

Led Zeppelin/Classic I/II Bass: Guitar Personality Book. 144p. (Orig.). 1992. pap. 24.95 (0-7692-0554-2, GF0490) Wrner Bros.

Led Zeppelin/Classic III Auth Guitar: Guitar Personality Book. 172p. (Orig.). 1991. pap. 24.95 (0-7692-0556-9, GF0460) Wrner Bros.

Led Zeppelin/Classic III/IV Bass: Guitar Personality Book. 140p. (Orig.). 1993. pap. 24.95 (0-7692-0557-7, GF0539) Wrner Bros.

Led Zeppelin/Classic II Auth Guitar: Guitar Personality Book. 116p. (Orig.). 1990. pap. 22.95 (0-7692-0555-0, GF0421) Wrner Bros.

Led Zeppelin/Classics Auth Guitar: Guitar Personality Book. 260p. (Orig.). 1993. pap. 24.95 (0-7692-0560-7, GF0585) Wrner Bros.

Led Zeppelin/Guitar Superstar Series: Guitar Personality Book. 100p. (Orig.). 1986. pap. 14.95 (0-7692-0561-5, GF0292) Wrner Bros.

Led Zeppelin's Zoso. Robert Godwin. (Making of Ser.). 1996. pap. 7.95 (1-896522-23-8) CN06.

LEDA: A Platform for Combinatorial & Geometric Computing. S. Naher & Kurt Mehlhorn. LC 99-24952. (Illus.). 500p. (C). 1999. text 80.00 (0-521-56329-1) Cambridge U Pr.

Leda the House of Spirits. Aaronna Griffith. (Orig.). 1997. mass mkt. 6.95 (1-56333-585-9, Rosebud) Masquerade.

L

L'Edera: C Level. Deledda. text 8.95 (*0-88436-884-X*) EMC-Paradigm.

Le/Desert est Fertile see Desert Is Fertile

***Ledge.** Michael Collier. LC 99-85997. 96p. 2000. 22.00 (*0-618-05014-0*) HM.

Ledge House: Bohlin Cywinski Jackson. Oscar Riera Ojeda. (Single Building Ser.). 1999. pap. text 19.99 (*1-56496-521-X*) Rockport Pubs.

Ledge, the Ledger, & the Legend. Paul Elliott. 28p. 1972. pap. 3.50 (*0-87129-636-5*, L15) Dramatic Pub.

Ledger. Robert Kroetsch. 32p. 1975. pap. 8.95 (*0-919626-11-4*, Pub. by Brick Bks) Genl Dist Srvs.

Ledger. fac. ed. F. Scott Fitzgerald. 1973. 150.00 (*0-910972-29-X*) Bruccoli.

Ledger of Fruitful Exchange. Peter Sirr. LC 96-105959. 94p. 1997. 24.95 (*1-85235-175-6*); pap. 14.95 (*1-85235-174-8*) Dufour.

Ledger of U. S. Coins. 3rd rev. ed. Coin World Staff. Ed. by Suellen Rattkay. (Illus.). 1998. pap. 9.95 (*0-944945-28-7*) Amos Ohio.

Ledgerbook of Thomas Blue Eagle. Jewel Grutman & Gaye Matthaei. LC 94-8966. (Illus.). 72p. (J). (gr. 2 up). 1994. 17.95 (*1-56566-063-3*) Thomasson-Grant.

Ledgers & Prices: Early Mesopotamian Merchant Accounts. Daniel C. Snell. LC 80-26604. (Near Eastern Researches Ser.: No. 8). (Illus.). 340p. 1982. 62.50 (*0-300-02517-3*) Yale U Pr.

Ledgers of Merit & Demerit: Social Change & Moral Order in Late Imperial China. Cynthia J. Brokaw. LC 90-9059. 299p. reprint ed. pap. 92.70 (*0-608-09112-X*, 206974400005) Bks Demand.

Ledges. 2nd ed. Michael Frederick. 334p. 1998. reprint ed. pap. 7.95 (*1-893794-00-8*) M Frederick.

Ledoux Heritage "The Collecting of Ukiyo-e Master Prints" Ed. by Donald Jenkins. (Illus.). 163p. 1973. 12.00 (*0-913304-02-6*) Japan Soc.

L'/Education du Travail see Education Through Work: A Model for Child-Centered Learning

LeDue Regole della Prospettiva Practica: Ed. I. Danti. Jiacomo B. Da Vignola. (ITA., Illus.). 176p. 1998. reprint ed. pap. 495.00 (*1-85297-025-1*, Pub. by Archival Facs) St Mut.

Lee. Douglas Freeman. 1997. per. 18.00 (*0-684-82953-3*) S&S Trade.

Lee. Otterman J. Hermen. LC 97-66793. 384p. 1998. 24.95 (*1-887750-62-2*) Rutledge Bks.

Lee. Tito Perdue. LC 91-9477. 145p. 1991. 18.95 (*0-941423-39-5*) FWEW.

Lee: A Biography of Robert E. Lee. Clifford Dowdey. (Illus.). 781p. 1991. reprint ed. 35.00 (*1-879664-09-7*); reprint ed. pap. 19.95 (*1-879664-10-0*) Stan Clark Military.

Lee: A Romance. Pamela Marvin. 1997. 27.95 (*0-571-19028-6*) Faber & Faber.

Lee: A Romance. Pamela Marvin. 512p. 1999. pap. 15.95 (*0-571-19550-4*) Faber & Faber.

Lee: An Abridgement. Douglas S. Freeman. 1982. pap. 19.95 (*0-685-46146-7*, Scribners Ref) Mac Lib Ref.

Lee: An Abridgement in One Volume of the Four-Volume R.E. Lee. Abr. by Douglas S. Freeman & Richard B. Harwell. LC 93-6528. (Illus.). 640p. 1993. reprint ed. pap. 18.00 (*0-02-013960-8*) Macmillan.

Lee: John Lee of Farmington, Hartford County, CT, & His Descendants, 1634-1897. L. Lee & S. F. Lee. (Illus.). 572p. 1993. reprint ed. pap. 87.00 (*0-8328-3698-2*); reprint ed. lib. bdg. 97.00 (*0-8328-3697-4*) Higginson Bk Co.

Lee: Selected Papers, 1. T. D. Lee. Ed. by Gerald Feinberg. (Contemporary Physicists Ser.). 1986. 109.50 (*0-8176-3341-3*) Birkhauser.

Lee: Selected Papers, 2. T. D. Lee. Ed. by Gerald Feinberg. (Contemporary Physicists Ser.). 1986. 109.50 (*0-8176-3342-1*) Birkhauser.

Lee: Selected Papers, 3. T. D. Lee. Ed. by Gerald Feinberg. (Contemporary Physicists Ser.). 1986. 109.50 (*0-8176-3343-X*) Birkhauser.

Lee: Selected Papers, Set. T. D. Lee. Ed. by Gerald Feinberg. (Contemporary Physicists Ser.). 1986. 273.50 (*0-8176-3344-8*) Birkhauser.

Lee: The Centennial Celebration & Centennial History of the Town of Lee, Massachusetts. C. M. Hyde & Alexander Hyde. (Illus.). 352p. 1992. reprint ed. lib. bdg. 41.00 (*0-8328-2520-4*) Higginson Bk Co.

Lee: The Last Years. Charles B. Flood. 320p. 1998. pap. 14.00 (*0-395-92974-1*) HM.

***Lee: The Last Years.** Charles B. Flood. 1999. 25.00 (*0-8446-7013-8*) Peter Smith.

Lee Adams Visualization. Lee Adams. 1991. 24.95 (*0-8306-0721-8*); 24.95 (*0-8306-0741-2*) McGraw-Hill Prof.

Lee after the War. Marshall W. Fishwick. LC 73-7102. (Illus.). 242p. 1973. reprint ed. lib. bdg. 35.00 (*0-8371-6911-9*, FILW, Greenwood Pr) Greenwood.

Lee. Ancestors & Descendants of Andrew Lee & Clarinda Knapp Allen. Gerald R. Fuller. Ed. by Esther F. Dial. (Illus.). 445p. 1997. reprint ed. pap. 67.50 (*0-8328-9463-X*); reprint ed. lib. bdg. 77.50 (*0-8328-9462-1*) Higginson Bk Co.

Lee & Grant. Gene Smith. 1989. 10.99 (*0-88394-073-6*) Promntory Pr.

***Lee & His Generals: The Ultimate Trivia Book.** Wendy Sauers. 120p. 2000. pap. 8.95 (*1-57249-196-5*, Burd St Pr) White Mane Pub.

Lee & His Generals in War & Memory. Gary W. Gallagher. LC 98-6215. (Illus.). 288p. 1998. 27.95 (*0-8071-2286-6*) La State U Pr.

Lee & His Men at Gettysburg: The Death of a Nation. Clifford Dowdey. LC 92-37872. (Illus.). 1999. pap. 16.95 (*0-8032-6616-2*) U of Nebr Pr.

Lee & Jackson. Paul D. Casdorph. 448p. 1994. pap. 24.95 (*1-56924-985-7*) Marlowe & Co.

Lee & Longstreet at Gettysburg. Glenn Tucker. LC 67-27229. 1968. 6.00 (*0-672-50734-X*, Bobbs) Macmillan.

Lee & Longstreet at Gettysburg. Glenn Tucker. 286p. 1989. reprint ed. 14.95 (*0-89029-764-9*) Morningside Bkshop.

Lee & Longstreet at High Tide: Gettysburg in the Light of the Official Records. Helen D. Longstreet. (Illus.). 360p. 1989. reprint ed. 35.00 (*0-916107-92-2*) Broadfoot.

Lee & Saralee Rosenberg's 50 Fabulous Places to Raise a Family. 2nd rev. ed. Melissa Giavagnoli. LC 96-28855. (Illus.). 320p. 1996. pap. 18.99 (*1-56414-261-2*) Career Pr Inc.

Lee at Appomattox. Charles F. Adams, Jr. (Works of Charles Francis Adams Jr. (1835-1915)). 1989. reprint ed. lib. bdg. 79.00 (*0-7812-1414-9*) Rprt Serv.

Lee at Appomattox, & Other Papers. 2nd ed. Charles F. Adams, Jr. LC 77-134047. (Essay Index Reprint Ser.). 1977. 28.95 (*0-8369-1901-7*) Ayer.

Lee Bailey's Cooking for Friends: Good Simple Food for Entertaining Friends Everywhere. Lee Bailey. LC 97-51779. 200p. 1998. 16.99 (*0-517-20307-3*) Random Hse Value.

Lee Bailey's Country Flowers: Gardening & Bouquets from Spring to Fall. Lee Bailey. LC 97-12225. 176p. 1997. pap. 14.99 (*0-517-18742-6*) Random Hse Value.

Lee Bailey's Country Weekends: Recipes for Good Food & Easy Living. Lee Bailey. LC 97-9759. 176p. 1997. 14.99 (*0-517-18746-9*) Wings Bks.

Lee Bailey's Desserts. Lee Bailey. LC 97-23983. 184p. 1998. 14.99 (*0-517-18749-3*) Random Hse Value.

Lee Bailey's Dinners at Home. Lee Bailey. 1995. 25.00 (*0-614-15464-2*) C Potter.

Lee Bailey's "The Way I Cook" A Collection of All My Recipes with More Than 90 New Favorites. Lee Bailey. LC 96-20757. 1996. 32.50 (*0-517-59751-9*) C Potter.

Lee Bailey's the Way I Cook: The Collected Lee Bailey. 1996. 30.00 (*0-614-19889-5*) C Potter.

Lee Blessing: Four Plays. Lee Blessing. LC 90-38989. 207p. (Orig.). (C). 1990. pap. 13.95 (*0-435-08601-4*, 08601) Heinemann.

Lee Chesney: Twenty-Five Years of Printmaking. Lee Chesney & Wayne Miyamoto. LC 78-13555. 96p. reprint ed. pap. 30.00 (*0-7837-4914-7*, 204457900004) Bks Demand.

Lee Chronicle: Studies of the Early Generations of the Lees of Virginia. Cazenove Gardner Lee. Ed. by Dorothy Mills Parker. LC 56-10782. 468p. reprint ed. pap. 145.10 (*0-608-10224-5*, 205025800058) Bks Demand.

Lee Considered: General Robert E. Lee & Civil War History. Alan T. Nolan. LC 90-48296. xii, 231p. (C). 1991. 29.95 (*0-8078-1956-5*) U of NC Pr.

Lee Considered: General Robert E. Lee & Civil War History. Alan T. Nolan. 243p. (C). 1996. pap. 16.95 (*0-8078-4587-6*) U of NC Pr.

Lee County, Iowa: A Pictorial History. Jerry Sloat. LC 92-46447. 1993. write for info. (*0-89865-857-8*) Donning Co.

Lee County, Kentucky: Births, Deaths, & Marriages, 1874-1878 & 1900-1910. Margaret M. Hayes. viii, 165p. (Orig.). 1992. pap. text 17.00 (*1-55613-661-7*) Heritage Bk.

Lee County, Kentucky, 1880: Annotated Census, Including the 1880 Mortality Schedule. Margaret M. Hayes. ix, 165p. (Orig.). 1993. pap. text 17.00 (*1-55613-779-6*) Heritage Bk.

***Lee County, Kentucky, 1990 Annotated Census.** annot. ed. Kay A. Spencer & Margaret Millar Hayes. 414p. 1999. pap. 31.50 (*0-7884-1308-2*, S616) Heritage Bk.

Lee County Library, Sanford, North Carolina. (PCI Journal Reprints Ser.). 7p. 1981. pap. 10.00 (*0-686-40147-6*, JR243) P-PCI.

Lee County Marriages, 1830-1836. John Vogt & T. William Kethley, Jr. 28p. 1984. pap. 5.95 (*0-935931-06-6*) Iberian Pub.

***Lee County, Texas.** Lee County Historical Commission. (Images of America Ser.). (Illus.). 128p. 1999. pap. 18.99 (*0-7385-0296-0*) Arcadia Publng.

***Lee Davis.** Lee Davis. (My First Steps to Reading Ser.). (Illus.). (ps-3). 1999. pap. 0.00 (*0-7894-4593-X*) DK Pub Inc.

Lee de Forest & the Fatherhood of Radio. James A. Hijiya. LC 91-76959. (Illus.). 184p. 1992. 32.50 (*0-934223-23-8*) Lehigh Univ Pr.

Lee Enfield Number Four Rifles. Alan M. Petrillo. (British Firearms Ser.: Vol. 1). (Illus.). 64p. (Orig.). 1992. pap. 10.95 (*1-880677-00-8*) Excalibur AZ.

This is a detailed look at the Number 4 series of rifles, used by British soldiers from World War II to Korea. The Lee Enfield Number 4 rifles is full of photos & illustrations showing full-length views of rifles & close-ups of actions & various parts. The book provides a general history of the series, with chapters on the various marks, plus the Number 4 Mark I (T) sniper rifle. Sniper instructions & No. 32 telescopic sight details also are included in the book. Contact Excalibur Publications, PO Box 35369, Tucson, AZ 85740-5369. Voice: (502) 575-9057. Fax: (520) 575-9068. *Publisher Paid Annotation.*

Lee Enfield Number One Rifles. Alan M. Petrillo. (British Firearms Ser.: Vol. 2). (Illus.). 64p. (Orig.). 1992. pap. 10.95 (*1-880677-01-6*) Excalibur AZ. This is the story of the rifles used by the British soldier during World War I - the Number 1 SMLE - Short Magazine Lee Enfield. The Lee Enfield Number 1 Rifles shows full-length views, close-ups of actions & parts of all Number 1 series rifles. The book has a general history of the series, with chapters on each mark, ranging from the Mark I through the Mark VI. Models converted from earlier rifles are included. The Lee Enfield Number 1 Rifles has 47 photographs & 5 illustrations to complement the test. Contact Excalibur Publications, PO Box 35369, Tucson, AZ 85740-5369. Voice: (520) 575-9057. Fax: (520) 575-9068. *Publisher Paid Annotation.*

Lee Evans. Perf. by Lee Evans. (Contemporary Christian Favorites Ser.). 48p. 1996. pap. 8.95 (*0-7935-6822-6*) H Leonard.

Lee Evans Arranges Beautiful Hymns & Spirituals - Piano Solo. Arranged by Lee Evans. 32p. 1989. pap. 6.95 (*0-7935-8443-4*) H Leonard.

Lee Evans Arranges Cole Porter. Cole Porter. 48p. 1985. pap. 7.95 (*0-7935-0932-7*, 00240176) H Leonard.

Lee Evans Arranges Frank Loesser. 64p. 1995. pap. 12.95 (*0-7935-4380-0*, 00385003) H Leonard.

Lee Evans Arranges Great Songs from the Movies. 80p. 1996. pap. 10.95 (*0-7935-5142-0*, 00290044) H Leonard.

Lee Evans Arranges Harold Arlen. 120p. 1995. otabind 14.95 (*0-7935-3343-0*, 00009088) H Leonard.

Lee Evans Arranges Hits of the Fifties. 40p. 1992. pap. 7.95 (*0-7935-1553-X*, 00221014) H Leonard.

Lee Evans Arranges Jerome Kern. 120p. 1992. per. 12.95 (*0-7935-1842-3*, 00009084) H Leonard.

Lee Evans Arranges Rodger & Hammerstein. Contrib. by Lee Evans. 64p. 1989. pap. 9.95 (*0-7935-3861-0*, 00009079) H Leonard.

Lee Evans Arranges Stephen Sondheim. Lee Evans & Stephen Sondheim. (Keyboard Ser.). 80p. 1989. per. 10.95 (*0-88188-837-0*, HL 00009636) H Leonard.

Lee Evans Arranges the Beatles, 1963-1965. 56p. 1992. pap. 8.95 (*0-7935-1740-0*, 00009645) H Leonard.

***Lee Friedlander.** Lee Friedlander. Ed. by Jeffrey Fraenkel. (Illus.). 88p. 2000. pap. 35.00 (*1-891024-19-1*) Dist Art Pubs.

***Lee Friedlander.** Lee Friedlander. Ed. by Jeffrey Fraenkel. (Illus.). 88p. 2000. 75.00 (*1-881337-08-1*, Pub. by Fraenkel Gal) Dist Art Pubs.

Lee Friedlander: Letters from the People. Lee Friedlander. (Illus.). 88p. 1993. 125.00 (*1-881616-05-3*) Dist Art Pubs.

Lee Friedlander: Photographs. Lee Friedlander. (Illus.). 108p. 30.00 (*0-686-28438-0*) Haywire Pr.

Lee Friedlander: The American Monument. limited ed. Lee Friedlander. (Illus.). 77p. 1976. 450.00 (*0-87130-043-5*, Pub. by Eakins) RAM Publications.

Lee Genealogy. Jonathan N. Smith. (Illus.). 37p. 1998. pap. 8.00 (*0-8328-7191-5*); lib. bdg. 18.00 (*0-8328-7190-7*) Higginson Bk Co.

Lee Girls. Mary P. Coulling. (Illus.). 242p. (Orig.). 1996. pap. 12.95 (*0-89587-147-5*) Blair.

***Lee, Grant & Sherman: A Study in Leadership in the 1864-1865 Campaign.** Alfred H. Burne. 2000. reprint ed. pap. 16.95 (*0-7006-1073-1*) U Pr of KS.

***Lee, Grant & Sherman: A Study in Leadership in the 1864-65 Campaign.** Alfred H. Burne. (Modern War Studies). 2000. 29.95 (*0-7006-1072-3*) U Pr of KS.

Lee Haney's Ultimate Bodybuilding Book. Lee Haney & Jim Rosenthal. LC 93-18819. (Illus.). 200p. (Orig.). 1993. pap. 16.95 (*0-312-09322-5*) St Martin.

Lee Iacocca. Darlene E. Resling & Albert Lindel. (Our Changing Lives Ser.). (Illus.). 64p. (YA). (gr. 4-12). 1997. pap. text 7.95 (*1-55596-169-X*, LW2020) Learning Well.

Lee Iacocca: Chrysler's Good Fortune. David R. Collins. Ed. by Richard G. Young. LC 91-31989. (Wizards of Business Ser.). (Illus.). 64p. (J). (gr. 4-8). 1992. lib. bdg. 17.26 (*1-56074-017-5*) Garrett Ed Corp.

Lee Iacocca: Standing up for America: A Biography of Lee Iacocca. Patricia Haddock. LC 86-32965. (People in Focus Ser.). (Illus.). 128p. (YA). (gr. 6 up). 1987. lib. bdg. 13.95 (*0-87518-362-X*, Dillon Silver Burdett) Silver Burdett Pr.

Lee Jaffe: Cordially Yours, Blind Willie McTell. Compiled by Craig A. Subler. (Illus.). 12p. (Orig.). (C). 1989. pap. 5.00 (*0-914489-06-2*) Univ Miss-KC Art.

Lee Kelly at Marylhurst. Paul Sutinen. (Illus.). 1993. pap. 2.00 (*0-914435-10-8*) Marylhurst Art.

Lee Kong Chian Art Museum Catalogue: Chinese Art: Ceramics, Bronze, Jade, Painting & Calligraphy. Ed. by Lu Yaw. (Illus.). 456p. 1990. 87.50 (*9971-69-155-8*, Pub. by Sngapore Univ Pr) Coronet Bks.

Lee Krasner. Robert Hobbs. LC 93-4141. (Modern Masters Ser.). (Illus.). 128p. 1993. 35.00 (*1-55859-651-8*); pap. 14.95 (*1-55859-283-0*) Abbeville Pr.

***Lee Krasner.** Robert Hobbs. 224p. 1999. 49.50 (*0-8109-6395-7*, Pub. by Abrams) Time Warner.

Lee Krasner: A Catalogue Raisonne. Ellen G. Landau. LC 94-41535. (Illus.). 336p. 1995. 150.00 (*0-8109-3513-9*, Pub. by Abrams) Time Warner.

Lee Krasner: Umber Paintings, 1959-1962. Lee Krasner & Richard Howard. Ed. by John Cheim. (Illus.). 70p. (Orig.). 1993. pap. 25.00 (*0-944680-43-7*) R Miller Gal.

Lee Krasner - Collages & Paintings. Edward Albee. Ed. by Mary B. Hynes. LC 98-60141. (Illus.). 34p. 1998. pap. 12.00 (*0-9655319-3-7*) Tasende Gallery.

***Lee Kuan Yew: The Beliefs Behind the Man.** Michael D. Barr. 288p. 2000. text 39.95 (*0-87840-816-9*) Georgetown U Pr.

Lee Marek's Soakin' Science: Book & Kit. Lee Marek et al. 48p. (J). (gr. 3-7). 1999. pap. 14.99 (*1-58184-029-2*) Somerville Hse.

Lee Marvin: His Films & Career. Robert J. Lentz. LC 99-43492. (Illus.). 238p. 1999. boxed set 45.00 (*0-7864-0723-9*) McFarland & Co.

***Lee Middleton Original Dolls Price Guide.** Larry Koon. (Illus.). 128p. 2000. pap. 24.95 (*0-87588-564-0*) Hobby Hse.

Lee Miller Photographs. Jane Livingston. 1989. 50.00 (*0-500-55413-7*) Thames Hudson.

***Lee Mingwei: The Living Room.** Jennifer R. Gross & Lewis Hyde. LC 99-89887. (Illus.). 68p. 2000. pap. 17.95 (*0-914660-13-6*, Pub. by I S Gardner Mus) U Pr of New Eng.

Lee Moor Tramway. R. M. Hall. (C). 1985. 39.00 (*0-85361-245-5*) St Mut.

Lee Moves North: Robert E. Lee on the Offensive. Michael A. Palmer. 189p. 1999. pap. 14.95 (*0-471-35059-1*) Wiley.

Lee of Virginia: A Biography. William E. Brooks. LC 75-16842. (Illus.). 361p. 1975. reprint ed. lib. bdg. 35.00 (*0-8371-8270-0*, BRLV, Greenwood Pr) Greenwood.

Lee Papers. Charles Lea. (Notable American Authors Ser.). 1999. reprint ed. lib. bdg. 125.00 (*0-7812-3785-8*) Rprt Serv.

Lee, Piensa, Corta y Pega. Joy Evans & Jo E. Moore. Tr. by Liz Wolfe & Dora Ficklin from ENG. (SPA., Illus.). 20p. (J). (gr. 1-3). 1990. pap. text 5.95 (*1-55799-183-9*, EMC 025) Evan-Moor Edu Pubs.

Lee Remick: A Bio-Bibliography, 64. Barry Rivadue. LC 95-12421. (Bio-Biographies in the Performing Arts Ser.: Vol. 64). 248p. 1995. lib. bdg. 55.00 (*0-313-28447-4*, Greenwood Pr) Greenwood.

Lee Restored: The General & His Critics. John M. Taylor. LC 99-29910. (Illus.). 268p. 1999. 24.95 (*1-57488-183-3*) Brasseys.

Lee, Shakespeare & a Tertium Quid. George Greenwood. LC 76-52449. (Studies in Shakespeare: No. 24). 1977. lib. bdg. 75.00 (*0-8383-2155-0*) M S G Haskell Hse.

Lee Smith. Dorothy C. Hill. (Twayne's United States Authors Ser.: No. 592). 170p. (C). 1992. 22.95 (*0-8057-7640-0*, Twyne) Mac Lib Ref.

***Lee Smith, Annie Dillard & the Hollins Group: A Genesis of Writers.** Nancy C. Parrish. LC 88-27632. (Southern Literary Studies). (Illus.). 256p. 1999. reprint ed. pap. text 16.95 (*0-8071-2434-6*) La State U Pr.

Lee Sr. Falls to the Floor. Leland Hickman. 90p. (Orig.). 1991. pap. text 7.95 (*0-9629903-1-0*) Jahbone Pr.

Lee Takes Command see Civil War Series

Lee Takes Command. (Civil War Ser.). (Illus.). 176p. 1984. lib. bdg. 25.93 (*0-8094-4805-X*) Time-Life.

Lee Takes Command, Gettysburg & Pursuit to Appomattox: 3-Book Set. (Illus.). 176p. 1999. 89.85 (*0-8094-9194-X*, Pub. by Mouse Works) Time Warner.

Lee Tanner. Phillip Underwood. 192p. 1989. 18.95 (*0-8027-4099-5*) Walker & Co.

Lee the American. Gamaliel Bradford. LC 98-71804. (Illus.). 324p. 1998. pap. 16.95 (*1-888295-06-6*) Elephant Books.

Lee, the Rabbit with Epilepsy. Deborah Moss. LC 88-40249. (Illus.). 32p. (J). (ps up). 1989. lib. bdg. 12.95 (*0-933149-32-8*) Woodbine House.

Lee the Soldier. Ed. by Gary W. Gallagher. LC 95-31874. (Illus.). 648p. 1996. text 45.00 (*0-8032-2153-3*) U of Nebr Pr.

***Lee the Soldier.** Ed. by Gary W. Gallagher. LC 95-31874. (Illus.). 648p. 1999. pap. 19.95 (*0-8032-7084-4*) U of Nebr Pr.

Lee Trevino. Jon Kramer. LC 95-45388. (Overcoming the Odds Ser.). 48p. (J). (gr. 4-6). 1996. lib. bdg. 24.26 (*0-8172-4124-8*) Raintree Steck-V.

Lee Trevino: Mexican-American Golfer. Thomas Gilbert. (Hispanics of Achievement Ser.). (Illus.). 120p. (YA). (gr. 5 up). 1992. lib. bdg. 19.95 (*0-7910-1256-5*) Chelsea Hse.

Lee Van Cleef: A Biographical, Film & Television Reference. Mike Malloy. LC 98-13033. 204p. 1998. lib. bdg. 35.00 (*0-7864-0437-X*) McFarland & Co.

Lee Versus Pickett: Two Divided by War. Richard F. Selcer. LC 98-84332. (Illus.). 144p. 1998. pap. 12.95 (*1-57747-030-3*) Thomas Publications.

Lee vs. McClellan: The First Campaign. Clayton R. Newell. (Illus.). 304p. 1996. 24.95 (*0-89526-452-8*) Regnery Pub.

Lee Wade's Korean Cookery. Joan Rutt. (Illus.). 64p. 1995. 16.95 (*0-930878-45-0*) Hollym Intl.

Lee Wulff on Flies. Lee Wulff. LC 79-5028. (Illus.). 160p. (Orig.). 1985. pap. 16.95 (*0-8117-2205-8*) Stackpole.

LeeAnn Rimes. Tamara L. Britton. LC 98-40385. (Young Profiles Ser.). 1998. 13.95 (*1-57765-325-4*) ABDO Pub Co.

LeeAnne, the Disposable Kid. VeraLee Wiggins. LC 94-32707. (J). (gr. 7-10). 1994. pap. 5.99 (*0-8280-0791-8*) Review & Herald.

Leech Biology & Behavior, 3 vols. Roy T. Sawyer. (Illus.). 1986. write for info. (*0-318-59208-8*) OUP.

Leech Lake, Yesterday & Today. Lund. 120p. 1998. pap. 9.95 (*1-885061-53-6*) Adventure Pubns.

Leechdoms, Wortcunning, & Starcraft of Early England: Being a Collection of Documents Illustrating the History of Science in This Country Before the Norman Conquest, 3 vols. Ed. by Oswald Cockayne. (Rolls Ser.: No. 35). 1969. reprint ed. 210.00 (*0-8115-1083-2*) Periodicals Srv.

Leeches. Patrick Merrick. LC 98-44320. (Illus.). 32p. (J). 1999. lib. bdg. write for info. (*1-56766-633-7*) Childs World.

Leeches. Lynn M. Stone. LC 95-16560. (Creepy Crawlers Discovery Library). 24p. (J). (gr. k-4). 1995. lib. bdg. 15.93 (*1-55916-162-0*) Rourke Bk Co.

An Asterisk (*) at the beginning of an entry indicates that the title is appearing for the first time.

Leechtime: Novel. Albert B. Davis. LC 88-27629. 184p. 1989. 17.95 (*0-8071-1494-4*) La State U Pr.

Leedy Drum Topics: Complete from 1923 to 1941. Rob Cook & John Aldridge. (Illus.). 300p. 1997. pap. 29.95 (*0-931759-78-1*) Centerstream Pub.

Leela. Harish Johari. 1986. 14.95 (*0-7100-0689-6*, Routledge Thoemms) Routledge.

Leela: The Game of Self-Knowledge, Set. Harish Johari. LC 93-4565. (Illus.). 144p. (Orig.). 1993. boxed set 24.95 (*0-89281-419-5*, Destiny Bks) Inner Tradit.

Leela Kaivalya Vahini (Stream of Cosmic Sport Divine) Sathya Sai Baba. 1988. pap. 1.50 (*1-57836-064-1*, BA-306) Sathya Sai Bk Ctr.

Leelanau Country Inn Cookery: Food & Wine from the Land of Delight. Linda Sisson & John Sisson. Ed. by Larry Mawby. LC 94-71255. (Illus.). 256p. (Orig.). 1994. pap. text 19.95 (*0-9640306-0-8*) Cairn Press.

***Leelanau Country Inn Cookery ... Continued Vol. 2: Food & Wine from the Land of Delight.** Linda Sisson & John Sisson. LC 99-68157. (Illus.). 240p. 1999. pap. 21.95 (*0-9676535-0-9*) Bucca Pr.

Leelanau County Postcard History. Lawrence M. Wakefield. (Illus.). (Orig.). 1994. pap. 12.00 (*0-9618903-4-7*) L M Wakefield.

Leena's Ribbon. Maysel Beck. 106p. 1995. pap. 10.00 (*0-87012-529-X*) McClain.
An educating children's book about a young girl & her desire to race her horse, Ribbon, in a real horse race. Leena shows her dedication to her dream & to her best friend, Ribbon, as she endures her daily chores on the Coy Ranch & the responsibility of working with her trainer to make her horse a winner.
Publisher Paid Annotation.

Leer para Escribir: Antologia de Lecturas para Practicar los Procesos de la Redaccion. 4th ed. Elsa Arroyo & Julia C. Ortiz. (SPA.). 448p. (C). 1996. reprint ed. pap. text 16.95 (*1-56328-065-5*) Edit Plaza Mayor.

Leer! Un Paso Mas: Reading Strategies & Communication. H. Villarreal & Gene S. Kupferschmid. 256p. (C). 1990. pap. 33.75 (*0-07-557643-0*) McGraw.

Leer y Escribir en Espanol. Marcia Weinstein. 1998. pap. 9.95 (*0-87594-366-7*); pap., teacher ed. 7.95 (*0-87594-367-5*) Book-Lab.

Leerboek Ansi SQL. Marcus. (C). 1993. pap. text. write for info. (*0-201-54516-0*) Addison-Wesley.

Lee's Adjutant: The Wartime Letters of Colonel Walter Herron Taylor, 1862-1865. Walter H. Taylor. Ed. by R. Lockwood Tower & John S. Belmont. LC 94-18751. 350p. 1995. 24.95 (*1-57003-021-9*) U of SC Pr.

***Lee's Aide-de-Camp.** Charles Marshall. Ed. by Frederick Maurice. 352p. 2000. pap. 14.95 (*0-8032-8262-1*, Bison Books) U of Nebr Pr.

Lee's Colonels: A Biographical Register of the Field Officers of the Army of Northern Virginia. 4th rev. ed. Robert K. Krick. (Illus.). 520p. 1996. reprint ed. pap. 25.00 (*0-89029-548-4*, Pr of Morningside) Morningside Bkshop.

Lee's Endangered Left. Richard R. Duncan. LC 98-33689. (Illus.). 400p. 1998. 29.95 (*0-8071-2291-2*) La State U Pr.

Lee's Ferry: Desert River Crossing. 3rd rev. ed. W. L. Rusho. (Illus.). 196p. (C). 1998. pap. 16.95 (*0-9656645-1-1*) Tower Prods.

Lee's Ferry: From Mormon Crossing to National Park. P. T. Reilly et al. Ed. by Robert H. Webb. LC 98-58050. (Illus.). 480p. 1998. 39.95 (*0-87421-261-8*) Utah St U Pr.

Lee's Ferry: From Mormon Crossing to National Park. P. T. Reilly et al. Ed. by Robert H. Webb. LC 98-58050. (Illus.). 542p. 1999. pap. 21.95 (*0-87421-260-X*) Utah St U Pr.

Lee's Grenadier Guard see Hood's Texas Brigade

Lee's Last Campaign: The Story of Lee & His Men Against Grant - 1864. Clifford Dowdey. LC 92-37872. (Illus.). xxii, 415p. (C). 1993. pap. 15.95 (*0-8032-6595-6*, Bison Books) U of Nebr Pr.

Lee's Last Major General: Bryan Grimes of North Carolina. T. Harrell Allen. (Illus.). 352p. 1998. 24.95 (*1-882810-23-6*) Savas Pub.

***Lee's Lieutenants.** Ed. by Lam Peng & Kevin Tan. 272p. 2000. 49.95 (*1-86508-172-8*, Pub. by Allen & Unwin Pty); 35.00 (*1-86448-639-2*, Pub. by Allen & Unwin Pty) Paul & Co Pubs.

Lee's Lieutenants, Vol. 1. Daniel B. Freeman. 832p. 1977. 60.00 (*0-684-15486-2*, Scribners Ref) Mac Lib Ref.

Lee's Lieutenants, Vol. 1. Douglas S. Freeman. LC 97-151696. 1997. 40.00 (*0-684-83783-8*, Scribners Ref) Mac Lib Ref.

Lee's Lieutenants, Vol. 2. Daniel B. Freeman. 784p. 1977. 60.00 (*0-684-15487-0*, Scribners Ref) Mac Lib Ref.

Lee's Lieutenants, Vol. 2. Douglas S. Freeman. LC 97-151696. 1997. 40.00 (*0-684-83784-6*, Scribners Ref) Mac Lib Ref.

Lee's Lieutenants, Vol. 3. Daniel B. Freeman. 896p. 1977. 65.00 (*0-684-15488-9*, Scribners Ref) Mac Lib Ref.

Lee's Lieutenants, Vol. 3. Douglas S. Freeman. LC 97-151696. 1997. 40.00 (*0-684-83785-4*, Scribners Ref) Mac Lib Ref.

Lee's Lieutenants: A Study in Command. Douglas S. Freeman. (Illus.). 912p. 1999. pap. 35.00 (*0-684-85979-3*, Fireside) S&S Trade Pap.

Lee's Lieutenants: A Study in Command, Vol. 1. Douglas S. Freeman. (Illus.). 773p. 1986. reprint ed. pap. 23.00 (*0-684-18748-5*, Scribners Ref) Mac Lib Ref.

Lee's Lieutenants: A Study in Command, Vol. 2. Douglas S. Freeman. 760p. 1986. reprint ed. per. 23.00 (*0-684-18749-3*, Scribners Ref) Mac Lib Ref.

Lee's Lieutenants: A Study in Command, Vol. 3. Douglas S. Freeman. 862p. 1986. reprint ed. per. 23.00 (*0-684-18750-7*, Scribners Ref) Mac Lib Ref.

Lee's Lieutenants Abridged. Douglas S. Freeman. LC 98-15416. 1998. 65.00 (*0-684-83309-3*) S&S Trade.

Lee's Maverick General: Daniel Harvey Hill. Hal Bridges. 323p. 1961. 30.00 (*1-56013-004-0*) Olde Soldier Bks.

Lee's Maverick General: Daniel Harvey Hill. Hal Bridges. LC 91-13093. (Illus.). xxii, 323p. 1991. reprint ed. pap. 13.95 (*0-8032-6096-2*, Bison Books) U of Nebr Pr.

Lees-McRae College Recipe Book. Ed. by Clarence A. Carder. (Illus.). 1984. 5.50 (*0-317-00834-X*) Puddingstone.

Lee's Miserables: Life in the Army of Northern Virginia from the Wilderness to Appomattox. J. Tracy Power. LC 97-17724. (Civil War America Ser.). (Illus.). 488p. 1998. 34.95 (*0-8078-2392-9*) U of NC Pr.

Lee's New School History of the United States. Susan R. Lee. (Johnson Ser.). (Illus.). 422p. 1996. pap. 17.95 (*0-9627989-0-8*) Grapevine ID.

***Lee's North Carolina Family Law, Vol. 2.** 5th ed. Kenneth Craig et al. 800p. 1999. write for info. (*0-327-04937-5*, 6427211) LEXIS Pub.

Lees of Virginia: Biography of a Family. Burton J. Hendrick. (Illus.). 455p. 1997. reprint ed. pap. 39.95 (*0-8063-4655-8*, Pub. by Clearfield Co) ACCESS Pubs Network.

Lee's Priceless Recipes. N. T. Oliver. (Classic Reprint Ser.). 370p. 1995. reprint ed. pap. 5.95 (*0-921335-17-2*, Pub. by LVTL) Veritas Tools.

Lee's Sharpshooters: Or The Forefront of Battle: A Story of Southern Valor That Never Has Been Told. W. S. Dunlop. (Illus.). 499p. 2000. reprint ed. 50.00 (*0-89029-064-4*) Morningside Bkshop.

Lees Synopsis of Anaesthesia. Rushman. 816p. pap. text. write for info. (*0-7506-1608-3*) Buttrwrth-Heinemann.

***Lee's Synopsis of Anaesthesia.** 12th ed. G. B. Rushman. LC 99-25482. 750p. 1999. pap. text 47.50 (*0-7506-3247-X*) Buttrwrth-Heinemann.

Lee's Tarnished Lieutenant: James Longstreet & His Place in Southern History. William G. Piston. LC 86-16025. (Brown Thrasher Bks.). 264p. 1990. pap. 15.95 (*0-8203-1229-0*) U of Ga Pr.

Lee's Tigers: The Louisiana Infantry in the Army of Northern Virginia. Terry L. Jones. LC 86-27627. (Illus.). 312p. 1987. 34.95 (*0-8071-1314-X*) La State U Pr.

Lee's Tough Time Rhyme. Susanne M. Swanson. (Illus.). 40p. (Orig.). (J). (gr. k-5). 1994. pap. 6.99 (*1-885101-09-0*) Writers Pr ID.

Lee's Young Artillerist: William R. J. Pegram. Peter S. Carmichael. (Nation Divided Ser.). 222p. 1998. reprint ed. pap. 15.95 (*0-8139-1828-6*) U Pr of Va.

Leese: The Lawrence Leese Family: Two Centuries in America (1741-1941) Charles Leese. (Illus.). 214p. 1993. reprint ed. pap. 34.00 (*0-8328-3362-2*); reprint ed. lib. bdg. 44.00 (*0-8328-3361-4*) Higginson Bk Co.

Leeshore. Robert Reed. 272p. 1988. mass mkt. 3.50 (*0-445-20616-0*, Pub. by Warner Bks) Little.

Leete: The Family of William Leete. E. Leete. (Illus.). 168p. 1990. reprint ed. pap. 26.00 (*0-8328-1487-3*); reprint ed. lib. bdg. 34.00 (*0-8328-1486-5*) Higginson Bk Co.

***Leeteg of Tahiti; Paintings from the Villa Velour.** John Turner & Greg Escalante. (Illus.). 96p. 2000. pap. 29.95 (*0-86719-489-8*) Last Gasp.

Leete's Island Legacy. Joel E. Helander. (Illus.). 66p. 1981. reprint ed. pap. 12.95 (*0-935600-08-6*, 81-82110) Helander.

Leet's Christmas. Elithe H. Kirkland. (Illus.). 64p. 1996. 16.95 (*1-57441-014-8*) UNTX Pr.

Leeuwenhoek Legacy. Brian J. Ford. (Illus.). 185p. 1991. lib. bdg. 59.00 (*0-948737-10-7*, Pub. by Biopress) Balogh.

Leeward Islands Restaurant Guide & Recipe Book. unabridged ed. Charles H. Eanes & Susan E. Eanes. LC 92-74722. (Illus.). 104p. (Orig.). 1992. pap. 14.95 (*1-890494-00-3*) Espichel Enterp.

Leeway: The Lee Morgan Discography. Roger Wernboe. 112p. 1998. pap. 13.00 (*1-881993-29-9*) Cadence Jazz.

Lef, Vol. 3. limited ed. James Humphrey. LC 98-121392. 85p. 1998. pap. 16.00 (*0-936641-22-3*) Poets Alive Pr.

LeFebvre, Love, & Struggle: Spatial Dialectics. Rob Shields. LC 98-20945. 1p. 1999. write for info. (*0-415-09369-4*); pap. write for info. (*0-415-09370-8*) Routledge.

Lefever: Guns of Lasting Fame. Robert W. Elliott & Jim Cobb. 174p. 1987. 29.95 (*0-9616575-0-2*) R W Elliott.

Lefevre: Pioneer of Ecclesiastical Renewal in France. Philip E. Hughes. LC 84-13739. 222p. (Orig.). reprint ed. pap. 68.90 (*0-608-17879-9*, 203273300080) Bks Demand.

Lefkandi III: The Toumba Cemetery : The Excavations of 1981, 1984, 1986 & 1992-4. Mervyn R. Popham et al. LC 97-189550. 1996. write for info. (*0-904887-27-8*) Brit Sch Athens.

Leflunomide: Proceedings of the Vienna Symposium, 12 October 1993. Ed. by R. R. Bartlett. LC 94-43800. 1994. write for info. (*3-7643-5150-0*); write for info. (*0-8176-5150-0*) Birkhauser.

Lefrancois: Psychologie Lernes. 1994. 39.95 (*0-387-57807-2*) Spr-Verlag.

Lefschetz Centennial Conference, Set, Pts. I[00ad]III. LC 86-14040. (Contemporary Mathematics Ser.: Vol. 58). 695p. 1986. pap. 85.00 (*0-8218-5065-2*, CONM/58) Am Math.

Lefschetz Centennial Conference: Differential Equations, Pt. III. Verjovsky. LC 86-14040. (Contemporary Mathematics Ser.: Vol. 58.3). 253p. 1987. pap. 37.00 (*0-8218-5064-4*, CONM/58.3) Am Math.

Lefschetz Centennial Conference: Proceedings on Algebraic Topology, Pt. II. S. Gitler. LC 86-14040. (Contemporary Mathematics Ser.: Vol. 58.2). 137p. 1987. reprint ed. pap. 26.00 (*0-8218-5063-6*, CONM/58.2) Am Math.

Lefschetz Centennial Conference Pt. 1: Proceedings on Algebraic Geometry. D. Sundararaman. LC 86-14040. (Contemporary Mathematics Ser.: Vol. 58.1). 275p. 1986. reprint ed. pap. 37.00 (*0-8218-5061-X*, CONM/58.1) Am Math.

***Left: The Sound of "L"** Alice K. Flanagan. LC 99-20958. (Wonder Books Ser.). (Illus.). 24p. (J). 1999. lib. bdg. 21.41 (*1-56766-702-3*) Childs World.

Left Academy: Marxist Scholarship on American Campuses, Vol. 2. Ed. by Bertell Ollman & Edward Vernoff. LC 81-12365. 290p. (Orig.). (C). 1984. 59.95 (*0-275-91237-X*, C12372, Praeger Pubs) Greenwood.

Left Academy: Marxist Scholarship on American Campuses, Vol. 3. Ed. by Bertell Ollman & Edward Vernoff. LC 86-9321. 322p. (Orig.). 1986. 59.95 (*0-275-92116-6*, C21163, Praeger Pubs) Greenwood.

Left Academy: Marxist Scholarship on American Campuses, Vol. 3. Ed. by Bertell Ollman & Edward Vernoff. LC 86-9321. 322p. (Orig.). 1986. pap. 19.95 (*0-275-92117-4*, B21173, Praeger Pubs) Greenwood.

Left Against Zion: Communism, Israel & the Middle East. Ed. by Robert Wistrich. 309p. 1979. 49.50 (*0-85303-193-2*, Pub. by M Vallentine & Co); pap. 24.50 (*0-85303-199-1*, Pub. by M Vallentine & Co) Intl Spec Bk.

Left Alive: After a Suicide Death in the Family. Linda Rosenfeld & Marilynne Prupas. 120p. 1984. text 31.95 (*0-398-04953-X*); pap. text 20.95 (*0-398-06650-7*) C C Thomas.

Left & Culture. 5th ed. Ed. by Willie Thompson. (Socialist History Ser.: Vol. 5). 64p. 1994. pap. 9.99 (*0-7453-0809-0*, Pub. by Pluto GBR) Stylus Pub VA.

Left & Israel. Edmunds. LC 99-38451. 1999. text 65.00 (*0-312-22605-5*) St Martin.

Left & Right. Norberto Bobbio. LC 96-26392. 1996. pap. text 14.95 (*0-226-06246-5*); lib. bdg. 34.95 (*0-226-06245-7*) U Ch Pr.

Left & Right: Selected Essays, 1954-1965. LC 71-172210. (Right Wing Individualist Tradition in America Ser.). 1972. reprint ed. 16.95 (*0-405-00426-5*) Ayer.

Left & Right: The Topography of Political Perceptions. J. A. Laponce. 284p. 1981. text 40.00 (*0-8020-5533-8*) U of Toronto Pr.

Left & the Erotic. Ed. by Eileen Phillips. (C). 1983. pap. 18.50 (*0-85315-583-6*, Pub. by Lawrence & Wishart) NYU Pr.

Left & the French Revolution. Morris Slavin. LC 93-25741. (Revolutionary Studies). 208p. (C). 1995. text 45.00 (*0-391-03843-5*) Humanities.

Left at East Gate. Larry Warren & Peter Robbins. LC 96-24996. 1996. 24.95 (*1-56924-759-5*) Marlowe & Co.

Left at East Gate: A First-Hand Account of the Bentwaters-Woodbridge UFO Incident, Its Cover-Up. Larry Warren & Peter Robbins. 512p. 1998. pap. 15.95 (*1-56924-668-8*) Marlowe & Co.

Left at the Altar. Justine Davis. 1994. per. 3.50 (*0-373-07596-0*, 1-07596-9) Harlequin Bks.

Left at the Altar! Kate William. (Sweet Valley High Ser.: No. 108). (YA). (gr. 7 up). 1994. 8.60 (*0-606-06781-7*, Pub. by Turtleback) Demco.

Left Back! Molly Mia Stewart. (Sweet Valley Kids Ser.: No. 32). (J). (gr. 1-3). 1992. 8.19 (*0-606-00641-9*, Pub. by Turtleback) Demco.

***Left Back: A Century of Failed School Reforms.** Diane Ravitch. LC 00-38067. 560p. 2000. 30.00 (*0-684-84417-6*) Simon & Schuster.

Left Bank: Writers, Artists, & Politics from the Popular Front to the Cold War. Herbert Lottman. LC 98-8786. 1998. pap. 17.00 (*0-226-49368-7*) U Ch Pr.

Left Bank & Other Stories. Jean Rhys. LC 79-134976. (Short Story Index Reprint Ser.). 1977. 26.95 (*0-8369-3698-1*) Ayer.

Left Behind see Dejados Atras

Left Behind see Que Se Quedaron

Left Behind. Carol Carrick. LC 88-1040. (Illus.). 32p. (J). (gr. k-3). 1988. text 16.60 (*0-89919-535-0*, Clarion Bks) HM.

Left Behind. Peter Lalonde & Patti Lalonde. (Orig.). 1995. pap. 9.99 incl. VHS (*1-56507-364-9*) Harvest Hse.

Left Behind: A Book of Comfort & Hope. Michael N. Darnell. Ed. by Carol Brown. (Illus.). 102p. (Orig.). 1991. pap. 8.95 (*1-56325-005-5*, TB001) Davis Pub Law.

Left Behind: A Mother's Grief. Carol J. Kifer. LC 98-91755. xii, 164p. 1999. pap. 12.95 (*0-9666014-0-8*, 117) PAZ Publns.

Left Behind: A Novel of the Earth's Last Days. Tim F. LaHaye & Jerry B. Jenkins. LC 95-19132. (Left Behind Ser.: Bk. 1). 468p. 1995. 19.99 (*0-8423-2911-0*) Tyndale Hse.

Left Behind: A Novel of the Earth's Last Days. Tim F. LaHaye & Jerry B. Jenkins. (Left Behind Ser.: Bk. 1). 320p. 1996. pap. 13.99 (*0-8423-2912-9*) Tyndale Hse.

***Left Behind: A Novel of the Earth's Last Days.** large type ed. Tim F. LaHaye & Jerry B. Jenkins. LC 99-87745. (Left Behind Ser.). 575p. 2000. 29.95 (*0-7862-2468-1*) Thorndike Pr.

Left Behind in Rosedale: Race Relations & the Collapse of Community Institutions. Scott Cummings. LC 97-32511. (C). 1998. pap. 24.00 (*0-8133-3421-7*, Pub. by Westview) HarpC.

***Left Behind: The Kids Boxed Set: The Vanishings; Second Chance; Facing the Future; Through the Flames; Nicolae High; The Underground, 6 vols.** Jerry B. Jenkins. (Left Behind: Bks. 1-6). 1999. pap., boxed set 29.97 (*0-8423-0907-1*) Tyndale Hse.

Left-Brain Finance for Right-Brain People: A Money Guide for the Creatively Inclined. 2nd rev. ed. Paula A. Monroe. LC 98-13241. (Illus.). 352p. 1998. pap. 18.95 (*1-57071-340-5*) Sourcebks.

Left Brain, Right Brain. 3rd ed. Sally P. Springer & Geog Deutsch. LC 88-30097. (Psychology Ser.). 384p. (C). 1989. pap. text 14.40 (*0-7167-2000-0*) W H Freeman.

Left Brain, Right Brain. 5th ed. Springer. 1997. 17.60 (*0-7167-3148-7*); write for info. (*0-7167-3149-5*) W H Freeman.

Left Brain, Right Brain. 5th ed. Sally P. Springer & Georg Deutsh. LC 97-27803. 368p. 1997. pap. 20.95 (*0-7167-3111-8*) W H Freeman.

Left Brain-Right Brain Differences: Inquiries, Evidence & New Approaches. James F. Iaccino. LC 92-49108. 288p. 1993. 69.95 (*0-8058-1340-3*); pap. 34.50 (*0-8058-1341-1*) L Erlbaum Assocs.

Left by the Indians. Emeline Fuller & Carl P. Schlicke. 81p. 1988. pap. 9.95 (*0-87770-452-X*) Ye Galleon.

Left Coast City: Progressive Politics in San Francisco, 1975-1991. Richard E. DeLeon. LC 92-14119. (Studies in Government & Public Policy). (Illus.). xii, 244p. 1992. 35.00 (*0-7006-0554-1*); pap. 14.95 (*0-7006-0555-X*) U Pr of KS.

Left Coast of Paradise: California & the American Heart. Judith Moore. LC 87-20481. 256p. 1987. 17.95 (*0-939149-03-6*) Soho Press.

Left Experiment in West Bengal. P. R. Choudhury. 1986. 19.00 (*0-8364-1833-6*, Pub. by Heritage IA) S Asia.

Left Extremist Movement in West Bengal. Amiya K. Samanta. 1985. 22.50 (*0-8364-1264-8*, Pub. by Mukhopadhyaya) S Asia.

Left Face: Soldier Unions & Resistance Movements in Modern Armies, 107. David Cortright & Max Watts. LC 90-46702. (Contributions in Military Studies Ser.: No. 107). 296p. 1991. 65.00 (*0-313-27626-9*, CLT/, Greenwood Pr) Greenwood.

Left Field Bear. Jean Rogers. LC 95-81527. (Illus.). 32p. (Orig.). (J). (gr. k-3). 1996. pap. 6.95 (*0-9641998-2-3*) Lapcat Pubns.

Left for Dead. Diane Langford. LC 98-86412. 208p. 1999. pap. 12.99 (*1-85242-369-2*, Pub. by Serpents Tail) Consort Bk Sales.

Left for Dead. Dick Quinn et al. (Illus.). 200p. (Orig.). 1992. pap. 12.95 (*0-9632839-0-1*) R F Quinn.

Left for Dead. Michael Tomasky. 240p. 1996. 23.00 (*0-684-82750-6*) Free Pr.

Left for Dead. Michael Tomasky. 1996. 23.00 (*0-02-874093-9*) Macmillan.

***Left for Dead: My Journey Home from Everest.** Beck Weathers & Stephen G. Michaud. LC 00-21503. (Illus.). 288p. 2000. 24.95 (*0-375-50404-4*) Villard Books.

Left for Dead: Poems by David Franks. David Franks. Ed. by R. D. Baker. (Poetry Chapbook Ser.). (Illus.). 28p. (Orig.). 1997. pap. 4.00 (*1-887641-08-4*) Argonne Hotel Pr.

Left Guide: A Guide to Left-of-Center Organizations. 2nd rev. ed. Ed. by Derk A. Wilcox. 662p. 1998. 74.95 (*0-914169-05-X*) Econ America.

Left Hand Chord Chart. Ron Middlebrook. (Illus.). 4p. 1982. pap. 2.50 (*1-57424-078-1*) Centerstream Pub.

Left Hand Like God: A History of Boogie Woogie Piano. Peter J. Silvester. (Quality Paperbacks Ser.). 332p. 1989. pap. 12.95 (*0-306-80359-3*) Da Capo.

Left-Hand Maps: San Francisco Bay Area Poets. Ed. by LeeAnn Heringer. (Illus.). 56p. (Orig.). 1998. pap. 3.00 (*1-888431-18-0*) ASGP.

Left Hand of Darkness. Ursula K. Le Guin. 304p. 1982. mass mkt. 6.99 (*0-441-47812-3*) Ace Bks.

***Left Hand of Darkness.** Ursula K. Le Guin. 320p. 2000. pap. 12.95 (*0-441-00731-7*) Ace Bks.

Left Hand of Darkness. 25th anniversary ed. Ursula K. Le Guin. LC 94-27147. 325p. 1994. 27.50 (*0-8027-1302-5*) Walker & Co.

Left Hand of Eden: Meditations on Nature & Human Nature. William Ashworth. LC 98-54935. 208p. 1999. pap. 19.95 (*0-87071-460-0*) Oreg St U Pr.

Left Hand of God. William E. Barrett. 23.95 (*0-685-10845-7*, Queens House) Amereon Ltd.

***Left Hand of God.** Hugh Holton. 416p. 2000. mass mkt. 6.99 (*0-8125-7084-7*, Pub. by Forge NYC) St Martin.

Left Hand of God. Hugh Holton. LC 98-47004. 384p. 1999. 24.95 (*0-312-86763-8*, Pub. by Tor Bks) St Martin.

Left Hand of God. William E. Barrett. 1990. reprint ed. lib. bdg. 19.95 (*0-89968-475-0*) Buccaneer Bks.

Left Hand of God: A Biography of the Holy Spirit. Adolf Holl. 368p. 1999. pap. 12.95 (*0-385-49285-5*, Anchor NY) Doubleday.

Left Hand of God: A Biography of the Holy Spirit. Adolf Holl. Tr. by John Cullen from ENG. LC 98-17994. 368p. 1998. reprint ed. 23.95 (*0-385-49284-7*) Doubleday.

Left Hand Solos, Vol. 2. Ed. by Carole Flatau. 24p. (YA). 1997. pap. text 5.95 (*0-7692-1552-1*, EL9742) Wrner Bros.

Left Hand Solos: And One Duet for Two Left Hands. Ed. by Carole Flatau. 24p. (Orig.). (C). 1997. pap. text 5.95 (*0-7692-0105-9*, EL9741) Wrner Bros.

Left-Handed. Lillian Cram. Ed. by Barry Lane. (Opening Doors Ser.: No. 1). (Illus.). 32p. (Orig.). 1989. pap. 4.00 (*1-877829-06-4*) Homegrown Bks.

Left-Handed Book. James T. de Kay. LC 66-23271. (Illus.). 64p. 1966. pap. 3.50 (*0-87131-156-9*) M Evans.

Left-Handed Calligraphy. Vance Studley. (Lettering, Calligraphy, Typography Ser.). (Illus.). 64p. 1991. reprint ed. pap. 3.95 (*0-486-26702-4*) Dover.

Left-Handed Designer. Seymour Chwast. Ed. by Steven Heller. LC 85-3922. (Illus.). 143p. 1985. 49.50 (*0-8109-1289-9*, Pub. by Abrams) Time Warner.

***Left-Handed Dreams.** Francesca Duranti. LC 00-22737. 2000. 20.00 (*1-883285-19-4*) Delphinium.

L

An Asterisk (*) at the beginning of an entry indicates that the title is appearing for the first time.

Left-Handed Green Beans. Ralph Sexton, Sr. (Illus.). 32p. (Orig.). 1997. pap. 9.95 (1-57090-057-4, Mountain Chrch) Alexander Dist.

Left Handed Guitar: Chords Especially for Lefties. Nicholas Clarke. (Illus.). 28p. 1992. pap. 12.95 (0-933224-99-0, T024) Bold Strummer Ltd.

***Left-handed Guitar: The Complete Method.** 80p. 1998. pap. 9.95 (0-7935-8788-3) H Leonard.

Left-Handed Happiness. Margo Lockwood. (Illus.). 60p. (Orig.). 1987. pap. 12.00 (0-9617521-0-6) Dirty Dish Pr.

Left-Handed in a Right-Handed World. Jeff Goldsmith. Ed. by Judy A. Noble et al. (Illus.). 212p. (Orig.). 1995. pap. write for info. (0-9648822-0-5) Left Hand Pub.

Left-Handed Kids. James T. de Kay. LC 89-36893. (Illus.). 96p. (J). 1989. pap. 5.95 (0-87131-591-2) M Evans.

Left-Handed Sewing. Sally Cowan. (Illus.). 64p. 1994. reprint ed. pap. text 2.95 (0-486-27752-6) Dover.

Left-Handed Shortstop. Patricia Reilly Giff. (Illus.). 128p. (J). (gr. k-6). 1989. pap. 3.99 (0-440-44672-4, YB BDD) BDD Bks Young Read.

Left-Handed Shortstop. Patricia Reilly Giff. (J). 1980. 9.09 (0-606-02895-1, Pub. by Turtleback) Demco.

Left Handed, Son of Old Man Hat: A Navaho Autobiography. Left Handed. LC 95-37149. 378p. 1967. pap. 14.95 (0-8032-7958-2, Bison Books) U of Nebr Pr.

Left-Handed Stitchery. Sally Cowan. LC 85-31175. (Illus.). 64p. 1986. pap. 9.95 (0-671-61393-6) P-H.

Left-Handed Stitchery. Sally Cowan. LC 87-61438. (Illus.). 64p. 1987. pap. 9.95 (0-88740-110-4) Schiffer.

Left-Handed Students: A Forgotten Minority. Evelyn B. Kelly. LC 96-67181. (Fastback Ser.: No. 399). 40p. (Orig.). 1996. pap. 3.00 (0-87367-599-1) Phi Delta Kappa.

***Left Handed Through Time.** John H. Baldwin. LC 00-190670. 191p. 2000. 25.00 (0-7388-1726-0); pap. 18.00 (0-7388-1727-9) Xlibris Corp.

Left-Handedness: Behavioral Implications & Anomalies. Ed. by Stanley Coren. (Advances in Psychology Ser.: No. 67). xviii,574p. 1990. 201.50 (0-444-88438-6, North Holland) Elsevier.

Left-Hander Syndrome: The Causes & Consequences of Left-Handedness. Stanley Coren. (Illus.). 375p. 1991. 27.95 (0-02-906682-4) Free Pr.

Left-Hander Syndrome: The Causes & Consequences of Left-Handedness. Stanley Coren. LC 92-50646. 1993. pap. 14.00 (0-679-74468-1) Vin Bks.

Left-Handers. Hubert Moore. 72p. 1996. pap. 15.95 (1-870612-42-6, Pub. by Enitha Pr) Dufour.

Left-Hander's Book of Days. Leigh W. Rutledge. LC 98-54340. (Illus.). 320p. 1999. 16.95 (0-525-94348-X) NAL.

Left-Handers Guide & Reference Manual. John Diana. LC 92-70141. (Illus.). 126p. 1992. 12.95 (1-880896-00-1) Left-Handed Sol.

Left-Hander's Guide to Life. Leigh W. Rutledge & Richard Donley. (Illus.). 128p. (Orig.). 1992. pap. 9.95 (0-452-26845-1, Plume) Dutton Plume.

Left-Hander's Handbook. James T. DeKay. 408p. 1997. 9.98 (1-56731-229-2) Fine Comms.

***Left Hander's 2001 Desk Calendar.** Charles Koegle & Donald Koegle. 640p. 2000. pap. 10.99 (0-8431-7572-9) Peng Put Young Read.

Left in France: Towards the Socialist Republic. Ed. by D. S. Bell & Eric Shaw. 192p. 1983. pap. 57.50 (0-85124-349-5, Pub. by Spokesman) Coronet Bks.

Left in History. Willie Thompson. 288p. (C). 1997. pap. 24.95 (0-7453-0891-0, Pub. by Pluto GBR); text 59.95 (0-7453-0892-9, Pub. by Pluto GBR) Stylus Pub VA.

Left in Search of a Center. Ed. by Michael Crozier & Peter Murphy. LC 95-16648. 224p. 1996. text 39.95 (0-252-02199-1); pap. text 16.95 (0-252-06497-6) U of Ill Pr.

***Left in the Care of: A Novel of Suspense.** Dinah L. Kung. 270p. 1999. 29.95 (0-7351-0224-4) Replica Bks.

Left in Trust. Kay Thorpe. (Presents Ser.). 1993. per. 2.99 (0-373-11571-7, 1-11571-6) Harlequin Bks.

Left Intellectuals & Popular Culture in Twentieth-Century America. Paul R. Gorman. LC 95-14387. (Illus.). 256p. (C). 1996. pap. 18.95 (0-8078-4556-6); lib. bdg. 49.95 (0-8078-2248-5) U of NC Pr.

Left Is Right: The Survival Guide for Living Lefty in a Right-Handed World. Rae Lindsay. LC 96-94650. (Illus.). 96p. (Orig.). 1996. pap. 9.95 (0-9653753-0-7, Gilmour Hse) R&R Writers.

Left Leg. Theodore F. Powys. LC 72-140337. (Short Story Index Reprint Ser.). 1977. 18.95 (0-8369-3729-5) Ayer.

Left Leg. Phoebe Atwood Taylor. (Leonidas Witherall Mystery Ser.). 275p. 1988. reprint ed. pap. 5.95 (0-88150-121-2, Foul Play) Norton.

Left Letters: The Culture Wars of Mike Gold & Joseph Freeman. James D. Bloom. 160p. 1992. text 44.00 (0-231-07690-8) Col U Pr.

***Left-Libertarianism & Its Critics: The Contemporary Debate.** Peter Vallentyne & Hillel Steiner. LC 00-34788. 2000. write for info. (0-312-23699-9) St Martin.

Left Margins: Cultural Studies & Composition Pedagogy. Ed. by Karen Fitts & Alan W. France. LC 94-32677. 369p. (C). 1995. text 59.50 (0-7914-2537-1); pap. text 23.95 (0-7914-2538-X) State U NY Pr.

***Left of the Middle.** 64p. 1998. per. 16.95 (0-7935-9596-7) H Leonard.

***Left on Center.** rev. ed. Mark Marks. LC 99-93229. 56p. 1999. 15.00 (1-57579-158-7) Pine Hill Pr.

Left on the Field to Die Pt. 1: Timothy Richardson. Ira Rosenstein. LC 84-242659. 27p. (Orig.). 1980. pap. 3.00 (0-9605438-0-5) Starlight Pr.

Left on the Field to Die Pt. 2: Yehudi Weismann. Ira Rosenstein. LC 84-242659. 42p. (Orig.). 1982. pap. 4.00 (0-9605438-1-3) Starlight Pr.

Left on the Field to Die Pt. 3: Peter Koslov. Ira Rosenstein. LC 84-242659. 30p. (Orig.). 1984. pap. 3.00 (0-9605438-2-1) Starlight Pr.

Left Opposition in the U. S. Writings & Speeches, 1928 to 1931. James P. Cannon. Ed. by Frederick Stanton. LC 81-83236. 446p. (C). 1981. pap. 22.95 (0-913460-87-7); lib. bdg. 60.00 (0-913460-86-9) Pathfinder NY.

Left or Right? Karl M. Rehm. (J). 1991. 10.15 (0-606-07778-2) Turtleback.

***Left Out.** (Angelwings 0). (gr. 4-6). 2000. per. 3.99 (0-689-83971-5) Aladdin.

Left Out: A Political Journey. Martin Duberman. 16.00 (0-465-01745-2) Basic.

***Left Out: A Political Journey.** Martin Duberman. 466p. 1999. 30.00 (0-465-01744-4, Pub. by Basic) HarpC.

Left Out: By Rosie. unabridged ed. Maureen Holohan. LC 98-128326. (Broadway Ballplayers Ser.: Bk. 2). (J). (gr. 4-8). 1998. pap. 6.95 (0-9659091-1-5) Broadway Ballplayers.

Left Out: Pragmatism, Exceptionalism, & the Poverty of American Marxism, 1890-1922. Brian Lloyd. LC 96-47995. (New Studies in American Intellectual & Cultural History). 456p. 1997. text 45.00 (0-8018-5541-1) Johns Hopkins.

Left-Out Elizabeth. Created by Francine Pascal. (Sweet Valley Kids Ser.: No. 25). 80p. (J). (gr. 1-3). 1991. pap. 2.99 (0-553-15921-6) Bantam.

Left-Out Elizabeth. Molly Mia Stewart. (Sweet Valley Kids Ser.: No. 25). (J). (gr. 1-3). 1991. 8.19 (0-606-00554-4, Pub. by Turtleback) Demco.

Left Out in the Rain. Gary Snyder. LC 86-60994. 210p. (J). 1986. pap. 12.00 (0-86547-268-8) N Point Pr.

Left-Over Louie. Carol Olsen. (Illus.). 169p. (Orig.). (J). 1993. 29.95 (1-883078-75-X) Gig Harbor Pr.

Left-Over Louie. 2nd ed. Carol Olsen. (Illus.). 168p. (Orig.). (J). (gr. 2 up). 1993. pap. 11.95 (1-883078-76-8) Gig Harbor Pr.

***Left Overs.** Rose Stauffer. 28p. 1999. pap. 3.95 (1-930354-03-7) Bean Burner.

Left Parties & Social Policy in Post-Communist Europe. Ed. by Marilyn Rueschemeyer et al. (Eastern Europe after Communism Ser.). 280p. 1999. pap. 25.00 (0-8133-3569-8, Pub. by Westview); text 69.00 (0-8133-3568-X, Pub. by Westview) HarpC.

Left Politics & the Literary Profession. Ed. by Lennard J. Davis & M. Bella Mirabella. (Social Foundations of Aesthetic Forms Ser.). 320p. 1990. text 57.50 (0-231-06566-3) Col U Pr.

Left Review, 1934-1938, 8 vols., Set. Ed. by M. Slater. 1968. 350.00 (0-7146-2111-0, Pub. by F Cass Pubs) Intl Spec Bk.

Left, Right, & Babyboom: America's New Politics. Ed. by David Boaz. 119p. 1986. pap. 2.00 (0-932790-57-7) Cato Inst.

Left, Right, & Center. Atwan. 620p. 1996. pap. text 38.95 (0-312-10200-3) St Martin.

Left, Right, & Center. White. 1996. pap. text, teacher ed. 5.00 (0-312-14228-5) St Martin.

Left, Right & Center: Essays on Liberalism & Conservatism in the United States. Frank S. Meyer et al. Ed. by Robert A. Goldwin. LC 70-156679. (Essay Index Reprint Ser.). 1977. reprint ed. 20.95 (0-8369-2777-X) Ayer.

Left Right Center. 2nd ed. Atwan. 1995. pap. text. write for info. (0-312-17152-8) St Martin.

Left Side of Paradise: The Screenwriting of John Howard Lawson. Gary Carr. Ed. by Diane Kirkpatrick. LC 84-2551. (Studies in Cinema: No. 26). 137p. reprint ed. 42.50 (0-8357-1570-1, 207047000095) Bks Demand.

Left Side, Right Side. Alan Beaton. LC 85-52037. 370p. 1986. 47.50 (0-300-03549-7) Yale U Pr.

Left Strikes Back: Class Conflict in Latin America in the Age of Neoliberalism. James Petras. LC 98-20772. (Latin American Perspectives Ser.: No. 19). 232p. 1998. text 69.00 (0-8133-3554-X, Pub. by Westview) HarpC.

***Left to Die.** Frank Roderus. 2000. mass mkt. 5.99 (0-425-17637-1) Berkley Pub.

Left to Die: The Story of the U. S. S. Juneau. Dan Kurzman. (Illus.). 352p. (J). 1995. mass mkt. 6.99 (0-671-74874-2) PB.

Left to Go to Hell! But Bouncing Back. Larry Hunter. 90p. 1996. pap. write for info. (1-57502-153-6, P00745) Morris Pubng.

Left Unraveled: Social Democracy & the New Left Challenge in Britain & West Germany. Thomas A. Koelble. LC 90-45573. 176p. 1991. text 42.95 (0-8223-1108-9) Duke.

Left Ventricular Dysfunction. Ed. by J. J. Kellermann & David H. Spodick. (Advances in Cardiology Ser.: Vol. 34). (Illus.). viii, 212p. 1986. 152.25 (3-8055-4349-2) S Karger.

Left Ventricular Hypertrophy. Sheridan. (C). 1999. text 89.00 (0-443-06361-3) Harcrt Hlth Sci Grp.

***Left Ventricular Hypertrophy - Physiology Versus Pathology.** Ernst E. Van der Wall et al. 192p. 1999. 75.00 (0-7923-6038-9) Kluwer Academic.

Left-Wing Communism, an Infantile Disorder. Vladimir Il'ich Lenin. 95p. 1988. reprint ed. pap. 2.50 (0-7178-0107-1) Intl Pubs Co.

Left Wing Conspiracy Theories. 1996. lib. bdg. 251.95 (0-8490-6932-7) Gordon Pr.

Left-Wing Democracy in the English Civil War. David W. Petegorsky. LC 72-2021. (British History Ser.: No. 30). 1972. reprint ed. lib. bdg. 75.00 (0-8383-1472-4) M S G Haskell Hse.

Left-Wing Democracy in the English Civil War: Gerrard Winstanley & the Digger Movement. David W. Petegorsky. 352p. 1996. pap. 26.95 (0-7509-1053-4, Pub. by Sutton Pub Ltd) Intl Pubs Mktg.

Left-Wing Dramatic Theory in the American Theatre. Ira A. Levine. LC 84-28018. (Theater & Dramatic Studies: No. 24). (Illus.). 249p. reprint ed. pap. 77.20 (0-8357-1599-X, 207055700001) Bks Demand.

Left-Wing Nietzscheans: The Politics of German Expressionism, 1919-1920. Seth Taylor. (Monographien und Texte zur Nietzscge-Forschung Ser.: Vol. 22). x, 254p. (C). 1990. lib. bdg. 83.10 (3-11-012457-2) De Gruyter.

Left Wings over Europe. Wyndham Lewis. LC 72-82186. 1972. reprint ed. lib. bdg. 250.00 (0-87968-004-0) Gordon Pr.

***Lefties: A Book for Southpaws, Mini Edition.** Andrews & McMeel Publishing Staff. (Illus.). 2000. 4.95 (0-7407-0512-1) Andrews & McMeel.

Leftism Revisited: From de Sade & Marx to Hitler & Pol Pot. Erik Von Kuehnelt-Leddihn. LC 90-8821. 544p. 1990. 29.95 (0-89526-537-0) Regnery Pub.

Leftisms. Anne Martens. 1994. 15.00 (0-614-18205-0) Visual Studies.

Leftist Politics in India: M. N. Roy & the Radical Democratic Party. Dipti K. Roy. (C). 1989. 25.50 (81-85195-18-8, Pub. by Minerva) S Asia.

Leftist Theories of Sport: A Critique & Reconstruction. William J. Morgan. LC 93-24135. (Sport & Society Ser.). 288p. 1994. text 49.50 (0-252-02068-5); pap. text 17.95 (0-252-06361-9) U of Ill Pr.

Lefton China. Ruth McCarthy. LC 97-80252. (Illus.). 180p. 1998. pap. 29.95 (0-7643-0415-1) Schiffer.

Lefton China Price Guide. Loretta DeLozier. LC 99-208408. 96p. 1999. 9.95 (1-57432-113-7) Collector Bks.

Lefton Learning Community: An Interactive Site for Users. Lester A. Lefton. (C). 1996. write for info. (0-205-26859-5, T6859-7) Allyn.

***Leftover Dreams.** Charlotte Vale Allen. 592p. 1999. reprint ed. pap. 23.00 (1-892738-29-5) Isld Nation.

Leftover Kid. Joanne Stanbridge. LC 96-910776. (Northern Lights Young Novels Ser.). 160p. (J). (gr. 4-9). 1997. pap. 7.95 (0-88995-160-8, Pub. by Red Deer) Genl Dist Srvs.

Leftover Lefse. Art Lee. (Illus.). 224p. (Orig.). 1987. pap. 7.95 (0-934860-48-3) Adventure Pubns.

Leftover Lily. Sally Warner. (Illus.). 128p. (gr. k-3). 2000. pap. 3.99 (0-375-80347-5) Knopf.

***Leftover Lily.** Sally Warner. LC 98-11669. (Illus.). 80p. (J). (gr. k-3). 1999. 15.00 (0-679-89139-0, Pub. by Knopf Bks Yng Read); lib. bdg. 16.99 (0-679-99139-5, Pub. by Knopf Bks Yng Read) Random.

***Leftover Lily.** Sally Warner. (Illus.). (J). 2000. 9.34 (0-606-18238-1) Turtleback.

Leftover Love. Janet Dailey. 1993. per. 6.99 (0-671-87507-8, PB Trade Paper) PB.

Leftover Lutefisk. Art Lee. 224p. 1984. pap. 7.95 (0-934860-32-7) Adventure Pubns.

Leftover Magic. Wendy Rotton et al. 96p. (Orig.). 1994. pap. 15.95 (1-56721-084-8) Twnty-Fifth Cent Pr.

Leftovers. Kathy Gunst. LC 88-4258. 1990. 21.45 (0-13-528134-2) P-H.

Leftovers. Toni L. Lozowick. LC 98-89521. 375p. 1998. text 25.00 (0-7388-0207-7); pap. text 15.00 (0-7388-0208-5) Xlibris Corp.

Leftovers Catch Flies! Tristan Howard. 1996. 8.70 (0-606-09534-9, Pub. by Turtleback) Demco.

Leftovers Use Their Heads. Tristan Howard. 1996. 8.19 (0-606-09535-7, Pub. by Turtleback) Demco.

Left's Dirty Job: The Politics of Industrial Restructuring in France & Spain. W. Rand Smith. LC 97-45319. (Pitt Series in Policy & Institutional Studies). 363p. 1998. pap. 22.95 (0-8229-5658-6); text 50.00 (0-8229-4053-1) U of Pittsburgh Pr.

Left's Dirty Job: The Politics of Industrial Restructuring in France & Spain. W. Rand Smith. (Studies in Comparative Political Economy & Public Policy Ser.). (Illus.). 416p. 1998. pap. text 29.95 (0-8020-8231-9) U of Toronto Pr.

Leftward Ho! V. F. Calverton & American Radicalism, 315. Philip Abbott. LC 92-21363. (Contributions in Political Science Ser.: No. 315). 248p. 1993. 62.95 (0-313-28568-3, ALH, Greenwood Pr) Greenwood.

Leftward Journey: The Education of Vietnamese Students in France, 1919-1939. Scott McConnell. 220p. 1988. 44.95 (0-88738-238-X) Transaction Pubs.

Lefty. John Benton. 192p. (Orig.). (J). (gr. 7-12). 1981. pap. 3.50 (0-8007-8401-4) J Benton Bks.

Lefty: A Handbook for Left-Handed Kids, 7 vols. Planet Dexter Editors. (J). 1997. pap. 54.75 (0-201-30439-2) Addison-Wesley.

Lefty: On Handbook for Left-Handed Kids. Beth W. Singer. LC 97-199930. (Illus.). 64p. (J). (gr. 3). 1997. spiral bd. 10.95 (0-201-15143-X) Addison-Wesley.

***Lefty Carmichael Has a Fit.** Don Trembath. LC 99-65155. 215p. (YA). (gr. 8-12). 2000. pap. 6.95 (1-55143-166-1) Orca Bk Pubs.

***Lefty Carmichael Has a Fit.** Don Trembath. (Illus.). (J). 2000. 13.30 (0-606-18328-0) Turtleback.

***Lefty Grove: American Original.** Jim Kaplan. (Illus.). 225p. 2000. pap. 12.95 (0-910137-80-3) U of Nebr Pr.

Lefty Meets Hefty. Ronald Reepen. (Illus.). 40p. (J). (gr. 2-7). 1987. 6.95 (0-930905-02-4) Platypus Bks.

Lefty O'Doul - The Legend That Baseball Nearly Forgot: The Story of the Hall of Fame's Missing Star. Richard Leutzinger. (Illus.). 170p. (Orig.). 1997. pap. 19.95 (1-883532-03-5) Carmel Bay.

Lefty's 101 Fly Fishing Tips. Lefty Kreh. (Illus.). 96p. 1999. pap. 12.00 (1-893342-01-8) K&D Ltd.

Leg. John M. Bennett. 5p. (Orig.). 1992. pap. 2.00 (0-935350-76-4) Luna Bisonte.

Leg Ours - The Bears: Gardiens du People D'Arbonie - Guardiens of the People of Arbonia. Caroline Lamarche & Jephan De. (FRE.). 64p. 1976. 40.00 (0-9672487-0-1) R Koener Art Gall.

Leg to Stand On. Oliver W. Sacks. LC 98-13410. 224p. 1998. pap. 13.00 (0-684-85395-7, Touchstone) S&S Trade Pap.

Leg Ulcers. Christine J. Moffatt & Peter Harper. LC 97-22896. (Access to Clinical Education Ser.). 1997. pap. text 42.00 (0-443-05533-5) Church.

Leg Ulcers: Diagnosis & Treatment. Ed. by Wiete Westerhof. LC 93-28116. 422p. 1993. 361.25 (0-444-81427-2) Elsevier.

Lega: The Making of a Successful Cooperative Network. Piero Ammirato. 376p. 1996. text 82.95 (1-85521-839-9, Pub. by Dartmth Pub) Ashgate Pub Co.

Legacies. Grant Antrews. 1997. mass mkt. 7.95 (1-56333-587-5, Rhinoceros) Masquerade.

Legacies. Suzanne E. Berger. LC 84-70353. 72p. 1984. 6.95 (0-914086-48-0); pap. 3.95 (0-914086-49-9) Alice James Bks.

Legacies. Janet Dailey. 1995. 22.95 (0-614-15482-0) Little.

Legacies. Janet Dailey. 400p. 1996. mass mkt. 6.99 (0-446-60348-1, Pub. by Warner Bks) Little.

Legacies. Alexander Darke. 1997. pap. 3.50 (0-87129-714-0, L86) Dramatic Pub.

***Legacies, 4 vols.** Anita Ganeri. (Illus.). 32p. (J). 1999. lib. bdg. 63.80 (1-929298-53-6, Pub. by Thameside Pr) Smart Apple.

Legacies. Starling Lawrence. 243p. 1996. text 20.00 (0-374-18474-7) FS&G.

Legacies. Alison Sinclair. 448p. 1996. mass mkt. 5.50 (0-06-105699-5, HarperPrism) HarpC.

Legacies. F. Paul Wilson. LC 98-14322. 352p. 1998. text 24.95 (0-312-86414-0) St Martin.

***Legacies.** F. Paul Wilson. 2000. mass mkt. 6.99 (0-8125-7199-1, Pub. by Tor Bks) St Martin.

Legacies. large type ed. Janet Dailey. (Wheeler Large Print Bks.). 1996. 26.95 (1-56895-295-3) Wheeler Pub.

***Legacies** 2nd ed. Bogarad. (C). 2001. pap. text. write for info. (0-15-506953-5) Harcourt.

Legacies: A Chinese Mosaic. Bette Bao Lord. 256p. 1991. pap. 10.00 (0-449-90620-5) Fawcett.

Legacies: A Chinese Mosaic. large type ed. Bette Bao Lord. (General Ser.). 375p. 1991. lib. bdg. 20.95 (0-8161-5065-6, G K Hall Lrg Type) Mac Lib Ref.

Legacies: A Chinese Mosaic. Bette Bao Lord. 245p. 1997. reprint ed. text 20.00 (0-7881-5039-1) DIANE Pub.

Legacies: A History of Women & the Family in America, 1607-1870. Adams et al. 1987. 65.00 (0-938545-04-3) Jennings & Keefe.

Legacies: Children Celebrate Their Grandmothers. Sally Koppinger & Libbey Koppinger. LC 97-41157. (Illus.). 108p. (Orig.). 1998. pap. 6.00 (1-57601-058-9) Martz.

Legacies: Fiction, Poetry, Drama. Bogarad. (C). 1994. pap. text 49.00 (0-15-500213-9, Pub. by Harcourt Coll Pubs) Harcourt.

Legacies: Fiction, Poetry, Drama. Bogarad. (C). 1994. pap. text, teacher ed. 4.00 (0-15-500215-5) Harcourt Coll Pubs.

Legacies: Kansas' Older County Courthouses. 2nd ed. Julie A. Wortman & David P. Johnson. LC 81-84055. (Illus.). 64p. 1982. pap. 3.00 (0-87726-025-7) Kansas St Hist.

Legacies: Stories. Starling Lawrence. 256p. 1998. pap. 13.00 (0-393-31869-9, Norton Paperbks) Norton.

Legacies: Stories. Nancy Potter. LC 86-30851. (Illinois Short Fiction Ser.). 144p. 1987. 14.95 (0-252-01428-6) U of Ill Pr.

Legacies: Using Children's Literature in the Classroom. Anita M. Meinbach & Liz C. Rothlein. LC 94-34987. (C). 1995. pap. text, teacher ed. 18.00 (0-673-55344-2) Addson-Wesley Educ.

Legacies & Ambiguities: Postwar Fiction & Culture in West Germany & Japan. Ed. by Ernestine Schlant & J. Thomas Rimer. 323p. 1991. text 35.00 (0-943875-30-7); pap. text 13.95 (0-943875-32-3) Johns Hopkins.

Legacies & Lies Bk. 2. Nancy Holder. 292p. 1999. mass mkt. 5.99 (0-380-79313-X, Eos) Morrow Avon.

Legacies Book: A Companion Volume to the Audiocourse. Elizabeth H. Pleck et al. 288p. (Orig.). 1987. pap. 25.00 (0-89776-206-1) Jennings & Keefe.

***Legacies for Libraries: A Practical Guide to Planned Giving.** Amy Sherman Smith & Matthew D. Lehrer. LC 00-25923. 2000. write for info. (0-8389-0784-9) ALA.

Legacies for the Future: Contemporary Architecture in Islamic Societies. Ed. by Cynthia Davidson. LC 98-61186. (Illus.). 176p. 1999. pap. 27.50 (0-500-28087-8, Pub. by Thames Hudson) Norton.

Legacies from Ancient China. Anita Ganeri. LC 99-21086. (J). 1999. write for info. (0-382-42228-7, Dillon Silver Burdett) Silver Burdett Pr.

***Legacies from Ancient China.** Anita Ganeri. (Legacies Ser.). (Illus.). 32p. (J). 1999. lib. bdg. 15.95 (1-929298-51-X, Pub. by Thameside Pr) Smart Apple.

***Legacies from Ancient Egypt.** Anita Ganeri. (Legacies Ser.). (Illus.). 32p. (J). 1999. lib. bdg. 15.95 (1-929298-52-8, Pub. by Thameside Pr) Smart Apple.

Legacies from Ancient Greece. Anita Ganeri. LC 99-19770. (J). 1999. write for info. (0-382-42229-5, Dillon Silver Burdett) Silver Burdett Pr.

***Legacies from Ancient Greece.** Anita Ganeri. (Legacies Ser.). (Illus.). 32p. (J). 1999. lib. bdg. 15.95 (1-929298-49-8, Pub. by Thameside Pr) Smart Apple.

***Legacies from Ancient Rome.** Anita Ganeri. (Legacies Ser.). (Illus.). 32p. (J). 1999. lib. bdg. 15.95 (1-929298-50-1, Pub. by Thameside Pr) Smart Apple.

Legacies of a French Empire in North America. Veronique Deplanne. LC 98-44502. 1998. write for info. (1-57864-075-X) Donning Co.

Legacies of Anti-Semitism in France. Jeffrey Mehlman. LC 83-3685. 155p. reprint ed. pap. 48.10 (0-7837-2934-0, 205752000006) Bks Demand.

An Asterisk (*) at the beginning of an entry indicates that the title is appearing for the first time.

Legacies of Change: Transformations of Postcommunist European Economies. Ed. by John L. Campbell & Ove K. Pedersen. (Sociology & Economics Ser.). 270p. 1996. pap. text 26.95 (*0-202-30559-7*); lib. bdg. 52.95 (*0-202-30558-9*) Aldine de Gruyter.

Legacies of Childhood: Growing up Chinese in a Time of Crisis, 1890-1920. Jon L. Saari. (East Asian Monographs). 390p. 1990. 32.50 (*0-674-52160-9*) HUP.

Legacies of Communism in Eastern Europe. Ed. by Zoltan Barany & Ivan Volgyes. LC 94-43245. 272p. 1995. text 48.00 (*0-8018-4997-7*); pap. text 15.95 (*0-8018-4998-5*) Johns Hopkins.

Legacies of Fear: Law & Politics in Quebec in the Era of the French Revolution. F. Murray Greenwood. (Illus.). 440p. 1993. pap. text 20.00 (*0-8020-6974-6*) U of Toronto Pr.

Legacies of Fear: The Impact of the French Revolution on the Politics of Law in Quebec - Lower Canada, 1789-1811. F. Murray Greenwood. (Illus.). 440p. 1993. text 40.00 (*0-8020-0534-9*) U of Toronto Pr.

Legacies of Greatness: An Exposition on the Eight Most Influential & Significant Black Male Leaders of 20th Century. Areeb Malik Shabazz. (Illus.). 76p. 1999. reprint ed. pap. 8.00 (*1-56411-215-2*, Kitabu Pub) Untd Bros & Sis.

Legacies of Literacy: Continuities & Contradictions in Western Culture & Society. Harvey J. Graff. LC 85-46029. (Interdisciplinary Studies in History). (Illus.). 506p. (Orig.). 1991. pap. 15.95 (*0-253-20598-0*, MB-598) Ind U Pr.

***Legacies of Love.** Jayne Ann Krentz. 1999. per. 9.99 (*0-373-83430-6*) Harlequin Bks.

Legacies of Maoist Economic Development in Sichuan. Chris Bramall. LC 92-44066. 408p. 1993. 69.00 (*0-19-828790-9*, Clarendon Pr) OUP.

Legacies of Mary Ellen Pleasant: Mother of Civil Rights in California. unabridged ed. Susheel Bibbs. (Illus.). 28p. (YA). (gr. 9 up). 1998. mass mkt. 9.95 (*1-892516-01-2*) MEP Publications.

Legacies of Perfume No. 7: Monsen & Baer Perfume Bottle Auction. Randall B. Monsen et al. (Illus.). 128p. 1997. 45.00 (*0-9636102-5-2*) Monsen & Baer.

Legacies of the American Revolution. Ed. by Larry R. Gerlach et al. LC 78-5888. (Illus.). 254p. reprint ed. pap. 78.80 (*0-8357-6187-8*, 203460400090) Bks Demand.

Legacies of the Collapse of Marxism. Ed. by John H. Moore. 276p. (C). 1994. 62.50 (*0-913969-71-0*); pap. 26.50 (*0-913969-72-9*) Univ Pub Assocs.

Legacies of the Comfort Women of World War II. Ed. by Margaret D. Stetz & Bonnie B. Oh. 232p. 2000. 55.00 (*0-7656-0543-0*, East Gate Bk) M E Sharpe.

***Legacies of the 1964 Civil Rights Act.** Ed. by Bernard Grofman. 320p. 2000. 55.00 (*0-8139-1920-7*); pap. 16.50 (*0-8139-1921-5*) U Pr of Va.

Legacies of the St. Louis World's Fair. Bert Minkin. (Illus.). 100p. 1998. pap. 9.95 (*1-891442-05-8*) VA Pub Corp.

Legacies of the Sword: The Kashima-Shinryu & Samurai Martial Culture. Karl F. Friday & Seki Humitake. LC 96-33624. (Illus.). 1997. text 34.00 (*0-8248-1847-4*); pap. text 14.95 (*0-8248-1879-2*) UH Pr.

Legacies of Woodrow Wilson. Ed. by James M. Morris. LC 94-47449. 1995. pap. write for info. (*0-943875-70-6*) W Wilson Ctr Pr.

***Legacy.** Rick Albrecht & Wendy Albrecht. Ed. by Pete Boethcher et al. 320p. 2000. pap. 19.95 (*0-9700389-0-9*) Visions of Help.

Legacy. Evelyn Anthony. LC 98-17591. 361 p. 1998. write for info. (*0-7540-2118-1*) Chivers N Amer.

Legacy. Jeanette Baker. 1996. mass mkt. 5.99 (*0-671-53674-5*) PB.

Legacy. Greg Bear & Olmy A. Sennon. 1996. pap. 6.99 (*0-614-98100-X*) Tor Bks.

***Legacy.** Josep M. Beneti Jornet. Ed. by Phyllis Zatlin. Tr. by Janet De Cesaris from CAT. LC 99-71172. (Contemporary Spanish Plays Ser.: Vol. 17). (Illus.). xiv, 50p. 2000. pap. 8.00 (*1-888463-09-0*) Estreno.

Legacy. Leigh Bristol. 352p. 1993. mass mkt. 4.99 (*0-446-35081-8*) Warner Bks.

Legacy. Marian Coe. LC 92-64095. (Illus.). 373p. 1993. pap. 14.95 (*0-9633341-0-7*) SouthLore Pr.

This award winning suspense/mystery (second printing June 94) has won favorable reviews for both its story suspense, sense of place & blend of wisdom & passion. Winner of the FALLOT LITERARY AWARD FOR FICTION given by the National Assoc. Independent Publishers also cited as 1st in Florida, 3rd in nation 1993 NFPW awards (National Federation of Press Women). "In this intriguing novel set during the closing months of World War II, a young woman, surrounded by mystery, is determined to learn the truth about herself & her family...(Florida's Gulf waterfront) sets the stage for intrigue as the mystery unfolds..."--PUBLISHER'S WEEKLY. "Remarkable insights & imagery evoking the time...excitement...& a healthy romance."--THE TAMPA TRIBUNE. "Lelia's discovery deliciously involves the reader. A lush & seductive mystery..."--BOOK READER REVIEWS. "LEGACY paints vivid pictures of a Florida that once was..."--Patrick Smith, author, A LAND REMEMBERED. "Traditional elements of a good mystery taken to a deeper level. A satisfying read," NEW AGE RETAILER. "Suspenseful metaphysical mystery, "LEADING EDGE REVIEW. SouthLore Press, 730 Grouse Moor Drive, Banner Elk, NC 28604, www.mariancoe.com. Order: Ingram, Baker & Taylor, Enfield Distrib. Phone 603-632-7377, Fax: 603-632-5611. *Publisher Paid Annotation.*

Legacy. Howard Fast. 2001. pap. 12.00 (*0-15-600508-5*) Harcourt.

Legacy. Michael J. Friedman. Ed. by Dave Stern. (Star Trek Ser.: No. 56). 256p. (Orig.). 1991. mass mkt. 4.95 (*0-671-74468-2*) PB.

Legacy. Shirley Hailstock. 304p. 1997. mass mkt. 4.99 (*0-7860-0415-0*, Pinncle Kensgtn) Kensgtn Pub Corp.

Legacy. Susan Kay. 656p. 1987. mass mkt. 4.50 (*0-380-70322-X*, Avon Bks) Morrow Avon.

Legacy. Jayne Ann Krentz. (Mira Bks.). 1996. per. 5.99 (*1-55166-148-9*, 1-66148-7, Mira Bks) Harlequin Bks.

Legacy. Al Lacy. LC 98-39759. 1998. 22.95 (*0-7862-1651-4*) Thorndike Pr.

Legacy. Steve Lawson. LC 97-36396. (What Every Father Wants to Leave His Child Ser.). 216p. 1998. 12.99 (*1-57673-329-7*) Multnomah Pubs.

Legacy. James A. Michener. 288p. 1988. mass mkt. 6.99 (*0-449-21641-1*, Crest) Fawcett.

Legacy. Linda Lael Miller. Ed. by Linda Marrow. 336p. 1994. mass mkt. 6.99 (*0-671-79792-1*, Pocket Star Bks) PB.

Legacy. Mel Odom. (Journey of Allen Strange Ser.: No. 4). (J). (gr. 3-6). 1999. pap. 3.99 (*0-671-02512-0*) PB.

Legacy. Wendy Pini. (Elfquest Reader's Collection: Vol. 11). (Illus.). 1998. pap. text 11.95 (*0-936861-45-2*, Pub. by Warp Graphics) Midpt Trade.

***Legacy.** Elinor Stuyvesant. 1999. pap. write for info. (*1-58235-286-0*) Watermrk Pr.

Legacy. Steve White. 320p. (Orig.). 1995. mass mkt. 5.99 (*0-671-87643-0*) Baen Bks.

Legacy. Robert J. Yborra. 1998. pap. write for info. (*1-57553-971-3*) Watermrk Pr.

Legacy. large type ed. Leigh Bristol. LC 93-22679. 413p. 1993. lib. bdg. 21.95 (*0-8161-5828-2*, G K Hall Lrg Type) Mac Lib Ref.

Legacy. large type ed. Jan Butlin. 1994. 27.99 (*0-7089-3144-8*) Ulverscroft.

Legacy. large type ed. Stephen W. Frey. LC 98-35882. 1998. 24.95 (*1-56895-664-9*) Wheeler Pub.

Legacy. large type ed. Linda Lael Miller. LC 94-29353. 488p. 1995. 20.95 (*0-7862-0326-9*) Thorndike Pr.

Legacy. large type ed. Claire Rayner. (Charnwood Large Print Ser.). 608p. 1998. 29.99 (*0-7089-9006-1*, Charnwood) Ulverscroft.

***Legacy.** Sybille Bedford. LC 75-34600. (Neglected Books of the 20th Century Ser.). 380p. 1999. reprint ed. pap. 8.50 (*0-912946-26-1*, Ecco Press) HarperTrade.

Legacy. Marian Coe. LC 92-64095. (Illus.). 373p. 1993. reprint ed. 19.95 (*0-9633341-1-5*) SouthLore Pr.

Legacy. Stephen Frey. 373p. 1999. reprint ed. mass mkt. 6.99 (*0-451-19015-7*, Onyx) NAL.

Legacy. Peter L. Macnair et al. (Illus.). 194p. 1984. reprint ed. pap. 29.95 (*0-295-96166-X*) U of Wash Pr.

Legacy. R. A. Salvatore. (Forgotten Realms Ser.). 368p. 1993. reprint ed. pap. 6.99 (*1-56076-640-9*, Pub. by TSR Inc) Random.

Legacy, Vol. 1. Greg Bear. 1996. mass mkt. 6.99 (*0-8125-2481-0*, Pub. by Tor Bks) St Martin.

Legacy, Vol. 1. Al Lacy. (Journeys of the Stranger Ser.: Bk. 1). 320p. 1994. pap. 10.99 (*0-88070-619-8*, Multnomah Bks) Multnomah Pubs.

Legacy: A Biography of Moses & Walter Annenberg. Christopher Ogden. LC 98-51441. 624p. (YA). (gr. 8). 1999. 29.95 (*0-316-63379-8*) Little.

***Legacy: A Conversation with Dad.** Ross Gray & Claire Gray. LC 99-68202. 154p. 2000. pap. 18.95 (*0-9671794-2-4*) Mens Studies.

Legacy: A History of the Tuskegee University School of Veterinary Medicine. Eugene W. Adams. LC 94-74577. (Illus.). 312p. 1995. 32.50 (*0-9645067-1-8*) Media Ctr.

Legacy: A Portrait of the Young Men & Women of Kamehameha Schools 1887-1987. Sharlene Chun-Lum & Lesley Agard. (Illus.). 150p. 1987. 24.95 (*0-87336-009-5*) Kamehameha Schools.

Legacy: A Step-by-Step Guide to Writing Personal History. Linda Spence. LC 97-23680. (Illus.). 182p. 1997. 24.95 (*0-8040-1002-1*); pap. 14.95 (*0-8040-1003-X*) Swallow.

Legacy: A Story of Your Family History to Pass down from Generation to Generation & Keep the History Alive. Cheryl Pryor. (Illus.). 200p. (Orig.). 1995. pap. 18.00 (*1-886541-09-4*) Higher Priority.

***Legacy: Bill Evans Reaching Out from the Regional Southwest.** Jennifer Noyer. (Choreography & Dance Archives Ser.: Vol. 2). (Illus.). 112p. 1999. pap. text 49.00 incl. VHS (*90-5755-115-2*, Harwood Acad Pubs); pap. text 49.00 incl. VHS (*90-5755-118-7*, Harwood Acad Pubs) Gordon & Breach.

Legacy: Challenging Lessons in Civics & Citizenship. Legacy Classroom Teachers Staff et al. LC 95-69628. 258p. (Orig.). 1995. pap. 18.00 (*1-879953-07-2*) CRD Law-Related.

Legacy: Engineering at Kansas State University. Cheryl May. (Illus.). 105p. (Orig.). 1983. pap. text 5.00 (*0-9609342-0-0*) College Engineering KS.

Legacy: Frank Frazetta. Arnie Fenner. 1999. 35.00 (*1-887424-49-0*) Underwood Bks.

Legacy: Frank Frazetta. deluxe ed. Arnie Fenner. 1999. 150.00 (*1-887424-48-2*) Underwood Bks.

Legacy: Gifts from a Grandmother. Elizabeth Koppinger. LC 95-18683. 96p. (Orig.). 1995. pap. 6.00 (*0-918949-68-8*) Martz.

Legacy: Making Wishes Come True. Lurlene McDaniel. (One Last Wish Ser.: No. 7). 224p. (YA). 1993. mass mkt. 4.50 (*0-553-56134-0*) Bantam.

Legacy: Making Wishes Come True. Lurlene McDaniel. (One Last Wish Ser.). (J). 1993. 9.60 (*0-606-05422-7*, Pub. by Turtleback) Demco.

Legacy: New Perspectives on the Battle of the Little Bighorn. Ed. by Charles E. Rankin. LC 96-24512. (Illus.). 132p. 1996. 20.00 (*0-917298-41-7*); pap. 19.95 (*0-917298-42-X*) MT Hist Soc.

Legacy: Poems from Hollywood. Mark Dunster. 11p. 1998. pap. 5.00 (*0-89642-554-1*) Linden Pubs.

***Legacy: Portrait of an Ancestor.** unabridged ed. Edward Bruce Bynum et al. Ed. by Kitty Axelson-Berry. (Illus.). 74p. 1999. write for info. (*0-9662602-2-8*) Modern Memoirs.

Legacy: Southwest Indian Art at the School of American Research. Duane Anderson. LC 98-36554. 224p. 1998. pap. 49.95 (*0-933452-57-8*) Schol Am Res.

Legacy: Southwest Indian Art at the School of American Research. Duane Anderson. LC 98-36554. 3p. 1998. 100.00 (*0-933452-54-3*) Schol Am Res.

Legacy: The Giving of Life's Greatest Treasures. Barrie Greiff. 256p. 1999. 22.00 (*0-06-039283-5*, ReganBks) HarperTrade.

Legacy: The Myers Park Story. Mary N. Kratt & Tom Hanchett. Ed. by Pat Heol. (Illus.). 200p. 1986. 25.00 (*0-318-22192-6*) Myers Park Found.

Legacy: The Poetic Works of Robert C. Hillyard. Robert C. Hillyard. 188p. 1998. pap. 10.00 (*1-57502-856-5*, PO2584) Morris Pubng.

Legacy: The Search for Ancient Cultures. Michael Wood. (Illus.). 224p. 1995. pap. 16.95 (*0-8069-0863-7*) Sterling.

Legacy: The Story of Talula Gilbert Bottoms & Her Quilts. Nancilu B. Burdick. LC 88-11534. (Illus.). 1993. pap. 18.95 (*1-55853-236-6*) Rutledge Hill Pr.

Legacy: The Story of the Permian Basin Region of West Texas & Southeast New Mexico. Gus Clemens. (Illus.). 256p. 1983. 25.95 (*0-938036-04-1*) Mulberry Ave Bks.

***Legacy: The Treaty of Little Big Horn. Ward Garing & Linda Baker. 320p. 2000. 17.95 (*1-891571-06-0*) Easy Break.**

Legacy: The Treaty of Little Big Horn is a tale of one Lakota Indian determined to change the Native American destiny. Lincoln Long Trail, a graduate student in physics at US Berkeley & radical member of the Native American Nation (NAN), is involved with the classified "Project I" research, which will enable human time travel. In the year 2021 he realizes his opportunity to go back in time, attempt to stop history's pivotal massacre of Custer at Little Big Horn & in negotiations between the Lakota & US Government to create a sovereign Lakota Nation. Linc's cousins (Charlie & Ruth), join Linc on his journey to avoid capture for a crime of which they were wrongfully accused. As their adventure begins in the past, he FBI uncovers documents which detail Linc's plans to reshape the past. Fearing Linc will alter history the FBI sends Major Jamison Partridge III to pursue & foil any plans the fugitives have of changing history. While in pursuit he too, is caught within the web of time & indecision. In the end history is altered, but did anything change for the Lakota Nation? Order Toll-free 888-777-9899 or visit our web site at http//publisher.easybreak.com/ products *Publisher Paid Annotation.*

Legacy: War of Ages. Brandon Blackmoor & Susan Blackmoor. 252p. (YA). (gr. 10 up). 1994. pap. 25.00 (*0-9641722-0-8*) Black Gate.

Legacy & History of Roswell Park Cancer Institute, 1898-1998. Edwin A. Mirand. LC 98-18365. 216p. 1998. 35.00 (*1-57864-036-9*) Donning Co.

Legacy & Leadership: USF&G's First Century. Russ Banham. LC 95-82396. (Illus.). 112p. 1995. write for info. (*0-944641-18-0*) Greenwich Pub Group.

Legacy & Other Short Stories. Tariq Rahman. Ed. by Harish Narang. (C). 1989. 29.00 (*0-8364-2472-7*) S Asia.

Legacy & Testament: The Story of Columbia River Gillnetters. Irene Martin. LC 94-14431. (Illus.). 184p. (Orig.). 1994. pap. 19.95 (*0-87422-109-9*) Wash St U Pr.

Legacy & the Glory: Greatest Moments in Kentucky Basketball History. Ed. by Francis J. Fitzgerald. (Illus.). 232p. 1995. pap. 19.95 (*1-887761-01-2*) AdCraft.

***Legacy & the Testament.** Francois Villon. Tr. by Louis Simpson from FRE. 256p. 2000. 32.00 (*1-885266-00-7*, Pub. by Story Line); pap. 17.95 (*1-885266-99-5*, Pub. by Story Line) Consort Bk Sales.

Legacy Builders: Dad, What Does Your Life Say to Your Wife & Children? Jim Burton. LC 96-60586. 208p. 1996. pap. 11.99 (*1-56384-117-7*, Vital Issue Pr) Huntington Hse.

Legacy Continues: The Manley Years at Spelman College, 1953-1976. Albert E. Manley. (Illus.). 246p. (C). 1995. lib. bdg. 39.00 (*0-8191-9880-3*) U Pr of Amer.

Legacy for a Doctor. Elizabeth Seifert. 1974. reprint ed. lib. bdg. 22.95 (*0-88411-048-6*) Amereon Ltd.

Legacy for Maine: The November Collection of Elizabeth B. Noyce. Jessica Nicoll et al. (Illus.). 80p. 1997. pap. 14.95 (*0-916857-11-5*) Port Mus Art.

Legacy for Our Children. Steven J. Bolen. Ed. & Intro. by Lynne E. Lewis. LC 93-85582. 239p. (Orig.). 1995. pap. write for info. (*1-885487-07-X*) Brownell & Carroll.

Legacy from Beyond the Seventh Star. (Illus.). 176p. 1997. pap. 14.95 (*0-9661029-0-8*) Revelation OK.

Legacy from Luxembourg: A Historical Guide to the Early Settlement of Rollingstone, Minnesota. Mary E. Nilles. 154p. (Orig.). 1986. pap. 9.95 (*0-9616845-0-X*) M E Nilles.

Legacy from Tenerife. large type ed. Robert MacLeod. 1985. 27.99 (*0-7089-1351-2*) Ulverscroft.

Legacy from the Stars. Dolores Cannon. LC 96-67899. 320p. (Orig.). 1996. pap. 23.95 (*0-9632776-9-3*) Ozark Mountn.

Legacy I Leave: A Personal Account of Sixty Years (1839-1899) Mark Hunt. LC 84-90589. (Illus.). 212p. 1984. 26.95 (*0-943480-59-0*); pap. 15.95 (*0-943480-60-4*) Friis-Pioneer Pr.

Legacy in Bricks & Mortar: African-American Landmarks in Allegheny County. Frank E. Bolden et al. Ed. by Louise Sturgess. LC 95-67169. (Illus.). 84p. 1995. pap. text 8.95 (*0-916670-17-1*) Pitt Hist & Landmks Found.

Legacy in Light: Photographic Treasures from Philadelphia Area Public Collections. Contrib. by Kenneth Finkel & Photography Sesquicentennial Project Staff. (Illus.). 72p. 1990. pap. 10.00 (*0-914076-83-3*) Lib Co Phila.

Legacy in Song - Harry Chapin (Piano-Vocal) Harry Chapin. Ed. by Milton Okun. (Illus.). 180p. (Orig.). (YA). 1990. pap. text 24.95 (*0-89524-327-X*, Pub. by Cherry Lane) H Leonard.

Legacy in Stone: The Rideau Corridor. Barbara Humphreys & Fiona Spalding-Smith. 96p. 1997. 19.95 (*1-55046-213-X*, Pub. by Boston Mills) Genl Dist Srvs.

Legacy in the Sand: The U. S. Army Armament, Munitions & Chemical Command in Operations Desert Shield & Desert Storm. 240p. (Orig.). (C). 1994. pap. text 65.00 (*0-7881-0475-6*) DIANE Pub.

Legacy in the Sand: United States Army Armament, Munitions & Chemical Command in Operations Desert Shield & Desert Storm. Kimberly K. Porter. 240p. 1993. per. 23.00 (*0-16-061106-7*) USGPO.

***Legacy Leadership: The 5 Best Practices.** Lee Smith et al. (Illus.). 36p. 1999. pap. 15.00 (*0-9672175-1-2*) CoachWorks.

Legacy Lived: Your Enduring Influence for Future Generations. 2nd rev. ed. L. Allen Morris. Ed. by Barbara R. Thompson et al. Orig. Title: Dreams, Deals, Dividends & Donuts. 139p. 1998. pap. text 10.00 (*0-9640852-7-5*, 1006) Look Gl Bks.

Legacy of a Divided Nation: India's Muslims Since Independence to Ayodhya. Mushirul Hasan. LC 97-3721. 368p. (C). 1997. pap. text 32.00 (*0-8133-3340-7*, Pub. by Westview) HarpC.

Legacy of a Gentle Genius: The Life of A. M. O. Smith Tuncer Cebeci. LC 99-24379. 1999. write for info. (*0-9668461-1-7*) Horizons Pubg.

Legacy of a Hunter: A Novel. Emery Barrus. 256p. (Orig.). 1995. pap. 10.95 (*0-931832-88-8*) Fithian Pr.

Legacy of a Master Potter: Nampeyo & Her Descendants. Mary Ellen Blair & Laurence Blair. (Illus.). 1999. pap. 29.95 (*1-887896-06-6*, Rio Nuevo) Treas Chest Bks.

Legacy of a Shared Vision: The History of Calcot. Catherine M. Merlo. 192p. 1995. lib. bdg. 32.00 (*0-9645117-0-3*) Calcot.

Legacy of a Spy. 248p. 1998. pap. 14.95 (*0-9666289-0-X*) Southwick Hse.

Legacy of a Stranger. David Thayer. LC 99-35241. 192p. 1999. pap. 12.95 (*1-882897-38-2*) Lost Coast.

Legacy of a Village: Italian Swiss Colony & the People of Asti. Jack W. Florence, Sr. (Illus.). 308p. 1999. 24.95 (*0-9673081-0-0*) Raymond Ct Pr.

Legacy of a War: The American Soldier in Vietnam. Ellen Frey-Wouters & Robert Laufer. LC 85-10913. 472p. (gr. 13). 1986. 81.95 (*0-87332-354-8*); pap. 35.95 (*0-87332-562-1*) M E Sharpe.

Legacy of Achille Martino. Martin Sampierre. 120p. 1988. 13.95 (*0-8453-4812-4*, Cornwall Bks) Assoc Univ Prs.

Legacy of African Methodism. Taylor T. Thompson. (Illus.). 204p. 1988. text. write for info. (*0-929386-00-0*) AMEC Sunday Schl Union.

Legacy of Aging: Inheritance & Disinheritance in Social Perspective. Jeffrey P. Rosenfeld. LC 78-24209. (Modern Sociology Ser.). (Illus.). 152p. 1979. text 73.25 (*0-89391-011-2*) Ablx Pub.

Legacy of Albert Kahn. W. Hawkins Ferry. LC 87-13295. (Great Lakes Bks.). (Illus.). 184p. 1987. reprint ed. 29.95 (*0-8143-1888-6*); reprint ed. pap. 19.95 (*0-8143-1889-4*) Wayne St U Pr.

Legacy of Albion Small. Vernon K. Dibble. LC 74-16686. (Heritage of Sociology Ser.). x, 288p. 1996. lib. bdg. 24.00 (*0-226-14520-4*) U Ch Pr.

Legacy of Ancient Egypt. Charles Freeman & John D. Ray. LC 96-30041. (Illus.). 224p. 1997. 45.00 (*0-8160-3656-X*) Facts on File.

Legacy of Andrew Jackson: Essays on Democracy, Indian Removal, & Slavery. Robert V. Remini. LC 87-24137. (Walter Lynwood Fleming Lectures in Southern History). 117p. 1988. pap. text 12.95 (*0-8071-1642-4*) La State U Pr.

Legacy of Anomie Theory. Ed. by Freda Adler & William S. Laufer. (Advances in Criminological Theory Ser.: Vol. 6). 370p. (C). 1994. text 49.95 (*1-56000-125-9*) Transaction Pubs.

Legacy of Anomie Theory Vol. 6: Advances in Criminological Theory. Ed. by Freda Adler & William S. Laufer. 449p. 1999. pap. 32.95 (*0-7658-0662-2*) Transaction Pubs.

Legacy of Arctic Art. Dorothy J. Ray. LC 95-36452. (Illus.). 208p. 1996. pap. 24.95 (*0-295-97518-0*); text 40.00 (*0-295-97507-5*) U of Wash Pr.

Legacy of B. F. Skinner: Concepts & Perspectives, Controversies & Misunderstandings. Robert D. Nye. LC 91-21644. 145p. (C). 1991. pap. 18.25 (*0-534-16944-9*) Brooks-Cole.

L

Legacy of Bitterness: Ethiopia & Fascist Italy. Alberto Sbacchi. LC 96-5384. 390p. (C). 1994. 69.95 (*0-932415-73-3*); pap. 19.95 (*0-932415-74-1*) Red Sea Pr.

Legacy of Boadicea: Gender & Recovery of Native Origins in Early Modern England. Jodi Mikalachki. LC 97-39148. (Illus.). 218p. (C). (gr. 13). 1998. 75.00 (*0-415-18263-8*); pap. 24.99 (*0-415-18264-6*) Routledge.

Legacy of Buford Pusser: A Pictorial History of the "Walking Tall" Sheriff. W. R. Morris. LC 94-61035. (Illus.). 144p. Date not set. 29.95 (*1-56311-164-0*) Turner Pub KY.

Legacy of Cain: A Novel see Works of Wilkie Collins

Legacy of Caring: The Impassioned Mission of Sisters of the Holy Family. Charlotte M. Hall. LC 97-93185. (Illus.). vi, 120p. 1997. 32.95 (*0-9657486-0-X*) Hall Media Grp.

Legacy of Caring: The Society of Memorial Sloan-Kettering Cancer Center. Joan S. Straus. (Illus.). xiv, 298p. 1996. 44.95 (*0-9653303-0-3*); pap. 24.95 (*0-9653303-1-1*) Soc Mem Sloan-Kettering.

Legacy of Cell Fusion. Ed. by Siamon Gordon. (Illus.). 318p. 1994. text 125.00 (*0-19-854772-2*) OUP.

Legacy of Champions: The Story of the Men Who Built Kentucky Basketball. Louisville Courier Journal Staff. 1997. 99.95 (*1-57028-179-3*, Mstrs Pr) NTC Contemp Pub Co.

Legacy of Champions: The Story of the Men Who Built University of Michigan Football. Angelique Chengelis et al. (Illus.). 224p. 1996. 29.95 (*0-9654671-0-4*) C T C Sports.

Legacy of Change: Historic Human Impact on Vegetation in the Arizona Borderlands. Conrad J. Bahre. LC 90-39777. (Illus.). 231p. 1991. 36.00 (*0-8165-1204-3*) U of Ariz Pr.

Legacy of Chernobyl. Zhores A. Medvedev. (Illus.). 376p. 1992. pap. 10.95 (*0-393-30814-6*) Norton.

Legacy of China. Ed. by Raymond Dawson. LC 90-83185. (C & T Asian Language Ser.). 460p. (C). 1990. reprint ed. pap. 18.95 (*0-88727-152-9*) Cheng & Tsui.

Legacy of Conquest: The Unbroken Past of the American West. Patricia N. Limerick. LC 86-23883. 1988. pap. 13.95 (*0-393-30497-3*) Norton.

***Legacy of Courage: A Brave Woman's Search for Her Mother's Killer & Her Own Identity - A True Story.** Paula Mints. LC 99-70157. 324p. 2000. 24.95 (*0-88282-186-5*,) New Horizon NJ.

Legacy of Custer's 7th U. S. Cavalry in Korea. Edward L. Daily. LC 90-70004. (Illus.). 128p. 1990. 39.95 (*0-938021-84-2*) Turner Pub KY.

Legacy of Daedalus. Eugenia Macer-Story. 94p. 1995. pap. 6.00 (*1-879980-05-3*) Magick Mirror.

Legacy of D'Arcy McNickle: Writer, Historian, Activist. Ed. by John L. Purdy. LC 95-25863. (American Indian Literature & Critical Studies Ser.: Vol. 21). 288p. 1996. 29.95 (*0-8061-2806-2*) U of Okla Pr.

Legacy of Democritus Junior, Robert Burton: An Exhibition to Commemorate the 350th Anniversary of the Death of Robert Burton (1577-1640) Nicolas K. Kiessling & Bodleian Library Staff. LC 92-168891. x, 123p. 1990. pap. write for info. (*1-85124-018-7*) Bodleian Lib.

Legacy of Demons. Pat Molloy. 214p. (C). 1989. pap. 27.00 (*0-86383-615-1*, Pub. by Gomer Pr) St Mut.

Legacy of Design: An Historical Survey of the Kansas City, Missouri, Parks & Boulevards System, 1893-1940. Ed. by Janice Lee et al. (Illus.). 296p. 1995. write for info. (*0-9648063-0-4*) KCC Design Educ.

Legacy of Diamond. Andrea Kane. 1997. mass mkt. 5.99 (*0-614-20517-4*, PB Trade Paper); per. 5.99 (*0-671-53485-8*) PB.

***Legacy of Discord: Voices of the Vietnam Era.** Gil Dorland. 2001. 26.95 (*1-57488-215-5*) Brasseys.

Legacy of Dissent: Forty Years of Writing from Dissent Magazine. Ed. by Nicolaus Mills. 464p. 1994. pap. 16.00 (*0-671-88879-X*, Touchstone) S&S Trade Pap.

***Legacy of Doc Watson.** Steve Kaufman. 152p. 1999. pap. 25.00 (*0-7866-3393-X*, 95742) Mel Bay.

Legacy of Dr. Ambedkar. D. C. Ahir. (C). 1990. 140.00 (*0-89771-212-9*) St Mut.

Legacy of Dr. Ambedkar (Bharat Ratna) D. C. Ahir. 1990. 42.00 (*81-7018-603-X*, Pub. by BR Pub) S Asia.

Legacy of Dreams: The Life & Contributions of Dr. William Venoid Banks. Ed. by Sheila T. Gregory. 176p. 1999. 32.50 (*0-7618-1285-7*) U Pr of Amer.

Legacy of Egypt. Stephen R. Glanville. LC 76-44448. (Illus.). 424p. 1977. reprint ed. lib. bdg. 35.00 (*0-8371-9092-4*, GLLE, Greenwood Pr) Greenwood.

Legacy of Egypt. 2nd ed. Ed. by J. R. Harris. (Legacy Ser.). (Illus.). 552p. 1987. 39.95 (*0-19-821912-1*) OUP.

Legacy of Erich Fromm. Daniel Burston. LC 90-5348. (Illus.). 288p. 1991. 43.50 (*0-674-52168-4*, BURLEG) HUP.

***Legacy of Ernest Mandel.** Gilbert Achcar. 1999. 45.00 (*1-85984-703-X*, Pub. by Verso) Norton.

Legacy of Erskine Caldwell. Stanley W. Lindberg. (Georgia Humanities Council Publications). (Illus.). 64p. 1991. pap. 9.95 (*0-8203-1315-7*) U of Ga Pr.

Legacy of Excellence: Orthodox Theological Seminary, 1938-1988. (Illus.). 96p. (Orig.). 1991. pap. 10.95 (*0-88141-074-8*) St Vladimirs.

Legacy of Excellence: The Story of Villa Tatti. William Weaver. LC 96-31347. (Illus.). 152p. 1997. 49.50 (*0-8109-3587-2*, Pub. by Abrams) Time Warner.

Legacy of Exile: Life, Letters, Literature. Ed. by Deborah Vietor Englander. LC 98-47711. 192p. 1999. pap. 29.95 (*0-631-21454-2*) Blackwell Pubs.

***Legacy of Failure: The Inability of the Federal-State Vocational Rehabilitation System to Serve People with Sevre Mental Illnesses.** John H. Noble, Jr. (Illus.). 125p. (C). 2000. reprint ed. pap. text 20.00 (*0-7881-8667-1*) DIANE Pub.

***Legacy of Faith.** William Chazonof. LC 99-69427. 100p. 2000. 21.95 (*1-888160-00-4*) Ice Cube.

***Legacy of Faith.** Lester Sumrall. 1999. 24.95 (*1-58568-168-7*) Sumrall Pubng.

Legacy of Fear. Evelyn A. Crowe. LC 95-13687. (Superromance Ser.). 297p. 1995. per. 3.75 (*0-373-70646-4*, 1-70646-4) Harlequin Bks.

Legacy of Fear: American Race Relations to 1900, 4. Michael J. Cassity. LC 84-8981. (Grass Roots Perspectives on American History Ser.: No. 4). (Illus.). 248p. 1985. 59.95 (*0-313-24553-3*, CLF/, Greenwood Pr) Greenwood.

***Legacy of Felix Hintemeyer.** Paschal Michael Baumstein. (Illus.). 20p. 2000. pap. 15.00 (*1-890763-26-8*) Archives Belmont.

Legacy of Five Wives. Shirley S. Howe. (Illus.). 200p. 1988. 15.00 (*0-9616538-2-5*); pap. 10.00 (*0-9616538-3-3*) Heritage Val Pub.

Legacy of Francis Bacon. Ed. by William A. Sessions. (Georgia State Literary Studies: No. 5). 1988. 55.00 (*0-404-63205-X*) AMS Pr.

***Legacy of Friedrich Von Hayek, 3 vols.** Ed. by Peter J. Boettke et al. LC 99-49358. (Intellectual Legacies in Modern Economics Ser.). 1624p. 2000. 575.00 (*1-85898-299-5*) E Elgar.

Legacy of Genghis Khan & Other Essays on Russia's Identity. Nikolai S. Trubetzkoy. (Michigan Slavic Materials Ser.: No. 33). 1991. 28.50 (*0-930042-70-0*) Mich Slavic Pubns.

Legacy of Geo Mason. 1983. 15.00 (*0-913969-00-1*) Univ Pub Assocs.

Legacy of George Partridgeberry. J. Lansing Shubert. Ed. by Robert Steele. (Illus.). 381p. (Orig.). (YA). (gr. 9-12). 1990. pap. 12.95 (*0-9627015-0-5*) J L Shubert.

Legacy of Gird. Elizabeth Moon. 864p. 1996. per. 15.00 (*0-671-87747-X*) Baen Bks.

Legacy of Grace. Elizabeth N. Nagle. LC 85-96921. 1986. 10.00 (*0-87212-191-7*) Libra.

Legacy of Greece: A New Appraisal. Moses I. Finley. (Illus.). 496p. (C). 1984. pap. text 32.00 (*0-19-285136-5*) OUP.

Legacy of Hans Freudenthal. Ed. by Leen Streefland. LC 93-43583. 164p. (C). 1994. lib. bdg. 78.00 (*0-7923-2653-9*) Kluwer Academic.

***Legacy of Hate: A Short History of Ethnic, Religious & Racial Prejudice in America.** Philip Perlmutter. LC 99-11648. 344p. 1999. text 34.95 (*0-7656-0406-X*) M E Sharpe.

Legacy of Hatred Continues: A Response to Hal Lindsey's "The Road to Holocaust" Gary DeMar & Peter J. Leithart. 68p. 1989. pap. 3.95 (*0-930464-29-X*) Inst Christian.

Legacy of Heorot. Larry Niven & Jerry Pournelle. Ed. by Dave Stern. 400p. 1989. mass mkt. 6.99 (*0-671-69532-0*) PB.

Legacy of Hiroshima. Edward Teller & Allen Brown, Jr. LC 75-23264. 325p. 1975. reprint ed. lib. bdg. 65.00 (*0-8371-8344-8*, TELH, Greenwood Pr) Greenwood.

Legacy of Hiroshima: Its Past, Our Future. Naomi Shohno. Tr. by Tomoko Nakamura from JPN.Tr. of Hiroshima wa Mukashibanashi ka. (Illus.). 150p. 1986. pap. 9.95 (*4-333-01234-1*, Pub. by Kosei Pub Co) Tuttle Pubng.

Legacy of Holmes & Brandeis. Samuel J. Konefsky. LC 78-157828. (American Constitutional & Legal History Ser). 316p. 1974. reprint ed. lib. bdg. 37.50 (*0-306-70215-0*) Da Capo.

Legacy of Homes & Families: Princeton-Athens Area West Virginia. LC 85-51221. 1985. 25.00 (*0-685-35684-1*) W Sanders.

Legacy of Honor: President Grover Cleveland & Son Francis. Naomi G. Topalian. Ed. by Barbara Merguerian. LC 95-81157. (Illus.). 294p. 1995. 29.95 (*0-936893-12-5*); write for info. (*0-614-29558-0*) N G Topalian.

Legacy of Honor: The Life of Rafael Chacon, a Nineteenth-Century New Mexican. Rafael Chacon. Ed. by Jacqueline D. Meketa. LC 86-16018. (Illus.). 451p. 1986. reprint ed. pap. 139.90 (*0-608-04125-4*, 206485800011) Bks Demand.

Legacy of Horace M. Kallen. Ed. by Milton R. Konvitz. LC 85-46028. 128p. 1987. 29.50 (*0-8386-3291-2*) Fairleigh Dickinson.

Legacy of Human Rights Violations in the Southern Cone: Argentina, Chile & Uruguay. Mario Sznajder & Luis Roniger. LC 99-10365. (Oxford Studies in Democratization Ser.). 384p. 1999. text 82.00 (*0-19-829615-0*) OUP.

Legacy of Ibo Landing: Gullah Roots of African-American Culture. Ed. by Marquetta L. Goodwine. (Illus.). 208p. 1998. 27.95 (*0-932863-25-6*) Clarity Pr.

Legacy of Inherited Wealth: Interviews with Heirs. rev. ed. Ed. by Barbara Blouin et al. LC 95-232932. 185p. 1995. pap. 17.95 (*0-9699195-0-6*) Trio Pr.

Legacy of Injustice: Exploring the Cross-Generational Impact of the Japanese American Internment. D. K. Nagata. (Critical Issues in Social Justice Ser.). (Illus.). 298p. (C). 1993. 45.00 (*0-306-44425-9*, Plenum Trade) Perseus Pubng.

Legacy of Islam. 2nd ed. Ed. by Joseph Schacht & C. E. Bosworth. (Legacy Ser.). (Illus.). 554p. (C). 1974. text 45.00 (*0-19-821913-X*) OUP.

***Legacy of J. C. Kapteyn: Studies on Kapteyn & the Development of Modern Astronomy.** J. C. Kapteyn et al. LC 00-31328. (Astrophysics & Space Science Library). 2000. write for info. (*0-7923-6393-0*) Plenum.

Legacy of James Bowdoin, III. Kenneth E. Carpenter et al. LC 93-79512. (Illus.). 268p. 1994. 39.95 (*0-916606-27-9*) Bowdoin Coll.

Legacy of Jewish Migration, 1881: And Its Impact. David Berger. (Social Science Monographs). 189p. 1983. text 61.00 (*0-88033-026-0*, Pub. by East Eur Monographs) Col U Pr.

***Legacy of John Cyclone.** Andy Weiner & Rick Whipple. LC 99-56242. (Publish-a-Book Ser.). (Illus.). 24p. (J). (ps-3). 2000. write for info. (*0-7398-2370-1*) Raintree Steck-V.

***Legacy of John Paul II: His Contribution to Catholic Thought.** John F. Crosby. LC 99-53600. 2000. write for info. (*0-8245-1850-0*) Crossroad NY.

Legacy of John von Neumann. James Glimm et al. LC 90-33765. (Proceedings of Symposia in Pure Mathematics Ser.: Vol. 50). 334p. 1990. text 39.00 (*0-8218-1487-7*, PSPUM/50) Am Math.

Legacy of Joseph A. Schumpeter, 2 vols., Set. Ed. by Horst Hanusch. LC 99-47652. (Intellectual Legacies in Modern Economics Ser.). 1040p. 2000. 360.00 (*1-85898-505-6*) E Elgar.

Legacy of Joy: A Devotional for Fathers. Mike Nappa & Norm Wakefield. 224p. 1998. 14.99 (*1-57748-379-0*) Barbour Pub.

Legacy of Kafka in Contemporary Austrian Literature. Ed. by Frank Pilipp. LC 97-9314. (Studies in Austrian Literature, Culture, & Thought). 231p. 1997. 29.50 (*1-57241-044-2*) Ariadne CA.

Legacy of Kain. Tim Bogenn. (Brady Games Strategy Guides Ser.). (Illus.). 191p. 1999. pap. 7.99 (*1-56686-874-2*, BradyGAMES) Brady Pub.

***Legacy of Kain: Soul Reaver (DC)** Prima Development Staff. LC 98-73122. (Official Strategy Guides Ser.). (Illus.). 128p. (YA). 2000. pap. 14.99 (*0-7615-2757-5*, Prima Tech) Prima Pub.

Legacy of Kain: Soul Reaver: Prima's Unauthorized Game Secrets. Prima Publishing Staff. 96p. 1999. per. 12.99 (*0-7615-1796-0*, Prima Games) Prima Pub.

Legacy of Kenneth Burke. Ed. by Herbert W. Simons & Trevor Melia. LC 88-40197. 324p. (C). 1988. pap. text 18.95 (*0-299-11834-7*) U of Wis Pr.

Legacy of Keynes & Friedman: Economic Analysis, Money, & Ideology. William Frazer. LC 93-23490. 304p. 1994. 65.00 (*0-275-94731-9*, Praeger Pubs) Greenwood.

Legacy of Language: A Tribute to Charlton Laird. Ed. by Phillip C. Boardman. LC 86-30840. 224p. 1987. 24.95 (*0-87417-121-0*) U of Nev Pr.

***Legacy of Laughter.** Linda Raye Settle. 304p. 1999. pap. 14.95 (*0-9674478-0-1*) L R Settle.

Legacy of Lawrence Kohlberg. Ed. by Dawn E. Schrader. LC 85-644581. (New Directions for Child Development Ser.: No. CD 47). 1990. pap. 25.00 (*1-55542-824-X*) Jossey-Bass.

***Legacy of Leadership.** Bert Lunan. LC 99-47655. 1999. write for info. (*0-9675005-0-8*) S C Bus Hall of Fame.

Legacy of Leadership: Lessons from Admiral Lord Nelson. Joseph F. Callo. LC 99-47211. 154p. 2000. 17.95 (*1-55571-510-9*) PSI Resch.

Legacy of Leadership: Presidential Addresses from the Superintendents' Society & the National League for Nursing 1894-1952. Ed. by Nettie Birnbach & Sandra B. Lewenson. 416p. (C). 1993. pap. text 29.95 (*0-88737-575-8*, 14-2514) Natl League Nurse.

Legacy of Leadership: The History of Lee Enterprises, Inc. Wilbur Cross. Ed. by Ceila D. Robbins. (Illus.). 176p. 1990. write for info. (*0-944641-00-8*) Greenwich Pub Group.

Legacy of Learning: A History of Western Education. Edward J. Power. LC 90-37218. (SUNY Series, the Philosophy of Education). 400p. (C). 1991. text 64.50 (*0-7914-0610-5*); pap. text 21.95 (*0-7914-0611-3*) State U NY Pr.

Legacy of Learning: The History of the West Chester Area Schools. Florence S. Miller. LC 94-60393. 339p. 1994. text 25.00 (*0-9640745-0-8*) W Chester Area.

***Legacy of Learning: Your Stake in Standards & New Kinds of Public Schools.** David T. Kearns & James Harvey. LC 99-50467. 2000. 24.95 (*0-8157-4894-9*) Brookings.

Legacy of Lehr. Katherine Kurtz. 224p. 1988. pap. 3.50 (*0-380-70454-4*, Avon Bks) Morrow Avon.

Legacy of Lehr. Katherine Kurtz. (Millennium Series, a Byron Priess Bk.). (Illus.). 240p. 1986. 15.95 (*0-8027-6661-7*) Walker & Co.

***Legacy of Leon Van Hove.** Ed. by Alberto Giovannini. (Series in 20th Century Physics). 600p. 2000. 88.00 (*981-02-4330-8*) World Scientific Pub.

Legacy of Leonardo: Painters in Lombardy, 1480-1530. David A. Brown et al. (Illus.). 304p. 1999. 90.00 (*88-8118-463-X*, Pub. by Skira IT) Abbeville Pr.

Legacy of Lies. Joann Ross. 378p. 1995. per. 4.99 (*1-55166-018-0*, Mira Bks) Harlequin Bks.

Legacy of Lies & Love: The True Story of Gerda Daub O'Dey. Jean M. Tiedtke. (Illus.). 329p. 1991. text 23.50 (*1-880272-00-8*) J M Tiedtke.

***Legacy of Lies, Dark Secrets, Vol. 1.** Elizabeth Chandler. 176p. 2000. 4.99 (*0-7434-0028-3*, Archway) PB.

Legacy of Life: Readings & Exercises. W. Britt Leatham. 438p. (C). 1997. pap. text, per. 59.95 (*0-7872-2750-1*) Kendall-Hunt.

Legacy of Light: A History of the Idaho Power Company. Susan M. Stacy. (Illus.). 226p. (Orig.). 1991. pap. write for info. (*0-9631822-0-X*) Idaho Power.

Legacy of Lions, History of University City, MO. NiNi Harris. Ed. by John Lindenbusch. (Illus.). 192p. 1981. 18.00 (*0-9606674-0-7*); pap. 12.00 (*0-9606674-1-5*) Hist Univ City.

Legacy of Logical Positivism in the Philosophy of Science. Ed. by Peter Achinstein & Stephen F. Barker. LC 69-15396. 10p. reprint ed. pap. 30.00 (*0-608-10079-X*, 200628500056) Bks Demand.

Legacy of Longevity: Health & Health Care in Later Life. Ed. by Sidney M. Stahl. 342p. (C). 1990. text 52.00 (*0-8039-4001-7*); pap. text 24.50 (*0-8039-4002-5*) Sage.

Legacy of Love. Hazel Graves. LC 96-97072. 87p. (Orig.). 1996. pap. 10.00 (*0-9654219-0-2*) H Graves.

Legacy of Love. Ed. by Lynn Guise. 100p. 1995. pap. 14.95 (*1-888257-01-6*) Cameron Press.

Legacy of Love. Caroline Harvey. 1993. mass mkt. 8.99 (*0-552-13872-X*) Bantam.

***Legacy of Love.** Caroline Harvey. 2000. 24.95 (*0-670-89181-9*, Viking) Viking Penguin.

Legacy of Love. Marianne K. Martin. LC 97-10005. 240p. (Orig.). 1997. pap. 11.95 (*1-56280-184-8*) Naiad Pr.

Legacy of Love. unabridged ed. Gerry Samuels. (Illus.). 176p. 1999. 24.95 (*0-9665315-0-7*) Alger Pr.

Legacy of Love: A Biography of Rose Hawthorne Lathrop, 3 pts. Alberta Hapenney. 176p. 1999. pap. 14.00 (*0-8059-4580-6*) Dorrance.

Legacy of Love - Captive Desire, 2 vols. in 1. Tate McKenna. 368p. 1992. pap. text, mass mkt. 4.50 (*0-8439-3326-7*) Dorchester Pub Co.

Legacy of Lucian Van Zandt. Kate Chambers. LC 99-60491. (Diana Winthrop Detective Ser.). 200p. (YA). (gr. 5-12). 1999. reprint ed. pap. 16.00 (*1-892323-45-1*) Vivisphere.

***Legacy of Luna: The Story of a Tree, a Woman & the Struggle to Save the Redwoods.** Julia Butterfly Hill. LC 99-88633. (Illus.). 256p. 2000. 25.00 (*0-06-251658-2*, Pub. by Harper SF) HarpC.

***Legacy Of Luna: The Story of aTree, a Woman & the Struggle to Save the Redwoods.** Julia Butterfly Hill. LC 99-88633. 2000. pap. write for info. (*0-06-251659-0*) Harper SF.

Legacy of Luther: Martin Luther & the Reformation in the Estimation of the German Lutherans from Luther's Death to the Beginning of the Age of Goethe. Ernest W. Zeeden. Tr. by Ruth M. Bethell from GER. LC 83-45685. reprint ed. 39.50 (*0-404-19865-1*) AMS Pr.

Legacy of Mark Rothko. rev. ed. Lee Seldes. LC 96-11368. (Illus.). 432p. 1996. pap. 15.95 (*0-306-80725-4*) Da Capo.

Legacy of Medieval Persian Sufism. Ed. by Leonard Lewisohn. (Illus.). 434p. 1992. pap. 29.95 (*0-933546-46-7*) KNP.

Legacy of Medieval Persian Sufism. Ed. by Leonard Lewisohn. 434p. 1996. pap. 29.95 (*0-614-21301-0*, 707) Kazi Pubns.

Legacy of Mesoamerica: History & Culture of a Native American Civilization. Ed. by Robert M. Carmack et al. LC 94-31722. (Exploring Cultures Ser.). 494p. 1995. pap. text 42.00 (*0-13-337445-9*) P-H.

Legacy of Mesopotamia. Stephanie Dalley et al. LC 97-12948. (Illus.). 248p. (C). 1998. text 105.00 (*0-19-814946-8*) OUP.

***Legacy of Michael Kalecki, 2 vols.** Ed. by Malcolm C. Sawyer. LC 99-47553. (Intellectual Legacies in Modern Economics Ser.). 985p. 2000. 360.00 (*1-84064-055-3*) E Elgar.

Legacy of Michael Sattler. Ed. by John H. Yoder. LC 72-6333. (Classics of the Radical Reformation Ser.: Vol. 1). 208p. 1973. 17.99 (*0-8361-1187-7*) Herald Pr.

Legacy of Muslim Rule in India. K. S. Lal. (C). 1992. 34.00 (*81-85689-03-2*, Pub. by Aditya Prakashan) S Asia.

Legacy of Muslim Spain. Ed. by Salma K. Jayyusi. LC 92-29604. (Handbook of Oriental Studies, the Near & Middle East: Vol. 12). xx, 1106p. 1994. 342.50 (*90-04-09599-3*); pap. 106.00 (*90-04-09954-9*) Brill Academic Pubs.

Legacy of Names: British Places in the New World. Elaine Borish. (Illus.). 260p. 1996. pap. 15.95 (*0-9524881-2-4*, Pub. by Fidelio Pr) IPG Chicago.

***Legacy of Nazi Occupation: Patriotic Memory & National Recovery in Western Europe, 1945-1965.** Pieter Lagrou. (Studies in the Social & Cultural History of Modern Warfare: No. 8). (Illus.). 342p. (C). 2000. 59.95 (*0-521-65180-8*) Cambridge U Pr.

Legacy of Nehru: A Centennial Assessment. Ed. by D. R. SarDesai & Anand Mohan. x, 420p. (C). 1992. 39.95 (*1-881338-00-2*) Nataraj Bks.

Legacy of Norbert Wiener: A Special Symposium in Honor of the 100th Anniversary of Norbert Wiener's Birth, October 8-14, 1994, Massachusetts Institute of Technology, Cambridge, Massachusetts. Norbert Wiener et al. LC 97-297. (Proceedings of Symposia in Pure Mathematics Ser.: No. 60). 405p. 1997. text 80.00 (*0-8218-0415-4*, PSPUM/60) Am Math.

***Legacy of Norman Rockwell.** Ben Sonder. (Illus.). 144p. 1998. 24.98 (*1-57717-014-8*) Todtri Prods.

Legacy of North Dakota's Country Schools. Ed. by Warren A. Henke & Everett C. Albers. LC 97-75977. (Illus.). 320p. 1997. 27.49 (*0-9654579-2-3*); pap. 19.95 (*0-9654579-1-5*) N Dakota Hum.

Legacy of Northrop Frye. Ed. by Alvin A. Lee & Robert D. Denham. 354p. 1994. text 55.00 (*0-8020-0632-9*); pap. text 24.95 (*0-8020-7588-6*) U of Toronto Pr.

Legacy of Olaf Stapledon: Critical Essays & an Unpublished Manuscript, 34. Ed. by Patrick A. McCarthy et al. LC 88-25097. (Contributions to the Study of Science Fiction & Fantasy Ser.: No. 34). 140p. 1989. 49.95 (*0-313-26114-8*, MLC/, Greenwood Pr) Greenwood.

Legacy of Oliver Wendell Holmes, Jr. Ed. by Robert W. Gordon. LC 91-43265. (Jurists: Profiles in Legal Theory Ser.). 336p. (C). 1992. 45.00 (*0-8047-1989-6*) Stanford U Pr.

Legacy of Pain. Grosskopf. 1997. 22.50 (*0-02-874132-3*) Macmillan.

An Asterisk (*) at the beginning of an entry indicates that the title is appearing for the first time.

Legacy of Paradise: Marriage, Motherhood & Woman in Carolingian Edifying Literature. Katrien Heene. LC 97-11957. 338p. 1997. pap. 57.95 (3-631-30932-5) P Lang Pubng.

Legacy of Paradise: Marriage, Motherhood & Woman in Carolingian Edifying Literature. Katrien Heene. LC 97-11957. 338p. 1997. pap. 57.95 (0-8204-3226-1) P Lang Pubng.

***Legacy of Parmenides: Eleatic Monism & Later Presocratic Thought.** Patricia Curd. LC 97-8636. 280p. 1998. text 45.00 (0-691-01182-6, Pub. by Princeton U Pr) Cal Prin Full Svc.

Legacy of Passion. Catherine Kay. 512p. 1993. per. 23.12 (0-373-97002-1) Harlequin Bks.

Legacy of Penn's Woods: A History of the Pennsylvania Bureau of Forestry. Lester A. DeCoster. (Illus.). 70p. 1995. pap. 12.95 (0-89271-066-7, 0425) Pa Hist & Mus.

***Legacy of Percy Gray: A Collection of Biographical Essays & Photos from 1998 Exhibition.** Ed. & Intro. by Janet Howell. LC 99-74267. (Illus.). 180p. 1999. pap. 29.95 (1-885666-09-8); text 75.00 (1-885666-08-X) Carmel Art.

***Legacy of Pope John Paul II: His Contribution to Catholic Thought.** John F. Crosby. LC 99-53600. 2000. pap. 12.95 (0-8245-1831-4, Herdr & Herdr) Crossroad NY.

***Legacy of Prometheus.** Eric Kotani & John Maddox Roberts. LC 99-89840. 272p. 2000. 24.95 (0-312-87298-4, Pub. by Forge NYC) St Martin.

Legacy of Promises: Agriculture, Politics, & Ritual in the Morelos Highlands of Mexico. Guillermo De la Pena. (Texas Pan American Ser.). 299p. (C). 1982. text 25.00 (0-292-74630-X) U of Tex Pr.

Legacy of Promises for a Godly Man. Tony Evans. Date not set. 12.99 (0-8499-5438-X) Word Pub.

Legacy of Raul Prebisch. Ed. by Enrique V. Iglesias. 204p. 1993. 14.50 (0-940602-70-9) IADB.

***Legacy of Reginald Perrin.** large type unabridged ed. David Nobbs. 336p. 1999. 25.95 (0-7531-5507-9, 155079, Pub. by ISIS Lrg Prnt) ISIS Pub.

***Legacy of Robert Penn Warren.** Ed. by David Madden. LC 00-28726. (Southern Literary Studies). 200p. 2000. 34.95 (0-8071-2592-X) La State U Pr.

Legacy of Roman Law in the German Romantic Era: Historical Vision & Legal Change. James Q. Whitman. (Illus.). 309p. 1990. text 52.50 (0-691-05560-2, Pub. by Princeton U Pr) Cal Prin Full Svc.

Legacy of Rome. Ed. by Cyril Bailey. (Legacy Ser.). (Illus.). 1923. 49.95 (0-19-821906-7) OUP.

Legacy of Rome. Ed. & Contrib. by Cyril Bailey. xii, 512p. 1998. reprint ed. 158.00 (1-56169-368-5) Gaunt.

Legacy of Ronald Coase in Economic Analysis, 2 vols., Set. Ed. by Steven G. Medema. LC 94-32261. (Intellectual Legacies in Modern Economics Ser.). 1088p. 1995. 400.00 (1-85898-010-0) E Elgar.

Legacy of Rousseau. Ed. by Clifford Orwin & Nathan Tarcov. LC 96-8908. 296p. 1997. pap. text 17.95 (0-226-63856-1) U Ch Pr.

Legacy of Rousseau. Ed. by Clifford Orwin & Nathan Tarcov. LC 96-8908. 296p. 1998. lib. bdg. 45.00 (0-226-63855-3) U Ch Pr.

Legacy of Roxaboxen: A Collection of Voices. Alice McLerran. 72p. 1998. 19.95 (1-888842-08-3) Absey & Co.

Legacy of Sacco & Vanzetti. Louis Joughlin & Edmund M. Morgan. LC 88-122147. 608p. 1948. reprint ed. pap. 188.50 (0-608-07651-1, 205996900010) Bks Demand.

Legacy of Sandor Ferenczi. Ed. by Lewis Aron & Adrienne Harris. LC 93-6594. 320p. 1996. reprint ed. 49.95 (0-88163-149-3) Analytic Pr.

Legacy of Scholasticism in Economic Thought: Antecedents of Choice & Power. Odd Langholm. LC 97-26895. (Historical Perspectives on Modern Economics Ser.). 226p. (C). 1998. text 59.95 (0-521-62159-3) Cambridge U Pr.

Legacy of Scottish Missionaries in Malawi. Harvey J. Sindima. LC 92-21917. (Studies in the History of Missions: Vol. 8). 164p. 1992. text 79.95 (0-7734-9574-6) E Mellen.

Legacy of Secrets. Elizabeth A. Adler. LC 92-37239. 624p. 1994. mass mkt. 6.99 (0-440-21657-5) Dell.

Legacy of Secrets. Judith Arnold. (Delta Justice Ser.). 1998. per. 4.50 (0-373-82571-4) Harlequin Bks.

Legacy of Secrets. Pamela Pacotti. 1988. 3.95 (0-517-00036-9) Random Hse Value.

Legacy of Secrets. large type ed. Elizabeth A. Adler. LC 93-26431. 916p. 1993. lib. bdg. 23.95 (1-56054-753-7) Thorndike Pr.

Legacy of Secrets. large type ed. Elizabeth A. Adler. LC 93-26431. 916p. 1994. pap. 16.95 (1-56054-798-7) Thorndike Pr.

Legacy of Sedona Schnebly. Kate R. Thorne. Ed. by Aliza Caillou. (Regional History Ser.). (Illus.). 44p. (Orig.). 1994. pap. 5.95 (0-9628329-9-5) Thorne Enterprises.

Legacy of Shadows. Virginia Brown. 1987. mass mkt. 3.95 (0-446-32954-1, Pub. by Warner Bks) Little.

Legacy of Shadows. Lillian Moats. LC 98-96937. (Illus.). 173p. 1999. 18.00 (0-9669576-0-1) Three Arts.
Legacy of Shadows, Lillian Moats, 192 pages. Hardcover. $18.00. ISBN: 0966957601 Robert Coles: "This book will hold its readers close & tight, will teach them its remarkable, affecting & important lesson: that experiences live & last over a family's generations as memories that shape hearts & minds." Booklist: "Moats...has written a poetic, fictionalized memoir that recounts the most bewildering & frightening of experiences, the onslaught of mental illness....Moats' sequencing of scenes & gift for metaphor & distillation render her psychologically acute narrative as supple as film without sacrificing the beauty unique to language." The Bloomsbury Review: " This is a beautiful, brief book in which the reader is not told about the lives or complexes that 'funneled' into her own, but rather is shown, subtly, how grief, guilt & unassuageable fear can find & wind their way, unintentionally, through the psyches & emotions of three generations....Its genre, a novel written as if a journal. Its pace, compelling. Its images & descriptions, haunting. Its story human.....Lillian Moats is...a brave & generous woman." Kathleen McCrone, PhD., University of Windsor: Legacy of Shadows is a beautiful & profoundly moving tapestry of crisis & connection, forgiveness & healing....likely to be of immense benefit to more readers that (Moats) would ever have imagined. Ingram, Baker & Taylor or Bookmasters Distribution Services: Phone: (800) 247-6553 Fax: (419) 281-6883 E-mail: order@bookmaster.com
Publisher Paid Annotation.

Legacy of Shadows. large type ed. Marion Lennox. 259p. 1996. 27.99 (0-7505-0818-3, Pub. by Mgna Lrg Print) Ulverscroft.

Legacy of Shadows: Selected Poems. David Lee. LC 99-6401. 440p. 1999. 28.00 (1-55659-098-9, Pub. by Copper Canyon); pap. 16.00 (1-55659-097-0, Pub. by Copper Canyon) SPD-Small Pr Dist.

Legacy of Shame. Diana Hamilton. 1994. per. 2.99 (0-373-11690-X, 1-11690-4) Harlequin Bks.

Legacy of Shame. large type ed. Diana Hamilton. (Harlequin Romance Ser.). 1994. lib. bdg. 19.95 (0-263-13713-9) Thorndike Pr.

Legacy of Shingwaukonse: A Century of Native Leadership. Janet Chute. LC 98-205034. (Illus.). 400p. 1998. text 60.00 (0-8020-4273-2); pap. text 24.95 (0-8020-8108-8) U of Toronto Pr.

Legacy of Sigmund Freud. Jacob A. Arlow. LC 56-9746. 1956. 35.00 (0-8236-2980-5) Intl Univs Pr.

Legacy of Silence. Belva Plain. 432p. 1999. mass mkt. 7.99 (0-440-22640-6) Dell.

Legacy of Silence. Belva Plain. LC 98-23619. 1998. 28.95 (0-7862-1511-9) Thorndike Pr.

Legacy of Silence. large type ed. Belva Plain. LC 98-23619. 1998. pap. 26.95 (0-7862-1512-7) Thorndike Pr.

Legacy of Silence: Belva Plain. Belva Plain. LC 98-2934. 352p. 1998. 24.95 (0-385-31689-5) Doubleday.

Legacy of Silence: Encounters with Children of the Third Reich. Dan Baron. LC 89-7484. 354p. 1989. 37.00 (0-674-52185-4) HUP.

Legacy of Silence: Encounters with Children of the Third Reich. Dan Baron. 352p. (C). 1991. pap. text 12.95 (0-674-52186-2) HUP.

Legacy of Slabodka: The Life & Thought of Hagaon Rav Mardechai Shulman. Reuven Grossman. Tr. by Moshe Dombey from HEB. 192p. 1989. 13.95 (0-944070-11-6) Targum Pr.

Legacy of Solomon Asch: Essays in Cognition & Social Psychology. Ed. by Irvin Rock. 320p. 1990. text 69.95 (0-8058-0440-4) L Erlbaum Assocs.

Legacy of Sonya Kovalevskaya. Ed. by Linda Keen. LC 86-32032. (Contemporary Mathematics Ser.: Vol. 64). 297p. 1987. pap. 37.00 (0-8218-5067-9, CONM/64) Am Math.

***Legacy of Sovereign Joy: God's Triumphant Grace in the Lives of Augustine, Luther, & Calvin.** John Piper. (Swans Are Not Silent Ser.: Vol. 1). 176p. 2000. 17.99 (1-58134-173-3) Crossway Bks.

Legacy of St. Vladimir: Byzantium, Russia, America. Ed. by John Meyendorff et al. LC 90-32389. 324p. 1990. pap. 11.95 (0-88141-078-0) St Vladimirs.

Legacy of Steel. Mary H. Herbert. (DragonLance Bridges of Time Ser.: Vol. 2). 1998. pap. 5.99 (0-7869-1187-5, Pub. by TSR Inc) Random.

Legacy of Stewardship: The Ohio Department of Natural Resources, 1949-1989. Ed. by Charles C. King. 272p. (Orig.). 1990. pap. write for info. (0-931079-03-9) Ohio Nat Res.

***Legacy of Supranationalism.** Paul Close. LC 00-36899. 2000. write for info. (0-312-23524-0) St Martin.

***Legacy of Tamar: Courage & Faith in an African American Family.** Raye Springfield. LC 99-50585. (Illus.). 296p. 2000. pap. 17.50 (1-57233-078-3, Pub. by U of Tenn Pr); lib. bdg. 40.00 (1-57233-077-5, Pub. by U of Tenn Pr) U Ch Pr.

Legacy of Tethys. F. D. Por. (Monographiae Biologicae). (C). 1989. text 160.00 (0-7923-0189-7) Kluwer Academic.

Legacy of the Ancient Hebrews: Unveils the Truth of Black History & the Bible. Delaney E. Smith, Jr. (Illus.). 1998. pap. 19.95 (0-9646568-1-7) Truth in Pubng.

Legacy of the Ancients, Vol. 2. Ron Sarti. 448p. 1997. mass mkt. 5.99 (0-380-73025-1, Avon Bks) Morrow Avon.

Legacy of the Blues: Art & Lives of Twelve Great Bluesmen. SamuelB. Charters. LC 76-51809. (Roots of Jazz Ser.). (Illus.). 1977. 25.00 (0-306-70847-7); pap. 9.95 (0-306-80054-3) Da Capo.

Legacy of the Brass Plates of Laban: A Comparison of Biblical & Book of Mormon Isaiah Texts. H. Clay Gorton. 304p. 1994. 19.98 (0-88290-511-2, 1056) Horizon Utah.

Legacy of the Burger Court & the Schools, 1969-1986. H. C. Hudgins, Jr. & Richard S. Vacca. 143p. 1991. 20.00 (1-56534-026-4) Ed Law Assn.

Legacy of the Cat. Gloria Stephens. 144p. 1990. 29.95 (0-87701-728-X) Chronicle Bks.

***Legacy of the Cat.** rev. expanded ed. Gloria Stephens. (Illus.). 2000. pap. 22.95 (0-8118-2910-3) Chronicle Bks.

Legacy of the Cat: The Ultimate Illustrated Guide. Gloria Stephens. (Illus.). 1997. pap. 18.95 (0-8118-1661-3) Chronicle Bks.

Legacy of the Civil War. Robert Penn Warren. LC 97-47290. xvii, 109p. 1998. pap. 9.00 (0-8032-9801-3, Bison Books) U of Nebr Pr.

Legacy of the Constitution: An Assessment for the Third Century. William S. Livingston. (Symposia Ser.). 164p. 1987. pap. 12.00 (0-89940-421-9) LBJ Sch Pub Aff.

Legacy of the Cowbird. Betty S. Baird. LC 94-67722. 280p. 1995. 22.00 (1-886029-00-8) Spider Hill Pr.

Legacy of the DC-3. Henry M. Holden. (Illus.). 365p. 1997. pap. 29.95 (1-879630-39-7, Wind Canyon Bks) Wind Canyon.

***Legacy of the Dead: An Inspector Ian Rutledge Mystery.** Charles Todd. LC 00-36076. 320p. 2000. pap. 24.95 (0-553-80168-6) Bantam.

Legacy of the Dog: The Ultimate Illustrated Guide to Over 200 Breeds. Tetsu Yamazaki.Tr. of Sekai no inu Zukan. (Illus.). 344p. 1995. 45.00 (0-8118-1123-9); pap. 24.95 (0-8118-1069-0) Chronicle Bks.

Legacy of the 4th Armored Division. Turner Publishing Company Staff. LC 90-70159. (Illus.). 112p. 1990. 39.95 (0-938021-88-5) Turner Pub KY.

Legacy of the French Revolution. Ed. by Ralph C. Hancock & L. Gary Lambert. 328p. (Orig.). (C). 1996. pap. text 26.95 (0-8476-7842-3) Rowman.

Legacy of the French Revolution. Ed. by Ralph C. Hancock & L. Gary Lambert. 328p. (Orig.). (C). 1996. lib. bdg. 71.00 (0-8476-7841-5) Rowman.

Legacy of the Great Oklahoma Land Rush: A Photographic History of Hoffman Townsite & School in Okmulgee County. Mickey J. Martin. LC 93-72854. 489p. 1993. 88.00 (0-9638279-0-1) Fowble Pr.

Legacy of the Heart: The Spiritual Advantages of a Painful Childhood. Wayne Muller. 224p. 1992. pap. 20.00 (0-671-76119-6) S&S Trade.

Legacy of the Heart: The Spiritual Advantages of a Painful Childhood. Wayne Muller. 224p. 1993. per. 11.00 (0-671-79784-0) S&S Trade Pap.

Legacy of the Hollywood Empire. John W. Cones. (Hollywood Ser.). 335p. 1996. pap. 24.95 (1-890341-07-X) Rivas Canyon.

Legacy of the Holocaust: Psychohistorical Themes in the Second Generation. Robert M. Prince. LC 84-24036. (Research in Clinical Psychology Ser.: No. 12). 239p. reprint ed. pap. 74.10 (0-8357-1627-9, 207041100088) Bks Demand.

Legacy of the Holocaust: Psychohistorical Themes in the Second Generation. Robert M. Prince. LC 99-25641. 223p. 1999. reprint ed. pap. 25.00 (1-892746-26-3, 46263) Other Pr LLC.

Legacy of the Honorable Elijah Muhammad. H. Khalif Khalifah. 32p. (Orig.). 1988. pap. 3.95 (1-56411-108-3) Untd Bros & Sis.

Legacy of the Land: 250 Years of Agriculture in Carroll County, Maryland. Carol Lee. LC 82-83567. (Illus.). 177p. 1982. 6.00 (0-685-33351-5) Hist Soc Carroll.

Legacy of the Landscape: An Illustrated Guide to Hawaiian Archaeological Sites. Patrick V. Kirch. LC 95-41637. (Illus.). 1996. text 45.00 (0-8248-1816-4); pap. text 29.95 (0-8248-1739-7) UH Pr.

Legacy of the Meek. W. Basil Wehrle. 212p. 1997. pap. 10.95 (0-9659064-0-X) Schakett Bks.

***Legacy of the Mexican & Spanish-American Wars: Legal, Literacy, & Historical Perspectives.** Ed. by Gary D. Keller & Cordelia Candelaria. LC 99-58432. 126p. 2000. pap. 15.00 (0-927534-90-8, Pub. by Biling Rev-Pr) SPD-Small Pr Dist.

Legacy of the Middle Ages. Ed. by C. G. Crump & Ernest F. Jacob. (Legacy Ser.). (Illus.). 1938. 48.00 (0-19-821907-5) OUP.

Legacy of the Ming. Tr. by Peter Y. K. Lam & Yau Hok-wa. 143p. 1996. pap. 120.00 (962-7101-32-X, Pub. by Chinese Univ of Hong Kong) St Mut.

Legacy of the Mongol Empire. Ed. by D. O. Morgan. 320p. 1997. 85.00 (0-7007-0665-8, Pub. by Curzon Pr Ltd) Paul & Co Pubs.

Legacy of the 90th Bombardment Group: The Jolly Rogers. Wiley O. Woods. LC 94-60850. 144p. 1994. 49.95 (1-56311-151-9) Turner Pub KY.

Legacy of the Past. large type ed. Anne Mather. 316p. 1993. 27.99 (0-7505-0551-6, Pub. by Mgna Lrg Print) Ulverscroft.

***Legacy of the Priest.** Stephen P. Matava. LC 00-190300. 396p. 2000. 25.00 (0-7388-1721-X); pap. 18.00 (0-7388-1722-8) Xlibris Corp.

Legacy of the Purple Heart. 3rd ed. Turner Publishing Company Staff. LC 95-60322. 356p. 1996. 52.50 (1-56311-186-1) Turner Pub KY.

Legacy of the Revolution: The Story of the Valentine-Varian House. Lloyd Ultan. (Illus.). 130p. 1983. pap. 20.00 (0-941980-12-X) Bronx County.

Legacy of the Rose. Kasey Michaels. Ed. by Claire Zion. 448p. (Orig.). 1992. mass mkt. 5.99 (0-671-73180-7) PB.

Legacy of the Rose: The Story of Beauty & the Beast. Brian Kral. 1997. pap. 3.50 (1-57514-294-5, 1006) Encore Perform Pub.

***Legacy of the Scottish Harpers.** Robin Williamson. 104p. 1999. spiral bd. 24.95 incl. audio compact disk (0-7866-4453-2, 98142BCD) Mel Bay.

Legacy of the Somme: The Battle in Fact, Film & Fiction. Gerald Gliddon. LC 97-157642. (Illus.). 256p. 1996. 35.95 (0-7509-1160-3, Pub. by Sutton Pub Ltd) Intl Pubs Mktg.

Legacy of the Soviet Block. Ed. by Jane S. Zacek & Ilpyong J. Kim. LC 96-16351. (Illus.). 328p. 1997. 49.95 (0-8130-1475-1) U Press Fla.

Legacy of the Swamp Rat: Tennessee Quarterbacks Who Just Said No to Alabama. Chris Cawood. LC 94-76938. 224p. 1994. 15.95 (0-9642231-6-3) Magnolia Hill.

Legacy of the Sword. Jennifer Roberson. (Chronicles of the Cheysuli Ser.: Bk. III). (Orig.). 1986. mass mkt. 4.99 (0-88677-316-4, Pub. by DAW Bks) Penguin Putnam.

Legacy of the Tetons: Homesteading in Jackson Hole. Candy V. Moulton. LC 95-105717. 237p. (Orig.). 1994. pap. 15.95 (0-9634839-4-3) Tamarack Bks.

Legacy of the Tubingen School: The Relevance of Nineteenth-Century Theology for the Twenty-First Century. Ed. by Donald J. Dietrich & Michael J. Himes. LC 97-30950. 228p. 1997. pap. text 24.95 (0-8245-1700-8) Crossroad NY.

Legacy of the Vienna Circle: Modern Appraisals. Sahotra Sarkar. LC 95-50328. (Science & Philosophy in the Twentieth Century Ser.: Vol. 6). 400p. 1996. text 80.00 (0-8153-2267-4) Garland.

Legacy of the War Orphans: How We Lost World War II. Owen W. Dykema. 37p. 1998. pap. 9.95 (0-9660705-1-8) Dykema Pub Co.

Legacy of the West. David C. Hunt. LC 82-10109. (Illus.). 157p. (Orig.). 1982. 27.95 (0-936364-11-4); pap. 17.95 (0-936364-08-4) Joslyn Art.

Legacy of the 1956 Hungarian Revolution: 5 Participants 40 Years Later. Andras Fodor et al. Ed. by Peter Pastor. LC 96-79363. 46p. 1996. 8.00 (0-910539-07-3) Hungarian Alumni.

Legacy of Tiananmen: China in Disarray. James A. Miles. LC 95-52804. (China in Disarray Ser.). 408p. 1996. 37.50 (0-472-10731-3, 10731) U of Mich Pr.

Legacy of Tiananmen: China in Disarray. James A. Miles. 408p. (C). 1997. pap. 19.95 (0-472-08451-8, 08451) U of Mich Pr.

Legacy of Trust: Life after the Sudbury Valley School Experience. Daniel Greenberg & Mimsy Sadofsky. 332p. (Orig.). 1992. pap. 10.00 (1-888947-04-7) Sudbury Valley.

Legacy of Truth: Great Minds That Made Great Lives. 2nd ed. J. Kennedy Shultz. 160p. 1990. reprint ed. pap. 9.95 (0-87516-622-9) DeVorss.

***Legacy of Valor.** Jed L. Babbin. LC 99-80018. 320p. 2000. write for info. (1-57197-213-7, Pub. by Pentland Pr) Assoc Pubs Grp.

Legacy of Vengeance. John Armistead. 256p. 1994. 19.95 (0-7867-0059-9) Carroll & Graf.

Legacy of Vietnam: Veterans & Their Families, 2 vols. 1997. lib. bdg. 600.99 (0-8490-6161-X) Gordon Pr.

Legacy of Vietnam Veterans & Their Families: Survivors of War: Catalysts for Change. Ed. by Dennis K. Rhoades et al. LC 95-7814. 520p. (Orig.). 1995. write for info. (0-9647667-0-1); pap. 34.00 (0-9647667-1-X) Agent Orange.

Legacy of Vietnam Veterans & Their Families: Survivors of War: Catalysts for Change. Ed. by Dennis K. Rhoades et al. (Illus.). 520p. (Orig.). (C). 1996. pap. text 40.00 (0-7881-3255-5) DIANE Pub.

Legacy of Vietnam Veterans & Their Families: Survivors of War, Catalysts for Change, Papers from the 1994 National Symposium. Dennis K. Rhoades. 518p. 1995. per. 36.00 (0-16-048205-4) USGPO.

Legacy of Virtue: A Devotional for Mothers. Amy Nappa. LC 99-212484. 1999. 14.99 (1-57748-493-2) Barbour Pub.

Legacy of Wildness: The Photographs of Robert Glenn Ketchum. Pref. by Robert Redford. 120p. 1993. 76.00 (0-89381-498-9) Aperture.

Legacy of William Carey: A Model for the Transformation of a Culture. Vishal Mangalwadi & Ruth Mangalwadi. LC 99-25218. 160p. 1999. reprint ed. pap. 10.99 (1-58134-112-1) Crossway Bks.

***Legacy of William R. Plum: Civil War Telegrapher, Lawyer, & Horticulturist** Gerry R. Watts & Lombard Historical Society Staff. LC 99-71443. xii, 216p. 1999. write for info. (1-886372-04-7) Graphic Prodns Inc.

Legacy of William Schwartz: Group Practice As Shared Interaction. Ed. by Alex Gitterman & Lawrence Shulman. LC 85-17586. (Social Work with Groups Ser.: Vol. 8, No. 4). 120p. 1986. text 39.95 (0-86656-520-5) Haworth Pr.

Legacy of Wings: The Harold F. Pitcairn Story. 2nd rev. ed. Frank K. Smith. Tr. by Harry Plank. (Illus.). 371p. 1987. reprint ed. 12.95 (0-9618221-0-4) S Pitcairn.

***Legacy of Winnicott: Essays on Infant & Child Mental Health.** Ed. by Brett Kahr. 256p. 2000. pap. 31.95 (1-85575-236-0, Pub. by H Karnac Bks Ltd) Other Pr LLC.

Legacy of Winning: It Doesn't All Happen on Game Day. Phillip Fulmer & Gerald C. Sentell. LC 96-69656. (Illus.). 288p. 1996. 24.95 (1-883999-06-5) Pressmark Intl.

***Legacy of Wisdom: Great Thinkers & Journalism.** John C. Merrill. LC 99-462344. 200p. 2000. pap. 24.95 (0-8138-2040-5) Iowa St U Pr.

Legacy of Wisdom: The Egyptian Contribution to the Wisdom of Israel. Glendon E. Bryce. LC 74-4984. 336p. 1979. 38.50 (0-8387-1576-1) Bucknell U Pr.

Legacy of Women's Uplift in India: Contemporary Women Leaders in the Arya Samaj. J. E. Llewellyn. LC 98-5351. 1998. write for info. (0-7619-9252-9); pap. write for info. (0-7619-9253-7) Sage.

Legacy of Wood & Woodworking. Ed. by G. Lister Sutcliffe. (Modern Carpenter Joiner & Cabinet-Maker Ser.: Vol. 2). (Illus.). 128p. 1990. reprint ed. 24.95 (0-918678-56-0) Natl Hist Soc.

Legacy of Woodrow Wilson: American War Aims in World War I. David M. Esposito. LC 95-43729. 176p. 1996. 47.95 (0-275-95493-5, Praeger Pubs) Greenwood.

L

L

Legacy of Words: Texas Women's Stories, 1850-1920. Ed. by Ava E. Mills. LC 98-96325. (Illus.). viii, 174p. 1999. pap. 16.95 (0-9658789-2-9, 096587) Doss Bks.
Legacy on Stone: Rock Art of the Colorado Plateau & Four Corners Region. Sally J. Cole. LC 90-45715. (Illus.). 280p. (Orig.). 1990. pap. 15.95 (1-55566-074-6) Johnson Bks.
***Legacy or Love.** William D. Coughlan. 240p. 2000. pap. 15.00 (0-9678341-0-4) Coughlan & Assocs.
Legacy Plan, Protect & Preserve Your Estate. Ed. by Robert A. Esperti & Renno L. Peterson. LC 96-77472. xvi, 542p. 1996. 30.00 (0-922943-09-5, nn1-232bk) Esperti Petrsn.
Legacy Recorded: Martyrdom & Resistance. Ed. by Harvey Rosenfeld & Eli Zborowski. 368p. 1994. lib. bdg. 25.00 (0-9619503-0-7) Martyrdom & Resist Found.
Legacy Remembered: One Hundred Years of Medical Missions. Sophie M. Crane. LC 98-65983. (Illus.). 512p. 1998. 34.95 (1-57736-091-5) Providence Hse.
Legacy Series. 1995. pap. 15.00 incl. VHS (1-888361-05-0) Power Publns.
Legacy Through the Lens. Janet W. Foster. Ed. by Robert P. Guter. LC 86-50972. (Illus.). 171p. 1986. 29.95 (0-931661-00-5) Mendham Publ Lib.
***Legacy to Liberation: Politics & Culture of Revolutionary Asian/Pacific America.** Fred W. Ho. 2000. pap. text 22.95 (1-902593-24-3) AK Pr.
Legacy to the World: A Study of America's Political Ideas. Max J. Skidmore. XIII, 412p. (C). 1998. pap. text 35.95 (0-8204-3968-1) P Lang Pubng.
Legacy West: Reading, Vol. 2. Ed. by David B. Mock. LC 94-26316. 288p. (C). 1997. pap. text 48.00 (0-673-99000-1) Addson-Wesley Educ.
Legacy West, Vol. 1. Ed. by David B. Mock. LC 94-26316. 288p. (C). 1997. pap. text 49.00 (0-673-46999-9) Addson-Wesley Educ.
***Legacy Workbook: Teacher's Edition.** F. M. Avey. (Illus.). 50p. 2000. pap., teacher ed., wbk. ed. 34.95 (1-930758-61-8, Legacy Kids) Yeva Corp.
Legado de Raul Prebisch. Ed. by Enrique V. Iglesias. 208p. 1993. 14.50 (0-940602-62-8) IADB.
Legado, Poesias y Sonetos. Paulino S. Rodriguez. (SPA.). 144p. 1995. lib. bdg. write for info. (1-888598-01-8) P S Rodriguez.
Legal - The Code of Civil of North Carolina. Albion W. Tourgee. (Notable American Authors). 1999. reprint ed. lib. bdg. 125.00 (0-7812-9789-3) Rprt Serv.
Legal Abuse Syndrome. Karin Huffer. 234p. 1995. pap. 19.95 (0-9641786-0-5) Fulkort Pr.
Legal Accounting Principles & Applications. Douglas C. Michael. LC 97-9147. (Paralegal). 556p. 1997. text 36.50 (0-314-21136-5) West Pub.
***Legal Administrative Texts from the Reign of Nabonidus.** Paul-Alain Beaulieu. LC 99-88525. (Oriental Ser.: Vol. 19). (Illus.). 288p. 2000. 60.00 (0-300-05770-9) Yale U Pr.
Legal Adoption Guide: Safety Navigating the System. Colleen Alexander-Roberts. 208p. (Orig.). 1996. pap. 12.96 (0-87833-933-7) Taylor Pub.
Legal Advertising: The Illinois Experiment. ABA, Commission on Law & the Economy. 37p. 1985. pap. 12.50 (0-685-14368-6, 406-0008) Amer Bar Assn.
Legal Advocacy: Lawyers & Nonlawyers at Work. Herbert M. Kritzer. LC 98-19708. (Illus.). 288p. 1998. text 44.50 (0-472-10935-9, 10935) U of Mich Pr.
Legal Advocacy in the Roman World. J. A. Crook. 224p. 1995. text 52.50 (0-8014-3158-1) Cornell U Pr.
Legal Affairs: Essential Advice. Hertz. LC 97-41750. 283p. 1998. pap. 17.95 (0-8050-5224-0, Owl) H Holt & Co.
Legal Affairs Specialist. (Career Examination Ser.: C-3668). pap. 34.95 (0-8373-3668-6) Nat Learn.
Legal Aid - the New Framework. Duncan Matheson. 180p. 1988. pap. 34.00 (0-406-50295-1, UK, MICHIE) LEXIS Pub.
Legal Aid Board - Report on the Operation & Finance of Legal Aid Act 1988 for 1995-96. 130p. 1996. pap. 40.00 (0-10-277296-7, HM72967, Pub. by Statnry Office) Bernan Associates.
Legal Aid Clients with General Assistance Problems: A Study of Housing Conditions. R. K. Piper et al. 14p. (Orig.). 1984. pap. 1.50 (1-55719-077-1) U NE CPAR.
Legal Aid Handbook, Vol. 1. 1994. pap. text 20.00 (0-421-52730-7, Pub. by Sweet & Maxwll) Gaunt.
Legal Aid in Canada: From Charity to Public Policy. Dieter Hoehne. LC 88-12705. (Canadian Studies: Vol. 2). 388p. 1989. 99.95 (0-88946-198-8) E Mellen.
Legal Aid in the Criminal Courts. James L. Wilkins. LC 75-16176. (Canadian Studies in Criminology: No. 3). 166p. reprint ed. pap. 51.50 (0-608-16661-8, 202637400049) Bks Demand.
Legal Alchemy: The Use & Misuse of Science in the Law. David L. Faigman. LC 99-31292. 1999. pap. text 24.95 (0-7167-3143-6) W H Freeman.
***Legal Alchemy: The Use & Misuse of Science in the Law.** David L. Faigman. 2000. pap. 14.95 (0-7167-4169-5) W H Freeman.
Legal Analysis: The Fundamental Skill. David Romantz & Kathy Vinson. LC 98-26063. 160p. 1998. pap. 15.00. (0-89089-905-3) Carolina Acad Pr.
Legal Analysis & Writing: 1997 Edition. Robin Wellford. LC 97-61095. 208p. 1997. pap. text. write for info. (1-55834-577-9, 12915-10, MICHIE) LEXIS Pub.
Legal Analysis & Writing for Paralegals. William Putnam. LC 97-10303. 384p. (C). 1997. mass mkt. 45.95 (0-314-12830-1) West Pub.
Legal Analysis & Writing for Paralegals, IML. Putman. 160p. 1997. teacher ed. 17.95 (0-314-13022-5) Delmar.
Legal Analysis of the Free Trade Agreement of 1975 Between the European Community & the State of Israel. Daphna Kapeliuk-Klinger. (Law Ser.). 36p. (Orig.). 1995. pap. 16.50 (90-6186-688-X, Pub. by Leuven Univ) Coronet Bks.
Legal & Administrative Documents of the Time of Hammurabi & the Samsuiluna (Mainly from Lagaba) W. F. Leemans. vi, 120p. 1960. pap. text 28.00 (0-614-04002-7, Pub. by Netherlands Inst) Eisenbrauns.
Legal & Administrative Texts in the Reign of Samsu-Iluna. Samuel I. Feigin. LC 78-4032. (Yale Oriental Series, Babylonian Texts: Vol. 12). (Illus.). 83p. 1979. 52.50 (0-300-01963-7) Yale U Pr.
Legal & Business Aspects of the Advertising Industry, 1989. 490p. 1989. 17.50 (0-685-69456-9) PLI.
***Legal & Business Strategies for Year 2000 & Beyond.** Holland & Knight, LLP Staff. 650p. 1999. ring bd. 248.00 (1-56726-087-X) Mgmt Concepts.
Legal & Commercial Dictionary. L. Mastellone. (ENG & ITA.). 173p. 1980. write for info. (0-8288-0397-8, F 22010) Fr & Eur.
Legal & Commercial Dictionary. M. Mitra. (C). 1990. 180.00 (0-89771-130-0) St Mut.
Legal & Constitutional Phases of the WRA Program see U. S. War Relocation Authority
Legal & Contractual Limitations to Working-Time in the European Community Member States. Ed. by Roger Blanpain & E. Kohler. 466p. 1988. 84.00 (90-6544-364-9) Kluwer Law Intl.
Legal & Contractual Procedures for Architects. 4th ed. Bob Greenstreet & David Chappell. LC 93-5253. (Illus.). 110p. 1995. pap. text 47.95 (0-7506-1617-2) Buttrwrth-Heinemann.
Legal & Economic Aspects of Gray Market Goods. Seth E. Lipner. LC 90-30008. 240p. 1990. 65.00 (0-89930-466-4, LLC/, Quorum Bks) Greenwood.
Legal & Economic Basis of International Trade. Grady Miller. LC 95-44348. 256p. 1996. 67.95 (0-89930-918-6, Quorum Bks) Greenwood.
Legal & Economic Dictionary see Dictionnaire Juridique et Economique Doucet
Legal & Economic Records from the Kingdom of Larsa. W. F. Leemans. viii, 103p. 1954. pap. text 28.00 (0-614-03986-X, Pub. by Netherlands Inst) Eisenbrauns.
Legal & Economic Regulations in Marketing: A Practitioner's Guide. Ray O. Werner. LC 88-39909. 204p. 1989. 49.95 (0-89930-287-4, WLL, Quorum Bks) Greenwood.
Legal & Ethical Aspects of Fetal Tissue Transplantation. Arthur R. Bauer. LC 93-42908. (Medical Intelligence Unit Ser.). 128p. 1993. 99.00 (1-57059-021-4) Landes Bioscience.
Legal & Ethical Aspects of HIV-Related Research. Sana Loue. LC 95-34011. (Illus.). 214p. 1995. 47.00 (0-306-45055-0, Plenum Trade) Perseus Pubng.
***Legal & Ethical Aspects of Organ Transplantation.** David Price. 350p. (C). 2000. text Price not set. (0-521-65164-6) Cambridge U Pr.
Legal & Ethical Bases for Educational Leadership. M. Donald Thomas & E. E. Davis. LC 98-65074. (Fastback Ser.: No. 426). 51p. 1998. pap. 3.00 (0-87367-626-2, FB#426) Phi Delta Kappa.
***Legal & Ethical Considerations for Dental Hygienists & Assistants.** Judith A. Davison. (Illus.). 320p. 1999. text. write for info. (1-55664-422-1) Mosby Inc.
Legal & Ethical Dimensions for Mental Health Professionals. Patrick B. Malley. LC 98-31545. 367p. 1999. pap. 29.95 (1-56032-687-5) Hemisp Pub.
Legal & Ethical Environment of Business. Edwin W. Tucker & Jan W. Henkel. (Illus.). 728p. (C). 1998. reprint ed. text 25.00 (0-7881-5154-1) DIANE Pub.
***Legal & Ethical Issues.** Killion & Dempsi. (Quick Look Nursing Ser.). 2000. 18.95 (1-889325-48-1, Pub. by Fence Crk Pubng) Blackwell Sci.
Legal & Ethical Issues in Acquisitions. Ed. by Katina Strauch & Bruce Strauch. LC 90-35841. (Acquisitions Librarian Ser.: Vol. 3). 146p. 1990. text 39.95 (1-56024-007-5) Haworth Pr.
Legal & Ethical Issues in Health. Aiken. 1999. pap. text. write for info. (0-7216-6525-X, W B Saunders Co) Harcrt Hlth Sci Grp.
Legal & Ethical Issues in Physical Therapy. Dolly Swisher & Carol Krueger-Brophy. LC 97-23859. 272p. 1998. text 40.00 (0-7506-9788-1) Buttrwrth-Heinemann.
Legal & Ethical Issues in Presentation/Desktop Publishing. Robin B. McAllister. 1997. pap. 12.95 (0-8273-7922-6) Delmar.
Legal & Ethical Issues in Surreptitious Recording. Thomas E. Murray et al. LC 90-26320. (Publications of American Dialect Society: No. 76). 88p. 1992. pap. text 11.00 (0-8173-0540-8) U of Ala Pr.
Legal & Ethical Issues in the Management of the Dementing Elderly, Vol. 3. Mary Gilhooley. (Medico-Legal Issues Ser.). 1994. text 69.95 (1-85521-027-4, Pub. by Dartmth Pub) Ashgate Pub Co.
Legal & Ethical Perspectives in Healthcare: An Integrated Approach. Raymond S. Edge. LC 97-6627. (Allied Health Ser.). 288p. (C). 1997. mass mkt. 34.95 (0-8273-7684-7) Delmar.
Legal & Ethical Text for Telemarketers. Franklin S. Forbes. 1991. pap. text. write for info. (0-9632666-0-8) Intl Ctr Telecomm.
Legal & Financial Issues on Alzheimer[0012]s Disease: An Annotated List of Resources. 33p. pap. text 20.00 (0-7881-3861-8) DIANE Pub.
Legal & Healthcare Ethics for the Elderly. George P. Smith, 2nd. 207p. 1996. 69.95 (1-56032-452-X); pap. 29.95 (1-56032-453-8) Hemisp Pub.
Legal & Historical Commentary to Cicero's Oratio Pro C. Rabirio perduellionisreo. W. B. Tyrrell. 152p. 1978. pap. text 30.00 (0-317-54480-2, Pub. by AM Hakkert) Coronet Bks.
Legal & Institutional Aspects of the International Monetary System: Selected Essays, 2 Vols. Joseph Gold. Ed. by Jane B. Evensen & Jai K. Oh. xx, 633p. 1984. 50.00 (0-685-02616-7) Intl Monetary.
Legal & Institutional Aspects of the International Monetary System: Selected Essays, 2 Vols., Vol. 1. Joseph Gold. Ed. by Jane B. Evensen & Jai K. Oh. xx, 633p. 1979. 17.50 (0-939934-13-2) Intl Monetary.
Legal & Institutional Aspects of the International Monetary System: Selected Essays, Vol. 1. Joseph Gold. Ed. by Jane B. Evensen & Jai K. Oh. LC 79-10168. 653p. reprint ed. pap. 200.00 (0-608-13766-9, 202060500018) Bks Demand.
Legal & Institutional Aspects of the International Monetary System: Selected Essays, 2 Vols., Vol. 2. Joseph Gold. Ed. by Jane B. Evensen & Jai K. Oh. xviii, 947p. 1984. 40.00 (0-939934-34-5) Intl Monetary.
Legal & Institutional Aspects of the International Monetary System: Selected Essays, Vol. 2. Joseph Gold. LC 79-10168. 965p. reprint ed. pap. 180.00 (0-608-12346-3, 2024271) Bks Demand.
Legal & Institutional Factors Affecting the Implementation of the International Drinking Water Supply & Sanitation Decade (IDWSSD), No. 23. (Natural Resources-Water Ser.). 121p. 1988. 15.50 (92-1-104305-0, E.88.II.A.21) UN.
Legal & Judicial History of New York, 3 vols., Set. Alden Chester. LC 83-82570. 1983. reprint ed. 140.00 (0-89941-297-1, 303000) W S Hein.
***Legal & Justice Studies Workbook.** Scott Beattie. 151p. 1999. pap. 25.00 (1-86287-319-4, Pub. by Federation Pr) Gaunt.
Legal & Legislative Information Processing. Ed. by Beth K. Eres. LC 79-7063. (Illus.). 299p. 1980. lib. bdg. 42.95 (0-313-21343-7, ERL/, Greenwood Pr) Greenwood.
Legal & Management Dictionary: Fachwoerterbuch fur Recht und Verwaltung. 2nd ed. Crescencio Antolinez Quijano. (GER & SPA.). 427p. 1983. 150.00 (0-8288-0979-8, M7398) Fr & Eur.
Legal & Medical Liability in Health Sciences: Index of New Information & Research Bible. Roy R. Zimmerman. 180p. 1994. 47.50 (0-7883-0098-9); pap. 44.50 (0-7883-0099-7) ABBE Pubs Assn.
Legal & Moral Aspects of International Trade: Freedom & Trade, Vol. 3. Asif H. Qureshi et al. LC 97-30853. 272p. (C). 1998. 85.00 (0-415-15526-6) Routledge.
Legal & Paralegal Services on Your Home-Based PC: Entrepreneurial PC Series. Rick Benzel & Katherine Sheehy-Hussey. LC 93-48742. 1994. pap. 16.95 (0-07-005109-7, Windcrest) TAB Bks.
***Legal & Political Interpretation of Article 215 of the Treaty of Rome: The Individual Strikes Back.** Constantin Stefanou & Helen Xanthaki. LC 99-68585. 236p. 2000. 69.95 (1-84014-428-9, Pub. by Ashgate Pub) Ashgate Pub Co.
Legal & Political Interpretation of Articles 224 & 225 of the Treaty of Rome: The Former Yugoslav Republic of Macedonia. Constantin Stefanou & Helen Xanthaki. LC 97-7847. 160p. 1997. text 82.95 (1-85521-894-1, Pub. by Ashgate Pub) Ashgate Pub Co.
Legal & Political Obligation: Classic & Contemporary Texts & Commentary. R. George Wright. 298p. (Orig.). (C). 1992. pap. text 27.50 (0-8191-8596-5); lib. bdg. 56.00 (0-8191-8595-7) U Pr of Amer.
Legal & Political Structure of an Islamic State: Implications for Iran & Pakistan. Ayatollah Y. Noori. 144p. 1987. 60.00 (0-946706-31-X, Pub. by Royston Ltd) St Mut.
Legal & Practical Aspects of Doing Business in the Soviet Republics. (Commercial Law & Practice Ser.). 494p. 1992. pap. text 70.00 (0-685-56865-2, A4-4364) PLI.
Legal & Practical Guide to the Use of the ECU. Ed. by ECU Institute Staff. LC 95-40686. 1995. 427.50 (90-411-0859-9) Kluwer Law Intl.
Legal & Procedural Application of Mobile Videotaping to Criminal Interdiction Patrol Jim Kuboviak. LC 98-148199. 1997. write for info. (1-884566-28-6) Inst Police Tech.
Legal & Regulatory Affairs Manual. Ed. by Ted Nelson et al. 1982. pap. 15.00 (0-686-37426-6) Coun NY Law.
***Legal & Regulatory Enviornment.** 2nd ed. Simon & Schuster Staff. (C). 2000. write for info. (0-13-013739-1) S&S Trade.
***Legal & Regulatory Environment: Contemporary Perspectives in Business.** 2nd ed. Henry R. Cheeseman. LC 99-24455. (Illus.). 692p. 1999. text 94.00 incl. cd-rom, audio compact disk (0-13-012954-2) P-H.
Legal & Regulatory Environment of Business. 4th ed. Jennings. LC 96-9283. (LA - Business Law Ser.). 1996. 61.00 (0-538-85441-3) S-W Pub.
Legal & Regulatory Environment of Business. 4th ed. Jennings. (LA - Business Law Ser.). 1996. student ed. 20.00 (0-538-86034-0) S-W Pub.
Legal & Regulatory Environment of Business. 10th ed. Robert N. Corley & Lee O. Reed. (C). 1995. pap., student ed. 27.50 (0-07-013390-5) McGraw.
Legal & Regulatory Environment of Business. 10th rev. ed. Robert N. Corley et al. LC 95-11279. 752p. (C). 1995. 84.37 (0-07-013337-9) McGraw.
Legal & Regulatory Environment of Business. 11th ed. Robert N. Corley. LC 98-20992. 572p. 1998. 86.25 (0-07-365429-9) McGraw.
Legal & Regulatory Environment of Business: Case Brief. 10th ed. Robert N. Corley & Lee O. Reed. 1995. pap. text. write for info. (0-07-013340-9) McGraw.
Legal & Regulatory Environment Today: Changing Perspectives for Business. Roger L. Miller & Frank B. Cross. LC 92-18824. 650p. (C). 1993. text 68.50 (0-314-01046-7) West Pub.
Legal & Regulatory Issues in International Aviation. R. I. Abeyratne. LC 95-37807. 1996. 125.00 (1-57105-010-8) Transnatl Pubs.
Legal & Scientific Uncertainties of Weather Modification: Proceeding of a Symposium Convened at Duke University, March 11-12, 1976, by the National Conference of Lawyers & Scientists. Ed. by William A. Thomas. LC 77-82058. 163p. reprint ed. pap. 50.60 (0-608-15260-9, 205220600060) Bks Demand.
Legal & Social Environment of Business. 4th ed. Susan E. Grady. (C). 1994. pap. text, student ed. 24.37 (0-07-070008-7) McGraw.
Legal & Social Environment of Business. 4th ed. Douglas Whitman & John W. Gergacz. LC 93-31671. (C). 1994. text 67.00 (0-07-070005-2) McGraw.
Legal & Tax Guide. Lefebvre. 1992. pap. text 102.50 (90-6544-624-9) Kluwer Academic.
Legal Answer Book. Bruce R. Hopkins. LC 95-53194. (Nonprofit Law, Finance, & Management Ser.). 320p. 1996. pap. 79.95 (0-471-10606-2) Wiley.
Legal Answer Book for Managed Care. Aspen Health Law Center Staff. 368p. 1995. 70.00 (0-8342-0700-1) Aspen Pub.
Legal Anthropology. Norbert Rouland. Tr. by Philippe G. Planel from FRE. 364p. 1995. 45.00 (0-8047-1931-4) Stanford U Pr.
Legal Antiquities: A Collection of Essays upon Ancient Laws & Customs. Edward J. White. 349p. 1986. reprint ed. 42.50 (0-8377-2730-8, Rothman) W S Hein.
Legal Approach to Verification in Disarmament or Arms Limitation. (United Nations Institute for Disarmament Research (UNIDIR) Publications). 71p. 1988. 15.00 (92-9045-029-0, EGV.88.0.5) UN.
Legal Arguments: 1993 Edition. James Gardner. 168p. 1993. pap. text 14.00 (1-55834-129-3, 11495-10, MICHIE) LEXIS Pub.
Legal Aspect of Money. 5th ed. F. A. Mann. 662p. 1992. text 195.00 (0-19-825650-7) OUP.
Legal Aspects of Agriculture in the European Community. John A. Usher. (Oxford European Community Law Ser.). 206p. 1988. text 55.00 (0-19-825565-9) OUP.
Legal Aspects of AIDS. Donald H. Hermann & William P. Schurgin. LC 90-19718. (Civil Rights Ser.). 1991. ring bd. 130.00 (0-685-59811-X) West Group.
Legal Aspects of Anaesthesia. Ed. by J. F. Crul. (Developments in Critical Care, Medicine, & Anesthesiology Ser.). 146p. (C). 1989. lib. bdg. 80.00 (0-7923-0393-8) Kluwer Academic.
Legal Aspects of Architecture, Engineering & the Construction Process. 5th ed. Justin Sweet. Ed. by Hannan. LC 93-34741. 889p. (C). 1994. mass mkt. 70.75 (0-314-02706-8) West Pub.
***Legal Aspects of Architecture, Engineering & the Construction Process.** 6th ed. Justin Sweet. LC 99-28878. 996p. 2000. 104.95 (0-534-95323-9) Brooks-Cole.
***Legal Aspects of Bank Insolvency: A Comparative Analysis of Western Europe, the United States & Canada.** Eva H. G. Hupkes. LC 00-33058. (Studies in Comparative Corporate & Financial Law). 2000. write for info. (90-411-9769-9) Kluwer Law Intl.
Legal Aspects of Building Code Enforcement in North Carolina. 2nd ed. Phillip P. Green, Jr. 188p. (C). 1987. 13.00 (1-56011-094-5) Institute Government.
Legal Aspects of California Real Estate. 3rd ed. Louis B. Hansotte. LC 95-44354. 494p. (C). 1995. 39.20 (0-13-180266-6) P-H.
Legal Aspects of Child Abuse. Elizabeth Butler-Sloss & A. E. Levy. (Waterlow Practitioner's Library). 256p. 1991. 40.01 (0-08-036906-5) Macmillan.
Legal Aspects of Child Health Care. J. Hendrick. (Illus.). 224p. (Orig.). 1996. pap. 47.75 (1-56593-340-0, 0670) Singular Publishing.
Legal Aspects of Code Administration. 1986. 25.00 (1-884590-12-8, 230S00) Intl Conf Bldg Off.
Legal Aspects of Collecting in Health Care. Zimmerman & Associates Staff. 48p. 1996. 55.00 (0-8342-0690-0) Aspen Pub.
Legal Aspects of Complementary Therapy Practice: A Guide for Health Care Professionals. Bridgit Dimond. LC 98-20834. (C). 1998. text. write for info. (0-443-05615-3) Church.
Legal Aspects of Corporate Finance. Richard T. McDermott. 1995. write for info. (0-8205-2917-6) Bender.
***Legal Aspects of Corporate Finance.** 3rd ed. Richard T. McDermott. LC 99-462254. (Analysis & Skills Ser.). 2000. write for info. (0-8205-4372-1) Bender.
Legal Aspects of Corrections Management. Clair A. Cripe. LC 97-1322. 350p. 49.00 (0-8342-0866-0, 8660) Aspen Pub.
Legal Aspects of Documenting Patient Care. Ronald W. Scott. LC 93-34851. 258p. 1994. 59.00 (0-8342-0549-1) Aspen Pub.
***Legal Aspects of Documenting Patient Care.** 2nd ed. Ronald W. Scott. LC 99-55592. 240p. 2000. 65.00 (0-8342-1630-2) Aspen Pub.
Legal Aspects of Doing Business in Africa. Ed. by Dennis Campbell. (International Business Ser.: Vol. 4). 1992. 146.00 (90-6544-932-9) Kluwer Law Intl.
Legal Aspects of Doing Business in Asia & the Pacific. Ed. by Dennis Campbell. (International Business Ser.: Vol. 3). 1992. ring bd. 203.00 (90-6544-982-5) Kluwer Law Intl.
Legal Aspects of Doing Business in Europe. Ed. by Dennis Campbell. (International Business Ser.: Vol. 1). 1992. ring bd. 260.00 (90-6544-970-1) Kluwer Law Intl.
Legal Aspects of Doing Business in Latin America. Ed. by Dennis Campbell. (International Business Ser.: Vol. 2). 1992. 212.00 (90-6544-930-2) Kluwer Law Intl.
Legal Aspects of Doing Business in North America & Canada, Set. Ed. by Dennis Campbell. (International Business Ser.: Vols. 6 & 7). 1992. ring bd. 206.00 (90-6544-999-X) Kluwer Law Intl.
Legal Aspects of Doing Business in Singapore. Toh See Kiat. Ed. by George T. Shenoy. LC 95-39460. 1996. write for info. (0-201-88911-0) Addison-Wesley.

An Asterisk (*) at the beginning of an entry indicates that the title is appearing for the first time.

Legal Aspects of Doing Business in the Middle East. Ed. by Dennis Campbell. LC 92-9683. (International Business Ser.: Vol. 5). 1992. 146.00 (*90-6544-917-5*) Kluwer Law Intl.

Legal Aspects of Drug Control & Treatment of Drug-Dependent Persons Within the European Community. Syamal Chatterjee. (European Community Law Ser.). 240p. (C). 1995. text 85.00 (*0-485-70008-5*, Pub. by Athlone Pr) Humanities.

Legal Aspects of Emergency Medical Services. Bruce M. Cohn & Alan J. Azzara. LC 98-9780. (Illus.). 208p. (C). 1998. pap. text 18.00 (*0-7216-7014-8*, W B Saunders Co) Harcrt Hlth Sci Grp.

Legal Aspects of Engineering. 5th ed. Richard C. Vaughn-Borgman. 480p. 1995. pap., per. 42.95 (*0-8403-5257-3*) Kendall-Hunt.

Legal Aspects of Engineering. 6th ed. Richard Vaughn. LC 98-75481. 416p. 1999. per. 47.95 (*0-7872-5641-2*, 41564101) Kendall-Hunt.

Legal Aspects of European Space Policy. Hans W. Micklitz & Norbert Reich. 151p. 1989. pap. 36.00 (*3-7890-1875-9*, Pub. by Nomos Verlags) Intl Bk Import.

Legal Aspects of Exporting, an Introduction. 275p. 1984. pap. text 10.00 (*1-56986-207-9*) Federal Bar.

Legal Aspects of Foreign Direct Investment. Alfred Escher & Daniel D. Bradlow. LC 99-27524. 1999. 180.00 (*90-411-1214-6*) Kluwer Law Intl.

Legal Aspects of Foreign Investment in the Socialist Republic of Vietnam. Anne C. Schot. LC 95-51309. 1996. 163.00 (*90-411-0905-6*) Kluwer Law Intl.

Legal Aspects of Geology. Ronald W. Tank. LC 83-2246. 596p. 1983. 85.00 (*0-306-41159-8*, Plenum Trade); pap. 45.00 (*0-306-41215-2*, Plenum Trade) Perseus Pubng.

Legal Aspects of Global Information Infrastructure. Brotman. Date not set. write for info. (*90-411-0965-X*) Kluwer Law Intl.

***Legal Aspects of Globalisation: Conflicts of Laws, Internet, Capital Markets & Insolvency in a Global Economy.** Ed. by Jurgen Basedow & Toshiyuki Kono. 244p. 2000. text 66.25 (*90-411-1332-0*) Kluwer Law Intl.

Legal Aspects of Health Care. Olf. 1995. pap. text 53.00 (*0-443-05359-6*, W B Saunders Co) Harcrt Hlth Sci Grp.

Legal Aspects of Health Care Administration. 6th ed. George D. Pozgar & Nina S. Pozgar. 768p. 1996. 50.00 (*0-8342-0741-9*, 20741) Aspen Pub.

Legal Aspects of Health Care Administration. 7th ed. George D. Pozgar. teacher ed. write for info. (*0-8342-1648-5*, 16485) Aspen Pub.

Legal Aspects of Health Care Administration. 7th ed. George D. Pozgar. LC 98-39361. 600p. 1998. 50.00 (*0-8342-1197-1*, 11971) Aspen Pub.

Legal Aspects of Health Care for the Elderly: An Annotated Bibliography, 7. Compiled by Marshall B. Kapp. LC 88-15428. (Bibliographies & Indexes in Gerontology Ser.: No. 7). 174p. 1988. lib. bdg. 62.95 (*0-313-26159-8*, KLG/, Greenwood Pr) Greenwood.

Legal Aspects of Health Information Management. Dana C. McWay. LC 96-8394. (Nursing Education Ser.). 300p. (C). 1996. mass mkt. 49.95 (*0-8273-5576-9*) Delmar.

Legal Aspects of Health Policy: Issues & Trends. Ed. by Ruth Roemer & George McKray. LC 79-8583. (Illus.). 473p. 1980. lib. bdg. 59.95 (*0-313-21430-1*, RIH/, Greenwood Pr) Greenwood.

***Legal Aspects of High Voltage Direct Current (HVDC) Cables.** Rainer Lagoni. 120p. 1999. pap. 32.95 (*3-8258-3888-9*, Pub. by CE24) Transaction Pubs.

Legal Aspects of Home Health Care. William D. Cabin & James C. Pyles. LC 87-28974. 1987. write for info. (*0-87189-897-7*) Aspen Pub.

Legal Aspects of Horse Farm Operations. 2nd ed. James H. Newberry, Jr. (Illus.). vii, 173p. 1995. pap. 43.00 (*1-58757-006-8*, HM019) Univ of KY.

Legal Aspects of Hospitality Management Student Manual. 2nd ed. Educational Foundation of the National Restaurant. 96p. (Orig.). 1993. boxed set. write for info. (*0-915452-74-X*) Educ Found.

Legal Aspects of Hotel, Motel, & Restaurant Operation. Nathan Kalt. LC 78-142504. 1971. write for info. (*0-672-96089-3*); teacher ed. write for info. (*0-672-96091-5*); student ed. write for info. (*0-672-96090-7*) Macmillan.

Legal Aspects of Implementing International Telecommunication Links: Institutions, Regulations & Instruments. Jan M. Smits. (Utrecht Studies in Air & Space Law). 260p. (C). 1991. lib. bdg. 114.00 (*0-7923-1432-8*) Kluwer Academic.

Legal Aspects of Installment Credit see Installment Credit Series

Legal Aspects of Integration in the European Union. Emiliou. 1997. write for info. (*90-411-0689-8*) Kluwer Law Intl.

Legal Aspects of International Art Trade: Aspects Juridiques Du Commerce International De l'Art. Ed. by Martine Briat et al. LC 93-32026. (International Sales of Works of Art - la Vente Internationale d'Oeuvres d'Art Ser.: Vol. 4). 1993. 109.00 (*90-6544-691-5*) Kluwer Law Intl.

Legal Aspects of International Drug Control. S. K. Chatterjee. 612p. 1981. 117.00 (*90-286-2091-5*) Kluwer Academic.

Legal Aspects of International Drug Control. S. K. Chatterjee. 612p. 1981. lib. bdg. 286.50 (*90-247-2556-9*) Kluwer Academic.

Legal Aspects of International Investment. Ed. by Stephen Gorove. (L. Q. C. Lamar Society of International Law, University of Mississippi Law Center Monograph Ser.: No. 1). viii, 79p. 1977. pap. 25.00 (*0-8377-0607-6*, Rothman) W S Hein.

Legal Aspects of International Sourcing, No. A32. 500p. 1986. ring bd. 115.00 (*0-929576-09-8*) Busn Laws Inc.

Legal Aspects of International Terrorism. Ed. by Studies & Research in International Law & Internat. (C). 1989. pap. text 35.00 (*0-7923-0214-1*) Kluwer Academic.

Legal Aspects of International Terrorism: Summary Report of an International Conference, No. 19. John F. Murphy. (Studies in Transnational Legal Policy). 80p. 1980. 4.00 (*0-318-13186-2*) Am Soc Intl Law.

Legal Aspects of International Trade in Art: Les Aspects Juridiques du Commerce International de l'Art. Martine Briat et al. LC 96-36288. (ENG & FRE.). 1996. pap. 150.00 (*90-411-0295-7*) Kluwer Law Intl.

Legal Aspects of Investment & Trade with the Republic of China, No. 1. Ed. by John T. McDermott. 94p. 1991. 6.00 (*0-925153-13-3*, 102) Occasional Papers.

Legal Aspects of Managing Technology. Lee B. Burgunder. LC 94-37946. (Illus.). 448p. (C). 1994. mass mkt. 60.95 (*0-538-82664-9*) S-W Pub.

Legal Aspects of Medical Practice. 5th ed. Bernard Knight. (Illus.). 386p. 1992. pap. text 34.00 (*0-443-04568-2*) Church.

Legal Aspects of Medicare & Medicaid Reimbursement: Payment for Hospital & Physician Services. Ed. by Terry S. Coleman. 199p. 1990. 35.00 (*0-918945-05-4*) Am Hlth Lawyers.

Legal Aspects of Medicare & Medicaid Reimbursement: Payment for Hospital & Physician Services. Terry S. Coleman. Ed. by Susan K. Chambers. LC 90-61619. (NHLA Focus Ser.). 216p. 1990. pap. 45.00 (*0-918945-06-2*) Am Hlth Lawyers.

Legal Aspects of Medicare & Medicaid Reimbursement: Payment for Hospital & Physician Services; Supplement RBRVS & the New Medicare Physician Fee Schedule. Ed. by Terry S. Coleman. 44p. 1990. 35.00 (*0-918945-13-5*) Am Hlth Lawyers.

Legal Aspects of Medicine. Ed. by J. R. Vevaina et al. 330p. 1989. 135.00 (*0-387-96831-8*) Spr-Verlag.

Legal Aspects of Midwifery Workbook. Dimond & Walters. LC 97-181671. 80p. 1997. pap. text, wbk. ed. 32.00 (*1-898507-43-0*) Buttrwrth-Heinemann.

Legal Aspects of Nonpublic Schools: A Casebook. Lyndon G. Gurst & Charles J. Russo. LC 93-71089. 484p. (C). 1993. text 39.99 (*0-943872-72-3*) Andrews Univ Pr.

Legal Aspects of Nuclear Regulatory Commission's Provisional Policy Statement on GESMO. see Plutonium Recycle: Reports of 3 Contract Studies

Legal Aspects of Occupational Therapy. Bridgit C. Dimond. LC 96-9284. (Illus.). 400p. (Orig.). 1997. pap. text 34.95 (*0-632-04074-2*) Blackwell Sci.

Legal Aspects of Optometry. John G. Classe. (Illus.). 764p. 1989. text 95.00 (*0-409-95043-2*) Buttrwrth-Heinemann.

***Legal Aspects of Optometry.** 2nd ed. John G. Classe. (Illus.). 764p. 2000. 95.00 (*0-7506-7265-X*) Buttrwrth-Heinemann.

***Legal Aspects of Personal Fitness Training.** 2nd ed. Brian E. Koeberle. LC 97-75494. 186p. (Orig.). 1998. pap. 39.95 (*0-944183-24-7*) PRC Pub.

***Legal Aspects of Physiotherapy.** Bridgit Dimond. LC 99-89275. 2000. pap. write for info. (*0-632-05108-6*) Blackwell Sci.

Legal Aspects of Police Supervision. Isaac T. Avery & Mary Easley. LC 97-65224. 150p. (C). 1997. pap. 24.95 (*0-942728-80-7*) Copperhouse.

Legal Aspects of Police Supervision: Legal Resource Book. Isaac T. Avery & Mary Easley. LC 97-65244. 206p. (C). 1997. pap. 24.95 (*0-942728-81-5*) Copperhouse.

Legal Aspects of Preventive, Rehabilitative & Recreational Exercise Programs. 3rd ed. David L. Herbert & William G. Herbert. 384p. 1993. reprint ed. pap. 39.95 (*0-944183-17-4*) PRC Pub.

Legal Aspects of Privatisation: (Proceedings of the 21st Colloquy on European Law, Budapest, 1991) 1993. 21.00 (*92-871-2198-2*, Pub. by Council of Europe) Manhattan Pub Co.

Legal Aspects of Product Liability. (C). 1994. write for info. (*0-8087-5185-9*) Pearson Custom.

Legal Aspects of Real Property Investment in the Asia-Pacific Region. LC 96-945640. xvi, 168p. 1995. pap. write for info. (*0-409-99753-6*, MICHIE) LEXIS Pub.

Legal Aspects of Recreational Marina Operations in Florida. Richard G. Hamann & Bram D. Canter. iv, 92p. 1982. write for info. (*0-318-58258-9*) U Fla Law.

Legal Aspects of Special Education & Pupil. Julie K. Underwood & Julie F. Mead. LC 94-39877. 384p. 1995. 67.00 (*0-205-13777-6*) Allyn.

Legal Aspects of Sport Entrepreneurships. Dianne B. O'Brien & James O. Overby. 468p. (C). 1997. text 46.00 (*1-885693-08-7*) Fit Info Tech.

Legal Aspects of Sports Medicine. 2nd ed. David L. Herbert & William G. Herbert. LC 94-92196. 280p. 1995. pap. 39.95 (*0-944183-18-2*) PRC Pub.

***Legal Aspects of Stallion Management & Syndication.** Laura A. D'Angelo & Robert M. Beck, Jr. 194p. 2000. pap. 50.00 (*1-58757-033-5*, HM038) Univ of KY.

Legal Aspects of the Civil Rights Movement. Ed. by Donald B. King & Charles W. Quick. LC 64-25183. 457p. reprint ed. pap. 141.70 (*0-7837-3825-0*, 204364500010) Bks Demand.

Legal Aspects of the Conservation of Wetlands (EPLP 25) Jean Untermaier. Ed. by Hugh Synge. 212p. 1991. 20.00 (*2-8317-0073-6*, B115, Pub. by IUCN) Island Pr.

Legal Aspects of the Fire Service. Lawrence J. Hogan. LC 95-94446. 462p. (Orig.). 1995. pap. 49.95 (*0-9659174-0-1*) Amlex.

***Legal Aspects of the Fire Service.** 3rd rev. ed. Lawrence J. Hogan. 496p. (Orig.). 2000. pap. text 49.95 (*0-9659174-4-4*) Amlex.

Legal Aspects of the Medical & Nursing Service. Michael H. Whincup. (C). 1987. pap. 89.00 (*0-901812-47-1*) St Mut.

Legal Aspects of the Medical & Nursing Service. Michael H. Wincup. (C). 1987. 125.00 (*0-901812-48-X*) St Mut.

Legal Aspects of the Music Industry. Richard Schulenberg. LC 99-14471. (Illus.). 494p. 1998. pap. 29.95 (*0-8230-8327-6*) Watsn-Guptill.

Legal Aspects of the Purchase & Sale of Oil & Gas Properties. LC 92-73650. 104p. 1992. pap. 39.95 (*0-89707-802-0*, 535-0034, ABA Natl Res) Amer Bar Assn.

Legal Aspects of Trade Preferences for Developing States. Abdulqawi A. Yusuf. 1982. lib. bdg. 101.00 (*90-247-2583-6*) Kluwer Academic.

Legal Aspects of Transnational Marketing & Sales Contracts. Charles Chatterjee. 141p. 1996. pap. 40.00 (*1-85941-035-9*, Pub. by Cavendish Pubng) Gaunt.

Legal Aspects of Waivers in Sport, Recreation & Fitness Activities. Doyice J. Cotten & Mary B. Cotten. 200p. 1997. pap. 39.95 (*0-944183-25-5*) PRC Pub.

Legal Assistance to Developing Countries: Swedish Perspectives on the Rule of Law. Ed. by Per Sevastik. LC 97-32494. 277p. 1998. pap. text 83.00 (*90-411-0520-4*) Kluwer Academic.

Legal Assistant. Jack Rudman. (Career Examination Ser.: C-2980). 1994. pap. 27.95 (*0-8373-2980-9*) Nat Learn.

Legal Assistant I. Jack Rudman. (Career Examination Ser.: C-2988). 1994. pap. 27.95 (*0-8373-2988-4*) Nat Learn.

Legal Assistant Trainee. Jack Rudman. (Career Examination Ser.: C-2979). 1994. pap. 23.95 (*0-8373-2979-5*) Nat Learn.

Legal Assistant II. Jack Rudman. (Career Examination Ser.: C-2989). 1994. pap. 29.95 (*0-8373-2989-2*) Nat Learn.

Legal Assistant's Guide to Alternative Dispute Resolution. Judy Quan. LC 93-49766. (Paralegal Ser.). (C). 1995. ring bd. 52.75 (*0-87632-990-3*) Thomson Learn.

Legal Assistant's Handbook. 2nd ed. Thomas W. Brunner et al. 248p. 1988. trans. 44.00 (*0-87179-590-6*, 0590) BNA Books.

Legal Assistant's Letter Book. Sonia Von Matt Stoddard. LC 95-3025. 354p. 1995. pap. text 42.00 (*0-13-533084-X*) P-H.

Legal Assistant's Notebook Vol. 1: So. California. Sandra L. Quarles. 305p. 1992. ring bd. 85.00 (*0-9629697-5-3*) ASAP Pubng.

Legal Assistant's Notebook Vol. 2: No. California. Sandra L. Quarles. 505p. 1992. ring bd. 90.00 (*0-9629697-6-1*) ASAP Pubng.

Legal Assistant's Practical Guide to Professional Responsibility. Arthur Garwin & Carole Mostow. LC 98-15119. 1998. write for info. (*1-57073-564-6*) Amer Bar Assn.

Legal Assistants Update, Vol. 5. American Bar Association Standing Commission on La. LC 80-647738. 180p. 1986. pap. 6.00 (*0-89707-260-X*, 423-0021) Amer Bar Assn.

Legal Atlas of the United States. Julius Fast & Tim Fast. LC 97-5621. (Illus.). 208p. 1997. 80.00 (*0-8160-3128-2*) Facts on File.

***Legal Audit Assessment.** Nicholas Trott Long & Kent M. Weeks. 46p. (C). 1998. 25.00 (*1-881434-16-8*) Coll Legal Info.

Legal Barriers to Solar Heating & Cooling of Buildings. Environmental Law Institute Staff. LC 82-177261. 361p. reprint ed. pap. 112.00 (*0-7837-2410-1*, 204009500006) Bks Demand.

Legal Bases: Baseball & the Law. Roger I. Abrams. LC 97-28823. 240p. 1998. 27.95 (*1-56639-599-2*) Temple U Pr.

Legal Basics: A Handbook for Educators. Evelyn B. Kelly. LC 98-66095. 120p. 1998. pap. 11.00 (*0-87367-806-0*) Phi Delta Kappa.

Legal Basis of Corporate Governance in Publicly Held Corporations: A Comparative Approach. Ed. by Arthur R. Pinto & Gustavo Visentini. LC 98-309995. (Studies in Comparative Corporate & Financial Law). 328p. 1998. 116.00 (*90-411-9663-3*) Kluwer Academic.

***Legal Battles That Shaped the Computer Industry.** Lawrence D. Graham. LC 99-13620. (Illus.). 264p. 1999. 59.95 (*1-56720-178-4*, Q178, Quorum Bks) Greenwood.

Legal Beagle: Diary of a Canine Counselor. Linda A. Cawley. LC 96-68928. 256p. 1996. 21.95 (*0-88282-146-6*) New Horizon NJ.

Legal Bermuda Triangle: Avoiding Employee Lawsuits When ADA, FMLA & WC Collide. Inc Alexander Hamilton Institute, Inc. Staff. LC 97-228939. (Executive Strategy Briefings Ser.). v, 102p. 1997. write for info. (*0-86604-350-0*) Hamilton Inst.

Legal Bibliographic & Research Reprint Series, 12 vols., Set. R. A. Daly. Ed. by Richard H. Surles. LC 94-76711. vi, 226p. 1980. reprint ed. write for info. (*0-89941-031-6*, 301600) W S Hein.

Legal Bibliographies--General & International: An Evaluation. Juergen C. Goedan. Tr. by John E. Pickron. 388p. 1991. lib. bdg. 95.00 (*0-941320-09-X*) Transnatl Pubs.

Legal Bibliography: Tradition, Transitions, & Trends. Ed. by Scott B. Pagel. (Legal Reference Services Quarterly Ser.: Vol. 9, Nos. 1-2). 183p. 1989. 39.95 (*0-86656-932-4*) Haworth Pr.

Legal Bibliography Index (1985) Ed. by Win-Shin S. Chiang & Lance E. Dickson. 273p. 1986. 35.00 (*0-317-01337-8*) LSU Law Center.

Legal Bibliography Index, 1986. Ed. by Win-Shin S. Chiang & Lance E. Dickson. 278p. 1987. 40.00 (*0-318-32983-2*) LSU Law Center.

Legal Bibliography of European Integration, 1995. 731p. 1996. pap. 60.00 (*92-829-0298-6*, CY95-96-326-1FC, Pub. by Comm Europ Commun) Bernan Associates.

Legal Bibliography: or A Thesaurus of American, English, Irish & Scotch Law Books. J. G. Marvin. (Marvin's Legal Bibliography Ser.). vii, 800p. 1992. reprint ed. lib. bdg. 78.00 (*0-89941-349-8*, 502150) W S Hein.

***Legal Blame: How Jurors Think & Talk about Accidents.** Neal Feigenson. LC 00-20770. (Law & Public Policy Ser.). 392p. 2000. text 49.95 (*1-55798-677-0*, 431-5190) Am Psychol.

***Legal Blunders.** Geoff Tibballs. 384p. 2000. pap. 12.95 (*0-7867-0746-1*, Pub. by Carroll & Graf) Publishers Group.

Legal Boundaries of California Nursing Practice. 5th ed. Robert Anderson. 300p. 1997. pap. 20.00 (*0-942028-50-3*) Andrsn Cont Educ.

Legal Briefs. Michael Shook & Jeffrey D. Meyer. 208p. 1995. 9.95 (*0-02-860042-8*) Macmillan.

Legal Briefs: Stories by Today's Best Thriller Writers. Ed. by William Bernhardt. 352p. 1999. mass mkt. 6.99 (*0-440-22571-X*) Dell.

Legal Canons. Jack Balkin. 1999. text 50.00 (*0-8147-9857-8*) NYU Pr.

Legal Canons. Jack Balkin & Lev. pap. text. write for info. (*0-8147-9870-5*) NYU Pr.

Legal Capital. 3rd ed. Bayless Manning & James J. Hanks, Jr. (University Textbook Ser.). 213p. 1990. pap. text 17.95 (*0-88277-799-8*) Foundation Pr.

Legal Care for Your Software. rev. ed. Daniel Remer & Robert Dunaway. 368p. 1993. pap. 39.95 (*0-9636256-0-8*) RDS Pub.

Legal Career Guide: From Law Student to Lawyer. Gary A. Munneke. 1993. pap. text 14.95 (*0-89707-763-6*) Amer Bar Assn.

Legal Careers. Jack Rudman. (Career Examination Ser.: C-3284). 1994. pap. 27.95 (*0-8373-3284-2*) Nat Learn.

Legal Challenges to Solid Waste Flow Control Ordinances. Anne S. Kim. (Special Ser.: No. 12). 24p. (Orig.). (C). 1993. pap. text 9.00 (*1-56011-263-8*) Institute Government.

Legal Change: Essays in Honour of Julius Stone. A. R. Blackshield. (Essay in Honour of Julius Stone Ser.). 391p. 1983. boxed set 82.00 (*0-409-49130-6*, Austral, MICHIE) LEXIS Pub.

Legal Checklists, 1965-1991, 2 vols. Benjamin M. Becker et al. LC 82-4513. 1989. 240.00 (*0-685-09240-2*) West Group.

Legal Checklists Specially Selected Forms, 1977-1990. Benjamin M. Becker et al. LC 76-56745. 130.00 (*0-317-12018-2*) West Group.

Legal Citation Directory. Marion D. Powers. LC 75-25703. 302p. 1971. lib. bdg. 42.00 (*0-9600482-0-0*) Franas Pr.

Legal Clerk. Jack Rudman. (Career Examination Ser.: C-3394). 1994. pap. 23.95 (*0-8373-3394-6*) Nat Learn.

Legal Code of Aelfred the Great see Great Britain, Laws, Statutes: England, Laws & Statutes

Legal Community Internet Skills. DDC Publishing Staff. 1999. pap. text 18.00 (*1-56243-839-5*) DDC Pub.

Legal Community of Mankind. Walter Schiffer & Max Radin. LC 74-152603. 367p. 1972. reprint ed. lib. bdg. 69.50 (*0-8371-6038-3*, SCLC, Greenwood Pr) Greenwood.

Legal Competence in Environmental Health. T. Moran. 208p. 1997. text. write for info. (*0-412-71580-5*, Chap & Hall NY) Chapman & Hall.

Legal Competence in Environmental Health. Terence Moran. LC 98-171432. (Illus.). 352p. (C). (gr. 13). 1998. 75.00 (*0-419-23000-9*, D5809, E & FN Spon) Routledge.

Legal Compliance Auditing & the Federal Sentencing Guidelines. James S. Fargason. Ed. by Lee A. Campbell. (Briefing Ser.). 43p. 1993. 20.00 (*0-89413-298-9*, A856) Inst Inter Aud.

Legal Compliance Checkups: Business Clients, 4 vols. annuals Robert Hughes. LC 84-15516. 1990. suppl. ed. 495.00 (*0-685-09047-7*) West Group.

Legal Concept of Art. Paul Kearns. LC 98-198211. 304p. 1998. 60.00 (*1-901362-50-7*, Pub. by Hart Pub) Northwestern U Pr.

***Legal Concepts & Issues in Emergency Care.** Lee. 2000. pap. write for info. (*0-7216-8324-X*, W B Saunders Co) Harcrt Hlth Sci Grp.

Legal Concepts in Sport: A Primer. Linda J. Carpenter. 124p. (Orig.). 1995. pap. 25.00 (*0-88314-567-7*, 302-10006) AAHPERD.

Legal Concepts of Conspiracy: A Law Review Trilogy, 1922-1970. Ed. by Phyllis O. Flug & Michael J. Miller. LC 71-39304. (Conspiracy: Historical Perspectives Ser.). 1972. 22.95 (*0-405-04156-X*) Ayer.

Legal Connection. Compiled by Spencer P. Harris. 1982. 87.00 (*0-685-90845-3*) Data Financial.

Legal Considerations in Business Financing: A Guide for Corporate Management. Alan S. Gutterman. LC 93-49033. 288p. 1994. 65.00 (*0-89930-799-X*, Quorum Bks) Greenwood.

Legal Considerations in Healthcare Delivery. M. Cronin. 210p. (C). 1993. spiral bd. write for info. (*0-933195-26-5*) CA College Health Sci.

Legal Constraints on Methane Gas Development. Sarah K. Farnell. 1982. write for info. (*0-318-57212-5*) U AL Law.

Legal Constraints on Public Hospitals: Purchasing Requirements, Property Disposal, & Conflicts of Interest; Open Meetings & Public Records. Warren J. Wicker & David M. Lawrence. (Hospital Law in North Carolina Ser.: Chap. 7). 52p. (C). 1986. ring bd. 10.50 (*1-56011-079-1*, 85.03G) Institute Government.

Legal Construct, Social Concept: A Macrosociological Perspective on Law. Larry D. Barnett. LC 92-42409. (Social Institutions & Social Change Ser.). 190p. 1993. lib. bdg. 49.95 (*0-202-30479-5*) Aldine de Gruyter.

***Legal Consulting in the Civil Law Tradition.** Mario Ascheri et al. LC 99-56417. (Studies in Comparative Legal History). 1999. write for info. (*1-882239-11-3*) Robbins Collection.

Legal Context of Teaching. Nevilles Harris. 1992. pap. text. write for info. (*0-582-03956-8*, Pub. by Addison-Wesley) Longman.

L

Legal Control of Mergers in the European Communities. T. Antony Downes & Julian Ellison. 316p. 1991. pap. 58.00 (*1-85431-071-2*, Pub. by Blackstone Pr) Gaunt.

Legal Control of the Administration of Public School Expenditures. Ralph Yakel. LC 78-177618. (Columbia University. Teachers College. Contributions to Education Ser.: No. 388). reprint ed. 37.50 (*0-404-55388-5*) AMS Pr.

Legal Control of the Multinational Enterprise. Cynthia D. Wallace. 1982. lib. bdg. 146.00 (*90-247-2668-9*) Kluwer Academic.

Legal Control of Water Resources, Cases & Materials. 2nd ed. Joseph L. Sax et al. (American Casebook Ser.). 987p. (C). 1991. 65.00 (*0-314-86228-5*) West Pub.

Legal Control of Water Resources, Teacher Manual to Accompany Cases & Materials On. Joseph L. Sax et al. (American Casebook Ser.). 241p. (C). 1991. pap. text. write for info. (*0-314-93302-6*) West Pub.

Legal Control over Property Rights: England & Belgium: A Comparison. B. Siman. (C). 1988. 45.00 (*0-7855-3824-0*, Pub. by Oxford Polytechnic) St Mut.

***Legal Convergence in the Enlarged Europe of the New Millennium.** Ed. by Paul L. C. Torremans. 376p. 2000. text 117.00 (*90-411-1337-1*) Kluwer Law Intl.

Legal Coordinator. Jack Rudman. (Career Examination Ser.: C-2651). 1994. pap. 39.95 (*0-8373-2651-6*) Nat Learn.

Legal Core: Curiosities of Law & Lawyers. Ed. by William Andrews. xii, 117p. 1982. reprint ed. 32.50 (*0-8377-0212-7*, Rothman) W S Hein.

Legal Costing: How to Cost for Profitable File & Practice Management. Ed. by John White. 100p. (C). 1989. 100.00 (*1-875114-00-9*, Pub. by Blackstone Pr) Gaunt.

Legal Costs - Victoria: Compendium of Superseded Materials. J. Grace & R. A. Allen. 372p. 1994. pap. write for info. (*0-409-30079-9*, MICHIE) LEXIS Pub.

Legal Culture & the Legal Profession. Ed. by Lawrence M. Friedman & Harry N. Scheiber. LC 96-219431. 192p. (C). 1996. pap. 65.00 (*0-8133-8935-6*, Pub. by Westview) HarpC.

Legal Culture in the Early Medieval West: Law as Text, Image & Experience. Patrick Wormald. LC 99-32560. 1999. 70.00 (*1-85285-175-9*) Hambledon Press.

Legal Decisions Affecting Bankers 1879-1990. Ed. by T. G. Reeday & P. E. Smart. 1987. write for info. (*0-406-99887-6*, LDABVASET, MICHIE) LEXIS Pub.

Legal Decisions Affecting Insurance, 4 vols., Set. Ed. by Ray W. Hodgin. 1992. 1140.00 (*0-406-00289-4*, MICHIE) LEXIS Pub.

Legal Defense of Pathological Intoxication with Related Issues of Temporary & Self-Inflicted Insanity. Lawrence P. Tiffany & Mary Tiffany. LC 89-49429. 560p. 1990. 99.50 (*0-89930-548-2*, TPA/, Greenwood Pr) Greenwood.

Legal Definition of Death. Robert A. Carter. 25p. 1982. 5.00 (*0-318-01522-6*) NYS Library.

Legal Desk Reference for Healthcare Professionals: Connecticut. Robert S. Walzer. 687p. 1999. pap. 129.95 (*1-58244-044-1*) Rutledge Bks.

Legal Deskbook for Administrators of Colleges & Universities. 2nd ed. Ed. by Kent M. Weeks & Derek Davis. LC 93-80255. 455p. 1993. ring bd. 49.50 (*0-929182-21-9*) Baylor U J M Dawson.

Legal Determination of International Maritime Boundaries. G. J. Tanja. 382p. 1990. pap. 79.00 (*90-6544-478-5*) Kluwer Law Intl.

Legal Development & Comparative Law, 1986: Selected Essays for the 12th International Congress of Comparative Law. Z. Peteri & V. Lamm. (FRE.). 330p. (C). 1986. 90.00 (*963-05-4434-2*, Pub. by Akade Kiado) St Mut.

Legal Development & Constitutional Change in Sierra Leone (1797-1971) W. S. Jones. 330p. (C). 1989. pap. 59.00 (*0-7223-2210-0*, Pub. by A H S Ltd) St Mut.

Legal Development in Arabia: A Selection of Addresses & Articles. W. M. Ballantyne. 148p. 1980. lib. bdg. 84.50 (*0-86010-167-3*) Kluwer Law Intl.

Legal Dictation Machine Transcription Typewriting Practice. Rhoda Erickson et al. (Machine Transcription Ser.). 208p. 1982. spiral bd. 20.00 (*0-936862-13-0*, D-5) DDC Pub.

Legal Dictionary. E. A. Geissler. (ENG & GER.). 199p. 1989. 45.00 (*0-8288-7763-7*, M15068) Fr & Eur.

Legal Dictionary. H. P. Kniepkamp. (ENG & GER.). 47.95 (*3-7678-0013-6*); 59.95 (*3-89166-795-7*) Adlers Foreign Bks.

Legal Dictionary. Durval Noronha. (ENG & POR.). 510p. 1993. 175.00 (*0-7859-9549-8*); 195.00 incl. audio compact disk (*0-7859-9550-1*) Fr & Eur.

Legal Dictionary: Diccionario Juridico, 4 vols. 3rd rev. ed. Leon G. Fernandez. (SPA.). 2794p. 1982. 195.00 (*0-8288-1530-5*, S19892) Fr & Eur.

Legal Dictionary: Dictionnaire Juridique. Ibrahim Najjar. (ARA & FRE.). 292p. 1983. 75.00 (*0-8288-0971-2*, F48378) Fr & Eur.

***Legal Dictionary: German/English - English/German.** Collin & Janssen. (ENG & GER.). 471p. 1998. 99.00 (*0-320-02134-3*) Fr & Eur.

Legal Dictionary: Juridisk Ordbok. O. Hellberg. (FRE & SWE.). 1983. 95.00 (*0-8288-0983-6*, F22181) Fr & Eur.

Legal Dictionary: Rechtswoerterbuch. 7th ed. Hanns P. Kniepkamp. (ENG & GER.). 216p. 1981. 65.00 (*0-8288-0392-7*, M7598) Fr & Eur.

Legal Dictionary Dutch - French: With French - Dutch Index. G. Hessling. (DUT & FRE.). 514p. 1992. 195.00 (*0-8288-9434-5*) Fr & Eur.

Legal Dictionary Dutch - German. Ed. by Hans Langendorf. 1991. text 46.00 (*90-6544-563-3*) Kluwer Law Intl.

Legal Dictionary Dutch - Spanish: With Spanish - Dutch Index. M. C. Raparaz & Oosterveld-Egas. (DUT & SPA.). 371p. 1992. 295.00 (*0-8288-9435-3*) Fr & Eur.

Legal Dictionary English - Welsh. Ed. by Robyn Lewis. 500p. 1992. 114.00 (*0-86383-534-1*, Pub. by Gomer Pr) St Mut.

Legal Dictionary, English-Danish. H. P. Frandsen. (DAN & ENG.). Date not set. 68.00 (*0-7859-9738-5*) Fr & Eur.

Legal Dictionary English-Danish. H. Pals Frandsen. (DAN & ENG.). 208p. 1994. 68.00 (*87-12-02026-5*, Pub. by GAD) IBD Ltd.

Legal Dictionary, English-Spanish-French. Jose R. CanoRico. (ENG, FRE & SPA.). Date not set. 150.00 (*0-7859-9585-4*) Fr & Eur.

Legal Dictionary for Bad Spellers. Joseph Krevisky & Jordan L. Linfield. LC 95-182785. 246p. 1995. pap. 12.95 (*0-471-31068-9*) Wiley.

Legal Dictionary for Businessmen: Russian-English, English-Russian. 6th rev. ed. M. A. Baskakova. 640p. (C). 1995. 35.00 (*0-8285-5199-5*) Firebird NY.

Legal Dictionary for Everyone: German/English/German. 2nd ed. Gerhard Kobler. (ENG & GER.). 268p. 1997. 39.95 (*0-320-00466-X*) Fr & Eur.

Legal Dictionary German - Dutch. Matthias K. Scheer. 462p. 1989. 55.00 (*90-6544-350-9*) Kluwer Law Intl.

Legal Dictionary in Four Languages French-Dutch-English-German. Edgard Le Docte. 800p. 1988. 150.00 (*90-6215-163-9*, Pub. by Maklu Uitgev) Gaunt.

Legal Dictionary in Four Languages. E. LeDocte. (ENG, FRE, GER & SPA.). 822p. 1987. 195.00 (*3-7890-3961-6*) IBD Ltd.

Legal Dictionary in Four Languages. 3rd ed. Edgard Le Docte. (DUT, ENG, FRE & GER.). 758p. 1982. 195.00 (*0-8288-1532-1*, M6349) Fr & Eur.

Legal Dictionary in Four Languages. 4th ed. Edgard Le Docte. (DUT, ENG, FRE & GER.). 822p. 1987. 295.00 (*0-8288-0412-5*, M15088) Fr & Eur.

Legal Dictionary of the Penal System: Diccionario de Derecho Procesal Penal y Terminos Usuales En el Proceso Penal, 2 vols. M. A. Diaz de Leon. (SPA.). 2249p. 1986. 175.00 (*0-8288-1529-1*, S608) Fr & Eur.

Legal Dictionary, Spanish-English/English-Spanish. Francisco Ramos-Bossini. (ENG & SPA.). 568p. 1997. 150.00 (*0-7859-9643-5*) Fr & Eur.

Legal Directory of Children's Rights: State Statuses, Alabama-Kansas, 4 vols., Set. Ed. by Thomas A. Jacobs. LC 84-27111. 1200p. 1985. lib. bdg. 120.00 (*0-313-27100-3*, U7100) Greenwood.

Legal Directory of Children's Rights: State Statuses, Alabama-Kansas, 4 vols., Vol. 1. Ed. by Thomas A. Jacobs. LC 84-27111. 364p. 1985. lib. bdg. 42.95 (*0-313-27101-1*, U7101) Greenwood.

Legal Directory of Children's Rights: State Statuses, Alabama-Kansas, 4 vols., Vol. 2. Ed. by Thomas A. Jacobs. LC 84-27111. 364p. 1989. lib. bdg. 42.95 (*0-313-27102-X*, U7102) Greenwood.

Legal Directory of Children's Rights: State Statuses, Kentucky-North Carolina, 4 vols., Vol. 3. Ed. by Thomas A. Jacobs. LC 84-27111. 384p. 1989. lib. bdg. 42.95 (*0-313-27103-8*, U7103) Greenwood.

Legal Directory of Children's Rights: State Statuses, North Dakota-Wyoming, 4 vols., Vol. 4. Ed. by Thomas A. Jacobs. LC 84-27111. 378p. 1989. lib. bdg. 42.95 (*0-313-27104-6*, U7104) Greenwood.

Legal Doctrine & Social Progress. Frank Parsons. 219p. 1982. reprint ed. 37.00 (*0-8377-1014-6*, Rothman) W S Hein.

Legal Document Preparation. Bilz. 1988. teacher ed. write for info. (*0-8273-3617-9*) Thomson Learn.

Legal Document Preparation: The Guide for Preparing & Handling Legal Documents. Reed K. Bilz & Polly A. McGlew. 172p. (C). 1990. pap. text 19.95 (*1-885477-05-8*) Fut Horizons.

Legal Document Production. Tracy R. Johnston. LC 95-33081. 382p. 1996. pap. 51.00 incl. disk (*0-13-190703-4*) P-H.

Legal Document Production. Smith. 1996. pap. text. write for info. (*0-13-234857-8*) Allyn.

Legal Documents: Form, Content, & Style. write for info. (*0-318-61923-7*) Natl Educ Corp.

Legal Documents for Employers: Sample Contracts, Forms & Checklists for Hiring, Firing & Day-to-Day Operations. Steven Mitchell Sack. LC 94-96619. 416p. 1996. 199.00 (*0-9636306-2-8*) Legal Strat.

Legal Documents for HR Professionals. Steven Mitchell Sack. 1p. (C). 1997. pap. text, ring bd. 69.95 incl. disk (*0-13-889056-0*) P-H.

Legal Documents from Erech, Dated in the Seleucid Era (312-65 B.C.) Albert T. Clay. LC 78-63517. (Babylonian Records in the Library of J. Pierpont Morgan: 2). reprint ed. 34.50 (*0-404-60122-7*) AMS Pr.

Legal Drafting. S. Brody. LC 93-80291. 416p. 1994. pap. text 28.95 (*0-316-10908-8*, Aspen Law & Bus) Aspen Pub.

Legal Drafting. Susan Brody et al. 416p. 1994. teacher ed. write for info. (*0-316-10425-6*, 04256) Aspen Law.

Legal Drafting: Civil Proceedings. Peter Van Blerk. LC 98-213845. xvi, 110 p. 1998. write for info. (*0-7021-4578-5*) Juta & Co.

***Legal Drafting: Practical Exercises & Problem Materials.** Haggard. LC 99-175064. (Paralegal Ser.). (C). 1999. pap. 9.75 (*0-314-23362-8*) West Pub.

Legal Drafting: Practical Exercises & Problem Materials. Thomas R. Haggard. LC 99-175064. (American Casebook Ser.). 146 p. 1999. write for info. (*0-314-23405-5*) West Pub.

Legal Drafting : In a Nutshell: Nutshell Series. Thomas R. Haggard. LC 96-169917. (Paralegal). (C). 1996. pap. text 15.00 (*0-314-09853-4*) West Pub.

Legal Eagle: A Novel about Lawyers, Eggs, & Dangerous Women. Mick Thomas. LC 92-29291. 192p. (Orig.). 1993. pap. 9.95 (*1-56474-038-2*) Fithian Pr.

Legal Eagle Series, 5 novels, Set. Michel Lipman & Cathy Furniss. Ed. by Betty Lou Kratoville. (Illus.). 240p. (Orig.). (J). (gr. 4-12). 1988. pap. 17.00 (*0-87879-594-4*) High Noon Bks.

Legal Eagles. Martin Owens. (Illus.). 192p. (Orig.). 1986. pap. 7.95 (*0-918432-74-X*) Baseline Bks.

***Legal-Ease.** Andrea Campbell. 2001. pap. 18.95 (*0-936085-67-3*) Blue Heron OR.

Legal Ease. Michael H. Wald. 190p. 1995. pap. text 10.95 (*0-9661251-1-8*) Sound Advice Pubns.

Legal Ease: Fresh Insights into Lawyering. James C. Freund. LC 84-5651. 206p. 1984. 35.00 (*0-15-004373-2*) Harcourt.

Legal-Ease: Fresh Insights into Lawyering. James C. Freund. 216p. 1984. 65.00 (*0-13-528761-8*) Aspen Law.

Legal, Economic & Social Status of the Indian Child. Neel K. Sharda. (C). 1988. 38.00 (*81-85135-31-2*, Pub. by Natl Bk Orgn) S Asia.

Legal Edge for Homeowners, Buyers & Renters. Michel J. Bryant. (Illus.). 200p. 1999. pap. 16.95 (*1-58063-066-9*, Pub. by Renaissance) St Martin.

Legal Education. Martin Levine. LC 93-27764. (International Library of Essays in Law & Legal Theory: Vol. 5). (C). 1993. lib. bdg. 150.00 (*0-8147-5065-6*) NYU Pr.

Legal Education Division Brochure. Date not set. pap. text. write for info. (*0-314-06810-4*) West Pub.

Legal Education for the 21st Century. Stacy Alexander. Ed. by Donald B. King. LC 98-38655. xxviii, 585p. 1999. 79.95 (*0-8377-0784-6*, 322350, Rothman) W S Hein.

Legal Education in a Changing World: Report of the Committee on Legal Education in the Developing Countries. 94p. 1975. write for info. (*91-7106-092-8*, Pub. by Nordic Africa) Transaction Pubs.

Legal Education in Colonial New York. Paul L. Hamlin. LC 70-129082. (American Constitutional & Legal History Ser). (Illus.). 1970. reprint ed. lib. bdg. 32.50 (*0-306-70062-X*) Da Capo.

Legal Education in the United States: A Report Prepared for the Survey of the Legal Profession. Albert J. Harno. LC 80-23717. 211p. 1980. reprint ed. lib. bdg. 59.50 (*0-313-22425-0*, HALG, Greenwood Pr) Greenwood.

Legal Education, Law Practice & the Economy: A New England Study. Thomas C. Fischer. LC 90-42813. xx, 149p. 1990. reprint ed. 37.50 (*0-8377-0579-7*, Rothman) W S Hein.

Legal Education, 2000. Ed. by J. P. Grant et al. 200p. 1988. text 76.95 (*0-566-05472-8*) Ashgate Pub Co.

Legal Effects of Fluctuating Exchange Rates. Joseph Gold. LC 90-21406. xviii, 473p. 1990. pap. 37.50 (*1-55775-173-0*) Intl Monetary.

***Legal Effects of War.** 3rd ed. Arnold D. McNair. xxiii, 458p. 1999. reprint ed. 145.00 (*1-56169-470-3*) Gaunt.

Legal Elements of Boundaries. 2nd ed. Barlow & Voncannon. LC 97-76677. 675p. 1997. 65.00 (*1-55834-676-7*, 66925-11, MICHIE) LEXIS Pub.

Legal Env Of Bus: Text & Cases. 2nd ed. Frank B. Cross & Roger L. Miller. LC 94-39004. (SWC-Business Law). 1100p. (C). 1994. mass mkt. 58.25 (*0-314-04517-1*) West Pub.

Legal Envir Busn Qkprint. Jackson. 1999. pap. text 38.25 (*0-536-02352-2*) Pearson Custom.

Legal Environment. Miller. Date not set. pap. text, student ed. 10.25 (*0-314-01947-2*); pap. text, suppl. ed. write for info. (*0-314-02160-4*) West Pub.

Legal Environment. 3rd ed. Herbert M. Bohlman. 1996. pap., student ed. 21.75 (*0-314-09634-5*) West Pub.

Legal Environment: Answers. Miller. Date not set. pap. text, suppl. ed. write for info. (*0-314-02069-1*) West Pub.

Legal Environment: Printouts. Miller. Date not set. pap. text. write for info. (*0-314-02070-5*) West Pub.

Legal Environment for Foreign Direct Investment. Robert Goodwin. Ed. by Michael Calabrese. 1994. 55.00 (*0-935328-73-4*) Intl Law Inst.

Legal Environment for Foreign Direct Investment. 3rd ed. Ed. by Robert Goodwin & Michael Calabrese. 200p. 1993. 75.00 (*90-411-0991-9*) Kluwer Law Intl.

Legal Environment for Foreign Direct Investment in the United States. 2nd ed. Ed. by Rudolph S. Houck, III & Nancy L. Caywood. LC 81-82212. 318p. 1981. lib. bdg. 62.50 (*0-935328-05-X*) Intl Law Inst.

Legal Environment Handbook. Miller. Date not set. pap. text 5.75 (*0-314-02071-3*); pap. text. write for info. (*0-314-02072-1*) West Pub.

Legal Environment of Busines. 6th ed. Meiners & Ringleb. (LA - Business Law Ser.). (C). 1996. mass mkt., student ed. 18.25 (*0-314-20770-8*) S-W Pub.

***Legal Environment of Business.** 444p. (C). 1999. 46.89 (*0-536-60233-6*) Pearson Custom.

***Legal Environment of Business.** 2000. write for info. (*0-9700050-0-8*) Abbott Pubng.

Legal Environment of Business. John R. Allison. LC 92-70971. 1993. 13.50 (*0-685-75613-0*) Dryden Pr.

***Legal Environment of Business.** Michael B. Bixby et al. 832p. 2000. pap. 94.00 (*0-13-019492-1*, Prentice Hall) P-H.

Legal Environment of Business. Michael B. Bixby et al. LC 96-9283. (C). 1995. mass mkt. 102.95 (*0-538-84484-1*) S-W Pub.

Legal Environment of Business. Blair J. Kolasa. LC 83-12322. (Illus.). 752p. 1984. write for info. (*0-201-10604-3*); student ed. write for info. (*0-201-10607-8*) Addison-Wesley.

Legal Environment of Business. Victor D. Lopez. LC 95-53338. 480p. (C). 1996. 67.00 (*0-13-125386-7*) P-H.

***Legal Environment of Business.** 2nd ed. Leonard Bierman et al. 2000. 74.95 (*1-57879-012-3*) E Bowers Pub.

Legal Environment of Business. 2nd ed. Edward J. Conry et al. 650p. 1989. text 54.00 (*0-205-12192-6*, H21926) Allyn.

Legal Environment of Business. 2nd ed. Edward J. Conry et al. 650p. 1989. teacher ed. write for info. (*0-318-66388-0*, H21934); student ed. 19.00 (*0-685-29841-8*, H21942); write for info. (*0-318-66389-9*, H21959) P-H.

Legal Environment of Business. 2nd ed. McAdams- Pincus. 1999. 58.00 (*0-07-230335-2*) McGraw.

Legal Environment of Business. 3rd ed. (C). 1993. pap. 10.67 (*0-205-15612-6*, Macmillan Coll) P-H.

Legal Environment of Business. 3rd ed. (C). 1993. pap. 10.67 (*0-205-15597-9*, Macmillan Coll) P-H.

Legal Environment of Business. 3rd ed. Cross. LC 97-22498. (LA - Business Law Ser.). (C). 1997. mass mkt. 98.95 (*0-538-87965-3*) S-W Pub.

Legal Environment of Business. 3rd ed. Cross. (LA - Business Law Ser.). (C). 1997. mass mkt., student ed. 25.95 (*0-538-87970-X*) S-W Pub.

Legal Environment of Business. 3rd ed. Charles McGuire. 616p. (C). 1998. per. 49.95 (*0-7872-4558-5*, 41455801) Kendall-Hunt.

Legal Environment of Business. 3rd ed. Warner. 750p. 1998. pap. 61.00 (*0-536-00261-4*) Pearson Custom.

Legal Environment of Business. 4th ed. John R. Allison & Robert A. Prentice. 798p. (C). 1993. 13.50 (*0-318-70110-3*); 17.75 (*0-03-098059-3*); 17.75 (*0-03-098058-5*) Dryden Pr.

***Legal Environment of Business.** 4th ed. Cross & Miller. (SWC-General Business Ser.). (C). 2000. text, student ed. 23.00 (*0-324-05279-0*) Sth-Wstrn College.

***Legal Environment of Business.** 5th ed. Blackburn. 708p. 1998. pap. text 45.00 (*0-536-01714-X*) Pearson Custom.

Legal Environment of Business. 5th ed. Meiners. (LA - Business Law Ser.). 1994. pap. write for info. (*0-314-03378-5*) West Pub.

Legal Environment of Business. 5th ed. Roger E. Meiners et al. Ed. by Fenton. LC 93-33086. (SWC-Business Law). 825p. (C). 1993. mass mkt. 58.00 (*0-314-02690-8*) West Pub.

Legal Environment of Business. 6th ed. Roger E. Meiners et al. LC 96-26926. 800p. 1996. mass mkt. 84.95 (*0-314-09953-0*) West Pub.

***Legal Environment of Business.** 7th ed. Roger E. Meiners. LC 99-23199. 1999. pap. 99.95 (*0-324-00423-0*) Thomson Learn.

***Legal Environment of Business: A Critical-Thinking Approach.** 2nd ed. Nancy Kubasek et al. LC 98-23947. 644p. (C). 1998. pap. 96.00 (*0-13-922253-7*) P-H.

Legal Environment of Business: Cases & Principles. 2nd ed. George W. Spiro. LC 92-28825. 832p. 1992. text 82.60 (*0-13-529884-9*) P-H.

***Legal Environment of Business Custom Edition.** 380p. (C). 1999. pap. text 36.00 (*0-536-02509-6*) Pearson Custom.

Legal Environment of Business: Ethical & Public Policy Contexts. Tony McAdams & Laura B. Pincus. 704p. (C). 1996. text 70.75 (*0-256-17051-7*, Irwn McGrw-H) McGrw-H Hghr Educ.

Legal Environment of Business: Regulatory Law & Contracts. Douglas Whitman & John W. Gergacz. (C). 1991. text 68.00 (*0-07-069997-6*) McGraw.

***Legal Environment of Business - Faculty Guide.** (C). 2000. pap., teacher ed. write for info. (*1-58313-103-5*) Univ Access.

***Legal Environment of Business - Student Guide.** 249p. (C). 2000. pap., student ed. write for info. (*1-58313-102-7*) Univ Access.

Legal Environment of Business & Study Guide Package. John D. Blackburn. (C). 1992. text 59.95 (*0-256-13149-X*, Irwn McGrw-H) McGrw-H Hghr Educ.

Legal Environment of Business Environmental Issues in Marketing. 5th ed. John D. Blackburn et al. (C). 1994. text 32.95 (*0-256-17397-4*, Irwn McGrw-H) McGrw-H Hghr Educ.

***Legal Environment of Business Quickprint.** 40p. (C). 1999. write for info. (*0-536-60492-4*) Pearson Custom.

Legal Environment of Computing. Peter Knight. (C). 1990. pap. text 36.33 (*0-201-41701-4*) Addison-Wesley.

Legal Environment of Insurance, 2 vols., Vol. 1. 4th ed. James J. Lorimer et al. LC 93-71085. 342p. (C). 1993. text 41.00 (*0-89463-064-4*) Am Inst FCPCU.

Legal Environment of Insurance (For CPCU 6) rev. ed. R. Robert Rackley. (CPCU Ser.). 1998. 160.00 (*1-57195-167-9*) Insurance Achiev.

Legal Environment of Social Work. Leila O. Schroeder. 382p. (C). 1995. 34.95 (*0-87101-235-9*, 2359) Natl Assn Soc Wkrs.

Legal Environment of the Hospitality Industry. Raymond W. Knab & Patricia E. Bruen. 496p. (C). 2001. 54.00 (*0-13-749193-X*, Macmillan Coll) P-H.

Legal Environment Today. Miller. Date not set. pap. text, teacher ed. write for info. (*0-314-08863-6*) West Pub.

Legal Environment Today: Business in Its Ethical, Regulatory & International Setting. Roger L. Miller. (SWC-Business Law). 1996. pap., student ed. 19.00 (*0-314-08915-2*) West Pub.

Legal Environment Today: Business in Its Ethical, Regulatory & International Setting. Roger L. Miller & Frank B. Cross. (SWC-Business Law). 700p. (C). 1996. pap. 69.75 (*0-314-06425-7*) West Pub.

Legal Environment Today: Business in Its Ethical, Regulatory & International Setting. 2nd ed. Roger L. Miller & Frank B. Cross. LC 98-5809. 1998. pap. 98.95 (*0-538-88534-3*) S-W Pub.

Legal, Environmental & Social Perspectives of Surface Mining Law & Reclamation by Landfilling: Getting Maximum Yield from Surface Mines. R. Lee Aston. LC 98-54446. 410p. 1999. 78.00 (*1-86094-123-0*) World Scientific Pub.

Legal Environmental Business 370p. (C). 1997. text 46.00 (*0-536-00343-2*) Pearson Custom.

Legal Environmental Business Answers. Miller. Date not set. pap. text. write for info. (*0-314-09147-5*) West Pub.

An Asterisk (*) at the beginning of an entry indicates that the title is appearing for the first time.

Legal Environmental Business Statistics Handbook. Miller. Date not set. pap. text. write for info. (*0-314-09154-8*) West Pub.

Legal Essays. James B. Thayer. (Illus.). xvi, 402p. 1972. reprint ed. 65.00 (*0-8377-2627-1*, Rothman) W S Hein.

Legal, Ethical & International Environment of Business. 2nd ed. Herbert M. Bohlman & Mary J. Dundas. Ed. by Clyde Perlee. LC 92-15448. 680p. (C). 1993. text 68.50 (*0-314-00905-1*) West Pub.

Legal, Ethical & International Environment of Business. 3rd ed. Herbert M. Bohlman & Mary J. Dundas. LC 95-35003. 620p. (C). 1996. pap. 69.75 (*0-314-06456-7*) West Pub.

Legal, Ethical, & Political Issues in Nursing. Tonia D. Aiken. LC 93-46312. 297p. 1994. pap. 31.95 (*0-8036-0081-X*) Davis Co.

Legal, Ethical, & Political Issues in Nursing. 2nd ed. Tonia D. Aiken. 320p. pap. text 29.95 (*0-8036-0571-4*) Davis Co.

Legal, Ethical & Regulatory Environment of Business. 4th ed. Herbert M. Bohlman. LC 98-19537. (SWC-Business Law Ser.). 1998. pap. 98.95 (*0-538-88492-4*) S-W Pub.

Legal, Ethical & Regulatory Environment of Business. 6th ed. Bruce D. Fisher & Michael J. Phillips. LC 97-14938. 1997. mass mkt. 98.95 (*0-538-87880-0*) S-W Pub.

***Legal, Ethical, & Regulatory Environment of Business.** 7th ed. Bruce D. Fisher. 2000. pap. 67.75 (*0-324-02042-2*) Thomson Learn.

Legal Ethical & Regulatory Envof Business 5. 5th ed. Bruce D. Fisher & Michael J. Phillips. LC 94-4427. (SWC-Business Law). 972p. (C). 1994. mass mkt. 57.25 (*0-314-03920-1*) West Pub.

Legal-Ethical Considerations, Restrictions, & Obligations for Clinicians Who Treat Communicative Disorders. 2nd ed. Franklin H. Silverman. (Illus.). 258p. 1992. pap. 35.95 (*0-398-06429-6*); text 51.95 (*0-398-05783-4*) C C Thomas.

Legal Ethics. 2nd ed. David Luban & Deborah L. Rhode. (University Casebook Ser.). 930p. 1995. text 43.00 (*1-56662-249-2*) Foundation Pr.

Legal Ethics. 2nd ed. Charles W. Wolfram. (Hornbook Ser.). Date not set. text, student ed. write for info. (*0-314-06608-X*) West Pub.

Legal Ethics: An Annotated Bibliography & Resource Guide. Frederick A. Elliston & Jane Van Schaick. viii, 199p. 1984. 38.50 (*0-8377-0545-2*, Rothman) W S Hein.

Legal Ethics: Cases & Materials. David J. Luban & Deborah L. Rhode. (University Casebook Ser.). 1040p. (C). 1991. text 42.95 (*0-88277-939-7*) Foundation Pr.

Legal Ethics: The Law of Professional Responsibility. 3rd ed. L. Ray Patterson & Thomas B. Metzloff. 1989. teacher ed. 54.50 (*0-8205-2909-5*) Bender.

Legal Ethics & Legal Education. Michael J. Kelly. LC 80-10825. (Teaching of Ethics Ser.). 69p. 1980. pap. 4.00 (*0-916558-06-1*) Hastings Ctr.

Legal Ethics & Legal Practice: Contemporary Issues. Ed. by Stephen Parker & Charles Sampford. 278p. 1996. text 69.00 (*0-19-825945-X*) OUP.

Legal Ethics & Professional Responsibility. Ed. by Ross Cranston. LC 95-39861. 242p. 1996. text 65.00 (*0-19-825931-X*) OUP.

***Legal Ethics & Professional Responsibility.** Allan C. Hutchinson. (Essentials of Canadian Law Ser.). xvii, 268p. 1999. pap. 35.95 (*1-55221-030-8*, Pub. by Irwin Law) Gaunt.

Legal Ethics & Professional Responsibility. Jonathan S. Lynton & Terri M. Lyndall. LC 92-36136. (Illus.). 392p. (C). 1993. pap. 30.25 (*0-8273-5504-1*) Delmar.

Legal Ethics & Professional Responsibility: Instructor's Guide. Jonathan S. Lynton & Terri M. Lyndall. 34p. 1993. 12.50 (*0-8273-5506-8*) Delmar.

***Legal Ethics for Management & Their Counsel: 1999 Edition.** Len Biernat & R. Hunter Manson. 420p. 1999. 100.00 (*0-327-10014-1*, 6056114) LEXIS Pub.

Legal Ethics for Management & Their Counsel, 1998 Edition. Len Biernat & R. Hunter Mason. LC 99-461912. 410p. 1998. write for info. (*0-327-00715-X*, 6056113) LEXIS Pub.

Legal Ethics For Paralegals. Laura L. Morrison & Gina DeCiani. LC 94-27670. (Paralegal). 368p. (C). 1994. mass mkt. 48.95 (*0-314-04173-7*) West Pub.

Legal Ethics in the Practice of Law: Rules, Statutes & Comparisons 1999. Zitrin & Langford. 291p. 1999. pap. write for info. (*0-327-00926-8*, 1347411) LEXIS Pub.

Legal Ethics in the Practice of Law: 1995 Edition, Incl. Rules suppl. Richard A. Zitrin & Carol M. Langford. LC 95-76054. 687p. 1995. text 55.00 (*1-55834-223-0*, 13470-10, MICHIE) LEXIS Pub.

Legal Ethics Management & Their Counsel: 1997 Edition. Biernat & Manson. LC 97-73751. 416p. 1997. pap. text 90.00 (*1-55834-591-4*, 60561-12, MICHIE) LEXIS Pub.

Legal Ethics Teacher's Manual. Deborah L. Rhode & David J. Luban. (University Casebook Ser.). 177p. 1991. pap. text. write for info. (*0-88277-979-6*) Foundation Pr.

Legal Ethics Teacher's Manual to Accompany Problems. 3rd ed. Mortimer D. Schwartz & Richard C. Wydick. Ed. by Rex R. Perschbacher. (American Casebook Ser.). 260p. 1992. pap. text, teacher ed. write for info. (*0-314-01942-1*) West Pub.

***Legal Executions in New England: A Comprehensive Reference, 1622-1960.** Daniel A. Hearn. LC 98-49841. 452p. 1999. lib. bdg. 75.00 (*0-7864-0670-4*) McFarland & Co.

Legal Executions in New York State: A Comprehensive Reference, 1639-1963. Daniel A. Hearn. LC 97-26161. 373p. 1997. lib. bdg. 65.00 (*0-7864-0386-1*) McFarland & Co.

Legal Expense Defense: How to Control Your Business' Legal Costs & Problems. Dennis M. Powers. Ed. by Linda Pinkham. LC 95-34833. (Successful Business Library). (Illus.). 346p. (Orig.). 1998. pap. 19.95 (*1-55571-348-3*, Oasis Pr) PSI Resch.

Legal Expense Insurance: The European Experience in Financing Legal Services. American Bar Foundation Staff. LC 75-996. ix, 117p. 1975. pap. 25.00 (*0-910058-69-5*, 765-0016-01) W S Hein.

Legal Expenses Insurance. Michael Feldman. 112p. 1998. pap. 41.00 (*1-85811-188-9*, Pub. by CLT Prof) Gaunt.

Legal Facetiae: Satirical & Humorous. John Willock. 442p. 1982. reprint ed. 35.00 (*0-8377-1324-2*, Rothman) W S Hein.

Legal Feminisms: Theory & Practice. Clare McGlynn. LC 97-41408. 242p. 1998. text 77.95 (*1-85521-927-1*, Pub. by Ashgate Pub) Ashgate Pub Co.

Legal Fiction. Bob Huffman. LC 97-78450. 200p. 1999. pap. 13.95 (*0-88739-205-9*) Creat Arts Bk.

Legal Fiction. large type ed. E. X. Ferrars. (Nightingale Series Large Print Bks.). 287p. 1992. pap. 14.95 (*0-8161-5257-8*, G K Hall Lrg Type) Mac Lib Ref.

Legal Fictions. Lon L. Fuller. xvi, 142p. 1967. pap. 8.95 (*0-8047-0328-0*) Stanford U Pr.

Legal Fictions. V. K. Varadachari. (C). 1979. 45.00 (*0-7855-5498-X*) St Mut.

Legal Fictions: A Series of Cases from the Classics. A. Laurence Polak. (Illus.). 127p. 1995. reprint ed. 40.00 (*1-56169-105-4*) Gaunt.

Legal Fictions: Short Stories about Lawyers & the Law. Intro. by Jay Wishingrad. 410p. 1994. pap. 14.95 (*0-87951-540-6*, Pub. by Overlook Pr) Penguin Books.

Legal Fictions No. 32: Fall 1997. Ed. by Sally Ledger & Stella Swain. 192p. 1998. pap. 19.50 (*0-85315-847-9*, Pub. by Lawrence & Wishart) NYU Pr.

Legal-Financial Planning Guide for Families. 2nd ed. Tim Nay. 100p. 1990. pap. text 15.00 (*1-877592-14-5*) GSH&MC.

Legal Forms & Worksheets. Florida Bar Members. 492p. 1997. ring bd. write for info. (*0-945979-98-3*, 290) FL Bar Legal Ed.

Legal Forms Binder, Ready-to-Use. Timothy J. Smith. (Illus.). 125p. 1991. 29.95 (*0-9625456-2-7*) SJT Enterprises.

Legal Forms, Contracts & Advice for Horse Owners. 2nd ed. Sue E. Marder. 1997. pap. text 26.50 (*0-914327-69-0*); pap. text 39.95 incl. cd-rom (*0-914327-71-2*) Breakthrgh NY.

Legal Forms, Do-it-Yourself Assorted Kit. Timothy J. Smith. 1992. 9.95 (*1-880398-01-X*) SJT Enterprises.

Legal Foundations of Capitalism. John R. Commons. LC 75-184663. (Reprints of Economic Classics Ser.). x, 394p. 1974. reprint ed. lib. bdg. 49.50 (*0-678-00897-3*) Kelley.

Legal Foundations of Capitalism. rev. ed. John R. Commons. LC 94-12484. 438p. (C). 1994. pap. 29.95 (*1-56000-781-8*) Transaction Pubs.

Legal Foundations of Post. Rogers. Date not set. 22.95 (*0-465-03903-0*); pap. write for info. (*0-465-03904-9*) Basic.

Legal Foundations of the Single European Market. Nicholas Green et al. 384p. 1992. pap. text 45.00 (*0-19-825628-0*) OUP.

Legal Foundations of the Welfare State. Ross Cranston. (Law in Context Ser.). 490p. (C). 1994. pap. text 33.95 (*0-297-78534-6*) Northwestern U Pr.

Legal Foundations of the Welfare State. Ross Cranston. (Law in Context Ser.). (Illus.). xxxiv, 453p. 1985. 26.00 (*0-297-78487-0*) W S Hein.

Legal Foundations Public Administration. 2nd ed. Donald B. Barry & Howard R. Whitcomb. (Paralegal). 384p. (C). 1986. mass mkt. 53.50 (*0-314-30387-1*) West Pub.

Legal Framework & Social Consequences of Free Movement of Persons in the European Union. Elspeth Guild. LC 98-36788. (Studies in Law). 192p. 1998. 54.00 (*90-411-1073-9*) Kluwer Law Intl.

Legal Framework for Bioethics. Cosimo M. Mazzoni. LC 97-32491. (Nijhoff Law Specials Ser.). 256p. 1998. pap. text 81.00 (*90-411-0523-9*) Kluwer Academic.

Legal Framework for Water Users' Associations: A Comparative Study. Salman M. Salman. LC 97-6339. (Technical Paper Ser.: No. 360R). 112p. 1997. pap. 22.00 (*0-8213-3908-7*, 13908) World Bank.

Legal Framework for Water Users' Associations: A Comparative Study. Salman M. Salman. (Technical Paper Ser.: No. 360R). (RUS.). 109p. 1998. pap. 22.00 (*0-8213-4287-8*, 14287) World Bank.

Legal Framework of Education in the Organization of Eastern Caribbean States (OECS) Kenny Anthony. LC 93-44090. (Coleccion Interamer Ser.: No. 35). 1994. write for info. (*0-8270-3301-X*) OAS.

Legal Framework of English Feudalism. S. F. Milsom. LC 85-82332. (Cambridge Studies in English Legal History). 212p. 1986. reprint ed. 55.00 (*0-912004-58-4*) Gaunt.

Legal Framework of English Feudalism: The Maitland Lectures Given in 1972. Stroud Milsom. LC 75-2351. (Cambridge Studies in English Legal History). 212p. reprint ed. pap. 60.50 (*0-608-15754-6*, 2031693) Bks Demand.

Legal Framework of Police Powers. Leonard Jason-Lloyd. LC 96-26294. (Legal Framework Ser.). 64p. (C). 1996. 22.50 (*0-7146-4775-6*, Pub. by F Cass Pubs); pap. 14.50 (*0-7146-4286-X*, Pub. by F Cass Pubs) Intl Spec Bk.

Legal Framework of the Church of England: A Critical Study in a Comparative Context. Norman Doe. 618p. 1996. text 110.00 (*0-19-826220-5*, Clarendon Pr) OUP.

Legal Framework of the Constitution. Leonard Jason-Lloyd. (Legal Framework Ser.). 112p. (Orig.). (C). 1996. 22.50 (*0-7146-4779-9*, Pub. by F Cass Pubs) Intl Spec Bk.

Legal Framework of the Constitution: Leonard Jason-Lloyd. Leonard Jason-Lloyd. LC 96-26293. (The Legal Framework Ser.: Vol. 0965-3473). 112p. (Orig.). (C). 1996. pap. 14.50 (*0-7146-4290-8*, Pub. by F Cass Pubs) Intl Spec Bk.

Legal Framework of the European Union. Leonard Jason-Lloyd & Sukhwinder Bajwa. (Legal Framework Ser.). 64p. (Orig.). (C). 1996. 22.50 (*0-7146-4780-2*, Pub. by F Cass Pubs); pap. 14.50 (*0-7146-4291-6*, Pub. by F Cass Pubs) Intl Spec Bk.

Legal Framework of the Modern Company. Leonard Jason-Lloyd & Larry Mead. (Legal Framework Ser.). 72p. (Orig.). (C). 1996. 22.50 (*0-7146-4777-2*, Pub. by F Cass Pubs); pap. 14.50 (*0-7146-4288-6*, Pub. by F Cass Pubs) Intl Spec Bk.

***Legal Framework of the Single European Currency.** Ed. by Paul Beaumont & Neil Walker. 224p. 1999. 54.00 (*1-84113-001-X*) Hart Pub.

Legal Framework of the U. S. Securities Market. Kaj Hober. 96p. 1988. pap. 45.00 (*91-7598-195-5*) Coronet Bks.

Legal Framework of Trade. George Ginsburgs. 1976. pap. text 51.00 (*90-247-1850-3*) Kluwer Academic.

Legal Frameworks for Forest Management in Asia: Case Studies of Community/State Relations. Ed. by Jefferson Fox et al. LC 93-11400. (Occasional Paper Ser.: Vol. 16). 226p. 1993. reprint ed. pap. 70.10 (*0-608-03577-7*, 206440000009) Bks Demand.

Legal Frameworks for the Built Environment. J. Badman. 200p. (C). (gr. 13). 1996. pap. 29.99 (*0-419-21270-1*) Routledge.

Legal Frontiers. Ed. by Philip A. Thomas. (Applied Legal Philosophy Ser.). 330p. 1996. text 87.95 (*1-85521-262-5*, Pub. by Dartmth Pub) Ashgate Pub Co.

Legal Frontiers of Death & Dying. Norman L. Cantor. LC 86-45502. (Medical Ethics Ser.). 220p. 1987. reprint ed. pap. 68.20 (*0-608-01053-7*, 205936100001) Bks Demand.

Legal Future of Employee Representation. Ed. by Matthew W. Finkin. LC 94-13490. 264p. 1994. text 32.50 (*0-87546-330-4*, ILR Press) Cornell U Pr.

Legal Guide for Connecticut Entrepreneurs. Nan Barnes et al. 104p. 1994. pap. text 9.95 (*1-886277-00-1*) CT Small Busn.

Legal Guide for Day-to-Day Church Matters: A Handbook for Pastors & Church Members. Cynthia S. Mazur & Ronald K. Bullis. LC 94-7401. 148p. (Orig.). 1994. pap. 6.95 (*0-8298-0990-2*) Pilgrim OH.

Legal Guide for Handling Toxic Substances in the Workplace, No. A79. Lawrence Postol. 600p. 1990. ring bd. 125.00 (*0-929576-54-3*) Busn Laws Inc.

Legal Guide for Lesbian & Gay Couples. 10th ed. Hayden Curry. LC 98-28122. 344p. 1999. 25.95 (*0-87337-495-9*) Nolo com.

Legal Guide for Lesbian & Gay Couples. 10th ed. Hayden Curry et al. LC 96-15945. 344p. 1999. pap. 24.95 (*0-87337-336-7*) Nolo com.

***Legal Guide for Long-Term Care Administrators.** Peter J. Buttaro. LC 99-32771. (Long Term Care Administration Ser.). 240p. 1999. pap. 59.00 (*0-8342-1370-2*) Aspen Pub.

Legal Guide for Physicians. Joseph M. Taraska. 1300p. 1987. text 140.00 (*1-887515-01-1*) AHAB Press.

Legal Guide for Police: Constitutional Issues. 5th ed. John C. Klotter. LC 98-28118. 1998. pap. 24.95 (*0-87084-534-9*) Anderson Pub Co.

Legal Guide for Practicing Psychotherapy in Colorado. Louie V. Larimer, Jr. 1992. pap. 34.95 (*0-963550-0-7*) Ctr Prof Develop.

Legal Guide for Small Business. Charles P. Lickson. Ed. by Beverly Manber. LC 93-72970. (Crisp Small Business & Entrepreneurship Ser.). 210p. 1996. pap. 15.95 (*1-56052-266-6*) Crisp Pubns.

Legal Guide for Starting & Running a Small Business, Vol. 1. 3rd ed. Fred S. Steingold. Ed. by Ralph E. Warner. LC 97-13003. (Illus.). 416p. 1996. reprint ed. pap. 24.95 (*0-87337-374-X*) Nolo com.

Legal Guide for Starting & Running a Small Business, Vol. 1. 5th ed. Fred Steingold. LC 99-30244. 1999. pap. 24.95 (*0-87337-527-0*) Nolo com.

Legal Guide for Starting & Running a Small Business: Legal Forms, Vol. 2. Fred S. Steingold. Ed. by Ralph E. Warner. (Illus.). 340p. (Orig.). 1998. pap. 29.95 (*0-87337-379-0*) Nolo com.

Legal Guide for Student Affairs Professionals. William A. Kaplin & Barbara A. Lee. LC 96-51218. 1997. 39.95 (*0-7879-0862-2*) Jossey-Bass.

Legal Guide for the Family. Donald Very & Eugene F. Keefe. 370p. 1993. write for info. (*0-89434-131-6*) Ferguson.

Legal Guide for the Visual Artist. 3rd ed. Tad Crawford. LC 94-72263. 256p. 1994. pap. 19.95 (*0-927629-11-9*) Allworth Pr.

Legal Guide for the Visual Artist. 4th ed. Tad Crawford. LC 98-72761. (Illus.). 256p. 1999. pap. 19.95 (*1-58115-003-2*) Allworth Pr.

Legal Guide to Buying & Selling Art & Collectibles. Armen R. Vartian. LC 96-51959. 200p. (Orig.). 1997. pap. 12.95 (*1-56625-079-X*) Bonus Books.

Legal Guide to Computer Software: A Practical Handbook on Copyrights, Trademarks, Publishing & Trade Secrets. Thorne D. Harris, III. (Illus.). 19.95 (*0-317-13079-X*) P-H.

Legal Guide to EDP Management. Michael C. Gemignani. LC 88-18503. 270p. 1989. 65.00 (*0-89930-347-1*, GLG/, Quorum Bks) Greenwood.

Legal Guide to Employee Relations. Laurence S. Zakson. 334p. 1990. text 135.00 (*0-89982-366-1*) Am Bankers.

***Legal Guide to Independent Contractor Status, 1.** 3rd ed. Robert W. Wood. LC 99-46354. 880p. 1999. boxed set 165.00 (*0-7355-1078-4*) Panel Pubs.

Legal Guide to Public Employee Free Speech in North Carolina. 2nd ed. Stephen Allred. 58p. (C). 1995. pap. text 12.00 (*1-56011-239-5*) Institute Government.

Legal Guide to Purchasing & Contracting for North Carolina Local Governments. Frayda S. Bluestein. LC 99-185173. (C). 1998. ring bd. 28.00 (*1-56011-330-8*) Institute Government.

Legal Guide to Religion & Public Education. 2nd rev. ed. Benjamin A. Sendor. 96p. 1997. text 20.00 (*1-56534-094-9*) Ed Law Assn.

Legal Guide to Starting & Managing a Nonprofit Organization. 2nd ed. Bruce R. Hopkins. (Nonprofit Law, Finance, & Management Ser.). 320p. 1993. pap. 26.95 (*0-471-58506-8*) Wiley.

Legal Guidelines for Covert Surveillance. John D. Hartman. LC 92-5688. 235p. 1992. 49.95 (*0-7506-9021-6*) Buttrwrth-Heinemann.

Legal Guidelines for Curbing School Violence. NSBA Council of School Attorneys Members. 162p. 1995. pap. 30.00 (*0-88364-195-X*, 06-152) Natl Sch Boards.

Legal Guidelines for Reporters in Michigan. rev. ed. Jane Briggs-Bunting. LC 98-73481. 58 p. (C). 1998. pap. text 8.00 (*0-9649083-2-8*) Blck Riv Trad.

Legal Guidelines for the Use of Force in the Private Sector. John D. Hartman. LC 96-26445. 268p. 1998. 45.00 (*0-7506-9562-5*, Focal) Buttrwrth-Heinemann.

Legal Guidelines for Unlicensed Practitioners. Lawrence D. Wilson. 62p. (Orig.). 1998. pap. text 11.95 (*0-9628657-2-9*) L D Wilson Cnstls.

Legal Handbook for Community Development Organizations. Ed. by Council of New York Law Associates Staff. 67p. 1983. pap. 25.00 (*0-318-03110-8*) Coun NY Law.

Legal Handbook for the New York State Journalists. J. B. Wright & Brad Carr. LC 86-60850. 1987. 20.00 (*0-317-59726-4*) NYS Bar.

Legal Handbook for Trainers, Speakers & Consultants: The Essential Guide to Keeping Your Company & Your Clients Out of Court. Patricia S. Eyres. LC 97-48502. 464p. 1998. 39.95 (*0-07-063512-9*) McGraw.

Legal Handbook of Business Transactions: A Guide for Managers & Entrepreneurs. E. C. Lashbrooke, Jr. & Michael I. Swygert. LC 86-30595. 599p. 1987. 95.00 (*0-89930-179-7*, LLH/, Quorum Bks) Greenwood.

Legal Handbook of Texas Nurses. Susan S. Murphy. LC 94-27848. 256p. 1995. pap. 17.95 (*0-292-75176-1*); text 35.00 (*0-292-75161-3*) U of Tex Pr.

Legal Handbook on School Athletics. NSBA Council of School Attorneys Members. 120p. 1997. pap. text 35.00 (*0-88364-206-9*, 06-160) Natl Sch Boards.

Legal Help for Battered Women. 3rd rev. ed. Lisa G. Lerman. 12p. 1989. pap. 4.00 (*1-877966-02-9*) Ctr Women Policy.

Legal Hermeneutics: History, Theory, & Practice. Intro. by Gregory Leyh. LC 90-19397. 335p. 1991. 55.00 (*0-520-07283-9*, Pub. by U CA Pr); pap. 18.95 (*0-520-07284-7*, Pub. by U CA Pr) Cal Prin Full Svc.

Legal Highs: A Concise Encyclopedia of Legal Herbs & Chemicals with Psychoactive Properties. 2nd ed. Adam Gottlieb. (Twentieth Century Alchemist Ser.). (Illus.). 64p. 1995. pap. 10.95 (*0-914171-82-8*) Ronin Pub.

Legal History: A European Perspective. R. C. Van Caenegem. 256p. 1991. 55.00 (*1-85285-049-3*) Hambledon Press.

Legal History & Comparative Law: Essays in Honour of Albert Kiralfy. Ed. by Richard Plender. 239p. 1990. text 40.00 (*0-7146-3397-6*, Pub. by F Cass Pubs) Intl Spec Bk.

Legal History in the Making. Ed. by William Gordon. 256p. 1991. 60.00 (*1-85285-054-X*) Hambledon Press.

Legal History of Asian Americans, 1790-1990, 34. Hyung-chan Kim. LC 93-31625. (Contributions in Ethnic Studies: No. 34). 216p. 1994. 59.95 (*0-313-29142-X*, Greenwood Pr) Greenwood.

Legal History of India, 1600-1990. S. G. Mishra. (C). 1992. 22.00 (*81-85565-21-X*, Pub. by Uppal Pub Hse) S Asia.

Legal History of Money in the United States, 1774-1970. James W. Hurst. LC 72-86019. 385p. reprint ed. pap. 119.40 (*0-7837-1477-7*, 205717200023) Bks Demand.

Legal Homicide: Death As Punishment in America, 1864-1982. William J. Bowers. LC 81-11309. 648p. 1984. text 65.00 (*0-930350-25-1*) NE U Pr.

Legal Ideology & Politics in South Africa: A Social Science Approach. John Hund & Hendrik W. Van Der Merwe. 132p. (Orig.). (C). 1986. pap. text 24.00 (*0-8191-5353-2*) U Pr of Amer.

Legal Imagination. abr. ed. James B. White. LC 85-5860. 328p. 1985. pap. text 16.95 (*0-226-89493-2*) U Ch Pr.

Legal Imagination. abr. ed. James B. White. LC 85-5860. 330p. 1994. lib. bdg. 33.00 (*0-226-89492-4*) U Ch Pr.

Legal Imagination: Studies in the Nature of Legal Thought & Expression. James B. White. 1024p. 1973. 45.00 (*0-316-93602-2*, Aspen Law & Bus) Aspen Pub.

Legal Immigration: Setting Priorities. Barbara Jordan & Susan Martin. (Illus.). 245p. (Orig.). 1996. pap. text 35.00 (*0-7881-2819-1*) DIANE Pub.

Legal Impacts upon the Profession of Architecture: The Liability of the Architect in Wisconsin. Robert Greenstreet. (Publications in Architecture & Urban Planning: No. R85-6). (Illus.). iv, 51p. 1985. 10.00 (*0-938744-41-0*) U of Wis Ctr Arch-Urban.

Legal Impediments to Effective Rural Land Relations in Eastern Europe & Central Asia: A Comparative Perspective. Ed. by Roy Prosterman & Tim Hanstad. LC 99-28652. (Technical Paper Ser.: No. 436). 330p. 1999. pap. 30.00 (*0-8213-4501-X*, 14501) World Bank.

Legal Imperialism: American Lawyers & Foreign Aid in Latin America. James A. Gardner. LC 79-5406. 415p. 1980. reprint ed. pap. 128.70 (*0-608-07002-5*, 206721000009) Bks Demand.

An Asterisk (*) at the beginning of an entry indicates that the title is appearing for the first time.

L

Legal Implications for Banking, 1992. C. Cranston. Ed. by Ross Cranston. 188p. (C). 1990. 150.00 (*0-85297-243-1*, Pub. by Chartered Bank) St Mut.

***Legal Implications of Purchasing.** Renbe Sacasas. LC 98-180780. 127p. 1998. write for info. (*0-87622-770-1*) Aspen Pub.

***Legal Implications of the Millennium Bug.** Ed. by Dennis Campbell. (Comparative Law Yearbook of International Business Ser.: Vol. 21A). 480p. 1999. text 165.00 (*90-411-9776-1*) Kluwer Law Intl.

Legal Incompetents' Need for Guardians in Florida. W. Schmidt & R. Peters. 1983. write for info. (*0-318-58135-3*) FSU CSP.

Legal Incubus. Dian Kastl. 330p. mass mkt. 4.99 (*1-55197-264-6*) Picasso Publ.

Legal Indeterminacy & Constitutional Interpretation. Josep J. Moreso. LC 98-19233. (Law & Philosophy Library). xiii, 200 p. 1998. write for info. (*0-7923-5156-8*) Kluwer Academic.

Legal Industrial Espionage. Eurofi Staff. 160p. (C). 1988. 395.00 (*0-907304-12-5*, Pub. by Eurofi) St Mut.

Legal Information: How to Find It, How to Use It. Kent Olson. 344p. 1998. pap. 39.50 (*0-89774-963-4*); boxed set 59.95 (*0-89774-961-8*) Oryx Pr.

Legal Information Buyer's Guide & Reference Manual, 1996. Kendall F. Svengalis. (Illus.). viii, 582p. (Orig.). 1996. pap. 79.95 (*0-9651032-0-X*, 96-01) Rhode Isl LawPress.

Legal Information Buyers Guide & Reference Manual, 1998-1999. 3rd ed. Kendall F. Svengalis. 650p. 1998. 88.00 (*0-9651032-2-6*) Rhode Isl LawPress.

Legal Information for the 1980's: Meeting Needs of the Legal Profession - American Association of Law Libraries Proceedings of the Annual Meeting June 27-July 2, 1981, Washington, D. C. Ed. by Betty W. Taylor. (AALL Publications Ser.: No. 17). xii, 593p. 1982. 45.00 (*0-8377-0114-7*, Rothman) W S Hein.

Legal Information System Markets (U. S.) Market Intelligence Staff. 262p. 1992. 2250.00 (*1-56753-666-2*, A2502) Frost & Sullivan.

Legal Insanity: Disorder in the Court. Steve Rushing. (Illus.). 90p. (Orig.). 1993. pap. 10.00 (*0-88092-076-9*) Royal Fireworks.

Legal Insights to International Business in Spain. LC 91-76076. viii, 392p. 1991. pap. 249.00 (*0-9630929-0-1*, 307480) W S Hein.

Legal, Institutional, & Social Aspects of Irrigation & Drainage & Water Resources Planning & Management. 909p. 1979. pap. 55.00 (*0-87262-140-5*) Am Soc Civil Eng.

Legal, Institutional, Financial, & Environmental Aspects of Water Issues. Ed. by George R. Baumli. 232p. 1989. pap. text 5.00 (*0-87262-715-2*, 715) Am Soc Civil Eng.

Legal Instruments of Foundations. Ed. by F. Emerson Andrews. LC 58-9443. 318p. 1958. 45.00 (*0-87154-020-7*) Russell Sage.

Legal Insurrection. Ken Hunter. LC 97-75655. 800p. 1998. 43.00 (*1-57197-100-9*) Pentland Pr.

Legal Interventions in Family Violence: Research Findings & Policy Implications. Ed. by Jeremy Travis. 78p. (C). 1999. pap. text 25.00 (*0-7881-7798-2*) DIANE Pub.

Legal Interviewing: Theory, Tactics & Techniques. K. A. Lauchland & M. J. Le Brun. (Butterworths Skills Ser.). 200p. 1996. pap. write for info. (*0-409-30809-9*, MICHIE) LEXIS Pub.

Legal Interviewing & Counseling: A Client-Centered Approach. David A. Binder & Susan C. Price. (Miscellaneous Ser.). 217p. (C). 1979. pap. text. write for info. (*0-314-51174-1*) West Pub.

Legal Interviewing & Counselling: A Client-Centered Approach. David A. Binder & Susan C. Price. LC 77-84550. (Hornbook Ser.). 232p. (C). 1977. reprint ed. pap. 21.25 (*0-314-33557-9*) West Pub.

Legal Interviewing & Counselling in a Nutshell. 2nd ed. Thomas L. Shaffer & James R. Elkins. (Nutshell Ser.). 487p. (C). 1987. reprint ed. pap. text 17.00 (*0-314-36474-9*) West Pub.

Legal Interviewing /Counseling In a Nutshell. 3rd ed. Thomas L. Shaffer & James R. Elkins. LC 97-37787. (Paralegal). 418p. (C). 1997. pap. text, suppl. ed. 15.00 (*0-314-21164-0*) West Pub.

Legal Interviewing in Practice. Allan Chay & Judith Smith. 402p. 1996. pap. 49.00 (*0-455-21413-1*, Pub. by LawBk Co) Gaunt.

Legal Inversions: Lesbians, Gay Men & the Politics of the Law. Ed. by Didi Herman & Carl F. Stychin. LC 95-40370. 240p. (C). 1995. pap. text 22.95 (*1-56639-377-9*) Temple U Pr.

Legal Inversions: Lesbians, Gay Men & the Politics of the Law. Ed. by Didi Herman & Carl F. Stychin. LC 95-40370. 240p. (C). 1995. lib. bdg. 69.95 (*1-56639-376-0*) Temple U Pr.

Legal Investigation Training Manual. Ralph D. Thomas. 200p. 1990. pap. text 38.00 (*0-918487-32-3*) Thomas Investigative.

Legal Issue, 1965. Paul A. Freund. LC 65-26011. 1965. write for info. (*0-318-53172-0*) HUP.

Legal Issues. 9th ed. Katsh. 384p. 2000. pap. 18.44 (*0-07-237139-0*) McGraw.

Legal Issues Affecting Interstate Disposal. W. Victoria Becker. Ed. by Karen Glass. (Hazardous Waste Management in the States Ser.). 48p. (Orig.). 1989. pap. text 15.00 (*1-55877-045-3*) Natl Governor.

Legal Issues & Education Technology: A School Leader's Guide. Ronald Wenkart et al. 100p. 1999. pap. 35.00 (*0-88364-222-0*) Natl Sch Boards.

Legal Issues & Ethical Dilemmas in Respiratory Care. Charles Carroll. LC 95-44083. (Illus.). 163p. (C). 1996. pap. text 19.95 (*0-8036-0126-3*) Davis Co.

Legal Issues & Older Adults. Linda Josephson-Millman & Sallie C. Birket. LC 92-31475. (Choices & Challenges Ser.). 300p. 1992. lib. bdg. 45.00 (*0-87436-594-5*) ABC-CLIO.

Legal Issues & Religious Counseling. Ronald K. Bullis & Cynthia S. Mazur. 112p. (Orig.). 1993. pap. 15.95 (*0-664-25386-5*) Westminster John Knox.

Legal Issues & the Integrated Delivery System: An Executive Guide. American Academy of Healthcare Attorneys of the Am. Ed. by Deborah A. Randall. LC 96-8090. 104p. 1996. pap. 40.00 (*1-55648-159-4*, 118119) AHPI.

Legal Issues Facing the Nontraditional Family. (Tax Law & Estate Planning Course Handbook Ser.). Date not set. pap. 99.00 (*0-614-17283-7*, D4-5263) PLI.

Legal Issues for Correctional Staff Correspondence Course, 2 vols. rev. ed. American Correctional Association Staff. Ed. & Illus. by Capitol Communication Systems, Inc. Staff. LC 96-116620. 321p. 1999. pap. 70.00 (*1-56991-107-X*) Am Correctional.

Legal Issues for Industrial Educators. Forrest Gathercoal & Sam Stern. LC 86-60598. 200p. (Orig.). 1987. text 15.95 (*0-911168-64-8*); pap. text 10.95 (*0-911168-65-6*) Prakken.

Legal Issues for Managers: Essential Skills for Avoiding Your Day in Court. Mike Deblieux. Ed. by Karen M. Miller. LC 95-80142. (How-to Book Ser.). 120p. (Orig.). 1996. pap. 12.95 (*1-884926-49-5*, BEYON) Amer Media.

Legal Issues for Non-Profit Associations. Ed. by M. McGregor-Loundes et al. LC 96-170375. 224p. 1996. pap. 85.00 (*0-455-21401-8*, Pub. by Cavendish Pubng) Gaunt.

Legal Issues for Probation & Parole Officers Correspondence Course, 2 bks., Set. American Correctional Association Staff. Ed. by Rosalie Rosetti & Diane Geiman. (Illus.). 1988. pap. 70.00 (*0-929310-03-9*, 169) Am Correctional.

Legal Issues in Athletic Training. Richard T. Ball. 300p. 2000. pap. 19.95 (*0-8036-0339-8*) Davis Co.

Legal Issues in Biotechnology & Human Reproduction. Warren Freedman. LC 90-20709. 240p. 1991. 67.95 (*0-89930-635-7*, FLI/, Quorum Bks) Greenwood.

Legal Issues in Child Abuse & Neglect Practice. John B. Myers. (Interpersonal Violence: the Practice Ser.: Vol. 1). (Illus.). 184p. (C). 1992. 48.00 (*0-8039-4231-1*); pap. 21.50 (*0-8039-4232-X*) Sage.

Legal Issues in Child Abuse & Neglect Practice. 2nd ed. John E. Myers. LC 98-9022. (Interpersonal Violence Ser.). 1998. 68.50 (*0-7619-1665-2*); pap. 31.95 (*0-7619-1666-0*) Sage.

Legal Issues in Clinical Supervision. M. Janelle Disney & Anthony M. Stephens. LC 93-36194. (ACA Legal Ser.: Vol. 10). 90p. 1994. pap. text 18.95 (*1-55620-128-1*, 72310) Am Coun Assn.

Legal Issues in Compensating Victims of Violent Crime. W. Schmidt. 1976. write for info. (*0-318-58133-7*) FSU CSP.

Legal Issues in Foodservice Management Skillbook. Educational Foundation of the National Restaurant. (Management Skills Program Ser.). 50p. (Orig.). 1992. pap. 10.95 (*0-915452-96-0*) Educ Found.

***Legal Issues in Health Care for Prenant Adolescents: A Guide for North Carolina Providers.** Anne M. Dellinger. (C). 2000. pap. write for info. (*1-56011-378-2*) Institute Government.

Legal Issues in Health Care Fraud & Abuse: Navigating the Uncertainties. Ed. by Carrie S. Valiant. 288p. 1994. 50.00 (*0-918945-16-X*) Am Hlth Lawyers.

Legal Issues in Healthcare Fraud & Abuse: Navigating the Uncertainties. 2nd ed. David E. Matyas. LC 96-70114. (NHLA Focus Ser.). 403p. 1997. 75.00 (*0-918945-19-4*) Am Hlth Lawyers.

Legal Issues in Human Reproduction. Sheila A. McLean. (Medico-Legal Issues Ser.: Vol. 1). 1989. text 87.95 (*0-566-05393-4*, Pub. by Dartmth Pub) Ashgate Pub Co.

Legal Issues in Human Reproduction. Sheila A. McLean. (Medico-Legal Issues Ser.: Vol. 1). 1990. pap. 39.95 (*1-85521-008-6*, Pub. by Dartmth Pub) Ashgate Pub Co.

Legal Issues in International Trade. Ed. by Peter Sarcevic & Hans Van Houtte. (C). 1990. lib. bdg. 107.00 (*1-85333-360-3*) Kluwer Academic.

Legal Issues in Licensure. Donald Anderson & Carl D. Swanson. LC 93-33196. (ACA Legal Ser.: Vol. 11). 67p. 1994. pap. text 18.95 (*1-55620-129-X*, 72311) Am Coun Assn.

Legal Issues in Marriage & Family Counseling. Patricia Stevens-Smith & Marcia M. Hughes. LC 92-31486. (ACA Legal Ser.: Vol. 7). 61p. 1993. pap. text 18.95 (*1-55620-104-4*, 72307) Am Coun Assn.

Legal Issues in Medicine. Ed. by Sheila A. McLean. 234p. 1981. text 76.95 (*0-566-00428-3*) Ashgate Pub Co.

Legal Issues in Mental Health Care. R. Wettstein & Barbara A. Weiner. (Illus.). 432p. (C). 1993. 60.00 (*0-306-43867-4*, Plenum Trade) Perseus Pubng.

Legal Issues in Nursing. 2nd ed. Ginny Walker Guido. LC 96-17338. 416p. (C). 1996. pap. text 34.95 (*0-8385-5647-7*, A5647-1) Appleton & Lange.

Legal Issues in Nursing. 3rd ed. 528p. (C). 2000. pap. 35.95 (*0-8385-5659-0*) Appleton & Lange.

Legal Issues in Nursing: Instructors Manual. 2nd ed. Ginny W. Guido. 133p. 1997. teacher ed. write for info. (*0-8385-5648-5*, A5648-9) Appleton & Lange.

Legal Issues in Obstetrics. Vivienne Harpwood. (Medico-Legal Issues Ser.). (Illus.). 320p. 1996. text 91.95 (*1-85521-313-3*, Pub. by Dartmth Pub) Ashgate Pub Co.

Legal Issues in Pediatrics & Adolescent Medicine. 2nd enl. rev. ed. Angela R. Holder. LC 85-2410. 512p. 1985. 55.00 (*0-300-03384-2*) Yale U Pr.

Legal Issues in Property Valuation & Taxation: Cases & Materials. Joan Youngman. LC 94-77048. 1994. 75.00 (*0-88329-154-1*); pap. 60.00 (*0-88329-153-3*) IAAO.

Legal Issues in Social Work, Counseling, & Mental Health. Robert G. Madden. LC 97-45285. (Sourcebooks for the Human Services). 1998. write for info. (*0-7619-1232-0*); pap. write for info. (*0-7619-1233-9*) Sage.

Legal Issues in Special Education. Allan G. Osborne, Jr. LC 95-24024. 336p. 1995. 61.00 (*0-205-18442-1*) Allyn.

Legal Issues in Sport & Physical Education Management. John N. Drowatzky. Ed. by Earle F. Zeigler. (Monograph Series on Sport & Physical Education Management). (Illus.). 44p. 1993. pap. text 4.80 (*0-87563-426-5*) Stipes.

Legal Issues in the Private Practice of Psychiatry. Joel I. Klein. LC 84-6506. (Private Practice Monograph Ser.). 116p. reprint ed. pap. 36.00 (*0-8357-7843-6*, 203621800002) Bks Demand.

Legal Issues of Cross Border Banking. C. Cranston. Ed. by Ross Cranston. 158p. (C). 1990. 150.00 (*0-85297-232-6*, Pub. by Chartered Bank) St Mut.

Legal Issues of European Integration. Ed. by D. J. Gijlstra et al. 120p. 1978. pap. 33.00 (*90-268-1079-2*) Kluwer Law Intl.

Legal Issues of European Integration. Ed. by D. J. Gijlstra et al. (Law Review of the Europa Instituut (University of Amsterdam) Ser.: No. 2). 120p. 1979. 36.00 (*90-268-1178-0*) Kluwer Law Intl.

Legal Issues of European Integration. Ed. by Edmond L. Volker et al. (Law Review of the Europa Instituut (University of Amsterdam) Ser.: No. 1). 124p. 1974. 42.00 (*90-268-0738-4*) Kluwer Law Intl.

Legal Issues of European Integration. Ed. by Edmond L. Volker et al. (Law Review of the Europa Instituut (University of Amsterdam) Ser.: No.2). 148p. 1974. 50.00 (*90-268-0774-0*) Kluwer Law Intl.

Legal Issues of European Integration. Ed. by Edmond L. Volker et al. (Law Review of the European Instituut (University of Amsterdam) Ser.: No. 2). 160p. 1975. pap. 50.00 (*90-268-0848-8*) Kluwer Law Intl.

Legal Issues of European Integration. Ed. by Edmond L. Volker et al. (Law Review of the Europa Instituut (University of Amsterdam) Ser.: No. 1). 134p. 1976. 38.00 (*90-268-0905-0*) Kluwer Law Intl.

Legal Issues of European Integration. Ed. by Edmond L. Volker et al. (Law Review of the Europa Instituut (University of Amsterdam) Ser.: No. 2). 106p. 1976. pap. 46.00 (*90-268-0874-7*) Kluwer Law Intl.

Legal Issues of European Integration. Ed. by Edmond L. Volker et al. (Law Review of the Europa Instituut (University of Amsterdam) Ser.: No. 1). 134p. 1977. 46.00 (*90-268-0960-3*) Kluwer Law Intl.

Legal Issues of European Integration. Ed. by Edmond L. Volker et al. (Law Review of the Europa Instituut (University of Amsterdam) Ser.: No. 2). 76p. 1977. 30.00 (*90-268-0964-6*) Kluwer Law Intl.

Legal Issues of European Integration. Ed. by Edmond L. Volker et al. (Law Review of the Europa Instituut (University of Amsterdam) Ser.: No. 1). 98p. 1978. 38.00 (*90-268-1028-8*) Kluwer Law Intl.

Legal Issues of European Integration, 1982. D. J. Gijlstra. 1983. lib. bdg. 42.00 (*90-6544-140-9*) Kluwer Law Intl.

Legal Issues of European Integration, 1982-1983. D. J. Gijlstra. 1984. lib. bdg. 65.00 (*90-6544-210-3*) Kluwer Law Intl.

Legal Issues of European Integration, 1983-1: Law Review of the University of Amsterdam. Gijlstra-Lauwaars et al. 1984. pap. text 48.00 (*90-6544-161-1*) Kluwer Law Intl.

Legal Issues of European Integration, 1984. D. J. Gijlstra. 1984. pap. text 60.00 (*90-6544-205-7*) Kluwer Law Intl.

Legal Issues of European Integration, 1988, No. 2. D. J. Gijlstra et al. (Legal Issues of European Integration Ser.). 108p. 1989. pap. 52.00 (*90-6544-424-6*) Kluwer Law Intl.

***Legal Issues of the Amsterdam Treaty.** Ed. by Patrick Twomey & David O'Keeffe. 500p. 1999. 80.00 (*1-84113-002-8*, Pub. by Hart Pub) Intl Spec Bk.

Legal Issues Surrounding Safe Schools. Reed B. Day. 90p. 1994. text 30.00 (*1-56534-066-3*) Ed Law Assn.

Legal Job Interview. Clifford R. Ennico. 176p. (Orig.). 1992. pap. 17.95 (*0-9632835-5-3*) Biennix.

Legal Justice & Social Change, a Philosophy of Law. E. Levine. 256p. 1990. 67.00 (*965-09-0125-6*, 73865, Pub. by R Mass Ltd) Lambda Pubs.

Legal Keyboarding: Typewriters, Electric Typewriters, Word Processors. Mary A. Baumann & Mary A. Bahntge. 286p. 1985. pap. text 21.95 (*0-471-88590-8*) P-H.

Legal Keys: Keyboard Drills. Bedford. (C). 1991. pap. text. write for info. (*0-7730-5032-9*) Addison-Wes.

Legal Knowledge & Analogy: Fragments of Legal Epistemology, Hermeneutics & Linguistics. Ed. by Patrick Nerhot. 250p. (C). 1991. lib. bdg. 135.00 (*0-7923-1065-9*, Pub. by Kluwer Academic) Kluwer Academic.

Legal Knowledge Engineering: A Modelling Approach. (Frontiers in Artificial Intelligence & Applications Ser.: Vol. 30). (YA). (gr. 12). 1995. 72.00 (*90-5199-230-0*, 230-0) IOS Press.

Legal Knowledge Representation: Automatic Text Analysis in Public International & European Law. Erich Schweighofer. LC 98-54694. (Law & Electronic Commerce Ser.). 1999. 183.00 (*90-411-1148-4*) Kluwer Law Intl.

Legal L. C. Subject Headings Weekly Lists: Cumulation. Compiled by Melody B. Lembke. LC 86-529. (AALL Publications Ser.: No. 26). viii, 38p. 1986. ring bd. 57.50 (*0-8377-0125-2*, Rothman) W S Hein.

Legal Language. Peter M. Tiersma. LC 98-19367. 1999. 26.00 (*0-226-80302-3*) U Ch Pr.

***Legal Language.** Peter M. Tiersma. (Illus.). 2000. pap. text 17.00 (*0-226-80303-1*) U Ch Pr.

Legal Language & Legal Writing (Including Legal Maxims) M. A. Khan. (C). 1988. 40.00 (*0-7855-3705-8*) St Mut.

Legal Latin. Rudolph Masciantonio. (ENG, GRE & LAT.). 82p. 1992. spiral bd. 7.75 (*0-939507-22-6*, B312) Amer Classical.

Legal Laughs: A Joke for Every Jury. Gus C. Edwards. LC 93-79765. lii, 437p. 1993. reprint ed. text 48.50 (*0-89941-854-6*, 307800) W S Hein.

***Legal Liabilities at Bayshore Science.** Debra D. Burke & Sheila M. Brown-Walker. LC 00-44608. 2000. write for info. (*0-13-012500-8*) P-H.

***Legal Liabilities in Emergency Medical Services.** Thomas D. Schneid. LC 00-33762. 2000. write for info. (*1-56032-899-1*) Taylor & Francis.

Legal Liability: A Guide for Safety & Loss Prevention Professionals. Thomas D. Schneid & Michael S. Schumann. LC 97-21725. 307p. 1997. 59.00 (*0-8342-0984-5*) Aspen Pub.

Legal Liability & Malpractice in Health Sciences: Index of New Information with References. Brian H. Armstrong. 150p. 1996. 47.50 (*0-7883-0814-9*); pap. 44.50 (*0-7883-0815-7*) ABBE Pubs Assn.

Legal Liability & Risk Management for Public & Private Entities. Betty Van Der Smissen. 860p. 1990. pap. 38.50 (*0-87084-914-X*) Anderson Pub Co.

Legal Liability for Claims Arising from Hospital Treatment. Ravenswood Publ. Ltd. Staff. (C). 1987. pap. 89.00 (*0-7855-3752-X*); write for info. (*0-901812-14-5*) St Mut.

Legal Liability in Recreation & Sports. Bruce Hronek & John Spengler. 1997. pap. 44.95 (*1-57167-129-3*) Sagamore Pub.

Legal Limericks. Donald S. Altschul. (Illus.). 96p. (Orig.). 1993. pap. 7.95 (*1-882278-05-4*) Survival Series.

Legal Limits on the Use of Chemical & Biological Weapons. Ann V. Thomas & A. J. Thomas. LC 78-128123. (SMU Law School Study Ser.). 342p. reprint ed. pap. 106.10 (*0-8357-8938-1*, 203342800086) Bks Demand.

Legal List: Internet Desk Reference. Erik J. Heels. Ed. by Lisa K. Gregory. LC 95-76104. (Law-Related Resources on the Internet & Elsewhere Ser.). 300p. 1995. text 29.95 (*0-7620-0000-7*) West Group.

Legal List, Law-Related Resources on the Internet & Elsewhere: Version 5.1. 5th ed. Erik J. Heels. 278p. 1994. pap. 29.95 (*0-9643637-0-4*) Legal List.

Legal Literacy: A Tool for Women's Empowerment. Ed. by Margaret Schuler & Sakuntala Kadirgamar-Rajasingham. 340p. (Orig.). 1992. pap. 24.00 (*0-912917-25-3*) UNIFEM.

Legal Literature of Accounting: On Accounts by Diego del Castillo. Diego Del Castillo. Tr. by Patti A. Mills from SPA. (Foundations of Accounting Ser.: No. 12).Tr. of Tratado de Cuentas. 120p. 1988. text 10.00 (*0-8240-6118-7*) Garland.

Legal Looseleafs in Print 1999. Ed. by Arlene L. Eis. 440p. 1999. pap. text 99.00 (*0-939486-54-7*) Infosources.

Legal Lunacies 1996. Robert Pelton. 13.95 (*0-939251-50-7*) Accord CO.

Legal Lynching: The Plight of Sam Jennings. Perry T. Ryan. LC 89-92805. (Illus.). 230p. (Orig.). 1989. pap. 9.95 (*0-9625504-2-6*) P T Ryan.

Legal Malpractice, Vol. 1. 4th ed. Ronald E. Mallen & Jeffrey M. Smith. LC 95-5502. 700p. (C). 1995. text. write for info. (*0-314-05492-8*) West Pub.

Legal Malpractice, Vol. 2. 4th ed. Ronald E. Mallen & Jeffrey M. Smith. LC 95-5502. 700p. (C). 1995. text. write for info. (*0-314-05493-6*) West Pub.

Legal Malpractice, Vol. 3. 4th ed. Ronald E. Mallen & Jeffrey M. Smith. LC 95-5502. 700p. (C). 1995. text. write for info. (*0-314-05494-4*) West Pub.

Legal Malpractice No. 24: A Research Guide for Lawyers & Law Students. Patrick G. Reavey. LC 95-15352. Vol. 24. xix, 94p. 1995. 42.00 (*0-89941-933-X*, 308680) W S Hein.

Legal Manual for Programming Professionals. Robert J. Shoop & Dennis R. Darklee. 206p. 119.00 (*0-914951-66-1*) LERN.

Legal Marketing. Martin Davies. (Legal Practice Course Guides Ser.). 120p. 1995. pap. 26.00 (*1-85431-376-2*, Pub. by Blackstone Pr) Gaunt.

Legal Marketing of Drugs. Harrison Johnson. 69.95 (*1-85521-341-9*) Ashgate Pub Co.

Legal Masterpieces: Specimens of Argumentation & Exposition by Eminent Lawyers, 2 bks. in 1 vol., Set. Van V. Veeder. LC 74-82121. (Classics in Legal History Reprint Ser.: Vols. 24 & 25). 1994. 165.00 (*1-57588-322-8*, 308870) W S Hein.

Legal Measures for the Conservation of Natural Areas. (Nature & Environment Ser.: No. 82). 1996. 18.00 (*92-871-3070-1*, Pub. by Council of Europe) Manhattan Pub Co.

Legal Medical Quarterly, 1977-1980, 19 vols. 1995. 525.00 (*0-8377-9106-5*, Rothman) W S Hein.

Legal Medicine. 4th ed. American College of Legal Medicine. LC 97-43320. (Illus.). 688p. (C). (gr. 13). 1998. text 145.00 (*0-8151-3669-2*, 31390) Mosby Inc.

Legal Medicine in History. Ed. by Michael Clark & Catherine Crawford. LC 93-11582. (Cambridge History of Medicine Ser.). 378p. (C). 1994. text 69.95 (*0-521-39514-3*) Cambridge U Pr.

Legal Medicine, 1985. Ed. by Cyril H. Wecht. 416p. 1985. 99.50 (*0-275-90182-3*, C0182, Praeger Pubs) Greenwood.

Legal Medicine, 1987. Ed. by Cyril H. Wecht. LC 80-647751. 226p. 1988. 75.00 (*0-275-92595-1*, C2595, Praeger Pubs) Greenwood.

An Asterisk (*) at the beginning of an entry indicates that the title is appearing for the first time.

L

Legal Medicine, 1986. Ed. by Cyril H. Wecht. LC 86-47751. 267p. 1986. 75.00 (*0-275-92551-X*, C2551, Praeger Pubs) Greenwood.

Legal Medicine, 1994. Ed. by Cyril H. Wecht. 1994. boxed set 85.00 (*0-250-47780-7*, MICHIE) LEXIS Pub.

Legal Medicine, 1993. Ed. by Cyril H. Wecht. 1993. boxed set 85.00 (*0-685-71121-8*, MICHIE) LEXIS Pub.

Legal Memorandum Before the Council of State: Concerning the Skete of the Prophet Elias. Ed. by Monk of the Skete of the Propher Elias Staff. 65p. 1995. pap. 10.00 (*0-912927-64-X*, D031) St John Kronstadt.

Legal Memories & Amnesias in America's Rhetorical Culture. Arshag Hasian. 2000. 60.00 (*0-8133-6601-1*) Westview.

***Legal Method.** Sharon Hanson. 357p. 1999. pap. 32.50 (*1-85941-424-9*, Pub. by Cavendish Pubng) Gaunt.

Legal Method: Cases & Text Materials. Harry W. Jones et al. LC 80-13230. (University Casebook Ser.). 785p. 1991. reprint ed. text 31.95 (*0-88277-004-7*) Foundation Pr.

Legal Method & Writing. 2nd ed. Charles R. Calleros. 576p. 1994. teacher ed. write for info. (*0-316-13280-2*, 32802) Aspen Law.

Legal Method & Writing. 2nd ed. Charles R. Calleros. LC 94-75305. 576p. 1994. pap. 26.50 (*0-316-12505-9*, Aspen Law & Bus) Aspen Pub.

Legal Method & Writing. 3rd ed. Charles R. Calleros. LC 97-51907. 1998. pap. text 32.95 (*1-56706-647-X*) Aspen Law.

Legal Method Writing. Calleros. 1990. 22.00 (*0-316-12502-4*, Aspen Law & Bus) Aspen Pub.

Legal Methods. Jones Staff. Date not set. pap. text, teacher ed. write for info. (*0-88277-489-1*) Foundation Pr.

Legal Methods: Cases & Materials (University Casebook Series) Jane C. Ginsburg. (Paralegal). 523p. 1996. text 30.75 (*1-56662-339-1*) Foundation Pr.

Legal Methods, Cases & Materials, Teacher's Manual to Accompany. Jane C. Ginsburg. (University Casebook Ser.). 68p. 1996. pap. text. write for info. (*1-56662-418-5*) Foundation Pr.

Legal Mind: Essays for Tony Honore. Ed. by D. Neil MacCormick & Peter B. H. Birks. 336p. 1986. text 79.00 (*0-19-876196-1*) OUP.

Legal Miscellanies: Six Decades of Change & Progress. Henry W. Taft. (Illus.). 218p. 1977. 18.95 (*0-8369-2864-4*) Ayer.

Legal Modernism. David Luban. (Law, Meaning, & Violence Ser.). 424p. (C). 1994. text 59.50 (*0-472-10380-6*, 10380) U of Mich Pr.

Legal Modernism. David Luban. 424p. (C). 1997. pap. text 25.95 (*0-472-08439-9*, 08439) U of Mich Pr.

Legal Monograph - A New Dilemma: Reference Letters & Checks. Rochelle K. Kaplan. 1988. pap. 25.00 (*0-913936-22-7*) Coll Placement.

Legal Monograph - EEO & the Employment Process. Rochelle K. Kaplan. 1990. 25.00 (*0-913936-23-5*) Coll Placement.

Legal Monograph - Understanding the Buckley Amendment. Stephen Sivulich. 1988. pap. 25.00 (*0-913936-21-9*) Coll Placement.

Legal Naturalism: A Marxist Theory of Law. Olufemi Taiwo. 240p. 1995. text 32.50 (*0-8014-2851-3*) Cornell U Pr.

Legal Nature of Corporations. Ernst Freund. 1980. lib. bdg. 49.95 (*0-8490-3106-0*) Gordon Pr.

Legal Nature of the Unit Trust. Kam F. Sin. 398p. 1998. text 105.00 (*0-19-876468-5*) OUP.

Legal Needs & Civil Justice: A Survey of Americans. LC 94-196949. 30p. 1994. pap. 17.95 (*0-89707-970-1*, 429-0016) Amer Bar Assn.

Legal Needs of Children. 191p. 1988. 22.50 (*0-685-30179-6*, 43,900) NCLS Inc.

Legal Needs of the Public: The Final Report of a National Survey. American Bar Foundation Staff & Barbara A. Curran. LC 77-85325. (American Bar Foundation Publication Ser.). xxxvi, 382p. 1977. 38.50 (*0-910058-82-2*, 304900) W S Hein.

Legal Negotiation. 2nd ed. Williams. Date not set. pap. text. write for info. (*0-314-06606-3*) West Pub.

Legal Negotiation: Theory & Applications. Donald G. Gifford. 225p. (C). 1989. reprint ed. 25.50 (*0-314-50511-3*) West Pub.

Legal Negotiation & Settlement. Gerald R. Williams. LC 82-19975. 207p. (C). 1982. 25.50 (*0-314-68093-4*) West Pub.

Legal Negotiation & Settlement. Gerald R. Williams. LC 82-19975. 183p. (C). 1983. pap. text, teacher ed. write for info. (*0-314-73521-6*) West Pub.

Legal Negotiation in a Nutshell. Larry L. Teply. (Nutshell Ser.). 282p. (C). 1991. pap. 21.00 (*0-314-92147-8*) West Pub.

Legal Neurology & Malingering: Cases & Techniques. Warren F. Gorman. 420p. 1993. pap. 40.00 (*0-87527-507-9*) Green.

Legal Newsletters in Print 1999. Ed. by Arlene L. Eis. 393p. 1999. pap. 97.00 (*0-939486-52-0*) Infosources.

Legal Norms of Delinquency: A Comparative Study. (N. Y. U. Criminal Law Education & Research Center, Monograph Ser.: Vol. 1). 76p. 1969. reprint ed. pap. 18.50 (*0-8377-0800-1*, Rothman) W S Hein.

Legal Novels: An Annotated Bibliography. rev. ed. Karen L. Kretschman. (Legal Bibliography Ser.: No. 13A). 27p. 1979. pap. 10.00 (*0-935630-03-1*) U of Tex Tarlton Law Lib.

Legal Nurse Consulting. Weishapple. (Paralegal Ser.). (C). 2001. pap. 34.50 (*0-7668-1052-6*) Delmar.

Legal Nurse Consulting: Principles & Practice. Ed. by American Association of Legal Nurses Staff. LC 97-50089. 800p. 1997. boxed set 75.00 (*1-57444-123-X*, SL123X) St Lucie Pr.

Legal Obligations Arising Out of Treaty Relations Between China & Other States. Min-Ch'ien T. Tyan. Ed. by Igor I. Kavass et al. LC 72-76347. (International Military Law & History Ser.: Vol. 3). 304p. 1972. reprint ed. lib. bdg. 45.00 (*0-930342-40-2*, 301700) W S Hein.

Legal Obligations of Nonprofit Boards No. 39: A Guidebook for Board Members. Jacqueline C. Leifer & Michael B. Glomb. 44p. 1997. reprint ed. pap. text 28.00 (*0-925299-79-0*) Natl Ctr Nonprofit.

Legal Obstacles to the Application of Nature Conservation Legislation. (Nature & Environment Ser.: No. 89). 1997. 15.00 (*92-871-3303-4*, Pub. by Council of Europe) Manhattan Pub Co.

Legal Office Administration. Polly McClew. LC 89-78038. (C). 1994. pap. text 24.95 (*0-8273-3975-5*) Delmar.

Legal Office Document's Process. Diane M. Gilmore. 320p. pap. 38.95 (*0-538-71918-4*) S-W Pub.

Legal Office Procedures. 2nd ed. Marjorie D. Bate & Mary C. Casey. (Illus.). 544p. 1980. text 56.76 (*0-07-004058-3*) McGraw.

Legal Office Procedures. 3rd ed. (C). 1989. pap. text 29.25 (*0-538-70052-1*, KK41CC) S-W Pub.

Legal Office Procedures. 4th ed. Joyce Morton. LC 97-25108. 406p. 1997. pap. text 51.00 (*0-13-261017-5*) P-H.

***Legal Office Procedures.** 5th ed. Joyce Morton. LC 00-24719. 400p. 2000. pap. 44.67 (*0-13-015597-7*) P-H.

Legal Office Typing with Practical Applications. 2nd ed. Garland C. Dupree & Dorothy C. Namanny. (C). 1984. mass mkt. 19.25 (*0-538-11970-5*, K97) S-W Pub.

Legal 100: A Ranking of the Individuals Who Have Most Influenced the Law. Darien A. McWhirter. LC 97-17536. (Illus.). 416p. 1997. 27.50 (*0-8065-1860-X*, Citadel Pr) Carol Pub Group.

Legal Opinion, Set. Scott Fitzgibbon. 1504p. 1992. boxed set 170.00 (*0-316-28447-5*, Aspen Law & Bus) Aspen Pub.

***Legal Opinions: The Impact of the Tribar Committee's New Report on Legal Opinion Practice.** Arthur Norman Field et al. LC 98-166402. (Corporate Law & Practice Course Handbook Ser.). 456p. 1998. 129.00 (*0-87224-460-1*) PLI.

Legal Opinions in Commercial Transactions. Estey. 350p. 1989. boxed set 113.00 (*0-409-80904-7*, MICHIE) LEXIS Pub.

Legal Opinions in Corporate Transactions. Scott FitzGibbon & Donald W. Glazer. 1989. write for info. (*0-318-63267-5*, Aspen Law & Bus) Aspen Pub.

Legal Opinions in Corporate Transactions. Reade H. Ryan & Arthur Field. Vol. C6. text 82.00 (*0-8205-2412-3*) Bender.

Legal Opinions in International Transactions: Report of the Subcommittee on Legal Opinions of the Committee on Banking Law of the Section on Business Law of the International Bar Association, Vol. IBAS. 3rd ed. Ed. by Michael Gruson et al. LC 97-472. 272p. 1997. 118.00 (*90-411-0944-7*) Kluwer Academic.

Legal Order & Mental Disorder. Amita Dhanda. LC 99-17486. 1999. write for info. (*0-7619-9324-X*) Sage.

Legal Origins & Legal Change. Alan Watson. 320p. 1991. 60.00 (*1-85285-048-5*) Hambledon Press.

Legal Outlines. David Hoffman. Ed. by R. H. Helmholz & Bernard D. Reams, Jr. LC 80-84859. (Historical Writings in Law & Jurisprudence Ser.: No. 19, Bk. 27). 636p. 1981. reprint ed. lib. bdg. 58.00 (*0-89941-079-0*, 302270) W S Hein.

Legal Pages. rev. ed. Skinder-Strauss Staff. 307p. 1995. pap. 15.00 (*1-57741-006-8*) Skinder-Strauss.

Legal Papers of Andrew Jackson. James W. Ely, Jr. & Theodore Brown, Jr. LC 82-2635. 486p. 1987. lib. bdg. 60.00 (*0-87049-355-8*) U of Tenn Pr.

Legal Periodical Management Data. Ed. by Richard H. Surles, Jr. & Jatin N. Mukerji. LC 77-81317. 167p. 1977. lib. bdg. 37.50 (*0-930342-06-2*, 301610) W S Hein.

Legal Periodicals in English, 6 vols., Set. annuals Daniel L. May. LC 75-42308. 1976. ring bd., suppl. ed. 525.00 (*0-87802-054-3*) Glanville.

Legal Philosophies of Russian Liberalism. Andrzej Walicki. LC 92-50407. (C). 1992. reprint ed. pap. text 23.00 (*0-268-01298-9*) U of Notre Dame Pr.

Legal Philosophy. Timothy C. Shiell. (C). 1993. pap. text 57.50 (*0-03-076843-8*, Pub. by Harcourt Coll Pubs) Harcourt.

Legal Philosophy from Plato to Hegel. Huntington Cairns. LC 49-7752. 599p. reprint ed. pap. 185.70 (*0-608-10103-6*, 200495700048) Bks Demand.

Legal Philosophy from Plato to Hegel. Huntington Cairns. LC 79-12703. 583p. 1980. reprint ed. lib. bdg. 47.50 (*0-313-21499-9*, CALP, Greenwood Pr) Greenwood.

Legal Pitfalls for Health Care Managers. J. Fiesta. (Professional Reference - Nursing Ser.). 1996. 31.50 (*0-8273-7479-8*, VNR) Wiley.

Legal Planning for the Elderly in Massachusetts. William J. Brisk & William G. Talis. 530p. 1994. spiral bd. 125.00 (*0-88063-775-7*, MICHIE) LEXIS Pub.

***Legal Planning for Your Parents.** Martha N. O'Toole & Mary B. Payne. LC 98-170423. vi, 36p. 1998. pap. 9.95 (*0-9664247-0-0*) Sndwch Pr.

Legal Pluralism: Toward a Multicultural Conception of Law. Warwick Tie. LC 99-25150. 285p. 1999. text 87.95 (*1-84014-725-3*, Pub. by Ashgate Pub) Ashgate Pub Co.

Legal Pluralism & the Colonial Legacy. Kayleen M. Hazlehurst. LC 95-23818. (Illus.). 320p. (C). 1995. text 77.95 (*1-85972-078-1*, Pub. by Avebry) Ashgate Pub Co.

***Legal Pluralism in the Arab World.** Baudouin Dupret et al. (Arab & Islamic Laws Ser.: Vol. 18). 304p. 1999. 105.00 (*90-411-1105-0*) Kluwer Law Intl.

Legal Polycentricity: Consequences of Pluralism in Law. Ed. by Hanne Petersen & Henrik Zahle. (Illus.). 248p. 1995. text 81.95 (*1-85521-662-0*, Pub. by Dartmth Pub) Ashgate Pub Co.

Legal Polycentricity & International Law. Surya P. Sinha. LC 95-68004. 228p. (C). 1996. lib. bdg. 40.00 (*0-89089-929-0*) Carolina Acad Pr.

Legal Portraits. Lord Denning. pap. text 14.00 (*0-406-03250-5*, UK, MICHIE) LEXIS Pub.

Legal Portraits. Lord Hailsham. pap. text 14.00 (*0-406-03251-3*, UK, MICHIE) LEXIS Pub.

Legal Position of Aliens, Vol. 1. 1987. 348.95 (*0-387-16990-3*) Spr-Verlag.

Legal Position of Intergovernmental Organizations. Peter H. Bekker. (Legal Aspects of International Organizations Ser.). 284p. 1994. lib. bdg. 86.00 (*0-7923-2904-X*, Pub. by M Nijhoff) Kluwer Academic.

***Legal Positivism.** Ed. by Tom D. Campbell. LC 99-72416. (International Library of Essays in Law & Legal Theory). 500p. 1999. text 175.95 (*1-84014-732-6*, Pub. by Ashgate Pub) Ashgate Pub Co.

Legal Positivism. Ed. by Mario Jori. (International Library of Essays in Law & Legal Theory). 550p. (C). 1992. lib. bdg. 150.00 (*0-8147-4189-4*) NYU Pr.

Legal Positivism in American Jurisprudence. Anthony Sebok. LC 97-52780. (Studies in Philosophy & Law). 352p. (C). 1998. 59.95 (*0-521-48041-8*) Cambridge U Pr.

Legal Positivism, Its Scope & Limitations. Samuel I. Shuman. LC 62-14874. 272p. reprint ed. pap. 84.40 (*0-608-16607-3*, 202767700055) Bks Demand.

Legal Power: A Software Executive's Guide to Key Legal Practices. John C. Yates & Paul H. Arne. Ed. by H. Grady Thrasher, IV. 177p. 1995. pap. 295.00 (*1-58128-000-9*, LF) Culpepper.

Legal Power for Small Business Owners & Managers. Raymond J. Munna. LC 91-8838. 309p. (Orig.). 1991. pap. 19.95 (*0-935669-10-8*) A Granite Pubs.

Legal Practice & Management in Nigeria. Oluwatoyin Doherty. xxv, 398p. 1998. pap. 54.00 (*1-85941-178-9*, Pub. by Cavendish Pubng) Gaunt.

Legal Practice Book. Oates. 944p. 1993. 15.00 (*0-316-62197-8*) Little.

Legal Practice Companion, 1998-99. Gerald Montagu & Mark Weston. LC 99-199726. 435p. 1998. pap. 58.00 (*1-85431-862-4*) Gaunt.

Legal Practice Handbook. Stuart J. Faber. 556p. (Orig.). 1981. pap. text 49.50 (*0-89074-087-9*) Lega Bks.

Legal Practice in the 90s. David Stein & Charis Stein. LC 95-115509. 330p. 1994. pap. 49.00 (*0-455-21281-3*, Pub. by LawBk Co) Gaunt.

Legal Primer on Managing Museum Collections. Marie C. Malaro. LC 84-23497. 366p. 1987. pap. text 19.95 (*0-87474-697-3*, MALPP) Smithsonian.

Legal Primer on Managing Museum Collections. 2nd ed. Marie C. Malaro. LC 97-11780. 544p. 1998. text 55.00 (*1-56098-762-6*); pap. text 29.95 (*1-56098-787-1*) Smithsonian.

Legal Principles for Citizen Participation: Towards a Legal Framework for Civil Society Organizations. International Center for Not-for-Profit Law Staff. 40p. 1997. pap. 15.00 (*0-9644001-3-8*) CIVICUS.

Legal Problem Solver for Foodservice Operators. 7th rev. ed. Clyde L. Smith. Ed. by Robert Palmer. 1995. ring bd. 44.95 (*0-317-57855-3*, MG415) Natl Restaurant Assn.

Legal Problem Solving: A Guide for Law Students. Patrick Keyzer. 150p. 1994. pap. 35.00 (*0-409-30896-X*, Austral, MICHIE) LEXIS Pub.

Legal Problem Solving: Analysis, Research & Writing. 5th ed. Marjorie Dick-Rombauer. LC 83-9860. (American Casebook Ser.). 524p. (C). 1991. pap. 45.50 (*0-314-84243-8*) West Pub.

Legal Problem Solving: Analysis, Research & Writing, Teacher's Manual & 1991-92 Problem Supplement. 5th ed. Marjorie D. Rombauer. (American Casebook Ser.). 69p. (C). 1992. reprint ed. pap. text. write for info. (*0-314-00076-3*) West Pub.

Legal Problems & the Citizen. Brian Abel-Smith. 1973. text 26.00 (*0-435-82865-7*) Ashgate Pub Co.

Legal Problems in Advertising. Douglas Wood & Felix Kent. Vol. IP4. text 82.00 (*0-8205-2391-7*) Bender.

Legal Problems in Emergency Medicine. Alan P. Montague. (Illus.). 176p. 1996. text 54.00 (*0-19-262497-0*) OUP.

Legal Problems in Emergency Medicine. Alan P. Montague & Andrew Hopper. (Illus.). 176p. 1996. pap. text 49.95 (*0-19-262496-2*) OUP.

Legal Problems in Nursing Practice. 2nd ed. Ann P. Young. (Illus.). 264p. (Orig.). (C). (gr. 13). 1989. pap. text 34.95 (*0-412-44550-6*, Chap & Hall NY) Chapman & Hall.

Legal Problems in the Arctic Regions. Ed. by Terttu Utriainen. 100p. (Orig.). 1990. pap. 79.00 (*951-640-491-X*) Coronet Bks.

Legal Problems in the Far Eastern Conflict. Quincy Wright. LC 75-30104. (Institute of Pacific Relations Ser.). reprint ed. 42.50 (*0-404-59573-1*) AMS Pr.

Legal Problems of Codes of Conduct for Multinational Enterprises. Ed. by Norbert Horn. (International Transportational Economic Law Studies: No. 1). 520p. 1980. lib. bdg. 148.00 (*90-268-1127-6*) Kluwer Law Intl.

Legal Problems of International Economic Relations, Cases, Materials & Text on the National & International Regulation of Transnational Economic Relations. 3rd ed. John H. Jackson et al. LC 77-89401. (American Casebook Ser.). 1248p. (C). 1995. 68.50 (*0-314-04688-7*) West Pub.

Legal Problems of International Organizations. 163p. 1993. text 59.95 (*0-521-46325-4*) Cambridge U Pr.

Legal Problems of International Organizations. Felice Morgenstern. 163p. (C). 1986. 140.00 (*0-906496-24-1*, Pub. by Grotius Pubns Ltd) St Mut.

***Legal Problems of Religious & Private Schools.** 4th ed. Ralph D. Mawdsley. 300p. 2000. write for info. (*1-56534-101-5*) Ed Law Assn.

Legal Problems of Seabed Boundary Delimitation in the East China Sea. Ying-jeou Ma. 308p. 1984. 15.00 (*0-942182-63-4*); pap. 10.00 (*0-942182-62-6*) Occasional Papers.

Legal Problems of Woodland Operations: Seminar Proceedings, October 16-17, 1980. William R. Sizemore. LC SD0565.L43. 122p. reprint ed. pap. 37.90 (*0-7837-6038-8*, 204585100008) Bks Demand.

Legal Procedure of Cicero's Time, 1901. A. H. J. Greenidge. LC 99-26771. 1999. reprint ed. 85.00 (*1-886363-99-4*) Lawbk Exchange.

Legal Procedures & Terminology for Court Reporters & Paralegals. Mike Eskew & Nancy Patterson. LC 92-28453. 224p. (C). 1992. pap. text 25.40 (*0-13-529215-8*) P-H.

Legal Proceedings of Harold Weisberg vs. General Services Administration Civil Action 2052-73 Together with the January 22 & 27 Warren. Ed. by David R. Wrone. (Freedom of Information Act & Political Assassinations Ser.: Vol. 1). (Illus.). (Orig.). pap. 8.95 (*0-932310-00-1*) U of Wis-Stevens Point.

Legal Process: Basic Problems in the Making & Application of Law. William N. Eskridge, Jr. & Philip P. Frickey. (University Casebook Ser.). 1387p. 1994. text 49.95 (*1-56662-236-0*) Foundation Pr.

Legal Profession: Responsibility & Regulation. 3rd ed. Geoffrey C. Hazard, Jr. Ed. by Deborah L. Rhode. LC 93-36631. 500p. 1993. pap. text 23.00 (*1-56662-128-3*) Foundation Pr.

Legal Profession & the Common Law: Historical Essays. J. H. Baker. 450p. 1986. 70.00 (*0-907628-62-1*) Hambledon Press.

Legal Profession in the United States, 2 vols. in 1. American Bar Foundation Staff. (American Bar Foundation Publication Ser.). (RUS.). 1985. pap. 25.00 (*0-910058-21-0*, 304910) W S Hein.

Legal Profession in the United States. 3rd ed. American Bar Foundation Staff. LC 85-72996. (American Bar Foundation Publication Ser.). ix, 79p. 1985. pap. 22.00 (*0-910059-08-X*, 304910) W S Hein.

Legal Profession, 1996. Ed. by Jonathan Grosvenor. 272p. (C). 1996. 70.00 (*1-870757-19-X*) St Mut.

Legal Profession, Teacher's Manual to Accompany Cases & Materials on the Rules of The. Robert F. Cochran & Teresa S. Collett. (American Casebook Ser.). 148p. (C). 1996. pap. text. write for info. (*0-314-22379-7*) West Pub.

***Legal Professional Privilege: Law & Theory.** Jonathan Auburn. 288p. 2000. 54.00 (*1-84113-101-6*, Pub. by Hart Pub) Intl Spec Bk.

Legal Professions in the New Europe. 2nd ed. Alan Tyrrell & Zahd Yaqub. LC 96-188398. 600p. 1996. 115.00 (*1-85941-193-2*, Pub. by Cavendish Pubng) Gaunt.

Legal Property Relations of Married Parties: A Study in Comparative Legislation. Isidor Loeb. LC 68-56668. (Columbia University Studies in the Social Sciences Ser.: No. 34). reprint ed. 29.50 (*0-404-51034-5*) AMS Pr.

***Legal Protection Against Breaches of Duty on the Part of the German Works Council--Fata Morgana?** Detlev Belling. LC 99-87787. (Potsdamer Rechtswissenschaftliche Reihe Ser.: Bd. 8). x, 96p. 2000. 46.95 (*3-540-66835-7*) Spr-Verlag.

Legal Protection for the Individual Employee. 2nd ed. Matthew W. Finkin et al. (Paralegal). 871p. (C). 1999. text 48.00 (*0-314-06544-X*) West Pub.

Legal Protection for the Individual Employee: 1996 Statutory Supplement. 2nd ed. Matthew W. Finkin et al. (American Casebook Ser.). 871p. (C). 1995. pap. 22.50 (*0-314-07738-3*) West Pub.

Legal Protection of Biotechnological Inventions in Europe & in the United States: Current Framework & Future Developments Technical & Ethical Approach. Geertrui Van Overwalle. (Leuven Law Ser.: Vol. 10). 79p. 1997. pap. 37.50 (*90-6186-846-7*, Pub. by Leuven Univ) Coronet Bks.

Legal Protection of Children Against Sexual Exploitation in Taiwan: A Socio-Legal Perspective. Amy H. Shee. LC 97-38122. (Law, Social Change & Development Ser.). 280p. 1997. text 76.95 (*1-85521-869-0*, Pub. by Ashgate Pub) Ashgate Pub Co.

Legal Protection of Civil Liberties: The Legal Protection of Civil Liberties. R. C. Austin et al. 500p. 1994. pap. text 60.00 (*0-406-55511-7*, UK, MICHIE) LEXIS Pub.

Legal Protection of Computer Hardware & Software Marketed in Europe. JJ & J Consultants. (Illus.). 220p. 1986. 950.00 (*0-914849-05-0*) TBC Inc.

Legal Protection of Encrypted Television Services (Recommendation & Explanatory Memorandum), No. R(91)14. 1995. 12.00 (*92-871-2710-7*, Pub. by Council of Europe) Manhattan Pub Co.

Legal Protection of Know-How in the United States of America. 2nd ed. Francois Dessemontet. Tr. by H. W. Clarke from FRE. (Studies in Researches of the Institute of Comparative Law, Faculty of Law of the University of Lausanne). 487p. 1976. reprint ed. pap. 30.00 (*0-8377-0504-5*, Rothman) W S Hein.

Legal Protection of Literature, Art & Music. Stanley Rothenberg. xiii, 367p. 1988. reprint ed. 47.50 (*0-8377-2538-0*, Rothman) W S Hein.

***Legal Protection of the Underwater Cultural Heritage: National & International Perspectives.** Sarah Dromgoole. LC 99-36398. 1999. 96.00 (*90-411-9762-1*) Kluwer Law Intl.

Legal Provision in the Rural Environment: Legal Services, Criminal Justice & Welfare Provision in Rural Areas. Ed. by Christopher Harding & John Williams. 144p. 1994. pap. 29.95 (*0-7083-1228-4*, Pub. by Univ Wales Pr) Paul & Co Pubs.

An Asterisk (*) at the beginning of an entry indicates that the title is appearing for the first time.

L

Legal Psychology. M. Ralph Brown. (Historical Foundations of Forensic Psychiatry & Psychology Ser.). (Illus.). 346p. 1980. reprint ed. lib. bdg. 39.50 (*0-306-76065-7*) Da Capo.

Legal Queeries: Lesbian, Gay & Transgender Legal Studies. Leslie J. Moran et al. LC 97-52265. 1998. 69.95 (*0-304-33863-X*); pap. 24.95 (*0-304-33864-8*) Continuum.

Legal Realism: American & Scandinavian. Michael Martin. LC 96-30774. (American University Studies V: No. 179). IX, 242p. (C). 1997. text 44.95 (*0-8204-3462-0*) P Lang Pubng.

Legal Realism & Justice. Edwin N. Garlan. LC 81-13811. xii, 161p. 1981. reprint ed. lib. bdg. 55.00 (*0-8377-0614-9*, Rothman) W S Hein.

Legal Reason. 2nd ed. Steven J. Burton. 192p. 1995. pap. text 24.95 (*0-316-11489-8*, Aspen Law & Bus) Aspen Pub.

Legal Reasoning, Set, Vols. I & II. Ed. by Aulis Aarnio & D. Neil MacCormick. (International Library of Essays in Law & Legal Theory). 1200p. (C). 1992. lib. bdg. 250.00 (*0-8147-0608-8*) NYU Pr.

Legal Reasoning, Vol. I. Aulis Aarnio. (C). 1992. lib. bdg. 125.00 (*0-8147-0606-1*) NYU Pr.

Legal Reasoning, Vol. II. Ed. by Aulis Aarnio & D. Neil MacCormick. (C). 1992. lib. bdg. 125.00 (*0-8147-0607-X*) NYU Pr.

Legal Reasoning & Legal Theory. D. Neil MacCormick. (Clarendon Law Ser.). 322p. 1994. pap. text 32.00 (*0-19-876384-0*) OUP.

Legal Reasoning & Legal Writing. Neumann. 1990. 22.00 (*0-316-60379-1*, Aspen Law & Bus) Aspen Pub.

Legal Reasoning & Legal Writing: Structure, Strategy, & Style. 2nd ed. Richard K. Neumann, Jr. 512p. 1994. teacher ed. write for info. (*0-316-57151-2*, 71512) Aspen Law.

Legal Reasoning & Legal Writing: Structure, Strategy, & Style. 3rd ed. Richard K. Neumann. LC 97-50018. 1998. pap. text 34.95 (*1-56706-694-1*) Aspen Law.

Legal Reasoning & Legal Writing: Structure, Strategy, & Style, Vol. 2. 2nd ed. Richard K. Neumann, Jr. LC 93-80973. 512p. 1994. pap. 26.50 (*0-316-60390-2*, 03902) Aspen Law.

Legal Reasoning & Political Conflict. Cass R. Sunstein. 240p. 1996. 25.00 (*0-19-510082-4*) OUP.

Legal Reasoning & Political Conflict. Cass R. Sunstein. 240p. 1998. pap. 14.95 (*0-19-511804-9*) OUP.

Legal Record & Historical Reality. Ed. by Thomas G. Watkin. 256p. 1989. 60.00 (*1-85285-028-0*) Hambledon Press.

Legal Records in the Commonwealth. William Twining & Emma Quick. 344p. (C). 1994. text 87.95 (*1-85521-448-2*, Pub. by Dartmth Pub) Ashgate Pub Co.

***Legal Reductionism & Freedom.** Martin Van Hees. LC 00-44376. (Law & Philosophy Library). 2000. write for info. (*0-7923-6491-0*) Kluwer Academic.

Legal Reelism: Movies As Legal Texts. Ed. by John Denvir. LC 95-32511. (Illus.). 336p. 1996. text 39.95 (*0-252-02231-9*); pap. text 19.95 (*0-252-06535-2*) U of Ill Pr.

Legal Reference for Design & Construction. Charles R. Heuer. 1989. 109.95 (*0-87629-145-0*, 67266) R S Means.

***Legal References for California School Administrators, 2000.** Donald R. Wilson. 123p. 2000. pap. 12.00 (*0-939136-33-3*) School Admin.

Legal References for Texas School Administrators, 1999-2001. 4th ed. Donald R. Wilson. 124p. 1999. 12.00 (*0-939136-32-5*) School Admin.

Legal Reform in Post-Communist Europe: The View from Within. Ed. by Stanislaw Frankowski & Paul B. Stephan, III. 1994. lib. bdg. 187.50 (*0-7923-3218-0*) Kluwer Academic.

Legal Reform in Taiwan under Japanese Colonial Rule, 1895-1945: The Reception of Western Law. Tai-sheng Wang. LC 99-26277. Vol. 15. (Illus.). 392p. 1999. 65.00 (*0-295-97827-9*) U of Wash Pr.

Legal Reform in the Muslim World: The Anatomy of a Scholarly Dispute in the 19th & the Early 20th Centuries over the Usage of Ijtihad As a Legal Tool. Muneer G. Fareed. LC 96-13518. 206p. (Orig.). 1996. 69.95 (*1-57292-003-3*); pap. 49.95 (*1-57292-002-5*) Austin & Winfield.

Legal Reforms Affecting Child & Youth Services. Ed. by Gary B. Melton. LC 82-6204. (Child & Youth Services Ser.: Vol. 5, Nos. 1 & 2). 150p. 1983. text 49.95 (*0-86656-105-6*); pap. text 19.95 (*0-86656-216-8*) Haworth Pr.

Legal Regime for Transboundary Water Pollution: Between Discretion & Constraint. Andre Nollkaemper. LC 93-31558. (International Environmental Law & Policy Ser.). 408p. (C). 1993. lib. bdg. 149.00 (*0-7923-2476-5*) Kluwer Academic.

Legal Regime of International Rivers & Lakes. Ralph Zacklin & Lucius Caflisch. 442p. 1981. lib. bdg. 170.00 (*90-247-2565-8*) Kluwer Academic.

Legal Regime of the Protection of the Mediterranean Against Pollution from Landbased Sources. S. Kuwabara. 248p. 1984. text 90.00 (*0-907567-82-7*, Tycooly Pub) Weidner & Sons.

Legal Regulation of Employment Relations Within International Organizations: With Special Reference to the Jurisprudence of International Administrative Tribunals & the Practice of the United Nations. Woonsang Choi. 2000. text 85.00 (*0-379-21397-4*) Oceana.

Legal Regulation of the Competitive Process, Cases, Materials & Notes, Etc. 3rd rev. ed. Edmund W. Kitch & Harvey S. Perlman. (University Casebook Ser.). 252p. 1986. pap. text, teacher ed. write for info. (*0-88277-556-1*) Foundation Pr.

Legal Regulation of the Competitive Process, Cases, Materials & Notes on Unfair Business Practices, Trademarks, Copyright & Patents. 4th rev. ed. Edmund W. Kitch & Harvey S. Perlman. (University Casebook Ser.). 305p. 1993. pap. text 11.95 (*1-56662-140-2*) Foundation Pr.

Legal Regulation of the Competitive Process, Cases, Materials & Notes on Unfair Business Practices, Trademarks, Copyrights & Patents. 4th rev. ed. Edmund W. Ketch & Harvey S. Perlman. (University Casebook Ser.). 320p. 1994. 12.50 (*1-56662-204-2*) Foundation Pr.

Legal Regulation of the Competitive Process, Cases, Materials & Notes on Unfair Business Practices, Trademarks, Copyrights & Patents. 4th rev. ed. Edmund W. Kitch & Harvey S. Perlman. (University Casebook Ser.). 1080p. 1991. text 43.95 (*0-88277-887-0*) Foundation Pr.

Legal Regulation of the European Community's External Relations after the Completion of the Internal Market. Malcolm Evans & Stratos Konstadinidis. LC 96-83206. (EC International Law Forum Ser.: Vol. 1). (Illus.). 416p. 1996. text 96.95 (*1-85521-695-7*, Pub. by Dartmth Pub) Ashgate Pub Co.

Legal Relations Between Transnational Corporations & Host States. P. Ebow Bondzi-Simpson. LC 90-8389. 240p. 1990. 69.50 (*0-89930-590-3*, BZL, Quorum Bks) Greenwood.

Legal Relations of Infants, Parent & Child & Guardian & Ward: And a Particular Consideration of Guardianship in the State of New York. G. W. Field. xx, 376p. 1981. reprint ed. 42.00 (*0-8377-0537-1*, Rothman) W S Hein.

Legal Remedies. V. M. Shukla & Avtar Singh. (C). 1990. 38.00 (*0-89771-324-9*) St Mut.

Legal Requirements for Business Records: Federal Requirements. Donald S. Skupsky. 1994. 770.00 (*0-929316-11-8*) Info Requirements.

Legal Requirements for Business Records: State Requirements. Donald S. Skupsky. 1994. 670.00 (*0-929316-12-6*) Info Requirements.

Legal Requirements for Microfilm, Computer & Optical Disk Records: Evidence, Regulation, Government & International Requirements. Donald S. Skupsky. 528p. (Orig.). 1994. pap. text 75.00 (*0-929316-04-5*) Info Requirements.

Legal Research. (Quick Study Law School Ser.). 4p. pap. 4.95 (*1-57222-300-6*) Barcharts.

Legal Research. 1992. lib. bdg. 77.95 (*0-8490-5282-3*) Gordon Pr.

Legal Research. Barber. (C). 1996. text 39.95 (*0-8273-7971-4*) Delmar.

Legal Research. Barber. (Paralegal Ser.). 128p. 1996. teacher ed. 12.95 (*0-8273-7475-5*) Delmar.

Legal Research. Harris. 1996. pap. text, student ed., wbk. ed. 13.33 (*0-13-442492-1*) P-H.

Legal Research. Myra A. Harris. LC 96-5089. 470p. 1996. pap. text 49.00 (*0-13-437922-5*) P-H.

Legal Research. Walston. Date not set. pap. text, student ed. 13.75 (*0-314-04952-5*) West Pub.

Legal Research. David Stott. Ed. by Julie MacFarlane. (Essential Legal Skills Ser.). 159p. 1994. reprint ed. pap. 22.00 (*1-874241-40-6*, Pub. by Cavendish Pubng) Gaunt.

Legal Research. rev. ed. Steve Barber & Mark McCormick. LC 95-21728. (Paralegal Ser.). 448p. (C). 1995. mass mkt. 44.95 (*0-8273-7474-7*) Delmar.

Legal Research, No. 2, Chap. 2. Chanin. 1989. 23.50 (*0-316-13635-2*, Aspen Law & Bus) Aspen Pub.

Legal Research, No. 7, Ch. 5. Chanin. 1992. 30.00 (*0-316-13653-0*, Aspen Law & Bus) Aspen Pub.

Legal Research, No. 7, Ch. 7. Chanin. 1992. 27.00 (*0-316-13654-9*, Aspen Law & Bus) Aspen Pub.

Legal Research, No. 7, Ch. 8. Chanin. 1992. 17.00 (*0-316-13655-7*, Aspen Law & Bus) Aspen Pub.

Legal Research, No. 8, Ch. 9. Chanin. 1993. 35.00 (*0-316-13657-3*, Aspen Law & Bus) Aspen Pub.

Legal Research, No. 8, Ch. 10. Chanin. 1993. 35.00 (*0-316-13658-1*, Aspen Law & Bus) Aspen Pub.

Legal Research, No. 9, Ch. 12. Chanin. 1994. 35.00 (*0-316-13623-9*, Aspen Law & Bus) Aspen Pub.

Legal Research, No. 9, Ch. 13. Chanin. 1994. 35.00 (*0-316-13624-7*, Aspen Law & Bus) Aspen Pub.

Legal Research, No. 10, Chapter 1. Leah F. Chanin. 1995. 30.00 (*0-316-13617-4*, Aspen Law & Bus) Aspen Pub.

Legal Research, No. 10, Chapter 3. Leah F. Chanin. 1995. 30.00 (*0-316-13661-1*, Aspen Law & Bus) Aspen Pub.

Legal Research, No. 10, Chapter 4. Leah F. Chanin. 1995. 30.00 (*0-316-13619-0*, Aspen Law & Bus) Aspen Pub.

Legal Research: A Guide for Hong Kong Students. Jill Cottrell. 320p. (Orig.). 1997. pap. 42.50 (*962-209-430-9*, Pub. by HK Univ Pr) Coronet Bks.

Legal Research: A Practical Guide & Self-Instructional Workbook. Ruth A. Mckinney. LC 95-48934. (Paralegal). 264p. (C). 1996. pap. text 17.00 (*0-314-08244-1*) West Pub.

Legal Research: A Practical Guide & Self-Instructional Workbook. Ruth A. McKinney. (Miscellaneous Ser.). 79p. 1995. pap. text, teacher ed. write for info. (*0-314-09000-2*) West Pub.

Legal Research: Historical Foundations of the Electronic Age. Ed. by George S. Grossman. LC 93-23403. (Illus.). 384p. (C). 1994. text 60.00 (*0-19-508637-6*); pap. text 24.95 (*0-19-508638-4*) OUP.

Legal Research: How to Find & Understand the Law. Suzanne McKie. 220p. 1994. pap. 30.00 (*1-874241-50-3*, Pub. by Cavendish Pubng) Gaunt.

Legal Research: How to Find & Understand the Law. 6th ed. Stephen Elias. LC 98-15509. 1998. pap. 21.95 (*0-87337-468-1*) Nolo com.

Legal Research: How to Find & Understand the Law. 7th ed. Stephen Elias. LC 99-20584. 1999. 24.95 (*0-87337-525-4*) Nolo com.

***Legal Research: How to Find & Understand the Law.** 7th ed. Stephen Elias. 2000. pap. 34.95 (*0-87337-589-0*) Nolo com.

Legal Research: Materials & Methods. 3rd ed. Enid Campbell et al. xii, 326p. 1988. pap. 38.50 (*0-455-20803-4*, Pub. by LawBk Co) Gaunt.

Legal Research: Materials & Methods. 4th ed. Enid Campbell et al. LC 97-136079. 400p. 1996. pap. 60.00 (*0-455-21411-5*, Pub. by Cavendish Pubng) Gaunt.

Legal Research: Skill & Strategies for the Legal Assistant. Beth Walston-Dunham. LC 94-22668. 330p. (C). 1994. mass mkt. 44.95 (*0-314-04388-8*) West Pub.

Legal Research: Techniques & Strategies for Associates. (Commercial Law & Practice Ser.). 398p. 1991. pap. text 17.50 (*0-685-56854-7*, A4-4351) PLI.

***Legal Research: Traditional Sources, New Technologies.** Colleen Kristl Pauwels et al. LC 99-70205. 97p. 1999. pap. 12.00 (*0-87367-814-1*) Phi Delta Kappa.

Legal Research: Without Losing Your Mind. C. Edward Good. (Illus.). 280p. (C). 1997. reprint ed. pap. 29.95 (*0-9648247-2-8*) Word Store.

Legal Research & Citation. 4th ed. Larry L. Teply. (American Casebook Ser.). 462p. (C). 1992. pap. text 24.50 (*0-314-01047-5*); pap. text 16.00 (*0-314-01048-3*) West Pub.

Legal Research & Law Library Management. Julius J. Marke & Richard Sloane. 750p. 1986. reprint ed. ring bd. 90.00 (*0-318-21438-5*, 00572) NY Law Pub.

Legal Research & Materials: Ohio Edition. Ervin H. Pollack. LC 85-60265. (Legal Bibliographic & Research Reprint Ser.: Vol. 8). vii, 216p. 1985. reprint ed. lib. bdg. 42.00 (*0-89941-401-X*, 303680) W S Hein.

Legal Research & Writing. Bast. (Paralegal Ser.). 80p. 1995. text, teacher ed. 12.50 (*0-8273-7186-1*) Delmar.

Legal Research & Writing. Carol M. Bast. LC 94-29908. 400p. (C). 1995. mass mkt. 49.95 (*0-8273-6215-3*) Delmar.

Legal Research & Writing. Cohen. (C). 2000. pap. 26.50 (*0-314-12578-7*) Thomson Learn.

***Legal Research & Writing.** Edwards. (C). 2002. text 40.75 (*0-7668-2272-9*) Delmar.

Legal Research & Writing. Smith. (C). 1996. text 39.95 (*0-8273-7979-X*) Delmar.

Legal Research & Writing. Smith. (Paralegal Law Library). 1996. pap., teacher ed. 14.00 (*0-8273-6356-7*, VNR) Wiley.

Legal Research & Writing. David J. Smith. (Paralegal Ser.). 576p. (C). 1995. mass mkt. 52.95 (*0-8273-6355-9*) Delmar.

Legal Research & Writing. 4th ed. Statsky. (Paralegal Ser.). 1993. 17.00 (*0-314-01618-X*) Delmar.

Legal Research & Writing. 5th ed. Statsky. 150p. 1998. text 17.95 (*0-314-12977-4*) Delmar.

Legal Research & Writing. 5th ed. Statsky. LC 98-8346. (Paralegal Ser.). 325p. (C). 1998. text 50.95 (*0-314-12901-4*) Delmar.

Legal Research & Writing: Some Starting Points. 4th ed. William P. Statsky. Ed. by Hannan. LC 92-32549. 270p. (C). 1993. mass mkt. 30.25 (*0-314-01207-9*) West Pub.

Legal Research & Writing: Workbook/Study Guide. 5th ed. Statsky. (Paralegal Ser.). 250p. (C). 1998. text, student ed. 16.00 (*0-314-12978-2*) Delmar.

Legal Research & Writing Exercises for Paralegals. Charles P. Nemeth. (Illus.). 171p. (Orig.). (C). 1992. pap., student ed. 8.95 (*0-916951-00-6*) Adams & Ambrose.

Legal Research & Writing Exercises for Paralegals: Teacher's Answer Key. Charles P. Nemeth. 41p. (Orig.). (C). 1992. pap., student ed. 7.50 (*0-916951-01-4*) Adams & Ambrose.

Legal Research & Writing for Paralegals. Deborah E. Bouchoux. LC 93-80970. 656p. 1994. pap. 34.00 (*0-316-10366-7*, Aspen Law & Bus) Aspen Pub.

Legal Research & Writing for Paralegals. Joanne B. Hames & Yvonne Ekern. LC 98-54398. (Illus.). 480p. (C). 1999. pap. text 56.00 (*0-13-244799-1*, Macmillan Coll) P-H.

Legal Research & Writing for Paralegals. Ellyn Moscowitz. LC 93-72659. 315p. (C). 1993. pap. 29.95 (*0-87084-132-7*) Anderson Pub Co.

Legal Research & Writing for Paralegals. 2nd ed. Deborah E. Bouchoux. LC 97-39358. 1998. pap. text 40.95 (*1-56706-639-9*) Aspen Law.

Legal Research & Writing Handbook: A Basic Approach for Paralegals. Andrea B. Yelin & Hope V. Samborn. 528p. 1995. pap. write for info. (*0-316-96809-9*, 968099) Aspen Law.

Legal Research & Writing Handbook: A Basic Approach for Paralegals. 2nd ed. Andrea B. Yelin & Hope V. Samborn. LC 99-13631. 1999. write for info. (*0-7355-0188-2*) Panel Pubs.

***Legal Research & Writing Workbook: Including Instructor's Manual.** Helewitz. (C). 2002. 35.25 (*0-7668-1352-5*, AutoDesk Pr) Delmar.

Legal Research & Writing Workbook: Including Instructor's Manual. Jeffrey A. Helewitz & Maria K. Montgomery. 200p. 1997. pap. text, teacher ed., wbk. ed. 22.95 (*0-316-17706-7*, 177067) Aspen Law.

Legal Research Checklist for International Petroleum Operations. LC 94-70788. 88p. 1994. pap. 39.95 (*0-89707-988-4*, 535-0042, ABA Natl Res) Amer Bar Assn.

Legal Research Exercises. 4th rev. ed. Nancy P. Johnson. 259p. 1995. pap. text 14.00 (*0-314-06540-7*) West Pub.

Legal Research Exercises. 5th ed. Nancy P. Johnson & J. Wesley Cochran. 214p. (C). 1996. pap. text 14.00 (*0-314-09753-8*) West Pub.

Legal Research Exercises. 6th ed. Johnson. (Paralegal Ser.). (C). 1999. pap. 12.75 (*0-314-23742-9*) West Pub.

Legal Research Exercises: Accompany Cohen, Berring & Olson's How to Find the Law, Ninth Edition & Finding the Law. 4th ed. Lynn Foster & Nancy P. Johnson. 253p. 1992. pap. text. write for info. (*0-314-00947-7*) West Pub.

Legal Research Exercises, Instructor's Manual. 4th rev. ed. Nancy P. Johnson. 259p. 1995. pap. text, teacher ed. write for info. (*0-314-06541-5*) West Pub.

Legal Research for Beginners. John Bourdeau & Sonja Larsen. LC 96-39398. 272p. 1997. pap. 12.95 (*0-8120-9768-8*) Barron.

Legal Research For Paralegals. Edward H. Hein. LC 95-26179. (Paralegal). 500p. (C). 1996. mass mkt. 31.25 (*0-314-06740-X*) West Pub.

***Legal Research Guide: Patterns & Practice.** 4th ed. Bonita K. Roberts & Linda L. Schlueter. LC 99-87993. 2000. 18.00 (*0-8205-4378-0*) Bender.

Legal Research Guide for California Practice. Thomas S. Dabagh. LC 85-60262. (Legal Bibliographic & Research Reprint Ser.: Vol. 5). 66p. 1985. reprint ed. lib. bdg. 35.00 (*0-89941-398-6*, 303650) W S Hein.

Legal Research Guide, 1996. 3rd ed. Michele Roberts & Schlueter. 134p. 1996. pap. text 18.00 (*1-55834-381-4*, 12991-11, MICHIE) LEXIS Pub.

Legal Research Guide to Mechanical Patent Litigation. Adam V. Floyd. LC 95-7263. (Legal Research Guides Ser.: Vol. 21). xiv, 76p. 1995. 37.00 (*0-89941-906-2*, 308480) W S Hein.

Legal Research Guide to Post-Traumatic Stress Disorder As Related to Veterans. Steven R. Thorpe. LC 96-18839. (Legal Research Guides Ser.: Vol. 27). xiii, 56p. 1996. 42.00 (*1-57588-112-8*, 310640) W S Hein.

Legal Research Guide to Television Broadcasting & Program Syndication. Teresa Lee. LC 95-33965. (Legal Research Guides Ser.: Vol. 22). vi, iii, 42p. 1995. 35.00 (*0-89941-978-X*, 308650) W S Hein.

Legal Research Guide to Thoroughbred Racing Law for Scholars, Practitioners & Participants. Joan Howland. LC 98-87603. (Legal Research Guides Ser.: Vol. 31). xiii, 239p. 1998. 55.00 (*1-57588-486-0*) W S Hein.

Legal Research Guides, 29 vols., Set. 1985. write for info. (*0-89941-452-4*, 303690) W S Hein.

***Legal Research Guides of Texas Tech University.** W T. D. Myers & Douglas W. Gardner. LC 98-87658. Vol. 32. x, 84p. 1998. 42.00 (*1-57588-451-8*, 311820) W S Hein.

Legal Research Handbook. Douglass T. MacEllven. 440p. 1993. pap. text, student ed. 35.00 (*0-409-91116-X*, MICHIE) LEXIS Pub.

Legal Research Illustrated. 6th abr. ed. J. Myron Jacobstein & Donald J. Dunn. LC 94-60946. Orig. Title: Fundamentals of Legal Research. (Illus.). 488p. 1994. pap. text 24.95 (*1-56662-167-4*) Foundation Pr.

Legal Research Illustrated. 7th abr. ed. J. Myron Jacobstein et al. LC 98-39664. (Paralegal). Orig. Title: Fundamentals of Legal Research. (Illus.). 500p. 1998. pap. text 28.95 (*1-56662-712-5*) Foundation Pr.

Legal Research in a Nutshell. Morris L. Cohen & Kent C. Olson. (Nutshell Ser.). 361p. (C). 1996. pap. text 22.50 (*0-314-09589-6*) West Pub.

Legal Research in a Nutshell. 5th ed. Morris L. Cohen & Kent C. Olson. LC 92-15829. (Nutshell Ser.). 500p. (C). 1992. pap. text 17.00 (*0-314-00783-0*) West Pub.

Legal Research in Law Firms, Vol. 19. Terry Hutchinson. LC 94-17176. (Legal Research Guides Ser.: Vol. 19). xii, 173p. 1994. 38.00 (*0-89941-894-5*, 308370) W S Hein.

Legal Research in the District of Columbia, Maryland & Virginia. Leah F. Chanin et al. LC 94-16191. 420p. 1995. 45.00 (*0-89941-884-8*, 308140) W S Hein.

***Legal Research in the District of Columbia, Maryland & Virginia.** 2nd ed. Leah F. Chanin et al. LC 00-26782. 452p. 2000. ring bd. 65.00 (*1-57588-532-8*, 323530) W S Hein.

Legal Research Made Easy. 2nd ed. Suzan Herskowitz. (Legal Survival Guides Ser.). 128p. 1998. pap. 14.95 (*1-57071-400-2*) Sourcebks.

Legal Research Made Easy: A Roadmap Through the Law Library Maze. Nolo Staff Editors & Legal Star Communications Staff. 336p. 1996. pap., student ed. 89.95 incl. VHS (*0-87337-138-0*) Nolo com.

Legal Research Manual: A Game Plan for Legal Research & Analysis. 2nd ed. Christopher G. Wren & Jill R. Wren. LC 88-14437. (Illus.). 242p. (C). 1986. pap. text 9.95 (*0-916951-16-2*) Adams & Ambrose.

***Legal Research Manual: A Game Plan for Legal Research & Analysis.** 2nd ed. Christopher G. Wren & Jill R. Wren. LC 99-14787. 1999. pap. 12.95 (*1-57862-029-5*) State Bar WI.

Legal Research Manual for Law Students, 1988. Brigham Young University, Provo, Utah, Law Library. 1988. pap. write for info. (*0-318-63119-9*, BYU Law) Brigham.

***Legal Research on the Internet: A Compilation of Websites to Access United States Federal, State, Local & International Laws.** Antje Mays. LC 99-62273. (Legal Research Guide Ser.: Vol. 33). 58p. 1999. 45.00 (*1-57588-499-2*, 322910) W S Hein.

***Legal Research Online & in the Library** 2nd ed. Stephen Elias & Susan Levinkind. LC 99-22570. 1999. write for info. (*0-87337-526-2*) Nolo com.

Legal Research Using the Internet. Henry. (Paralegal Ser.). (C). 2001. pap. 19.50 (*0-7668-1136-0*) Delmar.

***Legal Research Using the Internet.** Long. LC 99-38664. (C). 1999. pap. 24.95 (*0-7668-1335-5*) Delmar.

Legal Research via the Internet. Atkinson. (Paralegal Ser.). 1996. teacher ed. 12.95 (*0-8273-7451-8*) Delmar.

Legal Research Workbook. Brian J. McCully & Grace I. Robinson. 224p. (C). 1995. pap. 21.95 (*0-87084-556-X*) Anderson Pub Co.

Legal Research Workbook: California Supplement. Brian J. McCully & Grace I. Robinson. 88p. (C). 1995. pap. text 5.00 (*0-87084-555-1*) Anderson Pub Co.

An Asterisk (*) at the beginning of an entry indicates that the title is appearing for the first time.

Legal Researcher's Desk Reference, 1998-99. Ed. by Arlene L. Eis. 424p. 1998. pap. 58.00 (*0-939486-48-2*) Infosources.

Legal Research/paralegals Study Guide. Hein. (Paralegal). (C). 1996. mass mkt., student ed. 14.75 (*0-314-06971-2*) West Pub.

Legal Resource Directory: Your Guide to Help Hotlines & Hot Websites. Theresa M. Rudy. 185p. 1997. 10.00 (*0-910073-23-6*) HALT DC.

Legal Response to Violence Against Women. Ed. & Intro. by Karen Maschke. LC 96-39890. (Gender & American Law Ser.: Vol. 5). 368p. 1997. text 80.00 (*0-8153-2519-3*) Garland.

Legal Responses to Aids in Comparative Perspective Balancing Individual Rights & Societal Interests. Stanis A. Frankowski. LC 98-29923. (Current Issues in International & Comparative Law Ser.). 1998. 105.00 (*90-411-1037-2*, Pub. by M Nijhoff) Kluwer Academic.

Legal Responses to Indoor Air Pollution. Frank B. Cross. LC 90-8963. 224p. 1990. 69.50 (*0-89930-519-9*, CAP/, Quorum Bks) Greenwood.

Legal Responses to Wife Assault: Current Trends & Evaluation. Ed. by N. Zoe Hilton. (Illus.). 272p. 1993. 52.00 (*0-8039-4552-3*); pap. 23.95 (*0-8039-4553-1*) Sage.

Legal Responsibilities & Rights of Public Accountants. Wiley D. Rich. Ed. by Richard P. Brief. LC 80-1514. (Dimensions of Accounting Theory & Practice Ser.). 1980. reprint ed. lib. bdg. 28.95 (*0-405-13539-4*) Ayer.

Legal Responsibilities of Company Directors. John Field. 250p. 1993. 96.00 (*0-7855-7037-3*, Pub. by Tolley Pubng) St Mut.

Legal Responsibilities of the Local Zoning Administrator. 2nd ed. Philip P. Green. 124p. 1987. pap. 12.00 (*1-56011-097-X*) Institute Government.

Legal Responsibility for Housing the Poor: Report to Westchester 2000 Subcommittee on Special Housing Needs. 49p. 1985. pap. 5.00 (*0-685-30166-4*, 38,788) NCLS Inc.

Legal Responsibility in Aquatics. Annie Clement. 230p. 1997. pap. text 40.00 (*0-9678874-0-5*) Sport & Law.

Legal Restraints on the Use of Force 40 Years after the U. N. Charter. Ed. by A. Cassese. (C). 1986. lib. bdg. 191.00 (*90-247-3247-6*) Kluwer Academic.

Legal Review. Graziano. Date not set. pap. text, teacher ed. write for info. (*0-314-89445-4*) West Pub.

Legal Review of the Case of Dred Scott see Dred Scott Case

Legal Revolution of 1902. William S. Child. LC 75-154434. (Utopian Literature Ser.). 1976. reprint ed. 26.95 (*0-405-03517-9*) Ayer.

Legal Right & Social Democracy: Essays in Legal & Political Philosophy. D. Neil MacCormick. 1984. pap. 18.95 (*0-19-825502-0*) OUP.

Legal Rights: Historical & Philosophical Perspectives. Ed. by Austin Sarat & Thomas R. Kearns. 328p. (C). 1997. reprint ed. pap. text 22.95 (*0-472-08471-2*, 08471) U of Mich Pr.

Legal Rights: The Guide for Deaf & Hard of Hearing People. 4th rev. ed. National Association of the Deaf Staff. LC 91-44372. (Illus.). 282p. 1992. pap. 19.95 (*1-56368-000-9*) Gallaudet Univ Pr.

Legal Rights, Duties, & Liabilities of Criminal Justice Personnel: History & Analysis. 2nd ed. Cyril D. Robinson. 516p. 1992. pap. 58.95 (*0-398-06405-9*) C C Thomas.

Legal Rights, Duties, & Liabilities of Criminal Justice Personnel: History & Analysis. 2nd ed. Cyril D. Robinson. 516p. (C). 1992. text 79.95 (*0-398-05779-6*) C C Thomas.

Legal Rights for Seniors: A Guide to Health Care, Income Benefits & Senior Legal Services. Wesley J. Smith. 215p. 1993. 10.00 (*0-910073-17-1*) HALT DC.

Legal Rights, Liabilities & Duties of Women. Edward D. Mansfield. LC 78-72352. (Free Love in America Ser.). reprint ed. 45.00 (*0-404-60951-1*) AMS Pr.

Legal Rights Manual: A Guide for Social Workers & Advice Centres. 2nd ed. Jeremy Cooper. 448p. 1994. pap. 36.95 (*1-85742-136-1*, Pub. by Arena) Ashgate Pub Co.

Legal Rights of Chemists & Engineers. Ed. by Warren D. Niederhauser & E. Gerald Meyer. LC 77-9364. (Advances in Chemistry Ser.: No. 161). 1977. 24.95 (*0-8412-0357-1*); pap. 14.95 (*0-8412-0537-X*) Am Chemical.

Legal Rights of Chemists & Engineers. Ed. by Warren D. Niederhauser & E. Gerald Meyer. LC 77-9364. (Advances in Chemistry Ser.: Vol. 161). 119p. 1977. reprint ed. pap. 36.90 (*0-608-03864-4*, 206431100008) Bks Demand.

Legal Rights of Children. Robert M. Horowitz & Howard A. Davidson. LC 84-1224. (Family Law Ser.). 674p. 1984. text 70.00 (*0-07-015429-5*) Shepards.

Legal Rights of Children: An Orginal Anthology. Ed. by Robert H. Bremner. LC 74-1692. (Children & Youth Ser.: Vol. 5). 1979. 29.95 (*0-405-05968-X*) Ayer.

Legal Rights of Citizens with Mental Retardation. Ed. by Lawrence A. Kane, Jr. et al. LC 88-19159. 360p. (Orig.). (C). 1988. lib. bdg. 37.00 (*0-8191-7110-7*) U Pr of Amer.

Legal Rights of Minors: Rental Housing in Massachusetts. 121p. 1984. pap. 9.75 (*0-685-30180-X*, 38,962) NCLS Inc.

Legal Rights of Persons with Disabilities: An Analysis of Federal Law. Bonnie P. Tucker & Bruce A. Goldstein. LC 90-47698. 1991. ring bd. 115.00 (*0-934753-46-6*) LRP Pubns.

Legal Rights of Persons with Epilepsy. Epilepsy Foundation of America Staff. 124p. 1992. pap. 14.95 (*0-916570-02-9*) Epilepsy Foundation of America.

Legal Rights of Prisoners. Ed. by Geoffrey P. Alpert. LC 80-17241. (Sage Criminal Justice System Annuals Ser.: No. 14). 280p. reprint ed. pap. 86.80 (*0-8357-8466-5*, 203473400091) Bks Demand.

Legal Rights of the Elderly: Everything You & Your Family Need to Know about Government Benefits, Health Care, Social Security, Veteran's Benefits, Medicare & Medicaid, & Guardianship. Sia Arnason et al. 319p. 1995. pap. 15.95 (*0-87224-079-7*, K1-1500) PLI.

Legal Rights of the Mentally Disordered Prison Inmate see Mentally Disordered Inmate & the Law

*__Legal Rights of Union Stewards.__ 3rd rev. ed. Robert M. Schwartz. LC 98-61577. (Illus.). 204p. (Orig.). 1999. pap. 9.95 (*0-945902-08-5*) Work Rights Pr.

Legal Rights of Women: Adapted for Use in Every State by Means of a Brief Synopsis of the Laws Relating to Property Rights, Dower, Divorce, the Rights of a Widow in the Estate of Her Husband, Etc. Containing Also Much Other Helpful Information, Advice & Direction for Women in Every Walk of Life. Lemuel H. Foster. 295p. 1986. reprint ed. 48.50 (*0-8377-2131-8*, Rothman) W S Hein.

Legal Risk Management for Associations: A Legal Compliance Guide for Volunteers & Employees of Trade & Professional Associations. Jerald A. Jacobs & David W. Ogden. LC 95-5868. 150p. (Orig.). 1995. text. write for info. (*1-55798-304-6*, 431-6580); pap. text. write for info. (*1-55798-312-7*, 431-6581) Am Psychol.

Legal Risks in the Long-Term Care Facility. Charlotte K. Eliopoulos. 52p. 1991. pap. text 14.95 (*1-882515-04-8*) Hlth Educ Netwk.

Legal Road Map for Consultants. Judy Gedge. LC 98-24138. 100p. 1998. pap. 18.95 (*1-55571-460-9*, LRMCP, Oasis Pr) PSI Resch.

*__Legal Rules & International Society.__ Anthony Clark Arend. LC 98-44260. 224p. 1999. 35.00 (*0-19-512710-2*); pap. 17.95 (*0-19-512711-0*) OUP.

*__Legal Rules & Legal Reasoning.__ Larry Alexander. LC 99-38741. (Collected Essays in Law Ser.). 275p. (C). 2000. text 101.95 (*0-7546-2004-2*) Ashgate Pub Co.

Legal Scholarship & Doctrines of Private Law, 13th-18th Centuries. Robert Feenstra. LC 96-20070. (Collected Studies: No. CS556). 352p. (C). 1996. text 115.95 (*0-86078-616-1*, Pub. by Variorum) Ashgate Pub Co.

Legal Scholarship, Microcomputers, & Super-Optimized Decision-Making. Stuart S. Nagel. LC 92-44684. 232p. 1993. 67.95 (*0-89930-444-3*, NLA, Quorum Bks) Greenwood.

*__Legal Seafoods Cookbook.__ George Berkowitz & Jane Doerfer. 1999. 26.00 (*0-8446-7018-9*) Peter Smith.

Legal Seafoods Cookbook: Simply Perfect Recipes from Boston's Favorite Seafood Restaurant. George Berkowitz & Jane Doerfer. LC 87-8922. (Illus.). 192p. 1988. pap. 15.95 (*0-385-23183-0*) Doubleday.

Legal Secretarial Assistant. Jack Rudman. (Career Examination Ser.: C-3545). 1994. pap. 23.95 (*0-8373-3545-0*) Nat Learn.

Legal Secretarial; Typewriting & Dictation: Syllabus. Virginia B. Schoepfer. 1974. pap. text 9.50 (*0-89420-014-3*, 290055); audio 102.55 (*0-89420-159-X*, 290000) Natl Book.

Legal Secretary. Jack Rudman. (Career Examination Ser.: C-1343). 1994. pap. 23.95 (*0-8373-1343-0*) Nat Learn.

Legal Secretary. 3rd ed. Clyde Welter. (KK - Legal Secretary Studies). 1990. 19.50 (*0-538-60142-6*) S-W Pub.

Legal Secretary: Fernandez, Payne, & Weber. 3rd ed. Clyde Welter. (KK - Legal Secretary Studies). 1991. 65.25 (*0-538-60371-2*) S-W Pub.

Legal Secretary: Terminology & Transcription. Dorothy Adams & Margaret A. Kurtz. (Illus.). 1981. text 76.50 (*0-07-000330-0*) McGraw.

Legal Secretary Federal Litigation. 1997. pap. write for info. (*1-58012-005-9*) James Pub Santa Ana.

Legal Secretary Federal Litigation. 4th ed. Pamela I. Everett. LC 87-114236. 1996. 89.98 (*0-938065-22-X*) James Pub Santa Ana.

Legal Secretary's Complete Handbook. 4th ed. Mary A. De Vries. LC 92-8332. 656p. (C). 1992. text 29.95 (*0-13-529876-8*) P-H.

Legal Secretary's Concise Dictionary. M. Roshton. 1974. 8.00 (*0-87511-099-1*) Claitors.

Legal Secretary's Concise Dictionary. 8th ed. 1990. 7.00 (*0-87511-739-2*) Claitors.

Legal Secretary's Desk Guide to Punctuation & Spelling. Prentice-Hall Staff. 32p. (C). 1992. 5.95 (*0-13-010786-7*, Macmillan Coll) P-H.

Legal Secretary's Guide. Ann Cheyne. 272p. (C). 1991. 46.00 (*1-85431-116-6*, Pub. by Blackstone Pr) Gaunt.

Legal Secretary's Guide. 2nd ed. Ann Cheyne. 278p. 1996. pap. 48.00 (*1-85431-548-X*, Pub. by Blackstone Pr) Gaunt.

*__Legal Secretary's Guide.__ 3rd ed. Ann Cheyne. 363p. 1999. pap. 48.00 (*1-85431-897-7*, Pub. by Blackstone Pr) Gaunt.

Legal Secrets: Equality & Efficiency in the Common Law. Kim L. Scheppele. (Illus.). 368p. 1988. pap. text 22.00 (*0-226-73779-9*); lib. bdg. 65.00 (*0-226-73778-0*) U Ch Pr.

Legal Semiotics Monographs . . . Making Sense in Law Vol. 4: Linguistic, Psychological & Semiotic Perspectives. Bernard S. Jackson. xii, 516p. 1995. 84.50 (*0-9513793-6-4*) Gaunt.

Legal Service Plans: Approaches to Regulation. American Bar Foundation Staff. Ed. by Werner Pfennigstorf & Spencer L. Kimball. LC 77-87182. xxiv, 662p. 1977. 35.00 (*0-910058-86-5*, 765-0018-01) W S Hein.

Legal Services Authorities Act: A Critique. V. R. Iyer & R. Krishna. (C). 1988. 65.00 (*0-7855-3678-7*) St Mut.

*__Legal Services Directory: Handbuch uber das Amerikanische Amwaltssystem.__ rev. ed. Ute M. Stockheim. (GER.). 1999. mass mkt. 50.00 (*0-86640-074-5*) German Am Chamber.

Legal Services for the Poor: A Comparative & Contemporary Analysis of Interorganizational Politics, 6. Mark Kessler. LC 86-27138. (Studies in Social Welfare Policies & Programs: No. 6). (Illus.). 200p. 1987. 52.95 (*0-313-25508-3*, KLS/) Greenwood.

Legal Services for the Poor: Time for Reform. Ed. by Douglas J. Besharov. 283p. 1990. 31.25 (*0-8447-3689-9*, AEI Pr) Am Enterprise.

Legal Services Marketing: A Planning Approach. Robert E. Stevens & David L. Loudon. (Illus.). 220p. (Orig.). 1989. pap. 19.95 (*0-923892-00-1*) Prof Mktg Systs.

Legal Services to the Poor: The Dream, the Reality, the Future. Jeff E. Rusk. (Institute & Seminar Proceedings Ser.). 120p. 1992. pap. 10.50 (*0-89940-103-1*) LBJ Sch Pub Aff.

Legal Side of Private Security: Working Through the Maze. Leo F. Hannon. LC 92-15685. 256p. 1992. 67.95 (*0-89930-790-6*, HPV, Quorum Bks) Greenwood.

Legal Side of Supervision. Bureau of Business Practice Staff. (C). 1992. pap. 11.95 (*0-13-529934-9*, Macmillan Coll) P-H.

Legal Skills & System. Ed. by Robert Clark. 322p. 1996. pap. 110.00 (*0-7510-0276-3*, Pub. by HLT Pubns) St Mut.

Legal Socialization: A Study of Norms & Rules. E. S. Cohn & S. O. White. 200p. 1990. 89.95 (*0-387-97213-7*) Spr-Verlag.

Legal Solution to Government Gridlock: The Enforcement Strategy of the Securities & Exchange Commission. rev. ed. Billy R. Hall, Jr. & Stuart Bruchey. LC 97-32974. (Financial Sector of the American Economy Ser.). 200p. 1997. text 50.00 (*0-8153-3062-6*) Garland.

Legal Soup: Wages, Civil Lawsuits, a Crooked Cop, a Corrupt Prosecutor, a Biased Judge, 3 vols. 1999. pap. 25.00 (*0-9671063-0-3*) N Thomas.

Legal Speller with Useful Medical Terms. 2nd ed. Sheila B. Sloane & John L. Dusseau. 366p. 1982. pap. text 23.25 (*0-314-69679-2*) West Pub.

Legal Status & Employment Conditions of Local Authorities' Staff in the Countries of Central & Eastern Europe. (Local & Regional Authorities in Europe Ser.: No. 62). 1997. 15.00 (*92-871-3213-5*, Pub. by Council of Europe) Manhattan Pub Co.

*__Legal Status & Remedies for Women in India.__ Roma Mukherjee. 1998. 30.00 (*81-7100-997-2*) Deep & Deep Pubns.

Legal Status of Adolescents. George Thomas et al. 408p. 1980. 12.50 (*0-318-16354-3*, B28) Regional Inst Social Welfare.

Legal Status of Berlin. 410p. 1993. text 100.00 (*0-521-46336-X*) Cambridge U Pr.

Legal Status of Berlin. I. D. Hendry & M. C. Wood. 410p. (C). 1987. 200.00 (*0-949009-05-9*, Pub. by Grotius Pubns Ltd) St Mut.

Legal Status of British Dependent Territories: The West Indies & North Atlantic Region. Elizabeth W. Davies. (Illus.). 410p. (C). 1995. text 95.00 (*0-521-48188-0*) Cambridge U Pr.

Legal Status of Church-State Relationships in the United States: With Special Reference to the Public Schools. Alvin W. Johnson. ix, 332p. 1982. reprint ed. 42.00 (*0-8377-0739-0*, Rothman) W S Hein.

Legal Status of Indians in Bolivia. Cecilia Medina. 10.00 (*0-944253-63-6*) Inst Dev Indian Law.

Legal Status of Indians in Brazil. Cecilia Medina. 10.00 (*0-944253-64-4*) Inst Dev Indian Law.

Legal Status of Indians in Chile. Cecilia Medina. 10.00 (*0-944253-65-2*) Inst Dev Indian Law.

Legal Status of Indians in Columbia. Cecilia Medina. 10.00 (*0-944253-66-0*) Inst Dev Indian Law.

Legal Status of Indians in Guatemala. Cecilia Medina. 15.00 (*0-944253-67-9*) Inst Dev Indian Law.

Legal Status of Indians in Paraguay. Cecilia Medina. 10.00 (*0-944253-68-7*) Inst Dev Indian Law.

Legal Status of International Institutions: SITA, INMARSAT & Eurocontrol Examined. Amir A. Majid. (Illus.). 276p. 1996. text 82.95 (*1-85521-761-9*, Pub. by Dartmth Pub) Ashgate Pub Co.

Legal Status of Israel & the Occupied Territories. Muhammad Farah. (Information Papers: No. 15). 60p. (Orig.). (C). 1975. pap. 1.00 (*0-937694-31-2*) Assn Arab-Amer U Grads.

Legal Status of Prisoners. American Bar Association Staff. 106p. 1983. 30.00 (*0-316-03720-6*); pap. 10.00 (*0-316-03722-2*) Aspen Pub.

Legal Status of Rural High Schools in the United States with Special Reference to the Methods Employed in Extending State Aid to Secondary Education in Rural Communities. Edwin R. Snyder. LC 77-177761. (Columbia University. Teachers College. Contributions to Education Ser.: No. 24). reprint ed. 37.50 (*0-404-55024-X*) AMS Pr.

Legal Status of the Indian. Robert Weil. LC 74-9015. reprint ed. 29.50 (*0-404-11912-3*) AMS Pr.

Legal Status of the Muslims in Singapore. Ibrahim. 1965. pap. 13.00 (*0-685-60632-5*, MICHIE) LEXIS Pub.

*__Legal Status of the Negro, 1940.__ fac. ed. Charles S. Mangum. LC 99-88240. 2000. 85.00 (*1-58477-081-3*) Lawbk Exchange.

*__Legal Status of Third Country Nationals Resident in the European Union.__ Helen Staples. LC 99-47999. (European Monographs: Vol. 22). 448p. 1999. pap. 126.00 (*90-411-1277-4*) Kluwer Law Intl.

Legal Status of Women & Poverty in Tanzania. Magdalena K. Rwebangira. (Scandinavian Institute of African Studies: No. 100). 58p. (Orig.). 1996. pap. 20.00 (*91-7106-391-9*) Coronet Bks.

Legal Status Pupils. De Groff. LC 98-181053. 1998. lib. bdg. 118.00 (*90-411-0521-2*) Kluwer Law Intl.

Legal Stenographer. Jack Rudman. (Career Examination Ser.: C-1344). 1994. pap. 23.95 (*0-8373-1344-9*) Nat Learn.

Legal Structure for Effective Income Tax Administration. Leon Yudkin. LC 78-172244. (Tax Technique Handbook Ser.). 124p. (Orig.). 1971. pap. 5.00 (*0-915506-13-0*) Harvard Law Intl Tax.

Legal Structure of Collective Bargaining in Education, 23. Kenneth H. Ostrander. LC 87-8470. (Contributions to the Study of Education Ser.). 164p. 1987. 49.95 (*0-313-24474-X*, OLS/, Greenwood Pr) Greenwood.

Legal Structure of International Textile Trade. Henry R. Zheng. LC 87-24936. 239p. 1988. 59.95 (*0-89930-334-X*, ZLS/, Quorum Bks) Greenwood.

Legal Structures. Buckley. 1996. text 184.95 (*0-471-96631-2*) Wiley.

Legal Studies: Terminology/Transcription. 4th ed. Wanda Frederick-Bolton. (KK - Legal Secretary Studies). (Illus.). 480p. 1996. pap. 41.95 (*0-538-71530-8*) S-W Pub.

Legal Studies As Cultural Studies: A Reader in (Post)Modern Critical Theory. Ed. by Jerry D. Leonard. LC 94-9240. 392p. (C). 1995. text 59.50 (*0-7914-2295-X*); pap. text 19.95 (*0-7914-2296-8*) State U NY Pr.

Legal Studies for New South Wales. 2nd ed. R. M. Duncan & D. Roberts. 504p. 1992. pap. 47.00 (*0-409-30432-8*, Austral, MICHIE) LEXIS Pub.

Legal Studies for Queensland, Vol. 1. 2nd ed. M. J. Evans. 480p. 1992. pap. 40.00 (*0-409-30780-7*, Austral, MICHIE) LEXIS Pub.

Legal Studies for Queensland, Vol. 2. 2nd ed. M. J. Evans. 480p. 1992. pap. 42.00 (*0-409-30668-1*, Austral, MICHIE) LEXIS Pub.

Legal Studies for South Australia Years 11 & 12. M. G. Nicholls et al. 1989. pap. 31.00 (*0-409-49471-2*, AT, MICHIE) LEXIS Pub.

Legal Studies for Tasmania. 3rd ed. Dalzell R. Chalmers. 1992. pap. 47.00 (*0-409-30489-1*, Austral, MICHIE) LEXIS Pub.

Legal Studies for Victoria, Vol. 1. 2nd ed. N. Bates & M. Bates. pap. 40.00 (*0-409-31047-6*, Austral, MICHIE) LEXIS Pub.

Legal Studies for Victoria, Vol. 2. 2nd ed. N. Bates & M. Bates. 1995. pap. 41.00 (*0-409-31048-4*, Austral, MICHIE) LEXIS Pub.

Legal Studies In Business. Douglas Whitman & John W. Gergacz. LC 96-49178. (SWC-Business Law). 650p. 1997. mass mkt. 98.95 (*0-314-20572-1*) West Pub.

Legal Studies to Wit: Basic Legal Terminology & Transcription. 2nd ed. Wanda W. Roderick. 1984. write for info. (*0-538-11360-X*, K36) S-W Pub.

Legal System. 2nd ed. Meridith B. Cox. (Introduction to the Law, Legal System & Legal Liability Ser.: Vol. I). (Illus.). (C). 1988. pap. text 35.00 (*0-912665-18-1*) BusinessWatch.

Legal System: A Social Science Perspective. Lawrence M. Friedman. LC 74-25855. 338p. 1975. 34.95 (*0-87154-296-X*) Russell Sage.

Legal System: Between Order & Disorder. Francois Ost & Michel Van de Kerchove. Tr. by Iain Stewart. 216p. 1994. text 48.00 (*0-19-825692-2*) OUP.

Legal System: Opposing Viewpoints. Tamara L. Roleff. 1996. pap. 16.20 (*1-56510-404-8*); lib. bdg. 26.20 (*1-56510-405-6*) Greenhaven.

Legal System & Criminal Responsibility of Intellectuals in the People's Republic of China 1949-1982. Carlos Wing-hung Lo. (Occasional Papers-Reprints Series in Contemporary Asian Studies: No. 2). 125p. (Orig.). 1985. pap. text 5.00 (*0-942182-69-3*) Occasional Papers.

Legal System in America: A Look at Lawyers, Judges, Courts & Jury. 1992. lib. bdg. 79.95 (*0-8490-5422-2*) Gordon Pr.

Legal System of Iraq. S. H. Amin. 1987. 90.00 (*0-946706-32-8*, Pub. by Royston Ltd) St Mut.

Legal System of Singapore. Helena H. Chan. LC 96-945765. xxiv, 194p. 1995. pap. write for info. (*0-409-99789-7*, MICHIE) LEXIS Pub.

*__Legal Systems in Conflict: Property & Sovereignty in Missouri, 1750-1860.__ Stuart Banner. LC 99-36236. (Legal History of North America Ser.). 224p. 2000. 39.95 (*0-8061-3182-9*) U of Okla Pr.

Legal Systems of the PRC. Thomas Chiu et al. vii, 134p. 1991. pap. 27.50 (*962-359-427-5*, Pub. by Longman Far East) Gaunt.

*__Legal Systems of the World: A Political, Social, & Cultural Encyclopedia, 4 Vols.__ Herbert M. Kritzer. 2001. lib. bdg. 375.00 (*1-57607-231-2*) ABC-CLIO.

Legal Tactics: Self-Defense for Tenants in Massachusetts. Ed. by Annette R. Duke et al. LC 92-82124. 576p. 1993. pap. text 29.00 (*0-944490-51-4*) Mass CLE.

Legal Tax Avoidance under Russian Law Through Off-Shore Business Operations: The Russian Off-Shore Book. Vladimir Momitko. (RUS., Illus.). 300p. 40.00 (*0-9643334-2-2*) Holland Pubng.

Legal Tender. Marion Foster. LC 92-4453. 240p. (Orig.). 1992. pap. 9.95 (*1-56341-010-9*); lib. bdg. 20.95 (*1-56341-011-7*) Firebrand Bks.

Legal Tender. Kelsey Roberts. (Intrigue Ser.). 1993. mass mkt. 2.99 (*0-373-22248-3*, 1-22248-8) Harlequin Bks.

Legal Tender. Lisa Scottoline. 464p. 2000. mass mkt. 6.99 (*0-06-109412-9*, Harp PBks) HarpC.

Legal Tender. large type ed. Lisa Scottoline. LC 96-39747. (Large Print Bks.). 1997. pap. 23.95 (*1-56895-413-1*) Wheeler Pub.

Legal Tender. Deirdre Shanahan. 78p. 1988. reprint ed. pap. 11.95 (*1-870612-10-8*, Pub. by Enitha Pr) Dufour.

***Legal Tender Acts Considered in Relation to their Constitutionality & their Political Economy.** Samuel T. Spear. LC 99-61888. 104p. 1999. reprint ed. 45.00 (*1-57588-503-4*) W S Hein.

***Legal Terminology.** Gordon W. Brown. LC 99-195589. 240p. (C). 1999. pap. text 15.00 (*0-536-02034-5*) Pearson Custom.

Legal Terminology. Condon. (C). 1998. 28.95 (*1-56253-355-X*) Milady Pub.

Legal Terminology. Cathy J. Okrent. 96p. 1995. pap. text 15.50 (*0-8273-6522-5*) Delmar.

***Legal Terminology.** 2nd ed. 236p. (C). 2000. 17.00 (*0-536-60772-9*) Pearson Custom.

Legal Terminology. 3rd ed. Gordon W. Brown. LC 97-25589. 444p. 1997. pap. text 44.00 (*0-13-260373-X*) P-H.

Legal Terminology: A Programmed Approach. Mary H. Knapp. (C). 1981. pap. 29.95 (*0-937112-00-3*); pap. text 29.95 (*0-685-31739-0*) Stenograph Corp.

Legal Terminology & Transcription. (Prentice Hall College Titles Ser.). (C). 1996. text 46.67 (*0-13-228131-7*, Macmillan Coll) P-H.

Legal Terminology & Transcription. Wallis. 1995. pap. text, teacher ed. write for info. (*0-13-227919-3*) Allyn.

Legal Terminology & Transcription. Marilynn K. Wallis. LC 95-16843. 212p. 1995. pap. text 42.00 (*0-13-190711-5*) P-H.

Legal Terminology & Transcription: Word Processing. Mary A. Baumann & Mary A. Bahntge. 176p. (C). 1986. pap. text 26.25 (*0-471-82042-3*) P-H.

Legal Terminology English & German. Rudiger Renner & Jeffery Tooth. (ENG & GER.). 76.00 (*3-19-006201-3*) Adlers Foreign Bks.

Legal Terminology Flash. Delmar, Inc., Staff. (Paralegal Ser.). 1996. 15.95 (*0-8273-7816-5*) Delmar.

Legal Terminology with Flashcards. Cathy J. Okrent. LC 94-38109. 384p. (C). 1994. mass mkt. 46.95 (*0-8273-6521-7*) Delmar.

Legal Terminology/Legal Dict/ Thesaurus Package. O'Krent. (Paralegal Law Library). (C). 1995. 52.00 (*0-8273-7295-7*, VNR) Wiley.

Legal Terms for Secretaries. Ed. by Educational Research Associates Staff. 1974. 6.75 (*0-89420-096-8*, 299900) Natl Book.

***Legal Texts: The Results of the Uruguay Round of Multilateral Trade Negotiations.** Ed. by World Trade Organization Staff. (World Trade Organization Legal Texts Ser.). 506p. (C). 2000. 90.00 (*0-521-78094-2*); pap. 40.00 (*0-521-78580-4*) Cambridge U Pr.

Legal Texts & Legal Issues: Proceedings of the Second Meeting of the International Organization for Qumran Studies, Cambridge, 1995: Published in Honour of Joseph M. Baumgarten. International Organization for Qumran Studies Staf et al. LC 97-22048. (Studies on the Texts of the Desert of Judah). 1997. 184.00 (*90-04-10829-7*) Brill Academic Pubs.

Legal Theory. 5th ed. Wolfgang G. Friedmann. LC 67-26509. 607p. 1967. text 113.00 (*0-231-03100-9*) Col U Pr.

Legal Theory: A Text Book of Jurisprudence & Comparative Law. Kalyan Chaudhuri. (C). 1989. 40.00 (*0-89771-457-1*, Pub. by Current Dist) St Mut.

Legal Theory - Comparative Law: Studies in Honour of Professor Imre Szabo. Z. Peteri. (ENG & FRE.). 463p. (C). 1984. 125.00 (*963-05-3992-6*, Pub. by Akade Kiado) St Mut.

Legal Theory & Legal History: Essays on the Common Law. A. W. Simpson. LC 87-7447. 1988. 60.00 (*0-907628-83-4*) Hambledon Press.

***Legal Theory in the Crucible of Constitutional Justice: A Study of Judges & Political Morality in Canada, Ireland & Italy.** Rory O'Connell. LC 00-34253. 2000. write for info. (*0-7546-2097-2*, Pub. by Ashgate Pub) Ashgate Pub Co.

Legal Theory of Ethical Positivism. Tom D. Campbell. (Applied Legal Philosophy Ser.). (Illus.). 304p. 1996. text 87.95 (*1-85521-171-8*, Pub. by Dartmth Pub) Ashgate Pub Co.

Legal Thesaurus. 2nd ed. Ed. by William C. Burton. 1024p. 1992. 27.00 (*0-02-897079-9*) Macmillan.

Legal Thesaurus-Dictionary. William P. Statsky. 813p. (Orig.). 1985. pap. text 35.75 (*0-314-85305-7*) West Pub.

***Legal Thriller.** Marcus McGee. 430p. 2000. 27.99 (*0-9673123-3-7*, Pegasus Books) Marcus McGee Med.

***Legal Thrillers: A Reader's Checklist & Reference Guide.** CheckerBee Publishing Staff. 1999. pap. text 4.95 (*1-58598-003-X*) CheckerBee.

Legal Time Limits. Peter Chainey. 100p. (C). 1991. text 30.00 (*1-85431-140-9*, Pub. by Blackstone Pr) Gaunt.

Legal Times of Washington D.C. Circuit Handbook. Ed. by Law & Business Inc. Staff. 1061p. 1980. ring bd. 55.00 (*0-686-89148-1*, H39867) Harcourt.

Legal Times of Washington D.C. Circuit Handbook. Ed. by Law & Business Inc. Staff. 1061p. 1982. suppl. ed. 35.00 (*0-686-89149-X*) Harcourt.

Legal Topics in Boundary Surveying. Ed. by Wendy R. Lathrop. 264p. 1990. pap. 65.00 (*0-614-06110-5*, S293) Am Congrs Survey.

Legal Traditions & Systems: An International Handbook. Ed. by Alan M. Katz. LC 85-27158. 461p. 1986. lib. bdg. 95.00 (*0-313-23830-8*, KLT/, Greenwood Pr) Greenwood.

***Legal Traditions of the World.** H. Patrick Glenn. 550p. 2000. pap. text 29.95 (*0-19-876575-4*) OUP.

Legal Transactions of the Royal Court of Ninevah, Pt. 1. T. Kwasman. (State Archives of Assyria Ser.: Vol. 6). (Illus.). xliv, 369p. 1992. text 85.00 (*951-570-093-0*, Pub. by Helsinki Univ Pr); pap. text 63.00 (*951-570-092-2*, Pub. by Helsinki Univ Pr) Eisenbrauns.

Legal Transcription. Linda Lyle & Howard Doty. 1994. text 150.00 incl. audio (*1-56118-673-2*) Paradigm MN.

Legal Transcription. Linda Lyle & Howard Doty. 500p. 1994. pap. text 25.95 (*1-56118-671-6*) Paradigm MN.

Legal Transcription. Linda Lyle & Howard Doty. 200p. 1995. teacher ed. 8.00 (*1-56118-672-4*) Paradigm MN.

Legal Transcription: Instructor's guide with forms disk, 3.5 IBM. Linda R. Lyle & Howard G. Doty. 69.00 (*1-56118-847-6*) EMC-Paradigm.

Legal Transfer Guide. Martin Torosian. 1987. 34.00 (*0-9603592-4-9*) MTA Financial Servs.

Legal Transplants: An Approach to Comparative Law. Alan Watson. LC 73-94276. (Virginia Legal Studies). 120p. reprint ed. pap. 37.20 (*0-608-15892-5*, 203078700074) Bks Demand.

Legal Transplants: An Approach to Comparative Law. Alan Watson. LC 92-42139. 144p. (C). 1993. reprint ed. 27.00 (*0-8203-1532-X*) U of Ga Pr.

Legal Treatment of Foreign Investment: The "World Bank Guidelines" Ibrahim F. Shihata. LC 93-32403. (International Studies in Human Rights). 484p. (C). 1993. lib. bdg. 149.00 (*0-7923-2525-7*) Kluwer Academic.

Legal Tutor on Sales. Ron Taylor. (C). 1992. text 24.95 (*0-538-81477-2*, LA81AH81) S-W Pub.

Legal Typewriting. 2nd ed. Norma Curchak et al. (Illus.). 1981. text 34.29 (*0-07-014940-2*) McGraw.

Legal Typing for Word Processing. Rhoda Erickson et al. 71p. 1984. 10.00 (*0-936862-14-9*, LT-48) DDC Pub.

***Legal U. S. Immigration: Influences on Gender, Age & Skill.** Michael J. Greenwood & John M. McDowell. LC 99-38679. (C). 1999. text 39.00 (*0-88099-190-9*); pap. text 21.00 (*0-88099-189-5*) W E Upjohn.

Legal Uncertainty & Land Disputes in Peri-Urban Areas of Mozambique: Land Markets in Transition. Steve Boucher et al. (Research Paper Ser.: Vol. 121). (Illus.). xxvi, 111p. (C). 1995. pap. 7.00 (*0-934519-33-1*, RP121) U of Wis Land.

Legal Visions of the New Europe. Ed. by Bernard S. Jackson. 380p. (C). 1993. lib. bdg. 107.50 (*1-85333-904-0*, Pub. by Graham & Trotman) Kluwer Academic.

Legal Visions of the 21st Century: Essays in Honour of Judge Christopher Weeramantry. C. G. Weeramantry et al. LC 98-46645. xx, 791 p. 1998. 208.00 (*90-411-1116-6*) Kluwer Law Intl.

Legal Vocabulary: Vocabulario Juridico, 4 vols., Set. 7th ed. P. E. Silva. (ENG & POR.). 1039p. 1982. 150.00 (*0-8288-1525-9*, M14434) Fr & Eur.

Legal-Wise: Self-Help Legal Guide for Everyone. 3rd rev. ed. Carl W. Battle. LC 96-84661. 208p. 1996. pap. 18.95 (*1-880559-52-8*) Allworth Pr.

Legal Word Book. 3rd rev. ed. Rev. by Frank S. Gordon. 368p. 1991. 12.00 (*0-395-59521-5*) HM.

Legal Word Processing Exercises. Sandra Muehlman-Shortt. 192p. (C). 1991. pap. text 22.40 (*0-13-964545-4*, 180101) P-H.

Legal Writing. (Quick Study Law School Ser.). 4p. pap. 4.95 (*1-57222-249-2*) Barcharts.

Legal Writing. Margot Costanzo. (Legal Skills Ser.). 171p. 1994. pap. 22.00 (*1-874241-43-0*, Pub. by Cavendish Pubng) Gaunt.

Legal Writing. Myra A. Harris. LC 96-5091. (Illus.). 240p. 1996. pap. text 36.40 (*0-13-238627-5*) P-H.

Legal Writing. Irwell. Date not set. pap. text, teacher ed. write for info. (*0-314-06116-9*) West Pub.

Legal Writing. Lecercq. 3024p. 1993. suppl. ed. 695.00 (*0-316-16136-5*, Aspen Law & Bus) Aspen Pub.

Legal Writing. 2nd ed. Barber. (Paralegal Ser.). 1997. teacher ed. 16.95 (*0-8273-7541-7*) Delmar.

Legal Writing. 2nd ed. Steve Barber. LC 96-21164. (Paralegal Ser.). 416p. (C). 1997. mass mkt. 42.95 (*0-8273-7539-5*) Delmar.

Legal Writing: A Systematic Approach. 2nd ed. Diana V. Pratt. LC 93-9682. (American Casebook Ser.). 426p. 1993. pap. 20.50 (*0-314-01843-3*) West Pub.

Legal Writing: A Systematic Approach, Teacher's Manual to Accompany. 2nd ed. Diana V. Pratt. (American Casebook Ser.). 138p. (C). 1993. pap. text 20.00 (*0-314-02394-1*) West Pub.

Legal Writing: Getting It Right & Getting It Written. 2nd ed. Mary B. Ray & Jill J. Ramsfield. 361p. (C). 1993. pap. 25.50 (*0-314-02255-4*) West Pub.

Legal Writing: Process, Analysis, & Organization. Linda H. Edwards. LC 95-81927. 420p. 1996. pap., teacher ed. write for info. (*0-316-21240-7*, 12407) Aspen Law.

Legal Writing: Process, Analysis & Organization. Linda H. Edwards. LC 99-21258. 1999. 32.95 (*0-7355-0311-7*) Panel Pubs.

***Legal Writing: Systematic Approach.** 3rd ed. Pratt. LC 99-202123. (Paralegal Ser.). (C). 1999. pap. 18.75 (*0-314-22803-9*) West Pub.

Legal Writing: The Strategy of Persuasion. 3rd ed. Norman Brand & John O. White. 224p. 1994. pap. text 25.50 (*0-312-08972-4*) St Martin.

Legal Writing, Analysis & Oral Argument. Larry L. Teply. (American Casebook Ser.). 576p. (C). 1989. pap. 31.50 (*0-314-70250-4*) West Pub.

Legal Writing, Analysis & Oral Argument. Larry L. Teply. (American Casebook Ser.). 155p. 1990. pap. text. write for info. (*0-314-76286-8*) West Pub.

Legal Writing & Other Lawyering Skills. 3rd ed. Nancy L. Schultz & Louis J. Sirico. LC 98-10240. 1998. 35.00 (*0-8205-3120-0*) Bender.

***Legal Writing by Design: A Guide to Great Briefs & Memos.** Teresa J. Reid Rambo & Leanne J. Pflaum. 2000. pap. text. write for info. (*0-89089-910-X*) Carolina Acad Pr.

Legal Writing for Paralegals. Steve Barber. 1993. 48.00 (*0-538-70631-7*) S-W Pub.

Legal Writing Handbook. L. Oates. 944p. 1993. 33.00 (*0-316-62194-3*, Aspen Law & Bus) Aspen Pub.

Legal Writing Handbook: Research, Analysis, & Writing. annot. ed. Laurel Oates et al. 944p. 1993. write for info. (*0-316-62198-6*, 21986) Aspen Law.

Legal Writing Handbook: Research, Analysis & Writing. 2nd ed. Laurel C. Oates et al. LC 97-49350. 1998. pap. text 38.00 (*1-56706-695-X*) Aspen Law.

Legal Writing in a Nutshell. Lynn B. Squires et al. LC 96-8963. (Paralegal). 347p. (C). 1996. pap. text 21.00 (*0-314-09900-X*) West Pub.

Legal Writing in a Nutshell. Lynn B. Squires & Marjorie D. Rombauer. LC 82-7082. (Nutshell Ser.). 294p. (C). 1993. reprint ed. pap. text 14.00 (*0-314-65346-5*) West Pub.

***Legal Writing in Plain English.** Bryan A. Garner. 1999. 30.00 (*0-226-28417-4*); pap. 13.00 (*0-226-28418-2*) U Ch Pr.

Legal Writing-Sense & Nonsense: Sense & Nonsense. David Mellinkoff. 242p. (C). 1981. reprint ed. pap. text 19.00 (*0-314-63275-1*) West Pub.

Legal Writing Syle. 2nd ed. Henry Weihofen. LC 79-23662. 332p. (C). 1979. reprint ed. 29.50 (*0-8299-2066-8*) West Pub.

Legal Writings see Complete Works of Henry Fielding

Legalidad y Derechos Humanos En Cuba. Domingo J. Delgado. (SPA.). 164p. (Orig.). 1991. pap. 10.00 (*0-917049-51-9*) Saeta.

Legalines Administrative Law-Schwartz. 4th ed. Spectra. 1996. pap. text 17.95 (*0-15-900171-4*) Harcourt Legal.

Legalines Antitrust-Areeda. 4th ed. Spectra. 1989. pap. text 17.95 (*0-15-900046-7*) Harcourt Legal.

Legalines Antitrust-Areeda. 5th ed. Spectra. 1998. pap. text 19.95 (*0-15-900405-5*) Harcourt Legal.

Legalines Antitrust-Handler. 4th ed. Spectra. 2000. pap. text 18.95 (*0-15-900390-3*) Harcourt.

Legalines Civil Procedure-Field. 6th ed. Spectra. 1991. pap. text 21.95 (*0-15-900048-3*) Harcourt Legal.

Legalines Civil Procedure-Rosenberg. 5th ed. Spectra. 1993. pap. text 19.95 (*0-15-900052-1*) Harcourt Legal.

Legalines Civil Procedure-Yeazell. 3rd ed. Spectra. 1993. pap. text 18.95 (*0-15-900053-X*) Harcourt Coll Pubs.

Legalines Civil Procedure-Yeazell. 4th ed. Spectra. 1997. pap. text 18.95 (*0-15-900241-9*) Harcourt Legal.

Legalines Commercial Law-Farnsworth. 5th ed. Spectra. 1996. pap. text 17.95 (*0-15-900176-5*) Harcourt Legal.

Legalines Constitutional Law-Barrett. 3rd ed. Spectra. 1989. pap. text 20.95 (*0-15-900058-0*) Harcourt Legal.

Legalines Constitutional Law-Gunther. 12th ed. Spectra. 1992. pap. text 23.95 (*0-15-900060-2*) Harcourt Legal.

Legalines Constitutional Law-Lockhart. 7th ed. Spectra. 1992. pap. text 20.95 (*0-15-900062-9*) Harcourt Legal.

Legalines Constitutional Law-Lockhart. 8th ed. Spectra. 1997. pap. text 20.95 (*0-15-900242-7*) Harcourt Legal.

Legalines Constitutional Law-Rotunda. 4th ed. Spectra. 1995. pap. text 19.95 (*0-15-900315-6*) Harcourt Legal.

Legalines Constitutional Law-Stone. 3rd ed. Spectra. 1997. pap. text 19.95 (*0-15-900236-2*) Harcourt Legal.

Legalines Contracts - Fuller. 5th ed. Spectra. 1992. pap. text 17.95 (*0-15-900069-6*) Harcourt Legal.

Legalines Contracts-Calamari. 2nd ed. Spectra. 1990. pap. text 21.95 (*0-15-900065-3*) Harcourt Legal.

Legalines Contracts-Dawson. 6th ed. Ed. by Spectra. 1995. pap. text 21.95 (*0-15-900268-0*) Harcourt Legal.

Legalines Contracts-Farnsworth. 5th ed. Ed. by Spectra. 1995. pap. text 19.95 (*0-15-900332-6*) Harcourt Legal.

Legalines Contracts-Fuller. 6th ed. Spectra. 1998. pap. text 17.95 (*0-15-900237-0*) Harcourt Legal.

Legalines Contracts-Kessler. 3rd ed. Spectra. 1987. pap. text 20.95 (*0-15-900070-X*) Harcourt Legal.

Legalines Contracts-Murphy. 4th ed. Spectra. 1992. pap. text 19.95 (*0-15-900072-6*) Harcourt Legal.

Legalines Contracts-Murphy. 5th ed. Spectra. 1997. pap. text 19.95 (*0-15-900387-3*) Harcourt Legal.

Legalines Corporations-Hamilton. 5th ed. Ed. by Spectra. LC 95-212750. 1995. pap. text 21.95 (*0-15-900313-X*) Harcourt Legal.

Legalines Corporations-Vagts. 3rd ed. Ed. by Spectra. 1991. pap. text 18.95 (*0-15-900078-5*) Harcourt Legal.

Legalines Criminal Law-Boyce. 7th ed. Spectra. 1991. pap. text 19.95 (*0-15-900080-7*) Harcourt Legal.

Legalines Criminal Law-Dix. 3rd ed. Spectra. 1988. pap. text 15.95 (*0-15-900081-5*) Harcourt Legal.

Legalines Criminal Law-Kadish. Ed. by Spectra. LC 96-104843. 1995. pap. text 18.95 (*0-15-900333-4*) Harcourt Legal.

Legalines Criminal Law-Lafave. 2nd ed. Ed. by Spectra. 1989. pap. text 20.95 (*0-15-900084-X*) Harcourt Legal.

Legalines Domestic Rel-Wadling. 3rd ed. Wadlington. 1997. pap. text 18.95 (*0-15-900377-6*) Harcourt Legal.

Legalines Domestic Relations-Clark. 4th ed. Spectra. 1992. pap. text 16.95 (*0-15-900090-4*) Harcourt Legal.

Legalines Evidence-Sutton. 8th ed. Spectra. LC 97-113437. 1996. pap. text 19.95 (*0-15-900096-3*) Harcourt Legal.

Legalines Evidence-Waltz. 8th ed. Spectra. LC 96-104863. 1995. pap. text 17.95 (*0-15-900334-2*) Harcourt Legal.

Legalines Evidence-Weinstein. 8th ed. Spectra. 1989. pap. text 18.95 (*0-15-900097-1*) Harcourt Legal.

Legalines Family Law-Areen. 3rd ed. Spectra. LC 95-107395. 1994. pap. text 19.95 (*0-15-900263-X*) Harcourt Legal.

Legalines Federal Courts-McCormick. 9th ed. Spectra. 1993. pap. text 17.95 (*0-15-900101-3*) Harcourt Legal.

Legalines Income Tax-Freeland. 8th ed. Spectra. 1996. pap. text 17.95 (*0-15-900222-2*) Harcourt Legal.

Legalines Income Tax-Freeland. 9th ed. Spectra. 1998. pap. text 17.95 (*0-15-900361-X*) Harcourt Legal.

Legalines Income Tax-Klein. 11th ed. Spectra. (C). 1998. pap. text 17.95 (*0-15-900383-0*) Harcourt Legal.

Legalines Labor Law-Cox. 12th ed. Spectra. 1997. pap. text 17.95 (*0-15-900238-9*) Harcourt Legal.

Legalines Labor Law-Merrifield. 8th ed. Spectra. 1992. pap. text 17.95 (*0-15-900108-0*) Harcourt Legal.

Legalines Property-Browder. 5th ed. Spectra. 1992. pap. text 19.95 (*0-15-900110-2*) Harcourt Legal.

Legalines Property-Casner. 3rd ed. Spectra. 1989. pap. text 19.95 (*0-15-900111-0*) Harcourt Legal.

Legalines Property-Cribbet. 3rd ed. Spectra. 1991. pap. text 20.95 (*0-15-900112-9*) Harcourt Legal.

Legalines Property-Cribbet. 7th ed. Spectra. 1999. pap. text 20.95 (*0-15-900239-7*) Harcourt.

Legalines Property-Dukeminier. 3rd ed. Ed. by Spectra. LC 94-232938. (C). 1994. pap. text 18.95 (*0-15-900264-8*) Harcourt Legal.

Legalines Property-Nelson. Spectra. 1998. pap. text 24.95 (*0-15-900228-1*) Harcourt Legal.

Legalines Remedies. 4th rev. ed. Spectra. LC 97-126775. 1997. pap. text 22.95 (*0-15-900116-1*) Harcourt.

Legalines Remedies-York. 5th ed. Spectra. LC 95-136267. 1994. pap. text 19.95 (*0-15-900118-8*) Harcourt Legal.

Legalines Securities Regul-Jennings. 7th ed. Spectra. LC 95-102750. 1994. pap. text 20.95 (*0-15-900253-2*) Harcourt Legal.

Legalines Torts - Franklin. 6th ed. Spectra. 1998. pap. text 17.95 (*0-15-900240-0*) Harcourt Legal.

Legalines Torts-Epstein. 6th ed. Spectra. 1995. pap. text 18.95 (*0-15-900335-0*) Harcourt Legal.

Legalines Torts-Franklin. 5th ed. Spectra. 1993. pap. text 17.95 (*0-15-900122-6*) Harcourt Legal.

Legalines Torts-Henderson. 2nd ed. Spectra. 1988. pap. text 17.95 (*0-15-900123-4*) Harcourt Legal.

Legalines Torts-Henderson. 4th ed. Spectra. 1996. pap. text 17.95 (*0-15-900174-9*) Harcourt Legal.

Legalines Torts-Keeton. 3rd ed. Spectra. 1990. pap. text 19.95 (*0-15-900124-2*) Harcourt Legal.

Legalines Torts-Keeton. 3rd ed. Spectra. 2000. pap. text 19.95 (*0-15-900406-3*) Harcourt Legal.

Legalines Torts-Prosser. 9th ed. Spectra. 1995. text 20.95 (*0-15-900301-6*) Harcourt Legal.

Legalines Wills-Dukeminier. 5th ed. Spectra. LC 96-104857. 1995. pap. text 19.95 (*0-15-900337-7*) Harcourt Legal.

Legalised Lawlessness: Soviet Revolutionary Justice. Richard Pipes. (C). 1990. 50.00 (*0-907967-73-6*, Pub. by Inst Euro Def & Strat) St Mut.

Legalism: Law, Morals, & Political Trials. Judith N. Shklar. LC 85-27496. 264p. 1986. pap. 13.95 (*0-674-52351-2*) HUP.

Legalistic Organization. Ed. by Sim B. Sitkin & Robert J. Bies. LC 93-41636. 368p. (C). 1994. text 55.00 (*0-8039-4863-8*); pap. text 26.00 (*0-8039-4864-6*) Sage.

Legality & Illegality: Semiotics, Postmodernism & Law. Ed. by W. Richard Janikowski & Dragan Milovanovic. (Critic of Institutions Ser.: Vol. 3). 288p. (Orig.). (C). 1995. text 52.95 (*0-8204-2512-5*) P Lang Pubng.

Legality & Legitimacy: Carl Schmitt, Hans Kelsen & Hermann Heller in Weimar Republic. David Dyzenhaus. LC 97-11502. 304p. 1997. text 75.00 (*0-19-826062-8*) OUP.

Legality & Legitimacy: Carl Schmitt, Hans Kelsen & Hermann Heller in Weimar Republic. David Dyzenhaus. 304p. 1999. pap. text 29.95 (*0-19-829846-3*) OUP.

Legality & Local Politics. Lee Bridges et al. LC 87-366. 150p. 1987. text 87.95 (*0-566-05430-2*, Pub. by Dartmth Pub) Ashgate Pub Co.

Legality & Locality: The Role of the Law in Central-Local Government Relations. Martin Loughlin. LC 96-13511. 460p. (C). 1996. text 99.00 (*0-19-826015-6*, Clarendon Pr) OUP.

Legality of Non-Forcible Counter-Measures in International Law. Omer Y. Elagab. LC 87-22913. (Oxford Monographs in International Law). (Illus.). 288p. 1988. 75.00 (*0-19-825590-X*, Clarendon Pr) OUP.

Legality of the Threat or Use of Nuclear Weapons (Request for Advisory Opinion) 740p. 1996. 50.00 (*92-1-070743-5*) UN.

Legality of the Threat or Use of Nuclear Weapons (Request for Advisory Opinion) Order of 1 February, 1995. (Reports of Judgments, Advisory Opinions & Orders). 5p. 1995. 5.00 (*92-1-070719-2*) UN.

Legality of the Use by a State of Nuclear Weapons in Armed Conflict. 326p. 1996. 25.00 (*92-1-070742-7*) UN.

Legality of the Use by a State of Nuclear Weapons in Armed Conflict (Request for Advisory Opinion) Order of 13 September, 1993. (Reports of Judgments, Advisory Opinions & Orders). 5p. 1993. 5.00 (*92-1-070700-1*) UN.

Legality of the Use by a State of Nuclear Weapons in Armed Conflict (Request for Advisory Opinion) Order of 20 June, 1994. (Reports of Judgments, Advisory Opinions & Orders). 5p. Date not set. 6.00 (*92-1-070710-9*) UN.

Legality of Threat or Use of Nuclear Weapons: A Guide to the Historic Opinion of the International Court of Justice. John Burroughs. 169p. 1998. pap. 24.95 (*3-8258-3516-2*) Transaction Pubs.

Legalize It? Debating American Drug Policy. Arnold S. Trebach & James A. Inciardi. 230p. (C). 1993. pap. text 16.00 (*1-879383-14-4*) Am Univ Pr.

Legalized Casino Gaming in the United States: The Economic & Social Impact. Ed. by Cathy H. Hsu. LC 98-37326. (Illus.). 270p. (C). 1999. lib. bdg. 49.95 (*0-7890-0640-5*) Haworth Pr.

Legalized Crime of Banking. Silas W. Adams. 1979. lib. bdg. 250.00 (*0-8490-2957-0*) Gordon Pr.

Legalized Gambling. William N. Thompson. LC 94-21258. (Contemporary World Issues Ser.). 209p. 1994. lib. bdg. 39.50 (*0-87436-729-8*) ABC-CLIO.

Legalized Gambling. Ed. by Mary E. Williams. LC 98-11807. (Contemporary Issues Ser.). 187p. (YA). (gr. 9-12). 1998. pap. 17.45 (*1-56510-898-1*) Greenhaven.

An Asterisk (*) at the beginning of an entry indicates that the title is appearing for the first time.

L

***Legalized Gambling.** Ed. by Mary E. Williams. LC 98-11807. (Contemporary Issues Ser.). (YA). (gr. 9-12). 1998. lib. bdg. 20.96 (*1-56510-899-X*) Greenhaven.

Legalized Gambling. 2nd ed. William N. Thompson. LC 97-23954. 298p. 1997. lib. bdg. 45.00 (*0-87436-947-9*) ABC-CLIO.

Legalized Gambling: Curse or Salvation? Andy Hjelmeland. LC 97-10336. (J). 1998. 14.96 (*0-8225-2615-8*, Lerner Publctns) Lerner Pub.

Legalized Gambling: For & Against. Ed. by Rod Evans & Mark Hance. LC 97-36501. 480p. 1997. pap. 19.95 (*0-8126-9354-X*) Open Court.

Legalized Gambling No. 2: For & Against. Ed. by Rod L. Evans & Mark E. Hance. LC 97-36501. 480p. 1997. 36.95 (*0-8126-9353-1*) Open Court.

***Legalized Racism: Federal Indian Policy & the End of Equal Rights for All Americans.** A. R. Eguiguren. LC 99-96819. (Illus.). 244p. 2000. pap. 14.99 (*1-883378-60-5*) Sun on Earth.

Legalized Stealing: The American Way of Life. Seymour Rauch. (American University Studies: Economics: Ser. XVI, Vol. 2). X, 334p. (C). 1989. text 43.00 (*0-8204-0625-2*) P Lang Pubng.

Legalizing Drugs. Ed. by Karin L. Swisher. LC 95-24105. (At Issue Ser.). 128p. (J). (gr. 5-12). 1996. pap. text 11.20 (*1-56510-378-5*) Greenhaven.

Legalizing Drugs. Ed. by Karin L. Swisher. LC 95-24105. (At Issue Ser.). 128p. (J). (gr. 5-12). 1996. lib. bdg. 18.70 (*1-56510-379-3*) Greenhaven.

Legalizing Gender Inequality: Courts, Markets & Unequal Pay for Women in America. Robert L. Nelson & William P. Bridges. LC 98-38432. (Structural Analysis in the Social Sciences Ser.: No. 16). (Illus.). 368p. (C). 1999. text 59.95 (*0-521-62169-0*); pap. text 19.95 (*0-521-62750-8*) Cambridge U Pr.

***Legalizing Moves: Salvadoran Immigrants' Struggle for U.S. Residency.** Susan Bibler Coutin. LC 99-6550. 248p. (C). 2000. text 44.50 (*0-472-11012-8*, 11012) U of Mich Pr.

Legalizing the Flow of Temporary Migrant Workers from Mexico: A Policy Proposal. Wayne A. Cornelius. (Research Reports: No. 7). 17p. (Orig.). (C). 1981. ring bd. 5.00 (*0-935391-06-1*, RR-07) UCSD Ctr US-Mex.

Legally: Contemporary American Culture & the Law. Helle Porsdam. LC 98-54186. 288p. 1999. pap. 16.95 (*1-55849-208-9*) U of Mass Pr.

Legally Binding. Jessica Hart. LC 96-480. 188p. 1995. mass mkt. 2.99 (*0-373-03382-6*, 1-03382-8) Harlequin Bks.

Legally Correct Fairy Tales. David Fisher. 1996. pap. write for info. (*0-446-67226-2*) Warner Bks.

Legally Correct Fairy Tales. David Fisher. LC 96-3491. 128p. 1996. 9.95 (*0-446-52075-6*, Pub. by Warner Bks) Little.

***Legally Correct Fairy Tales: Bedtime Classics Translated into the Legalese.** David Fisher. 116p. 1999. text 10.00 (*0-7881-6837-1*) DIANE Pub.

Legally Safe Mental Health Practice: Psycholegal Questions & Answers. Robert H. Woody. LC 96-3083. 121p. 1996. pap. 24.95 (*1-887841-04-0*, Psychosocial) Intl Univs Pr.

Legally Speaking: Contemporary American Culture & the Law. Helle Porsdam. LC 98-54186. 288p. 1999. 50.00 (*1-55849-207-0*) U of Mass Pr.

Legally Wed: Same-Sex Marriage & the Constitution. Mark P. Strasser. LC 96-50344. 256p. 1996. text 25.00 (*0-8014-3406-8*) Cornell U Pr.

Legally Wed: Same-Sex Marriage & the Constitution. Mark P. Strasser. LC 96-50344. 256p. 1997. pap. text 16.95 (*0-8014-8429-4*) Cornell U Pr.

Legat Saga: An Anecdotal Study of the Life & Times of Nicolai Legat. John Gregory. (Illus.). 188p. (C). 1994. 60.00 (*0-9518864-0-1*, Pub. by Javog Pubg Assocs) Princeton Bk Co.

Legates of Galatia from Augustus to Diocletian. Robert K. Sherk. LC 78-64216. (Johns Hopkins University. Studies in the Social Sciences. Thirtieth Ser. 1912: 2). reprint ed. 39.50 (*0-404-61320-9*) AMS Pr.

Legatio & De Resurrectione. Athenagoras. Ed. by William R. Schoedel. (Oxford Early Christian Texts Ser.). 1972. 45.00 (*0-19-826808-4*) OUP.

Legatus Divinae Pietatis see Herald of God's Loving-Kindness

Legend. Jude Deveraux. LC 96-216382. 416p. 1996. 23.00 (*0-671-74461-5*, PB Hardcover) PB.

Legend. Jude Deveraux. 1997. 23.00 (*0-671-00170-1*, Pocket Books) PB.

Legend. David Gemmell. 1994. mass mkt. 3.99 (*0-345-37906-3*) Ballantine Pub Grp.

Legend. Robert J. Randisi et al. 400p. 1999. mass mkt. 5.99 (*0-8439-4496-X*) Dorchester Pub Co.

Legend. Samuel Taylor. 1976. pap. 5.25 (*0-8222-0649-8*) Dramatists Play.

***Legend.** Cassandra Ward. Ed. by Lori Williams. 275p. 1999. pap. 12.99 (*1-58365-751-7*, Timeless Romance) BT Pub.

***Legend.** ed. Jude Deveraux. 1998. per. 23.00 (*0-671-03694-7*, Pocket Books) PB.

Legend. large type ed. Jude Deveraux. LC 96-39756. (Large Print Bks.). 1997. 26.95 (*1-56895-395-X*) Wheeler Pub.

Legend. large type ed. Patricia Robins. (Dales Large Print Ser.). 343p. 1997. pap. 18.99 (*1-85389-677-2*) Ulverscroft.

Legend, Vol. 1. Laura Baker. 288p. 1998. pap. 5.99 (*0-312-96662-8*, Pub. by Tor Bks) St Martin.

Legend: A Novel. Barry Maher & Bernard J. Garber. LC 83-83169. 304p. (Orig.). 1987. pap. 12.95 (*0-8334-0024-X*, Spir Lit Lib) Garber Comm.

Legend: Arctic Cat's First Four Decades. 2nd rev. ed. C. J. Ramstad. LC 99-60936. (Illus.). 1999. 49.95 (*0-9603786-3-4*) PPM Bks.

Legend: Frank Sinatra & the American Dream. Ethlie A. Vare. 256p. (Orig.). 1995. pap. 13.00 (*1-57297-027-8*) Blvd Books.

Legend: The Arthurian Tarot. Anna-Marie Ferguson. 1997. 14.95 (*1-56718-265-8*) Llewellyn Pubns.

Legend: The Arthurian Tarot. Anna-Marie Ferguson. (Illus.). 276p. 1999. pap., boxed set 34.95 (*1-56718-267-4*) Llewellyn Pubns.

Legend: The Life & Death of Marilyn Monroe. Fred L. Guiles. 534p. 1984. pap. 16.95 (*0-8128-8525-2*, Scrbrough Hse) Madison Bks UPA.

Legend: The Story of Neengay, a Libretto. Janet Lewis. LC 86-32863. 72p. (Orig.). 1987. pap. 8.95 (*0-936784-26-1*) J Daniel.

Legend & Cult of Upagupta: Sanskrit Buddhism in North India & Southeast Asia. John S. Strong. (Illus.). 414p. 1991. text 57.50 (*0-691-07389-9*, Pub. by Princeton U Pr) Cal Prin Full Svc.

Legend & Its Image: The Aerial Flight of Alexander the Great in Medieval Art. Victor M. Schmidt. (Mediaevalia Groningana Ser.: Vol. XVII). xiv, 294p. 1995. pap. 62.00 (*90-6980-053-5*, Pub. by Egbert Forsten) Hod1der & Stoughton.

Legend & Lore of the Americas Before 1492. Ronald H. Fritze. LC 93-13367. 319p. 1993. lib. bdg. 65.00 (*0-87436-664-X*) ABC-CLIO.

Legend Begins: The Texas Rangers, 1823-1845. Frederick Wilkins. LC 96-8497. 256p. 1996. 24.95 (*1-880510-40-5*); pap. 16.95 (*1-880510-41-3*) State House Pr.

Legend Days. Jamake Highwater. LC 82-48852. (Charlotte Zolotow Bk.). 160p. (YA). (gr. 7 up). 1984. 12.95 (*0-06-022303-0*) HarpC Child Bks.

Legend for the Legendary: The Origin of the Baseball Hall of Fame. James A. Vlasich. LC 90-81497. 266p. 1990. 41.95 (*0-87972-493-5*); pap. 20.95 (*0-87972-494-3*) Bowling Green Univ Popular Press.

Legend in Green Velvet. Elizabeth Peters, pseud. 1989. mass mkt. 4.50 (*0-8125-2441-1*, Pub. by Tor Bks) St Martin.

Legend in Green Velvet. Elizabeth Peters, pseud. 256p. 1995. reprint ed. 20.00 (*0-7278-4721-X*) Severn Hse.

Legend in Missouri. Matt Chaney. Ed. by John R. Stanard. LC 97-206848. 160p. 1997. 14.95 (*0-9639316-2-8*) Four Walls.

***Legend in Missouri.** Matt Chaney. 160p. 2000. (*0-9639316-3-6*) Four Walls.

Legend in the Dust. large type ed. Dwight B. Newton. (Sagebrush Large Print Westerns Ser.). 272p. 1996. lib. bdg. 17.95 (*1-57490-020-X*) T T Beeler.

Legend into History & Did Custer Disobey Orders at the Battle of the Little Big Horn? Charles Kuhlman. (Custer Library). (Illus.). 368p. 1994. 19.95 (*0-8117-0453-X*) Stackpole.

Legend into Language: Myths & Legends as a Springboard for Language & Artwork with Children from Five to Eleven Years. Moira Andrew. (Illus.). 72p. (J). (gr. k-4). 1998. pap. 15.95 (*0-947882-69-3*, IP 342-6) Incentive Pubns.

***Legend Logbook.** 2nd ed. Glenn Murray. (Illus.). ii, 75p. 1999. 79.95 (*1-58527-006-7*) Legend Pubns NY.

Legend MacKinnon. Donna Kauffman. 416p. 1999. mass mkt. 5.99 (*0-553-57923-1*) Bantam.

Legend Makers. Catherine Lanigan. 384p. 1999. mass mkt. 5.99 (*1-55166-517-4*, 1-66517-3, Mira Bks) Harlequin Bks.

Legend, Myth & Magic in the Image of the Artists: A Historical Experiment. Ernst Kris & Otto Kurz. 1979. pap. 14.00 (*0-300-02669-2*) Yale U Pr.

Legend of a Bad Man. Ray Hogan. LC 97-9309. 243p. 1997. lib. bdg. 17.95 (*0-7862-0747-7*) Five Star.

Legend of a Bad Man: A Western Quintet. large type ed. Ray Hogan. LC 98-24418. 1999. 19.95 (*0-7862-0770-1*) Thorndike Pr.

Legend of a Badman, 1. Ray Hogan. 240p. 1999. mass mkt. 4.50 (*0-8439-4560-5*) Dorchester Pub Co.

Legend of a Musical City: Music Book Index. Max Graf. 302p. 1993. reprint ed. lib. bdg. 89.00 (*0-7812-9566-1*) Rprt Serv.

Legend of Aleister Crowley. Israel Regardie & P. R. Stephensen. LC 83-81836. 192p. 1983. pap. 14.95 (*1-56184-114-5*) New Falcon Pubns.

Legend of Altazar: A Fragment of the True History of Planet Earth. Solara. 238p. (Orig.). 1990. reprint ed. pap. text 12.95 (*1-878246-02-X*) Star-Borne.

Legend of American Standard. Jeffrey L. Rodengen. 1999. 39.95 (*0-945903-48-0*) Write Stuff Syndicate.

Legend of AMP. Jeffrey L. Rodengen. Ed. by Karen Nitken. LC 96-61251. (Illus.). 1998. 39.95 (*0-945903-33-2*) Write Stuff Syndicate.

Legend of Annie Murphy. Frank E. Peretti. LC 96-41694. (Cooper Kids Adventure Ser.). (J). (gr. 5-9). 1997. pap. 5.99 (*0-8499-3645-4*) Tommy Nelson.

Legend of Applied Materials. Jeffrey L. Rodengen. Ed. by Karen Nitkin. LC 96-62226. (Illus.). 160p. 1997. 39.95 (*0-945903-14-6*) Write Stuff Syndicate.

Legend of Arthur in British & American Literature. Jennifer R. Goodman. (Twayne's English Authors Ser.: Vol. 461). 176p. (C). 1988. 32.00 (*0-8057-6965-X*, Twyne) Mac Lib Ref.

Legend of Baby Doe: The Life & Times of the Silver Queen of the West. John Burke. LC 89-32800. (Illus.). xiii, 256p. 1989. pap. 13.95 (*0-8032-6103-9*, Bison Books) U of Nebr Pr.

Legend of Bagger Vance: A Novel. Steven Pressfield. LC 94-32223. 245p. 1995. 20.00 (*0-688-14048-3*, Wm Morrow) Morrow Avon.

***Legend of Bagger Vance: A Novel of Golf & the Game of Life.** Steven Pressfield. LC 94-32223. 272p. 1999. pap. 12.50 (*0-380-72751-X*, Avon Bks) Morrow Avon.

***Legend of Bagger Vance: A Novel of Golf & the Game of Life.** Steven Pressfield. 304p. 2000. mass mkt. 6.99 (*0-380-81744-6*, Avon Bks) Morrow Avon.

Legend of Bear Bryant. Mickey Herskowitz. 256p. 1993. pap. 15.95 (*0-89015-910-6*) Sunbelt Media.

Legend of Bearby the Knight: A Sports Fable. Terry Whittaker. (Illus.). 36p. 1993. pap. 7.95 (*0-930899-12-1*) Fanatic Pubng.

Legend of Being Irish: A Collection of Irish-American Poetry. Ed. by David Lampe. 120p. 1988. pap. 9.00 (*0-934834-23-7*) White Pine.

Legend of Belle Starr. 3rd ed. Stoney Hardcastle. 255p. 1979. reprint ed. mass mkt. 6.95 (*0-9653874-0-2*) Indian Nations.

Legend of Bernardo Del Carpio: From Chronicle to Drama. David G. Burton. 150p. 1990. 30.00 (*0-916379-54-X*) Scripta.

Legend of Bill & Vince Dooley. Rosie S. Seaman. LC 81-50805. (College Sports Bks.). 1981. pap. 7.95 (*0-87397-187-6*, Strode Pubs) Circle Bk Service.

Legend of Bluebonnet. Houghton Mifflin Company Staff. (Literature Experience 1993 Ser.). (J). (gr. 2). 1992. pap. 9.48 (*0-395-61778-2*) HM.

Legend of Briggs & Stratton. Jeffrey L. Rodengen. Ed. by Karen Nitkin. LC 95-60793. (Illus.). 176p. 1995. 39.95 (*0-945903-11-1*) Write Stuff Syndicate.

Legend of Brittany & Other Miscellaneous Poems & Sonnets. James Russell Lowell. (Notable American Authors Ser.). 1999. reprint ed. lib. bdg. 125.00 (*0-7812-3877-3*) Rprt Serv.

Legend of Broken Saddle. large type ed. Will Black. (Linford Western Large Print Ser.). 224p. 1998. pap. 17.99 (*0-7089-5281-X*, Linford) Ulverscroft.

Legend of Burning Water. Sigmund Brouwer. LC 96-3452. (Winds of Light Ser.: No.3). 130p. (Orig.). (J). 1992. pap. 5.99 (*0-89693-117-X*, 6-1117, Victor Bks) Chariot Victor.

Legend of Cactus Eddie. Brian Gold. LC 97-217685. 60p. 1996. pap. 11.95 (*0-929385-74-8*, Strchld Pr) Light Tech Pubng.

***Legend of Catfish & Little Bream.** Ronnie Wells. 2000. 17.95 (*0-925417-26-2*) Acadian Hse Pub.

Legend of Catlantis. Gayle Middleton. (Illus.). 112p. 1989. text 24.95 (*0-685-29046-8*, 47025) Willitts Designs.

Legend of Cessna. Jeffrey L. Rodengen. Ed. by Karen Nitken. LC 97-60423. (Illus.). 1997. 39.95 (*0-945903-30-8*) Write Stuff Syndicate.

Legend of Chris-Craft. Jeffrey L. Rodengen. (Illus.). 304p. 1988. 49.95 (*0-945903-02-2*) Write Stuff Syndicate.

Legend of Chris-Craft, Vol. 3. 3rd rev. ed. Jeffrey L. Rodengen. LC 93-60544. (Illus.). 268p. 1998. 49.95 (*0-945903-20-0*) Write Stuff Syndicate.

Legend of Colin Kelly: America's First Hero of WWII. Dennis E. McClendon & Wallace F. Richards. (Illus.). 72p. 1994. pap. 8.95 (*0-929521-92-7*) Pictorial Hist.

Legend of Coyote Ford. large type ed. Marshall Grover. (Linford Western Library). 272p. 1993. pap. 16.99 (*0-7089-7435-X*, Linford) Ulverscroft.

Legend of Crazy Horse. Harry Combs. 320p. 1997. mass mkt. 6.50 (*0-440-21732-6*) Dell.

Legend of Crazy Horse Clan. Moses N. Crow. Ed. by Renee S. Flood. (Illus.). 36p. (Orig.). (J). (gr. 3 up). 1987. pap. 4.95 (*1-877976-03-2*, 406-0010) Tipi Pr.

Legend of Cropsey Vol. 1: A Legacy of Terror at Summer Camp. Hugo Furst. 208p. (YA). 1997. 15.95 (*0-9657781-7-7*) Full Mn Bks.

Legend of Crossbones Key. Steve Englehart. (Dnagers Ser.). (J). 1997. 9.09 (*0-606-11264-2*, Pub. by Turtleback) Demco.

***Legend of Crystal Lake.** Sally A. Roberts. LC 99-49996. 2000. write for info. (*1-57168-369-0*, Eakin Pr) Sunbelt Media.

Legend of Cushetunk: The Nathan Skinner Manuscript & the Early History of Cochecton. Barbara J. Sivertsen & Barbara L. Covey. 127p. (Orig.). 1993. pap. text 17.00 (*1-55613-787-7*) Heritage Bk.

Legend of Deadman's Mine. Joan Lowery Nixon. LC 94-71792. (Disney Adventures: No. 2). (Illus.). 96p. (J). (gr. 2-4). 1995. 13.95 (*0-7868-3047-6*, Pub. by Disney Pr) Little.

Legend of Deadman's Mine. Joan Lowery Nixon. LC 94-71792. (Disney Adventures: No. 2). (J). (gr. 2-4). 1995. 9.15 (*0-606-09128-9*, Pub. by Turtleback) Demco.

Legend of Death Walker. David Gemmell. 1997. mass mkt. 8.99 (*0-552-14252-2*) Bantam.

Legend of Deathwalker. David Gemmell. 1999. mass mkt. 6.99 (*0-345-40800-4*) Ballantine Pub Grp.

Legend of Desire. Kathleen Drymon. 320p. 1998. pap. 5.99 (*0-8217-5924-8*, Zebra Kensgtn) Kensgtn Pub Corp.

Legend of Doll Fin. Dan Parisi. LC 96-95274. (Illus.). 32p. (Orig.). (J). (ps-3). 1997. pap. 5.95 (*0-9655066-0-6*, 1) A&D Publishing.

***Legend of Dornar Caule: A Fable for the Modern Age.** Hilary Milton. 1999. 15.95 (*1-57359-023-1*, Starrhill Press) Black Belt Communs.

Legend of Dr. Markland. large type ed. Anna Ramsay. 257p. 1992. 11.50 (*0-7505-0391-2*) Ulverscroft.

Legend of Dr. Pepper - 7-Up. Jeffrey L. Rodengen. Ed. by Karen Nitkin. LC 95-60796. (Illus.). 142p. 1995. 39.95 (*0-945903-49-9*) Write Stuff Syndicate.

Legend of Dragon Hame. Benjamin Thorpe. 200p. 2000. pap. (*1-57532-260-9*) Press-Tige Pub.

***Legend of Dragoon: Prima's Official Strategy Guide.** Dimension Publishing Staff. 2000. pap. 14.99 (*0-7615-3007-X*) Prima Pub.

Legend of Duke Ernst. Herzog Ernst. Tr. by J. W. Thomas & Carolyn Dussere. LC 79-19843. 136p. 1979. reprint ed. pap. 42.20 (*0-7837-8900-9*, 204961100001) Bks Demand.

Legend of Eddie Bauer. Robert Spector & Ceila D. Robbins. (Illus.). 96p. 1994. pap. 15.00 (*0-944641-06-7*) Greenwich Pub Group.

Legend of El Chivato. Elizabeth Fackler. (Billy the Kid Ser.). 1997. mass mkt. 6.99 (*0-8125-3340-2*, Pub. by Tor Bks) St Martin.

Legend of Etana. J. V. Wilson. 1992. reprint ed. pap. write for info. (*0-85668-258-6*, Pub. by Aris & Phillips) David Brown.

Legend of Federal-Mogul, 1. Jeffrey L. Rodengen. 1999. 39.95 (*0-945903-44-8*) Write Stuff Syndicate.

Legend of Fire. Lee Roddy. (Ladd Family Adventure Ser.: Vol. 2). 148p. (J). (gr. 3-6). 1989. reprint ed. pap. 5.99 (*0-929608-17-8*) Focus Family.

Legend of Fleetwood. Jeffrey L. Rodengen. 1997. 39.95 (*0-945903-47-2*) Write Stuff.

Legend of Food Mountain (La Montana del Alimento) Illus. by Graciela Carrillo. LC 81-71634. 24p. (J). (gr. k-8). 1982. 14.95 (*0-89239-022-0*) Childrens Book Pr.

Legend of Frango Chocolate. Robert Spector. LC 93-73903. 1993. pap. 11.95 (*0-935503-14-5*) Document Bk.

Legend of Fredbird. Steven P. Kveton. (Illus.). 16p. (Orig.). (J). (ps up). 1986. pap. text 2.95 (*0-9616799-0-5*) Water St Missouri.

***Legend of Freedom Hill.** Linda Altman. (Illus.). 32p. (J). (ps-5). 2000. 15.95 (*1-58430-003-5*, Pub. by Lee & Low Bks) Publishers Group.

***Legend of Freud.** Samuel Weber. (Illus.). 180p. 1999. pap. 14.95 (*0-8047-3121-7*) Stanford U Pr.

Legend of Gold & Other Stories. Ishikawa Jun. Tr. by William J. Tyler. LC 98-16636. 312p. 1998. text 46.00 (*0-8248-1968-3*); pap. text 27.95 (*0-8248-2070-3*) UH Pr.

Legend of Gomek. William R. Adams. 32p. 1998. pap. text 6.95 (*1-881470-05-9*) So Herit FL.

Legend of Good Women. Geoffrey Chaucer. Ed. by Janet Cowen & George Kane. (Medieval Texts & Studies: No. 16). 360p. 1995. 95.00 (*0-937191-34-5*) Mich St U Pr.

Legend of Goodyear: The First 100 Years. Jeffrey L. Rodengen. Ed. by Alex Lieber. LC 96-61249. (Illus.). 208p. 1997. 39.95 (*0-945903-35-9*) Write Stuff Syndicate.

Legend of Green-Eye. James M. Kemp. LC 93-91558. (Illus.). 150p. (Orig.). 1993. pap. 9.95 (*0-9630899-1-9*) J M Kemp.

Legend of Greenmantle. Jocelyne Villeneuve. (Illus.). 80p. (J). (ps-8). 1988. 9.95 (*0-920806-95-3*, Pub. by Penumbra Pr) U of Toronto Pr.

Legend of Guy of Warwick. Velma B. Richmond. LC 95-17168. (Studies in Medieval Literature: Vol. 14). (Illus.). 632p. 1995. text 109.00 (*0-8153-2085-X*, H1929) Garland.

Legend of Halliburton. Jeffrey L. Rodengen. LC 95-62227. (Illus.). 208p. 1997. 39.95 (*0-945903-16-2*) Write Stuff Syndicate.

Legend of Hamlet, Prince of Denmark. George P. Hansen. LC 70-144634. reprint ed. 32.50 (*0-404-03105-6*) AMS Pr.

Legend of Hammie-Downz. large type ed. Timothy M. Dinan. LC 97-94844. (Illus.). 33p. (J). (gr. 3-6). 1997. 14.95 (*0-9664361-0-5*, 9864) ITF Bks Co.

Legend of Herostratus: Existential Envy in Rousseau & Unamuno. Gregory L. Ulmer. LC 77-22363. (University of Florida Humanities Monographs: No. 45). 92p. reprint ed. pap. 30.00 (*0-7837-5064-1*, 204475900004) Bks Demand.

Legend of Hiram. A. D. Wright. (Illus.). 300p. 1997. 55.00 (*1-897763-06-9*, Pub. by Adam Hart); pap. 24.95 (*1-897763-07-7*, Pub. by Adam Hart) Intl Spec Bk.

Legend of Holly Boy. Frank Latino. (Illus.). 38p. (J). (ps-12). 1993. 15.95 (*0-9640474-0-3*); pap. 7.95 (*0-9640474-1-1*) F Latino Pub Co.

Legend of Holly Boy. rev. ed. Illus. by Jack B. Hood. 38p. (J). (ps-12). pap. 3.95 (*0-9640474-2-X*) F Latino Pub Co.

Legend of Holy Women: A Translation of Osbern Bokenham's Legends of Holy Women. Sheila Delany. LC 91-51117. (Notre Dame Texts in Medieval Culture Ser.: Vol. 1). (C). 1992. text 34.50 (*0-268-01294-6*); pap. text 17.50 (*0-268-01295-4*) U of Notre Dame Pr.

Legend of Honeywell. Jeffrey L. Rodengen. Ed. by Karen Nitkin. (Illus.). 240p. 1995. 39.95 (*0-945903-25-1*) Write Stuff Syndicate.

Legend of Hua Mu Lan. Song N. Zhang. Tr. by Paulina Kobylinski & Nguyen N. Ngan. (ENG & SPA., Illus.). 32p. (J). (gr. 2-4). 1998. 16.95 (*1-57227-055-1*) Pan Asian Pubns.

Legend of Huma. Richard A. Knaak. LC 87-51254. (DragonLance Heroes Trilogy: Vol. 1). (Illus.). 352p. (Orig.). 1988. pap. 5.99 (*0-88038-548-0*, Pub. by TSR Inc) Random.

Legend of IBP, 1. Jeffrey L. Rodengen. 1999. 39.95 (*0-945903-52-9*) Write Stuff Syndicate.

Legend of Indian Mary & Umpqua Joe. Percy T. Booth. 70p. 1994. pap. 7.95 (*1-885813-01-5*) B & B Pubng.

Legend of Ingersoll-Rand. Jeffrey L. Rodengen. Ed. by Karen Nitkin. LC 95-60794. (Illus.). 208p. 1995. 39.95 (*0-945903-08-1*) Write Stuff Syndicate.

Legend of Injun Joe Brady. large type ed. J. D. Kincaid. (Linford Western Large Print Ser.). 224p. 1998. pap. 17.99 (*0-7089-5284-4*, Linford) Ulverscroft.

Legend of Inter-Tel. Jeffrey L. Rodengen. 1999. 39.95 (*0-945903-31-6*) Write Stuff Syndicate.

Legend of Jesse Owens. Hank Nuwer. LC 96-51188. (Impact Biograpies Ser.). 176p. (YA). (gr. 5-9). 1997. lib. bdg. 24.00 (*0-531-11356-6*) Watts.

Legend of Jimmy Spoon. Kristaina Gregory. (J). (gr. 4-7). 1991. 11.10 (*0-606-12391-1*, Pub. by Turtleback) Demco.

Legend of Jimmy Spoon. Kristiana Gregory. 165p. (J). (gr. 3-7). 1990. 15.95 (*0-15-200506-4*, Harcourt Child Bks) Harcourt.

Legend of Jimmy Spoon. Kristiana Gregory. LC 89-26863. (Great Episodes Ser.). 144p. (J). (gr. 4-7). 1991. pap. 6.00 (*0-15-243812-2*, Gulliver Bks) Harcourt.

An Asterisk (*) at the beginning of an entry indicates that the title is appearing for the first time.

L

Legend of Joaquin Murrieta, California's Gold Rush Bandit. James F. Varley. LC 95-91474. (Illus.). 230p. (Orig.). 1995. pap. 17.95 (*0-9647747-0-4*) Big Lost River Pr.

Legend of Job in the Middle Ages. Lawrence L. Besserman. LC 78-14936. 191p. 1979. reprint ed. pap. 59.30 (*0-7837-2224-9*, 205731400004) Bks Demand.

***Legend of Johnny Cloud.** large type ed. John Brand. 224p. 1999. pap. 20.99 (*1-85389-915-1*, Dales) Ulverscroft.

Legend of Jonah. Bowers. 1971. lib. bdg. 57.00 (*90-247-5132-2*, Pub. by M Nijhoff) Kluwer Academic.

Legend of Jonah & the Two Great Fish. Mordicai Gerstein. LC 96-31971. (Illus.). 32p. (J). (gr. 4-6). 1997. 16.00 (*0-689-81373-2*) S&S Bks Yung.

***Legend of Kamui.** Sanpei Shirato. (Perfect Collection: Vol. 1). (Illus.). 264p. 1999. pap. text 16.95 (*1-56931-318-0*, Cadence Bks) Viz Commns Inc.

Legend of Kamui, Vol. 2. Sanpei Shirato. (Perfect Collection Ser.). (Illus.). 224p. 1999. pap. text 16.95 (*1-56931-323-7*, Viz Comics) Viz Commns Inc.

Legend of Kamui Pt. 1: The Island of Sugaru. Sanpei Shirato. Ed. by Seiji Horibuchi. Tr. by Satoru Fujii & Toren Smith from JPN. (Illus.). 268p. (Orig.). 1990. pap. 16.95 (*0-929279-65-4*) Viz Commns Inc.

Legend of Kamui Pt. 2: The Island of Sugaru. Sanpei Shirato. Ed. by Seiji Horibuchi. Tr. by Satoru Fujii & Toren Smith from JPN. (Illus.). 268p. (Orig.). 1990. pap. 16.95 (*0-929279-66-2*) Viz Commns Inc.

Legend of Killer Noon. David J. Daly. LC 99-94273. 223p. 2000. pap. 14.95 (*0-9671411-0-9*, Pub. by Green Boat Pr) ACCESS Pubs Network.

Legend of King Arthur: A Young Reader's Edition of the Classic Story by Howard Pyle. Francesca D'Ottari. LC 94-74315. (Illus.). 56p. (J). 1996. 9.98 (*1-56138-503-4*, Courage) Running Pr.

Legend of King Piast. Babara Seidler. Tr. by Jane Kedron. (Kosciuszko Young People's Ser.). (Illus.). (J). (gr. 2-8). 1977. pap. 2.00 (*0-917004-08-6*) Kosciuszko.

***Legend of Kittyfish: The Weavus Family.** large type ed. Jonas O. Brumett. (Illus.). 26p. (J). (gr. k-2). 1999. pap. 7.95 (*1-892812-52-5*) Critters Kids.

***Legend of Kittyfish: The Weavus Family.** large type ed. Jonas O. Brumett. (Illus.). 26p. (J). (ps-2). 1999. pap. 9.95 incl. audio (*1-892812-57-6*) Critters Kids.

Legend of Kyrandia, Bk. 3. Joe Hutsko. 1995. pap. 19.95 (*1-55958-782-2*) Prima Pub.

Legend of Lagaia: Prima's Official Strategy Guide. Bart Farkas. LC 99-70258. 128p. 1999. per. 14.99 (*0-7615-2088-0*) Prima Pub.

Legend of Landsee. Harwell G. Davis. LC 76-40829. 1976. 10.95 (*0-87397-106-X*, Strode Pubs) Circle Bk Service.

***Legend of Lemnear, Vol. 1.** Kinji Yoshimoto. Tr. by Laura Jackson & Yoko Kobayashi from JPN. (Illus.). 158p. 1999. pap. 15.95 (*1-56219-912-9*, CMX 06161) Central Pk Media.

***Legend of Lemnear, Vol. 2.** Kinji Yoshimoto. Tr. by Laura Jackson & Yoko Kobayashi from JPN. (Illus.). x, 166p. 1999. pap. 15.95 (*1-56219-925-0*, CMX 06102) Central Pk Media.

Legend of Light. Bob Hicok. LC 95-15836. (Felix Pollak Prize in Poetry Ser.). 90p. 1995. pap. 11.95 (*0-299-14914-5*) U of Wis Pr.

Legend of Lightning Larry. Aaron Shepard. LC 91-43779. (Illus.). 32p. (J). (gr. 1-3). 1993. 14.95 (*0-684-19433-3*) Scribner.

Legend of Little Deer. Wade Blevins. LC 96-7033. (Cherokee Indian Legend Ser.: No. 3). (Illus.). 49p. (J). (gr. 2 up). 1993. lib. bdg. 12.95 (*1-56763-073-1*) Ozark Pub.

Legend of Little Nessie. Ramon P. Cassinari. (Illus.). 24p. (J). (gr. k-4). 1997. 14.95 (*0-9654002-0-4*) Little Lochness.

Legend of Litton Industries, 1. Jeffrey L. Rodengen. 1999. 39.95 (*0-945903-51-0*) Write Stuff Syndicate.

Legend of LoneStar Bear Bk. I: How LoneStar Got His Name. Remi Kramer. (Illus.). 64p. (J). 1988. lib. bdg. 15.00 (*0-945887-01-9*) Northwind Pr.

Legend of LoneStar Bear Bk. III: Mystery of the Walking Cactus. Remi Kramer. (Illus.). 80p. (J). (gr. 2-8). 1994. reprint ed. pap. 8.00 (*0-945887-16-7*) Northwind Pr.

Legend of LoneStar Bear Bk. 3: Mystery of the Walking Cactus. Remi Kramer. (Illus.). 80p. (Orig.). (J). (gr. 2-8). 1994. reprint ed. bds. 13.00 (*0-945887-15-9*) Northwind Pr.

Legend of LoneStar Bear Bk. III: The Mystery of the Walking Cactus. Remi Kramer. (Illus.). 80p. (J). (gr. 2-8). 1990. lib. bdg. 14.95 (*0-945887-03-5*) Northwind Pr.

Legend of LoneStar Bear Bk. IV: Soaring with Eagles. Remi Kramer. (Illus.). 64p. (J). 1994. pap., bds. 13.00 (*0-945887-02-7*) Northwind Pr.

Legend of LoneStar Bear Bk. IV: Soaring with Eagles. rev. ed. Remi Kramer. (Illus.). 64p. (J). (gr. 2-8). 1994. pap. 8.00 (*0-945887-14-0*) Northwind Pr.

Legend of Lostwithiel. E. F. Wells. (Illus.). (Orig.). 1979. mass mkt. 1.95 (*0-89083-446-6*, Zebra Kensgtn) Kensgtn Pub Corp.

Legend of Lotfiya: Who's after You? Andy Smart. (Illus.). 32p. (J). (gr. 2-6). 1997. pap. 6.95 (*977-5325-71-4*, Pub. by Hoopoe Bks) AMIDEAST.

Legend of Love. large type ed. Melinda Cross. (Harlequin Ser.). 1993. lib. bdg. 19.95 (*0-263-13351-6*) Mac Lib Ref.

***Legend of Luke.** Brian Jacques. LC 99-33891. (Redwall Ser.). (Illus.). 374p. (J). (gr. 4-7). 2000. 22.95 (*0-399-23490-X*, Philomel) Peng Put Young Read.

***Legend of Luke.** large type ed. Brian Jacques. LC PZ7.J15317LE 2000. (Redwall Ser.). (Illus.). 534p. (J). (gr. 8-12). 2000. 23.95 (*0-7862-2662-5*) Thorndike Pr.

Legend of Mackinac Island. Kathy-Jo Wargin. LC 98-56194. (Illus.). 48p. (J). (gr. k-5). 1999. 17.95 (*1-886947-12-0*) Sleepng Bear.

Legend of Mammy Jane. 3rd ed. Sibyl J. Pischke. 405p. 1994. pap. 14.95 (*0-9608532-2-7*) S J Pischke.

***Legend of Mana Official Strategy Guide.** Games Brady. 224p. 2000. pap. 14.99 (*1-56686-986-2*, BradyGAMES) Brady Pub.

Legend of Marguerite de Roberval. Arthur P. Stabler. LC 72-169728. (Illus.). 87p. reprint ed. pap. 30.00 (*0-8357-4568-6*, 203747800008) Bks Demand.

Legend of Mary the Egyptian: In Medieval Insular Hagiography. Ed. by Erich Poppe & Bianca Ross. LC 96-156997. 220p. 1996. boxed set 55.00 (*1-85182-187-2*, Pub. by Four Cts Pr) Intl Spec Bk.

Legend of Maya Deren, a Documentary & Collected Works Vol. 1, Pt. 2: Chambers, 1942-1947. (Illus.). 684p. 1988. 40.00 (*0-911689-18-4*); pap. 22.40 (*0-911689-17-6*) Anthology Film.

Legend of Maya Deren, a Documentary & Collected Works, Vol. 1, Pt. 1 Vol. 1, Pt. 1: Signatures, 1917-1942. VeVe A. Clark et al. Ed. by Hollis Melton. (Illus.). 514p. 1984. 40.00 (*0-911689-16-8*); pap. 22.50 (*0-911689-15-X*) Anthology Film.

Legend of Mel & Nin: How People Got the Color of Their Skin. Bill Grimmette. 1997. 17.95 (*0-9629978-1-1*) Sights Prods.

Legend of Mercury, 1. Jeffrey L. Rodengen. LC 98-61061. (Illus.). 207p. 1999. 39.95 (*0-945903-23-5*) Write Stuff Syndicate.

Legend of Mexicatl see Leyenda de Mexicatl

Legend of Mexicatl. Jo Harper. LC 97-42222. (Illus.). 32p. (YA). (ps up). 1998. 15.95 (*1-890515-05-1*, Pub. by Turtle Bks) Publishers Group.

***Legend of Mexicatl.** Jo Harper. 2000. pap. 7.95 (*1-890515-21-3*) Turtle Bks.

Legend of Minna Lamourrie. Nellie McCaslin. LC 93-2603. 20p. (J). 1993. pap. 5.00 (*0-88734-438-0*) Players Pr.

Legend of Montrose see Works of Sir Walter Scott

Legend of Mother Sarah: Tunnel Town. unabridged ed. Kat S. Otomo. Tr. by Dana Lewis & Toren Smith from JPN. (Illus.). 224p. (Orig.). (YA). (gr. 7 up). 1996. pap. 18.95 (*1-56971-145-3*) Dark Horse Comics.

Legend of Motley Mansion. David L. Cannon. (Appleseed Books for Children). (Illus.). 96p. (J). (gr. 4-5). 1994. 9.95 (*0-9631028-3-4*) Comm Just Foun TX.

Legend of Mu Lan: A Heroine of Ancient China see Tnuyen Thuyet Moc Lan: Anh Thu Eva Co Dai Trung Quoc

***Legend of Mulan: A Folding Book Inspired by the Disney Animated Film.** (Illus.). 96p. (J). 1998. 19.45 (*0-7868-6389-7*, Pub. by Hyperion) Time Warner.

***Legend of Mulan Gift Set.** 1998. 31.89 incl. audio (*1-878217-10-0*) Victory Press.

***Legend of Nance Dude.** Maurice Stanley. LC 99-66819. 264p. 1999. pap. 9.95 (*0-943335-16-7*) Marblehead Pub.

Legend of Natural Tunnel: La Leyenda del Tunel Natural. Clara T. Fugate. Ed. by Elizabeth C. Calvera. Tr. by Gilda Socarras-Roufagalas. LC 85-30068. (Tales of the Virginia Wilderness Ser.: No. 1). (ENG & SPA., Illus.). 78p. (Orig.). (YA). (gr. 6-12). 1986. pap. 5.95 (*0-936015-02-0*) Pocahontas Pr.

Legend of Nightfall. Mickey Z. Reichert. 496p. (Orig.). 1993. mass mkt. 6.99 (*0-88677-587-6*, Pub. by DAW Bks) Penguin Putnam.

Legend of Noah: Renaissance Rationalism in Art, Science, & Letters. fac. ed. Don C. Allen. LC 49-49065. (Illus.). 243p. 1949. reprint ed. pap. 75.40 (*0-7837-8067-2*, 204782000008) Bks Demand.

Legend of Nucor. Jeffrey L. Rodengen. Ed. by Karen Nitken. LC 96-61248. (Illus.). 144p. 1997. 39.95 (*0-945903-36-7*) Write Stuff Syndicate.

Legend of Old Befana. Tomie De Paola. LC 80-12293. (Illus.). 32p. (J). (gr. 4-7). 1980. pap. 6.00 (*0-15-243817-3*, Voyager Bks) Harcourt.

Legend of Old Befana. Tomie De Paola. LC 80-12293. (Illus.). 32p. (J). (ps-3). 1980. 16.00 (*0-15-243816-5*, Harcourt Child Bks) Harcourt.

Legend of Old Faithful. L. Walker Arnold. LC 86-50716. 364p. 1986. 12.95 (*0-931117-05-4*) Univ Pub.

Legend of Pan Phillips. 5th rev. ed. Darlene E. Brown & Jack Brown. (Illus.). 198p. (Orig.). 1986. reprint ed. pap. 11.95 (*0-9617572-1-3*) Times Journal Pub.

Legend of Perseus: A Study of Tradition in Story, Custom & Belief, 3 vols. Edwin S. Hartland. LC 77-139165. (Grimm Library: Nos. 2, 3, & 5). reprint ed. 84.50 (*0-404-53570-4*) AMS Pr.

Legend of Pfizer, 1. Jeffrey L. Rodengen. 1999. 39.95 (*0-945903-37-5*) Write Stuff Syndicate.

Legend of Pope Joan: In Search of the Truth. Peter Stanford. LC 98-39373. (Illus.). 205p. 1999. 26.00 (*0-8050-3910-4*) H Holt & Co.

***Legend of Pope Joan: In Search of the Truth.** Peter Stanford. 2000. pap. text 13.00 (*0-425-17347-X*) Berkley Pub.

Legend of Queen Cama: Bodhiramsi's Camadevivamsa, a Translation & Commentary. Donald K. Swearer & Sommai Premchit. LC 98-15911. (SUNY Series in Buddhist Studies). (Illus.). 192p. (C). 1998. pap. text 19.95 (*0-7914-3776-0*) State U NY Pr.

Legend of Queen Cama: Bodhiramsi's Camadevivamsa, a Translation & Commentary. Donald K. Swearer & Sommai Premchit. LC 98-15911. (SUNY Series in Buddhist Studies). (Illus.). 192p. (C). 1998. text 59.50 (*0-7914-3775-2*) State U NY Pr.

Legend of Rainbow Bridge. William N. Britton. (Illus.). 24p. (Orig.). 1994. pap. 9.95 (*0-9645018-0-5*) Savannah Pub.

Legend of Rama: Artistic Visions. Ed. by Vidya Dehejia. LC 93-901178. (C). 1994. 53.00 (*81-85026-24-6*, Pub. by Marg Publns) Art Media Resources.

***Legend of Red Clydeside.** Iain McLean. 2000. pap. 29.95 (*0-85976-516-4*, Pub. by J Donald) Dufour.

Legend of Red Horse Cavern. Gary Paulsen. 80p. (J). 1994. pap. 3.99 (*0-440-41023-1*) Dell.

Legend of Red Horse Cavern. Gary Paulsen. (Gary Paulsen's World of Adventure Ser.). 1994. 8.70 (*0-606-07141-5*, Pub. by Turtleback) Demco.

***Legend of Robin Hood.** Richard Rutherford-Moore. LC 99-488071. (Illus.). 1999. pap. 21.95 (*1-86163-069-7*, Pub. by Capall Bann Pubng) Holmes Pub.

Legend of Rosa's Window. Mark Tezel. LC 99-490000. (Illus.). 36p. (J). (gr. k-7). 1999. pap. 6.95 (*0-9667687-1-X*) Assaca Pr.

Legend of Rosepetal. Clemens Brentano. Tr. by Anthea Bell. LC 95-6621.Tr. of Marchen von Rosenblattchen. (Illus.). 32p. (J). (gr. k-3). 1995. 16.95 (*1-55858-484-6*, Pub. by North-South Bks NYC) Chronicle Bks.

Legend of Rowan. Jeffrey L. Rodengen. LC 97-62154. (Illus.). 183p. 1998. 39.95 (*0-945903-45-6*) Write Stuff Syndicate.

Legend of Rudolfo. Alan M. Hofmeister et al. (Reading for All Learners Ser.). (Illus.). (J). pap. write for info. (*1-56861-218-4*) Swift Lrn Res.

Legend of St. Helier, Hermit of the Isle of Jersey. 1998. pap. 3.95 (*0-89979-110-7*) British Am Bks.

Legend of Saint Julian Hospitator see Three Tales

Legend of Saint Nicholas: A Child's Pictorial Legend. 2nd large type rev. ed. Bernice Krasovec. (Children's Pictorial Legends Ser.: No. 1). (Illus.). 31p. (J). (gr. k-6). 1985. spiral bd. 5.95 (*0-9661627-0-6*) Childrens Pict.

Legend of Saint Peter: A Contribution to the Mythology of Christianity. Arthur Drews. Tr. by Frank R. Zindler from GER. LC 97-46189. Orig. Title: Die Petruslegende. (Illus.). vii, 182p. 1997. pap. 12.00 (*1-57884-951-9*, 5580) Am Atheist.

***Legend of Saladin in Western Literature & Historiography.** Margaret A. Jubb. LC 00-30921. (Studies in Comparative Literature: Vol. 34). 284p. 2000. 89.95 (*0-7734-7686-5*) E Mellen.

***Legend of Santa & His Brother Fred.** Donald G. Henkel. (Illus.). 46p. 2000. write for info. (*0-9673504-0-9*) Quillpen.

Legend of Scarface: A Blackfeet Indian Tale. Daniel San Souci. (Illus.). (J). (ps-3). 1987. 7.00 (*0-385-13247-6*) BDD Bks Young Read.

Legend of Senorita Scorpion. large type ed. Les Savage, Jr. 1996. lib. bdg. 18.95 (*1-57490-043-9*, Sagebrush LP West) T T Beeler.

Legend of Shamballa. 2nd ed. Torkom Saraydarian. LC 76-12895. 1988. 18.00 (*0-911794-68-9*) Saraydarian Inst.

Legend of Simon of Cyrene. Leon A. Michaud. 224p. (Orig.). 1995. pap. 15.95 (*1-885001-07-X*) Via Press.

Legend of Sinter Klaas. Great Aunt Adeline, pseud. (Illus.). 32p. (Orig.). (J). (gr. k-4). 1992. pap. text 5.95 (*0-9632863-0-7*) Ebner & Steffes.

Legend of Sir Gawain: Studies upon Its Original Scope & Significance. Jessie L. Weston. LC 73-144521. (Grimm Library: No. 7). reprint ed. 24.50 (*0-404-53552-6*) AMS Pr.

Legend of Sir Lancelot Du Lac: Studies upon Its Origin, Development & Position in the Arthurian Romantic Cycles. Jessie L. Weston. LC 78-144525. (Grimm Library: No. 12). reprint ed. 27.50 (*0-404-53555-0*) AMS Pr.

Legend of Sir Miguel. Michael Cain. Ed. by Nancy R. Thatch. LC 90-5927. (Books for Students by Students). (Illus.). 26p. (J). (gr. 3-6). 1990. lib. bdg. 15.95 (*0-933849-26-5*) Landmark Edns.

Legend of Sir Perceval: Studies upon Its Origin, Development & Position in the Arthurian Cycle, 2 vols. in 1. Jessie L. Weston. LC 74-144540. (Grimm Library: Nos. 17 & 19). reprint ed. 55.00 (*0-404-53560-7*) AMS Pr.

Legend of Slappy Hooper: An American Tall Tale. Retold by Aaron Shepard. LC 92-18153. (Illus.). 32p. (J). (gr. k-3). 1993. 14.95 (*0-684-19535-6*) Scribner.

Legend of Sleeping Bear. Kathy-jo Wargin. LC 98-14246. (Illus.). 48p. (J). (ps-5). 1998. 16.95 (*1-886947-35-X*) Sleepng Bear.

Legend of Sleepy Hollow. (Classics Illustrated Study Guides Ser.). (Illus.). 1997. mass mkt. 5.25 (*1-57840-047-3*, Pub. by Acclaim Bks) Penguin Putnam.

Legend of Sleepy Hollow. Washington Irving. 1976. 16.95 (*0-8488-1381-2*) Amereon Ltd.

Legend of Sleepy Hollow. Washington Irving. LC 91-77606. (Illus.). 64p. (J). 1996. pap. 8.95 (*1-56397-605-6*) Boyds Mills Pr.

Legend of Sleepy Hollow. Washington Irving. Ed. by Michael P. Jones. (Illus.). 50p. 1985. text 13.00 (*0-89904-166-3*); pap. text 8.00 (*0-89904-167-1*) Crumb Elbow Pub.

Legend of Sleepy Hollow. Washington Irving. 1994. pap. 3.95 (*0-87129-346-3*, L76) Dramatic Pub.

Legend of Sleepy Hollow. Washington Irving. 1997. pap. 2.95 (*0-89375-348-3*) NAL.

Legend of Sleepy Hollow. Washington Irving. Ed. by Joshua Hanft. (Great Illustrated Classics Ser.: Vol. 45). (Illus.). 240p. (J). (gr. 3-6). 1995. 9.95 (*0-86611-996-5*) Playmore Inc.

Legend of Sleepy Hollow. Washington Irving. (J). 1991. pap. 2.50 (*0-8125-0475-5*, Pub. by Tor Bks) St Martin.

Legend of Sleepy Hollow. Washington Irving. (Illustrated Classics Ser.). (Illus.). 48p. (J). (gr. 3-6). 1990. lib. bdg. 19.95 (*0-8167-1869-5*) Troll Communs.

Legend of Sleepy Hollow. Washington Irving. (Illustrated Classics Ser.). (Illus.). 48p. (J). (gr. 3-6). 1996. pap. 5.95 (*0-8167-1870-9*) Troll Communs.

Legend of Sleepy Hollow. Washington Irving. LC 93-21910. (Illus.). 48p. (J). (gr. 1 up). 1995. 18.95 (*0-399-22687-7*, Philomel) Peng Put Young Read.

Legend of Sleepy Hollow. Carla Jablonski. Ed. by Kevin Ryan. (Super Adventures of Wishbone Ser.: No. 2). (Illus.). 233p. (J). (gr. 3-7). 1998. pap. 3.99 (*1-57064-374-1*, Big Red) Lyrick Pub.

Legend of Sleepy Hollow. Patricia A. Jensen. LC 93-24803. (First-Start Tall Tale Ser.). (Illus.). (J). (gr. k-3). 1996. pap. 3.50 (*0-8167-3169-1*) Troll Communs.

Legend of Sleepy Hollow. Patricia A. Jensen & Washington Irving. LC 93-24803. (First-Start Tall Tales Ser.). (Illus.). (J). (gr. k-3). 1997. lib. bdg. 17.25 (*0-8167-3168-3*, BL266) Troll Communs.

***Legend of Sleepy Hollow.** Will Moses. 1999. pap. 6.99 (*0-698-11648-8*, PapStar) Peng Put Young Read.

Legend of Sleepy Hollow. Random House Value Publishing Staff & Washington Irving. LC 97-51194. 112p. (J). 1998. 6.99 (*0-517-20303-0*) Random Hse Value.

Legend of Sleepy Hollow. Daniel San Souci. (Illus.). 32p. 1995. pap. 6.99 (*0-440-41074-6*) Bantam.

Legend of Sleepy Hollow. adapted ed. Washington Irving. LC 91-72020. (Illus.). 32p. (J). (gr. k-4). 1992. pap., per. 6.95 (*0-8249-8574-5*, Ideals Child) Hambleton-Hill.

Legend of Sleepy Hollow. adapted ed. Washington Irving. LC 88-33375. (Illus.). 36p. (J). (gr. 2 up). 1995. mass mkt. 10.95 incl. audio (*0-689-80202-1*, Rabbit Ears) Litle Simon.

Legend of Sleepy Hollow. Washington Irving. 1982. reprint ed. lib. bdg. 17.95 (*0-89966-410-5*) Buccaneer Bks.

Legend of Sleepy Hollow. Washington Irving. LC 90-591. (Books of Wonder). (Illus.). 112p. (J). (gr. 2-7). 1990. reprint ed. 21.95 (*0-688-05276-2*, Wm Morrow) Morrow Avon.

***Legend of Sleepy Hollow, Vol. 2.** Lyrick Studios Staff. (Super Adventures of Wishbone Ser.). (Illus.). (J). 2000. pap. text 1.99 (*1-57064-967-7*) Lyrick Pub.

Legend of Sleepy Hollow: Found Among the Papers of the Late Diedrich Knickerbocker. Washington Irving. Ed. by Patricia Pingry. LC 99-12379. (Illus.). 1999. 16.95 (*0-8249-4160-8*, Candy Cane Pr) Ideals.

Legend of Sleepy Hollow: Minibook Edition. Washington Irving. LC 93-12153. (Illus.). (J). 1993. audio 9.95 (*0-88708-321-8*, Rabbit Ears) Litle Simon.

Legend of Sleepy Hollow & Other Selections from Washington Irving. Washington Irving. Ed. by Austin M. Fox. 288p. 1982. pap. 3.99 (*0-671-46211-3*, WSP) PB.

***Legend of Sleepy Hollow & Other Stories.** Washington Irving. (Penguin Classics Ser.). 368p. (J). 1999. pap. 8.95 (*0-14-043769-X*, Penguin Classics) Viking Penguin.

Legend of Sleepy Hollow & Other Tales. Washington Irving. Ed. by Michael J. Marshall. (Core Classics Ser.: Vol. 7). (Illus.). 132p. (J). (gr. 4-6). 1999. pap. 6.95 (*1-890517-14-3*) Core Knowledge.

Legend of Sleepy Hollow & Rip Van Winkle see New Method Supplementary Readers

Legend of Sleepy Hollow & Rip Van Winkle. unabridged ed. Washington Irving. (Children's Thrift Classics Ser.). (Illus.). 80p. (J). 1995. reprint ed. pap. 1.00 (*0-486-28828-5*) Dover.

***Legend of Sleepy Hollow Collection Book.** W. Irving. (J). 2000. pap. 2.95 (*0-486-41041-2*) Dover.

Legend of Sleepy Hollow, Rip Van Winkle, President Van Buren & Brom. J. P. Evanns & Edward R. Welles. LC 84-878. 1984. reprint ed. pap. 4.00 (*0-913692-10-7*) Learning Inc.

***Legend of Sleepy Hollow Stained Glass Coloring Book.** Marty Noble. (Little Activity Bks.). (Illus.). (J). 2000. pap. 1.00 (*0-486-40971-6*) Dover.

Legend of Snowshoes. Kimmel. LC 95-40989. (J). 1995. 15.95 (*0-8050-3137-5*) H Holt & Co.

Legend of Spinoza: The Bear Who Speaks from the Heart. Robert Talltree. (Illus.). 64p. (J). 1995. 18.95 (*0-9643529-0-7*) Universal Tradewinds.

***Legend of Squanto: An Unknown Hero Who Changed the Course of American History, 2.** 1999. audio 16.97 (*1-56179-617-4*) Bethany Hse.

Legend of Stanley. Jeffrey L. Rodengen. Ed. by Karen Nitkin. LC 95-60795. (Illus.). 192p. 1996. 39.95 (*0-945903-13-8*) Write Stuff Syndicate.

Legend of Starcrash. Dolores Cannon. LC 94-65021. 250p. 1994. pap. 21.95 (*0-9632776-7-7*) Ozark Mountn.

Legend of Storey County. Brock Thoene. 256p. 1996. pap. 10.99 (*0-7852-7367-0*, J Thoma Bks) Nelson.

Legend of Story Cazaunoux: A New Orleans Novel. C. J. Murray. 310p. 1998. pap. 14.95 (*1-57502-883-2*, PO1996) Morris Pubng.

Legend of Tarik. Walter Dean Myers. 192p. (J). (gr. 7-9). 1991. pap. 3.50 (*0-590-44426-3*) Scholastic Inc.

Legend of Tenet Healthcare, 1. Jeffrey L. Rodengen. 1999. 39.95 (*0-945903-54-5*) Write Stuff Syndicate.

Legend of the African Bao-Bab Tree. Bobbie D. Hunter. (Illus.). 32p. (J). (gr. 3-6). 1994. 16.95 (*0-86543-421-2*); pap. 8.95 (*0-86543-422-0*) Africa World.

Legend of the Baal-Shem. Martin Buber. Tr. by Maurice Friedman. LC 94-42486. (Mythos Ser.). 223p. 1995. pap. text 13.95 (*0-691-04389-2*, Pub. by Princeton U Pr) Cal Prin Full Svc.

Legend of the Bells & Other Tales: Stories of the Human Spirit. John Shea. 192p. (Orig.). 1996. pap. 12.95 (*0-87946-147-0*, 256) ACTA Pubns.

Legend of the Blue Unicorn: Land of OSM. Sandi Johnson & Sybrina Durant. Ed. by Britt Johnson. (Little Choo-Choo Bks.). (Illus.). 24p. (J). (ps-6). 1988. 8.99 (*1-929063-09-1*, 109) Moons & Stars.

Legend of the Bluebonnet see Leyenda de la Flor "El Conejo": Una Antigua Leyenda de Texas

***Legend of the Bluebonnet.** (J). 1999. 9.95 (*1-56137-328-1*) Novel Units.

Legend of the Bluebonnet. Tomie De Paola. LC 82-12391. (Illus.). 40p. (J). (ps-3). 1996. pap. 5.99 (*0-698-11359-4*, PapStar) Peng Put Young Read.

Legend of the Bluebonnet: A Study Guide. Garrett Christopher. Ed. by J. Friedland & R. Kessler. (Novel-Ties Ser.). (J). (gr. k-2). 1998. pap. text, student ed. 14.95 (*0-7675-0325-2*) Lrn Links.

An Asterisk (*) at the beginning of an entry indicates that the title is appearing for the first time.

Legend of the Bluebonnet: An Old Tale of Texas. Illus. & Retold by Tomie De Paola. LC 82-12391. 32p. (J). (ps-3). 1983. 15.95 (*0-399-20937-9*, G P Putnam) Peng Put Young Read.

Legend of the Bluebonnet: An Old Tale of Texas. Tomie De Paola. (J). 1983. 11.15 (*0-606-01690-2*, Pub. by Turtleback) Demco.

Legend of the Brewery Vol. 1: A Brief History of the Minneapolis Brewing Heritage. Jeff R. Lonto. (Illus.). 52p. 1998. pap. 9.95 (*0-9660213-3-9*) Studio Z-Seven.

Legend of the Buddha. L. Adams Beck. (C). 1993. text 26.00 (*81-7305-022-8*, Pub. by Aryan Bks Intl) S Asia.

Legend of the Bushwhacker Basket. Martha Wetherbee & Nathan Taylor. Ed. by Mary L. Ray. LC 86-50114. (Illus.). 64p. (Orig.). 1986. pap. 19.95 (*0-9609384-1-9*) M Wetherbee.

Legend of the Candy Cane. 1998. 14.99 (*0-310-23033-0*) Zondervan.

Legend of the Candy Cane: The Inspirational Story of Our Favorite Christmas Candy. Lori Walburg. LC 96-40087. (Illus.). 32p. (J). (ps-3). 1997. 14.99 (*0-310-21247-2*) Zondervan.

Legend of the Celtic Stone. Michael Phillips. LC 99-6432. (Caledonia Ser.). 576p. 1999. pap. 13.99 (*0-7642-2217-1*) Bethany Hse.

***Legend of the Celtic Stone.** Michael Phillips. No. 1. 576p. 1999. 19.99 (*0-7642-2250-3*) Bethany Hse.

***Legend of the Christmas Rose.** William H. Hooks. LC 98-45565. (Illus.). 32p. (J). (gr. k-4). 1999. lib. bdg. 14.89 (*0-06-027103-5*) HarpC.

Legend of the Christmas Rose. William H. Hooks. LC 98-45565. (Illus.). 32p. (J). (gr. k-4). 1999. 14.95 (*0-06-027102-7*) HarpC Child Bks.

Legend of the Corrib King. Tom McCaughren. 106p. 1993. pap. 8.95 (*0-947962-60-3*) Dufour.

Legend of the Desert Bigfoot. Jake Thoene & Luke Thoene. LC 95-47389. (Last Chance Detectives Ser.: No. 2). (J). 1996. pap. 5.99 (*0-8423-2084-9*) Tyndale Hse.

Legend of the Devil's Hoofprints. Carole Marsh. (Carole Marsh Bks.). (Illus.). (Orig.). (J). (gr. 2 up). 1994. pap. 19.95 (*0-935326-57-X*); lib. bdg. 29.95 (*1-55609-177-X*) Gallopade Intl.

***Legend of the Dogwood.** Brenda Gough. (Illus.). 32p. (J). (gr. 1-7). 2001. 22.95 (*1-57532-280-3*) Press-Tige Pub.

Legend of the Duelist. Rutledge Etheridge. 256p. (Orig.). 1993. mass mkt. 4.99 (*0-441-47962-6*) Ace Bks.

Legend of the Eagle Clan. Cathleen Cramer. 281p. (Orig.). 1995. pap. 12.95 (*0-929385-68-3*) Light Tech Pubng.

Legend of the Easter Egg Game. Lori Walburg. LC 98-47180. (J). 1999. 14.99 (*0-310-22447-0*) HarpC.

Legend of the Easter Egg Game. Lori Walburg. (J). Date not set. 14.99 (*0-310-22741-0*) Zondervan.

***Legend of the Emerald Lady.** Carolyn Keene. (Nancy Drew Mystery Stories Ser.: No. 154). 160p. (J). (gr. 3-6). 2000. per. 3.99 (*0-671-04262-9*, Minstrel Bks) PB.

Legend of the Firedrake, Vol. 2. Ian A. Montgomery. 2000. pap. write for info. (*1-890538-21-3*) Rhiannon Pubns.

Legend of the Firedrake, Vol. 3. Ian A. Montgomery. 2000. pap. write for info. (*1-890538-22-1*) Rhiannon Pubns.

Legend of the Firedrake: To Find a Dragon, Vol. 1. Ian A. Montgomery. Ed. by Jacalyn A. Spafford. 143p. (Orig.). 1995. pap. 9.95 (*1-890538-20-5*) Rhiannon Pubns.

Legend of the Flying Hotdog. White. (J). 1998. 11.95 (*0-671-75291-X*) S&S Bks Yung.

Legend of the Flying Hotdog. Celeste White. (Illus.). 32p. (J). 1991. 11.95 (*0-88138-131-4*, Green Tiger S&S) S&S Childrens.

Legend of the Founding Fathers. Wesley F. Craven. LC 82-25241. (New York University, Stokes Foundation, Anson G. Phelps Lectureship on Early American History Ser.). 222p. 1983. reprint ed. lib. bdg. 59.50 (*0-313-23840-5*, CRLE) Greenwood.

Legend of the Fourth King. Edzard Schaper. LC 99-31366. 1999. 14.95 (*0-8245-1814-4*) Crossroad NY.

Legend of the Free State of Jones. Rudy H. Leverett. LC 84-7513. (Illus.). 151p. (Orig.). reprint ed. pap. 46.90 (*0-7837-1070-4*, 204159300021) Bks Demand.

***Legend of the Ghost Pokemon.** Terry West. (Illus.). 128p. (J). (gr. 4-7). 2000. pap. 4.50 (*0-439-15419-7*) Scholastic Inc.

Legend of the Giant Panda. A. B. Curtiss. LC 97-65548. (Illus.). 40p. (J). (gr. k-4). 1997. 18.95 (*0-932529-59-3*) Oldcastle.

***Legend of the Golden Boat: Regulation, Trade & Traders in the Borderlands of Laos, Thailand, China, & Burma.** Andrew Walker. LC 99-28886. (Anthropology of Asia Ser.). (Illus.). 256p. 1999. text 45.00 (*0-8248-2255-2*); pap. text 21.95 (*0-8248-2256-0*) UH Pr.

Legend of the Golden Hawk. (Illus.). 57p. (Orig.). (J). (gr. 3-7). 1994. pap. 4.95 (*0-9632074-1-5*) Azimuth GA.

Legend of the Golden Key. Tom McCaughren. 144p. 1993. pap. 8.95 (*0-947962-36-0*) Dufour.

Legend of the Golden Scrolls: Ageless Secrets for Building Wealth. Glenn Bland. 144p. 1996. pap. text 12.00 (*0-7615-0666-7*) Prima Pub.

Legend of the Golden Scrolls: Ageless Secrets of Building Wealth. Glenn Bland. 144p. 1995. 15.95 (*1-55958-705-9*) Prima Pub.

Legend of the Great Stupa. Guru Padmasambhava. LC 73-79059. (Tibetan Translation Ser.: Vol. 2). (Illus.). 140p. 1973. pap. 12.95 (*0-913546-03-8*) Dharma Pub.

Legend of the Holy Fina, Virgin of Santo Gemignano. Giovanni Di Coppo. Tr. by M. Mansfield. LC 66-25699. (Medieval Library). (ENG & ITA., Illus.). reprint ed. 42.00 (*0-8154-0054-3*) Cooper Sq.

Legend of the Hummingbird: A Tale from Puerto Rico. Michael R. Ramirez. LC 96-38004. (Illus.). 32p. (J). (gr. k-4). 1998. pap. 4.95 (*1-57255-232-8*) Mondo Pubng.

Legend of the Indian Paintbrush see Leyenda del Pincel Indio

Legend of the Indian Paintbrush. Ed. & Illus. by Tomie De Paola. LC 87-20160. 40p. (J). (ps-3). 1988. 15.95 (*0-399-21534-4*, G P Putnam) Peng Put Young Read.

Legend of the Indian Paintbrush. Tomie De Paola. (J). 1991. 11.15 (*0-606-04963-0*, Pub. by Turtleback) Demco.

Legend of the Jack-O-Lantern: A Child's Pictorial Legend. large type ed. Bernice Krasovec et al. (Children's Pictorial Legends Ser.: No. 2). (Illus.). 24p. (J). (gr. k-6). 1996. spiral bd. 5.95 (*0-9661627-1-4*, 12588) Childrens Pict.

Legend of the Jesus Candy. Vicki Corona. (Celebrate the Cultures Ser.: Vol. X, Bk. 10). (Illus.). 26p. (J). (ps-7). 1990. pap. 14.95 (*1-58513-999-8*) Dance Fantasy.

***Legend of the Kite: A Story of China.** Jiang Hong Chen. LC 99-28855. Orig. Title: La Legende du Cerf-Volant. (Illus.). 32p. (J). (gr. k-3). 1999. pap. 5.95 (*1-56899-811-2*) Soundprints.

***Legend of the Kite: A Story of China.** Jiang Hong Chen. LC 99-28855. Orig. Title: La Legende du Cerf-Volant. (Illus.). 32p. (J). (ps-3). 1999. 15.95 (*1-56899-810-4*) Soundprints.

Legend of the Kite: A Story of China - Includes Doll. Jiang Hong Chen. Orig. Title: La Legende du Cerf-Volant. (Illus.). 32p. (J). (gr. k-3). 1999. pap. 16.95 (*1-56899-814-7*) Soundprints.

Legend of the Lady Slipper. Lise Lunge-Larsen & Margi Preus. LC 97-47209. (Illus.). 32p. (J). (ps-3). 1999. 15.00 (*0-395-90512-5*) HM.

Legend of the Lake: The 22-Gun Brig-Sloop Ontario, 1780. A. Britton Smith. LC 98-108860. (Illus.). 160p. 1997. 27.95 (*1-55082-186-5*, Pub. by Quarry Pr) LPC InBook.

Legend of the Laughing Gecko: A Hawaiian Fantasy. Bruce Hale. (Illus.). 32p. (Orig.). (J). (ps-3). 1989. pap. 8.95 (*0-9621280-0-7*) Wrds & Picts Pubng.

Legend of the Lepraclone. Ann Cannon. LC 95-92714. (Illus.). 32p. (J). (ps-3). 1998. lib. bdg. 14.95 (*0-9649539-0-0*) Star Chaser.

Legend of the Lighter. A. M. Van Weert. LC 95-197444. (Illus.). 192p. 1994. 45.00 (*1-55859-854-5*) Abbeville Pr.

Legend of the Little People: Brought Forth from Obscurity with Full-Hearted Devotion & in Spite of the Scoffing Protests of Non-Believers. Gary Clinton. LC 91-65736. 36p. 1991. write for info. (*1-879495-25-2*) United Design.

***Legend of the Loon.** Kathy-Jo Wargin. LC 00-25960. (Illus.). 48p. (J). (ps-3). 2000. 17.95 (*1-886947-97-X*) Sleepng Bear.

Legend of the Lost Gold. Carolyn Keene. (Nancy Drew Mystery Stories Ser.: No. 138). 160p. (J). (gr. 3-6). 1997. per. 3.99 (*0-671-00049-7*) S&S Trade.

Legend of the Lost Gold. Carolyn Keene. (Nancy Drew Mystery Stories Ser.: No. 138). (J). (gr. 3-6). 1997. 9.09 (*0-606-13640-1*, Pub. by Turtleback) Demco.

Legend of the Lost Legend. R. L. Stine, pseud. LC 00-5896. (Goosebumps Ser.: No. 47). (J). (gr. 3-7). 1996. pap. text 3.99 (*0-590-56884-1*) Scholastic Inc.

Legend of the Lost Legend. R. L. Stine, pseud. (Goosebumps Ser.: No. 47). 1996. 9.09 (*0-606-09537-3*, Pub. by Turtleback) Demco.

Legend of the Maneater. Arjan Singh. (C). 1993. 20.00 (*0-86311-450-4*, Pub. by Ravi Dayal) S Asia.

Legend of the Margil Vine: A Story of Old San Antonio as Retold. Mark Tezel. LC 99-167952. 1998. write for info. (*0-9667687-0-1*) Assaca Pr.

Legend of the Master. Simon Nowell-Smith. (BCL1-PS American Literature Ser.). 176p. 1993. reprint ed. lib. bdg. 69.00 (*0-7812-6980-6*) Rprt Serv.

Legend of the Milky Way. Jeanne M. Lee. LC 81-6906. (Illus.). 32p. (J). (ps-2). 1995. pap. 5.95 (*0-8050-1361-X*, Owlet BYR) H Holt & Co.

Legend of the Moon Maiden. Tr. by Kott Kok Kiang. (Illus.). 104p. 1996. pap. 9.95 (*981-3068-47-7*, Pub. by Asiapac) China Bks.

Legend of the Mutilated Victory: Italy, the Great War, & the Paris Peace Conference, 1915-1919, 38. H. James Burgwyn. LC 92-45082. (Contributions to the Study of World History Ser.: No. 38). 368p. 1993. 57.95 (*0-313-28885-2*, GM8885, Greenwood Pr) Greenwood.

Legend of the Muy Grande: The Search Continues, Vol. III. F. M. Faulkner et al. 84p. pap. write for info. (*0-9645016-0-0*) Muy Grande.

Legend of the 9 Talents. Joan Hutson. LC 92-26957. (Illus.). 58p. (J). 1992. 4.95 (*0-8198-4468-3*) Pauline Bks.

Legend of the North. Paul Sullivan. 200p. (YA). (gr. 7 up). 1995. pap. 9.99 (*0-88092-308-3*, 3083) Royal Fireworks.

Legend of the Painted Horse. Harry Combs. 1997. mass mkt. write for info. (*0-614-27735-3*) Dell.

Legend of the Painted Horse. large type ed. Harry Combs. LC 96-50222. 1997. pap. 22.95 (*1-56895-402-6*) Wheeler Pub.

Legend of the Panda. Linda Granfield. LC 97-62238. (Illus.). 24p. (J). (gr. 3-6). 1998. 15.95 (*0-88776-421-5*) Tundra Bks.

Legend of the Persian Carpet. Illus. by Claire Ewart. LC 91-45816. 32p. (J). (ps-3). 1993. 14.95 (*0-399-22415-7*, G P Putnam) Peng Put Young Read.

Legend of the Phantom Highwayman. Tom McCaughren. 112p. 1993. pap. 8.95 (*0-947962-58-1*) Dufour.

Legend of the Poinsettia. Illus. & Retold by Tomie De Paola. LC 92-20459. 32p. (J). (ps-3). 1994. lib. bdg. 15.95 (*0-399-21692-8*, G P Putnam) Peng Put Young Read.

Legend of the Poinsettia. Illus. & Retold by Tomie De Paola. 1997. 11.15 (*0-606-12753-4*, Pub. by Turtleback) Demco.

Legend of the Ragged Boy. Wes Magee. (Illus.). 32p. (J). (ps-3). 1993. 14.45 (*1-55970-228-1*, Pub. by Arcade Pub Inc) Time Warner.

Legend of the Red Wolf. 2nd ed. Valerie Ozeta. 34p. (J). 1999. pap. 5.95 (*0-9661687-1-2*, Pub. by Red Wolf Pub) ACCESS Pubs Network.

Legend of the Redneck Frog. large type ed. Robert J. Jones. LC 96-61610. (Illus.). 32p. (Orig.). (J). (ps-4). 1996. pap. 9.95 (*1-56664-112-8*) WorldComm.

Legend of the Rhine, Cornhill to Cairo & The Book of Snobs see Complete Works of William Makepeace Thackeray

***Legend of the Rock.** Steve Stout. (Illus.). 32p. (J). (gr. k-6). 1999. pap. 5.95 (*0-9609296-2-2*) Utica Hse.

***Legend of the Rockhills & Other Stories.** Funso Aiyejiana. 212p. 1999. pap. 15.95 (*0-920661-78-5*, Pub. by TSAR Pubns) SPD-Small Pr Dist.

Legend of the Sea Wolf. Vickie Britton. 358p. 1984. 11.95 (*0-89697-193-7*) Intl Univ Pr.

Legend of the Slain Soldiers. Marcia Muller. 192p. 1996. mass mkt. 5.99 (*0-446-40421-7*, Pub. by Warner Bks) Little.

***Legend of the Sleeping Giant of Steamboat Springs.** Trenia Sanford & Evelyn Senotan. (Illus.). 36p. 1999. 7.95 (*0-9676605-0-5*) Sleeping Giant.

***Legend of the Sorcerer.** Donna Kauffman. 384p. 2000. mass mkt. 5.99 (*0-553-57921-5*) Bantam Dell.

Legend of the South Meadow: Stories for Readers of All Ages. Fanny K. DeVine. LC 94-80120. 1996. 15.50 (*1-886796-02-5*) DEramo Pub.

Legend of the Sun Stone: In Search of the Lost City. Eduardo A. Robles. LC 98-94026. 193p. 1997. write for info. (*0-9661738-0-5*) Sun King.

Legend of the SunaKorn. Judy Woodard & Martha Tucker. LC 89-50138. 40p. (J). 1989. 12.95 (*0-938021-41-9*) Turner Pub KY.

***Legend of the Three Trees.** Tommy Nelson Publishers Staff. (Illus.). (J). 2000. 7.99 (*0-8499-7595-6*) Tommy Nelson.

Legend of the Topes. Tr. by B. C. Law. (C). 1986. 13.50 (*81-7069-000-5*, Pub. by M Manoharial) S Asia.

***Legend of the Tumbleweed.** Kirby Jonas. 288p. 1999. pap. 12.95 (*1-891423-02-9*) Howling Wolf ID.

Legend of the Veery Bird. Kathleen Hague. LC 84-19732. (Illus.). 32p. (J). (ps up). 1985. 13.95 (*0-15-243824-6*, Harcourt Child Bks) Harcourt.

Legend of the Villa Della Luna. Jana Kolpen. LC 97-65597. (Illus.). 90p. 1997. 19.95 (*1-55670-628-6*) Stewart Tabori & Chang.

***Legend of the Wandering Jew: True Stories of Encounters with the Man Who Cannot Die.** unabridged ed. Dana Edwards. LC 98-48604. 76p. 1998. pap. 10.00 (*0-941599-41-8*, Pub. by Piccadilly Bks) Empire Pub Srvs.

Legend of the Wars of Montrose. Sir Walter Scott. Ed. by J. H. Alexander. 271p. 1996. 44.50 (*0-231-10570-3*) Col U Pr.

Legend of the Whistle Pig Wrangler. Kate Allen. LC 95-79690. (Illus.). 32p. (J). (ps-4). 1996. 14.95 (*1-887218-00-9*) Kumquat Pr.

Legend of the White Buffalo Woman. Paul Goble. 32p. (YA). (gr. k up). 1998. 16.95 (*0-7922-7074-6*, Pub. by Natl Geog) S&S Trade.

Legend of the White Raccoon. Lee Roddy. (D. J. Dillon Ser.: No. 6). 144p. (J). (gr. 3-7). 1986. pap. 5.99 (*0-89693-500-0*, 6-2500, Victor Bks) Chariot Victor.

Legend of the Zuni Stallion. Allison Estes. (Short Stirrup Club Ser.: No. 7). (J). (gr. 3-7). 1996. pap. 3.99 (*0-671-00101-9*) PB.

***Legend of Thornbush.** Michael L. Laughlin. LC 99-37002. (Illus.). 32p. (J). (ps-2). 2000. 12.99 (*0-8499-5968-3*) Tommy Nelson.

***Legend of Thunder Moon.** Max Brand. 256p. 1999. mass mkt. 4.50 (*0-8439-4583-4*, Pub. by Dorchester Pub Co) CMG.

Legend of Thunder Moon. Max Brand. LC 95-26142. xvi, 162p. 1996. text 30.00 (*0-8032-1269-0*) U of Nebr Pr.

Legend of Thunder Moon. large type ed. Max Brand. LC 97-17581. (Sagebrush Large Print Westerns Ser.). 1997. lib. bdg. 19.95 (*1-57490-090-0*) T T Beeler.

Legend of Tico Bk. 1: The Synthesis of Religions. Terrence C. O'Brien. 80p. 1996. pap. 6.00 (*0-9648456-0-1*) Tico Enter.

Legend of Trinity Industries, Inc., 1. Jeffrey L. Rodengen. 1999. 39.95 (*0-945903-53-7*) Write Stuff Syndicate.

Legend of VF Corporation. Jeffrey L. Rodengen. LC 96-61246. 1998. 39.95 (*0-945903-38-3*) Write Stuff Syndicate.

Legend of Wappato: Chief Cassino of the Multnomah. Donald Bruner & Marilyn Bruner. LC 99-53593. (Illus.). 224p. 2000. pap. 16.95 (*1-58151-039-X*, Pub. by BookPartners) Midpt Trade.

Legend of Whiskey City. Robin Gibson. (Whiskey City Ser.: No. 3). 192p. 1995. 18.95 (*0-8034-9113-1*, Avalon Bks) Bouregy.

Legend of White Raccoon. rev. ed. Lee Roddy. (D.J. Dillon Adventure Ser.). 132p. (J). 1996. pap. 5.99 (*1-56476-507-5*, 6-3507, Victor Bks) Chariot Victor.

Legend of Willow Wood Springs. Terry Ellis. LC 85-63828. (Willow Wood Springs Ser.: No. 1). (Illus.). 180p. (Orig.). (J). (gr. 4 up). 1989. pap. 4.75 (*0-915677-30-X*) Roundtable Pub.

Legend of Worthington Industries, 1. Jeffrey L. Rodengen. 1999. 39.95 (*0-945903-55-3*) Write Stuff Syndicate.

Legend of Yore. Brennan Taylor. (Galileo Games System Ser.). (Illus.). 240p. (Orig.). 1996. pap. 26.95 (*1-887920-00-5*) Galileo Games.

Legend of York. Jeffrey L. Rodengen. Ed. by Karen Nitkin. LC 96-60604. (Illus.). 208p. 1997. 39.95 (*0-945903-17-0*) Write Stuff Syndicate.

Legend of Zelda: A Link to the Past Game Secrets/NES. Zach Meston. (Secrets of the Games Ser.). (Illus.). 224p. (Orig.). 1992. pap. 9.99 (*1-55958-204-9*) Prima Pub.

***Legend of Zelda: Link's Awakening DX: Official Strategy Guide.** James M. Ratkos. LC 99-63282. (Illus.). 112p. 1999. pap. 12.99 (*0-7615-2240-9*, Prima Games) Prima Pub.

***Legend of Zelda: Ocarina of Time Pathways to Adventure.** Jason Rich. LC 98-89151. 112p. 1998. pap. 9.99 (*0-7821-2478-X*) Sybex.

Legend of Zelda: Ocarina of Time Strategy Guide. Bradygames Staff. 1998. pap. text 11.99 (*1-56686-808-4*) Brady Pub.

Legend of Zelda 64 Ultimate Strategy Guide. Tiberius Wolf. 128p. 1998. pap. text 9.99 (*0-7821-2117-9*) Sybex.

Legend of Zias. Barbara Cordoves, pseud & Gladys M. Cordoves. (Zias' Adventures Ser.). (Illus.). 44p. (J). (gr. k). pap. 7.99 (*0-9637252-0-3*) B & G Cordoves.

Legend on the Road: Bobby Fischer's 1964 SimulTour. John Donaldson. Ed. by Eric Woro. (Illus.). 128p. 1994. 26.95 (*1-879479-15-X*); pap. 16.95 (*1-879479-14-1*) ICE WA.

Legend Reborn. Steven Frankos. 384p. 1997. mass mkt. 5.99 (*0-441-00419-9*) Ace Bks.

***Legend That Was Earth.** James P. Hogan. 2000. write for info. (*0-671-31945-0*) PB.

Legenda. A. H. Nash-Williams. 88p. (C). 1982. pap. text 39.00 (*0-900269-18-9*, Pub. by Old Vicarage) St Mut.

Legenda Aurea: A Reexamination of Its Paradoxical History. Sherry L. Reames. LC 84-40502. (Illus.). 336p. 1985. 40.00 (*0-299-10150-9*) U of Wis Pr.

Legenda of the Ancient & Accepted Scottish Rite of Freemasonry. Albert Pike. 436p. 1993. reprint ed. pap. 45.00 (*1-56459-309-6*) Kessinger Pub.

Legendary Abs II. Health for Life Staff. (Illus.). 48p. 1989. pap. 14.95 (*0-944831-20-6*) Health Life.

Legendary America. Henry Mahler. LC 95-60855. (YA). (gr. 7-12). 1995. 10.00 (*0-9638455-2-7*) Warwick Hse.

Legendary Baseball Stars Paper Dolls. 81st ed. Tom Tierney. (J). 1985. pap. 4.95 (*0-486-24846-1*) Dover.

Legendary Bells Vol. II: World of Bells. Dorothy Anthony. (Illus.). 50p. (Orig.). 1997. pap. 13.95 (*0-9607944-9-2*) World of Bells.

Legendary Blobshocker. Ryan Wilson. (Illus.). 20p. (gr. 1-4). 1999. pap. 16.95 (*1-885477-51-1*) Fut Horizons.

***Legendary Brides: The World's Most Celebrated Weddings & How to Recreate Their Magic.** Letitia Baldrige. 176p. 2000. 50.00 (*0-06-019559-2*, HarpCollins) HarperTrade.

Legendary Bruce Lee. Black Belt Magazine Editors. Ed. by Mike Lee & Jack Vaughn. LC 86-42770. (Specialties Ser.). 160p. (Orig.). 1986. pap. 10.95 (*0-89750-106-3*, 446) Ohara Pubns.

Legendary Characters. Ben T. Traywick. 14.95 (*1-889468-02-9*) Coastwide T L C.

Legendary Comedies. Peter Guttmacher. 128p. 1996. 16.98 (*1-56799-239-0*, MetroBooks) M Friedman Pub Grp Inc.

Legendary Connecticut. David Philips. LC 92-24532. (Illus.), 303p. 1992. pap. 15.95 (*1-880684-05-5*) Curbstone.

Legendary Cuisine of Persia. Margaret Shaida. (Illus.). xiii, 326p. 1992. 35.00 (*0-9519918-1-7*, Pub. by Lieuse Pubns) Bosphorus Bks.

Legendary Deaths. Emma Walling. 107p. 1995. pap. 12.95 (*0-9648437-0-6*) E Walling.

Legendary Dolls of Madame Alexander: 1945-1965. Cynthia Gaskill. (Illus.). 96p. 1995. pap. 39.00 (*0-912823-57-7*, BT-159, Pub. by Gold Horse) Dollmasters.

Legendary Fictions of the Irish Celts. Patrick Kennedy. LC 69-16321. 372p. 1972. reprint ed. 18.95 (*0-405-08695-4*, Pub. by Blom Pubns) Ayer.

Legendary Figures: Ancient History in Modern Novels. Clayton Koelb. LC 98-3643. xxviii, 186p. 1998. text 45.00 (*0-8032-2739-6*) U of Nebr Pr.

Legendary Four Horsemen of the A. M. E. Church. Albert P. Marshall. 24p. (Orig.). 1995. pap. text 5.00 (*1-885066-10-4*) Four-G Pubs.

Legendary Golf Clubs of Scotland, England, Wales & Ireland. Anthony Edgeworth & John De St. Jorre. (Illus.). 312p. 1999. 65.00 (*0-9658904-1-4*) Edgeworth Editions.

Legendary Heroes of the Wild West Series, 12 vols., Set. William R. Sanford & Carl R. Green. (Illus.). (J). (gr. 4-10). 1996. lib. bdg. 180.40 (*0-89490-777-8*) Enslow Pubs.

Legendary History of Britain. John S. Tatlock & S. Perry. LC 74-18288. 545p. 1975. reprint ed. 100.00 (*0-87752-168-9*) Gordian.

Legendary Horror Films. Peter Guttmacher. 128p. 1995. 16.98 (*1-56799-171-8*, MetroBooks) M Friedman Pub Grp Inc.

Legendary Illinois Cookbook: Historic & Culinary Lore from the Prairie State. Agnes M. Feeney & John L. Leckel. Ed. by Robin Browder. (Illus.). 352p. 1982. pap. 7.95 (*0-89865-199-9*, Pub. by Donning Co) Schiffer.

Legendary Ireland. Peter Somerville-Large. (Illus.). 155p. 1995. 35.00 (*1-57098-048-9*) Roberts Rinehart.

Legendary Ireland. Peter Somerville-Large. (Illus.). 155p. 1996. pap. 24.95 (*1-57098-095-0*) Roberts Rinehart.

Legendary Islands of the Atlantic: Study in Medieval Geography. William H. Babcock. LC 72-8459. (Select Bibliographies Reprint Ser.). 1977. reprint ed. 20.95 (*0-8369-6963-4*) Ayer.

Legendary Islands of the Ocean Sea. Robert H. Fuson. LC 94-41928. (Illus.). 230p. 1995. 24.95 (*1-56164-078-6*) Pineapple Pr.

Legendary Jackrabbit Johannsen. Alice E. Johannsen. (Illus.). 312p. 1993. 49.95 (*0-7735-1123-7*, Pub. by McG-Queens Univ Pr); pap. 19.95 (*0-7735-1151-2*, Pub. by McG-Queens Univ Pr) CUP Services.

Legendary King of San Miguel. Elizabeth Lester. 1979. pap. 6.50 (*0-87461-027-3*) McNally & Loftin.

L

L

Legendary Labor Leaders. Thomas Streissguth. LC 97-29017. (Profiles Ser.). (Illus.). 160p. (YA). (gr. 5-12). 1998. lib. bdg. 18.95 (*1-881508-44-7*) Oliver Pr MN.

Legendary Ladies of Texas. Ed. by Francis E. Abernethy. LC 94-16318. (Texas Folklore Society Publications: Vol. 43). (Illus.). 249p. (Orig.). 1994. reprint ed. pap. 17.95 (*0-929398-75-0*) UNTX Pr.

Legendary, Lexical, Loquacious Love. Eve Rhymer. Ed. by Sally Alatalo. 343p. 1996. pap. 16.00 (*1-888636-09-2*) Sara Ranchouse.

Legendary Lighthouses. John Grant & Ray Jones. LC 98-34417. (Illus.). 208p. 1998. pap. 24.95 (*0-7627-0325-3*) Globe Pequot.

Legendary Lives. 2nd ed. Joe Williams & Kathleen Williams. 272p. 1993. pap. 22.00 (*0-9625166-4-3*) Marquee Pr.

Legendary Lives in 'La Princesse de Cleves' Janet Letts. LC 97-31021. (EMF Monographs). 286p. 1998. lib. bdg. 49.95 (*1-886365-08-3*) Rookwood Pr.

Legendary Love Stories. Peter Guttmacher. LC 97-7237. (Illus.). 128p. 1997. 17.98 (*1-56799-489-X*, MetroBooks) M Friedman Pub Grp Inc.

***Legendary Lover.** Susan Johnson. 384p. 2000. mass mkt. 5.99 (*0-553-57867-7*) Bantam Dell.

Legendary Lovers. Debbie Macomber. 1995. per. 5.50 (*0-373-20114-1*) Harlequin Bks.

Legendary Mizners. Alva Johnston. (Illus.). 320p. 2000. pap. 15.00 (*0-374-51928-5*) FS&G.

Legendary Model A Ford. Peter Winnewisser. LC 99-61148. 272p. 1999. 34.95 (*0-87341-615-5*) Krause Pubns.

Legendary Monarchs & Nationalism in Renaissance France. R. E. Asher. (Illus.). 269p. 1993. text 76.50 (*0-7486-0407-3*, Pub. by Edinburgh U Pr) Col U Pr.

Legendary Norden Bombsight. Albert L. Pardini. LC 98-87635. (Illus.). 352p. 1999. 29.95 (*0-7643-0723-1*) Schiffer.

Legendary Northwoods Animals: A Field Guide. Galen Winter. (Illus.). 126p. 1999. text 17.00 (*0-7881-5963-1*) DIANE Pub.

Legendary Outlaws & Lawmen of the West. E. L. Reedstrom. 1991. pap. 2.95 (*0-486-25995-1*) Dover.

Legendary Peace Officers of Modern Arizona. Daniel Byram. (Legendary Peace Officers Ser.: No. 1). (Illus.). 120p. 1998. pap. 14.95 (*1-892798-04-2*) Sierra West.

Legendary Persian Rug & the Other High-Value Civil War Revenue Stamps. Thomas C. Kingsley. (C. & S. Revenue Ser.). (Illus.). 152p. 1993. 55.00 (*1-879767-03-1*) Castenholz Sons.

Legendary Pioneers of Black Radio. Gilbert A. Williams. LC 97-38995. 224p. 1998. 35.00 (*0-275-95888-4*, Praeger Pubs) Greenwood.

Legendary Sci-Fi Movies. Peter Guttmacher. LC 97-7235. (Illus.). 128p. 1997. 17.98 (*1-56799-490-3*, MetroBooks) M Friedman Pub Grp Inc.

Legendary Singing Cowboys. Friedman-Fairfax & Sony Music Staff. (CD Ser.). 1995. pap. 16.98 incl. audio, audio compact disk (*1-56799-230-7*, Friedman-Fairfax) M Friedman Pub Grp Inc.

Legendary Sporting Guns: Shotguns & Rifles. Eric Joly. LC 98-51424. (Illus.). 228p. 1999. 65.00 (*0-7892-0495-9*) Abbeville Pr.

Legendary Sporting Rifles. Sam Fadala. (Illus.). 288p. (Orig.). 1992. pap. 16.95 (*0-88317-167-8*) Stoeger Pub Co.

Legendary Stardust Boys. D. B. Gilles. 1981. pap. 5.25 (*0-8222-0650-1*) Dramatists Play.

Legendary Texians, Vol. I. Joe T. Davis. (Illus.). 192p. 1982. 15.95 (*0-89015-336-1*) Sunbelt Media.

Legendary Texians, Vol. II. Joe T. Davis. (Illus.). 200p. 1985. 15.95 (*0-89015-473-2*) Sunbelt Media.

Legendary Texians, Vol. III. Joe T. Davis. (Illus.). 224p. 1987. 15.95 (*0-89015-559-3*) Sunbelt Media.

Legendary Texians, Vol. IV. Joe T. Davis. (Illus.). 224p. 1989. 15.95 (*0-89015-669-7*) Sunbelt Media.

Legendary Voices. Nigel Douglas. LC 94-23927. (Illus.). 306p. 1995. pap. 20.00 (*0-87910-187-3*) Limelight Edns.

Legendary War Films. Peter Guttmacher. 128p. 1996. 16.98 (*1-56799-240-4*) M Friedman Pub Grp Inc.

Legendary Westerns. Peter Guttmacher. 128p. 1995. 16.98 (*1-56799-172-6*, MetroBooks) M Friedman Pub Grp Inc.

Legendary Whitetails: Stories & Photos of 40 of the Greatest Bucks of All Time. Dick Idol et al. Ed. by David Morris & Gordon Whittington. LC 95-62041. (Illus.). 224p. 1996. 39.95 (*0-9633315-3-1*) Venture Pr MT.

Legendary Wichita Bill: A Retrospective Exhibition of Paintings by John Noble. Howard D. Spencer. LC 82-61985. (Illus.). 44p. 1982. pap. 10.00 (*0-939324-06-7*) Wichita Art Mus.

Legendary Wild West: A Sourcebook on the American West. Ed. by Carter Smith. LC 91-31126. (American Albums from the Collections of the Library of Congress). (Illus.). 96p. (YA). (gr. 5-8). 1992. lib. bdg. 25.90 (*1-56294-133-X*) Millbrook Pr.

Legendary Wild West: A Sourcebook on the American West. Ed. by Carter Smith. (American Albums from the Collections of the Library of Congress). (Illus.). 96p. (J). (gr. 5-8). 1996. 8.95 (*0-7613-0153-4*) Millbrook Pr.

Legendary Wild West a Sourcebook on the American West. C. Carter Smith. LC 91-31126. (American Albums from the Collections of the Library of Congress). 1992. 14.15 (*0-606-09538-1*, Pub. by Turtleback) Demco.

***Legendary Yachts.** Illus. by Francois Chevalier. LC 99-88024. 200p. (J). 2000. 55.00 (*0-7892-0637-4*, Abbeville Kids) Abbeville Pr.

Legende Arthurienne, 3 vols., Set. Ed. by Edmond Faral. LC 75-178511. (FRE.). reprint ed. 185.25 (*0-404-56515-8*) AMS Pr.

Legende de la Mort en Basse-Bretagne see Celtic Legends of the Beyond: A Celtic Book of the Dead

Legende de Prakhriti: Ossements. Le Bestiaire Spirituel. Paul Claudel. 216p. 1972. 25.00 (*0-686-54398-X*) Fr & Eur.

Legende de Roland dans l'Art du Moyen Age. F. Lejeune & Stiennon. 125.00 (*0-685-34014-7*) Fr & Eur.

Legende de Saint Julien l'Hospitalier. Georges Duhamel. (FRE., Illus.). 256p. 1974. 125.00 (*0-7859-1176-6*, 2225384126) Fr & Eur.

Legende des Milles Taureaux. Yachar Kemal. (FRE.). 416p. 1987. pap. 12.95 (*0-7859-2524-4*, 2070377962) Fr & Eur.

Legende des Siecles, Vol. 1. Victor Hugo. Ed. by Alexandre Dumas. 1967. pap. 13.95 (*0-7859-2961-4*) Fr & Eur.

Legende des Siecles, Vol. 2. Victor Hugo. 1967. pap. 12.95 (*0-7859-2962-2*) Fr & Eur.

Legende des Siecles: Avec La Fin de Satan, Dieu. deluxe ed. Victor Hugo. (FRE.). 1344p. 1950. 105.00 (*0-7859-4681-0*) Fr & Eur.

Legende des Siecles: Fragments. Alphonse Daudet. (FRE., Illus.). 31p. 1977. 13.95 (*0-7859-1174-X*, 2203131241) Fr & Eur.

Legende du Cerf-Volant see Legend of the Kite: A Story of China

Legende du Cerf-Volant see Legend of the Kite: A Story of China - Includes Doll

Legende von Sankt Clemens in den Skandinavischen Landern im Mittelalter. Dietrich Hofmann. (Beitrage zur Skandinavistik: Bd. 13). (GER., Illus.). 374p. 1997. 82.95 (*3-631-32154-6*) P Lang Pubng.

Legendes Africaines. Bernard B. Dadie. (FRE.). 1982. pap. 10.95 (*0-7859-3225-9*, 2266028545) Fr & Eur.

Legendes & Chants Esquimaux du Groenland. William C. Thalbitzer. LC 78-20152. (Collection de contes et de chansons populaires: Vol. 45). reprint ed. 21.50 (*0-404-60395-5*) AMS Pr.

Legendes du Guatemala. Miguel Angel Asturias. (FRE.). 192p. 1985. pap. 10.95 (*0-7859-2007-2*, 2070376249) Fr & Eur.

Legendes Epiques: Recherches sur la formation des chansons de geste, 4 vols., Set. Joseph Bedier. LC 78-63487. reprint ed. 159.00 (*0-404-17130-3*) AMS Pr.

Legendes et Curiosites des Metiers. Paul Sebillot. Ed. by Richard M. Dorson. LC 80-749. (Folklore of the World Ser.). (FRE., Illus.). 1981. reprint ed. lib. bdg. 63.95 (*0-405-13323-5*) Ayer.

Legendes Grecques des Saints Militaires. Hippolyte Delehaye. LC 75-7314. (Roman History Ser.). (FRE.). 1975. reprint ed. 30.95 (*0-405-07196-5*) Ayer.

Legendes Religieuses Bulgares. L. Schismanoff. LC 78-20130. (Collection de contes et de chansons populaires: Vol. 21). reprint ed. 34.50 (*0-404-60371-8*) AMS Pr.

Legendes Rustiques. George Sand. (FRE., Illus.). 159p. 1985. pap. 24.95 (*0-7859-1618-0*, 286881008X) Fr & Eur.

Legendes Rustiques: Avec: Les Visions de la Nuit dans les Campagnes. George Sand. (Illus.). 210p. 1975. pap. 4.95 (*0-686-54933-3*) Fr & Eur.

Legendlore: Tainted Soul. Joe Martin. (Illus.). 112p. 1997. pap. 12.95 (*0-941613-94-1*, Caliber Comics) Stabur Pr.

Legendmaker. Howard I. Scott, III. (Illus.). 240p. 1998. pap. 19.95 (*0-9665044-0-2*) Chaos Enter.

Legends. Jonathan Bliss. LC 93-42816. (Hockey Heroes Ser.). 48p. (J). (gr. 3-8). 1994. lib. bdg. 22.60 (*1-55916-015-2*) Rourke Bk Co.

Legends. Ed. by Margaret Weis. (Tales from the Eternal Archives Ser.: 1). 320p. 1999. pap. 6.99 (*0-88677-823-9*, Pub. by DAW Bks) Penguin Putnam.

Legends. limited ed. Ed. by Robert Silverberg. 1998. text 250.00 (*0-312-86863-4*) St Martin.

Legends. Amy Lowell. (Collected Works of Amy Lowell). 259p. 1999. reprint ed. lib. bdg. 88.00 (*1-58201-757-3*, c0757) Classic Bks.

***Legends, Vol. 1.** Ed. by Robert Silverberg. (Illus.). (J). 1999. 12.34 (*0-606-18646-8*) Turtleback.

***Legends, Vol. 2.** Ed. by Robert Silverberg. LC 98-23593. Vol. 2. 400p. 1999. mass mkt. 6.99 (*0-8125-7523-7*, Pub. by Tor Bks) St Martin.

***Legends, Vol. 2.** Ed. by Robert Silverberg. (Illus.). (J). 1999. 12.34 (*0-606-18647-6*) Turtleback.

***Legends, Vol. 3.** Ed. by Robert Silverberg. 448p. 2000. mass mkt. 6.99 (*0-8125-6664-5*, Pub. by Tor Bks) St Martin.

***Legends, Vol. 3.** Ed. by Robert Silverberg. (Illus.). (J). 2000. 12.34 (*0-606-18648-4*) Turtleback.

Legends: Autobiographical Sketches. August Strindberg. LC 72-2120. (Studies in Fiction: No. 34). 1972. reprint ed. lib. bdg. 75.00 (*0-8383-1479-1*) M S G Haskell Hse.

Legends: How to Play & Compose Like the World's Greatest Guitarists, 1. Adrian Clarke. 1998. pap. text 21.95 (*1-86074-220-3*) Music Sales.

Legends: Reading Level 2-3. (Timeless Tales Ser.). 1993. audio 9.95 (*0-88336-269-4*) New Readers.

Legends: Reading Level 2-3. Tana Reiff. (Timeless Tales Ser.). 1993. 4.95 (*0-88336-273-2*) New Readers.

Legends: Short Novels by the Masters of Modern Fantasy. Stephen King et al. Ed. & Intro. by Robert Silverberg. LC 98-23593. (Illus.). 715p. 1998. 27.95 (*0-312-86787-5*, Pub. by Tor Bks) St Martin.

***Legends: Short Novels by the Masters of Modern Fantasy, Vol. 1.** Robert Silverberg et al. 1999. mass mkt. 6.99 (*0-8125-6663-7*, Pub. by Tor Bks) St Martin.

Legends: The BMW Battle of the Legends, 1992-1996. Ed. & Intro. by Don Emde. (Illus.). 128p. 1997. 24.95 (*0-9627434-2-9*) Infosport.

Legends: The Collected Edition. John Ostrander & Len Wein. Ed. by Bob Kahan. (Illus.). 160p. 1993. pap. 9.95 (*1-56389-095-X*, Pub. by DC Comics) Warner Bks.

Legends: The Official Book of the Hockey Hall of Fame. Michael McKinley. (Illus.). 224p. 1996. 40.00 (*1-57243-135-0*) Triumph Bks.

***Legends: Tsoutsouvas,&Sam, Vol. 3.** unabridged ed. Ed. by Robert Silverberg. 1999. audio 34.95 (*0-694-52083-7*) HarperAudio.

***Legends: Tsoutsouvas,&Sam, Vol. 4.** Anne McCaffrey. 1999. audio 34.95 (*0-694-52113-2*) HarperAudio.

Legends: Women Who Have Changed the World Through the Eyes of Great Women Writers. Ed. by John Miller. LC 98-16225. (Illus.). 128p. 1998. 29.95 (*1-57731-042-X*) New Wrld Lib.

Legends Vol. 1: Outstanding Quarter Horse Stallions & Mares. Diane C. Simmons. Ed. by Pat Close. (Illus.). 167p. 1993. pap. 12.95 (*0-911647-26-0*) Western Horseman.

Legends Vol. 3: Outstanding Quarter Horse Stallions & Mares. 3rd ed. Diane Ciarloni et al. (Illus.). 207p. 1997. pap. 15.95 (*0-911647-40-6*) Western Horseman.

***Legends Vol. 4: Outstanding Quarter Horse Stallions & Mares.** Mike Boardman et al. (Legends Ser.). (Illus.). 216p. 2000. pap. 17.95 (*0-911647-49-X*) Western Horseman.

Legends & Fables Papercrafts. Jerome C. Brown. 1991. 8.99 (*0-8224-4234-5*) Fearon Teacher Aids.

Legends & Folk Beliefs in a Swedish American Community, 2 vols. Barbro S. Klein. 1980. 42.95 (*0-405-13317-0*) Arno Press.

Legends & Folk Beliefs in a Swedish American Community: A Study in Folklore & Acculturation, 2 vols., Set. Barbro S. Klein. Ed. by Richard M. Dorson. LC 80-730. (Folklore of the World Ser.). 1981. lib. bdg. 85.95 (*0-405-13343-X*) Ayer.

Legends & Folklore of Holland. Ed. by Adele De Leeuw. (Illus.). 157p. (YA). (gr. 4 up). 1999. 12.50 (*0-7818-0743-3*) Hippocrene Bks.

Legends & Legacies: A Look Inside: Four Decades of Surgery at the University of North Carolina at Chapel Hill, 1952-1993. Colin G. Thomas, Jr. & Mary J. Kagarise. LC 96-30175. (Illus.). 1997. lib. bdg. 65.00 (*0-9653036-0-8*) U NC School Med.

Legends & Legacies: (Memories) Pearl K. Ahnen. LC 95-95288. (Illus.). 200p. (Orig.). 1995. pap. 16.95 (*0-9649930-0-7*) Legna Pr.

Legends & Legacies: Pacesetters in the Profession of Dietetics. Connie E. Vickery & Nancy Cotugna. 352p. (C). 1990. per. 39.95 (*0-8403-6146-7*) Kendall-Hunt.

Legends & Letters. Gustavo A. Becquer. Tr. by Robert M. Fedorchek from SPA. LC 95-10321. (Illus.). 1996. 38.50 (*0-8387-5307-8*) Bucknell U Pr.

Legends & Lies. 2nd ed. Dale L. Walker. LC 98-50738. 320p. (Orig.). 1999. pap. 13.95 (*0-312-86848-0*, Pub. by Tor Bks) St Martin.

Legends & Lies: Great Mysteries of the American West. Dale L. Walker. LC 97-20792. 288p. 1997. text 22.95 (*0-312-86311-X*) St Martin.

Legends & Lies of World History. Richard Shenkman. LC 92-56210. 320p. 1994. pap. 14.00 (*0-06-092255-9*) HarpC.

***Legends & Losers: Trivia from the South Bend & Notre Dame Region.** Andy Jones. LC 99-620095. (Illus.). 1999. pap. 12.95 (*0-89708-221-4*) And Bks.

Legends & Lovers: Fourteen Profiles. William F. Nolan. LC 88-36791. (Borgo Bioviews Ser.: No. 4). 152p. (C). 1997. reprint ed. pap. 19.00 (*0-89370-440-7*) Millefleurs.

Legends & Lyrics. Paul H. Hayne. (Notable American Authors Ser.). 1992. reprint ed. lib. bdg. 75.00 (*0-7812-3061-6*) Rprt Serv.

Legends & Mysteries of the Maori. Charles A. Wilson. LC 78-63233. (Folktale Ser.). reprint ed. 39.50 (*0-404-16177-4*) AMS Pr.

Legends & Myths of Hawaii. David Kalakaua. 576p. 1990. reprint ed. mass mkt. 7.95 (*0-935180-86-9*) Mutual Pub HI.

Legends & Myths of Hawaii: The Fables & Folk-Lore of a Strange People. David Kalakaua. Ed. & Illus. by R. M. Daggett. LC 72-77519. 530p. (YA). (gr. 9 up). 1972. reprint ed. pap. 12.95 (*0-8048-1032-X*) Tuttle Pubng.

Legends & Myths of the Aboriginal Indians of British Guiana. William H. Brett. LC 78-67691. (Folktale Ser.). reprint ed. 39.50 (*0-404-16059-X*) AMS Pr.

Legends & Other Voices: Selected & New Poems. Mary Shumway. (W.N.J. Ser.: No. 27). 1992. pap. 12.00 (*1-55780-118-5*) Juniper Pr ME.

Legends & Popular Tales of the Basque People. Mariana Monteiro. LC 72-173115. 274p. 1972. reprint ed. 18.95 (*0-405-08796-9*, Pub. by Blom Pubns) Ayer.

Legends & Reality: Stories from Chenango, Delaware & Otsego Counties in New York State. Shirley B. Goerlich. LC 90-92242. v, 55p. 1991. pap. text 12.00 (*0-9614858-3-3*) RSG Pub.

***Legends & Reality of the AK: A Behind-the-Scenes Look at the History, Design & Impact of the Kalashnikov Family of Weapons.** Charlie Cutshaw & Valery Shilin. (Illus.). 192p. 2000. pap. 35.00 (*1-58160-069-0*, 10011351) Paladin Pr.

Legends & Romances of Brittany. Lewis Spence. LC 96-54004. (Illus.). 448p. 1997. reprint ed. pap. text 11.95 (*0-486-29660-1*) Dover.

Legends & Romances of Brittany. Lewis Spence. 486p. 1997. reprint ed. pap. 35.00 (*0-7661-0089-8*) Kessinger Pub.

Legends & Stories of the Finger Lakes Region: The Heart of New York State. Emerson Klees. LC 95-60906. (Illus.). 152p. (Orig.). 1995. pap. 17.00 (*0-9635990-5-4*) Frnds Finger Lks.

Legends & Tales of Homeland on the Kankakee. B. E. Burroughs. 1923. 16.95 (*0-917914-65-1*) Lindsay Pubns.

Legends & Tales of the American West. Richard Erdoes. LC 98-15793. 464p. 1998. pap. 16.00 (*0-375-70266-0*) Random.

Legends & Theories of the Buddhists Compared with History & Science: With Introductory Notices of the Life & System of Gotama Buddha. R. Spence Hardy. (C). 1993. reprint ed. text 17.00 (*81-206-0733-3*, Pub. by Asian Educ Servs) S Asia.

Legends & Traditions of Christmas: Devotional Ideas for Family & Group Use During Advent & Christmas. Trudie W. Revoir & John H. Pipe. LC 98-36794. (Illus.). 96p. 1998. pap. 12.00 (*0-8170-1286-9*) Judson.

Legends Begins. (J). 1996. 6.98 (*1-57082-394-4*, Pub. by Mouse Works) Time Warner.

***Legends by the Lake: The Cleveland Browns at Municipal Stadium.** John Keim. LC 99-25712. (Ohio History & Culture Ser.). (Illus.). 1999. 35.95 (*1-884836-47-X*); pap. 17.95 (*1-884836-48-8*) U Akron Pr.

Legends, Customs & Social Life of Seneca Indians. John W. Sanborn. 1998. lib. bdg. 22.95 (*1-56723-130-6*) Yestermorrow.

Legends, Customs & Traditions of Christmas: A Collection. L. Peter Wren. (Illus.). 62p. 1986. pap. 4.95 (*0-9622084-0-X*) L P Wren.

Legends! Early Poems. Vladimir Mayakovsky. Tr. by Maria Enzensberger from RUS. 64p. (Orig.). 1991. pap. 5.95 (*0-87286-255-0*) City Lights.

Legends from Camp. Lawson F. Inada. LC 92-38871. 112p. (Orig.). 1993. pap. 11.95 (*1-56689-004-7*) Coffee Hse.

Legends from the Forest. Thomas Fiddler & James R. Stevens. 119p. 1985. 7.95 (*0-920806-64-3*, Pub. by Penumbra Pr) U of Toronto Pr.

Legends from the Frosty Sons of Thunder. William T. Doncaster, Jr. LC 98-30765. 156p. 1999. pap. 13.95 (*1-883911-25-7*) Brandylane.

Legends in Action: Ten Plays of Ten Lands. Nellie McCaslin. LC 93-22161. (J). Date not set. pap. 20.00 (*0-88734-633-2*) Players Pr.

Legends in Limestone. Seidel. LC 98-52488. 1998. pap. text 20.00 (*0-226-74516-3*) U Ch Pr.

Legends in Limestone: Lazarus, Gislebertus, & the Cathedral of Autun. Linda Seidel. LC 98-52488. (Illus.). 200p. 1999. 32.50 (*0-226-74515-5*) U Ch Pr.

Legends in Music. Prod. by Zobeida Perez. 12p. (Orig.). 1994. pap. 17.00 (*0-89898-746-6*, BMR05072) Wrner Bros.

Legends in the Life Divine. M. P. Pandit. 284p. 1988. 16.00 (*0-941524-34-5*) Lotus Pr.

Legends in Their Own Time: A Popular Biographical Dictionary. Coral Amende. 378p. 1998. pap. text 14.00 (*0-7881-5746-9*) DIANE Pub.

Legend's Lady. Kathryn Hockett. 352p. 1998. mass mkt. 4.99 (*0-8217-5847-0*, Zebra Kensgtn) Kensgtn Pub Corp.

Legends, Lies & Cherished Myths of American History. large type ed. Richard Shenkman. (General Ser.). 317p. 1990. lib. bdg. 19.95 (*0-8161-4867-8*, G K Hall Lrg Type) Mac Lib Ref.

Legends, Lies, & Cherished Myths of American History. Richard Shenkman. LC 89-45163. 224p. 1996. reprint ed. pap. 13.00 (*0-06-097261-0*, PL 7261, Perennial) HarperTrade.

Legends Live On: Interviews with the Cowboy Stars of the Silver Screen. Charlie LeSueur. 136p. 1999. pap. 11.95 (*1-885162-25-1*, CL-25-1) Norseman.

Legends Lost. Betty Dunn. (Illus.). 98p. (Orig.). 1995. pap. 6.50 (*0-9640603-8-8*) Badger Pubns.

***Legends Men of Falcon.** Ed. by Falcon Press Staff. 1999. pap. 42.95 (*3-86187-145-9*) B Gmunder.

Legends of a Log Cabin. Chandler Gilman. LC 75-104466. (C). 1987. reprint ed. pap. text 7.95 (*0-8290-2132-9*); reprint ed. lib. bdg. 22.50 (*0-8398-0661-2*) Irvington.

Legends of Africa. Mwizenge Tembo. (Myths of the World Ser.). (Illus.). 112p. 1996. 15.98 (*1-56799-352-4*, MetroBooks) M Friedman Pub Grp Inc.

Legends of Alexander the Great. Ed. by Richard Stoneman. 336p. 1994. 8.50 (*0-460-87514-0*, Everyman's Classic Lib) Tuttle Pubng.

***Legends of American Dance & Choreography.** Carin Ford. LC 99-38818. (Collective Biographies Ser.). (Illus.). 128p. (gr. 6 up). 2000. lib. bdg. 20.95 (*0-7660-1378-2*) Enslow Pubs.

***Legends of Ancient Egypt.** M. A. Murray. LC 99-54804. 96p. 2000. pap. 5.95 (*0-486-41137-0*) Dover.

Legends of Atlantis & the Lost Lemuria. W. Scott-Elliot. LC 90-50203. (Illus.). 174p. 1990. pap. 16.00 (*0-8356-0664-3*, Quest) Theos Pub Hse.

Legends of Babylon & Egypt in Relation to Hebrew Tradition. L. W. King. (British Academy, London, Schweich Lectures on Biblical Archaeology Series, 1930). 1969. reprint ed. pap. 25.00 (*0-8115-1258-4*) Periodicals Srv.

Legends of BAKA. Lawrence J. Lalonde. 52p. 1984. pap. write for info. (*0-9608136-0-8*) L J Lalonde.

Legends of Charlemagne. Thomas Bulfinch. (Works of Thomas Bulfinch). 1989. reprint ed. lib. bdg. 79.00 (*0-7812-2165-X*) Rprt Serv.

***Legends of Charlemagne: The Illustrated Bullfinch's Mythology.** Thomas Bullfinch. (Illus.). 160p. (YA). (gr. 9-12). 2000. reprint ed. pap. text 19.00 (*0-7881-6913-0*) DIANE Pub.

Legends of Chief Bald Eagle. Harry Bullshows & Hap Gilliland. (J). (gr. 2-10). 1997. pap. 1.95 (*0-89992-052-7*) Coun India Ed.

***Legends of Chivalry: Medieval Myth.** 144p. 2000. 29.95 (*0-7054-3673-X*) Time-Life Educ.

Legends of Christmas. Georgianna Summers. 1990. pap. 3.95 (*1-55673-256-2*, 9044) CSS OH.

Legends of Christmas. large type ed. Michael J. Matteson. (Illus.). 144p. (J). (gr. 3-8). 1998. pap. 9.50 (*1-890740-05-5*) Remnant Pr.

Legends of Cork. James Lyons. 144p. 1992. pap. 8.95 (*0-947962-29-8*) Dufour.

Legends of Country Blues Guitar. Stefan Grossman. 116p. 1997. 22.95 incl. audio compact disk (*0-7866-2856-1*, MB95269BCD) Mel Bay.

Legends of Country Guitar. 112p. 1998. otabind 16.95 (*0-7935-4420-3*, 00690084) H Leonard.

Legends of Dracula. Thomas Streissguth. LC 98-8428. (A&E Biography Ser.). (J). 1998. 25.26 (*0-8225-4942-5*) Lerner Pub.

***Legends of Dracula.** Tom Streissguth. 112-128p. 1999. pap. text 7.95 (*0-8225-9682-2*) Lerner Pub.

Legends of Flight: With the National Aviation Hall of Fame. Bill Yenne. LC 97-215873. 216p. 1997. write for info. (*0-7853-1910-7*) Pubns Intl Ltd.

Legends of French Canada. Edward C. Woodley. LC 75-174354. (Illus.). 1979. reprint ed. 23.95 (*0-405-09102-8*) Ayer.

***Legends of Genesis: The Israelite Literature.** Hermann Gunkel. (Biblical Encyclopaedia Library: Vol. XVI). (HEB.). iii, 192p. 1998. pap. text 29.00 (*965-342-692-3*, Pub. by Bialik) Eisenbrauns.

Legends of Gertrud von Le Fort: Text & Audience. Margaret K. Devinney. (Studies in Modern German Literature: Vol. 27). 223p. (C). 1989. text 34.00 (*0-8204-0719-4*) P Lang Pubng.

Legends of Golf. rev. ed. Louis T. Stanley. (Illus.). 128p. 1999. 14.98 (*0-7651-1656-1*) Smithmark.

Legends of Guitar Rock, the '50s: With Notes & Tablature, Vol. 1. 1994. pap. 19.95 incl. audio (*0-7935-1849-0*, 00694851) H Leonard.

Legends of Guitar Rock, the 60's, Vol. 1. 1994. pap. 24.95 (*0-7935-2961-1*, 00694902) H Leonard.

Legends of Health & Fitness, 10 vols., Set. (Illus.). 1280p. (YA). (gr. 6-12). 2000. lib. bdg. 249.50 (*1-58415-052-1*) M Lane Pubs.

***Legend's of Health & Fitness: Complete Set.** 960p. (YA). (gr. 5-12). 2000. 249.50 (*1-58415-062-9*) M Lane Pubs.

Legends of Home. Lenka Vodicka. LC 92-90937. 103p. 1992. pap. 9.95 (*0-9633779-0-6*) Milavel.

Legends of Israel. S. Z. Kahana. Ed. by Leo Gartnberg. Tr. by J. M. Lerman. 256p. 1987. 13.95 (*0-943688-58-2*); pap. 12.95 (*0-943688-62-0*) Res Ctr Kabbalah.

Legends of Journeys. O. J. Norris. (Illus.). 32p. 1988. 16.95 (*0-521-32181-6*) Cambridge U Pr.

Legends of King Arthur in Art. Muriel Whitaker. (Illus.). 408p. (C). 1995. pap. 55.00 (*0-85991-486-0*, DS Brewer) Boydell & Brewer.

Legends of Konkan. Arthur Crawford. 1986. reprint ed. 20.00 (*0-8364-1740-2*, Pub. by Manohar) S Asia.

Legends of Landforms: Native American Lore & the Geology of the Land. Carole Vogel. LC 98-30676. (Illus.). 96p. (J). (gr. 4-8). 1999. lib. bdg. 27.90 (*0-7613-0272-7*, Copper Beech Bks) Millbrook Pr.

Legends of Lehigh-Lafayette: College Football's Most-Played Rivalry. Todd Davidson & Bob Donchez. LC 95-92244. 256p. 1995. 39.95 (*0-9640341-1-5*) Successful Concepts.

Legends of Liverpool: 25 Classics Recorded by the Beatles. Ed. by Carol Cuellar. 84p. (Orig.). 1996. pap. text 12.95 (*1-57623-433-9*, MF9630) Wrner Bros.

Legends of Long Ago. Gottfried Keller. Tr. by Charles H. Handschin from GER. LC 71-167456. (Short Story Index Reprint Ser.). 1977. reprint ed. 15.95 (*0-8369-3982-4*) Ayer.

Legends of Long Beach Island. Charles J. Adams, III & David J. Seibold. (Illus.). 110p. 1985. pap. 7.95 (*0-9610008-2-1*) Exeter Hse.

Legends of Lost Treasure. C. A. Mills. 86p. 1987. pap. 5.00 (*0-945598-04-1*) Apple Cheeks Pr.

Legends of Loudoun Valley. Joseph V. Nichols. 117p. 1996. pap. 12.00 (*1-888265-09-4*) Willow Bend.

Legends of Maui, a Demi God of Polynesia, & of His Mother Hina. William D. Westervelt. LC 75-35217. reprint ed. 37.50 (*0-404-14240-0*) AMS Pr.

Legends of Maui & Tahaki. J. F. Stimson. (BMB Ser.). 1969. reprint ed. 25.00 (*0-527-02233-0*) Periodicals Srv.

Legends of Modernity. Czeslaw Milosz. text. write for info. (*0-374-18499-2*) FS&G.

Legends of Motorsport. Dave Friedman. Ed. by Ernest T. Nagamatsu. (Illus.). 350p. 1992. 150.00 (*0-9632751-0-0*) Motor Racing Images.

Legends of New England. John Greenleaf Whittier. LC 65-12302. 158p. 1972. reprint ed. 50.00 (*0-8201-1108-2*) Schol Facsimiles.

Legends of New York State. 2nd ed. Catherine H. Ainsworth. LC 78-54873. (Folklore Bks.). 99p. (J). (ps-12). 1983. 12.00 (*0-933190-11-5*) Clyde Pr.

***Legends of Origin of the Castes & Tribes of Eastern India.** G. K. Ghosh. 2000. 30.00 (*81-7102-046-1*, Pub. by Firma KLM) S Asia.

***Legends of Our Times: Native Cowboy Life.** Morgan Baillargeon & Leslie Tepper. LC 98-3001. (Illus.). 265p. 2000. pap. 24.95 (*0-295-97729-9*) U of Wash Pr.

Legends of Our Times: Native Cowboy Life. Leslie H. Tepper & Morgan Baillargeon. LC 98-3001. (Illus.). x, 254 p. 1998. 38.95 (*0-295-97728-0*) U of Wash Pr.

Legends of People, Myths of State: Violence, Intolerance & Political Culture in Sri Lanka & Australia. Bruce Kapferer. (Illus.). 288p. 1998. pap. 18.95 (*1-56098-573-9*) Smithsonian.

Legends of Pirate Gold. C. A. Mills. 92p. 1986. pap. 5.00 (*0-945598-03-3*) Apple Cheeks Pr.

Legends of Porthcawl & the Glamorgan Coast. Alun Morgan. 120p. (C). 1989. 45.00 (*0-9504475-0-1*, Pub. by D Brown & Sons Ltd) St Mut.

Legends of Rock Guitar. Pete Prown & H. P. Newquist. 300p. 1996. 19.95 (*0-614-20105-5*, 00330019) H Leonard.

Legends of Rock Guitar. Artie Traum & Arti Funaro. (Illus.). 72p. 1986. pap. 12.95 (*0-8256-0309-9*, OK64790, Oak) Music Sales.

Legends of Rock Guitar: The Essential Reference of Rock's Greatest Guitarists. Pete Prown & H. P. Newquist. LC 97-180000. (Illus.). 264p. (Orig.). 1997. per. 22.95 (*0-7935-4042-9*, HL00330019) H Leonard.

Legends of Rock Guitar Fake Book with Tablature. 416p. 1994. spiral bd. 24.95 (*0-7935-2216-1*, 00240023) H Leonard.

***Legends of Santa Claus.** H. Paul Jeffers. LC 99-27240. (A&E Biography Ser.). (Illus.). 128p. (YA). (ps up). 2000. lib. bdg. 25.26 (*0-8225-4983-2*, Lerner Publctns) Lerner Pub.

Legends of Smokeover. Lawrence P. Jacks. LC 70-125222. (Short Story Index Reprint Ser.). 1977. 23.95 (*0-8369-3589-6*) Ayer.

Legends of Steam. Colin Garratt. (Illus.). 256p. 1999. 40.00 (*1-56649-035-9*) Welcome Rain.

Legends of Stock Car Racing. John Craft. (Illus.). 160p. 1995. pap. 19.95 (*0-7603-0144-1*) MBI Pubg.

Legends of Texas. J. Frank Dobie. 1993. reprint ed. lib. bdg. 75.00 (*0-7812-5875-8*) Rprt Serv.

Legends of Texas Vol. I: Lost Mines & Buried Treasure. J. Frank Dobie. LC 91-32367. 208p. 1992. reprint ed. pap. 4.95 (*0-88289-909-0*) Pelican.

Legends of Texas, Vol. 2: Pirates Gold & Other Tales. Ed. by J. Frank Dobie. 208p. 1995. pap. 4.95 (*1-56554-073-5*) Pelican.

Legends of Texas' Heroic Age. Francis E. Abernethy. (Texas History Ser.). (Illus.). 108p. (C). 1984. pap. text 9.95 (*0-89641-143-5*) American Pr.

Legends of the Air 6: Boeing 707 Douglas DC-8 & Vickers VC10. Stewart Wilson. (Illus.). 180p. 1998. pap. 21.95 (*1-875671-36-6*, Pub. by Australian Aviation) Motorbooks Intl.

Legends of the American Desert: Sojourns in the Greater Southwest. Alex Shoumatoff. 544p. 1999. pap. 15.00 (*0-06-097769-8*) HarpC.

Legends of the American Revolution, 1776 see Washington & His Generals: or Legends of the American Revolution

Legends of the Animal World. Rosalind Kerven. (Illus.). 32p. (J). (gr. 3-7). 1986. 16.95 (*0-521-30576-4*) Cambridge U Pr.

Legends of the Ash. Brendan Fullam. 1999. pap. 15.95 (*0-86327-667-9*) Wolfhound Press.

Legends of The Ash. Brendan Fullam. (Illus.). 256p. 1998. 29.95 (*0-86327-619-9*, Pub. by Wolfhound Press) Irish Amer Bk.

Legends of the Batman. Ed. by Martin H. Greenberg. 528p. 1997. 10.98 (*1-56731-219-5*, MJF Bks) Fine Comms.

Legends of the Beothuk: White Indians of Canada. Ay Simiminha. Ed. by James Templar. LC 93-61068. (Illus.). 110p. 1993. 15.00 (*1-883147-12-3*); 15.00 (*1-883147-11-5*) Intern Guild ASRS.

Legends of the Bible. Louis Ginzberg. LC 56-9915. 686p. 1992. reprint ed. pap. text 21.95 (*0-8276-0404-1*) JPS Phila.

Legends of the California Bandidos. Angus MacLean. (Illus.). 256p. 1989. reprint ed. 12.50 (*0-939919-21-4*); reprint ed. pap. 8.95 (*0-939919-20-6*) Bear Flag Bks.

Legends of the Chinese Jews of Kaifeng. Xu Xin. (Illus.). 140p. (J). 1995. 19.95 (*0-88125-528-9*) Ktav.

Legends of the City of Mexico. Thomas A. Janvier. (Mexico Ser.). 1979. lib. bdg. 59.95 (*0-8490-2958-9*) Gordon Pr.

Legends of the Cowlitz Indian Tribe. Roy I. Wilson. LC 98-219915. 401 P. ;p. 1998. write for info. (*0-7880-0983-4*, Express Pr) CSS OH.

Legends of the Delaware Indians & Picture Writing. Richard C. Adams. Ed. & Intro. by Deborah Nichols. LC 97-23740. 128p. 1997. 25.95 (*0-8156-0487-4*) Syracuse U Pr.

***Legends of the Delaware Indians & Picture Writing.** Richard C. Adams. (The Iroquois & their Neighbors Ser.). (Illus.). 168p. 2000. pap. 15.95 (*0-8156-0639-7*) Syracuse U Pr.

Legends of the Earth, Sea & Sky: An Encyclopedia of Nature Myths. Ed. by Tamra Andrews. LC 98-40603. (Illus.). 336p. 1998. lib. bdg. 65.00 (*0-87436-963-0*, AD-EASKYC) ABC-CLIO.

Legends of the Egyptian Gods: Hieroglyphic Texts & Translations. E. A. Wallis Budge. LC 93-49097. Orig. Title: Egyptian Literature, Vol. I: Legends of the Gods, the Egyptian Texts, Edited with Translations. (Illus.). 352p. 1994. reprint ed. pap. 8.95 (*0-486-28022-5*) Dover.

Legends of the Fairway: Great Women Golfers Tell How to Play the Game. Geoff Russell. 1997. 22.00 (*0-671-54510-8*) PB.

Legends of the Fall. Jim Harrison. 288p. 1980. pap. 12.95 (*0-385-28596-5*, Delta Trade) Dell.

Legends of the Field: Famous Early Hunters in Africa. limited ed. W. Robert Foran. LC 97-60108. (Illus.). 340p. 1997. 100.00 (*1-882458-15-X*) Trophy Rm Bks.

Legends of the Forest. Henry H. Sloan. 16p. 1999. pap. 3.50 (*1-888181-10-9*) NW Law Pubng.

Legends of the Golden Era. Illus. by Jim Murray. (Baseball Legends Ser.). 64p. (J). (gr. 3 up). 1995. 203.80 (*0-7910-3563-8*) Chelsea Hse.

Legends of the Great Chiefs. Emerson N. Matson. (Illus.). 144p. (YA). (gr. 8-12). 1984. reprint ed. pap. 6.95 (*0-9609940-0-9*) Storypole.

Legends of the Hasidim: An Introduction to Hasidic Culture & Oral Tradition in the New World. Jerome R. Mintz. LC 95-6046. 494p. 1996. pap. 40.00 (*1-56821-530-4*) Aronson.

Legends of the Hasidim: An Introduction to Hasidic Culture & Oral Tradition in the New World. Jerome R. Mintz. LC 68-16707. 504p. 1993. reprint ed. pap. text 14.95 (*0-226-53103-1*, P612) U Ch Pr.

***Legends of the Heisman: Berwanger to Dayne, 1935 to 1999.** unabridged ed. Don Gwaltney. Ed. by John L. Gwaltney. (Illus.). 120p. 2000. 24.95 (*0-9639591-6-6*) Apple Core Pr.

Legends of the Hero-Kings. Ed Stark. 1996. 20.00 (*0-7869-0419-4*, Pub. by TSR Inc) Random.

Legends of the Holy Grail. Alfred T. Nutt. LC 78-139176. (Popular Studies in Mythology, Romance & Folklore: No. 14). reprint ed. 12.50 (*0-404-53514-3*) AMS Pr.

Legends of the Holy Rood: Symbols of the Passion & Cross-Poems. Ed. by Richard Morris. (EETS, OS Ser.: No. 46). 1969. reprint ed. 54.00 (*0-527-00043-4*) Periodicals Srv.

Legends of the Iroquois. William W. Canfield. 1998. lib. bdg. 26.95 (*1-56723-131-4*) Yestermorrow.

Legends of the Iroquois. Ray Fadden. LC 98-33967. 112p. 1998. pap. 9.95 (*1-57067-056-0*) Book Pub Co.

Legends of the Iroquois. William W. Canfield. 211p. 1993. reprint ed. lib. bdg. 79.00 (*0-7812-5157-5*) Rprt Serv.

Legends of the Jews, 6 vols. Louis Ginzberg. (GER.). 2723p. 1997. reprint ed. 950.00 (*3-487-10395-8*) G Olms Pubs.

Legends of the Jews, 7 vols., Set. Louis Ginzberg. LC 76-58650. 1956. 250.00 (*0-8276-0148-4*) JPS Phila.

Legends of the Jews, 7 vols., Vol. 1. Louis Ginzberg. LC 76-58650. 424p. 1956. 39.95 (*0-8276-0340-1*) JPS Phila.

Legends of the Jews, 7 vols., Vol. 2. Louis Ginzberg. LC 76-58650. 376p. 1956. 39.95 (*0-8276-0341-X*) JPS Phila.

Legends of the Jews, 7 vols., Vol. 3. Louis Ginzberg. LC 76-58650. 482p. 1956. 39.95 (*0-8276-0342-8*) JPS Phila.

Legends of the Jews, 7 vols., Vol. 5. Louis Ginzberg. LC 76-58650. 446p. 1956. 39.95 (*0-8276-0344-4*) JPS Phila.

Legends of the Jews, 7 vols., Vol. 6. Louis Ginzberg. LC 76-58650. 490p. 1956. 39.95 (*0-8276-0345-2*) JPS Phila.

Legends of the Jews, 7 vols., Vol. 7. Louis Ginzberg. LC 76-58650. 612p. 1956. 39.95 (*0-8276-0346-0*) JPS Phila.

Legends of the Jews Vol. 1: From the Creation to Jacob. Louis Ginzberg. Tr. by Paul Radin & Henrietta Szold from GER. LC 97-46024. 448p. 1998. pap. 15.95 (*0-8018-5890-9*) Johns Hopkins.

Legends of the Jews Vol. 2: From Joseph to the Exodus. Louis Ginzberg. 384p. pap. 15.95 (*0-8018-5891-7*) Johns Hopkins.

Legends of the Jews Vol. 3: Moses in the Wilderness. Louis Ginzberg. 494p. pap. 15.95 (*0-8018-5892-5*) Johns Hopkins.

Legends of the Jews Vol. 4: From Joshua to Esther. Louis Ginzberg. 456p. pap. 15.95 (*0-8018-5893-3*) Johns Hopkins.

Legends of the Jews Vol. 5: Notes for Volumes 1 & 2. Louis Ginzberg. 460p. pap. 18.95 (*0-8018-5894-1*) Johns Hopkins.

Legends of the Jews Vol. 6: Notes for Volumes 3 & 4. Louis Ginzberg. 504p. pap. 18.95 (*0-8018-5895-X*) Johns Hopkins.

Legends of the Jews Vol. 7: Index. Louis Ginzberg. 622p. pap. 18.95 (*0-8018-5896-8*) Johns Hopkins.

Legends of the Kings of Akkade - The Texts. Joan G. Westenholz. LC 96-45516. (Mesopotamian Civilizations Ser.: Vol. 7). 423p. 1998. text 54.50 (*0-931464-85-4*) Eisenbrauns.

Legends of the Lost. John Robinson. 160p. (Orig.). 1989. pap. 12.95 (*1-882021-07-X*) Summer.

Legends of the Madonna As Represented in the Fine Arts. Anna Brownell Jameson. (Illus.). lxxv, 344p. 1990. reprint ed. lib. bdg. 42.00 (*1-55888-277-4*) Omnigraphics Inc.

Legends of the Maori, 2 vols., Set. Maui Pomare et al. LC 75-35265. (Illus.). 1976. reprint ed. 125.00 (*0-404-14350-4*) AMS Pr.

Legends of the Mighty Sioux. Writers Program, South Dakota Staff. LC 73-3652. (American Guide Ser.). reprint ed. write for info. (*0-404-57952-3*) AMS Pr.

Legends of the Monastic Orders As Represented in the Fine Arts. Anna Brownell Jameson. LC 75-41154. xv, 489p. 1976. reprint ed. 62.50 (*0-404-14767-4*) AMS Pr.

Legends of the 1930s & 1940s. Intro. by Jim Murray. (Baseball Legends Ser.). (Illus.). 64p. (J). (gr. 3 up). 1995. 104.65 (*0-7910-3562-X*) Chelsea Hse.

Legends of the Old West. 24p. Date not set. pap. text 3.99 (*1-56944-148-0*) Terrell Missouri.

Legends of the Old West: Trailblazers, Desperadoes, Wranglers, & Yarn-Spinners. Kent Alexander. LC 94-8758. (Illus.). 120p. 1994. pap. 14.95 (*1-56799-109-2*, Friedman-Fairfax) M Friedman Pub Grp Inc.

Legends of the Outer Banks & Tar Heel Tidewater. Charles H. Whedbee. LC 66-23049. (Illus.). 165p. (YA). (gr. 5 up). 1979. reprint ed. 12.95 (*0-910244-41-3*) Blair.

Legends of the Panjab, 3 vols., Set. Richard C. Temple. Ed. by Richard M. Dorson. LC 77-70627. (International Folklore Ser.). 1977. reprint ed. 139.95 (*0-405-10128-7*) Ayer.

Legends of the Panjab, 3 vols., Vol. 1. Richard C. Temple. Ed. by Richard M. Dorson. LC 77-70627. (International Folklore Ser.). 1977. reprint ed. lib. bdg. 47.95 (*0-405-10129-5*) Ayer.

Legends of the Panjab, 3 vols., Vol. 2. Richard C. Temple. Ed. by Richard M. Dorson. LC 77-70627. (International Folklore Ser.). 1977. reprint ed. lib. bdg. 43.00 (*0-405-10130-9*) Ayer.

Legends of the Panjab, 3 vols., Vol. 3. Richard C. Temple. Ed. by Richard M. Dorson. LC 77-70627. (International Folklore Ser.). 1977. reprint ed. lib. bdg. 47.95 (*0-405-10131-7*) Ayer.

Legends of the Plumed Serpent: Biography of a Mexican God. Neil Baldwin. LC 98-36524. (Illus.). 224p. 1998. text 37.50 (*1-891620-03-7*, Pub. by PublicAffairs NY) HarpC.

***Legends of the Pond--Stories of Big Island Pond, Atkinson, Derry & Hampstead.** Alfred E. Kayworth. Ed. by Adolph Caso. (Illus.). 280p. 2000. pap. 15.95 (*0-8283-2053-5*) Branden Bks.

Legends of the Rabbis, 2 vol. set. Ed. by Judah Nadich. LC 94-1942. 776p. 1994. pap. 45.00 (*1-56821-129-5*) Aronson.

Legends of the Rabbis Vol. 1: Jewish Legends of the Second Commonwealth. Judah Nadich. LC 94-208. 512p. 1994. pap. 25.00 (*1-56821-130-9*) Aronson.

Legends of the Rabbis Vol. 2: The First Generation after the Destruction of the Temple & Jerusalem. Judah Nadich. LC 94-209. 264p. 1994. pap. 20.00 (*1-56821-131-7*) Aronson.

***Legends of the Rhine.** Joanne Asala. Ed. by Eberhardt Reichmann et al. (Illus.). 128p. 2000. pap. 12.95 (*1-57216-040-3*) Penfield.

Legends of the Sages: The Image of the Sage in Rabbinic Literature. Chaim Licht. 25.00 (*0-88125-361-8*) Ktav.

Legends of the Saints. Hippolyte Delehaye. Tr. by Donald Attwater. LC 61-18761. 272p. reprint ed. pap. 84.40 (*0-7837-0442-9*, 204076500018) Bks Demand.

Legends of the Saints. Hippolyte Delehaye. 288p. 1998. reprint ed. pap. 39.95 (*1-85182-370-0*, Pub. by Four Cts Pr) Intl Spec Bk.

Legends of the Samurai. Hiroaki Sato. 432p. 1995. 29.95 (*0-87951-619-4*, Pub. by Overlook Pr) Penguin Putnam.

Legends of the Sasquatch: An Introduction to the Private World of Bigfoot. Steve Heinzen. 148p. 1995. pap. 9.95 (*1-881147-20-7*) Lowell Print.

Legends of the Seminoles. Betty M. Jumper & Peter Gallagher. LC 93-50571. (Illus.). 96p. 1994. 24.95 (*1-56164-033-6*); pap. 17.95 (*1-56164-040-9*) Pineapple Pr.

Legends of the Shawangunk & Its Environs, Including Historical Sketches, Biographical Notices & Thrilling Border Incidents & Adventures Relating to Those Portions of Orange, Ulster & Sullivan Counties Lying in the Shawangunk Region. Philip H. Smith. 168p. 1997. reprint ed. lib. bdg. 25.00 (*0-8328-6082-4*) Higginson Bk Co.

Legends of the Sufis. Shams U. Din & E. Ahmed. Ed. by Idries Shah. Tr. by James W. Redhouse. 1977. pap. 10.95 (*0-7229-5051-9*) Theos Pub Hse.

***Legends of the Tribe: An Illustrated History of the Cleveland Indians.** Morris Eckhouse. (Illus.). 2000. 39.95 (*0-87833-197-2*) Taylor Pub.

Legends of the Wagner Drama. Jessie L. Weston. LC 74-24255. reprint ed. 47.50 (*0-404-13132-8*) AMS Pr.

***Legends of the Warring States: Persuasions, Romances, & Stories from "Chan-kuo Ts'e"** J. I. Crump. LC 98-36393. (Michigan Monographs in Chinese Studies: Vol. 83). (Illus.). xiv, 189p. 1999. text 45.00 (*0-89264-127-4*) Ctr Chinese Studies.

Legends of the Warring States: Persuasions, Romances & Stories from "Chan-Kuo Ts'e" J. I. Crump. LC 98-36393. (Michigan Monographs in Chinese Studies: Vol. 83). (Illus.). xiv, 189p. 1999. pap. 20.00 (*0-89264-129-0*) Ctr Chinese Studies.

Legends of the West. James A. Hall. (Notable American Authors Ser.). 1992. reprint ed. lib. bdg. 75.00 (*0-7812-2984-7*) Rprt Serv.

***Legends of the Wolf Creek Basin.** Illus. by Ralph E. Posey, Jr. 222p. 1999. pap. 12.95 (*0-9700565-0-8*) Ponto Hist Soc.

Legends of the World's Finest. Walter Simonson. LC 96-159689. (Illus.). 160p. 1995. mass mkt. 14.95 (*1-56389-179-4*, Pub. by DC Comics) Time Warner.

Legends of the Yosemite Miwok. 2nd rev. ed. Ed. by Craig D. Bates & Steven P. Medley. (Illus.). 1993. reprint ed. pap. 11.95 (*0-939666-57-X*) Yosemite Assn.

Legends of Vancouver. E. Pauline Johnson-Tekahionwake. 160p. 1998. pap. 12.95 (*1-55054-553-1*, Pub. by DGL) Orca Bk Pubs.

Legends of Vancouver. E. Pauline Johnson-Tekahionwake. (Illus.). 160p. Date not set. 13.95 (*1-55082-024-9*); pap. 7.95 (*1-55082-025-7*) LPC InBook.

Legends of Woburn, 1642-1892, Second Series. Parker L. Converse. (Illus.). 252p. 1995. reprint ed. lib. bdg. 35.00 (*0-8328-4699-6*) Higginson Bk Co.

Legends of Woburn, 1642-1892: Now First Written & Preserved in Collected Form...to Which Is Added a Chrono-Indexical History of Woburn. Parker L. Converse. (Illus.). 174p. 1995. reprint ed. lib. bdg. 29.00 (*0-8328-4700-3*) Higginson Bk Co.

Legends of Zion. S. Z. Kahana. Ed. by Leo Gartenberg. Tr. by S. M. Lehrman from HEB. 264p. 1987. 13.95 (*0-943688-59-0*); pap. 12.95 (*0-943688-63-9*) Res Ctr Kabbalah.

Legends on the Screen: The Narrative Film in Australia, 1919-1929. John Tulloch. 487p. (C). 1981. pap. 17.95 (*0-86819-057-8*, Pub. by Currency Pr) Accents Pubns.

Legends, Plain Truths, & Profanities: A Crawford/McWilliams Chronicle. George Pettett. LC 97-92617. (Illus.). 316p. 1997. 25.00 (*0-9624353-1-7*) Lochaber Bks.

Legends Told by the Old People. Adolf Hungrywolf. LC 90-42388. (Illus.). 80p. 1990. pap. 6.95 (*0-913990-71-X*) Book Pub Co.

Legends Told in Canada. Edith Fowke. (Illus.). 96p. 1994. 19.95 (*0-88854-410-3*) U of Toronto Pr.

Legends, Traditions & History in Medieval England. Antonia Gransden. 361p. 1992. 60.00 (*1-85285-016-7*) Hambledon Press.

Legends, Traditions & Laws of the Iroquois: or Six Nations, & History of the Tuscacora Indians. Elias Johnson. LC 76-43755. reprint ed. 24.50 (*0-404-15596-0*) AMS Pr.

***Legends Walking: A Novel of the Athanor.** Jane Lindskold. 416p. 1999. mass mkt. 6.99 (*0-380-78850-0*, Avon Bks) Morrow Avon.

Legends Worth Living. Nathan Drazin. 14.95 (*0-88125-381-2*) Ktav.

Leger. Ed. by Jose M. Faerna. (Great Modern Masters Cameo Bks.). (Illus.). 64p. 1996. pap. 11.98 (*0-8109-4688-2*, Pub. by Abrams) Time Warner.

Leger Felicite Sonthonax: The Lost Sentinel of the Republic. Robert Stein. LC 84-47548. (Illus.). 240p. 1985. 35.00 (*0-8386-3218-1*) Fairleigh Dickinson.

Leger, Our Contemporary. Institute for the Arts Staff. Ed. by Amy Goldin. (Illus.). 1978. pap. 5.00 (*0-914412-13-2*, Inst Arts Catalogues) Menil Found.

Leger's Le Grand Dejeuner. Minneapolis Institute of Arts Staff. LC 80-80235. (Illus.). 1980. 8.00 (*0-912964-11-1*) Minneapolis Inst Arts.

Leges Graecorum Sacrae. I. DePrott & L. Ziehen. (GER & GRE.). 372p. (Orig.). 1988. reprint ed. pap. 35.00 (*0-89005-478-9*) Ares.

Leges Palatinae. James, King of Majorca, 3rd. 164p. 1994. text 64.95 (*0-253-33110-2*) Ind U Pr.

Leges Publicae Populi Romani. Giovanni Rotondi. (Olms Paperbacks Ser.: Bd. 25). vii, 544p. 1990. reprint ed. pap. write for info. (*3-487-01173-5*) G Olms Pubs.

LeGettes Calorie Encyclopedia. Bernard LeGette. 448p. 1988. mass mkt. 5.99 (*0-446-35679-4*, Pub. by Warner Bks) Little.

LeGette's Cholesterol Encyclopedia. Bernard LeGette. 256p. (Orig.). 1989. mass mkt. 3.95 (*0-446-35092-3*, Pub. by Warner Bks) Little.

LeGette's Guide to Fresh Food Shopping. Bernard LeGette. 192p. 1985. mass mkt. 2.95 (*0-446-32421-3*, Pub. by Warner Bks) Little.

Legg Calve-Perthes Disease. Ed. by John A. Herring. (Illus.). 72p. 1996. pap. 35.00 (*0-89203-122-0*) Amer Acad Ortho Surg.

Legg-Calve-Perthes Disease. Jacob F. Katz. LC 83-24780. 252p. 1984. 55.00 (*0-275-91437-2*, C1437, Praeger Pubs) Greenwood.

Legged Robots That Balance. Marc Raibert. (Artificial Intelligence Ser.). (Illus.). 256p. 1986. 35.00 (*0-262-18117-7*) MIT Pr.

***Legged Robots That Balance.** Marc Raibert. (Illus.). 233p. 2000. pap. 35.00 (*0-262-68119-6*) MIT Pr.

Leggende e Racconti Italiani: An Easy Reader for Beginners. Luigi Borelli & Mary Borelli. (C). 1989. 10.95 (*0-913298-03-4*) S F Vanni.

***Leggetts' Antiques Atlas 2000: East.** Kim Leggett. LC 98-34759. (Illus.). 418p. 1999. pap. 18.00 (*0-609-80490-1*, Three Riv Pr) Crown Pub Group.

***Leggetts' Antiques Atlas West 2000: The Guide to Antiquing in America.** Kim Leggett. (Illus.). 512p. 1999. pap. 18.00 (*0-609-80492-8*, Three Riv Pr) Crown Pub Group.

Leggetts' Antiques Atlas West, 2000 Edition: The Guide to Antiquing in America. Kim Leggett & David Leggett. (Illus.). 512p. 1999. pap. 18.00 (*0-609-80498-7*, Three Riv Pr) Crown Pub Group.

***Leggs United: The Phantom Footballer.** large type ed. Alan Durant. (Illus.). (J). 1999. pap. write for info. (*0-7540-6084-5*, Galaxy Child Lrg Print) Chivers N Amer.

Legh Family of England: The House of Lyme, from Its Foundation to the End of the 18th Century. Lady Newton. 423p. 1994. reprint ed. pap. 64.00 (*0-8328-4142-0*); reprint ed. lib. bdg. 74.00 (*0-8328-4141-2*) Higginson Bk Co.

Legi de Compozitie Interna: Poeme Cu . . . Probleme! 2nd ed. Florentin Smarandache. Ed. by Xiquan Publishing House Staff. (RUM.). 120p. (Orig.). (C). 1992. reprint ed. pap. 13.99 (*1-879585-06-5*) Erhus Univ Pr.

***Legibilities: Poems from Hollywood.** Mark Dunster. 11p. 1999. pap. 5.00 (*0-89642-663-7*) Linden Pubs.

Legibility of Print. Miles A. Tinker. LC 63-16674. 339p. reprint ed. pap. 105.10 (*0-608-14882-2*, 202614400048) Bks Demand.

Legion. Jonathan Gage. 1063p. 1995. 26.95 (*0-9639608-3-0*) Higher Ground Pub.

Legion: Civic Choruses. William Harmon. LC 72-11053. (Wesleyan Poetry Ser.). 61p. 1973. pap. 12.95 (*0-8195-1065-3*, Wesleyan Univ Pr) U Pr of New Eng.

Legion Condor, 1936-1939: A History of the Luftwaffe in the Spanish Civil War. rev. ed. Karl Ries & Hans Ring. Tr. by David Johnston from GER. LC 91-62741. (Illus.). 288p. 1992. 37.50 (*0-88740-339-5*) Schiffer.

Legion Fifty: The American Legion in Minnesota. Ben Gimmestad. 1970. 10.00 (*0-87018-022-3*) Ross.

Legion of Decency: A Sociological Analysis of the Emergence & Development of a Social Pressure Group. Paul W. Facey. LC 73-21596. (Dissertations on Film Ser.). 1974. 18.95 (*0-405-04871-8*) Ayer.

Legion of Honor. 1995. write for info. (*1-56476-928-3*, Victor Bks) Chariot Victor.

Legion of Honor. David Horton. 324p. 1995. pap. 9.99 (*1-56476-540-7*, 6-3540, Victor Bks) Chariot Victor.

Legion of Liberty & Force of Truth, Containing the Thoughts, Words, & Deeds of Some Prominent Apostles, Champions, & Martyrs. American Anti-Slavery Society Staff. LC 71-82199. (Anti-Slavery Crusade in America Ser.). (Illus.). 1970. reprint ed. 18.95 (*0-405-00605-5*) Ayer.

Legion of Super-Hero Archives, Vol. 5. Ed. by Bob Kahan. (Illus.). 224p. 1994. 49.95 (*1-56389-154-9*, Pub. by DC Comics) Time Warner.

Legion of Super-Heroes: The Beginning of Tomorrow. Mark Waid et al. (Illus.). 240p. 1999. pap. text 17.95 (*1-56389-515-3*, Pub. by DC Comics) Time Warner.

Legion of Super-Heroes Archives, Vol. 1. Ed. by Michael C. Hill. (Illus.). 256p. 1991. 49.95 (*1-56389-020-8*, Pub. by DC Comics) Time Warner.

Legion of Super-Heroes Archives, Vol. 2. Ed. by Bob Kahan. (Illus.). 224p. 1992. 49.95 (*1-56389-057-7*, Pub. by DC Comics) Time Warner.

Legion of Super-Heroes Archives, Vol. 3. Edmond Hamilton & Jerry Siegel. Ed. by Bob Kahan. (Illus.). 224p. 1993. 39.95 (*1-56389-102-6*, Pub. by DC Comics) Time Warner.

Legion of Super-Heroes Archives, Vol. 4. Jerry Siegel et al. Ed. by Bob Kahan. (Illus.). 224p. 1994. 39.95 (*1-56389-123-9*, Pub. by DC Comics) Time Warner.

Legion of Super-Heroes Archives, Vol. 6. Ed. by Bob Kahan. (Illus.). 224p. 1996. 49.95 (*1-56389-277-4*, Pub. by DC Comics) Time Warner.

Legion of Super-Heroes Archives, Vol. 7. Jim Shooter. Ed. by Bob Kahan. (Illus.). 240p. 1997. 49.95 (*1-56389-398-3*, Pub. by DC Comics) Time Warner.

Legion of Super-Heroes Archives, Vol. 9. Jim Shooter. (Illus.). 256p. 1999. mass mkt. 49.95 (*1-56389-514-5*, Pub. by DC Comics) Time Warner.

Legion of Superhero Archives, Vol. 8. Jim Shooter & Nelson Bridwell. (Illus.). 224p. 1998. 49.95 (*1-56389-430-0*, Pub. by DC Comics) Time Warner.

Legion of Superheroes, Vol. 1. Paul Levitz. 1989. pap. 10.00 (*0-912771-52-6*) Mayfair Games.

Legion of the Damned. William C. Dietz. 352p. (Orig.). 1993. mass mkt. 6.50 (*0-441-48040-3*) Ace Bks.

Legion of the Rear Guard. Conor Foley. 256p. (C). 1992. pap. 19.95 (*0-7453-0686-1*, Pub. by Pluto GBR) Stylus Pub VA.

Legion of the Rearguard. Foley. (C). 54.95 (*0-7453-0685-3*, Pub. by Pluto GBR) Stylus Pub VA.

Legionary. 2nd ed. Peter Connolly. (The Roman World Ser.). (Illus.). 32p. (J). 1998. reprint ed. pap. 9.95 (*0-19-910425-5*) OUP.

Legionella: Current Status & Emerging Perspectives. Ed. by James M. Barbaree et al. LC 92-48890. (Illus.). 390p. 1993. 79.00 (*1-55581-055-1*) ASM Pr.

Legionella: Proceedings of the 2nd International Symposium. American Society for Microbiology Staff. Ed. by Clyde Thornsberry et al. LC 83-21499. (Illus.). 385p. reprint ed. pap. 119.40 (*0-8357-7511-9*, 203600300097) Bks Demand.

Legionella & Building Services. Geoffrey W. Brundrett. LC 91-36049. (Illus.). 426p. 1992. reprint ed. pap. 132.10 (*0-608-07926-X*, 206790000012) Bks Demand.

Legionella Environmental Sampling Guide. Matthew R. Freije. LC 98-96025. 32p. 1998. pap. 24.00 (*0-9649926-6-3*, 306) HC Info Res.

Legionellae Control in Health Care Facilities: A Guide for Minimizing Risk. Matthew R. Freije. Ed. by James M. Barbaree & Rex N. Olsen. LC 95-82252. 144p. 1996. pap. 79.00 (*0-9649926-4-7*, 104) HC Info Res.

Legionellosis, Vol. I. Ed. by Sheila M. Katz. LC 85-416. 232p. 1985. 132.00 (*0-8493-5233-9*, RC152, CRC Reprint) Franklin.

Legionellosis, Vol. II. Ed. by Sheila M. Katz. 224p. 1985. 127.00 (*0-8493-5234-7*, CRC Reprint) Franklin.

Legionnaire: An Erotic Gay Novel. Tom Kvaale. 160p. (Orig.). 1996. pap. 14.95 (*0-943595-62-2*) Leyland Pubns.

Legionnaires' Disease. (Euro Reports & Studies Ser.: No. 72). 100p. 1983. pap. text 4.00 (*92-890-1238-2*) World Health.

Legionnaires' Disease: Facts, Legal Issues, Risk. Matthew R. Freije. LC 98-96023. 20p. 1998. pap. 14.00 (*0-9649926-0-4*, 301) HC Info Res.

Legionnaires' Disease: Prevention & Control. Frank Rosa. LC 92-45807. 1993. 29.95 (*0-912524-79-0*) Busn News.

Legionnaire's Journey. Leslie Aparvary. (Illus.). 324p. (Orig.). 1989. pap. 17.95 (*0-920490-93-X*) Temeron Bks.

Legion's Ladies. Judith A. Lansdowne. 304p. 1996. mass mkt. 4.50 (*0-8217-5465-3*, Zebra Kensgtn) Kensgtn Pub Corp.

Legions of Fire: The Long Night of Centauri Prime. 4th ed. Peter David. 1999. mass mkt. 6.50 (*0-345-42718-1*, Del Rey) Ballantine Pub Grp.

***Legions of Light, Armies of Darkness: From Hybrid.** Rick Smith. 1999. pap. 24.95 (*0-9655816-6-7*) Wings of Dawn.

***Legions of the Empire.** Ed. by Bill Bridges. (Illus.). 128p. 1999. pap. 19.95 (*1-888906-16-2*) Holistic Design.

Legis Law & Process. Hetzel et al. 1388p. 1992. text 52.00 (*1-55834-025-4*, 11651-10, MICHIE) LEXIS Pub.

Legiserve: Botswana. Butterworths Editorial Staff. write for info. (*0-7021-1743-9*, R177,84, Pub. by Juta & Co) Gaunt.

Legiserve: Lesotho. Butterworths Editorial Staff. write for info. (*0-7021-1745-5*, R177,84, Pub. by Juta & Co) Gaunt.

Legiserve: Namibia. Butterworths Editorial Staff. write for info. (*0-7021-1750-1*, R238,26, Pub. by Juta & Co) Gaunt.

Legiserve: Swaziland. Butterworths Editorial Staff. write for info. (*0-7021-1746-3*, R238,26, Pub. by Juta & Co) Gaunt.

Legislacion de Aguas en America Central, Caribe y Mexico Vol. 1: El Salvador, Haiti, Honduras, Jamaica, Mexico, Nicaragua, Panama, Republica Dominicana. (SPA.). 204p. 1983. 30.00 (*92-5-301981-6*, F1021, Pub. by FAO) Bernan Associates.

Legislating Bureaucratic Change: The Civil Service Reform Act of 1978. Ed. by Patricia W. Ingraham & Carolyn Ban. LC 83-26937. (SUNY Series in Public Administration). 406p. (C). 1985. text 74.50 (*0-87395-886-1*); pap. text 24.95 (*0-87395-885-3*) State U NY Pr.

Legislating Death: Socio-Legal Studies on the Brain Death Controversy in Sweden. Dimitris Michailakis. (Studia Sociologica Upsaliensia: No. 40). 254p. 1995. pap. 47.50 (*91-554-3500-9*) Coronet Bks.

Legislating for Conflict. Simon Auerbach. (Oxford Monographs on Labour Law). (Illus.). 288p. 1991. 75.00 (*0-19-825275-7*) OUP.

Legislating for Harmony: Partnership Under the Children Act, 1989. Ed. by Felicity Kaganas & Michael King. LC 95-211369. 200p. 1995. pap. 29.95 (*1-85302-328-0*) Taylor & Francis.

Legislating Medical Ethics: A Study of the New York State Do-Not-Resuscitate Law. Ed. by Robert Baker. LC 94-19575. (Philosophy & Medicine Ser.: 48). 476p. (C). 1995. lib. bdg. 220.50 (*0-7923-2995-3*, Pub. by Kluwer Academic) Kluwer Academic.

Legislating Morality. Norman L. Geisler. LC 99-6384. 272p. 1999. pap. text 11.99 (*0-7642-2228-7*) Bethany Hse.

Legislating Morality: Private Choices on the Public Agenda. Ed. by Kim E. Shienbaum. 256p. 1988. 32.95 (*0-87073-689-2*); pap. 22.95 (*0-87073-690-6*) Schenkman Bks Inc.

Legislating Privacy: Technology, Social Values, & Public Policy. Priscilla M. Regan. LC 94-49544. 1995. 39.95 (*0-8078-2226-4*) U of NC Pr.

Legislating Revolution: The Contract with America in its First 100 Days. James G. Gimpel. LC 95-38907. 224p. (C). 1995. pap. text 31.60 (*0-205-18887-7*) Allyn.

Legislating the Criminal Code: Corruption. (Law Commission Consultation Papers: Series 81022805, No. 248). 1998. 40.00 (*0-10-288298-3*, HM82983, Pub. by Statnry Office) Bernan Associates.

Legislating the Criminal Code: Misuse of Trade Secrets: Law Commission Consultation, Paper No. 150. LC 98-193670. (Law Commission (Gt Britain) Consultation Papers Ser.: No. 81022805). 1997. 45.00 (*0-11-730235-X*, HM0235X, Pub. by Statnry Office) Bernan Associates.

***Legislating the Holocaust.** Schleunes. 2000. 55.00 (*0-8133-3775-5*, Pub. by Westview) HarpC.

Legislating the Revolution: The Contract with America in Its First 100 Days. James G. Gimpel. 180p. (C). 1996. 25.00 (*0-205-19935-6*) Allyn.

Legislating Together: The White House & Capitol Hill from Eisenhower to Reagan. Mark A. Peterson. 1990. pap. 19.50 (*0-674-52416-0*) HUP.

Legislating Together: The White House & Capitol Hill from Eisenhower to Reagan. Mark A. Peterson. (Illus.). 352p. 1990. 46.50 (*0-674-52415-2*) HUP.

Legislation: Statutes & the Creation of Public Policy. William N. Eskridge, Jr. & Philip P. Frickey. 937p. (C). 1992. reprint ed. teacher ed. write for info. (*0-318-62701-9*) West Pub.

***Legislation & Background of the Indian Reorganization Act.** Elmer R. Rusco. LC 00-8554. (Wilbur S. Shepperson Series in History & Humanities). 360p. 2000. 44.95 (*0-87417-345-0*) U of Nev Pr.

Legislation & Justice. Ed. by Antonio Padoa-Schioppa. (The Origins of the Modern State in Europe Ser.). 454p. 1997. text 95.00 (*0-19-820546-5*) OUP.

Legislation & the Courts. Ed. by Michael D. Freeman. LC 96-39522. (Issues In Law & Society Ser.). 176p. 1997. text 76.95 (*1-85521-846-1*, Pub. by Dartmth Pub); pap. text 28.95 (*1-85521-853-4*, Pub. by Dartmth Pub) Ashgate Pub Co.

Legislation & the Public Schools: Making It Work. Lawrence A. Wiget. LC 97-69146. (Fastback Ser.: No. 420). 45p. 1997. pap. 3.00 (*0-87367-620-3*, FB#420) Phi Delta Kappa.

Legislation by Members in the Indian Parliament. R. C. Bhardwaj. LC 95-900347. (C). 1994. 30.00 (*81-7023-409-3*, Pub. by Allied Pubs) S Asia.

Legislation Civile de la Revolution, 1789-1804. Philippe Sagnac. LC 75-174800. reprint ed. 55.00 (*0-404-07168-6*) AMS Pr.

Legislation Concerning Immigrant Issues: Hearing Before the Subcommittee on Immigration & Claims of the Committee on the Judiciary, House of Representatives, One Hundred Fifth Congress, First Session, On H.r. 231, H.r. 429, H.r. 471 & H.r. 1493, May 13, 1997. LC 98-160859. iv, 110 p. 1997. write for info. (*0-16-056240-6*) USGPO.

Legislation for Europe, 1992. Ed. by Jurgen Schwarze. (ENG & FRE.). 162p. 1989. pap. 54.00 (*3-7890-1827-9*, Pub. by Nomos Verlags) Intl Bk Import.

Legislation for Personnel Managers: A Checklist. Compiled by Erich Suter. 96p. (C). 1985. 35.00 (*0-85292-350-3*, Pub. by IPM Hse) St Mut.

Legislation for Press, Film & Radio: Comparative Study of the Main Types of Regulations Governing the Information Media. Fernand Terrou & Lucien Solal. LC 72-4680. (International Propaganda & Communications Ser.). 420p. 1972. reprint ed. 29.95 (*0-405-04764-9*) Ayer.

Legislation Forestiere au Cap-Vert, en Ethiopie, en Gambie, au Mali & en Mauritanie, au Niger, au Rwanda & au Senegal. (FRE.). 105p. 1986. 14.00 (*92-5-202309-7*, FF24, Pub. by FAO) Bernan Associates.

***Legislation of Congress for the Government of the Organized Territories of the United States 1789-1895.** Max Farrand. iv,101p. 2000. reprint ed. 45.00 (*1-57588-637-5*) W S Hein.

Legislation of Direct Elections to the European Parliament. Valentine Herman & Mark Hagger. 336p. 1980. text 82.95 (*0-566-00247-7*) Ashgate Pub Co.

Legislation on Dangerous Substances: Classification & Labelling in the European Communities, 2 vols., Vol. 1-2. Ed. by D. Perry. (C). 1987. lib. bdg. 153.00 (*0-86010-960-7*, Pub. by Graham & Trotman) Kluwer Academic.

Legislation on Dispute Resolution: 1990/1991 Addendum to the 1989 Dispute Resolution Legislative Monograph. 88p. 1992. pap. 20.00 (*0-89707-808-X*, 474-0048) Amer Bar Assn.

Legislation on Equal Opportunities & Full Participation in Development for Disabled Persons Examples from the Escap Region. Economic Commission for Europe. 522p. 1997. pap. 60.00 (*92-1-119789-9*) UN.

***Legislation on Foreign Relations Through 1996, Current Legislation & Related Executive Orders, November 1997, Vol.3.** Government Printing Office Staff. 1461p. 1998. per. 60.00 (*0-16-055861-1*) USGPO.

Legislation on Foreign Relations Through 1997 Vol. 1-B: Current Legislation & Related Executive Orders, April 1998. 1266p. 1998. pap. 62.00 (*0-16-056579-0*) USGPO.

***Legislation on Foreign Relations Through 1997, March 1998, Current Legislation & Related Executive Orders.** Dianne E. Rennack. 820p. 1998. per. 37.00 (*0-16-056344-5*) USGPO.

***Legislation on Foreign Relations Through 1998, March 1999, Current Legislation & Related Executive Orders.** Diane E. Rennack. 881p. 1999. per. 41.00 (*0-16-058495-7*) USGPO.

***Legislation on Foreign Relations Through 1999: Current Legislation & Related Executive Orders, March 2000, Vol. 1a.** Dianne E. Rennack. 937p. 2000. per. 47.00 (*0-16-060502-4*) USGPO.

Legislation on Insanity. George L. Harrison. LC 96-77453. ii, iv, 1119p. 1996. reprint ed. 105.00 (*1-57588-119-5*, 310700) W S Hein.

Legislation on the Rehabilitation of Disabled People in Sixteen Member States of the Council of Europe. 4th ed. Council of Europe Staff. 1990. 25.00 (*92-871-1870-1*, Pub. by Council of Europe) Manhattan Pub Co.

Legislation on the Rehabilitation of People with Disabilities in Sixteen Member States of the Council of Europe. 5th ed. 1993. 25.00 (*92-871-2316-0*, Pub. by Council of Europe) Manhattan Pub Co.

Legislation on Vacccination in the Member States of the European Economic Community. R. Senault & M. Manciaux. (International Digest of Health Legislation Offprints: Vol. 16, No. 2). 32p. 1965. 3.00 (*92-4-169162-X*) World Health.

Legislation on Women's Employment in Latin America: A Comparative Study. M. D. Calvo. LC 97-109125. (Occasional Papers: Vol. 11). iv, 57p. 1996. pap. 13.50 (*92-2-109509-6*) Intl Labour Office.

Legislation Statutes & the Creation of Public Policy. 2nd ed. William N. Eskridge & Philip P. Frickey. (American Casebook Ser.). 150p. (C). 1995. pap. text, teacher ed. write for info. (*0-314-05984-9*) West Pub.

Legislation sur l'Homologation des Pesticides. (FRE.). 104p. 1994. 12.00 (*92-5-203137-5*, FF1375, Pub. by FAO) Bernan Associates.

Legislation to Preempt State Motor Carrier Regulations Pertaining to Rates, Routes, & Services: Hearing Before the Subcommittee on Surface Transportation of the Committee on Public Works & Transportation, House of Representatives, One Hundred Third Congress, Second Session, July 20, 1994. USGPO Staff. LC 95-164930. xvi, 570p. 1994. write for info. (*0-16-046432-3*) USGPO.

Legislations: The Politics of Deconstruction. Geoffrey Bennington. LC 93-46858. 256p. (C). 1994. pap. 20.00 (*0-86091-668-5*, Pub. by Verso) Norton.

Legislative Action to Combat the World Tobacco Epidemic. 2nd ed. R. Roemer. (ENG, FRE & SPA.). xiii, 297p. 1993. pap. text 59.00 (*92-4-156157-2*, 1152202) World Health.

Legislative Actions in Forests Policy & Planning: Four States' Experiences. 12p. 1985. 4.00 (*0-317-45860-4*, RM 751) Coun State Govts.

Legislative Activities of the House Banking Committee, 1989-1994 United States Staff. LC 95-131756. 16 p. 1994. write for info. (*0-16-046031-X*) USGPO.

Legislative Analysis & Drafting. William P. Statsky. (Illus.). 217p. (C). 1984. pap. text, teacher ed. write for info. (*0-314-76096-2*) West Pub.

Legislative Analysis & Drafting. 2nd ed. William P. Statsky. (Illus.). 217p. (C). 1984. text 42.50 (*0-314-77815-2*) West Pub.

Legislative Analyst. Jack Rudman. (Career Examination Ser.: C-3065). 1994. pap. 34.95 (*0-8373-3065-3*) Nat Learn.

Legislative & Administrative Processes. 2nd ed. Hans A. Linde et al. LC 81-4738. (University Casebook Ser.). 887p. 1991. reprint ed. text 37.00 (*0-88277-026-8*) Foundation Pr.

Legislative & Documentary History of the Bank of the United States: Including the Original Bank of North America. Compiled by Matthew S. Clarke & D. A. Hall. LC 67-23017. (Library of Money & Banking History). 832p. 1967. reprint ed. 87.50 (*0-678-00269-X*) Kelley.

Legislative & Judicial History of the 15th Amendment. John M. Matthews. LC 77-129081. (American Constitutional & Legal History Ser). 1971. reprint ed. 22.50 (*0-306-70063-8*) Da Capo.

Legislative & Policy Environment. Ed. by Sergio Haddad. 192p. 1998. pap. text 44.00 (*0-7923-4658-0*) Kluwer Academic.

***Legislative & Regulatory Initiatives for the 106th Congress.** 96p. 1999. pap. 19.95 (*1-55810-145-4*, 9904LR) Am Nurses Pub.

Legislative Assemblies. Robert Luce. LC 73-5617. (American Constitutional & Legal History Ser). 692p. 1974. reprint ed. lib. bdg. 75.00 (*0-306-70583-4*) Da Capo.

Legislative Authority over the Enacted Budget. Corina L. Eckl. 100p. 1992. pap. text 25.00 (*1-55516-551-6*, 5319) Natl Conf State Legis.

Legislative Base: Maternal & Child Health Services Block Grant. National Center for Education in Maternal and Child Health (U.S.). 608p. 1996. pap. write for info. (*1-57285-036-1*) Nat Ctr Educ.

***Legislative Budget Procedures: A Guide to Appropriations & Budget Processes in the States, Commonwealths & Territories.** Jennifer Grooters et al. LC 98-222508. 1998. write for info. (*1-55516-791-8*) Natl Conf State Legis.

An Asterisk (*) at the beginning of an entry indicates that the title is appearing for the first time.

Legislative Budget Procedures in the 50 States: A Guide to Appropriations & Budget Processes. Tony Hutchison & Kathy James. Ed. by Sharon Schwoch. (C). 1988. pap. text 25.00 (*1-55516-542-7*, 5312) Natl Conf State Legis.

Legislative Connection: The Politics of Representation in Kenya, Korea & Turkey. Chong Lim Kim et al. LC 83-20725. (Duke Press Policy Studies). (Illus.). xvii, 237p. 1984. text 54.95 (*0-8223-0534-8*) Duke.

Legislative Control of the Elementary Curriculum. Jesse K. Flanders. LC 75-176777. (Columbia University, Teachers College, Contributions to Education Ser.: No. 195). 1995. reprint ed. 37.50 (*0-404-55195-5*) AMS Pr.

Legislative Council in the American States, 18. William J. Siffin. LC 82-1016. (Indiana University Publications Social Science: No. 18). 266p. 1982. reprint ed. lib. bdg. 65.00 (*0-313-23486-8*, SILE, Greenwood Pr) Greenwood.

Legislative Districts on Profile: A Demographic & Socio-Economic Data Book. Jennifer Shultz. 90p. 1993. pap. write for info. (*0-939667-27-4*) Penn State Data Ctr.

Legislative Drafter's Desk Reference. Lawrence Filson. LC 92-16062. 450p. 1992. 112.00 (*0-87187-670-1*) Congr Quarterly.

Legislative Drafter's Desk Reference. Lawrence Filson. LC 92-16062. 450p. 1994. pap. text 45.95 (*1-56802-008-2*) Congr Quarterly.

Legislative Drafting. V. C. Crabbe. 318p. 1994. 60.00 (*1-874241-15-5*, Pub. by Cavendish Pubng) Gaunt.

Legislative Drafting. 4th ed. G. C. Thornton. 470p. 1996. 118.00 (*0-406-04521-6*, MICHIE) LEXIS Pub.

Legislative Drafting for Market Reform: Some Lessons from China. Robert B. Seidman et al. LC 97-1720. (International Political Economy Ser.). 208p. 1997. text 55.00 (*0-312-17456-X*) St Martin.

Legislative Education Leadership in the States. Alan Rosenthal & Susan Fuhrman. 118p. 1981. pap. 8.00 (*0-318-03014-4*); lib. bdg. 14.00 (*0-318-03013-6*) Inst Educ Lead.

Legislative Elections in 1996 & the Democratic Crisis in Lebanon. LCPS Staff. (ARA., Illus.). 680p. 1998. pap. write for info. (*1-886604-16-9*) Lebanese Ctr.

***Legislative Entrepreneurship in the U.S. House of Representatives.** Gregory Wawro. (Illus.). 208p. (C). 2000. text 39.50 (*0-472-11153-1*, 11153) U of Mich Pr.

Legislative Guidance for Comprehensive State Groundwater Protection Programs. Larry Morandi. (State Legislative Reports: Vol. 19, No. 3). 10p. 1994. 15.00 (*1-55516-405-6*, 7302-1903) Natl Conf State Legis.

Legislative Handbook for the Practice of Acupuncture & Oriental Medicine. Barbara B. Mitchell. 62p. 1995. 18.00 (*0-9670262-4-5*) Natl Acup Fndt.

Legislative Hearing on H. R. 3267--The "Sonny Bono Memorial Salton Sea Reclamation Act" Hearing Before the Subcommittee on Water & Power of the Committee on Resources, House of Representatives, 105th Congress, Second Session, March 12, 1998, Washington, D. C. LC 98-176462. iv, 169p. 1998. write for info. (*0-16-056489-1*) USGPO.

Legislative History: Research for the Interpretation of Laws. Gwendolyn B. Folsom. viii, 136p. 1979. reprint ed. 25.00 (*0-8377-0532-0*, Rothman) W S Hein.

Legislative History & Analysis of the Civil Rights Restoration Act, 9 vols. Compiled by Jon S. Schultz. 5632p. 1989. 750.00 (*0-8377-1155-X*, Rothman) W S Hein.

Legislative History of America's Economic Policy Toward the Philippines. Jose S. Reyes. LC 23-11140. (Columbia University. Studies in the Social Sciences: No. 240). reprint ed. 20.00 (*0-404-51240-2*) AMS Pr.

Legislative History of Federal Rules of Evidence: Legislative Histories & Related Documents. Ed. by Oscar M. Trelles. LC 79-57110. 1980. lib. bdg. 120.00 (*0-89941-051-0*) W S Hein.

Legislative History of Naturalization in the United States from the Revolutionary War to 1861. Frank G. Franklin. LC 69-18776. (American Immigration Collection. Series 1). 1969. reprint ed. 16.95 (*0-405-00524-5*) Ayer.

Legislative History of Naturalization in the United States from the Revolutionary War to 1861. Frank G. Franklin. LC 75-119538. lx, 309p. 1971. reprint ed. 15.00 (*0-678-00689-X*) Kelley.

Legislative History of New York Consumer Law. 32p. 1987. pap. 3.75 (*0-317-03752-8*, 42,454) NCLS Inc.

Legislative History of Public Law. 1991. lib. bdg. 79.95 (*0-8490-5108-8*) Gordon Pr.

***Legislative History of Recent Primary Safety Belt Laws.** N. Russell. 76p. 1999. per. 6.00 (*0-16-049930-5*) USGPO.

***Legislative History of Recent Primary Safety Belt Laws.** N. Russell et al. 62p. (C). 2000. pap. text 20.00 (*0-7881-8857-7*) DIANE Pub.

Legislative History of Reconstruction see Political History of Slavery in the United States

Legislative History of the Americans with Disabilities Act. Ed. by G. John Tysse. 903p. 1990. 100.00 (*0-916559-28-9*, 2022-MO-4035) EPF.

Legislative History of the Americans with Disabilities Act. Ed. by G. John Tysse. LC 91-23121. 915p. 1991. reprint ed. ring bd. 85.00 (*0-934753-54-7*) LRP Pubns.

***Legislative History of the Balanced Budget Act of 1997.** Ed. by Pitman B. Potter. LC 99-48877. 2000. 4295.00 (*1-57588-557-3*) W S Hein.

Legislative History of the Carriage of Goods by Sea Act: And the Travaux Preparatoires of the Hague Rules, 3 vols. Tr. by Caroline Boyle. 1991. 225.00 (*0-8377-1166-5*, Rothman) W S Hein.

Legislative History of the Carriage of Goods by Sea Act & the Travaux Preparatoires of the Hague Rules, 3 vols., Set. Ed. by Michael F. Sturley. Tr. by Caroline Boyle. 1991. lib. bdg. 225.00 (*0-8377-1163-0*, Rothman) W S Hein.

Legislative History of the Clean Air Act Amendments of 1990, 6 vols. in 11 bks. U. S. Government Printing Office Staff. LC 98-35698. 1998. reprint ed. 995.00 (*1-57588-430-5*, 311700) W S Hein.

Legislative History of the Communications Act of 1934. Ed. by Max D. Paglin. (Illus.). 1008p. 1990. text 125.00 (*0-19-504915-2*) OUP.

***Legislative History of the Employee Retirement Income Security Act of 1974, 3.** Committee on Labor & Public Welfare Staff. 2000. reprint ed. 550.00 (*1-57588-623-5*, 324220) W S Hein.

Legislative History of the Financial Institutions Reform, Recovery, & Enforcement Act of 1989, 39 vols. Ed. by Bernard D. Reams, Jr. 1998. 4250.00 (*1-57588-416-X*, 310950) W S Hein.

Legislative History of the Immigration Act of 1990 Public Law 101-649, 23 vols. Ed. by Igor I. Kavass & Bernard D. Reams, Jr. LC 97-70276. 1997. 2100.00 (*1-57588-205-1*, 311100) W S Hein.

Legislative History of the International Antitrust Enforcement Assistance Act of 1994, Pub. L. No. 103-438, 3 vols. Ed. by Bernard D. Reams, Jr. & William H. Manz. LC 97-80026. 1997. 295.00 (*1-57588-392-9*, 310970) W S Hein.

Legislative History of the Model Rules of Professional Conduct: Their Development in the ABA House of Delegates. ABA, House of Delegates. 216p. 1987. 39.95 (*0-318-36467-0*, 561-0078); pap. 29.95 (*0-318-36468-9*) Amer Bar Assn.

Legislative History of the 1909 Copyright Act, 6 vols., Set. Ed. by E. Fulton Brylawski & Abe Goldman. 1976. text 325.00 (*0-8377-0806-0*, Rothman) W S Hein.

Legislative History of the Pennsylvania Solid Waste Management Act of 1980. Joel Fishman & Ann Orsag. Vol. 2. 1982. write for info. (*0-318-58240-6*) Allegheny Co Bar.

Legislative History of the Prison Litigation Reform Act of 1996 Public Law 104-134, 2 vols. Ed. by Bernard D. Reams, Jr. & William H. Manz. LC 97-80292. 1997. 195.00 (*1-57588-405-4*, 310980) W S Hein.

Legislative History of the Taiwan Relations Act Vol. 3: An Analytic Compilation with Documents on Subsequent Developments. rev. ed. Illus. by Lester L. Wolff et al. ixii, 440p. 1999. 14.95 (*0-9671650-0-8*) Pacific Community.

Perhaps the most overlooked element of U.S. China policy, the Taiwan Relations Act requires this country to maintain traditional relations with the Republic of China on Taiwan. It was passed & enacted on April 10, 1979, signed into law by President Jimmy Carter, whose recognition of the People's Republic of China made the TRA necessary. Since then, the TRA as the law of the land has governed the U.S. special relationship with the ROC on Taiwan. The Taiwan Relations Act is significant because of the complex issues surrounding American withdrawal of recognition from the Republic of China, & Taiwan's status in American & international law. This Legislative History contains excerpts from the Congressional Record pertaining to the Taiwan Relations Act during the 103rd, 104th & 105th terms of Congress. Includes original text of the TRA, President Carter's Executive Order of June 22, 1979, on "Maintaining unofficial relations with the people on Taiwan, " indices, & recent assessments of Taiwan's political-military situation. Despite domestic political differences, the TRA has maintained a bipartisan Congressional approach to U.S. - Taiwan relations, stabilizing U.S. policy toward East Asia Paper. ISBN 0-9671650-0-8. US$ $14.95 plus $4.00 shipping/handling. Order from the International Information Agency, Inc., 2111 Jeff Davis Highway Suite 505N, Arlington, VA 22202. 703/415-0947 fax 703/415-0585 *Publisher Paid Annotation.*

Legislative History of United States Tax Conventions, 18 vols., Set. Sidney I. Roberts. (Roberts & Holland Collection). 1986. ring bd. 2295.00 (*0-89941-379-X*, 303850) W S Hein.

***Legislative Institutions & Ideology in Chile.** John B. Londregan. (Political Economy of Institutions & Decisions Ser.). (Illus.). 328p. (C). 2000. 59.95 (*0-521-77084-X*) Cambridge U Pr.

Legislative Intent & Other Essays on Politics, Law, & Morality. Gerald C. MacCallum, Jr. Ed. by Marcus G. Singer & Rex Martin. LC 93-841. 288p. (C). 1993. text 45.00 (*0-299-13860-7*) U of Wis Pr.

Legislative Intent in New York State. Robert A. Carter. 57p. 1981. 5.00 (*0-318-01525-0*) NYS Library.

Legislative Journals of the Council of Colonial Virginia. 2nd ed. Ed. by Henry R. McIlwaine. LC 79-13108. xii, 1646p. 1979. reprint ed. 50.00 (*0-88490-078-9*) Library of VA.

Legislative-Judicial Relations: Seeking a New Partnership. (State Legislative Reports: Vol. 15, No. 14). 10p. 1990. 15.00 (*1-55516-270-3*, 7302-1514) Natl Conf State Legis.

Legislative Law & Process: Cases & Materials. 2nd ed. Otto J. Hetzel. 1993. write for info. (*0-318-69713-0*, MICHIE) LEXIS Pub.

Legislative Law & Process in a Nutshell. 2nd ed. Jack Davies. LC 86-7768. (Nutshell Ser.). 346p. (C). 1986. reprint ed. pap. 21.00 (*0-314-21437-2*) West Pub.

Legislative Leadership in the American States. Malcolm E. Jewell & Marcia L. Whicker. LC 94-3064. 240p. (C). 1994. text 47.50 (*0-472-10517-5*, 10517) U of Mich Pr.

Legislative Learning: The 104th Republican Freshmen in the House. Timothy J. Barnett. (Politics & Policy in American Institutions Ser.: Vol. 3). 256p. 1999. 60.00 (*0-8153-3362-5*, SS1414) Garland.

Legislative Leviathan: Party Government in the House. Gary W. Cox & Mathew D. McCubbins. 289p. 1993. pap. 17.95 (*0-520-07220-0*, Pub. by U CA Pr) Cal Prin Full Svc.

Legislative Leviathan: Party Government in the House. Gary W. Cox & Mathew D. McCubbins. 289p. 1994. 55.00 (*0-520-07219-7*, Pub. by U CA Pr) Cal Prin Full Svc.

Legislative Modernization: A Choice for South Dakota Voters in 1974. Michael P. Ortner. 1974. 1.00 (*1-55614-060-6*) U of SD Gov Res Bur.

Legislative Options for Cannabis in Australia David McDonald. LC 96-132275. (Monograph Series). xviii, 110 p. 1994. write for info. (*0-644-35086-5*) AGPS Pr.

Legislative Origins of American Foreign Policy, 5 vols. Ed. by Richard D. Challener. Incl. Vol. 1. Proceedings, April 7, 1913 to March 7, 1923. 415p. 1979. lib. bdg. 53.00 (*0-8240-3030-3*); Vol. 2. Proceedings, December 3, 1923 to March 3, 1933. 279p. 1979. lib. bdg. 37.00 (*0-8240-3031-1*); Vol. 3. Legislative Origins of the Truman Doctrine, March to April, 1947. 235p. 1979. 30.00 (*0-8240-3032-X*); Vol. 4. Foreign Relief Aid, 1947. 401p. 1979. lib. bdg. 48.00 (*0-8240-3033-8*); Vol. 5. Foreign Relief Assistance Act of 1948. 809p. 1979. lib. bdg. 86.00 (*0-8240-3034-6*); 1979. write for info. (*0-318-52530-5*) Garland.

Legislative Origins of the National Aeroneutics & Space Act of 1958: Proceedings of an Oral History Workshop Conducted April 3, 1992. John M. Logsdon. (Monographs in Aerospace History: No. 8). (Illus.). 84p. 1998. pap. 7.00 (*0-16-049641-1*) USGPO.

Legislative Origins of the Truman Doctrine, March to April, 1947 see Legislative Origins of American Foreign Policy

Legislative Oversight of Federal Funds. Arturo Perez. (Legislative Finance Papers: No. 5101-98). 13p. 1995. 10.00 (*0-614-10575-7*) Natl Conf State Legis.

Legislative Participation in Implementation: Policy Through Politics. Marcus E. Ethridge. LC 85-6496. 188p. 1985. 57.95 (*0-275-90095-9*, C0095, Praeger Pubs) Greenwood.

Legislative Party Campaign Committees in the American States. Anthony Gierzynski. LC 91-26935. 160p. 1992. text 28.00 (*0-8131-1771-2*) U Pr of Ky.

Legislative Performance in the States: Explorations of Committee Behavior. Alan Rosenthal. LC 73-10576. 1974. 14.95 (*0-02-927300-5*) Free Pr.

Legislative Perspectives: A 150-Year History of the Oregon Legislatures from 1843-1993. Douglas Heider & David Dietz. LC 95-10673. (Illus.). 227p. (Orig.). 1995. pap. 15.95 (*0-87595-257-7*) Oregon Hist.

***Legislative Politics in the Arab World: The Resurgence of Democratic Institutions.** Abdo Baaklini et al. LC 98-46654. 278p. 1999. pap. 22.50 (*1-55587-840-7*); lib. bdg. 59.95 (*1-55587-839-3*) L Rienner.

Legislative Power & Healthy People. Vigdor Schreibman. LC 87-6206. (Essays on the Impact of the Constitution & Legal System on American Life & Government Ser.: No. 5). (Illus.). 81p. (Orig.). 1987. pap. 19.00 (*0-942539-10-9*) Amicas Pubns.

Legislative Precedents, Vol. II. Justice Crabbe. 268p. 1998. 117.00 (*1-85941-421-4*) Gaunt.

Legislative Priorities for Policy Assistance. Ed. by Randy Huwa & Alan Rosenthal. 59p. 1976. pap. text 19.95 (*0-685-54931-3*) Transaction Pubs.

Legislative Problems. Robert Luce. LC 76-152834. (American Constitutional & Legal History Ser). 1971. reprint ed. lib. bdg. 75.00 (*0-306-70153-7*) Da Capo.

Legislative Process. Abner J. Mikva. LC 94-74421. 1104p. 1995. 62.00 (*0-316-56987-9*) Aspen Pub.

Legislative Process. Abner J. Mikva & Eric Lane. 1104p. 1995. teacher ed. write for info. (*0-316-56968-2*, 69682) Aspen Law.

Legislative Process. abr. ed. John M. Kernochan. LC 80-70768. 64p. (C). 1991. reprint ed. pap. text 8.95 (*0-88277-023-3*) Foundation Pr.

Legislative Process & Drafting U. S. Law Schools. Bernard Lammers. LC 77-79655. ix, 86p. 1977. 20.00 (*0-910058-87-3*, 304940) W S Hein.

Legislative Process in the European Community. Philip Raworth. LC 93-7393. 1993. 68.00 (*90-6544-690-7*) Kluwer Law Intl.

Legislative Proposals about Crime & Criminal Justice: Special Edition of the Texas Crime Poll, 1980. Glen A. Kercher et al. 61p. 1981. write for info. (*0-318-57033-5*) S Houston Corrections.

Legislative Proposals Relating to Counterintelligence: Hearing Before the Permanent Select Committee on Intelligence, House of Representatives, One Hundred Third Congress, Second Session, May 4, 1994. United States. LC 95-177676. 166 p. 1995. write for info. (*0-16-047073-0*) USGPO.

Legislative Reference Services & Sources. Kathleen Low. LC 93-39408. 100p. 1994. lib. bdg. 39.95 (*1-56024-891-2*) Haworth Pr.

Legislative Reform. Ed. by Leroy N. Rieselbach. 272p. (C). 1978. pap. 15.00 (*0-918592-21-6*) Pol Studies.

Legislative Reform: The Policy Impact. Ed. by Leroy N. Rieselbach. 272p. 1985. reprint ed. lib. bdg. 42.00 (*0-8191-5157-2*) U Pr of Amer.

Legislative Report on the Minnesota Compulsive Gambling Treatment Program. (Illus.). 105p. (Orig.). (C). 1994. pap. text 35.00 (*0-7881-1079-9*) DIANE Pub.

Legislative Representation in the Contemporary South. Malcolm E. Jewell. LC 67-26487. 151p. reprint ed. pap. 46.90 (*0-608-12750-7*, 202340500033) Bks Demand.

Legislative Requirement under the Clear Air Act Amendments of 1990. Jackie Cummins. (State Legislative Reports: Vol. 18, No. 2). 7p. 1993. 15.00 (*1-55516-299-1*, 7302-1802) Natl Conf State Legis.

Legislative Responses to AIDS. Ed. by World Health Organization Staff. (C). 1989. lib. bdg. 113.50 (*0-7923-0128-5*) Kluwer Academic.

Legislative Responses to Organ Transplantation. Ed. by World Health Organization Staff. LC 92-48521. 534p. (C). 1994. lib. bdg. 187.50 (*0-7923-2147-2*) Kluwer Academic.

Legislative Responses to Tobacco Use. Ed. by World Health Organization Staff. 264p. 1991. lib. bdg. 104.00 (*0-7923-1149-3*) Kluwer Academic.

Legislative Review of Administrative Rules & Regulations. 42p. 1990. 10.00 (*1-55516-736-5*, 7129) Natl Conf State Legis.

Legislative Role in Revenue & Demographic Forecasting. Tony Hutchinson. (Legislative Finance Papers: No. 58). (C). 1987. pap. 6.25 (*1-55516-058-1*, 5101-58) Natl Conf State Legis.

Legislative Sourcebook on the Environment. Jeffrey Tryens. 300p. 1986. 14.95 (*0-89788-089-7*) CPA Washington.

Legislative Sourcebook on Toxics. Ed. by David Jones. 250p. 1986. 14.95 (*0-89788-092-7*) CPA Washington.

Legislative Strategy: Shaping Public Policy. Edward V. Schneier & Bertram M. Gross. LC 92-50019. 289p. (C). 1993. pap. text 25.95 (*0-312-05192-1*) St Martin.

Legislative Struggle: A Study in Social Combat. Bertram M. Gross. LC 77-18784. 472p. 1978. reprint ed. lib. bdg. 79.50 (*0-313-20205-2*, GRLS, Greenwood Pr) Greenwood.

Legislative Television Programming in the States. Mary Renstrom. (State Legislative Reports: Vol. 17, No. 13). 16p. 1992. pap. text 15.00 (*1-55516-284-3*, 7302-1713) Natl Conf State Legis.

Legislative Term Limits: Public Choice Perspectives. Ed. by Bernard N. Grofman. LC 95-52837. (Studies in Public Choice: Vol. 10). 416p. (C). 1996. lib. bdg. 139.00 (*0-7923-9702-9*) Kluwer Academic.

Legislative Theatre: Using Performance to Make Politics. Augusto Boal. LC 98-37221. (Illus.). 224p. (C). (gr. 13). 1998. 75.00 (*0-415-18240-9*, D6202) Routledge.

Legislative Theatre: Using Performance to Make Politics. Augusto Boal. Tr. by Adrian Jackson. LC 98-37221. xiv, 254 p. 1999. pap. 22.99 (*0-415-18241-7*, D6206) Routledge.

Legislative Trends in Insurance Regulation. Douglas Caddy. LC 84-40562. 256p. 1986. 19.95 (*0-89096-222-7*) Tex A&M Univ Pr.

Legislative Turnover. Janet Gates & Charles O. Jones. 1957. write for info. (*0-318-56131-X*) U of SD Gov Res Bur.

Legislative Way of Life: Being the Course of Lectures Delivered at Westminster College, Fulton, Missouri, 1940. Thomas Smith. LC JF0511.S57. (Midway Reprint Ser.). 111p. reprint ed. pap. 34.50 (*0-608-16152-7*, 202406800035) Bks Demand.

Legislative Zoning Decisions: Legal Aspects. 2nd ed. David W. Owens. LC 99-229827. (C). 1999. text 42.00 (*1-56011-341-3*); pap. text 36.00 (*1-56011-336-7*) Institute Government.

Legislator: German Parliament As a Centre of Political Decision-Making. Klaus Von Beyme. LC 98-18565. (Illus.). 180p. 1998. text 72.95 (*1-84014-433-5*, JN3971.A71B44, Pub. by Ashgate Pub) Ashgate Pub Co.

Legislator of the World: Writings in Codification, Law & Education. Jeremy Bentham. Ed. by Philip Schofield & Jonathan Harris. LC 99-198145. (The Collection Works of Jeremy Bentham). 508p. 1999. text 110.00 (*0-19-820747-6*) OUP.

Legislators & Interpreters: On Modernity, Post-Modernity, & Intellectuals. Zygmunt Bauman. LC 87-47721. 226p. (C). 1987. 45.00 (*0-8014-2104-7*) Cornell U Pr.

Legislators & Politicians: Iowa's Women Lawmakers. Suzanne O. Schenken. LC 95-14434. (Illus.). 256p. 1995. text 32.95 (*0-8138-2277-7*) Iowa St U Pr.

Legislators, Law, & Public Policy: Political Change in Mississippi & the South, 267. Mary D. Coleman. LC 90-38422. (Contributions in Political Science Ser.: No. 267). 200p. 1993. 52.95 (*0-313-27271-9*, CPJ, Greenwood Pr) Greenwood.

Legislators, Leaders, & Lawmaking: The U. S. House of Representatives in the Postreform Era. Barbara Sinclair. LC 94-33953. 320p. 1995. text 39.95 (*0-8018-4955-1*) Johns Hopkins.

Legislators, Leaders, & Lawmaking: The U. S. House of Representatives in the Postreform Era. Barbara Sinclair. 392p. 1998. reprint ed. pap. text 17.95 (*0-8018-5712-0*) Johns Hopkins.

Legislators of the Massachusetts General Court: A Biographical Dictionary. John A. Schutz. LC 97-5651. 608p. 1997. text 75.00 (*1-55553-304-3*) NE U Pr.

Legislature: California's School for Politics. William K. Muir, Jr. LC 82-16128. xvi, 220p. 1995. pap. text 9.95 (*0-226-54626-8*) U Ch Pr.

Legislature As an Organization: A Study of the Kansas Legislature. Marvin A. Harder & Raymond G. Davis. LC 78-25721. x, 186p. 1979. pap. 12.95 (*0-7006-0187-2*) U Pr of KS.

L

An Asterisk (*) at the beginning of an entry indicates that the title is appearing for the first time.

Legislature Comes of Age: Hong Kong's Search for Influence & Indentity. Kathleen Cheek-Milby. 334p. 1995. text 55.00 (*0-19-585955-3*) OUP.

Legislature of the Province of Virginia. Elmer I. Miller. LC 08-1371. (Columbia University. Studies in the Social Sciences: No. 76). reprint ed. 32.50 (*0-404-51076-0*) AMS Pr.

Legislatures. Ed. by Philip Norton. (Oxford Readings in Politics & Government Ser.). (Illus.). 352p. 1990. 65.00 (*0-19-827582-X*) OUP.

Legislatures & Legislators. Ed. by Philip Norton. LC 97-39112. (International Library of Politics & Comparative Government). 571p. 1998. text 162.95 (*1-85521-357-5*, Pub. by Ashgate Pub) Ashgate Pub Co.

Legislatures & the New Democracies in Latin America. Ed. by David Close. LC 94-42491. 270p. 1995. pap. text 45.00 (*1-55587-475-4*) L Rienner.

Legislatures in the Policy Process: The Dilemmas of Economic Policy. Ed. by David M. Olson & Michael L. Mezey. (Advances in Political Science Ser.). (Illus.). 237p. (C). 1991. text 65.00 (*0-521-38103-7*) Cambridge U Pr.

***Legitima Defensa.** John Grisham. 1998. pap. text 11.95 (*84-08-02237-7*) Planeta.

Legitima Defensa. John Grisham. (SPA.). 1997. 17.30 (*0-606-18349-3*) Turtleback.

Legitimacy & Commitment in the Military, 100. Ed. by Thomas C. Wyatt & Reuven Gal. LC 90-2944. (Contributions in Military Studies Ser.: No. 100). 232p. 1990. 59.95 (*0-313-26815-0*, GLE/, Greenwood Pr) Greenwood.

Legitimacy & Force: State Papers & Current Perspectives, 1981-1985, 2 vols., Set. Jeane J. Kirkpatrick. Incl. Vol. 1. 485p. 1987. 44.95 (*0-88738-099-9*); Vol. 1. 485p. 1987. pap. 24.95 (*0-88738-646-6*); Vol. 2. 420p. 1987. 44.95 (*0-88738-100-6*); Vol. 2. 420p. 1987. pap. 24.95 (*0-88738-647-4*); 1987. 69.95 (*0-88738-111-1*) Transaction Pubs.

Legitimacy & History: Self-Government in American Constitutional Theory. Paul W. Kahn. LC 92-13116. 272p. (C). 1992. 37.50 (*0-300-05499-8*) Yale U Pr.

Legitimacy & History: Self-Government in American Constitutional Theory. Paul W. Kahn. 1995. pap. 20.00 (*0-300-06307-5*) Yale U Pr.

Legitimacy & Symbols: The South Asian Writings of F. W. Buckler. Ed. by M. N. Pearson. LC 82-72446. (Michigan Papers on South & Southeast Asia: No. 26). xiii, 193p. 1985. 11.95 (*0-89148-032-3*); pap. 4.99 (*0-89148-033-1*) Ctr S&SE Asian.

Legitimacy & the European Union. Ed. by Thomas Banchoff & Mitchell Smith. LC 98-38355. 208p. (C). 1999. pap. 24.99 (*0-415-18189-5*, D6207) Routledge.

Legitimacy & the European Union. Ed. by Thomas Banchoff & Mitchell Smith. LC 98-38355. (Illus.). 208p. (C). (gr. 13). 1999. 80.00 (*0-415-18188-7*, D6203) Routledge.

Legitimacy & the Military: The Yugoslav Crisis. James Gow. Date not set. write for info. (*1-85567-031-3*) St Martin.

Legitimacy & the Military: The Yugoslav Crisis. James Gow. 224p. 1994. pap. 19.00 (*1-85567-245-6*) St Martin.

Legitimacy in International Law of the Detention & Internment of Aliens & Minorities in the Interest of National Security. LaRae Larkin. LC 96-41016. (Symposium Ser.: Vol. 40). 508p. 1996. text 119.95 (*0-7734-8755-7*) E Mellen.

Legitimacy in International Relations & the Rise & Fall of Yugoslavia. John Williams. LC 97-30356. 272p. 1998. text 69.95 (*0-312-21081-7*) St Martin.

Legitimacy in Public Administration: A Discourse Analysis. O. C. McSwite. LC 96-51270. (Advances in Public Administration Ser.: Vol. 4). 288p. 1997. 49.95 (*0-7619-0273-2*); pap. 21.50 (*0-7619-0274-0*) Sage.

Legitimacy in the Modern State. John H. Schaar. 1989. pap. 26.95 (*0-88738-772-1*) Transaction Pubs.

Legitimacy-Legitimate: Proceedings of the Conference Held in Florence, June 3-4, 1982 (Actes de Colloque de Florence 3 et 4 June 1982) Ed. by Athanasios Moulakis. (European University Institute, Series C (Political & Social Science): No. 3). vi, 105p. 1985. 36.55 (*3-11-010063-0*) De Gruyter.

Legitimacy of the Business Corporation in the Law of the United States, 1780-1970. Willard J. Hurst. LC 79-110750. (Page-Barbour Ser). 208p. reprint ed. 64.50 (*0-8357-9807-0*, 201111900074) Bks Demand.

Legitimacy of the Modern Age. Hans Blumenberg. Ed. by Tom McCarthy. Tr. by Robert M. Wallace from GER. (German Social Thought Ser.). 728p. 1985. pap. text 32.50 (*0-262-52105-9*) MIT Pr.

Legitimate Acts & Illegal Encounters: Law & Society in Antigua & Barbuda. Mindie Lazarus-Black. LC 93-11005. (Series in Ethnographic Inquiry). 424p. (C). 1994. pap. text 24.95 (*1-56098-326-4*) Smithsonian.

Legitimate Corporation: Essential Readings in Business Ethics & Corporate Governance. Ed. by Brenda Sutton. LC 92-47388. (Illus.). 320p. 1993. pap. 37.95 (*0-631-18748-0*) Blackwell Pubs.

Legitimate Differences: Interpretation in the Abortion Controversy & Other Public Debates. Georgia Warnke. LC 98-41409. 212p. 1999. 40.00 (*0-520-21633-4*, Pub. by U CA Pr) Cal Prin Full Svc.

***Legitimate Expectations & Proportionality in Administrative Law.** Robert Thomas. 320p. 2000. 54.00 (*1-84113-086-9*, Pub. by Hart Pub) Intl Spec Bk.

Legitimate Histories: Scott, Gothic & the Authorities of Fiction. Fiona Robertson. LC 93-27024. (Oxford English Monographs). 336p. 1994. text 60.00 (*0-19-811224-6*, Clarendon Pr) OUP.

Legitimate Sisters. Gwen Mercer & Maxine Mercer. 84p. 1994. pap. 7.00 (*0-9649112-0-5*) RghtBrain.

Legitimate Use of Military Force Against State-Sponsored International Terrorism. 1993. lib. bdg. 256.95 (*0-8490-8935-2*) Gordon Pr.

Legitimate Use of Military Force Against State-Sponsored International Terrorism, 2 vols. Ed. by Richard J. Erickson. 274p. (Orig.). 1989. pap. text 45.00 (*1-57979-149-2*) DIANE Pub.

Legitimate Use of Military Force Against State-Sponsored International Terrorism. Richard J. Erickson. 279p. (Orig.). (C). 1992. pap. text 40.00 (*1-56806-028-9*) DIANE Pub.

Legitimating the Chinese Economic Reforms: A Rhetoric of Myth & Orthodoxy. Alan R. Kluver. LC 95-36331. (SUNY Series in Speech Communication). 172p. (C). 1996. text 57.50 (*0-7914-2991-1*); pap. text 18.95 (*0-7914-2992-X*) State U NY Pr.

Legitimation Crisis. Jurgen Habermas. Tr. by Thomas McCarthy from GER. LC 74-17586. Orig. Title: Legitimationsprobleme Im Spatkapitalismus. (ENG.). 192p. 1975. reprint ed. pap. 15.50 (*0-8070-1521-0*) Beacon Pr.

Legitimation of a Revolution: The Yugoslav Case. Bogdan D. Denitch. LC 75-18170. 272p. 1976. 42.50 (*0-300-01906-8*) Yale U Pr.

Legitimation of Belief. Ernest Gellner. LC 74-14337. 220p. reprint ed. pap. 62.70 (*0-608-16443-7*, 2026340) Bks Demand.

Legitimationsprobleme Im Spatkapitalismus see Legitimation Crisis

Legitimism & the Reconstruction of French Society, 1852-1883. Steven D. Kale. LC 92-9207. (Illus.). 416p. (C). 1992. text 57.50 (*0-8071-1727-7*) La State U Pr.

Legitimitat der Freiheit: Zur Rolle der Politisch Alternativen Gruppen in der DDR. Ed. by Detlef Pollack. (Forschungen zur Praktischen Theologie Ser.: Bd. 8). (GER.). 245p. 1990. 53.80 (*3-631-42989-4*) P Lang Pubng.

Legitimization of Violence. Apter. 448p. 1998. pap. text 20.00 (*0-8147-0649-5*) NYU Pr.

Legitimization of Violence. Ed. by David E. Apter. 448p. (C). 1997. text 55.00 (*0-8147-0648-7*) NYU Pr.

Legless in Flight. Laurel Trivelpiece. LC 78-50961. 1978. 6.95 (*0-913506-05-2*) Woolmer-Brotherson.

L'Eglise en Priere see Church at Prayer, Vol. III, The Sacraments

L'Eglise en Priere: L'eucharistie see Church at Prayer, Vol. II, The Eucharist

***Lego City: Level 1.** DK Publishing Staff. (Readers Ser.). (Illus.). 32p. (ps-3). 2000. 12.95 (*0-7894-6699-6*); pap. 3.95 (*0-7894-6700-3*) DK Pub Inc.

Lego Crazy Action Contraptions: A LEGO Inventions Book. Dan Rathjen. Ed. by Editors of Klutz. (Illus.). 66p. (J). (gr. 4-7). 1998. pap. 19.95 (*1-57054-157-4*) Klutz.

Lego Creator: Official Activity Book. Bradygames. 1999. pap. text 14.99 (*1-56686-835-1*) Brady Pub.

***Lego Game Books Mixed Counter Display.** DK Publishing Staff. 1999. pap. text 118.80 (*0-7894-4993-5*) DK Pub Inc.

***Lego Space Port: Level 2.** DK Publishing Staff. (Readers Ser.). (Illus.). 32p. (ps-3). 2000. 12.95 (*0-7894-6701-1*) DK Pub Inc.

***Lego Space Port: Level 2.** DK Publishing Staff. (Illus.). 32p. (ps-3). 2000. pap. 3.95 (*0-7894-6702-X*) DK Pub Inc.

***Legs.** Carlton Books Staff. (Objects of Desire Ser.). (Illus.). 128p. 2000. 14.95 (*1-85868-870-1*, Pub. by Carlton Bks Ltd) Natl Bk Netwk.

***Legs.** William Kennedy. LC 99-54772. 2000. 28.95 (*0-7838-8860-0*, G K Hall & Co) Mac Lib Ref.

Legs. William Kennedy. 1983. pap. 12.95 (*0-14-006484-2*, Penguin Bks) Viking Penguin.

Legs: The Story of a Giraffe. Phyllis Barber. LC 90-47679. (Illus.). 80p. (J). (gr. 4-7). 1991. text 13.95 (*0-689-50526-4*) McElderry Bks.

Legs & All. Shirley Greenway. LC 92-245109. (Illus.). 16p. (J). (ps-k). 1992. bds. 3.95 (*1-879085-52-6*, Whispering Coyote) Charlesbridge Pub.

Legs & Bizou. Frances Cherry. (Illus.). 36p. (J). (ps-8). 1986. 7.95 (*0-920806-60-0*, Pub. by Penumbra Pr) U of Toronto Pr.

Legs & Thighs. Fit Magazine Editors. (Fit Self-Improvement Ser.: No. 3). 96p. 1983. pap. 7.95 (*0-89037-260-8*) Anderson World.

Legs Benedict: A Bed-&-Breakfast Mystery. Mary R. Daheim. LC 98-93760. (Bed & Breakfast Mystery Ser.). 320p. 1999. mass mkt. 6.50 (*0-380-80078-0*, Avon Bks) Morrow Avon.

Legs That Dance to Elmer's Tune. Elmer Batters. (Photo & Sexy Bks.). (Illus.). 216p. 1997. 69.69 (*3-8228-8188-0*) Taschen Amer.

Legs the Caterpillar. Ben Rosenbaum. Ed. by Inter Continental Publishers Staff. Orig. Title: The Insect Brigade. (Illus.). 32p. (J). (gr. k-3). 1995. 19.95 incl. audio (*0-9650244-0-7*, 125) Inter Contntl Pubs.

Legs the Caterpillar. Ben Rosenbaum. Ed. by Inter Continental Publishers Staff. Orig. Title: The Insect Brigade. (Illus.). 32p. (J). (ps-3). 1995. pap. 9.95 (*0-9650244-4-X*, 125) Inter Contntl Pubs.

Legs the Caterpillar. abr. large type ed. Ben Rosenbaum. Ed. by Inter Continental Publishers Staff. Orig. Title: The Insect Brigade. (Illus.). 32p. (J). (ps-3). 1995. pap. 9.95 (*0-9650244-3-1*, 125) Inter Contntl Pubs.

Legs the Caterpillar. abr. large type ed. Ben Rosenbaum. Ed. by Inter Continental Publishers Staff. Orig. Title: The Insect Brigade. (Illus.). 32p. (J). (ps-3). 1995. 14.95 (*0-9650244-2-3*, 125); lib. bdg. 14.95 incl. audio (*0-9650244-1-5*, 125) Inter Contntl Pubs.

Legszebb Verseim: Muforditas-Gyuitemeny: Collection of Poetry Translations. Tr. & Intro. by Robert Hetzron. (HUN.). viii, 53p. 1988. pap. text 4.00 (*0-9621254-0-7*) R Hetzron.

LeGuin & Identity in Contemporary Fiction. Bernard Selinger. 185p. 1988. 79.95 (*0-7734-2006-1*) E Mellen.

Legume-Based Fermented Foods. N. R. Reddy et al. 272p. 1986. 151.00 (*0-8493-6286-5*, TX558, CRC Reprint) Franklin.

Legumes: Chemistry, Technology, & Human Nutrition. Matthews. (Food Science & Technology Ser.: Vol. 32). (Illus.). 408p. 1989. text 155.00 (*0-8247-8042-6*) Dekker.

Legumes & Oilseed Crops I. Ed. by Y. P. S. Bajaj. (Biotechnology in Agriculture & Forestry Ser.: Vol. 10). (Illus.). 785p. 1990. 432.95 (*0-387-50786-8*) Spr-Verlag.

Legumes for Milk & Meat. Roger Sheldrick et al. (Illus.). 108p. (Orig.). 1988. pap. text 15.75 (*0-948617-07-1*, Pub. by Chalcombe Pubns) Scholium Intl.

Legumes in Crop Rotations--Bibliography, January 1990-December 1993. Mary V. Gold. 121p. (Orig.). (C). 1994. pap. text 35.00 (*0-7881-1448-4*) DIANE Pub.

Legumes in Farming Systems. P. Plansquaert & R. Haggar. (Developments in Plant & Soil Sciences Ser.). (C). 1989. text 101.50 (*0-7923-0134-X*) Kluwer Academic.

Legumes of Africa: A Check-List. J. M. Lock. vii, 619p. 1989. pap. 30.00 (*0-947643-10-9*, Pub. by Royal Botnic Grdns) Balogh.

Legumes of Bahia. G. P. Lewis. (Illus.). xvi, 369p. 1987. pap. 24.00 (*0-947643-05-2*, Pub. by Royal Botnic Grdns) Balogh.

Legumes of Indo-China: A Check-List. J. M. Lock & J. Heald. vi, 164p. 1994. pap. 22.00 (*0-947643-66-4*, Pub. by Royal Botnic Grdns) Balogh.

Legumes of Northern Eurasia. G. P. Yakovlev et al. x, 724p. 1996. pap. 60.00 (*0-947643-97-4*, Pub. by Royal Botnic Grdns) Balogh.

Legumes of the Ilha de Maraca. G. P. Lewis & P. E. Owen. (Illus.). xvi, 95p. 1989. pap. 15.00 (*0-947643-15-X*, Pub. by Royal Botnic Grdns) Balogh.

Legumes of the World. (Illus.). 1800p. (C). (gr. 13). 1996. text 152.50 (*0-412-46980-4*, Chap & Hall NY) Chapman & Hall.

Legumes of West Asia: A Check-List. J. M. Lock & K. Simpson. xi, 263p. 1991. pap. 30.00 (*0-947643-29-X*, Pub. by Royal Botnic Grdns) Balogh.

***Leguminosae.** Ed. by V. I. Grubov. (Plants of Central Asia Ser.: Vol. 8A). (Illus.). 2002. text. write for info. (*1-57808-119-X*) Science Pubs.

Leguminosae: A Source Book of Characteristics, Uses & Nodulation. O. N. Allen & Ethel K. Allen. LC 80-5104. (Illus.). 878p. 1981. 75.00 (*0-299-08400-0*) U of Wis Pr.

Leguminosae: Astragalus, Moskva. Tr. by Israel Program for Scientific Translations Staff from RUS. (Flora of the U. S. S. R. (Flora SSSR) Ser.: Vol. 12). (Illus.). xxviii, 681p. 1986. reprint ed. 250.00 (*3-87429-232-0*, 003933, Pub. by Koeltz Sci Bks) Lubrecht & Cramer.

Leguminosae: Osytropis, Hedysarum. Tr. by Israel Program for Scientific Translations Staff from RUS. (Flora of the U. S. S. R. (Flora SSSR) Ser.: Vol. 13). (Illus.). xxiii, 455p. 1986. reprint ed. 210.00 (*3-87429-233-9*, 020980, Pub. by Koeltz Sci Bks) Lubrecht & Cramer.

Leguminosae of the United States: Subfamily Caesalpinioideae. Duane Isely. LC 66-6394. (Memoirs Ser.: Vol. 25, No. 2). (Illus.). 228p. 1975. pap. 20.00 (*0-89327-054-7*) NY Botanical.

Leguminosae of the United States: Subfamily Caesalpinioideae. Duane Isely. LC 66-6394. (Memoirs Ser.: Vol. 25, No. 2). (Illus.). 228p. 1975. pap. 20.00 (*0-89327-080-6*) NY Botanical.

Leguminosae of the United States Pt. III: Subfamily Papilionoideae-Tribes Sophoreae, Podalyreae, Loteae. Duane Isely. LC 81-38317. (Memoirs Ser.: Vol. 25, No. 3). (Illus.). 264p. 1981. pap. 35.00 (*0-89327-232-9*) NY Botanical.

Legwork. Ellen Burstein. (Illus.). 288p. 1994. 22.00 (*0-02-578110-3*) S&S Trade.

Legwork. David Gitin. 1977. 3.00 (*0-685-88996-3*) Oyez.

Legwork. Katy Munger. LC 96-95492. 240p. 1997. mass mkt. 5.50 (*0-380-79136-6*, Avon Bks) Morrow Avon.

Legwork. deluxe ed. David Gitin. 1977. 15.00 (*0-685-88995-5*) Oyez.

Legwork: An Inspiring Journey Through a Chronic Illness. Ellen B. MacFarlane & Patricia Burstein. LC 94-11726. 1994. write for info. (*0-02-578001-8*) Macmillan.

Leh & Trekking in Ladakh. Charlie Loram. 1996. pap. text 14.95 (*1-873756-09-7*, Pub. by Trailblazer) Seven Hills Bk.

Lehavin Ulehaskil. 1982. 15.95 (*0-87306-975-7*); pap. 13.95 (*0-685-01631-5*) Feldheim.

Leheutre (Gustave) Catalogue Raisonne of the Graphic Work. Loys Delteil. (FRE., Illus.). 192p. 1969. reprint ed. 95.00 (*1-55660-037-2*) A Wofsy Fine Arts.

Lehi in the Desert & the World of the Jaredites. Hugh Nibley. 9.95 (*0-88494-022-5*) Bookcraft Inc.

Lehi in the Desert & the World of There Were Jaredites. Hugh Nibley. LC 87-32941. (Collected Works of Hugh Nibley). xviii, 464p. 1988. reprint ed. 26.95 (*0-87579-132-8*) Deseret Bk.

Lehi Jones, a Man of Grace. Reid. 7.95 (*1-56684-249-2*) Evans Bk Dist.

Lehi Tree: A Novel. Katherine Myers. 188p. 1996. pap. text 7.95 (*1-57636-026-1*) SunRise Pbl.

Lehigh & New England. Fred Kramer & John Krause. (Hobby Bks.: No. C81). (Illus.). 80p. 1992. pap. 13.95 (*0-911868-81-X*, C81) Carstens Pubns.

Lehigh & New England Railroad: A Color Retrospect. Douglas E. Lilly. LC 88-82320. (Illus.). viii, 136p. 1988. 45.00 (*0-9620844-0-9*) Garrigues Hse.

Lehigh University: A History of Education in Engineering, Business, & the Human Condition. Ed. by W. Ross Yates. LC 91-60581. (Illus.). 336p. 1992. 48.50 (*0-934223-17-3*) Lehigh Univ Pr.

***Lehigh Valley: A Natural & Environmental History.** Robert Halma & Carl S. Oplinger. LC 00-32673. 2001. pap. write for info. (*0-271-02094-6*) Pa St U Pr.

Lehigh Valley Dine-a-Mate Book. 248p. 1996. pap. text 30.00 (*1-57393-058-X*) Dine-A-Mate.

***Lehigh Valley Entertainment, 2000.** (Illus.). 821p. 1999. pap. 35.00 (*1-58553-034-4*, 0062) Enter Pubns.

Lehigh Valley, in Color. Robert J. Yanosey. (Illus.). 128p. 1989. 45.00 (*0-9619058-5-9*) Morning NJ.

Lehigh Valley, in Color, No. 2. Robert J. Yanosey. LC 91-60918. (Illus.). 128p. 1991. 45.00 (*1-878887-03-3*) Morning NJ.

Lehigh Valley Memories: A Tour of the Lehigh Valley Railroad in New York's Finger Lakes Region, 1941-1959. David Marcham et al. Ed. by John Marcham. LC 98-26025. (Illus.). 88p. 1998. pap. 19.95 (*0-942690-40-0*) DeWitt Hist.

Lehigh Valley Railroad. Robert F. Archer. LC 93-61333. (Illus.). 372p. 1993. 44.95 (*0-911581-29-4*) Heimburger Hse Pub.

Lehigh Valley Railroad, the New York Division: An Illustrated Operational History Covering the Last Twenty Years of the Railroad & the People Who Were There. Mike Bednar. LC 93-38099. xiv, 138p. 1993. 52.50 (*0-9620844-5-X*) Garrigues Hse.

Lehigh Valley-3 in Color. Jeremy F. Plant & Richard T. Steinbrenner. LC 99-186852. (Illus.). 128p. 1999. 49.95 (*1-58248-013-3*) Morning NJ.

Lehi's Isle of Promise: A Scriptural Account. Arthur J. Kocherhans. (Illus.). 200p. 1989. pap. text 16.95 (*0-944329-02-0*) KOBO Ent.

Lehman A. Monk Ferris: Life of a Busy Man--Recollections of My Work As an Architect, Building Inspector, & Civic Leader. Ed. by Mary E. Glass. 395p. 1971. lib. bdg. 57.50 (*1-56475-100-7*); fiche. write for info. (*1-56475-101-5*) U NV Oral Hist.

Lehman Brothers: The WetFeet.com Insider Guide. 4th ed. WetFeet.com Staff. (Insider Guides Ser.). 65p. 1999. per. 25.00 (*1-58207-027-X*) WetFeet.

Lehman Families of Langnau, Switzerland. David Habegger. (Illus.). 42p. (Orig.). pap. 6.95 (*1-883294-13-4*) Masthof Pr.

Lehman, Smith, Wiseman & Associates: Design as Fluid Logic. Anthony Iannacci. LC 98-230677. 1999. pap. 40.00 (*88-7838-026-1*) L'Arca IT.

Lehmann & Coleman: Taxation Law in Australia. 3rd ed. G. Lehmann & C. Coleman. (Butterworths Australia Ser.). 1994. pap. write for info. (*0-409-30524-3*, MICHIE) LEXIS Pub.

Lehmann Haggadah. Marcus Lehmann. 384p. 1983. 19.95 (*0-87306-326-0*) Feldheim.

Lehmann-Prins Pirkei Avos. Marcus Lehmann & Eliezer Prins. 1992. 24.95 (*0-87306-589-1*); pap. 20.95 (*0-87306-593-X*) Feldheim.

Lehmanns Erzahlungen: C level. Lenz. text 8.95 (*0-8219-0852-9*) EMC-Paradigm.

Lehmbruck (Wilhelm) The Complete Graphic Work. Erwin Petermann. (GER., Illus.). 428p. 1985. 275.00 (*1-55660-005-4*) A Wofsy Fine Arts.

Lehner's Encyclopedia of U. S. Marks on Pottery, Porcelain & Clay. Lois Lehner. (Illus.). 636p. 1996. 24.95 (*0-89145-365-2*, 2379) Collector Bks.

Lehr-, Ubungs- und Testbuch der Schachkombinationen. Karl Colditz. (GER.). 184p. 1992. 20.00 (*3-283-00302-5*) G Olms Pubs.

Lehr- und Arbeitsbuch. (GER., Illus.). 224p. 1997. pap. write for info. (*3-468-49895-0*) Langenscheidt.

Lehratlanten der Radiologischen Diagnostik see Teaching Atlas of Urologic Radiology

Lehrbare Religion? Studien Ueber die Scientistische Theorieueberlierung und Ihr Weiterwirken in den Theologischreligionspaedagogischen Entwuerfen Richard Kabischs und Friedrich Niebergalls. Matthias Heesch. (Theologische Bibliothek Toepelmann Ser.: Vol. 80). (GER.). 240p. (C). 1997. lib. bdg. 95.00 (*3-11-015576-1*) De Gruyter.

Lehrbuch der Algebra, Vol. 3. 3rd ed. Heinrich Weber. LC 61-6890. 1979. reprint ed. text 65.00 (*0-8284-0144-6*) Chelsea Pub.

Lehrbuch der Anorganischen Chemie. A. F. Holleman & Egon Wiberg. (GER., Illus.). xxx, 1451p. 1984. 92.35 (*3-11-007511-3*) De Gruyter.

Lehrbuch der Biologischen Heilmittel. Gerhard Madaus. (GER.). 1997. reprint ed. 498.00 (*3-487-05889-8*) G Olms Pubs.

Lehrbuch der Finanzwissenschaft. Lorenz Von Stein. (GER.). lxix, 1899p. 1975. reprint ed. write for info. (*3-487-05351-9*) G Olms Pubs.

Lehrbuch der Geschichte der Medizin und der Epidemischen Krankheiten, 3 vols. Heinrich Haeser. lvii, 2992p. 1971. reprint ed. write for info. (*3-487-04016-6*); reprint ed. write for info. (*0-318-70751-9*); reprint ed. write for info. (*0-318-70753-5*) G Olms Pubs.

Lehrbuch der Geschichte der Medizin und der Epidemischen Krankheiten, 3 vols., Bd. II. Heinrich Haeser. lvii, 2992p. 1971. reprint ed. write for info. (*0-318-70752-7*) G Olms Pubs.

Lehrbuch der Hydrologie Band 1: Allgemeine Hydrologie. Quantitative Hydrologie. Albert Baumgartner & Hans-Juergen Liebscher. (GER.). xl, 694p. 1996. 93.00 (*3-443-30002-2*, Pub. by Gebruder Borntraeger) Balogh.

Lehrbuch der Logik: Auf positivistischer Grundlage mit Beruecksichtigung der Geschichte der Logik. Theodor Ziehen. viii, 866p. (C). 1974. reprint ed. 226.95 (*3-11-003305-4*) De Gruyter.

Lehrbuch der Naturphilosophie. Lorenz Oken. (GER.). 1997. reprint ed. 128.00 (*3-487-09453-3*) G Olms Pubs.

Lehrbuch der Pflanzenphysiologie see Plant Physiology

Lehrbuch der Phytotherapie see Herbal Medicine

Lehrbuch der Politischen Oekonomie. Karl H. Rau. 1997. write for info. (*3-487-10335-4*) G Olms Pubs.

An Asterisk (*) at the beginning of an entry indicates that the title is appearing for the first time.

***Lehrbuch der Salinenkunde.** C. Karsten. 1673p. 1999. 436.00 (3-487-10961-1) G Olms Pubs.

Lehrbuch der Thetafunktionen. Adolph Krazer. LC 75-113132. 1970. reprint ed. 35.00 (0-8284-0244-2) Chelsea Pub.

Lehrbuch der Topologie. Herbert Seifert & W. Threlfall. 19.95 (0-8284-0031-8) Chelsea Pub.

Lehrbuch der Wirtschaftssoziologie. Eugen Buss. (GER.). xii, 272p. 1985. pap. 34.65 (3-11-008897-5) De Gruyter.

Lehrbuch 2. (GER.). 1997. pap. write for info. (3-468-96778-0) Langenscheidt.

Lehre der Alten: II Das Testament als Literaturgattung im Alten Testament und im Alten Vorderen Orient. Eckhard Von Nordheim. (Arbeiten zur Literatur und Geschichte des Hellenistischen Judentums Ser.: No. 18). (GER.). xii, 184p. 1986. 45.50 (90-04-07313-2) Brill Academic Pubs.

Lehre der "Proprietates Terminorum" Sinn & Referenz in Mittelalterlicher Logik. Carlos A. Dufour. (Analytica Ser.). (GER.). 320p. (C). 1989. 99.00 (3-88405-063-X) Philosophia Pr.

***Lehre Vom Indizienbeweis im 19, Jahrhundert.** Rene Poltl. (Europaische Hochschulschriften Rechtswissenschaft Ser.). XXV, 547p. 1999. 79.95 (3-631-35361-8) P Lang Pubng.

Lehre Vom Unbewubten Im System Von Leibniz. Richard Herbertz. (Abhandlungen Zur Philosophie und Ihrer Geschichte Ser.: Vol. 20). (GER.). 1980. reprint ed. write for info. (3-487-06778-1) G Olms Pubs.

Lehre Von den Ideen Bei Malebranche. James Lewin. (Abhandlungen Zur Philosophie und Ihrer Geschichte Ser.: No. 35). viii, 165p. 1981. reprint ed. write for info. (3-487-06787-0) G Olms Pubs.

Lehre Von den Kegelschnitten Im Altertum. Hieronymus G. Zeuthen. xvi, 521p. 1966. reprint ed. write for info. (0-318-70847-7) G Olms Pubs.

Lehre von den Privaturkunden. Otto Posse. (GER., Illus.). viii, 242p. (C). 1974. reprint ed. 350.00 (3-11-002301-6) De Gruyter.

Lehre Von der Abstraktion Bei Plato und Aristoteles. Paul E. Gohlke. 118p. 1972. reprint ed. write for info. (3-487-04154-5) G Olms Pubs.

Lehre von der Sunde und vom Versohner - Tholucks Theologische Entwicklung in Seiner Berliner Zeit. Sung-Bong Kim. (Europaische Hochschulschriften Ser.: Reihe 23, Bd. 440). (GER.). V, 211p. 1992. 41.80 (3-631-44421-4) P Lang Pubng.

Lehre von Gottes Eigenschaften Bei Friedrich Schleiermacher und Karl Barth. Claus-Dieter Osthovener. (Theologische Bibliothek Toepelmann Ser.: Vol. 76). (GER.). ix, 232p. (C). 1996. lib. bdg. 124.45 (3-11-015055-7) De Gruyter.

Lehren des Ani: Ein Neuagyptischer Weisheitstext in Seinem Kulturellen Umfeld. Joachim F. Quack. (Orbis Biblicus et Orientalis Ser.: Vol. 141). (GER.). 338p. 1994. text 68.75 (3-7278-0984-1, Pub. by Presses Univ Fribourg) Eisenbrauns.

***Lehrerbildung fur Morgen: Wissenschaftlicher Nachwuchs Stellt Sich Vor.** Sabine Andresen & Barbel Schon. (Erziehungskonzeptionen und Praxis. Bd. 40 Ser.). 170p. 1999. 31.95 (3-631-35672-2) P Lang Pubng.

Lehrerhandbuch see Deutsch Aktiv, Level 3

Lehrerhandbuch 3: Teacher's Manual. Von H. Funk et al. (Sowieso Ser.: No. 3). (GER.). 176p. 1997. pap., teacher ed. write for info. (3-468-47692-2) Langenscheidt.

Lehrerhandreichungen. (Neuer Start 2 Ser.). (GER.). 104p. 1997. pap. write for info. (3-468-49967-1); pap. write for info. (3-468-49896-9) Langenscheidt.

Lehrerhandreichungen: Teacher's Manual/Exercise Book. Von E. Dehmel et al. (GER.). 40p. 1997. pap., teacher ed., wbk. ed. 8.95 (3-468-49696-6) Langenscheidt.

Lehrplanentwicklung im Fach Evangelische Religion in Schleswig-Holstein. Gudrun Philipp. (Beitrage zur Erziehungswissenschaft und Biblischen Bildung Ser.: Bd. 2). (GER.). 210p. 1997. 42.95 (3-631-30922-8) P Lang Pubng.

Lehrstuhl fur Poesie an der Universitat Helmstedt. Ingrid Henze. write for info. (0-318-70713-6) G Olms Pubs.

Lehrstuhl fur Poesie an der Universitat Helmstedt Bis Zum Tode Heinrich Meiboms des Alteren (1625) Ingrid Henze. (Beitrage Zur Altertumswissenschaft Ser.: Band 9). (GER.). x, 228p. 1990. write for info. (3-487-09329-4) G Olms Pubs.

Lei for Tutu. Rebecca N. Fellows. LC 98-9319. (Illus.). 32p. (J). (gr. 1-3). 1998. lib. bdg. 14.95 (0-8075-4426-4) A Whitman.

Lei Mele No Pauahi see Music, Past & Present, at Kamehameha Schools: Lei Mele No Pauahi

Lei of Love. Annette Mahon. LC 95-96218. 192p. 1996. 18.95 (0-8034-9165-4, Avalon Bks) Bouregy.

***Leib.** Raabenstein. (Illus.). 48p. 2000. 24.95 (3-9803212-3-1, Pub. by Vice Versa Verlag) Nazraeli Press.

Leiber Alex see Dear Alexandra: A Story of Switzerland

Leiber Alex see Dear Alexandra: A Story of Switzerland - Including Doll

Leiber & Stoller. Warner. (Great Pop Songwriters Ser.). 1998. 45.00 (0-02-864843-9) S&S Trade.

Leiber & Stoller Songbook. Leonard, Hal, Corporation Staff. 160p. 1997. pap. 22.95 (0-7935-8073-0, HL00313079) H Leonard.

Leiber & Stoller Songbook. Warner. 1995. pap. 22.95 (0-89724-695-0, VF1919) Wrner Bros.

Leibhaftigkeit: Jakob Bohmes Inkarnationsmorphologie. Christian Bendrath. 430p. 1998. 111.00 (3-11-016237-7) De Gruyter.

Leiblichkeit der Sprache Sprachlichkeit des Leibes: Wort, Gebarde, Tanz Bei Hugo von Hofmannsthal. Bettina Rutsch. (Europaische Hochschulschriften Ser.: Reihe 1, Bd. 1675). 312p. 1998. 51.95 (3-631-33306-4) P Lang Pubng.

Leibniz. Wilson. 166.95 (1-84014-705-9) Ashgate Pub Co.

Leibniz: An Introduction to His Philosophy. Nicholas Rescher. (Modern Revivals in Philosophy Ser.). 176p. 1994. 51.95 (0-7512-0275-4, Pub. by Gregg Revivals) Ashgate Pub Co.

Leibniz: Critical & Interpretive Essays. Ed. by Michael Hooker. LC 82-7010. 383p. reprint ed. pap. 118.80 (0-8357-8939-X, 203323000085) Bks Demand.

Leibniz: Determinist, Theist, Idealist. Robert M. Adams. 448p. 1994. text 65.00 (0-19-508460-8) OUP.

Leibniz: Determinist, Theist, Idealist. Robert Adams. 448p. 1998. reprint ed. pap. 19.95 (0-19-512649-1) OUP.

Leibniz: New Essays on Human Understanding. Gottfried Wilhelm Leibniz. Ed. by Peter Remnant & Jonathan Bennett. LC 82-1334. (Cambridge Texts in the History of Philosophy Ser.). 648p. (C). 1996. text 59.95 (0-521-57211-8); pap. text 21.95 (0-521-57660-1) Cambridge U Pr.

Leibniz: Perception, Apperception, & Thought. Robert F. McRae. LC 76-6084. 158p. reprint ed. pap. 49.00 (0-8357-3647-4, 203637400003) Bks Demand.

Leibniz: Philosophie des Panlogismus. Aron Gurwitsch. LC 73-88298. (GER.). 1974. 150.00 (3-11-004358-0) De Gruyter.

Leibniz: Representation, Continuity, & the Spatio-Temporal. Dionysios Anapolitanos. LC 98-47229. (Science & Philosophy Ser.). 1p. 1998. 96.00 (0-7923-5476-1) Kluwer Academic.

Leibniz & Clarke: A Study of Their Correspondence. Ezio Vailati. LC 96-45589. 268p. (C). 1997. text 49.95 (0-19-511399-3) OUP.

Leibniz & Confucianism, the Search for Accord. David E. Mungello. LC 77-4053. 220p. 1977. reprint ed. pap. 62.70 (0-608-00528-2, 2061407) Bks Demand.

Leibniz & Ludolf on Things Linguistic: Excerpts from Their Correspondence, 1688-1703. Gottfried Wilhelm Leibniz. Ed. & Tr. by John T. Waterman. LC 77-83104. (University of California Publications in Social Welfare: No. 88). 101p. reprint ed. pap. 31.40 (0-608-15272-2, 202959300061) Bks Demand.

Leibniz & Philosophical Analysis. Robert M. Yost. LC 54-9554. (California University Publications in Philosophy: Vol. 27). 220p. reprint ed. pap. 68.20 (0-608-11116-3, 202117500021) Bks Demand.

Leibniz & Strawson. Clifford Brown. (Introductiones Ser.). 120p. 1990. 33.00 (0-685-38867-0) Philosophia Pr.

Leibniz & the Kabbalah, 142. Allison P. Coudert. LC 94-32967. (International Archives of the History of Ideas Ser.). 1995. lib. bdg. 121.50 (0-7923-3114-1) Kluwer Academic.

Leibniz & the Rational Order of Nature. Donald Rutherford. 317p. (C). 1995. text 64.95 (0-521-46155-3) Cambridge U Pr.

Leibniz & the Rational Order of Nature. Donald Rutherford. 317p. 1998. pap. text 19.95 (0-521-59737-4) Cambridge U Pr.

Leibniz' Auffassung des Menschlichen Verstandes (Intellectus) Werner Schuessler. (Quellen und Studien zur Philosophie: Bd. 32). (GER.). xviii, 256p. 1992. lib. bdg. 106.15 (3-11-013645-7) De Gruyter.

Leibniz-Clarke Correspondence. I. Bernard Cohen. LC 80-2100. (Development of Science Ser.). (Illus.). 1981. lib. bdg. 55.95 (0-405-13865-2) Ayer.

***Leibniz-Clarke Correspondence: With Extracts from Newton's Principia Opticks.** Gottfried Wilhelm Leibniz et al. LC 98-18298. 256p. 1998. pap. 24.95 (0-7190-0669-4, Pub. by Manchester Univ Pr) St Martin.

Leibniz' Doctrine of Necessary Truth. Margaret D. Wilson & Margaret Dauler. (Harvard Dissertations in Philosophy Ser.). 152p. 1992. reprint ed. text 10.00 (0-8240-3767-7) Garland.

Leibniz-Faksimiles, Bekanntes und Unbekanntes Aus Seinem Nachlass. Gottfried Wilhelm Leibniz. (GER.). 1971. write for info. (3-487-06525-8) G Olms Pubs.

Leibniz, Humbold, & the Origins of Comparativism: Proceedings of the International Conference, Rome, 25-28 September 1986. Ed. by Tullio De Mauro & Lia Formigari. LC 89-17687. (Studies in the History of the Language Sciences: No. 49). vii, 329p. 1990. 97.00 (90-272-4532-0) J Benjamins Pubng Co.

***Leibniz in 90 Minutes.** Paul Strathern. (Philosophers in 90 Minutes Ser.). 96p. 2000. 14.95 (1-56663-330-3, Pub. by I R Dee); pap. 6.95 (1-56663-331-1, Pub. by I R Dee) Natl Bk Netwk.

Leibniz, Language, Signs & Thought: A Collection of Essays. Marcelo Dascal. LC 86-15017. (Foundations of Semiotics Ser.: No. 10). xi, 203p. 1987. 59.00 (90-272-3280-6) J Benjamins Pubng Co.

Leibniz, Mysticism & Religion. Allison Coudert et al. LC 98-27908. (International Archives of the History of Ideas Ser.). 1998. write for info. (0-7923-5223-8) Kluwer Academic.

***Leibniz on Freedom & Determinism in Relation to Aquinas & Molina.** Didier Njirayamanda Kaphagawani. LC 99-72850. (Avebury Series in Philosophy). 151p. 1999. 65.95 (0-7546-1032-2, Pub. by Ashgate Pub) Ashgate Pub Co.

Leibniz on Individuals & Individuation: The Persistence of Premodern Ideas in Modern Philosophy. Lawrence B. McCullough. LC 95-46629. (Philosophical Studies in Contemporary Culture: Vol. 3). 232p. (C). 1996. text 140.00 (0-7923-3864-2) Kluwer Academic.

Leibniz on the Mental Lives of Humans & Brutes. Mark Kulstad. (Analytica Ser.). 176p. (C). 1991. 66.00 (3-88405-069-9) Philosophia Pr.

Leibniz' System in Seinen Wissenschaftlichen Grundlagen. Ernst Cassirer. (GER.). 1980. reprint ed. write for info. (3-487-00318-X) G Olms Pubs.

Leibniz' Universal Jurisprudence: Justice As the Charity of the Wise. Patrick Riley. 368p. 1996. 43.00 (0-674-52407-1) HUP.

Leibnizian Inquiries: A Group of Essays. Ed. by Nicholas Rescher. LC 88-37059. (CPS Publications in Philosophy of Science). 196p. (Orig.). (C). 1989. pap. text 19.50 (0-8191-7359-2); lib. bdg. 37.00 (0-8191-7358-4) U Pr of Amer.

***Leibniz's Metaphysics: Its Origins & Development.** Christia Mercer. 448p. (C). 1999. 64.95 (0-521-40301-4) Cambridge U Pr.

Leibniz's Metaphysics of Nature: A Group of Essays. Nicholas Rescher. (University of Western Ontario Series in Phylosophy of Science: No. 18). 140p. 1981. pap. text 59.00 (90-277-1253-0); lib. bdg. 70.50 (90-277-1252-2) Kluwer Academic.

Leibniz's 'New System' & Associated Contemporary Texts. Ed. by R. S. Woolhouse & Richard Francks. LC 96-33601. 278p. 1997. text 65.00 (0-19-824846-6) OUP.

Leibstandarte, Vol. 1. Rudolf Lehmann. Tr. by Nick Olcott from GER. (Illus.). 400p. 1987. 30.00 (0-921991-01-0) J J Fedorowicz.

Leica Vol. 3-Accessories: An Illustrated History. James L. Lager. (Illus.). 352p. 1997. write for info. (0-9636973-3-1) Lager Ltd Edits.

Leica - An Illustrated History, Vol. 1: Cameras. James L. Lager. (Illus.). 320p. 1993. 149.95 (0-9636973-1-5) Lager Ltd Edits.

Leica - An Illustrated History, Vol. 2: Lenses. James L. Lager. (Illus.). 320p. 1995. 149.95 (0-9636973-2-3) Lager Ltd Edits.

Leica Camera Repair. Edward H. Romney. 64p. 1985. pap. text 29.00 (1-886996-56-3) Hillcrst Pub.

Leica Camera Repair Handbook. Thomas Tomosy. (Illus.). 144p. 1999. pap. 39.95 (0-936262-87-7) Amherst Media.

Leica in Colour. Paul-Henry Van Hasbroeck. (Illus.). 160p. 1997. 50.00 (0-85667-487-7, Pub. by P Wilson) Antique Collect.

Leica Lens Book. Brian Bower. LC 99-209695. (Illus.). 1999. 45.00 (0-7153-0817-3, Pub. by D & C Pub) Sterling.

Leica M. Photography. Bower. (Illus.). 160p. 1998. pap. 24.95 (0-7153-0842-4, Pub. by D & C Pub) Sterling.

Leica M Photography. Brian Bower. (Illus.). 160p. 1996. 39.95 (0-7153-0318-X, Pub. by D & C Pub) Sterling.

Leica M2 Military Camera Repair Manual. Signal Corps U. S. Army Staff. 117p. 1982. pap. text 35.00 (1-886996-60-1) Hillcrst Pub.

Leica Reflex Photography: New Edition Featuring the Leica R8. Brian Bower. LC 97-183392. (Illus.). 152p. 1997. pap. 24.95 (0-7153-0627-8) Sterling.

Leicester Engineering Department Building: Leicester University, 1959-1963, Sirling & Gowan. John McKean. (Architecture in Detail Ser.). (Illus.). 60p. (Orig.). (C). 1994. pap. 29.95 (0-7148-3154-9, Pub. by Phaidon Press) Phaidon Pr.

Leicestershire Community Colleges & Centres. A. N. Fairbairn. 112p. (C). 1978. text 30.00 (0-7855-3189-0, Pub. by Univ Nottingham) St Mut.

Leicestershire Community Colleges & Centres. Ed. by A. N. Fairbairn. (C). 1979. 35.00 (0-902031-42-2, Pub. by Univ Nottingham) St Mut.

Leicestershire Words, Phrases & Proverbs. Arthur B. Evans & Sebastian Evans. (English Dialect Society Publications: No. 31). 1969. reprint ed. pap. 40.00 (0-8115-0458-1) Periodicals Srv.

Leich, Lieder, Sangsprueche. rev. ed. Walther Von der Vogelweide. Ed. by Christoph Cormeau & Karl Lachmann. (GER.). lxv, 344p. (C). 1996. lib. bdg. 41.50 (3-11-014821-8) De Gruyter.

Leich, Lieder, Sangsprueche. 14th rev. ed. Walther Von der Vogelweide. Ed. by Christoph Cormeau & Karl Lachmann. (GER.). lxv, 344p. (C). 1996. pap. text 22.10 (3-11-013608-2) De Gruyter.

Leicht Verwechselbare Worter. (Duden-Taschenbucher Ser.: No. 17). 334p. 1973. 14.00 (3-411-01147-5, Pub. by Bibliogr Inst Brockhaus) Langenscheidt.

Leichte Aufgaben (Arbeitsheft) see Deutsch Fuer Auslaender: Grundstufe

Leichte Erzaelungen (Leseband) see Deutsch Fuer Auslaender: Grundstufe

Leichte Panzers in Action. Uwe Feist. (Armor in Action Ser.: Vol. 10). (Illus.). 50p. 2000. reprint ed. pap. 9.95 (0-89747-043-5, 2010) Squad Sig Pubns.

Leichter als Luft see Lighter Than Air: Moral Poems

Leichter Anfang (Lehrbuch) see Deutsch Fuer Auslaender: Grundstufe

***Leid im Werk Alfred Doblins: Eine Analyse der Spaten Romane in Beziehung Zum Gesamtwerk.** Friedrich Wambsganz. (Europaische Hochschulschriften Ser.). 289p. 1999. 48.95 (3-631-35466-5) P Lang Pubng.

Leiden des Jungen Werther. Johann Wolfgang Von Goethe. Ed. by Katharina Mommsen & Richard A. Koc. LC 85-12554. (Suhrkamp/Insel Ser.). (ENG & GER., Illus.). xviii, 216p. (C). 1987. pap. 15.00 (3-518-02971-1, Pub. by Suhr Verlag) Intl Bk Import.

Leiden des Jungen Werther, Vol. 1. Johann Wolfgang Von Goethe. (Cloth Bound Pocket Ser.). (GER.). 1999. 7.95 (3-89508-662-2) Konemann.

Leiden des Jungen Werthers. unabridged ed. Johann Wolfgang Von Goethe. (World Classic Literature Ser.). (GER.). pap. 5.95 (3-89507-000-9, Pub. by Bookking Intl) Distribks Inc.

Leiden Oriental Connections, 1850 to 1940. Ed. by Willem Otterspeer. (Studies in the History of Leiden University: Vol. 5). (Illus.). viii, 391p. 1989. pap. 110.50 (90-04-09022-3) Brill Academic Pubs.

Leiden und Gerechtigkeit: Studien Zu Theologie und Textgeschichte des Sirachbuches. Lutz Schrader. (Beitrage zur Biblischen Exegese und Theologie Ser.: Bd. 27). (GER.). 327p. 1994. 52.95 (3-631-47279-X) P Lang Pubng.

Leidenschaft der Erkenntnis: Philosophie und Aesthetische Lebensgestaltung Bei Nietzsche Von "Morgenroethe" Bis "Also Sprach Zarathustra" Marco Brusotti. (Monographien und Texte Zur Nietzsche-Forschung Ser.: Vol. 37). (GER.). xiii, 702p. (C). 1997. lib. bdg. 236.00 (3-11-014563-4) De Gruyter.

***Leider's Lecture: A Complete Course in Understanding Financial Aid.** 19th ed. Anna Leider & Robert Leider. 40p. 1999. pap. 15.00 (1-57509-054-6) Octameron Assocs.

Leif Sverdrup: Engineer Soldier at His Best. Gregory M. Franzwa & William J. Ely. LC 80-361. (Illus.). 435p. 1980. pap. 14.95 (0-935284-44-3) Patrice Pr.

Leif the Lucky. John Dandola. (Learning & Coloring Bks.). (Illus.). 24p. (J). (gr. k up). 1991. pap. 3.95 (1-878452-05-3, Tory Corner) Quincannon.

Leif the Lucky. Ingri D'Aulaire & Edgar P. D'Aulaire. LC 94-74546. (Illus.). 64p. (J). (gr. k-6). 1995. pap. 13.95 (0-9643803-0-7) Beautiful Feet.

Leif's Saga. Jonathan Hunt. LC 94-14233. 32p. (J). 1995. mass mkt. write for info. (0-02-745780-X) Macmillan.

Leif's Saga: A Viking Tale. Jonathan Hunt. LC 94-14233. (Illus.). 40p. (J). (gr. k-5). 1996. mass mkt. 16.00 (0-689-80492-X) S&S Bks Yung.

Leigh: Police Powers in England & Wales. 2nd ed. L. H. Leigh. 1985. pap. 46.00 (0-406-84542-5, MICHIE) LEXIS Pub.

Leigh Bowery. S. Tilley. (Illus.). 1997. mass mkt. 15.95 (0-340-69311-8, Pub. by Hodder & Stought Ltd) Trafalgar.

Leigh Bowery. Robert Violette et al. LC 99-231000. (Illus.). 240p. 1998. 45.00 (1-900828-04-9) Dist Art Pubs.

Leigh Brackett: American Writer. John L. Carr. (Booklet Ser.: No. 22). 67p. (Orig.). 1986. pap. 3.00 (0-936055-23-5) C Drumm Bks.

Leigh Hunt. James R. Thompson. LC 77-6803. (Twayne's English Authors Ser.). 176p. (C). 1977. lib. bdg. 20.95 (0-8057-6679-0) Irvington.

Leigh Hunt. Ed. by Reginald Johnson. LC 73-115182. (English Literature Ser.: No. 33). 1970. reprint ed. lib. bdg. 75.00 (0-8383-1010-9) M S G Haskell Hse.

Leigh Hunt: A Life in Letters - Together with Some Correspondence of William Hazlitt. Eleanor M. Gates. LC 98-74287. (Illus.). xxxi, 693p. 1999. 44.95 (0-9668258-3-7) Falls River Pubns.

Leigh Hunt & Charles Dickens: The Skimpole Caricature. L. Brewer. LC 72-160466. (English Literature Ser.: No. 33). 1971. reprint ed. lib. bdg. 75.00 (0-8383-1301-9) M S G Haskell Hse.

Leigh Hunt & His Circle. Edmund C. Blunden. (BCL1-PR English Literature Ser.). 402p. 1992. reprint ed. lib. bdg. 99.00 (0-7812-7570-9) Rprt Serv.

Leigh Hunt & the Poetry of Fancy. Rodney S. Edgecombe. LC 94-20741. 1994. 41.50 (0-8386-3571-7) Fairleigh Dickinson.

Leigh Hunt's London Journal & the Printing Machine, 2 vols. in 1. Leigh Hunt. reprint ed. 225.00 (0-404-19530-X) AMS Pr.

Leigh Weimers' Guide to Silicon Valley: An Insider's Tips for Techies & Tourists. Leigh Weimers. (Illus.). (Orig.). 1993. pap. 12.95 (0-934136-52-1) Good Life.

Leighton: Memorials of the Leightons of Ulishaven, Forfarshire, & Other Scottish Families of the Name, A. D. 1260-1518 (with Added Pedigress Through 1920's) Clarence F. Leighton. 126p. 1993. reprint ed. pap. 27.00 (0-8328-3364-9); reprint ed. lib. bdg. 37.00 (0-8328-3363-0) Higginson Bk Co.

Leighton. Ancestors & Descendants of George Leighton & Jean Guthrie Who Lived in West Ogil, Tannadice Parish, Angus Shire (Forfarshire) Scotland in the 18th Century, with Related Families. Margaret K. Bowman et al. (Illus.). 718p. 1997. pap. 105.00 (0-8328-7006-4); lib. bdg. 115.00 (0-8328-7005-6) Higginson Bk Co.

Leighton Buzzard & Linslade: With Heath & Reach, Eggington, Stanbridge & Billington. Maureen Brown & June Masters. LC 97-130920. (Britain in Old Photographs Ser.). 126p. 1998. write for info. (0-7509-0871-8) Sutton Pub Ltd.

Leighton Genealogy: Dscendants of Thomas Leighton of Dover New Hampshire, 2 vols. Compiled by Perly Leighton. 1054p. 1989. 60.00 (0-88082-023-3, S3-33650) New Eng Hist.

Leila. Robin Jenkins. 1995. pap. 18.00 (0-7486-6204-9, Pub. by Polygon) Subterranean Co.

Leila: Further in the Life & Destinies of Darcy Dancer, Gentleman. J. P. Donleavy. LC 89-28307. 432p. 1990. 12.00 (0-87113-288-5, Atlntc Mnthly) Grove-Atltic.

Leila Amoung the Mountains. Lucy Larcom. (Notable American Authors Ser.). 1999. lib. bdg. 125.00 (0-7812-3745-9) Rprt Serv.

***Leila or the Siege of Granada.** Edward Bulwer Lytton. 86p. 1999. reprint ed. pap. 14.95 (0-7661-0792-2) Kessinger Pub.

Leimon Tario see Spiritual Meadow

Leinster Street Ghosts. Dermot Bolger. 32p. 1990. pap. 7.95 (1-85186-067-3) Dufour.

Leipzig: Buildings 1989-1999. Ingeborg Flagge & Anette Hellmuth. Ed. by Engelbert L. Daldrup. (Illus.). 216p. 1999. 60.00 (3-7643-5957-9, Pub. by Birkhauser) Princeton Arch.

Leipzig Connection. Paolo Lionni. (Basics of Education Ser.: No. 1). (Illus.). xii, 119p. (Orig.). (C). 1980. pap. 4.95 (0-89739-001-6) Heron Bks OR.

Leipzig, Eighteen Thirteen. Peter Hofschroer. (Campaign Ser.). (Illus.). 96p. 1993. pap. 14.95 (1-85532-354-0, 9524, Pub. by Ospry) Stackpole.

Leipzig Manuscript. large type ed. Angus Ross. (Lythway Ser.). 256p. 1991. 21.95 (0-7451-1277-3, G K Hall Lrg Type) Mac Lib Ref.

Leipziger Beitrage Zur Bachforschung Vol. 1: Bericht Uber die Wissenschaftliche Konferenz Anlablich des 69. Bach-Festes der Neuen Bachgesellschaft Leipzig, Marz 1994. Ed. by Bach-Archiv Leipzig. (GER.). 280p. 1995. write for info. (3-487-09974-8) G Olms Pubs.

Leipziger Studien zur Classischen Philologie, 20 vols. in 10, Set. Ed. by Georg Curtius et al. lxxx, 7348p. 1972. reprint ed. 1360.00 (*3-487-04335-1*) G Olms Pubs.

Leirner, Jac. Text by Jac Leirner. (Illus.). 1991. pap. 30.00 (*0-905836-74-X*, Pub. by Museum Modern Art) St Mut.

***Leis: Poems from Hollywood.** Mark Dunster. 11p. 1999. pap. 5.00 (*0-89642-744-7*) Linden Pubs.

Leise Settings of the Renaissance & Reformation Era. Jacob Regnart et al. Ed. by Johannes Riedel. (Recent Researches in Music of the Renaissance Ser.: Vol. RRR35). (Illus.). xxvi, 100p. 1980. pap. 40.00 (*0-89579-130-7*, RRR35) A-R Eds.

Leishmaniases: Clinical Aspects & Control, Vol. 2. Ed. by W. Peters & R. Killick-Kendrick. 400p. 1987. text 104.00 (*0-12-552102-2*) Acad Pr.

Leishmaniases in Biology & Medicine, 2 vols. Peters. 1987. 157.00 (*0-12-552103-0*) Acad Pr.

Leishmaniases I: Biology & Epidemiology, Vol. 1. Ed. by W. Peters & R. Killick-Kendrick. 550p. 1987. text 104.00 (*0-12-552101-4*) Acad Pr.

Leishmaniasis: The Current States & New Strategies for Control. Ed. by D. T. Hart. (NATO ASI Series A, Life Sciences: Vol. 163). (Illus.). 1056p. 1989. 185.00 (*0-306-43146-7*, Plenum Trade) Perseus Pubng.

***Leisler Papers, 1689-1691: Files of the Provincial Secretary of New York Relating to the Administration of Lieutenant-Governor Jacob Leisler.** Ed. by Peter R. Christoph. LC 99-48622. 656p. 1999. 90.00 (*0-8156-2820-X*) Syracuse U Pr.

Leisler's Rebellion. Charles H. McCormick. (Outstanding Studies in Early American History). 417p. 1989. reprint ed. 25.00 (*0-8240-6190-X*) Garland.

Leiston Abbey Cartulary & Butley Priory Charters. Richard Mortimer. (Suffolk Charters Ser.: No. I). 187p. 1979. 45.00 (*0-85115-106-X*) Boydell & Brewer.

Leistungsermittlung und Leistungsbewertung Im Muttersprachunterrich der DDR: Klassen 5 Bix 10 - Determinanten und Tendenzen. Marina Kreisel. (Beitrage Zur Geschichte des Deutschunterrichts Ser.: Bd. 32). (GER., Illus.). 258p. 1996. 51.95 (*3-631-48852-1*) P Lang Pubng.

Leistungsmotivation Methoden, Soziale Erwunschtheit und das Konstrukt: Ansatzpunkte Zur Entwicklung Eines Neuen Eignungsdiagnostischen Verfahrens. Michael Prochaska. (Psychologie Ser.: Bd. 612). (GER., Illus.). VIII, 182p. 1998. 37.95 (*3-631-33162-2*) P Lang Pubng.

Leisure. 2nd ed. Kenneth Roberts. LC 80-42055. (Aspects of Modern Sociology: the Social Structure of Modern Britain Ser.). 146p. reprint ed. pap. 45.30 (*0-608-13118-0*, 202522300043) Bks Demand.

Leisure. 3rd ed. John R. Kelly. LC 95-1087. 448p. 1995. text 63.00 (*0-13-110561-2*) Allyn.

Leisure: The Basis of Culture. Josef Pieper. Tr. by Alexander Dru from GER. LC 98-40641. Orig. Title: Musse und Kult - Was Heisst Philosophieren?. 158p. 1999. 17.00 (*0-86597-210-9*) Liberty Fund.

Leisure: Toward a Theory & Policy. Hillel Ruskin. LC 83-48608. 192p. 1984. 33.50 (*0-8386-3134-7*) Fairleigh Dickinson.

Leisure & Aging: A Practical & Theoretical Guide. 2nd ed. Carolyn Love. 96p. (C). 1997. pap. text, per. 35.95 (*0-7872-3324-2*, 41332401) Kendall-Hunt.

Leisure & Aging: Ulyssean Living in Later Life. Francis A. McGuire et al. 286p. 1995. text 15.00 (*1-57167-014-9*) Sagamore Pub.

Leisure & Ancient Rome. J. P. Toner. 1999. pap. 29.95 (*0-7456-2198-8*) Blackwell Pubs.

Leisure & Ancient Rome. J. P. Toner. LC 95-16182. (Illus.). 250p. (C). 1996. 66.95 (*0-7456-1432-9*, Pub. by Polity Pr) Blackwell Pubs.

Leisure & Class in Victorian England: Rational Recreation & the Contest for Control, 1830-1885. Peter Bailey. (Illus.). 288p. 1987. pap. 16.95 (*0-416-02142-5*) Routledge.

Leisure & Crime. Mohammad M. Hussinat. LC 97-905778. 236p. 1997. 30.00 (*81-7033-411-X*, Pub. by Rawat Pubns) Nataraj Bks.

Leisure & Culture. Rojek. LC 99-15308. 2000. text 65.00 (*0-312-22591-1*) St Martin.

Leisure & Entertainment Facilities. Lawson. 1999. pap. 79.95 (*0-7506-3377-8*) Buttrwrth-Heinemann.

Leisure & Entertainment in America Donna R. Braden & Henry Ford Museum & Greenfield Village Staff. LC 88-80580. 367p. 1988. write for info. (*0-933728-32-8*) Henry Ford Mus.

Leisure & Ethics: Reflections on the Philosophy of Leisure, Vol. I. Ed. by Gerald S. Fain. 352p. (Orig.). 1991. pap. text 27.00 (*0-88314-489-1*, A4891) AAHPERD.

Leisure & Ethics: Reflections on the Philosophy of Leisure, Vol. II. Ed. by Gerald S. Fain. 330p. (Orig.). 1995. pap. text 27.00 (*0-88314-850-1*, 300-10006) AAHPERD.

Leisure & Family Fun. Mary Atteberry-Rogers. LC 92-62934. (Illus.). 95p. 1993. pap. 19.95 (*0-910251-59-2*) Venture Pub PA.

***Leisure & Feminist Theory.** Betsy Wearing. LC 98-61180. xvi, 207 p. 1999. 24.95 (*0-8039-7537-6*) Sage.

Leisure & Human Behavior. 3rd ed. Gene Bammel & Lei L. Bammel. LC 95-75475. 528p. (C). 1995. text. write for info. (*0-697-23330-8*) Brown & Benchmark.

Leisure & Human Behavior. 4th ed. Gene Bammel. 1999. pap. text 35.78 (*0-697-29496-X*) McGraw.

Leisure & Leisure Services in the 21st Century. Geoffrey Godbey. LC 97-61792. 272p. 1997. text 24.95 (*0-910251-92-4*, GEO96) Venture Pub PA.

Leisure & Life Satisfaction. 2nd ed. Ed. by Christopher R. Edginton. LC 97-15843. 464p. 1997. 54.69 (*0-697-29498-6*) McGraw.

Leisure & Life Satisfaction: Foundational Perspectives. Christopher R. Edginton et al. 456p. (C). 1995. text. write for info. (*0-697-13232-3*) Brown & Benchmark.

Leisure & Lifestyle in Selected Writings of Karl Marx: A Social & Theoretical History. Glen Eker. LC 91-29470. 140p. 1991. pap. 24.95 (*0-7734-9866-4*) E Mellen.

Leisure & Play in Therapy. McCree. 1998. pap. text 36.00 (*0-12-784562-3*) Acad Pr.

Leisure & Play in Therapy: Theory, Goals & Activities. Suesetta T. McCree. 140p. 1993. pap. text 38.00 (*0-7616-4281-1*) Commun Skill.

Leisure & Recreation: Introduction & Overview. Clayne R. Jensen. LC 77-22992. 303p. reprint ed. pap. 94.00 (*0-608-17763-6*, 205651500069) Bks Demand.

Leisure & Recreation, Case Study No. 6: The Peterborough Experience. Ed. by Barry Symonds. (C). 1988. text 75.00 (*0-85406-374-9*, Pub. by Surveyors Pubns) St Mut.

***Leisure & Recreation for Advanced GNVQ.** Rob Saipe. (Illus.). 320p. 2000. pap. 42.50 (*0-7487-5309-5*, Pub. by S Thornes Pubs) Trans-Atl Phila.

Leisure & Recreation Management. 4th ed. G. Torkildsen. 1998. pap. 32.99 (*0-419-22940-X*, E & FN Spon) Routledge.

***Leisure & Recreational Facilities in Taiwan: A Strategic Entry Report, 2000.** Compiled by Icon Group International. (Illus.). 121p. 1999. ring bd. 1210.00 incl. audio compact disk (*0-7418-2196-6*) Icon Grp.

Leisure & Society, Future Trends: Papers from Scola I, an Interdisciplinary Conference. Jay S. Shivers. LC GV0004.L4. 112p. reprint ed. pap. 34.80 (*0-7837-1532-3*, 204181300024) Bks Demand.

Leisure & the American Dream. Compton & Ellis. (Illus.). 425p. (C). (gr. 13). 2000. 22.95 (*0-8016-1028-1*, 01028) Mosby Inc.

Leisure & the Environment. John Spink. LC 95-129209. 96p. 1995. pap. 31.95 (*0-7506-0687-8*) Buttrwrth-Heinemann.

Leisure & the Future. A. J. Veal. (Leisure & Recreation Studies: No. 4). 220p. 1987. text 55.00 (*0-04-790006-7*) Routledge.

Leisure & the Future. A. J. Veal. LC 86-22191. (Leisure & Recreation Studies: No. 4). 207p. (C). 1987. pap. 24.99 (*0-04-790007-5*) Routledge.

Leisure & Tourism Assignments, Vol. 1. 2nd ed. John Ward. 104p. (Orig.). 1996. pap. 29.50 (*0-7487-2428-1*, Pub. by S Thornes Pubs) Trans-Atl Phila.

***Leisure & Tourism Geographies: Leisure/Tourism Practices & Geographical Knowledge.** Ed. by David Crouch. LC 99-45586. 304p. (C). 2000. text. write for info. (*0-415-18108-9*) Routledge.

***Leisure & Tourism Geographies: Practices & Geographical Knowledge.** David Crouch. LC 99-45586. (Critical Geographies Ser.). (Illus.). 304p. 1999. pap. 31.99 (*0-415-18109-7*) Routledge.

***Leisure & Tourism Landscapes: Social & Cultural Geographies.** Cara Aitchison et al. LC 00-30820. (Illus.). 2000. write for info. (*0-415-17060-5*) Routledge.

Leisure & Unemployment. Sue Glyptis. 176p. 1989. 113.00 (*0-335-15883-8*); pap. 36.95 (*0-335-15882-X*) OpUniv Pr.

Leisure & Urbanism in Nineteenth-Century Nice. C. James Haug. LC 81-15780. (Illus.). xviii, 168p. 1982. 25.00 (*0-7006-0221-6*) U Pr of KS.

***Leisure & Wellness Facilities.** Ed. by Shotenkenchiku-Sha Editorial Staff. (Illus.). 180p. 2000. 69.95 (*4-7858-0260-X*, Pub. by Shotenkenchiku-Sha) Bks Nippan.

Leisure Arts Best 250 Christmas Quickies. Leisure Arts Staff. 140p. 1995. pap. 19.95 (*0-942237-76-5*) Leisure AR.

Leisure Class in America, 41 vols., Set. Ed. by Leon Stein. (Illus.). 1975. 1126.50 (*0-405-06900-6*) Ayer.

Leisure Craft. Barbara Hemmings. (C). 1990. pap. 30.00 (*0-908175-88-4*, Pub. by Boolarong Pubns) St Mut.

Leisure Diagnostic Battery: User's Manual & Sample Forms. Peter Witt & Gary Ellis. LC 87-50934. 93p. (Orig.). 1985. spiral bd. 19.95 (*0-910251-22-3*) Venture Pub PA.

Leisure Education: A Manual of Activities & Resources. Steve R. Thompson. Ed. by Norma J. Stumbo. 462p. 1988. ring bd. 21.95 (*0-910251-25-8*) Venture Pub PA.

Leisure Education: Program Materials for Persons with Developmental Disabilities. Kenneth F. Joswiak. LC 89-51383. 141p. (C). 1989. 15.95 (*0-910251-33-9*) Venture Pub PA.

Leisure Education: Theory & Practice. 2nd ed. Jean Mundy. (Illus.). 270p. (C). 1997. 44.95 (*1-57167-035-1*) Sagamore Pub.

***Leisure Education, Community Development & Population with Special Needs.** Ed. by A. A. Sivan & H. Ruskin. LC 99-59522. 256p. 2000. text 70.00 (*0-85199-444-X*) OUP.

Leisure Education III: More Goal-Oriented Activities. Norma J. Stumbo. LC 97-61628. 392p. 1997. ring bd. 24.95 (*0-910251-91-6*, MG095) Venture Pub PA.

Leisure Education Program Planning: A Systematic Approach. John Dattilo & William D. Murphy. LC 91-66103. 485p. 1991. 34.95 (*0-910251-49-5*) Venture Pub PA.

***Leisure Education Program Planning: A Systematic Approach.** 2nd rev. ed. John Dattilo. LC 99-62854. 355p. (C). 1999. text 31.95 (*1-892132-05-2*, LPP108) Venture Pub PA.

Leisure Education Towards the 21st Century. Ed. by Hillel Ruskin & Atara Sivan. 289p. (Orig.). (C). 1995. pap. text 19.45 (*0-9648003-0-6*, Dept Rec Mgmt) Brigham.

Leisure Education II: More Activities & Resources. Norma J. Stumbo. LC 91-68520. (Illus.). 428p. (C). 1992. ring bd. 24.95 (*0-910251-54-1*) Venture Pub PA.

Leisure Enhancement. Ed. by Sara F. Leitner. LC 89-15549. (Illus.). 412p. 1989. pap. text 24.95 (*0-86656-847-6*) Haworth Pr.

Leisure Enhancement. Ed. by Sara F. Leitner. LC 89-15549. (Illus.). 412p. 1989. text 49.95 (*0-86656-892-1*) Haworth Pr.

Leisure Enhancement. 2nd ed. Michael J. Leitner et al. LC 95-36990. (Illus.). 447p. (C). 1996. 49.95 (*1-56024-958-7*); pap. 24.95 (*1-56024-959-5*) Haworth Pr.

Leisure Environment. Marcus Colquhoun. 208p. (Orig.). 1993. pap. 41.50 (*0-273-03752-8*, Pub. by Pitman Pub) Trans-Atl Phila.

***Leisure Ethic: Work & Play in American Literature, 1840-1940.** William A. Gleason. LC 98-35016. 1999. 60.00 (*0-8047-3399-6*); pap. 19.95 (*0-8047-3434-8*) Stanford U Pr.

Leisure Experience & Human Development. Douglas Kleiber. LC 98-43804. (Lives in Context Ser.). 256p. (C). 1999. text 65.00 (*0-8133-3148-X*, Pub. by Westview); pap. text 22.00 (*0-8133-3149-8*, Pub. by Westview) HarpC.

Leisure for Leisure: Critical Essays. Ed. by Chris Rojek. 256p. 1989. text 32.50 (*0-415-90065-4*) Routledge.

Leisure, Gender & Poverty: Working-Class Culture in Salford & Manchester, 1900-1939. Andrew Davies. (Themes in the Twentieth Century Ser.). 192p. 1992. pap. 40.95 (*0-335-15637-1*) OpUniv Pr.

Leisure Guide: Horse Riding. British Tourist Board Staff. 1994. pap. text 30.00 (*1-85253-294-7*, Pub. by Quiller Pr) St Mut.

Leisure Hive. 1993. pap. 5.95 (*0-426-20147-7*) Carol Pub Group.

Leisure Identities & Interactions. John R. Kelly. (Leisure & Recreation Studies: No. 1). (Illus.). 216p. 1985. text 37.95 (*0-04-301150-0*); pap. text 14.95 (*0-04-301203-5*) Routledge.

Leisure in a Changing America: Trends & Issues for the Twenty-First Century. 2nd ed. Richard Kraus. LC 99-53932. 384p. (C). 2000. pap. text 37.00 (*0-205-31456-2*) Allyn.

Leisure in Contemporary Society. Ken Roberts. LC 99-22426. (CABI Publishing Ser.). 256p. 1999. text 30.00 (*0-85199-338-9*) OUP.

Leisure in Europe. Ed. by Eric Corijn. 200p. 1994. pap. 29.50 (*90-5487-073-7*, Pub. by VUB Univ Pr) Paul & Co Pubs.

Leisure in Later Life. 2nd ed. Michael J. Leitner & Sara F. Leitner. LC 95-45915. (Illus.). 466p. (C). 1996. pap. 24.95 (*1-56024-966-8*) Haworth Pr.

Leisure in Later Life. 2nd ed. Michael J. Leitner & Sara F. Leitner. LC 95-45915. (Illus.). 466p. 1996. 49.95 (*1-56024-965-X*) Haworth Pr.

Leisure in Later Life: A Sourcebook for the Provision of Recreation Services for Elders. Michael J. Leitner & Sara F. Leitner. LC 85-17635. (Activities, Adaptation & Aging Ser.: Vol. 7, Nos. 3-4). 341p. 1986. text 49.95 (*0-86656-452-7*); pap. text 24.95 (*0-86656-476-4*) Haworth Pr.

Leisure in Society: A Comparative Approach. Hilmi Ibrahim. 304p. (C). 1990. text. write for info. (*0-697-05374-1*) Brown & Benchmark.

Leisure in Society: A Network Structural Perspective. Patricia A. Stokowski. (Tourism, Leisure & Recreation Ser.). (Illus.). 156p. 1995. pap. 33.95 (*0-7201-2311-9*) Continuum.

Leisure in the Modern World. Cecil D. Burns. 1982. 19.95 (*0-8434-0434-5*) McGrath NH.

Leisure in Your Life: An Explanation. 3rd ed. Geoffrey C. Godbey. LC 90-71133. 285p. 1990. 24.95 (*0-910251-36-3*) Venture Pub PA.

Leisure in Your Life: An Exploration. 4th ed. Geoffrey C. Godbey. LC 94-60095. (Illus.). 373p. (C). 1994. text 28.95 (*0-910251-65-7*, LEI04) Venture Pub PA.

***Leisure in Your Life: An Exploration.** 5th ed. Geoffrey Godbey. LC 99-64557. xviii, 428p. (C). 1999. text 35.95 (*1-892132-06-0*, LE105) Venture Pub PA.

Leisure, Lifestyle & the New Middle Class: A Case Study. Derek Wynne. LC 97-21482. 184p. (C). 1998. 80.00 (*0-415-03834-0*) Routledge.

Leisure Management: Issues & Applications. Ed. by M. F. Collins & I. S. Cooper. LC 97-22231. (A CAB International Publication). 336p. (C). 1998. 75.00 (*0-85199-215-3*) OUP.

Leisure Migration: A Sociological Study on Tourism. Jozsef Borocz. (Tourism Social Science Ser.). 230p. 1996. text 69.00 (*0-08-042560-7*, Pergamon Pr) Elsevier.

Leisure of One's Own: A Feminist Perspective on Women's Leisure. Karla Henderson et al. LC 89-50208. 195p. 1989. 22.95 (*0-910251-29-0*) Venture Pub PA.

Leisure Operations Management: People, Vol. 2. Badmin. 1988. pap. text. write for info. (*0-582-02326-2*, Pub. by Addison-Wesley) Longman.

Leisure Opportunities for Individuals with Disabilities: Legal Issues. Ed. by Susan J. Grosse & Donna Thompson. 112p. (Orig.). 1993. pap. 23.00 (*0-88314-553-7*) AAHPERD.

Leisure Pen: A Book for Elderwriters. Joyce S. Steward & Mary K. Croft. LC 88-82602. (Illus.). 206p. (Orig.). 1988. pap. 10.95 (*0-9621354-0-2*) Keepsake Pubs.

Leisure Policies in Europe. Ed. by P. Bramham et al. (Illus.). 288p. 1993. text 80.00 (*0-85198-819-9*) OUP.

Leisure Programming: Concepts, Trends, & Professional Practice. 3rd ed. Christopher R. Edginton et al. LC 96-86582. 496p. (C). 1997. text. write for info. (*0-697-23332-4*, WCB McGr Hill) McGrw-H Hghr Educ.

Leisure, Recreation & Tourism. Ed. by John B. Goddard. (Journal of Regional Studies: No. 15). (Illus.). 96p. 1981. pap. 18.75 (*0-08-028945-2*, Pergamon Pr) Elsevier.

Leisure Research in Europe: Methods & Traditions. Ed. by H. Mommaas et al. LC 97-144800. (CAB International Publication Ser.). (Illus.). 304p. 1997. text 70.00 (*0-85198-773-7*) OUP.

Leisure Resources. Dan McLean et al. LC 98-85172. (Illus.). 5p. (C). 1998. text 44.95 (*1-57167-025-4*) Sagamore Pub.

Leisure Service Delivery System: A Modern Perspective. James F. Murphy et al. LC 73-7851. (Health Education, Physical Education, & Recreation Ser.). 224p. reprint ed. pap. 69.50 (*0-608-12679-9*, 205600400043) Bks Demand.

Leisure Services in Canada: An Introduction. Mark S. Searle & Russell E. Brayley. LC 93-61300. 273p. (C). 1993. text 29.95 (*0-910251-64-9*) Venture Pub PA.

***Leisure Services in Canada: An Introduction.** 2nd ed. Mark S. Searle & Russell E. Brayley. LC 99-67805. xx, 300p. 2000. text 29.95 (*1-892132-11-7*, CAN114) Venture Pub PA.

Leisure Services in Hungary & Illinois: A Comparative Study. Allen V. Sapora. 258p. (Orig.). 1981. pap. text 14.80 (*0-87563-206-8*) Stipes.

Leisure Services with the Elderly. Joseph E. Teaff. (Illus.). 360p. (C). 1990. reprint ed. text 34.95 (*0-88133-571-1*) Waveland Pr.

Leisure Settings: Bourgeois Culture, Medicine & the Spa in Modern France. Douglas P. Mackaman. LC 98-15570. 256p. 1998. pap. text 18.00 (*0-226-50075-6*) U Ch Pr.

***Leisure Settings: Bourgeois Culture, Medicine & the Spa in Modern France.** Douglas P. Mackaman. LC 98-15570. 256p. 1998. lib. bdg. 46.00 (*0-226-50074-8*) U Ch Pr.

Leisure Step Up: Healthy Choices. Dave Dehn. (Illus.). 134p. 1995. pap. 50.00 (*1-882883-07-1*, 276) Idyll Arbor.

Leisure Step up Workbook: Healthy Choices. Dave Dehn. (Illus.). 46p. 1995. pap., wbk. ed. 4.00 (*1-882883-18-7*, 277) Idyll Arbor.

***Leisure Studies: Prospects for the 21st Century.** Ed. by Edgar L. Jackson & Thomas L. Burton. LC 98-89987. 584p. 1999. text 47.95 (*1-892132-03-6*, JB107) Venture Pub PA.

Leisure Suit Larry: Love for Sail!: The Official Strategy Guide, Vol. 7. Mel Odom. LC 96-70479. 240p. 1996. per. 19.99 (*0-7615-0876-7*) Prima Pub.

Leisure, the Basis of Culture (Musse und Kult & Was Heisst Philesephieren) Josef Pieper. Tr. by Gerald Malsbary from GER. LC 98-15340. 176p. 1998. pap. text 12.00 (*1-890318-35-3*) St Augustines Pr.

Leisure Time Activities for Deaf-Blind Children. California State Department of Health Staff. LC 75-70066. 24.95 (*0-917002-06-7*) Joyce Media.

Leisure Travel. Education Systems Staff. 269p. (C). 1997. pap. text 35.00 (*1-879982-56-0*) Educ Systs.

Leisure Travel: Making It a Growth Market... Again! Stanley C. Plog. 256p. 1991. 69.95 (*0-471-52952-4*) Wiley.

Leisure Wellness Series. C. Forrest McDowell. Incl. Assessing Your Leisurestyle & Formulating Strategies. 1983. 2.25 (*0-942064-06-2*); Concepts & Principles. 1.50 (*0-942064-02-X*); Coping Strategies & Managing Stress. 1983. 1.75 (*0-942064-07-0*); Identity & Social Roles. 1983. 1.75 (*0-942064-04-6*); Intimate Relationships. 1983. 1.00 (*0-942064-03-8*); Introduction. 1983. 2.25 (*0-942064-01-1*); Managing Attitudes, Affirmation & Assertion. 1983. 2.00 (*0-942064-08-9*); Managing Economics, Time & Cultural Forces. 1983. 1.75 (*0-942064-09-7*); Strategies for Fitness. 1983. 1.50 (*0-942064-05-4*); 1983. 12.95 (*0-942064-00-3*); 1983. write for info. (*0-318-57603-1*) Cortesia Pr.

Leisure Workbook. Ed. by Stephen J. Page & Roy Wood. (Tourism & Hospitality Management Ser.). 304p. 1995. 59.00 (*0-415-09963-3*); pap. 22.95 (*0-415-09964-1*) Routledge.

***Leisured Ladies.** Karla Walters. 300p. 2000. 55.00 (*0-8153-2053-1*) Garland.

Leisuregrams. Francis R. Lalor. LC 80-83525. 1981. 7.95 (*0-87212-144-5*) Libra.

Leisuretronics: A Statistical Typing Practice Set. G. Weathers. 168p. 1985. text 7.36 (*0-07-068693-9*) McGraw.

Leite Lopez Festschrift. Ed. by N. Fleury et al. 672p. 1989. text 139.00 (*9971-5-0693-9*) World Scientific Pub.

Leiter der Erinnerung. David Koenig. LC 93-79443. (GER.). 100p. pap. write for info. (*0-9637357-1-3*) Harp Song Pr.

Leitfaden der Deutschen Grammatik. Gerhard Helbig & Joachim Buscha. (GER.). 287p. 1996. 21.95 (*3-324-00047-5*) Langenscheidt.

Leitfaden der Kardiotokographie. F. Jaisle. (Illus.). viii, 112p. 1982. pap. 28.75 (*3-8055-3444-2*) S Karger.

Leitfaden fur Fachbergriffe des Futures und Optionsmarktes. Tr. by Jorg Gruhler. (GER.). 71p. 1990. pap. 3.95 (*0-915513-30-7*) Ctr Futures Ed.

Leitfaden fur Fachbergriffe des Futures und Optionsmarktes. Tr. by Jorg Gruhler. (GER.). 71p. 1997. pap. 3.95 (*0-915513-81-1*) Ctr Futures Ed.

Leitfaden fur Novell Netware, Vol. 2. 2nd ed. Andreas Zenk. (GER.). (C). 1991. text. write for info. (*0-201-56573-0*) Addison-Wesley.

Leitfaden Zu Perelandra Rosen- und Garten- Essenzen. Machaelle S. Wright. Tr. by Sabine Groote.Tr. of Perelandra Guide to Rose & Garden Essences. (ENG & GER., Illus.). 56p. 1997. pap. 3.00 (*0-927978-35-0*) Perelandra Ltd.

Leitfaden zur Systematischen Bearbeitung des Campagneund Gebrauchspferdes. E. F. Seidler. (Illus.). xx, 397p. 1977. write for info. (*3-487-08148-2*) G Olms Pubs.

An Asterisk (*) at the beginning of an entry indicates that the title is appearing for the first time.

Leitfossilien der Mikropalaeontologie. W. Simon et al. viii, 432p. 1962. 106.00 (*3-443-39027-7*, Pub. by Gebruder Borntraeger) Balogh.

Leith Hospital. D. H. Boyd. 180p. 1989. 40.00 (*0-7073-0584-5*, Pub. by Mercat Pr Bks) St Mut.

***Leithen Stories: The Power House - John Macnab - Dancing Floor - Sick Heart River.** John Buchan. 2000. pap. 16.00 (*0-86241-995-6*, Pub. by Canongate Books) Interlink Pub.

***Leith's Latin-American Cooking.** Valeria V. Sisti. (Illus.). 288p. 2000. 29.95 (*0-7624-0770-0*) Running Pr.

Leitmotifs in Natural Morphology. Wolfgang U. Dressler et al. LC 87-21791. (Studies in Language Companion: No. 10). ix, 168p. 1988. 43.00 (*90-272-3009-9*) J Benjamins Pubng Co.

Leitmotiv & Drama: Wagner, Brecht, & the Limits of "Epic" Theatre. Hilda M. Brown. (Illus.). 232p. 1991. 65.00 (*0-19-816227-8*) OUP.

Leitner: Geometry of Sound. Bernhard Leitner. (Illus.). 80p. 1999. pap. 16.95 (*3-89322-936-1*) Dr Cantz sche Druckerei GmbH.

Leittext Als (Fach-)Textlinguistisches Phanomen: Analyse und Optimierungsmoglichkeiten Einer Betriebsinternen Textsorte. Johann Bauer. (Forum Linguisticum Ser.: No. 34). (Illus.). 418p. 1997. 63.95 (*3-631-31709-3*) P Lang Pubng.

Lejeune, 1867-1942: A Marine's Life. Merrill L. Bartlett. LC 96-17123. (Bluejacket Bks.). (Illus.). 256p. 1996. pap. 16.95 (*1-55750-063-0*) Naval Inst Pr.

Lejeuneaceae (Hepaticae): Subfamily Ptychanthoideae. Barbara M. Thiers & S. Rob Gradstein. LC 88-34572. (Memoirs Ser.: No. 52). (Illus.). 82p. 1989. pap. text 13.00 (*0-89327-339-2*) NY Botanical.

***Lejos del Polvo.** Karen Hesse. (SPA., Illus.). (gr. 4-7). 1999. pap. 11.95 (*84-241-5928-4*) Everest SP.

Leks. Jacob Hoglund & Rauno V. Alatalo. LC 94-41218. (Monographs in Behavior & Ecology). 224p. 1995. text 60.00 (*0-691-03728-0*, Pub. by Princeton U Pr); pap. text 26.95 (*0-691-03727-2*, Pub. by Princeton U Pr) Cal Prin Full Svc.

Leksel Gamma Knife Society: Proceedings. Ed. by J. C. Ganz et al. (Journal Ser.: Vol. 64, Suppl. 1, 1995). (Illus.). vi, 274p. 1995. pap. 68.00 (*3-8055-6266-7*) S Karger.

***Leksell Gamma Knife?? Society: Proceedings of the 9th International Meeting, Hong Kong, November, 1998.** Ed. by J. C. Ganz et al. (Stereotactic & Functional Neurosurgery Ser.: Vol. 72, Suppl. 1). (Illus.). vi, 188p. 1999. pap. 45.25 (*3-8055-6982-3*) S Karger.

Leksell Gamma Knife Society: Proceedings, 7th International Meeting, Island of Lana'i, Hawaii, November 1995. Ed. by Jeremy C. Ganz et al. (Journal Ser.: Vol. 66, Supplement 1, 1996). (Illus.). vi, 374p. 1997. pap. 115.75 (*3-8055-6446-5*) S Karger.

Leksell Gamma Knife Society: 8th International Meeting, Marseille, June 1997 - Proceedings. Ed. by J. C. Ganz et al. (Stereotactic & Functional Neurosurgery Ser.: Vol. 70, Suppl. 1). (Illus.). vi, 252p. 1998. pap. 78.25 (*3-8055-6793-6*) S Karger.

Leksikon Prava Medjunarodnih Privrednih Odnosa. Zutora Crupa. (ENG, FRE, GER, RUS & SER.). 560p. 1982. 39.95 (*0-8288-0581-4*, F78530) Fr & Eur.

Lektionar Von St. Petersburger. fac. limited ed. Comment by Elena Schwarz. (Codices Selecti A Ser.: Vol. XCVIII). (ENG & GER.). 42p. 1994. lthr. 2064.00 (*3-201-01613-6*, Pub. by Akademische Druck-und) Balogh.

Lektsii Po Istoriji Russkoi Slovjesnosti, 2 Vols. Konstatine Zaitsev.Tr. of Lectures on the History of Russian Philology. 203p. 1968. pap. text 11.00 (*0-685-10968-2*) Holy Trinity.

Lektsii Po Kvantovoi Elektronike see Lectures on Quantum Electronics

Lektsii Po Struktural'noe Poetike: Vvedenie, Teoriia Stikha. Iu M. Lotman. LC 68-10643. (Brown University Slavic Reprint Ser.: 5). 203p. reprint ed. pap. 63.00 (*0-608-16795-9*, 200897900055) Bks Demand.

Lektsii Po Teorii Atomnogo Iadra see Lectures on Nuclear Theory

Lele of the Kasai. Mary Douglas. LC GN0654.D66. 309p. reprint ed. pap. 95.80 (*0-8357-6951-8*, 203901000009) Bks Demand.

Lelia. Mark Dunster. 24p. (Orig.). 1993. pap. 5.00 (*0-89642-217-8*) Linden Pubs.

Lelia, 2 vols. George Sand. (FRE.). 247p. 1988. pap. 24.95 (*0-7859-1577-X*, 2903950210) Fr & Eur.

Lelia, 2 vols., Set. George Sand. (FRE.). 237p. 1988. pap. 24.95 (*0-7859-1576-1*, 2903950202) Fr & Eur.

Lelia ou la Vie de George Sand. Andre Maurois. 22.95 (*0-685-36943-9*) Fr & Eur.

Lelu Stone Ruins (Kosrae, Micronesia), 1978-81: Historical & Archaeological Research. Ross Cordy. (Asian & Pacific Archaeology Ser.: No. 10). 472p. (C). 1993. pap. text 36.00 (*0-8248-1134-8*) U HI SSRI.

Lem Reader. Stanislaw Lem & Peter Swirski. LC 97-23102. (Rethinking Theory Ser.). 1997. 49.95 (*0-8101-1494-1*); pap. 14.95 (*0-8101-1495-X*) Northwestern U Pr.

Lemaitre, Big Bang, & the Quantum Universe: With His Original Manuscript. Michael Heller. LC 94-65476. (History of Astronomy Ser.: Vol. 10). 108p. (Orig.). 1996. pap. 37.00 (*0-88126-285-4*) Pachart Pub Hse.

Lemas para Vivir. Ed. by Susan Polis Schutz.Tr. of Mottos to Live By. (ENG & SPA.). 64p. 1997. pap. 7.95 (*0-88396-453-8*) Blue Mtn Art.

Lembra Archaeological Project Vol. I: Excavations at Lembra Lakkous, 1976-1983. E. J. Peltenburg. (Studies in Mediterranean Archaeology: Vol. LXX:1). (Illus.). 356p. (Orig.). 1985. pap. 165.00 (*91-86098-27-6*, Pub. by P Astroms) Coronet Bks.

Lembra Archaeological Project Vol. II.2: A Ceremonial Area at Kissonerga. Edgar Peltenburg et al. (Studies in Mediterranean Archaeology: Vol. LXX:3). (Illus.). 135p. (Orig.). 1991. pap. 97.50 (*91-7081-011-7*, Pub. by P Astroms) Coronet Bks.

Lemegeton: King Solomon's Lesser Key. Robert Blanchard. (Illus.). 76p. 1997. 55.00 (*1-57179-063-2*) Intern Guild ASRS.

***Lemegeton: The Complete Lesser Key of Solomon.** Ed. by Mitch Henson. (Illus.). 145p. 1999. pap. 14.95 (*0-9672797-0-4*) Metatron Bks.

Lemegeton, Clavicula Salomonis: or The Complete Lesser Key of Solomon the King. 2nd ed. Ed. by Nelson H. White. LC 94-60532. (Illus.). 138p. (Orig.). (C). 1994. pap. 50.00 (*1-877884-10-3*) Tech Group.

Lemenager Family History: America's Wastines Legacy. Charles R. LeMenager. (Illus.). 150p. 1998. pap. text 19.95 (*0-9611102-6-0*) Eagle Peak Pub.

Lemhi: Sacajawea's People. Brigham D. Madsen. LC 78-53137. (Illus.). (Orig.). 1980. pap. 7.95 (*0-87004-267-X*) Caxton.

Lemhi: Sacajawea's People. Brigham D. Madsen. LC 78-53137. (Illus.). 214p. (Orig.). reprint ed. pap. 66.40 (*0-8357-4120-6*, 203695100005) Bks Demand.

Lemme Tell You Where I Used to Live. Diana Schooler. (Folk Literature Ser.). 23p. (Orig.). 1991. pap. 4.95 (*1-878781-04-9*) Free River Pr.

Lemming Condition. Alan Arkin. LC 75-6296. (Illus.). 64p. (J). (gr. 4 up). 1976. 13.00 (*0-06-020133-9*) HarpC Child Bks.

Lemming Condition. Alan Arkin. LC 89-7418. 64p. 1989. pap. 9.00 (*0-06-250048-1*, Perennial) HarperTrade.

Lemming Condition. Alan Arkin. (J). 1976. 14.20 (*0-606-04266-0*, Pub. by Turtleback) Demco.

Lemming Conspiracy: How to Redirect Your Life from Stress to Balance. Don Hutcheson et al. LC 97-71930. xiii, 240 p. 1997. 22.00 (*1-56352-423-6*) Longstreet.

***Lemming Dilemma: Living with Purpose, Leading with Vision.** David Hutchens. LC 99-36522. (Illus.). 86p. 2000. pap. 19.95 (*1-883823-45-5*, FT006) Pegasus Comm.

Lemming Shepherds Vol. 1: Symphony for the Census. Rick Costello & K. K. Roberts. (Illus.). 40p. (J). (gr. 4-12). 1997. pap. 5.00 (*0-9655201-0-2*, EMCD9904-96); pap. 29.95 incl. cd-rom (*0-9655201-2-9*, EMCD9904-96); cd-rom 24.95 (*0-9655201-1-0*, EMCD9904-96) Exzel Music.

Lemmings: The Official Companion. Mark Tsai. (Illus.). 304p. (Orig.). 1993. pap. 24.95 (*1-55958-188-3*) Prima Pub.

Lemnitzer: A Soldier for His Time. L. James Binder, II. LC 97-19134. (Association of the U. S. Army Book Ser.). 400p. 1997. 32.95 (*1-57488-107-8*) Brasseys.

***Lemnitzer: A Soldier for His Time.** L. James Binder. (Illus.). 386p. 2000. text 33.00 (*0-7881-9028-8*) DIANE Pub.

Lemon. Mohammed Mrabet. Tr. by Paul Bowles. 192p. (Orig.). 1986. reprint ed. pap. 8.95 (*0-87286-181-3*) City Lights.

Lemon Aid: Use Cars, 1999. Phil Edmonston. 432p. 1998. pap. 19.95 (*0-7737-5961-1*) Stoddart Publ.

***Lemon-Aid Car Guide 2000: Secret Bulletins, Government Tests & Owners' Ratings of 1981-98 Cars & Minivans.** Phil Edmonston. 496p. (Orig.). 2000. pap. 17.95 (*0-7737-6084-9*) Stoddart Publ.

Lemon-Aid Used Cars 1999: Secret Bulletins, Government Tests & Owners' Ratings of 1980-97 Cars & Minivans. Phil Edmonston. 1999. pap. 17.95 (*0-7737-6022-9*, Pub. by Stoddart Publ) Genl Dist Srvs.

***Lemon-Aid Used Cars 2001.** annuals rev. ed. Phil Edmonston. (Illus.). 496p. 2000. 24.99 (*0-7737-6122-5*) Stoddart Publ.

***Lemon-Aid Used 4x4s, Vans & Trucks 2001.** annuals rev. ed. Phil Edmonston. (Illus.). 352p. 2000. 24.99 (*0-7737-6123-3*) Stoddart Publ.

***Lemon Balm.** Kathleen L. Brown. LC 00-30781. (Country Wisdom Bulletin Ser.). 2000. pap. write for info. (*1-58017-319-5*) Storey Bks.

Lemon Belly Up: An Introduction to Economics. 4th ed. Bruce L. Beatty. 272p. (C). 1995. per. 37.95 (*0-7872-1785-9*, 41178501) Kendall-Hunt.

Lemon Book. 4th rev. ed. Ralph Nader & Clarence Ditlow. LC 96-39310. 396p. (Orig.). 1990. pap. 16.95 (*1-55921-196-2*) Moyer Bell.

Lemon City, 1850-1925: Pioneering on Biscayne Bay. Thelma Peters. LC 76-48058. (Illus.). 1976. 14.95 (*0-916224-12-0*) Banyan Bks.

Lemon County Chronicles. Tom Moon. 180p. 1992. pap. 7.95 (*0-9632808-0-5*) Lemon Seed Pr.

***Lemon Dilemna.** Kerri Mabee. Ed. by Noreen Wise. (Book-a-Day Collection). 32p. (YA). (ps up). 2000. pap. 5.95 (*1-58584-430-6*) Huckleberry CT.

Lemon Drop. Jane Weinberger. LC 85-62023. (Illus.). 64p. (J). (gr. 1-3). 1985. reprint ed. pap. 4.95 (*0-932433-10-3*) Windswept Hse.

Lemon Drop Jar. Christine Widman. LC 91-11209. (Illus.). 32p. (J). (gr. k-3). 1992. text 16.00 (*0-02-792759-8*, Mac Bks Young Read) S&S Childrens.

Lemon Jelly Cake. Madeline B. Smith. LC 97-25198. (Prairie State Bks.). 240p. 1998. 14.95 (*0-252-06163-2*) U of Ill Pr.

Lemon Lovers Cookbook. Peg Bailey. LC 96-76510. (Illus.). 160p. 1996. 18.95 (*1-56352-324-8*) Longstreet.

Lemon Magic: 200Beauty & Household Uses for Lemons & Lemon Juice. Patty Moosbrugger. LC 98-28900. 1999. pap. 10.00 (*0-609-80340-9*) Crown Pub Group.

Lemon Meringue Dog see Hero

Lemon Pie & Lemon Juice: Sketches & Memories of Frances R. Kester Frances R. Kester & John G. Kester. LC 98-67478. ix, 147 p. 1998. write for info. (*0-9660956-1-8*) New Elm Pr.

Lemon Sky. Lanford Wilson. 1970. pap. 5.25 (*0-8222-0652-8*) Dramatists Play.

Lemon Swamp & Other Places: A Carolina Memoir. Mamie G. Fields & Karen E. Fields. (C). 1985. pap. 16.95 (*0-02-910550-1*) Free Pr.

Lemon Twist: No Salt Added Cookbook. Ree. LC 87-92238. 204p. 1989. 19.45 (*0-929622-02-2*); pap. text 14.95 (*0-929622-00-6*) Nutrit Unltd Pubns.

Lemon Uses: Uses for the Lemon. rev. ed. Recycling Consortium Staff. 1992. ring bd. 19.95 (*0-317-04795-7*) Prosperity & Profits.

***Lemon V. Kurtzman: The Religion & Public Funds Case.** Leah Farish. LC 99-40316. (Landmark Supreme Court Cases Ser.). (Illus.). 128p. (gr. 6 up). 2000. lib. bdg. 20.95 (*0-7660-1339-1*) Enslow Pubs.

Lemon Verbena & Other Essays. Edward V. Lucas. LC 76-84320. (Essay Index Reprint Ser.). 1977. 18.95 (*0-8369-1090-7*) Ayer.

Lemonade, Vol. 4472. Rosa Drew. Ed. by Joel Kupperstein. (Learn to Read Math Ser.). (Illus.). 16p. (J). 1998. pap. 2.75 (*1-57471-379-5*, 4472) Creat Teach Pr.

***Lemonade: Poems from Hollywood.** Mark Dunster. 11p. 1999. pap. 5.00 (*0-89642-879-6*) Linden Pubs.

Lemonade, & the Autograph Hound: Two Short Plays. James Prideaux. 1969. pap. 5.25 (*0-8222-0081-3*) Dramatists Play.

Lemonade for Sale. Bettina Ling. LC 97-31370. (Real Kids Readers Ser.). (Illus.). 48p. (J). (gr. 1-3). 1998. pap. 3.99 (*0-7613-2035-0*); lib. bdg. 17.90 (*0-7613-2010-5*) Millbrook Pr.

Lemonade for Sale. Stuart J. Murphy. LC 96-52063. (MathStart Ser.). (Illus.). 40p. (J). (gr. 2-5). 1998. 15.95 (*0-06-027440-9*); pap. 4.95 (*0-06-446715-5*) HarpC.

Lemonade for Sale. Stuart J. Murphy. LC 96-52063. (MathStart Ser.). (Illus.). 40p. (J). (gr. 2 up). 1998. lib. bdg. 15.89 (*0-06-027441-7*) HarpC.

Lemonade Gravy. Eugene Marks. 1994. pap. 4.95 (*0-9644648-0-2*) ideaReserve.

Lemonade Handbook: Seeing Everyday Lemons in a Positive Light. Cathi Duran. Ed. by Patrick Caton. LC 97-71653. 168p. 1997. pap. 5.95 (*1-56245-307-6*) Great Quotations.

Lemonade Raid. Carolyn Keene. (Nancy Drew Notebooks: No. 19). (Illus.). (J). (gr. 2-4). 1997. pap. 3.99 (*0-671-56863-9*) PB.

Lemonade Raid. Carolyn Keene. (Nancy Drew Notebooks: No. 19). 1997. 9.09 (*0-606-11672-9*, Pub. by Turtleback) Demco.

Lemonade Stand. Bryan Harnetiaux. 17p. 1989. pap. 3.50 (*0-87129-773-6*, L60) Dramatic Pub.

***Lemonade Stand.** Steck-Vaughn Company Staff. (Read All about It Ser.). (Illus.). (J). 2000. pap. 4.95 (*0-8114-3800-7*) Raintree Steck-V.

Lemonade Stand, 1 vol. Marcia K. Vaughan. LC 98-49203. (All Aboard Reading Ser.). (Illus.). 32p. (ps-1). 1999. pap. text 3.99 (*0-448-41977-7*) Putnam Pub Group.

Lemonade Stand: A Guide to Encouraging the Entrepreneur in Your Child. rev. ed. Emmanuel Modu. Ed. by Andrea Walker. LC 95-78201. 352p. 1996. pap. 19.95 (*1-887646-03-5*) Gateway Pubs.

Lemonade Sun: And Other Summer Poems. Rebecca K. Dotlich. LC 97-74192. (Illus.). 32p. (J). (ps-3). 1998. pap. 15.95 (*1-56397-660-9*, Wordsong) Boyds Mills Pr.

Lemonade Trick. Scott Corbett. (J). 1960. 9.09 (*0-606-03600-8*, Pub. by Turtleback) Demco.

Lemonade Trick. Scott Corbett. LC 59-7361. (Illus.). 112p. (J). (gr. 4-7). 1988. reprint ed. pap. 2.99 (*0-590-32197-8*, Apple Paperbacks) Scholastic Inc.

LemonAid! A Layperson's Guide to the Automotive Lemon Laws. Andrew Faglio. 150p. 1992. pap. 12.95 (*0-9635081-0-5*) LemonAid.

Lemonas Tale. Wiwa K. Saro. 160p. pap. 13.95 (*0-14-026086-2*, Pub. by Pnguin Bks Ltd) Trafalgar.

Lemonheads: It's a Shame. 56p. pap. 15.95 (*0-8256-1406-6*, AM92049) Music Sales.

***Lemonheads Car Button Cloth.** 72p. 1998. otabind 14.95 (*0-7935-8132-X*) H Leonard.

Lemons. Kent Broadhurst. 1984. pap. 5.25 (*0-8222-0651-X*) Dramatists Play.

Lemons: A Country Garden Cookbook. Christopher Idone. LC 92-43715. (Illus.). 96p. 1993. 14.95 (*0-00-255165-9*) Collins SF.

Lemons, Cherries & Bell-Fruit-Gum: Illustrated History of Automatic Payout Slot Machines. Richard M. Bueschel. (Illus.). 352p. 1995. text 39.95 (*0-9647836-0-6*) Royal Bell Bks.

Lemont & It's People. Sonia Kallick. 384p. 1997. pap. 25.00 (*1-886094-62-4*) Chicago Spectrum.

Le/Morale d'Epicure see Epicurus's Morals

LeMoyne Stars Made Easy. Sharyn S. Craig. Ed. by Nancy Roberts et al. LC 97-48541. (Illus.). 32p. 1998. pap. 12.95 (*1-885588-19-4*) Chitra Pubns.

L'Empreinte de l'ange see Mark of the Angel

L'Empreinte de l'ange see Mark of the Angel: A Novel

L'Empreinte de l'ange see Mark of the Angel

Lempriere's Classical Dictionary of Proper Names Mentioned in Ancient Authors. 3rd rev. ed. 708p. 1986. pap. 25.00 (*0-7102-0843-X*, Routledge Thoemms) Routledge.

Lemuel: A Love Story. Beverly B. Kelly. 198p. (Orig.). 1990. pap. 7.95 (*0-9627838-2-X*) B B Kelly.

Lemuel C. Shattuck: A Little Mining, a Little Banking, a Little Beer. Isabel S. Fathauer & Lemuel C. Shattuck. (Illus.). 1991. 34.95 (*0-87026-079-0*) Westernlore.

Lemuel Haynes: A Bio-Bibliography. Richard Newman. LC 83-24877. 160p. 1995. 40.00 (*0-931186-04-8*); 40.00 (*0-03-118604-1*) Carlson Pub.

Lemuel Shaw, Chief Justice of the Supreme Court of Massachusetts, 1830-1860. Frederic H. Chase. 1977. 17.95 (*0-8369-7104-3*, 7938) Ayer.

Lemur Behavior: A Madagascar Field Study. Alison Jolly. LC 66-23690. 213p. reprint ed. pap. 66.10 (*0-608-12559-8*, 202405000035) Bks Demand.

Lemur Social Systems & Their Ecological Basis. P. M. Kappeler & J. U. Ganzhorn. (Illus.). 282p. (C). 1993. text 95.00 (*0-306-44576-X*, Kluwer Plenum) Kluwer Academic.

Lemuria: The Lost Continent of the Pacific. Wishar S. Cerve. LC 31-34377. 197p. 1931. pap. 12.95 (*0-912057-97-1*, 510728) GLELJ AMORC.

Lemuria Rising, 1. Ruth E. Norman et al. (Illus.). 199p. 1976. pap. 7.00 (*0-932642-37-3*) Unarius Acad Sci.

Lemuria Rising, 2. Ruth E. Norman et al. (Illus.). 372p. 1976. pap. 9.00 (*0-932642-38-1*) Unarius Acad Sci.

Lemuria Rising, 4. Ruth E. Norman et al. 1977. pap. 9.00 (*0-932642-40-3*) Unarius Acad Sci.

Lemurian Atlantean Vision Wheel Book. David Jungclaus. 267p. 1991. pap. 12.00 (*1-883682-01-0*) Lost Wrld Pub.

Lemurian Scrolls: Angelic Prophecies Revealing Human Origins. Satguru Sivaya Subramuniyaswami. LC 98-70384. (Illus.). 396p. 1998. 29.85 (*0-945497-70-9*) Himalayan Acad.

***Lemurian Way.** Lauren O. Thyme. LC 99-47224. 1999. pap. write for info. (*1-880090-91-0*) Galde Pr.

Lemurs. John M. Bennett & Jake Berry. 10p. 1993. pap. 5.00 incl. audio (*0-935350-40-3*) Luna Bisonte.

Lemurs. Mary Ann McDonald. LC 97-44649. (Illus.). 32p. (J). 1998. lib. bdg. 22.79 (*1-56766-495-4*) Childs World.

Lemurs: On Location. Kathy Darling. LC 97-36250. (Illus.). 40p. 1998. 16.00 (*0-688-12539-5*); lib. bdg. 15.93 (*0-688-12540-9*) Lothrop.

Lemurs & Other Animals of the Madagascar Rain Forest see Animals & the Environment

Lemurs, Lorises, & Other Lower Primates. Patricia A. Martin. LC 99-17066. (Illus.). 48p. (gr. 3-5). 2000. 21.50 (*0-516-21575-2*) Childrens.

***Lemurs, Lorises & Other Lower Primates.** Patricia A. Fink Martin. (True Bks.). (Illus.). 48p. (J). (gr. 3-5). 2000. pap. 6.95 (*0-516-27015-X*) Childrens.

Lemurs of Madagascar. Roderic B. Mast et al. LC 94-72352. (Illus.). 360p. 1995. pap. 25.00 (*1-881173-08-9*, Pub. by Conser Intl) U Ch Pr.

Lemurs of Madagascar & the Comorans: Windows Version. Ed. by F. McIntyre. (World Biodiversity Database Ser.). 1997. 72.00 incl. cd-rom (*3-540-14551-6*) Spr-Verlag.

Lemurs of Madagascar & the Comoros. Caroline Harcourt & Jane Thornback. (IUCN Red Data Bks.). (Illus.). 248p. 1990. 38.00 (*0-685-54767-1*, Pub. by IUCN) Island Pr.

Lemurs of the Madagascar & the Comorans. Ed. by F. McIntyre & Expert-Center for Taxonomic Identification (ETI) S. (World Biodiversity Database Ser.). 1997. 71.95 incl. cd-rom (*3-540-14552-4*) Spr-Verlag.

Le/Mystere Waldheim see Waldheim

Len Cabral's Storytelling Book. Len Cabral & Mia Manouca. LC 96-30376. 275p. 1996. pap. 32.95 (*1-55570-253-8*) Neal-Schuman.

Len Deighton: An Annotated Bibliography, 1954-1985. Edward Milward-Oliver. 100p. 1988. 85.00 (*0-944166-02-4*) Santa Teresa Pr.

Lena. Audrey Evans. LC 98-55786. 1999. pap. 5.00 (*0-88734-793-2*) Players Pr.

Lena. Margaret T. Jensen. 150p. (Orig.). 1996. pap. 8.99 (*1-56507-508-0*) Harvest Hse.

Lena. Jacqueline Woodson. LC 98-24317. 128p. (YA). (gr. 5 up). 1999. 15.95 (*0-385-32308-5*) BDD Bks Young Read.

***Lena.** Jacqueline Woodson. 128p. (YA). (gr. 5). 2000. mass mkt. 4.99 (*0-440-22669-4*, LLL BDD) BDD Bks Young Read.

Lena: A Biography of Lena Horne. James S. Haskins & Kathleen Benson. 242p. 1991. pap. 10.95 (*0-8128-8524-4*, Scrbrough Hse) Madison Bks UPA.

Lena & the Whale. Deirdre Kessler. (NFS Canada Ser.). (Illus.). 24p. (J). (ps-3). 1991. pap. 5.95 (*0-921556-13-6*, Pub. by Gynergy-Ragweed) U of Toronto Pr.

Lena Horne: Entertainer. Leslie Palmer. Ed. by Nathan I. Huggins. (Black Americans of Achievement Ser.). (Illus.). 124p. (YA). (gr. 5 up). 1989. lib. bdg. 19.95 (*1-55546-594-3*) Chelsea Hse.

Lena Horne: Singer & Actress. Brett Howard. (Black American Ser.). (Illus.). 192p. (Orig.). (YA). 1991. mass mkt. 3.95 (*0-87067-572-9*, Melrose Sq) Holloway.

Lena Rivers. Mary J. Holmes. 1897. 25.00 (*0-403-00023-8*) Scholarly.

Lena Rivers. Mary J. Holmes. (BCL Ser. I). reprint ed. 49.50 (*0-404-03315-6*) AMS Pr.

Lena Rivers. Mary J. Holmes. (BCL1-PS American Literature Ser.). 416p. 1992. reprint ed. lib. bdg. 99.00 (*0-7812-6740-4*) Rprt Serv.

Lena Rivers. Mary J. Holmes. (Notable American Authors Ser.). 1992. reprint ed. lib. bdg. 75.00 (*0-7812-3144-2*) Rprt Serv.

Lena Taku Waste (These Good Things) Selections from the Elizabeth Cole Butler Collection of Native American Art. Bill Mercer. LC 98-180312. (Illus.). 127p. 1997. pap. 20.00 (*1-883124-05-0*) Portland Art Mus.

Lenape. unabridged ed. Nora T. Dean. 60p. 1979. pap. text 39.95 incl. audio (*0-88432-285-8*, AFLE10) Audio-Forum.

Lenape & the Colony of New Sweden. Bill Albensi. LC 87-15207. 183p. 1987. 14.75 (*0-930950-17-8*); pap. 8.75 (*0-930950-18-6*) Nopoly Pr.

Lenape & Their Legends. Ed. by Daniel G. Brinton. LC 77-102641. (Library of Aboriginal American Literature: No. 5). reprint ed. 37.50 (*0-404-52185-1*) AMS Pr.

***Lenape & Their Legends: With the Complete Text & Symbols of the Walum Olum.** Daniel Brinton. LC 99-61172. (Great Pennsylvania Frontier Ser.: Vol. 11). (Illus.). 262p. 1999. reprint ed. 39.95 (1-889037-16-8) Wennawoods.

Lenape-English Dictionary. Ed. by Daniel G. Brinton & Albert S. Anthony. LC 76-43670. (ENG.). reprint ed. 49.50 (0-404-15764-5) AMS Pr.

Lenape Indian Teaching Kits Kit 1: Introduction to the Lenape, Incl. tchr's. guide, posters, portfolio. Ed. by Karen Waldauer. (Illus.). 24.95 (0-912608-07-2) Mid Atlantic.

Lenape Indian Teaching Kits Kit 2: Lenape Lore/Folk Medicines, Incl. tchr's. guide, charts, quizzes. Ed. by Karen Waldauer. (Illus.). 24.95 (0-912608-08-0) Mid Atlantic.

Lenape Indian Teaching Kits No. 3: Lenape Lore/Clothing, Shelter, Crafts, Weapons, Tools & Specialties. Ed. by Karen Waldauer. (Illus.). teacher ed. 24.95 (0-912608-09-9) Mid Atlantic.

Lenape Indians see Junior Library of American Indians

Lenape or Delaware Indians: The Original People of New Jersey, Southeastern New York State, Eastern Pennsylvania. 6th rev. ed. Herbert C. Kraft. (Illus.). (J). (gr. 2-7). 1996. pap. 5.95 (0-935137-01-7) Seton Hall Univ Museum.

Lenape Trails. Clifton Lisle. 1993. reprint ed. lib. bdg. 89.00 (0-7812-5482-5) Rprt Serv.

Lenapes see Indians of North America

Lenardo und Blandine: Munich, 1779. Peter Winter. Ed. by Thomas Bauman. (German Opera Ser., 1770-1800). 275p. 1986. lib. bdg. 15.00 (0-8240-8859-X) Garland.

Lenbachhaus, Munich. Ed. by Helmut Friedel. (Museum Guides Ser.). (Illus.). 112p. (Orig.). 1996. pap. 14.95 (3-7913-1623-0, Pub. by Prestel) te Neues.

Lenchen see Dilek

Lenchens Geheimnis: A Level. Ende. 7.95 (0-8219-1219-4) EMC-Paradigm.

***L'encyclopedie de l'Islam: Livraison 169-170.** 1999. pap. 73.50 (90-04-11404-1) Brill Academic Pubs.

Lend-Lease Aircraft in World War II: An Operational History. Arthur Pearcy. (Illus.). 176p. 1996. 19.98 (0-7603-0259-6) MBI Pubg.

Lend Me a Tenor: A Comedy. Ken Ludwig. LC 87-209454. ii, 81p. 1986. write for info. (0-573-01640-2) S French Trade.

Lend Me an Ear: The Temperament, Selection & Training of the Hearing Dog. Martha Hoffman. Ed. by Mark Anderson. LC 99-60289. (Illus.). 285p. 1999. pap. 21.95 (0-944875-56-4) Doral Pub.

Lend Me Your Ear: Rhetorical Constructions of Deafness. Brenda J. Brueggemann. LC 99-20807. xii, 290p. 1999. 49.95 (1-56368-079-3) Gallaudet Univ Pr.

Lend Me Your Ears: A Guide to Orchestral Music from Vivaldi to Bernstein. Arthur Jacobs. 400p. (Orig.). 1990. pap. 8.95 (0-380-71020-X, Avon Bks) Morrow Avon.

Lend Me Your Ears: Great Speeches in History. 2nd expanded rev. ed. Ed. by William Safire. LC 96-43423. 1056p. 1997. 39.95 (0-393-04005-4) Norton.

Lend Me Your Ears: Telephone Jokes. Illus. by Dana Fradon. 40p. (J). (gr. 2-5). 1994. lib. bdg. 13.95 (0-945912-23-4) Pippin Pr.

Lend the Eye a Terrible Aspect: A Collection of Essays & Fiction. Ed. by Loren Rhoads & Mason Jones. LC 93-72388. (Illus.). 165p. (Orig.). 1994. pap. 9.99 (0-9636794-0-6) Automatism Pr.

Lend Thy Guiding Hand: A Provocative Collection of Religious Verse. (C). 1989. 45.00 (1-871014-02-6, Pub. by Desk Top Bks) St Mut.

Lend Your Way to Wealth: Private Lending in Real Estate. James C. Allen. 1990. pap. 14.95 (0-8306-9019-0) McGraw-Hill Prof.

Lender & Successor Liability for Hazardous Waste Cleanup. (State Legislative Reports: Vol. 19, No. 15). 18p. 1994. 15.00 (1-55516-383-1, 7302-1915) Natl Conf State Legis.

Lender Liability. A. Barry Cappello & Frances E. Komoroske. 1987. ring bd. 80.00 (1-55943-164-4, MICHIE) LEXIS Pub.

Lender Liability. 2nd ed. A. Barry Cappello & Frances E. Komoroske. 800p. 1993. spiral bd. 130.00 (0-250-40702-7, MICHIE) LEXIS Pub.

Lender Liability. 2nd ed. Cappello & Frances E. Komoroske. 1996. ring bd. 115.00 (0-327-03900-0, 81389-10, MICHIE) LEXIS Pub.

***Lender Liability.** 3rd ed. A. Barry Cappello & Frances E. Komoroske. 800p. 1999. ring bd. write for info. (0-327-04967-7, 8138911) LEXIS Pub.

Lender Liability, Issue 5. 2nd ed. 325p. 1998. ring bd. write for info. (0-327-00502-5, 8139115) LEXIS Pub.

Lender Liability, No. 1. A. Barry Cappello & Frances E. Komoroske. 1987. suppl. ed. 34.00 (0-685-66651-4, MICHIE) LEXIS Pub.

Lender Liability, No. 2. A. Barry Cappello & Frances E. Komoroske. 1987. suppl. ed. 32.50 (1-55943-064-8, MICHIE) LEXIS Pub.

Lender Liability, No. 3. A. Barry Cappello & Frances E. Komoroske. 1987. suppl. ed. 28.00 (1-55943-864-9, MICHIE) LEXIS Pub.

Lender Liability, No. 4. A. Barry Cappello & Frances E. Komoroske. 1987. suppl. ed. 34.00 (1-55943-765-0, MICHIE) LEXIS Pub.

Lender Liability: A Special Collection from the Journal of Commercial Bank Lending. Intro. by Charlotte Weisman. LC 88-4195. (Illus.). 96p. (Orig.). 1988. pap. 45.00 (0-936742-49-6, 36034) Robt Morris Assocs.

Lender Liability: Definitions - Theories - Applications. Dennis M. Patterson. 350p. 1990. boxed set 75.00 (0-88063-279-8, 81394-10, MICHIE) LEXIS Pub.

Lender Liability: Environmental Risk & Debt. John Jarvis & Michael Fordham. (Environmental Law Ser.). 280p. 1993. 95.00 (1-874698-05-8, Pub. by Cameron May) Gaunt.

Lender Liability: Protecting Officers & Directors: Expanding Theories. Joseph J. Johnston & John F. Olson. 525p. write for info. (0-318-61658-0) Harcourt.

Lender Liability: Strategies of Litigation. Ed. by Arnold J. Wolf. LC 89-50571. 856p. 1990. lib. bdg. 100.00 (0-9621125-0-X) Trial Law Pr.

Lender Liability & Banking Litigation. Edward F. Mannino. 700p. 1989. ring bd. 98.00 (0-317-05405-8, 00611) NY Law Pub.

Lender Liability for Contaminated Sites: Issues for Lenders & Investors in Canada. 48p. (Orig.). 1996. pap. text 35.00 (0-7881-2798-5) DIANE Pub.

Lender Liability in Secured Financing: Major Causes & Effective Cures. 4th ed. Steve H. Nickles. 456p. 1989. pap. 35.00 (0-943380-04-9) PEG MN.

Lender Liability Law, 2 vols. Joseph J. Norton. 1989. ring bd. 195.00 (0-8205-1488-8, 488) Bender.

Lender Liability Law, Practice & Prevention, 3 vols. Gerald Blanchard. 1992. 350.00 (0-685-30640-2) West Group.

Lender-of-Last Resort Function in an International Context. Jack M. Guttentag & Richard J. Herring. LC 83-8444. (Essays in International Finance Ser.: No. 151). 30p. 1983. pap. text 10.00 (0-88165-058-7) Princeton U Int Finan Econ.

Lender to the Lords, Given to the Poor. Gerry Black. 389p. 1992. text 30.00 (0-85303-249-1, Pub. by M Vallentine & Co) Intl Spec Bk.

Lenders & Landlords: A Guide to Tenant Organizing in Financially Distressed Housing. Northwest Bronx Community & Clergy Coalition Staff & New York Community Service Society Staff. (Illus.). 73p. (Orig.). 1996. mass mkt. 10.00 (0-88156-172-X) Comm Serv Soc NY.

Lenders Guide to Developing an Environmental Risk Program. Elizabeth Ward. LC 95-71141. 336p. (Orig.). 1995. pap. text, student ed. 59.95 incl. disk (0-9628098-2-9) RTM Comns.

Lender's Handbook. Richard T. Nassberg. 316p. 1986. 17.50 (0-8318-0480-7, B480) Am Law Inst.

Lender's Toolkit: The Pocket Guide to the Essential Formulas, Ratios & Tables. Kenneth R. Pirok. 150p. (C). 1995. text 24.95 (1-55738-756-7, Irwn Prfssnl) McGraw-Hill Prof.

Lending. Keith Checkley. 214p. 1999. pap. 130.00 (0-85297-474-4, Pub. by Chartered Bank) St Mut.

Lending. Peter McGregor. 247p. 1990. pap. 125.00 (0-85297-352-7, Pub. by Chartered Bank) St Mut.

Lending. Alan Selby. 1997. pap. 90.00 (0-85297-425-6, Pub. by Chartered Bank) St Mut.

Lending. Robert Souster. 129p. 1990. pap. 125.00 (0-85297-366-7, Pub. by Chartered Bank) St Mut.

Lending a Hand in Holland, 1945-1946. Joan Hewitt. 1999. pap. 21.00 (1-85072-075-4, Pub. by W Sessions) St Mut.

Lending & Diversity Handbook. Lee Gardenswartz & Anita Rowe. LC 96-33882. (Illus.). 256p. (C). 1996. text 50.00 (0-7863-0843-5, Irwn Prfssnl) McGraw-Hill Prof.

Lending & Diversity Training Workbook: Hands-On Guide to Increasing Profits, Meeting Regulatory Requirements, Expanding Markets by Meeting Diverse Needs of Your Community. Lee Gardenswartz & Anita Rowe. 88p. (C). 1996. text 9.95 (0-7863-0855-9, Irwn Prfssnl) McGraw-Hill Prof.

***Lending & Securities: A Practical Guide to the Principles of Good Lending.** Christopher Parry. 208p. 1999. pap. 80.00 (0-85297-510-4, Pub. by Chartered Bank) St Mut.

Lending for Electric Power in Sub-Saharan Africa. Alvaro J. Covarrubias & World Bank Staff. LC 96-1958. (Operations Evaluation Studies). 120p. 1996. pap. 22.00 (0-8213-3644-4) World Bank.

Lending Hand: Credit Union Executives Share Loan-Generating Success Stories. Eileen Courter et al. 91p. (Orig.). 1994. pap. 79.00 (1-889394-14-9) Credit Union Execs.

Lending Opportunities in Real Estate: A High-Profit Strategy for Every Inventor. James C. Allen. (Illus.). 192p. 1988. 24.95 (0-8306-1819-8, 30019H) McGraw-Hill Prof.

Lending to Different Industries. (Illus.). 224p. (Orig.). 1995. pap. 85.00 (1-57070-011-7, 36059) Robt Morris Assocs.

Lending to Different Industries, Vol. 2. 2nd ed. Ed. by Joan H. Behr & Sarah A. Burke. (Illus.). 396p. 1990. pap. 85.00 (0-936742-77-1, 36030) Robt Morris Assocs.

Lending to Different Industries, Vol. 3. Ed. by Joan H. Behr. LC 90-5900. 232p. 1992. pap. 85.00 (0-936742-91-7, 36058) Robt Morris Assocs.

***L'Enfant Cow-boy.** Gilles Tibo. (FRE., Illus.). 24p. (J). (gr. k-2). 2000. 16.95 (0-88776-511-4) Tundra Bks.

L'Enfant Derriere la Porte: Level B. Bisson & de Schonen. text 8.95 (0-8219-1459-6) EMC-Paradigm.

L'Enfant Ideal see Ideal Child

Leng Yen Ching Wu Shih Yin Mo Chien Shih see Shurangama Sutra: The Fifty Skandha-Demon States

Length. Peter Patilla. LC 98-49372. (Measuring up Ser.). 1999. write for info. (0-382-42233-3) Silver Burdett Pr.

Length. Henry Pluckrose. (Math Counts Ser.). (Illus.). 32p. (J). 1995. pap. 4.95 (0-516-45453-6) Childrens.

Length & Area. Tibor Rado. LC QA0461.R3. (American Mathematical Society, Colloquium Publications: Vol. 30). 579p. reprint ed. pap. 179.50 (0-608-30949-4, 200493600048) Bks Demand.

Length-Based Methods in Fisheries Research. Ed. by Daniel Pauly & G. R. Morgan. (Conference Proceedings Ser.: No. 13). 1986. text 32.50 (971-10-2228-1, Pub. by ICLARM) Intl Spec Bk.

Length of an Afternoon. James Cushing. 100p. 1999. pap. 12.00 (0-9649240-6-4) Cahuenga Pr.

Length of Civil & Criminal Proceedings in the Case-Law of the European Court of Human Rights. (Human Rights Files Ser.: No. 16). 1996. 15.00 (92-871-3028-0, Pub. by Council of Europe) Manhattan Pub Co.

Length of Service of Pennsylvania High School Teachers. Lyman H. Van Houten. LC 70-177680. (Columbia University. Teachers College. Contributions to Education Ser.: No. 522). reprint ed. 37.50 (0-404-55522-5) AMS Pr.

Length of Stay by Diagnosis & Operation, North Central. 1995. write for info. (1-57372-004-6) HCIA.

Length of Stay by Diagnosis & Operation, North Central. 1996. write for info. (1-57372-037-2) HCIA.

Length of Stay by Diagnosis & Operation, North Central Region, 1986. Commission on Professional & Hospital Activities S. LC 73-173193. 314p. pap. 97.40 (0-8357-8610-2, 203503500091) Bks Demand.

Length of Stay by Diagnosis & Operation, North Central Region, 1987. Commission on Professional & Hospital Activities S. LC 73-173193. 336p. reprint ed. pap. 104.20 (0-8357-6831-7, 203551800095) Bks Demand.

Length of Stay by Diagnosis & Operation, North Central Region, 1988. Commission on Professional & Hospital Activities S. LC 73-173193. 361p. reprint ed. pap. 112.00 (0-7837-1811-X, 204201100001) Bks Demand.

Length of Stay by Diagnosis & Operation, Northeastern. 1995. write for info. (1-57372-003-8) HCIA.

Length of Stay by Diagnosis & Operation, Northeastern. 1996. write for info. (1-57372-036-4) HCIA.

Length of Stay by Diagnosis & Operation, Northeastern Region, 1986. Commission on Professional & Hospital Activities S. LC 73-173193. 314p. reprint ed. pap. 97.40 (0-8357-8609-9, 203503400091) Bks Demand.

Length of Stay by Diagnosis & Operation, Northeastern Region, 1987. Commission on Professional & Hospital Activities S. LC 73-173193. 336p. reprint ed. pap. 104.20 (0-8357-6832-5, 203551900095) Bks Demand.

Length of Stay by Diagnosis & Operation, Northeastern Region, 1988. Commission on Professional & Hospital Activities S. LC 73-173193. 361p. reprint ed. pap. 112.00 (0-7837-1812-8, 204201200001) Bks Demand.

Length of Stay by Diagnosis & Operation, Southern. 1995. write for info. (1-57372-005-4) HCIA.

Length of Stay by Diagnosis & Operation, Southern. 1996. write for info. (1-57372-038-0) HCIA.

Length of Stay by Diagnosis & Operation, Southern Region, 1986. Commission on Professional & Hospital Activities S. LC 73-173193. 314p. reprint ed. pap. 97.40 (0-8357-8611-0, 203503600091) Bks Demand.

Length of Stay by Diagnosis & Operation, Southern Region, 1987. Commission on Professional & Hospital Activities S. LC 73-173193. 336p. reprint ed. pap. 104.20 (0-8357-6830-9, 203551700095) Bks Demand.

Length of Stay by Diagnosis & Operation, Southern Region, 1988. Commission on Professional & Hospital Activities S. LC 73-173193. 361p. reprint ed. pap. 112.00 (0-7837-1810-1, 204201000001) Bks Demand.

Length of Stay by Diagnosis & Operation, United States. 1996. write for info. (1-57372-035-6) HCIA.

Length of Stay by Diagnosis & Operation, United States, 1986. Commission on Professional & Hospital Activities S. LC 73-173193. 314p. reprint ed. pap. 97.40 (0-8357-8608-0, 203503300091) Bks Demand.

Length of Stay by Diagnosis & Operation, United States, 1987. Commission on Professional & Hospital Activities S. LC 73-173193. 336p. reprint ed. pap. 104.20 (0-8357-6299-8, 203551500097) Bks Demand.

Length of Stay by Diagnosis & Operation, United States, 1988. Commission on Professional & Hospital Activities S. LC 73-173193. 361p. reprint ed. pap. 112.00 (0-7837-1808-X, 204200800001) Bks Demand.

Length of Stay by Diagnosis & Operation, Western. 1995. write for info. (1-57372-006-2) HCIA.

Length of Stay by Diagnosis & Operation, Western. 1996. write for info. (1-57372-039-9) HCIA.

Length of Stay by Diagnosis & Operation, Western Region, 1986. Commission on Professional & Hospital Activities S. LC 73-173193. 314p. reprint ed. pap. 97.40 (0-8357-8612-9, 203503700091) Bks Demand.

Length of Stay by Diagnosis & Operation, Western Region, 1987. Commission on Professional & Hospital Activities S. LC 73-173193. 336p. reprint ed. pap. 104.20 (0-8357-6829-5, 203551600095) Bks Demand.

Length of Stay by Diagnosis & Operation, Western Region, 1988. Commission on Professional & Hospital Activities S. LC 73-173193. 361p. reprint ed. pap. 112.00 (0-7837-1809-8, 204200900001) Bks Demand.

Length of Stay by Diagnosis & Operation, Workers' Compensation. 1995. write for info. (1-57372-014-3) HCIA.

Length of Stay by Diagnosis & Procedure, 1997: Geriatric. 1997. pap. 295.00 (1-57372-074-7) HCIA.

Length of Stay by Diagnosis & Procedure, 1997: North Central. 1997. pap. 295.00 (1-57372-070-4) HCIA.

Length of Stay by Diagnosis & Procedure, 1997: Northeastern. 1997. pap. 295.00 (1-57372-069-0) HCIA.

Length of Stay by Diagnosis & Procedure, 1997: Pediatric. 1997. pap. 295.00 (1-57372-073-9) HCIA.

Length of Stay by Diagnosis & Procedure, 1997: Southern. 1997. pap. 295.00 (1-57372-071-2) HCIA.

Length of Stay by Diagnosis & Procedure, 1997: United States. 1997. pap. 295.00 (1-57372-068-2) HCIA.

Length of Stay by Diagnosis & Procedure, 1997: Western. 1997. pap. 295.00 (1-57372-072-0) HCIA.

Length of Stay by Diagnosis, 1998: Geriatric. 1998. pap. 295.00 (1-57372-110-7) HCIA.

Length of Stay by Diagnosis, 1998: North Central. 1998. pap. 295.00 (1-57372-106-9) HCIA.

Length of Stay by Diagnosis, 1998: Northeastern. 1998. pap. 295.00 (1-57372-107-7) HCIA.

Length of Stay by Diagnosis, 1998: Southern. 1998. pap. 295.00 (1-57372-108-5) HCIA.

Length of Stay by Diagnosis, 1998: United States. 1998. pap. 295.00 (1-57372-105-0) HCIA.

Length of Stay by Diagnosis, 1998: Western. 1998. pap. 295.00 (1-57372-109-3) HCIA.

Length of Stay by DRG & Payment Source, North Central. 1995. write for info. (1-57372-017-8) HCIA.

Length of Stay by DRG & Payment Source, North Central. 1996. write for info. (1-57372-060-7) HCIA.

Length of Stay by DRG & Payment Source, Northeastern. 1995. write for info. (1-57372-016-X) HCIA.

Length of Stay by DRG & Payment Source, Northeastern. 1996. write for info. (1-57372-059-3) HCIA.

Length of Stay by DRG & Payment Source, Southern. 1995. write for info. (1-57372-018-6) HCIA.

Length of Stay by DRG & Payment Source, Southern. 1996. write for info. (1-57372-061-5) HCIA.

Length of Stay by DRG & Payment Source, United States. 1995. write for info. (1-57372-015-1) HCIA.

Length of Stay by DRG & Payment Source, United States. 1996. write for info. (1-57372-058-5) HCIA.

Length of Stay by DRG & Payment Source, Western. 1995. write for info. (1-57372-019-4) HCIA.

Length of Stay by DRG & Payment Source, Western. 1996. write for info. (1-57372-062-3) HCIA.

Length of Stay by DRG & Payment Source, 1997: North Central. 1997. pap. 195.00 (1-57372-082-8) HCIA.

Length of Stay by DRG & Payment Source, 1997: Northeastern. 1997. pap. 195.00 (1-57372-081-X) HCIA.

Length of Stay by DRG & Payment Source, 1997: Southern. 1997. pap. 195.00 (1-57372-083-6) HCIA.

Length of Stay by DRG & Payment Source, 1997: United States. 1997. pap. 195.00 (1-57372-080-1) HCIA.

Length of Stay by DRG & Payment Source, 1997: Western. 1997. pap. 195.00 (1-57372-084-4) HCIA.

Length of Stay by Dx & Op, 1998: North Central. 1998. pap. 295.00 (1-57372-118-2) HCIA.

Length of Stay by Dx & Op, 1998: Northeastern. 1998. pap. 295.00 (1-57372-119-0) HCIA.

Length of Stay by Dx & Op, 1998: Southern. 1998. pap. 295.00 (1-57372-120-4) HCIA.

Length of Stay by Dx & Op, 1998: United States. 1998. pap. 295.00 (1-57372-117-4) HCIA.

Length of Stay by Dx & Op, 1998: Western. 1998. pap. 295.00 (1-57372-121-2) HCIA.

Length of Stay by Procedure, 1998: Geriatric. 1998. pap. 295.00 (1-57372-116-6) HCIA.

Length of Stay by Procedure, 1998: North Central. 1998. pap. 295.00 (1-57372-112-3) HCIA.

Length of Stay by Procedure, 1998: Northeastern. 1998. pap. 295.00 (1-57372-113-1) HCIA.

Length of Stay by Procedure, 1998: Southern. 1998. pap. 195.00 (1-57372-114-X) HCIA.

Length of Stay by Procedure, 1998: United States. 1998. pap. 295.00 (1-57372-111-5) HCIA.

Length of Stay by Procedure, 1998: Western. 1998. pap. write for info. (1-57372-115-8) HCIA.

Length of Wire & Other Stories. Megan Staffel. 1983. 12.50 (0-913219-39-8); pap. 6.00 (0-913219-40-1) Pym-Rand Pr.

Lengthen Your Smile: A Year's Supply of Stories for Latter-Day Saints. Richard N. Nash. LC 96-19527. 1996. pap. 9.95 (1-57345-046-4) Deseret Bk.

Lengthening Legacy: Eula Mae Henderson. Amelia Bishop. LC 98-28405. 1998. 15.95 (1-57168-261-9, Eakin Pr) Sunbelt Media.

Lengthening Shadows: Status of Women in India. Poonam S. Chauhan. LC 96-904811. (Illus.). 237p. 1996. 29.00 (81-86562-01-X, Pub. by Manak Pubns Pvt Ltd) Nataraj Bks.

Lengthening Shadows Before Nightfall. John Dugdale. 104p. 1995. 50.00 (0-944092-30-6) Twin Palms Pub.

Lengthening the Day: A History of Lighting Technology. Brian Bowers. (Illus.). 238p. 1998. 45.00 (0-19-856548-8) OUP.

Lengthening the Stride: Employing Peace Officers from Newly Arrived Ethnic Groups. Ed. by Judy Kirby. 50p. 1995. pap. 14.95 (0-934513-22-8) Natl Crime DC.

Lengua Abipona, 2 vols., Set. Elena Najlis. 1966. 60.00 (0-7859-0703-3, S-33069) Fr & Eur.

Lengua e Historia. Aurelio Tio. LC 83-1369. (Coleccion Mente y Palabra). (SPA.). 225p. (Orig.). 1983. pap. text 6.00 (0-8477-0586-2) U of PR Pr.

Lengua Espanola. Antonio Onieva. 299p. 1969. 9.95 (0-8288-7480-8) Fr & Eur.

Lengua Florida (The Flowery Language) Ed. by Angelina Muniz-Huberman. (SPA.). 303p. 1992. reprint ed. pap. 14.99 (968-16-3292-3, Pub. by Fondo) Continental Bk.

Lengua, Literatura y Comunicacion: Antologia de Lecturas, Ejercicios Gramaticales y Destrezas Linguisticas. 8th ed. Ileana Canetti-Mirabal. (Textbook Ser.). (SPA., Illus.). 260p. (Orig.). (C). 1991. reprint ed. pap. text 14.95 (1-56328-008-6) Edit Plaza Mayor.

Lengua Mataca, 2 vols., Set. M. T. Vinas L'Rquiza. 1975. 75.00 (0-7859-0704-1, S-33070) Fr & Eur.

Lengua Mayor: Ensayos Sobre el Espanol de Aqui y de Alla. Salvador Tio. (Biblioteca de Autores de Puerto Rico Ser.). (SPA.). 200p. 1991. pap. 7.95 (1-56328-017-5) Edit Plaza Mayor.

Lengua Mentirosa. Tr. of Tattletale Tongue. (SPA.). 24p. 1990. pap. write for info. (0-614-27070-7) Editorial Unilit.

Lengua Mentirosa. Barbara Davoll.Tr. of Tattletale Tongue. (SPA.). (J). 1990. 6.99 (1-56063-123-6, 490375) Editorial Unilit.

An Asterisk (*) at the beginning of an entry indicates that the title is appearing for the first time.

Lengua Muerta: Poesia, Post Litertura & Erotismo en Enrique Linn. Luis Correa-Diaz. (SPA.). 120p. (Orig.). 1996. pap. 15.00 (1-888135-00-X) Ediciones Inti.
Lengua Practica y Procesamiento Electronico de Texto. Gloria Butron et al. (SPA.). 114p. 1991. pap. 8.25 (0-8477-3673-3) U of PR Pr.
***Lengua Que Heredamos: Curso de Espanol para Bilinques.** 4th ed. Sarah Marques. LC 99-33528.Tr. of Spanish for Bilinguals. 464p. 1999. pap. 64.95 (0-471-29746-1) Wiley.
Lengua Sagrada de los Nanigos. Lydia Cabrera. LC 86-82213. (Coleccion del Chichereku). (SPA.). 530p. (Orig.). 1988. pap. 30.00 (0-89729-488-2) Ediciones.
Lenguaje. Edward Sapir. (Breviarios Ser.). (SPA.). pap. 8.99 (968-16-0550-0, Pub. by Fondo) Continental Bk.
Lenguaje de las Piedras. Roman P. Chan. (SPA.). pap. 11.99 (968-16-3990-1, Pub. by Fondo) Continental Bk.
Lenguaje de los Animales. Kyle Carter. (Que Hacen los Animales?).Tr. of Animals That Talk. 24p. (J). (gr. k-4). 1994. lib. bdg. 17.27 (1-55916-148-5) Rourke Bk Co.
Lenguaje de los Chicanos: Regional & Social Characteristics Used by Mexican Americans. Ed. by Eduardo Hernandez-Chavez et al. LC 75-18946. 274p. reprint ed. pap. 85.00 (0-8357-3338-6, 203956600013) Bks Demand.
Lenguaje de Programacion C++ 2nd ed. Bjarne Stroustrup. (SPA.). (C). 1993. pap. text 33.66 (0-201-60104-4) Addison-Wesley.
Lenguaje De Programacion Java. (C). 1997. pap. 16.00 (0-201-65314-1) HEPC Inc.
Lenguaje de Programacion Lisp. (C). 1991. text 27.33 (0-201-62937-2) Addison-Wesley.
Lenguaje del Corazon: Los Escritos de Bill W. Para el Grapevine. Bill W.Tr. of Language of the Heart: Bill W's Grapevine Writings. (SPA.). 435p. pap. 12.00 (0-933685-27-0) A A Grapevine.
Lenguaje del Cuerpo (Body Language) Pierre Guiraud. (Breviarios Ser.). (SPA.). 120p. 1986. pap. 5.99 (968-16-4022-5, Pub. by Fondo) Continental Bk.
Lenguaje Del Nino. Paule Aimard. (SPA.). pap. 7.99 (968-16-4074-8, Pub. by Fondo) Continental Bk.
***Lenguaje es la Clave: El Hablar y los Libros & El Hablar y el Jugar, Vol. II.** Ed. by Mary Maddox et al. (SPA.). 92p. 1999. student ed. 95.00 (1-930690-01-0) Wash Resrch Instit.
Lenguaje por Senas Simplificado. Edgar D. Lawrence. LC 91-39463. (Illus.). 240p. 1992. kivar 13.95 (0-88243-300-8, 02-0300) Gospel Pub.
Lenguaje Secreto de Su Cuerpo. Ed. by Malvin Kristos & Frank Cabrera. (SPA., Illus.). 160p. 1993. pap. 4.95 (0-939193-10-8) Edit Concepts.
Lenguaje Secreto de Su Cuerpo. Malvin Kristus. (SPA.). (Orig.). 1990. pap. write for info. (0-944499-81-3) Editorial Amer.
Lenguaje y Significado (Language & Meaning) Alejandro Rossi. (Breviarios Ser.). (SPA.). 157p. 1997. pap. 7.99 (968-16-4013-6, Pub. by Fondo) Continental Bk.
Lenguajes de Programacion: Conceptos y Construccion. Ravi Sethi. (C). 1992. pap. text 27.33 (0-201-51858-9) Addison-Wesley.
***Lenguajes Gramaticas Y Automatas Un Enfoques Practico.** (C). 1998. pap. 15.33 (0-201-65323-0) HEPC Inc.
Lenguas Sueltas: Poemas Anthology of 17 Poets Chicano Latino Chapbooks. Cherrie Moraga et al. (Chicano Latino Chapbooks Ser.). (ENG & SPA., Illus.). 32p. (Orig.). 1994. pap. 5.00 (0-939952-19-X) Moving Parts.
Lengue Espanola: Grammatica y Cultura. 3rd ed. Matilda O. De Castells & Harold E. Lionetti. (SPA.). 592p. (C). 1983. text 47.20 (0-13-524489-7) P-H.
Leni Riefenstahl: A Memoir. Leni Riefenstahl. LC 94-45089. 669p. 1995. pap. 16.00 (0-312-11926-7) St Martin.
***Leni Riefenstahl - Five Lives.** Taschen America Staff. Ed. by Angelika Taschen. (Illus.). 2000. pap. 4.99 (3-8228-6221-5) Taschen Amer.
***Leni Riefenstahl - Five Lives.** Ed. by Angelika Taschen. 2000. 39.99 (3-8228-6216-9) Taschen Amer.
Leni Riefenstahl & Olympia. Cooper C. Graham. LC 86-6715. (Filmmakers Ser.: No. 13). (Illus.). 347p. 1986. 37.00 (0-8108-1896-5) Scarecrow.
Leni Stern: Composing & Compositions. Ed. by Aaron Stang & Kenn Chipkin. (New Jazz Directions Ser.). 48p. (Orig.). (YA). (gr. 9-12). 1994. pap. text 19.95 incl. audio compact disk (0-89898-960-4, F3419GTXCD) Wrner Bros.
Leni Stern: Composing & Compositions. Ed. by Aaron Stang & Kenn Chipkin. (New Jazz Directions Ser.). 48p. (Orig.). (YA). (gr. 9-12). 1994. pap. text 17.95 incl. audio (0-89898-961-2, F3419GTXAT) Wrner Bros.
Lenihan: His Life & Loyalties James Downey. LC 98-229543. xii, 251p. 1998. write for info. (1-874597-34-0) New Island Books.
***Lenihan: His Life & Loyalties.** James Downey. (Illus.). 1999. pap. (1-874597-97-9, Pub. by New Island Books) Dufour.
***Lenin.** Helene Carrere d'Encausse. Tr. by George Holoch. 512p. 2001. 45.00 (0-8419-1412-5) Holmes & Meier.
Lenin. Michael Morgan. 1972. 20.00 (0-8214-0094-0) Lib Soc Sci.
***Lenin.** Beryl Williams. LC 99-45967. (Profiles in Power Ser.). 232p. (C). 1999. pap. 21.20 (0-582-03331-4) Longman.
***Lenin.** Beryl Williams. LC 99-45967. (Profiles in Power Ser.). 240p. (C). 1999. 69.95 (0-582-03330-6) Longman.
Lenin: A New Biography. Dmitri Volkogonov. (Illus.). 600p. 1994. 30.00 (0-02-933435-7) Free Pr.
Lenin: A New Biography. Dmitri Volkogonov. 1996. pap. 18.00 (0-02-874123-4) Free Pr.
Lenin: A Study in the Unity of His Thought. Georg Lukacs. 1998. pap. 15.00 (1-85984-174-0, Pub. by Verso) Norton.
Lenin: Against Imperialist War. Vladimir Il'ich Lenin. 1978. pap. 24.95 (0-8464-0554-7) Beekman Pubs.
Lenin: Against Liquidationism. Vladimir Il'ich Lenin. 1978. 29.95 (0-8464-0553-9) Beekman Pubs.
Lenin: Dedicated Marxist or Revolutionary Pragmatist. Stanley W. Page. LC 77-76608. (Problems in Civilization Ser.). 1977. pap. text 7.95 (0-88273-402-4) Forum Pr IL.
Lenin: Genesis & Development of a Revolutionary. Rolf H. Theen. LC 79-87768. 192p. 1979. reprint ed. pap. 59.60 (0-7837-8183-0, 204788800008) Bks Demand.
Lenin: On Utopian & Scientific Socialism. Vladimir Il'ich Lenin. 1978. pap. 24.95 (0-8464-0558-X) Beekman Pubs.
Lenin: Thinker, Fighter. Vince Copeland. 26p. 1989. pap. 0.50 (0-89567-095-X) World View Forum.
Lenin - A Political Life Vol. 1: The Strengths of Contradiction. Robert W. Service. LC 84-43044. 256p. 1985. 26.95 (0-253-33324-5) Ind U Pr.
Lenin - A Political Life Vol. 2: Worlds in Collision. Robert W. Service. LC 84-43044. (Illus.). 440p. 1991. 41.95 (0-253-33325-3) Ind U Pr.
Lenin - A Political Life Vol. 3: The Iron Ring, Vol. 3. Robert W. Service. LC 84-43044. 352p. 1995. text 29.95 (0-253-35181-2) Ind U Pr.
***Lenin--A Biography.** Robert Service. LC 00-21394. (Illus.). 592p. 2000. 35.00 (0-674-00330-6) HUP.
Lenin & Gandhi. Rene Fulop-Miller. Tr. by F. S. Flint & D. F. Tait from GER. LC 72-7057. (Select Bibliographies Reprint Ser.). 1977. reprint ed. 23.95 (0-8369-6932-4) Ayer.
Lenin & Gorky: Letters, Reminiscences, Articles. Ed. by MIR Publishers Staff. (Illus.). 429p. 1973. 26.95 (0-8464-0555-5) Beekman Pubs.
Lenin & His Rivals: The Struggle for Russia's Future, 1898-1906. Donald W. Treadgold. LC 76-28338. 291p. 1976. reprint ed. lib. bdg. 55.00 (0-8371-9045-2, TRLR, Greenwood Pr) Greenwood.
Lenin & Philosophy & Other Essays. Louis Althusser. Tr. by Ben Brewster from FRE. LC 78-178710. 256p. 1972. pap. 16.00 (0-85345-213-X, Pub. by Monthly Rev) NYU Pr.
Lenin & the Problems of Literature: Twentieth Century Progress in the Arts & Aesthetic Ideas & Literary Phenomena. Vladimir Sheherbina. 396p. (C). 1975. pap. 25.00 (0-8464-0556-3) Beekman Pubs.
Lenin & the Revolutionary Party. Paul Le Blanc. LC 88-18067. 456p. (C). 1993. pap. 25.00 (0-391-03742-0) Humanities.
Lenin & the Russian Revolution. Donald W. Mack. Ed. by Marjorie Reeves. (Then & There Ser.). (Illus.). 104p. (Orig.). (gr. 7-12). 1970. pap. text 8.76 (0-582-20457-7, 70766) Longman.
Lenin & the Twentieth Century: A Bertram D. Wolfe Retrospective. Compiled by Lennard D. Gerson. (Publication Ser.: No. 293). xvii, 216p. 1984. pap. 3.18 (0-8179-7932-8); lib. bdg. 11.18 (0-8179-7931-X) Hoover Inst Pr.
Lenin & Trotsky: Mini-Play & Activities. Lawrence Stevens. (World History Ser.). (YA). (gr. 7 up). 1981. 6.50 (0-89550-347-6) Stevens & Shea.
Lenin Anthology. Ed. by Robert C. Tucker. (C). 1975. pap. text 19.50 (0-393-09236-4) Norton.
Lenin As Election Campaign Manager. Doug Jenness. 15p. 1971. pap. 3.50 (0-87348-201-8) Pathfinder NY.
Lenin Era. Stuart A. Kallen. Ed. by Rosemary Wallner. LC 92-13473. (Rise & Fall of the Soviet Union Ser.). (J). 1992. lib. bdg. 14.98 (1-56239-101-1) ABDO Pub Co.
Lenin, Hegel, & Western Marxism: A Critical Study. Kevin Anderson. LC 94-45414. 344p. 1995. text 49.95 (0-252-02167-3) U of Ill Pr.
Lenin, Hegel, & Western Marxism: A Critical Study. Kevin Anderson. 344p. (C). 1995. pap. text 17.95 (0-252-06503-4) U of Ill Pr.
Lenin Lives! The Lenin Cult in Soviet Russia. Nina Tumarkin. (Illus.). 352p. 1983. 42.00 (0-674-52430-6) HUP.
Lenin Lives! The Lenin Cult in Soviet Russia. enl. ed. Nina Tumarkin. LC 96-6522. (Illus.). 384p. 1997. pap. 17.95 (0-674-52431-4) HUP.
Lenin on War & Peace: Three Articles. Vladimir Il'ich Lenin. 107p. 1966. pap. 1.95 (0-8351-0130-4) China Bks.
Lenin, Red Dictator. Georgii Vernadskii. Tr. by Davis W. Malcolm. LC 76-119660. reprint ed. 29.50 (0-404-06758-1) AMS Pr.
Lenin to Gorbachev: Three Generations of Soviet Communists Supplement. Joan F. Crowley & Dan Vaillancourt. 216p. (C). 1989. pap. text, suppl. ed. 14.95 (0-88295-863-1) Harlan Davidson.
Lenin, Trotsky, & Stalin: The Intelligentsia & Power. Philip Pomper. 456p. 1990. text 61.50 (0-231-06906-5) Col U Pr.
Lenin Trotsky Stalin. Philip Pomper. 1991. pap. 17.50 (0-685-62548-6) Col U Pr.
Leningrad. Trudy J. Hanmer. LC 92-14. (Cities at War Ser.). (Illus.). 96p. (J). (gr. 6 up). 1992. text 18.00 (0-02-742615-7, Mac Bks Young Read) S&S Childrens.
Leningrad. Marsha Nordby. (Soviet Guides Ser.). (Illus.). 160p. 1994. pap. 14.95 (0-8442-9678-3, Passprt Bks) NTC Contemp Pub Co.
Leningrad: A Guide. P. Kann. (Illus.). 384p. (C). 1988. 90.00 (0-7855-5197-2, Pub. by Collets) St Mut.
Leningrad: American Writers in the Soviet Union. Michael Davidson et al. LC 90-23186. (Illus.). 160p. 1991. pap. 9.95 (1-56279-005-6) Mercury Hse Inc.
Leningrad: Art & Architecture. Gubanov Gennady. 300p. 1985. 285.00 (0-7855-0927-5, Pub. by Collets) St Mut.
Leningrad: Art & Architecture. G. Gubanov. 300p. (C). 1985. 250.00 (0-89771-893-3, Pub. by Collets) St Mut.
Leningrad: Shaping a Soviet City. Blair A. Ruble. 1990. 55.00 (0-520-06534-4, Pub. by U CA Pr) Cal Prin Full Svc.
Leningrad, Aug. 9, 1991-Aug. 24, 1991: St. Petersburg, 1903. Louise O. Neaderland. (Illus.). 65p. 1992. 35.00 (0-942561-19-8) Bone Hollow.
Leningrad Codex. fac. ed. Astrid Beck. Ed. by David N. Freedman & James A. Sanders. 1072p. 1998. 255.00 (0-8028-3786-7) Eerdmans.
Leningrad Codex: A Facsimile Edition. fac. ed. Ed. by Astrid B. Beck et al. (Illus.). 1024p. 1997. 250.00 (90-04-10854-8) Brill Academic Pubs.
Leningrad Diary: One Surprise after Another in the U. S. S. R. Jim Luntzel. LC 91-90331. (Illus.). 180p. (Orig.). 1991. pap. 8.00 (0-9629878-0-8, Samizdat Press) Luntzel Enterp.
Leningrad Dutch. Jaan Ehlvest. 144p. 1995. pap. 17.95 (0-8050-2944-3, Pub. by Batsford Chess) H Holt & Co.
Leningrad Dutch: Strategy & Tactics. John Hall. 148p. 1997. pap. 16.95 (1-880673-14-2) Hays Pub.
Leningrad Mathematical Olympiads, 1987-1991. Dmitry Fomin & Alexey Kirichenko. LC 93-86579. (Contests in Mathematics Ser.: Vol. 1). (Illus.). 224p. (Orig.). 1994. pap. 24.00 (0-9626401-4-X) MathPro Pr.
Leningrad Oblast: Economy, Industry, Government, Business. 2nd rev. ed. Russian Information & Business Center, Inc. Staff. (Russian Regional Business Directories Ser.). (Illus.). 200p. 1997. pap. 99.00 (1-57751-415-7) Intl Business Pubns.
***Leningrad Oblast Regional Investment & Business Guide.** Global Investment & Business Center, Inc. Staff. (Russian Regional Investment & Business Guides Ser.: Vol. 42). (Illus.). 350p. 1999. pap. 99.00 (0-7397-0846-5) Intl Business Pubns.
***Leningrad Oblast Regional Investment & Business Guide.** Contrib. by Global Investment & Business Center, Inc. Staff. (Russian Regional Investment & Business Guides Ser.: Vol. 26). (Illus.). 350p. 2000. pap. 99.95 (0-7397-2990-X) Intl Business Pubns.
Leningrad's Modernists: Studies in Composition & Musical Thought, 1917-1932. David Haas. (American University Studies: Vol. 31, No. XX). XIV, 301p. (C). 1998. text 49.95 (0-8204-3073-0) P Lang Pubng.
Leninism. Neil Harding. LC 96-3874. 360p. 1996. text 49.95 (0-8223-1875-X); pap. text 17.95 (0-8223-1867-9) Duke.
Leninism: Political Economy As Pseudoscience. Folke Dovring. LC 95-43770. 168p. 1996. 52.95 (0-275-95464-1, Praeger Pubs) Greenwood.
Leninism & the Battle of Ideas. Yelena Modrezhinskaya. 1972. pap. 24.95 (0-8464-4448-8) Beekman Pubs.
Leninism under Lenin. Marcel Liebman. (C). 1985. pap. 9.95 (0-85036-261-X, Pub. by MRLN) Paul & Co Pubs.
Leninist Strategy of Party Building: The Debate on Guerrilla Warfare in Latin America. Joseph Hansen. Ed. by Evans et al. LC 79-89423. 608p. 1979. reprint ed. pap. 26.95 (0-87348-571-8); reprint ed. lib. bdg. 65.00 (0-87348-570-X) Pathfinder NY.
Lenin's Brain. Tilman Spengler. Tr. by Shaun Whiteside. 1993. text 23.00 (0-374-18502-6) FS&G.
Lenin's Doctrine on National Liberation: Revolutions & Modern World. V. I. Zotov. (Library of Political Knowledge: No.7). 152p. 1983. 22.00 (0-7855-1225-X, Pub. by Collets) St Mut.
***Lenin's Embalmers.** Ilya Zbarsky & Samuel Hutchinson. Tr. by Barbara Bray. 224p. 2000. reprint ed. pap. 12.00 (1-86046-655-9) Harvill Press.
Lenin's Embalmers: Translated from the French. Ilya Zbarsky & Samuel Hutchinson. 208p. 1999. text 20.00 (1-86046-515-3, Pub. by Harvill Press) FS&G.
Lenin's Final Fight see Ultima Lucha de Lenin: Discursos Y Escritos
Lenin's Final Fight: Speeches & Writings, 1922-1923. Vladimir Il'ich Lenin. Ed. by George Fyson. LC 95-68455. 320p. 1995. pap. 19.95 (0-87348-807-5); lib. bdg. 50.00 (0-87348-808-3) Pathfinder NY.
Lenin's Geneva Addresses. Ed. by A. Kudryavtsev et al. pap. 20.00 (0-8464-0559-8) Beekman Pubs.
Lenin's Government: Sovnarkom, 1917 to 1922. Thomas H. Rigby. LC 78-18754. (Soviet & East European Studies). 336p. reprint ed. pap. 95.80 (0-608-15606-X, 2031718) Bks Demand.
***Lenin's Legacy: A Concise History & Guide to Soviet Collectibles+** Martin J. Goodman. (Illus.). 192p. 2000. 59.95 (0-7643-1019-4) Schiffer.
Lenin's Legacy: The Story of the CPSU. Robert Wesson. LC 77-92341. (Publication Series: Histories of Ruling Communist Parties: No. 192). 318p. 1978. pap. 9.95 (0-8179-6922-5) Hoover Inst Pr.
Lenin's Struggle for a Revolutionary International: Documents: 1907-1916, the Preparatory Years. 2nd ed. Vladimir Il'ich Lenin. Ed. by John Riddell. LC 84-61519. 604p. 1986. pap. 32.95 (0-913460-95-8); lib. bdg. 75.00 (0-913460-94-X) Pathfinder NY.
Lenin's Teaching on the World Economy. K. Mikulsky. Tr. by Jim Riordan from RUS. 1975. pap. 25.00 (0-8464-0560-1) Beekman Pubs.
Lenin's Tomb: The Last Days of the Soviet Empire. David Remnick. 1994. pap. 14.00 (0-679-75125-4) Vin Bks.
Lenin's Will: Falsified & Forbidden. Yuri Buranov. LC 94-15108. (Illus.). 241p. (C). 1994. 33.95 (0-87975-886-4) Prometheus Bks.
Lenitives: Poems from Hollywood. Mark Dunster. 13p. 1998. pap. 5.00 (0-89642-430-8) Linden Pubs.
Lenk's Audio Handbook: Operation & Troubleshooting. John D. Lenk. 350p. 1991. 39.50 (0-07-037503-8) McGraw.
Lenk's Audio Handbook: Operation & Troubleshooting. John D. Lenk. 1992. pap. text 22.95 (0-07-004276-4) McGraw.
Lenk's Audio Handbook: Operation & Troubleshooting. John D. Lenk. 304p. 1992. pap. 22.95 (0-8306-4276-5, 4309) McGraw-Hill Prof.
Lenk's Laser Handbook: Featuring CD, CDV, & CD-Rom Technology. John D. Lenk. 1993. pap. 22.95 (0-8306-4429-6) McGraw-Hill Prof.
Lenk's Laser Handbook: Featuring CD, CDV & CD-Rom Technology. John D. Lenk. 352p. 1992. 39.50 (0-07-037505-4) McGraw.
Lenk's Video Handbook. 2nd ed. John D. Lenk. LC 96-34523. 1996. pap. text 29.95 (0-07-037617-4) McGraw.
Lenk's Video Handbook: Operation & Troubleshooting. John D. Lenk. 384p. 1992. pap. 22.95 (0-8306-4072-X) McGraw.
Lenk's Video Handbook: Operation & Troubleshooting. 2nd ed. John D. Lenk. LC 96-34523. (Illus.). 512p. 1996. 49.50 (0-07-037616-6) McGraw.
***Lennart Anderson: Recent Paintings.** Text by Louis Finkelstein & Steven Harvey. (Illus.). 25p. 1999. pap. 23.00 (1-58821-003-0) Salander OReilly.
Lennon: The Definitive Biography. Ray Coleman. LC 92-52621. 784p. 1992. pap. 20.00 (0-06-098608-5, Perennial) HarperTrade.
Lennon & McCartney. Geoffrey Giuliano. LC 96-50894. 1999. pap. 27.95 (0-670-84730-5) Viking Penguin.
Lennon & McCartney. O'Grady. (Great Pop Songwriters Ser.). 1998. 45.00 (0-02-864769-6) S&S Trade.
Lennon & McCartney: Their Magic & Their Music. Bruce Glassman. LC 94-48459. (Partners II Ser.). 112p. (J). (gr. 5 up). 1995. lib. bdg. 12.95 (1-56711-135-1) Blackbirch.
***Lennon & McCartney for the Harp: Arranged for All Harps.** Sylvia Woods. 144p. 1998. pap. 24.95 (0-936661-23-2) Woods Mus Bks.
Lennon & McCartney Piano Solos. 96p. 1995. per. 14.95 (0-7935-4817-9, 00294023) H Leonard.
Lennon & McCartney 60 Greatest Hits: Violin. Lennon & McCartney. 64p. 1986. pap. 9.95 (0-7935-3300-7, 00844286) H Leonard.
Lennon & McCartney 60 Greatest Hits: Clarinet. Lennon & McCartney. 64p. 1986. pap. 6.95 (0-7935-3294-9, 00844282) H Leonard.
Lennon & McCartney 60 Greatest Hits: Flute. Lennon & McCartney. 64p. 1986. pap. 6.95 (0-7935-3299-X, 00844281) H Leonard.
Lennon & McCartney's #1 Hits. 48p. 1970. pap. 5.95 (0-7935-3546-8, 00699035) H Leonard.
***Lennon in America, 1971-1980: Based in Part on the Lost Lennon Diaries.** Geoffrey Giuliano. 300p. 2000. 27.95 (0-8154-1073-5) Cooper Sq.
***Lennon Remembers: The Famous Rolling Stone Interviews.** Jann Wenner. 2000. 19.00 (1-85984-600-9) Verso.
Lennon, the Solo Years. 112p. 1983. per. 12.95 (0-7935-2147-5, 00700850) H Leonard.
***Lennox Berkeley: A Source Book.** Stewart R. Craggs. LC 99-36002. 300p. 1999. text 70.95 (0-85967-933-0) Ashgate Pub Co.
Lenny Breau Fingerstyle Jazz. John Knowles & Lenny Breau. 60p. 1997. pap. 19.95 incl. audio compact disk (0-7866-2956-8, 93972BCD) Mel Bay.
***Lenny Kravitz.** 5th ed. 88p. 1999. otabind 16.95 (1-57560-145-1, Pub. by Cherry Lane) H Leonard.
Lenny Kravitz - Are You Gonna Go My Way. Ed. by Milton Okun. 1994. pap. 14.95 (0-89524-776-3) Cherry Lane.
Lenny Kravitz - Mama Said. Ed. by Milton Okun. pap. 14.95 (0-89524-634-1) Cherry Lane.
Lenny Kravitz Just the Riffs. 1997. pap. 9.95 (1-57560-008-0, Pub. by Cherry Lane) H Leonard.
Lenny, Lefty & the Chancellor: The Len Bias Tragedy & the Search for Reform in Big-Time College Basketball. C. Fraser Smith. 304p. 1991. pap. 12.95 (0-9631246-0-9) Bancroft MD.
Lenny Long Legs. Kathy Wuertz. (Illus.). 32p. (Orig.). 1997. pap. 7.00 (1-890655-03-1) Red Hen Pr AZ.
***Lenny the Lazy Puppy.** Jenny Dale. (Puppy Friends Ser.: No. 4). (Illus.). 64p. (J). (gr. k-3). 2000. pap. 3.99 (0-689-83552-3) Aladdin.
Lenny the Sign Man - Signs of Love: A Keepsake Coloring Book. large type unabridged ed. Judith E. Nichols. (Illus.). 17p. (J). (ps-5). 1997. 19.50 (1-57529-061-8) Kabel Pubs.
Lenoir. Ken Greenhall. 246p. 1999. pap. 13.00 (1-58195-013-6, Pub. by Zoland Bks) SPD-Small Pr Dist.
***Lenore: Noogies.** Roman Dirge. (Illus.). 112p. (C). 1999. pap. 11.95 (0-943151-03-1) Slave Labor Bks.
***Lenore: Noogies.** Roman Dirge. (Lenore Collection: No. 1). (Illus.). 112p. 1999. pap. 11.95 (0-943151-16-3) Slave Labor Bks.
***Lenore's Natural Cuisine: Your Essential Guide to Wholesome, Vegetarian Cooking.** Lenore Y. Baum. LC 99-90885. (Illus.). 256p. 2000. pap. 17.95 (0-9674627-3-8) Culinary Pubns.
Lenox China: Celebrating a Century of Quality. Ellen P. Denker. (Illus.). 92p. (Orig.). 1990. pap. 22.95 (0-8122-1327-0) NJ State Mus.
Lenox (Mass.) & the Berkshire Highlands. R. DeWitt Mallary. (Illus.). 363p. 1995. reprint ed. lib. bdg. 42.50 (0-8328-4465-9) Higginson Bk Co.
Lens: Poems from Hollywood. Mark Dunster. 27p. 1998. pap. 5.00 (0-89642-390-5) Linden Pubs.
Lens: Proceedings of the Workshop on Aging of the Lens, Bonn, July 1977. Aging of the Lens Workshop Staff. Ed. by Otto Hockwin. (Interdisciplinary Topics in Gerontology Ser.: Vol. 12). (Illus.). 1978. 121.00 (3-8055-2876-0) S Karger.
***Lens & the Land: Photographing South Texas Wildlife.** Valley Land Fund Staff. Ed. by Ron Smith. (Illus.). 192p. 1999. write for info. (0-9660013-1-1) Chachalaca Pr.

L

Lens Book: Choosing & Using Lenses for Your SLR. Roger Hicks & Frances Schultz. (Illus.). 160p. (Orig.). 1996. pap. 19.95 (*0-7153-0470-4*, Pub. by D & C Pub) Sterling.

Lens Design. Ed. by W. J. Smith. (Critical Reviews Ser.). 1992. pap. 63.00 (*0-8194-0808-5*) SPIE.

Lens Design. 2nd expanded rev. ed. Milton Laikin. LC 94-44816. (Optical Engineering Ser.: Vol. 48). (Illus.). 464p. 1995. text 135.00 (*0-8247-9602-0*) Dekker.

Lens Design: A Resource Manual. Warren J. Smith. 471p. 1992. 75.00 (*0-07-059178-4*) McGraw.

Lens Design Fundamentals. Rudolph Kingslake. 1978. text 59.00 (*0-12-408650-0*) Acad Pr.

Lens Design, Illumination & Optomechanical Modeling. Ed. by R. Barry Johnson et al. 32p. 1997. pap. 69.00 (*0-8194-2552-4*) SPIE.

Lens Disorders: A Clinical Manual of Cataract Diagnosis. Nicholas P. Brown & Anthony J. Bron. LC 94-32580. (Illus.). 256p. 1996. text 125.00 (*0-7506-1482-X*) Buttrwrth-Heinemann.

Lens Implant Power Calculation: A Manual for Ophthalmologists & Biometrists. 3rd ed. John A. Retzlaff et al. LC 90-53345. 58p. 1990. pap. 25.00 (*1-55642-186-9*) SLACK Inc.

Lens, Light & Landscape: The Art & Technique of Scenic Photography. Brian Bower. (Illus.). 192p. 1996. pap. 19.95 (*0-7153-0463-1*, Pub. by D & C Pub) Sterling.

Lens of Perception. rev. ed. Hal Z. Bennett. (Field Guides to Inner Resources Ser.). 180p. (Orig.). 1995. pap. 11.95 (*0-89087-723-8*) Celestial Arts.

Lens of the World. R. A. MacAvoy. 288p. 1991. reprint ed. mass mkt. 4.99 (*0-380-71016-1*, Avon Bks) Morrow Avon.

Lens of the World Bk. 3: The Belly of the Wolf. R. A. MacAvoy. 224p. 1995. mass mkt. 4.99 (*0-380-71018-8*, Avon Bks) Morrow Avon.

Lens Surfacing Handbook. Clifford W. Brooks. (Illus.). 144p. 1992. spiral bd. 37.50 (*0-7506-9186-7*) Buttrwrth-Heinemann.

***L'enseignement de l'Histoire en Republique Democratique du Congo (Ex-Zaire)** Augustin O. Omakoko. xv, 339p. 1999. 47.95 (*3-906762-42-4*) P Lang Pubng.

Lenses! Take a Closer Look. Siegfried Aust. (Illus.). 32p. (J). 1996. pap. text 7.95 (*0-8225-9732-2*) Lerner Pub.

Lenses for 35mm Photography. Artur Landt. LC 95-73080. (Kodak Workshop Ser.). (Illus.). 112p. (C). 1998. pap. 22.95 (*0-87985-765-X*, KW-18, Kodak) Saunders Photo.

Lenses of Gender: Transforming the Debate on Sexual Inequality. Sandra L. Bem. LC 92-26345. 256p. (C). 1993. 35.00 (*0-300-05676-1*) Yale U Pr.

Lenses of Gender: Transforming the Debate on Sexual Inequality. Sandra Lipsitz-Bem. 256p. 1994. pap. 16.00 (*0-300-06163-3*) Yale U Pr.

Lenses on the World of Higher Education in Indiana. Ed. by Lisa J. Walker. 56p. (Orig.). 1985. pap. 3.95 (*0-937846-92-9*) Inst Educ Lead.

L'Ensorcellement Bk. 1: The Haunting. Rodman Philbrick & Lynn Harnett.Tr. of Maison de la Rue du Cerisier: L'Ensorcellement. (FRE.). (YA). mass mkt. 5.99 (*0-590-24674-7*) Scholastic Inc.

Lent. (St. Joseph's Coloring Bks.). (Illus.). 32p. (J). (ps-3). 1989. pap. 0.99 (*0-89942-697-2*, 697/00) Catholic Bk Pub.

Lent, 2 vols. Megan McKenna. Incl. Vol. II. Lent: The Daily Readings: Reflections & Stories. LC 96-26922. 200p. (Orig.). 1996. pap. 13.00 (*1-57075-103-X*); Vol. II. The Sunday Readings Reflections & Stories. LC 96-26922. 176p. (Orig.). 1996. pap. 13.00 (*1-57075-102-1*); LC 96-45059. 1996. 23.00 (*1-57075-104-8*) Orbis Bks.

Lent: The Daily Readings: Reflections & Stories see Lent

Lent: The Season of Sacred Stories. Elaine M. Ward. 1990. pap. 7.95 (*0-940754-86-X*) Ed Ministries.

Lent: The Slow Fast. Starkey Flythe, Jr. LC 89-29989. (Iowa Short Fiction Award Ser.). 164p. 1990. 10.00 (*0-87745-274-1*) U of Iowa Pr.

Lent - Proclamation 6A Series. Peter Gomes. 1993. pap. 5.00 (*0-8006-4209-0*, 1-4209) Augsburg Fortress.

Lent & Easter see St. Joseph Liturgy of the Hours: Liturgy of the Hours

Lent & Easter: Meditation & Prayer. Date not set. 2.95 (*0-88271-170-9*, 1507) Regina Pr.

Lent & Eastertide see In Conversation with God

Lent Begins at Home: Family Prayers & Activities. Pat Ryan & Rosemary Ryan. 64p. 1978. pap. 3.95 (*0-89243-101-6*) Liguori Pubns.

Lent Book. Ed. by Lonnie C. Pratt. LC 98-50326. (ML Book Ser.). (Illus.). 176p. 1999. pap. 29.95 (*0-89390-446-5*) Resource Pubns.

Lent Daily Missal. Veritas Publications Staff. 156p. 1989. pap. 22.00 (*1-85390-080-X*, Pub. by Veritas Pubns) St Mut.

Lent Easter Ascension. Concordia House Staff. 1995. pap. 5.50 (*0-570-09460-7*) Concordia.

Lent-Easter Meditations & Prayers. Hoagland. 1994. pap. 2.95 (*0-9626119-1-3*) Passionist Pr.

Lent, Good Friday & Easter. Ralph Becker. pap. 0.99 (*0-87377-011-0*) GAM Pubns.

Lent, Holy Week, Easter, & the Great 50 Days: A Ceremonial Guide. Leonel L. Mitchell & Howard Galley. LC 96-24910. 144p. 1996. pap. 13.95 (*1-56101-134-7*) Cowley Pubns.

Lent Instructor: Reflections & Symbols. Kenneth A. Mortonson. LC 95-94163. 1997. pap. text 6.95 (*1-55673-993-1*) CSS OH.

Lent Is for Children: Stories, Activities, Prayers. rev. ed. Julie Kelemen. LC 92-75934. (Illus.). 80p. (J). 1993. pap. 3.95 (*0-89243-532-1*) Liguori Pubns.

Lent Is for Remembering. Donna R. Rathert. LC 56-1613. 24p. (Orig.). (J). (ps-1). 1987. pap. 2.99 (*0-570-04147-3*, 56-1613) Concordia.

Lent Sourcebook, 2 vols., Set. Ed. by Peter Mazar et al. (Orig.). 1991. pap. 28.00 (*0-929650-36-0*, 2/LENT) Liturgy Tr Pubns.

Lent, Triduum, & Easter Answer Book: ML Answers the 101 Most Asked Questions. Paul J. Niemann. LC 98-39648. (ML Answers the 101 Most-Asked Questions Ser.). 152p. 1998. pap. 29.95 (*0-89390-447-3*) Resource Pubns.

Lent, 2000. Mark Link. 64p. 1997. pap. text 1.95 (*0-88347-353-4*) Tabor Pub.

Lent 2000 - Year A. Mark S. Link. 1998. pap. 1.95 (*0-88347-401-8*, 661-139 7401) T More.

Lent, 2000/Year B. Mark Link. 64p. 1997. pap. text 1.95 (*0-88347-373-9*) Res Christian Liv.

Lent with Evelyn Underhill. 2nd ed. Ed. by George M. Belshaw. LC 89-28659. 112p. 1990. pap. 9.95 (*0-8192-1449-3*) Morehouse Pub.

Lent with the Fathers. Bruce Harbert. 1994. pap. 34.00 (*1-85390-202-0*, Pub. by Veritas Pubns) St Mut.

Lenten Alphabet. Phyllis Wezeman & Jude Fournier. 53p. 1993. pap. 8.50 (*1-877871-46-X*, 2680) Ed Ministries.

Lenten & Easter Drama Resources. Compiled by Paul M. Miller. 1982. 4.99 (*0-685-68678-7*, ME-227) Lillenas.

Lenten Cookbook for Orthodox Christians. Ed. by Neketas S. Palassis. 260p. 1982. pap. 9.00 (*0-913026-13-1*) St Nectarios.

Lenten Hobo Honeymoon: Daily Reflections for the Journey of Lent. Edward Hays. LC 98-43672. 1999. pap. text 12.95 (*0-939516-43-8*) Forest Peace.

Lenten Hymns. (Harp Preludes for the Church Ser.: Vol. II). 18p. 1997. pap. 10.00 (*1-882712-04-8*) Dragonflower.

Lenten Journal. Anne McConney. 112p. 2000. pap. 9.95 (*0-8192-1787-5*, 5980) Morehouse Pub.

Lenten Journey, Cycle B. Joanne Simcik. 32p. 1996. pap. text 2.95 (*1-55612-407-4*, LL1407) Sheed & Ward WI.

Lenten Journey: Travels in the Spiritual Life Based on the Gospel of Mark. Larry R. Kalajainen. LC 90-70324. 112p. 1990. pap. 10.00 (*0-8358-0616-2*) Upper Room Bks.

Lenten Journey: Travels in the Spiritual Life Based on the Gospel of Mark. Larry R. Kalajainen. 1990. pap. 9.95 (*0-687-60638-1*) Abingdon.

Lenten Kitchen. Barbara Benjamin & Alexandria D. Vali. LC 94-33152. 96p. 1995. pap. 6.95 (*0-8091-3542-6*) Paulist Pr.

Lenten Labyrinth: Daily Reflections for the Journey of Lent. Edward Hays. 136p. 1994. pap. 10.95 (*0-939516-22-5*) Forest Peace.

Lenten Lands: My Childhood with Joy Davidman & C. S. Lewis. Douglas H. Gresham. LC 94-4366. 256p. 1994. pap. 12.00 (*0-06-063447-2*, Pub. by Harper SF) HarpC.

Lenten Longings: Let Yourself Be. Catherine T. Nerney. pap. 2.25 (*0-7648-0444-8*) Liguori Pubns.

Lenten Love Letters. Lucy D. Blount. LC 98-232050. 215p. 1998. write for info. (*0-9630017-9-5*) Light-Bearer.

Lenten Lunches: Reflections on the Weekday Readings for Lent & Easter Week. Daniel E. Pilarczyk. LC 95-222975. 112p. 1995. pap. 7.95 (*0-86716-243-0*) St Anthony Mess Pr.

Lenten Parish Programme: Renewal of Personal & Community Life Through Prayer & Scripture. Seamus Heaney. 1989. pap. 25.00 (*1-85390-075-3*, Pub. by Veritas Pubns); pap. 22.00 (*1-85390-031-1*, Pub. by Veritas Pubns) St Mut.

Lenten Reflections "A" Karen S. Smith & Donna L. Ciangio. (Follow Me! Ser.). (Illus.). 48p. 1998. pap. 2.60 (*1-881307-08-5*, B7085) Natl Pastoral LC.

Lenten Reflections "C" Karen S. Smith & Donna L. Ciangio. (Follow Me! Ser.). (Illus.). 48p. 1997. pap. 2.60 (*1-881307-07-7*, B7077) Natl Pastoral LC.

Lenten Resources for Worship Leaders: An Anthology. Alexander H. Wales. LC 96-38676. 98p. (Orig.). 1997. pap. 10.95 (*0-7880-0716-5*) CSS OH.

Lenten Scriptures: Cycle A. Joanne Simcik. 32p. 1989. pap. text 2.95 (*1-55612-309-4*) Sheed & Ward WI.

Lenten Spring. Thomas Hopko. LC 83-4278. 229p. 1983. pap. text 9.95 (*0-88141-014-4*) St Vladimirs.

Lenten Studies: Life Defeats Death. Marilyn Kunz & Catherine Schell. (Neighborhood Bible Studies). 40p. 1995. pap. text 5.99 (*1-880266-15-6*) Neighborhood Bible.

Lenten Walk. James A. Griffin. 64p. 1999. mass mkt. 1.95 (*0-8189-0857-2*) Alba.

Lenten Worship for Young Adults. Ellery Lane. 56p. (Orig.). 1997. pap. 7.95 (*0-7880-1015-8*) CSS OH.

Lentes, Quien Los Necesita? Lane Smith.Tr. of Glasses, Who Needs 'Em. 36p. 1995. 12.99 (*968-16-4419-0*, Pub. by Fondo) Continental Bk.

Lenticle: Two Radio Interviews with Fritz Faiss. deluxe limited ed. Ed. by Fritz W. Faiss. (Illus.). 63p. 1972. pap. 15.00 (*0-916678-08-3*); pap. 9.00 (*0-916678-09-1*) Green Hut.

Lentil. Robert McCloskey. (Illus.). (J). (gr. k-3). 1940. 16.99 (*0-670-42357-2*, Viking Child) Peng Put Young Read.

Lentil. Robert McCloskey. (J). (ps-3). 1978. pap. 5.99 (*0-14-050287-4*, PuffinBks) Peng Put Young Read.

Lentil. Robert McCloskey. (Picture Puffin Ser.). (Illus.). (J). 1978. 10.19 (*0-606-02156-6*, Pub. by Turtleback) Demco.

***Lentil Science: Intermediate.** Ron Marson. (Science with Simple Things Ser.: No. 72). (Illus.). 136p. 1999. teacher ed. 26.00 (*0-941008-52-5*) Tops Learning.

***Lentil Science: Primary.** Ron Marson. (Science with Simple Things Ser.: No. 72). (Illus.). 136p. 1999. teacher ed. 26.00 (*0-941008-51-7*) Tops Learning.

Lentil Soup for the Arab American Soul: Fighting Back: A Handbook for Arab Americans to Confront Bigotry & Discrimination. Ray Hananra. 100p. 1999. spiral bd. 29.95 (*0-9654761-1-1*) U S G Pub.

Lenya: A Life. Donald Spoto. (Illus.). 416p. 1989. 19.95 (*0-316-80725-7*) Little.

Lenya the Legend: A Pictorial Autobiography. Ed. & Compiled by David Farneth. LC 98-10625. (Illus.). 256p. 1998. 45.00 (*0-87951-825-1*, Pub. by Overlook Pr) Penguin Putnam.

Lenz. Georg Buchner. Tr. by Hedwig Rappolt from GER. 96p. (C). 1983. pap. text 6.00 (*0-939858-04-5*) T S L Pr.

Lenz Family: History of the American Branch Established at Stone Arabia, N.Y., in 1854, by Friedrich Konrad Lenz of Werdorf, Germany. E. E. Lenz. (Illus.). 187p. 1993. reprint ed. pap. 31.00 (*0-8328-3700-8*); reprint ed. lib. bdg. 41.00 (*0-8328-3699-0*) Higginson Bk Co.

Lenzkirch Clocks, 1994 Edition: European Industrial Clockmaking, 1866-1933. Winterhalden et al. (Illus.). 133p. 1985. pap. 22.50 (*0-933396-16-3*) Antique Clocks.

Leo. (Total Horoscopes, 1995 Ser.). 272p. 1994. pap. text 4.50 (*0-515-11415-4*, Jove) Berkley Pub.

Leo. (Parker's Love Signs Ser.). 1996. 8.95 (*0-614-20705-3*) DK Pub Inc.

Leo. (Cosmopolitan a Bedside Astrologer Book Ser.). (Illus.). 24p. (J). 1997. pap. write for info. (*1-56144-964-4*, Honey Bear Bks) Modern Pub NYC.

Leo. Ariel Books Staff. (Tiny Tomes Ser.). 128p. 1997. 3.95 (*0-8362-2667-4*, Arie Bks) Andrews & McMeel.

Leo. Lucille Callard. (Astro-Pups: Your Sign, Your Dogs Ser.). (Illus.). 60p. 1991. pap. 9.95 (*1-881038-04-1*) Penzance Pr.

Leo. Jove Publications Incorporated, Staff. (Total Horoscopes Ser.). 272p. 1997. mass mkt. 5.99 (*0-515-12112-6*, Jove) Berkley Pub.

Leo. Jove Publications Staff. (Total Horoscopes Ser.). 1998. mass mkt. 5.99 (*0-515-12308-0*, Jove) Berkley Pub.

Leo. Teresa Moorey. (Reach Your Potential Ser.). 96p. 1998. pap. 9.95 (*0-340-69713-X*, Pub. by Headway) Trafalgar.

Leo. Derek Parker & Julia Parker. LC 92-52788. (Sun & Moon Signs Library). (Illus.). 58p. 1992. 8.95 (*1-56458-088-1*) DK Pub Inc.

Leo. Julia Parker & Derek Parker. (Love Signs Library). 64p. 1996. 8.95 (*0-7894-1093-1*) DK Pub Inc.

Leo: Astro-Numerogia. Michael J. Kurban. Tr. by Loretta Hilsher-Kurban from ENG. LC 86-91271. (SPA., Illus.). (Orig.). 1992. pap. 8.00 (*0-938863-49-5*) HCI Pr.

Leo: Astro-Numerology. 2nd ed. Michael J. Kurban. (Illus.). 50p. 1991. pap. 8.00 (*0-938863-13-4*) HCI Pr.

Leo: Astrological Horoscopes for 1999. Teri King. (Teri King Ser.). 1998. pap. 4.95 (*1-86204-278-0*, Pub. by Element MA) Penguin Putnam.

Leo: Little Birth Sign. Andrews & McMeel. (Illus.). 80p. 1994. 4.95 (*0-8362-3074-4*) Andrews & McMeel.

***Leo: Secrets of the Sun Signs.** Ed. by Jennifer Fox. (Illus.). 272p. (J). 2000. pap. 5.95 (*0-7407-1074-5*) Andrews & McMeel.

Leo: The Incredible Story of the World's First Business Computer. David Caminer et al. LC 97-37095. 392p. 1997. 22.95 (*0-07-009501-9*) McGraw.

Leo: The Lion (July 24-August 23) Sterling Publishing Staff. 1999. 4.95 (*0-8069-3144-2*) Sterling.

***Leo: Your Personal Horoscope.** rev. ed. American Astroanalysts Institute Staff. (Astroanalysis Ser.). 2000. pap. 12.95 (*0-425-17562-6*) Berkley Pub.

Leo: Your Sun-&-Moon Guide to Love & Life. Ariel Books Staff. 374p. (Orig.). 1997. pap. 5.95 (*0-8362-3561-4*, Arie Bks) Andrews & McMeel.

Leo: 2000. Jove Books Publishing Staff. (Total Horoscopes Ser.). 1999. mass mkt. 5.99 (*0-515-12540-7*, Jove) Berkley Pub.

Leo Mini Edition. Ariel. (Women's Astrology Library). 1999. 4.95 (*0-8362-7889-5*) Andrews & McMeel.

Leo Africanus. Amin Maalouf. 360p. 1992. reprint ed. pap. 15.95 (*1-56131-022-0*, Pub. by I R Dee) Natl Bk Netwk.

Leo & Blossom's Sukkah. Jane Breskin Zalben. LC 89-24596. (Illus.). 32p. (J). (ps-2). 1995. 13.95 (*0-8050-1226-5*, Bks Young Read) H Holt & Co.

Leo & His Friends. Elizabeth Kontoyiannaki. (Illus.). 12p. (J). (gr. 1-4). 1992. pap. 12.95 (*1-56606-011-7*) Bradley Mann.

Leo & Julio. Louise Leblanc. (First Novels Ser.). (Illus.). 64p. (J). (gr. 1-4). 1999. mass mkt. 3.99 (*0-88780-478-0*, Pub. by Formac Publ Co) Orca Bk Pubs.

***Leo & Julio.** Louise LeBlanc. (First Novels). (Illus.). 62p. (J). 2000. bds. write for info. (*0-88780-479-9*, Pub. by Formac Publ Co) Formac Dist Ltd.

***Leo@fergusrules.com.** Arne E. Tangherlini. LC 99-19411. 216p. 1999. pap. 14.95 (*0-9654578-7-7*, Pub. by Leapfrog Pr) Consort Bk Sales.

Leo Baeck: A Radio Play Based on Authentic Texts. Erwin Sylvanus. Tr. by David Dowdey & Wolfgang Rhee. (Literature & the Sciences of Man Ser.: Vol. 10). (GER.). 151p. (C). 1996. text 40.95 (*0-8204-2806-X*) P Lang Pubng.

Leo Baeck: Teacher of Theresienstadt. Albert Friedlander. 294p. 1992. pap. 13.95 (*0-87951-441-8*, Pub. by Overlook Pr) Penguin Putnam.

Leo Brouwer's 20 Estudios Sencillos. David Tanenbaum. Ed. & Intro. by Jim Ferguson. (Essential Studies). (Illus.). 37p. (Orig.). (C). 1992. pap. text 14.95 (*0-9627832-3-4*) Guitar Solo.

Leo Buscagila's Love Cookbook. Leo F. Buscaglia. 88p. 1995. 29.50 (*0-8050-3725-X*) H Holt & Co.

Leo Castelli: Portraits of Art. Goldman. Date not set. 30.00 (*0-8050-5839-7*) H Holt & Co.

Leo Cockroach... Toy Tester. Kevin O'Malley. LC 98-27989. (Illus.). 32p. (J). (ps-2). 1999. 15.95 (*0-8027-8689-8*); lib. bdg. 16.85 (*0-8027-8690-1*) Walker & Co.

Leo Days. large type ed. Patricia Wendorf. 320p. 1986. 11.50 (*0-7089-1437-3*) Ulverscroft.

Leo, el Retono Tardio. Robert Kraus. Tr. by Teresa Mlawer.Tr. of Leo the Late Bloomer. (SPA., Illus.). 32p. (J). (gr. k-2). 1998. 15.95 (*1-880507-38-2*) Lectorum Pubns.

Leo Frank Case. Leonard Dinnerstein. 1999. pap. text 15.95 (*0-8203-2145-1*) U of Ga Pr.

Leo Gasperl. Fulvio Ferrari. 1998. pap. text 45.00 (*88-422-0700-4*, Pub. by U Allemandi) Antique Collect.

Leo Gross' Selected Essays on International Law & Organization. Leo Gross. LC 92-33197. 1993. 145.00 (*0-941320-75-8*) Transnatl Pubs.

Leo Hamilton Presents: Children's Dream Adventures, large type ed. Leo Hamilton. LC 99-63911. (Illus.). 40p. (J). (ps-5). 2000. pap. 8.99 (*0-9671660-2-0*) The Story Pl.

Leo Hamilton Presents: The Hill. large type ed. Leo Hamilton. 32p. (J). (ps-5). Date not set. pap. 8.99 (*0-9671660-5-5*) The Story Pl.

Leo Hamilton's Odd Collection of Animal & Insect Stories, Vol. I. large type ed. Leo Hamilton. LC 99-63911. (Illus.). 36p. (J). (ps-5). 2000. pap. 7.99 (*0-9671660-0-4*) The Story Pl.

Leo Hamilton's Odd Collection of Animal & Insect Stories, Vol. II. large type ed. Leo Hamilton. LC 99-63911. (Illus.). 40p. (J). (ps-5). 2000. pap. 8.99 (*0-9671660-1-2*) The Story Pl.

Leo Hamilton's Odd Collection of Animal & Insect Stories, Vol. III. large type ed. Leo Hamilton. (Illus.). 24p. (J). (ps-5). 2000. pap. 8.99 (*0-9671660-3-9*) The Story Pl.

Leo Kennedy. Francis Zichy. (Canadian Author Studies). 55p. 1997. pap. 9.95 (*1-55022-023-3*, Pub. by ECW) LPC InBook.

***Leo Kenney, a Retrospective: Celebrating the Mysteries.** Sheila Farr. (Illus.). 100p. 2000. pap. 25.00 (*0-295-97961-5*) U of Wash Pr.

***Leo Kenney, a Retrospective: Celebrating the Mysteries.** Leon F. Kenney et al. LC 00-25518. (Illus.). 100p. 2000. 40.00 (*0-295-97960-7*) U of Wash Pr.

Leo Kottke 8 Songs. 96p. 1986. pap. 14.95 (*0-88188-536-3*, 00699215) H Leonard.

***Leo Kottke Transcribed.** Mark Hanson. 64p. (C). 2000. 19.95 (*0-936799-19-6*, T302, Pub. by Accent Music) Music Sales.

Leo McCarey & the Comic Anti-Hero in American Film. Wes D. Gehring. Ed. by Garth S. Jowett. LC 79-6677. (Dissertations on Film, 1980 Ser.). 1980. lib. bdg. 18.95 (*0-405-12911-4*) Ayer.

Leo Melamed: Escape to the Futures. Leo Melamed & Bob Tamarkin. LC 96-15316. 480p. 1996. 27.95 (*0-471-11215-1*) Wiley.

Leo Melamed on the Markets: Twenty Years of Financial History As Seen by the Man Who Revolutionized the Markets. Leo Melamed. LC 95-22150. 304p. 1992. 29.95 (*0-471-57524-0*) Wiley.

***Leo, My Big Brother.** Norman D. Kisamore. LC 98-68270. 288p. 1999. 22.95 (*1-57197-151-3*) Pentland Pr.

Leo, 1995 Love Signs. 1995. mass mkt. 1.29 (*0-440-22124-2*) Dell.

Leo, 1995 Purse Book. 1994. mass mkt. 0.99 (*0-440-60235-1*) Dell.

Leo, 1994 Purse Book. 1994. mass mkt. 1.25 (*0-440-60228-9*) Dell.

Leo, 1996 Purse Book. 1995. mass mkt. 1.19 (*0-440-60250-5*) Dell.

Leo '98. Berkley Publishing Staff. (Berkley Super Horoscopes Ser.). 256p. 1997. pap. 6.99 (*0-425-15890-X*) Berkley Pub.

Leo '99. Astrology World Staff. (Super Horoscopes Ser.). 256p. 1998. pap. 7.99 (*0-425-16328-8*) Berkley Pub.

Leo Ornstein: The Man, His Ideas, & His Work. Frederick H. Martens. LC 74-29505. (Modern Jewish Experience Ser.). (Illus.). 1975. reprint ed. 16.95 (*0-405-06732-1*) Ayer.

Leo Rising. Douglas M. Baker. (Esoteric Astrology: The Rising Signs Ser.). 1978. pap. 7.50 (*0-906006-33-3*, Pub. by Baker Pubns) New Leaf Dist.

Leo Rosten's Carnival of Wit: From Aristotle to Woody Allen. Leo Rosten. 560p. 1996. pap. 15.95 (*0-452-27099-5*, Plume) Dutton Plume.

Leo Smith: A Biographical Sketch. Pearl McCarthy. LC 76-383510. 64p. reprint ed. pap. 30.00 (*0-608-10857-X*, 201427700089) Bks Demand.

Leo Spitzer: Representative Essays. Ed. by Alban K. Forcione et al. LC 87-10100. 512p. 1988. 55.00 (*0-8047-1367-7*); pap. 19.95 (*0-8047-1801-6*) Stanford U Pr.

Leo Spitzer on Language & Literature: A Descriptive Bibliography. E. Kristina Baer & Daisy E. Shenholm. LC 91-9845. vi, 172p. 1991. lib. bdg. 50.00 (*0-87352-195-1*, T124C) Modern Lang.

Leo Strauss: Political Philosopher & Jewish Thinker. Ed. by Kenneth L. Deutsch & Walter Nicgorski. 406p. (C). 1993. lib. bdg. 64.50 (*0-8476-7837-7*) Rowman.

Leo Strauss: Political Philosopher & Jewish Thinker. Ed. by Kenneth L. Deutsch & Walter Nicgorski. 406p. (C). 1994. pap. text 24.95 (*0-8476-7838-5*) Rowman.

Leo Strauss: The Straussians & the Study of the American Regime. Ed. by Kenneth L. Deutsch & John A. Murley. LC 99-22578. 472p. 1999. 70.00 (*0-8476-8691-4*); pap. 29.95 (*0-8476-8692-2*) Rowman.

Leo Strauss & Judaism: Jerusalem & Athens Revisited. Ed. by David Novak. 208p. (C). 1996. pap. text 23.95 (*0-8476-8147-5*); lib. bdg. 55.50 (*0-8476-8146-7*) Rowman.

Leo Strauss & Nietzsche. Laurence Lampert. LC 95-10467. 238p. 1995. 22.50 (*0-226-46825-9*) U Ch Pr.

Leo Strauss & Nietzsche. Laurence Lampert. x, 230p. 1997. pap. text 16.95 (*0-226-46826-7*) U Ch Pr.

Leo Strauss & the American Right. Shadia B. Drury. LC 97-11580. 256p. 1997. text 35.00 (*0-312-12689-1*) St Martin.

***Leo Strauss & the American Right.** Shadia B. Drury. 256p. 1999. pap. 18.95 (*0-312-21783-8*) St Martin.

Leo Strauss's Thought: Toward a Critical Engagement. Ed. by Alan Udoff. LC 90-24002. 327p. 1991. lib. bdg. 49.95 (*1-55587-232-8*) L Rienner.

An Asterisk (*) at the beginning of an entry indicates that the title is appearing for the first time.

Leo Sun Sign. Douglas M. Baker. (Astrological Sun Sign Ser.). 1972. pap. 5.50 (*0-906006-21-X*, Pub. by Baker Pubns) New Leaf Dist.

Leo Szilard: Science As a Mode of Being. David A. Grandy. LC 96-13768. 204p. (C). 1996. lib. bdg. 39.50 (*0-7618-0308-4*) U Pr of Amer.

Leo the Late Bloomer see Leo, el Retono Tardio

Leo the Late Bloomer. Robert Kraus. LC 70-159154. (Illus.). 32p. (J). (ps-3). 1971. 15.95 (*0-87807-042-7*); lib. bdg. 15.89 (*0-87807-043-5*) HarpC Child Bks.

Leo the Late Bloomer. Robert Kraus. LC 70-159154. (Trophy Picture Bk.). (Illus.). 32p. (J). (ps-3). 1994. pap. 6.95 (*0-06-443348-X*, HarpTrophy) HarpC Child Bks.

Leo the Late Bloomer. Robert Kraus. (My Little Library Board Book Ser.). (Illus.). (J). (ps). 1998. bds. 19.95 (*0-694-01183-5*, HarpFestival) HarpC Child Bks.

Leo the Late Bloomer. Robert Kraus. (J). 1971. 11.15 (*0-606-05904-0*, Pub. by Turtleback) Demco.

Leo the Late Bloomer: A Study Guide. Garrett Christopher. Ed. by Joyce Friedland & Rikki Kessler. (Little Novel-Ties Ser.). (J). (gr. k-2). 1991. pap. text 14.95 (*0-88122-591-6*) Lrn Links.

Leo the Late Bloomer Board Book. Robert Kraus. (Illus.). 17p. (J). (ps up). 1998. 6.95 (*0-694-00980-6*) HarpC Child Bks.

***Leo the Late Bloomer Board Book & Tape.** Robert Kraus. (My First Book & Tape Ser.). (Illus.). (J). (ps up). 1999. 9.95 incl. audio (*0-694-70098-3*, HarpFestival) HarpC Child Bks.

***Leo the Lion.** Sanduik Bokforlag. (Illus.). 6p. (J). 1999. 12.98 (*1-58048-093-4*) Sandvik Pub.

Leo the Lion. Gerda Wagener. Tr. by Nina Ignatowicz from GER. LC 90-46272. (Illus.). 32p. (J). (gr. k-3). 1991. 14.95 (*0-06-021656-5*) HarpC Child Bks.

Leo the Lion. Gerda Wagener. Tr. by Nina Ignatowicz from GER. LC 90-46272. (Illus.). 32p. (J). (gr. k-3). 1991. lib. bdg. 14.89 (*0-06-021657-3*) HarpC Child Bks.

Leo, the Littlest Lion. Christine H. Tangvald. LC 95-859. (Shaped Paperback Bks.). (Illus.). 24p. (J). (ps-k). 1995. pap. 2.99 (*0-7847-0167-9*, 03927) Standard Pub.

Leo the Lop. Stephen Cosgrove. LC 94-21448. (Serendipity Bks.). (Illus.). 32p. (J). (gr. 1-4). 1995. pap. 4.99 (*0-8431-3820-3*, Price Stern) Peng Put Young Read.

Leo the Lop. Stephen Cosgrove. (Serendipity Bks.). 1978. 9.15 (*0-606-06122-3*, Pub. by Turtleback) Demco.

Leo the Lop. Stephen Cosgrove. (J). 1995. 9.15 (*0-606-02402-6*, Pub. by Turtleback) Demco.

Leo the Lop: Tail Three. Stephen Cosgrove. (Serendipity Bks.). (Illus.). 32p. (J). (ps-3). 1980. pap. 4.99 (*0-8431-0577-1*, Price Stern) Peng Put Young Read.

Leo the Lop: Tail Two. Stephen Cosgrove. (Serendipity Bks.). (J). 1978. 9.15 (*0-606-02403-4*, Pub. by Turtleback) Demco.

Leo the Magnificat. Ann M. Martin. (J). 1996. pap. write for info. (*0-590-94219-0*) Scholastic Inc.

Leo the Magnificat. Ann M. Martin. LC 95-33640. (Illus.). 32p. (J). (gr. k-3). 1996. 15.95 (*0-590-48498-2*) Scholastic Inc.

***Leo the Magnificat.** Ann M. Martin. (Illus.). 32p. (J). (gr. k-3). 2000. mass mkt. 5.99 (*0-439-13647-4*) Scholastic Inc.

***Leo the Magnificent.** Ann Matthews Martin. (Illus.). (J). 2000. 11.44 (*0-606-18573-9*) Turtleback.

Leo Tolstoi: Fables, Tales, Stories, 2 cass. 84p. pap. 39.50 incl. audio (*1-57970-011-X*, SRU1115) Audio-Forum.

Leo Tolstoy. John Bayley. (Writers & Their Work Ser.). 95p. (Orig.). 1996. pap. text 17.00 (*0-7463-0744-6*, Pub. by Northcote House) U Pr of Miss.

***Leo Tolstoy.** Lynne F. Chapman. LC 93-10629. (Notebooks Ser.). (J). 1999. spiral bd. 23.95 (*1-56846-156-9*, Creative Eds) Creative Co.

Leo Tolstoy. Aylmer Maude. LC 75-20491. (Studies in Tolstoy: No. 62). 1974. lib. bdg. 75.00 (*0-8383-2001-5*) M S G Haskell Hse.

Leo Tolstoy. William W. Rowe. (Twayne's World Authors Ser.: No. 772). 160p. 1986. 32.00 (*0-8057-6623-5*, 416, Twyne) Mac Lib Ref.

Leo Tolstoy: A Chronology. V. Munoz. Tr. by W. Scott Johnson. (Libertarian & Anarchist Chronology Ser.). 1979. lib. bdg. 59.95 (*0-8490-3034-X*) Gordon Pr.

Leo Tolstoy: Great Short Stories from Around the World I. Illus. by James McConnell. LC 94-75342. (Classic Short Stories Ser.). 80p. 1994. pap. 5.95 (*0-7854-0655-7*, 40063) Am Guidance.

Leo Tolstoy, a Signature on a Portrait, Highlights of Tolstoy's Thought. 2nd ed. Michael L. Levin. (Illus.). 136p. (Orig.). 1995. per. 9.95 (*0-9628473-2-1*) Levin Pr.

Leo Tolstoy & His Works. Aylmer Maude. LC 74-6377. (Studies in Tolstoy: No. 62). 1974. lib. bdg. 75.00 (*0-8383-2009-0*) M S G Haskell Hse.

***Leo Tolstoy & the Oriental Religious Heritage: Influences & Parallels.** Dragan Milivojevic. 200p. 1998. text 28.00 (*0-88033-416-9*, 518, Pub. by East Eur Monographs) Col U Pr.

Leo Tolstoy, Resident & Stranger: A Study in Fiction & Theology. Richard F. Gustafson. LC 85-43286. (Sources & Translations Series of the Harriman Institute, Columbia University). 503p. reprint ed. pap. 156.00 (*0-608-06361-4*, 206672200008) Bks Demand.

***Leo 2001.** Ed. by Jove Books Publishing Staff. (Total Horoscopes Ser.). 272p. 2000. mass mkt. 5.99 (*0-515-12819-8*, Jove) Berkley Pub.

***Leo 2001.** Teri King. (Astrological Horoscopes Ser.). 2000. pap. 4.95 (*1-86204-780-4*, Pub. by Element MA) Penguin Putnam.

Leo White: Rocket Man. Ralph Roberts. LC 96-61839. (Illus.). 112p. (Orig.). 1996. pap. 9.95 (*1-56664-042-3*) WorldComm.

Leo XIII & the Rise of Socialism. Lillian P. Wallace. LC 66-16033. 474p. reprint ed. pap. 147.00 (*0-608-15051-7*, 202621700048) Bks Demand.

Leo y Entiendo, 7 levels. Gary D. Keller. Incl. Level A - Miro y Escucho. (J). (gr. k). 1983. pap. text 5.70 (*0-8077-5995-3*); Level A - Miro y Escucho. (J). (gr. k). 1983. 12.45 (*0-8077-6027-7*); Level B - Comenzando a Leer. (J). (gr. 1). 1983. pap. text 5.70 (*0-8077-5996-1*); Level C - Ya Me Gusta Leer. (J). (gr. 1). 1983. pap. text 5.70 (*0-8077-5997-X*); Level C - Ya Me Gusta Leer. (J). (gr. 1). 1983. 13.70 (*0-8077-6028-5*); Level D - Avanzando en la Lectura. (J). (gr. 2). 1983. pap. text 5.70 (*0-8077-5998-8*); Level E - Mira Cuanto Entiendo! (J). (gr. 2). 1983. pap. text 5.70 (*0-8077-5999-6*); Level E - Mira Cuanto Entiendo! (J). (gr. 2). 1983. 13.70 (*0-8077-6029-3*); Level F - Avanzando en la Comprension. (J). (gr. 3). 1983. pap. text 5.70 Level G - Que Bien Entiendo! (J). (gr. 3). 1983. pap. text 5.70 (*0-8077-6026-9*); Level G - Que Bien Entiendo! (J). (gr. 3). 1983. 13.70 (*0-8077-6030-7*); (Bilingual Education Ser.). (Orig.). (J). (gr. k-3). 1983. pap. text. write for info. (*0-318-55916-1*) Tchrs Coll.

Leo, Zack & Emmie. Amy Ehrlich. (Illus.). 64p. (J). (gr. 1-4). 1997. pap. 3.99 (*0-14-036199-5*, PuffinBks) Peng Put Young Read.

***Leo, Zack & Emmie Together Again.** Amy Ehrlich. (Puffin Easy-to-Read Program Ser.). 56p. (J). (gr. 1-4). 1998. pap. 3.99 (*0-14-037946-0*, PuffinBks) Peng Put Young Read.

Leocadia see Pieces Roses

Leocadia. Jean Anouilh. Ed. by Bettina L. Knapp & Alba Della Fazia. LC 66-17601. (FRE., Illus.). 1965. pap. text 7.95 (*0-89197-273-0*) Irvington.

Le/Occasion see Occasions

Leocolor. Caleb Gattegno. (SPA.). (Orig.). (gr. k-12). 1971. pap. 0.25 (*0-87825-092-1*) Ed Solutions.

Leocolor. Caleb Gattegno. (SPA.). (Orig.). (J). (gr. k-12). 1971. 7.50 (*0-87825-089-1*); 50.00 (*0-87825-094-8*) Ed Solutions.

Leocolor, Incl. worksheets 1-6. Caleb Gattegno. (SPA.). (Orig.). (J). (gr. k-12). 1971. pap. 3.00 (*0-87825-028-X*) Ed Solutions.

Leocolor, Libro 1. Caleb Gattegno. (SPA.). (Orig.). (gr. k-12). 1971. pap. 0.45 (*0-87825-090-5*) Ed Solutions.

Leocolor, Libro 2. Caleb Gattegno. (SPA.). (Orig.). (gr. k-12). 1971. pap. 0.55 (*0-87825-091-3*) Ed Solutions.

Leod: Six Old English Poems: A Handbook. B. J. Muir. xxxvi, 162p. 1989. 43.00 (*2-88124-357-6*) Gordon & Breach.

***Leola & the Honeybears.** Melodye Rosales. (Illus.). (J). 1999. 95.70 (*0-439-11756-9*) Scholastic Inc.

Leola & the Honeybears. Melodye Benson Rosales. LC 97-31871. (Illus.). 40p. (J). (ps-3). 1999. 15.95 (*0-590-38358-2*, Pub. by Scholastic Inc) Penguin Putnam.

***Leominster.** Leominster Historical Society Staff. (Images of America Ser.). 1999. pap. 18.99 (*0-7524-0996-4*) Arcadia Publng.

Leominster Book (Massachusetts) William A. Emerson. (Illus.). 304p. 1993. reprint ed. lib. bdg. 37.50 (*0-8328-3166-2*) Higginson Bk Co.

Leominster, Massachusetts of Today: Over Two Hundred Choice Photographical Views of Its Churches, Public Buildings, Streets, Residences, Factories, Reservoirs, Parks & Other Scenes of Interest. Compiled by Kate E. Nichols. (Illus.). 361p. 1998. reprint ed. lib. bdg. 42.00 (*0-8328-7119-2*) Higginson Bk Co.

Leominster Traditions. William A. Emerson. (Illus.). 99p. 1993. reprint ed. lib. bdg. 20.00 (*0-8328-3167-0*) Higginson Bk Co.

Leon & Albertine. Christine Davenier. Tr. by Dominic Barth. LC 97-25399. (Illus.). 32p. (J). (ps-1). 1998. 15.95 (*0-531-30072-2*) Orchard Bks Watts.

Leon & Bob. Simon James. LC 96-2684. (Illus.). 32p. (J). (gr. 1-4). 1997. 15.99 (*1-56402-991-3*) Candlewick Pr.

Leon Bakst: The Theater Art. Alexander Schouvaloff. 272p. 1991. 115.00 (*0-85667-391-9*) Sothebys Pubns.

***Leon Battista Alberti: Master Builder of the Italian Renaissance.** Anthony Grafton. (Illus.). 304p. 2000. text 30.00 (*0-8090-9752-4*) Hill & Wang.

Leon Battista Alberti, Dinner Pieces: A Translation of the "Intercenales" David Marsh. (Medieval & Renaissance Texts & Studies: Vol. 45).Tr. of Intercenales. (Illus.). 288p. 1987. 25.00 (*0-86698-028-8*, MR45) MRTS.

Leon Battista Alberti's Hypnerotomachia Poliphili: Eros, Furore, & Humanism in the Early Italian Renaissance. Liane Lefaivre. LC 96-40960. (Illus.). 340p. 1997. 49.50 (*0-262-12204-9*) MIT Pr.

Leon Blum. Stephen E. Bronner. (World Leaders Past & Present Ser.). (Illus.). 120p. (YA). (gr. 5 up). 1987. lib. bdg. 19.95 (*0-87754-511-1*) Chelsea Hse.

Leon Blum. Jean Lacouture. Tr. by George Holoch from FRE. LC 81-20083. 571p. 1982. 49.95 (*0-8419-0775-7*); pap. 29.50 (*0-8419-0776-5*) Holmes & Meier.

Leon Blum: Humanist in Politics. Joel Colton. LC 73-21892. (Illus.). xxv, 523p. 1987. pap. text 24.95 (*0-8223-0762-6*) Duke.

Leon Blum, 1872-1914: The Formative Years. William Logue. LC 72-7515. 345p. 1973. 32.00 (*0-87580-030-0*) N Ill U Pr.

Leon Boca Negra. Fiqureos Vasquez. 1995. 17.95 (*84-01-01172-8*) Plaza.

Leon C. Metz: Legendary Southwestern Historian. 2nd rev. ed. Deen Underwood. (Illus.). 132p. 1996. 39.95 (*0-944551-08-4*) Sundance Pr TX.

Leon D. Adams' Commonsense Book of Wine. Leon D. Adams. LC 75-6805. 240p. 1975. pap. 7.95 (*0-685-42192-9*) HM.

Leon de Santa Rita: El General Vicente Garcia y la Guerra de los Diez Anos, Cuba 1868-1878. Florencio Garcia-Cisneros. LC 88-82972. (Coleccion Cuba y sus Jueces). (SPA., Illus.). 231p. (Orig.). 1989. pap. 15.00 (*0-89729-514-5*) Ediciones.

Leon Dolice: Old New York Remembered & Other Etchings, 1920-1951. Joseph L. Dolice. LC 85-91514. (Illus.). 24p. (Orig.). 1987. pap. 5.00 (*0-935901-01-9*) Dolice Graphics.

Leon Edel & Literary Art. Lyall H. Powers. Ed. by A. Walton Litz. LC 87-19211. (Studies in Modern Literature: No. 84). (Illus.). 206p. reprint ed. 63.90 (*0-8357-1839-5*, 207075300004) Bks Demand.

Leon Felipe: El Hombre y el Poeta. Amelia A. De Del Rio. (SPA.). 1980. pap. 7.80 (*84-499-4047-8*) Edit Mensaje.

Leon Felipe the Last Troubador: Selected Poems. Leon Felipe. Ed. by Robert Houston & Criss Cannady. Tr. by John Franklin et al from SPA. LC 78-73996. 1980. 14.95 (*0-933188-09-9*); pap. 6.95 (*0-933188-08-0*) Blue Moon Pr.

Leon Forrest: Introductions & Interpretations. John G. Cawelti. LC 96-39151. 322p. 1997. 44.95 (*0-87972-733-0*); pap. 19.95 (*0-87972-734-9*) Bowling Green Univ Popular Press.

Leon Fremaux's New Orleans Characters. Ed. by Patrick J. Geary. (Illus.). 156p. 1987. 27.50 (*0-88289-495-1*) Pelican.

Leon Galatoire's Cookbook. Leon Galatoire. LC 93-37308. (Illus.). 224p. 1994. 23.95 (*0-88289-999-6*) Pelican.

Leon Garfield. Roni Natov. (Twayne's English Authors Ser.: No. 505). 176p. 1994. 22.95 (*0-8057-7042-9*, Twyne) Mac Lib Ref.

Leon Gaspard: Exhibition of Paintings. Margaret Morris. (Illus.). 31p. 1984. pap. 10.00 (*0-935037-08-X*) G Peters Gallery.

Leon Golub & Nancy Spero: War & Memory. Katy Kline & Helaine Posner. (Illus.). 104p. 1994. pap. 20.00 (*0-938437-48-8*) MIT List Visual Arts.

Leon Golub, 1987-1992: Paintings. (Illus.). (C). 1992. pap. 15.00 (*0-88454-066-9*) U of Pa Contemp Art.

Leon H. Rockwell: Recollections of Life in Las Vegas, Nevada, 1906-1968. Intro. by Mary E. Glass. 161p. 1969. lib. bdg. 38.50 (*1-56475-063-9*); fiche. write for info. (*1-56475-064-7*) U NV Oral Hist.

Leon Kossoff. Ed. by Paul Moorhouse. LC 96-60370. (Illus.). 176p. 1996. 45.00 (*0-500-09264-8*, Pub. by Thames Hudson) Norton.

Leon Krier: Houses, Palaces, Cities: An Architectural Design Profile. Ed. by Demetri Porphyrios. (Illus.). 128p. 1985. pap. 21.95 (*0-312-47990-5*) St Martin.

Leon Kroll, a Spoken Memoir. Leon Kroll. Ed. by Nancy Hale & Fredson Bowers. LC 83-3529. 289p. 1983. reprint ed. pap. 89.60 (*0-608-01441-9*, 206220400002) Bks Demand.

Leon, La Bruja y El Armario. C. S. Lewis. (Chronicles of Narnia Ser.). 1996. 17.05 (*0-606-10412-7*, Pub. by Turtleback) Demco.

Leon Levinstein/Moment of Exposure. Max Kozloff & Bob Shamis. (Illus.). 108p. 1999. pap. 27.50 (*0-88884-640-1*) U Ch Pr.

Leon Morin, Pretre. Beatrix Beck. (FRE.). 192p. 1972. pap. 10.95 (*0-7859-1711-X*, 2070362175) Fr & Eur.

Leon Rausch: The Voice of the Texas Playboys. John E. Perkins, Jr. LC 94-12045. (Illus.). 266p. 1996. 29.95 (*0-9654101-0-2*) Swing Pubng.

Leon Rooke & His Works. Keith Garebian. (Canadian Author Studies). 61p. (C). 1989. pap. text 9.95 (*1-55022-035-7*, Pub. by ECW) Genl Dist Srvs.

Leon Rosenfeld: Selected Papers. Ed. by R. S. Cohen & J. J. Stachel. (Synthese Library: No. 100). 963p. 1978. pap. text 115.50 (*90-277-0652-2*, D Reidel); lib. bdg. 245.50 (*90-277-0651-4*, D Reidel) Kluwer Academic.

Leon sans Son Chapeau - Follow That Hat! Pierre Pratt. (Picture Bks.). (FRE., Illus.). 32p. (J). (ps-2). 1992. lib. bdg. 16.95 (*1-55037-263-7*, Pub. by Annick) Firefly Bks Ltd.

Leon sans Son Chapeau - Follow That Hat! Pierre Pratt. (FRE., Illus.). 32p. (J). (ps-2). 1996. pap. 6.95 (*1-55037-262-9*, Pub. by Annick) Firefly Bks Ltd.

Leon Trotsky: The Portrait of a Youth. Max Eastman. LC 73-124774. (BCL Ser. I). reprint ed. 32.50 (*0-404-02235-9*) AMS Pr.

Leon Trotsky & the Art of Insurrection, 1905-1917. Harold W. Nelson. 250p. 1986. 49.50 (*0-7146-3272-4*, Pub. by F Cass Pubs); pap. text 22.50 (*0-7146-4065-4*, Pub. by F Cass Pubs) Intl Spec Bk.

Leon Trotsky & the Fate of Socialism in the 20th Century: A Reply to Professor Eric Hobsbawm. David North. (SEP Lecture Ser.). 56p. 1998. 5.00 (*1-875639-22-5*, Pub. by Mehring Bks) Mehring Bks.

***Leon Trotsky & World War One: August 1914-February 1917.** Ian D. Thatcher. LC 00-27151. 2000. write for info. (*0-312-23487-2*) St Martin.

Leon Trotsky on Black Nationalism & Self-Determination. 2nd ed. Leon Trotsky. Ed. by George Breitman. LC 78-59358. 96p. 1978. pap. 10.95 (*0-87348-557-2*); lib. bdg. 30.00 (*0-87348-556-4*) Pathfinder NY.

Leon Trotsky on Britain. Leon Trotsky. pap. 23.95 (*0-87348-850-4*) Pathfinder NY.

Leon Trotsky on Britain. Leon Trotsky. LC 72-92147. 334p. 1973. pap. 23.95 (*0-913460-13-3*); lib. bdg. 65.00 (*0-913460-12-5*) Pathfinder NY.

Leon Trotsky on China. Leon Trotsky. LC 76-25692. 687p. 1976. pap. 34.95 (*0-87348-835-0*); lib. bdg. 75.00 (*0-913460-45-1*) Pathfinder NY.

Leon Trotsky on France. Leon Trotsky. Ed. by David Salner. LC 78-59267. (Illus.). 271p. 1979. pap. 21.95 (*0-87348-836-9*); lib. bdg. 60.00 (*0-913460-65-6*) Pathfinder NY.

Leon Trotsky on Literature & Art see Art & Revolution

Leon Trotsky on the Paris Commune. Leon Trotsky. LC 75-143589. (Illus.). 63p. (Orig.). 1970. reprint ed. pap. 4.50 (*0-87348-174-7*) Pathfinder NY.

Leon Trotsky Speaks. Leon Trotsky. Ed. by Sarah Lovell. LC 72-186686. 332p. 1972. reprint ed. lib. bdg. 65.00 (*0-87348-221-2*) Pathfinder NY.

Leon Trotsky Speaks. Leon Trotsky. Ed. by Sarah Lovell. LC 72-186686. 332p. 1972. reprint ed. pap. 25.95 (*0-87348-222-0*) Pathfinder NY.

Leon Uris: A Critical Companion. Kathleen S. Cain. LC 97-52324. (Critical Companions to Popular Contemporary Writers Ser.). 232p. 1998. 29.95 (*0-313-30231-6*, Greenwood Pr) Greenwood.

Leon Vaudoyer: Historicism in the Age of Industry. Barry Bergdoll. (Architectural History Foundation Ser.). (Illus.). 416p. 1994. 65.00 (*0-262-02380-6*) MIT Pr.

Leon Walras: Critical Assessments, 4 vols., 1. Ed. by John C. Wood. LC 92-14261. (Critical Assessments of Leading Economists Ser.). 944p. 1993. write for info. (*0-415-07483-5*) Routledge.

Leon Walras, 1834-1910. Ed. by Mark Blaug. (Pioneers in Economics Ser.: Vol. 25). 480p. 1992. 190.00 (*1-85278-488-1*) E Elgar.

Leon y el Grillito see Lion & the Cricket

Leon y el Raton. Aesop.Tr. of Lion & the Mouse, (J). 1997. pap. 3.95 (*0-8167-3065-2*) Troll Communs.

Leona, a Love Story. Elizabeth Borton de Trevino. LC 93-38751. 176p. (J). 1994. 15.00 (*0-374-34382-9*) FS&G.

Leona Devours Books. Laurence Herbert. (Child's World Library). (Illus.). 32p. (J). (gr. k-5). 1992. lib. bdg. 18.50 (*0-89565-755-4*) Childs World.

Leonard & Gertrude. Johann H. Pestalozzi. 1976. lib. bdg. 250.00 (*0-8490-0507-8*) Gordon Pr.

Leonard & Virginia Woolf As Publishers, 1917-1941: The Hogarth Press. J. H. Willis, Jr. 472p. (C). 1992. text 35.00 (*0-8139-1361-6*) U Pr of Va.

Leonard Bacon: New England Reformer & Antislavery Moderate. Hugh Davis. LC 98-24710. (Illus.). 392p. 1998. text 60.00 (*0-8071-2287-4*) La State U Pr.

Leonard Baskin's Miniature Natural History. Leonard Baskin. (Illus.). 28p. (J). (gr. k up). 1993. reprint ed. 14.95 (*0-88708-265-3*, Picture Book Studio) S&S Childrens.

Leonard Bernstein. Paul Myers. LC 99-182081. (Twentieth Century Composers Ser.). (Illus.). 240p. 1998. pap. 19.95 (*0-7148-3701-6*, Pub. by Phaidon Press) Phaidon Pr.

Leonard Bernstein. Meryle Secrest. 496p. 1995. pap. 16.00 (*0-679-73757-X*) Random.

Leonard Bernstein. Mike Venezia. LC 96-53125. (Getting to Know the World's Greatest Composers Ser.). (J). 1997. lib. bdg. 21.00 (*0-516-20492-0*) Childrens.

Leonard Bernstein. Mike Venezia. (J). 1998. pap. text 6.95 (*0-516-26244-0*) Childrens.

Leonard Bernstein: A Complete Catalog of His Works: Life, Musical Compositions & Writings. (Illus.). 96p. 1998. pap. write for info. (*0-913932-82-5*) Leonard Bernstein.

Leonard Bernstein: A Life. Meryle Secrest. (Borzoi Reader Ser.). (Illus.). 496p. 1994. 30.00 (*0-679-40731-6*) Knopf.

Leonard Bernstein: A Passion for Music. Johanna Hurwitz. (Illus.). 80p. (J). (gr. 4 up). 1993. 12.95 (*0-8276-0501-3*) JPS Phila.

***Leonard Bernstein: Conductor & Composer.** Jean F. Blashfield. LC 00-37580. (Career Biographies Ser.). 2000. write for info. (*0-89434-337-8*) Ferguson.

Leonard Bernstein: The Harvard Years (1935-39) Leonard Bernstein. 1999. 30.00 (*0-9648083-4-X*) Eos Music.

***Leonard Bernstein: The Last 10 Years.** Thomas H. Seiler. 1999. 49.95 (*3-908161-98-3*) Abbeville Pr.

Leonard Bernstein Vol. 1: A Complete Catalog of His Works: Life, Musical Compositions & Writings. 3rd rev. ed. Jack Gottlieb. (Illus.). 100p. 1998. pap. 18.95 (*0-913932-21-3*) Leonard Bernstein.

Leonard Bernstein/I Hate Music! Ed. by Carol Cuellar. 20p. (Orig.). (C). 1995. pap. text 7.95 (*0-7692-0225-X*, VF0513) Wrner Bros.

Leonard Bloomfield: Critical Assessments. John G. Fought. LC 98-43354. 1999. write for info. (*0-415-17446-5*) Routledge.

Leonard Bloomfield Anthology. Leonard Bloomfield. Ed. by Charles F. Hockett. xii, 328p. (C). 1987. pap. text 17.95 (*0-226-06071-3*) U Ch Pr.

Leonard Bloomfield Anthology. Leonard Bloomfield. Ed. by Charles F. Hockett. LC 78-98981. (Indiana University Studies in the History & Theory of Linguistics). 585p. reprint ed. pap. 181.40 (*0-608-18475-6*, 205673500081) Bks Demand.

Leonard Bloomfield, Essays on His Life & Work. Ed. by Robert A. Hall, Jr. LC 87-6413. (Studies in the History of the Language Sciences: No. 47). x, 237p. (C). 1987. 65.00 (*90-272-4530-4*) J Benjamins Pubng Co.

***Leonard Bourdon: The Career of a Revolutionary, 1754-1807.** Michael J. Sydenham. LC 98-93282. (Illus.). 419p. 1999. 49.95 (*0-88920-319-9*) Wilfrid Laurier.

Leonard Calvert & the Maryland Adventure. Ann Jensen. LC 97-39052. (Illus.). 96p. (J). 1998. pap. 9.95 (*0-87033-502-2*, Tidewtr Pubs) Cornell Maritime.

***Leonard Cohen.** David Sheppard. (Kill Your Idols Ser.). (Illus.). 152p. 2000. pap. 13.95 (*1-56025-270-7*, Thunders Mouth) Avalon NY.

Leonard Cohen: A Life in Art. Ira B. Nadel. LC 94-232066. (Illus.). 160p. 1994. pap. 9.95 (*1-55022-210-4*, Pub. by ECW) LPC InBook.

Leonard Cohen: A Life in Art. large type ed. Ira Nadel. (Illus.). 190p. 1996. pap. 15.95 (*1-55022-267-8*, Pub. by ECW) Genl Dist Srvs.

Leonard Cohen: Anthology. Leonard Cohen. (Illus.). 208p. pap. 24.95 (*0-8256-1238-1*, AM 80060) Omnibus NY.

Leonard Cohen: Every Style of Passion. Jim Devlin. (Illus.). 392p. 1996. pap. 24.95 (*0-7119-5496-8*) Omnibus NY.

Leonard Cohen: In His Own Words. Jim Devlin. (Illus.). 96p. 1998. pap. 15.95 (*0-7119-6878-0*, op 48 63) Omnibus NY.

L

L

Leonard Cohen: Prophet of the Heart. L. S. Dorman & C. L. Rawlins. (Illus.). 384p. pap. 24.95 (*0-7119-2774-X*, OP 46614) Omnibus NY.
Leonard Cohen & His Works (Fiction) Linda Hutcheon. 41p. (C). 1989. pap. text 9.95 (*0-920763-86-3*, Pub. by ECW) Genl Dist Srvs.
Leonard Cohen & His Works (Poetry) Linda Hutcheon. (Canadian Author Studies). 45p. (C). 1992. pap. text 9.95 (*1-55022-074-8*, Pub. by ECW) Genl Dist Srvs.
Leonard Cohen Collection. (Illus.). 88p. 1991. pap. 19.95 (*0-8256-1314-0*, AM85549) Music Sales.
Leonard Covello: A Study of an Immigrants Contribution to New York City. Robert W. Peebles. Ed. by Francesco Cordasco. LC 77-90551. (Bilingual-Bicultural Education in the U. S. Ser.). 1978. lib. bdg. 41.95 (*0-405-11090-1*) Ayer.
Leonard E. Read, Philosopher of Freedom. Mary Sennholz. 207p. (Orig.). 1993. pap. 9.95 (*0-910614-85-7*) Foun Econ Ed.
***Leonard Everett Fisher: A Life of Art.** Leonard Everett Fisher. Ed. by Norman D. Stevens et al. (Illus.). 85p. 1998. 75.00 (*0-917590-10-4*) Univ Conn Lib.
Leonard L. Milberg Collection of American Poetry. Compiled by J. Howard Woolmer. LC 94-216149. (Illus.). 432p. 1995. 35.00 (*0-87811-038-0*, Pub. by Princeton Lib) Oak Knoll.
Leonard L. Milberg Collection of Irish Poetry. Ed. by John L. Logan & Patricia H. Marks. (Illus.). 338p. 1998. 40.00 (*0-87811-043-7*, Pub. by Princeton Lib) Oak Knoll.
***Leonard Lee Rue III's Way of the Whitetail.** Leonard Lee Rue, III. LC 00-24654. (Illus.), 160p. 2000. 35.00 (*0-89658-417-8*) Voyageur Pr.
Leonard Lee Rue III's Whitetails: Answers to All Your Questions on Life Cycle, Feeding Patterns, Antlers, Scrapes & Rubs, Behavior During the Rut, & Habitat. Leonard L. Rue, III. LC 90-27656. (Illus.). 288p. 1991. 34.95 (*0-8117-1938-3*) Stackpole.
Leonard M. Savoie: Words from the Past, Thoughts for Today. Ed. by Donald E. Tidrick. LC 95-32849. (New Works in Accounting History). (Illus.). 288p. 1995. reprint ed. text 61.00 (*0-8153-2242-9*) Garland.
Leonard Maltin's Family Film Guide. Leonard Maltin. LC 99-219505. 653p. 1999. mass mkt. 6.99 (*0-451-19714-3*, Sig) NAL.
Leonard Maltin's Movie & Video Guide, 1998. Ed. by Leonard Maltin. 1632p. 1997. pap. 19.95 (*0-452-27914-3*) NAL.
Leonard Maltin's Movie & Video Guide 2000: 2000 Edition. Leonard Maltin. 1999. mass mkt. 7.99 (*0-451-19837-9*, Sig) NAL.
***Leonard Maltin's Movie & Video Guide 2000.** Leonard Maltin. 1999. pap. 19.95 (*0-452-28123-7*, Plume) Dutton Plume.
***Leonard Maltin's Movie & Video Guide 2001.** Leonard Maltin. 2000. pap. 20.00 (*0-452-28187-3*, Plume) Dutton Plume.
***Leonard Maltin's Movie & Video Guide 2001.** Leonard Maltin. (Leonard Maltin's Movie & Video Guide Ser.). (Illus.). 2000. mass mkt. 8.99 (*0-451-20107-8*) Signet.
Leonard Maltin's Movie Encyclopedia: Career Profiles of More Than 2,000 Actors & Filmmakers, Past & Present. Leonard Maltin. 992p. 1995. pap. 21.95 (*0-452-27058-8*, Plume) Dutton Plume.
Leonard Maltin's 1999 Movie-a-Day Calendar. Leonard Maltin. 1998. pap. 10.95 (*0-525-94360-9*) NAL.
Leonard Maltin's 1999 Movie & Video Guide. rev. ed. Leonard Maltin. 1998. pap. 19.95 (*0-452-27992-5*, Plume) Dutton Plume.
Leonard Memorial: Genealogy, History, & Biography of Solomon Leonard; 1637, of Duxbury & Bridgewater, Mass., & Some of His Descendants. M. Leonard. (Illus.). 454p. 1989. reprint ed. pap. 68.00 (*0-8328-0766-4*); reprint ed. lib. bdg. 76.00 (*0-8328-0765-6*) Higginson Bk Co.
Leonard Nimoy: A Stars Trek. John Michlos, Jr. LC 87-32457. (Taking Part Ser.). (Illus.). 64p. (J). (gr. 3 up). 1988. lib. bdg. 13.95 (*0-87518-376-X*, Dillon Silver Burdett) Silver Burdett Pr.
Leonard Nimoy's Primortals: Target Earth. Steve Perry. 304p. 1998. mass mkt. 6.50 (*0-446-60510-7*, Pub. by Warner Bks) Little.
Leonard Nimoy's Primortals Vol. 1, No. 1: Origins. Leonard Nimoy. Ed. by James Chambers et al. (Illus.). 36p. (Orig.). (YA). pap. 2.25 (*0-9645175-1-5*) Big Enter Inc.
Leonard Nimoy's Primortals Chronicles, 2 vols. Leonard Nimoy. Incl. Vol. II. (Illus.). 144p. 1996. reprint ed. pap. 14.95 (*1-57780-004-4*); Vol. I. (Illus.). 144p. 1996. reprint ed. pap. 14.95 (*1-57780-003-6*); (Primortals Chronicles Ser.). 25.00 (*1-57780-002-8*) Big Enter Inc.
Leonard of Pisa & the New Mathematics of the Middle Ages. Frances Gies & Joseph Gies. LC 71-81952. (Illus.). 128p. 1983. pap. 13.00 (*0-932750-48-6*) New Classics Lib.
***Leonard Peltier.** Hill. 2000. 25.00 (*0-8133-3763-1*, Pub. by Westview) HarpC.
Leonard Shoun & His Wife Barbara Slemp of Johnson County, Tennessee & Their Descendants. Carl B. Neal. 283p. 1985. reprint ed. 28.95 (*0-932807-10-0*); reprint ed. pap. 21.95 (*0-932807-09-7*) Overmountain Pr.
Leonard Stromberg: A Swedish-American Writer. rev. ed. Rita Strombeck. Ed. by Franklyn D. Scott. LC 78-15848. (Scandinavians in America Ser.). 1979. lib. bdg. 28.95 (*0-405-11660-8*) Ayer.
Leonard Swain, D. D. First Minister of Central Congregational Church Providence, R.I., 1852-1869. Raymond E. Gibson. LC 95-75478. (Illus.). 150p. 1995. write for info. (*0-9645595-0-1*) Monadnock Pubs.
Leonard the Doolit. Doven Hayes. Ed. by Roberta Munro. (Tatterman Ser.). (Illus.). 1977. pap. 2.95 (*0-918774-02-0*) Fig Leaf.
***Leonard Warren: American Baritone.** Mary Jane Phillips-Matz. LC 99-40444. (Opera Biography Ser.: Vol. 13). (Illus.). 478p. 2000. 39.95 (*1-57467-053-0*, Amadeus Pr) Timber.
Leonard William Blumstrom: Life at the Nevada State Orphans' Home in Carson City, Nevada, from 1913-1928. Intro. by Carol M. Blumstrom. (Illus.). 55p. 1981. lib. bdg. 24.50 (*1-56475-205-4*); fiche. write for info. (*1-56475-206-2*) U NV Oral Hist.
Leonard Woolf: A Bibliography. Leila Luedeking & Michael Edmonds. (Illus.). 310p. 1992. 78.00 (*0-938768-41-7*) Oak Knoll.
***Leonardismus und Symbolistische Asthetik: Ein Beitrag Zur Wirkungsgeschichte Leonardo Da Vincis In Paris und Brussel.** Isa Bickmann. (GER., Illus.). 295p. 1999. 57.00 (*3-631-34146-6*) P Lang Pubng.
Leonardo. Peter Hohenstatt. (Masters of Italian Art Ser.). (Illus.). 140p. 1998. 19.95 (*3-8290-0251-3*, 520531) Konemann.
Leonardo. Victoria Looseleaf. LC 98-38013. 1998. pap. 8.95 (*0-345-43222-3*) Ballantine Pub Grp.
***Leonardo.** Michael White. (Illus.). 384p. 2000. text 27.95 (*0-312-20333-0*) St Martin.
Leonardo. Roger Whitiny. 1992. 29.98 (*1-55521-796-6*) Bk Sales Inc.
***Leonardo.** Frank Zöllner. 1999. pap. text 9.99 (*3-8228-7025-0*) Benedikt Taschen.
Leonardo: A Portrait of the Renaissance Man. Roger Whiting. (Illus.). 192p. 1998. pap. 25.95 (*1-57715-031-7*) Knckerbocker.
Leonardo: A Scrapbook in Words & Pictures. Doubleday Publishing Staff & Grace Catalano. LC 99-182116. (Illus.). 32p. (YA). 1998. pap. 7.95 (*0-440-22795-X*) Dell.
Leonardo: The Artist & the Man. Serge Bramly. Tr. by Sian Reynolds. (Illus.). 512p. 1995. pap. 21.95 (*0-14-023175-7*, Penguin Bks) Viking Penguin.
***Leonardo: The Last Supper.** Federico Zeri. (One Hundred Paintings Ser.). (Illus.). 48p. 2000. 14.95 (*1-55321-000-X*, Pub. by NDE Pub) IPG Chicago.
Leonardo Almanac: International Resources in Art, Science, & Technology. Ed. by Craig Harris. (Leonardo Book Ser.). (Illus.). 255p. 1993. pap. text 35.00 (*0-262-58125-6*) MIT Pr.
***Leonardo & His Times.** Ed. by Dorling Kindersley Staff. (Eyewitness Books). (Illus.). (J). (gr. 4-7). 2000. 19.99 (*0-7894-6819-0*) DK Pub Inc.
***Leonardo & His Times.** Andrew Langley. (Eyewitness Books). (J). (gr. 4-7). 2000. 15.95 (*0-7894-6290-7*) DK Pub Inc.
***Leonardo & the Flying Boy.** Laurence Anholt. 2000. 13.95 (*0-7641-5225-4*) Barron.
Leonardo Cremonini, 1976-1986: Paintings & Watercolors. Umberto Eco. LC 87-70909. (Illus.). 52p. 1987. 10.00 (*0-936827-06-8*) C Bernard Gallery Ltd.
Leonardo Da Vinci. Daniel Arasse. (Illus.). 560p. 1998. 40.00 (*1-56852-198-7*, Konecky & Konecky) W S Konecky Assocs.
Leonardo da Vinci. Kenneth Clark. 1989. pap. 21.95 (*0-14-016982-2*) Viking Penguin.
***Leonardo Da Vinci.** Sean Connolly. LC 99-10151. (Life & Work of...Ser.). (Illus.). 32p. (J). (gr. k-3). 1999. lib. bdg. 13.95 (*1-57572-954-X*) Heinemann Lib.
***Leonardo da Vinci.** Leonardo da Vinci. (Illus.). 96p. 2000. pap. 4.95 (*3-8290-4152-7*) Konemann.
Leonardo da Vinci. Tony Hart. LC 93-2385. (Famous Children Ser.). (Illus.). 24p. (J). (ps-3). 1994. pap. 5.95 (*0-8120-1828-1*) Barron.
***Leonardo da Vinci.** Stuart A. Kallen. (Importance of...Ser.). (Illus.). 128p. (YA). (gr. 6-9). 2000. lib. bdg. 23.70 (*1-56006-604-0*) Lucent Bks.
***Leonardo Da Vinci.** Rachel Kaplan. LC 95-52781. 384p. 2000. 85.00 (*0-8109-3581-3*, Pub. by Abrams) Time Warner.
Leonardo da Vinci. Lepscky. (Famous People Ser.). (Illus.). 28p. (gr. k-3). 1984. 9.95 (*0-8120-5512-8*) Barron.
Leonardo da Vinci. Ibi Lepscky. (Famous People Ser.). (Illus.). 28p. (J). (gr. k-3). 1992. pap. 4.95 (*0-8120-1451-0*) Barron.
Leonardo da Vinci. Ibi Lepscky. (Children of Genius Ser.). (J). 1992. 10.15 (*0-606-05423-5*, Pub. by Turtleback) Demco.
***Leonardo Da Vinci.** Fiona MacDonald. (World in the Time of... Ser.). (Illus.). (J). 2000. 17.95 (*0-7910-6032-2*) Chelsea Hse.
Leonardo da Vinci. John Malam. LC 98-8489. (Tell Me about Ser.). 24p. (J). (gr. k-3). 1999. 19.93 (*1-57505-367-5*, Carolrhoda) Lerner Pub.
Leonardo da Vinci. Norman F. Marshall & Aldo Ripamonti. (What Made Them Great Ser.). (Illus.). 104p. (J). (gr. 5-8). 1990. 12.95 (*0-382-09982-6*); pap. 5.95 (*0-382-24007-3*) Silver Burdett Pr.
Leonardo Da Vinci. Antony Mason. (Famous Artists Ser.). 1994. 11.15 (*0-606-07023-0*, Pub. by Turtleback) Demco.
Leonardo da Vinci. Antony Mason & Andrew S. Hughes. (Famous Artists Ser.). (Illus.). 32p. (YA). (gr. 5 up). 1994. 10.95 (*0-8120-6460-7*) Barron.
Leonardo da Vinci. Antony Mason et al. (Famous Artists Ser.). (Illus.). 32p. (YA). (gr. 5 up). 1994. pap. 6.95 (*0-8120-1997-0*) Barron.
Leonardo da Vinci. Richard B. McLanathan. (First Impressions Ser.). (Illus.). 72p. (YA). (gr. 7 up). 1990. 19.95 (*0-8109-1256-2*, Pub. by Abrams) Time Warner.
Leonardo Da Vinci. Nancy Plain. LC 97-46943. (Biographies Ser.). (J). 1999. write for info. (*0-7614-0790-1*) Benchmark Books.
Leonardo Da Vinci. Random House Value Publishing Staff. 80p. 1998. 9.99 (*0-517-16062-5*) Random Hse Value.
Leonardo da Vinci. Bruno Santi. (Library of Great Masters). (Illus.). 80p. (Orig.). 1990. pap. 12.99 (*1-878351-10-9*) Riverside NY.
Leonardo da Vinci. Bruno Santi. (Grandes Maestros del Arte Ser.). (SPA., Illus.). 80p. (Orig.). 1995. pap. 12.99 (*1-878351-39-7*) Riverside NY.
Leonardo da Vinci. Diane Stanley. 48p. (J). (gr. 2 up). 1996. 16.00 (*0-688-10437-1*, Wm Morrow) Morrow Avon.
Leonardo da Vinci. Diane Stanley. LC 95-35227. (Illus.). 48p. (J). (gr. 2). 1996. 15.89 (*0-688-10438-X*, Wm Morrow) Morrow Avon.
Leonardo da Vinci. Diane Stanley. LC 95-35227. (Illus.). 48p. (J). (gr. 2 up). 2000. mass mkt. 6.95 (*0-688-16155-3*, Wm Morrow) Morrow Avon.
Leonardo da Vinci. Jack Wassermann. (Masters of Art Ser.). (Illus.). 128p. 1984. 24.95 (*0-8109-1285-6*, Pub. by Abrams) Time Warner.
Leonardo da Vinci. Peter Amey et al. Ed. by Malcolm Yapp et al. (World History Program Ser.). (Illus.). (J). (gr. 6-11). 1980. reprint ed. pap. text 5.90 (*0-89908-016-2*) Greenhaven.
Leonardo da Vinci. V. P. Zubov. Tr. by David Kraus. LC 67-27096. (Illus.). 355p. reprint ed. 110.10 (*0-8357-9164-5*, 201726400003) Bks Demand.
***Leonardo da Vinci: A Penguin Life.** Sherwin B. Nuland. (Illus.). 2000. 19.95 (*0-670-89391-9*, Viking) Viking Penguin.
Leonardo da Vinci: A Singular Vision. Martin Clayton. (Illus.). 168p. 1996. 50.00 (*0-7892-0156-9*) Abbeville Pr.
Leonardo Da Vinci: A Singular Vision. Martin Clayton. (Illus.). 168p. 1996. 24.98 (*0-89660-101-3*, Artabras) Abbeville Pr.
Leonardo da Vinci: Artist - Scientist - Inventor. Leonardo da Vinci. (Illus.). 224p. 1996. pap. 35.00 (*3-7757-0625-9*, 620162, Pub. by Gerd Hatje) Dist Art Pubs.
Leonardo da Vinci: Artist, Inventor & Scientist of the Renaissance. Francesca Romei. (Masters of Art Ser.). (Illus.). 64p. (J). (gr. 5). 1994. lib. bdg. 22.50 (*0-87226-313-4*, 63134B, P Bedrick Books) NTC Contemp Pub Co.
***Leonardo da Vinci: Artist, Inventor & Scientist of the Renaissance.** 2nd ed. Francesca Romei et al. LC 00-39745. (Masters of Art Ser.). (Illus.). (YA). 2000. write for info. (*0-87226-640-0*, P Bedrick Books) NTC Contemp Pub Co.
Leonardo da Vinci: Dreams, Schemes & Flying Machines. Heinz Kaehue. (Adventures in Art Ser.). (Illus.). 30p. (YA). (gr. 3-10). 1999. 14.95 (*3-7913-2166-8*, Pub. by Prestel) te Neues.
Leonardo Da Vinci: Nature Studies from the Royal Library at Windsor Castle. Carlo Pedretti. 1981. pap. 14.95 (*0-15-149848-2*) Harcourt.
Leonardo da Vinci: Origins of a Genius. David A. Brown. LC 98-15164. (Illus.). 248p. 1998. 55.00 (*0-300-07246-5*) Yale U Pr.
Leonardo Da Vinci: Psychoanalytic Notes on the Enigma. K. R. Eissler. LC 61-11610. (Illus.). 379p. 1961. 55.00 (*0-8236-3000-5*) Intl Univs Pr.
Leonardo da Vinci: The Anatomy of Man: Drawings from the Collection of Her Majesty Queen Elizabeth II. Martin Clayton & Ron Philo. (Illus.). 141p. 1992. 40.00 (*0-8212-1916-2*, Pub. by Bulfinch Pr) Little.
Leonardo da Vinci: The Daedalian Myth-Maker. Giancarlo Maiorino. (Illus.). 320p. 1992. text 40.00 (*0-271-00817-2*) Pa St U Pr.
Leonardo da Vinci: The Man & the Mystery. Anna Rosstad. (Illus.). 139p. 1995. 42.00 (*82-560-0972-1*, Pub. by Solum Verlag) Intl Spec Bk.
Leonardo da Vinci: The Mind of the Renaissance. Alessandro Vezzosi. LC 97-5747. (Discoveries Ser.). (Illus.). 160p. 1997. pap. 12.95 (*0-8109-2809-4*, Pub. by Abrams) Time Warner.
Leonardo da Vinci: The Royal Palace at Romorantin. Carlo Pedretti. LC 76-102673. 176p. 1972. 45.00 (*0-674-52455-1*) Belknap Pr.
Leonardo Da Vinci: Una Biografia. Luis Antonio De Villena. LC 93-205010. (Memoria de La Historia Ser.). (Illus.). 1998. pap. 15.95 (*84-08-00284-8*) Planeta.
Leonardo da Vinci & a Memory of His Childhood. Sigmund Freud. 16.95 (*0-89190-688-6*) Amereon Ltd.
Leonardo da Vinci & a Memory of His Childhood. Sigmund Freud. Ed. by James Strachey. Tr. by Alan Tyson. 1990. pap. 7.95 (*0-393-00149-0*) Norton.
***Leonardo da Vinci & the Renaissance in World History.** Allison Lassieur. LC 99-50571. (In World History Ser.). (Illus.). 128p. (YA). (gr. 5 up). 2000. lib. bdg. 20.95 (*0-7660-1401-0*) Enslow Pubs.
Leonardo da Vinci As a Musician. Emanuel Winternitz. LC 81-16475. 267p. 1982. reprint ed. pap. 82.80 (*0-7837-3333-X*, 205774000007) Bks Demand.
Leonardo da Vinci, Codex Leicester: A Masterpiece of Science. Claire Farago. (Illus.). 1996. pap. write for info. (*0-913424-19-6*) Am Mus Natl Hist.
Leonardo da Vinci Drawings. Leonardo da Vinci. (Illus.). 64p. 1980. pap. 4.95 (*0-486-23951-9*) Dover.
Leonardo da Vinci Programme: Vade-Mecum. European Commission. LC 98-222873. 22 p. 1996. (*92-827-6990-9*) Bernan Associates.
Leonardo da Vinci's "Paragone" A Critical Interpretation with a New Edition of the Text in the Codex Urbinas. Claire J. Farago. LC 91-17966. (Brill's Studies in Intellectual History: Vol. 25). (Illus.). xvii, 472p. 1992. 154.50 (*90-04-09415-6*) Brill Academic Pubs.
Leonardo da Vinci's Psychology of the Twelve Types. H. S. Burgers. Tr. by A. Van Rood. LC 84-90396. 1984. 10.95 (*0-87212-184-4*) Libra.
Leonardo da Vinci's Sforza Monument Horse - the Art & the Engineering: Proceedings of the Symposium Held Apr. 18-19, at Lafayette College & Lehigh University, & the Dent Projet Studio, Fogelsville, Pa. Diane C. Ahl. LC 94-36557. (Illus.). 152p. 1995. 55.00 (*0-934223-33-5*) Lehigh Univ Pr.
Leonardo DaVinci for Kids: His Life & Times. Janis Herbert. LC 98-25690. (Illus.). 136p. (J). (gr. 3-8). 1998. pap. 16.95 (*1-55652-298-3*) Chicago Review.
Leonardo DiCaprio see Galaxy of Superstars
Leonardo DiCaprio. Andrews & McMeel Staff. LC 98-85112. (Illus.). 80p. 1998. 4.95 (*0-8362-6986-1*) Andrews & McMeel.
***Leonardo Dicaprio, 1.** Paul Joseph. LC 98-39494. 1999. pap. 5.95 (*1-57765-334-3*) ABDO Pub Co.
Leonardo DiCaprio. Lori Kinstad-Pupeza. LC 98-39494. (Young Profiles Ser.). (J). 1999. 13.95 (*1-57765-322-X*) ABDO Pub Co.
***Leonardo DiCaprio.** Kristin McCracken. (Illus.). (J). 2000. 19.00 (*0-516-23323-8*) Childrens.
***Leonardo DiCaprio.** Kristin McCracken. (High Interest Bks.). (Illus.). 48p. (J). (gr. 4-7). 2000. pap. 6.95 (*0-516-23523-0*) Childrens.
***Leonardo Dicaprio.** Contrib. by Miniature Book Collection Staff. LC 99-183227. (Pocket Romeos Ser.). (Illus.). 48p. (gr. 5 up). 1998. 4.98 (*0-7651-0941-7*) Smithmark.
Leonardo DiCaprio. Kieran Scott. (Scene Ser.: No. 1). (Illus.). 32p. (J). (gr. 4-9). 1998. pap. 6.99 (*0-689-82404-1*) S&S Childrens.
Leonardo DiCaprio. Stacey Stauffer. (Galaxy of Superstars Ser.). (Illus.). 64p. (YA). (gr. 3 up). 1999. 16.95 (*0-7910-5151-X*) Chelsea Hse.
Leonardo DiCaprio. Douglas Thompson. 1998. pap. 11.95 (*0-425-16752-6*) Berkley Pub.
Leonardo DiCaprio: Modern Day Romeo. Grace Catalano. LC 97-127572. 144p. (YA). 1997. mass mkt. 4.99 (*0-440-22701-1*) Dell.
Leonardo DiCaprio: Romantic Hero. Mark Bego. 96p. 1998. pap. 10.95 (*0-8362-6972-1*) Andrews & McMeel.
***Leonardo DiCaprio: The Illustrated Story.** rev. ed. Caroline Westbrook. (Illus.). (YA). 2000. pap. 9.95 (*0-600-59883-7*) P HM.
***Leonardo DiCaprio: The Top Ten Movies.** Andy Black. 96p. 1999. pap. 14.95 (*1-902588-05-3*, Pub. by Glitter Bks) Subterranean Co.
Leonardo Dicaprio: Unofficial Biography. Martin Noble. LC 99-172617. 1998. pap. 5.99 (*0-7894-4405-4*) DK Pub Inc.
Leonardo DiCaprio Album. John Berry. (Illus.). 80p. 1997. pap. 15.95 (*0-85965-242-4*, Pub. by Plexus) Publishers Group.
Leonardo Dicaprio Trivia Book. Krulik. LC 99-208426. (J). 1998. per. 4.50 (*0-671-02771-9*, PB Trade Paper) PB.
***Leonardo Drew.** Sara Krajewski. LC 99-88737. (Illus.). 64p. 1999. pap. 19.95 (*0-913883-27-1*) Madison Art.
Leonardo el Leon y Ramon el Raton. Dorothy S. Bishop et al.Tr. of Lion & The Mouse. (Illus.). 64p. 6.95 (*0-8442-7445-3*, 74453) NTC Contemp Pub Co.
Leonardo el Leon y Ramon el Raton (Leonard the Lion & Raymond the Mouse) Dorothy S. Bishop. (Bilingual Ser.). (ENG & SPA.). (J). 1986. 10.15 (*0-606-01306-7*, Pub. by Turtleback) Demco.
***Leonardo Forever.** Troll Communications Staff & Miniature Book Collection Library of Congress Staff. LC 99-180775. 1998. write for info. (*0-8167-4987-6*) Troll Communs.
Leonardo Lives: The Codex Leicester & Leonardo da Vinci's Legacy of Art & Science. Trevor Fairbrother & Chiyo Ishikawa. LC 97-30954. (Illus.). 70p. 1997. pap. 19.95 (*0-295-97688-8*) U of Wash Pr.
Leonardo Lives: The Codex Leicester & Leonardo Da Vinci's Legacy of Art & Science. Trevor J. Fairbrother et al. LC 97-30954. 1997. pap. 19.95 (*0-932216-48-X*) Seattle Art.
Leonardo, Michelangelo & Raphael, 1500-1508: In Renaissance Florence. Ed. by Serafina Hager. LC 91-13359. (ITA., Illus.). 136p. (Orig.). 1992. pap. text 25.00 (*0-87840-219-5*) Georgetown U Pr.
Leonardo Nierman, 1987-1994. Illus. by Edward L. Smith. 216p. 1996. 75.00 (*970-91356-0-0*) U of Ariz Pr.
Leonardo on Painting. Martin Kemp. 328p. 1989. pap. 16.00 (*0-300-04509-3*) Yale U Pr.
Leonardo on the Human Body. Leonardo da Vinci. (Fine Art Ser.). (Illus.). 506p. 1983. reprint ed. pap. 21.95 (*0-486-24483-0*) Dover.
Leonardo, Psychoanalysis, & Art History. Bradley Collins. LC 97-3215. 1997. 30.00 (*0-8101-1419-4*) Northwestern U Pr.
Leonardo Sciascia. Joseph Farrell. (Writers of Italy Ser.). 192p. 1996. 69.50 (*0-7486-0620-3*, Pub. by Edinburgh U Pr) Col U Pr.
Leonardo-Studien. Hans Ost. (Beitraege zur Kunstgeschichte Ser.: Vol. 11). (GER., Illus.). xii, 750p. (C). 1975. 165.40 (*3-11-005727-1*) De Gruyter.
Leonardo Thoughts. Mark Dunster. 10p. (Orig.). 1995. pap. 4.00 (*0-89642-257-7*) Linden Pubs.
Leonardo Trivia Book. Lynn Valentine & Michelle Bubnis. LC 98-67500. (Illus.). 128p. 1998. pap. 6.95 (*1-887654-60-7*) Premium Pr TN.
Leonardo Was Right. Roland Topor. Tr. by Barbara Wright from FRE. (Orig.). 1989. pap. 7.95 (*0-7145-3671-7*) Riverrun NY.
Leonardo's ABC: Sharing Leonardo da Vinci with Children. Carolyn C. DeCristofano. (Illus.). 29p. (J). (ps-2). 1997. 12.95 (*0-918866-00-6*) Museum of Science.
Leonardo's Dessert: No Pi. Herbert Wills, III. LC 84-27185. (Illus.). 28p. 1985. pap. 8.95 (*0-87353-221-X*) NCTM.
Leonardo's Equestrian Statuette. Ed. by M. Agghazy. (C). 1989. 145.00 (*0-7855-4522-0*, Pub. by Collets) St Mut.
***Leonardo's Flight: A Fantastic Novel.** Philippe Blais. 340p. 2000. 21.00 (*1-929953-00-3*) Gates & Bridges.
***Leonardo's Hand.** Warwick Downing. LC 00-32034. (Illus.). (J). 2001. write for info. (*0-618-07893-2*) HM.
Leonardo's Hands. Alois Hotschnig. Tr. by Peter Filkins from GER. LC 98-8780. 144p. 1999. pap. 12.00 (*0-8032-7317-7*) U of Nebr Pr.

An Asterisk (*) at the beginning of an entry indicates that the title is appearing for the first time.

Leonardo's Hands. Alois Hotsching. Tr. by Peter Filkins from GER. LC 98-8780. 144p. 1999. text 40.00 (*0-8032-2387-0*) U of Nebr Pr.
Leonardo's Horse. R. M. Berry. (Illus.). 317p. (Orig.). 1997. pap. 13.95 (*1-57366-031-0*) Fiction Coll.
Leonardo's Incessant Last Supper. Leo Steinberg. write for info. (*1-890951-18-8*); pap. write for info. (*1-890951-19-6*) Zone Bks.
Leonardo's Ink Bottle: The Artist's Way of Seeing. Roberta Weir. LC 97-46731. 192p. 1998. pap. 14.95 (*0-89087-854-4*) Celestial Arts.
Leonardo's Mountain of Clams & the Diet of Worms: Essays on Natural History. Stephen Jay Gould. LC 98-11500. (Illus.). 432p. 1998. 25.00 (*0-609-60141-5*, Three Riv Pr) Crown Pub Group.
***Leonardo's Mountain of Clams & the Diet of Worms: Essays on Natural History, Vol. 1.** Stephen Jay Gould. 1999. pap. 15.00 (*0-609-80475-8*, Three Riv Pr) Crown Pub Group.
Leonardo's Nephew: Essays in the History of Art & Artists. James Fenton. LC 98-34079. (Illus.). 283p. 1998. 25.00 (*0-374-18505-0*) FS&G.
***Leonardo's Nephew: Essays on Art & Artists.** James Fenton. LC 99-55666. (Illus.). 2000. pap. 15.00 (*0-226-24147-5*) U Ch Pr.
Leonardo's Projects, c. 1500-1519, 3. Ed. by Claire Farago. LC 99-32157. (Leonardo Da Vinci Ser.: Vol. 3). (Illus.). 432p. 1999. reprint ed. text 100.00 (*0-8153-2935-0*) Garland.
Leonardo's Science & Technology: Essential Readings for the Non-Scientist. Ed. by Claire Farago. LC 99-31614. (Leonardo Da Vinci Ser.: Vol. 5). (Illus.). 456p. 1999. reprint ed. text 100.00 (*0-8153-2937-7*) Garland.
***Leonardo's Studio: A Pop-up Experience.** Bob Hersey. (Illus.). (J). 2000. 24.95 (*0-7893-0387-6*, Pub. by Universe) St Martin.
Leonardo's Writings & Theory of Art. Ed. by Claire Farago. LC 99-28385. (Leonardo Da Vinci Ser.: Vol. 4). (Illus.). 488p. 1999. reprint ed. text 100.00 (*0-8153-2936-9*) Garland.
Leonard's Annual Price Index of Art Auctions, 1980-1981 Auction Season, 1982 Edition, Vol. 1. Susan Theran. (Books on Auction Records Ser.). 454p. 1982. lib. bdg. 175.00 (*0-918819-03-2*) Auction Index.
Leonard's Annual Price Index of Art Auctions, 1981-1982 Auction Season, 1983 Edition, Vol. 2. Susan Theran. (Books on Auction Records Ser.). 456p. 1983. lib. bdg. 175.00 (*0-918819-02-4*) Auction Index.
Leonard's Annual Price Index of Art Auctions, 1982-1983 Auction Season, 1984 Edition, Vol. 3. Susan Theran. (Books on Auction Records Ser.). 440p. 1984. lib. bdg. 175.00 (*0-918819-01-6*) Auction Index.
Leonard's Annual Price Index of Art Auctions, 1983-1984 Auction Season, 1985 Edition, Vol. 4. Susan Theran. 551p. 1985. lib. bdg. 175.00 (*0-918819-00-8*) Auction Index.
Leonard's Annual Price Index of Art Auctions, 1984-1985 Auction Season, 1986 Edition, Vol. 5. Susan Theran. 553p. 1986. lib. bdg. 175.00 (*0-918819-04-0*) Auction Index.
Leonard's Annual Price Index of Art Auctions, 1985-1986 Auction Season, 1987 Edition, Vol. 6. Susan Theran. 586p. 1987. lib. bdg. 195.00 (*0-918819-05-9*) Auction Index.
Leonard's Annual Price Index of Art Auctions, 1986-1987 Auction Season, 1988 Edition, Vol. 7. Susan Theran. (Books on Auction Records Ser.). 598p. 1988. lib. bdg. 195.00 (*0-918819-06-7*) Auction Index.
Leonard's Annual Price Index of Art Auctions, 1987-1988 Auction Season, 1989 Edition, Vol. 8. Susan Theran. (Books on Auction Records Ser.). 690p. 1989. lib. bdg. 195.00 (*0-918819-07-5*) Auction Index.
Leonard's Annual Price Index of Art Auctions, 1988-1989 Auction Season, 1990 Edition, Vol. 9. Susan Theran. (Books on Auction Records Ser.). 760p. 1990. lib. bdg. 195.00 (*0-918819-08-3*) Auction Index.
Leonard's Annual Price Index of Art Auctions, 1989-1990 Auction Season, 1991 Edition, Vol. 10. Susan Theran. (Books on Auction Records Ser.). 745p. 1991. lib. bdg. 210.00 (*0-918819-10-5*) Auction Index.
Leonard's Annual Price Index of Art Auctions, 1990-1991 Auction Season, 1992 Edition, Vol. 11. Susan Theran. (Books on Auction Records Ser.). 631p. 1992. lib. bdg. 245.00 (*0-918819-11-3*) Auction Index.
Leonard's Annual Price Index of Art Auctions, 1991-1992 Auction Season, 1993 Edition, Vol. 12. Susan Theran. (Books on Auction Records Ser.). 595p. 1993. lib. bdg. 245.00 (*0-918819-12-1*) Auction Index.
Leonard's Annual Price Index of Art Auctions, 1992-1993 Auction Season, 1994 Edition, Vol. 13. Susan Theran. 592p. 1994. lib. bdg. 245.00 (*0-918819-13-X*) Auction Index.
Leonard's Annual Price Index of Art Auctions, 1993-1994 Auction Season, 1995 Edition, Vol. 14. Susan Theran. 610p. 1995. lib. bdg. 245.00 (*0-918819-14-8*) Auction Index.
Leonard's Annual Price Index of Art Auctions, 1994-1995 Auction Season, 1996 Edition, Vol. 15. Susan Theran. 645p. 1996. lib. bdg. 245.00 (*0-918819-15-6*) Auction Index.
Leonard's Annual Price Index of Art Auctions, 1995-1996 Auction Season, 1997 Edition, Vol. 16. Susan Theran. 670p. 1997. lib. bdg. 245.00 (*0-918819-16-4*) Auction Index.
***Leonard's Annual Price Index of Art Auctions, 1996-1997 Auction Season, 1998 Edition, Vol. 17.** Susan Theran. 715p. 1998. lib. bdg. 245.00 (*0-918819-17-2*) Auction Index.
Leonard's Annual Price Index of Posters & Photographs, 1994-1995 Auction Season, 1996 Edition, Vol. 4. Susan Theran. 342p. 1996. lib. bdg. 185.00 (*0-918819-34-2*) Auction Index.
Leonard's Annual Price Index of Prints, Posters & Photographs, 1991-1992 Auction Season, 1993 Edition, Vol. 1. Susan Theran. 765p. 1993. lib. bdg. 195.00 (*0-918819-31-8*) Auction Index.
Leonard's Annual Price Index of Prints, Posters & Photographs, 1992-1993 Auction Season, 1994 Edition, Vol. 2. Susan Theran. 1125p. 1994. lib. bdg. 215.00 (*0-918819-32-6*) Auction Index.
Leonard's Annual Price Index of Prints, Posters & Photographs, 1993-1994 Auction Season, 1995 Edition, Vol. 3. Susan Theran. 1062p. 1995. lib. bdg. 215.00 (*0-918819-33-4*) Auction Index.
Leonard's Combined Price Index of Art Auctions, Vol. III. 1997. 995.00 (*0-918819-25-3*) Auction Index.
Leonard's Lizard, His Body & Himself: The Nature of Little Boys. Jack L. Fadely & Virginia Hosler. (Illus.). 43p. 1985. pap. text 3.50 (*0-934293-01-5*) Huber-Copeland Pub.
Leonard's Price Index of Latin American Art at Auction. Susan Theran. LC 98-94934. (Illus.). 556p. 1999. lib. bdg. 149.95 (*0-918819-98-9*) Auction Index.
Leona's Sanctuary: Her Story & Recipes. Patsy Swendson. (Illus.). 68p. 1998. pap. write for info. (*0-9666658-5-6*) PS Hospitality.
Leonberger. Angela White. 1999. 39.95 (*1-85279-064-4*) TFH Pubns.
Leonce & Lena: A Comedy. Georg Buchner. Tr. by Hedwig Rappolt from GER. LC 83-70614. 96p. (C). 1983. pap. text 6.00 (*0-939858-03-7*) T S L Pr.
Leonce & Lena; Lenz; Woyzeck. Incl. Woyzeck. LC 78-184507. LC 78-184507. (German Literary Classics in Translation Ser.). xiii, 99p. 1973. Set pap. text 10.00 (*0-226-07842-6*, P467) U Ch Pr.
Leonce & Lena, Lenz, Woyzeck. Georg Buchner. Tr. & Intro. by Michael Hamburger. LC 78-184507. (German Literary Classics in Translation Ser.). 120p. 1972. lib. bdg. 9.00 (*0-226-07841-8*) U Ch Pr.
Leonce & Lena, Lenz, Woyzeck. Georg Buchner. Tr. & Intro. by Michael Hamburger. LC 78-184507. (German Literary Classics in Translation Ser.). 115p. Date not set. reprint ed. pap. 35.70 (*0-608-20669-5*, 207210600003) Bks Demand.
Leone Leoni. 2nd ed. George Sand. Tr. by George B. Ives from FRE. LC 77-28240. 175p. 1997. reprint ed. pap. 12.00 (*0-915864-61-4*) Academy Chi Pubs.
Leonel - Roque. Jim Smith. 84p. 1998. pap. 10.95 (*1-55050-128-3*, Pub. by Coteau) Genl Dist Srvs.
Leone's Italian Cookbook. Gene Leone. 1994. lib. bdg. 37.95 (*1-56849-509-9*) Buccaneer Bks.
Leones Marinos. Sarah Palmer. (Mamifero Marino Ser.).Tr. of Sea Lions. 24p. (J). (gr. k-4). 1991. lib. bdg. 14.60 (*0-86592-674-3*) Rourke Enter.
Leonhard Classification of Endogenous Psychoses: Cycloid Psychoses, Differentiated Nosology, Differentiated Therapy & Historical Aspects - Journal: Psychopathology, 1990, Vol. 23, Nos. 4-6. Ed. by H. Beckmann & M. Lanczik. (Illus.). 164p. 1991. pap. 106.25 (*3-8055-5373-0*) S Karger.
Leonhard Euler, 1707-1783. Ed. by Emil Fellmann. (Opera Omnia, Complete Works of Leonhard Euler). (ENG, FRE & GER.). 500p. 1983. 61.50 (*0-8176-1343-9*) Birkhauser.
Leonhard Rauwolf: Sixteenth-Century Physician, Botanist, & Traveler. Karl H. Dannenfeldt. LC 68-15634. (Monographs in the History of Science). (Illus.). 329p. 1968. 29.95 (*0-674-52500-0*) HUP.
Leonhardi Euleri Opera Omnia. Ed. by C. Blanc. (Series Secunda: Vol. 24). 356p. 1990. 202.00 (*0-8176-1454-0*) Birkhauser.
Leonhardt Thurneysser Zum Thurn, Kaa 'Eounveia, 2 vols., Set. reprint ed. write for info. (*0-318-72079-5*) G Olms Pubs.
Leonid Andreyev. Alexander S. Kaun. LC 70-75509. (Select Bibliographies Reprint Ser.). 1977. 29.95 (*0-8369-5009-7*) Ayer.
Leonid Andreyev. Alexander S. Kaun. LC 68-57191. 372p. 1972. reprint ed. 30.95 (*0-405-08685-7*, Pub. by Blom Pubns) Ayer.
Leonid Andreyev, a Critical Study. Alexander S. Kaun. LC 75-126652. (BCL Ser.). (Illus.). reprint ed. 27.50 (*0-404-03638-4*) AMS Pr.
Leonid Brezhnev. Ina Navazelskis. (World Leaders Past & Present Ser.). (Illus.). 120p. (YA). (gr. 5 up). 1987. lib. bdg. 19.95 (*0-87754-513-8*) Chelsea Hse.
Leonid I. Brezhnev: His Life & Work, 1906-1982. Ed. by Leonid I. Brezhnev. LC 82-19510. (Illus.). 214p. 1982. 29.95 (*0-943071-03-8*) Sphinx Pr.
Leonid Pasternak Vol. I: Text: The Russian Years, 1875-1921. A Critical Study & Catalogue, 2 vols., vol. II: Plates. Rimgaila Salys. LC N6999.P375S26 1999. (Illus.). 1,012p. 1999. text 675.00 (*0-19-817516-7*) OUP.
***Leonid Stein: Master of Risk Strategy.** Eduard Gufeld. 2000. pap. text 24.95 (*0-938650-54-8*) Thinkers Pr.
Leonide Massine: A Bio-Bibliography. Leslie Norton. Ed. by Joan Stahl. (Garland Library of Dance). 250p. Date not set. text 37.50 (*0-8153-1733-6*) Garland.
Leonides. Romain Rolland. (FRE.). 252p. 1928. pap. 8.95 (*0-7859-5565-8*) Fr & Eur.
Leonidov: Complete Works. V. Volboudt. (C). 1990. 350.00 (*0-7855-4462-3*, Pub. by Collets) St Mut.
Leonie. Elizabeth A. Adler. 592p. 1987. mass mkt. 6.99 (*0-440-14662-3*) Dell.
Leonie. Declan Burke-Kennedy. LC 96-101809. 270p. 1995. 28.00 (*1-85371-501-8*, Pub. by Poolbeg Pr) Dufour.
Leonie. Declan Burke-Kennedy. 304p. 1996. pap. 14.95 (*1-85371-542-5*, Pub. by Poolbeg Pr) Dufour.
Leonie Martin: A Difficult Life. Marie Baudouin-Croix. Tr. by Mary F. Mooney. 120p. 1993. pap. text 29.95 (*1-85390-281-0*, Pub. by Veritas Pubns) St Mut.
Leonie's Luck: (Kids & Kisses) Emma Goldrick. (Romance Ser.). 1995. per. 2.99 (*0-373-03351-6*, 1-03351-3) Harlequin Bks.
Leonine Union of the Order of Friars Minor, 1897. Maurice Carmody. (History Ser.). 234p. 1994. pap. 20.00 (*1-57659-084-4*) Franciscan Inst.
Leonis. George Theotokas. Tr. by Donald E. Martin from GRE. (Modern Greek History & Culture Ser.). (Illus.). 164p. 1985. 20.00 (*0-932963-01-3*) Nostos Bks.
Leonor Fini: Italian Painter. Esther Selsdon. (Reveries Ser.). 120p. 1991. 14.95 (*1-85995-466-9*) Parkstone Pr.
Leonor Park. Nash Candelaria. LC 91-20652. 168p. 1991. 25.00 (*0-927534-18-5*); pap. 15.00 (*0-927534-19-3*) Biling Rev-Pr.
Leonora. Arnold Bennett. LC 74-5379. (Collected Works of Arnold Bennett: Vol. 43). 1977. reprint ed. 22.95 (*0-518-19124-9*) Ayer.
Leonora: The Buried Story of Guadeloupe. Dany Bebel-Gisler. Tr. by Andrea Leskes from CRP. 284p. (C). 1994. text 50.00 (*0-8139-1515-5*) U Pr of Va.
Leonora: The Buried Story of Guadeloupe. Dany Bebel-Gisler. Tr. by Andrea Leskes from CRP. 320p. (C). 1995. pap. 18.50 (*0-8139-1518-X*) U Pr of Va.
Leonora Carrington: The Mexican Years, 1943-1985. Mexican Museum Staff. Ed. by Patricia Draher. 48p. 1991. 20.00 (*1-880508-00-1*) Mexican Museum.
Leonora O'Grady. Leah Komaiko. LC 91-23208. (Laura Geringer Bks.). (Illus.). 32p. (J). (gr. k-3). 1992. 15.00 (*0-06-021766-9*); lib. bdg. 14.89 (*0-06-021767-7*) HarpC Child Bks.
Leonora's Last Act: Essays in Verdian Discourse. Roger Parker. LC 97-5487. 208p. 1997. text 32.50 (*0-691-01557-0*, Pub. by Princeton U Pr) Cal Prin Full Svc.
Leon's Story. Leon W. Tillage. LC 96-43544. (Illus.). 107p. (J). (gr. 4 up). 1997. 14.00 (*0-374-34379-9*) FS&G.
***Leon's Story.** Leon W. Tillage. (Illus.). 112p. (J). (gr. 3-7). 2000. pap. 4.95 (*0-374-44330-0*) FS&G.
Leon's Story, Homework. unabridged ed. Leon W. Tillage. (J). 1997. 30.70 incl. audio (*0-7887-1833-9*, 40613) Recorded Bks.
Leontiev. Nicolas Berdiaev. (Russian Ser.: Vol. 15). 1968. reprint ed. pap. 25.00 (*0-87569-004-1*) Academic Intl.
***Leontyne Price.** Joseph D. McNair. LC 99-44229. (YA). 2000. lib. bdg. write for info. (*1-56766-720-1*) Childs World.
Leontyne Price: Opera Superstar. Richard Steins. LC 92-40333. (Library of Famous Women). (Illus.). 64p. (J). (gr. 4-7). 1993. lib. bdg. 17.95 (*1-56711-009-6*) Blackbirch.
Leonwohlhage. Ed. by Friederike Schneider. (Illus.). 128p. 1997. pap. 45.00 (*3-7643-5604-9*, Pub. by Birkhauser) Princeton Arch.
Leopard. Richard La Plante. 336p. 1995. 5.99 (*0-8125-3020-9*, Pub. by Tor Bks) St Martin.
Leopard. V. S. Reid. (Caribbean Writers Ser.). 110p. (C). 1980. pap. 7.95 (*0-435-98660-0*, 98660) Heinemann.
Leopard. Giuseppe Tomasi Di Lampedusa. 1976. 23.95 (*0-8488-0985-8*) Amereon Ltd.
Leopard. Giuseppe Tomasi Di Lampedusa. 304p. 1991. 17.00 (*0-679-40757-X*) Everymns Lib.
Leopard. Giuseppe Tomasi Di Lampedusa. Tr. by Archibald Colquhoun from ITA. LC 90-53443. 320p. 1991. pap. 12.00 (*0-679-73121-0*) Pantheon.
Leopard. V. S. Reid. 159p. 1972. reprint ed. 15.00 (*0-911860-08-8*) Chatham Bkseller.
***Leopard & Fat-Tailed Geckos.** R. D. Bartlett & Patricia Bartlett. LC 99-14653. (Illus.). 48p. 1999. pap. write for info. (*0-7641-1119-1*) Barron.
Leopard Family. Michael Scheibert. Ed. by Edward Force. LC 88-63995. (Illus.). 52p. 1989. pap. 9.95 (*0-88740-167-8*) Schiffer.
***Leopard Family Book.** Jonathan Scott. (Animal Family Ser.). (Illus.). 56p. (J). (gr. 1-5). 1999. pap. 8.95 (*0-7358-1212-8*, Pub. by North-South Bks NYC) Chronicle Bks.
Leopard IV: Bearing Witness. Christopher Maclehose. 352p. 1999. pap. text 15.00 (*1-86046-067-4*) Harvill Press.
***Leopard Gecko: An Owner's Guide to a Happy, Healthy Pet.** Puente. (Illus.). 128p. 2000. 12.95 (*1-58245-165-6*) Howell Bks.
Leopard Gecko Manual. Philippe De Vosjoli. 1999. pap. text 8.95 (*1-882770-44-7*, Pub. by Adv Vivarium) IPG Chicago.
Leopard Geckos. R. Hunziker. (Illus.). 64p. 1995. pap. text 9.95 (*0-7938-0258-X*, RE106) TFH Pubns.
Leopard I Main Battle Tank, 1965-95. Michael Jerchel. (Elite Ser.). (Illus.). 48p. 1995. pap. 12.95 (*1-85532-520-9*, Pub. by Ospry) Stackpole.
***Leopard in Exile.** Rosemary Edghill & Andre Norton. 2001. text 22.95 (*0-312-86428-0*) St Martin.
***Leopard in the Sun.** Laura Restrepo. (International Ser.). 256p. 2000. pap. 12.00 (*0-375-70508-2*) Vin Bks.
***Leopard in the Sun.** Laura Restrepo. LC 99-13509. 256p. 1999. 22.00 (*0-609-60386-8*, Crown) Crown Pub Group.
Leopard Lord. Alanna Morland. 272p. 1999. mass mkt. 5.99 (*0-441-00606-X*) Ace Bks.
Leopard Lounge. Courage Books Staff. 160p. 1997. 5.98 (*0-7624-0226-1*, Courage) Running Pr.
Leopard Radio. Jacqueline Disler. 64p. (Orig.). 1989. pap. 6.00 (*0-942582-15-2*) Erie St Pr.
Leopard Son. Discovery Channel Staff. (Illus.). 29p. (J). (ps-3). 1996. 14.95 (*0-07-016061-9*) McGraw.
Leopard Speaks about Changes in Life. Barbara P. Avent. Ed. by Nelson G. Alston. LC 93-72214. (Illus.). 64p. (Orig.). (YA). 1993. pap. 9.95 (*0-9632202-1-7*) Alpha Bk N Pr.
***Leopard Tortoise Guide: She Says; He Says.** unabridged ed. Richard C. Paull & Liz Palika. (Tortoises of the World Ser.: Vol. 8). (Illus.). 107p. 1999. pap. text 37.95 (*1-888089-42-3*) Green Nature Bks.
Leopard 2 Main Battle Tank, 1972-1998. Michael Jerchel. (New Vanguard Ser.: No. 24). (Illus.). 48p. 1998. pap. 12.95 (*1-85532-691-4*, Pub. by Ospry) Stackpole.
Leopardi: A Study in Solitude. Iris Origo. 396p. (Orig.). 1999. pap. 16.95 (*1-885983-44-1*, Helen Mx) Turtle Point Pr.
Leopardi: Poems & Prose. Giacomo Leopardi. Ed. by Angel Flores. LC 86-29460. 256p. 1987. reprint ed. lib. bdg. 77.50 (*0-313-25769-8*, FLLE, Greenwood Pr) Greenwood.
Leopardi: Poems: Bilingual. 2nd ed. Giacomo Leopardi. Tr. & Intro. by Arturo Vivante. 85p. 1994. pap. 12.00 (*0-9620305-0-3*) Delphinium Pr.
Leopardi: Selected Poems. Giacomo Leopardi. Tr. by Eamon Grennan from ITA. LC 96-47721. (Lockert Library of Poetry in Translation). 104p. 1997. pap. 9.95 (*0-691-01644-5*, Pub. by Princeton U Pr); text 27.50 (*0-691-01643-7*, Pub. by Princeton U Pr) Cal Prin Full Svc.
Leopardi Reader. fac. ed. Giacomo Leopardi. Ed. & Tr. by Ottavio M. Casale. LC 80-29068. 288p. 1994. pap. 89.30 (*0-7837-7611-X*, 204736300007) Bks Demand.
Leopards see Endangered! - Group 2
Leopards. Mary A. McDonald. LC 95-30899. (Nature Books Ser.). (Illus.). 32p. (J). (gr. 2-6). 1995. lib. bdg. 22.79 (*1-56766-211-0*) Childs World.
Leopards. Don Middleton. LC 97-44840. 24p. (J). (gr. k-4). 1999. 15.93 (*0-8239-5209-6*, PowerKids) Rosen Group.
Leopards. Lynn M. Stone. (Big Cat Discovery Library). (Illus.). 24p. (J). (gr. k-5). 1989. 8.95 (*0-685-58630-8*) Rourke Corp.
Leopards. Lynn M. Stone. (Big Cat Discovery Library). (Illus.). 24p. (J). (gr. k-4). 1989. lib. bdg. 14.60 (*0-86592-502-X*) Rourke Enter.
Leopards. Anne Welsbacher. LC 98-12652. (Wild Cats Ser.). (Illus.). 24p. (J). 2000. lib. bdg. 18.60 (*1-57765-088-3*, Checkerboard Library) ABDO Pub Co.
Leopard's Claw. George W. Ellis. LC 71-144605. reprint ed. 12.50 (*0-404-00156-4*) AMS Pr.
Leopard's Drum: An Asante Tale from West Africa. Jessica Souhami. LC 94-76697. (Illus.). 32p. (J). (gr. k-3). 1996. 14.95 (*0-316-80466-5*) Little.
Leopards in the Temple: Studies in American Popular Culture. Steven Carter. LC 97-20352. 152p. 1997. 74.95 (*1-57309-170-7*); pap. 54.95 (*1-57309-169-3*) Intl Scholars.
Leopards in the Temple: Studies in American Popular Culture. 2nd ed. Steven Carter. LC 98-20478. 172p. 1998. 74.95 (*1-57309-326-2*, Cath Scholar Pr); pap. 54.95 (*1-57309-325-4*, Cath Scholar Pr) Intl Scholars.
Leopard's Lady. Mary Gillgannon. 480p. 1995. mass mkt. 4.99 (*0-7860-0153-4*, Pinncle Kensgtn) Kensgtn Pub Corp.
Leopards of Londolozi. 1997. pap. text 80.00 (*0-947430-22-9*, Pub. by New5 Holland) BHB Intl.
Leopard's Spots: A Romance of the White Man's Burden. Thomas Dixon, Jr. LC 67-29265. (Americans in Fiction Ser.). (Illus.). 481p. 1979. reprint ed. lib. bdg. 49.50 (*0-8398-0366-4*) Irvington.
Leopard's Spots: Biblical & African Wisdom in Proverbs. Friedemann W. Golka. 160p. 1993. text 37.95 (*0-567-09636-X*, Pub. by T & T Clark) Bks Intl VA.
Leopard's Spots: Scientific Attitudes Toward Race in America, 1815-1859. William R. Stanton. LC 59-11625. (Midway Reprint Ser.). 256p. reprint ed. pap. 79.40 (*0-608-09537-0*, 205433900005) Bks Demand.
Leopard's Spots: Scientific Attitudes Toward Race in America, 1815-1859. William R. Stanton. LC 59-11625. (Midway Reprint Ser.). 1993. reprint ed. pap. text 16.95 (*0-226-77124-5*) U Ch Pr.
Leopold & Brink No. 1: Introductions. Christopher Fink. (Illus.). 24p. (YA). 1997. pap. 2.50 (*1-930281-00-5*) FINK Inc.
Leopold & Brink No. 2: Orbit. Christopher Fink. (Illus.). 32p. (YA). 1997. pap. 2.95 (*1-930281-01-3*) FINK Inc.
***Leopold & Brink No. 3, Pt. 2: Orbit.** Christopher Fink. 32p. (YA). 1998. pap. 2.95 (*1-930281-02-1*) FINK Inc.
Leopold & Loeb: The Crime of the Century. Hal Higdon. LC 99-10745. 384p. 1999. pap. 18.95 (*0-252-06829-7*) U of Ill Pr.
Leopold Frog: Bookshelf Buddies. Jerry Smath. (J). (ps-3). 1997. pap. 3.95 (*0-8167-3585-9*) Troll Communs.
Leopold Hirschfeldt & James Robert Davis Memorial Lecture: Reflections on the Growth & Changes of the Private Practice of Geotechnical Engineering. Elio D'Appolonia. 25.00 (*0-614-05239-4*, LHML04831.5M) ASFE.
Leopold Kozeluch: 6 String Quartets, Opus 32 & Opus 33. Leopold Kozeluch. Ed. by Roger Hickman. (Recent Researches in Music of the Classic Era Ser.: Vol. RRC42). xiv, 262p. 1994. pap. 85.00 (*0-89579-299-0*) A-R Eds.
Leopold Sedar Senghor. Janice Spleth. (Twayne's World Authors Ser.: No. 765). 216p. 1985. 29.95 (*0-8057-6616-2*, Twyne) Mac Lib Ref.
Leopold Sedar Senghor: From Politics to Poetry. William Kluback. LC 96-45380. XI, 117p. (C). 1997. pap. text 24.95 (*0-8204-3488-4*) P Lang Pubng.
Leopold Sedar Senghor: The Collected Poetry. Leopold S. Senghor. Tr. & Intro. by Melvin Dixon. (CARAF: Caribbean & African Literature Ser.). 1991. text 45.00 (*0-8139-1275-X*) U Pr of Va.
***Leopold Sedar Senghor: The Collected Poetry.** Leopold S. Senghor. Tr. & Intro. by Melvin Dixon. (CARAF Bks.). (ENG & SPA.). 598p. 1998. reprint ed. pap. 20.00 (*0-8139-1832-4*) U Pr of Va.
Leopold Sedar Senghor et la Defense et Illustration de la Civilisation Noire. S. Okechukwu Mezu. 19.50 (*0-685-36567-0*) Fr & Eur.

An Asterisk (*) at the beginning of an entry indicates that the title is appearing for the first time.

L

Leopold von Ranke & the Shaping of the Historical Discipline. Ed. by Georg G. Iggers & James M. Powell. LC 89-34028. (Illus.). 245p. 1990. reprint ed. pap. 76.00 (0-608-07611-2, 205992600010) Bks Demand.

Leopold Von Ranke Manuscript Collection of Syracuse University: The Complete Catalogue. Edward Muir. 240p. 1983. text 75.00 (0-8156-2294-5) Syracuse U Pr.

Leopoldo Alas: Great Short Stories from Around the World I. Illus. by James Balkovek. (Classic Short Stories Ser.). 80p. 1994. pap. 5.95 (0-7854-0646-8, 40067) Am Guidance.

Leopold's Bibliography of Child Language. Ed. by Dan I. Slobin. LC 79-184526. (Indiana University Studies in the History & Theory of Linguistics). 220p. reprint ed. 68.20 (0-8357-9222-6, 201583300097) Bks Demand.

Leopold's Way: Detective Stories by Edward D. Hoch. Ed. by Francis M. Nevins, Jr. & Martin H. Greenberg. LC 84-27554. (Mystery Makers Ser.). 359p. 1985. 26.95 (0-8093-1233-6) S Ill U Pr.

***Leopoldville Troopship Disaster in Memoriam.** unabridged ed. Allan Andrade. LC 99-75433. (Illus.). VIII, 72p. 1999. pap. 19.95 (0-9675950-0-2) A Andrade.

Leo's Amazing Paws & Jaws. David R. Collins. (Illus.). (J). (ps-2). 1987. pap. 5.10 (0-8136-5682-6); lib. bdg. 7.95 (0-8136-5182-4) Modern Curr.

Leota Foreman, RN. large type ed. Peggy Gaddis. (Linford Romance Library). 288p. 1993. pap. 16.99 (0-7089-7396-5, Linford) Ulverscroft.

***Leota's Garden.** Francine Rivers. LC 99-25963. 425p. 1999. 17.97 (0-8423-3572-2); audio 15.99 (0-8423-5211-2) Tyndale Hse.

Leota's Garden Francine Rivers. LC 99-25963. 1999. pap. 12.99 (0-8423-3498-X) Tyndale Hse.

Le/Patron des traducteurs see Homage to Jerome

Lepchas & Their Heritage. Tapan Chattopadhyay. 1990. 24.00 (81-7018-571-8, Pub. by BR Pub) S Asia.

Le/Pelerinage De Vie Humaine see Pilgrimage of the Lyf of the Manhode

***Leper & Other Strangers.** Guy Bates. (Illus.). vi, 136p. 2000. 24.95 (0-9679472-0-0) Wysiwyg Pubng.

***Leper Colony.** Khanh Ha. LC 00-190566. 388p. 2000. 25.00 (0-7388-1832-1); pap. 18.00 (0-7388-1833-X) Xlibris Corp.

Leper Hospitals in Medieval Ireland. Gerard Lee. 72p. 1996. 15.00 (1-85182-271-2, Pub. by Four Cts Pr) Intl Spec Bk.

Leper Hospitals in Medieval Ireland. limited ed. Gerard Lee. 72p. 1996. 75.00 (1-85182-285-2, Pub. by Four Cts Pr) Intl Spec Bk.

***Leper in Blue.** Amalia Gladhart. (North Carolina Studies in the Romance Languages & Literatures Ser.: Vol. 226). 240p. 2000. pap. text 32.50 (0-8078-9270-X) U of NC Pr.

***Leper King & His Heirs: Baldwin IV & the Crusader Kingdom of Jerusalem.** Bernard Hamilton. (Illus.). 284p. (C). 2000. 59.95 (0-521-64187-X) Cambridge U Pr.

Leper of St. Giles. Ellis Peters. 1995. mass mkt. 5.99 (0-446-40437-3, Pub. by Warner Bks) Little.

Leper of St. Giles: The Fifth Chronicle of Brother Cadfael. large type ed. Ellis Peters. LC 97-42553. 1998. 22.95 (0-7862-1375-2) Thorndike Pr.

***Leper Priest of Moloka'i: The Father Damien Story.** Richard Stewart. LC 00-20266. 2000. pap. write for info. (0-8248-2322-2) UH Pr.

Leper Ship. large type ed. Peter Tonkin. LC 94-2974. 494p. 1994. pap. 17.95 (0-7862-0181-9) Thorndike Pr.

***Leper's Companion.** Julia Blackburn. (International Ser.). 208p. 2000. pap. 12.00 (0-679-75838-0) Vin Bks.

Leper's Companion. Julia Blackburn. LC 98-27026. 208p. 1999. 22.00 (0-679-43984-6) Pantheon.

Lepers of Molokai. Charles W. Stoddard. (Notable American Authors Ser.). 1999. reprint ed. lib. bdg. 125.00 (0-7812-8943-2) Rprt Serv.

***Leper's Return.** Michael Jecks. 350p. 1999. pap. 9.95 (0-7472-5951-8, Pub. by Headline Bk Pub) Trafalgar.

Le/Petit Prince see Kleine Prinz

Lepidoptera: Annotated Catalogue see Fauna of New Zealand Series

Lepidoptera: Butterflies, Vol. I. 2nd ed. G. Talbot. (Fauna of British India Ser.). (Illus.). xxx, 612p. 1978. reprint ed. 50.00 (0-88065-199-7) Scholarly Pubns.

Lepidoptera: Butterflies, Vol. II. 2nd ed. (Fauna of British India Ser.). (Illus.). 510p. 1986. reprint ed. 50.00 (0-88065-215-2) Scholarly Pubns.

Lepidoptera: Form, Function & Diversity. Malcolm J. Scoble. (Illus.). 416p. 1995. pap. text 50.00 (0-19-854952-0) OUP.

Lepidoptera of Norfolk Island. J. D. Holloway. (Series Entomologica: No. 13). (Illus.). 1977. text 121.50 (90-6193-123-1) Kluwer Academic.

Lepidoptera of Taiwan Series, Set. pap. write for info. (0-945417-75-6) Sci Pubs.

Lepidopteran Anatomy. John L. Eaton. LC 87-25226. (Insect Morphology Ser.). 257p. 1988. 150.00 (0-471-05862-9) Wiley.

Lepidopterorum Catalogus, Fascicle 118, Noctuidae, 3 vols., Set. Robert W. Poole. (New Ser.). xii, 500p. 1988. 195.00 (0-916846-45-8) Sandhill Crane.

Lepidopterorum Catalogus, Fascicle 118, Noctuidae, Vol. 2. Robert W. Poole. (New Ser.). 1988. write for info. (0-916846-46-6) Sandhill Crane.

Lepidopterorum Catalogus, Fascicle 118, Noctuidae, Vol. 3. Robert W. Poole. (New Ser.). 1988. write for info. (0-916846-47-4) Sandhill Crane.

Lepidopterorum Catalogus Series. Ed. by J. B. Heppner. 1989. pap. write for info. (0-945417-50-0) Sci Pubs.

Lepidus: The Tarnished Triumvir. Richard D. Weigel. 192p. (C). (gr. 13). 1992. 80.00 (0-415-07680-3, A7938) Routledge.

Lepidus the Centurion: A Roman of Today. Edwin L. Arnold. Ed. by R. Reginald & Douglas Melville. LC 77-84196. (Lost Race & Adult Fantasy Ser.). 1978. reprint ed. lib. bdg. 29.95 (0-405-10954-7) Ayer.

***L'Epithete Pindarique.** Pascale Hummel. (Sapheneia Ser.: Bd. 3). 677p. 1999. 70.95 (3-906763-12-9, Pub. by P Lang) P Lang Pubng.

Leplace's Mecanique Celeste. Nathaniel Bowditch. (Works of Nathaniel Bowditch). 1989. reprint ed. lib. bdg. 79.00 (0-7812-2022-X) Rprt Serv.

L'epopee Du Siosnisme see Zionism: The Saga of a National Liberation Movement

Lepopee Napoleonienne. F&G Hourtelle Staff. 1997. 55.00 (2-908182-69-6, Pub. by Histoire) Combined Pub.

Le/Postmoderne Explique Aux Enfants see Postmodern Explained

***Leprechaun & His Bag of Gold.** Nancy Carpino. LC 00-91172. (Illus.). 50p. (J). (gr. k-4). 2000. 8.95 (1-928675-03-4) N Carpino.

Leprechaun Cake & Other Tales: A Vegetarian Story-Cookbook. Vonnie W. Crist & Debra Wasserman. Ed. by Charles Stahler. LC 94-61558. (Illus.). 128p. (Orig.). (J). (gr. 1-5). 1995. pap. text 9.95 (0-931411-13-0) Vegetarian Resc.

Leprechaun Gold. Teresa Bateman. LC 97-19111. (Illus.). 32p. (J). (gr. k-2). 1998. lib. bdg. 16.95 (0-8234-1344-6) Holiday.

***Leprechaun Gold.** Teresa Bateman. (Illus.). (J). 1998. pap. 6.95 (0-8234-1514-7) Holiday.

Leprechaun in the Basement. Kathy Tucker. LC 98-9318. (Illus.), 32p. (J). (gr. k-3). 1999. lib. bdg. 15.95 (0-8075-4450-7) A Whitman.

***Leprechaun Tales.** Yvonne Carroll. (Illus.). 64p. (J). (gr. k-5). 1999. 15.95 (0-7171-2698-6, Pub. by Gill & MacMill) Irish Bks Media.

***Leprechaun Who Wished He Wasn't.** Siobhan Parkinson. (Illus.). 80p. (J). 2000. pap. 6.95 (0-86278-334-8, Pub. by OBrien Pr) IPG Chicago.

***Leprechauns.** Craig Shaw Gardner. 1999. mass mkt. 5.99 (1-57566-535-2) Kensgtn Pub Corp.

***Leprechauns.** Craig Shaw Gardner. (Illus.). 1999. 20.00 (1-57566-534-4) Kensgtn Pub Corp.

Leprechauns Don't Play Basketball. Debbie Dadey et al. (Adventures of the Bailey School Kids Ser.: No. 4). (Illus.). 71p. (J). (gr. 2-5). 1992. pap. 3.99 (0-590-44822-6) Scholastic Inc.

Leprechauns Never Lie. Lorna Balian. (Illus.). 32p. (J). (ps-5). 1994. lib. bdg. 14.95 (1-881772-07-1) Humbug Bks.

Leprechaun's St. Patrick's Day. Sarah K. Blazek. LC 96-22490. (Illus.). 32p. (J). (gr. 1-4). 1997. 14.95 (1-56554-237-1) Pelican.

Lepreuses, Les Jeunes Filles. Henry De Montherlant. (Jeunes Filles Ser.: Vol. 4). (FRE.). 1972. pap. 10.95 (0-8288-3721-X, F115740) Fr & Eur.

Le/Probleme de l'Ethique dans l'Evolution de la Pense Humaine see Difficulty of Ethics in the Evolution of Human Thought

Leprosy. 2nd ed. Ed. by Robert C. Hastings & Diltor V. Opromolla. LC 93-16295. (Medicine in the Tropics Ser.). 488p. 1994. text 179.00 (0-443-04405-8) Church.

Leprosy, Vol. 2. Dharmendra. (Illus.). 900p. 1985. 52.95 (0-318-36371-2) Asia Bk Corp.

Leprosy in Children. F. M. Noussitou et al. 1976. pap. text 8.10 (92-4-154053-2, 1150095) World Health.

Leprosy in Five Young Men. George J. Hill. LC 79-125621. (Illus.). 224p. reprint ed. pap. 69.50 (0-8357-5502-9, 203511700093) Bks Demand.

Leprosy in Rural India. K. Venkateswara Rao. (Illus.). xii, 500p. 1992. 34.00 (81-85445-43-5, Pub. by Manak Pubns Pvt Ltd) Nataraj Bks.

Leptiminus (Lamta). A Roman Port City in Tunisia, No. 1. N. Ben Lazreg & D. J. Mattingly. (JRA Supplementary Ser.: No. 4). (ENG, FRE & ITA., Illus.). 334p. 1992. 79.50 (1-887829-04-0) Jour Roman Arch.

Leptoceratops. John Acorn & Dale Russell. (Tiny Perfect Dinosaur Ser.: No. 1). (Illus.). 32p. (J). (gr. 1-7). pap. 12.95 (0-921051-50-6) Somerville Hse.

Leptodactylid Frogs of the Genus Eleutherodactylus from the Andes of Southern Ecuador. John D. Lynch. (Miscellaneous Publications: No. 66). 62p. 1979. pap. 3.25 (0-686-80375-2) U KS Nat Hist Mus.

Leptodactylid Frogs of the Genus Eleutherodactylus in the Andes of Northern Ecuador & Adjacent Colombia. John D. Lynch. (Miscellaneous Publications: No. 72). 46p. 1981. 2.75 (0-317-04880-5) U KS Nat Hist Mus.

Lepton & Baryon Number Violation in Particle Physics, Astrophysics & Cosmology: Proceedings of the 1st International Symposium on Lepton & Baryon Number Violation (Lepton-Baryon 98), European Centre for Theoretical Physics, Trento, Italy, 20-25 April, 1998. International Symposium on Lepton & Baryon Number Violation Staff et al. LC 99-25997. 1999. 320.00 (0-7503-0616-5) IOP Pub.

Lepton & Photon Interaction at High Energies. M. Riordan. 556p. (C). 1990. pap. 48.00 (981-02-0216-4); text 130.00 (981-02-0104-4) World Scientific Pub.

Lepton & Photon Interactions: XVI International Symposium. Ed. by Persis Dvell & David Rubin. LC 94-70079. (AIP Conference Proceedings Ser.: No. 302). 837p. 1994. text 830.00 (1-56396-106-7) Am Inst Physics.

Lepton & Photon Interactions at High Energies: Proceedings of the XVIII International Symposium Hamburg, Germany 28 July-1 August, 1997. Ed. by A. De Roeck & A. Wagner. 700p. 1998. 136.00 (981-02-3393-0) World Scientific Pub.

Lepton & Photon Interactions at High Energies: Proceedings of the 1985 International Symposium, Kyoto, Japan, August 19-24, 1985. Ed. by M. Konoma & Koichiro Takahashi. 984p. 1986. text 163.00 (4-9900055-1-1) World Scientific Pub.

Lepton Nucleon Interactions at High Energies: Proceedings of the XVth Winter Meeting on Fundamental Physics. Ed. by F. Barreiro & J. L. Sanchez-Gomez. 384p. (C). 1988. text 100.00 (9971-5-0469-3) World Scientific Pub.

Lepton-Photon Interactions: Proceedings of the XVII International Symposium. Zhi-Peng Zheng & He-Sheng Chen. LC 96-217083. 839 p. 1996. text 158.00 (981-02-2285-8) World Scientific Pub.

***Lepton-Photon Interactions at High Energies: Proceedings of the XIX International Symposium.** John Jaros. 2000. 148.00 (981-02-4189-5) World Scientific Pub.

Lepton Physics at CERN & Frascati. Ed. by Nicola Cabibbo. (Series in 20th Century Physics: Vol. 8). 396p. 1995. text 86.00 (981-02-2078-2) World Scientific Pub.

Leptonia & Related Genera of the West Coast. D. L. Largent. 1976. 52.00 (3-7682-1114-2) Lubrecht & Cramer.

Leptons & Quarks. L. B. Okun. (North-Holland Personal Library: Vol. 2). xiv, 362p. 1987. reprint ed. pap. 68.00 (0-444-86924-7, North Holland) Elsevier.

Leptons, Hadrons, & Nuclei see Electroweak & Strong Interaction: An Introduction to Theoretical Particle Physics: with 80 Exercises & Solutions

Leptophlebiidae (Insecta: Ephemeroptera) see Fauna of New Zealand Series

Leptospermum Scoparium J. R. et G. Forst: Isolierung, Strukturaufklaerung und Analytik Von Flavonoiden und Harzestem Mit In-Vitro-Affinitaet Zum GABAA-Rezeptor-Chloridkanalkomplex. Klaus-Peter Tschiersch. (Dissertationes Botanicae Ser.: Band 241). (Illus.). x, 204p. 1995. pap. 48.00 (3-443-64153-9, Pub. by Gebruder Borntraeger) Balogh.

Leptospira & Leptospirosis. Solomon Faine. 368p. 1993. lib. bdg. 189.00 (0-8493-6994-0, QR729) CRC Pr.

***Learn MS SQL 7.0 Care & Maintenance.** Jeffrey Garbus. (Illus.). 250p. (C). 2000. pap. 29.95 (1-55622-747-7) Wordware Pub.

LERA Writer's Guide: The Ultimate Guide to Writing & Your Career As a Writer. 2nd rev. ed. (Illus.). 354p. 1995. pap. 30.00 (0-9660063-0-5, LERA-WG) Lnd of Enchantmnt.

Lerche Motivgeschichtliche Untersuchung Zur Deutschen Literatur, Insbesondere Zur Deutschen Lyrik. Verena Doebele-Fluegel. (C). 1977. 167.70 (3-11-005909-6) De Gruyter.

Le/Remede Dans le Mal see Blessings in Disguise, or, the Morality of Evil

Le/Reve et l'existence; Traum und Existenz see Dream & Existence

Lerida or the Long Shadow. Alexander Giese. Tr. by Lowell A. Bangerter. (Studies in Austrian Literature, Culture, & Thought. Translation Ser.). 1994. pap. 21.50 (0-929497-72-4) Ariadne CA.

Lermontov: Demon. Ed. by D. Ward. (Bristol Russian Texts Ser.). (RUS.). 104p. 1992. pap. 18.95 (1-85399-316-6, Pub. by Brist Class Pr) Focus Pub-R Pullins.

***Lermontov's "A Hero of Our Time" A Critical Companion.** Ed. by Lewis Bagby. 2001. pap. 18.95 (0-8101-1680-4) Northwestern U Pr.

Lermontov's Narratives of Heroism. Vladimir Goldstein. (Studies in Russian Literature & Theory). 272p. 1998. text 59.95 (0-8101-1611-1) Northwestern U Pr.

Lern Im Auto: Englisch, Level 1, set. unabridged ed. Henry N. Raymond.Tr. of Learn in Your Car: English. (ENG & GER.). pap. 16.95 incl. audio (1-56015-153-6) Penton Overseas.

Lerna in the Argolid. 2nd rev. ed. John L. Caskey & E. T. Blackburn. LC 98-161669. (Illus.). 32p. 1997. pap. text 4.00 (0-87661-680-5) Am Sch Athens.

***Lernen mit Allen Sinnen.** Brigitte Jonen-Dittman. (Illus.). 68p. 1999. ring bd. 36.00 (0-942017-69-2, 4-6486) Amer Assn Teach German.

***Lernen Mit Seelisch Behinderten Erwachsenen in der Beruflichen Rehabilitation: Ein Handlungsorientierter Sonderpadagogischer Forderansatz.** Tilmann Fischer. (Europaische Hochschulschriften: Reihe 11, Padagogik Ser.). 338p. 1999. 48.95 (3-631-35438-X) P Lang Pubng.

Lernen und Realitatsverlust in der Schule. Eva Novotny. 190p. 1996. 38.95 (3-631-49752-0) P Lang Pubng.

***Lernen unter Veranderten Lebensbedingungen: Fachdidaktiken und Lehrerbildung auf dem Weg Ins Nachste Jahrhundert.** Peter Schulz-Hageleit. 279p. 1999. 45.95 (3-631-34509-7) P Lang Pubng.

Lerner Survey of Health Care in New York: Your Consumer Guide to HMOs, Health Insurance Plans, Hospitals, Free & Low-Cost Services & Your Legal Rights. Julie Lerner & Paul Lerner. LC 99-94087. 320p. 1999. pap. 17.95 (0-9669999-1-6) Lerner.

***Lerner's Consumer Guide to Health Care: How to Get the Best Health Care for Less.** Paul Lerner & Julie Lerner. 224p. 2000. pap. 13.95 (0-9669999-2-4, Pub. by Lerner) IPG Chicago.

Lerner's Dictionary of English Idioms. 2nd ed. Oxford University Press Staff. 350p. 1995. pap. text 10.95 (0-19-431277-1) OUP.

Lernexpress II: German Grammar Companion. Gudrun Clay. 160p. (C). 1996. spiral bd. 15.95 (0-7872-2033-7) Kendall-Hunt.

Lernfahigkeit von Unternehmen: Grundlagen Organisationaler Lernprozesse & Unterstutzungstechnologien fur Lernen im Strategischen Management. Jurgen Greschner. (GER., Illus.). XLIX, 249p. 1996. 57.95 (3-631-30818-3) P Lang Pubng.

Lernheft Deutsch Zusammn. Donahue Tharp & Watzinger Tharp. 640p. (C). 1998. pap. text 28.80 (0-536-01178-8) Pearson Custom.

Lernt Aktiv! Live Action German. 2nd ed. Contee Sealy. Tr. by Alexandra Kristall from ENG. (Live Action Ser.). (GER., Illus.). xlviii, 152p. (Orig.). 1999. pap. text 12.95 (0-929724-03-8) Command Performance.

Lernziel Glauben: Einfuhrung in die Theologie. Johannes Wirsching. (GER., Illus.). 239p. 1995. 38.95 (3-631-48053-9) P Lang Pubng.

Lernziel Sozialkompetenz Vol. VIII: Ein Bildungskonzept fur die Erstausbildung in den Industriellen Metallberufen. Rainer Schlomer-Helmerking. (Europaische Hochschulschriften: Reihe 11: Bd. 685). (GER., Illus.). VIII, 263p. 1996. pap. 51.95 (3-631-30091-3) P Lang Pubng.

LeRoi Jones - Amiri Baraka Reader. Amiri Imamu Baraka, pseud. Ed. by William J. Harris. 544p. 1991. pap. 16.95 (1-56025-007-0, Thunders Mouth) Avalon NY.

***LeRoi Jones - Amiri Baraka Reader.** 2nd ed. Amiri Imamu Baraka, pseud. LC 99-32364. 560p. 1999. pap. 16.95 (1-56025-238-3, Thunders Mouth) Avalon NY.

Leroy & the Old Man. W. E. Butterworth, pseud. 168p. (YA). (gr. 7-9). 1989. pap. 3.99 (0-590-42711-3) Scholastic Inc.

Leroy & the Old Man. W. E. Butterworth, pseud. (Point Ser.). (J). 1980. 9.09 (0-606-01139-0, Pub. by Turtleback) Demco.

Leroy Anderson: Almost Complete. 128p. (YA). 1985. pap. 14.95 (0-7692-1453-3, 11696) Wrner Bros.

LeRoy Neiman on Safari. LeRoy Neiman. LC 96-25980. (Illus.). 168p. 1997. 60.00 (0-8109-6332-9, Pub. by Abrams) Time Warner.

Leroy Potts Meets the McCrooks. Vivian Sathre. LC 95-53285. (Illus.). 48p. (J). 1997. pap. 3.99 (0-440-41137-8) BDD Bks Young Read.

Leroy Robertson: Music Giant from the Rockies. Marian R. Wilson. LC 96-1123. (Illus.). 384p. 1996. text 14.95 (0-9634732-2-0, Blue Ribbon Books) Freethinker.

Leroy, the Lizard Coloring Book. Claudia Cherness. (ENG, FRE & SPA.). 24p. (J). (ps-2). 1993. pap. 3.95 (0-943864-66-6) Davenport.

Leroy the Lobster & Crabby Crab. Edward Harriman. (Illus.). 42p. (J). (gr. k-2). 1967. pap. 9.95 (0-89272-000-X) Down East.

Leroy's Zoo: Featuring the Folk Art Carvings of Leroy Ramon Archuleta. Warren Lowe et al. LC 97-7696. (Illus.). (J). 1997. 21.00 (1-881320-87-1, Black Belt) Black Belt Communs.

Lertfaden Zur Kriegsschuldfrage see Versaille Verdic

Les: Kel, Pt. 1. Mark Dunster. (Rin Ser.: Pt. 28). 60p. 1981. pap. 4.00 (0-89642-075-2) Linden Pubs.

Les & the Laundry. Gwenda Smyth. LC 93-26219. (Illus.). (J). 1994. 4.25 (0-383-03757-3) SRA McGraw.

Les Arteres des Muscles des Membres et du Tronc, Les Vois Anastomotiques Arterielles des Membres see Michel Salmon Anatomic Studies: Arterial Anastomotic Pathways of the Extremities

Les Arteres des Muscles des Membres et du Tronc, Les Vois Anastomotiques Arterielles des Membres see Michel Salmon Anatomic Studies

Les Blessures Que Guerit l'Armour see Wounds Healed by Love Alone: A Charismatic Interview with St. Therese of Lisieux

Les Boucs see Butts

Les Catilinaires see Stranger Next Door

Les Chemins de Loco-Miroir see Reflections of Loko Miwa

Les Choses see Things: A Story of the Sixties

Comedies-Ballets, I 1664-1665, Tome 1, Le Mariage force; L'Amour medecin see Oeuvres Completes de Jean-Baptiste Lully

Comedies-Ballets, III 1669-1670, Tome 3, Monsieur de Pourceaugnac; Le Bourgeois Gentilhomme; Les Amants magnifiques see Oeuvres Completes de Jean-Baptiste Lully

Comedies-Ballets, II 1666-1668, Tome 2, Les Plaisirs de l'Ile enchantee; La Pastorale comique; Le Sicilien; Le Grand Di see Oeuvres Completes de Jean-Baptiste Lully

Les 'Confessions' de Kurt Gerstein see "Confessions" of Kurt Gerstein

Les Crimes de la Police Montee see Crimes of the Secret Police

Cris de Paris, 1529 see Florilege du Concert Vocal de la Renaissance

Les Diaconesses essai Historique see Deaconesses: An Historical Study

Les Dons du Ministere see Ministry Gifts: Apostles, Prophets, Evangelists, Pastors, Teachers

Les Enfants du Limon see Children of Clay

Les Heros de l'Equinoxe see Heroes of the Equinox: Valerjan Spatiotemporal Agent

Les Litteratures de l'Exquite see Exiguity: Reflections on the Margins of Literature

Les Morales de L'Histoire see Morals of History

***Les Murray: A Life in Progress.** Peter F. Alexander. (Illus.). 304p. 2000. 30.00 (0-374-11310-6) FS&G.

Les Mythes Fondateurs de la Politique Israelienne see Founding Myths of Modern Israel

Primitifs du XIIIe. Jacques Prevert & P. Guilbaud. (FRE.). 5.95 (0-686-54917-1) Fr & Eur.

Les Relations entre les Negociations Bilaterales et Multilaterales sur le Desarmement (Baku (U. S. S. R.), 2-4 June, 1987) see Interrelationship of Bilateral & Multilateral Disarmament Negotiations

7 Ponts de Sati. 1993. 18.50 (2-920083-71-6) Edns Roseau.

Lesabendio ein Asteroidenroman. unabridged ed. Scheerbart. (World Classic Literature Ser.). (GER.). pap. 5.95 (3-89507-033-5, Pub. by Bookking Intl) Distribks Inc.

***Lesage.** Lydia Kamitsis. (Illus.). 80p. 2000. text 18.95 (*0-7893-0470-8*) Universe.

Les/Anciens Combattants et la Societe Francaise see In the Wake of War: Les Anciens Combattants & French Society

Lesarten: Festschrift fur Athanasios Kambylis zum 70. Geburstag. 396p. 1998. 185.35 (*3-11-015894-9*) De Gruyter.

Lesbian Adventure Stories. Ed. by Mara Wild & Mikaya Heart. LC 94-60743. 280p. 1994. pap. 11.95 (*0-9615129-3-8*) Tough Dove.

Lesbian Almanac: The Most Comprehensive Reference Source Available. Lesbian & Gay Community Services, National Museum & Program of the Lesbian & Gay Community Community S. 534p. 1996. pap. 16.95 (*0-425-15301-0*) Berkley Pub.

Lesbian & Bisexual Identities: Constructing Communities, Constructing Selves. Kristin G. Esterberg. LC 96-35409. 216p. 1997. 49.95 (*1-56639-509-7*); pap. 18.95 (*1-56639-510-0*) Temple U Pr.

Lesbian & Gay Almanac & Events of 1990: Gay Games Edition. Ed. by Danni Munson. (Illus.). 160p. (Orig.). 1989. pap. 9.95 (*0-945043-02-3*) Envoy Enter.

Lesbian & Gay Book of Love & Marriage: Creating the Stories of Our Lives. Paula Martinac. LC 97-43996. (Illus.). 304p. 1998. pap. 18.00 (*0-7679-0162-2*) Broadway BDD.

Lesbian & Gay Christian Movement: Campaigning for Justice, Truth & Love. Sean Gill. 256p. 1998. 69.95 (*0-304-33778-1*); pap. 19.95 (*0-304-33779-X*) Continuum.

Lesbian & Gay Counseling: A Practice Primer. Barret & Logan. (Counseling Ser.). 2001. pap. text 27.00 (*0-534-55084-3*) Wadsworth Pub.

Lesbian & Gay Families: Redefining Parenting in America. Jill S. Pollack. (Changing Family Ser.). 128p. (YA). (gr. 9-12). 1995. lib. bdg. 24.00 (*0-531-11207-1*) Watts.

Lesbian & Gay Families: Redefining Parenting in America. Jill S. Pollack. (Changing Family Ser.). (Illus.). 144p. (YA). (gr. 9 up). 1995. pap. 9.00 (*0-531-15749-0*) Watts.

Lesbian & Gay Images: An Entertainment Media Resource. GLAAD Staff. 88p. 1995. 14.95 (*0-9648910-0-X*) GLAAD.

Lesbian & Gay Issues: A Resource Manual for Social Workers. Ed. by Hilda Hidalgo et al. LC 84-25585. 220p. 1984. pap. text 20.95 (*0-87101-127-1*) Natl Assn Soc Wkrs.

Lesbian & Gay Issues in the English Classroom: The Importance of Being Honest. Simon Harris. (English, Language & Education Ser.). 160p. 1990. 31.95 (*0-335-15194-9*) OpUniv Pr.

Lesbian & Gay Liberation in Canada: A Selected Annotated Chronology, 1964-75. Donald W. McLeod. (Illus.). 320p. 1996. pap. 30.00 (*1-55022-273-2*, Pub. by ECW) LPC InBook.

Lesbian & Gay Lifestyles: A Guide for Counseling & Education. Ed. by Natalie J. Woodman et al. LC 92-1135. 300p. 1992. pap. 14.95 (*0-685-50058-6*) Irvington.

Lesbian & Gay Marriage: Private Commitments, Public Ceremonies. Ed. by Suzanne Sherman. LC 92-9299. (Illus.). 288p. (C). 1992. 34.95 (*0-87722-974-0*); pap. 19.95 (*0-87722-975-9*) Temple U Pr.

Lesbian & Gay Memphis: Building Communities Behind the Magnolia Curtain. Daneel Buring. LC 97-41476. (Studies in American Popular History & Culture). 284p. 1997. text 61.00 (*0-8153-2990-3*) Garland.

Lesbian & Gay Nurses. Jeffrey Zurlinden. (Professional Reference - Nursing Ser.). 256p. 1996. pap. 34.95 (*0-8273-6970-0*) Delmar.

Lesbian & Gay Parenting Handbook: Creating & Raising Our Families. April Martin. LC 92-54782. 416p. 1993. pap. 16.00 (*0-06-096929-6*, Perennial) HarperTrade.

Lesbian & Gay Psychology: Theory, Research & Clinical Applications. Ed. by Beverly Greene & Gregory M. Herek. LC 94-155258. (Contemporary Prespectives on Lesbian & Gay Issues Ser.: Vol. 1). (C). 1994. text 52.00 (*0-8039-5311-9*); pap. text 23.95 (*0-8039-5312-7*) Sage.

Lesbian & Gay Rights: The Legal Controversies. Patricia A. Cain. (New Perspectives on Law, Culture & Society Ser.). 288p. 2000. pap. text 24.00 (*0-8133-2617-6*) Westview.

Lesbian & Gay Studies: A Critical Introduction. Andy Medhurst & Sally Munt. LC 98-101793. (Illus.). 400p. 1997. 69.95 (*0-304-33881-8*); pap. 22.95 (*0-304-33882-6*) Continuum.

***Lesbian & Gay Studies & the Teaching of English: Positions, Pedagogies & Cultural Politics.** Ed. by William J. Spurlin. 288p. 2000. pap. write for info. (*0-8141-2794-0*, 27940) NCTE.

Lesbian & Gay Studies Reader. Ed. by Henry Abelove et al. 800p. (gr. 13). 1993. pap. 28.99 (*0-415-90519-2*, A6621) Routledge.

Lesbian & Gay Visions of Ireland: Towards the Twenty-First Century. Ed. by Ide O'Carroll & Eoin Collins. (Lesbian & Gay Studies). 288p. 1996. pap. 21.95 (*0-304-33229-1*) Continuum.

Lesbian & Gay Visions of Ireland: Towards the Twenty-First Century. Ed. by Ide O'Carroll & Eoin Collins. (Lesbian & Gay Studies). 288p. 1997. 69.95 (*0-304-33227-5*) Continuum.

***Lesbian & Gay Voices: An Annotated Bibliography & Guide to Literature for Children & Young Adults.** Frances Ann Day. LC 00-21074. 296p. 2000. 35.00 (*0-313-31162-5*, GR1162, Greenwood Pr) Greenwood.

Lesbian & Gay Wedding Album: A Documentary Planner for Lesbian & Gay Couples. Ed. by Phillip Lynch. LC 96-40112. (Illus.). 1998. 23.00 (*0-934172-23-4*) WIM Pubns.

Lesbian & Gay Wedding Album: An All-in-One Photo Documentary Planner. Ed. by Phillip Lynch. LC 96-40112. (Illus.). 1998. 45.00 (*0-934172-24-2*) WIM Pubns.

Lesbian & Gay Writing: An Anthology of Critical Essays. Ed. by Mark Lilly. 220p. 1990. 27.95 (*0-87722-706-3*) Temple U Pr.

Lesbian & Gay Youth: Care & Counseling. Caitlin Ryan & Donna Futterman. 256p. 1998. 47.50 (*0-231-11190-8*); pap. 22.50 (*0-231-11191-6*) Col U Pr.

***Lesbian Art in America: A Contemporary History.** Harmony Hammond. (Illus.). 208p. 2000. text 50.00 (*0-8478-2248-6*) Rizzoli Intl.

Lesbian Bedtime Stories. Ed. by Terry Woodrow. 272p. (Orig.). 1989. pap. 9.95 (*0-9615129-1-1*) Tough Dove.

Lesbian Bedtime Stories, No. 2. Ed. by Terry Woodrow. 280p. (Orig.). 1990. pap. 10.95 (*0-9615129-2-X*) Tough Dove.

Lesbian Body. Monique Wittig. Tr. by David Le Vay from FRE. LC 85-47943. 165p. 1986. reprint ed. pap. 13.00 (*0-8070-6307-X*) Beacon Pr.

Lesbian Choices. Claudia Card. LC 94-12527. (Between Men - Between Women Ser.). 320p. 1994. 41.00 (*0-231-08008-5*) Col U Pr.

Lesbian Choices. Claudia Card. 1995. pap. 19.00 (*0-231-08009-3*) Col U Pr.

Lesbian Configurations. Renee C. Hoogland. LC 96-38895. (Between Men - Between Women Ser.). 168p. 1997. 47.50 (*0-231-10906-7*); pap. 17.50 (*0-231-10907-5*) Col U Pr.

***Lesbian Couples: A Guide to Creating Healthy Relationships.** 3rd ed. D. Merilee Clunis & G. Dorsey Green. 288p. 2000. pap. 15.95 (*1-58005-041-7*, Pub. by Seal Pr WA) Publishers Group.

Lesbian Couples Guide. J. McDaniel. LC 95-14601. 288p. 1995. pap. 14.00 (*0-06-095021-8*) HarpC.

***Lesbian Crossword.** 160p. 2000. pap. 9.95 (*1-892514-35-4*) Hill St Pr.

Lesbian Desire in India. Giti Thadani. (Sexual Politics Ser.). 256p. 1996. pap. 17.95 (*0-304-33452-9*) Continuum.

Lesbian Desire in the Lyrics of Sappho. Jane M. Snyder. LC 96-31981. 1997. 47.50 (*0-231-09994-0*) Col U Pr.

***Lesbian Desire in the Lyrics of Sappho.** Jane M. Snyder. (Between Men - Between Women Ser.). 347p. 1998. pap. 17.50 (*0-231-09995-9*) Col U Pr.

Lesbian Epiphanies: Women Coming Out in Later Life. Karol L. Jensen. LC 99-13599. 230p. 1999. pap. 19.95 (*1-56023-964-6*, Harrington Park) Haworth Pr.

***Lesbian Epiphanies: Women Coming Out in Later Life.** Karol L. Jensen. LC 99-13599. 230p. 1999. 49.95 (*1-56023-963-8*, Harrington Park) Haworth Pr.

Lesbian Erotic Cookbook. Ffiona Morgan. LC 98-71933. (Illus.). 218p. 1998. pap. 22.95 (*1-880130-08-4*) Daughters Moon.

Lesbian Erotic Dance: Butch, Femme, Androgyny, & Other Rhythms. Jo Ann Loulan. LC 90-10177. 304p. (Orig.). 1990. pap. 12.95 (*0-933216-76-9*) Spinsters Ink.

Lesbian Erotics. Ed. by Karla Jay. (The Cutting Edge: Lesbian Life & Literature Ser.). (Illus.). 320p. (C). 1995. text 50.00 (*0-8147-4221-1*); pap. text 18.50 (*0-8147-4225-4*) NYU Pr.

Lesbian Ethics: Toward New Value. Sarah L. Hoagland. (Series in Lesbian & Feminist Theory). 368p. (Orig.). 1988. pap. 14.95 (*0-934903-03-4*) Inst Lesbian.

Lesbian Family Life Cycle. Suzanne Slater. 1995. 25.00 (*0-02-920895-5*) Free Pr.

Lesbian Family Life Cycle. Suzanne Slater. LC 98-29598. 272p. 1999. pap. 14.95 (*0-252-06783-5*) U of Ill Pr.

Lesbian Family Relationships in American Society: The Making of an Ethnographic Film. Maureen A. Asten. LC 96-36314. 160p. 1997. 52.95 (*0-275-95642-3*, Praeger Pubs) Greenwood.

Lesbian Film Guide: An Essential A-Z guide to the Celluloid Lesbian. Alison Darren. LC 99-43640. (Sexual Politics Ser.). (Illus.). 224p. 1999. pap. 15.95 (*0-304-33376-X*) Continuum.

Lesbian Friendships: For Ourselves & Each Other. Ed. by Jacqueline S. Weinstock & Esther D. Rothblum. LC 96-10114. (Illus.). 300p. (C). 1996. text 50.00 (*0-8147-7472-5*); pap. text 19.00 (*0-8147-7473-3*) NYU Pr.

Lesbian, Gay, & Bisexual Identities in Families: Psychological Perspectives. Ed. by Charlotte J. Patterson & Anthony R. D'Augelli. LC 97-44736. 320p. 1998. pap. 29.95 (*0-19-511050-1*); text 60.00 (*0-19-511049-8*) OUP.

Lesbian, Gay & Bisexual Identities over the Lifespan: Psychological Perspectives. Ed. by Anthony R. D'Augelli & Charlotte J. Patterson. 472p. 1996. reprint ed. pap. 27.50 (*0-19-510899-X*) OUP.

Lesbian, Gay, & Bisexual Youths & Adults: Knowledge for Human Services Practice. Ski Hunter. LC 98-8872. 232p. 1998. 32.00 (*0-8039-5886-2*); pap. 14.99 (*0-8039-5887-0*) Sage.

Lesbian, Gay, Bisexual & Transgender Campus Organizing: A Comprehensive Manual. Curtis F. Shepard. 1996. pap. 24.00 (*0-9652779-0-9*) Natl Gay & Lesbian.

Lesbian Gothic: Transgressive Fictions. Paulina Palmer. LC 99-12385. 160p. 1999. 49.95 (*0-304-70153-X*); pap. 19.95 (*0-304-70154-8*) Continuum.

Lesbian Health. Institute of Medicine Staff. LC 99-6101. 200p. 1999. 34.95 (*0-309-06093-1*); pap. 19.95 (*0-309-06567-4*) Natl Acad Pr.

Lesbian Health: What Are the Issues? Ed. by Phyllis N. Stern. LC 93-3686. 1993. 20.95 (*1-56032-299-3*) Hemisp Pub.

Lesbian Health Book: Caring for Ourselves. Ed. by Jocelyn C. White & Marissa C. Martinez. LC 97-18091. (Illus.). 392p. (Orig.). 1997. pap. 18.95 (*1-878067-31-1*) Seal Pr WA.

Lesbian Heresy. Shelia Jeffreys. 208p. 1993. pap. 17.95 (*1-875559-17-5*, Pub. by SpiniFex Pr) LPC InBook.

Lesbian Idol: Martina, K. D. & the Consumption of Lesbian Masculinity. Louise Allen. LC 97-224836. (Sexual Politics Ser.). 184p. 1997. pap. text 18.95 (*0-304-33819-2*) Continuum.

Lesbian Idol: Martina, K. D. & the Consumption of Lesbian Masculinity. Louise Allen. LC 97-224836. (Sexual Politics Ser.). 1997. 69.95 (*0-304-33818-4*) Continuum.

Lesbian Images. Ann Rule. (C). 1989. pap. 16.95 (*0-7453-0366-8*) Westview.

Lesbian Issue: Essays from Signs. Ed. by Estelle B. Freedman et al. LC 84-16246. 326p. 1985. pap. 22.95 (*0-226-26152-2*) U Ch Pr.

Lesbian Land. Ed. by Joyce Cheney. (Illus.). 200p. 1985. pap. 15.00 (*0-9615605-0-9*) Word Weavers.

Lesbian Lifestyles: Women's Work & the Politics of Sexuality. Gillian A. Dunne. 240p. 1996. text 50.00 (*0-8020-4104-3*); pap. text 18.95 (*0-8020-7951-2*) U of Toronto Pr.

***Lesbian Lives: Identity & Autobiography in the Twentieth Century.** Nicky Hallett. LC 99-15330. 240p. 1999. 59.95 (*0-7453-1132-6*, Pub. by Pluto GBR); pap. 18.95 (*0-7453-1131-8*, Pub. by Pluto GBR) Stylus Pub VA.

Lesbian Lives: Psychoanalytic Narratives Old & New. Maggie Magee & Diana C. Miller. LC 97-35034. 448p. 1997. 55.00 (*0-88163-269-4*) Analytic Pr.

Lesbian Looks: Postcards from the Edge. Ed. by Belinda Budge. (Illus.). 88p. 1994. pap. 14.95 (*1-85727-096-7*, Pub. by Scarlet Pr) LPC InBook.

Lesbian Love Advisor. Celeste West. (Illus.). 216p. 1989. pap. 9.95 (*0-939416-26-3*) Cleis Pr.

Lesbian Love Advisor: The Sweet & Savory Arts of Lesbian Courtship. Celeste West. (Illus.). 190p. (Orig.). 1997. reprint ed. pap. 12.00 (*0-912932-17-1*) Booklegger Pubng.

Lesbian Love Companion: How To Survive Everything From Heartthrob to Heartbreak. Marny Hall. LC 97-33290. 240p. 1998. pap. 15.00 (*0-06-251431-8*) HarpC.

Lesbian Love Signs: An Astrological Guide to Women Loving Women. Aurora. (Illus.). 130p. 1991. pap. 8.95 (*0-89594-467-7*) Crossing Pr.

Lesbian Menace: Ideology, Identity, & the Representation of Lesbian Life. Sherrie A. Inness. LC 96-53173. 272p. 1997. pap. 17.95 (*1-55849-091-4*); text 40.00 (*1-55849-090-6*) U of Mass Pr.

Lesbian Motherhood: An Exploration of Canadian Lesbian Families. Fiona Nelson. 176p. 1996. text 50.00 (*0-8020-0765-1*) U of Toronto Pr.

Lesbian Motherhood: An Exploration of Canadian Lesbian Families. Fiona Nelson. 176p. 1996. pap. text 18.95 (*0-8020-7135-X*) U of Toronto Pr.

Lesbian Motherhood in Europe. Ed. by Kate Griffin & Lisa Mulholland. LC 97-182812. (Sexual Politics Ser.). 227p. 1997. pap. 21.95 (*0-304-33312-3*) Continuum.

Lesbian Mothers: Accounts of Gender in American Culture. Ellen Lewin. LC 92-54977. (Anthropology of Contemporary Issues Ser.). 256p. 1993. text 39.95 (*0-8014-2857-2*); pap. text 15.95 (*0-8014-8099-X*) Cornell U Pr.

Lesbian Nuns. Rosemary Curb & Nancy Manahan. 400p. 1986. mass mkt. 5.95 (*0-446-32659-3*, Pub. by Warner Bks) Little.

Lesbian Origins. rev. ed. Susan Cavin. LC 85-18158. Orig. Title: An Hystorical & Cross-Cultural Analysis of Sex Ratios, Female Sexuality, & Homosexual Segregation Versus Heterosexual Integration Patterns in Relation to the Liberation of Women. (Illus.). 288p. 1985. 18.00 (*0-910383-16-2*); pap. 12.00 (*0-910383-15-4*) Ism Pr.

Lesbian (Out) Law: Survival under the Rule of Law. Ruthann Robson. LC 92-8333. 188p. (Orig.). 1992. pap. 9.95 (*1-56341-012-5*); lib. bdg. 20.95 (*1-56341-013-3*) Firebrand Bks.

Lesbian Panic: Homoerotics in Modern British Women's Fiction. LC 96-48366. (Between Men - Between Women Ser.). 1997. 52.00 (*0-231-10620-3*) Col U Pr.

Lesbian Panic: Homoerotics in Modern British Women's Fiction. Patricia J. Smith. LC 96-48366. (Between Men - Between Women Ser.). 1997. pap. 17.50 (*0-231-10621-1*) Col U Pr.

Lesbian Parenting. Ed. by Katherine Arnup. LC 95-188265. 432p. 1995. pap. 16.95 (*0-921881-33-9*) LPC InBook.

Lesbian Parenting Book: A Guide to Creating Families & Raising Children. D. Merilee Clunis & G. Dorsey Green. LC 95-14905. 396p. (Orig.). 1995. pap. 16.95 (*1-878067-68-0*) Seal Pr WA.

Lesbian Passages: True Stories Told by Women over 40. rev. ed. Marcy Adelman. Orig. Title: Long Time Passing: Lives of Older Lesbians. 256p. 1996. pap. text 11.95 (*1-55583-365-9*) Alyson Pubns.

Lesbian Passion: Loving Ourselves & Each Other. Jo Ann Loulan. LC 87-60781. 325p. (Orig.). 1987. pap. 12.95 (*0-933216-29-7*) Spinsters Ink.

Lesbian Path. enl. rev. ed. Ed. by Margaret L. Cruikshank. LC 85-12519. 232p. 1985. reprint ed. pap. 10.95 (*0-912516-96-8*) Grey Fox.

Lesbian Philosophies & Cultures. Ed. by Jeffner Allen. LC 90-9554. (SUNY Series in Feminist Philosophy). 410p. (C). 1990. text 44.50 (*0-7914-0383-1*); pap. text 16.95 (*0-7914-0384-X*) State U NY Pr.

Lesbian Philosophy: Explorations. Jeffner Allen. (Series in Lesbian & Feminist Theory). 120p. (Orig.). 1986. pap. 9.95 (*0-934903-86-7*) Inst Lesbian.

Lesbian Photo Album: The Lives of Seven Lesbian Feminists. Cathy Cade. LC 87-50503. (Illus.). 144p. (Orig.). 1987. pap. 14.95 (*0-9618453-2-5*) Waterwomen Bks.

***Lesbian Polyamory Reader: Open Relationships, Non-Monogamy & Casual Sex.** Ed. by Marcia Munson & Judith P. Stelboum. LC 99-10965. 242p. 1999. 49.95 (*0-7890-0660-X*) Haworth Pr.

Lesbian Polyamory Reader: Open Relationships, Non-Monogamy & Casual Sex. Ed. by Marcia Munson & Judith P. Stelboum. LC 99-10965. 274p. 1999. pap. 24.95 (*1-56023-120-3*, Harrington Park) Haworth Pr.

Lesbian Polyfidelity: How to Keep Nonmonogamy Safe, Sane, Honest & Laughing, You Rogue. Celeste West. (Illus.). 352p. 1996. 25.00 (*0-912932-16-3*); pap. 15.00 (*0-912932-15-5*) Booklegger Pubng.

Lesbian Portraits. MQ Publications Staff. (Infatuations Ser.). 1998. 12.95 (*1-897954-92-1*, Pub. by Mus Quilts Pub) Sterling.

Lesbian Postmodern. Laura Doan. LC 94-187096. (Between Men - Between Women Ser.). 267p. 1994. 61.00 (*0-231-08410-2*); pap. 19.00 (*0-231-08411-0*) Col U Pr.

Lesbian Psychologies: Explorations & Challenges. Ed. by Boston Lesbian Psychologies Collective. LC 86-30736. 384p. (C). 1987. 16.95 (*0-252-01404-9*); text 34.95 (*0-252-01403-0*) U of Ill Pr.

***Lesbian Pulp.** Susan Stryker. 142p. 2000. pap. 12.95 (*0-8118-2183-8*) Chronicle Bks.

Lesbian Reader. Ed. by Gina Covina & Laurel Galana. 1975. pap. 8.95 (*0-9609626-0-3*, Amazon Pr) Barn Owl Bks.

Lesbian S-M Safety Manual. Ed. by Pat Califia. 80p. 1988. pap. 7.95 (*1-55583-301-2*) Alyson Pubns.

Lesbian Sacred Sexuality. Diane Mariechild. LC 94-4125. (Illus.). 144p. (Orig.). 1995. pap. 27.50 (*0-914728-81-4*) Wingbow Pr.

Lesbian Sex. Jo Ann Loulan. LC 84-52008. (Illus.). 320p. (Orig.). 1984. pap. 12.95 (*0-933216-13-0*) Spinsters Ink.

Lesbian Sex: An Oral History. Susan Johnson. 336p. (Orig.). 1996. pap. 14.95 (*1-56280-142-2*) Naiad Pr.

Lesbian Sex Book: A Guide for Women Who Love Women. Wendy Caster. LC 93-71122. (Illus.). 192p. 1998. pap. 15.95 (*1-55583-211-3*) Alyson Pubns.

Lesbian Sex Scandals: Sexual Practices, Identities, & Politics. Ed. by Dawn Atkins. 145p. 1998. 39.95 (*0-7890-0547-6*, Harrington Park) Haworth Pr.

Lesbian Sex Scandals: Sexual Practices, Identities & Politics. Ed. by Dawn Atkins. LC 98-34517. 150p. 1998. 49.95 (*0-7890-0548-4*, Harrington Park); pap. 19.95 (*1-56023-118-1*, Harrington Park) Haworth Pr.

***Lesbian Sex Secrets for Men: What Every Man Wants to Know about Making Love to a Woman & Never Asks.** Amy Jo Goddard et al. 256p. 2000. pap. 12.95 (*0-452-28133-4*, Plume) Dutton Plume.

Lesbian Social Services: Research Issues. Ed. by Carol T. Tully. LC 95-32130. (Journal of Gay & Lesbian Social Services: Vol. 3, No. 1). 106p. 1995. 29.95 (*1-56024-750-9*); pap. 9.95 (*1-56023-071-1*, Harrington Park) Haworth Pr.

Lesbian Sources: A Bibliography of Periodical Articles, 1970-1990. Linda Garber. LC 92-21941. (Gay & Lesbian Studies: Vol. 9). 736p. 1992. text 30.00 (*0-8153-0782-9*, H1557) Garland.

Lesbian Speaker's Bureau. Janell Moon. Ed. by Clarinda Harriss. (Illus.). 28p. (Orig.). 1996. pap. 8.00 (*0-932616-53-4*, 932616) Brick Hse Bks.

Lesbian Stages: Plays by Sarah Dreher. Sarah Dreher. LC 88-61508. 300p. (Orig.). 1988. pap. 9.95 (*0-934678-15-4*) New Victoria Pubs.

Lesbian Step Families: An Ethnography of Love. Janet M. Wright. LC 97-46157. 262p. 1998. lib. bdg. 39.95 (*0-7890-0436-4*) Haworth Pr.

Lesbian Step Families: An Ethnography of Love. Janet M. Wright. LC 97-46157. 262p. 1998. pap. 19.95 (*1-56023-928-X*) Haworth Pr.

Lesbian Studies: Setting an Agenda. Tamsin Wilton. LC 95-6689. 272p. (C). (gr. 13). 1995. 80.00 (*0-415-08655-8*, B4206); pap. 25.99 (*0-415-08656-6*, B4210) Routledge.

Lesbian Subjects: A Feminist Studies Reader. Martha Vicinus. LC 95-34788. (Illus.). 284p. 1996. pap. text 16.95 (*0-253-21038-0*) Ind U Pr.

Lesbian Subjects: A Feminist Studies Reader. Martha Vicinus. LC 95-45054. (Illus.). 284p. (C). 1996. 39.95 (*0-253-33060-2*) Ind U Pr.

Lesbian Teachers: An Invisible Presence. Madiha D. Khayatt. LC 91-30545. (SUNY Series, Feminist Theory in Education). 304p. (C). 1992. text 21.50 (*0-7914-1171-0*) State U NY Pr.

Lesbian Texts & Contexts: Radical Revisions. Ed. by Karla Jay & Joanne Glasgow. (Feminist Crosscurrents Ser.). 420p. (C). 1990. pap. text 19.50 (*0-8147-4177-0*) NYU Pr.

Lesbian Therapists & Their Therapy: From Both Sides of the Couch. Ed. by Nancy D. Davis et al. LC 96-13471. (Women & Therapy Ser.: Vol. 18, No. 2). 80p. 1996. pap. 9.95 (*1-56023-082-7*, Harrington Park) Haworth Pr.

Lesbian Therapists & Their Therapy: From Both Sides of the Couch. Ed. by Nancy D. Davis et al. LC 96-13471. (Women & Therapy Ser.: Vol. 18, No. 2). 80p. 1996. 39.95 (*1-56024-800-9*, Haworth Pastrl) Haworth Pr.

Lesbian Travels: A Literary Companion. Ed. by Lucy J. Bledsoe. LC 98-37807. 218p. 1998. pap. 14.95 (*1-883513-07-3*) Whereabouts.

Lesbian Triptych. Jovette Marchessault. Tr. by Yvonne M. Klein. 150p. pap. 8.95 (*0-88961-088-6*, Pub. by Womens Pr) LPC InBook.

Lesbian Utopics. Annamarie Jagose. 224p. (C). 1994. pap. 19.99 (*0-415-91019-6*, B3837) Routledge.

Lesbian Utopics. Annamarie Jagose. 224p. (C). (gr. 13). 1994. 70.00 (*0-415-91018-8*, B3833) Routledge.

Lesbian Voices from Latin America: Breaking Ground. Elena M. Martinez. LC 95-37411. (Latin American Studies: Vol. 7). 248p. 1995. text 50.00 (*0-8153-1349-7*, SS907) Garland.

L

An Asterisk (*) at the beginning of an entry indicates that the title is appearing for the first time.

L

Lesbian Words: State of the Art. Ed. by Randy Turoff. LC 96-228060. 1995. pap. 10.95 (*1-56333-340-6*, R Kasak Bks) Masquerade.
Lesbianism. Ed. by Wayne R. Dynes & Stephen Donaldson. LC 92-15643. (Studies in Homosexuality: Vol. 7). 416p. 1992. text 77.00 (*0-8153-0552-4*) Garland.
Lesbianism: Affirming Nontraditional Roles. Esther D. Rothblum & Ellen Cole. LC 88-32028. (Women & Therapy Ser.: Vol. 8, Nos. 1-2). (Illus.). 224p. 1989. text 49.95 (*0-86656-809-3*) Haworth Pr.
Lesbianism: An Annotated Bibliography & Guide to the Literature, 1976-1986. 2nd ed. Dolores J. Maggiore. LC 92-34699. 271p. 1992. 34.50 (*0-8108-2617-8*) Scarecrow.
Lesbianism: Index of New Information. Gina S. Loggerwit. 140p. 1995. 47.50 (*0-7883-0478-X*); pap. 44.50 (*0-7883-0479-8*) ABBE Pubs Assn.
Lesbianism: Index of New Information & Bibliography. Gloria T. Werth. 150p. 1996. 47.50 (*0-7883-1012-7*); pap. 44.50 (*0-7883-1013-5*) ABBE Pubs Assn.
Lesbianism & Feminism in Germany, 1895-1910: An Original Anthology. Ed. by Jonathan N. Katz. LC 75-12332. (Homosexuality Ser.). 1975. reprint ed. 36.95 (*0-405-07369-0*) Ayer.
Lesbians & Bisexual Fiction Writers. Ed. by Harold Bloom. LC 97-4113. (Women Writers & Their Works Ser.). (Illus.). 180p. (C). 1997. 29.95 (*0-7910-4478-5*); pap. 16.95 (*0-7910-4494-7*) Chelsea Hse.
Lesbians & Child Custody: A Casebook, Vol. 8. Ed. by Dolores J. Maggiore. LC 92-5398. (Gay & Lesbian Studies). 280p. 1992. text 15.00 (*0-8153-0229-0*) Garland.
Lesbians & Gay Men: Chemical Dependency Treatment Issues. 2nd ed. Intro. by Dava L. Weinstein. LC 92-31975. (Journal of Chemical Dependency Treatment: Vol. 5, No. 1). (Illus.). 175p. 1993. pap. 14.95 (*1-56023-036-3*, Harrington Park); lib. bdg. 54.95 (*1-56024-393-7*, Harrington Park) Haworth Pr.
Lesbians & Gay Men As Foster Parents. Wendell Ricketts. (Orig.). 1991. pap. write for info. (*0-939561-09-3*) Univ South ME.
Lesbians & Gays & Sports. Perry D. Young. Ed. by Martin Duberman. LC 93-43170. (Issues in Gay & Lesbian Life Ser.). (Illus.). 154p. (YA). (gr. 9 up). 1995. 24.95 (*0-7910-2611-6*); pap. 12.95 (*0-7910-2951-4*) Chelsea Hse.
Lesbians & Gays in Couples & Families: A Handbook for Therapists. Ed. by Joan Laird & Robert-Jay Green. (Psychology Ser.). 352p. 1996. 40.95 (*0-7879-0222-5*) Jossey-Bass.
Lesbians & Lesbian Families: Reflections on Theory & Practice. Joan Laird. LC 98-36503. 363p. 1999. 49.50 (*0-231-10252-6*); 21.50 (*0-231-10253-4*) Col U Pr.
Lesbians & Lesbianisms: A Post-Jungian Perspective. Claudetta Kulkarni. LC 96-52975. 256p. (C). 1997. 75.00 (*0-415-15510-X*) Routledge.
Lesbians & Lesbianisms: A Post-Jungian Perspective. Claudette Kulkarni. LC 96-52975. 256p. (C). 1997. pap. 24.99 (*0-415-15511-8*) Routledge.
Lesbians & Psychoanalysis: Revolutions in Theory & Practice. Ed. by Judith M. Glassgold & Suzanne Iasenza. LC 95-13612. 352p. 1995. 35.00 (*0-02-874006-8*) Free Pr.
Lesbians at Midlife: The Creative Transition. Ed. by Barbara Sang et al. LC 90-24743. 288p. (Orig.). 1991. pap. 12.95 (*0-933216-77-3*) Spinsters Ink.
Lesbians, Gay Men & the Law: Cases & Materials. 2nd ed. William B. Rubenstein. LC 96-46482. (American Casebook Ser.). 918p. (C). 1996. 60.25 (*0-314-20383-4*) West Pub.
***Lesbians, Gays & the Empowerment Perspective.** Carol T. Tully. LC 99-87520. (Empowering the Powerless Ser.). 2000. pap. 22.50 (*0-231-10959-8*) Col U Pr.
***Lesbians, Gays & the Empowerment Perspective.** Carol T. Tully. LC 99-87520. (Empowering the Powerless Ser.). 2000. 49.50 (*0-231-10958-X*) Col U Pr.
***Lesbians Guide to Spain.** Perez. (Illus.). 2000. pap. text 13.00 (*84-605-9197-2*) Fundacion EFE.
Lesbians in Academia: Degrees of Freedom. Ed. by Beth Mintz & Esther D. Rothblum. LC 97-16999. 304p. (C). 1997. 75.00 (*0-415-91701-8*); pap. 21.99 (*0-415-91702-6*) Routledge.
Lesbians in Print: A Bibliography of 1500 Books with Synopses. Ed. by Margaret Gillon. LC 95-77022. 480p. (Orig.). 1995. pap. 19.50 (*1-887237-13-5*) Odd Girls Pr.
***Lesbians, Levis & Lipstick: The Meaning of Beauty in Our Lives.** Ed. by Jeanine Cogan & Joanie Erickson. LC 99-31178. (Journal of Lesbian Studies: Vol. 3, No. 4). 154p. (C). 1999. 39.95 (*0-7890-0661-8*, Harrington Park); pap. 14.95 (*1-56023-121-1*) Haworth Pr.
Lesbians of Color: Social & Human Services. Ed. by Hilda Hidalgo. LC 95-36538. 85p. 1995. 9.95 (*1-56023-072-X*, Harrington Park); 29.95 (*1-56024-751-7*) Haworth Pr.
Lesbians over Sixty Speak for Themselves. Intro. by Monika Kehoe. LC 88-24304. (Journal of Homosexuality: Vol. 16, Nos. 3-4). (Illus.). 111p. 1989. text 39.95 (*0-86656-816-6*) Haworth Pr.
Lesbians over Sixty Speak for Themselves. Intro. by Monika Kehoe. LC 88-21352. (Journal of Homosexuality Ser.: Vol. 16, Nos. 3-4). (Illus.). 111p. 1994. pap. text 9.95 (*0-918393-55-8*, Harrington Park) Haworth Pr.
Lesbians Raising Sons: An Anthology. Ed. by Jess Wells. LC 97-1109. 232p. (Orig.). 1997. pap. 14.95 (*1-55583-410-8*) Alyson Pubns.
Lesbians Talk Age & Attitude. Spike Katz. 64p. 1996. pap. text 8.95 (*1-85727-078-9*, Pub. by Scarlet Pr) LPC InBook.
Lesbians Talk Detonating the Nuclear Family. Julia Brosnan. 1996. pap. 8.95 (*1-85727-028-2*, Pub. by Scarlet Pr) LPC InBook.
Lesbians Talk Left Politics. Kristina Studinski. 1994. pap. 8.50 (*1-85727-012-6*, Pub. by Scarlet Pr) LPC InBook.
Lesbians Talk Making Black Waves. Valerie Mason-John & Ann Khambatta. 64p. 1994. pap. 8.50 (*1-85727-007-X*, Pub. by Scarlet Pr) LPC InBook.
Lesbians Talk (Safer) Sex. Sue O'Sullivan & Pratibha Parmar. 64p. (Orig.). 1992. pap. 8.50 (*1-85727-020-7*, Pub. by Scarlet Pr) LPC InBook.
Lesbians Talk Transgender. Zachary I. Nataf. Date not set. pap. 8.95 (*1-85727-008-8*, Pub. by Scarlet Pr) LPC InBook.
Lesbians Talk Violent Relationships. Joelle Taylor & Tracey Chandler. 1995. pap. 8.50 (*1-85727-032-0*) LPC InBook.
Lesbiot. Ed. by Tracy Moore. 1995. pap. 21.95 (*0-304-33158-9*) LPC InBook.
Lesbomania. Jorjet Harper. LC 94-809. (Illus.). 160p. (Orig.). 1994. pap. 9.95 (*0-934678-53-7*) New Victoria Pubs.
Lesbos - 3000 Years on an Aeolian Island. Konstantin I. Fallieros. LC 96-132462. (Illus.). 498p. (Orig.). 1995. pap. 22.95 (*0-9627950-1-1*) ISOS PC.
Les/Cabines de Bain see Bathing Huts
Leschetizky Method: A Guide to Fine & Correct Piano Playing. Malwine Bree. Tr. by Arthur Elson. (Illus.). 96p. 1997. reprint ed. pap. text 8.95 (*0-486-29596-6*, 706640Q) Dover.
Leschi, Last Chief of the Nisquallies. Cecelia S. Carpenter. (Illus.). 56p. 1986. reprint ed. pap. 5.00 (*0-945433-11-5*) Herit Quest.
Les/Convertisseurs de l'Electronique de Puissance see Power Electronic Converters: DC-DC Conversion
Les/Dernieres Nuits de Paris see Last Nights of Paris
Lese der Deutschen Lyrik: Von Klopstock bis Rilke. Ed. by Friedrich Bruns. (GER.). (Orig.). 1961. pap. text 22.95 (*0-89197-274-9*) Irvington.
Lesebogen, 25 units. Van Eunen et al. 192p. 1990. 56.00 (*3-468-49476-9*) Langenscheidt.
Lesebuchgeschichten: Traditionelle Erzaehlstoffe in Deutschsprachigen Schullesebuechern 1770-1920. Ingrid Tomkowiak. (GER.). viii, 370p. (C). 1993. lib. bdg. 160.00 (*3-11-014077-2*) De Gruyter.
Les/Eglises particulieres & La maternite de l'eglise see Motherhood of the Church
Lesekurs Deutsch. Peter F. Hainy & Horst Wirbelauer. (Lehrbuch Ser.). 108p. 1983. 14.95 (*3-468-49885-3*); 14.95 (*3-468-49888-8*); 8.95 (*3-468-49890-X*) Langenscheidt.
Lesekurs fuer Geisteswissenschaftler: Anfaenger. M. L. Brandi & B. Momenteau. (GER.). 80p. (C). 1992. pap. text 19.75 (*3-12-675360-4*, Pub. by Klett Edition) Intl Bk Import.
Lesekurs fuer Geisteswissenschaftler: Anhang Englisch. M. L. Brandi & B. Momenteau. (GER.). 72p. (C). 1992. pap. text 17.25 (*3-12-675363-9*, Pub. by Klett Edition) Intl Bk Import.
Lesekurs fuer Geisteswissenschaftler: Fortgeschrittene. M. L. Brandi & B. Momenteau. (GER.). 209p. (C). 1992. pap. text 33.25 (*3-12-675361-2*, Pub. by Klett Edition) Intl Bk Import.
Lesen Als Verstehen. Swantje Ehlers. Ed. by Gerd Neuner. (Fernstudienangebot Ser.). (GER.). 112p. 1996. 11.25 (*3-468-49678-8*) Langenscheidt.
Lesen, na Und? Boschma et al. 104p. 1987. 13.00 (*3-468-49466-1*) Langenscheidt.
Lesen und Sprechen. 144p. 1996. 13.00 (*3-468-49462-9*) Langenscheidt.
Leser und Lekture des 18: Jahrnunderts Die Ausleibucher der Herzog August Bibliothek Wolfenbuttel, 1715-1800, 4 vols. Compiled by Mechthild Raabe. (GER.). 400p. 1987. write for info. (*0-318-61906-7*); write for info. (*0-318-61907-5*); write for info. (*0-318-61908-3*) K G Saur Verlag.
Leser und Lekture des 18: Jahrnunderts Die Ausleibucher der Herzog August Bibliothek Wolfenbuttel, 1715-1800, 4 vols., Band 1: Einleitung-Alphabetischer Katalog. Compiled by Mechthild Raabe. (GER.). 400p. 1987. lib. bdg. 160.00 (*3-598-10651-3*) K G Saur Verlag.
Lesespass. Boog et al. 88p. 1989. text 19.25 (*3-468-49467-X*); text, teacher ed. 11.25 (*3-468-49468-8*) Langenscheidt.
Lesestoff Nach Wahl, Vol. 3. Ursula Thomas & Freeman Twaddell. LC 76-11321. (GER.). 117p. 1977. reprint ed. pap. 36.30 (*0-608-02212-8*, 206251400003) Bks Demand.
Lesestoff Nach Wahl, Vol. 4. Ursula Thomas & Freeman Twaddell. LC 76-11321. (GER.). 116p. 1977. reprint ed. pap. 36.00 (*0-608-02213-6*, 206251400004) Bks Demand.
Lesestoff Nach Wahl, Vol. 5. Ursula Thomas & Freeman Twaddell. LC 76-11321. (GER.). 144p. 1977. reprint ed. pap. 44.70 (*0-608-02214-4*, 206251400005) Bks Demand.
Lesestoff Nach Wahl, Vol. 6. Ursula Thomas & Freeman Twaddell. LC 76-11321. (GER.). 214p. 1977. reprint ed. pap. 66.40 (*0-608-02210-1*, 206251400006) Bks Demand.
Lesestoff Nach Wahl Vol. 1: Einfuhrung. Ursula Thomas. LC 76-11321. (GER., Illus.). 175p. 1977. reprint ed. pap. 54.30 (*0-7837-9797-4*, 206251400001) Bks Demand.
Lesestoff Nach Wahl Vol. 2: Physik & Chemie. Ursula Thomas & Freeman Twaddell. LC 76-11321. (GER.). 111p. 1977. reprint ed. pap. 34.50 (*0-608-02211-X*, 206251400002) Bks Demand.
Les/Etats-Unis et la Strategie Alimentaire Mondiale see American Green Power
Les/Fourrures et les Grands lacs cahier a colorier see Great Lakes Fur Trade Coloring Book
Les/Georgiques see Georgics
Les/Grandes Marees see Spring Tides
Les/Hommes Dans la Prison see Men in Prison
Lesikar's Basic Business Communication. 7th ed. Raymond Vincent Lesikar et al. 128p. (C). 1995. text, student ed. 23.43 (*0-256-14079-0*, Irwn McGrw-H) McGrw-H Hghr Educ.
Lesikar's Basic Business Communication. 8th ed. Raymond Vincent Lesikar & Marie E. Flatley. LC 98-21173. 1998. 77.00 (*0-07-292990-1*) McGraw.
Lesikar's Basic Business Communication. 8th ed. Raymond Vincent Lesikar & John D. Pettit. 640p. 1998. pap., student ed. 71.88 (*0-07-561942-3*) McGraw.
Lesion Analysis in Neuropsychology. Hanna Damasio & Antonio R. Damasio. (Illus.). 256p. 1989. text 59.50 (*0-19-503919-X*) OUP.
Lesionado en el Trabajo: Una Guia del Sistema de Compensacion Laboral en Massachusetts. Philip S. Korman. Tr. by Translation Center, U Mass. Staff. (SPA.). 200p. (Orig.). 1996. pap. 9.95 (*0-9648873-1-2*) Wstrn MassCOSH.
Lesions. Flora Durham. 36p. (Orig.). 1996. pap. 4.00 (*1-882550-17-X*) Quiet Lion Pr.
***Lesions of Genetic Sin.** limited ed. Bruce Boston. (Illus.). 1999. 4.00 (*0-9676666-0-0*) Miniature Sun Pr.
Lesions of the Jawbone: Radiographic Features. Vivian J. Harris. (Illus.). 192p. 1983. 32.50 (*0-87527-212-6*) Green.
Lesiure & Society in Colonial Brazzaville. Phyllis M. Martin. (African Studies: No. 87). (Illus.). 295p. (C). 1996. text 64.95 (*0-521-49551-2*) Cambridge U Pr.
Lesko's Info-Power, Vol. 2. Matthew Lesko. 1600p. 1993. pap. 29.95 (*0-8103-9485-5*) Visible Ink Pr.
Leskos Info-Power III: Special Edition. 1996. 29.95 (*0-7876-1049-6*) Gale.
Lesko's Info-Power III. 3rd ed. Matthew Lesko. Ed. by Andrew Naprawa. 1519p. 1996. pap. text 39.95 (*1-878346-37-7*) Info USA.
Lesko's Info Power III, Vol. III. 3rd ed. Matthew Lesko. 1600p. 1996. 29.95 (*0-7876-0880-7*) Visible Ink Pr.
Les/Larmes d'Eros see Tears of Eros
***Leslie.** Walter J. Frazier. 1999. pap. write for info. (*1-58235-327-1*) Watermrk Pr.
Leslie: Historical Records of the Family of Leslie, 3 vols. K. H. Leslie. 1991. reprint ed. pap. 134.50 (*0-8328-2159-4*); reprint ed. lib. bdg. 144.50 (*0-8328-2158-6*) Higginson Bk Co.
Leslie: History of the Early Life & Business Interests of the Village & Township of Leslie, Ingham County. Arranged & Compiled by Mina A. Vliet et al. (Illus.). 120p. 1997. reprint ed. pap. 17.50 (*0-8328-6769-1*); reprint ed. lib. bdg. 27.50 (*0-8328-6768-3*) Higginson Bk Co.
Leslie Bassett: A Bio-Bibliography, 52. Ellen S. Johnson. LC 93-44461. (Bio-Bibliographies in Music Ser.: No. 52). 192p. 1994. lib. bdg. 65.00 (*0-313-25851-1*, Greenwood Pr) Greenwood.
***Leslie Beck's Coordinated Kitchen: Creative Projects You Can Make.** Leslie Beck. (Illus.). 128p. 2000. pap. 27.95 (*1-56477-350-7*) Martingale & Co.
***Leslie Bricusse Book of Love Songs: Cherry Lane Music.** Cherry Lane Music Company Staff. 1998. otabind 19.95 (*1-57560-101-X*, Pub. by Cherry Lane) H Leonard.
Leslie Bricusse Christmas Songbook. Ed. by Milton Okun. 94p. (YA). Date not set. pap. 17.95 (*1-57560-025-0*, Pub. by Cherry Lane) H Leonard.
Leslie Bricusse Movie Songbook. Leslie Bricusse. pap. 19.95 (*0-685-75232-1*) Cherry Lane.
Leslie Bricusse Theatre Book. Ed. by Milton Okun. 224p. (YA). pap., per. 24.95 (*0-89524-882-4*, 02502148) Cherry Lane.
***Leslie County, Kentucky Marriages 1884-1894.** Richard E. Sampson. 99p. 2000. pap. 14.50 (*0-7884-1380-5*, 1380) Heritage Bk.
***Leslie Fiedler & American Culture.** Steven G. Kellman & Irving Malin. LC 99-18961. 1999. write for info. (*0-87413-689-X*) U Delaware Pr.
Leslie Lewis Doud: His Family & Ancestors. Robert D. Martin & Laurel M. Doud. LC 93-80964. (Illus.). 33p. reprint ed. pap. 30.00 (*0-7837-6970-9*, AU0044800004) Bks Demand.
Leslie Lindsey Mason Collection. Boston Museum of Fine Arts Staff. (Music Book Index Ser.). 503p. 1992. reprint ed. lib. bdg. 99.00 (*0-685-59992-2*) Rprt Serv.
Leslie Linsley's Country Christmas Crafts: More Than 70 Quick & Easy Projects. Leslie Linsley. (Illus.). 160p. 1995. pap. 18.95 (*0-312-13535-1*) St Martin.
Leslie Linsley's 15-Minute Decorating Ideas. Leslie Linsley. (Illus.). 269p. 1996. pap. 12.95 (*0-312-14117-3*, St Martin Griffin) St Martin.
Leslie Linsley's High-Style, Low-Cost Decorating Ideas. Leslie Linsley. LC 99-26230. 237p. 1999. pap. 12.95 (*0-312-19908-2*, St Martin Griffin) St Martin.
Leslie Linsley's Quick Christmas Decorating Ideas. Leslie Linsley. LC 96-18925. (Illus.). 160p. 1996. pap. 9.95 (*0-312-14643-4*) St Martin.
Leslie Marmon Silko. Salyer. LC 97-37697. 1997. 32.00 (*0-8057-1624-6*) Mac Lib Ref.
Leslie Marmon Silko. Per Seyersted. LC 80-70460. (Western Writers Ser.: No. 45). (Illus.). 50p. 1980. pap. 4.95 (*0-88430-069-2*) Boise St U W Writ Ser.
***Leslie Marmon Silko: A Collection of Critical Essays.** Ed. by Louise K. Barnett & James L. Thorson. LC 98-58048. 296p. 1999. 45.00 (*0-8263-2033-3*) U of NM Pr.
Leslie Marmon Silko: A Study of the Short Fiction. Jaskoski. LC 97-36410. 1998. 29.00 (*0-8057-0868-5*) Macmillan.
Leslie Moren: Fifty Years an Eldo County Doctor. Intro. by Owen C. Bolstad. (Great Basin History of Medicine Ser.: No. 2). (Illus.). 182p. 1992. lib. bdg. 42.00 (*1-56475-353-0*) U NV Oral Hist.
***Leslie Neumann: The Temporal & the Celestial.** Daniel E. Stetson. (Illus.). 16p. 1999. pap. 1.00 (*0-9619219-7-8*) Polk Mus Art.
Leslie Nielsen: The Naked Truth. Leslie Nielsen. 1994. pap. 10.00 (*0-671-79578-3*) PB.
Leslie Nielsen's Stupid Little Golf Book. Leslie Nielsen. 144p. 1995. 17.50 (*0-385-47598-5*) Doubleday.
Leslie S. Kofoed: Kofoed's Meanderings in Lovelock Business, Nevada Government, the U. S. Marshal's Office, & the Gaming Industry. Jerome E. Edwards. 370p. 1972. lib. bdg. 55.50 (*1-56475-115-5*); fiche. write for info. (*1-56475-116-3*) U NV Oral Hist.
Leslie Scalopino. Joan L. Scalopino. 1988. 5.00 (*0-944521-11-8*) Dia Ctr Arts.
Leslie Stephen: His Thought & Character in Relation to His Time. Noel G. Annan. Ed. by Walter P. Metzger. LC 76-55199. (Academic Profession Ser.). (Illus.). 1977. reprint ed. lib. bdg. 29.95 (*0-405-10028-0*) Ayer.
Leslie Stephen: The Godless Victorian. Noel G. Annan. LC 85-24714. (Illus.). 448p. 1986. pap. 17.95 (*0-226-02106-8*) U Ch Pr.
Leslie Stephen & Matthew Arnold As Critics of Wordsworth. John D. Wilson. LC 72-2060. (English Biography Ser.: No. 31). 1972. reprint ed. lib. bdg. 75.00 (*0-8383-1455-4*) M S G Haskell Hse.
Leslie Stephen, His Thought & Character in Relation to His Time. Noel G. Annan. LC 75-30015. reprint ed. 52.50 (*0-404-14021-1*) AMS Pr.
Leslie Stephen's Life in Letters. Gillian Fraser. 476p. 1993. 104.95 (*0-85967-912-8*, Pub. by Scolar Pr) Ashgate Pub Co.
Leslie Weatherhead's the Will of God a Workbook. Rebecca Laird. 96p. (Orig.). 1995. pap. 7.95 (*0-687-00840-9*) Abingdon.
Leslie's Famous Leaders & Battle Scenes of the Civil War. 2nd ed. (Illus.). 540p. 1998. reprint ed. 295.00 (*0-938530-65-8*) Lexikos.
***Leslie's Journal.** Allan Stratton. 176p. (YA). (gr. 8 up). 2000. 18.95 (*1-55037-665-9*, Pub. by Annick Pr); per. 6.95 (*1-55037-664-0*, Pub. by Annick Pr) Firefly Bks Ltd.
Leslie's Story: A Book about a Girl with Mental Retardation. Text by Martha McNey. LC 95-35621. (Illus.). (J). 1996. lib. bdg. 21.27 (*0-8225-2576-3*, Lerner Publctns) Lerner Pub.
Lesly's Handbook of Public Relations & Communications. 35th ed. Philip Lesley. LC 96-40864. (Illus.). 224p. 1997. 100.00 (*0-8442-3257-2*, 35272) NTC Contemp Pub Co.
Les/Mervelles De Rigomer see Marvels of Rigomer: Les Mervelles de Rigomer
Les/Mots Pour le Dire see Words to Say It
Les/Murailles de Samaris see Story of Fantastic: The Great Walls of Samaris
Lesney's Matchbox Toys: Regular Wheel Years, 1947-1969. Charlie Mack. LC 92-60637. (Illus.). 144p. 1992. pap. 16.95 (*0-88740-434-0*) Schiffer.
Lesney's Matchbox Toys: The Superfast Years, 1969-1982. Charlie Mack. LC 92-63103. (Illus.). 128p. (Orig.). 1993. pap. 19.95 (*0-88740-463-4*) Schiffer.
Lesney's Matchbox Toys: The Superfast Years, 1969-1982. 2nd rev. ed. Charlie Mack. (Illus.). 128p. (Orig.). 1999. pap. 19.95 (*0-7643-0772-X*) Schiffer.
Lesniewski's Systems: Ontology & Mereology. Ed. by Jan T. Srzednicki & V. F. Rickey. 262p. 1986. lib. bdg. 153.00 (*90-247-2879-7*, Pub. by M Nijhoff) Kluwer Academic.
Le/Soldat Oublie see Forgotten Soldier
Lesotho, Vol. 3. 2nd rev. ed. Deborah Johnston. LC 97-181195. (World Bibliographical Ser.). 238p. 1997. lib. bdg. 74.00 (*1-85109-247-1*) ABC-CLIO.
***Lesotho: A Country Study Guide.** Global Investment & Business Center, Inc. Staff. (World Country Study Guides Library: Vol. 96). (Illus.). 350p. 2000. pap. 59.00 (*0-7397-2394-4*) Intl Business Pubns.
Lesotho - A Country Study Guide: Basic Information for Research & Pleasure. Global Investment Center, USA Staff. (World Country Study Guide Library: Vol. 96). (Illus.). 350p. 1999. pap. 59.00 (*0-7397-1493-7*) Intl Business Pubns.
***Lesotho Business Intelligence Report, 190 vols.** Global Investment & Business Center, Inc. Staff. (World Business Intelligence Library: Vol. 96). (Illus.). 350p. 2000. pap. 99.95 (*0-7397-2594-7*) Intl Business Pubns.
***Lesotho Foreign Policy & Government Guide.** Global Investment & Business Center, Inc. Staff. (World Foreign Policy & Government Library: Vol. 92). (Illus.). 350p. 1999. pap. 99.00 (*0-7397-3590-X*) Intl Business Pubns.
***Lesotho Foreign Policy & Government Guide.** Global Investment & Business Center, Inc. Staff. (World Foreign Policy & Government Library: Vol. 92). (Illus.). 350p. 2000. pap. 99.95 (*0-7397-3794-5*) Intl Business Pubns.
Lesotho Herders Video Project: Explorations in Visual Anthropology. Chuck Scott. (Illus.). 126p. 1994. 21.00 (*87-89825-04-7*, Pub. by Intervention Pr) Smyrna.
***Lesotho Investment & Business Guide.** Global Investment & Business Center, Inc. Staff. (Global Investment & Business Guide Library: Vol. 96). (Illus.). 2000. pap. 99.95 (*0-7397-1794-4*) Intl Business Pubns.
***Lesoto Business Law Handbook, 190 vols.** Global Investment & Business Center, Inc. Staff. (Global Business Law Handbooks Library: Vol. 96). (Illus.). 350p. 2000. pap. 99.95 (*0-7397-1993-9*) Intl Business Pubns.
***Lesoto Business Opportunity Yearbook.** Global Investment & Business Center, Inc. Staff. (Global Business Opportunity Yearbooks Library: Vol. 96). (Illus.). 2000. pap. 99.95 (*0-7397-2194-1*) Intl Business Pubns.

An Asterisk (*) at the beginning of an entry indicates that the title is appearing for the first time.

*Lesoto Business Opportunity Yearbook: Export-Import, Investment & Business Opportunities. International Business Publications, U. S. A. Staff & Global Investment Center, U. S. A. Staff. (Global Business Opportunity Yearbooks Library: Vol. 96). (Illus.). 350p. 1999. pap. 99.95 (0-7397-1294-2) Intl Business Pubns.
Les/Penetenciers: Un Systeme a Abattre see Prisons in Canada
L'Esprit de Famille: Level B. Janine Boissard. text 8.95 (0-8219-1065-5) EMC-Paradigm.
L'Esprit du don see World of the Gift
Less: Minimalist Design. Mel Byars. (Pro-Design Ser.). 1998. pap. text 39.50 (0-8230-6793-9) Watsn-Guptill.
Less Common Metals in Proteins & Nucleic Acid Probes. C. B. Allan et al. Ed. by M. J. Clarke. LC 99-164802. (Structure & Bonding Ser.: Vol. 92). (Illus.). 170p. 1998. 139.00 (3-540-63925-X) Spr-Verlag.
Less Competitive College Grants & Loans. Student College Aid Staff. Ed. by Barbara E. Komer. 240p. (Orig.). 1992. pap. 16.95 (0-932495-05-2) Student Coll.
Less Developed Countries & the World Trading System. Diana Tussie. LC 86-20399. 250p. 1987. text 35.00 (0-312-48158-6) St Martin.
Less Expensive Spread: The Delights & Dilemmas of a Weekend Cowboy. Irving Townsend. (Illus.). 1990. reprint ed. pap. 11.95 (0-9617426-3-1) J N Townsend.
Less Garbage Overnight: A Waste Prevention Guide for the Lodging Industry. John P. Winter & Sharene L. Azimi. 1996. pap. 30.00 (0-918780-66-7) INFORM NY.
Less Important Than Opulence the Conservatives & Dence. Christopher Coker. (C). 1990. 55.00 (0-907967-92-2, Pub. by Inst Euro Def & Strat) St Mut.
Less Is More: Every Creature Can Make a World of Difference. Alison Klassen. (Illus.). 32p. (J). (gr. k-5). 1994. 15.95 (1-880092-20-4) Bright Bks TX.
Less Is More: Simple, Healthful Recipes with Less Fuss. Julee Rosso. LC 96-31767. 1998. pap. 18.95 (0-517-88524-7, Crown) Crown Pub Group.
Less Is More: Simple, Healthful Recipes with Less Fuss. Julee Rosso. LC 96-31767. 1999. 30.00 (0-517-70285-1) Random Hse Value.
Less Is More: The Art of Voluntary Poverty. Ed. by Goldian VandenBroeck. LC 94-44249. 336p. 1996. pap. text 14.95 (0-89281-554-X) Inner Tradit.
*Less Is More: The New Simplicity in Graphic Design. Steven Heller & Anne Fink. LC 99-22715. (Illus.). 160p. 1999. 34.99 (0-89134-899-9, 31369, North Lght Bks) F & W Pubns Inc.
*Less Legible Meanings: Between Poetry & Philosophy in the Work of Emerson. Pamela J. Schirmeister. LC 99-39450. (Illus.). 242p. 1999. 39.50 (0-8047-3015-6) Stanford U Pr.
Les's Life: A Prairie Boyhood, 1914-1929. Lester D. Kirkham. Ed. by Shirley F. McDermott. LC 95-118225. (Illus.). 126p. (Orig.). 1994. pap. 9.95 (0-9641688-0-4) Uncommon Buffalo.
Les's Life: A Prairie Manhood, 1929-1940. Lester D. Kirkhart. Ed. by Shirley F. McDermott. LC 98-11943. (Illus.). 15p. 1998. pap. 9.95 (0-9641688-2-0) Uncommon Buffalo.
Less Noble Sex: Scientific, Religious, & Philosophical Conceptions of Woman's Nature. Nancy Tuana. LC 92-47411. (Race, Gender, & Science Ser.). 240p. 1993. pap. 13.95 (0-253-20830-0) Ind U Pr.
*Less of Her: (Poems) Paula McLain. (New Issues Press Poetry Ser.). 64p. 1999. 22.00 (0-932826-81-4, Pub. by WMU Poetry & Prose); pap. 12.00 (0-932826-82-2, Pub. by WMU Poetry & Prose) Partners Pubs Grp.
Less of the Same: A Guide for the Bored, the Unappreciated, & the Unemployed. Dale Dauten. 1996. 22.00 (0-614-15442-1, Wm Morrow) Morrow Avon.
Less Stress, More Happiness. Hua-Ching Ni. (Healthy Living Ser.). 32p. (Orig.). 1994. pap. 3.00 (0-937064-55-6) SevenStar Comm.
Less Stress, Please. (Dialog Ser.). 128p. 1992. pap. 6.50 (0-8341-1407-0); pap., teacher ed. 5.50 (0-8341-1406-2) Beacon Hill.
Less Suffering for Everybody: An Introduction to Panetics. R. G. Siu. LC 93-61384. 243p. 1994. pap. 25.00 (1-884437-01-X) Intl Soc Panetics.
Less-Taxation & More Democracy, the Amendment 6 Prescription for Prosperity Looking at the Pros & Cons. Duane Parde. 16p. 1988. pap. text 8.00 (1-57655-115-6) Independ Inst.
Less Than Entirely Sanctified. Doug Hall. LC 91-44964. (Illus.). 104p. (Orig.). 1992. pap. 6.99 (0-8308-1833-2, 1833) InterVarsity.
Less Than Forever: The Rise & Decline of Union Solidarity in Western Pennsylvania, 1914-1948. Carl I. Meyerhuber, Jr. LC 86-62504. 240p. 1987. 39.50 (0-941664-27-9) Susquehanna U Pr.
Less Than Half, More Than Whole. Kathleen LaCapa. (gr. 1-3). 1998. pap. text. write for info. (0-87358-734-0) Northland AZ.
Less Than Half, More Than Whole. Kathleen Lacapa & Michael Lacapa. LC 94-13132. (Illus.). 40p. (J). (gr. 1-3). 1994. lib. bdg. 14.95 (0-87358-592-5, Rising Moon Bks) Northland AZ.
Less Than Half, More Than Whole. Kathleen LaCapa & Michael LaCapa. (Illus.). 40p. (J). (gr. 1-3). 1998. pap. 7.95 (0-87358-731-6, Rising Moon Bks) Northland AZ.
Less Than Human. Gary Raisor. Ed. by Lauri Hinchberger. (Illus.). 256p. (C). 1992. 29.95 (0-9633397-0-2) Overlook Connect.
Less Than Human. aut. limited ed. Gary Raisor. Ed. by Lauri Hinchberger. (Illus.). 256p. (C). 1992. boxed set 45.00 (0-9633397-1-0) Overlook Connect.
Less Than Kind. large type ed. David Armstrong. (Linford Mystery Large Print Ser.). 336p. 1998. pap. 17.99 (0-7089-5262-3, Linford) Ulverscroft.
Less Than Meets the Eye: Foreign Policymaking & the Myth of the Assertive Congress. Barbara Hinckley. LC 93-36084. 264p. (C). 1994. pap. 13.95 (0-226-34144-5); lib. bdg. 34.95 (0-226-34143-7) U Ch Pr.
Less Than Nothing Is Really Something. Robert Froman. LC 72-7546. (Young Math Ser.). (Illus.). (J). (gr. 1-5). 1973. 11.06 (0-690-48862-9) HarpC Child Bks.
Less Than One: Selected Essays. Joseph Brodsky. 501p. 1986. text 30.00 (0-374-18503-4) FS&G.
Less Than One: Selected Essays. Joseph Brodsky. 448p. 1987. pap. 16.00 (0-374-52055-0) FS&G.
Less Than Overweight. Bern Porter. 500p. 1993. 30.00 (0-9638236-0-4) Plaster Cramp.
Less Than Perfect Horse: Problems Encountered & Solutions Explained. Jane Wallace. (Illus.). 288p. 1991. pap. 29.95 (1-872119-13-1) Half Halt Pr.
Less Than Perfect Rider: Overcoming Common Riding Problems. Lesley Bayley & Caroline Davis. LC 93-33471. (Illus.). 160p. 1994. per. 29.95 (0-87605-976-0) Howell Bks.
Less Than Sharp Show. Ed. by Howard Kaplan. LC 77-77524. 1977. pap. 4.00 (0-932026-01-X) Columbia College Chi.
Less Than Slaves: Jewish Forced Labor & the Quest for Compensation. Benjamin B. Ferencz. LC 79-10690. 275p. reprint ed. pap. 85.30 (0-7837-2257-5, 205734500004) Bks Demand.
Less Than Zero. Bret Easton Ellis. LC 97-53236. 1998. pap. 12.00 (0-679-78149-8) Vin Bks.
Less Than Zero: The Case for a Falling Price Level in a Growing Economy. George Selgin. (IEA Hobart Paper Ser.: No. 132). 82p. 1997. pap. 22.50 (0-255-36402-4, Pub. by Inst Economic Affairs) Coronet Bks.
Less Time to Do More: Psychotherapy on the Short-Term Inpatient Unit. Ed. by Ellen Leibenluft et al. LC 93-20081. 321p. 1993. text 19.95 (0-88048-512-4, 8512) Am Psychiatric.
Less-Toxic Alternatives. Carolyn P. Gorman. LC 99-189650. 176 p. 1997. write for info. (1-57397-009-3) Optimum Pubng.
Less Traveled Road & the Bible: A Scriptural Critique of the Philosophy of M. Scott Peck. H. Wayne House & Richard Abanes. (And the Bible Ser.: Bk. 3). 248p. (Orig.). 1995. pap. 10.99 (0-88965-117-5, 0021175, Pub. by Horizon Books) Chr Pubns.
L'Essai Therapeutiques Chez L'Homme see Clinical Trials
Lessening Political Violence in South Africa: The CODESSA Decision. Daniel R. Kempton. (Pew Case Studies in International Affairs). 50p. 1994. pap. text 3.50 (1-56927-366-9, GU Schl Foreign) Geo U Inst Dplmcy.
Lesser Antilles: Barbados & Grenada to the Virgin Islands. R. C. C. Pilotage Foundation/SHOM Staff. Ed. by O. Robinson. (Illus.). 256p. 1991. 125.00 (0-85288-153-3, Pub. by Laurie Norie & Wilson Ltd) St Mut.
Lesser Antilles: Grenada to the Virgin Islands. Wilson Ltd. Staff & Imray L. Norie. (C). 1991. 194.00 (0-7855-5908-6, Pub. by Laurie Norie & Wilson Ltd) St Mut.
Lesser Antilles in the Age of European Expansion. Ed. by Robert L. Paquette & Stanley L. Engerman. LC 95-45478. (Illus.). 432p. (C). 1996. 49.95 (0-8130-1428-X) U Press Fla.
Lesser Bird of Paradise: Selected Poems, 1979-1989. Timothy M. Riordan. (Illus.). 115p. (Orig.). 1990. pap. 19.95 (0-9625817-0-4) In Hse Bks.
Lesser Brother. Jeri Massi. 124p. (Orig.). (YA). (gr. 11). 1989. pap. 5.95 (1-877778-02-8) Llama Bks.
Lesser Bushbaby (Galago) As an Animal Model: Selected Topics. Ed. by Duane E. Haines. 376p. 1982. 200.00 (0-8493-6321-7, QL737, CRC Reprint) Franklin.
Lesser Child: An Autobiography. Karen Gershon et al. (Illus.). 198p. 1994. 33.00 (0-7206-0899-6, Pub. by P Owen Ltd) Dufour.
Lesser Eastern Churches. Adrian Fortescue. LC 79-168124. reprint ed. 45.00 (0-404-02517-X) AMS Pr.
Lesser Evil: The Democratic Party. Lenni Brenner. 1988. 19.95 (0-8184-0482-5) Carol Pub Group.
Lesser Goods & Other Poems. Coburn Britton. 64p. 1988. pap. 8.95 (0-86316-106-5) Writers & Readers.
Lesser Key of Solomon. L. W. De Laurence. 15.95 (0-685-22016-8) Wehman.
*Lesser Key of Solomon. Ed. by L. W. De Laurence. 90p. 1999. reprint ed. pap. 12.95 (0-7661-0776-0) Kessinger Pub.
*Lesser Kindred. Elizabeth Kerner. 2001. text 22.95 (0-312-89066-4) St Martin.
Lesser-Known Aircraft & Projects. (Illus.). (Orig.). 1992. pap. 2.50 (0-9618861-1-0) BCFK Pubns.
Lesser Known Areas of the National Park System. (Illus.). 49p. (Orig.). (C). 1994. pap. text 15.00 (0-7881-0327-X) DIANE Pub.
Lesser Known 16 or 20 Pages. Mark Sonnenfeld. 28p. 1997. pap. 3.00 (1-887379-13-4) M Sonnenfeld.
Lesser-Known Women: A Biographical Dictionary. Beverly E. Golemba. LC 91-41182. 380p. 1992. lib. bdg. 29.95 (1-55587-301-4) L Rienner.
Lesser Life. Hewlett. 1987. mass mkt. 10.95 (0-446-38511-5, Pub. by Warner Bks) Little.
Lesser Life: The Myth of Women's Liberation in America. Sylvia A. Hewlett. 464p. 1987. pap. 10.95 (0-446-39122-0) Warner Bks.
Lesser Lives. Diane Johnson. 256p. 1999. pap. 10.95 (0-452-27738-8) Viking Penguin.
Lesser Metaphysical Poets: A Bibliography, 1961-1980. William E. McCarron. LC 83-448. (Checklists in the Humanities & Education Ser.: No. 7). 64p. reprint ed. pap. 30.00 (0-8357-6351-X, 203562600096) Bks Demand.
Lesser of 2 Evils: Eastern European Jewry under Soviet Rule. Dov Levin. 1995. 29.95 (0-8276-0518-8) JPS Phila.
Lesser People: America's Real Problem. Jim Means. 104p. (Orig.). 1997. pap. 9.95 (1-880710-03-X) Monterey Pacific.
Lesser Terror: Soviet State Security, 1939-1953. Michael Parrish. LC 94-38565. 456p. 1996. 69.50 (0-275-95113-8, Praeger Pubs) Greenwood.
Lesser Vehicle. John Drew. 1986. pap. 10.95 (0-906427-71-1, Pub. by Bloodaxe Bks) Dufour.
Lessico Dei Romanzieri Greci, Band 1. Ed. by F. Conca et al. (GER.). 167p. 1983. 60.00 (0-318-70474-9) G Olms Pubs.
Lessico Dei Romanzieri Greci, Band 3. Ed. by F. Conca et al. (GER.). 250p. 55.00 (3-487-09749-4) G Olms Pubs.
Lessico Dei Romanzieri Greci, Band 4. Ed. by F. Conca et al. (Alpha-Omega, Reihe A Ser.: Bd. LXXVIII). (GER.). 250p. write for info. (0-318-70477-3) G Olms Pubs.
Lessico Dei Romanzieri Greci, 4 vols., Set. Ed. by Fabrizio Conca et al. (Alpha-Omega, Reihe A Ser.: Bd. LXXVIII). (GER.). ii, 289p. 1989. 55.00 (3-487-09080-5) G Olms Pubs.
Lessico Dei Romanzieri Greci, Vol. 4. Ed. by Simone Beta. (Alpha-Omega, Reihe A Ser.: Vol. LXXVIII). (GER.). 378p. 1997. write for info. (3-487-10556-X) G Olms Pubs.
Lessing, 2 vols. in 1. Erich Schmidt. xii, 1311p. 1983. reprint ed. write for info. (3-487-07317-X) G Olms Pubs.
Lessing Als Wegbereiter der Emanzipation der Frau. Beate Sturges. (Enlightment: Vol. 1). 180p. (C). 1990. text 44.80 (0-8204-0801-8) P Lang Pubng.
Lessing & the Drama. F. J. Lamport. 254p. (C). 1982. text 39.00 (0-19-815767-3) OUP.
Lessing & the Enlightenment. Ed. by Alexej Ugrinsky. LC 66-11080. (Contributions to the Study of World Literature Ser.: No. 15). 230p. reprint ed. pap. 71.30 (0-608-30787-4, 201004100072) Bks Demand.
Lessing & the Enlightenment, 15. Ed. by Alexej Ugrinsky. LC 85-27251. (Contributions to the Study of World Literature Ser.: No. 15). 196p. 1986. 52.95 (0-313-25313-7, ULE/, Greenwood Pr) Greenwood.
Lessing in Heutiger Sicht: Supplement to Lessing Yearbook. Ed. by E. P. Harris & Richard E. Schade. 348p. 1977. 20.00 (3-87447-231-0) Lessing Soc.
Lessing und die Toleranz: Supplement to the Lessing Yearbook. Ed. by Peter Freimark et al. 374p. 1986. 20.00 (3-88377-248-8) Lessing Soc.
Lessing und Zinzendorf: Eine vergleichende Studie zu Lessings Glauben. Peter Willmer. (American University Studies: Germanic Languages & Literature: Ser. I, Vol. 72). VI, 224p. (C). 1988. text 33.00 (0-8204-0837-9) P Lang Pubng.
*Lessing Yearbook. Ed. by Georg Braungart et al. 2000. 39.95 (3-89244-325-4) Wayne St U Pr.
Lessing Yearbook. Ed. by Richard E. Schade. 1998. 39.95 (3-89244-288-6) Wayne St U Pr.
Lessing Yearbook, Vol. XXIX. Ed. by Richard E. Schade. 1998. 39.95 (0-8143-2814-8) Wayne St U Pr.
*Lessing Yearbook, Vol. XXX. Ed. by Georg Braungart et al. 1999. 39.95 (0-8143-2847-4) Lessing Soc.
*Lessing Yearbook, Vol. XXXI. Ed. by Richard Schade. 2000. 39.95 (0-8143-2930-6) Wayne St U Pr.
Lessing Yearbook VIII. Ed. by E. P. Harris. 322p. 1976. 15.00 (3-19-006797-X) Lessing Soc.
Lessing Yearbook XVIII. Ed. by Richard E. Schade. 301p. 1986. 37.50 (0-8143-1822-3) Lessing Soc.
Lessing Yearbook XI. Ed. by E. P. Harris. 278p. 1979. 15.00 (3-19-006919-0) Lessing Soc.
Lessing Yearbook XV. Ed. by E. P. Harris. 309p. 1983. 37.50 (0-8143-1759-6) Lessing Soc.
Lessing Yearbook V. Ed. by J. Glenn. 291p. 1973. 12.50 (0-318-20527-0, 6753) Lessing Soc.
Lessing Yearbook IV. Ed. by Markus F. Motsch. 247p. 1972. 12.50 (0-318-20524-6, 6741) Lessing Soc.
Lessing Yearbook XIV. Ed. by E. P. Harris & L. W. Wucherpfennig. 300p. 1982. 37.50 (0-8143-1733-2) Lessing Soc.
Lessing Yearbook Index to Volumes I-XX & the Supplements. Contrib. by Edward Dvoretzky. 30p. 1994. 29.95 (0-317-05917-3) Lessing Soc.
Lessing Yearbook Index to Volumes I-XX & the Supplements. Ed. by Edward Dvoretzky. 298p. 1994. text 34.95 (0-8143-2521-1) Wayne St U Pr.
Lessing Yearbook IX. Ed. by E. P. Harris. 302p. 1977. 15.00 (3-19-006904-2) Lessing Soc.
Lessing Yearbook XIX. Ed. by Richard E. Schade. (Illus.). 368p. 1988. 42.50 (0-8143-1963-7) Lessing Soc.
Lessing Yearbook I. Ed. by J. Glenn. 294p. 1969. 10.50 (0-318-20520-3, 6682) Lessing Soc.
Lessing Yearbook VII. Ed. by E. P. Harris. 278p. 1975. 15.00 (3-19-006792-9) Lessing Soc.
Lessing Yearbook XVII. Ed. by Richard E. Schade. 319p. 1986. 37.50 (0-8143-1799-5) Lessing Soc.
Lessing Yearbook VI. Ed. by J. Glenn. 260p. 1974. 12.50 (3-19-006767-8) Lessing Soc.
Lessing Yearbook XVI. Ed. by E. P. Harris & Richard E. Schade. 378p. 1984. 37.50 (0-8143-1787-1) Lessing Soc.
Lessing Yearbook X. Ed. by Richard E. Schade & J. Glenn. 261p. 1978. 15.00 (3-19-006913-1) Lessing Soc.
Lessing Yearbook XIII. Ed. by Richard E. Schade. 345p. 1982. 15.00 (0-8143-1681-6) Lessing Soc.
Lessing Yearbook III. Ed. by J. Glenn. 281p. 1971. 10.50 (0-318-20523-8, 6724) Lessing Soc.
Lessing Yearbook XII. Ed. by E. P. Harris. 300p. 1981. 37.50 (0-614-07852-0) Lessing Soc.
Lessing Yearbook XX. Ed. by Richard E. Schade. 378p. 1989. 18.00 (0-8143-2113-5) Lessing Soc.
Lessing Yearbook XXVIII. Ed. by Katharina Gerstenberger & Richard E. Schade. 1997. 42.50 (0-8143-2680-3) Wayne St U Pr.
Lessing Yearbook XXV. Ed. by Richard E. Schade. 1994. 24.00 (0-8143-2487-8) Lessing Soc.
Lessing Yearbook XXIV. Ed. by Richard E. Schade. 223p. 1993. 24.00 (0-8143-2462-2) Lessing Soc.
Lessing Yearbook XXI. Ed. by Richard E. Schade. 322p. 1990. 18.00 (0-8143-2251-4) Lessing Soc.
Lessing Yearbook XXVII. Ed. by Richard E. Schade & Katharina Gerstenberger. 1996. 24.00 (0-8143-2628-5) Lessing Soc.
Lessing Yearbook XXVI. Ed. by Richard E. Schade & Susanne Kord. 1995. 24.00 (0-8143-2569-6) Lessing Soc.
Lessing Yearbook XXII. Ed. by Richard E. Schade. 311p. 1992. 24.00 (0-8143-2371-5) Lessing Soc.
Lessing Yearbook II. Ed. by J. Glenn. 261p. 1970. 10.50 (0-318-20522-X, 6698) Lessing Soc.
Lessings Anglophilie. Jutta Meise. (Europaische Aufklarung in Literatur und Sprache Ser.: No. 10). XI, 238p. 1997. 51.95 (3-631-31301-2) P Lang Pubng.
Lessings Denkmal. W. Gustav Grossmann. 360p. 1997. reprint ed. 90.00 (3-487-10258-7) G Olms Pubs.
Lessing's Dramatic Theory. Ed. by John G. Robertson. LC 63-14713. (Illus.). 1972. 36.95 (0-405-08894-9) Ayer.
Lessing's Education of the Human Race. John D. Haney. LC 77-176835. (Columbia University. Teachers College. Contributions to Education Ser.: No. 20). reprint ed. 37.50 (0-404-55020-7) AMS Pr.
Lessings Philotas: Aesthetisches Experiment mit satirischer Wirkungsabsicht. Ein Beitrag zur Quellenforschung, Text-und Wirkungsgeschichte. Jutta G. Schmidt. (GER.). 253p. (C). 1988. text 39.00 (0-8204-0746-1) P Lang Pubng.
Lessings Saemtliche Schriften, 23 vols., Set. 3rd ed. Gotthold Ephraim Lessing. Ed. by Karl Lachmann. (C). 1968. reprint ed. 1523.10 (3-11-005161-3) De Gruyter.
Lessing's Theological Writings: Selections in Translation. Gotthold Ephraim Lessing. Tr. by Henry Chadwick. 110p. 1957. reprint ed. pap. 10.95 (0-8047-0335-3) Stanford U Pr.
Lessing's "Ugly Ditch" A Study of Theology & History. Gordon E. Michalson, Jr. LC 84-42991. 224p. (C). 1985. 29.50 (0-271-00385-5) Pa St U Pr.
*Lesslie Newbigin: A Theological Life /c Geoffrey Wainwright. Geoffrey Wainwright. LC 99-45907. 480p. 2000. text 65.00 (0-19-510171-5) OUP.
Lesson see Four Plays
*Lesson: A Fable for Our Times. Carol L. Pearson. LC 98-4353. (Fable for Our Times Ser.). (Illus.). 32p. 1998. 9.95 (0-87905-862-5) Gibbs Smith Pub.
*Lesson Before Dying. Cliffs Notes Staff. (Cliffs Notes Ser.). 80p. 1999. 4.95 (0-7645-8503-7) IDG Bks.
Lesson Before Dying. Ernest J. Gaines. 1997. 25.00 (0-679-45561-2) Random.
Lesson Before Dying. Ernest J. Gaines. (Vintage Contemporaries Ser.). 1994. 17.10 (0-606-07150-4, Pub. by Turtleback) Demco.
Lesson Before Dying. Ernest J. Gaines. LC 93-42201. 272p. 1994. pap. 12.00 (0-679-74166-6) Vin Bks.
Lesson Before Dying. Ernest J. Gaines. 256p. 1997. pap. 12.00 (0-375-70270-9) Vin Bks.
Lesson Book: Level C, Willard A. Palmer et al. (Alfred's Basic Piano Library). 1990. pap. 5.95 (0-88284-828-3) Alfred Pub.
Lesson Book Level 1: God's Full Salvation. Living Street Ministry Staff. 113p. 1990. per. 6.00 (0-87083-521-1, 16-018-001) Living Stream Ministry.
Lesson Book Level 1B: Teacher's Guide. Willard A. Palmer et al. (Basic Piano Library). 48p. 1986. pap. write for info. (0-7390-0864-1, 8650) Alfred Pub.
Lesson Book Level 2: Teacher's Guide. Willard A. Palmer et al. (Basic Piano Library). 48p. 1986. pap., teacher ed. write for info. (0-7390-0865-X, 9180) Alfred Pub.
Lesson Book Level 2: Triune God & the Person & Work of Christ. Living Street Ministry Staff. 131p. 1990. per. 6.25 (0-87083-522-X, 16-019-001) Living Stream Ministry.
Lesson Book Level 3: 2 Spirits - Divine Spirit & the Human Spirit. Living Street Ministry Staff. 181p. 1990. per. 7.50 (0-87083-523-8, 16-020-001) Living Stream Ministry.
Lesson Book Level 5: Vision & Building of the Church. Living Street Ministry Staff. 294p. 1990. per. 10.50 (0-87083-525-4, 16-022-001) Living Stream Ministry.
Lesson Book Level 6 - Bible: The Word of God. Living Street Ministry Staff. 342p. 1991. per. 11.75 (0-87083-594-7, 16-023-001) Living Stream Ministry.
Lesson-Drawing in Public Policy: A Guide to Learning Across Time & Space. Richard Rose. LC 92-36205. 192p. (C). 1993. pap. text 21.95 (0-934540-32-2, Chatham House Pub) Seven Bridges.
Lesson for Janie. Dorothy Simpson. 190p. Date not set. 20.95 (0-8488-2617-5) Amereon Ltd.
*Lesson Forgotten: Minority Protection under the League of Nations: The Case of the German Minority in Poland, 1920-1934. Christian Raitz von Frentz. LC 99-52701. 2000. text 65.00 (0-312-23111-3) St Martin.
Lesson from Aloes. Athol Fugard. LC 80-6040. 96p. 1989. reprint ed. pap. 6.95 (1-55936-001-1) Theatre Comm.
Lesson from History: The Integration of Immigrants in the Pastoral Practice of the Church in the United States see Pastoral Series
Lesson from the Past: The Silver Panic of 1893. Lawrence W. Reed. 93p. (Orig.). 1993. pap. 7.95 (0-910614-90-3) Foun Econ Ed.
Lesson in Dying. large type ed. Ann Cleeves. 336p. 1992. 27.99 (0-7089-2566-9) Ulverscroft.
Lesson in Music: Poems. Jean Daive. Tr. by Julie Kalendek from FRE. (Serie d'Ecriture: No. 6). 64p. 1992. pap. 6.00 (0-930901-80-0) Burning Deck.

L

An Asterisk (*) at the beginning of an entry indicates that the title is appearing for the first time.

L

Lesson in School Reform from Great Britain. John E. Chubb & Terry M. Moe. 76p. (C). 1992. pap. 8.95 (*0-8157-1411-4*) Brookings.

Lesson in Seduction. Susan Napier. (Presents Ser.). 1997. per. 3.50 (*0-373-11870-8*, 1-11870-8) Harlequin Bks.

Lesson in Seduction. large type ed. Susan Napier. (Harlequin Romance Ser.). 1997. 20.95 (*0-263-15069-0*) Thorndike Pr.

Lesson of Balzac see Works of Henry James Jr.: Collected Works

Lesson of Her Death. Jeffery Deaver. 528p. 1994. mass mkt. 6.50 (*0-553-56020-4*) Bantam.

Lesson of Life. Mother. 180p. 1985. pap. 6.00 (*0-89071-322-7*, Pub. by SAA) Acrpls Bks CO.

Lesson of Life. Mother. 182p. 1997. pap. 6.95 (*81-7058-474-4*, Pub. by SAA) E-W Cultural Ctr.

Lesson of Love: Revelations of Julian of Norwich. John Julian. 1988. 12.95 (*0-8027-1029-8*) Walker & Co.

Lesson of Moogoo-Maagooville. Karen Jensen. LC 97-15739. (Illus.). 32p. (J). (gr. k-4). 1997. 16.95 (*1-880090-49-X*) Galde Pr.

Lesson of the Ancient Bones. Eric Wiggin. (Hannah's Island Ser.: Bk. 4). 150p. (Orig.). (J). (gr. 3-7). 1996. pap. 5.99 (*1-883002-27-3*) Emerald WA.

Lesson of the Master: The Death of the Lion; The Next Time & Other Tales. Henry James. LC 77-158794. (Novels & Tales of Henry James Ser.: Vol. 15). xvii, 367p. 1978. reprint ed. 39.50 (*0-678-02815-X*) Kelley.

Lesson of the 1965 Indonesian Coup. Terri Cavanagh. 58p. 1995. reprint ed. 3.00 (*1-875639-00-4*) Mehring Bks.

Lesson of the Spanish War. Alfred Thayer Mahan. (Notable American Authors Ser.). 1999. reprint ed. lib. bdg. 125.00 (*0-7812-3921-4*) Rprt Serv.

Lesson of This Century: With Two Talks on Freedom & the Democratic State. Karl R. Popper. Tr. by Patrick Camiller. LC 96-5656. 112p. (C). 1996. 30.00 (*0-415-12958-3*) Routledge.

***Lesson of This Century: With Two Talks on Freedom & the Democratic State.** Karl R. Popper. 176p. 2000. pap. 16.95 (*0-415-12959-1*) Routledge.

Lesson on Analytic Sublime. Jean-Francois Lyotard. LC 96-37014. (Deridian Ser.). 1997. pap. 24.95 (*0-8047-2763-5*) Stanford U Pr.

Lesson Plan: Coaching Students to Study the Cover Card Way. Robert Katrein. 40p. 1986. pap. 7.95 (*0-9607324-1-1*) Mr Coach.

***Lesson Plan & Record Book.** 160p. 2000. pap., teacher ed. 10.95 (*0-7439-3008-8*, TCM 3008) Tchr Create Mat.

***Lesson Plan & Record Book.** Ed. by Walter Kelly. 160p. 1999. pap., teacher ed. 10.95 (*1-57690-390-7*, TCM2390) Tchr Create Mat.

Lesson Plan Book. Teacher Created Materials Staff. (Illus.). 96p. 1998. pap., teacher ed. 7.95 (*1-57690-122-X*, TCM2122) Tchr Create Mat.

Lesson Plan for Children. 54p. 14.95 (*0-9679866-2-1*) Sq Ft Garden.

Lesson Plan for Murder. Richard L. Baldwin. LC 97-78341. (Louis Searing & Margaret McMillan Mystery Ser.). 253p. 1998. pap. 12.95 (*0-9660685-0-5*) Buttonwood.

Lesson Planning for Meaningful Variety in Teaching. 2nd ed. Richard M. Henak. 128p. 1984. reprint ed. pap. 11.95 (*0-8106-1515-0*) NEA.

Lesson Planning for Student Teachers. Peter D. John. LC 92-42793. (Education Ser.). 96p. 1993. spiral bd. 37.95 (*0-304-32625-9*) Continuum.

Lesson Plans & Modifications for Inclusion & Collaborative Classrooms. Master Teacher Staff. LC 95-79721. 203p. 1995. ring bd. 59.95 (*0-914607-37-5*) Master Tchr.

Lesson Plans & Modifications for Inclusion & Collaborative Classrooms, Bk. 2. 300p. 1996. ring bd. 59.95 (*0-914607-42-1*, 1716) Master Tchr.

Lesson Plans & Reproduction Masters Used for Teaching Children the Art of Inventing. Melvin L. Fuller & Maggie Weisberg. 100p. 1989. student ed., ring bd. 50.00 (*1-877782-01-7*) MGM & Assocs.

Lesson Plans for a Women's Guide to Business & Social Success. Ruth Tolman. 1984. pap. 23.95 (*0-87350-184-5*) Thomson Learn.

Lesson Plans for a Women's Guide to Business & Social Success. Ruth Tolman. 2001. 23.95 (*0-87350-183-7*) Thomson Learn.

***Lesson Plans for Character Education: Elementary Edition.** 210p. 1998. ring bd. 59.95 (*0-914607-53-7*, 1728) Master Tchr.

***Lesson Plans for Character Education: Secondary Edition.** 140p. 1998. ring bd. 59.95 (*0-914607-54-5*, 1729) Master Tchr.

Lesson Plans for Classroom Teachers: Kindergarten Through 2nd Grade. Robert P. Pangrazi. LC 96-46298. 87p. (C). 1996. pap. text 17.00 (*0-205-19363-3*) Allyn.

Lesson Plans for Cosmetology. 480p. 1991. text 49.95 (*1-56253-013-5*) Milady Pub.

***Lesson Plans for Dynamic Physical Education for Elementary School Children.** 4th ed. Robert P. Pangrazi. 291p. 2000. pap. 21.33 (*0-205-32631-5*) Allyn.

Lesson Plans for Dynamic Physical Education for Secondary Sc: Dynamic Physic Education. 3rd ed. Darst. 308p. 1997. pap. 26.00 (*0-205-26267-8*) Allyn.

***Lesson Plans for Integrating Technology into the Classroom: Elementary Edition.** 200p. 1998. ring bd. 49.95 (*0-914607-59-6*, 1738) Master Tchr.

***Lesson Plans for Integrating Technology into the Classroom: Secondary Edition.** 250p. 1998. ring bd. 49.95 (*0-914607-60-X*, 1739) Master Tchr.

Lesson Plans for Milady's Professional Barber-Styling. 3rd ed. Milady Staff. (Cosmetology Ser.). 216p. (C). 1998. student ed. 74.95 (*1-56253-369-X*) Milady Pub.

Lesson Plans for Professional Estheticians. Bobbi R. Madry. 1982. student ed. 17.95 (*0-87350-357-0*) Milady Pub.

Lesson Plans for Professional Estheticians: Lesson Plans. Young. (Skin Ser.). 1992. text 55.00 (*1-56253-039-9*) Milady Pub.

Lesson Plans for Salon Management for Cosmetology Students. 4th ed. Edward J. Tezak. 76p. 1992. teacher ed., ring bd. 34.95 (*1-56253-069-0*) Milady Pub.

***Lesson Plans for Service Learning.** xi, 212p. 1999. ring bd. 49.95 (*0-914607-70-7*, 1752) Master Tchr.

Lesson Plans for the Standard Textbook of Professional Barber-Styling. 164p. 1.60 (*0-87350-863-7*) Milady Pub.

Lesson Plans for the Standard Textbook of Professional Barber-Styling. 164p. 1989. ring bd. 54.95 (*0-87350-525-5*) Milady Pub.

Lesson Plans for the Van Dean Manual. Dorothy Mankiw. Ed. by Israel Rubenstein. 1977. ring bd., vinyl bd. 51.00 (*0-87350-074-1*) Milady Pub.

***Lesson Plans Incorporating Multiple Intelligences into the Curriculum & the Classroom: Elementary Edition.** 180p. 1998. ring bd. 49.95 (*0-914607-63-4*, 1741) Master Tchr.

***Lesson Plans Incorporating Multiple Intelligences into the Curriculum & the Classroom: Secondary Edition.** 280p. 1998. ring bd. 49.95 (*0-914607-64-2*, 1742) Master Tchr.

Lesson Plans to Accompany Milady's Standard Textbook of Cosmetology. Milady Publishing Company Staff. 404p. 1995. text, teacher ed. 49.95 (*1-56253-234-0*) Milady Pub.

Lesson to Learn. Penny Jordan. (Presents Ser.). 1994. per. 2.99 (*0-373-11673-X*, 1-11673-0) Harlequin Bks.

Lesson Workbook for Spending Time with the Lord. Bill Freeman. 33p. (Orig.). 1992. pap. 1.50 (*0-914271-35-0*) Mnstry Pubns.

LessonMaker - New Testament: Create Your Own Customized Bible Study on Any Passage in the New Testament in Minutes. Ed. by Navigators Staff. LC 92-81117. 432p. (Orig.). 1992. pap. 26.00 (*0-89109-688-4*) NavPress.

Lessonpack: For Creative & Critical Thinking. Vincent R. Ruggiero. 327p. 1990. 380.00 (*0-9629083-0-4*) Mindbuilding.

Lessons. Barbara Bache-Wiig. (Illus.). ii, 51p. 1997. pap. 5.00 (*1-890644-00-5*) Union Cnty.

Lessons. Mirkalice Gore. 19p. pap. 3.00 (*0-942494-43-1*) Coleman Pub.

Lessons. Melanie McAllester. LC 94-2770. 240p. 1994. pap. 9.95 (*0-933216-99-8*) Spinsters Ink.

Lessons. Myrtle R. Williams. (Illus.). 125p. 1996. pap. 10.95 (*1-884778-12-7*) Old Mountain.

Lessons. rev. ed. C. Alexander West. 312p. 1994. pap. text 25.00 (*0-942683-12-9*) Four-G Pubs.

Lessons: An Autobiography. An Wang & Eugene Linden. 288p. 1988. 17.26 (*0-201-09400-2*); pap. 9.57 (*0-201-07408-7*) Addison-Wesley.

Lessons: For Where There Is Love, There Is Hope - from a Mother Who Lost Her Child to Cancer. Susan S. Abbott. LC 96-14424. (Illus.). 1996. 4.95 (*1-56123-092-8*, LESC) Centering Corp.

Lessons All Around You. Bonnie Ronson. LC 98-67322. 76p. (C). 1998. per. 20.95 (*0-7872-5148-8*, 41514801) Kendall-Hunt.

***Lessons All Around You.** Bonnie Ronson. 348p. (C). 1999. pap. text 62.95 (*0-7872-6450-4*, 41645001) Kendall-Hunt.

Lessons & Adventures in Sales. Lloyd Allard. LC 93-8933. 296p. 1994. 17.95 (*1-56554-001-8*) Pelican.

Lessons & Legacies: Farewell Addresses from the Senate. Norman J. Ornstein. Ed. by Henning Gutmann. LC 96-46021. 240p. (Orig.). 1996. pap. 12.00 (*0-201-69579-0*) Addison-Wesley.

Lessons & Legacies: The Meaning of the Holocaust in a Changing World. Intro. by Peter Hayes. 373p. (Orig.). 1991. 49.95 (*0-8101-0955-7*); pap. 16.95 (*0-8101-0956-5*) Northwestern U Pr.

Lessons & Legacies Vol. 2: Teaching the Holocaust. Ed. by Donald G. Schilling. LC 98-154438. (Jewish & Holocaust Studies). 264p. 1998. text 59.95 (*0-8101-1562-X*); pap. text 16.95 (*0-8101-1563-8*) Northwestern U Pr.

Lessons & Legacies Vol. III: Memory, Memorialization, & Denial. Ed. by Peter Hayes. (Illus.). 280p. 1999. pap. text 24.95 (*0-8101-1666-9*) Northwestern U Pr.

Lessons & Legacies III: Memory, Memorialization, & Denial. Ed. by Peter Hayes. (Illus.). 280p. 1999. 69.95 (*0-8101-1665-0*) Northwestern U Pr.

Lessons & Questions: A Gathering of Poetic Reflections. Julia Fisher. LC 98-96472. (Illus.). v, 120p. 1998. pap. 14.95 (*0-9664837-0-7*, 0001) Crow & Elk.

Lessons & the Legacy of the Pew Health Policy Program. Institute of Medicine Staff. Ed. by Jon A. Chilingerian & Corrine M. Kay. LC 97-210200. 360p. (C). 1997. pap. text 59.50 (*0-309-05825-2*) Natl Acad Pr.

Lessons at the Fence Post. Paul D. Cummings. (Orig.). 1999. pap. 7.95 (*0-345-43287-8*, Ballantine) Ballantine Pub Grp.

Lessons at the Fence Post. Paul D. Cummings. 208p. (Orig.). 1996. pap. 7.95 (*0-9655098-0-X*) Trning Strategies.

Lessons at the Halfway Point: Wisdom for Midlife. Michael Levine. 150p. 1995. bds. 12.95 (*0-89087-744-0*) Celestial Arts.

Lessons for a 4th Grade Class. Mary Molyneux. (Illus.). 13p. 1982. 7.50 (*0-915124-74-2*) Coffee Hse.

***Lessons for Citizens of a New Democracy.** Peter C. Ordeshook. LC 97-38257. (Shaftesbury Papers: Vol. 10). 144p. (C). 1998. pap. 15.00 (*1-85898-545-5*) E Elgar.

Lessons for Leaders. A. McShane. 1996. 21.99 (*0-946351-23-6*, Pub. by John Ritchie) Loizeaux.

***Lessons for Leaders.** Homer Rice. LC 00-105059. 208p. 2000. 22.00 (*1-56352-632-8*) Longstreet.

Lessons for Life: A Complete Career Development Curriculum for Busy Educators. Bette A. Buchan & Zark Vanzandt. LC 97-28088. (Illus.). 244p. 1997. pap. text 28.95 (*0-87628-514-0*) Ctr Appl Res.

***Lessons for Life: Career Development Activities Library.** Zark Vanzandt. 1999. pap. 28.95 (*0-87628-515-9*) Ctr Appl Res.

Lessons for Life: Education & Learning. Marianne Pickering. Ed. by Beth Steinhorn. LC 94-47413. (Our Human Family Ser.). (Illus.). 80p. (YA). (gr. 7 up). 1995. lib. bdg. 22.45 (*1-56711-127-0*) Blackbirch.

***Lessons for Life: Ruthie Bolton-Holifield, 100.** Good News Publishing Company Staff. 1999. pap. 8.50 (*5-550-09544-0*) Nairi.

Lessons for Life Bk. A: Bible History Lessons & Workbook, Bk. A. Gunnar Salmonson. Ed. by David Rinden. (Lessons for Life Confirmation Instruction Ser.: Bks. A & B). (Illus.). 80p. 1997. wbk. ed. 5.95 (*0-943167-40-X*) Faith & Fellowship Pr.

Lessons for Little Ones: Language Arts & Cooperative Learning. rev. ed. Lorna Curran. (Illus.). 248p. 1994. pap. 25.00 (*1-879097-09-5*) Kagan Cooperative.

Lessons for Little Ones: Mathematics & Cooperative Learning. Lorna Curran. (Illus.). 285p. 1994. pap. text 25.00 (*1-879097-19-2*) Kagan Cooperative.

Lessons for Living from an Ugly Old Man. Richard N. Diggs. (Illus.). 178p. 1997. pap. 12.95 (*0-937157-16-3*) Progressive Pubns.

Lessons for New Believers see Lecciones para Nuevo Creyentes: Edicion Juvenil

Lessons for New Teachers. Perron. LC 99-32561. 208p. 1999. pap. 29.36 (*0-07-232446-5*) McGraw.

Lessons for Nurseries for English-Speaking Children. 2nd rev. ed. Vira Andrushkiw.Tr. of Prohrama Zajriat u Svitlychkac Dlia Ditej. 68p. 1978. pap. 3.00 (*0-317-36111-2*) UNWLA.

Lessons for Science from the Seven Countries Study. Ed. by A. Keys. 236p. 1995. 70.00 (*0-387-70140-0*) Spr-Verlag.

Lessons for Science from the Seven Countries Study: A 35-Year Collaborative Experience. H. Blackburn et al. 240p. 1994. write for info. (*4-431-70140-0*) H Blackburn.

Lessons for the Children of Godly Ancestors. Ed. by Ronald A. Bosco. LC 82-5844. (Sermon in America Ser.). 416p. 1982. 75.00 (*0-8201-1381-6*) Schol Facsimiles.

Lessons for the Future: Minorities in Math, Science, & Engineering at Community Colleges. Ed. by Enid B. Jones. 89p. 1993. pap. 15.00 (*0-87117-256-9*, 1355) Comm Coll Pr Am Assn Comm Coll.

Lessons for the Professional Actor. Michael Chekhov. Ed. by D. Deirdre Hurst. 1985. pap. 14.95 (*0-933826-80-X*) PAJ Pubns.

Lessons for the Right Brain: Complete Kit, 5 bks. Kathleen Anderson & Pamela C. Miller. 64p. 1984. pap. text 44.00 (*0-88120-212-6*, 2700) PRO-ED.

Lessons for the Right Brain: Memory Workbook. Kathleen Anderson & Pamela C. Miller. 64p. 1984. pap. text 44.00 (*0-88120-213-4*, 2701) PRO-ED.

Lessons for the Right Brain: Reading & Writing Workbook. Kathleen Anderson & Pamela C. Miller. 64p. 1984. pap. text 44.00 (*0-88120-214-2*, 2702) PRO-ED.

Lessons for the Right Brain: Self Perception-Organizing Functional Information Workbook. Kathleen Anderson & Pamela C. Miller. 64p. 1984. pap. text 44.00 (*0-88120-217-7*, 2705) PRO-ED.

Lessons for the Right Brain: Thought Organization Workbook. Kathleen Anderson & Pamela C. Miller. 64p. 1984. pap. text 44.00 (*0-88120-216-9*, 2704) PRO-ED.

Lessons for the Right Brain: Visual Perception & Attention Workbook. Kathleen Anderson & Pamela C. Miller. 64p. 1984. pap. text 44.00 (*0-88120-215-0*, 2703) PRO-ED.

Lessons for the Stage: An Approach to Acting. Julian S. Schlusberg. LC 93-37695. (Illus.). xix, 245p. (C). 1994. lib. bdg. 29.50 (*0-208-02373-9*, Archon Bks) Shoe String.

***Lessons for the Trail of Life Conversations Starters for Parents & Children.** Brian J. Cunningham. 80p. 1999. pap. 13.00 (*1-55833-223-5*) Natl Cath Educ.

Lessons for the Young. unabridged ed. Rufus Babcock. (Children's Heritage Ser.). 135p. (J). (gr. 4-6). 1996. pap. 6.98 (*1-58339-107-X*, D7) Triangle Press.

Lessons for Today. Russ. 1999. text. write for info. (*0-312-48168-3*) St Martin.

Lessons for Welfare Reform: An Analysis of the AFDC Caseload & Past Welfare-to-Work. Dave M. O'Neill & June E. O'Neill. LC 97-20524. 134p. 1997. 32.00 (*0-88099-180-1*); pap. 13.00 (*0-88099-179-8*) W E Upjohn.

Lessons from a Child: On the Teaching & Learning of Writing. Lucy M. Calkins. LC 83-8599. (Illus.). 192p. (Orig.). (C). 1983. pap. 18.00 (*0-435-08206-X*, 08206) Heinemann.

Lessons from a Father to His Son. John Ashcroft. LC 98-10178. 240p. 1998. 14.99 (*0-7852-7540-1*) Nelson.

Lessons from a Mother's Heart: Reflecting God's Love. Pamela J. Kennedy. LC 98-45943. 208p. 1999. 12.99 (*0-570-05338-2*, 12-3386GJ) Concordia.

Lessons from a Secret War. G. W. Potter. LC 97-90286. 224p. 1997. pap. 12.95 (*0-533-12355-0*) Vantage.

Lessons from a Sheepdog. W. Phillip Keller. 125p. 1988. pap. 8.99 (*0-8499-3130-4*) Word Pub.

Lessons from Abroad: Fresh Ideas from Fund-Raising Experts in the United Kingdom. Judith E. Nichols. LC 96-48040. (Illus.). 298p. 1997. 40.00 (*1-56625-080-3*) Bonus Books.

Lessons from Abroad: How Other Countries Educate Their Children. Richard McAdams. LC 93-60192. 340p. 1998. text 39.95 (*0-87762-986-2*) Scarecrow.

Lessons from Africa. Ed. by Merry M. Merryfield. (Illus.). 99p. 1989. pap. text 12.00 (*0-941339-07-6*) Ind U SSDC.

Lessons from an Ever-Evolving Therapist. Irvin Cohen, Jr. LC 96-26290. 192p. (Orig.). 1996. pap. 28.95 (*1-56887-021-3*, EETBP, Prof Resc Pr) Pro Resource.

Lessons from an Optical Illusion: On Nature & Nurture, Knowledge & Values. Edward M. Hundert. (Illus.). 288p. 1995. 24.95 (*0-674-52540-X*, HUNLES) HUP.

Lessons from an Optical Illusion: On Nature & Nurture, Knowledge & Values. Edward M. Hundert. 1995. 24.95 (*0-674-27018-5*) HUP.

Lessons from an Optical Illusion: On Nature & Nurture, Knowledge & Values. Edward M. Hundert. (Illus.). 272p. 1997. pap. text 18.00 (*0-674-52541-8*) HUP.

Lessons from Animal Diabetes: 75th Anniversary of the Insulin Industry. Ed. by Eleazar Shafrir. LC 96-216799. (Hormones in Health & Disease Ser.: Vol. 6). (Illus.). 440p. 1996. 132.00 (*0-8176-3876-8*) Birkhauser.

Lessons from Bosnia. Larry K. Wentz. LC 97-38128. 1997. write for info. (*1-57906-004-8*) Natl Defense.

Lessons from Cost-Recovery in Health No. 2: Forum on Health Sector Reform, Discussion Paper. 28p. 1995. pap. 10.80 (*0-614-32408-4*, 1932076) World Health.

Lessons from Dad: A Tribute to Fatherhood. Joan A. Ryan. 200p. 1997. pap. 10.95 (*1-55874-479-7*) Health Comm.

Lessons from Dam Incidents, U. S. A. II. 236p. 1988. 21.00 (*0-87262-661-X*) Am Soc Civil Eng.

Lessons from Defeated Presidential Candidates. Ed. by Kenneth W. Thompson. LC 94-13978. 196p. (Orig.). 1994. pap. 23.50 (*0-8191-9378-X*, Pub. by White Miller Center); pap. 52.50 (*0-8191-9377-1*, Pub. by White Miller Center) U Pr of Amer.

Lessons from Disaster. Trevor A. Kletz. 180p. 1993. 49.00 (*0-88415-154-9*) Gulf Pub.

Lessons from East Asia. Ed. by Danny M. Leipziger. LC 96-35267. 608p. (C). 1997. text 90.00 (*0-472-10679-1*, 10679) U of Mich Pr.

***Lessons from East Asia.** Ed. by Danny M. Leipziger. (Studies in International Trade Policy). (Illus.). 608p. (C). 2000. pap. text 32.95 (*0-472-08722-3*, 08722) U of Mich Pr.

Lessons from Esther. Jerri M. Lucas. 1991. pap. 6.95 (*0-89137-459-0*) Quality Pubns.

Lessons from Experience: Experiential Learning in Administrative Reforms in Eight Democracies. Ed. by Johan P. Olsen & B. Guy Peters. 339p. (C). 1996. pap. text 41.00 (*82-00-22565-8*) Scandnvan Univ Pr.

Lessons from High-Performing Hispanic Schools: Creating Learning Communities. Pedro Reyes et al. LC 98-51496. (Critical Issues in Educational Leadership Ser.). 240p. 1999. pap. text 23.95 (*0-8077-3830-1*) Tchrs Coll.

Lessons from High-Performing Hispanic Schools: Creating Learning Communities, Vol. #5. Pedro Reyes et al. Ed. by Alicia Paredes Scribner. LC 98-51496. 5. 240p. 1999. 52.00 (*0-8077-3831-X*) Tchrs Coll.

Lessons from History: A Celebration in Blackness. Jawanza Kunjufu. 108p. (J). (gr. 1-5). 1987. pap. 6.95 (*0-913543-04-7*) African Am Imag.

Lessons from History: A Celebration in Blackness. Jawanza Kunjufu. 116p. (J). (gr. 6-12). 1987. pap. 7.95 (*0-913543-06-3*) African Am Imag.

Lessons from History: A Celebration in Blackness. Jawanza Kunjufu. 108p. (J). (gr. 1-5). 1987. 12.95 (*0-913543-05-5*) African Am Imag.

Lessons from History: A Celebration in Blackness. Jawanza Kunjufu. 116p. (J). (gr. 6-12). 1987. 13.95 (*0-913543-07-1*) African Am Imag.

***Lessons from Indian Country: McGruff & Scruff's Drug & Violence Prevention Story & Activity Book & Leaders Guide.** Jean O'Neil. Ed. by Judy Kirby. (Illus.). 21p. (Orig.). (J). 1998. pap. Price not set. (*0-934513-75-9*) Natl Crime DC.

Lessons from Islam: Ta'alim-i-Asmani Islam. rev. ed. S. M. Suhufi. Ed. by A. A. Aini & S. M. Hyder. Tr. by M. Fazal Haq from PER. 390p. 1991. reprint ed. pap. 10.00 (*0-941724-44-1*) Islamic Seminary.

Lessons from Japanese Development: An Analytical Economic History. Allen C. Kelley & Jeffrey G. Williamson. LC 73-90945. 300p. 1998. pap. text 9.00 (*0-226-42984-9*) U Ch Pr.

Lessons from Lamentations. Iverna M. Tompkins. 36p. (Orig.). 1987. pap. 2.50 (*0-9611260-5-1*) I Tompkins.

Lessons from Laron Syndrome (LS), 1966-1992: A Model of GH & IGF-I Action & Interaction. Ed. by Z. Laron & J. S. Parks. (Pediatric & Adolescent Endocrinology Ser.: Vol. 24). (Illus.). x, 368p. 1993. 321.75 (*3-8055-5671-3*) S Karger.

Lessons from Leaders Vol. 1: Politicians. Jason Meyers. (Illus.). 1985. pap. 4.95 (*0-913290-83-1*) Camaro Pub.

Lessons From Learner. Sheelagh Deller. (Pilgrims Resource Bks.). 79p. 1990. pap. text 17.95 (*0-582-07004-X*, 78671) Longman.

Lessons from Learning: Proceedings of the IFIP TC3 - WG3.3 Wording Conference on Lessons from Learning, Archamps, France. Ed. by Robert Lewis & Patrick Mendelsohn. LC 94-7739. (IFIP Transactions Ser.). 256p. 1994. 94.00 (*0-444-81832-4*) Elsevier.

***Lessons from Library Power: Enriching Teaching & Learning.** Douglas L. Sweizig & Dianne M. Hopkins. LC 99-52025. 1999. pap. 37.50 (*1-56308-833-9*, TIP) Libs Unl.

Lessons from Life: Studies of Old Testament. Tom Adcox. 138p. 1993. pap. write for info. (*0-9636261-1-6*) Abund Life Bks.

An Asterisk (*) at the beginning of an entry indicates that the title is appearing for the first time.

*Lessons from Littleton: Levelling - A Guide to Positive Parenting. Brian Brody & Sandy Petersen. (Illus.). 145p. 2000. pap. 19.95 (0-9618074-9-0, Pub. by IFIT) Partners Pubs Grp.

Lessons from Littleton: Levelling: A Guide to Positive Parenting. Brian Brody. Ed. by Institute for Integration Therapy Staff. (Illus.). 109p. 1985. pap. text 27.00 (0-9618074-8-2) IFIT.

Lessons from Mom: A Tribute to Loving Wisdom. Joan A. Ryan. 200p. 1996. pap. 10.95 (1-55874-386-3, 3863) Health Comm.

Lessons from Mother Goose. Elaine Commins. LC 87-30130. (Illus.). 164p. (Orig.). 1989. lib. bdg. 28.95 (0-89334-177-0, 177-0) Humanics Ltd.

*Lessons from Mount Kilimanjaro: Schooling, Community & Gender in East Africa. Amy Stambach. 2000. 80.00 (0-415-92582-7); pap. 19.99 (0-415-92583-5) Routledge.

Lessons from Nature: Learning to Live Sustainably on the Earth. Daniel D. Chiras. LC 91-39156. 289p. 1992. text 40.00 (1-55963-107-4); pap. text 22.00 (1-55963-106-6) Island Pr.

Lessons from Nature: Poems for Boys & Girls. John Bunyan. Ed. by Gary Sanseri & Wanda Sanseri. LC 98-70028. (Illus.). 124p. (J). 1998. reprint ed. 19.95 (1-880045-19-2) Back Home Indust.

Lessons from Nature for Youth. Charles Williams. (Illus.). 96p. (Orig.). (J). (gr. 1 up). 1995. reprint ed. pap. 4.95 (0-925279-46-3) Wallbuilders.

Lessons from Nebraska Football: Inspirational Stories & Lessons from the Gridiron. Gordon Thiessen & Mark Todd. 160p. 1999. pap. 8.95 (1-887002-98-7) Cross Trng.

Lessons from New American Schools Development Corporation's Demonstration. Susan Bodilly. LC 96-19822. 150p. 1996. pap. text 15.00 (0-8330-2369-1, MR-729-NASDC) Rand Corp.

Lessons from New American Schools' Scale-Up Phase: Prospects for Bringing Designs to Multiple Schools. Susan J. Bodilly et al. LC 98-20629. (Illus.). 140p. 1998. pap. 15.00 (0-8330-2632-1) Rand Corp.

*Lessons from Nothing: Activities for Language Teaching with Limited Time & Resources. Bruce Marsland. LC 98-24907. 1998. write for info. (0-521-62765-6) Cambridge U Pr.

*Lessons from Our Children: A Tribute to the Wisdom of Kids. Joan Aho Ryan. LC 99-31723. 200p. 1999. pap. 10.95 (1-55874-691-9) Health Comm.

Lessons from Our Living Past. Kelly Cherry. (J). 1995. pap., teacher ed. 14.95 (0-87441-086-X) Behrman.

Lessons from Our Living Past. Seymour Rossel. Ed. by Jules Harlow. (J). (gr. 2-3). 1997. reprint ed. pap. 8.95 (0-87441-085-1) Behrman.

Lessons from Our Living Past, No. 1. Morissa Lipstein. (J). (gr. 2-3). 1995. pap., wbk. ed. 3.95 (0-87441-087-8) Behrman.

Lessons from Our Living Past, No. 2. Morissa Lipstein. (J). (gr. 2-3). 1995. pap., wbk. ed. 3.95 (0-87441-088-6) Behrman.

Lessons from Privatization: Labor Issues in Developing & Transitional Countries. LC 98-121958. 191p. (Orig.). 1997. pap. 24.75 (92-2-109452-9) Intl Labour Office.

Lessons from Privilege: The American Prep School Tradition. Arthur G. Powell. LC 96-9157. 304p. 1996. 36.50 (0-674-52549-3) HUP.

Lessons from Privilege: The American Prep School Tradition. Arthur G. Powell. 320p. 1998. pap. text 16.95 (0-674-52553-1) HUP.

Lessons from Restructuring Experiences: Stories of Change in Professional Development Schools. Ed. by Nancy E. Hoffman et al. LC 96-34720. (SUNY Series, Restructuring & School Change). 326p. (C). 1997. text 59.50 (0-7914-3407-9); pap. text 19.95 (0-7914-3408-7) State U NY Pr.

Lessons from Rural America: A Case History. John M. Cornman & Barbara Kincaid. LC 84-14107. 160p. 1984. 13.95 (0-932020-24-0) Seven Locks Pr.

*Lessons from Schools: The History of Education in Banaras Nita Kumar. LC 99-37979. 1999. write for info. (0-7619-9378-9) Sage.

Lessons from South Africa: A New Perspective on Public Policy & Productivity. Oren Harari & David T. Beaty. 240p. 1989. text 34.95 (0-88730-249-1, HarpBusn) HarpInfo.

Lessons from Structural Failures. Ed. by M. Drdacky. 160p. 1991. pap. text 59.00 (0-685-59661-3, CZ1) Am Soc Civil Eng.

Lessons from Team Leaders: A Team Fitness Companion. Jane E. Henry. LC 97-50123. 188p. 1998. pap., wbk. ed. 21.00 (0-87389-382-4, H0971) ASQ Qual Pr.

Lessons from the Ayurveda: Health for Devotees. Navayauvana Das. Ed. by Nityananda Das. 150p. 1989. pap. write for info. (0-923519-04-1) New Jaipur.

*Lessons from the Beach Chair: Nature's Wisdom for Teaching Character. Deb Austin Brown. 75p. 1999. pap. 9.95 (1-892056-05-4) Character Dev.

Lessons from the Big House: One Family's Passage Through the History of the South. Frye Gaillard. Ed. by Jerry Bledsoe. LC 94-67915. (Illus.). 156p. 1994. 19.95 (1-878086-35-9, Pub. by Down Home NC) Blair.

Lessons from the Cloth: 501One-Minute Motivators for Leaders. Bo Prosser & Charles Qualls. LC 98-30883. 96p. 1999. pap. 10.00 (1-57312-252-1) Smyth & Helwys.

Lessons from the Coaches. Rita M. Fisher. LC 97-65164. (All Star Moments Ser.: Vol. 5). 104p. 1997. 9.95 (0-89221-342-6) New Leaf.

Lessons from the Damned: Class Struggle in the Black Community. 2nd ed. Frwd. by Lamar Hoover. LC 90-10969. (Illus.). viii, 156p. 1990. pap. 7.95 (0-87810-036-9) Times Change.

Lessons from the Damned: Queers, Junkies & Whores Respond to AIDS. Nancy E. Stoller. LC 97-21462. (Illus.). 320p. (C). 1997. pap. 19.99 (0-415-91961-4) Routledge.

Lessons from the Damned: Queers, Junkies & Whores Respond to AIDS. Nancy E. Stoller. LC 97-21462. (Illus.). 320p. (C). 1998. 75.00 (0-415-91960-6) Routledge.

Lessons from the Dead: The Graveyard As a Classroom for the Study of the Life Cycle. Roberta Halporn. LC 78-70538. (Illus.). 64p. (Orig.). 1979. pap. 4.95 (0-930194-01-2) Ctr Thanatology.

Lessons from the Diamond. R. McKenzie Fisher. LC 95-69889. (All Star Moments Ser.: Vol. 1). (Illus.). 104p. (YA). (gr. 6 up). 1995. 9.95 (0-89221-292-6) New Leaf.

Lessons from the Dying. Rodney Smith. LC 98-11990. 224p. 1998. pap. 16.95 (0-86171-140-8) Wisdom MA.

Lessons from the Economic Transition: Central & Eastern Europe in the 1990's. Ed. by Salvatore Zecchini. LC 96-49917. 624p. (C). 1997. pap. text 66.00 (0-7923-9857-2); lib. bdg. 129.95 (0-7923-9852-1) Kluwer Academic.

*Lessons from the Edge: Extreme Athletes Show You How to Take on High Risk & Succeed. Maryann Karinch. LC 99-57396. 240p. 2000. per. 14.00 (0-684-86215-8) S&S Trade.

Lessons from the Fairway. R. McKenzie Fisher. LC 95-72880. (All Star Moments Ser.: Vol. 3). 106p. 1996. 9.95 (0-89221-312-4) New Leaf.

Lessons from the Farmyard. Emilie Poulsson. (Illus.). 45p. (J). (gr. k-1). 1992. pap. text 3.50 (1-930092-25-3, CLP29605) Christian Liberty.

Lessons from the Field: Applying Appreciative Inquiry. Sue A. Hammond & Cathy Royal. 299p. 1998. pap. 22.00 (0-9665373-0-0, Practical Pr) Thin Bk Pubg.

Lessons from the Field: Head Start Mental Health Strategies to Meet Changing Needs. Hirokazu Yoshikawa & Jane Knitzer. 103p. 1997. pap. 15.95 (0-926582-21-6) NCCP.

Lessons from the Field: Unlocking Economic Potential with an Environmental Key - 20 Case Studies. Edith Pepper. 230p. 1997. pap. 40.00 (1-882061-64-0) Northeast-Midwest.

Lessons from the First 20 Years of Medicare: Research Implications for Public & Private Sector Policy. Ed. by Mark V. Pauly et al. LC 88-17368. (Health Economics, Health Management, & Health Policy Ser.). 412p. (C). 1989. text 45.00 (0-8122-8118-7) U of Pa Pr.

Lessons from the Fish: An Anthology of Fishing Experiences. Len Colclough. (Illus.). 192p. 1997. 35.95 (1-85310-818-9, Pub. by Swan Hill Pr) Voyageur Pr.

Lessons from the Front Line: Market Tools & Investing Tactics from the Pros. Michael Brush. LC 99-32876. (Investments Ser.). 272p. 1999. 29.95 (0-471-35017-6) Wiley.

Lesson's from the Garden - Harvest of Reflections. Justin Matott. LC 97-46879. 1998. 19.95 (0-345-42091-8) Ballantine Pub Grp.

Lessons from the Good Old Days. Cliff Schimmels. LC 94-5076. 208p. 1994. 10.99 (1-56476-329-3, 6-3329, Victor Bks) Chariot Victor.

Lessons from the Great Depression. Peter Temin. (Lionel Robbins Lectures). 200p. 1989. 28.00 (0-262-20073-2) MIT Pr.

Lessons from the Great Depression. Peter Temin. (Illus.). 212p. 1991. reprint ed. pap. text 14.00 (0-262-70044-1) MIT Pr.

Lessons from the Gridiron. R. McKenzie Fisher. LC 95-69894. (All Star Moments Ser.: Vol. 2). (Illus.). 104p. (YA). 1995. 9.95 (0-89221-298-5) New Leaf.

Lessons from the Ground Up: African Development That Works. Peter G. Veit et al. LC 95-61917. 50p. 1995. pap. 20.00 (1-56973-038-5) World Resources Inst.

Lessons from the Hardwoods. R. McKenzie Fisher. LC 95-72881. (All Star Moments Ser.: Vol. 4). 106p. 1996. 9.95 (0-89221-311-6) New Leaf.

Lessons from the Heart. Lighten Up Enterprises Staff. (Places of the Heart Ser.). 366p. 1994. spiral bd. 8.50 (1-879127-35-0) Lighten Up Enter.

Lessons from the Heart: Individualizing Physical Education with Heart Rate Monitors. Beth Kirkpatrick & Burton H. Birnbaum. LC 96-53062. (Illus.). 136p. 1997. pap. text 19.00 (0-88011-764-8, BKIR0764) Human Kinetics.

*Lessons from the Heart of American Business: A Roadmap for Managers in the 21st Century. Gerald Greenwald & Charles Madigan. 288p. 2001. 25.95 (0-446-52544-8, Pub. by Warner Bks) Little.

Lessons from the Hill: The Legislative Journey of an Education Program. Janet M. Martin. 222p. 1993. text 39.95 (0-312-10685-8) St Martin.

Lessons from the 100-Acre Wood. Kathleen Zoehfeld. 208p. 1999. 12.99 (0-7868-3243-6, Pub. by Disney Pr) Time Warner.

Lessons from the Intersexed. Suzanne J. Kessler. LC 97-39342. 193p. (C). 1998. text 48.00 (0-8135-2529-2); pap. text 18.00 (0-8135-2530-6) Rutgers U Pr.

*Lessons from the Legends of Wall Street: How Warren Buffet, Phil Fisher, Benjamin Graham, T. Rowe Price & John Templeton Can Help You Grow Rich. Nikki Ross. 2000. 22.00 (0-7931-3715-2) Dearborn.

Lessons from the Life of Moody. George Sweeting & Donald Sweeting. 145p. pap. 9.99 (0-8024-4686-8, 202) Moody.

*Lessons from the Light: Extraordinary Messages of Comfort & Hope from the Other Side. George Anderson & Andrew Barone. 336p. 2000. pap. text 12.95 (0-425-17416-6) Berkley Pub.

Lessons from the Light: Extraordinary Messages of Love & Comfort from the Other Side. George Anderson & Andrew Barone. LC 98-56039. 320p. 1999. 23.95 (0-399-14510-9, G P Putnam) Peng Put Young Read.

Lessons from the Light: Insights from a Journey to the Other Side. Sandra H. Rogers. 112p. 1995. mass mkt. 4.99 (0-446-60277-9, Pub. by Warner Bks) Little.

*Lessons from the Light: What We Can Learn from the Near-Death Experience. Kenneth Ring & Evelyn Elsaesser Valarino. LC 99-59665. 364p. 2000. pap. 16.95 (0-9661327-8-5, Pub. by Moment Pt Pr) ACCESS Pubs Network.

Lessons from the Lion's Den: Therapeutic Management of Children in Psychiatric Hospitals & Treatment Centers. Nancy S. Cotton. LC 93-3623. (Social & Behavioral Sciences Ser.). 345p. 1993. text 36.95 (1-55542-575-5) Jossey-Bass.

*Lessons from the Logbook: Flying Techniques from the Best Teachers of All: Experience. Ron Fowler. 230p. 1999. pap. write for info. (0-916413-27-6) Aviation.

Lessons from the Masters: Seven Keys to Peak Performance & Inner Peace. Jim Brault. Ed. by Jennifer Resnick. 160p. 1998. pap. 13.50 (0-9663482-0-6) Ctr Line Pr.

*Lessons from the Mississippi Freedom School. Kathy Emery & Linda Gold. 2001. pap. 18.95 (1-56584-630-3, Pub. by New Press NY) Norton.

*Lessons from the Nordstrom Way: How Companies Are Emulating the #1 Customer Service Company. Robert Spector. 224p. 2000. 24.95 (0-471-35594-1) Wiley.

Lessons from the Oklahoma City Bombing: Defensive Design Techniques. Eve E. Hinman & David J. Hammond. LC 96-49992. 80p. 1997. pap. 44.00 (0-7844-0217-5, ASCE Press) Am Soc Civil Eng.

Lessons from the Past. Fred Fedler. 264p. 1999. pap. 17.95 (1-57766-067-6) Waveland Pr.

*Lessons from the Past. Peter Gordon. 192p. 1999. 32.50 (0-7130-0208-5) Intl Spec Bk.

Lessons from the Past: Issues for Social Work Theory. 224p. 1989. pap. 18.95 (0-415-00819-0, A3707) Routledge.

*Lessons from the Pit: A Successful Veteran of the Chicago Mercantile Exchange Shows Executives How to Thrive in a Competitive Environment. Joseph E. Leininger & Terry Whalin. LC 98-49104. 224p. 1999. 14.99 (0-8054-1699-4) Broadman.

*Lessons from the Political Economy of Small Islands: The Resourcefulness of Jurisdiction. Godfrey Baldacchino & David Milne. LC 99-55726. 2000. 69.95 (0-312-23195-4) St Martin.

Lessons from the Recession: A Management & Communication Perspective. Ed. by Sarah S. King & Donald P. Cushman. LC 96-48281. (SUNY Series in International Management). 330p. (C). 1997. text 74.50 (0-7914-3291-2); pap. text 24.95 (0-7914-3292-0) State U NY Pr.

Lessons from the Rocking Chair: Timeless Stories for Teaching Character. Deb A. Brown. 70p. 1997. pap. 8.95 (0-9653163-3-5) Character Dev.

Lessons from the Source. Tom Johnson. LC 91-11613. 160p. 1991. 19.95 (0-941992-27-6); pap. 12.95 (0-941992-24-1) Los Arboles Pub.

Lessons from the South. Susan King. 1986. pap. 75.00 (0-932526-24-1) Nexus Pr.

Lessons from the Spelling Doctor Pt. 1: Essays on the Way Words Work. Raymond E. Laurita. 117p. (YA). (gr. 6-12). 1991. pap. 12.95 (0-914051-19-9) Leonardo Pr.

Lessons from the Stories of the Quran. M. R. Muhajir. 1991. pap. 16.50 (1-56744-120-3) Kazi Pubns.

Lessons from the Swaps Litigation. Ed. by Peter Birks. 188p. 1999. 74.00 (0-9526499-3-4, Pub. by Hart Pub) Northwestern U Pr.

Lessons from the Top: The Search of America's Best Business Leaders. Thomas J. Neff et al. LC 99-21724. 448p. 1999. 24.95 (0-385-49343-6) Doubleday.

Lessons from the Torah: A Child's Bible Gamebook, Bk. 1. Seymour Rossel. 1997. reprint ed. 4.95 (0-87441-512-8) Behrman.

Lessons from the Varsity of Life. Lord Baden-Powell. (Illus.). 320p. 1992. pap. 17.95 (0-9632054-7-1) Stevens Pub.

*Lessons from the Window Seat: Achieving Shared Vision in the Workplace. David Specht. LC 99-64657. (Illus.). 160p. 2000. pap. 14.95 (0-9664624-8-3) Telos Pubns.

Lessons from the Wolverine. Barry H. Lopez. LC 96-54705. (Illus.). 1997. 15.95 (0-8203-1927-9) U of Ga Pr.

Lessons in Beauty: Art & Adult Education. Bastiaan Van Gent. Ed. by Franz Poggeler. (Studies in Pedagogy, Andragogy & Gerontagogy: Vol. 35). (Illus.). 145p. 1997. pap. 35.95 (3-631-31585-6) P Lang Pubng.

Lessons in Beauty: Art & Adult Education. Bastiaan Van Gent. Ed. by Franz Poggeler. LC 97-24643. (Studies in Pedagogy, Andragogy & Gerontagogy: Vol. 35). (Illus.). 145p. 1997. pap. 35.95 (0-8204-3271-7) P Lang Pubng.

*Lessons in Being Chinese: Minority Education & Ethnic Identity in Southwest China. Mette Halskov Hansen. LC 98-49028. (Studies on Ethnic Groups in China). (Illus.). 248p. 1999. pap. text 22.50 (0-295-97788-4) U of Wash Pr.

Lessons in Bobbin Lacemaking. Southard. (Illus.). 224p. reprint ed. pap. 12.95 (0-486-27122-6) Dover.

Lessons in Chess. Garry Kasparov. 1997. pap. text 19.95 (1-85744-164-8, Pub. by Cadgn Bks) Macmillan.

Lessons in Classical Dance: For Teachers & Students. Sophia N. Golovkina. (Illus.). 144p. 1991. 29.95 (1-85273-024-2) Princeton Bk Co.

Lessons in Colloquial Egyptian Arabic. rev. ed. Richard S. Harrell et al. LC 64-2973. (Arabic Ser.: No. 2). 250p. reprint ed. pap. 77.50 (0-7837-6326-3, 204604100010) Bks Demand.

Lessons in Cultural Change: The Utility Industry Experience. Ed. & Intro. by Philip R. Theibert. (Illus.). 375p. 1994. pap. text 47.00 (0-910325-52-9) Public Util.

Lessons in Dadhood from the Father Who Really Knows Best. Tim Wesemann. LC 96-45187. 240p. 1997. 12.99 (0-570-04885-0, 12-3302) Concordia.

Lessons in Death & Life. Dave LaBelle. Ed. by Alan Judd & Rex Perry. (Illus.). 112p. (C). 1994. text 24.95 (0-9630770-0-7) D LaBelle.

*Lessons in Democracy. Ed. by Ewa Hauser & Jacek Wasilewski. LC 99-47180. 250p. 1999. pap. 24.95 (1-58046-049-6) Univ Rochester Pr.

Lessons in Development: A Comparative Study of Asia & Latin America. Ed. by Seiji Naya et al. LC 89-19996. 361p. 1989. 34.95 (1-55815-051-X); pap. 19.95 (1-55815-052-8) ICS Pr.

Lessons in Dying: Learning How to Live. Maggie Lane. LC 96-61543. 144p. (Orig.). 1997. pap. 9.95 (1-883893-78-X) WinePress Pub.

Lessons in Economic Policy for Eastern Europe from Latin America. Ed. by Gary McMahon. LC 95-2566. (International Political Economy Ser.). 256p. 1996. text 65.00 (0-312-12647-6) St Martin.

Lessons in EKG Interpretation: A Basic Self-Instructional Guide. Charles P. Summerall. LC 84-21025. 216p. reprint ed. pap. 67.00 (0-7837-1376-2, 204152400021) Bks Demand.

Lessons in EKG Interpretation: A Basic Self-Instructional Guide. 2nd ed. Charles P. Summerall, III. (Illus.). 214p. 1991. pap. text 36.95 (0-443-08778-4) Church.

Lessons in Estimation Theory. 2nd ed. Jerry M. Mendel. LC 94-15781. (Signal Processing Ser.). 592p. 1995. 90.00 (0-13-120981-7) P-H.

Lessons in Excellence from Charlie Trotter: 75 Ways One Visionary is Setting a New Standard. Paul Clarke. 208p. 1999. pap. 19.95 (0-89815-908-3) Ten Speed Pr.

Lessons in Fear: A Carter Colborn Mystery. Diana Shaw. (J). (gr. 7 up). 1987. 12.95 (0-316-78341-2, Joy St Bks) Little.

Lessons in Formal Writing. Edward Johnston. Ed. by Heather Child & Justin Howes. (Illus.). 248p. 1986. reprint ed. pap. 19.95 (0-8008-4642-7) Taplinger.

*Lessons in Goddess Spirituality: Wicca. Athena Gardner. 267p. 2000. pap. 17.00 (1-893774-19-8) Star Rising.

Lessons in Islam, 5. Ashraf. (J). 1995. pap. 8.50 (1-56744-121-1) Kazi Pubns.

Lessons in Laughter: The Autobiography of a Deaf Actor. Bernard Bragg & Eugene Bergman. LC 89-1493. (Illus.). 237p. 1989. 19.95 (0-930323-46-7) Gallaudet Univ Pr.

Lessons in Leadership: Fifty Respected Evangelical Leaders Share Their Wisdom on Ministry. Ed. by Randal Roberts. 288p. 1998. pap. text 13.99 (0-8254-3630-3) Kregel.

Lessons in Leadership: Mostly Learned the Hard Way. Duane R. Lund & Lewis W. Finch. 96p. (Orig.). (C). 1987. pap. 8.95 (0-934860-47-5) Adventure Pubns.

Lessons in Leadership from the Bible. Kenneth O. Gangel. 1980. pap. 7.99 (0-88469-109-8) BMH Bks.

*Lessons in Leadership from the Ground Up: Turning Dreams into Success. Larry Holman & Bunny Holman. (Lessons in Leadership Ser.). (Illus.). 304p. 1999. 19.95 (0-9648829-9-X) Wyncom.

Lessons in Leaving. Sheila Raeschild. 1974. pap. 2.50 (0-912786-30-2) Know Inc.

*Lessons in Life's Valleys, 2. Justine Toms & Iyanla Vanzant. 1999. audio 16.95 (1-56170-696-5, 4010) Hay House.

Lessons in Living. Susan L. Taylor. 176p. 1998. pap. 11.95 (0-385-48379-1, Anchor NY) Doubleday.

Lessons in Love. Akhileshwar Jha. 1988. 16.50 (81-7001-038-1, Pub. by Chanakya) S Asia.

Lessons in Love. B. J. RanDelle & Sandra Marshburn. LC 24-476. (Illus.). 64p. (J). (gr. k-4). 1982. text 5.95 (0-910445-00-1) Randelle Pubns.

Lessons in Love. Kate Trask. LC 73-94745. (Short Story Index Reprint Ser.). 1977. 16.95 (0-8369-3125-4) Ayer.

Lessons in Love: The Transformation of Spirit Through Intimacy. Guy Corneau. LC 98-20668. 224p. 1999. 22.50 (0-8050-6024-3) H Holt & Co.

Lessons in Love: The Transformation of Spirit Through Intimacy. Guy Corneau. 320p. 2000. pap. 14.00 (0-8050-6397-8, Owl) H Holt & Co.

Lessons in Love: World's Greatest Dad, House Calls, A Knight in Tarnished Armor. Marie Ferrarella et al. 1997. per. 5.99 (0-373-20139-7, 1-20139-1) Harlequin Bks.

Lessons in Modern Hebrew, 2 vols., I. Edna A. Coffin. LC 76-49149. 544p. 1977. pap. text 21.95 (0-472-08225-6, 08225) U of Mich Pr.

Lessons in Modern Hebrew, 2 vols., II. Edna A. Coffin. LC 76-49149. 496p. 1978. pap. text 21.95 (0-472-08226-4, 08226) U of Mich Pr.

Lessons in Murder. Claire McNab. (Carol Ashton Mystery Ser.). 216p. 1988. pap. 11.95 (0-941483-14-2) Naiad Pr.

Lessons in Music Form. Percy Goetschius. LC 79-109735. 146p. 1970. reprint ed. lib. bdg. 49.50 (0-8371-4225-3, GOMF, Greenwood Pr) Greenwood.

Lessons in Music Form: A Manual of Analysis of All the Structural Factors & Designs Employed in Musical Composition. Percy Goetschius. 146p. 1990. reprint ed. lib. bdg. 59.00 (0-7812-9145-3) Rprt Serv.

Lessons in Perspective Drawing. Illus. by Lester Showalter. 40p. 1993. pap. 2.35 (0-7399-0238-5, 2560) Rod & Staff.

Lessons in Persuasion: Creative Nonfiction/Pittsburgh Connections. Ed. by Lee Gutkind. LC 99-6834. (Illus.). 256p. 1999. pap. 17.95 (0-8229-5715-9) U of Pittsburgh Pr.

Lessons in Professional Liability: A Notebook for Certified Public Accountants. DPIC Companies Staff. Ed. by Alison E. Edwards. 76p. (Orig.). 1990. spiral bd. 20.00 (0-932056-05-9) Design Prof Ins.

An Asterisk (*) at the beginning of an entry indicates that the title is appearing for the first time.

Lessons in Professional Liability: A Notebook for Design Professionals. 1988. 20.00 (*0-932056-04-0*) Design Prof Ins.

*__Lessons in Progress: State Universities & Progressivism in the New South, 1880-1920.__ Michael Dennis. LC 00-9308. 2001. write for info. (*0-252-02617-9*) U of Ill Pr.

Lessons in Religion. 2nd ed. Garrett Kenney. 194p. (C). 1998. spiral bd. 28.95 (*0-7872-1948-7*, 41194801) Kendall-Hunt.

Lessons in Religion for a Skeptical World. Rodney Collin. 1991. pap. 7.95 (*1-55818-178-4*) Holmes Pub.

Lessons in Restructuring Defense Industry: The French Experience. (Illus.). 35p. (Orig.). (C). 1992. pap. text 25.00 (*1-56806-099-8*) DIANE Pub.

Lessons in School Funding. 2nd ed. Terry N. Whitney & Amy Hightower. (State Legislative Reports: Vol. 17, No. 3). 8p. 1992. pap. text 15.00 (*1-55516-275-4*) Natl Conf State Legis.

Lessons in Seismic Computing. M. M. Slotnick. Ed. by Richard A. Geyer. (Illus.). 268p. 1959. 17.00 (*0-931830-07-9*, 311A) Soc Expl Geophys.

Lessons in Sign Writing Textbook. Valerie J. Sutton. (Illus.). 260p. 1995. ring bd. 50.00 (*0-914336-55-X*) Ctr Sutton Movement.

Lessons in Sign Writing Video Series, 2 cass.; set. Deaf Action Committee Staff & Valerie J. Sutton. 1996. 75.00 incl. VHS (*0-914336-72-X*) Ctr Sutton Movement.

Lessons in Soaring. James Applewhite. LC 88-3148. 64p. 1989. pap. 6.95 (*0-8071-1540-1*); text 15.95 (*0-8071-1539-8*) La State U Pr.

Lessons in Space. Cathleen Calbert. LC 96-49005. (Contemporary Poetry Ser.). 88p. 1997. 19.95 (*0-8130-1502-2*); pap. 10.95 (*0-8130-1503-0*) U Press Fla.

Lessons in Spoken Cornish. A. S. Smith. (C). 1989. 40.00 (*0-907566-78-2*, Pub. by Dyllansow Truran) St Mut.

Lessons in Success from the NBA's Top Players. Michael T. Glenn. 144p. 1997. pap. 14.95 (*0-9649795-5-1*) Visions Three-Thousand.

Lessons in Success from the Silent Performer: Walt's Friday Inspirations The Book. 160p. 1998. 14.95 (*0-9629202-7-4*) Co Called W.

Lessons in Survival. Laramie Dunaway. 1995. pap. write for info. (*0-446-67067-7*) Warner Bks.

*__Lessons in System Safety: Proceedings of the Eighth Safety-Critical Systems Symposium, Southampton, UK, 2000.__ Ed. by Felix Redmill & Tom Anderson. LC 99-56289. x, 302p. 2000. pap. text 89.95 (*1-85233-249-2*) Spr-Verlag.

Lessons in Tanya. Schneur Zalman Baruchovitch. Ed. by Uri Kaploun. Tr. by Sholom B. Wineberg. (Lessons in Tanya Ser.: Vol. 3). 320p. 1991. 17.00 (*0-8266-0543-5*) Kehot Pubn Soc.

Lessons in Tanya. Schneur Zalman-Baruchovitch. Ed. by Uri Kaploun. Tr. by Sholom B. Wineberg. (Lessons in Tanya Ser.: Vol. 4). 424p. 1992. 17.00 (*0-8266-0544-3*) Kehot Pubn Soc.

Lessons in Tanya, 5 vols., Set. 2nd ed. Yosef Wineberg. Ed. by Uri Kaploun. Tr. by Levi Wineberg & Sholom B. Wineberg from YID. 1998. 75.00 (*0-8266-0546-X*) Kehot Pubn Soc.

Lessons in Tanya, Vols. 1-34. Schneur Zalman. Ed. by Uri Kaploun. Tr. by Sholom B. Wineberg. (Lessons in Tanya Ser.: Vol. 1). 480p. 1987. 17.00 (*0-8266-0541-9*) Kehot Pubn Soc.

Lessons in Tanya, Vols. 35-53. Schneur Zalman. Ed. by Uri Kaploun. Tr. by Sholom B. Wineberg. (Lessons in Tanya Ser.: Vol. 2). 374p. 1988. reprint ed. 17.00 (*0-8266-0542-7*) Kehot Pubn Soc.

Lessons in Tanya: Kuntres Acharon (Essays 1-9) Schneur Zalman-Baruchovitch. Ed. by Uri Kaploun. Tr. by Sholom B. Wineberg. (Lessons in Tanya Ser.: Vol. 5). 412p. 1993. 17.00 (*0-8266-0545-1*) Kehot Pubn Soc.

Lessons in Terror: The Cheater; College Weekend; Final Grade. 8th ed. R. L. Stine, pseud. (Fear Street Collector's Edition Ser.: No. 8). (J). (gr. 7 up). 1998. mass mkt. 6.99 (*0-671-02304-7*, Archway) PB.

Lessons in the Catholic Faith. Ed. by Kevin Vaillancourt. 120p. 1993. pap. text 10.00 (*1-883511-00-3*) Veritas Pr CA.

Lessons in the Law. Frank Schaffer Publications, Inc. Staff. (Middle School Bks.). (Illus.). 1996. wbk. ed. 12.95 (*0-7647-0054-5*, FS-10206) Schaffer Pubns.

*__Lessons in the Tall Grasses.__ Stanley Hahn. 1998. pap. 9.95 (*0-9628733-2-2*, Pub. by Legacy Pub FL) BookWorld.

Lessons in Trade Policy Reform. Vinod Thomas et al. (Policy & Research Ser.: No. 10). 24p. 1990. 22.00 (*0-8213-1464-5*, 11464) World Bank.

Lessons in Truth. rev. ed. H. Emilie Cady. LC 95-6534. 194p. 2000. 12.95 (*0-87159-108-1*) Unity Bks.

Lessons in Truth Instructors' Course Guide. 175p. 1996. ring bd. 17.95 (*0-87159-999-6*, 2100, Unity Schl Relgs Studies) Unity Bks.

Lessons in Truth Learners' Workbook. 164p. (Orig.). 1996. pap. text 14.95 (*0-87159-998-8*, 2101, Unity Schl Relgs Studies) Unity Bks.

Lessons Jesus Taught: The Savior's Teachings Retold for Children. Bessie Dean. (Children's Inspirational Coloring Bks.). (Illus.). 72p. (J). (gr. k-5). 1980. reprint ed. pap. 6.98 (*0-88290-671-2*) Horizon Utah.

Lessons Learned. John N. McNamara. (Illus.). 32p. (Orig.). 1984. pap. 4.00 (*0-932770-05-3*) McNamara Pubns.

Lessons Learned. Katie C. O'Connell et al. Ed. by Jane Weber. (Anthology of Teachers' Writing Ser.: Vol. 3). 1998. pap. 9.95 (*0-9666573-2-2*) Plymouth Writers.

Lessons Learned. Dale Ritterbusch. write for info. (*1-885215-08-8*, Viet Nam Gnrtn) Burning Cities Pr.

Lessons Learned. Nora Roberts. (NR Flowers Ser.: No. 25). 1993. per. 3.59 (*0-373-51025-X*, 1-51025-4) Silhouette.

Lessons Learned: Dispelling the Myths of Downsizing. Right Associates Staff. 84p. (Orig.). 1992. pap. 25.00 (*0-9628438-1-4*) Right Assocs.

Lessons Learned: Provision of Technical Assistance to States. P. Pizzo et al. Ed. by Noelle Beatty. 90p. (Orig.). 1993. pap. 9.00 (*0-943657-29-6*) ZERO TO THREE.

Lessons Learned: Students with Learning Disabilities, Ages 7-19, Share What They've Learned about Life & Learning. Dave Fullen. (Learning Disability Ser.). (Illus.). 40p. (Orig.). (J). (gr. 1 up). 1993. pap. 6.95 (*1-881650-02-2*) Mntn Bks.

Lessons Learned: The Iran-Iraq War. Stephen C. Pelletiere & Douglas V. Johnson, II. (Illus.). 119p. (Orig.). (C). 1994. pap. text 35.00 (*0-7881-0601-5*) DIANE Pub.

*__Lessons Learned by a Farmgirl.__ Beth Wehr. 51p. 2000. pap. write for info. (*0-7880-1612-1*, Fairway Pr) CSS OH.

Lessons Learned During a Wasted Youth: Selected Writings by Judd Arnett. Judd Arnett. 376p. (Orig.). 1995. pap. 17.95 (*0-9625276-1-0*) T P Stewart Pub.

Lessons Learned form Accidents in Industrial Irradiation Facilities. International Atomic Energy Agency Staff. LC 97-124492. 52p. 1996. pap. 30.00 (*92-0-102696-X*, STI/PUB/1015, Pub. by IAEA) Bernan Associates.

*__Lessons Learned from Accidental Exposures in Radiotherapy.__ (Safety Report Ser.: No. 17). 2000. 35.00 (*92-0-100200-9*, STI/PUB/1084, Pub. by IAEA) Bernan Associates.

Lessons Learned from Accidents in Industrial Radiography. International Atomic Energy Agency. (Safety Report Ser.). 595p. 1997. 30.00 (*92-0-103098-3*, Pub. by IAEA) Bernan Associates.

Lessons Learned from Design, Construction & Performance of Hydraulic Structures. (Task Committee Report Ser.). 265p. 1986. 26.00 (*0-87262-542-7*) Am Soc Civil Eng.

Lessons Learned from High-Performance Organizations in the Federal Government. 1995. lib. bdg. 250.00 (*0-8490-5861-9*) Gordon Pr.

Lessons Learned from High-Performing Organizations in the Federal Government. Michele Hunt. 93p. (Orig.). (C). 1995. pap. text 30.00 (*0-7881-1566-9*) DIANE Pub.

Lessons Learned from Implemented Software Architectures for Physical Agents: Papers from the 1995 Spring Symposium. Ed. by Henry Hexmoor & David Kortenkamp. (Technical Reports). (Illus.). 223p. 1995. spiral bd. 30.00 (*0-929280-85-7*) AAAI Pr.

Lessons Learned from the California Drought (1987-1992) National Study of Water Management During Drought. Benedykt Dziegielewski et al. (Illus.). 277p. (C). 1997. reprint ed. pap. text 40.00 (*0-7881-4163-5*) DIANE Pub.

Lessons Learned from the Clementine Mission. National Research Council Staff. LC 97-196894. 38p. (C). 1997. pap. text 10.00 (*0-309-05839-2*) Natl Acad Pr.

Lessons Learned from the Design, Construction & Operation of Dams & Reservoirs: Proceedings for the 1st USCOLD Technical Conference. Ed. by Wayne D. Edwards. LC 94-60236. (Illus.). 387p. (Orig.). 1994. pap. 56.00 (*1-884575-01-3*) US Cttee Dams.

Lessons Learned from the Design, Construction, & Operation of Hydroelectric Facilities. Ed. by Task Committee on Lessons Learned from the Design,. LC 94-7387. 120p. 1994. 17.00 (*0-7844-0000-8*) Am Soc Civil Eng.

Lessons Learned from the Gullah Experience: Powerful Focus in Educating African-American Youth. Thomas J. Brown & Kitty K. Green. LC 98-92835. 96p. 1998. pap. 12.95 (*1-891404-00-8*, BA001) Brown & Assocs.

Lessons Learned in Global Environmental Governance. Peter H. Sand. 60p. 1990. pap. 15.00 (*0-915825-56-2*, SALLP) World Resources Inst.

Lessons Learned in the D. C. Public Schools: Hearing Before the Subcommittee on Oversight of Government Management, Restructuring & the District of Columbia of the Committee on Governmental Affairs, United States Senate, 105th Congress, Second Session, March 9, 1998. LC 98-212672. (S. Hrg. Ser.). iii, 134p. 1998. write for info. (*0-16-057197-9*) USGPO.

*__Lessons Learned, Lessons Shared: Texas Immigrant Education Collaborative.__ Pam McCollum. 60p. 1999. pap. 24.95 (*1-878550-66-7*) Inter Dev Res Assn.

*__Lessons Learned Looking Back.__ Laura Sowers & Todd Linaman. 2001. pap. 10.99 (*0-8054-2057-6*) Broadman.

*__Lessons Learned over Time.__ Christopher Arnold et al. (Illus.). 118p. 1998. pap. 15.00 (*0-943198-67-4*, 99-01) Earthquake Eng.

Lessons Learned the Hard Way: A Personal Report. Newt Gingrich. LC 98-16518. (Illus.). 224p. 1998. 25.00 (*0-06-019106-6*) HarpC.

Lessons Life Has Taught Me. (Illus.). 160p. (Orig.). 1996. pap. 15.00 (*0-9654249-0-1*) Lees Summit Educ.

Lessons My Sled Dog Taught Me: Humor & Heartwarming Tails from Alaska's Mushers. Ed. by Tricia Brown. (Illus.). 160p. 1998. 9.95 (*0-945397-69-0*) Epicenter Pr.

*__Lessons of a Century.__ Education Week Staff. (Illus.). 2000. pap. 24.95 (*0-9674795-0-9*) Editorial Proj.

*__Lessons of Aloha: Stories of the Human Spirit.__ Noland. LC 99-75822. (Illus.). xvi, 128p. 1999. pap. 18.95 (*0-9631154-8-0*) Watermark.

Lessons of Azikwelwa: The Bus Boycott in South Africa. 2nd ed. Dan Mokonyane. 119p. (Orig.). 1995. pap. 11.00 (*0-614-09359-7*, Pub. by Nakong Ya Rena) AK Pr Dist.

Lessons of Azusa Street on Revival. Larry Keefauver. 76p. 1997. pap. 6.99 (*0-88419-499-X*) Creation House.

Lessons of Buffalo: The Strategy & Tactics That Booted "Operation Rescue" Out of Buffalo. 1992. pap. 2.50 (*0-89567-109-3*) World View Forum.

Lessons of Chile: The Chilean Group & the Future of Socialism. Ed. by John Gitting. 91p. 1975. 23.50 (*0-85124-111-5*, Pub. by Spkesman) Coronet Bks.

Lessons of East Asia: An Overview of Country Experience - Experiencia de Asia Oriental. Danny M. Leipziger & Vinod Thomas. (SPA.). 52p. 1994. pap. 22.00 (*0-8213-2743-7*, 12743) World Bank.

Lessons of East Asia: An Overview of Country Experience - Experiencia de Asia Oriental. Danny M. Leipziger & Vinrod Thomas. 48p. 1993. pap. 22.00 (*0-8213-2607-4*, 12607) World Bank.

Lessons of East/South-East Asian Growth Experience Particularly for South Asia. LC 95-947939. (Development Papers: No. 17). 100p. 25.00 (*92-1-119676-0*, E.95.II.F.11) UN.

Lessons of Economic Stabilization & Its Aftermath. Ed. by Michael Bruno et al. (Illus.). 436p. 1991. 46.00 (*0-262-02324-5*) MIT Pr.

Lessons of Experience: How Successful Executives Develop on the Job. Morgan W. McCall, Jr. et al. LC 87-46405. 212p. 1988. 27.50 (*0-669-18095-5*) Free Pr.

Lessons of Experience Vol. VI: Financial Institutions. World Bank Staff et al. 150p. 1998. pap. 22.00 (*0-8213-4343-2*) World Bank.

Lessons of History. Will Durant & Ariel Durant. 118p. 1993. 7.98 (*1-56731-024-9*, MJF Bks) Fine Comms.

Lessons of History. Will Durant & Ariel Durant. LC 68-19949. 128p. 1968. 22.00 (*0-671-41333-3*) S&S Trade.

Lessons of History. Michael C. Howard. 248p. (C). 1992. reprint ed. pap. 15.00 (*0-300-05665-6*) Yale U Pr.

Lessons of History for the Nigerian Republic & Other World Essays. P. Bodunrin Adeniji. LC 98-61098. (Illus.). 72p. 1998. pap. 9.95 (*1-890306-13-4*) Warwick Hse.

Lessons of Israel's Great Inflation. Haim Barkai. LC 95-7984. 264p. 1995. 69.50 (*0-275-95146-4*, Praeger Pubs) Greenwood.

Lessons of Japan: Assayings of Some Intercultural Stances. Darko Suvin. 247p. 1997. pap. 23.95 (*0-944624-37-5*) Maisonneuve Pr.

Lessons of John G. Lake on Prayer. Larry Keefauver. 76p. 1997. pap. 6.99 (*0-88419-497-3*) Creation House.

Lessons of Love. Susan Phillips. (Serenade Serenata Ser.: No. 35). 1986. pap. 1.49 (*0-310-47232-6*, 15569P) Zondervan.

Lessons of Love: Rediscovering Our Passion for Life When It All Seems Too Hard to Take. Melody Beattie. LC 94-14158. 240p. 1995. pap. 12.00 (*0-06-251078-9*, Pub. by Harper SF) HarpC.

Lessons of Love: Rediscovering Our Passion for Life When It All Seems Too Hard to Take. large type ed. Melody Beattie. 224p. 1995. pap. 12.95 (*0-8027-2685-2*) Walker & Co.

Lessons of Love from Daughters of Faith. Debbie S. Goodwin. LC 97-30451. 52p. 1998. pap. 2.99 (*0-8341-1728-2*) Beacon Hill.

Lessons of Maria Woodworth-Etter on Miracles. Larry Keefauver. LC 98-218016. 76p. 1997. pap. 6.99 (*0-88419-498-1*) Creation House.

Lessons of Modern War: The Gulf War, Vol. 4. Anthony H. Cordesman. (C). 1998. pap. 40.00 (*0-8133-8602-0*, Pub. by Westview) HarpC.

Lessons of Monetary Experience: Essays in Honor of Irving Fisher. Ed. by Arthur D. Gayer. LC 70-86089. (Library of Money & Banking History). (Illus.). xii, 450p. 1970. reprint ed. 49.50 (*0-678-00643-1*) Kelley.

Lessons of Romanticism: A Critical Companion. Thomas Pfau & Robert F. Gleckner. LC 97-31426. 1998. 22.95 (*0-8223-2077-0*) Duke.

Lessons of Romanticism: A Critical Companion. Ed. by Thomas Pfau & Robert F. Gleckner. LC 97-31426. 475p. 1998. pap. 22.95 (*0-8223-2091-6*) Duke.

Lessons of Smith Wigglesworth on Faith. Larry Keefauver. 76p. 1997. pap. 6.99 (*0-88419-496-5*) Creation House.

Lessons of St. Francis: How to Bring Simplicity & Spirituality into Your Daily Life. John M. Talbot & Steve Rabey. (Illus.). 288p. 1998. pap. 11.95 (*0-452-27834-1*, Plume) Dutton Plume.

Lessons of St. Francis: How to Bring Simplicity & Spirituality into Your Daily Life. John M. Talbot & Steve Rabey. LC 97-8709. (Illus.). 288p. 1997. 22.95 (*0-525-94314-5*) NAL.

Lessons of Struggle: South African Internal Opposition, 1960-1990. Anthony W. Marx. (Illus.). 384p. (C). 1992. pap. text 23.95 (*0-19-507348-7*) OUP.

Lessons of Tax Reform. World Bank Staff. 92p. 1991. 22.00 (*0-8213-1906-X*, 11906) World Bank.

Lessons of the Bush Defeat. Ed. by Peter W. Schramm. (Essay Ser.: No. 6). 77p. 1993. pap. text 3.00 (*1-878802-16-X*) J M Ashbrook Ctr Pub Affairs.

Lessons of the Future: Thriving Today By Understanding Tomorrow. Andrew Duggan & David J. Murcott. LC 98-86065. 112p. 1999. pap. 9.95 (*0-9665329-0-2*, STS0210) Strtgc Tech Sltns.

Lessons of the Game. Diane G. Bertrand. LC 98-28340. 192p. (YA). (gr. 6 up). 1998. pap. 9.95 (*1-55885-245-X*, Pinata Bks) Arte Publico.

*__Lessons of the Game: The Betrayal of an All-American Football Star.__ Derek Sparks. (Illus.). 232p. 1999. pap. 19.95 (*0-9671471-1-5*) Game Time Pub.

Lessons of the Grandfather, Vol. 1. unabridged ed. Richard L. Oldham. 35p. 1997. pap. 6.30 (*0-9655710-4-1*) With Heart Bks.

Lessons of the Grandfather, Vol. 2. unabridged ed. Richard L. Oldham. 35p. 1997. pap. 6.30 (*0-9655710-5-X*) With Heart Bks.

Lessons of the Grandfather, Vol. 3. 3rd ed. Richard L. Oldham. 1997. pap. 6.30 (*0-9655710-6-8*) With Heart Bks.

Lessons of the Gulf War: Ascendant Technology & Declining Capability. Gene I. Rochlin & Chris C. Demchak. LC 91-77818. (Policy Papers in International Affairs: No. 39). 42p. (Orig.). (C). 1991. pap. text 5.50 (*0-87725-539-3*) U of Cal IAS.

*__Lessons of the Heart.__ Kristin Billerbeck et al. 352p. 2000. 4.97 (*1-57748-792-3*) Barbour Pub.

Lessons of the Heart: Celebrating the Rhythms of Life. Patricia H. Livingston. LC 92-72924. 128p. (Orig.). 1992. pap. 7.95 (*0-87793-486-X*) Ave Maria.

Lessons of the Locker Room: The Myth of School Sports. Andrew W. Miracle, Jr. & C. Roger Rees. LC 93-48666. 243p. (C). 1994. 26.95 (*0-87975-879-1*) Prometheus Bks.

Lessons of the Lotus: Practical Spiritual Teachings of a Traveling Buddhist Monk. Bhante Y. Wimala. LC 97-13258. (Illus.). 224p. 1997. pap. 12.95 (*0-553-37855-4*) Bantam.

Lessons of the Master & Other Stories see Works of Henry James Jr.: Collected Works

Lessons of the Past: The Use & Misuse of History in American Foreign Policy. Ernest R. May. LC 73-82670. 236p. 1975. reprint ed. pap. text 10.95 (*0-19-501890-7*) OUP.

Lessons of the Pipeline Negotiations. Nil Ozergene. (CISA Working Papers: No. 40). 45p. (Orig.). 1983. pap. 15.00 (*0-86682-052-3*) Ctr Intl Relations.

Lessons of the Rainforest. Ed. by Suzanne Head & Robert Heinzman. LC 89-27661. (Illus.). 256p. 1990. 24.95 (*0-87156-678-8*, Pub. by Sierra); pap. 15.00 (*0-87156-682-6*, Pub. by Sierra) Random.

Lessons of the Venezuelan Experience. Ed. by Louis W. Goodman et al. 576p. 1995. text 70.00 (*0-943875-65-X*); pap. text 24.95 (*0-943875-66-8*) Johns Hopkins.

Lessons of the Vietnam War. 4th ed. Ed. by Jerold M. Starr. 364p. (Orig.). 1999. pap. text, teacher ed. 22.95 (*0-945919-21-2*) Ctr Social Studies.

Lessons of the War with Spain. Alfred Thayer Mahan. LC 79-133526. (Select Bibliographies Reprint Ser.). 1977. reprint ed. 23.95 (*0-8369-5558-7*) Ayer.

Lessons of War: The Civil War in Children's Magazines. James A. Marten. LC 98-15798. 259p. 1998. 55.00 (*0-8420-2654-1*, SR Bks); pap. 18.95 (*0-8420-2656-8*, SR Bks) Scholarly Res Inc.

*__Lessons of War: The Play.__ Fred Leo Brown. LC 99-93476. 70p. 1999. write for info. (*0-942551-11-7*) Combat Ready.

Lessons on Assurance see Seguridad en Cristo

Lessons on Assurance: Learn God's Promises for Salvation, Answered Prayer, Victory over Sin, Forgiveness & Guidance. rev. ed. Navigators Staff. (Growing in Christ Ser.). 32p. 1980. pap. 3.00 (*0-89109-160-2*) NavPress.

Lessons on Christian Living: Learn & Apply God's Principles for Maturing in the Christian Life. rev. ed. Navigators Staff. (Growing in Christ Ser.). 48p. 1980. pap. 3.00 (*0-89109-162-9*) NavPress.

Lessons on Faith. A. T. Jones & E. J. Waggoner. LC 94-61189. 160p. 1994. per. 6.95 (*1-57258-012-7*) Teach Servs.

Lessons on Living from Abraham. Woodrow Kroll. 1999. pap. text 3.99 (*0-8474-0685-7*) Back to Bible.

Lessons on Living from Daniel. Woodrow Kroll. (Giants of the Old Testament Ser.). 1999. pap. text 3.99 (*0-8474-0692-X*) Back to Bible.

Lessons on Living from David. Woodrow Kroll. (Giants of the Old Testament Ser.). 1999. pap. text 3.99 (*0-8474-0690-3*) Back to Bible.

Lessons on Living from Elijah: A Devotional Woodrow Michael Kroll. LC 99-159032. (Giants of the Old Testament Ser.). 65 p. 1998. write for info. (*0-8474-0686-5*) Back to Bible.

Lessons on Living from Esther: Living Courageously. Woodrow Kroll. 1999. pap. text 3.99 (*0-8474-0679-2*) Back to Bible.

Lessons on Living from Isaiah. Woodrow Kroll. 1999. pap. text 3.99 (*0-8474-0683-0*) Back to Bible.

Lessons on Living from Jeremiah: A Devotional. Woodrow Michael Kroll. LC 98-228017. (Giants of the Old Testament Ser.). 65 p. 1998. 3.99 (*0-8474-0689-X*) Back to Bible.

Lessons on Living from Job. Woodrow Kroll. (Giants of the Old Testament Ser.). 1999. pap. text 3.99 (*0-8474-0693-8*) Back to Bible.

Lessons on Living from Joseph. Woodrow Kroll. (Giants of the Old Testament Ser.). 1999. pap. text 3.99 (*0-8474-0694-6*) Back to Bible.

Lessons on Living from Joshua. Woodrow Kroll. 1999. pap. text 3.99 (*0-8474-0684-9*) Back to Bible.

Lessons on Living from Ruth: A Devotional Woodrow Michael Kroll. LC 99-159034. (Giants of the Old Testament Ser.). 65 p. 1998. 3.99 (*0-8474-0688-1*) Back to Bible.

Lessons on Living from Solomon. Woodrow Kroll. (Giants of the Old Testament Ser.). 1999. pap. text 3.99 (*0-8474-0691-1*) Back to Bible.

Lessons on Love: Following Christ's Example. Bill Hybels. (Interactions). 96p. 1996. pap., student ed. 5.99 (*0-310-20680-4*) Zondervan.

Lessons on Prayer. Witness Lee. 247p. 1981. per. 10.00 (*0-87083-045-7*, 07-011-001) Living Stream Ministry.

Lessons on Security & Disarmament from the History of the League of Nations. James T. Shotwell & Marina Salvin. LC 74-15557. 149p. 1975. reprint ed. lib. bdg. 65.00 (*0-8371-7824-X*, SHSD, Greenwood Pr) Greenwood.

Lessons on Teaching. 3rd ed. Leigh Chiarelott. LC 97-74037. (C). 1997. pap. text 33.50 (*0-15-505470-8*, Pub. by Harcourt Coll Pubs) Harcourt.

An Asterisk (*) at the beginning of an entry indicates that the title is appearing for the first time.

Lessons on the Analytic of the Sublime. Jean-Francois Lyotard. LC 93-10683. 208p. (C). 1993. 39.50 (*0-8047-2241-2*); pap. 14.95 (*0-8047-2242-0*) Stanford U Pr.

Lessons on the Analytic of the Sublime, Sections 23-29: Kant's Critique of Judgment. Jean-Francois Elyotard. LC 93-10683. 264p. (C). 1994. 40.00 (*0-8047-2022-3*); pap. 14.95 (*0-8047-2023-1*) Stanford U Pr.

Lessons on the Constitution: Supplements to High School Courses in American History, Government & Civics. John J. Patrick & Richard C. Remy. 302p. (Orig.). 1985. pap. 13.50 (*0-89994-302-0*) Soc Sci Ed.

Lessons on the Federalist Papers. John J. Patrick & Clair W. Keller. (Illus.). 95p. (gr. 9-12). 1987. pap. text 10.00 (*0-941339-00-9*) Ind U SSDC.

Lessons on the Human Body. Susan Brecht Hibbard. 1994. 4.95 (*1-55708-429-7*, MCR750) McDonald Pub Co.

Lessons on the Journey. Dave Nimmer. 1996. 17.95 (*0-931714-72-9*, Pub. by Nodin Pr) Bookmen Inc.

Lessons on the Northwest Ordinance of 1787. John J. Patrick. (Illus.). 84p. (YA). (gr. 9-12). 1987. spiral bd. 8.50 (*0-941339-02-5*) Ind U SSDC.

Lessons on the Northwest Ordinance of 1787: Learning Materials for Secondary School Courses in American History, Government, & Civics. John J. Patrick. 1987. pap. 6.95 (*1-885323-52-2*) IN Hist Bureau.

Lessons Plans for Classroom Teachers: Third & Fourth Grades. Robert P. Pangrazi. LC 96-46651. 88p. (C). 1996. pap. text 17.00 (*0-205-19364-1*) Allyn.

Lessons That Rhyme . . . Stay in the Mind: The Little Rhyme Book. rev. ed. Charles Sorrell & Paul DeVere. LC 96-92885. (Illus.). 100p. (Orig.). (J). 1996. pap. 14.95 (*0-9650791-3-9*, 1012SP) Saron Pr.

Lessons to Be Learned Just in Time. James J. Cammarano. LC 97-18858. (Illus.). 290p. 1997. 34.95 (*0-89806-162-8*, LESSON) Eng Mgmt Pr.

Lessons to Share: Workbook for a Healthy Family. 3rd rev. ed. Chas Ridley. (Illus.). 120p. 1987. pap. 15.00 (*1-890894-00-1*, 97001) Chas HotBooks.

Lessons to Share on Teaching Grammar in Context. Ed. by Constance Weaver. LC 97-51626. 323p. 1998. pap. text 29.50 (*0-86709-394-3*, Pub. by Boynton Cook Pubs) Heinemann.

Lessons with Eisenstein. Vladimir Nizhny. LC 78-27394. (Quality Paperbacks Ser.). 1979. reprint ed. pap. 9.95 (*0-306-80100-0*) Da Capo.

Lest Darkness Fall & To Bring the Light. L. Sprague De Camp & David Drake. 368p. 1996. mass mkt. 5.99 (*0-671-87736-4*) Baen Bks.

Lest I Forget. Martha B. Downs. 110p. 1997. pap. 7.00 (*0-89540-401-X*, SB-401) Sun Pub.

Lest I Shall Be Forgotten: Anecdotes & Traditions of Quilts. Nancy Roan & Donald Roan. LC 93-78780. (Illus.). 96p. 1993. per. 10.00 (*1-883801-02-8*) Goschenhopn Hist.

Lest Memory Cease: Finding Meaning in the American Jewish Past. Henry L. Feingold. LC 96-25659. (Modern Jewish History Ser.). 224p. 1996. 44.95 (*0-8156-2710-6*, FELM); pap. 18.95 (*0-8156-0400-9*, FELMP) Syracuse U Pr.

Lest We Forget. Margaret Eck. 72p. pap. 1.50 (*0-686-29125-5*); pap. 2.00 (*0-686-29126-3*) Faith Pub Hse.

Lest We Forget. Harry O. Nawroth. 97p. 1993. pap. 4.95 (*1-883537-51-7*) Nawroth Pub.

Lest We Forget. S. Wahrman. 1991. 16.99 (*0-89906-870-7*); pap. 13.99 (*0-89906-871-5*) Mesorah Pubns.

Lest We Forget. large type ed. Raji H. Sahyoun. 288p. (Orig.). 1997. pap. 14.95 (*0-9656607-0-2*) Intl Printers.

Lest We Forget: A Guide to the Civil War Monuments in Maryland. Susan C. Soderberg. LC 94-37410. 195p. 1995. 29.95 (*0-942597-76-1*) White Mane Pub.

Lest We Forget: A Personal Reflection on the Formation of the Orthodox Presbyterian Church. 3rd ed. Robert K. Churchill. (Illus.). 135p. 1997. reprint ed. pap. 7.95 (*0-934688-34-6*) Comm Hist Orthodox.

Lest We Forget: A POW Memoir of World War II. Dan McCullen. (Illus.). 208p. 1997. 22.95 (*1-56474-191-5*) Fithian Pr.

Lest We Forget: Howard Beach & Other Racial Atrocities. Alphonso Pinkney. 300p. (Orig.). (C). 1993. pap. 14.95 (*0-88378-088-7*) Third World.

Lest We Forget: Nanjing Massacre, 1937. Xu Zhigeng. Tr. by Zhang Tingquan & Lin Wusun from CHI. (Illus.). 307p. 1996. pap. 14.95 (*0-8351-3149-1*) China Bks.

Lest We Forget: Orthopaedics at the Massachusetts General Hospital, 1900-1995. Carter R. Rowe. LC 96-5704. 1996. 30.00 (*0-87233-119-9*) Bauhan.

Lest We Forget: Passage from Africa to Slavery. Velma M. Thomas. LC 96-54240. 31p. (YA). (gr. 7 up). 1997. 29.95 (*0-609-60030-3*) Random Hse Value.

Lest We Forget: Remembrances of Cheyenne's Jews. Mark Elliott & Marie Still. LC 90-80775. (Illus.). 196p. (Orig.). 1990. pap. 11.95 (*0-9625760-0-X*) Aaron Mntn Pub.

Lest We Forget: Report of Japanese Air Raid on Pearl Harbor. Ed. by Gary Gibson & Bill Berger. LC 91-72699. (Illus.). 463p. 1991. lib. bdg. 45.00 (*0-9629483-0-6*) GB Pub OK.

***Lest We Forget: The Kingsmen, 101st Aviation Battalion 1968.** William C. Meacham. 1999. mass mkt. 6.99 (*0-8041-1917-1*) Ivy Books.

Lest We Forget: The Signs of Jah's Coming Increases Daily. Ricardo A. Scott & Giancarlo T. Scott. (Ras Cardo Speaks to the Heathen in Babylon Ser.). (Illus.). 100p. (Orig.). 1995. pap. 9.95 (*1-883427-77-0*) Crnerstone GA.

Lest We Forget . . . John Raymond Wildman, 1878-1938. Gary J. Previts & Richard F. Taylor. (Monograph Series of the Academy of Accounting Historians: Monograph 2). 84p. 1978. pap. 5.00 (*1-879750-00-7*) Acad Acct Hist.

***Lest We Forget: or Character Gems Gleaned from South Arkansas.** J. D. Riggin. (Illus.). 230p. 1999. reprint ed. pap. 18.00 (*1-56546-145-2*) Arkansas Res.

Lest We Forget: or Character Gems Gleaned from South Arkansas. J. H. Riggins. 224p. 1978. reprint ed. 20.00 (*0-89308-072-1*) Southern Hist Pr.

Lester Beall: Trailblazer of American Graphic Design. R. Roger Remington. (Illus.). 320p. 1996. 60.00 (*0-393-73002-6*) Norton.

Lester Ben Benny Binion: Some Recollections of a Texas & Las Vegas Gaming Operator. Intro. by Mary E. Glass. 99p. 1976. lib. bdg. 30.50 (*1-56475-146-5*); fiche. write for info. (*1-56475-147-3*) U NV Oral Hist.

Lester Dent: The Man, His Craft & His Market. M. Martin McCarey-Laird. LC 94-76268. 120p. (Orig.). 1994. pap. 11.95 (*0-9641004-9-5*) Hidalgo Pubng.

Lester Horton: Modern Dance Pioneer. Larry Warren. 265p. 1992. pap. 15.95 (*0-87127-165-6*) Princeton Bk Co.

Lester Horton, Modern Dance Pioneer. Larry Warren. LC 76-23364. (Dance Program Ser.: Vol. 3). 288p. reprint ed. pap. 89.30 (*0-608-16715-0*, 202782000054) Bks Demand.

Lester J. Hilp: Reminiscences of a White Pine County Native, Reno Pharmacy Owner, & Civic Leader. Intro. by Mary E. Glass. 80p. 1968. lib. bdg. 28.50 (*1-56475-053-1*); fiche. write for info. (*1-56475-054-X*) U NV Oral Hist.

***Lester Piggott Autobiography.** Lester Piggott. 2000. pap. 10.95 (*0-552-14153-4*, Pub. by Transworld Publishers Ltd) Trafalgar.

Lester Sumrall: The Life Story of Lester Sumrall. Lester Sumrall & Tim Dudley. LC 92-64449. 240p. 1993. 14.95 (*0-89221-229-2*) New Leaf.

***Lester the Lazy Lion.** Jean Christie. (Felt Lift the Flap Bks.). (Illus.). (J). 2000. 4.95 (*1-58646-007-2*) Polka Dot.

Lester Ward & the Welfare State. Ed. by Henry S. Commager. LC 66-22579. 1967. 52.50 (*0-672-50998-9*) Irvington.

Lester Young Reader. Ed. by Lewis Porter. LC 90-24922. (Smithsonian Readers in American Music Ser.). (Illus.). 344p. 1991. pap. 19.95 (*1-56098-065-6*) Smithsonian.

Lester Young Solos. unabridged ed. Robert A. Luckey. 39p. 1994. pap. 10.00 (*0-9667047-0-3*, 02) Olympia LA.

Lester's Dog. Karen Hesse. LC 92-27674. (Illus.). 32p. (J). (ps-2). 1993. 16.00 (*0-517-58357-7*, Pub. by Crown Bks Yng Read); lib. bdg. 16.99 (*0-517-58358-5*, Pub. by Crown Bks Yng Read) Random.

Lesters Luck. Horatio Alger, Jr. (Works of Horatio Alger Jr.). 1989. reprint ed. lib. bdg. 79.00 (*0-685-44746-4*) Rprt Serv.

Lester's Progress. Harry M. Caudill. LC 86-82569. 106p. (Orig.). 1986. pap. 6.95 (*0-935680-29-2*) Kentucke Imprints.

Lestorie des Engles Solum la Translacion Maistre Geffrei Gaimar: Text & Translation, 2 vols., Vol. 1. Ed. by Thomas D. Hardy & Charles T. Martin. (Rolls Ser.: No. 91). 1969. reprint ed. write for info. (*0-8115-1167-7*) Periodicals Srv.

Lestorie des Engles Solum la Translacion Maistre Geffrei Gaimar: Text & Translation, 2 vols., Vol. 2. Ed. by Thomas D. Hardy & Charles T. Martin. (Rolls Ser.: No. 91). 1969. reprint ed. write for info. (*0-8115-1168-5*) Periodicals Srv.

***Lestrade & the Brother of Death.** M. J. Trow. LC 99-41316. (Lestrade Mystery Ser.: Vol. 7). 224p. 1999. 19.95 (*0-89526-268-1*) Regnery Pub.

***Lestrade & the Dead Man's Hand.** M. J. Trow. LC 99-59916. (Lestrade Mystery Ser.: Vol. XI). 224p. 2000. 19.95 (*0-89526-288-6*, Gateway Editions) Regnery Pub.

Lestrade & the Deadly Game. M. J. Trow. LC 99-23799. (Lestrade Mystery Ser.: Vol. 5). 208p. 1999. 19.95 (*0-89526-312-2*, Pub. by Regnery Pub) Natl Bk Netwk.

***Lestrade & the Gift of the Prince.** M. J. Trow. LC 99-59357. (Lestrade Mysteries Ser.). 208p. 2000. 19.95 (*0-89526-253-3*, Gateway Editions) Regnery Pub.

***Lestrade & the Guardian Angel.** M. J. Trow. LC 99-41315. (Lestrade Mystery Ser.: Vol. 8). 240p. 1999. 19.95 (*0-89526-267-3*) Regnery Pub.

Lestrade & the Hallowed House. M. J. Trow. (Lestrade Mystery Ser.: Vol. 3). 208p. 1999. 19.95 (*0-89526-341-6*, Pub. by Regnery Pub) Natl Bk Netwk.

Lestrade & the Leviathan. M. J. Trow. (Lestrade Mystery Ser.: Vol. 4). 208p. 1999. 19.95 (*0-89526-340-8*, Pub. by Regnery Pub) Natl Bk Netwk.

***Lestrade & the Magpie.** M. J. Trow. LC 99-59915. (Lestrade Mystery Ser.: Vol. X). 224p. 2000. 19.95 (*0-89526-289-4*, Gateway Editions) Regnery Pub.

Lestrade & the Ripper. M. J. Trow. LC 99-15926. (Lestrade Mystery Ser.: Vol. 6). 208p. 1999. 19.95 (*0-89526-311-4*, Pub. by Regnery Pub) Natl Bk Netwk.

***Lestrade & the Sawdust Ring, Vol. 13.** M. J. Trow. (Lestrade Mystery Ser.). 2000. 19.95 (*0-89526-245-2*) Regnery Pub.

***Lestrade & the Sign of Nine, Vol. 12.** M. J. Trow. (Lestrade Mystery Ser.). 224p. 2000. 19.95 (*0-89526-246-0*) Regnery Pub.

LeStrange Records: A Chronicle of the Early LeStranges of Norfolk, England, & the March of Wales, 1100-1310. H. LeStrange. (Illus.). 407p. 1993. reprint ed. pap. 61.00 (*0-8328-3702-4*); reprint ed. lib. bdg. 71.00 (*0-8328-3701-6*) Higginson Bk Co.

Lestriad. Steve Katz. LC 86-71804. 96p. 1987. 15.00 (*0-917453-08-5*); pap. 8.00 (*0-917453-09-3*) Bamberger.

Lestriad. deluxe ed. Steve Katz. LC 86-71804. 96p. 1987. 25.00 (*0-917453-10-7*) Bamberger.

Lestvitsa. Saint John Climacus.Tr. of Ladder. 363p. reprint ed. 18.00 (*0-317-28895-4*); reprint ed. pap. 13.00 (*0-317-28896-2*) Holy Trinity.

Let a Single Flower Blossom. Gary Kizer. 1977. 3.00 (*0-912678-30-5*, Greenfld Rev Pr) Greenfld Rev Lit.

Let All Creation Sing. Paul Tate. 1998. pap. 7.00 (*0-937690-68-6*, 7473) Wrld Lib Pubns.

Let All Creation Sing Music Collection. Paul Tate. 1999. pap. 15.00 (*1-58459-007-6*, 7475) Wrld Lib Pubns.

Let All God's Glory Through. Peter G. Van Breemen. LC 94-34867. 208p. 1995. pap. 14.95 (*0-8091-3525-6*) Paulist Pr.

Let All of Them Take Heed: Mexican Americans & the Campaign for Educational Equality in Texas, 1910-1981. Guadalupe San Miguel. LC 86-30777. (Mexican American Monograph Ser.: Vol. 11). 278p. reprint ed. pap. 86.20 (*0-608-08649-5*, 2069172) Bks Demand.

Let All the Earth Keep Silence. Phil Sanders. 176p. (Orig.). 1988. pap. 7.95 (*0-940999-36-6*, C-2148) Star Bible.

Let All the People Praise You. 1999. pap. 12.00 (*0-8100-0904-8*) Northwest Pub.

Let All Within Us Praise! Dramatic Resources for Worship. Patricia J. Shelly. LC 96-84113. 210p. 1996. pap. 15.95 (*0-87303-208-X*) Faith & Life.

Let All Within Us Praise! Songs for Worship & Celebration. Patricia J. Shelly. 52p. 1996. pap. 4.95 (*0-87303-209-8*) Faith & Life.

Let an Earthworm Be Your Garbage Man. Home, Farm & Garden Research Association Staff. (Illus.). 1954. pap. 8.00 (*0-9600102-6-2*) Shields.

Let Conscience Speak. David Fountain. pap. 0.99 (*0-85479-810-2*) Revival Lit.

Let Contention Cease: The Dynamics of Dissent in the Reorganized Church of Jesus Christ of Latter Day Saints. Ed. by Roger D. Launius & W. B. Spillman. 304p. (Orig.). 1991. pap. text 3.00 (*0-8309-0592-8*) Herald Pub Hse.

Let Dead Enough Alone: A Captain Heimrich Mystery. large type ed. Richard Lockridge & Frances Lockridge. LC 94-33676. 232p. 1995. pap. 18.95 (*0-7838-1159-4*, G K Hall Lrg Type) Mac Lib Ref.

Let Evening Come. Jane Kenyon. 80p. (C). 1990. pap. 11.00 (*1-55597-131-8*) Graywolf.

***Let Evening Come: Reflections on Aging.** Mary C. Morrison. LC 97-19578. 144p. 1998. 14.95 (*0-385-49086-0*) Doubleday.

Let Every Child Be Wanted: How Social Marketing is Revolutionizing Contraceptive Use Around the World. Philip D. Harvey. LC 99-13697. 264p. 1999. 59.95 (*0-86569-282-3*, Auburn Hse) Greenwood.

Let Every Heart: A Family Devotional for the Advent Season. Thomas Pless. (Illus.). 112p. 1999. 14.99 (*1-57748-573-4*) Barbour Pub.

Let Every Heart Prepare: Meditations for Advent & Christmas. Barbara C. Crafton. LC 98-27850. 96p. 1998. pap. 7.95 (*0-8192-1755-7*) Morehouse Pub.

Let Faith Change Your Life. Becky Tirabassi. 1996. 19.99 (*0-345-40070-4*, Moorings) Ballantine Pub Grp.

Let Faith Change Your Life. Becky Tirabassi. LC 96-35397. 192p. 1997. 17.99 (*0-7852-7235-6*) Nelson.

Let Farmers Judge: Experiences in Assessing Agricultural Innovations. Wim Hiemstra et al. LC 99-939619. (ILEIA Readers in Sustainable Agriculture Ser.). 208p. 1992. pap. 25.00 (*1-85339-149-2*, Pub. by Intermed Tech) Stylus Pub VA.

Let Food Be Thy Medicine: 750 Scientific Studies on the Personal & Planetary Benefits of Whole Foods. 3rd rev. ed. Alex Jack. 302p. 1999. pap. 15.95 (*1-882984-35-8*) One Peaceful World.

Let Freedom Reign. Leonard E. Read. 167p. 1969. 6.95 (*0-910614-40-7*) Foun Econ Ed.

Let Freedom Ring. Arthur Garfield Hays. LC 71-166329. (Civil Liberties in American History Ser.). (Illus.). 1972. reprint ed. lib. bdg. 57.50 (*0-306-70227-4*) Da Capo.

Let Freedom Ring: A Documentary History of the Modern Civil Rights Movement. Ed. by Peter B. Levy. LC 91-27717. 296p. 1992. pap. 19.95 (*0-275-93434-9*, B3434, Praeger Pubs) Greenwood.

Let Freedom Ring: A History of the Jews in the United States. Seymour Rossel. Ed. by Ruby G. Strauss. LC 96-132650. (Illus.). 96p. (J). (gr. 5-7). 1995. pap. text 5.95 (*0-87441-582-9*) Behrman.

Let Freedom Ring! Patriotic Poems. Patricia Tingry. (Illus.). 16p. 1998. pap. 1.95 (*0-8249-5010-0*) Ideals.

Let Go. Francois Fenelon. 96p. 1973. mass mkt. 5.99 (*0-88368-010-6*) Whitaker Hse.

Let Go & Let God. Ed. by Albert Cliffe. (C). 1990. pap. 30.00 (*0-85305-233-6*, Pub. by Arthur James) St Mut.

Let Go & Let God: Steps in Victorious Living. rev. ed. Albert Cliffe. 176p. 1992. pap. 10.00 (*0-671-76396-2*) Simon & Schuster.

Let Go, Let God: Surrendering Self-Centered Delusions in the Costly Journey of Faith. John E. Keller. LC 85-11048. 128p. 1985. pap. 12.99 (*0-8066-2162-1*, 10-3815, Augsburg) Augsburg Fortress.

Let Go, My Love. 2nd ed. Dorothy G. Hellman. 1996. reprint ed. lib. bdg. 22.00 (*0-8197-0613-2*) Bloch.

Let Go, My Love. 2nd ed. Dorothy G. Hellman. 168p. 1996. reprint ed. pap. 10.95 (*0-8197-0612-4*) Bloch.

Let Go of Fear: Tackling Our Worst Emotion. Carlos G. Valles. LC 90-46506. 224p. 1993. pap. text 9.95 (*0-89243-554-2*, Liguori Triumph) Liguori Pubns.

Let Go of My Ear! I Know What I'm Doing. LC 99-93885. 288p. 1999. pap. 12.95 (*0-9672126-0-X*) Sulisa Pubg.

Let Go of That Toe! Gary Hogg. (Spencer's Adventures Ser.). (J). 1997. pap. text 3.50 (*0-590-93940-8*, Little Apple) Scholastic Inc.

Let Go of the Ring: The Hope Chapel Story. 3rd rev. ed. Ralph E. Moore & Dan Beach. 200p. Date not set. mass mkt. 13.95 (*0-9628127-1-4*) Straight St.

***Let Go of the Ring: The Hope Chapel Story.** 4th ed. Ralph E. Moore & Dan Beach. (Illus.). 240p. 2000. pap. text 12.95 (*0-9628127-2-2*) Straight St.

Let Go of the Struggle. Joan Fericy. (Illus.). 52p. (Orig.). 1989. pap. 3.95 (*0-9622371-1-6*) J Fericy.

Let Go of Whatever Makes You Stop see Sueltese de Lo Que le Detiene

Let Go of Your Baggage & Travel Light: A Manual for Changing Your Life. Cecil McLaughlin. 64p. 1991. pap. 5.95 (*1-879838-00-1*) Travel Light.

Let Go the Glass Voice: A Novel. unabridged ed. Maureen McCafferty. LC 97-71805. (Illus.). 128p. 1997. 19.95 (*0-942979-27-3*, 942979); pap. 9.95 (*0-942979-28-1*, 942979) Livingston U Pr.

***Let God & Let Go.** S. M. Henriques & Criswell Freeman. 128p. 2000. pap. 4.95 (*1-58334-081-5*, Pub. by Walnut Gr Pr) Midpt Trade.

Let God Arise. Richard Holloway. LC 73-160038. x, 171 p. 1972. write for info. (*0-264-64598-7*) A R Mowbray.

***Let God Be God: A Study of the Attributes of God - Student Worktext.** ACSI Staff. 116p. (YA). (gr. 9-11). 1999. student ed. 13.00 (*1-58331-119-X*) Assn Christ Sch.

Let God Be God: An Interpretation of the Theology of Martin Luther. Philip S. Watson. LC 83-45675. reprint ed. 39.50 (*0-404-19864-3*) AMS Pr.

Let God Comfort You. Esther Armstrong. 16p. 1996. pap. 1.50 (*0-88243-936-7*) Gospel Pub.

Let God Guide You Daily. Wesley L. Duewel. 224p. (Orig.). 1988. pap. 10.99 (*0-310-36171-0*, 17094P) Duewel Lit.

Let God Help You Choose: Learning to Make Decisions That Honor God. Roger C. Palms. 163p. 1998. reprint ed. pap. 10.99 (*0-89367-231-9*) Light & Life Comm.

Let God Love You. Malcolm Smith. 1995. mass mkt. 4.99 (*1-880089-18-1*) Albury Pub.

Let God Speak: Let Us Listen. Edmund R. McDavid, III. 382p. 1991. 14.95 (*0-9630447-0-2*); pap. 10.95 (*0-9630447-1-0*) Hope AL.

Let Good Fortune Jump on You. Paul Reps. (Illus.). 75p. 1990. reprint ed. pap. 7.95 (*0-9620812-7-2*) Good Karma.

Let Grassroots Speak. Aditee N. Chowdhury. (C). 1989. 28.00 (*81-85054-79-7*, Pub. by Manohar) S Asia.

Let Heaven & Earth Unite! Stephen M. Weglian & Miriam A. Weglian. LC 95-72448. 160p. 1996. pap. 9.00 (*1-877678-40-6*) Queenship Pub.

Let Heaven Fall. large type ed. Freda Davies. (Linford Mystery Large Print Ser.). 400p. 1998. pap. 17.99 (*0-7089-5288-7*, Linford) Ulverscroft.

Let Her Keep It Vol. 1: Jesus' Ordination of Mary of Bethany. large type unabridged ed. Thomas W. Butler. Ed. by Barbara Hope. LC 98-65357. (Illus.). 360p. 1998. pap. 22.00 (*0-9627161-1-1*) QLP CA.

***Let Heroes Speak: Antarctic Explorers, 1772-1922.** Michael H. Rosove. LC 99-56907. (Illus.). 320p. 2000. 34.95 (*1-55750-967-0*) Naval Inst Pr.

Let Him Go! Lili W. Blumenstein. (Illus.). 240p. 1996. 13.00 (*0-8059-3904-0*) Dorrance.

Let Him Have His Way with Thee. Craig Tappe. 1994. pap. 8.80 (*0-89137-828-6*) Quality Pubns.

Let Him Live. Lurlene McDaniel. (One Last Wish Ser.: No. 6). 192p. (YA). 1993. mass mkt. 4.50 (*0-553-56067-0*) Bantam.

Let Him Live. Lurlene McDaniel. (One Last Wish Ser.). (J). 1993. 9.09 (*0-606-02706-8*, Pub. by Turtleback) Demco.

Let Him That Is Without Sin . . . Tom Allen. 1998. pap. 1.59 (*0-87509-748-0*) Chr Pubns.

Let History Judge: The Origins & Consequences of Stalinism. enl. rev. ed. Roy A. Medvedev. Ed. & Tr. by George Shriver. 891p. 1989. text 87.50 (*0-231-06350-4*) Col U Pr.

Let History Judge: The Origins & Consequences of Stalinism. rev. ed. Roy A. Medvedev. 1990. pap. text 29.00 (*0-231-06351-2*) Col U Pr.

Let It Be. Sri Chinmoy. (Little Books of Wisdom: Vol. 18). (Illus.). 1999. pap. 4.95 (*1-893161-01-3*, BK-18) Jharna Kala.

Let It Be: Advent & Christmas Meditations for Women. Ed. by Therese J. Burchard. LC 98-18349. 112p. 1998. pap. 9.95 (*0-8245-1767-9*, Crsrd) Crossroad NY.

Let It Be a Dance. Ric Masten. 176p. 1997. pap. 12.95 (*0-931104-45-9*) SunInk Pubn.

Let It Be Hot. unabridged ed. Terry L. Christopherson. 80p. 1998. pap. 7.95 (*0-9666898-0-1*) IFF Inc.

Let It Bleed. Ian Rankin. 1996. 20.00 (*1-883402-76-X*) S&S Trade.

Let It Bleed. Ian Rankin. LC 96-30535. 288p. 1996. 20.50 (*0-684-83055-8*) S&S Trade.

Let It Bleed. Ian Rankin. 320p. 1998. pap. 5.99 (*0-312-96665-2*, Pub. by Tor Bks) St Martin.

***Let It Bleed: An Inspector Rebus Novel.** large type ed. Ian Rankin. LC 00-37764. 530p. 2000. pap. 26.95 (*0-7862-2677-3*) Thorndike Pr.

Let It Bleed: Essays, 1985-95. Gary Indiana. LC 95-71068. 300p. (Orig.). (C). 1997. pap. 16.00 (*1-85242-332-3*) Serpents Tail.

***Let It Blurt: The Life & Times of Lester Bangs, America's Greatest Rock Critic.** Jim DeRogatis. (Illus.). 331p. 2000. pap. 15.95 (*0-7679-0509-1*) Broadway BDD.

Let It Come Down. Paul Bowles. LC 80-24825. 296p. 1994. reprint ed. 20.00 (*0-87685-480-3*); reprint ed. pap. 15.00 (*0-87685-479-X*) Black Sparrow.

Let It Go. unabridged ed. Marilyn Halverson. 240p. (YA). (gr. 7-11). 1985. pap. 5.95 (*0-7736-7347-4*) STDK.

Let It Just Happen. Albert Krassner. 77p. (Orig.). 1986. pap. 4.95 (*0-912061-08-1*) Veridon Edns.

Let It Rain. David W. Christner. 105p. 1980. pap. 5.50 (*0-87129-179-7*, L42) Dramatic Pub.

Let It Ride. Samuel F. Pickering, Jr. 192p. (C). 1991. 24.95 (*0-8262-0801-0*) U of Mo Pr.

Let It Ride. Samuel F. Pickering, Jr. 192p. 1992. reprint ed. pap. 14.95 (*0-8262-0869-X*) U of Mo Pr.

Let It Ride & Caribbean Stud Poker for Women. Denise Richards. Ed. by Debby Frerichs. 54p. (Orig.). 1996. per. 10.95 (*1-890244-04-X*) D&D Pubns.

Let It Rip. Greg Daniells. (Illus.). 128p. 1997. 12.98 (*0-7858-0656-3*) Bk Sales Inc.

Let It Rot! The Gardener's Guide to Composting. rev. ed. Stu Campbell. Ed. by Kim Foster. LC 90-50354. (Illus.). 160p. 1990. pap. 8.95 (*0-88266-635-5*) Storey Bks.

Let It Rot! The Gardener's Guide to Composting. 3rd rev. ed. Stu Campbell. LC 97-36405. (Illus.). 1998. 11.95 (*1-58017-023-4*, Garden Way Pub) Storey Bks.

Let It Shine: A Meditation Coloring Book. A. J. Wolff. (Illus.). 64p. (Orig.). 1997. pap. 7.95 (*0-931481-07-4*) Rosebush Pub.

Let It Shine: A Tribute To . . . Emily G. DeCarlo. LC 92-53713. 37p. (Orig.). 1993. pap. 6.95 (*0-936026-31-6*) R&M Pub Co.

Let It Shine: Quiet Time Book for Teens. Ed. by Sheila Jones & Tom Jones. 133p. (YA). 1994. pap. 7.99 (*1-884553-48-6*) Discipleshp.

***Let It Shine: Stories of Black Women Freedom Fighters.** Andrea Pinkney. (Illus.). 2000. 32.83 (*0-7398-3073-2*) Raintree Steck-V.

***Let It Shine: The Stories of Ten Black Women Freedom Fighters.** Andrea Davis Pinkney & Stephen Alcorn. LC 99-42806. (Illus.). 128p. (J). (ps up). 2000. 20.00 (*0-15-201005-X*, Harcourt Child Bks) Harcourt.

***Let It Snow!** 64p. 1999. pap. 10.95 (*0-634-00918-4*) H Leonard.

Let It Snow. Sherry Lewis. (Harlequin Super Romance Ser.). 1998. per. 4.25 (*0-373-70816-5*) Silhouette.

Let Jasmine Rain Down. Shelemay. LC 98-10938. 1998. pap. text 25.00 (*0-226-75212-7*); lib. bdg. 65.00 (*0-226-75211-9*) U Ch Pr.

Let Jorge Do It: An Approach to Rural Nonformal Education. James Hoxeng. 221p. (Orig.). (C). 1973. spiral bd. 6.00 (*0-932288-30-8*) Ctr Intl Ed U of MA.

Let Justice Be Done: Crime & Politics in Early San Francisco. Kevin J. Mullen. LC 89-4750. (Wilbur S. Shepperson Series in History & Humanities). (Illus.). 336p. 1989. 24.95 (*0-87417-146-6*) U of Nev Pr.

Let Justice Be Done: New Light on the Jim Garrison Investigation. 341p. 1999. pap. 14.95 (*0-9669716-0-4*) Jordan Pubg.

***Let Justice Flow: A Black Woman's Struggle for Equality in Bermuda.** Muriel Wade-Smith. LC 98-61304. 160p. 1999. pap. 12.99 (*1-57921-147-X*) WinePress Pub.

Let Justice Roll: Prophetic Challenges in Religion, Politics, & Society. Ed. by Neal Riemer. (Religious Forces in the Modern Political World). 244p. (C). 1996. pap. text 25.95 (*0-8476-8193-9*); lib. bdg. 66.00 (*0-8476-8192-0*) Rowman.

Let Justice Roll Down: The Old Testament, Ethics, & Christian Life. Bruce C. Birch. 320p. (Orig.). 1991. pap. 32.95 (*0-664-24026-7*) Westminster John Knox.

Let Justice Roll down Like Waters: Biblical Justice Homilies Throughout the Year. Walter J. Burghardt. LC 97-37897. 320p. 1998. pap. 19.95 (*0-8091-3765-8*) Paulist Pr.

Let Justice Sing: Hymnody & Justice. Paul Westermeyer. LC 98-19837. (American Essays in Liturgy Ser.). 118p. 1998. pap. 9.95 (*0-8146-2505-3*) Liturgical Pr.

Let Life Be Like This! 2nd ed. Marcus Bach. LC 63-22126. 199p. 1997. reprint ed. pap. 12.95 (*0-87516-707-1*) DeVorss.

Let Loose on Mother Goose. Terry Graham. LC 81-80248. (Illus.). 96p. (J). (ps-3). 1982. pap. text 10.95 (*0-86530-030-5*, IP 30-5) Incentive Pubns.

Let Love Change Your Life see How to Live with Them Since You Can't Live Without Them: Developing the Skills, Understanding, & Insights for Successful Relationships

Let Love Come Last. Taylor Caldwell. 1974. reprint ed. lib. bdg. 27.95 (*0-88411-160-1*) Amereon Ltd.

Let Love Preside see Dejad Que el Amor Presida

Let Me Alone. Anna Kavan. 320p. 1974. 30.00 (*0-7206-0243-2*, Pub. by P Owen Ltd) Dufour.

Let Me Be a Woman. Elisabeth Elliott. 190p. 1977. pap. 8.99 (*0-8423-2161-6*) Tyndale Hse.

Let Me Be a Woman. Elisabeth Elliott. 185p. 1982. mass mkt. 4.99 (*0-8423-2162-4*) Tyndale Hse.

Let Me Be Free. Sarah Sam & Rose Atkinson. 28p. 1998. pap. 6.00 (*0-8059-4195-9*) Dorrance.

***Let Me Be Free: The Nez Perce Tragedy.** David Sievert Lavender. LC 99-24427. 432p. 1999. 17.95 (*0-8061-3190-X*) U of Okla Pr.

Let Me Be Los: A Code Book for Finnegans Wake. Frances Phipps. Ed. by George Quasha. LC 87-6451. (Illus.). 211p. (C). 1987. reprint ed. pap. 16.95 (*0-88268-042-0*) Station Hill Pr.

Let Me Be LOS: Codebook for Finnegans Wake. Frances Phipps. (Illus.). 1987. 43.50 (*0-9606540-5-4*) Classic Nonfic.

Let Me Be the Boss. Brod Bagert. LC 91-91408. (Illus.). 48p. (J). (gr. 3-7). 1992. 14.95 (*1-56397-099-6*, Wordsong) Boyds Mills Pr.

Let Me Be... The Boss: Poems for Kids to Perform. Brod Bagert. LC 91-91408. (Illus.). 48p. (J). (gr. 3-7). 1995. pap. 6.95 (*1-56397-524-6*, Wordsong) Boyds Mills Pr.

Let Me Be... The Boss: Poems for Kids to Perform. Brod Bagert. 1996. pap. 9.95 incl. audio (*1-56397-540-8*, Wordsong) Boyds Mills Pr.

Let Me Be Your Friend . . . Jane S. Pasley. (Illus.). 52p. (Orig.). 1989. pap. text 6.95 (*0-685-29398-X*) J S Pasley.

Let Me Build Your Dreams. Roosevelt Wright, Jr. 21p. (Orig.). (C). 1995. pap. text 3.00 (*0-943751-02-0*) Free Pr LA.

Let Me Call You Sweetheart. Mary Higgins Clark. 320p. 1996. per. 7.50 (*0-671-56817-5*) Thorndike Pr.

Let Me Call You Sweetheart. Mary Higgins Clark. LC 95-7331. 1996. 12.60 (*0-606-09540-3*, Pub. by Turtleback) Demco.

Let Me Call You Sweetheart. Nancy Gideon. 1998. per. 4.25 (*0-373-07851-X*, 1-07851-8) Silhouette.

Let Me Call You Sweetheart. enl. ed. Mary Higgins Clark. 1995. 7.50 (*0-684-80396-8*) Thorndike Pr.

***Let Me Call You Sweethearts: A Thriller with a Touch of Polyamory.** Eddie L. Phelts. 309p. 1999. pap. 16.95 (*0-7414-0227-0*) Buy Books.

Let Me Count the Ways. Leigh Michaels. (Romance Ser.: No. 3023). 1989. per. 2.50 (*0-373-03023-1*) Harlequin Bks.

Let Me Count the Ways. large type ed. Leigh Michaels. (Magna Large Print Ser.). 287p. 1996. 27.99 (*0-7505-0989-9*, Pub. by Mgna Lrg Print) Ulverscroft.

Let Me Count the Ways: Discovering Great Sex Without Intercourse. Marty Klein & Riki Robbins. LC 98-42900. 224p. 1999. 24.95 (*0-87477-956-1*, Tarcher Putnam) Putnam Pub Group.

***Let Me Count the Ways: Practical Innovations for Jewish Teachers.** Carol Oseran Starin. LC 99-36310. 192p. 1999. pap. 8.95 (*0-933873-97-2*) Torah Aura.

Let Me Decide: The Health Care Directive That Speaks for You When You Can't. William Molloy & Virginia Mepham. LC 94-61128. 72p. 1994. 4.95 (*0-934104-09-3*) Woodland.

Let Me Die in Ireland: The True Story of Patrick. David W. Bercot. LC 99-210833. 1999. pap. text 8.95 (*0-924722-08-8*) Scroll Pub.

Let Me Do It! Janice Gibala-Broxholm. LC 92-12856. (Illus.). 32p. (J). (ps-k). 1994. text 14.95 (*0-02-735827-5*, Bradbury S&S) S&S Childrens.

Let Me Do It! rev. ed. Anne Rogovin. LC 90-30226. 160p. 1990. pap. 5.48 (*0-687-21376-2*) Abingdon.

Let Me Entertain You. Merlin R. Carothers. 1992. 6.95 (*0-943026-21-0*) Carothers.

Let Me Entertain You: Conversations with Show People. Jordan R. Young. LC 88-9152. (Illus.). 176p. (Orig.). 1988. pap. 9.95 (*0-940410-83-4*, Moonstone Pr) Past Times.

Let Me Explain: A Story about Donor Insemination. Jane T. Schnitter. LC 94-417837. (Illus.). 32p. (J). (gr. 2-5). 1995. 14.00 (*0-944934-12-9*) Perspect Indiana.

Let Me Grieve, but Not Forever. Verdell Davis. LC 97-5643. Orig. Title: Riches Stored in Secret Places. 160p. 1997. 12.99 (*0-8499-1425-6*) Word Pub.

Let Me Hear You Whisper, & the Ladies Should Be in Bed: 2 Plays. Paul Zindel. 1973. pap. 5.25 (*0-8222-0626-9*) Dramatists Play.

Let Me Hear Your Voice: A Family's Triumph over Autism. Catherine Maurice. 1994. reprint ed. pap. 12.00 (*0-449-90664-7*, Columbine) Fawcett.

***Let Me Help!** Louise Tidd. LC 98-52515. (Illus.). 32p. (J). 1999. 16.90 (*0-7613-2067-9*, Copper Beech Bks) Millbrook Pr.

Let Me Help! Louise Vitellaro Tidd & Dorothy Handelman. LC 98-52515. (Real Kids Readers Ser.). (Illus.). 32p. (J). (gr. k-2). 1999. pap. 3.99 (*0-7613-2092-X*, Copper Beech Bks) Millbrook Pr.

***Let Me Help You with Your Business: How I Made a Fortune by Following These Three Steps Motivation, Marketing, Management.** Rosita Almes. LC 00-90140. 210p. 2000. pap. write for info. (*0-9679083-0-2*) Brand Wayn Pubns.

Let Me Hold the World. Genevieve Stiles. pap. 3.50 (*0-686-00948-7*) Wagon & Star.

Let Me Illustrate: More Than 400 Stories, Anecdotes & Illustrations. Donald Grey Barnhouse. (Illus.). 384p. 1994. pap. 12.99 (*0-8007-5508-1*) Revell.

Let Me Introduce You to My Father: A Study on the Nature of God. Dale E. Phillips. 120p. 1992. pap. 6.50 (*0-9633335-1-8*) Dryden Pubs.

Let Me Introduce You to the Bible. William MacDonald. 1980. pap. 4.00 (*0-937396-22-2*) Walterick Pubs.

Let Me Keep Laughter. Audre Pitts. 112p. 1985. pap. 7.99 (*0-8341-1090-3*) Beacon Hill.

Let Me Learn. Christine A. Johnston. LC 98-19722. 240p. 1998. wbk. ed. 61.95 (*0-8039-6764-0*); pap., wbk. ed. 27.95 (*0-8039-6765-9*) Corwin Pr.

Let Me Live. Angelo Herndon. LC 69-18566. (American Negro: His History & Literature. Series 2). 1969. reprint ed. 22.95 (*0-405-01869-X*) Ayer.

Let Me Live. Angelo Herndon. (American Biography Ser.). 409p. 1991. reprint ed. lib. bdg. 89.00 (*0-7812-8178-4*) Rprt Serv.

Let Me Live Again. Angel Nunez. 1998. pap. 10.99 (*1-56043-310-8*, Treasure Hse) Destiny Image.

Let Me Make It Good: A Chronicle of My Life with Borderline Personality Disorder. Jane Wanklin. (Orig.). 1996. pap. 17.95 (*0-88962-627-8*) Mosaic.

Let Me Make Myself Plain. Catherine Cookson. pap. 10.95 (*0-552-13407-4*, Pub. by Transworld Publishers Ltd) Trafalgar.

Let Me off This Spaceship! Gery Greer & Robert Ruddick. LC 90-32045. (Illus.). 64p. (J). (gr. 2-5). 1991. 12.95 (*0-06-021605-0*) HarpC Child Bks.

Let Me Que You In. Diane McLeod. (Illus.). 135p. 1998. pap. 29.95 (*0-9664594-0-7*) McLeo.

Let Me Say That Again: Maxims for Spiritual Living. Maxie Dunnam. 128p. 1996. 12.00 (*0-8358-0769-X*) Upper Room Bks.

Let Me See Your Body Talk. Jan Latiolas Hargrave. 1994. pap. text 19.95 (*0-7872-2851-6*) Kendall-Hunt.

Let Me See Your Eyes: Mrs. Johns' School. Ed. by Calvert W. Tazewell. LC 90-80407. 74p. (Orig.). 1991. pap. 8.00 (*1-878515-11-X*) W S Dawson.

Let Me Show to the World My Eyes (The American Years) Ludwig J. Marek. LC 98-30724. 68p. 1998. pap. 14.95 (*0-7734-3086-5*, Mellen Poetry Pr) E Mellen.

Let Me Show You My World. Katy Tartakoff. (Illus.). 54p. (Orig.). (J). student ed. 14.95 (*0-9629365-2-9*) Childrens Lgcy.

Let Me Speak! Testimony of Domitila, a Woman of the Bolivian Mines. Domitila B. De Chungara & Moema Viezzer. Tr. by Victoria Ortiz. LC 77-91757. 235p. 1979. pap. 15.00 (*0-85345-485-X*, Pub. by Monthly Rev) NYU Pr.

Let Me Stand at Your Side. M. Basilea Schlink. 1975. 3.50 (*3-87209-614-1*) Evang Sisterhood Mary.

Let Me Survive: A True Story. Louise Longo. LC 96-8897. 160p. 1996. 17.95 (*1-57409-006-2*) Sheridan.

Let Me Take You Down. Jack Jones. 376p. 1994. mass mkt. 5.99 (*0-446-60043-1*, Pub. by Warner Bks) Little.

***Let Me Tell You a Story.** Anthony Campolo. LC 00-34985. 224p. 2000. pap. 12.99 (*0-8499-4205-5*) Word Pub.

Let Me Tell You about Jesus. Lucile Bechdolt. 1990. 4.35 (*0-89137-058-7*) Quality Pubns.

Let Me Tell You Everything: Memoirs of a Lovesick Intellectual. Barbara Bottner. LC 88-22066. 160p. (YA). (gr. 7 up). 1989. 12.95 (*0-06-020596-2*) HarpC Child Bks.

Let Me Tell You How I Died. Sinclair Smith. 160p. (YA). (gr. 7-9). 1994. pap. 3.50 (*0-590-47786-2*) Scholastic Inc.

Let Me Tell You Where I've Been: Photographs & Interviews with Seven Vietnam Veterans by Janice Rogovin. Ed. by John Grady & Sarah Rogovin. LC 88-90819. (Illus.). 48p. (Orig.). 1988. pap. 8.95 (*0-9621783-0-6*) Stonybrook Pr.

Let Me Think! Activities to Develop Problem-Solving Abilities in Young Children. Sue Dinwiddie. (Illus.). 70p. 1997. spiral bd. 10.95 (*0-9660573-1-7*) Better World.

Let Me Touch You. Joyce Tyre. LC 78-59563. 1978. pap. 2.95 (*0-88435-010-X*) Chateau Pub.

Let Me Walk Beside You. Margie Domingo. 60p. (Orig.). (C). 1993. pap. 10.00 (*0-9631826-1-7*) Exist InVerse.

***Let Me Whisper in Your Ear.** Mary Jane Clark. 304p. 2000. 22.95 (*0-312-26191-8*) St Martin.

Let Me Write. (Key Words Readers Ser.: C Series, No. 641-3c). (Illus.). (J). (ps-5). pap. 3.50 (*0-7214-0027-2*, Ladybrd) Penguin Putnam.

Let Me Write, No. 3. (Key Words Readers Ser.: Series S705). (Illus.). (J). (ps-5). student ed. 1.95 (*0-317-04758-2*, Ladybrd) Penguin Putnam.

Let Mercy Abound: Social Concern in the Greek Orthodox Church. Stanley S. Harakas. 188p. (C). 1983. text 10.95 (*0-916586-60-X*, Pub. by Holy Cross Orthodox); pap. text 5.95 (*0-916586-61-8*, Pub. by Holy Cross Orthodox) BookWorld.

Let Ministry Teach: A Guide to Theological Reflection. Robert L. Kinast. 152p. 1996. pap. 14.95 (*0-8146-2374-3*, Liturg Pr Bks) Liturgical Pr.

Let My Babies Go! A Passover Story. Sarah Willson. (Rugrats (tv) Ser.). (Illus.). 32p. (J). (ps-3). 1998. mass mkt. 5.99 (*0-689-81979-X*) S&S Childrens.

Let My Existence Be Born. Margie Domingo. LC 92-90122. 80p. (Orig.). (C). 1992. pap. 10.00 (*0-9631826-0-9*) Exist InVerse.

***Let My Heart Attack Save Your Life: A Simple, Sound, Workable Weight Management Plan.** Joseph Mason. 240p. 1998. pap. 14.95 (*0-471-34745-0*) Wiley.

***Let My Heart Attack Save Your Life: A Simple, Sound, Workable Weight Management Plan.** Joseph W. Mason. LC 98-230249. 240p. 1998. pap. 14.95 (*1-56561-134-9*) Wiley.

Let My Name Stand Fair. Elizabeth Seifert & Shirley Seifert. Date not set. reprint ed. lib. bdg. 17.95 (*0-89190-134-5*, Am Repr) Amereon Ltd.

***Let My Nation Go.** Yosef Deutsch. LC 99-220860. 404p. 1998. 21.95 (*0-87306-818-1*) Feldheim.

Let My People Eat! Passover Seders Made Simple. Zell Schulman. LC 97-38973. (Illus.). 288p. 1998. 27.50 (*0-02-861259-0*, Pub. by Macmillan) S&S Trade.

Let My People Go. Chofetz Chaim Staff. 168p. 1993. 17.95 (*1-58330-096-1*) Feldheim.

Let My People Go! Moses C. Chow & Leona Choy. 180p. (Orig.). 1995. pap. 13.95 (*1-882324-13-7*) Ambssdrs Christ.

Let My People Go. Tom Hess. 178p. (Orig.). 1987. pap. 9.95 (*1-878327-66-6*, THI-001) Morning NC.

Let My People Go: African-American Women Writers, 1910-1940 by Lillian E. Wood. Gates. 1996. 25.00 (*0-7838-1429-1*, Hall Reference) Macmillan.

Let My People Go: African-Americans, 1804-1860 see Young Oxford History of African Americans

Let My People Go: Bible Stories Told by a Freeman of Color. Patricia C. McKissack & Fredrick McKissack. LC 97-19983. (Illus.). 144p. (YA). (gr. 3 up). 1998. 20.00 (*0-689-80856-9*) S&S Bks Yung.

Let My People Go: Cairo, Illinois, 1967-1973. Ed. by Jan P. Roddy. LC 96-7578. (Illus.). 124p. (C). 1996. 49.95 (*0-8093-2085-1*); pap. 19.95 (*0-8093-2086-X*) S Ill U Pr.

Let My People Go: Empowering Laity for Ministry. Alvin J. Lindgren & Norman Shawchuck. 144p. (Orig.). (C). 1989. reprint ed. pap. text 12.95 (*0-938180-15-0*) Spiritual Growth.

Let My People Go: The Story of the Underground Railroad & the Growth of the Abolitionist Movement. Henrietta Buckmaster. Ed. by John G. Sproat. LC 92-16843. (Southern Classics Ser.). 424p. (C). 1992. reprint ed. pap. 16.95 (*0-87249-865-4*) U of SC Pr.

Let My People Go: The True Story of Present-Day Persecution & Slavery. Cal Bombay. LC 98-226464. 170p. 1998. pap. 12.99 (*1-57673-459-5*) Multnomah Pubs.

Let My People Go Vol. 1: The Life of Robert A. Jaffray. rev. ed. A. W. Tozer. LC 90-80076. (Jaffray Collection of Missionary Portraits: Bk. 1). 128p. (YA). 1990. pap. 9.99 (*0-87509-427-9*) Chr Pubns.

Let My People Go Haggadah. Chofetz Chaim Staff. 168p. 1994. 14.95 (*1-58330-095-3*) Feldheim.

Let My People Grow! Tim Massengale. LC 88-31269. (Illus.). 304p. (Orig.). 1989. pap. 8.99 (*0-932581-41-2*) Word Aflame.

***Let My People Know: A Manual for Understanding the Black Presence in the Bible.** John Terry Allen. (Illus.). 80p. 2000. pap. 9.95 (*0-936369-76-0*) Son-Rise Pubns.

Let My People Know . . . And Go. Ed. by Jennifer L. Pratt et al. LC 96-68906. (Illus.). 85p. (Orig.). 1996. pap. 4.00 (*0-9652533-0-9*) Presby Ctr Mission.

Let My People Laugh. Martha Bolton. 58p. 1989. 15.99 (*0-8341-9009-5*, MP-653) Lillenas.

Let My People Learn: The Biography of Wil Lou Gray. Maria E. Ayres. 228p. 1988. 16.95 (*0-87921-078-8*) Attic Pr.

Let My People Live: Faith & Struggle in Central America. Gordon J. Spykman et al. LC 88-11294. 287p. 1988. reprint ed. pap. 89.00 (*0-7837-6570-3*, 204613500011) Bks Demand.

***Let My Spirit Move: Churches Becoming Free by the Work of the Spirit.** Steven Sampson. 128p. 1999. pap. text 10.99 (*1-85240-233-4*) SOV5.

Let My Spirit Soar! Narratives of Diverse Women in School Leadership. Maenette K. Nee-Benham & Joanne E. Cooper. LC 97-33952. (1-Off Ser.). 176p. 1998. 51.95 (*0-8039-6671-7*); pap. 22.95 (*0-8039-6672-5*) Corwin Pr.

Let My Words Be Sweet & Tender . . . 'Cause I May Have to Eat Them Tomorrow! Ron Wheeler. LC 97-136681. (Adventures of Jeremiah Ser.: No. 4). (Illus.). 96p. (Orig.). (YA). 1996. pap. 7.99 (*0-8341-1594-8*) Beacon Hill.

Let Myself Shine. S. R. Lavin. 7.00 (*0-686-65484-6*); pap. 3.50 (*0-686-65485-4*) Kulchur Foun.

Let Nature Do the Growing: The Fertilizer-Free Vegetable Garden. Gajin Tokuno. LC 86-80219. (Illus.). 256p. (Orig.). 1987. pap. 24.00 (*0-87040-668-X*) Japan Pubns USA.

Let Newton Be! Ed. by John Fauvel et al. (Illus.). 280p. 1989. 29.95 (*0-685-47299-X*) OUP.

Let Night Touch You. unabridged ed. Marion C. Carion. (Message from Yin Ser.: Vol. 2). 32p. 1999. pap. 6.00 (*1-890185-02-7*) Half-Moon.

Let No Man Deceive You: Responses to Objections about the Church of Jesus Christ of Latter-Day Saints. Bruce Richardson. 308p. 1998. pap. 14.95 (*1-890828-09-2*, 09-2, Pub. by Camden Ct) Origin Bk Sales.

Let No Man Put Asunder: The Control of Marriage in the German Southwest, 1550-1600. Thomas Max Safley. (Sixteenth Century Essays & Studies: Vol. II). 210p. 1984. 40.00 (*0-940474-02-6*, SCJP) Truman St Univ.

Let No One Deceive You. Michael L. Brown. LC 97-220120. 312p. 1997. pap. 13.99 (*1-56043-693-X*, Revival Pr) Destiny Image.

Let Nobody Turn Me 'Round: Reading Level 3. (Sundown Fiction Collection). 1993. 3.95 (*0-88336-764-5*); audio 17.95 (*0-88336-797-1*) New Readers.

Let Nobody Turn Us Around: Voices of Resistance, Reform & Renewal: An African American Anthology. Ed. by Manning Marable & Leith Mullings. LC 99-49099. 600p. 1999. 35.00 (*0-8476-8345-1*) Rowman.

***Let Nobody Turn Us Around: Voices of Resistance, Reform & Renewal: An African American Anthology.** Ed. by Manning Marable & Leith Mullings. 560p. 1999. 35.00 (*0-8476-9930-7*, Pub. by Rowman) Natl Bk Netwk.

Let Not Your Heart Be Troubled. Boyd K. Packer. 1991. 19.95 (*0-88494-787-4*) Bookcraft Inc.

Let Not Your Heart Be Troubled. Edward J. Saleska. 16p. 1967. pap. 1.49 (*0-570-03676-3*, 74-1001) Concordia.

***Let Not Your Heart Be Troubled: Living with God in the Worst of Times & the Best of Times.** Roosevelt McPherson. LC 98-74731. 85p. 1999. pap. 12.00 (*1-878647-59-8*) APU Pub Grp.

Let Not Your Heat Be Troubled. Norvel Hayes. (Mini-Bks.). 48p. pap. 1.00 (*0-89274-640-8*, HH-640) Harrison Hse.

Let Nothing Disturb You: A Journey to the Center of the Soul with Teresa of Avila. John Kirvan. LC 95-80886. (Thirty Days with a Great Spiritual Teacher Ser.). 216p. (Orig.). 1996. pap. 6.95 (*0-87793-570-X*) Ave Maria.

Let Nothing Trouble You. Compiled by Heidi S. Hess. LC 98-5141. (Saints Speak Today Ser.). 1998. pap. text 9.99 (*1-56955-062-X*) Servant.

Let Nothing You Dismay. Mark O'Donnell. LC 98-15883. 224p. 1998. 22.00 (*0-375-40103-2*) Knopf.

Let Nothing You Dismay. Mark O'Donnell. 208p. 1999. 12.00 (*0-375-70096-X*, Vin) Random.

Let O. J. Heart! abr. ed. Eric Fortmeyer. 64p. 1999. pap. 25.00 (*1-928620-18-3*, EFX-999105M0384, Poms Healing) AGI Prods.

Let Ocean Seethe & Terra Slide: A History of the Sonoma Coast & the State Park That Shares It's Name. Rex Grady. (Illus.). 288p. 1998. pap. 15.00 (*0-9662058-1-2*) Lilburne Pr.

Let Peace Disturb You. Michael Buckley. 128p. (C). 1991. 39.00 (*0-85439-410-9*, Pub. by St Paul Pubns) St Mut.

***Let Peace Surround You.** Lawrence A. Kacmarcik. LC 99-91683. 2000. 25.00 (*0-7388-1194-7*); pap. 18.00 (*0-7388-1195-5*) Xlibris Corp.

Let Prayer Change Your Life. Becky Tirabassi. 160p. 1995. pap. 10.99 (*0-7852-7721-8*) Nelson.

***Let Prayer Change Your Life: Discover the Awesome Power of, Empowering Discipline of & Ultimate Design for Prayer.** rev. ed. Becky Tirabassi. 2000. pap. 10.99 (*0-7852-6885-5*) Tommy Nelson.

Let Prayer Change Your Life Workbook: An Easy-to-Use, Exciting, & Fulfilling Approach to Developing a Prayer Life That Works. Becky Tirabassi. 256p. (Orig.). 1995. pap., student ed. 15.99 (*0-7852-7746-3*) Nelson.

An Asterisk (*) at the beginning of an entry indicates that the title is appearing for the first time.

L

Let Sleeping Afghans Lie. Michael Thall. 192p. 1990. 18.95 (*0-8027-5755-3*) Walker & Co.

Let Sleeping Dogs Lie see Deja Que Los Perros Dormidos Descansen

Let Sleeping Dogs Lie. John R. Erickson. (Hank the Cowdog Ser.: No. 6). (Illus.). 19p. (J). (gr. 2-5). 1986. 9.95 (*0-916941-15-9*); pap. 6.95 (*0-916941-14-0*) Maverick Bks.

Let Sleeping Dogs Lie. John R. Erickson. (Hank the Cowdog Ser.: No. 6). (Illus.). (J). (gr. 2-5). 1989. 12.05 (*0-606-01398-9*, Pub. by Turtleback) Demco.

Let Sleeping Dogs Lie. John R. Riggs. 1993. mass mkt. 4.50 (*0-515-11211-9*, Jove) Berkley Pub.

Let Sleeping Dogs Lie. large type ed. Janet Edmonds. (Ulverscroft). 336p. 1994. 27.99 (*0-7089-3023-9*) Ulverscroft.

Let Sleeping Dogs Lie. unabridged ed. John R. Erickson. (Hank the Cowdog Audio Ser.: No. 6). (Illus.). 19p. (J). (gr. 2-5). 1986. 13.95 incl. audio (*0-916941-16-7*) Maverick Bks.

Let Sleeping Dogs Lie, Vol. 6. John R. Erickson. (Hank the Cowdog Ser.: N0. 6). (Illus.). (J). (gr. 2-5). 1989. pap. 12.25 (*0-8335-6819-1*) Econo-Clad Bks.

Let Sleeping Dogs Lie & Other Proverbs from Around the World. Axel Scheffler. LC 97-8289. 128p. 1997. 12.95 (*0-7641-5056-1*) Barron.

Let Someone Hold You: The Journey of a Hospice Priest. Paul F. Morrissey. LC 93-45874. 240p. (Orig.). 1994. pap. 16.95 (*0-8245-1408-4*) Crossroad NY.

Let the Advice Be Good: A Defense of Madison's Democratic Nationalism. William B. Allen. LC 93-1608. 76p. (Orig.). (C). 1993. pap. text 18.50 (*0-8191-9155-8*); lib. bdg. 39.50 (*0-8191-9154-X*) U Pr of Amer.

Let the Ancestors Speak: Removing the Veil of Mysticism from Medu Netcher. James E. Laws, 3rd. Ed. by Diane M. Laws & Gilberta D. Grimball. (Illus.). 288p. (Orig.). (C). 1995. pap. text 19.95 (*0-9640661-1-4*) J E Laws.

***Let the Art of Medicine Flourish: The Centennial History of the Rochester Academy of Medicine.** Teresa K. Lehr. LC 00-27483. (Illus.). 2000. write for info. (*0-9665228-4-2*) Q Pubng VA.

Let the Authors Speak: A Guide to Worthy Books Based on Historical Setting. Carolyn Hatcher. LC 94-65916. 120p. 1995. pap. 18.95 (*0-9640681-2-5*) Old Pinnacle.

Let the Band Play Dixie. Lawrence Wells. LC 86-32816. 391p. 1989. reprint ed. 17.95 (*0-916242-61-7*) Yoknapatawpha.

Let the Band Play Dixie, & Other Stories. Roark Bradford. LC 70-128721. (Short Story Index Reprint Ser.). 1977. 26.95 (*0-8369-3612-4*) Ayer.

Let the Bible Speak about Tongues see Deje Que la Biblia Hable Sobre las Lenguas

Let the Bible Speak... About Tongues. Richard C. Schwab. LC 85-8098. 144p. 1985. pap. 8.99 (*0-8254-3753-9*) Kregel.

***Let the Big Dog Eat.** Hubert Pedroli. LC 99-58054. (Illus.). 96p. 2000. 18.00 (*0-688-17576-7*, Hearst) Hearst Commns.

***Let the Boonta Race Begin.** Fontes & Justine Korman. (ps-3). 2000. pap. 3.99 (*0-375-80431-5*) Random Hse Chldrns.

Let the Brother Go If... Phyllis Akers. LC 99-37848. 1999. pap. text 7.95 (*1-890194-38-7*) Pines One.

Let the Bunker Burn: The Final Battle with MOVE. Charles W. Bowser. LC 89-505. 192p. 1989. 17.50 (*0-940159-08-2*) Camino Bks.

Let the Celebrations Begin! Margaret Wild. LC 90-21606. (Illus.). 32p. (J). (ps-1). 1991. lib. bdg. 16.99 (*0-531-08537-6*) Orchard Bks Watts.

Let the Celebrations Begin! Margaret Wild. LC 90-21606. (Illus.). 32p. (J). (ps-1). 1996. pap. 6.95 (*0-531-07076-X*) Orchard Bks Watts.

Let the Celebrations Begin! Margaret Wild. LC 90-21606. 1996. 12.15 (*0-606-09541-1*, Pub. by Turtleback) Demco.

Let the Children Come: A New Approach to Children's Sermons. Brent D. Baker. LC 91-8876. 80p. (Orig.). 1991. pap. 9.99 (*0-8066-2545-7*, 9-2545, Augsburg) Augsburg Fortress.

. . . Let the Children Come: Fifty-Two Object Lessons for Children in Worship. Robert B. Lantz. LC 96-52554. 90p. (Orig.). 1997. pap. 10.95 (*0-7880-1059-X*) CSS OH.

***Let the Children Pray.** Esther Ilnisky. 2000. pap. 10.99 (*0-8307-2524-5*, Regal Bks) Gospel Lght.

***Let the Children Sing.** Cathedral Choir. 1999. pap. text 14.98 (*5-555-32727-7*) ISNM.

***Let the Children Sing.** Cathedral Choir Staff. 1999. pap. text 16.98 (*5-550-00644-8*) Nairi.

Let the Church Counsel Together. M. A. Tomlinson. 1978. pap. 2.95 (*0-934942-10-2*) White Wing Pub.

***Let the Circle Be Unbroken.** (J). 1999. 9.95 (*1-56137-660-4*) Novel Units.

Let the Circle Be Unbroken. Mildred D. Taylor. LC 81-65854. 432p. (J). (gr. 7 up). 1981. 16.99 (*0-8037-4748-9*, Dial Yng Read) Peng Put Young Read.

Let the Circle Be Unbroken. Mildred D. Taylor. (J). (gr. 4-7). 1991. pap. 4.99 (*0-14-034892-1*, PuffinBks) Peng Put Young Read.

Let the Circle Be Unbroken. Mildred D. Taylor. 1991. 10.09 (*0-606-00558-7*, Pub. by Turtleback) Demco.

Let the Circle Be Unbroken: A Study Guide. Diana Sergis. Ed. by J. Friedland & R. Kessler. (Novel-Ties Ser.). (J). (gr. 6-8). 1995. pap. text, student ed. 15.95 (*1-56982-323-5*) Lrn Links.

Let the Circle Be Unbroken: The Implications of African Spirituality in the Diaspora. Richards. 1994. per. 6.95 (*0-932415-25-3*) Red Sea Pr.

Let the Cow Wander: Modeling the Metaphors in Veda & Vedanta. Michael W. Myers. LC 95-16070. (Monographs of the Society for Asian & Comparative Philosophy: No. 14). 144p. 1995. pap. text 12.00 (*0-8248-1753-2*) UH Pr.

Let the Cowboy Ride: Cattle Ranching in the American West. Paul F. Starrs. LC 97-21744. (Creating the North American Landscape Ser.). (Illus.). 460p. 1998. 35.95 (*0-8018-5684-1*) Johns Hopkins.

***Let the Cowboy Ride: Cattle Ranching in the American West.** Paul F. Starrs. 2000. pap. 18.95 (*0-8018-6351-1*) Johns Hopkins.

Let the Crazy Child Write! Finding Your Creative Writing Voice. Clive Matson. LC 98-21570. 256p. 1998. pap. 14.00 (*1-880032-35-X*) New Wrld Lib.

Let the Daughters Live! The Literary Architecture of Exodus 1-2 as a Key for Interpretation. Jopie Siebert-Hommes. LC 98-37777. (Biblical Interpretation Ser.). xii, 148p. 1998. 50.00 (*90-04-10778-9*) Brill Academic Pubs.

Let the Dead Bury Their Dead: Bad Company. Ras Cardo. (Ras Cardo Speaks Ser.). 110p. 1995. pap. 30.95 (*1-883427-93-2*, RAS9949-C) Crnerstone GA.

Let the Dead Bury Their Dead & Other Stories. Randall Kenan. 360p. 1993. pap. 13.00 (*0-15-650515-0*) Harcourt.

Let the Dead Speak of Their Lives see Psychic

Let the Dog Drive. David Bowman. LC 92-31757. (C). 1993. 19.95 (*0-8147-1205-3*) NYU Pr.

Let the Dog Drive. David Bowman. 1994. reprint ed. pap. 10.95 (*0-14-023724-0*, Penguin Bks) Viking Penguin.

Let the Drum Beat: A History of the Detroit Light Guard. Stanley D. Solvick. LC 87-34634. (Great Lakes Bks.). (Illus.). 174p. 1988. 29.95 (*0-8143-1886-X*) Wayne St U Pr.

Let the Drum Speak. Linda L. Shuler. 496p. 1997. mass mkt. 6.99 (*0-451-19095-5*, Sig) NAL.

Let the Eagle Soar! The Foreign Policy of Andrew Jackson. John M. Belohlavek. LC 85-1007. 338p. reprint ed. pap. 104.80 (*0-7837-4727-6*, 204438500002) Bks Demand.

Let the Earth Bless the Lord: God's Creation & Our Responsibility. United States Catholic Conference Staff. Ed. by Walter Grazer & Jill Ortman-Fouse. (Illus.). 40p. (Orig.). 1996. pap. 3.95 (*1-57455-085-3*) US Catholic.

***Let the Earth Rejoice: A Biblical Theology of Holistic Mission.** William A. Dyrness. 224p. 1998. pap. 20.00 (*1-57910-125-9*) Wipf & Stock.

Let the Earth Rejoice: A Biblical Theology of Holistic Mission. William A. Dyrness. LC 84-82346. 216p. (C). 1991. reprint ed. pap. 18.00 (*0-9602638-3-7*) Fuller Seminary.

***Let the Earth Rejoice! Prayers for Life, Prayers for Love.** Joseph T. Nolan. 128p. 2000. pap. 14.95 (*0-88347-466-2*, Pub. by T More) BookWorld.

***Let the Earth Resound: SoundPax Instrumental Accompaniment Packet.** Sally Albrecht & Jay Althouse. 1999. pap. 20.00 (*0-7390-0748-3*, 18650) Alfred Pub.

Let the Earth Teach You Torah. Ellen Bernstein & Dan Fink. (Illus.). 184p. (Orig.). 1992. teacher ed. 22.50 (*0-9632848-1-9*) Shomrei Adamah.

Let the Fire Fall. Michael Scanlan & James Manney. 226p. 1997. pap. 9.95 (*0-940535-97-1*) Franciscan U Pr.

Let the Future Come: Perspectives for a Planetary Peace. Wilfrid Desan. LC 87-3. (Planetary Man Ser.: No. 3). 164p. reprint ed. pap. 50.90 (*0-7837-6316-6*, 204603100010) Bks Demand.

***Let the Games Begin!** Maya Ajmera. (Illus.). (J). 2000. 12.40 (*0-606-18804-5*) Turtleback.

***Let the Games Begin!** Maya Ajmera & Michael J. Regan. LC 99-24032. (Illus.). 32p. 2000. pap. 6.95 (*0-88106-068-2*) Charlesbridge Pub.

***Let the Games Begin!** Maya Ajmera & Michael J. Regan. LC 99-24032. (Illus.). 32p. (J). 2000. 16.95 (*0-88106-067-4*) Charlesbridge Pub.

Let the Gas Flow: A Marketing, Sales, & Equipment Handbook for the Natural Gas Industry. Richard Karg. LC 97-92923. 288p. (Orig.). 1997. pap. 29.95 (*0-9656706-0-0*) R J Karg Assocs.

Let the Good Times Roll! A Guide to Cajun & Zydeco Music. Pat Nyhan et al. LC 97-90429. (Illus.). 232p. 1998. pap. 16.95 (*0-9658232-0-2*) Upbeat Bks.

Let the Good Times Roll: Prostitution & the U. S. Military in Asia. Saundra P. Sturdevant & Brenda Stoltzfus. LC 92-53736. (Illus.). 352p. 1993. pap. 24.95 (*1-56584-049-6*, Pub. by New Press NY) Norton.

Let the Good Times Roll: Prostitution & the U. S. Military in Asia. Saundra P. Sturdevant & Brenda Stolzfus. Ed. by Lois Keith. LC 92-53736. (Illus.). 240p. 1996. 22.50 (*1-56584-025-9*, Pub. by New Press NY) Norton.

Let the Good Times Roll: The Story of Louis Jordan & His Music. John Chilton. 320p. (C). 1997. reprint ed. pap. 21.95 (*0-472-08478-X*, 08478) U of Mich Pr.

Let the Guns Roar. large type ed. Charles N. Heckelmann. (Linford Western Library). 368p. 1988. pap. 16.99 (*0-7089-6609-8*, Linford) Ulverscroft.

***Let the Healing Begin.** Deborah Cox-Stubblefield. 26p. 1998. pap. 12.00 (*1-930183-04-6*, DR-0002A-99) Anyanwu.

Let the Ice Speak: Poems by Wendy Barker. Wendy Barker. 72p. 1990. 9.95 (*0-87886-134-3*) Greenfld Rev Lit.

Let the Inner Knower Lead the Way. Judith A. Baldwin. 132p. 1996. pap. 11.95 (*1-56519-000-9*) Human Relations.

Let the Inside Be Sweet: The Interpretation of Music Event among the Kpelle of Liberia. Ruth M. Stone. LC 81-48628. (Illus.). 204p. reprint ed. pap. 63.30 (*0-8357-6682-9*, 205686100094) Bks Demand.

Let the Journey Begin. 1998. 9.99 (*0-8499-5416-9*) Word Pub.

***Let the Journey Begin: God's Roadmap for New Beginnings.** Max Lucado. LC 98-182743. (Illus.). 120p. 1998. 12.99 (*0-8499-5342-1*) Word Pub.

Let the Kids Do It! Using Rebus Task Cards. J. Christine Catalani & Cathleen F. McAuliffe. 176p. (J). (ps-3). 1996. 14.99 (*1-56417-858-7*, FE7858) Fearon Teacher Aids.

Let the Laughs Begin! Humor Writing in the Classroom. Karen Jennings. 1997. pap. text 8.95 (*0-673-36351-1*) Addson-Wesley Educ.

***Let the Lion Eat Straw.** 5th ed. Ellease Southerland & Ebele Oseye. 181p. 2000. reprint ed. pap. 11.95 (*1-929454-00-7*, 727180) Eneke.

Let the Lions Roar! The Evolution of Brookfield Zoo. Andrea F. Ross. Ed. by Christopher Howes. LC 97-66395. (Illus.). 276p. 1997. 40.00 (*0-913934-24-0*) Chicago Zoo.

Let the Lynx Come In. Jonathan London. LC 95-34548. (Illus.). 32p. (J). (gr. k-3). 1996. 15.99 (*1-56402-531-4*) Candlewick Pr.

Let the Magic. Mary Engelbreit. 1999. 4.95 (*0-8362-8347-3*) Andrews & McMeel.

Let the Magic Begin. Cathy Lee Crosby. LC 96-49405. 304p. 1997. 22.50 (*0-684-80280-5*) S&S Trade.

Let the Mocking Bird Sing Herbal Praise. Sandy Bradley. LC 96-61231. 416p. 1996. otabind 29.95 (*1-57258-123-9*) Teach Servs.

***Let the Mountains Talk, Let the Rivers Run: A Call to Those Who Would Save the Earth.** David Brower & Steve Chapple. 208p. 2000. reprint ed. pap. 14.95 (*0-86571-411-8*, Pub. by New Soc Pubs) Consort Bk Sales.

Let the Nations Be Glad! The Supremacy of God in Missions. John Piper. LC 93-14327. 240p. 1993. pap. 12.99 (*0-8010-7124-0*) Baker Bks.

Let the Niggers Burn: The Sir George Williams University Affair & Its Caribbean Aftermath. Ed. by Dennis Forsythe. LC 73-164258. (Black Rose Bks.: Vol. B4). 211p. 1971. reprint ed. pap. 65.50 (*0-608-00464-2*, 206128300007) Bks Demand.

Let the Part Play You: A Practical Approach to the Actors' Creative Process. 4th rev. ed. Anita Jesse. LC 97-61944. 152p. 1998. pap. 16.95 (*0-9639655-2-2*) Wolf Creek CA.

Let the People Decide: Neighborhood Organizing in America. Robert Fisher. LC 94-4261. (Social Movements Past & Present Ser.). 320p. 1994. 33.00 (*0-8057-3859-2*, Twyne) Mac Lib Ref.

Let the People Decide Neighborhood Organizing In America Updated Edition: Neighborhood Organizing in America, Vol. 1. Robert Fisher. (Social Movements Past & Present Ser.). 1994. pap. 20.00 (*0-8057-3860-6*, Twyne) Mac Lib Ref.

Let the People Judge: A Reader on the Wise Use Movement. John Echeverria & Ray Eby. LC 93-43331. 1995. text 55.00 (*1-55963-276-3*) Island Pr.

Let the People Judge: A Reader on the Wise Use Movement. John Echeverria & Raymond B. Eby. LC 93-43331. 1995. pap. text 29.95 (*1-55963-277-1*) Island Pr.

Let the People Sing! A Story of Craigmillar. Ed. by Helen Crummy. 240p. (C). 1992. pap. 40.00 (*0-9518593-0-7*, Pub. by Argyll Pubng) St Mut.

Let the Prophets Speak. Kevin Van der Westhuizen. 80p. 1993. pap. text. write for info. (*0-9638586-0-2*) Van der Westhuizen.

Let the Prophets Speak Vol. 1: Commissioning & Calling Forth the New Guard. Vincom Publishing Company Staff. 1996. pap. text. write for info. (*0-927936-90-9*) Vincom Pubng Co.

Let the Record Show: A Legal History of Ingham County. Richard Frazier & David Thomas. LC 97-23218. 1997. 29.95 (*0-87013-425-6*) Mich St U Pr.

Let the Record Show: The Hackneys, Two Early, Prominent Black Families of Chatham & Orange Counties, NC. Louise C. Hackney. Ed. by Gentrace Assocs., Inc. LC 86-83003. (Illus.). 340p. 1987. text 46.00 (*0-936065-04-4*) Gentrace Assocs.

Let the Redeemed of the Lord Say So: Expressing Your Faith Through Witnessing. H. Eddie Fox. 1991. pap. 8.95 (*0-687-21380-0*) Abingdon.

***Let the Redeemed of the Lord Say So: Invitational Witnessing for the New Millennium.** rev. ed. Ed. by H. Eddie Fox & George E. Morris. LC 99-65726. 228p. 1999. pap. 15.95 (*1-57736-158-X*) Providence Hse.

Let the River Flow. L. Charles Burlage. (Illus.). 500p. (Orig.). 1986. pap. 14.95 (*0-9616208-0-3*) Burlage Corp.

Let the River Flow. Roger Helland. LC 96-78632. 1996. pap. 10.99 (*0-88270-732-9*) Bridge-Logos.

***Let the Rivers Flow, Vol. 3, Pt. 2.** unabridged ed. Ed. by Lana Wegeng. (Illus.). 75p. 1999. pap. 10.95 (*1-892651-21-1*) Columbia Pubns.

Let the Rivers Run: Stewardship & the Biblical Story. fac. ed. Eugene F. Roop. LC 91-26338. (Library of Christian Stewardship). 120p. (Orig.). 1991. reprint ed. pap. 37.20 (*0-7837-7972-0*, 204772800008) Bks Demand.

***Let the Scriptures Speak: Reflections on the Sunday Readings, Year C.** Dennis Hamm. 120p. 2000. pap. 11.95 (*0-8146-2557-6*) Liturgical Pr.

Let the Scriptures Speak: Reflections on the Sunday Readings, Year B. M. Dennis Hamm. LC 99-19050. 1999. 11.95 (*0-8146-2556-8*) Liturgical Pr.

Let the Seasons Change: Four Introspections on God's Providence. Robert D. Papa. 100p. (Orig.). 1993. pap. 5.95 (*0-9638855-0-2*) Prisoners Web.

Let the Shadows Speak: Developing Childrens' Language Through Shadow Puppetry. Franzeska G. Ewart. 150p. 1998. pap. 19.95 (*1-85856-099-3*, Trentham Bks) Stylus Pub VA.

***Let the Storm Burst.** Barry Cohen. LC 99-96860. 2000. pap. 12.95 (*0-533-13363-7*) Vantage.

Let the Sun Go. Alan P. Akmakjian. Ed. by Ken Stone. LC 93-145132. (Illus.). (Orig.). 1992. pap. 3.50 (*0-930715-11-X*) M F Pr.

***Let the Sun Shine: Stories & Poems for Reading Aloud.** Ed. by Kaye Webb. (Illus.). 72p. (J). (ps-3). 1998. pap. 9.99 (*0-7112-1247-3*) F Lincoln.

Let the Symbols Speak: Liturgical Clip-Art. Illus. by Francis M. George. 92p. (Orig.). 1989. pap. 20.00 (*1-878268-05-8*) Lit Comm Pubs.

Let the Trumpet Sound: The Life of Martin Luther King, Jr. Stephen B. Oates. (Illus.). 592p. 1994. reprint ed. pap. 17.00 (*0-06-092473-X*, Perennial) HarperTrade.

Let the Walls Fall Down. Phillip H. Porter. LC 95-83906. 180p. (Orig.). 1996. pap. 11.99 (*0-88419-424-8*) Creation House.

Let the Whole World Sing: The Story Behind the Music of Lausanne II. Corean Bakke. LC 94-24994. 286p. 1994. pap. 13.00 (*0-940895-18-8*) Cornerstone IL.

Let the Wind Speak. Juan Carlos Onetti. Tr. by Helen Lane from SPA. (Extraordinary Classics Ser.). (SPA.). 288p. (Orig.). (C). 1997. pap. 15.99 (*1-85242-196-7*) Serpents Tail.

Let the Witness Die. large type ed. Isobel Lambot. 240p. 1990. 19.95 (*0-7451-1144-0*, G K Hall Lrg Type) Mac Lib Ref.

Let Them All Talk: Elvis Costello. Brian Hinton. 1998. pap. text 19.95 (*1-86074-196-7*, Pub. by Sanctuary Pubng) Music Sales.

Let Them Be Remembered. Elizabeth B. Losey. LC 97-91114. 761p. 2000. 29.95 (*0-533-12572-3*) Vantage.

Let Them Be Themselves. 3rd ed. Lee B. Hopkins. LC 91-19119. 224p. (J). 1992. 21.00 (*0-06-023852-6*); pap. 10.95 (*0-06-446126-2*, HarpTrophy) HarpC Child Bks.

"Let Them Eat Cheesecake" The Art of Olivia. Olivia De Berardinis. Ed. by Joel Beren. (Illus.). 108p. 1993. 29.95 (*0-929643-06-2*) Ozone Prodns.

***Let Them Eat Data: How Computers Affect Education, Cultural Diversity & the Prospects of Ecological Sustainability.** C. A. Bowers. LC 00-26718. 2000. write for info. (*0-8203-2230-X*) U of Ga Pr.

Let Them Eat Ketchup! The Politics of Poverty & Inequality. Sheila D. Collins. (Cornerstone Ser.). (Illus.). 144p. 1995. text 26.00 (*0-85345-904-5*, Pub. by Monthly Rev); pap. text 13.00 (*0-85345-905-3*, Pub. by Monthly Rev) NYU Pr.

Let Them Go Free: A Ritual & Guidelines for the Withdrawal of Life Support Systems. Thomas A. Shannon & Charles N. Faso. LC 87-50321. 42p. 1987. pap. 3.95 (*1-55612-064-8*) Sheed & Ward WI.

Let Them Live. Huw Morgan. 1985. pap. 0.99 (*0-85234-199-7*, Pub. by Evangelical Pr) P & R Pubng.

Let Them Serve Me. Chofetz Chaim Staff. 272p. 1995. 17.95 (*1-58330-097-X*) Feldheim.

Let Them Show Us the Way: Fostering Independent Learning in the Elementary Classroom. Anne Green. (Illus.). 154p. 1995. pap., teacher ed. 13.00 (*1-895411-76-9*) Peguis Pubs Ltd.

Let Them Speak for Themselves: Women in the American West, 1849-1900. Ed. by Christiane Fischer. LC 77-5094. 346p. (C). 1990. reprint ed. pap. 23.50 (*0-208-02311-9*, Archon Bks) Shoe String.

Let There Be a Forest. A. Arnold. 95p. 1986. pap. 125.00 (*81-7089-097-7*, Pub. by Intl Bk Distr) St Mut.

Let There Be... Blacklight. Todd Liebenow & Dave Privett. Ed. by Liz VonSeggen. (Illus.). 32p. 1998. pap. 15.00 (*1-58302-136-1*) One Way St.

Let There Be Blood. J. Jakeman. 1997. mass mkt. 11.95 (*0-7472-5603-9*, Pub. by Headline Bk Pub) Trafalgar.

Let There Be Clothes: 40,000 Years of Fashion. Lynn Schnurnberger. LC 91-315. (Illus.). 512p. (Orig.). 1991. pap. 19.95 (*0-89480-833-8*, 833) Workman Pub.

***Let There Be Laughter.** Richard W. Bimler & Robert D. Bimler. LC 99-20570. 128p. 1999. pap. 9.99 (*0-570-05356-0*, 12-3407) Concordia.

Let There Be Life. Noel Brooks. 1975. pap. 3.95 (*0-911866-88-4*) LifeSprings Res.

Let There Be Life. Pam Campbell & Stan Campbell. LC 92-487. (BibleLog Ser.). 180p. (Orig.). 1992. pap. 7.99 (*0-89693-871-9*, 6-1871, Victor Bks) Chariot Victor.

Let There Be Life! Animating with the Computer. Christopher W. Baker. LC 96-23289. (Illus.). 48p. (J). (gr. 3-7). 1997. 16.95 (*0-8027-8472-0*); lib. bdg. 17.85 (*0-8027-8473-9*) Walker & Co.

Let There Be Light see Es Werde Licht: Praktischer Leitfaden fur Dinshahs 12-Farben Chromotherapie

Let There Be Light. Roger Oakland & Dan Wooding. 176p. 1993. pap. write for info. (*0-9637797-0-2*) Understand Times.

Let There Be Light. Jane Ray. LC 97-29456. (Illus.). 96p. (J). 1997. 19.99 (*0-525-45925-1*, Dutton Child) Peng Put Young Read.

Let There Be Light. David Conrad Taylor & Harry S. Scales. (Illus.). 180p. (C). 1994. text 34.50 (*0-930329-79-1*) Kabel Pubs.

Let There Be Light. Thomas-Cochran. (What a Wonderful World Intro Ser.). 1993. pap. text. write for info. (*0-582-91089-7*, Pub. by Addison-Wesley) Longman.

Let There Be Light! Marilyn J. Wright. (Illus.). 74p. (C). 1997. pap. 20.00 (*1-886232-41-5*) Majesty Pubns.

Let There Be Light. 4th ed. Darius Dinshah. (Illus.). 164p. 1997. 12.00 (*0-933917-17-1*) Dinshah Hlth Soc.

Let There Be Light, Vol. II. Helena E. Ruhnau. (Illus.). (Orig.). 1990. 13.95 (*0-941036-70-7*) Colleasius Pr.

Let There Be Light, Vol. III. Helena E. Ruhnau. (Illus.). 183p. (Orig.). 1991. pap. 13.95 (*0-941036-99-5*) Colleasius Pr.

Let There Be Light: A Book about Windows. James C. Giblin. LC 87-35052. (Illus.). 176p. (J). (gr. 3-7). 1988. 16.00 (*0-690-04693-6*) HarpC Child Bks.

An Asterisk (*) at the beginning of an entry indicates that the title is appearing for the first time.

L

Let There Be Light: Based on the Visionary Spirituality of Hildegard of Bingen. John Kirvan. LC 96-49862. (Thirty Days with a Great Spiritual Teacher Ser.). 216p. (Orig.). 1997. pap. 6.95 (*0-87793-602-1*) Ave Maria.

Let There Be Light: Creation & Evolution in the Bible. Elyse Curtis. LC 97-93213. (Illus.). 145p. (Orig.). 1997. pap. 14.95 (*0-9657282-0-X*, 100) Astral Projections.

***Let There Be Light: How to Transform Personal & Environmental Toxins.** Sandra Ingerman. 2001. pap. 14.00 (*0-609-80517-7*, Three Riv Pr) Crown Pub Group.

Let There Be Light: The Old Testament Metaphysically Interpreted. Elizabeth S. Turner. LC 89-51026. 302p. 2000. reprint ed. 12.95 (*0-87159-194-4*) Unity Bks.

Let There Be Light: The Rwanda Project. Alfredo Jaar. 1998. pap. text 35.00 (*84-89698-44-9*) Actar.

Let There Be Light: The Rwanda Project. Photos by Alfredo Jaar. (Illus.). 200p. 1998. pap. 35.00 (*84-89698-45-7*, 811041, Pub. by Actar) Dist Art Pubs.

Let There Be Light: The 7 Keys. Rocco A. Errico. 272p. (Orig.). 1994. pap. 17.95 (*0-9631292-4-X*) Noohra Found.

Let There Be Light: Unlocking the Mysteries in The Books of Genesis & Luke of the Holy Bible. 2nd ed. Dan L. Hopper. (Illus.). 304p. (Orig.). 1995. pap. 14.95 (*0-9646124-0-2*) Dancy Co.

Let There Be Light - Living Waters of Life for the New Age. Helena E. Ruhnau. (Illus.). 190p. (Orig.). 1987. pap. 13.95 (*0-941036-60-X*) Colleasius Pr.

Let There Be Light, Words & Music. Daniel Polin. LC 95-94209. (Illus.). 153p. (Orig.). 1995. pap. 29.95 (*0-9645795-0-2*) Light Words & Music.

Let There Be Lights. Camille Kress. LC 97-228608. (Illus.). 10p. (J). 1997. bds. 5.95 (*0-8074-0642-2*, 102007) UAHC.

Let There Be Limericks. Ramona Demerey. pap. 6.95 (*1-55517-399-3*) CFI Dist.

Let There Be Lite! An Illuminating Guide to Delicious Low-Fat Cooking. Jay Disney. (Illus.). 300p. 1995. 23.95 (*0-87951-576-7*, Pub. by Overlook Pr) Penguin Putnam.

Let There Be Lite! An Illuminating Guide to Delicious Low-Fat Cooking. Jay Disney. LC 94-37368. (Illus.). 300p. 1997. reprint ed. pap. 15.95 (*0-87951-758-1*, Pub. by Overlook Pr) Penguin Putnam.

Let There Be Towns: Spanish Municipal Origins in the American Southwest, 1610-1810. Gilbert R. Cruz. LC 87-33553. (Illus.). 256p. (C). 1997. pap. 16.95 (*0-89096-677-X*) Tex A&M Univ Pr.

Let This Cup Pass. Jane McWhorter. (Illus.). 1979. pap. 7.15 (*0-89137-414-0*) Quality Pubns.

Let This Life Speak: The Legacy of Henry Joel Cadbury. Margaret H. Bacon. LC 86-14669. (Illus.). 272p. 1987. text 43.95 (*0-8122-8045-8*) U of Pa Pr.

Let This Mind Be in You: A Practical Guide to Servanthood. Harold D. Gingerich. 54p. (Orig.). 1987. pap. 2.95 (*0-9619701-0-3*) Vessel Pub.

Let This Mind Be in You: A Quest for Identity Through Oedipus to Christ. Sebastian Moore. 192p. 1985. 13.95 (*0-86683-797-3*, 8597) Harper SF.

***Let This Mind Be in You: Thinking the Thoughts of Jesus.** Frances G. Hunter. LC 00-9595. 2000. write for info. (*0-88368-626-0*) Whitaker Hse.

***Let Those Who Receive the Benefits Pay the Costs: An Analysis of the Colorado State Government's Flawed Plan.** Stephen R. Mueller & Dennis Polhill. 1999. pap. write for info. (*1-57655-187-3*) Independ Inst.

Let Thy Breeze Refresh Them: Baha'i Prayers & Tablets for Children. 48p. (J). 1983. 8.00 (*0-900125-36-5*) Bahai.

Let Thy Words Be Few. J. V. Cunningham. 17p. (Orig.). 1986. 45.00 (*0-936576-11-1*) Symposium Pr.

Let Time Tick Softly. Dorothy E. Ward. LC 96-68074. (Illus.). 64p. 1996. 4.95 (*0-932529-51-8*) Oldcastle.

Let Tomorrow Come. Rebecca Lang. 1999. mass mkt. 3.50 (*0-373-17409-8*, 1-17409-3, Mira Bks) Harlequin Bks.

***Let Tomorrow Come.** large type ed. Rebecca Lang. 288p. 1999. 25.99 (*0-263-15906-X*, Pub. by Mills & Boon) Ulverscroft.

Let Us Abide: How to Adjust Your Will & Stay in God's Presence. Judson Cornwall. 155p. 1977. pap. 7.99 (*0-88270-626-8*) Bridge-Logos.

Let Us All Sleep, Nature's Way. NaiKang Chang. (Illus.). (Orig.). 1989. pap. 12.95 (*0-9622374-0-X*) Jupiter Pub.

Let Us Be Holy. Judson Cornwall. LC 87-70993. 1978. pap. 7.99 (*0-88270-278-5*) Bridge-Logos.

Let Us Begin: The Sha'ar Zahav Haggadah. CSZ Membership. (ENG & HEB., Illus.). 64p. (Orig.). 1996. pap. 10.00 (*0-9619242-1-7*) Cong Shaar Zahav.

Let Us Build Us a City: 11 Lost Towns. Donald Harington. (Illus.). 512p. 1986. 19.95 (*0-15-150100-9*) Harcourt.

Let Us Commit Ourselves & One Another & Our Whole Life to Christ Our God. Anthony M. Coniaris. LC 97-73558. 75p. 1997. write for info. (*1-880971-30-5*) Light&Life Pub Co MN.

***Let Us Converse in Arabic.** Syed Ali. 1998. pap. 11.50 (*81-7476-145-4*, Pub. by UBS Pubs) S Asia.

Let Us Draw in Patterns. G. G. Thomson. LC 97-67237. (Children's Library of Visual Literacy: Vol. 2). (Illus.). 28p. (Orig.). (J). 1997. pap. 6.95 (*1-887003-99-1*) Dancng Jester.

Let Us Draw in Perspective. G. G. Thomson. LC 97-66533. (Children's Library of Visual Literacy: Vol. 3). (Illus.). 28p. (J). 1997. pap. 6.95 (*1-887003-98-3*) Dancng Jester.

Let Us Draw Near: Spiritual Symbolism of the Old Testament Tabernacle. Judson Cornwall. LC 77-24832. 168p. 1977. pap. 8.99 (*0-88270-226-2*) Bridge-Logos.

Let Us Enjoy Forgiveness. Judson Cornwall. 159p. 1992. reprint ed. pap. 8.99 (*0-88270-708-6*) Bridge-Logos.

Let Us Go... see Salgamos Pues...

Let Us Go on to Maturity see Going on to Maturity

Let Us Have Music for Flute. Ed. by Richard Drake. (Illus.). 79p. 1963. pap. 9.95 (*0-8258-0156-7*, 0-4077) Fischer Inc NY.

Let Us Have Music for Organ. Bill Simon. (Illus.). 64p. 1958. pap. 7.95 (*0-8258-0246-6*, 0-4106) Fischer Inc NY.

Let Us Have Music for Piano: 74 Famous Melodies, Vol. 1. Ed. by Maxwell Eckstein. (Let Us Have Music Ser.). 112p. (J). 1940. pap. 10.95 (*0-8258-0047-1*, 02942) Fischer Inc NY.

Let Us Have Music for Piano: 74 Famous Melodies, Vol. 2. Ed. by Maxwell Eckstein. (Let Us Have Music Ser.). 111p. (J). 1940. pap. 9.95 (*0-8258-0048-X*, 03127) Fischer Inc NY.

Let Us Have Music for Violin, Vol. 2. Pulman. (Illus.). 80p. 1944. pap. 10.95 (*0-8258-0247-4*, 0-3207) Fischer Inc NY.

Let Us Have Peace: Ulysses S. Grant & the Politics of War & Reconstruction, 1861-1868. Brooks D. Simpson. LC 91-50256. xx, 339p. (C). 1991. 45.00 (*0-8078-1966-2*) U of NC Pr.

Let Us Have Peace: Ulysses S. Grant & the Politics of War & Reconstruction, 1861-1868. Brooks D. Simpson. LC 91-50256. 359p. (C). 1997. pap. 19.95 (*0-8078-4629-5*) U of NC Pr.

Let Us Highly Resolve. Gene S. Porter. 39.50 (*0-8488-1529-7*) Amereon Ltd.

Let Us Highly Resolve: Preparing Families to Enter the 21st Century. David Quine & Shirley Quine. 128p. 1997. pap. text. write for info. (*0-9656512-0-7*) Crnrstone Curriculum.

***Let Us Honor the Creator & Other Poems.** Alex F. Osborn. 2000. write for info. (*1-58235-490-1*) Watermrk Pr.

Let Us Make a Wedding! A Guidebook for Creating Your Own Ceremony. Henry S. Basayne & Linda R. Janowitz. (Illus.). 200p. (Orig.). 1993. pap. 15.95 (*0-9637071-0-8*) Basayne-Janowitz.

Let Us Make Man. Linleigh J. Roberts. 168p. (Orig.). (C). 1988. pap. 11.99 (*0-85151-525-8*) Banner of Truth.

Let Us Make Man. Decker Tapscott. Ed. by Kepler Nigh. 1997. pap. 7.99 (*1-884369-69-3*, EBED Pubns) McDougal Pubng.

Let Us March On! Selected Civil Rights Photographs of Ernest C. Withers, 1955-1968. Michele Furst & Ronald W. Bailey. (Illus.). 90p. (Orig.). 1992. pap. 15.00 (*0-9628905-1-0*) MA Collge Art.

Let Us Not Blame Foolish Women. Dotty LeMieux. (Desert Island Chapbook Ser.). 32p. 1983. pap. text 3.50 (*0-939180-26-X*) Tombouctou.

Let Us Now Praise Famous Men. James Agee. (Illus.). 460p. 1989. pap. 16.95 (*0-395-48897-4*) HM.

Let Us Now Praise Famous Men. James Agee. LC 88-18110. (Illus.). 432p. 2000. 30.00 (*0-395-95771-0*) HM.

Let Us Praise: Principles & Practices of Scriptural Praise. Judson Cornwall. LC 73-75957. 159p. 1973. pap. 9.99 (*0-88270-039-1*) Bridge-Logos.

Let Us Pray see Oremos

Let Us Pray. Alfonso T. Delany. (Illus.). 52p. 1999. pap. 9.95 (*0-7392-0189-1*, PO3161) Morris Pubng.

Let "Us" Pray. Charles Gallagher. (Celebrate Love Ser.). 72p. (Orig.). 1990. pap. text 3.95 (*0-911905-36-7*) Past & Mat Rene Ctr.

Let Us Pray. Leisure Arts Staff. LC 96-77626. 96p. 1997. 24.95 (*1-57486-047-X*) Leisure AR.

Let Us Pray. Watchman Nee. Tr. by Stephen Kaung from CHI. 87p. 1977. pap. 3.50 (*0-935008-26-8*) Christian Fellow Pubs.

Let Us Pray: A Book of Uncommon Prayers. Tom Bagnal. LC 98-66926. 64p. 1998. pap. 11.95 (*1-57736-115-6*) Providence Hse.

***Let Us Pray: A Plea for Prayer in Our Schools.** William J. Murray. 205p. 1999. reprint ed. text 20.00 (*0-7881-6651-4*) DIANE Pub.

Let Us Pray: Contemporary Prayers for the Seasons of the Church. Israel Galindo. LC 98-43237. 1999. pap. 13.00 (*0-8170-1296-6*) Judson.

Let Us Pray! The Reasons, Models, Facets, Result, Power, Help & Joy. M. L. Smith. LC 96-93106. 76p. (Orig.). 1997. pap. 7.00 (*1-882581-16-4*) Campbell Rd Pr.

Let Us Prey. large type ed. Gerald Hammond. (Mystery Ser.). 256p. 1993. 27.99 (*0-7089-2893-5*) Ulverscroft.

Let Us Prey. large type ed. Bill Branon. LC 94-9239. 466p. 1994. reprint ed. lib. bdg. 24.95 (*0-8161-7432-6*, G K Hall Lrg Type) Mac Lib Ref.

Let Us Prey. Dorothy Eden. 216p. 1995. reprint ed. 20.00 (*0-7278-4760-0*) Severn Hse.

Let Us Prey: The Public Trial of Jimmy Swaggart. Hunter Lundy. 1999. pap. 25.95 (*1-885478-70-4*, Pub. by Genesis Press) BookWorld.

Let Us Proclaim the Mystery of Faith. Veritas Publications Staff. 1989. pap. 22.00 (*0-86217-010-9*, Pub. by Veritas Pubns) St Mut.

Let Us Rejoice. 1995. pap. 1.35 (*0-8341-9429-5*, AG-1009) Lillenas.

Let Us Remember Vol. 1: The Vietnam Veterans Memorial. Louise Graves. (Illus.). 30p. (Orig.). 1984. pap. 5.00 (*1-887878-00-9*) Pks & Hist.

***Let Us See, Is This Real?** Ansuya Blom. 112p. 2000. 35.00 (*90-5662-137-8*) NAi Uitgevers.

Let Us See Jesus. Judson Cornwall. LC 80-20645. 160p. 1981. pap. 7.99 (*0-88270-628-4*) Bridge-Logos.

Let Us Serve Them All Their Days: Young Volunteers Serving Homebound Elderly Persons. Ed. by Larry Couch. 170p. 1992. pap. 15.00 (*0-910883-66-1*, 2051) Natl Coun Aging.

Let Us Sing unto the Lord. Armando Di Robbio et al. (Illus.). 92p. (Orig.). 1997. spiral bd. 30.00 (*0-9661540-0-2*) Far Memory.

***Let Us Talk of Many Things: The Collected Speeches.** William F. Buckley, Jr. 608p. 2000. 30.00 (*0-7615-2551-3*) Prima Pub.

Let Us Tell It . . . How it Was, How It Is, & How It Will Be in the Future. Turner Publishing Company Staff. LC 95-60323. 144p. 1995. 24.95 (*1-56311-187-X*) Turner Pub KY.

Let Us Worship. Judson Cornwall. LC 82-75089. 177p. 1983. pap. 9.99 (*0-88270-542-3*) Bridge-Logos.

Let Us Worship. D. Marsh. 1993. pap. 6.95 (*1-55897-498-9*) Brentwood Music.

***Let Wisdom Sing: Stories of Profound Insight & the Songs They Inspired.** Azra Simonetti. Tr. by Chris Marietta Rhyne. LC 00-105564. (Illus.). 80p. (YA). (gr. 5-12). 2000. pap. 19.99 incl. cd-rom (*0-9701062-7-0*) N S P Pubng.

Let Women Vote! Marlene T. Brill. (Spotlight on American History Ser.). (Illus.). 64p. (J). (gr. 4-6). 1995. lib. bdg. 21.90 (*1-56294-589-0*) Millbrook Pr.

Let Your Alcoholic Suffer! A Battle Plan for Families of Alcoholics. Donald M. Lazo. Ed. by Erik Fair. (Illus.). 128p. (Orig.). 1999. pap. 11.95 (*0-913581-12-7*) Publitec.

***Let Your Artist Out.** William Denning. 64p. 1999. 22.00 (*1-85608-185-0*, Pub. by Hunt GBR) St Mut.

Let Your Attitude Be Gratitude: The Basis of Human Happiness. Alice W. Johnson. 112p. (Orig.). 1997. pap. 10.00 (*0-9648271-3-1*) Mal-Jonal Prodns.

Let Your Body Interpret Your Dreams. Eugene T. Gendlin. LC 85-26920. 200p. (Orig.). (C). 1986. pap. 17.95 (*0-933029-01-2*) Chiron Pubns.

***Let Your Dreams Take Flight.** Sandra Magsamen. 96p. 1999. text 8.95 (*1-55670-898-X*) Stewart Tabori & Chang.

Let Your Heart Answer. large type ed. Clarissa Ross. 1994. 27.99 (*0-7089-3210-X*) Ulverscroft.

Let Your Ideas Speak Out: A Guide to Preparing & Marketing Spoken Words on Audiotape & CDs. Eugene D. Wheeler & Rennie Mau. LC 91-17889. 96p. 1991. pap. 8.95 (*0-934793-33-6*) Pathfinder CA.

Let Your Life Speak: A Study of Politics, Religion & Antinuclear Weapons Activism. Robert D. Holsworth. LC 88-40436. (History of American Thought & Culture Ser.). (Illus.). 235p. reprint ed. pap. 72.90 (*0-608-09910-4*, 206924800003) Bks Demand.

Let Your Life Speak: Listening for the Voice of Vocation. Parker J. Palmer. LC 99-6467. 112p. 1999. 18.00 (*0-7879-4735-0*) Jossey-Bass.

Let Your Light Shine: Pioneer Women Educators of Wyoming. 2nd ed. Ed. by Priscilla McKim. LC 84-63062. (Illus.). 182p. 1985. write for info. (*0-930535-01-4*) Rustler Print & Pub.

***Let Your Light Shine: Raising Awareness about Your Church.** James H. Heine. LC 99-14397. 64p. 1999. 4.99 (*0-570-03570-8*) Concordia.

Let Your Light Shine: 99 Easy Ways to Witness. Donald R. Key. LC 98-70873. (Illus.). 168p. 1998. pap. 10.00 (*0-944019-25-0*) Empire NC.

Let Your Lives Speak. Elfrida V. Foulds. (C). 1953. pap. 4.00 (*0-87574-071-5*) Pendle Hill.

Let Your Mind Alone. James Thurber. reprint ed. lib. bdg. 22.95 (*0-89190-266-X*) Amereon Ltd.

Let Your Mind Alone. James Thurber. 1977. reprint ed. lib. bdg. 26.95 (*0-89244-058-9*) Queens Hse-Focus Serv.

Let Your Money Do the Talking! The Christian Witness Through Material Resources. Raymond B. Knudsen. LC 87-70104. 77p. (Orig.). 1987. pap. 6.95 (*0-9618108-0-7*) Counselor Assn.

Let Your Sink So Shine: A Missionary Quick Cleaning Guide. Don Aslett. (Illus.). 40p. (Orig.). 1994. pap. 5.00 (*0-937750-10-7*) Marsh Creek Pr.

Let Your Soul Roam: Towards the Liberation of the Spirit. Slightly Off Center Writers Group Staff. (Orig.). 1995. pap. 9.95 (*1-56721-130-5*) Twnty-Fifth Cent Pr.

Let your Spirit Breathe: Living with Joy & Peace. Timothy E. O'Connell. 144p. 1999. pap. 12.95 (*0-88347-439-5*, Pub. by T More) BookWorld.

Let Your Spirit Soar (365 Inspirational Flights) C. S. Lovett. (Illus.). 560p. 1994. pap. 19.95 (*0-938148-47-8*) Prsnl Christianity.

Let Your Voice Be Heard! Songs from Ghana & Zimbabwe: (Call-&-Response, Multipart & Game Songs Arranged & Annotated for Grades K-12) 10th anniversary ed. Abraham K. Adzinyah et al. (Illus.). 167p. (Orig.). 1997. pap. 26.95 incl. audio (*0-937203-76-9*) World Music Pr.

Let Your Voice Be Heard! Songs from Ghana & Zimbabwe: Multipart & Game Songs Arranged & Annotated for Grades K-12. Abraham K. Adzenyah et al. (Illus.). 167p. 1997. pap. 26.95 incl. audio compact disk (*0-937203-75-0*) World Music Pr.

Let Your Worries Go. Jessica Hurley. pap. 18.95 (*0-312-26531-X*) St Martin.

Let Yourself Be Loved. Phillip Bennett. LC 97-21394. (Illumination Bks.). 96p. (Orig.). 1997. pap. 5.95 (*0-8091-3736-4*, 3736-4) Paulist Pr.

Leta Stetter Hollingworth: A Biography. Harry L. Hollingworth. Ed. by Stephanie A. Shields. 224p. (C). 1990. reprint ed. 30.95 (*0-9627042-0-2*) Anker Pub.

L'Etabli see Assembly Line

Letany of J. Bastwick. John Bastwick. LC 76-57354. (English Experience Ser.: No. 773). 1977. reprint ed. lib. bdg. 9.50 (*90-221-0773-6*) Walter J Johnson.

Letargo. Frank Samperi. LC 79-64921. 82p. 1980. pap. 9.95 (*0-930794-14-1*) Station Hill Pr.

Letarouilly on Renaissance Rome: An American Student Edition. abr. ed. Paul Letarouilly. Ed. by John B. Bayley. (Classical America Series in Art & Architecture). (Illus.). xiv, 160p. 1984. pap. text 14.95 (*0-8038-9250-0*) Archit CT.

Let'em Eat Cake. Susan Jedren. 1996. pap. 14.00 (*0-679-76805-X*) Random.

Let'em Holler: A Political Biography of J. Bracken Lee. Dennis L. Lythgoe. LC 82-60039. (Illus.). xii, 343p. 1982. 17.50 (*0-913738-33-6*) Utah St Hist Soc.

Le/Temple de Jerusalem see Temple of Jerusalem

Le/Temps et L'Autre see Time & the Other

***Letena, Forever A-Flutter.** Dayne Hillcrest. (J). (gr. k-4). 1999. pap. 6.95 (*0-533-12757-2*) Vantage.

Lethal Agent. Don Pendleton. (Executioner Ser.). 1994. per. 3.50 (*0-373-61182-X*, 1-61182-1) Harlequin Bks.

Lethal Aid: The Illusion of Socialism & Self-Reliance in Tanzania. Severine M. Rugumamu. LC 96-20933. 256p. 1996. 69.95 (*0-86543-512-X*); pap. 21.95 (*0-86543-513-8*) Africa World.

Lethal Arrhythmias Resulting from Myocardial Ischemia & Infarction: Proceedings of Second Rappaport Symposium Haifa, Israel, March 13-16, 1988. Ed. by Michael R. Rosen & Yoram Palti. (Developments in Cardiovascular Medicine Ser.). (C). 1988. text 170.00 (*0-89838-401-X*) Kluwer Academic.

Lethal Arrogance. Alexandre Dumas. LC 99-31677. 416p. 1999. text 29.95 (*0-312-22251-3*) St Martin.

Lethal Attraction. Rebecca King. (Presents Ser.). 1994. per. 2.99 (*0-373-11638-1*, 1-11638-3) Harlequin Bks.

***Lethal Combination.** Anne Marie Duquette. 2000. mass mkt. 9.95 (*1-55279-018-5*, Pub. by Picasso Publ) Baker & Taylor.

Lethal Commerce: The Global Trade in Small Arms & Light Weapons. Ed. by Michael T. Klare et al. LC 94-74471. 160p. (C). 1995. pap. text 10.00 (*0-87724-000-0*) Am Acd Arts Sciences.

***Lethal Delivery, Postage Prepaid.** Kathleen A. Barrett. (Thumbprint Mysteries Ser.). 128p. 1999. pap. 5.95 (*0-8092-0645-5*, 064550) NTC Contemp Pub Co.

Lethal Dose. Steven L. Snodgrass. LC 36-67650. 350p. 1996. 22.95 (*0-9642463-1-7*) ICAM Pub Co.

Lethal Exposure. Kevin J. Anderson. 1998. mass mkt. 5.99 (*0-441-00536-5*) Ace Bks.

Lethal Fixation. large type ed. Stella Shepherd. (Dales Large Print Ser.). 352p. 1996. pap. 18.99 (*1-85389-681-0*, Dales) Ulverscroft.

Lethal Frequencies. James Galvin. LC 94-31305. 80p. 1995. pap. 11.00 (*1-55659-069-5*) Copper Canyon.

Lethal Frontiers: A Soviet View of Nuclear Strategy, Weapons, & Negotiations. Alexei G. Arbatov. Tr. by Kent D. Lee. LC 88-15538. 313p. 1988. 59.95 (*0-275-93017-3*, C3017, Praeger Pubs) Greenwood.

Lethal Genes. Linda Grant. 272p. 1996. 20.50 (*0-684-82653-4*) S&S Trade.

Lethal Glory: Dramatic Defeats of the Civil War. Philip Katcher. (Illus.). 240p. 1997. pap. 16.95 (*1-85409-378-9*, Pub. by Arms & Armour) Sterling.

Lethal Glory: Dramatic Defeats of the Civil War. Philip Katcher. 1999. pap. text 9.99 (*0-304-35131-8*) Continuum.

***Lethal Harvest.** William Cutrer & Sandra Glahn. 400p. 2000. pap. 10.99 (*0-8254-2371-6*) Kregel.

Lethal Heritage: Blood of Kerensky Trilogy, Vol. 1. Michael A. Stackpole. 288p. 1995. mass mkt. 6.99 (*0-451-45383-2*) NAL.

Lethal Hero: The Mel Gibson Biography. Roland Perry. 256p. 1993. 22.95 (*1-870049-79-9*) Oliver Bks.

Lethal Imagination: Violence & Brutality in American History. Ed. by Michael A. Bellesiles. 485p. 1999. pap. 24.95 (*0-8147-1296-7*) NYU Pr.

***Lethal Imagination: Violence & Brutality in American History.** Ed. by Michael A. Bellesiles. LC 98-37696. 485p. 1999. text 65.00 (*0-8147-1295-9*) NYU Pr.

Lethal Impact. Don Pendleton. 1992. per. 4.99 (*0-373-61429-2*, 1-61429-6) Harlequin Bks.

Lethal Innocence: The Cinema of Alexander MacKendrick. Philip Kemp. (Illus.). 298p. (C). 1991. pap. write for info. (*0-413-64980-6*, A0540, Methuen Drama) Methn.

Lethal Involvement. large type ed. Clive Egleton. (Charnwood Large Print Ser.). 528p. 1997. 27.99 (*0-7089-8932-2*, Charnwood) Ulverscroft.

***Lethal Judgments: Assisted Suicide & American Law.** Melvin I. Urofsky. LC KF3827.E87U755 2000. 192p. 2000. text 29.95 (*0-7006-1010-3*); pap. text 12.95 (*0-7006-1011-1*) U Pr of KS.

Lethal Ladies II. Christine Matthews. 1998. mass mkt. 6.99 (*0-425-16268-0*) Berkley Pub.

Lethal Laws: Animal Testing, Human Health & Environmental Policy. Alix Fano. LC 97-9182. (C). 1997. text 19.95 (*1-85649-498-5*) Zed Books.

Lethal Laws: "Gun Control" is the Key to Genocide. Jay Simkin et al. 350p. (Orig.). 1994. pap. 24.95 (*0-9642304-0-2*) Jews Preserv Firearms.

Lethal Legacy. Louise Hendricksen. 288p. 1995. mass mkt. 4.99 (*0-8217-4965-X*, Pinncle Kensgtn) Kensgtn Pub Corp.

Lethal Lessons. Karen H. Stuyck. 272p. 1997. mass mkt. 5.99 (*0-425-15723-7*, Prime Crime) Berkley Pub.

Lethal Losses. Crimmins. 1999. pap. 60.00 (*0-8133-3352-0*) Westview.

Lethal Love: Feminist Literary Readings of Biblical Love Stories. Mieke Bal. LC 86-45592. (Illus.). 152p. 1987. pap. 11.95 (*0-253-20434-8*, MB 434) Ind U Pr.

Lethal Lover (Dangerous Men) Laura Gordon. LC 95-22383. 251p. 1995. per. 3.50 (*0-373-22345-5*) Harlequin Bks.

Lethal Lovers & Poisonous People: How to Protect Your Health from Relationships That Make You Sick. Harriet B. Braiker. Ed. by Judith Regan. 272p. 1993. reprint ed. mass mkt. 5.99 (*0-671-72423-1*, Pocket Star Bks) PB.

Lethal Marriage. Nick Pron. 1996. mass mkt. 5.99 (*0-345-39055-5*) Ballantine Pub Grp.

Lethal Marriage: The Unspeakable Crimes of Paul Bernardo & Karla Homolka. Nick Pron. LC 97-201464. 352p. 1995. pap. 8.99 (*0-7704-2710-3*) Bantam.

***Lethal Measures: A Novel of Medical Suspense.** Leonard S. Goldberg. LC 99-43711. 336p. 2000. 24.95 (*0-525-94528-8*, Dutt) Dutton Plume.

Lethal Medicine: The Epidemic of Medical Malpractice in America. Harvey F. Wachsman. 240p. 1995. 22.50 (*0-8050-2513-8*) H Holt & Co.

Lethal Medicine: The Story of America's Worst Drug Disaster. Moore. 1995. 23.00 (*0-671-87016-5*) S&S Trade.

Lethal Mercy. Harry L. Kraus, Jr. LC 96-38742. 384p. 1997. pap. 12.99 (*0-89107-921-1*) Crossway Bks.

Lethal Mists: An Introduction to the Natural & Military Science of Chemical, Biological Warefare & Terrorism. Eric R. Taylor. 217p. 1998. lib. bdg. 55.00 (*1-56072-459-5*) Nova Sci Pubs.

Lethal Mutation. D. Gordon Johnston. 248p. 1999. pap. 13.00 (*1-890461-09-1*) Winlock Publng Co.

Lethal Origins the 6 1 Digest. Fabian Nicieza et al. (J). 1997. per. 3.99 (*0-671-01167-7*) PB.

Lethal Passage. Erik Larson. 1995. 22.95 (*0-8050-2531-6*) H Holt & Co.

Lethal Passage: The Journey of a Gun. Erik Larson. LC 97-189011. 1995. pap. 12.00 (*0-679-75927-1*) Vin Bks.

Lethal Politics: Soviet Genocide & Mass Murder since 1917. R. J. Rummel. 172p. (C). 1990. 39.95 (*0-88738-333-5*) Transaction Pubs.

Lethal Politics: Soviet Genocide & Mass Murder since 1917. R. J. Rummel. 172p. 1996. pap. text 24.95 (*1-56000-887-3*) Transaction Pubs.

Lethal Practice. Peter Clement. 1997. mass mkt. 6.99 (*0-345-40776-8*) Ballantine Pub Grp.

Lethal Practice. Peter Clement. 1998. mass mkt. 6.99 (*0-449-00281-0*, GM) Fawcett.

Lethal Practice. Peter Clement. 1998. mass mkt. 6.99 (*0-8041-1781-0*) Ivy Books.

***Lethal Secrets.** rev. ed. Annette Baran & Reuben Pannor. LC 93-20015. (Illus.). 187p. 1999. reprint ed. pap. 11.95 (*1-56743-020-1*, Amistad) HarperTrade.

***Lethal Seduction.** Jackie Collins. 480p. 2000. 25.50 (*0-684-85031-1*) Simon & Schuster.

***Lethal Seduction.** large type ed. Jackie Collins. 720p. 2000. 26.00 (*0-7432-0425-5*) S&S Trade.

Lethal Shadow: The Inside Story of America's Most Dangerous Criminal. Stephen G. Michaud. 360p. (Orig.). 1994. mass mkt. 6.50 (*0-451-40530-7*, Onyx) NAL.

Lethal Silence. rev. ed. John Preston. (Mission of Alex Kane Ser.). (Orig.). 1993. mass mkt. 4.95 (*1-56333-125-X*, Badboy) Masquerade.

Lethal Vintage. Martin Sylvester. 1989. mass mkt. 3.95 (*1-55817-283-1*, Pinncle Kensgtn) Kensgtn Pub Corp.

Lethal Violence: A Sourcebook on Fatal Domestic, Acquaintance, & Stranger Aggression. Harold V. Hall. LC 98-37992. 736p. 1998. boxed set 134.95 (*0-8493-7003-5*) CRC Pr.

Lethal Violence, 2000: A Sourcebook on Fatal Domestic, Acquaintance & Stranger Aggression. Ed. by Harold V. Hall. (Illus.). 800p. 1997. text 125.00 (*0-9649535-0-1*) Pac Inst Conflict.

Lethal Yellowing: Research & Practical Aspects, Vol. 5. Ed. by C. Oropeza et al. LC 95-37539. (Developments in Plant Pathology Ser.). 268p. (C). 1995. text 121.50 (*0-7923-3723-9*) Kluwer Academic.

Letham or Leatham Family Book of Remembrance: The Story of Robert Letham & His Wife J net Urquhart with Historical-Genealogical & Biographical Data on Their Ancestry & Descendants. Louis S. Leatham. (Illus.). 1072p. 1995. reprint ed. lib. bdg. 145.00 (*0-8328-4921-9*) Higginson Bk Co.

Letham or Leatham Family Book of Remembrance: The Story of Robert Letham & His Wife Janet Urquhart with Historical-Genealogical & Biographical Data on Their Ancestry & Descendants. Louis S. Leatham. (Illus.). 1072p. 1995. reprint ed. pap. 135.00 (*0-8328-4922-7*) Higginson Bk Co.

***Lethe; Forgetting & Memory in Literature.** Harald Weinrich. 2000. text 26.95 (*0-312-20556-2*, St Martins Paperbacks) St Martin.

Lethe's Adolescence. Kiki Dimoula & Theofanis G. Stavrou. LC 96-72137. (Modern Greek History & Culture Ser.: Vol. 20). 102p. 1996. 25.00 (*0-932963-08-0*) Nostos Bks.

Leticia's Secret. Ofelia D. Lachtman. LC 97-24772. 128p. (YA). 1997. 14.95 (*1-55885-208-5*, Pinata Bks) Arte Publico.

Leticia's Secret. Ofelia D. Lachtman. LC 97-24772. 128p. (YA). (gr. 3-7). 1997. pap. text 7.95 (*1-55885-209-3*, Pinata Bks) Arte Publico.

Letitia. Cathleen Clare. (Regency Romance Ser.). 256p. (Orig.). 1994. mass mkt. 3.99 (*0-380-77667-7*, Avon Bks) Morrow Avon.

Letitia Baldrige's Complete Guide to the New Manners for the '90s. Letitia Baldrige. (Illus.). 672p. 1990. 30.00 (*0-89256-320-6*) S&S Trade.

Letitia Baldrige's More Than Manners. Letitia Baldrige. LC 96-50980. 1997. 23.00 (*0-684-81875-2*, Scribners Ref) Mac Lib Ref.

Letitia Baldrige's New Complete Guide to Executive Manners. rev. ed. Letitia Baldrige. 672p. 1993. 40.00 (*0-89256-362-1*, Rawson Assocs) Macmillan.

Letitia Elizabeth Landon: Selected Writings. Ed. by Jerome J. McGann & Daniel M. Riess. LC 98-219517. (Broadview Literary Texts Ser.). 400p. (C). 1997. pap. 14.95 (*1-55111-135-7*) Broadview Pr.

***Letitia's Home in the Valley.** Virginia Gilbert. (J). (gr. 3-7). 2000. pap. 9.99 (*0-88092-449-7*) Royal Fireworks.

Letizia Battaglia: Passion, Justice, Freedom: Photographs of Sicily. Contrib. by Alexander Stille et al. LC 98-89091. (Illus.). 144p. 1999. 45.00 (*0-89381-805-4*) Aperture.

***L'Etoile de la Chance.** Kathleen Creighton. (Amours d'Aujourd'Hui Ser.: No. 348). (FRE.). 2000. mass mkt. 5.50 (*0-373-38348-7*, 1-38348-8, Harlequin French) Harlequin Bks.

Letourneau's Used Auto Parts. Carolyn Chute. LC 94-37243. (Harvest American Writing Ser.). 256p. 1995. pap. 11.00 (*0-15-600189-6*, Harvest Bks) Harcourt.

Letourneau's Used Auto Parts. Carolyn Chute. 224p. 1988. 16.45 (*0-89919-500-8*, Pub. by Ticknor & Fields) HM.

Letra Escarlata. Nathaniel Hawthorne. 1998. pap. text 8.95 (*84-8327-002-1*) E Martinez Roca.

Letra Muerta, Level 4. Adapted by Juan J. Millas. (Leer en Espanol Ser.). (SPA.). (C). 1998. pap. 6.95 (*84-294-3487-9*) Santillana.

Letra Roja. Nathaniel Hawthorne. (Nueva Austral Ser.: Vol. 34). (SPA.). 1991. pap. text 24.95 (*84-239-1834-3*) Elliots Bks.

***Letras.** Alma Flor Ada. (SPA., Illus.). 1999. pap. text 4.95 (*1-58105-402-5*) Santillana.

Letras: The Letters. Maribel Suarez. (Albores Ser.). (Illus.). 14p. (J). (ps-1). 1990. 10.75 (*970-05-0094-2*) Hispanic Bk Dist.

Letras, I. Carlos P. Otero. (Monagrafias A Ser.: Vol. VIII). (SPA.). 202p. (Orig.). (C). 1966. pap. 51.00 (*0-900411-47-3*, Pub. by Tamesis Bks Ltd) Boydell & Brewer.

Let's Abolish Government: An Original Arno Press Compilation. Lysander Spooner. LC 73-172232. (Right Wing Individualist Tradition in America Ser.). 1978. reprint ed. 33.95 (*0-405-00441-9*) Ayer.

Let's All Be Friends! Chris Gilmer & June M. Milam. (Drugless Douglass Tales Ser.). (Illus.). 20p. (Orig.). (J). (ps). 1994. pap. text 32.95 (*1-884307-09-4*); student ed. 6.95 (*1-884307-10-8*) Dev Res Educ.

Let's All Be Friends! Chris Gilmer & June M. Milam. Ed. by Charlotte C. Daley. Tr. by Carmen Miranda. (Drugless Douglass Tales Ser.). (SPA., Illus.). 24p. (Orig.). (J). (ps). 1997. pap. 32.95 (*1-884307-28-0*); pap., student ed. 6.95 (*1-884307-29-9*) Dev Res Educ.

Let's All Dig & Burrow! Anna Nilsen & Anni Axworthy. LC 99-161890. (Animals on the Move Ser.). (J). 1998. 10.95 (*1-84089-003-7*) Zero to Ten.

Let's All Hang & Dangle! Anna Nilsen & Anni Axworthy. LC 98-60346. (Animals on the Move Ser.). (J). 1998. 10.95 (*1-84089-002-9*) Zero to Ten.

***Let's All Have Fun!** large type ed. WeWrite Kids Staff. (WeWrite Kids! Ser.). (Illus.). 50p. (J). (gr. 1-7). 2000. pap. 3.95 (*1-57635-056-8*) WeWrite.

Let's All Leap & Jump! Anna Nilsen. (Illus.). 24p. (J). 1999. 10.95 (*1-84089-157-2*) LKC.

Let's All Sleep, Nature's Way, Vol. 1. Naikang Chang. (Illus.). (Orig.). 1989. pap. write for info. (*0-318-64861-X*) Jupiter Pub.

***Let's All Swim & Dive!** Anna Nilsen. (Illus.). 24p. (J). 1999. 10.95 (*1-84089-156-4*) LKC.

Let's Always Make Love Last: Promises to Make Love Last. Susan Newman. LC 94-16788. 194p. (Orig.). 1995. pap. 8.00 (*0-399-51901-7*, Perigee Bks) Berkley Pub.

Let's Articulate: Reproducible Drill Sheets for Therapy & Carryover. Bonita L. Martin & Greta C. Momeier. 410p. 1983. student ed., spiral bd. 39.00 (*0-7616-4646-9*) Commun Skill.

Let's Bake a Cake. Helen Drew & Angela Wilkes. LC 97-12534. (Illus.). (J). 1997. write for info. (*0-7894-1560-7*) DK Pub Inc.

***Let's Bake Cookies.** (Tami & Moishy Ser.: Vol. 2). 1999. bds. 6.95 (*0-87306-963-3*) Feldheim.

Let's Ban Smoking Outright! Patrick Griffin. 56p. (Orig.). 1995. pap. 4.95 (*0-89815-685-8*) Ten Speed Pr.

Let's Be Animals. Ann Turner. LC 97-75051. (Illus.). 24p. (J). (ps-k). 1998. 9.95 (*0-694-01154-1*) HarpC.

Let's Be Better Friends: The Peer Intergration Program. Mary B. Delaney et al. (Illus.). 1997. spiral bd. 34.95 (*1-890265-01-2*, 0950) Janelle Pubns.

Let's Be Circus Animals. Kathy Christensen. Ed. by Barbara B. Linse. (Using Themes Ser.). (Illus.). 60p. 1988. pap. text 6.95 (*0-9607458-9-0*) Arts Pubns.

Let's Be Circus Stars. Kathy Christensen. Ed. by Barbara B. Linse. (Using Themes Ser.). (Illus.). 57p. 1988. pap. text 6.95 (*0-685-45616-1*) Arts Pubns.

Let's Be Circus Stars. Kathy Christensen. (Illus.). 60p. 1990. 6.95 (*1-878079-13-1*) Arts Pubns.

Let's Be Enemies. Janice M. Udry. LC 61-5777. (Illus.). 32p. (J). (ps-1). 1961. lib. bdg. 14.89 (*0-06-026131-5*) HarpC Child Bks.

Let's Be Enemies. Janice M. Udry. LC 61-5777. (Illus.). 32p. (J). (ps-1). 1961. 13.00 (*0-06-026130-7*) HarpC Child Bks.

Lets Be Enemies. Janice M. Udry. LC 61-5777. (Trophy Picture Bk.). (Illus.). 32p. (J). (ps-2). 1988. pap. 5.95 (*0-06-443188-6*, HarpTrophy) HarpC Child Bks.

Let's Be Enemies. Janice May Udry. (J). 1961. 11.15 (*0-606-03844-2*, Pub. by Turtleback) Demco.

***Let's Be Frank, Pt. 2.** Shery L. Williams. (YA). 1999. pap. 6.95 (*1-56794-192-3*) Star Bible.

Let's Be Frank, Okay! Talibah F. Modupe. Ed. by T. Munirah Harris. (Illus.). 94p. (Orig.). 1994. pap. 7.95 (*1-887442-01-4*) Modupe Pr.

Let's Be Friends. Morrell Gipson & Lene Mayer. Ed. by Rebecca Stefoff. LC 90-13795. (Magic Mountain Fables Ser.). (Illus.). 24p. (J). (gr. k-3). 1990. lib. bdg. 14.60 (*0-944483-92-5*) Garrett Ed Corp.

Let's Be Friends. Read Alone Books Staff. (Read Alone Bks.). (Illus.). (J). (ps). 1997. pap. 15.95 (*0-395-88090-4*) HM.

Let's Be Friends: A Friends History & Doctrine Course for Youth. Carol Spencer et al. 124p. (YA). (gr. 7-12). 1993. ring bd. 9.95 (*0-943701-21-X*) George Fox Pr.

Let's Be Heard. Bob Grant. 1997. per. 14.00 (*0-671-53721-0*, PB Trade Paper) PB.

Let's Be Heard: The King of Conservative Talk Radio Speaks Out to America! Bob Grant. 256p. 1996. 22.00 (*0-671-53487-4*) S&S Trade.

Let's Be Organized: How to Organize Your Entire Life with 5 x 8 Cards. Olive D. Osmond. (Illus.). (Orig.). 1990. pap. text 5.95 (*0-929786-00-9*) Know Unltd UT.

Let's Be Thankful. Matt Mitter. (Little Golden Bks.). 24p. (J). 1998. 2.29 (*0-307-96022-6*, 96022, Goldn Books) Gldn Bks Pub Co.

Let's Become Internationally Minded. John R. Terry. (Illus.). 184p. 1990. pap. 8.95 (*0-933704-85-2*) Dawn Pr.

Let's Begin: On the Path to School Readiness. Rose M. Sicoli-Ostler. (Illus.). vii, 112p. (Orig.). 1996. pap. 9.95 (*0-9654489-6-7*) Lets Begin.

***Let's Begin Reading.** (Richard Scarry Bks.). (Illus.). 32p. (J). (gr. k-2). 1998. pap. 4.95 (*0-88724-489-0*, CD-5853) Carson-Dellos.

Let's Begin Reading Right: A Developmental Approach to Emergent Literacy. 4th ed. Marjorie V. Fields. LC 99-13650. 398p. (C). 1999. pap. text 39.00 (*0-13-011291-7*) P-H.

Let's Begin with Prayer: 130 Prayers for Junior & Senior High Schools. Mitch Finley. LC 97-20174. 128p. (YA). (gr. 7-12). 1997. pap. 8.95 (*0-87793-615-3*) Ave Maria.

Let's Blow Thru Europe. rev. ed. Thomas Neenan & Greg Hancock. LC 91-50886. (Illus.). 256p. 1992. pap. 12.95 (*0-914457-46-2*) Mustang Pub.

Let's Build a Bridge. Carson Koonce & John Farmer. (Illus.). 4p. 1994. 5.00 (*1-880994-28-3*) Mt Olive Coll Pr.

Let's Build a Car. Margaret A. Schaefer. LC 89-29426. (Illus.). 32p. (J). (gr. 1-5). 1992. pap., per. 4.95 (*0-8249-8536-2*, Ideals Child) Hambleton-Hill.

Let's Build Airplanes & Rockets! en P. Millspaugh. LC 96-22405. (Illus.). 128p. (J). (gr. 3-6). 1996. pap., teacher ed. 16.95 (*0-07-042952-9*, Lrng Triangle) McGraw-Hill Prof.

Let's Build an Airport. Kath Mellentin. LC 98-25776. (J). (gr. 1-5). 1998. 14.95 (*1-84089-026-6*) Zero to Ten.

Let's Build an Invention. Jack Challoner et al. LC 97-12560. (Illus.). (J). (gr. k up). 1997. write for info. (*0-7894-1558-5*) DK Pub Inc.

Let's Buy & Sell in Spanish! Lucero Alatriste.Tr. of Compremos y Vendamos en Espanol!. (SPA.). 800p. 1995. pap. 35.00 (*0-9648353-0-4*) L Alatriste.

Let's Call Him Lau-Wili-Wili-Humu-Humu-Nukunuku-Nukunuku-Apuaa-Oioi. Tim Myers. LC 93-72767. (Illus.). 24p. (J). (ps-3). 1993. pap. 6.95 (*1-880188-66-X*) Bess Pr.

Let's Care about Sharing! P. K. Hallinan. LC 96-38781. (Illus.). 24p. (Orig.). (J). (ps-3). 1997. pap. 3.25 (*1-57102-105-1*, Ideals Child) Hambleton-Hill.

Let's Carve Wooden Plaques. Harold L. Enlow. LC 77-81439. 48p. 1977. pap. 6.00 (*1-882475-00-3*) Enlow Wood Carv.

Let's Celebrate see Celebremos

Let's Celebrate. (Let's Celebrate Series). 1995. pap., teacher ed. 16.95 (*0-87441-573-X*) Behrman.

Let's Celebrate. Veritas Publications Staff. 1989. pap. 21.00 (*0-86217-129-6*, Pub. by Veritas Pubns) St Mut.

Let's Celebrate! large type ed. Nancy N. Bijan. (Second Ser.). (Illus.). 22p. (J). (ps-6). 1998. pap. 6.95 (*1-880710-19-6*) Monterey Pacific.

Let's Celebrate, 7 bks., Set. Behrman House, Inc. Staff. (Illus.). 112p. pap. 8.50 (*0-614-06077-X*) Behrman.

Let's Celebrate! A Public Relations & Special Events Guide for Nonprofit Homes & Services for the Aging. Ed. by Deborah A. Cloud. LC 88-70046. 100p. (Orig.). 1988. pap. 38.50 (*0-943774-39-X*) Am Assn Homes.

Let's Celebrate! Canada's Special Days. Caroline Parry. (Illus.). 256p. (J). 1987. pap. 18.95 (*0-921103-40-9*) Kids Can Pr.

Let's Celebrate: Festival Poems. Compiled by John Foster. (Illus.). 112p. (J). (gr. 3 up). 1997. reprint ed. pap. 11.95 (*0-19-276085-8*) OUP.

Let's Celebrate Christmas. Peter Roop & Connie Roop. LC 97-4268. (Illus.). 32p. (J). (gr. k-3). 1997. lib. bdg. 19.90 (*0-7613-0115-1*) Millbrook Pr.

Let's Celebrate Christmas. Peter Roop et al. LC 97-4268. (Illus.). 32p. (J). (gr. k-3). 1997. pap. 5.95 (*0-7613-0283-2*) Millbrook Pr.

Let's Celebrate Christmas: A Book of Drawing Fun. Roseanna Pistolesi. (J). 1988. 7.15 (*0-606-03601-6*, Pub. by Turtleback) Demco.

Let's Celebrate Easter. (Easter Coloring & Activity Ser.). (Illus.). 32p. (J). (gr. k-2). 1997. pap. write for info. (*1-56144-909-1*, Honey Bear Bks) Modern Pub NYC.

Let's Celebrate Halloween. Peter Roop & Connie Roop. LC 96-36466. (Illus.). 32p. (J). (gr. k-3). 1997. pap. 5.95 (*0-7613-0284-0*); lib. bdg. 19.90 (*0-7613-0113-5*) Millbrook Pr.

Let's Celebrate Halloween: A Book of Drawing Fun. Roseanna Pistolesi. (J). 1968. 7.15 (*0-606-03602-4*, Pub. by Turtleback) Demco.

Let's Celebrate Kwanzaa. Universal Language Staff & Gwen Jackson. Ed. by Alan L. Jackson. (Illus.). 18p. (J). (ps-6). 1997. pap. 14.95 (*0-9663978-0-0*) Unilan Pub.

Let's Celebrate Kwanzaa: An Activity Book for Young Readers. Helen Davis-Thompson. (Illus.). 32p. (J). (ps-5). 1993. pap. 5.95 (*0-936073-07-1*) Gumbs & Thomas.

Let's Celebrate Math. Claire Patterson. (Illus.). 80p. 1991. pap. 4.95 (*0-9623835-6-2*, CLC0053) Pieces of Lrning.

Let's Celebrate Our Differences. Mary L. Williams. LC 94-1521. (Illus.). 48p. (Orig.). 1994. pap. 8.95 (*1-55874-294-8*, 2948) Health Comm.

Let's Celebrate Our Jewish Holidays! Alfred J. Kolatch. LC 96-49289. (Illus.). 64p. (J). (ps-3). 1997. 14.95 (*0-8246-0394-X*) Jonathan David.

Let's Celebrate Series, 6 vols., Set. Jacqueline Woodson et al. (Illus.). 192p. (J). (gr. k-2). 1990. lib. bdg. 41.70 (*0-671-31230-8*, Silver Pr NJ) Silver Burdett Pr.

***Let's Celebrate Shabbat.** Madeline Wikler. LC 99-94433. (Illus.). 12p. (J). (ps). 1999. bds. 4.95 (*1-58013-055-0*) Kar-Ben.

***Let's Celebrate Thanksgiving.** Connie Roop. LC 98-51380. (Illus.). 32p. (J). (gr. 1-3). 1999. 19.90 (*0-7613-0973-X*, Copper Beech Bks) Millbrook Pr.

***Let's Celebrate Thanksgiving.** Connie Roop et al. LC 98-51380. (Books for Halloween & Thanksgiving Ser.). 32p. (J). (gr. k-3). 1999. 5.95 (*0-7613-0429-0*, Copper Beech Bks) Millbrook Pr.

***Let's Celebrate Thanksgiving.** Peter Roop. (Illus.). (J). 1999. 11.40 (*0-606-18293-4*) Turtleback.

Let's Celebrate Thanksgiving: A Book of Drawing Fun. Janice Kinnealy. (J). 1988. 7.15 (*0-606-03604-0*, Pub. by Turtleback) Demco.

Let's Celebrate Today: Calendars, Events, & Holidays. Diana F. Marks. LC 98-26745. 350p. 1998. pap. 35.00 (*1-56308-558-5*) Teacher Ideas Pr.

Let's Celebrate Valentine's Day. Connie Roop. LC 98-13971. (Illus.). 32p. (J). (gr. k-3). 1999. lib. bdg. 21.90 (*0-7613-0972-1*, Copper Beech Bks) Millbrook Pr.

Let's Celebrate Valentine's Day. Connie Roop & Peter Roop. LC 98-13971. (Illus.). 32p. (J). (gr. k-3). 1999. pap. 5.95 (*0-7613-0428-2*, Copper Beech Bks) Millbrook Pr.

Let's Chant, Let's Sing, Bk. 3. Carolyn Graham. 1996. pap., student ed. 6.95 (*0-19-434753-2*) OUP.

Let's Chant, Let's Sing, Bk. 4. Carolyn Graham. 1996. pap., student ed. 6.95 (*0-19-434894-6*) OUP.

Let's Chant, Let's Sing, Vol. 2. Carolyn Graham. (Illus.). 1995. pap., student ed. 6.95 (*0-19-434652-8*) OUP.

Let's Chant, Let's Sing 1. Carolyn Graham. (Illus.). 1994. student ed. 6.95 (*0-19-434648-X*) OUP.

Let's Chant, Let's Sing 1-2. 1995. write for info. (*0-19-470062-3*) OUP.

Let's Chat. Panush. 1995. 28.00 (*0-7616-3218-2*) Commun Skill.

Let's Choose the Right. Bessie Dean. 1993. reprint ed. 3.98 (*0-88290-072-2*, 1337) Horizon Utah.

Let's Clean up Our Act: Songs for the Earth. Perf. by Tom Callinan & Ann Shapiro. (gr. 1-6). 1990. 3.50 (*1-879305-06-2*, AM-B-106) Am Melody.

Let's Collect Coins! 3rd unabridged ed. Albert Whitman Publishing Staff. LC 96-210610. (Illus.). 96p. 1996. pap. text 3.50 (*0-307-99381-7*, Whitman Coin) St Martin.

Let's Collect Scotch Whiskey. Ed. by Jarrold Publishing Staff. 32p. 1999. pap. 3.95 (*0-7117-0222-5*) JARR UK.

Lets Color & Count: Colorions et Comptons. Nancy Palumbo. (Illus.). 32p. (J). (gr. k-6). 1989. student ed. 0.45 (*0-927024-09-8*) Crayons Pubns.

Let's Color Chicago. Gary Grimm & Associates Staff. (Illus.). 40p. (Orig.). (J). (ps-6). 1993. student ed. 4.00 (*1-56490-000-2*) G Grimm Assocs.

Let's Color Korea, 3 vols., Set. (J). 1990. 32.85 (*1-56591-050-8*) Hollym Intl.

Let's Color Korea: Everyday Life in Traditional. B. J. Jones. 24p. (J). (gr. k-3). 1990. pap. 10.95 (*0-930878-98-1*) Hollym Intl.

Let's Color Korea: Traditional Games. M. Mueller. 24p. (J). (gr. k-3). 1989. pap. 10.95 (*0-930878-95-7*) Hollym Intl.

Let's Color Korea: Traditional Lifestyles. Suzanne C. Han. 24p. (J). (gr. k-3). 1989. pap. 10.95 (*0-930878-94-9*) Hollym Intl.

Let's Communicate. Roger Campbell. (Orig.). 1977. pap. 4.50 (*0-87508-060-X*) Chr Lit.

Let's Communicate. Paul E. Herman & Sheila H. Ihde. 1979. teacher ed. 6.96 (*0-88334-123-9*, 76097); teacher ed. 9.28 (*0-8013-0086-X*, 75750); pap. text 12.30 (*0-685-45047-3*, 76097) Longman.

Let's Communicate: A Self-Help Program on Writing Letters & Memos. George W. Martin. LC 71-109516. (Supervisory Management Ser.). 1970. pap. text. write for info. (*0-201-04500-1*) Addison-Wesley.

Let's Communicate! Breaking the Cycle of Non-Communication. Dee Frances. 255p. Date not set. lib. bdg. 24.95 (*1-885519-14-1*) DDDD Pubns.

Let's Communicate: Using Grammar Effectively. Paul E. Herman & Sheila H. Ihde. 233p. (J). (gr. 4-7). 1979. reprint ed. pap. text 16.00 (*1-877653-48-9*) Wayside Pub.

Let's Cook. Dr. Oetker. (Illus.). 48p. (J). (gr. 4-10). 1993. pap. 5.95 (*0-8069-8533-X*) Sterling.

Let's Cook, America: Traditional American Cooking. Joleen W. Mullins. LC 91-91371. 265p. (Orig.). 1992. pap. text 14.95 (*0-9631418-0-5*) W Mullins Pubs.

Let's Cook Dutch! A Complete Guide for the Dutch Oven Chef. Robert L. Ririe. LC 79-89360. (Illus.). 104p. 1979. pap. 8.98 (*0-88290-120-6*) Horizon Utah.

Let's Cook Fish: A Complete Guide to Fish Cookery. 1984. lib. bdg. 79.95 (*0-87700-545-1*) Revisionist Pr.

Let's Cook Fish: Complete Guide to Fish Cookery. 1986. lib. bdg. 79.95 (*0-8490-3790-5*) Gordon Pr.

Let's Cook International. Canadian Red Cross Society Staff. 189p. (Orig.). 1989. pap. 11.95 (*0-920581-02-1*) Gordon Soules Bk.

Let's Cook It Metric. Elizabeth Read. LC 75-5395. (Illus.). 1975. pap. 5.00 (*0-9600996-1-1*) E Read.

Let's Cook Microwave! Barbara Harris. 1987. ring bd., vinyl bd. 11.95 (*0-9601060-2-2*) B Harris.

Let's Cook Microwave!, Vol. 1. 4th ed. Barbara Harris. 1987. pap. 5.95 (*0-9601060-0-6*); spiral bd. 7.95 (*0-9601060-1-4*) B Harris.

Let's Cook Once - Eat Twice: A Cookbook for Busy Families. Cynthia Hillson. Ed. by Jan Teel. (Illus.). 96p. Date not set. pap. 16.95 (*0-9649267-3-3*) Up on the Hill.

***Let's Cook Pasta.** Jeni Wright. 128p. 2000. 17.95 (*1-84215-104-5*) Anness Pub.

Let's Cook with Nora. Nora V. Daza. (Illus.). 279p. 1979. 15.95 (*0-318-36296-1*) Asia Bk Corp.

L

Let's Count. Deni Bown. (Tab Board Bks.). 8p. (J). 1995. 3.95 (0-7894-0232-7, 5-70644) DK Pub Inc.

Let's Count. DiCicco Digital Arts Staff. LC 98-208280. 1998. write for info. (0-7853-2705-3) Pubns Intl Ltd.

Let's Count. Illus. by Lynn A. Grundy. 28p. (J). (ps). 1992. pap. 3.50 (0-7214-1509-1, Ladybrd) Penguin Putnam.

Let's Count. Tana Hoban. LC 98-44739. (Illus.). 48p. (J). (ps-k). 1999. 16.00 (0-688-16008-5, Grenwillow Bks) HarpC Child Bks.

***Let's Count.** Tana Hoban. LC 98-44739. (Illus.). 48p. (J). (ps-k). 1999. 15.89 (0-688-16009-3, Grenwillow Bks) HarpC Child Bks.

Let's Count at Old MacDonald's Farm. (Illus.). 10p. (J). (ps-1). 1996. 29.99 (1-888074-47-7) Pckts Lrning.

Let's Count Baby. Cheryl W. Hudson. (Illus.). 10p. 1995. 3.95 (0-590-94922-5, Cartwheel) Scholastic Inc.

Let's Count, Dracula: A Chubby Board Book. Alan Benjamin. (Illus.). 16p. (J). (ps up). 1992. 3.95 (0-671-77008-X) Litle Simon.

Let's Count It Out, Jesse Bear. Nancy W. Carlstrom. (Illus.). 32p. (J). (ps-1). 1996. per. 15.00 (0-689-80478-4) S&S Childrens.

Let's Create a Story. Ed. by Amanda Robinson. (J). (gr. 4-7). 1997. wbk. ed. 9.95 (0-9653035-0-0) Huckleberry CT.

Let's Create with Paint. Dawn Sirett et al. LC 97-12558. (Illus.). (J). (gr. k up). 1997. write for info. (0-7894-1559-3) DK Pub Inc.

Let's Curtoon! with Curt Visca. rev. ed. Curtis Visca & Kelley V. Visca. (Illus.). 64p. (J). (ps-6). 1990. pap. 14.95 (1-890796-00-X) Curtz Cartoon.

***Let's Cut the Small Talk: The Adult Party Game for the 21st Century.** Jeff Reuter. 304p. 2000. 6.95 (0-9663303-0-7) Corporate Designs.

Let's Dance. George Ancona. LC 97-29436. (J). 1998. 15.99 (0-525-67536-1, Dutton Child) Peng Put Young Read.

***Let's Dance!** George Ancona. LC 97-52022. (Illus.). 40p. (J). (ps-3). 1998. 16.00 (0-688-16211-8, Wm Morrow); 15.89 (0-688-16212-6, Wm Morrow) Morrow Avon.

Let's Dance: Learn to Salsa, Fox-Trot, Rumba, Tango, Line Dance, Lambada, Cha-Cha, Waltz, Two-Step. Paul Bottomer. 256p. 1998. 19.98 (1-57912-046-6) Blck Dog & Leventhal.

Let's Dance: Popular Music in the 1930s. Arnold Shaw. Ed. by Bill Willard. LC 97-45584. 256p. 1998. 30.00 (0-19-505307-9) OUP.

Let's Dance: The Greek Way. Theoni Pappas. (Illus.). 1977. pap. 2.95 (0-933174-07-1) Wide World-Tetra.

Let's Dance No. 4: Country Western Line Dancer's Reference Handbook. Jean Y. Woolman. 145p. (Orig.). Date not set. pap. text 9.95 (0-9638125-3-X) Wild & Wooly.

Let's Debate! Kathy M. Littlefield & Robert S. Littlefield. (Illus.). 36p. (Orig.). (J). (gr. 3-6). 1989. pap. text 8.95 (1-879340-03-8, K0104) Kidspeak.

Let's Design, Cut, Sew, & Fit with George W. Trippon. George W. Trippon. LC 85-51714. (Illus.). 139p. 1985. 14.95 (0-935245-03-0) Trippon Fash.

Let's Develop! A Guide to Continuous Personal Growth. Fred Newman et al. LC 94-68612. 272p. 1994. pap. 11.95 (0-9628621-6-9) Castillo Intl.

Let's Discover Bryce & Zion National Parks. Lynell Diamond. (Children's Activity Bks. for Ages 6-11). (Illus.). 32p. (J). (gr. 1-6). 1990. pap. 4.95 (0-89886-253-1) Mountaineers.

Let's Discover Canada, 14 vols. Suzanne LeVert. (Illus.). (J). (gr. 3 up). 1991. lib. bdg. 237.30 (0-7910-1021-X) Chelsea Hse.

Let's Discover Capitol Reef, Arches, & Canyonlands National Parks: A Children's Activity Book for Ages 6-11. Lynnell Diamond. (Let's Discover Ser.). (Illus.). 32p. (J). (gr. 1-6). 1991. pap. 4.95 (0-89886-285-X) Mountaineers.

Let's Discover Cold-Blooded Animals. LC 80-24150. (Illus.). 80 p. 1981. write for info. (0-8172-1752-5) Raintree Steck-V.

Let's Discover Computers! Barbara R. Hamm. LC 97-7188. 350p. (J). 1997. pap. text, teacher ed. 28.95 (0-87628-520-5) Ctr Appl Res.

Let's Discover Computers! Ready-to-Use Lessons & Activities for. Barbara R. Hamm. LC 97-7188. 350p. 1997. pap., teacher ed. 28.50 (0-87628-271-0) Ctr Appl Res.

Let's Discover Crayon. Jenean Romberg. (Arts & Crafts Discovery Units Ser.). (Illus.). 64p. 1994. reprint ed. pap. text 9.95 (0-87628-523-X) Ctr Appl Res.

Let's Discover Mobiles. Jenean Romberg. (Arts & Crafts Discovery Units Ser.). (Illus.). 64p. 1994. reprint ed. pap. text 9.95 (0-87628-524-8) Ctr Appl Res.

Let's Discover Paper. Jenean Romberg. (Arts & Crafts Discovery Units Ser.). (Illus.). 64p. 1994. reprint ed. pap. text 9.95 (0-87628-526-4) Ctr Appl Res.

Lets Discover Petrified Forest: A Children's Activity Book for Ages 6-11. Lynnell Diamond. (Let's Discover Ser.). (Illus.). 32p. (J). (gr. 1-6). 1991. pap. 4.95 (0-89886-286-8) Mountaineers.

Let's Discover Puppets. Jenean Romberg. (Arts & Crafts Discovery Units Ser.). (Illus.). 64p. 1994. reprint ed. pap. text 9.95 (0-87628-528-0) Ctr Appl Res.

Let's Discover Tempera. Jenean Romberg. (Arts & Crafts Discovery Units Ser.). (Illus.). 64p. 1994. reprint ed. pap. text 9.95 (0-87628-529-9) Ctr Appl Res.

Let's Discover the Bible, Vol. 1. Shirley Rose. (Illus.). 64p. (J). (gr. k-2). pap. 4.75 (0-87441-538-1) Behrman.

Let's Discover the Grand Canyon. Lynnell Diamond. 32p. (J). (gr. 1-6). 1990. pap. 4.95 (0-89886-252-3) Mountaineers.

Let's Discover the San Juan Islands. Lynnell Diamond & Marge Mueller. (Illus.). 32p. (Orig.). (J). 1989. pap. 4.95 (0-89886-220-5) Mountaineers.

Let's Discover Tissue. Jenean Romberg. (Arts & Crafts Discovery Units Ser.). (Illus.). 64p. 1994. reprint ed. pap. text 9.95 (0-87628-530-2) Ctr Appl Res.

Let's Discover Weaving. Jenean Romberg. (Arts & Crafts Discovery Units Ser.). (Illus.). 64p. 1994. pap. text 9.95 (0-87628-532-9) Ctr Appl Res.

Let's Do Fingerplays. Marion Grayson. LC 62-10217. (Illus.). (J). (ps-3). 1962. 14.95 (0-88331-003-1) R B Luce.

Let's Do It: A Fundamental Guide to Slow-Pitch Softball. Richard J. Aligo. (Illus.). 194p. (Orig.). 1987. spiral bd. 14.95 (0-9615760-7-3) Nel-Mar Pub.

Let's Do Lunch Southern California Style. Betty B. Simm & Mary J. Bennett. 96p. 1995. 19.95 (0-9647560-4-8) Simm-Bennett.

Let's Do Something. J. G. Malphurs. 1958. pap. 0.60 (0-88027-099-3) Firm Foun Pub.

***Let's Do Something! Educational Crafts & Activities for Juniors & Intermediates.** Elizabeth A. Showalter. (Illus.). 112p. (YA). (gr. 4-9). 1999. 8.95 (0-87813-582-0) Christian Light.

Let's Do the Vowel Sounds. DeeAnn Champlin. (Little Lyrics Short Vowel Collection: Vol. 6). (Illus.). 11p. (J). (gr. k-2). 1998. pap. 12.00 (1-893429-30-X) Little Lyrics.

Let's Dough It Again. Paulette S. Jarvey. (Illus.). 80p. (Orig.). 1982. pap. 6.95 (0-9605904-1-2) Hot off Pr.

Let's Draw in Dots. G. G. Thomson. LC 97-67236. (Children's Library of Visual Literacy). (Illus.). 28p. (Orig.). (J). 1997. pap. 6.95 (1-887003-97-5) Dancng Jester.

Lets Draw Monsters. (High Q Wipe-Off Bks.). 24p. (J). (ps-1). 1999. mass mkt. 4.99 (0-7681-0130-1, McClanahan Book) Learn Horizon.

Let's Drive Con Artists Out of Business. Ed. by Jean O'Neil. 24p. 1992. pap. 7.95 (0-934513-42-2, R11A) Natl Crime DC.

***Let's Eat!** Andrea Posner. (Illus.). (J). 2000. 3.99 (0-307-14530-1) Gldn Bks Pub Co.

***Let's Eat.** Random House Staff. (Pictureback Ser.). 24p. (J). 2000. pap. 3.25 (0-375-80435-8, Pub. by Random Bks Yng Read) Random.

Let's Eat! Ana Zamorano. LC 96-25928. (Illus.). 32p. (J). (ps-2). 1997. 15.95 (0-590-13444-2) Scholastic Inc.

Let's Eat! Ana Zamorano. (Illus.). 32p. (ps-2). 1999. pap. 5.99 (0-439-06758-8) Scholastic Inc.

Let's Eat. Gyo Fujikawa. (Illus.). 16p. (J). (ps). 1989. reprint ed. bds. 6.95 (1-55987-005-2, Sunny Bks) J B Comns.

Let's Eat: Vamos a Comer. Alan Benjamin. LC 93-151091. (Chubby Board Book in English & Spanish Ser.). (ENG & SPA., Illus.). 16p. (J). (ps-1). 1992. pap. 3.95 (0-671-76927-8) Litle Simon.

Let's Eat Chinese at Home! Wendy Wei & Ku Yue-Mei. (Let's Eat...at Home! Ser.). 160p. 1995. pap. 5.95 (0-572-01748-0, Pub. by Foulsham UK) Assoc Pubs Grp.

Let's Eat French at Home! Jean Conil. (Let's Eat...at Home! Ser.). 160p. 1995. pap. 5.95 (0-572-01834-7, Pub. by Foulsham UK) Assoc Pubs Grp.

Let's Eat Greek at Home! Candida Tofallis. (Let's Eat...at Home! Ser.). 160p. 1995. pap. 5.95 (0-572-01800-2, Pub. by Foulsham UK) Assoc Pubs Grp.

Let's Eat In: Menus, Recipes, Grocery Lists for Singles & Couples. Eileen Hulsey. 260p. 1997. ring bd. 19.95 (0-9651830-2-5) Blackberry.

Let's Eat Indian at Home! Das Gupta. (Let's Eat...at Home! Ser.). 160p. 1995. pap. 5.95 (0-572-01728-6, Pub. by Foulsham UK) Assoc Pubs Grp.

Let's Eat Italian at Home! Angelo Capistrani. (Let's Eat...at Home! Ser.). 160p. 1995. pap. 5.95 (0-572-01747-2, Pub. by Foulsham UK) Assoc Pubs Grp.

Let's Eat Mexican at Home! Juana M. Del Campo. (Let's Eat...at Home! Ser.). 160p. 1995. pap. 5.95 (0-572-01729-4, Pub. by Foulsham UK) Assoc Pubs Grp.

Let's Eat Out in Montgomery County. 4th ed. Joyce Rogers & Alan Rogers. Ed. by A. Siegel & Joyce Siegel. 256p. 1997. pap. 11.95 (1-883720-02-8) A Siegel Assocs.

Let's Eat Spanish at Home! Therese Avila-Lupe. (Let's Eat...at Home! Ser.). 160p. 1995. pap. 5.95 (0-572-01835-5, Pub. by Foulsham UK) Assoc Pubs Grp.

Let's Eat Stars. Nanao Sakaki. (Orig.). 1997. pap. 11.95 (0-942396-76-6) Blackberry ME.

Let's Eat Thai at Home! Supenn Vudinantha. (Let's Eat...at Home! Ser.). 160p. 1995. pap. 5.95 (0-572-01799-5, Pub. by Foulsham UK) Assoc Pubs Grp.

Let's Enjoy English. John R. Terry. (Illus.). 106p. 1979. pap. 6.00 (0-933704-35-6) Dawn Pr.

***Let's Entertain: Life's Guilty Pleasures.** Philippe Vergne et al. LC 99-59395. (Illus.). 320p. 2000. 29.95 (0-935640-66-5, Pub. by Walker Art Ctr) Dist Art Pubs.

***Let's Exercise.** Elizabeth Vogel. LC 00-39177. (Readers Clean & Healthy All Day Long Ser.). (Illus.). (YA). 2000. write for info. (0-8239-5687-3, PowerKids) Rosen Group.

Let's Experiment! Natalie Lunis & Nancy White. (Thinking Like a Scientist Ser.). (Illus.). 20p. (J). Date not set. pap. 16.95 (1-58273-111-X) Newbridge Educ.

Lets Explore . . . Aquatic Animals. Bob Kaminski. (Illus.). 24p. (J). 1997. 9.95 (1-890716-02-2) K & M Intl.

Lets Explore . . . Dinosaurs. Bob Kaminski. (Illus.). 24p. (J). 1997. write for info. (1-890716-01-4) K & M Intl.

Lets Explore . . . Space. Bob Kaminski. (Illus.). 24p. (J). 1997. 9.95 (1-890716-03-0) K & M Intl.

Lets Explore . . . the Rainforest, 4 vols. Bob Kaminski. (Illus.). 24p. (J). 1997. 9.95 (1-890716-00-6) K & M Intl.

Let's Explore Being Jewish Ser., 8 vols., Set. Sarah Feldman. (Illus.). (J). (gr. 1-2). 1996. pap. 8.50 (0-87441-611-6) Behrman.

Let's Explore Central America. Stuart J. Faber. 100p. 1975. pap. 1.95 (0-89074-013-5) Charing Cross.

Let's Explore Inside the Bible: An Activity, Information & Story Book. Fiona Walton. LC 94-70893. (Illus.). 64p. (J). (gr. 4-7). 1994. pap. 11.99 (0-8066-2745-X, Augsburg) Augsburg Fortress.

Let's Explore Israel: A City Tour. Sarah Feldman. (Let's Explore Being Jewish Ser.). (Illus.). 16p. (J). (gr. 1-2). 1995. pap. 2.25 (0-87441-586-1) Behrman.

Let's Explore Israel: People & Places. Sarah Feldman. (Let's Explore Being Jewish Ser.). (Illus.). 16p. (J). (gr. 1-2). 1995. pap. 2.25 (0-87441-587-X) Behrman.

Let's Explore Jewish Symbols. Sarah Feldman. (Let's Explore Being Jewish Ser.). (Illus.). 16p. (J). (gr. 1-2). 1996. pap. 2.25 (0-87441-603-5) Behrman.

Let's Explore Mitzvot. Sarah Feldman. (Let's Explore Being Jewish Ser.). (Illus.). 16p. (J). (gr. 1-2). 1996. pap. 2.25 (0-87441-598-5) Behrman.

Let's Explore the Airport! (Junior Field Trip Bks.). (J). (ps-2). 1996. 4.99 (0-614-15719-6) Random.

Let's Explore the Bible. Sarah Feldman. (Let's Explore Being Jewish Ser.). (Illus.). 16p. (J). (gr. 1-2). 1996. pap. 2.25 (0-87441-602-7) Behrman.

Let's Explore the Farm! (Junior Field Trip Bks.). (J). (ps-2). 1996. 4.99 (0-614-15718-8) Random.

Let's Explore the Life Cycle. Sarah Feldman. (Let's Explore Being Jewish Ser.). (Illus.). 16p. (J). (gr. 1-2). 1996. pap. 2.25 (0-87441-604-3) Behrman.

Let's Explore the Shore. Ilka Maidoff. (Illus.). (J). (gr. 5 up). 1962. 9.95 (0-8392-3017-6) Astor-Honor.

Let's Explore the Synagogue. Sarah Feldman. (Let's Explore Being Jewish Ser.). (Illus.). 16p. (J). (gr. 1-2). 1996. pap. 2.25 (0-87441-599-3) Behrman.

Let's Face It! Marie-Christine Forester. (Illus.). 100p. (Orig.). 1984. pap. 6.95 (0-917043-05-7) Press on Pr.

Let's Face It. Chris Harrison. Ed. by Judith Moretz. (Illus.). Date not set. write for info. (0-614-30360-5) C Harrison Prods.

***Let's Face It: Bg Beading Hearts Designs Inc.** Adrienne E. Anderson & Dona S. Anderson. (Beading Heart Designs). (Illus.). 34p. (C). 2000. pap. text 22.00 (1-892980-01-0) Buckaroo Pr.

Let's Face It: The Complete Facial Exercise Program for a Youthful, Healthier Face. unabridged ed. Christopher L. Harrison. Ed. by Judith Moretz. (Illus.). 166p. 1991. pap. 19.95 (0-9631512-0-7) C Harrison Prods.

Let's Face It: The Ultimate Skin Care Consultation. Nancy Purvis. 70p. 1998. pap. 8.95 (0-9664402-0-X) N Purvis.

Let's Face It, Men Are @$$#$$ What Women Can Do about It. Joseph W. Rock & Barry L. Duncan. LC 98-34228. 300p. 1998. pap. 12.95 (1-55874-625-0) Health Comm.

***Let's Face the Music: The Golden Age of Popular Songs.** Benny Green. (Illus.). 240p. 1999. pap. 22.95 (1-86205-314-6, Pub. by Pavilion Bks Ltd) Trafalgar.

Let's Face the Music & Die: A Lauren Laurano Mystery. Sandra Scoppettone. LC 96-95409. (Lauren Laurano Mystery Ser.). 312p. 1997. mass mkt. 5.99 (0-345-41225-7) Ballantine Pub Grp.

Let's Fall in Love. Carol Hill. 288p. 1996. pap. 11.00 (0-393-31408-1, Norton Paperbks) Norton.

Let's Fall in Love 'til Wednesday: An Adventure of the Heart. Joan Wendland. LC 94-69511. (Illus.). 112p. (Orig.). 1995. pap. 9.95 (0-9644369-0-6) Dandelion.

***Let's Fill up the House with Stories & Songs.** unabridged ed. Rives Collins & Julie Shannon. (J). (gr. k-6). 1999. audio 10.00 (1-888019-03-4) L M Alleycat Mus.

***Let's Find Digimon.** Ellen Sullivan. (Digimon Ser.). (Illus.). (J). 2000. pap. 5.99 (0-439-21664-8) Scholastic Inc.

Let's Find Out see Vamos a Descubrir

Let's Find Out. (Fisher-Price Preschool Workbooks Ser.). (Illus.). 72p. (J). (ps). 1996. pap. write for info. (1-56144-766-8, Honey Bear Bks) Modern Pub NYC.

Let's Find Out. Karen M. Rogers. LC 98-71342. (Think-Kids Book Collection). (Illus.). 16p. (J). (gr. 1-4). 1998. pap. 2.95 (1-58237-003-6) Creat Think.

Let's Find Out about Florida! In the Yellow Pages, Dictionary, Encyclopedia, Almanac, Atlas, Who's Who, Bartlett's Quotations & Other Reference Sources! Carole Marsh. 36p. (J). (gr. 3-5). 1994. pap. 19.95 (0-7933-7350-6); lib. bdg. 29.95 (0-7933-7349-2); disk 29.95 (0-7933-7351-4) Gallopade Intl.

Let's Find Out about Ice Cream. Mary E. Reid. (Let's Find Out Library Ser.). 24p. (J). (ps-2). 1997. pap. text 4.95 (0-590-73800-3) Scholastic Inc.

Let's Find Out about Money. Kathy Barabas. LC 96-44077. (Let's Find Out Library Ser.). (Illus.). 24p. (J). (ps-2). 1997. 4.95 (0-590-73803-8) Scholastic Inc.

Let's Find Out about Toothpaste. Kathy Barabas. LC 96-47546. (Let's Find Out Library Ser.). (Illus.). (J). 1997. write for info. (0-590-73804-6) Scholastic Inc.

***Let's Find Pokemon.** Kazunori Aihara. (Illus.). 22p. (J). (ps-3). 1999. pap. 11.95 (1-56931-390-3, Pub. by Viz Commns Inc) Publishers Group.

***Let's Find Pokemon!, No. 2.** Kazunori Aihara. (Illus.). 32p. (ps-3). 2000. 11.95 (1-56931-414-4, Pub. by Viz Commns Inc) Publishers Group.

***Let's Find Pokemon! 3.** Kazunori Aihara. (Let's Find Pokemon Ser.). (Illus.). (J). 2000. 11.95 (1-56931-503-5) Viz Commns Inc.

Let's Find Teddy. Tony Potter. (J). (ps). 1998. 9.95 (1-902553-00-4, Pub. by Grimond) BHB Intl.

Let's Fix America! Alan B. Jones. LC 94-208700. 239p. 1994. pap. 15.00 (0-9640848-0-5) ABJ Press.

Let's Fix the Kids! Complete Parenting Program: LDS Version. 6th unabridged ed. James J. Jones. 374p. 1997. pap. 199.00 incl. audio (0-9666984-4-4) Familyhood Inc.

Let's Fix the Kids! Complete Parenting Program: Standard Version. 6th unabridged ed. James J. Jones. 374p. 1997. pap. 199.00 incl. audio (0-9666984-3-6) Familyhood Inc.

Lets Fix the Kids! Complete Parenting Resource Manual: Creating a New Environment at Home. 6th unabridged ed. James J. Jones. 374p. 1997. pap. 29.00 (0-9666984-0-1) Familyhood Inc.

Let's Flip the Script: An African American Discourse on Language, Literature, & Learning. Keith Gilyard. LC 96-16292. (African American Life Ser.). 160p. (Orig.). 1996. pap. 16.95 (0-8143-2645-5) Wayne St U Pr.

***Let's Fly a Kite.** Stuart J. Murphy. LC 99-26550. (MathStart Ser.). (Illus.). 40p. (J). (gr. 1-4). 2000. 15.95 (0-06-028034-4); lib. bdg. 15.89 (0-06-028035-2) HarpC Child Bks.

***Let's Fly a Kite.** Stuart J. Murphy. LC 99-26550. (MathStart Ser.). (Illus.). 40p. (J). (gr. 1 up). 2000. pap. 4.95 (0-06-446737-6, HarpTrophy) HarpC Child Bks.

***Let's Fly Backward: Barnstorming the Grand Traverse Bay Region.** Al Barnes. LC 75-39182. (Illus.). 206p. 2000. pap. 14.95 (0-915937-07-7) Hor Bks MI.

Let's Folk Dance. Herbert Rothgarber. 16p. 1980. pap. 3.25 (0-918812-10-0, SE 0440) MMB Music.

Let's Get a Pet. Rose Greydanus. LC 87-10938. (Illus.). 32p. (J). (gr. k-2). 1988. lib. bdg. 3.05 (0-8167-0986-6) Troll Communs.

Let's Get a Pet. Rose Greydanus. LC 87-10938. (Illus.). 32p. (J). (gr. k-2). 1997. pap. 2.50 (0-8167-0987-4) Troll Communs.

Let's Get a Pet. Houghton Mifflin Company Staff. (Literature Experience 1991 Ser.). (J). 1990. pap. write for info. (0-395-55017-3) HM.

Lets Get a Pet. Houghton Mifflin Company Staff. (Literature Experience 1993 Ser.). (J). 1992. pap. 4.48 (0-395-62568-8) HM.

***Let's Get a Pet.** Harriet Ziefert. (Illus.). (J). 1999. pap. text 13.40 (0-7857-7844-6) Econo-Clad Bks.

Let's Get a Pet. Harriet Ziefert. LC 91-48458. 1996. 11.19 (0-606-09542-X, Pub. by Turtleback) Demco.

Let's Get Acquainted. Kenneth McFarland. LC 86-30397. (Outreach Ser.). 32p. 1987. pap. 0.99 (0-8163-0691-5) Pacific Pr Pub Assn.

Let's Get America Moving Again. William J. McMillan. LC 81-85202. 101p. 1981. spiral bd. 12.95 (0-918214-08-4) F E Peters.

Let's Get at the Roots of Crime. rev. ed. Philip R. Wheeler. (Illus.). 1994. write for info. (0-9615763-1-6) Pussy Willow.

Let's Get Better (Anglais), Bk. 2: English for French Speakers. Assimil Staff. (ENG & FRE.). 28.95 (0-8288-4475-5, M10746) Fr & Eur.

Let's Get Closer: Selected Articles about Women by Chinese & Foreign Authors. Zhao Ning. 272p. 1995. pap. 9.95 (7-80005-287-7, Pub. by New World Pr) China Bks.

Let's Get Cooking. Judy Pemberton. (Illus.). 103p. (Orig.). (J). (gr. 3-12). 1984. text 7.95 (0-317-02695-X) King Fisher Pr.

Let's Get Criminal. 2nd ed. Lev Raphael. LC 96-48910. 244p. 1997. pap. 11.95 (0-312-15160-8) St Martin.

***Let's Get Down to Business.** Donald Burgis. Ed. by Anthony Noresta. (Illus.). 148p. 2000. spiral bd. 20.00 (0-9701633-0-4) Hisp Inst for Res.

Let's Get Dressed! Barbara Brenner et al. Ed. by Bank Street College Media Group Staff. (Illus.). 32p. (Orig.). (J). (ps). 1986. write for info. (0-9617460-0-9) Levi Strauss.

Let's Get Dressed. Harriet Ziefert. (J). (ps). 1988. 3.95 (0-671-65539-6) S&S Bks Yung.

Let's Get Going! Arthur M. Smith, Jr. & Robert T. King. (Illus.). 238p. 1996. 21.95 (1-56475-371-9) U NV Oral Hist.

Let's Get Growing: A Dirt-under-the-Nails Primer on Raising Vegetables, Fruits & Flowers Organically. Crow Miller. (Illus.). 388p. 1995. 23.95 (0-87596-640-3) Rodale Pr Inc.

Let's Get Growing: Twenty-Five Quick & Easy Gardening Projects for Kids. Joel Rapp. (J). 1992. pap. 7.00 (0-517-58880-3, Crown) Crown Pub Group.

***Lets Get Interpersonal Concordance Wisconsin.** 210p. (C). 1999. 31.27 (0-201-57551-5) Addison-Wesley.

Let's Get into Hydraulics. (Illus.). Date not set. reprint ed. pap. 3.50 (0-87288-028-1, IT-1) Intertec Pub.

Let's Get Invisible see Volvamonos Invisibles

Let's Get Invisible! Adapted by Megan Stine. LC 49-248960. (Goosebumps Presents Ser.: No. 11). (Illus.). 64p. (gr. 2-5). 1997. pap. 3.99 (0-590-93968-8, Apple Paperbacks) Scholastic Inc.

Let's Get Invisible! Adapted by Megan Stine. (Goosebumps Presents Ser.: No. 11). 1997. 9.19 (0-606-11405-X, Pub. by Turtleback) Demco.

Let's Get Invisible! R. L. Stine, pseud. (Goosebumps Ser.: No. 6). 160p. (J). (gr. 3-7). 1993. pap. 3.99 (0-590-45370-X) Scholastic Inc.

Let's Get Invisible! R. L. Stine, pseud. (Goosebumps Ser.: No. 6). (J). 1993. 9.09 (0-606-02707-6, Pub. by Turtleback) Demco.

Let's Get Invisible! see Goosebumps

Let's Get It On: The Politics of Black Performance. Ed. by Catherine Ugwu. LC 95-15190. (Illus.). 224p. (Orig.). 1995. pap. 18.95 (0-941920-33-X) Bay Pr.

Let's Get Lost: Adventures in the Great Wide Open. Craig Nelson. LC 98-49256. 320p. 1999. 24.00 (0-446-52366-6, Pub. by Warner Bks) Little.

***Let's Get Lost: Adventures in the Great Wide Open.** Craig Nelson. 384p. 2000. pap. 14.95 (0-446-67603-9) Warner Bks.

Let's Get Mommy Married. Marie Ferrarella. (Yours Truly Ser.). 1996. per. 3.50 (0-373-52019-0, 1-52019-6) Silhouette.

An Asterisk (*) at the beginning of an entry indicates that the title is appearing for the first time.

Let's Get Moving: The Joy of Movement for Small Children. Lisa Fitterman. (Funtasy League Ser.). (Illus.). 32p. (J). 1999. 9.95 (*1-896933-93-9*) C&B Co.
Let's Get Moving - Movement in the Classroom: Video Manual. 3rd ed. Diane Berry. (Illus.). 22p. (C). 1994. pap. text 5.00 (*1-878631-19-5*) S Kovalik.
Let's Get Organized. Beverly Jones. (Illus.). 58p. (Orig.). 1990. pap. 7.95 (*0-9627939-0-6*) Lockwood Pr.
Let's Get Organized: Protect Your Loved Ones with an Organized Account of Affairs. unabridged ed. Katrina A. Durdy. 1998. pap. 9.95 (*1-887430-48-2*) Global Inc.
Let's Get Ready for Christmas: Advent Activities for Preschool Children. Sandra M. Anderson. (Illus.). 32p. 1993. pap. 7.99 (*0-8066-2662-3*, 10-26623) Augsburg Fortress.
Let's Get Real. Donna Richardson & David Peden. LC 98-156081. 1998. per. 16.00 (*0-671-53883-7*, PB Trade Paper) PB.
*__Let's Get Real or Let's Not Play: The Demise of 20th Century Selling & the Advent of Helping Clients Suceed.__ Mahan K. Khalsa. 1999. pap. 19.95 (*1-883219-50-7*) Franklin Covey.
Let's Get Rich! The Pre-Millionaire's Guide to Music & Business. Rych McCain. Ed. by Janeska Smith. (Illus.). 175p. (Orig.). 1984. pap. text 6.95 (*0-9611904-1-8*) Street Wise Pubns.
Let's Get Rid of Social Security: How Americans Can Take Charge of Their Own Future. E. J. Myers. LC 95-47520. 273p. 1996. 26.95 (*1-57392-015-0*) Prometheus Bks.
*__Let's Get Rowdy!__ Michael James Martineau. 300p. 2000. pap. 12.98 (*1-930739-17-6*) Internet Bk CA.
Let's Get Serious. Jack Havey. (Illus.). 101p. (C). 1993. 19.95 (*0-9639530-0-1*) Good Little.
Let's Get Serious about Teaching Children to Write. Jerral R. Hicks. 136p. (Orig.). (C). 1993. pap. text 18.50 (*0-8191-8945-6*) U Pr of Amer.
Let's Get Started. Martha A. Lane. (Passport to the World of English Ser.: Bk. 1). (Illus.). 142p. 1996. teacher ed., ring bd. 18.00 incl. audio (*1-877596-21-3*); student ed., ring bd. 15.00 incl. audio (*1-877596-22-1*) Literacy & Evangelism.
Let's Get the Rhythm of the Band. Cheryl Mattox & Cheryl W. Mattox. (J). 1997. pap. 19.95 incl. audio (*0-938971-96-4*) JTG Nashville.
Let's Get the Rhythm of the Band. Cheryl W. Mattox. (J). (ps-3). 1993. pap. 8.95 (*0-938971-97-2*) JTG Nashville.
*__Let's Get This Straight: A Gay & Lesbian Affirming Approach to Child Welfare.__ Gerald P. Mallon. 2000. 49.50 (*0-231-11136-3*) Col U Pr.
*__Let's Get This Straight: A Gay & Lesbian Affirming Approach to Child Welfare.__ Gerald P. Mallon. 2000. pap. text 22.00 (*0-231-11137-1*) Col U Pr.
Let's Get to Know Each Other. Tony Evans. 180p. 1995. pap. 10.99 (*0-7852-8134-7*) Nelson.
Let's Get to Know Each Other: A Compatibility Quiz for Breaking the Ice. Andy Zubko & Andrew William. (Radiant Life Ser.). 125p. (Orig.). 1997. pap. 4.95 (*1-889606-01-4*) Radiant Summit.
Let's Get to Know the Bahama Parrot. Rosemarie Gnam. (Illus.). 20p. (J). (gr. 1-3). 1991. write for info. (*0-9629613-0-2*) Isld Conser Effort.
Let's Get to Know the Bahama Parrot. Rosemarie Gnam. (Illus.). 24p. (J). (gr. k-4). 1996. pap. 5.95 (*0-9643786-1-2*) Media Pubng.
*__Let's Get to Work.__ Merry North. (Giant Flap Bks.). (Illus.). 10p. (J). (ps-k). 1999. bds. write for info. (*1-57584-345-5*, Pub. by Rdrs Digest) Random.
Let's Get to Work: A Collection of Ideas & Proposals. Norma Phillips. 25p. (Orig.). 1996. mass mkt. 3.00 (*0-9622758-2-4*) Little Bridge.
Let's Get Together! C. Lynn Fox. LC 92-75715. 192p. (J). (gr. k-6). 1993. pap. 21.95 (*0-915190-99-0*, JP9099-0) Jalmar Pr.
Let's Get Together. Julie A. Gorman. (Groupbuilders Series for Adults). 144p. 1991. pap. 6.50 (*0-89693-299-0*, 6-1299, Victor Bks) Chariot Victor.
Let's Get Well. Adelle Davis. 480p. 1972. mass mkt. 7.99 (*0-451-15463-0*, Sig) NAL.
Let's Give Thanks, Vol. 2. Shirley A. Barone. (My Give Away Coloring Bk.). (Illus.). 44p. (Orig.). (J). (ps-2). 1989. pap. 1.75 (*0-685-30448-5*) Toad Hse Bks.
Let's Go! see **Ivamos!**
Let's Go! Karin L. Badt. LC 94-36911. (World of Difference Ser.). (Illus.). 32p. (J). (gr. 3-7). 1995. lib. bdg. 21.00 (*0-516-08195-0*) Childrens.
Let's Go! Karin L. Badt. (World of Difference Ser.). (Illus.). 32p. (J). (gr. 3-7). 1995. pap. 6.95 (*0-516-48195-9*) Childrens.
*__Let's Go.__ Brighter Vision Publishing Staff. (Little Books to Make & Read). (Illus.). (J). 2000. pap. 1.49 (*1-55254-067-7*) Brighter Vision.
Let's Go. Margie Burton et al. Ed. by Susan Evento. (Early Connections Ser.). 16p. (J). (gr. k-2). 1998. pap. 4.25 (*1-892393-45-X*) Benchmark Educ.
Let's Go. Otto R. Castillo. Tr. by Margaret Randall. LC 84-9397. 96p. 1996. pap. 11.95 (*0-915306-44-1*) Curbstone.
Let's Go. Griffin Trade Paperbacks Staff. LC 98-38082. (Let's Go 2000 Ser.). (Illus.). 976p. 1999. pap. 22.99 (*0-312-24485-1*) St Martin.
Let's Go! Barbara Shook Hazen. (Whole-Language Big Bks.). (Illus.). 16p. (Orig.). (J). (ps-2). 1994. pap. 16.95 (*1-56784-056-6*) Newbridge Educ.
Let's Go. Amy MacDonald. LC 92-46095. (Let's Explore Board Bks.). (Illus.). 12p. (J). (ps up). 1994. bds. 5.95 (*1-56402-202-1*) Candlewick Pr.
Let's Go. Burton Marks. LC 91-9986. (Read-a-Picture Ser.). (Illus.). 24p. (J). (gr. k-2). 1997. pap. 2.50 (*0-8167-2414-8*) Troll Communs.
Let's Go. Kees Moerbeek. LC 91-38117. 9p. (J). 1992. 5.99 (*0-85953-542-8*) Childs Play.
Let's Go. Ritsuko Nakata. (Illus.). 64p. 1992. pap. text, wbk. ed. 5.95 (*0-19-434395-5*) OUP.
Let's Go. Anna Pomaska. (Illus.). 32p. (J). pap. 1.00 (*0-486-40163-4*) Dover.
Let's Go, Bk. 3. 3rd ed. Ritsuko Nakata & Karen Frazier. (Illus.). 80p. 1994. pap. text, student ed. 9.25 (*0-19-434401-0*) OUP.
Let's Go, Bk. 3. 3rd ed. Ritsuko Nakata & Karen Frazier. (Illus.). 78p. 1994. pap. text, wbk. ed. 5.95 (*0-19-434403-7*) OUP.
Let's Go, Bk. 3. 3rd ed. Ritsuko Nakata & Karen Frazier. (Illus.). 114p. 1994. pap. text, teacher ed. 16.95 (*0-19-434402-9*) OUP.
Let's Go, Level 5. B. Hoskins. (Illus.). 116p. 1996. pap. text, teacher ed. 16.95 (*0-19-434671-4*) OUP.
Let's Go, Vol. 5. S. Wilkinson. (Illus.). 78p. 1996. pap. text, wbk. ed. 5.95 (*0-19-434672-2*) OUP.
Let's Go, Vol. 6. Ritsuko Nakata & Karen Frazier. (Illus.). 116p. 1997. teacher ed., spiral bd. 16.95 (*0-19-434675-7*) OUP.
Let's Go! A Guide to Outings & Adventures in Dallas - Ft. Worth with Children Ages 1-5. 2nd rev. ed. Lynda T. Morley. LC 97-94060. 200p. 1998. pap. 15.95 (*0-9662888-0-7*) Morley Pr.
Let's Go: Book & Doll. Balloon Books Staff. 1999. pap. text 6.95 (*0-8069-5926-6*) Sterling.
Let's Go: Britain & Ireland, 1999. annuals rev. ed. Harvard Student's Staff. (Let's Go Ser.). (Illus.). 736p. 1998. pap. 19.99 (*0-312-19476-5*) St Martin.
Let's Go: California, 1999. annuals rev. ed. Harvard Student's Staff. (Let's Go Ser.). (Illus.). 512p. 1998. pap. 18.99 (*0-312-19477-3*) St Martin.
Let's Go: Creative Ways to Ask - Dates & Proposals - Illustrated. Leone R. Creager. (Illus.). (Orig.). 1990. pap. write for info. (*0-9624638-2-5*) L R Creager.
Let's Go: Eastern Europe, 1999. annuals rev. ed. Harvard Student's Staff. (Let's Go Ser.). (Illus.). 864p. 1998. pap. 21.99 (*0-312-19479-X*) St Martin.
Let's Go: Ecuador & The Galapagos Islands, 1999. annuals rev. ed. Harvard Student's Staff. (Let's Go Ser.). (Illus.). 384p. 1998. pap. 18.99 (*0-312-19480-3*) St Martin.
Let's Go: France, 1999. annuals rev. ed. Harvard Student's Staff. (Let's Go Ser.). (Illus.). 736p. 1998. pap. 19.99 (*0-312-19482-X*) St Martin.
Let's Go: Greece, 1999. annuals rev. ed. Harvard Student's Staff. (Let's Go Ser.). (Illus.). 544p. 1998. pap. 18.99 (*0-312-19484-6*) St Martin.
Let's Go: India & Nepal, 1999. annuals rev. ed. Harvard Student's Staff. (Let's Go Ser.). (Illus.). 848p. 1998. pap. 22.99 (*0-312-19485-4*) St Martin.
Let's Go: Ireland, 1999. annuals rev. ed. Harvard Student's Staff. (Let's Go Ser.). (Illus.). 528p. 1998. pap. 18.99 (*0-312-19486-2*) St Martin.
Let's Go: Israel & Egypt, 1999. annuals rev. ed. Harvard Student's Staff. (Let's Go Ser.). (Illus.). 848p. 1998. pap. 19.99 (*0-312-19487-0*) St Martin.
Let's Go: Level 4 Student Book. 4th ed. Ritsuko Nakata & Karen Frazier. (Illus.). 80p. 1994. pap. text, student ed. 9.25 (*0-19-434405-3*) OUP.
Let's Go: Level 4 Teacher's Book. 4th ed. Ritsuko Nakata & Karen Frazier. (Illus.). 110p. 1995. pap. text, teacher ed. 16.95 (*0-19-434406-1*) OUP.
Let's Go: Level 4 Workbook. 4th ed. Ritsuko Nakata & Karen Frazier. (Illus.). 78p. 1995. pap. text, wbk. ed. 5.95 (*0-19-434407-X*) OUP.
Let's Go: Level 5. K. Frazier. (Illus.). 80p. 1995. pap. text 9.25 (*0-19-434670-6*) OUP.
Let's Go: Level 6. K. Frazier. (Illus.). 78p. 1996. pap. text, wbk. ed. 5.95 (*0-19-434676-5*) OUP.
Let's Go: Mexico, 1999. annuals rev. ed. Harvard Student's Staff. (Let's Go Ser.). (Illus.). 640p. 1998. pap. 19.99 (*0-312-19490-0*) St Martin.
Let's Go: New York, 1999. annuals rev. ed. St. Martin's Press Staff. (Let's Go Ser.). (Illus.). 368p. 1998. pap. 15.99 (*0-312-19491-9*) St Martin.
Let's Go: New Zealand, 1999. annuals rev. ed. Harvard Student's Staff. (Let's Go Ser.). (Illus.). 368p. 1998. pap. 15.99 (*0-312-19492-7*) St Martin.
Let's Go: Paris, 1999. annuals rev. ed. Harvard Student's Staff. (Illus.). 352p. 1998. pap. 15.99 (*0-312-19493-5*) St Martin.
Let's Go: Rome, 1999. annuals rev. ed. Harvard Student's Staff. (Let's Go Ser.). (Illus.). 336p. 1998. pap. 15.99 (*0-312-19496-X*) St Martin.
Let's Go: South Africa, 1999. annuals rev. ed. Harvard Student's Staff. (Let's Go Ser.). (Illus.). 544p. 1998. pap. 17.99 (*0-312-19497-8*) St Martin.
Let's Go: Southeast Asia, 1999. annuals rev. ed. Harvard Student's Staff. (Illus.). 912p. 1998. pap. 22.99 (*0-312-19498-6*) St Martin.
Let's Go: Spain, Portugal & Morocco 1991. Harvard Student Agencies. 1990. pap. text. write for info. (*0-312-05120-4*) St Martin.
Let's Go: Student Cards 4. Ritsuko Nakata & Karen Frazier. 1994. student ed. 11.95 (*0-19-434537-8*) OUP.
Let's Go: Student's Book 2. R. Nakata. (Illus.). 80p. 1993. pap. text 9.25 (*0-19-434397-9*) OUP.
Let's Go: Teacher's Book 1. K. Frazier. (Illus.). 110p. 1993. spiral bd. 16.95 (*0-19-434394-4*) OUP.
Let's Go: Teacher's Book 2. B. Hoskins. (Illus.). 116p. 1994. spiral bd. 16.95 (*0-19-434398-7*) OUP.
Let's Go: Teacher's Cards 4. Ritsuko Nakata & Karen Frazier. 1994. teacher ed. 49.95 (*0-19-434493-2*) OUP.
Let's Go: Turkey, 1999. annuals rev. ed. Harvard Student's Staff. (Let's Go Ser.). (Illus.). 448p. 1998. pap. 17.99 (*0-312-19500-1*) St Martin.
Let's Go: Washington DC, 1999. annuals rev. ed. Harvard Student's Staff. (Let's Go Ser.). (Illus.). 320p. 1998. pap. 15.99 (*0-312-19502-8*) St Martin.
Let's Go: Workbook 2. S. Wilkinson. (Illus.). 80p. 1993. pap. text, wbk. ed. 5.95 (*0-19-434399-5*) OUP.
Let's Go! 85 Years of Adventure. Carl M. Dunrud et al. (Illus.). 112p. 1998. pap. 19.95 (*0-9652942-1-8*) WordsWorth.
Let's Go Level 3: Teacher's Cards 3. Ritsuko Nakata & Karen Frazier. 1994. teacher ed. 11.95 (*0-19-434536-X*) OUP.
Let's Go Level 3: Teacher's Cards 3. Ritsuko Nakata & Karen Frazier. 1994. student ed. 49.95 (*0-19-434492-4*) OUP.
Let's Go Level 6. K. Frazier. (Illus.). 80p. 1997. pap. text, student ed. 9.25 (*0-19-434674-9*) OUP.
Let's Go a Wondering. (Tell-a-Story Sticker Bks.). (J). 3.29 (*0-307-07616-4*, 07616) Gldn Bks Pub Co.
Let's Go Alaska & the Pacific Northwest. Griffin Trade Paperbacks Publishing Staff. (Illus.). 560p. 1999. pap. 19.99 (*0-312-24137-2*, St Martin Griffin) St Martin.
Let's Go Anthropology. Joan Ferrante. LC 98-131362. (Anthropology Ser.). (C). 1997. 13.95 (*0-534-53113-X*) Wadsworth Pub.
*__Let's Go Baby-o!__ Marcia Leonard. LC 99-66434. (Hanna Bks.). 24p. (J). 2000. 7.95 (*0-694-01367-6*, HarpFestival) HarpC Child Bks.
Lets Go Back to the Piano. (YA). 1985. pap. 19.95 (*0-910957-55-X*, FDL00877) Wrner Bros.
Let's Go Baroque Golden Threads Carden. Susan Ogilvy. 1996. pap. 24.95 (*0-7935-6465-4*) H Leonard.
Let's Go, Britain & Ireland. Griffin Trade Paperbacks Publishing Staff. (Let's Go 2000 Ser.). (Illus.). 768p. 1999. pap. 21.99 (*0-312-24452-5*, St Martin Griffin) St Martin.
Let's Go, California. Griffin Trade Paperbacks Publishing Staff. (Illus.). 544p. 1999. pap. 19.99 (*0-312-24453-3*, St Martin Griffin) St Martin.
Let's Go Caroling. 16p. 1963. 0.99 (*0-8341-9372-8*, MC-219) Lillenas.
Let's Go, Central America. Griffin Trade Paperbacks Publishing Staff. (Let's Go 2000 Ser.). 560p. 1999. pap. 19.99 (*0-312-24454-1*, St Martin Griffin) St Martin.
Let's Go Dear Dragon. Margaret Hillert. (Illus.). (J). (ps). 1981. pap. 5.10 (*0-8136-5525-0*, TK2323); lib. bdg. 7.95 (*0-8136-5025-9*, TK2322) Modern Curr.
Let's Go Dinosaur Tracking! Miriam Schlein. LC 90-39632. (Illus.). 48p. (J). (gr. 2-5). 1991. 14.95 (*0-06-025138-7*) HarpC Child Bks.
Let's Go down to the Beach: Poems & Translations of Four Caribbean Writers. William Lawlor. 128p. (Orig.). 1996. pap. text 13.95 (*0-9641986-9-X*) Poetry Harbor.
Let's Go, Eastern Europe. Griffin Trade Paperbacks Publishing Staff. (Let's Go 2000 Ser.). (Illus.). 864p. 1999. pap. 22.99 (*0-312-24461-4*, St Martin Griffin) St Martin.
Let's Go Eat: The Kansas Guide to Good Dining. Bobbie A. Pray & Glennis A. Mann. LC 91-66141. 200p. (Orig.). 1991. pap. 18.00 (*0-9627361-1-2*) Turn Century Pr.
Lets' Go Etats-Unis Cote Est. Harvard Student Agencies. 600p. 1996. pap. 39.95 (*0-7859-9469-6*) Fr & Eur.
Let's Go Etats-Unis Cote Ouest. Harvard Student Agencies Staff. (Orig.). 1998. pap. text 24.95 (*2-910932-03-6*) Distribks Inc.
Let's Go Exploring. Ed. by Better Homes & Gardens. (Max the Dragon Project Book Ser.). (Illus.). 32p. (J). (gr. k-3). 1991. lib. bdg. 12.95 (*1-878363-58-1*) Forest Hse.
Let's Go Fishing. Trevor Wilson. LC 93-26220. (Illus.). (J). 1994. 4.25 (*0-383-03758-1*) SRA McGraw.
Let's Go Fishing: A Book for Beginners. Gerald D. Schmidt. (Illus.). 92p. 1990. pap. 11.95 (*0-911797-84-X*) Roberts Rinehart.
Let's Go Fishing: A Fish & Fishing Project. Daniel J. Decker et al. (Four-H Ser.). (Illus.). 36p. (YA). (gr. 7-11). 1993. pap. 3.00 (*1-57753-205-8*, 147L-5-6) Corn Coop Ext.
Let's Go Fishing for a Living. George Travis. LC 97-51885. (Let's Go Fishing Ser.). (J). 1998. 17.43 (*0-86593-462-2*) Rourke Corp.
Let's Go Fishing for Shellfish. George Travis. LC 97-49078. (Let's Go Fishing Ser.). (J). 1998. (*0-86593-466-5*) Rourke Corp.
Let's Go Fishing in a Tournament. George Travis. LC 97-51917. (Let's Go Fishing Ser.). (J). 1998. (*0-86593-467-3*) Rourke Corp.
Let's Go Fishing in Streams, Rivers & Lakes. George Travis. LC 97-51918. (Let's Go Fishing Ser.). (J). 1998. (*0-86593-465-7*) Rourke Corp.
Let's Go Fishing in the Ocean. George Travis. LC 97-49076. (Let's Go Fishing Ser.). (J). 1998. (*0-86593-463-0*) Rourke Corp.
Let's Go Fishing on the Ice. George Travis. LC 97-49077. (Let's Go Fishing Ser.). (J). 1998. (*0-86593-464-9*) Rourke Corp.
*__Let's Go for a Ride!__ rev. ed. Diana James. (My Turn Ser.). (Illus.). (J). 2000. bds. 4.95 (*1-58728-005-1*) Two Can Pub.
Let's Go for Great Photos. Rod Vahl. 1991. 10.00 (*0-317-06093-7*) Quill & Scroll.
Let's Go Fossil Shark Tooth Hunting: A Guide for Identifying Sharks & Where & How to Find Their Superbly Formed Fossilized Teeth. B. Clay Cartmell. (Search Series Bk.). (Illus.). 76p. (Orig.). 1978. pap. 3.50 (*0-930498-01-1*) Nat Sci Res.
Let's Go Froggy! Jonathan London. (Illus.). 32p. (J). (ps-1). 1996. pap. 5.99 (*0-14-054991-9*, PuffinBks) Peng Put Young Read.
Let's Go, Froggy! Jonathan London. LC 93-24059. (Illus.). 32p. (J). (ps-1). 1994. 15.99 (*0-670-85055-1*, Viking Child) Peng Put Young Read.
Let's Go, Froggy! Jonathan London. LC 93-24059. 1996. 10.19 (*0-606-09543-8*, Pub. by Turtleback) Demco.
Let's Go, Gaels: A Novella by Jim LaBate. Jim LaBate. LC 98-165634. (Illus.). 60p. (YA). (gr. 7-12). 1998. pap. 5.95 (*0-9662100-4-2*) Mohawk River Pr.
Let's Go Gardening: A Young Person's Guide to the Garden. Ursula Kruger. LC 95-82213. (Illus.). 95p. (J). (gr. 1 up). 1996. 16.95 (*0-7188-2879-8*, Lutterworth-Parkwest) Parkwest Pubns.
*__Let's Go Ghana: A Visitor's Guide to Business Opportunities, Networking & Tourism in Ghana.__ Kwasi Bosompem. (Illus.). 96p. 2000. pap. 10.00 (*0-9649351-3-9*) PRDC Pubng.
Let's Go Git a Pint an' Be's Somebody: A Poetic Journey from Slavery to Forgiveness. Lydia F. Williams. LC 96-94013. (Illus.). 88p. (Orig.). 1996. pap. 12.95 (*0-9648045-0-6*) LFW Ent.
Let's Go, Greece. Griffin Trade Paperbacks Publishing Staff. (Illus.). 592p. 1999. pap. 19.99 (*0-312-24469-X*, St Martin Griffin) St Martin.
Let's Go Hippo. Kenn Hayes. (J). (ps). 1993. 14.95 (*1-56729-025-6*) Newport Pubs.
*__Let's Go Home: The Wonderful Things about a House.__ Illus. by Cynthia Rylant & Wendy Anderson Halperin. LC 99-22574. 2000. 20.01 (*0-689-82326-6*) S&S Childrens.
Let's Go Home, Little Bear. Martin Waddell. LC 92-53003. (Illus.). 32p. (J). (ps-3). 1993. 15.99 (*1-56402-131-9*) Candlewick Pr.
Let's Go Home, Little Bear. Martin Waddell. LC 92-53003. (Illus.). 32p. (J). (ps up). 1995. pap. 5.99 (*1-56402-447-4*) Candlewick Pr.
Let's Go Home, Little Bear. Martin Waddell. (Little Book Cards Ser.). 32p. (J). (gr. 1-4). 1997. pap. text 3.29 (*0-7636-0216-7*) Candlewick Pr.
Let's Go Home, Little Bear. Martin Waddell. 1995. 11.19 (*0-606-08797-4*, Pub. by Turtleback) Demco.
Let's Go Ice Fishing. Ronald A. Howard, Jr. & H. David Greene. (Four-H Ser.). (Illus.). 24p. (YA). (gr. 7-11). 1993. pap. 2.75 (*1-57753-206-6*, 147L5-15) Corn Coop Ext.
*__Let's Go into Business Together: Eight Secrets to Successful Business Partnering.__ rev. ed. Azriela Jaffe. 288p. 2001. pap. 14.99 (*1-56414-513-1*) Career Pr Inc.
Let's Go Let's Go: Biography of Lorrin "Whitey" Harrison, Californias Legendary Surf Pioneer. Rosie H. Clark. (Illus.). 176p. 1997. 35.00 (*0-9660153-1-2*); pap. 20.00 (*0-9660153-2-0*) R H Clark.
Let's Go! Let's Publish! Katharine Graham & the Washington Post. Nancy Whitelaw. LC 98-46284. (Makers of the Media Ser.). 112p. (YA). (gr. 5 up). 1999. lib. bdg. 18.95 (*1-883846-37-4*) M Reynolds.
Let's Go Map Guide: Berlin. Harvard Student's Staff. (Map Ser.). (Illus.). 40p. 1997. pap. 7.95 (*0-312-15567-0*) St Martin.
Let's Go Map Guide: Boston. Harvard Student's Staff. (Illus.). 32p. 1998. pap. 7.95 (*0-312-18468-9*) St Martin.
*__Let's Go Map Guide: Boston.__ 3rd ed. Let's Go Staff. 2000. pap. 8.95 (*0-312-24632-3*) St Martin.
Let's Go Map Guide: Los Angeles. Harvard Student's Staff. (Let's Go Ser.). (Illus.). 40p. 1997. pap. 7.95 (*0-312-15162-4*) St Martin.
Let's Go Map Guide: Madrid. Harvard Student's Staff. (Map Ser.). (Illus.). 32p. 1997. pap. 7.95 (*0-312-15568-9*) St Martin.
Let's Go Map Guide: New Orleans. Harvard Student's Staff. (Let's Go Ser.). (Illus.). 24p. 1997. pap. 7.95 (*0-312-15370-8*) St Martin.
Let's Go Map Guide: Rome. Harvard Student's Staff. (Let's Go Ser.). (Illus.). 32p. 1997. pap. 7.95 (*0-312-15163-2*) St Martin.
Let's Go Map Guide: San Francisco. Harvard Student's Staff. 24p. 1998. pap. 7.95 (*0-312-18469-7*) St Martin.
*__Let's Go Map Guide: San Francisco.__ 3rd ed. Lets Go Inc. Staff. 20p. 2000. pap. 8.95 (*0-312-24642-0*) St Martin.
Let's Go Map Guide: Washington DC. Harvard Student's Staff. 32p. 1998. pap. 7.95 (*0-312-18467-0*) St Martin.
*__Let's Go Map Guide: Washington DC.__ 3rd ed. Lets Go Inc. Staff. 2000. pap. 8.95 (*0-312-24643-9*) St Martin.
*__Lets Go Map Guide Florence.__ Let's Go Staff. 32p. 2000. pap., student ed. 8.95 (*0-312-24633-1*) St Martin.
*__Lets Go Map Guide Hong Kong.__ Lets Go Inc. Staff. 2000. pap. 8.95 (*0-312-24638-2*) St Martin.
*__Lets Go Map Guide London.__ Let's Go Staff. 32p. 2000. pap., student ed. 8.95 (*0-312-24635-8*) St Martin.
*__Lets Go Map Guide New York City.__ Let's Go Staff. 32p. 2000. pap., student ed. 8.95 (*0-312-24636-6*) St Martin.
*__Lets Go Map Guide Paris.__ 32p. 2000. pap., student ed. 8.95 (*0-312-24641-2*) St Martin.
Let's Go Map Guide, Prague; Know It Like a Native: Complete Street Locator & City Guide ... Addresses. 2nd ed. (Let's Go Map Guides Ser.). 32p. 1999. pap. 8.95 (*0-312-20273-3*) St Martin.
Let's Go Map Guides: Amsterdam. 24p. 1998. pap. 7.95 (*0-312-18470-0*) St Martin.
*__Let's Go Map Guides: Amsterdam.__ 2nd ed. Let's Go Staff. 16p. 2000. pap. 8.95 (*0-312-24631-5*) St Martin.
Lets Go Newsletter. 1999. pap. write for info. (*0-312-17197-8*) St Martin.
Let's Go, 1986: The Budget Guide to Spain. Harvard Student Agencies Incorporated Staff. 1985. 9.95 (*0-317-43360-1*) St Martin.
Let's Go, 1986: The Budget Guide to the U. S. A. Harvard Student Agencies Incorporated Staff. (Let's Go Ser.). (Illus.). 928p. 1985. 9.95 (*0-317-44004-7*) St Martin.
Let's Go, 1992: The Budget Guide to Italy Including Tunisia & Malta. rev. ed. Harvard Student Agencies Incorporated Staff. (Illus.). 608p. 1991. 14.95 (*0-685-48107-7*) St Martin.
Let's Go On: Pacific Northwest Ballet at 25. Wayne Johnson. LC 97-33586. 1997. 24.95 (*0-935503-20-X*) Document Bk.

L

An Asterisk (*) at the beginning of an entry indicates that the title is appearing for the first time.

Let's Go on Vacation. Pam Howard. (HRL Little Book Ser.). (Illus.). 8p. (Orig.). (J). (ps-k). 1996. pap. text 10.95 (1-57332-044-7) HighReach Lrning.

Let's Go on Vacation. large type ed. Pam Howard. (HRL Big Bks.). (Illus.). 8p. (Orig.). (J). (ps-k). 1996. pap. text 10.95 (1-57332-045-5) HighReach Lrning.

***Let's Go Out & About.** rev. ed. David James. (Talk Together Ser.). (Illus.). (J). 2000. 9.95 (1-58728-016-7); pap. 4.95 (1-58728-020-5) Two Can Pub.

***Let's Go Outside! Designing the Early Childhood Playground.** Tracy Theemes. LC 99-34787. (Illus.). 144p. 1999. 19.95 (1-57379-082-6) High-Scope.

Let's Go, Philadelphia! Patricia Reilly Giff. (Polk Street Special Ser.: No. 11). (Illus.). 128p. (J). (gr. 1-4). 1998. pap. 3.99 (0-440-41368-0, YB BDD) BDD Bks Young Read.

***Let's Go, Philadelphia!, 11.** Patricia Reilly Giff. (Polk Street Special Ser.). 1998. 9.09 (0-606-13567-7, Pub. by Turtleback) Demco.

Let's Go Picture Dictionary. Ritsuko Nakata. (Illus.). 110p. 1999. 12.50 (0-19-435865-8) OUP.

***Let's Go Potty.** Karen Fung. 2000. pap. text 7.95 (0-7641-5288-2) Barron.

Let's Go Riding. Nancy Parent. (Barbie Glittery Window Bks.). (Illus.). 12p. (J). (gr. k-3). 2000. bds. 4.99 (1-57584-409-5, RD Childrens) Rdrs Digest.

Let's Go Riding in Our Strollers. Fran Manushkin. LC 92-72935. (Illus.). 32p. (J). (ps-k). 1993. lib. bdg. 13.89 (1-56282-391-4, Pub. by Hyprn Child) Little.

Let's Go Riding in Our Strollers. Fran Manushkin. LC 92-72935. (Illus.). 32p. (J). (ps-k). 1995. pap. 4.95 (0-7868-1038-6, Pub. by Hyprn Ppbks) Little.

Let's Go Rock Collecting. Roma Gans. (Let's Read-&-Find-Out Science Ser.). (J). 1997. 10.15 (0-606-11553-6, Pub. by Turtleback) Demco.

Let's Go Rock Collecting. 2nd rev. ed. Roma Gana. LC 95-44999. (Let's-Read-&-Find-Out Science Bks.: Level 2). (Illus.). 32p. (J). (gr. k-4). 1997. 15.95 (0-06-027282-1); lib. bdg. 15.89 (0-06-027283-X) HarpC Child Bks.

Let's Go Rock Collecting. 2nd rev. ed. Roma Gans. LC 95-44999. (Let's-Read-&-Find-Out Science Bks.: Stage 2). (Illus.). 32p. (J). (gr. k-4). 1997. pap. 4.95 (0-06-445170-4, HarpTrophy) HarpC Child Bks.

***Let's Go Shopping!** Ed. by Chris Angelli. (J). 2000. pap. 2.99 (0-375-80493-5, Pub. by Random Bks Yng Read) Random.

Let's Go Shopping. Snapshot Staff. (Tab Board Bks.). (Illus.). 8p. (J). (ps). 1996. 3.95 (0-7894-1133-4) DK Pub Inc.

Let's Go Skiing with a Psychiatrist: The Mental Game of Sensational Skiing. Ned R. Harley. Ed. by Mary E. Gililand. LC 93-61803. (Illus.). 210p. (Orig.). 1994. pap. text 12.95 (0-9635493-2-4, TX 3-971-736) Vail Pr.

Let's Go Sociology. 2nd ed. Ferrante. LC 98-222507. (Sociology-Introduction Level Ser.). 1998. pap. 7.95 (0-534-53666-2) Wadsworth Pub.

***Let's Go Sociology.** 3rd ed. Ferrante. 2001. pap. 5.25 (0-534-54190-9) Thomson Learn.

Let's Go Sociology: Travels on the Internet. Joan Ferrante & Angela Vaughn. LC 97-142315. (Sociology Ser.). (C). 1996. pap. 9.50 (0-534-53109-1) Wadsworth Pub.

Let's Go! Soft Cube with Rattle. Chris L. Demarest. (J). (ps-k). 1997. bds. 8.95 (0-614-28821-5, Red Wagon Bks) Harcourt.

Let's Go Soul Winning. Jack Hyles. 1999. pap. 2.00 (0-87398-503-6) Dake Pub.

Let's Go Soul Winning - Chinese Edition. Jack Hyles. Tr. by K. H. Chen. (CHI.). 112p. 1974. pap. 4.00 (1-56582-052-5) Christ Renew Min.

Let's Go Starter. Ritsuko Nakata. (Illus.). 64p. 1998. pap. text, student ed. 9.25 (0-19-435290-0) OUP.

Let's Go Starter. Ritsuko Nakata. (Illus.). 80p. 1998. pap. text, teacher ed. 16.95 (0-19-435292-7) OUP.

Let's Go Story Knifing see Yaaruiyarluk

Let's Go Story Knifing see Yaaruiyarciqukug

Let's Go Storyknifing. large type ed. Kelly J. Lincoln. (Illus.). 12p. (J). (gr. k-3). 1999. pap. text 17.00 (1-58084-066-3) Lower Kuskokwim.

Let's Go Swimming with Mr. Sillypants. Mary Kay Brown. (Reading Rainbow Bks.). (J). 1992. 11.19 (0-606-01556-6, Pub. by Turtleback) Demco.

Let's Go! Teddy Bear. Lynne Bertrand. LC 93-71172. (Illus.). 24p. (J). (ps). 1993. pap. 9.95 (1-881527-15-8, Chapters Bks) HM.

Let's Go to Africa & Nigeria: A Poetic Profile. Augustine A. Amanzeh. 70p. (Orig.). 1998. pap. 9.00 (1-890606-04-9) A A Amanzeh.

Let's Go to Church. Bessie Dean. LC 76-3995. (Books for LDS Children). (Illus.). 63p. (J). (ps-3). 1993. reprint ed. pap. 3.98 (0-88290-062-5) Horizon Utah.

Let's Go to Grammy's. Aunt Eeebs. LC 94-67656. (Dino-Buddies Ser.). (Illus.). 160p. (Orig.). (J). (ps-2). 1994. pap. 3.95 (1-878908-06-5) Rivercrest Indus.

Let's Go to Meherabad. Bhau Kalchuri. 120p. 1981. pap. 6.95 (0-940700-11-5) Meher Baba Info.

***Let's Go to Rainbow Canyon.** Random House Staff. (Painting Time Ser.). (Illus.). 32p. (J). (ps-3). 2000. pap. 3.99 (0-375-80638-5, Pub. by Random Bks Yng Read) Random.

Let's Go to School. Michelle Petty. LC 95-20411. (First Start Easy Reader Ser.). (Illus.). 32p. (J). (gr. k-3). 1995. pap. text 2.95 (0-8167-3853-X); lib. bdg. 13.05 (0-8167-3852-1) Troll Communs.

Let's Go to School, Big Book ed. Michelle Petty. 1999. pap. text 16.95 (0-8167-3955-2); pap. text 16.95 (0-8167-3985-4) Troll Communs.

***Let's Go to School with Thomas.** Random House Staff. (Toddler Bks.). (Illus.). 12p. (J). (ps). 2000. bds. 2.99 (0-375-80279-7, Pub. by Random Bks Yng Read) Random.

Let's Go to the Airport. Barbara Bazaldua. LC 97-70005. (Little Golden Bks.). 24p. (J). (ps-k). 1998. 2.29 (0-307-98833-3, 98833, Goldn Books) Gldn Bks Pub Co.

Let's Go to the Arctic: A Story & Activities Book about Arctic People & Animals. Charlotte F. Mateer & Louise Craft. (Illus.). 60p. (J). (gr. 4-6). 1993. pap. text 7.95 (1-879373-24-6) Roberts Rinehart.

Let's Go to the Balloon Show! Judy Mullican. (HRL Big Bks.). (Illus.). 8p. (J). (ps-k). 1994. pap. text 10.95 (1-57332-004-8) HighReach Lrning.

Let's Go to the Beach. Elizabeth Van Steenwyk. 1950. text 16.95 (0-8050-6235-1) St Martin.

Let's Go to the Carnival! Grosset & Dunlap Staff. 16p. 1999. pap. 4.99 (0-448-42079-1, G & D) Peng Put Young Read.

Let's Go to the Country Fair. Pam Howard. (HRL Little Bks.). (Illus.). 8p. (Orig.). (J). (ps-k). 1996. pap. text 10.95 (1-57332-070-6) HighReach Lrning.

Let's Go to the Country Fair. large type ed. Pam Howard. (HRL Big Bks.). (Illus.). 8p. (Orig.). (J). (ps-k). 1996. pap. text 10.95 (1-57332-072-2) HighReach Lrning.

Let's Go to the Dairy Farm. Barbara Bazaldua. LC 97-76886. (Little Golden Bks.). (Illus.). 24p. (J). 1998. 2.29 (0-307-98224-6, 98224, Goldn Books) Gldn Bks Pub Co.

Let's Go to the Farm. (J). (gr. k-2). 1996. 14.95 (1-885958-05-6) VT Story Works.

***Let's Go to the Firehouse.** Random House U. K. Ltd. (J). 2001. mass mkt. 4.99 (0-375-80312-2, Pub. by Random Bks Yng Read) Random.

Let's Go to the Moon see Books for Young Explorers

Let's Go to the Movies. Iris Barry. LC 79-169357. (Arno Press Cinema Program Ser.). (Illus.). 318p. 1978. reprint ed. 20.95 (0-405-03911-5) Ayer.

Let's Go to the Movies for Young Adults: Alternative Studies for Christian Growth. Edward N. McNulty. Ed. by Vincent Patton. LC 98-52040. 16p. 2000. 5.95 (1-57895-028-7) Curriculm Presbytrn KY.

Let's Go to the Movies for Younger & Older Youth: Alternative Studies for Christian Growth. Edward N. McNulty. Ed. by Vincent Patton. LC 98-52001. 16p. (YA). (gr. 7-12). 1999. 5.95 (1-57895-029-5) Curriculm Presbytrn KY.

Let's Go to the Park. Rosanne Boettiger. LC 98-30219. (J). 1998. write for info. (1-56763-422-2); pap. write for info. (1-56763-423-0) Ozark Pub.

Let's Go to the Tackle Store & Fondle the Plugs. Joann Phillips. 1994. pap. text 8.95 (0-913507-58-X) New Forums.

Let's Go to the Vet! Cathy Hapka & Zoe Lewis. LC 97-70001. (Little Golden Bks.). (Illus.). 24p. (J). (ps-k). 1997. 2.29 (0-307-98804-X, 98804, Goldn Books) Gldn Bks Pub Co.

***Let's Go to the Video Tape! All the Plays - & Replays - From My Life in Sports.** Warner Wolf. LC 99-39614. (Illus.). 320p. 2000. 24.95 (0-446-52559-6, Pub. by Warner Bks) Little.

Let's Go to Video Tape. Warner Wolf. pap. 13.95 (0-698-11187-7) Putnam Pub Group.

Let's Go Traveling in Mexico. Robin R. Krupp. LC 95-18206. (Illus.). (J). (ps-3). 1996. 16.00 (0-688-12367-8, Wm Morrow) Morrow Avon.

***Lets Go (Vamos)** Rebecca Emberley. 28p. (J). (ps-3). 2000. pap. 5.95 (0-316-23033-2) Little.

***Let's Go-Vamos: A Book in Two Languages.** Rebecca Emberley. (Illus.). (J). 2000. 11.40 (0-606-18259-4) Turtleback.

Let's Go Visiting. Sue Williams. 1998. 90.00 (0-15-202036-5, Gulliver Bks) Harcourt.

Let's Go Visiting. Sue Williams. LC 97-34398. (Illus.). 32p. (J). 1998. 15.00 (0-15-201823-9) Harcourt.

***Let's Go Visiting.** Sue Williams. (Illus.). 32p. (ps-k). 2000. pap. 7.00 (0-15-202410-7, Harcourt Child Bks) Harcourt.

Let's Grow! Children's Gardening Fun Kit. Linda Tilgner. (J). (ps-5). 1988. pap. 19.95 (0-88266-537-5, Garden Way Pub) Storey Bks.

Let's Grow! Seventy-Two Gardening Adventures with Children. Linda Tilgner. Ed. by Deborah Burns. LC 87-45581. (Illus.). 216p. (Orig.). (J). (ps up). 1988. pap. 10.95 (0-88266-470-0, Garden Way Pub) Storey Bks.

Let's Grow! Seventy-Two Gardening Adventures with Children. Linda Tilgner. Ed. by Deborah Burns. LC 87-45581. (Illus.). 216p. (Orig.). (J). (ps up). 1988. 21.95 (0-88266-471-9, Garden Way Pub) Storey Bks.

Let's Grow a Garden. Angela Wilkes. LC 97-12559. (Illus.). (J). 1997. write for info. (0-7894-1557-7) DK Pub Inc.

Let's Grow a Garden. Gyo Fujikawa. (Illus.). 16p. (J). (ps). 1989. reprint ed. bds. 6.95 (1-55987-010-9, Sunny Bks) J B Comns.

Let's Grow & Make Disciples! Charles L. Sattenfield. 92p. (Orig.). 1980. 2.75 (0-88027-080-2) Firm Foun Pub.

Let's Grow It! Funstation, 5 vols. (Illus.). 48p. (J). (gr. 3-7). 1998. 17.95 (1-57145-348-2, Silver Dolph) Advantage Pubs.

Let's Grow Raspberries! David R. Beach. LC 90-93433. (Illus.). 90p. (Orig.). 1991. pap. 8.00 (0-9621195-1-2) D R Beach.

Let's Grow Tomatoes. Jacob R. Mittleider. LC 80-84563. (Illus.). 142p. 1986. mass mkt. 16.95 (1-929982-01-1) Food For Every.

Let's Guess Flap Book: Baa! Richard Powell. LC 97-100808. (Illus.). 6p. (J). 1995. 4.50 (0-689-80039-8) Litle Simon.

Let's Guess Flap Book: Grr! Richard Powell. LC 97-124273. (Illus.). 6p. (J). 1995. 4.50 (0-689-80040-1) Litle Simon.

Let's Have a Baby! Wed in the West. Christy Lockhart. 1999. per. 3.75 (0-373-76212-7, 1-76212-9) Silhouette.

Let's Have a Banquet: Or Will One Dollar & Thirty-Six Cents Be Enough. Joyce Landorf. 1968. pap. 5.95 (0-310-27131-2, 9994P) Zondervan.

Let's Have a Ceilidh: A Guide to Scottish Dancing. Robbie Shepherd. (Canongate Classic Ser.). (Illus.). 128p. 1996. pap. 11.95 (0-86241-513-6, Pub. by Canongate Books) Interlink Pub.

Let's Have a Circus. Kathy Christensen. Ed. by Barbara B. Linse. (Using Themes Ser.). (Illus.). 70p. 1988. pap. text 6.95 (0-685-45615-3) Arts Pubns.

Let's Have a Circus. Kathy Christensen. (Illus.). 70p. 1990. 7.95 (1-878079-12-3) Arts Pubns.

Let's Have a Drink: A Complete Guide to Ethyl Alcohol. Paul A. Nickas. Ed. by Katerine Harvey. LC 98-55563. (Illus.). 256p. 1999. 29.95 (0-9634155-0-6) Sigma Pub Assocs.

Let's Have a Meeting: A Comprehensive Guide to Making Your Meetings Work. Leslie Rae. LC 93-43264. 1994. 19.95 (0-07-707628-1) McGraw.

Let's Have a Musical Rhythm Band. Phoebe Diller. 32p. 1976. pap., student ed. 5.95 (0-7390-0609-6, 270) Alfred Pub.

***Let's Have a Parade!** large type ed. Judy Mullican. (HRL Cuddle Bks.). (Illus.). 7p. (J). (ps-k). 1999. pap. text 10.95 (1-57332-139-7) HighReach Lrning.

Let's Have a Party! Ron Fritz. LC 92-28560. (Singalongs Ser.). (Illus.). 32p. (J). (gr. k-2). 1992. pap. text 4.95 (0-8167-2985-9) Troll Communs.

Lets Have a Party. Honey Zisman et al. LC 97-31755. 192p. 1998. pap. 10.95 (0-312-18126-4) St Martin.

Let's Have a Play. Margaret Hillert. (Illus.). (J). (ps). 1981. pap. 5.10 (0-8136-5594-3, TK2169); lib. bdg. 7.95 (0-8136-5094-1, TK2168) Modern Curr.

Let's Have a Reunion! A How-to-Do-It Guide for Your Class Reunion. Philip A. Hannema. LC 77-78512. 1978. write for info. (0-9601286-1-1); pap. 4.95 (0-9601286-2-X) Second Thoughts.

Let's Have a Sauna. M. Herva. (Illus.). 24p. 1978. pap. 5.00 (0-318-19013-3) Sauna Soc.

Let's Have a Seder! Madeline Wikler. LC 96-79324. (HEB., Illus.). 12p. (J). (ps). 1997. bds. 4.95 (0-929371-41-0) Kar-Ben.

Let's Have a Show! (A Guideline for Having a Pigeon Show) rev. ed. J. A. Fancier. (Illus.). 74p. 1989. 9.95 (0-9622998-0-4) WFancier Pubns.

Let's Have a Sleepover. Bonnie Lasser. (Look-Look Bks.). (Illus.). 24p. (J). (ps-3). 1998. pap. 3.29 (0-307-12963-2, 12963, Goldn Books) Gldn Bks Pub Co.

Let's Have a Tea Party! Emilie Barnes. LC 97-8362. (Illus.). 32p. (J). (gr. 1-7). 1997. 14.99 (1-56507-679-6) Harvest Hse.

Let's Have an Evangelist! Preparing Your Church for Revival. Charles A. Kempf. 91p. (Orig.). 1987. pap. 8.25 (0-89084-369-4, 031989) Bob Jones Univ.

***Let's Have Fun.** (Furby Coloring & Activity Bks.). (Illus.). 32p. 1999. pap. write for info. (0-7666-0415-2, Honey Bear Bks) Modern Pub NYC.

Let's Have Fun. Ed. by Brigitta Geltrich. (Humor Ser.). (Illus.). 68p. 1997. pap. 10.00 (0-936945-82-6) Creat with Wds.

***Let's Have Fun with Barney.** Lyrick Publishing Staff. (J). (ps-3). 2000. pap. text 9.99 (1-57064-953-7) Lyrick Pub.

Let's Have Healthy Children. Adelle Davis. 1995. reprint ed. lib. bdg. 28.95 (1-56849-622-2) Buccaneer Bks.

Let's Hear It: Shrupps. Jim O'Connor. LC 95-73062. (Illus.). (J). 1996. pap. 3.99 (0-679-87909-9) McKay.

Let's Hear It for Herps! LC 97-35980. (Illus.). 96p. (J). (gr. k-8). 1998. pap., teacher ed. 12.95 (0-07-047099-5) McGraw.

Let's Hear It for Herps. National Wildlife Federation Staff. (J). (gr. k-8). 1991. pap. 7.95 (0-945051-42-5, 75034) Natl Wildlife.

Let's Hear It for Herps! All about Reptiles & Amphibians. National Wildlife Federation Staff. LC 97-51602. (Ranger Rick's Naturescope Ser.). (Illus.). 96p. (J). (gr. 1-7). 1999. lib. bdg. 19.95 (0-7910-4835-7) Chelsea Hse.

Let's Hear It for the Boys! Supporting Sex & Relationships Education for Boys & Young Men. Ed. by Gill Lenderyou & Caroline Ray. LC 98-180602. 64p. 1998. pap. 22.00 (1-900990-15-6, Pub. by Natl Childrens Bur) Paul & Co Pubs.

Let's Hear It for the Girls: 375 Great Books for Readers 2-14. Erica Bauermeister & Holly Smith. LC 96-9791. 240p. (C). 1999. pap. 10.95 (0-14-025732-2) Viking Penguin.

Let's Hear It for the Shrumps! Jim Oconnor. (No Stars Ser.). 1996. 9.09 (0-606-10897-1, Pub. by Turtleback) Demco.

Let's Hit the Road. Richard Tommaso. pap. 9.95 (1-56097-273-4, Pub. by Fantagraph Bks) Seven Hills Bk.

***Let's Hop & Skip.** rev. ed. Diana James. (My Turn Ser.). (Illus.). (J). 2000. 4.95 (1-58728-010-8) Two Can Pub.

Let's Hug! Once Upon a Planet, Inc. Staff. (Illus.). 32p. 1994. 2.50 (0-88009-071-5) Once Upon A Planet.

Let's Illustrate: The Whys & Hows of Illustrating a Sermon. Eldon Weisheit. LC 98-24656. 144p. 1998. pap. 12.99 (0-570-05331-5) Concordia.

Let's Improvise: Becoming Creative, Expressive & Spontaneous Through Drama. Milton E. Polsky. LC 97-28482. (Illus.). 315p. 1998. pap. 18.95 (1-55783-307-9) Applause Theatre Bk Pubs.

Let's Investigate, 12 Vol. Catherine J. Bernardy et al. (Illus.). 384p. (J). 167.40 (0-88682-667-5) Creative Co.

Let's Investigate - Group 1, 6 bks. Marion Smoothey. Incl. Area & Volume. LC 92-10579. (Illus.). 64p. (YA). (gr. 4 up). 1992. lib. bdg. 25.64 (1-85435-460-4); Circles. LC 92-7159. (Illus.). 64p. (YA). (gr. 4-7). 1992. lib. bdg. 25.64 (1-85435-456-6); Number Patterns. LC 92-4629. (Illus.). 64p. (YA). (gr. 4-7). 1992. lib. bdg. 25.64 (1-85435-458-2); Numbers. (Illus.). 64p. (YA). (gr. 4 up). 1992. lib. bdg. 25.64 (1-85435-457-4); Quadrilaterals. LC 92-10436. (Illus.). 64p. (YA). (gr. 4-7). 1992. lib. bdg. 25.64 (1-85435-459-0); Triangles. LC 92-12156. (Illus.). 64p. (YA). (gr. 4-7). 1992. lib. bdg. 25.64 (1-85435-461-2); 153.86 (1-85435-455-8, Benchmark NY) Marshall Cavendish.

Let's Investigate - Group 2, 6 bks. Marion Smoothey. Incl. Angles. LC 92-36222. (Illus.). 64p. (YA). (gr. 4 up). 1993. lib. bdg. 25.64 (1-85435-466-3); Shape Patterns. LC 92-36223. (Illus.). 64p. (YA). (gr. 4-7). 1993. lib. bdg. 25.64 (1-85435-465-5); Shapes. LC 92-36224. (Illus.). 64p. (YA). (gr. 4-7). 1993. lib. bdg. 25.64 (1-85435-464-7); Solids. LC 92-36220. (Illus.). 64p. (YA). (gr. 4-7). 1993. lib. bdg. 25.64 (1-85435-469-8); Statistics. LC 92-35574. (Illus.). 64p. (YA). (gr. 4 up). 1993. lib. bdg. 25.64 (1-85435-468-X); Time, Distance, & Speed. LC 92-36225. (Illus.). 64p. (YA). (gr. 4-7). 1993. lib. bdg. 25.64 (1-85435-467-1); 153.86 (1-85435-463-9, Benchmark NY) Marshall Cavendish.

Let's Investigate - Group 3, 6 bks. Marion Smoothey. Incl. Codes & Sequences. Illus. by Ann Baum. LC 94-13134. 64p. (YA). (gr. 4-7). 1994. lib. bdg. 25.64 (1-85435-774-3); Estimating. Illus. by Ann Baum. LC 94-19142. 64p. (YA). (gr. 4 up). 1994. lib. bdg. 25.64 (1-85435-779-4); Graphs. Illus. by Ann Baum. LC 94-13133. 64p. (YA). (gr. 4 up). 1994. lib. bdg. 25.64 (1-85435-775-1); Maps & Scale Drawing. LC 94-22463. (Illus.). 64p. (YA). (gr. 4-7). 1996. lib. bdg. 25.64 (1-85435-778-6); Ratio & Proportion. LC 94-17995. (Illus.). 64p. (YA). (gr. 4 up). 1996. lib. bdg. 25.64 (1-85435-776-X); 153.86 (1-85435-773-5, Benchmark NY) Marshall Cavendish.

Let's Investigate Beautiful, Bouncy Balloons. Madelyn Carlisle. (Illus.). 32p. (J). (gr. 4-7). 1992. pap. 4.95 (0-8120-4734-6) Barron.

Let's Investigate Magical, Mysterious Meteorites. Madelyn Carlisle. LC 92-12776. (Illus.). 32p. (J). (gr. 4-7). 1992. pap. 4.95 (0-8120-4733-8) Barron.

Let's Investigate Series, 8 vols. Incl. Australia. Adele Richardson. (Illus.). 32p. (J). 2000. pap. 10.60 (0-89812-002-0, Creative Paperbks); Bats. Nancy J. Shaw. (Illus.). 32p. (J). 2000. pap. 10.60 (0-89812-003-9, Creative Paperbks); Fossils. Nancy J. Shaw & Melissa Gish. (Illus.). 32p. (J). 2000. pap. 10.60 (0-89812-004-7, Creative Paperbks); Japan. Adele Richardson. (Illus.). 32p. (J). 2000. pap. 10.60 (0-89812-005-5, Creative Paperbks); Mexico. Adele Richardson. (Illus.). 32p. (J). 2000. pap. 10.60 (0-89812-006-3, Creative Paperbks); Russia. Adele Richardson. (Illus.). 32p. (J). 2000. pap. 10.60 (0-89812-007-1, Creative Paperbks); Seashells. Adele Richardson. (Illus.). 32p. (J). 2000. pap. 10.60 (0-89812-008-X, Creative Paperbks); Snakes. Melissa Gish. (Illus.). 32p. (J). 2000. pap. 10.60 (0-89812-009-8, Creative Paperbks); (Illus.). (J). Set pap. 84.80 (0-89812-011-X, Creative Paperbks) Creative Co.

Let's Investigate Series, 6 vols., Set. Madelyn W. Carlisle. (Illus.). 192p. (J). (gr. 2-6). 1997. lib. bdg. 86.70 (1-56674-929-8) Forest Hse.

Let's Investigate Sparkling, Silent Snow. Madelyn Carlisle. (Illus.). 32p. (J). (gr. 4-7). 1992. pap. 4.95 (0-8120-4736-2) Barron.

Let's Join In: Four Stories. Shirley Hughes. LC 98-21931. (Illus.). 64p. (J). (ps-1). 1999. 17.99 (0-7636-0824-6, Pub. by Candlewick Pr) Penguin Putnam.

Let's Jump! Houghton Mifflin Company Staff. (J). 1992. pap. 4.48 (0-395-62573-4) HM.

Let's Jump In! Susan Hood. LC 99-18494. (Fisher-Price All-Star Readers Ser.). (Illus.). 32p. (J). (gr. k-3). 1999. pap. 3.99 (1-57584-320-X, Pub. by Rdrs Digest) Random.

***Let's Jump Rope.** Sarah Hughes. (Welcome Bks.). (Illus.). (J). 2000. 13.50 (0-516-23114-6) Childrens.

***Let's Jump Rope.** Sarah Hughes. LC 00-25909. (Play Time Ser.). (Illus.). 24p. (J). (ps-2). 2000. pap. write for info. (0-516-23039-5) Childrens.

Let's Keep Christmas. Peter Marshall. LC 53-10628. (Illus.). 48p. (gr. 10). 1995. reprint ed. 9.99 (0-8007-9134-7) Chosen Bks.

Let's Keep Singing! John Langstaff Sings with Children Ages 6-10. Elizabeth L. Mayer. (Making Music with John Langstaff Ser.). (J). (gr. 2-5). 1997. pap. 4.95 (1-886380-23-6) Langstaff Vid.

Let's Kill 'Em: Understanding & Controlling Violence in Sports. Jon Leizman. LC 99-14399. 144p. 1999. pap. text 24.50 (0-7618-1378-0) U Pr of Amer.

***Let's Kill 'Em: Understanding & Controlling Violence in Sports.** Jon Leizman. LC 99-14399. 144p. 1999. 42.00 (0-7618-1377-2) U Pr of Amer.

Let's Learn: Spanish Word Book. Passport Books Staff. (SPA., Illus.). 16p. (J). 1996. pap. 7.95 (0-8442-7885-8, 78858) NTC Contemp Pub Co.

Let's Learn a Little Hawaiian. W. Ray Helbig. (ENG & HAW.). 1970. pap. 3.95 (0-930492-07-2) Hawaiian Serv.

Let's Learn About . . . Language Arts. Elaine Commins. LC 90-30477. (Illus.). 32p. (J). (gr. k-3). 1990. pap. 4.95 (0-89334-147-9) Humanics Ltd.

Let's Learn about Aging: A Book of Readings. Ed. by John R. Barry & C. Ray Wingrove. 350p. 1977. text 18.95 (0-87073-673-6) Schenkman Bks Inc.

Let's Learn about Getting Along with Others. Jeri A. Carroll. 64p. (J). (ps-2). 1988. student ed. 8.99 (0-86653-439-3, GA1042) Good Apple.

Let's Learn about Good Health. Kay W. Springate. 64p. (J). (ps-2). 1988. student ed. 6.99 (0-86653-438-5, GA1041) Good Apple.

***Let's Learn about Jesus: The Life of Christ Retold for Children.** Bessie Dean. (Children's Inspirational Coloring Bks.). (Illus.). 72p. (J). (ps-6). 1999. reprint ed. pap. 6.98 (0-88290-669-0) Horizon Utah.

Let's Learn about Jewish Symbols. Joyce Fishman. (Illus.). (J). (gr. k-3). 1995. pap., student ed., wbk. ed. 7.00 (0-8074-0171-4, 101050) UAHC.

An Asterisk (*) at the beginning of an entry indicates that the title is appearing for the first time.

***Let's Learn about Kosher Food.** large type ed. Ze'ev Greenwald. 1999. 16.95 (*0-87306-894-7*) Feldheim.

Let's Learn about Magnificent Me. Jeri Carroll. (Illus.). 64p. (J). (ps-2). 1987. pap. 8.99 (*0-86653-384-2*, GA1010) Good Apple.

Let's Learn about Maryland. 5th rev. ed. Rita G. Cameron. (Illus.). 96p. (J). (gr. 4). 1995. pap. text 9.99 (*1-55596-166-5*, 00092) Learning Well.

Let's Learn about Outer Space. Meg Jansen et al. LC 91-61949. (Illus.). 112p. (Orig.). 1991. teacher ed. 9.95 (*1-880038-08-0*) Learn-Abouts.

Let's Learn about Safety. Diana Courson. (Illus.). 64p. (J). (ps-2). 1987. pap. 7.99 (*0-86653-382-6*, GA1011) Good Apple.

Let's Learn about Spain. Sacha De Frisching. (Let's Learn about Ser.). (Illus.). 32p. (J). (gr. 4 up). 1991. pap. 5.95 (*0-8442-7631-6*, Passprt Bks) NTC Contemp Pub Co.

Let's Learn about Story Elements: Character. Michelle O'Brien-Palmer. 64p. 1998. pap. 9.95 (*0-590-10717-8*) Scholastic Inc.

Let's Learn about Story Elements: Plot. Michelle O'Brien-Palmer. 64p. 1998. pap. 9.95 (*0-590-10716-X*) Scholastic Inc.

Let's Learn about Story Elements: Setting. Michelle O'Brien-Palmer. 64p. 1998. pap. 9.95 (*0-590-10715-1*) Scholastic Inc.

Let's Learn about the Church & Celebrate Its Message. Mary C. Senger. (Illus.). 64p. (J). (gr. 4-6). 1990. pap. 4.95 (*0-8146-1888-X*) Liturgical Pr.

Let's Learn about Tithing. Jan Clawson. (Illus.). 24p. (J). (gr. k-6). 1988. pap. 4.98 (*0-88290-339-X*) Horizon Utah.

Let's Learn Aleph-Beis. (Yoni Gold Board Book Ser.). bds. 4.95 (*1-58330-149-6*) Feldheim.

Let's Learn All We Can, 1. P. K. Hallinan. 1999. 6.95 (*1-57102-156-6*) Hambleton-Hill.

Let's Learn American English. Ed. by Passport Books Staff. LC 97-44570. (Let's Learn...Picture Dictionary Ser.). (Illus.). 72p. (J). 1995. 9.95 (*0-8442-5453-3*, 54533, Passprt Bks) NTC Contemp Pub Co.

Let's Learn Arabic. A. Ashurakis. 72p. 1984. pap. 45.00 (*1-85077-007-7*, Pub. by Darf Pubs Ltd) St Mut.

Let's Learn at the Treasure House. (Captain Kangaroo Coloring & Activity Bks.: Vol. 4). (Illus.). 32p. (J). 1998. pap. write for info. (*0-7666-0226-5*, Honey Bear Bks) Modern Pub NYC.

Let's Learn Bible. Dona Z. Meilach et al. LC 98-164997. 1991. 7.95 (*0-88125-399-5*) Ktav.

***Let's Learn Colors.** Joanie Ellering. (J). (ps-3). 1999. write for info. (*1-929343-00-0*) Peer Tutor Pr.

Let's Learn English: Second Language Activities for the Primary Grades, K-3. G. Yvonne Perez et al. (Illus.). 91p. (Orig.). 1987. pap. 9.95 (*0-673-18371-8*, GoodYrBooks) Addson-Wesley Educ.

Let's Learn English Coloring Book. Anne-Francoise Hazzan. (Illus.). 64p. (J). 1994. pap. 3.95 (*0-8442-5451-7*, Passprt Bks) NTC Contemp Pub Co.

***Let's Learn First Skills!** (Illus.). 32p. (J). (ps-2). 1998. pap. 4.95 (*0-88724-491-2*, CD-5855) Carson-Dellos.

Let's Learn French. Ed. by Passport Books Staff. (Let's Learn...Picture Ser.). (FRE., Illus.). 72p. (J). 1995. 9.95 (*0-8442-1392-6*, 13926, Natl Textbk Co) NTC Contemp Pub Co.

Let's Learn French Coloring Book. Anne-Francoise Pattis. (Let's Learn...Coloring Books Ser.). (FRE., Illus.). 16p. (J). (gr. 4 up). 1994. pap. 3.95 (*0-8442-1389-6*, 13896, Passprt Bks) NTC Contemp Pub Co.

Let's Learn French Coloring Book with Crayons. Contrib. by Anne-Francoise Hazzan. (Let's Learn Ser.). (FRE., Illus.). 64p. (J). 1992. pap. 9.95 incl. audio (*0-8442-9183-8*) NTC Contemp Pub Co.

Let's Learn French Multimedia Picture Dictionary Package. (Let's Learn...Multimedia Ser.). (FRE., Illus.). 16p. (J). 1995. 39.95 incl. cd-rom (*0-8442-1373-X*, 1373X, Passprt Bks) NTC Contemp Pub Co.

Let's Learn French Word Book. (Let's Learn...Multimedia Ser.). (FRE., Illus.). 16p. (J). 1996. pap. 7.95 (*0-8442-1374-8*, 13748) NTC Contemp Pub Co.

Let's Learn from the Holy Qur'an: An Activity Book for Children. large type ed. Tasneema Ghazi. (Illus.). 56p. (J). (ps-1). 1999. ring bd., wbk. ed. 6.00 (*1-56316-122-2*) Iqra Intl Ed Fdtn.

Let's Learn German. (Let's Learn...Multimedia Ser.). (Illus.). 16p. (J). 1997. pap. 39.95 incl. audio (*0-8442-2197-X*, 2197X); pap. 7.95 (*0-8442-2198-8*, 21988) NTC Contemp Pub Co.

Let's Learn German. Ed. by Passport Books Staff. (Let's Learn...Picture Ser.). (GER., Illus.). 72p. (J). 1995. 9.95 (*0-8442-2167-8*, 21678, Passprt Bks) NTC Contemp Pub Co.

Let's Learn German Coloring Book. Anne-Francoise Hazzan & Anne-Francoise Pattis. (Let's Learn Ser.). (GER., Illus.). 64p. (J). 1993. pap. 9.95 incl. audio (*0-8442-9274-5*) NTC Contemp Pub Co.

Let's Learn German Coloring Book. S. William Pattis. (Let's Learn...Coloring Books Ser.). (GER., Illus.). 16p. (J). (gr. 4 up). 1994. pap. 4.95 (*0-8442-2164-3*, 21643, Passprt Bks) NTC Contemp Pub Co.

Let's Learn God's Plan see Aprendamos el Plan de Dios

Let's Learn God's Plan. Bessie Dean. LC 78-52114. (Illus.). (J). 1978. pap. 3.98 (*0-88290-092-7*) Horizon Utah.

Let's Learn Hebrew. Ed. by Passport Books Staff. LC 97-38801. (Let's Learn...Picture Dictionary Ser.). (HEB., Illus.). 72p. (J). (gr. 4-7). 1995. 11.95 (*0-8442-8490-4*, 84904, Passprt Bks) NTC Contemp Pub Co.

Let's Learn Hiragana. Yasuko K. Mitamura. LC 84-82275. 72p. (Orig.). 1985. pap. 13.00 (*0-87011-709-2*) Kodansha.

Let's Learn Italian Coloring Book. Anne-Francoise Hazzan. (ITA., Illus.). 16p. (J). (ps-3). 1993. pap. 4.95 (*0-8442-8060-7*, 80607, Natl Textbk Co) NTC Contemp Pub Co.

Let's Learn Japanese Picture Dictionary: Elementary Through Junior High. Ed. by Passport Books Staff. LC 97-38795. (Let's Learn...Picture Dictionary Ser.). (JPN., Illus.). 80p. (J). (gr. 4-7). 1992. 11.95 (*0-8442-8494-7*, 84947, Natl Textbk Co) NTC Contemp Pub Co.

Let's Learn Kanji: An Introduction to Radicals, Components, & 250 Very Basic Kanji. Yasuko K. Mitamura & Joyce Y. Mitamura. Ed. by Paul Hulbert. LC 97-36398. (JPN., Illus.). 256p. 1998. pap. 22.00 (*4-7700-2068-6*) Kodansha.

Let's Learn Katakana. Yasuko K. Mitamura. LC 85-40059. (Illus.). 88p. (Orig.). 1986. pap. 13.00 (*0-87011-719-X*) Kodansha.

Let's Learn Korean. 2nd rev. ed. B. J. Jones. LC 85-60068. (Illus.). 64p. 1998. pap. 14.50 incl. audio (*0-930878-41-8*) Hollym Intl.

Let's Learn Language Development Transparencies. (Illus.). 1992. teacher ed. 11.25 (*0-8442-9126-9*) NTC Contemp Pub Co.

***Let's Learn Letters.** Mary Clingan. (J). (ps-3). 1999. write for info. (*1-929343-03-5*) Peer Tutor Pr.

Let's Learn Maori. rev. ed. Bruce Biggs. LC 98-215797. 208p. 1998. pap. 18.95 (*1-86940-186-7*, Pub. by Auckland Univ) Paul & Co Pubs.

Let's Learn More Kanji: Family Groups, Learning Strategies, & 300 Complex Kanji. Yasuko K. Mitamura. 1998. pap. text 30.00 (*4-7700-2069-4*, Pub. by Kodansha Intl) Kodansha.

***Let's Learn Number Skills.** (Richard Scarry Bks.). (Illus.). 32p. (J). (gr. 1-3). 1998. pap. 4.95 (*0-88724-490-4*, CD-5854) Carson-Dellos.

***Let's Learn Numbers.** Kathy Nolan. (J). (ps-3). 1999. write for info. (*1-929343-02-7*) Peer Tutor Pr.

Let's Learn of God's Love. Bessie Dean. LC 79-89367. (Books for LDS Children). (Illus.). 64p. (J). (ps-3). 1979. pap. 3.98 (*0-88290-124-9*) Horizon Utah.

***Let's Learn Our Numbers!** (Richard Scarry Bks.). (Illus.). 32p. (J). (ps-1). 1998. pap. 4.95 (*0-88724-488-2*, CD-5852) Carson-Dellos.

Let's Learn Portuguese. Ed. by Passport Books Staff. LC 97-41121. (Let's Learn...Picture Dictionary Ser.). (POR., Illus.). 72p. (J). (gr. 4-7). 1995. 11.95 (*0-8442-4699-9*, 46999, Passprt Bks) NTC Contemp Pub Co.

Let's Learn Prayer. Sol Scharfstein. LC 99-178722. 160p. 1985. 8.95 (*0-88125-189-5*) Ktav.

Let's Learn Set. Incl. Alphabet Sounds & Pictures. 1984. Capital & Lower Case Letters. 1984. Color Words. 1984. Consonants. 1984. pap. Fun with Numbers. Letters & the Sounds They Make. 1984. pap. Numbers, Number Words, & Sets. 1984. pap. Positions. 1984. pap. Pre-School & Kindergarten Skills. 1984. pap. Printing Practice. 1984. pap. Shapes. 1984. pap. 32p. (J). 1984. Set pap. 285.12 (*0-88724-099-2*) Carson-Dellos.

***Let's Learn Shapes.** Joanie Ellering. (J). (ps-3). 1999. write for info. (*1-929343-01-9*) Peer Tutor Pr.

Let's Learn Spanish. Anne-Francoise Pattis. (Let's Learn...Coloring Books Ser.). (SPA., Illus.). 16p. (J). (gr. 4 up). 1995. pap. 4.95 (*0-8442-7549-2*, 75492, Passprt Bks) NTC Contemp Pub Co.

Let's Learn Spanish Coloring Book with Crayons. Contrib. by Anne-Francoise Hazzan. (Let's Learn Ser.). (SPA., Illus.). 64p. (J). 1993. pap. 9.95 incl. audio (*0-8442-9172-2*) NTC Contemp Pub Co.

Let's Learn Spanish Multimedia Picture Dictionary Package. (SPA., Illus.). 16p. (J). 1995. 39.95 incl. cd-rom (*0-8442-7884-X*, 7884X, Passprt Bks) NTC Contemp Pub Co.

Let's Learn the Alef Bet: Reading Readiness Book for the Hebrew Primer. Ruby G. Strauss. (Hebrew Primer Ser.). (Illus.). 94p. (J). (gr. 4-7). 1987. pap. text 5.45 (*0-87441-439-3*) Behrman.

Let's Learn the First Principles. Bessie Dean. LC 78-70366. (Books for LDS Children). (Illus.). 64p. (J). (ps-3). 1993. reprint ed. pap. 3.98 (*0-88290-104-4*) Horizon Utah.

Let's Learn the Hawaiian Alphabet. Patricia A. Murray. (Illus.). 24p. (J). (ps). 1987. 10.95 (*0-89610-075-8*) Island Heritage.

Let's Learn the Hawaiian Alphabet. Patricia A. Murray. (Illus.). 24p. (J). (ps). 1988. audio 13.95 (*0-89610-079-0*) Island Heritage.

Let's Learn the Hawaiian Alphabet Coloring & Activity Book. Patricia Murray. 1988. pap. 2.95 (*0-89610-022-7*) Island Heritage.

Let's Learn to Count in Hawaiian. Keiki C. Kawai'ae'a. (Illus.). 24p. (J). (ps). 1988. 10.95 (*0-89610-076-6*); audio 13.95 (*0-89610-080-4*) Island Heritage.

Let's Learn to Count in Hawaiian Coloring & Activity Book. Keiki Kawaiaea. 1988. pap. 2.95 (*0-89610-021-9*) Island Heritage.

Let's Learn to Write Letters. (Illus.). 24p. (J). (ps-3). 1996. pap. 12.95 (*0-8167-3172-1*) Troll Communs.

Let's Learn to Write Numbers. (Illus.). 24p. (J). (ps-3). 1997. pap. 12.95 (*0-8167-3171-3*) Troll Communs.

Let's Learn to Write Script. (Illus.). (J). 1997. pap. 12.95 (*0-8167-3547-6*) Troll Communs.

***Let's Learn Twi - Ma Yensua Twi.** Paul A. Kotey. 260p. 2000. pap. 24.95 (*0-86543-854-4*) Africa World.

Let's Lindy. Simon Selmon. (Illus.). 60p. 1993. pap. 12.95 (*1-85273-039-0*, Pub. by Dance Bks) Princeton Bk Co.

Let's Listen: Communicating with Your Youth about Faith & Sexuality, Parent Resource. (Teen Sexuality Resources Ser.). 32p. 1998. pap. 6.95 (*0-687-72215-2*) Abingdon.

Let's Listen to Jesus: A Bible Study on John 13-17. Reuben R. Welch. 112p. (Orig.). 1988. pap. 5.95 (*0-310-75271-X*, 17046P) Zondervan.

Let's Listen to Jesus: Reflections on the Farewell Discourse. Reuben R. Welch. 144p. (Orig.). 1985. pap. 2.70 (*0-310-75101-2*, 17044P) Zondervan.

Let's Look at Animals: Preschool Picture & First Word Books. Lorenz Books Staff. (Illus.). 24p. (J). 1996. 4.95 (*1-85967-265-5*, Lorenz Bks) Anness Pub.

Let's Look at Art. Darla Linerode. (Illus.). (Orig.). (J). (gr. 1-6). 1992. pap. write for info. (*0-935493-30-1*) Modern Learn Pr.

Let's Look at Art, 9 vols., Set. Darla Linerode. (Illus.). 168p. (Orig.). pap. text 410.00 (*1-56762-044-2*) Modern Learn Pr.

Let's Look at Colors: Preschool Picture & First Word Books. Lorenz Books Staff. (Illus.). 24p. (J). 1996. 3.95 (*1-85967-270-1*, Lorenz Bks) Anness Pub.

Let's Look at Dance! Using Professional Dance on Video. Linda Rolfe & Mary Harlow. LC 97-204498. 80p. 1997. pap. 24.95 (*1-85346-430-9*, Pub. by David Fulton) Taylor & Francis.

Let's Look at Dinosaurs. Illus. by Mario Gomboli. (Poke & Look Learning Ser.). 16p. (J). (ps-3). 1999. bds. 9.99 (*0-448-42047-3*, G & D) Peng Put Young Read.

Let's Look at Faces. Darla Linerode. (Illus.). 18p. 1991. pap. text 49.50 (*1-56762-042-6*) Modern Learn Pr.

Let's Look at Families (Poke & Look Learning Books) Laura Driscoll. (Poke & Look Learning Ser.). (Illus.). 16p. (J). (ps-3). 1999. bds. 9.99 (*0-448-41990-4*, G & D) Peng Put Young Read.

Let's Look at Flowers: Preschool Picture & First Word Books. Lorenz Books Staff. (Illus.). 24p. (J). 1996. 3.95 (*1-85967-314-7*, Lorenz Bks) Anness Pub.

Let's Look at Fruit: Preschool Picture & First Word Books. Lorenz Books Staff. (Illus.). 24p. (J). 1996. 3.95 (*1-85967-275-2*, Lorenz Bks) Anness Pub.

Let's Look at Indonesia. David Ellis. 1987. pap. 1.95 (*9971-83-824-9*) OMF Bks.

Let's Look at It Another Way. (Shorewood Art Programs for Education Ser.). 12p. 1975. teacher ed. 107.00 (*0-88185-052-7*); 143.00 (*0-685-07227-4*) Shorewood Fine Art.

Let's Look at Landscapes. Darla Linerode. (Illus.). 18p. 1991. pap. text 49.50 (*1-56762-043-4*) Modern Learn Pr.

Let's Look at Line. Darla Linerode. (Illus.). 18p. 1991. pap. text 49.50 (*1-56762-039-6*) Modern Learn Pr.

Let's Look at Malaysia. Miriam Dunn. 1986. pap. 1.95 (*9971-972-48-4*) OMF Bks.

***Let's Look at Nature.** Anness Publishing Staff. (J). (-8). 2000. bds. 4.95 (*0-7548-0709-6*) Anness Pub.

Let's Look at Numbers: Preschool Picture & First Word Books. Lorenz Books Staff. (Illus.). 24p. (J). 1996. 4.95 (*1-85967-280-9*, Lorenz Bks) Anness Pub.

Let's Look at Opposites. Lorenz Books Staff. (Illus.). 24p. (J). 1996. 3.95 (*1-85967-315-5*, Lorenz Bks) Anness Pub.

Let's Look at Our Bodies: Preschool Picture & First Word Books. Lorenz Books Staff. (Illus.). 24p. (J). 1998. 4.95 (*1-85967-316-3*, Lorenz Bks) Anness Pub.

***Let's Look at Patterns.** Anness Publishing Staff. (J). 2000. bds. 4.95 (*0-7548-0710-X*) Anness Pub.

***Let's Look at Pets.** Anness Publishing Staff. (J). (-7). 2000. bds. 4.95 (*0-7548-0711-8*) Anness Pub.

Let's Look at Portraits. Darla Linerode. (Illus.). 18p. 1991. pap. text 49.50 (*1-56762-041-8*) Modern Learn Pr.

Let's Look at Shapes: Preschool Picture & First Word Books. Lorenz Books Staff. (Illus.). 24p. (J). 1998. 4.95 (*1-85967-317-1*, Lorenz Bks) Anness Pub.

Let's Look at the Law. Lee M. Tan & J. Bollen. 1985. pap. 11.00 (*0-409-49264-7*, AT, MICHIE) LEXIS Pub.

Let's Look at the Planets. Laura Driscoll. (Poke & Look Learning Ser.). (Illus.). 16p. (J). (ps-3). 1999. bds. 9.99 (*0-448-42066-X*, G & D) Peng Put Young Read.

Let's Look at Things That Go. (Let's Look Ser.). (Illus.). 20p. (J). (ps). 1998. 4.95 (*1-85967-599-9*) Anness Pub.

Let's Look at Transportation. Darla Linerode. (Illus.). 18p. 1991. pap. text 49.50 (*1-56762-040-X*) Modern Learn Pr.

Let's Look Inside a Tepee. Betsy Warren. (Illus.). 28p. (Orig.). (J). (gr. 3 up). 1989. pap. 3.50 (*0-9618660-2-0*) Ranch Gate Bks.

Let's Look Inside the Red Car. Amanda Leslie. LC 96-84555. (Illus.). 10p. (J). (ps up). 1997. 9.99 (*0-7636-0089-X*) Candlewick Pr.

Let's Look Inside the Yellow Truck. Amanda Leslie. LC 96-84560. (Illus.). 10p. (J). (ps up). 1997. 8.99 (*0-7636-0104-7*) Candlewick Pr.

Let's Love One Another. Bessie Dean. LC 77-74492. (Books for LDS Children). (Illus.). 64p. (J). (ps-3). 1993. reprint ed. pap. 3.98 (*0-88290-077-3*) Horizon Utah.

Let's Make a Baby. Jacqueline Diamond. 1999. per. 3.99 (*0-373-16763-6*, Harlequin) Harlequin Bks.

Let's Make a Deal: Collaborating on a Full-Service School with Your Community. Susan Hoover & Charles M. Achilles. LC 95-47185. (Illus.). 64p. 1996. pap. 14.95 (*0-8039-6346-7*) Corwin Pr.

Let's Make a Deal: Family Negotiation in Recovery. rev. ed. Sandra Inskeep-Fox. 1998. pap. 0.50 (*0-89230-213-5*) Do It Now.

Let's Make a Deal: Understanding the Negotiation Process in Ordinary Litigation. Herbert M. Kritzer. LC 90-50648. 220p. 1991. pap. text 14.95 (*0-299-12824-5*) U of Wis Pr.

Let's Make a Garden. Tamara A. Lobe. LC 95-78436. (Illus.). 40p. (Orig.). (J). (ps-3). 1995. pap. 7.99 (*0-8361-9021-1*) Herald Pr.

Let's Make a Jesse Tree. Darcy James. 32p. (J). (gr. k-3). 1988. pap. 6.95 (*0-687-21439-4*) Abingdon.

Let's Make a Law. Edward Dye. (Illus.). 12p. (gr. 4-12). 1983. 9.95 (*0-910141-03-7*, KP117) Kino Pubns.

Let's Make a Memory: Great Ideas for Building Family Traditions & Togetherness. rev. ed. Gloria Gaither et al. LC 94-30402. (Illus.). 1994. pap. 15.99 (*0-8499-3517-2*) Word Pub.

***Let's Make a Move! A Creative Visualization Activity Book for Children.** rev. ed. Beverly D. Roman. Ed. by Dalene Bickel. (Illus.). 32p. (J). (gr. k-7). 1999. pap. 7.45 (*1-888891-04-1*) BR Anchor.

Let's Make a Movie. Giovanni Belgrano. LC 72-90235. (Illus.). 48p. (J). (gr. 4-9). 1973. 12.95 (*0-87592-028-4*) Scroll Pr.

Let's Make a Patchwork Quilt. LC 80-500. 1984. 15.95 (*0-685-08404-3*) Farm Journal.

Let's Make a Present! Easy to Make Gifts for Friends & Relatives of Any Age. Andrea Cheng. (Projects for Parents Ser.). (Illus.). 128p. (J). (gr. k-5). 1991. pap. 9.95 (*1-878767-16-X*) Murdoch Bks.

Let's Make a Scene. Betty Carney & Keith Adams. LC 89-60299. 52p. (Orig.). 1989. pap. 8.95 (*0-916809-28-5*) Scott Pubns MI.

Let's Make a Summer Memory. Gloria Gaither. 1995. 4.99 (*0-8499-5109-7*) Word Pub.

Let's Make Banners. Valerie J. Lund. (Illus.). 8p. (Orig.). 1995. pap. text 14.95 (*0-9622405-2-4*) V J Lund.

Let's Make Books. Sandra Brady. 176p. (C). 1992. per. 25.95 (*0-8403-7334-1*, 40733401) Kendall-Hunt.

***Let's Make Butter.** Eleanor Christian & Lyzz Roth-Singer. LC 00-36475. (Illus.). (J). 2000. write for info. (*0-7368-0728-4*) Capstone Pr.

Let's Make Cookies. unabridged ed. Joan B. Smith. (Illus.). 14p. (J). (gr. k-4). 1990. mass mkt. 3.00 (*0-9665509-0-0*) Smiths Commun.

Let's Make Country Wine. Sylvia Fisher. (Illus.). 96p. (Orig.). 1991. pap. 5.95 (*0-914875-06-X*) Bright Mtn Bks.

Let's Make Disciples see Manual Del Discipulado: Hagamos Discipulos

Let's Make It Legal. Trisha Alexander. 1994. per. 3.50 (*0-373-09924-X*, 1-09924-1) Harlequin Bks.

Let's Make Jesus Happy. Mack Thomas & Bruce Day. 256p. (J). (ps-2). 1993. 12.99 (*0-945564-76-7*, Gold n Honey) Zondervan.

Let's Make Magic: Over Forty Tricks You Can Do. Jon Day. LC 92-53093. (Illus.). 96p. (J). (gr. 2-6). 1992. pap. 12.95 (*1-85697-806-0*, Kingfisher) LKC.

Let's Make Music. Pam Howard. (HRL Little Bks.). (Illus.). 8p. (Orig.). (J). (ps-1). 1996. pap. text 10.95 (*1-57332-037-4*) HighReach Lrning.

***Let's Make Music.** Random House U. K. Ltd. 80p. (J). 2001. mass mkt. 2.99 (*0-375-81145-1*) Random Bks Yng Read.

Let's Make Music. large type ed. Pam Howard. (HRL Big Bks.). (Illus.). 8p. (Orig.). (J). (ps-1). 1996. pap. text 10.95 (*1-57332-038-2*) HighReach Lrning.

Let's Make Music! Multicultural Songs & Activities: An Interactive Musical Trip Around the World. Perf. by Ronny Susan Schiff & Heather Harris. 80p. (J). 1995. pap., teacher ed. 15.95 incl. audio (*0-7935-4056-9*) H Leonard.

Let's Make Piano Music with Marvin, Bk. 1. Ann Patrick. 40p. (J). (gr. k-7). 1985. pap. text 6.95 (*0-931759-06-4*) Centerstream Pub.

Let's Make Piano Music with Marvin, Bk. 2. Ann Patrick. (Illus.). 48p. (J). (gr. k-7). 1986. pap. text 6.95 (*0-931759-13-7*) Centerstream Pub.

Let's Make Piano Music with Marvin, Bk. 3. Ann Patrick. 40p. (J). (gr. k-7). 1985. pap. text 6.95 (*0-931759-05-6*) Centerstream Pub.

Let's Make Piano Music with Marvin, Bk. 4. 1988. pap. 7.95 (*0-931759-23-4*) Centerstream Pub.

Let's Make Seasonal Windsocks. Valerie J. Lund. (Illus.). 70p. (Orig.). 1992. pap. text 10.95 (*0-9622405-1-6*) V J Lund.

Let's Make Up. Esther E. Olson. 1945. pap. 3.25 (*0-8222-0653-6*) Dramatists Play.

Let's Make Windsocks. rev. ed. Valerie J. Lund. (Illus.). 70p. (C). 1995. pap. text 10.95 (*0-9622405-0-8*) V J Lund.

Let's Measure It!, Vol. 3735. Luella Connelly. (Emergent Reader Bks.). (Illus.). 16p. (J). (gr. k-2). 1995. pap. 2.75 (*1-57471-006-0*) Creat Teach Pr.

Let's Measure It!, Vol. 3978. Luella Connelly. (Emergent Reader Big Bks.). (Illus.). 16p. (J). (gr. k-2). 1996. pap. 12.98 (*1-57471-116-4*) Creat Teach Pr.

Let's Meet Allosaurus: And Other Jurassic Dinosaurs. Winky Adam. (Illus.). 14p. (J). (ps-1). 1998. 4.99 (*0-689-81595-6*) Litle Simon.

Let's Meet Famous Artists: A Creative Art Activity Book. Harriet Kinghorn. (Illus.). (J). 1998. pap. text 9.95 (*0-513-02050-0*) Denison.

Let's Meet the Triceratops: And Other Cretaceious Dinosaurs. Winky Adam. (Illus.). 14p. (J). (ps-1). 1998. 4.99 (*0-689-81596-4*) Litle Simon.

***Let's Motivate Our People!** J. R. Roman. 1999. pap. text 8.99 (*0-8297-2170-3*) Vida Pubs.

Let's Move Overseas: The International Edition of Let's Make a Move! Beverly D. Roman. Ed. by Dalene Bickel. (Illus.). 32p. (J). (gr. 2-6). 1999. pap., mass mkt. 8.45 (*1-888891-16-5*) BR Anchor.

***Let's Move Together.** Carol M. Schubeck. (Illus.). 52p. (J). (ps-6). 2000. pap. 15.95 (*0-9675567-0-8*) Suitcase Pr.

Let's Name It: Ten Thousand Boat Names, an Ingenious Reference Source for Beginners & "Old Salts" Alike. John Corcoran & Lewis R. Hackler. LC 87-90745. (Illus.). 144p. 1987. 9.95 (*0-931595-02-9*) Seascape Enters.

Let's Name It: Ten Thousand Boat Names for All Types of Watercraft. John Corcoran & Lewis R. Hackler. 1987. pap. text 9.95 (*0-07-155340-1*) Intl Marine.

Let's Name the Baby. C. R. Gibson. 1977. pap. 4.95 (*0-8378-5099-1*) Gibson.

Let's Not Reinvent the Wheel: Profiles of School-Business Collaboration. Ed. by Ian McNett. 72p. (Orig.). 1983. pap. 6.95 (*0-937846-97-X*) Inst Educ Lead.

An Asterisk (*) at the beginning of an entry indicates that the title is appearing for the first time.

L

Let's Obraize Our Activities! Mary C. Crittenden. Ed. by Linda Faber-Czingula. 134p. 1996. ring bd. 49.00 (*1-890118-06-0*, QualityCare Pub) Convalescnt Cnslts.
Let's Obraize Our Careplans! 9th rev. ed. Linda Faber-Czingula. 179p. 1991. ring bd. 49.00 (*1-890118-00-1*, QualityCare Pub) Convalescnt Cnslts.
Let's Obraize Our Lesson Plans! 4th rev. ed. Linda Faber-Czingula. 194p. 1994. ring bd. 59.00 (*1-890118-01-X*, QualityCare Pub) Convalescnt Cnslts.
Let's Obraize Our Social Services! 2nd rev. ed. Linda Faber-Czingula. 114p. 1995. ring bd. 49.00 (*1-890118-03-6*, QualityCare Pub) Convalescnt Cnslts.
Let's Open the Bible see Abramos la Biblia: Antiguo Testamento
Let's Paint a Rainbow. Eric Carle. (Play-&-Read Book Ser.). (Illus.). 12p. (YA). (ps). 1998. bds. 6.95 (*0-590-32844-1*, Cartwheel) Scholastic Inc.
Let's Party. Jacqueline Ball. (Looking Good Ser.). (Illus.). 32p. (J). (gr. 5 up). 1990. lib. bdg. 11.95 (*0-685-36382-1*) Rourke Corp.
Let's Party. Jacqueline A. Ball. (Looking Good Ser.: Set II). (Illus.). 32p. (YA). (gr. 5 up). 1990. lib. bdg. 19.93 (*0-86625-418-8*) Rourke Pubns.
***Let's Party!** Judy Katschke. (Two of a Kind Ser.: No. 8). 112p. (J). (gr. 3-7). 1999. pap. 4.25 (*0-06-106578-1*) HarpC.
Let's Party. Kady Martin. Ed. by William Martin. (Illus.). 160p. (Orig.). 1986. pap. 8.95 (*0-942752-02-3*) C A M Co.
Let's Party! How to Plan Special Events & Raise Money in Early Childhood Programs. Judith A. Rice. LC 97-34166. (Illus.). (Orig.). 1997. pap. 13.95 (*1-884834-41-8*, 5320) Redleaf Pr.
Let's Party: Themes, Recipes & Activities. Marguerite Furlong. 84p. (C). pap. text 15.00 (*1-882541-15-4*) Food Allergy.
Let's Party! Chicago: A Quite Martini to an Outrageous Soiree. Scott Power. LC 96-53306. 192p. 1997. pap. 14.95 (*1-57034-073-0*) Globe Pequot.
Let's Pattern Block It. Peggy McLean et al. (Illus.). 170p. (Orig.). (J). (gr. 2-8). 1973. pap. 13.95 (*0-918932-26-2*, A-1118) Activity Resources.
Let's Play see Juguemos
Let's Play. (My Big Little Fat Bks.). 20p. (J). 1994. bds. 2.98 (*0-86112-990-3*) Brimax Bks.
Let's Play. (Read with Me Key Words to Reading Ser.: No. 9010-1). (Illus.). (J). (ps-2). 1990. teacher ed. 3.95 (*0-317-04025-1*, Ladybrd) Penguin Putnam.
Let's Play. Carla Dijs & Kees Moerbeek. 9p. (J). (gr. 3 up). 1990. 9.99 (*0-85953-224-0*) Childs Play.
Let's Play. Yvonne Enoch. 1977. pap. text 5.80 (*0-87563-138-X*) Stipes.
Let's Play. Lisa Heath Jinkins. 1999. pap. text 3.99 (*0-7868-4324-1*, Pub. by Hyperion) Time Warner.
Let's Play. Ladybird Books Staff. (Read with Me Key Words to Reading Ser.: No. 9010-1). (Illus.). (J). (ps-2). 1990. 3.50 (*0-7214-1314-5*, Ladybrd) Penguin Putnam.
Let's Play. Amy MacDonald. LC 91-71838. (Let's Explore Board Bks.). (Illus.). 12p. (J). (ps). 1992. bds. 5.95 (*1-56402-023-1*) Candlewick Pr.
Let's Play! Photos by Margaret Miller. (Illus.). (J). (ps-k). 1997. 4.99 (*0-614-29106-2*) Litle Simon.
Let's Play. Illus. by Tony Tallarico. (Activity & Coloring Bks.). 48p. (J). (ps-1). 1990. 1.39 (*0-89828-164-4*, Tuffy) Putnam Pub Group.
Let's Play. Gyo Fujikawa. (Illus.). 16p. (J). (ps). 1989. reprint ed. bds. 6.95 (*0-317-93045-1*, Sunny Bks) J B Comns.
Let's Play, Vol. 1. (Read with Me Key Words to Reading Ser.: Series 9011-1, No. 1). (Illus.). (J). (ps-2). 1990. student ed. 1.95 (*0-7214-3220-4*, Ladybrd) Penguin Putnam.
Let's Play: A Story Rhyme. Golden Books Staff. (Disney Babies Ser.). (Illus.). (J). 1997. pap. text 1.09 (*0-307-08711-5*, 08711, Goldn Books) Gldn Bks Pub Co.
***Let's Play: I Can Do It.** Debbie Mackinnon. (Illus.). 8p. (J). (ps-3). 1999. 7.95 (*0-316-64897-3*) Little.
Let's Play: Traditional Games of Childhood. Camilla Gryski. (Illus.). 48p. (J). 1995. 16.95 (*1-55074-256-6*) Kids Can Pr.
***Let's Play: Traditional Games of Childhood.** Camilla Gryski. (Illus.). (J). 2000. pap. 6.95 (*1-55074-817-3*, Pub. by Kids Can Pr) Genl Dist Srvs.
Let's Play: Traditional Games of Childhood. unabridged ed. Camilla Gryski. (Illus.). 48p. (J). (ps-3). 1998. 14.95 (*1-55074-497-6*, Pub. by Kids Can Pr) Genl Dist Srvs.
Let's Play: Vamos a Jugar. Alan Benjamin. (Chubby Board Book in English & Spanish Ser.). (ENG & SPA., Illus.). 16p. (J). (ps-1). 1992. pap. 4.99 (*0-671-76928-6*) Litle Simon.
Let's Play a Bible Game! 48 Reproducible Scripture Games & Puzzles for the Overhead Projector. Ed Dunlop. Ed. by Rhonda Wray. LC 95-36395. (Illus.). 208p. 1995. pap. 14.95 (*1-56608-013-4*, B183) Meriwether Pub.
Let's Play a Game. LC 97-73202. (Big Comfy Couch Ser.). 24p. (Orig.). (J). (ps). 1997. pap. 3.99 (*0-448-41639-5*, G & D) Peng Put Young Read.
Let's Play a Game Everyone Wins. 2-9. 36p. (J). (ps-4). 1985. audio. write for info. (*0-318-59511-7*) Listen USA.
Let's Play a Game Everyone Wins. Joseph Currier. (WellinWorld Ser.: 2-9). 36p. (J). (ps-4). 1985. 8.95 incl. audio (*0-88684-178-X*, TC:114604) Listen USA.
Let's Play a Rhyme: Ready-to-Use Rhymes to Promote Early Learning Skills. Christine Branch. Ed. by Jan Keeling. LC 94-75266. (Illus.). 64p. (Orig.). (J). (ps). 1994. pap. text 8.95 (*0-86530-288-X*, 270-3) Incentive Pubns.
Let's Play As a Team! P. K. Hallinan. LC 96-22458. (Illus.). 24p. (Orig.). (J). (ps-3). 1996. pap. 3.25 (*1-57102-099-3*, Ideals Child) Hambleton-Hill.
Let's Play Ball. Marty Allen. (Illus.). 32p. (J). (ps-6). 1999. text 14.99 (*0-9672972-0-6*) Kids Bks Pub.
Let's Play Ball. Gina C. Erickson. (Get Ready - Get Set - Read! Ser.). (J). 1996. 9.15 (*0-606-11558-7*, Pub. by Turtleback) Demco.
Let's Play Ball. Kelli C. Foster & Gina C. Erickson. LC 96-18018. (Get Ready...Get Set...Read! Ser.). (Illus.). 26p. (J). (gr. k-3). 1996. pap. 3.95 (*0-8120-9435-2*) Barron.
Let's Play Ball, Set 5. Kelli C. Foster & Gina C. Erickson. (Get Ready...Get Set...Read! Ser.). (Illus.). (J). 1996. lib. bdg. 11.95 (*1-56674-198-X*) Forest Hse.
Let's Play Basketball see Set 6
Let's Play Bible Detective. R. P. Daniel. 36p. pap. 2.95 (*0-88172-017-8*) Believers Bkshelf.
Let's Play Cards. Elizabeth Silbaugh. (J). 1996. mass mkt. 3.99 (*0-689-80801-1*) S&S Bks Yung.
Let's Play Cards. Elizabeth Silbaugh. (Illus.). 48p. (J). (gr. 1-4). 1996. 14.00 (*0-689-80802-X*) S&S Childrens.
Let's Play Dreidel. Roz Grossman & Gladys Gewirtz. LC 89-34892. (Illus.). 16p. (J). (ps-3). 1989. pap. 6.95 incl. audio (*0-929371-00-3*) Kar-Ben.
Let's Play Games. Maria Rosato. (Stickers 'n' Shapes Ser.). (Illus.). 24p. (J). (gr. k-3). 1997. per. 3.99 (*0-689-81303-1*) S&S Childrens.
Let's Play Games in Chinese. Tao-chung Yao & Scott McGinnis. 164p. 1989. pap. 19.95 (*0-8442-8560-9*) NTC Contemp Pub Co.
Let's Play Games in Japanese. Scott McGinnis et al. 178p. Date not set. 20.95 (*0-8442-8414-9*) NTC Contemp Pub Co.
Let's Play Games in Spanish. (SPA.). 160p. 1985. pap. 15.50 (*0-8442-7600-6*) NTC Contemp Pub Co.
Let's Play Games in Spanish. (SPA.). 128p. 1986. pap. 15.50 (*0-8442-7601-4*) NTC Contemp Pub Co.
"Let's Play!" Group Games for Preschoolers: More Than 140 All New Easy-to-Play, Everyone-Wins Games Your Preschoolers Will Love! Group Publishing Staff. 1996. pap. 16.99 (*1-55945-613-2*) Group Pub.
Let's Play Hide & Seek! Betty Birney. (Lift-the-Flap Bk.). (Illus.). 24p. (J). (ps). 1997. bds. 9.95 (*0-590-92960-7*) Scholastic Inc.
***Let's Play Hide-&-Seek.** Sarah Hughes. (Welcome Bks.). (Illus.). (J). 2000. 13.50 (*0-516-23111-1*) Childrens.
***Let's Play Hide & Seek.** Sarah Hughes. (Play Time Ser.). (Illus.). 24p. (J). (ps-2). 2000. pap. write for info. (*0-516-23036-0*) Childrens.
***Let's Play Hopscotch.** Sarah Hughes. (Welcome Bks.). (Illus.). (J). 2000. 13.50 (*0-516-23112-X*) Childrens.
***Let's Play Hopscotch.** Sarah Hughes. (Play Time Ser.). (Illus.). 24p. (J). (ps-2). 2000. pap. 4.95 (*0-516-23037-9*) Childrens.
***Let's Play Jacks.** Sarah Hughes. (Welcome Bks.). (Illus.). (J). 2000. 13.50 (*0-516-23113-8*) Childrens.
***Let's Play Jacks.** Sarah Hughes. LC 00-23356. (Play Time Ser.). (Illus.). 24p. (J). (ps-2). 2000. pap. write for info. (*0-516-23038-7*) Childrens.
Let's Play Math! Number Games with a Deck of Cards. Denise Gaskins. LC 00-190133. (Homeschool Math Manuals: Vol. 5). 100p. 2001. pap. 10.95 (*1-892083-10-8*) Tabletop Acad.
Let's Play Nintendo Hits. 48p. 1991. pap. 8.95 (*0-7935-0733-2*, 00110002) H Leonard.
***Let's Play Pokemon!** Ed. by Wizards of the Coast Staff. (Pokemon Ser.). (Illus.). 128p. (J). 2000. pap. 12.95 (*0-7869-1763-6*) TSR Inc.
Let's Play Rough! Lynne Jonell. LC 99-10624. (Illus.). 32p. (J). (ps-1). 2000. 13.99 (*0-399-23039-4*, G P Putnam) Peng Put Young Read.
Let's Play Sand. Satomi Ichikawa. Date not set. pap. 5.95 (*0-399-22513-7*) Putnam Pub Group.
***Let's Play Tag.** Sarah Hughes. (Play Time Ser.). (Illus.). 24p. (J). (ps-2). 2000. pap. 4.95 (*0-516-23041-7*) Childrens.
***Let's Play Tag.** Sarah Hughes. (Welcome Bks.). (Illus.). (J). 2000. 13.50 (*0-516-23116-2*) Childrens.
Let's Play Take the Coat off the Dead Guy. John Hulse. 16p. 1996. pap. 3.00 (*1-885710-13-5*) Geekspeak Unique.
Let's Play the Autoharp. Meg Peterson. 40p. 1981. 6.95 (*0-87166-524-7*, 93701) Mel Bay.
Let's Play the Recorder. Robert Bouchard. (J). (gr. 6 up). 9.95 (*0-8283-1471-3*) Branden Bks.
Let's Play Today. Mary Becker et al. (Teddy Ruxpin Tell Me Again Ser.). (Illus.). 24p. (J). 1995. pap. 11.95 incl. audio (*0-934323-83-6*) Alchemy Comms.
***Let's Play Tug-of-War.** Sarah Hughes. (Play Time Ser.). (Illus.). 24p. (J). (ps-2). 2000. pap. 4.95 (*0-516-23040-9*) Childrens.
***Let's Play Tug-of-War.** Sarah Hughes. (Welcome Bks.). (Illus.). (J). 2000. 13.50 (*0-516-23115-4*) Childrens.
***Let's Play with Winnie the Pooh.** Mary Hogan. 10p. 1999. 9.99 (*0-7364-0185-7*, Pub. by Mouse Works) Time Warner.
Let's Playland Learn: Over 160 Fun & Easy Activities. 1999. pap. text 7.95 (*1-56822-812-0*) Instruct Fair.
Let's Practice Hospitality. 1978. 3.50 (*0-918403-04-9*) Agape Ministries.
Let's Praise & Play: Children's Christian Mini-Piano Book. Advance Cal-Tech Inc. Staff. Ed. by Edward Kung. (Illus.). 36p. (J). (ps-6). text. write for info. (*0-943759-00-5*) Advance Cal Tech.
Let's Pray! Illus. by Leon Baxter. 128p. (J). (ps-1). 1998. 9.99 (*0-8054-1684-6*) Broadman.
***Let's Pray: Catholic Prayers & the Mass.** Francine M. O'Connor. Ed. by Jean Larkin. (Active Learning for Catholic Kids Ser.). (Illus.). 28p. (J). (gr. 1-3). 1999. pap. 9.95 (*0-937997-54-4*, 3403) Hi-Time Pflaum.
Let's Pretend see I Hagamos De Cuenta!
Let's Pretend. Debbie Bailey. (Talk about Bks.: Vol. 13). (Illus.). 14p. (J). (ps). 1999. bds. 5.95 (*1-55037-558-X*, Pub. by Annick Pr) Firefly Bks Ltd.
Let's Pretend. Rose Greydanus. LC 81-2357. (Illus.). 32p. (J). (gr. k-2). 1981. lib. bdg. 17.25 (*0-89375-545-1*) Troll Communs.
Let's Pretend. Cedric Hardwicke. LC 78-93165. 259p. 1972. 18.95 (*0-405-08598-2*, Pub. by Blom Pubns) Ayer.
Lets Pretend. Margaret Miller. (Super Chubby Board Bks.). (Illus.). 26p. (J). (ps-k). 1998. 4.99 (*0-689-80042-8*) Litle Simon.
***Let's Pretend.** Random House Staff. (Sticker Time Ser.). (Illus.). 16p. (J). (ps-3). 2000. pap. 2.99 (*0-375-81064-1*) Random.
Let's Pretend. Kiki Thorpe. (Bear in the Big Blue House Ser.). (Illus.). 8p. (J). 2000. pap. 9.99 (*1-57584-402-8*, Pub. by Rdrs Digest) S&S Trade.
Let's Pretend. Ed. & Frwd. by Robert Wolf. (Folk Literature Ser.). 60p. 1994. pap. 6.50 (*1-878781-15-4*) Free River Pr.
Let's Pretend. large type ed. Illus. & Created by Clare Beaton. (Craft & Project Books for Children). 48p. (J). (ps-4). 1998. lib. bdg. 17.95 (*1-56674-243-9*) Forest Hse.
Let's Pretend: My Coloring Book. Golden Books Family Entertainment Staff. (Walt Disney's Cinderella Ser.). (Illus.). (J). 1998. pap. text 1.09 (*0-307-08945-2*, 08945, Goldn Books) Gldn Bks Pub Co.
Let's Pretend: My Jesus Pocketbook. Jeannie Harmon. Date not set. pap. text 0.79 (*1-55513-379-7*) Chariot Victor.
***Let's Pretend! The Why & How of Dramatic Play.** Melanie Bazarte. (Illus.). 32p. 1998. pap. 9.95 (*0-9664365-3-9*) Dr Melanie.
Let's Pretend Board Book. Dessie Moore. LC 95-128173. (Jump at the Sun Board Bks.). (Illus.). 16p. (J). (ps up). 1994. 5.95 (*0-694-00591-6*) HarpC Child Bks.
Let's Pretend You're Dead. Vincent Courtney. 1991. mass mkt. 4.50 (*1-55817-557-1*, Pinncle Kensgtn) Kensgtn Pub Corp.
Let's Put Kids First, Finally: Getting Class Size Right. Charles M. Achilles. LC 99-6240. (One-Off Ser.). (Illus.). 216p. 1999. pap. 23.95 (*0-8039-6807-8*) Corwin Pr.
***Let's Put Kids First, Finally: Getting Class Size Right.** Charles M. Achilles. LC 99-6240. (One-Off Ser.). (Illus.). 216p. 1999. 53.95 (*0-8039-6806-X*) Corwin Pr.
Let's Put on a Musical! How to Choose the Right Show for Your School, Community, or Professional Theater. Peter Filichia. 384p. 1997. pap. 14.95 (*0-8230-8817-0*, Back Stage Bks) Watsn-Guptill.
Let's Put on a Musical! How to Choose the Right Show for Your School, Community or Professional Theatre. Peter Filichia. 256p. (Orig.). 1993. pap. 10.00 (*0-380-77045-8*, Avon Bks) Morrow Avon.
***Lets Put on a Show!** Elizabeth Winfrey. (Full House Sisters Ser.). 160p. (J). (gr. 4-6). 2000. per. 3.99 (*0-671-04088-X*, Minstrel Bks) PB.
Let's Put on a Show! A Beginner's Theatre Handbook for Young Actors. Adrea Gibbs. LC 99-38372. 160p. (YA). (gr. 7-8). 1999. pap. 16.95 (*1-56608-052-5*, U-B231) Meriwether Pub.
Let's Put the Future Behind Us. Jack Womack. 320p. 1997. pap. 12.00 (*0-8021-3503-X*, Grove) Grove-Atltic.
Let's Put the World Right Together. F. Fremer. (C). 1989. 25.00 (*0-7223-2332-8*, Pub. by A H S Ltd) St Mut.
Let's Quilt: A First Book on Quilt Making. Darcy Pattison. LC 96-33615. (J). 1997. write for info. (*0-8442-2629-7*, Quilt Dgst Pr) NTC Contemp Pub Co.
Let's Quilt Alabama & Stuff It Topographically! Carole Marsh. (Carole Marsh Alabama Bks.). (Illus.). (YA). (gr. 3-12). 1994. pap. 19.95 (*1-55609-073-0*); lib. bdg. 29.95 (*1-55609-462-0*); disk 29.95 (*0-7933-1328-7*) Gallopade Intl.
Let's Quilt Alaska & Stuff It Topographically! Carole Marsh. (Carole Marsh Alaska Bks.). (Illus.). (YA). (gr. 3-12). 1994. pap. 19.95 (*1-55609-094-3*); lib. bdg. 29.95 (*1-55609-475-2*); disk 29.95 (*0-7933-1344-9*) Gallopade Intl.
Let's Quilt Arizona & Stuff It Topographically! Carole Marsh. (Carole Marsh Arizona Bks.). (Illus.). (YA). (gr. 3-12). 1994. pap. 19.95 (*1-55609-128-1*); lib. bdg. 29.95 (*1-55609-499-X*); disk 29.95 (*0-7933-1360-0*) Gallopade Intl.
Let's Quilt Arkansas & Stuff It Topographically! Carole Marsh. (Carole Marsh Arkansas Bks.). (Illus.). (YA). (gr. 3-12). 1994. pap. 19.95 (*1-55609-078-1*); lib. bdg. 29.95 (*1-55609-486-8*); disk 29.95 (*0-7933-1376-7*) Gallopade Intl.
Let's Quilt California & Stuff It Topographically! Carole Marsh. (Carole Marsh California Bks.). (Illus.). (YA). (gr. 3-12). 1994. pap. 19.95 (*1-55609-512-0*); lib. bdg. 29.95 (*1-55609-513-9*); disk 29.95 (*0-7933-1392-9*) Gallopade Intl.
Let's Quilt Colorado & Stuff It Topographically! Carole Marsh. (Carole Marsh Colorado Bks.). (Illus.). (YA). (gr. 3-12). 1994. pap. 19.95 (*1-55609-126-5*); lib. bdg. 29.95 (*1-55609-526-0*); disk 29.95 (*0-7933-1408-9*) Gallopade Intl.
Let's Quilt Connecticut & Stuff It Topographically! Carole Marsh. (Carole Marsh Connecticut Bks.). (Illus.). (YA). (gr. 3-12). 1994. lib. bdg. 29.95 (*1-55609-539-2*); disk 29.95 (*0-7933-1424-0*) Gallopade Intl.
Let's Quilt Connecticut & Stuff It Topographically! Carole Marsh. (Carole Marsh Connecticut Bks.). (Illus.). (J). (gr. 3-12). 1997. pap. 19.95 (*1-55609-061-7*) Gallopade Intl.
Let's Quilt Delaware & Stuff It Topographically! Carole Marsh. (Carole Marsh Delaware Bks.). (Illus.). (YA). (gr. 3-12). 1994. pap. 19.95 (*1-55609-063-3*); lib. bdg. 29.95 (*1-55609-552-X*); disk 29.95 (*0-7933-1440-2*) Gallopade Intl.
Let's Quilt Florida & Stuff It Topographically! Carole Marsh. (Carole Marsh Florida Bks.). (Illus.). (YA). (gr. 3-12). 1994. pap. 19.95 (*1-55609-055-2*); lib. bdg. 29.95 (*1-55609-419-1*); disk 29.95 (*0-7933-1488-7*) Gallopade Intl.
Let's Quilt Georgia & Stuff It Topographically! Carole Marsh. (Carole Marsh Georgia Bks.). (Illus.). (YA). (gr. 3-12). 1994. pap. 19.95 (*1-55609-054-4*); lib. bdg. 29.95 (*1-55609-382-9*); disk 29.95 (*0-7933-1507-7*) Gallopade Intl.
Let's Quilt Hawaii & Stuff It Topographically! Carole Marsh. (Carole Marsh Hawaii Bks.). (Illus.). (YA). (gr. 3-12). 1994. pap. 19.95 (*1-55609-093-5*); lib. bdg. 29.95 (*1-55609-569-4*); disk 29.95 (*0-7933-1526-3*) Gallopade Intl.
Let's Quilt Idaho & Stuff It Topographically! Carole Marsh. (Carole Marsh Idaho Bks.). (Illus.). (YA). (gr. 3-12). 1994. pap. 19.95 (*1-55609-139-7*); lib. bdg. 29.95 (*1-55609-584-8*); disk 29.95 (*0-7933-1545-X*) Gallopade Intl.
Let's Quilt Illinois & Stuff It Topographically! Carole Marsh. (Carole Marsh Illinois Bks.). (Illus.). (YA). (gr. 3-12). 1994. pap. 19.95 (*1-55609-097-8*); lib. bdg. 29.95 (*1-55609-408-6*); disk 29.95 (*0-7933-1585-9*) Gallopade Intl.
Let's Quilt Indiana & Stuff It Topographically! Carole Marsh. (Carole Marsh Indiana Bks.). (Illus.). (YA). (gr. 3-12). 1994. pap. 19.95 (*1-55609-096-X*); lib. bdg. 29.95 (*1-55609-429-9*); disk 29.95 (*0-7933-1604-9*) Gallopade Intl.
Let's Quilt Iowa & Stuff It Topographically! Carole Marsh. (Carole Marsh Iowa Bks.). (Illus.). (YA). (gr. 3-12). 1994. pap. 19.95 (*1-55609-072-2*); lib. bdg. 29.95 (*1-55609-451-5*); disk 29.95 (*0-7933-1623-5*) Gallopade Intl.
Let's Quilt Kansas & Stuff It Topographically! Carole Marsh. (Carol Marsh Kansas Bks.). (J). (gr. 3-12). 1994. pap. 19.95 (*1-55609-357-8*); lib. bdg. 29.95 (*1-55609-356-X*); disk 29.95 (*1-55609-358-6*) Gallopade Intl.
Let's Quilt Louisiana & Stuff It Topographically! Carole Marsh. (Carole Marsh Louisiana Bks.). (Illus.). (J). (gr. 3-8). 1994. pap. 19.95 (*1-55609-075-7*); lib. bdg. 29.95 (*1-55609-397-7*); disk 29.95 (*0-7933-1664-2*) Gallopade Intl.
Let's Quilt Maine & Stuff It Topographically! Carole Marsh. (Carole Marsh Maine Bks.). (Illus.). (J). (gr. 3-8). 1994. pap. 19.95 (*1-55609-068-4*); lib. bdg. 29.95 (*1-55609-599-6*); disk 29.95 (*1-55609-601-1*) Gallopade Intl.
Let's Quilt Maryland & Stuff It Topographically! Carole Marsh. (Carole Marsh Maryland Bks.). (Illus.). (J). (gr. 3-8). 1994. pap. 19.95 (*1-55609-058-7*); lib. bdg. 29.95 (*1-55609-622-4*); disk 29.95 (*1-55609-623-2*) Gallopade Intl.
Let's Quilt Massachusetts & Stuff It Topographically! Carole Marsh. (Carole Marsh Massachusetts Bks.). (Illus.). (J). (gr. 3-8). 1994. pap. 19.95 (*1-55609-685-2*); lib. bdg. 29.95 (*1-55609-684-4*); disk 29.95 (*1-55609-686-0*) Gallopade Intl.
Let's Quilt Michigan & Stuff It Topographically! Carole Marsh. (Carole Marsh Michigan Bks.). (Illus.). (J). (gr. 3 up). 1994. pap. 19.95 (*1-55609-138-9*); lib. bdg. 29.95 (*1-55609-669-0*); disk 29.95 (*1-55609-670-4*) Gallopade Intl.
Let's Quilt Minnesota & Stuff It Topographically! Carole Marsh. (Carole Marsh Minnesota Bks.). (Illus.). (J). (gr. 3 up). 1994. pap. 19.95 (*1-55609-099-4*); lib. bdg. 29.95 (*1-55609-645-3*); disk 29.95 (*1-55609-647-X*) Gallopade Intl.
Let's Quilt Mississippi & Stuff It Topographically! Carole Marsh. (Carole Marsh Mississippi Bks.). (Illus.). (J). (gr. 3 up). 1994. pap. 19.95 (*1-55609-074-9*); lib. bdg. 29.95 (*1-55609-710-7*); disk 29.95 (*1-55609-716-6*) Gallopade Intl.
Let's Quilt Missouri & Stuff It Topographically! Carole Marsh. (Carole Marsh Missouri Bks.). (Illus.). (J). (gr. 3 up). 1994. pap. 19.95 (*1-55609-734-4*); lib. bdg. 29.95 (*1-55609-733-6*); disk 29.95 (*1-55609-735-2*) Gallopade Intl.
Let's Quilt Montana & Stuff It Topographically! Carole Marsh. (Carole Marsh Montana Bks.). (Illus.). (J). (gr. 3 up). 1994. pap. 19.95 (*1-55609-131-1*); lib. bdg. 29.95 (*1-55609-757-3*); disk 29.95 (*1-55609-759-X*) Gallopade Intl.
Let's Quilt Nebraska & Stuff It Topographically! Carole Marsh. (Carole Marsh Nebraska Bks.). (Illus.). (J). (gr. 3 up). 1994. lib. bdg. 29.95 (*1-55609-781-6*); disk 29.95 (*1-55609-783-2*) Gallopade Intl.
Let's Quilt Nebraska & Stuff It Topographically! Carole Marsh. (Carole Marsh Nebraska Bks.). (Illus.). (J). (gr. 3 up). 1997. pap. 19.95 (*1-55609-779-4*) Gallopade Intl.
Let's Quilt Nevada & Stuff It Topographically! Carole Marsh. (Carole Marsh Nevada Bks.). (Illus.). (J). 1994. pap. 19.95 (*1-55609-130-3*); lib. bdg. 29.95 (*1-55609-805-7*); disk 29.95 (*1-55609-807-3*) Gallopade Intl.
Let's Quilt New Hampshire & Stuff It Topographically! Carole Marsh. (Carole Marsh New Hampshire Bks.). (Illus.). (J). 1994. pap. 19.95 (*1-55609-067-6*); lib. bdg. 29.95 (*1-55609-829-4*); disk 29.95 (*1-55609-831-6*) Gallopade Intl.
Let's Quilt New Jersey & Stuff It Topographically! Carole Marsh. (Carole Marsh New Jersey Bks.). (Illus.). (J). 1994. pap. 19.95 (*1-55609-069-2*); lib. bdg. 29.95 (*1-55609-853-7*); disk 29.95 (*1-55609-855-3*) Gallopade Intl.

An Asterisk (*) at the beginning of an entry indicates that the title is appearing for the first time.

Let's Quilt New Mexico & Stuff It Topographically! Carole Marsh. (Carole Marsh New Mexico Bks.). (Illus.). (J). 1994. pap. 19.95 (*1-55609-127-3*); lib. bdg. 29.95 (*1-55609-877-4*); disk 29.95 (*1-55609-879-0*) Gallopade Intl.

Let's Quilt New York & Stuff It Topographically! Carole Marsh. (Carole Marsh New York Bks.). (Illus.). (J). 1994. pap. 19.95 (*1-55609-060-9*); lib. bdg. 29.95 (*1-55609-904-5*); disk 29.95 (*1-55609-905-3*) Gallopade Intl.

Let's Quilt North Carolina & Stuff It Topographically! Carole Marsh. (Carole Marsh North Carolina Bks.). (Illus.). (J). 1994. pap. 19.95 (*1-55609-050-1*); lib. bdg. 29.95 (*1-55609-925-8*); disk 29.95 (*1-55609-926-6*) Gallopade Intl.

Let's Quilt North Dakota & Stuff It Topographically! Carole Marsh. (Carole Marsh North Dakota Bks.). (Illus.). (J). 1994. pap. 19.95 (*1-55609-135-4*); lib. bdg. 29.95 (*1-55609-946-0*); disk 29.95 (*1-55609-947-9*) Gallopade Intl.

Let's Quilt Ohio & Stuff It Topographically! Carole Marsh. (Carole Marsh Ohio Bks.). (Illus.). (J). 1994. pap. 19.95 (*1-55609-095-1*); disk 29.95 (*1-55609-985-1*) Gallopade Intl.

Let's Quilt Ohio & Stuff It Topographically! Carole Marsh. (Carole Marsh Ohio Bks.). (Illus.). (J). 1997. lib. bdg. 29.95 (*1-55609-984-3*) Gallopade Intl.

Let's Quilt Oklahoma & Stuff It Topographically! Carole Marsh. (Carole Marsh Oklahoma Bks.). (Illus.). (J). 1994. pap. 19.95 (*0-7933-1861-0*); lib. bdg. 29.95 (*0-7933-1860-2*); disk 29.95 (*0-7933-1862-9*) Gallopade Intl.

Let's Quilt Oregon & Stuff It Topographically! Carole Marsh. (Carole Marsh Oregon Bks.). (Illus.). (J). 1994. pap. 19.95 (*1-55609-132-X*); lib. bdg. 29.95 (*0-7933-1893-9*); disk 29.95 (*0-7933-1894-7*) Gallopade Intl.

Let's Quilt Our Alabama County. Carole Marsh. (Carole Marsh Alabama Bks.). (J). 1994. pap. text 19.95 (*0-7933-6935-5*); lib. bdg. 29.95 (*0-7933-6936-3*); disk 29.95 (*0-7933-6937-1*) Gallopade Intl.

Let's Quilt Our Alabama Town. Carole Marsh. (Carole Marsh Alabama Bks.). (J). 1994. pap. text 19.95 (*0-7933-6932-0*); lib. bdg. 29.95 (*0-7933-6933-9*); disk 29.95 (*0-7933-6934-7*) Gallopade Intl.

Let's Quilt Our Alaska County. Carole Marsh. (Carole Marsh Alaska Bks.). (J). 1994. pap. text 19.95 (*0-7933-7117-1*); lib. bdg. 29.95 (*0-7933-7116-3*); disk 29.95 (*0-7933-7118-X*) Gallopade Intl.

Let's Quilt Our Alaska Town. Carole Marsh. (Carole Marsh Alaska Bks.). (J). 1994. pap. text 19.95 (*0-7933-6967-3*); lib. bdg. 29.95 (*0-685-60854-9*); disk 29.95 (*0-7933-6968-1*) Gallopade Intl.

Let's Quilt Our Arizona County. Carole Marsh. (Carole Marsh Arizona Bks.). (J). 1994. pap. text 19.95 (*0-7933-7120-1*); lib. bdg. 29.95 (*0-7933-7119-8*); disk 29.95 (*0-7933-7121-X*) Gallopade Intl.

Let's Quilt Our Arizona Town. Carole Marsh. (Carole Marsh Arizona Bks.). (J). 1994. pap. text 19.95 (*0-7933-6970-3*); lib. bdg. 29.95 (*0-7933-6969-X*); disk 29.95 (*0-7933-6971-1*) Gallopade Intl.

Let's Quilt Our Arkansas County. Carole Marsh. (Carole Marsh Arkansas Bks.). (J). 1994. pap. text 19.95 (*0-7933-7123-6*); lib. bdg. 29.95 (*0-7933-7122-8*); disk 29.95 (*0-7933-7124-4*) Gallopade Intl.

Let's Quilt Our Arkansas Town. Carole Marsh. (Carole Marsh Arkansas Bks.). (J). 1994. pap. text 19.95 (*0-7933-6973-8*); lib. bdg. 29.95 (*0-7933-6972-X*); disk 29.95 (*0-7933-6974-6*) Gallopade Intl.

Let's Quilt Our Black Heritage. Carole Marsh. (Our Black Heritage Ser.). 1994. 29.95 (*1-55609-324-1*); pap. 19.95 (*1-55609-323-3*); disk 29.95 (*1-55609-325-X*) Gallopade Intl.

Let's Quilt Our California County. Carole Marsh. (Carole Marsh California Bks.). (J). 1994. pap. text 19.95 (*0-7933-7126-0*); lib. bdg. 29.95 (*0-7933-7125-2*); disk 29.95 (*0-7933-7127-9*) Gallopade Intl.

Let's Quilt Our California Town. Carole Marsh. (Carole Marsh California Bks.). (J). 1994. pap. text 19.95 (*0-7933-6976-2*); lib. bdg. 29.95 (*0-7933-6975-4*); disk 29.95 (*0-7933-6977-0*) Gallopade Intl.

Let's Quilt Our Colorado County. Carole Marsh. (Carole Marsh Colorado Bks.). (J). 1994. pap. text 19.95 (*0-7933-7129-5*); lib. bdg. 29.95 (*0-7933-7128-7*); disk 29.95 (*0-7933-7130-9*) Gallopade Intl.

Let's Quilt Our Colorado Town. Carole Marsh. (Carole Marsh Colorado Bks.). (J). 1994. pap. text 19.95 (*0-7933-6979-7*); lib. bdg. 29.95 (*0-7933-6978-9*); disk 29.95 (*0-7933-6980-0*) Gallopade Intl.

Let's Quilt Our Connecticut County. Carole Marsh. (Carole Marsh Connecticut Bks.). (J). 1994. pap. text 19.95 (*0-7933-7132-5*); lib. bdg. 29.95 (*0-7933-7131-7*); disk 29.95 (*0-7933-7133-3*) Gallopade Intl.

Let's Quilt Our Connecticut Town. Carole Marsh. (Carole Marsh Connecticut Bks.). (J). 1994. pap. text 19.95 (*0-7933-6982-7*); lib. bdg. 29.95 (*0-7933-6981-9*); disk 29.95 (*0-7933-6983-5*) Gallopade Intl.

Let's Quilt Our Delaware County. Carole Marsh. (Carole Marsh Delaware Bks.). (J). 1994. pap. text 19.95 (*0-7933-7135-X*); lib. bdg. 29.95 (*0-7933-7134-1*); disk 29.95 (*0-7933-7136-8*) Gallopade Intl.

Let's Quilt Our Delaware Town. Carole Marsh. (Carole Marsh Delaware Bks.). (J). 1994. pap. text 19.95 (*0-7933-6985-1*); lib. bdg. 29.95 (*0-7933-6984-3*); disk 29.95 (*0-7933-6986-X*) Gallopade Intl.

Let's Quilt Our Florida County. Carole Marsh. (Carole Marsh Florida Bks.). (J). 1994. pap. text 19.95 (*0-7933-7141-4*); lib. bdg. 29.95 (*0-7933-7140-6*); disk 29.95 (*0-7933-7142-2*) Gallopade Intl.

Let's Quilt Our Florida Town. Carole Marsh. (Carole Marsh Florida Bks.). (J). 1994. pap. text 19.95 (*0-7933-6991-6*); lib. bdg. 29.95 (*0-7933-6990-8*); disk 29.95 (*0-7933-6992-4*) Gallopade Intl.

Let's Quilt Our Georgia County. Carole Marsh. (Carole Marsh Georgia Bks.). (J). 1994. pap. text 19.95 (*0-7933-7144-9*); lib. bdg. 29.95 (*0-7933-7143-0*); disk 29.95 (*0-7933-7145-7*) Gallopade Intl.

Let's Quilt Our Georgia Town. Carole Marsh. (Carole Marsh Georgia Bks.). (J). 1994. pap. text 19.95 (*0-7933-6994-0*); lib. bdg. 29.95 (*0-7933-6993-2*); disk 29.95 (*0-7933-6995-9*) Gallopade Intl.

Let's Quilt Our Hawaii County. Carole Marsh. (Carole Marsh Hawaii Bks.). (J). 1994. pap. text 19.95 (*0-7933-7147-3*); lib. bdg. 29.95 (*0-7933-7146-5*); disk 29.95 (*0-7933-7148-1*) Gallopade Intl.

Let's Quilt Our Hawaii Town. Carole Marsh. (Carole Marsh Hawaii Bks.). (J). 1994. pap. text 19.95 (*0-7933-6997-5*); lib. bdg. 29.95 (*0-7933-6996-7*); disk 29.95 (*0-7933-6998-3*) Gallopade Intl.

Let's Quilt Our Idaho County. Carole Marsh. (Carole Marsh Idaho Bks.). (J). 1994. pap. text 19.95 (*0-7933-7150-3*); lib. bdg. 29.95 (*0-7933-7149-X*); disk 29.95 (*0-7933-7151-1*) Gallopade Intl.

Let's Quilt Our Idaho Town. Carole Marsh. (Carole Marsh Idaho Bks.). (J). 1994. pap. text 19.95 (*0-7933-7000-0*); lib. bdg. 29.95 (*0-7933-6999-1*); disk 29.95 (*0-7933-7001-9*) Gallopade Intl.

Let's Quilt Our Illinois County. Carole Marsh. (Carole Marsh Illinois Bks.). (J). 1994. pap. text 19.95 (*0-7933-7153-8*); lib. bdg. 29.95 (*0-7933-7152-X*); disk 29.95 (*0-7933-7154-6*) Gallopade Intl.

Let's Quilt Our Illinois Town. Carole Marsh. (Carole Marsh Illinois Bks.). (J). 1994. pap. text 19.95 (*0-7933-7003-5*); lib. bdg. 29.95 (*0-7933-7002-7*); disk 29.95 (*0-7933-7004-3*) Gallopade Intl.

Let's Quilt Our Indiana County. Carole Marsh. (Carole Marsh Indiana Bks.). (J). 1994. pap. text 14.95 (*0-7933-7156-2*); lib. bdg. 29.95 (*0-7933-7155-4*); disk 29.95 (*0-7933-7157-0*) Gallopade Intl.

Let's Quilt Our Indiana Town. Carole Marsh. (Carole Marsh Indiana Bks.). (J). 1994. pap. text 19.95 (*0-7933-7006-X*); lib. bdg. 29.95 (*0-7933-7005-1*); disk 29.95 (*0-7933-7007-8*) Gallopade Intl.

Let's Quilt Our Iowa County. Carole Marsh. (Carole Marsh Iowa Bks.). (J). 1994. pap. text 19.95 (*0-7933-7159-7*); lib. bdg. 29.95 (*0-7933-7158-9*); disk 29.95 (*0-7933-7160-0*) Gallopade Intl.

Let's Quilt Our Iowa Town. Carole Marsh. (Carole Marsh Iowa Bks.). (J). 1994. pap. text 19.95 (*0-7933-7009-4*); lib. bdg. 29.95 (*0-7933-7008-6*); disk 29.95 (*0-7933-7010-8*) Gallopade Intl.

Let's Quilt Our Kansas County. Carole Marsh. (Carole Marsh Kansas Bks.). (J). 1994. pap. text 19.95 (*0-7933-7162-7*); lib. bdg. 29.95 (*0-7933-7161-9*); disk 29.95 (*0-7933-7163-5*) Gallopade Intl.

Let's Quilt Our Kansas Town. Carole Marsh. (Carole Marsh Kansas Bks.). (J). 1994. pap. text 19.95 (*0-7933-7012-4*); lib. bdg. 29.95 (*0-7933-7011-6*); disk 29.95 (*0-7933-7013-2*) Gallopade Intl.

Let's Quilt Our Kentucky County. Carole Marsh. (Carole Marsh Kentucky Bks.). (J). 1994. pap. text 19.95 (*0-7933-7165-1*); lib. bdg. 29.95 (*0-7933-7164-3*); disk 29.95 (*0-7933-7166-X*) Gallopade Intl.

Let's Quilt Our Kentucky Town. Carole Marsh. (Carole Marsh Kentucky Bks.). (J). 1994. pap. text 19.95 (*0-7933-7015-9*); lib. bdg. 29.95 (*0-7933-7014-0*); disk 29.95 (*0-7933-7016-7*) Gallopade Intl.

Let's Quilt Our Louisiana Parish. Carole Marsh. (Carole Marsh Louisiana Bks.). (J). 1994. pap. text 19.95 (*0-7933-7168-6*); lib. bdg. 29.95 (*0-7933-7167-8*); disk 29.95 (*0-7933-7169-4*) Gallopade Intl.

Let's Quilt Our Louisiana Town. Carole Marsh. (Carole Marsh Louisiana Bks.). (J). 1994. pap. text 19.95 (*0-7933-7018-3*); lib. bdg. 29.95 (*0-7933-7017-5*); disk 29.95 (*0-7933-7019-1*) Gallopade Intl.

Let's Quilt Our Maine County. Carole Marsh. (Carole Marsh Maine Bks.). (J). 1994. pap. text 19.95 (*0-7933-7171-6*); lib. bdg. 29.95 (*0-7933-7170-8*); disk 29.95 (*0-7933-7172-4*) Gallopade Intl.

Let's Quilt Our Maine Town. Carole Marsh. (Carole Marsh Maine Bks.). (J). 1994. pap. text 19.95 (*0-7933-7021-3*); lib. bdg. 29.95 (*0-7933-7020-5*); disk 29.95 (*0-7933-7022-1*) Gallopade Intl.

Let's Quilt Our Maryland County. Carole Marsh. (Carole Marsh Maryland Bks.). (J). 1994. pap. text 19.95 (*0-7933-7174-0*); lib. bdg. 29.95 (*0-7933-7173-2*); disk 29.95 (*0-7933-7175-9*) Gallopade Intl.

Let's Quilt Our Maryland Town. Carole Marsh. (Carole Marsh Maryland Bks.). (J). 1994. pap. text 19.95 (*0-7933-7024-8*); lib. bdg. 29.95 (*0-7933-7023-X*); disk 29.95 (*0-7933-7025-6*) Gallopade Intl.

Let's Quilt Our Massachusetts County. Carole Marsh. (Massachuseets Bks.). (J). 1994. pap. text 19.95 (*0-7933-7177-5*); lib. bdg. 29.95 (*0-7933-7176-7*); disk 29.95 (*0-7933-7178-3*) Gallopade Intl.

Let's Quilt Our Massachusetts Town. Carole Marsh. (Massachuseets Bks.). (J). 1994. pap. text 19.95 (*0-7933-7027-2*); lib. bdg. 29.95 (*0-7933-7026-4*); disk 29.95 (*0-7933-7028-0*) Gallopade Intl.

Let's Quilt Our Michigan County. Carole Marsh. (Carole Marsh Michigan Bks.). (J). 1994. pap. text 19.95 (*0-7933-7180-5*); lib. bdg. 29.95 (*0-7933-7179-1*); disk 29.95 (*0-7933-7181-3*) Gallopade Intl.

Let's Quilt Our Michigan Town. Carole Marsh. (Carole Marsh Michigan Bks.). (J). 1994. pap. text 19.95 (*0-7933-7030-2*); lib. bdg. 29.95 (*0-7933-7029-9*); disk 29.95 (*0-7933-7031-0*) Gallopade Intl.

Let's Quilt Our Minnesota County. Carole Marsh. (Carole Marsh Minnesota Bks.). (J). 1994. pap. text 19.95 (*0-7933-7183-X*); lib. bdg. 29.95 (*0-7933-7182-1*); disk 29.95 (*0-7933-7184-8*) Gallopade Intl.

Let's Quilt Our Minnesota Town. Carole Marsh. (Carole Marsh Minnesota Bks.). (J). 1994. pap. text 19.95 (*0-7933-7033-7*); lib. bdg. 29.95 (*0-7933-7032-9*); disk 29.95 (*0-7933-7034-5*) Gallopade Intl.

Let's Quilt Our Mississippi County. Carole Marsh. (Carole Marsh Mississippi Bks.). (J). 1994. pap. text 19.95 (*0-7933-7186-4*); lib. bdg. 29.95 (*0-7933-7185-6*); disk 29.95 (*0-7933-7187-2*) Gallopade Intl.

Let's Quilt Our Mississippi Town. Carole Marsh. (Carole Marsh Mississippi Bks.). (J). 1994. pap. text 19.95 (*0-7933-7036-1*); lib. bdg. 29.95 (*0-7933-7035-3*); disk 29.95 (*0-7933-7037-X*) Gallopade Intl.

Let's Quilt Our Missouri County. Carole Marsh. (Carole Marsh Missouri Bks.). (J). 1994. pap. text 19.95 (*0-7933-7189-9*); lib. bdg. 29.95 (*0-7933-7188-0*); disk 29.95 (*0-7933-7190-2*) Gallopade Intl.

Let's Quilt Our Missouri Town. Carole Marsh. (Carole Marsh Missouri Bks.). (J). 1994. pap. text 19.95 (*0-7933-7039-6*); lib. bdg. 29.95 (*0-7933-7038-8*); disk 29.95 (*0-7933-7040-X*) Gallopade Intl.

Let's Quilt Our Montana County. Carole Marsh. (Carole Marsh Montana Bks.). (J). 1994. pap. text 19.95 (*0-7933-7192-9*); lib. bdg. 29.95 (*0-7933-7191-0*); disk 29.95 (*0-7933-7193-7*) Gallopade Intl.

Let's Quilt Our Montana Town. Carole Marsh. (Carole Marsh Montana Bks.). (J). 1994. pap. text 19.95 (*0-7933-7042-6*); lib. bdg. 29.95 (*0-7933-7041-8*); disk 29.95 (*0-7933-7043-4*) Gallopade Intl.

Let's Quilt Our Nebraska County. Carole Marsh. (Carole Marsh Nebraska Bks.). (J). 1994. pap. text 19.95 (*0-7933-7195-3*); lib. bdg. 29.95 (*0-7933-7194-5*); disk 29.95 (*0-7933-7196-1*) Gallopade Intl.

Let's Quilt Our Nebraska Town. Carole Marsh. (Carole Marsh Nebraska Bks.). (J). 1994. pap. text 19.95 (*0-7933-7045-0*); lib. bdg. 29.95 (*0-7933-7044-2*); disk 29.95 (*0-7933-7046-9*) Gallopade Intl.

Let's Quilt Our Nevada County. Carole Marsh. (Carole Marsh Nevada Bks.). (J). 1994. pap. text 19.95 (*0-7933-7198-8*); lib. bdg. 29.95 (*0-7933-7197-X*); disk 29.95 (*0-7933-7199-6*) Gallopade Intl.

Let's Quilt Our Nevada Town. Carole Marsh. (Carole Marsh Nevada Bks.). (J). 1994. pap. text 19.95 (*0-7933-7048-5*); lib. bdg. 29.95 (*0-7933-7047-7*); disk 29.95 (*0-7933-7049-3*) Gallopade Intl.

Let's Quilt Our New Hampshire County. Carole Marsh. (Carole Marsh New Hampshire Bks.). (J). 1994. pap. text 19.95 (*0-7933-7201-1*); lib. bdg. 29.95 (*0-7933-7200-3*) Gallopade Intl.

Let's Quilt Our New Hampshire County. Carole Marsh. (Carole Marsh New Hampshire Bks.). (J). 1997. disk 29.95 (*0-7933-7202-X*) Gallopade Intl.

Let's Quilt Our New Hampshire Town. Carole Marsh. (Carole Marsh New Hampshire Bks.). (J). 1994. pap. text 19.95 (*0-7933-7051-5*); lib. bdg. 29.95 (*0-7933-7050-7*); disk 29.95 (*0-7933-7052-3*) Gallopade Intl.

Let's Quilt Our New Jersey County. Carole Marsh. (Carole Marsh New Jersey Bks.). (J). 1994. pap. text 19.95 (*0-7933-7204-6*); lib. bdg. 29.95 (*0-7933-7203-8*); disk 29.95 (*0-7933-7205-4*) Gallopade Intl.

Let's Quilt Our New Jersey Town. Carole Marsh. (Carole Marsh New Jersey Bks.). (J). 1994. pap. text 19.95 (*0-7933-7054-X*); lib. bdg. 29.95 (*0-7933-7053-1*); disk 29.95 (*0-7933-7055-8*) Gallopade Intl.

Let's Quilt Our New Mexico County. Carole Marsh. (Carole Marsh New Mexico Bks.). (J). 1994. pap. text 19.95 (*0-7933-7207-0*); lib. bdg. 29.95 (*0-7933-7206-2*); disk 29.95 (*0-7933-7208-9*) Gallopade Intl.

Let's Quilt Our New Mexico Town. Carole Marsh. (Carole Marsh New Mexico Bks.). (J). 1994. pap. text 19.95 (*0-7933-7057-4*); lib. bdg. 29.95 (*0-7933-7056-6*); disk 29.95 (*0-7933-7058-2*) Gallopade Intl.

Let's Quilt Our New York County. Carole Marsh. (Carole Marsh New York Bks.). (J). 1994. pap. text 19.95 (*0-7933-7210-0*); lib. bdg. 29.95 (*0-7933-7209-7*); disk 29.95 (*0-7933-7211-9*) Gallopade Intl.

Let's Quilt Our New York Town. Carole Marsh. (Carole Marsh New York Bks.). (J). 1994. pap. text 19.95 (*0-7933-7060-4*); lib. bdg. 29.95 (*0-7933-7059-0*); disk 29.95 (*0-7933-7061-2*) Gallopade Intl.

Let's Quilt Our North Carolina County. Carole Marsh. (Carole Marsh North Carolina Bks.). (J). 1994. pap. text 19.95 (*0-7933-7213-5*); lib. bdg. 29.95 (*0-7933-7212-7*); disk 29.95 (*0-7933-7214-3*) Gallopade Intl.

Let's Quilt Our North Carolina Town. Carole Marsh. (Carole Marsh North Carolina Bks.). (J). 1994. pap. text 19.95 (*0-7933-7063-9*); lib. bdg. 29.95 (*0-7933-7062-0*); disk 29.95 (*0-7933-7064-7*) Gallopade Intl.

Let's Quilt Our North Dakota County. Carole Marsh. (Carole Marsh North Dakota Bks.). (J). 1994. pap. text 19.95 (*0-7933-7216-X*); lib. bdg. 29.95 (*0-7933-7215-1*); disk 29.95 (*0-7933-7217-8*) Gallopade Intl.

Let's Quilt Our North Dakota Town. Carole Marsh. (Carole Marsh North Dakota Bks.). (J). 1994. pap. text 19.95 (*0-7933-7066-3*); lib. bdg. 29.95 (*0-7933-7065-5*); disk 29.95 (*0-7933-7067-1*) Gallopade Intl.

Let's Quilt Our Ohio County. Carole Marsh. (Carole Marsh Ohio Bks.). (J). 1994. pap. text 19.95 (*0-7933-7219-4*); lib. bdg. 29.95 (*0-7933-7218-6*); disk 29.95 (*0-7933-7220-8*) Gallopade Intl.

Let's Quilt Our Ohio Town. Carole Marsh. (Carole Marsh Ohio Bks.). (J). 1994. pap. text 19.95 (*0-7933-7069-8*); lib. bdg. 29.95 (*0-7933-7068-X*); disk 29.95 (*0-7933-7070-1*) Gallopade Intl.

Let's Quilt Our Oklahoma County. Carole Marsh. (Oklahoma Bks.). (J). 1994. pap. text 19.95 (*0-7933-7222-4*); lib. bdg. 29.95 (*0-7933-7221-6*); disk 29.95 (*0-7933-7223-2*) Gallopade Intl.

Let's Quilt Our Oklahoma Town. Carole Marsh. (Carole Marsh Oklahoma Bks.). (J). 1994. pap. text 19.95 (*0-7933-7072-8*); lib. bdg. 29.95 (*0-7933-7071-X*); disk 29.95 (*0-7933-7073-6*) Gallopade Intl.

Let's Quilt Our Oregon County. Carole Marsh. (Oregon Bks.). (J). 1994. pap. text 19.95 (*0-7933-7225-9*); lib. bdg. 29.95 (*0-7933-7224-0*); disk 29.95 (*0-7933-7226-7*) Gallopade Intl.

Let's Quilt Our Oregon Town. Carole Marsh. (Carole Marsh Oregon Bks.). (J). 1994. pap. text 19.95 (*0-7933-7075-2*); lib. bdg. 29.95 (*0-7933-7074-4*); disk 29.95 (*0-7933-7076-0*) Gallopade Intl.

Let's Quilt Our Pennsylvania County. Carole Marsh. (Pennsylvania Bks.). (J). 1994. pap. text 19.95 (*0-7933-7228-3*); lib. bdg. 29.95 (*0-7933-7227-5*); disk 29.95 (*0-7933-7229-1*) Gallopade Intl.

Let's Quilt Our Pennsylvania Town. Carole Marsh. (Carole Marsh Pennsylvania Bks.). (J). 1994. pap. text 19.95 (*0-7933-7078-7*); lib. bdg. 29.95 (*0-7933-7077-9*); disk 29.95 (*0-7933-7079-5*) Gallopade Intl.

Let's Quilt Our Rhode Island County. Carole Marsh. (Rhode Island Bks.). (J). 1994. pap. text 19.95 (*0-7933-7231-3*); lib. bdg. 29.95 (*0-7933-7230-5*); disk 29.95 (*0-7933-7232-1*) Gallopade Intl.

Let's Quilt Our Rhode Island Town. Carole Marsh. (Carole Marsh Rhode Island Bks.). (J). 1994. pap. text 19.95 (*0-7933-7081-7*); lib. bdg. 29.95 (*0-7933-7080-9*); disk 29.95 (*0-7933-7082-5*) Gallopade Intl.

Let's Quilt Our South Carolina County. Carole Marsh. (South Carolina Bks.). (J). 1994. pap. text 19.95 (*0-7933-7234-8*); lib. bdg. 29.95 (*0-7933-7233-X*); disk 29.95 (*0-7933-7235-6*) Gallopade Intl.

Let's Quilt Our South Carolina Town. Carole Marsh. (Carole Marsh South Carolina Town). (J). 1994. pap. text 19.95 (*0-7933-7084-1*); lib. bdg. 29.95 (*0-7933-7083-3*); disk 29.95 (*0-7933-7085-X*) Gallopade Intl.

Let's Quilt Our South Dakota County. Carole Marsh. (South Dakota Bks.). (J). 1994. pap. text 19.95 (*0-7933-7237-2*); lib. bdg. 29.95 (*0-7933-7236-4*); disk 29.95 (*0-7933-7238-0*) Gallopade Intl.

Let's Quilt Our South Dakota Town. Carole Marsh. (Carole Marsh South Carolina Bks.). (J). 1994. pap. text 19.95 (*0-7933-7087-6*); lib. bdg. 29.95 (*0-7933-7086-8*); disk 29.95 (*0-7933-7088-4*) Gallopade Intl.

Let's Quilt Our Tennessee County. Carole Marsh. (Tennessee Bks.). (J). 1994. pap. text 19.95 (*0-7933-7240-2*); lib. bdg. 29.95 (*0-7933-7239-9*); disk 29.95 (*0-7933-7241-0*) Gallopade Intl.

Let's Quilt Our Tennessee Town. Carole Marsh. (Carole Marsh Tennessee Bks.). (J). 1994. pap. text 19.95 (*0-7933-7090-6*); lib. bdg. 29.95 (*0-7933-7089-2*); disk 29.95 (*0-7933-7091-4*) Gallopade Intl.

Let's Quilt Our Texas County. Carole Marsh. (Texas Bks.). (J). 1994. pap. text 19.95 (*0-7933-7243-7*); lib. bdg. 29.95 (*0-7933-7242-9*); disk 29.95 (*0-7933-7244-5*) Gallopade Intl.

Let's Quilt Our Texas Town. Carole Marsh. (Carole Marsh Texas Bks.). (J). 1994. pap. text 19.95 (*0-7933-7093-0*); lib. bdg. 29.95 (*0-7933-7092-2*); disk 29.95 (*0-7933-7094-9*) Gallopade Intl.

Let's Quilt Our Utah County. Carole Marsh. (Utah Bks.). (J). 1994. pap. text 19.95 (*0-7933-7246-1*); lib. bdg. 29.95 (*0-7933-7245-3*); disk 29.95 (*0-7933-7247-X*) Gallopade Intl.

Let's Quilt Our Utah Town. Carole Marsh. (Carole Marsh Utah Bks.). (J). 1994. pap. text 19.95 (*0-7933-7096-5*); lib. bdg. 29.95 (*0-7933-7095-7*); disk 29.95 (*0-7933-7097-3*) Gallopade Intl.

Let's Quilt Our Vermont County. Carole Marsh. (Vermont Bks.). (J). 1994. pap. text 19.95 (*0-7933-7249-6*); lib. bdg. 29.95 (*0-7933-7248-8*); disk 29.95 (*0-7933-7250-X*) Gallopade Intl.

Let's Quilt Our Vermont Town. Carole Marsh. (Carole Marsh Vermont Bks.). (J). 1994. pap. text 19.95 (*0-7933-7099-X*); lib. bdg. 29.95 (*0-7933-7098-1*); disk 29.95 (*0-7933-7100-7*) Gallopade Intl.

Let's Quilt Our Virginia County. Carole Marsh. (Virginia Bks.). (J). 1992. pap. text 19.95 (*0-7933-7252-6*); lib. bdg. 29.95 (*0-7933-7251-8*); disk 29.95 (*0-7933-7253-4*) Gallopade Intl.

Let's Quilt Our Virginia Town. Carole Marsh. (Carole Marsh Virginia Bks.). (J). 1994. pap. text 19.95 (*0-7933-7102-3*); lib. bdg. 29.95 (*0-7933-7101-5*); disk 29.95 (*0-7933-7103-1*) Gallopade Intl.

Let's Quilt Our Washington County. Carole Marsh. (Washington Bks.). (J). 1994. pap. text 19.95 (*0-7933-7255-0*); lib. bdg. 29.95 (*0-7933-7254-2*); disk 29.95 (*0-7933-7256-9*) Gallopade Intl.

Let's Quilt Our Washington Town. Carole Marsh. (Carol Marsh Washington Bks.). (J). 1994. pap. text 19.95 (*0-7933-7105-8*); lib. bdg. 29.95 (*0-7933-7104-X*); disk 29.95 (*0-7933-7106-6*) Gallopade Intl.

Let's Quilt Our West Virginia County. Carole Marsh. (West Virginia Bks.). (J). 1994. pap. text 19.95 (*0-7933-7258-5*); lib. bdg. 29.95 (*0-7933-7257-7*); disk 29.95 (*0-7933-7259-3*) Gallopade Intl.

Let's Quilt Our West Virginia Town. Carole Marsh. (Carole Marsh West Virginia Bks.). (J). 1994. pap. text 19.95 (*0-7933-7108-2*); lib. bdg. 29.95 (*0-7933-7107-4*); disk 29.95 (*0-7933-7109-0*) Gallopade Intl.

Let's Quilt Our Wisconsin County. Carole Marsh. (Wisconsin Bks.). (J). 1994. pap. text 19.95 (*0-7933-7261-5*); lib. bdg. 29.95 (*0-7933-7260-7*); disk 29.95 (*0-7933-7262-3*) Gallopade Intl.

Let's Quilt Our Wisconsin Town. Carole Marsh. (Carole Marsh Wisconsin Bks.). (J). 1994. pap. text 19.95 (*0-7933-7111-2*); lib. bdg. 29.95 (*0-7933-7110-4*); disk 29.95 (*0-7933-7112-0*) Gallopade Intl.

Let's Quilt Our Wyoming County. Carole Marsh. (Wyoming Bks.). (J). 1994. pap. text 19.95 (*0-7933-7264-X*); lib. bdg. 29.95 (*0-7933-7263-1*); disk 29.95 (*0-7933-7265-8*) Gallopade Intl.

Let's Quilt Our Wyoming Town. Carole Marsh. (Carole Marsh Wyoming Bks.). (J). 1994. pap. text 19.95 (*0-7933-7114-7*); lib. bdg. 29.95 (*0-7933-7113-9*); disk 29.95 (*0-7933-7115-5*) Gallopade Intl.

L

L

Let's Quilt Pennsylvania & Stuff It Topographically! Carole Marsh. (Carole Marsh Pennsylvania Bks.). (Illus.). (J). 1994. pap. 19.95 (*1-55609-059-5*); lib. bdg. 29.95 (*0-7933-1925-0*); disk 29.95 (*0-7933-1926-9*) Gallopade Intl.

Let's Quilt Rhode Island & Stuff it Topographically! Carole Marsh. (Carole Marsh Rhode Island Bks.). (Illus.). (J). 1994. pap. 19.95 (*1-55609-065-X*); lib. bdg. 29.95 (*0-7933-1957-9*); disk 29.95 (*0-7933-1958-7*) Gallopade Intl.

Let's Quilt South Carolina & Stuff It Topographically! Carole Marsh. (Carole Marsh South Carolina Bks.). (Illus.). (J). 1994. pap. 19.95 (*1-55609-053-6*); lib. bdg. 29.95 (*0-7933-1987-0*); disk 29.95 (*0-7933-1988-9*) Gallopade Intl.

Let's Quilt South Dakota & Stuff It Topographically! Carole Marsh. (Carole Marsh South Dakota Bks.). (Illus.). (J). 1994. pap. 19.95 (*1-55609-136-2*); lib. bdg. 29.95 (*0-7933-2018-6*); disk 29.95 (*0-7933-2019-4*) Gallopade Intl.

Let's Quilt Tennessee & Stuff It Topographically! Carole Marsh. (Tennessee Bks.). (Illus.). (J). 1994. pap. 19.95 (*1-55609-079-X*); lib. bdg. 29.95 (*0-7933-2048-8*); disk 29.95 (*0-7933-2049-6*) Gallopade Intl.

Let's Quilt Texas & Stuff It Topographically! Carole Marsh. (Carole Marsh Texas Bks.). (Illus.). (J). 1994. pap. 19.95 (*1-55609-077-3*); lib. bdg. 29.95 (*0-7933-2078-X*); disk 29.95 (*0-7933-2079-8*) Gallopade Intl.

Let's Quilt Utah & Stuff It Topographically! Carole Marsh. (Carole Marsh Utah Bks.). (Illus.). (J). 1994. pap. 19.95 (*1-55609-129-X*); lib. bdg. 29.95 (*0-7933-2109-3*); disk 29.95 (*0-7933-2110-7*) Gallopade Intl.

Let's Quilt Vermont & Stuff It Topographically! Carole Marsh. (Carole Marsh Vermont Bks.). (Illus.). (J). 1994. pap. 19.95 (*1-55609-066-8*); lib. bdg. 29.95 (*0-7933-2141-7*); disk 29.95 (*0-7933-2142-5*) Gallopade Intl.

Let's Quilt Virginia & Stuff It Topographically! Carole Marsh. (Carole Marsh Virginia Bks.). (Illus.). (J). 1994. pap. 19.95 (*1-55609-051-X*); lib. bdg. 29.95 (*0-7933-2171-9*); disk 29.95 (*0-7933-2172-7*) Gallopade Intl.

Let's Quilt Washington & Stuff It Topographically! Carole Marsh. (Carole Marsh Washington Bks.). (Illus.). (J). 1994. pap. 19.95 (*1-55609-133-8*); lib. bdg. 29.95 (*0-7933-2204-9*); disk 29.95 (*0-7933-2205-7*) Gallopade Intl.

Let's Quilt Washington, D. C. & Stuff It Topographically! Carole Marsh. (Carole Marsh Washington, D. C. Bks.). (Illus.). (J). (gr. 3-12). 1994. lib. bdg. 29.95 (*1-55609-564-3*); disk 29.95 (*0-7933-1461-5*) Gallopade Intl.

Let's Quilt Washington, D. C. & Stuff It Topographically! Carole Marsh. (Carole Marsh Washington, D. C. Bks.). (Illus.). (J). (gr. 3-12). 1997. pap. 19.95 (*1-55609-563-5*) Gallopade Intl.

Let's Quilt West Virginia & Stuff It Topographically! Carole Marsh. (Carole Marsh West Virginia Bks.). (Illus.). (J). 1994. pap. 19.95 (*1-55609-052-8*); lib. bdg. 29.95 (*0-7933-2236-7*); disk 29.95 (*0-7933-2237-5*) Gallopade Intl.

Let's Quilt Wisconsin & Stuff It Topographically! Carole Marsh. (Carole Marsh Wisconsin Bks.). (Illus.). (J). 1994. pap. 19.95 (*1-55609-098-6*); lib. bdg. 29.95 (*0-7933-2268-5*); disk 29.95 (*0-7933-2269-3*) Gallopade Intl.

Let's Quilt Wyoming & Stuff It Topographically! Carole Marsh. (Carole Marsh Wyoming Bks.). (Illus.). (J). 1994. pap. 19.95 (*1-55609-134-6*); lib. bdg. 29.95 (*1-55609-290-3*); disk 29.95 (*1-55609-291-1*) Gallopade Intl.

***Let's Raise Those Test Scores! The 21st Century Guide for Teachers, Administrators & Parents.** (Illus.). vi, 70p. 2000. pap. 20.00 (*0-9700039-0-0*) Osborn Innov.

Let's Reach for the Sun: Thirty Original Solar & Earth Sheltered Home Designs. rev. ed. George Reynoldson. (Illus.). 144p. 1981. pap. 12.95 (*0-9603570-1-7*) Space-Time WA.

***Let's Read.** 2000. 28.50 (*0-13-032019-6*) P-H.

Let's Read. Maralene Wesner. LC 88-51801. 47p. (Orig.). 1988. pap., teacher ed. 4.95 (*0-936715-18-9*) Diversity Okla.

Let's Read a Horoscope. Doris C. Doane. 78p. 1994. 12.95 (*0-86690-440-9*, D3512-014) Am Fed Astrologers.

Let's Read, a Linguistic Approach. Leonard Bloomfield & Clarence L. Barnhart. LC 61-9080. (Illus.). 474p. 1961. 21.95 (*0-8143-1115-6*) Wayne St U Pr.

Let's Read & Write. (Fisher-Price Kindergarten Learning Pads Ser.). (Illus.). 48p. (J). (gr. k). 1998. pap., wbk. ed. write for info. (*0-7666-0138-2*, Honey Bear Bks) Modern Pub NYC.

Let's Read & Write Arabic, Vol. 1. 2nd ed. Fadel Abdallah. Ed. by Assad Busool & Khalil Tahrawi. 4p. (J). (gr. 1-5). 1996. reprint ed. pap. 4.00 (*1-56316-005-6*) Iqra Intl Ed Fdtn.

Let's Read & Write Arabic, Vol. 2. 2nd ed. Fadel Abdallah. Ed. by Assad Busool & Khalil Tahrawi. (J). (gr. 1-5). 1996. reprint ed. pap. 4.00 (*1-56316-006-4*) Iqra Intl Ed Fdtn.

Let's Read English, Bk. 4. J. M. Fuste & S. N. Rizvi. 136p. 1990. pap. 28.00 (*81-209-0298-X*, Pub. by Pitambar Pub) St Mut.

Let's Read English: Pre-Primer. C. B. Hammond & S. N. Rizvi. (Illus.). 1997. pap. 20.00 (*81-209-0293-9*, Pub. by Pitambar Pub) St Mut.

Let's Read English: Pre-Primer, Primer Books, Bk. I. Greg J. Fuste & S. N. Rizvi. 1997. pap. 30.00 (*81-209-0295-5*, Pub. by Pitambar Pub) St Mut.

Let's Read English: Pre-Primer, Primer Books, Bk. II. Greg J. Fuste & S. N. Rizvi. 96p. 1997. pap. 35.00 (*81-209-0296-3*, Pub. by Pitambar Pub) St Mut.

Let's Read English: Pre-Primer, Primer Books, Bk. III. Greg J. Fuste & S. N. Rizvi. 128p. 1997. pap. 40.00 (*81-209-0297-1*, Pub. by Pitambar Pub) St Mut.

Let's Read English: Pre-Primer, Primer Books, Bk. V. Greg J. Fuste & S. N. Rizvi. 136p. 1997. pap. 45.00 (*81-209-0299-8*, Pub. by Pitambar Pub) St Mut.

Let's Read English: Primer. Greg J. Fuste & S. N. Rizvi. 1997. pap. 25.00 (*81-209-0294-7*, Pub. by Pitambar Pub) St Mut.

Let's Read Hebrew. rev. ed. Anna P. Koch. 1974. reprint ed. pap. 6.95 (*0-8197-0029-0*) Bloch.

Let's Read Latin. Ralph McInerny. 170p. (Orig.). (C). 1995. pap. text 29.95 incl. audio (*1-883357-25-X*) Dumb Ox Bks.

Let's Read the Arabic Newspapers: Arabic Reader. Howard Rowland. 1997. pap. 19.95 (*0-86685-673-0*) Intl Bk Ctr.

Let's Read Together, 15 bks. Barbara DeRubertis. (Illus.). 480p. (J). (ps-3). 1998. pap. 134.25 incl. audio (*1-57565-087-8*) Kane Pr.

Let's Read Together: Long & Short Vowel Books, 10 vols., Set. Barbara DeRubertis. (Illus.). (Orig.). (J). (ps-2). 1997. pap. 49.50 (*1-57565-020-7*) Kane Pr.

Let's Read Together: Safe at Home. Clairece B. Feagin. 1991. pap. 6.40 (*0-8092-4012-2*) NTC Contemp Pub Co.

Let's Read Together: Short Vowel Packages. Barbara DeRubertis. (Let's Read Together Ser.: No. 3). (Illus.). 32p. (J). (ps-2). 1996. pap. 44.75 incl. audio (*1-57565-040-1*) Kane Pr.

Let's Read Together: What Will School be Like? Clairece B. Feagin. 1991. pap. 6.40 (*0-8092-4013-0*) NTC Contemp Pub Co.

Let's Read Together: Why Is Daddy Leaving? Feagin. 1991. pap. 6.40 (*0-8092-4014-9*) NTC Contemp Pub Co.

Let's Read Together Set 1: Short Vowel Book Set. Barbara De Rubertis. (Illus.). 32p. (Orig.). (J). (ps-2). 1996. pap. 24.75 (*1-57565-037-1*) Kane Pr.

Let's Read Together Set 2: Long Vowel Book Set. Barbara De Rubertis. (Illus.). 32p. (Orig.). (J). (ps-2). 1997. pap. 24.75 (*1-57565-038-X*) Kane Pr.

Let's Read Together Set 5: Vowel Team Books. Barbara DeRubertis. (Illus.). 32p. (J). (ps-3). 1998. pap. 24.75 (*1-57565-079-7*) Kane Pr.

Let's Read Together Set 6: Vowel Team Book & Tape Packages. Barbara DeRubertis. (Illus.). 32p. (J). (ps-3). 1998. pap. 44.75 incl. audio (*1-57565-080-0*) Kane Pr.

Let's Read Together Series: Long Vowel Book & Tape Packages. Barbara DeRubertis. (Let's Read Together Ser.: No. 4). (Illus.). 32p. (J). (ps-1). 1997. pap. 44.75 incl. audio (*1-57565-041-X*) Kane Pr.

Let's Read Together Series: Set 7 (5 Short Vowel, 5 Long Vowel, 5 Vowel Team Book Titles), 15 bks. Barbara DeRubertis. (Illus.). 480p. (J). (ps-3). 1998. pap. 74.25 (*1-57565-086-X*) Kane Pr.

Let's Read Together Series: Short & Long Vowel Book & Tape Packages. Barbara DeRubertis. (Illus.). 32p. (J). (ps-2). 1997. pap. 89.50 incl. audio (*1-57565-039-8*) Kane Pr.

Let's Really Make Love: Sex, the Family, & Education in the Twenty-First Century. Robert H. Rimmer. LC 95-2877. 296p. 1995. pap. 18.95 (*0-87975-964-X*) Prometheus Bks.

Let's Reduce & Recycle: Curriculum for Solid Waste Awareness. 144p. pap. text 30.00 (*0-941375-41-2*) DIANE Pub.

Let's Remember. 2nd rev. ed. Donna Martin. (Love 'n Hug Notes Ser.). (Illus.). 10p. (J). 1993. write for info. (*1-879127-42-3*) Lighten Up Enter.

Let's Remember . . . Indians of Texas. Betsy Warren. (Illus.). 32p. (J). (gr. 3-7). 1981. pap. 6.95 (*0-937460-03-6*) Hendrick-Long.

Let's Remember . . . Texas, the Twenty-Eighth State. Betsy Warren. (Illus.). 32p. (J). (gr. 3-7). 1984. pap. 6.95 (*0-937460-13-3*) Hendrick-Long.

Let's Remember . . . When Texas Belonged to Mexico. Betsy Warren. (Illus.). 32p. (J). (gr. 3-7). 1982. pap. 6.95 (*0-937460-07-9*) Hendrick-Long.

Let's Remember . . . When Texas Belonged to Spain. Betsy Warren. (Illus.). 32p. (J). (gr. 3-7). 1982. pap. 6.95 (*0-937460-04-4*) Hendrick-Long.

Let's Remember . . . When Texas Was a Republic. Betsy Warren. (Illus.). 32p. (J). (gr. 3-7). 1983. pap. 6.95 (*0-937460-09-5*) Hendrick-Long.

Let's Research Native Americans: Eastern Woodland Tribes Primary. Cindy Sheldon & Virginia Morse. (IIM Integrated Thematic Units Ser.). (Illus.). (Orig.). 1996. pap. text 13.95 (*1-57652-009-9*) Active Lrng NH.

Let's Research Native Americans: North American Tribes Intermediate/Advanced. Cindy Sheldon & Virginia Morse. (IIM Integrated Thematic Units Ser.). (Illus.). (Orig.). 1997. pap. 19.95 (*1-57652-002-1*) Active Lrng NH.

Let's Return to Christian Unity. Kokichi Kurosaki. LC 91-73463. 82p. 1991. pap. 14.95 (*0-940232-45-6*) Seedsowers.

Let's Review: Biology. 2nd ed. G. Scott Hunter. LC 95-37737. (Barron's Review Course Ser.). 440p. 1995. pap. 11.95 (*0-8120-9077-2*) Barron.

Let's Review: Earth Science. Edward J. Denecke. 1995. pap., student ed. 12.95 (*0-8120-1568-1*) Barron.

***Let's Review: Global History & Geography.** 3rd ed. Mark Willner. (Let's Review Ser.). (Illus.). 624p. 2000. pap. 11.95 (*0-7641-1207-4*) Barron.

***Let's Review: Math A.** Lawrence S. Leff. LC 99-53233. (Review Course Ser.). (Illus.). 624p. 2000. pap. 11.95 (*0-7641-1202-3*) Barron.

Let's Review: Sequential Mathematics, Course I. 2nd ed. Lawrence S. Leff. LC 95-2341. (Review Course Ser.). 464p. 1995. pap. 10.95 (*0-8120-9036-5*) Barron.

Let's Review: Sequential Mathematics, Course II. 2nd ed. Lawrence S. Leff. (Barron's Review Course Ser.). 480p. 1996. pap. 10.95 (*0-8120-9051-9*) Barron.

Let's Review: Spanish Power Pack, 2 vols. Jose M. Diaz & Maria F. Nadel. (ENG & SPA.). 1998. pap. 19.95 (*0-7641-7161-5*) Barron.

Let's Review: Spanish with Compact Disk. Jose M. Diaz & Maria Nadel. (Let's Review Ser.). (ENG & SPA.). 500p. 1998. pap. 11.95 (*0-7641-0133-1*, 835991Q) Barron.

Let's Review: Spanish with Compact Disk. Jose M. Diaz & Maria F. Nadel. (Let's Review Ser.). 500p. 1998. pap. 16.95 incl. audio compact disk (*0-7641-7216-6*) Barron.

Let's Review: U. S. History & Government. 2nd ed. John McGeehan & Morris Gall. LC 94-29829. (Review Course Ser.). 1995. pap. 12.95 (*0-8120-1962-8*) Barron.

***Let's Review: U. S. History & Government.** 3rd ed. John McGeehan & Morris Gall. LC 00-31243. (Review Course Ser.). 2001. write for info. (*0-7641-1346-1*) Barron.

Let's Review Physics. Miriam A. Lazar. 1996. pap. text 11.95 (*0-8120-9606-1*) Barron.

Let's Ride! with Linda Tellington-Jones: Fun & Teamwork with Your Horse or Pony. Linda Tellington-Jones & Andrea Pabel. LC 97-60007. (Illus.). 117p. 1997. 19.95 (*1-57076-085-3*, Trafalgar Sq Pub) Trafalgar.

***Let's Rock.** (Rock & Pop Classics: Vol. 19). (Illus.). 30p. 2000. write for info. (*1-892207-48-6*) Intl Masters Pub.

Let's Rodeo! Young Buckaroos & the World's Wildest Sport. Robert Crum. LC 95-43540. (Illus.). 48p. (J). (gr. 2-9). 1996. mass mkt. 17.00 (*0-689-80075-4*) S&S Bks Yung.

***Let's Run Our Schools Together.** D. J. Mathews. 101p. 1999. pap. 9.95 (*0-7414-0006-5*) Buy Books.

Let's Salve Today's Family see Salvemos la Familia de Hoy

Let's Say Grace: Mealtime Prayers for Family Occasions Throughout the Year. Robert M. Hamma. LC 95-78470. (Illus.). 120p. 1995. pap. 9.95 (*0-87793-555-6*) Ave Maria.

Let's Scare 'Em! Grand Interviews & a Filmography of Horrific Proportions, 1930-1961. Rick Atkins. LC 97-12580. (Illus.). 260p. 1997. boxed set 48.50 (*0-7864-0373-X*) McFarland & Co.

Let's Scare the Teacher to Death! Tom B. Stone. (Graveyard School Ser.: No. 8). (J). (gr. 3-7). 1995. pap. 4.75 (*0-553-54232-X*) BDD Bks Young Read.

Let's Scare the Teacher to Death! Tom B. Stone. (Graveyard School Ser.: No. 8). (J). (gr. 3-7). 1995. 8.60 (*0-606-07597-6*, Pub. by Turtleback) Demco.

Let's Sew. Nancy L. Zieman. Ed. by Pat Hahn. LC 91-62364. (Illus.). 76p. 1991. pap. 4.95 (*0-931071-54-2*) Nancys Notions.

Let's Share. Michelle Foerder. LC 96-78350. (Look-Look Bks.). (Illus.). 24p. (J). (ps-3). 1997. pap. text 3.29 (*0-307-12960-8*, 12960, Goldn Books) Gldn Bks Pub Co.

Let's Share: Friendship: Sharing. Betty Gouge et al. Ed. by J. Thomas Morse et al. LC 86-81270. (KidSkills Interpersonal Skill Ser.). (Illus.). 48p. (J). (ps). 1986. lib. bdg. 8.95 (*0-934275-13-0*) Fam Skills.

Let's Share a Devotion: A Book of Daily Meditations for Couples. Ed. by Ralph L. McIntyre. 526p. 1986. pap. text 7.95 (*0-89827-032-4*) Wesleyan Pub Hse.

Let's Shop for Hanukkah. Sol Scharfstein. 1985. 3.95 (*0-88125-182-8*) Ktav.

Let's Sing! John Langstaff Sings with Children Ages 3-7. Elizabeth L. Mayer. (Making Music with John Langstaff Ser.). (J). (ps-2). 1997. pap. 4.95 (*1-886380-22-8*) Langstaff Vid.

Let's Sing about America. Andrew Belling. LC 92-763081. (Singalongs Ser.). (Illus.). 32p. (J). (gr. k-2). 1992. pap. text 4.95 (*0-8167-2983-2*) Troll Communs.

Let's Sing about Animals. George James. LC 91-763080. (Singalongs Ser.). (Illus.). 32p. (J). (gr. k-2). 1992. pap. text 4.95 (*0-8167-2981-6*) Troll Communs.

***Let's Sing about Math: Teacher Planner.** Colleen Pinar. (Illus.). 4p. 1998. teacher ed., spiral bd. 20.95 (*1-881641-70-8*) Pencil Point.

Let's Sing about Silly People. Steve Charney. LC 92-24713. (Singalongs Ser.). (Illus.). 32p. (J). (gr. k-2). 1992. pap. text 4.95 (*0-8167-2979-4*) Troll Communs.

Let's Sing & Learn in French. Neraida Smith. (FRE., Illus.). 64p. (J). 1994. pap. 4.95 (*0-8442-1455-8*, Natl Textbk Co) NTC Contemp Pub Co.

Let's Sing & Learn in French. Neraida Smith. (Let's Sing & Learn Ser.). (FRE., Illus.). 64p. (J). 1994. audio 9.95 (*0-8442-1454-X*, 1454X, Passprt Bks) NTC Contemp Pub Co.

Let's Sing & Learn in Spanish. Neraida Smith. (SPA., Illus.). 32p. 1994. pap. 4.95 (*0-8442-7079-2*, Natl Textbk Co) NTC Contemp Pub Co.

Let's Sing & Learn in Spanish! Neraida Smith. (ENG & SPA., Illus.). 32p. (YA). 1994. pap., pap. text 9.95 incl. audio (*0-8442-7075-X*, 326448, Natl Textbk Co) NTC Contemp Pub Co.

Let's Sing & Let's Keep Singing! John Langstaff Sings with Children, 2 vols., Set. Elizabeth L. Mayer. (Making Music with John Langstaff Ser.). (J). (gr. k-5). 1997. pap. 8.95 (*1-886380-24-4*) Langstaff Vid.

Let's Sing & Make Music: Developing a Music Ministry. Eric A. Thorn. (C). 1989. 25.00 (*0-9510086-6-8*, Pub. by Jay Bks) St Mut.

Let's Sing & Play: Easy-to-Learn Letter Notation Method for Recorder, "Flutes," Keyboard. 4th ed. Peg Hoenack. (Recorder & "Flute" Ser.: Bk. 1). (Illus.). 64p. (J). (gr. 2-7). 1991. student ed., spiral bd. 5.25 (*0-913500-43-7*, L-1) Peg Hoenack MusicWorks.

Let's Sing & Play: Easy-to-Learn Letter Notation Method for Recorder, "Flutes," Keyboard, Set 1. 4th ed. Peg Hoenack. (Recorder & "Flute" Ser.: Bk. 1). (Illus.). 32p. (J). (gr. 2-7). 1991. teacher ed. 54.95 incl. trans. (*0-913500-40-2*, L-ITRA) Peg Hoenack MusicWorks.

Let's Sing & Play an Opera: Hansel & Gretel, Humperdinck Arr. 2nd ed. Peg Hoenack. (Recorder & "Flute" Ser.). (Illus.). 16p. (J). (gr. 2-6). 1972. pap., student ed. 4.50 (*0-913500-19-4*, L-4) Peg Hoenack MusicWorks.

Let's Sing & Play an Opera: Hansel & Gretel, Humperdinck Arr., Piano Accompaniment Book. 2nd ed. Peg Hoenack et al. (Recorder & "Flute" Ser.). (Illus.). 16p. (J). (gr. 2-6). 1972. teacher ed. 4.50 (*0-913500-07-0*, L-5) Peg Hoenack MusicWorks.

Let's Sing & Play Carols & Holiday Songs: Thanksgiving, Hanukkah, Christmas, New Year's: Easy-to-Read Letter Notation for Recorder, "Flutes," Keyboard, any Melody Instrument. 2nd ed. Peg Hoenack. (Recorder & "Flute" Ser.). (Illus.). 48p. (J). (gr. 2-7). 1978. pap. text 8.95 (*0-913500-18-6*, L-3) Peg Hoenack MusicWorks.

Let's Sing & Play While Learning Rhythm Notation Bk. 2: Easy Transition from Letter Notes to Rhythm Symbols. 2nd ed. Peg Hoenack & Kay Jones. (Recorder & "Flute" Ser.). (Illus.). 32p. (J). (gr. 2-7). 1992. student ed., spiral bd. 5.25 (*0-913500-44-5*, L-2) Peg Hoenack MusicWorks.

***Let's Sing! Japanese Songs for Kids.** Tr. by Janet Jensen Sono from JPN. (Illus.). 38p. (ps-12). 1998. pap. 24.00 incl. audio compact disk (*1-893533-00-X*) Kamish for Kids.

Let's Sing, Listen & Learn, Bk. 1. Ed. by Debbie Cavalier. 16p. (Orig.). (YA). 1992. pap. text 9.95 (*1-57623-721-4*, BSM1001) Wrner Bros.

Let's Sing, Listen & Learn, Bk. 2. Ed. by Debbie Cavalier. 16p. (Orig.). (YA). 1992. pap. text 9.95 (*1-57623-722-2*, BSM1002) Wrner Bros.

Let's Sing, Listen & Learn, Bk. 3. Ed. by Debbie Cavalier. 16p. (Orig.). (YA). 1992. pap. text 9.95 (*1-57623-723-0*, BSM1003) Wrner Bros.

Let's Sing, Listen & Learn, Bk. 4. Ed. by Debbie Cavalier. 16p. (Orig.). (YA). 1992. pap. text 9.95 (*1-57623-724-9*, BSM1004) Wrner Bros.

Let's Sing Songs. (J). 1986. pap. 6.99 (*0-88207-469-5*, Victor Bks) Chariot Victor.

Let's Sing Songs. (J). (gr. 1-3). 1984. pap. 6.99 (*0-88207-471-7*) SP Pubns.

Let's Sing Together. Ed. by Walford Davies. 1987. pap. 40.00 (*0-946095-13-2*, Pub. by Gresham Bks) St Mut.

Let's Sing Together: Favorite Primary Songs. Ed. by Frances B. Perry. (Illus.). 96p. (J). (ps-6). 1984. 12.98 (*0-941518-02-7*) Perry Enterprises.

Let's Sing Together: Favorite Primary Songs of Members of the Church of Jesus Christ of Latter-day Saints. Ed. by Frances B. Perry. (Illus.). 96p. (J). (ps-6). 1981. 10.98 (*0-941518-00-0*) Perry Enterprises.

Let's Sit This One Out. Mimi Tate. 1973. pap., teacher ed. 3.25 (*0-685-51735-7*, LSTTM); pap., wbk. ed. 2.35 (*0-685-51734-9*, LSTWB) Quality Pubns.

Let's Skate Minnesota! Where to Roll Outdoors & Indoors. Squarest Wheels Staff & Barbara J. Shotwell. (Illus.). 128p. (Orig.). 1992. pap. 9.95 (*0-9632311-5-4*) WOW Pub MN.

Let's Slice the Ice: A Collection of Black Children's Ring Games & Chants. Eleanor Fulton & Pat Smith. (Illus.). 56p. (J). (ps-k). 1978. pap. 7.95 (*0-918812-02-X*, SE 0409) MMB Music.

Let's Smock It. Patricia Munoz-Timmins. (Illus.). 64p. 1997. pap. 21.95 (*0-9583873-8-9*, Pub. by Triple T Pubng) Quilters Res.

Let's Solve Your Problem: Answers to the Most Frequently Asked Questions about Electromechanical Repair. Electrical Apparatus Magazine Editors. Ed. by Ann Coles & Kevin Jones. (Illus.). 158p. (Orig.). 1993. pap. 29.95 (*0-943876-07-9*) Barks Pubns.

Let's Speak Business English, Set. Linda Cypres. 256p. pap. 18.95 incl. audio (*0-7641-7306-5*) Barron.

Let's Speak Chinese. Jing Luo. LC 99-37502. (Illus.). 180p. 2000. pap. 27.50 (*1-57524-082-3*) Krieger.

Let's Speak Creole, Set. unabridged ed. Albert Valdman. (CRP.). 264p. pap. 215.00 incl. audio (*0-88432-720-5*, SCR100) Audio-Forum.

Let's Speak French! A First Book of Words. rev. ed. Ed. by Katherine Farris. LC 92-41737. (ENG & FRE., Illus.). 48p. (J). (ps-5). 1993. 11.99 (*0-670-85042-X*, Viking Child) Peng Put Young Read.

Let's Speak Hawaiian - E Kama'ilio Hawai'i Kakou. rev. ed. Dorothy M. Kahananui & Alberta P. Anthony. (Illus.). 452p. (C). 1985. pap. text 18.00 (*0-8248-0283-7*) UH Pr.

Let's Speak Ilokano. Precy Espiritu. 320p. 1984. pap. text 16.00 (*0-8248-0822-3*) UH Pr.

Let's Speak Spanish, Bk. 1. 2nd ed. Conrad J. Schmitt. LC 77-8914. (Illus.). 1978. text, student ed. 17.96 (*0-07-055481-1*) McGraw.

Let's Speak Spanish, Bk. 2. 2nd ed. Conrad J. Schmitt. LC 77-8916. (Illus.). 1978. text, student ed. 17.96 (*0-07-055483-8*) McGraw.

Let's Speak Spanish, Bk. 3. 2nd ed. Conrad J. Schmitt. 1978. text, student ed. 17.52 (*0-07-055485-4*) McGraw.

Let's Speak Spanish, Bk. 4. 2nd ed. Conrad J. Schmitt. LC 77-8915. (Illus.). 1978. text, student ed. 17.52 (*0-07-055487-0*) McGraw.

***Let's Speak Tuvan.** Kaadyr-ool A. Bicheldei et al. Ed. by J. Eric Slone. LC 99-69185. 110p. 2000. pap. 40.00 (*1-58490-029-6*) Scientific Consulting.

Let's Start Alphabet. (Illus.). 32p. (J). (gr. k-4). 1999. 12.95 (*1-57145-387-3*, Silver Dolph) Advantage Pubs.

Let's Start (Anglais), Bk. 1: English for French Speakers. Assimil Staff. (ENG & FRE.). 28.95 (*0-8288-4473-9*, M10945) Fr & Eur.

An Asterisk (*) at the beginning of an entry indicates that the title is appearing for the first time.

Let's Start Collage, 4 vols. Silver Dolphin Staff. (Let's Start Bks.). (Illus.). 32p. (J). (gr. k-4). 1998. 12.95 (*1-57145-331-8*, Silver Dolph) Advantage Pubs.

Let's Start Drawing, 4 vols. Silver Dolphin Staff. (Let's Start Bks.). (Illus.). 32p. (J). (gr. k-4). 1998. 12.95 (*1-57145-332-6*, Silver Dolph) Advantage Pubs.

Let's Start Learning Phonetics. Dina Anastasio. (J). 1992. pap. 1.95 (*0-590-45272-X*) Scholastic Inc.

Let's Start Modeling with Clay, 4 vols. Silver Dolphin Staff. (Let's Start Bks.). (Illus.). 32p. (J). (gr. k-4). 1998. 12.95 (*1-57145-333-4*, Silver Dolph) Advantage Pubs.

Let's Start Numbers. (Illus.). 32p. (gr. k-4). 1999. 12.95 (*1-57145-386-5*, Silver Dolph) Advantage Pubs.

Let's Start Painting, 4 vols. Silver Dolphin Press Staff. (Let's Start Bks.). (Illus.). 32p. (J). (gr. k-4). 1998. 12.95 (*1-57145-334-2*, Silver Dolph) Advantage Pubs.

Let's Start Sand Art. (Let's Start Ser.). (Illus.). 32p. (J). (gr. k). 1999. spiral bd. 12.95 (*1-57145-381-4*, Silver Dolph) Advantage Pubs.

***Let's Start Shapes.** (Let's Start Ser.). (J). 2000. 12.95 (*1-57145-403-9*, Silver Dolph) Advantage Pubs.

Let's Start Something! Riddles to Get You Going. Mark Dantzler. (Illus.). 64p. (Orig.). (J). (gr. 2 up). 1994. pap. 3.95 (*0-9643953-0-4*) G T Bks.

Let's Start Stamp Art. (Let's Start Ser.). (Illus.). 32p. (J). (gr. k). 1999. spiral bd. 12.95 (*1-57145-380-6*, Silver Dolph) Advantage Pubs.

Let's Start Talking: Conversation for High Beginning & Low Intermediate Students of English. George M. Rooks. LC 93-41508. 160p. (J). 1994. mass mkt. 15.00 (*0-8384-4825-9*) Heinle & Heinle.

Let's Stir It Up! Kids' Cookbook & Earth Friendly Fun. Dianne Pratt. Ed. by Sherri Eldridge. (Illus.). 40p. (J). (gr. k-8). 1998. pap. 4.95 (*1-886862-29-X*, MN KIDS) Harv Hill ME.

Let's Stop Fighting . . . Let's Start Playing. Felicia S. Siegel. 42p. (J). (gr. 2-8). 1988. spiral bd. 4.95 (*0-9631627-0-5*) Social Skills.

Let's Stop Putting Each Other Down. Thelma Williams. (Illus.). 10p. (Orig.). 1988. pap. 4.00 (*0-945768-01-X*) A-Town Pub Co.

Let's Study Japanese. Jun Maeda. LC 64-24949. (JPN., Illus.). 130p. (YA). (gr. 9 up). 1965. pap. 6.95 (*0-8048-0362-5*) Tuttle Pubng.

Let's Study Mark. Sinclair B. Ferguson. 303p. 1999. pap. 14.99 (*0-85151-755-2*) Banner of Truth.

Let's Study Philippians. Sinclair B. Ferguson. 136p. 1997. reprint ed. pap. 9.99 (*0-85151-714-5*) Banner of Truth.

***Let's Study Second Corinthians.** Derek Prime. 151p. 2000. pap. 10.99 (*0-85151-779-X*) Banner of Truth.

Let's Study the Holy Spirit. Richard Perkins. 96p. (C). 1995. pap. 7.95 (*1-883893-09-7*) WinePress Pub.

Let's Switch: Poems. Photos by Oliver Brown. 40p. 1998. pap. 8.00 (*0-9665390-0-1*) Emerick Bell.

Let's Take a Field Trip to a Cave. Kathy Furgang. LC 99-17076. (Neighborhoods in Nature Ser.). 24p. (J). 1999. 18.60 (*0-8239-5447-1*, PowerKids) Rosen Group.

Let's Take a Field Trip to a Coral Reef. Kathy Furgang. LC 98-53285. (Neighborhoods in Nature Ser.). 24p. (J). 1999. lib. bdg. 18.60 (*0-8239-5445-5*, PowerKids) Rosen Group.

***Let's Take a Field Trip to a Deep Sea Community.** Kathy Furgang. LC 99-18065. (Neighborhoods in Nature Ser.). 24p. (J). 1999. lib. bdg. 18.60 (*0-8239-5448-X*, PowerKids) Rosen Group.

Let's Take a Field Trip to a Tide Pool. Kathy Furgang. LC 98-55734. (Neighborhoods in Nature Ser.). 24p. (J). 1999. lib. bdg. 18.60 (*0-8239-5446-3*, PowerKids) Rosen Group.

Let's Take a Field Trip to an Ant Colony. Kathy Furgang. LC 98-52906. (Neighborhoods in Nature Ser.). 24p. (J). 2000. lib. bdg. 18.60 (*0-8239-5444-7*, PowerKids) Rosen Group.

Let's Take a Trip. Frank A. Arnold. (Illus.). 135p. 1998. write for info. (*0-7541-0040-5*, Pub. by Minerva Pr) Unity Dist.

***Let's Take a Trip.** In-House Staff. 2000. pap. 2.99 (*0-375-80494-3*, Pub. by Random Bks Yng Read) Random.

Let's Take a Trip. Susan R. Simms. (Sound Doodles Ser.). 16p. (J). (ps-2). 1994. write for info. (*1-883366-47-X*) YES Ent.

Let's Take a Trip to a Beehive. Kathy Furgang. LC 98-49452. (Neighborhoods in Nature Ser.). 24p. (J). 1999. lib. bdg. 18.60 (*0-8239-5443-9*, PowerKids) Rosen Group.

***Let's Take a Trip to Mexico.** large type ed. Pam Jerrell & Judy Mullican. (BB Ser.). (Illus.). 8p. (J). (ps-1). 2000. pap. text 10.95 (*1-57332-177-X*) HighReach Lrning.

Let's Take a Walk: Discovering the Habitats, Adaptations, Uses & Folklore of Some Common Wild Plants of Eastern United States. Gale W. Carter. LC 90-93571. (Illus.). 175p. (Orig.). 1991. pap. 14.95 (*0-9628153-0-6*) G W Carter.

Let's Take a Walk Through Our Orthodox Church. Anthony M. Coniaris. LC 98-92087. (Illus.). 100p. (J). (gr. 3-6). 1998. pap. 16.95 (*1-880971-39-9*) Light&Life Pub Co MN.

Let's Take a Wingwalk. Lisa D. Pardue. (Illus.). 48p. (Orig.). (J). (gr. 2 up). 1994. pap. 8.99 (*1-877633-25-9*) Luthers.

Let's Take Care of Earth, Vol. 3532. Rozanne L. Williams. (Emergent Reader Science Ser.). 16p. 1994. pap. 2.75 (*0-916119-42-4*, 3532) Creat Teach Pr.

Let's Take Care of Earth, Vol. 3576. Rozanne L. Williams. (Emergent Reader Big Bks.). 16p. (J). (gr. k-2). 1995. pap. 12.98 (*0-916119-81-5*) Creat Teach Pr.

Let's Take Care of the Earth, Vol. 4056. Rozanne L. Williams. (Spanish Emergent Reader Bks.). (SPA., Illus.). 16p. (J). (gr. k-2). 1995. pap. 2.49 (*1-57471-039-7*) Creat Teach Pr.

Let's Take the Bus. Chris Economos. (Real Reading Ser.: Level Red). (Illus.). 32p. (J). (gr. 1-4). 1989. pap. 4.95 (*0-8114-6702-3*) Raintree Steck-V.

Let's Take the Kids: Great Places to Go with Children in New York's Hudson Valley. 5th ed. Mary Barile. LC 97-8949. 1997. pap. 14.95 (*0-312-15569-7*) St Martin.

Let's Take Turns. (Young Dragon Readers 2 Ser.). (J). 1995. pap. text. write for info. (*962-359-532-8*) Addison-Wesley.

Let's Talk! Ruth I. Dowell. (Illus.). 24p. (J). (ps-6). 1986. pap. 8.00 (*0-945842-03-1*) Pollyanna Prodns.

Let's Talk. Leo Jones. (Illus.). 80p. (C). 1997. pap. text, teacher ed. 16.95 (*0-521-46752-7*) Cambridge U Pr.

Let's Talk! Marc Rosen. 425p. (Orig.). 1992. pap. 14.95 (*0-9629821-0-5*) Baron Pied.

Let's Talk! A Discussion of Group Dynamics. Mark D. Ross. 208p. (C). 1993. pap. text 29.95 (*0-8403-8237-5*) Kendall-Hunt.

Let's Talk: A Resource Guide to Good Speaking. Dionne M. Celebre. 1996. 10.00 (*1-878276-24-7*) Educ Systs Assocs Inc.

Let's Talk: An Introduction to Interpersonal Communication. 3rd ed. Freda S. Eldon. 224p. (C). 1991. pap. text 45.00 (*0-536-58048-0*) Pearson Custom.

***Let's Talk: Communication Skills & Conflict Transformation.** Barry C. Bartel. 80p. 1999. pap. 8.95 (*0-87303-340-X*) Faith & Life.

***Let's Talk... Conversation, Goals, Service, Teams, Conflict.** Beth M. Harwood. 159p. 2000. pap. 15.95 (*1-928854-01-X*) Harray Pubns.

Let's Talk: Early Separation & Divorce Activity Book. Jim Boulden & Joan Boulden. (Illus.). (J). (gr. 3-5). 1991. pap., student ed. 5.95 (*1-878076-05-1*) Boulden Pub.

***Let's Talk... Friendship, Family, Romance, Marriage, Money,** Beth M. Harwood. 159p. 2000. pap. 15.95 (*1-928854-00-1*) Harray Pubns.

Let's Talk: Helping Couples, Groups & Individuals Communicate. Robert L. Randall. LC 97-25732. 112p. (Orig.). 1997. pap. 12.95 (*0-8298-1214-8*) Pilgrim OH.

Let's Talk! Music Therapy Strategies to Facilitate Communication. Cathy Knoll & Dellinda Henry. 37p. 1994. pap. text, ring bd. 30.00 incl. VHS (*0-9617272-3-3*) Music Works.

Let's Talk: Speaking & Listening Activities for Intermediate Students. Leo Jones. LC 95-26524. (Illus.). 98p. (C). 1996. pap. text, student ed. 15.95 (*0-521-46753-5*) Cambridge U Pr.

Let's Talk About: Stepfamilies. Fred Rogers. LC 96-34176. (Let's Talk about It Ser.). (Illus.). 32p. 1997. 15.95 (*0-399-23144-7*, G P Putnam) Peng Put Young Read.

Let's Talk About: Stepfamilies. Fred Rogers. LC HQ759.92.R64 1997. (Let's Talk about It Ser.). (Illus.). 32p. (J). 1997. pap. 7.95 (*0-399-23145-5*, G P Putnam) Peng Put Young Read.

Let's Talk about . . . S-E-X: A Read & Discuss Guide for People 9 to 12 & Their Parents. rev. ed. Sam Gitchel & Lorri Foster. (Illus.). 64p. (J). (gr. 4-8). 1995. pap. 5.95 (*0-9610122-2-6*) Plan Par Ctrl CA.

***Let's Talk about Accepting "No" An Early Social Skills Book.** rev. ed. Joy Berry. (Let's Talk about Ser.: Vol. 5). (Illus.). 36p. (J). (ps-3). 2000. pap. 3.95 (*1-58634-058-1*) Goldstar.

***Let's Talk about Adoption.** Diana S. Helmer. LC 97-47362. (Let's Talk Library). 24p. (J). (gr. k-4). 1999. 15.93 (*0-8239-5201-0*, PowerKids) Rosen Group.

Let's Talk about Alcohol Abuse. Marianne Johnston. LC 95-26714. (Let's Talk about Library: Set 1). (Illus.). 24p. (J). (gr. k-4). 1996. lib. bdg. 15.93 (*0-8239-2303-7*, PowerKids) Rosen Group.

Let's Talk about Alcohol Abuse. Marianne Johnston. (PowerKids Ser.). 24p. (J). (gr. k-3). 1998. reprint ed. pap. 6.95 (*1-56838-221-9*) Hazelden.

Let's Talk about Alcoholism. Robert A. Liebelt & Edward B. Truitt, Jr. (Illus.). 248p. (Orig.). 1989. pap. 15.95 (*0-926719-00-9*) Platte River Pr.

***Let's Talk about Being a Good Friend.** Susan Kent. LC 98-46465. (Let's Talk Library). 24p. (J). 1999. lib. bdg. 17.26 (*0-8239-5419-6*, PowerKids) Rosen Group.

Let's Talk about Being Afraid. Anna Kreiner. (Let's Talk about Library: Set 1). (Illus.). 24p. (J). (gr. k-4). 1996. lib. bdg. 15.93 (*0-8239-2305-3*, PowerKids) Rosen Group.

Let's Talk about Being Afraid. Anna Kreiner. (PowerKids Ser.). 24p. (J). (gr. k-3). 1998. reprint ed. pap. 6.95 (*1-56838-223-5*) Hazelden.

***Let's Talk About Being Fair: An Early Social Skills Book.** Joy Berry. (Let's Talk about Ser.: Vol. 6). 36p. (J). (ps-2). 2000. 3.95 (*1-58634-059-X*) Goldstar.

***Let's Talk about Being Good: An Early Social Skills Book.** rev. ed. Joy Berry. (Let's Talk about Ser.: Vol. 4). (Illus.). 36p. (J). (ps-2). 1999. pap. 3.95 (*1-58634-057-3*, 01-0204-04) Goldstar.

Let's Talk about Being Helpful. Joy W. Berry. (J). (ps-3). 1996. pap. text 3.50 (*0-590-62385-0*) Scholastic Inc.

Let's Talk about Being Helpful. Joy Wilt Berry. 1996. 8.70 (*0-606-09544-6*, Pub. by Turtleback) Demco.

Let's Talk about Being Overweight. Melanie A. Gordon. LC 98-45439. (Let's Talk Library). (J). 1998. lib. bdg. 17.26 (*0-8239-5413-7*, PowerKids) Rosen Group.

***Let's Talk about Being Patient: An Early Social Skills Book.** rev. ed. Joy Berry. (Let's Talk about Ser.: Vol. 2). (Illus.). 36p. (J). (ps-2). 1999. pap. 3.95 (*1-58634-055-7*, 01-0204-02) Goldstar.

Let's Talk about Being Shy. Marianne Johnston. (Let's Talk about Library: Set 1). (Illus.). 24p. (J). (gr. k-4). 1997. lib. bdg. 15.93 (*0-8239-2304-5*, PowerKids) Rosen Group.

Let's Talk about Being Shy. Marianne Johnstone. (PowerKids Ser.). 24p. (J). (gr. k-3). 1998. reprint ed. pap. 6.95 (*1-56838-222-7*) Hazelden.

Let's Talk about Children Around the World. Debby Anderson. Ed. by LoraBeth Norton. LC 94-9161. (Illus.). 32p. (J). (ps-2). 1994. 9.99 (*0-7814-0178-X*, Chariot Bks) Chariot Victor.

Let's Talk about Church Staff Relationships. Ronald W. Wiebe & Bruce A. Rowlison. 64p. 1983. pap. 4.95 (*0-938462-12-1*) Green Leaf CA.

Let's Talk about Clearcutting: A Forestry Book for Youth. large type unabridged ed. Shelby E. Chunko & Jane M. Madsen. (Illus.). v, 32p. (J). (gr. 4-9). 1998. pap. 7.50 (*0-9661896-1-2*) PA Forestry.

Let's Talk about Deafness. Melanie A. Gordon. LC 97-48363. (Let's Talk Library). 24p. (J). 1999. 17.26 (*0-8239-5198-7*, PowerKids) Rosen Group.

Let's Talk about Diabetes. Melanie A. Gordon. LC 97-38705. (Let's Talk Library). 24p. (J). 1999. 17.26 (*0-8239-5196-0*, PowerKids) Rosen Group.

***Let's Talk about Down Syndrome.** Melanie A. Gordon. LC 97-46860. (Let's Talk Library). 24p. (J). 1999. 17.26 (*0-8239-5197-9*, PowerKids) Rosen Group.

Let's Talk about Drug Abuse. Anna Kreiner. LC 95-48384. (Let's Talk about Library: Set 1). (Illus.). 24p. (J). (gr. k-4). 1996. lib. bdg. 15.93 (*0-8239-2302-9*, PowerKids) Rosen Group.

Let's Talk about Drug Abuse. Anna Kreiner. (PowerKids Ser.). 24p. (J). (gr. k-3). 1998. reprint ed. pap. 6.95 (*1-56838-219-7*) Hazelden.

Let's Talk about Dyslexia. Melanie Apel Gordan. 1999. pap. text 6.95 (*1-56838-275-8*) Hazelden.

Let's Talk about Dyslexia. Melanie A. Gordon. LC 97-44744. (Let's Talk Library). 24p. (YA). (gr. 2-8). 1999. 13.95 (*0-8239-5199-5*, PowerKids) Rosen Group.

Let's Talk about Epilepsy. Melanie A. Gordon. LC 98-39850. (The Let's Talk Library). 24p. (J). 1999. 17.26 (*0-8239-5414-5*, PowerKids) Rosen Group.

Let's Talk about Feeling Afraid. Joy W. Berry. (Let's Talk About Ser.). (Illus.). (J). (ps-1). 1996. pap. 3.50 (*0-614-15764-1*) Scholastic Inc.

Let's Talk about Feeling Afraid. Joy W. Berry. (J). (ps-3). 1996. pap. text 3.50 (*0-590-62384-2*) Scholastic Inc.

Let's Talk about Feeling Angry. Joy W. Berry. LC 96-147738. (J). (ps-1). 1996. pap. text 3.50 (*0-590-62386-9*) Scholastic Inc.

Let's Talk about Feeling Angry. Joy Wilt Berry. 1995. 8.70 (*0-606-09546-2*, Pub. by Turtleback) Demco.

***Let's Talk about Feeling Confused.** Melanie A. Apel. LC 00-36711. (Let's Talk about Library). (Illus.). (J). 2000. write for info. (*0-8239-5623-7*, PowerKids) Rosen Group.

***Let's Talk about Feeling Defeated: A Personal Feelings Book.** rev. ed. Joy Berry. (Let's Talk about Ser. : Vol. 4). (Illus.). 36p. (J). (ps-2). 2000. pap. 3.95 (*1-58634-035-2*) Goldstar.

***Let's Talk about Feeling Disappointed: An Interpersonal Feelings Book.** rev. ed. Joy Berry. (Let's Talk about Ser.: Vol. 4). (Illus.). 36p. (J). (ps-2). 1999. pap. 3.95 (*1-58634-043-3*, 01-0202-04) Goldstar.

***Let's Talk about Feeling Embarrassed: An Interpersonal Feelings Book.** rev. ed. Joy Berry. (Let's Talk about Ser.: Vol. 1). (Illus.). 36p. (J). (ps-2). 2000. pap. 3.95 (*1-58634-040-9*) Goldstar.

***Let's Talk about Feeling Frustrated: A Personal Feelings Book.** rev. ed. Joy Berry. (Let's Talk about Ser. : Vol. 3). (Illus.). 36p. (J). (ps-2). 1999. pap. 3.95 (*1-58634-034-4*, 01-0201-03) Goldstar.

***Let's Talk about Feeling Inferior: An Interpersonal Feelings Book.** rev. ed. Joy Berry. (Let's Talk about Ser.: Vol. 2). (Illus.). 36p. (J). (ps-3). 2000. pap. 3.95 (*1-58634-041-7*) Goldstar.

***Let's Talk about Feeling Jealous: An Interpersonal Feelings Book.** rev. ed. Joy Berry. (Let's Talk about Ser.: Vol. 3). (Illus.). 36p. (J). (ps-2). 1999. pap. 3.95 (*1-58634-042-5*, 01-0202-03) Goldstar.

***Let's Talk about Feeling Lonely.** Melanie Ann Apel. LC 00-23838. 2000. write for info. (*0-8239-5620-2*, PowerKids) Rosen Group.

Let's Talk about Feeling Nervous. Susan Kent. LC 98-44976. (Let's Talk Library). (J). 1998. lib. bdg. 17.26 (*0-8239-5420-X*, PowerKids) Rosen Group.

Let's Talk about Feeling Sad. Joy W. Berry. (ps-3). 1996. pap. text 3.50 (*0-590-62387-7*) Scholastic Inc.

Let's Talk about Feeling Sad. Joy Wilt Berry. 1996. 8.70 (*0-606-09547-0*, Pub. by Turtleback) Demco.

Let's Talk about Feeling Sad. Diana S. Helmer. LC 98-3524. (Let's Talk Library). 24p. (J). (gr. k-4). 1999. 17.26 (*0-8239-5193-6*, PowerKids) Rosen Group.

***Let's Talk about Feeling Worried.** Melanie Ann Apel. LC 00-24769. (Let's Talk about Library). (Illus.). (J). 2000. write for info. (*0-8239-5622-9*, PowerKids) Rosen Group.

***Let's Talk about Feeling Worried: A Personal Feelings Book.** rev. ed. Joy Berry. (Let's Talk about Ser. : Vol. 2). (Illus.). 36p. (J). (ps-3). 2000. pap. 3.95 (*1-58634-033-6*) Goldstar.

Let's Talk about Foster Homes. Elizabeth Weitzman. LC 95-26715. (Let's Talk about Library: Set 2). (Illus.). 24p. (J). (gr. k-4). 1996. lib. bdg. 15.93 (*0-8239-2310-X*, PowerKids) Rosen Group.

Let's Talk about Going to the Dentist. Marianne Johnston. LC 96-27193. (Let's Talk about Library: Set.1). (Illus.). 24p. (J). (gr. k-4). 1997. lib. bdg. 15.93 (*0-8239-5034-4*, PowerKids) Rosen Group.

Let's Talk about Going to the Doctor. Marianne Johnston. LC 96-27205. (Let's Talk Library). (Illus.). 24p. (J). (gr. k-4). 1997. lib. bdg. 15.93 (*0-8239-5035-2*, PowerKids) Rosen Group.

Let's Talk about Going to the Hospital. M. Johnston. LC 96-27206. (Let's Talk Library). 24p. (J). 1997. lib. bdg. 15.93 (*0-8239-5036-0*, PowerKids) Rosen Group.

Let's Talk about Having a Broken Bone. Elizabeth Weitzman. LC 96-46974. (Let's Talk Library). (J). (gr. k-4). 1997. lib. bdg. 15.93 (*0-8239-5028-X*, PowerKids) Rosen Group.

Let's Talk about Having a New Brother or Sister. Diana S. Helmer. LC 98-3525. (Let's Talk Library). (J). 1998. 17.26 (*0-8239-5191-X*, PowerKids) Rosen Group.

Let's Talk about Having Allergies. Elizabeth Weitzman. (Let's Talk about Library). (Illus.). 24p. (J). (gr. k-4). 1998. pap. 6.95 (*1-56838-273-1*) Hazelden.

Let's Talk about Having Allergies. Elizabeth Weitzman. LC 96-18004. (Let's Talk Library). (Illus.). 24p. (J). (gr. k-4). 1997. lib. bdg. 15.93 (*0-8239-5033-6*, PowerKids) Rosen Group.

Let's Talk about Having Asthma. Elizabeth Weitzman. (Let's Talk about Library). (Illus.). 24p. (J). (gr. k-4). 1998. pap. 6.95 (*1-56838-272-3*) Hazelden.

Let's Talk about Having Chicken Pox. Elizabeth Weitzman. LC 96-43326. (Let's Talk Library). (J). (gr. k-4). 1997. lib. bdg. 15.93 (*0-8239-5031-X*, PowerKids) Rosen Group.

Let's Talk about Having Lyme Disease. Elizabeth Weitzman. LC 96-47210. (Let's Talk Library). (J). (gr. k-4). 1997. lib. bdg. 15.93 (*0-8239-5029-8*, PowerKids) Rosen Group.

Let's Talk about Having the Flu. Elizabeth Weitzman. LC 96-43325. (Let's Talk Library). (J). (gr. k-4). 1997. lib. bdg. 15.93 (*0-8239-5030-1*, PowerKids) Rosen Group.

Let's Talk about Head Lice. Melanie A. Gordon. LC 97-46758. 24p. (J). 1999. pap. 13.95 (*1-56838-276-6*) Hazelden.

***Let's Talk about Head Lice.** Melanie A. Gordon. LC 97-46758. (Let's Talk Library). 24p. (YA). (gr. k-8). 1999. 17.26 (*0-8239-5200-2*, PowerKids) Rosen Group.

Let's Talk about Heaven. Debby Anderson. Ed. by Julie Smith. LC 91-312. 32p. (J). (gr. 1-2). 1991. 9.99 (*1-55513-531-5*) Chariot Victor.

Let's Talk about Heaven. Debby Anderson. 32p. (J). (ps-2). 1998. 12.99 (*0-7814-3077-1*) Chariot Victor.

Let's Talk about Heaven, No. 3. 32p. (J). 1999. write for info. (*0-7814-0195-X*, Chariot Bks) Chariot Victor.

Let's Talk about Heaven, No. 4. 32p. (J). 1996. write for info. (*0-7814-0196-8*, Chariot Bks) Chariot Victor.

Let's Talk about It. 38p. 1987. pap. text 3.95 (*0-910796-10-6*) Intl Students Inc.

Let's Talk about It! Joe Wayman. (Illus.). 96p. (J). (gr. 1-8). 1986. student ed. 11.99 (*0-86653-372-9*, GA 799) Good Apple.

Let's Talk about It: Adoption. Fred Rogers. LC 92-15607. (Mister Rogers' Neighborhood Ser.). (Illus.). 32p. (J). (ps-1). 1998. pap. 6.99 (*0-698-11625-9*, PapStar) Peng Put Young Read.

Let's Talk about It: Divorce. Fred Rogers. LC 94-2312. (Illus.). 32p. (J). (ps-3). 1996. 15.95 (*0-399-22449-1*, G P Putnam) Peng Put Young Read.

Let's Talk about It: Divorce. Fred Rogers. (Mister Rogers' Neighborhood Ser.). (Illus.). 32p. (J). (ps-3). 1998. pap. 6.99 (*0-698-11670-4*, PapStar) Peng Put Young Read.

Let's Talk about It: Sharing Values with Your Kids. Allan H. Jahsmann. LC 98-9250. 1998. 14.00 (*1-57683-059-4*) NavPress.

Let's Talk about It: Stories about Sensitive Issues, Dilemmas & Ethical Decision Making, Vol. I. large type ed. Judith Campbell. Ed. by Joanne Howard. (Illus.). 64p. (J). (gr. 2-6). 1998. pap. 10.00 (*1-891180-51-7*) Campbell & Lockwood.

Let's Talk about Life: Advanced Russian Conversation-An Integrated Approach. Emily Tall & Valentina Vlasikova. LC 95-52906. 304p. 1996. pap., pap. text 42.95 (*0-471-30939-7*) Wiley.

***Let's Talk about Life! An Integrated Approach to Russian Conversation.** Emily Tall. 1998. pap. text 40.50 (*0-471-15756-2*) Wiley.

Let's Talk about Life! An Integrated Approach to Russian Conversation Emily Tall & Valentina Vlasikova. LC 95-52906. viii, 274 p. 1996. write for info. incl. audio (*0-471-02093-1*) Wiley.

Let's Talk about Life Skills I. Janie Haugen. 250p. 1995. text 89.95 (*1-884074-25-1*, PCI 213) PCI Educ Pubg.

Let's Talk about Life Skills Set, 2 vols., Set. Janie Haugen. 500p. 1995. text 162.00 (*1-884074-24-3*, PCI 215) PCI Educ Pubg.

Let's Talk about Life Skills II. Janie Haugen. 250p. 1995. text 89.95 (*1-884074-26-X*, PCI 214) PCI Educ Pubg.

Let's Talk about Living in a Blended Family. Elizabeth Weitzman. LC 96-3334. (Let's Talk about Library: Set 2). (Illus.). 24p. (J). (gr. k-4). 1996. lib. bdg. 15.93 (*0-8239-2312-6*, PowerKids) Rosen Group.

Let's Talk about Living in a World with Violence: An Activity Book for School-Age Children. James Garbarino. Tr. by Sonia Csaszar. (SPA., Illus.). 48p. (J). (gr. k-8). 1993. student ed. 10.00 (*0-9639159-0-8*) Erikson Inst.

***Let's Talk about Living with a Grandparent.** Susan Kent. LC 98-44975. (Let's Talk Library). 24p. (J). 1999. lib. bdg. 17.26 (*0-8239-5421-8*, PowerKids) Rosen Group.

Let's Talk about Living with a Single Parent. Elizabeth Weitzman. (Let's Talk about Library: Set 2). (Illus.). 24p. (J). (gr. k-4). 1996. lib. bdg. 15.93 (*0-8239-2314-2*, PowerKids) Rosen Group.

***Let's Talk about Living with Your Single Dad.** Melanie Ann Apel. LC 99-88251. (Let's Talk Library). 2000. lib. bdg. write for info. (*0-8239-5619-9*) Rosen Group.

***Let's Talk about Love, Marriage & Family Life.** Vanessa Destiny. LC 99-93954. 106p. 1999. per. 10.00 (*0-9665098-1-1*) Universal Express.

Let's Talk about Me: A Girl's Personal, Private & Portable Instruction Book for Life. Ed. by Girlgames Staff. (J). 1997. per. 12.00 (*0-671-01521-4*) PB.

Let's Talk about Moving to a New Place. Diana S. Helmer. LC 97-46975. (Let's Talk Library). 24p. (J). (gr. k-4). 1999. 15.93 (*0-8239-5194-4*, PowerKids) Rosen Group.

L

Let's Talk about Needing Attention. Joy W. Berry. LC 96-201787. (J). (ps-3). 1996. pap. text 3.50 (*0-590-62424-5*) Scholastic Inc.

Let's Talk about Needing Attention. Joy Wilt Berry. 1996. 9.19 (*0-606-09548-9*, Pub. by Turtleback) Demco.

Let's Talk about Needing Extra Help in School. Susan Kent. LC 99-12550. (Let's Talk Library). 24p. (J). 1999. 17.26 (*0-8239-5422-6*, PowerKids) Rosen Group.

Let's Talk about Needing Glasses. Diane Shaughnessy. LC 96-41651. (Let's Talk Library). (J). (gr. k-4). 1997. lib. bdg. 15.93 (*0-8239-5042-5*, PowerKids) Rosen Group.

***Let's Talk about Playing with Others: An Early Social Skills Book.** rev. ed. Joy Berry. (Let's Talk about Ser.: Vol. 7). (Illus.). 36p. (J). (ps-2). 1999. pap. 3.95 (*1-58634-060-3*, 01-0204-07) Goldstar.

Let's Talk about Race. Julius Lester. 32p. (J). 15.95 (*0-06-028596-6*); 15.89 (*0-06-028598-2*); 5.95 (*0-06-446226-9*) HarpC.

***Let's Talk... about Relationships: A Guided, Interactive Process for You to Discover Your Needs.** Barry Spilchuk. 1999. pap. 149.00 (*0-9657536-3-8*) Creat Alternat.

Let's Talk about Relationships: Cases in Study. 2nd rev. ed. Thomas L. Veenendall & Marjorie C. Feinstein. (Illus.). 379p. (C). 1995. pap. text 21.95 (*0-88133-864-8*) Waveland Pr.

Let's Talk about Rocks. Dunning. 1966. 5.95 (*0-87505-125-1*) Borden.

Let's Talk about Salvation. Robert B. Burnette. 56p. 1990. pap. 3.95 (*1-881202-06-2*) Anointed Pubns.

Let's Talk about Salvation. Elaine Cole & David Cole. 36p. (Orig.). (J). (gr. 1-6). 1994. pap. 11.95 incl. audio (*1-883426-14-6*) Chldrns Outrch.

Let's Talk about Saying No. Joy W. Berry. (Illus.). (J). (ps-1). 1996. pap. 3.50 (*0-614-15765-X*) Scholastic Inc.

Let's Talk about Saying No. Joy W. Berry. LC 96-134281. (Illus.). (J). (ps-3). 1996. pap. text 3.50 (*0-590-62425-3*) Scholastic Inc.

Let's Talk about Saying No. Joy Wilt Berry. LC 96-134281. 1996. 8.70 (*0-606-09549-7*, Pub. by Turtleback) Demco.

***Let's Talk about Scratches, Scabs, & Bug Bites.** Melanie A. Gordon. (Let's Talk Library). 24p. (J). 2000. lib. bdg. 17.26 (*0-8239-5416-1*, PowerKids) Rosen Group.

Let's Talk about Sex & Loving. rev. ed. Gail J. Sanchez. 69p. (J). (gr. 1-6). 1994. pap. 9.95 (*0-9640252-0-5*) Empty Nest.

***Let's Talk about Sex & Relationships: A Policy Framework for Working with Children & Young People in Public Care.** Hansa Patel-Kanwal & Gill Lenderyou. 66p. 1999. spiral bd. 24.95 (*1-900990-36-9*, Pub. by Natl Childrens Bur) Paul & Co Pubs.

***Let's Talk about Sickle Cell Anemia.** Melanie Gordon. LC 98-39855. (Let's Talk Library). (J). 1998. 2.50 (*0-8239-5417-X*, PowerKids) Rosen Group.

Let's Talk about Smoking. Elizabeth Weitzman. LC 96-14327. (Let's Talk about Library: Set 1). (Illus.). 24p. (J). (gr. k-4). 1996. lib. bdg. 15.93 (*0-8239-2307-X*, PowerKids) Rosen Group.

Let's Talk about Smoking. Elizabeth Weitzman. (PowerKids Ser.). 24p. (J). (gr. k-3). 1998. reprint ed. pap. 6.95 (*1-56838-220-0*) Hazelden.

Let's Talk about Staying in a Shelter. Elizabeth Weitzman. LC 95-26713. (Let's Talk about Library: Set 2). (Illus.). 24p. (J). (gr. k-4). 1996. lib. bdg. 15.93 (*0-8239-2311-8*, PowerKids) Rosen Group.

Let's Talk about Strength of Materials & Structures. Elliott. 1991. pap. text 54.95 (*0-409-10661-5*) Buttrwrth-Heinemann.

***Let's Talk About Stuttering.** Susan Kent. LC 98-50160. (Let's Talk Library). 24p. (J). 1999. lib. bdg. 17.26 (*0-8239-5423-4*, PowerKids) Rosen Group.

Let's Talk about the Bible. Robert B. Burnette. 68p. 1990. pap. 3.95 (*1-881202-07-0*) Anointed Pubns.

Let's Talk about the Church. Robert B. Burnette. 56p. 1990. pap. 3.95 (*1-881202-05-4*) Anointed Pubns.

Let's Talk about the Sabbath. Dorothy K. Kripke. LC 98-56053. (Illus.). 56p. 1999. 16.95 (*1-881283-18-6*) Alef Design.

Let's Talk about the Weather. Marin Sorescu. Tr. by A. Deletant & B. Walker. LC 85-70247. 84p. 1987. reprint ed. pap. 16.95 (*0-9509487-8-0*, Pub. by Forest Bks) Dufour.

Let's Talk about Tongues. Allan Fowler. LC 96-28765. (Rookie Read-About Science Ser.). (J). 1997. lib. bdg. 18.50 (*0-516-20324-X*) Childrens.

Let's Talk about Tongues. Allan Fowler. LC 96-28765. (Rookie Read-About Science Ser.). (J). 1997. pap. 4.95 (*0-516-26157-6*) Childrens.

Let's Talk about Visiting Your Parent in Prison. M. Wittbold. LC 96-53427. (Let's Talk Library). (J). (gr. k-4). 1997. lib. bdg. 15.93 (*0-8239-5043-3*, PowerKids) Rosen Group.

Let's Talk about When a Parent Dies. Elizabeth Weitzman. LC 96-3335. (Let's Talk about Library: Set 2). (Illus.). 24p. (J). (gr. k-4). 1996. lib. bdg. 15.93 (*0-8239-2309-6*, PowerKids) Rosen Group.

Let's Talk about When Kids Have Cancer. Melanie Apel Gorden. 1999. pap. text 6.95 (*1-56838-274-X*) Hazelden.

Let's Talk about When Kids Have Cancer. Melanie A. Gordon. LC 97-38704. (Let's Talk Library). 24p. (J). 1999. 17.26 (*0-8239-5195-2*, PowerKids) Rosen Group.

Let's Talk about When Someone You Love Has Alzheimer's Disease. Elizabeth Weitzman. LC 95-50794. (Let's Talk about Library: Set 1). (Illus.). 24p. (J). (gr. k-4). 1996. lib. bdg. 15.93 (*0-8239-2306-1*, PowerKids) Rosen Group.

Let's Talk about When Someone You Love Has Alzheimer's Disease. Elizabeth Weitzman. (PowerKids Ser.). 24p. (J). (gr. k-3). 1998. reprint ed. pap. 6.95 (*1-56838-224-3*) Hazelden.

Let's Talk about When Someone You Love Is in a Nursing Home. Diana S. Helmer. LC 97-41241. (Let's Talk Library Ser.). 24p. (J). (ps-2). 1999. 15.93 (*0-8239-5190-1*, PowerKids) Rosen Group.

Let's Talk about When You Have Asthma. Elizabeth Weitzman. LC 96-27202. (Let's Talk Library). (J). (gr. k-4). 1997. lib. bdg. 15.93 (*0-8239-5032-8*, PowerKids) Rosen Group.

***Let's Talk About When You Have to Have Your Tonsils Out.** Melanie A. Gordon. (Let's Talk Library). (J). 1998. 17.26 (*0-8239-5418-8*, PowerKids) Rosen Group.

Let's Talk about When You Have Trouble Going to Sleep. Susan Kent. LC 98-50163. (Let's Talk Library). 24p. (J). 1999. lib. bdg. 17.26 (*0-8239-5424-2*, PowerKids) Rosen Group.

Let's Talk about When Your Mom or Dad Is Unhappy. Diana S. Helmer. LC 98-11548. (Let's Talk Library). (J). 1998. 15.93 (*0-8239-5192-8*, PowerKids) Rosen Group.

Let's Talk about When Your Mom or Dad Is Unhappy. Diana Star Helmer. 1999. pap. text 6.95 (*1-56838-277-4*) Hazelden.

Let's Talk about When Your Parent Doesn't Speak English. Maureen Wittbold. LC 96-53428. (Let's Talk Library). (Illus.). 24p. (J). (gr. k-4). 1997. lib. bdg. 15.93 (*0-8239-5044-1*, PowerKids) Rosen Group.

Let's Talk about When Your Pet Dies. Marianne Johnston. LC 96-32582. (Let's Talk about Library). 1997. lib. bdg. 15.93 (*0-8239-5039-5*, PowerKids) Rosen Group.

Let's Talk about Witnessing. Robert B. Burnette. 68p. 1992. pap. 3.95 (*1-881202-10-0*) Anointed Pubns.

Let's Talk about You. Gene E. Clark. 109p. 1982. reprint ed. pap. 3.50 (*0-87516-478-1*) DeVorss.

Let's Talk about Your Parent's Divorce. Elizabeth Weitzman. LC 96-1513. (Let's Talk about Library: Set 2). (Illus.). 24p. (J). (gr. k-4). 1996. lib. bdg. 15.93 (*0-8239-2313-4*, PowerKids) Rosen Group.

Let's Talk about Your Wedding & Marriage. 3rd ed. Bruce A. Rowlison & George Hinn. 48p. 1994. pap. 3.95 (*0-938462-17-2*) Green Leaf CA.

Let's Talk Advanced American English. Victoria Liu & Joseph B. Durra. (Let's Talk Ser.). 100p. 1992. 108.00 incl. audio (*1-881906-02-7*) JBD Pub.

Let's Talk American English: Beginning & Intermediate. rev. ed. Victoria Liu & Joseph B. Durra. (Let's Talk Ser.). (CHI & ENG.). 100p. 1992. reprint ed. 218.00 incl. VHS (*1-881906-01-9*) JBD Pub.

Let's Talk an Oil Deal: Your Key to Oil Patch Lingo. John Orban, III. (Illus.). 120p. (Orig.). 1989. pap. 13.50 (*0-9615776-2-2*) Meridian Oklahoma.

Let's Talk Business. Vetrano & Whalley. (College ESL Ser.). 160p. (J). 1995. mass mkt. 33.95 (*0-8384-4005-3*) Heinle & Heinle.

Let's Talk Business. Vetrano & Whalley. (College ESL Ser.). 48p. (J). 1995. mass mkt., teacher ed. 7.95 (*0-8384-4266-8*) Heinle & Heinle.

Let's Talk Cantonese. Victoria Liu & Joseph Durra. (CHI & ENG., Illus.). 251p. 1994. pap. 49.95 incl. audio (*1-881906-04-3*) JBD Pub.

Let's Talk Cantonese. Victoria Liu & Joseph B. Durra. (CHI & ENG., Illus.). 251p. 1994. pap. 16.95 (*1-881906-03-5*) JBD Pub.

Let's Talk Cheyenne: An Audio Cassette Tape Course of Instruction in the Cheyenne Language. Ted Risingsun & Wayne Leman. 57p. 1999. pap. 18.95 incl. audio (*0-9658014-1-1*) WinterSun Pr.

Let's Talk D P: Dictionary of Data Processing. J. P. Drieux & A. Jarlaud. (ENG & FRE.). 160p. 1986. pap. 31.95 (*0-7859-4821-X*) Fr & Eur.

Let's Talk Decorating: Professional's Guide to Smart Design. Mark McCauley. Ed. by Patrick Caton. 168p. (Orig.). 1996. pap. 5.95 (*1-56245-226-6*) Great Quotations.

Let's Talk French Today. Penton Overseas Inc. Staff. (Immersion Plus Ser.). (FRE.). 1994. pap. 10.95 incl. audio (*1-56015-550-7*) Penton Overseas.

Let's Talk German Today. Penton Overseas Inc. Staff. (Immersion Plus Ser.). (ENG & GER.). 1995. pap. 10.95 incl. audio (*1-56015-552-3*) Penton Overseas.

Let's Talk Hair! Vol. 1: Every Woman's Personal Consultation for Healthy Growing Hair. Pamela Ferrell. Ed. by Lurma Rackley. LC 96-85919. (Illus.). 240p. (Orig.). (YA). 1996. pap. 24.95 (*0-939183-02-1*) Cornrows & Co.

Let's Talk in Korean. Pong K. Lee & Chi S. Ryu. LC 78-72953. 312p. 1998. 14.95 (*0-930878-10-8*) Hollym Intl.

***Lets Talk It Over: Interpersonal Common In Relationship.** 5th ed. 488p. (C). 2000. 35.95 (*0-536-60264-6*) Pearson Custom.

Let's Talk Italian Today. Penton Overseas Inc. Staff. (Immersion Plus Ser.). (ENG & ITA.). 1995. pap. 10.95 incl. audio (*1-56015-553-1*) Penton Overseas.

Let's Talk, Let's Play. Jane Eliot. Ed. by David Mitchell. 82p. 1997. pap. 12.00 (*0-9623978-9-X*) Assn Waldorf Schls.

Let's Talk Lisp. Laurent Siklossy. 456p. (C). 1975. pap. text 28.00 (*0-13-532762-8*) P-H.

Let's Talk Math: Encouraging Children to Explore Ideas. Pat Lilburn & Pam Rawson. LC 93-44870. 120p. 1994. pap. text 16.00 (*0-435-08348-1*, 08348) Heinemann.

Let's Talk Money: Your Complete Personal Finance Guide. Dee Lee. (Illus.). 411p. 1999. pap. 16.95 (*1-886284-40-7*, Pub. by Chandler Hse) Natl Bk Netwk.

Let's Talk of Graves, of Worms, of Epitaphs. Robert Player. 1996. 19.50 (*0-7451-8690-4*, Black Dagger) Chivers N Amer.

Let's Talk of Wills. large type ed. Sarah J. Mason. (Linford Mystery Large Print Ser.). 416p. 1995. pap. 16.99 (*0-7089-7731-6*, Linford) Ulverscroft.

Let's Talk Pay. Vernon A. Stone. 194p. 1993. 29.95 (*1-56625-031-5*) Bonus Books.

Let's Talk Spanish Today. Penton Overseas Inc. Staff. (Immersion Plus Ser.). (SPA.). 1994. pap. 10.95 incl. audio (*1-56015-551-5*) Penton Overseas.

***Let's Talk Tails.** June A. English. (Illus.). (J). 2000. 3.99 (*0-307-11006-0*) Gldn Bks Pub Co.

Let's Talk Terror. Carolyn Keene. LC 93-222444. (Nancy Drew Files: No. 86). 151p. (YA). (gr. 6 up). 1993. mass mkt. 3.99 (*0-671-79478-7*, Archway) PB.

Let's Talk Terror. Carolyn Keene. (Nancy Drew Files: No. 86). (YA). (gr. 6 up). 1993. 9.09 (*0-606-05500-2*, Pub. by Turtleback) Demco.

Let's Talk to Teens about Chastity: For Public School Audience. Center for Learning Network Staff. (Molly Kelly Ser.). 42p. 1994. pap. text, teacher ed. 5.95 (*1-56077-559-9*) Ctr Learning.

***Let's Talk to Teens about Chastity: Molly Kelly Catholic Program.** Center for Learning Network Staff. 57p. 1998. pap. text, teacher ed. 5.95 (*1-56077-560-2*) Ctr Learning.

***Let's Talk to Teens about Chastity: Molly Kelly Christian Program.** Center for Learning Network Staff. 57p. 1998. pap. text, teacher ed. 5.95 (*1-56077-558-0*) Ctr Learning.

Let's Talk Together. Frank Endersby. (Duckling Ser.). (Illus.). 32p. (J). (ps). 1993. 15.95 (*0-460-88059-4*, Pub. by J M Dent & Sons) Trafalgar.

Let's Talk Trash: The Kids' Book about Recycling. Kelly McQueen & David Fassler. LC 90-21400. (Illus.). 168p. (J). (ps-6). 1991. pap. 14.95 (*0-914525-19-0*); 18.95 (*0-914525-20-4*) Waterfront Bks.

Let's Talk Turkey. Delgadillo. 1989. text 14.62 (*0-673-19448-5*) Addison-Wesley.

Let's Talk Turkey. Mary A. Trombold. (Illus.). 174p. (Orig.). 1985. 12.95 (*0-9615262-0-3*) Yearround Pr.

Let's Talk Turkey: Answer Key. Delgadillo. 1997. text 15.66 (*0-673-19449-3*) Addison-Wesley.

Let's Talk Turkey (about Japanese Turkey) And Other Tales from the Asian Wall Street Journal. Ed. by Urban Lehner. LC 95-61323. (Illus.). 192p. (Orig.). 1996. pap. 9.95 (*0-8048-2051-1*) Tuttle Pubng.

***Let's Talk with the World: A Child's Guide to Art & the Natural World.** Karla Cikanova. (Illus.). 128p. 1998. text 22.50 (*90-5703-311-9*, Harwood Acad Pubs) Gordon & Breach.

Let's Teach Music in the Elementary School. Maurine Timmerman. LC 58-7733. 225p. reprint ed. pap. 69.80 (*0-608-10975-4*, 200355700035) Bks Demand.

Let's Teach with Puppets see Ensenemos con Titeres

Let's Tell a Story. (Shorewood Art Programs for Education Ser.). 4p. 1974. teacher ed. 107.00 (*0-88185-010-1*); 143.00 (*0-685-07211-8*) Shorewood Fine Art.

Let's Tell Time. Melissa Getzoff. LC 95-20409. (First Start Easy Reader Ser.). (Illus.). 32p. (J). (gr. k-3). 1995. pap. text 2.95 (*0-8167-3855-6*); lib. bdg. 13.05 (*0-8167-3854-8*) Troll Communs.

Let's Tell Time: Spanish. enl. ed. Melissa Getzoff. 1999. pap. text 16.95 (*0-8167-3984-6*) Troll Communs.

Let's Tell Time, Big Book. Melissa Getzoff. 1999. pap. text 16.95 (*0-8167-3956-0*) Troll Communs.

Let's Think. (Fisher-Price Kindergarten Learning Pads Ser.). (Illus.). 48p. (J). (gr. k). 1998. pap., wbk. ed. write for info. (*0-7666-0137-4*, Honey Bear Bks) Modern Pub NYC.

Let's Think About . . . Educational Activities for the First & Second Grade Student. T. L. Smith. (Illus.). 53p. 1991. spiral bd. 4.95 (*1-880825-00-7*) Tracey Smith.

Let's Think About . . . Educational Activities for the Third & Fourth Grade Student. T. L. Smith. (Illus.). 53p. 1991. spiral bd. 4.95 (*1-880825-01-5*) Tracey Smith.

Let's Think about Japan. Akemi Morioka. (C). 1997. pap. 23.44 (*0-07-289936-0*) McGrw-H Hghr Educ.

***Let's Think Urban Education.** 4th ed. Stephanie Evans. 60p. (C). 2000. 30.95 (*0-7872-7189-6*) Kendall-Hunt.

Let's Trade. Harriet Ziefert. LC 88-62150. (Puffin Easy-to-Read Ser.). (J). 1996. 8.70 (*0-606-09550-0*, Pub. by Turtleback) Demco.

Let's Travel Pathways Through Iowa: A Compilation of the Best in Iowa Travel. Ed. by Alexander Marshall. (Let's Travel Pathways Through America Ser.). (Illus.). 450p. (Orig.). 1995. reprint ed. pap. 16.95 (*0-9626647-3-1*) Clark & Miles.

Let's Travel Pathways Through Missouri. Alexander Marshall. (Let's Travel Pathways Through America Ser.). (Illus.), 600p. (Orig.). 1998. pap. 16.95 (*0-9626647-4-X*) Clark & Miles.

Let's Travel Pathways Through Wisconsin: A Compilation of the Best in Wisconsin Travel. Ed. by Alexander Marshall. (Let's Travel Pathways Through America Ser.). (Illus.). 640p. (Orig.). 1995. reprint ed. pap. 16.95 (*0-9626647-2-3*) Clark & Miles.

Let's Try. Amy MacDonald. LC 91-71839. (Let's Explore Board Bks.). (Illus.). 12p. (J). (ps). 1992. bds. 5.95 (*1-56402-022-3*) Candlewick Pr.

Let's Try a Workshop with Teen Women. 23p. 1974. pap. 0.50 (*0-686-14084-2*) YWCA.

Let's Try It Out in the Air. Seymour Simon & Nicole Fauteux. LC 99-20370. (J). 2001. 15.00 (*0-689-82918-3*) S&S Childrens.

Let's Try It Out in the Water. Seymour Simon & Nicole Fauteux. LC 99-20371. (J). 2001. 15.00 (*0-689-82919-1*) S&S Childrens.

Let's Try Math. (Fisher-Price Kindergarten Learning Pads Ser.). (Illus.). 48p. (J). (gr. k). 1998. pap., wbk. ed. write for info. (*0-7666-0140-4*, Honey Bear Bks) Modern Pub NYC.

Let's Try Phonics. (Fisher-Price Kindergarten Learning Pads Ser.). (Illus.). 48p. (J). (gr. k). 1998. pap., wbk. ed. write for info. (*0-7666-0139-0*, Honey Bear Bks) Modern Pub NYC.

Let's Try Some Scottish Cooking. Ed. by Jarrold Publishing Staff. 32p. 1999. pap. 3.95 (*0-7117-0231-4*) JARR UK.

Let's Try Sumi Painting. T. Mikami. 1996. 23.95 (*4-07-972938-3*) Shufu No.

Let's Try This Way. Clifford Fuller. 1961. pap. 1.00 (*0-87516-196-0*) DeVorss.

Let's Tune Up. John W. Travis. Ed. by R. Annabel Rathman. LC 68-14025. (Illus.). (C). 1974. reprint ed. 20.00 (*0-9600394-2-2*); reprint ed. pap. 17.50 (*0-9600394-3-0*) Travis.

Let's Turn Back the Years. Barbara Kaye. (Crystal Creek Ser.). 1994. per. 3.99 (*0-373-82530-7*, 1-82530-6) Harlequin Bks.

Let's "Unhook" the French Verbs & 77 Quick Grammar, Syntax & Pronunciation "Tips" 2nd rev. ed. Helene Ranieri. LC 77-85156. (Illus.). 1974. 10.50 (*0-686-24866-X*) H Ranieri.

Let's Us Go down to the River An' . . . B. Faaborg et al. (Illus.). 191p. 1993. pap. 9.95 (*1-878488-82-1*) Quixote Pr IA.

***Let's Use It Again!** Steck-Vaughn Company Staff. (Read All about It Ser.). (Illus.). (J). 2000. pap. 4.95 (*0-8114-3740-X*) Raintree Steck-V.

Let's Visit a Space Camp. Edith Alston. LC 89-34373. (Let's Visit Ser.). (Illus.). 32p. (J). (gr. 2-4). 1990. pap. text 3.50 (*0-8167-1744-3*); lib. bdg. 15.35 (*0-8167-1743-5*) Troll Communs.

Let's Visit a Spaghetti Factory. Melinda Corey. LC 89-5110. (Let's Visit Ser.). (Illus.). 32p. (J). (gr. 2-4). 1990. lib. bdg. 15.35 (*0-8167-1741-9*) Troll Communs.

Let's Visit Korea. Suzanne C. Han. (Illus.). 40p. (J). 1993. 16.95 (*1-56591-010-9*) Hollym Intl.

Let's Visit Seoul. Suzanne C. Han. (Illus.). 40p. (J). 1993. 16.95 (*1-56591-009-5*) Hollym Intl.

Let's Visit Some Islands. Allan Fowler. LC 97-17896. (Rookie Read-About Science Ser.). 32p. (J). 1998. 18.50 (*0-516-20807-1*) Childrens.

Let's Visit Some Islands. Allan Fowler. Ed. by Dana Rau. (Rookie Read-About Science Ser.). (Illus.). 32p. (J). (gr. 1-2). 1998. pap. 4.95 (*0-516-26366-8*) Childrens.

Let's Visit South Korea. Patricia Shepheard. 1988. 14.95 (*0-333-45696-3*, Pub. by Macmillan) Humanities.

Let's Visit Texas Missions. Margaret M. Maxwell. (Illus.). xi, 68 p. (J). (gr. 4-5). 1998. 13.95 (*1-57168-197-3*) Sunbelt Media.

Let's Visit the Bank. Marianne Johnston. LC 99-19102. (Our Community Ser.). 24p. (J). 1999. lib. bdg. 17.26 (*0-8239-5432-3*, PowerKids) Rosen Group.

***Let's Visit the Fire Station.** Marianne Johnston. LC 99-19176. (Our Community Ser.). 24p. (J). 1999. lib. bdg. 17.26 (*0-8239-5435-8*) Rosen Group.

***Let's Visit the Library.** Marianne Johnston. LC 99-19101. (Our Community Ser.). 24p. (J). 1999. lib. bdg. 17.26 (*0-8239-5431-5*, PowerKids) Rosen Group.

Let's Visit the Police Station. Marianne Johnston. LC 99-21296. (Our Community Ser.). 24p. (J). 1999. lib. bdg. 17.26 (*0-8239-5434-X*, PowerKids) Rosen Group.

Let's Visit the Post Office. Marianne Johnston. LC 99-18010. (Our Community Ser.). 24p. (J). 1999. 17.26 (*0-8239-5433-1*, PowerKids) Rosen Group.

***Let's Visit the Supermarket.** Marianne Johnston. LC 99-20154. (Our Community Ser.). (Illus.). 24p. (J). 1999. lib. bdg. 17.26 (*0-8239-5436-6*, PowerKids) Rosen Group.

Let's Wait for Korea to Decide: An Essay on the Hoover Conference "A New Economic Relationship: the United States & Korea" Jongryn Mo. LC 96-4419. (Essays in Public Policy Ser.: No. 66). 15p. (Orig.). 1996. pap. 5.00 (*0-8179-5712-X*) Hoover Inst Pr.

Let's Walk Safely. Richard G. Boyer. LC 80-82953. (Safety Ser.). (Illus.). 32p. (J). (gr. 1-6). 1981. lib. bdg. 9.95 (*0-87783-159-9*) Oddo.

Let's Weave Color into Baskets. Pat Laughridge. LC 85-63237. (Illus.). 58p. 1986. pap. 12.95 (*0-88740-056-6*) Schiffer.

Let's Weigh the Evidence. Barry Burton. LC 83-71271. 95p. 1983. pap. 4.50 (*0-937958-17-4*) Chick Pubns.

Let's Work It Out. Lila Swell. 48p. (C). 1994. teacher ed., per. 9.95 (*0-8403-9535-3*, 40953501); per. 9.95 (*0-8403-9526-4*, 40952601) Kendall-Hunt.

Let's Work It Out: Topics for Parents, Reading 2-6. 1993. teacher ed. 6.50 (*0-88336-573-1*) New Readers.

Let's Work It Out! A Conflict Resolution Workbook. Hennie M. Shore. (Illus.). 113p. (J). (gr. k-3). 1995. pap. 17.95 (*1-882732-34-0*) Childswork.

Let's Work It Out! A Conflict Resolution Workbook. Hennie M. Shore. (Illus.). 110p. (J). (gr. 4-6). 1995. pap. 17.95 (*1-882732-35-9*) Childswork.

Let's Work It Out, Level 1: Topics for Parents, Reading Level 2-3, 8 bks. 1993. 2.25 (*0-88336-284-8*); 2.25 (*0-88336-285-6*); 2.25 (*0-88336-286-4*); 2.25 (*0-88336-287-2*); 2.25 (*0-88336-288-0*); 2.25 (*0-88336-289-9*); 2.25 (*0-88336-290-2*); 2.25 (*0-88336-291-0*) New Readers.

Let's Work It Out, Level 1: Topics for Parents, Reading Level 2-3, 8 bks., Set. 1993. 14.25 (*0-88336-593-6*) New Readers.

Let's Work It Out, Level 2: Topics for Parents, Reading Level 4-6, 8 bks. 1993. 2.25 (*0-88336-292-9*); 2.25 (*0-88336-293-7*); 2.25 (*0-88336-294-5*); 2.25 (*0-88336-295-3*); 2.25 (*0-88336-296-1*); 2.25 (*0-88336-297-X*); 2.25 (*0-88336-298-8*); 2.25 (*0-88336-299-6*) New Readers.

Let's Work It Out, Level 2: Topics for Parents, Reading Level 4-6, 8 bks., Set. 1993. 14.25 (*0-88336-594-4*) New Readers.

Let's Work Safely! English Language Skills for Safety in the Workplace. Linda Mrowicki. (Illus.). 114p. (Orig.). 1984. pap. text 7.50 (*0-916591-00-X*); 4.50 (*0-916591-01-8*) Linmore Pub.

Let's Work Smarter, Not Harder: How to Engage Your Entire Organization in the Execution of Change. Michael Caravatta. LC 97-3241. 283p. 1997. pap. 32.00 (*0-87389-386-7*, H0975) ASQ Qual Pr.

An Asterisk (*) at the beginning of an entry indicates that the title is appearing for the first time.

Let's Work Together! Kathy M. Littlefield & Robert S. Littlefield. (Illus.). 32p. (Orig.). (J). (gr. 3-6). 1991. pap. text 8.95 (*1-879340-08-9*, K0109) Kidspeak.

*__Let's Work Together.__ Steck-Vaughn Company Staff. (Read All about It Ser.). (Illus.). (J). 2000. pap. 4.95 (*0-8114-3797-3*) Raintree Steck-V.

*__Let's Write.__ 2000. 27.50 (*0-13-032010-2*) P-H.

Let's Write. Professional Books Staff. LC 97-198078. 1997. pap. text 15.95 (*0-590-93102-4*) Scholastic Inc.

Let's Write, Bk. C. Ed. by Scholastic, Inc. Staff. 1993. pap., teacher ed. 5.25 (*0-590-49520-8*) Scholastic Inc.

Let's Write, Bk. C. Scholastic Professional Books Staff. Vol. C. (J). 1993. pap. 3.50 (*0-590-49514-3*) Scholastic Inc.

Let's Write, Bk. D. Ed. by Scholastic, Inc. Staff. 1993. pap., teacher ed. 5.25 (*0-590-49521-6*) Scholastic Inc.

Let's Write, Bk. D. Ed. by Scholastic, Inc. Staff. (J). 1993. pap. 3.50 (*0-590-49515-1*) Scholastic Inc.

Let's Write, Bk. A. Ed. by Scholastic, Inc. Staff. 1993. pap., teacher ed. 5.25 (*0-590-49518-6*) Scholastic Inc.

Let's Write, Bk. A. Ed. by Scholastic, Inc. Staff. (J). 1993. pap. 3.50 (*0-590-49512-7*) Scholastic Inc.

Let's Write, Bk. B. Ed. by Scholastic, Inc. Staff. 1993. pap., teacher ed. 5.25 (*0-590-49519-4*) Scholastic Inc.

Let's Write, Bk. B. Ed. by Scholastic, Inc. Staff. Vol. B. (J). 1993. pap. 3.50 (*0-590-49513-5*) Scholastic Inc.

Let's Write, Bk. E. Ed. by Scholastic, Inc. Staff. 1993. pap., teacher ed. 5.25 (*0-590-49522-4*) Scholastic Inc.

Let's Write, Bk. E. Ed. by Scholastic, Inc. Staff. Vol. E. (J). 1993. pap. 3.50 (*0-590-49516-X*) Scholastic Inc.

Let's Write, Bk. F. Ed. by Scholastic, Inc. Staff. 1993. pap., teacher ed. 5.25 (*0-590-49523-2*) Scholastic Inc.

Let's Write, Bk. F. Ed. by Scholastic, Inc. Staff. Vol. F. (J). 1993. pap. 3.50 (*0-590-49517-8*) Scholastic Inc.

Let's Write! A Ready-to-Use Activities Program for Learners with Special Needs. Cynthia Stowe & Center for Applied Research in Education Staff. LC 97-25821. 1997. pap. text 29.95 (*0-87628-521-3*) Ctr Appl Res.

Let's Write about It: The Indiana Experience. Ed. by Brian O'Neill. x, 124p. (Orig.). 1989. pap. 10.95 (*0-9624180-0-5*) Stone Hills Area Lib Servs.

Let's Write about It Vol. 2: The Indiana Experience. Ed. by Brian F. O'Neill. 170p. (Orig.). 1991. pap. 10.95 (*0-9624180-2-1*) Stone Hills Area Lib Servs.

Let's Write & Read Music: An Easy-to-Learn Method for Reading Music Through Writing Music. Vicki Jorgensen. (Recorder & "Flute" "Let's Sing & Play" Ser.). (Illus.). 152p. 1988. teacher ed., ring bd. 49.95 (*0-913500-29-1*, L-7TE) Peg Hoenack MusicWorks.

Let's Write English: Pre-Primer. Greg J. Fuste & S. N. Rizvi. 1997. pap. 20.00 (*81-209-0554-7*, Pub. by Pitambar Pub) St Mut.

Let's Write English: Pre-Primer, Primer Books, Bk. I. Greg J. Fuste & S. N. Rizvi. 1997. pap. 20.00 (*81-209-0285-8*, Pub. by Pitambar Pub) St Mut.

Let's Write English: Pre-Primer, Primer Books, Bk. II. Greg J. Fuste & S. N. Rizvi. 1997. pap. 25.00 (*81-209-0286-6*, Pub. by Pitambar Pub) St Mut.

Let's Write English: Pre-Primer, Primer Books, Bk. III. Greg J. Fuste & S. N. Rizvi. 1997. pap. 22.00 (*81-209-0287-4*, Pub. by Pitambar Pub) St Mut.

Let's Write English: Pre-Primer, Primer Books, Bk. IV. Greg J. Fuste & S. N. Rizvi. 1997. pap. 22.00 (*81-209-0288-2*, Pub. by Pitambar Pub) St Mut.

Let's Write English: Pre-Primer, Primer Books, Bk. V. Greg J. Fuste & S. N. Rizvi. 72p. 1997. pap. 22.00 (*81-209-0289-0*, Pub. by Pitambar Pub) St Mut.

Let's Write English: Primer. Greg J. Fuste & S. N. Rizvi. 1997. pap. 20.00 (*81-209-0308-0*, Pub. by Pitambar Pub) St Mut.

*__Lets' Write! Grades 2-3: Reading, Writing, & Oral Language Experiences to Promote Creative Expression.__ Robynne Eagan & Tracey Ann Schofield. Ed. by Judy Mitchell. 128p. (J). (gr. 2-3). 1999. 12.95 (*1-57310-202-4*) Teachng & Lrning Co.

*__Let's Write! Grades 4-6: Reading, Writing, Thinking, Spelling & Grammer Activities to Promote Creative Expression.__ Robynne Eagan & Tracey Ann Schofield. Ed. by Judy Mitchell. (Illus.). 128p. (J). (gr. 4-6). 1999. 12.95 (*1-57310-203-2*) Teachng & Lrning Co.

Let's Write, Grades 4-6: Writing & Study Activities. Troll Books Staff. (Teacher Time-Savers Ser.). 80p. (gr. 4). 1999. pap. text 11.95 (*0-8167-3944-7*) Troll Communs.

Let's Write Japanese in Japanese, Custom Pub. 2nd ed. Nomura. (C). 1994. pap. 31.88 (*0-07-047075-8*) McGraw.

*__Let's Write! K-1: Thinking, Reading, Writing, Speaking & Using Activites to Promote Creative Expression.__ Robynne Eagan & Tracey Ann Schofield. Ed. by Judy Mitchell. (Illus.). 128p. (J). (gr. k-1). 1999. 12.95 (*1-57310-201-6*) Teachng & Lrning Co.

Let's Write Right: Manuscript & Cursive, Student Edition. Don McCabe. 82p. 1995. pap., student ed. 12.95 (*1-56400-036-2*) AVKO Educ Res.

Let's Write Right: Manuscript & Cursive Teacher Edition AVKO Sequential Handwriting. Don McCabe. 164p. 1995. pap., teacher ed. 19.95 (*1-56400-030-3*) AVKO Educ Res.

Let's Write Your Business Plan. 5th ed. Ginny L. Kuebler. 117p. 1996. wbk. ed. 12.00 (*0-9633127-3-1*) GLK Pub.

Letter see Modern Russian Classics

Letter. Richard Paul Evans. 1999. per. 5.99 (*0-671-00422-0*) PB.

Letter. Richard Paul Evans. LC 97-34444. (Christmas Box Trilogy Ser.). (Illus.). 335p. 1997. 17.95 (*0-684-83472-3*) S&S Trade.

Letter. Donald M. Smith. Ed. by Diane Parker et al. LC 83-91201. (Illus.). 217p. 20.00 (*0-914731-00-9*) DMS Publishing Co.

Letter. large type ed. Richard Paul Evans. 240p. 1997. 16.45 (*0-684-84283-1*) S&S Trade.

Letter: A Play in Three Acts. W. Somerset Maugham. LC 75-25389. (Works of W. Somerset Maugham). 1977. reprint ed. 23.95 (*0-405-07841-2*) Ayer.

Letter: Interview: What Is M. A. M.?: Statement to the Press. Augusta E. Stetson. LC 91-815614. 27p. 1989. reprint ed. pap. 5.00 (*1-879135-02-7*) Emma Pub Soc.

Letter: Read-Along. Spirn. (Illus.). 32p. (J). (ps-2). 1984. pap. 9.95 (*0-87386-260-0*) Jan Prods.

Letter & Report Writing Skills see Ready-to-Use Writing Workshop Activities Kits

Letter & Spirit in Hispanic Writers-Renaissance to Civil War. Alan S. Trueblood. 1986. 69.00 (*0-7293-0249-0*, Pub. by Tamesis Bks Ltd) Boydell & Brewer.

Letter & the Spirit: A History of Interpretation from Origen to Luther, Vol. 167. Wai-Shing Chau. LC 93-32451. (American University Studies: Series VII). VIII, 250p. (C). 1995. text 48.95 (*0-8204-2328-9*) P Lang Pubng.

Letter & the Spirit: A Selection from His Addresses. Monroe E. Deutsch. (Essay Index Reprint Ser.). 1977. 23.95 (*0-8369-0372-2*) Ayer.

Letter at the End of Winter. Don Stap. LC 87-2093. (University of Central Florida Contemporary Poetry Ser.). 70p. 1988. pap. 10.95 (*0-8130-0859-X*) U Press Fla.

Letter B. S. Bruckner & L. Kingman. (Consonant Easy Readers Ser.). 8p. (J). (ps-1). 1997. pap. 1.99 (*1-57690-289-7*) Tchr Create Mat.

Letter Bandits. Daniel L. Polonsky. (Illus.). 72p. (J). (gr. 3 up). 1991. 14.95 (*0-931474-41-8*) TBW Bks.

Letter Bomb: Nuclear Holocaust & the Exploding Word. Peter Schwenger. LC 92-18277. (Parallax Ser.). (Illus.). 181p. reprint ed. pap. 56.20 (*0-608-06128-X*, 206646100008) Bks Demand.

Letter Book. Rough Notes Co., Inc., Staff. 211p. 1991. 38.25 (*1-877723-77-0*, 29008) Rough Notes.

*__Letter Book: Ideas for Teaching College English.__ Ed. by Toby Fulwiler & Sue Dinitz. LC 99-58139. 167p. 2000. pap. text 18.00 (*0-86709-496-6*, Pub. by Boynton Cook Pubs) Heinemann.

Letter Book of James Abercromby, Colonial Agent, 1751-1773. Ed. by John C. Van Horne & George H. Reese. vi, 471p. 1991. 40.00 (*0-88490-170-X*) Library of VA.

Letter Book of James Brown of Providence, Merchant, 1735-1738. James Brown. (American Biography Ser.). 66p. 1991. reprint ed. lib. bdg. 59.00 (*0-7812-8043-5*) Rprt Serv.

Letter Book of James Brown of Providence, Merchant, 1735-1738. James Browne. LC 75-164613. (Select Bibliographies Reprint Ser.). 1977. reprint ed. 15.95 (*0-8369-5897-7*) Ayer.

Letter-Book of John, Viscount Mordaunt, 1658-60. M. Coate. (Camden Third Ser.). 35.00 (*0-86193-069-X*) David Brown.

Letter-Book of Samuel Sewall, 1685-1729, 2 vols. Samuel Sewall. LC 75-31101. reprint ed. 125.00 (*0-404-13580-3*) AMS Pr.

Letter-Box Man. large type ed. Alan Sewart. (Linford Mystery Library). 1991. pap. 16.99 (*0-7089-7024-9*, Linford) Ulverscroft.

Letter Box Mechanic (USPS) Jack Rudman. (Career Examination Ser.: C-3367). 1994. pap. 27.95 (*0-8373-3367-9*) Nat Learn.

Letter C: Consonant Easy Readers. S. Bruckner & L. Kingman. (Consonant Easy Readers Ser.). 8p. (J). (ps-1). 1997. pap. 1.99 (*1-57690-290-0*) Tchr Create Mat.

Letter Carrier: Autobiography of William J. Leonard, S.J. William J. Leonard. LC 93-18887. 384p. (Orig.). 1993. 29.95 (*1-55612-651-4*); pap. 15.95 (*1-55612-671-9*) Sheed & Ward WI.

*__Letter Carriers.__ Alice K. Flanagan. (Community Workers Ser.). (Illus.). 32p. (J). (gr. 1-2). 2000. write for info. (*0-7565-0010-9*) Compass Point.

Letter Collection of Arnulf of Lisieux. Tr. by Carolyn P. Schriber from LAT. LC 97-12629. (Texts & Studies in Religion: No. 72). 352p. 1997. text 99.95 (*0-7734-8689-5*) E Mellen.

Letter Concerning Toleration. John Locke. 91p. 1997. pap. 15.00 (*0-9627423-6-8*, LCT) Candlestick.

Letter Concerning Toleration. John Locke. Ed. by James Tully. LC 83-281. (HPC Classics Ser.). 72p. (C). 1983. pap. text 4.95 (*0-915145-60-X*); lib. bdg. 24.95 (*0-87220-100-7*) Hackett Pub.

Letter Concerning Toleration. John Locke. LC 89-64199. (Great Books in Philosophy). 78p. (C). 1990. reprint ed. pap. 5.95 (*0-87975-598-9*) Prometheus Bks.

Letter Concerning Toleration: Locke. Patrick Romanell. 64p. (C). 1955. pap. text 3.80 (*0-02-403400-2*, Macmillan Coll) P-H.

Letter D. S. Bruckner & L. Kingman. (Easy Readers Ser.). 8p. (J). (ps-1). 1997. pap. 1.99 (*1-57690-291-9*) Tchr Create Mat.

Letter Dice. Jock Gunter & Carla Clason. (Technical Notes Ser.: No. 6). 17p. (Orig.). 1973. pap. 2.00 (*0-932288-14-6*) Ctr Intl Ed U of MA.

Letter Dice, No. 6. Jock Gunter & Carla Clason. (Technical Notes Ser.). (SPA.). 17p. (Orig.). 1973. pap. 2.00 (*0-932288-15-4*) Ctr Intl Ed U of MA.

Letter Does Not Blush. Parsons. 1985. write for info. (*0-907675-21-2*) Random House.

Letter Excerpts, Statements on Christian Science. Herbert W. Eustace. 36p. 1976. pap. 3.00 (*0-9611156-1-0*) H W Eustace.

Letter F. S. Bruckner & L. Kingman. (Easy Readers Ser.). 8p. (J). (ps-1). 1997. pap. 1.99 (*1-57690-292-7*) Tchr Create Mat.

Letter for Daria. Ekaterina Gordeeva. LC 98-65144. 96p. (J). (ps-4). 1998. 12.95 (*0-316-32994-0*) Little.

Letter for the Ages: Iggeres Haramban. Avrohom C. Feuer. (ArtScroll Mesorah Ser.). 128p. 1989. 15.99 (*0-89906-218-0*); pap. 12.99 (*0-89906-219-9*) Mesorah Pubns.

Letter Form & the French Enlightenment: The Epistolary Paradox. John W. Howland. LC 90-42184. (American University Studies: Romance Languages & Literature: Ser. II, Vol. 126). 197p. (C). 1991. text 95.00 (*0-8204-1132-9*) P Lang Pubng.

Letter Forms: 110 Complete Alphabets. Frederick Lambert. 110p. 1972. pap. 6.95 (*0-486-22872-X*) Dover.

Letter Forms & Type Designs of Eric Gill. Ed. by Robert Harling. (Illus.). 64p. (C). 1989. 100.00 (*0-903696-08-8*, Pub. by Hurtwood Pr Ltd) St Mut.

Letter from a Busy Street: Traffic vs. People. Peter Saint James. 128p. 1997. pap. 12.95 (*1-887936-50-5*) Khabir Pr.

Letter from a Clergyman to His Friend, with an Account of the Travels of Capt. Lemuel Gulliver: And a Character of the Author. Intro. by Martin Kallich. LC 92-2375. (Augustan Reprints Ser.: No. 143). 1970. reprint ed. 14.50 (*0-404-70143-4*, PR3724) AMS Pr.

Letter from a Great-Uncle & Other Stories. Richard Hall. LC 84-15798. 180p. (Orig.). 1985. pap. 7.95 (*0-912516-88-7*) Grey Fox.

Letter from Aida. pap. 0.69 (*1-56632-017-8*) Revival Lit.

Letter from an Outlying Province. Patricia Cumming. LC 76-19884. 80p. 1976. pap. 3.95 (*0-914086-14-6*) Alice James Bks.

Letter from an Unknown Woman: Rutgers Films in Print. Ed. by Virginia W. Wexman. 250p. (C). 1986. text 30.00 (*0-8135-1159-3*) Rutgers U Pr.

Letter from Benjamin Franklin to a Young Friend on the Choice of a Mistress. deluxe limited ed. Benjamin Franklin. 21p. 1993. 135.00 (*1-886015-03-1*) Sandlins Bks.

Letter from Casablanca. Antonio Tabucchi. Tr. by Janice M. Thresher from ITA. LC 85-28380.Tr. of Il Gioco del Rovescio. 128p. 1986. 17.95 (*0-8112-0985-7*, Pub. by New Directions) Norton.

Letter from Dad/Letter from Mom. David Novak. (Illus.). 32p. 1994. pap. 6.95 (*0-9625261-7-7*) Medicott Pr.

Letter from Dr. Samuel L. Mitchill of New York to Samuel M. Burnside. Samuel Latham Mitchill. (LC History-America-E). 1820. reprint ed. lib. bdg. 99.00 (*0-7812-4391-2*) Rprt Serv.

Letter from Governor Pownall to Adam Smith: Being an Examination of Several Points of Doctrine Laid down in His Inquiry. Thomas Pownall. LC 66-15563. (Reprints of Economic Classics Ser.). 48p. 1967. reprint ed. 19.50 (*0-678-00258-4*) Kelley.

Letter from James: A Simplified Version of the Bible Book of James. Ed. by Laurie Penner. (Illus.). 20p. 1992. reprint ed. pap. text 3.50 (*1-893916-01-4*, 1003) Project Pr.

Letter from Koln, Christmas, 1935. Marilynn Hoffman. Ed. by Malachi McCormick. 32p. 1987. 10.00 (*0-943984-25-4*) Stone St Pr.

Letter from Los Angeles. Charles Gullans. LC 89-27908. 80p. (Orig.). 1990. pap. 8.95 (*0-936784-79-2*) J Daniel.

*__Letter from Lydia.__ large type ed. Mollie Chappell. 320p. 1999. pap. 20.99 (*1-85389-868-6*) Ulverscroft.

Letter from McCarty's Farm. Ellen Kort. (Fox Sense Collection). (Illus.). 32p. (Orig.). 1994. pap. 24.95 (*1-885520-02-6*) Fox Print.

Letter from Mr. Cibber, to Mr. Pope. Colley Cibber. LC 92-25030. (Augustan Reprints Ser.: No. 158). 1973. reprint ed. 14.50 (*0-404-70158-2*, PR3347) AMS Pr.

*__Letter from Moses: Mysticism That Leads One to the Brink of Experience of God.__ Ben Gilberti. 144p. 2000. pap. 14.95 (*1-893075-12-5*, Pub. by Spirit Pr OR) ACCESS Pubs Network.

Letter from New York: BBC Woman's Hour Broadcasts. Helene Hanff. LC 92-54842. 148p. 1992. 10.95 (*1-55921-064-8*) Moyer Bell.

Letter from New York: BBC Woman's Hour Broadcasts. large type ed. Helene Hanff. 153p. 1995. 19.95 (*1-85695-006-9*, Pub. by ISIS Lrg Prnt) Transaction Pubs.

Letter from Phoenix Farm. Jane Yolen. LC 92-7795. (Meet the Author Ser.). (Illus.). 32p. (J). (gr. 2-5). 1992. 14.95 (*1-878450-36-0*, 701) R Owen Pubs.

Letter from the Secretary of the Interior - Information in Relation to the Early Labors of the Missionaries. 90p. 1988. pap. 9.95 (*0-87770-451-1*) Ye Galleon.

Letter from the Snow. Ellen B. Obed. (Illus.). 36p. (J). (gr. 1-4). 1999. pap. 10.00 (*0-9618592-8-8*) Maine Writers.

Letter from the West. James A. Hall. (Notable American Authors Ser.). 1992. reprint ed. lib. bdg. 75.00 (*0-7812-2983-9*) Rprt Serv.

Letter from Toto. Mary Van Duyn Hill. 115p. 1990. pap. 14.99 (*0-9648622-0-4*) Pine Grve Pr.

*__Letter from Washington, 1863-1865.__ Evelynn M. Leasher. LC 98-46253. 1999. 39.95 (*0-8143-2798-2*) Wayne St U Pr.

Letter G: Consonant Easy Readers. S. Bruckner & L. Kingman. (Easy Readers Ser.). 8p. (J). (ps-1). 1997. pap. 1.99 (*1-57690-293-5*) Tchr Create Mat.

Letter Getters: For Language Development & Thinking Fun. Greta Rasmussen & Ted Rasmussen. LC 98-90339. (Illus.). 112p. 1998. pap. 11.95 (*0-936110-20-1*, 055) Tin Man Pr.

Letter H: Consonant Easy Readers. S. Bruckner & L. Kingman. (Easy Readers Ser.). 8p. (J). (ps-1). 1997. pap. 1.99 (*1-57690-294-3*) Tchr Create Mat.

Letter Home. Jerry Gildemeister. LC 87-1151. (Illus.). 120p. (J). (gr. 4-12). 1987. 24.50 (*0-936376-04-X*) Bear Wallow Pub.

Letter Idea Book. 3rd ed. American Society of Association Executives Staff. 246p. (Orig.). 1989. pap. 75.00 (*0-88034-034-7*) Am Soc Assn Execs.

Letter Idea Book: Sample Business Letters That Communicate Clearly to Customers, Employees, & Vend. Barbara Darraugh. 1996. pap. 50.00 (*1-892725-09-6*, RP123) Building Serv.

Letter in a Bottle. Elaine Goolsby & Graham Campbell. (Illus.). 338p. (Orig.). 1991. pap. 17.50 (*0-932112-32-3*) Carolina Wren.

Letter in a Klein Bottle. Photos by John Menapace. LC 84-80980. (Illus.). 1984. 30.00 (*0-912330-56-2*) Jargon Soc.

Letter J. S. Bruckner & L. Kingman. (Easy Readers Ser.). 8p. (J). (ps-1). 1997. pap. 1.99 (*1-57690-295-1*) Tchr Create Mat.

Letter Jesters. Cathryn Falwell. LC 93-22739. (Illus.). 48p. (J). (gr. k-3). 1994. 14.95 (*0-395-66898-0*) Ticknor & Flds Bks Yng Read.

Letter-Journal of George Canning, 1793-1795. Peter Jupp. (Camden Fourth Ser.). 316p. (C). 35.00 (*0-86193-126-2*) David Brown.

Letter K: Consonant Easy Readers. S. Bruckner & L. Kingman. (Easy Readers Ser.). 8p. (J). (ps-1). 1997. pap. 1.99 (*1-57690-296-X*) Tchr Create Mat.

Letter Kills but the Spirit Gives Life: The Smiths--Abolitionists, Suffragists, Bible Translators. Kathleen L. Housley. (Illus.). 256p. (Orig.). 1992. pap. 18.00 (*0-9610676-2-4*) Hist Soc Glastonbury.

Letter L: Consonant Easy Readers. S. Bruckner & L. Kingman. (Easy Readers Ser.). 8p. (J). (ps-1). 1997. pap. 1.99 (*1-57690-297-8*) Tchr Create Mat.

Letter Letter. Gerrit Noordzij. (Illus.). 160p. 2000. pap. 19.95 (*0-88179-175-X*, Pub. by Hartley & Marks) Andrews & McMeel.

Letter Liveth: The Life, Work & Library of August Friedrich Pott (1802-1887) Joan Leopold. (Library & Information Sources in Linguistics: 9). clii, 438p. 1983. 130.00 (*90-272-3733-6*) J Benjamins Pubng Co.

Letter M. S. Bruckner & L. Kingman. (Easy Readers Ser.). 8p. (J). (ps-1). 1997. pap. 1.99 (*1-57690-298-6*) Tchr Create Mat.

Letter N: Consonant Easy Readers. S. Bruckner & L. Kingman. (Easy Readers Ser.). 8p. (J). (ps-1). 1997. pap. 1.99 (*1-57690-299-4*) Tchr Create Mat.

Letter Notations in the Middle Ages. Alma C. Santosuosso. (Wissenschaftliche Abhandlungen-Musicological Studies: Vol. 52). (ENG.). 400p. 1990. 97.00 (*0-685-59015-1*) Inst Mediaeval Mus.

Letter of Ammon & Pachomian Monasticism. James E. Goehring. (Patristische Texte und Studien: Vol. 27). xii, 307p. 1985. 161.55 (*0-89925-134-X*) De Gruyter.

Letter of Application & Resume. Jackson. (CA - Career Development Ser.). 1989. pap. 11.95 (*0-538-60118-3*) S-W Pub.

Letter of Columbus on His Discovery of the New World. Christopher Columbus. Tr. by Samuel Eliot Morison. LC 88-21730. (Illus.). 51p. 1989. 320.00 (*0-944585-01-9*) Bieler.

Letter of Consolation, A - Reissue. Henri J. M. Nouwen. LC 81-48212. 96p. 1998. pap. 11.00 (*0-06-066314-6*, Pub. by Harper SF) HarpC.

Letter of Consolation to the Bereaved. Augoustinos N. Kantiotes. 21p. 1993. pap. 2.00 (*0-914744-99-2*) Inst Byzantine.

Letter of James. J. W. Roberts. LC 76-51637. 1984. 12.95 (*0-915547-35-X*) Abilene Christ U.

Letter of John Adams, Addressed to His Wife. John Adams. (Works of John Adams). 286p. 1985. reprint ed. lib. bdg. 69.00 (*0-932051-15-4*) Rprt Serv.

Letter of John Bright, Esq., M. P., on the War see Crimean War: Pro & Con

Letter of Marque. Patrick O'Brian. 1999. 28.95 (*0-7862-1925-4*) Mac Lib Ref.

Letter of Marque. Patrick O'Brian. 1990. 24.00 (*0-393-02874-7*) Norton.

Letter of Marque. Patrick O'Brian. 288p. 1992. pap. 13.95 (*0-393-30905-3*) Norton.

Letter of Mary: A Mary Russell Novel. Laurie R. King. LC 96-22424. 336p. 1998. reprint ed. mass mkt. 6.50 (*0-553-57780-8*) Bantam.

Letter of Meric Casaubon to Peter du Moulin Concerning Natural Experimental Philosophie. Meric Casaubon. LC 76-47045. 600p. 1976. reprint ed. 90.00 (*0-8201-1284-4*) Schol Facsimiles.

Letter of Paul to the Ephesians. rev. ed. Francis Foulkes. (Tyndale New Testament Commentaries Ser.). 190p. (C). 1989. pap. 12.00 (*0-8028-0312-1*) Eerdmans.

Letter of Paul to the Philippians. Patrick E. Harrell. LC 79-134688. 1984. 12.95 (*0-915547-31-7*) Abilene Christ U.

Letter of Paul to the Romans. Richard A. Batey. LC 68-58865. 1984. 12.95 (*0-915547-26-0*) Abilene Christ U.

Letter of Private Direction. Tr. by James Walsh. 77p. 1979. pap. 5.95 (*0-87243-083-9*) Templegate.

Letter of the Churches of Vienne & Lyons to the Churches of Asia & Phrygia in 177 A. D. T. Herbert Bindley. 1991. reprint ed. pap. 2.95 (*0-89981-220-1*) Eastern Orthodox.

*__Letter of the Law.__ Tim Green. 352p. 2000. 24.95 (*0-446-52299-6*) Warner Bks.

Letter of the Law: Bonnie Indermill Mystery. Carole Berry. 1995. mass mkt. 4.99 (*0-425-15105-0*) Berkley Pub.

Letter of Unity: A Woman's Workshop on Ephesians. Martha Hook. (Woman's Workshop Ser.). 1987. pap. 5.99 (*0-310-26181-3*, 11685P); mass mkt. 5.99 (*0-310-26191-0*, 11686P) Zondervan.

Letter on Shakespeare's Authorship of the Two Noble Kinsmen. William Spalding. (New Shakespeare Society, London, Ser. 8: Nos. 1 & 4). 1969. reprint ed. pap. 80.00 (*0-8115-0248-1*) Periodicals Srv.

L

An Asterisk (*) at the beginning of an entry indicates that the title is appearing for the first time.

L

Letter on the Political Obligations of Abolitionists, by James G. Birney: With a Reply by William Lloyd Garrison. James G. Birney. LC 71-82172. (Anti-Slavery Crusade in America Ser.). 1969. reprint ed. 7.50 (*0-405-00613-6*) Ayer.

Letter Openers - Advertising & Figural. (Illus.). 144p. (Orig.). 1996. pap. 12.00 (*0-89538-044-7*) L-W Inc.

Letter P: Consonant Easy Readers. S. Bruckner & L. Kingman. 8p. (J). (ps-1). 1997. pap. 1.99 (*1-57690-300-1*) Tchr Create Mat.

Letter Perfect: A Guide to Practical Proofreading. Peggy Smith. LC 95-20246. 230p. (Orig.). Date not set. pap. 24.95 (*0-935012-17-6*) E E I Pr.

Letter Perfect: An ABC for Business Writers. Daniel D. Pearlman & Anita Dubose. 112p. (Orig.). (C). 1985. pap. text. write for info. (*0-672-61623-8*) Macmillan.

Letter Princess. Peter D. Hays. 41p. (J). (gr. 1-5). 1998. pap. 4.95 (*1-885554-05-2*) P D Hays.

Letter Q: Consonant Easy Readers. S. Bruckner & L. Kingman. (Easy Readers Ser.). 8p. (J). (ps-1). 1997. pap. 1.99 (*1-57690-301-X*) Tchr Create Mat.

Letter R: Consonant Easy Readers. S. Bruckner & L. Kingman. (Easy Readers Ser.). 8p. (J). (ps-1). 1997. pap. 1.99 (*1-57690-302-8*) Tchr Create Mat.

Letter Recognition Workbook: Lowercase Letters. Melissa Delhomme. (Tutor Bks.). (Illus.). 96p. (YA). (gr. k up). 1997. pap. 8.95 (*1-56565-760-8*, 07608W, Pub. by Lowell Hse) NTC Contemp Pub Co.

***Letter Recognition Workbook: Uppercase & Lowercase Letters.** Melissa Del'Homme. (Tutor Bks.). (Illus.). 160p. (YA). (ps up). 2000. pap. 12.95 (*0-7373-0455-3*, 04553W, Pub. by Lowell Hse Juvenile) NTC Contemp Pub Co.

Letter S. S. Bruckner & L. Kingman. (Easy Readers Ser.). 8p. (J). (ps-1). 1997. pap. 1.99 (*1-57690-303-6*) Tchr Create Mat.

Letter Sent into England from the Summer Islands. Lewis Hughes. LC 70-171766. (English Experience Ser.: No. 391). 14p. 1971. reprint ed. 10.00 (*90-221-0391-9*) Walter J Johnson.

Letter Sounds - Phonics for Beginners. rev. ed. Brad Caudle & Richard Caudle. (Rock 'N Learn Ser.). (Illus.). 28p. (J). (gr. k-2). 1997. pap. 12.99 incl. audio (*1-878489-11-9*, RL911) Rock N Learn.

Letter Symbols & Glossary for Hydraulics: With Special Reference to Irrigation Hydraulics. American Society of Civil Engineers, Special Commi. LC 42-233. (American Society of Civil Engineers Manuals of Engineering Practice Ser.: No. 11). 42p. reprint ed. pap. 30.00 (*0-608-14328-6*, 205200000027) Bks Demand.

Letter T: Consonant Easy Readers. S. Bruckner & L. Kingman. (Easy Readers Ser.). 8p. (J). (ps-1). 1997. pap. 1.99 (*1-57690-304-4*) Tchr Create Mat.

Letter, the Witch & the Ring. John Bellairs. LC 92-31361. (Illus.). 208p. (J). (gr. 3 up). 1993. pap. 4.99 (*0-14-036338-6*, PuffinBks) Peng Put Young Read.

Letter, the Witch & the Ring. John Bellairs. (J). 1993. 9.09 (*0-606-05424-3*, Pub. by Turtleback) Demco.

***Letter to Philemon: A New Translation with Notes & Commentary.** Markus Barth. LC 00-28776. (Critical Commentary Ser.). 2000. write for info. (*0-8028-3829-4*) Eerdmans.

Letter to a Comrade. Joy Davidman. LC 75-144744. (Yale Series of Younger Poets: No. 37). reprint ed. 18.00 (*0-404-53837-1*) AMS Pr.

Letter to a Distant Father. Kenneth Radu. 1987. pap. 9.95 (*0-919626-32-7*, Pub. by Brick Bks) Genl Dist Srvs.

Letter to a Fallen Away Catholic. 2nd ed. Ed. by Catholic Treasures Staff. (Illus.). 109p. 1994. reprint ed. pap. 4.95 (*0-9620994-5-7*) Cath Treas.

Letter to a Jewish Friend: The Simple & Extraordinary Story of Pope John Paul II & His Jewish School Friend. Gian F. Svidercoschi. 108p. 1995. 12.95 (*0-8245-1482-3*) Crossroad NY.

Letter to a Lonesome Cowboy: Montana Mavericks: Return to Whitehorn. Jackie Merritt. (Special Edition Ser.: No. 1154). 1998. per. 4.25 (*0-373-24154-2*, 1-24154-6) Silhouette.

***Letter to a Man in the Fire.** large type ed. 2000. 30.00 (*0-7838-8835-X*, G K Hall Lrg Type) Mac Lib Ref.

Letter to a Member of the National Assembly. Edmund Burke. LC 90-36404. 84p. 1990. reprint ed. 40.00 (*1-85477-037-3*) Continuum.

Letter to a Non-Believer. Cosmatom Staff. (C). 1992. pap. 25.00 (*1-874686-05-X*, Pub. by Cosmatom) St Mut.

Letter to a Respected Psychiatrist. Harvey Jackins. 1970. pap. 2.00 (*0-911214-25-9*) Rational Isl.

***Letter to a Son.** Koffi Addo. 112p. 2000. pap. 11.00 (*0-8059-4779-5*) Dorrance.

Letter to a Stranger. Elswyth Thane. 1974. reprint ed. lib. bdg. 22.95 (*0-88411-954-8*) Amereon Ltd.

Letter to a Universalist. John Punshon. LC 89-60789. (Orig.). 1989. pap. 4.00 (*0-87574-285-8*) Pendle Hill.

Letter to a Young Man in the Fire: Does God Exist & Does He Care? Reynolds Price. LC 98-54197. 108p. 1999. 20.00 (*0-684-85626-3*) S&S Trade.

Letter to American Workers. Vladimir Il'ich Lenin. 1970. pap. 0.45 (*0-87898-047-4*) New Outlook.

Letter to Amy. Ezra Jack Keats. LC 97-49433. (Picture Puffin Ser.). (Illus.). 40p. (J). 1998. pap. 5.99 (*0-14-056442-X*, PuffinBks) Peng Put Young Read.

Letter to Amy. Ezra Jack Keats. LC 97-49433. (Illus.). 40p. (J). (ps-3). 1998. 15.99 (*0-670-88063-9*) Viking Penguin.

Letter to an Arab Friend. Andre N. Chouraqui. Tr. by William V. Gugli. LC 72-77573. 284p. 1972. 32.50 (*0-87023-108-1*) U of Mass Pr.

Letter to an Imaginary Friend, Pts. I-IV. Thomas McGrath. LC 97-33929. 1997. 35.00 (*1-55659-077-6*); pap. text 20.00 (*1-55659-078-4*) Copper Canyon.

Letter to an Unknown Woman. deluxe ed. Ascher-Straus. (Treacle Story Ser.: No. 6). (Illus.). 48p. 1979. 12.50 (*0-914232-21-5*) McPherson & Co.

***Letter to Artists.** John Paul, II, pseud. 1999. pap. 5.00 (*1-56854-338-7*) Liturgy Tr Pubns.

Letter to Bugenhagen: Supplication of Souls' & Letter Against Frith. Thomas More. Ed. by Frank Manley. (Yale Edition of the Complete Works of St. Thomas More Ser.: Vol. 7). xxx, 752p. (C). 1990. 90.00 (*0-300-03809-7*) Yale U Pr.

Letter to C. M. Ingleby . . . Containing Notes & Conjectural Emendations on Shakespeare's Cymbaline. Karl Elze. LC 76-166026. reprint ed. 19.50 (*0-404-02326-6*) AMS Pr.

Letter to Christopher Columbus: And Other Poems. Carlos Moreno. 64p. (Orig.). 1993. pap. 4.95 (*1-880365-55-3*) Prof Pr NC.

Letter to College Students from the Catholic Bishop of the United States. U. S. Catholic Bishops Staff. (Illus.). 8p. (Orig.). (C). 1996. pap. 0.75 (*1-57455-084-5*) US Catholic.

Letter to Daniel: Despatches from the Heart. Fergal Keane. 208p. 1997. pap. 13.95 (*0-14-026289-X*, Pub. by Pnguin Bks Ltd) Trafalgar.

Letter to Earth. Elia Wise. LC 97-90695. (Illus.). 250p. 1998. 34.00 (*0-9625678-1-7*) Inspired Co.

***Letter to Earth: Who We Are Becoming & What We Need to Know.** Elia Wise. LC 99-34134. 256p. 2000. 24.00 (*0-609-60526-7*) Harmony Bks.

Letter to Einstein Beginning Dear Albert. Paul Hoover. LC 79-12329. 1979. pap. 3.00 (*0-916328-12-0*) Yellow Pr.

Letter to Families from Pope John Paul II. John Paul, II, pseud. 95p. pap. 2.95 (*0-8198-4471-3*) Pauline Bks.

Letter to George Steevens. James Boaden. LC 74-39459. reprint ed. 31.50 (*0-404-00916-6*) AMS Pr.

Letter to George Washington. Thomas Paine. (Notable American Authors Ser.). 1999. reprint ed. lib. bdg. 125.00 (*0-7812-4724-1*) Rprt Serv.

Letter to Harvey Milk. Leslea Newman. LC 88-3923. 176p. (Orig.). 1988. pap. 9.95 (*0-932379-43-5*); lib. bdg. 20.95 (*0-932379-44-3*) Firebrand Bks.

Letter to His Countryman. James Fenimore Cooper. (Works of James Fenimore Cooper). 1990. reprint ed. lib. bdg. 79.00 (*0-7812-2381-4*) Rprt Serv.

Letter to Hon. Charles Sumner. Hamilton W. Pierson. LC 78-38018. (Black Heritage Library Collection). reprint ed. 12.50 (*0-8369-8985-6*) Ayer.

Letter to Isis. James Knight. (Illus.). 77p. 1998. pap. 10.00 (*0-9663929-0-6*) Blue Knight.

Letter to Jefferson. unabridged ed. S. Gianinazzi. 1998. pap. 14.95 (*1-893336-15-8*) B Newton.

Letter to Juvenal. Martial & Peter Whigham. 120p. 1985. 21.95 (*0-85646-141-5*, Pub. by Anvil Press); pap. 14.95 (*0-85646-092-3*, Pub. by Anvil Press) Dufour.

***Letter to "Kids" A Guide to Self-Defense & Survival.** 208p. 1999. pap. 15.00 (*0-9677645-0-5*) L W Stark.

Letter to Louis Kossuth, Concerning Freedom & Slavery in the United States in Behalf of the American Anti-Slavery Society. William L. Garrison et al. LC 76-82204. (Anti-Slavery Crusade in America Ser.). 1970. reprint ed. 11.95 (*0-405-00630-6*) Ayer.

Letter to Maxine. Mark Weiss. (Illus.). 1974. write for info. (*0-685-78962-4*); 20.00 (*0-686-67809-5*) Heron Pr.

Letter to Mother - With Love: From the Boy with the Bean in His Ear. Thorn Bacon. (Illus.). 48p. 2000. pap. 9.95 (*1-58151-052-7*) BookPartners.

***Letter to Mrs. Roosevelt.** C. Coco De Young. 112p. (J). (gr. 3-7). 2000. pap. 4.50 (*0-440-41529-2*, Yearling) BDD Bks Young Read.

Letter to Mrs. Roosevelt. C. Coco De Young. LC 98-22254. 112p. (YA). (gr. 2-8). 1999. 14.95 (*0-385-32633-5*) BDD Bks Young Read.

Letter to My Children: From Romania to America via Auschwitz. Rudolph Tessler. (Illus.). 248p. 1999. 29.95 (*0-8262-1244-1*) U of Mo Pr.

Letter To My Dad. Jan Marino. (J). 1997. write for info. (*0-316-54615-1*) Little.

Letter to My Daughter, 1687 with Essays from a New England College Town. Phoebe Taylor et al. 104p. 1992. pap. 14.95 (*0-9617481-4-1*) Oyster River Pr.

Letter to My Descendents. Niels A. Skov. LC 98-232726. 435p. 1998. 36.50 (*87-7838-329-3*, Pub. by Odense Univ) Intl Spec Bk.

***Letter to My Descendants.** Niels A. Skov. (Illus.). 450p. 1999. pap. 12.99 (*87-7838-473-7*, Pub. by Odense Univ) Intl Spec Bk.

Letter to My Grandchild. Ed. by Liv Ullmann. LC 98-26864. 128p. 1998. 20.00 (*0-87113-728-3*, Atlntc Mnthly) Grove-Atltic.

Letter to My Grandchildren. Harold Drimmer. (Illus.). 224p. 1989. write for info. (*0-318-66599-9*) Drimmer Pr.

Letter to My Grandchildren. William F. Miller. 579p. 1998. write for info. (*1-86106-620-1*, Pub. by Minerva Pr) Unity Dist.

Letter to My Mother: Reflections on the Christian Reformed Church in North America. Edward Heerema. LC 90-93205. 144p. (Orig.). 1990. pap. 6.95 (*0-9626955-0-5*) E Heerema.

Letter to Our Son. Peter Carey. LC 95-119184. 1994. 19.95 (*0-7022-2764-1*, Pub. by Univ Queensland Pr) Intl Spec Bk.

***Letter to Philemon: A New Translation with Introduction & Commentary.** Joseph A. Fitzmyer. LC 00-29501. (Anchor Bible Ser.). (Illus.). 2001. pap. write for info. (*0-385-49629-X*) Broadway BDD.

Letter to Pope Hadrian about the Novelties of the Day. Gerhoch Reichersberg. Ed. by Nikolaus M. Haring. (LAT.). 125p. 16.57 (*0-88844-024-3*) Brill Academic Pubs.

Letter to Santa. Janet A. Craig. LC 93-2214. (Let's Celebrate Holidays Library). (Illus.). 32p. (J). (gr. k-2). 1993. lib. bdg. 17.25 (*0-8167-3252-3*, BL025) Troll Communs.

Letter to Santa. Janet A. Craig. LC 93-2214. (Giant First Start Reader Ser.). (Illus.). 32p. (J). (gr. k-2). 1997. pap. 3.95 (*0-8167-3253-1*) Troll Communs.

***Letter to Santa Claus.** Brigitte Weninger. (Illus.). 32p. (gr. k-3). 2000. 15.95 (*0-7358-1359-0*); lib. bdg. 15.88 (*0-7358-1360-4*) North-South Bks NYC.

Letter to Teachers: Reflections on Schooling & the Art of Teaching. Vito Perrone. LC 90-19890. (Education-Higher Education Ser.). 166p. 1991. pap. text 17.95 (*1-55542-313-2*) Jossey-Bass.

Letter to the Bishops of Catholic Church on the Pastoral Care of Homosexual Persons. Sacred Congregation for the Doctrine of the Faith. 16p. (Orig.). 1986. pap. 2.95 (*1-55586-148-2*) US Catholic.

Letter to the Bishops of the United States & Essential Elements in the Church's Teaching on Religious Life As Applied to Works of the Apostolate. Congregation for Institutes of Consecrated Life St & Societies of Apostolic Life Staff. 55p. pap. 0.50 (*0-8198-2323-6*) Pauline Bks.

Letter to the Colossians. Adrienne Von Speyr. LC 97-76851. 1998. pap. 12.95 (*0-89870-661-0*) Ignatius Pr.

***Letter to the Editor.** Arno Froese. 2001. 18.99 (*0-937422-49-5*, 1045, Olive Pr SC) Midnight Call.

Letter to the Editor of the Letters on "The Spirit of Patriotism," "The Idea of a Patriot-King," & "The State of Parties, & C." And a Familiar Epistle to the Most Impudent Man Living. William Warburton & Henry S. Bolingbroke. LC 92-25499. (Augustan Reprints Ser.: No. 192). 1978. reprint ed. 14.50 (*0-404-70192-2*, PR3633) AMS Pr.

***Letter to the Ephesians.** Peter T. O'Brien. (Pillar New Testament Commentary Ser.). 608p. 1999. 40.00 (*0-8028-3736-0*) Eerdmans.

Letter to the Ephesians. Adrienne Von Speyr. LC 95-79889. 268p. (Orig.). 1996. pap. 12.95 (*0-89870-570-3*) Ignatius Pr.

Letter to the Friars Minor & Other Writings. William Ockham. Ed. by John Kilcullen & Arthur S. McGrade. (Cambridge Texts in the History of Political Thought Ser.). (Illus.). 433p. (C). 1995. text 64.95 (*0-521-35243-6*) Cambridge U Pr.

Letter to the Ghosts. W. B. Patrick. LC 77-17153. 53p. 1977. 3.50 (*0-87886-091-6*, Greenfld Rev Pr) Greenfld Rev Lit.

Letter to the Hebrews see Daily Study Bible for the New Testament

Letter to the Hebrews. James Thompson. LC 70-163750. 1984. 12.95 (*0-915547-34-1*) Abilene Christ U.

Letter to the Interior. Muska Nagel. Ed. by Constance Hunting. 80p. (Orig.). 1996. pap. 10.95 (*0-913006-63-7*) Puckerbrush.

Letter to the King. Leong Va. Tr. by James Anderson from CHI. LC 91-9469. (Illus.). 32p. (J). (gr. k-3). 1991. lib. bdg. 14.89 (*0-06-020070-7*) HarpC Child Bks.

Letter to the King of Spain: Being a Description of the Ancient Provinces of Guazacapan, Izalco, Cuscatlan & Chiquimula & a Description of the Ruins of Copan. Diego Garcia De Palacios. Ed. by Frank E. Comparato. LC 84-81821. Orig. Title: Carta Dirijida al Rey de Espana. (Illus.). 72p. 1985. reprint ed. pap. 20.00 (*0-911437-04-5*) Labyrinthos.

Letter to the Lake. Susan M. Swanson. LC 97-34107. (Illus.). 32p. (J). (ps-3). 1998. 15.95 (*0-7894-2483-5*) DK Pub Inc.

Letter to the People of the U. S. Touching the Matter of Slavery. Theodore Parker. LC 76-92450. 120p. 1972. reprint ed. 13.00 (*0-403-00180-3*) Scholarly.

Letter to the People of the United States: Touching the Matter of Slavery. Theodore Parker. LC 76-154086. (Black Heritage Library Collection). 1977. 17.95 (*0-8369-8797-7*) Ayer.

Letter to the People of the United States Touching the Matter of Slavery. rev. ed. Theodore Parker. 122p. 1991. pap. text 34.95 (*0-9627882-5-2*) Bradley Mann.

Letter to the President on Crime Control. Norval Morris & Gordon J. Hawkins. LC 76-54657. 1993. pap. text 1.95 (*0-226-53998-9*) U Ch Pr.

Letter to the Right Reverend Father in God, John, Lord Bishop of Landatt. William Livingston. (Notable American Authors Ser.). 1999. reprint ed. lib. bdg. 125.00 (*0-7812-3798-X*) Rprt Serv.

Letter to the Romans see Daily Study Bible for the New Testament

Letter to the Sheriffs of Bristol: A Speech at Bristol on Parliamentary Conduct; a Letter to a Noble Lord. Edmund Burke. Ed. by W. Murison. LC 76-29423. reprint ed. 34.00 (*0-404-15344-5*) AMS Pr.

Letter to the Twenty-Second Century. William E. Knight. LC 98-92510. (Illus.). 195p. 1998. 19.00 (*0-9636778-3-7*) Araluen Pr.

Letter to the Twenty-Second Century: An American Family's Odyssey. William E. Knight. LC 98-92510. (Illus.). 195p. 1998. pap. 9.00 (*0-9636778-4-5*) Araluen Pr.

Letter to the West Wind. Jonathan Welsh. 63p. 1980. 12.95 (*0-920806-24-4*, Pub. by Penumbra Pr); pap. 6.95 (*0-920806-15-5*, Pub. by Penumbra Pr) U of Toronto Pr.

Letter to the Women of England on the Injustice of Mental Subordination 1799. Mary Robinson. LC 97-28632. (Revolution & Romanticism Ser.). 116p. 1998. 55.00 (*1-85477-211-2*) Continuum.

Letter to the World. Isma'il Fassih. LC 94-32357. (PER.). 272p. (Orig.). 1995. pap. 15.95 (*0-936347-54-6*) IBEX.

***Letter to the World: Seven Women Who Shaped the American Century.** Susan Ware. 2000. pap. text 17.95 (*0-674-52545-0*) HUP.

Letter to the World: Seven Women Who Shaped the American Century. Susan Ware. LC 97-45923. (Illus.). 320p. 1998. 25.95 (*0-393-04652-4*) Norton.

Letter to the World: The Life & Dances of Martha Graham. Trudy Garfunkel. (Illus.). 92p. (YA). (gr. 7-12). 1999. reprint ed. text 17.00 (*0-7881-6064-8*) DIANE Pub.

Letter to Titus: A New Translation with Notes & Commentary, Vol. 35. Jerome D. Quinn. 384p. 1990. 28.00 (*0-385-05900-0*) Doubleday.

Letter to Women. John Paul, II, pseud. 19p. (Orig.). 1995. pap. text 2.95 (*1-57455-052-7*) US Catholic.

Letter to Young Black Men: You Won't Find Role Models on Street Corners. Eliot F. Battle. LC 97-61435. (YA). 1997. write for info. (*0-923950-18-4*) Tucker IL.

Letter Tracking, Bk. 1. large type ed. Ed. by W. Edwards & S. Edwards. 1975. 15.00 (*0-87879-851-X*) Acad Therapy.

Letter Tracking: Reusable Edition. Ed. by W. Edwards & S. Edwards. (Large Type Tracking Ser.). 1973. student ed. 9.00 (*0-89039-019-3*, Ann Arbor Div) Acad Therapy.

Letter Tracking Bks. 1-2: Reusable Edition. Ed. by W. Edwards & S. Edwards. (Ann Arbor Tracking Program Ser.). 1975. 12.00 (*0-87879-866-8*, Ann Arbor Div); 12.00 (*0-87879-865-X*, Ann Arbor Div); 15.00 (*0-87879-735-1*, Ann Arbor Div) Acad Therapy.

Letter Tracking Bks. 1-2: Reusable Edition, Bk. 1. Ed. by W. Edwards & S. Edwards. (Ann Arbor Tracking Program Ser.). 1975. 15.00 (*0-87879-736-X*, Ann Arbor Div) Acad Therapy.

Letter Tracking Bks. 1-2: Reusable Edition, Bk. 1. Ed. by W. Edwards & S. Edwards. (Ann Arbor Tracking Program Ser.). (J). (gr. 3-8). 1975. 15.00 (*0-87879-737-8*, Ann Arbor Div) Acad Therapy.

Letter Tracking Bks. 1-2: Reusable Edition, Bk. 2. Ed. by W. Edwards & S. Edwards. (Ann Arbor Tracking Program Ser.). 1975. 15.00 (*0-87879-868-4*, Ann Arbor Div); 15.00 (*0-87879-883-8*, Ann Arbor Div) Acad Therapy.

Letter V: Consonant Easy Readers. S. Bruckner & L. Kingman. (Easy Readers Ser.). 8p. (J). (ps-1). 1997. pap. 1.99 (*1-57690-305-2*) Tchr Create Mat.

Letter W. S. Bruckner & L. Kingman. (Easy Readers Ser.). 8p. (J). (ps-1). 1997. pap. 1.99 (*1-57690-306-0*) Tchr Create Mat.

Letter Within a Letter. unabridged ed. S. Gianinazzi. 1998. pap. 14.95 (*1-893336-07-7*) B Newton.

Letter Writer Starter Set. rev. ed. Reader's Digest Editors & Nancy Cobb. (Illus.). 64p. (J). (gr. 2-6). 1999. pap. text 8.99 (*1-57584-326-9*, Pub. by Rdrs Digest) Random.

Letter Writing. Louise B. Lang. 1994. pap. 10.00 (*0-00-470702-8*) Collins.

Letter Writing As a Social Practice. Ed. by David Barton & Nigel Hall. Date not set. write for info. (*1-85359-413-X*, Pub. by Multilingual Matters); pap. write for info. (*1-85359-412-1*, Pub. by Multilingual Matters) Taylor & Francis.

***Letter Writing as a Social Practice.** David Barton & Nigel Hall. LC 99-39098. (Studies in Written Language & Literacy: Vol. 9). vi, 262p. 2000. pap. 29.95 (*1-55619-208-8*) J Benjamins Pubng.

***Letter Writing as a Social Practice.** Ed. by David Barton & Nigel Hall. LC 99-39098. (Studies in Written Language & Literacy: Vol. 9). vi, 262p. 2000. text 70.00 (*1-55619-207-X*) J Benjamins Pubng.

Letter Writing for the Office: Syllabus. 2nd ed. Carl W. Salser. 1975. pap. text 10.65 (*0-89420-026-7*, 216720); audio 194.90 (*0-89420-160-3*, 110800) Natl Book.

Letter Writing in English. Brian Deakin. 254p. (C). 1986. 50.00 (*81-7002-016-6*, Pub. by Himalayan Bks) St Mut.

Letter Writing in Greco-Roman Antiquity. Stanley K. Stowers. LC 86-9082. (Library of Early Christianity: Vol. 5). 188p. (C). 1986. pap. 24.95 (*0-664-25015-7*) Westminster John Knox.

Letter Writing Made Easy! Featuring More Sample Letters for Hundreds of Common Occasions!, Vol. 2. Margaret McCarthy. 224p. 1998. pap. 12.95 (*1-891661-00-0*, 1-00-0) Snta Monica.

Letter Writing Made Easy! Featuring Sample Letters for Hundreds of Common Occasions! Margaret McCarthy. 224p. (Orig.). 1995. pap. 12.95 (*0-9639946-2-X*) Snta Monica.

Letter Writing Skills: Letter Writing. David James & Anthony Masters. LC 99-160212. (Teach Yourself Ser.). (Illus.). 208p. 1998. pap. 9.95 (*0-8442-0013-1*, 00131) NTC Contemp Pub Co.

Letter X: Consonant Easy Readers. S. Bruckner & L. Kingman. (Easy Readers Ser.). 8p. (J). (ps-1). 1997. pap. 1.99 (*1-57690-307-9*) Tchr Create Mat.

Letter Y: Consonant Easy Readers. S. Bruckner & L. Kingman. (Easy Readers Ser.). 8p. (J). (ps-1). 1997. pap. 1.99 (*1-57690-308-7*) Tchr Create Mat.

Letter Z: Consonant Easy Readers. S. Bruckner & L. Kingman. (Easy Readers Ser.). 8p. (J). (ps-1). 1997. pap. 1.99 (*1-57690-309-5*) Tchr Create Mat.

Letterbook of Eliza Lucas Pinckney, 1739-1762. rev. ed. Eliza L. Pinckney. Ed. by Marvin R. Zahniser. LC 96-51677. (Illus.). 230p. 1977. reprint ed. pap. 16.95 (*1-57003-186-X*) U of SC Pr.

***Letterbook of Greg & Cunningham, 1756-57: Merchants of New York & Belfast.** Ed. by Thomas M. Truxes. (Records of Social & Economic History, New Ser.: Vol. 28). (Illus.). 440p. 2000. text 85.00 (*0-19-726219-8*) OUP.

Lettercarving in Wood: A Practical Course. Chris Pye. LC 98-110394. (Illus.). 256p. 1997. pap. text 18.95 (*1-86108-043-3*, Pub. by Guild Master) Sterling.

Lettere Dall'Italia: Beginning Through Intermediate. (ITA.). (C). 8.40 (*0-8442-8040-2*, X8040-2) NTC Contemp Pub Co.

Lettere Di Clemente Rebora, 1897-1930, Vol. I. Ed. by Margherita Marchione. 680p. 1976. pap. 20.00 (*0-916322-17-3*) Am Inst Ital Stud.

An Asterisk (*) at the beginning of an entry indicates that the title is appearing for the first time.

Lettere Di Clemente Rebora, 1930-1957, Vol. 2. Ed. by Margherita Marchione. 410p. 1982. pap. 20.00 (*0-916322-13-0*) Am Inst Ital Stud.

Lettered City. Angel Rama. LC 96-13996. (Post-Contemporary Interventions Ser.). 176p. 1996. text 39.95 (*0-8223-1757-5*); pap. text 14.95 (*0-8223-1766-4*) Duke.

Letterforms. rev. ed. Stanley Morison. LC 96-18636. (Illus.). 128p. 1997. pap. 19.95 (*0-88179-136-9*) Hartley & Marks.

***Letterforms - Bawdy, Bad & Beautiful: The Evolution of Hand-Drawn, Humorous, Vernacular & Experimental Type.** Steven Heller & Christine Thompson. (Illus.). 192p. 2000. pap. 35.00 (*0-8230-0464-3*) Watsn-Guptill.

LetterFun ABC Book. Eleanor D. Reynolds. (Illus.). 32p. (J). 1999. pap. 5.95 (*0-9660157-1-1*) FunStuff Prodns.

***Lettergrams Favorite Hymns.** Ken Stiles. Ed. by Pat Fittro. 48p. 1999. pap. 1.49 (*0-7847-1073-2*, 02804) Standard Pub.

***Lettergrams Find-a-Bible Word.** Michael Leonard. Ed. by Pat Fittro. 48p. 1999. pap. 1.49 (*0-7847-1072-4*, 02803) Standard Pub.

Letterhead & Logo Design, No. 4. Ed. by Rockport Publishers Editorial Staff. (Illus.). 192p. 1996. 44.99 (*1-56496-257-1*) Rockport Pubs.

Letterhead & Logo Design Vol. 3: Creating the Corporate Image. Compiled by Rockport Publishers Staff. (Illus.). 256p. 1998. pap. 35.00 (*1-56496-228-8*) Rockport Pubs.

Letterhead & Logo Design 5. Compiled by Rockport Publishers Staff. (Illus.). 192p. 1998. pap. text 39.99 (*1-56496-405-1*) Rockport Pubs.

Letterhead & Logo Design 5, Vol. 5. Compiled by Rockport Publishers Staff. (Illus.). 192p. 1998. pap. 49.99 incl. cd-rom (*1-56496-366-7*) Rockport Pubs.

Letterhead & Logo Design 4. Compiled by Rockport Publishers Editors. (Illus.). 192p. 1997. pap. 34.99 (*1-56496-398-5*) Rockport Pubs.

***Letterhead & Logo Design 6.** Stoltze Design Staff. (Letterhead & Logo Design 6 Ser.). (Illus.). 208p. 1999. 45.00 (*1-56496-618-6*) Rockport Pubs.

Letterhead & Logo Designs: Creating the Corporate Image. Lisa Walker & Steve Blount. (Illus.). 256p. 1991. reprint ed. pap. 34.99 (*0-935603-97-2*) Rockport Pubs.

Letterhead & Logo Designs 2: Creating the Corporate Image. Rockport Book Editors. (Illus.). 256p. 1995. pap. 29.99 (*1-56496-121-4*) Rockport Pubs.

Letterheads. 4th ed. (TA - Typing/Keyboarding Ser.). 1987. 8.00 (*0-538-20470-2*) S-W Pub.

Letterheads, No. 3. David E. Carter. LC 81-65825. (Illus.). 326p. 1981. 32.50 (*0-910158-71-1*) Art Dir.

Letterheads, No. 4. Ed. by David E. Carter. LC 78-58439. (Letterheads Ser.). 304p. 1984. 32.50 (*0-88108-002-0*) Art Dir.

Letterheads, No. 5. David E. Carter. LC 78-58439. 342p. 1985. 35.00 (*0-88108-018-7*) Art Dir.

Letterheads, No. 6. David E. Carter. LC 78-640636. 302p. 1987. 39.50 (*0-88108-038-1*) Art Dir.

Letterheads, No. 7. David E. Carter. LC 89-80318. 300p. 1989. 55.00 (*0-88108-065-9*) Art Dir.

Letterheads, No. 8. Ed. by Don Barron. LC 78-640636. (Illus.). 274p. 1992. text 59.95 (*0-88108-104-3*) Art Dir.

Letterheads: The International Annual of Letterhead Design, No. 1. Ed. by David E. Carter. LC 78-58439. (Illus.). 1977. 32.50 (*0-910158-42-8*) Art Dir.

Letterheads: The Second International Annual of Letterhead Design, No. 2. Ed. by David E. Carter. LC 78-58439. (Letterheads Ser.). (Illus.). 1979. 32.50 (*0-910158-57-6*) Art Dir.

Letterheads: 100 Years of Great Designs. Leslie Cabarga. 16.99 (*0-8118-2253-2*) Rockport Pubs.

Letterheads & Business Cards. Chris Foges. 1999. pap. 35.00 (*2-88046-390-4*, Rotovision) Watsn-Guptill.

***Letterheads Gone Digital.** Carter. 1999. 39.95 (*0-688-16476-5*, Wm Morrow) Morrow Avon.

Letterheads Gone Digital. David E. Carter. 1998. pap. 39.95 (*0-8230-6624-X*) Watsn-Guptill.

Letterheads in the 3rd Dimension. David E. Carter. (Illus.). 192p. 1997. pap. text 39.95 (*0-8230-2753-8*) Watsn-Guptill.

Lettering: Make Your Own Cards, Signs, Gifts & More. Amanda Lewis. (Kids Can Crafts Ser.). (Illus.). 48p. (J). 1996. 16.99 (*1-55074-312-0*) Kids Can Pr.

Lettering: Make Your Own Cards, Signs, Gifts & More. unabridged ed. Amanda Lewis. (Kids Can Crafts Ser.). (Illus.). 48p. (J). (gr. 3 up). 1997. pap. 5.95 (*1-55074-232-9*, Pub. by Kids Can Pr) Genl Dist Srvs.

Lettering: Modes of Writing in Western Europe. Hermann Degering. (Illus.). 1978. pap. 9.95 (*0-8008-4727-X*) Taplinger.

Lettering: Studies & Research on the Evolution of Writing & Print Typefaces. Antonio Tubaro & Ivana Tubaro. Tr. by Stuart A. THom from ITA. (Illus.). 96p. (Orig.). 1995. pap. 14.95 (*0-9627985-0-9*) Idea Bks.

Lettering & Alphabets. Cavanaugh. (Illus.). 121p. pap. 6.95 (*0-486-20053-1*) Dover.

Lettering & Calligraphy. Instructional Fair Staff. 1998. pap. 7.95 (*1-56822-771-X*) Instruct Fair.

Lettering & Calligraphy Workbook. Diagram Group Staff. LC 98-3576. (Illus.). 288p. 1998. 14.95 (*0-8069-4273-8*) Sterling.

Lettering & Graphic Design of F. G. Cooper. Leslie E. Cabarga. LC 96-84614. (Illus.). 128p. 1996. pap. 16.95 (*0-88108-192-2*) Art Dir.

Lettering As Drawing. Nicolete Gray. LC 81-84750. (Illus.). 195p. 1982. pap. 9.95 (*0-8008-4729-6*) Taplinger.

Lettering for Advertising. Mortimer Leach. LC 56-10596. 244p. reprint ed. pap. 75.70 (*0-608-11285-2*, 200578900060) Bks Demand.

Lettering for Architects & Designers. 2nd ed. Martha Sutherland. 144p. 1989. pap. 39.95 (*0-471-28955-8*, VNR) Wiley.

Lettering for Architects & Designers. 2nd ed. Martha Sutherland. (Illus.). 146p. 1989. pap. 36.95 (*0-442-28214-1*, VNR) Wiley.

Lettering for Students & Craftspeople. Graily Hewitt. LC 92-35684. (Illus.). 336p. 1993. reprint ed. pap. 8.95 (*0-486-27518-3*) Dover.

Lettering for Woodworkers. 208p. Date not set. text 22.95 (*0-921335-20-2*, Pub. by LVTL) Veritas Tools.

Lettering of an Athenian Mason. Stephen V. Tracy. LC 74-8130. (Hesperia Supplement Ser.: No. 15). (Illus.). xxiii, 134p. 1975. pap. 15.00 (*0-87661-515-9*) Am Sch Athens.

Lettering: The History & Technique of Lettering As Design see History & Technique of Lettering

Letterman Wit: His Life & Humor. Bill Adler, Jr. 144p. 1994. 14.95 (*0-7867-0075-0*) Carroll & Graf.

Letterman Wit: His Life & Humor. Bill Adler, Jr. (Illus.). 160p. 1995. pap. 8.95 (*0-7867-0210-9*) Carroll & Graf.

Letterman's Guide to International Business, 4 vols. G. Gregory Letterman. LC 96-18160. (International Business & Law Ser.). 1996. ring bd. write for info. (*0-8366-1045-8*) West Group.

Letterman's Law of Private International Business, 3 vols., Set. annuals rev. ed. G. Gregory Letterman. LC 89-64180. (International Business & Law Ser.). 1990. suppl. ed. 375.00 (*0-685-59810-1*) West Group.

Lettermen: Album Guide: The Recording History of the World's Foremost Practitioners of Peace, & Harmony. Patrick S. Fullerton & Tony Butala. LC 94-90450. (Illus.). 100p. (Orig.). 1995. pap., spiral bd. 15.00 (*0-9634122-9-9*) Feather Fables.

Lettermen-Backstage-Onstage! Tony Butala et al. LC 94-71316. (Illus.). 28p. (Orig.). 1994. pap. 12.95 (*0-9634122-7-2*) Feather Fables.

Letterpress - Visual Aid Kit. Pira Staff. 1998. 95.00 (*1-85802-057-3*, Pub. by Pira Pub) Bks Intl VA.

Letterpress Pressman. Jack Rudman. (Career Examination Ser.: C-437). 1994. pap. 27.95 (*0-8373-0437-7*) Nat Learn.

Letters see Centennial Edition of the Works of Sidney Lanier

Letters see Little Mouse's Learn-&-Play

Letters. Nicky Burbidge. 142p. 1996. pap. text 13.95 (*0-19-442149-X*) OUP.

Letters. William S. Burroughs. 1993. pap. 25.00 (*0-670-77285-2*) Viking Penguin.

Letters. Ray Di Palma. (Littoral Bks.). 63p. 1998. pap. 10.95 (*1-55713-374-3*) Sun & Moon CA.

Letters. Marrissa R. Dick. Date not set. pap. 14.95 (*1-893979-02-4*) Nubian Romance.

Letters, 3 vols. Emily Dickinson. Ed. by Thomas H. Johnson & Theodora Ward. LC 58-5594. (Illus.). 1042p. 1958. boxed set 74.50 (*0-674-52625-2*) Belknap Pr.

***Letters.** Keith Douglas. 360p. 2000. pap. 29.95 (*1-85754-477-3*, Pub. by Carcanet Pr) Paul & Co Pubs.

Letters. Educational Development Corporation Staff & Carolyn B. Mitchell. (First Learning Ser.). (Illus.). 24p. (J). (ps-3). 1992. pap. 3.50 (*0-7460-1036-2*) EDC.

Letters. Golden Books Staff. (My First Book & Disk Ser.). 48p. (J). 1998. 14.95 (*0-307-19860-X*, Goldn Books) Gldn Bks Pub Co.

Letters. Jon Hamilton. 118p. (Orig.). 1997. pap. 11.95 (*1-57502-444-6*, PO1337) Morris Pubng.

Letters. Leo the Great. Tr. by Edmund Hunt. LC 63-18826. (Fathers of the Church Ser.: Vol. 34). 312p. 1957. 17.95 (*0-8132-0034-2*) Cath U Pr.

Letters. Lady Mary Wortley Montagu. LC 92-52913. 592p. 1992. 20.00 (*0-679-41747-8*) Everymns Lib.

Letters. Tobias George Smollett. Ed. by Edward S. Noyes. LC 77-99671. (Select Bibliographies Reprint Ser.). 1977. 25.95 (*0-8369-5100-X*) Ayer.

Letters. Baruch Spinoza. Tr. by Samuel Shirley. LC 95-23700. 414p. (C). 1995. lib. bdg. 34.95 (*0-87220-275-5*) Hackett Pub.

Letters. Katie Yates & Cassandra Terman. 32p. (Orig.). 1996. pap. 5.00 (*1-887289-17-8*) Rodent Pr.

Letters see Complete Works of Algernon Charles Swinburne

Letters. Henry (Brooks) Adams. (Works of Henry Adams). 1989. reprint ed. lib. bdg. 79.00 (*0-7812-1447-5*) Rprt Serv.

Letters. John Barth. LC 94-8761. 772p. 1994. reprint ed. pap. 14.95 (*1-56478-061-9*) Dalkey Arch.

Letters. Bernard of Clairvaux. Tr. by Bruno S. James. LC 78-63344. (Crusades & Military Orders Ser.: Second Series). reprint ed. 82.50 (*0-404-17004-8*) AMS Pr.

Letters. Ambrose Bierce. Ed. by B. C. Pope. LC 67-30702. 252p. 1967. reprint ed. 50.00 (*0-87752-009-7*) Gordian.

Letters. Ambrose Bierce. (BCL1-PS American Literature Ser.). 204p. 1992. reprint ed. lib. bdg. 79.00 (*0-7812-6675-0*) Rprt Serv.

Letters, 2 vols. James Boswell. reprint ed. 59.00 (*0-403-04137-6*) Somerset Pub.

Letters. Charles F. Browne. (Works of Charles Farrar Browne). 1989. reprint ed. lib. bdg. 79.00 (*0-7812-2097-1*) Rprt Serv.

Letters. John Dryden. Ed. by Charles E. Ward. LC 74-164791. reprint ed. 27.50 (*0-404-02186-7*) AMS Pr.

Letters. John G. Dundee. Ed. by George Smythe. LC 76-164808. (Bannatyne Club, Edinburgh. Publications: No. 15). reprint ed. 34.50 (*0-404-52715-9*) AMS Pr.

Letters. William James. Ed. by H. James. (Notable American Authors Ser.). 1992. reprint ed. lib. bdg. 75.00 (*0-7812-3484-0*) Rprt Serv.

Letters. Sarah Orne Jewett. (American Biography Ser.). 186p. 1991. reprint ed. lib. bdg. 59.00 (*0-7812-8219-5*) Rprt Serv.

Letters. Sidney Lanier. (Notable American Authors Ser.). 1999. reprint ed. lib. bdg. 125.00 (*0-7812-3725-4*) Rprt Serv.

Letters. James Russell Lowell. (Notable American Authors Ser.). 1999. reprint ed. lib. bdg. 125.00 (*0-7812-3900-1*) Rprt Serv.

Letters. Tobias George Smollett. (BCL1-PR English Literature Ser.). 260p. 1992. reprint ed. lib. bdg. 79.00 (*0-7812-7404-4*) Rprt Serv.

Letters. Edward J. Trelawny. Ed. by H. Buxton Forman. LC 74-177570. reprint ed. 42.00 (*0-404-07439-1*) AMS Pr.

Letters. Daniel Webster. (Notable American Authors Ser.). 1999. reprint ed. lib. bdg. 125.00 (*0-7812-9916-0*) Rprt Serv.

Letters, 2 vols., 1. Ed. by Betty Radice. (Loeb Classical Library: No. 55, 59). 596p. 1969. text 18.95 (*0-674-99061-7*) HUP.

Letters, 4 Vols, 1. St. Basil. LC 65-18318. (Loeb Classical Library: No. 190, 215, 243, 270). 422p. 1926. 18.95 (*0-674-99209-1*) HUP.

Letters, 2 vols., 2. Tr. by Betty Radice. (Loeb Classical Library: No. 55, 59). 592p. 1969. text 18.95 (*0-674-99066-8*) HUP.

Letters, 4 Vols, 2. St. Basil. LC 65-18318. (Loeb Classical Library: No. 190, 215, 243, 270). 492p. 1928. 18.95 (*0-674-99237-7*) HUP.

Letters, 4 Vols, 3. Caesarea Basil. LC 65-18318. (Loeb Classical Library: No. 190, 215, 243, 270). 504p. 1930. 19.95 (*0-674-99268-7*) HUP.

Letters, 4 Vols, 4. Tr. by Roy J. Deferrari. LC 65-18318. (Loeb Classical Library: No. 190, 215, 243, 270). 472p. 1934. 18.95 (*0-674-99298-9*) HUP.

Letters, 2 vols., Set. James Boswell. 1988. reprint ed. lib. bdg. 99.00 (*0-7812-0083-0*) Rprt Serv.

Letters, 2 Vols., Set. Edward Fitzgerald. Ed. by William A. Wright. LC 72-5597. (Select Bibliographies Reprint Ser.). 1977. reprint ed. 46.95 (*0-8369-6906-5*) Ayer.

Letters, 2 vols., Set. Franz Liszt & La Mara. Tr. by Constance Bache. LC 69-13973. 1970. reprint ed. lib. bdg. 65.00 (*0-8371-1104-8*, LILE) Greenwood.

Letters, 2 vols., Set. Robert Louis Stevenson. (American Biography Ser.). 1991. reprint ed. lib. bdg. 148.00 (*0-7812-8361-2*) Rprt Serv.

Letters, 4 vols., Set. Robert Louis Stevenson. (BCL1-PR English Literature Ser.). 1992. reprint ed. lib. bdg. 300.00 (*0-7812-7668-3*) Rprt Serv.

Letters, Vol. 1. Said Nursi. 281p. 1993. pap. 8.95 (*0-9521497-2-9*) Fountain Pub.

Letters, 2 vols., Vol. 1. Franz Liszt & La Mara. Tr. by Constance Bache. LC 69-13973. 1970. reprint ed. lib. bdg. 45.00 (*0-313-21285-6*, LILA) Greenwood.

Letters, 2 vols., Vol. 1: 1906-1950. C. G. Jung. Ed. by Gerhard Adler & Aniela Jaffe. LC 74-166378. (Bollingen Ser.: No. 95). 624p. reprint ed. pap. 193.50 (*0-8357-6703-5*, 202503600001) Bks Demand.

Letters, Vol. 1, Nos. 1-82. Augustine, Saint. Tr. by Wilfrid Parsons. LC 64-19948. (Fathers of the Church Ser.: Vol. 12). 420p. 1951. 34.95 (*0-8132-0012-1*) Cath U Pr.

Letters, Vol. 1, Nos. 1-185. Caesarea Basil. Tr. by Agnes C. Way. LC 65-18318. (Fathers of the Church Ser.: Vol. 13). 345p. 1951. 20.95 (*0-8132-0013-X*) Cath U Pr.

Letters, Vol. 2. Said Nursi. 330p. 1993. pap. 8.95 (*975-7388-44-0*) Fountain Pub.

Letters, 2 vols., Vol. 2. Franz Liszt & La Mara. Tr. by Constance Bache. LC 69-13973. 1970. reprint ed. lib. bdg. 45.00 (*0-8371-1105-6*, LILB) Greenwood.

Letters, 2 vols., Vol. 2: 1951-1961. C. G. Jung. Ed. by Gerhard Adler & Aniela Jaffe. LC 74-166378. (Bollingen Ser.: No. 95). 764p. reprint ed. pap. 200.00 (*0-8357-6704-3*, 202503600002) Bks Demand.

Letters, Vol. 2, Nos. 186-368. Caesarea Basil. Tr. by Agnes C. Way. LC 65-18318. (Fathers of the Church Ser.: Vol. 28). 369p. 1955. 21.95 (*0-8132-0028-8*) Cath U Pr.

Letters, Vol. 3, Nos. 131-164. Augustine, Saint. Tr. by Wilfrid Parsons. LC 64-19948. (Fathers of the Church Ser.: Vol. 20). 402p. 1953. 36.95 (*0-8132-0020-2*) Cath U Pr.

Letters, Vol. 4, 1877-1882. Algernon Charles Swinburne. Ed. by Cecil Y. Lang. LC 59-12698. 331p. reprint ed. pap. 102.70 (*0-8357-8207-7*, 203379500004) Bks Demand.

Letters, Vol. 4, Nos. 165-203. Augustine, Saint. Tr. by Wilfrid Parsons. LC 64-19948. (Fathers of the Church Ser.: Vol. 30). 421p. 1955. 36.95 (*0-8132-0030-X*) Cath U Pr.

Letters, Vol. 5, Nos. 204-270. Augustine, Saint. Tr. by Wilfrid Parsons. LC 64-19948. (Fathers of the Church Ser.: Vol. 32). 317p. 1956. 31.95 (*0-8132-0032-6*) Cath U Pr.

Letters, Vol. 6, Nos. 1-29. Augustine, Saint. Tr. by Robert B. Eno. LC 64-19948. (Fathers of the Church Ser.: Vol. 81). 208p. 1989. 31.95 (*0-8132-0081-4*) Cath U Pr.

Letters see Centennial Edition of the Works of Sidney Lanier

Letters, Vols. 5-6. Eleanor Roosevelt. 25.00 (*0-674-52802-6*) HUP.

Letters: Inventing the Cinema. Auguste Lumiere & Louis Lumiere. Tr. by Pierre Hodgson. (Illus.). 336p. 1997. 33.95 (*0-571-17545-7*) Faber & Faber.

Letters: Selections from His Correspondence. Sidney Lanier. Ed. by Henry W. Lanier. LC 71-37890. (Select Bibliographies Reprint Ser.). 1977. reprint ed. 23.95 (*0-8369-6727-5*) Ayer.

***Letters: Text Library System.** Edwin P. Morrow. 1999. per. write for info. (*1-893717-04-6*) Finan Plan.

Letters . . . Regarding the Absence of Consideration in Our Present Form of Government for Our Coloured Population (1906) Joseph Baynes. (Colin Webb Natal & Zululand Ser.: No. 2). 44p. 1992. pap. 11.95 (*0-86980-878-8*, Pub. by Univ Natal Pr) Intl Spec Bk.

Letters a Stendhal, 1810-1842. Stendhal, pseud. Ed. by Henri Martineau. pap. 5.95 (*0-685-35014-2*) Fr & Eur.

Letters: A Study in Friendship see Latin Letters of C. S. Lewis

Letters A-Z, 5 bks. Cynthia Muller et al. (Apples for Teachers Ser.). 96p. 11.99 (*0-8224-0456-7*, FE0456) Fearon Teacher Aids.

Letters about Shelley Interchanged by Three Friends-Edward Dowden, Richard Garnett & William Michael Rossetti. William M. Rossetti. LC 77-168058. reprint ed. 24.50 (*0-404-05444-7*) AMS Pr.

Letters about the Hudson River & Its Vicinity. Freeman Hunt. 252p. 1993. reprint ed. lib. bdg. 79.00 (*0-7812-5127-3*) Rprt Serv.

Letters about the Hudson River, 1835-1837. pap. 12.95 (*0-941567-31-1*) J C & A L Fawcett.

Letters Addressed to H. R. H. the Grand Duke of Saxe Coburg & Gotha, on the Theory of Probabilities. Adolphe J. Quetelet. Ed. by I. Bernard Cohen. LC 80-2143. (Development of Science Ser.). (Illus.). 1981. lib. bdg. 33.95 (*0-405-13950-0*) Ayer.

Letters, Addressed to Sir John Sinclair, Bart. William Creech. LC 78-67652. (Scottish Enlightenment Ser.). reprint ed. 39.50 (*0-404-17187-7*) AMS Pr.

Letters Addressed to the People of Pennsylvania: Respecting the Internal Improvement of the Commonwealth by Means of Roads & Canals. William J. Duane. LC 68-18218. (Reprints of Economic Classics Ser.). 125p. 1968. reprint ed. 35.00 (*0-678-00381-5*) Kelley.

***Letters & Asceticism in Fourth-Century Egypt.** Bernadette McNary-Zak. LC 99-88553. 160p. 2000. 42.50 (*0-7618-1621-6*) U Pr of Amer.

Letters & Autobiographical Writings C. Wright Mills et al. LC 99-29106. 2000. write for info. (*0-520-22072-2*) U CA Pr.

Letters & Charters of Cardinal Guala Bicchieri, Papal Legate in England, 1216-1218. Ed. by Nicholas Vincent. (Canterbury & York Society Ser.: Vol. 83). (Illus.). 290p. 1996. 45.00 (*0-907239-53-6*) Boydell & Brewer.

Letters & Contracts from Erech Written in the Neo-Babylonian Period. Clarence E. Keiser. LC 78-63521. (Babylonian Inscriptions in the Collection of James B. Nies Ser.: 1). reprint ed. 27.50 (*0-404-60131-6*) AMS Pr.

***Letters & Diaries of a Combat Rifleman.** Charles Davis. 2000. pap. 18.00 (*0-8059-5047-8*) Dorrance.

Letters & Diaries of John Henry Cardinal Newman. Incl. Vol. 23. Defeat at Oxford-Defence at Rome, January to December, 1867. John Henry Newman. Ed. by Charles S. Dessain & Thomas Gornall. 454p. 1973. text 38.50 (*0-19-920040-8*); Vol. 27. Controversy with Gladstone, January 1874-December 1875. 476p. 1975. text 38.50 (*0-19-920057-2*); Vol. 28. Fellow of Trinity, January 1876-December 1878. 496p. 1975. text 38.50 (*0-19-920058-0*); write for info. (*0-318-54854-2*) OUP.

Letters & Diaries of John Henry Cardinal Newman. Incl. Vol. 23. Defeat at Oxford-Defence at Rome, January to December, 1867. John Henry Newman. Ed. by Charles S. Dessain & Thomas Gornall. 454p. 1973. text 38.50 (*0-19-920040-8*); Vol. 27. Controversy with Gladstone, January 1874-December 1875. 476p. 1975. text 38.50 (*0-19-920057-2*); Vol. 28. Fellow of Trinity, January 1876-December 1878. 496p. 1975. text 38.50 (*0-19-920058-0*); 1973. write for info. (*0-318-54853-4*) OUP.

Letters & Diaries of John Henry Cardinal Newman Vol. 1: Ealing, Trinity, Oriel, February 1801 to December 1826. John Henry Newman. Ed. by Ian Ker & Thomas Gornall. 364p. 1978. text 52.00 (*0-19-920102-1*) OUP.

Letters & Diaries of John Henry Cardinal Newman Vol. 2: Tutor of Oriel, January 1827 to December 1831. John Henry Newman. Ed. by Ian Ker & Thomas Gornall. 436p. 1979. text 55.00 (*0-19-920108-0*) OUP.

Letters & Diaries of John Henry Cardinal Newman Vol. 3: New Bearings, January 1832 to June 1833. John Henry Newman. Ed. by Ian Ker & Thomas Gornall. 364p. 1979. text 52.00 (*0-19-920109-9*) OUP.

Letters & Diaries of John Henry Cardinal Newman Vol. 4: The Oxford Movement, July 1833 to December 1834. John Henry Newman. Ed. by Ian Ker & Thomas Gornall. 428p. 1980. text 55.00 (*0-19-920112-9*) OUP.

Letters & Diaries of John Henry Cardinal Newman Vol. 5: Liberalism in Oxford, January 1835 to December 1836. John Henry Newman. Ed. by Thomas Gornall. 440p. 1981. text 65.00 (*0-19-920117-X*) OUP.

Letters & Diaries of John Henry Cardinal Newman Vol. 6: The Via Media & Froude's Remains, January 1837 to December 1838. John Henry Newman. Ed. by Gerard Tracey. 438p. 1984. text 70.00 (*0-19-920141-2*) OUP.

Letters & Diaries of John Henry Cardinal Newman Vol. 7: Editing the British Critic, January 1839 - December 1840. Ed. by Gerard Tracey. 576p. 1995. text 105.00 (*0-19-920402-0*) OUP.

Letters & Diaries of John Henry Cardinal Newman Vol. 29: The Cardinalate, January 1878-September 1881. John Henry Newman. Ed. by Charles S. Dessain & Thomas Gornall. 496p. 1976. text 47.00 (*0-19-920059-9*) OUP.

Letters & Diaries of John Henry Cardinal Newman Vol. 30: A Cardinal's Apostolate, October 1881-December 1884. John Henry Newman. Ed. by Charles S. Dessain & Thomas Gornall. 504p. 1976. text 47.00 (*0-19-920060-2*) OUP.

Letters & Diaries of John Henry Cardinal Newman Vol. 31: The Last Years, January 1885 to August 1890. John Henry Newman. Ed. by Charles S. Dessain & Thomas Gornall. 458p. 1977. text 52.00 (*0-19-920083-1*) OUP.

Letters & Diaries of John Henry Newman Vol. VIII: Tract 90 & the Jerusalem Bishopric. John Henry Newman. Ed. by Gerard Tracey. 672p. 2000. text 120.00 (*0-19-920403-9*) OUP.

Letters & Diary of John Rowe: Boston Merchant, 1759 to 1762. John Rowe. Ed. by Anne R. Cunningham. LC 76-76564. (Eyewitness Accounts of the American Revolution Ser.). (Illus.). 453p. 1969. reprint ed. 28.95 (*0-405-01148-2*) Ayer.

Letters & Diary of Laura M. Towne: Written from the Sea Islands of South Carolina, 1862-1884. Laura M. Towne. (American Biography Ser.). 310p. 1991. reprint ed. lib. bdg. 79.00 (*0-7812-8395-7*) Rprt Serv.

Letters & Dispatches, 1924-1944. Raoul Wallenberg. Tr. by Kjersti Board. (Illus.). 320p. 1996. pap. 12.45 (*1-55970-320-2*, Pub. by Arcade Pub Inc) Time Warner.

Letters & Dispatches, 1924-1945. Raoul Wallenberg. Tr. by Kjersti Board from SWE. (Illus.). 256p. 1995. 24.45 (*1-55970-275-3*, Pub. by Arcade Pub Inc) Time Warner.

Letters & Dispatches of John Churchill, First Duke of Marlborough from 1702-1712, 5 vols., Set. John C. Marlborough. Ed. by George Murray. LC 68-54801. 1969. reprint ed. lib. bdg. 295.00 (*0-8371-2663-0*, MUJC) Greenwood.

Letters & Dispatches of John Churchill, First Duke of Marlborough from 1702-1712, 5 vols., Vol. 2. John C. Marlborough. Ed. by George Murray. LC 68-54801. 1969. reprint ed. lib. bdg. 75.00 (*0-8371-0829-2*, MUJE) Greenwood.

Letters & Dispatches of John Churchill, First Duke of Marlborough from 1702-1712, 5 vols., Vol. 3. John C. Marlborough. Ed. by George Murray. LC 68-54801. 1969. reprint ed. lib. bdg. 75.00 (*0-8371-0830-6*, MUJF) Greenwood.

Letters & Dispatches of John Churchill, First Duke of Marlborough from 1702-1712, 5 vols., Vol. 4. John C. Marlborough. Ed. by George Murray. LC 68-54801. 1969. reprint ed. lib. bdg. 75.00 (*0-8371-0831-4*, MUJG) Greenwood.

Letters & Dispatches of John Churchill, First Duke of Marlborough from 1702-1712, 5 vols., Vol. 5. John C. Marlborough. Ed. by George Murray. LC 68-54801. 1969. reprint ed. lib. bdg. 75.00 (*0-8371-0832-2*, MUJH) Greenwood.

Letters & Documents. Soren Kierkegaard. Tr. by Henrik Rosenmeier from DAN. LC 77-85897. (Kierkegaard's Writings: No. XXV). (Illus.). 518p. 1978. text 85.00 (*0-691-07228-0*, Pub. by Princeton U Pr) Cal Prin Full Svc.

Letters & Documents in the Enoch Pratt Free Library. Edgar Allan Poe & Lambert A. Wilmer. LC 41-10640. 192p. 1978. 50.00 (*0-8201-1199-6*) Schol Facsimiles.

Letters & Documents of Armand De Gontaut, Baron De Biron, Marshal of France, 1524-1592, 2 vols., Set. Armand D. Biron. Ed. by Sidney H. Ehrman. LC 76-29405. reprint ed. 82.50 (*0-404-15351-8*) AMS Pr.

Letters & Essays, 1886-1913. Mirza Abu'l-Fadl. Tr. by Juan R. Cole from PER. (Illus.). 210p. 1985. 19.95 (*0-933770-36-7*) Kalimat.

Letters & Essays of a Pope. Frank C. Hughes. 1989. 12.50 (*0-936128-35-6*) De Young Pr.

Letters & Friendships of Sir Cecil Spring Rice, 2 vols, Set. Cecil A. Rice. Ed. by Stephen L. Gwynn. LC 73-110868. (Illus.). 1971. reprint ed. lib. bdg. 85.00 (*0-8371-4545-7*, SPLE) Greenwood.

Letters & Friendships of Sir Cecil Spring Rice, 2 vols, Vol. 1. Cecil A. Rice. Ed. by Stephen L. Gwynn. LC 73-110868. (Illus.). 1971. reprint ed. lib. bdg. 45.00 (*0-8371-4546-5*, SPLF) Greenwood.

Letters & Friendships of Sir Cecil Spring Rice, 2 vols, Vol. 2. Cecil A. Rice. Ed. by Stephen L. Gwynn. LC 73-110868. (Illus.). 1971. reprint ed. lib. bdg. 45.00 (*0-8371-4547-3*, SPLG) Greenwood.

Letters & Friendships of Sir Cecil Spring Rice: A Record, 2 Vols., Set. Cecil A. Rice. Ed. by Stephen L. Gwynn. LC 79-37912. (Select Bibliographies Reprint Ser.). 1977. reprint ed. 58.95 (*0-8369-6750-X*) Ayer.

Letters & Heads. W. S. Graham. 72p. 1993. pap., boxed set 400.00 (*0-907664-37-7*, Pub. by Old Stiles) St Mut.

Letters & Inscriptions of Hammurabi, King of Babylon, About B. C. 2200, 3 vols. in 2. Hammurabi. LC 73-18853. (Luzac's Semitic Text & Translation Ser.: Nos. 2, 3, & 8). reprint ed. 74.50 (*0-404-11265-X*) AMS Pr.

Letters & Instructions of Francis Xavier. Francis Xavier. Tr. & Intro. by M. Joseph Costelloe. LC 92-73954. (Jesuit Primary Sources in English Translation Series I: No. 10). xxx, 488p. 1992. 34.95 (*1-880810-00-X*); pap. 27.95 (*1-880810-01-8*) Inst Jesuit.

Letters & Journal of a Civil War Surgeon. Stewart J. Petrie. LC 97-75508. 208p. 1998. 21.95 (*1-57197-095-9*) Pentland Pr.

Letters & Journals, 3 vols. Robert Baillie. Ed. by David Laing. LC 70-161745. (Bannatyne Club, Edinburgh. Publications: No. 73). reprint ed. 295.00 (*0-404-52800-7*) AMS Pr.

Letters & Journals, Vol. 2. James Fenimore Cooper. Ed. by James F. Beard. LC 60-5388. (Illus.). 442p. 1960. reprint ed. pap. 137.10 (*0-7837-3082-9*, 205746500002) Bks Demand.

Letters & Journals, Vol.1. James Fenimore Cooper. Ed. by James F. Beard. LC 60-5388. (Illus.). 500p. 1994. reprint ed. pap. 155.00 (*0-7837-3081-0*, 205746500001) Bks Demand.

Letters & Journals: Literary Correspondence L. Ron Hubbard. LC 97-222982. 88p. 1997. write for info. (*1-57318-130-7*) Bridge Pubns Inc.

Letters & Journals: Paula Modersohn-Becker. Paula Modersohn-Becker. Ed. by Gunter Busch & Liselotte Von Reinken. LC 98-155373. (Illus.). 576p. 1998. pap. text 24.95 (*0-8101-1644-8*) Northwestern U Pr.

Letters & Journals: The Dianetics Letters L. Ron Hubbard. LC 98-134881. 73 p. 1997. write for info. (*1-57318-094-7*) Bridge Pubns Inc.

Letters & Journals of James Fenimore Cooper, 6 vols. James Fenimore Cooper. Ed. by James F. Beard. Incl. Set. JF Cooper's Letters, 8 Journals. 895p. 1968. 80.00 (*0-674-52552-3*); Set. 992p. 1964. 79.95 (*0-674-52551-5*); (Illus.). write for info. (*0-318-53093-7*) Belknap Pr.

Letters & Journals of Paula Modersohn-Becker. Paula Modersohn-Becker. LC 80-18993. 370p. 1980. 29.50 (*0-8108-1344-0*) Scarecrow.

Letters & Journals of Samuel Gridley Howe, 2 vols. Samuel G. Howe. Ed. by Laura E. Richards. LC 75-169451. reprint ed. 115.00 (*0-404-03357-1*) AMS Pr.

Letters & Journals of Samuel Gridley Howe: The Greek Revolution, 2 vols., Set. Samuel G. Howe. (American Biography Ser.). 1991. reprint ed. lib. bdg. 148.00 (*0-7812-8201-2*) Rprt Serv.

Letters & Journals of Thomas Wentworth Higginson. Thomas W. Higginson. (Notable American Authors Ser.). 1992. reprint ed. lib. bdg. 75.00 (*0-7812-3116-7*) Rprt Serv.

Letters & Journals of Thomas Wentworth Higginson, 1846-1906. Thomas W. Higginson. Ed. by Mary T. Higginson. LC 73-87489. (American Public Figures Ser.). 1969. reprint ed. lib. bdg. 42.50 (*0-306-71495-7*) Da Capo.

Letters & Journals of Thomas Wentworth Higginson, 1846-1906. Thomas W. Higginson. Ed. by Mary T. Higginson. LC 73-88435. (Illus.). 358p. 1970. reprint ed. lib. bdg. 59.50 (*0-8371-1843-3*, HIH&) Greenwood.

Letters & Journals Relating to the War of the American Revolution, & the Capture of the German Troops at Saratoga. Frederick A. Riedesel. LC 67-29035. (Eyewitness Accounts of the American Revolution Ser.). 1968. reprint ed. 19.95 (*0-405-01120-2*) Ayer.

Letters & Labyrinths: Women Writing/Cultural Codes. Diane Cousineau. LC 96-53198. 232p. 1997. 36.50 (*0-87413-627-X*) U Delaware Pr.

Letters & Lectures of Idries Shah. Ed. by Adam Musa. 40p. 1981. pap. 9.00 (*0-86304-010-1*, Pub. by Octagon Pr) ISHK.

Letters & Literary Memorials of Samuel J. Tilden, 2 Vols., Set. Samuel J. Tilden. Ed. by John Bigelow. LC 74-164629. (Select Bibliographies Reprint Ser.). 1977. reprint ed. 51.95 (*0-8369-5913-2*) Ayer.

Letters & Literary Remains of Edward Fitzgerald, 7 vols. Edward Fitzgerald. Ed. by William A. Wright. LC 78-168035. reprint ed. 535.00 (*0-404-02440-8*) AMS Pr.

***Letters & Mailing.** Joshua Mostafa. LC 99-54212. (Essential Computers Ser.). 72p. 2000. pap. text 6.95 (*0-7894-5529-3*, D K Ink) DK Pub Inc.

Letters & Memorials of Emanuel Swedenborg, Set, Vols. I & II. Ed. & Tr. by Alfred Acton. 1948. 16.00 (*0-915221-04-7*) Swedenborg Sci Assn.

Letters & Memorials of Emanuel Swedenborg, Vol. 1. Ed. & Tr. by Alfred Acton. 508p. 1948. 8.50 (*0-915221-29-2*) Swedenborg Sci Assn.

Letters & Memorials of Emanuel Swedenborg, Vol. 2. Ed. & Tr. by Alfred Acton. 803p. 1948. 8.50 (*0-915221-30-6*) Swedenborg Sci Assn.

Letters & Memorials of Jane Welsh Carlyle, 3 vols., Set. Jane B. Carlyle. LC 79-37683. 1168p. 1983. reprint ed. 230.00 (*0-404-56709-6*) AMS Pr.

Letters & Memorials of State, in the Reigns of Queen Mary, Queen Elizabeth, King James, King Charles the First, Part of the Reign of King Charles the Second, & Oliver's Usurpation, 2 vols. Arthur Collins. LC 72-997. reprint ed. lib. bdg. 185.00 (*0-404-01631-6*) AMS Pr.

Letters & Memos Just Like That! Dave Davies. LC 97-67311. (Self-Study Sourcebook Ser.). 164p. 1997. pap. 15.95 (*1-57294-095-6*, 13-0037) SkillPath Pubns.

Letters & Notebooks of Mary Devlin Booth, 23. Ed. by L. Terry Oggel. LC 87-130. (Contributions in Drama & Theatre Studies: No. 23). 200p. 1987. 55.00 (*0-313-25468-0*, OCE/, Greenwood Pr) Greenwood.

Letters & Notes on the Manners, Customs & Conditions of the North American Indians, Vol. 1. George Catlin. LC 64-18844. (Illus.). 264p. 1973. reprint ed. pap. 9.95 (*0-486-22118-0*) Dover.

Letters & Notes on the Manners, Customs & Conditions of the North American Indians, Vol. 2. George Catlin. LC 64-18844. (Illus.). 266p. 1973. reprint ed. pap. 9.95 (*0-486-22119-9*) Dover.

***Letters & Notes on the North American Indians.** George Catlin. (Illus.). 290p. 1999. reprint ed. text 30.00 (*0-7881-6659-X*) DIANE Pub.

Letters & Numbers. (Early Learning Ser.). (J). Price not set. incl. audio NewSound.

Letters & Numbers. Kim Thompson et al. (Early Childhood Ser.). Orig. Title: A Little Rhythm, Rhyme & Read, Letters & Numbers. (Illus.). 24p. (J). (ps-1). 1993. student ed. 9.98 incl. audio (*1-882331-15-X*, TWIN 407) Twin Sisters.

Letters & Numbers. Contrib. by Twin Sisters Productions Staff. 1997. 19.95 incl. audio compact disk (*1-57583-030-2*) Twin Sisters.

Letters & Numbers: Full Size Designs, Ready to Cut. John A. Nelson. (Scroll Saw Pattern Bks.). (Illus.). 96p. 1996. pap. 14.95 (*0-8117-3075-1*) Stackpole.

Letters & Numbers for Me. Janice Z. Olsen. (Illus.). 72p. (J). (gr. k-1). 1999. pap. text, wbk. ed. 4.75 (*1-891627-10-4*) Handwriting.

***Letters & Orations.** Cassandra Fedele & Diana M. Robin. LC 99-51321. (Other Voice in Early Modern Europe Ser.). 208p. 2000. pap. text 15.00 (*0-226-23932-2*) U Ch Pr.

Letters & Other Documents Illustrating the Relations Between England & Germany at the Commencement of the Thirty Years' War, 2 vols. Ed. by Samuel R. Gardiner. LC 70-168100. (Camden Society, London. Publications, First Ser.: Nos. 90 & 98). reprint ed. 105.00 (*0-404-50211-3*) AMS Pr.

Letters & Other Materials from the Moscow & Prague Linguistic Circles, 1912-1945. Ed. & Tr. by Toman Jindrich. LC 94-31979. (Cahiers Roman Jakobson Ser.). 1995. write for info. (*0-930042-75-1*) Mich Slavic Pubns.

Letters & Papers. Patrick G. Gray. Ed. by Thomas Thomson. LC 72-168184. (Bannatyne Club, Edinburgh. Publications: No. 48). reprint ed. 37.50 (*0-404-52758-2*) AMS Pr.

Letters & Papers from Prison. Dietrich Bonhoeffer. 1981. 17.95 (*0-02-513110-9*) Macmillan.

Letters & Papers Illustrative of the Reigns of Richard III & Henry VII, 2 vols. Ed. by James Gairdner. (Rolls Ser.: No. 24). 1969. reprint ed. 140.00 (*0-8115-1040-9*) Periodicals Srv.

Letters & Papers Illustrative of the Wars of the English in France During the Reign of Henry VI, 2 vols. in 3, Vol. 1. Ed. by Joseph Stevenson. (Rolls Ser.: No. 22). 1969. reprint ed. write for info. (*0-8115-1035-2*) Periodicals Srv.

Letters & Papers Illustrative of the Wars of the English in France During the Reign of Henry VI, 2 vols. in 3, Vol. 2. Ed. by Joseph Stevenson. (Rolls Ser.: No. 22). 1969. reprint ed. write for info. (*0-8115-1036-0*) Periodicals Srv.

Letters & Papers Illustrative of the Wars of the English in France During the Reign of Henry VI, 2 vols. in 3, Vol. 3. Ed. by Joseph Stevenson. (Rolls Ser.: No. 22). 1969. reprint ed. write for info. (*0-8115-1037-9*) Periodicals Srv.

Letters & Papers Illustrative to the Reigns of Richard III & Henry VII, 2 vols., Set. Ed. by James Gairdner. LC 75-41107. reprint ed. 115.00 (*0-404-14910-3*) AMS Pr.

Letters & Papers of Benjamin Franklin & Richard Jackson. Benjamin Franklin. (American Autobiography Ser.). 222p. 1995. reprint ed. lib. bdg. 79.00 (*0-7812-8522-4*) Rprt Serv.

Letters & Papers of Benjamin Franklin & Richard Jackson, 1753-1785. Benjamin Franklin. (History - United States Ser.). 222p. 1993. reprint ed. lib. bdg. 79.00 (*0-7812-4877-9*) Rprt Serv.

Letters & Papers of Cadwallader Colden. Cadwallader Colden. (Works of Cadwallader Colden). 1990. reprint ed. lib. bdg. 79.00 (*0-7812-2310-5*) Rprt Serv.

Letters & Papers of Cadwallader Colden, 1711-1775, 9 vols., Set. Cadwallader Colden. LC 72-996. reprint ed. 795.00 (*0-404-01690-1*) AMS Pr.

Letters & Papers of Chaim Weizmann, 23 vols. Ed. by Meyer W. Weisgal & Barnet Litvinoff. Incl. July 1933-August 1935. 29.95 (*0-87855-256-1*); July 1929-December 1930. 29.95 (*0-87855-254-5*); Vol. 1. Childhood & Student Years. 29.95 (*0-87855-194-8*); Vol. 2. Early Zionist Activities. 29.95 (*0-87855-195-6*); Vol. 3. In Opposition. 29.95 (*0-87855-196-4*); Vol. 4. First Steps in England. 29.95 (*0-87855-197-2*); Vol. 5. Science & Zionism. 29.95 (*0-87855-198-0*); Vol. 6. Towards a Hebrew University. 29.95 (*0-87855-199-9*); Vol. 7. Prelude to Balfour Declaration. 29.95 (*0-87855-200-6*); Vol. 8. Head of Zionist Commision to Palestine. 29.95 (*0-87855-224-3*); Vol. 9. Presenting Zionist Case at Paris & San Remo Conferences. 29.95 (*0-87855-249-9*); Vol. 10. Conquest of America & Leadership of World Zionist Organization. 29.95 (*0-87855-250-2*); Vol. 15. January 1931 - June 1933. 29.95 (*0-87855-255-3*); Vol. 17. August 1935-December 1936. 29.95 (*0-87855-257-X*); Vol. 18. January 1937 - December 1938. 29.95 (*0-87855-258-8*); Vol. 11. 29.95 (*0-87855-251-0*); Vol. 12. 29.95 (*0-87855-252-9*); Vol. 13. 29.95 (*0-87855-253-7*); Vol. 19. 29.95 (*0-87855-259-6*); Vol. 20. 29.95 (*0-87855-260-X*); Vol. 21. 29.95 (*0-87855-261-8*); Vol. 22. 29.95 (*0-87855-262-6*); Vol. 23. 29.95 (*0-87855-263-4*); Set ring bd. 500.00 (*0-87855-222-7*) Transaction Pubs.

Letters & Papers of Chaim Weizmann, 1898-1931, Vol. I. Barnet Litvinoff. (Series B Papers). 700p. 1984. 59.95 (*0-87855-279-0*) Transaction Pubs.

Letters & Papers of Chaim Weizmann, 1931-1952, Vol. II. Barnet Litvinoff. (Series B Papers). 750p. 1984. 64.95 (*0-87855-297-9*) Transaction Pubs.

Letters & Papers of Jan Hendrik Oortas Archived in the University Library, Leiden. J. K. Katgert-Merkelijn. LC 97-6837. 1997. text 53.50 (*0-7923-4542-8*) Kluwer Academic.

Letters & Papers of John Singleton Copley & Henry Pelham, 1739-1776. John S. Copley. LC 78-100615. (Library of American Art). (Illus.). 1970. reprint ed. lib. bdg. 49.00 (*0-306-71406-X*) Da Capo.

Letters & Papers of John Singleton Copley & Henry Pelham, 1739-1776. John S. Copley. (American Biography Ser.). 253p. 1991. reprint ed. lib. bdg. 69.00 (*0-7812-8091-5*) Rprt Serv.

Letters & Papers of John Singleton Copley & Henry Pelham, 1739-1776. John S. Copley & Henry Pelham. LC 72-456. reprint ed. 54.00 (*0-404-01719-3*) AMS Pr.

Letters & Papers of Major-General John Sullivan, Continental Army, 3 vols. John Sullivan. Ed. by Otis G. Hammond. LC 75-176462. reprint ed. 80.00 (*0-404-06310-1*) AMS Pr.

Letters & Papers of Sir John Hill, 1714-1775. Ed. by G. S. Rousseau. LC 81-68993. (Studies in the Eighteenth Century: No. 6). (Illus.). 264p. 1990. 39.50 (*0-404-61472-8*) AMS Pr.

Letters & Papers of the Verney Family down to the End of the Year, 1639. Verney Family Staff. Ed. by John Bruce. (Camden Society, London. Publications, First Ser.: No. 56). reprint ed. 72.50 (*0-404-50156-7*) AMS Pr.

Letters & Passages Restored from the Original Manuscript of the History of Clarissa. Samuel Richardson. LC 92-9737. (Clarissa Project Ser.: Vol. 10). 1992. 76.50 (*0-404-64110-5*) AMS Pr.

Letters & People of the Spanish Indies. James Lockhart & E. Otte. LC 75-6007. (Cambridge Latin American Studies: No. 22). 267p. 1976. pap. text 19.95 (*0-521-09990-0*) Cambridge U Pr.

***Letters & Personal Writings.** Jonathan Edwards. Ed. by George S. Claghorn. LC 97-26557. (Works of Jonathan Edwards Ser.: Vol. 16). (Illus.). 896p. 1998. 80.00 (*0-300-07295-3*) Yale U Pr.

Letters & Private Papers of William Makepeace Thackeray, 2 vols., Set. William Makepeace Thackeray. Ed. by Edgar F. Harden. LC 94-19104. 1780p. 1994. text 80.00 (*0-8240-3646-8*, H946) Garland.

Letters & Prose Writings of William Cowper, 5 vols. William Cowper. Ed. by James King & Charles Ryskamp. (Illus.). 640p. 1979. text 115.00 (*0-19-811863-5*) OUP.

Letters & Prose Writings of William Cowper, 5 vols., Vol. II: Letters, 1782-1786. William Cowper. Ed. by James King & Charles Ryskamp. (Illus.). 680p. 1981. text 155.00 (*0-19-812607-7*) OUP.

Letters & Prose Writings of William Cowper: Letters, 1792-1799, Vol. 4. William Cowper. Ed. by Charles Ryskamp & James King. (Illus.). 532p. 1984. text 175.00 (*0-19-812681-6*) OUP.

Letters & Prose Writings of William Cowper Vol. 3: Letters, 1787-1791. William Cowper. Ed. by James King & Charles Ryskamp. (Illus.). 664p. 1983. text 110.00 (*0-19-812608-5*) OUP.

Letters & Prose Writings of William Cowper Vol. 5: Prose, 1756-1798 & Cumulative Index. William Cowper. Ed. by James King & Charles Ryskamp. 272p. (C). 1986. text 72.00 (*0-19-812690-5*) OUP.

Letters & Recollections of John Murray Forbes. John M. Forbes & S. Forbes Hughes. LC 80-1319. (Illus.). 1981. reprint ed. lib. bdg. 66.95 (*0-405-13790-7*) Ayer.

Letters & Reflections from Poland. Carolyn Wedin. 203p. (Orig.). 1993. pap. 8.95 (*0-9637385-1-8*) R & R Wedin Pr.

Letters & Religion. John J. Chapman. 1988. reprint ed. lib. bdg. 59.00 (*0-7812-0052-0*) Rprt Serv.

Letters & Religion. John J. Chapman. 1977. reprint ed. 45.00 (*0-403-07361-8*) Scholarly.

Letters & Sketches from Northern Nigeria. Martin S. Kisch. (Modern Revivals in African Studies). 224p. 1993. 74.25 (*0-7512-0087-5*, Pub. by Gregg Pub) Ashgate Pub Co.

Letters & Social Aims. Ralph Waldo Emerson. (Notable American Authors Ser.). 1992. reprint ed. lib. bdg. 75.00 (*0-7812-2815-8*) Rprt Serv.

Letters & Sounds see Early Learning Mastery Masters

Letters & Sounds. Ed. by Lois Bottoni & Patti Reynolds. (Golden Step Ahead Workbooks Ser.). (Illus.). 36p. 1985. 2.09 (*0-307-23536-X*, 03536) Gldn Bks Pub Co.

Letters & Sounds. Ellen B. Church. 1996. pap. text 3.95 (*0-590-97695-8*) Scholastic Inc.

Letters & Sounds. Beth A. Wise. (J). (gr. k-1). 1997. pap. text, wbk. ed. 2.25 (*1-56293-965-3*, McClanahan Book) Learn Horizon.

Letters & Sounds, Grades K-1: Decoding Activities. Troll Books Staff. (Teacher Time-Savers Ser.). 80p. (J). (gr. k-1). 1999. pap. text 11.95 (*0-8167-3937-4*) Troll Communs.

Letters & the Sounds They Make see Let's Learn Set

Letters & Their Sounds. (Home Workbooks Ser.). (Illus.). 64p. (Orig.). (J). (gr. k-1). 1995. pap., wbk. ed. 2.49 (*0-88724-315-0*, CD6812) Carson-Dellos.

Letters & Times of the Tylers, 3 vols. Lyon G. Tyler. LC 71-75267. (American Public Figures Ser.). 1970. reprint ed. lib. bdg. 145.00 (*0-306-71316-0*) Da Capo.

Letters & Transactions from Cappadocia. Albert T. Clay. LC 78-63523. (Babylonian Inscriptions in the Collection of James B. Nies Ser.: 4). reprint ed. 30.00 (*0-404-60134-0*) AMS Pr.

Letters & Words. Illus. by Pam Adams. (Motivation Ser.). 16p. (Orig.). (J). (ps-2). 1975. pap. 1.99 (*0-85953-046-9*, Pub. by Childs Play) Random House.

Letters & Works of Lady Mary Wortley Montagu, 2 vols., Set. Lady Mary Wortley Montagu & Jame A. Wharncliffe. Ed. by Lord Wharncliffe. LC 70-115358. reprint ed. 125.00 (*0-404-04378-X*) AMS Pr.

Letters & Writings of George Frideric Handel. George Frideric Handel. Ed. by Erich H. Muller. LC 70-114882. (Select Bibliographies Reprint Ser.). 1977. 18.95 (*0-8369-5286-3*) Ayer.

Letters & Writings of George Friedrich Handel. George Frideric Handel. (Music Book Index Ser.). 98p. 1992. reprint ed. lib. bdg. 59.00 (*0-7812-9481-9*) Rprt Serv.

Letters Are Lost! Lisa C. Ernst. LC 95-42209. (Illus.). 32p. (J). (ps-1). 1996. 15.99 (*0-670-86336-X*, Viking Child) Peng Put Young Read.

Letters Are Lost. Lisa Campbell Ernst. 32p. (YA). (ps-1). 1999. pap. 5.99 (*0-14-055663-X*, PuffinBks) Peng Put Young Read.

Letters at Christmas: And Other Poems. Ann Hayes. 239p. 1995. 29.95 (*0-9646150-1-0*); pap. 14.95 (*0-9646150-0-2*) Badger Pr PA.

Letters at the Zoo. (Super Sticker Bks.). (Illus.). 16p. (J). (gr. k-2). 1996. pap. write for info. (*1-56144-452-9*, Honey Bear Bks) Modern Pub NYC.

Letters at Three a.m. Reports on Endarkenment. Michael Ventura. LC 93-23203. 248p. 1993. pap. 19.50 (*0-88214-361-1*) Spring Pubns.

Letters Back to Ancient China. Herbert Rosendorfer. Tr. by Mike Mitchell from GER. (Europe 1997 Ser.). 274p. 1998. pap. 15.99 (*1-873982-97-6*, Pub. by Dedalus) Subterranean Co.

Letters Between Edward Weston & Willard Van Dyke. Contrib. by Leslie S. Calmes. (Illus.). 76p. 1992. pap. 15.00 (*0-938262-23-8*) Ctr Creat Photog.

An Asterisk (*) at the beginning of an entry indicates that the title is appearing for the first time.

Letters Between Katherine Mansfield & John Middleton Murry. Katherine Mansfield. Ed. by Cherry A. Hankin. 425p. (Orig.). 1990. pap. 16.95 (*0-941533-76-X*, NAB) I R Dee.

Letters (Brieven) Catharose De Petri. 151p. 1997. 22.50 (*90-6732-197-4*) Rosycross Pr.

Letters By Henry Miller to Hoki Tokuda Miller. Henry Miller. Ed. by Joyce Howard. LC 86-8874. 208p. 1987. 19.95 (*0-88191-038-4*) Freundlich.

Letters by Inez Perry on Using the Cell Salts. Lorena Gardenhire. 350p. 1996. reprint ed. spiral bd. 29.50 (*0-7873-0342-9*) Hlth Research.

Letters by Lamplight: A Woman's View of Everyday Life in South Texas, 1873-1883. Lois E. Myers. LC 90-85476. (Illus.). 240p. 1991. 23.95 (*0-918954-53-3*) Baylor Univ Pr.

Letters by Lamplight: A Woman's View of Everyday Life in South Texas, 1873-1883. Lois E. Myers. LC 90-85476. (Illus.). 240p. 1999. pap. 14.95 (*0-918954-69-X*) Baylor Univ Pr.

Letters by the Lubavitcher Rebbe. Menachem M. Schneerson. 138p. (Orig.). 1981. 9.00 (*0-8266-0456-0*) Kehot Pubn Soc.

Letters by the Lubavitcher Rebbe Vol. 1: Tishre - Adar. Menachem M. Schneerson. 368p. 1979. 10.00 (*0-8266-0451-X*); 8.00 (*0-8266-0452-8*) Kehot Pubn Soc.

Letters Concerning the English Nation. Voltaire. Ed. by Nicholas Cronk. (Oxford World's Classics Ser.). (Illus.). 233p. 1999. pap. 9.95 (*0-19-283708-7*) OUP.

Letters Dipped in Honey: Jewish Children's Literature from the Moldovan Family Collection. Yeshiva University Museum Staff. (Illus.). 36p. (Orig.). 1995. text 10.99 (*0-945447-06-X*) Yesh Mus.

Letters Dropt from God: When Life Overwhelms, Look For . . . Ruth Vaughn. LC 94-202327. 132p. 1994. pap. 8.99 (*0-8341-1497-6*) Beacon Hill.

Letters, 1857-1864. Nathaniel Hawthorne. LC 83-27336. (Centenary Edition of the Works of Nathaniel Hawthorne: Vol. XVIII). 732p. 1987. text 95.00 (*0-8142-0383-3*) Ohio St U Pr.

Letters, 1853-1856. Nathaniel Hawthorne. LC 83-27336. (Centenary Edition of the Works of Hawthorne: Vol. XVII). 667p. 1988. text 80.00 (*0-8142-0365-5*) Ohio St U Pr.

Letters, 1843-1853. Nathaniel Hawthorne. Ed. by Thomas Woodson et al. LC 83-27336. (Centenary Edition of the Works of Nathaniel Hawthorne: Vol. XVI). 775p. 1985. text 95.00 (*0-8142-0364-7*) Ohio St U Pr.

Letters, 1802-1823, Vol. 6. Washington Irving. Ed. by Ralph M. Aderman et al. 1978. 35.50 (*0-8057-8522-1*, Twyne) Mac Lib Ref.

Letters, 1813-1843. Nathaniel Hawthorne. Ed. by Thomas Woodson et al. LC 83-27336. (Centenary Edition of the Works of Nathaniel Hawthorne: Vol. XV). 785p. 1985. text 95.00 (*0-8142-0363-9*) Ohio St U Pr.

Letters, 1831-1857, Vols. 1 & 2. James G. Birney. Ed. by Dwight L. Dumond. 1990. 29.00 (*0-8446-1078-X*) Peter Smith.

Letters: 1826-1836 : vol. 1/2 : 1826-1832 : 1832-1836 : 2 vol. in 1, 2 vols. in 1. Thomas Carlyle. Ed. by Charles E. Norton. (Anglistica & Americana Ser.: No. 171). (Illus.). viii, 841p. 1977. reprint ed. 160.00 (*3-487-06285-2*) G Olms Pubs.

Letters, Fictions, Lives: James-Howells Correspondences. Henry James & William Dean Howells. Ed. by Michael Anesko. LC 97-11832. (Illus.). 512p. 1997. text 65.00 (*0-19-506119-5*) OUP.

Letters, 51-110. St. Cyril of Alexandria. Tr. by John McEnerney. LC 85-5692. (Fathers of the Church Ser.: Vol. 77). 204p. 1987. 31.95 (*0-8132-0077-6*) Cath U Pr.

Letters for All Occasions. Alfred S. Myers. 272p. (Orig.). 1996. mass mkt. 6.50 (*0-06-109283-5*, Harp PBks) HarpC.

Letters for All Occasions: Revised edition. rev. ed. Alfred S. Myers. Ed. by Lynn Ferrari. LC 92-34472. (Illus.). 208p. (Orig.). 1993. pap. 13.00 (*0-06-273177-7*) HarperTrade.

Letters for All Seasons: A Year of Letters Designed to Increase Giving in Your Church. Herbert Mather. LC 93-12892. 80p. (Orig.). 1993. pap. 6.95 (*0-687-39343-4*) Abingdon.

Letters for Eternity: Collected from the Correspondence of Charles Rich with Ronda Chervin 1985-1993. Ed. by Rhonda D. Chervin. LC 94-67778. 112p. (Orig.). 1994. pap., pap. text 11.95 (*1-879007-11-8*) St Bedes Pubns.

Letters for Every Occasion: A Pastor's Sourcebook. Thomas J. Tozer. 160p. (Orig.). 1992. pap. 12.95 (*0-687-21424-6*) Abingdon.

Letters for Everyday Use. Angelica W. Cass. pap. write for info. (*0-671-09224-3*, Arco) Macmillan Gen Ref.

Letters for God's Name. Gail Ramshaw-Schmidt. (Illus.). 1986. 5.95 (*0-86683-880-5*, 7458) Harper SF.

Letters for Lawyers: Essential Communications for Clients, Prospects, & Others. LC 95-83635. 144p. 1996. pap. 64.95 (*1-57073-304-X*, 515-0244, ABA Genl Prac) Amer Bar Assn.

Letters for Literary Ladies. Maria Edgeworth. Ed. by Claire Connolly. 128p. 1993. pap. 7.95 (*0-460-87250-8*, Everyman's Classic Lib) Tuttle Pubng.

Letters for Our Children: Fifty Americans Share Lessons in Living. Ed. by Erica Goode. 1996. 19.00 (*0-614-97011-3*) Random.

Letters for Special Situations: Letters to Use in the Special Situations in Life. Ed. by Anne McKinney. LC 99-11353. (Anne McKinney Career Ser.). 256p. 1999. pap. 25.00 (*1-885288-09-3*, Pub. by PREP Pubng) BookWorld.

Letters for the Living: Teaching Writing in a Violent Age. Michael Blitz & C. Mark Hurlbert. LC 98-13637. (Refiguring English Studies). 181p. 1998. pap. 25.95 (*0-8141-2803-3*) NCTE.

Letters for Tomorrow: A Journal for Expectant Moms & Dads. Robin F. Bernstein & Cathy Moore. LC 94-9466. 160p. 1995. pap. 20.00 (*0-385-47515-2*) Doubleday.

Letters for Young Lovers. Ellen Gould Harmon White. 1984. pap. 8.99 (*0-8163-0528-5*) Pacific Pr Pub Assn.

Letters from a Candidate's Wife: or It Looks Like a Rough Ride but There's a Rainbow in Sight. Lucy D. Blount. (Illus.). 294p. (Orig.). 1994. pap. text. write for info. (*0-9630017-4-4*) Light-Bearer.

Letters from a Candidate's Wife: or It Looks Like a Rough Ride but There's a Rainbow in Sight. Lucy D. Blount. (Illus.). 294p. (Orig.). 1995. write for info. (*0-9630017-6-0*) Light-Bearer.

Letters from a Convert: Missionary Letters from an Orthodox Convert to Her Protestant Parents. Marianna Friesel. Ed. by Gregory Williams. (Illus.). 64p. (Orig.). 1985. pap. 4.00 (*0-912927-01-1*, X001) St John Kronstadt.

Letters from a Farmer in Pennsylvania to the Inhabitants of the British Colonies. John Dickinson. LC 03-20873. 49.00 (*0-403-00186-2*) Scholarly.

Letters from a Farmer in Pennsylvania to the Inhabitants of the British Colonies. John Dickinson. 1988. reprint ed. lib. bdg. 59.00 (*0-7812-0534-4*) Rprt Serv.

Letters from a Farmer in Pennsylvania to the Inhabitants of the British Colonies. John Dickinson. 1993. reprint ed. lib. bdg. 89.00 (*0-7812-5446-9*) Rprt Serv.

Letters from a Headmaster's Study (1949-1977) enl. rev. ed. Charles Martin. Ed. by Louise D. Piazza. (Illus.). 302p. 1986. reprint ed. pap. text 26.50 (*0-8191-5387-7*) U Pr of Amer.

Letters from a Headmaster's Study (1949-1977) 2nd enl. rev. ed. Charles Martin. Ed. by Louise D. Piazza. (Illus.). 302p. 1986. reprint ed. lib. bdg. 48.00 (*0-8191-5386-9*) U Pr of Amer.

Letters from a Hermit. William Paulsell & Matthew Kelty. 128p. 1978. 7.95 (*0-87243-086-3*) Templegate.

Letters from a Lady Rancher. Monica Hopkins. 169p. 1981. mass mkt. 4.95 (*0-88780-115-3*; Pub. by Formac Publ Co) Formac Dist Ltd.

Letters from a Landscape Painter. Charles Lanman. (Notable American Authors Ser.). 1999. reprint ed. lib. bdg. 125.00 (*0-7812-3730-0*) Rprt Serv.

Letters from a Life: Selected Letters & Diaries of Benjamin Britten, 2 vols., Vol. Set. Ed. by Donald Mitchell & Philip Reed. LC 90-42998. (Illus.). 1403p. 1991. 195.00 (*0-520-06520-4*, Pub. by U CA Pr) Cal Prin Full Svc.

Letters from a Little Girl Addict. Rae S. Stewart. 224p. (Orig.). 1990. mass mkt. 2.95 (*0-87067-337-8*) Holloway.

Letters from a Long Illness with the World: The D. H. Lawrence Poems. Barry Dempster. 64p. 1993. pap. 11.95 (*0-919626-64-5*, Pub. by Brick Bks) Genl Dist Srvs.

Letters from a Lost Generation: First World War Letters of Vera Brittain & Four Friends. Vera Brittain et al. LC 98-42383. (Illus.). 448p. 1999. text 29.95 (*1-55553-379-5*) NE U Pr.

Letters from a Modernist. J. Weaver. 1990. pap. 70.00 (*0-7220-4917-X*) St Mut.

Letters from a "Modernist" The Letters of George Tyrrell to Wilfrid Ward, 1893-1908. Ed. by Mary J. Weaver. LC 80-28372. xxxiv, 194p. 1981. 35.00 (*0-915762-12-9*) Patmos Pr.

Letters from a New Campus. Daniel Bliss. (Illus.). 256p. (Orig.). (C). 1997. 18.95 (*0-8156-6087-1*) Syracuse U Pr.

Letters from a New World: Amerigo Vespucci's Discovery of America. Tr. by David Jacobson from ITA. LC 92-82639. (Illus.). 150p. 1992. 24.00 (*0-941419-62-2*) Marsilio Pubs.

***Letters from a Nut.** Ted L. Nancy. LC 96-47610. 192p. 1999. 15.00 (*0-380-97354-5*, Avon Bks) Morrow Avon.

Letters from a Peruvian Woman. Francoise De Graffigny. Tr. by David Kornacker from FRE. LC 93-37517. (Texts & Translations Ser.: No. 2b). Orig. Title: Letters of a Peruvian Princess. xxviii, 174p. (Orig.). 1993. pap. 5.95 (*0-87352-778-X*, P002P) Modern Lang.

Letters from a Serial Killer. Pablo Eskimo. 72p. (Orig.). 1992. pap. write for info. (*0-9632130-1-6*) Lysander.

Letters from a Sharpshooter: The Civil War Letters of Private William B. Greene, Co. G, 2nd United States Sharpshooters, Berdan's, Army of the Potomac 1861-1865. William H. Hastings. LC 93-61358. (Illus.). 336p. 1993. pap. 24.95 (*0-9638744-0-3*) Historic Pubns.

Letters from a Skeptic. Gregory A. Boyd & Edward K. Boyd. LC 93-33314. 180p. 1993. 10.99 (*1-56476-244-0*, 6-3244, Victor Bks) Chariot Victor.

Letters from a Slave Girl: The Story of Harriet Jacobs. Mary E. Lyons. (J). (gr. 7). 1996. mass mkt. 3.95 (*0-689-80015-0*) Aladdin.

Letters from a Slave Girl: The Story of Harriet Jacobs. Mary E. Lyons. LC 91-45778. (Illus.). 176p. (YA). (gr. 7 up). 1992. 16.00 (*0-684-19446-5*) Scribner.

Letters from a Slave Girl: The Story of Harriet Jacobs. Mary E. Lyons. LC 91-45778. 1996. 9.05 (*0-606-09551-9*, Pub. by Turtleback) Demco.

Letters from a Stoic. Lucius Annaeus Seneca. Tr. by Robin Campbell. (Classics Ser.). 256p. 1969. pap. 11.95 (*0-14-044210-3*, Penguin Classics) Viking Penguin.

***Letters from a Stranger.** James Tipton. LC 98-73866. 82p. 1998. 17.50 (*0-9657159-2-2*); pap. 12.00 (*0-9657159-3-0*) Conundrum Pr.

Letters from a Wandering Jew: A Study of the Pauline Epistles. Richard J. Dickson. (Dickson Study Ser.). 80p. 2001. pap. text 6.95 (*0-916010-13-9*, DS-6) Crkside Weems.

Letters from a War Zone. Andrea Dworkin. LC 93-13114. 344p. 1992. reprint ed. pap. 14.95 (*1-55652-185-5*, Lawrence Hill) Chicago Review.

Letters from a World War I Aviator. Josiah P. Rowe, Jr. Ed. by Genevieve B. Rowe & Diana R. Doran. LC 86-90456. (Illus.). 200p. 1986. 15.95 (*0-9616886-0-2*) Sinclaire Pr.

Letters from a World War II G. I. Judith E. Greenberg & Helen C. McKeever. (In Their Own Words Ser.). (Illus.). 144p. (YA). (gr. 7-12). 1995. lib. bdg. 24.00 (*0-531-11212-8*) Watts.

***Letters from a Wounded Heart: Reflections to Stregthen & Comfort the Soul.** Gerard F. Baumbach. 96p. 2000. pap. 8.95 (*0-8091-3988-X*) Paulist Pr.

Letters from a Young Shaker: William S. Byrd at Pleasant Hill. William J. Byrd. Ed. by Stephen J. Stein. LC 84-27014. 176p. 1985. 19.00 (*0-8131-1542-6*) U Pr of Ky.

Letters from Africa. Homer T. Rosenberger. LC 65-16638. 209p. 1965. pap. 3.50 (*0-917264-04-5*) Rose Hill.

Letters from Africa, 1914-1931. Isak Dinesen. Ed. by Frans Lasson. Tr. by Anne Born. LC 80-25856. (Phoenix Fiction Ser.). (Illus.). xiii, 516p. (C). 1984. pap. 18.95 (*0-226-15311-8*) U Ch Pr.

Letters from Africa, 1914-1931. Isak Dinesen. Ed. by Frans Lasson. Tr. by Anne Born. LC 80-25856. (Phoenix Fiction Ser.). (Illus.). xiii, 530p. (C). 1992. 25.00 (*0-226-15309-6*) U Ch Pr.

Letters from Alabama, (U. S.) Chiefly Relating to Natural History. Philip H. Gosse. LC 92-27936. (Library of Alabama Classics). 360p. 1993. reprint ed. pap. text 19.95 (*0-8173-0683-8*) U of Ala Pr.

Letters from Alaska. John Muir. Ed. by Robert Engberg & Bruce Merrell. LC 93-18845. (Illus.). 128p. (Orig.). (C). 1993. pap. 14.95 (*0-299-13954-9*); lib. bdg. 30.00 (*0-299-13950-6*) U of Wis Pr.

Letters from America Pt. 1: September 1860-January 1863. David Powell. 135p. 1995. pap. 14.95 (*1-85756-246-1*) Paul & Co Pubs.

Letters from an American Farmer. J. Hector St. John de Crevecoeur. Ed. & Intro. by Susan Manning. (Oxford World's Classics Ser.). (Illus.). 288p. 1999. pap. 11.95 (*0-19-283898-9*) OUP.

Letters from an American Farmer. Michel-Guillaume Jean De Crevecoeur. (Works of Michel-Guillaume Jean de Crevecoeur Ser.). 1990. reprint ed. lib. bdg. 79.00 (*0-685-44765-0*) Rprt Serv.

Letters from an American Farmer: The Eastern European & Russian Correspondence of Roswell Garst. Roswell Garst. Ed. by Richard Lowitt & Harold Lee. 1987. 35.00 (*0-87580-123-4*) N Ill U Pr.

Letters from an American Farmer & Sketches of Eighteenth-Century America. J. Hector. Ed. & Intro. by Albert E. Stone. (American Library). 496p. 1981. pap. 13.95 (*0-14-039006-5*, Penguin Classics) Viking Penguin.

Letters from an Other. Lise Gauvin. Tr. by Susanne De Lotbiniere-Harwood. 160p. pap. 8.95 (*0-88961-126-2*, Pub. by Womens Pr) LPC InBook.

Letters from an Understanding Friend: Jesus on the Way to Jerusalem. Isaias Powers. LC 84-50409. 96p. 1985. pap. 7.95 (*0-89622-413-9*) Twenty-Third.

Letters from Andover to Hogarp, Sweden, 1858-1898. Ed. & Tr. by Conrad Bergendoff. LC 88-80478. (Augustana College Library Occasional Papers, Wallin Lecture: No. 17). 53p. 1988. pap. 4.00 (*0-910182-44-2*) Augustana Coll.

Letters from Annapolis: Midshipmen Write Home, 1848-1969. Ed. by Anne Marie Drew. LC 98-4956. (Illus.). 256p. 1998. 29.95 (*1-55750-170-X*) Naval Inst Pr.

Letters from Archibald, Earl of Argyll, to John, Duke of Lauderdale. Archibald C. Argyll. Ed. by George Sinclair & C. K. Sharpe. LC 75-38489. (Bannatyne Club, Edinburgh: Publications: No. 33). reprint ed. 49.50 (*0-404-52739-6*) AMS Pr.

Letters from Atlantis. Robert Silverberg. (Illus.). 144p. 1992. mass mkt. 4.99 (*0-446-36286-7*, Pub. by Warner Bks) Little.

Letters from Baltimore: The Mencken-Cleator Correspondence. Ed. by P. E. Cleator. LC 78-75176. 280p. 1982. 38.50 (*0-8386-3075-8*) Fairleigh Dickinson.

Letters from Barbary, 1576-1774: Arabic Documents in the Public Record Office. J. F. Hopkins. (Oriental Documents Ser.: Vol. VI). 1983. 45.00 (*0-19-726010-1*) OUP.

Letters from Barcelona. Ed. by Billy Mills. (C). 1990. 23.00 (*0-948268-71-9*, Pub. by Dedalus) St Mut.

Letters from Bethelem: Five Dramatic Monologues for Advent. Wayne L. Tilden. 16p. (Orig.). 1997. pap. 4.50 (*0-7880-1027-1*) CSS OH.

Letters from Beyond the Sambatyon: The Myth of the Ten Lost Tribes. Ed. by Simcha Shtull-Trauring. LC 96-94695. (Illus.). 64p. 1997. 24.95 (*1-888297-03-4*, TLT-02) Maxima New Media.

Letters from Bonaire. Marion West. 156p. (Orig.). 1990. pap. 9.95 (*0-85398-294-5*) G Ronald Pub.

Letters from "Buffalo Bill" Stella Foote. LC 90-71190. (Montana & the West Ser.: Vol. 8). (Illus.). 160p. 1990. 30.00 (*0-912783-18-4*) Upton & Sons.

Letters from "Buffalo Bill" deluxe limited ed. Stella Foote. LC 90-71190. (Montana & the West Ser.: Vol. 8). (Illus.). 160p. 1990. 125.00 (*0-912783-22-2*) Upton & Sons.

Letters from Burma. Aung S. Suu Kyi. (Illus.). xi, 209p. 1998. pap. 13.95 (*0-14-026403-5*) Viking Penguin.

Letters from California: He Married Me for My Drapes. Norma Davidson. LC 96-71030. 352p. 1997. pap. 14.95 (*0-88739-113-3*) Creat Arts Bk.

Letters from Camp. Kate Klise. LC 98-52315. (Avon Camelot Bks.). (Illus.). 192p. (J). (gr. 3-7). 1999. 15.00 (*0-380-97539-4*, Avon Bks) Morrow Avon.

***Letters from Camp.** Kate Klise. LC 98-52315. (Illus.). 192p. (J). (gr. 4-7). 2000. mass mkt. 4.95 (*0-380-79348-2*, Avon Bks) Morrow Avon.

Letters from Chickadee Hill. Winston O. Abbott. (Illus.). 1978. 9.95 (*0-918114-04-7*) Inspiration Conn.

Letters from China: The Canton-Boston Correspondence of Robert Bennet Forbes, 1838-1840. Ed. by Phyllis F. Kerr. (Illus.). 317p. 1996. 39.95 (*0-913372-77-3*) Mystic Seaport.

Letters from China & India & Other Barnyard Rememberances. Ralph W. Phillips. 1990. 22.50 (*0-9613620-1-4*) McClain.

Letters From Cicely. Ellis Weiner. 1992. pap. 10.00 (*0-671-77735-1*) PB.

***Letters from Cleo & Tyrone: A Feline Perspective on Love, Life & Litter.** L. Virginia Browne et al. LC 00-40515. (Illus.). 2000. write for info. (*0-312-26706-1*, St Martin Griffin) St Martin.

***Letters from Colorado 1887.** rev. ed. H. L. Wason. x, 111p. 1999. pap. 12.95 (*1-928878-04-0*) Temporal Mech Pr.

Letters from Cuba: Kindness, Friendliness & Simple Living in the Face of Adversity. Adolf Hungry-Wolf. (Illus.). 316p. 1997. pap. 17.95 (*0-920698-52-2*) Can Cab Pr.

Letters from Dublin, Easter, 1916: The Diary of Alfred Fannin. Ed. by Sally Warwick-Haller & Adrian Warwick-Haller. (Illus.). 64p. 1995. pap. 10.50 (*0-7165-2559-3*, Pub. by Irish Acad Pr) Intl Spec Bk.

Letters from Dwight. Gary Kern. LC 98-10463. 1998. pap. 13.00 (*1-879378-35-3*) Xenos Riverside.

Letters from Egypt: A Journey on the Nile, 1849-1850. Florence Nightingale. LC 87-21637. 1992. 24.95 (*0-8021-1532-2*, Grove) Grove-Atltic.

Letters from Egypt & Palestine. Maltbie D. Babcock. Ed. by Moshe Davis. LC 77-70662. (America & the Holy Land Ser.). (Illus.). 1977. reprint ed. lib. bdg. 21.95 (*0-405-10223-2*) Ayer.

Letters from Egypt, 1863-1865. 2nd ed. Lucie Duff-Gordon. LC 75-164794. (BCL Ser. I). reprint ed. 49.50 (*0-404-02189-1*) AMS Pr.

Letters from England. Jackson Bryce. 1998. 20.00 (*0-939394-06-5*) Blck Willw Pr.

Letters from Exile: The Correspondence of Martha Hughes Cannon & Angus M. Cannon, 1886-1888. limited ed. Martha H. Cannon & Angus M. Cannon. Ed. by Constance L. Lieber & John Sillito. LC 89-32696. (Significant Mormon Diaries Ser.: No. 3). (Illus.). 344p. 1989. 60.00 (*0-941214-77-X*) Signature Bks.

Letters from Father Christmas. J. R. R. Tolkien. Ed. by Baillie Tolkien. LC 95-224701. (Illus.). 48p. (J). (ps-3). 1995. 18.95 (*0-395-74132-7*) HM.

Letters from Felix: A Little Rabbit on a World Tour. Annette Langen. LC 94-29355. (Illus.). 32p. (J). 1994. 16.95 (*1-55859-886-3*, Abbeville Kids) Abbeville Pr.

Letters from 1536, Notes, Index see **Life & Letters of Thomas Cromwell**

Letters from Forest Place: A Plantation Family's Correspondence, 1846-1881. Ed. by E. Grey Dimond & Herman Hattaway. LC 93-25041. (Illus.). 512p. 1993. text 35.00 (*0-87805-653-X*) U Pr of Miss.

Letters from France, 8 vols. in 2. Helen M. Williams. LC 75-22224. 2048p. 1975. 200.00 (*0-8201-1158-9*) Schol Facsimiles.

Letters from France & Italy, 1847-1852. Aleksandr Herzen. Tr. by Judith E. Zimmerman from FRE. LC 95-10700. (Pitt Series in Russian & East European: No. 24). 304p. 1995. text 59.95 (*0-8229-3890-1*) U of Pittsburgh Pr.

Letters from Freedom: Post-Cold War Realities & Perspectives. Adam Michnik. LC 98-22701. (Society & Culture in East Central Europe Ser.). 346p. 1998. 48.00 (*0-520-21759-4*, Pub. by U CA Pr); pap. 18.95 (*0-520-21760-8*, Pub. by U CA Pr) Cal Prin Full Svc.

Letters from Friends see **Dialogue with Friends**

Letters from George Lord Carew to Sir Thomas Roe. George C. Totnes. Ed. by John Maclean. (Camden Society, London. Publications, First Ser.: No. 76). reprint ed. 40.00 (*0-404-50176-1*) AMS Pr.

Letters from George Third to Lord Bute, 1756 to 1766. George III. Ed. by Romney Sedgwick. LC 81-4155. (Studies in Modern History). 277p. 1981. reprint ed. lib. bdg. 65.00 (*0-313-23039-0*, SELG, Greenwood Pr) Greenwood.

Letters from Grandma's Attic. Arleta Richardson. LC 96-102123. (In Grandma's Attic Ser.). (Illus.). 24p. (J). (gr. 3-6). 1995. 14.99 (*0-7814-0229-8*) Chariot Victor.

Letters from Greenroom Ghosts. John M. Brown. LC 67-23187. (Essay Index Reprint Ser.). 1977. reprint ed. 20.95 (*0-8369-0258-0*) Ayer.

Letters from Hanusse: The Structure of Deconstruction. Joshua Haigh. (Green Integer Bks.: No. 30). 176p. 1999. pap. text 12.95 (*1-892295-30-X*, Pub. by Green Integer) Consort Bk Sales.

Letters from Heaven. Hope MacDonald. LC 98-22233. 1998. 13.00 (*1-57683-098-5*) NavPress.

Letters from Home. Marilyn Johnson. (Illus.). 113p. 1995. 22.00 (*0-9641149-2-5*) Main Graphics.

Letters from Home. Marilyn Johnson. (Illus.). 113p. 1996. reprint ed. pap. 12.00 (*0-9641149-6-8*) Main Graphics.

Letters from Home: A Guide to Your Symbols - Awake or Dreaming. Patricia Troyer. LC 96-67360. 400p. (Orig.). 1996. pap. 19.95 (*1-885975-02-3*) Stone People.

***Letters from Home: Loving Messages from the Family.** Lee Carroll. Ed. by Jill Kramer. 1999. pap. 14.00 (*1-888053-12-7*) Kryon Writings.

Letters from Honeyhill: A Woman's View of Homesteading, 1914-1922. abr. ed. Cecilia H. Hendricks. Ed. by Cecilia Wahl. LC 90-43238. (Illus.). 361p. 1990. pap. 13.95 (*0-87108-764-2*) Pruett.

L

L

Letters from India, Describing a Journey in the British Dominions of India: Tibet, Lahore, & Cashmere During the Years 1828, 1829, 1820, 1831, 2 vols., Set. Victor Jac. (C). 1994. reprint ed. text 64.00 (81-206-0830-5, Pub. by Asian Educ Servs) S Asia.

Letters from Ireland During the Famine of 1847. Alexander Somerville. Ed. by K. D. Snell. LC 94-217634. 224p. 1994. 42.50 (0-7165-2530-5, Pub. by Irish Acad Pr); pap. 19.50 (0-7165-2545-3, Pub. by Irish Acad Pr) Intl Spec Bk.

Letters from Irish Australia, 1825-1925. Patrick O'Farrell. 244p. 1990. pap. 24.95 (0-86840-235-4, Pub. by New South Wales Univ Pr) Intl Spec Bk.

Letters from Irish College. Ed. by Rose Doyle. (Illus.). 128p. 1996. pap. 11.95 (1-86023-036-9, Pub. by Martello Bks) Irish Amer Bk.

Letters from Italy & Switzerland. Felix Mendelssohn. Tr. by Lady Wallace. LC 70-114866. (Select Bibliographies Reprint Ser.). 1977. 26.95 (0-8369-5271-5) Ayer.

Letters from Jamaica the Lands of Streams & Woods. Charles J. Rampini. 1977. text 17.95 (0-8369-9246-6, 9100) Ayer.

*__Letters from James.__ Ruth D. Layng. 352p. 2000. pap. write for info. (1-887905-23-5) Pkway Pubs.

Letters from James, Earl of Perth, Lord Chancellor of Scotland, to His Sister the Countess of Erroll, & Other Members of His Family. James D. Perth. Ed. by William Jerdan. (Camden Society, London. Publications, First Ser.: No. 33). reprint ed. 30.00 (0-404-50133-8) AMS Pr.

Letters from Japan. Joan Mondale. (Illus.). iv, 148p. 1997. pap. 24.95 (0-9662220-0-8) J Mondale.

Letters from Jenny. Ed. by Gordon W. Allport. LC 65-18327. (Illus.). 238p. (Orig.). (C). 1965. pap. 7.95 (0-15-650700-5, Harvest Bks) Harcourt.

Letters from Jerusalem. Ed. by Majid Tehranian. (Occasion Paper Ser.: No. 4). 88p. (C). 1990. 2.00 (1-880309-01-7) S M Matsunaga.

Letters from Jerusalem, 1922-1925. Eunice Holliday. Ed. by John Holliday. (Illus.). 256p. 1998. text 39.50 (1-86064-130-X) I B T.

Letters from Jerusalem, 1922-1925: During the Palestine Mandate. Eunice Holliday. Ed. by John Holliday. LC 97-177426. (Illus.). 224p. 1997. text 39.50 (1-86064-085-0) St Martin.

Letters from John Galsworthy, 1900-1932. John Galsworthy. Ed. by Edward Garnett. LC 79-131714. 1971. 59.00 (0-403-00601-5) Scholarly.

Letters from John Galsworthy, 1900-1932. John Galsworthy. 1988. reprint ed. lib. bdg. 49.00 (0-7812-0395-3) Rprt Serv.

*__Letters from Jonathan.__ Pamela James. 2000. pap. write for info. (1-928781-47-0) Hollis Bks.

Letters from Julio. Hedwig J. Trost. LC 98-90628. 1999. 12.50 (0-533-12868-4) Vantage.

Letters from Kartini. Tr. by Cote. pap. 5.99 (0-7326-0267-X, Pub. by Jarrold Pub) Seven Hills Bk.

Letters from Kiev. Solomea Pavlychko. Tr. by Myrna Kostash. 150p. 1992. text 35.00 (0-312-07588-X) St Martin.

Letters from Lady Margaret Burnet. Margaret Burnet. LC 74-39562. (Bannatyne Club, Edinburgh. Publications: No. 24). reprint ed. 32.50 (0-404-52730-2) AMS Pr.

Letters from Laura. Barbara B. Hixon. LC 97-67006. 104p. 1997. per. 10.00 (1-55856-242-7, 156) Closson Pr.

Letters from Lee's Army. Anno. by Susan L. Blackford & Charles M. Blackford. LC 98-29020. xx, 312p. 1998. pap. 15.00 (0-8032-6149-7) U of Nebr Pr.

Letters from Lexington: Reflections on Propaganda. Noam Chomsky. LC 93-2687. 1993. pap. 10.95 (1-56751-010-8); lib. bdg. 29.95 (1-56751-011-6) Common Courage.

Letters from Liselotte: Elizabeth-Charlotte, Princess Palatine & Duchess of Orleans. M. Kroll. 272p. 1999. pap. text 17.95 (0-7490-0373-1) Allison & Busby.

Letters from London. Julian Barnes. 352p. 1995. pap. 14.00 (0-679-76161-6) Random.

Letters from Lord Sydenham, Governor General of Canada, 1839-41, to Lord John Russell. C. Sydenham & E. P. Thomson. Ed. by Paul Knaplund. LC 73-83139. 185p. 1973. reprint ed. 35.00 (0-678-00737-3) Kelley.

*__Letters from Lost Thyme: Two Decades of Letters from John Joseph to Patricia Larsen.__ John Joseph & Patricia Larsen. 137p. 2000. pap. 15.95 (1-885586-52-3, Pub. by Turtle Point Pr) Dist Art Pubs.

Letters from Louisa: The Experiences of Louisa MacDonald. Jeanette Beaumont & W. Vere Hole. xiii, 202 p. 1996. pap. 24.95 (1-86448-054-8, Pub. by Allen & Unwin Pty) Paul & Co Pubs.

Letters from Maine. May Sarton. 1997. pap. 10.00 (0-614-29435-5) Norton.

Letters from Maine: Poems. May Sarton. 64p. 1997. pap. 10.00 (0-393-31716-1) Norton.

Letters from Managua: Meditations on Politics & Art. Gary Geddes. 112p. 1990. pap. 12.95 (1-55082-006-0, Pub. by Quarry Pr) LPC InBook.

Letters from Medjugorje. Wayne Weible. LC 91-62101. (Illus.). 193p. 1991. pap. 10.95 (1-55725-021-9, 930-012, Pub. by Paraclete MA) BookWorld.

Letters from Mexico. Hernan Cortes. Ed. & Tr. by Anthony Pagden. LC 86-50363. 640p. 1986. 65.00 (0-300-03724-4) Yale U Pr.

Letters from Mexico. Hernan Cortes. Ed. & Tr. by Anthony Pagden. LC 86-50363. 640p. 1986. pap. 25.00 (0-300-03799-6) Yale U Pr.

Letters from Mexico. David Romtvedt. (Illus.). 55p. (Orig.). 1988. pap. 50.00 (0-937459-04-6) Kutenai Pr.

Letters from Motherless Daughters: Words of Courage, Grief, & Healing. Intro. by Hope Edelman. LC 95-4116. 1995. 18.00 (0-201-48357-2) Addison-Wesley.

Letters from Motherless Daughters: Words of Courage, Grief, & Healing. Ed. by Hope Edelman. 162p. 1998. text 18.00 (0-7881-5745-0) DIANE Pub.

Letters from Motherless Daughters: Words of Courage, Grief & Healing. Ed. by Hope Edelman. 240p. 1996. pap. 9.95 (0-385-31522-8, Delta Trade) Dell.

Letters from Mrs. Elizabeth Carter to Mrs. Montagu Between the Years 1755-1800, 3 vols., Set. Elizabeth Carter. LC 73-178402. reprint ed. 210.00 (0-404-56720-7) AMS Pr.

Letters from My Mill & Letters to an Absent One. Alphonse Daudet. LC 72-37266. (Short Story Index Reprint Ser.). 1980. reprint ed. 20.95 (0-8369-4077-6) Ayer.

Letters from New France: The Upper Country, 1686-1783. Ed. & Tr. by Joseph L. Peyser. (Illus.). 264p. 1992. text 34.95 (0-252-01853-2) U of Ill Pr.

Letters from New York. Lydia M. Child. Ed. by Bruce Mills. LC 98-19480. 304p. 1999. 45.00 (0-8203-2038-2); pap. 19.95 (0-8203-2077-3) U of Ga Pr.

Letters from New York. 3rd ed. Lydia Maria Child. LC 79-137726. (American Fiction Reprint Ser.). 1977. 21.95 (0-8369-7025-X) Ayer.

Letters from Nigeria, 1899-1900. David W. Carnegie. Ed. by Ann O'Hear. LC 92-41951. (C). 1992. 30.00 (0-942615-16-6) U Wis African Stud.

*__Letters from Nin: Wisdom, Advice & Encouragement for a First-Time Mother.__ Eleanor Weisberger. 224p. 2001. pap. 14.95 (1-56474-344-6) Fithian Pr.

Letters from North America, Vol. 2. Janos Xantus. Tr. by Theodore Schoenman & Helen B. Schoenman. LC 75-25679. 199p. 1975. reprint ed. pap. 61.70 (0-7837-3662-2, 204353300009) Bks Demand.

Letters from Occupied Japan. Henry Zylstra. LC 81-16852. 1982. pap. 6.95 (0-931940-05-2) Middleburg Pr.

*__Letters from Otto Frank.__ Cara Weiss Wilson. Orig. Title: Love, Otto: The Legacy of Anne Frank. 176p. 2000. pap. 14.95 (1-880823-23-3, Pub. by N Star Pubns) Midpt Trade.

Letters from Palazzo Barbaro. Henry James. 222p. 2000. pap. 12.95 (1-885586-04-3, Pub. by Turtle Point Pr) Dist Art Pubs.

Letters from Palenque. Wizard Marks. (U. S. A. Poetry Chapbook Ser.: No. 5). (Illus.). 16p. (Orig.). 1985. pap. 3.00 (0-937724-06-8) Shadow Pr.

Letters from Paulos: A Leader in Wisdom to HUS Pupils 10 Korinthos, 1920. Omikron. 304p. 1998. reprint ed. pap. 24.95 (0-7661-0610-1) Kessinger Pub.

Letters from Pemberley: The First Year. Jane Dawkins. LC 98-56074. 200p. 1999. pap. 12.00 (1-893337-00-6) Chicken Soup.

Letters from Percy Bysshe Shelley to Elizabeth Hitchener. Percy Bysshe Shelley & Elizabeth Hitchener. 1977. 19.95 (0-8369-7169-8, 8001) Ayer.

Letters from Port Royal, 1862-1868. Ed. by Elizabeth W. Pearson. LC 69-18547. (American Negro: His History & Literature. Series 2). 1968. reprint ed. 17.95 (0-405-01886-X) Ayer.

Letters from President Longstreet to the Know-Nothing Preachers of the Methodist Church South. Augustus Baldwin Longstreet. (Notable American Authors Ser.). 1999. reprint ed. lib. bdg. 125.00 (0-7812-3856-0) Rprt Serv.

*__Letters from Priests to the Kings Esarhaddon & Assurbanipal.__ Ed. by Steven W. Cole & Peter Machinist. xxx, 221p. 1999. text 50.00 (951-570-437-5); pap. text 44.00 (951-570-436-7) Eisenbrauns.

Letters from Prison. Marquis De Sade, pseud. Tr. & Intro. by Richard Seaver. LC 97-43150. 7p. 1999. 25.45 (1-55970-411-X, Pub. by Arcade Pub Inc) Time Warner.

Letters from Prison. Lauren W. Orchard. (Spiritual Discovery Ser.). 128p. 1997. pap., teacher ed. 9.95 (0-88243-221-4, 02-0221); pap., student ed. 4.95 (0-88243-121-8) Gospel Pub.

Letters from Prison, 2 vols., Set. Antonio Gramsci. Ed. by Frank Rosengarten. Tr. by Raymond Rosenthal. (Illus.). 1994. 99.00 (0-231-07558-8) Col U Pr.

Letters from Prison, Vol. I. Antonio Gramsci. 1994. 52.50 (0-231-07552-9) Col U Pr.

Letters from Prison, Vol. II. Antonio Gramsci. 1994. 52.50 (0-231-07554-5) Col U Pr.

Letters from Prison: A Cry for Justice. George B. Palermo & Maxine A. White. LC 97-51866. (American Series in Behavioral Science & Law: Vol. 1095). 276p. 1998. text 55.95 (0-398-06851-8); pap. text 41.95 (0-398-06852-6) C C Thomas.

Letters from Prison: A Revolutionary Party Prepares for Post-World War II Labor Battles. James P. Cannon. Ed. by George Lavan. LC 73-79781. 362p. 1973. lib. bdg. 55.00 (0-87348-006-6) Pathfinder NY.

Letters from Prison: A Revolutionary Party Prepares for Post-World War II Labor Battles. 2nd ed. James P. Cannon. Ed. by George L. Weissman. LC 73-79781. (Illus.). 362p. 1973. pap. 21.95 (0-87348-307-3) Pathfinder NY.

Letters from Prison & Other Essays. Adam Michnik. Tr. by Maya Latynski. LC 85-1196. (Societies & Culture in East-Central Europe Ser.: No. 2). 371p. 1986. pap. 19.95 (0-520-06175-6, Pub. by U CA Pr) Cal Prin Full Svc.

Letters from Quebec: A Philosophy for Peace & Justice. Howard Richards. LC 93-37945. 448p. 1994. 74.95 (1-883255-17-1); pap. 44.95 (1-883255-16-3) Intl Scholars.

Letters from Ralph Waldo Emerson to a Friend, 1838-1853. Ralph Waldo Emerson. (American Biography Ser.). 81p. 1991. reprint ed. lib. bdg. 59.00 (0-7812-8124-5) Rprt Serv.

*__Letters from Rifka.__ 2000. 11.95 (1-56137-880-1) Novel Units.

Letters from Rifka. Karen Hesse. LC 91-48007. 160p. (J). (gr. 4-7). 1995. 14.95 (0-8050-1964-2, Bks Young Read) H Holt & Co.

Letters from Rifka. Karen Hesse. (J). 1993. 9.60 (0-606-05905-9, Pub. by Turtleback) Demco.

*__Letters from Rifka.__ Jean Jamieson. 44p. 1999. 9.95 (1-56137-842-9) Novel Units.

Letters from Rifka. Karen Hesse. LC 93-7486. 148p. (J). (gr. 3-7). 1993. reprint ed. pap. 4.99 (0-14-036391-2, PuffinBks) Peng Put Young Read.

Letters from Ring. Ring Lardner, Jr. Ed. by Clifford M. Caruthers. 1979. 10.95 (0-685-05275-3); pap. 5.95 (0-911938-09-5) Walden Pr.

*__Letters from Robben Island: A Selection of Ahmed Kathrada's Prison Correspondence, 1964-1989.__ Ahmed Kathrada. Ed. by Robert D. Vassen. LC 99-6515. 296p. 1999. pap. 22.95 (0-87013-527-9) Mich St U Pr.

Letters from Rome on the Council, by Quirinus, 2 vols. in 1. Johann J. Von Dollinger. LC 78-127193. (Europe 1815-1945 Ser.). 856p. 1973. reprint ed. lib. bdg. 85.00 (0-306-70040-9) Da Capo.

Letters from Roundhead Officers. Ed. by John Y. Akerman. LC 73-158237. (Bannatyne Club, Edinburgh. Publications: No. 101). reprint ed. 57.50 (0-404-52849-X) AMS Pr.

Letters from Russia. Vladimir N. Orlov. (Illus.). 48p. (Orig.). 1993. 5.95 (1-878116-19-3) JVC Bks.

Letters from Russia. William Vigor. LC 70-115594. (Russia Observed, Series I). 1970. reprint ed. 17.95 (0-405-03070-3) Ayer.

Letters from Ruth. Ruth S. Fajfr. 1984. pap. 5.99 (1-56632-026-7) Revival Lit.

Letters from s Sufi Teacher. Baijnath Singh. 1987. pap. 5.75 (81-7059-045-0, 7545, Quest) Theos Pub Hse.

Letters from Saints to Sinners. Ed. by John Cumming. LC 95-43599. 288p. (Orig.). 1996. pap. 19.95 (0-8245-1560-9) Crossroad NY.

Letters from Sarajevo: Voices under Siege. Anna Catalci. 1994. text 19.95 (1-85230-500-2, Pub. by Element MA) Penguin Putnam.

Letters from Sardis. George M. Hanfmann. LC 77-174542. (Illus.). 380p. 1972. 55.00 (0-674-52579-5) HUP.

Letters from Saudi Arabia. Abdul Bel-Ka. (Illus.). 120p. (Orig.). 1987. pap. 29.50 (0-930329-17-1) Kabel Pubs.

Letters from Sea, 1882-1901: Joanna & Lincoln Colcord's Seafaring Childhood. Parker Bishop Albee, Jr. LC 99-43369. (Illus.). 224p. 1999. 35.00 (0-88448-214-6) Tilbury Hse.

Letters from Side Lake: A Chronicle of Life in the North Woods. Peter M. Leschak. LC 92-8713. 208p. 1992. pap. 14.95 (0-8166-2243-4) U of Minn Pr.

Letters from Simon. I. H. Paul. LC 96-444465. 270p. (Orig.). 1996. pap. 29.95 (0-8236-8130-0, 23011) Intl Univs Pr.

Letters from Sir Robert Cecil to Sir George Carew. Robert C. Salisbury. Ed. by John MacLean. LC 17-1256. (Camden Society, London, Publications: No. 88). reprint ed. 40.00 (0-404-50188-5) AMS Pr.

Letters from Slave Girl. Lyons. (J). 1998. pap. 3.95 (0-87628-518-3) Ctr Appl Res.

Letters from Sunnyside & Spain. Washington Irving. (American Biography Ser.). 80p. 1991. reprint ed. lib. bdg. 59.00 (0-7812-8207-1) Rprt Serv.

Letters from Tarsus, 2 vols., Set. Harry A. Poole. 1995. 85.00 (1-887189-09-2); pap. text 55.00 (1-887189-10-6) Symi Pub.

Letters from Tarsus: From Pythagoras to Paul, Vol. I. Harry A. Poole. 324p. 1995. 45.00 (1-887189-11-4); pap. text 29.50 (1-887189-12-2) Symi Pub.

Letters from Tarsus: From Pythagoras to Paul, Vol. II. Harry A. Poole. 296p. 1995. 45.00 (1-887189-13-0); pap. text 29.50 (1-887189-14-9) Symi Pub.

Letters from Tehran: An Ambassador in World War II Persia. Reader Bullard. Ed. by E. C. Hodgkin. 300p. 1991. 49.50 (0-685-38701-1, Pub. by I B T) St Martin.

Letters from Tel Mond Prison: An Israeli Settler Defends His Act of Terror. Era Rapaport. 280p. 1996. 22.50 (0-684-83180-5) S&S Trade.

Letters from the Alleghany Mountains. Charles Lanman. (Notable American Authors Ser.). 1999. reprint ed. lib. bdg. 125.00 (0-7812-3733-5) Rprt Serv.

*__Letters from the Attic.__ Gregg Condon. (Illus.). 248p. 1999. pap. 14.95 (0-9637697-1-5) Marsh Lake.

Letters from the Avant-Garde: Modern Graphic Design. Ellen Lupton & Elaine L. Cohen. (Illus.). 128p. 1996. pap. 24.95 (1-56898-052-3) Princeton Arch.

Letters from the Backwoods & the Adirondacks. Joel T. Headley. 105p. 1993. reprint ed. lib. bdg. 69.00 (0-7812-5125-7) Rprt Serv.

Letters from the Bird Barge. Owen W. Dykema. (Illus.). 214p. 1997. pap. 19.95 (0-9660705-0-X) Dykema Pub Co.

Letters from the Camp/Lettres du Camp/Scrisori din Lagar. Florentin Smarandache. Ed. by Xiquan Publishing House Staff. (ENG, FRE & RUM.). 500p. (C). 1991. pap. 39.99 (1-879585-21-9) Erhus Univ Pr.

Letters from the Canyon (Grand Canyon) Kathleen McAnally. LC 95-78447. (Illus.). 32p. (Orig.). (J). (gr. 2-4). 1995. pap. 8.95 (0-938216-52-X) GCA.

Letters from the Carlist War, 1874-1876. Kennett-Barrington. Ed. by Lascelles & Alberich. (Exeter Hispanic Text Ser.: No. 43). 133p. Date not set. pap. text 17.95 (0-85989-264-6, Pub. by Univ Exeter Pr) Northwestern U Pr.

Letters from the Children: From the Mouths of Babes & Sucklings. Ricardo A. Scott. (Reggae Book of Light Ser.). (Illus.). 65p. 1995. pap. 19.95 (1-883427-27-4) Crnerstone GA.

Letters from the Cosmos. Carol J. Swiedler & Edward B. Swiedler. LC 93-86875. 200p. 1993. per. 10.95 (0-9638986-0-4) Clermont Pr.

Letters from the Cosmos. 2nd ed. Carol J. Swiedler & Edward B. Swiedler. LC 93-86875. 200p. 1993. spiral bd. 14.95 (0-9638986-1-2) Clermont Pr.

*__Letters from the Country.__ Carol Bly. LC 98-53291. 208p. 1999. pap. 14.95 (0-8166-3322-3) U of Minn Pr.

*__Letters from the Dead: Poems from Hollywood.__ Mark Dunster. 11p. 1999. pap. 5.00 (0-89642-936-9) Linden Pubs.

Letters from the Desert. Carlo Carretto. Tr. by Rose Hancock from ITA. LC 72-85791. Orig. Title: Lettres dal deserto. 146p. (Orig.). 1982. pap. 11.00 (0-88344-280-9) Orbis Bks.

Letters from the Doomed: Concentration Camp Correspondence, 1940-1945. Ed. & Tr. by Richard S. Geehr. 88p. (C). 1991. lib. bdg. 38.50 (0-8191-8414-4) U Pr of Amer.

Letters From the Ear. Ed. by Bernard A. De Voto. LC 90-56427. 320p. 1991. reprint ed. pap. 13.00 (0-06-092105-6, Perennial) HarperTrade.

Letters from the Earth. Mark Twain, pseud. 1996. lib. bdg. 22.95 (0-8488-1770-2) Amereon Ltd.

Letters from the Earth. Mark Twain, pseud. 1991. reprint ed. lib. bdg. 21.95 (1-56849-069-0) Buccaneer Bks.

Letters from the East. William C. Bryant. (Works of William Cullen Bryant). 1989. reprint ed. lib. bdg. 79.00 (0-685-44808-8) Rprt Serv.

Letters from the End of the World: A Firsthand Account of the Bombing of Hiroshima. Ogura Toyofumi. Tr. by Kisaburo Murakami & Shigeru Fujii. LC 97-36072. 1997. 25.00 (4-7700-2147-X, Pub. by Kodansha Intl) Kodansha.

Letters from the English Abbots to the Chapter at Citeaux, 1442-1521. C. H. Talbot. (Camden Fourth Ser.: No. 4). 200p. 27.00 (0-901050-64-4) David Brown.

Letters from the Equator. C. H. Gervais. 79p. 1986. 7.95 (0-920806-87-2, Pub. by Penumbra Pr) U of Toronto Pr.

*__Letters from the Fens.__ large type unabridged ed. Edward Storey. 1999. 25.95 (0-7531-5090-5, 150905, Pub. by ISIS Lrg Prnt) ISIS Pub.

*__Letters from the Field: Wallace at the Little Big Horn.__ Douglas Westfall. Ed. by James Willert. (Illus.). 200p. 2000. pap. 18.76 (1-891030-01-9) Paragon Agency.

Letters from the Field: Wallace at the Little Big Horn. Douglas P. Westfall. Ed. by James Willert. (Special Bks.). xii, 86p. 1997. pap. 18.76 (1-891030-00-0) Paragon Agency.

*__Letters from the Field 1925-75.__ Margaret Mead. 2000. pap. 13.00 (0-06-095804-9) HarpC.

Letters from the Floating World: Selected & New Poems. Siv Cedering. LC 84-5222. (Pitt Poetry Ser.). 195p. 1984. pap. 60.50 (0-608-05083-0, 206563700005) Bks Demand.

*__Letters from the Front.__ Sharon S. Bardsley. 80p. 2000. pap. text 9.95 (0-89827-207-6) Wesleyan Pub Hse.

Letters from the Front: Boys Town on the Battlefield from Pearl Harbor to the Persian Gulf. Hugh J. Reilly & Terry L. Hyland. Ed. by Barbara A. Lonnborg & David Manley. (Illus.). 272p. (Orig.). 1995. pap. 10.99 (0-938510-51-7, 19-007) Boys Town Pr.

Letters from the Front, 1898-1945. Ed. by Michael E. Stevens et al. LC 92-27598. (Voices of the Wisconsin Past Ser.). (Illus.). 187p. 1992. pap. 12.95 (0-87020-268-5, LEFR) State Hist Soc Wis.

Letters from the Frontiers: A Facsimile Reproduction of the 1868 Edition with an Introduction & Index by John K. Mahon. George A. McCall. LC 74-22038. (Bicentennial Floridian Facsimile Ser.). (Illus.). 591p. reprint ed. pap. 183.30 (0-7837-0596-4, 204094400019) Bks Demand.

Letters from the Gold Rush. Francis T. Sherman & Henry A. Ballentine. Ed. by Robert T. Sherman, Jr. LC 80-52965. (Illus.). 63p. (Orig.). 1982. pap. 4.00 (0-9613031-0-7) R T Sherman.

Letters from the Good War: A Young Man's Discovery of the World. Hugh Aaron. Ed. by Ramon De Rosas. LC 96-68798. 750p. (Orig.). 1997. pap. 20.00 (1-882521-04-8) Stones Pt Pr.

Letters from the Grand Tour. Joseph Spence. Ed. by Slava Klima. LC 73-79098. 508p. reprint ed. pap. 157.50 (0-608-12528-8, 202385500034) Bks Demand.

*__Letters from the Grave.__ Deborah Cox-Stubblefield. 2000. pap. 12.00 (1-930183-09-7, DR-0004-99) Anyanwu.

Letters from the Great Turke. I. Ahmad. LC 72-164. (English Experience Ser.: No. 292). 16p. 1971. reprint ed. 10.00 (90-221-0292-0) Walter J Johnson.

Letters from the Gulag: The Life, Letters & Poetry of Michael Dray-Khmara. Oksana Dray-Khmara Asher. (Illus.). 164p. 1983. 15.00 (0-8315-0187-1) Speller.

Letters from the Heart. James Cloutier. LC 86-62945. 64p. 1986. pap. 5.95 (0-918966-11-6) Image West.

*__Letters from the Heart: A Celebration of Letters to Absolutely Incredible Kids.__ unabridged ed. Ed. by Stewart Smith. 126p. 2000. pap. 11.95 (0-9674529-0-2) Camp Fire Pr.

Letters from the Highlands. Robert Somers. 203p. (C). 1989. pap. 40.00 (0-9505884-0-7, Pub. by Mercat Pr Bks) St Mut.

Letters from the Hill Country: The Correspondence Between Rebekah & Lyndon Baines Johnson. Ed. by Philip R. Rulon. LC 82-19369. 1982. 17.00 (0-914476-97-1) Thorp Springs.

*__Letters from the Holy Ground: Seeing God Where You Are.__ Loretta Ross-Gotta. 296p. 2000. pap. 16.95 (1-58051-084-1) Sheed & Ward WI.

Letters from the Horse Latitudes: Short Fiction. C. W. Smith. LC 94-6504. 160p. (C). 1994. 19.95 (0-87565-131-3) Tex Christian.

Letters from the Inside. John Marsden. LC 95-174528. 160p. (YA). (gr. 7 up). 1996. mass mkt. 4.99 (0-440-21951-5) Dell.

Letters from the Inside. John Marsden. LC 93-41185. 37p. (J). 1994. 14.95 (0-395-68985-6) HM.

An Asterisk (*) at the beginning of an entry indicates that the title is appearing for the first time.

Letters from the Inside. John Marsden. LC 95-174528. 1996. 9.09 (*0-606-09552-7*, Pub. by Turtleback) Demco.

Letters from the Inside John Marsden. LC 95-174528. 146 p. (J). 1992. write for info. (*0-330-27314-0*, Pub. by Pan) Trafalgar.

Letters from the Iron Brigade: George W. Partridge, Jr., 1839-1863 - Civil War Letters to His Sister. Hugh Whitehouse. LC 94-77600. 117p. 1994. 21.95 (*1-878208-47-0*) Guild Pr IN.

Letters from the Leelanau: Essays of People & Place. Kathleen Stocking. LC 90-35596. (Illus.). 182p. 1990. 29.95 (*0-472-09445-9*, 09445); pap. 18.95 (*0-472-06445-2*, 06445) U of Mich Pr.

Letters from the Levant: During the Embassy to Constantinople, 1716-18. Lady Mary Wortley Montagu. LC 71-135825. (Eastern Europe Collection). 1971. reprint ed. 32.95 (*0-405-02767-2*) Ayer.

Letters from the Light: An Afterlife Journal from the Self-Lighted World. 2nd ed. Elsa Barker. Ed. by Katherine Hart. LC 94-43637. 296p. (C). 1995. reprint ed. 18.95 (*1-885223-08-0*) Beyond Words Pub.

Letters from the Lord of Heaven: The Seven Churches of Asia (Revelation 2-3) Edward P. Myers. (Small Group Studies). 90p. 1996. pap. 5.99 (*0-89900-705-8*, T96-705-8) College Pr Pub.

Letters from the Lost Generation: Gerald & Sara Murphy & Friends. Ed. by Linda P. Miller. LC 90-42139. (Illus.). 362p. 1993. pap. 16.95 (*0-8135-1966-7*) Rutgers U Pr.

*__Letters from the Lost Soul: A Five Year Voyage of Discovery & Adventure.__ Bob Bitchin. LC 00-36555. (Illus.). 272p. 2000. 29.95 (*1-57409-112-3*) Sheridan.

Letters from the Mandali of Avatar Meher Baba, Vol. I. Compiled by Jim Mistry. LC 83-142831. 152p. (Orig.). 1981. pap. 7.95 (*0-913078-42-5*) Sheriar Pr.

Letters from the Mandali of Avatar Meher Baba, Vol. II. Jim Mistry. LC 83-142831. 176p. (Orig.). 1983. pap. 7.95 (*0-913078-46-8*) Sheriar Pr.

Letters from the Masters of the Wisdom. C. Jinarajadasa. 1988. pap. 6.95 (*81-7059-039-6*, 7612, Quest) Theos Pub Hse.

Letters From the Masters of the Wisdom, Vol. 1. C. Jinarajadasa. (Series 1). 1988. 10.95 (*81-7059-040-X*) Theos Pub Hse.

Letters from the Middle. Kathernie V. Goerss et al. 46p. 1993. pap. text 9.00 (*1-56090-074-1*) Natl Middle Schl.

Letters from the Middle East by an Occasional Archaeologist. R. W. Hamilton. 252p. (C). 1989. text 75.00 (*1-872795-69-2*, Pub. by Pentland Pr) St Mut.

Letters from the Middle Years: Reflections on Life & Faith for the Middle Generation. deluxe ed. Martha M. Kern. LC 98-164569. 207p. 1998. pap. 10.99 (*0-7459-3850-7*, Lion) Chariot Victor.

Letters from the Mountain. Sherry Garland. LC 96-2257. 256p. (J). 1996. 12.00 (*0-15-200661-3*); pap. 6.00 (*0-15-200659-1*) Harcourt.

Letters from the Mughal Court: The First Jesuit Mission to Akbar (1580-1583) Ed. & Tr. by John Correia-Afonso. LC 81-81766. (Jesuit Primary Sources in English Translation Series I: No. 4). (Illus.). xvi, 136p. 1981. 4.50 (*0-912422-57-2*) Inst Jesuit.

Letters from the Nevada Frontier: Correspondence of Tasker L. Oddie, 1898-1902. Tasker L. Oddie. Ed. by William A. Douglass & Robert A. Nylen. LC 92-54132. (Illus.). 416p. 1992. 45.00 (*0-8061-2448-2*) U of Okla Pr.

Letters from the New World: Selected Correspondence of Don Diego de Vargas to His Family, 1675-1706. John L. Kessell. LC 92-7560. (Illus.). 237p. 1992. pap. 22.50 (*0-8263-1354-X*) U of NM Pr.

Letters from the Other Side. Kay Saunders. LC 98-96479. (Illus.). 48p. 1998. pap. write for info. (*0-9666146-0-7*) Saunders Ents.

Letters from the Other Side: With Love, Harry & Helen. Mary B. White. Ed. by Stephen Carlson. (Illus.). 195p. (Orig.). 1988. 15.95 (*0-942679-02-4*); pap. 10.95 (*0-942679-03-2*) Upper Access.

*__Letters from the Pacific: A Combat Chaplain in World War II.__ Russell Cartwright Stroup. Ed. & Intro. by Richard Cartwright Austin. LC 99-85994. 224p. 2000. 24.95 (*0-8262-1288-3*) U of Mo Pr.

Letters from the Paris Peace Conference. Charles Seymour. Ed. by Harold B. Whiteman. LC 65-22336. (Illus.). 321p. reprint ed. pap. 99.60 (*0-608-30148-5*, 202203700024) Bks Demand.

Letters from the Past (Allegheny County) Wainwright Family. C. Saddler. 73p. 1989. per. 7.50 (*1-55856-012-2*, 193) Closson Pr.

Letters from the Peninsula: The Civil War Letters of General Philip Kearny. Philip Kearny & William B. Styple. (Illus.). 241p. (Orig.). 1988. 25.00 (*0-9622053-2-X*); pap. 15.95 (*0-9622053-1-1*) Belle Grv Pub.

Letters from the Peninsula: 1808-1812. William Warre. Ed. by William Atcheson Warre. 304p. 1997. 80.00 (*1-86227-037-6*, Pub. by Spellmnt Pubs) St Mut.

Letters from the Promised Land: Swedes in America, 1840-1914. H. Arnold Barton. LC 74-22843. (Illus.). 256p. 1980. pap. 16.95 (*0-8166-1009-6*) U of Minn Pr.

Letters from the Raven, Being the Correspondence of Lafcadio Hearn with Henry Watkin. Lafcadio Hearn. 1977. 16.95 (*0-8369-6977-4*, 7856) Ayer.

Letters from the Right Honourable Lady Mary Wortley Montagu, 1709-1762. Lady Mary Wortley Montagu. (BCL1-PR English Literature Ser.). 551p. 1992. reprint ed. lib. bdg. 99.00 (*0-7812-7391-9*) Rprt Serv.

Letters from the Sandwich Islands. Mark Twain, pseud. LC 72-2113. (American Literature Ser.: No. 49). (C). 1972. reprint ed. lib. bdg. 75.95 (*0-8383-1471-6*) M S G Haskell Hse.

Letters from the Sandwich Islands. Mark Twain, pseud. (American Biography Ser.). 224p. 1991. reprint ed. lib. bdg. 69.00 (*0-7812-8074-5*) Rprt Serv.

Letters from the Sea: Written Aboard the Sailboat "Northern Light" During a 61-Day Ocean Voyage. Deborah Shapiro & Lea Daniel. (Illus.). 96p. (J). (gr. 4-7). 1997. pap. 12.95 (*0-939837-03-X*) Paradise Cay Pubns.

Letters from the Shores of the Baltic. Elizabeth Rigby. LC 73-115533. (Russia Observed, Series I). 1970. reprint ed. 33.95 (*0-405-03023-1*) Ayer.

Letters from the Soul: Unsent Letters & Stories for Spiritual Growth. Rose Offner. (Illus.). 72p. (Orig.). 1997. pap. 19.95 (*0-87905-793-9*) Gibbs Smith Pub.

Letters from the South: By a Northern Man. James K. Paulding. (Notable American Authors Ser.). 1999. reprint ed. lib. bdg. 125.00 (*0-7812-4741-1*) Rprt Serv.

Letters from the South Pacific: A World War II Chronicle. Robert P. Gregory. (Illus.). 128p. (Orig.). 1996. pap. 10.95 (*1-56474-168-0*) Fithian Pr.

Letters from the South, Written During an Excursion in the Summer of 1816, 2 vols. in 1. James K. Paulding. LC 75-173933. reprint ed. 59.50 (*0-404-00280-3*) AMS Pr.

Letters from the Southwest. Charles Lummis. Ed. by James W. Byrkit. LC 88-27793. 309p. 1989. 39.00 (*0-8165-1039-3*) U of Ariz Pr.

Letters from the Streets of Exile. Salah M. Abood. LC 97-93567. (Illus.). vi, 52p. 1997. pap. text. write for info. (*0-9658362-0-7*) Salah M Abood.

Letters from the West. James A. Hall. LC 67-10123. 406p. 1967. reprint ed. 50.00 (*0-8201-1024-8*) Schol Facsimiles.

Letters from Thirty-One Artists. Ed. by Ethel Moore. (Gallery Notes Ser.). (Illus.). (Orig.). 1970. pap. 1.50 (*0-914782-97-5*, C214) Buffalo Fine-Albrght-Knox.

Letters from Togo. Susan Blake. LC 91-20943. (Singular Lives: The Iowa Series in North American Autobiography). (Illus.). 203p. 1991. pap. 13.95 (*0-87745-340-3*) U of Iowa Pr.

Letters from Turkey. Keleman Mikes. Tr. by Bernard Adams from HUN. LC 97-51369. 61p. 1998. 110.00 (*0-7103-0610-5*, Pub. by Kegan Paul Intl) Col U Pr.

Letters from Turkey, 1939-1946. G. Maynard. LC 94-69122. (Illus.). viii, 298p. 1994. pap. text 20.00 (*0-918986-96-6*) Orient Inst.

Letters from Two Brothers, 1870-1873: William Anderson Patrick & Beverly Prior Patrick. Mary Collie-Cooper. LC 88-70358. (Illus.). 155p. (Orig.). 1988. pap. 12.50 (*0-943553-05-9*) Collie-Cooper Ent.

Letters from Two Women: Poems. Evelyn C. Appelbee & Violette Newton. 25p. (Orig.). 1990. pap. write for info. (*0-9626347-0-0*) Harp & Quill Pr.

Letters from Vienna. Mary Wagner. LC 99-70089. 272p. 1999. 22.95 (*1-57197-167-X*) Pentland Pr.

*__Letters from Vietnam.__ Morley Safer. 2000. 25.00 (*0-06-019865-6*); pap. 14.00 (*0-06-095823-5*) HarpC.

Letters from Vinnie. Maureen S. Sappey. LC 98-52337. 248p. (J). (gr. 8 up). 1999. 16.95 (*1-886910-31-6*, Pub. by Front Str) Publishers Group.

*__Letters from Wales.__ Ed. by Joan Abse. 324p. 2000. 42.95 (*1-85411-270-8*, Pub. by Seren Bks) Dufour.

Letters from Windermere, 1912-1914. Ed. by R. Cole Harris & Elizabeth Phillips. (Pioneers of British Columbia Ser.). (Illus.). 277p. 1984. pap. 15.95 (*0-7748-0394-0*) U of Wash Pr.

Letters from Wingfield Farm. Dan Needles. 160p. 1990. pap. 7.99 (*0-7704-2386-8*) Bantam.

Letters from Women Who Love Too Much. Robin Norwood. 1989. mass mkt. 6.50 (*0-671-73342-7*) PB.

Letters from Wupatki. Courtney R. Jones. Ed. by Lisa Rappoport. LC 94-18756. (Illus.). 151p. 1995. 27.95 (*0-8165-1530-1*); pap. 14.95 (*0-8165-1507-7*) U of Ariz Pr.

Letters from Yellowstone. Jim Carrier. 150p. 1987. 16.95 (*0-911797-37-8*); pap. 8.95 (*0-911797-38-6*) Roberts Rinehart.

*__Letters from Yellowstone.__ Diane Smith. 240p. 2000. pap. 12.95 (*0-14-029181-4*) Viking Penguin.

Letters Home. (Illus.). 27p. 1996. pap. 3.00 (*1-890541-01-X*) Americana Souvenirs & Gifts.

Letters Home. Michael Andre. 24p. 1979. pap. 1.50 (*0-916696-14-6*) Cross Country.

Letters Home. Britt Barker. (Illus.). 64p. (Orig.). 1990. pap. 5.50 (*0-945097-09-3*) Home Educ Pr.

Letters Home. William B. Bruce. Ed. by Joan Murray. 254p. 1982. 24.95 (*0-920806-36-8*, Pub. by Penumbra Pr) U of Toronto Pr.

*__Letters Home.__ Donald R. Hunt. 373p. 2000. pap. 29.92 (*0-7884-1478-X*, 1478) Heritage Bk.

*__Letters Home.__ Brian Johnston. 1998. 40.00 (*0-297-84127-0*, Pub. by Weidenfeld & Nicolson) Trafalgar.

*__Letters Home.__ Terry Vance. 1999. pap. 13.00 (*0-375-70902-9*) Pantheon.

Letters Home. William Dean Howells. (Notable American Authors Ser.). 1992. reprint ed. lib. bdg. 75.00 (*0-7812-3256-2*) Rprt Serv.

Letters Home: A Soldier's Legacy. Roger L. Shaffer. (Military History Ser.). 208p. 1996. pap. 12.95 (*1-55622-488-5*, Rep of TX Pr) Wordware Pub.

Letters Home: Celebrated Authors Write to Their Mothers. Ed. by Reid Sherline. LC 92-43125. (Illus.). 108p. 1993. 14.95 (*0-943221-16-1*) Timken Pubs.

Letters Home: Correspondence, 1950-1963. Sylvia Plath. LC 91-58567. (Illus.). 512p. 1992. reprint ed. pap. 17.00 (*0-06-097491-5*, Perennial) HarperTrade.

Letters Home: Genealogical & Family-Historical Data on Nineteenth-Century German Settlers in Australia, Bermuda, Brazil, Canada, & the United States. Tr. by Clifford N. Smith. (German-American Genealogical Research Monographs: No. 25, Pt. 1). ii, 36p. 1989. pap. 20.00 (*0-915162-90-3*) Westland Pubns.

Letters Home: Henry Matrau of the Iron Brigade. Henry Matrau. Ed. by Marcia M. Reid-Green. LC 92-26862. (Illus.). xix, 170p. 1993. text 30.00 (*0-8032-3151-2*) U of Nebr Pr.

Letters Home: Henry Matrau of the Iron Brigade. Henry Matrau. Ed. by Marcia Reid-Green. LC 92-26862. (Illus.). xix, 170p. 1998. pap. 11.00 (*0-8032-8242-7*, Bison Books) U of Nebr Pr.

*__Letters Home: Memoirs of One Army Nurse in the Southwest Pacific in WWII.__ 2nd ed. (Illus.). 163p. 1998. reprint ed. spiral bd. 20.00 (*0-9673257-0-6*) S H Pullman.

Letters Home: Sage Advice from Wise Men & Women of the Ages to Their Friends & Loved Ones. George Grant & Karen Grant. LC 97-29581. 224p. (Orig.). (YA). (gr. 10 up). 1997. pap. 12.95 (*1-888952-48-2*) Cumberland Hse.

Letters Home: The True Story of Lt. Harry Frank Hunt, Veterinary Reserve Corps, AEF, WWI. Faye C. Brown. LC 98-160279. (Illus.). 108p. 1998. pap. 22.95 (*0-9661807-0-4*) Daphne Pub.

Letters Home from Brazil. Marcia S. Gresko. LC 99-23480. (Letters Home from... Ser.). (Illus.). 32p. (J). (gr. 3-5). 1999. lib. bdg. 16.95 (*1-56711-407-5*) Blackbirch.

*__Letters Home from Canada.__ Marcia S. Gresko. (Letters Home from... Ser.). (Illus.). 32p. (J). (gr. 3-5). 2000. lib. bdg. 16.95 (*1-56711-410-5*) Blackbirch.

Letters Home from China. Marcia S. Gresko. LC 98-52405. (Letters Home from... Ser.). (Illus.). 32p. (J). (gr. 3-5). 1999. lib. bdg. 16.95 (*1-56711-400-8*) Blackbirch.

Letters Home from Egypt. Marcia S. Gresko. LC 99-23118. (Letters Home from... Ser.). (Illus.). 32p. (J). (gr. 3-5). 1999. lib. bdg. 16.95 (*1-56711-401-6*) Blackbirch.

Letters Home from Greece. Marcia S. Gresko. LC 99-25618. (Letters Home from... Ser.). (Illus.). 32p. (J). (gr. 3-5). 1999. lib. bdg. 16.95 (*1-56711-406-7*) Blackbirch.

Letters Home from India. Marcia S. Gresko. LC 99-22795. (Letters Home from... Ser.). (Illus.). 32p. (J). (gr. 3-5). 1999. lib. bdg. 16.95 (*1-56711-403-2*) Blackbirch.

Letters Home from Israel. Marcia S. Gresko. LC 98-10913. (Letters Home from... Ser.). (Illus.). 32p. (J). (gr. 3-5). 1999. lib. bdg. 16.95 (*1-56711-404-0*) Blackbirch.

*__Letters Home from Japan.__ Marcia S. Gresko. LC 99-45467. (Letters Home from... Ser.). 32p. (J). (gr. 3-5). 2000. lib. bdg. 16.95 (*1-56711-409-1*) Blackbirch.

Letters Home from Kenya. Marcia S. Gresko. LC 99-27024. (Letters Home from... Ser.). (Illus.). 32p. (J). (gr. 3-5). 1999. lib. bdg. 16.95 (*1-56711-405-9*) Blackbirch.

Letters Home from Mexico. Marcia S. Gresko. LC 99-24507. (Letters Home from... Ser.). (Illus.). 32p. (J). (gr. 3-5). 1999. lib. bdg. 16.95 (*1-56711-402-4*) Blackbirch.

*__Letters Home from Russia.__ Marcia S. Gresko. LC 99-56774. (Letters Home from... Ser.). 32p. (J). (gr. 3-5). 2000. lib. bdg. 16.95 (*1-56711-411-3*) Blackbirch.

*__Letters Home from Scotland.__ Marcia S. Gresko. LC 99-41814. (Letters Home from... Ser.). (Illus.). 32p. (J). (gr. 3-5). 2000. lib. bdg. 16.95 (*1-56711-408-3*) Blackbirch.

Letters Home from the Crimea: A Young Cavalryman's Campaign. Philip Warner. 1999. pap. text 21.95 (*1-900624-24-9*) W1indrush Pr.

*__Letters Home from the Grand Canyon.__ Marcia S. Gresko & Lisa Halvorsen. LC 99-50075. (Letters Home from National Parks Ser.). 32p. (J). (gr. 3-5). 2000. lib. bdg. 16.95 (*1-56711-463-6*) Blackbirch.

Letters Home from the Lafayette Flying Corps. Alan Nichols, Sr. Ed. by Nancy A. Nichols. LC 92-28089. (Illus.). 320p. 1993. 24.95 (*0-9630274-0-9*); pap. 14.95 (*0-9630274-7-6*) J D Huff.

*__Letters Home from Turkey.__ Lisa Halvorsen. (Letters Home From... Ser.). (Illus.). 32p. 2000. 16.95 (*1-56711-415-6*) Blackbirch.

*__Letters Home from Yosemite.__ Lisa Halvorsen. LC 99-44255. (Letters Home from National Parks Ser.). 32p. (J). (gr. 3-5). 2000. lib. bdg. 16.95 (*1-56711-462-8*) Blackbirch.

*__Letters Home from Zimbabwe.__ Lisa Halvorsen. (Illus.). 32p. 2000. 16.95 (*1-56711-412-1*) Blackbirch.

Letters Home, the Ohio Veterans Plaza. 186p. 1998. 12.95 (*0-9669903-0-7*) D Meeks.

Letters Home to Minnesota: Second Minnesota Volunteers. Joan Albertson. 270p. 1992. pap. 27.95 (*0-9630286-1-8*) PD Enter.

Letters I: 1721-1739 see Works of John Wesley

Letters II: 1740-1755 see Works of John Wesley

Letters in a Mahratta Camp During the Year, 1809. Thomas D. Broughton. (C). 1995. reprint ed. 28.00 (*81-206-1008-3*, Pub. by Asian Educ Servs) S Asia.

Letters in Gold: Ottoman Calligraphy from the Sakip Sabanci Collection, Istanbul. M. Ugur Derman. LC 98-21945. (Illus.). 208p. 1998. 65.00 (*0-8109-6526-7*, Pub. by Abrams) Time Warner.

Letters in Gold: Ottoman Calligraphy from the Sak P. Sabanc Collection, Istanbul. M. Ugur Derman et al. LC 98-21945. 196p. 1998. 50.00 (*0-87099-873-0*); pap. 35.00 (*0-87099-874-9*) Metro Mus Art.

Letters in Search of Love: And Other Essays. Ronald L. Donaghe. LC 98-87848. 325p. 1998. 25.00 (*0-7388-0119-4*); pap. 15.00 (*0-7388-0120-8*) Xlibris Corp.

Letters in the British Museum. Tr. by Wilfred H. Van Soldt. (Altbabylonische Briefe im Umschrift und Ubersetzung Ser.: No. 12). x, 155p. 1989. 44.00 (*90-04-09208-0*) Brill Academic Pubs.

Letters in the British Museum, Band II. Ed. by Wilfred H. Van Soldt. (Altbabylonische Briefe im Umschrift und Ubersetzung Ser.: No. 13). 150p. 1993. 57.50 (*90-04-09948-4*, NLG85) Brill Academic Pubs.

Letters Inside the Journey. Amatullah Armstrong. 206p. 1996. pap. 17.00 (*0-614-21302-9*, 1398) Kazi Pubns.

Letters, Lies & Alibis. Sandy Steen. (Delta Justice Ser.). 1997. per. 4.50 (*0-373-82562-5*) Harlequin Bks.

Letters-Lights - Words for Adelle. Jack Foley. LC 87-60436. (Mucho Somos Ser.: No. 10). 32p. (Orig.). 1987. pap. 1.50 (*0-914370-55-3*) Mothers Hen.

Letters-Lines-Images: International Contemporary Calligraphy Exhibition. Intro. by Donald Jackson. LC 90-83441. (Illus.). 120p. (Orig.). 1990. pap. 29.95 (*0-9622349-1-5*) CRE Norman.

Letters Lost & Found. Elaine Goolsby. LC 98-51175. (Illus.). 100p. 1999. pap. 10.95 (*0-932112-39-0*) Carolina Wren.

Letters Make Words see Mortimer's Fun with Words

Letters Mostly Unpublished. Robert V. Keeley. 72p. 1997. pap. 5.00 (*1-892379-04-X*) Five & Ten.

Letters Never Sent: One Woman's Cathartic Release in Poetry. Paula Curci. (Illus.). 24p. (Orig.). 1996. pap. 9.00 (*0-9654831-0-X*) P Curci.

Letters Never Sent: One Woman's Journey from Hurt to Wholeness. 2nd rev. ed. Ruth E. Van Reken. 176p. (Orig.). 1995. pap. 7.95 (*0-9646423-0-1*) Letters IN.

Letters, 1961-1968. Karl Barth. Ed. by Jurgen Fangmeier & Hinrich Stoevesand. LC 80-29140. 398p. reprint ed. pap. 123.40 (*0-608-14659-5*, 202320800032) Bks Demand.

Letters, 91-120. Peter Damian. Tr. by Owen J. Blum from LAT. (Fathers of the Church Ser.: No. 5). 440p. 1998. text 42.95 (*0-8132-0816-5*) Cath U Pr.

Letters Notes, on the Manners, Customs & Condition of the North American Indians. George Catlin. (Works of George Catlin). 1990. reprint ed. lib. bdg. 79.00 (*0-7812-2247-8*) Rprt Serv.

Letters, Numbers & Shapes: An Early Childhood Book, Ps-1. Karen Sevaly & Debra Teel. (Illus.). 144p. (Orig.). 1989. pap. 10.95 (*0-943263-11-5*, TF-1301) Teachers Friend Pubns.

Letters of a Civil War Nurse: Cornelia Hancock, 1863-1865. Cornelia Hancock. Ed. by Henrietta Stratton Jaquette. LC 98-10011. (Illus.). xx, 179p. 1998. pap. 9.95 (*0-8032-7312-6*, Bison Books) U of Nebr Pr.

Letters of a Civil War Surgeon. William Watson. Ed. by Paul Fatout. LC 96-19912. 145p. 1996. pap. 14.95 (*1-55753-092-0*) Purdue U Pr.

Letters of a Confederate Officer to His Family in Europe During the Last Year of the War of Secession. Richard W. Corbin. 99p. (C). 1993. text 22.50 (*0-935523-34-0*) Butternut & Blue.

Letters of a Diplomat's Wife, 1883-1900. Mary A. Waddington. (American Biography Ser.). 417p. 1991. reprint ed. lib. bdg. 89.00 (*0-7812-8398-1*) Rprt Serv.

Letters of A. E. Housman. Henry Maas. 1979. 25.00 (*0-8464-0090-1*) Beekman Pubs.

*__Letters of a German American Farmer: Juernjakob Swehn Travels to America.__ Johannes Gillhoff. Tr. by Richard Lorenz August Trost from GER. LC 99-88016. (Bur Oak Ser.). Orig. Title: Jurnjakob Swehn der Amerikafahrer. (Illus.). 186p. 2000. reprint ed. pap. 16.95 (*0-87745-706-9*); reprint ed. text 32.95 (*0-87745-719-0*) U of Iowa Pr.

Letters of a Hindoo Rajah. Elizabeth Hamilton. Ed. by P. Perkins & S. Russell. (Literary Texts Ser.). 340p. 1999. pap. 12.95 (*1-55111-175-6*) Broadview Pr.

Letters of a Japanese Schoolboy. Wallace Irwin. LC 77-96889. (Illus.). 385p. reprint ed. pap. text 9.95 (*0-8290-1681-3*); reprint ed. lib. bdg. 32.50 (*0-8398-0851-8*) Irvington.

Letters of a Javanese Princess. Adjeng K. Raden. Ed. by Hildred Geertz. Tr. by Agnes L. Symmers from DUT. 246p. 1985. reprint ed. pap. text 22.00 (*0-8191-4758-3*) U Pr of Amer.

Letters of a Lifetime. Sally K. Babinat. iii, 235p. 1999. 38.50 (*0-9672966-0-9*) Babblins.

Letters of a Love Hungry Farmer. John B. Keane. 390p. 1997. 24.95 (*1-57098-166-3*); pap. 14.95 (*1-57098-183-3*) Roberts Rinehart.

Letters of a Loyalist Lady, Ann Hulton, Sister of Henry Hulton, Commissioner of Customs at Boston, 1767-1776. Ann Hulton. LC 79-140868. (Eyewitness Accounts of the American Revolution Ser.). (Illus.). 1975. reprint ed. 19.95 (*0-405-01204-7*) Ayer.

Letters of a Malcontent: A Collection of Thoughtful, Absurd, & Bizarre Correspondence. James W. Fagan. 170p. (Orig.). 1996. pap. write for info. (*1-57502-228-1*) Morris Pubng.

Letters of a Matchmaker. John B. Keane. 1990. pap. 10.95 (*0-85342-826-3*) Dufour.

Letters of a Nation: A Collection of Extraordinary American Letters. Andrew Carroll. LC 98-38061. 496p. 1999. pap. 15.00 (*0-7679-0331-5*) Broadway BDD.

Letters of a Nation: A Collection of Extraordinary American Letters. Ed. by Andrew Carroll. LC 97-25510. 512p. 1997. 27.00 (*1-56836-196-3*) Kodansha.

Letters of a New Market Cadet. 32.95 (*0-8488-1543-2*, Evergreen NY) Amereon Ltd.

Letters of a Peruvian Princess see Letters from a Peruvian Woman

Letters of a Russian Traveler, 1789-1790. Nikolai Karamzin. Tr. by Florence Jonas. LC 75-46515. (Columbia Slavic Studies). (Illus.). 351p. 1976. reprint ed. lib. bdg. 35.00 (*0-8371-8725-7*, KART, Greenwood Pr) Greenwood.

Letters of a Self-Made Merchant to His Son: An American Father Gives Timeless Advice to His Son on How to Succeed in Life. George H. Lormer. 260p. 16.95 (*0-89526-475-7*) Regnery Pub.

L

An Asterisk (*) at the beginning of an entry indicates that the title is appearing for the first time.

L

Letters of a Successful T. D. John B. Keane. 1990. pap. 10.95 (*0-85342-824-7*) Dufour.

***Letters of a Sufi Master.** Shaikh A. Ad-Darqawi. 1998. pap. text 11.95 (*1-887752-16-1*) Fons Vitae.

Letters of a Sufi Master: The Shaikh Al-'Arabi Ad-Darqawi. 2nd ed. Shaikh A. Ad-Darqawi. Tr. by Titus Burckhardt from FRE. 38p. 1987. pap. 9.95 (*0-900588-00-4*) S Perennis.

Letters of a Traveller. William C. Bryant. (Works of William Cullen Bryant). 1989. reprint ed. lib. bdg. 79.00 (*0-7812-2137-4*) Rprt Serv.

Letters of a Victorian Madwoman. Ed. by John S. Hughes. LC 92-27442. (Women's Diaries & Letters of the Nineteenth-Century South Ser.). 273p. 1993. text 24.95 (*0-87249-840-9*) U of SC Pr.

Letters of A. W. Pink. Arthur W. Pink. 1978. pap. 4.99 (*0-85151-262-3*) Banner of Truth.

Letters of a Westchester Farmer, 1774-1775. Samuel Seabury. Ed. by Clarence H. Vance. LC 70-103943. (Era of the American Revolution Ser.). 1970. reprint ed. lib. bdg. 25.00 (*0-306-71868-5*) Da Capo.

Letters of a Woman Homesteader. Elinore P. Stewart. 310p. 1998. pap. 13.00 (*0-395-91151-6*, Mariner Bks) HM.

Letters of a Woman Homesteader. Elinore P. Stewart. LC 88-20764. xii, 282p. 1990. pap. 9.95 (*0-8032-5193-9*, Bison Books) U of Nebr Pr.

Letters of a Woman Homesteader. Elinore P. Stewart. (American Biography Ser.). 281p. 1991. reprint ed. lib. bdg. 69.00 (*0-7812-8365-5*) Rprt Serv.

Letters of Abelard & Heloise. Betty Radice et al. LC 74-177112. (Classics Ser.). 312p. 1998. pap. text 6.67 (*0-14-044297-9*) Addison-Wesley Educ.

Letters of Adam of Perseigne. Tr. by Grace Perigo. LC 76-15486. (Cistercian Fathers Ser.: No. 21). 1976. 12.95 (*0-87907-621-6*) Cistercian Pubns.

Letters of Ahmad Ibn Idris. Ed. by Einor Thomassen & Bernd Radtke. Tr. by Albrech Hofheinz et al. LC 92-39183. (Islam & Society in Africa Ser.). 1993. 59.95 (*0-8101-1070-9*) Northwestern U Pr.

Letters of al-Ghazali. Muhammad Al-Ghazali. Tr. by Abdul Qayyum. 150p. (Orig.). 1986. pap. 4.50 (*1-56744-322-2*) Kazi Pubns.

Letters of Alfred Lord Tennyson, 1871-1892, Vol. 3. Alfred Lord Tennyson. Ed. by Cecil Y. Lang & Edgar F. Shannon, Jr. 534p. 1991. text 140.00 (*0-19-812692-1*) OUP.

Letters of Alfred Lord Tennyson, 1821-1850, Vol. I. Alfred Lord Tennyson. Ed. by Cecil Y. Lang & Edgar F. Shannon, Jr. LC 80-25764. 400p. (C). 1981. 51.95 (*0-674-52583-3*) HUP.

Letters of Alfred Lord Tennyson, 1851-1870, Vol. 2. Alfred Lord Tennyson. Ed. by Cecil Y. Lang & Edgar F. Shannon, Jr. LC 80-25764. 608p. 1987. 50.00 (*0-674-52584-1*) Belknap Pr.

Letters of an Altrurian Traveller. William Dean Howells. LC 61-5081. 128p. 1979. reprint ed. 50.00 (*0-8201-1255-0*) Schol Facsimiles.

Letters of an Irish Publican. John B. Keane. 1990. pap. 10.95 (*0-85342-949-9*) Dufour.

Letters of Anna Seward Written Between the Years 1784-1807, 6 vols., Set. Anna Seward. LC 76-37721. (Woman of Letters Ser.). reprint ed. 450.00 (*0-404-56840-8*) AMS Pr.

***Letters of Anne Gilchrist & Walt Whitman.** Walt Whitman. (Notable American Authors Ser.). 1999. reprint ed. lib. bdg. 125.00 (*0-7812-9957-8*) Rprt Serv.

Letters of Anne Gilchrist & Walt Whitman. Walt Whitman & Anne Gilchrist. Ed. by Thomas B. Harned. LC 72-6286. (Studies in Whitman: No. 28). (Illus.). 282p. 1972. reprint ed. lib. bdg. 75.00 (*0-8383-1630-1*) M S G Haskell Hse.

Letters of Anthony Trollope. Anthony Trollope. Ed. by Bradford A. Booth. LC 78-12349. 519p. 1979. reprint ed. lib. bdg. 48.50 (*0-313-21156-6*, TRLE, Greenwood Pr) Greenwood.

Letters of Anthony Trollope, 2 vols., Set. Anthony Trollope. Ed. by N. John Hall & Nina Burgis. LC 79-64213. (Illus.). xxxviii, 1,082p. 1983. 125.00 (*0-8047-1076-7*) Stanford U Pr.

Letters of Anton Chehov to Olga Knipper. Anton Chekhov. Tr. by Constance Garnett. LC 65-16232. 415p. 1972. 26.95 (*0-405-08354-8*, Pub. by Blom Pubns) Ayer.

Letters of Arabella Stuart. Arabella Stuart. Ed. by Sara J. Steen. (Women Writers in English Ser.). (Illus.). 320p. 1994. pap. text 24.95 (*0-19-508718-6*) OUP.

Letters of Armand Jean de Rance, Abbot & Reformer of La Trappe, 2 vols., I. Ed. by Alban J. Krailsheimer. 1984. 29.95 (*0-87907-880-4*) Cistercian Pubns.

Letters of Armand Jean de Rance, Abbot & Reformer of La Trappe, 2 vols., II. Ed. by Alban J. Krailsheimer. 1984. 29.95 (*0-87907-881-2*) Cistercian Pubns.

Letters of Artemus Ward to Charles E. Wilson, 1858-1861. Charles F. Brown. 1971. 59.95 (*0-8490-0511-6*) Gordon Pr.

Letters of Arthur Henry Hallam. Arthur H. Hallam. Ed. by Jack Kolb. LC 79-13490. 861p. 1981. reprint ed. pap. 200.00 (*0-608-00916-4*, 206171000011) Bks Demand.

Letters of Aubrey Beardsley. Ed. by Henry Maas et al. LC 68-11571. (Illus.). 472p. 1975. 65.00 (*0-8386-6884-4*) Fairleigh Dickinson.

Letters of Ayn Rand. Ayn Rand. 720p. 1997. pap. 17.95 (*0-452-27404-4*, Plume) Dutton Plume.

Letters of Bede Jarrett. Ed. by Bede Bailey et al. (Dominican Sources in English Ser.: Vol. 5). 282p. 1989. write for info. (*0-9502759-6-4*, Pub. by Downside Abbey); lib. bdg. write for info. (*0-9511202-4-7*, Pub. by Downside Abbey) Parable.

Letters of Benjamin Disraeli, 1842-1847, Vol. IV. Ed. by M. G. Wiebe et al. 480p. 1989. text 75.00 (*0-8020-5810-8*) U of Toronto Pr.

Letters of Benjamin Disraeli, 1848-1851, Vol. V. Ed. by M. H. Wiebe et al. 592p. 1993. text 95.00 (*0-8020-2927-2*) U of Toronto Pr.

Letters of Benjamin Disraeli, 1831-1841, Vol. III. Ed. by M. G. Wiebe. 1987. text 60.00 (*0-8020-5736-5*) U of Toronto Pr.

Letters of Bliss Carman. Ed. by H. Pearson Gundy. (Illus.). 416p. 1981. 49.95 (*0-7735-0364-1*, Pub. by McG-Queens Univ Pr) CUP Services.

Letters of Brendan Behan. Brendan Behan. Ed. by E. H. Mikhail. (Illus.). 272p. 1991. 60.00 (*0-7735-0888-0*, Pub. by McG-Queens Univ Pr) CUP Services.

Letters of Bret Harte. Bret Harte. LC 70-161761. reprint ed. 42.50 (*0-404-09024-9*) AMS Pr.

Letters of Bret Harte. Bret Harte. (American Biography Ser.). 515p. 1991. reprint ed. lib. bdg. 99.00 (*0-7812-8170-9*) Rprt Serv.

Letters of Bret Harte: Assembled & Ed. by Geoffrey Bret Harte. Bret Harte. (BCL1-PS American Literature Ser.). 515p. 1992. reprint ed. lib. bdg. 99.00 (*0-7812-6721-8*) Rprt Serv.

Letters of Brunswick & Hessian Officers During the American Revolution. Ed. by William L. Stone. LC 76-112706. (Era of the American Revolution Ser.). 1970. reprint ed. lib. bdg. 35.00 (*0-306-71919-3*) Da Capo.

Letters of C. P. E. Bach. Carl P. Bach. Ed. & Tr. by Stephen L. Clark. LC 97-5414. (Illus.). 370p. (C). 1997. text 98.00 (*0-19-816238-3*) OUP.

Letters of C. S. Lewis. C. S. Lewis. Ed. by Walter Hooper & W. H. Lewis. 528p. 1994. pap. 14.95 (*0-15-650871-0*) Harcourt.

Letters of Capt. Geo. Hamilton Perkins, U. S. N. George H. Perkins. LC 78-107825. (Select Bibliographies Reprint Ser.). 1977. 23.95 (*0-8369-5219-7*) Ayer.

Letters of Capt. Geo. Hamilton Perkins, U. S. N. George H. Perkins. (American Biography Ser.). 254p. 1991. reprint ed. lib. bdg. 69.00 (*0-7812-8311-6*) Rprt Serv.

Letters of Carl van Vechten & Gertrude Stein, 1913-1946, 2 vols., Set. Ed. by Edward Burns. LC 85-24343. (Illus.). 901p. 1986. text 145.00 (*0-231-06308-3*) Col U Pr.

Letters of Caroline Norton to Lord Melbourne. Caroline Sheridan Norton. Ed. by James O. Hoge & Clarke Olney. LC 74-12344. (Illus.). 200p. reprint ed. pap. 62.00 (*0-608-09687-3*, 206980200006) Bks Demand.

Letters of Catharine Cottam Romney, Plural Wife. Ed. by Jennifer M. Hansen. (Illus.). 360p. 1992. text 29.95 (*0-252-01868-0*) U of Ill Pr.

***Letters of Catherine of Siena: Vol. 1: Letters 1-70.** 2nd ed. Catherine & Suzanne Noffke. LC 99-54886. (Medieval & Renaissance Texts & Studies: Vol. 202). 1999. write for info. (*0-86698-244-2*) MRTS.

Letters of Centinel. Samuel Bryan. Ed. by Warren Hope. LC 98-74072. 160p. 1998. reprint ed. pap. 21.99 (*1-892355-01-9*) Fifth Season.

Letters of Charles & Mary Anne Lamb, 3 vols. Charles Lamb & Mary Lamb. Ed. by E. V. Lucas. LC 68-59268. reprint ed. write for info. (*0-404-03840-9*) AMS Pr.

Letters of Charles & Mary Anne Lamb, Vol. I: 1796-1801. Charles Lamb & Mary A. Lamb. Ed. by Edwin W. Marrs, Jr. (Illus.). 352p. 1975. text 59.95 (*0-8014-0930-6*) Cornell U Pr.

Letters of Charles & Mary Anne Lamb, Vol. II: 1801-1809. Charles Lamb et al. (Illus.). 336p. 1976. text 59.95 (*0-8014-0977-2*) Cornell U Pr.

Letters of Charles & Mary Anne Lamb, Vol. III: 1809-1817. Charles Lamb & Mary A. Lamb. Ed. by Edwin W. Marrs, Jr. (Illus.). 320p. 1978. text 59.95 (*0-8014-1129-7*) Cornell U Pr.

Letters of Charles Baudelaire to His Mother, 1833-1866. Charles Baudelaire. Tr. by Arthur Symons. LC 70-173184. 1972. reprint ed. 24.95 (*0-405-08242-8*, Pub. by Blom Pubns) Ayer.

Letters of Charles Baudelaire to His Mother, 1833-1866: Eighteen Thirty-Three - Eighteen Sixty-Six. Charles Baudelaire. Ed. by Arthur Symons. LC 73-153490. (Studies in French Literature: No. 45). 1971. reprint ed. lib. bdg. 75.00 (*0-8383-1241-1*) M S G Haskell Hse.

***Letters of Charles Demuth, American Artist, 1883-1935.** Ed. by Bruce Kellner. LC 99-461967. (Illus.). 232p. 2000. pap. 19.95 (*1-56639-781-2*) Temple U Pr.

***Letters of Charles Demuth, American Artist, 1883-1935.** Ed. by Bruce Kellner. LC 99-461967. (Illus.). 232p. 2000. 54.50 (*1-56639-780-4*) Temple U Pr.

Letters of Charles Dickens. Charles Dickens et al. 1977. 52.95 (*0-8369-7100-0*, 7934) Ayer.

Letters of Charles Dickens: The Pilgrim Edition, Vol. 1, 1820-1839. Charles Dickens. Ed. by Madeline House & Graham Story. 796p. (C). 1982. reprint ed. text 140.00 (*0-19-811447-8*) OUP.

Letters of Charles Dickens: The Pilgrim Edition, Vol. 2, 1840-1841. Charles Dickens. Ed. by Madeline House & Graham Storey. (Illus.). 570p. 1969. text 110.00 (*0-19-811478-8*) OUP.

Letters of Charles Dickens: The Pilgrim Edition, Vol. 3, 1842-1843. Charles Dickens. Ed. by Madeline House et al. (Illus.). 720p. (C). 1974. text 120.00 (*0-19-812474-0*) OUP.

Letters of Charles Dickens: The Pilgrim Edition, Vol. 5, 1847-1849. Charles Dickens. Ed. by Graham Storey & Kenneth J. Fielding. (Illus.). 778p. (C). 1981. 150.00 (*0-19-812514-3*) OUP.

Letters of Charles Dickens: The Pilgrim Edition, Vol. 6, 1850-1852. Charles Dickens. Ed. by Nina Burgis & Graham Storey. (Illus.). 928p. 1988. text 175.00 (*0-19-812617-4*) OUP.

Letters of Charles Dickens: 1862-1864, Vol. 10. Charles Dickens. Ed. by Graham Storey & Margaret Brown. (Illus.). 530p. 1998. text 130.00 (*0-19-812294-2*) OUP.

Letters of Charles Dickens: 1865-1867; The Pilgrim Edition, Vol. 11. Charles Dickens. Ed. by Graham Storey et al. (British Academy Ser.). (Illus.). 602p. 2000. text 120.00 (*0-19-812295-0*) OUP.

Letters of Charles Dickens Vol. 4: The Pilgrim Edition, 1844-1846. Charles Dickens. Ed. by Kathleen Tillotson & Nina Burgis. (Illus.). 798p. 1978. text 140.00 (*0-19-812475-9*) OUP.

Letters of Charles Dickens Vol. 8: The Pilgrim Edition, 1856-1858. Charles Dickens. Ed. by Graham Storey & Kathleen Tillotson. (Illus.). 834p. 1995. text 170.00 (*0-19-812662-X*) OUP.

Letters of Charles Dickens: The Pilgrim Edition Vol. 9: 1859-1861. Charles Dickens. Ed. by Graham Storey & Margaret Brown. (British Academy Ser.). (Illus.). 634p. 1998. text 140.00 (*0-19-812293-4*) OUP.

Letters of Charles Dickens to Wilkie Collins. Charles Dickens. LC 73-20382. (Studies in Dickens: No. 52). 1974. lib. bdg. 75.00 (*0-8383-1823-1*) M S G Haskell Hse.

Letters of Charles Eliot Norton with Biographical Comment, 2 vols. Charles E. Norton. Ed. by Sara Norton & M. A. Howe. LC 76-148817. reprint ed. 125.00 (*0-404-04800-5*) AMS Pr.

Letters of Charles Haddon Spurgeon. Charles H. Spurgeon. Ed. by Iain H. Murray. 224p. 1992. pap. 6.99 (*0-85151-606-8*) Banner of Truth.

Letters of Charles O'Conor of Belanagare: A Catholic Voice in Eighteenth-Century Ireland. Charles O'Conor. Ed. by Robert E. Ward et al. LC 87-32563. 571p. 1988. reprint ed. pap. 177.10 (*0-7837-9104-6*, 204990600004) Bks Demand.

***Letters of Charlotte Bronte 1848-1851, Vol. II.** Charlotte Bronte. Ed. by Margaret Smith. (Illus.). 650p. 2000. text 110.00 (*0-19-818598-7*) OUP.

Letters of Charlotte Bronte, 1829-1847, Vol. I. Charlotte Bronte. Ed. by Margaret Smith. (Illus.). 644p. 1995. text 98.00 (*0-19-818597-9*) OUP.

Letters of Chauncey Wright: With Some Account of His Life, by James Bradley Thayer. Chauncey Wright. (American Biography Ser.). 392p. 1991. reprint ed. lib. bdg. 79.00 (*0-7812-8430-9*) Rprt Serv.

Letters of Christina Rosetti, 1843-1873, Vol. 1. Christina Georgina Rossetti. Ed. by Antony H. Harrison. LC 96-26707. (Victorian Literature & Culture Ser.). 544p. (C). 1997. text 49.50 (*0-8139-1686-0*) U Pr of Va.

***Letters of Christina Rossetti, Vol. 3.** Ed. by Antony H. Harrison. 352p. 2000. 60.00 (*0-8139-1929-0*) U Pr of Va.

Letters of Christina Rossetti Vol. 2: 1874-1881. Ed. by Antony H. Harrison. (Victorian Literature & Culture Ser.). 384p. 1999. text 60.00 (*0-8139-1783-2*) U Pr of Va.

Letters of Claudio Monteverdi. Denis Stevens. LC 80-66219. 432p. 1980. text 89.95 (*0-521-23591-X*) Cambridge U Pr.

Letters of Composers: An Anthology, 1603-1945. Ed. by Gertrude Norman & Mirian L. Shrifte. LC 78-11483. 422p. 1979. reprint ed. lib. bdg. 79.50 (*0-313-20664-3*, NOLC, Greenwood Pr) Greenwood.

Letters of Conrad Aiken & Malcolm Lowry, 1929-1954. Conrad Aiken & Malcolm Lowry. Ed. by Cynthia Conchita Sugars. (Illus.). 350p. (C). 1992. pap. text 25.00 (*1-55022-168-X*, Pub. by ECW) Genl Dist Srvs.

Letters of Creation. Marcia Prager. 2003. 21.00 (*0-517-70362-9*) Random Hse Value.

Letters of Credit. Burton V. McCullough. 1987. ring bd. 215.00 (*0-8205-1387-3*) Bender.

Letters of Credit. Gerald T. McLaughlin. 500p. 1985. suppl. ed. 70.00 (*0-317-29394-X*, #H4397X) Harcourt.

Letters of Credit. 2nd ed. Michael Rowe. 311p. 1997. pap. 215.00 (*1-85564-579-3*, Pub. by Euromoney) Am Educ Systs.

Letters of Credit Series, Bks. I-V. 3rd ed. 1985. teacher ed. 22.00 (*0-685-63170-2*, 230101); teacher ed. 15.00 (*0-685-63171-0*, 230101) Am Bankers.

Letters of Credit Series, Set, Bks. I-V. 3rd ed. 1985. 189.00 (*0-89982-343-2*, 230100); 125.00 (*0-318-69882-X*, 230100) Am Bankers.

Letters of D. H. Lawrence, 7 vols., Vol. 1: 1901-1913. D. H. Lawrence. Ed. by James T. Boulton. LC 78-7531. (Cambridge Edition of the Works of D. H. Lawrence). (Illus.). 624p. 1979. text 105.00 (*0-521-22147-1*) Cambridge U Pr.

Letters of D. H. Lawrence, 7 vols., Vol. 2: 1913-1916. D. H. Lawrence. Ed. by James T. Boulton. LC 78-7531. (Cambridge Edition of the Works of D. H. Lawrence). (Illus.). 710p. 1982. text 105.00 (*0-521-23111-6*) Cambridge U Pr.

Letters of D. H. Lawrence, 7 vols., Vol. 5: March 1924-March 1927. D. H. Lawrence. Ed. by James T. Boulton. LC 78-7531. (Cambridge Edition of the Works of D. H. Lawrence). (Illus.). 736p. 1989. text 105.00 (*0-521-23114-0*) Cambridge U Pr.

Letters of D. H. Lawrence, 7 vols., Vol. 7: Nov. 1928-Feb. 1930. D. H. Lawrence. Ed. by James T. Boulton. LC 78-7531. (Cambridge Edition of the Works of D. H. Lawrence). (Illus.). 713p. 1993. text 105.00 (*0-521-23116-7*) Cambridge U Pr.

Letters of D. H. Lawrence Vol. 3: October 1916-June 1921. 776p. 1985. text 105.00 (*0-521-23112-4*) Cambridge U Pr.

Letters of D. Martyn Lloyd-Jones. D. Martyn Lloyd-Jones. 248p. 1994. 25.99 (*0-85151-674-2*) Banner of Truth.

Letters of Daniel Webster. D. Webster. LC 68-25003. (American Biography Ser.: No. 32). 1969. reprint ed. lib. bdg. 75.00 (*0-8383-0255-6*) M S G Haskell Hse.

Letters of Daniel Webster. Daniel Webster. LC 02-26743. 1902. reprint ed. 59.00 (*0-403-00261-3*) Scholarly.

Letters of Daniel Webster: From Documents Owned Principally by the New Hampshire Historical Society. Daniel Webster. (American Biography Ser.). 769p. 1991. reprint ed. lib. bdg. 119.00 (*0-7812-8405-8*) Rprt Serv.

Letters of Daniel Webster: From Documents Owned Principally by the New Hampshire Historical Society. Daniel Webster. (BCL1 - U. S. History Ser.). 769p. 1992. reprint ed. lib. bdg. 109.00 (*0-7812-6149-X*) Rprt Serv.

Letters of Delegates to Congress, 1774-1789 Sept.-Dec. 1775, Vol. 2. Paul H. Smith. 585p. 1992. boxed set 36.00 (*0-16-061797-9*, Library of Cong) USGPO.

Letters of Delegates to Congress, 1774-1789, Vol. 17, Mar. 1-Aug. 31, 1781. Ed. by Paul H. Smith. LC 76-2592. 647p. 1991. text 44.00 (*0-16-025828-6*, 030-000-00225-3) USGPO.

***Letters of Delegates to Congress, 1774-1789, March 1, 1788-july 25, 1789, With Supplement, 1774-87, Vol. 25.** Paul H. Smith. 873p. 1998. boxed set 62.00 (*0-16-061806-1*, Library of Cong) USGPO.

Letters of Delegates to Congress, 1774-1789 Vol. 23: November 7, 1785 - November 5, 1786. Ed. by Paul H. Smith & Ronald M. Gephart. (Illus.). 691p. (*0-16-048407-3*) USGPO.

Letters of Delegates to Congress, 1774-1789 Vol. 24: November 6, 1786 - February 29, 1788. Ed. by Paul H. Smith & Ronald M. Gephart. (Illus.). 721p. (*0-16-048369-7*) USGPO.

Letters of Delegates to Congress, 1774-1789 Vol. 25: March 1, 1788-July 25, 1789, with Supplement, 1774-87. Ed. by Paul H. Smith et al. Incl. Ibid: October 1, 1783-October 31, 1784. LC 76-2592. 861p. 41.00 March 12-September 30, 1783. LC 76-2592. 791p. 1993. 41.00 Vol. 1. August Seventeen Seventy-Four to August Seventeen Seventy-Five. LC 76-2592. (Illus.). xxxvii, 751p. 1976. 33.00 (*0-8444-0191-9*, 030-000-00076-5); Vol. 2. September to December, 1775. LC 76-2592. (Illus.). xxvii, 735p. 1977. 27.00 (*0-8444-0230-3*, 030-000-00077-3); Vol. 3. January 1 to May 15, 1976. LC 76-2592. (Illus.). xxix, 735p. 1978. 18.00 (*0-8444-0259-1*, 030-000-00083-8); Vol. 4. May 16th to August 15th, 1776. LC 76-2592. (Illus.). xxviii, 739p. 1979. 18.00 (*0-8444-0260-5*, 030-000-00103-6); Vol. 5. August Sixteenth to December Thirty-First, Seventeen Seventy-Six. LC 76-2592. (Illus.). xxx, 767p. 1979. 19.00 (*0-8444-0276-1*, 030-000-00111-7); Vol. 6. January 1 to April 30, 1777. LC 76-2592. (Illus.). xxviii, 760p. 1980. 19.00 (*0-8444-0310-5*, 030-000-00101-0); Vol. 7. May 1st to September 18, 1777. LC 76-2592. (Illus.). xxvi, 749p. 1981. 15.00 (*0-8444-0350-4*, 030-000-00107-9); Vol. 8. September Nineteenth, Seventeen Seventy-Seven to January Thirty First, Seventeen Seventy-Eight. LC 76-2592. (Illus.). xxxii, 745p. 1981. 17.00 (*0-8444-0356-3*, 030-000-00119-2); Vol. 9. February 1 to May 31, 1978. LC 76-2592. (Illus.). xxviii, 844p. 1982. 19.00 (*0-8444-0388-1*, 030-000-00140-1); Vol. 10. June 1 to September 30, 1978. LC 76-2592. (Illus.). xxix, 766p. 1983. 27.00 (*0-8444-0434-9*, 030-000-00151-6); Vol. 11. October 1, 1778 to January 31, 1779. LC 76-2592. (Illus.). xxxi, 587p. 1985. 18.00 (*0-8444-0454-3*, 030-000-00157-5); Vol. 12. February 1 to May 31, 1779. LC 76-2592. (Illus.). xxix, 595p. 1985. 20.00 (*0-8444-0505-1*, 030-000-00161-3); Vol. 13. June 1 to September 30, 1779. LC 76-2592. (Illus.). 647p. 1987. 27.00 (*0-8444-0524-8*, 030-000-00173-7); Vol. 14. October 1, 1779 to March 31, 1780. LC 76-2592. (Illus.). 600p. 1987. 28.00 (*0-8444-0562-0*, 030-000-00192-3); Vol. 15. April 1 to August 31, 1780. LC 76-2592. (Illus.). 678p. 1988. 37.00 (*0-8444-0577-9*, 030-000-00186-9); Vol. 16. September 1, 1780 to February 28, 1781. LC 76-2592. (Illus.). 804p. 1989. 38.00 (*0-8444-0616-3*, 030-000-00200-8); Vol. 17. March 1 to August 31, 1781. LC 76-2592. (Illus.). 617p. 1990. 34.00 (*0-8444-0679-1*, 030-000-00225-3); Vol. 18. September 1781 to July 31, 1782. LC 76-2592. (Illus.). 749p. 1991. 37.00 (*0-8444-0725-9*, 030-000-00231-8); Vol. 19. August 1, 1782 to March 11, 1783. LC 76-2592. (Illus.). 827p. 1992. 35.00 (*0-8444-0740-2*, 030-000-00239-3); LC 76-2592. (Illus.). 841p. 1998. Set boxed set 56.00 (*0-8444-0177-3*) Lib Congress.

Letters of Denise Levertov & William Carlos Williams. Denise Levertov & William Carlos Williams. Ed. by Christopher MacGowan. LC 98-34194. 192p. 1998. 24.95 (*0-8112-1392-7*, Pub. by New Directions) Norton.

Letters of Dennys De Berdt, 1757-70. Dennys De Berdt. (Select Bibliographies Reprint Ser.). 1977. reprint ed. 19.95 (*0-8369-5931-0*) Ayer.

Letters of Direction. Abbe De Tourville. LC 84-60628. 111p. 1993. reprint ed. pap. 5.95 (*0-8192-1346-2*) Morehouse Pub.

Letters of Dominique Chaix, Botanist-Cur E. Dominique Chaix & Roger L. Williams. LC 97-19829. (International Archives of the History of Ideas Ser.). 1997. lib. bdg. 174.00 (*0-7923-4615-7*) Kluwer Academic.

Letters of Dorothy L. Sayers: 1937-1943: From Novelist to Playwright, Vol. II. Dorothy L. Sayers. Ed. by Barbara Reynolds. (Illus.). 450p. 1998. text 27.95 (*0-312-18127-2*) St Martin.

Letters of Dorothy Wordsworth. Dorothy Wordsworth. Ed. by Alan G. Hill. (Oxford Letters & Memoirs). 224p. 1985. text 7.95 (*0-19-818539-1*) OUP.

Letters of Dr. John McLoughlin. John McLoughlin. (American Autobiography Ser.). 376p. 1995. reprint ed. lib. bdg. 89.00 (*0-7812-8587-9*) Rprt Serv.

Letters of Dr. Richard Maurice Bucke to Walt Whitman. Artem Lozynsky. LC 77-58. 317p. reprint ed. 98.30 (*0-8357-9829-1*, 201553900001) Bks Demand.

Letters of Edgar Allan Poe, 2 vols., Set. Edgar Allan Poe. Ed. by John Ostrom. LC 66-20025. 731p. 1966. reprint ed. 150.00 (*0-87752-085-2*) Gordian.

An Asterisk (*) at the beginning of an entry indicates that the title is appearing for the first time.

Letters of Edward Fitzgerald, Vol. 1: 1830-1850. Edward FitzGerald. Ed. by Alfred M. Terhune & Annabelle B. Terhune. LC 78-23221. (Illus.). 773p. 1980. reprint ed. pap. 200.00 (*0-8357-3705-5*, 203643000001) Bks Demand.

Letters of Edward Fitzgerald, Vol. 2: 1851-1866. Edward FitzGerald. Ed. by Alfred M. Terhune & Annabelle B. Terhune. LC 78-23221. (Illus.). 671p. 1980. reprint ed. pap. 200.00 (*0-8357-3706-3*, 203643000002) Bks Demand.

Letters of Edward Fitzgerald, Vol. 3: 1867-1876. Edward FitzGerald. Ed. by Alfred M. Terhune & Annabelle B. Terhune. LC 78-23221. (Illus.). 793p. 1980. reprint ed. pap. 200.00 (*0-8357-3707-1*, 203643000003) Bks Demand.

Letters of Edward Fitzgerald, Vol. 4: 1877-1883. Edward FitzGerald. Ed. by Alfred M. Terhune & Annabelle B. Terhune. LC 78-23221. (Illus.). 687p. 1980. reprint ed. pap. 200.00 (*0-8357-3708-X*, 203643000004) Bks Demand.

Letters of Edward Fitzgerald to Fanny Kremble, 1871-1883. Edward Fitzgerald. LC 72-2502. (Select Bibliographies Reprint Ser.). 1977. reprint ed. 21.95 (*0-8369-6854-9*) Ayer.

Letters of Edward Jenner & Other Documents Concerning the Early History of Vaccination. Ed. by Genevieve Miller. LC 82-21295. (Henry E. Sigerist Supplements to the Bulletin of the History of Medicine, New Ser.). 176p. (C). 1983. text 28.50 (*0-8018-2962-3*) Johns Hopkins.

Letters of Edward Lear to Chichester Fortescue & Frances Countess Waldegrave. Edward Lear. LC 70-107812. (Select Bibliographies Reprint Ser.). 1977. 27.95 (*0-8369-5208-1*) Ayer.

Letters of Eliza Wilkinson During the Invasion & Possession of Charleston, S. C. by the British in the Revolutionary War. Eliza Wilkinson. LC 70-76242. (Eyewitness Accounts of the American Revolution Ser.). 1980. reprint ed. 14.95 (*0-405-01157-1*) Ayer.

Letters of Ellen Tucker Emerson, 2 vols., Vol. 1. Ellen T. Emerson. Ed. by Edith E. Gregg. LC 82-10069. 730p. 1982. reprint ed. pap. 200.00 (*0-7837-0573-5*, 204091700001) Bks Demand.

Letters of Ellen Tucker Emerson, 2 vols., Vol. 2. Ellen T. Emerson. Ed. by Edith E. Gregg. LC 82-10069. 692p. 1982. reprint ed. 200.00 (*0-7837-2028-9*, 204091700002) Bks Demand.

Letters of Emily Dickinson. Ed. by Thomas H. Johnson & Theadora Ward. 1056p. 1996. 78.00 (*0-674-52627-9*) HUP.

Letters of Emily Dickinson. Emily Dickinson. (Notable American Authors Ser.). 1992. reprint ed. lib. bdg. 75.00 (*0-7812-2630-9*) Rprt Serv.

Letters of Emma & Florence Hardy. Emma Hardy & Florence E. Hardy. Ed. by Michael Millgate. 390p. (C). 1996. text 80.00 (*0-19-818609-6*) OUP.

Letters of Eric Gill. Eric Gill. (Illus.). 10.00 (*0-8159-6106-5*) Devin.

Letters of Ernest Dowson. Ernest Dowson. Ed. by Desmond Flower & Henry Maas. LC 67-29136. (Illus.). 470p. 1975. 65.00 (*0-8386-6747-3*) Fairleigh Dickinson.

Letters of Eugene V. Debs, 1874-1926, 3 vols., Vols. 1-3. Eugene V. Debs. Ed. by J. Robert Constantine. (Illus.). 1952p. 1991. text 120.00 (*0-252-01742-0*) U of Ill Pr.

Letters of Euler on Different Subjects in Natural Philosophy, 2 vols. Leonhard Euler. LC 74-26260. (History, Philosophy & Sociology of Science Ser.). 1975. reprint ed. 65.95 (*0-405-06588-4*) Ayer.

Letters of Euler to a German Princess: On Different Subjects in Physics & Philosophy, 2 vols. Leonhard Euler. Tr. by Henry Hunter from FRE. 1137p. 1997. reprint ed. 265.00 (*1-85506-507-X*) Thoemmes Pr.

Letters of Ezra Pound. Ezra Pound. LC 74-11145. (Studies in Pound: No. 103). 1974. lib. bdg. 75.00 (*0-8383-1991-2*) M S G Haskell Hse.

Letters of Ezra Pound to Alice Corbin Henderson. Ezra Pound. Ed. by Ira B. Nadel. LC 93-9162. (Illus.). 296p. (C). 1993. 34.95 (*0-292-71134-4*) U of Tex Pr.

Letters of F. Scott Fitzgerald. F. Scott Fitzgerald. (Hudson River Editions Ser.). 616p. 1981. 60.00 (*0-684-16476-0*, Scribners Ref) Mac Lib Ref.

Letters of Fanny Mendelssohn Hensel to Felix Mendelssohn. Marcia J. Citron. LC 84-26364. (ENG & GER.). 600p. 1987. lib. bdg. 83.00 (*0-918728-52-5*) Pendragon NY.

Letters of Father Payeras: The Last Days of Spain in California. Tr. & Intro. by Donald C. Cutter. 380p. 1995. 29.95 (*0-88388-187-X*) Bellerophon Bks.

Letters of Felix Mendelssohn-Bartholdy from 1833-1847. Felix Mendelssohn. Ed. by Paul Mendelssohn-Bartholdy & C. Mendelssohn-Bartholdy. LC 73-114867. (Select Bibliographies Reprint Ser.). 1977. 29.95 (*0-8369-5272-3*) Ayer.

Letters of Felix Mendelssohn to Ignaz & Charlotte Moscheles. Felix Mendelssohn. Ed. & Tr. by Felix Moscheles. LC 77-107822. (Select Bibliographies Reprint Ser.). 1977. 29.95 (*0-8369-5217-0*) Ayer.

Letters of Felix Mendelssohn to Ignaz & Charlotte Moscheles. Felix Mendelssohn. Ed. by Felix Moscheles. LC 76-173116. (Illus.). 1972. reprint ed. 30.95 (*0-405-08786-1*, Pub. by Blom Pubns) Ayer.

Letters of Fire: Mystical Insights into the Hebrew Language. Matityahu Glazerson. 1991. 19.95 (*0-87306-565-4*) Feldheim.

Letters of Frances Hodgkins. Ed. by Linda Gill. (Illus.). 594p. 1993. 45.00 (*1-86940-081-X*, Pub. by Auckland Univ) Paul & Co Pubs.

Letters of Francis Parkman, 2 Vols, 1. Francis Parkman. Ed. by Wilbur R. Jacobs. LC 60-8754. (Illus.). 284p. 1960. reprint ed. pap. 88.10 (*0-8357-9730-9*, 201010000068) Bks Demand.

Letters of Francis Parkman, 2 Vols, 2. Francis Parkman. Ed. by Wilbur R. Jacobs. LC 60-8754. (Illus.). 342p. 1960. reprint ed. pap. 106.10 (*0-608-08255-4*, 201010000069) Bks Demand.

Letters of Franklin K. Lane, Personal & Political. Franklin K. Lane. (American Biography Ser.). 473p. 1991. reprint ed. lib. bdg. 89.00 (*0-7812-8237-3*) Rprt Serv.

Letters of Franz Liszt, 2 vols. Franz Liszt. 1990. reprint ed. lib. bdg. 140.00 (*0-7812-0410-0*) Rprt Serv.

Letters of Franz Liszt, 2 Vols, Set. Franz Liszt. LC 68-25294. (Studies in Music: No. 42). 1969. reprint ed. lib. bdg. 150.00 (*0-8383-0307-2*) M S G Haskell Hse.

Letters of Franz Liszt, 2 vols., Set. Franz Liszt. 1980. reprint ed. lib. bdg. 95.00 (*0-403-00360-1*) Scholarly.

Letters of Franz Liszt to Marie Zu Sayn-Wittgenstein. Franz Liszt. Ed. & Tr. by Howard E. Hugo from FRE. LC 71-142931. 376p. 1971. reprint ed. lib. bdg. 69.50 (*0-8371-1428-4*, LILM, Greenwood Pr) Greenwood.

Letters of Franz Liszt to Olga von Meyendorff, 1871-1886: In the Mildred Bliss Collection at Dumbarton Oaks. Franz Liszt. Tr. by William R. Tyler. (Illus.). 553p. (C). 1979. text 32.50 (*0-685-02129-7*) HUP.

Letters of Franz Liszt to Olga Von Meyendorff, 1871-1886: In the Mildred Bliss Collection at Dumbarton Oaks. Franz Liszt. 553p. (C). 1979. 32.50 (*0-88402-078-9*) HUP.

Letters of Freeman, Etc. William H. Drayton. LC 75-31089. reprint ed. 19.50 (*0-404-13507-2*) AMS Pr.

Letters of Frida Kahlo: Cartas apasionadas. Ed. by Martha Zamora. LC 95-14227. (Illus.). 160p. 1995. 17.95 (*0-8118-1124-7*) Chronicle Bks.

Letters of Gamaliel Bradford, 1918-1931. Gamaliel Bradford. (American Biography Ser.). 377p. 1991. reprint ed. lib. bdg. 79.00 (*0-7812-8035-4*) Rprt Serv.

Letters of George Catlin & His Family: A Chronicle of the American West. Marjorie C. Roehm. LC 66-13090. (Illus.). 485p. reprint ed. pap. 150.40 (*0-608-17987-6*, 202906100058) Bks Demand.

Letters of George Gissing to Members of His Family. George R. Gissing. 1927. 21.00 (*0-685-38424-1*) Scholarly.

Letters of George Gissing to Members of His Family. George R. Gissing. LC 77-130257. (English Literature Ser.: No. 33). 1970. reprint ed. lib. bdg. 75.00 (*0-8383-1158-X*) M S G Haskell Hse.

Letters of George Gissing to Members of His Family. George R. Gissing. (BCL1-PR English Literature Ser.). 414p. 1992. reprint ed. lib. bdg. 99.00 (*0-7812-7538-5*) Rprt Serv.

Letters of George Meredith, 3 vols., Set. Ed. by C. L. Cline. 1786p. 1970. 75.00 (*0-87959-123-4*) U of Tex H Ransom Ctr.

Letters of George Meredith, 2 vols., Set. George Meredith. (BCL1-PR English Literature Ser.). 1992. reprint ed. lib. bdg. 150.00 (*0-7812-7594-6*) Rprt Serv.

Letters of George Sand. George Sand. 1976. lib. bdg. 300.00 (*0-87968-451-8*) Gordon Pr.

Letters of George Sand, 3 vols. George Sand. Ed. & Tr. by Raphael L. De Beaufort. LC 76-7889. reprint ed. 85.00 (*0-404-15230-9*) AMS Pr.

Letters of Gerhard Marcks & Marguerite Wildenhain, 1970-1981: A Mingling of Souls. Gerhard Marcks. LC 90-48292. (Illus.). 285p. 1991. reprint ed. pap. 88.40 (*0-608-06874-8*, 206708200009) Bks Demand.

Letters of Gertrude Stein & Thornton Wilder. Ed. by Edward M. Burns et al. LC 96-17169. (Illus.). 384p. 1997. 35.00 (*0-300-06774-7*) Yale U Pr.

Letters of Giacomo Puccini. Giacomo Puccini. Ed. by Ena Makin. LC 71-140038. reprint ed. 32.50 (*0-404-05149-9*) AMS Pr.

Letters of Giovanni Garzoni: Bolognese Humanist & Physician (1419-1505) L. R. Lind. (American Philological Association Philological Monographs). 600p. 1992. 69.95 (*1-55540-111-2*, 400033) OUP.

Letters of Gregory Akindynos. Tr. by Angela C. Hero. LC 82-24263. (Dumbarton Oaks Texts: Vol. 7). 520p. 1983. text 50.00 (*0-88402-107-6*) Dumbarton Oaks.

Letters of Groucho Marks. Groucho Marx. 1976. 24.95 (*0-8488-1092-9*) Amereon Ltd.

Letters of Grover Cleveland, 1850-1908. Grover Cleveland. (American Biography Ser.). 640p. 1991. reprint ed. lib. bdg. 109.00 (*0-7812-8079-6*) Rprt Serv.

Letters of Grover Cleveland, 1850-1908. Ed. by Allan Nevins. LC 70-123752. (American Public Figures Ser.). 1970. reprint ed. lib. bdg. 75.00 (*0-306-71982-7*) Da Capo.

Letters of Gustaf Nordenskiold & Articles from Ymer & the Photographic Times. Gustaf E. Nordenskiold. Ed. by Irving L. Diamon & Daniel M. Olson. (Illus.). 99p. (Orig.). 1991. pap. 9.95 (*0-937062-16-2*) Mesa Verde Museum.

Letters of Gustave Courbet. Gustave Courbet. LC 91-21917. (Illus.). 738p. 1992. 63.50 (*0-226-11653-0*) U Ch Pr.

Letters of Gustave Flaubert & John E. Woods. Gustave Flaubert. Ed. by Francis Steegmuller. 328p. 1984. pap. text 10.95 (*0-674-52641-4*) Belknap Pr.

Letters of Gustave Flaubert & John E. Woods, Vol. II. Gustave Flaubert. Ed. & Tr. by Francis Steegmuller from FRE. (Illus.). 328p. 1982. 33.50 (*0-674-52640-6*) Belknap Pr.

Letters of Gustave Flaubert, 1830-1857. Gustave Flaubert. Ed. by Francis Steegmuller. LC 79-13503. (Harvard Paperbacks Ser.). 267p. 1981. pap. text 9.95 (*0-674-52637-6*) Belknap Pr.

Letters of H. P. Blavatsky to A. P. Sinnett. Compiled by A. Trevor Barker. LC 73-84138. 420p. 1973. reprint ed. 23.95 (*0-911500-23-5*) Theos U Pr.

Letters of Hans Von Bulow to Richard Wagner & Others. Hans Von Bulow. Ed. by Scott Goddard. LC 78-31972. (Music Reprint Ser.). 470p. 1979. reprint ed. 55.00 (*0-306-79539-6*) Da Capo.

Letters of Harold Ross. Ed. by Thomas Kunkel. 1998. write for info. (*0-679-45727-5*) Random.

Letters of Hart Crane & His Family. Hart Crane. Ed. by Thomas S. Lewis. LC 73-21675. 699p. reprint ed. pap. 200.00 (*0-8357-4575-9*, 203748400008) Bks Demand.

Letters of Hartley Coleridge. Hartley Coleridge. Ed. by Grace E. Griggs & Earl L. Griggs. LC 75-41063. reprint ed. 30.00 (*0-404-14524-8*) AMS Pr.

Letters of Hawthorne to William D. Ticknor, 1851-1864, 2 vols. in 1. Nathaniel Hawthorne. (American Biography Ser.). 1991. reprint ed. lib. bdg. 99.00 (*0-7812-8172-5*) Rprt Serv.

Letters of Heinrich & Thomas Mann, 1900-1949. Thomas Mann et al. Ed. by Heinrich Mann & Hans Wysling. Tr. by Richard Winston & Clara Winston from GER. LC 96-38461. (Weimar & Now Ser.). (Illus.). 700p. 1997. 50.00 (*0-520-07278-2*, Pub. by U CA Pr) Cal Prin Full Svc.

Letters of Helena Roerich, Vol. I. 1979. reprint ed. 16.00 (*0-933574-14-2*) Agni Yoga Soc.

Letters of Helena Roerich, Vol. II. 1982. reprint ed. 16.00 (*0-933574-15-0*) Agni Yoga Soc.

Letters of Henry Adams, 1883-1895, Vol. 3. Henry James. Ed. by Leon Edel. LC 74-77181. (Illus.). 601p. 1980. 56.00 (*0-674-38782-1*) Belknap Pr.

Letters of Henry Adams, 1858-1892, Vols. 1-3. Henry (Brooks) Adams. Ed. by J. C. Levenson et al. (Illus.). 2016p. 1983. 165.00 (*0-674-52685-6*) Belknap Pr.

Letters of Henry James, 1843-1875, Vol. 1. Henry James. Ed. by Leon Edel. LC 74-77181. (Illus.). 493p. 1974. 56.00 (*0-674-38780-5*) Belknap Pr.

Letters of Henry James, 1895-1916, Vol. 4. Henry James. Ed. by Leon Edel. LC 74-77181. (Illus.). 864p. 1984. 56.00 (*0-674-38783-X*) Belknap Pr.

Letters of Henry Adams, 1892-1918, Vols. 4-6. Henry (Brooks) Adams. Ed. by J. C. Levenson et al. LC 82-14673. (Illus.). 2400p. 1988. 225.00 (*0-674-52686-4*) HUP.

Letters of Henry James, 1875-1883, Vol. 2. Henry James. Ed. by Leon Edel. LC 74-77181. (Illus.). 438p. 1975. 56.00 (*0-674-38781-3*) Belknap Pr.

Letters of Henry Handel Richardson to Nettie Palmer. Karl-Johan Rossing. (Essays & Studies on English Language & Literature: Vol. 14). 1953. pap. 25.00 (*0-8115-0212-0*) Periodicals Srv.

Letters of Henry James, 2 vols., Set. Henry James. (BCL1-PS American Literature Ser.). 1992. reprint ed. lib. bdg. 150.00 (*0-7812-6768-4*) Rprt Serv.

Letters of Henry Miller & Wallace Fowlie, 1943-1972 Henry Miller & Wallace Fowlie. LC 74-24859. 184 p. 1975. 9.50 (*0-394-49737-6*) Random.

Letters of Henry Venn. Henry Venn. 594p. 1993. reprint ed. 29.99 (*0-85151-653-X*) Banner of Truth.

Letters of Henry Wadsworth Longfellow, 6 vols. Henry Wadsworth Longfellow. Ed. by Andrew R. Hilen. Incl. Set. Longfellows Letters Vols. 1-2: 1814-1836 & 1837-1843., **2 vols.** LC 66-18248. 1164p. 1967. 95.00 (*0-674-52725-9*); Set. Longfellows Letters Vols. 3-4: 1844-1856 & 1857-1865., **2 vols.** LC 66-18248. 1126p. 1972. 95.00 (*0-674-52728-3*); Set. 1866-1875 & 1876-1882., **2 vols.** LC 66-18248. 1792p. 1983. 127.50 (*0-674-52729-1*); LC 66-18248. write for info. (*0-318-53094-5*) Belknap Pr.

Letters of Hildegard of Bingen, Vol. I. Hildegard of Bingen. Tr. by Joseph L. Baird & Radd K. Ehrman. 248p. 1998. reprint ed. pap. 19.95 (*0-19-512117-1*) OUP.

Letters of Hildegard of Bingen, Vol. II. Hildegard of Bingen. Ed. & Tr. by Joseph L. Baird & Radd K. Ehrman. 240p. 1998. text 45.00 (*0-19-512010-8*) OUP.

Letters of Hope: Living after the Loss of Your Child. Teresa Griffin. LC 91-72709. 79p. (Orig.). 1991. pap. 9.95 (*0-9629584-0-9*) Cedarbrook Pr.

Letters of Horatio Greenough. Ed. by Frances Greenough. LC 70-96437. (Library of American Art). 1970. reprint ed. lib. bdg. 39.50 (*0-306-71828-6*) Da Capo.

Letters of Horatio Greenough, American Sculptor. Horatio Greenough. Ed. by Nathalia Wright. LC 77-176417. 494p. reprint ed. pap. 153.20 (*0-8357-6786-8*, 203546300095) Bks Demand.

Letters of Horatio Greenough to His Brother, Henry Greenough. Horace Bender, pseud. (American Biography Ser.). 250p. 1991. reprint ed. lib. bdg. 69.00 (*0-7812-8156-3*) Rprt Serv.

Letters of Horatio Greenough to His Brother, Henry Greenough. Horatio Greenough. Ed. by Frances B. Greenough. LC 78-168199. reprint ed. 37.50 (*0-404-02897-7*) AMS Pr.

Letters of Horatio Greenough to His Brother Henry Greenough (Ed. by F. B. Greenough) Ed. by Horatio Greenough. (Notable American Authors Ser.). 1992. reprint ed. lib. bdg. 75.00 (*0-7812-2955-3*) Rprt Serv.

Letters of Humfrey Wanley: Palaeographer, Anglo-Saxonist, Librarian, 1694-1726. Humfrey Wanley. Ed. by Peter Heyworth. (Illus.). 556p. 1989. text 135.00 (*0-19-812477-5*) OUP.

Letters of Ignatius Sancho. Ed. by Paul Edwards & Pauline Rewt. (Early Black Writers Ser.). 308p. 1994. 60.00 (*0-7486-0453-7*, Pub. by Edinburgh U Pr) Col U Pr.

Letters of Ignatius Sancho. Ignatius Sancho. LC 97-23377. 1998. pap. 11.95 (*0-14-043637-5*) Viking Penguin.

Letters of Insurgents. Sophia Nachalo & Yarostan Vochek. 1976. pap. 7.50 (*0-934868-13-1*) Black & Red.

***Letters Of Intent: Women Cross the Generations to Talk About Family, Work, Sex, Love, & the Future of Feminism.** Anna Bondoc & Meg Daly. LC 98-51896. 256p. 1999. 23.00 (*0-684-85624-7*) S&S Trade.

Letters of Intent & Other Precontractual Documents: Comparative Analysis & Forms. 2nd ed. Ralph B. Lake & Ugo Draetta. 350p. 1994. 95.00 (*0-250-40740-X*, MICHIE) LEXIS Pub.

Letters of J. N. Darby, 3 vols., Set. J. N. Darby. 22.00 (*0-88172-060-7*) Believers Bkshelf.

***Letters of J. R. R. Tolkien.** Humphrey Carpenter. LC 00-36939. (Illus.). 480p. 2000. pap. 15.00 (*0-618-05699-8*) HM.

Letters of J. R. R. Tolkien, 001. J. R. R. Tolkien. Ed. by Humphrey Carpenter & Christopher Tolkien. 464p. 1981. 24.95 (*0-395-31555-7*) HM.

Letters of J. R. R. Tolkien. J. R. R. Tolkien. Ed. by Humphrey Carpenter & Christopher Tolkien. 463p. 1981. write for info. (*0-04-826005-3*, Pub. by Allen & Unwin Pty) Paul & Co Pubs.

Letters of Jack London, 3 vols., Set. Jack London. Ed. by Earle G. Labor et al. LC 83-45346. (Illus.). 1768p. 1988. 149.50 (*0-8047-1227-1*); 199.50 (*0-8047-1507-6*) Stanford U Pr.

Letters of Jacob Burckhardt. Jacob Burckhardt. Tr. by Alexander Dru from GER. LC 75-8821. (Illus.). 242p. 1975. reprint ed. lib. bdg. 65.00 (*0-8371-8114-3*, BULE, Greenwood Pr) Greenwood.

***Letters of James.** Douglas J. Moo. 2000. 28.00 (*0-8028-3730-1*) Eerdmans.

Letters of James & Peter see Daily Study Bible for the New Testament

Letters of James Joyce, 3 vols. James Joyce. 1966. 40.00 (*0-670-42695-4*) Viking Penguin.

Letters of James Murray, Loyalist. James Murray. (American Biography Ser.). 324p. 1991. reprint ed. lib. bdg. 79.00 (*0-7812-8293-4*) Rprt Serv.

Letters of James Murray, Loyalist. Ed. by Nina M. Tiffany & Susan I. Lesley. LC 72-10762. (American Revolutionary Ser.). 384p. 1979. reprint ed. lib. bdg. 40.50 (*0-8398-1976-5*) Irvington.

Letters of James R. Lowell, 2 vols. James Russell Lowell. Ed. by Charles E. Norton. LC 76-172754. 1894. 115.00 (*0-404-00080-0*) AMS Pr.

Letters of James Whitcomb Riley. James Whitcomb Riley. Ed. by William L. Phelps. LC 78-153348. reprint ed. 49.50 (*0-404-05336-X*) AMS Pr.

Letters of James Whitcomb Riley. James Whitcomb Riley. (American Biography Ser.). 349p. 1991. reprint ed. lib. bdg. 79.00 (*0-7812-8323-X*) Rprt Serv.

Letters of Jan Swammerdam to Melchisedec Thevenot, with English Translation & a Biographical Sketch. G. A. Lindeboom. 202p. 1975. text 94.50 (*90-265-0222-2*) Swets.

Letters of Jessie Benton Fremont. Ed. by Pamela Herr & Mary L. Spence. (Illus.). 656p. (C). 1992. text 39.95 (*0-252-01942-3*) U of Ill Pr.

Letters of Jews Through the Ages, Vol. 1. Ed. by Franz Kobler. 1978. pap. 9.95 (*0-85222-212-2*) Hebrew Pub.

Letters of Jews Through the Ages, Vol. 2. Franz Kobler. 1978. pap. 9.95 (*0-85222-213-0*) Hebrew Pub.

Letters of John. Gary M. Burge. (NIV Application Commentary Ser.). 256p. 1996. 22.99 (*0-310-48620-3*) Zondervan.

***Letters of John.** Colin G. Kruse. (Pillar New Testament Commentary Ser.). 2000. 28.00 (*0-8028-3728-X*) Eerdmans.

Letters of John. John Painter. (Sacra Pagina Ser.). Date not set. write for info. (*0-8146-5812-1*, M Glazier) Liturgical Pr.

Letters of John. J. W. Roberts. 1984. 12.95 (*0-915547-37-6*) Abilene Christ U.

Letters of John: An Introduction & Commentary. 22nd ed. John R. Stott. LC 88-772. (Tyndale New Testament Commentaries Ser.). 1988. pap. 13.00 (*0-8028-0368-7*) Eerdmans.

Letters of John Addington Symonds, 3 vols. John A. Symonds. Ed. by Herbert M. Schueller & Robert L. Peters. LC 67-11765. 869p. reprint ed. pap. 200.00 (*0-608-18520-5*, 202767800001) Bks Demand.

Letters of John & James. Ed. by Ronald R. Williams. (Cambridge Bible Commentary on the New English Bible, New Testament Ser.). 152p. (Orig.). (C). 1965. pap. text 21.95 (*0-521-09250-7*) Cambridge U Pr.

Letters of John & Jude see Daily Study Bible for the New Testament

Letters of John Baptist de La Salle. John B. De La Salle. Ed. by Augustine Loes. Tr. by Colman Molloy from FRE. LC 87-83220. (Lasallian Sources, the Complete Works of John Baptist de La Salle: Vol. 1). (Illus.). xviii, 301p. 1988. 20.00 (*0-944808-00-X*); pap. 15.00 (*0-944808-01-8*) Lasallian Pubns.

Letters of John Calvin. John Calvin. 1980. pap. 10.99 (*0-85151-323-9*) Banner of Truth.

Letters of John Clare. John Clare. Ed. by Mark Storey. 748p. 1986. text 79.00 (*0-19-812669-7*) OUP.

Letters of John Cowper Powys to Louis Wilkinson. 400p. text 32.50 (*0-912568-14-3*) Colgate U Pr.

Letters of John Davenport, Puritan Divine. John Davenport, Jr. Ed. by Isabel M. Calder. 1937. 100.00 (*0-685-69794-0*) Elliots Bks.

Letters of John Greenleaf Whittier, 3 vols., Set. John Greenleaf Whittier. Ed. by John B. Pickard. LC 73-8805. (Illus.). 2080p. 1975. 165.50 (*0-674-52830-1*) Belknap Pr.

Letters of John Hamilton Reynolds. John H. Reynolds. Ed. by Leonidas M. Jones. LC 72-90342. 122p. reprint ed. pap. 37.90 (*0-8357-3811-6*, 203653800003) Bks Demand.

Letters of John Hay & Extracts from His Diary, 3 vols., Set. John Hay. LC 71-93245. 1139p. (C). 1969. reprint ed. 200.00 (*0-87752-051-8*) Gordian.

Letters of John Holmes: To James Russell Lowell & Others. Ed. by William R. Thayer. LC 72-21. (Select Bibliographies Reprint Ser.). 1977. reprint ed. 22.95 (*0-8369-9973-8*) Ayer.

Letters of John Keats: A New Selection. John Keats. Ed. by Robert Gittings. LC 87-12263. (Oxford Letters & Memoirs). 448p. 1970. pap. 19.95 (*0-19-281081-2*) OUP.

***Letters of John Keats, 1814-1821.** John Keats. Ed. by Hyder Edward Rollins. LC 98-51920. 1999. write for info. (*0-674-52702-X*) HUP.

Letters of John Keats, 1814-1821, 2 vols., Set. John Keats. Ed. by Hyder E. Rollins. LC 58-5597. (Illus.). 918p. 1958. boxed set 79.95 (*0-674-52700-3*) HUP.

Letters of John Marin. John Marin. Ed. by Herbert J. Seligmann. LC 77-109780. 1971. reprint ed. lib. bdg. 45.00 (*0-8371-4270-9*, MALE, Greenwood Pr) Greenwood.

Letters of John McLoughlin in from Fort Vancouver to the Governor & Committee: First Series, 1825-1838. Ed. by E. E. Rich. (Hudson's Bay Record Society Publications: Vol. 4). 1969. reprint ed. pap. 65.00 (*0-8115-3178-3*) Periodicals Srv.

Letters of John McLoughlin in from Fort Vancouver to the Governor & Committee: Second Series, 1839-1844. Ed. by E. E. Rich. (Hudson's Bay Record Society Publications: Vol. 6). 1969. reprint ed. pap. 65.00 (*0-8115-3180-5*) Periodicals Srv.

Letters of John McLoughlin in from Fort Vancouver to the Governor & Committee: Third Series, 1844-1846. Ed. by E. E. Rich. (Hudson's Bay Record Society Publications: Vol. 7). 1969. reprint ed. pap. 65.00 (*0-8115-3181-3*) Periodicals Srv.

Letters of John of Salisbury Vol. 1: The Early Letters (1153-1161) John of Salisbury. Ed. by W. J. Millor & C. N. Brooke. (Oxford Medieval Texts Ser.). 624p. 1986. text 95.00 (*0-19-822239-4*) OUP.

Letters of John of Salisbury Vol. 2: The Later Years (1163-1180), Vol. 2. John of Salisbury. Ed. by W. J. Millor & C. N. Brooke. (Oxford Medieval Texts Ser.). 950p. 1979. text 118.00 (*0-19-822240-8*) OUP.

Letters of John Quinn to William Butler Yeats. John Quinn. Ed. by Alan Himber. LC 83-9207. (Studies in Modern Literature: No. 28). 316p. reprint ed. pap. 98.00 (*0-8357-1464-0*, 207055300001) Bks Demand.

Letters of John Ramsay McCulloch to David Ricardo. John R. McCulloch et al. 1979. 17.95 (*0-405-10625-4*) Ayer.

Letters of John Ruskin, Pt. 1, 1827-1869 see Complete Works of John Ruskin

Letters of John Ruskin, Pt. 2, 1870-1889 see Complete Works of John Ruskin

Letters of John Sutherland, 1942-1956. 6th ed. John Sutherland. Ed. by Bruce Whiteman. 362p. (C). 1992. pap. 25.00 (*1-55022-170-1*, Pub. by ECW) Genl Dist Srvs.

Letters of John Wilmot, Earl of Rochester. John Wilmot. Ed. by Jeremy Treglown. LC 80-20592. 1995. 31.50 (*0-226-81181-6*) U Ch Pr.

Letters of John Wilmot, Earl of Rochester. John W. Rochester. Ed. by Jeremy Treglown. LC 80-20592. (Illus.). 292p. reprint ed. pap. 90.60 (*0-608-09552-4*, 205435400005) Bks Demand.

Letters of Jonathan Oldstyle. Washington Irving. (BCL1-PS American Literature Ser.). 67p. 1993. reprint ed. lib. bdg. 59.00 (*0-7812-6972-5*) Rprt Serv.

Letters of Jonathan Swift to Charles Ford. Jonathan Swift. Ed. by David N. Smith. LC 76-29410. reprint ed. 43.50 (*0-404-15325-9*) AMS Pr.

Letters of Joseph Jones of Virginia, 1777-1787. Joseph Jones. Ed. by Worthington Ford. LC 77-140862. (Eyewitness Accounts of the American Revolution Ser.). 1971. reprint ed. 13.95 (*0-405-01253-5*) Ayer.

Letters of Junius. Junius. 1976. lib. bdg. 75.00 (*0-8490-2153-7*) Gordon Pr.

Letters of Junius. Junius. (C). 1970. reprint ed. 25.00 (*0-87266-047-8*) Argosy.

***Letters of Kate Duncan Smith & John Harrington, 1894-1907.** Lillie Frances Harrington Davis. 112p. 2000. 22.00 (*0-937194-42-5*, Deepak Heritage Bks) A Deepak Pub.

Letters of Katherine Anne Porter. Katherine Anne Porter. LC 89-31240. (Illus.). 642p. 1981. pap. 16.95 (*0-87113-453-5*, Atlntc Mnthly) Grove-Atltic.

Letters of Lafayette & Jefferson. Marie J. Lafayette et al. LC 78-19274. 1979. 35.95 (*0-405-10593-2*) Ayer.

Letters of Lanfranc, Archbishop of Canterbury. Lanfranc. Ed. by Helen Clover & Margaret Gibson. (Oxford Medieval Texts Ser.). (Illus.). 220p. 1980. text 65.00 (*0-19-822235-1*) OUP.

Letters of Leonard Woolf. Ed. by Frederic Spotts. 640p. 1989. 29.95 (*0-15-150915-8*) Harcourt.

Letters of Letitia Hargrave, Vol. 28. Letitia M. Hargrave. Ed. by Margaret A. Macleod. LC 69-14502. 310p. 1969. reprint ed. lib. bdg. 65.00 (*0-8371-5065-5*, HALE, Greenwood Pr) Greenwood.

Letters of Liam O'Flaherty. Ed. by A. A. Kelly. LC 94-122200. 464p. 1997. 55.00 (*0-86327-380-7*, Pub. by Wolfhound Press) Irish Amer Bk.

Letters of Life. Lydia H. Sigourney. Ed. by Annette K. Baxter. LC 79-8814. (Signal Lives Ser.). (Illus.). 1980. reprint ed. lib. bdg. 48.95 (*0-405-12859-2*) Ayer.

***Letters of Life in an Aristocratic Russian Household Before & After the Revolution: Amy Coles & Princess Vera Urusov.** Nicholas Tyrras. LC 99-57957. (Studies in Russian History: Vol. 3). 448p. 2000. text 109.95 (*0-7734-7776-4*) E Mellen.

Letters of Lincoln Steffens, 2 vols., Set. Lincoln Steffens. LC 74-11989. (Illus.). 1974. reprint ed. lib. bdg. 95.00 (*0-8371-7710-3*, STLLS) Greenwood.

Letters of Lincoln Steffens, 2 vols., Vol. 1. Lincoln Steffens. LC 74-11989. (Illus.). 1974. reprint ed. lib. bdg. 55.00 (*0-8371-7711-1*, STLLT) Greenwood.

Letters of Lincoln Steffens, 2 vols., Vol. 2. Lincoln Steffens. LC 74-11989. (Illus.). 1974. reprint ed. lib. bdg. 55.00 (*0-8371-7713-8*, STLLU) Greenwood.

Letters of Long Ago. 4th rev. ed. Agnes J. Reid. Ed. by Rick Just et al. (Illus.). 132p. 1997. pap. 13.95 (*0-9653539-4-X*) Cedar Creek ID.

Letters of Lord Hood, 1781-1782. David Hannay. (C). 1987. 100.00 (*0-7855-4018-0*) St Mut.

Letters of Louis D. Brandeis, Vol. 2. Louis D. Brandeis. Ed. by Melvin I. Urofsky & David W. Levy. LC 73-129640. 610p. (C). 1972. text 59.50 (*0-87395-091-7*) State U NY Pr.

Letters of Louis D. Brandeis, Vol. 3. Louis D. Brandeis. Ed. by Melvin I. Urofsky & David W. Levy. LC 73-129640. 750p. (C). 1973. text 59.50 (*0-87395-231-6*) State U NY Pr.

Letters of Louis D. Brandeis, Vol. 4. Louis D. Brandeis. Ed. by Melvin I. Urofsky & David W. Levy. LC 73-129640. 587p. (C). 1975. text 59.50 (*0-87395-297-9*) State U NY Pr.

Letters of Louis D. Brandeis, Vol. 5. Louis D. Brandeis. Ed. by Melvin I. Urofsky & David W. Levy. LC 73-129640. 770p. (C). 1978. text 59.50 (*0-87395-330-4*) State U NY Pr.

Letters of Louise Imogen Guiney. Louise I. Guiney & Grace C. Guiney. 1977. 37.95 (*0-8369-6975-8*, 7855) Ayer.

Letters of Louise Imogen Guiney, 2 vols. Louise I. Guiney. (American Biography Ser.). 1991. reprint ed. lib. bdg. 148.00 (*0-7812-8160-1*) Rprt Serv.

Letters of Louise Ritter from 1893-1925. Darlene M. Ritter. (Illus.). 178p. (Orig.). (C). 1980. pap. 10.00 (*0-9609372-0-X*) Siegenthaler-Ritter.

Letters of Love. Andrew Cohen Students. Ed. by Andrew Cohen. LC 92-60070. 155p. (Orig.). 1992. pap. 10.95 (*0-9622678-5-6*) Moksha Pr.

***Letters of Love.** Margaret A. Meginnis. LC 99-75268. (Illus.). 190p. 1999. 32.00 (*1-883122-17-1*) Pearce Pub.

Letters of Love, Bk. 34. Judy Kaye. (Born in the U. S. A. Ser.). 1997. mass mkt. 4.50 (*0-373-47184-X*, 1-47184-6) Harlequin Bks.

***Letters of Love: Stories from the Heart.** Ed. by Salvatore Caputo et al. LC 99-89590. 2000. pap. 12.95 (*1-877749-35-4*) Five Star AZ.

Letters of Love & Duty: The Correspondence of Susanna & John Moodie. Ed. by Carl Ballstadt et al. LC 92-95697. 360p. 1993. text 35.00 (*0-8020-5708-X*) U of Toronto Pr.

Letters of Love & War: A World War II Correspondence. Helen D. Stringer. LC 97-12897. 256p. 1997. 26.95 (*0-8156-0472-6*) Syracuse U Pr.

Letters of Love & War, 1944-1945: A True Story. Harry O. Lang, Jr. LC 98-85079. 144p. 1998. pap. 12.95 (*1-890394-26-2*, Sage Creek) Rhodes & Easton.

Letters of Lucien to Camille Pissarro, 1883-1903. Ed. by Anne Thorold. (Studies in the History of Art). (Illus.). 818p. (C). 1993. text 200.00 (*0-521-39034-6*) Cambridge U Pr.

Letters of Lydia Maria Child. Lydia Maria Child. LC 72-82183. (Anti-Slavery Crusade in America Ser.). 1970. reprint ed. 15.95 (*0-405-00622-5*) Ayer.

Letters of Lydia Maria Child. Lydia Maria Child. LC 73-92740. 280p. 1969. reprint ed. lib. bdg. 52.50 (*0-8371-2189-2*, CHL&) Greenwood.

Letters of Lydia Maria Child. Lydia Maria Child & John Whittier Greenleaf. LC 73-165169. reprint ed. 37.50 (*0-404-00141-6*) AMS Pr.

Letters of Machiavelli: A Selection. Niccolo Machiavelli. Ed. & Tr. by Allan H. Gilbert. 252p. 1988. pap. text 13.50 (*0-226-50041-1*) U Ch Pr.

Letters of Margaret Fuller, 1850 & Undated, Vol. V. Margaret Fuller. Ed. by Robert N. Hudspeth. (Illus.). 440p. 1995. text 47.50 (*0-8014-3069-0*) Cornell U Pr.

Letters of Margaret Fuller, 1842-1844, Vol. III. Margaret Fuller. Ed. by Robert N. Hudspeth. LC 82-22098. (Illus.). 269p. 1984. text 47.50 (*0-8014-1707-4*) Cornell U Pr.

Letters of Margaret Fuller, 1845-1847, Vol. IV. Margaret Fuller. Ed. by Robert N. Hudspeth. LC 86-22098. (Illus.). 328p. 1987. text 47.50 (*0-8014-1972-7*) Cornell U Pr.

Letters of Margaret Fuller, 1848-1849, Vol. V. Margaret Fuller. Ed. by Robert N. Hudspeth. LC 88-22098. (Illus.). 320p. 1988. text 47.50 (*0-8014-2174-8*) Cornell U Pr.

Letters of Margaret Fuller, 1817-1838, Vol. I. Margaret Fuller. Ed. by Robert N. Hudspeth. LC 82-22098. (Illus.). 384p. 1983. text 47.50 (*0-8014-1386-9*) Cornell U Pr.

Letters of Margaret Fuller, 1839-1841, Vol. II. Margaret Fuller. Ed. by Robert N. Hudspeth. LC 82-22098. (Illus.). 272p. 1983. text 47.50 (*0-8014-1575-6*) Cornell U Pr.

Letters of Mari Sandoz. Mari Sandoz. Ed. by Helen W. Stauffer. LC 91-46762. (Illus.). xxxvi, 493p. 1992. text 75.00 (*0-8032-4206-9*) U of Nebr Pr.

***Letters of Marina Tsvetaeva.** Marina I. Tsvetaeva. 2000. 42.00 (*0-87501-119-5*) Ardis Pubs.

Letters of Marsilio Ficino, Vol. 1. 248p. 1993. text 27.00 (*0-85683-010-0*, Pub. by Shepheard-Walwyn Pubs) Paul & Co Pubs.

Letters of Marsilio Ficino, Vol. 2. 144p. 1993. text 25.00 (*0-85683-036-4*, Pub. by Shepheard-Walwyn Pubs) Paul & Co Pubs.

Letters of Marsilio Ficino, Vol. 3. 176p. 1993. text 25.00 (*0-85683-045-3*, Pub. by Shepheard-Walwyn Pubs) Paul & Co Pubs.

Letters of Marsilio Ficino, Vol. 4. Marsilio Ficino. (Illus.). 208p. 1993. reprint ed. text 27.00 (*0-85683-070-4*, Pub. by Shepheard-Walwyn Pubs) Paul & Co Pubs.

Letters of Marsilio Ficino, Vol. 5. Marsilio Ficino. 1994. text 39.95 (*0-85683-129-8*, Pub. by Shepheard-Walwyn Pubs) Paul & Co Pubs.

Letters of Martin Buber: A Life of Dialogue. Ed. by Nahum N. Glatzer & Paul R. Mendes-Flohr. LC 96-29029. (Martin Buber Library). 722p. 1996. pap. 24.95 (*0-8156-0420-3*, BUMLP) Syracuse U Pr.

Letters of Mary Baker Eddy to Augusta E. Stetson, C. S. D., 1889-1909. Mary Baker Eddy. LC 90-84301. (Illus.). xiii, 113p. 1990. 14.00 (*1-879135-07-8*) Emma Pub Soc.

Letters of Mary Wollstonecraft Shelley: A Part of the Elect, Vol. 1. Mary Wollstonecraft Shelley. Ed. by Betty T. Bennett. LC 79-24190. 1980. 55.00 (*0-8018-2275-0*) Johns Hopkins.

Letters of Mary Wollstonecraft Shelley: Treading in Unknown Paths, Vol. 2. Mary Wollstonecraft Shelley. Ed. by Betty T. Bennett. LC 79-24190. 416p. 1983. text 55.00 (*0-8018-2645-4*) Johns Hopkins.

Letters of Mary Wollstonecraft Shelley Vol. III: "What Years I Have Spent" Ed. by Betty T. Bennett. LC 79-24190. 520p. 1988. text 55.00 (*0-8018-2646-2*) Johns Hopkins.

Letters of Matthew Arnold, 1848-1888, 2 vols., Set. Matthew Arnold. (BCL1-PR English Literature Ser.). 1992. reprint ed. lib. bdg. 150.00 (*0-7812-7424-9*) Rprt Serv.

Letters of Matthew Arnold, 1848-1888, 2 vols., Set. Matthew Arnold. Ed. by George W. Russell. LC 04-13997. 1969. reprint ed. 59.00 (*0-403-00141-2*) Scholarly.

Letters of Matthew Arnold, 1866-1870. Matthew Arnold. Ed. by Cecil Y. Lang. (Victorian Literature & Culture Ser.: Vol. 3). 544p. 1998. 60.00 (*0-8139-1765-4*) U Pr of Va.

Letters of Matthew Arnold, 1860-1865, Vol. II. Matthew Arnold. Ed. by Cecil Y. Lang. (Victorian Literature & Culture Ser.). 560p. (C). 1997. text 60.00 (*0-8139-1706-9*) U Pr of Va.

Letters of Matthew Arnold, 1829-1859, Vol. I. Ed. by Cecil Y. Lang. LC 95-50448. (Victorian Literature & Culture Ser.). 600p. (C). 1996. text 60.00 (*0-8139-1651-8*) U Pr of Va.

***Letters of Matthew Arnold, 1871-1878, Vol. 4.** Ed. by Cecil Y. Lang. (Victorian Literature & Cultural Ser.). 496p. 2000. 60.00 (*0-8139-1896-0*) U Pr of Va.

Letters of Members of the Continental Congress, 1774-1789, Vols. 3, 4, 5, & 6. E. C. Burnett. 1990. 74.00 (*0-8446-1095-X*) Peter Smith.

Letters of Mercurius. 116p. 1990. 18.95 (*0-674-52832-8*) HUP.

Letters of Michelangelo, Vols. 1 & 2. Tr. by E. H. Ramsden. (Illus.). 1963. 125.00 (*0-8047-0183-0*) Stanford U Pr.

***Letters of Milton H. Erickson.** Ed. by Jeffrey K. Zeig & Brent Geary. 393p. 2000. 50.00 (*1-891944-11-8*) Zeig Tucker.

Letters of Mina Harker. Dodie Bellamy & Sam D'Allesandro. LC 98-12241. (Lingo Magazine Ser.). 221p. 1998. pap. text 13.95 (*1-889097-14-4*) Hard Pr MA.

Letters of Mistress Henley Published by Her Friend. Isabelle De Charriere. Tr. by Philip Stewart & Jean Vache from FRE. LC 93-26862. (MLA Texts & Translations Ser.: No. 1b). xxix, 42p. (Orig.). 1993. pap. 3.95 (*0-87352-776-3*, P001P) Modern Lang.

Letters of Mozart & His Family. J. Chrysostom & Wolfgang Amadeus Mozart. 2p. reprint ed. lib. bdg. 108.00 (*0-685-14765-7*) Rprt Serv.

Letters of Mozart & His Family. 2nd rev. ed. Emily Anderson. (Illus.). 1986. 75.00 (*0-393-02248-X*) Norton.

Letters of Mrs. Adams: The Wife of John Adams. Abigail S. Adams. (Works of Abigail (Smith) Adams). 1989. reprint ed. lib. bdg. 79.00 (*0-685-27360-1*) Rprt Serv.

Letters of Mrs. Elizabeth Montagu, with Some of the Letters of Her Correspondents, 4 vols. Elizabeth R. Montagu. LC 72-37704. 1813. reprint ed. 295.00 (*0-404-56800-9*) AMS Pr.

Letters of Mrs. Gaskell. J. A. Chapple & Arthur Pollard. 1040p. 1997. pap. 24.95 (*1-901341-03-8*) St Martin.

Letters of Mrs. Gaskell. Elizabeth Gaskell. Ed. by John A. Chapple & Arthur Pollard. LC 67-3154. 1034p. 1966. 95.00 (*0-674-52675-9*) HUP.

Letters of Mrs. Gaskell & Chalres Eliot Norton, 1855-1865. Elizabeth Gaskell. (Anglistica & Americana Ser.: No. 141). xxxii, 131p. 1973. reprint ed. 37.70 (*3-487-04768-3*) G Olms Pubs.

Letters of Mrs. John Adams. Mrs. John Adams. 1988. reprint ed. lib. bdg. 75.00 (*0-7812-1401-7*) Rprt Serv.

Letters of Narcissa Whitman. 2nd ed. Narcissa P. Whitman. 267p. 1996. pap. 16.95 (*0-87770-386-8*) Ye Galleon.

Letters of Nichiren. Ed. by Philip B. Yampolsky. Tr. by Burton Watson et al. (Columbia Asian Studies). 1996. 50.00 (*0-231-10384-0*) Col U Pr.

Letters of Ogier Ghislain De Busbecq to the Holy Roman Emperor Maximillian II. J. B. Howaert. Ed. & Tr. by Robert E. Jones & Bernerd C. Weber from LAT. LC 61-17940. 180p. 1980. reprint ed. 32.50 (*0-8290-0182-4*) Irvington.

Letters of Old Age: Rerum Senilium Libri, No. I-XVIII, 2 vols. Francesco Petrarca. Tr. by Aldo S. Bernardo et al from LAT. 368p. 1992. text 95.00 (*0-8018-4212-3*) Johns Hopkins.

Letters of Owen Wangensteen to a Surgical Fellow - With a Memoir. Stacey B. Day. LC 96-78241. (Illus.). 240p. 1996. 59.50 (*0-934314-25-X*, B10-10) Intl Found Biosocial Dev.

Letters of P. H. Pearse. Ed. by Seamas O'Buachalla. 532p. 1980. 50.00 (*0-901072-87-7*, Pub. by Smyth) Dufour.

Letters of Pacificus & Helvidius. Alexander Hamilton. LC 76-41676. 144p. 1976. reprint ed. 50.00 (*0-8201-1279-8*) Schol Facsimiles.

Letters of Paul. Comment by John S. Spong. LC 98-18588. (Riverhead Sacred Text Ser.). 256p. (Orig.). 1998. pap. 12.95 (*1-57322-683-1*, Riverhd Trade) Berkley Pub.

Letters of Paul. Ed. by Gene M. Tucker & Charles B. Cousar. (Interpreting Biblical Texts Ser.). 176p. 1996. pap. 18.95 (*0-687-00852-2*) Abingdon.

Letters of Paul: A New Spiritual World View. Hilarion. Ed. by Lewis E. Durham & Sylvia M. Schechter. LC 89-51921. 352p. (Orig.). 1990. pap. 12.95 (*0-9625281-0-2*) Triad Pubs CA.

Letters of Paul: An Introduction. Charles B. Puskas, Jr. (Good News Studies: Vol. 25). 232p. (Orig.). 1993. pap. 14.95 (*0-8146-5690-0*, M Glazier) Liturgical Pr.

Letters of Paul: Conversations in Context. 3rd ed. Calvin J. Roetzel. LC 74-21901. 240p. 1991. pap. 22.95 (*0-664-25201-X*) Westminster John Knox.

Letters of Paul: Conversations in Context. 4th ed. Calvin J. Roetzel. LC 98-37903. 248p. 1998. pap. 20.00 (*0-664-25782-8*) Westminster John Knox.

Letters of Paul Gauguin to Georges Daniel De Monfried see Gauguin's Letters from the South Seas

Letters of Paul to the Ephesians, Colossians, & Philemon. Michael R. Weed. LC 79-134688. 1979. 12.95 (*0-915547-30-9*) Abilene Christ U.

Letters of Paul to the Thessalonians. Raymond Kelcy. LC 68-55947. 1984. 12.95 (*0-915547-32-5*) Abilene Christ U.

Letters of Pelagius: Celtic Soul Friend. Ed. by Robert Van de Weyer. (Little Gidding Bks.). 96p. 1997. 8.95 (*0-85305-335-9*, 743, Pub. by Arthur James) Morehouse Pub.

***Letters of Peter & Jude.** David G. Horrell. 208p. 2000. pap. 17.00 (*0-7162-0523-8*) Epworth Pr.

Letters of Peter & Jude. Raymond Kelcy. LC 78-179612. 1984. 12.95 (*0-915547-36-8*) Abilene Christ U.

Letters of Peter Damian, 61-90. Peter Damian. Tr. by Owen J. Blum from LAT. LC 88-25802. (Fathers of the Church: Mediaeval Continuation Ser.: Vol. 3). 397p. 1992. text 42.95 (*0-8132-0750-9*) Cath U Pr.

Letters of Peter Plymley. Sydney Smith. LC 72-11. (Select Bibliographies Reprint Ser.). 1977. reprint ed. 19.95 (*0-8369-9972-X*) Ayer.

Letters of Peter the Venerable, 2 vols., Set. Peter The Venerable. Ed. by Giles Constable. LC 67-10086. (Historical Studies: No. 78). 897p. 1967. 60.00 (*0-674-52775-5*) HUP.

Letters of Phillip Dormer Stanhope, 4th Earl of Chesterfield, 6 vols. Phillip D. Stanhope. Ed. by Bonamy Dabree. LC 68-59007. reprint ed. 475.00 (*0-404-06230-X*) AMS Pr.

Letters of Pliny: A Historical & Social Commentary. Ed. by A. N. Sherwin-White. 824p. 1985. text 125.00 (*0-19-814435-0*) OUP.

Letters of Queen Elizabeth & King James Sixth of Scotland. H. R. M. Queen Elizabeth I & H. R. M. King James VI. Ed. by John Bruce. LC 75-166015. (Camden Society, London. Publications, First Ser.: No. 46). reprint ed. 49.00 (*0-404-50146-X*) AMS Pr.

Letters of Queen Elizabeth I. Ed. by George B. Harrison. LC 81-6819. (Illus.). 323p. 1981. reprint ed. lib. bdg. 59.75 (*0-313-23157-5*, HALQ, Greenwood Pr) Greenwood.

Letters of Queen Margaret of Anjou & Bishop Beckington & Others. Ed. by Cecil Monro. LC 17-1255. (Camden Society, London. Publications, First Ser.: No. 86). reprint ed. 45.00 (*0-404-50186-9*) AMS Pr.

Letters of Quintus Curtius Snodgrass: American Autobiography. Mark Twain, pseud. 76p. 1995. lib. bdg. 69.00 (*0-7812-8481-3*) Rprt Serv.

Letters of Ralph Waldo Emerson. Ralph Waldo Emerson. Ed. by R. L. Rusk. LC 39-12289. 1939. 572.50 (*0-231-00724-8*) Col U Pr.

Letters of Ralph Waldo Emerson, Vol. 7. Ed. by Eleanor M. Tilton. 623p. 1990. text 115.50 (*0-231-06870-0*) Col U Pr.

Letters of Ralph Waldo Emerson, Vol. 8. Ed. by Eleanor M. Tilton. 653p. 1991. text 115.50 (*0-231-07516-2*) Col U Pr.

Letters of Ralph Waldo Emerson, 1860-1869, Vol. 9. Ed. by Eleanor M. Tilton. 360p. 1993. 115.50 (*0-231-08102-2*) Col U Pr.

Letters of Ralph Waldo Emerson, 1870-1881 Vol. 10: With an Index of Proper Names for Volumes Seven to Ten. Eleanor M. Tilton. 515p. 1995. 110.50 (*0-231-10183-X*) Col U Pr.

Letters of Randolph Bourne: A Comprehensive Edition. Eric J. Sandeen. LC 79-57326. xvi, 454p. 1981. 49.00 (*0-87875-190-4*) Whitston Pub.

Letters of Rebecca Gratz. Rebecca Gratz. LC 74-27987. (Modern Jewish Experience Ser.). 1975. reprint ed. 42.95 (*0-405-06714-3*) Ayer.

Letters of Richard Cumberland. Ed. by Richard J. Dircks. LC 87-45799. (Studies in the Eighteenth Century: No. 13). 1989. 49.50 (*0-404-63513-X*) AMS Pr.

Letters of Richard D. Arnold, M. D., 1808-1876. Richard D. Arnold. Ed. by Richard H. Shryock. LC 71-115999. (Duke University. Trinity College Historical Society. Historical Papers: Nos. 18-19). reprint ed. 30.00 (*0-404-51768-4*) AMS Pr.

Letters of Richard Watson Gilder. Richard W. Gilder. 1977. 28.95 (*0-8369-7137-X*, 7970) Ayer.

Letters of Richard Watson Gilder. Richard W. Gilder. (American Biography Ser.). 515p. 1991. reprint ed. lib. bdg. 99.00 (*0-7812-8144-X*) Rprt Serv.

Letters of Ring Lardner. rev. ed. Ed. by Clifford M. Caruthers. LC 94-42459. (Illus.). 300p. 1995. reprint ed. 29.95 (*0-914061-52-6*) Orchises Pr.

Letters of Robert Burns, 2 vols., Vol. 1. 2nd ed. Robert Burns. Ed. by De Lancey Ferguson & G. Ross Roy. (Illus.). 558p. (C). 1986. text 130.00 (*0-19-812478-3*) OUP.

An Asterisk (*) at the beginning of an entry indicates that the title is appearing for the first time.

Letters of Robert Burns, 2 vols., Vol. 2. 2nd ed. Robert Burns. Ed. by De Lancey Ferguson & G. Ross Roy. (Illus.). 550p. (C). 1986. text 110.00 (*0-19-812321-3*) OUP.

Letters of Robert Louis Stevenson see Works of Robert Louis Stevenson, Valima Edition

Letters of Robert Louis Stevenson Vol. 1: 1854-July 1874, 2 vols., Set. abr. ed. Ed. by Bradford A. Booth & Ernest Mehew. LC 93-45419. 640p. 1994. 50.00 (*0-300-05183-2*) Yale U Pr.

Letters of Robert Louis Stevenson Vol. 2: April 1874-July 1879, Vol. 2. Robert Louis Stevenson. Ed. by Bradford A. Booth & Ernest Mehew. LC 93-45419. Vol. 2. 1994. 50.00 (*0-300-06021-1*) Yale U Pr.

Letters of Robert Louis Stevenson Vol. 3: August 1879-September 1882, Vol. III. Ed. by Bradford A. Booth & Ernest Mehew. LC 93-45419. Vol. III. 352p. 1994. 50.00 (*0-300-06187-0*) Yale U Pr.

Letters of Robert Louis Stevenson Vol. 4: October 1882-June 1884, Vol. IV. Ed. by Bradford A. Booth & Ernest Mehew. LC 93-45419. Vol. IV. 352p. 1994. 50.00 (*0-300-06188-9*) Yale U Pr.

Letters of Robert Louis Stevenson Vol. 5: October 1882-June 1884, Vol. V. Ed. by Bradford E. Booth & Ernest Mehew. LC 93-45419. Vol. V. 544p. 1994. 50.00 (*0-300-06190-0*) Yale U Pr.

Letters of Robert Louis Stevenson Vol. 6: October 1882-June 1884, Vol. VI. Ed. by Bradford A. Booth & Ernest Mehew. LC 93-45419. Vol. VI. 544p. 1994. 50.00 (*0-300-06191-9*) Yale U Pr.

Letters of Robert Louis Stevenson Vol. 7: April 1874-July 1879. Robert Louis Stevenson. LC 93-45419. 8p. 1995. 55.00 (*0-300-06213-3*) Yale U Pr.

Letters of Robert Louis Stevenson Vol. 8, 8. Robert Louis Stevenson. LC 93-45419. Vol. 8. 1995. 55.00 (*0-300-06214-1*) Yale U Pr.

Letters of Robert MacKay to His Wife. Robert Mackay. (American Autobiography Ser.). 325p. 1995. reprint ed. lib. bdg. 89.00 (*0-7812-8584-4*) Rprt Serv.

Letters of Robert Molloy, 1971-1977. Melvin B. Yoken. LC 88-12711. (Studies in American Literature: Vol. 1). 150p. 1989. lib. bdg. 69.95 (*0-88946-167-8*) E Mellen.

Letters of Robert Schumann. Robert Schumann. Ed. by Karl Storck. LC 79-173122. 1979. reprint ed. 30.95 (*0-405-08939-2*) Ayer.

Letters of Robert Southey. Robert Southey. LC 75-41260. reprint ed. 55.00 (*0-404-14608-2*) AMS Pr.

Letters of Robert Southey: A Selection. Robert Southey. (BCL1-PR English Literature Ser.). 552p. 1992. reprint ed. lib. bdg. 99.00 (*0-7812-7660-8*) Rprt Serv.

Letters of Roger Ascham. Roger Ascham. Ed. & Tr. by Alvin Vos from LAT. Tr. by Maurice Hatch from LAT. 322p. (C). 1989. 52.95 (*0-8204-0205-2*) P Lang Pubng.

Letters of Rosa Luxemburg. Tr. by Eric Bronner. LC 92-33137. 320p. (C). 1993. reprint ed. pap. 18.50 (*0-391-03789-7*) Humanities.

Letters of Roy Bedichek. Ed. by William A. Owens & Lyman Grant. 600p. 1985. 24.95 (*0-292-70742-8*) U of Tex Pr.

Letters of Rudyard Kipling Vol. 3: 1900-10. Rudyard Kipling. Ed. by Thomas Pinney. LC 90-70525. (Illus.). 376p. 1995. text 49.95 (*0-87745-495-7*) U of Iowa Pr.

***Letters of Rudyard Kipling Vol. 4: 1911-19.** Rudyard Kipling. Ed. by Thomas Pinney. LC 90-70525. (Illus.). 620p. 1999. text 62.95 (*0-87745-657-7*) U of Iowa Pr.

***Letters of Ruth Draper: Self-Portrait of an Actress, 1920-1956.** Ruth Draper. Ed. by Dorothy M. Warren. LC 99-25456. 374p. 1999. pap. 19.95 (*0-8093-2188-2*) S Ill U Pr.

Letters of Sacco & Vanzetti. Nicola Sacco. (American Biography Ser.). 414p. 1991. reprint ed. lib. bdg. 89.00 (*0-7812-8334-5*) Rprt Serv.

Letters of Saint Anselm of Canterbury. Anselm, Abbot of BEC. Tr. by Walter Frohlich from LAT. (Cistercian Studies: Vol. 2). (Illus.). 1993. 42.95 (*0-87907-897-9*) Cistercian Pubns.

Letters of Saint Anselm of Canterbury, Vol. 3. 2nd ed. Anselm, Saint of Canterbury. Tr. by Walter Frohlich from LAT. (Cistercian Studies). 1994. 42.95 (*0-87907-742-5*) Cistercian Pubns.

Letters of St. Antony: Monasticism & the Making of a Saint. Samuel Rubenson. LC 95-24837. (Studies in Antiquity & Christianity). 256p. (C). 1998. pap. 22.00 (*0-8006-2910-8*) TPI PA.

***Letters of St. Boniface.** Thomas F. Noble. (Foundations of Social Work Knowledge Ser.). 2000. 45.00 (*0-231-12092-3*); pap. text 16.50 (*0-231-12093-1*) Col U Pr.

Letters of St. Cyprian. Tr. by Graehme W. Clarke. (Ancient Christian Writers Ser.: Nos. 43 & 44). 416p. 1983. 24.95 (*0-8091-0341-9*) Paulist Pr.

Letters of St. Cyprian. Tr. by Graeme W. Clarke. (Ancient Christian Writers Ser.: No. 44). 352p. 1983. 22.95 (*0-8091-0342-7*) Paulist Pr.

Letters of St. Cyprian Vol. 3: Letters 55-66. Ed. by Graeme W. Clarke. (Ancient Christian Writers Ser.: No. 46). 352p. 1986. 24.95 (*0-8091-0369-9*) Paulist Pr.

Letters of St. Cyprian of Carthage, Vol. IV. Ed. by G. W. Clarke. (Ancient Christian Writers Ser.: No. 47). 1988. 24.95 (*0-8091-0370-2*) Paulist Pr.

Letters of Saint Evremond. Charles S. De Saint-Evremond. Ed. by John Hayward. LC 72-83506. (Illus.). 436p. 1972. 30.95 (*0-405-08908-2*) Ayer.

Letters of Saint Evremond. Charles S. De Saint-Evremond. LC 76-164624. (Select Bibliographies Reprint Ser.). 1977. reprint ed. 27.95 (*0-8369-5907-8*) Ayer.

Letters of Saint Ignatius of Loyola. Tr. by William J. Young. LC 59-13459. 450p. 1959. 14.95 (*0-8294-0085-0*, Jesuit Way) Loyola Pr.

Letters of Saint Jerome, Vol. 1. Jerome. Ed. by Burqhardt & J. Quasten. (Ancient Christian Writers Ser.: No. 33). 1963. 18.95 (*0-8091-0087-8*) Paulist Pr.

Letters of Saint Paulinus of Nola, Vol. 1. J. Quasten & Nola Paulinus. (Ancient Christian Writers Ser.: Nos. 35-36). 1966. 18.95 (*0-8091-0088-6*) Paulist Pr.

Letters of Saint Paulinus of Nola, Vol. 2. J. Quasten & Nola Paulinus. (Ancient Christian Writers Ser.: Nos. 35-36). 1967. 24.95 (*0-8091-0089-4*) Paulist Pr.

Letters of Samuel Johnson, Vol. I: 1731-1772. Ed. by Bruce Redford. LC 90-8806. (Illus.). 431p. 1992. text 47.50 (*0-691-06881-X*, Pub. by Princeton U Pr) Cal Prin Full Svc.

Letters of Samuel Johnson, Vol. II: 1773-1776. Ed. by Bruce Redford. (Illus.). 389p. 1992. text 47.50 (*0-691-06928-X*, Pub. by Princeton U Pr) Cal Prin Full Svc.

Letters of Samuel Johnson, Vol. III: 1777-1781. Ed. by Bruce Redford. (Illus.). 399p. 1992. text 47.50 (*0-691-06929-8*, Pub. by Princeton U Pr) Cal Prin Full Svc.

Letters of Samuel Johnson, Vol. IV: 1782-1784. Ed. by Bruce Redford. (Illus.). 488p. 1993. text 47.50 (*0-691-06977-8*, Pub. by Princeton U Pr) Cal Prin Full Svc.

Letters of Samuel Johnson, Vol. V: Appendices & Comprehensive Index. Ed. by Bruce Redford. (Illus.). 202p. 1993. text 47.50 (*0-691-06978-6*, Pub. by Princeton U Pr) Cal Prin Full Svc.

Letters of Samuel Johnson: Volume I: 1731-1772, Volume II: 1773-1776, Volume III: 1777-1781, 3 vols. Ed. by Bruce Redford. 1909p. 1993. text 175.00 (*0-691-03389-7*, Pub. by Princeton U Pr) Cal Prin Full Svc.

Letters of Samuel Johnson, LLD, 2 Vols. Samuel Johnson. 1977. text 47.95 (*0-8369-8187-1*, 8325) Ayer.

Letters of Samuel Rutherford. Samuel Rutherford. 206p. 1997. reprint ed. pap. 4.99 (*0-85151-163-5*) Banner of Truth.

Letters of Sarah, Duchess of Marlborough. Sarah J. Marlborough. LC 77-37708. reprint ed. 29.50 (*0-404-56766-5*) AMS Pr.

Letters of Sarah Harriet Burney. Sarah H. Burney. Ed. by Lorna J. Clark. LC 94-49167. 1997. 85.00 (*0-8203-1746-2*) U of Ga Pr.

Letters of Sarah Orne Jewett. Annie Fields. (Notable American Authors Ser.). 1992. reprint ed. lib. bdg. 75.00 (*0-7812-2830-1*) Rprt Serv.

Letters of Sarah Orne Jewett, 1879-1904. Sarah Orne Jewett. (American Autobiography Ser.). 75p. 1995. reprint ed. lib. bdg. 69.00 (*0-7812-8567-4*) Rprt Serv.

Letters of Sean O'Casey. Sean O'Casey. Ed. by David Krause. LC 74-11442. 640p. reprint ed. pap. 198.40 (*0-608-20716-0*, 207181400004) Bks Demand.

Letters of Sean O'Casey, 1955-1958, Vol. 3. Ed. by David Krause. LC 74-11442. 688p. 1989. 49.95 (*0-8132-0651-0*) Cath U Pr.

Letters of Sean O'Casey, 1959-1964, Vol. 4. Sean O'Casey. Ed. by David Krause. LC 74-11442. (Illus.). 610p. 1992. 49.95 (*0-8132-0678-2*) Cath U Pr.

Letters of Sean O'Casey, 1910-1941, Vol. I. Ed. by David Krause. LC 74-11442. 972p. 1975. 49.95 (*0-02-566660-6*) Cath U Pr.

Letters of Shahcoolen: A Hindu Residing in Philadelphia. Benjamin Silliman. LC 62-7013. 174p. 1962. reprint ed. 40.00 (*0-8201-1041-8*) Schol Facsimiles.

Letters of Sidney Hook: Democracy, Communism, & the Cold War. Ed. by Edward S. Shapiro. LC 94-43873. 416p. (gr. 13). 1995. 87.95 (*1-56324-487-X*) M E Sharpe.

Letters of Sigmund Freud. Sigmund Freud. (Illus.). xii, 470p. 1992. reprint ed. pap. 9.95 (*0-486-27105-6*) Dover.

Letters of Sigmund Freud to Eduard Silberstein, 1871-1881. Ed. by Walter Boehlich. Tr. by Arnold J. Pomerans. 204p. 1994. 32.50 (*0-317-03028-0*) Belknap Pr.

Letters of Sigmund Freud to Eduard Silberstein, 1871-1881. Ed. by Walter Boehlich. Tr. by Arnold J. Pomerans. LC 90-39119. (Illus.). 204p. 1990. text 39.00 (*0-674-52827-1*) HUP.

Letters of Sigmund Freud to Eduard Silberstein, 1871-1881. Ed. by Walter Boehlich. Tr. by Arnold J. Pomerans. (Illus.). 240p. 1992. pap. 17.50 (*0-674-52828-X*) HUP.

Letters of Sir John Hackett, 2 vols. Ed. by Elizabeth F. Rogers. LC 70-105570. (Archives of British History & Culture Ser). 419p. 1971. 15.00 (*0-937058-05-X*) West Va U Pr.

***Letters of Sir Joseph Banks.** Ed. by Neil Chambers. LC 99-89844. 200p. 2000. 46.00 (*1-86094-204-0*) World Scientific Pub.

***Letters of Sir Joshua Reynolds.** Ed. by John Ingamells & John Edgcumbe. (Illus.). 224p. 2000. 40.00 (*0-300-08733-0*) Yale U Pr.

Letters of Sir Walter Ralegh. Ed. by Agnes Latham & Joyce Youings. (Illus.). 464p. 1999. 89.95 (*0-85989-527-0*, Pub. by Univ Exeter Pr) Northwestern U Pr.

Letters of Sir Walter Scott, 12 vols. Sir Walter Scott. Ed. by H. J. Grierson. LC 72-144431. reprint ed. 360.00 (*0-404-05650-4*) AMS Pr.

Letters of Sister Nivedita. Nivedita. 1982. 25.00 (*0-87481-228-3*, Pub. by Advaita Ashrama) Vedanta Pr.

Letters of St. Ignatius of Anioch & of St.Polycarp of Smyrna see Paslanije Svatago Ignatija Aniokhiskago I Sviatago Polykarpa Smirnskago

Letters of St. Ignatius of Antioch & of St. Polycarp of Smirna see Poslanije Saviatago Ignatija Antiokhiskago i Sviatago Polykarpa Smirnskago

Letters of St. Margaret Mary Alacoque. St. Margaret M. Alacoque. Tr. by Clarence A. Herbst from FRE. LC 97-60910. 285p. 1997. reprint ed. pap. 13.50 (*0-89555-605-7*, 1526) TAN Bks Pubs.

Letters of St. Oliver Plunkett. Oliver Plunkett. Ed. by John Hanly. 624p. 1979. 85.00 (*0-85105-344-0*, Pub. by Smyth) Dufour.

Letters of St. Therese of Lisieux Vol. I: General Correspondence I, 1877-1890. Intro. by John Clarke. LC 81-6474. 700p. (Orig.). 1982. pap. 16.95 (*0-9600876-9-9*) ICS Pubns.

Letters of St. Therese of Lisieux Vol. II: General Correspondence II. Tr. by John Clarke from FRE. LC 81-6474. (Illus.). 688p. (Orig.). 1988. pap. 16.95 (*0-935216-10-3*) ICS Pubns.

Letters of Stephen Gardiner. Stephen Gardiner. Ed. by James A. Muller. 1990. reprint ed. lib. bdg. 85.00 (*0-8371-4223-7*, GALE, Greenwood Pr) Greenwood.

Letters of Still. William Still. (Religious Ser.). 192p. (Orig.). 1984. pap. 8.99 (*0-85151-378-6*) Banner of Truth.

Letters of Susan Hale. Susan Hale. (American Biography Ser.). 472p. 1991. reprint ed. lib. bdg. 89.00 (*0-7812-8161-X*) Rprt Serv.

Letters of Swami Vivekananda. 2nd ed. Swami Vivekananda. 1960. 8.95 (*0-87481-093-0*); pap. 8.95 (*0-87481-192-9*) Vedanta Pr.

Letters of T. S. Eliot, 1898-1922, Vol. 1. T. S. Eliot. Ed. by Valerie Eliot. 900p. 1988. 29.95 (*0-15-150885-2*) Harcourt.

Letters of Teilhard de Chardin & Lucile Swan. Ursula King. (Teilhard Studies: No. 32). 1995. pap. write for info. (*0-89012-074-9*) Am Teilhard.

Letters of the Alphabet. (High Q Wipe-Off Bks.). (Illus.). 24p. (J). (ps-k). 1998. pap. 4.99 (*0-7681-0038-0*, McClanahan Book) Learn Horizon.

Letters of the Alphabet see Reading Readiness Program

Letters of the British Spy. William Wirt. LC 76-104599. 224p. reprint ed. pap. text 9.95 (*0-8290-1680-5*); reprint ed. lib. bdg. 32.00 (*0-8398-2172-7*) Irvington.

Letters of the Brownings to George Barrett. Elizabeth Barrett Browning. Ed. by Paul Landis & Ronald E. Freeman. LC 57-6950. (Illus.). 402p. reprint ed. pap. 124.70 (*0-608-17988-4*, 201503500098) Bks Demand.

***Letters of the Cedar Tree.** (Illus.). 121p. 1999. pap. 9.95 (*1-880906-20-1*) IDI Pub.

Letters of the Century: America: 1900-1999. Ed. by Lisa Grunwald & Stephen J. Adler. LC 99-16808. 768p. 1999. 35.00 (*0-385-31590-2*, Dial Pr) Dell.

Letters of the Dragon: AN Anthology of Bruce Lee's Correspondence with Family, Friends & Fans, 1958-1973. Bruce Lee. Ed. by John Little. LC 98-36553. (Bruce Lee Library: Vol. 5). (Illus.). 190p. 1998. pap. 14.95 (*0-8048-3111-4*) Tuttle Pubng.

Letters of the First Viscount Hardinge of Lahore, 1844-1847. B. S. Singh. (Camden Fourth Ser.: No. 32). 266p. 27.00 (*0-86193-110-6*) David Brown.

Letters of the Holy Prophet. Prophet of Islam. Tr. by Ahmed Qureshi. 125p. (Orig.). 1985. pap. 7.50 (*1-56744-323-0*) Kazi Pubns.

Letters of the Lady Brilliana Harley, Wife of Sir Robert Harley, of Brampton Bryan, Knight of the Bath. Brilliana Harley. Ed. by Thomas T. Lewis. LC 73-6768. (Camden Society, London. Publications, First Ser.: No. 58). reprint ed. 72.50 (*0-404-50158-3*) AMS Pr.

Letters of the Late Edward Bulwer, Lord Lytton, to His Wife. Edward Bulwer Lytton & Louisa Devey. LC 79-148815. reprint ed. 49.50 (*0-404-08884-8*) AMS Pr.

Letters of the Late Ignatius Sancho, an African. Ignatius Sancho. LC 74-154080. (Black Heritage Library Collection). 1977. 22.95 (*0-8369-8791-8*) Ayer.

Letters of the Law. Tom Mandel. LC 94-4020. (New American Poetry Ser.: No. 15). 128p. (Orig.). 1994. pap. 10.95 (*1-55713-164-3*) Sun & Moon CA.

Letters of the Lewis & Clark Expedition, with Related Documents, 1783-1854, 2 vols. 2nd ed. Ed. by Donald Jackson. LC 78-15288. 832p. 1978. text 100.00 (*0-252-00697-6*) U of Ill Pr.

Letters of the Master, Vol. 3. Ram Chandra & Parthasarathi Rajagopalachari. Ed. by Rajendrasinh N. Rathod. 448p. 1996. 20.00 (*0-945242-30-1*) Shri Ram Chandra.

Letters of the Queens of England, 1100-1547. Ed. by Anne Crawford. LC 93-33709. 250p. 1994. 33.95 (*0-86299-726-7*, Pub. by Sutton Pub Ltd) Intl Pubs Mktg.

Letters of the Queens of England, 1100-1547. Ed. by Anne Crawford. (Illus.). 256p. 1997. pap. 22.95 (*0-7509-1606-0*, Pub. by Sutton Pub Ltd) Intl Pubs Mktg.

Letters of the Republic: Publication & the Public Sphere in Eighteenth-Century America. Michael Warner. 224p. 1990. 32.00 (*0-674-52785-2*) HUP.

Letters of the Republic: Publication & the Public Sphere in Eighteenth-Century America. Michael Warner. 224p. 1992. pap. 18.00 (*0-674-52786-0*) HUP.

Letters of the Scattered Brotherhood. Mary Strong. LC 90-55802. 256p. (gr. 1). 1991. pap. 13.00 (*0-06-067758-9*, Pub. by Harper SF) HarpC.

Letters of the Soul: From the Silence of the Mind. Jack Cuthrell. (Illus.). 208p. (Orig.). 1997. per. 11.95 (*0-9650525-6-7*) Spiritual Quest.

Letters of the Tsar's Family from Captivity see Pisoma Tsarskoj Semji iz Zatotchenija

Letters of the Wadsworth Family, 1787-1855, 3 vols., Set. William Wadsworth. 1981. reprint ed. lib. bdg. 89.00 (*0-686-71928-X*) Scholarly.

Letters of the Wordsworth Family from, 1787-1855, 3 Vols, Set. William Wordsworth. Ed. by William Knight. LC 68-24927. (Studies in Wordsworth: No. 29). (Illus.). 1969. reprint ed. lib. bdg. 199.00 (*0-8383-0177-0*) M S G Haskell Hse.

Letters of the Wordsworth Family from, 1787-1855, 3 vols., Set. William Wordsworth. (BCL1-PR English Literature Ser.). 1992. reprint ed. lib. bdg. 225.00 (*0-7812-7647-0*) Rprt Serv.

Letters of the Younger Pliny. Betty Radice. (Classics Ser.). 320p. 1963. pap. 11.95 (*0-14-044127-1*, Penguin Classics) Viking Penguin.

Letters of Themistokles. rev. ed. Norman A. Doenges. Ed. by W. R. Connor. LC 80-2648. (Monographs in Classical Studies). 1981. lib. bdg. 38.95 (*0-405-14035-5*) Ayer.

Letters of Theodore Dwight Weld, Angelina Grimke & Sarah Grimke, 1822-1844, Vols. 1 & 2. Ed. by Gilbert H. Barnes & Dwight L. Dumond. 1934. 33.00 (*0-8446-1055-0*) Peter Smith.

Letters of Theodore Dwight Weld, Angelina Grimke Weld, & Sarah Grimke. Ed. by Gilbert H. Barnes & Dwight L. Dumond. LC 77-121103. (American Public Figures Ser.). 1970. reprint ed. lib. bdg. 95.00 (*0-306-71981-9*) Da Capo.

Letters of Theodore Roosevelt & Brander Matthews. Ed. by Lawrence J. Oliver. LC 94-18766. (Illus.). 272p. (C). 1995. text 28.00 (*0-87049-894-0*) U of Tenn Pr.

Letters of Third Viscount Palmerston to Laurence & Elizabeth Sullivan 1804-1863. K. Bourne. (Camden Fourth Ser.: Vol. 23). 362p. 27.00 (*0-901050-55-5*) David Brown.

Letters of Thomas Carlyle. Thomas Carlyle. 1971. reprint ed. 39.00 (*0-403-00897-2*) Scholarly.

Letters of Thomas Carlyle, 1826-1836, 2 vols, Set. Thomas Carlyle. Ed. by Charles E. Norton. LC 70-39194. (Select Bibliographies Reprint Ser.). 1977. 53.95 (*0-8369-6796-8*) Ayer.

Letters of Thomas Carlyle to His Brother Alexander: With Related Family Letters. Thomas Carlyle. Ed. by Edwin W. Marrs, Jr. LC 68-21978. 848p. reprint ed. pap. 200.00 (*0-7837-2058-0*, 204233300004) Bks Demand.

Letters of Thomas Carlyle to John Stuart Mill, John Sterling & Robert Browning. Thomas Carlyle. Ed. by Alexander Carlyle. LC 77-95420. (English Biography Ser.: No. 31). 1969. reprint ed. lib. bdg. 75.00 (*0-8383-0964-X*) M S G Haskell Hse.

Letters of Thomas Carlyle to John Stuart Mill, John Sterling & Robert Browning. Thomas Carlyle. (BCL1-PR English Literature Ser.). 311p. 1992. reprint ed. lib. bdg. 89.00 (*0-7812-7486-9*) Rprt Serv.

Letters of Thomas Love Peacock, 1. Ed. by Nicholas A Joukovsky. 512p. 1999. 130.00 (*0-19-812658-1*) OUP.

Letters of Thomas Love Peacock, 2. Ed. by Francois Joukovsky. 512p. 1999. 130.00 (*0-19-818633-9*) OUP.

Letters of Thomas Lovell Beddoes. Thomas L. Beddoes. Ed. by Edmund W. Gosse. LC 70-173168. 270p. 1972. reprint ed. 24.95 (*0-405-08250-9*, Pub. by Blom Pubns) Ayer.

Letters of Thomas Lovell Beddoes. Thomas L. Beddoes. (Anglistica & Americana Ser.: No. 142). viii, 270p. 1973. reprint ed. 50.00 (*3-487-04828-0*) G Olms Pubs.

Letters of Thomas Mann, 1889-1955. Thomas Mann. Ed. & Tr. by Richard Winston & Clara Winston. 1990. 50.00 (*0-520-07004-6*, Pub. by U CA Pr); pap. 15.95 (*0-520-06968-4*, Pub. by U CA Pr) Cal Prin Full Svc.

Letters of Thomas Nelson & Benjamin Harrison. Ed. by Henry R. McIlwaine. LC 27-2700. (Official Letters of the Governors of Virginia Ser: Vol. 3). xii, 510p. 1929. 19.95 (*0-88490-020-7*) Library of VA.

Letters of Thomas Wolfe. Elizabeth Nowell. (Hudson River Editions Ser.). 1984. 52.00 (*0-684-18269-6*, Scribners Ref) Mac Lib Ref.

Letters of Transit. Edward W. Said. Ed. by Andre Aciman. 135p. 1999. 18.95 (*1-56584-504-8*, Pub. by New Press NY) Norton.

***Letters of Transit: Reflections on Exile, Identity, Language & Loss.** Ed. by Andre Aciman. 2000. pap. 12.95 (*1-56584-607-9*, Pub. by New Press NY) Norton.

Letters of Travel (1892-1913) Rudyard Kipling. reprint ed. lib. bdg. 23.95 (*0-88411-820-7*) Amereon Ltd.

Letters of Vincent Van Gogh. Roskill. 1997. per. 12.00 (*0-684-84300-5*) S&S Trade.

Letters of Vincent Van Gogh. Vincent Van Gogh. Ed. by Mark Roskill. LC 63-13069. 360p. 1963. pap. 10.95 (*0-689-70167-5*, 39) Atheneum Yung Read.

Letters of Virginia Woolf, 1911-1922, Vol. II. Ed. by Nigel Nicolson & Joanne Trautmann. LC 76-40422. (Illus.). 672p. 1978. pap. 5.95 (*0-15-650882-6*, Harvest Bks) Harcourt.

Letters of Virginia Woolf, 1923-1928, Vol. III. Ed. by Nigel Nicolson & Joanne Trautmann. LC 76-40422. (Illus.). 632p. 1980. pap. 5.95 (*0-15-650883-4*, Harvest Bks) Harcourt.

Letters of Virginia Woolf, 1929-1931, Vol. IV. Ed. by Nigel Nicolson & Joanne Trautmann. LC 76-40422. Vol. IV. 442p. 1981. pap. 10.95 (*0-15-650884-2*, Harvest Bks) Harcourt.

Letters of Wallace Stevens. Ed. by Holly Stevens. LC 96-17104. (Illus.). 960p. (C). 1996. pap. 27.50 (*0-520-20668-1*, Pub. by U CA Pr) Cal Prin Full Svc.

Letters of Wanda Tinasky, Vol. 1. TR Factor & Bruce Anderson. (Illus.). 224p. 1996. pap. 22.00 (*0-9652881-0-2*) vers libre pr.

Letters of Warwick Greene, 1915-1928. Warwick Greene. Ed. by Richard W. Hale. LC 77-179522. (Select Bibliographies Reprint Ser.). 1977. reprint ed. 25.95 (*0-8369-6651-1*) Ayer.

Letters of Washington Irving, 1839-1846, Vol. III. Ed. by Ralph M. Aderman et al. (Critical Editions Program Ser.). (C). 1982. 60.00 (*0-8057-8524-8*, Twyne) Mac Lib Ref.

***Letters of Wilkie Collins.** William Baker. LC 99-19642. 1999. text 55.00 (*0-312-22343-9*) St Martin.

***Letters of Wilkie Collins, Vol.2.** Baker. LC 99-19642. 1999. text 55.00 (*0-312-22344-7*) St Martin.

Letters of William Allen White & a Young Man. William White. (American Autobiography Ser.). 116p. 1995. reprint ed. lib. bdg. 69.00 (*0-7812-8662-X*) Rprt Serv.

L

An Asterisk (*) at the beginning of an entry indicates that the title is appearing for the first time.

Letters of William & Dorothy Wordsworth Vol. III, Pt.1: The Later Years, 1821-1828, Vol. 4. 2nd ed. William Wordsworth & Dorothy Wordsworth. Ed. by Alan G. Hill. (Illus.). 762p. 1978. text 115.00 (*0-19-812481-3*) OUP.

Letters of William & Dorothy Wordsworth Vol. V, Pt. 2: The Later Years, 1829-1835, Vol. 5. 2nd ed. William Wordsworth & Dorothy Wordsworth. Ed. by Alan G. Hill. (Letters of William & Dorothy Wordsworth Ser.). (Illus.). 812p. 1980. text 150.00 (*0-19-812482-1*) OUP.

Letters of William & Dorothy Wordsworth Vol. VI, Pt. III: The Later Years, 1835-1839, Vol. 6. 2nd ed. William Wordsworth & Dorothy Wordsworth. Ed. by Alan G. Hill. 1982. 120.00 (*0-19-812483-X*) OUP.

Letters of William & Dorothy Wordsworth Vol. VII, Pt. IV: The Later Years, 1840-1853. 2nd ed. William Wordsworth & Dorothy Wordsworth. Ed. by Alan G. Hill. (Illus.). 976p. 1988. text 185.00 (*0-19-812606-9*) OUP.

Letters of William & Dorothy Wordsworth Vol. VIII: A Supplement of New Letters. William Wordsworth & Dorothy Wordsworth. Ed. by Alan G. Hill. 328p. 1993. text 65.00 (*0-19-818523-5*) OUP.

Letters of William Carlos Williams & Charles Tomlinson. William Carlos Williams & Charles Tomlinson. Ed. by Barry Magid & Hugh Witemeyer. 64p. 1992. 150.00 (*1-891472-00-3*) Dim Gray.

Letters of William Carlos Williams & Charles Tomlinson. deluxe ed. William Carlos Williams & Charles Tomlinson. Ed. by Barry Magid & Hugh Witemeyer. 64p. 1992. lthr. 300.00 (*1-891472-01-1*) Dim Gray.

Letters of William Cowper, 2 Vols, Set. William Cowper. Ed. by James George Frazer. LC 70-103647. (Select Bibliographies Reprint Ser.). 1977. 60.95 (*0-8369-5147-6*) Ayer.

Letters of William Cullen Bryant, 6 vols., Set, Vols. 1-6. Ed. by William C. Bryant & Thomas G. Voss. (Illus.). 1993. 300.00 (*0-8232-0997-0*) Fordham.

Letters of William Cullen Bryant, 6 vols., Vol. VI: 1872-1878. Ed. by William C. Bryant & Thomas G. Voss. (Illus.). 474p. 1993. 65.00 (*0-8232-0996-2*) Fordham.

Letters of William Cullen Bryant, 1809-1836, Vol. 1. Ed. by William C. Bryant & Thomas G. Voss. LC 74-27169. (Illus.). viii, 501p. 1975. 65.00 (*0-8232-0991-1*) Fordham.

Letters of William Cullen Bryant, 1836-1849, Vol. 2. Ed. by William C. Bryant & Thomas G. Voss. LC 74-27169. (Illus.). viii, 567p. 1977. 65.00 (*0-8232-0992-X*) Fordham.

Letters of William Cullen Bryant, 1849-1857, Vol. 3. Ed. by William C. Bryant. LC 74-27169. (Illus.). 564p. 1981. 65.00 (*0-8232-0993-8*) Fordham.

Letters of William Cullen Bryant, 1858-1864, Vol. 4. Ed. by William C. Bryant & Thomas G. Voss. LC 74-27169. (Illus.). 450p. 1984. 65.00 (*0-8232-0994-6*) Fordham.

Letters of William Cullen Bryant, 1865-1871, 6 vols., Vol. 5. Ed. by William C. Bryant & Thomas G. Voss. LC 74-27169. (Illus.). 462p. 1993. 65.00 (*0-8232-0995-4*) Fordham.

Letters of William G. Butler & Other Tales of Saugatuck. Kit Lane. LC 94-66962. (Illus.). 80p. (Orig.). 1994. pap. 5.50 (*1-877703-23-0*) Pavilion Pr.

Letters of William James & Theodore Flournoy. William James. Ed. by Robert C. Le Clair. LC 66-13803. 272p. reprint ed. pap. 84.40 (*0-608-09915-5*, 206925300003) Bks Demand.

Letters of William Lee, 1766-1783, 3 vols., Set. William Lee. Ed. by Worthington Ford. LC 70-140863. (Eyewitness Accounts of the American Revolution Ser.). (Illus.). 1971. reprint ed. 69.95 (*0-405-01254-3*) Ayer.

Letters of William Lloyd Garrison, 6 vols. Incl. Vol. 1. I Will Be Heard 1822-1835. Ed. by Walter M. Merrill. LC 75-133210. (Illus.). 646p. 1971. 72.00 (*0-674-52660-0*); Vol. 2. House Dividing Against Itself, 1836-1840. Ed. by Louis Ruchames. LC 75-133210. (Illus.). 802p. 1971. 80.00 (*0-674-52661-9*); Vol. 3. No Union with Slaveholders, 1841-1849. Ed. by Walter M. Merrill. LC 75-133210. 595p. 1974. 72.00 (*0-674-52662-7*); Vol. 4. From Disunionism to the Brink of War. Ed. by Louis Ruchames. LC 75-133210. 318p. 1976. 60.00 (*0-674-52663-5*); Vol. 6. To Rouse the Slumbering Land, 1868-1879. Ed. by Walter M. Merrill & Louis Ruchames. LC 75-133210. 657p. 1981. 72.00 (*0-674-52666-X*); LC 75-133210. write for info. (*0-318-53095-3*) Belknap Pr.

Letters of William Lloyd Garrison: Let the Oppressed Go Free, 1861-1867, Vol. 5. William L. Garrison. Ed. by Walter M. Merrill. LC 75-133210. (Letters of William Lloyd Garrison Ser.: Vol. V). (Illus.). 656p. 1979. 72.00 (*0-674-52665-1*) Belknap Pr.

Letters of William Morris to His Family & Friends. William Morris. Ed. by Philip Henderson. LC 75-41199. reprint ed. 69.50 (*0-404-14711-9*) AMS Pr.

Letters of William S. Burroughs, 1945-1959. Intro. by Oliver Harris. 512p. 1994. pap. 14.95 (*0-14-009452-0*, Penguin Bks) Viking Penguin.

Letters of William Shenstone. William Shenstone. LC 75-41250. reprint ed. 75.00 (*0-404-14601-5*) AMS Pr.

Letters of William Wordsworth: A New Selection. William Wordsworth. Ed. by Alan G. Hill. (Oxford Letters & Memoirs). 360p. (C). 1985. text 45.00 (*0-19-818529-4*) OUP.

Letters of Wolfgang Amadeus Mozart. Wolfgang Amadeus Mozart. Ed. by Hans Mersman. Tr. by M. M. Bozman. (Illus.). 276p. 1972. pap. 7.95 (*0-486-22859-2*) Dover.

Letters of World War I Pilot in the Army Air Corps. Gardner Dunton. 252p. 1977. pap. text 36.95 (*0-89126-028-5*) MA-AH Pub.

Letters on a Solitary Wanderer. Charlotte Smith. LC 94-24514. (Revolution & Romanticism, 1789-1834 Ser.). 1995. 85.00 (*1-85477-193-0*) Continuum.

Letters on American Slavery, Addressed to Mister Thomas Rankin, Merchant at Middlebrook, Augusta County, Virginia. John Rankin. LC 73-82214. (Anti-Slavery Crusade in America Ser.). 1970. reprint ed. 13.95 (*0-405-00653-5*) Ayer.

Letters on an Elk Hunt by a Woman Homesteader. Elinore P. Stewart. LC 79-13840. (Illus.). xv, 164p. 1979. reprint ed. pap. 9.95 (*0-8032-9112-4*, Bison Books) U of Nebr Pr.

Letters on Cezanne. Rainer Maria Rilke. Ed. by Clara Rilke. Tr. by Joel Agee from GER. LC 85-16014. 98p. 1988. pap. 10.00 (*0-88064-107-X*) Fromm Intl Pub.

Letters on Christian Education. 1992. write for info. (*0-9622508-7-2*) Simpson NJ.

Letters on Dance & Choreography. August Bournonville & Knud Arne Jurgensen. (Illus.). 77p. 19.95 (*1-85273-073-0*) Princeton Bk Co.

Letters on Demonology & Witchcraft. Sir Walter Scott. 1973. 250.00 (*0-87968-180-2*) Gordon Pr.

Letters on Demonology & Witchcraft. Sir Walter Scott. 320p. 1994. reprint ed. pap. 24.95 (*1-56459-430-0*) Kessinger Pub.

***Letters on England.** Voltaire. Tr. & Intro. by Leonard W. Tancock. (Classics Ser.). 160p. 2000. pap. 5.33 (*0-14-044386-X*, Prentice Hall) P-H.

Letters on Equality of the Sexes & the Condition of Woman, Addressed to Mary S. Parker. Sarah M. Grimke. (American Biography Ser.). 128p. 1991. reprint ed. lib. bdg. 59.00 (*0-7812-8158-X*) Rprt Serv.

Letters on Familiar Matters: Rerum Familiarum Libri I-XXIV, 3 vols. Francesco Petrarca. Tr. by Aldo S. Bernardo from LAT. LC 75-2418. 352p. 1985. text 50.00 (*0-8018-2750-7*); text 50.00 (*0-8018-2902-X*); text 50.00 (*0-8018-2287-4*) Johns Hopkins.

Letters on Familiar Matters: Rerum Familiarum Libri I-XXIV, 3 vols., Set. Francesco Petrarca. Tr. by Aldo S. Bernardo from LAT. LC 75-2418. 1985. 135.00 (*0-8018-2768-X*) Johns Hopkins.

Letters on Huna: The Fundamentals of Huna Psychology. E. Otha Wingo. 1980. pap. write for info. (*0-910764-00-X*) Huna Res Inc.

Letters on Irish Emigration. Edward E. Hale. LC 70-39376. (Select Bibliographies Reprint Ser.). 1977. reprint ed. 15.95 (*0-8369-9910-X*) Ayer.

Letters on Landscape Photography. Henry P. Robinson. LC 72-9229. (Literature of Photography Ser.). 1973. reprint ed. 17.95 (*0-405-04935-8*) Ayer.

Letters on Literature. Andrew Lang. LC 68-54277. reprint ed. 37.50 (*0-404-03836-0*) AMS Pr.

Letters on Occult Meditation. Alice A. Bailey. LC 26-8569. 1922. 26.00 (*0-85330-011-9*) Lucis.

Letters on Occult Meditation. Alice A. Bailey. LC 26-8569. 1972. pap. 13.00 (*0-85330-111-5*) Lucis.

Letters on Paraguay Comprising an Account of a Four Years' Residence in That Republic, under the Government of the Dictator Francia, 3 vols. 2nd ed. John P. Robertson & W. P. Robertson. LC 74-128429. reprint ed. 155.00 (*0-404-05390-4*) AMS Pr.

Letters on Poetry, Literature & Art. Sri Aurobindo. 271p. 1994. 6.95 (*81-7058-351-9*, Pub. by SAA); pap. 5.95 (*81-7058-098-6*, Pub. by SAA) E-W Cultural Ctr.

Letters on Practical Subjects to a Daughter. Wiliam B. Sprague. 1992. 19.99 (*0-87377-946-0*) GAM Pubns.

Letters on Practical Subjects to a Daughter. Wiliam B. Sprague. 1993. pap. 16.99 (*0-87377-192-3*) GAM Pubns.

Letters on Sanctification. John Hunt. pap. 9.99 (*0-88019-166-X*) Schmul Pub Co.

Letters on Scientific Subjects. Ed. by James O. Halliwell. 280p. 1965. 29.00 (*0-8464-1472-4*) Beekman Pubs.

Letters on Slavery. William Dickson. LC 79-111573. 1970. reprint ed. 25.00 (*0-8371-4598-8*, DLS&) Greenwood.

Letters on Slavery from the Old World. James D. Williams. LC 74-83884. (Black Heritage Library Collection). 1977. 22.95 (*0-8369-8693-8*) Ayer.

Letters on Slavery from the Old World. James D. Williams. LC 71-97445. 321p. 1970. reprint ed. lib. bdg. 59.50 (*0-8371-2718-1*, WIO&) Greenwood.

Letters on Smith's History of New York. Cadwallader Colden. (Works of Cadwallader Colden). 1990. reprint ed. lib. bdg. 79.00 (*0-7812-2309-1*) Rprt Serv.

Letters on South America Comprising Travels on the Banks of the Parana & the Rio De la Plata, 3 vols., Set. John P. Robertson. LC 70-128428. reprint ed. 145.00 (*0-404-05380-7*) AMS Pr.

Letters on the American Rebellion, 1860 to 1865. Samuel A. Goddard. LC 73-179521. (Select Bibliographies Reprint Ser.). 1977. reprint ed. 45.95 (*0-8369-6650-3*) Ayer.

Letters on the Epistle of Paul to Philemon or, The Connection of Apostolic Christianity with Slavery. Augustus Baldwin Longstreet. (Notable American Authors Ser.). 1999. reprint ed. lib. bdg. 125.00 (*0-7812-3854-4*) Rprt Serv.

Letters on the Improvement of the Mind, 1773: An Enquiry into the Duties of the Female Sex, 1797. Hester Chapone & Thomas Gisborne. LC 96-33667. (Female Education in the Age of Enlightenment Ser.: No. 2). 1996. write for info. (*1-85196-276-X*, Pub. by Pickering & Chatto) Ashgate Pub Co.

Letters on the League of Nations: From the Files of Raymond B. Fosdick. Raymond B. Fosdick. LC 66-10271. (Supplementary Volumes to the Papers of Woodrow Wilson). 185p. 1966. reprint ed. pap. 57.40 (*0-7837-9338-3*, 206007900004) Bks Demand.

Letters on the Political Condition of the Gold Coast since the Exchange of Territory between the English & Dutch Governments on January 1, 1868: Together with a Short Account of the Ashantee War, 1862-1864 & the Awoonan War, 1866. Africanus B. Horton. 178p. 1970. reprint ed. 50.00 (*0-7146-1758-X*, Pub. by F Cass Pubs) Intl Spec Bk.

Letters on the Religious Revivals Which Prevailed about the Beginning of the Present Century: With Supplementary Material Compiled by Kurt R. Linde. Ebenezer Porter et al. xx, 316p. 1992. reprint ed. pap. 6.95 (*0-9631745-0-9*) Linde Pubns.

Letters on the Short Story. Anton Chekhov. 1973. 59.95 (*0-8490-0513-2*) Gordon Pr.

Letters on the Spanish Inquisition. Tr. by Joseph M. De Maistre. LC 77-24949. 184p. 1977. reprint ed. 50.00 (*0-8201-1293-3*) Schol Facsimiles.

Letters on the State of Christianity in India: To Which Is Added a Vindication of the Hindus Male & Female. Abbe J. Dubois. (C). 1995. reprint ed. 17.50 (*81-206-0624-8*, Pub. by Asian Educ Servs) S Asia.

Letters on the Sufi Path. Ibn Abbad. Tr. by John Renard. 238p. 1996. 14.50 (*0-614-21303-7*, 715) Kazi Pubns.

Letters on Turkey, 2 vols. M. A. Ubicini. Tr. by Lady Easthope. LC 73-6306. (Middle East Ser.). 1973. reprint ed. 63.95 (*0-405-05367-3*) Ayer.

Letters on Unified Field Theory. 4th rev. ed. James A. Green. LC 96-94732. (Field Physics Ser.). (Illus.). 238p. 1999. 49.00 (*1-890121-02-9*, 01-03-08) Grnwd Resch.

Letters on Various Interesting & Important Subjects. Philip Freneau. (BCL1-PS American Literature Ser.). 142p. 1993. reprint ed. lib. bdg. 69.00 (*0-7812-6939-3*) Rprt Serv.

Letters on Various Interesting & Important Subjects. Philip M. Freneau. LC 43-6720. 152p. 1976. reprint ed. lib. bdg. 50.00 (*0-8201-1205-4*) Schol Facsimiles.

Letters on West Africa & the Slave Trade: Paul Erdmann Isert's Journey to Guinea & the Caribbean Islands in Columbia, 1788, Vol. 7. Paul E. Isert. Ed. & Tr. by Selena A. Winsnes. (Fontes Histroiae Africanae Series Varia Seven British Academy). (Illus.). 288p. 1992. text 75.00 (*0-19-726105-1*) OUP.

Letters on Yoga, 2 vols. Sri Aurobindo. (Life Companion Library). 1984p. 29.90 (*0-89744-014-5*) Auromere.

Letters on Yoga. 3rd ed. Sri Aurobindo. 502p. 1996. 18.95 (*81-7058-438-8*, Pub. by SAA) E-W Cultural Ctr.

Letters on Yoga, Vol. I. Sri Aurobindo. 502p. 1979. 16.00 (*0-89744-984-3*, Pub. by Sri Aurob Ashram Trust); pap. 14.00 (*0-89744-985-1*, Pub. by Sri Aurob Ashram Trust) Acrpls Bks CO.

Letters on Yoga, Vol. 1. 3rd ed. Sri Aurobindo. 502p. 1988. pap. 13.00 (*81-7058-007-2*, Pub. by SAA) E-W Cultural Ctr.

Letters on Yoga, Vol. II. Sri Aurobindo. 587p. 1979. 16.50 (*0-89744-986-X*); pap. 15.00 (*0-89744-987-8*) Auromere.

Letters on Yoga, Vol. 2. 3rd ed. Sri Aurobindo. 587p. 1988. pap. 14.50 (*81-7058-008-0*, Pub. by SAA) E-W Cultural Ctr.

Letters on Yoga, Vol. 2. 3rd ed. Sri Aurobindo. 587p. 1996. 21.95 (*81-7058-439-6*, Pub. by SAA) E-W Cultural Ctr.

Letters on Yoga, Vol. III. Sri Aurobindo. 720p. 1979. 20.00 (*0-89744-988-6*, Pub. by Sri Aurob Ashram Trust); pap. 18.50 (*0-89744-989-4*, Pub. by Sri Aurob Ashram Trust) Acrpls Bks CO.

Letters on Yoga, Vol. 3. 3rd ed. Sri Aurobindo. 719p. 1988. pap. 16.50 (*81-7058-009-9*, Pub. by SAA) E-W Cultural Ctr.

Letters on Yoga, Vol. 3. 3rd ed. Sri Aurobindo. 719p. 1996. 24.95 (*81-7058-440-X*, Pub. by SAA) E-W Cultural Ctr.

Letters, 1-81. St. Cyprian of Carthage. Tr. by Rose B. Donna. LC 65-12906. (Fathers of the Church Ser.: Vol. 51). 352p. 1964. 21.95 (*0-8132-0051-2*) Cath U Pr.

Letters, 1-91. Ambrose. LC 67-28583. (Fathers of the Church Ser.: Vol. 26). 515p. 1954. 36.95 (*0-8132-0026-1*) Cath U Pr.

Letters, 1-30. St. Peter Damian. Tr. by Owen Blum. LC 88-25802. (Fathers of the Church: Mediaeval Continuation Ser.: Vol. 1). 312p. 1989. 39.95 (*0-8132-0702-9*) Cath U Pr.

Letters Papers from Prison. Dietrich Bonhoeffer. 1997. per. 13.00 (*0-684-83827-3*) S&S Trade.

Letters Plus: Communications on the Job. C. E. Reynolds. 136p. 1987. pap. text 7.56 (*0-07-052057-7*) McGraw.

Letters, Poetry & Other Thoughts from Ellas, Israel, & Egypt. Lana R. Fishergerlach. 56p. 1993. per. 25.00 (*0-8403-8379-7*) Kendall-Hunt.

Letters, Principal Doctrine & Vatican Sayings: Epicurus. Russell M. Geer. 144p. (C). 1964. pap. text 5.60 (*0-02-341200-3*, Macmillan Coll) P-H.

Letters Received by the Attorney General, 1809-1870: Western Law & Order. Frederick S. Calhoun et al. LC 96-3287. (Research Collections in American Legal History). 1996. 1515.00 (*1-55655-634-9*) U Pubns Amer.

Letters Slate Cut. David Kindersley & Lida L. Cardozo. LC 80-54744. (Illus.). 96p. 1981. pap. 9.95 (*0-8008-4741-5*) Taplinger.

Letters, Speeches & Tracts on Irish Affairs. Edmund Burke. Ed. by Matthew Arnold. LC 75-28809. reprint ed. 72.50 (*0-404-13802-0*) AMS Pr.

Letters Sticker Book. Karen Bryant-Mole. (First Learning Ser.). (Illus.). 16p. (J). (ps-3). 1996. pap. 6.95 (*0-7460-2429-0*, Usborne) EDC.

Letters Sticker Book Kid Kit. Educational Development Staff. (J). (ps-3). 1998. pap. 18.95 (*1-58086-137-7*, Usborne) EDC.

Letters, Summer 1926. Rainer Maria Rilke et al. Ed. by Yevgeny Pasternak et al. Tr. by Margaret Wettlin & Walter Arndt. LC 85-865. (Helen & Kurt Wolff Bk.). (Illus.). 384p. 1985. 24.95 (*0-15-150871-2*) Harcourt.

Letters That Get Results: A Practical Guide to Business Letter Writing. Peter M. Stephan. LC 85-51896. 43p. (Orig.). 1985. pap. 4.95 (*0-931705-01-0*) Wredco Pr.

Letters That Have Helped Me, 2 vols. in 1. William Q. Judge. LC 81-52614. 209p. 1981. 17.95 (*0-911500-41-3*); pap. 11.95 (*0-911500-42-1*) Theos U Pr.

Letters That Have Helped Me. William Q. Judge. Ed. & Intro. by Jasper Niemand. (Illus.). x, 300p. 1946. 7.00 (*0-938998-08-0*) Theosophy.

Letters That Have Helped Me (1891) Compiled by Jasper Niemand. 94p. 1998. reprint ed. pap. 12.95 (*0-7661-0571-7*) Kessinger Pub.

Letters That Help Churches Grow. Elizabeth W. Crisci. (Illus.). 160p. 1987. ring bd. 24.95 (*0-89265-113-X*) Randall Hse.

Letters That Sell. Edward W. Werz. 176p. 1987. pap. 14.95 (*0-8092-4684-8*, 468480, Contemporary Bks) NTC Contemp Pub Co.

Letters, 31-60. St. Peter Damien. Tr. by Owen J. Blum. LC 88-25802. (Fathers of the Church: Mediaeval Continuation Ser.: Vol. 2). 422p. 1990. 39.95 (*0-8132-0707-X*) Cath U Pr.

Letters to a Beginner: On Giving One's Life to God. Abbess Thaisia. LC 93-83750. (Modern Matericon Ser.). (Illus.). 112p. 1993. pap. 7.95 (*0-938635-43-3*) St Herman Pr.

Letters to A. C. Benson. Henry James. 1972. 250.00 (*0-87968-031-8*) Gordon Pr.

Letters to A. C. Benson & Auguste Monod: Now First Published, & Edited with an Introduction by E. F. Benson. Henry James. (American Biography Ser.). 118p. 1991. reprint ed. lib. bdg. 59.00 (*0-7812-8212-8*) Rprt Serv.

Letters to a Dear Baby. Beth Garbo. (Illus.). 76p. 1998. spiral bd. 18.95 (*1-892373-08-4*, 99-06) Especially Bks.

***Letters to a Devasted Christian.** Gene Edwards. 45p. 2000. write for info. (*0-940232-69-3*) Seedsowers.

Letters to a Dying Friend: Helping Those You Love Make a Conscious Transition. rev. ed. Anton Grosz. LC 97-22259. 170p. 1997. pap. 12.00 (*0-8356-0765-8*, Quest) Theos Pub Hse.

Letters to a Fiction Writer. Frederick Busch. LC 98-54320. 291p. 1999. 25.00 (*0-393-04735-0*) Norton.

***Letters to a Fiction Writer.** Frederick Busch. 304p. 2000. pap. 13.95 (*0-393-32061-8*) Norton.

Letters to a Lady. Gail Whitaker. (Regency Romance Ser.). 1993. per. 2.99 (*0-373-31206-7*, 1-31206-5) Harlequin Bks.

Letters to a Lady. Gail Whitiker. (Promo Ser.). 1999. per. 3.75 (*0-373-31230-X*, 1-31230-5) Harlequin Bks.

Letters to a Lady. large type ed. Gail Whitiker. (Mills & Boon Large Print Ser.). 350p. 1998. 24.99 (*0-263-15496-3*, Pub. by Mills & Boon) Ulverscroft.

Letters to a Lady in the Country, Together with Her Replies. Stuart P. Sherman. (American Biography Ser.). 232p. 1991. reprint ed. lib. bdg. 69.00 (*0-7812-8352-3*) Rprt Serv.

Letters to a Mormon Elder. James R. White. 382p. 1991. pap. write for info. (*0-925703-59-1*) Crown MA.

Letters to a Mormon Elder: Challenging Eye-Opening Information for Mormons & the Christians. James R. White. LC 93-25153. 34p. 1993. reprint ed. pap. 10.99 (*1-55661-344-X*) Bethany Hse.

Letters to a Mother on Faith. Emmanuel. 1995. pap. 4.25 (*0-935952-25-X*) Angelus Pr.

Letters to a New Elder: The Melchizedek Priesthood, Its Duty & Fulfillment. Robb Russon. pap. 3.95 (*0-89036-144-4*) Liahona Pub Trust.

***Letters to a Niece.** Friedrich von Hugel. 172p. 1998. reprint ed. pap. 18.95 (*1-57383-103-4*, Regent Coll Pub) Regent College.

Letters to a Niece & Prayer to the Virgin of Chartres. Henry (Brooks) Adams. 1988. reprint ed. lib. bdg. 49.00 (*0-7812-1446-7*) Rprt Serv.

Letters to a Niece & Prayer to the Virgin of Chartres. Henry (Brooks) Adams. Ed. by Mabel La Farge. 1970. reprint ed. 29.00 (*0-403-00490-X*) Scholarly.

Letters to a Nobleman, on the Conduct of the War in the Middle Colonies. Joseph Galloway. LC 72-10707. (American Revolutionary Ser.). reprint ed. lib. bdg. 21.50 (*0-8398-0673-6*) Irvington.

Letters to a Qu[00e9]b[00e9]cois Friend. Philip Resnick & Daniel Latouche. 136p. (C). 1990. pap. 17.95 (*0-7735-0777-9*, Pub. by McG-Queens Univ Pr) CUP Services.

Letters to a Quibicois Friend. Philip Resnick & Daniel Latouche. 136p. (C). 1990. 55.00 (*0-7735-0772-8*, Pub. by McG-Queens Univ Pr) CUP Services.

Letters to a Roman Catholic Priest. 2nd ed. Henry A. Ironside. LC 89-36834. 40p. 1989. pap. 2.99 (*0-87213-349-4*) Loizeaux.

Letters to a Serious Education President. Seymour B. Sarason. LC 92-37817. 152p. 1992. 49.95 (*0-8039-6063-8*); pap. 21.95 (*0-8039-6064-6*) Corwin Pr.

Letters to a Sex Therapist. A. Alexander. 1990. pap. 21.00 (*1-85461-000-7*, Pub. by Northcote House) St Mut.

Letters to a Soul. Hubert Van Zeller. 121p. 1976. 12.95 (*0-87243-067-7*) Templegate.

Letters to a Stranger. Beate Goldman. LC 81-50429. (Series Six). 50p. (Orig.). 1981. pap. text 7.00 (*0-931846-18-8*) Wash Writers Pub.

Letters to a Student Revolutionary. Elizabeth Wong. 61p. 1996. pap. 5.50 (*0-87129-645-4*, L74) Dramatic Pub.

Letters to a Young Doctor. Richard Selzer. 208p. (C). 1996. pap. 13.00 (*0-15-600399-6*, Harvest Bks) Harcourt.

Letters to a Young Doctor. Richard Selzer. 1995. reprint ed. lib. bdg. 24.95 (*1-56849-580-3*) Buccaneer Bks.

Letters to a Young Feminist. Phyllis Chesler. LC 97-42846. 176p. 1998. 18.00 (*1-56858-093-2*) FWEW.

***Letters to a Young Feminist.** Phyllis Chesler. (Women's Studies). 176p. 1999. pap. 11.00 (*1-56858-151-3*) FWEW.

Letters to a Young Lady 1811, Vol. 1. Jane West. LC 96-33668. (Female Education in the Age of Enlightenment Ser.: No. 4-6). 1996. write for info. (*1-85196-278-6*, Pub. by Pickering & Chatto) Ashgate Pub Co.

An Asterisk (*) at the beginning of an entry indicates that the title is appearing for the first time.

Letters to a Young Lady 1811, Vol. 2. Jane West. LC 96-33668. (Female Education in the Age of Enlightenment Ser.: Nos. 4-6). 1996. write for info. (*1-85196-279-4*, Pub. by Pickering & Chatto) Ashgate Pub Co.

Letters to a Young Lady 1811, Vol. 3. Jane West. LC 96-33668. (Female Education in the Age of Enlightenment Ser.: Nos. 4-6). 1996. write for info. (*1-85196-280-8*, Pub. by Pickering & Chatto) Ashgate Pub Co.

Letters to a Young Lady on the Art of Playing the Pianoforte. Charles C. Czerny. Tr. by J. A. Hamilton from GER. (Music Ser.). vii, 82p. 1982. reprint ed. lib. bdg. 24.50 (*0-306-76123-8*) Da Capo.

Letters to a Young Poet. Rainer Maria Rilke. Tr. & Frwd. by Stephen Mitchell. 128p. 1986. pap. 9.00 (*0-394-74104-8*) Vin Bks.

Letters to a Young Poet. Rainer Maria Rilke. Tr. & Frwd. by Stephen Mitchell. LC 93-20169. (Pocket Classics Ser.). 112p. 1993. reprint ed. pap. 6.00 (*0-87773-946-3*, Pub. by Shambhala Pubns) Random.

***Letters to a Young Poet.** rev. ed. Rainer Maria Rilke. Tr. by Joan M. Burnham. LC 91-42157. 128p. 2000. 15.00 (*1-57731-155-8*, Pub. by New Wrld Lib) Publishers Group.

Letters to a Young Poet. rev. ed. Rainer Maria Rilke. Tr. by M. D. Norton. LC 91-42157. 128p. 1993. pap. 7.95 (*0-393-31039-6*) Norton.

Letters to a Young Priest from a Laicised Priest. Anton Grabner-Haider. 1989. pap. 22.00 (*0-901810-88-6*, Pub. by Veritas Pubns) St Mut.

Letters to a Young Teacher. Grace S. Treet. 113p. pap. 9.95 (*0-932720-40-4*) New Plays Inc.

Letters to African-Americans: Chiefly on Orthodox Christianity. Larry E. Johnson. 138p. (Orig.). 1996. pap. 6.40 (*1-888704-00-4*) Aksum.

***Letters to Alice on First Reading Jane Austen.** Fay Weldon. 160p. 1999. pap. text 9.95 (*0-7867-0688-0*) Carroll & Graf.

Letters to Amanda: The Civil War Letters of Marion Hill Fitzpatrick, Army of North Virginia. Ed. by Jeffrey C. Lowe & Sam Hodges. LC 98-36817. (Civil War Georgia Ser.). 256p. 1998. text 29.95 (*0-86554-591-X*, H444) Mercer Univ Pr.

Letters to America: Contemporary American Poetry on Race. Ed. by Jim Daniels. LC 95-19996. 230p. (Orig.). (C). 1995. pap. 21.95 (*0-8143-2542-4*) Wayne St U Pr.

Letters to an Alien. Robert Caisley. 39p. 1996. pap. 5.50 (*0-87129-682-9*, L58) Dramatic Pub.

Letters to an American Lady. C. S. Lewis. Ed. by Clyde S. Kilby. 128p. 1967. pap. 8.00 (*0-8028-1428-X*) Eerdmans.

Letters to an Ex-Priest. Emmett McLoughlin. 1965. 4.95 (*0-8184-0050-1*) Carol Pub Group.

Letters to Anais Nin. Henry Miller. 1996. pap. 14.00 (*0-15-600387-2*) Harcourt.

Letters to & from Caesar Rodney. George H. Ryden. LC 75-107417. (Era of the American Revolution Ser.). 1970. reprint ed. lib. bdg. 55.00 (*0-306-71881-2*) Da Capo.

Letters to Annie: The Letters of Jehan Rictus to Annie & Paul Vulliaud. Tr. by Herbert W. Kitson from FRE. LC 87-31693. 96p. (C). 1988. lib. bdg. 29.50 (*0-8191-6822-X*) U Pr of Amer.

Letters to Atticus, 3 vols., Bks. 1-6. Marcus Tullius Cicero. (Loeb Classical Library: No. 7, 8, 97). 570p. 1912. 18.95 (*0-674-99008-0*) HUP.

Letters to Atticus, 3 vols., Bks. 7-11. Marcus Tullius Cicero. (Loeb Classical Library: No. 7, 8, 97). 458p. 1913. 18.95 (*0-674-99009-9*) HUP.

Letters to Atticus, 3 vols., Bks. 12-16. Marcus Tullius Cicero. (Loeb Classical Library: No. 7, 8, 97). 470p. 1918. 18.95 (*0-674-99108-7*) HUP.

Letters to Bab: Sherwood Anderson to Marietta D. Finley, 1916-33. Sherwood Anderson. Ed. by William A. Sutton. LC 83-18258. 376p. 1985. text 29.95 (*0-252-00979-7*) U of Ill Pr.

***Letters to Baby: A Keepsake of Blessings & Wisdom for New Babies.** Chaz Corzine. 137p. 2000. reprint ed. 17.00 (*0-7881-9244-2*) DIANE Pub.

Letters to Barbara. Leo Meter. Tr. by Joel Agee. (Illus.). 62p. 1996. pap. 16.95 (*0-87951-589-9*, Pub. by Overlook Pr) Penguin Putnam.

Letters to Barbara. Glenn Meeter. LC 81-15235. 274p. reprint ed. pap. 85.00 (*0-608-14505-X*, 202533600043) Bks Demand.

Letters to Barbara Bush. Margaret E. Phillips. 152p. (Orig.). 1992. pap. 9.95 (*0-943487-38-2*) Sevgo Pr.

Letters to Beethoven & Other Correspondence. Ed. & Tr. by Theodore Albrecht. LC 95-43793. (North American Beethoven Studies: Vol. 1). lii, 279p. 1996. text 65.00 (*0-8032-1033-7*) U of Nebr Pr.

Letters to Beethoven & Other Correspondence, Vol. 2. Ed. & Tr. by Theodore Albrecht. LC 95-43793. (North American Beethoven Studies). (Illus.). xxiv, 302p. 1996. text 65.00 (*0-8032-1039-6*) U of Nebr Pr.

Letters to Beethoven & Other Correspondence, Vol. 3. Ed. & Tr. by Theodore Albrecht. LC 95-43793. (North American Beethoven Studies). (Illus.). xxiv, 365p. 1996. text 65.00 (*0-8032-1040-X*) U of Nebr Pr.

Letters to Benjamin Franklin, from His Family & Friends, 1751-1790. Ed. by William Duane. (Select Bibliographies Reprint Ser.). 1977. 20.95 (*0-8369-5325-8*) Ayer.

Letters to Bill: On University Administration. George L. Cross. LC 83-47832. 225p. 1983. 22.95 (*0-8061-1850-4*) U of Okla Pr.

***Letters to Brian: Brian Learns to Cook.** (Illus.). 93p. 1999. pap. 11.95 (*0-7414-0168-1*) Buy Books.

Letters to Bridgie. Melvin R. Bloom. (Illus.). 88p. (Orig.). 1996. pap. 6.95 (*1-886203-95-4*) Pubs Paradigm.

Letters to Burke, 1791. Joseph Priestley. LC 96-34849. (Revolution & Romanticism Ser.). 1997. 65.00 (*1-85477-215-5*) Continuum.

Letters to Callie. Miller. 1999. pap. write for info. (*0-671-52103-9*) S&S Trade.

Letters to Callie. Dawn Miller. 1999. 25.01 (*0-671-52102-0*) S&S Trade.

Letters to Cassite Kings from the Temple Archives of Nippur. LC 08-33646. (University of Pennsylvania, Babylonian Expedition, Series A: Cuneiform Texts: Vol. 17, Pt. 1). 273p. reprint ed. pap. 84.70 (*0-608-13646-8*, 205201800027) Bks Demand.

Letters to Catherine E. Beecher. Angelina E. Grimke. LC 71-138338. (Black Heritage Library Collection). 1977. 21.95 (*0-8369-8730-6*) Ayer.

Letters to Catherine E. Beecher, in Reply to an Essay on Slavery & Abolitionism. Angelina E. Grimke. LC 70-82196. (Anti-Slavery Crusade in America Ser.). 1975. reprint ed. 21.95 (*0-405-00636-5*) Ayer.

Letters to Charlie . . . And One to Jane. Fred Snyder. 187p. (Orig.). 1996. pap. 9.95 (*0-9653227-1-8*) Bon Temps.

Letters to Che. Melba J. Boyd. 36p. 1996. pap. text 8.00 (*1-56439-055-1*) Ridgeway.

Letters to Chief Ministers, 1947-1964 Vol. 1: 1947-1949. Jawaharlal Nehru. Ed. by G. Parthasarathi. (Illus.). 584p. 1988. 36.00 (*0-19-561881-5*) OUP.

Letters to Chief Ministers, 1947-1964 Vol. 2: 1950-1952. Jawaharlal Nehru. (Illus.). 600p. 1987. 36.00 (*0-19-562012-7*) OUP.

Letters to Chief Ministers, 1947-1964 Vol. 3: 1952-1954. Jawaharlal Nehru. (Illus.). 706p. 1988. 36.00 (*0-19-562180-8*) OUP.

Letters to Chief Ministers, 1947-1964 Vol. 4: 1954-1957, Vol. 4. Jawaharlal Nehru. (Illus.). 684p. 1990. text 36.00 (*0-19-562338-X*) OUP.

Letters to Chief Ministers, 1947-1964 Vol. 5: 1958-1964, Vol. 5. Jawaharlal Nehru. (Illus.). 664p. 1990. text 36.00 (*0-19-562512-9*) OUP.

***Letters to Children.** C. S. Lewis. (J). 1999. pap. 8.00 (*0-8054-2043-6*) Broadman.

Letters to Children. Beatrix Potter. (Illus.). 48p. (J). (gr. 2 up). 1986. pap. 5.95 (*0-8027-7293-5*) Walker & Co.

Letters to Churches: Timeless Lessons for the Body of Christ. Charles R. Swindoll. 91'p. 1998. pap., student ed. 5.95 (*1-57972-185-0*) Insight Living.

***Letters to Colleen.** Bobby McGee. (Illus.). 170p. 1999. pap. 14.95 (*1-930499-02-7*) Bobbysez Pub.

Letters to Contemplatives. William Johnston. 1991. reprint ed. pap. 12.00 (*0-88344-784-3*) Orbis Bks.

Letters to Copy. Ed. by Lisa Miles. (Sticker Learning Bks.). (Illus.). 18p. (J). (ps-3). 1999. pap. 6.95 (*0-7460-3110-6*, Usborne) EDC.

Letters to Corinth. Charles Harris. (Spiritual Discovery Ser.). 128p. 1997. pap., teacher ed. 9.95 (*0-88243-216-8*, 02-0216); pap., student ed. 4.95 (*0-88243-116-1*) Gospel Pub.

Letters to Cristina: Reflections on My Life & Work. Paulo Freire. Tr. by Donaldo Macedo. 260p. (C). 1996. pap. 17.99 (*0-415-91097-8*) Routledge.

Letters to Cristina: Reflections on My Life & Work. Pavlo Freire. 259p. (C). 1996. 70.00 (*0-415-91096-X*) Routledge.

Letters to Dead Authors. Andrew Lang. LC 68-59284. reprint ed. 37.50 (*0-404-03819-0*) AMS Pr.

Letters to Dean. Paul Rosenfels. LC 87-402040. (Ninth Street Center Monographs). (Orig.). 1981. pap. 3.95 (*0-932961-07-X*) Ninth St Ctr.

***Letters to Doctor Laura: And Other Struggles Against Demagoguery & Fundamentalism.** Jim Terr. LC 99-76148. (Illus.). 110p. 1999. pap. 12.95 (*0-929830-04-0*) Blue Canyon Bks.

Letters to Dolcidia, 1954-1983. Carlo Carretto. Ed. by Gian C. Sibilia. Tr. by Michael J. Smith. LC 91-28836. 224p. reprint ed. pap. 69.50 (*0-608-20247-9*, 207150600012) Bks Demand.

Letters to Dotty B: World War II in the South Pacific. Ed. by Frederick Lankard. LC 98-134884. (Illus.). 300p. 1998. pap. 22.95 (*0-89745-218-6*) Sunflower U Pr.

Letters to Elvis. P. K. McLemore. LC 97-2742. 124p. 1997. pap. 9.95 (*0-312-16906-X*) St Martin.

Letters to Emil. Henry Miller & Emil Schnellock. Ed. by George Wickes. LC 88-36470. 192p. 1989. reprint ed. 21.95 (*0-8112-1092-8*, Pub. by New Directions) Norton.

Letters to Emil. Henry Miller & Emil Schnellock. Ed. by George Wickes. LC 88-36470. 192p. 1991. reprint ed. pap. 12.95 (*0-8112-1170-3*, NDP717, Pub. by New Directions) Norton.

Letters to Emma Lazarus in the Columbia University Library. Emma Lazarus. Ed. by Ralph L. Rusk. LC 39-14112. 1984. reprint ed. 20.00 (*0-404-05459-5*) AMS Pr.

Letters to Eva in Heaven. Russell Shull. 4.95 (*0-910924-51-1*) Macalester.

Letters to Father Aristotle: A Journey Through Contemporary American Orthodoxy. Francis A. Schaeffer. 230p. 1995. pap. 22.95 (*0-9649141-0-7*) Regina Orthodox.

Letters to Friends. Beredene Jocelyn. 10.00 (*0-929979-20-6*, 1584) Merc Pr NY.

***Letters to Gabriel: The True Story of Gabriel Michael Santorum.** Karen G. Santorum. LC 98-159752. 132p. 1998. 14.99 (*1-56814-528-4*) CCC of America.

Letters to George. Max S. Clark. 208p. 1997. pap. 22.95 (*1-85459-317-X*) N Hern Bks.

Letters to Gilbert Imlay. Mary Wollstonecraft Shelley. LC 77-158203. (English Literature Ser.: No. 33). 1971. lib. bdg. 75.00 (*0-8383-1269-1*) M S G Haskell Hse.

Letters to God. Nadene C. King. LC 98-90857. 1999. pap. 8.95 (*0-533-12957-5*) Vantage.

Letters to Graduates: From Billy Graham, Pope John Paul II, Madeleine L'Engle, Alan Paton, & Others. Compiled by Myrna Grant. LC 90-38371. 64p. 1991. 7.98 (*0-687-21563-3*) Abingdon.

Letters to Harry: The True Story of a Daughter's Love & a Mother's Final Journey. Janet F. Graham. LC 98-32221. (Illus.). 208p. (YA). (gr. 5). 1999. 18.95 (*0-7370-0046-5*) T-L Custom Pub.

Letters to Harry, 1872-1874: A Man of Letters. Prudence Taylor Palmer & Theodore J. Palmer. (Illus.). 208p. 1999. pap. write for info. (*0-9634150-1-8*) Paper Rock Pub.

***Letters to Helen.** Edward Thomas. Ed. & Intro. by R. George Thomas. 192p. 2000. pap. 24.95 (*1-85754-447-1*, Pub. by Carcanet Pr) Paul & Co Pubs.

Letters to Henry. Les Moore. LC 95-206434. 356p. (Orig.). (C). 1995. pap. 15.95 (*0-9647111-0-9*) Little Lion.

Letters to Hildegard Jone & Josef Humplik. Anton Webern. Ed. by Josef Polnauer. Tr. by Cornelius Cardew. Orig. Title: Briefe an Hildegard Jone und Josef Humplik. 1967. pap. 19.00 (*3-7024-0031-1*, UE14230) Eur-Am Music.

Letters to His Brother Llewelyn, 1902-1925, Vol. I. John Cowper Powys. Ed. by Malcolm Elwin. 367p. 1975. pap. text 12.95 (*0-912568-06-2*) Colgate U Pr.

Letters to His Brother Llewelyn, 1925-1939, Vol. II. John Cowper Powys. Ed. by Malcolm Elvin. 284p. 1975. pap. text 12.95 (*0-912568-07-0*) Colgate U Pr.

Letters to His Brother Quintus. Marcus Tullius Cicero. (Loeb Classical Library: No. 462). 15.50 (*0-674-99509-0*) HUP.

Letters to His Excellency Governor Manning on the Lunatic Asylum. Daniel H. Trezevant. LC 73-2423. (Mental Illness & Social Policy; the American Experience Ser.). 1973. reprint ed. 16.95 (*0-405-05232-4*) Ayer.

Letters to His Friends, 3 vols., Bks. 1-6. Marcus Tullius Cicero. (Loeb Classical Library: No. 205, 216, 230). 562p. 1927. 18.95 (*0-674-99225-3*) HUP.

Letters to His Friends, 3 vols., Bks. 7-12. Marcus Tullius Cicero. (Loeb Classical Library: No. 205, 216, 230). 670p. 1929. 18.95 (*0-674-99238-5*) HUP.

Letters to His Friends, 3 vols., Bks. 13-16. Marcus Tullius Cicero. (Loeb Classical Library: No. 205, 216, 230). 424p. 1929. 18.95 (*0-674-99253-9*) HUP.

Letters to His Parents, 1839-1864. Rudolph Virchow. Ed. by L. Rather. (Resources in Medical History Ser.). 200p. 1990. 20.00 (*0-88135-090-7*, Sci Hist) Watson Pub Intl.

Letters to His Son Lucien. Camille Pissarro. Ed. by John Rewald. Tr. by Lionel Abel from FRE. LC 94-49368. (Illus.). 431p. 1995. reprint ed. pap. 15.95 (*0-306-80631-2*) Da Capo.

Letters to His Son Lucien. 3rd enl. rev. ed. Ed. by Camille Pissarro et al. (Illus.). 399p. 37.50 (*0-911858-22-9*) Appel.

Letters to His Wife. Ferruccio Busoni. Tr. by Rosamond Ley. LC 74-34378. (Music Reprint Ser.). (Illus.). 319p. 1975. reprint ed. lib. bdg. 37.50 (*0-306-70732-2*) Da Capo.

Letters to His Wife. Ferruccio B. Busoni. (Music Book Index Ser.). 319p. 1992. reprint ed. lib. bdg. 89.00 (*0-7812-9489-4*) Rprt Serv.

Letters to His Youngest Sister. Thomas Carlyle. Ed. by C. T. Copeland. (Anglistica & Americana Ser.: No. 30). 284p. 1968. reprint ed. 80.00 (*0-685-25148-9*, 05102208) G Olms Pubs.

Letters to Hon. William Prescott. Jimmy Carter. 1977. lib. bdg. 59.95 (*0-8490-2156-1*) Gordon Pr.

***Letters to Hyun A: Bridging Two Cultures.** Chi S. Rhee. 1999. pap. 8.95 (*1-57087-480-8*) Prof Pr NC.

Letters to Ibbotson. Ezra Pound. LC 78-55724. (Ezra Pound Scholarship Ser.). 145p. 1979. 15.00 (*0-915032-10-4*) Natl Poet Foun.

***Letters to Ida: Farm Life in the Early 1900's.** Ed. by Iris W. Swenson. (Illus.). 207p. 1999. pap. 14.95 (*0-9653934-1-0*) Access Midwest.

Letters to Jack Wilson, the Paiute Prophet, Written Between 1908 & 1911. fac. ed. Ed. by Grace M. Dangberg. (Smithsonian Institution, Bureau of American Ethnology, Bulletins Ser.: No. 164, Paper 55). 18p. (C). 1957. reprint ed. pap. text 2.19 (*1-55567-803-3*) Coyote Press.

Letters to Jacob. Sadie Lancellotti. LC 98-85371. 192p. 1999. pap. 11.95 (*1-56315-199-5*, Pub. by SterlingHse) Natl Bk Netwk.

Letters to Jeannine. Charlotte M. Savignac. LC 94-69485. 232p. (Orig.). 1995. pap. 12.95 (*0-87516-671-7*) DeVorss.

Letters to Jenny. Piers Anthony. Ed. by Alan Riggs. 288p. 1994. pap. 4.99 (*0-8125-2282-6*, Pub. by Tor Bks) St Martin.

Letters to Jill. Pati Hill. LC 79-55883. (Illus.). 128p. 1979. pap. 7.50 (*0-89822-009-2*) Visual Studies.

Letters to Jonas Gilman Clark. G. Stanley Hall. (American Autobiography Ser.). 38p. 1995. reprint ed. lib. bdg. 69.00 (*0-7812-8543-7*) Rprt Serv.

Letters to Judy: What Your Kids Wish They Could Tell You. Judy Blume. 320p. 1987. mass mkt. 4.50 (*0-671-62696-5*) PB.

Letters to Judy: What Your Kids Wish They Could Tell You. Judy Blume. (J). 1987. 9.60 (*0-606-03246-0*, Pub. by Turtleback) Demco.

Letters to Julia. Holmes. LC 96-34804. (Illus.). 320p. (YA). (gr. 7-12). 1999. pap. 5.95 (*0-06-447215-9*) HarpC Child Bks.

Letters to Karen: On Keeping Love in Marriage. Charlie W. Shedd. 1990. mass mkt. 5.95 (*0-687-21565-X*) Abingdon.

Letters to Karen: On Keeping Love in Marriage. Charlie W. Shedd. 160p. 1976. mass mkt. 4.99 (*0-380-00207-8*, Avon Bks) Morrow Avon.

Letters to Karl & Luise Kautsky, 1896-1918. Rosa Luxemburg. 1974. 250.00 (*0-87968-190-X*) Gordon Pr.

Letters to Ken. Harvey Sarner. 60p. 1997. 25.00 (*1-888521-10-4*) Brunswick Pr.

Letters to Kennedy. John Kenneth Galbraith. Ed. by James Goodman. LC 97-38839. 192p. 1999. text 25.95 (*0-674-52837-9*) HUP.

Letters to King James the Sixth. James First King of England. Ed. by Alexander Macdonald. LC 70-170840. (Maitland Club, Glasgow. Publications: No. 35). reprint ed. 32.50 (*0-404-53005-2*) AMS Pr.

Letters to Lalage: The Letters of Charles Williams to Lois Lang-Sims. Lois Lang-Sims. LC 89-33241. 97p. 1990. pap. 16.50 (*0-87338-398-2*) Kent St U Pr.

Letters to Laura: A Confederate Surgeon's Impressions of Four Years of War. Ed. by Sadye T. Wilson et al. LC 96-43689. (Illus.). 304p. (C). 1997. 28.00 (*0-9616526-3-2*) Tunstede.

Letters to Lisa: Conversations with a Christian Teacher. John Van Dyk. (Illus.). 197p. (Orig.). 1997. pap. 11.95 (*0-932914-37-3*) Dordt Coll Pr.

***Letters to Lithopolis from O. Henry to Mabel Wagnalls.** O. Henry & Mabel Wagnalls. LC 99-48763. 1999. write for info. (*1-57168-355-0*, Eakin Pr) Sunbelt Media.

Letters to Lorenzo. Amanda Prantera. 258p. 1999. 24.95 (*1-58234-018-8*) Bloomsbury Pubg.

Letters to Lou: A Midshipman's Odyssey. Donald F. Hogan. Ed. by Richard Boles. LC 98-96552. 238p. 1998. pap. 25.00 (*0-9666798-0-6*) Lines & Designs.

Letters to Louise: The Answers Are Within You. Louise L. Hay. LC 97-39212. xi, 295p. 1999. pap. 12.95 (*1-56170-468-7*, 119) Hay House.

Letters to Malcolm: Chiefly on Prayer. C. S. Lewis. LC 64-11536. 136p. 1973. reprint ed. pap. 9.00 (*0-15-650880-X*, Harvest Bks) Harcourt.

Letters to Marc about Jesus. Henri J. M. Nouwen. 96p. 1988. 16.00 (*0-06-066315-4*, Pub. by Harper SF) HarpC.

Letters to Marc About Jesus: Living a Spiritual Life in a Material World. Henri J. M. Nouwen. 96p. 1998. pap. 10.00 (*0-06-066367-7*, Pub. by Harper SF) HarpC.

Letters to Maria Regina see Cartas a Maria Regina: Letters to Maria Regina

Letters to May, 1917-1948. Mabel E. Sarton. Ed. by Constance Hunting. (Illus.). 120p. (Orig.). 1986. pap. 16.95 (*0-913006-35-1*) Puckerbrush.

Letters to Mead: A Mother's Extraordinary Gift to Her Son. 1995. 14.95 (*1-57071-087-2*) Login Pubs Consort.

Letters to Molly: John Millington Synge to Maire O'Neill. Ed. by Ann Saddlemyer. 374p. 1984. pap. text 7.95 (*0-674-52833-6*) HUP.

Letters to Molly: John Millington Synge to Maire O'Neill, 1906-1909. John Millington Synge. Ed. by Ann Saddlemyer. LC 75-143231. (Illus.). 374p. 1971. 37.50 (*0-674-52834-4*) Belknap Pr.

Letters to Mother: Expressions of Love from Famous People. Ed. by Elizabeth Belew. LC 96-203667. (Illus.). 96p. 1996. boxed set 15.95 (*1-889116-00-9*) Penbrooke Pub.

Letters to Mr. Urban of the Gentleman's Magazine, 1751-1811. Arthur Sherbo. LC 97-40796. (Studies in British History: Vol. 44). 260p. 1997. 89.95 (*0-7734-8427-2*) E Mellen.

Letters to Mrs. Z. Kazimierz Brandys. Tr. by Morris Edelson. LC 87-70598. 176p. 1987. pap. 15.00 (*0-913204-19-6*) December Pr.

Letters to Mrs. Z. Kazimierz Brandys. Tr. by Morris Edelson. 1986. pap. 5.00 (*0-317-17750-8*) Quixote.

Letters to My Angel. Gay Bark. 85p. 1999. pap. 7.99 (*1-57532-183-1*) Press-Tige Pub.

Letters to My Brother. Joseph Katz. LC 97-77318. 176p. 1998. 26.95 (*0-913559-47-4*) Birch Brook Pr.

Letters to My Brother. Joseph Katz. LC 97-77318. (Illus.). 172p. 1998. pap. 16.95 (*0-913559-46-6*) Birch Brook Pr.

Letters to My Brother Priests. rev. ed. John Paul, II, pseud. 288p. 2000. pap. 9.95 (*0-933932-61-8*) Scepter Pubs.

Letters to My Brothers & Sisters: Living by the Rule of St. Benedict. Denis Huerre. Tr. by Sylvester Houedard. (FRE.). 152p. (Orig.). 1994. pap. 11.95 (*0-8146-2241-0*) Liturgical Pr.

***Letters to My Children: A Father Passes on His Values.** Daniel Taylor. LC 99-48729. 174p. 2000. pap. 11.99 (*0-8308-2238-0*) InterVarsity.

Letters to My Daughter: A Father Writes about Torah & the Jewish Woman. Walter Orenstein. LC 94-45801. 280p. 1995. 30.00 (*1-56821-387-5*) Aronson.

Letters to My Daughters. Judith Minty. 24p. (Orig.). 1981. pap. 5.00 (*0-932412-03-3*) Mayapple Pr.

Letters to My Friends: On Social & Personal Crisis in Today's World. Silo. Tr. by Paul Tooby from SPA. LC 94-20708. 160p. (Orig.). 1994. pap. 8.95 (*1-878977-23-7*) Latitude Pr.

Letters to My Government: Dear, Dear Government . . . Not Famous. (Illus.). 165p. (Orig.). 1998. lib. bdg. 12.95 (*0-9662733-0-3*) Goldy Pub.

***Letters to My Grandchildren.** George Friedman. LC 99-93936. 1999. 14.95 (*0-533-13197-9*) Vantage.

Letters to My Grandchildren. Charlie W. Shedd. LC 98-25027. 1998. pap. text 15.95 (*0-8027-2734-4*) Walker & Co.

Letters to My Husband. Fern F. Brooks. LC 93-81264. (Illus.). 250p. 1993. pap. 14.95 (*0-9638683-0-6*) Hall-Sloane.

Letters to My Mother: A Daughter's Journey Through Grief & Recovery. rev. ed. Betty J. Holt. Ed. by Human Services Press. 40p. reprint ed. pap. 5.95 (*0-9623335-0-6*) HSP IL.

Letters to My Parents. Brassai. 1998. pap. 16.00 (*0-226-07147-2*) U Ch Pr.

Letters to My Patients: A Guide to Healthy & Happy Living. Harlan O. Wright. 256p. 1995. 18.95 (*0-9648404-0-5*) Shallowater.

L

An Asterisk (*) at the beginning of an entry indicates that the title is appearing for the first time.

L

Letters to My Son: A Father's Wisdom on Manhood, Life & Love. 2nd rev. ed. Kent Nerburn. LC 98-51499. 240p. 1999. pap. 12.95 (*1-57731-031-4*, Pub. by New Wrld Lib) Publishers Group.

***Letters to My Teenage Friends.** Gary Hutchison. 55p. 1999. pap. 12.50 (*1-885631-39-1*, 39-1, Family Of Man Pr) G F Hutchison.

Letters to My Wife. Finley McDiarmid. LC 97-28200. 1997. 19.95 (*0-87770-472-4*); pap. 14.95 (*0-87770-609-3*) Ye Galleon.

Letters to My Wife: A Civil War Diary from the Western Front. Sharon L. Kraynek. 110p. 1995. per. 9.75 (*1-55856-199-4*, 434) Closson Pr.

Letters to Myself on Dying: A Journal of Hope, Pain & Courage. MIRTH VOS. LC 99-16359. 160p. 1999. 12.99 (*0-8010-1189-2*) Baker Bks.

***Letters to Myself on Dying: A Journal of Hope, Pain & Courage.** MIRTH VOS. LC 99-16359. 1999. 12.99 (*1-56212-456-0*) CRC Pubns.

Letters to New Disciples: Practical Advice for Those Who Have Decided to Follow Jesus. Thomas A. Jones. 130p. 1998. pap. 8.99 (*1-57782-048-7*) Discipleship.

Letters to Obscure Men. Gerald Burns. LC 75-40540. (Lucky Heart Bk.). 68p. 1975. reprint ed. pap. 30.00 (*0-7837-9097-X*, 204984700003) Bks Demand.

Letters to Olga: June 1979 to September 1982. Vaclav Havel. 88p. 1995. pap. 16.95 (*0-8050-0973-6*, Owl) H Holt & Co.

Letters to Oma: A Young German Girl's Account of Her First Year in Texas, 1847. Marjorie A. Gurasich. LC 88-38747. (Chaparral Bks.). (Illus.). 162p. (J). (gr. 4-8). 1989. pap. 12.95 (*0-87565-037-6*) Tex Christian.

Letters to Our Daughters: Mothers' Words of Love. Molly Davis. LC 99-18779. (Illus.). 144p. 1999. 18.00 (*0-7868-6528-8*, Pub. by Disney Pr) Time Warner.

Letters To Parents. Bye. (C). 1996. 58.00 (*0-13-459488-6*, Macmillan Coll) P-H.

***Letters to Parents - ESL.** Diane Pinkley. (Illus.). 1999. pap. 11.95 (*0-673-59232-4*, GoodYrBooks) Addson-Wesley Educ.

***Letters to Parents in Math: 30 Ready-To-Use Letters in English & Spanish.** Lisa C. Kircher. 1999. pap. text 11.95 (*0-673-58660-X*) Addson-Wesley Educ.

Letters to Parents in Math Grades. Janet K. Razionale & Lisa C. Kircher. (Illus.). 128p. 1997. 11.95 (*0-673-36370-8*, 757192Q, GoodYrBooks) Addson-Wesley Educ.

Letters to Parents in Reading. Anthony Fredericks & Elaine Le Blanc. LC 97-222266. (ENG & SPA., Illus.). 144p. 1997. 11.95 (*0-673-36392-9*, GoodYrBooks) Addson-Wesley Educ.

Letters to Parents in Science. Anthony D. Fredericks. (Illus.). 152p. (Orig.). (J). (gr. 3-6). 1993. pap. 9.95 (*0-673-36079-2*, GoodYrBooks) Addson-Wesley Educ.

Letters to Parents of Preschool Children. Mary Demovek. 39p. 1989. 3.00 (*1-55833-012-7*) Natl Cath Educ.

Letters to Paul Amann, 1915-1952. Thomas Mann. Ed. by Herbert Wegener. Tr. by Richard Winston & Clara Winston. LC 60-7258. 196p. reprint ed. pap. 60.80 (*0-608-30825-0*, 200195500011) Bks Demand.

Letters to Paul's Delegates: I Timothy, 2 Timothy, Titus. Luke T. Johnson. Ed. by Howard C. Kee & J. Andrew Overman. LC 96-42303. (New Testament in Context Ser.). 256p. (Orig.). 1996. pap. 20.00 (*1-56338-144-3*) TPI PA.

***Letters to Penthouse XI.** Penthouse Magazine Editors. 2000. mass mkt. 7.99 (*0-446-60850-5*) Warner Bks.

Letters to Penthouse III. Penthouse Magazine Editors. 240p. (Orig.). 1992. mass mkt. 7.50 (*0-446-36296-4*, Pub. by Warner Bks) Little.

Letters to Penthouse IV. Penthouse Magazine Editors. 224p. (Orig.). 1994. mass mkt. 7.99 (*0-446-60056-3*, Pub. by Warner Bks) Little.

Letters to Penthouse IX. Penthouse Magazine Editors. 352p. 1999. mass mkt. 7.50 (*0-446-60640-5*, Pub. by Warner Bks) Little.

***Letters to Penthouse X.** Penthouse Magazine Editors. 352p. 2000. mass mkt. 7.99 (*0-446-60641-3*) Warner Bks.

Letters to Penthouse V. Penthouse Magazine Editors. 224p. (Orig.). 1995. mass mkt. 7.50 (*0-446-60195-0*, Pub. by Warner Bks) Little.

Letters to Penthouse VIII. Penthouse Magazine Editors. 352p. (Orig.). 1998. mass mkt. 7.50 (*0-446-60419-4*, Pub. by Warner Bks) Little.

Letters to Phil, Memories of a New York Boyhood, 1848-1856. Gene Schermerhorn. (Illus.). 96p. 1982. 10.95 (*0-9608788-0-7*) NY Bound.

Letters to Philip. Charlie W. Shedd. (Orig.). 1986. mass mkt. 5.99 (*0-515-09078-6*, Jove) Berkley Pub.

Letters to Rebecca. William B. Moore, Jr. (Illus.). 378p. (Orig.). 1995. pap. 27.50 (*0-7884-0304-4*) Heritage Bk.

Letters to Reggie Turner. Max Beerbohm. Ed. by Rupert Hart-Davis. LC 79-8052. reprint ed. 39.50 (*0-404-18362-X*) AMS Pr.

Letters to Rollins. R. K. Overton. (Illus.). 96p. (Orig.). 1994. pap. 10.00 (*1-880985-20-9*) Two Thirteen Sixty-one.

Letters to Sarah. Katharine O. Elsom. LC 89-11554. (Illus.). 128p. 1989. 15.95 (*0-915010-35-6*) Sutter House.

Letters to Sarah - from God: A Gift of Love. unabridged ed. Dave Grams. v, 68p. 1998. spiral bd. 9.50 (*0-9663002-1-1*) Court Jester.

Letters to Sarah - From God Vol. II: Growing in the Lord. David L. Grams. ii, 110p. (YA). (gr. 7 up). 1998. spiral bd. 9.50 (*0-9663002-2-X*) Court Jester.

Letters to Sarah - From God Vol. III: Hearing His Call. David L. Grams. ii, 110p. (YA). (gr. 7 up). 1999. 9.50 (*0-9663002-3-8*) Court Jester.

Letters to Sartre. Simone de Beauvoir. Ed. & Tr. by Quintin Hoare from FRE. 544p. (C). 1993. reprint ed. pap. 12.45 (*1-55970-212-5*, Pub. by Arcade Pub Inc) Time Warner.

Letters to Several Persons of Honour. John Donne. (Anglistica & Americana Ser.: No. 148). 318p. 1974. reprint ed. 63.70 (*3-487-04484-6*) G Olms Pubs.

Letters to Several Persons of Honour. John Donne. LC 77-10078. 352p. 1977. reprint ed. lib. bdg. 75.00 (*0-8201-1296-8*) Schol Facsimiles.

Letters to Stephen: A Father's Journey of Grief & Recovery. 2nd ed. James Taylor. 224p. 1996. pap. 14.50 (*1-55145-054-2*) NStone Publ.

Letters to Strongheart. J. Boone. 1980. pap. 10.00 (*0-933062-19-2*) R H Sommer.

Letters to Students. 4th ed. Max Heindel. Ed. by Rosicrucian Fellowship Staff. 237p. 1975. reprint ed. pap. text 12.50 (*0-911274-09-X*) Rosicrucian.

Letters to Teens: Hopeful Words from an Archbishop. Rembert G. Weakland. 48p. (YA). (gr. 8-12). 1988. pap. 3.95 (*0-89243-290-X*) Liguori Pubns.

Letters to Teresa. Samuel Fisk. 91p. 1973. pap. 2.95 (*0-914012-14-2*) Sword of Lord.

Letters to the Argyll Family from Elizabeth Queen of England, Mary Queen of Scots, & Others. Ed. by Alexander Macdonald. LC 77-12765. (Maitland Club, Glasgow. Publications: No. 50). reprint ed. 37.50 (*0-404-53031-1*) AMS Pr.

Letters to the Brain. John B. Keane. 160p. (Orig.). 1993. pap. 11.95 (*0-86322-157-2*, Pub. by Brandon Bk Pubs) Irish Bks Media.

Letters to the Children. John T. Ferrier. (Illus.). 238p. 1949. text 11.00 (*0-900235-48-9*) Order Of The Cross.

Letters to the Churches. M. L. Andreasen. LC 96-60002. 96p. 1996. reprint ed. per. 7.95 (*1-57258-074-7*) Teach Servs.

Letters to the Corinthians see Daily Study Bible for the New Testament

Letters to the Dead. Simon Perchik. 64p. 1994. pap. 8.95 (*1-879934-08-6*) St Andrews Pr.

Letters to the Editor. James P. Massey. Ed. by Carole J. Massey-Reyner & David B. Reyner. LC 96-94329. (Collective Works of James P. Massey Ser.: Vol. II). 125p. (Orig.). 1996. pap. 14.95 (*0-9650514-1-2*) Massey-Reyner.

Letters to the Editor. Gerard Stropnicky. LC 98-10198. (Illus.). 256p. 1998. mass mkt. 14.00 (*0-684-84853-8*, Touchstone) S&S Trade Pap.

Letters to the Galatians & Ephesians see Daily Study Bible for the New Testament

Letters to the Hinterland. Roy McFadden. (C). 1986. pap. 15.00 (*0-948268-15-8*, Pub. by Dedalus) St Mut.

Letters to the Home Circle: The North Carolina Service of Pvt. Henry A. Clapp, 1862-1863. Ed. by John R. Barden. LC 99-229793. (Illus.). 252p. 1999. pap. 28.00 (*0-86526-270-5*) NC Archives.

Letters to the Honorable William Prescott, LL.D., on the Free Schools of New England. James G. Carter. LC 77-89161. (American Education: Its Men, Institutions, & Ideas. Series 1). 1975. reprint ed. 16.95 (*0-405-01400-7*) Ayer.

Letters to the Martyrs. Helen Homan. LC 79-148220. (Biography Index Reprint Ser.). 1977. 23.95 (*0-8369-8067-0*) Ayer.

Letters to the People on Health & Happiness. Catharine E. Beecher. LC 70-180554. (Medicine & Society in America Ser.). (Illus.). 228p. 1972. reprint ed. 18.95 (*0-405-03934-4*) Ayer.

Letters to the People on Health & Happiness. Catherine E. Beecher. (Works of Catherine E. Beecher). vi, 222p. reprint ed. lib. bdg. 49.00 (*0-932051-03-0*) Rprt Serv.

Letters to the Philippians, Colossians & Thessalonians see Daily Study Bible for the New Testament

Letters to the Precious Group. Lucy D. Blount. (Illus.). 176p. 1990. 19.95 (*0-9630017-X*) Light-Bearer.

Letters to the Precious Group. Lucy D. Blount. LC 91-90462. (Illus.). 176p. 1991. 13.98 (*0-9630017-0-1*) Light-Bearer.

Letters to the Quick - Letters to the Dead. unabridged ed. Shirley Cochrane. LC 98-17252. 152p. 1998. pap. 12.00 (*0-930095-33-2*) Signal Bks.

Letters to the Right Rev. John Hughes, Roman Catholic Bishop of New York. Nicholas Murray. Ed. by Gerald N. Grob. LC 76-46091. (Anti-Movements in America Ser.). 1977. reprint ed. 31.95 (*0-405-09964-9*) Ayer.

Letters to the School. Oscar Ichazo. LC 88-71178. 107p. 1988. pap. 12.00 (*0-916554-17-1*) Arica Inst Pr.

Letters to the Seven Churches. rev. ed. W. M. Ramsay. Ed. by Mark W. Wilson. LC 94-33869. (Illus.). 320p. 1994. pap. 19.95 (*1-56563-059-9*) Hendrickson MA.

Letters to the Thessalonians. Margaret Fromer & Sharrel Keyes. LC 75-33441. (Fisherman Bible Studyguide Ser.). 47p. 1975. pap. 4.99 (*0-87788-489-7*, H Shaw Pubs) Waterbrook Pr.

***Letters to the Thessalonians.** Abraham J. Malherbe. LC 00-21363. (Anchor Bible Ser.). 2000. 50.00 (*0-385-18460-3*) Doubleday.

Letters to the Thessalonians. rev. ed. William McDonald. 1982. pap. 6.00 (*0-937396-43-5*) Walterick Pubs.

Letters to the Thessalonians - Chinese Edition. Margaret Fromer & Sharrel Keyes. Tr. by Jen-Chi Chang. (CHI.). 47p. 1995. pap. 5.00 (*1-56582-008-8*) Christ Renew Min.

Letters to the Third Millennium: An Experiment in East-West Communication. Clinton C. Gardner. LC 81-12689. 272p. 1981. 10.00 (*0-912148-11-X*); pap. 5.00 (*0-912148-12-8*) Argo Bks.

Letters to the Thirsty: For Vision... For Life... For Rest. Edward P. Miller. 208p. 1998. 14.95 (*1-57856-047-0*) Waterbrook Pr.

Letters to the Wizard. 2nd large type ed. K. Vernon Davis. 280p. (YA). 1998. pap. 12.50 (*1-878431-12-9*) Artist Profile Pub.

Letters to Thomas & Adele Seltzer. D. H. Lawrence. Ed. by Gerald M. Lacy. LC 76-10782. (Illus.). 283p. (Orig.). 1976. pap. 9.00 (*0-87685-224-X*) Black Sparrow.

Letters to Three Friends. William H. White. (BCL1-PR English Literature Ser.). 404p. 1992. reprint ed. lib. bdg. 99.00 (*0-7812-7576-8*) Rprt Serv.

Letters to Timothy: Discipleship in Action. Margaret Fromer & Sharrel Keyes. LC 74-19763. (Fisherman Bible Studyguide Ser.). 80p. 1974. pap. 4.99 (*0-87788-490-0*, H Shaw Pubs) Waterbrook Pr.

Letters to Timothy, Titus & Philemon see Daily Study Bible for the New Testament

Letters to Tomasito: Poems. Thomas McGrath. Ed. by James Perlman. 1977. pap. 2.00 (*0-930100-01-8*) Holy Cow.

Letters to Twenty-Two Astrologers. Mae R. Wilson-Ludlam. 1989. pap. 25.95 (*0-86690-299-6*, 3091-014) Am Fed Astrologers.

Letters to Uncle Mike. Michael Burgess. 172p. 1998. pap. 10.95 (*0-9657638-0-3*) Saddle Mtn.

***Letters to Uncle Mike.** 2nd ed. Michael Burgess. 172p. 2000. pap. 14.00 (*0-9657638-5-4*) Saddle Mtn.

Letters to Vanessa: On Opening to Life & Meaning in an Enchanted World. Jeremy W. Hayward. LC 97-2051. 1997. pap. 15.00 (*1-57062-077-6*, Pub. by Shambhala Pubns) Random.

Letters to Various Persons. Henry David Thoreau. (American Biography Ser.). 229p. 1991. reprint ed. lib. bdg. 69.00 (*0-7812-8388-4*) Rprt Serv.

Letters to Vermont Vol. 1: From Her Civil War Soldier Correspondents to the Home Press. Ed. by Donald Wickman. LC 98-12293. (Illus.). 256p. 1998. 30.00 (*1-884592-10-4*); pap. 19.95 (*1-884592-11-2*) Images from the Past.

Letters to Vermont Vol. 2: From the Civil War Soldier Correspondents to the Home Press. Ed. by Donald Wickman. LC 98-12293. (Illus.). 272p. 1998. 30.00 (*1-884592-16-3*); pap. 19.95 (*1-884592-17-1*) Images from the Past.

Letters to Vernon Watkins. Dylan Thomas. LC 82-15823. (Illus.). 145p. 1982. reprint ed. lib. bdg. 49.50 (*0-313-23746-8*, THLV, Greenwood Pr) Greenwood.

Letters to Virgins. Gwen P. Aseltine. LC 79-65034. 1979. pap. 3.95 (*0-917182-13-8*) Triumph Pub.

Letters to War Criminals: The War in the Gulf. Garry De Young. 1992. 27.50 (*0-936128-24-0*) De Young Pr.

Letters to William Allingham. Ed. by Helen Allingham & E. Baumer Williams. LC 70-148739. reprint ed. 42.50 (*0-404-00343-5*) AMS Pr.

Letters to William Blackwood & David S. Meldrum. Joseph Conrad. LC 58-12588. 247p. reprint ed. pap. 76.60 (*0-608-15091-6*, 202619300048) Bks Demand.

Letters to X. Harold J. Massingham. LC 67-26763. (Essay Index Reprint Ser.). 1977. 19.95 (*0-8369-0691-8*) Ayer.

Letters to Young Men. William B. Sprague. 1992. 17.99 (*0-87377-945-2*) GAM Pubns.

Letters via Chinook: Life in Montana in the 20s & 30s. J. Philip Ambuel & Louise Ambuel. (Illus.). xiv, 219p. (Orig.). 1996. pap. 10.00 (*0-9652972-0-9*) J & L Ambuel.

***Letters Workbook.** Landoll. (Beginners Bible Ser.). 2000. pap. text 14.95 (*1-56189-620-9*) Amer Educ Pub.

Letters Written by John Chamberlain During the Reign of Queen Elizabeth. John Chamberlain. Ed. by Sarah Williams. (Camden Society, London. Publications, First Ser.: No. 79). reprint ed. 45.00 (*0-404-50179-6*) AMS Pr.

Letters Written by Walt Whitman to His Mother, 1866-1872. Walt Whitman. (American Biography Ser.). 71p. 1991. reprint ed. lib. bdg. 59.00 (*0-7812-8416-3*) Rprt Serv.

Letters Written During a Residence in Sweden, Norway, & Denmark. Mary Wollstonecraft Shelley. Ed. by Carol H. Poston. LC 75-38056. (Illus.). 202p. 1976. text 25.00 (*0-8032-0862-6*); pap. text 6.95 (*0-8032-5832-1*, Bison Books) U of Nebr Pr.

Letters Written During the President's Tour 'Down East' Seba Smith. LC 78-76929. (American Fiction Reprint Ser.). 1977. 13.95 (*0-8369-7008-X*) Ayer.

***Letters Written in Black & White.** David Anderson & Brent Zuercher. 2001. pap. 12.99 (*0-8010-6343-4*) Baker Bks.

Letters Written in the Interior of Cuba. Abiel Abbot. LC 75-37299. (Black Heritage Library Collection). 1977. reprint ed. 22.95 (*0-8369-8936-8*) Ayer.

Letters You Write. Richard H. Turner. (Follet Success Skills Ser.). 48p. 1988. pap. text 5.00 (*0-8428-2263-1*) Cambridge Bk.

Lettershop Calligraphy Project Kit. Joanne Fink & Cheryl O. Adams. (Illus.). 116p. 1994. text 29.99 (*0-9631532-2-6*); pap. text 9.99 (*0-9631532-1-8*) Speedball Art.

Letterwork: Creative Letterforms in Graphic Design. Brody Neuenschwander. (Illus.). 160p. (C). 1993. pap. 29.95 (*0-7148-2909-9*, Pub. by Phaidon Press) Phaidon Pr.

Lettie Lane Paper Doll. Sheila Young. (J). 1981. pap. 4.95 (*0-486-24089-4*) Dover.

Lettin' It All Hang Out: An Autobiography. RuPaul. (Illus.). 240p. (J). 1995. 19.45 (*0-7868-6156-8*, Pub. by Hyperion) Time Warner.

Lettin' It All Hang Out: An Autobiography. RuPaul. Ed. by David Cashion. LC 94-43503. (Illus.). 240p. (J). 1996. reprint ed. pap. 10.45 (*0-7868-8165-8*, Pub. by Hyperion) Time Warner.

Letting Girls Learn: Promising Approaches in Primary & Secondary Education. Barbara K. Herz et al. (Discussion Paper Ser.: No. 133). 112p. 1991. pap. 22.00 (*0-8213-1937-X*, 11937) World Bank.

Letting Girls Learn: Promising Approaches in Primary & Secondary Edution. Barbara Kerz et al. (Discussion Papers: No. 133F). (FRE.). 124p. 1993. pap. 22.00 (*0-8213-2373-3*, 12373) World Bank.

Letting Go. 1999. 414.00 (*0-671-71839-8*) S&S Trade.

Letting Go. Laurie Adams. 1980. 10.95 (*0-02-500270-8*) Macmillan.

Letting Go. Ann O'Leary. LC 97-10006. 256p. (Orig.). 1997. pap. 11.95 (*1-56280-183-X*) Naiad Pr.

Letting Go. Veronica Ray. (A Moment to Reflect Ser.). pap. 2.50 (*0-89486-569-2*) Hazelden.

Letting Go. Philip Roth. LC 97-6675. 1997. pap. 15.00 (*0-679-76417-8*) Vin Bks.

Letting Go. Lauraine Snelling. LC 99-6450. (High Hurdles Ser.: No. 8). 160p. (YA). (gr. 6-9). 1999. pap. text 5.99 (*0-7642-2036-5*) Bethany Hse.

Letting Go. Zev Wanderer & Tracy Cabot. 320p. 1987. reprint ed. mass mkt. 6.50 (*0-440-14730-1*) Dell.

Letting Go: A Parent's Guide to Understanding the College Years. 3rd rev. ed. Karen L. Coburn. LC 97-5901. 384p. 1997. pap. 13.00 (*0-06-095244-X*, Perennial) HarperTrade.

Letting Go: A Practical Theory of Relationship Disengagement & Re-engagement. Dudley D. Cahn, Jr. LC 86-14549. (SUNY Series, Human Communication Processes). 243p. (C). 1987. text 64.50 (*0-88706-452-3*); pap. text 21.95 (*0-88706-454-X*) State U NY Pr.

Letting Go: Cost-Based Productivity Soared 106 Percent When Management Loosened the Reins at the GE Business Information Center. James R. Burnside. LC 92-73013. (Illus.). 132p. (Orig.). 1992. pap. 12.95 (*0-9624923-1-0*) High Peaks Pr.

Letting Go: Death, Dying, & the Law. Melvin I. Urofsky. LC 93-31027. 224p. 1994. reprint ed. pap. 14.95 (*0-8061-2635-3*) U of Okla Pr.

Letting Go: From the Writings of the Rev. Dr. Edmund D. Campbell, Jr. Edmund D. Campbell, Jr. 1998. pap. 1.95 (*0-88028-201-0*, 1488) Forward Movement.

Letting Go: Morrie's Reflections on Living While Dying. Morrie Schwartz. 144p. 1997. pap. 9.95 (*0-385-31879-0*) Doubleday.

Letting Go: Reflections & Prayers for Midlife. Judy Esway. LC 90-70622. 88p. (Orig.). 1990. pap. 7.95 (*0-89622-434-1*) Twenty-Third.

Letting Go: The Grief Experience. unabridged ed. Francis P. Conner. 126p. 1996. pap. text 16.00 (*0-9656373-0-1*) AUM Prods.

Letting Go - Deregulating the Process of Deregulation: Temptation of the Kleptocrats & the Political Economy of Regulatory Disingenuousness. Alfred E. Kahn. (Public Utilities Papers). 146p. 1998. pap. 19.95 (*0-87744-182-0*) MSU Inst Pub.

***Letting Go & Learning to Live.** Treana Holsey. LC 98-89510. 120p. 1998. pap. 4.99 (*1-893181-09-X*) Le Gesse Stevens.

Letting Go of Anger: The Ten Most Common Anger Styles & What to Do about Them. Ronald T. Potter-Efron & Patricia S. Potter-Efron. LC 94-73923. 168p. 1995. pap. 12.95 (*1-57224-001-6*) New Harbinger.

Letting Go Of Clutter. Schechter. 2000. 16.95 (*0-07-135122-1*) McGraw.

***Letting Go of Debt: Meditations on Growing Richer One Day at a Time.** Karen Casanova. 372p. 2000. pap. 12.00 (*1-56838-367-3*) Hazelden.

Letting Go of Loneliness: A Positive Approach. Gina Levete. 1993. pap. 12.95 (*1-85230-398-0*, Pub. by Element MA) Penguin Putnam.

Letting Go of Mother: Overcoming Dependence & Finding Authentic Intimacy as an Adult. James M. McMahon. LC 96-1338. 128p. 1996. pap. 8.95 (*0-8091-3662-7*) Paulist Pr.

Letting Go of Shame see Verguenza

Letting Go of Shame: Understanding How Shame Affects Your Life. Ronald Potter-Efron & Patrica Potter-Efron. 192p. (Orig.). pap. 12.00 (*0-89486-635-4*) Hazelden.

Letting Go of Stuff. Darren Johnson. (Change-N-U Ser.). 1999. 14.95 (*0-9652307-2-4*, Change-N-U Lrning) InsideOut Learning.

Letting Go of Suffering. Karuna Poole. (Orig.). 1994. pap. 12.95 (*0-9643629-0-2*) K Poole.

Letting Go with Love: The Grieving Process. Nancy O'Connor. 1994. mass mkt. 4.95 (*0-553-85040-7*) Bantam.

Letting Go with Love: The Grieving Process. Nancy D. O'Connor. LC 84-61538. 186p. (C). 1985. 24.95 (*0-9613714-1-2*); pap. 14.95 (*0-9613714-0-4*) La Mariposa.

Letting Go with Love: The Grieving Process. Nancy O'Connor & Nancy D. O'Connor. LC 84-61538. 186p. (C). 1985. 15.95 incl. audio (*0-9613714-3-9*) La Mariposa.

Letting God: Christian Meditations for Recovering Persons. A. Philip Parham. LC 86-45835. (Illus.). 384p. 1987. pap. 14.00 (*0-06-250669-2*, Pub. by Harper SF) HarpC.

Letting God Bless You: The Beatitudes for Today. John Killinger. LC 92-11245. 144p. (Orig.). 1992. pap. 7.95 (*0-687-21569-2*) Abingdon.

Letting God Create Your Day Vol. 1, No. 1: Scripts from the International Broadcast Creation Moments. Paul A. Bartz. 84p. (Orig.). (YA). 1989. pap. write for info. (*0-318-65237-4*) Colorsong Prodns.

Letting God Free Us. Carlo M. Martini. 128p. 1993. 26.00 (*0-85439-452-4*, Pub. by St Paul Pubns) St Mut.

Letting God Free Us: Meditations on Ignatian Spiritual Exercises. Carlo M. Martini. Tr. by Richard Arnandez from ITA. LC 93-15187. 128p. (Orig.). 1993. pap. 9.95 (*1-56548-053-8*) New City.

Letting in the Night. Joan Lindau. LC 89-1331. 180p. (Orig.). 1989. pap. 8.95 (*0-932379-59-1*); lib. bdg. 18.95 (*0-932379-60-5*) Firebrand Bks.

Letting Loose. Sue Civil-Brown. 384p. 1998. mass mkt. 5.99 (*0-380-72775-7*, Avon Bks) Morrow Avon.

Letting Loose. Christopher T. Leland. LC 96-16396. 384p. 1996. 23.95 (*0-944072-69-0*) Zoland Bks.

Letting Loose the Hounds. Brady Udall. 1998. per. 12.00 (*0-671-01702-0*, PB Trade Paper) PB.

An Asterisk (*) at the beginning of an entry indicates that the title is appearing for the first time.

Letting Loose the Hounds: Stories. Brady Udall. LC 96-18642. 192p. 1997. 22.00 (*0-393-04033-X*) Norton.

Letting off Steam: The Story of Geothermal Energy. Linda Jacobs. (Earth Watch Bks.). (Illus.). 48p. (J). (gr. 1-4). 1989. lib. bdg. 19.95 (*0-87614-300-1*, Carolrhoda) Lerner Pub.

Letting Rip: Fast Bowling from Lillee to Wagar. Simon Wilde. (Illus.). 240p. 1995. pap. 15.95 (*0-85493-244-5*) Trafalgar.

Letting Swift River Go. Jane Yolen. (Illus.). 32p. (J). (gr. k-3). 1995. pap. 4.95 (*0-316-96860-9*) Little.

Letting Swift River Go. Jane Yolen. (J). 1992. 10.40 (*0-606-07783-9*) Turtleback.

***Letting the Heart Lead: The King Family Story.** Suzanne Barnett. 263p. 1999. 19.95 (*0-9630632-4-3*) Abbott-Sterling.

Letting the Lion Loose: C. H. Spurgeon & the Bible. Eric W. Hayden. 1984. mass mkt. 6.00 (*0-907927-05-X*) Pilgrim Pubns.

Letting the People Decide: The Dynamics of a Canadian Election. Richard Johnston et al. LC 91-68213. 288p. (C). 1992. 42.50 (*0-8047-2077-0*); pap. 15.95 (*0-8047-2078-9*) Stanford U Pr.

Lettische Sprache & Ihre Dialekte. Gaters. 1977. 76.15 (*90-279-3126-7*) Mouton.

Lettre a Francisque Michel, 1848-1870. Prosper Merimee & Pierre Trahard. (FRE.). 238p. 1930. pap. 79.95 (*0-7859-5385-X*) Fr & Eur.

Lettre a Laurence. Jacques De Bourbon Busset. (FRE.). 118p. 1989. pap. 10.95 (*0-7859-2110-9*, 2070381080) Fr & Eur.

Lettre a M. d'Alembert sur les Spectacles. Jean-Jacques Rousseau. (FRE.). 254p. 1967. pap. 10.95 (*0-7859-1420-X*, 2080701606) Fr & Eur.

Lettre a Mme la Comtesse. Chesnaye Des Bois. Ed. by Adams. 48p. Date not set. pap. text 19.95 (*0-85989-159-3*, Pub. by Univ Exeter Pr) Northwestern U Pr.

Lettre a Moi-Meme. Francoise Mallet-Joris. (FRE.). 304p. 1970. 6.95 (*0-8288-9839-1*, F110761) Fr & Eur.

Lettre a Mon Chien. Francois Nourissier. (FRE.). 1976. pap. 8.95 (*0-7859-4068-5*) Fr & Eur.

Lettre a Mon Pere Qui Aurait Eu Cent Ans. Alain Bosquet. (FRE.). 283p. 1990. pap. 11.95 (*0-7859-2154-0*, 2070383210) Fr & Eur.

Lettre au General Franco. Fernando Arrabal. (FRE.). 192p. 1984. pap. 16.95 (*0-7859-4708-6*, F83490) Fr & Eur.

Lettre aux Americains. Jean Cocteau. (FRE.). 102p. 1949. 14.95 (*0-8288-9127-3*) Fr & Eur.

Lettre aux Anglais: Essai. Georges Bernanos. pap. 12.95 (*0-685-37221-9*, F87770) Fr & Eur.

Lettre D'Affaires: Initiation. 2nd ed. P. Godaert. (FRE.). 160p. 1982. pap. 29.95 (*0-7859-5080-X*) Fr & Eur.

Lettre D'Affaires: Le Courrier Quotidien. 2nd ed. P. Godaert. (FRE.). 148p. 1981. pap. 29.95 (*0-7859-4938-0*) Fr & Eur.

Lettre des Iles Baladar. Jacques Prevert. (FRE.). pap. 3.40 (*0-685-37051-8*) Fr & Eur.

Lettre des Iles Baladar. Jacques Prevert. (FRE., Illus.). 93p. 1977. pap. 10.95 (*0-7859-1361-0*, 2070330257) Fr & Eur.

Lettre du Pretre Jean: Edition des Versions en Ancien Francais et en Ancien Occitan Textes et Commentaires. Ed. by Martin Gosman. (Mediaevalia Groningana Ser.: Vol. II).Tr. of Fasciculus II. (FRE.). xi, 637p. 1982. 74.00 (*90-6088-080-3*, Pub. by Boumas Boekhuis) Gen Publ ON.

Lettre d'un Patissier Anglios, et Autres Contributions a une Polemique Gastronom. Ed. by Mennell. 95p. Date not set. pap. text 19.95 (*0-85989-172-0*, Pub. by Univ Exeter Pr) Northwestern U Pr.

Lettre Ecarlate. Nathaniel Hawthorne. (FRE.). 306p. 1982. pap. 11.95 (*0-7859-2664-X*, 208070382X) Fr & Eur.

Lettre Ouverte a Harlem Desir see Nations Without Nationalism

Lettre Ouverte a un Jeune Homme sur la Conduite de la Vie. Andre Maurois. (Coll. Lettre Ouverte). pap. 9.95 (*0-685-36944-7*) Fr & Eur.

Lettre Ouverte Contre une Vaste Conspiration. Jules Romains, pseud. (FRE.). 176p. 1965. pap. 10.95 (*0-7859-5472-4*) Fr & Eur.

Lettres sur la Danse, et sur les Ballets. fac. ed. Jean-Georges Noverre. (Monuments of Music & Music Literature in Facsimile, II Ser.: Vol. 47). (Illus.). 1967. lib. bdg. 35.00 (*0-8450-2247-4*) Broude.

Lettre sur les Aveugles a l'Usage de ceux qui Voient. 2nd ed. Denis Diderot. (FRE.). 124p. 1973. 14.95 (*0-8288-9956-8*, F46880) Fr & Eur.

Lettres. Joachim Du Bellay & Pierre de Nolhac. (Illus.). 120p. 1974. 49.95 (*0-7859-5527-5*) Fr & Eur.

Lettres. Jean Giraudoux & Jacques Body. (FRE.). 290p. 1975. 45.00 (*0-7859-0100-0*, M3512) Fr & Eur.

Lettres. Voltaire. (FRE.). 96p. 1968. pap. 14.95 (*0-7859-5513-5*) Fr & Eur.

Lettres a Bibesco. Marcel Proust. (FRE.). 11.95 (*0-685-37066-6*) Fr & Eur.

Lettres a Brizeux. Alfred De Vigny. 5.95 (*0-686-55710-7*) Fr & Eur.

Lettres a Fanny Lagden. Prosper Merimee. 12.50 (*0-686-54756-X*) Fr & Eur.

Lettres a Jean Rousselot (1949-1954) Avec: Rousselot, Jean. Pierre Reverdy Romancier, ou quand le Poete Se Dedouble. Pierre Reverdy. Ed. by Jean Rousselot. 87p. 1973. 9.95 (*0-686-54722-5*) Fr & Eur.

Lettres a Julie Victoire Dauble (1824-1874) La Premiere Bacheliere de France et son Temps. Ed. by Raymonde A. Bulger. LC 91-3695. (Writing about Women: Feminist Literary Studies: Vol. 2). (FRE., Illus.). 329p. (C). 1992. text 55.95 (*0-8204-1621-5*) P Lang Pubng.

Lettres a la Presidente: Avec: Poesies Libertines. Theophile Gautier. (FRE., Illus.). 292p. 1970. 32.95 (*0-8288-9987-8*, F62980) Fr & Eur.

Lettres a Leontine Zanta. Pierre Teilhard De Chardin. pap. 10.50 (*0-685-36594-8*) Fr & Eur.

Lettres a Lou. Guillaume Apollinaire. (FRE.). 528p. 1990. pap. 28.95 (*0-7859-2942-8*, 2070178549) Fr & Eur.

Lettres a Madame la Marquise de Pompadour sur l'Opera. Gabriel B. De Mably. LC 76-43925. (Music & Theatre in France in the 17th & 18th Centuries Ser.). reprint ed. 39.50 (*0-404-60169-3*) AMS Pr.

Lettres a Milorad, 1955-1963. Jean Giono. (FRE.). 238p. 1987. 15.95 (*0-7859-1178-2*, 2246123127) Fr & Eur.

Lettres a Quelques-uns. Paul Valery. pap. 6.25 (*0-685-36617-0*) Fr & Eur.

Lettres a Regius et Remarques sur l'Explication de l'Esprit Humain. Rene Descartes. (FRE.). 216p. 1959. 20.95 (*0-8288-9575-9*, F36630) Fr & Eur.

Lettres a Reynaldo Hahn. Marcel Proust. (FRE.). pap. 6.50 (*0-685-37068-2*) Fr & Eur.

Lettres a Roger Blin see Oeuvres Completes

Lettres a Sa Fille. Sidonie-Gabrielle Colette. (FRE.). 1984. pap. 46.95 (*0-7859-3303-4*, 2721002643) Fr & Eur.

Lettres a Sa Marraine (1915-1918) Guillaume Apollinaire. pap. 8.95 (*0-685-37173-5*) Fr & Eur.

Lettres a Sa Mere. Antoine de Saint-Exupery. (Gallimard Ser.). (FRE.). pap. 27.95 (*2-07-022726-X*) Schoenhof.

Lettres a Sartre, 1940 a 1963, Tomo 2. Simone de Beauvoir. (Gallimard Ser.). (FRE.). 1990. pap. 35.95 (*2-07-071864-6*) Schoenhof.

Lettres a Sartre, 1940-1963, Vol. 2. Simone de Beauvoir. (FRE.). 448p. 1990. 49.95 (*0-8288-9674-7*, 2070718646) Fr & Eur.

Lettres a Sartre, 1930 a 1939, Tome 1. Simone de Beauvoir. (Gallimard Ser.). (FRE.). 1990. pap. 35.95 (*2-07-071829-8*) Schoenhof.

Lettres a Sartre, 1930-1939, Vol. 1. Simone de Beauvoir. (FRE.). 404p. 1990. 49.95 (*0-8288-9673-9*, 2070718298) Fr & Eur.

Lettres a Ses Pairs: Correspondances Inedite de Colette a Marcel Proust, Alfred Jarry, Paul Leautaud. Sidonie-Gabrielle Colette. (FRE.). 456p. 1973. 41.95 (*0-8288-9150-8*, M3330) Fr & Eur.

Lettres a son Frere Theo. Vincent Van Gogh. (Imaginaire Ser.). (FRE.). pap. 20.95 (*2-07-071448-9*) Schoenhof.

Lettres a Sophie Volland. Denis Diderot. (FRE.). 416p. 1984. pap. 16.95 (*0-7859-1993-7*, 2070375471) Fr & Eur.

Lettres a Sophie Volland. Denis Diderot. (Folio Ser.: No. 1547). (FRE.). 405p. 1984. pap. 14.95 (*2-07-037547-1*) Schoenhof.

Lettres a Theodore Hannon (1876-1886) J. K. Huysmans. Ed. by Pierre Cogny & Christian Berg. (FRE., Illus.). 295p. 1995. pap. 74.95 (*0-614-14015-3*) Intl Scholars.

Lettres a un Ami, 1. Jules Romains, pseud. (FRE.). 238p. 1964. pap. 4.95 (*0-686-55316-0*, 2080506137) Fr & Eur.

Lettres a un Ami, 2. Jules Romains, pseud. (FRE.). 238p. 1964. pap. 10.95 (*0-7859-1400-5*) Fr & Eur.

Lettres a un Ami: 1880-1886, avec le Fac-Simile d'Une Lettre Inedite a Stephane Mallarme. Jules Laforgue. LC 77-10274. 240p. reprint ed. 47.50 (*0-404-16326-2*) AMS Pr.

Lettres a un Ami Allemand. Albert Camus. (FRE.). 1945. pap. 10.95 (*0-8288-3666-3*, F90640) Fr & Eur.

Lettres a un Ami Allemand. Albert Camus. (FRE.). 1991. pap. 10.95 (*0-7859-2924-X*, 2070383261) Fr & Eur.

Lettres a un Ami Allemand. Albert Camus. (Folio Ser.: No. 2226). (FRE.). 1948. pap. 8.95 (*2-07-038326-1*) Schoenhof.

Lettres a un Otage. Antoine de Saint-Exupery. (FRE.). 128p. 1974. pap. 10.95 (*0-7859-1366-1*, 2070353176) Fr & Eur.

Lettres Acadiennes. Don Goodrum. LC 92-5124. (Illus.). 32p. (J). (ps-3). 1992. 14.95 (*0-88289-899-X*) Pelican.

Lettres au Castor et a quelques autres see Witness to My Life: The Letters of Jean-Paul Sartre to Simone de Beauvoir, 1926-1939

Lettres au Castor et a Quelques Autres, 1926-1939, Vol. 1. Simone de Beauvoir. (FRE.). 528p. 1983. 59.95 (*0-8288-9687-9*, 207026078X) Fr & Eur.

Lettres au Castor et a Quelques Autres, 1940-1963, Vol. 2. Simone de Beauvoir. (FRE.). 372p. 1983. 39.95 (*0-8288-9688-7*, 2070700399) Fr & Eur.

Lettres au Petit Corsaire. Sidonie-Gabrielle Colette. 153p. 1963. 19.95 (*0-8288-7465-4*) Fr & Eur.

Lettres Choisies. Mme De Sevigne. (Folio Ser.: No. 1935). (FRE.). pap. 12.95 (*2-07-037935-3*) Schoenhof.

Lettres Choisis. Mme De Sevigne. 127p. 1967. 19.95 (*0-8288-7477-8*) Fr & Eur.

Lettres dal deserto see Letters from the Desert

Lettres d'Alsace. rev. ed. Voltaire. (FRE.). 292p. 1938. pap. 15.95 (*0-7859-1334-3*, 2070265889) Fr & Eur.

Lettres de Cachet & Social Control in the Ancient Regime, 1659-1789. Brian E. Strayer. LC 91-30742. (American University Studies: History: Ser. IX, Vol. 118). (Illus.). 247p. (C). 1992. text 40.95 (*0-8204-1706-8*) P Lang Pubng.

Lettres de Cavelier de la Salle et Correspondance Relative a ses Entreprises (1678-1685) see Decouvertes et Establissements des francais dans l'ouest et dans le sud de l'Amerique septentrional: 1614-1754

Lettres de France: Intermediate. (FRE.). (C). 1985. pap. 6.99 (*0-8442-1023-4*, VF1023-4) NTC Contemp Pub Co.

Lettres de Jeunesse a l'Amie Inventee. Antoine de Saint-Exupery. (FRE.). 1976. pap. 10.95 (*0-8288-3731-7*, F123540) Fr & Eur.

Lettres de Jeunesse de 1777 a Aout, 1788 see Correspondance Generale

Lettres de Jeunesse (1923-1931) Antoine de Saint-Exupery. (FRE.). pap. 9.95 (*0-685-37089-5*) Fr & Eur.

Lettres de la Vie Litteraire. Arthur Rimbaud. (Imaginaire Ser.). (FRE.). 1990. pap. 11.95 (*2-07-072009-8*) Schoenhof.

Lettres de Leibniz a Arnauld D'Apres un Manuscrit Inedit. Gottfried Wilhelm Leibniz. LC 84-48423. (Philosophy of Leibniz Ser.). 111p. 1985. text 15.00 (*0-8240-6536-0*) Garland.

Lettres de Margry a Parkman, 1872-1892. Pierre Margry & Louis-Philippe Cormier. LC 78-377587. (Cahiers du Centre de Recherche en Civilisation Canadienne-Francaise: Vol. 11). (FRE.). 217p. 1977. reprint ed. pap. 67.30 (*0-608-02204-7*, 206287400004) Bks Demand.

Lettres de Mezery et de Coppet (16 Mai 1794-16 Mai 1795) see Correspondance Generale

Lettres de Mistriss Henley Publiees par son Amie. Isabelle De Charriere. Ed. by Philip Stewart. LC 93-26864. (MLA Texts & Translations Ser.: No. 1a). (FRE.). xxx, 45p. (Orig.). 1993. pap. 3.95 (*0-87352-775-5*, Q001P) Modern Lang.

Lettres de Mon Moulin. 7.95 (*0-8219-1469-3*) EMC-Paradigm.

Lettres de Mon Moulin. Daudet. (FRE.). (C). 1985. pap. 8.95 (*0-8442-1828-6*, VF1828-6) NTC Contemp Pub Co.

Lettres de Mon Moulin. Alphonse Daudet. (Illus.). write for info. (*0-318-52036-2*, 848); 428.00 (*0-685-34889-X*) Fr & Eur.

Lettres de Mon Moulin. Alphonse Daudet. (FRE.). 1984. pap. 11.95 (*0-7859-1988-0*, 2070375331) Fr & Eur.

Lettres de Mon Moulin. Alphonse Daudet. (Folio Ser.: No. 1533). (FRE., Illus.). 1962. 9.95 (*2-07-037533-1*) Schoenhof.

Lettres de Mon Moulin. unabridged ed. Daudet. (FRE.). pap. 6.95 (*2-87714-135-7*, Pub. by Bookking Intl) Distribks Inc.

Lettres de Russie (La Russie en 1839) Astolphe M. De Custine. (FRE.). 1975. pap. 11.95 (*0-7859-1807-8*, 2070366898) Fr & Eur.

Lettres de sa Vie Litteraire, 1870-1875. Arthur Rimbaud. (FRE.). 236p. 1931. pap. 10.95 (*0-7859-1302-5*, 2070254356) Fr & Eur.

Lettres de 1289 et 1305 des Ilkhan Argun et Oljeitu A. Philippe Le Bel. Ed. by Antoine Mostaert & Francis W. Cleaves. LC 62-19219. (Harvard-Yenching Institute, Scripta Mongolica Ser.: No. 1). (FRE., Illus.). 111p. 1962. pap. 10.00 (*0-674-52850-6*) HUP.

Lettres de Voyage (1923-1955) Pierre Teilhard De Chardin. 232p. 1956. pap. 24.95 (*0-7859-5284-5*) Fr & Eur.

Lettres d'Egypte. Gustave Flaubert & Antoine Y. Naaman. (FRE.). 480p. 1965. 10.95 (*0-7859-0126-4*, M62334) Fr & Eur.

Lettres d'Egypte (1905-1908) Pierre Teilhard De Chardin. pap. 7.95 (*0-685-36595-6*) Fr & Eur.

Lettres d'Hastings et de Paris (1908-1914) Pierre Teilhard De Chardin. 15.75 (*0-685-36596-4*) Fr & Eur.

Lettres d'Indochine. Guy de Chaumont Guitry. LC 79-179177. (South & Southeast Asia Studies). reprint ed. 37.50 (*0-404-54807-5*) AMS Pr.

Lettres Diverses de 1792 a Mai 1794 see Correspondance Generale

Lettres du Voyant, 13 et 15 Mai 1871. Arthur Rimbaud. Ed. by Gerard Schaeffer. (FRE.). 195p. 1975. pap. 49.95 (*0-7859-5380-9*) Fr & Eur.

Lettres d'un Bourgeois de Paris a un Ami de Province. Adrien-Joseph Colson. (FRE.). 200p. 1995. pap. 69.95 (*2-86808-079-0*) Intl Scholars.

Lettres d'un Dernier Amour: Correspondance Inedit avec Augusta. Alfred De Vigny. (FRE.). 152p. 1952. pap. 13.95 (*0-7859-5501-1*) Fr & Eur.

Lettres d'un Voyageur. George Sand. (FRE.). 320p. 1971. pap. 10.95 (*0-7859-1426-9*, 2080702416) Fr & Eur.

Lettres d'une Nouvelle Republicaine see Correspondance Generale

Lettres d'une Peruvienne. Francoise De Graffigny. LC 93-34826. (MLA Texts & Translations Ser.: No. 2a). (FRE.). xxviii, 168p. (Orig.). 1993. pap. 5.95 (*0-87352-777-1*, Q002P) Modern Lang.

Lettres d'Uzes. Jean Racine. (FRE., Illus.). 118p. 1991. pap. 24.95 (*0-7859-1557-5*, 2869713746) Fr & Eur.

Lettres et de la Vie de Descartes par Baillet. Denis Diderot. (FRE.). 192p. 1967. 10.95 (*0-7859-1170-7*, 2080701649) Fr & Eur.

Lettres et Entretiens. Charles Peguy. 13.95 (*0-685-37027-5*) Fr & Eur.

Lettres et Opuscules Inedits. Gottfried Wilhelm Leibniz. cxii, 336p. 1975. reprint ed. write for info. (*3-487-05321-7*) G Olms Pubs.

Lettres Francises dans les Revues Allemandes du XVIIIe Siecle: Die Franzosische Literatur in Den Deutschen Zeitschriften des 18. Jahrhunderts. Ed. by Pierre-Andre Bois et al. (Convergences Ser.: Vol. 4). (FRE.). xii, 388p. 1997. 51.95 (*3-906758-14-1*, Pub. by P Lang) P Lang Pubng.

Lettres Inedites a Arif Prins, 1885-1907. deluxe ed. Joris-Karl Huysmans. (FRE.). 415p. 1977. 110.00 (*0-7859-0032-2*, F88070) Fr & Eur.

Lettres Inedites a Charles Morice. Paul M. Verlaine & G. Zayed. (FRE.). 154p. 1970. pap. 18.95 (*0-7859-5408-2*) Fr & Eur.

Lettres Inedites a Divers Correspondants. Paul M. Verlaine & G. Zayed. (FRE.). 305p. 1976. pap. 65.00 (*0-7859-5409-0*) Fr & Eur.

Lettres Inedites a E. de Goncourt. Joris-Karl Huysmans. (FRE.). 140p. 1956. 14.95 (*0-7859-0009-8*, F65250) Fr & Eur.

Lettres Inedites a Jules Destree. Joris-Karl Huysmans & Gustave Vanwelkenhuyzen. (FRE.). 192p. 1966. 22.95 (*0-7859-0010-1*, F65254) Fr & Eur.

Lettres Inedites a Louis de Norbonne see Correspondance Generale

Lettres Inedites a Son Imprimeur Gabriel Cramer. Voltaire. (FRE.). 316p. 1952. pap. 13.95 (*0-7859-5514-3*) Fr & Eur.

Lettres Inedites et Manuscripts: Bulletins de la Societe Chateaubriand, Vol. 15. Francois-Rene de Chateaubriand. (FRE., Illus.). 96p. 1972. pap. 79.95 (*0-7859-5362-0*) Fr & Eur.

Lettres Inedites Publiees Par G. Chinard. Pierre De Beaumarchais. (FRE.). 130p. 1929. pap. 39.95 (*0-7859-5345-0*) Fr & Eur.

Lettres, Instructions et Memoires de Colbert, 8 vols. Jean B. Colbert. (FRE.). 1969. reprint ed. pap. 1080.00 (*0-8115-3817-6*) Periodicals Srv.

L

Lettres Intimes a Auguste Valensin Bruno de Solages et Hanri de Labac. Pierre Teilhard De Chardin & De Labac. 18.95 (*0-685-36597-2*) Fr & Eur.

Lettres Pastorales. Pierre Jurieu. (Bayle, Pierre, Volumes Supplementaires aux Oeuvres Diverses Ser.: No. 2). lxxvii, 604p. 1988. reprint ed. write for info. (*3-487-07977-1*) G Olms Pubs.

Lettres Persanes. Charles-Louis De Montesquieu. Ed. by Paul Verniere. (Coll. Prestige). 49.95 (*0-685-34047-3*); pap. 24.95 (*0-685-34046-5*) Fr & Eur.

Lettres Persanes. Charles-Louis De Montesquieu. 1984. pap. 10.95 (*0-7859-3061-2*) Fr & Eur.

Lettres Persanes. Montesquieu. (Folio Ser.: No. 475). (FRE.). pap. 9.95 (*2-07-036475-5*) Schoenhof.

Lettres Persanes. unabridged ed. Montesquieu. (FRE.). pap. 7.95 (*2-87714-141-1*, Pub. by Bookking Intl) Distribks Inc.

Lettres Philosophiques. Voltaire. Ed. by Rene Pomeau. (FRE.). 192p. 1964. pap. 10.95 (*0-7859-1418-8*, 2080700154) Fr & Eur.

Lettres Philosophiques. Voltaire. (Folio Ser.: No. 1703). (FRE.). pap. 9.95 (*2-07-037703-2*) Schoenhof.

Lettres Philosphiques. Jean-Jacques Rousseau. (FRE.). 232p. 1974. pap. 29.95 (*0-686-55353-5*, 271106666X) Fr & Eur.

Lettres Portugais suivi de Guilleragues par Lui-Meme. Gabriel J. Guilleragues. (FRE.). 220p. 1990. pap. 11.95 (*0-7859-2588-0*, 2070382443) Fr & Eur.

Lettres Portugaises. Guilleragues Par Lui-Meme. Gabriel J. Guilleragues. (Folio Ser.: No. 2154). (FRE.). 1990. pap. 10.95 (*2-07-038244-3*) Schoenhof.

Lettres Retrouvees. Marcel Proust. (FRE.). 6.95 (*0-685-37069-0*) Fr & Eur.

Lettrines, 2 vols. Julien Gracq. 1967. 26.50 (*0-685-73296-7*) Fr & Eur.

Lettrines, Vol. 1. Alexandre Dumas. (FRE.). 288p. 1977. 16.95 (*0-7859-1200-2*, 2859560262) Fr & Eur.

Lettrines, Vol. 2. 5th ed. Julien Gracq. (FRE.). 256p. 1989. pap. 32.95 (*0-7859-4773-6*) Fr & Eur.

Lettuce & Greens see NGA Garden Library

Lettuce & Greens. National Gardening Association Staff. LC 86-40343. 1987. pap. 4.95 (*0-317-56625-3*) Villard Books.

Lettuce, Endive & Chicory. Edward J. Ryder. LC 98-34438. (Crop Production Science in Horticulture Ser.). 224p. 1999. 50.00 (*0-85199-285-4*) OUP.

Lettuce in Your Kitchen: Flavorful And Unexpected Main-Dish Salads And Dressings. Chris Schlesinger & John Willouohby. Ed. by Justin Schwartz. (Illus.). 272p. 1998. pap. 10.00 (*0-688-16062-X*, Wm Morrow) Morrow Avon.

Lettuce in Your Kitchen: 100 Innovative Salads & 100 Versatile Dressings. Chris Schlesinger & John Willoughby. LC 95-46765. (Illus.). 1996. write for info. (*0-614-11015-7*, Wm Morrow) Morrow Avon.

Lettuce Leaf. 2nd rev. ed. Menelaos Stefanidis. (Folk Tales from Greece Ser.: Vol. 7). (Illus.). 32p. (J). (gr. 1-6). 1996. lib. bdg. 19.95 (*960-425-046-9*, Pub. by Sigma Publns) Cosmos.

Lettura e Conversazione. Salvatore Bancheri et al. 116p. (Orig.). (C). 1987. pap. text 17.95 (*0-8020-6641-0*) U of Toronto Pr.

Letty & the Law. Faith Baldwin. 1976. reprint ed. lib. bdg. 22.95 (*0-88411-610-7*) Amereon Ltd.

L'Etude Moderne de la Harpe see Modern Study of the Harp: L'Etude Moderne de la Harpe

***Letzte Gaben von Annette von Droste-Hulshoff 1860: Zum Editionsphilologischen Umgang Mit einer Fruhen Nachla & Beta; Edition eine Exemplarische Untersuchung Mit Dem Faksimiledruck der Letzten Gaben Als Beigabe.** Rudiger Nutt-Kofoth. (Arbeiten Zur Editionswissenschaft Ser.). 910p. 1999. 120.95 (*3-906763-46-3*) P Lang.

Letzten Dinge, Vol. 4. Ed. by Clive Brown. LC 87-75818. (Selected Works of Louis Spohr, 1784-1859). 248p. 1987. text 25.00 (*0-8240-1503-7*) Garland.

Leuchter Report. Fred Leuchter. 67p. 1989. pap. 20.00 (*1-872197-00-0*, Pub. by Focal Pt) Legion Survival.

Leuchter Report: A Dissection. rev. ed. Mitchell Jones. 118p. 1995. pap. 9.95 (*1-882719-03-4*) Twnty-Frst Cent Logic.

Leucocyte Antigen Factsbook. 2nd ed. Ed. by A. Neil Barclay et al. LC 97-15939. (Illus.). 640p. 1997. pap. text 49.95 (*0-12-078185-9*) Morgan Kaufmann.

Leucocyte Culture Conference: Proceedings, 4th, 1969, Hanover. Leucocyte Culture Conference Staff. Ed. by O. Ross McIntyre. LC 69-19545. 607p. reprint ed. pap. 188.20 (*0-608-16616-2*, 202630200049) Bks Demand.

Leucocyte Depletion & Its Clinical Usefulness: Proceedings of the 33rd Hokkaido Symposium on Transfusion Medicine. Thirty-third Hokkaido Symposium on Transfusion Med. Ed. by Sadayoshi Sekiguchi. LC 92-48510. (Illus.). 256p. 1993. 85.00 (*0-632-03716-4*) Blackwell Sci.

Leucocyte Depletion of Blood Components: Present Trends & the Future. Claes F. Hogman. 160p. 1994. 27.50 (*90-5383-275-0*, Pub. by VU Univ Pr) Paul & Co Pubs.

Leucocyte Typing. Ed. by A. J. Bernard et al. (Illus.). 820p. 1984. 139.00 (*0-387-12056-4*) Spr-Verlag.

L

Leucocyte Typing III: White Cell Differentiation Antigens. Ed. by A. J. McMichael et al. (Illus.). 1088p. 1987. 175.00 (*0-19-261552-1*) OUP.
Leucocyte Typing IV: White Cell Differentiation Antigens. Ed. by W. Knapp et al. (Illus.). 1208p. 1990. text 195.00 (*0-19-261867-9*) OUP.
Leucocyte Typing V: White Cell Differentiation Antigens, 2 vols., Set. Stuart F. Schlossman. (Illus.). 1995. text 325.00 (*0-19-262376-1*) OUP.
Leucocyte Typing VI: White Cell Differentiation Antigens. Ed. by Tadamitsu Kishimoto et al. LC 97-33315. 1376p. 1997. text 330.00 (*0-8153-2745-5*) Garland.
Leukaemia. 2nd ed. J. A. Whittaker. (Illus.). 704p. 1992. 235.00 (*0-632-02945-5*) Blackwell Sci.
Leukaemia & Related Disorders. 3rd ed. J. A. Whittaker. LC 97-31481. (Illus.). 1998. 299.95 (*0-86542-607-4*) Blackwell Sci.
Leukaemia Diagnosis. 2nd ed. Barbara J. Bain. LC 98-28846. (Illus.). 1999. 99.95 (*0-632-05165-5*) Blackwell Sci.
***Leukemia.** Judith Peacock. LC 99-15709. (Perspectives on Disease & Illness Ser.). (Illus.). 64p. (YA). 1999. 22.60 (*0-7368-0282-7*) Capstone Pr.
Leukemia. Dorothy S. Siegel & David E. Newton. LC 94-15517. (Venture Bks.). (Illus.). 112p. (YA). (gr. 9-12). 1994. lib. bdg. 24.00 (*0-531-12509-2*) Watts.
***Leukemia.** Alvin Silverstein et al. LC 99-50698. (Diseases & People Ser.). (Illus.). 128p. (YA). (gr. 6 up). 2000. lib. bdg. 20.95 (*0-7660-1310-3*) Enslow Pubs.
***Leukemia.** Sue Vander Hook. LC 99-39172. (Understanding Illness Ser.). (J). 2000. lib. bdg. 22.60 (*1-58340-027-3*) Smart Apple.
Leukemia. 6th rev. ed. Edward S. Henderson et al. LC 95-11494. (Illus.). 608p. 1996. text 215.00 (*0-7216-5381-2*, W B Saunders Co) Harcrt Hlth Sci Grp.
***Leukemia.** 7th ed. Edward S. Henderson. 2001. text. write for info. (*0-7216-9060-2*) Harcrt Hlth Sci Grp.
Leukemia: A Research Report. 2nd ed. Ed. by Barry Leonard. 63p. (C). 1998. pap. text 15.00 (*0-7881-7189-5*) DIANE Pub.
Leukemia: Advances in Research & Treatment. Ed. by Emil J. Freireich & Hagop Kantarjian. LC 92-49282. (Cancer Treatment & Research Ser.: No. 64). 432p. (C). 1993. text 280.50 (*0-7923-1967-2*) Kluwer Academic.
Leukemia: Just a Shadow. Mary A. Croskey. LC 97-221872. 80p. (Orig.). 1996. pap. 14.95 (*0-9654678-0-5*) Life Shadows.
Leukemia & Lymphoma Reviews, No. 1. Ed. by Aaron Polliack. 372p. 1992. text 176.00 (*3-7186-5251-X*, Harwood Acad Pubs) Gordon & Breach.
Leukemia & Lymphoma Reviews, No. 2. Ed. by Aaron Polliack. 294p. 1993. 78.00 (*3-7186-5374-5*) Kluwer Academic.
Leukemia & Lymphoma Reviews, No. 3. Ed. by Aaron Polliack. (Leukemia & Lymphoma Reviews Ser.). 296p. 1994. text 116.00 (*3-7186-5490-3*, Harwood Acad Pubs) Gordon & Breach.
Leukemia & Lymphoma Reviews, No. 4. Ed. by Aaron Polliack. (Leukemia & Lymphoma Reviews Ser). 304p. 1995. text 105.00 (*3-7186-5760-0*, Harwood Acad Pubs) Gordon & Breach.
Leukemia & Lymphoma Reviews, Vol. 5. Ed. by Aaron Polliack. (Leukemia & Lymphoma Reviews Ser.). 360p. 1997. text 72.00 (*90-5702-197-8*, Harwood Acad Pubs) Gordon & Breach.
Leukemia & Lymphoma Reviews, Vol. 6. Contrib. by Aaron Polliack. (Leukemia & Lymphoma Reviews Ser.). 408p. 1997. text 84.00 (*90-5702-198-6*, Harwood Acad Pubs) Gordon & Breach.
Leukemia & Lymphoma Reviews, Vol. 7. Contrib. by Aaron Polliack. (Leukemia & Lymphoma Reviews Ser.). 358p. 1997. text 75.00 (*90-5702-199-4*, Harwood Acad Pubs) Gordon & Breach.
Leukemia Cell. Arnold Rubin & Samuel Waxman. (Uniscience Ser.). 192p. 1979. 112.00 (*0-8493-5009-3*, RC643, CRC Reprint) Franklin.
Leukemia Reviews International, 2 vols., Vol. 1. Ed. by Marvin A. Rich. LC 88-659642. (Illus.). 367p. 1983. reprint ed. pap. 113.80 (*0-7837-0620-0*, 204096500001) Bks Demand.
Leukemia Reviews International, 2 vols., Vol. 2. Ed. by Marvin A. Rich. LC 88-659642. (Illus.). 201p. 1984. reprint ed. pap. 57.30 (*0-7837-0621-9*) Bks Demand.
Leukemias. Ed. by J. Fleischer. LC 92-48828. 1993. 129.00 (*0-387-54782-7*) Spr-Verlag.
Leukemias & Lymphomas. Ed. by Peter H. Wiernik. LC 84-17519. (Contemporary Issues in Clinical Oncology Ser.: No. 4). 303p. reprint ed. pap. 94.00 (*0-7837-6256-9*, 204596800010) Bks Demand.
Leukemic Cell. Ed. by Daniel Catovsky. LC 80-41107. (Methods in Hematology Ser.: No. 2). (Illus.). 293p. reprint ed. pap. 90.90 (*0-8357-3065-4*, 203932100012) Bks Demand.
Leukemic Cell. 2nd ed. Ed. by D. Catovsky. (Methods in Hematology Ser.). (Illus.). 428p. 1991. text 152.00 (*0-443-03867-8*) Church.
Leukocyte Adhesion Molecules. Ed. by Timothy A. Springer et al. (Illus.). 272p. 1991. 161.00 (*0-387-96983-7*) Spr-Verlag.
Leukocyte Chemotaxis: Methods, Physiology, & Clinical Implications. fac. ed. Ed. by John I. Gallin & Paul G. Quie. LC 76-58053. (Kroc Foundation Ser.: No. 9). (Illus.). 443p. pap. 137.40 (*0-7837-7533-4*, 204697100005) Bks Demand.
Leukocyte-Depleted Blood Products. Ed. by T. A. Lane & G. Myllylae. (Current Studies in Hematology & Blood Transfusion: No. 60). (Illus.). viii, 150p. 1994. 149.75 (*3-8055-5862-7*) S Karger.
Leukocyte Emigration & Its Sequelae. Ed. by H. Z. Movat. (Illus.). vi, 186p. 1987. 121.00 (*3-8055-4489-8*) S Karger.
Leukocyte Integrins: Structure, Expression & Function. Angel L. Corbi. LC 96-22039. (Molecular Biology Intelligence Unit Ser.). 200p. 1996. 99.00 (*1-57059-358-2*) Landes Bioscience.
Leukocyte Integrins in the Immune System & Malignant Disease. Ed. by B. Holzmann et al. (Current Topics in Microbiology & Immunology Ser.). (Illus.). viii, 189p. 1997. 135.00 (*3-540-63609-9*) Spr-Verlag.
Leukocyte Typing II: Human B Lymphocytes, Vol. 2. Ed. by E. L. Reinherz et al. (Illus.). 530p. 1985. 215.00 (*0-387-96176-3*) Spr-Verlag.
Leukocyte Typing II: Human Myeloid & Hematopoietic Cells, Vol. 3. Ed. by E. L. Reinherz et al. (Illus.). xvi, 366p. 1985. 174.00 (*0-387-96177-1*) Spr-Verlag.
Leukocyte Typing II: Human T Lymphocytes, Vol. 1. Ed. by E. L. Reinherz et al. (Illus.). 575p. 1985. 215.00 (*0-387-96175-5*) Spr-Verlag.
Leukolysins & Cancer. Ed. by Janet H. Ransom & John R. Ortaldo. LC 87-17221. (Contemporary Biomedicine Ser.: Vol. 8). (Illus.). 344p. 1988. 125.00 (*0-89603-125-X*) Humana.
Leukotrienes: New Concepts & Targets for Therapy. Ed. by Ian Rodger et al. 160p. 1998. 85.00 (*0-7923-8738-4*) Kluwer Academic.
Leukotrienes: Their Biological Significance: a Biological Council Symposium. Ed. by Priscilla J. Piper. LC 86-6643. 235p. 1986. reprint ed. pap. 72.90 (*0-608-00424-3*, 206113900007) Bks Demand.
Leukotrienes & Other Lipoxygenase Products: Proceedings of the Annual Symposium of the Institute of Basic Medical Sciences, Royal College of Surgeons of England, 25-26 October 1982. Royal College of Surgeons of England, Institute of. Ed. by Priscilla J. Piper. LC 83-175919. (Prostaglandins Ser.: No. 3). (Illus.). 367p. reprint ed. pap. 113.80 (*0-8357-7081-8*, 203334600085) Bks Demand.
Leukotrienes & Prostanoids in Health & Disease. Ed. by Z. Naor et al. (New Trends in Lipid Mediators Research Ser.: Vol. 3). (Illus.). x, 346p. 1989. 278.50 (*3-8055-5011-1*) S Karger.
Leukotrienes & Prostanoids in Health & Disease. Ed. by Uriel Zor et al. LC 85-43512. (Advances in Prostaglandin, Thromboxane, & Leukotriene Research Ser.: No. 16). (Illus.). 423p. 1986. reprint ed. pap. 131.20 (*0-608-00675-0*, 206126200007) Bks Demand.
Leukotrienes As Mediators of Asthma & Inflammation: Basic & Applied Research - 2nd International Symposium on Trends in Eicosanoid Biology, Interlaken, Switzerland, 1992. International Symposium on Trends in Eicosanoid Biology Staff. Ed. by Sven-Erik Dahlen et al. LC 94-69543. (Advances in Prostaglandin, Thromboxane, & Leukotriene Research Ser.: Vol. 22). (Illus.). 373p. 1994. reprint ed. pap. 115.70 (*0-608-07269-9*, 206749700009) Bks Demand.
Leukotrinenes: Development of Assay Methodology in Biologic Fluids & Evaluation of Antagonists In Vitro & In Vivo in Man. M. Depre. No. 91. 185p. (Orig.). 1994. pap. 44.50 (*90-6186-633-2*, Pub. by Leuven Univ) Coronet Bks.
Leukozytenseparation und Transfusion. V. Kretschmer. (Beitraege zur Infusionstherapie und Klinische Ernaehrung Ser.: Vol. 6). (Illus.). viii, 188p. 1981. 43.50 (*3-8055-1946-X*) S Karger.
Leutebuch Ein Leichtes Lese 2E. 2nd ed. Albrecht Holschuh. (GER., Illus.). 179p. (C). 1988. pap. text 35.50 (*0-15-550602-1*) Harcourt Coll Pubs.
***Leuven in Books - Books in Leuven: The Oldest University of the Low Countries & Its Library.** Ed. by Christian Coppens. Tr. by Ardis Dreisbach. (Illus.). 323p. 1999. pap. 77.50 (*90-6186-951-X*, Pub. by Leuven Univ) Coronet Bks.
LEV - ULEV Emission Technologies: SAE International Congress & Exposition 1994, 12 papers. (Special Publications). 149p. 1994. pap. 44.00 (*1-56091-496-3*, SP-1044) Soc Auto Engineers.
Lev Krevza's Defense of Church Unity & Zaxarija Kopystens'kyj's Palinodia Or, Book of Defense of the Holy Catholic Apostolic Eastern Church & the Holy Patriarchs: Texts, Zaxarija Kopystens'kyj. Ed. by William R. Veder & Dana R. Miller. Tr. & Frwd. by Bohdan A. Struminsky. (Harvard Library of Early Ukrainian Literature). 953p. 1995. 58.00 (*0-916458-29-6*) Harvard Ukrainian.
Lev Krevza's Obrona iednosci cerkiewney & Zaxarija Kopystens'kyj's Palinodija. Ed. by Omeljan Pritsak. LC 87-81952. (Harvard Library of Early Ukrainian Literature: Vol. 3). (POL & UKR., Illus.). 596p. (C). 1987. text 15.00 (*0-916458-22-9*) Harvard Ukrainian.
Lev S. Vygotsky & Contemporary Educational Psychology Vol. 30, No. 2, 1995: A Special Issue of Educational Psychologist, Vol. 30, No. 2, 1995. J. P. Das & Boris Gindis. 56p. 1995. pap. 20.00 (*0-8058-9938-3*) L Erlbaum Assocs.
Lev Shestov & His Times: Encounters with Brandes, Tolstoy, Dostoevsky, Chekhov, Ibsen, Nietzsche, & Husserl. Andrius Valevicius. LC 93-391. (American University Studies: Theology & Religion: Ser. VII, Vol. 155). IX, 152p. 1993. write for info. (*0-8204-2146-4*) P Lang Pubng.
Lev the Lucky Lulav. Cheryl Gunsher. (Illus.). 24p. (J). (ps). 1993. 10.00 (*1-881602-01-X*) Prism NJ.
Lev Tolstoi I Russkaia Istoriia. Gordin Y. Arkadievich. LC 92-23259. (RUS.). 152p. (Orig.). 1992. pap. 12.00 (*1-55779-057-4*) Hermitage Pubs.
***LEV-II Emission Solutions.** (Special Publications). 88p. 2000. 49.00 (*0-7680-0560-4*, SP-1510) Soc Auto Engineers.
Lev Vygotsky: Critical Assessment, 4 vols. Ed. by Peter Lloyd & Charles Fermyhough. (Critical Assessments Ser.). (Illus.). 1536p. (C). (gr. 13). 1999. 700.00 (*0-415-11156-0*, D6205) Routledge.
Lev Vygotsky: Critical Assessments. Peter Lloyd & Charles Fernyhough. LC 98-9488. 1998. write for info. (*0-415-11152-8*); write for info. (*0-415-11153-6*); write for info. (*0-415-11154-4*); write for info. (*0-415-11155-2*) Routledge.
Lev Vygotsky: Revolutionary Scientist. Fred Newman & Lois Holzman. LC 92-28810. (Critical Psychology Ser.). 256p. (C). 1993. pap. 25.99 (*0-415-06442-2*, B0216) Routledge.
***L'Evangelisation.** Murriell McCulley. (Discovery Ser.).Tr. of Evangelism. (FRE.). 76p. 1999. pap. text. write for info. (*2-912377-04-8*, Editions SAFT) Africa Theolog Trng.
***Levant.** Koenemann Inc. Staff. 2000. 29.95 (*3-8290-0495-8*) Konemann.
Levantate y Pelea. Ken Abraham.Tr. of Stand up & Fight Back. (SPA.). 256p. (YA). 1995. 9.99 (*0-88113-298-5*, B067-2985) Caribe Betania.
Levantate y Se Sano. Benny Hinn.Tr. of Rise & Be Healed. (SPA.). 76p. 1995. 4.99 (*1-56063-379-4*, 550125) Editorial Unilit.
Levante. (Arte & Arquitectura Ser.). (Illus.). 400p. 2000. 39.95 (*3-8290-0498-2*, 540541) Konemann.
Levantemos el Cielo. Richard Vaughan.Tr. of Lift the Sky Up. (J). 1996. 2.95 (*0-673-36332-5*, GoodYrBooks) Addson-Wesley Educ.
Levanter. Eric Ambler. 24.95 (*0-88411-296-9*) Amereon Ltd.
Levantine Arabic for Non-Natives. Lutfi Hussein. LC 95-702507. (Language Ser.). (ARA.). (C). 1993. audio, digital audio 55.00 (*0-300-05635-4*) Yale U Pr.
Levantine Arabic for Non-Natives: A Proficiency-Oriented Approach. Lutfi Hussein. LC 93-15797. (Language Ser.). (ARA.). 117p. (C). 1993. pap. 27.00 (*0-300-05634-6*); pap., teacher ed. 35.00 (*0-300-05633-8*) Yale U Pr.
Levantine Arabic Pronunciation. unabridged ed. Foreign Service Institute Staff. (ARA.). 100p. pap. 185.00 incl. audio (*0-88432-038-3*, AFA244) Audio-Forum.
Levantine Trade & Hungary in the Middle Ages: Theses, Controversies, Arguments. Zsigmond P. Pach. LC 84-672719. (Studia Historica Academiae Scietiarum Hungaricae). (ENG & RUS.). 27p. 1975. write for info. (*963-05-0810-9*, Pub. by Akade Kiado) Intl Spec Bk.
L'Eve future see Eve of the Future Eden
Leve-Toi et Marche. Herve Bazin. (FRE.). 1958. pap. 12.95 (*0-7859-3408-1*) Fr & Eur.
Levee Site & the Knoll Site. Gary F. Fry & Gardiner F. Dalley. (Anthropological Papers: No. 100). (Illus.). (Orig.). 1979. pap. 15.00 (*0-87480-153-2*) U of Utah Pr.
Level. Kirk Woodburn. LC 98-90935. 1999. pap. 8.95 (*0-533-12990-7*) Vantage.
Level A see Be a Better Reader Series: Basic Skills Edition
Level A - Miro y Escucho see Leo y Entiendo
Level B - Comenzando a Leer see Leo y Entiendo
Level C - Ya Me Gusta Leer see Leo y Entiendo
Level Chemistry. 2nd ed. E. N. Ramsden. (C). 1990. text 97.50 (*0-7487-0154-0*, Pub. by S Thornes Pubs) Trans-Atl Phila.
Level D - Avanzando en la Lectura see Leo y Entiendo
Level E - Mira Cuanto Entiendo! see Leo y Entiendo
Level F - Avanzando en la Comprension see Leo y Entiendo
Level Five. large type ed. Duff Hart-Davis. 480p. 1983. 27.99 (*0-7089-0931-0*) Ulverscroft.
Level G - Que Bien Entiendo! see Leo y Entiendo
Level Green. Judith Vollmer. LC 90-50101. (Brittingham Prize in Poetry, 1990 Ser.). 96p. (Orig.). (C). 1990. pap. 11.95 (*0-299-12754-0*) U of Wis Pr.
Level II see Study Skills Workshop Kit
Level Law. Penny Booth et al. Ed. by Peter Shears & Paul Cappi. (Questions & Answers Ser.). 376p. 1995. 18.00 (*1-874241-32-5*, Pub. by Cavendish Pubng) Gaunt.
Level Law Paper, Vol. 2. Gordon McLeish et al. (Lecture Notes Ser.). 486p. 1995. pap. 28.00 (*1-874241-75-9*, Pub. by Cavendish Pubng) Gaunt.
***Level-Loading Production: A Common Sense Approach to Improving Margins & Eliminating Waste.** James Kirwan. LC 99-63292. (Illus.). 112p. 1999. 34.95 (*0-9673046-0-1*) J J K.
Level 1 see Classics of Spanish Literature
Level 1 CFA Candidate Readings, 1996. (Orig.). 1995. pap. text 40.00 (*1-879087-49-9*) RFICFA.
Level 1 Mix Design: Materials Selection, Compaction, & Conditioning. Ronald Cominsky et al. (SHRP Ser. A-408). (Illus.). 121p. (C). 1994. pap. text 10.00 (*0-309-05824-4*, PA408) Natl Res Coun.
***Level I Networking: Sair Linux & GNU Certification.** Tobin Maginnis. 304p. 2000. pap. text 34.99 (*0-471-36977-2*) Wiley.
Level Paper. Paul Cappi & Mary Collins. (Lecture Notes Ser.). 328p. 1995. pap. 28.00 (*1-874241-74-0*, Pub. by Cavendish Pubng) Gaunt.
Level Playing Field. John Kingston. 243p. (Orig.). 1996. pap. 6.95 (*0-9644574-7-4*) Shoeless Pub.
Level Playing Field: Sports & Race. Evaleen Hu. LC 94-31516. (J). (gr. 5 up). 1995. lib. bdg. 21.50 (*0-8225-3302-2*, Lerner Publctns) Lerner Pub.
***Level Playing Field: The Athletic Administrator's Guide to Title IX, Gender Equity in Sports & OCR Investigations.** Lee E. Green. 244p. 1998. 175.00 (*0-9671804-1-4*) Sports Law.
Level Set Methods: Evolving Interfaces in Geometry, Fluid Mechanics, Computer Vision, & Material Science. J. A. Sethian. LC 96-232397. (Monographs on Applied & Computational Mathematics: No. 3). (Illus.). 236p. (C). 1996. text 42.95 (*0-521-57202-9*) Cambridge U Pr.
Level Set Methods & Fast Marching Methods: Evolving Interfaces in Computational Geometry, Fluid Mechanics, Computer Vision & Materials Science. 2nd ed. J. A. Sethian. (Cambridge Monographs on Applied & Computational Mathematics: No. 3). 250p. (C). 1999. text 74.95 (*0-521-64204-3*); pap. text 29.95 (*0-521-64557-3*) Cambridge U Pr.
Level 3. 2nd ed. Gutierrez. (Secondary Spanish Ser.). (SPA.). 1997. mass mkt., suppl. ed. 196.95 (*0-8384-6241-3*) Heinle & Heinle.
Level III: Visual & Optical Testing Method. Greg Sayler. (Illus.). 126p. (C). 1998. student ed., ring bd. 39.00 (*1-57117-057-X*, 2263) Am Soc Nondestructive.
Level 3 CFA Candidate Readings, 1996. (Orig.). 1995. pap. text 40.00 (*1-879087-51-0*) RFICFA.
Level 3 Workbook Computer Lab. Joan Kimmelman & Sandra Seltzer. 128p. (C). 1995. spiral bd. 11.95 (*0-7872-1375-6*) Kendall-Hunt.
***Top Hits! Duet Book, Level 2.** Hal Leonard. (Alfred's Basic Piano Library). 1999. pap. 6.95 (*0-7390-0835-8*, 17166) Alfred Pub.
Level 2 CFA Candidate Readings, 1996. (Orig.). 1995. pap. text 40.00 (*1-879087-50-2*) RFICFA.
***Level II Study Guide: Utrasonic Testing.** William Spaulding & George C. Wheeler. (Illus.). 70p. 1999. pap. 30.00 (*1-57117-063-4*) Am Soc Nondestructive.
***Level II Study Guide: Visual & Optical Testing Method.** Douglas Krauss. (Illus.). 62p. 1998. pap. 30.00 (*1-57117-064-2*) Am Soc Nondestructive.
Level 4 Whats Story, 4 bks., Bk. 4, Advanced. Linda R. Markstein & Dorien Grunbaum. (English As a Second Language Bk.). 1981. pap. text 12.40 (*0-582-79786-1*, 75041) Longman.
***Leveling Books K-6: Matching Readers to Text.** Brenda M. Weaver. 2000. pap., teacher ed. 17.95 (*0-87207-267-3*, 267) Intl Reading.
Leveling Crowds: Ethno-Nationalist Conflicts & Collective Violence in South Asia. Stanely J. Tambiah. (Comparative Studies in Religion & Society: Vol. 10). (Illus.). 417p. (C). 1997. 55.00 (*0-520-20002-0*, Pub. by U CA Pr); pap. 22.50 (*0-520-20642-8*, Pub. by U CA Pr) Cal Prin Full Svc.
Leveling the Playing Field: Giving Girls an Equal Chance for Basic Education - Three Countries' Efforts. LC 96-12164. (EDI Learning Resources Ser.). 44p. 1996. pap. 22.00 (*0-8213-3601-0*, 13601) World Bank.
***Leveling the Playing Field: How the Law Can Make Sports Better for Fans.** Paul Weiler. LC 99-87304. 368p. 2000. text 29.95 (*0-674-00165-6*) HUP.
Leveling Wind: Politics, the Culture & Other News, 1990-1994. George F. Will. 446p. 1994. 19.95 (*0-02-934438-7*) Free Pr.
Leveling Wind: Politics, the Culture & Other News, 1990-1994. George F. Will. 496p. 1995. pap. 13.95 (*0-14-024702-5*, Penguin Bks) Viking Penguin.
Leveller Movement. T. C. Pease. 1988. 16.50 (*0-8446-1345-2*) Peter Smith.
Levels. Nancy M. Brannon. LC 96-84254. (Illus.). 80p. 1996. pap. 12.95 (*1-888341-00-9*) Enspirit Pr.
Levels & Trends of Contraceptive Use as Assessed in 1987. (Population Studies). 137p. 1989. pap. 15.00 (*92-1-151176-3*, E.89.XIII.4) UN.
Levels & Trends of Contraceptive Use As Assessed in 1994. Department for Economic & Social Information & Pol. LC 97-114933. (Population Studies: No. 146). 171p. pap. 17.50 (*92-1-151310-3*, RG133) UN.
Levels & Trends of Fertility & their Determinants for Small Geographic Areas in the ESCAP Region. Ed. by Economic & Social Commission for Asia & the Pacific Staff. (Asian Population Studies: No. 146). 164p. 1998. 25.00 (*92-1-119785-6*) UN.
Levels in Speech Communication: Relations & Interactions: A Tribute to Max Wajskop. Ed. by Christel Sorin et al. LC 94-48109. 296p. 1995. 191.50 (*0-444-81846-4*) Elsevier.
Levels of Analysis Paradigm: A Model for Individual & Systematic Therapy. Thomas A. Skurky. LC 89-16124. 172p. 1990. 52.95 (*0-275-93296-6*, C3296, Praeger Pubs) Greenwood.
Levels of Cognitive Complexity: An Approach to the Measurement of Thinking. E. McDaniel & C. Lawrence. (Recent Research in Psychology Ser.). (Illus.). xii, 97p. 1990. 58.95 (*0-387-97301-X*) Spr-Verlag.
Levels of Cognitive Development. Tracy S. Kendler. 208p. 1995. 45.00 (*0-8058-0680-6*) L Erlbaum Assocs.
Levels of Constituent Structure in New Testament Greek. Michael W. Palmer. LC 93-30457. (Studies in Biblical Greek: Vol. 4). X, 143p. (C). 1995. pap. text 24.95 (*0-8204-2115-4*) P Lang Pubng.
Levels of Edit. Robert Van Buren & Mary F. Buehler. 36p. 1991. pap. 23.00 (*0-19-454867-8*) Soc Tech Comm.
Levels of Knowing & Existence: Studies in General Semantics. Harry L. Weinberg. LC 73-80740. (C). 1973. reprint ed. pap. 8.95 (*0-910780-07-2*) Inst Gen Seman.
Levels of Living in the Ilocos Region. Horacio C. Lava. LC 75-30066. (Institute of Pacific Relations Ser.). reprint ed. 29.50 (*0-404-59538-3*) AMS Pr.
Levels of Personality. 2nd ed. Mark Cook. LC 88-47779. 276p. 1993. 85.00 (*0-304-32425-6*); pap. 40.00 (*0-304-32438-8*) Weidner & Sons.
Levels of Property Tax Exemption: Part I, Sources of Basic Data & Part II, Tax Exemption in Central Cities & Suburbs, a Comparison Across States, No. 840. John M. Quigley & Debra Stinson. 1975. 6.00 (*0-686-20363-1*, Sage Prdcls Pr) Sage.
Levels of Selection in Evolution. Laurent Keller. LC 99-22314. (Monographs in Behavior & Ecology). (Illus.). 272p. 1999. 16.95 (*0-691-00704-7*, Pub. by Princeton U Pr) Cal Prin Full Svc.

An Asterisk (*) at the beginning of an entry indicates that the title is appearing for the first time.

***Levels of Selection in Evolution.** Ed. by Laurent Keller. LC 99-22314. (Illus.). 272p. 1999. 59.50 (*0-691-00703-9*, Pub. by Princeton U Pr) Cal Prin Full Svc.

Levels of Social Behavior: Evolutionary & Genetic Aspects: Award Winning Papers from the Third T. C. Schneirla Conference: Evolution Social Behavior & Integrative Levels. Gary Greenberg & Ethel Tobach. 75p. (C). 1992. lib. bdg. write for info. (*0-9632568-0-7*) T C Schneirla.

Levels of Socio-Economic Development Theory. 2nd ed. David Jaffee. LC 97-50048. 240p. 1998. 65.00 (*0-275-95658-X*, Praeger Pubs); pap. 22.95 (*0-275-95659-8*, Praeger Pubs) Greenwood.

Levels of Syntactic Representation. Ed. by Robert May & Jan Koster. (Studies in Generative Grammar). 350p. 1981. pap. 69.25 (*90-70176-30-0*) Mouton.

Levels of the Game. John McPhee. 160p. 1969. text 18.95 (*0-374-18568-9*) FS&G.

Levels of the Game. John McPhee. 152p. 1979. pap. 9.00 (*0-374-51526-3*) FS&G.

Levels 1-5 see Guide to the Best in Contemporary Piano Music: An Annotated List of Graded Solo Piano Music Published Since 1950

Levels 6-8 see Guide to the Best in Contemporary Piano Music: An Annotated List of Graded Solo Piano Music Published Since 1950

Leven & Melville Papers. William L. Melville. LC 78-172725. (Bannatyne Club, Edinburgh. Publications: No. 77). reprint ed. 67.50 (*0-404-52798-1*) AMS Pr.

Levend Nederlands: Een Cursus Nederlands Voor Buitenlanders. 240p. 1984. pap. 36.95 (*0-521-27576-8*) Cambridge U Pr.

Levene's Colour Atlas of Dermatology. 2nd ed. White. 1997. 29.95 (*0-7234-2552-3*) Wolfe Pubng AZ.

Levenstein, 2 vols., Set. 1995. 60.00 (*0-19-521227-4*) OUP.

Lever. Patricia Armentrout. LC 97-15149. (Simple Machines Ser.). (J). 1997. lib. bdg. 17.27 (*1-57103-177-4*) Rourke Pr.

Lever Crosswords. Joseph. 1999. pap. write for info. (*0-8069-6201-1*) Sterling.

Lever of Riches: Technological Creativity & Economic Progress. Joel Mokyr. (Illus.). 368p. 1992. pap. text 16.95 (*0-19-507477-7*) OUP.

Leverage for the Environment: A Guide to the Private Financial Services Industry. John Ganzi et al. LC 98-87983. (Illus.). 107p. 1998. pap. 20.00 (*1-56973-267-1*) World Resources Inst.

Leverage of Labor: Managing the Cortes Haciendas in Tehuantepec, 1588-1688. Lolita G. Brockington. LC 88-25717. (Illus.). xxv, 246p. 1989. text 49.95 (*0-8223-0884-3*) Duke.

Leverage of Sea Power: The Strategic Advantage of Navies in War. Colin S. Gray. 372p. 1992. 29.95 (*0-02-912661-4*) Free Pr.

Leverage Your Time: Balance Your Life. 3rd ed. John Ingram Walker. xi, 128p. 1999. reprint ed. pap. 16.95 (*0-9621073-5-2*, Lifeworks Pub) Lynn Grove Pr.

Leveraged Buyout. Albert F. Gargiulo. LC 82-16473. 50p. reprint ed. pap. 30.00 (*0-608-15010-X*, 205608700047) Bks Demand.

Leveraged Buyouts. Stephen C. Diamond. LC 84-73255. 1985. 70.00 (*0-87094-579-3*, Irwn Prfssnl) McGraw-Hill Prof.

***Leveraged ESOPs & Employee Buyouts: How to Use an Employee Ownership Plan (ESOP)** 3rd rev. enl. ed. Scott S. Rodrick. (Illus.). viii, 272p. 2000. pap. 35.00 (*0-926902-62-8*) NCEO.

Leveraged Finance: How to Raise & Invest Cash. Mark Stevens. LC 79-23897. 220p. 1980. 19.95 (*0-13-535104-9*, Busn) P-H.

***Leveraged Grantmaking: Challenging Funders & Programs to Sustain National Service.** (Illus.). 130p. 2000. pap. 10.00 (*1-58534-037-5*) Points of Light.

Leveraged Innovation: Unlocking the Innovation Potential of Strategic Supply. Francis Bidault. LC 98-50469. 200p. 1999. text 40.00 (*0-312-22154-1*) St Martin.

Leveraged Management Buyouts: Causes & Consequences. Ed. by Yakov Amihud. 1989. 60.00 (*1-55623-208-X*, Irwn Prfssnl) McGraw-Hill Prof.

***Leveraging Competitive Advantage from the Euro.** Rupert Cook. (Management Briefings Ser.). (Illus.). 1999. pap. 127.50 (*0-273-64324-X*, Pub. by F T P-H) Trans-Atl Phila.

Leveraging Design: Finance & the Kitchen & Bathroom Specialist. Debi Bach. (Illus.). 106p. (Orig.). 1996. pap. text 30.00 (*1-887127-31-3*, 5301) Natl Kit Bath.

Leveraging Funds for Section 514/516 Farmworker Housing Development. Housing Assistance Council Staff. 38p. 1998. 5.50 (*1-58064-088-5*) Housing Assist.

Leveraging Information Systems Capabilities of Third Party Logistics Providers. David Waller. (Illus.). 15p. 1995. pap. 20.00 (*1-892663-05-8*) WERC.

Leveraging Japan: Marketing to the New Asia. George Fields et al. LC 99-6831. 352p. 1999. 32.00 (*0-7879-4663-X*) Jossey-Bass.

Leveraging Knowledge: A 17-Day Program for a Smarter Organization. Patrick J. Thurbin. 240p. 1995. 24.95 (*0-273-61896-2*) F T P-H.

Leveraging People & Profit: The Hard Work of Soft Management. Bernard A. Nagle & Perry Pascarella. LC 97-14579. 224p. 1997. pap. text 17.95 (*0-7506-9961-2*) Buttrwrth-Heinemann.

Leveraging the Benefits of Parks & Recreation: The Phoenix Project. 268p. 1994. 29.95 (*0-614-23166-3*) Venture Pub PA.

Leveraging the Corporate Brand. James R. Gregory & Jack G. Wiechmann. LC 96-48113. (Illus.). 256p. 1997. 44.95 (*0-8442-3444-3*, NTC Business Bks) NTC Contemp Pub Co.

Leveraging the Language of Work: Improving the Performance of People, Systems, & Organizations. Danny G. Langdon. LC 99-6755. 304p. 1999. 44.95 (*0-7879-4736-9*) Jossey-Bass.

Leveraging the Law: Using the Courts to Achieve Social Change. David A. Schultz & Stephen Gottlieb. LC 96-39624. (Teaching Texts in Law & Politics Ser.: Vol. 3). 354p. (C). 1998. pap. text 32.95 (*0-8204-3492-2*) P Lang Pubng.

Leveraging the New Infrastructure: How Market Leaders Capitalize on Information Technology. Peter Weill & Marianne Broadbent. LC 98-11335. 320p. 1998. 29.95 (*0-87584-830-3*) Harvard Busn.

Leveraging Visual Basic with ActiveX Controls. Wayne S. Freeze. LC 95-72671. 640p. 1996. pap., per. 45.00 incl. cd-rom (*0-7615-0901-1*) Prima Pub.

Leveraging with Legal Assistants: How to Maximize Team Performance, Improve Quality, & Boost Your Bottom Line. LC 93-72399. 224p. 1993. pap. 64.95 (*0-89707-897-7*, 511-0322) Amer Bar Assn.

***Leverett Letters: Correspondence of a South Carolina Family, 1851-1868.** Ed. by Frances Wallace Taylor et al. (Illus.). 2000. 49.95 (*1-57003-333-1*) U of SC Pr.

Leverett Saltonstall: Diary (Jan. 1806-April 1807) 54p. 1977. reprint ed. pap. 2.50 (*0-934909-10-5*) Mass Hist Soc.

Levering Avenue. Robert Daseler. LC 98-38948. x, 70p. 1998. 15.00 (*0-930982-50-9*); pap. 10.00 (*0-930982-51-7*) U of Evansville Pr.

Levering Fruit Cookbook: A Guide to Preparing Cherries, Peaches, Apples & Other Fruits. unabridged ed. Wanda Urbanska. 53p. 1994. pap. 5.95 (*0-9656330-2-0*) Orchard Gap Pr.

Levers see Simple Machines Series

Levers. David Glover. LC 96-15816. (Simple Machines Ser.). (J). 1998. (*1-57572-080-9*) Heinemann Lib.

***Levers.** Angela Royston. LC 00-35002. (Machines in Action Ser.). (Illus.). (J). 2000. lib. bdg. write for info. (*1-57572-319-0*) Heinemann Lib.

Levers. Caroline Suhr. LC 96-22824. (Simple Science Ser.). (Illus.). 32p. (J). (ps-4). 1996. lib. bdg. 19.97 (*0-8172-4501-4*) Raintree Steck-V.

***Levers.** Anne Welsbacher. (Understanding Simple Machines Ser.). 24p. (J). (ps-3). 2000. lib. bdg. 15.93 (*0-7368-0611-3*, Bridgestone Bks) Capstone Pr.

***Levers & Pulleys.** Stuart Matthews. (How Does It Work? Ser.). (Illus.). 24p. (J). (gr. 2-7). 2001. lib. bdg. 21.30 (*1-58340-068-0*) Smart Apple.

Lever's Histopathology of the Skin. 8th ed. David E. Elder et al. 1,104p. write for info. (*0-7817-2096-6*) Lppncott W & W.

Lever's Histopathology of the Skin. 8th ed. Walter F. Lever & David E. Elder. LC 96-30912. 1104p. 1997. text 173.00 (*0-397-51500-6*) Lppncott W & W.

Levers of Control. Simons. 240p. 1994. 29.95 (*0-07-103604-0*) McGraw.

Levers of Control: How Managers Use Control Systems to Drive Strategic Renewal. Robert Simons. LC 94-9073. 232p. 1994. 29.95 (*0-87584-559-2*) Harvard Busn.

Levi: The Smartest Boy in the World. Jeane H. Candido. (Illus.). 30p. (J). (gr. 1-5). 1998. pap. 9.95 (*1-886383-34-0*) Pride & Imprints.

Levi Ben Gerson's Prognostication for the Conjunction of 1345. Bernard R. Goldstein & David Pingree. LC 90-83198. (Transactions Ser.: Vol. 80, Pt. 6). 100p. (C). 1991. pap. 12.00 (*0-87169-806-4*, T806-GOB) Am Philos.

Levi Dust: Tales from the Kerry Patch. Steven J. Givens. (Illus.). 56p. (Orig.). (J). (gr. 2-4). 1997. pap. 4.25 (*1-889658-07-3*) New Canaan Pub.

Levi Parsons Morton: Banker, Diplomat & Statesman. Robert M. McElroy. LC 75-2646. (Wall Street & the Security Market Ser.). (Illus.). 1975. reprint ed. 33.95 (*0-405-06971-5*) Ayer.

Levi Scott: Oregon Trailblazer. Vira Cordano. LC 81-70857. (Illus.). 1982. pap. 7.50 (*0-8323-0400-X*) Binford Mort.

Levi Strauss: Blue Jean Tycoon. Meish Goldish. LC 93-11997. (Made in America Ser.). 48p. (J). (gr. 4-8). 1993. lib. bdg. 21.27 (*0-86592-070-2*) Rourke Enter.

Levi Strauss: The Blue Jeans Man. Elizabeth Van Steenwyk. LC 87-31809. 96p. (J). (gr. 4-7). 1988. lib. bdg. 14.85 (*0-8027-6796-6*) Walker & Co.

Levia-Pondera. Francis B. Bickerstaffe-Drew. LC 67-26715. (Essay Index Reprint Ser.). 1977. 23.95 (*0-8369-0210-6*) Ayer.

Leviatan: O la Materia, Forma Poder De una Republica, Eclesiastica y Civil. 4th ed. Thomas Hobbes. (Biblioteca De Cultura Basica Ser.). 1995. 3.00 (*0-8477-0707-5*) U of PR Pr.

Leviathan. Paul Auster. 272p. 1993. pap. 12.95 (*0-14-017813-9*, Penguin Bks); pap. 11.00 (*0-14-017958-5*) Viking Penguin.

Leviathan. Hugh Fox. LC 80-39823. 1981. pap. 12.50 (*0-914140-10-8*) Carpenter Pr.

Leviathan. Julien Green. (FRE.). 1985. pap. 16.95 (*0-7859-2704-2*) Fr & Eur.

Leviathan. Thomas Hobbes. Ed. & Intro. by J. C. Gaskin. LC 99-178169. (Oxford World's Classics Ser.). (Illus.). 564p. 1998. pap. 8.95 (*0-19-283498-3*) OUP.

Leviathan. Thomas Hobbes. 1997. per. 8.00 (*0-684-84295-5*) S&S Trade.

Leviathan. Thomas Hobbes. Ed. by C. B. Macpherson. (English Library). 736p. 1982. pap. 9.95 (*0-14-043195-0*, Penguin Classics) Viking Penguin.

Leviathan. Thomas Hobbes. LC 88-60150. (Great Books in Philosophy). 205p. (C). 1988. pap. 7.95 (*0-87975-445-1*) Prometheus Bks.

Leviathan. James B. Huggins. 396p. 1996. pap. text 12.99 (*0-7852-7263-1*) Nelson.

Leviathan. Ed. by O. A. Robinson & Joseph Bien. (Orig.). 1986. pap. write for info. (*0-934135-00-2*) Klare Ltd.

Leviathan, Vol. 4. Frank O. Braynard. 424p. 1978. 45.00 (*0-685-34209-3*) F O Braynard.

Leviathan: Authoritative text, backgrounds, interpretations. Thomas Hobbes. Ed. by Richard Flathman & David Johnston. LC 95-42021. (Critical Editions Ser.). (C). 1996. pap. text 11.25 (*0-393-96798-0*, Norton Paperbks) Norton.

Leviathan: Contemporary Responses to the Political Theory of Thomas Hobbes. Ed. & Intro. by G. A. Rogers. (Key Issues Ser.). 317p. 1995. 72.00 (*1-85506-407-3*); pap. 24.00 (*1-85506-406-5*) Bks Intl VA.

Leviathan: The Legacy of Boccaccio. Richard Calder et al. Ed. by Jeff Vandermeer & Rose Secrest. (Leviathan Anthology Ser.: Vol. II). 192p. 1998. pap. 10.99 (*1-890464-03-1*) Ministry of Whimsy.

Leviathan: With Selected Variants from the Latin Edition of 1668. Thomas Hobbes. Tr. & Intro. by Edwin Curley. LC 93-49690. (Hackett Classics Ser.). 672p. (Orig.). (C). 1994. pap. text 10.95 (*0-87220-177-5*); lib. bdg. 39.95 (*0-87220-178-3*) Hackett Pub.

Leviathan & Natural Law. Francis L. Windolph. LC 73-88975. 146p. 1970. reprint ed. lib. bdg. 55.00 (*0-8371-2520-0*, WILL, Greenwood Pr) Greenwood.

Leviathan & the Air Pump: Hobbes, Boyle, & the Experimental Life. Steven Shapin & Simon Schaffer. LC 85-42705. (Illus.). 475p. 1985. text 75.00 (*0-691-08393-2*, Pub. by Princeton U Pr) Cal Prin Full Svc.

Leviathan & the Air Pump: Hobbes, Boyle, & the Experimental Way of Life. Steven Shapin & Simon Schaffer. (Illus.). 455p. (C). 1985. pap. text 24.95 (*0-691-02432-4*, Pub. by Princeton U Pr) Cal Prin Full Svc.

Leviathan at War. Ed. by Edmund A. Opitz. (Freeman Classics Ser.). 195p. 1995. pap. 9.95 (*1-57246-009-1*) Foun Econ Ed.

Leviathan I & II Hobbes. Herbert W. Schneider. 320p. (C). 1958. pap. text 10.00 (*0-02-407750-X*, Macmillan Coll) P-H.

Leviathan in the State Theory of Thomas Hobbes: Meaning & Failure of a Political Symbol, 374. Carl Schmitt. Tr. by George Schwab & Erna Hilfstein. LC 96-3642. (Contributions in Political Science Ser.: No. 374). 160p. 1996. 49.95 (*0-313-30057-7*, Greenwood Pr) Greenwood.

Leviathan Revisited: The Growth of Government Spending in Canada Since 1961. G. C. Ruggeri & Derek Hermanutz. LC 97-18353. (Illus.). 112p. 1997. text 55.95 (*1-85972-447-7*, Pub. by Avebry) Ashgate Pub Co.

Levin & O'Neal's the Diabetic Foot. 6th ed. John H. Bowker & Michael A. Pfeifer. (Illus.). 600p. (C). 2001. text. write for info. (*1-55664-471-X*) Mosby Inc.

Levin Years: A Golden Era, 1929-1951 Dallas, Texas (Bet Ha-Sefer Ha-Ivre Ba-Dallas) Ginger C. Jacobs. (Illus.). 112p. 1989. lib. bdg. 29.95 (*0-9624207-0-0*) G C Jacobs.

Levin Years - A Golden Era 1929-1951 Dallas, Texas: Hebrew School of Dallas & Its Activities. Ginger C. Jacobs. (Illus.). 112p. 1989. lib. bdg. 29.95 (*0-685-29101-4*) G C Jacobs.

Levinas: An Introduction. Colin Davis. LC 96-46628. 1996. pap. 17.00 (*0-268-01314-4*) U of Notre Dame Pr.

Levinas & Lacan: The Missed Encounter. Ed. by Sarah Harasym. LC 97-48472. (Series in Psychoanalysis & Culture). 256p. (C). 1998. text 65.50 (*0-7914-3959-3*); pap. text 21.95 (*0-7914-3960-7*) State U NY Pr.

Levinas Between Ethics & Politics: For the Beauty that Adorns the Earth. Bettina Bergo. LC 99-24358. (Phaenomenologica Ser.). 1999. write for info. (*0-7923-5694-2*) Kluwer Academic.

Levinas Beyond the Horizons of Cartesianism: An Inquiry into the Metaphysics of Morals. Anthony F. Beavers. LC 93-35785. (American University Studies: Vol. 150). 146p. (C). 1995. text 34.95 (*0-8204-2173-1*) P Lang Pubng.

Levinas, Blanchot, Jabes: Figures of Estrangement. Gary D. Mole. LC 97-12250. (CrossCurrents). 240p. 1997. 49.95 (*0-8130-1505-7*) U Press Fla.

Levinas Reader. Sean Hand. 356p. 1989. pap. text 28.95 (*0-631-16447-2*) Blackwell Pubs.

Levine. Donald E. Westlake. LC 83-63034. 1987. 45.00 (*0-89296-064-7*, Pub. by Mysterious Pr) Little.

Levine: Paintings & Drawings. Tom Levine. (Illus.). 80p. 1999. pap. 35.00 (*3-89322-339-8*) Dr Cantz sche Druckerei GmbH.

Levine & Co. Wall Street's Insider Trading Scandal. Douglas Frantz. 384p. 1988. mass mkt. 4.50 (*0-380-70625-3*, Avon Bks) Morrow Avon.

Levine's Conservation Model: A Framework for Nursing Practice. Ed. by Karen M. Schaefer & Jane B. Pond. LC 91-9488. 282p. 1991. text 36.95 (*0-8036-7747-2*) Davis Co.

Levine's Guide to Knives & Their Values: The Complete Handbook of Knife Collecting. 4th ed. Bernard Levine. LC 85-71895. (Illus.). 512p. 1997. pap. 27.95 (*0-87349-189-0*, LGK4(DB19746)) Krause Pubns.

***Levine's Guide to Knives & Their Values: The Complete Handbook of Knife Collecting.** 5th rev. ed. Bernard Levine. LC 85-71895. (Illus.). 544p. 2000. pap. 29.95 (*0-87341-945-6*, LGK5) Krause Pubns.

Levine's Quick Review Torts. 2nd ed. Publishing West Staff. (Sum & Substance Quick Review Ser.). 1998. pap. 18.95 (*1-57793-010-X*) West Pub.

Levine's Real Estate Transactions. Mark L. Levine. 1991. pap. write for info. (*0-314-86700-7*) West Pub.

Levin's Mill. Johannes Bobrowski. Tr. by Janet Cropper from GER. Orig. Title: Levins Muhle. 240p. 1988. 16.95 (*0-7145-0020-8*) M Boyars Pubs.

Levin's Mill. Johannes Bobrowski. Tr. by Janet Cropper from GER. LC 95-47598. (A New Directions Classic Ser.). Orig. Title: Levins Muhle. 230p. 1996. pap. 12.00 (*0-8112-1329-3*, Pub. by New Directions) Norton.

Levins Muhle see Levin's Mill

Levinson I Can Read: Chapter Book. Nancy Smiler Levinson. 48p. (J). (gr. 2-4). 14.89 (*0-06-028002-6*) HarpC Child Bks.

Levi's. William Gould. LC 97-39124. (VGM's Business Portraits Ser.). (Illus.). 48p. 1997. 14.95 (*0-8442-4782-0*, VGM Career) NTC Contemp Pub Co.

***Levi's Children: Coming to Terms with Human Rights in the Global Marketplace.** Karl Schoenberger. LC 99-55104. 288p. 2000. 25.00 (*0-87113-809-3*, Pub. by Grove-Atltic) Publishers Group.

Levitan. A. Fyodorov-Davydov. (Illus.). (C). 1988. 190.00 (*0-569-54052-6*, Pub. by Collets) St Mut.

Levitan. T. Yurova. (Illus.). 188p. (C). 1988. text 200.00 (*0-7855-5833-0*, Pub. by Collets) St Mut.

Levitating the Pentagon: Evolutions in the American Theatre of the Vietnam War Era. J. W. Fenn. LC 91-50677. 288p. 1992. 39.50 (*0-87413-442-0*) U Delaware Pr.

Levitating Trains & Kamikaze Genes: Technological Literacy for the Future. Richard P. Brennan. 262p. 1994. pap. 12.95 (*0-471-07902-2*) Wiley.

Levitating Trains & Kamikaze Genes: Technological Literacy for the 1990s. Richard P. Brennan. LC 90-55492. 1991. pap. 53.70 (*0-06-097374-9*, Perennial) HarperTrade.

Levitation. Timothy Mason. 1984. pap. 5.25 (*0-8222-0654-4*) Dramatists Play.

Levitation: Five Fictions. Cynthia Ozick. (Library of Modern Jewish Literature). 158p. 1995. pap. 16.95 (*0-8156-0353-3*) Syracuse U Pr.

Leviticus see Daily Study Bible for the Old Testament

Leviticus. (People's Bible Commentary Ser.). 252p. 1996. pap. 10.99 (*0-570-04867-2*, 12-8045) Concordia.

Leviticus. Andrew A. Bonar. (Banner of Truth Geneva Series Commentaries). 1978. 25.99 (*0-85151-086-8*) Banner of Truth.

Leviticus. Philip J. Budd. (New Century Bible Ser.). 395p. 1996. pap. 19.95 (*0-551-02834-3*, Pub. by Sheffield Acad) CUP Services.

Leviticus. Gary Demarest. (Communicator's Commentary Ser.: Vol. 3). 286p. 1990. 22.99 (*0-8499-0408-0*) Word Pub.

Leviticus. Gary W. Demarest. (Mastering the Old & New Testament Ser.: Vol. 3). pap. 14.99 (*0-8499-3542-3*) Word Pub.

Leviticus. Lester L. Grabbe. (Old Testament Guides Ser.). 116p. 1993. pap. 12.50 (*1-85075-440-3*, Pub. by Sheffield Acad) CUP Services.

Leviticus. R. K. Harrison. Ed. by Donald J. Wiseman. LC 80-7985. (Tyndale Old Testament Commentary Ser.). 240p. 1980. pap. 12.99 (*0-87784-253-1*, 253) InterVarsity.

Leviticus. John Hartley. (Biblical Commentary Ser.: Vol. 4). 1992. 29.99 (*0-8499-0203-7*) Word Pub.

Leviticus. G. A. Knight. 184p. 1993. pap. 30.00 (*0-7152-0479-3*, Pub. by St Andrew) St Mut.

Leviticus. Mark J. Lenz. LC 88-61920. (People's Bible Ser.). 246p. 1988. pap. 10.99 (*0-8100-0298-1*, 15N0459) Northwest Pub.

Leviticus. Mark J. Lenz. (The People's Bible Ser.). 62p. 1989. pap. text, student ed. 5.00 (*0-938272-68-3*, 22-2214) WELS Board.

Leviticus. J. McGee. (Thru the Bible Commentary Ser.: Vol. 1). 1997. pap. text 6.97 (*0-7852-0315-X*) Nelson.

Leviticus. J. Mcgee. (Thru the Bible Commentary Ser.: Vol. 2). 1997. pap. text 6.97 (*0-7852-0329-X*) Nelson.

Leviticus. Wayne A. Turner. (Bible Commentary - Old Testament Ser.). 88p. 1985. pap. 4.95 (*0-8146-1372-1*) Liturgical Pr.

Leviticus. Gordon J. Wenham. (New International Commentary on the Old Testament Ser.). 375p. 1979. 35.00 (*0-8028-2522-2*) Eerdmans.

Leviticus: A Commentary. Erhard S. Gerstenberger. Tr. by Douglas W. Stott. LC 96-21399. (Old Testament Library). 456p. 1996. 42.00 (*0-664-22064-9*) Westminster John Knox.

Leviticus: An Economic Commentary. Gary North. LC 94-37832. 792p. 1994. 29.95 (*0-930464-72-9*) Inst Christian.

Leviticus: Bible Study Commentary. Louis Goldberg. (Study Guide Commentary Ser.). 128p. (Orig.). 1980. pap. 6.99 (*0-310-41813-5*, 18198P) Zondervan.

Leviticus: The/Jewish Children's Bible. Sheryl Prenzlau. (Jewish Children's Bible Ser.). (Illus.). 64p. (J). (gr. 2-5). 1998. 18.95 (*0-943706-33-5*) Pitspopany.

Leviticus & Numbers. Paul R. House. LC 99-11543. (Shepherd's Notes Ser.). 100p. 1999. pap. 5.95 (*0-8054-9069-8*) Broadman.

Leviticus & Numbers. Compiled by A. E. Knoch. 167p. 1983. pap. 3.50 (*0-910424-27-6*) Concordant.

Leviticus & Numbers. Norman H. Snaith. (New Century Bible Ser.). 224p. 1977. reprint ed. 8.95 (*0-551-00778-8*) Attic Pr.

***Leviticus As Literature.** Mary Douglas. LC 99-24071. 304p. 2000. text 35.00 (*0-19-815092-X*) OUP.

Leviticus-Deuteronomy. M. Goldsmith. (Bible Study Commentaries Ser.). 126p. 1981. pap. 4.95 (*0-87508-151-7*) Chr Lit.

Leviticus-Numbers, Vol. 3. Mark F. Rooker. (The New American Commentary Ser.). 2000. 29.99 (*0-8054-0103-2*) Broadman.

Leviticus, Numbers, Deuteronomy. Yaacov Peterseil. (Tell It from the Torah Ser.). 1998. 18.95 (*0-943706-97-1*); pap. text 12.95 (*0-943706-84-X*) Pitspopany.

***Leviticus, Numbers, Deuteronomy.** Stephen K. Sherwood. (Berit Olam (The Everlasting Covenant) Ser.). 2000. 0.00 (*0-8146-5046-5*) Liturgical Pr.

L

An Asterisk (*) at the beginning of an entry indicates that the title is appearing for the first time.

L

Leviticus 17-27. Jacob Milgrom. LC 99-89367. (Anchor Bible Ser.). 2000. write for info. (0-385-41255-X) Doubleday.

***Leviticus 23-27.** Jacob Milgrom. LC 99-86528. (Anchor Bible Ser.). 2000. 50.00 (0-385-50035-1) Doubleday.

Levitsky. (Masters of World Painting Ser.). 1982. pap. 24.00 (0-7855-1637-9) St Mut.

Levitt & Tapley's Technological Basis of Radiation Therapy. 2nd ed. S. H. Levitt et al. (Illus.). 414p. 1992. text 82.00 (0-8121-1466-3) Lppncott W & W.

Levitt & Tapley's Technological Basis of Radiation Therapy: Clinical Applications. 3rd ed. Ed. by Seymour H. Levitt et al. LC 98-3836. 560p. 1998. 89.00 (0-683-30123-3) Lppncott W & W.

Levitt on Marketing. Harvard Business Review Staff. 100p. 1991. pap. 19.95 (0-07-103344-0) McGraw.

Levittown. Margaret L. Ferrer. LC 97-158190. (Images of America Ser.). 1997. pap. 16.99 (0-7524-0465-2) Arcadia Publng.

Levittown, Vol. II. Margaret Lundrigan & Tova Navarra. (Images of America Ser.). (Illus.). 128p. 1998. pap. 16.99 (0-7524-0982-4) Arcadia Publng.

Levittown: The Way We Were. Susan Kirsch Duncan. (Illus.). 112p. 1999. pap. 10.95 (0-930545-18-4) Maple Hill Pr.

Levittowners: Ways of Life & Politics in a New Suburban Community. Herbert J. Gans. LC 82-4375. (Morningside Bk.). 512p. 1982. reprint ed. pap. text 22.00 (0-231-05571-4) Col U Pr.

***Levni & the Surname: The Story of an Eighteenth-Century Ottoman Festival.** Esin Atil. (Illus.). 252p. 2000. 75.00 (975-6845-03-1) U of Wash Pr.

Levoglucosenone & Levoglucosans, Chemistry & Applications. Ed. by Zbigniew J. Witczak. LC 96-86322. 220p. 1993. 167.00 (1-882360-14-1) ATL Pr Sci.

Levon West. Neil MacNeil. (Illus.). 16p. (Orig.). (C). 1968. pap. 6.00 (0-943526-33-7) Parrish Art.

Levora. Lee Witte. 103p. (Orig.). 1990. pap. text 12.95 (0-9627087-0-4) Mt Olive Coll Pr.

Levy Chapter Book. Elizabeth Levy. 96p. (J). (gr. 2-5). 14.89 (0-06-028593-1) HarpC Child Bks.

Levy Flights & Related Topics in Physics: Proceedings of the International Workshop Held at Nice, France, 27-30 June 1994. Ed. by Michael F. Shlesinger et al. LC 95-17873. (Lecture Notes in Physics Ser.: Vol. 450). 400p. 1995. 92.95 (3-540-59222-9) Spr-Verlag.

Levy Processes. Jean Bertoin. (Cambridge Tracts in Mathematics Ser.: No. 121). 275p. (C). 1998. pap. text 27.95 (0-521-64632-4) Cambridge U Pr.

***Levy Processes & Infinitely Divisible Distributions.** Ken-iti Sato. (Cambridge Studies in Advanced Mathematics: No. 68). 498p. (C). 1999. 80.00 (0-521-55302-4) Cambridge U Pr.

Lew & His New Cap see Early Phonetic Readers - Set C

Lew Burke's Dog Training. Lew Burke. (Illus.). 255p. 1976. 17.95 (0-87666-656-X, H-962) TFH Pubns.

Lew Hunter's Screenwriting, No. 434. Lew Hunter. LC 93-32927. Vol. 434. 352p. (Orig.). 1994. pap. 14.95 (0-399-51838-X, Perigee Bks) Berkley Pub.

Lew McCoy on Antennas. Lew McCoy. LC 94-69519. (Illus.). 128p. (Orig.). 1995. pap. 15.95 (0-943016-08-8) CQ Commns Inc.

***Lew Wallace: Boy Writer.** Martha Schaaf et al. (Illus.). 120p. (J). (gr. 2-7). 2000. 14.95 (1-882859-05-7) Patria Pr.

Lew Wallace: An Autobiography (1906) see Smoke, Sound & Fury: The Civil War Memoirs of Major-General Lew Wallace, U. S. Volunteers

Lewd & Notorious: Female Transgression in the Eighteenth Century. Ed. by Katharine Kittredge. (Illus.). (C). text. write for info. (0-472-11090-X) U of Mich Pr.

Lewes String Theory Workshop: Lewes, Delaware, July 6-27, 1985. Ed. by L. Clavelli & A. Halprin. 312p. 1986. text 127.00 (9971-5-0033-7) World Scientific Pub.

Lewesdon Hill. William Crowe, Jr. LC 90-119018. 44p. 1989. reprint ed. 40.00 (1-85477-005-5) Continuum.

Lewin Legacy. Ed. by E. H. Stivers & S. A. Wheelan. (Recent Research in Psychology Ser.). xix, 281p. 1989. 70.95 (0-387-96352-9) Spr-Verlag.

Lewin's Mead. large type ed. E. V. Thompson. (Charnwood Large Print Ser.). 672p. 1997. 27.99 (0-7089-8955-1, Charnwood) Ulverscroft.

Lewis: Australian Bankruptcy Law. 10th ed. Dennis Rose. 1994. write for info. (0-455-21236-8, Pub. by LawBk Co); pap. write for info. (0-455-21237-6, Pub. by LawBk Co) Gaunt.

Lewis Acid Chemistry: A Practical Approach. Ed. by Hisashi Yamamoto. LC 98-35182. (Practical Approach Series in Chemistry). (Illus.). 292p. 1999. text 135.00 (0-19-850099-8) OUP.

Lewis Album from the Collection of Historical Photographs of Angus M. Macdonald, A. R. P. S. Ed. by Acair Ltd. Staff. 1985. 65.00 (0-86152-011-4, Pub. by Acair Ltd) St Mut.

***Lewis & Clark.** Contrib. by Lara Rice Bergen. LC 99-55477. (Explorers & Exploration Ser.). 48p. (J). 2000. 22.83 (0-7398-1486-9) Raintree Steck-V.

Lewis & Clark. Lynda Hatch. (Pathways of America Ser.). (Illus.). 96p. (J). (gr. 4-8). 1994. 10.99 (0-86653-799-6, GA1474) Good Apple.

Lewis & Clark. National Geographic Staff. LC 98-20061. 256p. 1998. per. 35.00 (0-7922-7084-3) Natl Geog.

Lewis & Clark. Scholastic Professional Books Staff. 56p. (J). 1997. pap. text 9.95 (0-590-67480-3) Scholastic Inc.

Lewis & Clark. R. Conrad Stein. LC 96-50146. (Cornerstones to Freedom Ser.). (Illus.). 32p. (J). (gr. 4-6). 1997. lib. bdg. 19.50 (0-516-20461-0) Childrens.

Lewis & Clark. R. Conrad Stein. (Cornerstones to Freedom Ser.). (J). 1998. pap. text 5.95 (0-516-26228-9) Childrens.

***Lewis & Clark.** George Sullivan. LC 99-27629. (In Their Own Words Ser.). (Illus.). 128p. (J). (gr. 4-7). 2000. 4.50 (0-439-09553-0); 12.95 (0-439-14749-2) Scholastic Inc.

Lewis & Clark: A Photographic Journey. Bill Moeller & Jan Moeller. LC 99-34862. (Illus.). 116p. 1999. pap. 18.00 (0-87842-405-9) Mountain Pr.

Lewis & Clark: An American Journey. Daniel B. Thorp. LC 98-12948. (Illus.). 160p. 1998. 22.98 (1-56799-584-5, MetroBooks) M Friedman Pub Grp Inc.

Lewis & Clark: Explorers of the American West see Junior World Biographies

Lewis & Clark: Explorers of the American West. Steven Kroll. (Illus.). 32p. (J). (gr. 4-6). 1994. pap. 6.95 (0-8234-1273-3) Holiday.

Lewis & Clark: Explorers of the Far West. Steven Kroll. LC 92-40427. (Illus.). 32p. (J). (gr. 4-6). 1994. lib. bdg. 16.95 (0-8234-1034-X) Holiday.

Lewis & Clark: Explorers of the Louisiana Purchase. Richard Kozar. LC 99-35227. (Explorers of the New World Ser.). (Illus.). 64p. 1999. 16.95 (0-7910-5513-2) Chelsea Hse.

Lewis & Clark: Explorers of the Northwest. Thomas Streissguth. LC 97-18044. (Historical American Biographies Ser.). 128p. (YA). (gr. 6 up). 1998. lib. bdg. 20.95 (0-7660-1016-3) Enslow Pubs.

Lewis & Clark: Exploring North America. Clint Twist. LC 93-33624. (Beyond the Horizons Ser.). 48p. (J). 1994. lib. bdg. 24.26 (0-8114-7255-8) Raintree Steck-V.

Lewis & Clark: Historic Places Associated with Their Transcontinental Exploration (1804-1806) 2nd ed. Roy Appleman. (Illus.). 484p. (C). 1993. reprint ed. pap. text 14.95 (0-931056-09-8) Jefferson Natl.

Lewis & Clark: Partners in Discovery. unabridged ed. John E. Bakeless. LC 96-19433. (Illus.). 498p. 1996. reprint ed. pap. text 11.95 (0-486-29233-9) Dover.

Lewis & Clark: Pioneering Naturalists. Paul R. Cutright. LC 88-38522. (Illus.). xvi, 522p. 1989. reprint ed. pap. 24.00 (0-8032-6334-1, Bison Books) U of Nebr Pr.

***Lewis & Clark: The Journey of The Corps of Discovery.** Dayton Duncan. 1999. pap. 25.00 (0-375-70652-6) Knopf.

Lewis & Clark: The Journey of the Corps of Discovery. Dayton Duncan et al. LC 97-73823. (Illus.). 288p. 1997. 40.00 (0-679-45450-0) Knopf.

Lewis & Clark: The Journey West. Albert Salisbury. 256p. 1990. 12.98 (0-88394-080-9) Promntory Pr.

Lewis & Clark: Voyage of Discovery. Stephen E. Ambrose & Sam Abell. LC 98-20061. 1998. denim. write for info. (0-7922-7155-6); denim 41.95 (0-7922-7085-1) Natl Geog.

Lewis & Clark: Voyage of Discovery. Dan Murphy. LC 76-57451. (Illus.). 64p. (Orig.). 1977. pap. 7.95 (0-916122-50-6) KC Pubns.

Lewis & Clark: Voyage of Discovery. Dan Murphy. Tr. by Brigitte Morales. (GER., Illus.). 48p. (Orig.). 1997. pap. 8.95 (0-88714-816-6) KC Pubns.

***Lewis & Clark: 1801-1850.** Sally Senzell Isaacs. (America in the Time Of... Ser.). 48p. 1999. 7.95 (1-57572-976-8) Heinemann Lib.

Lewis & Clark among the Indians. James P. Ronda. LC 84-3544. (Illus.). xvii, 310p. 1984. pap. 15.00 (0-8032-8929-4, Bison Books) U of Nebr Pr.

Lewis & Clark & Davey Hutchins. Nolan Carlson. LC 93-80993. (Illus.). 158p. (Orig.). (J). (gr. 4-8). 1994. pap. 6.95 (1-882420-08-X, 1-882420-08-X) Hearth KS.

Lewis & Clark & the Image of the American Northwest. John L. Allen. Orig. Title: Passage Through the Garden. (Illus.). 448p. 1998. reprint ed. pap. 12.95 (0-486-26914-0) Dover.

Lewis & Clark & the Route to the Pacific. Seamus Cavan. (World Explorers Ser.). (J). 1991. 15.15 (0-606-07784-7) Turtleback.

Lewis & Clark & the Route to the Pacific. Gary Moulton. Ed. by William H. Goetzmann. (World Explorers Ser.). (Illus.). 120p. (YA). (gr. 5 up). 1991. lib. bdg. 19.95 (0-7910-1327-8) Chelsea Hse.

Lewis & Clark College. Stephen D. Beckham. LC 91-71222. (Illus.). 160p. 1991. 29.95 (0-9630866-1-8) L&C Coll.

Lewis & Clark (1801-1850) Sally S. Isaacs. (America in the Time...Ser.). 48p. (YA). 1999. pap. 7.95 (1-57572-935-0) Heinemann Lib.

Lewis & Clark (1800-1849) Sally Isaacs. LC 98-34485. 1998. 25.45 (1-57572-744-7) Heinemann Lib.

Lewis & Clark Expedition. Sanna Kiesling. LC 95-24435. (Highlights in American History Ser.). (Illus.). 30p. (gr. 4-7). 1990. pap. 6.95 (0-937959-60-X) Falcon Pub Inc.

Lewis & Clark Expedition. Patrick McGrath. LC 84-40381. (Turning Points in American History Ser.). (Illus.). 64p. (J). (gr. 5 up). 1984. lib. bdg. 14.95 (0-382-06828-9) Silver Burdett Pr.

Lewis & Clark Expedition. Patrick McGrath. LC 84-40381. (Turning Points in American History Ser.). (Illus.). 64p. (YA). (gr. 5 up). 1984. pap. 7.95 (0-382-09899-4) Silver Burdett Pr.

***Lewis & Clark Expedition.** Patricia Ryon Quiri. (We the People Ser.). (Illus.). 48p. (J). 2000. write for info. (0-7565-0044-3) Compass Point.

Lewis & Clark Expedition, Vol. 1. Barth. 240p. 1998. pap. text 11.95 (0-312-11118-5) St Martin.

Lewis & Clark Expedition: Selections from the Journals, Arranged By Topics. Gunther Barth. LC 97-74956. 240p. 1998. text 35.00 (0-312-12801-0) St Martin.

Lewis & Clark Expedition: 1804-1806. James A. Crutchfield. 39.00 (1-56696-098-3) Jackdaw.

Lewis & Clark Exploration of Central Montana: Marias River to the Gates of the Mountains. Ella M. Howard. (Illus.). 69p. (J). (gr. 4 up). 1993. pap. 7.00 (1-883844-00-2) Lewis & Clark.

***Lewis & Clark for Kids: Their Journey of Discovery with 21 Activities.** Janis Herbert. LC 99-48178. (J). 2000. 14.95 (1-55652-374-2) Chicago Review.

Lewis & Clark in Missouri. Ann Rogers. 1994. 14.95 (0-941088-01-4) Meredco.

Lewis & Clark in North Dakota. 2nd ed. Ed. by Russell Reid. (Illus.). 347p. 1988. reprint ed. pap. 15.95 (1-891419-08-0) State Hist ND.

***Lewis & Clark in the Bitterroot.** Jean O'Neill. 216p. 1998. 19.95 (0-912299-76-2); pap. 14.95 (0-912299-71-1) Stoneydale Pr Pub.

Lewis & Clark in the Three Rivers Valleys. Donald F. Nell & John E. Taylor. (Illus.). 299p. (Orig.). 1996. pap. text 23.40 (0-9651346-0-1) Headwaters Chapter.

Lewis & Clark in the Three Rivers Valleys, Montana, 1805-1806: From the Original Journals of the Lewis & Clark Expedition. Meriwether Lewis & William Clark. Ed. by Donald F. Nell & John E. Taylor. LC 96-35318. 1996. pap. 16.95 (1-880397-17-X) Patrice Pr.

Lewis & Clark in the Three Rivers Valleys, Montana, 1805-1806: From the Original Journals of the Lewis & Clark Expedition (Includes Sheets Containing Six Full Color Maps) Meriwether Lewis et al. (Illus.). 1996. pap., suppl. ed. 20.90 (1-880397-19-6) Patrice Pr.

***Lewis & Clark Meet the American Indians: As Told by Seaman the Dog.** Everett C. Albers. (Illus.). 32p. (J). (ps-11). 1999. pap. 3.95 (0-9674002-0-1) United Printing.

***Lewis & Clark on the Upper Missouri.** Discovery Writers Staff. LC 99-75624. (Illus.). 215p. 1999. 19.95 (0-912299-85-1); pap. 14.95 (0-912299-84-3) Stoneydale Pr Pub.

***Lewis & Clark Trail Maps Vol. I: A Cartographic Reconstruction.** Martin Plamondon. (Illus.). 176p. 2000. 65.00 (0-87422-232-X); pap. 45.00 (0-87422-233-8) Wash St U Pr.

***Lewis & Clark Travel Planner & Guide.** Barbara Fifer. (Illus.). 100p. 2000. pap. 3.95 (1-56037-159-5, Montana Magazine) Am Wrld Geog.

Lewis & Clark's Journey of Discovery in American History. Judy Edwards. LC 98-14484. (In American History Ser.). 128p. (YA). (gr. 5 up). 1999. lib. bdg. 20.95 (0-7660-1127-5) Enslow Pubs.

Lewis & Pappa: Adventure on the Santa Fe Trail. Barbara M. Joosse. LC 97-22572. (Illus.). 40p. (J). (gr. k-3). 1998. 14.95 (0-8118-1959-0) Chronicle Bks.

Lewis B. Hershey: Mr. Selective Service. George Q. Flynn. LC 84-10397. (Illus.). 402p. reprint ed. pap. 124.70 (0-608-06005-4, 206633300008) Bks Demand.

***Lewis Baltz: New Industrial Parks Near Irvine, California.** 2nd ed. Photos by Lewis Baltz. (Illus.). 112p. 2000. reprint ed. 35.00 (0-9630785-6-9) RAM Publications.

Lewis Carroll see Modern Critical Views Series

Lewis Carroll. Beverly L. Clark. Ed. by Roger C. Schlobin. LC 87-16032. (Starmont Reader's Guide Ser.: Vol. 47). viii, 96p. 1990. pap. 17.00 (1-55742-030-0) Millefleurs.

Lewis Carroll. Morton N. Cohen. 1996. pap. 17.00 (0-679-74562-9) Knopf.

Lewis Carroll. deluxe ed. Lewis Carroll, pseud. (Illus.). 896p. 1995. 19.99 (0-517-14781-5) Random Hse Value.

Lewis Carroll. Walter J. De La Mare. (English Literature Ser.: No. 33). 1972. reprint ed. lib. bdg. 75.00 (0-8383-1489-9) M S G Haskell Hse.

Lewis Carroll. Derek Hudson. LC 72-5453. 354p. 1972. reprint ed. lib. bdg. 69.50 (0-8371-6439-7, HULC, Greenwood Pr) Greenwood.

Lewis Carroll: A Biography. Michael Bakewell. LC 95-472. (Illus.). 400p. 1996. 27.50 (0-393-03906-4) Norton.

Lewis Carroll: A Biography. Morton N. Cohen. 12.95 (0-614-28402-3) Vin Bks.

Lewis Carroll: A Portrait with Background. Donald Thomas. (Illus.). 416p. 1998. 35.00 (0-7195-5323-7, Pub. by John Murray) Trafalgar.

Lewis Carroll: A Reference Guide. Rachel Fordyce. 400p. 1988. 50.00 (0-8161-8925-0, Hall Reference) Macmillan.

Lewis Carroll: An Annotated International Bibliography, 1960-1977. Edward Guiliano. LC 80-13975. 253p. 1980. 10.00 (0-8139-0862-0) L Carroll Soc.

Lewis Carroll: An Annotated International Bibliography, 1960-1977. Edward Guiliano. LC 80-13975. 263p. reprint ed. pap. 81.60 (0-7837-4352-1, 204406200012) Bks Demand.

Lewis Carroll: Revised Edition. Richard Kelly. (Twayne's English Authors Ser.: No. 212). 208p. (C). 1990. 32.00 (0-8057-6988-9, Twyne) Mac Lib Ref.

Lewis Carroll: Selected Poems. Ed. by Keith Silver. 128p. pap. 12.95 (1-85754-147-2, Pub. by Carcanet Pr) Paul & Co Pubs.

Lewis Carroll & His Camera. Roy Aspin. (C). 1989. text 60.00 (0-948706-04-X, Pub. by Brent Pubns) St Mut.

Lewis Carroll & the Kitchins. Lewis Carroll, pseud. Tr. by Morton N. Cohen. LC 79-92406. (Carroll Studies: No. 4). (Illus.). 80p. (Orig.). pap. 10.00 (0-930326-04-0) L Carroll Soc.

Lewis Carroll & the Kitchins. limited ed. Ed. by Morton N. Cohen. (Illus.). 64p. 1980. 37.50 (0-317-64759-8) Argosy.

Lewis Carroll & the Press. Charles Lovett. LC 98-52495. (Illus.). 135p. 1999. text 35.00 (1-884718-87-6, R53904) Oak Knoll.

***Lewis Carroll & the Press: An Annotated Bibliography of Charles Dodgson's Contributions to Periodicals** Charles C. Lovett. LC 98-52495. vi, 1117p. 1999. write for info. (0-7123-4627-9, Pub. by B23tish Library) S Asia.

Lewis Carroll at Texas. Compiled by Robert N. Taylor. (Illus.). 1985. pap. 25.00 (0-87959-104-8) U of Tex H Ransom Ctr.

Lewis Carroll in Russia: Translations of Alice in Wonderland 1879-1989. Fan Parker. 89p. 1994. pap. text 15.00 (0-9644886-0-4) Russian Hse.

Lewis Carroll in Wonderland: The Life & Times of Alice & Her Creator. Stephanie L. Stoffel. LC 96-39346. (Discoveries Ser.). (Illus.). 176p. 1997. pap. 12.95 (0-8109-2838-8, Pub. by Abrams) Time Warner.

Lewis Carroll's Alice: An Annotated Checklist of the Lovett Collection, 1965-1986. Charles C. Lovett & Stephanie B. Lovett. 565p. 1989. lib. bdg. 89.50 (0-313-27682-X, LLR/) Greenwood.

Lewis Carroll's Alice: An Annotated Checklist of the Lovett Collection, 1965-1986. Charles C. Lovett et al. LC 89-13494. xvii, 548p. 1990. write for info. (0-88736-166-8) Mecklermedia.

Lewis Carroll's Classic Photos of Children. Lewis Carroll, pseud. 1998. pap. 4.95 (0-486-29788-8) Dover.

Lewis Carroll's Games & Puzzles. 40th ed. Lewis Carroll, pseud. (Illus.). 128p. (Orig.). 1992. pap. 4.95 (0-486-26922-1) Dover.

Lewis Cass. Andrew C. McLaughlin. Ed. by John T. Morse, Jr. LC 70-128957. (American Statesmen Ser.: No. 24). reprint ed. 49.50 (0-404-50874-X) AMS Pr.

Lewis Cass & the Politics of Moderation. Willard C. Klunder. LC 95-37385. (Illus.). 440p. 1996. 39.00 (0-87338-536-5) Kent St U Pr.

Lewis Cass-Frontier Soldier. Virginia L. Burns. LC 80-81133. (Illus.). 1980. lib. bdg. 17.50 (0-9604726-1-4) Enterprise Pr.

Lewis Chessman & What Happened to Them. Irving Finkel. (J). (gr. 4-7). 1999. pap. text 16.95 (0-7141-0592-9) Brimax Bks.

Lewis Chessmen & the Enigma of the Hoard. Neil Stratford. LC 97-186380. 1999. pap. text. write for info. (0-7141-0587-2) British Mus Pr.

Lewis Collection, in Corpus Christi College, Cambridge Pt. I: The Greek & Hellenistic Coins. (Sylloge Nummorum Graecorum Ser.: Vol. VI). 1972. 45.00 (0-19-725924-3) David Brown.

Lewis Collection, in Corpus Christi College, Cambridge Pt. II: The Greek Imperial Coins. Ed. by Ian Carradice. (Sylloge Nummorum Graecorum Ser.: Vol. VI). (Illus.). 64p. 1992. text 115.00 (0-19-726089-6) OUP.

Lewis' Cork: A Topographical Dictionary of the Parishes, Towns & Villages of Cork City & County. Samuel Lewis. LC 99-176130. (Illus.). 360p. 1998. pap. 31.95 (1-898256-57-8, Pub. by Collins Press) Irish Bks Media.

Lewis County, MO Vols. 1-2: Index to Circuit Court Records, 1833-1841 & 1841-1851. Sherida K. Eddlemon. 121p. (Orig.). 1994. pap. text 16.50 (1-55613-984-5) Heritage Bk.

Lewis County, Tennessee. Turner Publishing Company Staff. LC 95-60268. 176p. 1995. 49.95 (1-56311-196-9) Turner Pub KY.

Lewis Creek Mound Culture in Virginia, No. M3. Howard A. MacCord, Sr. 92p. 1986. pap. 17.00 (1-884626-20-3) Archeolog Soc.

Lewis D. & Mary Ellen (Meader) Fry Family Genealogy. Arthur Fry. (Illus.). 410p. (Orig.). 1991. pap. write for info. (0-938041-07-X) Arc Pr AR.

Lewis DeSoto. Dan Cameron. (Illus.). 36p. 1998. pap. 10.00 (1-889195-19-7) Smart Art Pr.

***Lewis Dictionary of Occupational & Environmental Safety & Health.** Jeffrey W. Vincoli. LC 99-32640. 1104p. 1999. boxed set 89.95 (1-56670-399-9) Lewis Pubs.

Lewis Edmund Crook Jr. Architect, 1898-1967: A Twentieth-Century Traditionalist in the Deep South. William R. Mitchell. LC 84-6240. (Illus.). 144p. 1984. 45.00 (0-9614203-0-8) L C Crossley.

Lewis Evans: His Map of the Middle British Colonies in America. Harry N. Stevens. LC 70-146422. (First American Frontier Ser.). 1971. reprint ed. 13.95 (0-405-02892-X) Ayer.

Lewis Evans, to Which Is Added Evans', a Brief Account of Pennsylvania, Together with Facsimiles of His Geographical, Historical, Political, Philosophical, & Mechanical Essays, Nos. I & II. Ed. by Lawrence H. Gipson. (History - United States Ser.). 246p. 1993. reprint ed. lib. bdg. 79.00 (0-7812-4873-6) Rprt Serv.

Lewis Families of Putnam County, Missouri Vol. 2: Lewis Ancestors, Research Data, Maps & Obituaries. Gary G. Lloyd. LC 89-91322. (Illus.). 166p. 1989. pap. 15.00 (0-9622972-2-4) G G Lloyd.

Lewis-Gale Medical Center. Amy Phillips. Ed. by Phyllis Harholdt & Rodney Nelson. (Illus.). 250p. (C). 1993. 50.00 (0-929690-21-4) Herit Pubs AZ.

Lewis Grizzard: Two Blockbuster Best Sellers. Lewis Grizzard. LC 97-39742. 1997. write for info. (1-889372-68-4) Sweetwater Pr.

Lewis H. Morgan on Iroquois Material Culture. Elizabeth Tooker. (Illus.). 400p. (Orig.). 1994. lib. bdg. 76.00 (0-8165-1347-3) U of Ariz Pr.

Lewis Hayden & the War Against Slavery. Joel Strangis. LC 98-29406. (Illus.). xiv, 167p. (YA). (gr. 9 up). 1999. lib. bdg. 23.50 (0-208-02430-1, Linnet Bks) Shoe String.

Lewis Henry Morgan. Tooker. (Illus.). 400p. (Orig.). 1994. pap. 41.00 (0-8165-1462-3) U of Ariz Pr.

Lewis Henry Morgan, American Scholar. Carl Resek. LC 60-5468. (Midway Reprint Ser.). (Illus.). 196p. reprint ed. pap. 60.80 (0-608-09512-5, 205431300005) Bks Demand.

Lewis Henry Morgan, American Scholar. Carl Resek. (Midway Reprint Ser.). (Illus.). 1974. reprint ed. pap. text 8.00 (0-226-71012-2) U Ch Pr.

Lewis Henry Morgan & the Invention of Kinship. Thomas R. Trautman. LC 86-24941. (Illus.). 300p. 1987. pap. 16.95 (0-520-06457-7, Pub. by U CA Pr) Cal Prin Full Svc.

Lewis Hine: Passionate Journey: Photographs, 1905-1937. Lewis Hine. (Illus.). 240p. 1997. 55.00 (3-908162-55-6) Dist Art Pubs.

An Asterisk (*) at the beginning of an entry indicates that the title is appearing for the first time.

Lewis Howard Latimer. Glennette Turner. (Pioneers in Change Ser.). (Illus.). 144p. (J). (gr. 5-9). 1990. lib. bdg. 13.95 (*0-382-09524-3*) Silver Burdett Pr.

Lewis Is Dead & I Don't Feel So Good Myself! James T. Curtis. 208p. 1997. pap. 11.00 (*0-8059-4148-7*) Dorrance.

Lewis Land Struggle: Na Gaisgich. Joni Buchanan. LC 98-189059. 209 p. 1996. write for info. (*0-86152-166-8*) Acair Ltd.

Lewis Latimer: Creating Bright Ideas. Eleanor H. Ayer. LC 96-18930. (Innovative Minds Ser.). 112p. (J). 1997. lib. bdg. 27.11 (*0-8172-4407-7*) Raintree Steck-V.

Lewis Latimer: Scientist. Winifred L. Norman & Lily Patterson. Ed. by Nathan I. Huggins. LC 93-185. (Black Americans of Achievement Ser.). (Illus.). 124p. (J). (gr. 5 up). 1994. lib. bdg. 19.95 (*0-7910-1977-2*) Chelsea Hse.

Lewis Leffman: Ordnance Sergeant United States Army. Donald E. Loker. 64p. (Orig.). 1974. pap. 3.50 (*0-685-29131-6*) Niagara Cnty Hist Soc.

Lewis M. Terman: Pioneer in Educational Testing. Henry L. Minton. (American Social Experience Ser.: No. 12). (Illus.). 254p. (C). 1990. pap. text 20.00 (*0-8147-5452-X*) NYU Pr.

Lewis Management. Date not set. pap. text, teacher ed. write for info. (*0-314-05606-8*) West Pub.

Lewis Management. 1995. pap., student ed. 20.00 (*0-314-05409-X*) West Pub.

Lewis Management Modules. Date not set. pap. text. write for info. (*0-314-05410-3*) West Pub.

Lewis Management Multimedia Guide. Date not set. pap. text. write for info. (*0-314-05411-1*) West Pub.

Lewis Management Note Guide. 1994. pap. 13.75 (*0-314-05412-X*) West Pub.

Lewis Management Readings. LC 96-128197. 1995. pap. 13.75 (*0-314-05413-8*) West Pub.

Lewis Miller (Berry) Hendrick. 1998. lib. bdg. write for info. (*1-56723-121-7*) Yestermorrow.

Lewis Morley: Photographer of the '60s. Terence Pepper. (Illus.). 96p. 1989. pap. 29.50 (*1-85514-003-9*, Pub. by Natl Port Gall) Antique Collect.

Lewis Morris, Anglo-American Statesman, ca 1613-1691. Samuel S. Smith. (Illus.). 136p. 1983. 20.00 (*0-391-02767-0*) Morris Genealog Lib.

Lewis Morris, 1671-1746: A Study in Early American Politics. Eugene R. Sheridan. LC 81-14531. (New York State Study Ser.). 269p. 1981. reprint ed. pap. 83.40 (*0-608-07626-0*, 205994100010) Bks Demand.

Lewis Mumford. Novak. 1998. 23.95 (*0-8057-4548-3*, Twyne) Mac Lib Ref.

Lewis Mumford: A Life. Donald L. Miller. LC 91-29646. (Illus.). 672p. 1992. pap. 24.95 (*0-8229-5907-0*) U of Pittsburgh Pr.

Lewis Mumford: A Life. Donald L. Miller. 628p. 1999. reprint ed. pap. text 23.00 (*0-7881-6271-3*) DIANE Pub.

Lewis Mumford & American Modernism: Eutopian Theories for Architecture & Urban Planning. Robert Wojtowicz. LC 95-16564. (Illus.). 236p. (C). 1996. text 64.95 (*0-521-48215-1*) Cambridge U Pr.

Lewis Mumford & American Modernism: Eutopian Theories for Architecture & Urban Planning. Robert Wojtowicz. (Illus.). 236p. (C). 1998. reprint ed. pap. text 18.95 (*0-521-63924-7*) Cambridge U Pr.

Lewis Mumford & Patrick Geddes: The Correspondence. Ed. by Frank G. Novak, Jr. LC 94-41551. (Illus.). 408p. (C). (gr. 13). 1995. 75.00 (*0-415-11906-5*) Routledge.

Lewis Mumford & the Ecological Region: The Politics of Planning. Mark Luccarelli. LC 95-30860. (Critical Perspectives Ser.). 230p. 1995. lib. bdg. 35.00 (*1-57230-001-9*) Guilford Pubns.

Lewis Mumford & the Ecological Region: The Politics of Planning. Mark Luccarelli. LC 95-30860. (Critical Perspectives Ser.). 230p. 1997. pap. text 18.95 (*1-57230-228-3*, 0228) Guilford Pubns.

Lewis Mumford Reader. Mumford. 1986. 14.95 (*0-07-545025-9*) McGraw.

Lewis Mumford Reader. Ed. by Donald L. Miller. LC 94-29148. 400p. 1995. reprint ed. pap. 19.95 (*0-8203-1695-4*) U of Ga Pr.

Lewis Mumford/David Liebovitz Letters, 1923-1968. Bettina L. Knapp. LC 82-50418. viii, 249p. 1983. 40.00 (*0-87875-250-1*) Whitston Pub.

Lewis Mumford's Reception in German Translation & Criticism. Heinz Tschachler. 150p. (C). 1994. lib. bdg. 36.00 (*0-8191-9564-2*) U Pr of Amer.

Lewis Namier & Zionism. Norman Rose. 192p. 1980. text 29.95 (*0-19-822621-7*) OUP.

Lewis Patriarchs of Early Virginia & Maryland. 3rd ed. Robert J. Lewis. LC 99-159785. (Illus.). 176p. 1998. pap. 27.00 (*0-7884-0906-9*, L183) Heritage Bk.

Lewis Percy. Anita Brookner. LC 90-50482. 272p. 1991. pap. 14.00 (*0-679-72944-5*) Vin Bks.

*__Lewis Perdue 2.__ Lewis Perdue. 2001. text. write for info. (*0-312-85238-X*) St Martin.

Lewis Rubenstein: The Hudson Valley Painter. Frwd. by Nicolai Cikovsky, Jr. LC 93-19589. (Illus.). 1993. 29.95 (*0-87951-515-5*, Pub. by Overlook Pr) Penguin Putnam.

Lewis Tappan & the Evangelical War Against Slavery. Bertram Wyatt-Brown. (Illus.). 400p. 1997. pap. text 16.95 (*0-8071-2223-8*) La State U Pr.

Lewis the Story of an Island. Christine Macdonald. (C). 1992. text 45.00 (*0-86152-804-2*, Pub. by Acair Ltd) St Mut.

Lewis Theobald. Richard F. Jones. LC 19-6896. reprint ed. 27.50 (*0-404-03605-8*) AMS Pr.

Lewis Theobald & the Editing of Shakespeare. Peter Seary. 264p. 1990. text 75.00 (*0-19-812965-3*) OUP.

Lewis Thomas. Andrew J. Angyal. (United States Authors Ser.). 176p. 1989. text 24.95 (*0-8057-7536-6*, TUSAS 547, Twyne) Mac Lib Ref.

*__Lewis W. Hine: Children at Work.__ Vicki Goldberg. (Illus.). 104p. 1999. 39.95 (*3-7913-2156-0*, Pub. by Prestel) te Neues.

Lewis W. Hine: The Empire State Building. Ed. by Freddy Langer. LC 98-34624. (Illus.). 104p. 1998. 39.95 (*3-7913-1996-5*) te Neues.

Lewis Walker, Ninety-Day Wonder. 200p. 1989. 16.95 (*0-8187-0116-1*) Harlo Press.

Lewis Walker of Chester Valley & His Descendants, 1686-1896. P. W. Streets. (Illus.). 446p. 1989. reprint ed. pap. 67.00 (*0-8328-1219-6*); reprint ed. lib. bdg. 75.00 (*0-8328-1218-8*) Higginson Bk Co.

*__Lewis Watts: South to West Oakland.__ Lewis Watts. (Contact Sheet Ser.: Vol. 101). (Illus.). 32p. 1999. pap. write for info. (*0-935445-08-0*) Light Work.

Lewis Wetzel, Indian Fighter. rev. ed. C. B. Allman. (Illus.). 1961. 16.95 (*0-8159-6107-3*) Devin.

Lewisboro. Maureen Koehl. (Images of America Ser.). 128p. 1997. pap. 16.99 (*0-7524-0545-4*) Arcadia Publng.

Lewisburg United Methodist Church: A Bicentennial History. Otis K. Rice. 111p. 1988. pap. text. write for info. (*0-9620189-0-2*) Lewisburg United.

Lewises, Meriwethers & Their Kin. Sarah T. Anderson. LC 84-80082. (Illus.). 652p. 1995. reprint ed. 40.00 (*0-8063-1072-3*) Genealog Pub.

*__Lewisias.__ B. LeRoy Davidson. LC 99-53481. (Illus.). 238p. 2000. 34.95 (*0-88192-447-4*) Timber.

Lewiston & Auburn. H. Kenneth Dutille. (Images of America Ser.). 1995. pap. 16.99 (*0-7524-0220-X*) Arcadia Publng.

Lewiston Country: An Armchair History Margaret Day Allen & Ladd Hamilton. LC 90-60181. vi, 253p. 1990. write for info. (*0-9626050-0-X*) Nez Perce Cnty Hist Soc.

Lewitt Sol: Structures, 1962-1993. Photos by David Batchelor et al. (GER., Illus.). 128p. 1993. pap. 68.00 (*0-905836-78-2*, Pub. by Museum Modern Art) St Mut.

Lex & Yacc. 2nd ed. John Levine et al. (Computer Science). 366p. 1992. pap. 29.95 (*1-56592-000-7*) Thomson Learn.

Lex., Dictionary Industrial Measuring Technology. 3rd ed. P. Profos & Domeisen. (GER & ENG.). 251p. 1993. 120.00 (*0-320-03038-5*) Fr & Eur.

Lex et Evangelium: Untersuchungen Zur Jesajavorlesung von Johannes Bugenhagen. Volker Gummelt. (Arbeiten zur Kirchengeschichte Ser.: Vol. 62). (GER.). xi, 209p. (C). 1994. lib. bdg. 121.55 (*3-11-014204-X*) De Gruyter.

*__Lex et Romanitas: Essays for Alan Watson.__ Alan Watson & Michael H. Hoeflich. LC 00-20406. (Studies in Comparative Legal History). 2000. write for info. (*1-882239-10-5*) Robbins Collection.

Lex-I-Con. Robert L. Rucker. (Chaplets Ser.). 12p. 1996. pap. 2.50 (*0-916155-33-1*) Trout Creek.

Lex Mercatoria & Arbitration. Ed. by Thomas E. Carbonneau. 250p. 1990. 85.00 (*0-929179-35-8*) Juris Pubng.

Lex Mercatoria & Arbitration: A Discussion of the New Law Merchant. Thomas E. Carbonneau. LC 97-46193. 1997. 85.00 (*1-57823-023-3*) Juris Pubng.

Lex Mercatoria & Arbitration: A Discussion of the New Law Merchant. Thomas E. Carbonneau. LC 98-17861. 1998. 100.00 (*90-411-0586-7*) Kluwer Law Intl.

Lex Mercatoria & Legal Pluralism: A Late Thirteenth-Century Treatise & Its Afterlife. Mary E. Basile et al. (Ames Foundation Publications). (Illus.). 212,42,118p. 1998. 60.00 (*1-893606-12-0*) W S Hein.

Lex Mundi. Alexander Vincent. viii, 121p. 1993. reprint ed. 35.00 (*0-8377-2706-5*, Rothman) W S Hein.

Lex of Machine Assembling Tools. Gilles Boivin. (FRE & ENG.). 82p. 1994. pap. 24.95 (*0-320-02953-0*) Fr & Eur.

Lex Parliamentaria: Or, A Treatise of the Law & Custom of the Parliaments of England. B. Georgeson. Incl. Defense of the Parliament of England in the Case of James II., **2 vols. in 1** LC 72-83167. 1974. reprint ed. LC 72-83167. (English Studies). 1974. 33.00 (*0-8420-1420-9*) Scholarly Res Inc.

Lex Parliamentaria Americana: Elements of Law & Practice of Legislative Assemblies in the United States of America. Luther S. Cushing. (Lex Parliamentaria Americana Ser.). xxxvi, 1063p. 1989. reprint ed. 95.00 (*0-8377-2014-1*, Rothman) W S Hein.

Lex Publica: Gesetz und Recht in der roemischen Republik. Jochen Bleicken. (C). 1975. 146.15 (*3-11-004584-2*) De Gruyter.

Lex Rex. Samuel Rutherford. 1992. pap. 19.99 (*0-87377-951-7*) GAM Pubns.

Lex und Yacc. Helmut Herold. (GER.). (C). 1992. text. write for info. (*0-201-56577-3*) Addison-Wesley.

Lexeconics: The Interaction of Law & Economics. Ed. by Gerald Sirkin. (Social Dimensions of Economics, CCNY Ser.: Vol. 2). 272p. 1981. lib. bdg. 111.00 (*0-89838-053-7*) Kluwer Academic.

Lexeme-Morpheme Base Morphology: A General Theory of Inflection & Word Formation. Robert Beard. LC 94-30216. (SUNY Series in Linguistics). 433p. (C). 1995. text 89.50 (*0-7914-2471-5*); pap. text 29.95 (*0-7914-2472-3*) State U NY Pr.

Lexi-Hotel Francais-Anglais. Chantal Meyrier. 144p. 1993. pap. 22.95 (*0-7859-5637-9*, 2713512441) Fr & Eur.

Lexi-Tourisme Espagnol-Francais. Maria-Luisa Le Poullioun. 144p. 1993. pap. 22.95 (*0-7859-5636-0*, 2713512433) Fr & Eur.

Lexica Graeca Minora. xvii, 372p. 1992. 130.00 (*3-487-00997-8*) G Olms Pubs.

Lexica Graeca Minora. K. Latte & H. Erbse. xvii, 372p. 1965. write for info. (*0-318-72039-6*) G Olms Pubs.

Lexical Acculturation in Native American Languages. Cecil H. Brown. LC 98-13835. (Oxford Studies in Anthropological Linguistics: No. 19). 272p. 1999. text 55.00 (*0-19-512161-9*) OUP.

Lexical Acquisition: Exploiting On-Line Resources to Build a Lexicon. Ed. by Uri Zernik. 440p. 1991. pap. 45.00 (*0-8058-1127-3*); text 99.95 (*0-8058-0829-9*) L Erlbaum Assocs.

Lexical Affiliations of Vegliote. John Fisher. 249p. 1975. 20.00 (*0-8386-7796-7*) Fairleigh Dickinson.

Lexical Aids for Students of New Testament Greek. Bruce Metzger. 100p. 1990. pap. 12.95 (*0-567-29182-0*, Pub. by T & T Clark) Bks Intl VA.

Lexical Aids for Students of New Testament Greek. 3rd ed. Bruce M. Metzger. LC 98-17400. 112p. (C). (gr. 8 up). 1998. pap. 7.99 (*0-8010-2180-4*) Baker Bks.

Lexical Aids for Students of New Testament Greek. 3rd ed. Bruce M. Metzger. xi, 100p. 1969. pap. text 5.65 (*0-9644891-0-4*) Princeton Theol Sem.

Lexical Ambiguity in Poetry. Soon P. Su. LC 93-8248. (Studies in Language & Linguistics). 1994. write for info. (*0-582-10116-6*, Pub. by Addison-Wesley) Longman.

Lexical Ambiguity Resolution: Perspectives from Psycholinguistics, Neuropsychology, & Artificial Intelligence. Ed. by Steven Small et al. 518p. (C). 1988. text 38.95 (*0-934613-50-8*) Morgan Kaufmann.

Lexical Amiguity Poetry. Soon P. Su. LC 93-8248. (Studies in Language & Linguistics). 1995. pap. text 22.66 (*0-582-10114-X*, Pub. by Addison-Wesley) Longman.

*__Lexical Anaphors & Pronouns in Selected South Asian Languages.__ Barbara Lust. LC 99-52518. (Empirical Approaches to Language Typology Ser.). 950p. 1999. write for info. (*3-11-014388-7*) Mouton.

*__Lexical & Constructional Aspects of Linguistic Explanation.__ Ed. by Gert Webelhuth et al. LC 98-26881. (Studies in Constraint-Based Lexicalism (SCBL)). 378p. (C). 1999. pap. text 24.95 (*1-57586-152-6*) CSLI.

*__Lexical & Constructional Aspects of Linguistic Explanation.__ Ed. by Gert Webelhuth et al. LC 98-26881. (Studies in Constraint-Based Lexicalism (SCBL)). 378p. (C). 1999. 64.95 (*1-57586-153-4*) CSLI.

Lexical & Grammatical Variation in a Corpus: A Computer-Assisted Study of Discourse on the Environment. Andrea Gerbig. LC 97-42186. (Duisburg Papers for Research in Language & Culture: Vol. 33). (Illus.). 237p. (C). 1997. pap. text 44.95 (*0-8204-3278-4*) P Lang Pubng.

Lexical & Syntactical Constructions & the Construction of Meaning: Proceedings of the Bi-Annual ICLA Meeting in Albuquerque, July 1996. Kidong Yi. Ed. by Marjolijn Verspoor et al. LC 97-18868. (Current Issues in Linguistics Theory Ser.: Vol. 150). xii, 454p. 1997. lib. bdg. 99.00 (*1-55619-865-5*) J Benjamins Pubng Co.

Lexical Approach to Italian Cliticization. Paola Monachesi. (Lecture Notes Ser.: No. 84). 200p. 1999. text 64.95 (*1-57586-109-7*); pap. text 24.95 (*1-57586-108-9*) CSLI.

Lexical Atlas of the Hutsul Dialects of the Ukrainian Language. Ed. & Compiled by Janusz A. Rieger. LC 97-187357. (Illus.). 370p. 1996. pap. 39.95 (*83-86619-90-2*) Harvard Ukrainian.

Lexical Basis of the Russian Language: Learner's Dictionary. V. Morkovkin. (RUS.). 1168p. (C). 1984. 95.00 (*0-7855-6671-6*, Pub. by Collets) St Mut.

Lexical Borrowing in American Sign Language. Robbin M. Battison. LC 78-59164. (Illus.). 240p. 1978. pap. text 18.95 (*0-932130-02-X*) Linstok Pr.

Lexical Categories in Spanish: The Determiner. Linda M. McManness. LC 95-38845. 1995. 33.00 (*0-7618-0137-5*) U Pr of Amer.

Lexical Change & Variation in the Southeastern United States, 1930-1990. Ellen Johnson. LC 95-31808. 336p. 1996. pap. text 19.95 (*0-8173-0794-X*) U of Ala Pr.

Lexical Characteristics of the Estonian North Eastern Coastal Dialect. Tiina Soderman. (Studia Uralica Upsaliensia: Vol. 24). 184p. (Orig.). 1996. pap. 42.50 (*91-554-3695-1*) Coronet Bks.

Lexical Competence. Diego Marconi. LC 96-29014. (Language, Speech & Communication Ser.). (Illus.). 222p. 1997. 27.50 (*0-262-13333-4*, Bradford Bks) MIT Pr.

Lexical Concordance to the Poetical Works of Percy Bysshe Shelley. Frederick S. Ellis. (BCL1-PR English Literature Ser.). 818p. 1992. reprint ed. lib. bdg. 109.00 (*0-7812-7651-9*) Rprt Serv.

Lexical Expansion Due to Technical Change: As Illustrated by the Arabic of Al Hasa, Saudi Arabia. B. Hunter Smeaton. (Language Science Monographs: Vol. 10). 260p. 1973. pap. text 18.00 (*0-87750-167-X*) Res Inst Inner Asian Studies.

Lexical Field of Taste: A Semantic Study of Japanese Taste Terms. A. E. Backhouse. (Cambridge Studies in Linguistics: Supplementary Volumes). 210p. (C). 1994. text 52.95 (*0-521-44535-3*) Cambridge U Pr.

Lexical-Functional Grammar. George M. Horn. (Trends in Linguistics, Studies & Monographs: No. 21). ix, 394p. 1983. 134.65 (*90-279-3169-0*) Mouton.

Lexical Functions in Lexicography & Natural Language Processing. Ed. by Leo Wanner. LC 95-53207. (Studies in Language Companion Ser.: Vol. 31). xx, 355p. 1996. lib. bdg. 79.00 (*1-55619-383-1*) J Benjamins Pubng Co.

Lexical Help for Reading the Greek New Testament see Ayuda Lexica para la Lectura del Nuevo Testamento Griego

Lexical Innovation: A Study of Slang, Colloquialisms & Casual Speech. Karl Sornig. (Pragmatics & Beyond Ser.: II: 5). x, 117p. (Orig.). (C). 1981. pap. 29.00 (*90-272-2518-4*) J Benjamins Pubng Co.

Lexical Issues in Language Learning. Birgit Harley. LC 95-21039. (Best of Language Learning Ser.: No. 2). iv, 318p. 1995. pap. 32.95 (*1-55619-715-2*) J Benjamins Pubng Co.

Lexical Knowledge in the Organization of Language. Ed. by Arnim Von Stechow et al. LC 94-44090. (Current Issues in Linguistic Theory Ser.: No. 114). xiv, 367p. 1995. lib. bdg. 89.00 (*1-55619-568-0*) J Benjamins Pubng Co.

Lexical Matters. Farrell Ackerman et al. Ed. by Ivan A. Sag & Anna Szabolcsi. LC 90-28772. (Center for the Study of Language & Information-Lecture Notes Ser.). 328p. (Orig.). (C). 1992. 64.95 (*0-937073-65-2*); pap. 21.95 (*0-937073-66-0*) CSLI.

Lexical Passives in Modern Greek. Jane Smirniotopoulos. LC 92-13234. (Outstanding Dissertations in Linguistics Ser.). 312p. 1992. text 20.00 (*0-8153-0705-5*) Garland.

Lexical Perspectives on Transitivity & Ergativity: Causatives Constructions in English. Maarten Lemmens. LC 98-36270. (Current Issues in Linguistic Theory Ser.: Vol. 166). xii, 268p. 1998. 69.00 (*1-55619-882-5*) J Benjamins Pubng Co.

Lexical Phonology. Ed. by Sharon Hargus & Ellen M. Kaisse. LC 92-23535. (Phonetics & Phonology Ser.: Vol. 4). (Illus.). 415p. 1993. pap. text 59.95 (*0-12-325071-4*) Acad Pr.

*__Lexical Phonology & the History of English.__ April M. McMahon. (Cambridge Studies in Linguistics: No. 91). (Illus.). 300p. (C). 2000. 59.95 (*0-521-47280-6*) Cambridge U Pr.

Lexical Phonology of Masset Haida. John Enrico. (Alaska Native Language Center Research Papers Ser.: Vol. 8). 272p. (Orig.). (C). 1991. pap. text 20.00 (*1-55500-042-8*) Alaska Native.

Lexical Phonology of Sekani. Sharon Hargus. (Linguistics Ser.). 368p. 1988. text 20.00 (*0-8240-5187-4*) Garland.

Lexical Phonology of Slovak. Jerzy Rubach. LC 92-38746. (Phonology of the World's Languages Ser.). (Illus.). 328p. 1993. text 75.00 (*0-19-824000-7*, Clarendon Pr) OUP.

Lexical Phrases & Language Teaching. J. R. Nattinger & J. De Carrico. (Illus.). 236p. 1992. pap. text 21.95 (*0-19-437164-6*) OUP.

Lexical Relations. Jean-Pierre Koenig. LC 98-45562. (Stanford Monographs in Linguistics). 160p. (C). 1999. text 59.95 (*1-57586-177-1*); pap. text 18.95 (*1-57586-176-3*) CSLI.

Lexical Representation & Process. Ed. by William Marslen-Wilson. (Illus.). 588p. 1991. reprint ed. pap. text 32.50 (*0-262-63142-3*) MIT Pr.

Lexical Representations & Sentence Processing. Ed. by Maryellen C. MacDonald. LC 97-202451. (Illus.). 403p. 1997. write for info. (*0-86377-962-X*, Pub. by Psychol Pr) Taylor & Francis.

Lexical Semantics. D. A. Cruse. (Cambridge Textbooks in Linguistics Ser.). (Illus.). 310p. 1986. pap. text 24.95 (*0-521-27643-8*) Cambridge U Pr.

Lexical Semantics. Ed. by David Testen et al. 1984. pap. 8.00 (*0-914203-21-5*) Chicago Ling.

Lexical Semantics: The Problem of Polysemy. Ed. by James Pustejovsky & Branimir Boguraev. (Illus.). 220p. 1997. pap. text 32.00 (*0-19-823662-X*) OUP.

Lexical Semantics & Knowledge Representation: First SIGLEX Workshop, Berkeley, CA, U. S. A., June 1991, Proceedings. Ed. by James Pustejovsky et al. LC 92-26469. (Lecture Notes in Computer Science, Lecture Notes in Artificial Intelligence Ser.: Vol. 627). xiii, 381p. 1992. 57.00 (*0-387-55801-2*) Spr-Verlag.

*__Lexical Semantics & Knowledge Representation in Multilingual Text Generation.__ Manfred Stede. LC 98-51817. 11p. 1999. write for info. (*0-7923-8419-9*) Kluwer Academic.

Lexical Semantics Without Thematic Roles. Yael Ravin. 256p. 1990. 70.00 (*0-19-824831-8*) OUP.

Lexical Specialization in Russian. R. D. Schupbach. (UCLA Slavic Studies: Vol. 8). 102p. 1984. pap. 14.95 (*0-89357-128-8*) Slavica.

*__Lexical Specification & Insertion.__ Ed. by Peter Coopmans et al. LC 99-58274. (Current Issues in Linguistic Theory Ser.: Vol. 197). 458p. 2000. 85.00 (*1-55619-975-9*) J Benjamins Pubng Co.

*__Lexical Strata in English: Morphological Causes, Phonological Effects.__ Heinz J. Giegerich. LC 98-48367. (Studies in Linguistics: No. 89). 338p. (C). 1999. 64.95 (*0-521-55412-8*) Cambridge U Pr.

Lexical Structure of Spanish. William Patterson & Hector Urrutibeheity. LC 73-77744. (Janua Linguarum, Ser. Practica: No. 198). 162p. 1975. pap. text 42.35 (*90-279-3207-7*) Mouton.

Lexical Studies of Medieval Spanish Texts: A Bibliography of Concordances, Glossaries, Vocabularies & Selected Word Studies. 2nd expanded rev. ed. Steven N. Dworkin & David J. Billick. (Bibliographical Ser.: No. 11). xiii, 209p. 1993. 25.00 (*0-940639-89-0*) Hispanic Seminary.

Lexical Study of Raeto-Romance & Contiguous Italian Dialect Areas. James Redfern. LC 70-159469. (Janua Linguarum, Ser. Practica: No. 120). (Illus.). 105p. (Orig.). 1971. pap. text 76.95 (*90-279-1908-9*) Mouton.

Lexical Tools to the Syriac New Testament. George A. Kiraz. (Manuals Ser.: No. 7). 136p. 1994. pap. 25.00 (*1-85075-470-5*, Pub. by Sheffield Acad) CUP Services.

Lexical Usage in Southern Louisiana; Word List of Construction Terms. Mima Babington et al. (Publications of the American Dialect Society: No. 36). (Illus.). 31p. 1961. pap. 3.20 (*0-8173-0636-6*) U of Ala Pr.

Lexicarry: An Illustrated Vocabulary-Builder for Second Languages. 2nd rev. ed. Patrick R. Moran. LC 84-1007. (Supplementary Materials Handbook Ser.: No. 2). (Illus.). 128p. 1989. reprint ed. pap. text 11.00 (*0-86647-032-8*) Pro Lingua.

Lexicarry: French Word List. rev. ed. Patrick R. Moran. Tr. by Annie Suquet. LC 84-18026. (FRE.). 25p. 1991. pap. text 4.00 (*0-86647-045-X*) Pro Lingua.

An Asterisk (*) at the beginning of an entry indicates that the title is appearing for the first time.

L

Lexicarry: Japanese Word List. rev. ed. Ed. by Patrick R. Moran. Tr. by Tetsuo Nishizawa & Ryuko Kubota. (JPN.). 106p. 1991. pap. text 15.00 (*0-86647-054-9*) Pro Lingua.

Lexicarry: Spanish Word List. rev. ed. Patrick R. Moran. Tr. by Beatriz C. DeFantini. LC 84-17939. (SPA.). 26p. 1991. pap. text 4.00 (*0-86647-046-8*) Pro Lingua.

Lexicarry Posters: Twenty-Five Wall Charts. Patrick R. Moran. (Illus.). 26p. 1990. pap. text 25.00 (*0-86647-034-4*) Pro Lingua.

Lexico Basico del Contador: Basic Lexicon of Accounting. R. Enriquez Palomec. (ENG & SPA.). 160p. 1980. pap. 12.95 (*0-8288-0129-0*, S35128) Fr & Eur.

Lexico Castellano de los Vocabularios de Elio Antonio de Nebrija: Concordancia Lematizada, 3 vols. Elio A. De Nebrija. (SPA.). civ, 2117p. 1996. 400.00 (*3-487-10096-7*) G Olms Pubs.

Lexico-Concordancia Del Nuevo Testamento en Griego y Espanol: Greek-Spanish Lexicon Concord. of the N.T. George Parker. (SPA.). 1000p. 1991. pap. 35.50 (*0-311-42065-6*) Casa Bautista.

Lexico de Alarifes de los Siglos de Oro. Fernando Garcia Salinero. (SPA.). 280p. 1968. pap. 125.00 (*0-614-00228-1*) Elliots Bks.

Lexico de Antropologia. 3rd ed. Abelardo Martinez Cruz. (SPA.). 184p. 1975. pap. 9.95 (*0-8288-5913-2*, S50038) Fr & Eur.

Lexico de Economia: Talasa Ediciones, 1993. Andres Bilbao. (Illus.). 140p. 1993. 39.95 (*84-88119-16-X*) Fr & Eur.

Lexico de Politica. 6th ed. Jose M. Coloma. (SPA.). 200p. 1976. pap. 14.95 (*0-8288-5727-X*, S50039) Fr & Eur.

Lexico de Sociologia. 5th ed. Alain Birou. (SPA.). 114p. 1975. pap. 14.95 (*0-8288-5914-0*, S50041) Fr & Eur.

Lexico de Terminos Nucleares: Diccionario Vocabulario Triligue. (ENG, FRE & SPA.). 848p. 1974. 59.95 (*0-8288-6060-2*, S-50124) Fr & Eur.

Lexico Griego - Espanol del Nuevo Testamento. Alfredo Tuggy.Tr. of Greek-Spanish Lexicon of the New Testament. (SPA.). 1260p. (C). 1997. pap. text 54.99 (*0-311-03644-9*) Casa Bautista.

Lexico Hispanoamericano del Siglo XVI. Peter Boyd-Bowman. (Monografias A Ser.: Vol. XVI). (SPA.). 1004p. (C). 1971. 81.00 (*0-900411-28-7*, Pub. by Tamesis Bks Ltd) Boydell & Brewer.

Lexico Historico de Espana Moderna y Contemporanea (Siglos XVI-XX) 3rd ed. Bartholome Bennassar. 224p. 1990. 24.95 (*0-7859-4935-6*) Fr & Eur.

Lexico Historico de la Edad Media. 3rd ed. Rene Fedou. 170p. 1990. 15.95 (*0-7859-4936-4*) Fr & Eur.

Lexico-Logical Form: A Radically Minimalist Theory. Michael Brody. LC 95-8254. (Linguistic Inquiry Monographs: No. 27). 168p. 1995. 40.00 (*0-262-02390-3*); pap. text 20.00 (*0-262-52203-9*) MIT Pr.

Lexico Marinero: 6 Idiomas. N. Hollander et al. (SPA.). 128p. pap. 22.50 (*84-261-1668-X*, S-37657) Fr & Eur.

Lexico Marinero en 6 Idiomas: Marine Lexicon in 6 Languages. N. Hollander. (DUT, ENG, FRE, GER & ITA.). 128p. 1980. pap. 35.00 (*0-8288-0428-1*, S37657) Fr & Eur.

Lexico Sucinto Del Erotismo. Andre Breton. (SPA.). 110p. 1974. pap. 14.95 (*0-7859-0897-8*, S50153) Fr & Eur.

Lexico Tabacalero Cubano: Con Vocabulario Espanol-Ingles with Spanish-English Vocabulary. Jose E. Perdomo. (ENG & SPA., Illus.). 265p. 1998. pap. 24.95 (*0-89729-846-2*) Ediciones.

Lexicogrammar of Adjectives: A Systemic Functional Approach to Lexis. Gordon H. Tucker. LC 97-52313. (Functional Descriptions of Language Ser.). 1998. 79.95 (*0-304-33903-2*) Continuum.

Lexicographers & Their Work. Ed. by James. 236p. 1989. pap. text 21.95 (*0-85989-336-7*, Pub. by Univ Exeter Pr) Northwestern U Pr.

Lexicographic Description of English. Morton Benson et al. LC 86-17506. (Studies in Language Companion: No. 14). xiii, 275p. 1986. 81.00 (*90-272-3014-5*) J Benjamins Pubng Co.

Lexicographica Graeca: Contributions to the Lexicography of Ancient Greek. John Chadwick. LC 96-13436. 350p. 1997. text 85.00 (*0-19-814970-0*, Clarendon Pr) OUP.

Lexicography: Principles & Practice. Ed. by Reinhard R. Hartmann. (Applied Language Studies). 1983. text 105.00 (*0-12-328540-2*) Acad Pr.

Lexicography & Physicke: The Record of Sixteenth-Century English Medical Terminology. R. W. McConchie. LC 97-12359. (Oxford Studies in Lexicography). 460p. 1997. text 100.00 (*0-19-823630-1*) OUP.

Lexicography & the OED: Pioneers in the Untrodden Forest. Ed. by Lynda Mugglestone. (Oxford Studies in Lexicography & Lexicology). (Illus.). 480p. 2000. text 85.00 (*0-19-823784-7*) OUP.

Lexicography in Africa. Ed. by Hartmann. 112p. 1990. pap. text 15.95 (*0-85989-345-6*, Pub. by Univ Exeter Pr) Northwestern U Pr.

***Lexicography in Nepal: Proceedings of Institution on Lexicography 1995.** S. Yadav & S. Kansakar. 1998. pap. 22.00 (*0-7855-7607-X*) St Mut.

Lexicolabor: Diccionario Enciclopedico Ilustrado, 4 vols., Set. Labor Staff. (SPA.). 2216p. 1977. 395.00 (*0-8288-5484-X*, S50443) Fr & Eur.

***Lexicology, Semantics & Lexicography: Selected Papers from the Fourth G. L. Brook Symposium, Manchester, August 1998.** Ed. by Julie Coleman & Christian J. Kay. LC 99-88593. (Current Issues in Linguistic Theory Ser.: Vol. 194). xi, 240p. 2000. 75.00 (*1-55619-972-4*) J Benjamins Pubng Co.

Lexicon: A Cornucopia of Wonderful Words for the Inquisitive Word Lover. William F. Buckley, Jr. (Illus.). 176p. (C). 1998. pap. 9.00 (*0-15-600616-2*, Harvest Bks) Harcourt.

Lexicon: Combustion Engines. E. Freixa. (DUT, ENG, FRE, GER & ITA.). 94p. 1977. 39.95 (*0-8288-7751-3*, M15551) Fr & Eur.

Lexicon Aetherianum. Willem Van Oorde. viii, 219p. 1963. reprint ed. write for info. (*0-318-71188-5*) G Olms Pubs.

Lexicon Alchemiae. Martin Ruland. (GER.). 1997. reprint ed. 158.00 (*3-487-00631-6*) G Olms Pubs.

Lexicon Arabico-Latinum, 4 vols., Set. George W. Freytag. (ARA & LAT.). 2257p. 110.00 (*0-86685-124-0*, LDL1240, Pub. by Librairie du Liban) Intl Bk Ctr.

Lexicon Arabico-Latinum, 4 vols., Set. Georg W. Freytag. reprint ed. write for info. (*0-318-72023-X*) G Olms Pubs.

Lexicon Atticum, 2 vols. in 1. Moeris Atticista. (Illus.). cvii, 494p. 1969. reprint ed. write for info. (*0-318-70977-5*) G Olms Pubs.

Lexicon CAD, CAM, FMS, CIM: Numerical Control Lexicon. Yvonne H. Attiyate. (ENG, FRE & GER.). 939p. 1989. 95.00 (*0-8288-7594-4*, M6013) Fr & Eur.

Lexicon Caesarianum. R. Menge & S. Preuss. (GER.). 1972. 175.00 (*0-8288-6405-5*, M-7284) Fr & Eur.

Lexicon de Comunicologia - Diccinario para Audiologos, Audioprotesistas, Fonitras, Logopedas, Profesores de Sordos y Psicolinguistas: Lexicon of Communications Science. Jorge Perello. (ENG, FRE, GER & SPA.). 856p. 1977. 75.00 (*0-8288-5485-8*, S50096) Fr & Eur.

Lexicon der Seit Dem 15: Jahrhundert Verstorbenen und Jetzt Lebenden Oberlausitzischen Schriftsteller und Kunstler, 3 vols., Set. Gottlieb F. Otto. 1983. write for info. incl. fiche (*0-318-71937-1*) G Olms Pubs.

***Lexicon Development for Speech & Language Processing.** F. Van Eynde & Dafydd Gibbon. LC 00-30207. (Text, Speech & Language Technology Ser.). 2000. write for info. (*0-7923-6368-X*) Kluwer Academic.

Lexicon Diplomaticum. Johann L. Walther. 459p. 1973. reprint ed. write for info. (*3-487-04574-5*) G Olms Pubs.

***Lexicon-Encyclopedia Interface.** Peeters. 2000. 90.00 (*0-08-043591-2*, Pergamon Pr) Elsevier.

Lexicon Gregorianum. Ed. by F. Mannone. 1999. 291.00 (*90-04-11228-6*) Brill Academic Pubs.

***Lexicon Gregorianum, 2.** Ed. by Friedhelm Mann. (GER & GRE.). 600p. 1999. text 500.00 (*90-04-11450-5*) Brill Academic Pubs.

Lexicon Homericum. Apollonius Sophista. iv, 195p. 1967. reprint ed. 50.00 (*0-318-71996-7*) G Olms Pubs.

Lexicon Homericum. Apollonius Sophista. Ed. by Immanuel Bekker. iv, 195p. 1967. reprint ed. write for info. (*0-318-70853-1*) G Olms Pubs.

Lexicon Homericum, 2 vols., Set. H. Ebeling. Ed. by F. Albracht et al. ii, 1696p. 1987. reprint ed. write for info. (*3-487-05123-0*) G Olms Pubs.

Lexicon in Phonological Change. W. Wang. (Monographs on Linguistic Analysis: No. 5). 1977. 86.15 (*90-279-7814-X*) Mouton.

Lexicon Latinatatis Nederlandicae Medii Aevi: Woordenboek van het Middeleeuws Latijn van de Noordelijke Nederlanden, Fasc. 44. Johanne W. Fuchs et al. 80p. 1995. pap. 28.00 (*90-04-10411-9*) Brill Academic Pubs.

Lexicon Latinitatis, Fasc. 43. Johanne W. Fuchs et al. 80p. 1995. pap. 28.00 (*90-04-10286-8*) Brill Academic Pubs.

Lexicon Latinitatis Medii Aevi Hungariae Vol. 1-1: A, Ab, Abs-Aeternaliter. I. Boronkai. 102p. (C). 1987. pap. 60.00 (*963-05-4251-X*, Pub. by Akade Kiado) St Mut.

Lexicon Latinitatis Medii Aevi Hungariae Vol. 1-2: Aeternaliter-Assignatio. Tr. by I. Boronkai. 160p. (C). 1988. pap. 60.00 (*963-05-4252-8*, Pub. by Akade Kiado) St Mut.

Lexicon Latinitatis Medii Aevi Hungariae Vol. 1-3: Assignatio-Byzantius. Ed. by I. Boronkai. 101p. (C). 1989. pap. 60.00 (*963-05-4858-5*, Pub. by Akade Kiado) St Mut.

Lexicon Latinitatis Medii Aevi Hungariae Vol. 11-1: Cabalia-Cliciarius. Ed. by I. Bornokai. 152p. (C). 1991. pap. 75.00 (*963-05-5394-5*, Pub. by Akade Kiado) St Mut.

Lexicon Latinitatis Medii Aevi Hungariae Vol. 11-2: Cliciarius-Conor. I. Bornokai. 160p. (C). 1991. pap. 86.00 (*963-05-5780-0*, Pub. by Akade Kiado) St Mut.

Lexicon Latinitatis Medii Aevi Hungariae Vol. 11-3: Conor-Czwkarum. 148p. (C). 1991. pap. 66.00 (*963-05-5787-8*, Pub. by Akade Kiado) St Mut.

Lexicon Latinitatis Nederlandicae Medii Aevi. Olga Weijers & Marijke Gumbert-Hepp. (Fascicule Ser.: No. 47). 80p. 1997. pap. 37.00 (*90-04-10759-2*, NLG 56) Brill Academic Pubs.

Lexicon Latinitatis Nederlandicae Medii Aevi. Olga Weijers & Marijke Gumbert-Hepp. (Lexicon Latinitatis Nederlandicae Medii Aevi Ser.: No. 49). (DUT & LAT.). 80p. 1998. pap. 35.00 (*90-04-11055-0*) Brill Academic Pubs.

Lexicon Latinitatis Nederlandicae Medii Aevi, Fasc. 36. Ed. by J. W. Fuchs et al. (LAT.). 2807-2886p. 1991. pap. 28.50 (*90-04-09516-0*) Brill Academic Pubs.

Lexicon Latinitatis Nederlandicae Medii Aevi, Fasc. 37. Johanne W. Fuchs et al. 2887-2966p. 1992. pap. 28.50 (*90-04-09594-2*) Brill Academic Pubs.

Lexicon Latinitatis Nederlandicae Medii Aevi, Fascicule 48. Olga Weijers & Marijke Gumbert-Hepp. 80p. 1997. pap. 37.00 (*90-04-10780-0*) Brill Academic Pubs.

***Lexicon Latinitatis Nederlandicae Medii Aevi: Fasc. 53.** Composuerunt Johanne W. Fuchs et al. 80p. 2000. 32.00 (*90-04-11636-2*) Brill Academic Pubs.

***Lexicon Latinitatis Nederlandicae Medii Aevi: Fasc. 53.** Johanne W. Fuchs et al. 80p. 1999. 37.00 (*90-04-11593-5*) Brill Academic Pubs.

***Lexicon Latinitatis Nederlandicae Medii Aevi: Fascicule 51.** Olga Weijers & Marijke Gumbert-Hepp. 80p. 1999. pap. 37.00 (*90-04-11336-3*) Brill Academic Pubs.

Lexicon Latinitatis Nederlandicae Medii Aevi: Woordenboek Van Het Middeleeuws Latijn Van de Noordelijke Nederlanden. Johanne W. Fuchs et al. 80p. 1996. pap. 34.50 (*90-04-10570-0*) Brill Academic Pubs.

Lexicon Latinitatis Nederlandicae Medii Aevi: Woordenboek van het Middeleeuws Latijn van de Noordelijke Nederlanden, Vol. 3 D-Efasc 17-25. Johanne W. Fuchs et al. iv, 1235-1957p. 1986. 331.50 (*90-04-08081-3*) Brill Academic Pubs.

Lexicon Latinitatis Nederlandicae Medii Aevi, Vol. 4, Fascicle 34: Woordenboek Van Het Middeleeuws Latijn Van de Noordelijke Nederlanden, Vol. 4: Fascicle 26-34, Pts. F, G & I. Ed. by Marijke Gumbert-Hepp & Olga Weijers. (DUT & LAT.). 126p. 1990. pap. 342.00 (*90-04-08353-7*) Brill Academic Pubs.

Lexicon Latinitatis Nederlandicae Medii Aevi, Vol. 5, Fasc. 39: Woordenboek van het Middeleeuws Latijn van de Noordelijke Nederlanden. Marijke Gumbert-Hepp et al. (LAT.). 80p. 1993. pap. 27.00 (*90-04-09782-1*) Brill Academic Pubs.

Lexicon Latinitatis Nederlandicae Medii Aevi. Woordenboek van het Middeleeuws Latijn van de Noordelijke Nederlanden Fasc. 35 (L-Licite) Ed. by Olga Weijers & Marijke Gumbert-Hepp. (LAT.). 2727-2806p. 1991. pap. 28.50 (*90-04-09322-2*) Brill Academic Pubs.

Lexicon Manuale Ad Scriptores Mediae et Infimae Latinitatis, Ex Glossariis Caroli Dufresne D. Ducangii, D. P. Carnentarii, Adelungii, Latingii, et Aliorum, in Compendium Accuratissimi Redactum. W. H. D'Arnis. 1168p. 1977. reprint ed. write for info. (*3-487-06426-X*) G Olms Pubs.

Lexicon of Accadian Prayers in the Rituals of Expiation. Cecil J. Weir. LC 78-72774. (Ancient Mesopotamian Texts & Studies). reprint ed. 35.00 (*0-404-18236-4*) AMS Pr.

Lexicon of Agriculture & Horticultural Terms: Lexique des Termes Agricoles et Horticoles. Paul Habault. (FRE.). 152p. 1983. 39.95 (*0-8288-1176-8*, F80210) Fr & Eur.

Lexicon of Al-Farra's Terminology in His Quran Commentary: With Full Definitions, English Summaries, & Extensive Citations. Naphtali Kinberg. LC 95-49417. (Handbuch Der Orientalistik Ser.). 1995. 409.00 (*90-04-10421-6*) Brill Academic Pubs.

Lexicon of Al-Farra's Terminology in His Quran Commentary: With Full Definitions, English Summaries & Extensive Citations. Naphtali Kinberg. 900p. 1996. 267.75 (*0-614-21059-3*, 1413) Kazi Pubns.

Lexicon of Alchemy: or Alchemical Dictionary. Martinus Rulandus. 466p. 1992. reprint ed. pap. 30.00 (*0-922802-82-3*) Kessinger Pub.

Lexicon of Alcohol & Drug Terms. 65p. 1994. pap. text 17.00 (*92-4-154468-6*, 1150413) World Health.

Lexicon of Amateur Photography: Lexique de la Photagraphie d'Amateur: Appareils et Accessoires. R. J. Pollet. (FRE.). 127p. 1981. pap. 19.95 (*0-8288-2089-9*, M14196) Fr & Eur.

Lexicon of Ancient Greek: Lexico de la Antiquedad Griega. Claude Vial. (SPA.). 273p. 1983. pap. 17.95 (*0-8288-1499-6*, S27403) Fr & Eur.

Lexicon of Arabic Horse Terminology. Janet C. Watson. 70p. 1996. 129.50 (*0-7103-0542-7*, Pub. by Kegan Paul Intl) Col U Pr.

Lexicon of Astrology: Lexikon der Astrologie. Udo Becker. (GER.). 320p. 1986. 45.00 (*0-8288-1190-3*, M15271) Fr & Eur.

Lexicon of Borrowed Words: Fremdwoerter Lexicon. Gerhard Wahrig. (GER.). 928p. 1991. 45.00 (*0-8288-1985-8*, M7416) Fr & Eur.

Lexicon of Building & Several Other Related Fields. Gilles Boivin & France Michel. (ENG & FRE.). 51p. 1992. pap. 29.95 (*0-8288-9392-6*) Fr & Eur.

Lexicon of Carbonated Beverages: Lexiques des Boissons Gazeuses. Jacques Maurais. (ENG & FRE.). 40p. 1980. pap. 14.95 (*0-8288-4818-1*, M9241) Fr & Eur.

Lexicon of Christian Art: Lexikon Christlicher Kunst: Themen-Gestalten-Symbole. Jutta Seibert. (GER.). 352p. 1986. 110.00 (*0-8288-2312-X*, M15211) Fr & Eur.

Lexicon of Cichlids. 2nd ed. Herbert R. Axelrod. (TS Ser.). (Illus.). 864p. 1993. 100.00 (*0-7938-0026-9*, TS-190) TFH Pubns.

Lexicon of Comicana. Mort Walker. (Illus.). 96p. (C). 1980. pap. 4.95 (*0-940420-00-7*) Comicana.

Lexicon of Cross-Cultural Terms in Mental Health. WHO Staff. 1997. write for info. (*92-4-154505-4*) World Health.

Lexicon of Detergents, Cosmetics & Toiletries. G. Carriere. (DUT, ENG, FRE, GER & ITA.). 204p. 1966. 175.00 (*0-8288-9221-0*, M15543) Fr & Eur.

Lexicon of Economic & Commercial Terms: Lexique de Termes Economiques et Commerciaux. H. Bouillon. (FRE & GER.). 196p. 1988. pap. 45.00 (*0-7859-4736-1*) Fr & Eur.

Lexicon of Economic & Commercial Terms (Lexique des Termes Economiques et Commerciaux) Blavier-Paquot. (FRE & SPA.). 225p. 1988. pap. 24.95 (*0-7859-4659-4*) Fr & Eur.

Lexicon of Education: Lexique d'Education. Gaston Mialaret. (FRE.). 168p. 1981. pap. 12.95 (*0-8288-1389-2*, M14201) Fr & Eur.

Lexicon of Education Practice: Lexikon der Ausbildungspraxis. 3rd ed. Helmut Paulik. (GER.). 256p. 1982. pap. 49.95 (*0-8288-1394-9*, M7274) Fr & Eur.

Lexicon of Fishing Products: Lexique des Produits de la Peche Anglais-Francais. P. Vallieres. (ENG & FRE.). 35p. 1980. pap. 7.95 (*0-8288-0840-6*, M9223) Fr & Eur.

Lexicon of Food Chemistry: Lexique de la Chimie Alimentaire. 10th ed. Jacques Maurais. (ENG & FRE.). 119p. 1981. pap. 9.95 (*0-8288-0837-6*, M6656) Fr & Eur.

Lexicon of Freemasonry. Albert G. Mackey. 527p. 1994. reprint ed. pap. 39.95 (*1-56459-463-7*) Kessinger Pub.

Lexicon of French Borrowings in the German Vocabulary. William J. Jones. (Studia Linguistica Germanica: No. 12). (FRE & GER.). (C). 1976. 161.55 (*3-11-004769-1*) De Gruyter.

Lexicon of French Literature: Lexikon Der Franzoesischen Literatur. 2nd ed. Winfried Engler. (FRE & GER.). 1005p. 1984. 65.00 (*0-8288-1569-0*, M7259) Fr & Eur.

Lexicon of Geologic Names in the U. S., 2 vols., Set. Mary G. Wilmarth. 1968. reprint ed. 175.00 (*0-403-00128-5*) Scholarly.

Lexicon of Geological Terms for the Sudan. J. R. Vail. 208p. 1988. text 110.00 (*90-6191-705-0*, Pub. by A A Balkema) Ashgate Pub Co.

Lexicon of German History: Lexikon der Deutschen Geschichte. 2nd ed. Gerhard Taddey. (GER.). 1391p. 1983. 125.00 (*0-8288-1493-7*, M7263) Fr & Eur.

Lexicon of German Language Literature of the 20th Century: Autorenlexikon Deutschsprachiger Literatur des 20 Jahrhunderts. Manfred Brauneck. (GER.). 720p. 1984. pap. 59.95 (*0-8288-1568-2*, M14150) Fr & Eur.

Lexicon of Greek Personal Names: The Peloponnese, Western Greece, Sicily & Magna Graecia, Vol. 3 A. Ed. by Peter Fraser & Elaine Matthews. (British Academy Ser.). 552p. 1998. text 150.00 (*0-19-815229-9*) OUP.

Lexicon of Greek Personal Names Vol. 1: The Aegean Islands, Cyprus, & Cyrenaica. P. M. Fraser & E. Matthews. 528p. 1988. text 125.00 (*0-19-864222-9*) OUP.

Lexicon of Greek Personal Names Vol. II: Attica. Ed. by Michael J. Osborne et al. 532p. 1994. text 95.00 (*0-19-814990-5*) OUP.

Lexicon of Green Coin Inscriptions. A. Florence. LC 66-19173. (Illus.). 1966. pap. 15.00 (*0-932106-21-8*) S J Durst.

Lexicon of Internet-Speak, English to German. O. Rosenbaum. (ENG & GER.). 280p. 1996. 49.95 (*0-320-00502-X*) Fr & Eur.

Lexicon of Labor: More Than 500 Key Terms, Biographical Sketches, & Historical Insights Concerning Labor in America. R. Emmett Murray. LC 98-12783. (Illus.). 192p. 1998. pap. 13.95 (*1-56584-456-4*, Pub. by New Press NY) Norton.

Lexicon of Latin Derivatives in Italian, Spanish, French & English. James H. Dee. (Alpha-Omega, Reihe A Ser.; Bd. CXC). (ENG, FRE, ITA & SPA.). lvi, 1083p. 1997. write for info. (*3-487-10557-8*) G Olms Pubs.

Lexicon of Legal Terms: Lexique des Termes Juridiques. 9th ed. R. Guillien & J. Vincent. (FRE.). 448p. 1993. pap. 35.00 (*0-8288-1521-6*, M6304) Fr & Eur.

Lexicon of Library Sciences: Lexikon des Bibliothekswesens, 2 vols., Set. 2nd ed. Horst Kunze & Gotthard Rueckl. (GER.). 2112p. 1986. 275.00 (*0-8288-0872-4*, M7209) Fr & Eur.

Lexicon of Lunacy: Metaphoric Malady, Moral Responsibility, & Psychiatry. Thomas Szasz. 192p. (C). 1992. 34.95 (*1-56000-065-1*) Transaction Pubs.

Lexicon of Medical Radiological Engineering: Lexikon der Radiologischen Technik der Medizin. 4th ed. Wilfried Angerstein. (GER.). 576p. 1987. 95.00 (*0-8288-1834-7*, M15430) Fr & Eur.

Lexicon of Medical Terminology: Medicinsk Terminologi Lexikon. B. I. Lindskog & B. L. Zetterberg. 620p. 1981. 250.00 (*0-8288-1884-3*, F22400) Fr & Eur.

Lexicon of Medicine: Medicinski Leksikon. deluxe ed. Aleksandar Kostic. (CRO & SER.). 917p. 1981. 150.00 (*0-8288-4668-5*, M9706) Fr & Eur.

Lexicon of Molecular Biology: English-French, French-English. Nicolas Didier.Tr. of Lexique Biologie Moleculaire. (ENG & FRE.). 1990. pap. 39.95 (*0-7859-3917-2*) Fr & Eur.

***Lexicon of Musical Invective: Critical Assaults on Composers since Beethoven's Time.** Nicolas Slonimsky. 336p. 2000. pap. 14.95 (*0-393-32009-X*) Norton.

Lexicon of Musical Invective: Critical Assaults on Composers Since Beethoven's Time. 2nd ed. Nicolas Slonimsky. LC 65-26270. 331p. 1969. reprint ed. pap. 14.95 (*0-295-78579-9*, WP52) U of Wash Pr.

***Lexicon of Orthopaedic Etymology.** Mohammad Diab. 460p. 1999. text 92.00 (*90-5702-597-3*, Harwood Acad Pubs) Gordon & Breach.

Lexicon of Pasta, 1982. 3rd ed. Jacques Maurais et al. (ENG & FRE.). 43p. 1980. pap. 14.95 (*0-8288-0839-2*, M9243) Fr & Eur.

Lexicon of Political Terms: Lexique des Termes Politiques. 5th ed. J. Debbasch & Y. Daudet. (FRE.). 439p. 1988. pap. 49.95 (*0-7859-4781-7*) Fr & Eur.

Lexicon of Politics: Lexikon der Politik, UTB 431. 9th ed. Walter Theimer. (GER.). 309p. 1981. 35.00 (*0-8288-2260-3*, M15258) Fr & Eur.

Lexicon of Psychiatric & Mental Health Terms, Vol. 1. WHO Staff. 79p. 1989. 16.00 (*92-4-154242-X*) World Health.

Lexicon of Psychiatric & Mental Health Terms, Vol. 1. 2nd ed. WHO Staff. 108p. 1994. pap. text 25.00 (*92-4-154466-X*, 1152309) World Health.

Lexicon of Psychiatry, Neurology, & Neurosciences. 2nd ed. Frank J. Ayd, Jr. 1120p. pap. text 69.95 (*0-7817-2468-6*) Lppncott W & W.

Lexicon of Psychiatry, Neurology & the Neurosciences. 741p. pap. text 35.00 (*0-7881-6959-9*) DIANE Pub.

Lexicon of Psychiatry, Neurology, & the Neurosciences. Frank J. Ayd, Jr. LC 94-38956. 720p. 1995. pap. text 50.00 (*0-683-00298-8*) Lppncott W & W.

Lexicon of Psychology, Psychiatry & Psychoanalysis. Ed. by Jessica Kuper. (Social Science Lexicons Ser.). 384p. 1988. pap. text 19.95 (*0-415-00233-8*) Routledge.

An Asterisk (*) at the beginning of an entry indicates that the title is appearing for the first time.

Lexicon of Russian Literature Before 1917: Lexikon der Russischen Literatur AB 1917. Wolfgang Kasack. (GER.). 225p. 1986. 45.00 (*0-8288-1571-2*, M7230) Fr & Eur.

Lexicon of Safety Terminology in Chemistry: Lexikon Sicherheitstechnischer Begriffe in der Chemie. Werner Berthold & Ullrich Loffler. (GER.). 170p. 1981. 75.00 (*0-8288-1311-6*, M15296) Fr & Eur.

Lexicon of Scientific Terms: Lexikon der Sprachwissenschft. H. Bussmann. (GER.). 603p. 1983. 49.95 (*0-8288-1973-4*, M15150) Fr & Eur.

Lexicon of Sewage Processing: Lexikon der Abwassertechnik. 4th ed. W. Bischofsberger & W. Hegemann. (ENG & GER.). 671p. 1990. 125.00 (*0-685-53795-1*, F38010) Fr & Eur.

Lexicon of Social Sciences: Lexique des Sciences Sociales. 5th ed. Madeleine Grawitz. (FRE.). 399p. 1991. pap. 38.95 (*0-7859-4733-7*, M14145) Fr & Eur.

Lexicon of Spices & Seasonings: Lexique des Epices et Assaisonnements. Jacques Maurais. (ENG & FRE.). 44p. 1980. pap. 14.95 (*0-8288-4817-3*, M9236) Fr & Eur.

Lexicon of Tamil Literature. Kamil V. Zvelebil. 1994. 287.50 (*90-04-10072-5*) Brill Academic Pubs.

Lexicon of Terms Relating to the Assessment & Classification of Coal Resources. A. H. Todd. 136p. 1982. lib. bdg. 129.00 (*0-86010-403-6*) G & T Inc.

Lexicon of Terror: Argentina & the Legacies of Torture. Marguerite Feitlowitz. LC 97-16843. (Illus.). 320p. 1998. 30.00 (*0-19-510635-0*) OUP.

Lexicon of Terror: Argentina & the Legacies of Torture. Marguerite Feitlowitz. (Illus.). 302p. 1999. pap. 16.95 (*0-19-513416-8*) OUP.

Lexicon of the Bible: Lexikon Zur Bibel. 10th ed. Fritz Rienecker. (GER.). 968p. 1985. 95.00 (*0-8288-2311-1*, M7192) Fr & Eur.

Lexicon of the Bread Industry: Lexique de l'Industrie de la Boulangerie. F. Hudson. (ENG & FRE.). 123p. 1984. 9.95 (*0-8288-0836-8*, 837) Fr & Eur.

Lexicon of the Fourteenth-Century Aragonese Manuscripts of Juan Fernandez de Heredia. Jean G. Mackenzie. (Dialect Ser.: No. 8). xlii, 234p. 1984. 35.00 (*0-942260-48-1*) Hispanic Seminary.

Lexicon of the Greek & Roman Cities & Place Names in Antiquity ca 1500 BC-AD 500 Fascicule 3: Alga Minor - Anastasiupolis. Ed. by K. Branigan et al. 80p. 1995. pap. 45.00 (*90-256-0985-6*, Pub. by AM Hakkert) BookLink Distributors.

Lexicon of the Homeric Dialect. Richard J. Cunliffe. LC 63-17165. 456p. 1977. pap. 24.95 (*0-8061-1430-4*) U of Okla Pr.

Lexicon of the Sports & Racing Car Enthusiast: Includes Words Relating to Plants & Animals in the Mammoth Cave Region. Ann S. Haskell & Gordon Wilson. (Publications of the American Dialect Society Ser.). 200p. 1993. 24.95 (*0-8173-0642-0*) U of Ala Pr.

Lexicon of the Sports & Racing Car Enthusiast; Words Relating to Plants & Animals in the Mammoth Cave Region; Terms of Abuse for Some Chicago Social Groups. Ann S. Haskell et al. (Publications of the American Dialect Society: No. 42). 48p. 1964. pap. 4.80 (*0-8173-0918-7*) U of Ala Pr.

Lexicon of the Textile Industry: French-English, English-French. Roger Habert. (ENG & FRE.). 240p. 1974. pap. 24.95 (*0-8288-6067-X*, M9222) Fr & Eur.

Lexicon of Trial Law Techniques: Lexikon der Prozessrechnertechnik. 2nd ed. Peter Schafer & Martin Wiczorke. (GER.). 356p. 1981. 95.00 (*0-8288-1359-0*, M15285) Fr & Eur.

Lexicon of Usual Terms in Psychiatry, Neuropsychiatry & Psychopathology. 3rd ed. Lise Moor. (ENG, FRE & GER.). 236p. 1980. 49.95 (*0-8288-0584-9*, M 15383) Fr & Eur.

Lexicon Petronianum. Johannes Segebade & Ernst Lommatzsch. ix, 274p. 1965. reprint ed. write for info. (*0-318-72076-0*) G Olms Pubs.

Lexicon Petronianum. Johannes Segebade & Ernst Lommatzsch. ix, 274p. 1988. reprint ed. write for info. (*3-487-00337-6*) G Olms Pubs.

Lexicon Pharmaceutico-Chymicum Latino-Germanicum et Germanicolatinum. J. C. Sommerhoff. (GER.). 1997. 198.00 (*3-487-06373-5*) G Olms Pubs.

Lexicon Philosophicum Graecum. Rudolph Goclenius. vi, 390p. reprint ed. write for info. (*0-318-70750-0*) G Olms Pubs.

Lexicon Philosophicum Quo Tanquam Clave Philosophiae Fores Aperiuntur, Informantum Opera Et Studio Rodolphi Goclenii. Rudolph Goclenius. xii, 1143p. 1980. reprint ed. write for info. (*3-487-00607-3*) G Olms Pubs.

Lexicon Pindaricum. Johannes Rumpel. 498p. 1961. reprint ed. write for info. (*0-318-71017-X*) G Olms Pubs.

Lexicon Plutarcheum, 2 vols., Set. Daniel Wyttenbach. (GER.). iv, 1744p. 1962. reprint ed. write for info. (*0-318-70535-4*) G Olms Pubs.

Lexicon Pseudonymorum. Emil Weller. x, 627p. 1977. reprint ed. write for info. (*3-487-00414-3*) G Olms Pubs.

Lexicon Q. Ennii et Pacuvii Sermonis Scaenici, Band 61. Ennius. (Alpha-Omega, Reihe A Ser.: Bd. CLXII). (GER.). iv, 377p. 1996. write for info. (*3-487-10156-4*) G Olms Pubs.

Lexicon Quintilianeum. Eduard Bonnell. lxxxiv, 1043p. 1962. reprint ed. 240.00 (*0-318-71078-1*) G Olms Pubs.

Lexicon Scholasticum Philosophico-Theologicum: In Quo Termini, Definitiones, Distinctiones et Effata a Joanne Duns Scoto Exponuntur, Declarantur. 2nd ed. Mariano G. Fernandez. (GER.). xiv, 1055p. 1989. reprint ed. write for info. (*3-487-05221-0*) G Olms Pubs.

Lexicon Slavonicum, Vol. 1. Johan G. Sparwenfeld. Ed. by Ulla Birgegard. (Acta Bibliothecae R. Universitatis Upsaliensis Ser.: No. XXIV.1). 511p. 1987. lib. bdg. 202.00 (*91-554-2129-6*, Pub. by Uppsala Univ Acta Univ Uppsaliensis) Coronet Bks.

Lexicon Slavonicum, Vol. III. II-P. Johan G. Sparwenfeld. Ed. by Ulla Birgegard. 272p. 1989. 162.00 (*91-554-2444-9*) Coronet Bks.

Lexicon Slavonicum Vol. II: K-O. Johan G. Sparwenfeld. Ed. by Ulla Birgegard. 1988. 208.00 (*91-554-2296-9*) Coronet Bks.

Lexicon Sophocleum. Friedrich Ellendt. pap. write for info. (*0-318-70791-8*) G Olms Pubs.

Lexicon Sophocleum. Friedrich Ellendt. xvi, 812p. 1958. reprint ed. write for info. (*0-318-72015-9*) G Olms Pubs.

Lexicon Sophocleum. Friedrich Ellendt. (Olms GW Paperbacks Ser.: Bd. 8). (GER.). xvi, 812p. 1986. reprint ed. write for info. (*3-487-00038-5*); reprint ed. pap. write for info. (*3-487-00843-2*) G Olms Pubs.

Lexicon Spinozanum, Set. E. G. Boscherini. (International Archives of the History of Ideas Ser.: No. 28). 1411p. 1987. lib. bdg. 574.00 (*90-247-0205-4*) Kluwer Academic.

Lexicon Taciteum, 2 vols., Set. Arnold Gerber & Adolf Greef. 1962. reprint ed. write for info. (*0-318-72027-2*) G Olms Pubs.

Lexicon Tactieum, 2 vols. A. Gerber & A. Greef. (GER.). 1802p. 1975. reprint ed. write for info. (*3-487-00235-3*) G Olms Pubs.

Lexicon Technologiae Graecorum Rhetoricae. J. C. Ernesti. xxiv, 400p. 1962. reprint ed. write for info. (*0-318-72017-5*) G Olms Pubs.

Lexicon Technologiae Graecorum Rhetoricae. J. C. Ernesti. xxiv, 400p. 1983. reprint ed. write for info. (*3-487-00291-4*) G Olms Pubs.

Lexicon Technologiae Latinorum Rhetoricae. J. C. Ernesti. xxxii, 440p. 1962. reprint ed. write for info. (*0-318-72018-3*) G Olms Pubs.

Lexicon Technologiae Latinorum Rhetoricae. J. C. Ernesti. xxxii, 440p. 1983. reprint ed. write for info. (*3-487-00292-2*) G Olms Pubs.

Lexicon Theocriteum. Johannes Rumpel. 319p. 1961. reprint ed. write for info. (*0-318-72072-8*) G Olms Pubs.

Lexicon Theocriteum. Johannes Rumpel. 319p. 1973. reprint ed. write for info. (*3-487-71018-8*) G Olms Pubs.

Lexicon Theologicum Quo Tanquam Clave Theologicae Fores Aperiuntur et Omnium Fere Terminorum et Obsciorum Vocum, Quae es Theologicae Studiosos Facile Remorantur, Etymologiae, Ambiguitates, Defitiones, Etc. Johann Altensteig & Johann Tytz. (LAT.). xvi, 994p. 1974. reprint ed. lib. bdg. 320.00 (*3-487-04903-1*) G Olms Pubs.

Lexicon Thucydideum, 2 vols., Set. Elie A. Betant. 1969. reprint ed. 215.00 (*0-318-72001-9*) G Olms Pubs.

Lexicon to Achilles Tatius. Ed. by James N. O'Sullivan. (Untersuchungen zur Antiken Literatur und Geschichte Ser.: Vol. 18). (GER.). 442p. (C). 1980. text 176.95 (*3-11-007844-9*) De Gruyter.

Lexicon to Herodotus. J. Enoch Powell. (Olms Paperbacks Ser.: Vol. 26). x, 392p. 1977. reprint ed. pap. write for info. (*3-487-01149-2*); reprint ed. lib. bdg. 63.50 (*3-487-00036-9*) G Olms Pubs.

Lexicon to Pindar. Ed. by William J. Slater. (C). 1969. 238.50 (*3-11-002562-0*) De Gruyter.

Lexicon Topographicum Urbis Romae, Vol. 2. Ed. by Eva M. Steinby. (Illus.). 504p. 1995. 165.00 (*88-7140-073-9*) OUP.

Lexicon Topographicum Urbis Romae, Vol. 3, H-O. Ed. by Eva M. Steinby. (FRE & ITA., Illus.). 512p. 1997. 165.00 (*88-7140-096-8*) OUP.

***Lexicon Topographicum Urbis Romae, Vol. 5.** Eva M. Steinby. Vol. 5. (LAT., Illus.). 376p. 2000. 165.00 (*88-7140-162-X*) Edizioni Quasar.

Lexicon Topographicum Urbis Romae Volume Primo: A-C, Vol. 1. Ed. by Eva M. Steinby. (FRE & ITA., Illus.). 484p. 1995. 165.00 (*88-7097-019-1*) OUP.

Lexicon Typographicum Italiae: Dictionnaire Geographique D'Italie pour Servir a l'Histoire de l'Imprimerie Dan Ce Pays. Guiseppe Fumagalli. (FRE., Illus.). 587p. 1998. reprint ed. 85.00 (*1-57898-076-3*) Martino Pubng.

Lexicon Urthus: A Dictionary for the Urth Cycle. Michael Andre-Driussi. LC 95-120345. (Illus.). 304p. 1994. 39.95 (*0-9642795-9-2*) Sirius Fiction.

Lexicon Vindobonense. lvi, 404p. 1965. reprint ed. 110.00 (*0-318-70963-5*) G Olms Pubs.

Lexicon Vocum Platonicarum. Timaeus Sophista. Ed. by Georg A. Koch. xx, 260p. 1970. reprint ed. write for info. (*0-318-71054-4*) G Olms Pubs.

Lexicon Vocum Platonicarum. Timaeus Sophista. xx, 260p. 1970. reprint ed. write for info. (*0-318-72080-9*) G Olms Pubs.

Lexicon Xenophonteum, 4 vols., Set. F. W. Sturz. 3008p. 1964. reprint ed. write for info. (*0-318-71045-5*) G Olms Pubs.

Lexicon Xenophonteum, 4 vols., Set. Frid G. Sturz. 1964. reprint ed. write for info. (*0-318-72078-7*) G Olms Pubs.

Lexicostatistics in Genetic Linguistics: Proceedings of the Yale Conference, Yale University, April 3-4, 1971. Ed. by Isidore Dyen. (Janua Linguarum, Series Major: No. 69). 1973. 52.35 (*90-279-2497-X*) Mouton.

Lexigrow: A New & Easy Gardening Concept. Jack M. Langston. LC 82-90041. (Illus.). 160p. (Orig.). 1982. pap. 14.95 (*0-910387-00-1*) Lexigrow Intl.

Lexikalische Studien Zum Dialekt Im Wiener Volksstuck Vor Nestroy: Mit Einer Edition von Baeuerles "Die Fremden in Wien" (1814) Richard Reutner. Ed. by Peter Wiesinger. (Schriften zur Deutschen Sprache in Osterreich Ser.: Band 25). (GER.). 454p. 1998. pap. 67.95 (*3-631-32534-7*) P Lang Pubng.

Lexikbeziehungen im Text Als Systematisierungshilfen fur die Wortschatzarbeit. Steffi Simon-Ruttloff. (Europaische Hochschulschriften, Reihe 14: No. 332). (Illus.). 200p. 1997. 42.95 (*3-631-31828-6*) P Lang Pubng.

***Lexikologische Beschreibungen Zum Konzeptuell-semantischen Netz Intelligence im Heutigen Franzosisch.** Hans-Burkard Krause. (Rostocker Romanistische Arbeiten Ser.). 393p. 1999. 52.95 (*3-631-34779-0*) P Lang Pubng.

***Lexikon: Dictionary of Healthcare Terms, Organizations & Acronyms.** 2nd rev. ed. Joint Commission on Accreditation of Healthcare Organizations. 464p. 1998. 55.00 (*0-86688-549-8*, JC-600) Joint Comm Hlthcare.

Lexikon Aetherianum. Willem V. Oorde. viii, 219p. 1963. reprint ed. write for info. (*0-318-72061-2*) G Olms Pubs.

Lexikon Amerikanische Literatur. Alfred Hornung. (GER.). 366p. 1992. 49.95 (*0-7859-8351-1*, 3411077018) Fr & Eur.

Lexikon Angiologie, Kardiologie. Ulrich Busch. (GER.). 312p. 1992. 75.00 (*0-7859-8423-2*, 3541171413) Fr & Eur.

Lexikon Angloamerikanischer und Deutscher Managementbegriffe: Lexicon of Anglo-American & german Management Terminology. Peter Linnert. (GER.). 1972. 45.00 (*0-8288-6406-3*, M-7286) Fr & Eur.

Lexikon Baufinanzierung Von A Bis Z. 4th ed. Harald Gerhards. (GER.). 667p. 1993. 135.00 (*0-7859-8344-9*, 3409499180) Fr & Eur.

Lexikon Biochemie. H. D. Jakubke. (GER.). 1976. 75.00 (*0-8288-5728-8*, M7285) Fr & Eur.

Lexikon Buch, Bibliothek, Neue Medien. Margarete Rehm. (GER.). 294p. 1991. 195.00 (*0-7859-8447-X*, 3598108893) Fr & Eur.

Lexikon Buch, Bibliothek, Neue Medien. Margarete Rehm. (GER.). 294p. 1991. pap. text 30.00 (*3-598-10851-6*) K G Saur Verlag.

Lexikon Chemischer Kurzbezeichnungen Von Arzneistoffen. (GER.). 1970. pap. 24.95 (*0-8288-6544-2*, M-7283) Fr & Eur.

Lexikon Computerwissen Von A-Z: German-English, English-German. Gunter Rolle. 124p. 1990. 19.95 (*0-7859-8441-0*, 3572033500) Fr & Eur.

Lexikon der Abkurzungen see German Lexicon of Abbreviations

Lexikon der Abwassertechnik. W. Bischofsberger. (ENG & GER.). 717p. 1990. lib. bdg. 115.00 (*0-8288-3595-0*, F99120) Fr & Eur.

Lexikon der Aegyptischen Baukunst. Dieter Arnold. (GER.). 352p. 1994. 150.00 (*0-7859-8453-4*, 3760810993) Fr & Eur.

Lexikon der Aero und Astronautik Enischliesslich Raketentechnik. (GER.). 1972. write for info. (*0-8288-6409-8*, M-7282) Fr & Eur.

Lexikon der Alten Welt. Karl Andresen. (GER.). 1965. 495.00 (*0-8288-6749-6*, M7281) Fr & Eur.

Lexikon der Anstrichtechnik, Vol. 1. 3rd ed. Kurt Sponzel. (GER.). 1970. 30.00 (*0-7859-0948-6*, M-7279) Fr & Eur.

Lexikon der Anstrichtechnik, Vol. 2. Anton Brasholz. (GER.). 1975. 95.00 (*0-8288-5915-9*, M7280) Fr & Eur.

Lexikon der Arabischen Welt. Nandy Ronart. (GER.). 295.00 (*3-7608-0138-2*, M-7277); 295.00 (*0-8288-7969-9*, M7277) Fr & Eur.

Lexikon der Arbeits und Soziallere. Rainer Roth. (GER.). 1976. 65.00 (*0-8288-5729-6*, M7278) Fr & Eur.

Lexikon der Archaeologie, 2 vols., Set. Warwick Bray & David Trump. (GER.). 1975. pap. 49.95 (*0-8288-5916-7*, M7276) Fr & Eur.

Lexikon der Astronomie. Joachim Herrmann. (GER.). 405p. 1980. 85.00 (*0-7859-8443-7*, 3576005412) Fr & Eur.

Lexikon der Audio-Visuellen Bildungsmittel. Heribert Heinrichs. (GER.). 1971. 65.00 (*0-8288-6467-5*, M-7275) Fr & Eur.

Lexikon der Datenkommunikation. Klaus Lipiniski. (GER.). 380p. 1994. 185.00 (*0-7859-8541-7*, 3892380732) Fr & Eur.

Lexikon der Datenverarbeitung. Loebel & Peter Mueller. (GER.). 704p. 1975. 165.00 (*0-8288-5918-3*, M7264) Fr & Eur.

Lexikon der Datenverarbeitung. Peter Mueller. (GER.). 1968. 55.00 (*0-7859-0836-6*, M-7265) Fr & Eur.

Lexikon der Dentalen Technologie. Erich Korber. (GER.). 405p. 1986. 135.00 (*0-7859-8528-X*, 3876520967) Fr & Eur.

Lexikon der Deutschen Konzertliteratur, 2 vols., Set. Theodor Muller-Reuter. LC 70-171079. (Music Ser.). (GER.). 1972. reprint ed. lib. bdg. 110.00 (*0-306-70274-6*) Da Capo.

Lexikon der Deutschen Marinegeschichte: Lexicon of German Maritime History. Hans Witthoeft. (GER.). 1977. 59.95 (*0-8288-5486-6*, M7262) Fr & Eur.

Lexikon der Elektronischen Musik: The Lexicon of Electronic Music. Herbert Eimert. (GER.). 426p. 1973. 69.95 (*0-8288-6304-0*, M7260) Fr & Eur.

Lexikon der Englisch Wirtschaftsfachbegriffe: German-English. Michael Kummert. (ENG & GER.). 312p. 1991. 29.95 (*0-7859-7052-5*) Fr & Eur.

Lexikon der Englischen Antiquitaten. 2nd ed. Gordon Fellow. (GER.). 284p. 1991. 29.95 (*0-7859-8567-0*, 3927117706) Fr & Eur.

Lexikon der Englischen Literatur. Horst Drescher. (GER.). 534p. 1979. 49.95 (*0-7859-8410-0*, 3520465019) Fr & Eur.

Lexikon der Englischen Umgangssprache (Idioms) English-German. Cheri Booth. (ENG & GER.). 508p. 1989. 29.95 (*0-7859-8562-X*, 3927117323) Fr & Eur.

Lexikon der Esoterik. Helmut Werner. (GER.). 756p. 1991. 55.00 (*0-7859-8557-3*, 3925037578) Fr & Eur.

Lexikon der Europaischen Abkurzungen. Herald Kipp. (GER.). 306p. 1990. 29.95 (*0-7859-8565-4*, 3927117668) Fr & Eur.

Lexikon der Finanzinnovationen. 2nd ed. Guido Eilenberger. (GER.). 500p. 1993. 105.00 (*0-7859-8401-1*, 3486227033) Fr & Eur.

Lexikon der Forstbotanik. Peter Schutt. (GER.). 581p. 1992. 295.00 (*0-7859-8448-8*, 3609658002) Fr & Eur.

Lexikon der Franzoesischen Wirtschaftsfachbegriffe: German-French. Vicki Ebermann. (FRE & GER.). 312p. 1994. 29.95 (*0-7859-8513-1*, 3860470639) Fr & Eur.

Lexikon der Gastechnik. DVGW Staff. (GER.). 472p. 1990. 150.00 (*0-7859-8484-4*, 3802722868) Fr & Eur.

Lexikon der Geldenlage. Werner Schwilling. (GER.). 1974. 69.95 (*0-8288-6061-0*, M-7258) Fr & Eur.

Lexikon der Germanistischen Linguistik: Lexicon of German Linguistics. 2nd ed. Hans Althaus et al. (GER.). 870p. 1980. 195.00 (*0-8288-1965-3*, M7256) Fr & Eur.

Lexikon der Geschaeftsbriefe in Vier Sprachen, 3 vols. (ENG, FRE, GER & ITA.). 1972. 135.00 (*0-8288-6407-1*, M-7257) Fr & Eur.

Lexikon der Geschicte, 3 vols., Set. (GER.). 1976. pap. 250.00 (*0-8288-5730-X*, M7255) Fr & Eur.

Lexikon der Gesundheit: Medizinisches Fachwoerterbuch. Wolfhart Draeger. (GER.). 19.95 (*0-7859-8329-5*, 3404621190) Fr & Eur.

Lexikon der Grammatischen Terminologie: Lexicon of Grammar Technology. Otmar Bohusch. (GER.). 1972. 35.00 (*0-8288-6408-X*, M7254) Fr & Eur.

Lexikon der Graphischen Technik: Lexicon of Graphics Engineering. 4th ed. (GER.). 1977. 39.95 (*0-8288-5487-4*, M7253) Fr & Eur.

Lexikon der Griechischen und Roemischen Mythologie. H. Hunger. (GER.). 452p. 1974. pap. 17.95 (*0-8288-6062-9*, M-7252) Fr & Eur.

Lexikon der Guten Kuche. Ulrich Kuhn-Hein. (GER.). 400p. 1993. 39.95 (*0-7859-8449-6*, 3625108585) Fr & Eur.

Lexikon der Hamburgischen Schriftsteller Bis Zur Gegenwart, 8 vols., Set. Hans Schroder. 1983. write for info. incl. fiche (*0-318-71947-9*) G Olms Pubs.

Lexikon der Heraldik. Gert Oswald. (GER.). 478p. 1985. 79.95 (*0-7859-8349-X*, 3411021497) Fr & Eur.

Lexikon der Italienische Wirtschaftsfachbegriffe: German-Italian. Bernardo Romano. (GER & ITA.). 312p. 1991. 29.95 (*0-7859-7053-3*) Fr & Eur.

Lexikon der Keltischen Mythologie. Sylvia Botheroyd. (GER.). 378p. 1992. 105.00 (*0-7859-8356-2*, 3424010774) Fr & Eur.

Lexikon der Korrosion und des Korrosionsschutzes. H. Beneke. (GER.). 389p. 1992. 95.00 (*0-7859-8485-2*, 3802726979) Fr & Eur.

Lexikon der Kunst Vol. 1: A-Cim. Gerhard Strauss. (GER.). 850p. 1987. 250.00 (*0-7859-8323-6*, 3363000448) Fr & Eur.

Lexikon der Kunst Vol. 2: Cin-Gree. Gerhard Strauss. (GER.). 842p. 1989. 250.00 (*0-7859-8324-4*, 3363000456) Fr & Eur.

Lexikon der Kunst Vol. 3: Greg-Konv. Gerhard Strauss. (GER.). 850p. 1991. 250.00 (*0-7859-8325-2*, 3363000464) Fr & Eur.

Lexikon der Kunst Vol. 4: Kony-Mosa. Gerhard Strauss. (GER.). 850p. 1992. 250.00 (*0-7859-8326-0*, 3363000472) Fr & Eur.

Lexikon der Kunst Vol. 5: Mosb-Q. Gerhard Strauss. (GER.). 841p. 1993. 250.00 (*0-7859-8327-9*, 3363000480) Fr & Eur.

Lexikon der Kunstmotive: Antike und Christliche Welt. Gert Richter. (GER.). 319p. 1993. 29.95 (*0-7859-8689-8*, 357200554x) Fr & Eur.

Lexikon der Kunststile, 2 vols., Set. G. Lindemann. (GER.). 360p. 1980. pap. 24.95 (*0-8288-1421-X*, M7251) Fr & Eur.

Lexikon Der Lateinischen Wortformen. Karl E. Georges. iv, 758p. 1967. reprint ed. write for info. (*0-318-71126-5*) G Olms Pubs.

Lexikon der Lateinischen Wortformen. Karl E. Georges. iv, 758p. 1967. reprint ed. write for info. (*0-318-72026-4*) G Olms Pubs.

Lexikon der Lebensmitteltechnologie. Benno Kunz. (GER.). 520p. 1993. 225.00 (*0-7859-8684-7*, 354056215x) Fr & Eur.

Lexikon der Medizinischen Fachsprache, 2 vols., Set. Dagobert Tutsch. (GER.). 388p. 1970. pap. 19.95 (*0-7859-0840-4*, M-7249) Fr & Eur.

Lexikon der Medizinischen Psychologie: Lexicon of Medical Psychology. U. Tewes. (GER.). 1977. 24.95 (*0-8288-5488-2*, M7248) Fr & Eur.

Lexikon der Mikrobiologie und Infektologie. 2nd ed. Promod M. Shah. (GER.). 352p. 1993. 125.00 (*0-7859-8475-5*, 3794514386) Fr & Eur.

Lexikon der Mikroelektronik. Eugen-Georg Woschni. (GER.). 132p. 1992. 75.00 (*0-7859-8479-8*, 3800717921) Fr & Eur.

Lexikon der Missionstheologischer Grundergriffe see Dictionary of Mission: Theology, History, Perspectives

Lexikon der Modernen Konservation. Hanns Kurth. (GER.). 1973. 34.95 (*0-8288-6305-9*, M-7247) Fr & Eur.

Lexikon der Musiktherapie. Hans-Helmut Decker-Voight. (GER.). 400p. 1992. 150.00 (*0-7859-8481-X*, 3801706362) Fr & Eur.

Lexikon der Mykologie. H. Doerfelt. (GER., Illus.). 432p. 1989. lib. bdg. 33.00 (*3-437-20413-0*) Lubrecht & Cramer.

Lexikon der Mythologie der Eurpaeischen Voelker. Herbert Gottschalk. (GER.). 85.00 (*3-7934-1184-2*, M-7246); 85.00 (*0-8288-7771-8*, M7246) Fr & Eur.

L

An Asterisk (*) at the beginning of an entry indicates that the title is appearing for the first time.

L

Lexikon der Neuzeitlichen Landwirtschaft, 3 vols. 9th ed. (GER.). 1974. 25.00 (*0-8288-6064-5*, M-7244) Fr & Eur.

Lexikon der Neuzeitlichen Landwirtschaft, Vol. 1. 9th ed. (GER.). 1973. 25.00 (*0-7859-0849-8*, M-7242) Fr & Eur.

Lexikon der Niedersachsischen Schriftsteller Von Den Altesten Zeiten Bis Zur Gegenwart. Rudolf Eckart. vi, 181p. 1974. reprint ed. write for info. (*3-487-05409-4*) G Olms Pubs.

Lexikon der Numismatik: Numismatics Lexicon. Tyll Kroha. (GER.). 1977. 85.00 (*0-8288-5489-0*, M7241) Fr & Eur.

Lexikon der Offentichen Finanzwirtschaft. 3rd ed. Klaus Staender. (GER.). 423p. 1993. 55.00 (*0-7859-8460-7*, 3768519937) Fr & Eur.

Lexikon der PC-Abkurzungen. Jurgen Kiel. (GER.). 252p. 1994. 49.95 (*0-7859-8494-1*, 3806843902) Fr & Eur.

Lexikon der Philosophischen Begriffe. Alexander Ulfig. (GER.). 503p. 1993. 29.95 (*0-7859-8695-2*, 386047040x) Fr & Eur.

Lexikon der Planun und Organisation. Hans Niewerth. (GER.). 1968. 65.00 (*0-8288-6651-1*, M-7235) Fr & Eur.

Lexikon der Praktischen Psychologie. Knoll Ludwig. (GER.). 488p. 1993. 29.95 (*0-7859-8543-3*, 3893501657) Fr & Eur.

Lexikon der Psychologie: Lexicon of Psychology, 3 vols. W. Arnold. (GER.). 1306p. 1980. 495.00 (*0-8288-2207-7*, M7234) Fr & Eur.

Lexikon der Rechtsbegriffe. Thomas Montasser. (GER.). 512p. 1991. 29.95 (*0-7859-8566-2*, 3927117692) Fr & Eur.

Lexikon der Rechtsmedizin. Horst Hunger. (GER.). 309p. 1993. 225.00 (*0-7859-8315-5*, 3335002539) Fr & Eur.

Lexikon der Reproduktionstechnik. 2nd ed. Franz Bauer. (GER.). 634p. 1986. 75.00 (*0-7859-8533-6*, 3880133387) Fr & Eur.

Lexikon der Schleswig-Holstein-Lauenburgischen und Eutinischen Schriftsteller Von 1796 Bis 1828, Vols. 1-2. Detlev L. Lubker & Hans Schroder. xxxvii, 904p. 1983. write for info. (*0-318-71926-6*) G Olms Pubs.

Lexikon der Schleswig-Holstein-Lauenburgischen und Eutinischen Schriftsteller Von 1829-1882, 4 vols., Set. Eduard Alberti. 1983. write for info. incl. fiche (*0-318-71884-7*) G Olms Pubs.

Lexikon der Schulphysik: Atomphysik, Vol. 5. O. Hoefling. (GER.). 85.00 (*3-7614-0110-8*, M-7227) Fr & Eur.

Lexikon der Schulphysik: Elektrizitaet und Magnetismus A-K, Vol. 3A. Breitsameter. (GER.). 75.00 (*3-7614-0168-X*, M7224) Fr & Eur.

Lexikon der Schulphysik: Elektrizitaet und Magnetismus L-Z, Vol. 3B. Breitsameter. (GER.). 75.00 (*3-7614-0169-8*, M7225) Fr & Eur.

Lexikon der Schulphysik: Geschichte der Physik, Vol. 6. A. Hermann. (GER.). 75.00 (*3-7614-0131-0*, M-7228) Fr & Eur.

Lexikon der Schulphysik: Geschichte der Physik, Vol. 7. A. Hermann. (GER.). 75.00 (*3-7614-0153-1*, M-7229) Fr & Eur.

Lexikon der Schulphysik: Mechanik und Akustik, Vol. 1. K. Zita. (GER.). 85.00 (*3-7614-0107-8*, M-7222) Fr & Eur.

Lexikon der Schulphysik: Optik und Relativitaet, Vol. 4. W. Ruth. (GER.). 85.00 (*3-7614-0109-4*, M-7226) Fr & Eur.

Lexikon der Schulphysik: Waerme und Wetter, Vol. 2. W. Hein. (GER.). 75.00 (*3-7614-0108-6*, M-7223) Fr & Eur.

Lexikon der Schulphysik Vol. 1: Mechanik und Akustik. K. Zita. (GER.). 85.00 (*0-8288-8062-X*, M7222) Fr & Eur.

Lexikon der Schulphysik Vol. 2: Waerme und Wetter. W. Hein. (GER.). 75.00 (*0-8288-7802-1*, M7223) Fr & Eur.

Lexikon der Schulphysik Vol. 3A: Elektrizitaet und Magnetismus A-K. Breitsameter. (GER.). 75.00 (*0-8288-7625-8*, M7224) Fr & Eur.

Lexikon der Schulphysik Vol. 3B: Elektruzitaet und Magnetismus L-Z. (GER.). 75.00 (*0-8288-7626-6*, M7225) Fr & Eur.

Lexikon der Schulphysik Vol. 4: Optik und Relativitaet. W. Ruth. (GER.). 85.00 (*0-8288-7975-3*, M7226) Fr & Eur.

Lexikon der Schulphysik Vol. 5: Atomphysik. O. Hoefling. (GER.). 85.00 (*0-8288-7810-2*, M7227) Fr & Eur.

Lexikon der Schulphysik Vol. 6: Geschichte der Physik. A. Hermann. 75.00 (*0-8288-7806-4*, M7228) Fr & Eur.

Lexikon der Schulphysik Vol. 7: Geschichte der Physik. A. Hermann. 75.00 (*0-8288-7807-2*, M7229) Fr & Eur.

Lexikon der Sozialerziehung. Tobias Brocher. (GER.). 1972. 17.95 (*0-8288-6410-1*, M7221) Fr & Eur.

Lexikon der Spanischen Redewendungen: Expresiones Idiomaticas. Felipa Morena Torres. (GER & SPA.). 312p. 1990. 29.95 (*0-7859-8564-6*, 3927117498) Fr & Eur.

Lexikon der Spanischen Wirtschaftsfachbegriffe: German-Spanish. Vicki Ebermann. (GER & SPA.). 312p. 1994. 29.95 (*0-7859-8514-X*, 3860470647) Fr & Eur.

Lexikon der Staedte und Gemeinden. Fritz Siefert. (GER.). 561p. 1981. 79.95 (*0-8288-1395-7*, M7261) Fr & Eur.

Lexikon der Symbole. Udo Becker. (GER.). 352p. 1992. 150.00 (*0-7859-8376-7*, 3451224836) Fr & Eur.

Lexikon der Symbole. 14th ed. Wolfgang Bauer. (GER.). 580p. 1993. 39.95 (*0-7859-8551-4*, 3921695546) Fr & Eur.

Lexikon der Synonyme. Ines Schill. (GER.). 300p. 1993. 19.95 (*0-7859-8497-6*, 3809400955) Fr & Eur.

Lexikon der Telecommunikation. 2nd ed. Klaus-Rudiger Fellbaum. (GER.). 323p. 1985. 35.00 (*0-7859-8477-1*, 3800713977) Fr & Eur.

Lexikon der Textkommunikation und Datenkommunikation: Lexicon of Text & Data Communication. 3rd ed. Wolfgang W. Mache. (GER.). 580p. 1993. 195.00 (*0-8288-1358-2*, M15282) Fr & Eur.

Lexikon der Unternehmensfuehrung. Klaus Altfelder. (GER.). 1973. 85.00 (*0-8288-6307-5*, M7219) Fr & Eur.

Lexikon der Videotechnik. Heinz Bergmann. (GER.). 144p. 1992. 39.95 (*0-7859-8478-X*, 3800717735) Fr & Eur.

Lexikon der Voelker und Kulturen, 3 vols. W. Stoehr. (GER.). 1972. pap. 75.00 (*0-8288-6411-X*, M-7218) Fr & Eur.

Lexikon der Volkswirtschaft. 5th ed. Friedrich Geigant. (GER.). 832p. 1987. 75.00 (*0-8288-1278-0*, M7217) Fr & Eur.

Lexikon der Vom Jahre 1750-1800 Verstorbenen Teutschen Schriftsteller, 15 vols., Set. Johann G. Meusel. 1968. reprint ed. write for info. (*0-318-71929-0*) G Olms Pubs.

Lexikon der Vornamen. (Duden-Taschenbuch Ser.: No. 4). 239p. 1974. 12.25 (*3-411-01333-8*, Pub. by Bibliogr Inst Brockhaus) Langenscheidt.

Lexikon der Weine Italiens. Luigi Veronelli. (GER.). 374p. 1991. 59.95 (*0-7859-8560-3*, 3926763299) Fr & Eur.

Lexikon der Welt Literatur Vol. 2: Lexicon of World Literature. 2nd ed. Gero Von Wilpert. (GER.). 1359p. 1980. 150.00 (*0-8288-1573-9*, M7211) Fr & Eur.

Lexikon der Weltarchitektur. 3rd rev. ed. Nikolaus Pevsner. (GER.). 876p. 1992. pap. 295.00 (*0-8288-1195-4*, M7216) Fr & Eur.

Lexikon der Weltgeschichte: Lexicon of World History. (GER.). 1977. 27.95 (*0-8288-5490-4*, M7215) Fr & Eur.

Lexikon der Weltliteratur: Biographisch - Bibliographisches Handwoerterbuch, Vol. 1. 2nd ed. Gero Von Wilpert. (GER.). 1975. 195.00 (*0-8288-5921-3*, M7212) Fr & Eur.

Lexikon Des Controlling. 5th ed. Klaus Fassler. (GER.). 638p. 1991. 125.00 (*0-7859-8395-3*, 3478341957) Fr & Eur.

Lexikon des deutschen Widerstandes. Ed. by Wolfgang Benz & Walter H. Pehle. (GER.). 432p. 1994. 43.25 (*3-10-005702-3*, Pub. by S Fischer) Intl Bk Import.

Lexikon des Geheimwissens. Horst E. Miers. (GER.). 125.00 (*0-8288-7901-X*, M7214) Fr & Eur.

Lexikon des Geheimwissens. deluxe ed. Horst E. Miers. (GER.). 125.00 (*3-7626-0028-7*, M-7214) Fr & Eur.

Lexikon des Impressionismus. Maurice Serullaz. (GER.). 1975. 49.95 (*0-8288-5922-1*, M7208) Fr & Eur.

Lexikon des Marxismus, 3 vols, Set. Iring Fetscher. (GER.). 1976. 125.00 (*0-8288-5732-6*, M7207) Fr & Eur.

Lexikon des Mittelalters: Lexicon of the Middle Ages. Artemis Staff. (GER.). 1977. pap. 3500.00 (*0-8288-5492-0*, M7206) Fr & Eur.

Lexikon Des Nebenestrafrechts. 2nd ed. Erich Gohler. (GER.). 1986. pap. 110.00 (*0-8288-1523-2*, M7245) Fr & Eur.

Lexikon des Offsetdrucks. Wolfgang Walenski. (GER.). 352p. 1993. 105.00 (*0-7859-8534-4*, 3880134693) Fr & Eur.

Lexikon Des Rechts der Wirtschafts, Zur Fortsetzung. Hermann-Josef Bunte. (GER.). 1993. 195.00 (*0-7859-8394-5*, 3472001372) Fr & Eur.

Lexikon des Surrealismus. Rene Passeron. (GER.). 1975. 45.00 (*0-8288-5923-X*, M7220) Fr & Eur.

Lexikon des Tarot Sowie der Oracle und Selbsterfahrungsspiele. Eskhard Graf. (GER.). 224p. 1991. 39.95 (*0-7859-8568-9*, 3927913030) Fr & Eur.

Lexikon des Wirtschaftsrechnens. 2nd ed. Franz Kafitz. (GER.). 1976. 27.95 (*0-8288-5733-4*, M7210) Fr & Eur.

Lexikon des Zen von A-Z. Michael Diener. (GER.). 264p. 1992. 45.00 (*0-7859-8681-2*, 350267406x) Fr & Eur.

Lexikon des Zweites Weltkriegs: Lexicon of the Two World Wars. Cristian Zentner. (GER.). 1977. pap. 75.00 (*0-8288-5491-2*, M7213) Fr & Eur.

Lexikon Deutscher Dichter und Prosaisten, 6 vols., Set. Karl H. Jordens. 1970. reprint ed. write for info. (*0-318-71919-3*) G Olms Pubs.

Lexikon Deutscher Frauen der Feder, 2 vols., Set. Sophie Pataky. 1983. write for info. incl. fiche (*0-318-71938-X*) G Olms Pubs.

Lexikon Deutscher Konjunktionen. Joachim Buscha. 159p. 1986. 21.00 (*3-324-00486-1*) Langenscheidt.

Lexikon Deutscher Modalworter. Gerhard Helbig & Agnes Helbig. 300p. 1990. 21.00 (*3-324-00550-7*) Langenscheidt.

Lexikon Deutscher Partikeln. Gerhard Helbig. 258p. 1990. 21.00 (*3-324-00310-5*) Langenscheidt.

Lexikon Deutscher Prafixverben. Jochen Schroder. 288p. 1992. 21.00 (*3-324-00595-7*) Langenscheidt.

Lexikon Deutscher Prapositionen. Jochen Schroder. 268p. 1990. 21.00 (*3-324-00007-6*) Langenscheidt.

Lexikon Deutschprachiger Mundartautoren. Bernhard Sowinski. xxx, 797p. 1997. 110.00 (*3-487-10381-8*) G Olms Pubs.

Lexikon Deutschsprachiger Mundartautoren. Bernhard Sowinski. 797p. 1997. 125.00 (*3-487-10307-9*) G Olms Pubs.

Lexikon Deutschsprachiger Schriftsteller, Vol. 1. Guenther Albrecht. (GER.). 1974. 75.00 (*0-7859-0408-5*, M7204) Fr & Eur.

Lexikon Deutschsprachiger Schriftsteller, Vol. 2. Guenther Albrecht. (GER.). 1974. 75.00 (*0-7859-0409-3*, M7205) Fr & Eur.

Lexikon dt. Verben der Fortbewegung. Jochen Schroder. 224p. 1993. 21.00 (*3-324-00603-1*) Langenscheidt.

Lexikon EDV und Rechnungswesen. Kurt Nagel. (GER.). 1977. 59.95 (*0-8288-5493-9*, M7203) Fr & Eur.

Lexikon Elektronik und Mikroelektronik. 2nd ed. Dieter Sautter. (GER.). 1155p. 1993. 295.00 (*0-7859-8673-1*, 318401178x) Fr & Eur.

Lexikon Elektrotechnik. German Muller. (GER.). 1994. 195.00 (*0-7859-8416-X*, 3527281541) Fr & Eur.

Lexikon Esoterischen Wissens. Necill Drury. (GER.). 29.95 (*0-7859-8678-2*, 342604160x) Fr & Eur.

Lexikon Exotischer Fruechte (Lexicon of Exotic Fruits) Helmut Kratochvil. (Illus.). vii, 180p. 1995. 41.00 (*3-8263-8490-3*, Pub. by Blckwell Wissenschafts) Balogh.

Lexikon Feurden Bauherrn. Ernst Huerlimann. (GER.). 1975. 59.95 (*0-8288-5924-8*, M7202) Fr & Eur.

Lexikon Filmschauspieler International. Hans-Michael Bock. (GER.). 850p. 1994. 135.00 (*0-7859-8549-2*, 3894871997) Fr & Eur.

Lexikon Fuer die Graphische Industrie. Ernst Born. (GER.). 135.00 (*0-8288-7621-5*, M7201) Fr & Eur.

Lexikon Fuer die Graphische Industrie. 2nd ed. Ernst Born. (GER.). 125.00 (*3-87641-184-X*, M7201) Fr & Eur.

Lexikon Fuer Eisenbahnfreunde. Erhard Born. (GER.). 1977. pap. 59.95 (*0-8288-5494-7*, M7200) Fr & Eur.

Lexikon Fuer Eltern und Erzieher. Hans H. Groothoff. (GER.). 1973. 21.95 (*0-8288-6308-3*, M-7199) Fr & Eur.

Lexikon Fuer Mineralien - und Gesteins Freunde. Herrmann Harder. (GER.). 1977. 49.95 (*0-8288-5495-5*, M7198) Fr & Eur.

Lexikon Fuer Pferdefreunde. (GER.). 1976. 49.95 (*0-8288-5734-2*, M7197) Fr & Eur.

Lexikon Fuer Planetenbilder. Ilse Schnitzler. (GER.). 1975. 49.95 (*0-8288-5925-6*, M7196) Fr & Eur.

Lexikon Fuer Tennisfreunde. Ulrich Kaiser. (GER.). 1977. 49.95 (*0-8288-5496-3*, M7195) Fr & Eur.

Lexikon Fur Rechnungswesen und Controlling. Reinhard Heyd. (GER.). 525p. 1993. 150.00 (*0-7859-8476-3*, 3799207309) Fr & Eur.

***Lexikon fur Theologie und Kirche, Vol. 1.** Walter Kasper. (GER.). 1998. 285.00 (*0-8245-2175-7*) Crossroad NY.

Lexikon fur Theologie und Kirche, Vol. 2. Walter Kasper. (GER.). 1998. 285.00 (*0-8245-2176-5*) Crossroad NY.

Lexikon fur Theologie und Kirche, Vol. 3. Walter Kasper. (GER.). 1998. 285.00 (*0-8245-2177-3*) Crossroad NY.

Lexikon fur Theologie und Kirche, Vol. 4. Walter Kasper. (GER.). 1998. 285.00 (*0-8245-2178-1*) Crossroad NY.

***Lexikon fur Theologie und Kirche, Vol. 5.** Walter Kasper. (GER.). 1998. 285.00 (*0-8245-2179-X*) Crossroad NY.

***Lexikon fur Theologie und Kirche, Vol. 6.** Walter Kasper. (GER.). 1998. 285.00 (*0-8245-2180-3*) Crossroad NY.

Lexikon fur Wirtschaft, Recht, Steuern, Finanzen, Institutionen. Heinrich Weiler. (GER.). 280p. 1993. 75.00 (*0-7859-8520-4*, 3870814535) Fr & Eur.

Lexikon Informatik und Datenverarbeitung (Informatics & Dataprocessing Lexicon German-English with Eng-Ger Index) H. J. Schneider. 1060p. 1997. 141.00 (*3-486-22875-7*) IBD Ltd.

Lexikon Landwirtschaft. 2nd ed. Ingrid Alsing. (GER.). 703p. 1993. 225.00 (*0-7859-8333-3*, 3406135613) Fr & Eur.

Lexikon Lebensmittel-Mikrobiologie. Hanns K. Frank. (GER.). 312p. 1990. 175.00 (*0-7859-8559-X*, 3925673539) Fr & Eur.

Lexikon Lokaler Netzwerke: Fachbegriffe. Jurgen Aschenbrunner. (GER.). 232p. 1992. 95.00 (*0-7859-8692-8*, 377234691x) Fr & Eur.

Lexikon Management. Rudiger Pieper. (GER.). 418p. 1992. 105.00 (*0-7859-8338-4*, 3409132147) Fr & Eur.

Lexikon Manilianum. Pedro J. Del Real Francia. (Alpha-Omega, Reihe A Ser.). (GER.). xii, 584p. 1998. write for info. (*3-487-10640-X*) G Olms Pubs.

Lexikon Medicum. B. Zlotnicki. (ENG, FRE, GER, LAT & POL.). 1973. 95.00 (*0-8288-6309-1*, M-6576) Fr & Eur.

Lexikon Medizinisch-Wissenschaftlicher Abkurzungen. 3rd ed. Rolf Heister. (GER.). 424p. 1993. 69.95 (*0-7859-8509-3*, 3825215490) Fr & Eur.

Lexikon Messtechnikund Automatisierungstechnik. Elmar Schrufer. (GER.). 689p. 1992. 250.00 (*0-7859-8286-8*, 3184008959) Fr & Eur.

Lexikon Slovenskych Dejin (Lexicon of the Slovak History) D. Skvama et al. (SLO.). 360p. 1997. write for info. (*80-08-01131-9*, Pub. by Slov Pegagog Naklad); pap. 145.00 (*80-08-02478-X*, Pub. by Slov Pegagog Naklad); lthr. write for info. (*80-08-02477-1*, Pub. by Slov Pegagog Naklad) IBD Ltd.

Lexikon Svetovych Dejin (Lexicon of the World History) M. Kamenicky et al. (SLO.). 320p. 1997. write for info. (*80-08-01120-3*, Pub. by Slov Pegagog Naklad); pap. write for info. (*80-08-02479-8*, Pub. by Slov Pegagog Naklad); lthr. write for info. (*80-08-02480-1*, Pub. by Slov Pegagog Naklad) IBD Ltd.

Lexikon Technologie Metallverarbeitende Industri. 2nd ed. Gerhard Muller. (GER.). 699p. 1992. 125.00 (*0-7859-8694-4*, 380855102x) Fr & Eur.

Lexikon Uber die Formen der Griechischen Verba. Georg Traut. viii, 719p. 1968. reprint ed. write for info. (*0-318-72082-5*) G Olms Pubs.

Lexikon Uber die Formen der Griechischen Verba. Georg Traut. viii, 719p. 1986. reprint ed. write for info. (*3-487-02152-8*) G Olms Pubs.

Lexikon und Lexikographie. Ed. by Burkhard Schaeder & Burkhard Rieger. (Sprache und Computer Ser.: Vol. 11). (GER.). x, 184p. 1992. write for info. (*3-487-09433-9*) G Olms Pubs.

Lexikon Verstorbener Baierischer Schriftsteller des 18 und 19 Jahrhunderts, 2 vols., Set. Clemens A. Baader. (Schriftsteller- und Gelehrtenlexika des 17, 18 und 19 Jahrhunderts Ser.). 1971. reprint ed. 225.00 (*3-487-04048-4*) G Olms Pubs.

Lexikon Zu Den Philosophischen Schriften Cicero's, 3 vols. Ed. by Hugo Merguet. (Lexikon Zu den Schriften Cicero's Ser.: Pt. 2). 2715p. 1987. reprint ed. 700.00 (*3-487-00051-2*) G Olms Pubs.

Lexikon Zu Den Philosophischen Schriften Ciceros, 3 vols., Set. Hugo Merguet. 1971. reprint ed. write for info. (*0-318-72052-3*) G Olms Pubs.

Lexikon Zu Den Philosophischen Schriften Cicero's: Mit Angabe Saemtlicher Stellen, 3 vols., Set. Hugo Merguet. (GER & LAT.). 1987. reprint ed. lib. bdg. 575.00 (*3-487-00052-0*) G Olms Pubs.

Lexikon Zu Den Reden des Cicero, 4 vols., Set. Hugo Merguet. (Lexikon Zu den Schriften Cicero's Ser.: Teil 1). 3513p. 1973. write for info. (*3-487-05028-5*) G Olms Pubs.

Lexikon Zu Den Reden des Cicero, 4 vols., Set. Hugo Merguet. 1962. reprint ed. write for info. (*0-318-72051-5*) G Olms Pubs.

Lexikon Zu Den Schriften Casars, 2 vols., Set. Hugo Merguet. iv, 1142p. 1963. reprint ed. write for info. (*0-318-71175-3*); reprint ed. write for info. (*0-318-72049-3*) G Olms Pubs.

Lexikon Zu Den Schriften Casars. Entwicklung. Hugo Merguet. pap. write for info. (*0-318-70798-5*) G Olms Pubs.

Lexikon Zu Vergilius. Hugo Merguet. 786p. 1969. reprint ed. write for info. (*0-318-72053-1*) G Olms Pubs.

Lexikon Zu Vergilius Mit Angabe Samtlicher Stellen. Hugo Merguet. pap. write for info. (*0-318-70800-0*) G Olms Pubs.

Lexikon Zu Vergilius Mit Angabe Samtlicher Stellen. Hugo Merguet. 786p. 1969. reprint ed. write for info. (*0-318-71176-1*); reprint ed. pap. write for info. (*0-318-70519-2*); reprint ed. pap. write for info. (*0-318-71177-X*) G Olms Pubs.

Lexikon Zum Artikelgebrauch. Hans J. Grimm. 236p. 1989. 21.00 (*3-324-00149-8*) Langenscheidt.

Lexikon Zur - und Fruehgeschichtlicher Fundstaetten Oesterreichs. L. Franz. (GER.). 1965. 85.00 (*0-8288-6750-X*, M-7193) Fr & Eur.

Lexikon Zur Soziologie, 2 vols. 3rd ed. Werner Fuchs. (GER.). 890p. 1993. 59.95 (*0-8288-5926-4*, M7191) Fr & Eur.

Lexikon Zur Weltmission. S. E. Neill. (GER.). 95.00 (*3-7974-0054-3*, M-7190); 95.00 (*0-8288-7912-5*, M7190) Fr & Eur.

Lexikon 2000, 13 vols., Set. (GER.). 1970. 1295.00 (*0-8288-6543-4*, M-7189) Fr & Eur.

Lexilogus Oder Beitrage Zur Griechischen Worterklarung Hauptsachlich Fur Homer und Hesiod, 2 vols. in 1. Philipp K. Buttmann. xvi, 542p. 1968. reprint ed. 120.00 (*0-318-72004-3*) G Olms Pubs.

Lexilogus Xenophonteus. Gustav Sauppe. iv, 146p. 1971. reprint ed. write for info. (*3-487-04153-7*) G Olms Pubs.

Lexilogus Zu Homer. Friedrich Bechtel. viii, 314p. 1964. reprint ed. 80.00 (*0-318-70873-6*) G Olms Pubs.

Lexímed Compact: Dictionary of Clinical Medicine: Deutsch-Englisch. P. Reuter. 1997. 49.00 (*0-86577-735-7*) Thieme Med Pubs.

Lexímed Compact: Dictionary of Clinical Medicine: English-German. P. Reuter. 1997. 49.00 (*0-86577-734-9*) Thieme Med Pubs.

Lexington: A Century in Photographs. Bettie Kerr & John Wright, Jr. LC 84-81388. (Illus.). 256p. 1984. 27.50 (*0-912839-07-4*) Lexington-Fayette.

Lexington: Changes in the Twentieth Century. Wynelle Deese. LC 98-86344. (Images of America Ser.). (Illus.). 128p. 1998. pap. 16.99 (*0-7524-1386-4*) Arcadia Publng.

Lexington: Heart of the Bluegrass. John D. Wright, Jr. LC 82-82604. (Illus.). 232p. 1982. 23.75 (*0-912839-06-6*) Lexington-Fayette.

Lexington: Heart of the Bluegrass. deluxe ed. John D. Wright, Jr. LC 82-82604. (Illus.). 232p. 1982. ring bd. 69.00 (*0-912839-04-X*) Lexington-Fayette.

Lexington & Concord. Deborah Kent. (J). 1998. pap. 5.95 (*0-516-26229-7*) Childrens.

Lexington & Concord. David King. LC 97-27065. (Battlefields Across America Ser.). 64p. (YA). (gr. 5 up). 1997. 23.40 (*0-8050-5225-9*) TFC Bks NY.

***Lexington & Concord: The Beginning of the War of the American Revolution.** Arthur B. Tourtellot. (Illus.). 336p. 2000. pap. text 14.95 (*0-393-32056-1*) Norton.

Lexington & Kentucky's Inner Bluegrass Region. Ed. by Richard Ulack et al. LC 95-167203. (Pathways Site Guide Ser.: No. 16). (Illus.). 70p. 1994. pap. text 9.50 (*1-884136-02-8*) NCFGE.

Lexington & Rochbridge County in the Civil War. Robert J. Driver, Jr. (Virginia Civil War Battles & Leaders Ser.). (Illus.). 177p. 1989. 19.95 (*0-930919-84-X*) H E Howard.

Lexington-Class Carriers: A Technical History of America's Early Carriers. Robert C. Stern. (Illus.). 160p. 1993. 37.95 (*1-55750-503-9*) Naval Inst Pr.

***Lexington Entertainment, 2000.** (Illus.). 358p. 1999. pap. 25.00 (*1-58553-035-2*, 005H) Enter Pubns.

Lexington Goes Down: A Fighting Carrier's Last Hours in the Coral Sea. Adolph A. Hoehling. LC 93-17980. (Illus.). 208p. 1994. reprint ed. pap. 12.95 (*0-8117-2550-2*) Stackpole.

Lexington Industrial Automation. J. Bleux. (FRE & ENG.). 157p. 1996. 37.95 (*0-320-02481-4*) Fr & Eur.

Lexington Introduction to Literature: Reading & Responding to Texts. Gary F. Waller et al. LC 86-81356. 1278p. (C). 1987. pap. text 47.16 (*0-669-09556-7*); teacher ed. 2.66 (*0-669-09557-5*) HM Trade Div.

***Lexington, Kentucky, 1.** Rand McNally Staff. 1998. pap. 5.95 (*0-528-96762-2*) Rand McNally.

Lexington, Mass., Record of Births, Marriages & Deaths to January 1, 1898. 479p. 1898. reprint ed. lib. bdg. 49.00 (*0-8328-0838-5*, MA0066-7) Higginson Bk Co.

Lexington Reader. Lynn Z. Bloom. 828p. (C). 1987. teacher ed. 2.66 (*0-669-09559-1*) HM Trade Div.

Lexington School: Its Story, Its Community. Mary H. Bakeman. LC 98-19273. 50p. 1998. pap. 15.00 (*0-915709-62-7*) Pk Geneal Bk.

Lexington, 1779. Bettye L. Mastin. LC 79-90522. 137p. 1979. 12.50 (*0-912839-00-7*) Lexington-Fayette.

An Asterisk (*) at the beginning of an entry indicates that the title is appearing for the first time.

Lexington Who's Who Registry, 1998-1999. Lexington Who's Who, Inc. Staff. Date not set. write for info. (*0-9672740-0-1*) Lex Whos Who.

***Lexipedia.** Encyclopaedia Britannica Publishers, Inc. Staff. (SPA., Illus.). 2768p. 1998. text 250.00 (*1-56409-031-0*) EBP Latin Am.

Lexique: Machines a Combustion. Conseil International des Machines a Combustion St. (DUT, FRE, GER, ITA & SPA.). 96p. pap. 29.95 (*84-600-0836-3*, S-30858) Fr & Eur.

Lexique Anglais-Francais de la Banque et de la Monnaie: English - French Lexicon of Banking & Finance. Pierre Ricour. (ENG & FRE.). 40p. 1974. pap. 9.95 (*0-8288-6311-3*, M-6486) Fr & Eur.

Lexique Anglais-Francais de L'Aciere Electrique. B. Besse et al. (ENG & FRE.). 135p. 1975. pap. 8.95 (*0-8288-5927-2*, M9239) Fr & Eur.

Lexique Anglais-Francais du Compteur D'electricite: Principes et Pieces Composantes. Jean Mercier. (ENG & FRE.). 42p. 1973. pap. 9.95 (*0-8288-6312-1*, M-6407) Fr & Eur.

Lexique Anglais-Francais du Programmateur De Cuisiniere: Fonctionnement et Pieces Composantes. Jean Mercier. (ENG & FRE.). 29p. 1973. pap. 9.95 (*0-8288-6313-X*, M-6406) Fr & Eur.

Lexique Bilingue Comptabilite-Finance, Anglais-Francais-Francais-Anglais. Jean-Yves Eglem. (ENG & FRE.). 192p. 1996. 19.95 (*0-7859-9322-3*) Fr & Eur.

Lexique Bilingue de la Bureautique, Anglais-Francais-Francais-Anglais. Jean-Pierre Merle. (ENG & FRE.). 192p. 1996. 19.95 (*0-7859-9323-1*) Fr & Eur.

Lexique Bilingue de l'Anglais Juridique, Anglais-Francais-Francais-Anglais. (ENG & FRE.). 1996. 19.95 (*0-7859-9325-8*) Fr & Eur.

Lexique Bilingue des Techniques Commerciales, Anglais-Francais/Francais-Anglais. Jean-Michel Daube. (ENG & FRE.). write for info. (*0-7859-9324-X*) Fr & Eur.

Lexique Bilingue du Commerce Internationale, Anglais-Francais-Francais-Anglais. Jean-Michel Daube. (ENG & FRE.). 208p. 1996. 19.95 (*0-7859-9321-5*) Fr & Eur.

Lexique Biologie Moleculaire see Lexicon of Molecular Biology: English-French, French-English

Lexique Cinema Video Francais-Anglais/Anglais-Francais - Cinema & Video Dictionary French-English/ English-French. P. Le Moal. (ENG & FRE.). 1995. spiral bd. 60.00 (*2-85608-074-X*, Pub. by La Maison Du Dict) IBD Ltd.

Lexique Civilisation Germanique. H. Dupas. (FRE.). 1998. 65.00 (*0-320-00148-2*) Fr & Eur.

Lexique Comorien (Shindzuani)-Francais. Mohamed Ahmed-Chamanga. (FRE.). 240p. 1992. pap. 69.95 (*0-7859-1008-5*, 2738416632) Fr & Eur.

Lexique Compare de la Langue de Corneille et de la Langue du XVIie Siecle en General, 2 vols. Frederic Godefroy. 1990. reprint ed. 165.00 (*0-8115-3868-0*) Periodicals Srv.

Lexique de Commerce International. Ugo Brassart. 225p. 1993. pap. 32.95 (*0-7859-5576-3*, 2010200527) Fr & Eur.

Lexique de Comptabilite. 3rd ed. Pierre Lassegue. 404p. 1993. pap. 39.95 (*0-7859-5622-0*, 2247015328) Fr & Eur.

Lexique de Comptabilite et de Gestion. Colasse. (FRE.). 1979. pap. 29.95 (*0-8288-5928-0*, M6079) Fr & Eur.

Lexique de Droit Civil: Contrats, Responsabilite. Eric Colin & Beatrice Morin. 160p. 1993. pap. 32.95 (*0-7859-5577-1*, 2010200985) Fr & Eur.

Lexique de la Fabrication du Refrigerateur: Francais-Anglais. Hector Dupuis et al. (ENG & FRE.). 66p. 1975. pap. 5.95 (*0-8288-5929-9*, M9240) Fr & Eur.

Lexique de la Geographie en Cinq Langues. Presse Commerciale Staff. (FRE.). 2248p. 1993. 75.00 (*0-7859-5674-3*, 7100008379) Fr & Eur.

Lexique de la Langue de la Bruyere. Adolphe Regnier. lxxi, 380p. 1970. reprint ed. write for info. (*0-318-71399-3*) G Olms Pubs.

Lexique de la Langue de Malherbe. Adolphe Regnier. lxxxvii, 680p. 1970. reprint ed. write for info. (*0-318-71400-0*) G Olms Pubs.

Lexique de la Langue de Mme. Sevigne, 2 vols., Set. Jean E. Sommer. lxxxiv, 1099p. 1973. reprint ed. write for info. (*3-487-05001-3*) G Olms Pubs.

Lexique de la Langue de Moliere, 3 vols., Set. Charles L. Livet. xiii, 2022p. 1970. reprint ed. write for info. (*0-318-71373-X*) G Olms Pubs.

Lexique de la Langue de Pierre Corneille. Charles J. Marty-Laveaux. (Oeuvres De P. Corneille, Eleven - Les Grands Ecrivains De la France Ser.). xcvi, 1060p. 1971. reprint ed. write for info. (*3-487-04032-8*) G Olms Pubs.

Lexique de la Langue des Oeuvres Burlesques de Scarron. Leonard T. Richardson. lxv, 281p. 1976. reprint ed. write for info. (*3-487-05742-5*) G Olms Pubs.

Lexique de la Machine a Coudre Familiale. Francois Lanecki. Ed. by Celine Dupre. (FRE.). 12p. 1974. pap. 9.95 (*0-7859-0800-5*, M-9229) Fr & Eur.

Lexique de la Musique. Jean Queval. (FRE.). 130p. 1968. 19.95 (*0-7859-0774-2*, F-11890) Fr & Eur.

Lexique de la Philosophie. H. Vautrelle. (FRE.). 1998. 19.95 (*0-320-00158-X*) Fr & Eur.

Lexique de la Psychanalyse. A. Vanier. (FRE.). 1998. 19.95 (*0-320-00157-1*) Fr & Eur.

Lexique de la Restaurant Chinoise. Gilles Boivin. (ENG & FRE.). 58p. 1984. pap. 7.95 (*0-8288-1297-7*, M9587) Fr & Eur.

Lexique de la Scene. M. Ladj. (FRE.). 1998. 95.00 (*0-320-00151-2*) Fr & Eur.

Lexique de l'ancien Francais. Frederic Godefroy. (FRE.). 544p. 1982. reprint ed. pap. 69.95 (*0-7859-5098-2*) Fr & Eur.

Lexique de l'Anglais Comptable. Jean-Charles Khalifa. 240p. 1993. pap. 38.95 (*0-7859-5638-7*, 2729842225) Fr & Eur.

Lexique de l'Anglais Comptable et Financier. Jean-Charles Khalifa. 240p. 1992. 69.95 (*0-7859-9462-9*) Fr & Eur.

Lexique de l'Ecologie, Anglais-Francais, Francais-Anglais. Chantal Pierre & Maurande Pierre. (ENG & FRE.). 1989. pap. 49.95 (*0-7859-3918-0*) Fr & Eur.

Lexique de L'Education. Rene La Borderie. (FRE.). 1998. 24.95 (*0-320-00150-4*) Fr & Eur.

Lexique de l'Histoire de la France, Ancien Regine. G. Cabourdin. (FRE.). 1998. 79.95 (*0-320-00146-6*) Fr & Eur.

Lexique de l'Histoire et Civilisation Brittanique. P. Chassaigne. (FRE.). 1998. 45.00 (*0-320-00147-4*) Fr & Eur.

Lexique de l'Homme a Cheval. Marc De Saint-Riquier. (FRE.). 39.95 (*0-8288-7976-1*, M4669) Fr & Eur.

Lexique de l'Immobilier: French-English, English-French Dictionary of Property Dealing. N. Wilkins. (ENG & FRE.). 160p. 1991. 49.95 (*0-8288-6971-5*, 2856080413) Fr & Eur.

Lexique de l'Industrie Petroliere Rafinage: Anglais-Francais: English-French Dictionary of the Petroleum Refining Industry. Monique Heroux. (ENG & FRE.). 163p. 1979. pap. 19.95 (*0-8288-4816-5*, M9235) Fr & Eur.

Lexique de l'Informatique. Dominique Maillet. 205p. 1993. pap. 32.00 (*0-7859-5575-5*, 2010200519) Fr & Eur.

Lexique de L'Informatique. 3rd ed. Jean Guilhaumou. (FRE.). 122p. 1976. pap. 18.95 (*0-8288-5736-9*, F137140) Fr & Eur.

Lexique de L'Internet. J. Finidori. (FRE.). 1998. 34.95 (*0-320-00149-0*) Fr & Eur.

Lexique de Nutrition: Les Mots pour Comprendre. Jean-Pierre Ruasse. (FRE.). 45p. 1993. pap. 15.95 (*0-7859-5668-9*, 2908502100) Fr & Eur.

Lexique de Prevention des Accidents Anglais-Francais. M. Villiers et al. 130p. 1980. 9.95 (*0-8288-1787-1*) Fr & Eur.

Lexique de Ronsard. Louis Mellerio. lxxv, 250p. 1974. reprint ed. write for info. (*3-487-05248-2*) G Olms Pubs.

Lexique de Termes Juridiques. 9th ed. Serge Guinchard. 573p. 1993. pap. 36.95 (*0-7859-5623-9*, 2247015611) Fr & Eur.

Lexique de Transport International. Jean C. Bertin. (ENG & FRE.). 143p. 1992. 49.95 (*0-8288-7187-6*, 2729892176) Fr & Eur.

Lexique des Ascenceurs et Monte-Charge: Francais-Anglais, Anglais-Francais. D. Maranda & A. Daigle. (ENG & FRE.). 32p. 1978. pap. 7.95 (*0-8288-5249-9*, M9224) Fr & Eur.

Lexique des Industries Graphiques. R. Comte & A. Pernin. (FRE.). 128p. 1975. pap. 39.95 (*0-8288-5930-2*, M6082) Fr & Eur.

Lexique des Lois & des Reglements de l'Ontario. Centre de Traduction & de Documentation Juridiques. LC 89-90449. (FRE.). 976p. 1989. reprint ed. pap. 200.00 (*0-608-01996-8*, 206265200003) Bks Demand.

Lexique des Mots-Cles, Descripteurs et Identificateurs, Francais et Anglais, a Utiliser Pour la Recherche Documentaire, 3 vols., Set. Ed. by Centre de Documentation de l'Armement Staff. (ENG & FRE.). 2001p. 1976. pap. 95.00 (*0-8288-5737-7*, M6360) Fr & Eur.

Lexique des Outils de la Communication. (FRE.). 1998. 35.00 (*0-320-00159-8*) Fr & Eur.

Lexique des Sciences Biologiques. Philippe Bourbeau. (ENG & FRE.). 650p. 1996. 110.00 (*0-320-00028-1*) Fr & Eur.

Lexique des Terme de Prothese Dentaire (Lexicon of Dental Prothetics Terminology) 2nd ed. Evelyn Batarec. (FRE.). 90p. 1980. pap. 29.95 (*0-7859-4805-8*, M6024) Fr & Eur.

Lexique des Termes de Parodontologie de Microbiologie Parodontale et Buccale et de Sciences Fondamentales. Robert Sinsoilliez. (FRE.). 112p. 1973. pap. 29.95 (*0-8288-6315-6*, M-6518) Fr & Eur.

Lexique des Termes du Batiment. (FRE.). 212p. 1963. pap. 19.95 (*0-8288-6794-1*, M-6361) Fr & Eur.

Lexique des Termes Juridiques. Raymond Gullien. (FRE.). 574p. 1995. 49.95 (*0-7859-9269-3*) Fr & Eur.

Lexique des Termes Medicaux. (FRE.). pap. 35.00 (*0-686-56722-6*, M-6362) Fr & Eur.

Lexique des Termes Medicaux Avec Lexique Etymologique a L'Usage des Infirmiers. J. P. Harley. 116p. 1984. 35.00 (*0-8288-1810-X*) Fr & Eur.

Lexique des Termes Techniques Concernant le Material d'Une Usine d'Acetylene Dissous. (FRE.). 78p. 1970. pap. 39.95 (*0-7859-0726-2*, M-6363) Fr & Eur.

Lexique des Termes Usuels de Psychiatrie. Jean Carrere & Jacques Dessaigne. (FRE.). 114p. 1976. pap. 39.95 (*0-8288-5738-5*, M6061) Fr & Eur.

Lexique des Termes Utiles a l'Etude des Noms de Lieux. Henri Dorion & Jean Poirier. (FRE.). 162p. 1975. pap. 24.95 (*0-8288-5931-0*, M6168) Fr & Eur.

Lexique du Batiment. (FRE.). 19.95 (*0-686-57015-4*, M-6364) Fr & Eur.

Lexique du Marketing. Jean-Pierre Lacour. 128p. 1993. pap. 19.95 (*0-7859-5641-7*, 2735208230) Fr & Eur.

Lexique du Marketing. Hubert Nyssen. (FRE.). 86p. 1971. pap. 7.50 (*0-686-57064-2*, M-6435) Fr & Eur.

Lexique du Nouvel Age. Bernard Franck. 200p. 1993. pap. 28.95 (*0-7859-5634-4*, 2704106762) Fr & Eur.

Lexique Encyclopedique & Them. Iran. E. Peters. 1998. 28.95 (*90-6831-923-X*, Pub. by Peeters Pub) Bks Intl VA.

Lexique Encyclopedique Thematique de L'Iran: Nom Vallee Topoymes. M. Mokri. (FRE.). 1998. 69.95 (*0-320-00152-0*) Fr & Eur.

Lexique Francais-Anglais et Anglais-Francais des Termes d'usage Courant En Hydraulique et Pneumatique. P. Nichil. (ENG & FRE.). 42p. 1974. pap. 8.95 (*0-686-56790-0*, M-6426) Fr & Eur.

Lexique Francais de la Reparation Juridique du Dommage Corporel. Maurice A. Touati. (FRE.). 268p. 1976. 49.95 (*0-8288-5739-3*, M6534) Fr & Eur.

Lexique General. 4th ed. 700p. 75.00 (*92-1-000069-2*, 91.I.15) UN.

Lexique-Guide D'Acoustique Architecturale. Jean Pujolle. (FRE.). 152p. 1971. 59.95 (*0-8288-6470-5*, M-6470) Fr & Eur.

Lexique Historique du Moyen-Age. 2nd rev. ed. Rene Fedou. (FRE.). 176p. 1989. pap. 28.95 (*0-7859-4861-9*) Fr & Eur.

Lexique Ilustre du Machinisme et des Equipements Agricoles. C. Cedra. (FRE.). 350p. 1991. 85.00 (*0-8288-7258-9*, 2852067390) Fr & Eur.

Lexique International de Petrographie des Charbons. 2nd ed. (ENG & FRE.). 160p. 1963. 75.00 (*0-8288-6795-X*, M-6366) Fr & Eur.

Lexique International de Petrographie des Charbons: Supplement. (FRE.). 250p. 1971. pap. 49.95 (*0-8288-6469-1*, M-6367) Fr & Eur.

Lexique Inverse: Listes Grammaticales, Releves Divers. Plautus. Ed. by Albert Maniet. (GER.). viii, 201p. 1969. write for info. (*0-318-70440-4*) G Olms Pubs.

Lexique Mental et Morphologie Lexicale. Jean-Philippe Babin. (Sciences pour la Communication Ser.: Vol. 54). xiv, 257p. 39.95 (*3-906760-82-0*, Pub. by P Lang) P Lang Pubng.

Lexique Multiligue de la Linguistique et de la Philogie: Anglais-Russe-Allemand-Francais. Rose Nash & M. Alleyne. (ENG, FRE, GER & RUS.). 416p. 1968. pap. 99.50 (*0-8288-6654-6*, M-6422) Fr & Eur.

Lexique Occitan-Francais: Occitan-French Lexicon. 3rd ed. R. Barthe. (FRE.). 238p. 1984. pap. 35.00 (*0-8288-1038-9*, F45930) Fr & Eur.

Lexique Officiel des lampes Radios. 21st ed. Louis Gaudilat. (FRE.). 96p. 1963. pap. 19.95 (*0-8288-6796-8*, M-6263) Fr & Eur.

Lexique Patois/Francais: (marais sud-vendeen) L. Gaignet. (FRE.). 910p. 1997. 175.00 (*0-320-00908-4*) Fr & Eur.

Lexique Pedologique Trilingue. George Plaisance. (FRE.). 355p. 1958. pap. 39.95 (*0-8288-6851-4*, M-6458) Fr & Eur.

Lexique Quadrilingue des Affaires. Ivan de Renty. (ENG, FRE, GER & SPA.). 702p. 1977. 59.95 (*0-8288-5497-1*, M6483) Fr & Eur.

Lexique Quadrilingue de la Preparation des Minerais. Ed. by Congres International de la Preparation des Minera. (ENG, FRE, GER & RUS.). 260p. 1963. pap. 25.00 (*0-686-56795-1*) Fr & Eur.

Lexique Technique de l'Eau see Water Treatment Glossary French-English/English-French

Lexique Textile: Anglais-Francais. Pierre Hirsch. (ENG & FRE.). 224p. 1989. pap. 49.95 (*0-7859-4907-0*) Fr & Eur.

Lexique Textile: Francais-Anglais. Pierre Hirsch. (ENG & FRE.). 224p. 1989. pap. 49.95 (*0-685-67881-4*) Fr & Eur.

Lexique Thematique des Descripteurs et Identificateurs. Centre de Documentation de l'Armement Staff. (FRE.). 151p. 1976. pap. 35.00 (*0-8288-5740-7*, M6371) Fr & Eur.

Lexique Trilingue des Termes D'Usage Courant En Electrotechnique, Electronique, Acoustique, Optique et Controle Par Ultrasons. (FRE.). 340p. 1966. pap. 59.95 (*0-8288-6726-7*, M-6373) Fr & Eur.

Lexique Trilingue des Termes d'usage Courant En Machines Outils; les Tours, Pt. 1. (FRE.). 74p. 1961. pap. 19.95 (*0-8288-6826-3*, M-6374) Fr & Eur.

Lexique Trilingue des Termes de l'Eau. P. Johanet. (FRE.). 230p. 1988. pap. 145.00 (*0-7859-4891-0*) Fr & Eur.

Lexique Trilinque des Termes d'Usage Courant En Machines Outils, les Perceuses, Pt. 2. (FRE.). 96p. pap. 24.95 (*0-686-56792-7*, M-6375) Fr & Eur.

Lexique Usuel des Nouvelles Technologies de Communicacion: French-English-Arabic. A. Abbou. (ARA, ENG & FRE.). 173p. 1986. pap. 79.95 (*0-7859-7135-1*) Fr & Eur.

Lexiques-Grammaires Compares en Francais: Actes Du Colloque International De Montreal (3-5 Juin 1992) Ed. by Jacques Labelle & Christian LeClere. LC 95-15436. (Lingvisticae Investigationes Supplementa Ser.: No. 17). 217p. 1995. lib. bdg. 45.00 (*1-55619-257-6*) J Benjamins Pubng Co.

Lexis: Academic Vocabulary Study. (C). 1990. pap. 26.67 (*0-13-535048-4*) P-H.

Lexis: Academic Vocabulary Study for ESL Students. Arline Burgmeier et al. 240p. (C). 1990. pap. text 31.53 (*0-13-535022-0*) P-H.

Lexis: Dictionnaire de la Langue Francaise. Ed. by Jean Dubois. (FRE.). 2109p. 1992. 95.00 (*0-7859-4830-9*) Fr & Eur.

Lexis - Nexis: The Legal Basics. Ed. by Peter Adams. 52p. 1995. 9.95 (*0-926578-12-X*) LEXIS-NEXIS.

Lexis Companion: A Concise Guide to Effective Searching. Jean S. McKnight. LC 95-22398. 304p. (C). 1995. pap. text 19.95 (*0-201-48335-1*) Addison-Wesley.

Lexis Law Publishing Practice Code Series, Florida Civil 98. 1800p. 1998. 75.00 (*0-327-00277-8*, 6984010) LEXIS Pub.

Lexis Law Publishing Practice Code Series, Florida Statutes & Rules--Wills, Trust, Estates & Probate. 2060p. 1999. pap. write for info. (*0-327-01360-5*, 6990010) LEXIS Pub.

Lexis-Nexis for Law Students. 3rd rev. ed. Steven L. Emanuel. LC 97-25610. (C). 1997. pap. text. write for info. (*1-56542-002-0*) E Pub Corp.

Lexis-Nexis 7.X Unplugged: The User-Friendly Guide to Lexis-Nexis Version 7.X. Adam J. Piacente. (CALR Unplugged Ser.). (Illus.). (C). 1999. pap. 60.00 (*0-9662482-2-8*) Montag Multimedia.

Lexis, 1990 No. 5-6: Poetica, Retorica e Communicazione Nella Tradizione Classica. Ed. by Lorenzo Braccesi & Angelo Casanova. (FRE.). 252p. 1992. pap. 44.00 (*90-256-1018-8*, Pub. by AM Hakkert) BookLink Distributors.

Lexis Publishing's Research Guide to Nebraska Law, 1999 Edition. 120p. Price not set. (*0-327-09758-2*, 4520211) LEXIS Pub.

Lexis (R) Product Guide, 2 vols. Ed. by Peter Adams. 1992. ring bd. write for info. (*0-318-72160-0*); ring bd. write for info. (*0-318-72161-9*) LEXIS-NEXIS.

Lexis (R) Product Guide, 2 vols., Set. Ed. by Peter Adams. 1992. ring bd. 85.00 (*0-926578-07-3*) LEXIS-NEXIS.

***Lexis.com Unplugged: The User-Friendly Guide to Lexis.com.** Adam J. Piacente. (Illus.). 246p. (C). 1999. pap. 60.00 (*0-9662482-4-4*) Montag Multimedia.

Lexitect. Cynthia S. Dessen & Maria V. Abricka. (C). 1988. teacher ed. 32.50 incl. disk (*0-15-550626-9*, Pub. by Harcourt Coll Pubs) Harcourt.

Lexiwine - Lexivin: French - English, English - French Wine Dictionary. Paul Cadiau. (ENG & FRE.). 198p. 1987. pap. 29.95 (*0-7859-3656-4*, 2907080008) Fr & Eur.

L'Experience de la Nuit see Experience of the Night

Lexpo '93: Legal & Financial Aspects of Doing Business in India & the U. S. U. S. & Foreign Commercial Service Staff. LC 94-900651. (C). 1994. 38.00 (*81-204-0851-9*, Pub. by Oxford IBH) S Asia.

L'Express, Aujourd'hui la France. 2nd ed. Ross Steele & Jose Pavis. (FRE., Illus.). 256p. 1995. pap. 39.95 incl. audio (*0-8442-1275-X*, 1275X) NTC Contemp Pub Co.

***L'Expression Musicale.** Anne-Claire Desesquelles. (Publications Universitaires Europeennes Ser.: Vol. 591). xv, 281p. 1999. 44.95 (*3-906763-26-9*, Pub. by P Lang) P Lang Pubng.

***Lexus & the Olive Tree: Understanding Globalization.** Thomas L. Friedman. LC 99-59697. 490p. 2000. pap. 15.00 (*0-385-49934-5*, Anchor NY) Doubleday.

***Lexus & the Olive Tree: Understanding Globalization.** Thomas L. Friedman. LC 99-10742. 320p. 1999. 27.50 (*0-374-19203-0*) FS&G.

***Lexus & the Olive Tree: Understanding Globalization.** Thomas L. Friedman. LC 00-29411. (Illus.). (J). 2000. 30.00 (*0-374-18552-2*) FS&G.

***Lexus & the Olive Tree: Understanding Globalization.** large type ed. Thomas L. Friedman. LC 99-46181. 1999. 28.95 (*0-7862-2239-5*) Thorndike Pr.

***Lexus Legacy: Improving Democracy in the Age of the Mental Artisan.** B. D. Foose. Orig. Title: Records of the Concepts & Comments of Lexus. 880p. 2000. pap. 22.50 (*0-9672826-0-8*, Pub. by Pro Factor Inc) BookMasters.

Lexus Ludens: Wordplay & the Book of Micah. Anthony J. Petrotta. LC 91-16769. (American University Studies: Theology & Religion: Ser. VII, Vol. 105). 178p. 1991. 36.95 (*0-8204-1539-1*) P Lang Pubng.

***Lexus Story.** Brian Long. (Illus.). 192p. 2000. 49.95 (*1-901295-81-8*, 130696AE, Pub. by Vloce Pub) Motorbooks Intl.

Ley de La Calle. S. E. Hinton. 1994. 15.05 (*0-606-10439-9*, Pub. by Turtleback) Demco.

Ley de la Calle: Rumble Fish. S. E. Hinton. LC 49-125450. (SPA.). (gr. 7-12). 1995. pap. text 9.95 (*84-204-3923-1*) Santillana.

***Ley de Vehiculos y Transito: Edicion de 1999.** (SPA.). 410p. 1999. pap. write for info. (*0-327-09457-5*, 3180715) LEXIS Pub.

Ley de Vehiculos y Transito, 1993. Ed. by Butterworth Staff. 310p. 1993. pap. 30.00 (*0-88063-534-7*, MICHIE) LEXIS Pub.

Ley de Vehiculos y Transito, 1998: Con las Leyes de Propiedad Vehicular y Guardia Municipal Basada en los Titulos 9 y 21 de L. P. R. A. Ed. by Elsa Smith & Delta Star.Tr. of Vehicle Law. (SPA.). 416p. 1998. pap. write for info. (*0-327-06069-7*, 31807-14) LEXIS Pub.

Ley del Amor see Law of Love

Ley del Amor. Laura Esquivel. (SPA.). 1997. pap. 16.00 (*0-609-80149-X*, Crown) Crown Pub Group.

Ley Del Amor. Laura Esquivel. 1997. pap. 16.00 (*970-05-0517-0*) Grijalbo Edit.

Ley e Historia del Antiguo Testamento. Samuel J. Schultz. Tr. by Fernando P. Villalobos from ENG. (Curso para Maestros Cristianos Ser.: No. 1).Tr. of Broadening Your Biblical Horizons: Old Testament Survey. (SPA., Illus.). 122p. 1972. pap. 7.99 (*0-89922-008-8*) Caribe Betania.

Ley Foraker: Raices de la Politica Colonial de los Estados Unidos. 2nd ed. Lyman J. Gould. (UPREX, C. Sociales Ser.: No. 40). 284p. (C). 1975. pap. 1.50 (*0-8477-0040-2*) U of PR Pr.

Ley Hipotecaria y del Registro de la Propiedad: Con Su Reglamento, Legislaci/aon y Otros Reglamentos Relacionados al Registro de la Propiedad. Ed. by Elsa Smith & Delta Star.Tr. of Mortgage Law. (SPA.). 634p. 1998. pap. write for info. (*0-327-06066-2*, 31805-14) LEXIS Pub.

***Ley Hipotecaria y Del Registro de la Propiedad: Ediccion de 2000, 2 vols.** 650p. 2000. write for info. (*0-327-10525-9*, 3180516) LEXIS Pub.

***Ley Hipotecaria y del Registro de la Propiedad Ediccion de 1999, 2 vols., Set.** (SPA.). 643p. 1999. 42.50 (*0-327-09772-8*, 3180515) LEXIS Pub.

Ley Hipotecaria y del Registro de la Propiedad y su Reglamento, 1993. 540p. 1994. 38.00 (*0-88063-511-8*, MICHIE) LEXIS Pub.

Ley Moral de Dios: Un Estudio de los Diez Mondamientos. Thomas Montgomery. Tr. by Omar Ibanez Negrete. (SPA.). 142p. Date not set. pap. 3.10 (*1-928980-01-5*) Pub Faro.

L

An Asterisk (*) at the beginning of an entry indicates that the title is appearing for the first time.

Ley Notarial de Puerto Rico: Special Edition. 30p. 1987. pap. 15.00 (*0-88063-520-7*, MICHIE) LEXIS Pub.

Ley Uniforme de Instrumentos Negociables - Uniform Negotiable Instruments Act: Edicion Especial. Ed. by Butterworth Staff. (ENG & SPA.). 180p. 1990. pap. 20.00 (*0-88063-675-0*, 31819-10, MICHIE) LEXIS Pub.

Leyden Papyrus: An Egyptian Magical Book. Ed. by Francis L. Griffith & Herbert Thompson. LC 73-90639. 207p. 1974. reprint ed. pap. 8.95 (*0-486-22994-7*) Dover.

Leydig Cell. Anita Payne et al. Ed. by Lonnie D. Russell. (Illus.). 800p. (C). 1996. text 137.50 (*0-9627422-7-9*) Cache River Pr.

Leyenda de la Flor de Noche Buena. Tomie De Paola. (SPA., Illus.). (J). (ps-3). 1994. 15.95 (*0-399-22789-X*, G P Putnam) Peng Put Young Read.

Leyenda de la Flor de Noche Buena. Tomie De Paola. 1997. 11.15 (*0-606-12751-8*, Pub. by Turtleback) Demco.

Leyenda de la Flor "El Conejo" Una Antigua Leyenda de Texas. Tomie De Paola. Orig. Title: The Legend of the Bluebonnet. (SPA.). (J). 1993. 11.15 (*0-606-05402-2*, Pub. by Turtleback) Demco.

Leyenda de Los Soles. Homero Aridjis. (SPA.). 1993. pap. text 12.99 (*968-16-3952-9*) Fondo.

Leyenda de Mexicatl. Jo Harper.Tr. of Legend of Mexicatl. (SPA., Illus.). 40p. (J). 1998. 15.95 (*1-890515-06-X*, Pub. by Turtle Bks) Publishers Group.

***Leyenda de Mexicatl.** Jo Harper. 2000. pap. 7.95 (*1-890515-22-1*) Turtle Bks.

Leyenda del Anillo: Tallchief's Bride. Cait London. (Deseo Ser.: Vol. 119).Tr. of Ring's Legend. (SPA.). 1998. per. 3.50 (*0-373-35249-2*, 1-35249-1) Harlequin Bks.

Leyenda del Beisbol Cubano, 1878-1997. Angel Torres. (Illus.). 320p. 1997. pap. 19.95 (*0-9614110-1-5*) A Torres.

Leyenda del Castillo, Level 1. Elena Moreno. (Leer en Espanol Ser.). (SPA.). (C). 1998. pap. 5.95 (*84-294-4044-5*) Santillana.

Leyenda del Pincel Indio. Tomie De Paola. LC 87-20160. Orig. Title: The Legend of the Indian Paintbrush. (SPA., Illus.). 40p. (J). (ps-3). 1996. pap. 6.99 (*0-698-11362-4*, PapStar) Peng Put Young Read.

Leyenda del Pincel Indio. Tomie De Paola. Orig. Title: The Legend of the Indian Paintbrush. 1996. 11.15 (*0-606-09522-5*, Pub. by Turtleback) Demco.

Leyendas. Gustavo A. Bequer. Ed. by Estrada F. Lopez. (Nueva Austral Ser.: No. 36). (SPA.). 1991. pap. text 24.95 (*84-239-1836-X*) Elliots Bks.

Leyendas Cubanas. Olympia Gonzalez. LC 97-66223. (SPA & ENG.). 128p. 1997. pap. 16.56 (*0-8442-7236-1*, 72361) NTC Contemp Pub Co.

Leyendas de Espana. Genevieve Barlow. (SPA.). 128p. 1989. pap. 15.50 (*0-8442-7243-4*) NTC Contemp Pub Co.

Leyendas de Guatemala: Level C Books. Miguel Angel Asturias. text 8.95 (*0-88436-290-6*) EMC-Paradigm.

Leyendas de la Luna. Rosalie Ash. Orig. Title: Myths of the Moon. (SPA.). 1996. per. 3.50 (*0-373-33352-8*) Harlequin Bks.

Leyendas de Puerto Rico. Robert L. Muckley. (SPA.). 128p. 1993. pap. 15.50 (*0-8442-7275-2*) NTC Contemp Pub Co.

***Leyendas Del Mundo Hispano.** (C). 2000. 13.33 (*0-13-016535-2*) S&S Trade.

***Leyendas del Mundo Hispano.** Susan M. Bacon et al. LC 99-58934. (SPA.). 120p. 1999. pap. text 29.33 (*0-13-010010-2*) P-H.

Leyendas Latinoamericanas. 2nd ed. Barlow. (SPA.). 176p. 1996. pap. 15.50 (*0-8442-7239-6*) NTC Contemp Pub Co.

Leyendas Mexicanas. Nelinda Galvan Macias. 1996. pap. text 6.98 (*968-403-911-5*) Selector.

Leyendas Mexicanas. 2nd ed. (SPA.). 160p. 1996. pap. 15.50 (*0-8442-7238-8*) NTC Contemp Pub Co.

Leyendas Mexicanas de Antes y Despues de la Conquista. Franco Sodja. (SPA.). (gr. 7-11). 1997. pap. text 8.98 (*968-409-657-7*) Edamex.

Leyendas Puertorriquenas. rev. ed. Cayetano Coll Y Toste. Tr. by Jose Ramirez-Rivera. LC 78-73076. (SPA., Illus.). 120p. 1979. reprint ed. pap. 9.95 (*0-9601700-2-2*) Editl Libero.

Leyes. Marco Tulio Ciceron. (Biblioteca De Cultura Basica Ser.). 204p. 1968. 1.50 (*0-8477-0702-4*) U of PR Pr.

Leyes de Corporaciones Anotadas: Edicion Especial. Ed. by Butterworth Staff. 170p. 1986. pap. 25.00 (*0-88063-498-7*, 31817-10, MICHIE) LEXIS Pub.

Leyes de Puerto Rico. (ENG & SPA.). 1993. 85.00 (*0-88063-517-7*, MICHIE) LEXIS Pub.

Leyes de Puerto Rico. 24th ed. Ed. by Butterworth Staff. 1990. 85.00 (*0-614-05883-X*, MICHIE) LEXIS Pub.

Leyes de Puerto Rico: Puerto Rico Session Laws. Michie Editors Staff. (SPA.). 1993. ring bd. 85.00 (*0-327-01025-8*, 47578, MICHIE) LEXIS Pub.

Leyes de Puerto Rico Vols. 2-3: 1998 Spanish Replacement Volume. (SPA.). 830p. 1998. 47.50 (*0-327-05975-3*, 47462-11) LEXIS Pub.

Leyes de Puerto Rico Anotadas: Laws of Puerto Rico Annotated, 41 vols. annot. ed. Michie Editors Staff. (SPA.). 1994. 1319.00 (*0-327-01024-X*, 47460, MICHIE) LEXIS Pub.

***Leyes de Puerto Rico Anotadas: Poder Ejecutivo y Apendice, Vol. 4.** 470p. 2000. write for info. (*0-327-13189-6*, 4746311, Lexis Law PR) LEXIS Pub.

Leyes de Puerto Rico Anotadas No. 18-19: 1998 Replacement Volume. (SPA., Illus.). 660p. 1998. 47.50 (*0-327-05864-1*, 47477-11) LEXIS Pub.

Leyes de Puerto Rico Anotadas No. 20: 1998 Replacement Volume. (SPA.). 700p. 1998. 47.50 (*0-327-05863-3*, 47478-11) LEXIS Pub.

Leyes de Puerto Rico Anotadas Vol. 4apx: 1998 Spanish Replacement Volume. (SPA.). 640p. 1998. 47.50 (*0-327-05977-X*, 47465-11) LEXIS Pub.

***Leyes de Puerto Rico Anotadas - Seguridad Internationale.** 540p. 1999. write for info. (*0-327-08719-6*, 47483-11) LEXIS Pub.

***Leyes de Puerto Rico Anotadas Indice.** (SPA.). 1150p. 2000. write for info. (*0-327-11133-X*, 4750816) LEXIS Pub.

Leyes de Puerto Rico Anotadas, Indice Edicion, 1998. Tr. of Law of Puerto Rico, 1998 Index. (SPA.). 1125p. 1998. write for info. (*0-327-05355-0*, 47508-14) LEXIS Pub.

Leyes de Puerto Rico Anotadas, 1998 Supplement, 38 vols. Tr. of Laws of Puerto Rico Annotated, 1998 Supplement. (SPA.). 6154p. 1998. pap. write for info. (*0-327-05352-6*, 47505-14) LEXIS Pub.

Leyes de Puerto Rico Anotadas Servicio de Anataciones Provisionales. 65p. 1998. pap. write for info. (*0-327-06838-8*, 4751113) LEXIS Pub.

Leyes de Puerto Rico Anotadas T. 22 Replacement. annot. ed. (SPA.). 400p. 1999. write for info. (*0-327-08622-X*, 47480-11) LEXIS Pub.

***Leyes de Puerto Rico Anotadas T. 16 Elecciones e Inscripciones; T. 17 Hogares No. 16: Leyes de Puerto Rico Anotadas Elecciones/ Hogar.** (SPA.). 400p. 2000. write for info. (*0-327-13188-8*, 4747511) LEXIS Pub.

Leyes de Puerto Rico Anotados Documentos Historicos; Relaciones Federales; Constitution Titulo 1: LPRA t. 1 & Historical Docs. (SPA.). 645p. Price not set. (*0-327-09966-6*, 4746111) LEXIS Pub.

***Leyes de Puerto Rico 1999, 3 vols., Set.** (SPA.). 2990p. 1999. write for info. (*0-327-09950-X*, 4757815) LEXIS Pub.

Leyes de Puerto Rico, 1997-DNU. 2620p. 1998. write for info. (*0-327-05794-7*, 4757814) LEXIS Pub.

Leyes de Puerto Rico, 1997, Vol. 1. Ed. by Juan C. Rivera-Rodriguez.Tr. of Laws of Puerto Rico, 1997. (SPA.). 990p. 1998. write for info. (*0-327-05795-5*, 8460314) LEXIS Pub.

Leyes de Puerto Rico, 1997, Vol. 2. Ed. by Juan C. Rivera-Rodriguez.Tr. of Laws of Puerto Rico, 1997. (SPA.). 1082p. 1998. write for info. (*0-327-05796-3*, 8460414) LEXIS Pub.

Leyes de Puerto Rico, 1997, Vol. 3. Ed. by Juan C. Rivera-Rodriguez.Tr. of Laws of Puerto Rico, 1997. (SPA.). 600p. 1998. write for info. (*0-327-05797-1*, 8460514) LEXIS Pub.

Leyes del Amor: (The Laws of Love) Margaret Mayo. (Bianca Ser.: No. 132).Tr. of Love Laws. (SPA.). 1998. per. 3.50 (*0-373-33482-6*, 1-33482-0) Harlequin Bks.

Leyes del Trabajo: Basado en el Titulo 29 de L. P. R. A. Ed. by Elsa Smith & Delta Star.Tr. of Labor Law. (SPA.). 880p. 1998. pap. write for info. (*0-327-06068-9*, 31803-12) LEXIS Pub.

***Leyes Del Trabajo: 2000 Edicion.** 884p. 2000. write for info. (*0-327-10533-X*, 3180314) LEXIS Pub.

Leyes del Trabajo Anotadas, 1986: Edicion Especial. Ed. by Butterworth Staff. 740p. 1986. 45.00 (*0-88063-533-9*, MICHIE) LEXIS Pub.

Leyes del Trabajo Anotadas, 1986: Edicion Especial. Butterworth Staff. 1994. ring bd., suppl. ed. 30.00 (*0-614-03736-0*, MICHIE) LEXIS Pub.

***Leyes del Trabajo Edicion 1999.** (SPA.). 884p. 1999. Price not set. (*0-327-09634-9*, 3180313) LEXIS Pub.

Leyes Fiscales Anotadas: Edicion Especial. 1977. write for info. (*0-88063-507-X*, MICHIE) LEXIS Pub.

Leyes Selladas Del Ano. Ed. by Butterworth Staff. 1992. 140.00 (*0-685-66876-2*, MICHIE) LEXIS Pub.

***Leyes y Reglamentos de las Corporaciones Privadas.** 633p. 1999. 36.00 (*0-327-09968-2*, 3181712) LEXIS Pub.

Leyes y Reglamentos de los Municipios: 1998 Edition. Ed. by Elsa Smith. (SPA.). 111p. 1998. write for info. (*0-327-06452-8*, 31867-10) LEXIS Pub.

***Leyes y Reglamentos de Puerto Rico Municipal: 1999 Edition.** LEXIS Law Publishing Editors. (SPA.). 799p. 1999. pap. 80.00 (*0-327-10218-7*, 3183711) LEXIS Pub.

***Leyner: Novel, Vol. 2.** Mark Leyner. 2001. 20.00 (*0-517-70102-2*) Crown Pub Group.

Leyte: The United States Army Campaigns of World War 2. 35p. 1994. pap. 3.00 (*0-16-045114-0*) USGPO.

Leyte Gulf: The Death of the Princeton. Edwin P. Hoyt. 160p. 1987. pap. 3.50 (*0-380-75408-8*, Avon Bks) Morrow Avon.

***LFO.** Sarah Shelly. (Illus.). 80p. (J). 2000. 4.95 (*0-7407-0858-9*) Andrews & McMeel.

***LFO: Backstage Pass.** Scholastic, Inc. Staff. 1999. pap. 5.99 (*0-439-15967-9*) Scholastic Bk Fairs.

LFP, 94: Conference on LISP & Functional Programming. LC 95-192713. 336p. 1994. pap. text 48.00 (*0-89791-643-3*, 552940) Assn Compu Machinery.

LG MAP GD MADRID 2ND ED P. 2nd ed. (Let's Go Map Guides Ser.). 32p. 1999. pap. 8.95 (*0-312-20272-5*) St Martin.

LH-RH Agonists in Oncology. Ed. by K. Hoffken. (Illus.). 210p. 1988. 111.00 (*0-387-19070-8*) Spr-Verlag.

LH-RH & Its Analogues: Fertility & Anti-Fertility Aspects. Ed. by Manfred Schmidt-Gollwitzer & Rosemarie Schley. (New Developments in Biosciences Ser.). (Illus.). x, 357p. 1985. 89.25 (*3-11-010055-X*) De Gruyter.

LHA Phewa: The Thakali Twelve Year Festival. Michael Vinding. 1992. 45.00 (*0-7855-0230-0*, Pub. by Ratna Pustak Bhandar) St Mut.

Lhasa. Ganeri. (Illus.). (J). 1995. write for info. (*0-237-51457-5*) EVN1 UK.

Lhasa & Its Mysteries. L. Austine Waddell. (Illus.). 1988. pap. 11.95 (*0-486-25763-0*) Dover.

Lhasa & Its Mysteries: With a Record of the Expedition of 1903-1904. L. Austine Waddell. LC 70-39214. (Select Bibliographies Reprint Ser.). (Illus.). 1977. reprint ed. 66.95 (*0-8369-6816-6*) Ayer.

Lhasa Apso: An Owner's Guide to a Happy, Healthy Pet. Carolyn Herbel. LC 98-17604. (Owner's Guide to a Happy, Healthy Pet Ser.). 160p. 1998. 12.95 (*0-87605-228-6*) Howell Bks.

Lhasa Apso Champions, 1981-1986. Camino E. E. & Bk. Co. Staff. (Illus.). 75p. 1988. pap. 28.95 (*0-940808-64-1*) Camino E E & Bk.

Lhasa Apso Champions, 1952-1980. Jan L. Pata. (Illus.). 164p. 1981. pap. 36.95 (*0-940808-09-9*) Camino E E & Bk.

***Lhasa Apsos.** Nancy Plunkett. (New Owner's Guide to Ser.). 1999. 12.95 (*0-7938-2797-3*) TFH Pubns.

Lhasa Apsos. Steven Wehrman. LC 89-38540. (Illus.). 71p. (Orig.). 1990. pap. text 6.95 (*0-8120-3950-5*) Barron.

Lhasa Apsos: AKC Rank #33. Diane McCarty. (Illus.). 1997. pap. 9.95 (*0-7938-2316-1*, KW-076S) TFH Pubns.

Lhasa Moon Tibetan Cookbook. Tsering Wangmo & Zara Houshmand. LC 98-39575. (Illus.). 150p. 1999. pap. 14.95 (*1-55939-104-9*, Snow Lion) Snow Lion Pubns.

Lhasa the Holy City. F. Spencer Chapman. LC 75-37875. (Select Bibliographies Reprint Ser.). 1977. reprint ed. 35.95 (*0-8369-6712-7*) Ayer.

Lhasa, Tibet's Forbidden City. Christine J. Brignoli & Frank J. Brignoli. LC 89-108700. (Illus.). 107p. 1987. 25.00 (*0-9622122-0-2*) Creative Focus.

L'Herbe see Grass

L'Heresiarque et Cie see Heresiarch & Co.

L'Histoire de l'Oie see Tale of Teeka

L'Homme De Boue, Mini Bk. Ted Staunton & Brenda Clark. (FRE.). (J). mass mkt. 3.99 (*0-590-74821-1*) Scholastic Inc.

L'Homme Machine? Anthropologie im Umbruch. (Philosophische Texte und Studien: Bd. 45). (GER.). 310p. 1998. 68.00 (*3-487-10639-6*) G Olms Pubs.

L'Horreur Economique see Economic Horror

Lhota Nagas. James P. Mills. LC 76-44760. reprint ed. 55.00 (*0-404-15869-2*) AMS Pr.

LHRH & Its Analogs: Contraceptive & Therapeutic Applications, Pt. 1. Ed. by B. H. Vickery et al. 450p. 1984. text 244.50 (*0-85200-732-9*) Kluwer Academic.

LHRH & Its Analogs: Contraceptive & Therapeutic Applications, Pt. 2. Ed. by B. H. Vickery & J. J. Nestor, Jr. (C). 1987. text 255.50 (*0-85200-987-9*) Kluwer Academic.

L'Humanisme De L'Islam see Jihad: A Commitment to Universal Peace

L'Hypnotisme a la Portee de Tous see Hypnotism Made Easy

LH7 Ranch in Houston's Shadow: The E. H. Marks' Legacy from Longhorns to the Salt Grass Trail. Deborah L. Sizemore. LC 91-20920. (Illus.). 236p. 1991. 22.50 (*0-929398-28-5*) UNTX Pr.

***Li Be B, Cosmic Rays & Related X- & Gamma-Rays, Vol. 171.** Ed. by Renven Rumaty et al. (ASP Conference Series Proceedings). 279p. (C). 1999. text 52.00 (*1-886733-93-7*) Astron Soc Pacific.

Li Chih, Fifteen Twenty-Seven to Sixteen Hundred Two, in Contemporary Chinese Historiography: New Light on His LIfe & Works. Li Chih. LC 79-57496. 231p. reprint ed. pap. 71.70 (*0-608-18122-6*, 203277500081) Bks Demand.

Li-Ch'ing-Chao: Complete Poems. Li-Ching-Chao. Ed. by Kenneth Rexroth & Ling Chung. LC 79-15596. 1980. pap. 8.95 (*0-8112-0745-5*, NDP492, Pub. by New Directions) Norton.

***Li Dynasty: Hong Kong Aristocrats.** Francis D. K. Ching. LC 99-34979. (Illus.). 296p. 1999. text 35.00 (*0-19-590904-6*) OUP.

Li Hua Paintings. Li Hua et al. (Illus.). 22p. 1984. pap. 5.00 (*1-877921-24-6*) Pacific Asia.

Li Hung-Chang. John O. Bland. LC 77-175688. (Select Bibliographies Reprint Ser.). 1977. reprint ed. 23.95 (*0-8369-6603-1*) Ayer.

Li Hung-chang & China's Early Modernization. Ed. by Samuel C. Chu & Liu Kwang-Ching. LC 93-31417. (Illus.). 320p. (C). (gr. 13). 1994. text 77.95 (*1-56324-242-7*, East Gate Bk); pap. text 38.95 (*1-56324-458-6*, East Gate Bk) M E Sharpe.

***Li Ka-Shing: Hong Kong's Elusive Billionaire.** Anthony B. Chan. 251p. 2000. reprint ed. text 25.00 (*0-7881-6855-X*) DIANE Pub.

Li, Konprann, Ekri: Read, Understand & Write. Hyppo Lite. 244p. Date not set. wbk. ed. 17.00 (*1-881839-63-X*) Educa Vision.

Li Kung-Lin's Classic of Filial Piety. Richard M. Barnhart. (Illus.). 176p. 1994. 50.00 (*0-8109-6462-7*, Pub. by Abrams) Time Warner.

Li Kung-Lin's Classic of Filial Piety. Ed. by Richard M. Barnhart. LC 93-17578. (Illus.). 176p. 1993. 39.95 (*0-87099-679-7*, 0-8109-6462-7) Metro Mus Art.

Li-Lan: Stationary Images. Contrib. by Thomas P. Bruhn & Robert Berlind. (Illus.). 12p. 1990. 4.50 (*0-918386-42-X*) W Benton Mus.

Li Lun, Lad of Courage. Carolyn Treffinger. LC 95-11285. (Newbery Honor Roll Ser.). 1995. 11.15 (*0-606-09553-5*, Pub. by Turtleback) Demco.

Li Lun, Lad of Courage. Carolyn Treffinger. LC 95-11285. (Illus.). 96p. (J). (gr. 4-7). 1995. pap. 5.95 (*0-8027-7468-7*) Walker & Co.

Li Pei Kan & Chinese Anarchism: A Chronology. V. Munoz. 1976. 250.00 (*0-87700-242-8*) Revisionist Pr.

Li Po & Tu Fu: Poems. Li Po et al. Tr. & Intro. by Arthur Cooper. (Classics Ser.). (Illus.). 256p. (Orig.). 1973. pap. 10.95 (*0-14-044272-3*, Penguin Classics) Viking Penguin.

Li Proverbes au Conte de Bretaigne: A Critical Study. Michele G. Diaferia. LC 90-5985. (Currents in Romance Languages & Literature Ser.: Vol. 3). (FRE., Illus.). XIV, 166p. (C). 1990. text 40.95 (*0-8204-1231-7*) P Lang Pubng.

Li Ssu's Contributions to the Founding of China's First Empire. Joseph D. Lowe. LC 88-91009. (Illus.). xii, 80p. 1994. pap. 48.00 (*0-930325-02-8*) Lowe Pub.

Li Ti: A Study of the Chinese Painter Li Ti. Richard Edwards. (Occasional Papers: Vol. 3, No. 3). (Illus.). 1967. pap. 5.00 (*0-934686-07-6*) Freer.

Li Yong (1627-1705) & Epistemological Dimensions of Confucian Philosophy. Anne D. Birdwhistell. LC 95-31977. 300p. 1996. 45.00 (*0-8047-2605-1*) Stanford U Pr.

Lia a l Eimfidh Thar Tonnta see Stone That Will Leap over the Wave

LIA Guide to Medical Laser Safety. Ed. by Steven L. Trogel. (Illus.). 40p. 1997. pap. text 25.00 (*0-912035-07-2*) Laser Inst.

Lia Schorr's Skin Care Guide for Men. Lia Schorr. 185p. 1985. pap. 9.95 (*0-13-535113-8*, Busn) P-H.

Liabilities of Office: Indemnification & Insurance of Corporate Officers & Directors. Michael A. Schaeftler. 1978. 27.50 (*0-316-77276-3*, Aspen Law & Bus) Aspen Pub.

Liability. Preston Dilts. LC 98-90665. 1999. 18.95 (*0-533-12875-7*) Vantage.

Liability: A National Crisis in Insurance. 1992. lib. bdg. 94.96 (*0-8490-5384-6*) Gordon Pr.

Liability: Perspectives & Policy. Ed. by Robert E. Litan & Clifford M. Winston. LC 88-7254. 248p. 1988. 36.95 (*0-8157-5272-5*); pap. 16.95 (*0-8157-5271-7*) Brookings.

Liability: The Legal Revolution & Its Consequences. Peter W. Huber. 1990. pap. 15.00 (*0-465-03919-7*, Pub. by Basic) HarpC.

Liability & Responsibility: Essays in Law & Morals. Ed. by R. G. Frey & Christopher W. Morris. (Studies in Philosophy & Law). 442p. (C). 1991. text 89.95 (*0-521-39216-0*) Cambridge U Pr.

Liability & Risk Management in Home Health Care. F. A. Rozovsky. LC 97-44706. 368p. 1998. 149.00 (*0-8342-1067-3*) Aspen Pub.

Liability & Risk Management in Managed Care. Charles G. Benda & Fay A. Rozovsky. LC 98-131242. 1998. ring bd. 169.00 (*0-8342-1035-5*, S512) Aspen Pub.

Liability & Safety in Physical Education & Sport: A Practitioner's Guide to the Legal Aspects of Teaching & Coaching in Elementary & Secondary Schools. James E. Hart & Robert J. Ritson. 224p. (Orig.). 1993. pap. text 23.00 (*0-88314-546-4*) AAHPERD.

Liability Claims: Essential Information for the Insurance Claims Professional. Barry Zalma. 680p. 1998. pap. 125.95 (*1-884770-20-7*) ClaimSchool.

Liability Claims - Bad Faith. Barry Zalma. 80p. (Orig.). 1997. pap. 19.95 (*1-884770-12-6*) ClaimSchool.

Liability Claims - Basics. Barry Zalma. 50p. (Orig.). (C). 1997. pap. write for info. (*0-918487-99-4*) Thomas Investigative.

Liability Claims - Basics. 2nd rev. ed. Barry Zalma. 46p. (Orig.). 1996. pap. 19.95 (*1-884770-16-9*) ClaimSchool.

Liability Claims - Evaluation & Settlement. Barry Zalma. 61p. (Orig.). 1997. pap. 19.95 (*1-884770-13-4*) ClaimSchool.

Liability Claims - Fraud. Barry Zalma. 42p. (Orig.). 1996. pap. 19.95 (*1-884770-15-0*) ClaimSchool.

Liability Claims - Fraud Investigations. Barry Zalma. 43p. (Orig.). (C). 1997. pap. write for info. (*0-918487-98-6*) Thomas Investigative.

Liability Claims Supervisor. Jack Rudman. (Career Examination Ser.: C-3509). 1994. pap. 34.95 (*0-8373-3509-4*) Nat Learn.

Liability Environment. 1989. 20.90 (*0-9613459-4-2*, S291) Am Congrs Survey.

Liability Environment. Robert W. Foster. 264p. 1989. pap. 20.00 (*0-614-06111-3*, S291) Am Congrs Survey.

Liability Exposures. Dan Cassidy. 150p. (C). 1989. pap. 250.00 (*0-948691-75-1*, Pub. by Witherby & Co) St Mut.

Liability for Damage to Luggage in International Air Transport. P. Verwer. 256p. 1987. pap. 83.00 (*90-6544-281-2*) Kluwer Law Intl.

Liability for Damage to the Marine Environment. Ed. by Colin De la Rue. 268p. 1993. 110.00 (*1-85044-535-4*) LLP.

Liability for Employee Grievances: Mental Stress & Wrongful Termination. Ed. by Richard B. Victor. LC 88-27895. 1988. 35.00 (*0-935149-17-1*, WC-88-6) Workers Comp Res Inst.

***Liability for Environmental Damages: Incentives for Precaution & Risk Allocation.** Elga Bartsch. LC 99-197950. (Illus.). 220p. (C). 1999. text 69.50 (*3-16-146999-2*) JCB Mohr.

Liability for Negligence & Judicial Discretion. 2nd ed. Francesco Parisi. LC 92-13434. (Research Ser.: No. 82). 1992. pap. text 18.50 (*0-87725-702-7*) U of Cal IAS.

***Liability for Negligent Words.** Barbara Ann Hocking. 264p. 1999. 45.00 (*1-86287-297-X*, Pub. by Federation Pr) Gaunt.

Liability for Oil Pollution & Collisions. O. Oya Hozpcayir. LC 98-198432. lx, 573p. 1998. write for info. (*1-85978-179-9*) LLP.

Liability for Psychiatric Illness. (Law Commission/Scottish Law Commission Reports: No. 249 (HCP 525)). 1998. 40.00 (*0-10-288798-5*, HM87985, Pub. by Statnry Office) Bernan Associates.

Liability for Storage Tanks. 2nd ed. Michael L. Italiano et al. 634p. 1992. 120.00 (*0-685-69457-7*) PLI.

Liability Fraud. Greg Hauser. 1995. spiral bd. 19.95 (*1-882852-12-5*) Marinelli Publishing.

Liability Game. Stuart M. Bloch. 1988. pap. 59.95 (*0-318-42425-8*) Exec Ent Pubns.

An Asterisk (*) at the beginning of an entry indicates that the title is appearing for the first time.

L

Liability in Construction Management. Ed. by David M. Lee. 89p. 1983. pap. 5.00 (*0-87262-383-1*) Am Soc Civil Eng.
Liability in Medical Practice: A Reference for Physicians. N. S. Blackman & C. P. Bailey. x, 476p. 1990. text 77.00 (*3-7186-0506-6*); pap. text 38.00 (*3-7186-0512-0*) Gordon & Breach.
Liability in Negligence. J. C. Smith. (C). 1984. 250.00 (*0-7855-4101-2*, Pub. by Witherby & Co) St Mut.
Liability in the Public Sector: Defending & Challenging Government Action. Clifford M. Greene. 199p. 1996. pap. 35.00 (*0-943380-65-0*) PEG MN.
Liability Insurance: The Purchaser's Guide. Edith Merila. 36p. 1986. 5.00 (*0-932622-08-9*) Ctr Public Rep.
Liability Insurance Claims. Kenneth Cannar. 600p. 1983. 280.00 (*0-900886-80-3*, Pub. by Witherby & Co) St Mut.
Liability Issues for Public Safety Telecommunications: Student Manual. 57p. 1997. student ed., spiral bd. 60.00 (*1-57927-071-9*) APCO Inst.
Liability Issues for Supervisors. (Training in a Box Ser.). 50p. 1997. ring bd. 49.00 (*1-57927-029-8*) APCO Inst.
Liability Issues in Perinatal Nursing. Donna Miller-Slade. LC 98-27994. 416p. 1998. pap. text 39.95 (*0-397-55276-9*) Lppncott W & W.
Liability Maze: The Impact of Liability Law on Safety & Innovation. Ed. by Peter W. Huber & Robert E. Litan. 514p. 1991. 49.95 (*0-8157-3760-2*); pap. 22.95 (*0-8157-3761-0*) Brookings.
Liability of Businesses & Industries for Earthquake Hazards & Losses: Background Research Reports. 199p. 1984. 15.00 (*0-318-22688-X*) Assn Bay Area.
Liability of Corporate Groups: Autonomy & Control in Parent-Subsidiary Relationships in U. S., German & EEC Law: An International & Comparative Perspective. Jose E. Antunes. LC 93-42436. (Studies in Transnational Economic Law: Vol. 10). 1994. 178.50 (*90-6544-785-7*) Kluwer Law Intl.
Liability of Corporate Officers & Directors, 2 vols., Set. 5th ed. William E. Knepper & Dan A. Bailey. 1993. 165.00 (*1-55834-103-X*, 63962-11, MICHIE) LEXIS Pub.
Liability of Corporate Officers & Directors: 1989 Supplement. Knepper & Bailey. 1989. write for info. (*0-87473-525-4*, 63963-10, MICHIE) LEXIS Pub.
***Liability of Corporate Officers & Directors: 1998 Replacement Volumes, 2 vols.** 6th ed. Ed. by Lexis Law Publishing Staff. LC 98-88727. 1998. lib. bdg. 165.00 (*0-327-00730-3*) LEXIS Pub.
Liability of Corporate Officers & Directors Vol. 1: 1998 Replacement Volume. 6th ed. Dan A. Bailey. LC 98-88727. 1998. 165.00 (*0-327-00731-1*) LEXIS Pub.
Liability of Corporate Officers & Directors Vol. 2: 1998 Replacement Volume. 6th ed. Dan A. Bailey. LC 98-88727. 1998. 165.00 (*0-327-00732-X*, 6395811) LEXIS Pub.
Liability of Enterprises for Offences (Recommendation & Explanatory Memorandum), No. R(88)16. Council of Europe Staff. 1990. 12.00 (*92-871-1750-0*, Pub. by Council of Europe) Manhattan Pub Co.
Liability of Lawyers & Indemnity Insurance for the Legal Profession. Albert Rogers et al. Ed. by Karin C. Frikkee. LC 95-43581. 1995. 109.00 (*90-411-0876-9*) Kluwer Law Intl.
Liability of Local Governments for Earthquake Hazards & Losses: Report: A Guide to the Law & Its Impacts in the States of Alaska, California, Utah & Washington. 52p. 1989. 12.00 (*0-317-05681-6*, P88003PLN) Assn Bay Area.
Liability of Municipal Corporations for Tort: Treating Fully Municipal Liability for Negligence. Waterman L. Williams. xxxix, 345p. 1982. reprint ed. 42.50 (*0-8377-1321-8*, Rothman) W S Hein.
Liability of Security Personnel: How to Stay Out of Court. Donna Lea Hawley. 1998. pap. 29.95 (*0-7506-7031-2*, Newnes) Buttrwrth-Heinemann.
Liability of Tax Return Preparers. Ira L. Shafiroff. 529p. 1989. text 15.00 (*0-685-45795-8*, J1-1466) PLI.
Liability of the Crown. 2nd ed. Peter W. Hogg. xxxiv, 290p. 1989. 89.50 (*0-455-20969-3*, Pub. by LawBk Co) Gaunt.
Liability of the Holding Company for the Debts of Its Insolvent Subsidiaries. Andrew Muscat. LC 96-20667. (Illus.). 570p. 1996. text 115.95 (*1-85521-844-5*, Pub. by Dartmth Pub) Ashgate Pub Co.
Liability or Asset? A Policy for the Falkland Islands. Robert Miller. (C). 1990. 45.00 (*0-907967-80-9*, Pub. by Inst Euro Def & Strat) St Mut.
Liability Policy Wording & Cover. Peter Madge. 150p. 1973. 75.00 (*0-948691-04-2*, Pub. by Witherby & Co) St Mut.
Liability Policy Wording & Cover. 2nd ed. Peter Madge. (C). 1973. 85.00 (*0-7855-4100-4*, Pub. by Witherby & Co) St Mut.
Liability Regime of the International Air Carrier. Rene H. Mankiewicz. 288p. 1981. 104.00 (*90-268-1170-5*) Kluwer Law Intl.
LIAF 1st Year Set. Kimm Walton & Lazar Emanuel. (Law in a Flash Cards Ser.). 1999. pap. text 95.00 (*1-56542-596-0*) E Pub Corp.
Liaison, 2 vols. Ralph Hester et al. (FRE.). (C). 1992. text, teacher ed. 3.96 (*0-395-59191-0*) HM.
Liaison, 2 vols. 2nd ed. Ralph Hestor et al. (C). 1992. pap. text 52.36 (*0-395-47284-9*) HM.
Liaison, 2 vols. 2nd annot. ed. Ralph Hester et al. (FRE.). (C). 1992. pap. text, teacher ed. 53.56 (*0-395-59187-2*) HM.
***Liaison: Flood Tide.** C. Anderson. 1998. mass mkt. 6.95 (*0-7472-5826-0*, Pub. by Headline Bk Pub) Trafalgar.
Liaison Blindfold. S. Danson. 1997. mass mkt. 6.95 (*0-7472-5583-0*, Pub. by Headline Bk Pub) Trafalgar.
Liaison Curtain Calls. L. Carlyle. 1997. mass mkt. 6.95 (*0-7472-5579-2*, Pub. by Headline Bk Pub) Trafalgar.
***Liaison Driven by Desire.** L. Chester. 1998. mass mkt. 6.95 (*0-7472-5760-4*, Pub. by Headline Bk Pub) Trafalgar.
Liaison Family Affair. C. Mildenhall. mass mkt. 6.95 (*0-7472-5387-0*) Headline Bk Pub.
Liaison Heatwave. K. Cavendish. 1997. mass mkt. 6.95 (*0-7472-5652-7*, Pub. by Headline Bk Pub) Trafalgar.
Liaison Interpreting: A Handbook. Adolfo Gentile et al. LC 97-140719. 154p. 1996. pap. 24.95 (*0-522-84581-9*, Pub. by Melbourne Univ Pr) Paul & Co Pubs.
Liaison Intimate Disclosures. C. Mildenhall. 1997. mass mkt. 6.95 (*0-7472-5589-X*, Pub. by Headline Bk Pub) Trafalgar.
***Liaison Intoxication.** C. Cooper. 1998. mass mkt. 6.95 (*0-7472-5820-1*, Pub. by Headline Bk Pub) Trafalgar.
Liaison Island in the Sun. S. Sebastian. 1997. mass mkt. 6.95 (*0-7472-5689-6*, Pub. by Headline Bk Pub) Trafalgar.
Liaison Life Classes. S. Sebastian. mass mkt. 6.95 (*0-7472-5813-9*, Pub. by Headline Bk Pub) Trafalgar.
***Liaison Make Me an Offer.** I. Shaw. 1998. mass mkt. 6.95 (*0-7472-5866-X*, Pub. by Headline Bk Pub) Trafalgar.
Liaison Pleasure Points. C. Mildenhall. 1997. mass mkt. 6.95 (*0-7472-5590-3*, Pub. by Headline Bk Pub) Trafalgar.
***Liaison Pride & Prurience.** L. Campion. 1998. mass mkt. 6.95 (*0-7472-5768-X*) Headline Bk Pub.
Liaison Private Education. C. Anderson. 1997. mass mkt. 6.95 (*0-7472-5518-0*, Pub. by Headline Bk Pub) Trafalgar.
Liaison Private Performance. C. Anderson. 1997. mass mkt. 6.95 (*0-7472-5674-8*, Pub. by Headline Bk Pub) Trafalgar.
***Liaison Psychiatry & Teamwork.** Lynch et al. 256p. 2000. pap. text 40.00 (*0-7506-4298-X*) Buttrwrth-Heinemann.
Liaison Seduction. C. Cooper. 1997. mass mkt. 6.95 (*0-7472-5627-6*, Pub. by Headline Bk Pub) Trafalgar.
Liaison Slippery Slope. A. Geene. 1997. mass mkt. 6.95 (*0-7472-5714-0*, Pub. by Headline Bk Pub) Trafalgar.
Liaison Temptation. C. Cooper. 1997. mass mkt. 6.95 (*0-7472-5628-4*, Pub. by Headline Bk Pub) Trafalgar.
Liaison Tonight's the Night. Crewe & Wells. 1997. mass mkt. 6.95 (*0-7472-5626-8*, Pub. by Headline Bk Pub) Trafalgar.
Liaison True Colours. L. Chester. 1997. mass mkt. 6.95 (*0-7472-5629-2*, Pub. by Headline Bk Pub) Trafalgar.
Liaison Velvet Vices. L. Carlyle. 1997. mass mkt. 6.95 (*0-7472-5767-1*, Pub. by Headline Bk Pub) Trafalgar.
***Liaison Voyeurs.** C. Mildenhall. 1998. mass mkt. 6.95 (*0-7472-5814-7*, Pub. by Headline Bk Pub) Trafalgar.
Liaison Ways of a Woman. J. Duke. 1996. mass mkt. 6.95 (*0-7472-5443-5*, Pub. by Headline Bk Pub) Trafalgar.
***Liaison Wild Child.** S. Walker. 1998. mass mkt. 6.95 (*0-7472-5326-9*, Pub. by Headline Bk Pub) Trafalgar.
Liaisons, 2 vols. 2nd ed. Hester. (C). 1992. pap. text, wbk. ed. 29.56 (*0-395-59188-0*) HM.
Liaisons: Philosophy Meets the Cognitive & Social Sciences. Alvin I. Goldman. (Illus.). 344p. 1991. 50.00 (*0-262-07135-5*, Bradford Bks) MIT Pr.
Liaisons Dangereuses. Choderlos De Laclos. Tr. by Ernest C. Dowson from ENG. LC 98-6220. (New York Public Library Collector's Edition Ser.). (Illus.). 496p. 1998. 18.50 (*0-385-48733-9*) Doubleday.
Liaisons Dangereuses. Choderlos De Laclos. 448p. (C). 1987. pap. 17.99 (*0-415-09447-X*) Routledge.
Liaisons Dangereuses. Choderlos De Laclos. Tr. by P. W. Stone. (Classics Ser.). 400p. 1961. pap. 9.95 (*0-14-044116-6*, Penguin Classics) Viking Penguin.
Liaisons Dangereuses. Christopher Hampton. LC 85-6839. 96p. 1985. pap. 11.95 (*0-571-13724-5*) Faber & Faber.
Liaisons Dangereuses. Laclos. (FRE.). (C). 1987. pap. 11.95 (*0-8442-1971-1*, VF1971-1) NTC Contemp Pub Co.
Liaisons Dangereuses. Choderlos De Laclos. 1992. 17.00 (*0-679-41325-1*) Everymns Lib.
Liaisons Dangereuses. Choderlos De Laclos. (Coll. GF). pap. 8.95 (*0-685-34038-4*) Fr & Eur.
Liaisons Dangereuses. Choderlos De Laclos. (Coll. Prestige Ser.). 382p. 1958. pap. 10.95 (*0-7859-1417-X*) Fr & Eur.
Liaisons Dangereuses. Choderlos De Laclos. (Folio Ser.: No. 894). pap. 11.95 (*2-07-036894-7*) Schoenhof.
***Liaisons Dangereuses.** Choderlos de Laclos. Ed. by Douglas Parmee. (Oxford World's Classics Ser.). 442p. 1999. pap. 8.95 (*0-19-283867-9*) OUP.
Liaisons Dangereuses. unabridged ed. Choderlos De Laclos. (FRE.). pap. 7.95 (*2-87714-153-5*, Pub. by Bookking Intl) Distribks Inc.
Liaisons Dangereuses: A Study of Motive & Moral. Patrick Byrne. 186p. 1993. 59.00 (*0-85261-252-4*, Pub. by Univ of Glasgow) St Mut.
Liaisons Dangereuses, Laclos: Critical Monographs in English. Phillip Thody. 72p. 1993. pap. 32.00 (*0-85261-317-2*, Pub. by Univ of Glasgow) St Mut.
***Liam Gillick.** Michael Archer et al. Tr. by Brigitte Kalthoff from GER. (Illus.). 168p. 2000. pap. 25.00 (*0-9671802-3-6*) Lukas & Sternberg.
***Liam Gillick: Five or Six.** Liam Gillick. Ed. by Nicolaus Schafhausen & Caroline Schneider. 120p. 1999. pap. write for info. (*0-9671802-5-2*) Lukas & Sternberg.
Liam Neeson. I. Millar. 1998. mass mkt. 6.99 (*0-340-62831-6*) Hodder & Stought Ltd.
Liam O'Flaherty. James A. O'Brien. LC 78-126291. (Irish Writers Ser.). 124p. 1975. 8.50 (*0-8387-7772-4*); pap. 1.95 (*0-8387-7773-2*) Bucknell U Pr.
Liam O'Flaherty: A Study of the Short Fiction. James M. Cahalan. (Twayne's Studies in Short Fiction: No. 23). 184p. (C). 1991. 24.95 (*0-8057-8312-1*, Twyne) Mac Lib Ref.
Liam O'Flaherty: An Annotated Bibliography. Paul A. Doyle. LC 71-161085. iv, 68p. 1972. 7.50 (*0-87875-017-7*) Whitston Pub.
***Liam O'Flaherty: The Collected Stories, 3 vols.** A. A. Kelly. 1999. text 100.00 (*0-312-22906-2*) St Martin.
Liam O'Flaherty's Ireland. Peter Costello. LC 97-116148. (Illus.). 127p. 1997. 29.95 (*0-86327-550-8*) Irish Bks Media.
Liam Poems. Thomas Heffernan. LC 81-67497. (Living Poets' Library: Vol. 27). 1981. pap. 6.00 (*0-934218-22-6*) Dragons Teeth.
Liamado a la Pureza. Johann Christoph Arnold. (SPA.). 1997. pap. write for info. (*950-724-671-1*) Lumen ARG.
Lianas, Climber & Shrubby Climbers, Pt. III. A. B. Chaudhari. 89p. (C). 1985. pap. 40.00 (*81-7089-075-6*, Pub. by Intl Bk Distr) St Mut.
Lianas, Climber & Shrubby Climbers, Pt. III. A. B. Chaudhuri. 1985. 90.00 (*0-7855-3076-2*, Pub. by Intl Bk Distr) St Mut.
Lianda: A Chinese University in War & Revolution. John Israel. LC 98-7841. (Illus.). xv, 459p. 1998. 60.00 (*0-8047-2929-8*) Stanford U Pr.
Liang & Lin: Partners in Exploring China's Architectural Past. Wilma Fairbank. LC 94-16414. (Illus.). 256p. (C). 1994. text 32.50 (*0-8122-3278-X*) U of Pa Pr.
Liang & the Magic Paintbrush. Demi. LC 80-11351. (Illus.). 32p. (J). (ps-3). 1995. pap. 5.95 (*0-8050-0801-2*, Bks Young Read) H Holt & Co.
Liang & the Magic Paintbrush. Hitz Demi. 123p. (J). 1980. 11.15 (*0-606-03845-0*, Pub. by Turtleback) Demco.
Liang Ch'i-Ch'ao & Intellectual Transition in China, 1890-1907. Hao Chang. LC 75-162635. (Harvard East Asian Ser.: No. 64). 355p. reprint ed. pap. 110.10 (*0-7837-2233-8*, 205732300004) Bks Demand.
Liang Zhen Pu Eight Diagram Palm. Zi M. Li. 154p. 1993. pap. 17.95 (*1-883175-00-3*) High View Pubns.
***Lian's Lie.** Qumry Bnita. LC 99-96467. (Qumry Bnita's Scripts Ser.: Bk. II). (Illus.). 48p. (J). (gr. 3-9). 1999. pap. 6.50 (*1-891339-02-8*) Akebulan Ctr.
Liao Architecture. Nancy S. Steinhardt. LC 97-3096. (Illus.). 440p. 1998. text 55.00 (*0-8248-1843-1*) UH Pr.
Liar see London Life
Liar. Stephen Fry. LC 92-40407. 277p. 1994. pap. 12.00 (*1-56947-012-X*) Soho Press.
Liar. Carlo Goldoni. Tr. by Frederick H. Davies. (Orig.). 1963. pap. 3.50 (*0-87830-531-9*, Thtre Arts Bks) Routledge.
Liar. Carlo Goldoni. Tr. by Tunc Yalman. 1973. pap. 5.25 (*0-8222-0655-2*) Dramatists Play.
Liar. Winnifred Morris. LC 96-2465. 176p. (YA). 1996. 15.95 (*0-8027-8461-5*) Walker & Co.
***Liar.** Francine Pascal. (Fearless Ser.: No. 10). 240p. (YA). (gr. 7-12). 2000. per. 5.99 (*0-671-03951-2*, Pocket Pulse) PB.
Liar see Works of Henry James Jr.: Collected Works
Liar. Martin A. Hansen. Tr. by John J. Egglishaw from DAN. (Sun & Moon Classics Ser.: No. 111). (Illus.). 208p. 1995. reprint ed. pap. 12.95 (*1-55713-243-7*) Sun & Moon CA.
Liar: An Irene Kelly Mystery. Jan Burke. (Irene Kelly Mystery Ser.). 400p. 1999. mass mkt. 6.99 (*0-06-104440-7*) HarpC.
Liar: An Irene Kelly Mystery. Jan Burke. LC 98-10197. 320p. 1998. 23.00 (*0-684-80345-3*) S&S Trade.
Liar, Jones. Maggie Hannan. 62p. 1996. pap. 16.95 (*1-85224-308-2*, Pub. by Bloodaxe Bks) Dufour.
Liar, Liar. Barthe DeClements. LC 97-17716. 144p. (YA). (gr. 3-7). 1998. lib. bdg. 14.95 (*0-7614-5021-1*) Marshall Cavendish.
Liar, Liar, Pants on Fire! Miriam Cohen. (J). 1995. 10.19 (*0-606-07785-5*) Turtleback.
Liar, Liar, Pants on Fire. Gordon Korman. (Illus.). 96p. (gr. 2-4). 1999. pap. 3.99 (*0-590-27141-5*) Scholastic Inc.
Liar, Liar, Pants on Fire! Gordon Korman. LC 96-44317. (Illus.). 96p. (J). (gr. 2-4). 1997. 14.95 (*0-590-27142-3*) Scholastic Inc.
***Liar Moon.** Ben Pastor. 230p. 2001. 25.00 (*1-929871-01-5*) Van Neste.
Liar School of Herodotus. W. Kendrick Pritchett. 350p. 1993. 74.00 (*90-5063-088-X*, Pub. by Gieben) J Benjamins Pubng Co.
Liar Speaks the Truth: A Defense of the Revision Theory of Truth. Aladdin M. Yaqub. LC 92-37507. 168p. 1993. text 49.95 (*0-19-508343-1*) OUP.
Liars. P. J. Petersen. LC 91-28490. 176p. (YA). (gr. 7 up). 1992. 15.00 (*0-671-75035-6*) S&S Bks Yung.
Liars. P. J. Petersen. (J). 1995. 9.30 (*0-606-07786-3*) Turtleback.
Liars. P. J. Peterson. LC 91-28490. 176p. (J). (gr. 5-9). 1995. mass mkt. 3.95 (*0-689-80130-0*) Aladdin.
Liars & Tyrants & People Who Turn Blue. Barbara Paul. 179p. 1992. pap. 5.95 (*1-55882-110-4*) Intl Polygonics.
Liars' Book. Ed. by Jane Yolen & Linda Mannheim. LC 97-23482. (Illus.). 1999. 16.95 (*0-590-48999-2*, Blue Sky Press) Scholastic Inc.
Liar's Club. 1995. write for info. (*0-201-43896-8*) Addison-Wesley.
***Liars' Club: A Memoir.** Mary Karr. LC 94-41252. 320p. (C). 1998. pap. 6.67 (*0-14-017983-6*) Addson-Wesley Educ.
Liars' Club: A Memoir. Mary Karr. (C). 1997. pap. text 11.95 (*0-8013-3144-7*) Longman.
Liars' Club: A Memoir. large type ed. Mary Karr. (Wheeler Large Print Bks.). 1995. pap. 22.95 (*1-56895-273-2*) Wheeler Pub.
Liars Club Readers Guide. Mary Karr. 1996. pap. write for info. (*0-14-771137-1*) Viking Penguin.
Liar's Corner. Roger L. Welsch. 152p. 1988. pap. 4.95 (*0-317-93306-X*); text 11.95 (*0-317-93305-1*) Plains Heritage.
***Liar's Game.** Eric Jerome Dickey. LC 99-87739. 336p. 2000. 23.95 (*0-525-94483-4*) NAL.
Liar's Moon. Heather Graham. 288p. 1996. 24.00 (*0-7278-5120-9*) Severn Hse.
***Liar's Moon.** Philip Kimball. 2000. pap. 12.95 (*0-452-28183-0*, Plume) Dutton Plume.
Liar's Moon: A Long Story. Phillip Kimball. LC 99-27191. 288p. 1999. 23.00 (*0-8050-6148-7*) H Holt & Co.
Liar's Oath. Elizabeth Moon. 480p. (Orig.). 1992. mass mkt. 5.99 (*0-671-72117-8*) Baen Bks.
Liar's Poker. Michael Lewis. 1989. 21.95 (*0-393-02750-3*) Norton.
Liar's Poker: A Harry Garnish/Bridget O'Toole Mystery. Frank McConnell. LC 92-43525. 234p. 1993. 19.95 (*0-8027-3229-1*) Walker & Co.
Liar's Poker: Rising Through the Wreckage on Wall Street. Michael Lewis. 1990. pap. 12.95 (*0-14-014345-9*, Penguin Bks) Viking Penguin.
Liar's Prayer: A Grouch's Guide to Enlightenment. Gregory Flood. 208p. (Orig.). 1998. pap. 12.95 (*0-938407-03-1*) Brob Hse Bks.
Liar's Promise. Dana Ransom. 1990. mass mkt. 4.25 (*0-8217-2881-4*, Zebra Kensgtn) Kensgtn Pub Corp.
Liar's Too. Roger Welsch. 116p. 1993. pap. 5.95 (*0-934904-32-4*) J & L Lee.
Liasions. Hester. (C). 1992. pap., wbk. ed. 12.56 (*0-395-63075-4*) HM.
Liason: Love Hurts. L. Aspen. 1997. mass mkt. 6.95 (*0-7472-5588-1*, Pub. by Headline Bk Pub) Trafalgar.
Lib Parents, Lib Childre. Adele Faber & Elaine Mazlish. 270p. 1990. pap. 11.00 (*0-380-71134-6*, Avon Bks) Morrow Avon.
***Libanesische Immigranten in Ghana: Selbstwahrnehmungen und Rollenzuschreibungen in Autobiographischen Schriften.** Charlotte B. Looss. (Illus.). 193p. 1999. 39.95 (*3-631-34437-6*) P Lang Pubng.
Libanius: Autobiography & Selected Letters, 2 vols., Vol. I. Ed. & Tr. by A. F. Norman. (Loeb Classical Library: Nos. 478 & 479). 478p. 1993. 19.95 (*0-674-99527-9*) HUP.
Libanius: Autobiography & Selected Letters, 2 vols., Vol. 2. Ed. & Tr. by A. F. Norman. (Loeb Classical Library: Nos. 478 & 479). 479p. 1993. 19.95 (*0-674-99528-7*) HUP.
Libanius: Index Nominum Propriorum. E. Richsteig. 90p. 1963. reprint ed. write for info. (*0-318-72041-8*) G Olms Pubs.
Libanius Vol. 1: Concordantiae in Libanium. (Alpha-Omega Ser.: Reihe A, Bd. L). (GER.). xlvi, 894p. 1996. 260.00 (*3-487-10132-7*) G Olms Pubs.
Libanius - Concordantiae in Libanium: Pars Altera: Orationes, 3 vols., Set. Ed. by Georgios Fatouros et al. (Alpha-Omega, Reihe A Ser.: Vol. L). 1989. write for info. (*3-487-07689-6*) G Olms Pubs.
Libanius - Concordantiae in Libanium: Pars Prima: Epistulae, 2 vols., Set. Ed. by Georgios Fatouros et al. (Alpha-Omega, Reihe A Ser.: Vol. L). 1987. write for info. (*3-487-07686-1*) G Olms Pubs.
Libanius - Concordantiae in Libanium: Pars Tertia: Declamationes Et Progymnasmata. 225.00 (*0-318-70664-4*) G Olms Pubs.
Libanius & the Dancers. Margaret E. Molloy. LC 96-225402. 340p. 1996. write for info. (*3-487-10220-X*) G Olms Pubs.
***Libary Skills.** Sharon Upchurch. (Illus.). 80p. (YA). (gr. 5). 1999. pap. text 9.95 (*1-58037-098-5*, Pub. by M Twain Media) Carson-Dellos.
Libation. Estella C. Majoza. (Illus.). 105p. (Orig.). 1996. pap. 12.00 (*0-86316-024-7*) Writers & Readers.
Libation. Estella C. Majozo. 106p. (Orig.). 1992. 24.00 (*0-86316-303-3*) Writers & Readers.
Libation Bearers, Electra (Sophocles), Iphigenia in Tauris, Electra (Euripides), the Trojan Women see Greek Tragedies
Libation by Death. Dorian Yeager. LC 97-31622. 240p. 1998. text 21.95 (*0-312-18128-0*, 874692) St Martin.
Libbie. Libbie Braverman. (Illus.). 220p. 1986. 16.95 (*0-8197-0504-7*) Bloch.
Libbie: A Three-Act Play with Only One Character, Elizabeth Bacon Custer. Ray Kemble. 22.95 (*0-8488-0031-1*, J M C & Co) Amereon Ltd.
Libby: The Black Duck of Wadleigh Pond. Susan B. Pickford. LC 96-92539. (Illus.). 32p. (Orig.). (J). (gr. k-6). 1996. pap. 6.95 (*1-889664-03-0*) SBP.
Libby: The Sketches, Letters & Journal of Libby Meaman, Recorded in the Pribilof Islands, 1879-1880. 2nd ed. Elizabeth B. John. (Illus.). 206p. 1998. pap. 16.95 (*1-57178-067-X*) Coun Oak Bks.
Libby Bloom. Susan Rowan Masters. LC 94-43898. (Redfeather Bks.). (Illus.). (J). (gr. 2-4). 1995. 14.95 (*0-8050-3374-2*) H Holt & Co.
Libby Bloom. Illus. by Beata Szpura. 1998. pap. 6.95 (*0-8050-5799-4*) H Holt & Co.
***Libby Died: This Book Is for All Kids, but Especially My Sister, Libby.** Annette Dauphin Simon. (Illus.). 32p. (J). (ps-6). 2000. 15.99 (*0-9701853-0-8*, 00088AGPres) G S D & M.
Libby Family in America, 2 bks., Set, Vol. II. Ed. & Compiled by Libby, John, Family Association Members Staff. LC 87-125730. 1900p. 1993. 80.00 (*0-9636308-1-4*) Libby Homestead.
Libby Family in America, 1602-1881. Charles T. Libby. (Illus.). 628p. 1990. reprint ed. pap. 93.50 (*0-8328-1495-4*); reprint ed. lib. bdg. 101.50 (*0-8328-1494-6*) Higginson Bk Co.
Libby Life: Experiences of a Prisoner of War in Richmond, VA, 1863-64. F. F. Cavada. (Illus.). 232p. (Orig.). 1994. pap. text 20.00 (*0-7884-0051-7*) Heritage Bk.
Libby Meets the Bully. Elizabeth Connor & Mary Kinzler. (Illus.). 100p. (J). (gr. 2-7). 1997. 12.95 (*0-9658468-0-6*) Adbeth Pr.
Libby on Wednesday. Zilpha Keatley Snyder. 208p. (J). (gr. 4-7). 1991. pap. 4.99 (*0-440-40498-3*) Dell.

L

Libby on Wednesday. Zilpha Keatley Snyder. 1990. 9.09 (0-606-04964-9, Pub. by Turtleback) Demco.

Libby Prison & Beyond: A Union Staff Officer in the East, 1862-1865. Thomas M. Boaz. LC 99-11789. 225p. 1999. 24.95 (1-57249-123-X, Burd St Pr) White Mane Pub.

***Libby Saves Beauty's Colt.** limited large type ed. Elizabeth Connor & Mary Kinzler. LC 98-93720. (Illus.). 106p. (J). (gr. 2-6). 1999. 12.95 (0-9658468-1-4) Adbeth Pr.

Libby's Choice. Katharine E. Matchette. LC 94-69605. 157p. (YA). (gr. 6-12). 1995. pap. 8.75 (0-9645045-0-2) Deka Pr.

Libel: A Basic Program for Beginning Journalists. Jerome L. Nelson. LC 73-13006. 121p. reprint ed. pap. 37.60 (0-608-16266-3, 202665900051) Bks Demand.

Libel & Academic Freedom: A Lawsuit Against Political Extremists. Arnold M. Rose. LC 68-19743. 299p. reprint ed. pap. 92.70 (0-608-14155-0, 205590500039) Bks Demand.

Libel & Newsgathering Litigation: Getting & Reporting the News. David A. Schulz et al. LC 98-207459. (Patents, Copyrights, Trademarks & Literary Property Course Handbook Ser.). 1998. write for info. (0-87224-471-7) PLI.

Libel & Privacy. 2nd ed. Bruce W. Sanford. 1054p. 1991. ring bd. 110.00 (0-13-109174-3) Aspen Law.

Libel & Privacy. 2nd ed. Bruce W. Sanford. 1036p. 1991. ring bd. 156.00 (0-13-535816-7, 42842) Aspen Law.

Libel & Privacy Litigation: Prevention & Defenses. Bruce W. Sanford. 1983. suppl. ed. 70.00 (0-317-05989-0, H42841) Harcourt.

Libel & Slander in the Workplace. Kathleen B. Hayward et al. 72p. 1996. spiral bd. 47.00 (0-925773-25-5) M Lee Smith.

Libel & the First Amendment: Legal History & Practice in Print & Broadcasting. Richard E. Labunski. LC 85-24656. 327p. (Orig.). 1989. pap. 24.95 (0-88738-790-X) Transaction Pubs.

Libel Law & the Media: The Chilling Effect. Baren. LC 96-40026. 220p. 1997. pap. text (0-19-826234-5) OUP.

Libel Law & the Media: The Chilling Effect. Eric Barendt & Laurence Lustgarten. LC 96-40026. (Illus.). 224p. 1997. text 56.00 (0-19-826227-2) OUP.

Libel Law & the Press: Myth & Reality. Randall P. Bezanson et al. LC 86-33579. 1987. 55.00 (0-02-905870-8) Free Pr.

Libel Litigation, 1992. (Patents, Copyrights, Trademarks, & Literary Property Ser.). 890p. 1992. pap. 70.00 (0-685-69458-5); audio 175.00 (0-685-69459-3) PLI.

Libel Revolution: A New Look at Defamation & Privacy. Michael F. Mayer. 28.75 (0-317-67926-0) Law Arts.

Libel, Slander, & Related Problems. 2nd ed. Robert D. Sack & Sandra S. Baron. 1097p. 1994. 145.00 (0-614-17121-0, G1-1013) PLI.

Libel Suitors & Other Stories. M. R. Avena. v, 82p. (Orig.). (C). 1990. pap. 8.75 (971-10-0392-9, Pub. by New Day Pub) Cellar.

Libellen in Bayern (Dragonflies of Bavaria) K. Kuhn & K. Burbach. (GER., Illus.). 300p. 1998. 30.00 (3-8001-3495-0, Pub. by Eugen Ulmer) Balogh.

Libellus de Opificio Mundi. Philo Alexandrinus. Ed. by Leopold Cohn. lviii, 108p. 1967. reprint ed. 32.00 (0-318-70997-X) G Olms Pubs.

Libellus de Rudimentis Musices. fac. ed. Biagio Rossetti. (Monuments of Music & Music Literature in Facsimile, II Ser.: Vol. 136). (Illus.). 1968. lib. bdg. 35.00 (0-8450-2336-5) Broude.

Libellus de Sublimitate. 4th ed. Longinus. Ed. by Donald A. Russell. (Oxford Classical Texts Ser.). 1968. reprint ed. text 12.95 (0-19-814566-7) OUP.

Libellus Fabularum Latinarum. Sarah F. Roach. 200p. 1997. 49.00 (0-7618-0866-3); pap. 29.50 (0-7618-0867-1) U Pr of Amer.

Libellus Sanguinis: Keepers of the Word. Cynthia Summers. (Vampire Ser.). (Illus.). 1998. pap. 15.00 (1-56504-294-8, 2815) White Wolf.

Libellus Sanguinis: Masters of the State. Robert Hatch et al. (Vampire Ser.: Vol. 1). (Illus.). (Orig.). 1997. pap. 15.00 (1-56504-286-7, 2807) White Wolf.

Libelulas. R. Hugh Rice. Tr. by Raquel Torres. (Books for Young Learners).Tr. of Dragonflies. (SPA., Illus.). 12p. (J). (gr. k-2). 1996. pap. text 5.00 (1-57274-032-9, A2875) R Owen Pubs.

Liber Albus see Munimenta Gildhallae Londoniensis: Liber Albus, Liber Custumarum, et Liber Horn

Liber Aleph Vel CXI: The Book of Wisdom or Folly. Aleister Crowley. LC 91-8023. 254p. 1991. pap. 19.95 (0-87728-729-5) Weiser.

Liber Amicorum: Professor Ignaz Seidl-Hohenveldern in Honour of His 80th Birthday. Ignaz Seidl-Hohenveldern & Gerhard Hafner. LC 98-19236. 1998. 200.00 (90-411-1024-0) Kluwer Law Intl.

Liber Amicorum for Emil Alfred Loeliger. Ed. by E. Briet. (Journal: Haemostasis: Vol. 15, No. 4, 1985). (Illus.). 72p. 1985. pap. 51.50 (3-8055-4146-5) S Karger.

Liber Amicorum for Lord Wilberforce. Ed. by Maarten Bos & Ian Brownlie. 264p. 1987. text 69.00 (0-19-825595-0) OUP.

***Liber Amicorum "In Memoriam" of Judge Jose Maria Ruda.** Jose Maria Ruda & Calixto A. Armas Barea. LC 00-25768. 2000. write for info. (90-411-1367-3) Kluwer Law Intl.

Liber Amicorum John Steele: A Musical Tribute. Warren Drake. LC 96-39599. (Festschrift Ser.: No. 16). 1997. 54.00 (0-945193-80-7) Pendragon NY.

Liber Amicorum Leif Muten see International Studies in Taxation: Law & Economics

Liber Amicorum Presented to Prof. Dr. J. D. Mulder: Journal: Diagnostic Imaging in Clinical Medicine, Vol. 55, Nos. 4 & 5. J. L. Bloem. (Illus.). 100p. 1986. pap. 61.75 (3-8055-4480-4) S Karger.

Liber Amicorum Presented to Prof. Dr. J. R. Blickman. L. Penning & C. J. Thijn. (Journal: Diagnostic Imaging in Clinical Medicine: Vol. 53, No. 4). (Illus.). 56p. 1984. 38.50 (3-8055-3934-7) S Karger.

Liber Amoris. William C. Hazlitt. LC 92-33464. 208p. 1992. reprint ed. 48.00 (1-85477-119-1) Continuum.

Liber Amoris: or The New Pygmalion. William C. Hazlitt. (BCL1-PR English Literature Ser.). 130p. 1992. reprint ed. lib. bdg. 69.00 (0-7812-7556-3) Rprt Serv.

Liber Apologeticus de Omni Statu Humanae Naturae (1460) Thomas Chaundler. Ed. by Doris E. Shoukri. No. 5. 1974. write for info. (0-318-59382-3) Renaiss Soc Amer.

Liber Ardmachanus - The Book of Armagh. 2nd ed. Ed. by John Gwynn. (Illus.). 808p. 1996. 254.95 (1-85928-335-7, Pub. by Scolar Pr) Ashgate Pub Co.

Liber Augustalis: or Constitutions of Melfi Promulgated by the Emperor Frederick the Second for the Kingdom of Sicily in 1231. Ed. by James M. Powell. LC 76-150107. 201p. reprint ed. pap. 62.40 (0-608-17477-7, 202997000067) Bks Demand.

Liber Baal: Being Further Revelations Concerning King Solomon's Arte & Philosophy Known As Magick. Ed. by Frater Zarathustra. 48p. (Orig.). 1983. pap. 10.00 (0-939856-35-2) Tech Group.

Liber Canonis (Al-Qanun Fi't-Tibb, Lateinisch) Avicenne Revisus et ab Omni Errore Mendaque Purgatus Summaque Cum Diligentia Impressus. Ibn S. Avicenna. (GER.). 573p. 1998. write for info. (3-487-00594-8) G Olms Pubs.

Liber Cartarum. St. Andrews Priory Staff. Ed. by Thomas Thomson. LC 72-174802. (Bannatyne Club, Edinburgh. Publications: No. 69). reprint ed. 55.00 (0-404-52789-2) AMS Pr.

Liber Cartarum Sancte Crucis. Ed. by Cosmo N. Innes. LC 79-169479. (Bannatyne Club, Edinburgh. Publications: No. 70). reprint ed. 59.50 (0-404-52790-6) AMS Pr.

Liber Celestis of St. Bridget of Sweden: The Middle English Version in British Library MS Claudius BI, Together with a Life of the Saint from the Same Manuscript, Vol. I. Ed. by Roger Ellis. (OS 291 Ser.: No. 291). 520p. 1988. 69.00 (0-19-722293-5) OUP.

Liber Collegii Nostre Domine: Registrum Ecclesie B. V. Marie et S. Anne Infra Muros Civitatis Glasguensis. Ed. by Joseph Robertson. LC 71-168165. (Maitland Club, Glasgow. Publications: No. 65). reprint ed. 40.00 (0-404-53073-7) AMS Pr.

Liber Custumarum, with Extracts from the Cottonian Ms Claudius D II see Munimenta Gildhallae Londoniensis: Liber Albus, Liber Custumarum, et Liber Horn

Liber de Causis see Book of Causes

Liber de Diversis Medicinis. Ed. by Margaret S. Ogden. (EETS, OS Ser.: Vol. 207). 1969. reprint ed. 30.00 (0-8115-3383-2) Periodicals Srv.

Liber de Illustribus Henricis. John Capgrave. Ed. by Francis C. Hingeston. (Rolls Ser.: No. 7). 1969. reprint ed. 70.00 (0-8115-1008-5) Periodicals Srv.

Liber de Pomo: The Apple or Aristotle's Death. Tr. by Mary F. Rousseau. LC 68-28028. (Medieval Philosophical Texts in Translation Ser.: No. 18). 1968. pap. 5.00 (0-87462-218-2) Marquette.

Liber de Pulchritudine. Plotinus. cxlii, 574p. 1976. reprint ed. write for info. (3-487-06054-X) G Olms Pubs.

Liber des Goules - The Book of Ghouls. Cynthia Summers & Richard Dansky. (Mind's Eye Theater Ser.). (Illus.). 100p. (Orig.). 1997. pap. 10.95 (1-56504-507-6, 5006) White Wolf.

Liber Ecclesie de Scon. Scone Abbey Staff. Ed. by Cosmo N. Innes. LC 78-175585. (Maitland Club, Glasgow. Publications: No. 62). 1843. 42.50 (0-404-52799-X) AMS Pr.

Liber Famelicus of Sir James Whitelocke. James Whitelocke. Ed. by John Bruce. (Camden Society, London. Publications, First Ser.: No. 70). reprint ed. 35.00 (0-404-50170-2) AMS Pr.

Liber Gersumarum of Ramsey Abbey: A Calendar & Index. Edwin B. DeWindt. (Illus.). viii, 455p. pap. text 59.43 (0-88844-356-0) Brill Academic Pubs.

Liber Historae Francorum. Ed. by Bernard S. Bachrach. 123p. 1973. pap. 7.50 (0-87291-058-X) Coronado Pr.

Liber Insule Missarum. Inchaffray Abbey Staff. Ed. by Cosmo N. Innes. LC 70-170060. (Bannatyne Club, Edinburgh. Publications: No. 85). reprint ed. 45.00 (0-404-52814-7) AMS Pr.

Liber Ka. John R. Snead. Ed. by Sam Shirley & Kenneth Hite. (Nephilim Rolplaying Game Ser.). (Illus.). 96p. (Orig.). 1997. pap. 14.95 (1-56882-093-3, 3107) Chaosium.

Liber Kaos. Peter Carroll. LC 92-6241. (Illus.). 224p. (Orig.). 1992. reprint ed. pap. 14.95 (0-87728-742-2) Weiser.

Liber Lilliati. Ed. by Edward Doughtie. LC 84-40489. (Illus.). 232p. 1985. 40.00 (0-87413-267-3) U Delaware Pr.

Liber Manualis: Dhuoda's Handbook for Her Warrior Son. Ed. & Tr. by Marcelle Thiebaux. LC 97-28633. (Cambridge Medieval Classics: No. 8). 296p. 1998. 74.95 (0-521-39599-2) Cambridge U Pr.

Liber Miraculorum Sancte Fidis see Book of Sainte Foy

Liber Monasterii de Hyda: A Chronicle of the Affairs of England...Hampshire, 455-1203. Ed. by Edward Edwards. (Rolls Ser.: No. 45). 1969. reprint ed. 70.00 (0-8115-1104-9) Periodicals Srv.

Liber Null & Psychonaut. Peter Carroll. LC 86-24539. (Illus.). 222p. 1987. pap. 15.95 (0-87728-639-6) Weiser.

Liber Poenitentialis. Robert of Flamborough. Ed. by J. J. Firth. (ENG & LAT.). xxx, 364p. 51.43 (0-88844-018-9) Brill Academic Pubs.

Liber Quartus Madrigalium Quatuor Vocum see Complete Works of Philippe De Monte

Liber Quartus Motettorum Quinque Vocum see Complete Works of Philippe De Monte

Liber Quindecim Missarum, Pt. 1, Brumel: "Missa De Beata Virgine;" de la Rue: "Missa Ave Maria" see Maitres Musiciens de la Renaissance Francaise

Liber Quindecim Missarum, Pt. 2, Io. Mouton: Missa Alma redemtoris; Fevin: Missa Mente tota see Maitres Musiciens de la Renaissance Francaise

Liber S. Mariae de Dryburgh. Ed. by John Spottiswoode. LC 70-164790. reprint ed. 57.50 (0-404-52808-2) AMS Pr.

Liber S. Marie De Calchou, Registrum Abbacie Tironensis De Kelso, 1113-1567, 2 vols. Kelso Abbey Staff. Ed. by Cosmo N. Innes. LC 71-171552. (Bannatyne Club Publications: No. 82). reprint ed. 75.00 (0-404-52805-8) AMS Pr.

Liber S. Thome de Aberbrothoc, 2 vols. Arbroath Abbey Staff. Ed. by Cosmo N. Innes & Patrick Chalmers. LC 79-158268. (Bannatyne Club, Edinburgh. Publications: No. 86). reprint ed. 210.00 (0-404-52815-5) AMS Pr.

***Liber Sanctae Crucis' Di Rabano Mauro: Testo - Immagine - Contesto Prefazione Di Claudio Leonardi.** Michele C. Ferrari. xix, 527p. 1999. 75.95 (3-906762-17-3, Pub. by P Lang) P Lang Pubng.

Liber Sancte Marie de Melros, 2 vols. Melrose Abbey Staff. Ed. by Cosmo N. Innes. LC 77-172722. (Bannatyne Club, Edinburgh, Publications: No. 56). reprint ed. 115.00 (0-404-52910-0) AMS Pr.

Liber Septimus Motettorum Cum Quinque Vocibus see Complete Works of Philippe De Monte

Liber Thirty-One. Frater Achad. Ed. by T. Allen Greenfield. (Illus.). 80p. 1998. pap. 9.95 (1-891948-00-8) Luxor Press.

Libera. Robert Pinget. (FRE.). 224p. 1984. pap. 24.95 (0-7859-1516-8, 2707303488) Fr & Eur.

Libera Me Domine. Robert Pinget. Tr. by Barbara Wright from FRE. LC 78-53831. (New French Writing Ser.). 1979. 10.50 (0-87376-025-5) Red Dust.

Liberace see Notable Biographies

Liberace: A Bio-Bibliography, 65. Jocelyn Faris. LC 95-18176. (Bio-Bibliographies in the Performing Arts Ser.: No. 65). 320p. 1995. lib. bdg. 65.00 (0-313-29383-X, Greenwood Pr) Greenwood.

***Liberace: An American Boy.** Darden Asbury Pyron. LC 99-89031. (Illus.). 482p. 2000. 27.50 (0-226-68667-1) U Ch Pr.

Liberace - a Collecting Guide to the Recordings of Liberace & His Brother George. Karl B. Johnson. 190p. 1994. pap. 15.95 (0-9644176-5-0) J Carlson Pr.

Liberace Christmas Music. Karl B. Johnson. (Illus.). 56p. (Orig.). 1994. pap. 14.95 (0-9644176-2-6) J Carlson Pr.

Liberacion: El Evangelo de Dios. Jay Edward Adams. 1980. pap. 3.50 (0-85151-417-0) Banner of Truth.

Liberacion Del Espiritu. Watchman Nee.Tr. of Release of the Spirit. 112p. 1992. 6.99 (0-88113-255-1) Caribe Betania.

Liberacion Nacional in Costa Rica: The Development of a Political Party in a Transitional Society. Burt H. English. LC 73-107880. (Latin American Monographs: Ser. 2, No. 8). 196p. reprint ed. pap. 60.80 (0-7837-4962-7, 204462800004) Bks Demand.

Liberados de la Esclavitud. Kay Arthur. Tr. by Capstone Publishers Staff from CHI.Tr. of Free from Bondage God's Way. 87p. 1996. pap. 4.99 (1-888655-61-5) Precept Ministries.

Liberados de la Esclavitud. Kay Arthur. (International Inductive Study Ser.).Tr. of Free from Bondage God's Way. (SPA.). 1996. pap. 5.99 (0-8297-1503-7) Vida Pubs.

Liberal: Lord Byron, Leigh Hunt & the Liberal. Leslie Pickering. LC 68-763. (Studies in Byron: No. 5). 1972. lib. bdg. 75.00 (0-8383-0609-8) M S G Haskell Hse.

Liberal Adult Education: The End of an Era? Ed. by John Wallis. 179p. 1997. pap. 29.95 (1-85041-081-X, Pub. by U of Nottingham) Paul & Co Pubs.

Liberal Anglican Politics: Whiggery, Religion & Reform, 1830-1841. Richard Brent. LC 87-5567. (Oxford Historical Monographs). (Illus.). 352p. 1987. text 69.00 (0-19-822942-9) OUP.

Liberal Anxieties & Liberal Education. Alan Ryan. LC 97-38930. 199p. 1998. 22.00 (0-8090-6539-8) Hill & Wang.

Liberal Art of Science: Agenda for Action. LC 90-570. 142p. 1990. 12.95 (0-87168-378-4, 90-13S) AAAS.

***Liberal Arts.** Jordanna Bailkin. 1999. pap. text 18.00 (0-226-03551-4); lib. bdg. 50.00 (0-226-03550-6) U Ch Pr.

Liberal Arts. Blitzer. LC 99-88495. 740p. 1999. 86.00 (0-13-948845-6) P-H.

Liberal Arts: The Political Art of Tomi Ungerer. Tomi Ungerer. (Illus.). 168p. 1999. pap. 24.95 (1-57098-303-8, Pub. by Roberts Rinehart) Publishers Group.

***Liberal Arts: The Political Art of Tomi Ungerer.** Tomi Ungerer. (Illus.). 168p. 1999. 40.00 (1-57098-276-7, Pub. by Roberts Rinehart) Publishers Group.

Liberal Arts Advantage: How to Turn Your Degree into a Great Job. Gregory Giangrande. LC 97-49053. 208p. 1998. pap. 12.00 (0-380-79567-1, Avon Bks) Morrow Avon.

Liberal Arts & Community: The Feeding of the Larger Body. Marion Montgomery. LC 89-12792. 184p. 1990. text 30.00 (0-8071-1558-4) La State U Pr.

Liberal Arts & Sciences Test (LAST) Jack Rudman. (Admission Test Ser.: Vol. 119). 49.95 (0-8373-5869-8) Nat Learn.

Liberal Arts & Sciences Test (LAST) Jack Rudman. (Admission Test Ser.: Vol. ATS-119). 1997. pap. 29.95 (0-8373-5819-1) Nat Learn.

Liberal Arts & Social Sciences see Career Employment Opportunities Directory

Liberal Arts & the Future of Higher Education in the Middle East. 1979. 24.95 (0-8156-6052-9, Pub. by Am U Beirut) Syracuse U Pr.

Liberal Arts & the Jesuit College System. Aldo Scaglione. LC 86-17507. (Paperbacks Ser.: No. 6). (Illus.). v, 229p. 1986. 71.00 (0-915027-76-3); pap. 27.95 (0-915027-77-1) J Benjamins Pubng Co.

***Liberal Arts Chemistry.** Baird. 2001. pap. text. write for info. (0-7167-3902-X) W H Freeman.

Liberal Arts Chemistry: Worktext & Lab Manual. 4th ed. Rothenberger-Webb. 500p. (C). 1998. per., wbk. ed., lab manual ed. 32.95 (0-7872-5073-2) Kendall-Hunt.

Liberal Arts Classes. Marilyn Hariman. 32p. 14.95 (0-914951-19-X) LERN.

Liberal Arts College - 1960. Eugen Rosenstock-Huessy. (Eugen Rosenstock-Huessy Lectures: Vol. 22). 26p. 1997. pap. 15.00 incl. audio (0-912148-41-1) Argo Bks.

Liberal Arts College Adapting to Change: The Survival of Small Schools. Gary Bonvillian & Robert Murphy. LC 95-45053. (Studies in Higher Education: Vol. 09). (Illus.). 272p. 1996. text 50.00 (0-8153-1946-0, SS1011) Garland.

Liberal Arts College & the Ideal of Liberal Education: The Case of Radical Reform. Henry H. Crimmel. LC 93-11066. 390p. (Orig.). (C). 1993. pap. text 37.50 (0-8191-9174-4); lib. bdg. 64.00 (0-8191-9173-6) U Pr of Amer.

Liberal Arts Colleges: Thriving, Surviving, or Endangered? David W. Breneman. 184p. (C). 1994. 34.95 (0-8157-1062-3); pap. 14.95 (0-8157-1061-5) Brookings.

Liberal Arts in a Time of Crisis. Ed. by Barbara A. Scott. LC 89-48666. 256p. 1991. 55.00 (0-275-93295-8, C3295, Greenwood Pr) Greenwood.

Liberal Arts in Higher Education: Challenging Assumptions, Exploring Possibilities. Ed. by Diana Glyer & David L. Weeks. LC 98-22991. 192p. 1998. pap. 18.95 (0-7618-1164-8) U Pr of Amer.

Liberal Arts Jobs: Turning Your Learning into Earning Power. 3rd ed. Peterson's Guides Staff. (Peterson's Guides). 240p. 1998. pap. text 14.95 (0-7689-0148-0) Petersons.

Liberal Arts Mathematics. Wood. (C). 1996. text. write for info. (0-201-51499-0) Addison-Wesley.

Liberal Ascendancy, 1830-1886. T. A. Jenkins. LC 94-1160. 1994. text 49.95 (0-312-12167-9) St Martin.

Liberal Cage. Harry Clifton. 56p. 1988. pap. 12.95 (1-85235-026-1) Dufour.

Liberal Challenge. Joseph Grimond. LC 75-2696. 317p. 1975. reprint ed. lib. bdg. 65.00 (0-8371-8025-2, GRLC, Greenwood Pr) Greenwood.

Liberal City, Conservative State: Moscow & Russia's Urban Crisis, 1906-1914. Robert W. Thurston. LC 86-28648. (Illus.). 286p. 1987. text 65.00 (0-19-504331-6) OUP.

Liberal Civil War: Fraternity & Fratricide on the Left. Jim Tuck. LC 98-14350. 304p. 1998. 59.00 (0-7618-1087-0); pap. 39.50 (0-7618-1088-9) U Pr of Amer.

Liberal College. Alexander Meiklejohn. LC 79-89203. (American Education: Its Men, Institutions, & Ideas. Series 1). 1975. reprint ed. 18.95 (0-405-01441-4) Ayer.

Liberal Conspiracy: The Congress for Cultural Freedom & the Struggle for the Mind of Postwar Europe. Peter Coleman. 350p. 1989. 29.95 (0-02-906481-3) Free Pr.

Liberal Crusader: The Life of Sir Archibald Sinclair. Gerard J. De Groot. LC 92-39141. (C). 1993. text 45.00 (0-8147-1849-3) NYU Pr.

Liberal Democracy: A Critique of Its Theory. Andrew Levine. LC 81-1204. 224p. reprint ed. pap. 69.50 (0-608-15783-X, 203101500073) Bks Demand.

Liberal Democracy: Its Merits & Prospects. James R. Pennock. LC 77-13903. 403p. 1978. reprint ed. lib. bdg. 38.50 (0-8371-9865-8, PELD, Greenwood Pr) Greenwood.

Liberal Democracy & Its Critics: Perspectives in Contemporary Political Thought. April Carter & Geoff Stokes. LC 98-33638. 240p. 1998. 59.95 (0-7456-1919-3); pap. 26.95 (0-7456-1920-7) Blackwell Pubs.

Liberal Democracy & Political Science. James W. Ceaser. LC 89-27310. 224p. 1990. text 39.95 (0-8018-3985-8) Johns Hopkins.

Liberal Democracy & Political Science. James W. Ceaser. LC 89-27310. 224p. 1992. reprint ed. pap. text 15.95 (0-8018-4511-4) Johns Hopkins.

Liberal Democracy & the Bible. Ed. by Kim I. Parker. LC 92-23478. 196p. 1992. text 79.95 (0-7734-9154-6) E Mellen.

***Liberal Democracy & the Limits of Tolerance: Essays in Honor & Memory of Yitzhak Rabin.** Raphael Cohen-Almagor. 320p. (C). 2000. text 54.50 (0-472-11016-0, 11016) U of Mich Pr.

Liberal Democracy in Non-Western States. Ed. by Dennis Austin. LC 92-3014. 1995. pap. text 14.95 (0-943852-99-4) Prof World Peace.

Liberal Democracy in Non-Western States. Ed. by Dennis Austin. LC 92-3014. 256p. (C). 1995. text 24.95 (0-943852-98-6) Prof World Peace.

Liberal Democracy into 21st Century: Globalization, Integration & the Nation-State. Axtmann. LC 97-181935. (Political Analyses Ser.). 1997. pap. 24.95 (0-7190-4305-0, Pub. by Manchester Univ Pr) St Martin.

Liberal Democrats. Ed. by D. N. MacIver. LC 96-1620. 256p. (C). 1996. pap. text 32.00 (0-13-227802-2) P-H.

Liberal Democrats in the Weimar Republic: The History of the German Democratic Party & the German State Party. Bruce B. Frye. LC 84-22169. 256p. 1985. 26.95 (0-8093-1207-7) S Ill U Pr.

An Asterisk (*) at the beginning of an entry indicates that the title is appearing for the first time.

***Liberal Diplomacy & German Unification: The Early Career of Robert Morier.** Scott W. Murray. LC 99-59653. 304p. 2000. 65.00 (*0-275-96730-1*, C6730, Praeger Pubs) Greenwood.

Liberal Dreams & Nature'S Limits: Great Cities Of North America Since 1600. Ed. by James T. Lemmon. LC 97-141393. (Illus.). 342p. 1997. pap. text 42.00 (*0-19-540793-8*) OUP.

Liberal Economic Order, 2 vols. Gottfried Haberler. Ed. by Anthony Y. Koo. (Economists of the Twentieth Century Ser.). 704p. 1993. write for info. (*1-85278-650-7*) E Elgar.

Liberal Economics & Democracy: Keynes, Galbraith, Thurow, & Reich. Conrad P. Waligorski. LC 96-42442. 248p. 1996. 29.95 (*0-7006-0803-6*) U Pr of KS.

Liberal Education: Critical Essays on Professions, Pedagogy, & Structure. Frederick S. Weaver. 208p. (C). 1991. text 31.00 (*0-8077-3063-7*) Tchrs Coll.

Liberal Education & the Canon: Five Great Texts Speak to Contemporary Social Issues. Laura C. Ford. LC 94-21298. viii, 294p. 1994. 45.00 (*1-57113-013-6*); pap. 24.95 (*1-57113-059-4*) Camden Hse.

Liberal Education & the Corporation: The Hiring & Advancement of College Graduates. Michael Useem. (Social Institutions & Social Change Ser.). 243p. 1989. pap. text 27.95 (*0-202-30357-8*); lib. bdg. 48.95 (*0-202-30356-X*) Aldine de Gruyter.

Liberal Education & the Democratic Ideal & Other Essays. A. Whitney Griswold. LC 76-43025. 206p. 1977. reprint ed. lib. bdg. 59.50 (*0-8371-8977-2*, GRLE, Greenwood Pr) Greenwood.

Liberal Education & the Modern University. Charles Wegener. LC 78-6789. 172p. 1996. 13.50 (*0-226-87891-0*) U Ch Pr.

Liberal Education & the Modern University. Charles Wegener. LC 78-6789. 172p. reprint ed. pap. 53.40 (*0-608-09548-6*, 205435000005) Bks Demand.

Liberal Education & the New Scholarship on Women: Issues & Constraints in Institutional Change. Association of American Colleges Staff et al. vi, 56p. (Orig.). 1982. pap. 4.00 (*0-911696-12-1*) Assn Am Coll.

Liberal Education & the New Scholarship on Women: Issues & Constraints in Institutional Change, a Report of the Wingspread Conference, Racine, Wisconsin, Oct. 22-24, 1981. Association of American Colleges Staff. LC LC1576.L524. 64p. 1982. reprint ed. pap. 30.00 (*0-608-01793-0*, 206244600003) Bks Demand.

Liberal Education & the Small University in Canada. Ed. by Christine Storm. LC 97-159441. 248p. 1996. pap. 24.95 (*0-7735-1512-7*, Pub. by McG-Queens Univ Pr) CUP Services.

Liberal Education & the Small University in Canada. Ed. by Christine Storm. LC 97-159441. 248p. 1996. 60.00 (*0-7735-1424-4*, Pub. by McG-Queens Univ Pr) CUP Services.

Liberal Education & Value Relativism: A Guide to Today's B. A. Patrick Malcolmson et al. 111p. 1996. pap. text 19.95 (*0-7618-0337-8*) U Pr of Amer.

Liberal Education & Value Relativism: A Guide to Today's B. A. Patrick Malcolmson et al. LC 96-13032. 111p. 1996. lib. bdg. 39.00 (*0-7618-0336-X*) U Pr of Amer.

***Liberal Education of Charles Eliot Norton.** James Turner. LC 99-11498. 480p. 1999. 45.00 (*0-8018-6147-0*) Johns Hopkins.

Liberal Education Reconsidered: Reflections on Continuing Education for Contemporary Man. J. B. Whipple et al. LC 78-75207. (Notes & Essays Ser.: No. 60). (C). 1969. pap. text 2.50 (*0-87060-024-9*, NES 60) Syracuse U Cont Ed.

Liberal Future in America: Essays in Renewal, 123. Ed. by Philip Abbot & Michael B. Levy. LC 84-12834. (Contributions in Political Science Ser.: No. 123). (Illus.). 210p. 1985. 57.95 (*0-313-23761-1*, ALF/, Greenwood Pr) Greenwood.

Liberal Ideal & the Demons of Empire: Theories of Imperialism from Adam Smith to Lenin. Bernard Semmel. LC 92-36270. 240p. (C). 1993. text 36.00 (*0-8018-4540-8*) Johns Hopkins.

Liberal Imagination: Essays on Literature & Society. Lionel Trilling. LC 78-65749. 320p. 1979. 10.00 (*0-15-151197-7*) Harcourt.

Liberal Imperialists: The Ideas & Politics of a Post-Gladstonian Elite. H. C. Matthew. (Oxford Historical Monographs). 1973. 36.00 (*0-19-821842-7*) OUP.

Liberal International Economic Order: The International Monetary System & Economic Development. Deepak Lal. LC 80-22523. (Essays in International Finance Ser.: No. 139). 50p. reprint ed. pap. 30.00 (*0-608-18075-0*, 203211800078) Bks Demand.

Liberal Interpretation on the Prophecy of Israel-Disproved: Nostradamus Biblical Sage or Socerer. Philip N. Moore. LC 97-68229. (Illus.). 50p. (Orig.). 1997. pap. 5.00 (*1-57915-997-4*) Rams Head Pr.

Liberal Islam: A Sourcebook. Charles Kurzman. 360p. 1998. pap. 24.95 (*0-19-511622-4*); text 55.00 (*0-19-511621-6*) OUP.

Liberal Journalism & American Education, 1914-1941. James M. Wallace. LC 90-45946. 252p. (C). 1991. text 45.00 (*0-8135-1662-5*); pap. text 17.00 (*0-8135-1663-3*) Rutgers U Pr.

Liberal Judaism. Eugene B. Borowitz. LC 83-17997. 468p. (Orig.). 1984. pap. 12.00 (*0-8074-0264-8*, 386050) UAHC.

Liberal Judaism. Judy Shanks. LC 83-17997. 468p. (Orig.). 1984. pap., teacher ed. 5.00 (*0-8074-0325-3*, 203121) UAHC.

Liberal Judaism & Halakhah: Reform & Conservative Views of Jewish Law. Ed. by Walter Jacob. 162p. (Orig.). 1988. pap. 12.00 (*0-929699-00-9*) Rodef Shalom Pr.

Liberal Judaism at Home. rev. ed. Morrison David Bial. 1971. reprint ed. pap. 6.95 (*0-8074-0075-0*, 383110) UAHC.

Liberal Judaism at Home: The Practices of Modern Reform Judaism. rev. ed. Morrison David Bial. 1971. reprint ed. pap., teacher ed. 5.00 (*0-8074-0245-1*, 203110) UAHC.

Liberal Justice & the Marxist Critique of Education. Kenneth A. Strike. 200p. 1989. 29.95 (*0-415-90090-5*, A2560) Routledge.

Liberal Landslide: The General Election of 1906. A. K. Russell. 260p. 1973. 79.50 (*0-208-01389-X*) Elliots Bks.

Liberal Leadership: Great Powers & Their Challengers in Peace & War. Mark R. Brawley. 224p. 1994. text 39.95 (*0-8014-2808-4*) Cornell U Pr.

Liberal Leadership: Great Powers & Their Challenges in Peace & War. Mark R. Brawley. LC 93-4844. 221p. reprint ed. pap. 68.60 (*0-608-20088-3*, 207136000011) Bks Demand.

Liberal Learning American Experience. 262p. (C). 1996. pap. 59.00 (*0-536-59644-1*) Pearson Custom.

Liberal Learning & the Arts of Connection for the New Academy. American Commitments National Panel Staff. LC 95-80685. (American Commitments Ser.: Vol. 2). 41p. 1995. pap. 10.00 (*0-911696-66-0*) Assn Am Coll.

Liberal Learning & the World: A Banker's Perspective. Robert J. Callander. 7p. (Orig.). 1986. pap. text 2.00 (*0-911696-39-3*) Assn Am Coll.

***Liberal Man: Final Mission.** Marcus P. Meleton, Jr. (Illus.). 168p. 2000. pap. 14.95 (*0-9635826-5-8*) Sharkbait Pr.

***Liberal Mind.** Kenneth R. Minogue. LC 00-35409. 2000. write for info. (*0-86597-308-3*) Liberty Fund.

Liberal Mind in a Conservative Age: American Intellectuals in the 1940s & 1950s. 2nd ed. Richard H. Pells. LC 89-14676. 488p. 1989. pap. 24.95 (*0-8195-6225-4*, Wesleyan Univ Pr) U Pr of New Eng.

Liberal Modernism & Democratic Individuality: George Kateb & the Practices of Politics. Austin Sarat. LC 96-16565. 352p. 1996. pap. text 18.95 (*0-691-02595-9*, Pub. by Princeton U Pr) Cal Prin Full Svc.

Liberal Modernism & Democratic Individuality: George Kateb & the Practices of Politics. Ed. by Austin Sarat & Dana R. Villa. LC 96-16565. 352p. 1996. text 59.50 (*0-691-02596-7*, Pub. by Princeton U Pr) Cal Prin Full Svc.

Liberal Moment: Modernity, Security & the Making of Postwar International Order. Robert Latham. LC 96-53164. (New Directions in World Politics Ser.). (Illus.). 296p. 1997. pap. 19.50 (*0-231-10757-9*); lib. bdg. 52.00 (*0-231-10756-0*) Col U Pr.

Liberal Movement in English Literature. William J. Courthope. LC 72-458. reprint ed. 38.50 (*0-404-01784-3*) AMS Pr.

Liberal Nationalism. Yael Tamir. (Studies in Moral, Political, & Legal Philosophy). 232p. 1993. text 39.50 (*0-691-07893-9*, Pub. by Princeton U Pr); pap. text 16.95 (*0-691-00174-X*, Pub. by Princeton U Pr) Cal Prin Full Svc.

Liberal Nationalism for Israel: Towards an Israeli National Identity. Joseph Agassi. LC 99-74061. Orig. Title: Ben Dat U-Le'om. (Illus.). 328p. 1999. 24.95 (*965-229-190-0*) Gefen Bks.

Liberal Opposition in Hungary, 1919-1945. Z. L. Nagy. (Studia Historica Academiae Scientiarum Hungaricae: No. 185). 143p. (C). 1983. 30.00 (*963-05-2998-X*, Pub. by Akade Kiado) St Mut.

Liberal Papers. Ed. by James Roosevelt. LC 79-111861. (Essay Index Reprint Ser.). 1977. 26.95 (*0-8369-1716-2*) Ayer.

Liberal Parties in Western Europe. Ed. by Emil J. Kirchner. (Illus.). 528p. 1988. text 85.00 (*0-521-32394-0*) Cambridge U Pr.

Liberal Party in Alberta: A History of Politics in the Province of Alberta, 1905-1921. Lewis G. Thomas. LC 60-122. 242p. reprint ed. 75.10 (*0-8357-9769-4*, 201943800011) Bks Demand.

Liberal Party Politics. Vernon Bogdanor. 1983. 37.50 (*0-19-827465-3*) OUP.

Liberal Peace, Liberal War: American Politics & International Security. John M. Owen. LC 97-29419. (Studies in Security Affairs). 224p. 1997. 35.00 (*0-8014-3319-3*) Cornell U Pr.

***Liberal Peace, Liberal War: American Politics & International Security.** John M. Owen, IV. 2000. reprint ed. pap. 17.95 (*0-8014-8690-4*) Cornell U Pr.

Liberal Persuasion: Arthur Schlesinger, Jr., & the Challenge of the American Past. John P. Diggins. LC 97-18920. 310p. 1997. text 35.00 (*0-691-04829-0*, Pub. by Princeton U Pr) Cal Prin Full Svc.

Liberal Political Science of Raymond Aron: A Critical Introduction. Daniel J. Mahoney. 192p. 1991. pap. text 15.95 (*0-8476-7716-8*) Rowman.

Liberal Political Science of Raymond Aron: A Critical Introduction. Daniel J. Mahoney. 192p. (C). 1991. text 58.00 (*0-8476-7715-X*) Rowman.

Liberal Political Tradition: Contemporary Reappraisals. Ed. by James Meadowcroft. LC 95-19663. 208p. 1996. 85.00 (*1-85898-083-6*) E Elgar.

Liberal Politics in Britain. rev. ed. Arthur Cyr. 290p. 1988. 39.95 (*0-88738-209-6*) Transaction Pubs.

Liberal Professions & Illiberal Politics: Hungary from the Habsburgs to the Holocaust. Maria M. Kovacs. (Woodrow Wilson Press Co-Publication). (Illus.). 192p. 1994. text 52.00 (*0-19-508597-3*) OUP.

Liberal Promise: Anti-Discrimination Legislation in Australia. Margaret Thornton. 400p. 1994. 59.00 (*0-19-553204-X*) OUP.

Liberal Protestantism. Ed. by Bernard M. Reardon. 244p. 1968. 32.50 (*0-8047-0647-6*) Stanford U Pr.

Liberal Purposes: Goods, Virtues, & Diversity in the Liberal State. William A. Galston. (Studies in Philosophy & Public Policy). 348p. (C). 1991. pap. text 26.95 (*0-521-42250-7*) Cambridge U Pr.

Liberal Racism: How Fixating on Race Subverts the American Dream. Jim Sleeper. 208p. 1998. pap. 12.95 (*0-14-026378-0*) Viking Penguin.

Liberal Republican Movement. Earle D. Ross. LC 71-137286. reprint ed. 20.00 (*0-404-05407-2*) AMS Pr.

Liberal Revolution, Social Change, & Economic Development: The Region of Viana (NW Portugal) in the First Three Quarters of the 19th Century. Rui Feijo. LC 93-6578. (Modern European History Ser.: Spain & Portugal). 264p. 1993. text 20.00 (*0-8153-0736-5*) Garland.

Liberal Rights: Collected Papers, 1981-1991. Jeremy Waldron. LC 92-2390. (Studies in Philosophy & Public Policy). 494p. (C). 1993. text 69.95 (*0-521-43024-0*); pap. text 22.95 (*0-521-43617-6*) Cambridge U Pr.

Liberal Self: John Stuart Mill's Moral & Political Philosophy. Wendy Donner. LC 91-55065. 256p. 1992. text 45.00 (*0-8014-2629-4*); pap. text 16.95 (*0-8014-9987-9*) Cornell U Pr.

Liberal Socialism. Carlo Rosselli. Ed. by Nadia Urbinati. Tr. by William McCraig. LC 93-42365. 208p. (C). 1994. text 45.00 (*0-691-08650-8*, Pub. by Princeton U Pr); pap. text 14.95 (*0-691-02560-6*, Pub. by Princeton U Pr) Cal Prin Full Svc.

***Liberal Socialism: Four Essays on the Political Thought of Carlo Rosselli.** Paolo Bagnoli. 124p. 1999. pap. 7.00 (*0-913298-98-0*) S F Vanni.

Liberal State at War: English Politics & Economics During the Crimean War. Olive Anderson. (Modern Revivals in History Ser.). 320p. (C). 1994. text 63.95 (*0-7512-0279-7*, Pub. by Gregg Revivals) Ashgate Pub Co.

Liberal Theories of State: Contemporary Perspectives. Prakash Sarangi. (C). 1996. write for info. (*81-207-1835-6*) Sterling Pubs.

Liberal Trade & Japan: The Incompatibility Issue. M. F. Van Marion. (Contributions to Economics Ser.). (Illus.). xii, 298p. 1993. 71.95 (*0-387-91452-8*) Spr-Verlag.

Liberal Tradition: A Free People & a Free Economy. Lewis W. Douglas. LC 77-171382. (FDR & the Era of the New Deal Ser.). 136p. 1972. reprint ed. lib. bdg. 19.50 (*0-306-70376-9*) Da Capo.

Liberal Tradition in America: An Interpretation of American Political Thought Since the Revolution. 2nd ed. Louis Hartz. LC 55-5242. 346p. 1991. pap. 13.00 (*0-15-651269-6*, Harvest Bks) Harcourt.

Liberal Tradition in American Politics: Reassessing the Legacy of American Liberalism. David F. Ericson. LC 99-38659. 1999. pap. 24.99 (*0-415-92257-7*) Routledge.

***Liberal Tradition in American Politics: Reassessing the Legacy of American Liberalism.** David F. Ericson & Louisa Bertch Green. LC 99-38659. 1999. write for info. (*0-415-92256-9*) Routledge.

***Liberal Tradition in Focus: Problems & New Perspectives.** Ed. by Joao C. Espada et al. LC 99-48065. (Applications of Political Theory Ser.). 176p. 2000. 55.00 (*0-7391-0083-1*) Lxngtn Bks.

Liberal View of Texas Politics, 1890s-1930s. George N. Green. (Texas History Ser.). (Illus.). 45p. 1982. pap. text 9.95 (*0-89641-087-0*) American Pr.

Liberal View of Texas Politics since the 1930s. George N. Green. (Texas History Ser.). (Illus.). 52p. 1982. pap. text 9.95 (*0-89641-088-9*) American Pr.

Liberal Virtues: Citizenship, Virtue, & Community in Liberal Constitutionalism. Stephen Macedo. 320p. 1991. reprint ed. pap. 19.95 (*0-19-827872-1*) OUP.

Liberal Vocationalism. Harold Silver & John Brennan. 200p. 1988. pap. text 22.00 (*0-416-09262-4*) Routledge.

Liberalisation: European Telecommunications Standards & Liberalisation Guides. 1996. 595.00 (*0-614-18413-4*) Info Gatekeepers.

Liberalisation & Human Resource Management: Challenges for the Corporations of Tomorrow. Arun Monappa & Mahrukh Engineer. LC 98-20680. 1998. 38.00 (*0-7619-9273-1*); pap. 38.00 (*0-7619-9274-X*) Sage.

Liberalisation & Industrial Development in the Third World: A Comparison of the Indian & South Korean Engineering Industries. Staffan Jacobsson & Ghayur Alam. LC 94-16268. 256p. 1994. write for info. (*0-8039-9177-0*) Sage.

***Liberalisation & Protectionism in the World Trading System: 2nd Yearbook of the WTLA.** Ed. by Philip Ruttley et al. 1999. 100.00 (*1-874698-92-9*, Pub. by Cameron May) Gaunt.

***Liberalisation of International Insurance Operations: Cross-Border Trade & Establishment of Foreign Branches.** Hisaya Ishii. LC 99-228530. 240p. (Orig.). 1999. pap. 69.00 (*92-64-05846-X*, 21-1999-02-3 P, Pub. by Org for Econ) OECD.

Liberalisation of Public Procurement & Its Effects on the Common Market. Christopher Bovis. LC 98-20665. 229p. 1998. pap. 72.95 (*1-84014-440-8*, KJE5632.B678, Pub. by Ashgate Pub) Ashgate Pub Co.

Liberalising a Regulated Banking System: The Caribbean Case. Marion V. Williams. 336p. 1996. text 77.95 (*1-85972-432-9*, Pub. by Avebry) Ashgate Pub Co.

Liberalism. John Gray. (Concepts in Social Thought Ser.). 110p. 1995. pap. 14.95 (*0-8166-2801-7*) U of Minn Pr.

Liberalism. D. J. Manning. LC 76-15053. (Modern Ideologies Ser.). (C). 1976. pap. text 9.00 (*0-312-48335-X*) St Martin.

Liberalism. Harry Neumann. LC 91-70429. 359p. 1991. 29.95 (*0-89089-455-8*) Carolina Acad Pr.

Liberalism. Leonard T. Hobhouse. LC 80-10822. 130p. 1980. reprint ed. lib. bdg. 35.00 (*0-313-22332-7*, HOLI, Greenwood Pr) Greenwood.

Liberalism. Leonard T. Hobhouse. 136p. 1964. reprint ed. pap. text 16.95 (*0-19-500332-2*) OUP.

Liberalism. 2nd ed. John Gray. Ed. by Frank Parkin. (Concepts in the Social Sciences Ser.). 128p. 1995. 9.00 (*0-335-19475-3*); pap. 2.00 (*0-335-19422-2*) OpUniv Pr.

Liberalism, 3 vols., Set. Ed. by Richard J. Arneson. (Schools of Thought in Politics Ser.: Vol. 2). 2016p. 1992. 680.00 (*1-85278-348-6*) E Elgar.

L

Liberalism: Fatal Consequences. W. A. Borst. LC 98-75318. 304p. 1998. pap. 14.99 (*1-56384-153-3*) Huntington Hse.

Liberalism: Its Cause & Cure. Gregory L. Jackson. LC 90-61924. 182p. (Orig.). 1990. pap. 9.99 (*0-8100-0356-2*, 15N0474) Northwest Pub.

Liberalism: Politics, Ideology & the Market. John A. Hall. LC 88-40140. ix, 256p. (C). 1988. pap. 16.95 (*0-8078-4235-4*) U of NC Pr.

Liberalism: The Classical Tradition. 4th ed. Ludwig Von Mises. Tr. by Ralph Raico. 227p. 1996. pap. 14.95 (*1-57246-022-9*) Foun Econ Ed.

Liberalism after Communism. Jerzy Szacki. Tr. by Chester A. Kisiel. 224p. 1996. 21.95 (*1-85866-016-5*) Ctrl Europ Univ.

Liberalism after Communism. Jerzy Szacki. Tr. by Chester A. Kisiel. (Central European University Press Book Ser.). 224p. (C). 1996. 51.95 (*1-85866-015-7*) Ctrl Europ Univ.

Liberalism Against Populism: A Confrontation Between the Theory of Democracy & the Theory of Social Choice. William H. Riker. 311p. (C). 1988. reprint ed. pap. text 21.95 (*0-88133-367-0*) Waveland Pr.

Liberalism Ancient & Modern. Leo Strauss. LC 95-21951. xii, 276p. 1995. pap. text 15.95 (*0-226-77689-1*) U Ch Pr.

Liberalism & American Constitutional Law. Rogers M. Smith. 328p. 1983. 43.00 (*0-674-53015-2*) HUP.

Liberalism & American Constitutional Law. Rogers M. Smith. 344p. 1990. pap. 18.50 (*0-674-53016-0*) HUP.

Liberalism & American Identity. Patrick M. Garry. LC 91-30840. 232p. 1992. 32.00 (*0-87338-451-2*) Kent St U Pr.

Liberalism & Catholicism. A. Roussel. Tr. by Coenraad Daniels from FRE. LC 99-164535. Orig. Title: Liberalisme et Catholicisme. 135p. 1998. pap. 6.95 (*0-935952-53-5*) Angelus Pr.

Liberalism & Community. Steven Kautz. 240p. 1995. text 39.95 (*0-8014-2979-X*) Cornell U Pr.

Liberalism & Community. Steven Kautz. 248p. 1997. pap. 15.95 (*0-8014-8481-2*) Cornell U Pr.

Liberalism & Conservatism: The Nature & Structure of Social Attitudes. Fred N. Kerlinger. LC 84-10217. (Basic Studies in Human Behavior). (Illus.). 308p. 1984. reprint ed. pap. 95.50 (*0-608-01785-X*, 206244300003) Bks Demand.

***Liberalism & Crime: The British Experience.** Robert R. Sullivan. 240p. 2000. 65.00 (*0-7391-0130-7*) Lxngtn Bks.

Liberalism & Empire. Mehta. LC 98-40812. 1999. pap. text 17.00 (*0-226-51882-5*); lib. bdg. 45.00 (*0-226-51881-7*) U Ch Pr.

Liberalism & Its Challengers: From F.D.R. to Bush. 2nd ed. Alonzo L. Hamby. 448p. (C). 1992. pap. text 25.95 (*0-19-507030-5*) OUP.

Liberalism & Its Critics. Ed. by Michael J. Sandel. (Readings in Social & Political Theory Ser.). 256p. (C). 1984. pap. text 17.50 (*0-8147-7841-0*) NYU Pr.

Liberalism & Its Discontents. Alan Brinkley. LC 97-40654. 384p. 1999. text 29.00 (*0-674-53017-9*) HUP.

***Liberalism & Its Discontents.** Alan Brinkley. 2000. pap. 16.95 (*0-674-00185-0*) HUP.

Liberalism & Its Discontents. Patrick Neal. LC 97-8084. 1997. text 40.00 (*0-8147-5796-0*) NYU Pr.

Liberalism & Its Discontents. Patrick Neal. 1999. pap. text 20.00 (*0-8147-5798-7*) NYU Pr.

Liberalism & Its Practice. Dan Avnon & Avner De Shalit. LC 98-27628. 13p. 1999. write for info. (*0-415-19354-0*); pap. 27.99 (*0-415-19355-9*) Routledge.

Liberalism & Liberal Politics in Edwardian England. George L. Bernstein. 256p. (C). 1986. pap. text 18.95 (*0-04-942199-9*) Routledge.

Liberalism & Modern Society: A Historical Argument. Richard Bellamy. LC 92-7406. 330p. 1992. 50.00 (*0-271-00879-2*); pap. 19.95 (*0-271-00880-6*) Pa St U Pr.

Liberalism & Other Writings. Leonard T. Hobhouse. Ed. by James Meadowcroft. (Cambridge Texts in the History of Political Thought Ser.). 244p. (C). 1994. text 59.95 (*0-521-43112-3*); pap. text 19.95 (*0-521-43726-1*) Cambridge U Pr.

Liberalism & Paternalism in the 19th Century: Proceedings of the Tenth International Economic History Congress, Leuven, Belgium, August 1990. Ed. by E. Aerts et al. (Studies in Social & Economic History: No. 17). 137p. (Orig.). 1990. pap. 32.50 (*90-6186-389-9*, Pub. by Leuven Univ) Coronet Bks.

Liberalism & Pluralism: Towards a Politics of Compromise. Richard Bellamy. LC 99-20773. 1999. pap. write for info. (*0-415-19662-0*) Routledge.

***Liberalism & Pluralism: Towards Politics of Compromise.** Richard Bellamy. LC 99-20773. 240p. (C). 1999. text. write for info. (*0-415-19661-2*) Routledge.

Liberalism & Republicanism in the Historical Imagination. Joyce Appleby. 351p. (C). 1992. 45.00 (*0-674-53012-8*); pap. 23.50 (*0-674-53013-6*) HUP.

***Liberalism & Social Action.** John Dewey. LC 99-39280. (Great Books in Philosophy Ser.). 100p. 1999. pap. 9.95 (*1-57392-753-8*) Prometheus Bks.

L

***Liberalism & Social Justice: International Perspectives.** 256p. 2000. 69.95 (*0-7546-1053-5*) Ashgate Pub Co.

Liberalism & Social Reform: Industrial Growth & Progressiste Politics in France, 1880-1914, 55. David M. Gordon. LC 95-33981. (Contributions to the Study of World History Ser.: No. 55). 240p. 1996. 62.95 (*0-313-29811-4*, Greenwood Pr) Greenwood.

Liberalism & the Economic Order. Ed. by Ellen F. Paul et al. (Social Philosophy & Policy Ser.: No. 10: 2). 339p. (C). 1993. pap. text 24.95 (*0-521-45724-6*) Cambridge U Pr.

Liberalism & the Left. Ed. by Radical History Review Collective Staff. (Radical History Review Ser.: Vol. 71). 250p. (C). 1999. pap. text 21.95 (*0-521-64470-4*) Cambridge U Pr.

Liberalism & the Limits of Justice. 2nd ed. Michael J. Sandel. LC 98-4500. 250p. (C). 1998. text 54.95 (*0-521-56298-8*); pap. text 16.95 (*0-521-56741-6*) Cambridge U Pr.

Liberalism & the Modern Polity: Essays in Contemporary Political Theory. Ed. by Michael J. McGrath. LC 78-2583. (Political Science Ser.: No. 5). 319p. reprint ed. pap. 98.90 (*0-8357-6190-8*, 203455000090) Bks Demand.

Liberalism & the Moral Life. Ed. by Nancy L. Rosenblum. 312p. (C). 1989. pap. 18.50 (*0-674-53021-7*) HUP.

Liberalism & the Moral Life. Ed. by Nancy L. Rosenblum. LC 89-30983. 312p. 1989. 46.50 (*0-674-53020-9*) HUP.

Liberalism & the New Europe. Bob Breacher & Otakar Fleischmann. (Philosophy of Science Ser.). 205p. 1993. 64.95 (*1-85628-538-3*, Pub. by Avebry) Ashgate Pub Co.

Liberalism & the Origins of European Social Theory. Steven Seidman. LC 82-21802. 416p. (C). 1983. pap. 16.95 (*0-520-04986-1*, Pub. by U CA Pr) Cal Prin Full Svc.

***Liberalism & the Politics of Difference.** Andrea Baumeister. 224p. 2000. pap. text 25.00 (*0-7486-0909-1*) Col U Pr.

Liberalism & the Politics of Plunder: The Conscience of a Neo-Liberal. Robert Gillmore. LC 87-28994. (Orig.). 1987. pap. 12.00 (*0-87233-087-7*) Bauhan.

Liberalism & the Problem of Knowledge: A New Rhetoric for Modern Democracy. Charles A. Willard. (New Practices of Inquiry Ser.). 344p. 1996. pap. text 17.95 (*0-226-89846-6*); lib. bdg. 55.00 (*0-226-89845-8*) U Ch Pr.

Liberalism & the Quest for Islamic Identity in the Philippines. Kenneth E. Bauzon. LC 89-82249. xx, 219p. (Orig.). (C). 1991. pap. text 25.95 (*0-89386-028-X*) Acorn NC.

Liberalism & the Social Problem. Winston L. S. Churchill. LC 72-3299. (British History Ser.: No. 30). 1972. reprint ed. lib. bdg. 75.00 (*0-8383-1528-3*) M S G Haskell Hse.

Liberalism at the Crossroads: An Introduction to Contemporary Liberal Political Theory & Its Critics. Ed. by Christopher Wolfe & John Hittinger. 212p. (C). 1994. pap. text 22.95 (*0-8476-7876-8*); lib. bdg. 62.50 (*0-8476-7875-X*) Rowman.

Liberalism at Wit's End: The Libertarian Revolt Against the Modern State. Stephen L. Newman. LC 84-7108. 192p. 1984. text 37.50 (*0-8014-1747-3*) Cornell U Pr.

Liberalism at Work: The Rise & Fall of OSHA. Charles Noble. (Labor & Social Change Ser.). (Illus.). 304p. 1989. pap. 19.95 (*0-87722-665-2*) Temple U Pr.

Liberalism, Citizenship, & Autonomy. Ed. by David Milligan & William Watts-Miller. LC 92-9982. (Avebury Series in Philosophy). 260p. 1992. 82.95 (*1-85628-280-5*, Pub. by Avebry) Ashgate Pub Co.

Liberalism-Communitarianism Debate. Ed. by C. F. Delaney. LC 93-573. 260p. (C). 1994. pap. text 23.95 (*0-8476-7864-4*); lib. bdg. 59.50 (*0-8476-7863-6*) Rowman.

Liberalism, Community, & Culture. Will Kymlicka. 288p. 1991. reprint ed. pap. text 24.95 (*0-19-827871-3*) OUP.

Liberalism, Conservatism, & Catholicism: An Evaluation of Contemporary American Political Ideologies in Light of Catholic Social Teaching. Stephen M. Krason. 335p. (C). 1991. pap. text 14.95 (*1-879860-00-7*) Cath United Faith.

Liberalism, Constitutionalism, & Democracy. Russell Hardin. LC 99-36964. 400p. 2000. 29.95 (*0-19-829084-5*) OUP.

***Liberalism Defended: The Challenge of Post-Modernity.** Douglas B. Rasmussen & Douglas J. Den Uyl. LC 97-38258. (Shaftesbury Papers: Vol. 9). 96p. (C). 1998. pap. 15.00 (*1-85898-557-9*) E Elgar.

Liberalism, Democracy, & the State in Britain: Five Essays, 1862-1891. Ed. & Intro. by Julia Stapleton. (Primary Sources in Political Thought Ser.). 154p. 1997. 39.95 (*1-85506-534-7*); pap. 15.00 (*1-85506-535-5*) Thoemmes Pr.

Liberalism Divided: A Study in British Political Thought, 1914-1939 Religion. Michael Freeden. 410p. 1986. text 64.00 (*0-19-827432-7*) OUP.

Liberalism, Equality, & Cultural Oppression. Andrew Kernohan. LC 97-47477. 144p. (C). 1998. pap. 14.95 (*0-521-62753-2*); text 49.95 (*0-521-62164-X*) Cambridge U Pr.

Liberalism, Fascism, or Social Democracy: Social Classes & the Political Origins of Regimes in Interwar Europe. Gregory M. Luebbert. 432p. 1991. text 75.00 (*0-19-506610-3*); pap. text 26.00 (*0-19-506611-1*) OUP.

Liberalism in an Illiberal Age: New Culture Liberals in Republican China, 1919-1937, 5. Eugene Lubot. LC 81-13409. (Contributions in Intercultural & Comparative Studies: No. 5). 194p. 1982. 49.95 (*0-313-23256-3*, LUL/, Greenwood Pr) Greenwood.

***Liberalism in Australia.** Ian Cook. 272p. 2000. pap. text 22.00 (*0-19-553702-5*) OUP.

***Liberalism in Germany.** Dieter Langewiesche. 384p. 1999. pap. 24.95 (*0-691-01032-3*, Pub. by Princeton U Pr) Cal Prin Full Svc.

***Liberalism in Germany.** Dieter Langewiesche & John Breuilly. 384p. 1999. 65.00 (*0-691-01031-5*, Pub. by Princeton U Pr) Cal Prin Full Svc.

Liberalism in Mexico, 1857-1929. Wilfrid H. Callcott. 1976. lib. bdg. 59.95 (*0-8490-2157-X*) Gordon Pr.

Liberalism in Modern Times: Essays in Honour of Jose G. Merquior. Ernest Gellner & Cesar Cansino. LC 96-229039. 256p. 1996. pap. text 21.95 (*1-85866-053-X*) Ctrl Europ Univ.

Liberalism in Modern Times: Essays in Honour of Jose G. Merquior. Ed. by Ernest Gellner & Cesar Cansino. LC 96-229039. (Central European University Press Bk.). 256p. 1996. 51.95 (*1-85866-052-1*) Ctrl Europ Univ.

Liberalism in the Bedroom: Quarreling Spouses in Nineteenth-Century Lima. Christine Hhunefeldt. LC 98-55336. 440p. 1999. pap. text 75.00 (*0-271-01936-0*) Pa St U Pr.

***Liberalism in the Bedroom: Quarreling Spouses in Nineteenth-Century Lima.** Christine Hunefeldt. LC 98-55336. 1999. write for info. (*0-271-01935-2*) Pa St U Pr.

Liberalism in the South. Virginius Dabney. LC 77-128983. (BCL Ser. II). reprint ed. 49.50 (*0-404-00146-7*) AMS Pr.

Liberalism Is a Sin. Feliz S. Salvany. Tr. by Conde B. Pallen. LC 92-82526. 161p. 1993. reprint ed. pap. 7.50 (*0-89555-478-X*) TAN Bks Pubs.

Liberalism, Justice, & Markets: A Critique of Liberal Equality. Colin M. MacLeod. 248p. 1998. text 55.00 (*0-19-829397-6*) OUP.

Liberalism, Marxism & the Struggle for the State: Prolegomena to the Study of Public Administration. Ed. by Richard Bates. 152p. (C). 1985. 60.00 (*0-7300-0301-9*, Pub. by Deakin Univ) St Mut.

Liberalism, Multiculturalism, & Toleration. Ed. by John Horton. LC 93-10. 315p. 1993. text 49.95 (*0-312-09637-2*) St Martin.

Liberalism Old & New. Jose G. Merquior. Ed. by Michael Roth. (Studies in Intellectual & Cultural History: No. 1). 208p. 1991. pap. 14.95 (*0-8057-8627-9*, Twyne); text 24.95 (*0-8057-8602-3*, Twyne) Mac Lib Ref.

Liberalism, Oppression, & Empowerment. Ed. by Creighton Peden & Yeager Hudson. LC 94-17270. 306p. 1994. text 99.95 (*0-7734-9091-4*) E Mellen.

Liberalism, Perfectionism & Restraint. Steven Wall. LC 97-27917. 251p. (C). 1998. text 54.95 (*0-521-62411-8*) Cambridge U Pr.

Liberalism Proper & Proper Liberalism. Gottfried Dietze. LC 98-24554. 292p. 1998. pap. 32.00 (*0-7618-1191-5*) U Pr of Amer.

Liberalism Reconsidered. Ed. by Douglas MacLean & Claudia Mills. 1983. 55.75 (*0-317-05227-6*); pap. 24.00 (*0-317-05228-4*) IPPP.

Liberalism Reconsidered. Ed. by Douglas MacLean & Claudia Mills. LC 83-8623. (Maryland Studies in Public Philosophy). 160p. (C). 1983. 55.75 (*0-8476-7279-4*) IPPP.

Liberalism Reconsidered. Ed. by Douglas MacLean & Claudia Mills. LC 83-8623. (Maryland Studies in Public Philosophy). 160p. (C). 1983. pap. 26.50 (*0-8476-7280-8*) Rowman.

***Liberalism, Social Democracy & Fascism in Central Europe: Past & Present.** Ed. by Lene Bogh Sorensen & Leslie Eliason. 280p. 2000. 39.95 (*87-7288-719-2*, Pub. by Aarhus Univ Pr) David Brown.

***Liberalism, Socialism & Christian Social Order Bk. 1: The Philosophical Roots of Economic Liberalism.** Heinrich Pesch. Tr. by Rupert J. Ederer from GER. LC 99-88233. (Studies in Economics: Vol. 3). 300p. 2000. text 89.95 (*0-7734-7798-5*) E Mellen.

***Liberalism Versus Conservatism: A Bibliography with Indexes.** Ed. by Francois B. Gerard. 237p. 2000. lib. bdg. 49.00 (*1-56072-812-4*) Nova Sci Pubs.

Liberalism Without Illusions: Essays on Liberal Theory & the Political Vision of Judith N. Shklar. Contrib. by Tracy B. Stron et al. LC 95-18561. 304p. 1996. pap. text 16.95 (*0-226-94470-0*) U Ch Pr.

Liberalism Without Illusions: Essays on Liberal Theory & the Political Vision of Judith N. Shklar. Contrib. by Tracy B. Strong et al. LC 95-18561. 304p. 1996. lib. bdg. 42.00 (*0-226-94469-7*) U Ch Pr.

Liberalisme et Catholicisme see Liberalism & Catholicism

Liberalismes, la Theorie & l'Histoire: La France & les Pays-Bas, Vol. II. Ed. by Siep Stuurman. (FRE.). 250p. (Orig.). (C). 1994. pap. 34.50 (*90-5356-103-X*, Pub. by Amsterdam U Pr) U of Mich Pr.

Liberalismo Europeo. H. Laski. (Breviarios Ser.). (SPA.). pap. 8.99 (*968-16-0931-X*, Pub. by Fondo) Continental Bk.

Liberalisms: Essays in Political Philosophy. John Gray. 304p. 1989. 29.95 (*0-415-00744-5*, A3550) Routledge.

Liberalism's Crooked Circle: Letters to Adam Michnik. Ira Katznelson. 212p. 1996. pap. text 13.95 (*0-691-00447-1*, Pub. by Princeton U Pr) Cal Prin Full Svc.

Liberalism's Crooked Circle: Letters to Adam Michnik. Ira Katznelson. LC 95-43184. 232p. (C). 1996. text 22.95 (*0-691-03438-9*, Pub. by Princeton U Pr) Cal Prin Full Svc.

Liberalitsm & Affirmative Obligation. Patricia Smith. 272p. 1998. text 49.95 (*0-19-511528-7*) OUP.

Liberality & Civilization: Lectures Given at the Invitation of the Hibbert Trustees in the Universities of Bristol, Glasgow & Birmingham. Gilbert Murray. LC 77-27139. (Hibbert Lectures). reprint ed. 30.00 (*0-404-60430-7*) AMS Pr.

Liberalizacion Del Comercio en el Hemisferio Occidental. Ed. by CEPAL Staff & BID (Banco Interamericano De Desarrollo) Staff. (SPA.). 656p. (C). 1995. pap. text. write for info. (*0-9645938-1-5*) ECLAC.

Liberalization: India & Canadian Perspectives. Ed. by G. N. Ramu & Vishwas P. Govitrikar. (C). 1995. 17.50 (*81-7023-446-8*, Pub. by Allied Pubs) S Asia.

Liberalization & Crisis in Colombian Agriculture. Felipe Jaramillo. LC 98-35911. 192p. 1998. text 59.00 (*0-8133-3561-2*, Pub. by Westview) HarpC.

Liberalization & Democratization: Change in the Soviet Union & Eastern Europe. Ed. by Nancy Bermeo. 200p. 1992. pap. text 14.95 (*0-8018-4418-5*) Johns Hopkins.

Liberalization & Development in Nepal. Pandey & Arya. 1997. pap. 30.00 (*0-7855-7426-3*, Pub. by Ratna Pustak Bhandar) St Mut.

Liberalization & Entrepreneurship: Dynamics of Reform in Socialism & Capitalism. Branko Milanovic. LC 89-4196. 200p. (gr. 13). 1989. text 79.95 (*0-87332-568-0*) M E Sharpe.

Liberalization & Foreign Policy. Miles Kahler & Social Science Research Council (U. S.) Staff. LC 97-10996. 352p. 1997. pap. 18.50 (*0-231-10943-1*) Col U Pr.

Liberalization & Foreign Policy. Social Science Research Council (U. S.) Staff. Ed. by Miles Kahler. LC 97-10996. 325p. 1997. lib. bdg. 52.00 (*0-231-10942-3*) Col U Pr.

Liberalization & India's North East. Ed. by Gurudas Das & R. K. Purkayastha. LC 98-901510. 1998. 48.00 (*81-7169-498-5*, Commonwealth) S Asia.

***Liberalization & Industrial Transformation: Sri Lanka in International Perspective.** Prema-Chandra Athukorala & Sarath Rajapatirana. 280p. 2000. text 26.95 (*0-19-565179-0*) OUP.

***Liberalization & Its Consequences: A Comparative Perspective on Latin America & Eastern Europe.** Werner Baer & Joseph LeRoy Love. LC 00-37622. 2001. write for info. (*1-84064-436-2*) E Elgar.

Liberalization & Redemocratization in Latin America, 178. Ed. by George A. Lopez & Michael Stohl. LC 87-272. (Contributions in Political Science Ser.: No. 178). 287p. 1987. 65.00 (*0-313-25299-8*, LLB/, Greenwood Pr) Greenwood.

Liberalization & the Turkish Economy, 86. Ed. by Tevfik F. Nas & Mehmet Odekon. LC 88-9755. (Contributions in Economics & Economic History Ser.: No. 86). 231p. 1988. 59.95 (*0-313-26031-1*, NLZ/, Greenwood Pr) Greenwood.

Liberalization Attempts & Consequences. Anne O. Krueger. LC 77-14401. (National Bureau of Economic Research Ser.). 331p. 1978. reprint ed. pap. 102.70 (*0-608-08256-2*, 205609600049) Bks Demand.

***Liberalization, Growth & the Asian Financial Crisis: Lessons for Developing & Transitional Economies in Asia.** Mohamed Ariff & Ahmed M. Khalid. 544p. 2000. 120.00 (*1-85898-839-X*) E Elgar.

Liberalization in the Process of Economic Development. Ed. by Lawrence B. Krause. 1990. 48.00 (*0-520-06357-0*, Pub. by U CA Pr) Cal Prin Full Svc.

Liberalization of Abortion Laws: Implications. Ed. by Abdel R. Omran. LC 75-42005. 305p. 1976. pap. 5.00 (*0-89055-115-4*) Carolina Pop Ctr.

Liberalization of American Protestantism: A Case Study in Complex Organizations. Henry J. Pratt. LC 74-38837. 304p. reprint ed. pap. 94.30 (*0-7837-3618-5*, 204348400009) Bks Demand.

Liberalization of Capital Movements in Europe: The Monetary Committee & Financial Integration, 1958-1994. Age F. Bakker. LC 95-20404. (Financial & Monetary Policy Studies: Vol. 29). 340p. (C). 1996. lib. bdg. 110.50 (*0-7923-3591-0*) Kluwer Academic.

Liberalization of Cereals Marketing in Sub-Saharan Africa: Implementation Issues. J. Coulter & J. A. Compton. 1992. pap. 35.00 (*0-85954-280-7*, Pub. by Nat Res Inst) St Mut.

Liberalization of Cereals Marketing in Sub-Saharan Africa: Lessons from Experience. J. Coulter. 1994. pap. 30.00 (*0-85954-368-4*, Pub. by Nat Res Inst) St Mut.

Liberalization of Foreign Exchange Markets & Economic Growth in Sub-saharan Africa. Nguyuru H. Lipumba & World Institute for Development Economics Research. LC 98-178575. (Research for Action Ser.). viii, 60p. 1997. write for info. (*952-9520-52-2*) UN.

***Liberalization of Russian Foreign Trade: Problems & Prospects.** O. D. Davydov & V. A. Oreshkin. LC 99-49278. 2000. write for info. (*0-8232-1969-0*) Fordham.

***Liberalization of State Monopolies in the European Union & Beyond.** Ed. by Damien Geradin. (European Monographs: Vol. 23). 384p. 1999. pap. text 156.00 (*90-411-1264-2*) Kluwer Law Intl.

Liberalization of the Capital Account: Experiences & Issues. Donald J. Mathieson & Liliana Rojas-Suarez. LC 93-16797. (Occasional Paper - International Fund: No. 103). 39p. 1993. 15.00 (*1-55775-280-X*) Intl Monetary.

Liberalization, Productivity & Competition: A Panel Study on Indian Manufacturing. Vivek Srivastava. LC 96-900193. (Illus.). 176p. (C). 1996. text 19.95 (*0-19-563738-0*) OUP.

Liberalization with Stabilization in the Southern Cone of Latin America. V. Corbo & Jaime De Melo. 1985. pap. 26.00 (*0-08-033412-1*, Pub. by PPL) Elsevier.

Liberalized & Neglected? Food Marketing Policies in Eastern Africa. 154p. 12.00 (*952-9520-72-7*) UN.

Liberalized Depreciation & the Cost of Capital. Eugene F. Brigham & James L. Pappas. LC 77-631430. (MSU Public Utilities Studies: Vol. 1970). (Illus.). 136p. reprint ed. pap. 42.20 (*0-608-20491-9*, 207174300002) Bks Demand.

Liberalized Development in Tanzania: Studies on Accumulation Processes & Local Institutions. Peter Gibbon. 176p. 1995. pap. 42.50 (*91-7106-370-6*) Coronet Bks.

Liberalizing Finance in Interventionist States. Michael Loriaux et al. LC 96-23238. (Illus.). 256p. 1996. text 39.95 (*0-8014-3176-X*); pap. text 15.95 (*0-8014-8281-X*) Cornell U Pr.

Liberalizing International Transactions in Services: A Handbook. LC 95-175665. 180p. 45.00 (*92-1-104432-4*) UN.

Liberalizing Tanzania's Food Trade: The Public & Private Faces of Urban Marketing Policy, 1939-88. Bryceson. 306p. (C). 1993. text 65.00 (*0-435-08077-6*, 08077) Heinemann.

Liberalizing the European Media: Politics, Regulation, & the Public Sphere. Shalini Venturelli. 324p. 1999. text 65.00 (*0-19-823379-5*) OUP.

Liberals. Dean Jaensch. LC 93-210256. 224p. 1994. pap. 19.95 (*1-86373-361-2*, Pub. by Allen & Unwin Pty) Paul & Co Pubs.

Liberals. John H. Preston. LC 74-22803. (Labor Movement in Fiction & Non-Fiction Ser.). reprint ed. 45.00 (*0-404-58460-8*) AMS Pr.

Liberals among the Orthodox: Unitarian Beginnings in New York City, 1819-1839. Walter D. Kring. LC 73-21275. (Illus.). 288p. reprint ed. pap. 89.30 (*0-8357-3062-X*, 203931800012) Bks Demand.

Liberals & Communism: The "Red Decade" Revisited. Frank A. Warren. LC 93-15274. 276p. 1993. 57.50 (*0-231-08444-7*); pap. 20.00 (*0-231-08445-5*) Col U Pr.

Liberals & Communitarians. 2nd ed. Ed. by Stephen Mulhall & Adam Swift. 384p. (C). 1996. pap. 28.95 (*0-631-19819-9*) Blackwell Pubs.

Liberals & Ireland: The Ulster Question in British Politics to 1914. Patricia Jalland. (Modern Revivals in History Ser.). 304p. 1993. 63.95 (*0-7512-0182-0*, Pub. by Gregg Revivals) Ashgate Pub Co.

Liberals & J. Edgar Hoover: Rise & Fall of a Domestic Intelligence State. William W. Keller. LC 88-17828. 229p. reprint ed. pap. 71.00 (*0-608-06293-6*, 206665500008) Bks Demand.

Liberals & Other Born-Again Christians: Commentaries on Bleeding Hearts & Warmed Hearts Coming. Sally B. Geis. LC 97-22742. 144p. 1997. pap. 10.95 (*0-687-01797-1*) Abingdon.

Liberals & Social Democrats. Peter Clarke. (Modern Revivals in History Ser.). 360p. 1993. 72.95 (*0-7512-0212-6*, Pub. by Gregg Revivals) Ashgate Pub Co.

Liberals at the Crossroads: Germany Case Study, 1870-1878. J. D. Hunley. (Modern European History Ser.). 220p. 1987. text 15.00 (*0-8240-8048-3*) Garland.

Liberals, Church & Indian Peasants: Corporate Lands & the Challenge of Reform in Nineteenth-Century Spanish America. R. Jackson. LC 96-25225. 229p. 1997. 47.50 (*0-8263-1762-6*) U of NM Pr.

Liberals Face the Future. Ed. by G. Brandis et al. (C). 1985. pap. text 22.50 (*0-19-554505-2*) OUP.

Liberals on Liberalism. Ed. by Alfonso J. Damico. 240p. 1986. 39.50 (*0-8476-7484-3*); pap. 23.00 (*0-8476-7485-1*) Rowman.

Liberals, Politics, & Power: State Formation in Nineteenth-Century Latin America. Ed. by Vincent C. Peloso & Barbara A. Tenenbaum. LC 95-32602. (C). 1996. 50.00 (*0-8203-1777-2*); pap. 25.00 (*0-8203-1800-0*) U of Ga Pr.

Liberalsocialismo. Paolo Bagnoli. (ITA.). 151p. 1997. pap. 22.00 (*0-913298-40-9*) S F Vanni.

Liberando la Mente de los Recuerdos Que Atan. F. Littauer.Tr. of Freeing Your Mind from Memories That Bind. (SPA.). 330p. 1993. 8.99 (*1-56063-402-2*, 498513) Editorial Unilit.

Liberando la Tierra: Regeneracion O Revolucion? Gary North. Tr. by Paul Howden from ENG. (SPA.). 254p. 1989. pap. 5.95 (*0-930464-31-1*) Inst Christian.

Liberate! Anthony De Mello. 1997. pap. text 2.98 (*950-724-452-2*) Lumen ARG.

Liberate Yourself: How to Control Your Destiny & Achieve Greater Personal Success & Happiness in Your Life. Michael P. Sweeney. LC 93-93879. (Illus.). 199p. 1993. 19.95 (*1-883946-01-8*) Vision Pubng.

Liberated, Vol. 26. Daffyd Hugh. (Resistance Trilogy Ser.: Bk. 3). 238p. 1999. mass mkt. 6.50 (*0-671-01142-1*, Star Trek) PB.

Liberated Canvas: A Creative Approach to Canvas Embroidery. 2nd ed. Penny Cornell. (Illus.). 64p. 1995. reprint ed. pap. 19.95 (*0-9583873-5-4*, Pub. by Triple T Pubng) Quilters Res.

Liberated Cinderella: A One-Act Spoof of Fairy Tales. Rex Stephenson & Ginny Stephenson. (Illus.). 39p. 1974. pap. 3.25 (*0-88680-108-7*) I E Clark.

Liberated Cinderella: Director's Script. Rex Stephenson & Ginny Stephenson. (Illus.). 39p. 1974. pap. 7.50 (*0-88680-109-5*) I E Clark.

Liberated Imagination: Thinking Christianly about the Arts. Leland Ryken. (Wheaton Literary Ser.). 283p. 1989. pap. 12.99 (*0-87788-495-1*, H Shaw Pubs) Waterbrook Pr.

Liberated Mind. Edwin Derensbourg. 1997. pap. 8.99 (*1-56229-476-8*) Pneuma Life Pub.

Liberated No Longer Bound. M. Edwards. 1995. pap. 8.00 (*0-927936-16-X*) Vincom Pubng Co.

Liberated Orgasm: The Orgasmic Revolution. Herbert A. Otto. 268p. 1999. pap. 23.95 (*0-9671181-3-1*) Liberating Creations.

Liberated Parents Liberated Children. Adele Faber & Elaine Mazlish. 256p. 1976. mass mkt. 4.95 (*0-380-00466-6*, Avon Bks) Morrow Avon.

Liberated Quiltmaking. Gwen Marston. (Illus.). 192p. (Orig.). 1997. 24.95 (*0-89145-878-6*, 4751, Am Quilters Soc) Collector Bks.

Liberated Through Submission. P. B. Wilson. 192p. 1997. reprint ed. pap. 8.99 (*1-56507-720-2*) Harvest Hse.

An Asterisk (*) at the beginning of an entry indicates that the title is appearing for the first time.

Liberated Through Submission: The Essence of Power. Philomina B. Wilson. Ed. by Henry Soles, Jr. 128p. (Orig.). 1988. pap. text 8.95 (*0-685-74041-2*) New Dawn Pub.

***Liberated Voices: Contemporary Art from South Africa.** Frank Herreman. (Illus.). 1999. 70.00 (*3-7913-2195-1*) Prestel.

Liberated Woman: A Life of May Arkwright Hutton. James W. Montgomery. LC 85-8401. (Illus.). 407p. 1985. reprint ed. 21.95 (*0-87770-353-1*); reprint ed. pap. 16.95 (*0-87770-354-X*) Ye Galleon.

***Liberating Alternatives: The Founding Convention of the Cultural Environment Movement.** Kate Duncan & Cultural Environment Movement. LC 99-17257. (Hampton Press Communication Ser.). 1999. pap. 21.95 (*1-57273-199-0*) Hampton Pr NJ.

Liberating & Control: Reader: The Uses of Knowledge & Power. David W. Chambers et al. 276p. (C). 1984. 44.00 (*0-86828-273-1*, Pub. by Deakin Univ); student ed. 44.00 (*0-7855-6751-8*, Pub. by Deakin Univ) St Mut.

Liberating Children's Minds: Education, Citizenship & Critical Thinking. Patrick J. Costello. 1999. write for info. (*1-85359-382-6*, Pub. by Multilingual Matters); pap. write for info. (*1-85359-381-8*, Pub. by Multilingual Matters) Taylor & Francis.

Liberating Christ: Exploring Christologies of Contemporary Liberation Movements. Lisa Isherwood. LC 99-30822. 160p. (C). 1999. pap. 16.95 (*0-8298-1350-0*) Pilgrim OH.

Liberating Conscience: Feminist Explorations in Catholic Moral Theology. Anne E. Patrick. 176p. 1996. 24.95 (*0-8264-0891-5*) Continuum.

Liberating Conscience: Feminist Explorations in Catholic Moral Theology. Anne E. Patrick. 252p. 1997. pap. 16.95 (*0-8264-1051-0*) Continuum.

Liberating Cyberspace: Civil Liberties, Human Rights & the Internet. Ed. by Liberty National Council for Civil Liberties Staff. 256p. 1999. pap. 19.95 (*0-7453-1294-2*, Pub. by Pluto GBR) Stylus Pub VA.

Liberating Cyberspace: Civil Liberties, Human Rights & the Internet. Ed. by Liberty National Council for Civil Liberties Staff. LC 97-44923. 256p. 1999. 59.95 (*0-7453-1299-3*, Pub. by Pluto GBR) Stylus Pub VA.

Liberating Devotional: Daily Planner-Compact Pak. Dave Ray. 200p. 1993. ring bd. 24.95 (*1-57326-003-7*) Core Ministries.

Liberating Devotional: Intro-Pak. Dave Ray. 70p. 1994. pap. 6.95 (*1-57326-004-5*) Core Ministries.

Liberating Devotional: Six Month Spiral Bound Refill. 91p. 1994. spiral bd. 9.95 (*1-57326-006-1*) Core Ministries.

Liberating Devotional: Six Month Standard Refill. 91p. 1994. 6.95 (*1-57326-010-X*) Core Ministries.

Liberating Devotional: Soft Cover Pak. Dave Ray. 110p. 1993. spiral bd. 24.95 (*1-57326-001-0*) Core Ministries.

Liberating Devotional: Standard Version. Dave Ray. 200p. 1993. ring bd. 29.95 (*1-57326-000-2*) Core Ministries.

Liberating Devotional: The Executive Version. Dave Ray. 200p. 1993. ring bd. 79.95 (*1-57326-002-9*) Core Ministries.

Liberating Devotional: 6 Month Day Planner, Compact Refill. 182p. 1994. ring bd. 4.95 (*1-57326-008-8*) Core Ministries.

Liberating Disciplines see Disciplinas Libertadoras

Liberating Education. Zelda F. Gamson et al. LC 83-49260. (Jossey-Bass Higher Education Ser.). 277p. reprint ed. pap. 85.90 (*0-8357-4884-7*, 203781600009) Bks Demand.

Liberating Eschatology: Essays in Honor of Letty M. Russel. Ed. by Margaret A. Farley & Serene Jones. LC 99-23656. 296p. 1999. pap. 24.95 (*0-664-25788-7*) Westminster John Knox.

***Liberating Evangelism: Gospel Theology & the Dynamics of Communication.** Stephen L. Pickard. LC 99-26134. (CMMC Ser.). 120p. 1999. pap. 10.00 (*1-56338-279-2*) TPI PA.

Liberating Factor. Edward W. Brown, III. (Illus.). 136p. (Orig.). 1997. pap. 10.95 (*1-57502-440-3*, PO1331) Morris Pubng.

***Liberating Factor: Unmasking the Truth about Life.** 2nd ed. Edward S. Brown, III. LC 99-98074. (Illus.). 110p. 1999. pap. 9.95 (*0-9678208-0-4*) ESB Pubng.

Liberating Form: Mormon Essays on Religion & Literature. Marden J. Clark. LC 92-32725. 1992. pap. 9.95 (*1-56236-206-2*, Pub. by Aspen Bks) Origin Bk Sales.

Liberating Gospel in China: The Christian Faith among China's Minority Peoples. Ralph R. Covell. LC 94-42375. (Illus.). 320p. 1995. pap. 17.99 (*0-8010-2595-8*) Baker Bks.

Liberating Grammar. Clifford J. Vaida. LC 95-50462. 304p. 1996. 57.00 (*0-13-092859-3*) P-H.

Liberating Intimacy: Enlightenment & Social Virtuosity in Ch'an Buddhism. Peter D. Hershock. LC 95-38079. (SUNY Series in Chinese Philosophy & Culture). 236p. (C). 1996. text 62.50 (*0-7914-2981-4*); pap. text 20.95 (*0-7914-2982-2*) State U NY Pr.

Liberating Law. Beacon Hill Press Staff. (Dialog Ser.). 144p. 1999. pap. text, student ed. 6.50 (*0-8341-1708-8*) Beacon Hill.

Liberating Law: Leader's Guide. David Felter. 44p. 1998. pap., teacher ed. 5.50 (*0-8341-1709-6*) Beacon Hill.

Liberating Law: 10 Steps to Freedom. Gerard A. Reed. 208p. (Orig.). 1996. pap. 13.99 (*0-8341-1617-0*) Beacon Hill.

Liberating Leaders from the Superman Syndrome. J. Richard Love. 254p. (C). 1994. lib. bdg. 37.50 (*0-8191-9241-4*) U Pr of Amer.

Liberating Leadership. David Turner. 144p. 1998. pap. 19.95 (*1-85835-525-7*, Indust Soc) Stylus Pub VA.

Liberating Leadership: The Report. Mahen Tampoe. LC 99-488665. 128p. 1998. ring bd. 285.00 (*1-85835-516-8*, Indust Soc) Stylus Pub VA.

Liberating Life from Silence. Dale Marsh. LC 97-61157. 224p. 1997. pap. 13.25 (*1-57921-041-4*) WinePress Pub.

Liberating Literature: Feminist Fiction in America. Maria Lauret. LC 93-48839. 224p. (C). 1994. pap. 27.99 (*0-415-06516-X*, A7975) Routledge.

Liberating Liturgies, Vol. 1. Ed. by Ruth M. Fitzpatrick. (Illus.). 91p. (Orig.). (C). 1989. pap. 8.50 (*0-9623386-1-3*); pap. text 7.00 (*0-685-26436-X*) Women's Ord Conf.

Liberating Medicine. David Seedhouse. LC 90-12515. 198p. 1991. pap. 80.00 (*0-471-92844-5*) Wiley.

Liberating Memory: Our Work & Our Working-Class Consciousness. Intro. by Janet Zandy. LC 94-8042. (Illus.). 400p. (C). 1994. pap. 16.95 (*0-8135-2122-X*); text 45.00 (*0-8135-2121-1*) Rutgers U Pr.

Liberating Method: Feminism & Social Research. Marjorie L. DeVault. LC 98-31712. (Illus.). 256p. 1999. 59.50 (*1-56639-697-2*) Temple U Pr.

***Liberating Method: Feminism & Social Research.** Marjorie L. DeVault. LC 98-31712. (Illus.). 256p. 1999. pap. 19.95 (*1-56639-698-0*) Temple U Pr.

Liberating Minds: The Stories & Professional Lives of Gay, Lesbian & Bisexual Librarians & Their Advocates. Ed. by Norman G. Kester. LC 97-2117. 272p. 1997. lib. bdg. 42.50 (*0-7864-0363-2*) McFarland & Co.

Liberating Ministry from the Success Syndrome. rev. ed. Kent Hughes & Barbara Hughes. 204p. 1988. pap. 9.99 (*0-8423-2849-1*) Tyndale Hse.

***Liberating Narratives.** Stefanie Sievers. (Forecast Ser.: Vol. 2). 240p. 1999. pap. 29.95 (*3-8258-3919-2*, Pub. by CE24) Transaction Pubs.

Liberating Nature: Theology & Economics in a New Order. Paul G. King & David O. Woodyard. LC 98-45512. 160p. 1999. pap. 16.95 (*0-8298-1317-9*) Pilgrim OH.

Liberating Our Past. Ed. by Marc Miller. (Illus.). 120p. 1984. pap. 4.00 (*0-943810-18-3*) Inst Southern Studies.

Liberating Paul: The Justice of God & the Politics of the Apostle. Neil Elliott. LC 94-3540. (Bible & Liberation Ser.). 300p. (Orig.). 1994. pap. 20.00 (*0-88344-981-1*) Orbis Bks.

Liberating Paul: The Justice of God & the Politics of the Apostle. Neil Elliott. (Biblical Seminar Ser.: No. 27). 308p. (Orig.). 1995. pap. 28.50 (*1-85075-529-9*, Pub. by Sheffield Acad) CUP Services.

Liberating Pulpit. Justo L. Gonzalez & Catherine G. Gonzalez. LC 93-23500. 144p. (Orig.). 1994. pap. 13.95 (*0-687-33844-1*) Abingdon.

Liberating Rites: Understanding the Transformative Power of Ritual. Tom F. Driver. LC 97-43296. 296p. (C). 1997. pap. 27.00 (*0-8133-3455-1*, Pub. by Westview) HarpC.

Liberating Sojourn: Frederick Douglass & Transatlantic Reform. Ed. by Alan J. Rice & Martin Crawford. LC 99-23997. (Illus.). 217p. 1999. 45.00 (*0-8203-2102-8*); pap. 20.00 (*0-8203-2129-X*) U of Ga Pr.

Liberating Solutions to Alcohol Problems: Treating Problem Drinkers Without Saying No. Doug Cameron. LC 94-47466. 1995. reprint ed. 50.00 (*1-56821-462-6*) Aronson.

Liberating Systems Theory. R. L. Flood. LC 90-42963. (Contemporary Systems Thinking Ser.). (Illus.). 270p. (C). 1990. 59.50 (*0-306-43592-6*, Plenum Trade) Perseus Pubng.

Liberating the Adult Within: How to Be a Grown-Up for Good. Helen Kramer. 240p. 1995. per. 12.00 (*0-684-80060-8*, Fireside) S&S Trade Pap.

Liberating the Church: The Ecology of Church & Kingdom. Howard A. Snyder. 288p. 1996. pap. 20.00 (*1-57910-013-9*) Wipf & Stock.

Liberating the Corporate Soul: A Values-Driven Approach to Building a Visionary Organization. Richard Barrett. LC 98-29208. 248p. 1998. pap. text 18.95 (*0-7506-7071-1*) Buttrwrth-Heinemann.

Liberating the Early American Dream: A Way to Transcend the Capitalist-Communist Dilemma Nonviolently. Alfred F. Andersen. LC 85-51336. (Illus.). xiii, 273p. (Orig.). 1985. 12.00 (*0-931803-02-0*); pap. 10.00 (*0-931803-01-2*) T Paine Inst.

Liberating the Everyday Genius: A Revolutionary Guide for Identifying & Mastering Your Exceptional Gifts. Mary E. Jacobson. LC 99-30112. 416p. 1999. 24.00 (*0-345-42771-8*) Ballantine Pub Grp.

Liberating the Family: Gender & British Slave Emancipation in the Rural Western Cape, South Africa. P. Scully. LC 97-37305. (Social History of Africa Ser.). 1997. pap. text 23.95 (*0-435-07427-X*) Heinemann.

Liberating the Family? Gender & British Slave Emancipation in the Rural Western Cape, South Africa, 1823-1853. Pamela Scully. LC 97-37305. (Social History of Africa Ser.). 1997. text 60.00 (*0-435-07431-8*) Heinemann.

Liberating the Future: God, Mammon & Theology. Ed. by Joerg M. Rieger. 160p. 1998. pap. 14.00 (*0-8006-3143-9*, 1-3143) Augsburg Fortress.

Liberating the Ghosts: Photographs & Text from the March of the Living. Raphael Shevelev. LC 96-75505. 1996. audio compact disk. write for info. (*1-888803-03-7*) Lenswrk.

Liberating the Ghosts: Photographs & Text from the March of the Living. Raphael Shevelev. LC 96-75505. (Illus.). 144p. 1996. write for info. (*1-888803-01-0*); pap. 19.95 (*1-888803-00-2*) Lenswrk.

Liberating the Ghosts: Photographs & Text from the March of the Living. limited ed. Raphael Shevelev. LC 96-75505. (Illus.). 144p. 1996. write for info. (*1-888803-02-9*) Lenswrk.

Liberating the Gospels: Reading the Bible with Jewish Eyes. John S. Spong. LC 96-12598. 384p. 1997. pap. 13.00 (*0-06-067557-8*, Pub. by Harper SF) HarpC.

Liberating the Heart. Lawrence W. Jaffe. 176p. 1995. pap. 18.00 (*0-919123-43-0*, Pub. by Inner City Bks) BookWorld.

Liberating the Home, 2 bks., 1 vol. Incl. Domestic Problem: Work & Culture in the Household. Abby M. Diaz. LC 74-3988. 1974. reprint ed. Woman & Her Needs. Elizabeth Oakes Smith. LC 74-3988. 1974. reprint ed. LC 74-3988. (Women in America Ser.). 1974. 20.95 (*0-405-06107-2*) Ayer.

Liberating the Human Spirit in the Workplace. William Bickham. 2192p. 1995. 25.00 (*0-7863-0454-5*, Irwn Prfssnl) McGraw-Hill Prof.

Liberating the Laity. Paul Stevens. 177p. 1993. reprint ed. pap. 16.50 (*1-57383-012-7*) Regent College.

Liberating the Law: Creating Popular Justice in Mozambique. Albie Sachs & Gita H. Welch. LC 90-39968. 176p. (C). 1990. pap. 17.50 (*0-86232-921-3*, Pub. by Zed Books); text 55.00 (*0-86232-920-5*, Pub. by Zed Books) St Martin.

Liberating the Learner: Lessons for Professional Development in Education. Ed. by Guy Caxton et al. LC 95-36543. (Educational Management Ser.). 304p. (C). 1996. pap. 27.99 (*0-415-13127-8*) Routledge.

Liberating the Nations: Biblical Principles of Government, Education, Economics, & Politics. Stephen K. McDowell & Mark A. Beliles. 215p. 1993. pap. 12.95 (*1-887456-01-5*) Providence Found.

Liberating Theory. Michael Albert et al. LC 86-13032. 197p. 1986. 25.00 (*0-89608-307-1*) South End Pr.

Liberating Visions: Human Fulfillment & Social Justice in African-American Thought. Robert M. Franklin. LC 89-35979. 176p. (Orig.). 1990. pap. 17.00 (*0-8006-2392-4*, 1-2392) Augsburg Fortress.

Liberating Voices: Oral Tradition in African American Literature. Gayl Jones. LC 90-45559. 228p. 1991. 37.50 (*0-674-53024-1*, JONLIB) HUP.

Liberating Women from Modern Feminism. Ed. by Caroline Quest. (Choice in Welfare Ser.: No. 19). 101p. 1994. pap. 19.95 (*0-255-36353-2*, Pub. by Inst Economic Affairs) Coronet Bks.

Liberating Women's History: Theoretical & Critical Essays. Ed. by Berenice A. Carroll. 448p. 1976. pap. text 14.95 (*0-252-00569-4*) U of Ill Pr.

Liberating Words: Paul's Use of Rhetorical Maxims in First Corinthians 1-10. Rollin A. Ramsaran. LC 96-24733. 176p. 1996. pap. 17.00 (*1-56338-164-8*) TPI PA.

Liberating Young Children from Sex Roles: Experiences in Day Care Centers, Play Groups, & Free Schools. Phyllis T. Greenleaf. (Illus.). 22p. 1986. reprint ed. pap. text 6.95 (*0-940139-01-4*) Consortium RI.

Liberating Your Magnificence: 25 Keys to Loving & Healing Yourself. M. Scott Peck & Shannon Peck. 292p. 1999. pap. 13.95 (*0-9659976-5-0*, Pub. by Lifepath Pub) IPG Chicago.

Liberation: Marines in the Recapture of Guam. 1995. lib. bdg. 250.75 (*0-8490-6697-2*) Gordon Pr.

Liberation: Marines in the Recapture of Guam. Cyril J. O'Brien. (Illus.). 45p. 1996. reprint ed. pap. text 20.00 (*0-7881-3537-6*) DIANE Pub.

Liberation: Teens in the Concentration Camps & the Teen Soldiers Who Liberated Them see Teen Witnesses to the Holocaust

Liberation: The Canadians in Europe. Bill McAndrew et al. (Illus.). 160p. 1996. 50.00 (*2-920718-59-2*, Pub. by A4rt Global) Howell Pr VA.

***Liberation & Beyond: April 1946 - April 1947.** rev. ed. Ed. by John A. Hammerton. (Second World War : Vol. X). (Illus.). 814p. (YA). 2000. 35.00 (*1-58279-109-0*) Trident Pr Intl.

Liberation & Democratization: The South African & Palestinian National Movements. Mona M. Younis. LC 99-54991. (Social Movements, Protest, & Contention Ser.: Vol. 11). 240p. 1999. lib. bdg. 47.95 (*0-8166-3299-5*, Pub. by U of Minn Pr) Chicago Distribution Ctr.

***Liberation & Democratization: The South African & Palestinian National Movements.** Mona N. Younis. LC 99-54991. (Social Movements, Protest, & Contention Ser.). 240p. 1999. pap. 18.95 (*0-8166-3300-2*, Pub. by U of Minn Pr) Chicago Distribution Ctr.

Liberation & Ethics: Essays in Religious Social Ethics in Honor of Gibson Winter. Ed. by Charles Amjad-Ali & W. Alvin Pitcher. LC 83-73425. (Studies in Religion & Society). 233p. 1985. text 32.95 (*0-913348-22-8*) Ctr Sci Study.

Liberation & Orthodoxy: The Promise & Failures of Interconfessional Dialogue. Yacob Tesfai. LC 96-24932. 196p. (Orig.). 1996. pap. 20.00 (*1-57075-088-2*) Orbis Bks.

Liberation & Purity: Race, New Religious Movements & the Ethics of Postmodernity. Bhatt. LC 97-202060. 320p. 1997. 65.00 (*1-85728-423-2*, Pub. by UCL Pr Ltd); pap. 22.95 (*1-85728-424-0*, Pub. by UCL Pr Ltd) Taylor & Francis.

Liberation & Reconciliation: A Black Theology. rev. ed. J. Deotis Roberts. LC 93-38133. 150p. 1994. reprint ed. pap. 18.00 (*0-88344-951-X*) Orbis Bks.

Liberation & Reconciliation: A Black Theology. rev. ed. James D. Roberts. LC 93-38133. 141p. reprint ed. pap. 43.80 (*0-608-20270-3*, 207152900012) Bks Demand.

Liberation Christologies of Leonardo Boff & Jon Sobrino: Latin American Contributions to Contemporary Christology. Donald E. Waltermire. 150p. (C). 1993. lib. bdg. 39.50 (*0-8191-9018-7*) U Pr of Amer.

Liberation Cricket: West Indies Cricket Culture. Ed. by Hilary M. Beckles & Brian Stoddart. LC 94-11595. (Sport, Society, & Politics Ser.). 1995. text 29.95 (*0-7190-4315-8*, Pub. by Manchester Univ Pr) St Martin.

Liberation Debate: Rights at Issue. Ed. by Michael Leahy & Dan Cohn-Sherbok. LC 95-35993. 320p. (C). 1996. 70.00 (*0-415-11693-7*); pap. 25.99 (*0-415-11694-5*) Routledge.

Liberation Deferred? The Ideas of the English-Canadian Suffragists, 1877-1918. Carol L. Bacchi. (Social History of Canada Ser.). 222p. 1983. pap. text 17.95 (*0-8020-6466-3*) U of Toronto Pr.

Liberation Ecologies: Environment, Development, Social Movements. Ed. by Richard Peet & Michael Watts. LC 95-45381. 288p. (C). 1996. pap. 25.99 (*0-415-13362-9*) Routledge.

Liberation Ecologies: Environment, Development, Social Movements. Ed. by Richard Peet & Michael Watts. LC 95-45381. 288p. (C). 1996. 85.00 (*0-415-13361-0*) Routledge.

Liberation Ethics: Sources, Models, & Norms. Thomas L. Schubeck. 272p. 1993. pap. 18.00 (*0-8006-2755-5*, 1-2755, Fortress Pr) Augsburg Fortress.

Liberation from Class Oppression: Greek Translation. Harvey Jackins. 1997. pap. 2.00 (*1-885357-56-7*) Rational Isl.

Liberation from Karma & Rebirth. Sant Keshavadas. (Illus.). 164p. (Orig.). 1970. pap. 8.00 (*0-942508-02-5*) Vishwa.

Liberation from Self: A Theory of Personal Autonomy. Bernard Berofsky. 284p. (C). 1995. text 69.95 (*0-521-48045-0*) Cambridge U Pr.

Liberation Guide, Demonic Influence see Guia de Liberacion, Influencia Demoniaca

Liberation in Southern Africa-Regional & Swedish Voices: Interviews from Angola, Mozambique, Zimbabwe, Namibia, South Africa, the Frontline & Sweden. Ed. by Tor Sellstrom. 300p. 1999. pap. 31.95 (*91-7106-438-9*) Transaction Pubs.

Liberation in the Palm of Your Hand: A Concise Discourse on the Stages of the Path to Enlightenment. Pabongka Rinpoche. Ed. by Trijang Rinpoche. Tr. by Michael Richards from TIB. LC 97-19285. 1997. pap. 24.95 (*0-86171-126-2*) Wisdom MA.

Liberation Increases the Mind's Eye to See, Vol. 1. Wesley T. Ingram. Ed. & Illus. by Ricardo A. Black. 36p. (Orig.). 1996. pap. 10.00 (*0-939241-14-5*) Faith Print.

Liberation Lie. Crystal Wortman. 64p. (Orig.). 1995. pap. 5.99 (*0-89114-226-6*) Baptist Pub Hse.

Liberation Lyrics. Peggy A. Griffin. 1984. pap. text. write for info. (*1-884056-03-2*) Scribes Pubns.

Liberation Management. Tom Peters. 1994. pap. text 12.00 (*0-449-90910-7*) Fawcett.

Liberation Management: Necessary Disorganization for the Nanosecond Nineties. Tom Peters. 880p. 1994. pap. 15.00 (*0-449-90888-7*, Columbine) Fawcett.

Liberation Management: Necessary Disorganization for the Nanosecond Nineties. Tom Peters. LC 90-53071. 928p. 1992. 27.50 (*0-394-55999-1*) Knopf.

Liberation Ministry see Ministerio de Liberacion

Liberation Movements in Southern Africa. Nathan Shamuyarira. (Hans Wolff Memorial Lectures). 38p. (Orig.). 1978. pap. text 3.00 (*0-941934-21-7*) Indiana Africa.

Liberation, 1945. Ed. by Kevin Mahoney. 1995. pap. 24.95 (*0-89604-701-6*, Holocaust Library) US Holocaust.

Liberation, 1944: The Pictorial History of Guam. Don A. Farrell. Ed. by Phyllis Koontz. (Illus.). (J). (gr. 8-12). 1984. reprint ed. 15.95 (*0-930839-00-5*) Micronesian.

Liberation of Asians. Cheng Imm Tan. LC 98-183050. 1993. pap. 3.00 (*0-913937-82-7*) Rational Isl.

Liberation of Asians. Cheng I. Tan. (JPN.). 1996. pap. 3.00 (*1-885357-36-2*) Rational Isl.

Liberation of Christmas: The Infancy Narratives in Social Context. Richard A. Horsley. 202p. 1993. reprint ed. pap. 12.95 (*0-8264-0592-4*) Continuum.

Liberation of Class: P. R. Sarkar's Theory of Class & History. Tim Anderson. 72p. (Orig.). (C). 1984. pap. 3.50 (*0-9591792-2-4*) Proutist Universal.

Liberation of Dogma. Juan L. Segundo. LC 92-3654. 325p. 1992. pap. 20.00 (*0-88344-804-1*) Orbis Bks.

Liberation of France: Image & Event. Ed. by Harry R. Kedward et al. (French Studies). (Illus.). 369p. 1995. 65.00 (*1-85973-082-5*, Pub. by Berg Pubs); pap. 22.50 (*1-85973-087-6*, Pub. by Berg Pubs) NYU Pr.

Liberation of Guam: July 21-August 10, 1944. Harry Gailey. (Illus.). 256p. 1998. pap. 15.95 (*0-89141-651-X*) Presidio Pr.

Liberation of Intellect: Neo-Humanism. Prabhat Rainjan Sarkar. Tr. by Avadhutika Anamda Mitra Acarya & Acarya Vijayananda Avadhuta from BEN. 102p. (Orig.). (C). 1982. pap. 4.95 (*0-88476-011-1*) Ananda Marga.

Liberation of Italy. Luigi Villari. 1960. 10.00 (*0-8159-6108-1*) Devin.

Liberation of Italy, 1815-1870. Evelyn M. Cesaresco. LC 72-2563. (Select Bibliographies Reprint Ser.). 1980. reprint ed. 26.95 (*0-8369-6850-6*) Ayer.

Liberation of Jerusalem. 2nd ed. Uzi Narkiss. 285p. 1992. text 34.50 (*0-85303-209-2*, Pub. by M Vallentine & Co) Intl Spec Bk.

Liberation of Layla. Sarah Temple. (Special Edition Ser.: No. 736). 1992. per. 3.39 (*0-373-09736-0*, 5-09736-5) Harlequin Bks.

Liberation of Life: From the Cell to the Community. 2nd ed. Charles Birch & John B. Cobb, Jr. Ed. by Eugene C. Hargrove. 353p. (C). 1990. reprint ed. pap. 14.95 (*0-9626807-0-2*) Environ Ethics Bks.

Liberation of Little Heaven: And Other Stories. Mark Jacobs. LC 98-39432. 254p. 1999. 23.00 (*1-56947-135-5*, Pub. by Soho Press) FS&G.

Liberation of Margaret McCabe. Catherine Brophy. 168p. 1992. pap. 9.95 (*0-86327-067-0*) Dufour.

Liberation of Men. John Irwin et al. 1992. pap. 3.00 (*0-913937-59-2*) Rational Isl.

An Asterisk (*) at the beginning of an entry indicates that the title is appearing for the first time.

Liberation of Men. John Irwin et al. Tr. by Molnar Gabriella. (HUN.). 1994. 2.00 (1-885357-61-3) Rational Isl.

*Liberation of Pointe du Hoc: The 2nd Rangers at Normandy, June 6, 1944. Ed. by Joanna McDonald. 200p. 2000. pap. write for info. (1-888967-06-4) Rank & File.

Liberation of Southern Africa: Speeches of Olaf Palme. Ed. by E. S. Reddy. 1990. text 18.95 (0-7069-5317-7, Pub. by Vikas) Advent Bks Div.

Liberation of the Actor. Peter Bridgmont. 160p. 1992. pap. 16.95 (0-904693-33-3, Pub. by Temple Lodge) Anthroposophic.

Liberation of Theology. Juan L. Segundo. Tr. by John Drury. LC 76-7049. 249p. 1976. reprint ed. pap. 77.20 (0-7837-9865-2, 206059100005) Bks Demand.

*Liberation of Tolstoy: A Tale of Two Writers. Ivan Bunin. 2001. 35.00 (0-8101-1752-5) Northwestern U Pr.

Liberation of Women: A Document in the History of Egyptian Feminism. Qasim Amin. Tr. by Samiha S. Peterson from ARA. 128p. 1993. pap. 14.50 (977-424-343-9, Pub. by Am Univ Cairo Pr) Col U Pr.

Liberation of Women: A Study of Patriarchy & Capitalism. Roberta Hamilton. (Controversies in Sociology Ser.). 1978. pap. text 15.95 (0-04-301086-5) Routledge.

Liberation of Women Through Islam. Kaukab Siddique. 150p. (Orig.). (C). 1990. pap. 10.00 (0-942978-12-9) Am Soc Ed & Rel.

Liberation of Women Through Islam. Kaukab Siddique. 138p. (Orig.). 1996. pap. 10.00 (0-614-21390-8, 716) Kazi Pubns.

*Liberation Sociology. Feagin. 250p. 2000. pap. text 24.00 (0-8133-3323-7) Westview.

Liberation South, Liberation North. Novak. 100p. (Orig.). 1981. pap. 13.25 (0-8447-3464-0) Am Enterprise.

Liberation Struggles in International Law. Christopher O. Quaye. 358p. 1991. 69.95 (0-87722-712-8) Temple U Pr.

Liberation Theo.: God of ... Poor see O Deus Dos Pobres

Liberation Theologies: A Research Guide. annot. ed. Ronald G. Musto. LC 90-29156. 632p. 1991. text 25.00 (0-8240-3624-7, SS507) Garland.

Liberation Theologies: The Global Pursuit of Justice. Alfred T. Hennelly. LC 94-62051. 392p. (Orig.). 1995. pap. 19.95 (0-89622-647-6) Twenty-Third.

Liberation Theologies, Postmodernity & the Americas. Ed. by David Batstone & Eduardo Mendieta. LC 96-54817. 320p. (C). 1997. pap. 22.99 (0-415-91659-3) Routledge.

Liberation Theologies, Postmodernity & the Americas. Ed. by David Batstone & Eduardo Mendieta. LC 96-54817. 320p. (C). 1997. 75.00 (0-415-91658-5) Routledge.

Liberation Theology see Teologia de la Liberacion: Respuesta Pastoral

Liberation Theology. Berryman. 1987. pap. 6.95 (0-07-545051-8) McGraw.

Liberation Theology: A Study in Its Soteriology. Atilio R. Dupertuis. (Andrews University Seminary Doctoral Dissertation Ser.: Vol. 9). 376p. 1987. pap. 19.99 (0-943872-42-1) Andrews Univ Pr.

Liberation Theology: An Introductory Guide. Robert M. Brown. LC 92-30934. 160p. (Orig.). 1993. pap. 14.95 (0-664-25424-1) Westminster John Knox.

Liberation Theology: An Introductory Reader. Ed. by Curt Cadorette et al. LC 92-15666. 1992. 18.00 (0-88344-801-7) Orbis Bks.

Liberation Theology: Essential Facts about the Revolutionary Religious Movement in Latin America & Beyond. Phillip Berryman. 240p. 1987. 37.95 (0-87722-479-X) Temple U Pr.

Liberation Theology: Human Hope Confronts Christian History & American Power. Rosemary Radford Ruether. LC 72-92263. 202p. reprint ed. pap. 62.70 (0-8357-9487-3, 201521200092) Bks Demand.

Liberation Theology: The Church's Future Shock. Gerard Berghoef & Lester DeKoster. 197p. 1984. 15.95 (0-934874-06-9) Chr Lib Pr.

Liberation Theology: The Paradigm Shift. D. Litonjua. LC 97-39632. 84p. (C). 1997. 32.00 (0-7618-0928-7); pap. 17.50 (0-7618-0929-5) U Pr of Amer.

Liberation Theology & Critical Pedagogy in Today's Catholic Schools: Social Justice in Action. Thomas Oldenski. LC 96-51085. (Critical Education Practice Ser.: Vol. 11). (Illus.). 264p. 1997. text 44.00 (0-8153-2379-4); pap. text 22.95 (0-8153-2375-1) Garland.

Liberation Theology & Teilhard de Chardin. Eulalio Baltazar. (Teilhard Studies: No. 20). 1989. pap. 3.50 (0-89012-057-9) Am Teilhard.

Liberation Theology & the Message of Salvation: Proceedings of the Cerdic Colloquium, 4th, Strasbourg, May 10-12, 1973. Cerdic Colloquium Staff. Ed. by Rene Metz & Jean Schlick. Tr. by David G. Gelzer. LC 78-7540. (Pittsburgh Theological Monographs: No. 20). 1978. pap. 8.75 (0-915138-26-3) Pickwick.

Liberation Theology Debate. Rosino Gibellini. Tr. by John Bowden from ITA. LC 88-4854.Tr. of Il Dibattito sulla Teologia della Liberazione. 126p. 1988. reprint ed. pap. 39.10 (0-7837-9816-4, 206054500005) Bks Demand.

Liberation Theology for Quakers. Alice Lynd & Staughton Lynd. 1996. pap. 4.00 (0-87574-326-9) Pendle Hill.

*Liberation Totale. Stephen Bell.Tr. of Breaking Free. (FRE.). 32p. 1999. pap. 2.95 (1-891050-16-8) Key Ministries.

Liberations Contemporary Multimedia Art: Representation of Feeling. Alice Rubbini & Peter Weiermair. (Illus.). 144p. 1998. pap. 29.95 (88-8158-171-X, Pub. by Charta) Dist Art Pubs.

*Liberator. PAUL DENGELEGI. 1999. mass mkt. 5.99 (0-515-12689-6, Jove) Berkley Pub.

*Liberator: Voice of the Abolitionist Movement. Stephan Currie. LC 99-41296. (Words That Changed History Ser.). (Illus.). 144p. (YA). (gr. 6-9). 2000. lib. bdg. 23.70 (1-56006-672-5) Lucent Bks.

*Liberator Album: B-24s of the 2nd Air Division USAAF. Mike Bailey & Tony North. (Illus.). 192p. 1998. 39.95 (1-85780-060-5) Specialty Pr.

Liberator (Eleutherios) see Eleutherios (The Only Truth That Sets the Heart Free): The "Late Time" Avataric Revelation of the "Perfect Practice" of the Great Means to Worship & to Realize the True & Divine Spiritual Person

Liberator Pilot: The Cottontails' Battle for Oil. Vincent F. Fagan. LC 91-70428. (Illus.). 145p. (Orig.). 1991. pap. 9.95 (0-914379-02-X) CalAero.

Liberatore's Women. Liberatore. 96p. 1998. 24.95 (0-87816-617-3) Kitchen Sink.

Liberators. Notburga Tilt. 176p. (C). 1990. 42.00 (0-7223-2511-8, Pub. by A H S Ltd) St Mut.

Liberators: Exhibit & Catalog. LC 83-73114. (Center for Holocaust Studies, Documentation & Research). (Orig.). 1983. write for info. (0-9609970-3-2) Mus Jew Heritage.

Liberators: Eyewitness Accounts of the Liberation of Concentration Camps, Liberation Day Vol. I. Yaffa Eliach & Brana Gurewitsch. LC 81-70261. (Liberators Ser.). (Illus.). 59p. (Orig.). 1981. pap. 8.95 (0-9609970-1-6) Mus Jew Heritage.

Liberators: Fighting on Two Fronts in World War II. Lou Potter et al. LC 92-18791. 1992. write for info. (0-15-151283-3) Harcourt.

*Liberators: Latin America's Struggle for Independence. Robert Harvey. (Illus.). 524p. 2000. 40.00 (1-58567-072-3, Pub. by Overlook Pr) Penguin Putnam.

Liberators: Military Harley-Davidson Motorcycles Circa 1939-1952. 2nd ed. David Sarafan. Ed. by David Sarafan, Inc., Staff. (Illus.). 83p. (Orig.). 1986. pap. text. write for info. (0-9625507-0-1) D Sarafan.

Liberators & Heroes of Mexico & Central America. Marion F. Lansing. LC 72-152186. (Essay Index Reprint Ser.). 1977. reprint ed. 28.95 (0-8369-2237-9) Ayer.

Liberators & Heroes of South America. Marion F. Lansing. LC 76-156675. (Essay Index Reprint Ser.). 1977. reprint ed. 31.95 (0-8369-2321-9) Ayer.

Liberators & Patriots of Latin America: Biographies of 23 Leaders from Dona Marina (1505-1530) to Bishop Romero (1917-1980) Jerome R. Adams. LC 91-52511. (Illus.). 301p. (C). 1991. lib. bdg. 35.00 (0-89950-602-X) McFarland & Co.

Liberators from Wendling. 2nd ed. Robert E. Vickers, Jr. (Illus.). 287p. 1987. pap. text 30.00 (0-89126-033-1) MA-AH Pub.

Liberators of the Female Mind: The Shirreff Sisters, Educational Reform, & the Women's Movement, 7. Edward W. Ellsworth. LC 78-67910. (Contributions in Women's Studies: No. 7). (Illus.). 345p. 1979. 38.50 (0-313-20644-9, ELL, Greenwood Pr) Greenwood.

Liberese del Cancer. Sidney J. Minawer et al.Tr. of Cancer Free. (SPA.). 1995. per. 11.00 (0-684-81332-7, Fireside) S&S Trade Pap.

Liberia see Cultures of the World - Group 16

Liberia. D. Ellwood Dunn. LC 96-192637. (World Bibliographical Ser.). 252p. 1995. lib. bdg. 77.50 (1-85109-178-5) ABC-CLIO.

Liberia. Elwood D. Dunn & Byron S. Tarr. (Profiles of Africa Ser.). 1996. text 26.50 (0-86531-736-4) Westview.

Liberia. Martin Ford. (Profiles of Africa Ser.). 1996. text 35.00 (0-8133-1070-9) Westview.

Liberia: A Century of Survival, 1847-1947. Raymond L. Buell. (African Handbooks Ser.: Vol. 7). (Illus.). viii, 140p. 1947. pap. 10.00 (0-686-24090-1) U Museum Pubns.

Liberia: A Country Study. Ed. by Harold D. Nelson. LC 85-7393. (Army Department Pamphlet Area Handbook Ser.: No. 550-38). (Illus.). 371p. 1985. 16.00 (0-318-18782-5, S/N 008-020-01041-3) USGPO.

*Liberia: A Country Study Guide. Global Investment & Business Center, Inc. Staff. (World Country Study Guides Library: Vol. 97). (Illus.). 350p. 2000. pap. 59.00 (0-7397-2395-2) Intl Business Pubns.

Liberia: Anguish in a Divided Land. Physicians for Human Rights Staff. 12p. 1991. pap. 2.50 (0-614-14424-8) Phy Human Rights.

Liberia: History of the First African Republic, 2 vols., 1. Abayomi Cassell. (Illus.). 1988. 37.50 (0-8290-1307-5) Irvington.

Liberia: History of the First African Republic, 2 vols., 2. Abayomi Cassell. (Illus.). 1988. 39.50 (0-8290-1308-3) Irvington.

Liberia: History of the First African Republic, Vol. 1. Abayomi Cassell. (Illus.). 457p. 15.00 (0-685-41741-7) Fountainhead.

Liberia: The Evolution of Privilege. J. Gus Liebenow. LC 69-18359. (Africa in the Modern World Ser.). 269p. reprint ed. pap. 83.40 (0-608-18811-5, 203023000067) Bks Demand.

Liberia - A Country Study Guide: Basic Information for Research & Pleasure. Global Investment Center, USA Staff. (World Country Study Guide Library: Vol. 97). (Illus.). 350p. 1999. pap. 59.00 (0-7397-1494-5) Intl Business Pubns.

Liberia - Easy Prey: Child Soldiers in Liberia. Human Rights Watch Africa Staff & Human Rights Watch Children's Rights Project Staff. LC 94-78257. 88p. (Orig.). 1994. pap. 7.00 (1-56432-139-8) Hum Rts Watch.

Liberia - Flight from Terror: Testimony of Abuses in Nimba County. Africa Watch Staff. LC 90-82266. 30p. 1990. 5.00 (0-929692-58-6, Africa Watch) Hum Rts Watch.

Liberia & Sierra Leone: An Essay in Comparative Politics. Christopher S. Clapham. LC 75-32447. (African Studies: No. 20). 164p. reprint ed. pap. 46.80 (0-608-15705-8, 2031632) Bks Demand.

*Liberia Business Intelligence Report, 190 vols. Global Investment & Business Center, Inc. Staff. (World Business Intelligence Library: Vol. 97). (Illus.). 350p. 2000. pap. 99.95 (0-7397-2595-5) Intl Business Pubns.

*Liberia Business Law Handbook, 190 vols. Global Investment & Business Center, Inc. Staff. (Global Business Law Handbooks Library: Vol. 97). (Illus.). 350p. 2000. pap. 99.95 (0-7397-1994-7) Intl Business Pubns.

Liberia Business Law Handbook-98. Russian Information & Business Center, Inc. Staff. (World Business Law Library-98). (Illus.). 350p. 1998. pap. 99.00 (1-57751-839-X) Intl Business Pubns.

*Liberia Business Opportunity Yearbook. Global Investment & Business Center, Inc. Staff. (Global Business Opportunity Yearbooks Library: Vol. 97). (Illus.). 2000. pap. 99.95 (0-7397-2195-X) Intl Business Pubns.

*Liberia Business Opportunity Yearbook: Export-Import, Investment & Business Opportunities. International Business Publications, U. S. A. Staff & Global Investment Center, U. S. A. Staff. (Global Business Opportunity Yearbooks Library: Vol. 97). (Illus.). 350p. 1999. pap. 99.95 (0-7397-1295-0) Intl Business Pubns.

*Liberia Foreign Policy & Government Guide. Global Investment & Business Center, Inc. Staff. (World Foreign Policy & Government Library: Vol. 93). (Illus.). 350p. 1999. pap. 99.00 (0-7397-3591-8) Intl Business Pubns.

*Liberia Foreign Policy & Government Guide. Global Investment & Business Center, Inc. Staff. (World Foreign Policy & Government Library: Vol. 93). (Illus.). 350p. 2000. pap. 99.95 (0-7397-3795-3) Intl Business Pubns.

Liberia Genealogical Research. Roma J. Stewart. 50p. 1991. pap. 8.00 (0-9631578-0-9) Homeland IL.

Liberia in Pictures. rev. ed. Department of Geography, Lerner Publications. (Visual Geography Ser.). (Illus.). 64p. (YA). (gr. 5 up). 1988. lib. bdg. 19.93 (0-8225-1837-6, Lerner Publctns) Lerner Pub.

*Liberia Investment & Business Guide. Global Investment & Business Center, Inc. Staff. (Global Investment & Business Guide Library: Vol. 97). (Illus.). 2000. pap. 99.95 (0-7397-1795-2) Intl Business Pubns.

Liberia Investment & Business Guide: Economy, Export-Import, Business & Investment Climate, Business Contacts. Contrib. by Russian Information & Business Center, Inc. Staff. (Russia, NIS & Emerging Markets Investment & Business Library-98). (Illus.). 350p. 1998. pap. 99.00 (1-57751-896-9) Intl Business Pubns.

*Liberia Investment & Business Guide: Export-Import, Investment & Business Opportunities. International Business Publications, USA Staff & Global Investment Center, USA Staff. (World Investment & Business Guide Library-99: Vol. 97). (Illus.). 350p. 1999. pap. 99.95 (0-7397-0292-0) Intl Business Pubns.

Liberia: or Early History & Signal Preservation of the American Colony of Free Negroes on the Coast of Africa. Ed. by William Innes. LC 76-154078. (Black Heritage Library Collection). 1977. 23.95 (0-8369-8789-6) Ayer.

Liberia Will Rise Again: Reflections on the Liberian Civil Crisis. Arthur F. Kulah. LC 98-50431. 104p. 1999. pap. 10.00 (0-687-07594-7) Abingdon.

Liberian Civil War. Mark Huband. (Illus.). 256p. 1998. 49.50 (0-7146-4785-3, Pub. by F Cass Pubs); pap. 26.50 (0-7146-4340-8, Pub. by F Cass Pubs) Intl Spec Bk.

Liberian Dreams: Back-to-Africa Narratives from the 1850's. Miguel A. Centeno. Ed. by Wilson J. Moses. LC 97-37112. 272p. 1998. 50.00 (0-271-01710-4) Pa St U Pr.

Liberian Dreams: Back-to-Africa Narratives from the 1850s. Wilson J. Moses. LC 97-37112. 1998. pap. 16.95 (0-271-01711-2) Pa St U Pr.

Liberian Family. Stephen Chicoine. LC 96-16739. (Journey Between Two Worlds Ser.). (J). 1997. lib. bdg. 22.60 (0-8225-3411-8, Lerner Publctns) Lerner Pub.

Liberian Family. Stephen Chicoine. (Illus.). 56p. (gr. 3-6). 1997. pap. 8.95 (0-8225-9758-6) Lerner Pub.

Liberian Research Association Journal, No. 3. 1971. 10.00 (0-317-93946-7) Arden Assocs.

Liberian Research Association Journal, Vol. 1, No. 1. 1967. 10.00 (0-317-93942-4) Arden Assocs.

Liberian Research Association Journal, Vol. 2. 1971. 10.00 (0-317-93945-9) Arden Assocs.

Liberian Research Association Journal, Vol. 2, No. 1. 1968. 10.00 (0-317-93943-2) Arden Assocs.

Liberian Research Association Journal, Vol. 3, No. 1. 1971. 10.00 (0-317-93944-0) Arden Assocs.

Liberian Studies Journal, Vol. 1 & 2. 1971. 10.00 (0-317-93935-1) Arden Assocs.

Liberian Studies Journal, Vol. I, No. 2. 1969. 10.00 (0-317-93933-5) Arden Assocs.

Liberian Studies Journal, Vol. II. 1970. 10.00 (0-317-93934-3) Arden Assocs.

Liberian Studies Journal, Vol. IV, Nos. 1 & 2. 1972. 10.00 (0-317-93936-X) Arden Assocs.

Liberian Studies Journal, Vol. V, Nos. 1 & 2. 1974. 10.00 (0-317-93937-8) Arden Assocs.

Liberian Studies Journal, Vol. VI, Nos. 1 & 2. 1975. 10.00 (0-317-93938-6) Arden Assocs.

Liberian Studies Journal, Vol. VII, Nos. 1 & 2. 1977. 10.00 (0-317-93939-4) Arden Assocs.

Liberian Studies Journal, Vols. 1 - 7. Incl. Vol. 1. 1968-1969. 13.50 Vol. 3. 1970-1971. 13.50 Vol. 5. 1972-1974. 13.50 Vol. 2. 1969-1970. 13.50 Vol. 4. 1971-1972. 13.50 1977. 100.00 (0-318-54076-2) Arden Assocs.

Libero Bigiaretti Checkpoint: Poems of Death & Old Age: A Bilingual Edition of Posto di Blocco. Tr. by Gabriele Erasmi & Gerald Chapple. LC 91-33912. (Illus.). 240p. 1991. lib. bdg. 89.95 (0-7734-9630-0) E Mellen.

Liberta: Un Dialogo see Freedom: A Dialogue

Libertad a Traves del Perdon. Charles Stanley. (Serie Enfoque a la Familia - Focus on the Family Ser.).Tr. of Freedom Through Forgiveness. (SPA.). 199p. 1991. pap. 1.99 (1-56063-110-4, 497421) Editorial Unilit.

Libertad Bajo Palabra (Freedom on Parole) Obras Poetica (1935-1957) 2nd ed. Octavio Paz. (SPA.). 263p. 1968. 15.99 (968-16-4425-5, Pub. by Fondo) Continental Bk.

*Libertad Bajo Palabra (1935-1957) Octavio Paz. 1998. 10.95 (84-376-0775-2) Ediciones Catedra.

Libertad de Xavier Zubiri. Isabel E. Trio. LC 84-28101. (Estudios Filosoficos Ser.: No. 73). (SPA.). 204p. 1988. 5.00 (0-8477-0073-9) U of PR Pr.

Libertad del Temor. Kenneth Copeland. Tr. by Copeland, Kenneth, Publications Staff. (SPA.). 30p. (Orig.). 1985. pap. 1.00 (0-88114-309-X) K Copeland Pubns.

*Libertad en la Predicacion: A Los Cuatro Rincones Del Mundo. Barbara Bate. Tr. by Hugo L. Lopez. 116p. 1999. pap. 8.95 (0-88177-294-1) Discipleship Res.

Libertad Financiera. Larry Burkett. (Serie Conceptos Cristianos Financieros (Christian Financial Concepts) Ser.).Tr. of Financial Freedom. (SPA.). 82p. 1995. 3.29 (0-7899-0022-X, 497247) Editorial Unilit.

Libertad Incondicional. Laurie John. Tr. by Maruja Del Pozo. (Sweet Valley University Ser.: No. 2).Tr. of Love, Lies & Jessica Wakefield. (YA). (gr. 7 up). 1994. 15.60 (0-606-10530-1, Pub. by Turtleback) Demco.

Libertad Total. 4th ed. Stephen Bell.Tr. of Breaking Free. (ENG & SPA.). 21p. 1991. reprint ed. pap. 2.95 (1-891050-01-X) Key Ministries.

*Libertad y el Poder del Perdon. John F. MacArthur, Jr. (SPA.). 256p. 1999. pap. 9.99 (0-8254-1469-5, Edit Portavoz) Kregel.

Libertadores Osados. Ed. by Richard Meyer.Tr. of Daring Deliverers. (SPA., Illus.). 87p. 1997. pap., teacher ed. 5.50 (1-879892-60-X, SI-887) Editorial Bautista.

Libertando a Su Iglesia. N. Anderson.Tr. of Setting Your Church Free. 12.99 (0-7899-0168-4, 497454) Editorial Unilit.

Libertando A Su Iglesia - Setting Your Church Free. Anderson. pap. write for info. (0-7899-0379-2) Editorial Unilit.

Libertarian Anthology. Benjamin Tucker & Elbert Hubbard. 1980. lib. bdg. 250.00 (0-8490-3076-5) Gordon Pr.

Libertarian Dirt: Everything You're Not Supposed to Know about Murray Rothbard, Robert Poole, & Other Movement Icons. 73p. (Orig.). 1995. pap. 7.95 (1-886739-29-3) Socratic Pr.

Libertarian Forum, 1969-1971. Ed. by Murray N. Rothbard & Karl Hess. LC 77-172217. (Right Wing Individualist Tradition in America Ser.). 1979. reprint ed. 23.95 (0-405-00427-3) Ayer.

Libertarian Heritage Church: Constitution & Confession of Faith. 3rd ed. 81p. 1997. pap. 15.00 (0-9627423-8-4, LHC) Candlestick.

Libertarian Reader. David Boaz. LC 96-48122. 458p. 1997. 27.00 (0-684-83200-3) Free Pr.

Libertarian Theology of Freedom. Edmund A. Opitz & Charles Hallberg. LC 99-72105. 160p. 1999. 19.95 (0-87319-046-7) Hallberg Pub Corp.

Libertarianism: A Primer. David Boaz. LC 96-46012. 320p. 1997. 22.50 (0-684-83198-8) Free Pr.

Libertarianism: The Newest Oldest Movement in America & Why You Should Join. David Boaz. 1997. 21.00 (0-614-20400-3) Free Pr.

Libertarians & Liberalism: Essays in Honour of Gerard Radnitzky. Ed. by Hardy Bouillon. (Avebury Series in Philosophy). 360p. 1997. text 87.95 (1-85972-460-4, Pub. by Avebury) Ashgate Pub Co.

Libertarians & the Fight Revolution. Jason Alexander. 122p. (Orig.). 1988. pap. 9.95 (0-931826-03-9) Sitnalta Pr.

Libertas As a Political Idea at Rome. Chaim Wirszubski. (Cambridge Classical Studies). 194p. 1950. text 34.95 (0-521-06848-7) Cambridge U Pr.

*"Libertas Praestantissimum" On Human Liberty. Leo XIII, pseud. 34p. 1998. pap. 3.95 (0-935952-48-9) Angelus Pr.

Liberte: Negritude et Civilisation de l'Universal, Vol. 3. Leopold S. Senghor. (FRE.). 573p. 1977. pap. 75.00 (0-7859-1250-9, 2020046601) Fr & Eur.

Liberte, Egalite, Fratenite: The American Revolution & the European Response. Ed. by Charles W. Toth. LC 87-50833. x, 399p. 1989. 48.50 (0-87875-350-8) Whitston Pub.

Liberte en Democratie: L'Ethique Sociale et la Realite Politique en Afrique. Raymond B. Goudjo. (Publications Universitaires Europeennes Ser.: Series 23, Vol. 601). (FRE.). 281p. 1997. 54.95 (3-631-31587-2) P Lang Pubng.

Liberte et Civilisation chez les Grecs see Freedom & Civilization among the Greeks

Liberte et le Destin dans le Theatre de Jean Racine. Eleonore M. Zimmermann. (Stanford French & Italian Studies: Vol. 24). viii, 200p. 1982. pap. 56.50 (0-915838-15-X) Anma Libri.

Liberte Grande. Julien Gracq. (FRE.). 126p. 1990. reprint ed. pap. 28.95 (0-7859-4594-6) Fr & Eur.

Liberte Intericure: Un Auto-Enseignement. Suzanne Harvey. 204p. 1992. 19.95 (2-920083-65-1) Edns Roseau.

An Asterisk (*) at the beginning of an entry indicates that the title is appearing for the first time.

Liberte I: Negritude et Humanisme. Leopold S. Senghor. 21.95 (*0-685-35638-8*) Fr & Eur.

Liberte ou l'Amour. Robert Desnos. (FRE.). 168p. 1982. pap. 13.95 (*0-7859-4723-X*) Fr & Eur.

Liberte ou l'Amour & Deuil pour Deuil. Robert Desnos. (Imaginaire Ser.). (FRE.). pap. 10.95 (*2-07-027695-3*) Schoenhof.

Liberte, Pourquoi Faire? Essai. Georges Bernanos. pap. 8.95 (*0-685-37222-7*, F87780) Fr & Eur.

Liberte II: Nation et voie africaine du socialisme. Leopold S. Senghor. 16.50 (*0-685-35639-6*) Fr & Eur.

***Liberties.** Andrea Brady. 48p. 1999. pap. 7.00 (*1-893541-04-5*, Pub. by Potes Poets) SPD-Small Pr Dist.

Liberties & Communities in Medieval England: Collected Studies in Local Administration & Topography. Helen M. Cam. (C). 1963. text 17.00 (*0-85036-042-0*, Pub. by MRLN) Paul & Co Pubs.

Libertinage. Louis Aragon. (FRE.). 283p. 1977. pap. 17.95 (*0-7859-2750-6*, 2070297748) Fr & Eur.

Libertine. Louis Aragon. Tr. by Jo Levy from FRE. 160p. 1993. pap. 11.95 (*0-7145-4020-X*) Riverrun NY.

Libertine. Stephen Jeffreys. 115p. 1997. pap. 5.95 (*0-87129-756-6*, L88) Dramatic Pub.

Libertine. Stephen Jeffreys. 96p. 1995. pap. 14.95 (*1-85459-277-7*, Pub. by N Hern Bks) Theatre Comm.

Libertine, 4 vols., Set. Charlotte Dacre. LC 73-22761. 997p. 1979. reprint ed. 96.95 (*0-405-06012-2*) Ayer.

Libertine in Love. Caroline Courtney. 224p. 1984. mass mkt. 2.25 (*0-446-32591-0*, Pub. by Warner Bks) Little.

***Libertine Plays of the Restoration, Vol. 1.** Gillian Manning. 2000. pap. 12.50 (*0-460-87745-3*, Everyman's Classic Lib) Tuttle Pubng.

Libertine Reader: Eroticism & Enlightenment in Eighteenth Century France. Ed. by Michel Feher. LC 96-49079. 1324p. 1997. 54.00 (*0-942299-42-6*); pap. 32.50 (*0-942299-41-8*) Zone Bks.

Libertine's Progress: Seduction in the Eighteenth Century French Novel. Pierre Saint-Amand. Tr. by Jennifer C. Gage from FRE. LC 94-15409. 182p. 1994. 35.00 (*0-87451-686-2*) U Pr of New Eng.

***Liberty.** Lynn Curlee. LC 98-44732. (Illus.). 2000. 18.00 (*0-689-82823-3*) Atheneum Yung Read.

Liberty. Ed. by David Miller. (Oxford Readings in Politics & Government Ser.). 232p. 1991. 65.00 (*0-19-878041-9*, 12225) OUP.

Liberty! Arnold Bennett. LC 74-5300. (Collected Works of Arnold Bennett: Vol. 44). 1977. reprint ed. 19.95 (*0-518-19125-7*) Ayer.

Liberty: A Path to Its Recovery. 2nd ed. F. A. Harper. 159p. 1993. reprint ed. pap. 10.95 (*0-910614-95-4*) Foun Econ Ed.

Liberty: Contemporary Responses to John Stuart Mill. Ed. & Intro. by Andrew Pyle. LC 94-183793. (Key Issues Ser.). 466p. 1994. pap. 24.95 (*1-85506-245-3*) Bks Intl VA.

***Liberty: Contemporary Responses to John Stuart Mill.** Andrew Pyle. LC 99-52296. (Key Issues Ser.). 466p. 2000. pap. text 25.00 (*1-890318-43-4*) St Augustines Pr.

***Liberty: Its Meaning & Scope, 77.** Mordecai Roshwald. LC 99-54455. (Contributions in Philosophy Ser.). 216p. 2000. 65.00 (*0-313-31275-3*, Greenwood Pr) Greenwood.

Liberty: The Story of Cuba. Horatio S. Rubens. LC 72-111732. (American Imperialism: Viewpoints of United States Foreign Policy, 1898-1941 Ser.). 1970. reprint ed. 26.95 (*0-405-02049-X*) Ayer.

Liberty Vol. 2: Its Use & Abuse. Ignatius W. Cox. LC 36-23289. 280p. reprint ed. pap. 86.80 (*0-7837-5581-3*, 204536900002) Bks Demand.

Liberty--Liberte: The American & French Experiences. Ed. by Joseph Klaits & Michael H. Haltzel. 218p. 1991. text 29.50 (*0-943875-18-8*) Johns Hopkins.

Liberty Against Government: The Rise, Flowering, & Decline of a Famous Judicial Concept. Edward S. Corwin. LC 77-4090. 210p. 1979. reprint ed. lib. bdg. 59.50 (*0-8371-9589-6*, COLAG, Greenwood Pr) Greenwood.

Liberty Against Power: Essays by Roy A. Childs, Jr. Ed. by Joan K. Taylor. xviii, 290p. 1994. 24.95 (*0-930073-13-4*); pap. 14.95 (*0-930073-12-6*) Fox & Wilkes.

Liberty Against the Law: Some Seventeenth-Century Controversies. Christopher Hill. LC 98-130259. 368p. 1998. pap. 14.95 (*0-14-024033-0*, Penguin Bks) Viking Penguin.

Liberty & Community: Canadian Federalism & the Failure of the Constitution. Robert C. Vipond. LC 90-32115. 261p. (C). 1991. text 64.50 (*0-7914-0465-X*); pap. text 21.95 (*0-7914-0466-8*) State U NY Pr.

Liberty & Corruption - The Antulay Case & Beyond. Upendra Baxi. (C). 1989. 100.00 (*0-89771-757-0*, Pub. by Eastern Book) St Mut.

Liberty & Culture: Essays on the Idea of a Free Society. Tibor R. Machan. LC 88-32183. 288p. 1989. 27.95 (*0-87975-524-5*) Prometheus Bks.

Liberty & Free Soil Parties in the Northwest. Theodore C. Smith. LC 76-28555. (Anti-Slavery Crusade in America Ser.). 1970. reprint ed. 32.95 (*0-405-00661-6*) Ayer.

Liberty & Justice. Day. 240p. 1994. 53.95 (*0-7512-0305-X*) Ashgate Pub Co.

Liberty & Justice. J. P. Day. 256p. 1986. 49.95 (*0-7099-4523-X*, Pub. by C Helm) Routldge.

Liberty & Justice: Select Essays on Law & Lawyers in Rhode Island. Patrick T. Conley. LC 99-194540. (Illus.). 178p. 1998. 39.95 (*0-917012-99-2*) RI Pubns Soc.

Liberty & Justice - Why, How & for Whom. Amnon Katz. 16p. 1989. pap. 1.00 (*0-938245-10-4*) Inverted-A.

Liberty & Justice for Some. Matt R. Erickson. (Illus.). 232p. (Orig.). 1994. pap. 25.00 (*0-9646169-0-4*) M R Erickson.

Liberty & Law: Reflections on the Constitution in American Life & Thought. Ed. by Ronald A. Wells & Thomas A. Askew. LC 87-24582. 188p. (Orig.). reprint ed. pap. 58.30 (*0-7837-5563-5*, 204533800005) Bks Demand.

Liberty & Law under Federative Government. Britton A. Hill. 263p. 1987. reprint ed. 37.50 (*0-8377-2236-5*, Rothman) W S Hein.

Liberty & Legislation. Ed. by Richard Hoggart. 1989. 30.00 (*0-7146-3308-9*, Pub. by F Cass Pubs) Intl Spec Bk.

Liberty & Licence in the Indian Cinema. A. Vasudev. 221p. 1978. 12.95 (*0-7069-0625-X*) Asia Bk Corp.

Liberty & Locality: Parliament, Permissive Legislation & Ratepayers' Democracies in the Mid-Nineteenth Century. John Prest. 248p. 1990. 70.00 (*0-19-820175-3*) OUP.

Liberty & Morality: A Political Biography of Edward Bulwer-Lytton. Charles W. Snyder. LC 94-900. (American University Studies, Series IX: Vol. 162). 230p. (C). 1995. text 37.95 (*0-8204-2471-4*) P Lang Pubng.

Liberty & Nature: An Aristotelian Defense of Order. Douglas Rasmussen & Douglas Den Uyl. LC 90-20965. 284p. (C). 1991. 49.95 (*0-8126-9119-9*) Open Court.

Liberty & Order: Public Order Policing in a Capital City. Waddington. LC 94-33893. 224p. 1994. 65.00 (*1-85728-226-4*, Pub. by UCL Pr Ltd); pap. 24.95 (*1-85728-227-2*, Pub. by UCL Pr Ltd) Taylor & Francis.

Liberty & Order: The Theory & Practice of Italian Public Security, Policy 1848 to the Crisis of the 1890s. Richard B. Jensen. LC 91-3336. (Modern European History Outstanding Studies & Dissertations). 344p. 1991. text 20.00 (*0-8153-0472-2*) Garland.

Liberty & Poetics in Eighteenth Century England. Michael Meehan. LC 85-22404. 1985. 37.50 (*0-7099-4623-6*, Pub. by C Helm) Routldge.

Liberty & Power: The Politics of Jacksonian America. Harry Watson. LC 89-3424. 9600p. 1990. pap. 10.00 (*0-374-52196-4*) FS&G.

Liberty & Power: U. S. Diplomatic History, 1750-1945. 2nd expanded rev. ed. Walter LaFeber. (New American History Ser.). 20p. (C). 1997. reprint ed. pap. 5.00 (*0-87229-089-1*) Am Hist Assn.

Liberty & Property: Political Economy & Policymaking in the New Nation, 1789-1812. John R. Nelson. LC 86-21373. (Johns Hopkins University Studies in Historical & Political Science: 105th Series, No. 2). 240p. 1987. reprint ed. pap. 74.40 (*0-608-03739-7*, 206456400009) Bks Demand.

***Liberty & Religion: Church & State in Leiden's Reformation, 1572-1620.** Christine Kooi. LC 00-39817. (Studies in Medieval & Reformation Thought). 2000. write for info. (*90-04-11643-5*) Brill Academic Pubs.

Liberty & Sexuality: The Right to Privacy & the Making of Roe vs. Wade. David J. Garrow. LC 93-8231. 800p. 1994. 28.00 (*0-02-542755-5*, Lisa Drew) Scribner.

Liberty & Sexuality: The Right to Privacy & the Making of Roe vs. Wade. David J. Garrow. LC 97-52173. 1064p. 1998. pap. 35.00 (*0-520-21302-5*, Pub. by U CA Pr) Cal Prin Full Svc.

Liberty & Slavery: Southern Politics to 1860. William Cooper. LC 83-4311. 320p. (C). 1983. pap. 27.81 (*0-07-553588-2*) McGraw.

Liberty & Socialism: Writings of Libertarian & Socialists in Hungary, 1884-1919. Ed. by James M. Bak. 224p. (C). 1991. text 57.50 (*0-8476-7680-3*) Rowman.

Liberty & the Great Libertarians: An Anthology of Liberty, a Handbook of Freedom. Ed. by Charles T. Sprading. 362p. 1995. 24.95 (*0-930073-16-9*); pap. 14.95 (*0-930073-15-0*) Fox & Wilkes.

Liberty & the Great Libertarians: An Anthology on Liberty, a Handbook of Freedom. Ed. by Charles T. Sprading. LC 77-172233. (Right Wing Individualist Tradition in America Ser.). 1978. reprint ed. 36.95 (*0-405-00442-7*) Ayer.

Liberty & the News. Walter Lippmann. LC 94-44023. 92p. 1995. pap. 21.95 (*1-56000-809-1*) Transaction Pubs.

Liberty & the State. Charles K. Rowley. (Shaftesbury Papers: Vol. 4). 112p. 1993. pap. 13.00 (*1-85278-853-4*) E Elgar.

Liberty & Union. David Herbert Donald. 318p. (C). 1978. pap. text 31.16 (*0-669-01152-5*) HM Trade Div.

Liberty As a Way of Life: Understanding the U. S. Constitution As the Community's Formal Recognition of the Right to Exist for One's Own Good. John H. Zaugg. LC 96-95353. 127p. 1997. pap. text 8.50 (*0-9640241-2-8*) Basal Bks.

***Liberty at the Millennium.** Norris Hansell. 2000. pap. 12.95 (*0-89314-429-0*) Philos Res.

Liberty Before Liberalism. Quentin Skinner. LC 97-38824. 150p. (C). 1998. pap. text 9.95 (*0-521-63876-3*) Cambridge U Pr.

Liberty Bell. Gilbert Morris. (Liberty Bell Ser.: Vols. 1-3). 1996. boxed set 29.99 (*0-7642-8084-8*) Bethany Hse.

Liberty Bell. Gail Sakurai. LC 95-17740. (Cornerstones to Freedom Ser.). (Illus.). 32p. (J). (gr. 3-6). 1996. lib. bdg. 19.50 (*0-516-06634-X*) Childrens.

Liberty Bell. Gail Sakurai. LC 95-17740. (Cornerstones to Freedom Ser.). (Illus.). 32p. (J). (gr. 3-6). 1996. pap. 5.95 (*0-516-20067-4*) Childrens.

Liberty Bell: The Sounds of Freedom. Jon Wilson. LC 98-4332. (Illus.). 32p. (J). 1998. lib. bdg. 21.36 (*1-56766-543-8*) Childs World.

Liberty Blue: Liberty Blue. Robin L. Hatcher. 320p. 1995. mass mkt. 5.99 (*0-06-108389-5*) HarpC.

Liberty Campaign. Jonathan Dee. 288p. 1995. pap. 10.00 (*0-671-89085-9*, WSP) PB.

Liberty, Charity & Politics: Non-Profit Law & Freedom of Speech. Perri 6 & Anita Randon. (Illus.). 240p. 1995. text 82.95 (*1-85521-507-1*, Pub. by Dartmth Pub) Ashgate Pub Co.

Liberty, Charity, Fraternity: Lay Religious Confraternities at Bergamo in the Age of the Commune. Lester K. Little. LC 89-154929. (Studies in History: Vol. 51). (Illus.). 228p. 1989. pap. 25.00 (*0-87391-040-0*) Smith Coll.

***Liberty Circle.** Phil Campagna. 248p. (YA). (gr. 9-12). 2000. pap. 7.95 (*0-929141-69-5*) Napoleon Publ.

Liberty Corps No. 5: Poisoned Paradise. Mark K. Roberts. 224p. (Orig.). 1988. mass mkt. 3.95 (*0-445-20725-6*, Pub. by Warner Bks) Little.

Liberty Corps No. 6: Costa Rican Chaos. Mark K. Roberts. 208p. 1988. mass mkt. 3.95 (*0-445-20727-2*, Pub. by Warner Bks) Little.

Liberty County, Texas Cemeteries Pt. 2: East of the Trinity River. Mildred S. Wright. LC 77-75434. 1978. pap. 20.00 (*0-917016-08-4*) M S Wright.

Liberty Crisis. Bruce G. Siminoff. LC 94-76347. 275p. 1995. 24.95 (*0-944435-27-0*) Glenbridge Pub.

Liberty Defenced & Other Living Newspapers of the 1930's. Ed. by Lorraine Brown. LC 88-21425. 327p. (C). 1989. 69.00 (*0-913969-20-6*) Univ Pub Assocs.

Liberty Denied: The Current Rise of Censorship in America. rev. ed. Donna A. Demac. 180p. (Orig.). 1990. pap. 12.95 (*0-8135-1545-9*) Rutgers U Pr.

Liberty, Dominion, & the Two Swords: On the Origins of Western Political Theology (180-398) Lester L. Field, Jr. LC 94-15470. (Publications in Medieval Studies: Vol. 28). 560p. (C). 1999. text 95.00 (*0-268-01304-7*) U of Notre Dame Pr.

Liberty, 1881-1908: A Comprehensive Index. Compiled by Wendy McElroy. LC 82-1383. 162p. 1982. 30.00 (*0-9602574-2-X*) M E Coughlin.

Liberty Enlightening the World. Lionel Austone. (Illus.). 1986. 55.00 (*0-938237-04-7*) Gold Stein Pr.

Liberty, Equality . . . or Death: The French Revolution, 1789-1794. Michael L. Berkvam. (Illus.). 141p. 1989. pap. 10.00 (*1-879598-10-8*) IN Univ Lilly Library.

Liberty, Equality, & Efficiency: Apologia Pro Agathotopia Mea. J. E. Meade. LC 92-34923. (C). 1993. text 65.00 (*0-8147-5491-0*) NYU Pr.

Liberty, Equality, & Fraternity: Studies on the Era of the French Revolution & Napoleon. Joseph I. Shulim. (American University Studies: History: Ser. IX, Vol. 75). XI, 287p. (C). 1989. text 45.00 (*0-8204-0965-0*) P Lang Pubng.

Liberty, Equality & Fraternity in Wordsworth, 1791-1800. H. J. Wuscher. (Studia Anglistica Upsaliensia Ser.: No. 39). 204p. (Orig.). 1980. pap. 30.00 (*91-554-1090-1*) Coronet Bks.

Liberty, Equality, & Justice: Civil Rights, Women's Rights & the Regulation of Business, 1865-1932. Ross E. Paulson. LC 96-53409. 361p. 1997. pap. text 18.95 (*0-8223-1991-8*); lib. bdg. 54.95 (*0-8223-1982-9*) Duke.

Liberty, Equality & Modern Constitutionalism Vol. I: From Socrates & Pericles to Thomas Jefferson. George Anastaplo. (Focus Philosophical Library). 260p. 1999. pap. text 19.95 (*0-941051-62-5*) Focus Pub-R Pullins.

Liberty, Equality & Modern Constitutionalism Vol. II: From George III to Hitler & Stalin. George Anastaplo. (Focus Philosophical Library). 260p. 1999. pap. text 19.95 (*0-941051-66-8*) Focus Pub-R Pullins.

Liberty, Equality, & Plurality. Ed. by Larry May et al. LC 97-3124. 312p. 1997. 45.00 (*0-7006-0847-8*) U Pr of KS.

Liberty, Equality, & the Market: Essays by B. N. Chicherin. Ed. & Tr. by G. M. Hamburg from ENG. LC 98-13867. 440p. 1998. 45.00 (*0-300-07232-5*) Yale U Pr.

Liberty, Equality, Democracy. Ed. by Eduardo Nolla. 216p. (C). 1992. text 50.00 (*0-8147-5774-X*) NYU Pr.

Liberty, Equality, Democracy. Ed. by Eduardo Nolla. 216p. (C). 1996. pap. text 20.00 (*0-8147-5778-2*) NYU Pr.

Liberty, Equality, Fraternity. James F. Stephen. Ed. by Stuart D. Warner. LC 93-12505. 297p. 1993. 19.50 (*0-86597-110-2*); pap. 7.50 (*0-86597-111-0*) Liberty Fund.

Liberty, Equality, Fraternity: And Three Brief Essays. James F. Stephen. 312p. 1992. pap. text 17.95 (*0-226-77258-6*) U Ch Pr.

***Liberty, Equality, Fraternity: Exploring the French Revolution.** Jack Richard Censer & Lynn Avery Hunt. LC 00-33653. 2001. write for info. (*0-271-02088-1*) Pa St U Pr.

Liberty, Equality, Power, Vol. 1. 2nd ed. John M. Murrin. (C). 1998. pap. text 63.50 (*0-15-508097-0*) Harcourt.

Liberty, Equality, Power, Vol. 1. 2nd ed. John M. Murrin. (C). 1998. pap. text, teacher ed. 26.75 (*0-15-508103-9*); pap. text, student ed. 21.00 (*0-15-508099-7*, Pub. by Harcourt Coll Pubs) Harcourt.

Liberty, Equality, Power, Vol. 2. John M. Murrin. (C). 1996. pap. text, student ed. 21.00 (*0-15-500583-9*) Harcourt Coll Pubs.

***Liberty, Equality, Power, Vol. 2.** 2nd ed. John M. Murrin. (C). 1998. pap. text 57.50 (*0-15-508098-9*, Pub. by Harcourt Coll Pubs) Harcourt.

Liberty, Equality, Power, Vol. 2. 2nd ed. John M. Murrin. (C). 1998. pap. text, student ed. 21.00 (*0-15-508100-4*, Pub. by Harcourt Coll Pubs) Harcourt.

Liberty, Equality, Power: A History of the American People. John M. Murrin. (C). 1995. pap. text, teacher ed. 33.50 (*0-15-500584-7*, Pub. by Harcourt Coll Pubs) Harcourt.

Liberty, Equality, Power: A History of the American People. John M. Murrin. (C). 1996. pap. text 441.50 (*0-15-503612-2*) Harcourt Coll Pubs.

Liberty, Equality, Power: A History of the American People. 2nd ed. John M. Murrin. LC 98-84610. (C). 1998. text 76.50 (*0-15-508096-2*) Harcourt.

Liberty, Equality, Power: A History of the American People. 2nd ed. John M. Murrin. (C). 1998. pap. text 44.50 (*0-15-508104-7*, Pub. by Harcourt Coll Pubs); pap. text 44.50 (*0-15-507151-3*) Harcourt Coll Pubs.

Liberty, Equality, Power: A History of the American People, No. 1. John M. Murrin. (C). 1995. pap. text, student ed. 21.00 (*0-15-500582-0*) Harcourt Coll Pubs.

Liberty, Equality, Sisterhood: On the Emancipation of Women in Church & Society. Elizabeth Moltmann-Wendel. Tr. by Ruth Gritsch. LC 77-15240. 95p. reprint ed. pap. 30.00 (*0-608-16780-0*, 202691900053) Bks Demand.

***Liberty Falling.** Nevada Barr. LC 98-37343. (Anna Pigeon Mysteries Ser.). (Illus.). 384p. 2000. mass mkt. 6.99 (*0-380-72827-3*, Avon Bks) Morrow Avon.

Liberty Falling. Nevada Barr. LC 98-37343. (Anna Pigeon Mystery Ser.). 321p. 1999. 24.95 (*0-399-14459-5*) Putnam Pub Group.

***Liberty Falling.** large type ed. Nevada Barr. LC 99-18708. (Wheeler Large Print Bks.). 1999. 25.95 (*1-56895-711-4*, Wheeler) Wheeler Pub.

Liberty Financial Companies: Relationship Marketing on the Web. Patricia Seybold. (Illus.). 30p. 1997. pap. 295.00 (*1-892815-18-4*) Patricia Seybold.

Liberty for All? Joy Hakim. (History of US Ser.: Vol. 5). (Illus.). 192p. (YA). (gr. 5 up). 1994. pap. 10.95 (*0-19-507754-7*); text 14.95 (*0-19-507753-9*) OUP.

Liberty For All? Joy Hakim. (History of Us Ser.). 1994. 16.05 (*0-606-09420-2*, Pub. by Turtleback) Demco.

***Liberty for All.** Peter B. Kaplan & Lee A. Iacocca. LC 00-42358. 2000. write for info. (*0-9663337-1-3*) Miller Publng.

Liberty for All? (1800 - 1860) see History of U. S.

Liberty for the 21st Century: Contemporary Libertarian Thought. Ed. by Tibor R. Machan & Douglas B. Rasmussen. LC 95-19310. (Studies in Social, Political, & Legal Philosophy). 416p. (C). 1995. pap. text 26.95 (*0-8476-8058-4*); lib. bdg. 67.50 (*0-8476-8057-6*) Rowman.

Liberty Grove Site (CA-SBR-901) Archaeological Interpretations of a Late Millingstone Site on the Cucamonga Plain. Roy A. Salls. (Illus.). x, 233p. (C). 1983. pap. 25.63 (*1-55567-020-2*) Coyote Press.

Liberty in Absolutist Spain: The Habsburg Sale of Towns, 1516-1700. Helen Nader. (Johns Hopkins University Studies in Historical & Political Science). 400p. (C). 1993. reprint ed. pap. text 19.95 (*0-8018-4731-1*) Johns Hopkins.

Liberty in America. 120p. 1993. pap. 8.95 (*0-9631345-3-1*) Regal Direct.

***Liberty in Confinement: A Story of Faith in the Red Army.** Johannes Reimer.Tr. of Verweigerer. 164p. 2000. mass mkt. 3.95 (*0-921788-59-2*, Pub. by Kindred Prods) Spring Arbor Dist.

Liberty in Hume's History of England. Ed. by Nicholas Capaldi & Donald W. Livingston. 240p. (C). 1990. lib. bdg. 155.00 (*0-7923-0650-3*, Pub. by Kluwer Academic) Kluwer Academic.

***Liberty in Jesus! Evil Spirits & Exorcism - Simply Explained...** L. David Mitchell. xvi, 201p. 1999. pap. 13.95 (*1-85821-611-7*, Pub. by Pentland Pr) Pentland Pr.

Liberty in the Modern State. rev. ed. Harold J. Laski. LC 77-122064. xi, 175p. 1972. reprint ed. 35.00 (*0-678-03166-5*) Kelley.

Liberty, Justice & F'Rall: Sam Houston's Three Dogs. Marjorie Kutchinski. (Illus.). 152p. (J). (gr. k-5). 1998. pap. 9.95 (*1-57168-227-9*, Eakin Pr) Sunbelt Media.

Liberty, Justice & F'Rall: The Dog Heroes of the Texas Republic. Marjorie Kutchinski. LC 97-48558. 152p. (J). (gr. k-5). 1998. 15.95 (*1-57168-217-1*) Sunbelt Media.

Liberty, Justice & Morals: Contemporary Value Conflicts. 3rd ed. Burton M. Leiser. 579p. (C). 1985. pap. text 35.20 (*0-02-369530-7*, Macmillan Coll) P-H.

Liberty, Laughter & Tears: Reflections on the Relations of Comedy & Tragedy to Human Freedom. Horace M. Kallen. LC 68-26268. 402p. 1968. 28.00 (*0-87580-006-8*) N Ill U Pr.

Liberty Line: The Legend of the Underground Railroad. Larry Gara. LC 95-26336. 216p. 1996. pap. 17.00 (*0-8131-0864-0*) U Pr of Ky.

Liberty Line: The Legend of the Underground Railroad. Larry Gara. LC 61-6552. 211p. reprint ed. pap. 65.50 (*0-8357-4292-X*, 203709200007) Bks Demand.

Liberty Lobby & the American Right: Race, Conspiracy & Culture, 121. Frank P. Mintz. LC 84-10761. (Contributions in Political Science Ser.: No. 121). 251p. 1985. 65.00 (*0-313-24393-X*, MIL/, Greenwood Pr) Greenwood.

Liberty March: The Battle of Oriskany. Allan D. Foote. (Illus.). 1998. 35.00 (*0-925168-71-8*); pap. 20.00 (*0-925168-72-6*) North Country.

Liberty Men & Great Proprietors: The Revolutionary Settlement on the Maine Frontier, 1760-1820. Alan Taylor. LC 89-24790. (Institute of Early American History & Culture Ser.). (Illus.). xvi, 392p. (C). 1990. 49.95 (*0-8078-1909-3*); pap. 19.95 (*0-8078-4282-6*) U of NC Pr.

Liberty Nickels, 1883-1913. 1985. 17.95 (*0-307-09114-7*) St Martin.

***Liberty of Conscience: Roger Williams in America.** Edwin S. Gaustad. LC 99-17338. 248p. 1999. pap. 17.00 (*0-8170-1338-5*) Judson.

Liberty of Conscience: The History of a Puritan Idea. L. John Van Til. 200p. 1992. reprint ed. pap. 9.99 (*0-87552-460-5*) P & R Pubng.

Liberty of Conscience & the Growth of Religious Diversity in Early America, 1636-1786. Carla G. Pestana. (Illus.). 102p. 1986. pap. 30.00 (*0-916617-02-5*) J C Brown.

Liberty of Expression. Ed. by Philip S. Cook. 130p. (C). 1990. lib. bdg. 25.25 (*0-943875-14-5*) W Wilson Ctr Pr.

Liberty of London: Masters of Style & Decoration. Ed. by Stephen Calloway. LC 92-53855. (Illus.). 224p. 1992. 60.00 (*0-8212-1974-X*) Little.

Liberty of Man, Woman, & Child. unabridged ed. Robert G. Ingersoll. (Classic Reprint Ser.). 72p. 1997. reprint ed. 10.00 (0-936128-58-5) De Young Pr.

Liberty of Obedience. Elisabeth Elliot. 94p. 1987. reprint ed. pap. 4.99 (0-89283-358-0, Vine Bks) Servant.

Liberty of Rome, 2 vols., Set. Samuel Eliot. (Notable American Authors Ser.). 1992. reprint ed. lib. bdg. 75.00 (0-7812-2788-7) Rprt Serv.

Liberty of the Press, Speech & Public Worship: Being Commentaries on the Liberty of the Subject & Laws of England. James Paterson. xxxi, 568p. 1985. reprint ed. 52.00 (0-8377-1019-7, Rothman) W S Hein.

Liberty or Death. Ray Hemmings. pap. text 21.00 (0-85315-907-6) Lawrence & Wishart.

Liberty or Death: India's Journey to Independence & Division. Patrick French. 467p. 1999. 14.95 (0-00-655045-2, Pub. by HarpC) Trafalgar.

Liberty or Death: The Northern Campaigns in the American Revolutionary War. Gregory T. Edgar. 397p. (Orig.). 1994. pap. text 29.00 (0-7884-0023-1) Heritage Bk.

Liberty or Equality: The Challenge of Our Time. rev. ed. Erik Von Kuehnelt-Leddihn. 395p. 1993. pap. 14.95 (0-931888-51-4) Christendom Pr.

Liberty or Love! Robert Desnos. Tr. by Terry Hale from FRE. 1994. reprint ed. pap. 12.99 (0-947757-66-X, Pub. by Atlas Pr) Serpents Tail.

Liberty, Order & Justice: An Introduction to the Constitutional Principles of American Government. James McClellan. LC 89-10544. 1989. 16.95 (0-940973-08-1); pap. write for info. (0-940973-09-X) James River.

***Liberty, Order & Justice: An Introduction to the Constitutional Principles of American Government.** 2nd rev. ed. James McClellan. LC 99-46334. 2001. 25.00 (0-86597-255-9); pap. 15.00 (0-86597-256-7) Liberty Fund.

Liberty Pole. Maynard Hatcher. Ed. by Jane Weinberger. LC 87-50395. 200p. (Orig.). 1987. pap. 5.00 (0-932433-32-4) Windswept Hse.

Liberty Primer. 2nd ed. W. Alan Burris. LC 83-61673. (Illus.). 562p. (Orig.). (C). 1983. pap. 7.95 (0-9608490-1-7) Society Indiv Lib.

Liberty, Property, & Government: Constitutional Interpretation Before the New Deal. Ed. by Ellen F. Paul & Howard Dickman. LC 88-38771. (SUNY Series in the Constitution & Economic Rights). 303p. (C). 1989. text 64.50 (0-7914-0086-7); pap. text 21.95 (0-7914-0087-5) State U NY Pr.

Liberty, Property, & Privacy: Toward a Jurisprudence of Substantive Due Process. Edward Keynes. LC 95-12709. 256p. 1996. 45.00 (0-271-01509-8); pap. 18.95 (0-271-01510-1) Pa St U Pr.

Liberty, Property, & the Foundations of the American Constitution. Ed. by Ellen F. Paul & Howard Dickman. LC 88-11614. (SUNY Series in the Constitution & Economic Rights). 181p. (C). 1988. pap. text 19.95 (0-88706-915-0) State U NY Pr.

Liberty, Property, & the Future of Constitutional Development. Ed. by Ellen F. Paul & Howard Dickman. LC 89-21639. (SUNY Series in the Constitution & Economic Rights). 341p. (C). 1990. text 69.50 (0-7914-0303-3); pap. text 24.95 (0-7914-0304-1) State U NY Pr.

Liberty, Right & Nature: Individual Rights in Later Scholastic Thought. Annabel S. Brett. LC 96-15357. (Ideas in Context Ser.: No. 44). 243p. (C). 1997. text 59.95 (0-521-56239-2) Cambridge U Pr.

Liberty Rose. Stef Ann Holm. Ed. by Carolyn Tolley. 352p. (Orig.). 1993. per. 5.50 (0-671-74125-X) PB.

Liberty Secured? Britain Before & after 1688. Ed. by James R. Jones. LC 91-21532. (Making of Modern Freedom Ser.). 424p. (C). 1992. 49.50 (0-8047-1988-8) Stanford U Pr.

Liberty, Servitude & the Income Tax: A Concise Pocket Guide for the Tax Revolution. 22p. Date not set. pap. 5.00 (0-9671337-0-X) Freedom Pr PA.

Liberty Ship: The Voyages of the "John W. Brown," 1942-1946. Sherod Cooper. LC 97-1519. (Illus.). 264p. 1997. 34.95 (1-55750-135-1) Naval Inst Pr.

Liberty Ships. John G. Bunker. LC 79-6103. (Navies & Men Ser.). (Illus.). 1980. reprint ed. lib. bdg. 31.95 (0-405-13032-5) Ayer.

Liberty Ships. 2nd ed. L. A. Sawyer & W. H. Mitchell. 250p. 1985. pap. 40.00 (1-85044-049-2) LLP.

Liberty Ships Eastward. George Elliott. LC 95-42722. 1995. write for info. (0-931675-02-2) Prov Pr Maine.

Liberty Ships in Peacetime. I. G. Stewart. (Illus.). 300p. 1993. 75.00 (0-646-05987-4, Pub. by I Stewart Marine) Maiden Voyage.

Liberty Square: A Kate Delafield Mystery. Katherine V. Forrest. LC 95-46809. 256p. 1996. pap. 21.95 (0-425-15467-X, Prime Crime) Berkley Pub.

Liberty Square: A Kate Delafield Mystery. Katherine V. Forrest. 256p. 1997. mass mkt. 5.99 (0-425-15899-3, Prime Crime) Berkley Pub.

Liberty Street. William Andris. LC 80-51206. 460p. 1980. 14.95 (0-9604278-0-5) St Basil Pr.

Liberty, the Castle of Indolence & Other Poems. James Thomson. Ed. by James Sambrook. (Oxford English Texts Ser.). 462p. 1986. text 150.00 (0-19-812759-6) OUP.

Liberty, the Story of Cuba. Horatio S. Rubens. LC 79-107075. reprint ed. 21.50 (0-404-00633-7) AMS Pr.

***Liberty Through the Cross.** 136p. 2000. pap. 10.95 (1-885857-25-X) Four Wnds Pubng.

Liberty Tree: The Beginning of the American Revolution. Lucille R. Penner. LC 95-23715. (Picture Landmark Ser.). 1998. lib. bdg. 15.99 (0-679-93482-0) Random.

Liberty Tree: The Beginning of the American Revolution. Lucille R. Penner. LC 95-23715. (Picture Landmark Ser.). 48p. (J). (gr. 2-4). 1998. 14.00 (0-679-83482-6) Random.

Liberty under Law: American Constitutionalism, Yesterday, Today & Tomorrow. Ed. by Kenneth L. Grasso & Cecilia R. Castillo. LC 96-53643. 232p. 1997. 37.50 (0-7618-0691-1); pap. 18.95 (0-7618-0692-X) U Pr of Amer.

Liberty under Law: American Constitutionalism, Yesterday, Today & Tomorrow. 2nd ed. Cicelia R. Castillo. Ed. by Kenneth L. Grasso. LC 97-25976. 254p. (C). 1997. pap. 20.95 (0-7618-0852-3) U Pr of Amer.

Liberty under Siege: American Politics, 1976-1988. Walter Karp. 1993. pap. 14.95 (1-879957-11-6, Franklin Sq Pr) Harpers Mag Found.

Liberty, Utility & Anarchy: A Philosophical & Economic Reconciliation. J. C. Lester. (Studies in Social, Political, & Legal Philosophy: No. 70). 256p. 1998. 62.50 (0-8476-8451-2); pap. 23.95 (0-8476-8452-0) Rowman.

***Liberty, Virtue, & Happiness: The Story of Economic Freedom in America.** Edward W. Ryan. LC 98-37418. 1998. 34.00 (1-56072-620-2) Nova Sci Pubs.

Liberty, Virtue, & Progress: Northerners & Their War for the Union. 2nd ed. Earl J. Hess. LC 97-15035. (North's Civil War Ser.: No. 3). xx, 154p. 1997. 24.95 (0-8232-1798-1) Fordham.

Liberty We Seek: Loyalist Ideology in Colonial New York & Massachusetts. Janice Potter. 256p. 1983. 41.00 (0-674-53026-8) HUP.

***Liberty Worth the Name: Locke on Free Agency.** Gideon Yaffe. 200p. 2000. 49.50 (0-691-04966-1); pap. 16.95 (0-691-05706-0) Princeton U Pr.

Liberty's Daughters: The Revolutionary Experience of American Women, 1750-1800. Mary B. Norton. LC 96-12247. (Illus.). 400p. 1996. pap. text 16.95 (0-8014-8347-6) Cornell U Pr.

***Liberty's Excess: Short Fictions.** Lidia Yuknavitch. 175p. 2000. pap. 12.95 (1-57366-084-1) Fiction Coll.

Liberty's Five Flags. Forrest McDonald. Ed. by George F. Cahill. (Flag Plaza Standard Ser.: Special Edition: Vol. 4). (Illus.). 12p. (Orig.). 1988. pap. 2.50 (0-934021-06-6) Natl Flag Foun.

Liberty's Flame. Linda Covington. 432p. 1994. mass mkt. 4.50 (0-8217-4699-5, Zebra Kensgtn) Kensgtn Pub Corp.

Liberty's Impact: The World Views, 1776. Durand Echeverria et al. (Illus.). 76p. 1976. pap. 5.00 (0-685-54613-6) J C Brown.

Liberty's Lady. Karen Harper. (Mira Bks.). 1998. per. 5.50 (1-55166-433-X, 1-66433-3, Mira Bks) Harlequin Bks.

Liberty's Legacy: Our Celebration of the Northwest Ordinance & the United States Constitution. John C. Dann & Cecil K. Byrd. Ed. by Howard H. Peckham. 116p. 1987. pap. 5.00 (0-87758-020-0) Ohio Hist Soc.

Libesbegrieff bei Augustine see Love & Saint Augustine

Libi, Titi, Libri XXVIII-XXX. Ed. by Walsh. (LAT.). 1986. 23.95 (3-322-00269-1, T1497, Pub. by B G Teubner) U of Mich Pr.

Libidinal Currents. Joseph A. Boone. LC 97-30717. 528p. 1997. pap. text 18.95 (0-226-06467-0) U Ch Pr.

Libidinal Economy. Jean-Francois Lyotard. Tr. by Iain H. Grant. LC 91-32761. (Theories of Contemporary Culture Ser.). 320p. 1993. text 51.95 (0-253-33614-7); pap. text 22.95 (0-253-20728-2, MB-728) Ind U Pr.

Libidinal Jitters. L. D. Holcomb. 315p. 1983. pap. 8.95 (0-915413-00-0) Sunfisher Bks.

Libido: The French Existential Theories. Alphonso Lingis. LC 84-48483. (Studies in Phenomenology & Existential Philosophy). 144p. reprint ed. pap. 44.70 (0-7837-3715-7, 205789300009) Bks Demand.

Libido Breakthrough: A Doctor's Guide to Restoring Sexual Vigor & Peak Health. Stuart L. Fine. 1999. 23.00 (0-7871-1977-6) NewStar Media.

***Libido Dominandi: Sexual Liberation & Political Control.** E. Michael Jones. LC 99-51925. 672p. 2000. 40.00 (1-890318-37-X, Pub. by St Augustines Pr) Chicago Distribution Ctr.

Libido into Literature: The "Primera Epoca" of Benito Perez Galdos. Clark M. Zlotchew. LC 93-338. (Milford Series: Popular Writers of Today: Popular Writers of Today: Vol. 60). 136p. 1993. pap. 19.00 (0-89370-298-6) Millefleurs.

Libido Sexualis: Studies in the Psychosexual Laws of Love Verified by Clinical Sexual Case Histories. Albert Moll. Tr. by David Berger from GER. LC 72-11288. reprint ed. 36.00 (0-404-57481-5) AMS Pr.

Libio de las Hechos. S. Horton.Tr. of Book of Acts. (SPA.). 288p. 1983. pap. 9.99 (0-8297-1305-0) Vida Pubs.

Libra. (Total Horoscopes, 1995 Ser.). 272p. 1994. pap. text 4.50 (0-515-11417-0, Jove) Berkley Pub.

Libra. (Parker's Love Signs Ser.). 1996. 8.95 (0-614-20706-1) DK Pub Inc.

Libra. (Cosmopolitan a Bedside Astrologer Book Ser.). (Illus.). 24p. (J). 1997. pap. write for info. (1-56144-966-0, Honey Bear Bks) Modern Pub NYC.

Libra. Ariel Books Staff. (Tiny Tomes Ser.). 128p. 1997. 3.95 (0-8362-2668-2, Arie Bks) Andrews & McMeel.

Libra. Lucille Callard. (Astro-Pups: Your Sign, Your Dogs Ser.). (Illus.). 60p. 1991. pap. 9.95 (1-881038-06-8) Penzance Pr.

Libra. Don DeLillo. (Contemporay American Fiction Ser.). 464p. 1991. pap. 13.95 (0-14-015604-6, Penguin Bks) Viking Penguin.

Libra. Jove Publications Incorporated, Staff. (Total Horoscopes Ser.). 272p. 1997. mass mkt. 5.99 (0-515-12114-2, Jove) Berkley Pub.

Libra. Jove Publications Staff. (Total Horoscopes Ser.). 1998. mass mkt. 5.99 (0-515-12310-2, Jove) Berkley Pub.

Libra. Teresa Moorey. (Reach Your Potential Ser.). (Illus.). 96p. 1998. pap. 9.95 (0-340-69715-6, Pub. by Headway) Trafalgar.

Libra. Derek Parker & Julia Parker. LC 92-52790. (Sun & Moon Signs Library). (Illus.). 58p. 1993. 8.95 (1-56458-090-3) DK Pub Inc.

Libra. Julia Parker & Derek Parker. (Love Signs Library). 64p. 1996. 8.95 (0-7894-1095-8) DK Pub Inc.

Libra: Astro-Numerogia. Michael J. Kurban. Tr. by Loretta H. Kurban from ENG. LC 86-91273. (SPA., Illus.). (Orig.). 1992. pap. 8.00 (0-938863-51-7) HCI Pr.

Libra: Astro-Numerology. 2nd ed. Michael J. Kurban. (Illus.). 50p. 1991. pap. 8.00 (0-938863-15-0) HCI Pr.

Libra: Astrological Horoscopes for 1999. Teri King. (Teri King Ser.). 1998. pap. 4.95 (1-86204-281-0, Pub. by Element MA) Penguin Putnam.

Libra: Etudes Roumanies Offertes a Willem Noomen a L'Occasion de Son Soixantieme Anniversaire. Ed. by I. P. Culianu. (FRE.). 204p. (Orig.). (C). 1983. pap. text 46.15 (3-11-013319-9) Mouton.

***Libra: Learning & Inquiry-Based Reuse Adoption.** Sidney C. Bailin. LC 00-33487. 2000. write for info. (0-7803-6009-5) IEEE Standards.

Libra: Little Birth Sign. Andrews & McMeel. (Illus.). 80p. 1994. 4.99 (0-8362-3075-2) Andrews & McMeel.

***Libra: Secrets of the Sun Signs.** Ed. by Jennifer Fox. (Illus.). 272p. 2000. pap. 5.95 (0-7407-1075-3) Andrews & McMeel.

***Libra: Your Personal Horoscope.** rev. ed. American Astroanalysts Institute Staff. (Astroanalysis Ser.). 2000. pap. 12.95 (0-425-17564-2) Berkley Pub.

Libra: Your Sun-&-Moon Guide to Love & Life. Ariel Books Staff. 374p. (Orig.). 1997. pap. 5.95 (0-8362-3562-2, Arie Bks) Andrews & McMeel.

Libra: 2000 Edition, 1 vol. Jove Books Publishing Staff. 1999. mass mkt. 5.99 (0-515-12542-3, Jove) Berkley Pub.

Libra Mini Edition. Ariel. (Women's Astrology Library). 1999. 4.95 (0-8362-7890-9) Andrews & McMeel.

Libra, Angel or Vampire. Stephanie Queen. 304p. 1997. 21.95 (1-57087-336-4) Prof Pr NC.

Libra Love Signs, 1995. 1995. mass mkt. 1.29 (0-440-22126-9) Dell.

Libra '98. Berkley Publishing Staff. (Berkley Super Horoscopes Ser.). 256p. 1997. pap. 6.99 (0-425-15892-6) Berkley Pub.

Libra '99. Astrology World Staff. (Super Horoscopes Ser.). 1998. pap. 7.99 (0-425-16330-X) Berkley Pub.

Libra Purse Book, 1995. 1994. mass mkt. 0.99 (0-440-60238-6) Dell.

Libra Purse Book, 1994. 1994. mass mkt. 1.25 (0-440-60234-3) Dell.

Libra Purse Book, 1996. 1995. mass mkt. 1.19 (0-440-60252-1) Dell.

Libra Rising. Douglas M. Baker. (Esoteric Astrology: The Rising Signs Ser.). 1980. pap. 7.50 (0-906006-53-8, Pub. by Baker Pubns) New Leaf Dist.

Libra Sun Sign. Douglas M. Baker. (Astrological Sun Sign Ser.). 1972. pap. 5.50 (0-906006-23-6, Pub. by Baker Pubns) New Leaf Dist.

***Libra 2001.** Teri King. (Astrological Horoscopes Ser.). 2000. pap. 4.95 (1-86204-783-9, Pub. by Element MA) Penguin Putnam.

***Libra 2001.** Ed. by Jove Books Publishing Staff. (Total Horoscopes Ser.). 272p. 2000. mass mkt. 5.99 (0-515-12821-X, Jove) Berkley Pub.

Librairie Francaise, Tables Decennales, 7 tomes Incl. 1956-1965. 275.00 Set. 1946-1955., **3 tomes** 175.00 (Cercle de la Librairie). write for info. (0-318-52037-0) Fr & Eur.

Libranos del Mal. 2nd ed. Don Basham.Tr. of Deliver us from Evil. (SPA.). 240p. 1991. pap. text 7.99 (0-88113-313-2) Caribe Betania.

Librarian. Jack Rudman. (Career Examination Ser.: C-438). 1994. pap. 27.95 (0-8373-0438-5) Nat Learn.

Librarian & Reference Queries: A Systematic Approach. Gerald Jahoda & Judith S. Braunagel. LC 79-6939. (Library & Information Science Ser.). 192p. 1980. text 49.95 (0-12-379760-8) Acad Pr.

Librarian-Author: A Practical Guide on How to Get Published. Ed. by Betty-Carol Sellen. LC 85-4953. 250p. 1985. pap. 38.50 (0-918212-83-9) Neal-Schuman.

Librarian V. Jack Rudman. (Career Examination Ser.: C-2792). 1994. pap. 29.95 (0-8373-2792-X) Nat Learn.

Librarian IV. Jack Rudman. (Career Examination Ser.: C-2791). 1994. pap. 29.95 (0-8373-2791-1) Nat Learn.

Librarian from the Black Lagoon. Mike Thaler. 32p. (J). 1997. pap. text 2.99 (0-590-50311-1, Cartwheel) Scholastic Inc.

Librarian from the Black Lagoon. Mike Thaler. (J). 1997. 8.19 (0-606-11559-5, Pub. by Turtleback) Demco.

Librarian in the University: Essays on Membership in the Academic Community. Ed. by H. Palmer Hall & Caroline Byrd. LC 90-21791. 203p. 1991. 29.00 (0-8108-2399-3) Scarecrow.

Librarian-Library Educator: An Autobiography & Planning for the Future. Martha Boaz. LC 87-4349. 322p. 1987. 31.00 (0-8108-1988-0) Scarecrow.

Librarian of Congress Annual Report, 1995. Audrey Fischer. 186p. 1996. per. 8.00 (0-16-061802-9, Library of Cong) USGPO.

***Librarian of Congress Annual Report, 1997.** Audrey Fischer. 189p. 1998. per. 9.50 (0-16-061808-8, Library of Cong) USGPO.

Librarian of the Night. Avonelle Kelsey. 250p. 6.95 (1-885351-03-8) Cheval Intl.

Librarian I. Jack Rudman. (Career Examination Ser.: C-2788). 1994. pap. 27.95 (0-8373-2788-1) Nat Learn.

Librarian, the Scholar, & the Future of the Research Library, 66. Eldred Smith. LC 89-25665. (Contributions in Librarianship & Information Science Ser.: No. 66). 119p. 1990. 47.95 (0-313-27210-7, SLX/, Greenwood Pr) Greenwood.

Librarian III. Jack Rudman. (Career Examination Ser.: C-2790). 1994. pap. 29.95 (0-8373-2790-3) Nat Learn.

Librarian Trainee. Jack Rudman. (Career Examination Ser.: C-2864). 1994. pap. 23.95 (0-8373-2864-0) Nat Learn.

Librarian II. Jack Rudman. (Career Examination Ser.: C-2789). 1994. pap. 29.95 (0-8373-2789-X) Nat Learn.

Librarian Who Measured the Earth. Kathryn Lasky. LC 92-42656. (Illus.). 48p. (J). (gr. k-3). 1994. 16.95 (0-316-51526-4, Joy St Bks) Little.

Librarians see Community Helpers Series

Librarians. Dee Ready. (Community Helpers Ser.). (Illus.). 24p. (J). (gr. k-3). 1997. lib. bdg. 14.00 (0-516-20877-2) Childrens.

Librarians A to Z. Jean Johnson. (Walker's Community Helpers Ser.). (Illus.). 48p. (J). (gr. 1-3). 1989. 11.95 (0-8027-6841-5); lib. bdg. 12.85 (0-8027-6842-3) Walker & Co.

Librarians' Agreements: Bargaining for a Heterogeneous Profession. John W. Weatherford. LC 87-35605. 306p. 1988. 39.50 (0-8108-2073-0) Scarecrow.

Librarians & Labor Relations: Employment under Union Contracts, 35. Robert C. O'Reilly & Marjorie I. O'Reilly. LC 80-1049. (Contributions in Librarianship & Information Science Ser.: No. 35). 191p. 1981. 52.95 (0-313-22485-4, OLL/) Greenwood.

Librarians & Professional Status: Continuing Professional Development & Academic Libraries. Norman Roberts & Tania Konn. LC 91-230493. 222p. Date not set. reprint ed. pap. 68.90 (0-608-20729-2, 207182700002) Bks Demand.

Librarians & Publishers in the Scholarly Information Process: Transition in the Electronic Age: A Report from the Joint Working Group on Professional & Scholarly Information in the Electronic Age. Linda Scovill et al. LC 94-48709. 1994. 25.00 (0-933636-30-X) AAP.

Librarians & the Awakening from Innocence: Collected Papers. Herbert S. White. (Professional Librarian Ser.). 388p. 1989. 40.00 (0-8161-1892-2, Hall Reference) Macmillan.

Librarians & the Selection of Publications from Small Presses: Implications for Intellectual Freedom. Y. G. Lulat. 176p. 1996. pap. text 29.90 (0-944265-15-4, Cerebrum Bks); lib. bdg. 39.90 (0-944265-14-6, Cerebrum Bks) Librosmondiale.

Librarians Are Human: Memories in & Out of the Rare-Book World, 1907-1970. Margaret B. Stillwell. LC 73-85910. 441p. reprint ed. pap. 136.80 (0-608-11288-7, 200206400011) Bks Demand.

Librarians As Learners, Librarians As Teachers: The Diffusion of Internet Expertise in the Academic Library. Ed. by Patricia O'Brien Libutti. LC 99-13042. 308p. (C). 1999. pap. 27.00 (0-8389-8003-1) Assn Coll & Res Libs.

Librarian's Companion: A Handbook of Thousands of Facts & Figures on Libraries, Librarians, Books, Newspapers, Publishers, Booksellers. Vladimir F. Wertsman. LC 96-5802. 248p. 1996. lib. bdg. 67.95 (0-313-29975-7, Greenwood Pr) Greenwood.

Librarian's Complete Guide to Involving Parents Through Children's Literature: Grades K-6. Anthony D. Fredericks. LC 97-256. (Illus.). 180p. (Orig.). 1997. pap. 26.00 (1-56308-538-0) Libs Unl.

Librarian's Cookbook. Ed. by Betty-Carol Sellen. (Illus.). 445p. (Orig.). 1989. pap. text 27.50 (1-55570-042-X) Neal-Schuman.

Librarian's Genealogy Notebook: A Guide to Resources. D. Elizabeth Moore. LC 98-19110. x, 142 p. 1998. 32.00 (0-8389-0744-X) ALA.

Librarians Glossary. Leonard M. Harrod. (C). 1977. text 48.50 (0-89158-727-6) Westview.

Librarian's Guide to Genealogical Research. James Swan. LC 98-26997. (Handbook Ser.). (Illus.). 120p. 1998. pap. 19.00 (1-57950-011-0) Highsmith Pr.

Librarian's Guide to Homeschooling Resources. Susan G. Scheps. LC 98-6218. 156p. 1998. 25.00 (0-8389-0737-7) ALA.

Librarian's Guide to Microcomputer Technology & Applications. Lawrence A. Woods & Nolan F. Pope. LC 83-13548. 209p. 1983. pap. 27.50 (0-313-25778-7, Greenwood Pr) Greenwood.

Librarian's Guide to Partnerships. Ed. by Sherry Lynch. LC 99-14137. (Handbook Ser.). (Illus.). 99p. 1999. pap. 19.00 (1-57950-002-1, 95681) Highsmith Pr.

***Librarian's Guide to Public Records.** rev. ed. Ed. by Michael Sankey & James Flowers. (Public Record Research Library). 600p. 2000. per. 39.50 (1-879792-56-7) BRB Pubns.

Librarians Help Us Find Information. Carol Greene. LC 98-20331. (Community Helpers Ser.). (Illus.). 32p. (J). 1998. lib. bdg. 21.36 (1-56766-558-6, 65586) Childs World.

Librarian's Idea Book: Research, Innovations, Solutions from ALA Poster Sessions. Katherine J. Harig et al. LC 92-25508. 198p. (C). 1993. pap. text 9.00 (0-8389-0593-5) ALA.

Librarians in Fiction: A Critical Bibliography. Grant Burns. LC 98-10695. 191p. 1998. pap. 29.95 (0-7864-0499-X) McFarland & Co.

Librarians in Search of Science & Identity: The Elusive Profession. George E. Bennett. LC 88-14679. 231p. 1988. 29.00 (0-8108-2075-7) Scarecrow.

Librarian's Internet Companion. Timothy McLain. Ed. by Gregory Giagnocavo & Chris N. Sturm. (Illus.). 200p. (Orig.). 1995. pap. 39.95 (0-932577-25-3) Wentworth Worldwide.

Librarian's Legal Companion. Jonathan S. Tryon. LC 93-39607. 1994. 40.00 (0-8161-1961-9, G K Hall Lrg Type); 30.00 (0-8161-1962-7, G K Hall & Co) Mac Lib Ref.

An Asterisk (*) at the beginning of an entry indicates that the title is appearing for the first time.

Librarian's Manual. Ed. by Ferne L. Weimer & Kenneth D. Gill. 350p. 1994. pap. text 25.00 (*0-9638050-0-2*) Assn Chr Libs.

Librarians on the Internet: Impact on Reference Services. Ed. by Robin Kinder. LC 94-18593. (Reference Librarian Ser.: Nos. 41 & 42). (Illus.). 410p. 1994. lib. bdg. 69.95 (*1-56024-672-3*) Haworth Pr.

Librarian's Open Shelf: Essays on Various Subjects. Arthur E. Bostwick. LC 67-23182. (Essay Index Reprint Ser.). 1977. 23.95 (*0-8369-0226-2*) Ayer.

Librarian's Planning Handbook for a Read-to-Me Club. Julie Todaro-Cagle. (Illus.). 96p. (Orig.). (C). 1995. pap. text 20.00 (*0-7881-2357-2*) DIANE Pub.

Librarian's Psychological Commitments: Human Relations in Librarianship, 27. Florence E. DeHart. LC 79-7059. (Contributions in Librarianship & Information Science Ser.: No. 27). 208p. 1979. 49.95 (*0-313-21329-1*, DLC/, Greenwood Pr) Greenwood.

Librarian's Puzzle: MARC-CIP-ISBN-ISSN-RLIN. 2nd ed. Ursula R. Noher & F. O. Garcia. 130p. 1993. 15.00 (*0-929928-15-6*) Fog Pubns.

Librarian's Quick Guide to Internet Resources. Jenny Semenza. LC 99-36888. 88p. 1999. pap. 19.00 (*1-57950-035-8*) Highsmith Pr.

***Librarian's Secret Wish.** Carol Grace. (Silhouette Romance Ser.: Vol. 1473). 2000. mass mkt. 3.50 (*0-373-19473-0*, 1-19473-7) Harlequin Bks.

Librarians Thesaurus: A Concise Guide to Library & Information Terms. Mary E. Soper et al. LC 90-147. 225p. (C). 1990. pap. text 25.00 (*0-8389-0530-7*, 0530-7) ALA.

Librarian's Yellow Pages: Publications, Products & Services for Libraries & Information Centers. (Illus.). 310p. 1997. pap. text. write for info. (*0-9635270-4-5*) Garance.

Librarianship: A Third World Perspective, 59. Rosario G. De Horowitz. LC 87-17741. (Contributions in Librarianship & Information Science Ser.: No. 59). 150p. 1988. 47.95 (*0-313-25507-5*, HLY/, Greenwood Pr) Greenwood.

Librarianship: The Erosion of a Woman's Profession. Roma Harris. Ed. by Peter Hernon & Charles R. McClure. (Information Management, Policies & Services Ser.). 192p. (C). 1992. pap. 39.50 (*0-89391-941-1*); text 73.25 (*0-89391-840-7*) Ablx Pub.

Librarianship & Information Work Worldwide, 1998. Ed. by G. MacKenzie & Maurice B. Line. 1997. pap. 95.00 (*1-85739-169-1*) Bowker-Saur.

***Librarianship & Information Work Worldwide, 1999.** Ed. by Maurice Line et al. 353p. 1999. 175.00 (*1-85739-297-3*) Bowker-Saur.

Librarianship & Legitimacy: The Ideology of the Public Library Inquiry, 90. Douglas Raber. LC 97-9376. (Contributions in Librarianship & Information Science: Vol. 90). 184p. 1997. 52.95 (*0-313-30234-0*, Greenwood Pr) Greenwood.

Librarianship & Library Science in India: An Outline of Historical Perspectives. Mohamed Taher & Donald G. Davis, Jr. LC 94-905652. (C). 1995. 30.00 (*81-7022-524-8*, Pub. by Concept) S Asia.

Librarianship & the Information Paradigm. Richard A. Apostle & Boris Raymond. LC 96-40043. 192p. 1997. 32.00 (*0-8108-3273-9*) Scarecrow.

Librarianship Documentation. Coblans. (C). 1977. text 12.75 (*0-233-96596-3*) Westview.

Librarianship in Australia, New Zealand & Oceania. D. H. Borchardt & John Horacek. pap. write for info. (*0-08-019752-3*, Pergamon Pr) Elsevier.

Librarianship in Australia, New Zealand & Oceania. D. H. Borchardt & John Horacek. 1976. 24.00 (*0-08-019920-8*, Pergamon Pr) Elsevier.

Libraries. 1992. 36.00 (*0-86022-324-8*, Pub. by Build Servs Info Assn) St Mut.

Libraries. 1986. 49.95 (*0-85139-765-4*) Buttrwrth-Heinemann.

Libraries. Meisei Publications Editorial Staff. (New Concept in Architecture & Design Ser.). (Illus.). 224p. 1996. 85.00 (*4-938812-21-5*, Pub. by Puroto Gyarak) Bks Nippan.

Libraries. Lucia Raatma. LC 97-18052. (True Bks.). (Illus.). 48p. (J). (gr. 2-4). 1998. 21.00 (*0-516-20672-9*) Childrens.

Libraries. Lucia Raatma. Ed. by Shari Joffe. (True Bks.). (Illus.). 48p. (J). 1998. pap. 6.95 (*0-516-26380-3*) Childrens.

Libraries see Information Through the Printed Word The Dissemination of Scholarly, Scientific, & Intellectual Knowledge

Libraries: Addresses & Essays. John C. Dana. LC 67-22088. (Essay Index Reprint Ser.). 1977. 23.95 (*0-8369-1329-9*) Ayer.

Libraries: Addresses & Essays. John C. Dana. LC 67-22088. (Essay Index Reprint Ser.). 299p. 1982. reprint ed. lib. bdg. 20.00 (*0-8290-0476-9*) Irvington.

***Libraries: Global Reach, Local Touch.** Kathleen D. McCook et al. LC 98-4397. 256p. 1998. 42.00 (*0-8389-0738-5*) ALA.

Libraries: Index of Activities & Research. Alphonse R. Abell. 150p. 1990. 47.50 (*1-55914-112-3*); pap. 44.50 (*1-55914-113-1*) ABBE Pubs Assn.

Libraries: Partners in Adult Literacy. Jane Robbins et al. Ed. by Peter Hernon & Charles R. McClure. (Information Management, Policies & Services Ser.: Vol. 15). 248p. 1991. text 73.25 (*0-89391-614-5*) Ablx Pub.

Libraries, Access & Intellectual Freedom: Developing Policies for Public & Academic Libraries. Barbara M. Jones. LC 99-20937. 232p. 1999. pap. 40.00 (*0-8389-0761-X*) ALA.

Libraries & Archives: Design & Renovation with a Preservation Perspective. Susan Garretson et al. LC 98-8692. 235p. 1998. 28.50 (*0-8108-3560-6*) Scarecrow.

Libraries & Archives: Design & Renovation with a Preservation Perspective. Susan G. Swartzburg & Holly Bussey. LC 91-24415. 235p. 1991. 31.00 (*0-8108-2420-5*) Scarecrow.

Libraries & Bibliographic Centers in the Soviet Union. Paul L. Horecky. LC 59-63389. (Indiana University Russian & East European Ser.: No. 16). (Illus.). 305p. reprint ed. pap. 94.60 (*0-8357-9223-4*, 201762400007) Bks Demand.

Libraries & Copyright: A Guide to Copyright Law in the Nineties. Laura N. Gasaway & Sarah K. Wiant. LC 94-8694. 272p. 1994. pap. 59.00 (*0-87111-407-0*) SLA.

Libraries & Copyright Law see Libraries & the Law Series

Libraries & Cultural Change. Ronald C. Benge. LC 71-467778. 278p. reprint ed. pap. 86.20 (*0-7837-5315-2*, 204505400005) Bks Demand.

Libraries & Culture: 25-Year Cumulative Index, 1996-1990, Vols. 1-25. Ed. by Hermina G. Anghelescu & Elizabeth A. Dupuis. 312p. (Orig.). 1995. pap. 25.00 (*0-938729-02-0*) UTX SLIS.

Libraries & Environmental Information Centers in Central Eastern Europe: A Locator - Directory. Czeslaw J. Grycz et al. cviii, 331p. 1994. pap. 27.95 (*1-56513-003-0*) W Poniecki Charit.

Libraries & Information - Towards a Policy for Schools: Conference Proceedings of the 14th Annual Conference of the IASL. Ed. by Katie Mungo. 155p. 1985. pap. 25.00 (*1-890861-05-7*) IASL.

Libraries & Information Centres in Hong Kong. Ed. by Julia L. Chan. LC 97-146164. (Libraries Publications: No. 7). 554p. (Orig.). 1996. pap. 97.50 (*962-209-409-0*, Pub. by HK Univ Pr) Coronet Bks.

Libraries & Information in the Arab World: An Annotated Bibliography, 12. Compiled by Lokman I. Meho & Mona A. Nsouli. LC 99-10850. (Bibliographies & Indexes in Library & Information Science Ser.: Vol. 12). 368p. 1999. lib. bdg. 79.50 (*0-313-31098-X*) Greenwood.

***Libraries & Information Services in China.** Gong Yitai & G. E. Gorman. (Illus.). 215p. 2000. 65.00 (*0-8108-3782-X*) Scarecrow.

Libraries & Information Services Today: The Yearly Chronicle, 1991. Ed. by June Lester. LC Z 0731.L53. (Illus.). 318p. 1991. reprint ed. pap. 98.60 (*0-7837-9681-1*, 206041000005) Bks Demand.

Libraries & Librarianship in China. Sharon C. Lin. LC 97-49482. (Guides to Asian Librarianship Ser.). 272p. 1998. lib. bdg. 75.00 (*0-313-28937-9*, Greenwood Pr) Greenwood.

***Libraries & Librarianship in India.** Jashu Patel & Krishan Kumar. LC 00-35454. (Guides to Asian Librarianship Ser.). 2000. lib. bdg. write for info. (*0-313-29423-2*) Greenwood.

Libraries & Librarianship in Japan. Theodore F. Welch. LC 96-22010. (Guides to Asian Librarianship Ser.). 232p. 1997. lib. bdg. 75.00 (*0-313-29668-5*, Greenwood Pr) Greenwood.

Libraries & Librarianship in Korea. Pongsoon Lee & Young A. Um. LC 93-47094. (Guides to Asian Librarianship Ser.). 192p. 1994. lib. bdg. 59.95 (*0-313-28743-0*, Greenwood Pr) Greenwood.

Libraries & Literature. Marshall. (C). 1977. text 20.00 (*0-233-96604-8*) Westview.

Libraries & Living. Louis S. Jast. LC 72-76906. (Essay Index Reprint Ser.). 1977. 20.95 (*0-8369-0020-0*) Ayer.

Libraries & Other Academic Support Services for Distance Learning. Carolyn A. Snyder & James W. Fox. LC 97-9941. (Foundations in Library & Information Science: Vol. 39). 1997. 78.50 (*0-7623-0229-1*) Jai Pr.

Libraries & Philanthropy: Proceedings of Library History Seminar IX, University of Alabama, Tuscaloosa, 30 March-1 April, 1995. unabridged ed. Edward G. Holley et al. Ed. by Donald G. Davis, Jr. LC 96-78192. (Illus.). 548p. 1996. reprint ed. 25.00 (*0-938729-03-9*) UTX SLIS.

Libraries & Research: A Practical Approach. 3rd ed. Donald B. Collins. 260p. 1996. per. 23.95 (*0-8403-8480-7*) Kendall-Hunt.

Libraries & Scholarly Communication in the United States: The Historical Dimension, 2. Ed. by Phyllis Dain & John Y. Cole. LC 89-23248. (Beta Phi Mu Monograph: No. 2). 164p. 1990. 55.00 (*0-313-26807-X*, DLS/, Greenwood Pr) Greenwood.

Libraries & Special Collections on Latin America & the Caribbean: A Directory of European Resources. 2nd ed. R. MacDonald & C. Travis. LC 87-24114. (Institute of Latin American Studies Monographs). 256p. (C). 1988. text 75.00 (*0-485-17714-5*, Pub. by Athlone Pr) Humanities.

Libraries & Student Assistants: Critical Links. Ed. by William K. Black. 176p. 1995. 39.95 (*1-56024-755-X*) Haworth Pr.

Libraries & Subscription Agencies: Interactions & Innovations. Ed. by Peter Gellatly. LC 88-18803. (Serials Librarian Ser.: Vol. 14, Nos. 3-4). (Illus.). 177p. 1988. text 5.95 (*0-86656-842-5*) Haworth Pr.

Libraries & the Changing Face of Academia: Responses to Growing Multicultural Populations. Rebecca R. Martin. LC 93-42118. 273p. 1993. 32.50 (*0-8108-2824-3*) Scarecrow.

Libraries & the Future: Essays on the Library in the Twenty-First Century. Ed. by F. W. Lancaster. LC 92-42380. (Original Book Ser.). (Illus.). 195p. (C). 1994. lib. bdg. 49.95 (*1-56024-382-1*) Haworth Pr.

Libraries & the Handicapped. Marshall. (C). 1981. text 27.50 (*0-86531-056-4*) Westview.

Libraries & the Internet. Charles R. McClure. 500p. 1994. pap. 35.00 (*0-88736-824-7*) Mecklermedia.

Libraries & the Law Series, 6 vols. Arlene C. Bielefield. Incl. Libraries & Copyright Law. Lawrence Cheeseman. 148p. 1993. 45.00 (*1-55570-130-2*); Library Contracts & the Law. Lawrence Cheeseman. 150p. 1998. pap. 45.00 (*1-55570-134-5*); Library Employment Within the Law. Lawrence G. Cheeseman. LC 93-31839. 150p. 1993. pap. 45.00 (*1-55570-131-0*); Library Facilities & the Law. Lawrence Cheeseman. 150p. 1999. pap. 45.00 (*1-55570-133-7*); Library Patrons & the Law. Lawrence Cheeseman. 142p. (Orig.). 1995. pap. 45.00 (*1-55570-132-9*); Trustees, Friends, & the Law. Lawrence Cheeseman. 150p. 1998. pap. 45.00 (*1-55570-135-3*); Set pap. 220.00 (*1-55570-136-1*) Neal-Schuman.

Libraries & the Literacy Challenge - The Frontier of the 90's: Proceedings of the Mountain Plains Library Association Academic Section Research Forum. V. Sue Hatfield. 116p. (Orig.). 1987. pap. 7.50 (*0-934068-04-6*) Memorial Union.

Libraries & the National Information Infrastructure: Proceedings of the 1994 Forum on Library & Information Services Policy. 128p. (Orig.). (C). 1994. pap. text 30.00 (*0-7881-1390-9*) DIANE Pub.

Libraries & Universities: Addresses & Reports. Paul Buck. Ed. by E. E. Williams. LC 64-25053. 191p. 1964. 26.95 (*0-674-53050-0*) Belknap Pr.

Libraries Are for Children. rev. ed. 1971. pap. 8.95 (*0-913308-01-3*) Fordham Pub.

Libraries As Communication Systems, 17. J. M. Orr. LC 76-8739. (Contributions in Librarianship & Information Science Ser.: No. 17). 221p. 1977. 55.00 (*0-8371-8936-5*, ORL, Greenwood Pr) Greenwood.

Libraries As User-Centered Organizations: Imperatives for Organizational Change. Ed. by Meredith A. Butler. LC 93-49814. (Journal of Library Administration). (Illus.). 256p. 1994. lib. bdg. 49.95 (*1-56024-616-2*) Haworth Pr.

Libraries Betrayed Vol. 1, Pts. 1 & 2: The Hawaii Outsourcing Disaster. Ed. by Patricia D. Wallace & Earl Lee. (Illus.). 220p. 1997. pap. 20.00 (*0-9640119-6-4*) Crises Press.

Libraries Betrayed Vol. 2: The Hawaii Outsourcing Disaster. Ed. by Patricia D. Wallace & Earl Lee. (Illus.). 220p. 1997. pap. 20.00 (*0-9640119-7-2*) Crises Press.

Libraries, Books & Culture. Ed. by Donald G. Davis, Jr. LC 86-14821. 491p. 1986. 15.00 (*0-938729-00-4*) UTX SLIS.

Libraries, Coalitions & the Public Good. Ed. & Intro. by E. J. Josey. 175p. 1987. pap. text 38.50 (*1-55570-017-9*) Neal-Schuman.

Libraries for Children. Gwendolen Rees. (Library Science Ser.). 1980. lib. bdg. 55.00 (*0-8490-3131-1*) Gordon Pr.

Libraries for Small Museums. 3rd ed. Marcia R. Collins & Linda Anderson. Ed. by Lawrence Feldman. LC 78-620740. (Miscellaneous Publications in Anthropology Ser.: No. 4). iii, 48p. 1977. pap. text 2.50 (*0-913134-90-2*) Mus Anthro MO.

Libraries for Teaching, Libraries for Research: Essays for a Century. Ed. by Richard D. Johnson. LC 77-9097. (ACRL Publications in Librarianship: No. 39). (Illus.). 275p. reprint ed. pap. 85.30 (*0-7837-5962-2*, 204576200007) Bks Demand.

Libraries for the National Education Goals. Barbara K. Stripling. 125p. 1992. 10.00 (*0-937597-34-1*, IR-94) ERIC Clear.

Libraries for the New Millennium: Implications for Managers. David I. Raitt. LC 98-161128. 288p. 1997. 75.00 (*1-85604-257-X*, Pub. by Library Association) Bernan Associates.

Libraries, History, Diplomacy, & the Performing Arts: Essays in Honor of Carleton Sprague Smith. Intro. by Israel J. Katz. LC 91-20069. (Festschrift Ser.: No. 9). (Illus.). 470p. 1991. lib. bdg. 54.00 (*0-945193-13-0*) Pendragon NY.

Libraries, Immigrants & the American Experience, 92. Plummer A. Jones, Jr. LC 98-26439. (Contributions in Librarianship & Information Science: Vol. 92). 256p. 1999. 59.95 (*0-313-30769-5*, Greenwood Pr) Greenwood.

Libraries in Africa: Pioneers, Policies, Problems. Anthony Olden. 190p. 1995. 39.50 (*0-8108-3093-0*) Scarecrow.

Libraries in Croatia. Alexander Stipcevic. 83p. 1975. pap. 7.00 (*0-918660-48-3*) Ragusan Pr.

Libraries in East Africa. Anna B. Wallenius. LC 70-163924. 200p. 1971. 25.00 (*0-8419-0091-4*, Africana) Holmes & Meier.

Libraries in East Africa. Ed. by Anna-Britta Wallenius. 219p. 1971. write for info. (*91-7106-051-0*, Pub. by Nordic Africa) Transaction Pubs.

Libraries in New England. Margaret E. Haller. (Illus.). 188p. 1991. pap. 17.95 (*0-9629311-0-1*) Bookcraft MA.

Libraries in Prisons: A Blending of Institutions, 15. William J. Coyle. LC 86-25719. (New Directions in Information Management Ser.: No. 15). 153p. 1987. 49.95 (*0-313-24769-2*, CRO/, Greenwood Pr) Greenwood.

Libraries in the Age of Automation: A Reader for the Professional Librarian. Walt Crawford et al. LC 86-2724. (Professional Librarian Ser.). 160p. 1986. 40.00 (*0-86729-194-X*, Hall Reference); 30.00 (*0-86729-193-1*, Hall Reference) Macmillan.

Libraries in the Age of Mediocrity. Earl Lee. LC 98-24669. 159p. 1998. pap. 28.50 (*0-7864-0548-1*) McFarland & Co.

Libraries in the Political Scene: Georg Leyh & German Librarianship, 1933-53, 7. Tr. by Marta L. Dosa. LC 72-5218. (Contributions in Librarianship & Information Science Ser.: No. 7). 226p. 1974. 59.95 (*0-8371-6443-5*, DGL/, Greenwood Pr) Greenwood.

Libraries in the United Kingdom & the Republic of Ireland - Mailing Labels, 1999 Edition. 1998. 670.00 (*1-85604-026-7*, LAP267X) Library Association.

***Libraries in the United Kingdom & the Republic of Ireland, 2000.** Ed. by A. Harrold. 401p. 1999. pap. 75.00 (*1-85604-342-8*, LAP3428, Pub. by Library Association) Bernan Associates.

Libraries in the 80s: Papers in Honor of the Late Neal L. Edgar. Ed. by Dean H. Keller. LC 85-5862. (Technical Services Quarterly Ser.: Vol. 3, Nos. 1-2). 157p. 1985. 49.95 (*0-86656-459-4*) Haworth Pr.

Libraries in Utility Commissions: Creation, Evaluation & Use. Ed. by Diane Friese & Christine Westerlund. 63p. 1990. 15.00 (*0-9628889-1-5*) Pub Util Commsn.

L

Libraries Inside: A Practical Guide for Prison Librarians. Rhea J. Rubin & Daniel Suvak. Ed. & Illus. by Richard Lee. LC 94-43076. 243p. 1995. lib. bdg. 41.50 (*0-7864-0061-7*) McFarland & Co.

Libraries; Military; Parks & Recreation Areas see Rhode Island General Laws, 1998 Cumulative Supplement

Libraries of Bengal, 1700-1947. A. Kabir. 192p. 1987. pap. text 89.50 (*0-7201-1839-5*) Continuum.

Libraries of Bengal, 1700-1947: The Story of Bengali Renaissance. Abulfazal M. Kabir. (C). 1988. 17.50 (*81-85002-07-X*, Pub. by Promilla) S Asia.

Libraries of Scandinavia. Harrison. (C). 1977. text 12.00 (*0-233-95968-8*) Westview.

Libraries Serving Science-Oriented & Vocational High Schools. Ed. by Ellis Mount. LC 88-6597. (Science & Technology Libraries: Vol. 8, No. 3). (Illus.). 134p. 1989. text 4.95 (*0-86656-792-5*) Haworth Pr.

Libraries Take Us Far. Lee S. Hill. LC 97-16234. (Building Block Bks.). (Illus.). 32p. (J). (gr. 1-3). 1997. lib. bdg. 19.95 (*1-57505-072-2*, Carolrhoda) Lerner Pub.

Libraries, Technology & the Information Marketplace. Richard DeGennaro. (Professional Librarian Ser.). 410p. 1987. 40.00 (*0-8161-1855-8*, Hall Reference); 30.00 (*0-8161-1869-8*, Hall Reference) Macmillan.

***Libraries, the First Amendment & Cyberspace: What You Need to Know.** Robert B. Peck. LC 99-39455. 144p. 1999. pap. 32.00 (*0-8389-0773-3*) ALA.

Libraries Through the Ages. Fred Lerner. LC 99-33321. (Illus.). 1999. 17.95 (*0-8264-1201-7*) Continuum.

Libraries Through the Seasons Vol. 3: Winter, Spring, Summer & Fall. Ed. by Christine A. Olson. (Olson's Library Clip Art). (Illus.). 64p. (Orig.). 1995. pap. text 112.00 (*1-56984-020-2*) C Olson & Assocs.

Libraries Through the Seasons Vol. 3, Pt. 1: Winter. Ed. by Christine A. Olson. (Olson's Library Clip Art). (Illus.). 16p. (Orig.). 1995. pap. text 33.00 (*1-56984-008-3*) C Olson & Assocs.

Libraries Through the Seasons Vol. 3, Pt. 2: Spring. Christine A. Olson. (Olson's Library Clip Art). (Illus.). 16p. (Orig.). 1995. pap. text 33.00 (*1-56984-009-1*) C Olson & Assocs.

Libraries Through the Seasons Vol. 3, Pt. 3: Summer. Ed. by Christine A. Olson. (Olson's Library Clip Art). (Illus.). 16p. (Orig.). 1995. pap. text 33.00 (*1-56984-010-5*) C Olson & Assocs.

Libraries Through the Seasons Vol. 3, Pt. 4: Fall. Ed. by Christine A. Olson. (Olson's Library Clip Art). (Illus.). 16p. (Orig.). 1995. pap. text 33.00 (*1-56984-011-3*) C Olson & Assocs.

Libraries Without Limits: Changing Needs--changing Roles : Proceedings of the 6th European Conference of Medical & Health LibrariesUtrecht, 22-27 June 1998 / European Conference of Medical and Health Libraries et al. LC 99-10144. 25p. 1999. write for info. (*0-7923-5626-8*) Kluwer Academic.

Library. (National Teacher Examination Ser.: NT-17). pap. 23.95 (*0-8373-8407-9*) Nat Learn.

***Library.** John Malam. LC 99-57835. (Building Works Ser.). 32p. 2000. 16.95 (*0-87226-587-0*, 65870B, P Bedrick Books) NTC Contemp Pub Co.

Library. N. T. Morley. 1998. mass mkt. 6.95 (*1-56333-683-9*) Masquerade.

Library. Sarah Stewart. LC 94-30320. (Illus.). 32p. (J). (ps-3). 1995. 16.00 (*0-374-34388-8*) FS&G.

***Library.** Sarah Stewart. LC 94-30320. (Illus.). 32p. (J). (ps-3). 1999. pap. 5.95 (*0-374-44394-7*, Sunburst Bks) FS&G.

Library. Andrew Lang. LC 68-59288. reprint ed. 40.00 (*0-404-03816-6*) AMS Pr.

Library, 2 vols., 2. Tr. by J. G. Frazer. (Loeb Classical Library: No. 121, 122). 552p. 1921. 18.95 (*0-674-99136-2*) HUP.

Library, Set. Sarah Stewart. (Illus.). (J). (ps-3). 1996. 24.95 incl. audio (*0-87499-359-8*) Live Oak Media.

Library, 2 vols., Vol. 1, Bks. 1-3. Tr. by J. G. Frazer. (Loeb Classical Library: No. 121, 122). 464p. 1921. 18.95 (*0-674-99135-4*) HUP.

Library: The Drama Within. Photos by Diane A. Griliches. LC 95-41804. (Illus.). 132p. 1996. 35.00 (*0-8263-1693-X*) U of NM Pr.

***Library: The Drama Within.** (Illus.). 2000. reprint ed. pap. 18.95 (*0-8263-2285-9*) U of NM Pr.

Library: With a Chapter on Modern English Illustrated Books by Austin Dobson. 2nd enl. ed. Andrew Lang. LC 72-1657. reprint ed. 40.00 (*0-404-03844-1*) AMS Pr.

Library - Computer Lab - Classroom Connection: Linking Content, Thinking & Writing. M. Ellen Jay & Hilda L. Jay. LC 93-40271. 132p. 1993. 45.00 (*1-55570-169-8*) Neal-Schuman.

Library Acquisition Survey. 85p. 1988. write for info. (*0-933636-29-6*) AAP.

Library Acquisitions Special Reports. Ed. by Scott R. Bullard. 115p. 1981. pap. 31.00 (*0-08-026112-4*, Pergamon Pr) Elsevier.

Library Administration. S. R. Ranganathan. 678p. 1990. reprint ed. pap. 25.00 (*81-85273-22-7*, Pub. by Sarada Ranganathan Endowment for Library Science) Advent Bks Div.

Library Administrator's Automation Handbook. Richard W. Boss. LC 96-52791. 226p. 1997. 39.50 (*1-57387-038-2*) Info Today Inc.

L

Library, an Introduction for Library Assistants. Ed. by William C. Petru. LC 66-29578. 85p. reprint ed. pap. 30.00 (*0-8357-2605-3*, 201613700098) Bks Demand.

Library & Archives Conservation: 1980's & Beyond, Vol. I. George M. Cunha & Dorothy G. Cunha. LC 82-10806. 220p. 1983. 29.00 (*0-8108-1587-7*) Scarecrow.

Library & Community. S. N. Sahai. 216p. 1973. 8.00 (*0-88065-185-7*) Scholarly Pubns.

Library & Information Center Management. 5th rev. ed. Robert D. Stueart & Barbara B. Moran. LC 98-23574. (Library & Information Science Text Ser.). 509p. 1998. 65.00 (*1-56308-593-3*); pap. 47.50 (*1-56308-594-1*) Libs Unl.

***Library & Information Professional's Guide to the World Wide Web.** Alan Poulter et al. 133p. 1999. 40.00 (*1-85604-227-8*, Pub. by Library Association) Bernan Associates.

Library & Information Science Annual, 1998, Vol. 6. rev. ed. Ed. by Bohdan S. Wynar. 300p. 1998. 65.00 (*1-56308-609-3*) Libs Unl.

***Library & Information Science Annual, 1999, Vol. 7.** Ed. by Bohdan S. Wynar. 300p. 1999. 65.00 (*1-56308-785-5*) Libs Unl.

Library & Information Science Education: An International Symposium. Ed. by James S. Hu. 277p. 1988. 35.00 (*0-8108-2111-7*) Scarecrow.

Library & Information Science in China: An Annotated Bibliography, 3. Compiled by Karen T. Wei. LC 88-17767. 286p. 1988. lib. bdg. 75.00 (*0-313-25548-2*, WLN/, Greenwood Pr) Greenwood.

Library & Information Science in France: A 1983 Overview. Ed. by William V. Jackson & Benjamin Whitten. LC 83-51692. 212p. 1984. 15.00 (*0-614-14900-2*) UTX SLIS.

Library & Information Science Journals & Serials: An Analytical Guide, 1. Compiled by Mary A. Bowman. LC 84-15787. (Annotated Bibliographies of Serials: A Subject Approach Ser.: No. 1). 140p. 1985. lib. bdg. 55.00 (*0-313-23807-3*, BLF/, Greenwood Pr) Greenwood.

Library & Information Science Research: Perspectives & Strategies for Improvement. Charles R. McClure & Peter Hernon. LC 90-25018. (Information Management, Policies, & Services Ser.: Vol. 18). 416p. (C). 1991. pap. 42.50 (*0-89391-732-X*); text 78.50 (*0-89391-731-1*) Ablx Pub.

Library & Information Services in Astronomy III (Lisa III) Ed. by U. Grothkopf et al. LC 98-74288. (Conference Series Proceedings: Vol. 153). 356p. 1998. 52.00 (*1-886733-73-2*) Astron Soc Pacific.

Library & Information Services of Management Development Institutions. Ed. by Ken D. C. Vernon. (Management Development Ser.: No. 24). ix, 122p. (Orig.). 1986. pap. 20.25 (*92-2-105593-0*) Intl Labour Office.

Library & Its Users: The Communication Process, 71. John M. Budd. LC 91-42732. (Contributions in Librarianship & Information Science Ser.: No. 71). 216p. 1992. 57.95 (*0-313-28153-X*, BLX/, Greenwood Pr) Greenwood.

Library & Learning Resource Programs: Evaluation & Self-Study. Wanda K. Johnston & Association of College & Research Libraries Staff. LC 98-33959. (CJCLS Guide Ser.: No. 3). 224p. 1998. 31.00 (*0-8389-7989-0*) Assn Coll & Res Libs.

Library & Reference Bulletin Boards. Imogene Forte. (Easy-To-Make-&-Use Ser.). 64p. (J). (gr. k-6). 1986. pap. text 7.95 (*0-86530-136-0*, IP-112-5) Incentive Pubns.

Library & Society. Ed. by Arthur E. Bostwick. LC 68-54330. (Essay Index Reprint Ser.). 1977. 23.95 (*0-8369-0227-0*) Ayer.

Library & the Community. Harrison. (C). 1977. text 15.50 (*0-233-96875-X*) Westview.

Library Application Software see Essential Guide to the Library IBM PC

Library As a Learning Service Center. Patrick R. Penland & Aleyamma Mathai. LC 78-13491. (Books in Library & Information Science: No. 24). 255p. reprint ed. pap. 79.10 (*0-8357-6191-6*, 203456100090) Bks Demand.

Library As Literacy Classroom: A Program for Teaching. Marguerite C. Weibel. LC 92-24275. (Illus.). 300p. (C). 1992. pap. 30.00 (*0-8389-0596-X*) ALA.

Library Assistant. Jack Rudman. (Career Examination Ser.: C-1345). 1994. pap. 23.95 (*0-8373-1345-7*) Nat Learn.

Library Association Directory of Suppliers & Services, 1994-95. 2nd ed. Tony McSean. LC 94-55995. (Illus.). 113p. 1994. reprint ed. pap. 35.10 (*0-608-07778-X*, 206786600010) Bks Demand.

Library Association Guidelines for Secondary School Libraries. OECD Staff. LC 99-204565. 84p. 1998. 35.00 (*1-85604-278-2*, LAP2782, Pub. by Library Association) Bernan Associates.

Library Association Yearbook, 1998-99. Ed. by K. A. Beecroft & R. E. Palmer. 518p. 1998. pap. 80.00 (*1-85604-285-5*, LAP42855, Pub. by Library Association) Bernan Associates.

***Library Association Yearbook, 2000-2001.** Ed. by K. A. Beecroft & R. E. Palmer. 432p. 2000. pap. 80.00 (*1-85604-368-1*, LAP3681, Pub. by Library Association) Bernan Associates.

Library Automation: A State of the Art Review: Papers of the Preconference Institute on Library Automation, San Francisco, 1967. Preconference Institute on Library Automation Staf. Ed. by Stephen R. Salmon. LC 73-77283. 186p. reprint ed. pap. 57.70 (*0-608-14076-7*, 202420800035) Bks Demand.

Library Automation: A Systems & Software Sampler. Charlotte L. Levy & Sara Robbins. (CompuBibs Ser.: No. 11). 87p. 1985. pap. 15.50 (*0-914791-10-9*) Vantage Info.

Library Automation As a Source of Management Information: Proceedings of the Clinic on Library Applications of Data Processing, 1982. Ed. by F. W. Lancaster. LC 83-9110. 200p. 1983. 10.00 (*0-87845-068-8*) U of Ill Grad Sch.

Library Automation for Library Technicians: An Introduction. Joan I. Tracy. LC 85-26233. (Illus.). 171p. 1986. 29.00 (*0-8108-1865-5*) Scarecrow.

***Library Automation in Transitional Societies: Lessons from Eastern Europe.** Andrew Lasslo & Richard E. Quandt. LC 98-50384. (Illus.). 468p. 2000. text 55.00 (*0-19-513262-9*) OUP.

Library Bear. Date not set. 9.95 (*0-89868-293-2*); pap. 0.95 (*0-89868-292-4*) ARO Pub.

***Library Binding, Z39.78-2000.** National Information Standards Organization Staff. LC 99-88934. 40p. 2000. 59.00 (*1-880124-43-2*) NISO.

Library Book Selection. S. R. Ranganathan. 436p. 1990. reprint ed. text 50.00 (*81-85273-26-X*, Pub. by Sarada Ranganathan Endowment for Library Science) Advent Bks Div.

Library Boss: Thoughts on Library Personnel. Robert S. Alvarez. 322p. 1987. 19.95 (*0-9618247-0-0*) Admin Digest Pr.

Library Budgeting: Critical Challenges for the Future. Ed. by Sul H. Lee. LC 77-85231. (Library Management Ser.: No. 3). 111p. 1977. 24.50 (*0-87650-083-1*) Pierian.

Library Builders. Maggie Toy. (Builders Ser.: Vol. III). (Illus.). 224p. 1997. 75.00 (*1-85490-484-1*) Academy Ed UK.

Library Building Projects: Tips for Survival. Susan B. Hagloch. (Illus.). xiii, 151p. 1994. lib. bdg. 27.50 (*0-87287-980-1*) Libs Unl.

Library Buildings: Innovation for Changing Needs. fac. ed. American Library Association Staff. LC 73-39011. 303p. 1994. pap. 94.00 (*0-7837-7311-0*, 204723800007) Bks Demand.

Library Buildings & the California Earthquake Experience of October 1989. David C. Weber. 66p. 1990. pap. text 8.95 (*0-929722-41-8*) CA State Library Fndtn.

Library Buildings Consultant List 1999. Compiled by Jonathan LeBreton. 100p. 1999. pap. 12.50 (*0-8389-8016-3*) Library Admin.

Library Buildings, Equipment, & the ADA: Compliance Issues & Solutions. Library Administration & Management Association Pr. Ed. by Susan E. Cirillo & Robert E. Danford. LC 95-40196. 105p. 1996. pap. 27.00 (*0-8389-0673-7*, 0673-7-2045) ALA.

Library Card. Jerry Spinelli. LC 96-18412. 176p. (J). (gr. 3-9). 1997. 15.95 (*0-590-46731-X*) Scholastic Inc.

Library Card. Jerry Spinelli. 160p. (J). (gr. 3-9). 1998. pap. 3.99 (*0-590-38633-6*, Pub. by Scholastic Inc) Penguin Putnam.

***Library Card.** Jerry Spinelli. (YA). 1998. 9.09 (*0-606-13568-5*, Pub. by Turtleback) Demco.

Library Catalog of New York State School of Industrial & Labor Relation. 1994. 175.00 (*0-7838-2213-8*, G K Hall & Co) Mac Lib Ref.

Library Catalog of the Hoover Institution on War, Revolution & Peace: Catalog of the Japanese Collection, Supplement 1. Stanford University Staff. 1972. suppl. ed. 160.00 (*0-8161-1413-7*, G K Hall & Co) Mac Lib Ref.

Library Catalog of the Hoover Institution on War, Revolution & Peace: Catalog of the Japanese Collection, Supplement 2. Stanford University Staff. 1977. suppl. ed. 180.00 (*0-8161-1414-5*, G K Hall & Co) Mac Lib Ref.

Library Catalog of the Hoover Institution on War, Revolution & Peace: The Chinese Collection. Stanford University Staff. 1981. 375.00 (*0-8161-1318-1*, G K Hall & Co) Mac Lib Ref.

Library Catalog of the International Museum of Photography at George Eastman House, 4 vols., Set. International Museum of Photography, George Eastma. 1987. 480.00 (*0-8161-1733-0*, G K Hall & Co) Mac Lib Ref.

Library Catalog of the Martin P. Catherwood Library of the New York State School of Industrial & Labor Relations, 12 vols., Set. Cornell University, New York State School of Indus. 1970. 1365.00 (*0-8161-0757-2*, G K Hall & Co) Mac Lib Ref.

Library Catalog of the Martin P. Catherwood Library of the New York State School of Industrial & Labor Relations, Suppl. 2. 1978. 190.00 (*0-8161-0093-4*, G K Hall & Co) Mac Lib Ref.

Library Catalog of the Metropolitan Museum of Art. 1994. 175.00 (*0-7838-2235-9*, G K Hall & Co); 2580.00 (*0-7838-2302-9*, G K Hall & Co); 175.00 (*0-7838-2305-3*, G K Hall & Co) Mac Lib Ref.

Library Catalog of the Metropolitan Museum of Art. 2nd ed. Metropolitan Museum of Art Staff. 1994. 175.00 (*0-7838-2297-9*, G K Hall & Co) Mac Lib Ref.

Library Catalog of the Metropolitan Museum of Art. 2nd rev. ed. Metropolitan Museum of Art Staff. 1980. 5985.00 (*0-8161-1470-6*, G K Hall & Co) Mac Lib Ref.

Library Catalog of the Metropolitan Museum of Art, 3 vols., Suppl. 5. 2nd ed. Metropolitan Museum of Art Staff. 1994. 780.00 (*0-7838-2060-7*) Mac Lib Ref.

Library Catalog of the Metropolitan Museum of Art, Supplement 3. 2nd ed. Metropolitan Museum of Art Staff. 1989. suppl. ed. 755.00 (*0-8161-1560-5*, G K Hall & Co) Mac Lib Ref.

Library Catalog of the Metropolitan Museum of Art, Supplement 5. Metropolitan Museum of Art Staff. 1981. suppl. ed. 175.00 (*0-8161-1319-X*, G K Hall & Co) Mac Lib Ref.

Library Catalog of the Metropolitan Museum of Art, Supplement 6. Metropolitan Museum of Art Staff. 1981. suppl. ed. 175.00 (*0-8161-1320-3*, G K Hall & Co) Mac Lib Ref.

Library Catalog of the New York State School of Industrial & Labor Relation. 1994. 175.00 (*0-7838-2234-0*, G K Hall & Co); 175.00 (*0-7838-2243-X*, G K Hall & Co); 175.00 (*0-7838-2248-0*, G K Hall & Co); 175.00 (*0-7838-2285-5*, G K Hall & Co) Mac Lib Ref.

Library Catalog of the New York State School of Industrial & Labor Relations. 1994. 175.00 (*0-7838-2271-5*, G K Hall & Co); 175.00 (*0-7838-2273-1*, G K Hall & Co); 345.00 (*0-7838-2295-2*, G K Hall & Co); 375.00 (*0-7838-2296-0*, G K Hall & Co) Mac Lib Ref.

Library Catalog of the School of Oriental African Studies: University of London. 1994. 2610.00 (*0-7838-2291-X*, G K Hall & Co) Mac Lib Ref.

Library Catalog of the School of Oriental & African Studies of the University of London. School of Oriental African Studies Staff. 1980. 3355.00 (*0-8161-1225-8*, G K Hall & Co) Mac Lib Ref.

Library Catalog of the School of Oriental & African Studies of the University of London, Supplement 2. School of Oriental Studies of the University of Lo. 1980. suppl. ed. 2205.00 (*0-8161-1296-7*, G K Hall & Co) Mac Lib Ref.

Library Catalogs of the Hoover Institution on War, Revolution & Peace: Chinese Collection, Supplement 1. Stanford University Staff. 1992. suppl. ed. 1550.00 (*0-8161-1594-X*, G K Hall & Co) Mac Lib Ref.

Library Catalogs of the Hoover Institution: Catalog of Western Language Collection, Supplement 2. Stanford University Staff. 1977. suppl. ed. 1060.00 (*0-8161-1431-5*, G K Hall & Co) Mac Lib Ref.

Library Catalogs of the Hoover Institution on War, Revolution & Peace: Catalog of the Japanese Collection. Stanford University Staff. 1988. 880.00 (*0-8161-1547-8*, G K Hall & Co) Mac Lib Ref.

Library Catalogue: Fundamentals & Procedures. S. R. Ranganathan. (Library Science Ser.). 1980. lib. bdg. 75.00 (*0-8490-3168-0*) Gordon Pr.

Library Catalogue of the American Numismatic Association. 2nd ed. LC 77-93078. 1977. per. 25.00 (*0-89637-000-3*) American Numismatic.

Library Catalogue of the American Numismatic Association: Supplement, 1977-1984. LC 85-71656. 1985. per. 4.95 (*0-89637-004-6*) American Numismatic.

Library Catalogue of the Radzinowicz Library, 6 vols., Set. Institute of Criminology, University of Cambridge,. Ed. by R. Perry. (Library Reference Ser.). 1979. 720.00 (*0-8161-0242-2*, G K Hall & Co) Mac Lib Ref.

Library Catalogue of the School of Oriental & African Studies, Supplement 1. School of Oriental & African Studies Staff. 1981. suppl. ed. 2205.00 (*0-8161-1336-X*, G K Hall & Co) Mac Lib Ref.

Library Catalogue of the Scott Polar Research Institute. Scott Polar Research Institute Staff. 1981. 860.00 (*0-8161-0334-8*, G K Hall & Co) Mac Lib Ref.

Library Catalogue of the Scott Polar Research Institute, 19 vols., Set. Scott Polar Research Institute Staff. 1976. 2135.00 (*0-8161-1216-9*, G K Hall & Co) Mac Lib Ref.

Library Celebrations. Cindy Dingwall. LC 98-50401. 96p. (J). (gr. k-5). 1999. pap. 16.95 (*1-57950-027-7*, Alleyside) Highsmith Pr.

Library-Centered Approach to Learning. Marie Schuster. LC 76-54328. 1977. 15.95 (*0-88280-047-7*) ETC Pubns.

Library Classification for City & Regional Planning: A Revision of Pray & Kimball's City Planning Classification of 1913. Caroline Shillaber. LC 72-95456. (City Planning Studies: No. 18). 111p. 1973. 20.50 (*0-674-53055-1*) HUP.

Library-Classroom Connection. Silvana Carletti et al. 136p. (C). 1991. pap. text 18.00 (*0-435-08711-8*, 08711) Heinemann.

Library Classroom Connection. Silvana Carletti et al. 136p. (J). 1994. pap. 24.25 (*0-921217-66-8*) Pembroke Pubs.

Library-Classroom Partnership: Teaching Library Media Skills in Middle & Junior High Schools. Rosann Jweid & Margaret Rizzo. LC 88-31920. (Illus.). 247p. 1988. 34.00 (*0-8108-2191-5*) Scarecrow.

Library-Classroom Partnership: Teaching Library Media Skills in Middle & Junior High Schools. 2nd ed. Rosann Jweid & Margaret Rizzo. LC 98-21206. (Illus.). 256p. 1998. pap. 32.50 (*0-8108-3476-6*) Scarecrow.

Library Clerk. Jack Rudman. (Career Examination Ser.: C-1931). 1994. pap. 23.95 (*0-8373-1931-5*) Nat Learn.

Library Collection Development Policies: A Reference & Writers' Handbook. Richard J. Wood & Frank Hoffman. LC 95-15474. 500p. 1995. 52.00 (*0-8108-3039-6*) Scarecrow.

Library Communication: The Language of Leadership. Ed. by Donald E. Riggs. LC 91-34565. (Illus.). 198p. 1991. reprint ed. pap. 61.40 (*0-608-01737-X*, 206239400002) Bks Demand.

Library Connection: Essays Written in Praise of Public Libraries. Public Library Assn. Staff. LC 77-24687. 96p. reprint ed. pap. 30.00 (*0-608-17133-6*, 202735600055) Bks Demand.

Library Contracts & the Law see Libraries & the Law Series

Library Cooperation. Jewell Smith & Sara Parker. LC 84-12530. (Library Administration & Management Association Small Libraries Publications: No. 10). 8p. 1984. pap. 8.00 (*0-8389-5650-5*) ALA.

Library Cooperation & Networks: A Basic Reader. Anne Woodsworth & Thomas B. Wall. 200p. 1991. 45.00 (*1-55570-088-8*) Neal-Schuman.

Library Crime & Security: An International Perspective. Alan J. Lincoln & Carol Z. Lincoln. LC 87-12059. (Library & Archival Security Ser.: Vol. 8, Nos. 1-2). 163p. 1987. text 39.95 (*0-86656-480-2*) Haworth Pr.

Library Data Collection Handbook. Ed. by Mary J. Lynch & Helen M. Eckard. LC 82-147483. 236p. reprint ed. pap. 73.20 (*0-608-12586-5*, 202394800034) Bks Demand.

Library Development: A Future Imperative. Ed. by Dwight Burlingame. LC 89-33331. (Journal of Library Administration: Vol. 12, No. 4). 152p. 1990. text 39.95 (*1-56024-030-X*) Haworth Pr.

Library Development in Central & Eastern Europe - From Assistance to Cooperation. Rachel Roberts. 139p. 1994. pap. 25.00 (*92-826-2657-1*, CD-NA-15660-ENC, Pub. by Comm Europ Commun) Bernan Associates.

Library Director. Jack Rudman. (Career Examination Ser.: C-1346). 1994. pap. 34.95 (*0-8373-1346-5*) Nat Learn.

Library Director I. Jack Rudman. (Career Examination Ser.: C-1929). 1994. pap. 34.95 (*0-8373-1929-3*) Nat Learn.

Library Director II. Jack Rudman. (Career Examination Ser.: C-2779). 1994. pap. 34.95 (*0-8373-2779-2*) Nat Learn.

Library Director III. Jack Rudman. (Career Examination Ser.: C-2780). 1994. pap. 39.95 (*0-8373-2780-6*) Nat Learn.

Library Director IV. Jack Rudman. (Career Examination Ser.: C-2781). 1994. pap. 39.95 (*0-8373-2781-4*) Nat Learn.

Library Director V. Jack Rudman. (Career Examination Ser.: C-2782). 1994. pap. 39.95 (*0-8373-2782-2*) Nat Learn.

***Library Disaster Planning & Recovery Handbook.** 614p. 2000. pap. 75.00 (*1-55570-373-9*) Neal-Schuman.

Library Display Ideas. Linda C. Franklin. LC 80-17036. (Illus.). 244p. 1980. lib. bdg. 26.50 (*0-89950-008-0*) McFarland & Co.

Library Displays. Nancy Everhart et al. LC 88-35640. (Illus.). 124p. 1989. pap. 20.50 (*0-8108-2183-4*) Scarecrow.

Library Displays Handbook. Mark Schaeffer. 256p. (Orig.). 1991. 42.00 (*0-8242-0801-3*) Wilson.

Library Displays on a Shoestring: 3-Dimensional Techniques for Promoting Library Services. Wendy D. Barteluk. LC 93-4813. (Illus.). 128p. 1993. 29.00 (*0-8108-2662-3*) Scarecrow.

Library Dragon. Carmen A. Deedy. LC 94-14754. (Illus.). 32p. (J). (ps-3). 1994. 16.95 (*1-56145-091-X*) Peachtree Pubs.

Library Education & Employer Expectations. Ed. by E. Dale Cluff. LC 89-24511. (Journal of Library Administration: Vol. 11, Nos. 3-4). (Illus.). 242p. 1990. text 49.95 (*0-86656-896-4*) Haworth Pr.

Library Education & Leadership: Essays in Honor of Jane Anne Hannigan. Ed. by Sheila S. Intner & Kay E. Vandergrift. LC 90-21841. 426p. 1990. 52.00 (*0-8108-2398-5*) Scarecrow.

Library Education & Professional Issues: A Handbook for Library Management. David F. Kohl. LC 85-15833. (Handbooks for Library Management Ser.). 274p. 1986. lib. bdg. 49.00 (*0-87436-436-1*) ABC-CLIO.

Library Effectiveness: A State of the Art: Papers from a 1980 ALA Preconference, 1980. American Library Association Staff. LC Z 0665. 423p. reprint ed. pap. 131.20 (*0-608-12587-3*, 202394900034) Bks Demand.

Library, Elementary School. Jack Rudman. (Teachers License Examination Ser.: T-38). 1994. pap. 27.95 (*0-8373-8038-3*) Nat Learn.

Library Employment Within the Law see Libraries & the Law Series

Library Essays. Arthur E. Bostwick. LC 71-84299. (Essay Index Reprint Ser.). 1977. 24.95 (*0-8369-1076-1*) Ayer.

***Library Evaluation: A Casebook & Can-Do-Guide.** Danny P. Wallace & Connie Van Fleet. 250p. 2000. 45.00 (*1-56308-862-2*) Libs Unl.

Library Exhibits: Fish Convention. A. Doyle. (Illus.). 20p. 1999. ring bd. 69.95 (*1-56820-395-0*) Story Time.

Library Experience: Sharing the Responsibility. Lolee Daniels & Rita Pollard. (Illus.). 121p. (YA). (gr. 6-8). 1987. teacher ed. 64.95 (*0-935637-08-7*); student ed. 11.99 (*0-935637-09-5*) Cambridge Strat.

Library Experience: Sharing the Responsibility, Set. Lolee Daniels & Rita Pollard. (Illus.). 48p. (YA). (gr. 6-8). 1987. trans. 85.00 (*0-935637-10-9*) Cambridge Strat.

***Library Explorations: Activities for International Students.** Darlene Larson. (Illus.). 144p. (C). 2000. pap. text 16.95 (*0-472-08641-3*, 08641) U of Mich Pr.

Library Facilities & the Law see Libraries & the Law Series

Library Facility Siting & Location Handbook. Christine M. Koontz. LC 96-35014. (Greenwood Library Management Collection). 224p. 1997. lib. bdg. 62.95 (*0-313-28682-5*) Greenwood.

Library Flipper: A Dewey Decimal System Guide. Sybilla Cook. 49p. (YA). (gr. 5 up). 1988. 6.95 (*1-878383-08-6*) C Lee Pubns.

Library Forms Illustrated Handbook. Elizabeth Futas. LC 82-22362. (Illus.). 875p. 1984. ring bd. 125.00 (*0-918212-69-3*) Neal-Schuman.

Library Friends Guidelines. Jack Short. Ed. by Lissa Poincenot & Norma H. Short. LC 97-67734. 54p. (Orig.). 1997. pap. 25.00 (*0-9640976-2-1*) Cnslt Pubns.

Library Friends Operation Guide: Friends of the San Diego Public Library. 5th rev. ed. Betty G. Sherman. Ed. by Frances L. Pierce et al. 156p. pap. 40.00 (*0-9634530-0-9*, FSDPL Guide) B G Sherman.

Library Fundraising: Models for Success. Ed. by Dwight Burlingame. 95p. (Orig.). 1995. pap. 30.00 (*0-8389-0657-5*, 0657-5-2045) ALA.

Library Fundraising Guidelines. Jack Short. Ed. by Lissa Poincenot & Norma H. Short. LC 98-71237. 76p. 1999. pap. 25.00 (*0-9640976-3-X*) Cnslt Pubns.

Library Hi Tech Bibliography, Vol. 2. Ed. by C. Edward Wall. 147p. (Orig.). 1987. pap. 45.00 (*0-87650-235-4*) Pierian.

An Asterisk (*) at the beginning of an entry indicates that the title is appearing for the first time.

Library Hi Tech Bibliography, Vol. 8. Ed. by C. Edward Wall. 220p. (Orig.). 1993. 45.00 (*0-87650-325-3*) Pierian.

Library Hi Tech Bibliography, Vol. 9. Ed. by C. Edward Wall. 280p. (Orig.). 1994. pap. 45.00 (*0-87650-336-9*) Pierian.

Library Hi Tech Bibliography: Browsing in Information Systems: An Extensive Annotated Bibliography of the Literature, Vol. 10. Ed. by Martin Kurth & Thomas A. Peters. 288p. (Orig.). 1995. pap. 45.00 (*0-87650-341-5*) Pierian.

Library HiTech Bibliography, Vol. 1. Ed. by C. Edward Wall. 198p. 1986. pap. 45.00 (*0-87650-219-2*) Pierian.

Library HiTech Bibliography, Vol. 3. Ed. by C. Edward Wall. 160p. 1988. pap. 45.00 (*0-87650-247-8*) Pierian.

Library HiTech Bibliography, Vol. 4. Ed. by C. Edward Wall. 196p. 1989. pap. 45.00 (*0-87650-257-5*) Pierian.

Library HiTech Bibliography, Vol. 5. Ed. by C. Edward Wall. 213p. 1990. pap. 45.00 (*0-87650-262-1*) Pierian.

Library HiTech Bibliography, Vol. 6. Ed. by C. Edward Wall. 186p. 1991. pap. 45.00 (*0-87650-288-5*) Pierian.

Library HiTech Bibliography, Vol. 7. Ed. by C. Edward Wall. 190p. 1991. pap. 45.00 (*0-87650-297-4*) Pierian.

***Library in Alexandria & the Bible in Greek.** Nina L. Collins. 176p. 2000. 53.00 (*90-04-11866-7*) Brill Academic Pubs.

Library in Colonial New York. Austin B. Keep. 1976. lib. bdg. 59.95 (*0-8490-2158-8*) Gordon Pr.

Library Information Science Education for the 21st Century: The Tromso Conference. Ed. by Bendik Rugaas. LC 93-4497. 163p. 1993. 55.00 (*1-55570-148-5*) Neal-Schuman.

Library Information Skills & the High School English Program. 2nd ed. Mary H. Hackman. LC 98-53626. (Library & Information Problem-Solving Skills Ser.). 150p. 1999. pap. 25.00 (*1-56308-544-5*) Teacher Ideas Pr.

Library Information Technology & Networks. Audrey N. Grosch. LC 94-33628. (Books in Library & Information Science: Vol. 56). (Illus.). 384p. 1994. text 150.00 (*0-8247-8971-7*) Dekker.

Library Instruction: A Bibliography. Compiled by Deborah Lockwood. LC 78-20011. 166p. 1979. lib. bdg. 47.95 (*0-313-20720-8*, LLI/, Greenwood Pr) Greenwood.

***Library Instruction: A Peer Tutoring Model.** Susan Deese-Roberts. 185p. 2000. 46.00 (*1-56308-652-2*) Libs Unl.

Library Instruction & Reference Services. Ed. by Bill Katz & Ruth A. Fraley. LC 84-505. (Reference Librarian Ser.: No. 10). 254p. 1984. text 49.95 (*0-86656-288-5*) Haworth Pr.

Library Instruction in the '70s: State of the Art. Ed. by Hannelore B. Rader. LC 77-75678. (Library Orientation Ser.: No. 7). 135p. 1977. 25.00 (*0-87650-078-5*) Pierian.

Library Instruction Revisited: Bibliographic Instruction Comes of Age. Ed. by Lynne M. Martin. LC 95-23248. (Reference Librarian Ser.: Nos. 51 & 52). 480p. 1995. 59.95 (*1-56024-759-2*) Haworth Pr.

Library Internet Research Workbook. 2nd ed. Klein. 1997. wbk. ed. 14.25 (*0-07-303444-4*) McGraw.

Library Law & Legislation in the United States. Alex Ladenson. LC 81-23176. (Library Administration Ser.: No. 1). 203p. 1982. 24.00 (*0-8108-1513-3*) Scarecrow.

Library Lessons for Grades 7-9. Arden Druce. (School Library Media Ser.: No. 8). (Illus.). 329p. 1989. teacher ed. 24.00 (*0-9617595-2-6*) D Whittington Pr.

Library Lessons for Grades 7-9. rev. ed. Arden Druce. LC 95-46644. (School Library Media Ser.: No. 8). (Illus.). 356p. 1996. text 55.00 (*0-8108-3100-7*) Scarecrow.

Library Lightning: A Practical Approach to Library Skills. Sherry R. Crow. (Illus.). 128p. 1990. pap. 12.95 (*0-913839-72-8*, BL190) Pieces of Lrning.

Library Lil. Suzanne Williams. LC 95-23490. (Illus.). 32p. (J). (ps-3). 1997. 15.99 (*0-8037-1698-2*, Dial Yng Read) Peng Put Young Read.

Library Literacy Means Lifelong Learning. Carolyn Michaels & Dennette C. Leopold. LC 84-10705. 388p. 1985. 36.00 (*0-8108-1719-5*) Scarecrow.

Library Literate. Abraham M. Rudolph et al. 136p. 1996. spiral bd. 15.95 (*0-7872-1668-2*) Kendall-Hunt.

Library Literature: The Best of 1988. Ed. by Jane A. Hannigan. LC 78-154842. (Illus.). 387p. 1990. 31.00 (*0-8108-2276-8*) Scarecrow.

Library Literature No. 1: The Best of 1970. Ed. by William A. Katz & Joel J. Schwartz. LC 78-154842. 429p. 1971. 41.50 (*0-8108-0418-2*) Scarecrow.

Library Literature No. 2: The Best of 1971. Ed. by William A. Katz. LC 78-154842. 468p. 1972. 41.50 (*0-8108-0519-7*) Scarecrow.

Library Literature No. 3: The Best of 1972. Ed. by William A. Katz & Janet Klaessig. LC 78-154842. 456p. 1973. 41.50 (*0-8108-0613-4*) Scarecrow.

Library Literature No. 5: The Best of 1974. Ed. by William A. Katz & Robert Burgess. LC 78-154842. 443p. 1975. 41.50 (*0-8108-0808-0*) Scarecrow.

Library Literature No. 6: The Best of 1975. Ed. by William A. Katz. LC 78-154842. 344p. 1976. 41.50 (*0-8108-0923-0*) Scarecrow.

Library Literature No. 7: The Best of 1976. Ed. by William A. Katz. LC 78-154842. 355p. 1977. 41.50 (*0-8108-1017-4*) Scarecrow.

Library Literature No. 8: The Best of 1977. Ed. by William A. Katz. LC 78-154842. 339p. 1978. lib. bdg. 31.00 (*0-8108-1125-1*) Scarecrow.

Library Literature No. 9: The Best of 1978. Ed. by William A. Katz. LC 78-154842. 427p. 1979. 41.50 (*0-8108-1213-4*) Scarecrow.

Library Literature No. 10: The Best of 1979. Ed. by Bill Katz. LC 78-154842. 512p. 1980. 41.50 (*0-8108-1379-3*) Scarecrow.

Library Literature No. 11: The Best of 1980. Ed. by Bill Katz. LC 78-154842. 335p. 1981. 31.00 (*0-8108-1431-5*) Scarecrow.

Library Literature No. 12: The Best of 1981. Ed. by Bill Katz & Kathleen Weibel. LC 78-154842. 315p. 1982. 31.00 (*0-8108-1522-2*) Scarecrow.

Library Literature No. 13: The Best of 1982. Ed. by Bill Katz. LC 78-154842. 368p. 1983. 31.00 (*0-8108-1624-5*) Scarecrow.

Library Literature No. 15: The Best of 1984. Ed. by Bill Katz. LC 78-154842. 352p. 1985. 31.00 (*0-8108-1808-6*) Scarecrow.

Library Literature No. 16: The Best of 1985. Ed. by Bill Katz. LC 78-154842. 425p. 1988. 31.00 (*0-8108-1926-0*) Scarecrow.

Library Literature No. 17: The Best of 1986. Bill Katz. LC 78-154842. (Illus.). 376p. 1988. 31.00 (*0-8108-2089-7*) Scarecrow.

Library Literature No. 18: The Best of 1987. Ed. by Bill Katz. LC 78-154842. 385p. 1989. 31.00 (*0-8108-2163-X*) Scarecrow.

Library Literature No. 20: The Best of 1989. Ed. by Jane A. Hannigan. (Illus.). 485p. 1990. 31.00 (*0-8108-2374-8*) Scarecrow.

Library Literature No. 21: The Best of 1990. Ed. by Jane A. Hannigan. LC 78-154842. (Illus.). 516p. 1992. 39.50 (*0-8108-2534-1*) Scarecrow.

Library Log: The Diary of a Public Library Director. Robert S. Alvarez. 388p. 1991. 22.95 (*0-9618247-2-7*) Admin Digest Pr.

Library Management: Papers from the Management Workshops, Vol. 1. Ed. by Janette S. Closurdo. LC Z 0678.L52. 101p. reprint ed. pap. 31.40 (*0-608-11182-1*, 201728100005) Bks Demand.

Library Management & Technical Services: The Changing Role of Technical Services in Library Organizations. Ed. by Jennifer Cargill. LC 88-6824. (Journal of Library Administration: Vol. 9, No. 1). (Illus.). 154p. 1988. text 4.95 (*0-86656-779-8*) Haworth Pr.

Library Management in Review, Vol. 1. Ed. by Alice Bruemmer et al. LC 81-13562. 112p. pap. 34.80 (*0-7837-0266-3*, 204057500001) Bks Demand.

Library Management in the Information Technology Environment: Issues, Policies, & Practice for Administrators. Ed. by Brice G. Hobrock. LC 91-47676. (Journal of Library Administration: Vol. 15, Nos. 3-4). 155p. 1992. 39.95 (*1-56024-230-2*) Haworth Pr.

Library Management in the Information Technology Environment: Issues, Policies, & Practice for Administrators. Ed. by Brice G. Hobrock. LC 91-47676. (Journal of Library Administration: Vol. 15, Nos. 3-4). 155p. 1992. pap. 14.95 (*1-56024-231-0*) Haworth Pr.

Library Management Without Bias. Ching-Chih Chen. Ed. by Robert D. Stueart. LC 80-82482. (Foundations in Library & Information Science: Vol. 13). 225p. 1981. 78.50 (*0-89232-163-6*) Jai Pr.

Library Manager's Deskbook: 102 Expert Solutions to 101 Common Dilemmas. Paula P. Carson et al. 212p. (Orig.). 1995. pap. 32.00 (*0-8389-0655-9*, 0655-9-2045) ALA.

Library Manager's Guide to Automation. 3rd ed. Richard W. Boss. (Professional Librarian Ser.). 1990. 45.00 (*0-8161-1942-2*, Hall Reference) Macmillan.

Library Manager's Guide to the Physical Processing of Nonprint. Karen C. Driessen & Sheila A. Smyth. LC 94-17983. (Library Management Collection). 272p. 1995. lib. bdg. 67.95 (*0-313-27930-6*, Greenwood Pr) Greenwood.

***Library Manager's Internet Policy Handbook.** Mark Smith. LC 98-49487. 13p. 1998. pap. 55.00 (*1-55570-345-3*) Neal-Schuman.

Library Manpower: Needs & Utilization. Conference on Library Manpower (1967: Washington,. Ed. by Lester Asheim. LC 72-3089. 39p. reprint ed. pap. 30.00 (*0-608-14077-5*, 202420900035) Bks Demand.

***Library Manual.** 4th ed. Krishan Kumar. 1998. pap. 12.00 (*0-7069-7424-7*, Pub. by Vikas) S Asia.

Library Manual: For Library Authorities, Librarians & Library Workers. rev. ed. S. R. Ranganathan. 414p. (C). 1990. reprint ed. pap. 18.95 (*81-85273-03-0*, Pub. by Sarada Ranganathan Endowment for Library Science) Advent Bks Div.

Library Marketplace. Alpphonse F. Trezza. LC 97-15614. 1997. 29.95 (*0-8161-1622-9*, G K Hall & Co) Mac Lib Ref.

Library Materials Costs & Access to Information. Ed. by Sul H. Lee. LC 91-12604. (Journal of Library Administration: Vol. 12, No. 3). (Illus.). 114p. 1991. lib. bdg. 39.95 (*1-56024-146-2*) Haworth Pr.

Library Materials Guide, Spring 1997. 107p. 1997. pap. 27.50 (*0-87463-073-8*, 1700738) Chr Sch Intl.

Library Materials Preservation Manual: Practical Methods for Preserving Books, Pamphlets & Other Printed Materials. Hedi Kyle et al. LC 83-578. (Illus.). 160p. (C). Date not set. 22.50 (*0-935164-10-3*) NY Botanical.

Library, Media & Archival Preservation Glossary. John N. DePew. 200p. 1992. lib. bdg. 59.00 (*0-87436-576-7*) ABC-CLIO.

Library, Media & Archival Preservation Handbook. John N. DePew. LC 91-16501. 550p. 1991. lib. bdg. 51.50 (*0-87436-543-0*) ABC-CLIO.

Library Media & Information Skills. LMS Associate Staff. (School Library Media Ser.). 1992. pap. text 24.95 (*0-87436-665-8*) ABC-CLIO.

***Library Meeting Survival Manual.** George J. Soete. (Practical Library Management Ser.). iv, 145p. 2000. pap. 29.95 (*0-9701384-0-7*) Tulane Str.

Library Networking: Current Problems & Future Prospects. Ed. by Wilson Luquire. LC 83-18474. (Resource Sharing & Information Networks Ser.: Vol. 1, Nos. 1-2). 140p. 1983. text 49.95 (*0-86656-270-2*) Haworth Pr.

Library Networks, 1986-1987: Libraries in Partnership. Susan K. Martin. LC 86-7438. (Professional Librarian Ser.). 220p. 1986. 40.00 (*0-86729-128-1*, Hall Reference); 30.00 (*0-86729-127-3*, Hall Reference) Macmillan.

Library Notes. rev. ed. Addison P. Russell. LC 72-4599. (Essay Index Reprint Ser.). 1977. reprint ed. 24.95 (*0-8369-2971-3*) Ayer.

Library of Aboriginal American Literature, 8 vols., Set. Ed. by Daniel G. Brinton. 1977. reprint ed. 276.00 (*0-404-52180-0*) AMS Pr.

Library of Aboriginal Literature. Daniel G. Brinton. (Works of Daniel Garrison Brinton). 1989. reprint ed. lib. bdg. 79.00 (*0-7812-2056-4*) Rprt Serv.

Library of African American Arts & Culture, 8 vols. Incl. African-American Kitchen: Food for Body & Soul. George Erdosh. LC 98-51814. (Illus.). 64p. (YA). (gr. 7-12). 1998. lib. bdg. 17.95 (*0-8239-1850-5*); African-American Quilting: The Warmth of Tradition. Sule Greg C. Wilson. LC 99-18290. (Illus.). 64p. (YA). (gr. 7-13). 1999. lib. bdg. 17.95 (*0-8239-1854-8*); Blues: Its Birth & Growth. Howard Elmer. LC 98-43705. (Illus.). 64p. (YA). (gr. 7-12). 1999. lib. bdg. 17.95 (*0-8239-1853-X*); Capoeira: A Martial Art & a Cultural Tradition. Jane E. Atwood. LC 98-42448. (Illus.). 64p. (YA). (gr. 7-13). 1999. lib. bdg. 17.95 (*0-8239-1859-9*); Jam! The Story of Jazz Music. Jeanne Lee. LC 99-10973. (Illus.). 64p. (YA). (gr. 7-12). 1999. lib. bdg. 17.95 (*0-8239-1852-1*); Jazz Tap: From African Drums to American Feet. Anne E. Johnson. LC 98-29523. (Illus.). 64p. (YA). (gr. 7-12). 1999. lib. bdg. 17.95 (*0-8239-1856-4*); Kwanzaa! Africa Lives in a New World Festival. Sule G. Wilson. LC 98-37929. (Illus.). 64p. (YA). (gr. 7-12). 1999. lib. bdg. 17.95 (*0-8239-1857-2*); Rap & Hip Hop: The Voice of a Generation. Sherry Ayazi-Hashjin. LC 99-10972. (Illus.). 64p. (YA). (gr. 7-12). 1999. lib. bdg. 17.95 (*0-8239-1855-6*); (Illus.). (YA). (gr. 7-12). Set lib. bdg. 159.60 Rosen Group.

Library of Alexandria. Ed. by Roy MacLeod. 196p. 1999. text 55.00 (*1-86064-428-7*) St Martin.

Library of American Biography. Ed. by Youngs. (Douglas MacArthur Ser.). (C). 1993. text. write for info. (*0-673-52117-6*) Addison-Wesley.

Library of American Linguistics, 13 vols. Ed. by John G. Shea. reprint ed. 555.75 (*0-404-50980-0*) AMS Pr.

Library of American Literature from the Earliest Settlement to the Present Time, 11 vols., Set. Edmund C. Stedman & Ellen M. Cortissoz. (BCL1-PS American Literature Ser.). 1995. reprint ed. lib. bdg. 990.00 (*0-7812-6646-7*) Rprt Serv.

Library of American Puritan Writings: The Seventeenth Century, 27 vols., Set. Ed. by Sacvan Bercovitch. Incl. Vol. 1. Election Day Sermons: Massachusetts. LC 84-45975. lib. bdg. 76.50 (*0-404-60801-9*); Vol. 2. Election Day Sermons: Plymouth & Connecticut. LC 84-45975. 76.50 (*0-404-60802-7*); Vol. 3. Fast Day Sermons. LC 84-45975. 76.50 (*0-404-60803-5*); Vol. 4. Sermons on Conduct & Manners. LC 84-45975. 76.50 (*0-404-60804-3*); Vol. 5. Execution Sermons. LC 84-45975. 76.50 (*0-404-60805-1*); Vol. 6. Aspects of Puritan Religious Thought. LC 84-45975. Vol. 7. Puritan Personal Writings: Diaries. LC 84-45975. Vol. 8. Puritan Personal Writings: Autobiographies & Other Writings. LC 84-45975. 240p. Vol. 9. Histories & Narratives. LC 84-45975. 76.50 (*0-404-60809-4*); Vol. 10. Tracts Against New England. LC 84-45975. 76.50 (*0-404-60810-8*); Vol. 11. Orthodox Evangelist. John Norton. LC 84-45975. Vol. 12. John Cotton: The New England Way. LC 84-45975. 76.50 (*0-404-60812-4*); Vol. 13. John Cotton: The Way of Faith. LC 84-45975. 76.50 (*0-404-60813-2*); Vol. 14. John Cotton: The End of the World. LC 84-45975. 76.50 (*0-404-60814-0*); Vol. 15. Thomas Hooker: The Soules Preparation for Christ. LC 84-45975. Vol. 16. Thomas Hooker: The Soules Humiliation. LC 84-45975. Vol. 17. Thomas Hooker: The Soules Implantation. LC 84-45975. Vol. 18. Thomas Hooker: The Soules Exaltation. LC 84-45975. Vol. 19. Richard Mather: Life, Journal & Selected Writings. LC 84-45975. 76.50 (*0-404-60819-1*); Vol. 20. Increase Mather: Jeremiads. LC 84-45975. 76.50 (*0-404-60820-5*); Vol. 21. Increase Mather: Doctrine. LC 84-45975. 76.50 (*0-404-60821-3*); Vol. 22. Increase Mather: Two Tracts. LC 84-45975. 76.50 (*0-404-60822-1*); Vol. 23. Cotton Mather: Historical Writings. LC 84-45975. 76.50 (*0-404-60823-X*); Vol. 24. Cotton Mather: Apocalyptic Writings. LC 84-45975. 76.50 (*0-404-60824-8*); Vol. 25. Cotton Mather: Sermons on Church & State. LC 84-45975. 76.50 (*0-404-60825-6*); Vol. 26. Samuel Willard: Selected Sermons. LC 84-45975. 76.50 (*0-404-60826-4*); Vol. 27. Vision of New England: Selected Writings. Sacvan Bercovitch. LC 84-45975. 76.50 (*0-404-60827-2*); LC 84-45975. (American Puritan Writings Ser.). 1938. reprint ed. write for info. (*0-404-60800-0*) AMS Pr.

Library of Anglo-Catholic Theology, 18 titles in 81 vols., Set. Ed. by W. J. Copeland et al. reprint ed. write for info. (*0-404-52010-3*) AMS Pr.

Library of Application Data Models. Frank Sweet. (Illus.). 86p. 1988. pap. 6.50 (*0-939479-06-0*) Boxes & Arrows.

***Library of Babel.** Jorge Luis Borges. Tr. by Andrew Hurley from SPA. (Pocket Paragon Ser.). (Illus.). 36p. 2000. 20.00 (*1-56792-123-X*) Godine.

Library of Children's Piano Pieces. Amy Appleby. (Library Of...). 240p. pap. 19.95 (*0-8256-1455-4*, AM 92874) Omnibus NY.

Library of Christian Hymns, 3 vols. in 2. Ed. by John Dahle. LC 72-1649. reprint ed. 125.00 (*0-404-13202-2*) AMS Pr.

***Library of Christmas Songs.** Amy Appleby. (Illus.). 258p. (J). 1999. pap. 19.95 (*0-8256-1704-9*, AM948850, Pub. by Omnibus NY) Music Sales.

***Library of Classic Women's Literature.** Running Press Staff. 2000. pap. 15.95 (*0-7624-0873-1*) Running Pr.

Library of Congress. Allan Fowler. LC 96-13871. (True Bks.). 48p. (J). 1996. lib. bdg. 21.00 (*0-516-20137-9*) Childrens.

Library of Congress. Allan Fowler. (True Bks.). 48p. (J). (gr. 3-4). 1997. pap. 6.95 (*0-516-26107-X*) Childrens.

Library of Congress. Charles Goodrum. 337p. (C). 1987. 17.50 (*81-204-0197-2*, Pub. by Oxford IBH) S Asia.

Library of Congress. Gail Sakurai. LC 97-29722. (Cornerstones to Freedom Ser.). (Illus.). 32p. (J). (gr. 4-6). 1998. 19.50 (*0-516-20940-X*) Childrens.

Library of Congress. Gail Sakurai. (Cornerstones to Freedom Ser.). (Illus.). 32p. (J). (gr. 4-6). 1999. pap. text 5.95 (*0-516-26395-1*) Childrens.

Library of Congress: A Guide to Genealogical & Historical Research. James C. Neagles. 381p. 1990. 39.95 (*0-916489-48-5*) Ancestry.

***Library of Congress: A Tour in Words & Pictures.** Kurt Salomon Maier. LC 00-38654. (Illus.). 160p. 2000. pap. 8.99 (*0-517-16249-0*) Gramrcy Bks.

Library of Congress: America's Memory. Carol M. Highsmith & Ted Landphair. LC 94-19914. (Illus.). 120p. (Orig.). 1994. pap. 24.95 (*1-55591-188-9*) Fulcrum Pub.

***Library of Congress: An Architectural Alphabet.** Library of Congress Staff. LC 99-50105. (Illus.). 2000. 17.95 (*0-7649-1262-3*) Pomegranate Calif.

Library of Congress: Its Construction, Architecture & Decoration. Ed. by John Cole & Henrey H. Reed. LC 97-42115. (Illus.). 320p. 1998. 60.00 (*0-393-04563-3*) Norton.

Library of Congress: Opportunities to Improve General & Financial Management. 12p. pap. text 30.00 (*0-7881-4179-1*) DIANE Pub.

***Library of Congress Activity Brochure.** Martin W. Sandler. (J). 2000. pap. write for info. (*0-06-449263-X*, HarpTrophy) HarpC Child Bks.

Library of Congress Classification: A Content Analysis of the Schedules in Preparation for Their Conversion into Machine-Readable Form. Nancy J. Williamson et al. LC 94-49342. 1995. write for info. (*0-8444-0871-9*) Lib Congress.

Library of Congress Classification: Class H, Social Sciences: Cumulative Schedule & Index. 4th ed. Compiled by Larry D. Dershem. LC 95-30738. (AALL Publications: No. 48). 1995. write for info. (*0-8377-9299-1*, Rothman) W S Hein.

Library of Congress Classification: Class J, Political Science, Cumulative Schedule & Index. Larry D. Dershem. LC 86-51384. (LC Class Ser.: No. 1). 800p. 1987. 105.00 (*0-941235-00-9*) Time Saver Pubns.

Library of Congress Classification: Class J Political Science Cumulative Schedule & Index. Larry D. Dershem. 1987. ring bd. 105.00 (*0-318-39895-8*) W S Hein.

Library of Congress Classification: Class J Political Science, 1995 Edition Cumulative Schedule & Index. 1995th ed. American Association of Law Libraries Staff. LC 96-28994. (AALL Publications: No. 54). xiii, 884p. 1996. ring bd. 110.00 (*0-8377-9327-0*, Rothman) W S Hein.

Library of Congress Classification: Class K Subclass K Law (General) Cumulative Schedule & Index. Compiled by Larry D. Dershem. (AALL Publications Ser.: No. 24). 1985. ring bd. 60.00 (*0-8377-0122-8*, Rothman) W S Hein.

Library of Congress Classification: Class K Subclass KD Law of the United Kingdom & Ireland Cumulative Schedule & Index. Compiled by Larry D. Dershem. LC 85-25597. (AALL Publications Ser.: No. 25). xiv, 431p. 1985. ring bd. 75.00 (*0-8377-0124-4*, Rothman) W S Hein.

Library of Congress Classification: Class K Subclass KE Law of Canada Cumulative Schedule & Index. Compiled by Larry D. Dershem. (AALL Publications Ser.: No. 27). xiv, 460p. 1987. ring bd. 75.00 (*0-8377-0126-0*, 312090, Rothman) W S Hein.

Library of Congress Classification: Class KDZ, KG-KH Law of the Americas, Latin America & the West Indies Cumulative Schedule & Index. Compiled by Larry D. Dershem. (AALL Publications Ser.: No. 28). 1988. ring bd. 85.00 (*0-8377-0127-9*, Rothman) W S Hein.

Library of Congress Classification: Class KJV-KJW Law of France Cumulative Schedule & Index. Compiled by Larry D. Dershem. (AALL Publications Ser.: No. 30). 1999. ring bd. 85.00 (*0-8377-0131-7*, Rothman) W S Hein.

Library of Congress Classification: Class KL-KWX, Law of Asia & Eurasia, Africa, Pacific Area, & Antarctica Cumulative Schedule, 2 vols., 1. Compiled by Larry D. Dershem. 1992. write for info. (*0-318-69560-X*) W S Hein.

Library of Congress Classification: Class KL-KWX, Law of Asia & Eurasia, Africa, Pacific Area, & Antarctica Cumulative Schedule, 2 vols., 2. Compiled by Larry D. Dershem. LC 92-25906. 1992. write for info. (*0-8377-9285-1*, Rothman) W S Hein.

Library of Congress Classification: Cumulative Schedule & Index. 1997th ed. Library of Congress Staff & Larry D. Dershem. LC 98-8004. (AALL Publications Ser.). 1998. 67.50 (*0-8377-9330-0*, Rothman) W S Hein.

An Asterisk (*) at the beginning of an entry indicates that the title is appearing for the first time.

Library of Congress Classification: H Social Studies. Contrib. by Cataloging Policy & Support Office, Collections Se. 1994. write for info. (*0-614-32031-3*) Lib Congress.

Library of Congress Classification: R, Medicine. Cataloging Policy & Support Office, Collections Se. LC 95-13948. 1995. write for info. (*0-614-05431-1*) Lib Congress.

Library of Congress Classification: T Technology. Contrib. by Cataloging Policy & Support Office, Collections Se. LC 95-36131. 1995. write for info. (*0-614-08623-X*) Lib Congress.

Library of Congress Classification: 1995 Edition. Contrib. by Cataloging Policy & Support Office, Collections Se. 1995. write for info. (*0-614-08609-4*) Lib Congress.

***Library of Congress Classification: 1999 Edition.** Larry D. Dershem & American Association of Law Libraries Staff. LC 00-20491. (AALLI Publication Ser.). 2000. ring bd. write for info. (*0-8377-9339-4*, Rothman) W S Hein.

***Library of Congress Classification 1999: Class KF, Law of the United States: Cumulative Schedule.** Larry D. Dershem et al. LC 00-27726. 2000. ring bd. write for info. (*0-8377-9341-6*, Rothman) W S Hein.

***Library of Congress Classification - Class KF Law of the United States: Cumulative Index.** Library of Congress Staff & Larry D. Dershem. LC 00-27725. (AALL Publications). 2000. ring bd. write for info. (*0-8377-9340-8*, Rothman) W S Hein.

Library of Congress Classification. A. General Works Library of Congress. LC 98-49940. 1998. write for info. (*0-8444-0973-1*) Lib Congress.

***Library of Congress Classification Class H, Social Sciences, Cumulative Schedule & Index: 1997 Edition.** 1997th ed. Compiled by Larry D. Dershem. LC 98-8003. (AALL Publications: No. 48). 1998. ring bd. 125.00 (*0-8377-9328-9*, Rothman) W S Hein.

***Library of Congress Classification Class J Political Science Cumulative Schedule & Index: 1997 Edition.** 1997th ed. Compiled by Larry D. Dershem. LC 98-8005. (AALL Publications: No. 54). 1998. ring bd. 110.00 (*0-8377-9329-7*, Rothman) W S Hein.

***Library of Congress Classification Class K: Law in General Comparative & Uniform Law Jurisprudence Cumulative Schedule & Index 1998.** annuals Compiled by Larry D. Dershem. LC 99-42658. (AALL Publications: No. 24). 1998. ring bd. 62.00 (*0-8377-9335-1*) W S Hein.

Library of Congress Classification Class K Subclass KF Law of the United States Cumulative Schedule & Index. Compiled by Larry D. Dershem. (AALL Publications Ser.: No. 18). vii, 326p. 1982. ring bd. 75.00 (*0-8377-0115-5*, Rothman) W S Hein.

Library of Congress Classification Class K Subclass KF Law of the United States Cumulative Schedule & Index. Compiled by Larry D. Dershem. (AALL Publications Ser.: No. 20). 1984. ring bd. 82.00 (*0-8377-0118-X*, Rothman) W S Hein.

***Library of Congress Classification, Class KD Law of the United Kingdom & Ireland: Cumulative Schedule & Index.** Larry D. Dershem. LC 98-52339. No. 57. 1999. lib. bdg. 67.50 (*0-8377-9333-5*, Rothman) W S Hein.

Library of Congress Classification, Class KD Law of the United Kingdom & Ireland: Cumulative Schedule & Index. Library of Congress Staff & Larry D. Dershem. LC 99-12103. (AALL Publications Ser.: No. 25). 1999. ring bd. 75.00 (*0-8377-9334-3*, Rothman) W S Hein.

***Library of Congress Classification Class KE Law of Canada: Cumulative Schedule & Index.** Library of Congress Staff et al. LC 99-57328. (AALL Publications: No. 27). 1999. ring bd. 75.00 (*0-8377-9338-6*, Rothman) W S Hein.

Library of Congress Classification Class KJ-KKZ Law of Europe Cumulative Schedule & Index. Compiled by Larry D. Dershem. (AALL Publications Ser.: No. 37). 1988. ring bd. 95.00 (*0-8377-9259-2*, Rothman) W S Hein.

Library of Congress Classification Class KK-KKC Law of Germany Cumulative Schedule & Index. Compiled by Larry D. Dershem. (AALL Publications Ser.: No. 35). 1990. ring bd. 95.00 (*0-8377-9255-X*, Rothman) W S Hein.

Library of Congress Classification Class KL-KWX Law of Asia & Eurasia, Africa, Pacific Area & Antarctica Cumulative Schedule & Index, 2 vols., Set. Compiled by Larry D. Dershem. LC 92-25906. (AALL Publications Ser.: No. 43). 1992. ring bd. 130.00 (*0-8377-9283-5*, Rothman) W S Hein.

Library of Congress Classification Class R, Medicine Cumulative Schedule & Index. Compiled by Larry D. Dershem. LC 96-5206. (AALL Publications: No. 50). 916p. 1996. ring bd. 110.00 (*0-8377-9325-4*, Rothman) W S Hein.

Library of Congress Classification Class Z Bibliography & Library Science Cumulative Schedule & Index. Compiled by Larry D. Dershem. (AALL Publications Ser.: No. 40). 1996. ring bd. 110.00 (*0-8377-9261-4*, Rothman) W S Hein.

***Library of Congress Classification Class K Tables Forms Division Tables for Law.** Compiled by Larry D. Dershem. LC 99-51310. (AALL Publications Ser.: No. 59). 1999. ring bd. 35.00 (*0-8377-9336-X*, 323750, Rothman) W S Hein.

***Library of Congress Classification. M. Music, Books on Music.** Library of Congress Staff. LC 99-11719. 1999. write for info. (*0-8444-0981-2*) Lib Congress.

***Library of Congress Classification. R. Medicine, 1999.** Library of Congress Staff. LC 99-86967. 2000. write for info. (*0-8444-1004-7*) Lib Congress.

Library of Congress Collections Policy Statements. Compiled by Library of Congress, Collections Policy Office Sta. LC 94-40681. 1994. write for info. (*0-614-32185-9*) Lib Congress.

Library of Congress Geography & Maps: An Illustrated Guide. Library of Congress Staff. (Illus.). 84p. pap. 22.00 (*0-8444-0817-4*) Lib Congress.

Library of Congress Headings for Judaica. Daniel D. Stuhlman et al. LC 82-73398. (Orig.). 1983. pap. 5.00 (*0-934402-13-2*) BYLS Pr.

Library of Congress, Its Architecture & Decoration. Herbert Small. LC 82-14199. (Classical America Series in Art & Architecture). 215p. 1982. pap. write for info. (*0-393-30038-2*) Lib Congress.

Library of Congress Luso-Hispanic Collection: An Illustrated Guide. Library of Congress Staff. LC 95-18095. (Illus.). 84p. 1995. pap. 13.00 (*0-8444-0881-6*) Lib Congress.

Library of Congress Manuscripts: An Illustrated Guide. Library of Congress Staff. LC 93-2529. (Illus.). 64p. 1993. pap. 7.00 (*0-8444-0798-4*) Lib Congress.

Library of Congress Music, Theater, & Dance: An Illustrated Guide. Library of Congress Staff. LC 93-27720. (Illus.). 80p. 1993. pap. 13.00 (*0-8444-0801-8*) Lib Congress.

Library of Congress Online. Ed. by Robert S. Want. (Best of the Web Ser.). (Illus.). 50p. 1999. spiral bd. 9.95 (*0-942008-91-X*) Want Pub.

***Library of Congress Online.** 2nd rev. ed. Ed. by Robert S. Want. LC 98-90902. (Best of the Web Ser.). (Illus.). 50p. 2000. spiral bd. 9.95 (*0-942008-97-9*) Want Pub.

Library of Congress Prints & Photographs: An Illustrated Guide. Pref. by Stephen E. Ostrow. LC 94-17438. (Illus.). 80p. 1994. pap. 7.50 (*0-8444-0816-6*) Lib Congress.

Library of Congress Subject Headings: Philosophy, Practice & Prospects. William E. Studwell. (Cataloging & Classification Quarterly Ser.: No. 2). 120p. (C). 1990. text 39.95 (*1-56024-003-2*) Haworth Pr.

Library of Congress Subject Headings: Principles & Application. Lois M. Chan. LC 95-2664. xi, 541p. 1995. pap. text 45.00 (*1-56308-191-1*) Libs Unl.

Library of Congress Subject Headings: Principles & Application. 3rd ed. Lois M. Chan. LC 95-2664. xi, 541p. 1995. lib. bdg. 55.00 (*1-56308-195-4*) Libs Unl.

Library of Congress Subject Headings for Judaica. 3rd ed. Ed. by Daniel D. Stuhlman. LC 88-92698. 62p. 1988. spiral bd. 16.00 (*0-934402-23-X*); ring bd. 11.00 (*0-934402-24-8*); disk 12.00 (*0-934402-25-6*); disk 13.00 (*0-934402-26-4*) BYLS Pr.

Library of Congress Subject Headings in Philosophy: A Thesaurus. Ed. by Barbara Berman. 550p. 1999. 65.00 (*0-912632-64-X*) Philos Document.

Library of Drummond of Hawthornden. Robert H. MacDonald. LC 68-22845. xii, 245p. 1971. write for info. (*0-85224-019-8*) Edinburgh U Pr.

Library of Easiest Book of Piano Classics. Music Sales Publishing Staff. 352p. pap. 19.95 (*0-8256-1596-8*) Omnibus NY.

Library of Easy Guitar Classics. Amy Appleby. 238p. 1997. pap. text 19.95 (*0-8256-1617-4*, AMN943239) Music Sales.

Library of Easy Piano Classics. LC 94-100752. (Library Of...). (Illus.). 296p. 1991. pap. 19.95 (*0-8256-1284-5*, AM 80151) Omnibus NY.

Library of Easy Piano Classics, Vol. 2. Amsco Publications Staff. 1996. pap. 19.95 (*0-8256-1566-6*, AM940270) Music Sales.

Library of Easy Piano Favorites. 239p. 1998. pap. text 19.95 (*0-8256-1483-X*, AM931205) Music Sales.

Library of Emmanuel College, Cambridge, 1584-1637. 236p. 1987. text 90.00 (*0-521-30846-1*) Cambridge U Pr.

Library of Flute Classics with Book. (Illus.). 159p. 1998. pap. 19.95 (*0-8256-1707-3*, AM948882, Amsco Music) Music Sales.

***Library of Folk Songs.** Ed. by Amy Appleby. 239p. 1999. pap. text 19.95 (*0-8256-1770-7*, AM961521) Music Sales.

Encyclopedia of German Women Writers, 1900-1933: With Biographies & Bibliographies with Exemplary Readings. Ed. by Brian Keith-Smith. LC 97-29881. (German Women Writers Ser.: Vol. 1). (ENG & GER.). 255p. 1997. text 89.95 (*0-7734-8582-1*) E Mellen.

Library of Greek Mythology. Apollodorus. Tr. & Intro. by Robin Hard. (Oxford World's Classics Ser.). (Illus.). 336p. 1999. pap. 10.95 (*0-19-283924-1*) OUP.

Library of Greek Thought, 9 vols. Ed. by Ernest Barker. reprint ed. 321.50 (*0-404-07800-1*) AMS Pr.

***Library of Guitar Classics.** Jerry Willard. 2000. pap. text 19.95 (*0-8256-1620-4*) Music Sales.

Library of Helene Hanff: A Catalogue of the Books in Her Collection. unabridged ed. Helene Hanff & Stephen R. Pastore. 1998. pap. 19.95 (*1-893173-00-3*) YaleBooks.

Library of Henry James. Leon Edel & Adeline R. Tintner. LC 87-24371. (Studies in Modern Literature: No. 90). 116p. reprint ed. pap. 36.00 (*0-8357-1856-5*, 207064500012) Bks Demand.

Library of Hispanic America, 3 vols. 2nd ed. Date not set. 119.00 (*0-7876-1549-8*) Gale.

Library of History, 12 vols. Incl. Vol. 1. Tr. by C. H. Oldfather. 498p. 1933. 19.95 (*0-674-99307-1*); Vol. 2. Siculus Diodorus. 544p. 1935. 19.95 (*0-674-99334-9*); Vol. 3. Siculus Diodorus. 19.95 (*0-674-99375-6*); Vol. 4. Siculus Diodorus. 19.95 (*0-674-99413-2*); Vol. 5. Siculus Diodorus. 19.95 (*0-674-99422-1*); Vol. 6. Siculus Diodorus. 19.95 (*0-674-99439-6*); Vol. 7. Siculus Diodorus. 19.95 (*0-674-99428-0*); Vol. 8. Siculus Diodorus. 19.95 (*0-674-99464-7*); Vol. 9. Siculus Diodorus. 19.95 (*0-674-99415-9*); Vol. 10. Siculus Diodorus. 19.95 (*0-674-99429-9*); Vol. 11. Siculus Diodorus. 19.95 (*0-674-99450-7*); Vol. 12. Siculus Diodorus. 19.95 (*0-674-99465-5*); Nos. 279, 303, 340, 375, 384, 399, 422, 377, 390. write for info. (*0-318-53099-6*) HUP.

Library of Interior Detail - Casa: Southern Spanish Style. Elizabeth Hilliard. (Illus.). 80p. 1995. 18.45 (*0-8212-2174-4*, Pub. by Bulfinch Pr) Little.

Library of Interior Detail - Villa: Italian Country Style. Elizabeth Hilliard. LC 94-73028. (Illus.). 80p. 1995. 18.45 (*0-8212-2171-X*, Pub. by Bulfinch Pr) Little.

Library of Investment Banking, 7 vols. Robert L. Kuhn. 4400p. 1990. 475.00 (*1-55623-278-0*, Irwn Prfssnl) McGraw-Hill Prof.

Library of Investment Banking, Vol. III. Ed. by Robert L. Kuhn. 672p. 1990. text 100.00 (*1-55623-250-0*, Irwn Prfssnl) McGraw-Hill Prof.

Library of Investment Banking, Vol. IV. Ed. by Robert L. Kuhn. 800p. 1990. text 100.00 (*1-55623-251-9*, Irwn Prfssnl) McGraw-Hill Prof.

Library of Investment Banking, Vol. V. Ed. by Robert L. Kuhn. 576p. 1990. text 100.00 (*1-55623-252-7*, Irwn Prfssnl) McGraw-Hill Prof.

Library of Investment Banking, Vol. VI. Ed. by Robert L. Kuhn. 576p. 1990. text 100.00 (*1-55623-253-5*, Irwn Prfssnl) McGraw-Hill Prof.

Library of Investment Banking: Investing & Risk Management. Ed. by Robert L. Kuhn. 992p. 1990. text 100.00 (*1-55623-248-9*, Irwn Prfssnl) McGraw-Hill Prof.

Library of Investment Banking Vol. 2: Handbook of Capital Raising & Financial Structure. Ed. by Robert L. Kuhn. 786p. 1990. text 100.00 (*1-55623-249-7*, Irwn Prfssnl) McGraw-Hill Prof.

Library of Irish Music. Compiled by Amy Appleby. 239p. 1998. pap. 19.95 (*0-8256-1653-0*) Music Sales.

Library of James Logan of Philadelphia, 1674-1751. 2nd ed. Edwin Wolf. LC 73-84179. (Illus.). lvii, 578p. 1974. 45.00 (*0-914076-51-5*) Lib Co Phila.

***Library of John Montgomerie, Colonial Governor of New York & New Jersey.** Kevin J. Hayes. LC 99-55814. 216p. 2000. 35.00 (*0-87413-711-X*) U Delaware Pr.

Library of John Morris: The Reconstruction of a Seventeenth-Century Collection T. A. Birrell. LC 77-362673. xxiv, 83 p. 1976. write for info. (*0-7141-0365-9*) BRI5.

Library of Lesson Plans: Courtroom Demeanor. Bud Allen & Diana Bosta. 95p. 1982. vinyl bd. 39.95 (*0-939438-22-4*) Rae John.

Library of Lesson Plans: Creative Thinking & Problem Solving. Bud Allen & Diana Bosta. 80p. 1982. vinyl bd. 39.95 (*0-939438-19-4*) Rae John.

Library of Lesson Plans: Forty Hour Orientation Package. Bud Allen & Diana Bosta. 82p. 1981. vinyl bd. 39.95 (*0-9605226-4-6*) Rae John.

Library of Lesson Plans: How Administrators & Victims Can Handle a Hostage Situation. Bud Allen & Diana Bosta. 100p. 1982. ring bd. 49.95 (*0-939438-21-6*) Rae John.

Library of Lesson Plans: How to Handle Classroom Disturbances. Bud Allen & Diana Bosta. 64p. 1982. vinyl bd. 29.95 (*0-939438-20-8*) Rae John.

Library of Lesson Plans: Rape Prevention-How to Avoid It & What to Do If You Can't. Bud Allen & Diana Bosta. 41p. 1981. vinyl bd. 29.95 (*0-9605226-5-4*) Rae John.

Library of Lesson Plans: Stress Management. Bud Allen & Diana Bosta. 64p. 1981. vinyl bd. 49.95 (*0-939438-17-8*) Rae John.

Library of Lesson Plans: Team Building & Listening Workshop. Bud Allen & Diana Bosta. 90p. 1981. vinyl bd. 49.95 (*0-939438-16-X*) Rae John.

Library of Lesson Plans: The Anatomy of a Set Up. Bud Allen & Diana Bosta. 222p. 1981. ring bd. 59.95 (*0-939438-18-6*) Rae John.

Library of Lesson Plans Vol. 1: Career Development. Bud Allen & Diana Bosta. 285p. 1981. ring bd. 99.95 (*0-939438-02-X*) Rae John.

Library of Lesson Plans Vol. 1, No. 1: Professionalism - What It Really Means. Bud Allen & Diana Bosta. 50p. 1981. vinyl bd. 29.95 (*0-939438-00-3*) Rae John.

Library of Lesson Plans Vol. 1, No. 2: Report Writing. Bud Allen & Diana Bosta. 105p. 1981. 39.95 (*0-9605226-1-1*) Rae John.

Library of Lesson Plans Vol. 1, No. 3: How to Take Promotional Examinations & Oral Interviews. Bud Allen & Diana Bosta. 74p. 1981. vinyl bd. 29.95 (*0-9605226-3-8*) Rae John.

Library of Lesson Plans Vol. 1, No. 4: How to Reduce Sick Leave. Bud Allen & Diana Bosta. 57p. 1981. vinyl bd. 29.95 (*0-939438-01-1*) Rae John.

Library of Lesson Plans Vol. 2: Supervision in Depth. Bud Allen & Diana Bosta. 257p. 1981. ring bd. 99.95 (*0-939438-03-8*) Rae John.

Library of Lesson Plans Vol. 2, No. 1: Basic Supervision. Bud Allen & Diana Bosta. 73p. 1981. vinyl bd. 29.95 (*0-939438-09-7*) Rae John.

Library of Lesson Plans Vol. 2, No. 2: Discretionary Decision Making. Bud Allen & Diana Bosta. 61p. 1981. vinyl bd. 29.95 (*0-939438-10-0*) Rae John.

Library of Lesson Plans Vol. 2, No. 3: Corrective Interviewing for Supervisors. Bud Allen & Diana Bosta. 63p. 1981. vinyl bd. 29.95 (*0-939438-11-9*) Rae John.

Library of Lesson Plans Vol. 2, No. 4: Human Relations. Bud Allen & Diana Bosta. 67p. 1981. vinyl bd. 29.95 (*0-939438-12-7*) Rae John.

Library of Lesson Plans Vol. 3: Improving Staff-Inmate Relations. Bud Allen & Diana Bosta. 256p. 1981. ring bd. 99.95 (*0-939438-04-6*) Rae John.

Library of Lesson Plans Vol. 3, No. 1: How to Recognize & Handle Disturbed Inmates. Bud Allen & Diana Bosta. 41p. 1981. vinyl bd. 29.95 (*0-9605226-2-X*) Rae John.

Library of Lesson Plans Vol. 3, No. 2: Counseling & Interviewing. Bud Allen & Diana Bosta. 78p. 1981. vinyl bd. 29.95 (*0-939438-06-2*) Rae John.

Library of Lesson Plans Vol. 3, No. 3: Staff-Inmate Relations. Bud Allen & Diana Bosta. 82p. 1981. vinyl bd. 29.95 (*0-939438-07-0*) Rae John.

Library of Lesson Plans Vol. 3, No. 4: Recognizing Signs of a Riot & What to Do about Them. Bud Allen & Diana Bosta. 57p. 1981. vinyl bd. 29.95 (*0-939438-08-9*) Rae John.

Library of Lesson Plans Vol. 4: Techniques of Custodial Functions. Bud Allen & Diana Bosta. 227p. 1981. ring bd. 99.95 (*0-939438-05-4*) Rae John.

Library of Lesson Plans Vol. 4, No. 1: Custodial Competence & Expectations. Bud Allen & Diana Bosta. 79p. 1981. vinyl bd. 29.95 (*0-939438-13-5*) Rae John.

Library of Lesson Plans Vol. 4, No. 2: Transportation of Prisoners & How to Build a Transportation Kit. Bud Allen & Diana Bosta. 41p. 1981. vinyl bd. 29.95 (*0-9605226-6-2*) Rae John.

Library of Lesson Plans Vol. 4, No. 3: What Most People Don't Know about Court Procedure. Bud Allen & Diana Bosta. 42p. 1981. vinyl bd. 29.95 (*0-939438-14-3*) Rae John.

Library of Lesson Plans Vol. 4, No. 4: Search Techniques. Bud Allen & Diana Bosta. 67p. 1981. vinyl bd. 29.95 (*0-939438-15-1*) Rae John.

Library of Lewis Henry Morgan. Thomas R. Trautman & Karl S. Kabelac. LC 94-72123. (Transactions Ser.: Vol. 84, Pts. 6 & 7). (Illus.). 440p. (C). 1994. pap. 20.00 (*0-87169-846-3*, T846-trt) Am Philos.

Library of Life Skills Sixteen Educational Programs, 16 vols., Set. Janie Haugen. (Life Skills Series Educational Board Games). (Illus.). 800p. 1993. text 690.00 (*1-884074-12-X*, LSG 716) PCI Educ Pubg.

Library of Literary Criticism. Ed. by Harold Bloom. Incl. Beaumont & Fletcher to Sir Thomas Browne. 650p. 1986. 75.00 (*0-87754-792-0*); Critical Perspective Bibliographical Supplement & Index. Ed. by S. T. Joshi. 200p. 1989. text 50.00 (*1-55546-774-1*); Fanny Burney to Walter Savage Landor. 650p. 1988. 75.00 (*0-87754-796-3*); Izaak Walton to Henry Fielding. 650p. 1987. 75.00 (*0-87754-793-9*); Mary Wollstonecraft to William Godwin. 650p. 1988. 75.00 (*0-87754-795-5*); Nathaniel Hawthorne to Edward FitzGerald. 650p. 1989. 75.00 (*0-87754-797-1*); Vol. 1. Beowulf to Christopher Marlowe. 650p. 1985. 75.00 (*0-87754-790-4*); Vol. 1. Walter Abish to William S. Burroughs. 650p. 1985. 75.00 (*0-87754-801-3*); Vol. 2. Edmund Spenser & William Shakespeare. 650p. 1986. 75.00 (*0-87754-791-2*); Vol. 5. Jonathan Edwards to Edmund Burke. 650p. 1987. 75.00 (*0-87754-794-7*); Vol. 9. Emily Dickinson to Lewis Carroll. 650p. 1989. 75.00 (*0-87754-798-X*); 1988. Set pap. text 2600.00 (*0-7910-3592-1*) Chelsea Hse.

Library of Literary Criticism of English & American Authors, 8 vols. Charles W. Moulton. 1990. 360.00 (*0-8446-1318-5*) Peter Smith.

Library of Literary Criticism of English & American Authors, 8 vols., Set. Charles W. Moulton. (BCL1-PR English Literature Ser.). 1992. reprint ed. lib. bdg. 600.00 (*0-7812-7004-9*) Rprt Serv.

Library of Lord George Douglas (ca. 1667/8?-1693?) An Early Donation of the Advocates Library, Vol. 5: Libri Pertinentes. W. A. Kelly. (Medieval & Renaissance Texts & Studies: Vol. 179). 178p. 1997. 20.00 (*0-86698-221-3*, MR179) MRTS.

Library of Piano Classics. (Library Of...). 352p. pap. 19.95 (*0-8256-1111-3*, AM 66895) Omnibus NY.

Library of Piano Classics, Vol. 2. Amy Appleby. (Library Of...). 300p. pap. 19.95 (*0-8256-1377-9*, AM 91728) Omnibus NY.

Library of Piano Favorites. Compiled by Amy Appleby. 240p. 1997. pap. text 19.95 (*0-8256-1613-1*, AM943195, Amsco Music) Music Sales.

Library of Pico Della Mirandola. Pearl Kibre. LC 36-7980. reprint ed. 20.00 (*0-404-03667-8*) AMS Pr.

Library of Poetry & Song: Revised & Enlarged with Recent Authors & Dictionary of Poetical Quotations, 3 Vols., Set. Ed. by William C. Bryant. LC 72-3178. (Granger Index Reprint Ser.). 1977. reprint ed. 82.95 (*0-8369-8238-X*) Ayer.

***Library of Qumran: On The Essenes, Qumran, John The Baptist & Jesus.** Hartmut Stegemann. (Illus.). 278p. 1998. pap. text 30.50 (*90-04-11210-3*) Brill Academic Pubs.

Library of Qunuran: On the Essenes, Qunuran, John the Baptism, & Jesus. Hartmut Stegemann. LC 97-38525. 278p. (Orig.). 1998. pap. 23.00 (*0-8028-6167-9*) Eerdmans.

Library of Ragtime & Early Blues Piano. Amy Appleby. LC 96-704233. (Library Of...). 240p. (Orig.). 1995. pap. 21.95 (*0-8256-1458-9*, AM 92877) Omnibus NY.

Library of Robert Hooke: The Scientific Book Trade of Restoration England. Leona Rostenberg. (Illus.). 288p. (Orig.). 1989. pap. 18.00 (*0-929246-01-2*) Modoc Pr.

Library of Romantic Piano. 239p. 1998. pap. 19.95 (*0-8256-1710-3*, AM948915) Music Sales.

Library of Shopping Center Forms. 2nd ed. 160p. 1990. pap. 89.95 (*0-685-68041-X*) Intl Coun Shop.

Library of Shopping Center Forms. 2nd ed. 160p. 1990. pap. 119.95 (*0-913598-98-4*, 881) Intl Coun Shop.

Library of Songs & Arias. rev. ed. Compiled by Amy Appleby & Peter Rekon. (Library Of...). 240p. Date not set. 21.95 (*0-8256-1389-2*, AM91735) Music Sales.

Library of Specifications Sections, 4 vols., Set. Hans W. Meier. LC 82-10149. 1983. ring bd. 250.00 (*0-686-84600-1*, Busn) P-H.

Library of Specifications Sections, 4 vols., Set. 2nd ed. Hans W. Meier. 1568p. 1988. ring bd. 295.00 (*0-13-535352-1*, Busn) P-H.

An Asterisk (*) at the beginning of an entry indicates that the title is appearing for the first time.

Library of Specifications Sections, Vol. C. (C). 1988. pap. 250.00 (*0-13-535386-6*) P-H.

Library of Specifications Sections, Vol. D. (C). 1988. pap. 250.00 (*0-13-535410-2*) P-H.

Library of Specifications Sections, Vol. A. (C). 1988. pap. 250.00 (*0-13-535360-2*) P-H.

Library of Specifications Sections, Vol. B. (C). 1988. pap. 250.00 (*0-13-535378-5*) P-H.

Library of the College of William & Mary in Virginia, 1693-1793. John M. Jennings. LC 68-59130. 116p. reprint ed. 36.00 (*0-8357-9808-9*, 201139000075) Bks Demand.

Library of the Eighties: Swedish Public Library Buildings, 1980-89. Karin Monie et al. (Illus.). 78p. (Orig.). 1990. pap. 65.00 (*0-685-41471-X*) Coronet Bks.

Library of the Hoover Institution on War, Revolution & Peace. Ed. by Peter Duignan. LC 85-838. (Publication Ser.: No. 316). viii, 163p. 1985. lib. bdg. 22.95 (*0-8179-8161-6*) Hoover Inst Pr.

Library of the Late John Gerard Heckscher of New York City, Pts. I-III. John G. Heckscher. 89p. 1992. 75.00 (*1-882860-04-7*) J Cummins Bksell.

Library of the Oceans. Grolier Educational Corporation Staff. LC 97-42835. (J). 1998. lib. bdg. 305.00 (*0-7172-9180-4*) Grolier Educ.

Library of the Palestine Pilgrims' Text Society: Circa 1480-1483 A.D., 11 vols., Set. Palestine Pilgrims' Text Society Staff. Tr. by Aubrey Stewart et al. Incl. Vol. 12, 1895-1897., **3 pts.** reprint ed. 37.50 (*0-404-04902-8*); Vol. 4, 1893-1897., **3 pts.** reprint ed. 37.50 (*0-404-04894-3*); 1887-1891., **5 pts.** reprint ed. 37.50 (*0-404-04891-9*); 1890-1897., **4 pts.** reprint ed. 37.50 (*0-404-04892-7*); 1893-1897., **4 pts.** reprint ed. 37.50 (*0-404-04893-5*); 1896-1897., **5 pts.** reprint ed. 37.50 (*0-404-04895-1*); 1894-1897., **4 pts.** reprint ed. 37.50 (*0-404-04896-X*); 1892-1897., **4 pts. in 2 vols** reprint ed. 49.00: 1892-1897., **4 pts. in 2 vols.** reprint ed. (*0-404-04897-8*); Set. 1892-1897., **4 pts. in 2 vols** reprint ed. 98.00: 1895-1897., **2 pts.** reprint ed. 37.50 (*0-404-04901-X*); 1897. reprint ed. 37.50 (*0-404-04903-6*); LC 74-141802. (Palestine Pilgrim's Text Society Ser.: Nos. 7-10). reprint ed. 742.50 (*0-404-04890-0*) AMS Pr.

Library of the Thirteen Colonies & the Lost Colony, 14 bks. Incl. Colony of Connecticut. Susan Whitehurst. LC 98-32370. (Illus.). 24p. (J). (gr. 3). 1999. lib. bdg. 19.33 (*0-8239-5479-X*, PowerKids); Colony of Delaware. Susan Whitehurst. LC 98-32368. (Illus.). 24p. (J). (gr. 3). 1999. lib. bdg. 19.33 (*0-8239-5482-X*, PowerKids); Colony of Maryland. Brooke Coleman. LC 98-32364. (Illus.). 24p. (J). (gr. 3). 1999. lib. bdg. 19.33 (*0-8239-5483-8*, PowerKids); Colony of Massachusetts. Susan Whitehurst. LC 98-32369. (Illus.). 24p. (J). (gr. 3). 1999. lib. bdg. 19.33 (*0-8239-5475-7*, PowerKids); Colony of New Hampshire. Susan Whitehurst. LC 98-32367. (Illus.). 24p. (J). (gr. 3). 1999. lib. bdg. 19.33 (*0-8239-5477-3*, PowerKids); Colony of New Jersey. Susan Whitehurst. LC 99-14960. (Illus.). 24p. (J). (gr. 3). 1999. lib. bdg. 19.33 (*0-8239-5480-3*, PowerKids); Colony of New York. Susan Whitehurst. LC 99-14961. (Illus.). 24p. (J). (gr. 3). 1999. lib. bdg. 19.33 (*0-8239-5478-1*, PowerKids); Colony of North Carolina. Susan Whitehurst. LC 99-26038. (Illus.). 24p. (J). (gr. 3). 2000. lib. bdg. 19.33 (*0-8239-5485-4*, PowerKids); Colony of Pennsylvania. Susan Whitehurst. LC 99-14962. (Illus.). 24p. (J). (gr. 3). 1999. lib. bdg. 19.33 (*0-8239-5481-1*, PowerKids); Colony of Rhode Island. Susan Whitehurst. LC 99-26048. (Illus.). 24p. 2000. lib. bdg. 19.33 (*0-8239-5476-5*, PowerKids); Colony of South Carolina. Susan Whitehurst. LC 99-14963. (Illus.). 24p. (J). (gr. 3). 1999. lib. bdg. 19.33 (*0-8239-5486-2*, PowerKids); Colony of Virginia. Brooke Coleman. LC 98-32365. (Illus.). 24p. (J). (gr. 3). 1999. lib. bdg. 19.33 (*0-8239-5484-6*, PowerKids); Roanoke: The Lost Colony. Brooke Coleman. LC 98-32366. (Illus.). 24p. (J). (gr. 3). 1999. lib. bdg. 19.33 (*0-8239-5473-0*, PowerKids); (J). (gr. 3). Set lib. bdg. 270.62 (*0-8239-7005-1*, PowerKids) Rosen Group.

Library of the World's Best Literature. Charles D. Warner. (Notable American Authors Ser.). 1999. reprint ed. lib. bdg. 125.00 (*0-7812-9911-X*) Rprt Serv.

Library of the World's Best Literature, 30 vols, Set. Ed. by Charles D. Warner. 1975. lib. bdg. 3500.00 (*0-87968-365-1*) Gordon Pr.

Library of Thomas Rivka. Martin Nakell. LC 97-14755. (New American Fiction Ser.: No. 40). 86p. (Orig.). 1997. pap. 11.95 (*1-55713-089-2*) Sun & Moon CA.

Library of Violin Classics with Book. (Illus.). 159p. 1998. pap. 19.95 (*0-8256-1711-1*, AM948926, Amsco Music) Music Sales.

Library of William Byrd of Westover. Ed. by Kevin J. Hayes. xv, 654p. 1997. text 79.50 (*0-945612-41-9*) Madison Hse.

Library of World Poetry. William C. Bryant. LC 94-39050. (Illus.). 912p. 1995. 12.99 (*0-517-11892-0*) Gramrcy Bks.

Library Organization. Krishan Kumar. 1997. pap. 10.00 (*0-7069-9032-3*, Pub. by Vikas) S Asia.

Library Orientation: Syllabus. 2nd ed. Janet Bohlool. 1975. pap. text 9.50 (*0-89420-080-1*, 216788); audio 101.70 (*0-89420-161-1*, 140800) Natl Book.

***Library Outreach, Partnerships & Distance Education: Reference Librarians at the Gateway.** Ed. by Wendi Arant & Pixie Anne Mosely. LC 00-21759. 304p. 2000. 59.95 (*0-7890-0842-4*) Haworth Pr.

***Library Outreach, Partnerships & Distance Education: Reference Librarians at the Gateway.** Ed. by Wendi Arant & Pixey Anne Mosley. LC 00-21759. 304p. 2000. pap. text 24.95 (*0-7890-0953-6*) Haworth Pr.

Library Overdues: Analysis, Strategies & Solutions to the Problem. Ed. by Robert Burgin et al. LC 84-19736. (Library & Archival Security: Vol. 6, Nos. 2-3). 135p. 1985. text 39.95 (*0-86656-376-8*) Haworth Pr.

Library Paraprofessional: Notes from the Underground. Terry Rodgers. LC 96-26371. 367p. 1997. lib. bdg. 48.50 (*0-7864-0222-9*) McFarland & Co.

Library Patrons & the Law see Libraries & the Law Series

Library Patrons with Disabilities. Dayton R. Turner. Ed. by VeraLyn Kinzer. LC 96-60755. (Illus.). 300p. 1996. spiral bd. 55.00 (*0-9653037-0-5*) Whte Buffalo Pr.

Library Performance, Accountability & Responsiveness: Essays in Honor of Ernest R. DeProspo. Ed. by Charles C. Curran et al. LC 89-78242. (Information Management, Policies & Services Ser.: Vol. 11). 192p. (C). 1990. text 73.25 (*0-89391-597-1*) Ablx Pub.

Library Personnel Administration. Lowell A. Martin. LC 94-6569. (Library Administration: No. 11). (Illus.). 214p. 1994. text 31.00 (*0-8108-2839-1*) Scarecrow.

Library Personnel Management. Herbert S. White. LC 84-26146. (Professional Librarian Ser.). 214p. 1985. 35.00 (*0-86729-135-4*, G K Hall & Co) Mac Lib Ref.

Library Personnel Policies. American Library Association Staff. 1990. 30.00 (*0-8389-7468-6*) ALA.

Library Photocopying & the U. S. Copyright Law of 1976: An Overview for Librarians & Their Counsel. Special Libraries Association Staff. LC Z 0681.L5. 88p. reprint ed. pap. 30.00 (*0-608-11129-5*, 201613600001) Bks Demand.

Library Planning & Policy Making: The Legacy of the Public & Private Sectors. Redmond K. Molz. LC 90-8020. (Library Administration Ser.: No. 2). 233p. 1990. 24.00 (*0-8108-2272-5*) Scarecrow.

Library Policeman see Policia de la Biblioteca

Library Preservation & Conservation in the 90's: Proceedings of the Satellite Meeting of the IFLA Section on Preservation & Conservation, Budapest, Hungary- August 15-17, 1995. Ed. by Jean I. Whiffen & John Havermans. (IFLA Publications: 84). x, 181p. 1998. write for info. (*3-598-21809-5*) K G Saur Verlag.

Library Problems in Science & Technology. James M. Matarazzo. LC 70-164033. (Problem-Centered Approaches to Librarianship Ser.). 191p. reprint ed. 59.30 (*0-8357-9043-6*, 201758900007) Bks Demand.

Library Programming for Families with Young Children: A How-to-Do-It Manual. Sue M. Nespeca. LC 94-37894. (A How-to-do-it Manual Ser.: 45). 180p. 1994. 38.50 (*1-55570-181-7*) Neal-Schuman.

Library Programs for Children. Taffy Jones. LC 89-42726. (Illus.). 288p. 1989. pap. 30.00 (*0-89950-431-0*) McFarland & Co.

Library Public Relations, Promotions & Communications: A How-to-Do-It Manual. Lisa A. Wolfe. LC 97-1423. (How-to-Do-It Manuals Ser.). 101p. 1997. pap. 45.00 (*1-55570-266-X*) Neal-Schuman.

Library Puzzles & Word Games for Grades 7-12. Carol Smallwood. LC 90-52696. (Illus.). 196p. 1990. pap. 26.50 (*0-89950-536-8*) McFarland & Co.

Library Recommendations for Undergraduate Mathematics. Ed. by Lynn A. Steen. LC 91-67940. 200p. 1992. pap. text 9.60 (*0-88385-076-1*, LRU) Math Assn.

Library Records: A Retention & Confidentiality Guide. Shirley A. Wiegand. LC 93-14465. (Library Management Collection). 256p. 1994. lib. bdg. 69.50 (*0-313-28408-3*, Greenwood Pr) Greenwood.

Library Relocations & Collection Shifts. Dennis Tucker. LC 98-51898. (Illus.). 208p. 1999. 35.00 (*1-57387-069-2*) Info Today Inc.

Library Research Assignments: Photocopyable Worksheets Across-the-Curriculum for High Schools. Evelin Sanders. LC 95-2616. 191p. 1995. pap. 36.50 (*0-7864-0066-8*) McFarland & Co.

Library Research for the Analysis of Public Policy. Renee S. Captor. (Learning Packages in the Policy Sciences Ser.: No. 19). 36p. (Orig.). 1979. pap. text 8.50 (*0-936826-08-8*) PS Assocs Croton.

Library Research Guide to Education: Illustrated Search Strategy & Sources. James R. Kennedy, Jr. LC 79-88940. (Library Research Guides Ser.: No. 3). 1979. 25.00 (*0-87650-115-3*); pap. 15.00 (*0-87650-116-1*) Pierian.

Library Research Guide to Music: Illustrated Search Strategy & Sources. John E. Druesdow, Jr. LC 81-86634. (Library Research Guides Ser.: No. 6). (Illus.). 1982. 25.00 (*0-87650-138-2*) Pierian.

Library Research Guide to Nursing: Illustrated Search Strategy & Sources. 2nd ed. Katina Strauch et al. (Library Research Guides Ser.: No. 8). 86p. 1992. pap. 18.00 (*0-87650-253-2*) Pierian.

Library Research Guide to Philosophy: Illustrated Search Strategy & Sources. Ed. by Charles J. List & Stephen H. Plum. (Library Research Guides Ser.: No. 9). 104p. 1991. pap. 18.00 (*0-87650-264-8*) Pierian.

Library Research Guide to Psychology. Nancy E. Douglas & Nathan Baum. LC 84-60640. (Library Research Guides Ser.: No. 7). 1984. pap. 15.00 (*0-87650-175-7*) Pierian.

Library Research Guide to Religion & Theology: Illustrated Search Strategy & Sources. 2nd rev. ed. James R. Kennedy, Jr. LC 73-90317. (Library Research Guides Ser.: No. 1). 1984. 25.00 (*0-87650-185-4*); pap. 15.00 (*0-87650-184-6*) Pierian.

Library Research Guide to Sociology: Illustrated Search Strategy & Sources. Patricia McMillan & James R. Kennedy, Jr. LC 80-83513. (Library Research Guides Ser.: No. 5). 78p. 1981. 25.00 (*0-87650-121-8*) Pierian.

Library Research Models: A Guide to Classifications, Catalogs & Computers. Thomas Mann. LC 92-34311. (Illus.). 264p. 1993. text 30.00 (*0-19-508190-0*) OUP.

Library Research Models: A Guide to Classifications, Catalogs & Computers. Thomas Mann. (Illus.). 268p. (C). 1994. reprint ed. pap. 17.95 (*0-19-509395-X*) OUP.

Library Research Round Table: 1977 Research Forums Proceedings: Meetings Held at the 96th Annual Conference of the American Library Association, 1977. Ed. by Charles C. Curran. LC 79-15300. (Monograph Publishing). 299p. 1979. reprint ed. pap. 92.70 (*0-8357-0424-6*, 201985900015) Bks Demand.

Library Research Skills. Klein. 144p. 1999. pap., student ed. 16.88 (*0-07-229704-2*) McGraw.

Library Research Skills Handbook: Southwestern Oklahoma State University Edition. Pauline B. Travis & SOSU Staff. 320p. (C). 1993. per. 24.95 (*0-8403-9079-3*) Kendall-Hunt.

Library Resource Sharing: Proceedings of the 1976 Conference on Resource Sharing in Libraries, Pittsburgh, Pennsylvania. Conference on Resource Sharing in Libraries Staff. Ed. by Allen Kent & Thomas J. Galvin. LC 77-5399. (Books in Library & Information Science: No. 21). (Illus.). 368p. reprint ed. pap. 114.10 (*0-7837-0832-7*, 204114600019) Bks Demand.

Library Resources for German-Jewish Genealogy. Angelika Ellmann-Kruger & Edward D. Luft. LC 98-19521. 240p. 1968. text 20.00 (*1-886223-09-2*) Avotaynu.

Library Resources for Singers, Coaches & Accompanists: An Annotated Bibliography, 1970-1997, 71. Compiled by Ruthann B. McTyre. LC 98-23959. (Music Reference Collection: Vol. 71). 176p. 1998. lib. bdg. 65.00 (*0-313-30266-9*, Greenwood Pr) Greenwood.

Library Resources for the Blind & Physically Handicapped: A Directory with FY 1994 Statistics on Readership, Circulation, Budget, Staff, & Collections. (Illus.). 91p. (Orig.). (C). 1996. pap. text 25.00 (*0-7881-2732-2*) DIANE Pub.

Library Resources for the Blind & Physically Handicapped: A Directory with FY 1996 Statistics on Readership, Circulation, Budget, Staff, & Collections. Ed. by Barry Leonard. (Illus.). 96p. (C). 1998. pap. text 20.00 (*0-7881-7437-1*) DIANE Pub.

Library School Closings: Four Case Studies. Marion Paris. LC 88-7276. 176p. 1988. 25.00 (*0-8108-2130-3*) Scarecrow.

Library School Review, Vol. 16. Ed. by Marylouise D. Meder. 1976. pap. 2.00 (*0-941044-00-9*) Sch Lib Sci.

Library School Review, Vol. 18. Ed. by Marylouise D. Meder. 1979. pap. 2.00 (*0-686-26897-0*) Emporia State.

Library School Review, Vol. 18. Ed. by Marylouise D. Meder. 1979. pap. 2.00 (*0-941044-02-5*) Sch Lib Sci.

Library School Review, Vol. 19. Ed. by Marylouise D. Meder. 1980. pap. 2.00 (*0-941044-03-3*) Sch Lib Sci.

Library Science Dissertations, 1925-1960: An Annotated Bibliography of Doctoral Studies. Nathan M. Cohen. (Library Science Ser.). 1980. lib. bdg. 55.00 (*0-8490-3167-2*) Gordon Pr.

Library Science Research, 1974-1979. Shirley Magnotti. viii, 179p. 1983. 45.00 (*0-87875-235-8*) Whitston Pub.

Library, Secondary Schools. Jack Rudman. (Teachers License Examination Ser.: T-39). 1994. pap. 27.95 (*0-8373-8039-1*) Nat Learn.

Library Security & Safety Handbook: Prevention, Policies, & Procedures. Bruce A. Shuman. LC 99-18484. 276p. 1999. pap. 42.00 (*0-8389-0714-8*) ALA.

Library Service in Black & White: Some Personal Recollections, 1921-1980. Annie L. McPheeters. LC 88-1979. (Illus.). 184p. 1988. 27.50 (*0-8108-2104-4*) Scarecrow.

Library Service to Isolated Schools & Communities: IASL Occasional Paper. Ed. by Berres Colville. (Occasional Paper Ser.). 51p. 1981. pap. 25.00 (*0-9598398-7-9*) IASL.

Library Service to People with Disabilities: Ten Case Studies. Eunice G. Lovejoy. (Professional Librarian Ser.). 176p. 1989. 35.00 (*0-8161-1922-8*, Hall Reference); 25.00 (*0-8161-1923-6*, Hall Reference) Macmillan.

***Library Service to Spanish Speaking Patrons: A Practical Guide.** Sharon Chickering Moller. 200p. 2000. 28.00 (*1-56308-719-7*) Libs Unl.

Library Services & Construction Act: An Historical Overview from the Viewpoint of Major Participants. Edward G. Holley & Robert F. Schremser. LC 83-48088. (Foundations in Library & Information Science: Vol. 18). 165p. 1983. 78.50 (*0-89232-410-4*) Jai Pr.

Library Services for Adult Continuing Education & Independent Learning: A Guide. Raymond K. Fisher. LC 87-48828. (Library Association Pamphlet Ser.: No. 40). 116p. Date not set. reprint ed. pap. 36.00 (*0-608-20730-6*, 207182800002) Bks Demand.

Library Services for Career Planning, Job Searching & Employment Opportunities. Ed. by Byron Anderson. LC 92-11277. (Reference Librarian Ser.: No. 36). (Illus.). 183p. 1992. 39.95 (*1-56024-303-1*) Haworth Pr.

Library Services for Career Planning, Job Searching & Employment Opportunities. Ed. by Byron Anderson. LC 92-11277. (Reference Librarian Ser.: No. 36). 183p. 1996. reprint ed. pap. 19.95 (*0-7890-0054-7*) Haworth Pr.

Library Services for Children & Youth: Dollars & Sense. Ed. by Virginia H. Mathews. 68p. 1995. pap. 21.95 (*1-55570-176-0*) Neal-Schuman.

Library Services for Disabled Individuals. Rashelle S. Karp. (Professional Librarian Ser.). 128p. 1991. 30.00 (*0-8161-1928-7*, Hall Reference) Macmillan.

Library Services for Disabled Individuals. Rashelle S. Karp. (Professional Librarian Ser.). 128p. 1991. 45.00 (*0-8161-1927-9*, Hall Reference) Macmillan.

Library Services for Distance Learning. Sharon M. Edge & Denzil Edge. 1999. pap. write for info. (*0-939991-02-0*) Learning KY.

Library Services for Nonaffiliated Patrons. Compiled by Eugene S. Mitchell. (CLIP Note Ser.: Vol. 21). 151p. (Orig.). (C). 1995. pap. 33.00 (*0-8389-7781-2*) Assn Coll & Res Libs.

Library Services for Off-Campus & Distance Education: The Second Annotated Bibliography. Alexander L. Slade & Marie A. Kascus. LC 96-2546. 325p. 1996. lib. bdg. 65.00 (*1-56308-465-1*) Libs Unl.

***Library Services for Open & Distance Learning: The Third Annotated Bibliography.** 3rd ed. Alexander L. Slade & Marie A. Kascus. 360p. 2000. 75.00 (*1-56308-745-6*) Libs Unl.

***Library Services for People with Mental Retardation.** 1999. pap. 14.00 (*0-8389-8000-7*) ALA.

Library Services in Mental Health Settings. Mary E. Johnson & Medical Library Association Staff. LC 97-5801. 1997. 42.00 (*0-8108-3306-9*) Scarecrow.

Library Services in Theory & Context. Michael K. Buckland. 250p. 1983. text 39.00 (*0-08-030134-7*, Pergamon Pr); pap. text 15.75 (*0-08-030133-9*, Pergamon Pr) Elsevier.

Library Services in Theory & Context. 2nd ed. Michael K. Buckland. LC 88-17864. (Illus.). 268p. 1988. pap. text 22.00 (*0-08-035754-7*, Pergamon Pr) Elsevier.

Library Services to Household People. Ed. by Julia Ryder. LC 90-223190. (Illus.). 233p. Date not set. reprint ed. pap. 72.30 (*0-608-20731-4*, 207182900002) Bks Demand.

***Library Services to Latinos: An Anthology.** Salvador Ghuerena. LC 00-26849. 261p. 2000. pap. 45.00 (*0-7864-0911-8*) McFarland & Co.

Library Services to the Blind & Physically Handicapped. Mary Strom. LC 77-24686. 291p. 1977. 24.00 (*0-8108-1068-9*) Scarecrow.

***Library Services to Youth of Hispanic Heritage.** Ed. by Barbara Immroth & Kathleen de la Pena McCook. (Illus.). 207p. 2000. per. 42.50 (*0-7864-0790-5*) McFarland & Co.

Library Shakespeare. deluxe ed. William Shakespeare. (Illus.). 1800p. 1999. 70.00 (*1-888777-74-5*) Trident Pr Intl.

Library Skills Activities for the Primary Grades: Ready-to-Use Projects & Activities for Grades 1-4. Ruth Snoddon. LC 87-13235. 250p. 1987. pap. text 27.95 (*0-87628-106-4*) Ctr Appl Res.

Library Skills Activities Kit: Puzzles, Games, Bulletin Boards & Other Interest-Rousers for the Elementary School Library. Jerry J. Mallett. 1981. pap. text 24.95 (*0-87628-535-3*) Ctr Appl Res.

Library Space Planning: A How-to-Do-It Manual for Assessing, Allocating & Reorganizing Collections, Resources & Facilities. 2nd ed. Ruth A. Fraley & Carol L. Anderson. 195p. 1990. pap. 45.00 (*1-55570-040-3*) Neal-Schuman.

Library Sponsored Discussion Group. Robert E. Lee. LC 57-4833. 87p. reprint ed. pap. 30.00 (*0-608-12799-X*, 202421000035) Bks Demand.

Library Standards for Adult Correctional Institutions, 1992. American Correctional Association Staff & Association of Specialized and Cooperative Library Agencies, American Library Asssociation. 47p. 1992. 15.00 (*0-8389-7583-6*) ASCLA.

Library Standards for Jails & Detention Facilities. 8p. 1981. 1.50 (*0-8389-5598-3*) ASCLA.

Library Statistics Cooperative Program. 8p. 1997. pap. 1.25 (*0-16-063617-5*) USGPO.

Library Statistics, Z39.7-1995. National Information Standards Organization Staff. LC 97-27081. (National Information Standards Ser.). 1997. pap. 45.00 (*1-880124-27-0*) NISO.

Library Story: How to Market Your Library Through Story. Jim Fleck. (Illus.). 226p. (Orig.). 1994. pap. text 25.00 (*0-9643702-0-4*) FLC Pubng.

Library Story Book from A To Z: Ready-to-Use Alphabet Activities for Young Learners. Ellen K. Hasbrouck. LC 97-39859. 1997. pap. text 28.95 (*0-87628-895-6*) Ctr Appl Res.

Library Systems Analysis Guidelines. Edward A. Chapman et al. LC 75-109391. 242p. reprint ed. pap. 75.10 (*0-608-11298-4*, 201305500085) Bks Demand.

Library Systems in Europe: A Directory & Guide. Juliet Leeves et al. LC 94-222321. (Publication No. Eur 15494 En of the European Commission, Dissemination of Scientific & Technical Knowledge Unit, Directorate-General Telecommunications, Information Market & Exploitation of Research). v, 401p. 1994. write for info. (*1-870889-47-9*) TFPL.

Library Technical Services: A Selected, Annotated Bibliography. Ed. by Constance Rinehart. LC 76-27130. 238p. 1976. lib. bdg. 49.95 (*0-8371-9286-2*, MAB/, Greenwood Pr) Greenwood.

Library Technical Services: Operations & Management. 2nd ed. Ed. by Irene P. Godden. (Library & Information Science Ser.). (Illus.). 238p. 1991. text 69.95 (*0-12-287041-7*) Acad Pr.

Library Technician. Jack Rudman. (Career Examination Ser.: C-2544). 1994. pap. 23.95 (*0-8373-2544-7*) Nat Learn.

Library Techniques & Technologies Vols. 1-3: Perspectives in Multimedia Library Development, 3 vols. S. N. Paruthi. 1997. 725.00 (*81-7391-172-X*, Pub. by Print Hse) St Mut.

Library Technology Consortia: Case Studies in Design & Cooperation. Ed. by Jerry Kuntz. (Supplement to Computers in Libraries Ser.: No. 70). 165p. 1994. pap. 42.50 (*0-88736-886-7*) Mecklermedia.

***Library Training for Staff & Customers.** Ed. by Sara Ramser Beck. LC 00-23133. 108p. 2000. 39.95 (*0-7890-0965-X*); pap. text 14.95 (*0-7890-0983-8*) Haworth Pr.

L

L

Library Trustee: A Practical Guidebook. 4th ed. Ed. by Virginia G. Young. LC 88-6313. 240p. 1988. reprint ed. pap. 74.40 (0-608-01445-1, 206220800002) Bks Demand.
Library Trustee: A Practical Guidebook. 5th ed. Ed. by Virginia G. Young. 252p. 1995. 40.00 (0-8389-0659-1, 06591-1-2045) ALA.
Library Trustee & the Public Librarian: Partners in Service. Lorraine M. Williams. LC 93-15033. (Illus.). 178p. 1993. 24.00 (0-8108-2623-2) Scarecrow.
Library Trustee Guidelines. Jack Short. LC 94-94382. 54p. 1994. pap. 25.00 (0-9640976-0-5) Cnslt Pubns.
Library Use: A Handbook for Psychology. 2nd ed. Jeffrey G. Reed & Pam M. Baxter. 177p. (Orig.). (C). 1992. pap. text 19.95 (1-55798-144-2) Am Psychol.
Library Users & Reference Services. Ed. & Intro. by Jo B. Whitlatch. LC 94-48326. (Reference Librarian Ser.: Nos. 49 & 50). (Illus.). 304p. 1995. lib. bdg. 49.95 (1-56024-731-2) Haworth Pr.
Library Volunteers - Worth the Effort! A Program Manager's Guide. Sally G. Reed. LC 94-4568. 128p. 1994. pap. 27.50 (0-7864-0004-8) McFarland & Co.
Library Web. Ed. by Julie M. Still. LC 97-12454. (Illus.). 222p. 1997. 39.50 (1-57387-034-X) Info Today Inc.
***Library Web Site Policies.** Jeri L. Traw & Association of College & Research Libraries Staff. LC 00-30633. (Clip Note Ser.). (Illus.). 2000. pap. write for info. (0-8389-8088-0) ALA.
Library Without Walls: Plug in & Go. Susan Ardis. LC 93-47261. 216p. 1994. pap. 36.00 (0-87111-422-4) SLA.
Library's Public: A Report of the Public Library Inquiry. Bernard Berelson & Lester Ansheim. LC 75-31430. 174p. 1976. reprint ed. lib. bdg. 38.50 (0-8371-8499-1, BELP, Greenwood Pr) Greenwood.
Library's Public Revisited. Ed. by Mary Lee Bundy & Sylvia Goodstein. (Student Contribution Ser.: No. 1). 1967. pap. 3.00 (0-911808-01-9) U of Md Lib Serv.
Libre Comme l'Air. Jean-Marie Poupart. (Novels in the Roman Plus Ser.). (FRE.). 160p. (YA). (gr. 8 up). 1990. pap. 8.95 (2-89021-135-5, Pub. by La Courte Ech) Firefly Bks Ltd.
Libre de Addiciones. Maria E. De Castillo et al.Tr. of Free from Addictions. (SPA.). 248p. pap. 15.00 (968-39-0507-2) Hazelden.
Libre de Ataduras. Neil Anderson.Tr. of Released from Bondage. (SPA.). 271p. 1996. pap. text 10.99 (0-88113-283-7) Caribe Betania.
Libre de la Adiccion. N. Anderson & Mike Quarles.Tr. of Freedom from Addiction. 12.99 (0-7899-0321-0, 497514) Editorial Unilit.
Libre de las Ataduras del Pecado. H. Brandt.Tr. of Breaking Free from the Bondage of Sin. (SPA.). 198p. 1996. 8.99 (1-56063-969-5, 497388) Editorial Unilit.
Libre Echange, No. 1. 2nd ed. Janine Courtillon & Genevieve-Dominique De Salins. (FRE., Illus.). 255p. 1995. pap. text 23.95 (2-278-04461-3, Pub. by Edns Didier) Hatier Pub.
Libre Echange, No. 2. Janine Courtillon & Genevieve-Dominique De Salins. (FRE., Illus.). 271p. 1991. pap. text 23.95 (2-278-04022-7, Pub. by Edns Didier) Hatier Pub.
Libre Echange, No. 3. Janine Courtillon & Genevieve-Dominique De Salins. (FRE., Illus.). 255p. 1993. pap. text 24.95 (2-278-04026-X, Pub. by Edns Didier) Hatier Pub.
Libre para Decidir y Elegir lo Bueno: Edicion para Jovenes. Josh McDowell. (Es bueno Es Malo Ser.).Tr. of Setting You Free to Make Right Choices. (SPA.). 144p. (J). 1996. pap., student ed., wbk. ed. 11.95 (0-311-11085-1, Edit Mundo) Casa Bautista.
Libre para Decidir y Elegir lo Bueno: Guia para el Lider. Josh McDowell. (Right from Wrong Ser.).Tr. of Setting You Free to Make Right Choices. (SPA.). 48p. 1996. pap., teacher ed. 6.95 (0-311-11086-X) Casa Bautista.
Libre para Ser Delgado. Neva Coyle & Marie Chapian.Tr. of Free to Be Thin. (SPA.). 176p. (Orig.). 1992. pap. 8.99 (0-88113-247-0) Caribe Betania.
***Libres en Cristo.** Paolo Bottari. (SPA.). 1999. pap. 8.99 (0-88419-605-4) Casa Creacion.
Libres en Cristo. Warren W. Wiersbe. Ed. by Gary Hilliker. (New Testament Ser.). (SPA.). 152p. 1992. 7.95 (1-879892-07-3) Editorial Bautista.
Libres en Cristo, Vol. 1. Ed. by Richard Meyer.Tr. of Free in Christ (Romans 1-7). (SPA., Illus.). 100p. 1997. pap., teacher ed. 4.40 (1-879892-63-4, SS-961) Editorial Bautista.
Libres en Cristo, Vol. 2. Ed. by Richard Meyer.Tr. of Free in Christ (Romans 1-7). (SPA., Illus.). 99p. 1997. pap., teacher ed. 4.40 (1-879892-64-2, SS-962) Editorial Bautista.
Libreta de Suenos. Mirna Nieves. (Aqui y Ahora Ser.). 103p. 1997. pap. 6.95 (0-8477-0281-2) U of PR Pr.
***Libretti of Mozart's Completed Operas, Vol. 2.** Wolfgang Amadeus Mozart. LC 98-220275. (ITA, GER & ENG., Illus.). 1998. 75.00 (1-878617-22-2) Leyerle Pubns.
Libretto: Opera Society Menu Cookbook. Opera Society of Fort Lauderdale Staff. Ed. by Melanie Camp & Marion Gamble. 192p. 1987. 17.95 (0-9618686-0-0) Opera Soc Ft Lauderdale.
Libretto d'Autore, 1860-1930. Jone Gaillard Corsi. (VIA Folios Ser.: No. 12). (ITA.). 174p. 1997. pap. 17.00 (1-884419-12-7, Pub. by Bordighera) SPD-Small Pr Dist.
Librettos. Ernest Warburton. (Johann Christian Bach Ser.: Vol. 44). 335p. 1984. text 72.00 (0-8240-6093-8) Garland.
Librettos, Vol. III. Ernest Warburton. LC 83-48727. (Johann Christian Bach Ser.: Vol. 45). 325p. 1991. text 94.00 (0-8240-6094-6) Garland.
Librettos, Vol. IV. Ernest Warburton. (Johann Christian Bach Ser.). 280p. 1985. text 77.00 (0-8240-6095-4) Garland.
Librettos, Vol. V. Ernest Warburton. (Johann Christian Bach Ser.). 400p. 1987. text 105.00 (0-8240-6096-2) Garland.
Librettos 1. Ernest Warburton. (Johann Christian Bach Ser.: Vol. 45). 325p. 1987. text 99.00 (0-8240-6092-X) Garland.
Libri Annales Pontificum Maximorum: The Origins of Annalistic Tradition. Bruce W. Frier. 368p. (C). 1999. text 42.50 (0-472-10915-4, 10915) U of Mich Pr.
Libri Annales Pontificum Maximorum: The Origins of the Annalistic Tradition. Bruce W. Frier. (Papers & Monographs: No. 27). 330p. 1979. 38.00 (0-271-00475-4) Am Acad Rome.
Libri Annales Pontificum Maximorum: The Origins of the Annalistic Tradition. Bruce W. Frier. LC 98-11373. (Papers & Monographs of the American Academy in Rome). xix, 345 p. 1999. write for info. (0-04-721091-5) Routledge.
Libri Liturgici Bibliothecae Apostolicae Vaticanae Manu Scripti, Dig. Et Rec. Hugo Ehrensberger. xii, 591p. 1985. reprint ed. write for info. (3-487-07575-X) G Olms Pubs.
Libri Qui Supersunt. Sulpicius Severus. Ed. by Carolus Halm. xiv, 278p. 1983. reprint ed. write for info. (3-487-07305-6) G Olms Pubs.
Libri Tres de Institutione Harmonica. fac. ed. Pietro Aaron. (Monuments of Music & Music Literature in Facsimile, I Ser.: Vol. 67). (LAT.). 134p. 1976. lib. bdg. 35.00 (0-8450-2267-9) Broude.
Librito de Instrucciones de Dios, Bk. II. Honor Books Staff.Tr. of God's Little Instruction Book. (SPA.). 3.99 (0-7899-0369-5, 498347) Editorial Unilit.
Librito de Instrucciones de Dios, Vol. I. Jakes.Tr. of God's Little Instruction Book. (SPA.). 160p. 1997. pap. 3.99 (0-7899-0351-2, 198344) Editorial Unilit.
***Librito de Instrucciones de Dios III.** (SPA.). 2000. pap. 3.99 (0-7899-0698-8) Spanish Hse Distributors.
***Librito de Instrucciones de Dios para Hombres.** Honor Books Staff.Tr. of God's Little Instruction Book for Men. (SPA.). 2000. 3.99 (0-7899-0545-0, 498350) Editorial Unilit.
***Librito de Instrucciones de Dios para Jovenes.** Honor Books Staff.Tr. of God's Little Instruction Book for Couples. (SPA.). 2000. 3.99 (0-7899-0547-7, 498351) Editorial Unilit.
***Librito de Instrucciones de Dios Para Lideres.** (God's Little Instruction Books (Spanish)). (SPA.). 2000. pap. 3.99 (0-7899-0781-X) Spanish Hse Distributors.
***Librito de Instrucciones de Dios Para los Padres.** Various. (SPA.). 1999. pap. 3.99 (0-7899-0701-1) Spanish Hse Distributors.
Librito de Instrucciones de Dios para Madres. Honor Books Staff.Tr. of God's Little Instruction Book for Moms. (SPA.). 3.99 (0-7899-0544-2, 498349) Editorial Unilit.
Librito de Instrucciones de Dios para Mujeres. Jakes.Tr. of God's Little Instruction Book for Women. (SPA.). 156p. pap. 3.99 (0-7899-0352-0, 498345) Editorial Unilit.
Librito de Instrucciones de Dios para Ninos. Honor Books Staff.Tr. of God's Little Instruction Book for Kids. (SPA.). 1998. pap. text 3.99 (0-7899-0367-9, 498346) Editorial Unilit.
***Librito de Instrucciones de Dios para Parejas.** Honor Books Staff.Tr. of God's Little Instruction Book for Students. (SPA.). 2000. 3.99 (0-7899-0546-9, 498352) Editorial Unilit.
Librito de Instrucciones para la Vida. H. Jackson Brown, Jr. LC 91-9800. (SPA.). 160p. (Orig.). 1994. pap. 6.95 (1-55853-291-9) Rutledge Hill Pr.
Libro Apestoso (The Smelly Book) Babette Cole. Tr. by Francisco Segovia. (SPA., Illus.). 32p. (J). (gr. 1-3). 1994. 12.99 (968-16-4559-6, Pub. by Fondo) Continental Bk.
Libro Basico Ilustrado de Cienciologia. L. Ron Hubbard. 92p. 1991. pap. 18.00 (0-88404-743-1) Bridge Pubns Inc.
Libro Basico Ilustrado de Dianetica. L. Ron Hubbard. 82p. 1991. pap. 18.00 (0-88404-742-3) Bridge Pubns Inc.
Libro Catolico de Oraciones. large type ed. Maurus FitzGerald. (SPA., Illus.). 1984. vinyl bd. 8.50 (0-89942-438-4, 438/S) Catholic Bk Pub.
Libro Conplido en los Judizios de las Estrellas. Aly Aben Ragel. Ed. by Gerald Hilty. (SPA.). 273p. 1968. pap. 200.00 (0-614-00232-X) Elliots Bks.
Libro de Acciones. Barbara Saul. Tr. by Patricia Rodriguez-Kalson. (SPA.). (J). (gr. k-3). 1993. 12.50 (1-57842-105-5) Delmas Creat.
Libro de Actividades Biblicas, No. 1. G. Stowell.Tr. of Bible Story Puzzle Books. (SPA.). (J). 1.89 (1-56063-761-7, 497741) Editorial Unilit.
Libro de Actividades Biblicas, No. 2. G. Stowell.Tr. of Bible Story Puzzle Books. (SPA.). (J). 1.89 (1-56063-791-9, 497742) Editorial Unilit.
Libro de Actividades Biblicas, No. 3. G. Stowell.Tr. of Bible Story Puzzle Books. (SPA.). (J). 1.89 (1-56063-792-7, 497743) Editorial Unilit.
Libro de Actividades Biblicas, No. 4. G. Stowell.Tr. of Bible Story Puzzle Books. (SPA.). (J). 1.89 (1-56063-793-5, 497744) Editorial Unilit.
Libro de Alexandre: Medieval Epic & Silver Latin. Charles F. Fraker. LC 92-56387. (Studies in the Romance Languages & Literatures: No. 245). (C). 1993. 32.50 (0-8078-9249-1) U of NC Pr.
Libro de Alexandre: Texts of the Paris & the Madrid Manuscripts. Ed. by Raymond S. Willis, Jr. (Elliott Monographs: Vol. 32). 1934. 50.00 (0-527-02635-2) Periodicals Srv.
Libro de Alixandre. Alexander. (Gesellschaft Fur Romanische Literatur Ser.: Vol. 10). xxviii, 333p. 1978. reprint ed. 72.00 (3-487-06543-6) G Olms Pubs.
Libro de Apollonio, an Old Spanish Poem, 2 pts. Ed. & Contrib. by C. C. Marden. Incl. Vols. 11-12. 1969. reprint ed. pap. 25.00 (0-527-02615-8); (SPA.). 1969. Set pap. 25.00 (0-527-02610-7) Periodicals Srv.
Libro de Arena. Jorge Luis Borges. (SPA.). pap. 15.95 (84-206-3313-5, Pub. by Alianza Editorial) Continental Bk.
Libro de Arena. 2nd ed. Jorge Luis Borges. (SPA.). 128p. 1991. pap. 6.95 (0-7859-4974-7) Fr & Eur.
Libro de Arte para el Boletin de la Iglesia. Tr. of Church Bulletin Clip Art Book. 14.99 (1-56063-346-8, 498604) Editorial Unilit.
Libro de Arte para el Ministerio de la Iglesia. Tom Finley.Tr. of Church Ministry Clip Art Book. (SPA.). 100p. 1988. pap. 14.99 (1-56063-345-X, 498607) Editorial Unilit.
Libro de Arte para la Escuela Dominical. A. Huffaker.Tr. of Sunday School Clip Art Book. (SPA.). 100p. 1993. pap. 14.99 (1-56063-344-1, 498605) Editorial Unilit.
Libro de Astrologia y Numerologia de Zolar. Zolar Staff.Tr. of Zolar's Book of Dreams, Numbers & Lucky Days. (ENG & SPA.). 1995. per. 10.00 (0-684-81328-9, Fireside) S&S Trade Pap.
Libro de Ayudas Visuales Biblicas. Tr. of Bible Visual Resources Book. (SPA.). 320p. 1995. 18.99 (1-56063-547-9, 498602) Editorial Unilit.
***Libro de Bolsillo de Oraciones Catolicas.** Ed. by Catholic Book Publishing Staff.Tr. of Pocket Book of Catholic Prayers. 2000. pap. 4.95 (0-89942-332-9) Catholic Bk Pub.
Libro de Buen Amor. Arcipreste de Hita. (SPA.). 7.95 (84-241-5640-4) E Torres & Sons.
Libro de Buen Amor. Arcipreste de Hita. (Nueva Austral Ser.: No. 9). (SPA.). pap. 12.95 (84-239-1809-2) Elliots Bks.
Libro de Buen Amor: Edicion Facsimil del Manuscrito Gayoso (1389) Juan Ruiz. (Real Academia Ediciones Ser.). (SPA.). 1993. 500.00 (84-600-6149-3) Elliots Bks.
Libro de Buen Amor' Studies. Ed. by G. B. Gybbon-Moneypenny. (Monagrafias A Ser.: Vol. XII). 256p. 1970. pap. 51.00 (0-900411-04-X, Pub. by Tamesis Bks Ltd) Boydell & Brewer.
Libro de Caca de las Aves. Pero L. De Ayala. Ed. by John G. Cummins. 1986. 51.00 (0-7293-0258-X, Pub. by Tamesis Bks Ltd) Boydell & Brewer.
***Libro de Caligrafia.** Portavoz Editorial Staff. (Sabio & Prudente Ser.). 64p. 1999. pap. 4.99 (0-8254-0996-9, Edit Portavoz) Kregel.
Libro de Calo. rev. ed. Harry Polkinhorn et al. LC 86-4693. 95p. 1987. 19.95 (0-915745-10-0) Floricanto Pr.
Libro de Calo: The Dictionary of Chicano Slang. 2nd rev. ed. Harry Polkinhorn et al. 100p. 1988. pap. 19.95 (0-685-45617-X) Floricanto Pr.
Libro de Colores y Numeros. Delma Morton. Tr. by Patricia Rodriguez-Kalson. (SPA.). (J). (gr. k-2). 1993. 12.50 (1-57842-109-8) Delmas Creat.
Libro de Concordia. Ed. by Andres A. Melendez. (SPA.). 1989. 19.95 (0-570-09902-1, 16-1009) Concordia.
***Libro de Consulta Para el Orador.** Eleanor Doan. 1999. pap. write for info. (0-8297-0630-5) Vida Pubs.
Libro de Contar de los Chocolates Marca "M&M" Barbara B. McGrath. Tr. by Teresa Mlawer from ENG. LC 96-945. (SPA., Illus.). 32p. (J). (ps-3). 1996. pap. 6.95 (0-88106-903-5) Charlesbridge Pub.
Libro de Contar de Los Chocolates Marca M&M. Barbara Barbieri McGrath. 1996. 12.15 (0-606-10413-5, Pub. by Turtleback) Demco.
Libro de Contrarios. Carl Morton. Tr. by Angelita L. Aguilar. (SPA.). (J). (gr. k-3). 1995. 12.50 (1-57842-101-2) Delmas Creat.
Libro de Convocaciones I: Cervantes, Dostoyevski, Nietzsche, A. Machado. Jose Echeverria. 1987. 9.95 (0-317-58456-1) U of PR Pr.
Libro de Datacad 5 en Espanol. Leonard O. Nasman. Tr. by Raul Herrera. (SPA., Illus.). 120p. 1994. student ed. 15.95 (1-880544-37-7, DCAD5-2, Pub. by Micro Educ) Tech Ed Concepts.
Libro de Dio. 1989. 6.99 (0-311-48796-3) Baptist Spanish.
Libro de Ejercicios. (GER.). 1997. pap. write for info. (3-468-49407-6) Langenscheidt.
Libro de Ejercicios 1. (GER.). 1997. pap. write for info. (3-468-96812-4) Langenscheidt.
Libro de Ejercicios 2. (GER.). 1997. pap. write for info. (3-468-96824-8) Langenscheidt.
Libro de Estilo el Pais. (SPA.). 661p. 1996. pap. 28.00 (84-86459-69-9, Pub. by Pais Ediciones) IBD Ltd.
Libro de Exodo. Ernesto Trenchard & Antonio Ruiz. (SPA.). 400p. 1994. pap. 12.99 (0-8254-1750-3, Edit Portavoz) Kregel.
Libro de la Arena. Jorge Luis Borges. (SPA.). pap. 15.95 (84-206-1662-1, Pub. by Alianza Editorial) Continental Bk.
Libro de la Caza. Infant V. Juan Manuel. viii, 208p. 1984. reprint ed. write for info. (3-487-07346-3) G Olms Pubs.
Libro de la Escritura. Pinguino Tinto. Tr. by Isaac Goldemberg. (Illus.). 56p. 1989. pap. 8.95 (0-915924-65-X) Tchrs & Writers Coll.
Libro de la Navidad. (SPA., Illus.). 318p. 1996. 18.95 (0-86573-973-0) Creat Pub Intl.
Libro de la Risa y el Olvido. 8th ed. Milan Kundera. Tr. by Fernando De Valenzuela from CZE. (SPA.). 327p. 1991. pap. 29.95 (0-7859-0542-1, 8432204145) Fr & Eur.
Libro de la Selva (The Jungle Book) Mouse Works Staff. (SPA.). 96p. (J). 1996. 7.98 (1-57082-511-4, Pub. by Mouse Works) Time Warner.
Libro de la Vida Verdadera see Book of the True Life
Libro de las Arenas Movedizas. Tomie De Paola. Tr. by Teresa Mlawer. LC 93-18317. (SPA.). 32p. (J). (ps-3). 1993. lib. bdg. 15.95 (0-8234-1056-0) Holiday.
Libro de las Arenas Movedizas. Tomie De Paola. LC 93-18317. (SPA., Illus.). 32p. (J). (ps-3). 1993. pap. 5.95 (0-8234-1057-9) Holiday.
Libro de las Cruzes. Alfonso X. Ed. by Lloyd A. Kasten & Lawrence B. Kiddle. (Illus.). xlviii, 173p. 1961. pap. 10.00 (0-942260-03-1) Hispanic Seminary.
Libro de las Fundaciones. Teresa De Jesus. Ed. by Victor Garcia de la Concha. (Nueva Austral Ser.: Vol. 205). (SPA.). 1991. pap. text 24.95 (84-239-7205-4) Elliots Bks.
Libro de las Generaciones & The Book of Yashar. Ed. by Moshe Lazar & Robert Dilligan. LC 89-85090. (Sephardic Classical Library: No. 3). (ENG & SPA.). 515p. (C). 1990. lib. bdg. 90.00 (0-911437-51-7) Labyrinthos.
Libro de las Ideas Para Producir Mejor. Japan Management Association Staff. (SPA., Illus.). 255p. (Orig.). 1991. pap. 35.00 (84-86703-50-6) Productivity Inc.
Libro de las Inteferencia (The Book of Interferences) Rafael Bordao. Tr. by Louis Bourne. LC 94-61894. (SPA.). 53p. (Orig.). (C). 1995. pap. text 5.95 (0-9623552-7-5, Palmar Pr) Ed Arcas.
Libro de las Mejoras: Creacion de Areas de Trabajo Libres de Problemas. Tomo Sugiyama. (SPA., Illus.). 259p. (Orig.). 1991. pap. 50.00 (84-87022-75-8) Productivity Inc.
Libro de las Nubes. Tomie De Paola. Tr. by Teresa Mlawer. LC 93-18316. (SPA., Illus.). 32p. (J). (ps-3). 1993. pap. 6.95 (0-8234-1055-2) Holiday.
Libro de las Palomitas de Maiz. Tomie De Paola. Tr. by Teresa Mlawer. LC 93-18318. (SPA.). 32p. (J). (ps-3). 1993. lib. bdg. 15.95 (0-8234-1058-7) Holiday.
Libro de las Preguntas: Seleccion. Pablo Neruda. (Coleccion Estrella de los Andes). (SPA.). 1991. 12.70 (0-606-05257-7, Pub. by Turtleback) Demco.
Libro de las Profecias of Christopher Columbus: An en Face Edition. Tr. by August Kling from LAT. (Columbus Quincentenary Ser.). 274p. 1991. 49.95 (0-8130-1054-3) U Press Fla.
Libro de las Tahuererias. Ed. by Robert A. MacDonald. (Spanish Legal Texts Ser.). xii, 485p. 1995. 50.00 (1-56954-027-6) Hispanic Seminary.
Libro de lo Insolito (The Book of the Bizarre) Antologia (Anthology) 2nd ed. Emiliano Gonzalez & Beatriz A. Klein. (SPA.). 624p. 1994. pap. 10.99 (968-16-4468-9, Pub. by Fondo) Continental Bk.
Libro de los Afectos Culinarios. Carmen V. Arce. 1996. pap. text. write for info. (1-56758-042-4) Edit Cultl.
Libro de los Amigos. Andrew Matthews. (SPA.). 1997. pap. text 8.98 (968-403-604-3) Selector.
Libro de los Buenos Proverbios: A Critical Edition. Harlan Sturm. LC 72-111515. (Studies in Romance Languages: No. 5). 149p. 1970. reprint ed. pap. 46.20 (0-608-17480-7, 202997400067) Bks Demand.
Libro de los Cerdos. Anthony Browne.Tr. of Piggybook. (Illus.). 32p. 1995. 12.99 (958-9093-33-7, Pub. by Fondo) Continental Bk.
Libro de los Enganos. Ed. by John E. Keller. (Romance Monographs: No. 2). 1983. reprint ed. pap. 9.00 (0-317-01689-X) Romance.
Libro de los Hopis. Frank Waters. (SPA.). pap. 15.99 (968-16-3705-4, Pub. by Fondo) Continental Bk.
Libro de los Libros de Chilam Balam (The Book of Books of Chilam Balam) (SPA.). 213p. 1984. pap. 7.99 (968-16-0977-8, Pub. by Fondo) Continental Bk.
Libro de los Santos. (SPA., Illus.). 1985. 9.95 (0-89942-236-5, 236/22S) Catholic Bk Pub.
***Libro de los Signos Lunares para el Ano 2000.** Gloria Star. (SPA.). 559p. 1999. pap. 9.95 (968-19-0599-7) Santillana.
***Libro de los Signos Solares Para el Ano 2000.** Gloria Star. (SPA.). 2000. pap. 9.95 (968-19-0598-9) Aguilar.
***Libro De Magia De La Bruja Moderna.** Montse Osuna. 1999. pap. 17.95 (84-270-2418-5) Planeta.
Libro de Mapas Biblicos. Simon Jenkins.Tr. of Bible Map Book. (SPA.). 1985. 9.99 (1-56063-207-0, 490460); pap. write for info. (0-614-27071-5) Editorial Unilit.
Libro de McGruff - McGruff's Activity Book. Ed. by Jean O'Neil. (SPA., Illus.). 96p. 1993. pap. 22.95 (0-934513-50-3, K9) Natl Crime DC.
Libro de Mirdad. Mikhail Naimy. (SPA.). 248p. pap. 15.00 (84-404-1600-8) Rosycross Pr.
Libro de Musica de Vihuela de Mano Intitulado el Maestro. Luys Milan. (Publikationen Alterer Musik Ser.: No. II). xxx, 382p. 1976. reprint ed. write for info. (3-487-00629-4) G Olms Pubs.
Libro de Oraciones: Letra Grande. large type ed. Jerome Duesman. (SPA.). 48p. 1994. pap. 1.00 (0-8189-0705-3) Alba.
Libro de Oracyones: Ferrara Ladino Siddur. Ed. by Moshe Lazar & Robert Dilligan. LC 95-80477. (Sephardic Classical Library: Vol. 11). (LAD., Illus.). 612p. (C). 1995. 95.00 (0-911437-64-9) Labyrinthos.
***Libro de Pegatinas Banderas (Flags Sticker Book)** Lisa Miles. (Spotter's Guides Sticker Bks.). (SPA., Illus.). 32p. (gr. 2 up). 1999. pap. 7.95 (0-7460-3644-2, Usborne) EDC.
***Libro de Pegatinas Caballos y Ponis (Horses & Ponies Sticker Book)** (ENG & SPA., Illus.). 32p. (J). (gr. 2 up). 2000. pap. 7.95 (0-7460-3885-2, Usborne) EDC.
***Libro de Pegatinas Dinosaurios (Dinosaur Sticker Book)** (ENG & SPA., Illus.). 32p. (J). (gr. 2 up). 2000. pap. 7.95 (0-7460-3886-0, Usborne) EDC.
***Libro de Pegatinas Gatos (Cats Sticker Book)** Lisa Miles. (Spotter's Guide Sticker Bks.). (ENG & SPA., Illus.). 32p. (YA). (gr. 2 up). 2000. pap. 7.95 (0-7460-3884-4, Usborne) EDC.
***Libro de Pegatinas Perros.** A. Glover. (Spotter's Guides Sticker Bks.).Tr. of Dogs Sticker Book. (SPA., Illus.). 32p. (J). (gr. 2 up). 1999. pap. 7.95 (0-7460-3643-4, Usborne) EDC.
***Libro de Pegatinas Rocas y Minerales.** Lisa Miles. (Spotter's Guides Sticker Bks.). (SPA., Illus.). 32p. (gr. 2 up). 1999. pap. 7.95 (0-7460-3642-6, Usborne) EDC.

An Asterisk (*) at the beginning of an entry indicates that the title is appearing for the first time.

Libro de Piel de Tiburon. Manuel De Lope. 1996. pap. text 11.95 (*84-204-4853-2*) Santillana.

Libro de Poemas. Federico Garcia Lorca. Ed. & Intro. by Mario Hernandez. (SPA.). pap. 17.95 (*84-206-6114-7*, Pub. by Alianza Editorial) Continental Bk.

Libro de Poemas, Poema del Cante Jondo, Romancero Gitano, Poeta en Nueva York, Odas, Llanto por Sanchez Mejias, Bodas de Sangre, Yerma. Federico Garcia Lorca. (SPA.). 1999. pap. 9.95 (*970-07-1734-8*) Colton Bk.

Libro de Preludios. Jaume Cabre. Tr. by Enrique Sordo Lamadrid. (Nueva Austral Ser.: No. 62). (SPA.). 1991. pap. text 24.95 (*84-239-1862-9*) Elliots Bks.

Libro de Reencarnacion de Zolar el Libro de Reencarnacion de Zolar. Zolar Staff. (SPA.). 240p. 1996. per. 12.00 (*0-684-82669-0*) S&S Trade.

***Libro de Sinonimos y Antonimos para Estudiantes: Spanish Thesaurus for Students.** Joan Greisman & Harriet Wittels. (SPA.). 260p. 2000. pap. 9.95 (*0-7641-1447-6*) Barron.

Libro de Urantia. Ed. by Andite Corporation Staff. 1998. pap. 24.95 (*1-883395-01-1*) Andite IL.

***Libro de Urantia.** 5th ed. Andite Corporation Staff. (SPA.). lxvi, 2097p. 1999. reprint ed. 24.95 (*1-883395-03-8*) Andite IL.

***Libro de Urantia.** 6th ed. Ed. by Andite Corporation Staff. (SPA.). lxvi, 2097p. 1999. reprint ed. pap. 19.95 (*1-883395-02-X*) Andite IL.

Libro de Verdades Biblicas (Daily Book of Bible Truths) (SPA.). 1994. 1.99 (*1-56063-444-8*, 491403) Editorial Unilit.

Libro de Vida (E. V.) Tr. of Book of Hope - Edition E. V. (SPA.). 224p. 1990. pap. 1.95 (*0-8297-0416-7*) Life Pubs Intl.

Libro Degli Esecizi E Sintesi Di Grammatica. Gruppo Meta. (Illus.). 210p. 1996. pap. 29.95 (*0-521-57808-6*) Cambridge U Pr.

Libro Degli Esercizi 1. D. Balduzzi et al. (GER.). 128p. 1997. pap. write for info. (*3-468-96771-3*) Langenscheidt.

Libro Degli Esercizi 2. F. Bovo et al. (GER.). 128p. 1997. pap. write for info. (*3-468-96774-8*) Langenscheidt.

***Libro Dei Mori.** Ed. by Cristiana Grocometti. (Visions of the World Ser.). (ITA.). 1999. 29.95 incl. audio compact disk (*1-58214-128-2*) Mltilingl Bks.

***Libro Dei Mori, Vol. 2.** Ed. by Cristiana Grocometti. (Visions of the World Ser.). (ITA.). 1999. 19.95 incl. audio (*1-58214-127-4*) Mltilingl Bks.

Libro Del Ano - 1998. Encyclopaedia Britannica Publishers, Inc. Staff. (SPA., Illus.). 416p. 1998. write for info. (*1-56409-022-1*) EBP Latin Am.

***Libro del Ano 2000.** Encyclopaedia Britannica Publishers, Inc. Staff. (SPA., Illus.). 416p. 2000. write for info. (*1-56409-035-3*) EBP Latin Am.

Libro del Ano, 1999. Encyclopedia Britannica Publishers, Inc. Staff. (SPA., Illus.). 416p. 1999. text 39.95 (*1-56409-029-9*) EBP Latin Am.

Libro Del Ano, 1997. Encyclopedia Britannica Publishers, Inc. Staff et al. (SPA., Illus.). 416p. 1997. write for info. (*1-56409-019-1*) EBP Latin Am.

Libro Del Arcipreste, Tambien Llamado Libro de Buen Amor: Edicion Sinoptica. Juan Ruiz. (Spanish Ser.: No. 44). (SPA.). lxvi, 230p. (C). 1989. 20.00 (*0-940639-28-9*) Hispanic Seminary.

Libro Del Buen Amor. Arcipreste De Hita. (SPA.). 162p. 1979. 9.95 (*0-8288-7052-7*, S29007) Fr & Eur.

Libro del Conocimiento: Las Claves de Enoc. 2nd ed. J. J. Hurtak. 619p. 1982. 30.00 (*0-9603450-4-3*) Acad Future Sci.

Libro Del Conoscimiento de Todos Los Reinos: The Book of Knowledge of All Kingdoms. Ed. by Nancy F. Marino. LC 99-13118. (Medieval & Renaissance Texts & Studies: Vol. 198). (Illus.). 224p. 1999. 24.00 (*0-86698-240-X*, MR198) MRTS.

Libro del Mucho Amor (The Book of Love) Jose M. Unsain. (SPA., Illus.). 189p. 1997. 37.99 (*968-16-4992-3*, Pub. by Fondo) Continental Bk.

Libro del Osito. Anthony Browne. Tr. by Carmen Esteva.Tr. of Little Bear Book. (SPA., Illus.). 24p. 1995. 6.99 (*968-16-4529-4*, Pub. by Fondo) Continental Bk.

Libro del Padre. Frank Minirth et al. (Serie Minirth-Meier).Tr. of Father Book. (SPA.). 288p. 10.99 (*0-88113-231-4*, B001-2314) Caribe Betania.

***Libro del Pene.** Ed. by Konemann Inc. Staff. 2000. 9.95 (*3-8290-4106-3*) Konemann.

Libro del Tesoro: Version Castellana de Li Livres dou Tresor. Brunetto Latini. Ed. & Tr. by Spurgeon Baldwin. (Spanish Ser.: No. 46). (SPA.). viii, 260p. 1989. 25.00 (*0-940639-31-9*) Hispanic Seminary.

Libro del Trasoro. Ed. by Dawn E. Prince. (Dialect Ser.: No. 15). xxxii, 235p. 1995. 35.00 (*1-56954-040-3*) Hispanic Seminary.

Libro Dello Studente. Gruppo Meta. (Illus.). 243p. 1996. pap. 31.95 (*0-521-57809-4*) Cambridge U Pr.

Libro d'Esercizi. (GER.). 1997. pap. write for info. (*3-468-49405-X*) Langenscheidt.

Libro Despegable (Concertina Puzzle Book) Regalos en la Primera Navidad (The First Christmas Present) Lion Staff. (SPA.). 4.99 (*1-56063-202-X*, 494002) Editorial Unilit.

Libro Detext. NAUI Staff. (Illus.). 188p. 1994. pap. 24.95 (*0-916974-56-1*, 11003) NAUI.

Libro Ilustrado Sobre Martin Luther King, Hijo. David A. Adler. Tr. by Teresa Mlawer from ENG. Orig. Title: A Picture Book of Martin Luther King, Jr.. (SPA., Illus.). 32p. (J). (ps-3). 1992. reprint ed. pap. 6.95 (*0-8234-0991-0*); reprint ed. lib. bdg. 15.95 (*0-8234-0982-1*) Holiday.

Libro Ilustrado Sobre Martin Luther King, Hijo. unabridged ed. David A. Adler. Orig. Title: A Picture Book of Martin Luther King, Jr.. (SPA., Illus.). (J). (gr. 1-6). 1993. 24.95 incl. audio (*0-87499-297-4*); pap. 15.95 incl. audio (*0-87499-296-6*) Live Oak Media.

Libro Ilustrado Sobre Martin Luther King, Hijo, 4 bks., Set. unabridged ed. David A. Adler. Orig. Title: A Picture Book of Martin Luther King, Jr.. (SPA., Illus.). (J). (gr. 1-6). 1993. pap., teacher ed. 37.95 incl. audio (*0-87499-298-2*) Live Oak Media.

Libro Judio del por Que. Alfred J. Kolatch. LC 93-44620. 326p. 1994. 16.95 (*0-8246-0375-3*) Jonathan David.

Libro Llamado Fedron: Plato's Phaedo. Plato. Ed. by Nicholas G. Round. (Textos B Ser.: No. 39). (SPA.). 406p. 1993. 75.00 (*1-85566-024-5*) Boydell & Brewer.

Libro Mondiale di Cognomi. Numa Research Department Staff. 95p. 1994. 54.00 (*1-885808-11-9*); pap. text 48.00 (*1-885808-12-7*) Numa Corp.

Libro Mundial de los Apellidos Familiares. Numa Research Department Staff. 95p. 1994. 54.00 (*1-885808-09-7*); pap. text 48.00 (*1-885808-10-0*) Numa Corp.

Libro Para Amantes: Los Hombres Que Excitan a las Mujeres, las Mujeres Que Excitan a los Hombres. Carolyn Reynolds. LC 95-35995.Tr. of Book of Lovers: Men Who Excite Women Women Who Excite Men. (SPA.). 480p. 1999. pap. 20.00 (*1-56718-569-X*) Llewellyn Pubns.

Libro Para Parteras: Una Guia Para Comadronas y Parteras Tradicionales. Susan Klein et al.Tr. of Book for Midwives. (SPA., Illus.). 519p. 1998. pap. 22.00 (*0-942364-28-7*) Hesperian Found.

Libro Puertorriqueno de Nueva York: Handbook of the Puerto Rican Community. Federico R. Tovar. Ed. by Carlos E. Cortes. LC 79-6219. (Hispanics in the United States Ser.). (ENG & SPA., Illus.). 1981. reprint ed. lib. bdg. 62.95 (*0-405-13167-4*) Ayer.

Libro Quemado - Burnt Book. Leandro Katz. (Illus.). 1995. pap. 18.00 (*0-932526-54-3*) Nexus Pr.

Libro Rojo-Tratado de Paris: Documentos Presentados a la Cortes en la Legislatura de 1898 por el Ministros de Estado. LC 88-21236. 324p. 1988. 37.50 (*0-8477-1002-5*) U of PR Pr.

Libro Secreto de Daniel Torres, Level 2. Rosana Acquaroni. (Leer en Espanol Ser.). (SPA.). (C). 1998. pap. 5.95 (*84-294-4043-7*) Santillana.

***Libro Secreto de los Gitanos.** Gillian Kemp. 1999. pap. 14.95 (*84-270-2390-1*) E Martinez Roca.

***Libro Siembre Neuvo.** J. S. Delgado. (SPA.). 1999. 9.99 (*0-8297-0430-2*) Vida Pubs.

Libro Universal de Ilustraciones del Parto. Fran P. Hosken. (Childbirth Picture Bks.).Tr. of Universal Childbirth Picture Book. (SPA., Illus.). 76p. (Orig.). 1982. 7.00 (*0-942096-03-7*) WINNEWS.

Libros Californianos: or Five Feet of California Books. Phil T. Hanna. 1992. reprint ed. lib. bdg. 75.00 (*0-7812-5045-5*) Rprt Serv.

Libros de Cuentas de los Corrales de Comedias de Madrid: 1706-1719 Estudio y Documentos. Ed. by J. E. Varey & Charles Davis. (Fuentes para la Historia del Teatro en Espana Ser.: No. XVI). (SPA.). 445p. (C). 1992. pap. 72.00 (*1-85566-018-0*, Pub. by Tamesis Bks Ltd) Boydell & Brewer.

Libros de Diez Palabras Series, 4 bks., Set. Bob Reese & Pam Preece-Sandoval. Tr. by Gloria Schaffer-Melendez. (SPA., Illus.). (J). (gr. k-3). 1994. pap. 15.80 (*0-89868-279-7*, Read Res); lib. bdg. 39.80 (*0-89868-278-9*, Read Res) ARO Pub.

Libros de Oratore Tres see Rhetorica

Libros de Poemas. Guillermo Nunez. LC 78-1444. (UPREX, Poesia Ser.: No. 53). (SPA.). 231p. 1978. pap. 1.50 (*0-8477-3225-8*) U of PR Pr.

Libros de Viente Palabras Series: Libros de la Granja Loca, 4 bks., Set. Wendy Kanno. Tr. by Gloria Schaffer-Melendez. (SPA., Illus.). (J). (gr. k-3). 1994. pap. 15.80 (*0-89868-281-9*, Read Res); lib. bdg. 39.80 (*0-89868-280-0*, Read Res) ARO Pub.

Libros en Espanol para los Pequenos. (ENG & SPA.). 47p. 1993. 5.00 (*0-685-70977-9*, Branch Libraries) NY Pub Lib.

Libros en Venta en Hispanoamerica y Espana, 1990, 3 vols., Set. 5th ed. (SPA.). 4500p. 1990. 385.00 (*0-923737-04-9*) NISC Puerto Rico.

Libros en Venta en Hispanoamerica y Espana, 1990, 3 vols., Vol. 3: Materias. 5th ed. (SPA.). 4500p. 1990. pap. 138.00 (*0-923737-06-5*) NISC Puerto Rico.

Libros en Venta en Hispanoamerica y Espana, 1990, 3 vols., Vols. 1 & 2. 5th ed. (SPA.). 4500p. 1990. pap. 276.00 (*0-923737-05-7*) NISC Puerto Rico.

Libros Historicos Del A. T. P. Hoff.Tr. of Historical Books of the O. T.. (SPA.). 288p. 1983. pap. 9.99 (*0-8297-1359-X*) Vida Pubs.

Libros Infantiles y Juveniles en Espanol: Una Guia Anotada see Books in Spanish for Children & Young Adults: An Annotated Guide

***Libros Poeticos.** Pablo Hoff. 1998. 9.99 (*0-8297-1510-X*) Vida Pubs.

Libya see Cultures of the World - Group 6

Libya. (Arte & Arquitectura Ser.). (Illus.). 256p. 1999. 29.95 (*3-8290-3281-1*, 540509) Konemann.

Libya. Richard I. Lawless. LC 88-149408. (World Bibliographical Ser.: No. 79). 268p. 1987. lib. bdg. 65.00 (*1-85109-033-9*) ABC-CLIO.

Libya. Terri Willis. LC 98-28174. (Enchantment of the World Ser.). 144p. (YA). (gr. 5-9). 1999. 32.00 (*0-516-21008-4*) Childrens.

Libya: A Country Study. 4th ed. Contrib. by Defense Department, Army Staff. LC 88-600480. (Illus.). 379p. 1996. boxed set 25.00 (*0-16-001711-4*) USGPO.

***Libya: A Country Study Guide.** Global Investment & Business Center, Inc. Staff. (World Country Study Guides Library: Vol. 98). (Illus.). 350p. 2000. pap. 59.00 (*0-7397-2396-0*) Intl Business Pubns.

Libya: Lost Sites of the Roman Empire. Antonino Di Vita & Lidiano Bacchielli. (Illus.). 160p. 1999. 29.95 (*3-89508-844-7*, 520509) Konemann.

***Libya: Major World Nations.** Renfield Sanders. LC 99-19183. (Major World Nations Ser.). (Illus.). 144p. 1999. 19.95 (*0-7910-5388-1*) Chelsea Hse.

Libya: The Political Economy of Oil. Judith Gurney. LC 97-157037. (Illus.). 256p. (C). 1996. text 60.00 (*0-19-730017-0*) OUP.

Libya: The Struggle for Survival. Geoff Simons. LC 92-30624. 256p. 1993. text 35.00 (*0-312-08997-X*) St Martin.

Libya: The Struggle for Survival. 2nd ed. Geoff Simons. 422p. 1996. pap. 19.95 (*0-312-16002-X*) St Martin.

Libya - A Country Study Guide: Basic Information for Research & Pleasure. Global Investment Center, USA Staff. (World Country Study Guide Library: Vol. 98). (Illus.). 350p. 1999. pap. 59.00 (*0-7397-1495-3*) Intl Business Pubns.

Libya - In Pictures. Compiled by Lerner Publications, Department of Geography Staff. LC 95-39567. (Visual Geography Ser.). (Illus.). (J). 1996. lib. bdg. 19.93 (*0-8225-1907-0*, Lerner Publctns) Lerner Pub.

Libya, a Modern History. John L. Wright. LC 81-48183. 303p. 1982. reprint ed. pap. 94.00 (*0-608-03709-5*, 206453400009) Bks Demand.

Libya, Amnesty International's Prisoner Concerns in the Light of Recent Legal Reforms. 69p. 1991. 5.00 (*0-685-50860-9*, MDE 19-02-91) Amnesty Intl USA.

Libya & Egypt in the First Millennium BC. Anthony Leahy. 224p. 1988. lib. bdg. 39.95 (*0-415-00478-0*) Routledge.

***Libya Business Intelligence Report, 190 vols.** Global Investment & Business Center, Inc. Staff. (World Business Intelligence Library: Vol. 98). (Illus.). 350p. 2000. pap. 99.95 (*0-7397-2596-3*) Intl Business Pubns.

***Libya Business Law Handbook, 190 vols.** Global Investment & Business Center, Inc. Staff. (Global Business Law Handbooks Library: Vol. 98). (Illus.). 350p. 2000. pap. 99.95 (*0-7397-1995-5*) Intl Business Pubns.

***Libya Business Opportunity Yearbook.** Global Investment & Business Center, Inc. Staff. (Global Business Opportunity Yearbooks Library: Vol. 98). (Illus.). 2000. pap. 99.95 (*0-7397-2196-8*) Intl Business Pubns.

***Libya Business Opportunity Yearbook: Export-Import, Investment & Business Opportunities.** International Business Publications, U. S. A. Staff & Global Investment Center, U. S. A. Staff. (Global Business Opportunity Yearbooks Library: Vol. 98). (Illus.). 350p. 1999. pap. 99.95 (*0-7397-1296-9*) Intl Business Pubns.

Libya, Chad, & the Central Sahara. John L. Wright. 208p. (C). 1989. lib. bdg. 56.00 (*0-389-20860-4*, N8418) B&N Imports.

***Libya Foreign Policy & Government Guide.** Global Investment & Business Center, Inc. Staff. (World Foreign Policy & Government Library: Vol. 94). (Illus.). 350p. 1999. pap. 99.00 (*0-7397-3592-6*) Intl Business Pubns.

***Libya Foreign Policy & Government Guide.** Global Investment & Business Center, Inc. Staff. (World Foreign Policy & Government Library: Vol. 94). (Illus.). 350p. 2000. pap. 99.95 (*0-7397-3796-1*) Intl Business Pubns.

***Libya Investment & Business Guide.** Global Investment & Business Center, Inc. Staff. (Global Investment & Business Guide Library: Vol. 98). (Illus.). 2000. pap. 99.95 (*0-7397-1796-0*) Intl Business Pubns.

***Libya Investment & Business Guide: Export-Import, Investment & Business Opportunities.** International Business Publications, USA Staff & Global Investment Center, USA Staff. (World Investment & Business Guide Library-99: Vol. 98). (Illus.). 350p. 1999. pap. 99.95 (*0-7397-0293-9*) Intl Business Pubns.

Libya since Independence: Oil & State-Building. Dirk Vandewalle. LC 98-3461. (Illus.). 232p. 1998. pap. 16.95 (*0-8014-8535-5*); text 45.00 (*0-8014-3472-6*) Cornell U Pr.

Libya since the Revolution: Aspects of Social & Political Development. Marius K. Deeb & Mary J. Deeb. LC 81-19985. 156p. 1982. 57.95 (*0-275-90780-5*, C0780, Praeger Pubs) Greenwood.

Libyan Arena: The U. S., Britain & the Council of Foreign Ministers, 1945-1948. Scott L. Bills. LC 94-33134. (American Diplomatic History Ser.: No. 8). (Illus.). 232p. 1995. 30.00 (*0-87338-511-X*) Kent St U Pr.

Libyan Civil Code. I. M. Arif & M. O. Ansell. (Libya Past & Present Ser.: Vol. 4). 1976. 95.00 (*0-902675-00-1*) Oleander Pr.

Libyan Independence & the United Nations: A Case of Planned Decolonization. Adrian Pelt. LC 72-99836. 1046p. reprint ed. pap. 200.00 (*0-8357-8208-5*, 203385300087) Bks Demand.

Libyan Jamahiriya. M. B. Fergiani. 256p. 1987. 150.00 (*1-85077-001-8*, Pub. by Darf Pubs Ltd) St Mut.

Libyan Mammals. Ernst Hufnagl. (Libya Past & Present Ser.: Vol. 3). (Illus.). 1968. 18.95 (*0-902675-08-7*) Oleander Pr.

Libyan Notes: Essentially a Study of the Berber Tribes. David Randall-Maciver & Wilkin. 176p. 1990. 125.00 (*1-85077-169-3*, Pub. by Darf Pubs Ltd) St Mut.

Libyan Oil Industry. Frank C. Waddams. LC 80-13939. (Illus.). 336p. 1980. reprint ed. pap. 104.20 (*0-608-05319-8*, 206585700001) Bks Demand.

Libyan Revolution: A Sourcebook of Legal & Historical Documents, Vol. 1, Sept. 1, 1969 to Aug. 30, 1970. I. M. Arif & M. O. Ansell. (Libya Past & Present Ser.: Vol. 1). 1970. 45.00 (*0-902675-10-9*) Oleander Pr.

Libyan Sands: Travel in a Dead World. Ralph A. Bagnold. 228p. (C). 1995. pap. 24.00 (*0-907151-90-6*, Pub. by IMMEL Pubng) St Mut.

Libyan Stories. Ed. by Ahmed Fagih. LC 99-20638. 77p. 1999. 35.00 (*0-7103-0634-2*, Pub. by Kegan Paul Intl) Col U Pr.

Libya's Agricultural Growth. Allen. 1990. 48.50 (*0-7146-2946-4*, Pub. by F Cass Pubs) Intl Spec Bk.

Libya's Qaddafui: The Politics of Contradiction. Mansour O. El-Kikhia. LC 96-44107. (Illus.). 280p. 1997. 49.95 (*0-8130-1488-3*) U Press Fla.

Libya's Qaddafui: The Politics of Contradiction. Mansour O. El-Kikhia. 280p. 1998. pap. 19.95 (*0-8130-1585-5*) U Press Fla.

Lice. Blaise Cendrars. Tr. by Nina Rootes from FRE. 189p. 1973. pap. 17.95 (*0-7206-0634-9*, Pub. by P Owen Ltd) Dufour.

***Lice.** Patrick Merrick. LC 98-45209. (Illus.). 32p. (J). 1999. lib. bdg. write for info. (*1-56766-634-5*) Childs World.

***Lice & Pediculosis: Index of New Information with Authors, Subjects & Bibliographical References.** rev. ed. Donald L. Downey. 149p. 1999. 47.50 (*0-7883-2136-6*); pap. 44.50 (*0-7883-2137-4*) ABBE Pubs Assn.

Lice Are Lousy: All about Headlice. Margaret Tsubakiyama. LC 98-26730. (Illus.). 32p. (J). (gr. k-3). 1999. lib. bdg. 19.90 (*0-7613-1316-8*, Copper Beech Bks) Millbrook Pr.

Lice-Buster Book: What to Do When Your Child Comes Home with Head Lice. Lennie Copeland. (Illus.). 128p. (Orig.). 1996. mass mkt. 8.99 (*0-446-67249-1*, Pub. by Warner Bks) Little.

***Lice Out Case.** Gwen E. Staples. (Illus.). 24p. (J). (gr. k-6). 1999. pap. 6.95 (*0-9675824-0-7*) Wal-Med Inc.

Licence Denied. Ed. by Paul Cornell. (Virgin Ser.). (Orig.). 1997. pap. text 7.95 (*0-7535-0104-X*, Pub. by Virgin Bks) London Brdge.

License Agreements in Developing Countries. 108p. 1987. pap. 13.50 (*92-1-104215-1*, E.87.II.A.21) UN.

License Exam Manual. 18th ed. Dearborn Financial Institute Staff. (Passtrak Ser.). 1998. pap. 24.00 (*0-7931-2806-4*, 36060218) Dearborn.

License Exam Manual. 18th ed. Dearborn Financial Institute Staff. (Passtrak Ser.). 1998. pap. 35.00 (*0-7931-3004-2*) Dearborn.

License Exam Manual & Questions & Answers: Uniform Securities Agent State Law Exam. 14th ed. Dearborn Financial Institute Staff. 1998. pap. text 35.00 (*0-7931-3379-3*) Dearborn.

License for Empire: Colonialism by Treaty in Early America. Dorothy V. Jones. LC 81-19700. 270p. reprint ed. pap. 83.70 (*0-608-09414-5*, 205421400004) Bks Demand.

License Inspector. Jack Rudman. (Career Examination Ser.: C-439). 1994. pap. 27.95 (*0-8373-0439-3*) Nat Learn.

License Investigator. Jack Rudman. (Career Examination Ser.: C-449). 1994. pap. 27.95 (*0-8373-0449-0*) Nat Learn.

License Investigator (Spanish Speaking) Jack Rudman. (Career Examination Ser.: C-2286). 1994. reprint ed. pap. 29.95 (*0-8373-2286-3*) Nat Learn.

***License My Roving Hands.** Juanita Tobin. LC 00-44133. 2000. write for info. (*1-887905-26-X*) Pkway Pubs.

License Plate Book: How to Read & Decode Plates from All 50 States. 7th ed. Thomson C. Murray & Michael C. Wiener. (Illus.). 128p. (J). (gr. 2-12). 1992. reprint ed. pap. 12.95 (*0-87131-710-9*) M Evans.

License Plate Book: 1997 Edition. annuals rev. ed. Thomson C. Murray. (Annual Ser.). (Illus.). 130p. 1997. pap. 16.95 (*1-886777-01-2*) Inter Directory.

License Plate Games. Thomson C. Murray. 1993. pap. 3.95 (*0-87131-749-4*) M Evans.

***License Plates.** Tracy Maurer. LC 99-32996. (Guide to State Symbols Ser.). 48p. (J). (gr. 3-5). 1999. 19.45 (*1-57103-298-3*) Rourke Pr.

License Plates 4U2Read. Paul Taylor. (Illus.). 60p. 1983. 3.95 (*0-9612016-0-6*) Pubs Guild CA.

License Plates of the United States: A Pictorial History, 1903 to the Present. James K. Fox. (Illus.). 176p. 1994. 29.95 (*0-9629962-5-4*) Inter Directory.

License Plates of the United States: A Pictorial History, 1903 to the Present. James K. Fox. (Illus.). 190p. 1997. 34.95 (*1-886777-00-4*) Inter Directory.

License Renewal Demonstration Program: NRC Observations & Lessons Learned. R. J. Prato. 24p. 1996. pap. 4.25 (*0-16-062681-1*) USGPO.

License Tax Laws of North Carolina, 1997. 98p. pap. 18.00 (*1-55834-851-4*) LEXIS Pub.

License to Carry a Gun. Andrei Codrescu. LC 97-76748. (Classic Contemporaries Ser.). 80p. 1997. pap. 12.95 (*0-88748-280-5*) Carnegie-Mellon.

License to Cook Arizona Style: Grand Canyon State. Dianna Stevens. Ed. by Dorothy Crum. (Illus.). 160p. 1999. spiral bd. 6.95 (*1-57216-069-1*) Penfield.

License to Cook Iowa Style: Tasty Recipes for Iowa Foods. Michael Nagle Spencer. 160p. 1996. spiral bd. 6.95 (*1-57216-055-1*) Penfield.

License to Cook Kansas Style. Ed. by Linda Hubaler. 118p. 1994. spiral bd. 6.95 (*0-941016-96-X*) Penfield.

License to Cook Minnesota Style: Land of 10,000 Recipes. 2nd ed. Gerry Kangas. Ed. by Joan Liffring-Zug. (License to Cook Ser.). Orig. Title: Marvelous Minnesota Recipes. (Illus.). 160p. 1996. reprint ed. spiral bd. 6.95 (*1-57216-028-4*) Penfield.

License to Cook New Mexico Style. Esther Feske. 160p. 1988. spiral bd. 6.95 (*0-941016-58-7*) Penfield.

License to Cook Texas Style. Dianna Stevens. 160p. 1996. spiral bd. 6.95 (*1-57216-067-5*) Penfield.

License to Cook Wisconsin Style. 2nd ed. Ed. by Diane Heusinkveld. (License to Cook Ser.). Orig. Title: Wonderful Wisconsin Recipes. 160p. 1996. reprint ed. spiral bd. 6.95 (*1-57216-027-6*) Penfield.

License to Dream: A Rose to Rose Collection. Pat Brady. LC 97-71629. (Illus.). 128p. (Orig.). 1997. pap. 9.95 (*0-8362-3664-5*) Andrews & McMeel.

L

L

License to Drive. Alliance for Safe Driving Staff. 560p. 41.95 (0-7668-1351-7, Pub. by Delmar) Thomson Learn.
License to Drive. Alliance for Safe Driving Staff. LC 98-38549. 1999. 33.95 (0-7668-0302-3) Delmar.
***License to Drive.** Alliance for Safe Driving Staff. 2000. pap., wbk. ed. 11.21 (0-7668-2812-3) Delmar.
***License to Drive: California.** Alliance for Safe Driving Staff. LC 99-37572. (Career Education Ser.). 520p. 2000. 17.95 (0-7668-0311-2) Delmar.
***License to Drive: Florida.** Alliance for Safe Driving Staff. (Career Education Ser.). 2002. 31.50 (0-7668-2368-7) Delmar.
***License to Drive: Mississippi.** Alliance for Safe Driving Staff. (Career Education Ser.). 2000. 31.50 (0-7668-2287-7) Delmar.
***License to Drive: New Jersey.** (Career Education Ser.). 2000. 31.50 (0-7668-2281-8) Delmar.
***License to Drive: New Mexico.** Alliance for Safe Driving Staff. (Career Education Ser.). 2001. 31.50 (0-7668-2285-0) Delmar.
***License to Drive: Ohio.** Alliance for Safe Driving Staff. (Career Education Ser.). 2000. pap. 17.95 (0-7668-0309-0) Delmar.
***License to Drive: Texas.** Alliance for Safe Driving Staff. (Career Education Ser.). 2000. pap. 17.95 (0-7668-0310-4) Delmar.
***License to Drive - Alabama State Specific Text.** ASD Staff. LC 99-22615. 560p. 1999. 41.95 (0-7668-0312-0) Delmar.
***License to Drive in Arizona.** Contrib. by Alliance for Safe Driving (U.S.). LC 99-32336. 2000. pap. 41.95 (0-7668-0306-6) Delmar.
***License to Drive in New York.** Alliance for Safe Driving (U.S.). LC 99-37573. 2000. 41.95 (0-7668-0307-4) Delmar.
***License to Drive-Massachusetts State Specific Text.** Alliance for Safe Driving Staff. (Career Education Ser.). 2000. pap. 24.50 (0-7668-2022-X) Delmar.
License to Grill: Achieve Greatness At The Grill With 200 Sizzling Recipes. Chris Schlesinger et al. LC 96-46690. (Illus.). 416p. 1997. 27.50 (0-688-13943-4, Wm Morrow) Morrow Avon.
License to Kill: Israeli Undercover Operations Against Wanted & Masked Palestinians. Ed. by Human Rights Watch Staff. 288p. (Orig.). 1993. pap. 15.00 (1-56432-109-6) Hum Rts Watch.
License to Laugh: Humor in the Classroom. Richard A. Shade. 120p. 1996. pap. text 16.00 (1-56308-364-7) Teacher Ideas Pr.
License to Love. Barbara Boswell. (Desire Ser.: No. 685). 1992. per. 2.79 (0-373-05685-0) Harlequin Bks.
License to Rape: Sexual Abuse of Wives. David Finkelhor & Kersti Yllo. 258p. 1987. pap. 16.95 (0-02-910401-7) Free Pr.
***License to Sell: Professional Field Guide to Selling Skills & Market Trends.** Joseph C. Ilvento & Doug Price. 208p. 1999. pap. 19.95 (0-9654362-1-7) Applied Bus Comm.
***License to Sell: Professional Field Guide to Selling Skills & Market Trends.** 2nd ed. Joseph C. Ilvento & Doug Price. 206p. 1999. reprint ed. 29.95 (0-9654362-2-5) Applied Bus Comm.
License to Steal. Jeff Friedman. (Orig.). 1991. pap. 12.95 (0-9630406-0-X) Gumshoe Ent.
***License to Steal.** Scott Gilman. LC HG4928.5.G55 1999. 2000. 25.00 (0-88730-992-5, HarpBusn) HarpInfo.
***License to Steal: How Fraud Bleeds America's Health Care System.** expanded ed. Malcolm K. Sparrow. LC 00-20812. 272p. 2000. 25.00 (0-8133-6810-3, Pub. by Westview) HarpC.
***License to Steal: Nevada's Gaming Control System in the Megaresort Age.** Jeff Burbank. LC 99-50648. (The/Gaming Studies). (Illus.). 272p. 2000. 29.95 (0-87417-339-6) U of Nev Pr.
License to Steal: The Forfeiture of Property. Leonard W. Levy. LC 95-14497. (Illus.). 288p. (C). 1995. 39.95 (0-8078-2242-6) U of NC Pr.
License to Steal: Traveling Con Artists: Their Games, Their Rules - Your Money. Dennis Marlock & John Dowling. 304p. 1993. text 34.95 (0-87364-751-3) Paladin Pr.
License to Steal: Why Fraud Plagues America's Health Care System. Malcolm K. Sparrow. LC 96-16557. 256p. (C). 1996. pap. text 26.00 (0-8133-3068-8, Pub. by Westview) HarpC.
License to Steal II: More True Adventures of Sherlock, "The Repoman" Jeff Friedman. 112p. 1998. pap. 12.95 (0-9630406-1-8) Gumshoe Ent.
License to Teach: Raising Standards for Teaching. Linda Darling-Hammond. LC 98-53975. (Illus.). 225p. 1999. pap. 23.00 (0-7879-4680-X) Jossey-Bass.
License to Thrill. Elizabeth Cage. (Spy Girls Ser.: No. 1). (YA). (gr. 7 up). 1998. mass mkt. 4.50 (0-671-02286-5, Minstrel Bks) PB.
***License to Thrill: A Cultural History of the James Bond Films.** James Chapman. LC 99-50011. 2000. 27.95 (0-231-12048-6) Col U Pr.
License to Thrill: The Magnificent McCoy Men. Tori Carrington. (Temptation Ser.: Bk. 740). 1999. per. 3.75 (0-373-25840-2, 1-25840-9) Harlequin Bks.
License Your Invention: Take Your Great Idea to Market with a Solid Legal Agreement. Richard Stim. Ed. by Patti Gima. LC 97-31181. (Illus.). 500p. (Orig.). 1998. pap. 39.95 (0-87337-407-X) Nolo com.
***License Your Invention: Take Your Great Idea to Market with a Solid Legal Agreement.** 2nd ed. Richard Stim. LC 99-52189. (Orig.). 2000. pap. 44.95 (0-87337-564-5) Nolo com.
Licensed by Authority: Ben Jonson & the Discourses of Censorship. Richard Burt. LC 92-38020. 248p. 1993. text 39.95 (0-8014-2782-7) Cornell U Pr.
***Licensed Fuel Facility Status Report: Inventory Difference Data, July 1, 1995-June 30, 1996.** T. N. Pham. 18p. 1998. pap. 2.00 (0-16-062724-9) USGPO.
***Licensed Fuel Facility Status Report: Inventory Difference Data, July 1, 1996-June 30, 1997.** T. N. Pham. 18p. 1998. pap. 2.00 (0-16-062772-9) USGPO.
Licensed Practical Nurse. Jack Rudman. (Career Examination Ser.: C-440). 1994. pap. 27.95 (0-8373-0440-7) Nat Learn.
***Licensed Practical Nurse.** Rosemary Wallner. 1999. 19.93 (0-516-21888-3) Capstone Pr.
Licensed Practical Nurse. Rosemary Wallner. LC 99-24322. (Career Exploration Ser.). 48p. (YA). 2000. lib. bdg. 19.93 (0-7368-0329-7) Capstone Pr.
Licensed to Kill? The Nuclear Regulatory Commission & the Shoreham Power Plant. Joan Aron. LC 97-21163. 200p. 1998. pap. 18.95 (0-8229-5649-7); text 45.00 (0-8229-4044-2) U of Pittsburgh Pr.
Licensed to Practice. Sykes. 1985. text 18.95 (0-7216-9894-8, W B Saunders Co) Harcrt Hlth Sci Grp.
Licensed to Rape? John Sullivan. 224p. 1998. pap. 23.95 (1-55691-145-9, 459) Learning Pubns.
Licensed to Work. Barrie Sherman & Phil Judkins. 208p. 1996. 99.50 (0-304-33371-9); pap. 32.50 (0-304-33372-7) Continuum.
Licensee Contractor & Vendor Inspection Status Report. Government Printing Office Staff. per. 9.50 (0-16-012046-2) USGPO.
Licenses. 2nd ed. (C). 1987. 30.00 (0-7855-2048-1, Pub. by Birmingham Midland Soc) St Mut.
Licenses, Areas, Area-Coordinates, Exploration Wells. Norwegian Petroleum Directorate Staff. 1998. pap. 1000.00 (82-7257-429-2, Pub. by Oljedirektoratet) St Mut.
Licensing. Jay Dratler, Jr. (Intellectual Property Ser.). 1994. write for info. (0-614-32056-9) Law Journal.
Licensing: A Strategy for Profits. 289p. 1990. 30.00 (0-685-38418-7) KEW Licensing Pr.
Licensing: The International Sale of Patents & Technical Knowhow. Michael Z. Brooke & John M. Skilbeck. 452p. 1994. 131.95 (0-566-07461-3, Pub. by Gower) Ashgate Pub Co.
Licensing - A Strategy for Profits: Useful Business Strategies for Everything from Electronics, Biotechnology & Pharmaceuticals to Copy Machines, Lawn Sprinklers & Concrete Blocks. Edward P. White. 289p. (Orig.). 1990. pap. 30.00 (0-9626017-0-5) KEW Licensing Pr.
Licensing Act of 1737. Vincent J. Liesenfeld. LC 84-40153. (Illus.). 272p. 1984. text 29.95 (0-299-09810-9) U of Wis Pr.
Licensing Act of 1737. Vincent J. Liesenfeld. LC 84-40153. 275p. reprint ed. pap. 85.30 (0-608-20449-8, 207170200002) Bks Demand.
Licensing Agreements. Koyo Yelpaala et al. 442p. 1988. pap. 66.00 (90-6544-314-2) Kluwer Law Intl.
Licensing & Certification of Psychologists & Counselors. Bruce R. Fretz & David H. Mills. LC 80-8011. (Jossey-Bass Social & Behavioral Science Ser.). 208p. reprint ed. pap. 64.50 (0-8357-4974-6, 203790700009) Bks Demand.
Licensing Art & Design. rev. ed. Caryn Leland. LC 95-75288. (Illus.). 128p. 1995. pap. 16.95 (1-880559-27-7) Allworth Pr.
Licensing Business Handbook. 3rd ed. Karen Raugust. Ed. by Ira Mayer. (Illus.). 216p. 2000. pap. 59.95 (1-885747-00-4) EPM Communs.
***Licensing, Censorship & Authorship in Early Modern England.** Richard Dutton. LC 00-40452. 2000. write for info. (0-312-23624-7) St Martin.
Licensing Electronic Resources: Strategic & Practical Considerations for Signing Electronic Information Delivery Agreements. Patricia Brennan et al. 23p. 1997. pap. 10.00 (0-918006-41-4) Assn Res Lib.
Licensing Entertainment: The Elevation of Novel Reading in Britain, 1684-1750. William B. Warner. LC 97-30171. 325p. 1998. 48.00 (0-520-20180-9, Pub. by U CA Pr); pap. 22.50 (0-520-21296-7, Pub. by U CA Pr) Cal Prin Full Svc.
Licensing Exam Review Guide in Nursing Home Administration: 1000 Test Questions in the Nation Examination Format on the 1996 Domains of Practice. 3rd ed. James E. Allen. LC 96-47701. 208p. 1997. 34.95 (0-8261-5922-2) Springer Pub.
Licensing Exams for Refrigeration, Air Conditioning, & Heating: 4000 Questions & Answers. rev. ed. James L. Dundas. LC 94-4632. 1994. 29.95 (0-912524-89-8) Busn News.
Licensing Guidebook for Nutrition Professionals, 1990. American Dietetic Association Staff. LC 90-130121. 75p. 1990. reprint ed. pap. 30.00 (0-608-03029-5, 206348000006) Bks Demand.
Licensing in International Strategy: A Guide for Planning & Negotiations. Farok J. Contractor. LC 84-22756. (Illus.). 254p. 1985. 69.50 (0-89930-024-3, CLI/, Quorum Bks) Greenwood.
Licensing in the Federal Laboratory: A Discussion of the Main Subjects in Licensing As It Relates to the Transfer of Technology from the Federal Laboratory. 111p. (Orig.). (C). 1993. pap. text 35.00 (1-56806-509-4) DIANE Pub.
Licensing Inspector Trainee. Jack Rudman. (Career Examination Ser.: C-3122). 1994. pap. 23.95 (0-8373-3122-6) Nat Learn.
Licensing Intellectual Property: Legal, Business, & Market Dynamics. John W. Schlicher. LC 96-33703. (Intellectual Property Library Ser.). 464p. 1996. 150.00 (0-471-15312-5) Wiley.
Licensing Intellectual Property in the Digital Age. Kenneth L. Port et al. LC 99-22415. 604p. 1999. boxed set 80.00 (0-89089-891-X) Carolina Acad Pr.
***Licensing Intellectual Property 1998 1999 Supplement: International Regulation, Strategies, & Practices.** John W. Schlicher. 336p. 1999. pap. 95.00 (0-471-36128-3) Wiley.
Licensing Law Guide. J. Phillips. 286p. 1994. pap. text 55.00 (0-406-02878-8, UK, MICHIE) LEXIS Pub.
Licensing Law in Scotland. J. C. Cummins. 400p. 1993. boxed set 121.00 (0-406-11547-8, UK, MICHIE) LEXIS Pub.
Licensing of Family Homes in Child Welfare: A Guide for Instructors & Trainees. Lela B. Costin & Jennette R. Gruener. LC 65-12939. 160p. reprint ed. pap. 49.60 (0-608-16615-4, 202767900055) Bks Demand.
Licensing Parents: Can We Prevent Child Abuse & Neglect? Jack C. Westman. LC 94-22546. (Illus.). 366p. (C). 1994. 27.95 (0-306-44766-5, Plen Insight) Perseus Pubng.
Licensing Power in New York City. Milton M. Carrow. (Illus.). 223p. 1968. reprint ed. 25.00 (0-8377-0401-4, Rothman) W S Hein.
Licensing Practice & Procedure. Kenneth W. Pain. 202p. 1986. 125.00 (1-85190-009-8, Pub. by Fourmat Pub) St Mut.
Licensing Practice & Procedure. Kenneth W. Pain. 250p. 1990. 69.00 (1-85190-102-7, Pub. by Tolley Pubng) St Mut.
Licensing Practice & Procedure. 3rd ed. Kenneth W. Pain. 228p. (C). 1988. 90.00 (1-85190-059-4, Pub. by Fourmat Pub) St Mut.
Licensing Practice & Procedure. 5th ed. Ed. by Kenneth W. Pain. 295p. 1994. 90.00 (0-85459-890-1, Pub. by Tolley Pubng) St Mut.
Licensing Procedures for Industrial Plants & the Influence of EC-Directives. Ed. by Betty Gebers & Marga Robesin. LC 92-39892. VI, 166p. 1992. 37.00 (3-631-45580-1) P Lang Pubng.
Licensing, Registration & Regulations Affecting Contruction Contracting see Advantage Contractor TM Business Success Series
Licensing Services Aide. Jack Rudman. (Career Examination Ser.: C-3120). 1994. pap. 23.95 (0-8373-3120-X) Nat Learn.
Licensing Technology & Trademarks in the United States: Lizenzierung von Technologie und Warenzeichen in den U. S. A. David W. Detjen. (ENG & GER.). 1997. 60.00 (0-86640-068-0) German Am Chamber.
Licensing Theory & French Parasitic Gaps. Christine Tellier. (Studies in Natural Language & Linguistic Theory). 224p. 1991. text 140.50 (0-7923-1311-9) Kluwer Academic.
***Licensure & Certification Mission.** Craig G. Schoon. LC 99-54200. 258p. 2000. 59.00 (0-8281-1450-1) Forb Custom Pub.
Licensure & the L. A. R. E. Clarence L. Chaffee & James T. Penrod. 1993. 44.95 incl. VHS (1-882998-04-9) Coun Lndscape.
Licensure in Professional Psychology: Preparatory Techniques. Tony D. Crespi. LC 94-14145. 1994. 39.95 (1-56032-310-8) Taylor & Francis.
Licensure of School Administrators: Policy & Practice. Carl R. Ashbaugh & Katherine L. Kasten. 1992. 15.00 (0-89333-095-7) AACTE.
Licensure Testing. Ed. by James C. Impara. (Buros-Nebraska Series on Measurement & Testing). 350p. (C). 1995. text 69.95 (0-910674-39-6) Buros Inst Mental.
***Licentia Poetica (Poetic License)** Socrateez. (Illus.). 128p. (C). 2000. pap. 14.95 (1-930112-03-3) inchanted.
"Licentious Liberty" in a Brazilian Gold-mining Region: Slavery, Gender & Social Control in Eighteenth-Century Sabara, Minas Gerais. Kathleen J. Higgins. LC 98-43338. 1999. 23.00 (0-271-01911-5) Pa St U Pr.
***"Licentious Liberty" in a Brazilian Gold-Mining Region: Slavery, Gender, & Social Control In Eighteenth-Century Sabara, Minas Gerais.** Kathleen J. Higgins. LC 98-43338. 1999. 55.00 (0-271-01910-7) Pa St U Pr.
Lich Gate. Clayton Eshleman. 16p. 1980. pap. write for info. (0-930794-20-6) Station Hill Pr.
Lich Lords Game. Mayfair Games Staff. 1988. pap. 7.00 (0-912771-33-X) Mayfair Games.
Lichauco Paper: Imperialism in the Philippines. Alejandro Lichauco. LC 73-7953. 127p. 1973. reprint ed. pap. 39.40 (0-7837-9603-X, 206036000005) Bks Demand.
Lichee Tree. Christina Russell. LC 96-84678. (Illus.). 128p. (YA). (gr. 5 up). 1997. 14.95 (1-56397-629-3) Boyds Mills Pr.
Lichen Biology. Ed. by Thomas H. Nash, III. (Illus.). 315p. (C). 1996. text 74.95 (0-521-45368-2); pap. text 27.95 (0-521-45974-5) Cambridge U Pr.
***Lichen Dyes: The New Source Book.** Karen D. Casselman. 2000. pap. 6.95 (0-486-41231-8) Dover.
Lichen Flora of the Antarctic Continent & Adjacent Islands. Carroll W. Dodge. 399p. 1973. lib. bdg. 19.95 (0-318-41528-3) Lubrecht & Cramer.
Lichen-Forming Fungi. David L. Hawksworth & D. J. Hill. (Tertiary Level Biology Ser.). 192p. (C). 1984. pap. text 29.50 (0-412-00641-3, 9027, Chap & Hall NY) Chapman & Hall.
Lichen Genus Cladonia in North America. John W. Thomson. LC 68-85084. 216p. reprint ed. pap. 67.00 (0-608-13630-1, 201915800010) Bks Demand.
Lichen Genus Pertusaria in Australia. Alan W. Archer. (Bibliotheca Lichenologica Ser.: Vol. 69). (Illus.). 249p. 1997. 76.70 (3-443-58048-3, Pub. by Gebruder Borntraeger) Balogh.
Lichen Genus Physcia in North America. J. W. Thomson. (Illus.). 1963. pap. 48.00 (3-7682-5407-0) Lubrecht & Cramer.
Lichen Physiology & Cell Biology. Ed. by D. H. Brown. LC 85-24452. 374p. 1985. 85.00 (0-306-42200-X, Plenum Trade) Perseus Pubng.
Lichen Symbiosis. Vernon Ahmadjian. LC 92-42873. 264p. 1993. 79.95 (0-471-57885-1) Wiley.
Lichenicolous Heterobasidiomycetes. Paul Diederich. (Bibliotheca Lichenologica: No. 61). (Illus.). 198p. 1996. 82.60 (3-443-58040-8, Pub. by Gebruder Borntraeger) Balogh.
Lichenographia Thomsoniana: North American Lichenology in Honor of John W. Thomson. Ed. by M. G. Glenn et al. 448p. 1998. pap. 35.00 (0-930845-08-0) Mycotaxon Ltd.
Lichenological Papers, 1869-1887, 3 vols. William Nylander. Ed. & Pref. by Teuvo Ahti. (Collected Lichenological Papers: Vol. 3). (GER.). 560p. 1990. reprint ed. 200.00 (3-443-50015-3, Pub. by Gebruder Borntraeger) Balogh.
Lichenological Papers 1863-1868 with Addenda Nova Ad Lichenographiam Europaeam 1865-1887, 3 vols. Wiliam Nylander. Ed. & Pref. by Teuvo Ahti. (Collected Lichenological Papers: Vol. 2). (GER.). 850p. 1990. reprint ed. 200.00 (3-443-50014-5, Pub. by Gebruder Borntraeger) Balogh.
Lichenologische Ausfluege in Tirol see Gesammelte Lichenologische Schriften
Lichens. Jack R. Laundon. 1989. pap. 25.00 (0-85263-811-6, Pub. by Shire Pubns) St Mut.
Lichens. P. Ozenda. (Handbuch der Pflanzenanatomie Encyclopedia of Plant Anatomy - Traite d' Anatomie Vegetale Ser.: Vol. 6, Pt. 9). (GER., Illus.). xii, 200p. 1963. 62.00 (3-443-39010-2, Pub. by Gebruder Borntraeger) Balogh.
***Lichens.** William Purvis. LC 00-29146. (Illus.). 2000. pap. 14.95 (1-56098-879-7) Smithsonian.
Lichens. 2nd ed. Mason E. Hale et al. (Pictured Key Nature Ser.). 256p. (C). 1979. text. write for info. (0-697-04763-6) Brown & Benchmark.
Lichens & Lichenicolous Fungi from New Guinea. Ed. by Andre Aptroot et al. (Bibliotheca Lichenologica Ser.: Vol. 64). (Illus.). 220p. 1997. 94.40 (3-443-58043-2, Pub. by Gebruder Borntraeger) Balogh.
Lichens, Bryophytes & Air Quality. Ed. by Thomas H. Nash, III et al. (Bibliotheca Lichenologica: Vol. 30). (GER., Illus.). 297p. 1988. 53.00 (3-443-58009-2, Pub. by Gebruder Borntraeger) Balogh.
Lichens for Vegetable Dyeing. Eileen Bolton. 1991. 12.50 (1-56659-001-9) Robin & Russ.
Lichfield: The U. S. Army on Trial. Jack Gieck. LC 97-6216. 277p. 1997. 39.95 (1-884836-26-7); pap. 19.95 (1-884836-27-5) U Akron Pr.
Licht- und Elektronenmicroskipische Untersuchungen Zum Infektionsablauf der Gunnera-Nostoc-Symbiose. Hannelore Schmidt. (Dissertationes Botanicae Ser.: Band 171). (Illus.). ii, 204p. 1991. pap. 53.00 (3-443-64083-4, Pub. by Gebruder Borntraeger) Balogh.
Licht & Raum see Louis I. Kahn: Light & Space
Licht und Materie see Light & Matter
Lichtenberg: Essays Commemorating the 250th Anniversary of His Birth. Ed. by Charlotte M. Craig. LC 93-19264. (Enlightenment Ser.: Vol. 4). XV, 152p. (C). 1993. text 47.95 (0-8204-2132-4) P Lang Pubng.
Lichtenbergs Gedankensystem: Denkanweisung Fur Jedermann. Linde Katritzky. (Enlightenment Ser.: Vol. 6). (GER.). 146p. (C). 1995. text 36.95 (0-8204-2710-1) P Lang Pubng.
Lichtenberg's Visits to England. Georg C. Lichtenberg. Tr. by Margaret L. Mare & W. H. Quarrell. LC 71-91906. 130p. 1972. 24.95 (0-405-08747-0, Pub. by Blom Pubns) Ayer.
Lichtenstein. Janis Hendrickson. 1994. pap. 9.99 (3-8228-9633-0) Taschen Amer.
Lichtenstein. Janis Hendrickson. (SPA.). 1996. pap. 9.99 (3-8228-0215-8) Taschen Amer.
Lichtenstein Hernia Repairs, & How to Do Them . . . Right! Alex G. Shulman. (Illus.). 162p. 1996. spiral bd. 30.00 (0-9653526-0-9) Wagner Design.
Lichtenwalner - Lichtenwalter Family History, 1700-1950. Ed. by Harry W. Wichtenwalner. (Illus.). 501p. 1996. reprint ed. pap. 76.00 (0-8328-5308-9); reprint ed. lib. bdg. 86.00 (0-8328-5307-0) Higginson Bk Co.
Lichtenwalner Family History. Charles Lichtenwalner et al. (Illus.). 198p. 1996. reprint ed. pap. 32.00 (0-8328-5412-3); reprint ed. lib. bdg. 42.00 (0-8328-5411-5) Higginson Bk Co.
Lichtiger Kuk Fin der Baal Shem. Miriam Silberman. Ed. by Mordecai Scheiner. (Illus.). 80p. (Orig.). (J). (gr. 4-8). 1985. pap. text 4.50 (0-9618441-0-8) Beth Chana.
Lichtner-Aix: Arbeiten der Letzten Jahre Mit Vollstandigem Oeuvre-Verzeichnis der Druckgraphik Von 1984 Bis 1987. Intro. by Rainer Beck. (GER., Illus.). 144p. (C). 1988. 82.00 (3-8170-2013-9, Pub. by Knstvrlag Weingrtn) Intl Bk Import.
Lichtner-Aix, Malerei und Graphik: Mit Vollstandigem Oeuvre-Verzeichnis der Druckgraphik Von 1967 Bis 1983. Intro. by Rainer Beck. (GER., Illus.). 143p. (C). 1983. 82.00 (3-921617-77-4, Pub. by Knstvrlag Weingrtn) Intl Bk Import.
Lichtvolles Alter see Fulfillment of Old Age
Lichtwellenleiter: Glossar. H. Schwanhauser. (FRE & GER.). 308p. 1989. lib. bdg. 85.00 (0-8288-3836-4, F83230) Fr & Eur.
Lick Shot. Peter Kalu. 1997. pap. text 9.95 (1-874509-04-2, Pub. by X Pr) LPC InBook.
Lick the Sugar Habit: How to Break Your Sugar Addiction Naturally. 2nd ed. Nancy Appleton. LC 96-8296. 272p. (Orig.). 1996. mass mkt. 5.95 (0-89529-695-0, Avery) Penguin Putnam.
Lick the Sugar Habit: How to Break Your Sugar Addiction Naturally. 2nd ed. Nancy Appleton. 272p. (Orig.). 1997. pap. 11.95 (0-89529-768-X, Avery) Penguin Putnam.

An Asterisk (*) at the beginning of an entry indicates that the title is appearing for the first time.

Lickety-Split: A Truman Kicklighter Mystery. Kathy Hogan Trocheck. 272p. 1997. mass mkt. 5.99 (*0-06-109361-0*, Harp PBks) HarpC.

Lickety-Split Grocery List. Zonya Foco. 32p. pap. 11.95 (*1-890926-25-6*) Z H I Pub.

Lickety-Split Meals for Health Conscious People on the Go! Zonya Foco. 432p. 1998. 29.95 (*1-890926-00-0*) Z H I Pub.

Lickety-Split Meals for Health Conscious People on the Go! 2nd rev. ed. Zonya Foco. Ed. by Katie Enders. (Illus.). 400p. 1998. spiral bd. 23.95 (*1-890926-01-9*) Z H I Pub.

Licking County, Ohio: Records Indexes to Licking County, 1808-1822, Marriages & Isaac Smucker's Centennial History Index. Fay Maxwell. 117p. 1984. 25.00 (*1-885463-16-2*) Ohio Genealogy.

Licking Our Wounds. Elise D'Haene. 1998. mass mkt. 7.95 (*1-56333-605-7*, Hard Candy) Masquerade.

Licking Our Wounds. Elise D'Haene. 1997. 24.00 (*0-614-20642-1*) Perm Pr FL.

Licking Our Wounds. Elise D'Haene. LC 96-19008. 208p. 1997. 24.00 (*1-877946-81-8*) Permanent Pr.

Licking Your Wounds. Charles Sommer. 128p. 1992. pap. 8.95 (*0-87516-646-6*) DeVorss.

***Licks of Love: Short Stories & a Sequel, "Rabbit Remembered"** John Updike. 368p. 2000. 25.00 (*0-375-41113-5*) Knopf.

Licorice. Abby Frucht. 224p. (C). 1990. 18.95 (*1-55597-137-7*) Graywolf.

Licorice. Abby Frucht. LC 92-32105. 224p. 1993. pap. 10.95 (*0-8021-3350-9*, Grove) Grove-Atltic.

Licorice Chronicles. Ted Greenwald. 1979. 7.00 (*0-686-65486-2*); pap. 3.50 (*0-686-65487-0*) Kulchur Foun.

Licorice Chronicles. Ted Greenwood. (Green Integer Bks.: No. 32). 160p. 1999. pap. text 11.95 (*1-892295-19-9*, Pub. by Green Integer) Consort Bk Sales.

Licorice Root. Amanda M. Crawford. (Keats Good Herb Guide Ser.). 1998. mass mkt. 4.95 (*0-87983-930-9*, Keats Publng) NTC Contemp Pub Co.

Lictenberg Ettinger, Bracha. Matrix-Borderlines. Pref. by Griselda Pollock. 1993. pap. 28.00 (*0-905836-80-4*, Pub. by Museum Modern Art) St Mut.

Lid off the Cauldron: A Handbook for Witches. Patricia Crowther. LC 81-141202. 1985. pap. 7.95 (*0-08-772869-9*, Pergamon Pr) Elsevier.

Lid off the Cauldron: A Wicca Handbook. Patricia Crowther. (Illus.). 1998. pap. 22.95 (*1-86163-032-8*, Pub. by Capall Bann Pubng) Holmes Pub.

Lidantiu Faram. Ilia M. Zdanevich. (RUS.). 61p. 1995. reprint ed. pap. 8.00 (*1-57201-018-5*) Berkeley Slavic.

Lidar Atmospheric Monitoring, Vol. 3104. Ed. by Jean-Pierre Wolf. LC 97-200312. 316p. 1997. 99.00 (*0-8194-2525-7*) SPIE.

Liddell Hart: A Study of His Military Thought. Brian Bond. (Modern Revivals in Military History Ser.). 300p. 1992. 63.95 (*0-7512-0029-8*, Pub. by Gregg Revivals) Ashgate Pub Co.

Liddell Hart & the Weight of History. John J. Mearsheimer. LC 88-47748. (Cornell Studies in Security Affairs). 264p. 1988. text 37.50 (*0-8014-2089-X*) Cornell U Pr.

Liddell's Record. St. John R. Liddell. Ed. by Nathaniel C. Hughes, Jr. LC 97-21424. (Illus.). 224p. 1997. pap. 11.95 (*0-8071-2218-1*) La State U Pr.

Liddesdale: or The Border Chief. James Lawson. (Notable American Authors Ser.). 1999. reprint ed. lib. bdg. 125.00 (*0-7812-3761-0*) Rprt Serv.

Liddia's Big Mistake. Greg Kennedy. 1999. pap. text 5.99 (*1-893509-00-1*) Wall of Fire.

Liddia's Great Escape. Greg Kennedy. 1999. pap. text 5.99 (*1-893509-01-X*) Wall of Fire.

Liddle. Genealogy of the Liddle Family (Descendants of John & Robert Liddle Who Emigrated from Scotland & Settled in N. Y. State. Martha L. Gifford. (Illus.). 72p. 1996. reprint ed. lib. bdg. 24.50 (*0-8328-5339-9*) Higginson Bk Co.

Liddle. Genealogy of the Liddle Family (Descendants of John & Robert Liddle Who Emigrated from Scotland & Settled in N. Y. State) Martha L. Gifford. (Illus.). 72p. 1996. reprint ed. pap. 14.50 (*0-8328-5340-2*) Higginson Bk Co.

Liden Enfoldig Beretning om det Landskab Guinea og dets Beskaffenhed see Short & Simple Account of the Country Guinea & Its Nature

***Lider.** John Edmund Haggai.Tr. of Leader. (SPA.). 256p. 1999. pap. text 9.75 (*0-311-46169-7*, Edit Mundo) Casa Bautista.

***Lider Con Poder.** Calvin Miller.Tr. of Empowered Leader. (SPA.). 224p. 1999. pap. text 11.50 (*0-311-46163-8*, Edit Mundo) Casa Bautista.

Lider Conforme al Corazon de Dios. Raul C. Yoccou.Tr. of Leader after God's Own Heart. (SPA.). 164p. 1991. pap. 5.99 (*1-56063-142-2*, 490223) Editorial Unilit.

Lider Juvenil - Sus Caracteristicas y Su Capacitacion: The Youth Leader - His Characteristics & Training. Compiled by David F. Garces. (SPA.). 94p. (Orig.). 1993. reprint ed. pap. 6.50 (*0-311-12254-X*) Casa Bautista.

Lider No Nace, Se Hace. Ted W. Engstrom.Tr. of Making of a Christian Leader. 256p. 1980. 8.99 (*0-88113-330-2*) Caribe Betania.

Liderazgo: Ministerio y Batalla. Hector Torres.Tr. of Leadership: Ministry & Battle. (SPA.). 1997. 9.99 (*0-88113-465-1*, B098-4651) Caribe Betania.

Liderazgo Biblico Genuino. Carlos Jimenez.Tr. of Genuine Biblical Leadership. (SPA.). 1997. 9.99 (*0-89922-298-6*, C064-2986) Caribe Betania.

Liderazgo con Amor: Funcion Hombre Hogar. D. Merrill. (Serie Enfoque a la Familia - Focus on the Family Ser.).Tr. of Loving Leader: The Man's Role at Home. (SPA.). 1.99 (*1-56063-559-2*, 497443) Editorial Unilit.

Liderazgo de la Mujer en la Iglesia. S. Hunt.Tr. of Leadership for Women in the Church. (SPA.). 1996. pap. 6.99 (*0-8297-0555-4*) Vida Pubs.

Liderazgo en los Equipos de Trabajo. Robert Johansen. (SPA.). 240p. (C). 1992. pap. text 10.66 (*0-201-51873-2*) Addison-Wesley.

Liderazgo Espiritual. J. Oswald Sanders. (SPA.). 192p. 1995. pap. 7.99 (*0-8254-1650-7*, Edit Portavoz) Kregel.

Liderazgo Para las Escuelas del Manana. Jerry L. Patterson. LC 95-41279. (SPA.). 1996. pap. 14.95 (*0-87120-257-3*) ASCD.

Liderazgo y Amistad. Jesse Miranda. (SPA.). 1998. pap. 6.99 (*0-8297-0373-X*) Vida Pubs.

Liderazgode la Mujer en la Iglesia. W. Calderon.Tr. of Leadership & Church Administration. (SPA.). 176p. 1982. pap. 7.99 (*0-8297-1354-9*) Vida Pubs.

Lidge & the Pahana Legend. Carole O. Cole. (Illus.). 137p. (Orig.). 1996. pap. 13.95 (*0-945767-03-X*) Write Place.

Lidia: The Life of Lidia Zamenhof, Daughter of Esperanto. Wendy Heller. (Illus.). 312p. 1985. 33.95 (*0-85398-194-9*); pap. 15.95 (*0-85398-195-7*) G Ronald Pub.

Lidia's Italian Table: More than 200 Recipes from the First Lady of Italian Cooking. Lidia M. Bastianich. Ed. by Christopher Styler & Pam Hoenig. LC 98-2949. (Illus.). 320p. 1998. 26.00 (*0-688-15410-7*, Wm Morrow) Morrow Avon.

Lidingo. Chana Mantel. 243p. 1998. 19.95 (*0-87306-880-7*) Feldheim.

Lido Fleet: Italian Line Passenger Ships & Services. Peter C. Kohler. LC 98-60050. (Illus.). 438p. 1998. pap. 39.95 (*0-9663052-0-5*) Seadragon Pr.

Lids & Logs. Alan M. Hofmeister et al. (Reading for All Learners Ser.). (Illus.). (J). pap. write for info. (*1-56861-149-8*) Swift Lrn Res.

Lids & Nasolacrimal System: Optometric Procedures. Eric E. Schmidt. LC 96-50471. (Illus.). 119p. 1997. pap. text 42.00 (*0-7506-9621-4*) Buttrwrth-Heinemann.

***Lidya: El Clamor de la Patria y el Cantar de Coquies.** Nelson Santos. Ed. by Bomexi Iztaccihuatl. (SPA.). 155p. 1998. pap. text 9.99 (*1-929183-02-X*) Edit Fundacion.

Lie. Laura A. Sonnenmark. 176p. (J). (gr. 7-9). 1994. pap. 3.50 (*0-590-44741-6*) Scholastic Inc.

Lie. Kurt Vonnegut, Jr. 1992. pap. 3.50 (*0-87129-171-1*, L75) Dramatic Pub.

Lie. Michael Weaver. 464p. 1998. mass mkt. 6.50 (*0-446-60526-3*, Pub. by Warner Bks) Little.

Lie: Evolution. Kenneth Ham. 190p. (C). 1987. pap. 9.95 (*0-89051-158-6*) Master Bks.

Lie: Exposing the Satanic Plot Behind Anti-Semitism. Bruce R. Booker. LC 94-183266. vi, 73p. 1993. pap. 8.00 (*0-916573-05-2*) Brentwood Comm.

Lie - Cartan - Ehresmann Theory. Robert Hermann. 283p. 1993. 95.00 (*0-915692-44-9*) Math Sci Pr.

Lie Admissible Approach to the Hadronic Structure, 2 vols. Ruggero M. Santilli. (C). 1982. pap. text 100.00 (*0-911767-05-3*) Hadronic Pr Inc.

Lie Admissible Approach to the Hadronic Structure: Covering of the Galilei & Einstein Relativites, Vol. 2. Ruggero M. Santilli. 575p. 1982. pap. 50.00 (*0-911767-07-X*) Hadronic Pr Inc.

Lie Admissible Approach to the Hadronic Structure: Non Applicability of the Galilei & Einstein Relativities?, Vol.1. Ruggero M. Santilli. 485p. 1978. pap. 50.00 (*0-911767-06-1*) Hadronic Pr Inc.

Lie Algebra with Triangular Decompositions. Robert V. Moody & Arturo Pianzola. LC 92-46890. (Canadian Mathematical Society Ser. & Advanced Texts). 712p. 1995. text 118.00 (*0-471-63304-6*, Pub. by Interscience) Wiley.

Lie Algebraic Methods in Integrable Systems. A. R. Chowdhury. LC 96-35718. (Pitman Research Notes in Mathematics Ser.). 1997. write for info. (*0-582-30267-6*) Longman.

***LIE Algebraic Methods in Integrable Systems.** A. R. Chowdhury. (Research Notes in Mathematics Ser.). (Illus.). 1999. pap. text (*0-8493-0637-X*, Chap & Hall CRC) CRC Pr.

***LIE Algebraic Methods in Integrable Systems, Vol. 415.** A. R. Chowdhury. (C&H/CRC Research Notes in Mathematics Series). 368p. 1999. per. 74.95 (*1-58488-037-6*, Chap & Hall CRC) CRC Pr.

Lie Algebras. Nathan Jacobson. LC 79-52006. 331p. 1979. reprint ed. pap. 9.95 (*0-486-63832-4*) Dover.

***Lie Algebras: Theory & Algorithms.** Willem A. Graaf. LC 99-86891. (North-Holland Mathematical Library). 406p. 2000. 118.00 (*0-444-50116-9*, North Holland) Elsevier.

Lie Algebras Pt. 1: Finite & Infinite Dimensional Lie Algebras & Applications in Physics. G. G. Bauerle & E. A. De Kerf. (Studies in Mathematical Physics: Vol. 1). xvi, 394p. 1990. 135.50 (*0-444-88776-8*, North Holland) Elsevier.

Lie Algebras Pt. 2: Finite & Infinite Dimensional Lie Algebras & Applications in Physics. E. G. Bauerle & F. Ten Kroode. LC 98-163919. 564p. 1997. 152.50 (*0-444-82836-2*, North Holland) Elsevier.

Lie Algebras & Flexible Lie-Admissible Algebras. Hyo C. Myung. (Monographs in Mathematics). 351p. (Orig.). (C). 1983. pap. text 50.00 (*0-911767-00-2*) Hadronic Pr Inc.

Lie Algebras & Lie Groups. Armand Borel et al. LC 52-42839. (Memoirs Ser.: No. 1/14). 54p. 1972. reprint ed. pap. 17.00 (*0-8218-1214-9*, MEMO/1/14) Am Math.

Lie Algebras & Lie Groups: Five Papers Prepared in Connection with the First Summer Mathematical Institute. American Mathematical Society Staff. LC 52-42839. (American Mathematical Society: No. 14). 61p. 1972. reprint ed. pap. 30.00 (*0-608-03971-3*, 205256300011) Bks Demand.

Lie Algebras & Lie Groups: Lectures Given at Harvard University, 1964. 2nd ed. Jean-Pierre Serre et al. Ed. by A. Dold et al. (Lecture Notes in Mathematics Ser.: Vol. 1500). 168p. 1996. 35.00 (*0-387-55008-9*) Spr-Verlag.

Lie Algebras & Locally Compact Groups. Irving Kaplansky. LC 76-136207. (Chicago Lectures in Mathematics). 1971. pap. text 22.00 (*0-226-42453-7*) U Ch Pr.

Lie Algebras & Related Topics. Ed. by G. Benkart & J. Osborn. LC 90-44712. (Contemporary Mathematics Ser.: Vol. 110). 313p. 1990. pap. 46.00 (*0-8218-5119-5*, CONM/110) Am Math.

Lie Algebras & Related Topics: Conference Proceedings of the Canadian Mathematical Society, Vol. 5. Ed. by D. J. Britten et al. LC 85-26818. 382p. 1986. reprint ed. pap. 57.00 (*0-8218-6009-7*, CMSAMS/5) Am Math.

Lie Algebras & Their Representations: A Symposium on Lie Algebras & Representation Theory, January 23-27, 1995, Seoul National University, Seoul, Korea, Vol. 194. Ed. by Seok-Jin Kang et al. LC 96-13056. (Contemporary Mathematics Ser.). 232p. 1996. pap. 45.00 (*0-8218-0512-6*, CONM/194) Am Math.

Lie Algebras, Cohomology, & New Applications to Quantum Mechanics. Ed. by Niky Kamran & Peter J. Olver. LC 93-48322. (Contemporary Mathematics Ser.: Vol. 160). 310p. 1994. pap. 51.00 (*0-8218-5169-1*, CONM/160) Am Math.

Lie Algebras, Geometry, & Toda Type Systems. Alexander V. Razumov & Mikhail V. Saveliev. LC 96-46118. (Cambridge Lecture Notes in Physics Ser.: No. 7). (Illus.). 266p. (C). 1997. pap. text 34.95 (*0-521-47923-1*) Cambridge U Pr.

Lie Algebras in Particle Physics, Vol. 54. Howard Georgi. (C). 1994. pap. 45.00 (*0-201-41048-6*) Addison-Wesley.

Lie Algebras in Particle Physics: From Isospin to Unified Theories. Howard Georgi. 255p. (C). 1982. 39.95 (*0-8053-3153-0*) Addison-Wesley.

***Lie Algebras in Particle Physics: From Isospin to Unified Theories.** Howard Georgi. 344p. 1999. pap. text 39.00 (*0-7382-0233-9*, Pub. by Perseus Pubng) HarpC.

***Lie Algebras, Rings & Related Topics.** Yuen Fong et al. LC 00-29723. 2000. write for info. (*962-430-110-7*) Spr-Verlag.

Lie & a Libel: The History of "The Protocols of the Elders of Zion" Binjamin W. Segel. Ed. & Tr. by Richard S. Levy from GER. LC 95-10034. (Illus.). xv, 148p. 1995. text 30.00 (*0-8032-4243-3*) U of Nebr Pr.

Lie & a Libel: The History of the Protocols of the Elders of Zion. Binjamin W. Segel. Ed. & Tr. by Richard S. Levy. LC 95-10034. (Illus.). xv, 148p. 1995. pap. 10.00 (*0-8032-9245-7*, Bison Books) U of Nebr Pr.

Lie-Backlund Transformations in Applications. R. L. Anderson & N. H. Ibragimov. LC 78-78207. (Studies in Applied Mathematics: No. 1). x, 124p. 1979. text 32.50 (*0-89871-151-7*) Soc Indus-Appl Math.

Lie Direct. Sara Woods. 160p. 1989. pap. 3.95 (*0-380-70588-5*, Avon Bks) Morrow Avon.

Lie down in Darkness. William Styron. 1992. pap. 14.00 (*0-679-73597-6*) Vin Bks.

Lie down in Roses. Shannon Drake. 512p. 1994. mass mkt. 5.99 (*0-8217-4794-0*, Zebra Kensgtn) Kensgtn Pub Corp.

Lie down with Lions. Ken Follett. 1986. mass mkt. 7.99 (*0-451-16350-8*) NAL.

Lie down with Lions. Ken Follett. 1994. mass mkt. 5.99 (*0-451-18292-8*) NAL.

***Lie Down with Lions, Set.** abr. ed. Ken Follett. 1999. 14.95 incl. audio (*0-671-62147-5*, 391065, Pub. by S&S Audio) Lndmrk Audiobks.

Lie Equations Vol. 1: General Theory. Antonio Kumpera & Donald D. Spencer. LC 77-39055. (Annals of Mathematics Studies: No. 73). 309p. 1972. reprint ed. pap. 95.80 (*0-608-06493-9*, 206679000001) Bks Demand.

***Lie for the Truth.** Pierre Delfosse. LC 00-190104. 2000. 25.00 (*0-7388-1544-6*); 18.00 (*0-7388-1545-4*) Xlibris Corp.

Lie Group Presentations, I. Ed. by R. Herb et al. (Lecture Notes in Mathematics Ser.: Vol. 1024). 369p. 1983. 46.95 (*0-387-12725-9*) Spr-Verlag.

Lie Group Representations II. Ed. by R. Herb et al. (Lecture Notes in Mathematics Ser.: Vol. 1041). 340p. 1984. 42.95 (*0-387-12715-1*) Spr-Verlag.

Lie Group Representations III. Ed. by R. Herb et al. (Lecture Notes in Mathematics Ser.: Vol. 1077). xi, 454p. 1984. 59.95 (*0-387-13385-2*) Spr-Verlag.

***Lie Groups.** J. J. Duistermaat & Johan A. C. Kolk. LC 99-50197. (Universitext Ser.). viii, 334p. 2000. pap. 48.00 (*3-540-15293-8*) Spr-Verlag.

Lie Groups. I. D. Ado et al. (Translations Ser. 1: Vol. 9). 534p. 1991. reprint ed. pap. 60.00 (*0-8218-1609-8*, TRANS1/9) Am Math.

Lie Groups. American Mathematical Society Staff. LC QA0003,A5716. (American Mathematical Society: No. 9). (Illus.). 545p. 1962. reprint ed. pap. 169.00 (*0-608-03970-5*, 205256200011) Bks Demand.

Lie Groups & Algebraic Groups Springer-Verlag. A. L. Onishchik & Ernst B. Vinberg. (Illus.). 352p. 1990. 86.95 (*0-387-50614-4*) Spr-Verlag.

Lie Groups & Algebras with Applications to Physics, Geometry, & Mechanics. David H. Sattinger & O. L. Weaver. (Applied Mathematical Sciences Ser.: Vol. 61). (Illus.). 315p. 1996. 59.95 (*0-387-96240-9*) Spr-Verlag.

Lie Groups & Lie Algebra Three: Structure of Lie Groups & Lie Algebras. Ed. by A. L. Onischchik & Ernst B. Vinberg. LC 93-33446. (Encyclopedia of Mathematical Sciences Ser.: Vol. 41). 1994. write for info. (*0-387-54683-9*) Spr-Verlag.

Lie Groups & Lie Algebras, Chapters 1-3. N. Bourbaki. 470p. 1989. 111.95 (*0-387-50218-1*) Spr-Verlag.

Lie Groups & Lie Algebras: E. B. Dynkin's Seminar. LC 91-640741. (American Mathematical Society Translations Ser.: Series 2, Vol. 169). 202p. 1995. text 89.00 (*0-8218-0454-5*, TRANS2/169) Am Math.

Lie Groups & Lie Algebras No. II: Discrete Subgroups of Lie Groups, Cohomologies of Lie Groups & Lie Algebras. Ed. by A. I. Onishchik & E. B. Vinberg. (Encyclopedia of Mathematical Sciences Ser.: Vol. 21). 230p. 2000. 95.00 (*3-540-50585-7*) Spr-Verlag.

Lie Groups & Lie Algebras I. Ed. by A. L. Onishchik. LC 92-21600. (Encyclopedia of Mathematical Sciences Ser.: Vol. 20). 1993. 118.95 (*0-387-18697-2*) Spr-Verlag.

Lie Groups & Lie Algebras II: Discrete Subgroups of Lie Groups, Cohomologies of Lie Groups & Lie Algebras. Ed. by A. L. Onishchik & Ernst B. Vinberg. 250p. 1996. write for info. (*0-387-50585-7*) Spr-Verlag.

Lie Groups & Lie Algebras Their Representations, Generalisations & Applications. Ed. by B. P. Komrakov et al. LC 97-49850. 442p. 1998. lib. bdg. 194.00 (*0-7923-4916-4*) Kluwer Academic.

Lie Groups & Subsemigroups with Subjective Exponential Function. Karl H. Hofmann & Wolfgang Ruppert. LC 97-30686. (Memoirs of the American Mathematical Society Ser.). 174p. 1997. pap. 45.00 (*0-8218-0641-6*) Am Math.

Lie Groups Beyond an Introduction. A. W. Knapp. LC 96-17002. (Progress in Mathematics Ser.: Vol. 140). (Illus.). 604p. 1996. 49.50 (*0-8176-3926-8*) Birkhauser.

Lie Groups Beyond an Introduction. Anthony W. Knapp. LC 96-17002. (Progress in Mathematics Ser.). 1996. write for info. (*3-7643-3926-8*, Pub. by Birkhauser) Princeton Arch.

Lie Groups, Convex Cones, & Semigroups. Joachim Hilgert et al. (Oxford Mathematical Monographs). (Illus.). 688p. 1989. 110.00 (*0-19-853569-4*) OUP.

Lie Groups I & Lie Groups II. M. Ise et al. Tr. by Katsumi Nomizu. LC 90-24683. (MMONO Ser.: Vol. 85). 259p. 1991. text 93.00 (*0-8218-4544-6*, MMONO/85) Am Math.

Lie Groups, Lie Algebras. Melvin Hausner & Jacob T. Schwartz. LC 66-28064. (Notes on Mathematics & Its Applications Ser.). x, 230p. 1968. text 178.00 (*0-677-00280-7*) Gordon & Breach.

Lie Groups, Lie Algebras, & Some of Their Applications. Robert Gilmore. LC 92-13132. 608p. (C). 1994. reprint ed. lib. bdg. 94.50 (*0-89464-759-8*) Krieger.

Lie Groups, Lie Algebras, & Their Representations. V. S. Varadarajan. (Graduate Texts in Mathematics Ser.: Vol. 102). 430p. 1988. reprint ed. 54.95 (*0-387-90969-9*) Spr-Verlag.

Lie Groups, Lie Algebras, Cohomology & Some Applications in Physics. J. A. De Azcarraga & J. M. Izquierdo. (Monographs on Mathematical Physics). (Illus.). 473p. (C). 1996. text 110.00 (*0-521-46501-X*) Cambridge U Pr.

Lie Groups, Lie Algebras, Cohomology & Some Applications in Physics. Jose A. De Azcarraga & Jose M. Izquierdo. (Monographs on Mathematical Physics). (Illus.). 473p. (C). 1998. reprint ed. pap. text 49.95 (*0-521-59700-5*) Cambridge U Pr.

Lie Groups, Their Discrete Subgroups, & Invariant Theory. Ernst B. Vinberg. LC 91-640741. 204p. 1992. text 119.00 (*0-8218-4107-6*, ADVSOV/8) Am Math.

Lie in the Dark. Dan Fesperman. LC 98-49750. 288p. 1999. 24.00 (*1-56947-153-3*) Soho Press.

***Lie in the Dark.** Dan Fesperman. (Crime - Black Lizard Ser.). 288p. 2000. pap. text 12.00 (*0-375-70767-0*) Vin Bks.

Lie Is a Debt. June Stephenson. LC 83-71777. 200p. 1984. pap. 6.95 (*0-941138-02-X*) Diemer-Smith.

Lie Methods in Optics. Ed. by J. Sanchez Mondradon & K. B. Wolf. (Lecture Notes in Physics Ser.: Vol. 250). xiv, 249p. 1986. 39.00 (*0-387-16471-5*) Spr-Verlag.

Lie Methods in Optics II. Ed. by K. B. Wolf. (Lecture Notes in Physics Ser.: Vol. 352). xii, 197p. 1990. 44.95 (*0-387-52123-2*) Spr-Verlag.

Lie of Horizons: Poems. Desmond Graham. 64p. 1993. pap. 14.95 (*1-85411-084-5*, Pub. by Seren Bks) Dufour.

Lie of the Land. John J. Clanchy. 245p. (C). 1990. 35.00 (*0-9592104-6-6*, Pub. by Pascoe Pub) St Mut.

Lie of the Land: Challenging Received Wisdom on the African Environment. Melissa Leach & Robin Mearns. LC 96-49147. (African Issues Ser.). 1996. 80.00 (*0-435-07407-5*); pap. 24.00 (*0-435-07408-3*) Heinemann.

Lie of the Land: English Literary Studies in India. Ed. by Rajeswari S. Rajan. 320p. (C). 1992. 24.95 (*0-19-562829-2*) OUP.

Lie of the Land: English Literary Studies in India. Ed. by Rajeswari S. Rajan. 320p. 1994. reprint ed. pap. text 12.95 (*0-19-563361-X*) OUP.

Lie of the Land: Irish Identities. Fintan O'Toole. 172p. (C). 1998. 23.00 (*1-85984-821-4*, Pub. by Verso) Norton.

Lie of the Land: Irish Identities. Fintan O'Toole. LC 97-42223. 192p. 1998. pap. 14.00 (*1-85984-132-5*, Pub. by Verso) Norton.

***Lie of the Land: Journeys Through Literary Cork.** Mary Leland. (Illus.). 170p. 2000. pap. 15.95 (*1-85918-231-3*, Pub. by Cork Univ) Stylus Pub VA.

Lie of the Land: Migrant Workers & the California Landscape. Don Mitchell. LC 95-30081. 1996. pap. 21.95 (*0-8166-2693-6*); text 54.95 (*0-8166-2692-8*) U of Minn Pr.

Lie of the Mind. Sam Shepard. 1986. pap. 5.25 (*0-8222-0656-0*) Dramatists Play.

Lie of the Mind. Sam Shepard. 1987. pap. 12.95 (*0-452-26357-3*, Plume) Dutton Plume.

Lie of the Mind. limited ed. Sam Shepard. (Illus.). 144p. 1993. 400.00 (*0-910457-25-5*) Arion Pr.

Lie of the Storm. LC 97-93026. 368p. (Orig.). 1997. pap. 12.95 (*0-9658073-0-4*) Alpha OmeGa Pub.

L

Lie Pseudogroups & Mechanics. J. F. Pommaret. (Mathematics & Its Applications Ser.: Vol. 16). x, 592p. 1988. text 480.00 (*2-88124-213-8*) Gordon & Breach.

Lie Semigroups & Their Applications. J. Hilgert & Karl-Hermann Neeb. (Lecture Notes in Mathematics Ser.: Vol. 1552). (Illus.). xii, 315p. 1993. pap. write for info. (*3-540-56954-5*) Spr-Verlag.

Lie Semigroups & Their Applications. Joachim Hilgert & Karl-Hermann Neeb. LC 93-5231. (Lecture Notes in Mathematics Ser.: Vol. 1552). 1993. 60.95 (*0-387-56954-5*) Spr-Verlag.

Lie, Sit, Stand, Be Still. limited ed. Michael McClure. (Illus.). 52p. 1995. text 5000.00 (*0-910457-37-9*) Arion Pr.

Lie Sphere Geometry: With Applications to Submanifolds. T. E. Cecil. (Universitext Ser.). (Illus.). xii, 207p. 1991. 47.95 (*0-387-97747-3*) Spr-Verlag.

Lie-Theoretic ODE Numerical Analysis, Mechanics, & Differential Systems. Robert Hermann. LC 94-10816. (Interdisciplinary Mathematics Ser.: Vol. 29). 1994. write for info. (*0-915692-45-7*) Math Sci Pr.

Lie Theory & Geometry: In Honor of Bertram Kostant. Ed. by Jean-Luc Brylinski et al. LC 94-32297. (Progress in Mathematics Ser.: Vol. 123). xliii, 596p. 1994. 72.50 (*0-8176-3761-3*) Birkhauser.

Lie Theory & Geometry: In Honor of Bertram Kostant. Jean-Luc Brylinski et al. LC 94-32297. 123. 1994. write for info. (*3-7643-3761-3*) Birkhauser.

Lie Theory & Its Applications in Physics II: Proceedings of the Workshop Arnold Sommerfield. V. K. Dobrev. 1998. 78.00 (*981-02-3539-9*) World Scientific Pub.

Lie to Me. David Martin. 320p. 1991. reprint ed. per. 6.50 (*0-671-73876-3*, Pocket Star Bks) PB.

***LIE-2K: Why the Alleged End-of-the-World Year 2000 Computer Crisis Is Really Just a Hoax.** Sherman S. Smith. 192p. 1999. 19.95 (*0-9643136-4-2*) Meister Pr.

Liebe Deinen Nachsten Wie Dich Selbst: Untersuchungen zum Alttestamentlichen Gebot der Nachstenliebe (Lev 19, 18) 2nd ed. H. P. Mathys. (Orbis Biblicus et Orientalis Ser.). (GER.). 1990. text 45.00 (*3-7278-0357-6*, Pub. by Presses Univ Fribourg) Eisenbrauns.

Liebe im Expressionismus: Eine Untersuchung der Lyrik in den Zeitschriften Die Aktion und Der Sturm von, 1910-1914. Juergen Froehlich. LC 89-48737. (Studies in Modern German Literature: Vol. 38). (GER.). 214p. (C). 1991. text 39.95 (*0-8204-1229-5*) P Lang Pubng.

Liebe-Macht-Gerechtigkeit. Paul Johannes Tillich. (GER.). ii, 85p. (Orig.). 1991. pap. text 19.10 (*3-11-013383-0*, 224-91) De Gruyter.

***Liebe und Trennung: Charlotte Von Ahlefelds Briefe an Christian Friedrich Tieck Herausgegeben und Kommentiert Von James Trainer.** Charlotte Ahlefeld. 234p. 1999. pap. 42.95 (*3-906761-87-8*) P Lang Pubng.

Liebelei; Reigen. 32nd ed. Arthur Schnitzler. (GER.). 168p. 1997. pap. 13.50 (*3-596-27009-X*, Pub. by Fischer Tasch) Intl Bk Import.

Lieber on Pensions, 5 vols. William M. Lieber. 4200p. 1991. ring bd. 595.00 (*0-13-085821-8*) Aspen Law.

Lieber Prinz: Der Briefwechsel Zwischen Hermann Diels Und Ulrich von Wilamowitz-Moellendorff (1869-1921) Ed. by Maximilian Braun et al. (GER.). xxiv, 354p. 1995. 98.00 (*3-615-00173-7*, Pub. by Weidmann) Lubrecht & Cramer.

Lieberman's Day. Stuart M. Kaminsky. LC 93-22910. (Henry Holt Mystery Ser.). 260p. 1995. 19.95 (*0-8050-2575-8*) H Holt & Co.

Lieberman's Day. large type ed. Stuart M. Kaminsky. LC 94-12987. 286p. 1994. 23.95 (*1-56895-115-9*) Wheeler Pub.

Lieberman's Folly. Stuart M. Kaminsky. (Midwest Mysteries Ser.). 1992. mass mkt. 4.99 (*0-8041-0924-9*) Ivy Books.

Lieberman's Law. Stuart M. Kaminsky. LC 95-42537. (Henry Holt Mystery Ser.). 309p. 1995. 22.50 (*0-8050-3749-7*) H Holt & Co.

Lieberman's Partner. Stuart M. Kaminsky. 1998. 22.50 (*0-8050-5402-2*) H Holt & Co.

Lieberman's Thief. Stuart M. Kaminsky. LC 94-27304. (Henry Holt Mystery Ser.). 238p. 1995. 22.50 (*0-8050-2576-6*) H Holt & Co.

Lieber's Code & the Law of War. Richard S. Hartigan. 157p. 1983. 24.95 (*0-913750-25-5*) Transaction Pubs.

Liebesgebot und Altruismusforschung: Ein Exegetischer Beitrag Zum Dialog Zwischen Theologie und Naturwissenschaft. Hubert Meisinger. (Novum Testamentum et Orbis Antiquus Ser.: Vol. 33). (GER.). 336p. 1996. text 68.75 (*3-7278-1093-9*, Pub. by Presses Univ Fribourg) Eisenbrauns.

Liebeskampf see Spieltexte der Wanderbuehne

Liebestraume No3 A Flat Major. Franz Liszt. 12p. 1997. per. 4.95 (*0-7935-8322-5*) H Leonard.

Liebling Vocal Course for Mezzo-Soprano & Contralto. E. Liebling. 60p. 1981. pap. 9.95 (*0-7935-0635-2*, 00312243) H Leonard.

Lieblings-Lieder Unserer Vorvater. American Historical Society of Germans from Russia. (Illus.). 215p. 1982. pap. 14.50 (*0-914222-06-6*) Am Hist Soc Ger.

Lieblose Lieder: Und Fragst du Mich, Was Mit der Liebe Sei das Sozialkritische Liebeslied. Otto Holzapfel. (GER.). 1997. 36.95 (*3-906757-94-3*, Pub. by P Lang) P Lang Pubng.

Liebmann's Mexican Ferns. J. T. Mickel et al. LC 87-24791. (Contributions from the New York Botanical Garden Ser.: Vol. 19). 350p. 1987. pap. 13.90 (*0-89327-324-4*) NY Botanical.

***Liebman's Neuroanatomy Made Easy & Understandable.** 6th ed. S. David Gertz & Rina Tadmor. LC 99-29749. 236p. 1999. 31.00 (*0-8342-1632-9*) Aspen Pub.

Liecestershire Marriage Licences: Being Abstracts, 1570-1729. Ed. by Henry Hartopp. (British Record Society Index Library: Vol. 38). 1969. reprint ed. pap. 53.00 (*0-8115-1483-8*) Periodicals Srv.

Liechtenstein. Regula A. Meier. LC 94-160591. (World Bibliographical Ser.). 146p. 1993. lib. bdg. 63.00 (*1-85109-201-3*) ABC-CLIO.

***Liechtenstein: A Country Study Guide.** Global Investment & Business Center, Inc. Staff. (World Country Study Guides Library: Vol. 99). (Illus.). 350p. 2000. pap. 59.00 (*0-7397-2397-9*) Intl Business Pubns.

Liechtenstein: The Princely Collections. Reinhold Baumstark et al. (Illus.). 400p. 1985. pap. 50.00 (*0-87099-386-0*, 0-8109-6481-3) Metro Mus Art.

Liechtenstein - A Country Study Guide: Basic Information for Research & Pleasure. Global Investment Center, USA Staff. (World Country Study Guide Library: Vol. 99). (Illus.). 350p. 1999. pap. 59.00 (*0-7397-1496-1*) Intl Business Pubns.

***Liechtenstein Business Intelligence Report, 190 vols.** Global Investment & Business Center, Inc. Staff. (World Business Intelligence Library: Vol. 99). (Illus.). 350p. 2000. pap. 99.95 (*0-7397-2597-1*) Intl Business Pubns.

***Liechtenstein Business Law Handbook, 190 vols.** Global Investment & Business Center, Inc. Staff. (Global Business Law Handbooks Library: Vol. 99). (Illus.). 350p. 2000. pap. 99.95 (*0-7397-1996-3*) Intl Business Pubns.

***Liechtenstein Business Opportunity Yearbook.** Global Investment & Business Center, Inc. Staff. (Global Business Opportunity Yearbooks Library: Vol. 99). (Illus.). 2000. pap. 99.95 (*0-7397-2197-6*) Intl Business Pubns.

***Liechtenstein Business Opportunity Yearbook: Export-Import, Investment & Business Opportunities.** International Business Publications, U. S. A. Staff & Global Investment Center, U. S. A. Staff. (Global Business Opportunity Yearbooks Library: Vol. 99). (Illus.). 350p. 1999. pap. 99.95 (*0-7397-1297-7*) Intl Business Pubns.

Liechtenstein Company Law: The Prevalent Sections for the Personen-und Gesellschaftsrecht. Tr. by Bryan Jeeves from GER. 361p. 1992. 84.95 (*3-85789-901-8*) Austin & Winfield.

***Liechtenstein Country Review 2000.** Robert C. Kelly et al. (Illus.). 60p. 1999. pap. 39.95 (*1-58310-523-9*) CountryWatch.

***Liechtenstein Export-Import & Business Directory: Ultimate Directory for Conducting Export-Import Operations in the Country. Largest Exporters & Importers, Strategic Government & Business Contacts, Selected Export-Import Regulations & More.** International Business Publications, USA Staff & Global Investment Center, USA Staff. (World Export-Import & Business Library: 19). (Illus.). 250p. 2000. pap. 99.95 (*0-7397-3378-8*) Intl Business Pubns.

***Liechtenstein Foreign Policy & Government Guide.** Global Investment & Business Center, Inc. Staff. (World Foreign Policy & Government Library: Vol. 95). (Illus.). 350p. 1999. pap. 99.00 (*0-7397-3593-4*) Intl Business Pubns.

***Liechtenstein Foreign Policy & Government Guide.** Global Investment & Business Center, Inc. Staff. (World Foreign Policy & Government Library: Vol. 95). (Illus.). 350p. 2000. pap. 99.95 (*0-7397-3797-X*) Intl Business Pubns.

***Liechtenstein Investment & Business Guide.** Global Investment & Business Center, Inc. Staff. (Global Investment & Business Guide Library: Vol. 99). (Illus.). 2000. pap. 99.95 (*0-7397-1797-9*) Intl Business Pubns.

***Liechtenstein Investment & Business Guide: Export-Import, Investment & Business Opportunities.** International Business Publications, USA Staff & Global Investment Center, USA Staff. (World Investment & Business Guide Library-99: Vol. 99). (Illus.). 350p. 1999. pap. 99.95 (*0-7397-0294-7*) Intl Business Pubns.

Lied: Mirror of Late Romanticism. Edward F. Kravitt. LC 95-42761. (Illus.). 336p. 1996. 37.50 (*0-300-06365-2*) Yale U Pr.

Lied von der Erde in Full Score. Gustav Mahler. 160p. 1988. pap. 9.95 (*0-486-25657-X*) Dover.

Lied Von der Welt. Dionysios Von Alexandria. (GER.). 168p. 1994. write for info. (*3-487-09893-8*) G Olms Pubs.

Lieder & Gesange see Complete Song Cycles

Lieder der Hitlerjugend: Eine Psychologische Studie an Ausgewahlten Beispielen 2., Durchgesehene Auflage. 2nd ed. Richard Kloppfleisch. (Europaische Hochschulschriften, Reihe 36: Bd. 145). VIII, 280p. 1997. pap. 54.95 (*3-631-31424-8*) P Lang Pubng.

Lieder der Seele (Songs of the Soul) (GER.). 14.00 (*0-87612-250-0*) Self Realization.

Lieder des Bakchylides. H. Maehler. 440p. 1997. pap. 156.50 (*90-04-10761-4*) Brill Academic Pubs.

Lieder in der Nacht see Songs Ini the Night

***Lieder In Politik und Alltag Des Nationalsozialismus.** Gottfried Niedhart & George Broderick. (GER., Illus.). VI, 288p. 1999. 52.00 (*3-631-33611-X*) P Lang Pubng.

Lieder Line by Line No. 2: And Word for Word. 2nd rev. ed. Lois Phillips. 444p. 1996. pap. text 32.00 (*0-19-879017-1*) OUP.

Liederbuch des Konigs Denis von Portugal. Henry R. Llang. (GER.). cxviii, 174p. 1972. reprint ed. write for info. (*3-487-04245-2*) G Olms Pubs.

Liederbuch von 1512. Erhart Oeglin. Ed. by Robert Eitner & Jul J. Maier. (Publikation Alterer Praktischer und Theoretischer Musikweke Ser.: Vol. 9). (GER., Illus.). 1966. reprint ed. lib. bdg. 75.00 (*0-8450-1709-8*) Broude.

Liedermacher Biermann und Degenhardt. Peter Werres. (GER.). 385p. (Orig.). 1990. pap. text 19.95 (*0-9628161-0-8*) Goldstein Schatz.

Lieferbar Band I: Aal-Beschaffenheit. (GER.). 706p. 1992. write for info. (*3-487-09645-5*) G Olms Pubs.

Lieferbar Band II: Beschaffenheit-Erfindung. (GER.). 707p. 1992. write for info. (*3-487-09646-3*) G Olms Pubs.

Lieferung, Vol. 1. Jiri Ruzicka. (Desmidiaceen Mitteleuropas Ser.: Band I). (GER., Illus.). viii, 292p. 1977. 82.00 (*3-510-65078-6*, Pub. by E Schweizerbartsche) Balogh.

Lieferung, Vol. 2. Jiri Ruzicka. (Desmidiaceen Mitteleuropas Ser.: Band I). (GER., Illus.). ix, 444p. 1981. 116.00 (*3-510-65103-0*, Pub. by E Schweizerbartsche) Balogh.

Liege-Killer. Christopher Hinz. (Paratwa Saga Ser.: Bk. 2). 1995. reprint ed. 5.99 (*0-8125-3075-6*, Pub. by Tor Bks) St Martin.

Liege, Lord, & Lackey. Tim Byrd et al. (Vampire Ser.). (Illus.). 96p. (Orig.). 1997. pap. 15.00 (*1-56504-281-6*, 2806) White Wolf.

Liegenschaftskonversion in Rheinland-Pfalz: Geographische Untersuchung Zu Den Entwicklungschancen Bei Der Umnutzung Aufgelassener Militarischer Liegenschaften. Claudius Moseler. (Illus.). 246p. 1998. 45.95 (*3-631-33480-X*) P Lang Pubng.

Liegt Im Trend, 9. Jim Davis. 1999. pap. text 10.95 (*3-8105-0753-9*) W Kruger.

Lieh-hsien Chuan (Biographies of the Holy Immortals) Tr. by Gary Williams. 1999. pap. 17.00 (*1-883058-46-5*, Consort Bilingual) Global Pubns.

Lien d'Amour. Jennifer Mikels. (Amours d'Aujourd'Hui Ser.: Vol. 321). (FRE.). 1999. mass mkt. 4.99 (*0-373-38321-5*, 1-38321-5) Harlequin Bks.

Lien Law for Contruction Contracting see Advantage Contractor TM Business Success Series

Lien Priorities in New York. Robert H. Bowmar. LC 86-83245. 1991. 115.00 (*0-317-04606-3*) West Group.

Lien Priorities in New York. Robert H. Bowmar. LC 86-83245. 1993. suppl. ed. 50.00 (*0-317-04750-7*) West Group.

Liens: En Paroles. Lively et al. (Bridging the Gap Ser.). (FRE.). (C). 1994. mass mkt. 36.95 (*0-8384-4607-8*) Heinle & Heinle.

Liens: Lectures Diverses. James N. Davis. (Bridging the Gap Ser.). (FRE.). (C). 1994. mass mkt. 36.95 (*0-8384-4618-3*) Heinle & Heinle.

Liens: Par Ecrit. Joann Hammadou. (Bridging the Gap Ser.). (FRE.). (C). 1994. mass mkt. 36.95 (*0-8384-4615-9*) Heinle & Heinle.

Lienzo of Tulancingo: An Introductory Study of a Ninth Painted Sheet from the Coixtlahuaca Valley. Ross Parmenter. LC 93-73287. (Transactions Ser.: Vol. 83, Pt. 7). (Illus.). 86p. (C). 1994. pap. 15.00 (*0-87169-837-4*, T827-PAR) Am Philos.

***Lienzo y Papel.** Alma Flor Ada. (SPA., Illus.). 1999. pap. text 9.95 (*1-58105-423-8*) Santillana.

Lies. John L'Heureux. 1999. text 18.95 (*0-670-83908-6*) Viking Penguin.

***Lies: A Diary, 1986-1999.** Ned Rorem. 2000. 30.00 (*1-58243-057-8*, Pub. by Counterpt DC) HarpC.

Lies: The Whole Truth. Carmine DeSena. 128p. (Orig.). 1993. pap. 5.95 (*0-399-51820-7*, Perigee Bks) Berkley Pub.

Lies Across America: What Our Historic Sites Get Wrong. James W. Loewen. LC 99-14212. 416p. 1999. 26.95 (*1-56584-344-4*, Pub. by New Press NY) Norton.

***Lies Across America: What Our Historic Sites Get Wrong.** James W. Loewen. 2000. pap. 15.00 (*0-684-87067-3*, Touchstone) S&S Trade Pap.

Lies & Fallacies of the Encyclopedia Britannica: How Powerful & Shameless Clerical Forces Castrated a Famous Work of Reference. Joseph McCabe. 46p. 1996. reprint ed. spiral bd. 7.00 (*1-885395-64-7*) Book Tree.

Lies & Fiction in the Ancient World. Ed. by Christopher Gill & T. P. Wiseman. LC 93-18679. 288p. (C). 1993. text 32.50 (*0-292-72767-4*) U of Tex Pr.

***Lies & Lemons.** Donna Jo Napoli. LC 99-87417. (Angelwings Ser.: Vol. 9). 80p. (J). (gr. 4-7). 2000. pap. 3.99 (*0-689-83209-5*) Aladdin.

***Lies & Shadows.** large type ed. Pam Hart. 376p. 1999. pap. 18.99 (*0-7089-5577-0*, Linford) Ulverscroft.

***Lies, Damn Lies & Documentaries.** Brian Winston. 2000. pap. 19.95 (*0-85170-797-1*, Pub. by British Film Inst) Ind U Pr.

Lies, Damned Lies & Testimony: Tell It to the Magistrate! John Jasper. LC 97-41223. 272p. 1999. pap. 14.95 (*1-56825-069-X*, 069-X) Rainbow Books.

Lies Doch Mal. Grittner. (GER.). 1992. pap. text 16.95 (*0-8384-4062-2*) Heinle & Heinle.

Lies Doch Weiter. Grittner. (GER.). 1993. pap. text 16.95 (*0-8384-4060-6*) Heinle & Heinle.

Lies in the Family Album. Paddy J. Miller. 288p. 1994. pap. 12.95 (*0-89896-291-9*) Larksdale.

***Lies, Israel's Secret Service & the Rabin Murder.** David Morrison. 284p. 2000. 24.95 (*965-229-241-9*, Pub. by Gefen Pub Hse) Gefen Bks.

Lies, Language & Logic in the Late Middle Ages. Paul V. Spade. (Collected Studies: No. CS272). 312p. (C). 1988. reprint ed. text 115.95 (*0-86078-220-4*, Pub. by Variorum) Ashgate Pub Co.

Lies, Legends & Lore of the San Juans: And a Few True Tales. Roger Henning. LC 99-61618. (Illus.). 186p. 1999. pap. 12.95 (*1-890437-29-8*) Western Reflections.

Lies! Lies! Lies! A Journal More or Less of John C. Gardner. John Gardner. 1999. 22.95 (*0-9665639-1-3*, Pub. by Univ Rochestr Libs); pap. text 12.50 (*0-9665639-2-1*, Pub. by Univ Rochestr Libs) Consort Bk Sales.

Lies! Lies!! Lies!!! The Psychology of Deceit. Charles V. Ford. 352p. 1995. 24.95 (*0-88048-739-9*, 8739) Am Psychiatric.

***Lies! Lies!! Lies!!! The Psychology of Deceit.** Charles V. Ford. 333p. 1999. pap. 17.00 (*0-88048-997-9*, 8997) Am Psychiatric.

Lies My Music Teacher Told Me: Music Theory for Grownups. Gerald Eskelin. LC 94-66811. (Illus.). 176p. (Orig.). 1994. pap. 14.95 (*1-886209-11-1*) Stage Three.

Lies My Parents Told Me. Bernice Kanner. 1996. pap. 8.99 (*0-312-95999-0*) St Martin.

Lies My Teacher Told Me: Everything Your American History Textbook Got Wrong. James W. Loewen. (Illus.). 384p. 1995. 24.95 (*1-56584-100-X*, Pub. by New Press NY) Norton.

Lies My Teacher Told Me: Everything Your American History Textbook Got Wrong. James W. Loewen. LC 96-20050. (Illus.). 384p. 1996. pap. 14.00 (*0-684-81886-8*) S&S Trade.

Lies of Fair Ladies. large type ed. Jonathan Gash. (Large Print Ser.). 592p. 1994. 25.99 (*0-7089-3006-9*) Ulverscroft.

Lies of Silence. Brian Moore. Date not set. pap. write for info. (*0-582-08170-X*, Pub. by Addison-Wesley) Longman.

Lies of Silence. Brian Moore. 208p. 1991. pap. 9.00 (*0-380-71547-3*, Avon Bks) Morrow Avon.

Lies of Silence. large type ed. Brian Moore. 1991. 27.99 (*0-7089-8611-0*, Charnwood) Ulverscroft.

Lies of the Land: The Truth of the Matter. Dick Hoskins. 200p. 1998. pap. 11.95 (*0-9639816-3-3*) Polecat Pr.

Lies (People Believe) about Animals. Susan Sussman & Robert James. Ed. by Kathleen Tucker. LC 86-15949. (Illus.). 48p. (J). (gr. 2-7). 1987. lib. bdg. 13.95 (*0-8075-4530-9*) A Whitman.

Lies, Slander & Obscenity in Medieval English Narrative: Pastoral Rhetoric & the Deviant Speaker. Edwin D. Craun. LC 96-20416. (Cambrige Studies in Medieval Literature: No. 31). 270p. (C). 1997. text 64.95 (*0-521-49690-X*) Cambridge U Pr.

***Lie's Structural Approach to PDE Systems.** Olle Stormark. LC 99-54436. 520p. (C). 2000. text. write for info. (*0-521-78088-8*) Cambridge U Pr.

Lies They Tell. Read. (Sky Bks.). Date not set. pap. text. write for info. (*0-582-08109-2*, Pub. by Addison-Wesley) Longman.

Lies We Believe see Mentiras Que Creemos

Lies We Believe. Chris Thurman. (Minirth-Meier Ser.). 224p. 1991. pap. 11.99 (*0-8407-3192-2*) Nelson.

Lies We Believe Workbook. Chris Thurman. 1995. pap. 14.99 (*0-7852-8087-1*) Nelson.

***Lies We Live By: Defeating Doubletalk & Deception in Advertising Politics & Media.** Carl Hausman. LC 99-49263. 224p. 2000. 24.95 (*0-415-92280-1*) Routledge.

***Lies We Live By: The Art of Self-Deception.** Eduardo Gianetti. 2000. 23.95 (*1-58234-057-9*) Bloomsbury Pubg.

Lies We Tell Ourselves. Chris Thurman. LC 98-53699. 320p. 1999. pap. 14.99 (*0-7852-7343-3*) Nelson.

Lies Within. Michael Largo. LC 98-88028. 433p. 1999. pap. 14.95 (*0-9666173-0-4*) Tropical Pr.

Liesel: Under His Wings. Liesel Jensen. 1997. pap. text 8.95 (*1-888445-02-5*) Sonstar Pubns.

Lietest: Deception, Truth & the Polygraph. Leonard H. Harrelson et al. 172p. 1998. 16.95 (*0-9661788-1-5*); pap. 11.95 (*0-9661788-0-7*) Jonas Pub.

Lietuviai Gydytojai Sesiuose Kontinentuose. unabridged ed. Milda Budrys. Ed. by Skirmante Miglinas. LC 96-77016.Tr. of Lithuanian Physicians Across Six Continents. (LIT., Illus.). 283p. 1996. 25.95 (*0-929700-15-5*) Lith Res & Studies.

Lieu Commun du Moi: Identite Poetique dans l'Oeuvre d'Ernst Meister (1911-1979) Francoise Lartillot. (Etudes & Documents Serie III: Vol. 42). xx, 490p. 1998. 52.95 (*3-906759-57-1*) P Lang Pubng.

Lieu d'Asile. Georges Duhamel. (FRE.). 144p. 1940. pap. 10.95 (*0-7859-5418-X*) Fr & Eur.

Lieut. Gulliver Jones: His Vacation. Edwin L. Arnold. LC 74-15947. (Science Fiction Ser.). 304p. 1975. reprint ed. 25.95 (*0-405-06273-7*) Ayer.

Lieutenant. Rick Shelley. 272p. 1998. pap. 5.99 (*0-441-00568-3*) Ace Bks.

Lieutenant: An Epic Tale of Courage & Endurance on the High Seas Jack Bennett. LC 78-314502. 130p. 1977. write for info. (*0-207-13395-6*, Pub. by Angus & Roberts) HarpC.

Lieutenant Birnbaum: A Soldier's Story. M. Birnbaum & Yonoson Rosenblum. 1993. 19.99 (*0-89906-822-7*); 16.99 (*0-89906-823-5*) Mesorah Pubns.

Lieutenant Cameron RNVR. large type ed. Philip McCutchan. LC 95-11465. 256p. 1995. pap. 20.95 (*0-7862-0474-5*) Thorndike Pr.

Lieutenant Christopher. William P. Mack. LC 97-43810. 1998. 24.95 (*1-877853-53-4*) Nautical & Aviation.

***Lieutenant Christopher: A Novel of the Sea.** William P. Mack. 316p. 1999. reprint ed. pap. 19.95 (*1-877853-57-7*) Nautical & Aviation.

***Lieutenant Colonel.** Rick Shelley. (Dirigent Mercenary Corps Ser.: Vol. 5). 288p. 2000. mass mkt. 5.99 (*0-441-00722-8*) Ace Bks.

Lieutenant-Colonel Charles A. Court Repington: A Study in the Interaction of Personality, the Press & Power. W. Michael Ryan. (Modern European History Ser.). 248p. 1987. text 15.00 (*0-8240-7830-6*) Garland.

Lieutenant-Colonel de Maumort. Roger Martin du Gard. Tr. by Luc Brebion & Timothy Crouse from FRE. LC 98-50912. 848p. 1999. 35.00 (*0-679-43397-X*) Knopf.

Lieutenant Colonel Emily U. Miller: A Biography. Kathleen E. Smith. LC 84-61080. (Illus.). 174p. 1984. 25.00 (*0-917898-11-7*) NSU Pr LA.

An Asterisk (*) at the beginning of an entry indicates that the title is appearing for the first time.

Lieutenant, Fire Department. Jack Rudman. (Career Examination Ser.: C-441). 1994. pap. 34.95 (*0-8373-0441-5*) Nat Learn.

Lieutenant General Karl Strecker: The Life & Thought of a German Military Man. Ed. by Uli Haller. LC 94-16455. 256p. 1994. 65.00 (*0-275-94582-0*, Praeger Pubs) Greenwood.

Lieutenant Governor: The Office & Its Powers. Council of State Governments Staff. Ed. by Keith C. White. 68p. pap. 20.00 (*0-87292-954-X*, C-89) Coun State Govts.

Lieutenant Gustl. Arthur Schnitzler. Tr. by Richard L. Simon from GER. (Sun & Moon Classics Ser.: No. 37). 72p. 1993. pap. 9.95 (*1-55713-176-7*) Sun & Moon CA.

Lieutenant Hornblower. C. S. Forester. 1976. 24.95 (*0-8488-0489-9*, Queens House) Amereon Ltd.

Lieutenant Hornblower. C. S. Forester. (J). (gr. 7 up). 1952. 17.95 (*0-316-28907-8*) Little.

Lieutenant Hornblower. C. S. Forester. 306p. (YA). (gr. 7 up). 1984. pap. 14.95 (*0-316-28921-3*) Little.

Lieutenant Hornblower. large type ed. C. S. Forester. LC 94-26160. 458p. 1995. pap. 19.95 (*0-7862-0285-8*) Thorndike Pr.

Lieutenant Hornblower: A Novel. C. S. Forester. LC 84-81019. Vol. 2. 320p. 1998. pap. 13.00 (*0-316-29063-7*, Back Bay) Little.

Lieutenant James Moody's Narrative of His Exertions & Sufferings in the Cause of Government, Since the Year 1776. James Moody. LC 67-29040. (Eyewitness Accounts of the American Revolution Ser.). 1976. reprint ed. 17.95 (*0-405-01138-5*) Ayer.

Lieutenant Kije & Young Vitushishnikov. Yury Tynyanov. Tr. by Mirra Ginsburg from RUS. LC 89-83812. 140p. 1991. pap. 9.95 (*0-941419-77-0*, Eridanos Library) Marsilio Pubs.

Lieutenant Lamb. Kenneth Maynard. 176p. 1984. 10.95 (*0-312-48371-6*) St Martin.

***Lt. Leary, Commanding: RCS Princess Cecile.** David Drake. 448p. 2000. 24.00 (*0-671-57875-8*) PB.

Lieutenant Lee of Beale Street. David M. Tucker. LC 76-157743. 229p. 1971. reprint ed. pap. 71.00 (*0-7837-9885-7*, 206061100006) Bks Demand.

Lieutenant Nun: Memoir of a Basque Transvestite in the New World. Catalina De Erauso. Tr. by Michele Stepto & Gabriel Stepto.Tr. of Historia de la Monja Alferez. 1997. pap. 12.00 (*0-8070-7073-4*) Beacon Pr.

***Lieutenant Nun: Transgenderism, Lesbian Desire, & Catalina de Erauso.** Sherry M. Velasco. LC 00-22196. (Illus.). 248p. 2001. 35.00 (*0-292-78745-6*); pap. 17.95 (*0-292-78746-4*) U of Tex Pr.

Lieutenant of Cavalry in Lee's Army. George W. Beale. 231p. 1994. 25.00 (*0-935523-43-X*) Butternut & Blue.

Lieutenant, Police Department. Jack Rudman. (Career Examination Ser.: C-442). 1994. pap. 34.95 (*0-8373-0442-3*) Nat Learn.

Lieutenant Ramsey's War: From Horse Soldier to Guerrilla Commander. Edwin P. Ramsey & Stephen Rivele. (World War II Commemorative Ser.). (Illus.). 336p. 1996. reprint ed. pap. 17.95 (*1-57488-052-7*) Brasseys.

Lieutenant River. Susan H. Ely & Elizebeth B. Plimpton. Ed. by John E. Noyes & Debra A. Fillos. (Lymes' Heritage Ser.). (Illus.). 71p. (Orig.). 1991. pap. 8.95 (*1-880897-00-8*) Lyme Hist.

Lieutenant Who Never Was. Tom Smith. 327p. (Orig.). 1997. pap. 12.95 (*0-614-25434-5*, 0002, Wind Sock) Compass Rose.

Lieutenant Who Never Was. Tom Smith. (Orig.). 1997. pap. 12.95 (*1-890183-00-8*, Wind Sock) Compass Rose.

Lieutenant William Barton of Morris County, New Jersey, & His Descendants. William E. Barton. (Illus.). 148p. 1988. reprint ed. pap. 22.00 (*0-8328-0203-4*); reprint ed. lib. bdg. 30.00 (*0-8328-0202-6*) Higginson Bk Co.

Lieutenant Zagoskin's Travels in Russian America. Henry N. Michael. (ENG.). 358p. 1967. text 50.00 (*1-57833-015-7*) Todd Commns.

Lieutenant Zagoskin's Travels in Russian America, 1842-1844: The First Ethnographic & Geographic Investigations on the Yukon & Kuskokwim Valleys of Alaska. Lavrentii A. Zagoskin. Ed. by Henry N. Michael. LC 67-2141. (Anthropology of the North Ser.: No. 7). (Illus.). 282p. reprint ed. pap. 87.50 (*0-7837-0532-8*, 204086000019) Bks Demand.

Lieutenants. W. E. B. Griffin. (Brotherhood of War Ser.: Bk. 1). 416p. 1986. mass mkt. 7.50 (*0-515-09021-2*, Jove) Berkley Pub.

Lieutenants: The Evolution of Political Style. Michael Maher. LC 90-39105. 208p. 1990. 55.00 (*0-275-93461-6*, C3461, Praeger Pubs) Greenwood.

***Lieutenant's Lady.** Kate Huntington. (Zebra Regency Romance Ser.). 224p. 1999. mass mkt. 4.99 (*0-8217-6420-9*, Zebra Kensgtn) Kensgtn Pub Corp.

Lieutenant's Lady. Rae Muir. 298p. 1997. per. 4.99 (*0-373-28993-9*, 1-28993-4) Harlequin Bks.

Lieutenant's Lady. Bess S. Aldrich. 275p. 1975. reprint ed. lib. bdg. 24.95 (*0-88411-252-7*) Amereon Ltd.

Lieutenant's Lady. Bess S. Aldrich. LC 87-4994. iv, 277p. 1987. reprint ed. pap. 13.50 (*0-8032-5914-X*, Bison Books) U of Nebr Pr.

Lieux Communs du Roman: Stereotypes Grecs d'Aventure & d'Amour. Francoise Letoublon. (Mnemosyne Ser.: Supplement 123). (FRE., Illus.). 248p. 1993. 86.00 (*90-04-09724-4*) Brill Academic Pubs.

Lieux de Marguerite Duras. Marguerite Duras & Michelle Porte. (FRE., Illus.). 117p. 1977. 19.95 (*0-8288-9921-5*, F33080) Fr & Eur.

Lieux de Memoire & Identites Nationales: La France & las Pays-Bas, Vol. I. Ed. by Pim Den Boer & Willem Frijhoff. (FRE.). 284p. (Orig.). (C). 1993. pap. 34.95 (*90-5356-022-X*, Pub. by Amsterdam U Pr) U of Mich Pr.

Lieux du Non-Lieu: Eine Bestandsaufnahme in der zeitgenossischen Fotografie in Frankreich Un Etat de lieu dans la photographie contemporaine francaise. Hubertus Von Amelunxen & Ulrich Pohlmann. (GER., Illus.). 96p. 1997. text 28.00 (*90-5705-062-5*, Verlag Kunst) Gordon & Breach.

Lieux Interdits: Transgression & French Literature. Larry Duffy & Adrian Tudor. 180p. 1998. pap. 25.00 (*0-85958-672-3*, Pub. by Univ of Hull Pr) Paul & Co Pubs.

Lievens und Rembrandt: Studien zum Berhaltnis ihrer Kunst. Helga Gutbrod. Ed. by Rudolf Kuhn. (Ars Faciendi: Bd. 6). (GER., Illus.). 411p. 1996. 69.95 (*3-631-30516-8*) P Lang Pubng.

Life see **Images**

Life. DK Publishing Staff. (Eyewitness Books). 64p. (J). (gr. 4-7). 1999. 15.95 (*0-7894-4884-X*, D K Ink) DK Pub Inc.

Life. John Feinstein. 1997. write for info. (*0-316-27733-9*) Little.

Life. Alessandro Garassino. Tr. by Rocco Serini from ITA. LC 94-8582. (Beginnings Origins & Evolution Ser.). (Illus.). 40p. (J). (gr. 3-10). 1994. lib. bdg. 24.26 (*0-8114-3335-8*) Raintree Steck-V.

Life. Ricki Lewis. 832p. (C). 1991. text. write for info. (*0-697-14187-X*, WCB McGr Hill); text. write for info. (*0-697-12059-7*, WCB McGr Hill); text. write for info. (*0-697-14193-4*, WCB McGr Hill); text. write for info. (*0-697-14197-7*, WCB McGr Hill); text. write for info. (*0-697-14199-3*, WCB McGr Hill); text. write for info. (*0-697-14201-9*, WCB McGr Hill) McGrw-H Hghr Educ.

Life. Ken A. Pelt. (Pocket Library). 73p. (Orig.). 1987. pap. 4.95 (*0-943139-00-7*) Heritage Heirloom.

Life. Anne L. Peters. 1992. pap. 5.50 (*0-87129-143-6*, L73) Dramatic Pub.

Life. William K. Purves. (C). teacher ed. 16.00 (*0-7167-2705-6*) W H Freeman.

Life. Robert Snedden. LC 94-41163. (Science Horizons Ser.). 48p. (J). (gr. 3-12). 1995. lib. bdg. 16.95 (*0-7910-3027-X*) Chelsea Hse.

Life. St. Paul Publications Staff. (C). 1990. text 35.00 (*0-85439-354-4*, Pub. by St Paul Pubns) St Mut.

Life see **Complete Works of Algernon Charles Swinburne**

Life. 2nd ed. Ricki Lewis & Randall C. Moore. (C). 1994. text, student ed. write for info. (*0-697-26488-2*, WCB McGr Hill) McGrw-H Hghr Educ.

Life. 2nd ed. Ricki Lewis & Randall C. Moore. (C). 1995. text, student ed. write for info. (*0-697-26487-4*, WCB McGr Hill) McGrw-H Hghr Educ.

Life. 2nd ed. Ricki Lewis et al. (SPA.). 224p. (C). 1995. student ed. write for info. (*0-697-28041-1*, WCB McGr Hill) McGrw-H Hghr Educ.

Life, 6 pts. 2nd ed. Randall c. Moore & Ricki Lewis. 936p. 1994. boxed set. write for info. (*0-697-15925-6*, WCB McGr Hill) McGrw-H Hghr Educ.

Life. 3rd ed. Lewis. 1999. text 50.00 (*0-07-235234-5*) McGraw.

Life. 3rd ed. Ricki Lewis & Alice C. Jacklet. 192p. (C). 1997. text, lab manual ed. write for info. (*0-697-28568-5*, WCB McGr Hill) McGrw-H Hghr Educ.

Life. 3rd ed. Ricki Lewis et al. LC 97-15290. 976p. (C). 1997. text. write for info. (*0-697-28563-4*, WCB McGr Hill) McGrw-H Hghr Educ.

Life. 3rd ed. William K. Purves. (C). 1992. pap. text 20.00 (*0-7167-2329-8*) W H Freeman.

Life. 4th ed. Lewis. 2001. pap. 62.25 (*0-07-027134-8*) McGraw.

Life. 4th ed. William K. Purves. teacher ed. 16.80 (*0-7167-2656-4*) W H Freeman.

Life. 5th ed. Purves. 1997. 46.00 (*0-7167-3354-4*) W H Freeman.

Life. 5th ed. Purves. 1998. student ed. write for info. (*0-7167-3393-5*) W H Freeman.

Life see **Sarada Devi, Sri the Holy Mother**

Life, Lab Manual. 2nd ed. Ricki Lewis & Randall c. Moore. 192p. (C). 1994. text, student ed. write for info. (*0-697-15942-6*, WCB McGr Hill) McGrw-H Hghr Educ.

Life, Study Art Notebook. 2nd ed. Ricki Lewis & Randall c. Moore. 232p. (C). 1994. text, student ed. write for info. (*0-697-24548-9*, WCB McGr Hill) McGrw-H Hghr Educ.

Life, Study Guide. 2nd ed. Ricki Lewis & Randall c. Moore. 176p. (C). 1995. text, student ed. 18.75 (*0-697-15945-0*, WCB McGr Hill) McGrw-H Hghr Educ.

Life, Vol. 1. 4th ed. William K. Purves. Date not set. student ed. 30.00 (*0-7167-3011-1*) W H Freeman.

Life, Vol. 1, 3. 5th ed. PURVES. 1997. 50.00 (*0-7167-3353-6*) W H Freeman.

Life, Vol. 1 & 2. 5th ed. Purves. 1997. 50.00 incl. cd-rom (*0-7167-3351-X*) W H Freeman.

Life, Vol. II. 4th ed. William K. Purves. Date not set. student ed. 36.00 (*0-7167-3012-X*) W H Freeman.

Life, Vol. III. William K. Purves. Date not set. student ed. 36.00 (*0-7167-3013-8*) W H Freeman.

Life, Vols. 1, 2 & 3. 5th ed. Purves. 1998. student ed. 87.00 incl. cd-rom (*0-7167-3447-8*) W H Freeman.

***Life: A Century in Pictures (Books Are Fun Edition)** Richard Stolley. (Illus.). 2000. 65.00 (*0-8212-2714-9*, Pub. by Bulfinch Pr) Little.

Life: A Collection of Poems. Bob Whitfield. LC 77-87401. (Illus.). 180p. 1978. 8.95 (*0-930920-07-4*) Whitfield Bks.

***Life: A Complete Operating Manual.** Lauren Tratar. 400p. 1999. pap., wbk. ed. 25.00 (*1-891850-19-9*) Med Bear.

***Life: A Natural History of the First Four Billion Years.** Richard Fortey. (Illus.). (J). 1998. 20.35 (*0-606-18239-X*) Turtleback.

Life: A Natural History of the First Four Billion Years of Life on Earth. Richard Fortey. LC 97-49466. 346p. 1998. 30.00 (*0-375-40119-9*) Knopf.

Life: A Natural History of the First Four Billion Years of Life on Earth. Richard Fortey. (Illus.). 400p. 1999. pap. 15.00 (*0-375-70261-X*) Vin Bks.

Life: A User's Manual. Ed. by John Miller. LC 98-3733. 144p. 1998. 15.00 (*1-57731-067-5*) New Wrld Lib.

Life: A User's Manual. Georges Perec. Tr. by David Bellos from FRE. LC 87-8782. 600p. 1987. reprint ed. pap. 19.95 (*0-87923-751-1*) Godine.

Life: A Workback Schedule. Elizabeth Reese. 1997. mass mkt. 5.99 (*0-614-20508-5*) Harlequin Bks.

Life: Against Apion see **Works of Josephus**

Life: Before, During & After. Illus. by Gary Lund. (Celebration of Discovery Ser.: Vol. II). 192p. (Orig.). 1988. pap. 12.95 (*0-938283-01-4*) Spirit Speaks.

***Life: Century of Change: America in Pictures, 1900-2000.** Ed. by Richard B. Stolley & Tony Chiu. (Illus.). 400p. 2000. 60.00 (*0-8212-2697-5*) Bulfinch Pr.

Life: From Surviving to Thriving. Mark J. Britzman. 100p. (Orig.). 1997. pap. 4.95 (*0-9657284-0-4*) M J Britzman.

Life: God's Way. 2nd rev. ed. Nancy Murdoch & Linda Fassett. 80p. 1997. wbk. ed. 12.95 (*0-9658737-0-6*) Step Up To Life.

Life: Here? There? Elsewhere?: The Search for Life on Venus & Mars. SETI Institute Staff. (Life in the Universe Ser.). 288p. 1996. pap. text 90.00 incl. vdisk (*1-56308-327-2*, C272) Teacher Ideas Pr.

Life: His Acronyms Really Refresh You. Harry F. Castagna. 96p. 1997. pap. 9.95 (*0-9661950-0-0*) HP Pub.

Life: In the Glory of Its Radiating Manifestations, Bk. 1. anniversary ed. Ed. by Anna-Teresa Tymieniecka. LC 95-44239. (Analecta Husserliana Ser.: Vol. XLVIII). 592p. (C). 1996. lib. bdg. 198.00 (*0-7923-3825-1*) Kluwer Academic.

Life: Its Nature & Origin: Chemical Evolution & a Consciousness-Based Paradigm. T. D. Singh & Greg Anderson. LC 96-6213. (Illus.). 100p. (Orig.). 1997. pap. text 4.95 (*0-941525-11-2*) Bhaktvdnta Institute.

Life: Its Nature, Origins & Distribution. Josephine Marquand. (Contemporary Science Library). (Illus.). (C). 1971. reprint ed. pap. 2.00 (*0-393-00589-5*) Norton.

LIFE: Learning Independence Through Functional Experiences. Karen Levgers & Kathy Stangler. (Illus.). 204p. 1995. spiral bd. 24.00 (*1-884135-13-7*) Mayer-Johnson.

***Life: Our Century in Pictures.** Ed. by Richard B. Stolley. LC 99-64899. (Illus.). 400p. 1999. 65.00 (*0-8212-2633-9*, Pub. by Bulfinch Pr) Little.

***Life: Our Century in Pictures for Young People.** Ed. by Richard B. Stolley. (Illus.). 225p. (J). (gr. 5 up). 2000. 25.95 (*0-316-81589-6*) Little.

Life: Phenomenology of Life As the Starting Point of Philosophy. Anna-Teresa Tymieniecka. LC 96-23675. (Analecta Husserliana Ser.). 1996. lib. bdg. 156.00 (*0-7923-4126-0*) Kluwer Academic.

***Life: Ready Notes.** 3rd ed. Lewis. 1999. 9.06 (*0-07-234545-4*) McGraw.

Life! Reflections on Your Journey. Louise L. Hay. LC 95-11990. 192p. 1995. 17.95 (*1-56170-092-4*, 164) Hay House.

Life! Reflections on Your Journey. Louise L. Hay. LC 95-11990. 192p. 1996. reprint ed. pap. 12.00 (*1-56170-312-5*, 164T) Hay House.

Life: Science of Biology. 4th ed. Purves. 2000. 58.00 (*0-7167-3020-0*); lab manual ed. 78.00 (*0-7167-3037-5*) W H Freeman.

Life: Science of Biology. 4th ed. William K. Purves. (C). 1995. text 16.80 (*0-7167-2936-9*) W H Freeman.

Life: Science of Biology. 5th ed. Purves. 1997. pap. text 4.95 (*0-7167-3372-2*, Pub. by W H Freeman) VHPS.

Life: Science of Biology. 5th ed. Purves. 280p. 1997. 18.00 (*0-7167-3219-X*); teacher ed. 20.00 (*0-7167-3220-3*) Worth.

***Life: Science of Biology.** 6th ed. William K. Purves et al. 2000. pap. text, student ed. write for info. (*0-7167-3951-8*) W H Freeman.

Life: Science of Biology, 2. 4th ed. Purves. Date not set. 43.00 (*0-7167-3017-0*) W H Freeman.

Life: Science of Biology, Vol. I. Purves. 1997. pap. text 35.95 (*0-7167-3274-2*) W H Freeman.

Life: Science of Biology, Vol. 1. 4th ed. Purves. Date not set. 60.00 (*0-7167-3014-6*); 43.00 (*0-7167-3015-4*) W H Freeman.

Life: Science of Biology, Vol. 1. 5th ed. Purves. 1997. pap. 40.95 (*0-7167-3326-9*) W H Freeman.

Life: Science of Biology, Vol. 1. 5th ed. William K. Purves et al. (Illus.). 1997. pap. text 35.95 (*0-7167-3275-0*) W H Freeman.

Life: Science of Biology, Vol. 1 & 2. Purves. Date not set. 74.00 (*0-7167-3018-9*) W H Freeman.

Life: Science of Biology, Vol. 2. 4th ed. Purves. Date not set. 58.00 (*0-7167-3021-9*) W H Freeman.

Life: Study of Biology. 5th ed. Purves. (Illus.). 413p. 1997. pap. text, student ed. 24.95 (*0-7167-3221-1*) St Martin.

***Life: The Human Being Between Life & Death; A Dialogue Between Medicine & Philosophy, Recurrent Issues & New Approaches.** Anna-Teresa Tymieniecka & Zigniew Zalewski. LC 99-40299. (Analecta Husserliana Ser.). 352p. 2000. 154.00 (*0-7923-5962-3*) Kluwer Academic.

Life: The Humble Truth. Guy de Maupassant. Tr. by Roger Pearson from FRE. LC 98-32139. (Oxford World's Classics Ser.). 245p. 1999. pap. 8.95 (*0-19-283298-0*) OUP.

Life: The Love & Poetry of the Black Hustler. Murray B. Binderman et al. 224p. 1986. mass mkt. 3.50 (*0-87067-367-X*, BH367) Holloway.

Life: The Millennium: The 100 Most Important Events & People of the Past 1,000 Years. Life Magazine Editors. (Illus.). 192p. 1998. 29.95 (*0-8212-2557-X*, Pub. by Bulfinch Pr) Little.

***Life: The Movie; How Entertainment Conquered Reality.** Neal Gabler. 2000. pap. 14.00 (*0-375-70653-4*) Vin Bks.

Life: The Owner's Manual. Alan Fensin. LC 94-68119. (Illus.). 400p. (Orig.). 1995. per. 15.95 (*0-9622183-2-4*) Way Enterprises.

Life: The Science of Biology. William K. Purves et al. (Illus.). 1200p. (C). 1992. student ed. 40.00 (*0-7167-2279-8*); student ed. 6.40 (*0-7167-2280-1*) W H Freeman.

Life: The Science of Biology. rev. ed. William K. Purves et al. (Illus.). 1200p. (C). 1991. disk 48.00 (*0-7167-2330-1*); disk 48.00 (*0-7167-2277-1*) W H Freeman.

Life: The Science of Biology. rev. ed. William K. Purves et al. (Illus.). 360p. (C). 1992. 40.00 (*0-7167-2278-X*) W H Freeman.

Life: The Science of Biology. 3rd rev. ed. William K. Purves et al. (Illus.). 1200p. (C). 1992. text 52.00 (*0-7167-2276-3*) W H Freeman.

Life: The Science of Biology. 5th ed. William K. Purves. 1997. pap. text 83.95 (*0-7167-3325-0*) W H Freeman.

Life: The Science of Biology, Sampler. 4th ed. William K. Purves. 1994. write for info. (*0-7167-2737-4*) W H Freeman.

Life: The Sixties. Doris C. O'Neil. (Illus.). 1989. 35.00 (*0-8212-1752-6*) Little.

***Life: The Way We Were.** Life Editors. (Illus.). 192p. 2000. 29.95 (*0-8212-2634-7*, Pub. by Bulfinch Pr) Little.

Life: Voices from the Heart. William J. Crockett. 15p. 1985. pap. 3.00 (*0-934383-05-7*) Pride Prods.

Life: You Are the Dreamer. Joseph Mark. 20p. 1994. pap. text. write for info. (*1-885206-08-9*, Iliad Pr) Cader Pubng.

Life . . . An Event! Judith McArtor. LC 89-90275. (Illus.). 80p. (Orig.). 1989. pap. 6.95 (*0-9623782-0-8*) Cynosure Self Discovery.

Life . . . Scientific Philosophy: Phenomenology of Life & the Sciences of Life. Anna-Teresa Tymieniecka. LC 98-8187. (Analecta Husserliana Ser.). 1998. write for info. (*0-7923-5141-X*) Kluwer Academic.

Life . . . with No Strings Attached! Carlos G. Daniels, Jr. 155p. 1984. 7.95 (*0-89697-144-9*) Intl Univ Pr.

Life - It Can Make You or Break You - You Decide. Sharon Farner Youtsey. 1998. pap. write for info. (*1-57553-841-5*) Watermrk Pr.

Life - Stop Crowding Me. Leona Choy. 190p. (Orig.), 1994. pap. text 8.95 (*1-882324-05-6*) Ambssdrs Christ.

***Life - Tain't Nawthin' but Wind: Growing up Country in the Fifties & Dancing to a Different Drummer.** Joe Neil Steward. LC 00-190963. 360p. 2000. 25.00 (*0-7388-2140-3*); pap. 18.00 (*0-7388-2141-1*) Xlibris Corp.

Life - 25: Interviews with Prisoners Serving Life Sentences. Loyd Johnsen. Ed. by Peter J. Murphy. 218p. 1997. pap. 14.00 (*0-921586-55-8*, Pub. by New Star Bks) Genl Dist Srvs.

Life - Vocal Selections. Ed. by Sy Feldman. 1997. pap. 14.95 (*1-57623-954-3*) Wrner Bros.

Life? or Theatre? Charlotte Salomon. (Illus.). 832p. 1999. pap. text 50.00 (*90-400-9286-9*) Waandrs.

Life a Dream. Pedro Calderon de la Barca. Tr. by Edward Fitzgerald from SPA. LC 92-53872. 70p. (Orig.). 1992. pap. 7.00 (*0-88734-254-X*) Players Pr.

Life... A Soul's Journey Home. 2nd ed. Patricia Lehman. (Illus.). Date not set. write for info. (*1-928587-04-6*) RoverMedia.

Life A-ta Z. Jacob D. Carver. pap. 12.95 (*1-893504-00-X*) ThirdEye Poet.

***Life Ablaze: A Woman's Novena.** deluxe ed. Joan Chittister. LC 99-51454. 80p. 2000. pap. 10.95 (*1-58051-041-8*) Sheed & Ward WI.

Life above the Rim. Keith Brown. 184p. (Orig.). (YA). (gr. 6 up). 1994. pap. 8.95 (*1-887002-10-3*) Cross Trng.

***Life Abundant: Rethinking Theology & Economy for a Planet in Peril.** Sallie McFague. 2000. pap. 16.00 (*0-8006-3269-9*, Fortress Pr) Augsburg Fortress.

Life Abundant for You (1928) Louise B. Brownell. 248p. 1998. reprint ed. pap. 19.95 (*0-7661-0324-2*) Kessinger Pub.

Life According to Motown. Patricia Smith. 76p. 1991. pap. 6.95 (*0-9624287-2-8*) Tia Chucha Pr.

Life According to Trombla. 160p. 1983. 7.95 (*0-932834-49-3*) Prime Natl Pub.

Life, Adventures & Piracies of the Famous Captain Singleton. Daniel Defoe. LC 74-13433. (Illus.). xviii, 316p. 1974. reprint ed. write for info. (*0-404-07916-4*) AMS Pr.

Life-Adventures of Zamba, an African Negro King. Ed. by Peter Neilson. LC 70-133162. (Black Heritage Library Collection). 1977. 27.95 (*0-8369-8717-9*) Ayer.

***Life Affirming Acts.** Hector Vila. 2000. pap. text. write for info. (*0-86709-560-1*, Pub. by Boynton Cook Pubs) Heinemann.

Life after a Death: A Study of the Elderly Widowed. Ann Bowling & Ann Cartwright. 239p. 1982. 29.95 (*0-422-78230-0*, NO. 3712, Pub. by Tavistock) Routldge.

Life after a Heart Attack: Social & Psychological Factors Eight Years Later. Sydney Croog & Sol Levine. LC 81-6702. 328p. 1982. 45.95 (*0-89885-071-1*, Kluwer Acad Hman Sci) Kluwer Academic.

Life, after All. Suzanne Jacob. 136p. 1989. pap. 9.50 (*0-88974-017-8*, Pub. by Press Gang Pubs) LPC InBook.

***Life after Baby: From Professional Woman to Beginner Parent.** Wynn McClenahan Burkett. (Illus.). 2000. pap. write for info. (*1-885171-44-7*, Pub. by Wldcat Canyon) Publishers Group.

L

An Asterisk (*) at the beginning of an entry indicates that the title is appearing for the first time.

Life after Big Bang. Ed. by Simon Maclachlan. (C). 1988. lib. bdg. 68.50 (*0-86010-982-8*, Pub. by Graham & Trotman) Kluwer Academic.

Life after Billy. Brian Vallee. 352p. 1995. mass mkt. 7.99 (*0-7704-2622-0*) Bantam.

Life after Birth: Every Woman's Guide to the First Year of Motherhood. Wendy Blumfield. 144p. 1993. pap. 12.95 (*1-85230-351-4*, Pub. by Element MA) Penguin Putnam.

Life after Birth: Imagery in Samuel Beckett's Trilogy. Philip H. Solomon. LC 75-11625. (Romance Monographs: No. 15). 1975. 24.00 (*84-399-3763-6*) Romance.

Life after Birth: Spirituality for College Students. William Toohey. 112p. 1984. 4.95 (*0-8164-2290-7*) Harper SF.

Life after Brain Injury: Who Am I? 2nd rev. ed. Tampa General Rehabilitation Center Staff. (Coping Ser.: Vol. 4). 100p. (Orig.). 1996. pap. 9.50 (*1-882855-47-7*) HDI Pubs.

Life after Cancer. Ann Kent. 160p. 1996. pap. 14.95 (*0-7063-7458-4*, Pub. by WrLock) Sterling.

Life after CDs: A Practical Guide to Safe Investing. J. Michael Martin & Sean M. Martin. (Financial Advantage Ser.). (Illus.). 308p. 1999. reprint ed. pap. 19.95 (*1-882584-51-1*) HOMEFILE.

Life after Co-Dependency. LaDeane R. Hudspeth. LC 98-90251. 1999. pap. 8.95 (*0-533-12741-6*) Vantage.

Life after College. Anthony Tedesco. 1996. pap. 12.00 (*1-57566-034-2*) Kensgtn Pub Corp.

***Life after College: A Descriptive Summary of 1992-93 Bachelor's Degree Recipients in 1997 : with an Essay on Participation in Graduate & First-professional Education.** Alexander C. McCormick. LC 99-227863. (Illus.). 131p. 1999. write for info. (*0-16-050066-4*) USGPO.

Life after College: Lessons for Students in Transition. Will Keim. 160p. (Orig.). 1996. pap. 9.99 (*0-8272-2125-8*) Chalice Pr.

Life after Cutbacks: Tracking California's Aerospace Workers. Robert F. Schoeni et al. 88p. (Orig.). 1996. pap. text 15.00 (*0-8330-2356-X*, MR-688-OSD) Rand Corp.

Life after Death. Douglas M. Baker. 1982. pap. 12.50 (*0-906006-58-9*, Pub. by Baker Pubns) New Leaf Dist.

Life after Death. Mary T. Browne. 1995. mass mkt. 5.99 (*0-8041-1386-6*) Ivy Books.

Life after Death. Sidney L. Freeman. LC 97-28871. (Survey of the Cumulative Evidence Ser.). 314p. 1998. 23.95 (*1-56072-467-6*, Nova Kroshka Bks) Nova Sci Pubs.

Life after Death. S. D. Gordon. Ed. by Dan Harmon. 256p. 1998. lthr. 4.97 (*1-57748-181-X*) Barbour Pub.

Life after Death. Tom Harpur. 368p. 1997. pap. 7.99 (*0-7710-3938-7*) McCland & Stewart.

***Life after Death.** Charles W. Leadbeater. 94p. 1998. 6.95 (*81-7059-254-2*, Quest) Theos Pub Hse.

Life after Death. Gordon Lindsay. 1960. per. 3.95 (*0-89985-083-9*) Christ for the Nations.

Life after Death. Gordon Lindsay. (Literature Crusade Ser.). 1965. pap. 0.95 (*0-89985-351-X*) Christ for the Nations.

Life after Death. Albert J. Nevins. LC 83-61888. 156p. (Orig.). 1983. pap. 6.95 (*0-87973-612-7*, 612) Our Sunday Visitor.

Life after Death. Sayyid M. Tabataba'i. Tr. by Laleh Bakhtiar. 96p. (Orig.). 1989. pap. text 6.70 (*1-871031-22-2*) Abjad Bk.

Life after Death. rev. ed. Spiros Zodhiates. Orig. Title: What Happens after Death?. (Illus.). 256p. 1993. pap. 7.99 (*0-89957-525-0*) AMG Pubs.

Life after Death: A New Revelation. William A. LePar et al. LC 94-66952. (Illus.). 256p. (Orig.). 1994. pap. 14.95 (*1-885728-00-X*) Solar Press.

Life after Death: A Study of the Afterlife in World Religions. Farnaz Masumian. 200p. 1995. pap. 14.95 (*1-85168-074-8*, Pub. by Onewrld Pubns) Penguin Putnam.

Life after Death? Christian Interpretation of Personal Eschatology. Jay D. Robison. LC 92-32236. (American Univ. Studies, VII: Vol. 137). XI, 234p. (C). 1998. text 43.95 (*0-8204-1959-1*) P Lang Pubng.

Life after Death: The Case for Survival of Bodily Death. D. Scott Rogo. 144p. 1987. pap. 9.95 (*0-85030-504-7*, Pub. by Aqrn Pr) HarpC.

Life after Death? Sex? Dinner? The Lighter Side of the Occult. Al G. Manning. LC 83-60386. 144p. (Orig.). 1983. pap. 6.95 (*0-941698-07-6*) Pan Ishtar.

Life after Death & How Theosophy Unveils It. C. W. Leadbeater. 58p. 1996. reprint ed. spiral bd. 9.00 (*0-7873-1246-0*) Hlth Research.

Life after Death & How Theosophy Unveils It. C. W. Leadbeater. 73p. 1992. reprint ed. pap. 8.00 (*1-56459-156-5*) Kessinger Pub.

Life after Death & the World Beyond. Jenny Randles & Peter Hough. LC 98-176844. (Illus.). 160p. 1998. 12.95 (*0-8069-0719-3*) Sterling.

Life after Death & the World Beyond: Investing Heaven & Sporotual Dimension. Jenny Randles. 1998. text 24.95 (*0-7499-1681-8*, Pub. by Piatkus Bks) London Brdge.

Life after Death in the World Religions. Ed. by Harold Coward. LC 96-51083. (Faith Meets Faith Ser.). 125p. (Orig.). 1997. pap. 15.00 (*1-57075-119-6*) Orbis Bks.

Life after Death (Vida Despues De la Muerta) Gordon Lindsay. (Literature Crusade Ser.). (SPA.). 1965. pap. 0.95 (*0-89985-364-1*) Christ for the Nations.

Life after Debt. Kisluk. 1997. pap. 18.95 (*0-385-25588-8*) Doubleday.

***Life after Debt: Free Yourself from the Burden of Money Worries Once & for All.** 3rd ed. Bob Hammond. LC 99-59730. 256p. (Orig.). 2000. pap. 14.99 (*1-56414-421-6*) Career Pr Inc.

***Life after Debt: Is Personal Bankruptcy Your Best Solution?** rev. ed. Frank Kisluk. 160p. 1999. pap. write for info. (*0-385-25873-9*, Pub. by Doubleday) Random House.

Life after Debt: The Blueprint for Surviving in America's Credit Society. Benjamin F. Dover. Ed. by Sharon Hallberg & Linda Vanderwold. LC 93-21205. 336p. (Orig.). 1993. pap. 16.95 (*1-880925-03-6*) Equitable Media.

Life after Debt: The Complete Credit Restoration Kit. Bob Hammond. 464p. 1992. pap. 35.00 (*0-87364-684-3*) Paladin Pr.

Life after Divorce. Dorothy Payne. (Looking up Ser.). 24p. (Orig.). 1982. pap. 1.95 (*0-8298-0610-5*) Pilgrim OH.

Life after Divorce: Create a New Beginning. Sharon Wegscheider-Cruse. LC 93-46943. 210p. 1993. pap. 8.95 (*1-55874-282-4*) Health Comm.

Life after Divorce: How to Grow Through a Divorce. Bobbie Reed. 192p. (Orig.). 1993. pap. 10.99 (*0-570-04614-9*, 123199) Concordia.

Life after Doomsday. Bruce D. Clayton. (Illus.). 200p. 1980. 29.95 (*0-87364-175-2*) Paladin Pr.

Life after Early Retirement: The Experiences of Lower Level Workers. Dean W. Morse et al. LC 81-70970. (Conservation of Human Resources Ser.: Vol. 17). 206p. 1983. text 53.50 (*0-916672-62-X*) Rowman.

Life after Easter: Mystagogia for Everyone. Pamela Smith. LC 92-21195. 96p. 1993. pap. 4.95 (*0-8091-3379-2*) Paulist Pr.

Life after Fifty: A Positive Look at Aging in the Faith Community. Ed. by Katie F. Wiebe. LC 92-74439. 169p. (Orig.). 1993. pap. 10.95 (*0-87303-203-9*) Faith & Life.

***Life after 40.** Benjamin Breeze. 50p. 1999. 14.95 (*0-9675120-0-X*) Gloom & Doomb Bk.

Life after God. Douglas Coupland. Ed. by Amy Einhorn. 368p. 1995. per. 10.00 (*0-671-87434-9*) PB.

Life after Grief. Janet Rosauer. (Illus.). 120p. 1998. pap. 9.95 (*1-890676-25-X*) Beavers Pond.

Life after Grief: A Soul Journey after Suicide. Jack Clarke. LC 88-90968. 192p. (Orig.). 1989. pap. 9.95 (*0-929841-02-6*) Prsnl Pathways.

Life after Head Injury: The Experiences of Twenty Young People & Their Families. Jane Hubert. 128p. 1995. text 61.95 (*1-85972-148-6*, Pub. by Avebry) Ashgate Pub Co.

Life after Hockey. 2nd rev. ed. Michael A. Smith. 300p. 1996. pap. 20.00 (*1-884125-51-4*) Cooper Pubng.

Life after Layoff: How to Pick Yourself Up, Dust Yourself Off & Start Again. Dean Hoch & Nancy Hoch. (Illus.). 150p. (Orig.). 1999. pap. write for info. (*0-9624209-7-2*) Landmark ID.

Life after Life. Raymond A. Moody, Jr. 208p. 1979. mass mkt. 6.99 (*0-553-27484-8*) Bantam.

Life after Life. Raymond A. Moody, Jr. 176p. 1981. 14.95 (*0-89176-037-7*, Mckingbird) R Bemis Pub.

***Life after Life.** Fraser Smith. 2000. pap. 10.95 (*0-281-04718-9*, Pub. by Society Prom Christ Know) Intl Pubs Mktg.

Life after Life: The Investigation of a Phenomenon, Survival of Bodily Death. large type ed. Raymond A. Moody. 240p. 1988. pap. 9.95 (*0-8027-2599-6*) Walker & Co.

Life after Life: The Theory of Reincarnation. Eustace Miles. 180p. 1985. pap. 16.50 (*0-89540-126-6*, SB-126) Sun Pub.

Life after Life after Life. Kathryn P. Jones. 171p. (Orig.). 1994. pap. 9.95 (*0-9649712-0-8*) Soapbox Pubng.

Life after Loss. Dorn J. Wheatley. LC 96-116703. 140p. (Orig.). 1995. pap. 9.99 (*1-56043-842-8*, Treasure Hse) Destiny Image.

Life after Loss. Larry Yeagley. 32p. (Orig.). 1985. pap. 0.89 (*0-8280-0292-4*) Review & Herald.

Life after Loss: A Personal Guide Dealing with Death, Divorce, Job Change & Relocation. 3rd ed. Bob Deits. LC 99-47461. 272p. 1999. pap. 12.95 (*1-55561-189-3*) Fisher Bks.

Life after Loss: A Personal Guide to Dealing with Death, Divorce, Job Change & Relocation. rev. ed. Bob Deits. LC 92-29593. 256p. (Orig.). 1992. reprint ed. pap. 12.95 (*1-55561-049-8*) Fisher Bks.

Life after Lucy: The True Story of I Love Lucy's Little Ricky. Keith Thibodeaux & Audrey Hingley. LC 93-87255. 240p. (Orig.). 1994. pap. 10.95 (*0-89221-256-X*) New Leaf.

Life after Medical School: Thirty-Two Doctors Describe How They Shaped Their Medical Careers. Leonard Laster. 320p. (C). 1996. 29.95 (*0-393-71030-0*) Norton.

Life after Nuclear War: The Economic & Social Impacts of Nuclear Attacks on the United States. Arthur M. Katz. LC 81-1300. 464p. 1982. 18.95 (*0-88410-096-0*, HarpBusn); pap. 18.95 (*0-88410-907-0*, HarpBusn) HarpInfo.

Life after Pentecost. Ed. by Evangelical Press Staff. 1996. pap. 16.99 (*0-85234-344-2*, Pub. by Evangelical Pr) P & R Pubng.

Life after Postmodernism: Essays on Value & Culture. Ed. by John Fekete. LC 90-10152. 256p. 1988. text 19.95 (*0-312-00833-3*) St Martin.

Life after Prison. Al Wengerd. 48p. (Orig.). 1984. pap. 4.50 (*0-8361-3382-X*) Herald Pr.

Life after Psychotherapy. Todd Davison. 192p. 1997. 30.00 (*1-56821-849-4*) Aronson.

Life after School: A Social Skills Curriculum. James McGuire & Philip Priestley. (Illus.). 239p. 1981. pap. text 21.00 (*0-08-025193-5*, Pergamon Pr) Elsevier.

Life after Scott: A Grieving Journal for Parents. Cheryl Kimpel. LC 99-62965. 88p. 1999. pap. 14.95 (*0-9671977-0-8*) River Crossing.

Life after Sixty: A Report on Britain's Older Population. Gerontology Data Service Staff. (C). 1992. 125.00 (*1-872342-60-4*, Pub. by Age Concern Eng) St Mut.

Life after Stress. M. Shaffer. LC 81-17785. (Illus.). 288p. (C). 1982. 15.95 (*0-306-40869-4*, Plenum Trade) Perseus Pubng.

Life after Suicide: A Ray of Hope for Those Left Behind. E. Betsy Ross. LC 97-33703. (Illus.). 322p. (C). 1997. 27.95 (*0-306-45630-3*, Plen Insight) Perseus Pubng.

Life after Suicide: The Survivor's Grief Experience. Terence Barrett. 149p. 1989. pap. 10.95 (*0-9664758-0-1*) Aftermath Res.

Life after Survival: A Therapeutic Approach for Adult Children of Alcoholics. Patricia A. Mansmann & Patricia A. Neuhausel. (Illus.). 56p. 1986. pap. text 6.95 (*0-940967-00-6*) Genesis Pub PA.

Life after Survival: A Therapeutic Approach for Adult Children of Alcoholics. 2nd rev. ed. Patricia A. Mansmann & Patricia A. Neuhausel. (Illus.). 88p. 1989. pap. text 6.95 (*0-940967-01-4*) Genesis Pub PA.

Life after Television. George Gilder. 1990. 11.95 (*0-614-17720-0*) Hudson Instit IN.

Life after Television. George Gilder. 144p. 1992. 14.95 (*0-393-03385-6*) Norton.

Life after Television. George Gilder. 1994. pap. 11.00 (*0-393-31158-9*) Norton.

Life after the Divorce: Practical Guidance for Starting Over. Medard Laz. LC 97-75382. 80p. 1998. pap. 4.95 (*0-7648-0191-0*) Liguori Pubns.

Life after the Line. Josie Kearns. LC 90-11936. (Great Lakes Bks.). 226p. (C). 1990. 34.95 (*0-8143-2015-5*); pap. 19.95 (*0-8143-2016-3*) Wayne St U Pr.

***Life after the Pain: The Way, the Truth & the Life.** Blanca Rosa Wright. 110p. 1999. pap. 12.00 (*0-7392-0419-X*, PO3682) Morris Pubng.

Life after Trauma: A Workbook for Healing. Dena Rosenbloom & Mary Beth Williams. LC 99-203928. 352p. 1999. pap. text 18.95 (*1-57230-239-9*) Guilford Pubns.

Life after TV: Slaying the One-Eyed Monster. Teresa Olive. (Contemporary Christian Living Ser.). 51p. (Orig.). 1992. pap. 1.99 (*0-87509-470-8*) Chr Pubns.

Life after Vietnam. Delores A. Kuenning. 369p. 1994. 22.95 (*1-56924-942-3*) Marlowe & Co.

***Life After Work: Stories of Freedom, Opportunity & Change.** Zelda Curtis. 1999. pap. 17.95 (*0-7043-4597-8*, Pub. by Womens Press) Trafalgar.

Life after Youth: Making Sense of One Man's Journey Through the Transition at Mid-Life. Sean D. Sammon. LC 96-49472. 119p. (Orig.). 1997. pap. 7.95 (*0-8189-0778-9*) Alba.

Life Against Death: The Psychoanalytical Meaning of History. 2nd ed. Norman O. Brown. LC 85-17928. 387p. 1985. pap. 22.95 (*0-8195-6144-4*, Wesleyan Univ Pr) U Pr of New Eng.

Life Album 1997: Pictures of the Year. Time-Life Books Editors. 200p. (gr. 7). 1999. 29.95 (*1-883013-29-1*) Time-Life.

Life Album 1996: Pictures of the Year. 160p. 1998. 24.95 (*1-883013-11-9*, People Bks) Tme Inc.

Life along the Hudson. Allan Keller. LC 75-7155. (Illus.). 272p. 1985. reprint ed. pap. 11.95 (*0-912882-59-X*) Sleepy Hollow.

Life along the Hudson. 2nd rev. ed. Allan Keller. LC 97-25054. xix, 272p. 1997. 25.00 (*0-8232-1803-1*); pap. 16.50 (*0-8232-1804-X*) Fordham.

Life along the Hudson: Wood Engravings of Hudson River Subjects from Harper's Weekly, 1859-1903. Ed. by Valis F. Ruge. (Illus.). 180p. 1994. 45.00 (*0-87951-523-6*, Pub. by Overlook Pr) Penguin Putnam.

Life along the Mangrove Shore: A Guide to Common Estuarine Plants & Animals of Southern Florida. G. Alex Marsh & Leni L. Bane. (Orig.). 1995. pap. 9.95 (*0-912451-31-9*) Florida Classics.

Life Along the Mekong: Asia's River People from China to Vietnam. Stan Sesser. (Illus.). 300p. 2000. pap. text 16.95 (*1-57143-070-9*) RDR Bks.

Life along the Merrimac: Collected Histories of the Native Americans Who Lived on Its Banks. Ed. by John Pendergast. LC 95-81901. (Illus.). 192p. (Orig.). (C). 1996. pap. 19.95 (*0-9629338-2-1*) Merrimac River.

***Life along the Silk Road.** Susan Whitfield. 253p. 2000. 27.50 (*0-520-22472-8*, Pub. by U CA Pr) Cal Prin Full Svc.

Life along the South Manchurian Railway: The Memoirs of Ito Takeo. Tr. by Joshua A. Fogel from JPN. LC 87-32230. 272p. (C). (gr. 13). 1988. text 66.95 (*0-87332-465-X*, East Gate Bk) M E Sharpe.

Life among the Ancient Ones: The Accounts of an Anasazi Archaeological Research Project. Bob Greenlee. 156p. 1995. 16.95 (*0-9647320-0-9*); pap. 12.95 (*0-9647320-1-7*) Hardscrabble Pr.

Life among the Apaches. John C. Cremony. LC 82-16106. 322p. 1983. reprint ed. pap. 13.95 (*0-8032-6312-0*, Bison Books) U of Nebr Pr.

Life among the Choctaws. Henry C. Benson & Phillip A. Sperry. 324p. 1994. reprint ed. 36.95 (*1-56869-055-X*); reprint ed. pap. 21.95 (*1-56869-056-8*) Oldbuck Pr.

Life among the English. Rose Macaulay. (Writers' Britain Ser.). (Illus.). 96p. 1997. 11.95 (*1-85375-231-2*) Prion.

Life among the Great Plains Indians. Earle Rice, Jr. LC 97-27149. (Way People Live Ser.). (Illus.). 112p. (J). (gr. 6-9). 1997. lib. bdg. 22.45 (*1-56006-347-5*) Lucent Bks.

Life among the Ibo Women of Nigeria. Salome C. Nnoromele. LC 97-45172. (Other America Ser.). (Illus.). (J). (gr. 9 up). 1997. lib. bdg. 22.45 (*1-56006-344-0*) Lucent Bks.

Life among the Indian Fighters. James P. Reger. LC 97-28776. (Way People Live Ser.). (Illus.). (J). (gr. 4-12). 1997. lib. bdg. 22.45 (*1-56006-349-1*) Lucent Bks.

Life among the Indians: or Personal Reminiscences & Historical Incidents Illustrative of Indian Life & Character. James B. Finley. Ed. by D. W. Clark. LC 76-160972. (Select Bibliographies Reprint Ser.). 1977. reprint ed. 34.95 (*0-8369-5840-3*) Ayer.

Life among the Indians: or the Captivity of the Oatman Girls among the Apache & Mohave Indians see Captivity of the Oatman Girls among the Apache & Mohave Indians

Life among the Magars. Gary Shepherd. (Summer Institute of Linguistics International Museum of Cultures). (Illus.). 270p. (Orig.). 1982. pap. 14.00 (*0-88312-921-3*) S I L Intl.

Life among the Mobile Homers. Arthur F. Joy. (Illus.). 100p. pap. 3.50 (*0-317-28504-1*) Saturscent Pubns.

Life among the Muses: Papers in Honor of James S. Findley. James S. Findley et al. LC 96-43185. 1997. pap. 20.00 (*1-879824-03-5*) U of NM Mus Biol.

***Life among the Pirates.** Stuart A. Kallen. LC 98-15468. (Way People Live Ser.). (Illus.). 96p. (YA). (gr. 5-12). 1998. 17.96 (*1-56006-393-9*) Lucent Bks.

Life among the Piutes: Their Wrongs & Claims. Sarah W. Hopkins. (Vintage West Ser.). 272p. 1994. pap. 13.95 (*0-87417-252-7*) U of Nev Pr.

Life among the Piutes: Their Wrongs & Claims. Hopkins & Sarah Winnemucca. LC 71-102992. 1969. pap. 13.50 (*0-912494-06-9*) Commun Print.

Life among the Samurai. Eleanor J. Hall. LC 98-30574. (Way People Live Ser.). (Illus.). 112p. (YA). (gr. 4-12). 1998. lib. bdg. 23.70 (*1-56006-390-4*) Lucent Bks.

Life among the Savages. Shirley Jackson. 22.95 (*0-89190-624-X*) Amereon Ltd.

Life among the Savages. Shirley Jackson. 241p. 1997. pap. 13.00 (*0-14-026767-0*) Viking Penguin.

Life among the Savages. Shirley Jackson. 1995. reprint ed. lib. bdg. 21.95 (*1-56849-654-0*) Buccaneer Bks.

Life among the Scientists: An Anthropological Study of an Australian Scientific Community. Max Charlesworth et al. 304p. 1995. pap. 60.00 (*0-949823-27-9*, Pub. by Deakin Univ) St Mut.

***Life among the Soldiers & Cavalry (Civil War)** James A. Corrick. LC 99-28237. (American War Library). (Illus.). 144p. (YA). (gr. 6-9). 2000. lib. bdg. 23.70 (*1-56006-491-9*) Lucent Bks.

Life among the Texas Flora: Ferdinand Lindheimer's Letters to George Engelmann. Minetta A. Goyne. LC 90-39322. (Illus.). 256p. 1991. 44.50 (*0-89096-457-2*) Tex A&M Univ Pr.

Life among the Texas Indians: The WPA Narratives. David La Vere. LC 97-32891. (Elma Dill Russell Spencer Series in the West & Southwest: Vol. 18). (Illus.). 288p. 1998. 29.95 (*0-89096-809-8*) Tex A&M Univ Pr.

Life among the Trolls. Maura Stanton. LC 97-65558. (Poetry Ser.). 86p. 1998. 24.95 (*0-88748-266-X*); pap. 11.95 (*0-88748-267-8*) Carnegie-Mellon.

***Life among the Vikings.** Thomas Streissguth. LC 98-30344. (Way People Live Ser.). (Illus.). 112p. (YA). (gr. 7-9). 1999. lib. bdg. 23.70 (*1-56006-392-0*) Lucent Bks.

Life among the Yanomami. John F. Peters. LC 98-205033. 148p. 1998. pap. 16.95 (*1-55111-193-4*) Broadview Pr.

***Life Amongst the Indians. A Book for Youth.** George Catlin. (LC History-America-E). 339p. 1999. reprint ed. lib. bdg. 89.00 (*0-7812-4246-0*) Rprt Serv.

Life Amongst the Modocs: Unwritten History. Joaquin Miller. LC 85-52081. 447p. 1987. 19.95 (*0-913522-13-9*) Urion Pr CA.

Life Amongst the Modocs: Unwritten History. Joaquin Miller. 457p. 1996. reprint ed. pap. 15.95 (*0-930588-79-7*) Heyday Bks.

Life Amongst the Modocs: Unwritten History. Joaquin Miller. LC 68-57540. (Muckrakers Ser.). 460p. reprint ed. lib. bdg. 27.50 (*0-8398-1259-0*) Irvington.

Life Amongst the Modocs: Unwritten History. Joaquin Miller. (Muckrakers Ser.). 460p. 1984. reprint ed. pap. 6.95 (*0-8290-1565-5*) Irvington.

Life & Achievements of "Old Glory", Godfather to the U. S. Flag. Robert S. Gauron. 8p. 1979. 1.50 (*0-934021-38-4*) Natl Flag Foun.

Life & Activities of Sir John Hawkins: Musician, Magistrate & Friend of Johnson. Percy A. Scholes. LC 77-26652. (Music Reprint Ser.: 1978). (Illus.). 1978. reprint ed. lib. bdg. 37.50 (*0-306-77571-9*) Da Capo.

Life & Adventures of a Country Merchant. John B. Jones. (Notable American Authors Ser.). 1992. reprint ed. lib. bdg. 75.00 (*0-7812-3519-7*) Rprt Serv.

Life & Adventures of a 1924 German Immigrant. William Kathmann, Sr. 220p. 1993. text 24.95 (*1-881579-04-2*) Theophilus Pr.

Life & Adventures of a Quaker among the Indians. Thomas C. Battey. 339p. 1972. reprint ed. 26.95 (*0-87928-025-5*) Corner Hse.

Life & Adventures of an Arkansaw Doctor. David Rattlehead. Ed. by W. K. McNeil. LC 89-4692. 200p. 1989. pap. 16.00 (*1-55728-079-7*) U of Ark Pr.

Life & Adventures of Black Hawk: With Sketches of Keokuk, the Sac & Fox Indians, & the Late Black Hawk War. Benjamin Drake. (Notable American Authors Ser.). 1992. reprint ed. lib. bdg. 75.00 (*0-7812-2685-6*) Rprt Serv.

Life & Adventures of 'Buffalo Bill' William F. Cody. LC 74-169755. (Select Bibliographies Reprint Ser.). 1977. reprint ed. 28.95 (*0-8369-5975-2*) Ayer.

Life & Adventures of Buffalo Bill: Colonel William F. Cody. William F. Cody. (American Biography Ser.). 352p. 1991. reprint ed. lib. bdg. 79.00 (*0-7812-8080-X*) Rprt Serv.

Life & Adventures of Calamity Jane: By Herself. Marthy C. Burke. (Illus.). 14p. 1979. pap. 2.95 (*0-87770-220-9*) Ye Galleon.

An Asterisk (*) at the beginning of an entry indicates that the title is appearing for the first time.

Life & Adventures of Captain John Avery, the Famous English Pirate: And the Successful Pyrate, a Play. Charles Johnson. LC 92-25463. (Augustan Reprints Ser.: Nos. 203-204). 1980. reprint ed. 21.50 (0-404-70203-1, PR1136) AMS Pr.

Life & Adventures of Carl Laemmle. John Drinkwater. Ed. by Garth S. Jowett. LC 77-11374. (Aspects of Film Ser.). 1978. reprint ed. lib. bdg. 23.95 (0-405-11130-4) Ayer.

Life & Adventures of Daniel Boone. Michael A. Lofaro. LC 85-31513. 168p. 1986. 21.00 (0-8131-1593-0) U Pr of Ky.

Life & Adventures of Frank Grouard. Joe De Barthe. Ed. by Edgar I. Stewart. LC 58-11651. (Illus.). 298p. reprint ed. 92.40 (0-8357-9731-7, 201620900002) Bks Demand.

*__Life & Adventures of Henry Bibb: An American Slave.__ Henry Bibb. 2000. 40.00 (0-299-16890-5); pap. 16.95 (0-299-16894-8) U of Wis Pr.

Life & Adventures of James P. Beckwourth. James P. Beckwourth. LC 73-88092. 663p. reprint ed. pap. 200.00 (0-608-08690-8, 206921300003) Bks Demand.

Life & Adventures of James P. Beckwourth. James P. Beckwourth. (American Biography Ser.). 547p. 1991. reprint ed. lib. bdg. 99.00 (0-7812-8015-X) Rprt Serv.

Life & Adventures of James P. Beckwourth, 2 vols. T. D. Bonner. 537p. 1985. reprint ed. lib. bdg. 79.00 (0-932051-88-X) Rprt Serv.

Life & Adventures of James P. Beckwourth. rev. ed. T. D. Bonner. (Illus.). 400p. 1977. reprint ed. 31.95 (0-87928-085-9) Corner Hse.

Life & Adventures of James P. Beckwourth: Mountainman. T. D. Bonner. 1965. reprint ed. 25.00 (0-87018-003-7) Ross.

Life & Adventures of James P. Beckwourth, Mountaineer, Scout & Pioneer & Chief of the Crow Nation of Indians. Ed. by T. D. Bonner. LC 69-18563. (American Negro: His History & Literature. Series 2). 1968. reprint ed. 40.95 (0-405-01850-9) Ayer.

Life & Adventures of James R. Durand. James R. Durand. Ed. by George S. Brooks. (Illus.). 160p. 1995. pap. 9.95 (0-939218-08-9) Chapman Billies.

Life & Adventures of Joaquin Murieta, the Celebrated California Bandit. John R. Ridge. (Western Frontier Library: No. 4). (Illus.). 1977. reprint ed. pap. 10.95 (0-8061-1429-0) U of Okla Pr.

Life & Adventures of John A. Murel: The Great Western Land Pirate. Augustus Q. Walton. 77p. 1994. reprint ed. pap. 6.00 (0-9646846-1-6) Dogwood TX.

Life & Adventures of John Nicol, Mariner. Ed. & Intro. by Tim Flannery. LC 99-24704. 208p. 1999. 21.00 (0-87113-755-0, Atlntc Mnthly) Grove-Atltic.

*__Life & Adventures of John Nicol, Mariner.__ Tim Flannery. 2000. pap. text 13.00 (0-8021-3746-6, Grove) Grove-Atltic.

Life & Adventures of Kit Carson, the Nestor of the Rocky Mountains from Facts Narrated by Himself. DeWitt C. Peters. LC 76-109631. (Select Bibliographies Reprint Ser.). 1977. 36.95 (0-8369-5240-5) Ayer.

Life & Adventures of Martin Chuzzlewit see Oxford Illustrated Dickens

Life & Adventures of Monica Monarch. Jules R. Poirier. LC 97-73933. (Illus.). 32p. (J). 1998. boxed set 11.95 (0-89051-189-6) Master Bks.

Life & Adventures of Nat Love. Nat Love. LC 95-23385. (Blacks in the American West Ser.). (Illus.). xviii, 162p. 1995. pap. 9.00 (0-8032-7955-8, Bison Books) U of Nebr Pr.

Life & Adventures of Nat Love. Nat Love. (Illus.). 162p. 1988. reprint ed. pap. 11.95 (0-933121-17-2) Black Classic.

Life & Adventures of Nat Love, Better Known in the Cattle Country As Deadwood Dick. Nat Love. LC 68-29007. (American Negro: His History & Literature. Series 1). 1968. reprint ed. 25.95 (0-405-01827-4) Ayer.

Life & Adventures of Nat Love, Better Known in the Cattle Country As Deadwood Dick, by Himself. Nat Love. (American Biography Ser.). 162p. 1991. reprint ed. lib. bdg. 59.00 (0-7812-8252-7) Rprt Serv.

Life & Adventures of Nicholas Nickleby see Oxford Illustrated Dickens

Life & Adventures of Nicholas Nickleby, Vol. 1. adapted ed. Charles Dickens. 1982. pap. 5.25 (0-8222-0817-2) Dramatists Play.

Life & Adventures of Nicholas Nickleby, Vol. 2. adapted ed. Charles Dickens. 1982. pap. 5.25 (0-8222-0818-0) Dramatists Play.

Life & Adventures of Polk Wells (Charles Knox Polk Wells) the Notorious Outlaw... Charles K. Wells. (American Biography Ser.). 259p. 1991. reprint ed. lib. bdg. 69.00 (0-7812-8411-2) Rprt Serv.

Life & Adventures of Polk Wells, the Notorious Outlaw. Charles K. Wells. LC 77-164635. (Select Bibliographies Reprint Ser.). 1977. reprint ed. 23.95 (0-8369-5919-1) Ayer.

*__Life & Adventures of Robinson Crusoe.__ Daniel Defoe. Ed. & Intro. by Angus Ross. LC 90-46733. (English Library). 320p. (YA). (gr. 9 up). 1998. pap. 4.67 (0-14-043007-5) Addson-Wesley Educ.

Life & Adventures of Robinson Crusoe. abr. ed. Daniel Defoe. Ed. by Michael J. Marshall. (Core Classics Ser.: Vol. 2). (Illus.). 160p. (J). (gr. 4-6). 1997. pap. 5.95 (1-890517-02-X); lib. bdg. 10.95 (1-890517-03-8) Core Knowledge.

Life & Adventures of Santa Claus. L. Frank Baum. (J). 1988. 16.95 (0-8488-0428-7) Amereon Ltd.

Life & Adventures of Santa Claus. L. Frank Baum. Ed. by Greg S. Baisden. (Illus.). 96p. (J). 1992. text 24.95 (1-879450-76-3) Kitchen Sink.

Life & Adventures of Santa Claus. L. Frank Baum. LC 83-11529. 160p. (J). (gr. 7-12). 1986. mass mkt. 3.95 (0-451-52064-5, Sig Classics) NAL.

Life & Adventures of Santa Claus. L. Frank Baum. (Illus.). (J). (gr. 3-8). 1990. 21.75 (0-8446-5450-7) Peter Smith.

Life & Adventures of Santa Claus. L. Frank Baum. (J). 1999. 6.99 (0-517-20579-3) Random Hse Value.

Life & Adventures of Santa Claus. L. Frank Baum. (Illus.). (J). 1993. reprint ed. lib. bdg. 18.95 (1-56849-175-1) Buccaneer Bks.

Life & Adventures of Santa Claus. L. Frank Baum. (Illus.). 208p. 1976. reprint ed. pap. 6.95 (0-486-23297-2) Dover.

Life & Adventures of Santa Claus. rev. ed. Julie Lane. (Illus.). 154p. (J). 1985. pap. 10.00 (0-9615664-1-8) Parkhurst Brook Pubs.

Life & Adventures of Santa Claus: A Keepsake. rev. ed. Julie Lane. (Illus.). (J). (ps-8). 1995. 18.95 (1-56888-149-5) Tapestry MA.

Life & Adventures of Trobadora Beatrice As Chronicled by Her Minstrel Laura: A Novel in Thirteen Books & Seven Intermezzos. Irmtraud Morgner. Tr. & Intro. by Jeanette Clausen. Intro. by Silke Von Erde. LC 99-52824. (European Women Writers Ser.). 544p. 2000. text 65.00 (0-8032-3203-9); pap. text 25.00 (0-8032-8260-5) U of Nebr Pr.

Life & Adventures of Wilburn Waters: The Famous Hunter & Trapper of White Top Mountain. Charles B. Coale. 86p. 1994. pap. 5.95 (1-57072-003-7) Overmountain Pr.

Life & Adventures of William Buckley. Morgan. (Australian National University Press Ser.). 1996. write for info. (0-08-033015-0, Pergamon Pr) Elsevier.

Life & Adventures, Songs, Services & Speeches of Private Miles O'Reilly. Charles G. Halpine. LC 77-168232. (Illus.). reprint ed. 39.50 (0-404-04834-X) AMS Pr.

Life & Adventures, Songs, Services & Speeches of Private Miles O'Reilly. Charles G. Halpine. (Notable American Authors Ser.). 1992. reprint ed. lib. bdg. 75.00 (0-7812-2996-0) Rprt Serv.

Life & Ancestry of John Thistlewaite Baynes (1833-1891) Richard C. Baynes. LC 87-73152. 144p. 1988. 16.00 (0-9619743-0-3) R C Baynes.

Life & Anecdotes of George Washington for Young Readers. Mary L. Williamson. (YA). 1994. 21.99 (0-87377-178-8) GAM Pubns.

Life & Apostolic Labors of the Venerable Father Junipero Serra, Founder of the Franciscan Missions of California. Francisco Palou. 1992. reprint ed. lib. bdg. 75.00 (0-7812-5073-0) Rprt Serv.

Life & Art. Thomas Hardy. LC 68-751. (Studies in Thomas Hardy: No. 14). 1972. reprint ed. lib. bdg. 75.00 (0-8383-0650-0) M S G Haskell Hse.

Life & Art: Essays, Notes & Letters. Thomas Hardy. Ed. by E. Brennecke. LC 68-16937. (Essay Index Reprint Ser.). 1977. 18.95 (0-8369-0510-5) Ayer.

Life & Art of Albrecht Durer. Erwin Panofsky. (Illus.). 500p. 1955. pap. text 35.00 (0-691-00303-3, Pub. by Princeton U Pr) Cal Prin Full Svc.

*__Life & Art of Athos Menaboni.__ Barbara C. Taylor. 2000. 30.00 (0-86554-712-2, H528) Mercer Univ Pr.

Life & Art of Edwin Booth. enl. rev. ed. William Winter. LC 70-91919. 1972. 20.95 (0-405-09090-0) Ayer.

Life & Art of Edwin Booth. William Winter. LC 68-8939. (Illus.). 308p. 1969. reprint ed. lib. bdg. 65.00 (0-8371-0275-8, WIEB, Greenwood Pr) Greenwood.

Life & Art of Edwin Booth. William Winter. (Notable American Authors Ser.). 1999. reprint ed. lib. bdg. 125.00 (0-7812-7772-8) Rprt Serv.

Life & Art of Esphyr Slobodkina. Gail Stavitsky & Elizabeth Wylie. (Illus.). 80p. 1992. pap. 19.50 (1-880593-01-7) Tufts Univ Gallery.

Life & Art of Florine Stettheimer. Barbara J. Bloemink. LC 95-30528. (Illus.). 320p. 1995. 50.00 (0-300-06340-7) Yale U Pr.

Life & Art of George Cruikshank. Hilary Evans & Mary Evans. LC 77-19166. (Illus.). 1978. 58.95 (0-87599-227-7) S G Phillips.

Life & Art of James Barry. William L. Pressly. LC 80-29665. (Paul Mellon Centre for Studies in British Art). (Illus.). 320p. 1981. 90.00 (0-300-02466-5) Yale U Pr.

Life & Art of Kathleen Bridle. Carole Froude-Durix. Ed. by Helen L. Wood. LC 98-235426. 96p. 1998. pap. 19.95 (1-85182-419-7, Pub. by Four Cts Pr); boxed set 60.00 (1-85182-418-9, Pub. by Four Cts Pr) Intl Spec Bk.

Life & Art of Lois Mailou Jones. Tritobia H. Benjamin. LC 94-18441. (Illus.). 160p. 1994. pap. 25.00 (0-87654-104-X) Pomegranate Calif.

Life & Art of Richard Mansfield. William Winter. (Notable American Authors Ser.). 1999. reprint ed. lib. bdg. 125.00 (0-7812-7773-6) Rprt Serv.

Life & Art of Richard Mansfield, with Selections from His Letters, 2 Vols, Set. William Winter. LC 77-126264. (Select Bibliographies Reprint Ser.). 1977. 54.95 (0-8369-5491-2) Ayer.

Life & Art of William Vincent. Suzanne Deats. LC 97-70752. (Illus.). 120p. 1998. 65.00 (1-889741-14-0) Internatl Graphics.

Life & Arts of Martin Luther. Philip Melanchthon. Orig. Title: Hymns of the Reformation. 46p. 1997. pap. 3.00 (1-891469-10-X) Repristination.

Life & Astonishing Adventures of John Daniel. Ralph Morris. LC 74-16398. (Science Fiction Ser.). (Illus.). 276p. 1975. reprint ed. 26.95 (0-405-06307-5) Ayer.

Life & Astonishing Adventures of Peter Williamson Who Was Carried off as a Child from Aberdeen & Sold for a Slave. Peter Williamson. 1978. pap. 4.95 (0-87770-196-2) Ye Galleon.

Life & Ballets of Lev Ivanov: Choreographer of The Nutcracker & Swan Lake. Roland J. Wiley. (Illus.). 326p. 1997. text 69.00 (0-19-816567-6) OUP.

Life & Bible Times. Anne Gilbert. 1992. pap. 24.95 (1-877871-36-2, 5250) Ed Ministries.

Life & Botanical Accomplishments of Boris Alexander Krukoff. Leslie R. Landrum. LC 86-838. (Advances in Economic Botany Ser.: Vol. 2). (Illus.). 96p. (Orig.). 1986. 17.50 (0-89327-298-1) NY Botanical.

Life & Building As Portrayed in the Song of Songs. Witness Lee. 171p. 1979. per. 7.50 (0-87083-024-4, 07-012-001) Living Stream Ministry.

Life & Campaigns of Field Marshal Prince Blucher. Count Gneisenau. Tr. by J. E. Marston. (Illus.). 442p. 1996. reprint ed. 40.00 (0-9653284-0-6) On Military.

Life & Campaigns of Lt. Gen. T. J. "Stonewall" Jackson. R. L. Dabney. 1992. 34.99 (0-87377-982-7); pap. 23.99 (0-87377-981-9) GAM Pubns.

Life & Campaigns of the Black Prince. Tr. by Richard Barber. LC 97-23498. (Illus.). 152p. 1997. pap. 24.95 (0-85115-469-7, Boydell Pr) Boydell & Brewer.

*__Life & Career of Hung Ch'eng-Ch'ou, 1593-1665: Public Service in a Time of Dynastic Change.__ Cheng-mien Wang. LC 99-52253. (Monograph & Occasional Paper Ser.). 1999. write for info. (0-924304-40-5) Assn Asian Studies.

Life & Career of Major John Andre. Winthrop Sargent. 1972. reprint ed. 22.00 (0-8422-8106-1) Irvington.

*__Life & Career of P. A. McHugh, 1859-1909: A Foot-Soldier of the Party.__ Ide Ni Liathain. LC 99-29351. (Maynooth Studies in Local History). 64p. 1999. pap. 10.95 (0-7165-2677-8, Pub. by Irish Acad Pr) Intl Spec Bk.

Life & Careers of William Henry Gorrill, 1841-1874. R. Bruce Way. LC 96-12016. 244p. 1996. lib. bdg. 42.00 (0-7618-0325-4) U Pr of Amer.

Life & Character of Erasmus. Arthur R. Pennington. 1977. lib. bdg. 59.95 (0-8490-2159-6) Gordon Pr.

Life & Character of the Late Reverend, Learned, & Pious Mr. Jonathan Edwards, President of the College in New Jersey. Jonathan Edwards. LC 75-31090. reprint ed. 28.50 (0-404-13508-0) AMS Pr.

Life & Character of the Reverend Benjamin Colman, D. D. Ebenezer Turell. LC 72-4539. 256p. 1972. reprint ed. 50.00 (0-8201-1104-X) Schol Facsimiles.

Life & Characteristics of Right Reverend Alfred A. Curtis, D.D., Second Bishop of Wilmington see Bishop Curtis of Wilmington: The Life & Writings of Right Reverend Alfred Allen Curtis, D.D. Second Bishop

Life & Civilization of Ancient Greece: Ancient Greek History. George Thomas. (Illus.). 112p. 1996. pap. 9.95 (1-880971-20-8) Light&Life Pub Co MN.

Life & Complete Works in Prose & Verse of Robert Greene, 15 vols. Robert Greene. Incl. Alcida: Greenes Metamorphosis, Greenes Mourning Garment, Greenes Farewell to Folly, 1588-1591. 392p. 1999. reprint ed. lib. bdg. 88.00 (1-58201-119-2); Blacke Booke's Messenger; The Defence of Conny-Catching; Philomela, the Lady Fitzwaters Nightingale; A Quippe for an Upstart Courtier, 1592. 344p. 1999. reprint ed. lib. bdg. 88.00 (1-58201-121-4); Carde of Fancie; The Debate Between Follie & Love; Pandosto, The Triumph of Time, 1584-1588. 356p. 1999. reprint ed. lib. bdg. 88.00 (1-58201-114-1); Frier Bacon & Frier Bongay; The Historie of Orlando Furioso; The Scottish Historie of James the Fourth; The Comical Historie of Alphonsus; King of Arragon, 1594-1599. 416p. 1999. reprint ed. lib. bdg. 88.00 (1-58201-123-0); General Index - Index of Names, Special Lists of Plants, Animals, Etc., Thieves' Vocabulary, Occasional Notes & Illustrations. 244p. 1999. reprint ed. lib. bdg. 88.00 (1-58201-125-7); Greenes Neuer Too Late, Francescos Fortunes, 1590. 266p. 1999. reprint ed. lib. bdg. 88.00 (1-58201-118-4); Looking-Glass for London & England; George A. Greene, the Pinner of Wakefield; Selimus, Emperour of the Turkes; A Maidens Dreame, 1590-1599. 318p. 1999. reprint ed. lib. bdg. 88.00 (1-58201-124-9); Mamillia, Pts. 1 & 2; Anatomie of Flatterie, 1583-1593. 348p. 1999. reprint ed. lib. bdg. 88.00 (1-58201-112-5); Menaphon; Camillas Alarum to Slumbering Euphues; Euphues His Censure to Philautus, 1587-1589. 316p. 1999. reprint ed. lib. bdg. 88.00 (1-58201-116-8); Myrrour of Modestie: Incl: Morando: The Tritameron of Love, Pts. 1 & 2: Arbasto: The Anatomie of Fortune, 1584-1587. 282p. 1999. reprint ed. lib. bdg. 88.00 (1-58201-113-3); Notable Discovery of Coosnage; The Second Part of Conny-Catching; Thirde & Last Parte of Conny-Catching; A Disputation Betweene a Hee & Shee Conny-Catcher. 332p. 1999. reprint ed. lib. bdg. 88.00 (1-58201-120-6); Orpharion; Greens Groatsworth of Wit; The Repentance of Robert Greene; Greenes Vision, 1592-1599. 312p. 1999. lib. bdg. 88.00 (1-58201-122-2); Perimedes the Blacke-Smith, Ciceronis, Amor; or Tullies Loue, the Royal Exchange, 1589-1590. 352p. 1999. reprint ed. lib. bdg. 88.00 (1-58201-117-6); Planetomachia; Penelope's Web; The Spanish Masquerado, 1585-1589. 320p. 1999. reprint ed. lib. bdg. 88.00 (1-58201-115-X); Storojenko's Life of Robert Greene. 262p. 1999. reprint ed. lib. bdg. 88.00 (1-58201-111-7); (Life & Complete Works of Robert Greene). 1999. Set lib. bdg. 1320.00 (1-58201-110-9) Classic Bks.

Life & Complete Works in Prose & Verse of Robert Greene, 15 vols. Robert Greene. (BCL1-PR English Literature Ser.). 1992. reprint ed. pap. text 825.00 (0-685-52857-X); reprint ed. lib. bdg. 1125.00 (0-7812-7242-4) Rprt Serv.

Life & Condition of the People of Hindustan, 1200-1500 AD. Mohammad Ashraf. Tr. by K. M. Ashraf. 322p. 1970. text 26.50 (0-685-13407-5) Coronet Bks.

Life & Conditions of the People of Hindustan, 12 vols. 3rd ed. Kanwar M. Ashraf. 1988. 20.00 (81-215-0092-3, Pub. by M Manoharial) Coronet Bks.

Life & Confessions of a Psychologist. G. Stanley Hall. Ed. by Walter P. Metzger. (Academic Profession Ser.). 1977. lib. bdg. 53.95 (0-405-10008-6) Ayer.

*__Life & Consciousness.__ rev. ed. J. R. Ench. 185p. 2000. 19.95 (0-9672814-0-7) Life Engineer Fndt.

Life & Contribution of the Nepalese Princess Bhrikuti Devi to Tibetan History (from Tibetan Sources) Min B. Shakya. LC 98-904544. (C). 1997. 20.00 (81-7303-065-0, Pub. by Aryan Bks Intl) S Asia.

Life & (Cooking) Times of an American Missionary in India: Recipes & Adventures of Rosetta Gempler Bell. Barbara L. Lacy. (Illus.). 60p. 1993. pap. text 5.95 (0-9617721-2-3) Golightly Pubns.

Life & Correspondence of Francis Bacon, 2 vols. Francis Bacon. 1985. reprint ed. lib. bdg. 69.00 (0-932051-83-9) Rprt Serv.

Life & Correspondence of Henry Ingersoll Bowditch, 2 vols, Set. Vincent Y. Bowditch. LC 72-121501. (Select Bibliographies Reprint Ser.). 1977. reprint ed. 44.95 (0-8369-5459-9) Ayer.

Life & Correspondence of Henry Knox. Francis S. Drake. (Notable American Authors Ser.). 1992. reprint ed. lib. bdg. 75.00 (0-7812-2689-9) Rprt Serv.

Life & Correspondence of James McHenry. Bernard C. Steiner. Ed. by Richard H. Kohn. LC 78-22398. (American Military Experience Ser.). (Illus.). 1980. reprint ed. lib. bdg. 48.95 (0-405-11874-0) Ayer.

Life & Correspondence of Major Cartwright, 2 Vols, Set. John Cartwright. Ed. by F. D. Cartwright. LC 68-57728. 1969. reprint ed. 95.00 (0-678-00449-8) Kelley.

Life & Correspondence of Robert Southey, 6 vols., Set. Robert Southey. (BCL1-PR English Literature Ser.). 1992. reprint ed. lib. bdg. 450.00 (0-7812-7661-6) Rprt Serv.

Life & Correspondence of the Late Admiral Lord Rodney, 2 vols., Set. Godfrey B. Munday. LC 72-8677. (American Revolutionary Ser.). 970p. reprint ed. lib. bdg. 122.00 (0-8398-1271-X) Irvington.

Life & Correspondence of the Late Robert Southey, Set. Robert Southey. Ed. by Charles C. Southey. 1970. reprint ed. 125.00 (0-403-00232-X) Scholarly.

Life & Correspondence of the Rev. William Smith, 2 vols. Horace W. Smith. LC 79-38786. (Religion in America, Ser. 2). 1208p. 1972. reprint ed. 80.95 (0-405-04084-9) Ayer.

Life & Correspondence of Theodore Parker, 2 Vols. John Weiss. LC 69-16854. (Select Bibliographies Reprint Ser.). 1977. 53.95 (0-8369-5018-6) Ayer.

Life & Correspondence of Theodore Parker, 2 vols. John Weiss. LC 76-106987. (American Public Figures Ser.). 1864. lib. bdg. 115.00 (0-306-71874-X) Da Capo.

Life & Correspondence of Theodore Parker. John Weiss. LC 70-83446. (Religion in America, Ser. 1). 1970. reprint ed. 57.95 (0-405-00279-3) Ayer.

Life & Crimes of Agatha Christie. large type ed. Charles Osborne. (Charnwood Library). (Illus.). 1991. 27.99 (0-7089-8583-1, Charnwood) Ulverscroft.

Life & Crimes of Harry Lavender. large type ed. Marele Day. (Bolinda Large Print Ser.). 1997. 24.95 (1-86340-566-6) T T Beeler.

Life & Crucifixion of Julian & the Threat of Group-Entities. John Harland. LC 93-86939. 112p. (Orig.). 1994. pap. 8.00 (0-914752-33-2); text 16.00 (0-914752-34-0) Sovereign Pr.

Life & Culture in Orissa. Ed. by Binod S. Das. 1985. 17.50 (0-8364-1402-0, Pub. by Minerva) S Asia.

Life & Culture of the Hupa. fac. ed. P. E. Goddard. Ed. by Frederic W. Putnam. (University of California Publications in American Archaeology & Ethnology: Vol. 1: 1). (Illus.). 150p. (C). reprint ed. pap. text 16.25 (1-55567-158-6) Coyote Press.

Life & Death. Robert Creeley. LC 97-45805. 87p. 1998. 19.95 (0-8112-1384-6, Pub. by New Directions) Norton.

*__Life & Death.__ Robert Creeley. 2000. pap. 9.95 (0-8112-1449-4, Pub. by New Directions) Norton.

Life & Death. James Davies. LC 76-356587. (Elementary Go Ser.: Vol. 4). 1975. pap. 12.95 (4-87187-013-8, G13) Ishi Pr Intl.

Life & Death. Andrea Dworkin. LC 96-38335. 1997. 22.50 (0-684-83512-6) Free Pr.

Life & Death. Louis P. Pojman. (Philosophy Ser.). (C). 1992. 21.50 (0-534-54257-3) Wadsworth Pub.

*__Life & Death.__ Russell Simmons. 2001. 24.00 (0-609-60607-7, Pub. by Crown Pub Group) Random House.

Life & Death. Ed. by Jonathan Westphal & Carl Levenson. LC 93-11501. (Readings in Philosophy Ser.). 192p. (Orig.). (C). 1993. pap. text 8.95 (0-87220-208-9); lib. bdg. 29.95 (0-87220-209-7) Hackett Pub.

Life & Death: A Reader. Louis P. Pojman. (Philosophy Ser.). (C). 1992. 33.00 (0-534-54258-1) Wadsworth Pub.

Life & Death: A Reader in Moral Problems. 2nd ed. Louis P. Pojman. LC 98-55383. (Philosophy Ser.). 1999. mass mkt. 51.95 (0-534-50825-1) Wadsworth Pub.

Life & Death: A Study in Biology. E. Teichmann. Tr. by A. M. Simons from GER. (Science for the Workers Ser.). 158p. 1984. 15.95 (0-88286-086-0) C H Kerr.

Life & Death: Grappling with the Moral Dilemmas of Our Time. 2nd ed. Louis P. Pojman. LC 99-10720. (Philosophy). 190p. 1999. mass mkt. 32.95 (0-534-50824-3) Wadsworth Pub.

Life & Death: Philosophical Essays in Biomedical Ethics. Dan W. Brock. LC 92-20921. (Studies in Philosophy & Public Policy). 449p. (C). 1993. pap. text 23.95 (0-521-42833-5) Cambridge U Pr.

Life & Death: Philosophical Essays in Biomedical Ethics. Dan W. Brock. LC 92-20921. (Studies in Philosophy & Public Policy). 449p. (C). 1993. text 74.95 (0-521-41785-6) Cambridge U Pr.

Life & Death: The Pilgrimage of the Soul. Harvey A. Green. LC 97-35145. (ARE Membership Ser.). 1998. pap. 7.95 (0-87604-404-6) ARE Pr.

Life & Death: Widows in Pennsylvania, 1750-1850. Lisa Wilson. (American Civilization Ser.). (C). 1992. 49.95 (0-87722-883-3) Temple U Pr.

An Asterisk (*) at the beginning of an entry indicates that the title is appearing for the first time.

L

Life & Death Aboard the U. S. S. Essex. Richard W. Streb. (Illus.). 344p. 1999. pap. 23.00 (*0-8059-4605-5*) Dorrance.

Life & Death & the Edgar Cayce Readings. Raymond Ouellette. LC 82-70682. 256p. 1982. 8.95 (*0-936450-09-6*) Aero Pr.

Life & Death at Paloma: Society & Mortuary Practices in a Preceramic Peruvian Village. Jeffrey Quilter. LC 88-31276. (Illus.). 203p. 1989. text 29.95 (*0-87745-194-X*) U of Iowa Pr.

Life & Death at Work: Industrial Accidents As a Case of Socially Produced Error. T. Dwyer. (Studies in Work & Industry). (Illus.). 335p. (C). 1991. text 59.50 (*0-306-43949-2*, Kluwer Plenum) Kluwer Academic.

Life & Death Debate: Moral Issues of Our Time. J. P. Moreland & Norman L. Geisler. LC 90-37862. 192p. 1990. pap. 19.95 (*0-275-93702-X*, B3702, Praeger Pubs) Greenwood.

Life & Death Debate: Moral Issues of Our Time, 43. J. P. Moreland & Norman L. Geisler. LC 90-37842. (Contributions in Philosophy Ser.: No. 43). 192p. 1990. 55.00 (*0-313-27556-4*, MOO/, Greenwood Pr) Greenwood.

Life & Death Decision-Making. Baruch A. Brody. 274p. (C). 1988. text 39.95 (*0-19-505007-X*) OUP.

Life & Death in a Maya Community: The Ixil Testaments of the 1760s. Matthew Restall. LC 94-77123. (Illus.). 200p. (Orig.). 1995. pap. 20.00 (*0-911437-31-2*) Labyrinthos.

***Life & Death in a Venetian Convent: The Chronicle & Necrology of Corpus Domini, 1395-1436.** Bartolomea Riccoboni. Ed. & Tr. by Daniel Ethan Bornstein from ITA. LC 99-37584. (Other Voice in Early Modern Europe Ser.). (Illus.). 109p. 2000. pap. text 12.00 (*0-226-71789-5*); lib. bdg. 35.00 (*0-226-71788-7*) U Ch Pr.

***Life & Death in Ancient Egypt: Scenes from the Private Tombs in New Kingdom Thebes.** Sigrid Hodel-Hoenes. Tr. by David Warburton from GER. LC 99-59747. (Illus.). 2000. 40.00 (*0-8014-3506-4*) Cornell U Pr.

Life & Death in Early Colonial Equador. Linda A. Newson. LC 94-41571. (Civilization of the American Indian Ser.: Vol. 214). (Illus.). 505p. 1995. 47.50 (*0-8061-2697-3*) U of Okla Pr.

Life & Death in Fifteenth Century Florence. Ed. by Rona Goffen et al. LC 88-7924. (Duke Monographs in Medieval & Renaissance Studies: No. 10). 272p. (C). 1989. text 34.95 (*0-8223-0872-X*) Duke.

***Life & Death in Health Care Ethics.** Helen Watt. 2000. pap. 12.99 (*0-415-21574-9*) Routledge.

***Life & Death in Health Care Ethics: A Short Introduction.** Helen Watt. 112p. 2000. 50.00 (*0-415-21573-0*) Routledge.

Life & Death in Psychoanalysis. Jean Laplanche. LC 75-36928. 160p. reprint ed. pap. 49.60 (*0-608-12099-5*, 202413800035) Bks Demand.

Life & Death in Psychoanalysis. Jean Laplanche. Tr. by Jeffrey Mehlman from FRE. LC 75-36928. 160p. 1985. reprint ed. pap. text 12.95 (*0-8018-2730-2*) Johns Hopkins.

Life & Death in Rebel Prisons. Robert H. Kellogg. LC 75-168517. (Black Heritage Library Collection). 1977. reprint ed. 27.95 (*0-8369-8869-8*) Ayer.

Life & Death in Shanghai. Nien Cheng. ix, 547p. 1987. pap. 24.95 (*0-394-55548-1*) Random.

Life & Death in Shanghai. Nien Cheng. (Illus.). 560p. 1988. pap. 14.95 (*0-14-010870-X*, Penguin Bks) Viking Penguin.

Life & Death in the Ancient City of Teotihuacan: A Modern Paleodemographic Synthesis. Rebecca Storey. LC 91-17942. 328p. (C). 1992. pap. text 29.95 (*0-8173-0559-9*) U of Ala Pr.

Life & Death in the Executive Fast Lane: Essays on Irrational Organizations & Their Leaders. Kets Devries et al. LC 95-4952. (Management Ser.). 274p. 1995. 29.95 (*0-7879-0112-1*) Jossey-Bass.

***Life & Death in the Executive Fast Lane: Essays on Irrational Organizations & Their Leaders.** Manfred F. Kets DeVries. 252p. 1999. text 24.00 (*0-7881-5996-8*) DIANE Pub.

Life & Death in the Nervous System: Role of Neurothropic Factors & Their Receptors. Ed. by C. F. Ibanez et al. LC 95-22623. (Wenner-Gren International Ser.). 498p. 1995. 191.50 (*0-08-042527-5*, Pergamon Pr) Elsevier.

Life & Death in the Templo Mayor. Eduardo M. Moctezuma. Tr. by Bernard R. Ortiz De Montellano & Thelma Ortiz De Montellano. (Illus.). 160p. 1995. pap. 17.50 (*0-87081-400-1*) Univ Pr Colo.

Life & Death in the United States: Statistics on Life Expectancies, Diseases & Death Rates for the Twentieth Century. Russell O. Wright. LC 97-20045. 151p. 1997. pap. 30.00 (*0-7864-0320-9*) McFarland & Co.

Life & Death Matters: Human Rights & the Environment at the End of the Millennium. Ed. by Barbara R. Johnston. (Illus.). 352p. 1997. 65.00 (*0-7619-9184-0*); pap. 25.95 (*0-7619-9185-9*) AltaMira Pr.

Life & Death of a Joint Venture in China. 2nd rev. ed. Asia Law & Practice Staff. 310p. 1996. pap. 260.00 (*962-7708-86-0*, Pub. by Asia Law & Practice) Am Educ Systs.

Life & Death of a Polish Shtetl. Ed. by Feigl Bisberg-Youkelson & Rubin Youkelson. Tr. by Gene Bluestein from YID. LC 99-30394. 128p. 2000. pap. text 12.95 (*0-8032-6167-5*) U of Nebr Pr.

Life & Death of a Rural American High School: Farewell, Little Kanawha. Alan J. DeYoung. LC 94-22298. (Illus.). 360p. 1995. text 61.00 (*0-8153-0744-6*) Garland.

Life & Death of a Small Magazine (Modern Music, 1924-1946) Minna Lederman. LC 83-80057. (I.S.A.M. Monographs: No. 18). (Illus.). 211p. (Orig.). 1983. pap. 20.00 (*0-914678-20-5*) Inst Am Music.

Life & Death of a Spanish Town. Elliot H. Paul. LC 79-138171. 427p. (C). 1971. reprint ed. lib. bdg. 35.00 (*0-8371-5628-9*, PAST, Greenwood Pr) Greenwood.

Life & Death of Almost Everybody. David Campton. 1971. pap. 5.25 (*0-8222-0657-9*) Dramatists Play.

Life & Death of an Infrastructure Project. 2nd ed. Asia Law & Practice Staff. 330p. 1997. pap. 225.00 (*962-7708-60-7*, Pub. by Asia Law & Practice) Am Educ Systs.

Life & Death of an Oilman: The Career of E. W. Marland. John J. Mathews. LC 89-70455. 1974. reprint ed. pap. 14.95 (*0-8061-1238-7*) U of Okla Pr.

Life & Death of Andy Warhol: The Biography. Victor Bockris. LC 97-16881. (Illus.). 570p. 1997. reprint ed. pap. 17.95 (*0-306-80795-5*) Da Capo.

Life & Death of Anna Mae Aquash. Johanna Brand. (Illus.). 172p. 1995. reprint ed. pap. 14.95 (*1-55028-422-3*) Formac Dist Ltd.

Life & Death of Bobby Z. Dan Winslow. 1998. mass mkt. 6.99 (*0-8041-1610-5*) Ivy Books.

Life & Death of C. M. De Jesus. Robert M. Levine. (Dialogos Ser.). (Illus.). 162p. 1996. pap. 15.95 (*0-8263-1648-4*) U of NM Pr.

Life & Death of Cardinal Wolsey. George Cavendish. 1962. write for info. Yale U Pr.

Life & Death of Cardinal Wolsey by George Cavendish. Ed. by R. S. Sylvester. (EETS Original Ser.: Vol. 243). 1963. reprint ed. 30.00 (*0-19-722243-9*, Pub. by EETS) Boydell & Brewer.

Life & Death of Colonel Albert Jennings Fountain. Arrell M. Gibson. LC 65-11229. (Illus.). 1965. reprint ed. pap. 14.95 (*0-8061-1231-X*) U of Okla Pr.

Life & Death of Colonel Blimp. A. L. Kennedy. LC 97-216118. 1997. pap. text 10.95 (*0-85170-568-5*) U of Ill Pr.

Life & Death of Cormac the Skald. Tr. by W. G. Collingwood & Jon Steffanson. LC 76-43948. (Viking Society for Northern Research: Translation Ser.: Vol. 1). (Illus.). 416p. reprint ed. 39.50 (*0-404-60011-5*) AMS Pr.

Life & Death of Crazy Horse. Russell Freedman. LC 95-33303. (Illus.). 176p. (YA). (gr. 4-6). 1996. 21.95 (*0-8234-1219-9*) Holiday.

Life & Death of Doctor Faustus, Made into a Farce. William Mountfort. LC 92-22711. (Augustan Reprints Ser.: No. 157). 1972. reprint ed. 14.50 (*0-404-70157-4*, PR3605) AMS Pr.

Life & Death of Fritz the Cat. R. Crumb. 96p. 1993. per. 9.95 (*1-56097-117-7*) Fantagraph Bks.

Life & Death of Industrial Languedoc, 1700-1920. Christopher H. Johnson. (Illus.). 336p. 1995. text 75.00 (*0-19-504508-4*) OUP.

Life & Death of Jason see Collected Works of William Morris

Life & Death of Jay Gould & How He Made His Millions. John S. Ogilvie. Ed. by Stuart Bruchey. LC 80-1336. (Railroads Ser.). (Illus.). 1981. reprint ed. lib. bdg. 20.95 (*0-405-13809-1*) Ayer.

Life & Death of John of Barneveld, Advocate of Holland, with a View of the Primary Causes & Movements of the Thirty Years' War see Writings of John Lothrop Motley

Life & Death of King James the First of Scotland. Ed. by Joseph Stevenson. LC 76-144432. (Maitland Club, Glasgow. Publications: No. 42). reprint ed. 29.50 (*0-404-53019-2*) AMS Pr.

Life & Death of King John see New Variorum Edition of Shakespeare

Life & Death of King Richard II see Bibliographies to Supplement the New Variorum Editions of Shakespeare

Life & Death of King Richard II. M.H. Publications Staff. 1990. 95.00 (*1-872680-16-X*, Pub. by M H Pubns) St Mut.

Life & Death of King Richard II see New Variorum Edition of Shakespeare

Life & Death of Martin Luther King, Jr. James Haskins. Ed. by ALC Staff. LC 77-3157. (Illus.). 192p. (J). (gr. 3-7). 1992. mass mkt. 5.95 (*0-688-11690-6*, Wm Morrow) Morrow Avon.

Life & Death of Martin Luther King, Jr. James Haskins. 1992. 10.05 (*0-606-01387-3*, Pub. by Turtleback) Demco.

Life & Death of Mary Magdalene. T. Robinson. Ed. by H. Oskar Sommer. (EETS, ES Ser.: Vol. 78). 1969. reprint ed. 30.00 (*0-8115-3401-4*) Periodicals Srv.

Life & Death of Mr. Badman: Presented to the World in a Familiar Dialogue Between Mr. Wiseman & Mr. Attentive. John Bunyan. Ed. by James F. Forrest & Roger Sharrock. (Oxford English Texts Ser.). (Illus.). 232p. 1988. text 85.00 (*0-19-812742-1*) OUP.

Life & Death of NSSM 200: How the Destruction of Political Will Doomed a U. S. Population Policy. rev. ed. Stephen D. Mumford. LC 96-70965. xxii, 579p. (Orig.). 1996. 39.00 (*0-937307-04-1*); pap. 32.00 (*0-937307-05-X*) CRPS.

Life & Death of Oregon "Cattle King" Peter: French 1849-1897. Edward Gray. (Illus.). 204p. 1995. 35.00 (*0-9622609-8-3*); lib. bdg. 22.95 (*0-9622609-9-1*) E Gray.

Life & Death of Peter Sellers. Roger Lewis. (Illus.). 528p. 1996. 24.95 (*1-55783-248-X*) Applause Theatre Bk Pubs.

Life & Death of Peter Sellers. Roger Lewis. (Illus.). 528p. 1999. pap. 14.95 (*1-55783-357-5*) Applause Theatre Bk Pubs.

Life & Death of Peter Stubbe. Jesse Glass. (Illus.). 64p. (Orig.). 1995. pap. 12.00 (*0-913559-27-X*) Birch Brook Pr.

Life & Death of Petra Kelly. Sara Parkin. (Illus.). 320p. 1995. pap. 14.00 (*0-04-440940-0*, Pub. by Rivers Oram) NYU Pr.

Life & Death of Pretty Boy Floyd. Jeffery S. King. LC 97-36166. 1998. 28.00 (*0-87338-582-9*) Kent St U Pr.

***Life & Death of Pretty Boy Floyd.** Jeffery S. King. 1999. pap. 15.00 (*0-87338-650-7*) Kent St U Pr.

Life & Death of Saint Malachy the Irishman. Bernard of Clairvaux. (Cistercian Fathers Ser.: No. 10). 170p. 7.95 (*0-87907-910-X*) Cistercian Pubns.

Life & Death of Solitude. Dennis Bridgeforth. 184p. 1997. pap. 8.95 (*1-878561-62-6*) Seacoast AL.

Life & Death of St. Thomas More. Nicholas Harpsfield. 1988. reprint ed. lib. bdg. 99.00 (*0-7812-0274-4*) Rprt Serv.

Life & Death of St. Thomas More. Nicholas Harpsfield. reprint ed. 69.00 (*0-403-04140-6*) Somerset Pub.

Life & Death of That Reverend Man of God, Mr. Richard Mather. Increase Mather. (Notable American Authors Ser.). 1999. reprint ed. lib. bdg. 125.00 (*0-7812-3973-7*) Rprt Serv.

Life & Death of the Chesapeake Bay. J. R. Schubel. 1991. 4.95 (*0-685-58965-X*) MD Sea Grant Col.

Life & Death of the Chesapeake Bay. J.R. Schubel. 1993. pap. text 4.95 (*0-943676-23-1*) MD Sea Grant Col.

Life & Death of the Luftwaffe. Werner Baumbach. (War & Warriors Ser.). (Illus.). 224p. 1991. 12.95 (*0-939482-37-1*, 0166, Noontide Pr) Legion Survival.

Life & Death of the Mayor of Casterbridge: A Story of a Man of Character. Thomas Hardy. 1962. 10.05 (*0-606-01055-6*, Pub. by Turtleback) Demco.

Life & Death of the Salt Marsh. John Teal & Mildred Teal. (Ecological Main Event Ser.). 288p. 1983. mass mkt. 5.99 (*0-345-31027-6*, Ballantine) Ballantine Pub Grp.

Life & Death of the Solid South: A Political History. Dewey W. Grantham. LC 88-50. (New Perspectives on the South Ser.). 272p. 1992. pap. text 18.00 (*0-8131-0813-6*) U Pr of Ky.

Life & Death of Venus Johnson. Marsha Hunt. LC 99-176549. 291p. 1998. write for info. (*0-00-225686-X*) HarpC.

Life & Death of Whales. 2nd enl. rev. ed. Robert Burton. (Helix Bks.: No. 378). (Illus.). 186p. (C). 1983. pap. text 15.00 (*0-8226-0378-0*) Littlefield.

Life & Death of Yukio Mishima. Henry S. Stokes. LC 73-90519. 344p. 1982. pap. 8.95 (*0-374-51703-7*) FS&G.

***Life & Death of Yukio Mishima.** Henry Scott Stokes. 2000. reprint ed. pap. 18.95 (*0-8154-1074-3*, Pub. by Cooper Sq) Natl Bk Netwk.

Life & Death of Yukio Mishima. rev. ed. Henry S. Stokes. LC 95-2927. 314p. 1995. pap. 15.00 (*0-374-52464-5*) FS&G.

***Life & Death on Mt. Everest: Sherpas & Himalayan Mountaineering.** Sherry B. Ortner. LC 99-31247. 376p. 1999. 26.95 (*0-691-00689-X*, Pub. by Princeton U Pr) Cal Prin Full Svc.

Life & Death on the Internet: How to Protect Your Family on the World Wide Web. Keith A. Schroeder. LC 98-96530. 197p. 1998. pap. 20.00 (*0-9666442-0-4*) Supple Pubg.

Life & Death on the Ocean. Henry Howe. (Notable American Authors Ser.). 1992. reprint ed. lib. bdg. 75.00 (*0-7812-3205-8*) Rprt Serv.

***Life & Death Planning for Retirement Benefits: The Essential Handbook for Estate Planners.** 3rd rev. ed. Natalie B. Choate. 572p. 1999. pap. 89.95 (*0-9649440-3-0*, Pub. by Ataxplan) BookMasters.

Life & Death Tattoos. rev. ed. Intro. by Donald E. Hardy. (Tattootime Ser.). (Illus.). 96p. 1989. pap. text 15.00 (*0-945367-05-8*) Hardy Marks Pubns.

Life & Death under Stalin: Kalinin Province 1945-1953. Kees Boterbloem. 49.95 (*0-7735-1811-8*) McG-Queens Univ Pr.

Life & Deeds of Uncle Sam: A Satirical Look at U. S. History. Intro. by Paul Buhle. 80p. pap. 10.00 (*0-88286-064-X*) C H Kerr.

Life & Demography of the Side Blotched Lizard, Uta Stansburiana. Donald W. Tinkle. LC 67-65983. (University of Michigan, Museum of Zoology, Miscellaneous Publications: No. 132). (Illus.). 182p. reprint ed. pap. 56.50 (*0-608-07029-7*, 206723600009) Bks Demand.

Life & Destiny of Isak Dinesen. Frans Lasson. LC 75-40669. (Illus.). 232p. 1994. reprint ed. pap. 17.95 (*0-226-46916-6*, P686) U Ch Pr.

Life & Diary. David Brainerd. (American Autobiography Ser.). 384p. 1995. reprint ed. lib. bdg. 89.00 (*0-7812-8463-5*) Rprt Serv.

Life & Diary of David Brainerd. David Brainerd. Ed. & Compiled by Jonathan Edwards. 386p. (YA). (gr. 10). 1989. pap. 13.99 (*0-8010-0976-6*) Baker Bks.

Life & Doctrines of Jacob Boehme. Franz Hartmann. 336p. 1996. reprint ed. pap. 19.00 (*0-7873-0376-3*) Hlth Research.

Life & Doctrines of Jacob Boehme the God-Taught Philosopher. Franz Hartmann. 340p. 1992. reprint ed. pap. 18.00 (*1-56459-270-7*) Kessinger Pub.

Life & Eager Death of Emily Bronte. Virginia Moore. LC 78-173844. (English Biography Ser.: No. 31). 1971. reprint ed. lib. bdg. 75.00 (*0-8383-1345-0*) M S G Haskell Hse.

Life & Early Works. Ed. by William Wallace. LC 95-4441. (Michelangelo: Selected Scholarship in English Ser.: Vol. 1). (Illus.). 544p. 1995. text 109.00 (*0-8153-1823-5*) Garland.

Life & Earth Sciences. Andreas Mandelis & P. Hess. LC 96-48001. (Progress in Photothermal & Photoacoustic Science & Technology Ser.). 454p. 1996. 80.00 (*0-8194-2450-1*) SPIE.

Life & Economics of David Ricardo. LC 97-16305. 1997. lib. bdg. 187.00 (*0-7923-9937-4*) Kluwer Academic.

Life & Education of Laura Dewey Bridgman: The Deaf, Dumb & Blind Girl. Mary S. Lamson. LC 74-21419. (Classics in Child Development Ser.). (Illus.). 420p. 1975. lib. bdg. 36.95 (*0-405-06469-1*) Ayer.

***Life & Environment in the Mediterranean.** Ed. by Louis Trabaud. (Advances in Ecological Sciences Ser.: Vol. 3). 386p. 1999. 188.00 (*1-85312-680-2*, 6802, Pub. by WIT Pr) Computational Mech MA.

Life & Epistles of St. Paul. W. J. Conybeare & J. S. Howson. 1977. lib. bdg. 59.95 (*0-8490-2160-X*) Gordon Pr.

Life & Experiences on the LST-556. Al Urie. 192p. 1993. pap. 12.95 (*1-880365-75-8*) Prof Pr NC.

Life & Exploits of a Jehovah (1915) Contrib. by Henry M. Tichener. 224p. 1998. reprint ed. pap. 17.95 (*0-7661-0663-2*) Kessinger Pub.

Life & Exploits of Alexander the Great, 2 vols., Set. E. A. Wallis Budge. LC 68-56521. (Illus.). 1972. reprint ed. 72.95 (*0-405-08318-1*, Pub. by Blom Pubns) Ayer.

Life & Exploits of Alexander the Great, 2 vols., Vol. 1. E. A. Wallis Budge. LC 68-56521. (Illus.). 1972. reprint ed. 36.95 (*0-405-08319-X*, Pub. by Blom Pubns) Ayer.

Life & Exploits of Alexander the Great, 2 vols., Vol. 2. E. A. Wallis Budge. LC 68-56521. (Illus.). 1972. reprint ed. 36.95 (*0-405-08320-3*, Pub. by Blom Pubns) Ayer.

Life & Exploits of S. Glenn Young: A Reprint of the 1925 Biography of S. Glenn Young, Southern Illinois' Most Infamous Law Officer. Intro. by Gordon Pruett. (Illus.). 253p. 1989. reprint ed. 16.95 (*0-685-28059-4*); reprint ed. pap. 12.95 (*0-685-28060-8*) Crossfire Pr.

Life & Explorations of David Livingstone. John S. Roberts. 1988. reprint ed. lib. bdg. 75.00 (*0-7812-0204-3*) Rprt Serv.

Life & Extraordinary Adventures of Private Ivan Chonkin. Vladimir Voinovich. Tr. by Richard Lourie from RUS. 316p. 1982. pap. 10.95 (*0-374-51752-5*) FS&G.

Life & Extraordinary Adventures of Private Ivan Chonkin. Vladimir Voinovich. Tr. by Richard Lourie. LC 94-49114. (European Classics Ser.). 215p. 1995. reprint ed. pap. 15.95 (*0-8101-1243-4*) Northwestern U Pr.

Life & Faith: Psychological Perspectives on Religious Experience. fac. ed. William W. Meissner. LC 85-8026. 328p. 1987. reprint ed. pap. 101.70 (*0-7837-7782-5*, 204753700007) Bks Demand.

Life & Faith of Martin Luther. Adolph Fehlauer. (J). (gr. 6-9). 1981. pap. 8.50 (*0-8100-0125-X*, 15N0376) Northwest Pub.

Life & Faith of the Baptists. H. Wheeler Robinson. 158p. 1985. reprint ed. pap. 9.95 (*0-913029-09-2*) Stevens Bk Pr.

Life & Fate of Solomon Mikhoels see Zhizn' I Sud'ba Solomona Mikhoelsa: Documents, Speaches, Letters of Solomon Mikhoels

Life & Films of Buck Jones: The Silent Era. Buck Rainey. (Illus.). 263p. 1988. pap. 14.95 (*0-936505-07-9*) World Yesterday.

Life & Films of Buck Jones: The Sound Era. Buck Rainey. (Illus.). 388p. (Orig.). 1992. pap. 24.95 (*0-936505-08-7*) World Yesterday.

Life & Food in the Basque Country. Maria J. Sevilla. 170p. 1992. pap. 10.95 (*1-56131-035-2*, NAB) I R Dee.

Life & Food in the Caribbean. Christine Mackie. 188p. 1995. pap. 11.95 (*1-56131-064-6*, NAB) I R Dee.

Life & Food in the Caribbean. Cristine Mackie. 188p. 1996. pap. 15.95 (*976-8100-49-4*, Pub. by Ian Randle) Paul & Co Pubs.

Life & Food in the Dordogne. James Bentley. LC 87-20396. 184p. 1987. 18.95 (*0-941533-04-2*, NAB) I R Dee.

Life & Gabriella. Ellen Glasgow. (Collected Works of Ellen Glasgow). 2000. 1998. reprint ed. lib. bdg. 108.00 (*1-58201-636-4*) Classic Bks.

***Life & Games of Carlos Toree.** Gabriel Velasco. Tr. by Taylor Kingston. 302p. 2000. write for info. (*1-888690-07-0*) Russell Ent.

Life & Games of Mikhail Tal. Mikhail Tal. 1997. text 24.95 (*1-85744-202-4*) Macmillan.

Life & Genius of Shakespeare. T. Kenny. LC 75-171056. reprint ed. 55.00 (*0-404-03657-0*) AMS Pr.

Life & Glories of St. Joseph. Edward H. Thompson. LC 80-53744. 1980. reprint ed. pap. 15.00 (*0-89555-161-6*) TAN Bks Pubs.

Life & Goal Planner: How to Win the Achievement Game. James D. Akers. 117p. (Orig.). 1988. pap. 19.95 (*0-9621678-0-0*) J D Akers & Assocs.

Life & Gravity: Physiological & Morphological Responses: Proceedings of the F1.1 Meeting of COSPAR Scientific Commission F Which Was Held During the 30th COSPAR Scientific Assembly, Hamburg, Germany, 11-21 July, 1994. Ed. by P. Todd et al. (Advances in Space Research Ser.: Vol. 17). 300p. 1995. pap. 194.50 (*0-08-042649-2*, Pergamon Pr) Elsevier.

Life & Growth of Language. William D. Whitney. 333p. reprint ed. lib. bdg. 50.70 (*0-685-13760-0*, 05103088) G Olms Pubs.

Life & Habit see Shrewsbury Edition of the Works of Samuel Butler

Life & Hard Times of a Korean Shaman: Of Tales & the Telling of Tales. Laurel Kendall. LC 87-19152. 168p. 1988. pap. text 14.00 (*0-8248-1145-3*) UH Pr.

Life & Health: Target Wellness. Levy. 1992. pap. text, teacher ed. 13.43 (*0-07-037497-X*) McGraw.

Life & Health: Targeting Wellness. Mark Dignan et al. (C). 1991. text 44.54 (*0-07-037494-5*); pap. text, student ed. 19.00 (*0-07-037523-2*) McGraw.

Life & Health Insurance: License Exam Manual. 4th ed. Dearborn Financial Institute Staff. LC 97-31724. 1997. pap. 29.00 (*0-7931-2736-X*, 5312-0304) Dearborn.

Life & Health Insurance Law. William F. Meyer. LC 72-76891. 1972. 125.00 (*0-685-59870-5*) West Group.

An Asterisk (*) at the beginning of an entry indicates that the title is appearing for the first time.

Life & Health Insurance Law. 6th ed. Muriel L. Crawford & William T. Beadles. (C). 1988. text 21.00 (*0-256-07121-7*, Irwn McGrw-H) McGrw-H Hghr Educ.

Life & Health Insurance Law. 7th rev. ed. Muriel L. Crawford. LC 93-29936. (Series in Finance). 720p. (C). 1993. text 19.40 (*0-256-13567-3*, Irwn Prfssnl) McGraw-Hill Prof.

Life & Health Insurance Marketing. 2nd ed. Ed. by Sharon B. Allen et al. LC 97-72887. 733p. text 65.95 (*1-57974-008-1*, Pub. by Life Office) PBD Inc.

Life & Health Insurance Underwriting. Barbara F. Brown & Jane L. Brown. LC 98-73106. (Underwriting Life & Health Insurance Ser.). 392p. pap. text 74.95 (*1-57974-019-7*, Pub. by Life Office) PBD Inc.

***Life & History of North America's Indian Reservations.** Richard Parchemin. 192p. 1998. write for info. (*1-57215-255-9*) World Pubns.

Life & History of the Rev. Elijah P. Marrs. Elijah P. Marrs. LC 70-89395. (Black Heritage Library Collection). 1977. 16.95 (*0-8369-8625-3*) Ayer.

Life & History of the Rev. Elijah P. Marrs. Elijah P. Marrs. (American Biography Ser.). 146p. 1991. reprint ed. lib. bdg. 59.00 (*0-7812-8268-3*) Rprt Serv.

Life & Holiness. Thomas Merton. 128p. 1969. pap. 8.95 (*0-385-06277-X*, D183, Image Bks) Doubleday.

Life & Holiness. Thomas Merton. 160p. 1995. pap. 6.00 (*0-385-48048-2*, Image Bks) Doubleday.

Life & How to Survive It. Robin Skynner & John Cleese. (Illus.). 432p. 1996. pap. 13.00 (*0-393-31472-3*, Norton Paperbks) Norton.

Life & Humor of Robin Williams: A Biography. Bill Adler, Jr. LC 99-15806. (Illus.). 224p. 1999. pap. 12.00 (*0-688-15245-7*, Wm Morrow) Morrow Avon.

Life & Humor of Rosie O'Donnell. Gloria Goodman & Bill Adler, Jr. LC 98-2678. 224p. 1998. 22.00 (*0-688-15315-1*, Wm Morrow) Morrow Avon.

***Life & Humor of Rosie O'donnell: A Biography.** Gloria Goodman. 240p. 1999. reprint ed. pap. 12.00 (*0-688-16979-1*, Wm Morrow) Morrow Avon.

Life & I: An Autobiography of Humanity. Gamaliel Bradford. (American Biography Ser.). 307p. 1991. reprint ed. lib. bdg. 79.00 (*0-7812-8036-2*) Rprt Serv.

Life & Ideas of Robert Owen. Robert Owen. 256p. 1969. pap. 1.95 (*0-7178-0115-2*) Intl Pubs Co.

Life & Ideas of the Marquis de Sade. Geoffrey Gorer. LC 77-16240. 250p. 1978. reprint ed. lib. bdg. 69.50 (*0-313-20023-8*, GOMDS, Greenwood Pr) Greenwood.

Life & Illustrious Martyrdom of Sir Thomas More. Thomas Stapleton. LC 66-23617. xviii, 206p. 1984. 15.00 (*0-8232-0731-5*) Fordham.

Life & Its Mirrors: A Feminist Reading of L. M. Montgomery's Fiction. Gabriella Ahmansson. LC 91-164517. 1991. pap. 45.00 (*91-554-2673-5*, Pub. by Uppsala Univ Acta Univ Uppsaliensis) Coronet Bks.

***Life & It's Poetry.** Mary Ann Fleck Legacy. 48p. 2000. pap. 9.99 (*1-892668-17-3*) Prospect Pr.

Life & Its Spirals: History in the Light of Theosophy. E. W. Preston. 1990. pap. 9.50 (*81-7059-137-6*, 7161, Quest) Theos Pub Hse.

Life & Journals of Kah-Ke-Wa-Quo-Na-by. Peter Jones. LC 76-43759. reprint ed. 26.00 (*0-404-15601-0*) AMS Pr.

Life & Journey of a Rainbow. Judith Taylor. 40p. 2000. pap. 8.00 (*0-8059-4683-7*) Dorrance.

Life & Labor: Dimensions of American Working-Class History. Ed. by Charles Stephenson & Robert Asher. LC 86-14362. (SUNY Series in American Labor History). 343p. (C). 1986. text 21.50 (*0-88706-173-7*) State U NY Pr.

Life & Labor in Ancient Mexico: The Brief & Summary Relation of the Lords of New Spain. Alonso D. Zorita. Tr. & Intro. by Benjamin Keen. LC 94-14777. (Illus.). 328p. (Orig.). 1994. reprint ed. pap. 16.95 (*0-8061-2679-5*) U of Okla Pr.

Life & Labor on the Border: Working People of Northeastern Sonora, 1886-1986. Josiah M. Heyman. LC 91-12782. (Illus.). 249p. 1991. 44.00 (*0-8165-1225-6*) U of Ariz Pr.

Life & Labors of Rev. Jordan W. Early: One of the Pioneers of African Methodism in the West & South. Sarah J. Early. LC 72-164386. (Black Heritage Library Collection). 1977. reprint ed. 21.95 (*0-8369-8845-0*) Ayer.

Life & Labour of the People in London, 1890-1900, 17 vols. Charles Booth et al. LC 76-113561. reprint ed. write for info. (*0-404-00940-9*) AMS Pr.

Life & Labours of Hieroschemamonk Parthenius, Elder of the Kiev-Caves Monastery see Skazanije o zhizni i Podvigakh Ieroskimanakha Parthenija, startsa Kievo-Petcherskoj-Lavri

Life & Labours of Mister Brassey, 1805-1870. Arthur Helps. LC 69-17620. (Illus.). xxviii, 386p. 1969. reprint ed. 45.00 (*0-678-07500-X*) Kelley.

Life & Land: Farm Security Administration Photographers in Utah, from 1936 to 1941. Brian Q. Cannon. (Illus.). 64p. (Orig.). 1988. pap. 4.00 (*0-87421-132-8*) Utah St U Pr.

Life & Land of Burns. Allan Cunningham. LC 76-144554. reprint ed. 47.50 (*0-404-08512-1*) AMS Pr.

Life & Land Use on the Bahrain Islands: The Geoarcheology of an Ancient Society. Curtis E. Larsen. LC 83-5085. (Prehistoric Archeology & Ecology Ser.). (Illus.). 360p. 1984. pap. text 11.00 (*0-226-46906-9*) U Ch Pr.

Life & Land Use on the Bahrain Islands: The Geoarcheology of an Ancient Society. Curtis E. Larsen. LC 83-5085. (Prehistoric Archeology & Ecology Ser.). (Illus.). 320p. 1995. lib. bdg. 24.00 (*0-226-46905-0*) U Ch Pr.

Life & Laughter. Monohan. 1990. pap. text. write for info. (*0-582-86839-4*, Pub. by Addison-Wesley) Longman.

Life & Law: An Autobiography. Samuel Williston. ix, 347p. 1998. reprint ed. 134.00 (*1-56169-343-X*) Gaunt.

Life & Learning, Vol. II. Ed. by Joseph W. Koterski. (UFL Proceedings 1992 Ser.). 1993. pap. text 10.00 (*1-886387-00-1*) U Faculty For Life.

Life & Learning, Vol. III. Ed. by Joseph W. Koterski. (UFL Proceedings 1993 Ser.). 1993. pap. text 10.00 (*1-886387-01-X*) U Faculty For Life.

Life & Learning, Vol. IV. Ed. by Joseph W. Koterski. (UFL Proceedings 1994 Ser.). 1995. pap. text 10.00 (*1-886387-02-8*) U Faculty For Life.

Life & Learning Vol. 5: University Faculty for Life, Proceedings 1995. Ed. by Joseph W. Koterski. 400p. 1996. pap. 10.00 (*1-886387-03-6*) U Faculty For Life.

Life & Learning Vol. 6: University Faculty for Life, Proceedings 1996. Ed. by Joseph W. Koterski. 350p. 1997. pap. 10.00 (*1-886387-04-4*) U Faculty For Life.

Life & Learning in Ancient Athens. Richard W. Hibler. LC 88-22769. (Illus.). 146p. (Orig.). (C). 1988. pap. 17.50 (*0-8191-7150-6*); lib. bdg. 39.00 (*0-8191-7149-2*) U Pr of Amer.

Life & Legacy of Annie Oakley. Glenda Riley. LC 94-10260. (Oklahoma Western Biographies Ser.: Vol. 7). (Illus.). 272p. 1994. write for info. (*0-8061-2656-6*) U of Okla Pr.

Life & Legacy of Franz Xaver Hauser: A Leader in the Nineteenth-Century Bach Movement. Dale A. Jorgenson. LC 94-3476. 1995. 41.95 (*0-8093-1975-6*) S Ill U Pr.

Life & Legacy of Fred Newton Scott. Donald C. Stewart & Patricia L. Stewart. LC 97-21006. (Series in Composition, Literacy, & Culture). (Illus.). 400p. 1997. text 45.00 (*0-8229-3992-4*) U of Pittsburgh Pr.

Life & Legacy of G. I. Taylor. George K. Batchelor. (Illus.). 300p. (C). 1996. text 80.00 (*0-521-46121-9*) Cambridge U Pr.

Life & Legacy of the Reverend Phinehas Bailey. Jeffrey D. Marshall. (Occasional Papers: No. 9). (Illus.). 32p. 1985. pap. text 5.00 (*0-944277-14-4*, M37) U VT Ctr Rsch VT.

Life & Legend of Babe Didrikson Zaharias. Susan E. Cayleff. LC 94-35584. (Women in American History; Sport & Society Ser.). (Illus.). 370p. 1995. 29.95 (*0-252-01793-5*) U of Ill Pr.

***Life & Legend of E. H. Harriman.** Maury Klein. LC 99-28864. 544p. 2000. 34.95 (*0-8078-2517-4*) U of NC Pr.

Life & Legend of Jay Gould. Maury Klein. LC 85-24107. (Illus.). 614p. 1997. reprint ed. pap. 24.95 (*0-8018-5771-6*) Johns Hopkins.

Life & Legend of Leadbelly. Charles Wolfe & Kip Lornell. LC ML420.L277W6 1999. (Illus.). 360p. 1999. reprint ed. mass mkt. 15.95 (*0-306-80896-X*, Pub. by Da Capo) HarpC.

Life & Leisure in the Adirondack Backwoods. Harold K. Hochschild. (Illus.). 1962. pap. 7.95 (*0-8156-8022-8*) Syracuse U Pr.

Life & Leisure in the Adirondack Backwoods. rev. ed. Harold K. Hochschild. (Township Thirty-Four Ser.). (Illus.). 121p. 1990. reprint ed. 7.95 (*0-910020-08-6*) Adirondack Mus.

Life & Letters. Irving Feldman. LC 94-6747. 116p. 1994. pap. 11.95 (*0-226-24068-1*); lib. bdg. 26.00 (*0-226-24067-3*) U Ch Pr.

Life & Letters. John C. Squire. LC 72-3533. (Essay Index Reprint Ser.). 1977. reprint ed. 20.95 (*0-8369-2923-3*) Ayer.

Life & Letters of Anton Chekhov. Anton Chekhov. Tr. by Samuel S. Koteliansky & Phillip Tomlinson. LC 65-16230. (Illus.). 1972. 29.95 (*0-405-08355-6*, Pub. by Blom Pubns) Ayer.

Life & Letters of Bayard Taylor. Horace E. Scudder. (Notable American Authors Ser.). 1999. reprint ed. lib. bdg. 125.00 (*0-7812-8888-6*) Rprt Serv.

Life & Letters of Benjamin Franklin. Benjamin Franklin. Date not set. lib. bdg. 26.95 (*0-8488-2087-8*) Amereon Ltd.

Life & Letters of Benjamin Morgan Palmer. Thomas C. Johnson. 676p. 1987. reprint ed. 35.99 (*0-85151-522-3*) Banner of Truth.

Life & Letters of Charles Bulfinch, Architect. Charles Bulfinch. (American Biography Ser.). 323p. 1991. reprint ed. lib. bdg. 79.00 (*0-7812-8052-4*) Rprt Serv.

Life & Letters of Charles Bulfinch, Architect, with Other Family Papers. Ed. by Ellen S. Bulfinch. (Illus.). 323p. 1995. reprint ed. lib. bdg. 42.50 (*0-8328-4504-3*) Higginson Bk Co.

Life & Letters of Christopher Pearse Cranch. Christopher P. Cranch. LC 72-90096. (Illus.). reprint ed. 52.50 (*0-404-05641-5*) AMS Pr.

Life & Letters of Christopher Pearse Cranch. Christopher P. Cranch. (American Biography Ser.). 395p. 1991. reprint ed. lib. bdg. 79.00 (*0-7812-8093-1*) Rprt Serv.

Life & Letters of Christopher Pearse Cranch, by His Daughter Lenora Cranch Scott. Christopher P. Cranch. (BCL1-PS American Literature Ser.). 395p. 1992. reprint ed. lib. bdg. 89.00 (*0-7812-6695-5*) Rprt Serv.

Life & Letters of David Coit Scudder: Missionary in Southern India. Horace E. Scudder. (Notable American Authors Ser.). 1999. reprint ed. lib. bdg. 125.00 (*0-7812-8884-3*) Rprt Serv.

Life & Letters of Dr. Samuel Butler see Shrewsbury Edition of the Works of Samuel Butler

Life & Letters of Edmund Clarence Stedman, 2 vols., Set. Edmund C. Stedman. (BCL1-PS American Literature Ser.). 1992. reprint ed. lib. bdg. 150.00 (*0-7812-6865-6*) Rprt Serv.

Life & Letters of Edward Young. Henry C. Shelley. (BCL1-PR English Literature Ser.). 289p. 1992. reprint ed. lib. bdg. 79.00 (*0-7812-7406-0*) Rprt Serv.

Life & Letters of Edward Young. Henry C. Shelley. LC 70-131831. 1970. reprint ed. 19.00 (*0-403-00718-6*) Scholarly.

Life & Letters of Emily Dickinson. Martha D. Bianchi. LC 70-162296. 386p. 1972. reprint ed. 32.00 (*0-8196-0276-0*) Biblo.

Life & Letters of Emory Upton. Peter S. Michie. Ed. by Richard H. Kohn. LC 78-22388. (American Military Experience Ser.). 1980. reprint ed. lib. bdg. 40.95 (*0-405-11865-1*) Ayer.

Life & Letters of Erasmus. James A. Froude. LC 70-155628. reprint ed. 47.50 (*0-404-02627-3*) AMS Pr.

Life & Letters of Francis Lieber. Thomas S. Perry. (Notable American Authors Ser.). 1999. reprint ed. lib. bdg. 125.00 (*0-7812-8739-1*) Rprt Serv.

Life & Letters of Frederic Shields. Frederic Shields. Ed. by Ernestine Mills. LC 76-148281. reprint ed. 24.00 (*0-404-04344-5*) AMS Pr.

Life & Letters of G. Stratton-Porter. Meehan. 1976. 24.95 (*0-8488-0833-9*) Amereon Ltd.

Life & Letters of Gen. Robert E. Lee. J. William Jones. 1992. 25.99 (*0-87377-959-2*) GAM Pubns.

***Life & Letters of General W. H. L. Wallace.** Isabel Wallace & William Hervy Lamme Wallace. LC 00-38784. (Shawnee Classics). 2000. pap. write for info. (*0-8093-2348-6*) S Ill U Pr.

Life & Letters of George Bancroft, 2 vols. in 1. George Bancroft. Ed. by Mark D. Howe. LC 78-106990. (American Public Figures Ser.). 1970. reprint ed. lib. bdg. 79.50 (*0-306-71877-4*) Da Capo.

Life & Letters of George Cabot. Henry C. Lodge. (Notable American Authors Ser.). 1999. reprint ed. lib. bdg. 125.00 (*0-7812-3807-2*) Rprt Serv.

Life & Letters of George Darley. Claude C. Abbott. (BCL1-PR English Literature Ser.). 285p. 1992. reprint ed. lib. bdg. 79.00 (*0-7812-7507-5*) Rprt Serv.

Life & Letters of George Gordon Meade, Major-General United States Army. George Meade. Ed. by George G. Meade. (Army of the Potomac Ser.). (Illus.). 965p. (C). 1994. text 100.00 (*0-935523-38-3*) Butternut & Blue.

Life & Letters of Gilbert White of Selbourne, 2 vols. Rashleigh Holt-White. LC 76-109501. (Illus.). reprint ed. 74.50 (*0-404-00640-X*) AMS Pr.

Life & Letters of Harriet Beecher Stowe. Annie Fields. (Notable American Authors Ser.). 1992. reprint ed. lib. bdg. 75.00 (*0-7812-2827-1*) Rprt Serv.

Life & Letters of Henry Arthur Jones. Doris A. Jones. (BCL1-PR English Literature Ser.). 448p. 1992. reprint ed. lib. bdg. 99.00 (*0-7812-7572-5*) Rprt Serv.

Life & Letters of Henry Arthur Jones. Doris A. Jones. LC 79-145115. (Illus.). 1971. reprint ed. 24.00 (*0-403-01053-5*) Scholarly.

Life & Letters of Henry Lee Higginson. Bliss Perry. LC 72-37905. (Select Bibliographies Reprint Ser.). 1977. reprint ed. 35.95 (*0-8369-6743-7*) Ayer.

Life & Letters of Henry Lee Higginson: By Bliss Perry. Henry L. Higginson. (American Biography Ser.). 557p. 1991. reprint ed. lib. bdg. 99.00 (*0-7812-8182-2*) Rprt Serv.

Life & Letters of Henry Martyn. John Sargent. 496p. 1985. reprint ed. pap. 11.99 (*0-85151-468-5*) Banner of Truth.

Life & Letters of Horace Bushnell. Mary A. Cheney. LC 74-83415. (Religion in America, Ser. 1). 1975. reprint ed. 25.95 (*0-405-00236-X*) Ayer.

Life & Letters of J. Alden Weir. Dorothy W. Young. LC 76-146157. (Library of American Art). 1971. reprint ed. lib. bdg. 42.50 (*0-306-70097-2*) Da Capo.

Life & Letters of James Abram Garfield, 2 vols., Set. Theodore C. Smith. (History - United States Ser.). 1992. reprint ed. lib. bdg. 150.00 (*0-7812-6208-9*) Rprt Serv.

Life & Letters of James Abram Garfield, 2 vols., Set. Theodore C. Smith. 1993. reprint ed. lib. bdg. 150.00 (*0-7812-5404-3*) Rprt Serv.

Life & Letters of James Henry Thornwell. Benjamin M. Palmer. LC 78-83432. (Religion in America, Ser. 1). 1970. reprint ed. 43.95 (*0-405-00257-2*) Ayer.

Life & Letters of James MacPherson. Thomas B. Saunders. LC 68-24916. (English Biography Ser.: No. 31). 1969. lib. bdg. 75.00 (*0-8383-0238-6*) M S G Haskell Hse.

Life & Letters of James MacPherson. Thomas B. Saunders. (BCL1-PR English Literature Ser.). 327p. 1992. reprint ed. lib. bdg. 89.00 (*0-7812-7371-4*) Rprt Serv.

Life & Letters of Jesse Hill Ford, Southern Writer: With Annotations & Commentary. annot. ed. Anne Cheney. LC 95-20588. (Studies in American Literature: Vol. 19). (Illus.). 580p. 1996. 119.95 (*0-7734-8876-6*) E Mellen.

Life & Letters of Joel Chandler Harris. Julia F. Harris. LC 72-168247. (Illus.). reprint ed. 37.50 (*0-404-00059-2*) AMS Pr.

Life & Letters of Joel Chandler Harris. Julia F. Harris. (BCL1-PS American Literature Ser.). 620p. 1992. reprint ed. lib. bdg. 109.00 (*0-7812-6718-8*) Rprt Serv.

Life & Letters of John A. Broadus. A. T. Robertson. 1996. 22.99 (*0-87377-916-9*) GAM Pubns.

Life & Letters of John Brown. Franklin B. Sanborn. (Notable American Authors Ser.). 1999. reprint ed. lib. bdg. 125.00 (*0-7812-8855-X*) Rprt Serv.

Life & Letters of John Brown, Liberator of Kansas & Martyr of Virginia. Ed. by Franklin B. Sanborn. LC 69-18658. (Illus.). 645p. 1969. reprint ed. lib. bdg. 35.00 (*0-8371-4849-9*, SAL&) Greenwood.

Life & Letters of John Burroughs, 2 vols., Set. Clara Barrus. (BCL1-PS American Literature Ser.). 1992. reprint ed. lib. bdg. 150.00 (*0-7812-6682-3*) Rprt Serv.

Life & Letters of John Burroughs, 2 vols., Set. Clara Barrus. 1993. reprint ed. lib. bdg. 150.00 (*0-7812-5267-9*) Rprt Serv.

Life & Letters of John Donne, 2 vols., Set. Edmund W. Gosse. (BCL1-PR English Literature Ser.). 1992. reprint ed. lib. bdg. 150.00 (*0-7812-7204-1*) Rprt Serv.

Life & Letters of John Gibson Lockhart, 2 vols. Andrew Lang. LC 79-110131. 1970. reprint ed. 74.50 (*0-404-03849-2*) AMS Pr.

Life & Letters of John Greenleaf Whittier. Samuel T. Pickard. (BCL1-PS American Literature Ser.). 804p. 1992. reprint ed. lib. bdg. 119.00 (*0-7812-6903-2*) Rprt Serv.

Life & Letters of John Greenleaf Whittier, 2 vols., Set. Samuel T. Pickard. LC 68-24941. (American Biography Ser.: No. 32). 1969. reprint ed. lib. bdg. 150.00 (*0-8383-0191-6*) M S G Haskell Hse.

Life & Letters of John Hay, 2 vols., Set. William R. Thayer. (History - United States Ser.). 1992. reprint ed. lib. bdg. 150.00 (*0-7812-6198-8*) Rprt Serv.

Life & Letters of John Muir, 2 vols. William F. Bade. LC 77-153302. (BCL Ser.: No. I). reprint ed. 92.50 (*0-404-00444-X*) AMS Pr.

Life & Letters of John Winthrop, 2 vols., Set, Vols. I & II. Robert C. Winthrop. 1994. reprint ed. lib. bdg. 94.50 (*0-8328-3809-8*) Higginson Bk Co.

Life & Letters of Joseph Severn. William Sharp. LC 70-175852. reprint ed. 36.50 (*0-404-07438-3*) AMS Pr.

Life & Letters of Joseph Story, 2 Vols., Set. Ed. by William W. Story. LC 75-175710. (Select Bibliographies Reprint Ser.). 1977. reprint ed. 70.95 (*0-8369-6625-2*) Ayer.

Life & Letters of Lewis Carroll. Stuart D. Collingwood. (BCL1-PR English Literature Ser.). 448p. 1992. reprint ed. lib. bdg. 99.00 (*0-7812-7518-0*) Rprt Serv.

Life & Letters of Lord MaCaulay. George M. Trevelyan. 1978. pap. 14.95 (*0-19-822487-7*) OUP.

Life & Letters of Maria Edgeworth, 2 Vols. Maria Edgeworth. Ed. by Augustus J. Hare. LC 73-152982. (Select Bibliographies Reprint Ser.). 1977. reprint ed. 44.95 (*0-8369-5734-2*) Ayer.

Life & Letters of Mary Wollstonecraft Shelley, 2 vols., Set. Florence Marshall. LC 70-115181. (Studies in Shelley: No. 25). 1970. reprint ed. lib. bdg. 150.00 (*0-8383-1011-7*) M S G Haskell Hse.

***Life & Letters of Paul.** Broadman & Holman Publishing Staff. LC 99-54866. (Shepherd's Notes Bible Summary Ser.). 1999. pap. 5.95 (*0-8054-9385-9*) Broadman.

Life & Letters of Peter Ilyich Tchaikovsky, 2 vols., Set. Modeste Tchaikovsky. LC 72-95443. (Studies in Music: No. 42). 1970. reprint ed. lib. bdg. 150.00 (*0-8383-0997-6*) M S G Haskell Hse.

Life & Letters of Robert Browning. Alexandra L. Orr. (BCL1-PR English Literature Ser.). 431p. 1992. reprint ed. lib. bdg. 99.00 (*0-7812-7465-6*) Rprt Serv.

Life & Letters of Saint Paul. Ed. by David Smith. 1977. lib. bdg. 69.95 (*0-8490-2161-8*) Gordon Pr.

Life & Letters of Samuel Wells Williams, LLD: Missionary, Diplomat, Sinologue. Frederick W. Williams. LC 72-79841. (China Library). (Illus.). 1972. reprint ed. lib. bdg. 37.00 (*0-8420-1355-5*) Scholarly Res Inc.

Life & Letters of Sir Edmund Gosse. Evan Charteris. LC 72-2097. (English Literature Ser.: No. 33). 1972. reprint ed. lib. bdg. 75.00 (*0-8383-1456-2*) M S G Haskell Hse.

Life & Letters of Sir George Savile, First Marquis of Halifax, 2 vols., Set. H. C. Foxcroft. Ed. by Gerald M. Straka. LC 72-83170. (English Studies). 1972. reprint ed. lib. bdg. 70.00 (*0-8420-1427-6*) Scholarly Res Inc.

Life & Letters of Sir John Everett Millais, President of the Royal Academy, 2 vols. John G. Millais. LC 72-148280. reprint ed. 124.50 (*0-404-04326-7*) AMS Pr.

Life & Letters of Sir Joseph Dalton Hooker: Materials Collected & Arranged by Lady Hooker, 2 vols., Set. Leonard Huxley. Ed. by Keir B. Sterling. LC 77-81130. (Biologists & Their World Ser.). (Illus.). 1978. reprint ed. lib. bdg. 102.95 (*0-405-10726-9*) Ayer.

Life & Letters of Sir Joseph Dalton Hooker: Materials Collected & Arranged by Lady Hooker, 2 vols., Vol. 1. Leonard Huxley. Ed. by Keir B. Sterling. LC 77-81130. (Biologists & Their World Ser.). (Illus.). 1978. reprint ed. lib. bdg. 51.95 (*0-405-10727-7*) Ayer.

Life & Letters of Sir Joseph Dalton Hooker: Materials Collected & Arranged by Lady Hooker, 2 vols., Vol. 2. Leonard Huxley. Ed. by Keir B. Sterling. LC 77-81130. (Biologists & Their World Ser.). (Illus.). 1978. reprint ed. lib. bdg. 51.95 (*0-405-10728-5*) Ayer.

Life & Letters of Stuart P. Sherman, 2 Vols., Set. Jacob Zeitlin & Homer Woodbridge. LC 74-150207. (Select Bibliographies Reprint Ser.). 1977. reprint ed. 58.95 (*0-8369-5720-2*) Ayer.

Life & Letters of the Rev. John Philip Boehm: Founder of the Reformed Church in Pennsylvania, 1683-1749. Ed. by William J. Hinke. LC 71-38784. (Religion in America, Ser. 2). 572p. 1972. reprint ed. 38.95 (*0-405-04069-5*) Ayer.

Life & Letters of the Right Honourable Friedrich Max Mueller, 2 vols., Set. Friedrich M. Mueller. LC 73-18820. (Illus.). reprint ed. 115.00 (*0-404-11445-8*) AMS Pr.

Life & Letters of the Right Honourable Sir Charles Tupper, Bart, 2 vols., Set. Edward M. Saunders. (BCL1 - History - Canada Ser.). 1991. reprint ed. lib. bdg. 150.00 (*0-7812-6365-4*) Rprt Serv.

Life & Letters of Theoleptos of Philadelphia. Theoleptos of Philadelphia. Ed. by Angela C. Hero. LC 94-10870. (Archbishop Iakovos Library of Ecclesiastical & Historical Sources: Vol. 20). (ENG & GRE.). 121p. 1994. pap. 9.95 (*0-917653-43-2*) Hellenic Coll Pr.

Life & Letters of Thomas Campbell, 3 vols. William Beattie. LC 70-161729. reprint ed. 225.00 (*0-404-07630-0*) AMS Pr.

Life & Letters of Thomas Cromwell, 2 vols. Roger B. Merriman. Incl. Vol. 1. Life, Letters of 1535. 1902. Vol. 2. Letters from 1536, Notes, Index. 1902. 1969. 85.00 (*0-19-822305-6*) OUP.

An Asterisk (*) at the beginning of an entry indicates that the title is appearing for the first time.

L

Life & Letters of Thomas Henry Huxley (by his Son, Leonard Huxley), 2 vols. Thomas Henry Huxley. LC 75-41152. (BCL Ser. II). reprint ed. 155.00 (*0-404-14980-4*) AMS Pr.

Life & Letters of Walter H. Page, 3 vols., Set. Burton J. Hendrick. (History - United States Ser.). 1992. reprint ed. lib. bdg. 225.00 (*0-7812-6199-6*) Rprt Serv.

Life & Letters of Walter H. Page, 3 vols., Set. Burton J. Hendrick. LC 79-145079. (Illus.). 1971. reprint ed. 95.00 (*0-403-00769-0*) Scholarly.

Life & Letters of Washington Allston. Jared B. Flagg. LC 72-82002. (Illus.). 450p. 1972. reprint ed. 32.95 (*0-405-08520-6*, Pub. by Blom Pubns) Ayer.

Life & Letters of Washington Allston. Jared B. Flagg. LC 68-27719. (Library of American Art). 1969. reprint ed. lib. bdg. 59.50 (*0-306-71168-0*) Da Capo.

Life & Letters of William Barton Rogers, 2 vols., Set. Ed. by Emma Rogers. (Illus.). 874p. 1995. reprint ed. lib. bdg. 97.50 (*0-8328-4502-7*) Higginson Bk Co.

Life & Letters of William Dean Howells, 2 vols., Set. Mildred Howells. 1993. reprint ed. lib. bdg. 150.00 (*0-7812-5377-2*) Rprt Serv.

Life & Letters on the Roman Frontier: Vindolanda & Its People. Alan K. Bowman. LC 97-52950. 160p. (C). 1998. 75.00 (*0-415-92024-8*); pap. 20.99 (*0-415-92025-6*) Routledge.

Life & Liberation of Padmasambhava, 2 vols., Set. Yeshe Tsogyal. Tr. by G. C. Toussaint et al. LC 78-17445. (Tibetan Translation Ser.: Vol. 7). (Illus.). 803p. 1978. 108.00 (*0-913546-18-6*) Dharma Pub.

Life & Limb. Keith Reddin. 1985. pap. 5.25 (*0-8222-0658-7*) Dramatists Play.

Life & Limb: Selected Tales of Peril, Predicament, & Dire Distress. Ed. by Gilbert Alter-Gilbert. LC 96-76623. 224p. 1997. pap. 16.00 (*1-57650-047-0*) Hi Jinx Pr.

Life & Literary Pursuits of Allen Davenport. Allen Davenport & Ainge Devyr. Ed. by Dorothy Thompson. (Chartism, Working-Class Politics in the Industrial Revolution Ser.). 308p. 1987. lib. bdg. 26.00 (*0-8240-5595-0*) Garland.

Life & Literary Pursuits of Allen Davenport: With a Further Selection of the Author's Work. Ed. by Malcolm Chase. LC 94-5838. 1994. 69.95 (*1-85928-068-4*, Pub. by Scolar Pr) Ashgate Pub Co.

Life & Literature. Lafcadio Hearn. Ed. by John Erskine. LC 78-90644. (Essay Index Reprint Ser.). 1977. 24.95 (*0-8369-1206-3*) Ayer.

Life & Lore of Illinois Wildflowers. William E. Werner, Jr. (Illus.). 238p. (Orig.). 1988. pap. 11.95 (*0-89792-117-8*) Ill St Museum.

Life & Lore of the Elephant. Robert Delort. (Discoveries Ser.). (Illus.). 192p. 1992. pap. 12.95 (*0-8109-2848-5*, Pub. by Abrams) Time Warner.

Life & Love. Ray Garfield Staff. 184p. (Orig.). 1983. pap. 5.95 (*0-9609856-0-3*) Garfield Pubns.

Life & Love All Not Spectator Sports. Bob Perlman. 1986. write for info. (*0-318-62747-7*) Dan Eli Pr.

Life & Love & Everything. Claire Rayner. (Children's Questions Ser.). (Illus.). 96p. (J). (gr. 2-5). 1995. 9.95 (*1-85626-112-3*, Pub. by Cathie Kyle) Trafalgar.

Life & Love Before Consciousness. Michelle Jordan. LC 00-90065. pap. 11.95 (*0-9678076-0-3*) M Y Jordan.

Life & Love, Such As They Are. Anna Shapiro. 1994. 21.00 (*0-671-87114-5*) S&S Trade.

Life & Loves of a She-Devil. Fay Weldon. 288p. 1985. mass mkt. 6.99 (*0-345-32375-0*) Ballantine Pub Grp.

Life & Loyalty: A Study in the Socio-Religious Culture of Syria & Mesopotamia in the Graeco-Roman Period Based on Epigraphical Evidence. Klaas Dijkstra. (Religions in the Graeco-Roman World Ser.: No. 128). 402p. 1995. 142.00 (*90-04-09996-4*) Brill Academic Pubs.

Life & Major Writings of Thomas Paine. Philip S. Foner. (Illus.). 698p. 1999. reprint ed. 42.95 (*0-7351-0077-2*) Replica Bks.

Life & Manners in Madrid, 1750-1800. Charles E. Kany. LC 70-124773. reprint ed. 52.50 (*0-404-03634-1*) AMS Pr.

Life & Manners in the Frontier Army. Oliver Knight. LC 77-15457. 1993. pap. 15.95 (*0-8061-2517-9*) U of Okla Pr.

Life & Many Deaths of Harry Houdini. Ruth Brandon. Ed. by Philip Turner. (Kodansha Globe Ser.). (Illus.). 400p. 1995. pap. 14.00 (*1-56836-100-9*, Kodansha Globe) Kodansha.

Life & Martyrdom of Saint Anastasia & Those Who Were Martyred with Her. Tr. by Holy Transfiguration Monastery Staff from GRE. 1987. pap. 5.00 (*0-913026-65-4*) St Nectarios.

Life & Meaning: A Reader. Ed. by Oswald Hanfling. 1988. pap. text 28.95 (*0-631-15784-0*) Blackwell Pubs.

Life & Memorable Actions of George Washington. Mason L. Weems. (Notable American Authors Ser.). 1999. reprint ed. lib. bdg. 125.00 (*0-7812-9920-9*) Rprt Serv.

Life & Message of Sr. Mary of The Holy Trinity: Poor Clare of Jerusalem (1901-1942) Alain-Marie Duboin. Ed. by Poor Clares of Rockford & Raphael Brown. Tr. by Mary D. Chomeau from FRE. LC 87-50747. (Illus.). 254p. 1987. pap. 10.00 (*0-89555-318-X*) TAN Bks Pubs.

Life & Mind of Oriental Jones: Sir William Jones, the Father of Modern Linguistics. Garland Cannon. 431p. (C). 1991. text 64.95 (*0-521-39149-0*) Cambridge U Pr.

Life & Ministry of Jesus Christ - Chinese Edition, No. 1. (CHI.). 81p. 1986. pap. 6.00 (*1-56582-100-9*) Christ Renew Min.

Life & Ministry of Jesus Christ - Chinese Edition, No. 2. (CHI.). 77p. 1986. pap. 6.00 (*1-56582-101-7*) Christ Renew Min.

Life & Ministry of Jesus Christ - Chinese Edition, No. 3. (CHI.). 83p. 1986. pap. 6.00 (*1-56582-102-5*) Christ Renew Min.

Life & Ministry of the Messiah. Laan Ray Vander. 128p. 1999. pap., student ed. 6.99 (*0-310-67898-6*) Zondervan.

***Life & Ministry of the Messiah.** Ray L. Vander. 224p. 2000. pap., teacher ed. 27.99 (*0-310-67858-7*) Zondervan.

***Life & Ministry of William J. Seymour & a History of the Azusa Street Revival.** Larry E. Martin. LC 99-76361. (Complete Azusa Street Library: Vol. 1). (Illus.). 384p. 1999. pap. 12.99 (*0-9646289-4-5*) Christian Life Bks.

Life & Miracles of Pope Kirillos VI. Ernest T. Abdel-Massih. 139p. (Orig.). 1982. pap. text 3.00 (*0-932098-20-7*) St Mark Coptic Orthodox.

Life & Miracles of Saint Benedict: Book Two of Dialogues. Gregorius I. Tr. by Odo J. Zimmermann & Benedict R. Avery from LAT. LC 80-19624. 87p. 1980. reprint ed. lib. bdg. 45.00 (*0-313-22766-7*, GRLI, Greenwood Pr) Greenwood.

Life & Miracles of St. Luke. Carolyn Connor & Robert Connor. (Archbishop Iakovos Library of Ecclesiastical & Historical Sources: No. 18). 178p. 1994. pap. 14.95 (*0-917653-36-X*, Pub. by Hellenic Coll Pr) BookWorld.

Life & Miracles of Saint Luke of Steiris. Carolyn L. Connor & W. Robert Connor. Ed. by Nomikos M. Vaporis. LC 89-11153. (Archbishop Iacovos Library of Ecclesiastical & Historical Sources: No. 18). 178p. (C). 1994. 14.95 (*0-917653-35-1*, Pub. by Hellenic Coll Pr) BookWorld.

Life & Murder of Henry Morshead: A True Story of the Raj. Ian Morshead. (Illus.). 220p. 1982. 27.00 (*0-900891-76-9*) Oleander Pr.

Life & Music of Amy Beach. Compiled by Gail Smith. 104p. 1992. pap. 11.95 (*1-56222-317-8*, 94705) Mel Bay.

Life & Music of Bela Bartok. 3rd ed. Halsey Stevens. (Illus.). 382p. 1993. pap. text 26.00 (*0-19-816349-5*) OUP.

Life & Music of Edward MacDowell. Gail Smith. (Illus.). 180p. 1996. pap. 19.95 (*0-7866-2311-X*, MB96192) Mel Bay.

Life & Music of Edward MacDowell. Gail Smith. 180p. 1996. pap. 34.95 incl. cd-rom (*0-7866-2515-5*, 96192CDP) Mel Bay.

Life & Music of Edward MacDowell. Gail Smith. 180p. 1997. pap. 27.95 incl. audio (*0-7866-2514-7*, 96192P) Mel Bay.

Life & Music of George Antheil, 1900-1959. Linda Whitesitt. Ed. by George J. Buelow. LC 83-15545. (Studies in Musicology: No. 70). 373p. reprint ed. 115.70 (*0-8357-1462-4*, 207043900089) Bks Demand.

***Life & Music of Nick Cave.** Johannes Beck & Robert Clanton. 1999. pap. 39.99 (*3-931126-27-7*, Pub. by Die Gestalten) Consort Bk Sales.

Life & Music of Pierre Rode: Containing an Account of Rode, French Violinist. Arthur Pougin. (Illus.). 81p. 1994. 25.00 (*0-9641631-0-1*) Lyre of Orpheus.

***Life & Non-Life Insurance Products in Thailand: A Strategic Entry Report, 1996.** Compiled by Icon Group International Staff. (Illus.). 141p. 1999. ring bd. 1410.00 incl. audio compact disk (*0-7418-1277-0*) Icon Grp.

Life & Old Age: A Commonplace Book. Joan Rockwell. 234p. 1999. 42.50 (*1-85776-306-8*) Trans-Atl Phila.

Life & Opinion of Tom Collins: A Study of the Works of Joseph Furphy. Julian Croft. 1991. pap. 14.95 (*0-7022-2364-6*, Pub. by Univ Queensland Pr) Intl Spec Bk.

Life & Opinions of John de Wycliffe, D. D., 2 vols. 2nd ed. Robert Vaughan. LC 71-178561. reprint ed. 145.00 (*0-404-56678-2*) AMS Pr.

***Life & Opinions of the Tomcat Murr.** L. T. Hoffman. (Penguin Classics Ser.). 352p. 1999. pap. 12.95 (*0-14-044631-1*, Penguin Bks) Viking Penguin.

Life & Opinions of Tristram Shandy, Gentleman. Martin Rowson. LC 96-49506. (Illus.). 176p. 1997. 26.95 (*0-87951-768-9*, Pub. by Overlook Pr) Penguin Putnam.

Life & Opinions of Tristram Shandy, Gentleman, 001. Laurence Sterne. Ed. by Ian Watt. LC 65-9537. (C). 1965. pap. 13.96 (*0-395-05145-2*, RivEd) HM.

Life & Opinions of Tristram Shandy, Gentleman. Laurence Sterne. Ed. & Intro. by Ian C. Ross. (Oxford World's Classics Ser.). 626p. 1998. pap. 8.95 (*0-19-283470-3*) OUP.

Life & Opinions of Tristram Shandy, Gentleman. Laurence Sterne. (Classics Library). 1998. pap. 3.95 (*1-85326-291-9*, 2919WW, Pub. by Wrdsworth Edits) NTC Contemp Pub Co.

Life & Opinions of Tristram Shandy, Gentleman: The Notes. Laurence Sterne. Ed. by Melvyn New. LC 77-20683. (Florida Edition of the Works of Laurence Sterne: Vol. 3). (Illus.). 572p. 1984. 49.95 (*0-8130-0738-0*) U Press Fla.

Life & Opinions of Tristram Shandy, Gentleman: The Text, 2 vols., 2. Laurence Sterne. Ed. by Melvyn New & Joan New. LC 77-20621. (Florida Edition of the Works of Laurence Sterne). 475p. 1978. 49.95 (*0-8130-0599-X*) U Press Fla.

Life & Opinions of Walter Richard Sickert. Robert Emmons. (Illus.). 336p. (C). 1992. pap. 29.95 (*0-85331-635-X*, Pub. by Lund Humphries) Antique Collect.

Life, & Other Ways to Kill Time. Mike Nichols. 288p. 1988. 15.95 (*0-8184-0462-0*) Carol Pub Group.

Life & Papers of Frederick Bates, 2 vols. Ed. by Thomas M. Marshall. LC 75-109. (Mid-American Frontier Ser.). 1975. reprint ed. 57.95 (*0-405-06876-X*) Ayer.

Life & Passion of St. John (Pommer) of Riga & Latvia. Ludmila Keller. Tr. by German Ciuba. 64p. 1997. pap. 5.00 (*0-912927-81-X*, X052) St John Kronstadt.

Life & Philosophy of J. McT. E. McTaggart, 1866-1925. Gerald Rochelle. LC 91-27674. (Studies in the History of Philosophy: Vol. 22). (Illus.). 268p. 1991. lib. bdg. 89.95 (*0-7734-9692-0*) E Mellen.

***Life & Photography of Doris Ulmann.** Philip Walker Jacobs. (Illus.). 328p. 2001. 40.00 (*0-8131-2175-2*) U Pr of Ky.

Life & Poems of Edgar Allen Poe. E. L. Didier. LC 73-16344. (Studies in Poe: No. 23). 1974. lib. bdg. 75.00 (*0-8383-1726-X*) M S G Haskell Hse.

Life & Poems of Mirabeau B. Lamar. Philip Graham. 1993. reprint ed. lib. bdg. 75.00 (*0-7812-5966-5*) Rprt Serv.

***Life & Poetry.** Toni Stevens. 2000. write for info. (*1-58235-446-4*) Watermrk Pr.

***Life & Poetry of Adelaide Proctor: Poetry, Feminism & Fathers.** Gill Gregory. LC 98-33797. (Nineteenth Century Ser.). 293p. 1998. text 84.95 (*1-84014-670-2*, Pub. by Ashgate Pub) Ashgate Pub Co.

Life & Poetry of Manoah Bodman: Bard of the Berkshires. Ed. by Lewis Turco. LC 98-51958. 128p. 1999. 29.50 (*0-7618-1324-1*) U Pr of Amer.

***Life & Poetry of Miklos Radnoti: Essays.** Ed. by George Gomori & Clive Wilmer. LC 99-72632. (Eastern European Studies of Columbia University: No. 528). 200p. 1999. 28.50 (*0-88033-426-6*, 528, Pub. by East Eur Monographs) Col U Pr.

Life & Poetry of Sara Shagufta. Amrita Pritam. LC 93-911494. (Orig.). (C). 1994. 8.50 (*81-7018-771-0*, Pub. by BR Pub) S Asia.

Life & Political Economy of Lauchlin Currie: New Dealer, Presidential Adviser, & Development Economist. Roger S. Sandilands. LC 89-71472. 455p. (C). 1990. text 64.95 (*0-8223-1030-9*) Duke.

Life & Pontificate of Pope Leo the Tenth, 2 vols. 6th rev. ed. William Roscoe. Ed. by Thomas Roscoe. LC 75-174965. reprint ed. 125.00 (*0-404-05430-7*) AMS Pr.

Life & Power of the Blood Covenant. Bill Basansky, 96p. 1993. pap. 7.00 (*0-89274-824-9*, HH-824) Harrison Hse.

Life & Private History of Emily Bronte. Romer Wilson. LC 72-3230. (English Literature Ser.: No. 33). 1972. reprint ed. lib. bdg. 75.00 (*0-8383-1527-5*) M S G Haskell Hse.

Life & Professional Career of Emma Abbott. Sadie E. Martin. LC 80-2290. reprint ed. 34.50 (*0-404-18858-3*) AMS Pr.

Life & Progress of Henry Quick of Zennor. Illus. by Laura Rowe. (C). 1989. 22.00 (*0-907566-43-X*, Pub. by Dyllansow Truran) St Mut.

Life & Prophecies of Paracelsus Containing the Prophecies, Occult Symbols, & Magic Figures of Paracelsus & the Life & Teachings of Paracelsus. Philippus Aureolus Paracelsus & Franz Hartmann. (Illus.). 320p. 1996. reprint ed. pap. 24.95 (*1-56459-981-7*) Kessinger Pub.

Life & Public Services of Ambrose E. Burnside: Soldier - Citizen - Statesman. Benjamin P. Poore. (Notable American Authors Ser.). 1999. reprint ed. lib. bdg. 125.00 (*0-7812-8763-4*) Rprt Serv.

Life & Public Services of an Army Straggler. Kittrell J. Warren. Ed. by Floyd C. Watkins. LC 61-17536. 112p. reprint ed. pap. 34.80 (*0-608-15803-8*, 203108000073) Bks Demand.

Life & Public Services of George Luther Stearns. Frank P. Stearns. LC 70-82224. (Anti-Slavery Crusade in America Ser.). 1970. reprint ed. 32.95 (*0-405-00663-2*) Ayer.

Life & Public Services of Hon. Abraham Lincoln, with a Portrait on Steel, to Which Is Added a Biographical Sketch of Hon. Hannibal Hamlin. David W. Bartlett. LC 78-95064. (Select Bibliographies Reprint Ser.). 1977. 33.95 (*0-8369-5066-6*) Ayer.

Life & Public Services of James Logan. I. J. Cooper. 1993. reprint ed. lib. bdg. 89.00 (*0-7812-5443-4*) Rprt Serv.

Life & Public Services of John Sherman. Benjamin P. Poore. (Notable American Authors Ser.). 1999. reprint ed. lib. bdg. 125.00 (*0-7812-8762-6*) Rprt Serv.

Life & Public Services of Martin R. Delany, Sub-Assistant Commissioner, Bureau Relief of Refugees, Freedmen & of Abandoned Lands, & Late Major 104th U. S. Colored Troops. Frank A. Rollin. LC 77-92236. (American Negro: His History & Literature. Series 3). 1970. reprint ed. 19.95 (*0-405-01934-3*) Ayer.

Life & Public Services of Salmon Portland Chase. J. W. Schuckers. LC 73-89432. (Black Heritage Library Collection). 1977. 29.95 (*0-8369-8649-0*) Ayer.

Life & Public Services of Salmon Portland Chase. J. W. Schuckers. LC 76-118202. (American Constitutional & Legal History Ser). 1970. reprint ed. lib. bdg. 75.00 (*0-306-71934-7*) Da Capo.

Life & Public Services of Samuel Adams, Being a Narrative of His Acts & Opinions, & of His Agency in Producing & Forwarding the American Revolution, 3 Vols., Set. William V. Wells. LC 76-85458. (Select Bibliographies Reprint Ser.). 1977. 108.95 (*0-8369-5032-1*) Ayer.

Life & Pursuit of Successful Living: On the Threshold to the Impending Economic - Political Storm. Homer R. Wells. LC 90-84575. 304p. 1991. pap. 19.95 (*0-942963-09-1*) Distinctive Pub.

Life & Raigne of King Edward the Sixth by John Hayward. Ed. by Barrett L. Beer. LC 92-26984. (Illus.). 208p. 1993. lib. bdg. 35.00 (*0-87338-475-X*) Kent St U Pr.

Life & Reality. Louis Herman. 250p. 1996. pap. 9.95 (*0-9649592-0-8*) Garstang.

Life & Rebellious Times of Cicely Hamilton: Actress, Writer, Suffragist. Lis Whitelaw. LC 92-100556. x, 262 p. 1990. write for info. (*0-7043-4225-1*) Quartet.

Life & Regimen of The Blessed & Holy Teacher Syncletica. Pseudo-Athanasius. Tr. by Elizabeth B. Bongie. (Translation Ser.). 85p. 1996. pap. 10.00 (*0-920669-46-8*, Pub. by Peregrina Pubng) Cistercian Pubns.

Life & Reign of Edward the Fourth, 2 vols., Set. Cora L. Scofield. 85.00 (*0-7146-1047-X*, Pub. by F Cass Pubs) Intl Spec Bk.

Life & Religion. Friedrich M. Mueller. LC 73-18821. reprint ed. 39.50 (*0-404-11448-2*) AMS Pr.

Life & Religion: An Aftermath from the Writings of the Right Honourable Professor F. Max Muller. 2nd ed. Max Muller. 237p. (Orig.). 1995. reprint ed. pap. 14.95 (*1-885395-10-8*) Book Tree.

Life & Religion at Louisbourg, 1713-1758. A. J. Johnston. (Illus.). 256p. 1996. pap. text 19.95 (*0-7735-1525-9*, BX1424, Pub. by McG-Queens Univ Pr) CUP Services.

Life & Remains of Theodore Edward Hook, 2 vols., Set. Theodore E. Hook. LC 73-170045. reprint ed. 115.00 (*0-404-07907-5*) AMS Pr.

Life & Remarkable Adventures of Israel R. Potter. Israel R. Potter. 1987. 15.50 (*0-8446-2752-6*) Peter Smith.

Life & Rhymes of Michigan: A Poetic Trip Through a Great Great Lakes State. Harry Knitter. 96p. 1998. spiral bd. 8.95 (*0-9652333-3-2*) Kordene Publns.

Life & Rhymes of Ogden Nash. David Stuart. LC 91-22056. (Illus.). 240p. 2000. 24.95 (*1-56833-127-4*, Pub. by Madison Bks UPA) Natl Bk Netwk.

Life & Rhymes of Ogden Nash. David Stuart & Ogden Nash. LC 91-22056. 1991. 19.95 (*0-8128-4015-1*, Scrbrough Hse) Madison Bks UPA.

Life & Ritual in Old Siam: Three Studies of Thai Life & Customs. Rajadhon P. Anuman. Ed. by William J. Gedney. LC 78-23833. (Illus.). 109p. 1979. reprint ed. lib. bdg. 49.75 (*0-313-21193-0*, ARLF, Greenwood Pr) Greenwood.

Life & Sayings of Mrs. Partington. Benjamin P. Shillaber. LC 79-91092. (American Humorists Ser.). reprint ed. lib. bdg. 32.50 (*0-8398-1858-0*) Irvington.

Life & Scientific & Medical Career of Benjamin Waterhouse: With Some Account of the Introduction of Vaccination in America, Vol. 1. I. Bernard Cohen. 1980. 37.95 (*0-405-12522-4*) Ayer.

Life & Scientific & Medical Career of Benjamin Waterhouse: With Some Account of the Introduction of Vaccination in America, Vol. 2. I. Bernard Cohen. 1980. 37.95 (*0-405-12523-2*) Ayer.

Life & Scientific Work of Othniel Charles Marsh: An Original Anthology. Ed. by I. Bernard Cohen. LC 79-7973. (Three Centuries of Science in America Ser.). (Illus.). 1980. lib. bdg. 63.95 (*0-405-12555-0*) Ayer.

Life & Sculpture of Wah Ming Chang. David Barrow & Glen Chang. (Illus.). 90p. 1990. write for info. (*0-9625293-0-3*); pap. write for info. (*0-9625293-1-1*) W M Chang.

Life & Select Literary Remains of Sam Houston of Texas, 2 vols in 1. William C. Crane. LC 74-38348. (Select Bibliographies Reprint Ser.). 1977. reprint ed. 37.95 (*0-8369-6765-8*) Ayer.

Life & Select Literary Remains of Sam Houston of Texas. William C. Crane. 1993. reprint ed. lib. bdg. 75.00 (*0-7812-5872-3*) Rprt Serv.

Life & Selected Writings of Thomas Jefferson. Adrienne Koch. LC 98-21092. 1998. pap. 15.95 (*0-375-75218-8*) Modern Lib NY.

Life & Sermons of Edward D. Griffin, 2 vols., Set. William B. Sprague. 1193p. (C). 1987. reprint ed. 57.99 (*0-85151-513-4*) Banner of Truth.

Life & Society in the West. Constance B. Bouchard & Peter N. Stearns. (Orig.). (C). 1988. pap. text, teacher ed. 2.50 (*0-15-550728-1*) Harcourt Coll Pubs.

Life & Society in the West. Constance B. Bouchard & Peter N. Stearns. 512p. (Orig.). (C). 1988. pap. text 33.50 (*0-15-550726-5*, Pub. by Harcourt Coll Pubs) Harcourt.

Life & Society in the West. Constance B. Bouchard & Peter N. Stearns. 512p. (Orig.). (C). 1988. pap. text 35.50 (*0-15-550727-3*, Pub. by Harcourt Coll Pubs) Harcourt.

Life & Songs of Iain MacNeacail. Tom McKean. 320p. 1997. pap. 35.00 (*0-7486-6214-6*, Pub. by Polygon) Subterranean Co.

Life & Songs of the Baroness Nairne, with a Memoir & Poems of Caroline Oliphant the Younger. Carolina O. Nairne. LC 70-144571. (Illus.). reprint ed. 42.50 (*0-404-08577-6*) AMS Pr.

Life & Sorrows of Anne Hardwick. Anne Hardwick. LC 81-9146. 152p. 1981. reprint ed. 50.00 (*0-8201-1368-9*) Schol Facsimiles.

Life & Soul of Mortal Man. Charles Ozanne. 32p. (Orig.). 1995. pap. 3.00 (*1-880573-21-0*) Bible Search Pubns.

Life & Speeches of Henry Clay, 2 vols. (Illus.). 1987. reprint ed. 95.00 (*0-8377-2407-4*, Rothman) W S Hein.

Life & Speeches of the Hon. Henry Clay. Henry Clay & Daniel Mallory. 1977. 51.95 (*0-8369-6983-9*, 7861) Ayer.

Life & Spirituality of John Newton. John Newton & Bruce Hindmarsh. (C). 1998. reprint ed. pap. write for info. (*1-57383-118-2*, Regent Coll Pub) Regent College.

Life & Status of Professional Women: A Study of Varanasi. Kavita Sazena. (C). 1994. 18.50 (*81-7027-207-6*, Pub. by Radiant Pubs) S Asia.

Life & Stories of the Jaina Savior Pearpevaneatha. Bheavadevaseuri. 1979. 25.95 (*0-405-10583-5*) Ayer.

Life & Story: Autobiographies for a Narrative Psychology. Ed. by D. John Lee. LC 93-19093. 304p. 1993. 69.50 (*0-275-94095-0*, C4095, Praeger Pubs) Greenwood.

Life & Strange & Surprising Adventures of Robinson Crusoe, of York, Mariner. Daniel Defoe. LC 74-13442. (Illus.). reprint ed. write for info. (*0-404-07911-3*) AMS Pr.

Life & Strange Surprising Adventures of Robinson Crusoe, of York, Mariner. Daniel Defoe. Ed. & Intro. by Joseph Donald Crowley. (Oxford World's Classics Ser.). (Illus.). 346p. 1998. pap. 6.95 (*0-19-283382-0*) OUP.

Life & Study Guide. 3rd ed. Lewis. 1998. text 62.25 (*0-07-561735-8*) McGraw.

An Asterisk (*) at the beginning of an entry indicates that the title is appearing for the first time.

L

Life & Sufferings of Saint Catherine the Great Martyr. Tr. by Leonidas J. Papadopulos & Georgia Lizardos from GRE. (Illus.). 1986. pap. 2.00 (*0-913026-63-8*) St Nectarios.

Life & Teaching of Anandmayi Ma. Alexander Lipski. 1977. 9.95 (*0-89684-484-6*, Pub. by Motilal Bnarsidass) S Asia.

Life & Teaching of Jesus. Bentley. Date not set. pap. text. write for info. (*0-582-34312-7*, Pub. by Addison-Wesley) Longman.

Life & Teaching of Jesus Christ. J. S. Stewart. 192p. 1993. pap. 24.00 (*0-7152-0685-0*, Pub. by St Andrew) St Mut.

Life & Teaching of Jesus Christ. James S. Stewart. 1996. 13.90 (*0-7152-0705-9*, Pub. by St Andrew) St Mut.

Life & Teaching of Ludwig Hesser: Leader & Martyr of the Anabaptists, 1500-1529. Frederick L. Weis. LC 83-45633. reprint ed. 31.50 (*0-404-19875-9*) AMS Pr.

Life & Teaching of Naropa. Herbert V. Guenther. 1995. pap. 17.00 (*1-57062-101-2*, Pub. by Shambhala Pubns) Random.

***Life & Teaching of Pachomius.** Monks of Ampleforth Abbey. (Wellsprings of Life Ser.). 136p. 1999. pap. 6.95 (*0-85244-416-8*, 6115, Pub. by Gra1cewing) Morehouse Pub.

Life & Teaching of Satguru Sant Keshavadas. Sant Keshavadas. LC 77-81277. (Illus.). 150p. (Orig.). 1977. pap. 8.00 (*0-942508-12-2*) Vishwa.

Life & Teaching of Sri Anandamayi Ma. Alexander Lipski. (C). 1995. reprint ed. 12.00 (*81-208-0530-5*, Pub. by Motilal Bnarsidass) S Asia.

Life & Teaching of the Masters of the Far East, 6 vols., Set. Baird T. Spalding. 850p. 1996. pap. 47.95 (*0-87516-538-9*) DeVorss.

Life & Teaching of the Masters of the Far East, 6 vols., Vol. 1. Baird T. Spalding. 170p. 1979. pap. 9.95 (*0-87516-363-7*) DeVorss.

Life & Teaching of the Masters of the Far East, 6 vols., Vol. 2. Baird T. Spalding. 162p. 1989. pap. 9.95 (*0-87516-364-5*) DeVorss.

Life & Teaching of the Masters of the Far East, 6 vols., Vol. 3. Baird T. Spalding. 178p. 1989. pap. 9.95 (*0-87516-365-3*) DeVorss.

Life & Teaching of the Masters of the Far East, Vol. 4. Baird T. Spalding. 170p. 1989. pap. 9.95 (*0-87516-366-1*) DeVorss.

Life & Teaching of the Masters of the Far East, 6 vols., Vol. 5. Baird T. Spalding. 170p. 1989. pap. 9.95 (*0-87516-367-X*) DeVorss.

Life & Teaching of the Masters of the Far East, 6 vols., Vol. 6. Baird T. Spalding. Ed. by Arthur Vergara. LC 96-85608. (Illus.). 223p. 1996. pap. 9.95 (*0-87516-698-9*) DeVorss.

Life & Teachings of Buddha. Alexander C. Korosi. 143p. 1991. reprint ed. pap. 15.00 (*957-9482-41-1*, PRE013, Pub. by SMC Pub) Antique Collect.

Life & Teachings of Chokgyur Lingpa. Orgyen T. Rinpoche. 62p. 1996. pap. 7.95 (*962-7341-03-7*, Pub. by Rang Jung Yshe) Bookpeople.

Life & Teachings of Christ. James Stalker. (World Classic Reference Library). 483p. 1995. reprint ed. 19.99 (*0-529-10450-4*, LTC) World Publng.

Life & Teachings of Christ, Vol. 1. Gordon Lindsay. 1963. pap. 7.95 (*0-89985-967-4*) Christ for the Nations.

Life & Teachings of Christ, Vol. 2. Gordon Lindsay. 1963. per. 7.95 (*0-89985-968-2*) Christ for the Nations.

Life & Teachings of Christ, Vol. 3. Gordon Lindsay. 1963. reprint ed. per. 7.95 (*0-89985-969-0*) Christ for the Nations.

***Life & Teachings of Jesus.** Broadman & Holman Publishing Staff. LC 99-54018. (Shepherd's Notes Bible Summary Ser.). 1999. pap. 5.95 (*0-8054-9384-0*) Broadman.

Life & Teachings of Jesus: A Restatement of the Gospels. L. Preston Thomas. (Illus.). 256p. 1992. 17.00 (*0-9632517-0-8*) Einstein Schl.

Life & Teachings of Jesus: A Search. Duane J. Estes. (YA). (gr. 9-12). 1980. teacher ed. 16.25 (*1-881678-11-3*) CSEE.

Life & Teachings of Jesus of Nazareth. Daniel G. Samuels. 50p. 1989. pap. 5.00 (*1-887621-06-7*) Found Ch Divine Truth.

***Life & Teachings of Jesus of Nazareth: Includes the Four Gospels, Acts, Psalms & Proverbs.** American Bible Society Staff. 672p. 2000. pap. text 2.95 (*1-58516-095-4*) Am Bible.

Life & Teachings of Sai Baba of Shirdi. Antonio Rigopoulos. LC 91-40880. (SUNY Series in Religious Studies). 494p. (C). 1993. text 64.50 (*0-7914-1267-9*); pap. text 23.95 (*0-7914-1268-7*) State U NY Pr.

Life & Teachings of Sri Ma Anandamayi: A Bird on the Wing. Bithika Mukerji. LC 98-904654. (Sri Garib Das Oriental Ser.). viii, 347 p. 1998. write for info. (*81-7030-577-2*) Sri Satguru Pubns.

Life & Teachings of Two Immortals Vol. I: Kou Hong. Hua-Ching Ni. LC 91-62058. 176p. (Orig.). 1992. pap. 12.95 (*0-937064-47-5*) SevenStar Comm.

Life & Teachings of Two Immortals Vol. II: Chen Tuan. Hua-Ching Ni. LC 91-62484. 176p. (Orig.). 1993. pap. 12.95 (*0-937064-48-3*) SevenStar Comm.

Life & Terror in Stalin's Russia, 1934-1941. Robert W. Thurston. LC 95-41333. (Illus.). 296p. 1996. 32.50 (*0-300-06401-2*) Yale U Pr.

Life & Terror in Stalin's Russia, 1934-1941. Robert W. Thurston. (Illus.). 336p. 1996. pap. 17.00 (*0-300-07442-5*) Yale U Pr.

Life & Text of Julian of Norwich: The Poetics of Enclosure. M. Diane Krantz. LC 96-42974. (Studies in the Humanities: Vol. 32). X, 150p. (C). 1997. text 38.95 (*0-8204-3662-3*) P Lang Pubng.

Life & the Art of Change: A Journey to Consciousness, Awareness & Personal Growth. Gene David Oliver. LC 98-53163. 137p. 1999. 12.95 (*0-9668441-7-3*) LifeChange Pr.

Life & the Arts in the Baroque Palaces of Rome. Stefanie Walker. LC 98-50529. (Illus.). 320p. 1999. 70.00 (*0-300-07933-8*) Yale U Pr.

Life & the Arts in the Baroque Palaces of Rome. Stefanie Walker et al. LC 98-50529. 1999. write for info. (*0-300-07934-6*) Yale U Pr.

Life & the Doctrines of Paracelsus. Franz Hartmann. 367p. 1998. reprint ed. pap. 18.50 (*0-7873-0378-X*) Hlth Research.

Life & the Doctrines of Philippus Theophrastus, Bombast of Hohenheim Known As Paracelsus: Extracted from His Rare & Extensive Works & from Some Unpublished Manuscripts. Franz Hartmann. 387p. 1992. reprint ed. pap. 17.95 (*1-56459-185-9*) Kessinger Pub.

Life & the Poet. Stephen Spender. LC 74-7171. (Studies in Poetry: No. 38). (C). 1974. lib. bdg. 75.00 (*0-8383-1924-6*) M S G Haskell Hse.

Life & the Scientific & Medical Career of Benjamin Waterhouse: With Some Account of the Introduction of Vaccination in America, An Original Anthology, 2 vols., Set. Ed. by I. Bernard Cohen. LC 79-8004. (Three Centuries of Science in America Ser.). (Illus.). 1980. lib. bdg. 75.95 (*0-405-12591-7*) Ayer.

Life & Thought of Kanzo Uchimura, 1861-1930. Hiroshi Miura. LC 96-52638. 152p. 1997. pap. 22.00 (*0-8028-4205-4*) Eerdmans.

Life & Thought in the Early Middle Ages. Ed. by Robert S. Hoyt. LC 67-15065. 187p. reprint ed. pap. 58.00 (*0-8357-7666-2*, 205699400097) Bks Demand.

Life & Thought in the Greek & Roman World. Max Cary & Theodore J. Haarhoff. LC 85-14852. (Illus.). 355p. 1985. reprint ed. lib. bdg. 69.75 (*0-313-24986-5*, CLTG, Greenwood Pr) Greenwood.

Life & Thought in the Northern Church, C. 1100 - C. 1700. Ed. by Diana Wood. LC 98-32347. (Studies in Church History). (Illus.). 576p. 1999. 75.00 (*0-9529733-2-4*) Boydell & Brewer.

Life & Thought of Chang Hseuh-ch'eng (1738-1801) David S. Nivison. ix, 336p. 1966. 47.50 (*0-8047-0230-6*) Stanford U Pr.

Life & Thought of Henry Gerhard Appenzeller (1858-1902) Missionary to Korea. Daniel M. Davies. LC 87-11041. (Studies in the History of Missions). 512p. lib. bdg. 119.95 (*0-88946-069-8*) E Mellen.

Life & Thought of John Gill (1697-1771) A Tercentennial Appreciation. Michael A. Haykin. LC 97-27447. (Studies in the History of Christian Thought, 0081-8607: No. 77). (Illus.). xvi, 240p. 1997. 102.50 (*90-04-10744-4*, NLG 138) Brill Academic Pubs.

Life & Thought of Josiah Royce. rev. expanded ed. John Clendenning. LC 98-25325. (Library of American Philosophy). (Illus.). 432p. 1998. pap. 24.95 (*0-8265-1322-0*); lib. bdg. 49.95 (*0-8265-1312-3*) Vanderbilt U Pr.

Life & Thought of Kedarnath Dutta Bhaktivinoda: A Hindu Encounter with Modernity. Shukavak Das. 400p. (C). 1996. pap. 40.00 (*1-889756-25-3*) Sanskrit Relgns Inst.

Life & Thought of Michael Sattler. C. Arnold Snyder. LC 83-22835. (Studies in Anabaptist & Mennonite History: Vol. 27). 264p. 1984. 19.99 (*0-8361-1264-4*) Herald Pr.

Life & Thought of Orson Pratt. Breck England. LC 85-7478. (Illus.). 375p. reprint ed. pap. 116.30 (*0-7837-2605-8*, 204276900006) Bks Demand.

Life & Thought of Sankaracarya. Govind Chandra. (C). 1994. 22.50 (*81-208-1104-6*, Pub. by M Manoharial) S Asia.

Life & Thought of Siger of Brabant, Thirteenth-Century Parisian Philosopher: An Examination of His Views on the Relationship of Philosophy & Theology. Tony Dodd. LC 97-52349. 1998. 119.95 (*0-7734-8477-9*) E Mellen.

Life & Thought of Soren Kierkegaard. Timothy T. Lin. (Masterworks of Literature Ser.). 1974. pap. 13.95 (*0-8084-0377-X*) NCUP.

***Life & Thought Of St. Edith Stein.** Freda M. Oben. LC 00-44179. 2000. write for info. (*0-8189-0846-7*) Alba.

Life & Thought of Yeh Shih. Winston W. Lo. LC 73-92410. 216p. reprint ed. pap. 67.00 (*0-7837-5014-5*, 204468100004) Bks Demand.

Life & Time of Ambroise Pare, 1510-1590. Ambroise Pare. Ed. by Francis R. Packard. LC 79-160607. (Illus.). 1972. reprint ed. 23.95 (*0-405-08834-5*, Pub. by Blom Pubns) Ayer.

Life & Time of Niccolo Machiavelli, 2 vols., Set. Pasquale Villari. LC 68-25275. (World History Ser.: No. 48). 1969. reprint ed. lib. bdg. 150.00 (*0-8383-0175-4*) M S G Haskell Hse.

Life & Time of Oliver Goldsmith. John Forster. 1988. reprint ed. lib. bdg. 69.00 (*0-7812-0018-0*) Rprt Serv.

Life & Time of Sir Kai Ho Kai. rev. ed. G. H. Choa. (Illus.). 320p. (C). text 20.00 (*962-201-873-4*, Pub. by Chinese Univ) U of Mich Pr.

Life & Times: Recollections of Eliza Cox Carter. Ed. by Judith Baxter & Beth Quigley. (Mercury Ser.: History No. 48). (Illus.). 144p. 1997. pap. 19.95 (*0-660-15970-8*, Pub. by CN Mus Civilization) U of Wash Pr.

Life & Times from the Clay County Courier Newspaper, Published at Corning, Arkansas, 1902-1903. Cathy Barnes. 154p. 1997. pap. 23.00 (*1-56546-122-3*) Arkansas Res.

Life & Times from the Clay County Courier Newspaper, 1893-1899, Published in Corning, Arkansas. Cathy Barnes. 138p. 1997. pap. 21.00 (*1-56546-112-6*) Arkansas Res.

Life & Times from the Clay County Courier Newspaper, 1900-1901, Published in Corning, Arkansas. Cathy Barnes. 135p. 1997. pap. 21.00 (*1-56546-120-7*) Arkansas Res.

Life & Times from the Clay County Courier Newspaper, 1904-1905, Published in Corning, Arkansas. Cathy Barnes. 139p. 1998. pap. 21.00 (*1-56546-129-0*) Arkansas Res.

Life & Times from the Clay County Courier Newspaper, 1906-1907 Published in Corning, Arkansas. Cathy Barnes. 133p. 1998. pap. 21.00 (*1-56546-130-4*) Arkansas Res.

Life & Times from the Clay County Courier Newspaper, 1908-1909 Published in Corning, Arkansas. 157p. 1998. pap. 23.00 (*1-56546-131-2*) Arkansas Res.

Life & Times from the Clay County Courier Newspaper, 1910, Published in Corning, Arkansas. Cathy Barnes. 199p. 1999. pap. 26.00 (*1-56546-133-9*) Arkansas Res.

Life & Times from the Clay County Courier Newspaper, 1911, Published in Corning, Arkansas. Cathy Barnes. 190p. 1999. pap. 25.00 (*1-56546-134-7*) Arkansas Res.

Life & Times from the Clay County Courier Newspaper, 1912, Published in Corning, Arkansas. Cathy Barnes. 172p. 1999. pap. 25.00 (*1-56546-135-5*) Arkansas Res.

***Life & Times from the Clay County Courier Newspaper, 1913: Published in Corning, Arkansas.** Cathy Barnes. 139p. 2000. pap. 22.00 (*1-56546-163-0*) Arkansas Res.

***Life & Times from the Clay County Courier Newspaper, 1913: Published in Corning, Arkansas.** Cathy Barnes. 176p. 2000. pap. 25.00 (*1-56546-170-3*) Arkansas Res.

***Life & Times from the Clay County Courier Newspaper, 1915: Published in Corning, Arkansas.** Cathy Barnes. 176p. 2000. pap. 25.00 (*1-56546-173-8*) Arkansas Res.

Life & Times in Brunswick, Ohio. Sharon L. Kraynek. 199p. 1995. per. 16.95 (*1-55856-187-0*, 421) Closson Pr.

Life & Times of A. B. Durand. John Durand. 232p. 1993. reprint ed. lib. bdg. 79.00 (*0-7812-5269-5*) Rprt Serv.

Life & Times of a Country Doctor. James E. Albrecht. (Illus.). 280p. 1993. pap. 18.00 (*0-9639102-0-5*) Jjea enter.

***Life & Times of a Country Peddler.** Ira G. Carter. LC 99-93574. 117p. 1999. pap. 10.95 (*0-533-13070-0*) Vantage.

***Life & Times of A. K. Hangal.** A. K. Hangal. 1999. pap. 14.00 (*81-207-2163-2*, Pub. by Sterling Pubs) S Asia.

Life & Times of a Locomotive Engineer. Charles F. Steffes. 305p. 1993. 24.20 (*1-880365-13-8*) Prof Pr NC.

***Life & Times of a Locomotive Engineer.** Charles F. Steffes. (Illus.). 312p. 1998. pap. 19.95 (*0-911868-94-1*, C94) Carstens Pubns.

Life & Times of a Vietnam Vet: A Collection of War Poems. Pedro L. Pino. LC 96-85361. (Illus.). 56p. (Orig.). 1996. pap. 5.95 (*0-9646450-3-3*) DeeMar Commun.

Life & Times of Agnes Tait. Lydia M. Pena. (Illus.). (Orig.). 1983. pap. text 14.95 (*0-9612982-0-0*) Pena Lydia.

***Life & Times of Akhnaton: Pharaoh of Egypt.** Arthur Weigall. LC 00-34545. 2000. reprint ed. pap. 17.95 (*0-8154-1092-1*, Pub. by Cooper Sq) Natl Bk Netwk.

***Life & Times of Alan Dower Blumlein.** R. W. Burns. (IEE History of Technology Ser.: No. 24). 534p. 1999. boxed set 95.00 (*0-85296-773-X*) INSPEC Inc.

Life & Times of Alfred the Great. C. Plummer. LC 68-25261. (English Biography Ser.: No. 31). 1969. reprint ed. lib. bdg. 75.00 (*0-8383-0230-0*) M S G Haskell Hse.

Life & Times of Alfred the Great. Charles Plummer. LC 72-131802. 1970. reprint ed. 49.00 (*0-403-00689-9*) Scholarly.

Life & Times of Ali Ibn Isa: The Good Vizier. Harold Bowen. LC 77-180320. (Mid-East Studies). reprint ed. 42.50 (*0-404-56215-9*) AMS Pr.

Life & Times of Alvah Crocker. William B. Wheelwright. Ed. by Stuart Bruchey. LC 80-1351. (Railroads Ser.). (Illus.). 1981. reprint ed. lib. bdg. 18.95 (*0-405-13822-9*) Ayer.

Life & Times of an Ordinary Captain: Forty Years of Flying. Antti Tervasmaa. Tr. by Richard A. Impola from FIN. (Illus.). 183p. 1994. 16.00 (*1-880474-08-5*) FATA.

Life & Times of Ann Bailey: Pioneer Heroine of the Kanawha Valley. 2nd ed. Virgil Lewis. LC 98-88393. Orig. Title: Life & Times of Anne Bailey. (Illus.). 96p. 1998. reprint ed. pap. 9.95 (*0-9667246-0-7*) Discovery WV.

Life & Times of Anne Bailey see Life & Times of Ann Bailey: Pioneer Heroine of the Kanawha Valley

Life & Times of Anne Royall. Sarah H. Porter. LC 72-2619. (American Women Ser.: Images & Realities). 302p. 1974. reprint ed. 23.95 (*0-405-04472-0*) Ayer.

***Life & Times of Archbishop Fulton J. Sheen.** Myles P. Murphy. LC 99-87648. 2000. pap. 14.95 (*0-8189-0842-4*) Alba.

Life & Times of Augustus Rapp, the Small Town Showman: Written by Himself. Augustus Rapp. Ed. by Marcia Boggs. (Illus.). 201p. 1991. 28.95 (*0-916638-44-8*, D M Magic Bks); pap. 15.95 (*0-916638-45-6*) Meyerbooks.

Life & Times of Backus by Hovey. Alvah Hovey. 1993. 21.99 (*0-87377-918-5*) GAM Pubns.

Life & Times of Berwick-upon-Tweed. Raymond Lamont-Brown. 200p. (C). 1989. pap. text 30.00 (*0-85976-233-5*, Pub. by J Donald) St Mut.

Life & Times of Bobby Jones: Portrait of a Gentleman. Sidney L. Matthew. (Illus.). 454p. 1995. text 25.00 (*0-9634887-1-6*) Impreg Quadrilat.

Life & Times of Buck Hooey. Daniel Bruce. 1999. pap. 12.50 (*0-88739-195-8*) Creat Arts Bk.

***Life & Times of Byron O'Tool.** Joseph Maciaszek. LC 99-93749. 2000. 13.95 (*0-533-13132-4*) Vantage.

Life & Times of Captain George W. Ely, 1840-1922: Secretary of the New York Stock Exchange, 1874-1919. 3rd large type ed. Bruce Campbell Adamson. Ed. by George W. Ely, III et al. (Illus.). 140p. 1996. 15.00 (*1-892501-01-5*) B C Adamson.

Life & Times of Charles II, 1. Christopher Falkus. 2000. pap. 18.95 (*1-56649-014-6*) Welcome Rain.

Life & Times of Charles II. Christopher Falkus. Ed. by Antonia Fraser. (Kings & Queens of England Ser.). (Illus.). 224p. 1992. 24.95 (*1-55859-446-9*) Abbeville Pr.

Life & Times of Charles II. large type ed. Christopher Falkus. 24.95 (*1-85695-073-5*, Pub. by ISIS Lrg Prnt) Transaction Pubs.

Life & Times of Chester L. Simmons. Odie Hawkins. 208p. 1991. mass mkt. 3.50 (*0-87067-341-6*) Holloway.

Life & Times of Cleopatra, Queen of Egypt: A Study in the Origin of the Roman Empire. rev. ed. Arthur E. Weigall. LC 69-10168. (Illus.). 445p. 1968. reprint ed. lib. bdg. 48.50 (*0-8371-0261-8*, WECE, Greenwood Pr) Greenwood.

Life & Times of Col. James Fisk, Jr. R. W. McAlpine. Ed. by Stuart Bruchey. LC 80-1329. (Railroads Ser.). (Illus.). 1981. reprint ed. lib. bdg. 35.95 (*0-405-13803-2*) Ayer.

Life & Times of Commander E. C. "Zeke," Cortez: Not Just a "Scuttlebut" David Wilde. (Illus.). 200p. (Orig.). (C). 1996. pap. 10.00 (*1-882204-19-0*) Wilde Pub.

***Life & Times of Commander E.C. "Zeke" Cortez Jr. USNR: Not Just "Scuttlebutt"** David Wilde. (Illus.). 200p. 1999. text 45.00 (*1-882204-02-6*) Wilde Pub.

***Life & Times of Commander E.C. "Zeke" Cortez Jr. USNR: Not Just "Scuttlebutt"** rev. ed. David Wilde. (SPA.). 200p. 1999. 60.00 (*1-882204-33-6*) Wilde Pub.

Life & Times of Constantine the Great: The First Christian Emperor. D. G. Kousoulas. 511p. 1997. 24.95 (*1-887750-61-4*) Rutledge Bks.

Life & Times of Cotton Mather. Abijah P. Marvin. LC 72-1979. (American Biography Ser.: No. 32). 1972. reprint ed. lib. bdg. 75.00 (*0-8383-1454-6*) M S G Haskell Hse.

Life & Times of Darryl Sutter: Wit, Wisdom & Tougher Love. E. C. Mcenery. (Illus.). 128p. 1999. pap. 12.95 (*1-57098-288-0*) Roberts Rinehart.

Life & Times of David Humphreys, Soldier-Statesman-Poet: Belov'd of Washington, 2 vols., Set. Francis L. Humphreys. (BCL1 - U. S. History Ser.). 1991. reprint ed. lib. bdg. 150.00 (*0-7812-6126-0*) Rprt Serv.

Life & Times of David Zeisberger, the Western Pioneer & Apostle of the Indians. Edmund A. De Schweinitz. LC 70-146391. (First American Frontier Ser.). 1971. reprint ed. 42.95 (*0-405-02844-X*) Ayer.

Life & Times of Deshbandhu Chittaranjan Das. Rathindra N. Sen. 1989. 11.00 (*81-85119-55-4*, Pub. by Northern Bk Ctr) S Asia.

Life & Times of Dudsberry. Jan Dawson. 29p. 1995. pap. 4.95 (*0-9626939-9-5*) Janelle Pubns.

Life & Times of Dundee. Christopher Whatley et al. 220p. (C). 1996. pap. 30.00 (*0-85976-388-9*, Pub. by J Donald) St Mut.

Life & Times of Edward Alleyn. George L. Hosking. LC 78-128935. reprint ed. 27.50 (*0-404-03339-3*) AMS Pr.

Life & Times of Edward Fred Kermott, Vol. I. Edward F. Kermott. LC 93-91840. 304p. 1994. pap. 12.95 (*0-9641997-0-X*) E F Kermott.

Life & Times of Elizabeth I. Neville Williams. Ed. by Antonia Fraser. (Kings & Queens of England Ser.). (Illus.). 224p. 1992. 24.95 (*1-55859-448-5*) Abbeville Pr.

Life & Times of Ellen von Frankenberg, Vol. 1. Karen Bell-Kanner. (Choreography & Dance Studies). xvii, 167p. 1991. text 22.00 (*3-7186-5110-6*, Harwood Acad Pubs) Gordon & Breach.

Life & Times of Emile Zola. F. W. Hemmings. LC 77-73899. (Illus.). 1977. 4.95 (*0-685-04565-X*, Scribners Ref) Mac Lib Ref.

Life & Times of Emma Goldman: A Curriculum for Middle & High School Students: Primary Historical Documents. Candace S. Falk et al. LC 92-45687. 1992. 13.00 (*0-9635443-0-6*) E Goldman.

Life & Times of Ephraim Cutler Prepared from His Journals & Correspondence by His Daughter Julia Perkins Cutler with Biographical Sketches of Jervis Cutler & William Parker Cutler. Julia P. Cutler. LC 71-146389. (First American Frontier Ser.). (Illus.). 1971. reprint ed. 35.95 (*0-405-02840-7*) Ayer.

Life & Times of Esther Marie Ingold Stone. Esther Marie Stone. Ed. by Kami Spangenberg. 76p. 1995. 19.95 (*1-886701-01-6*) Lifescapes.

Life & Times of Falkirk. Ian Scott. 220p. 1996. pap. 30.00 (*0-85976-386-2*, Pub. by J Donald) St Mut.

Life & Times of Francis Marion & Her Friends. Beauchamp. 1995. 25.00 (*0-02-508105-5*) Macmillan.

Life & Times of Fray Junipero Serra. rev. ed. Francis J. Weber. (Illus.). 104p. 1989. reprint ed. pap. 6.95 (*0-945092-09-1*) EZ Nature.

Life & Times of Frederick Douglass. Frederick Douglass. (American Biography Ser.). 640p. 1991. reprint ed. lib. bdg. 109.00 (*0-7812-8110-5*) Rprt Serv.

Life & Times of Frederick Douglass. Frederick Douglass. (Notable American Authors Ser.). 1992. reprint ed. lib. bdg. 75.00 (*0-7812-2676-7*) Rprt Serv.

Life & Times of Frederick Douglass: The Complete Autobiography. Frederick Douglass. LC 62-12834. 640p. 1962. pap. 14.95 (*0-02-002350-2*) Macmillan.

Life & Times of Frederick Reynolds, 2 Vols., 1 bk. 2nd ed. Frederick Reynolds. LC 74-88489. 840p. 1972. 49.95 (*0-405-08882-5*, Pub. by Blom Pubns) Ayer.

Life & Times of G. V. Black. Charles N. Pappas. (Illus.). 128p. (Orig.). 1983. pap. text 38.00 (*0-931386-55-1*) Quint Pub Co.

Life & Times of Geoffrey Dowling. Charles Calnan. (Illus.). 304p. 1992. 85.00 (*0-632-03505-6*) Blackwell Sci.

An Asterisk (*) at the beginning of an entry indicates that the title is appearing for the first time.

Life & Times of Girolamo Savonarola, 2 vols., Set. Pasquale Villari. LC 68-25276. (World History Ser.: No. 48). 1969. reprint ed. lib. bdg. 150.00 (*0-8383-0174-6*) M S G Haskell Hse.

Life & Times of Girolamo Savonarola, 2 vols., Set. Pasquale Villari. 1988. reprint ed. lib. bdg. 75.00 (*0-7812-0799-1*) Rprt Serv.

Life & Times of Goethe. Herman Grimm. LC 78-152986. (Select Bibliographies Reprint Ser.). 1977. reprint ed. 31.95 (*0-8369-5738-5*) Ayer.

Life & Times of Gregorii Rasputin. Alex De Jonge. (Illus.). 363p. 1989. pap. 10.95 (*0-88184-484-5*) Carroll & Graf.

Life & Times of Gustav Likan. Scott Michaud. (Illus.). 192p. 1994. 49.95 (*1-880092-15-8*) Bright Bks TX.

Life & Times of Henry Bellmon. Henry Bellmon & Pat C. Bellmon. LC 91-73539. (Illus.). 381p. 1995. 3.00 (*0-933031-47-5*) Coun Oak Bks.

Life & Times of Henry Clarke of Jamaica, 1828-1907. James Walvin. LC 94-342. 240p. (Orig.). 1994. pap. 24.50 (*0-7146-4551-6*, Pub. by F Cass Pubs) Intl Spec Bk.

Life & Times of Henry Crabb Robinson. Edith J. Morley. LC 71-115396. 1970. reprint ed. 32.50 (*0-404-05368-8*) AMS Pr.

Life & Times of Henry VIII. Robert Lacey. Ed. by Antonia Fraser. (Kings & Queens of England Ser.). (Illus.). 224p. 1992. 24.95 (*1-55859-451-5*) Abbeville Pr.

Life & Times of Horatio Hornblower. C. Northcote Parkinson. LC 74-590381. 304p. (J). 1970. write for info. (*0-7181-0787-X*, M Joseph) Viking Penguin.

Life & Times of Horatio Hornblower. C. Northcote Parkinson. 1994. reprint ed. lib. bdg. 32.95 (*1-56849-318-5*) Buccaneer Bks.

Life & Times of Horatio Hornblower: A Fictional Biography of Horatio Hornblower. C. Northcote Parkinson. 1998. pap. 10.95 (*0-7509-2109-9*) Bks Intl VA.

Life & Times of Horst Wessel. Donald G. Brownlow. LC 94-68121. 1996. 22.95 (*0-8158-0507-1*) Chris Mass.

Life & Times of Indira Gandhi. O. P. Ralhan & S. K. Sharma. 1994. pap. 250.00 (*81-7451-003-6*, Pub. by Print Hse) St Mut.

Life & Times of Inverness. Ed. by N. S. Newton. LC 97-178126. 250p. 1996. pap. 45.00 (*0-85976-442-7*, Pub. by J Donald) St Mut.

Life & Times of James Willard Schultz (Apikuni) Warren L. Hanna. LC 85-40944. (Illus.). 400p. 1986. 28.95 (*0-8061-1985-3*) U of Okla Pr.

***Life & Times of Jesus.** William G. Luff. (Illus.). 1999. pap. 10.00 (*0-7880-1400-5*) CSS OH.

Life & Times of Jesus the Messiah. Alfred Edersheim. 1580p. 1990. 39.99 (*0-529-10085-1*, LTJN) World Publng.

Life & Times of Jesus the Messiah. rev. ed. Alfred Edersheim. (Illus.). 1114p. 1993. 29.95 (*0-943575-83-4*) Hendrickson MA.

Life & Times of Joe McCarthy. Thomas C. Reeves. LC 79-3730. 1981. 19.95 (*0-8128-2337-0*, Scrbrough Hse) Madison Bks UPA.

Life & Times of Joe McCarthy: A Biography. Thomas C. Reeves. LC 83-42968. (Illus.). 848p. 1983. pap. 14.95 (*0-8128-6200-7*, Scrbrough Hse) Madison Bks UPA.

Life & Times of Joe McCarthy: A Biography. Thomas C. Reeves. LC 97-26679. (Illus.). 832p. 1997. reprint ed. pap. 19.95 (*1-56833-101-0*) Madison Bks UPA.

Life & Times of John Barrymore. John Barrymore. 1978. reprint ed. 15.85 (*0-89966-250-1*) Buccaneer Bks.

Life & Times of John Calvin, 2 vols., Set. Paul E. Henry. Tr. by Henry Stebbing from GER. LC 83-45613. reprint ed. 95.00 (*0-404-19831-7*) AMS Pr.

Life & Times of John Calvin: With an Earnest Appeal for the Adoption of Open-Air Preaching. Charles W. Banks. LC 83-45599. reprint ed. 42.50 (*0-404-19867-8*) AMS Pr.

Life & Times of John Dickerson, 1732-1808. Charles J. Stille. 1993. reprint ed. lib. bdg. 89.00 (*0-7812-5838-3*) Rprt Serv.

Life & Times of John England. Peter K. Guilday. LC 70-83422. (Religion in America, Ser. 1). 1970. reprint ed. 59.95 (*0-405-00247-5*) Ayer.

Life & Times of John Hooper (c. 1500-1555) Bishop of Gloucester. E. W. Hunt. LC 92-23477. (Illus.). 396p. 1992. text 99.95 (*0-7734-9156-2*) E Mellen.

Life & Times of John Hus: The Bohemian Reformation of the Fifteenth Century, 2 vols., Set. Ezra H. Gillett. LC 77-85271. reprint ed. 94.50 (*0-404-16150-2*) AMS Pr.

Life & Times of John Manjiro. Donald R. Bernard. (C). 1992. text 29.68 (*0-07-004947-5*) McGraw.

Life & Times of John Trevisa, Medieval Scholar. David C. Fowler. LC 95-7886. 288p. 1995. 40.00 (*0-295-97427-3*) U of Wash Pr.

Life & Times of Joseph Warren. R. Frothingham. LC 72-146148. (Era of the American Revolution Ser.). 1971. reprint ed. lib. bdg. 59.50 (*0-306-70133-2*) Da Capo.

Life & Times of Juan Jose d'Elhuyar: Discoverer of Tungston in 18th Century New Granada. Bernardo J. Caycedo. (Illus.). 290p. 1981. 25.00 (*0-87291-149-7*) Coronado Pr.

Life & Times of Laurence Sterne, 2 vols., Set. Wilbur L. Cross. (BCL1-PR English Literature Ser.). 1992. reprint ed. lib. bdg. 150.00 (*0-7812-7410-9*) Rprt Serv.

Life & Times of Leith. Ed. by James Marshall. 220p. (C). 1989. text 45.00 (*0-85976-148-7*, Pub. by J Donald) St Mut.

Life & Times of Leith. James Marshall. 220p. (C). 1996. pap. 26.00 (*0-85976-128-2*, Pub. by J Donald) St Mut.

Life & Times of Lewis Wetzel. C. B. Allman. (Illus.). 244p. (Orig.). 1995. reprint ed. pap. text 18.00 (*0-7884-0204-8*) Heritage Bk.

Life & Times of Little Richard. rev. ed. Charles White. (Illus.). 337p. 1994. reprint ed. pap. 13.95 (*0-306-80552-9*) Da Capo.

Life & Times of Louis-Amadeus Rappe, First Bishop of Cleveland. John F. Lyons. (Illus.). 300p. 1997. 29.95 (*0-9656426-0-7*) Bishop Pr OH.

Life & Times of Lydia E. Pinkham. Robert C. Washburn. LC 75-39280. (Getting & Spending: The Consumer's Dilemma Ser.). (Illus.). 1976. reprint ed. 24.95 (*0-405-08055-7*) Ayer.

Life & Times of Maharaja Juddha Shumsher Jung Bahadur Rana of Nepal. Ishwari Prasad. viii, 358p. (C). 1996. 35.00 (*81-7024-756-X*, Pub. by Ashish Pub Hse) Nataraj Bks.

Life & Times of Major Fiction. Jonathan Baumbach. LC 86-29215. 208p. 1987. 15.95 (*0-932511-08-2*) Fiction Coll.

Life & Times of Mary Ann McCracken, 1770-1866: A Belfast Panorama. Mary McNeill. LC 98-114290. 328p. 1988. pap. 19.95 (*0-85640-603-1*, Pub. by Blackstaff Pr) Dufour.

Life & Times of Mary Ann McCracken, 1770-1866: A Belfast Panorama. Mary McNeill. 328p. 1988. reprint ed. pap. 11.95 (*0-85640-403-9*, Pub. by Blackstaff Pr) Dufour.

Life & Times of Master John Hus. Franz Lutzow. LC 77-84728. (Illus.). reprint ed. 57.50 (*0-404-16128-6*) AMS Pr.

Life & Times of Menelik II: Ethiopia 1844-1913. Harold G. Marcus. LC 94-48485. 1995. 49.95 (*1-56902-009-4*); pap. 16.95 (*1-56902-010-8*) Red Sea Pr.

Life & Times of Miami Beach. Ann Armbruster. LC 94-11572. 224p. 1995. 45.00 (*0-394-57052-9*) Knopf.

Life & Times of Michael K. J. M. Coetzee. LC 84-19085. 192p. 1985. pap. 11.95 (*0-14-007448-1*, Penguin Bks) Viking Penguin.

***Life & Times of Michael Lizza, Vol. 8.** unabridged ed. Michael Lizza. (Illus.). 410p. 1998. write for info. (*1-929326-51-3*) Hal Bar Pubg.

***Life & Times of Mr. Rip-Off.** David McHugh. 184p. 1999. pap. 15.00 (*0-8059-4770-1*) Dorrance.

Life & Times of Modern Physics: History of Physics II. Ed. by Melba Phillips. LC 92-12669. (Readings from Physics Today Ser.: No. 4). 1992. 44.95 (*0-88318-846-5*) Spr-Verlag.

Life & Times of Muhammad. John Glubb. LC 97-51893. 416p. 1998. pap. 17.95 (*1-56833-112-6*) Madison Bks UPA.

Life & Times of Muhammad. John Glubb. LC 74-87954. 1970. reprint ed. pap. 14.95 (*0-8128-1393-6*, Scrbrough Hse) Madison Bks UPA.

Life & Times of Nargis. T. J. George. (C). 1994. text 28.00 (*81-7223-149-0*, Pub. by Indus Pub) S Asia.

Life & Times of Niccolo Machiavelli, 2 vols. in 1. Pasquale Villari. Tr. by Linda Villari from ITA. LC 79-115284. (Illus.). 1058p. 1972. reprint ed. 39.00 (*0-403-00033-5*) Scholarly.

Life & Times of Oliver Goldsmith. John Forster. LC 70-145020. (Literature Ser.). (Illus.). 496p. 1972. reprint ed. 69.00 (*0-403-00967-7*) Scholarly.

Life & Times of One Room Country Schools. Donald Gruber. 92p. (Orig.). 1990. pap. 7.95 (*0-9625791-0-6*) D M Gruber.

Life & Times of Our Family. William W. McNeal. 65p. 1993. ring bd., vinyl bd. 34.50 (*0-9636747-0-6*) Wrthngton Hse.

Life & Times of Pancho Villa. Friedrich Katz. LC 97-47271. 1032p. 1998. pap. 29.95 (*0-8047-3046-6*) Stanford U Pr.

Life & Times of Pancho Villa. Friedrich Katz. LC 97-47271. (Illus.). 985p. 1998. 85.00 (*0-8047-3045-8*) Stanford U Pr.

Life & Times of Postmodernity. Keith Tester. LC 92-45840. 224p. (C). 1993. pap. 22.99 (*0-415-09832-7*) Routledge.

Life & Times of R. Crumb: Comments from Contemporaries. Monte Beauchamp. LC 98-18842. (Illus.). 192p. 1998. pap. 17.95 (*0-312-19571-0*) St Martin.

Life & Times of Rabin Fadl Allah. W. K. Hallam. 368p. 1987. 50.00 (*0-7223-0959-7*, Pub. by A H S Ltd) St Mut.

Life & Times of Ralf: Only a Dog. unabridged ed. Betty Webster Bishop. (Illus.). 20p. 1997. spiral bd. 4.00 (*1-929326-36-X*) Hal Bar Pubg.

***Life & Times of Reb Rephoel Soloveitchik of Brisk.** B. C. Glaberson. 1999. 19.95 (*1-58330-361-8*) Feldheim.

Life & Times of Red Jacket. J. Niles Hubbard. 356p. reprint ed. pap. 24.50 (*0-941567-49-4*) J C & A L Fawcett.

Life & Times of Red Jacket or Sa-Go-Ye-Wat-Ha. William L. Stone. LC 71-108543. (American Indian History Ser.). 1970. reprint ed. 49.00 (*0-403-00227-3*) Scholarly.

***Life & Times of Redd Foxx.** Dempsey J. Travis. LC 98-83243. (Illus.). 223p. 1999. 23.75 (*0-941484-29-7*) Urban Res Pr.

Life & Times of Richard III. Anthony Cheetham. Ed. by Antonia Fraser. (Kings & Queens of England Ser.). (Illus.). 224p. 1992. 24.95 (*1-55859-447-7*) Abbeville Pr.

Life & Times of Ridgeway, Virginia, 1728-1990. Ruth Pace & Mary P. McGee. LC 90-37899. (Illus.). 292p. 1990. 42.00 (*0-936015-25-X*) Pocahontas Pr.

Life & Times of Robert G. Fowler: The Greatest Aviator in the World. Maria Schell Burden. (Illus.). 160p. 1999. pap. 18.00 (*0-87505-369-6*) Borden.

Life & Times of Robert the Rhino Bk. 1: The First Encounter. Timothy Keeler. (Illus.). 40p. (J). (gr. 2). 1996. pap. 12.00 (*0-8059-3900-8*) Dorrance.

Life & Times of Rochelle A. Gray. Rochelle A. Gray. Ed. by Kami Spangenberg. (Illus.). 76p. 1995. 19.95 (*1-886701-00-8*) Lifescapes.

Life & Times of Ron Brown: A Memoir by His Daughter. Tracey L. Brown. LC 97-32016. (Illus.). 256p. 1998. 26.00 (*0-688-15320-8*, Wm Morrow) Morrow Avon.

Life & Times of Samuel Bowles, 2 vols. Samuel Bowles. Ed. by George S. Merriam. LC 75-87417. (American Scene Ser.). 1970. reprint ed. lib. bdg. 95.00 (*0-306-71562-7*) Da Capo.

Life & Times of Samuel Bowles, 2 vols., Set. George S. Merriam. LC 76-108512. 1970. reprint ed. 49.00 (*0-403-00220-6*) Scholarly.

Life & Times of Sergeant Smith Prentiss. Joseph D. Shields. LC 76-179538. (Select Bibliographies Reprint Ser.). 1977. reprint ed. 26.95 (*0-8369-6667-8*) Ayer.

Life & Times of Shaikh Salman Bin Hamad Al-Khalifa: Ruler of Bahrain, 1942-1961. Andrew Wheatcroft. LC 94-32908. (Illus.). 256p. 1995. 59.50 (*0-7103-0495-1*) Routledge.

Life & Times of Sir Alexander Tilloch Galt. Oscar D. Skelton. (BCL1 - History - Canada Ser.). 586p. 1991. reprint ed. lib. bdg. 99.00 (*0-7812-6359-X*) Rprt Serv.

Life & Times of Sir Alfred Chester Beatty. A. J. Wilson. 315p. 1985. text 36.00 (*0-947754-12-1*) Metal Bulletin.

Life & Times of Sir Goldsworthy Gurney: Gentleman Scientist & Inventor 1793-1875. Dale H. Porter. LC 97-31833. (Illus.). 288p. 1998. 43.50 (*0-934223-50-5*) Lehigh Univ Pr.

Life & Times of Sir Thomas Malory. P. J. Field. (Arthurian Studies). 230p. 1999. pap. 29.95 (*0-85991-566-2*, DS Brewer) Boydell & Brewer.

Life & Times of Soviet Socialism. Alex F. Dowlah & John E. Elliott. LC 96-24358. 296p. 1997. 65.00 (*0-275-95629-6*, Praeger Pubs) Greenwood.

Life & Times of St. Andrews. Raymond Lamont-Brown. 220p. (C). 1996. pap. 35.00 (*0-85976-236-X*, Pub. by J Donald) St Mut.

Life & Times of St. Bernard see St. Bernard of Clairvaux: Oracle of the 12th Century (1091-1153) Abbot, Confessor & Doctor of the Church

Life & Times of St. Bernard of Clairvaux. James C. Morison. 1977. lib. bdg. 59.95 (*0-8490-2162-6*) Gordon Pr.

Life & Times of Stein: or Germany & Prussia in the Napoleonic Age, 3 Vols. John R. Seeley. LC 68-26368. (World History Ser.: No. 48). 1969. reprint ed. lib. bdg. 150.00 (*0-8383-0179-7*) M S G Haskell Hse.

Life & Times of Stein: or Germany & Prussia in the Napoleonic Age, 3 vols., Set. John R. Seeley. LC 68-23324. 1968. reprint ed. lib. bdg. 125.00 (*0-8371-9950-6*, SELS) Greenwood.

Life & Times of Stein: or Germany & Prussia in the Napoleonic Age, 3 vols., Set. John R. Seeley. LC 70-108538. 1970. reprint ed. 45.00 (*0-403-00231-1*) Scholarly.

Life & Times of Stein: or Germany & Prussia in the Napoleonic Age, 3 vols., Vol. 1. John R. Seeley. LC 68-23324. 1968. reprint ed. lib. bdg. 45.00 (*0-8371-0215-4*, SELA) Greenwood.

Life & Times of Stein: or Germany & Prussia in the Napoleonic Age, 3 vols., Vol. 2. John R. Seeley. LC 68-23324. 1968. reprint ed. lib. bdg. 45.00 (*0-8371-0888-8*, SELB) Greenwood.

Life & Times of Stein: or Germany & Prussia in the Napoleonic Age, 3 vols., Vol. 3. John R. Seeley. LC 68-23324. 1968. reprint ed. lib. bdg. 45.00 (*0-8371-0889-6*, SELC) Greenwood.

Life & Times of Stephen Higginson. Thomas W. Higginson. (Notable American Authors Ser.). 1992. reprint ed. lib. bdg. 75.00 (*0-7812-3109-4*) Rprt Serv.

Life & Times of Sukarno. C. L. Penders. LC 74-369. 224p. 1974. 32.50 (*0-8386-1546-5*) Fairleigh Dickinson.

Life & Times of Sydney & Beatrice Webb. Harrison. LC 99-15616. 2000. text 75.00 (*0-312-22641-1*) St Martin.

Life & Times of Tennyson from 1809 to 1850. Thomas R. Lounsbury. (Notable American Authors Ser.). 1999. reprint ed. lib. bdg. 125.00 (*0-7812-3872-2*) Rprt Serv.

Life & Times of the Apostle Paul. rev. ed. Charles F. Ball. 200p. 1996. pap. 9.99 (*0-8423-3500-5*) Tyndale Hse.

Life & Times of the Apple. Charles Micucci. LC 90-22779. (Illus.). 32p. (J). (gr. k-3). 1996. pap. 5.95 (*0-531-07067-0*) Orchard Bks Watts.

Life & Times of the Apple. Charles Micucci. 1995. 11.15 (*0-606-08798-2*, Pub. by Turtleback) Demco.

Life & Times of the Equitable. John Rousmaniere. LC 98-127561. (Illus.). 496p. 1995. write for info. (*0-9648761-2-4*) D L & J.

Life & Times of the Honeybee. Charles Micucci. (J). 1997. pap. text 93.32 (*0-395-86149-7*) HM.

Life & Times of the Honeybee. Illus. & Text by Charles Micucci. LC 93-8135. 32p. (J). (gr. k-3). 1995. 15.00 (*0-395-65968-X*) Ticknor & Flds Bks Yng Read.

Life & Times of the Honeybee. Charles Micucci. LC 93-8135. (Illus.). 32p. (J). (gr. k-3). 1997. reprint ed. pap. 5.95 (*0-395-86139-X*) HM.

Life & Times of the Hotel Athenaeum. 2nd ed. Thomas A. Dorey. LC 90-93506. (Illus.). 85p. 1991. pap. 8.95 (*0-9627431-1-9*) T A Dorey.

Life & Times of the Peanut. Charles Micucci. LC 96-1290. (Illus.). 32p. (J). (gr. k-3). 1997. 16.00 (*0-395-72289-6*) HM.

***Life & Times of the Peanut.** Charles Micucci. (Illus.). (J). 2000. 11.40 (*0-606-18211-X*) Turtleback.

***Life & Times of the Peanut.** Charles Micucci. (Illus.). 32p. (J). 2000. pap. 5.95 (*0-618-03314-9*) HM.

Life & Times of the Right Honourable Cecil John Rhodes, 1853-1902, 2 vols. Lewis Michell. Ed. by Mira Wilkins. LC 76-29768. (European Business Ser.). 1977. reprint ed. lib. bdg. 63.95 (*0-405-09782-4*) Ayer.

Life & Times of the Swansea & Mumbles Railway. Gerald Gabb. 80p. (C). 1989. 49.00 (*0-905928-79-2*, Pub. by D Brown & Sons Ltd) St Mut.

Life & Times of Thomas Day, 1748-1789 - English Philanthropist & Author: Virtue Almost Personified. Peter Rowland. LC 95-31872. (Studies in British History: Vol. 39). (Illus.). 468p. 1996. text 109.95 (*0-7734-8844-8*) E Mellen.

Life & Times of Thomas Wakley. S. Squire Sprigge. LC 73-89696. 542p. 1974. reprint ed. 49.50 (*0-88275-134-4*) Krieger.

Life & Times of Thomas Waties, Patriot, Jurist, & Churchman (1760-1828) Alva M. Lumpkin. 128p. 1995. 24.50 (*0-9644928-0-6*) A M Lumpkin.

Life & Times of Thomas Wilson Dorr, with Outlines of the Political History of Rhode Island. Dan King. LC 74-95071. (Select Bibliographies Reprint Ser.). 1977. 30.95 (*0-8369-5071-2*) Ayer.

Life & Times of Victoria. Dorothy Marshall. Ed. by Antonia Fraser. (Kings & Queens of England Ser.). (Illus.). 224p. 1992. 24.95 (*1-55859-450-7*) Abbeville Pr.

Life & Times of Warren Hastings: Maker of British India. A. Mervyn Davies. (C). 1988. reprint ed. 72.50 (*81-212-0144-6*, Pub. by Gian Publng Hse) S Asia.

Life & Times of William I, 1. Maurice Ashley. 1999. pap. text 18.95 (*1-56649-009-X*) Welcome Rain.

Life & Times of William S. Kelly: His Descendants & Related Families. Compiled by Barbara Chase. LC 96-6967. 1996. write for info. (*0-87152-497-X*) Reprint.

Life & Times of William Samuel Johnson. E. Edwards Beardsley. LC 72-4207. (Select Bibliographies Reprint Ser.). 1977. reprint ed. 20.95 (*0-8369-6872-7*) Ayer.

Life & Times of William I. Maurice Ashley. Ed. by Antonia Fraser. (Kings & Queens of England Ser.). (Illus.). 224p. 1992. 24.95 (*1-55859-449-3*) Abbeville Pr.

Life & Tradition in Rural Hungary. Laszlo Kosa. 48p. 1984. 50.00 (*0-7855-0987-9*) St Mut.

Life & Travels of John Bartram: From Lake Ontario to the River St. John. Edmund Berkeley & Dorothy S. Berkeley. LC 81-4083. (Illus.). xv, 376p. 1990. pap. 18.95 (*0-8130-0995-2*) U Press Fla.

Life & Travels of John Bartram: From Lake Ontario to the River St. John. Edmund Berkeley & Dorothy S. Berkeley. LC 81-4083. (Florida State University Bks.). 392p. reprint ed. pap. 121.60 (*0-8357-6925-9*, 203798400009) Bks Demand.

Life & Travels of Vasco Da Gama. K. D. Madan. LC 98-909888. xxix, 140p. 1998. write for info. (*81-206-1360-0*) Asian Educ Servs.

Life & Voyages of Christopher Columbus. Washington Irving. LC 73-14451. (Heroes of the Nations Ser.). reprint ed. 49.50 (*0-404-58268-0*) AMS Pr.

Life & Voyages of Wm. M. Phillipson. William M. Phillipson. LC 71-99667. (Select Bibliographies Reprint Ser.). 1977. 20.95 (*0-8369-5096-8*) Ayer.

Life & Wars of Gideon J. Pillow. Nathaniel C. Hughes, Jr. & Roy P. Stonesifer, Jr. LC 93-3250. (Civil War America Ser.). (Illus.). xx, 455p. 1993. 45.00 (*0-8078-2107-1*) U of NC Pr.

Life & Way for the Practice of the Church Life. Witness Lee. 151p. 1994. per. 7.50 (*0-87083-785-0*, 07-042-001) Living Stream Ministry.

Life & Wisdom of Augustine of Hippocrene. 1998. pap. 7.50 (*0-340-70971-5*) Hodder & Stought Ltd.

Life & Wisdom of Benedict see Saints Alive Series

Life & Wisdom of Benedict. Lavinia Byrne. 1998. pap. 7.50 (*0-340-70974-X*, Pub. by Hodder & Stought Ltd) Trafalgar.

Life & Wisdom of Catherine of Siena see Saints Alive Series

Life & Wisdom of Catherine of Siena. Lavinia Byrne. 1998. pap. 7.50 (*0-340-70973-1*, Pub. by Hodder & Stought Ltd) Trafalgar.

Life & Wisdom of Francis of Assisi see Saints Alive Series

Life & Wisdom of Francis of Assisi. Lavinia Byrne. 1998. pap. 8.95 (*0-340-70968-5*, Pub. by Hodder & Stought Ltd) Trafalgar.

Life & Wisdom of Francis Xavier. Lavinia Byrne. 1998. pap. 7.50 (*0-340-70975-8*, Pub. by Hodder & Stought Ltd) Trafalgar.

***Life & Wisdom of Gwen Frostic.** Sheryl James. LC 99-33315. (Illus.). 124p. 1999. 17.95 (*1-886947-85-6*) Sleepng Bear.

Life & Wisdom of Helena, Mother of Constantine. Lavinia Byrne. 1998. pap. 4.99 (*0-340-70970-7*, Pub. by Hodder & Stought Ltd) Trafalgar.

Life & Wisdom of Margaret of Scotland see Saints Alive Series

Life & Wisdom of Margaret of Scotland. Lavinia Byrne. 1998. pap. 4.99 (*0-340-70972-3*, Pub. by Hodder & Stought Ltd) Trafalgar.

Life & Wisdom of Teresa of Avila. Lavinia Byrne. 1998. pap. 4.99 (*0-340-70969-3*, Pub. by Hodder & Stought Ltd) Trafalgar.

***Life & Women: A Guide to an Enjoyable Relationship with the Opposite Sex.** Charlie B. Simon & Randy L. Chavez. xiv, 114p. 2000. 22.00 (*0-9676044-0-0*) Amazing Female.

Life & Wonderful Adventures of Wild Bill (J. B. Hicock) J. W. Buel. Ed. by William R. Jones. (Illus.). 1977. reprint ed. pap. 2.00 (*0-89646-013-4*) Vistabooks.

Life & Words of Martin Luther King Jr. Ira Peck. (Illus.). 112p. (J). (gr. 3-7). 1991. mass mkt. 5.50 (*0-590-43827-1*) Scholastic Inc.

Life & Words of Martin Luther King, Jr. Ira Peck. 1968. 8.70 (*0-606-03106-5*, Pub. by Turtleback) Demco.

Life & Work of Robert Welch, Founder of the John Birch Society. G. Edward Griffin. LC 74-3311. (Illus.). 428p. 1975. 24.50 (*0-912986-07-7*) Am Media.

Life & Work: A Manager's Search for Meaning. James A. Autry. 304p. 1995. pap. 11.00 (*0-380-72564-9*, Avon Bks) Morrow Avon.

Life & Work in an Initiatic School Pt. 1: Training for the Divine. Omraam M. Aivanhov. (Complete Works: Vol. 30). (Illus.). 264p. 1996. pap. 14.95 (*1-895978-09-2*, Pub. by Prosveta) Prosveta USA.

Life & Work in Benares & Kumaon, 1839-1877. James Kennedy. (C). 1993. reprint ed. 28.00 (*81-206-0751-1*, Pub. by Asian Educ Servs) S Asia.

An Asterisk (*) at the beginning of an entry indicates that the title is appearing for the first time.

Life & Work in Medieval Europe: The Evolution of Medieval Economy from the Fifth to the Fifteenth Century. Prosper Boissonnade. Tr. by Eileen E. Power & Lynn White, Jr. from FRE. LC 82-11818. (Illus.). 395p. 1982. reprint ed. lib. bdg. 79.50 (0-313-23566-X, BOLW) Greenwood.

Life & Work of an Eminent Psychologist: Autobiography of Richard S. Lazarus. Richard S. Lazarus. LC 98-10419. 1998. 39.95 (0-8261-1179-3) Springer Pub.

Life & Work of Andrew Sloan Draper. Harlan H. Horner. LC 34-3207. (Illus.). 407p. reprint ed. pap. 126.20 (0-608-30550-2, 201503300094) Bks Demand.

Life & Work of Buddhaghosa. Bimala Churn Law. LC 98-905010. xii, 183 p. 1997. write for info. (81-206-1096-2) Asian Educ Servs.

Life & Work of C. R. Cockerell. David Watkin. Ed. by John Harris & Alastair Laing. (Studies in Architecture: No. XIV). (Illus.). 272p. 1986. 75.00 (0-302-02571-5, Pub. by Zwemmer Bks) Intl Spec Bk.

***Life & Work of Charles Bell.** Phillida B. Simons et al. LC 99-164564. 176p. 1998. write for info. (1-874950-36-9) Fernwood ZAF.

Life & Work of Charles Haddon Spurgeon. G. Holden Pike. 608p. 1992. reprint ed. 69.99 (0-85151-622-X) Banner of Truth.

Life & Work Of Christ. 1996. pap. 6.99 (1-85078-224-5, Pub. by Sheffield Acad) CUP Services.

Life & Work of Dennis Potter. W. Stephen Gilbert. (Illus.). 16p. 1998. 29.95 (0-87951-873-1, Pub. by Overlook Pr) Penguin Putnam.

Life & Work of Dr. J. Th. Van Der Kemp: Missionary Pioneer & Protagonist of Racial Equality in South Africa, 1747-1811. Ed. by Ido H. Enklaar. (South African Biographical & Historical Studies). (Illus.). 234p. 1988. text 47.00 (90-6191-757-3, Pub. by A A Balkema) Ashgate Pub Co.

Life & Work of Edward Lamson Henry N. A. Elizabeth McCausland. LC 74-100614. (Library of American Art). (Illus.). 1970. reprint ed. lib. bdg. 55.00 (0-306-71866-9) Da Capo.

Life & Work of Ephraim Luzzatto. David Mirsky. 1987. 25.00 (0-88125-139-9) Ktav.

Life & Work of Ernest M. Skinner. Dorothy J. Holden. (Illus.). x, 318p. 1985. lib. bdg. 28.00 (0-913499-00-5) Organ Hist Soc.

Life & Work of Fedor Abramov. Ed. by David C. Gillespie. LC 97-2245. (Studies in Russian Literature & Theory Ser.). 1997. 59.95 (0-8101-1452-6) Northwestern U Pr.

Life & Work of Fredson Bowers. G. Thomas Tanselle. 200p. 1993. 30.00 (1-883631-00-9) Biblgraph Soc.

Life & Work of Gerard Noodt (1647-1725) Dutch Legal Scholarship Between Humanism & Enlightenment. G. C. Van Den Bergh. (Illus.). 412p. 1988. 95.00 (0-19-825602-7) OUP.

Life & Work of Goethe, 1749-1832. John G. Robertson. LC 79-179536. (Select Bibliographies Reprint Ser.). 1977. reprint ed. 23.95 (0-8369-6665-1) Ayer.

Life & Work of Goethe, 1749-1832. John G. Robertson. LC 72-8646. (Studies in German Literature: No. 13). 1973. reprint ed. lib. bdg. 75.00 (0-8383-1671-9) M S G Haskell Hse.

Life & Work of Hans urs von Balthasar. Ed. by David Schindler. LC 91-73330. 318p. (Orig.). 1991. pap. 17.95 (0-89870-378-6) Ignatius Pr.

Life & Work of Harold Palmer. E. J. Perkins. 144p. (C). 1988. 90.00 (0-7855-2245-X, Pub. by Domino Bks Ltd); pap. 100.00 (1-85122-025-9, Pub. by Domino Bks Ltd) St Mut.

Life & Work of Harold Pinter. Michael Billington. (Illus.). 384p. 1997. 24.95 (0-571-17103-6) Faber & Faber.

Life & Work of Henry Scott Tuke 1858-1929. Emmanuel Cooper. 1995. 35.00 (0-85449-069-8, Pub. by Gay Mens Pr) LPC InBook.

Life & Work of Henry Scott Tuke, 1858-1929. Emmanuel Cooper. (Illus.). 72p. 1997. 30.00 (0-85449-068-X, Pub. by Gay Mens Pr) LPC InBook.

Life & Work of Jacques Hadamard. V. G. Mazia & T. O. Shaposhnikova. LC 97-36357. (History of Mathematics Ser.). 574p. 1998. text 79.00 (0-8218-0841-9) Am Math.

Life & Work of Jalaluddin Rumi. Afzal Iqbal. 360p. 1999. text 26.95 (0-19-577989-4) OUP.

Life & Work of Jalaluddin Rumi. Afzal Iqbal. 330p. 1999. pap. 16.95 (0-19-579067-7) OUP.

Life & Work of Jalaluddin Rumi. Afzal Iqbal. 330p. 1983. 30.00 (0-86304-033-0, Pub. by Octagon Pr) ISHK.

Life & Work of James Coleman. James Coleman & Mark Doyle. Ed. by Angela Eaton. LC 95-92276. (Illus.). 168p. 1995. 39.95 (0-9646447-0-3) J Coleman.

Life & Work of John Bird Sumner. Nigel Scotland & Michael Chandler. LC 95-234010. 193p. 1996. pap. 19.95 (0-85244-246-7, 943, Pub. by Gra1cewing) Morehouse Pub.

Life & Work of John Mason Neale. Michael Chandler. 241p. 1995. pap. 17.95 (0-85244-305-6, 944, Pub. by Gra1cewing) Morehouse Pub.

Life & Work of John Snetzler. Alan Barnes & Martin Renshaw. LC 93-1812. 1994. 113.95 (0-85967-932-2, Pub. by Scolar Pr) Ashgate Pub Co.

Life & Work of John Williamson Nevin. Theodore Appel. LC 71-83409. (Religion in America, Ser. 1). 1970. reprint ed. 39.95 (0-405-00203-3) Ayer.

Life & Work of Karl Polanyi, Vol. 1. Ed. by Kari Polanyi-Levitt. LC 90-83624. (Illus.). 265p. (Orig.). (C). 1990. 48.99 (0-921689-81-0, Pub. by Black Rose); pap. 19.99 (0-921689-80-2, Pub. by Black Rose) Consort Bk Sales.

Life & Work of Kwame Nkrumah. Ed. by Kwame Arhin. LC 93-30706. 395p. 1993. reprint ed. 49.95 (0-86543-395-X); reprint ed. pap. 16.95 (0-86543-396-8) Africa World.

Life & Work of Ludwig Lewisohn Vol. 1: "A Touch of Wildness" Ralph Melnick. LC 97-36411. (Illus.). 752p. 1998. 39.95 (0-8143-2692-7) Wayne St U Pr.

Life & Work of Ludwig Lewisohn Vol. II: This Dark & Desperate Age. Ralph Meinick. 1998. 39.95 (0-8143-2765-6, Great Lks Bks) Wayne St U Pr.

Life & Work of Luis Barragan. Jose M. Buendia Julbez et al. LC 97-67800. (Illus.). 248p. 1997. text 50.00 (0-8478-2057-2) St Martin.

***Life & Work of Martin Johnson Heade: A Critical Analysis & Catalogue Raisonne.** Theodore E. Stebbins. LC 99-36424. (Illus.). 496p. 2000. 75.00 (0-300-08183-9) Yale U Pr.

Life & Work of Mary Carpenter. 2nd ed. J. Estlin Carpenter. LC 77-172564. (Criminology, Law Enforcement, & Social Problems Ser.: No. 145). (Illus.). 420p. 1974. reprint ed. lib. bdg. 28.00 (0-87585-145-2) Patterson Smith.

Life & Work of Mary O'Hara, Author of My Friend Flicka. Sharon Whitehill. LC 94-41355. 492p. 1995. text 109.95 (0-7734-9014-0) E Mellen.

Life & Work of Michael Brenner, 1885-1969. J. C. Leissring. (Illus.). 191p. 1991. 95.00 (0-9630085-0-1) J C Leissring.

Life & Work of Morgan Edwards: First Baptist Historian in the United States. Thomas R. McKibbens, Jr. & Kenneth Smith. Ed. by Edwin S. Gaustad. LC 79-5269. (Baptist Tradition Ser.). 1980. lib. bdg. 25.95 (0-405-12438-4) Ayer.

Life & Work of Mother Louise Margaret. Ed. by Patrick O'Connell. LC 86-51579. 230p. 1989. reprint ed. pap. 12.50 (0-89555-311-2) TAN Bks Pubs.

Life & Work of Our Lord, 3, Set. Charles H. Spurgeon. (YA). (gr. 10). 1996. 75.00 (0-8010-1115-9) Baker Bks.

Life & Work of Owen Thomas, 1812-1891: A Welsh Preacher. D. Ben Rees. LC 91-4083. (Welsh Studies: Vol. 3). 336p. 1991. lib. bdg. 99.95 (0-7734-9710-2) E Mellen.

Life & Work of Roger Bacon. John H. Bridges. Ed. by H. Gordon Jones. LC 79-8597. reprint ed. 27.50 (0-404-18450-2) AMS Pr.

Life & Work of Roger Bacon: An Introduction to the Opus Majus. John H. Bridges. Ed. by H. Gordon Jones. LC 76-1120. 1977. reprint ed. lib. bdg. 15.00 (0-915172-14-3) Richwood Pub.

Life & Work of Rudolf Steiner: From the Turn of the Century to His Death. 2nd ed. Guenther Wachsmuth. Tr. by Olim D. Wanamaker & Reginald Raab from GER. LC 82-82476. (Illus.). 648p. 1988. reprint ed. lib. bdg. 45.00 (0-89345-036-7, Spir Sci Lib) Garber Comm.

Life & Work of Rumi. 4th ed. Afzal Iqbal. 1992. 16.95 (1-56744-122-X) Kazi Pubns.

Life & Work of S. M. Dubnov: Diaspora Nationalism & Jewish History. Sophie Dubnov-Erlich. LC 89-46342. (Modern Jewish Experience Ser.). (Illus.). 298p. 1991. 12.95 (0-253-31836-X) Ind U Pr.

Life & Work of Samuel Rutherford Crockett. I. M. Donaldson. 1989. text 39.00 (0-08-036597-3, Pergamon Pr) Elsevier.

Life & Work of Susan B. Anthony, 3 vols., Set. Ed. by Ida H. Harper. LC 70-79184. (Women's Rights & Liberation Ser.). (Illus.). 1969. reprint ed. 128.95 (0-405-00102-9) Ayer.

Life & Work of Susan B. Anthony, 3 vols., Set. Ida H. Harper. 1993. reprint ed. lib. bdg. 225.00 (0-7812-5184-2) Rprt Serv.

Life & Work of Susan B. Anthony, 3 vols., Vol. 1. Ed. by Ida H. Harper. LC 70-79184. (Women's Rights & Liberation Ser.). (Illus.). 1969. reprint ed. 42.95 (0-405-00103-7) Ayer.

Life & Work of Susan B. Anthony, 3 vols., Vol. 2. Ed. by Ida H. Harper. LC 70-79184. (Women's Rights & Liberation Ser.). (Illus.). 1969. reprint ed. 42.95 (0-405-00104-5) Ayer.

Life & Work of Susan B. Anthony, 3 vols., Vol. 3. Ed. by Ida H. Harper. LC 70-79184. (Women's Rights & Liberation Ser.). (Illus.). 1969. reprint ed. 42.95 (0-405-00105-3) Ayer.

Life & Work of William Pryor Letchworth, Student & Minister of Public Benevolence. Joseph N. Larned. LC 71-172592. (Criminology, Law Enforcement, & Social Problems Ser.: No. 182). (Illus.). 1974. reprint ed. 24.00 (0-87585-182-7) Patterson Smith.

Life & Work on the Mission Field. fac. ed. J. Herbert Kane. LC 80-65010. 350p. 1980. reprint ed. pap. 108.50 (0-608-01001-4, 206185900012) Bks Demand.

***Life & Worklife Expectancies.** Hugh Richards. LC 99-48922. 272p. 2000. 85.00 (0-913875-36-8, 5368-N) Lawyers & Judges.

Life & Works. Joseph R. Drake. Ed. by F. L. Pleadwell. (Notable American Authors Ser.). 1992. reprint ed. lib. bdg. 75.00 (0-7812-2694-5) Rprt Serv.

Life & Works, 3 bks., Set. Nicholas McDowell. (Illus.). 448p. (J). (gr. 7 up). 1989. lib. bdg. 75.80 (0-86592-295-0) Rourke Enter.

Life & Works, 6 bks., Set. Jane Phillimore et al. (Illus.). 672p. (YA). (gr. 7 up). 1990. lib. bdg. 89.70 (0-685-36350-3) Rourke Corp.

Life & Works, 6 bks., Set. Jim Reilly et al. (Illus.). 672p. (YA). (gr. 7 up). 1990. lib. bdg. 119.64 (0-86593-015-5) Rourke Corp.

Life & Works, 4 bks., Set I, Reading Level 8. Nicholas McDowell. (Illus.). 448p. (J). (gr. 7 up). 1989. 59.80 (0-685-58807-6) Rourke Corp.

***Life & Works of a Demographer: An Autobiography.** C. Chandrasekaran. LC 99-938314. (Illus.). 1999. write for info. (0-07-463065-2) McGrw-H Hghr Educ.

Life & Works of Andrew Sloan Draper. H. H. Horner. 291p. 1993. reprint ed. lib. bdg. 79.00 (0-7812-5319-5) Rprt Serv.

Life & Works of Augustus Saint Gaudens. Burke Wilkinson. Orig. Title: Uncommon Clay: The Life & Works of Augustus Saint Gaudens. (Illus.). 480p. 1992. reprint ed. pap. 14.95 (0-486-27149-8) Dover.

Life & Works of Beethoven: Music Book Index. John N. Burk. 483p. 1993. reprint ed. lib. bdg. 99.00 (0-7812-9572-6) Rprt Serv.

Life & Works of Bessie Head. Virginia U. Ola. LC 94-20128. 108p. 1994. text 59.95 (0-7734-9018-3) E Mellen.

Life & Works of Charles Sealsfield (Karl Postl), 1864-1973. Ed. by Charlotte L. Brancaforte. (Max Kade Institute Studies). 302p. 1993. 22.50 (0-924119-72-1) German-Am Cult Soc.

Life & Works of Christoper Dock. Martin G. Brumbaugh. LC 70-89154. (American Education: Its Men, Institutions, & Ideas. Series 1). 1977. reprint ed. 23.95 (0-405-01392-2) Ayer.

Life & Works of Edward Moore. John H. Caskey. LC 72-8823. (Yale Studies in English: No. 75). iv, 197p. 1973. reprint ed. 59.50 (0-208-01125-0) Elliots Bks.

Life & Works of Elizabeth Stuart Phelps: Victorian Feminist Writer. Lori D. Kelly. LC 81-52809. viii, 146p. 1983. 45.00 (0-87875-232-3) Whitston Pub.

Life & Works of Francis Hopkinson. George E. Hastings. (BCL1-PS American Literature Ser.). 516p. 1992. reprint ed. lib. bdg. 99.00 (0-7812-6662-9) Rprt Serv.

Life & Works of Frank Lloyd Wright. Maria Costantino. LC 97-77958. (Illus.). 160p. 1998. 19.98 (0-7624-0378-0, Courage) Running Pr.

Life & Works of Friedrich Schiller. Calvin Thomas. LC 73-119662. reprint ed. 34.50 (0-404-06369-1) AMS Pr.

Life & Works of Garci Sanchez de Badajoz. Patrick Gallager. (Monagrafias A Ser.: Vol. VII). (SPA.). 1224p. (Orig.). (C). 1968. pap. 45.00 (0-900411-00-7, Pub. by Tamesis Bks Ltd) Boydell & Brewer.

Life & Works of General Charles King, 1844-1933: Martial Spirit. John W. Bailey. LC 98-23275. 270p. 1998. text 99.95 (0-7734-8356-X) E Mellen.

Life & Works of Gerald Griffin, 8 vols. Gerald Griffin. LC 78-148792. reprint ed. 135.00 (0-404-08860-0) AMS Pr.

Life & Works of Harry Clarke. Nicola G. Bowe. (Illus.). 301p. 1989. reprint ed. 49.50 (0-7165-2452-X, Pub. by Irish Acad Pr); reprint ed. pap. 29.50 (0-7165-2534-8, Pub. by Irish Acad Pr) Intl Spec Bk.

Life & Works of His Beatitude Anthony, Metropolitan of Kiev & Galitch see Zhizneopisanie i Tvorenije Blazhennejshago Antonia, Mitropolita Kievskago i Galitzkago, v 17 tomakh

Life & Works of J. C. Kapteyn: An Annotated Translation. E. Robert Paul & Henrietta Hertzsprung-Kapteyn. 90p. (C). 1994. text 55.50 (0-7923-2603-2) Kluwer Academic.

Life & Works of Jacob Medinger: The Last of the Pennsylvania Potters. (Illus.). (Orig.). 1992. 15.00 (0-9624021-6-8) Ursinus College.

Life & Works of John Arbuthnot, M. D., Fellow of the Royal College of Physicians. George A. Aitken. (BCL1-PR English Literature Ser.). 516p. 1992. reprint ed. lib. bdg. 99.00 (0-7812-7318-8) Rprt Serv.

Life & Works of John Hay, 1838-1905: A Commemorative Catalogue of the Exhibition Shown at the John Jay Library of Brown University in Honor of the Centennial of His Graduation at the Commencement of 1858. Brown University Library Staff. LC 61-3289. 69p. reprint ed. pap. 30.00 (0-608-15235-8, 202750100055) Bks Demand.

Life & Works of John Heywood. Robert W. Bolwell. LC 21-22336. reprint ed. 20.00 (0-404-00934-4) AMS Pr.

Life & Works of John Knowles Paine. John C. Schmidt. Ed. by George Buelow. LC 80-22511. (Studies in Musicology: No. 34). 771p. 1980. reprint ed. pap. 200.00 (0-8357-1126-9, 207028800065) Bks Demand.

Life & Works of John Weaver. Richard Ralph. LC 82-83649. (Illus.). 1075p. 1985. 125.00 (0-87127-139-7, Dance Horizons) Princeton Bk Co.

Life & Works of Joseph Anton Steffan (1726-1797) With Special Reference to His Keyboard Concertos, 2 vols., Set. rev. ed. Howard J. Picton. LC 89-23792. (Outstanding Dissertations in Music from British Universities Ser.). 788p. 1990. text 10.00 (0-8240-2345-5) Garland.

Life & Works of Joseph Kinghorn. expanded ed. Ed. by Terry Wolever. (Particular Baptists in England Ser.: Vol. 1). (Illus.). vi, 530p. 1995. reprint ed. 24.50 (1-888514-00-0) Particular Baptist.

Life & Works of Joseph Rodman Drake (1795-1820) Joseph Drake. (BCL1-PS American Literature Ser.). 424p. 1993. reprint ed. lib. bdg. 99.00 (0-7812-6959-8) Rprt Serv.

Life & Works of Lili Boulanger. Leonie Rosenstiel. LC 75-18244. 408p. (C). 1978. 42.50 (0-8386-1796-4) Fairleigh Dickinson.

Life & Works of Otto Dix: German Critical Realist. Linda F. McGreevy. LC 81-1895. (Studies in the Fine Arts: The Avant-Garde: No. 12). (Illus.). 164p. reprint ed. pap. 50.90 (0-8357-1165-X, 207023500065) Bks Demand.

Life & Works of Phillis Wheatley. Phillis Wheatley. LC 70-83899. (Black Heritage Library Collection). 1977. 21.95 (0-8369-8685-7) Ayer.

Life & Works of Saadat Hasan Manto. Ed. by Alok Bhalla. LC 97-913701. xii, 219p. 1997. 20.00 (81-85952-48-5, Pub. by Indian Inst) Nataraj Bks.

Life & Works of Sarah Purser. John O'Grady. (Illus.). 292p. 1996. boxed set 45.00 (1-85182-241-0, Pub. by Four Cts Pr) Intl Spec Bk.

Life & Works of Sir Charles Barry. Alfred Barry. LC 72-83088. (Illus.). 420p. 1977. reprint ed. 31.95 (0-405-08239-8, Pub. by Blom Pubns) Ayer.

Life & Works of St. Cyprian of Carthage, 10 vols., Set. St. Cyprian of Carthage. pap. 15.00 (0-89981-040-3) Eastern Orthodox.

Life & Works of the Sisters Bronte, 7 vols. Charlotte Bronte. LC 77-148757. reprint ed. 510.00 (0-404-08830-9) AMS Pr.

Life & Works of the Troubadour Raimbaut D'Orange. W. T. Pattison. LC 80-2182. reprint ed. 35.00 (0-404-19015-4) AMS Pr.

Life & Works of Thomas Cole. Louis L. Noble. Ed. by Elliot S. Vesell. LC 64-22725. 401p. reprint ed. pap. 124.40 (0-608-11213-5, 200164400002) Bks Demand.

Life & Works of Thomas Cole. Louis L. Noble. Ed. by Elliot S. Vesell. LC 97-15713. (Illus.). 400p. 1997. reprint ed. pap. 21.95 (1-883789-13-3) Blk Dome Pr.

Life & Works of Thomas Sully. Edward Biddle & Mantle Fielding. LC 74-77716. (Library of American Art). 1970. reprint ed. lib. bdg. 52.50 (0-306-71354-3) Da Capo.

Life & World of Call Girls in India. Promilla Kapur. 364p. 1978. 19.95 (0-7069-0609-8) Asia Bk Corp.

Life & World-Work of Thomas Lake Harris, Written from Direct Personal Knowledge. Arthur A. Cuthbert. LC 72-2954. reprint ed. 42.50 (0-404-10719-2) AMS Pr.

Life & Worship: The Mystery of Christ among Us. (Illus.). 81p. (Orig.). 1986. pap. text 7.00 (1-887158-01-4) God With Us.

Life & Writings of Abraham Lincoln. Abraham Lincoln. Ed. by Jeffrey Morris. LC 99-12661. 1999. 22.95 (0-679-60329-8) Random.

***Life & Writings of Abraham Lincoln.** Abraham Lincoln. (Classics Ser.). 2000. pap. 14.95 (0-679-78329-6) Modern Lib NY.

Life & Writings of Abraham Lincoln. Abraham Lincoln. (History - United States Ser.). 863p. 1993. reprint ed. lib. bdg. 119.00 (0-7812-4899-X) Rprt Serv.

Life & Writings of Alexandre Dumas. H. A. Spurr. LC 72-3515. (Studies in European Literature: No. 56). 1972. reprint ed. lib. bdg. 75.00 (0-8383-1549-6) M S G Haskell Hse.

Life & Writings of Amelia Bloomer. D. C. Bloomer. LC 72-78650. 1895. reprint ed. 49.00 (0-403-01994-X) Somerset Pub.

Life & Writings of Charles Dickens. R. A. Hammond. LC 72-3998. (Studies in Dickens: No. 52). 1972. reprint ed. lib. bdg. 75.00 (0-8383-1606-9) M S G Haskell Hse.

Life & Writings of Francis Makemie, Father of American Presbyterianism (c. 1658-1708) Boyd S. Schlenther. LC 98-53801. (Studies in American Religion: Vol. 69). 304p. 1999. text 99.95 (0-7734-8174-5) E Mellen.

Life & Writings of Frederick Douglass: Supplementary Volume: 1844-1860, Vol. 5. Frederick Douglass. Ed. by Philip S. Foner. LC 50-7654. 1975. 17.00 (0-7178-0453-4); pap. 7.95 (0-7178-0454-2) Intl Pubs Co.

Life & Writings of George Gascoigne. Felix E. Schelling. (BCL1-PR English Literature Ser.). 131p. 1992. reprint ed. lib. bdg. 69.00 (0-7812-7210-6) Rprt Serv.

Life & Writings of Henry Pickering Bowditch, Vol. 2. Henry P. Bowditch. 1980. 44.95 (0-405-12536-4) Ayer.

Life & Writings of Henry Pickering Bowditch: An Original Anthology, 2 vols., Set. Henry P. Bowditch. Ed. by I. Bernard Cohen. LC 79-7950. (Three Centuries of Science in America Ser.). (Illus.). 1980. lib. bdg. 88.95 (0-405-12531-3) Ayer.

Life & Writings of Hugh Henry Brackenridge (1932) Claude M. Newlin. 335p. 1971. 15.00 (0-911858-20-2) Appel.

Life & Writings of James Owen Hannay (George A. Birmingham), 1865-1950. Brian Taylor. LC 94-37314. (Illus.). 312p. 1995. text 99.95 (0-7734-9123-6) E Mellen.

Life & Writings of Jared Sparks. Herbert B. Adams. (Principle Works of Herbert Baxter Adams). 1989. reprint ed. lib. bdg. 79.00 (0-7812-1477-7) Rprt Serv.

Life & Writings of Jared Sparks, 2 Vols, Set. Herbert B. Adams. LC 76-119924. (Select Bibliographies Reprint Ser.). 1977. 60.95 (0-8369-5367-3) Ayer.

Life & Writings of John Howard Payne. rev. ed. Gabriel Harrison. LC 70-91517. 1972. 31.95 (0-405-08600-8) Ayer.

Life & Writings of Major Jack Downing, of Downingville. Seba Smith. LC 71-164785. reprint ed. 39.50 (0-404-02168-9) AMS Pr.

Life & Writings of the Historical St. Patrick. R. P. Hanson. 144p. 1984. 11.95 (0-8164-0523-9) Harper SF.

Life & Writings of Tobias George Smollett. David Hannay. LC 74-154151. (Select Bibliographies Reprint Ser.). 1977. reprint ed. 19.95 (0-8369-5767-9) Ayer.

Life Animation Series. Alan C. Walter. Ed. by Beverly Miles. 63p. 1995. pap. text 19.97 (1-57569-013-6) Wisdom Pubng.

Life: Any Questions? see Vida: Que Quiere Saber?

Life Apart: Sequel to a Life in Her Hands. Shirlee Evans. LC 90-42762. 176p. (Orig.). 1990. pap. 6.99 (0-8361-3536-9) Herald Pr.

***Life Appliation Study Bible.** Life Application Study Staff. 2000. 84.99 (0-310-91164-8, Zondervan Bibles) Zondervan.

Life Application Family Devotions. Len Woods. LC 97-8873. 320p. 1997. pap. 9.99 (0-8423-3750-4) Tyndale Hse.

Life Application Study Bible. 1997. 46.99 (0-8423-4895-6); 52.99 (0-8423-4896-4) Tyndale Hse.

***Life Application Study Bible.** 2000. 69.99 (0-8423-4045-9) Tyndale Hse.

***Life Application Study Bible.** 2000. 74.99 (0-310-91146-X); 74.99 (0-310-91148-6); 84.99 (0-310-91160-5); 84.99 (0-310-91171-0) Zondervan.

***Life Application Study Bible.** 2000. 39.99 (0-310-90095-6) Zondervan.

Life Application Study Bible. Life Application Study Bible Staff. 1997. 89.99 (0-8423-2099-7) Tyndale Hse.

L

An Asterisk (*) at the beginning of an entry indicates that the title is appearing for the first time.

L

***Life Application Study Bible.** Life Application Study Bible Staff. 2000. 39.99 (*0-8423-4035-1*); 64.99 (*0-8423-4039-4*); 64.99 (*0-8423-4040-8*) Tyndale Hse.
***Life Application Study Bible.** Life Application Study Bible Staff. 2000. 69.99 (*0-8423-4041-6*) Tyndale Hse.
***Life Application Study Bible.** Life Application Study Bible Staff. 2000. 74.99 (*0-310-91101-X*); 74.99 (*0-310-91161-3*) Zondervan.
***Life Application Study Bible.** Life Application Study Bible Staff. (Illus.). 2000. 84.99 (*0-310-91172-9*) Zondervan.
***Life Application Study Bible.** Tyndale House Publishers Staff. 2000. 64.99 (*0-8423-3246-4*); 46.99 (*0-8423-3295-2*) Tyndale Hse.
***Life Application Study Bible.** Tyndale House Publishers Staff. 2000. 52.99 (*0-8423-3296-0*) Tyndale Hse.
Life Around Longreach. Sue Cottam. 64p. (C). 1990. pap. 50.00 (*0-646-08772-X*, Pub. by Boolarong Pubns) St Mut.
Life Around the Lake: The Feasts of Lake Patzcuaro. Maricel E. Presilla & Gloria Soto. LC 95-38429. (Illus.). 32p. (J). (gr. 3-6). 1995. 16.95 (*0-8050-3800-0*, Bks Young Read) H Holt & Co.
***Life Around Us.** large type ed. Heather Hughes-Calero & Winged Wolf. (Illus.). 34p. (J). (ps-3). 1999. spiral bd. write for info. (*0-932927-15-7*) Higher Consciousness.
Life Around Us: Selected Poems on Nature. Denise Levertov. LC 96-52901. 80p. 1997. 19.95 (*0-8112-1351-X*, Pub. by New Directions); pap. 8.95 (*0-8112-1352-8*, NDP843, Pub. by New Directions) Norton.
***Life as a Human.** Mary Katherine Jones. 32p. (C). 2000. pap. 5.95 (*1-929416-25-3*) Magner Pubg.
Life As a Man: Contemporary Male-Female Relationships in the Novels of Max Frisch. Claus Reschke. LC 89-39785. (Studies in Modern German Literature: Vol. 34). 409p. (C). 1990. text 72.95 (*0-8204-1163-9*) P Lang Pubng.
Life As a Nazi Soldier. Eleanor H. Ayer. (Way People Live Ser.). (Illus.). (YA). (gr. 4-12). 1998. lib. bdg. 22.45 (*1-56006-484-6*) Lucent Bks.
***Life as a Paratrooper.** Robert C. Kennedy. (High Interest Bks.). (Illus.). (J). 2000. 19.00 (*0-516-23344-0*) Childrens.
***Life as a Paratrooper.** Robert C. Kennedy. LC 00-23801. (High Interest Bks.). (Illus.). 48p. (J). (gr. 4-7). 2000. pap. write for info. (*0-516-23544-3*) Childrens.
Life As a Peace Corps Volunteer in the Federated States of Micronesia. Carol Coleman & Steve Smith. (Illus.). 28p. 1986. pap. text 6.95 (*0-936731-04-4*) Devel Self Rel.
Life As a Peace Corps Volunteer in the Republic of the Marshall Islands. Carol Coleman & Steve Smith. (Illus.). 28p. 1986. pap. text 6.95 (*0-936731-05-2*) Devel Self Rel.
***Life as a Precious Gift.** G. F. Hutchison. 72p. 1999. pap. 12.95 (*1-885631-26-X*, 26-X, Family Of Man Pr) G F Hutchison.
***Life as a POW (WWII)** John F. Wukovitx. LC 99-37695. (American War Library). (Illus.). 144p. (YA). (gr. 6-9). 2000. lib. bdg. 23.70 (*1-56006-665-2*) Lucent Bks.
***Life as an Air Force Fighter Pilot.** Robert C. Kennedy. (High Interest Bks.). (Illus.). (YA). 2000. 19.00 (*0-516-23345-9*) Childrens.
***Life as an Air Force Fighter Pilot.** Robert C. Kennedy. (High Interest Bks.). (Illus.). 48p. (J). (gr. 4-7). 2000. pap. 6.95 (*0-516-23545-1*) Childrens.
***Life as an Army Demolition Expert.** Robert C. Kennedy. (High Interest Bks.). (Illus.). 48p. (J). (gr. 4-7). 2000. pap. 6.95 (*0-516-23546-X*) Childrens.
***Life as an Army Demolition Expert.** Robert C. Kennedy. (High Interest Bks.). (Illus.). (YA). 2000. 19.00 (*0-516-23346-7*) Childrens.
Life As Carola. Joan Grant. 312p. 1988. pap. 9.95 (*0-89804-144-9*) Ariel GA.
Life As Carola. Joan M. Grant. 1980. 33.95 (*0-405-11784-1*) Ayer.
Life As Creation: A Jewish Way of Thinking about the World. Shalom Freedman. LC 92-41080. 160p. 1993. 25.00 (*0-87668-778-8*) Aronson.
Life As I Find It. Mark Twain, pseud. 415p. 1989. reprint ed. lib. bdg. 28.95 (*0-89966-592-6*) Buccaneer Bks.
***Life as I Find It: A Treasury of Mark Twain Rarities.** Charles Neider. LC 99-50204. 2000. pap. write for info. (*0-8154-1027-1*) Cooper Sq.
Life As I Saw It: 1916-Infinity. Ernest M. Guthery. Ed. by Imagene G. Boyd. 320p. 1994. 24.95 (*0-9643619-0-6*) Guthery Bks.
Life As I Saw It: 1916-Infinity. Ernest M. Guthery. Ed. by Imagene G. Boyd. 320p. 1994. pap. 14.95 (*0-9643619-2-2*) Guthery Bks.
Life As I See It. Sandra Pittman-Brown. 64p. 2000. pap. 8.00 (*0-8059-4800-7*) Dorrance.
Life As It Is. J. W. Breazeale. LC 74-17309. 1969. reprint ed. 60.00 (*0-918450-00-4*) C Elder.
Life As Liberty, Life As Trust. fac. ed. Ed. by J. Robert Nelson. LC 92-6287. 104p. 1992. reprint ed. pap. 32.30 (*0-7837-7968-2*, 204772400008) Bks Demand.
Life As Process - Freedom As Communion: Eastern Orthodox Christian Ontology & Ecumenics. Anastasios Zavales. 85p. (C). 1995. pap. 37.95 (*1-884090-00-1*) Ecumenics Intl.
Life As Theater: A Dramaturgical Sourcebook. 2nd ed. Ed. by Dennis Brissett & Charles Edgley. (Communication & Social Order Ser.). 477p. (C). 1990. pap. text 34.95 (*0-202-30363-2*); lib. bdg. 56.95 (*0-202-30362-4*) Aldine de Gruyter.
Life As We Know It. Michael Berube. 1998. pap. 14.00 (*0-679-75866-6*) Random.
Life As We Know It Vol. 2: Extraordinary Stories from Ordinary People - The Best of Bulletin Board, Vol. 2. Ed. by Dan Kelly. 192p. (Orig.). 1996. pap. 8.95 (*0-8362-1445-5*) Andrews & McMeel.
Life As Worship: Prayer & Praise in Jesus' Name. Theodore W. Jennings. LC 82-7283. 151p. reprint ed. pap. 46.90 (*0-608-14499-1*, 202532900043) Bks Demand.
Life, As Written by Himself in His Letters & Memoirs. Hector Berlioz. Tr. by Katharine F. Boult from FRE. LC 74-24042. reprint ed. 37.50 (*0-404-12865-3*) AMS Pr.
Life As Yoga: Discourses at Chorwad, 2 bks. Vimala Thakar. Tr. by Devendra Singh. 286p. 1977. 14.00 (*0-89684-242-8*, Pub. by Motilal Bnarsidass); pap. 10.95 (*0-89684-241-X*, Pub. by Motilal Bnarsidass) S Asia.
Life Assessment & Repair Technology for Combustion Turbine Hot Section Components: Proceedings of an International Conference, Phoenix, Arizona, U. S. A., 17-19 April 1990. ASM International Staff. Ed. by R. Viswanathan & J. M. Allen. LC 90-83068. (Illus.). 404p. pap. 125.30 (*0-7837-1867-5*, 204206800001) Bks Demand.
Life Assurance & Pensions Handbook: Taxbriefs. 4th ed. Chris Marshall. (C). 1988. 250.00 (*0-7855-6048-3*, Pub. by Witherby & Co) St Mut.
Life Assurance Medicine Congress, 9th, Tel Aviv, March 1967: Proceedings. Ed. by M. Leffkowitz & H. Steinitz. vi, 368p. 1968. pap. 99.25 (*3-8055-0910-3*) S Karger.
Life at a Snail's Pace. Roger Harris. Ed. by Elizabeth Lake. LC 95-69877. 64p. (Orig.). 1995. pap. 6.95 (*0-89716-570-5*, Peanut Btr Pubng) Elton-Wolf Pub.
Life at Blandings. P. G. Wodehouse. 608p. 1981. pap. 19.99 (*0-14-005903-2*, Penguin Bks) Viking Penguin.
Life at Four Corners: Religion, Gender, & Education in a German-Lutheran Community, 1868-1945. Carol K. Coburn. LC 92-11905. (Rural America Ser.). (Illus.). 224p. 1992. 29.95 (*0-7006-0557-6*) U Pr of KS.
Life at Four Corners: Religion, Gender, & Education in a German-Lutheran Community, 1868-1945. Carol K. Coburn. LC 92-11905. (Rural America Ser.). (Illus.). 224p. 1994. pap. 16.95 (*0-7006-0682-3*) U Pr of KS.
Life at Its Best. Meher Baba. LC 57-14432. 73p. 1995. reprint ed. 2.00 (*0-915828-04-9*) Sufism Reoriented.
***Life at Its Best: Enjoying the Fruits of the Spirit.** Kenton Beshore & Woody Young. 2000. write for info. (*0-939513-15-3*) Joy Pub SJC.
***Life at Its Best: Living Wisely in an Unwise World.** Ronald J. Chewning & Phyllis J. Chewning. Ed. by Lori Looker. (Illus.). 180p. 1999. pap. 13.99 (*0-9673463-0-4*) Stwardshp Adv Pubns.
Life at Laxton c. 1880-1903. Ed. by B. A. Wood. 1983. pap. 21.00 (*0-902031-89-9*, Pub. by Continuing Education Pr) St Mut.
Life at Laxton, 1880-1903: The Childhood Memories of Edith Hickson. B. A. Wood et al. (C). 1983. text 35.00 (*0-7855-3211-0*, Pub. by Univ Nottingham) St Mut.
Life at Puget Sound. Caroline Leighton. (Illus.). 139p. 1980. 24.95 (*0-87770-209-8*) Ye Galleon.
***Life at School.** P. Salmon. 1998. text 39.95 (*0-09-477450-1*, Pub. by Constable & Co) Trafalgar.
***Life at School, Vol. 7.** Kara Eckmann Powell. (Pulse Ser.). (Illus.). 2000. pap. 14.99 (*0-8307-2508-3*) Gospel Lght.
Life at Sixteen: Good Intentions. Cheryl Lanham. (Life at Sixteen Ser.). (YA). 1998. pap. 4.50 (*0-425-16521-3*, JAM) Berkley Pub.
Life at Small Scale: The Behavior of Microbes. David B. Dusenberry. LC 96-28629. (Illus.). 250p. 1996. text 32.95 (*0-7167-5060-0*) W H Freeman.
***Life at Southern Living: A Sort of Memoir.** John Logue & Gary McCalla. LC 00-37066. (Illus.). 328p. 2000. 24.95 (*0-8071-2561-X*) La State U Pr.
Life at the Border. Leland M. Heller. (Illus.). 244p. 1987. pap. 20.00 (*1-928947-01-8*) Dyslimbia Pr.
Life at the Court of Queen Victoria: Illustrated from the Collection of Lord Edward Pelham-Clinton, Master of the Household with Selections from the Journals of Queen Victoria. Ed. by Barry S. Nevill. (Illus.). 224p. (Orig.). 1997. pap. 26.95 (*0-7509-1481-5*, Pub. by Sutton Pub Ltd) Intl Pubs Mktg.
Life at the Dakota: New York's Most Unusual Address. Stephen Birmingham. 263p. (C). 1996. pap. 18.95 (*0-8156-0338-X*, BILDP) Syracuse U Pr.
Life at the Edge of Chaos: Creating the Quantum Organization. Mark D. Youngblood. Ed. by John Renesch. LC 97-65406. (Illus.). 352p. 1997. 27.50 (*1-889847-40-2*) Perceval Pub.
Life at the Edge of Science: An Anthology of Papers by Beverly Rubik. Beverly Rubik. LC 96-94315. (Illus.). 185p. (Orig.). 1996. pap. 16.00 (*0-9652401-0-X*, BR1) Inst Frontier Sci.
Life at the End of Time: Stories & Essays. Jerome Gold. 42p. 1992. pap. 8.00 (*0-930773-26-8*) Black Heron Pr.
***Life at the Extremes: The Science of Survival.** Frances M. Ashcroft. LC 00-28672. (Illus.). 320p. 2000. 27.50 (*0-520-22234-2*) U CA Pr.
Life at the Margins: Literacy, Language, & Technology in Everyday Life. Juliet Merrifield. LC 97-30137. (Language & Literacy Ser.). 1997. 49.00 (*0-8077-3665-1*) Tchrs Coll.
Life at the Margins: Literacy, Language, & Technology in Everyday Life. Juliet Merrifield et al. LC 97-30137. 256p. 1997. pap. 22.95 (*0-8077-3664-3*) Tchrs Coll.
Life at the Royal Ballet School. Camilla Jessel. LC 79-12162. (Illus.). 143p. (J). (gr. 4 up). 1979. 15.95 (*0-416-30191-6*, NO. 0137) Routledge.
Life at the Royal Ballet School. Camilla Jessel. 1985. 12.95 (*0-416-86320-5*) Routledge.
Life at the Texas State Lunatic Asylum, 1857-1997. Sarah C. Sitton. LC 98-45348. (Centennial Series of the Association of Former Students, Texas A&M University). (Illus.). 256p. 1999. 34.95 (*0-89096-859-4*) Tex A&M Univ Pr.
Life at the Top. John Braine. LC 79-24779. 1980. reprint ed. pap. 3.95 (*0-416-00591-8*, NO. 0185) Routledge.
***Life at the Top: Discoveries in a Tropical Rain Forest Canopy.** Ellen Doris. (Turnstone Rain Forest Pilot Bks.). (Illus.). (J). 2000. 27.12 (*0-7398-2220-9*); pap. 7.95 (*0-7398-2229-2*) Raintree Steck-V.
Life at the Top: Tales, Truths, & Trusted Recipes from the Mount Washington Observatory. Eric Pinder. LC 97-11519. (Illus.). 160p. (Orig.). 1997. pap. 14.95 (*0-89272-396-3*) Down East.
Life at Work -- A Case for Skill. Thomas Addington. (Life@work Ser.). 1997. pap. 5.99 (*0-8054-0183-0*) Broadman.
Life at Work -- Case for Calling. 1997. pap. 5.99 (*0-8054-0185-7*) Broadman.
Life Awareness Manual. Barbara Nash-Price. (Illus.). 98p. (Orig.). 1995. pap. 8.95 (*0-9634419-1-4*) Nash-Price Pubs.
***Life Awareness Manual: A Simple Recipe for Living Life.** rev. ed. Judith Orloff. 144p. 2000. 19.95 (*0-8129-3270-6*, Times Bks) Crown Pub Group.
Life-Balance. Linda Eyre. LC 96-28996. 224p. 1997. pap. 11.00 (*0-684-81128-6*) S&S Trade.
Life Basic Training Workbook. Ralph W. Neighbour, Jr. 1992. pap. text 7.95 (*1-880828-57-X*) Touch Pubns.
Life (Before &) after Monty Python: The Solo Flights of the Flying Circus. Kim H. Johnson. LC 92-41315. 1993. pap. 15.95 (*0-312-08695-4*) St Martin.
Life Before Birth. Gary E. Parker. LC 87-70955. 88p. (J). (gr. 5-7). 1997. boxed set 12.95 (*0-89051-164-0*, LIBEBI) Master Bks.
Life Before Birth: The Challenges of Fetal Development. Peter W. Nathanielsz. 250p. 1996. pap. 13.95 (*0-7167-3025-1*) W H Freeman.
Life Before Birth: The Moral & Legal Status of Embryos & Fetuses. Bonnie Steinbock. 272p. (C). 1996. pap. 22.50 (*0-19-510872-8*) OUP.
Life Before Birth & a Time to Be Born. Peter W. Nathanielsz. LC 92-26052. (Illus.). 250p. 1992. 25.00 (*0-916859-55-X*) Promethean Pr.
Life Before Death: A Novel. Abby Frucht. 240p. 2000. per. 12.00 (*0-684-84627-6*, Scribner Pap Fic) S&S Trade Pap.
Life Before Death: A Religion of the Body. Lawrence Meredith. 1999. 28.95 (*0-89334-292-0*, Humanics Pub) Humanics Ltd.
***Life Before Life: Origins of the Soul... Knowing Where You Came from & Who You Really Are.** Richard Eyre. 2000. 18.95 (*1-57345-782-5*, Shadow Mount) Deseret Bk.
Life Before Man. Margaret Atwood. 304p. 1984. mass mkt. 5.95 (*0-7704-2029-X*) Bantam.
Life Before Man. Margaret Atwood. 368p. 1995. pap. 10.95 (*0-553-37782-5*) Bantam.
Life Before Man. Margaret Atwood. LC 97-48288. 384p. 1998. pap. 12.00 (*0-385-49110-7*, Anchor NY) Doubleday.
***Life Before Man.** Reader's Digest Editors. LC 98-48673. (The Earth, Its Wonders, Its Secrets Ser.). 1999. write for info. (*0-7621-0138-5*) RD Assn.
Life Before Man. rev. ed. Zdenek V. Spinar. LC 94-60275. (Illus.). 256p. (J). (gr. 7). 1996. pap. 16.95 (*0-500-27796-6*, Pub. by Thames Hudson) Norton.
Life Before Us: Madame Rosa. Romain Gary. Tr. by Ralph Manheim from FRE. LC 85-21779. (New Directions Classics Ser.).Tr. of La/Vie Devant Soi. 192p. 1986. reprint ed. pap. 10.95 (*0-8112-0961-X*, NDP604, Pub. by New Directions) Norton.
Life Begins. Norman Donaldson. LC 98-52398. 1999. pap. 5.00 (*0-88734-826-2*) Players Pr.
Life Begins . . . Later! Margaret Cameron. 240p. 1995. pap. write for info. (*1-874640-06-8*, Pub. by Argyll Pubng) St Mut.
Life Begins at Fifty: A Handbook for Creative Retirement Planning. Leonard J. Hansen. 1989. pap. 12.95 (*0-8120-4329-4*) Barron.
Life Begins at Forty. Walter B. Pitkin. 1994. lib. bdg. 24.95 (*1-56849-381-9*) Buccaneer Bks.
Life Begins at Six-Forty: An Adam Collection. Brian Basset. (Illus.). 128p. (Orig.). 1993. pap. 8.95 (*0-8362-1721-7*) Andrews & McMeel.
Life Behind a Veil: Blacks in Louisville, Kentucky, 1865-1930. fac. ed. George C. Wright. LC 84-28838. 316p. 1985. reprint ed. pap. 98.00 (*0-7837-7753-1*, 204750900007) Bks Demand.
***Life Behind Glass: A Personal Account of Autism Spectrum Disorder.** Wendy Lawson. LC 00-40567. 2000. write for info. (*1-85302-911-4*, Pub. by Jessica Kingsley) Taylor & Francis.
Life Behind the Cottage Door. Valerie Porter. (Illus.). 128p. text 34.95 (*1-873580-01-0*, Pub. by Whittet Bks) Diamond Farm Bk.
Life Behind the Potted Plant. Miz M. (Illus.). 236p. 1999. mass mkt. 14.95 (*0-9622608-6-X*) Gabbard Pubns.
Life Being the Best & Other Stories. Kay Boyle. LC 87-32059. (New Directions Classics Ser.). 160p. 1988. pap. 8.95 (*0-8112-1053-7*, NDP654, Pub. by New Directions) Norton.
Life Belts. Jane Hosie-Bounar. (J). 1995. 9.09 (*0-606-07787-1*) Turtleback.
Life Beneath the Sea. V. Santhakumari. 96p. (C). 1989. 110.00 (*81-209-0030-8*, Pub. by Pitambar Pub); pap. 30.00 (*81-209-0736-1*, Pub. by Pitambar Pub) St Mut.
Life Between Azalea Festivals. Amy J. Wood. 112p. 1998. pap. 6.95 (*0-9654136-1-6*) MW Enter.
Life Between Death & Rebirth. Rudolf Steiner. Tr. by R. M. Querido from GER. LC 68-57429. 308p. 1975. pap. 12.95 (*0-910142-62-9*) Anthroposophic.
Life Between Life: Scientific Explorations into the Void Separating One Incarnation from the Next. Joel L. Whitton & Joe Fisher. 237p. 1988. mass mkt. 6.99 (*0-446-34762-0*, Pub. by Warner Bks) Little.
Life Between Seedtime & Harvest. Anthony L. Orier. LC 98-91103. 200p. 1999. pap. 12.95 (*1-889448-52-4*) NBN Publishers Group.
Life Between the Tides: The Natural History of the Common Seashore Life of Southern California. Jeffrey L. Brandon & Frank J. Rokop. LC 84-73217. (Illus.). 230p. (gr. 9-12). 1985. pap. text 19.95 (*0-933177-00-3*) Am Southwest Pub Co.
Life Between Wars. Robert H. Patton. LC 96-46357. 256p. 1997. 24.00 (*1-877946-97-4*) Permanent Pr.
Life Beyond. Joseph F. McConkie & Robert L. Millet. 1986. 13.95 (*0-88494-601-0*) Bookcraft Inc.
Life Beyond: Compelling Evidence for Past Lives & Existence after Death. Hans Holzer. (Illus.). 368p. 1994. pap. write for info. (*0-8092-3577-3*) NTC Contemp Pub Co.
Life Beyond Death. M. K. Ghosh. 398p. 1985. 29.95 (*0-318-36383-6*) Asia Bk Corp.
Life Beyond Death. Rudolf Steiner. Ed. & Intro. by Frank Teichmann. 249p. (Orig.). 1995. pap. 19.95 (*1-85584-017-0*, Pub. by R Steiner Pr) Anthroposophic.
Life Beyond Death. Yogi Ramacharaka. reprint ed. 15.00 (*0-911662-09-X*) Yoga.
Life Beyond Death: A Critical Study of Spiritualism. Swami Abhedananda. 1946. pap. 7.95 (*0-87481-616-5*, Pub. by Rama Ved Math) Vedanta Pr.
***Life Beyond Earth.** Simon & Schuster Staff & Ferris. 224p. 2000. 40.00 (*0-684-84937-2*) S&S Trade.
Life Beyond Headaches. Jeffry Finnigan. 1999. pap. 14.95 (*0-9662786-0-7*) Finnigan Clinic.
Life Beyond Loss: A Workbook for Incarcerated Men. 2nd ed. Beverly Welo. 74p. 1998. pap. 15.00 (*1-56991-095-2*) Am Correctional.
Life Beyond the Classroom: Transition Strategies for Young People with Disabilities. 2nd ed. Paul Wehman. 608p. 1996. pap. text 59.95 (*1-55766-248-7*, 2487) P H Brookes.
Life Beyond the Veil: Echoes from Eternity, Glimpses of Eternity, in Search of Angels-Finding Joy Midst the Bramble Bushes, 3 bks., Set. Arvin S. Gibson. 1994. 42.98 (*0-88290-494-9*) Horizon Utah.
Life Beyond Time Management: How High Achievers Balance & Succeed in a Rapidly Changing World. Kim Norup & Willy Norup. (Illus.). 176p. 1997. 21.95 (*1-890256-32-3*, 3501) Geodex Intl.
Life Beyond 85 Years: The Aura of Survivorship. Colleen L. Johnson & Barbara M. Barer. LC 96-35185. (Life Styles & Issues in Aging Ser.: Vol. 4). (Illus.). 280p. 1997. 44.95 (*0-8261-9540-7*) Springer Pub.
Life Blood. Caroline Llewellyn. 1994. mass mkt. 5.99 (*0-8041-1263-0*) Ivy Books.
Life Blood. large type ed. Caroline Llewellyn. LC 93-46458. 571p. 1994. lib. bdg. 21.95 (*0-8161-5940-8*, G K Hall Lrg Type) Mac Lib Ref.
***Life Board Guidebook.** Melody Ivory. (Illus.). 40p. 1999. pap. 10.00 (*0-9655918-6-7*) Living Innov Pub.
Life Boring? Try "Down Under" S. Myron Wright. LC 93-94053. (Illus.). 104p. (Orig.). 1993. pap. 9.95 (*0-9636377-0-3*) S L Wright.
***Life by Design: A Do-It-Yourself Approach to Achieving Happiness.** Nancy Hunter Denney. (Illus.). 224p. 2000. pap. 14.95 (*1-930463-00-6*) Victory Inc.
Life by Design: Making Wise Choices in a Mixed up World. Rick Kirschner & Rick Brinkman. (Illus.). 243p. 1999. pap. 14.95 (*0-07-034749-2*) McGraw.
Life by Design: Your Handbook for Transformational Living. unabridged ed. Kevin L. Hogan. LC 95-71776. (Illus.). 300p. (Orig.). 1996. pap. 19.95 (*0-9635085-3-9*) Network Three Thous.
Life by Drowning. Jeni Couzyn. 1985. pap. 17.95 (*0-906427-73-8*, Pub. by Bloodaxe Bks) Dufour.
Life by Drowning: Selected Poems. Jeni Couzyn. 174p. (Orig.). 1983. pap. 8.95 (*0-88784-098-1*, Pub. by Hse of Anansi Pr) Genl Dist Srvs.
Life by His Death see Vida por Su Muerte
Life by His Death. J. Owen. 1998. pap. text 5.99 (*0-9505476-3-8*) P & R Pubng.
Life by His Death. John Owen. 1992. pap. 4.99 (*0-85234-763-4*, Pub. by Evangelical Pr) P & R Pubng.
Life by the Numbers. Keith J. Devlin. LC 97-41059. 214p. 1998. 29.95 (*0-471-24044-3*) Wiley.
Life Can Be Hard Sometimes but It's Going to Be Okay see Veces, la Vida Puede Ser Dura...Pero Todo Saldra Bien
Life Can Be Hard Sometimes, But It's Going to Be Okay: A Collection of Poems. Ed. by Susan Polis Schutz. LC 90-80731. (Illus.). 64p. 1990. pap. 8.95 (*0-88396-281-0*) Blue Mtn Art.
Life Capsule: Preserving the Past for the Future. Ed. by Sharon A. Bauer & William E. Bauer. (Illus.). vi, 182p. 1999. pap. 29.50 (*0-9659729-0-9*) K & J Pub.
Life Care: The Inside Story. Elwood N. Chapman. Ed. by Follin Armfield. LC 94-70615. 136p. 1994. pap. 12.95 (*1-56052-290-9*) Crisp Pubns.
Life Care Planning for the Amputee: A Step-by-Step Guide. Roger O. Weed & Anne Sluis-Powers. (Life Care Planning Monograph Ser.). 162p. 1990. per. 26.95 (*1-878205-09-9*) St Lucie Pr.
Life Care Planning for the Brain Damaged Baby: A Step-by-Step Guide. Julie A. Kitchen et al. (Life Care Planning Monograph Ser.). 140p. (C). 1989. per. 26.95 (*1-878205-00-5*) St Lucie Pr.
Life Care Planning for the Spinal Cord Injured: A Step-by-Step Guide. Paul M. Deutsch. 88p. 1989. per. 26.95 (*0-945019-08-4*) St Lucie Pr.
Life Care Planning for the Ventilator Dependent Patient: A Step-by-Step Guide. Julie A. Kitchen et al. (Life Care Planning Monograph Ser.). 224p. 1990. per. 31.95 (*1-878205-05-6*) St Lucie Pr.
Life Career & Educational Planning. Maire Liberace. 150p. (C). 1990. 45.00 (*0-536-57807-9*) Pearson Custom.

An Asterisk (*) at the beginning of an entry indicates that the title is appearing for the first time.

Life Career & Educational Planning. 2nd ed. Maire Liberace. 154p. (C). 1996. text 33.60 (*0-536-59615-8*) Pearson Custom.
Life Carries On: Still More Classic Photographs from the Pages of America's Favorite Magazine. Life Magazine Editors. (Illus.). 192p. 1993. pap. 14.00 (*0-671-86852-7*, Fireside) S&S Trade Pap.
Life Cast: Behind the Mask. Willa Shalit. LC 92-14236. (Illus.). 128p. 1992. 29.95 (*0-941831-80-9*) Beyond Words Pub.
Life Centered Career Education: A Competency Based Approach. 5th ed. Donn E. Brolin & Council for Exceptional Children Staff. LC 97-3894. 175p. 1997. pap. text 30.00 (*0-86586-292-3*, P180G) Coun Exc Child.
Life Centered Career Education: Activity Book 1. 96p. 1986. pap. text 15.40 (*0-86586-162-5*, P303) Coun Exc Child.
Life Centered Career Education: Activity Book 2. 96p. 1986. pap. text 15.40 (*0-86586-163-3*, P304) Coun Exc Child.
Life Centered Career Education: Competency Assessment Knowledge Batteries. Donn E. Brolin. LC 93-11908. 152p. 1992. ring bd. 125.00 (*0-86586-239-7*, P370K) Coun Exc Child.
Life Centered Career Education: Competency Assessment Performance Batteries. Donn E. Brolin. LC 93-11908. 683p. 1992. ring bd. 225.00 (*0-86586-240-0*, P370P) Coun Exc Child.
Life Centered Career Education: Competency Units for Daily Living Skills. Donn E. Brolin. LC 92-17690. 1556p. 1992. ring bd. 400.00 (*0-86586-224-9*, P367) Coun Exc Child.
Life Centered Career Education: Competency Units for Occupational Guidance & Preparation. Richard T. Roessler & Donn E. Brolin. LC 92-18255. 670p. 1992. ring bd. 300.00 (*0-86586-226-5*, P369) Coun Exc Child.
Life Centered Career Education: Competency Units for Personal-Social Skills. Donn E. Brolin. LC 92-17680. 1348p. 1992. ring bd. 400.00 (*0-86586-225-7*, P368) Coun Exc Child.
Life Centered Career Education: Modified Curriculum for Individuals with Moderate Disabilities. Robert J. Loyd & Donn E. Brolin. LC 97-3896. 120p. 1997. pap. text 30.00 (*0-86586-293-1*, P5194) Coun Exc Child.
Life Challenge Inventory: A Self-Administered Life Stress Questionnaire & Handbook for Managing Life's Challenges in Personal, Family & Work Life. rev. ed. Ruth Schelkun. 84p. (Orig.). 1995. pap. 13.50 (*0-933933-00-2*) Human Netwrks.
Life Challenges for Men. Jerald Daffe. 195p. 1997. pap. 9.99 (*0-87148-039-5*) Pathway Pr.
Life Chances: Approaches to Social & Political Theory. Ralf Dahrendorf. LC 79-18685. x, 182p. (C). 1994. pap. text 8.95 (*0-226-13443-1*) U Ch Pr.
Life Chances: Approaches to Social & Political Theory. Ralf Dahrendorf. LC 79-18685. 192p. reprint ed. pap. 59.60 (*0-608-09440-4*, 205424000005) Bks Demand.
Life Change Events Research, 1966-1978: An Annotated Bibliography of the Periodical Literature. Thomas E. Holmes & Ella M. David. LC 83-19287. 331p. 1984. 59.95 (*0-275-91192-6*, C1192, Praeger Pubs) Greenwood.
Life Change, Life Events, & Illness: Selected Papers. Ed. by Thomas H. Holmes & Ella M. David. LC 88-28610. 361p. 1989. 69.50 (*0-275-92480-7*, C2480, Praeger Pubs) Greenwood.
Life-Changer: How You Can Experience Freedom Power & Refreshment in the Holy Spirit. 2nd rev. ed. Francis Martin. LC 98-20142. 170p. 1998. reprint ed. pap. 14.95 (*1-879007-30-4*) St Bedes Pubns.
***Life Changes with the Energy of the Chakras.** Ambika Wauters. LC 99-36231. 208p. 1999. pap. 14.95 (*1-58091-020-3*) Crossing Pr.
Life-Changing Camps & Retreats: Everything You Need to Lead. Student Impact Team Staff & Bo Boshers. LC 98-231188. (Student Impact Ser.). (Illus.). 128p. 1998. pap. 16.99 (*0-310-20123-3*) Zondervan.
Life Changing Messages for Busters. Glen Martin. Ed. by Cindy G. Spear. 9p. 1997. ring bd. 44.95 incl. audio (*1-57052-087-9*) Chrch Grwth VA.
Life Changing Solutions Through Inspiration. large type ed. Thomas H. Stephens. pap. text 12.95 (*1-890556-07-6*) T Stephens Pub.
***Life Changing Testimonies of the Lord Jesus Christ.** Marlena Tanya Muchnick. 230p. 1999. pap. 13.95 (*1-55517-394-2*) CFI Dist.
Life, Character & Influence of Desiderius Erasmus of Rotterdam, 2 vols. John J. Mangan. LC 73-147113. reprint ed. 78.50 (*0-404-04178-7*) AMS Pr.
Life Chemistry & Molecular Biology: An Introduction Text. E. J. Wood et al. (Illus.). 230p. (Orig.). (C). 1996. pap. text 27.00 (*1-85578-064-X*, Pub. by Portland Pr Ltd) Ashgate Pub Co.
Life Chemistry Reports, Vol. 1, Part 1. Ed. by A. M. Michelson & J. V. Bannister. 56p. 1982. pap. text 106.00 (*3-7186-0185-0*) Gordon & Breach.
Life Chemistry Reports, Vol. 1, Part 2. Ed. by A. M. Michelson & J. V. Bannister. 108p. 1982. pap. text 82.00 (*3-7186-0186-9*) Gordon & Breach.
Life Chemistry Reports, Vol. 1, Part 3. Ed. by J. V. Bannister & A. M. Michelson. 114p. 1983. pap. text 112.00 (*3-7186-0171-0*) Gordon & Breach.
Life Chemistry Reports, Vol. 2. Ed. by J. V. Bannister & A. M. Michelson. 120p. 1984. pap. text 98.00 (*3-7186-0270-9*) Gordon & Breach.
Life Chemistry Reports, Vol. 2. Ed. by A. M. Michelson & J. V. Bannister. 96p. 1983. pap. text 77.00 (*3-7186-0199-0*) Gordon & Breach.
Life Chemistry Reports, Vol. 2. Ed. by A. M. Michelson & J. V. Bannister. 84p. 1984. pap. text 69.00 (*3-7186-0220-2*) Gordon & Breach.
Life Chemistry Reports, Vol. 3. Ed. by J. V. Bannister & A. M. Michelson. 52p. 1985. pap. text 43.00 (*3-7186-0298-9*) Gordon & Breach.
Life Chemistry Reports, Vol. 3. Ed. by J. V. Bannister & A. M. Michelson. 78p. 1986. pap. text 58.00 (*3-7186-0340-3*) Gordon & Breach.
Life Chemistry Reports, Vol. 4. Ed. by J. V. Bannister & A. M. Michelson. 112p. 1986. text 190.00 (*3-7186-0379-9*) Gordon & Breach.
Life Chemistry Reports, Vol. 4. Ed. by J. V. Bannister & A. M. Michelson. 106p. 1987. pap. text 71.00 (*3-7186-0417-5*); pap. text 129.00 (*3-7186-0451-5*); pap. text 192.00 (*3-7186-0461-2*) Gordon & Breach.
Life Chemistry Reports, Vol. 6. Ed. by J. V. Bannister & A. M. Michelson. 142p. 1987. pap. text 203.00 (*3-7186-4803-2*) Gordon & Breach.
Life Chemistry Reports, Vol. 6. Ed. by J. V. Bannister & A. M. Michelson. 122p. 1988. pap. text 145.00 (*3-7186-4810-5*) Gordon & Breach.
Life Chemistry Reports, Vol. 7. Ed. by J. V. Bannister. 48p. 1989. pap. text 63.00 (*3-7186-4982-9*) Gordon & Breach.
Life Chemistry Reports, Vol. 8. Ed. by J. V. Bannister. 48p. 1990. pap. text 69.00 (*3-7186-5037-1*) Gordon & Breach.
Life Chemistry Reports, Vol. 12. Ed. by J. V. Bannister. (Life Chemistry Reports: Vol. 12, No. 2). 102p. 1994. pap. text 211.00 (*3-7186-5640-X*) Gordon & Breach.
Life Chemistry Reports: Proceedings of the International Meeting on Antioxidants, Inflammation, Cardiovascular & Ophthalmic Diseases. Francisco Romero. (Life Chemistry Reports: Vol. 12). 104p. 1994. pap. text 215.00 (*3-7186-5639-6*) Gordon & Breach.
Life Chemistry Reports Vol. 5, Pts. 1-4: The Active Site of Copper Proteins, Vol. 5, Nos. 1-4. Ed. by J. V. Bannister & A. M. Michelson. ii, 341p. 1987. pap. text 431.00 (*3-7186-0462-0*) Gordon & Breach.
Life Chemistry Reports Vol. 6, No. 3: A Special Issue, Vol. 6, No. 3. J. V. Bannister. 118p. 1988. pap. text 94.00 (*3-7186-4885-7*) Gordon & Breach.
Life Chemistry Reports Vol. 7, No. 1: Temperature Dependent Proteins, Vol. 7, No. 1. Ed. by J. V. Bannister. 64p. 1989. pap. text 92.00 (*3-7186-4969-1*) Gordon & Breach.
Life Chemistry Reports Vol. 7, No. 3: Heavy Metal Toxicity Contents, Vol. 7, No. 3. Ed. by J. V. Bannister. 176p. 1989. pap. text 244.00 (*3-7186-4998-5*) Gordon & Breach.
Life Chemistry Reports Vol. 10, No. 2: Proceedings of the Meeting Organised by the Italian Chemical Society, Vol. 10. Bruno Rindone. (Life Chemistry Reports). 120p. 1994. pap. text 247.00 (*3-7186-5533-0*) Gordon & Breach.
Life Chemistry Reports Vol. 11, No. 1: Aluminum in Chemistry, Biology & Medicine, Vol. 11. Paolo F. Zatta. (Life Chemistry Reports). 270p. 1994. pap. text 189.00 (*3-7186-5567-5*) Gordon & Breach.
Life Chemistry Reports Vol. 12, No. 3. Ed. by J. V. Bannister. (Life Chemistry Reports). 196p. 1995. pap. text 580.00 (*3-7186-5735-X*, Harwood Acad Pubs) Gordon & Breach.
Life Choices. Richard Bence & Dawn Bence. Ed. by Dan E. Kennedy. (Illus.). 108p. (Orig.). 1989. pap. 12.00 (*0-943529-04-2*) Empire Comms.
Life Choices. Cooley. LC 96-76884. (C). 1996. pap. text 28.76 (*0-395-73865-2*) HM.
Life Choices. Cooley. (C). 1997. pap., teacher ed. 11.96 (*0-395-73866-0*) HM.
Life Choices. annot. ed. Frances S. Sizer. Date not set. text, teacher ed. write for info. (*0-314-07047-8*) West Pub.
Life Choices. 2nd ed. Turner. Date not set. pap. text, teacher ed. write for info. (*0-314-93384-0*) West Pub.
***Life Choices: A Hastings Center Introduction to Bioethics.** 2nd rev. ed. Ed. by Joseph H. Howell & William F. Sale. LC 99-29971. (Hastings Center Studies in Ethics). 601p. 2000. pap. text 35.00 (*0-87840-757-X*) Georgetown U Pr.
Life Choices: Applying Sociology. 3rd ed. Dan E. Kennedy. (C). 1996. pap. text 20.00 (*0-03-049939-9*) Harcourt Coll Pubs.
Life Choices: Health Concepts & Strategies. 2nd ed. Lori Turner et al. Ed. by Marshall. 621p. (C). 1992. pap. text 46.50 (*0-314-93383-2*) West Pub.
Life Choices: Understanding Dilemmas & Decisions. Tod S. Sloan. (Lives in Context Ser.). (C). 1996. pap. 22.00 (*0-8133-2657-5*, Pub. by Westview) HarpC.
Life Choices, Life Changes: The Art of Developing Personal Vision Through Inagework, 1. Dina Glouberman. 1999. pap. 12.95 (*1-85538-499-X*) HarpCollins.
Life Choices Sampler. Frances S. Sizer. Date not set. pap. text. write for info. (*0-314-38487-1*) West Pub.
Life Christmas Sound Book. 32p. (J). 1999. pap. write for info. (*0-7814-0237-9*, Chariot Bks) Chariot Victor.
Life Class. Elizabeth James. 1991. 20.00 (*0-7278-4055-X*) Severn Hse.
Life Class. large type ed. Elizabeth James. 464p. 1988. 27.99 (*0-7089-8453-3*, Charnwood) Ulverscroft.
Life Class: The Academic Male Nude, 1820-1920. Edward Lucie-Smith. 1995. per. 25.00 (*0-85449-103-1*, Pub. by Gay Mens Pr) LPC InBook.
Life Classic Photographs: A Personal Interpretation Expanded Edition with New Photographs. John Loengard. (Illus.). 200p. 1996. pap. 19.95 (*0-8212-2263-5*, Pub. by Bulfinch Pr) Little.
Life Coach: A Guide for Winning Basketball & Successful Living. Kenneth D. Griffin & William G. Burgin. 66p. 1997. pap. 12.00 (*1-57502-570-1*, PO1646) Morris Pubng.
Life Coaching: A New Career for Helping Professionals. David B. Ellis. 157p. 1998. ring bd. 74.95 (*0-942456-15-7*) Breakthrgh Enter.
Life Colors. Pamala Oslie. LC 91-40295. 380p. 1991. pap. 14.95 (*0-931432-81-2*) New Wrld Lib.
***Life Colors: What the Colors in Your Aura Reveal.** rev. ed. Pamala Oslie. 384p. 2000. pap. 16.95 (*1-57731-169-8*, Pub. by New Wrld Lib) Publishers Group.
Life Colors Art: Fifty Years of Painting. Peter Busa. (Artists Ser.: Vol. 1). (Illus.). 72p. 1992. pap. 20.00 (*0-944854-05-2*) Provincetown Arts.
Life Comes from Life. Swami A. C. Bhaktivedanta. 140p. 1979. reprint ed. pap. 2.95 (*0-89213-100-4*) Bhaktivedanta.
***Life Complete: Emotional & Spiritual Growth for Midlife & Beyond.** Sallirae Henderson. 224p. 2000. 23.50 (*0-684-83775-7*) Scribner.
***Life Complete E Book: Finding Meaning & Purpose in the Later Years.** 2000. 24.00 (*0-7432-0588-X*) S&S Trade.
Life Conflictions. Benjamin Hicks. 60p. 1995. pap. 5.00 (*1-929883-00-5*, 95-1PB) Ingleside Pr MD.
***Life Connections: Pioneers in Ecology** Linda Leuzzi. LC 99-33075. (Lives in Science Ser.). 2000. 25.00 (*0-531-11566-6*) Watts.
Life Contingencies. Alistair Neill. LC 78-303002. (Illus.). 464p. reprint ed. pap. 143.90 (*0-608-09702-0*, 206986800007) Bks Demand.
Life Continues with a Disability: A Practical Guide for the Newly Diagnosed. large type ed. La Vonne Scott. LC 97-61363. 128p. 1998. pap. 10.95 (*0-9659501-1-5*) A D Tate.
Life, Conversion, Preaching, Travels & Suffering of Elias Smith. Elias Smith. Ed. by Edwin S. Gaustad. LC 79-52606. (Baptist Tradition Ser.). 1980. reprint ed. lib. bdg. 37.95 (*0-405-12471-6*) Ayer.
Life Course. John A. Clausen. 1985. pap. text 24.00 (*0-13-535907-4*) P-H.
Life Course & Generational Politics. Ed. by Richard G. Braungart & Margaret M. Braungart. LC 92-21177. 218p. (Orig.). (C). 1993. reprint ed. pap. text 21.50 (*0-8191-9006-3*) U Pr of Amer.
Life Course Approach to Chronic Disease Epidemiology: Tracing the Origins of Ill-Health from Early to Adult Life. Ed. by Diana Kuh & Yoav Ben-Shlomo. LC 97-9893. (Illus.). 336p. 1997. text 65.00 (*0-19-262782-1*) OUP.
Life Course Dynamics: Trajectories & Transitions, 1968-1980. Ed. by Glen H. Elder, Jr. LC 84-21503. (Illus.). 352p. (C). 1985. pap. text 27.50 (*0-8014-9323-4*) Cornell U Pr.
Life Course Perspectives on Adulthood & Old Age. Marsha M. Seltzer et al. LC 93-41155. 210p. (C). 1994. pap. text 35.00 (*0-940898-31-4*) Am Assn Mental.
Life Crises & Experiences of Loss in Adulthood. Ed. by Leo Montada et al. 560p. 1992. text 99.95 (*0-8058-1001-3*) L Erlbaum Assocs.
Life Culture Versus Death Culture & the Death of Literature. Patrick A. O'Dougherty. LC 95-95349. 50p. (C). 1995. lib. bdg. 10.99 (*0-9626665-3-X*) Irish Catholic.
***Life Cycle: Psychological & Theological Perceptions.** Richard Dayringer. LC 99-37919. 177p. 1999. 49.95 (*0-7890-0171-3*, Haworth Pastrl); pap. 22.95 (*0-7890-0905-6*, Haworth Pastrl) Haworth Pr.
Life Cycle - A Diversity in a Balance. J. R. Blueford et al. (J). (gr. k-6). 1992. 24.95 (*1-56638-157-6*) Math Sci Nucleus.
Life Cycle Analysis for Environmental Problem Solving. Arthur H. Purcell. Date not set. 59.95 (*0-87371-854-2*) Lewis Pubs.
Life Cycle & Failure Data, LB 11-82. BSRIA Staff. (C). 1982. 70.00 (*0-86022-165-2*, Pub. by Build Servs Info Assn) St Mut.
Life-Cycle Assessment: Inventory Guideline & Principles. Battelle Memorial Institute Staff. 144p. 1994. lib. bdg. 54.95 (*1-56670-015-9*) Lewis Pubs.
Life Cycle Assessment: What It Is & How to Do It. 96p. 21.00 (*92-807-1546-1*, TS170) UN.
***Life Cycle Assessment in Industry & Business: Adoption Patterns, Applications & Implications.** Paolo Frankl & Frieder Rubik. LC 99-48449. (Illus.). x, 279p. 2000. 79.00 (*3-540-66469-6*) Spr-Verlag.
Life Cycle Assessment (LCA) - Quo Vadis? Ed. by Stefan Schaltegger et al. LC 96-14891. 1997. 47.00 (*0-8176-5341-4*) Birkhauser.
***Life Cycle Assessment of Natural Gas Vehicles: Development & Application of Site-Dependent Impact Indicators.** K. M. Nigge. LC 00-39468. (Wissenschaftsethik und Technikfolgenbeurteilung Ser.). (Illus.). 2000. pap. write for info. (*3-540-67273-7*) Spr-Verlag.
Life Cycle Chapter Study Kit. pap. 3.00 (*0-686-96087-4*) USCJE.
Life Cycle Completed. Joan M. Erikson. LC 96-3462. 160p. 1997. 19.95 (*0-393-03934-X*) Norton.
Life Cycle Completed: Extended Version. Erik H. Erikson & Joan M. Erikson. 144p. 1998. pap. 11.00 (*0-393-31772-2*) Norton.
Life-Cycle Cost Analysis for Protection & Rehabilitation of Concrete Bridges Relative to Reinforcement Corrosion. Ronald L. Purvis et al. 289p. (C). 1994. pap. text 25.00 (*0-309-05755-8*, SHRP-S-377) SHRP.
Life-Cycle Cost Analysis of Pavements. (National Cooperative Highway Research Program Report Ser.: No. 122). 136p. 1985. 10.80 (*0-309-04006-X*) Transport Res Bd.
Life Cycle Cost Assessments for Military Transatmospheric Vehicles. Melvin Eisman et al. LC 97-34875. (Project Air Force Ser.). (Illus.). 45p. 1997. pap. 13.00 (*0-8330-2554-6*, MR-893-AF) Rand Corp.
Life Cycle Costing: Techniques, Models & Applications. B. S. Dhillon. xviii, 354p. 1989. text 101.00 (*2-88124-302-9*) Gordon & Breach.
Life Cycle Costing for Construction. Ed. by John W. Bull. (Illus.). 169p. 1993. text 144.95 (*0-7514-0056-4*, Pub. by B Acad & Prof) Routldge.
Life Cycle Costing for Construction. Roger Flanagan. Ed. by George Norman & J. David Furbur. (C). 1989. text 110.00 (*0-85406-194-0*) St Mut.
Life Cycle Design: A Manual for Small & Medium Sized Companies. Ed. by S. Behrendt et al. LC 97-30264. (Illus.). 204p. 1997. 99.95 incl. cd-rom (*3-540-62793-6*) Spr-Verlag.
Life Cycle Education Manual see Life Cycles: Activites for Helping Children Cope with Daily Change & Loss
Life Cycle Education Manual: A Guide for Teachers & Helping Professionals: To Help Children Cope with Daily Change & Loss. rev. ed. Jeanne Lagorio. 216p. (Orig.). 1992. pap. text 20.00 (*0-9633195-9-0*) Empower in Act.
Life Cycle Environment Impact Analysis for Forest Products. 130p. 1996. 40.00 (*0-935018-80-8*, 7294) Forest Prod.
Life Cycle Group Work in Nursing. E. H. Janosik & L. B. Phipps. 1983. reprint ed. 38.75 (*0-86720-388-9*, 80-71075) Jones & Bartlett.
Life Cycle Management for Dependability. Ed. by Felix Redmill & Chris Dale. LC 96-27350. (Illus.). xviii, 235p. 1997. pap. 62.00 (*3-540-76073-3*) Spr-Verlag.
***Life Cycle of a Chicken.** Angela Royston. LC 98-10754. (J). 1998. 19.92 (*1-57572-698-X*) Heinemann Lib.
Life Cycle of a Congregation. Martin F. Saarinen. pap. 7.95 (*1-56699-189-7*, OD124) Alban Inst.
***Life Cycle of a Dog.** Angela Royston. LC 99-46854. 2000. lib. bdg. write for info. (*1-57572-209-7*) Heinemann Lib.
Life Cycle of a Frog: Shadow, Stick or Rod Puppet Workshop. Laura Glusha & Karen Muldrew. (Illus.). 9p. (Orig.). (J). (gr. 2-6). 1996. pap., wbk. ed. 6.50 (*1-890972-08-8*, FR - 11) Natures Shadows.
***Life Cycle of a Mushroom.** Angela Royston. LC 99-46105. 2000. lib. bdg. write for info. (*1-57572-210-0*) Heinemann Lib.
***Life Cycle of a Salmon.** Angela Royston. LC 99-46104. 2000. lib. bdg. write for info. (*1-57572-212-7*) Heinemann Lib.
***Life Cycle of an Oak Tree.** Angela Royston. LC 99-46855. 2000. lib. bdg. write for info. (*1-57572-211-9*) Heinemann Lib.
Life Cycle of Butterflies: Complete Unit. National Science Resources Center Staff. (Science & Technology for Children Ser.). (Illus.). (J). (gr. 2). 1992. pap. write for info. (*0-89278-616-7*) Carolina Biological.
Life Cycle of Butterflies Student Notebook. National Science Resources Center Staff. (Science & Technology for Children Ser.). (Illus.). 20p. (J). (gr. 2). 1992. pap. text, student ed. write for info. (*0-89278-618-3*) Carolina Biological.
Life Cycle of Butterflies Teacher's Guide. National Science Resources Center Staff. (Science & Technology for Children Ser.). (Illus.). 124p. 1992. pap. text, teacher ed. write for info. (*0-89278-617-5*) Carolina Biological.
Life Cycle of Groups: Group Developmental Stage Theory. Roy B. Lacoursiere. LC 79-27112. 317p. 1980. 42.95 (*0-87705-469-X*, Kluwer Acad Hman Sci) Kluwer Academic.
Life-Cycle of Synagogue Membership: A Guide to Membership, Recruitment, Integration & Retention. UAHC Task Force on the Unaffiliated Staff. 144p. 1991. pap. 12.00 (*0-8074-0465-9*, 280058) UAHC.
***Life Cycle of the Alligator.** Sabrina Crewe. (Life Cycles Ser.). 1998. pap. 5.95 (*0-8172-6245-8*) Raintree Steck-V.
Life Cycle of the Bear. Sabrina Crewe. LC 96-4845. (Life Cycles Bks.). (Illus.). (J). (gr. 2-5). 1997. pap. 5.95 (*0-8172-6230-X*) Raintree Steck-V.
Life Cycle of the Beaver. Sabrina Crewe. 1999. pap. text 5.95 (*0-8172-4249-X*) Raintree Steck-V.
Life Cycle of the Bee. Sabrina Crewe. LC 96-4833. (Life Cycles Bks.). 32p. (J). (gr. 2-5). 1997. pap. 5.95 (*0-8172-6225-3*) Raintree Steck-V.
***Life Cycle of the Buffalo.** Sabrina Crewe. 1999. pap. text 5.95 (*0-8172-6238-5*) Raintree Steck-V.
***Life Cycle of the Career Teacher.** Ed. by Betty E. Steffy et al. LC 99-46010. 144p. (C). 1999. pap. 22.95 (*0-7619-7540-3*); lib. bdg. 49.95 (*0-7619-7539-X*) Corwin Pr.
Life Cycle of the Career Teacher: Maintaining Excellence for a Lifetime. Betty E. Steffy & Michael P. Wolfe. 24p. 1997. pap. 3.00 (*0-912099-27-5*, 490) Kappa Delta Pi.
Life Cycle of the Kangaroo. Sabrina Crewe. LC 96-4829. (Life Cycles Bks.). (J). (gr. 2-5). 1997. pap. 5.95 (*0-8172-6233-4*) Raintree Steck-V.
Life Cycle of the Mountain Lion. Sabrina Crewe. (Life Cycles Ser.). 1998. pap. 5.95 (*0-8172-6239-3*) Raintree Steck-V.
Life Cycle of the Pacific Gray Whale. John Klobas. (Life Cycles Ser.). (Illus.). 32p. (J). (gr. 6-9). 1993. 12.95 (*0-89346-532-1*) Heian Intl.
***Life Cycle of the Penguin.** Sabrina Crewe. (Life Cycles Ser.). (Illus.). 32p. (J). (gr. 2-5). 1998. pap. 5.95 (*0-8172-6240-7*) Raintree Steck-V.
Life Cycle of the Snake. Sabrina Crewe. LC 96-4827. (Life Cycles Bks.). (Illus.). (J). 1997. pap. 5.95 (*0-8172-6235-0*) Raintree Steck-V.
***Life Cycle of the Spider.** Sabrina Crewe. (Life Cycles Ser.). 1998. pap. 5.95 (*0-8172-6241-5*) Raintree Steck-V.
Life Cycle of the Union Bank of Scotland, 1830-1954. Norio Tamaki. 264p. 1983. text 42.00 (*0-08-030359-5*, Pergamon Pr) Elsevier.
Life Cycle of the Whale. Sabrina Crewe. LC 96-4846. (Life Cycles Bks.). (Illus.). 32p. (J). (gr. 2-5). 1997. pap. 5.95 (*0-8172-6226-1*) Raintree Steck-V.
Life Cycle Strategies: Software Support on the Front Line. Thomas M. Pigoski. 107p. 1994. pap. 45.00 (*1-884521-03-7*) Software Maint.

Life Cycles, 18 vols. (Life Cycles Ser.). (Illus.). (J). (gr. 2-5). 1997. lib. bdg. 269.64 (*0-8172-4381-X*) Raintree Steck-V.

Life Cycles. John T. Bonner. 222p. 1993. pap. text 14.95 (*0-691-00151-0*, Pub. by Princeton U Pr) Cal Prin Full Svc.

***Life Cycles.** Marco Ferrari. LC 98-9268. (Everyday Life of Animals Ser.). (Illus.). 64p. (YA). (gr. 5-8). 1999. lib. bdg. 27.12 (*0-8172-4197-3*) Raintree Steck-V.

***Life Cycles.** Sally Hewitt. (Discovering Nature Ser.). (Illus.). 32p. (J). (gr. 2-4). 2000. 21.90 (*0-7613-1156-4*, Copper Beech Bks) Millbrook Pr.

Life Cycles. Donna Schaffer. (Illus.). 144p. 84.00 (*0-7368-0298-3*) Capstone Pr.

Life Cycles: Activites for Helping Children Cope with Daily Change & Loss. rev. ed. Jeanne Lagorio. Orig. Title: Life Cycle Education Manual. 128p. (J). (ps-6). 1997. pap. 13.95 (*0-9633195-0-7*) Empower in Act.

***Life Cycles: Hands on Elementary School Science.** 2nd ed. (Illus.). 53p. 2000. teacher ed. 35.00 (*1-883410-35-5*) L Poore.

Life Cycles: Reflections of an Evolutionary Biologist. John T. Bonner. (Illus.). 192p. 1993. text 39.50 (*0-691-03319-6*, Pub. by Princeton U Pr) Cal Prin Full Svc.

Life Cycles: The Astrology of Inner Space & Its Application to the Rhythms of Life. Bill Anderton. LC 90-49411. (Illus.). 160p. 1999. reprint ed. pap. 9.95 (*0-87542-021-4*) Llewellyn Pubns.

***Life Cycles: Your Emotional Journey to Freedom & Happiness.** Christine DeLorey. LC 99-90582. 352p. 2000. pap. 18.99 (*0-9673130-9-0*, Pub. by Osmos Bks) New Leaf Dist.

Life Cycles & Long Waves. Ed. by T. Vasko et al. (Lecture Notes in Economics & Mathematical Systems Ser.: Vol. 340). (Illus.). xiv, 293p. 1990. 44.95 (*0-387-52473-8*) Spr-Verlag.

Life Cycles Big Books Set. Melvin Berger. Ed. by Susan Evento. (Macmillan Early Science Big Bks.). (Illus.). (J). (ps-2). 1995. pap. write for info. (*1-56784-172-4*) Newbridge Educ.

Life Cycles in Atchalan: The Diverse Careers of Certain Guatemalans. G. Alexander Moore. LC 72-93732. 232p. reprint ed. pap. 72.00 (*0-608-12762-0*, 202432900037) Bks Demand.

Life Cycles in England, 1560-1720: Cradle to Grave. Mary Abbott. LC 95-37392. 320p. (C). 1996. 85.00 (*0-415-10842-X*); pap. 24.99 (*0-415-10843-8*) Routledge.

Life Cycles in Jewish & Christian Worship. Ed. by Paul F. Bradshaw & Lawrence A. Hoffman. LC 95-18807. (Two Liturgical Traditions Ser.: Vol. 4). (C). 1997. text 32.95 (*0-268-01307-1*) U of Notre Dame Pr.

Life Cycles of a Dozen Diverse Creatures. Paul Fleisher. LC 95-52717. (Illus.). 80p. (J). (gr. 3-6). 1996. lib. bdg. 24.90 (*0-7613-0000-7*) Millbrook Pr.

Life Cycles of a Dozen Diverse Creatures. Paul Fleisher. (Illus.). 80p. (J). (gr. 3-6). 1998. pap. text 9.95 (*0-7613-0349-9*) Millbrook Pr.

***Life Cycles of Extratropical Cyclones.** Ed. by Melvyn Shapiro & Sigbjorn Gronas. (Illus.). 385p. 1999. 65.00 (*1-878220-35-7*) Am Meteorological.

***Life Cycles Resource Guide, Vol. 3086.** Marilyn Marks. Ed. by Joel Kupperstein. (Illus.). 80p. 1999. pap. text 8.98 (*1-57471-633-6*, 3086) Creat Teach Pr.

Life Cycles Set. Melvin Berger. Ed. by Susan Evento. (Macmillan Early Science Big Bks.). (Illus.). (J). (ps-2). 1995. pap. write for info. (*1-56784-171-6*) Newbridge Educ.

Life Dance. William P. Gassen. 184p. 1993. pap. 10.95 (*0-9636157-0-X*) Tracher Pr.

Life Dance: A Photography Album. Nell Dorr & Covington Hardee. (Illus.). 72p. 1975. pap. 9.75 (*0-911726-21-7*, CODE LDB) Alleluia Pr.

Life, Death & Art: The Medieval Stained Glass of Fairford Parish Church, a Multimedia Exploration. Ed. by Sarah Brown & Lindsay MacDonald. LC NK5344.F3L54 1997. (Illus.). 192p. 1997. 81.00 incl. cd-rom (*0-7509-1523-4*, Pub. by Sutton Pub Ltd) Intl Pubs Mktg.

Life, Death & Beyond. J. J. Turner. 1988. reprint ed. pap. 4.50 (*0-89315-138-6*) Lambert Bk.

Life, Death & Decisions: Doctors & Nurses Reflect. McHaffie. LC 97-142928. 304p. 1997. pap. text 37.50 (*1-898507-55-4*) Buttrwrth-Heinemann.

***Life, Death & Dreams.** Paul Startzman. LC 99-93748. 1999. pap. 7.95 (*0-533-13131-6*) Vantage.

Life, Death, & Entertainment in the Roman Empire. Ed. by D. S. Potter & D. J. Mattingly. LC 98-40201. (Illus.). 368p. 1999. text 49.50 (*0-472-10924-3*, 10924); pap. text 18.95 (*0-472-08568-9*, 08568) U of Mich Pr.

Life, Death & in Between: Tales of Clinical Neurology. Harold L. Klawans. 270p. 1994. 21.95 (*1-56924-871-0*) Marlowe & Co.

Life, Death & In-Between on the U. S./Mexico Border: Asi es la Vida. Ed. by Martha Oehmke Loustaunau & Mary Sanchez-Bane. LC 99-14380. 256p. 1999. 65.00 (*0-89789-568-1*, Bergin & Garvey); pap. 22.95 (*0-89789-569-X*, Bergin & Garvey) Greenwood.

Life, Death & Litigation in the Athenian Agora. Mabel L. Lang. (Excavations of the Athenian Agora Picture Bks.: No. 23). (Illus.). 32p. 1994. pap. 3.00 (*0-87661-637-6*) Am Sch Athens.

Life, Death & Miracles of St. Francois de Paule. Antoine Donde. (Printed Sources of Western Art Ser.). (FRE., Illus.). 258p. 1981. reprint ed. boxed set 50.00 (*0-915346-64-8*) A Wofsy Fine Arts.

Life, Death, & Money: Actuaries & the Development of Social & Financial Markets. Ed. by Derek Renn. LC 97-38759. 339p. 1998. 78.95 (*0-631-20906-9*) Blackwell Pubs.

Life, Death & Public Policy. Robert H. Blank. 187p. 1988. pap. 15.00 (*0-87580-540-X*) N Ill U Pr.

Life, Death & the Government. fac. ed. Ed. by Melinda Maidens. LC 80-29094. (Illus.). 200p. 1980. reprint ed. pap. 62.00 (*0-7837-8143-1*, 204795100008) Bks Demand.

Life, Death, & the Law: A Sourcebook on Autonomy & Responsibility in Medical Ethics, 2 vols., Set. W. Noel Keyes. LC 95-18793. (Illus.). 1076p. 1995. 187.95 (*0-398-06533-0*); pap. 137.95 (*0-398-06534-9*) C C Thomas.

Life, Death & the Law: Landmark Right-to-Die Decisions. Ed. by Maureen Harrison & Steve Gilbert. LC 97-60186. 240p. (Orig.). 1997. pap. 16.95 (*1-880780-13-5*) Excellent Bks.

Life, Death & Two Chickens. Charles E. Fager. 100p. (J). (gr. 3-6). 1990. pap. 10.95 (*0-945177-04-6*) Kimo Pr.

Life, Death, Burial & Resurrection of Jesus Christ. Willie Mewborn. Date not set. pap. write for info. (*1-930070-28-4*) Words of Faith.

Life-Death Decisions in Health Care. Ed. by Lesley F. Degner & Janet I. Beaton. (Death Education, Aging & Health Care Ser.). 159p. 1987. 63.95 (*0-89116-399-9*) Hemisp Pub.

Life Design: Curriculum - Instructors Guide. Kathy A. Shawl. Ed. by Janette Perry. (Life Design Ser.). (Illus.). 198p. (Orig.). 1996. pap. text 19.95 (*1-885477-33-3*) Fut Horizons.

Life Design: Instructor's Guide. 2nd rev. ed. Kathy A. Shawl. (Life Design Ser.). (Illus.). 198p. 1997. pap. 19.95 (*1-885477-38-4*) Fut Horizons.

Life-Design: Living Your Life by Choice Instead of Chance. Peggy Vaughan & James Vaughan. (Illus.). 106p. 1994. wbk. ed. 25.00 (*0-936390-02-6*) Dialog Pr.

Life-Design: Living Your Life by Choice Instead of Chance. 2nd ed. Peggy Vaughan & James Vaughan. (Illus.). 106p. 1995. wbk. ed. 25.00 (*0-936390-03-4*) Dialog Pr.

Life Design: Student Guide. Kathy A. Shawl. (Life Design Ser.). 83p. (Orig.). 1997. pap. 19.95 (*1-885477-37-6*) Fut Horizons.

Life Designs. Elaine Ford. LC 97-3163. 192p. (Orig.). 1997. 22.95 (*0-944072-80-1*) Zoland Bks.

***Life Directions.** Jane A. G. Kise. LC 99-6419. 208p. 1999. pap. text 10.99 (*1-55661-208-7*) Bethany Hse.

Life Distilled: Gwendolyn Brooks, Her Poetry & Fiction. Maria K. Mootry & Gary Smith. LC 86-11356. 286 P. ;p. 1987. write for info. (*0-252-01367-0*) U of Ill Pr.

Life Distilled: Gwendolyn Brooks, Her Poetry & Fiction. Ed. by Maria K. Mootry & Gary Smith. LC 86-11356. 296p. 1989. reprint ed. pap. text 15.95 (*0-252-06065-2*) U of Ill Pr.

Life Divine. 2nd ed. Sri Aurobindo. LC 89-63859. 1113p. 1990. 39.95 (*0-941524-62-0*); pap. 29.95 (*0-941524-61-2*) Lotus Pr.

Life Divine. 5th ed. Sri Aurobindo. 1113p. 1996. 34.95 (*81-7058-188-5*, Pub. by SAA) E-W Cultural Ctr.

***Life Divine.** 5th ed. Sri Aurobindo. 1113p. 1998. pap. 29.95 (*81-7058-187-7*, Pub. by SAA) E-W Cultural Ctr.

Life Divine: A Commentary on Isha Upanished. Sri Aurobindo. 108p. (Orig.). 1981. pap. 5.00 (*0-89744-230-X*, Pub. by Sri Aurob Ashram Trust) Acrpls Bks CO.

Life Divine: The Mother's Talks. Mother. 154p. (Orig.). 1989. pap. 4.95 (*0-317-99972-9*, Pub. by Sri Aurob Ashram Trust) Acrpls Bks CO.

Life Divine Concordance: A Word-Concordance of Sri Aurobindo's 'The Life Divine' Ed. by Prem Sobel & Jyoti Sobel. 655p. 1993. 15.00 (*81-7058-307-1*, Pub. by SAA) E-W Cultural Ctr.

Life Doesn't Frighten Me at All. John Agard. LC 89-26766. (Illus.). 88p. (YA). (gr. 6 up). 1995. 14.95 (*0-8050-1237-0*, Bks Young Read) H Holt & Co.

Life Doesn't Get Any Better Than This: The Holiness of Little Daily Dramas. Robert A. Alper. LC 96-12887. 224p. (Orig.). 1996. pap. 12.00 (*0-89243-932-7*, Liguori Triumph) Liguori Pubns.

Life, Don't Juggle It, Balance It!!! Cecelia Jones. Date not set. write for info. (*1-893569-03-9*) Accolade Pub Co.

***Life Downunder.** large type ed. David Burchell. 416p. 1999. 31.99 (*0-7089-9120-3*) Ulverscroft.

Life Drawing in Charcoal. enl. ed. Douglas R. Graves. LC 94-35240. (Illus.). 176p. 1994. pap. text 9.95 (*0-486-28268-6*) Dover.

Life Drawing Life: On Seeing-Drawing the Human Body. Frederick Franck. LC 89-30757. (Illus.). 178p. (Orig.). 1989. pap. 11.95 (*0-915556-19-7*) Great Ocean.

Life Drawings of Michelangelo. Michelangelo Buonarroti. (Fine Art Ser.). (Illus.). 48p. 1980. pap. 4.95 (*0-486-23876-8*) Dover.

***Life During the Black Death.** John M. Dunn. LC 99-23791. (Way People Live Ser.). (Illus.). 112p. (YA). (gr. 6-9). 2000. lib. bdg. 23.70 (*1-56006-542-7*) Lucent Bks.

Life During the Civil War. Frank Schaffer Publications, Inc. Staff. (Middle School Bks.). (Illus.). 1996. wbk. ed. 10.95 (*0-7647-0016-2*, FS-10192) Schaffer Pubns.

Life During the Crusades. Earle Rice, Jr. LC 97-27994. (Way People Live Ser.). (Illus.). 96p. (YA). (gr. 4-12). 1997. lib. bdg. 22.45 (*1-56006-379-3*) Lucent Bks.

Life During the French Revolution. Gail B. Stewart. (Way People Live Ser.). 112p. (J). (gr. 6-9). 1995. lib. bdg. 22.45 (*1-56006-078-6*) Lucent Bks.

Life During the Gold Rush. Victoria Sherrow. LC 98-15447. (Way People Live Ser.). (J). (gr. 4-12). 1998. lib. bdg. 22.45 (*1-56006-382-3*) Lucent Bks.

Life During the Great Depression. Dennis Nishi. LC 97-33030. (Way People Live Ser.). (Illus.). (YA). (gr. 5 up). 1997. lib. bdg. 22.45 (*1-56006-381-5*) Lucent Bks.

Life During the Middle Ages. Earle Rice. LC 97-48275. (Way People Live Ser.). (Illus.). 96p. (YA). (gr. 7 up). 1998. lib. bdg. 22.45 (*1-56006-386-6*) Lucent Bks.

Life During the Renaissance. Patricia D. Netzley. LC 97-39781. (Way People Live Ser.). (Illus.). (YA). (gr. 4-12). 1997. lib. bdg. 22.45 (*1-56006-375-0*) Lucent Bks.

Life During the Russian Revolution. Victoria Sherrow. LC 97-51181. (Way People Live Ser.). (Illus.). 96p. (J). (gr. 7-10). 1997. lib. bdg. 22.45 (*1-56006-389-0*) Lucent Bks.

Life During the Spanish Inquisition. Gail B. Stewart. LC 97-17709. (Way People Live Ser.). (Illus.). (YA). (gr. 4-12). 1997. lib. bdg. 22.45 (*1-56006-346-7*) Lucent Bks.

Life During Wartime. Keith Reddin. 1991. pap. 5.25 (*0-8222-0659-5*) Dramatists Play.

Life Energy: Using the Meridians to Unlock the Hidden Power of Your Emotions. John Diamond. (Illus.). 252p. 1990. reprint ed. pap. 12.95 (*1-55778-281-4*) Paragon Hse.

Life Enhancement One: Tips from Time Travelers from the Crysanthemum Kids. E. R. Porter. 172p. 1999. pap. 12.00 (*0-9666004-0-1*) EPC Publ.

Life Enhancement Through Music. John Diamond. 150p. (Orig.). 1999. pap. 14.95 (*1-890995-01-0*, 0011, Enhancement Bks) Vital Health.

***Life Enhancement's 5-HTP Archives** Gail Valentine & Will Block. LC 98-87054. 158p. 1998. write for info. (*0-9666430-0-3*) Livelong Pubg.

Life Enhancing Activities for Mentally Impaired Adults. Beverly A. Beisgen. 336p. 1989. pap. 39.95 (*0-8261-6790-X*) Springer Pub.

Life Essential: The Hope of the Gospel. 2nd ed. George MacDonald. Ed. by Rolland Hein. LC 74-16732. (Wheaton Literary Ser.). 104p. 1978. pap. 6.99 (*0-87788-499-4*, H Shaw Pubs) Waterbrook Pr.

***Life Essentials: A Guide for Spiritual Growth.** Moody Press Editors. 1999. 29.99 (*0-8024-4978-6*); 29.99 (*0-8024-4979-4*) Moody.

Life Estates. Shelby Hearon. LC 93-13977. 1994. 22.00 (*0-679-41539-4*) Knopf.

Life Estates. Shelby Hearon. 1995. pap. 11.00 (*0-679-75796-1*) Vin Bks.

Life Estates: A Novel. large type ed. Shelby Hearon. LC 94-13819. 337p. 1994. lib. bdg. 22.95 (*0-7862-0262-9*) Thorndike Pr.

Life Events & Illness. Ed. by George W. Brown & Tirril O. Harris. 496p. 1989. lib. bdg. 65.00 (*0-89862-723-0*) Guilford Pubns.

Life Events & Psychological Functioning: Theoretical & Methodological Issues. Lawrence H. Cohen. (Focus Editions Ser.: Vol. 90). 310p. 1988. text 59.95 (*0-8039-2821-1*); pap. text 26.00 (*0-8039-2822-X*) Sage.

Life Events & Psychological Functioning: Theoretical & Methodological Issues. Ed. by Lawrence H. Cohen. LC 87-28889. (Sage Focus Editions Ser.: No. 90). (Illus.). 280p. reprint ed. pap. 86.80 (*0-7837-4572-9*, 204410100003) Bks Demand.

Life Events & Your Retirement & Insurance Benefits (for Annuitants) 13p. 1998. pap. 1.25 (*0-16-049682-9*) USGPO.

Life Events As Stressors in Childhood & Adolescence. James H. Johnson. (Developmental Clinical Psychology & Psychiatry Ser.: Vol. 8). 160p. (Orig.). 1986. text 42.00 (*0-8039-2725-8*); pap. text 18.95 (*0-8039-2726-6*) Sage.

Life Events As Stressors in Childhood & Adolescence. James H. Johnson. LC 86-1948. (Developmental Clinical Psychology & Psychiatry Ser.: No. 8). 159p. (Orig.). 1986. reprint ed. pap. 49.30 (*0-608-01619-5*, 205959800003) Bks Demand.

Life Everlasting see Vida Sempiterna

Life Everlasting. Ferdinando Camon. Tr. by John Shepley from ITA. 192p. 1987. 29.95 (*0-910395-31-4*); pap. 10.95 (*0-910395-32-2*) Marlboro Pr.

Life Everlasting. Marie Corelli. 1966. pap. 13.00 (*0-87505-092-1*) Borden.

Life Everlasting. John Fiske. 88p. 1997. reprint ed. pap. 12.95 (*0-7661-0065-0*) Kessinger Pub.

Life Everlasting: A Definitive Study of Life after Death. rev. ed. Duane S. Crowther. LC 98-71163. 528p. 1997. 23.98 (*0-88290-615-1*, 528) Horizon Utah.

Life Everlasting: A Novel of the Eternal Life & How to Attain It, a Love Story. Marie Corelli. (Longevity Ser.). 1991. lib. bdg. 75.00 (*0-8490-4135-X*) Gordon Pr.

Life Everlasting: A Reality of Romance (1911) Marie Corelli. 439p. 1996. reprint ed. pap. 29.95 (*1-56459-728-8*) Kessinger Pub.

Life Everlasting, a Reality of Romance. Marie Corelli. 439p. 1973. reprint ed. spiral bd. 17.50 (*0-7873-0205-8*) Hlth Research.

Life Everlasting & the Immensity of the Soul: A Theological Treatise on the Four Last Things: Death, Judgment, Heaven, Hell. Reginald Garrigou-Lagrange. Tr. by Patrick Cummins from FRE. LC 82-51270. 270p. 1991. reprint ed. pap. 13.50 (*0-89555-203-5*) TAN Bks Pubs.

Life Examined. J. Gray Sweeney. Ed. by Robert Horvath. LC 98-60908. (Illus.). 16p. 1998. pap. 15.00 (*0-9665700-0-6*, 001) Anne Coe.

Life Example of Teachings of Prophet Muhammad: Uswai Rasool-i-Akram. Maulana M. Hai. 436p. (Orig.). 1995. text 15.95 (*1-56744-505-5*) Kazi Pubns.

Life Expectancy & Mental Retardation: A Longitudinal Study in a State Residential Facility. R. Eyman et al. (Monographs of the American Association on Mental Retardation: No. 7). 84p. (C). 1987. pap. 8.00 (*0-940898-14-4*) Am Assn Mental.

Life Expectancy of Fatigue Design: Problems & Solutions Manual. 29p. 1996. lib. bdg. write for info. (*0-8493-3168-4*) CRC Pr.

***Life Experiences.** Lela Pendergrass. 1999. pap. write for info. (*1-58235-273-9*) Watermrk Pr.

***Life, Experiences & Incidents of Rev. Gardner Dean, with Genealogies of the Gardner, Dean & Hinds Families.** G. Dean & Ebenezer W. Peirce. 307p. 1999. reprint ed. 56.00 (*0-8328-9935-6*) Higginson Bk Co.

***Life, Experiences of Rev. Gardner Dean, with Genealogies.** Gardner Dean & Ebenezer W. Peirce. 307p. 1999. reprint ed. pap. 46.00 (*0-8328-9936-4*) Higginson Bk Co.

Life Explored. Blamire. 1994. teacher ed. 14.06 (*0-697-24020-7*, WCB McGr Hill) McGrw-H Hghr Educ.

Life Explored. Blamire. 1994. pap. text 325.31 (*0-697-24024-X*, WCB McGr Hill) McGrw-H Hghr Educ.

Life Explored. John Blamire. 192p. (C). 1994. text, student ed. 16.25 (*0-697-24021-5*, WCB McGr Hill) McGrw-H Hghr Educ.

Life Explored: The Principles of Biology. John Blamire. (C). 1994. text, student ed. 16.50 (*0-697-24022-3*) McGraw.

Life Explored: The Principles of Biology. John Blamire. 528p. (C). 1994. text. write for info. (*0-697-23370-7*, WCB McGr Hill) McGrw-H Hghr Educ.

Life Expressions. Miguel A. Wilder. 106p. write for info. (*0-9676245-0-9*) M Wilder.

Life Extenders & Memory Boosters! Life Extension Innovations for a Healthier Longer Life. A. Glenn Braswell. 335p. 1993. 29.95 (*1-883201-01-2*) Hlth Quest.

Life Extension: A Practical Scientific Approach. Durk Pearson & Sandy Shaw. 1987. mass mkt. 16.99 (*0-446-38735-5*, Pub. by Warner Bks) Little.

Life Extension: Adding Years to Your Life & Life to Your Years: A Practical Scientific Approach. Durk Pearson & Sandy Shaw. LC 80-27589. (Illus.). 600p. (Orig.). 1983. mass mkt. 10.95 (*0-446-87990-8*, Pub. by Warner Bks) Little.

Life Extension & the End of Aging. (Longevity Ser.). 1992. lib. bdg. 250.00 (*0-8490-5377-3*) Gordon Pr.

Life Extension Companion. Durk Pearson & Sandy Shaw. LC 83-42592. (Illus.). 430p. (Orig.). 1986. mass mkt. 10.95 (*0-446-38560-3*, Pub. by Warner Bks) Little.

Life-Extension, Purposeful Relaxation, Differential (Multiple) "Feeling" (Psychophysiological) Awareness & Communication, Set. Russell E. Mason. 1975. 70.00 incl. audio (*0-89533-018-0*) F I Comm.

Life Extension Weight Loss Program. Durk Pearson & Sandy Shaw. 1994. reprint ed. lib. bdg. 29.95 (*1-56849-543-9*) Buccaneer Bks.

Life Fast - Die Young: My Life with James Dean. John Gilmore. (Illus.). 254p. 1998. reprint ed. pap. 13.95 (*1-56025-169-7*, Thunders Mouth) Avalon NY.

Life Favors. Kim Anderson. 1997. 6.99 (*0-676-54053-8*) Random.

Life File: Drugs. (J). 1995. pap. write for info. (*0-237-51632-2*) EVN1 UK.

Life File: Homeless. (J). 1996. pap. write for info. (*0-237-51633-0*) EVN1 UK.

Life File Drugs. 1995. text. write for info. (*0-237-51508-3*) EVN1 UK.

***Life Files: Racism.** Gandara & Hewitt. 64p. 1998. write for info. (*0-237-51512-1*) EVN1 UK.

Life Flavored by Planets & Stars. Elijah. 140p. (Orig.). 1993. pap. 3.95 (*0-9636520-0-1*) Lotus Pub Hse.

Life Flight. Robert L. Rocker. 56p. (Orig.). 1997. pap. 4.95 (*0-916155-34-X*) Trout Creek.

Life Flow One: The Solution for Heart Disease. Karl Loren. (Illus.). 300p. 1994. write for info. (*1-882537-02-5*) Bigelow Charter.

Life Flow One: The Solution for Heart Disease. rev. ed. Karl Loren. (Illus.). 400p. 1995. pap. 19.95 (*1-882537-05-X*) Bigelow Charter.

***Life for a Life.** Ernest Hill. LC 98-17554. 240p. 1998. 23.00 (*0-684-82278-4*) S&S Trade.

Life for a Life see Collected Works of Robert Herrick

Life for a Life. Robert Herrick. (Collected Works of Robert Herrick). 1988. reprint ed. lib. bdg. 59.00 (*0-7812-1271-5*) Rprt Serv.

Life for a Life? The Death Penalty on Trial. Vernon W. Redekop. LC 89-26709. (Peace & Justice Ser.: Vol. 9). 104p. (Orig.). 1990. pap. 6.99 (*0-8361-3516-4*) Herald Pr.

Life for a Life? The Problem of Capital Punishment. Ernest A. Gowers. LC 82-45666. (Illus.). reprint ed. 22.50 (*0-404-62416-2*) AMS Pr.

Life for Africa: The Story of Bram Fischer. Naomi Mitchison. (C). 1973. text 29.95 (*0-85036-170-2*, Pub. by MRLN) Paul & Co Pubs.

Life for Every Sleeper: A Pictorial Record of the Burma-Thailand Railway. Hugh V. Clarke. (Illus.). 144p. 1987. 24.95 (*0-04-909023-2*) Routledge.

Life for Language: A Biographical Memoir of Leonard Bloomfield. Robert A. Hall, Jr. LC 89-28891. (Studies in the History of the Language Sciences: Vol. 55). x, 129p. 1990. 33.00 (*1-55619-350-5*) J Benjamins Pubng Co.

Life for Liberty: Anti-Slavery & Other Letters of Sallie Holley. Sallie Holley. LC 71-97453. 292p. 1970. reprint ed. lib. bdg. 35.00 (*0-8371-2689-4*, HOL&) Greenwood.

Life for Liberty: Anti-Slavery & Other Letters of Sallie Holley. Sallie Holley. (American Biography Ser.). 292p. 1991. reprint ed. lib. bdg. 69.00 (*0-7812-8189-X*) Rprt Serv.

Life for Life's Sake: A Book of Reminiscences. Richard Aldington. LC 78-64003. (Des Imagistes Ser.). 416p. reprint ed. 55.00 (*0-404-17076-5*) AMS Pr.

Life for Me Ain't Been No Crystal Staircase: Three Generations of Children in Crisis. Susan Sheehan. 192p. 1994. pap. 12.00 (*0-679-75450-4*) Vin Bks.

Life for New Music: Selected Papers of Paul Fromm. Ed. by David Gable & Christoph Wolff. LC 88-34718. (Harvard Publications in Music). 200p. 1989. 24.95 (*0-674-53088-8*) HUP.

An Asterisk (*) at the beginning of an entry indicates that the title is appearing for the first time.

Life for the Confederacy: As Recorded in the Pocket Diaries of Pvt. Robert A. Moore, Co. G 17th Mississippi Regiment, Confederate Guards, Holly Springs, Mississippi. Robert A. Moore. Ed. by James W. Silver. (Illus.). 182p. 1992. reprint ed. 25.00 (*0-916107-38-8*) Broadfoot.

Life for the Preaching of the High Gospel. Witness Lee. 68p. 1994. pap. 4.00 (*0-87083-776-1*, 11-004-001) Living Stream Ministry.

Life for the Spirit: Rudolf Steiner in the Crosscurrents of Our Time. Henry Barnes. LC 97-22243. (Vista Ser.: Vol. 1). (Illus.). 320p. 1997. pap. 18.95 (*0-88010-395-7*, 1842) Anthroposophic.

Life for Today: Acts of the Apostles Edition. Andrew Wommack. (Illus.). 192p. (C). 1994. 15.95 (*1-881541-07-X*, 304) A Wommack.

Life for Today: Gospels Edition. deluxe ed. Andrew Wommack. 704p. 1991. 25.00 (*0-9623936-6-5*, 302) A Wommack.

Life for Today: Romans. Andrew Wommack. 1995. 15.95 (*1-881541-13-4*, 305) A Wommack.

Life for Today: Study Bible & Commentary - The I & II Corinthians Edition. Andrew Wommack & Don Krow. Ed. by Wendy Kroq. 246p. 1996. pap. text 15.95 (*1-881541-27-4*, 306) A Wommack.

Life for Unity: An Interview with Chiara Lubich. Franca Zambonini. Tr. by Margaret Coen from ITA. 181p. (Orig.). 1992. pap. 9.95 (*0-904287-45-9*) New City.

Life for Unity: Sister Maria Gabriella. Paul B. Quattrocchi. Tr. by Mary Jeremiah from ITA. 184p. 1990. pap. 9.95 (*0-911782-77-X*) New City.

Life for Us Is What We Make It: Building Black Community in Detroit, 1915-1945. Richard W. Thomas. LC 91-26518. (Blacks in the Diaspora Ser.). (Illus.). 384p. 1992. text 24.95 (*0-253-35990-2*) Ind U Pr.

Life Force. Will Eisner. Ed. by Dave Schreiner. LC 96-189570. (Illus.). 144p. 1988. pap. 12.95 (*0-87816-039-6*) Kitchen Sink.

Life Force. 3rd ed. Omraam M. Aivanhov. (Complete Works: Vol. 5). (Illus.). 262p. 1993. pap. 14.95 (*2-85566-419-5*, Pub. by Prosveta) Prosveta USA.

Life Force: Facing Challenges. National Textbook Company Staff. LC 98-51535. (Fiction-Topics & Types Ser.). 1998. pap. write for info. (*0-8442-0674-1*) NTC Contemp Pub Co.

Life Force: The Psycho-Historical Recovery of the Self. Jean Houston. LC 92-50567. 303p. (Orig.). 1993. pap. 14.00 (*0-8356-0687-2*, Quest) Theos Pub Hse.

***Life Force: The World of Jainism.** Michael Tobias. (Illus.). 120p. 2000. pap. 12.00 (*0-87573-080-9*) Jain Pub Co.

Life Forces from Anthroposophy. Carl Unger. 1982. reprint ed. pap. 2.50 (*0-916786-63-3*, Saint George Pubns) R Steiner Col.

Life Form. Alan Dean Foster. 320p. (Orig.). 1995. mass mkt. 6.50 (*0-441-00218-8*) Ace Bks.

Life Form. Alan Dean Foster. 320p. (Orig.). 1996. 24.00 (*0-7278-5104-7*) Severn Hse.

Life Form User's Guide. Fewer Tiers, Inc. Staff. 1995. 49.00 incl. disk (*0-9642857-0-3*); 12.95 (*0-9642857-1-1*) Fitnesoft.

Life Forms. Daniel J. Langton. 245p. 1995. pap. text 15.00 (*0-9615838-2-7*) Cheltenham Pr.

Life Forms of Plants & Statistical Plants Geography. Christen Raunkiaer. Ed. by Frank N. Egerton, 3rd. Tr. by H. Gilbert-Carter et al. LC 77-74249. (History of Ecology Ser.). (Illus.). 1978. reprint ed. lib. bdg. 56.95 (*0-405-10418-9*) Ayer.

Life from Death: The Organ & Tissue Donation & Transplantation Source Book, with Forms. Phillip Williams. LC 88-24461. (Current Issues in Medicine & Law Ser.: Vol. 2). 252p. 1989. pap. 19.95 (*0-936284-44-7*) P Gaines Co.

Life from Persia to the U. S. A. M. Mir. (Illus.). 140p. 1996. 20.00 (*0-9656415-0-3*) M Mir.

Life from Where I Stand. Louise F. Underhill. 1991. pap. 12.50 (*0-936204-80-X*) Underhill Ent.

Life from Within: Prayers by Brother Roger of Taize. Brother Roger of Taize. 32p. (Orig.). 1990. pap. 9.95 (*0-664-25162-5*) Westminster John Knox.

Life-Fulfillment Planning & Personal Decision-Making. Hans Bleiker & Annemarie Bleiker. 1988. ring bd. write for info. (*0-925368-04-0*) IPMP.

Life Fulfillment Training: A Comprehensive System for Creating a Fulfilling Life. John M. Howell. Ed. by James Baker. LC 87-80718. 353p. 1992. pap. 16.95 (*0-942819-08-X*) The Howell Co.

Life Fund. Tony Conran. 120p. (C). 1979. pap. 30.00 (*0-85088-651-1*, Pub. by Gomer Pr) St Mut.

Life-Giving Church. Ted Haggard. LC 98-27599. 236p. 1998. pap. 11.99 (*0-8307-2135-5*, Regal Bks) Gospel Lght.

***Life Giving Church.** Ted Haggard. 2001. pap. 13.99 (*0-8307-2659-4*, Regal Bks) Gospel Lght.

Life-Giving Church: Promoting Growth & Life from Within the Body of Christ. Ted Haggard. LC 98-27599. 236p. 1998. 17.99 (*0-8307-2134-7*, Regal Bks) Gospel Lght.

Life-Giving Secrets: For True Health, Happiness, & Success, 3 vols. Ellen Gould Harmon White. 1995. pap. 29.95 (*1-883012-68-6*) Remnant Pubns.

Life-Giving Vision: How to Be a Christian in Today's World. John Powell. LC 95-237591. (Illus.). 342p. (Orig.). 1995. pap. 17.95 (*0-88347-294-5*) Res Christian Liv.

Life-Giving Way: A Commentary on the Rule of St. Benedict. Esther De Waal. 224p. 1995. pap. 19.95 (*0-8146-2358-1*, Liturg Pr Bks) Liturgical Pr.

***Life-Giving Workplace Vol. 36: Proceedings of the 36th Annual Meeting, Eastern Academy of Management.** Ed. by Joel Harmon & Priscilla Elsass. 300p. 1999. write for info. (*0-916958-19-1*) Eastrn Acad Mgmt.

Life God Blesses. Gordon Macdonald. LC 94-28151. 1994. 18.99 (*0-8407-9155-0*, Oliver-Nelson) Nelson.

Life God Blesses: Weathering the Storms of Life That Threaten the Soul. Gordon MacDonald. LC 97-6538. 276p. 1997. pap. 12.99 (*0-7852-7160-0*) Nelson.

Life Goes On: Adult Poetry Concerned with Life Situations from Birth to Death. Eugene L. Vickery. 104p. 1987. 15.00 (*0-937775-07-X*); per. 9.95 (*0-937775-09-6*) Stonehaven Pubs.

Life Goes Sleeping. Reed F. Coleman. LC 90-53325. 271p. 1991. 22.00 (*1-877946-05-2*) Permanent Pr.

Life-Guard: A Woman's Personal Safety Guide. Susan Erling. Ed. by Ronda Wintheiser. 64p. (Orig.). 1992. pap. 5.95 (*0-9625379-3-4*) Safe & Sound Prodns.

Life Guidance Through Literature. Arthur Lerner & Ursula R. Mahlendorf. LC 91-27499. 236p. (C). 1992. text 25.00 (*0-8389-0580-3*) ALA.

Life Guide Series. Judie Brown. Incl. Facts about Birth Control. (Illus.). 74p. 1997. pap. 5.00 (*1-890712-13-2*, LG02); Facts about Title X: The Six Billion Dollar Scam. John Cavanaugh-O'Keefe. (Illus.). 84p. 1997. pap. 5.00 (*1-890712-11-6*, LG04); Facts of Life. (Illus.). 80p. 1998. pap. 2.95 (*1-890712-12-4*, LG01); pap. write for info. (*1-890712-23-X*) Amer Life League.

Life Happens: A Teenager's Guide to Friends, Failure, Sexuality, Love, Rejection, Addiction, Peer Pressure, Families, Loss, Depression, Change & Other Challenges of Living. Kathy McCoy & Charles Wibbelsman. LC 95-9647. 224p. (Orig.). (YA). 1996. pap. 11.00 (*0-399-51987-4*, Perigee Bks) Berkley Pub.

Life Happens: Get Ready. Barry St. Clair. LC 96-41905. 1996. pap. 7.99 (*0-8054-6294-5*) Broadman.

Life Happens: Help Your Teenager Get Ready. Barry St. Clair. LC 96-36514. (YA). 1996. pap. 10.99 (*0-8054-6295-3*) Broadman.

***Life Has Become More Joyous, Comrades: Celebrations in the Time of Stalin.** Karen Petrone. LC 00-23201. (Russian & East European Studies). 2000. pap. write for info. (*0-253-21401-7*) Ind U Pr.

Life Has No Blessing Like a Good Friend: Ten Commandments of Friendship. Mary Engelbreit. (Real Life Ser.). 1998. 12.95 (*0-8362-5198-9*) Andrews & McMeel.

Life, Health & Annuity Reinsurance. 2nd rev. ed. John E. Tiller, Jr. & Denise F. Tiller. LC 90-44071. 644p. 1995. 70.00 (*1-56698-183-2*) Actex Pubns.

Life, Health & the Pursuit of Happiness. Jim Polito. LC 97-30122. 1998. pap. 16.95 (*1-56072-466-8*, Nova Kroshka Bks) Nova Sci Pubs.

Life Here & Hereafter. F. Newton Howden. (Illus.). 256p. (Orig.). 1992. 22.50 (*0-9627687-3-1*); pap. 15.75 (*0-9627687-4-X*) Proctors Hall Pr.

Life Here & Hereafter: Kathopanishad. Swami Rama. LC 76-361129. 132p. 1976. pap. 10.95 (*0-89389-002-2*) Himalayan Inst.

Life Histories & Psychobiography: Explorations in Theory & Method. William M. Runyan. (Illus.). 302p. 1984. pap. text 21.95 (*0-19-503486-4*) OUP.

Life Histories of African Women. Ed. by Patricia W. Romero. LC 87-1441. (C). 1987. pap. 15.95 (*0-948660-05-8*, Pub. by Ashfield Pr) Humanities.

Life Histories of Central American Highland Birds. Alexander F. Skutch. (Publications of the Nuttall Ornithological Club: No. 7). (Illus.), 213p. 1967. 8.00 (*1-877973-17-3*) Nuttall Ornith.

Life Histories of 50 Familiar North American Birds. Arthur C. Bent. Ed. & Selected by Patricia Newforth. LC 95-26797. 1996. write for info. (*0-253-33051-3*); pap. write for info. (*0-253-21063-1*) Ind U Pr.

Life Histories of North American Birds: Their Breeding Habits & Eggs, 2 vols. Charles E. Bendire. LC 73-17802. (Natural Sciences in America Ser.). (Illus.). 1042p. 1974. reprint ed. 75.95 (*0-405-05720-2*) Ayer.

Life Histories of North American Gallinaceous Birds. Arthur C. Bent. (Illus.). 1963. pap. 10.95 (*0-486-21028-6*) Dover.

Life Histories of North American Marsh Birds. Arthur C. Bent. (Illus.). 1963. pap. 13.95 (*0-486-21082-0*) Dover.

Life Histories of North American Petrels & Pelicans & Their Allies. Arthur C. Bent. (Illus.). xiv, 335p. 1987. reprint ed. pap. 11.95 (*0-486-25525-5*) Dover.

Life Histories of North American Wagtails, Shrikes, Vireos & Their Allies. Arthur C. Bent. (Illus.). 1965. pap. 11.95 (*0-486-21085-5*) Dover.

Life Histories of North American Wild Fowl. Arthur C. Bent. 685p. 1987. reprint ed. pap. 15.95 (*0-486-25422-4*) Dover.

Life Histories of North American Woodpeckers: Deluxe Edition. Arthur C. Bent. LC 91-48014. (Illus.). 286p. 1992. 29.95 (*0-253-31160-8*) Ind U Pr.

Life-Histories of Northern Animals: An Account of the Mammals of Manitoba, 2 vols., Set. Ernest Thompson Seton. LC 73-17845. (Natural Sciences in America Ser.). (Illus.). 1514p. 1974. reprint ed. 113.95 (*0-405-05767-9*) Ayer.

Life-Histories of the Northern Animals: An Account of the Mammals of Manitoba, 2 vols., 1. Ernest Thompson Seton. LC 73-17845. (Natural Sciences in America Ser.). (Illus.). 1514p. 1974. reprint ed. 57.95 (*0-405-05768-7*) Ayer.

Life-Histories of the Northern Animals: An Account of the Mammals of Manitoba, 2 vols., Vol. 2. Ernest Thompson Seton. LC 73-17845. (Natural Sciences in America Ser.). (Illus.). 1514p. 1974. reprint ed. 57.95 (*0-405-05769-5*) Ayer.

Life History & Ecology of the Gray Whale (Eschrichteus Robustus) Dale W. Rice & Alan A. Wolman. (ASM Special Publications: No 3). (Illus.). viii, 142p. 1971. pap. 6.00 (*0-943612-02-0*) Am Soc Mammalogists.

Life History & Narrative. Ed. by J. Amos Hatch & Richard Wisniewski. (Qualitative Studies). 240p. 1995. pap. 27.95 (*0-7507-0405-5*, Falmer Pr) Taylor & Francis.

Life History & Narrative. Ed. by J. Amos Hatch & Richard Wisniewski. LC 95-211930. (Qualitative Studies: Vol. 1). 145p. 1995. 85.00 (*0-7507-0404-7*, Falmer Pr) Taylor & Francis.

***Life History Evolution in Plants** Timo O. Vuorissalo & Pia K. Mutikainen. LC 99-29974. 1999. write for info. (*0-7923-5818-X*) Kluwer Academic.

Life History Invariants: Some Explorations of Symmetry in Evolutionary Ecology. Eric L. Charnov. (Oxford Series in Ecology & Evolution). (Illus.). 184p. (C). 1993. text 45.00 (*0-19-854072-8*, 7608); pap. text 35.00 (*0-19-854071-X*) OUP.

Life History of a Fossil: An Introduction to Taphonomy & Paleoecology. Pat Shipman. (Illus.). 224p. 1981. 40.00 (*0-674-53085-3*) HUP.

Life History of a Fossil: An Introduction to Taphonomy & Paleoecology. Pat Shipman. (Illus.). 232p. 1991. pap. 24.50 (*0-674-53086-1*) HUP.

Life History of an Ethiopian Refugee (1944-1991) Sojourn in the Fourth World. Taddele S. Teshale. Ed. by Virginia L. Barnes. LC 91-43500. 116p. 1991. lib. bdg. 59.95 (*0-7734-9625-4*) E Mellen.

Life History of Shirdi Sai Baba. Ammula Sambasiva Rao. 1997. pap. 10.00 (*81-207-2033-4*, Pub. by Sterling Pubs) S Asia.

Life History of the Freckled Madtom, Noturus Nocturnus, in Mill Creek, Illinois: Pisces: Ictaluridae. Brooks M. Burr & Richard L. Mayden. (Occasional Papers: No. 98). 15p. 1982. 1.00 (*0-317-04823-6*) U KS Nat Hist Mus.

Life History of the Slender Madtom, Noturus Exilis, in Southern Illinois: Pisces: Ictaluridae. Richard L. Mayden & Brooks M. Burr. (Occasional Papers: No. 93). 64p. 1981. 1.00 (*0-317-04827-9*) U KS Nat Hist Mus.

Life History of the Toucan, Ramphastos Brevicarinatus. Josselyn Van Tyne. LC 29-27239. (University of Michigan, Museum of Zoology, Miscellaneous Publications: No. 19). (Illus.). 60p. reprint ed. pap. 30.00 (*0-608-07027-0*, 206723400009) Bks Demand.

Life History Studies of Woodpeckers of Eastern North America see Woodpeckers of Eastern North America

Life History Studies of Woodpeckers of Eastern North America. Lawrence Kilham. (Publications of the Nuttall Ornithological Club: No. 20). (Illus.). 240p. 1984. 19.00 (*1-877973-30-0*) Nuttall Ornith.

Life I Lead. Keith Banner. LC PS3552.A4948L54 1999. 272p. 1999. 23.00 (*0-375-40376-0*, KnopfC) Knopf.

Life Immortal. John T. Ferrier. 20p. 1936. pap. text 5.00 (*0-900235-58-6*) Order Of The Cross.

Life Immortal (1898) I. Pickering Miller. 386p. 1998. reprint ed. pap. 27.95 (*0-7661-0632-2*) Kessinger Pub.

***Life In..., 4 vols.** Incl. Clearing in the Forest. (Illus.). 32p. (J). (gr. 2-6). 2000. lib. bdg. (*1-929298-84-6*, Pub. by Thameside Pr); Giant Tree in the Rainforest. (Illus.). 32p. (J). (gr. 2-6). 2000. lib. bdg. (*1-929298-85-4*, Pub. by Thameside Pr); Pond in the Meadow. (Illus.). 32p. (J). (gr. 2-6). 2000. lib. bdg. (*1-929298-86-2*, Pub. by Thameside Pr); Rockpool on the Seashore. (Illus.). 32p. (J). (gr. 2-6). 2000. lib. bdg. 22.60 (*1-929298-87-0*, Pub. by Thameside Pr); (Illus.). (J). (gr. 2-6). 2000. Set lib. bdg. 90.40 (*1-929298-88-9*, Pub. by Thameside Pr) Smart Apple.

Life in a Blender. Varberg. 1998. 9.95 (*1-56570-046-5*) Meridian MI.

***Life in a Bucket of Soil.** A. Silverstein & V. Silverstein. 2000. pap. 3.95 (*0-486-41057-9*) Dover.

Life in a Business-Oriented Society: A Sociological Perspective. Richard J. Caston. LC 97-25014. 344p. 1997. pap. text 46.00 (*0-205-15975-3*) Allyn.

Life in a California Mission: Monterey in 1786. Jean F. De La Perouse. (Illus.). 112p. 1989. pap. 10.95 (*0-930588-39-8*) Heyday Bks.

***Life in a Colonial Town.** Sally Senzell Isaacs. LC 99-89884. (Picture the Past Ser.). (Illus.). 2000. lib. bdg. write for info. (*1-57572-312-3*) Heinemann Lib.

Life in a Coral Reef. Melvin Berger. Ed. by Natalie Lunis. (Ranger Rick Science Spectacular Ser.). 16p. (J). (gr. 2-4). 1994. pap. 16.95 (*1-56784-204-6*) Newbridge Educ.

Life in a Coral Reef: Student Book. Melvin Berger. Ed. by Natalie Lunis. (Ranger Rick Science Spectacular Ser.). (Illus.). 16p. (Orig.). (J). (gr. 2-4). 1996. pap. 3.95 (*1-56784-229-1*) Newbridge Educ.

Life in a Coral Reef: Theme Pack. Melvin Berger. Ed. by Natalie Lunis. (Ranger Rick Science Spectacular Ser.). (Illus.). (Orig.). (J). (gr. 2-4). 1996. pap. 36.90 (*1-56784-263-1*) Newbridge Educ.

Life in a Crowded Place: Making a Learning Community. Ralph Peterson. LC 92-16468. 142p. (C). 1992. pap. text 19.50 (*0-435-08736-3*, 08736) Heinemann.

Life in A. D. Fifty: The Book of Ephesians. Lester Sumrall. 80p. (C). 1986. pap. text 12.00 (*0-937580-91-0*) Sumrall Pubng.

Life in a Day. Doris Grumbach. LC 96-13837. 160p. 1997. pap. 10.00 (*0-8070-7089-0*) Beacon Pr.

Life in a Day. large type ed. Doris Grumbach. LC 96-48603. (Americana Series). 1997. 23.95 (*0-7862-0976-3*) Thorndike Pr.

Life in a Day of Black L. A. The Way We See It: L. A.'s Black Photographers Present a New Perspective on Their City. Ed. by Roland Charles & Toyomi Igus. (Special Publications: Vol. 8). (Illus.). 148p. 1992. 43.00 (*0-934934-38-X*); pap. 28.95 (*0-934934-39-8*) CAAS Pubns.

Life in a Garden. Janet Halfmann. LC 99-10293. (Lifeviews Ser.). 2000. lib. bdg. 22.60 (*1-58341-072-4*, Creat Educ) Creative Co.

Life in a German Town. (GER.). (C). 1988. 9.95 (*0-8442-2444-8*, X2444-8) NTC Contemp Pub Co.

Life in a Glass House: The Minister's Family in Its Unique Social Context. Cameron Lee & Jack Balswick. 304p. 1989. 16.95 (*0-310-28750-2*) Zondervan.

Life in a Gothic Novel. Barbara Drake. (WEP Poetry Ser.: No. 4). 24p. (Orig.). 1981. pap. 2.50 (*0-917976-09-6*, White Ewe Pr) Thunder Baas Pr.

Life in a Japanese American Internment Camp. Diane Yancey. LC 97-21422. (Way People Live Ser.). (Illus.). (J). (gr. 4-12). 1997. lib. bdg. 22.45 (*1-56006-345-9*) Lucent Bks.

Life in a Japanese Women's College: Learning to Be Ladylike. Brian J. McVeigh. LC 96-19652. (Nissan Institute/Routledge Japanese Studies Ser.). 288p. (C). 1997. 90.00 (*0-415-14456-6*) Routledge.

Life in a Jewish Family Vol. 1: An Autobiography. Tr. by Josephine Koeppel from GER. LC 84-25164. (Collected Works of Edith Stein). (Illus.). 576p. (Orig.). 1986. pap. 13.95 (*0-935216-04-9*) ICS Pubns.

***Life in a Medieval Castle.** Gary L. Blackwood. LC 99-26848. (Way People Live Ser.). (Illus.). 112p. (YA). (gr. 6-9). 2000. lib. bdg. 23.70 (*1-56006-582-6*) Lucent Bks.

Life in a Medieval Castle. Joseph Gies & Frances Gies. LC 74-13058. (Illus.). 288p. 1979. pap. 13.50 (*0-06-090674-X*, CN 674, Perennial) HarperTrade.

Life in a Medieval Castle Coloring Book. John Green. (Illus.). (J). (gr. 4-7). 1990. pap. 2.95 (*0-486-26542-0*) Dover.

Life in a Medieval City. Frances Gies & Joseph Gies. LC 74-13058. (Illus.). 288p. 1981. pap. 13.50 (*0-06-090880-7*, CN 880, Perennial) HarperTrade.

Life in a Medieval Monastery. 2nd ed. Anne Boyd. (Cambridge Introduction to World History Topic Bks.). (Illus.). 48p. (YA). (gr. 7 up). 1988. pap. 12.95 (*0-521-33724-0*) Cambridge U Pr.

Life in a Medieval Village. Frances Gies & Joseph Gies. LC 89-33759. (Illus.). 272p. 1991. reprint ed. pap. 14.00 (*0-06-092046-7*, Perennial) HarperTrade.

Life in a Mental Hospital. William J. Kurdi. Ed. by Kort Kurdi. LC 77-92103. 1978. pap. 8.95 (*957-616-491-5*) Med Nurs Educ.

***Life in a Nazi Concentration Camp.** Anne Grenn Saldinger. LC 00-8930. (Way People Live Ser.). 2000. lib. bdg. write for info. (*1-56006-485-4*) Lucent Bks.

Life in a New Dimension. Don Double. 192p. 1979. mass mkt. 5.99 (*0-88368-083-1*) Whitaker Hse.

Life in a New Land. Linda Bosch. (Open Door Bks.). (Illus.). 69p. (Orig.). 1992. pap. text 3.95 (*1-56212-016-6*, 1740-2160) CRC Pubns.

Life in a Northern Town. Jared Glovsky. 132p. 1998. pap. 12.00 (*1-889924-02-4*) Paradigm Pr WI.

***Life in a Nutshell: Ways to Crack It.** (Illus.). 128p. (Orig.). 1999. pap. 14.95 (*0-9673144-0-2*) Wllspring Pubs.

***Life in a Peaceful New World.** Edward Mycue. (Illus.). 64p. 1999. pap. 13.00 (*1-879457-64-4*) Norton Coker Pr.

Life in a Pond. Allan Fowler. LC 95-39661. (Rookie Read-About Science Ser.). (Illus.). 32p. (J). (ps-2). 1996. lib. bdg. 18.50 (*0-516-06053-8*) Childrens.

Life in a Pond. Allan Fowler. (Rookie Read-About Science Ser.). 32p. (J). (ps-3). 1996. pap. 3.95 (*0-516-20218-9*) Childrens.

Life in a Pond. Janet Halfmann. LC 99-10295. (Lifeviews Ser.). 2000. 22.60 (*1-58341-073-2*, Creat Educ) Creative Co.

Life in a Pond. Lisa Trumbauer. Ed. by Susan Evento. (Early Science Big Bks.). 16p. (Orig.). (J). (ps-2). 1996. pap. 16.95 (*1-56784-314-X*) Newbridge Educ.

Life in a Pond Theme Pack. (Early Science Ser.). (Illus.). (Orig.). (J). (ps-2). 1996. pap. 49.95 (*1-56784-364-6*) Newbridge Educ.

Life in a Putty Knife Factory. H. Allen Smith. 224p. reprint ed. lib. bdg. 22.95 (*0-89190-983-4*, Rivercity Pr) Amereon Ltd.

Life in a Putty Knife Factory. H. Allen Smith. 1993. reprint ed. lib. bdg. 18.95 (*1-56849-223-5*) Buccaneer Bks.

Life in a Rock Shelter: Prehistoric Indians of the Lower Pecos. G. Elaine Acker. LC 95-17291. (Illus.). (Orig.). 1996. pap. 19.95 (*0-937460-84-2*) Hendrick-Long.

Life in a Small Alaskan Bush Community. David R. Stovner. vi, 212p. 1994. 15.00 (*0-9679736-0-0*, 01) Musk Ox.

Life in a Technocracy: What It Might Be Like. Harold Loeb. (Utopianism & Communitarianism Ser.). 230p. (C). 1996. pap. 17.95 (*0-8156-0380-0*, LOLTP) Syracuse U Pr.

Life in a Teenage Jungle. William Coleman. LC 94-5741. 160p. (Orig.). (YA). (gr. 9-12). 1994. pap. 6.99 (*0-8007-5525-1*) Revell.

Life in a Thousand Worlds. W. S. Harris. LC 72-154444. (Utopian Literature Ser.). 1976. reprint ed. 28.95 (*0-405-03527-6*) Ayer.

Life in a Tidal Pool, Vol. 1. Alvin Silverstein. (J). (gr. 4-7). 1990. 14.95 (*0-316-79120-2*, Joy St Bks) Little.

Life in a Tide Pool. Allan Fowler. (Rookie Read-About Science Ser.). 32p. (J). 1996. lib. bdg. 18.50 (*0-516-20031-3*) Childrens.

Life in a Tide Pool. Allan Fowler. (Rookie Read-About Science Ser.). 32p. (J). (gr. 1-2). 1997. pap. 4.95 (*0-516-26083-9*) Childrens.

***Life in a Tidepool.** Janet Halfmann. LC 99-23823. (Lifeviews Ser.). (Illus.). 32p. (J). 2000. lib. bdg. 22.60 (*1-58341-076-7*, Creat Educ) Creative Co.

***Life in a Tree.** Janet Halfmann. LC 99-29966. (Lifeviews Ser.). (Illus.). 32p. (J). 2000. lib. bdg. 22.60 (*1-58341-077-5*, Creat Educ) Creative Co.

L

Life in a Tree. Lisa Trumbauer. Ed. by Susan Evento. (Early Science Photocards Ser.). (Illus.). (Orig.). (J). (ps-2). 1996. pap. 16.95 (*1-56784-358-1*) Newbridge Educ.

Life in a Tree: Mini Book. Melvin Berger. Ed. by Susan Evento. (Early Science Mini Bks.). 16p. (Orig.). (J). (ps-2). 1996. pap. 3.95 (*1-56784-338-7*) Newbridge Educ.

Life in a Tree Theme Pack. (Early Science Ser.). (Illus.). (Orig.). (J). (ps-2). 1996. pap. 49.95 (*1-56784-363-8*) Newbridge Educ.

Life in a Turkish Village. Joe E. Pierce. Ed. by Louise S. Spindler & George D. Spindler. (Case Studies in Cultural Anthropology). (Illus.). 1983. reprint ed. pap. text 7.95 (*0-8290-0278-2*) Irvington.

Life in a Welsh Countryside. Alwyn D. Rees. LC 97-102959. 200p. 1996. pap. 19.95 (*0-7083-1271-3*, Pub. by Univ Wales Pr) Paul & Co Pubs.

Life in a Wetland. Allan Fowler. LC 97-28660. (Rookie Read-About Science Ser.). (J). 1998. 18.50 (*0-516-20799-7*) Childrens.

Life in a Wetland. Allan Fowler. LC 97-28660. (Rookie Read-About Science Ser.). (Illus.). 32p. (YA). (gr. 1-2). 1999. pap. text 4.95 (*0-516-26417-6*) Childrens.

Life in a Wild West Show. Stephen Currie. LC 98-27233. (Way People Live Ser.). (Illus.). (YA). (gr. 4-12). 1998. lib. bdg. 23.70 (*1-56006-352-1*) Lucent Bks.

Life in Abyssinia: Being Notes Collected During Three Years' Residence & Travels in That Country. Mansfield Parkyns. (Illus.). 446p. 1966. 55.00 (*0-7146-1844-6*, Pub. by F Cass Pubs) Intl Spec Bk.

Life in Advertising & at War. James B. Cameron. (C). 1989. text 80.00 (*1-85821-020-8*, Pub. by Pentland Pr) St Mut.

*__Life in Al-Barzakh.__ unabridged ed. Muhummad Al-Jibaly. (Inevitable Journey Ser.: Vol. 414). 126p. 1998. pap. 7.00 (*1-891229-04-4*) Al-Kitaab & As-Sunnah.

Life in Alaska: The Reminiscences of a Kansas Woman, 1916-1919. May W. Lamb. Ed. by Dorothy W. Zimmerman. LC 87-30023. (Illus.). 181p. reprint ed. pap. 56.20 (*0-608-05994-3*, 206632200008) Bks Demand.

Life in All Its Fullness. Phillip Potter. LC 82-5079. 183p. reprint ed. pap. 56.80 (*0-608-14509-2*, 202534000043) Bks Demand.

Life in Amana, 1867-1935: Reporters' Views. Compiled by Joan L. Bourret. 204p. 1998. pap. 14.95 (*1-57216-050-0*) Penfield.

Life in Amber. George O. Poinar, Jr. LC 91-5045. (Illus.). 374p. (C). 1992. 59.50 (*0-8047-2001-0*) Stanford U Pr.

Life in America: A Special Loan Exhibition of Paintings Held During the Period of the New York World's Fair, April 24 to October 29. Metropolitan Museum of Art Staff. 1974. 18.95 (*0-405-02261-1*, 16138) Ayer.

Life in America 100 Years Ago, 11 vols. (Illus.). (YA). (gr. 5 up). 1995. 219.45 (*0-7910-2838-0*) Chelsea Hse.

Life in America 100 Years Ago. Gaillard Hunt. (Illus.). 298p. 1971. reprint ed. 24.95 (*0-87928-023-9*) Corner Hse.

Life in American Denmark. Alfred C. Nielsen. Ed. by Franklyn D. Scott. LC 78-15843. (Scandinavians in America Ser.). (Illus.). 1979. reprint ed. lib. bdg. 17.95 (*0-405-11655-1*) Ayer.

Life in American Public Schools. Joan S. Brown. 332p. 1991. pap. 13.95 (*0-9700118-0-6*) J&F Consult.

*__Life in America's First Cities.__ Sally Senzell Isaacs. LC 99-89882. (Picture the Past Ser.). 2000. lib. bdg. write for info. (*1-57572-315-8*) Heinemann Lib.

Life in an Indian Village. Marilyn Turkovich. (C). 1989. teacher ed., spiral bd. 50.00 (*1-56709-061-3*) Indep Broadcast.

Life in an Irish Country House. Mark Bence-Jones. (Illus.). 270p. 1996. 29.95 (*0-09-474680-X*, Pub. by Constable & Co) Trafalgar.

Life in an Italian Town. (ITA.). 9.95 (*0-8442-8045-3*, X8045-3) NTC Contemp Pub Co.

Life in Ancient Athena. Don Nardo. LC 99-24576. (Way People Live Ser.). (Illus.). 112p. (YA). (gr. 6-9). 2000. lib. bdg. 23.70 (*1-56006-494-3*) Lucent Bks.

Life in Ancient Britain. Norman Ault. LC 70-39667. (Select Bibliographies Reprint Ser.). 1977. reprint ed. 18.95 (*0-8369-9927-4*) Ayer.

Life in Ancient Egypt. Adolf Erman. Tr. by H. M. Tirard. (Illus.). 597p. 1971. pap. 11.95 (*0-486-22632-8*) Dover.

Life in Ancient Egypt. Adolph Erman. LC 68-56523. (Illus.). 570p. 1972. reprint ed. 27.95 (*0-405-08488-9*, Pub. by Blom Pubns) Ayer.

Life in Ancient Egypt. 2nd ed. Katriana Hazell. (Illus.). 32p. 1994. pap. 2.95 (*0-948636-17-3*, 6173, Pub. by Natl Mus Scotland) A Schwartz & Co.

Life in Ancient Greece. Don Nardo. LC 95-30504. (Way People Live Ser.). (Illus.). 112p. (J). (gr. 5-12). 1996. lib. bdg. 22.45 (*1-56006-327-0*) Lucent Bks.

Life in Ancient Greece: Coloring Book. John Green. (J). 1993. pap. 2.95 (*0-486-27509-4*) Dover.

Life in Ancient India. P. T. Iyengar. 150p. 1987. reprint ed. 16.00 (*0-8364-1718-6*, Pub. by Manohar) S Asia.

Life in Ancient India As Depicted in Jaina Canon & Commentaries. 2nd ed. J. Jain. 1984. text 34.00 (*0-685-13786-4*) Coronet Bks.

Life in Ancient Mexico Coloring Book. John Green. 48p. 1991. pap. 2.95 (*0-486-26705-9*) Dover.

Life in Ancient Rome. F. R. Cowell. 1976. pap. 12.95 (*0-399-50328-5*, Perigee Bks) Berkley Pub.

Life in Ancient Rome. William Kaufman. 48p. (J). 1997. pap. 2.95 (*0-486-29767-5*) Dover.

Life in Ancient Rome. Don Nardo. LC 96-14184. (Way People Live Ser.). (Illus.). 112p. (YA). 1996. lib. bdg. 22.45 (*1-56006-335-1*) Lucent Bks.

Life in Architecture. Minoru Yamasaki. LC 79-11561. (Illus.). 196p. 1979. 75.00 (*0-8348-0136-1*) Weatherhill.

*__Life in Army Basic Training.__ Gene Gartman. (High Interest Bks.). (Illus.). (YA). 2000. 19.00 (*0-516-23347-5*) Childrens.

*__Life in Army Basic Training.__ Robert C. Kennedy. LC 00-23306. (High Interest Bks.). (Illus.). 48p. (J). (gr. 4-7). 2000. pap. write for info. (*0-516-23547-8*) Childrens.

Life in Astrophysics: Selected Papers of Viktor Ambartsumian. V. A. Ambartsumian. LC 97-52237. 279p. 1998. 65.00 (*0-89864-082-2*) Allerton Pr.

*__Life in Balance.__ Page L. D. Creach. LC 99-59483. (Real Faith, Real Life Ser.). 64p. 2000. 5.95 (*1-57895-077-5*) Curriculm Presbytrn KY.

Life in Beijing: Easy Chinese Readings in 500 Characters. Qingsheng Ma. Ed. by Jian Zhu. Tr. by Molly Luethi from CHI. LC 97-74382. (CHI., Illus.). 262p. (C). 1997. pap. 14.95 (*1-891107-02-X*) BIGI Intl.

Life in Black America: Findings from a National Survey. James S. Jackson. (Illus.). 310p. 1991. text 52.00 (*0-8039-3537-4*); pap. text 24.00 (*0-8039-3538-2*) Sage.

Life in Black & White: Family & Community in the Slave South. Brenda E. Stevenson. (Illus.). 496p. 1996. 39.95 (*0-19-509536-7*) OUP.

Life in Black & White: Family & Community in the Slave South. Brenda E. Stevenson. (Illus.). 496p. 1997. pap. 16.95 (*0-19-511803-0*) OUP.

Life in Boats: The Concordia Years. Waldo Howland. (Illus.). 312p. 1988. 45.00 (*0-913372-45-5*) Mystic Seaport.

Life in California Before the Conquest. Alfred Robinson. LC 68-30553. (American Scene Ser.). (Illus.). 1969. reprint ed. lib. bdg. 39.50 (*0-306-71142-7*) Da Capo.

Life in California Before the Conquest. Alfred Robinson. 1992. reprint ed. lib. bdg. 75.00 (*0-7812-5081-1*) Rprt Serv.

Life in Camelot, Vol. 1. Philip B. Kunhardt, Jr. 1989. pap. 19.95 (*0-316-50602-8*) Little.

Life in Catalogues & Other Essays. George Sims. 164p. 35.00 (*0-9619693-5-0*, Pub. by Holmes Publishing Co) Oak Knoll.

Life in Caves. Glenn A. Cheney. 158p. (Orig.). (YA). (gr. 9-12). 1995. pap. 9.99 (*0-88092-127-7*) Royal Fireworks.

Life in Celtic Times. Smith. 1998. pap. 2.95 (*0-486-29714-4*) Dover.

Life in Charles Dicken's England. Diane Yancey. LC 98-19569. (Way People Live Ser.). (Illus.). 112p. (YA). (gr. 9 up). 1999. lib. bdg. 23.70 (*1-56006-098-0*) Lucent Bks.

Life in Christ. Margo A. LeBert. (Breaking Open the Catechism of the Catholic Church for Small Groups Ser.). 48p. (C). 1995. pap. 3.95 (*0-8091-9445-7*) Paulist Pr.

Life in Christ. Tony Salerno et al. 34p. (Orig.). 1986. pap. 14.99 (*0-87123-887-X*) Bethany Hse.

Life in Christ: A Catechism for Adult Catholics. Gerard Webber & James J. Killgallon. LC 95-52131. 320p. 1996. pap. 6.99 (*0-06-069318-5*, Pub. by Harper SF) HarpC.

Life in Civil War America. Catherine Clinton. (National Park Civil War Ser.). (Illus.). 51p. 1996. pap. 4.95 (*1-888213-02-7*) Eastern National.

Life in Classrooms. 2nd ed. Philip W. Jackson. 208p. (C). 1990. reprint ed. pap. text 16.95 (*0-8077-3034-3*) Tchrs Coll.

*__Life in Common: An Essay in General Anthropology.__ Tzvetan Todorov. Tr. by Katherine Golsan & Lucy Golsan. (European Horizons Ser.). 160p. 2001. text 45.00 (*0-8032-4420-7*); pap. text 19.95 (*0-8032-9444-1*, Bison Books) U of Nebr Pr.

Life in Custer's Cavalry: Diaries & Letters of Albert & Jennie Barnitz, 1867-1868. Albert Barnitz & Jennie Barnitz. Ed. by Robert Marshall Utley. LC 86-25104. (Illus.). xiv, 302p. 1987. reprint ed. pap. 13.95 (*0-8032-9553-7*, Bison Books) U of Nebr Pr.

Life in Custer's Cavalry: Diaries & Letters of Albert & Jennie Barnitz, 1867-1868. Albert T. Barnitz. Ed. by Robert Marshall Utley. LC 76-52425. (Yale Western Americana Ser.: No. 30). (Illus.). 316p. reprint ed. pap. 98.00 (*0-8357-8209-3*, 203390700087) Bks Demand.

Life in Dark Ages. Ernst Pawel. 1995. 20.95 (*0-88064-168-1*) Fromm Intl Pub.

Life in Double Time: Confessions of an American Drummer. Mike Lankford. 256p. 1997. 22.95 (*0-8118-0683-9*) Chronicle Bks.

Life in Double Time: Confessions of an American Drummer. Mike Lankford. 272p. 1999. pap. 12.95 (*0-8118-2321-0*) Chronicle Bks.

Life in Early Hawai'i: The Ahupua'a. 3rd ed. Hawaiian Studies Institute Staff. LC 96-130150. Orig. Title: The Ahupua'a. (Illus.). 73p. (J). (gr. 4-12). 1994. pap. text 9.95 (*0-87336-038-9*) Kamehameha Schools.

Life in Early Philadelphia: Documents from the Revolutionary & Early National Periods. Ed. by Billy G. Smith. LC 94-4933. 1995. 50.00 (*0-271-01454-7*); pap. 14.95 (*0-271-01455-5*) Pa St U Pr.

Life in Edwardian Colchester. Patrick Denney. (Illus.). 112p. (Orig.). 1991. pap. 15.00 (*0-86025-429-1*, Pub. by I Henry Pubns) Empire Pub Srvs.

Life in Egypt Coloring Book. John Green. (Illus.). (J). (gr. 4-7). 1989. pap. 2.95 (*0-486-26130-1*) Dover.

Life in Elizabethan England. A. H. Dodd. (Illus.). 230p. 1998. pap. 26.95 (*0-8464-4922-6*) Beekman Pubs.

Life in Elizabethan England. A. H. Dodd. (Illus.). 192p. pap. 17.95 (*1-871083-46-X*, Pub. by J Jones Pub) Dufour.

Life in Elizabethan Days. William S. Davis. 1988. pap. 25.00 (*0-8196-1201-4*) Biblo.

Life in Ellen H. Richards, 1842-1911. Carolina L. Hunt. 1980. 15.00 (*0-8461-5043-3*) AAFCS.

Life in England in Aquatint & Lithography, 1770-1860: A Bibliographical Catalogue. J. R. Abbey. (Illus.). 512p. 1991. reprint ed. 175.00 (*1-55660-129-8*) A Wofsy Fine Arts.

Life in Fabulous Florida. Jim Brandetsas. (Orig.). 1996. pap. 2.95 (*1-888672-08-0*) J Ciano Pubng.

Life in Faith & Freedom: An Essay Presenting Gaston Fessard's Analysis of the Dialectic of the Spiritual Exercises of St. Ignatius. Edouard Pousset. Tr. by E. L. Donahue. LC 79-84200. (Modern Scholarly Studies about the Jesuits, in English Translations Series II: No. 4). xxviii, 240p. 1980. 9.00 (*0-912422-41-6*); pap. 7.00 (*0-912422-39-4*) Inst Jesuit.

Life in Fragments: Essays in Postmodern Morality. Zygmunt Bauman. 256p. (Orig.). 1995. pap. text 28.95 (*0-631-19267-0*) Blackwell Pubs.

Life in Freedom: Liberation Theologies from Asia. Michael Amaladoss. LC 96-29694. 196p. (Orig.). 1997. pap. 24.00 (*1-57075-124-2*) Orbis Bks.

Life in Germany: or Scenes, Impressions & Everyday Life of the Germans. William Howitt. LC 74-94311. reprint ed. 55.00 (*0-404-03370-9*) AMS Pr.

Life in God. D. Martyn Lloyd-Jones. LC 92-2507. (Studies in First John: Bk. 5). 208p. 1994. pap. 10.99 (*0-89107-829-0*) Crossway Bks.

*__Life in Hand: Creating the Illuminated Journal.__ Hannah Hinchman. (Illus.). 160p. 1998. reprint ed. pap. 19.95 (*0-87905-882-X*) Gibbs Smith Pub.

Life in High Heels. Loni Anderson & Larkin Warren. (Illus.). 306p. 1998. text 23.00 (*0-7881-5944-5*) DIANE Pub.

Life in High Latitudes: A Study of Bird Life. S. M. Uspenskii. 401p. (C). 1984. text 110.00 (*90-6191-433-7*, Pub. by A A Balkema) Ashgate Pub Co.

Life in His Body. David Finnell. 1995. pap. text 9.95 (*1-880828-87-1*) Touch Pubns.

Life in Illisconsin, 1927-1951. Patricia S. Phillips. (Illus.). 224p. (Orig.). 1995. pap. 9.95 (*0-9647032-0-3*) Whispering Pn.

Life in Iran: The Library of Congress Drawings. Ardeshir Mohassess. LC 93-40224. (Illus.). 48p. 1993. pap. 20.00 (*0-934211-39-6*) Mage Pubs Inc.

Life in Iron Mills. Harding. LC 96-86795. 368p. 1997. pap. text 12.95 (*0-312-13360-X*) St Martin.

Life in Jesus: A Memoir of Mrs. Mary Winslow. Octavius Winslow. 339p. 1993. reprint ed. 29.95 (*1-877611-68-9*) Soli Deo Gloria.

Life in Jesus: Twelve Studies in John 12-21. annot. ed. Gracia Rinden. 116p. (Orig.). 1992. pap. 4.95 (*0-943167-10-8*) Faith & Fellowship Pr.

*__Life in Jesus, God's Son: Based on the Gospel of John.__ Ed. by Melvin E. Banks, Sr. 162p. 1999. pap. text 7.95 (*0-940955-51-2*, 1-11) Urban Ministries.

Life in Jewish Education: Essays in Honor of Louis L. Kaplan. Jack Fruchtman, Jr. LC 97-40138. (Studies & Texts in Jewish History & Culture, the Joseph & Rebecca Meyerhoff Center for Jewish Studies: No. 4). 293p. 1997. 35.00 (*1-883053-38-2*) Univ Pr MD.

Life in Language Immersion Classrooms. Ed. by Elizabeth B. Bernhardt. LC 92-15152. (Multilingual Matters Ser.: No. 86). 1992. 74.95 (*1-85359-151-3*, Pub. by Multilingual Matters); pap. 29.95 (*1-85359-150-5*, Pub. by Multilingual Matters) Taylor & Francis.

Life in Lesu: The Study of a Melanesian Society in New Ireland. Hortense Powdermaker. LC 76-44778. reprint ed. 40.00 (*0-404-15877-3*) AMS Pr.

Life in Letters: A New Collection Edited & Annotated by Matthew J. Bruccoli. F. Scott Fitzgerald. Ed. & Anno. by Matthew J. Bruccoli. 1995. per. 16.00 (*0-684-80153-1*, Touchstone) S&S Trade Pap.

Life in Letters of William Dean Howells, 2 vols., Set. William Dean Howells. (American Biography Ser.). 1991. reprint ed. lib. bdg. write for info. (*0-7812-8202-0*) Rprt Serv.

Life in London: or The Day & Night Scenes of Jerry Hawthorn, Esq. & Corinthian Tom. Pierce Egan. LC 79-8260. reprint ed. 44.50 (*0-404-61841-3*) AMS Pr.

Life in Los Alamos, New Mexico: A Kid's View. Los Alamos Young Writers Club. LC 97-75730. (Illus.). 110p. (J). (gr. 4-12). 1997. pap. text 11.98 (*0-9645703-5-1*) Otowi Crossing Pr.

Life in Medieval Northern Andhra. B. Hemalatha. (C). 1992. 22.50 (*81-7013-086-7*, Pub. by Navarang) S Asia.

Life in Medieval Times. Marjorie Rowling. 1973. pap. 10.95 (*0-399-50258-0*, Perigee Bks) Berkley Pub.

Life in Medieval Village. Gwyneth Morgan. 48p. 1975. pap. 11.95 (*0-521-20404-6*) Cambridge U Pr.

Life in Mexico. Frances Calderon de la Barca. (Illus.). 550p. (C). 1982. reprint ed. pap. 18.95 (*0-520-04662-5*, Pub. by U CA Pr) Cal Prin Full Svc.

Life in Mexico During a Residence of Two Years in That Country. Calderon De La Barca & E. Frances. LC 75-41046. reprint ed. 67.50 (*0-404-14517-5*) AMS Pr.

Life in Mexico under Santa Ana, 1822-1855. Ruth R. Olivera & Liliane Crete. LC 90-50693. (Illus.). 280p. 1991. 28.95 (*0-8061-2320-6*) U of Okla Pr.

Life in Modern America. Bromhead. LC 97-107887. 1989. pap. text. write for info. (*0-582-01838-2*, Pub. by Addison-Wesley) Longman.

Life in Modern Britain. Bromhead. 1991. pap. text. write for info. (*0-582-03642-9*, Pub. by Addison-Wesley) Longman.

Life in Modern Britain. 6th ed. Bromhead. 1985. pap. text. write for info. (*0-582-74919-0*, Pub. by Addison-Wesley) Longman.

*__Life in Moscow, Russia.__ Laurel Corona. LC 00-9164. (Way People Live Ser.). (Illus.). (YA). 2000. write for info. (*1-56006-795-0*) Lucent Bks.

*__Life in Movies.__ Michael Powell. (Illus.). 640p. 2001. pap. 25.00 (*0-571-20431-7*) Faber & Faber.

Life in Movies: An Autobiography. Michael Powell. 700p. 1998. 24.95 (*0-685-18173-1*) Knopf.

Life in Moving Fluids: The Physical Biology of Flow. Steven Vogel. LC 83-60465. (Illus.). 368p. 1983. reprint ed. pap. 114.10 (*0-7837-9468-1*, 206021000004) Bks Demand.

Life in Moving Fluids: The Physical Biology of Flow. 2nd enl. rev. ed. Steven Vogel. LC 93-46149. 488p. 1994. text 75.00 (*0-691-03485-0*, Pub. by Princeton U Pr) Cal Prin Full Svc.

Life in Moving Fluids: The Physical Biology of Flow. 2nd rev. ed. Steven Vogel. 484p. 1994. pap. text 23.95 (*0-691-02616-5*, Pub. by Princeton U Pr) Cal Prin Full Svc.

Life in Mr. Lincoln's Navy. Denis J. Ringle. LC 98-15352. 272p. 1998. 32.95 (*1-55750-736-8*) Naval Inst Pr.

Life in Napoleon's Army: The Memoirs of Captain Elzear Blaze. Comment by Charles J. Napier. (Napoleonic Library: Vol. 28). (Illus.). 208p. 1995. 35.00 (*1-85367-196-7*, Pub. by Greenhill Bks) Stackpole.

Life in Nelson's Navy. Dudley Pope. (Bluejacket Bks.). (Illus.). 296p. 1996. pap. 16.95 (*1-55750-516-0*) Naval Inst Pr.

*__Life in Neolithic Farming Communities: Social Organization, Identity & Differentiation.__ Ian Kuijt. LC 99-52091. (Fundamental Issues in Archaeology Ser.). 332p. 2000. 80.00 (*0-306-46122-6*, Kluwer Plenum) Kluwer Academic.

Life in Old Boise. Arthur A. Hart. 208p. 1989. 27.50 (*0-9631258-3-4*) Historic Idaho.

Life in Old Bulloch: The Story of a Wiregrass. Dorothy Brannen. 732p. 1992. write for info. (*0-9630924-0-5*) State Reg Lib.

Life in Old Hawaii see Stories of Life in Old Hawai'i

Life in Old Japan Coloring Book. John Green. (Illus.). (J). (ps-3). 1994. pap. 2.95 (*0-486-27743-7*) Dover.

*__Life in Outer Space.__ Kim McDonald. LC 00-31075. (Space Explorer Ser.). (Illus.). (J). 2000. write for info. (*0-7398-2213-6*) Raintree Steck-V.

*__Life in Outer Space: The Search for Extraterrestrials.__ Kim McDonald. (Space Explorer Ser.). (Illus.). (J). 2000. pap. 8.95 (*0-7398-2223-3*) Raintree Steck-V.

Life in Oxford. Anthony Kenny. 288p. 1998. 40.00 (*0-7195-5061-0*, Pub. by John Murray) Trafalgar.

Life in Peace & War. Brian Urquhart. 1991. pap. 12.95 (*0-393-30771-9*) Norton.

Life in Pieces: Reflections on Alexander Trocchi Allan Campbell & Tim Niel. LC 97-220379. xi, 307p. 1997. write for info. (*0-86241-680-9*, Pub. by Canongate Books) Interlink Pub.

Life in Poetry. Ruth D. Hadfield. 1998. pap. write for info. (*1-57553-846-6*) Watermrk Pr.

Life in Poetry. Donald R. Siegel. LC 94-93960. 72p. (Orig.). 1995. pap. 12.95 (*0-9644769-0-8*) D R Siegel.

Life in Poetry. William J. Courthope. LC 72-992. reprint ed. 49.50 (*0-404-01785-1*) AMS Pr.

Life in Ponds & Streams see Books for Young Explorers

Life in Ponds & Streams. William H. Amos. Ed. by Donald J. Crump. LC 81-47745. (Books for Young Explorers: Set 8). 32p. (J). (ps-3). 1981. lib. bdg. 16.95 (*0-87044-404-2*) Natl Geog.

Life in Prairie Land. Eliza W. Farnham. LC 88-14369. (Prairie State Bks.). 312p. 1988. 10.95 (*0-252-06039-3*) U of Ill Pr.

Life in Prairie Land. Eliza W. Farnham. LC 72-2601. (American Women Ser.: Images & Realities). 412p. 1974. reprint ed. 24.95 (*0-405-04457-7*) Ayer.

Life in Prison. Stan Williams et al. LC 97-52352. (Illus.). 144p. (YA). (gr. 3-7). 1998. 15.00 (*0-688-15589-8*, Wm Morrow) Morrow Avon.

Life in Process. Dennis Morgan. (Personal Growth Bookshelf). 192p. 1993. 11.99 (*1-56476-125-8*, 6-3125, Victor Bks) Chariot Victor.

Life in Provincial Mexico: National & Regional History As Seen from Mascota, Jalisco, 1867-1972. Carlos B. Gil. LC 82-620031. (Latin American Studies: Vol. 53). 1983. text 20.00 (*0-87903-053-4*) UCLA Lat Am Ctr.

Life in Rainforests. Lucy Baker. 32p. (J). (gr. 3-7). 1993. pap. 4.95 (*0-590-46131-1*) Scholastic Inc.

*__Life in Regency Harrogate.__ Prudence Bebb. 1999. pap. 21.00 (*1-85072-174-2*, Pub. by W Sessions) St Mut.

*__Life in Regency Scarborough, 1811-1820.__ Prudence Bebb. 1999. pap. 21.00 (*1-85072-194-7*, Pub. by W Sessions) St Mut.

Life in Regency York, 1811-1820. Prudence Bebb. 1999. pap. 21.00 (*1-85072-095-9*, Pub. by W Sessions) St Mut.

*__Life in Relation to Death.__ 2nd ed. Chagdud Tulku. LC 99-44722. 2000. write for info. (*1-881847-11-X*, Pub. by Padma Pub CA) Bookpeople.

Life in Renaissance France. Lucien Febvre. Tr. by Marian Rothstein from FRE. LC 77-7454. 192p. 1977. pap. 14.00 (*0-674-53180-9*) HUP.

Life in School. Jane Tompkins. 256p. 1997. pap. 12.00 (*0-201-32799-6*) Addison-Wesley.

Life in Schools. 3rd ed. Peter McLaren. 352p. (C). 1997. pap. 51.00 (*0-8013-1771-1*) Addison-Wesley.

Life in Schools: An Introduction to Critical Pedagogy in the Foundations of Education. 2nd ed. Peter McLaren. LC 93-17627. 272p. (C). 1994. pap. text 31.95 (*0-8013-0638-8*, 78573) Longman.

Life in Schools: An Introduction to Critical Pedagogy in the Foundations of Education. 3rd ed. Peter Mclaren. LC 97-18730. 1997. pap. write for info. (*0-8013-1772-X*) Longman.

Life in Science. Sir Nevill Francis Mott. 198p. 1995. pap. 29.95 (*0-7484-0434-1*, Pub. by Tay Francis Ltd) Taylor & Francis.

Life in Science: Papers in Honor of J. Lawrence Angel. Ed. by Jane E. Buikstra. LC 90-48080. (Scientific Papers: No. 6). (Illus.). 218p. (Orig.). 1990. pap. 12.50 (*0-942118-31-6*) Ctr Amer Arche.

Life in Shakespeare's England: A Book of Elizabethan Prose. John D. Wilson. LC 68-23765. xv, 291p. 1969. write for info. (*0-389-01168-1*) B&N Imports.

An Asterisk (*) at the beginning of an entry indicates that the title is appearing for the first time.

Life in Sierra Leone, West Africa. Richard Corby et al. (J). (gr. 6-9). 1991. pap., teacher ed. 21.95 (*0-943804-83-3*) U of Denver Teach.

Life in South Beach. Gary Monroe. (Illus.). 52p. 1989. pap. 18.00 (*0-9618986-3-1*) Forest & Trees.

Life in South Beach. Gary L. Monroe. (Illus.). 52p. 1989. 30.00 (*0-9618986-0-7*) Forest & Trees.

Life in Stone: A Natural History of British Columbia's Fossils. Ed. by Rolf Ludvigsen. LC 97-121468. (Illus.). 320p. 1996. 65.00 (*0-7748-0577-3*) U of Wash Pr.

Life in Stone: A Natural History of British Columbia's Fossils. Ed. by Rolf Ludvigsen. (Illus.). 320p. 1997. pap. 27.95 (*0-7748-0578-1*) U of Wash Pr.

Life in Stone: Fossils of the Southwest. Krista Sadler. (Plateau Ser.). 32p. 1993. pap. 6.95 (*0-89734-116-3*) Mus Northern Ariz.

Life in the Air Ocean. Sylvia Foley. LC 98-14212. 176p. 1999. 21.00 (*0-375-40063-X*) Knopf.

***Life in the Amazon Rain-Forest.** Stuart A. Kallen. LC 98-43616. (Way People Live Ser.). (Illus.). 112p. (J). (gr. 4-12). 1999. lib. bdg. 23.70 (*1-56006-387-4*) Lucent Bks.

Life in the American Colonies. Ruth Dean & Melissa Thompson. LC 98-28726. (Way People Live Ser.). (Illus.). 112p. (J). (gr. 4-12). 1998. lib. bdg. 23.70 (*1-56006-376-9*) Lucent Bks.

Life in the American Colonies: Daily Lifestyles of the Early Settlers. Jeanne M. Bracken. LC 95-68768. (Perspectives on History Ser.). 60p. (YA). (gr. 5 up). 1995. pap. 6.95 (*1-878668-37-4*) Disc Enter Ltd.

Life in the Ancient Near East, 3100-332 B. C. E. Daniel C. Snell. LC 96-32549. (Illus.). 296p. 1997. 35.00 (*0-300-06615-5*); pap. 16.00 (*0-300-07666-5*) Yale U Pr.

Life in the Antarctic. Lynn M. Stone. LC 95-6893. (Antarctica Discovery Library). 24p. (J). (gr. k-4). 1995. lib. bdg. 15.93 (*1-55916-143-4*) Rourke Bk Co.

Life in the Argentine Republic in the Days of the Tyrants. Domingo Faustino Sarmiento. 1976. 300.00 (*0-87968-403-8*) Gordon Pr.

Life in the Argentine Republic in the Days of the Tyrants, or Civilization & Barbarism. Domingo Faustino Sarmiento. Tr. by Mary T. Mann. (Library of Classics: No. 21). 448p. 1970. pap. 13.95 (*0-02-851650-8*) Hafner.

***Life in the Army Special Forces.** Robert C. Kennedy. (High Interest Bks.). (Illus.). (YA). 2000. 19.00 (*0-516-23350-5*) Childrens.

***Life in the Army Special Forces.** Robert C. Kennedy. LC 00-24377. (High Interest Bks.). (Illus.). 48p. (J). (gr. 4-7). 2000. pap. write for info. (*0-516-23550-8*) Childrens.

Life in the Arts: Practical Guidance & Inspiration for Creative & Performing Artists. Eric Maisel. LC 93-21257. (Inner Work Bks.). 272p. 1994. pap., student ed. 15.95 (*0-87477-766-6*, Tarcher Putnam) Putnam Pub Group.

Life in the Balance: A Professional Juggler & Comic's Story of Surviving Cancer with Laughter & a Passion for Living. Scott Burton. 1997. 15.00 (*0-9658815-0-4*) Inconvenience Prods.

Life in the Balance: Companion to the Audubon Television Specials. David R. Wallace. (Illus.). 1987. 29.95 (*0-15-151561-1*) Harcourt.

Life in the Balance: Emergency Medicine & the Quest to Reverse Sudden Death. Mickey S. Eisenberg. (Illus.). 320p. 1997. 30.00 (*0-19-510179-0*) OUP.

Life in the Balance: Humanity & the Biodiversity Crisis. Niles Eldredge. LC 97-52087. 224p. 1998. 24.95 (*0-691-00125-1*, Pub. by Princeton U Pr) Cal Prin Full Svc.

***Life in the Balance: Humanity & the Biodiversity Crisis.** Niles Eldredge. LC 97-52087. (Illus.). 224p. 2000. pap. text 16.95 (*0-691-05009-0*) Princeton U Pr.

***Life in the Balance: The Billy Wayne Sinclair Story.** Billy W. Sinclair & Jodie Sinclair. (Illus.). 2001. 25.95 (*1-55970-555-8*, Pub. by Arcade Pub Inc) Time Warner.

***Life in the Balance: The Memoirs of Stanley J. Winkelman.** Stanley J. Winkelman. (Illus.). 288p. 2000. 29.95 (*0-8143-2942-X*, Great Lks Bks) Wayne St U Pr.

Life in the Ballona: Archaeological Investigations at the Admiralty Site (CA-LAn-47) & the Channel Gateway Site (CA-LAn-1596-H) Jeffrey H. Altschul et al. (Statistical Research Technical Ser.: No. 33). (Illus.). 452p. 1992. per. 32.50 (*1-879442-31-0*) Stats Res.

Life in the Blood. Andrew Murray. (Vital Ser.). 1997. pap. 0.75 (*0-87508-510-5*) Chr Lit.

***Life... In the Blood of Jesus.** Charles W. Raley. Ed. by Dorothy Mason-Raley. 209p. 1999. spiral bd. 15.00 (*1-930479-00-X*) C R Pubs.

***Life in the Canine Lane Vol. 1: A Handbook on How to Get a Life with Your Dog.** Stephanie Huber. (Illus.). 72p. 1999. 9.95 (*0-9674796-1-4*) Legacy by.

Life in the Chesapeake Bay. Alice J. Lippson & Robert L. Lippson. LC 83-11278. 240p. 1984. text 39.95 (*0-8018-3012-5*); pap. text 16.95 (*0-8018-3013-3*) Johns Hopkins.

Life in the Chesapeake Bay. 2nd ed. Alice J. Lippson & Robert L. Lippson. LC 96-27103. (Illus.). 304p. 1997. pap. 19.95 (*0-8018-5475-X*); text 39.95 (*0-8018-5476-8*) Johns Hopkins.

Life in the City. Margie Burton et al. Ed. by Alison Adams. (Early Connections Ser.). 16p. (J). (gr. k-2). 1999. pap. 4.50 (*1-58344-069-0*) Benchmark Educ.

Life in the Clearings Versus the Bush. Susanna Moodie. 344p. 1996. pap. text 6.95 (*0-7710-9976-2*) McCland & Stewart.

Life in the Colchester Reef Lighthouse. Gordon P. Manning. (Illus.). (Orig.). 1958. pap. 4.00 (*0-939384-01-9*) Shelburne.

Life in the Cold: An Introduction to Winter Ecology. 3rd ed. Peter J. Marchand. LC 96-19460. (Illus.). 320p. 1996. pap. 22.00 (*0-87451-785-0*) U Pr of New Eng.

***Life in the Cold: Eleventh International Hibernation Symposium.** International Hibernation Symposium Staff et al. LC 00-41047. 2000. write for info. (*3-540-67410-1*) Spr-Verlag.

Life in the Colonial Prison Service. Ed. by S. E. Hutchings. 138p. 1989. pap. 38.00 (*0-7223-2151-1*, Pub. by A H S Ltd) St Mut.

Life in the Coming Millennium. Adrian Berry. LC 99-11772. 1999. 7.99 (*0-517-20374-X*) Random Hse Value.

Life in the Confederate Army, Being the Observations & Experiences of an Alien in the South During the American Civil War. William Watson. 470p. 1995. pap. 19.95 (*0-8071-2015-4*) La State U Pr.

Life in the Coral Reef see Sea Life

Life in the Country with Country Threads. Connie Tesene & Mary Tendall. Ed. by Ursula G. Reikes & Amy Shayne. LC 97-1048. (Illus.). 88p. (Orig.). 1997. pap. 21.95 (*1-56477-185-7*, B299) Martingale & Co.

Life in the Dark. Joyce Pope. LC 91-18646. (Curious Creatures Ser.). (Illus.). 48p. (J). 1992. lib. bdg. 5.00 (*0-8114-3150-9*) Raintree Steck-V.

Life in the Day of an Editor. Charles Walters, Jr. LC 86-81256. 249p. 1986. pap. 10.00 (*0-911311-11-4*) Acres USA.

Life in the Day of Gordon Freewalker. Max Bongielo. Ed. by John P. Schumake. (Orig.). 1992. pap. 12.00 (*0-9616789-4-1*) Earnest Pubns.

Life in the Deep Sea. Elizabeth T. Gowell. LC 97-52239. (First Book Ser.). (J). 1999. 22.50 (*0-531-20391-3*) Watts.

Life in the Deep Sea. Elizableth Tayntor\Gowell. (First Books Ser.). 1999. pap. text 6.95 (*0-531-15957-4*) Watts.

Life in the Desert. Melvin Berger. Ed. by Donna Schaffer. (Rnager Rick Science Spectacular Ser.). (Illus.). 16p. (Orig.). (J). (gr. 2-4). 1996. pap. 16.95 (*1-56784-217-8*) Newbridge Educ.

Life in the Desert. Andrew Clements. 1998. pap. 4.95 (*0-8172-7983-0*) Raintree Steck-V.

Life in the Desert: Student Book. Melvin Berger. Ed. by Donna Schaffer. (Ranger Rick Science Spectacular Ser.). (Illus.). 16p. (Orig.). (J). (gr. 2-4). 1996. pap. 3.95 (*1-56784-242-9*) Newbridge Educ.

Life in the Desert: Theme Pack. Melvin Berger. Ed. by Donna Schaffer. (Ranger Rick Science Spectacular Ser.). (Illus.). (Orig.). (J). 1996. pap. 36.90 (*1-56784-264-X*) Newbridge Educ.

Life in the Deserts. Lucy Baker. 32p. (J). (gr. 4-7). 1993. pap. 4.95 (*0-590-46129-X*) Scholastic Inc.

Life in the Deserts. Lucy Baker. (Life in the . . . Ser.). (J). 1990. 10.15 (*0-606-05425-1*, Pub. by Turtleback) Demco.

Life in the Deserts. Lucy Bakerna. Ed. by World Book Staff. LC 96-61738. (World Book Ecology Ser.). (Illus.). 32p. (J). (gr. 3-8). 1997. 9.95 (*0-7166-5200-5*) World Bk.

Life in the Elizabethan Theater. Diane Yancey. (Way People Live Ser.). (Illus.). 112p. (J). (gr. 4-12). 1996. lib. bdg. 22.45 (*1-56006-343-2*) Lucent Bks.

Life in the English Country Cottage. Adrian Tinniswood. (Illus.). 216p. 1998. pap. (*0-7538-0038-1*) Phoenix Hse.

Life in the English Country Cottage. Adrian Tinniswood. (Illus.). 216p. 1996. 35.00 (*0-297-83274-3*, Pub. by Weidenfeld & Nicolson) Trafalgar.

Life in the English Country House: A Social & Architectural History. Mark Girouard. LC 78-9088. (Illus.). 1978. pap. 30.00 (*0-300-05870-5*) Yale U Pr.

Life in the Face of Death: The Resurrection Message of the New Testament. Richard N. Longenecker. LC 99-161356. (McMaster New Testament Studies: Vol. 3). 288p. 1998. pap. 22.00 (*0-8028-4474-X*) Eerdmans.

***Life in the Family: An Oral History of the Children of God.** James D. Chancellor. LC 00-22544. 296p. 2000. 29.95 (*0-8156-0645-1*) Syracuse U Pr.

Life in the Far West. George F. Ruxton. 330p. 1972. 20.00 (*0-87380-098-2*) Popular E Commerce.

Life in the Far West. George F. Ruxton. Ed. by LeRoy R. Hafen. (American Exploration & Travel Ser.: Vol. 14). (Illus.). 1979. pap. 14.95 (*0-8061-1534-3*) U of Okla Pr.

Life in the Farce Lane. Brian Rix. (Illus.). 256p. 1996. 45.00 (*0-233-98936-6*, Pub. by Andre Deutsch); pap. 24.95 (*0-233-98963-3*, Pub. by Andre Deutsch) Trafalgar.

Life in the Fast-Food Lane. Brian Basset. (Illus.). 128p. (Orig.). 1991. pap. 8.95 (*0-8362-1873-6*) Andrews & McMeel.

Life in the Fat Lane. Cherie Bennett. 272p. (YA). 1999. mass mkt. 4.99 (*0-440-22029-7*) BDD Bks Young Read.

Life in the Fat Lane. Cherie Bennett. LC 97-24072. 272p. (YA). 1998. 15.95 (*0-385-32274-7*) Delacorte.

Life in the Fat Lane. Paul M. Kimelman & David Wolfson. (Illus.). 273p. (Orig.). 1991. pap. 6.25 (*0-9624540-0-1*) Fat Lane.

Life in the Father's House: A Member's Guide to the Local Church. Wayne A. Mack & David Swavely. LC 96-20257. 224p. (Orig.). 1996. pap. 9.99 (*0-87552-355-2*) P & R Pubng.

Life in the Fiction of Ford Madox Ford. Thomas C. Moser. LC 80-7548. 370p. reprint ed. pap. 114.70 (*0-8357-4645-3*, 203757600008) Bks Demand.

Life in the Fishbowl: Building up Church Workers. Tom Rogers. 160p. 1996. 10.99 (*0-570-04871-0*, 12-3360) Concordia.

***Life in the Foreign Legion: How to Join & What to Expect When You Get There.** Evan McGorman. 250p. 2000. 22.95 (*1-55571-532-X*, Pub. by PSI Resch) Midpt Trade.

Life in the Forest. Eileen Curran. LC 84-16455. (Illus.). 32p. (J). (gr. k-2). 1985. pap. 3.50 (*0-8167-0447-3*) Troll Communs.

Life in the Forest. Denise Levertov. LC 78-9356. 1978. pap. 7.95 (*0-8112-0693-9*, NDP461, Pub. by New Directions) Norton.

***Life in the French Country House.** Mark Girouard. LC 99-88541. 2000. 60.00 (*0-679-42711-2*) Knopf.

Life in the Future. Martin Caidin. (Buck Rogers Ser.). 1995. 19.95 (*0-7869-0144-6*, Pub. by TSR Inc) Random.

Life in the Gang: Family, Friends, & Violence. Steve Decker & Barrik Van Winkle. (Criminology Ser.). (Illus.). 314p. (C). 1996. text 59.95 (*0-521-56292-9*); pap. text 19.95 (*0-521-56566-9*) Cambridge U Pr.

Life in the Ghetto. Anika D. Thomas. Ed. by Nancy R. Thatch. LC 91-13944. (Books for Students by Students). (Illus.). 26p. (YA). (gr. 5 up). 1991. lib. bdg. 15.95 (*0-933849-34-6*) Landmark Edns.

Life in the Goat Lane. Linda Fink. (Illus.). 160p. (Orig.). 1991. pap. 7.95 (*0-943149-08-8*) Alpha Bks OR.

Life in the Goat Lane. Linda Fink. (Illus.). vi, 134p. (Orig.). 1991. reprint ed. pap. 8.00 (*0-9657048-1-5*) Triple F.

Life in the Good Ol' U. S. A. rev. unabridged ed. August C. Varga. 102p. 1995. write for info. (*0-9645382-0-2*) A C Varga.

Life in the Great Ice Age. Michael Oard & Beverly Oard. LC 93-77826. 72p. 1998. boxed set 13.95 (*0-89051-167-5*, LIGRIC) Master Bks.

***Life in the Hitler Youth.** Jennifer Keeley. LC 99-37017. (Way People Live Ser.). (Illus.). 112p. (YA). (gr. 6-9). 2000. lib. bdg. 23.70 (*1-56006-613-X*) Lucent Bks.

Life in the Homeric Age. Thomas D. Seymour. LC 63-12451. (Illus.). 1907. 30.00 (*0-8196-0125-X*) Biblo.

Life in the House of Death. Daniel Kemp. 105p. 1997. pap. 12.95 (*0-9627623-4-2*) Iraya Pubns.

Life in the Ice Age. Anthony J. Stuart. (Illus.). 64p. 1989. pap. 35.00 (*0-85263-929-5*, Pub. by Shire Pubns) St Mut.

Life in the Imperial & Loyal City of Mexico in New Spain. Francisco Cervantes de Salazar. Tr. by Minnie L. Shepard. LC 79-100224. 113p. 1970. reprint ed. lib. bdg. 55.00 (*0-8371-3033-6*, CELM, Greenwood Pr) Greenwood.

Life in the Iron Mills. Rebecca H. Davis. Ed. by Cecilia Tichi. LC 96-86795. 432p. 1997. text 35.00 (*0-312-16374-6*) St Martin.

Life in the Iron Mills & Other Stories. 2nd ed. Rebecca H. Davis. Ed. by Tillie Olsen. LC 84-25908. 248p. 1985. pap. 10.95 (*0-935312-39-0*) Feminist Pr.

Life in the Islands. Rosanne Hooper. 32p. (J). (gr. 4-7). 1994. pap. 4.95 (*0-590-48044-8*) Scholastic Inc.

Life in the Islands. Rosanne Hooper. (Life in the . . . Ser.). 1992. 10.15 (*0-606-06529-6*, Pub. by Turtleback) Demco.

Life in the Kingdom: Foundations of the Faith. Ed. by Jack W. Hayford. LC 94-166332. 1993. pap. 6.99 (*0-8407-8432-5*) Nelson.

Life in the Kornfield: My 25 Years at Hee Haw. Sam Lovullo & Marc Eliot. LC 97-117524. (Illus.). 288p. (Orig.). 1996. pap. 15.00 (*1-57297-028-6*) Blvd Books.

***Life in the Lab: A Manual for Non-Majors.** 4th ed. Helen R. Koepfer & Donald Abramson. 220p. (C). 1999. 26.95 (*0-7872-6201-3*, 41620101) Kendall-Hunt.

Life in the Lab: Shorter Edition. Humphrey. (C). 1969. 26.00 (*0-15-550718-4*) Harcourt.

Life in the Labyrinth. E. J. Gold. LC 86-82759. 250p. 1986. pap. 16.95 (*0-89556-048-8*) Gateways Bks & Tapes.

***Life in the Marines.** Robert C. Kennedy. (High Interest Bks.). (Illus.). (YA). 2000. 19.00 (*0-516-23348-3*) Childrens.

***Life in the Marines.** Robert C. Kennedy. (High Interest Bks.). (Illus.). 48p. (J). (gr. 4-7). 2000. pap. 6.95 (*0-516-23548-6*) Childrens.

Life in the Meadow. Eileen Curran. LC 84-12384. (Illus.). 32p. (J). (gr. k-2). 1997. pap. 3.50 (*0-8167-0344-2*) Troll Communs.

Life in the Mezzogiorno: Mongst Gazing Gargoyles. Anne Condra. LC 97-92577. (Illus.). 247p. 1997. pap. 14.00 (*0-9660568-0-9*) Messapici Pub.

Life in the Middle. Ed. by Sherry Willis & James D. Reid. LC 98-87563. (Illus.). 304p. (C). 1998. boxed set 59.95 (*0-12-757230-9*) Acad Pr.

Life in the Middle Ages. Barron's Educational Editors. (Megascope Ser.). (Illus.). 64p. (J). (gr. 5). 1998. 6.95 (*0-7641-5094-4*) Barron.

***Life in the Middle Ages, 4 vols.** Kathryn Hinds. 2001. 182.25 (*0-7614-1012-0*, Benchmark NY) Marshall Cavendish.

***Life in the Middle Ages, 4 vols.** Kathryn Hinds. (Illus.). 2001. 114.00 (*0-7614-1009-0*, Benchmark NY) Marshall Cavendish.

Life in the Middle Ages: From the Seventh to the Thirteenth Century. Hans-Werner Goetz. Ed. by Steven Rowan. Tr. by Albert Wimmer from GER. LC 92-56868. (C). 1993. text 52.00 (*0-268-01300-4*); pap. text 23.00 (*0-268-01301-2*) U of Notre Dame Pr.

***Life in the Middle Ages: The Church.** Kathryn Hinds. LC 00-37849. 2000. lib. bdg. write for info. (*0-7614-1008-2*, Benchmark NY) Marshall Cavendish.

***Life in the Middle Ages: The City.** Kathryn Hinds. LC 99-86689. 2000. 28.50 (*0-7614-1005-8*, Benchmark NY) Marshall Cavendish.

***Life in the Middle Ages: The Countryside.** Kathryn Hinds. LC 99-86687. (Illus.). 2000. 28.50 (*0-7614-1006-6*, Benchmark NY) Marshall Cavendish.

Life in the Middle of the Century. John Dranow. 150p. (Orig.). 1988. 15.95 (*0-913123-14-5*); pap. text 9.95 (*0-913123-15-3*) Galileo.

Life in the Millennium. rev. ed. Mona Johnian. 231p. (Orig.). 1994. pap., student ed. 8.99 (*0-88270-705-1*) Bridge-Logos.

Life in the Minor Leagues. Intro. by Jim Murray. LC 99-11980. (Baseball Legends Ser.). (Illus.). 64p. (YA). (gr. 3 up). 1999. 16.95 (*0-7910-5160-9*) Chelsea Hse.

Life in the Mountains. Catherine Bradley. LC 94-231881. 32p. (J). (gr. 4-7). 1993. pap. 4.99 (*0-590-47608-4*) Scholastic Inc.

***Life in the Mountains.** Monica Byles & World Book Staff. LC 97-62316. (Illus.). 32p. (J). (gr. 2-7). 1999. write for info. (*0-7166-5213-7*) World Bk.

Life in the Music Classroom. Music Educators National Conference Staff. 64p. (Orig.). (C). 1992. pap., teacher ed. 11.00 (*1-56545-010-8*, 1021) MENC.

Life in the New World. Dorothy Kawaguchi. LC 98-92060. 406p. 1998. pap. 24.95 (*1-57502-941-3*, P02582) Morris Pubng.

Life in the North During the Civil War. Timothy L. Biel. LC 96-34422. (Way People Live Ser.). (Illus.). 112p. (YA). 1996. lib. bdg. 22.45 (*1-56006-334-3*) Lucent Bks.

Life in the Ocean: Grades 1-3. Jo Ellen Moor. Ed. by Marilyn Evans. (Science Picture Cards Ser.: Vol. 3). (Illus.). 24p. 1998. pap., teacher ed. 12.95 (*1-55799-694-6*, 865) Evan-Moor Edu Pubs.

Life in the Oceans. Lucy Baker. 32p. (J). (gr. 4-7). 1993. pap. 4.95 (*0-590-46132-X*) Scholastic Inc.

Life in the Oceans. Lucy Baker. (Life in the . . . Ser.). (J). 1990. 10.15 (*0-606-05426-X*, Pub. by Turtleback) Demco.

***Life in the Oceans.** Lucy Bakerna. LC 96-61736. (World Book Ecology Ser.). (Illus.). 32p. (J). (gr. 3-8). 1999. write for info. (*0-7166-5202-1*) World Bk.

Life in the Oceans. HarBrace Staff. 1995. pap. text 13.10 (*0-15-305617-7*) Harcourt.

Life in the Old West Series. Bobbie Kalman. Incl. Bandanas, Chaps & Ten-Gallon Hats. LC 99-10311. (Illus.). 32p. (J). (gr. 1-9). 1998. pap. 7.95 (*0-7787-0105-0*); Bandanas, Chaps & Ten-Gallon Hats. LC 99-10311. (Illus.). 32p. (J). (gr. 1-9). 1998. lib. bdg. 19.96 (*0-7787-0073-9*); Boomtowns of the West. LC 99-11529. (Illus.). 32p. (J). (gr. 4-9). 1999. lib. bdg. 19.96 (*0-7787-0078-X*); Boomtowns of the West. LC 99-11529. (Illus.). 32p. (J). (gr. 4-7). 1999. pap. 7.95 (*0-7787-0110-7*); Gold Rush. LC 99-11520. (Illus.). 32p. (J). (gr. 4-9). 1999. lib. bdg. 19.96 (*0-7787-0079-8*); Gold Rush. LC 99-11520. (Illus.). 32p. (J). (gr. 4-7). 1999. pap. 7.95 (*0-7787-0111-5*); Homes of the West. LC 98-37626. (Illus.). 32p. (J). (gr. 1-9). 1998. pap. 7.95 (*0-7787-0106-9*); Homes of the West. LC 98-37626. (Illus.). 32p. (J). (gr. 1-9). 1998. lib. bdg. 19.96 (*0-7787-0074-7*); Life on the Ranch. LC 98-42366. (Illus.). 32p. (J). (gr. 1-9). 1998. pap. 7.95 (*0-7787-0103-4*); Life on the Ranch. LC 98-42366. (Illus.). 32p. (J). (gr. 3-8). 1998. lib. bdg. 19.96 (*0-7787-0071-2*); Life on the Trail. (Illus.). 32p. (J). (gr. 3-9). 1998. pap. 7.95 (*0-7787-0104-2*); Life on the Trail. LC 98-40375. (Illus.). 32p. (J). (gr. 3-8). 1998. lib. bdg. 19.96 (*0-7787-0072-0*); Railroad. LC 99-11530. (Illus.). 32p. (J). (gr. 4-9). 1999. lib. bdg. 19.96 (*0-7787-0076-3*); Railroad. LC 99-11530. (Illus.). 32p. (J). (gr. 4-7). 1999. pap. 7.95 (*0-7787-0108-5*); Wagon Train. LC 98-93229. (Illus.). 32p. (J). (gr. 1-9). 1998. pap. 7.95 (*0-7787-0102-6*); Wagon Train. LC 98-93229. (Illus.). 32p. (J). (gr. 3-8). 1998. lib. bdg. 19.96 (*0-7787-0070-4*); Who Settled the West? LC 99-11528. (Illus.). 32p. (J). (gr. 3-8). 1999. lib. bdg. 19.96 (*0-7787-0075-5*); Who Settled the West? LC 99-11528. (Illus.). 32p. (J). (gr. 4-7). 1999. pap. 7.95 (*0-7787-0107-7*); (J). pap. write for info. (*0-7787-0097-6*); lib. bdg. write for info. (*0-7787-0065-8*) Crabtree Pub Co.

Life in the Orphanage. Dave Foster. Ed. by Ida Percoco. (Illus.). 168p. (Orig.). 1997. pap. 12.95 (*0-9644613-1-5*) Top Tenn Pr.

Life in the Passionate Lane. Donald J. Maizys. LC 89-91457. 1990. 10.95 (*0-87212-230-1*) Libra.

Life in the Pee Dee: Prehistoric & Historic Research on the Roche Carolina Tract, Florence County, South Carolina. Michael Trinkley et al. LC 93-33726. (Research Ser.: No. 39). (Illus.). xii, 207p. 1993. pap. 45.00 (*1-58317-034-0*) Chicora Found.

***Life in the Polar Lands.** Monica Bylesna. Ed. by World Book Staff. LC 96-61735. (World Book Ecology Ser.). (Illus.). 32p. (J). (gr. 3-8). 1999. write for info. (*0-7166-5206-4*) World Bk.

Life in the Polar Lands. Monica Byles. (Illus.). 32p. (J). (gr. 4-7). 1993. reprint ed. pap. 4.95 (*0-590-46130-3*) Scholastic Inc.

Life in the Polar Regions. Melvin Berger. Ed. by Natalie Lunis. (Ranger Rick Science Spectacular Ser.). 16p. (J). (gr. 2-4). 1994. pap. 16.95 (*1-56784-210-0*) Newbridge Educ.

Life in the Polar Regions: Student Book. Melvin Berger. Ed. by Natalie Lunis. (Ranger Rick Science Spectacular Ser.). (Illus.). 16p. (Orig.). (J). (gr. 2-4). 1996. pap. 3.95 (*1-56784-235-6*) Newbridge Educ.

Life in the Polar Regions: Theme Pack. Melvin Berger. Ed. by Natalie Lunis. (Ranger Rick Science Spectacular Ser.). (Illus.). (Orig.). (J). (gr. 2-4). 1996. pap. 36.90 (*1-56784-265-8*) Newbridge Educ.

Life in the Pond. Eileen Curran. LC 84-16285. (Illus.). 32p. (J). (gr. k-2). 1985. pap. 3.50 (*0-8167-0453-8*) Troll Communs.

Life in the Pressure Cooker: Studies in James. Roy R. Roberts. pap. 5.99 (*0-88469-036-9*) BMH Bks.

Life in the Pueblo: Understanding the Past Through Archaeology. Kathryn Kamp. (Illus.). 224p. (C). 1997. pap. text 13.95 (*0-88133-964-4*) Waveland Pr.

Life in the Pueblos. Ruth M. Underhill. Ed. by Willard W. Beatty. LC 90-85644. (Illus.). 168p. 1991. reprint ed. pap. 15.95 (*0-941270-68-8*) Ancient City Pr.

Life in the Quaker Lane. Seth B. Hinshaw. 209p. 1990. pap. 15.00 (*0-942585-16-X*) NC Frnds Hist Soc.

Life in the Rain Forest. Melvin Berger. Ed. by Natalie Lunis. (Ranger Rick Science Spectacular Ser.). 16p. (J). (gr. 2-4). 1993. pap. 16.95 (*1-56784-200-3*) Newbridge Educ.

Life in the Rain Forest: Student Book. Melvin Berger. Ed. by Natalie Lunis. (Ranger Rick Science Spectacular Ser.). (Illus.). 16p. (Orig.). (J). (gr. 2-4). 1996. pap. 3.95 (*1-56784-225-9*) Newbridge Educ.

An Asterisk (*) at the beginning of an entry indicates that the title is appearing for the first time.

Life in the Rain Forest: Theme Pack. Melvin Berger. Ed. by Natalie Lunis. (Ranger Rick Science Spectacular Ser.). (Illus.). (Orig.). (J). (gr. 2-4). 1996. pap. 36.90 (1-56784-266-6) Newbridge Educ.

*__Life in the Rain Forests.__ Lucy Bakerna. LC 96-61737. (World Book Ecology Ser.). (Illus.). 32p. (J). (gr. 3-8). 1999. write for info. (0-7166-5204-8) World Bk.

Life in the Rainbow: A Novel. Richard Horan. LC 95-47954. 164p. 1996. 17.00 (1-883642-02-7) Steerforth Pr.

Life in the Rainforest. John Erbacher & Sue Erbacher. (Illus.). 63p. (C). 1993. 21.50 (0-521-43238-3) Cambridge U Pr.

Life in the Rainforest: Plants, Animals, & People. Melvin Berger & Gilda Berger. LC 98-21542. (Discovery Readers Ser.). (Illus.). 48p. (J). (gr. k up). 1999. lib. bdg. 15.95 (0-7910-5068-8) Chelsea Hse.

Life in the Rainforest: Plants, Animals, & People. Melvin Berger & Gilda Berger. LC 94-6006. (Discovery Readers Ser.). (Illus.). 48p. (J). (gr. k-4). 1994. pap., per. 4.50 (1-57102-007-1, Ideals Child) Hambleton-Hill.

Life in the Rainforests. Lucy Baker. (J). 1990. 10.15 (0-606-05427-8, Pub. by Turtleback) Demco.

Life in the Real World: 5-Minute Devotions for Teens. Eileen Ritter. LC 96-39219. 128p. (J). 1997. 6.99 (0-570-04888-5, 12-3305) Concordia.

Life in the Real World 2: 5-Minute Devotions for Teens. Eileen Ritter. LC 98-41223. 128p. (YA). 1999. 6.99 (0-570-05348-X, 12-3396GJ) Concordia.

Life in the Rocky Mountains. rev. ed. Warren Ferris. Ed. by LeRoy R. Hafen. 1984. 35.00 (0-912094-20-6) Old West.

Life in the Saddle. Frank Collinson. Ed. by Mary W. Clarke. LC 96-44366. (Western Frontier Library: Vol. 21). (Illus.). 256p. 1997. pap. 14.95 (0-8061-2923-9) U of Okla Pr.

Life in the Saddle. deluxe ed. Ed. by Gretel Ehrlich. (Wilderness Experience Ser.). (Illus.). 100p. 1996. 30.00 (1-887656-26-X) Tehabi Bks.

Life in the Sandwich Generation: Life in the Sandwich Generation. Kay Meyer. (Family Life Issues Ser.). 1995. pap. 4.50 (0-570-09490-9, 20-2702) Concordia.

Life in the Sea. Melvin Berger. Ed. by Lisa Trumbauer. (Early Science Big Bks.). (Illus.). 16p. (J). (ps-2). 1993. pap. 16.95 (1-56784-013-2) Newbridge Educ.

Life in the Sea. Eileen Curran. LC 84-16190. (Illus.). 32p. (J). (gr. k-2). 1997. pap. 3.50 (0-8167-0449-X) Troll Communs.

*__Life in the Sea.__ Janet Halfmann. LC 98-43884. (Lifeviews Ser.). (Illus.). 32p. (J). 2000. lib. bdg. 22.60 (1-58341-074-0, Creat Educ) Creative Co.

Life in the Sea. J. M. Parramon & Maria Rius. (Habitats Ser.).Tr. of La Vida en el Mar. (Illus.). 32p. (J). (gr. 3-5). 1987. pap. 6.95 (0-8120-3865-7) Barron.

Life in the Sea Theme Pack. Melvin Berger. Ed. by Susan Evento. (Macmillan Early Science Big Bks.). (Illus.). (J). (ps-2). 1995. pap. 49.95 (1-56784-145-7) Newbridge Educ.

*__Life in the Shadows: The Sports Photography of Hy Peskin.__ Hy Peskin & John Thorn. (Illus.). 192p. 2000. 40.00 (1-892129-40-X) Total Sprts.

Life in the Shadows of the Crystal Palace, 1910-1927: Ford Workers in the Model T Era. Clarence Hooker. LC 96-37556. (Illus.). 210p. 1997. 42.95 (0-87972-737-3); pap. 19.95 (0-87972-738-1) Bowling Green Univ Popular Press.

Life in the Shtetl. Ilex Beller. Tr. by Alastair D. Pannell from FRE. LC 86-19512. (Illus.). 145p. 1986. 49.50 (0-8419-1095-2) Holmes & Meier.

Life in the Shtetl. Lamed Shapiro. 0.99 (0-89906-642-9); pap. 0.99 (0-89906-643-7) Mesorah Pubns.

Life in the Slow Lane. Ruth Anderson. 36p. (Orig.). 1996. pap. 8.43 (0-9648461-2-8) Ebert Desgn.

Life in the Slow Lane. Arthur E. Martin. (Illus.). 304p. 1990. 25.00 (0-914339-30-3) P E Randall Pub.

Life in the Slow Lane. Ed. by Jerry Wiebel. LC 98-67448. 160p. 1998. 16.95 (0-89821-240-5) Reiman Pubns.

Life in the Slow Lane: Ecology & Conservation of Long-Lived Marine Animals. Ed. by John A. Musick. LC 99-61670. (AFS Symposium Ser.). (Illus.). 280p. 1999. pap. text 47.00 (1-888569-15-8, 540.23) Am Fisheries Soc.

Life in the Slow Lane: The Benefits of Not Getting What You Want When You Want It. Stan Gaede. 256p. 1991. pap. 9.99 (0-310-53201-9) Zondervan.

Life in the Son. Robert Shank. LC 89-14990. 4p. 1989. reprint ed. pap. 14.99 (1-55661-091-2) Bethany Hse.

Life in the South During the Civil War. James P. Reger. (Way People Live Ser.). (Illus.). 112p. (YA). 1996. lib. bdg. 22.45 (1-56006-333-5) Lucent Bks.

Life in the South from the Commencement of the War by a Blockaded British Subject: Being a Social History of Those Who Took Part in the Battles, 2 vols. Catherine C. Hopley. LC 79-130532. 1971. reprint ed. 95.00 (0-678-00768-3) Kelley.

Life in the Southern Colonies: Jamestown, Williamsburg, St. Marty's City & Beyond. Ed. by Jeanne M. Bracken. (Perspectives on History Ser.: Vol. 31). (Illus.). 64p. 1997. pap. 6.95 (1-878668-74-9) Disc Enter Ltd.

Life in the Spirit. Charles Dixon. 89p. 1996. pap., wbk. ed. 11.99 (1-889389-09-9) End-Time Wave.

*__Life in the Spirit.__ Robertson McQuilkin. LC 99-47243. 256p. 2000. pap. 12.99 (0-8054-2079-7) Broadman.

Life in the Spirit. Jessie Penn-Lewis. 1979. pap. 5.99 (0-87508-956-9) Chr Lit.

Life in the Spirit. Bramwell H. Tillsley. 109p. (Orig.). 1986. pap. 4.95 (0-86544-037-9) Salv Army Suppl South.

Life in the Spirit. unabridged ed. Richard S. Taylor. 221p. 1994. reprint ed. pap. 12.99 (0-88019-316-6) Schmul Pub Co.

Life in the Spirit see Mother Teresa Treasury: Mother Teresa of Calcutta

Life in the Spirit: A 30 Day Personal Bible Study. abr. ed. J. I. Packer. LC 96-13990. 144p. 1996. pap. 9.99 (0-89107-892-4) Crossway Bks.

Life in the Spirit: Understanding the Gifts & Operations of the Holy Spirit. Charles Dixon. 179p. (Orig.). 1996. pap. 4.99 (1-889389-01-3) End-Time Wave.

Life in the Spirit Vol. 3: Systematic Theology, 3 vols. Thomas C. Oden. LC 90-55805. 560p. 1994. reprint ed. pap. 26.00 (0-06-066362-6, Pub. by Harper SF) HarpC.

Life in the Spirit Seminars Team Manual: Catholic Edition. 187p. 1979. pap. 9.99 (0-89283-065-4) Servant.

Life in the Struggle: Ivory Perry & the Culture of Opposition. 2nd ed. George Lipsitz. (Illus.). 320p. 1995. pap. 22.95 (1-56639-321-3) Temple U Pr.

Life in the Sun: A Guide to Long-Stay Holidays & Living Abroad in Retirement. Nancy Tuft. (C). 1989. 55.00 (0-86242-085-7, Pub. by Age Concern Eng) St Mut.

Life in the Temperate Zone & Other Stories. Robert Wexelblatt. (Fiction Ser.). 275p. 1990. 18.95 (0-8135-1535-1) Rutgers U Pr.

Life in the Theatre. David Mamet. LC 77-91884. 96p. 1978. pap. 10.95 (0-8021-5067-5, Grove) Grove-Atltic.

Life in the Third Reich. Ed. by Richard Bessel. (Illus.). 144p. 1987. pap. 12.95 (0-19-285184-5) OUP.

Life in the Thirteen Colonies, 1650-1750. Stuart K. Kallen. Ed. by Rosemary Walner. LC 90-82617. (Building of a Nation Ser.). (Illus.). 64p. (J). (gr. 4). 1990. lib. bdg. 13.98 (0-939179-87-3) ABDO Pub Co.

Life in the Three Sixth Grades. John H. Lounsbury & J. Howard Johnston. 144p. (Orig.). 1988. pap. text 11.00 (0-88210-212-5) Natl Assn Principals.

Life in the Tomb. Strates Myriveles. Tr. by Peter Bien from GER. LC 86-40519. 352p. 1987. reprint ed. pap. 109.20 (0-608-02321-3, 206296200004) Bks Demand.

Life in the Trash Lane: Cash, Cars & Corruption, a Sports Agent's True Story. Mel Levine. LC 93-44457. 192p. 1993. pap. 9.95 (0-942963-48-2) Distinctive Pub.

Life in the Treetops: Adventures of a Woman in Field Biology. Margaret D. Lowman. LC 98-48691. (Illus.). 240p. 1999. 30.00 (0-300-07818-8) Yale U Pr.

*__Life in the Treetops: Adventures of a Woman in Field Biology.__ Margaret D. Lowman. (Illus.). 240p. 1999. pap. 13.95 (0-300-08464-1) Yale U Pr.

*__Life in the 20th Century: Innocent Beginnings, 1917-1950.__ Arthur Meier Schlesinger, Jr. (Illus.). 384p. 2000. 27.00 (0-395-70752-8) HM.

Life in the Twenty-First Century. Ed. by Viktoras Kulvinskas. (Illus.). 398p. 1981. pap. text 14.95 (0-933278-00-4) Twen Fir Cent.

Life in the U. S. A. R. Jordania. (Bk. 1). 1983. text 3.60 (0-07-033060-3) McGraw.

Life in the U. S. A. R. Jordania. (Bk. 2). 1985. audio 20.00 (0-07-033063-8) McGraw.

Life in the Universe. Jean Heidmann. 1992. pap. 11.95 (0-07-027887-3) McGraw.

Life in the Universe: A Scientific American Special Issue. Stephen Weinberg et al. (Illus.). 160p. 1994. pap. text 16.95 (0-7167-2651-3) W H Freeman.

Life in the Universe: Readings from Scientific American Magazine. Scientific American Staff & Carolyn B. Mitchell. LC 94-44733. (Illus.). 160p. (C). 1995. pap. 16.95 (0-7167-2714-5) W H Freeman.

Life in the Universe/Discovering the Universe. Kaufmann. 1994. 33.20 (0-7167-2614-9) W H Freeman.

Life in the Universe/Exploring Earth & Life. Steven M. Stanley. 1994. 55.00 (0-7167-2615-7) W H Freeman.

Life in the Universe/Understanding the Earth. Frank Press. 1994. 37.20 (0-7167-2616-5) W H Freeman.

Life in the Upanishads. Shubhra Sharma. 1985. 15.00 (81-7017-202-0, Pub. by Abhinav) S Asia.

Life in the Vatican with John Paul II. Luigi Accattoli. 216p. 1999. pap. 29.95 (0-7893-0252-7, Pub. by Universe) St Martin.

Life in the Warsaw Ghetto. Gail B. Stewart. LC 96-26353. (Way People Live Ser.). (Illus.). 112p. (J). (gr. 5-9). 1995. lib. bdg. 22.45 (1-56006-075-1) Lucent Bks.

Life in the Water. (Child's First Library of Learning). (Illus.). 88p. (J). (ps-3). 1989. lib. bdg. 21.27 (0-8094-4854-8) Time-Life.

Life in the Womb: The Origin of Health & Disease. Peter W. Nathanielsz. LC 98-51356. (Illus.). 363p. 1999. 27.50 (0-916859-56-8) Promethean Pr.

*__Life in the Woodlands.__ Monica Byles & World Book Staff. LC 97-62318. (Illus.). 32p. (J). (gr. 2-7). 1999. write for info. (0-7166-5215-3) World Bk.

Life in the Word Devotional. J. Meyer. LC 99-192638. 219 p. 1998. 14.99 (1-57794-038-5) Harrison Hse.

Life in the Word Devotional. Joyce Meyer. 272p. pap. 24.99 (1-57794-048-2, HH2-038-5) Harrison Hse.

Life in the Word Gift Book. Joyce Meyer. LC 97-224549. 160p. 1997. pap. 5.99 (1-57794-004-0) Harrison Hse.

Life in the Word Gift Set. Joyce Meyer. boxed set 14.99 (1-57794-044-X, IW-044) Harrison Hse.

Life in the Word Journal. Joyce Meyer. 160p. 7.99 (1-57794-046-6, HH2-046-6) Harrison Hse.

Life in the Word Journal. Joyce Meyer. 1999. 9.99 (1-57794-170-5) Harrison Hse.

Life in the World of Women: A Collection of Vile, Dangerous & Loving Stories. Maxim Jakubowski. LC 97-129768. 182p. 1997. pap. 13.95 (1-899344-06-3) Dufour.

Life in the World Unseen. Anthony Borgia. 202p. 1993. pap. 12.00 (0-9636435-0-9) M A P.

*__Life in the 20th Century, Pts. 1 & 2.__ Sigmund F. Zakrzewski. (Illus.). 91p. 2000. pap. write for info. (0-9639784-5-4) SFZ Pubng.

Life in These United States: True Stories & Humorous Glimpses from America's Most Popular Magazine. Reader's Digest Editors. LC 95-49496. (Illus.). 216p. 1996. pap. 9.95 (0-89577-855-6, Pub. by RD Assn) Penguin Putnam.

Life in Three Cities: Frankfurt, London, & Jerusalem. Fred S. Worms. 1997. 27.50 (1-870015-64-9, Pub. by P Halban) Intl Spec Bk.

Life in Three Parts, No. 1, No. 1000. Marene P. Fassina. 11p. 1992. mass mkt. 2.50 (1-892996-05-7) M Fassina.

Life in Tudor Times. Christine Counsell & Kate Howe. LC 97-158699. (Primary History Ser.). (Illus.). 49p. (C). 1997. pap. 9.95 (0-521-55758-5) Cambridge U Pr.

Life in 2030: Exploring a Sustainable Future in Canada. John B. Robinson et al. LC 97-121139. 224p. 1996. pap. 25.95 (0-7748-0569-2) U of Wash Pr.

Life in Two Worlds. Betty Powel-Skoog & Justine Kerfoot. LC 96-70457. 1996. pap. 14.95 (0-9653027-1-7) Paper Moon Pub.

Life in Two Worlds: An Experiment in Autobiography. Bernhard Blume. Tr. by Hildegarde Hannum from GER. LC 91-37695. (Literature & the Sciences of Man Ser.: Vol. 3). (Illus.). XII, 240p. 1993. 47.95 (0-8204-1765-3) P Lang Pubng.

Life in (Very) Minor Works: Poems. Ellen Pearce. 1968. 4.50 (0-8079-0073-7); pap. 1.95 (0-8079-0074-5) October.

Life in Victorian Ireland. Deirdre Brown et al. (Primary History Ser.). 48p. 1996. pap. 10.95 (0-85640-556-6, Pub. by Blackstaff Pr) Dufour.

Life in Wales see Short History of Wales: Welsh Life & Customs from Prehistoric Times to the Present Day

Life in War-Torn Bosnia. Diane Yancey. (Way People Live Ser.). 112p. (J). 1996. 22.45 (1-56006-326-2) Lucent Bks.

Life in Western America. Pace International Research, Inc. Staff. (AAA Video Ser.). (Illus.). 132p. 1984. text 8.95 (0-89209-049-9); pap. text 4.25 (0-89209-080-4); digital audio 3.25 (0-89209-081-2); VHS 60.00 (0-89209-046-4) Pace Grp Intl.

Life in Your Backyard. Natalie Lunis. (Ranger Rick Science Spectacular Ser.). 16p. (J). (gr. 2-4). 1996. pap. 16.95 (1-56784-223-2) Newbridge Educ.

Life in Your Backyard: Student Book. Natalie Lunis. (Ranger Rick Science Spectacular Ser.). (Illus.). 16p. (Orig.). (J). (gr. 2-4). 1996. pap. 3.95 (1-56784-248-8) Newbridge Educ.

Life in Your Backyard Theme Pack. Natalie Louis. (Ranger Rick Science Spectacular Ser.). (Illus.). 16p. (J). (gr. 2-5). 1996. pap. 36.90 (1-56784-284-4) Newbridge Educ.

Life in Zion: An Intimate Look at the Latter-Day Saints, 1820-1995. William W. Slaughter. LC 95-9140. (Illus.). x, 196p. 1995. 24.95 (0-87579-893-4) Deseret Bk.

Life Industry: Biodiversity, People & Profits. Ed. by Miges Baumann et al. 206p. 1996. pap. 18.95 (1-85339-341-X, Pub. by Intermed Tech) Stylus Pub VA.

Life Injections: Connecting Scripture to the Human Experience. Richard Zajac. 1998. pap. 13.95 (0-7880-1145-6) CSS OH.

Life Injections: Connecting Scripture to the Human Experience. Richard E. Zajac. LC 97-27333. 144p. 1998. pap. 13.95 (0-7880-1142-1) CSS OH.

*__Life Injections: Connecting Scripture to the Human Experience.__ Richard E. Zajac. 1998. cd-rom 13.95 (0-7880-1143-X, Fairway Pr); mac hd 13.95 (0-7880-1144-8, Fairway Pr) CSS OH.

Life Instead. Diane Bringgold. 128p. 1984. reprint ed. pap. 4.95 (0-9614225-0-5) Howard Pub.

Life Insurance. Buist M. Anderson. 1991. 145.00 (0-316-03961-6) Aspen Pub.

*__Life Insurance.__ 13th ed. Black & Dinger. LC 99-22004. (Illus.). 1072p. 1999. 84.00 (0-13-891250-5) P-H.

Life Insurance: A Consumer's Handbook. 2nd ed. Joseph M. Belth. LC 84-47705. (Illus.). 240p. 1985. pap. 6.95 (0-253-20346-5) Ind U Pr.

Life Insurance Agent. Jack Rudman. (Career Examination Ser.: C-443). 1994. pap. 29.95 (0-8373-0443-1) Nat Learn.

Life Insurance Analysis: Policy & Company Performance. James M. Carson & Mark D. Forster. (Illus.). 147p. 1996. 34.95 (0-9656041-0-1) Iona Pub.

Life Insurance Answer Book: For Qualified Plans & Estate Planning. annuals Ed. by Gary S. Lesser & Lawrence C. Starr. LC 97-202983. 1152p. 1999. boxed set 118.00 (1-56706-424-8, 64248) Panel Pubs.

Life Insurance Answer Book: For Qualified Plans & Estate Planning. 2nd ed. Gary S. Lesser & Lawrence C. Starr. LC 98-44299. (Panel Answer Book Ser.). 1997. boxed set 118.00 (1-56706-886-3) Aspen Law.

*__Life Insurance Boot Camp 2000: The Buyer's Guide with Respect to Life Insurance & Other Financial Issues.__ 2nd ed. William D. Brownlie. 2000. spiral bd. 44.95 (0-9662791-3-1) LIBC.

*__Life Insurance Boot Camp 2000: The Buyer's Guide with Respect to Life Insurance & Other Financial Issues.__ 2nd abr. ed. William D. Brownlie. 330p. 2000. disk 14.95 (0-9662791-1-5) LIBC.

Life Insurance Company Mergers & Consolidations. Marshall. (C). 1972. 12.95 (0-256-00653-9, Irwn McGrw-H) McGrw-H Hghr Educ.

Life Insurance Company Mortgage Lending to U. S. Agriculture: Challenges & Opportunities. Jerome M. Stam. (Illus.). 59p. (C). 1997. reprint ed. pap. text 25.00 (0-7881-3698-4) DIANE Pub.

Life Insurance Dictionary: Lebensversicherungstechnisches Woerterbuch. 3rd ed. Wolfgang Sachs & Gunter Drude. (ENG, FRE, GER, ITA & SPA.). 270p. 1983. 125.00 (0-8288-0970-4, M15244) Fr & Eur.

Life Insurance Enterprise, 1885-1910: A Study in the Limits of Corporate Power. Morton Keller. LC 63-10868. (Center for the Study of the History of Liberty in America Ser.). (Illus.). 350p. 1963. 32.00 (0-674-53150-7) Belknap Pr.

Life Insurance Fiasco: How to Avoid It. Peter C. Katt. LC 91-72305. 180p. (Orig.). 1991. 19.95 (0-9629957-0-3); pap. 19.95 (0-9629957-1-1) Dolphin MI.

Life Insurance in Estate Planning. James C. Munch, Jr. LC 80-84027. (C). 1981. text, suppl. ed. 80.00 (0-316-58932-2, Aspen Law & Bus) Aspen Pub.

Life Insurance in Italy: A Strategic Entry Report, 1997. Compiled by Icon Group International Staff. (Illus.). 129p. 1999. ring bd. 1290.00 incl. audio compact disk (0-7418-1042-5) Icon Grp.

Life Insurance Investment in Commercial Real Estate. H. Wayne Snider. (C). 1956. 9.50 (0-256-00679-2, Irwn McGrw-H) McGrw-H Hghr Educ.

Life Insurance Law (For 324) 2nd rev. ed. R. Robert Rackley. (CLU Ser.). 1999. 160.00 (1-57195-102-4) Insurance Achiev.

Life Insurance Law in the Commonwealth Caribbean. Claude H. Denbow. 1984. 50.00 (0-406-07630-8, U.K., MICHIE) LEXIS Pub.

Life Insurance Law in the Commonwealth Caribbean. Claude H. Denbow. (C). 1984. 175.00 (0-7855-6046-7, Pub. by Witherby & Co) St Mut.

Life Insurance Mathematics. H. U. Gerber. Tr. by W. Neuhaus from GER. xiii, 131p. 1990. 49.50 (0-387-52944-6) Spr-Verlag.

Life Insurance Mathematics. 3rd ed. Hans U. Gerber. LC 97-1007. 1997. 59.95 (3-540-62242-X) Spr-Verlag.

Life Insurance Mathematics, Vol. XIII. 2nd expanded ed. Hans U. Gerber et al. 190p. 1995. 59.00 (3-540-58858-2) Spr-Verlag.

Life Insurance Multiple Choice Practice Questions. Harold C. Luckstone. 100p. (Orig.). 1997. pap. text 14.95 (1-884803-12-1) Werbel Pub.

Life Insurance, 1993. Munch. 1993. suppl. ed. 52.50 (0-316-58961-6, Aspen Law & Bus) Aspen Pub.

*__Life Insurance Products & Finance: Charting a Clear Course.__ David B. Atkinson & James W. Dallas. (Illus.). 800p. (C). 2000. text. write for info. (0-938959-67-0) Soc Actuaries.

Life Insurance Set, Set. Anderson. 1992. 145.00 (0-316-03971-3) Aspen Pub.

Life Insurance, Spend It & Keep It: How to Make a Tax-Free Exchange of Your Life Insurance & Earn Tax-Deferred Interest. William L. Lance. (Illus.). 52p. 1980. pap. 8.00 (0-686-27280-3) Truth Pub AZ.

*__Life Insurance Suitability.__ Dearborn Financial Pub. Staff. LC 99-48277. (Illus.). 113p. 1999. pap. 29.00 (0-7931-3295-9) Dearborn.

Life Insurance Theory: Actuarial Perspectives. F. Etienne De Vylder. LC 97-30711. 248p. 1997. 110.00 (0-7923-9995-1) Kluwer Academic.

Life into Art: Isadora Duncan & Her World. Ed. by Doree Duncan et al. LC 93-1737. 1993. 40.00 (0-393-03507-7) Norton.

Life into Space: Space Life Sciences Experiments: NASA Ames Research Center, 1965-1990. Ed. by Kenneth Souza et al. (Illus.). 606p. (C). 1998. pap. text 50.00 (0-7881-7353-7) DIANE Pub.

Life into Story: The Courtship of Elizabeth Wiseman. Mary Chan. LC 97-50361. (Women & Gender in Early Modern England, 1500-1750 Ser.). 164p. 1998. text 61.95 (1-84014-212-X, Pub. by Ashgate Pub) Ashgate Pub Co.

Life Is... aut. ed. Roberta Mendel. (Enigma Ser.). (Illus.). 33p. 1997. pap. 10.00 (0-936424-23-0, 017) Pin Prick.

*__Life Is a B****... And Then You Get Your Period: (Everything You Might as Well Know about Being a Woman)__ Dorian Yeager. (Illus.). 96p. 1999. pap. 9.95 (0-9674495-0-2) Empress Imprints.

*__Life Is a Blessing.__ Dale Evans Rogers. 2000. 9.99 (0-88486-282-8, Inspirational Pr) Arrowood Pr.

Life Is a Blessing. Sylvia T. Young. 44p. (Orig.). 1996. pap. 8.50 (0-9652368-2-X) Wright Pub Co.

Life Is a Cabaret. 208p. (Orig.). 1993. per. 14.95 (0-7935-2357-5, 00311622) H Leonard.

*__Life is a Celebration: Are You Celebrating, Just Getting Along, Suffering?__ Russell E. Osnes & Carole Gesme. (Illus.). 304p. 2000. pap. 14.95 (1-890676-53-5, Pub. by Beavers Pond) Bookman Bks.

Life Is a Challenge, Meet It! Joy Thomas. (Illus.). 200p. 1991. pap. 9.95 (0-9624494-1-X) Ontic Bk Pubs.

*__Life Is a Circus.__ Shirley Carroll O'Connor. LC 99-91850. 103p. 1999. 25.00 (0-7388-1314-1); pap. 18.00 (0-7388-1315-X) Xlibris Corp.

Life Is a Contact Sport: The Ten Point Strategy to Turbo-Charge Your Career. Ken Kragen & Jefferson Graham. LC 93-46309. 1994. 23.00 (0-688-13282-0, Wm Morrow) Morrow Avon.

Life Is a Dance: You Should Only Know the Steps. Katie Brown. Tr. by Sydney Bacon & Rose Kashtan from YID. (Illus.). 87p. 1987. 20.00 (0-89304-060-6); pap. 10.00 (0-89304-061-4) Cross-Cultrl NY.

Life Is a Dream. Pedro Calderon de la Barca. Tr. by John Clifford. 96p. 1998. pap. 6.95 (1-85459-188-6, Pub. by Theatre Comm) Consort Bk Sales.

Life Is a Dream. Richard Curle. LC 78-106284. (Short Story Index Reprint Ser.). 1977. 21.95 (0-8369-3321-4) Ayer.

Life Is a Dream & Other Spanish Classics. Ed. by Eric Bentley. Tr. by Roy Campbell from SPA. LC 85-15671. (Eric Bentley's Dramatic Repertoire Ser.). 304p. 1985. pap. 24.95 (1-55783-005-3) Applause Theatre Bk Pubs.

Life Is a Dream & Other Spanish Classics. Ed. by Eric Bentley. Tr. by Roy Campbell. 1989. pap. 10.95 (1-55783-006-1) Applause Theatre Bk Pubs.

Life Is a Dream, Realize It! Joy Thomas. (Illus.). 204p. (Orig.). 1993. pap. 9.95 (0-9624494-2-3) Ontic Bk Pubs.

Life Is a Fatal Disease: Selected Poems, 1964-94. Paula Gunn Allen. 224p. (Orig.). 1997. pap. 16.95 (0-931122-85-6) West End.

*__Life is a Flower: New Poems.__ R. Pease. 66p. 1999. per. 9.95 (1-889455-05-9) Flagg Mtn Pr.

An Asterisk (*) at the beginning of an entry indicates that the title is appearing for the first time.

Life Is a Football Game. Troy Dunn. 1998. pap. 3.95 (*1-57734-138-4*, 01113151) Covenant Comms.

Life Is a Game of Choice. Jennifer James. (Illus.). (Orig.). 1983. reprint ed. pap. text 3.95 (*0-915423-00-6*) Jennifer J.

Life Is a Game, Play It! Joy Thomas. (Illus.). 322p. (Orig.). 1989. reprint ed. pap. 9.95 (*0-9624494-0-7*) Ontic Bk Pubs.

Life Is a Garden. Francine Swann. (Illus.). 56p. (Orig.). 1995. pap. 5.00 (*0-9645451-4-4*) F Swann Pubns.

Life Is a Gift. Rusty Berkus. (Illus.). 64p. (Orig.). 1982. pap. 19.95 (*0-9609888-0-7*) Red Rose Pr.

Life Is a Gold Mine - Can You Dig It? A Practical Guide to Help You Get Your Natural Resources Out of the Ground & into Your Life. John Stanko. 192p. 1995. pap. 9.95 (*0-9637311-2-2*) Genesis Comm Inc.

***Life Is a Joke & God Wrote It: Stop Stress from Stealing Your Happiness.** Jerry Stanecki. 160p. 2000. 14.95 (*0-9635129-9-4*, Spirit Canyon Pr) J Stanecki Prods.

Life Is a Maze. Richard Flint. (Illus.). 118p. (Orig.). 1985. pap. text 10.00 (*0-937851-14-0*) Pendelton Lane.

Life Is a Meatloaf Sandwich: A Devotional for Early Teens. Carolyn Larsen. LC 95-61689. 382p. (J). (gr. 5-9). 1995. pap. 11.99 (*0-529-10452-0*, LMS) World Publng.

***Life Is a Miracle: An Essay Against Modern Superstition.** Wendell Berry. 124p. 2000. text 21.00 (*1-58243-058-6*, Pub. by Counterpt DC) HarpC.

***Life Is a Mission.** John Garrett & Janet Garrett. 112p. 2000. pap. 12.00 (*0-8059-4814-7*) Dorrance.

Life Is a Moody Rainbow: A Collection of Modern Poetry. Ed. by Louisa Persing. LC 72-87102. (Illus.). 130p. 1972. 5.50 (*0-686-01303-4*) Palomar.

***Life Is a Movie Starring You: Guide to Living Your Dreams.** Jennifur Brandt. 2000. pap. 12.95 (*0-446-67633-0*) Warner Bks.

Life Is a Poem: Often Set to Music. Evelyn Brill Stark. LC 99-15109. (Illus.). 256p. 1999. 20.00 (*0-913337-34-X*) Southfarm Pr.

Life Is a Poem to God. Patricia Cruser. vii, 70p. 1998. pap. 12.50 (*0-9667465-0-3*) ArtWord.

Life Is a Shared Creation. Paul Brenner. 176p. (Orig.). 1981. pap. 6.95 (*0-87516-454-4*) DeVorss.

Life Is a State of Mind. Helen P. Barker. (Illus.). 76p. 1999. pap. 7.95 (*0-7392-0233-2*, P03272) Morris Publng.

Life Is a Stretch: Easy Yoga Anytime, Anywhere. Carol Blackman & Elise Browning Miller. LC 98-27724. (Illus.). 224p. 1999. 17.95 (*1-56718-067-1*, K067) Llewellyn Pubns.

Life Is a Sweeter Song: A Breast Cancer Survivor's Story. Frances Cross. 100p. 1995. pap. 9.95 (*1-886979-06-5*) Practicl Pr.

Life Is a Symphony. Frances J. Murphy. (Illus.). 36p. (Orig.). 1992. pap. 5.00 (*1-878149-21-0*) Counterpoint Pub.

Life Is a Test & You Will Pass. David W. Merrill. (Illus.). 40p. 1995. pap. 9.95 (*1-879418-96-7*) Audenreed Pr.

Life Is a Trust. Frederick A. Meyer. (Religious Ser.). 95p. 1986. 8.95 (*0-935087-09-5*) Wright Pub Co.

Life Is an Adventure: A Temporary Condition at Best. Bryan Townsend. 132p. 1995. 19.95 (*0-9661848-1-5*) B Townsend.

Life Is an Attitude see Actitud Ante la Vida

Life Is an Attitude! Elwood N. Chapman. Ed. by Michael G. Crisp. LC 91-44382. 171p. (Orig.). 1992. pap. 12.95 (*1-56052-138-4*) Crisp Pubns.

Life Is an Attitude: A Tragedy Turns to Triumph. Ron Heagy. LC 97-3132. 224p. 1997. pap. 12.99 (*1-57673-089-1*, Multnomah Bks) Multnomah Pubs.

Life Is an Attitude: How to Grow Forever Better. rev. ed. Dottie Billington. 276p. 2000. pap. text 12.95 (*0-9671837-5-8*) Lowell Leigh.

Life Is an Inside Job. John G. Bruhn. (Illus.). 87p. (Orig.). 1995. pap. 6.00 (*0-9616570-3-0*) J G Bruhn.

Life Is an Operetta: And Other Short Stories. Peter Ustinov. LC 97-12865. 258p. 1997. 24.95 (*1-57392-150-5*) Prometheus Bks.

Life Is Awareness. Joy Thomas. (Illus.). 200p. (Orig.). 1996. pap. 9.95 (*0-9624494-2-3*) Ontic Bk Pubs.

Life Is Beautiful (La Vita E Bella) A Screenplay. Roberto Benigni & Vicenzo Cerami. LC 98-43728. (Illus.). 173p. 1998. pap. 10.95 (*0-7868-8469-X*, Pub. by Hyperion) Time Warner.

Life Is Built from the Inside Out: Meditation on the Pronoun "It" Edward Mycue. (Illus.). 50p. 1999. pap. 10.00 (*1-879457-61-X*) Norton Coker Pr.

Life Is but a Dream: Wise Techniques for an Inspirational Journey. Marica Weider. 220p. 1996. 16.95 (*1-57101-058-0*) MasterMedia Pub.

Life Is Change: Poems by Legro Bennett. Legro Bennett. 65p. 1995. mass mkt. 13.30 (*0-9644321-4-5*) Camel Dung Writ.

Life Is Change, Growth Is Optional. Karen K. Clark. (Illus.). 247p. 1993. pap. 15.95 (*0-9626467-2-5*) Ctr Exec Planning.

Life Is Choices, Hope Is a Decision. R. Lee Muehlberg. ii, 86p. (Orig.). 1996. pap. 7.95 (*0-9653342-1-X*) Muehlberg Pr.

Life Is Easy: Dreams & Recipes for Happiness on Earth Nightly Lullabies. Delaila S. Segal. 61p. 1991. pap. 13.00 (*0-9631510-0-2*) Delaila.

Life Is Elsewhere. Milan Kundera. LC 99-86224. 432p. 2000. pap. 13.00 (*0-06-099702-8*, Perennial) HarperTrade.

Life Is for Everyone. John Sharp & John Wilson. 144p. (C). 1988. pap. text 65.00 (*0-7152-0613-3*) St Mut.

Life Is for Everyone: Source Book for Church Services. Ed. by John Sharp & John Wilson. 144p. (C). 1989. spiral bd. 39.00 (*0-7855-6817-4*, Pub. by St Andrew) St Mut.

***Life Is for the Living & the Dying: Anthology: Searching the Shadows.** BonnieMarie Goul Huffaker. 77p. 2000. 17.95 (*0-9702050-0-7*) RedRidge Pubng.

Life Is for the Living: Recovering & Rebuilding after Spousal Loss: Recovering & Rebuilding After Spousal Loss. Gil Blum. LC 98-90344. 1998. pap. text 12.95 (*0-9663921-0-8*) Timed Resources.

Life Is Fun! Nancy Carlson. (Illus.). 32p. (J). (ps-3). 1996. pap. 5.99 (*0-14-054445-3*, PuffinBks) Peng Put Young Read.

Life Is Fun. Nancy L. Carlson. LC 93-14666. 1996. 10.19 (*0-606-09554-3*, Pub. by Turtleback) Demco.

***Life Is Funny: A Novel.** E. R. Frank. LC 99-23452. 272p. (YA). 2000. 17.95 (*0-7894-2634-X*, D K Ink) DK Pub Inc.

Life Is Good. Letha Owens. 56p. 1999. pap. 12.95 (*1-892668-07-6*) Prospect Pr.

Life Is Good! Rob McCarter. LC 99-62258. 129p. 1999. reprint ed. pap. 11.95 (*0-937539-37-6*) Executive Bks.

Life Is Good - Except for This Cancer. unabridged ed. Peter Polishuk. Ed. by Adam Abramowitz. (Illus.). 80p. 1996. pap. 9.95 (*1-56851-107-8*) Info Gatekeepers.

Life Is Goodbye, Life Is Hello: Grieving Well Through All Kinds of Loss. Alla R. Bozarth. 256p. pap. 14.95 (*1-56838-057-7*) Hazelden.

Life Is Hard: Machismo, Danger & the Intimacy of Power in Nicaragua. Roger N. Lancaster. LC 91-45764. 1994. pap. 16.95 (*0-520-08929-4*, Pub. by U CA Pr) Cal Prin Full Svc.

Life Is Hard, but God Is Good! David Brown. LC 98-171508. (Illus.). 128p. 1997. pap. 6.95 (*0-9659263-0-3*) D Brown Pub.

Life Is Hot in Cracktown. Buddy Giovinazzo. LC 92-45666. 256p. 1993. 19.95 (*1-56025-054-2*, Thunders Mouth) Avalon NY.

Life Is Just a Bowl of Cherries: And Other Delicious Sayings. Anne Bertram. LC 96-51179. (Artful Wordsmith Ser.). (Illus.). 336p. 1997. pap. 12.95 (*0-8442-0900-7*, 09007) NTC Contemp Pub Co.

Life Is Just a Bunch of Ziggys. Tom Wilson. (Illus.). 96p. 1973. pap. 2.50 (*0-8362-0551-0*) Andrews & McMeel.

Life Is Just a Chair of Bowlies. Mary Engelbreit. (Illus.). 32p. 1992. 6.95 (*0-8362-4604-7*) Andrews & McMeel.

Life Is Just a Chair of Bowlies. Mary Engelbreit. (Illus.). 48p. 1993. 4.95 (*0-8362-4615-2*) Andrews & McMeel.

***Life Is Just a Dream.** Gloria Chadwick. 70p. 2000. pap. 9.95 (*1-883717-24-8*) Myst Mndscapes.

Life Is Just What You Make It: My Story So Far. Donny Osmond & Patricia Romanowski. LC 99-24543. (Illus.). 304p. 1999. 22.95 (*0-7868-6494-X*, Pub. by Disney Pr) Time Warner.

Life Is Just What You Make It: My Story So Far. Donny Osmond & Patty Romanowski. 2000. mass mkt. 6.99 (*0-7868-8971-3*, Pub. by Hyperion) Time Warner.

Life Is Life & Other Tales & Episodes. Gwendoline Keats. LC 79-101816. (Short Story Index Reprint Ser.). 1977. 21.95 (*0-8369-3204-8*) Ayer.

Life Is Like a Box of Chocolates. Fundco Staff. 160p. 1995. 5.95 (*1-885507-03-8*) Fundco Printers.

Life Is Like a Chicken Coop Ladder: A Study of German National Character Through Folklore. Alan Dundes. LC 88-27955. (Illus.). 192p. (C). 1989. reprint ed. pap. 15.95 (*0-8143-2038-4*) Wayne St U Pr.

Life Is Like a Dogsled Team . . . If You're Not the Lead Dog, the Scenery Never Changes: The Wit & Wisdom of Lewis Grizzard. Lewis Grizzard. LC 94-74231. 1995. 12.00 (*1-56352-214-4*) Longstreet.

Life Is Like Driver's Ed . . . Ya Gotta Buckle up, Stay to the Right, & Watch Those Turns! Devotions for Teens & Their Parents. Greg Johnson. 180p. (Orig.). 1996. pap. 10.99 (*0-89283-961-9*, Vine Bks) Servant.

Life Is Like the Stock Market. Karla C. Erickson. Ed. by Jeff Erickson. (Illus.). 140p. (Orig.). 1998. pap. 11.95 (*0-9655000-1-2*) Blue Chip Ent.

Life Is Love, Enjoy It! Joy Thomas. (Illus.). 198p. (Orig.). 1994. pap. 9.95 (*0-9624494-3-1*) Ontic Bk Pubs.

Life Is More Important Than Food. Rita J. Carmack. 39p. 1987. pap. 5.00 (*0-937093-05-X*) Jewel Pr.

***Life Is More Than a Moment: The Desegregation of Little Rock's Central High.** Photos & Intro. by Will Counts. (Illus.). 1999. 29.95 (*0-253-33637-6*) Ind U Pr.

Life Is More Than Your To-Do List: Blending Business Success with Personal Satisfaction. Maggie M. Bedrosian. (Illus.). 192p. (Orig.). 1995. pap. 12.95 (*1-884798-26-8*) B C I Press.

Life Is My Song see Autobiography of John Gould Fletcher

Life Is My Song: The Autobiography of John Gould Fletcher. John G. Fletcher. LC 78-64024. (Des Imagistes: Literature of the Imagist Movement Ser.). 416p. reprint ed. 55.00 (*0-404-17098-6*) AMS Pr.

Life Is Not a Carwash: Finding Gold, Glory & God Without Being Perfect. Jennie Halloran. Ed. by Elizabeth Kurtz. LC 98-71614. 328p. 1998. pap. 19.95 (*0-9664019-0-5*) Halloran & Co.

***Life Is Not a Dress Rehearsal.** Sheri Rose Shepherd. 2000. pap. 10.99 (*1-57673-747-0*) Multnomah Pubs.

Life is Not a Dress Size: Rita Farro's Guide to Attitude, Style & a New You. Rita Farro. LC 96-20455. (Illus.). 144p. 1996. pap. 16.95 (*0-8019-8758-X*) Krause Pubns.

Life is Not a Game of Perfect: Finding Your Real Talent & Making It Work for You. Bob Rotella & Bob Cullen. LC 98-54819. 224p. 1999. 21.50 (*0-684-84286-6*) S&S Trade.

Life Is Not a Rehearsal: A Memoir. David Brudney. LC 97-42972. 300p. 1998. pap. 15.95 (*0-571-19933-X*) Faber & Faber.

***Life Is Not a Spectator Sport: Getting It on with Life Rather Than Just Getting By.** Art McNeil. vi, 256p. 2000. pap. 13.95 (*0-9681590-1-X*) FGII.

Life is Not an Empty Dream: Or a Glass Half Full, 1. Gertrude E. Luce. LC 98-86129. 288p. pap. text 12.00 (*1-889131-34-2*, Casananda Pub) Padaran Pubns.

Life Is Our Choice. Joan Marshall. (Orig.). 1997. pap. write for info. (*1-57554-455-X*) Watermrk Pr.

Life Is Paradise: The Portraits of Francesco Clemente. Vincent Katz. LC 99-32085. (Illus.). 144p. 1999. 65.00 (*1-57687-053-7*, pwerHse Bks) pwerHse Cultrl.

Life is Real Only Then, When "I Am" G. I. Gurdjieff. (All & Everything 1st Ser.). 196p. 1999. pap. 12.95 (*0-14-019585-8*) Viking Penguin.

***Life Is Short - Don't Blow It! Finding Success at Work & at Home.** Susan George. 336p. 1999. pap. 14.99 (*0-9672995-0-0*) Service Excel.

Life Is Simple. Christine Tarantino. 12p. 1996. spiral bd. 1.95 (*1-887480-06-4*) Wrds Lght Intl.

Life Is Simple - First Cutting. Jerry Crownover. 180p. 1998. pap. text 14.95 (*1-890622-43-5*) Leathers Pub.

Life Is So Daily: A Collection of Recipes from the Kitchen of Ada Belle Stewart Stone, 1887-1982. Martha J. Stone. LC 88-93054. 1988. pap., spiral bd. 10.00 (*0-9617084-4-1*) Martha J Stone.

Life Is So Daily: Continued Writings to God's Glory. Grace O. Weindorf. Ed. by Laura Reynolds. 1998. 8.95 (*0-9661661-4-0*) Write Designs.

Life Is So Good. George Dawson & Richard Glaubman. LC 99-48834. 288p. 2000. 23.00 (*0-375-50396-X*) Random.

***Life Is So Good.** George Dawson & Richard Glaubman. 2000. write for info. (*0-375-75604-3*) Random.

Life Is Something Else. Elsie Gibson. LC 74-13755. 151 p. 1974. write for info. (*0-8298-0286-X*) Pilgrim OH.

***Life Is Sugar & Vinegar: Solving Life's Problems with Laughter & Wisdom, Enjoy Living!** Margaret Valone. 100p. 1999. pap. write for info. (*0-9675352-0-4*) Valmar Pubg.

Life Is the Destiny. large type ed. Alex Stuart. 352p. 1984. 27.99 (*0-7089-1192-7*) Ulverscroft.

***Life Is the Father Within, Vol. 2.** rev. ed. D. Nathan Seti. Ed. by Donald M. Decker & Victoria Graphics Staff. 320p. 1999. pap. 19.75 (*0-9658460-1-6*) Crescent Pub.

Life Is the Way It Is. Sondra Anice Barnes. LC 78-73124. (Illus.). 85p. 1978. pap. 7.50 (*0-9602534-0-8*) Brason-Sargar.

Life Is Too Short. Helen Bland et al. 112p. (Orig.). 1994. mass mkt. 6.99 (*0-446-39523-4*, Pub. by Warner Bks) Little.

Life Is Too Short. Margaret Foth. 144p. (Orig.). 1985. pap. 4.70 (*0-310-42681-2*, 12779P) Zondervan.

Life Is Too Short to Be Ordinary: 365 Ways to Live More Creatively at Home, at Work & Everywhere in Between. Jeanne H. Chambers. LC 96-90701. 160p. (Orig.). 1996. pap. 9.95 (*1-889771-07-4*) Full Moon Ink.

Life Is Too Short to Live Only for the Weekends: And 199 Other Timely Reminders for Joyful Living. Judy G. Morrow. LC 98-16684. 128p. 1998. pap. 5.99 (*0-8054-1244-1*) Broadman.

Life Is Tough, but God Is Faithful. Sheila Walsh. LC 99-10924. 256p. 1999. 14.99 (*0-7852-6914-2*) Nelson.

***Life Is Tough, but God Is Faithful.** Sheila Walsh. (EZ Lesson Plan Ser.). 1999. pap., student ed. 7.99 (*0-7852-9620-4*) Tommy Nelson.

Life Is Tremendous! see Vida Es Tremenda!

Life Is Tremendous. Charles E. Jones. 100p. 1966. 9.95 (*0-937539-06-6*) Executive Bks.

Life Is Tremendous. Charlie Jones. 107p. 1981. pap. 4.99 (*0-8423-2184-5*) Tyndale Hse.

Life Is Victorious: How to Grow Through Grief. Diane K. Pike. LC 76-17328. (Illus.). 209p. 1982. 11.95 (*0-916192-20-2*) L P Pubns.

Life Is War but You Can Win: A Vietnam Veteran's Survival Guide for Everyone. Tony Anthony. LC 93-80045. (Illus.). 96p. (Orig.). 1994. pap. 5.95 (*0-9630976-1-X*) Morgin Pr.

Life Is Weird: And Other Noble Truths. Laurie F. Huck. LC 97-9664. (Little Books with Big Ideas Ser.). (Illus.). 72p. 1997. pap. 5.95 (*0-8348-0385-2*) Weatherhill.

Life Is What You Make It. A. C. Kennett. 117p. (C). 1989. text 65.00 (*1-872795-74-9*, Pub. by Pentland Pr) St Mut.

Life Is What You Make It. Marion E. Young. 84p. 1992. pap. 6.95 (*0-9632108-0-7*) M E Young.

***Life Is What You Make It, Darlin'** Marlene Taylor. 126p. 2000. pap. 7.99 (*0-9677679-0-3*, 1001) Oshun Dynasty.

Life Is with People: Household Organization of the Contemporary Southern Paiute Indians. Martha C. Knack. Ed. by Lowell J. Bean et al. (Anthropological Papers: No. 19). (Illus.). 106p. 1980. pap. 12.50 (*0-87919-091-4*) Ballena Pr.

Life Is with People: The Jewish Little-Town of Eastern Europe. Mark Zborowski & Elizabeth Herzog. 456p. 1962. 67.50 (*0-8236-3020-X*) Intl Univs Pr.

Life Is Worth Living. 70p. 1998. pap. 10.95 (*0-9660092-1-5*) Puget Sound.

Life is Worth Living. Fulton J. Sheen. LC 98-74067. 1999. pap. text 14.95 (*0-89870-611-4*) Ignatius Pr.

Life Is Your Choice. Curtis A. Merriweather. 18p. (Orig.). (C). 1989. pap. 1.00 (*0-9623431-0-2*) Faith Christ Ch.

***Life Isn't All Ha Ha Hee Hee.** Meera Syal. LC 99-54390. 336p. 2000. 22.95 (*1-56584-614-1*, Pub. by New Press NY) Norton.

Life Isn't Always a Day at the Beach: A Book for All Children Whose Lives Are Affected by Cancer. Pam Ganz. (Illus.). 28p. (Orig.). (J). (gr. k-6). 1996. spiral bd., wbk. ed. 9.95 (*0-9653392-0-3*) High Five.

Life Isn't Fair: Murphy's Laws for Kids. Carole Marsh. (Quantum Leap Ser.). (Illus.). (J). (gr. 4-12). 1994. 29.95 (*0-935326-08-1*); lib. bdg. 29.95 (*0-7933-6916-9*) Gallopade Intl.

Life Isn't Just a Panic: Stories of Hope by Recovering Agoraphobics. Anita L. Pace et al. (Illus.). 256p. (Orig.). 1996. pap. 13.95 (*0-9631666-3-8*) Baby Steps Pr.

***Life Isn't Rocket Science.** Jeff Canfield. 144p. 2000. pap. 9.99 (*1-930027-13-3*, 921-029, Pub. by Insght Pub) BookWorld.

Life Isn't Weighed on the Bathroom Scales. Laura Rose. 185p. 1994. 18.95 (*0-9653369-0-5*) Rose Prods.

Life Issues. Wright. 1997. pap. 14.95 (*0-7459-3420-X*, Pub. by Lion Pubng) Trafalgar.

Life Issues. Wright. 1997. pap., teacher ed. 55.00 (*0-7459-3708-X*, Pub. by Lion Pubng) Trafalgar.

Life It Brings: One Physicist's Beginnings. Jeremy Bernstein. (Illus.). 1987. 16.45 (*0-89919-470-2*, Pub. by Ticknor & Fields) HM.

***Life, Italian Style: Quotes & Quips from Notable Italian Americans.** Erica Merino. LC 99-33500. 176p. 1999. pap. 12.00 (*0-380-79696-1*, Avon Bks) Morrow Avon.

***Life! It's More Than a Notion.** Marjorie Laura Burgess. LC 99-96748. 2000. pap. 7.95 (*0-533-13334-3*) Vantage.

Life Itself. Robert Rosen. (Illus.). 320p. 1991. text 55.50 (*0-231-07564-2*) Col U Pr.

Life Itself. Paco I. Taibo, II. Tr. by Beth Henson. 208p. 1995. mass mkt. 5.99 (*0-446-40331-8*, Pub. by Warner Bks) Little.

Life Itself: Exploring the Realm of the Living Cell. Boyce Rensberger. LC 96-33679. (Illus.). 304p. 1997. 30.00 (*0-19-510874-4*) OUP.

Life Itself: Exploring the Realm of the Living Cell. Boyce Rensberger. (Illus.). 304p. 1998. reprint ed. pap. 15.95 (*0-19-512500-2*) OUP.

Life Itself: "Messiness Is Next to Goddessness" & Other Essays. John Boe. LC 94-19711. 184p. (Orig.). 1994. pap. 14.95 (*0-933029-86-1*) Chiron Pubns.

Life I've Been Living. Moses Cruikshank. LC 86-51263. (Oral Biography Ser.: No. 1). (Illus.). 132p. 1986. pap. 9.95 (*0-912006-23-4*) U of Alaska Pr.

Life, Journals & Correspondence of Rev. Manasseh Cutler, 2 vols., Set. William P. Cutler. 1993. reprint ed. lib. bdg. 150.00 (*0-7812-5353-5*) Rprt Serv.

Life, Journals & Correspondence of Rev. Manasseh Cutler, L L.D., 2 vols., Set. William P. Cutler & Julia P. Cutler. LC 86-23894. (Illus.). 1032p. 1987. text 60.00 (*0-8214-0859-3*) Ohio U Pr.

Life Journals & Letters of Henry Alford, 2 vols., Set. Ed. by Mrs. Henry Alford. vii, 542p. reprint ed. 69.00 (*0-7812-0872-6*) Rprt Serv.

Life Journey: Literature & the Search for Meaning in the Stages of Life. Milton E. Ford. 250p. (Orig.). (C). 1987. 14.95 (*0-931515-11-4*); pap. 9.95 (*0-931515-12-2*) Triumph Pr.

Life Journey of a Quaker Artist. Dorothea Blom. LC 80-80916. 32p. (Orig.). 1980. 1.00 (*0-87574-232-7*) Pendle Hill.

Life Keeper Planners. 5.49 (*0-8024-7265-6*); 5.49 (*0-8024-7268-0*); 5.99 (*0-8024-7269-9*); 5.99 (*0-8024-7271-0*); 3.99 (*0-8024-7272-9*); 3.99 (*0-8024-7274-5*) Moody.

Life, Land & Water in Ancient Peru. Kosok. LC 65-14627. (Illus.). 1965. 37.50 (*0-913252-00-X*) LIU Univ.

Life, Land, & Water in Ancient Peru. Paul Kosok. Ed. by Richard P. Schaedel et al. LC 65-14627. (Illus.). 264p. 1966. 65.00 (*0-913252-01-8*) LIU Univ.

Life, Language, Law: Essays in Honor of Arthur F. Bentley. Ed. by Richard W. Taylor. LC 56-8248. (Illus.). 337p. reprint ed. 104.50 (*0-8357-9368-0*, 205129000001) Bks Demand.

Life, Language, Literature. Linda Robinson Fellag. LC 92-31731. 271p. (J). 1992. mass mkt. 25.95 (*0-8384-3965-9*) Heinle & Heinle.

Life Later On: Older People in the Church. Ann Webber. 1990. pap. 6.95 (*0-687-85682-5*) Abingdon.

Life Later On: Older People in the Church. Ann Webber. 1991. pap. text 4.95 (*0-281-04455-4*) Abingdon.

Life Laughs Last. Philip B. Kunhardt, Jr. 224p. 1989. pap. 14.00 (*0-671-68797-2*, Fireside) S&S Trade Pap.

Life Launch: A Passionate Guide to the Rest of Your Life. Frederic M. Hudson & Pamela D. McLean. 190p. 1994. pap. 19.95 (*1-884433-84-7*) Hudson Institute.

Life, Law & the Pursuit of Balance: A Lawyer's Guide to Quality of Life. Ed. by Julie M. Tamminen. LC 96-86599. 144p. 1996. pap. 69.95 (*1-57073-361-9*, 511-0379) Amer Bar Assn.

Life, Law & the Pursuit of Balance: Lawyer's Guide to Quality of Life. 2nd ed. Ed. by Jeffrey R. Simoroni. LC 97-72252. 281p. 1997. pap. 59.95 (*1-879454-05-X*) Maricopa Co Bar.

Life, Learning, Love & Loss: Poems. Altha Y. Diggs. 1998. pap. 8.95 (*0-533-12540-5*) Vantage.

Life Legends. Ed. by Life Magazine Staff. 176p. 1998. 27.95 (*0-8212-2504-9*, Pub. by Bulfinch Pr) Little.

Life Less Ordinary. John Hodge. 1997. pap. 13.95 (*0-571-19281-5*) Faber & Faber.

Life Less Ordinary. John Hodge. 1997. mass mkt. 5.99 (*0-451-19522-1*, Sig) NAL.

Life Lessons see Lecciones de Vida

***Life Lessons.** Elisabeth Kubler-Ross & David Kessler. 2000. 24.00 (*0-684-87074-6*) Scribner.

Life Lessons, 1. Witness Lee. 83p. 1987. per. 5.25 (*0-87083-276-X*, 15-010-001) Living Stream Ministry.

Life Lessons, 2. Witness Lee. 109p. 1987. per. 5.75 (*0-87083-277-8*, 15-011-001) Living Stream Ministry.

Life Lessons, 3. Witness Lee. 93p. 1987. per. 5.50 (*0-87083-278-6*, 15-012-001) Living Stream Ministry.

Life Lessons, 4. Witness Lee. 89p. 1987. per. 5.50 (*0-87083-279-4*, 15-013-001) Living Stream Ministry.

Life Lessons: A Guided Journal. Miranda Hith. (Illus.). 100p. 1998. 19.95 (*0-9653869-3-7*) Castle Pacific.

Life Lessons: An Inspirational Instruction Book. Robert C. Savage. (Illus.). 160p. 1993. 9.99 (*0-88486-082-5*) Arrowood Pr.

Life Lessons: Book of Acts. Max Lucado. (Life Lessons Ser.). 1997. pap. 6.99 (*0-8499-5300-6*) Word Pub.

L

An Asterisk (*) at the beginning of an entry indicates that the title is appearing for the first time.

Life Lessons: Book of Ephesians. Ed. by Max Lucado. (Inspirational Bible Study Guides Ser.). 120p. 1998. pap. 6.99 (*0-8499-5326-X*) Word Pub.

Life Lessons: Book of Luke. Ed. by Max Lucado. (Inspirational Bible Study Guides Ser.). 120p. 1998. pap. 6.99 (*0-8499-5325-1*) Word Pub.

Life Lessons: Book of Revelation. Max Lucado. (Inspirational Bible Study Guides: Vol. 12). 1997. pap. 6.99 (*0-8499-5323-5*) Word Pub.

Life Lessons: Book of 1 Corinthians. Max Lucado. (Inspirational Bible Study; Life Lessons Ser.). 1997. pap. 6.99 (*0-8499-5321-9*) Word Pub.

Life Lessons: Books of Ezra & Nehemiah. Ed. by Max Lucado. (Inspirational Bible Study Guides Ser.). 120p. 1998. pap. 6.99 (*0-8499-5324-3*) Word Pub.

Life Lessons: Books of 1 & 2 Peter. Max Lucado. (Inspirational Bible Study Guides: Vol. 11). 1997. pap. 6.99 (*0-8499-5322-7*) Word Pub.

Life Lessons: Fifty Things I Learned from My Divorce. Beth Joselow. 160p. (Orig.). 1994. pap. 10.00 (*0-380-77494-1*, Avon Bks) Morrow Avon.

Life Lessons: The Art of Jerome Witkin. Sherry Chayat. LC 93-38713. (Illus.). 160p. 1994. 39.95 (*0-8156-2617-7*) Syracuse U Pr.

Life Lessons: What Really Works When Life Doesn't. Albert T. Forkas. 175p. (Orig.). 1996. pap. 10.99 (*0-9654060-0-8*) Zerlaut Pub.

***Life Lessons & Reflections.** Montel Williams. (Illus.). 2000. 15.00 (*1-58825-001-6*, Pub. by Mtn Movers) Hay House.

Life Lessons for Couples. Cindy Francis. 128p. (Orig.). 1995. pap. 5.95 (*0-8362-0821-8*) Andrews & McMeel.

Life Lessons for Mothers. Cindy Francis. 128p. (Orig.). 1995. pap. 5.95 (*0-8362-0822-6*) Andrews & McMeel.

Life Lessons for Women. Cindy Francis. 128p. (Orig.). 1995. pap. 5.95 (*0-8362-0818-8*) Andrews & McMeel.

Life Lessons for Young Adolescents: An Advisory Guide for Teachers. Fred Schrumpf et al. LC 93-83884. 212p. (Orig.). 1993. pap. text 25.95 (*0-87822-343-6*, 4670) Res Press.

***Life Lessons from the Bible.** Erin Slonaker. 120p. 2000. 4.95 (*1-930408-05-6*) Lawrnce Teach.

Life Lessons from Xena, Warrior Princess: A Guide to Happiness, Success & Body Armor. Chris Kreski. LC 98-13635. (Illus.). 112p. 1998. pap. 9.95 (*0-8362-6767-2*) Andrews & McMeel.

***Life Lessons My Mother Taught Me: Universal Values from Extraordinary Times.** Andrea Young. LC 99-51694. (Illus.). 272p. 2000. 19.95 (*1-58542-007-7*, Tarcher Putnam) Putnam Pub Group.

Life Lessons, Pocket Size. Witness Lee. 361p. 1987. boxed set 18.00 (*0-87083-413-4*, 15-024-901) Living Stream Ministry.

Life Lessons Through the Sun Signs. Alphee Lavoie & Carol Lavoie. Date not set. pap. write for info. (*0-9645621-2-X*) AIR Soft.

Life, Letters & Journals. Maria Mitchell. LC 79-152989. (Select Bibliographies Reprint Ser.). 1977. reprint ed. 23.95 (*0-8369-5741-5*) Ayer.

Life, Letters & Journals, 2 vols., Set. Charles Lyell. Ed. by Katharine M. Lyell. LC 72-1728. (Darwin Ser.). (Illus.). 488p. (C). 1983. reprint ed. 115.00 (*0-404-08156-8*) AMS Pr.

Life, Letters & Journals of Lord Byron. Thomas Moore. 735p. reprint ed. lib. bdg. 99.00 (*0-7812-0248-5*) Rprt Serv.

Life, Letters, & Journals of Lord Byron, by Thomas Moore. George Gordon Byron. (BCL1-PR English Literature Ser.). 735p. 1992. reprint ed. lib. bdg. 109.00 (*0-7812-7473-7*) Rprt Serv.

Life, Letters & Lectures, 1834-1844. Frances W. D'Arusmont. LC 72-2598. (American Women Ser.: Images & Realities). 1974. 23.95 (*0-405-04454-2*) Ayer.

Life, Letters & Poetry. Michelangelo di Lodovico Buonarroti Simoni. (Oxford World Classics Ser.). 206p. 1999. pap. 9.95 (*0-19-283770-2*) OUP.

Life, Letters & Posthumous Works of Frederika Bremer. Frederika Bremer. LC 75-37682. (Women of Letters Ser.). reprint ed. 52.50 (*0-404-56708-8*) AMS Pr.

Life, Letters, & Sermons Vol. 42: Works, English, 1999. Ed. & Tr. by John P. Donnelly from ITA. LC 98-27725. (Sixteenth Century Essays & Studies: Vol. 5). 350p. 1999. 45.00 (*0-943549-61-2*) Truman St Univ.

Life, Letters, & Speeches. George Copway. Ed. by A. LaVonne Ruoff & Donald B. Smith. LC 96-35888. (American Indian Lives Ser.). x, 255p. (C). 1997. text 45.00 (*0-8032-1470-7*) U of Nebr Pr.

Life, Letters, & Speeches of James Louis Petigru the Union Man of South Carolina. James L. Petigru & James P. Carson. 1977. 24.95 (*0-8369-6969-3*, 7850) Ayer.

Life, Letters & Travels of Father Pierre Jean de Smet, 4 vols., Set. Pierre-Jean De Smet. LC 75-83418. (Religion in America, Ser. 1). 1970. reprint ed. 96.95 (*0-405-00237-8*) Ayer.

Life, Letters & Travels of Father Pierre Jean de Smet, 4 vols., Vol. 1. Pierre-Jean De Smet. LC 75-83418. (Religion in America, Ser. 1). 1976. reprint ed. 24.95 (*0-405-00238-6*) Ayer.

Life, Letters & Travels of Father Pierre Jean de Smet, 4 vols., Vol. 2. Pierre-Jean De Smet. LC 75-83418. (Religion in America, Ser. 1). 1976. reprint ed. 24.95 (*0-405-00239-4*) Ayer.

Life, Letters & Travels of Father Pierre Jean de Smet, 4 vols., Vol. 3. Pierre-Jean De Smet. LC 75-83418. (Religion in America, Ser. 1). 1976. reprint ed. 24.95 (*0-405-00240-8*) Ayer.

Life, Letters & Travels of Father Pierre Jean de Smet, 4 vols., Vol. 4. Pierre-Jean De Smet. LC 75-83418. (Religion in America, Ser. 1). 1976. reprint ed. 24.95 (*0-405-00241-6*) Ayer.

Life, Letters & Work of Frederic Baron Leighton, 2 vols. Emilie I. Barrington. LC 70-140032. (Illus.). reprint ed. 127.50 (*0-404-00659-0*) AMS Pr.

Life, Letters & Writings of Charles Lamb, 6 vols, Set. Charles Lamb. Ed. by Percy H. Fitzgerald. LC 77-148887. (Select Bibliographies Reprint Ser.). 1977. reprint ed. 192.95 (*0-8369-5654-0*) Ayer.

Life, Letters of 1535 see Life & Letters of Thomas Cromwell

Life, Liberty, & Property: A Story of Conflict & a Measurement of Conflicting Rights. 2nd ed. Alfred W. Jones. Ed. by Daniel Nelson. 397p. 1999. reprint ed. pap. 27.95 (*1-884836-40-2*) U Akron Pr.

Life, Liberty & Property: The Scope & Nature of Our Fundamental Rights. 3rd rev. ed. Charles A. Weisman. 120p. 1997. reprint ed. pap. 8.00 (*0-9668921-9-4*) Weisman Pubns.

Life, Liberty, & the Pursuit of Holiness. Stuart Briscoe & Jill Briscoe. 192p. (Orig.). 1993. pap. 8.99 (*1-56476-064-2*, 6-3064, Victor Bks) Chariot Victor.

Life, Liberty & the Pursuit of Land: The Plunder of Early America. Daniel M. Friedenberg. LC 91-42160. (Illus.). 423p. (J). 1992. 31.95 (*0-87975-722-1*) Prometheus Bks.

Life, Liberty & the Pursuit of My Steve Sax Connection: The Politics of Abuse & Rigors of Recovery. Alan B. Waldman. 272p. (Orig.). 1993. pap. 12.95 (*0-9626298-6-3*) Astor Street Pub.

Life Line. Robert A. Heinlein. 23.95 (*0-89190-847-1*) Amereon Ltd.

Life Line: A Journal for Parents Grieving a Miscarriage, Stillbirth or Other Early Infant Death. Joanie Reid. LC 93-86825. 100p. 1994. 15.95 (*1-878526-30-8*) Pineapple MI.

***Life Line: The Merchant Navy at War, 1939-1945.** Peter Elphick. LC 99-491021. 1999. 36.95 (*1-86176-100-7*, Chatham Pubg) G Duckworth.

Life Line for Gladys. Nona Freeman. Ed. by Nell Perry. 214p. reprint ed. write for info. (*1-878366-14-9*) Nonas Bk Sales.

Life-Line of the Lone One. Warren Chase. LC 72-2950. reprint ed. 49.50 (*0-404-10715-X*) AMS Pr.

Life-Line of the Lone One. Warren Chase. (American Biography Ser.). 310p. 1991. reprint ed. lib. bdg. 79.00 (*0-7812-8067-2*) Rprt Serv.

Life Line Series, 5 in 1 set, Set. Julano Miller. (Illus.). 48p. (J). (gr. 3-9). 1985. pap. 17.00 (*0-87879-484-0*) High Noon Bks.

Life Lines. Jill Ireland. 1990. mass mkt. 5.99 (*0-446-35939-4*, Pub. by Warner Bks) Little.

Life Lines. Barbara Weiner. 1990. mass mkt. 4.50 (*0-8217-3043-6*, Zebra Kensgtn) Kensgtn Pub Corp.

***Life Lines.** Wendell Zehel. LC 98-87117. 192p. 1999. pap. 11.95 (*1-56315-146-4*) SterlingHse.

Life Lines. large type ed. Jill Ireland. LC 89-37867. 546p. 1989. lib. bdg. 18.95 (*0-89621-883-X*) Thorndike Pr.

Life Lines: An Introduction to Palmistry. Peter West. 1998. pap. 14.95 (*0-572-02412-6*, Pub. by W Foulsham) Trans-Atl Phila.

Life Lines: Collection of Poems. Regina Wachtel. Ed. by Tikvah Feinstein. (Illus.). 84p. (Orig.). 1991. pap. 8.50 (*1-890269-00-X*, 5) Taproot Press.

Life Lines: Community, Family & Assimilation among Chicago's Asian Indians. Jean Bacon. 320p. 1997. text 70.00 (*0-19-509972-9*); pap. text 22.00 (*0-19-509973-7*) OUP.

Life Lines: Holding on (And Letting Go) Forrest Church. LC 96-12620. 192p. 1996. 18.00 (*0-8070-2722-7*) Beacon Pr.

Life Lines: Holding on (And Letting Go) Forrest Church. LC 96-12620. 192p. 1997. pap. 11.00 (*0-8070-2723-5*) Beacon Pr.

Life Lines: Quotations from the Work of Eugen Rosenstock-Huessy. Eugen Rosenstock-Huessy. Ed. by Clinton C. Gardner. LC 88-19392. 1988. pap. 8.00 (*0-912148-16-0*) Argo Bks.

Life Lines: The Secrets of Your Character in Your Hands. Peter West. (Illus.). 128p. (Orig.). 1987. 5.95 (*0-85030-661-2*, Pub. by Aqrn Pr) HarpC.

Life Lines: The Story of the New Genetics. J. S. Kidd & Renee A. Kidd. LC 98-22219. (Science & Society Ser.). (Illus.). 160p. (gr. 7-12). 1998. 19.95 (*0-8160-3586-5*) Facts on File.

Life Link: Transition Lab. (C). 2000. pap. text. write for info. (*0-13-016300-7*) P-H.

Life List: Remembering the Birds of My Years. John N. Cole. LC 97-26445. (Illus.). 208p. 1997. 21.95 (*0-89272-415-3*) Down East.

***Life Live It or Lose It.** Betty Smith. 1999. pap. write for info. (*1-58235-325-5*) Watermrk Pr.

Life Lived Like a Story: Life Stories of Three Yukon Native Elders. Julie Cruikshank. LC 89-49361. (American Indian Lives Ser.). (Illus.). xvi, 404p. 1991. text 60.00 (*0-8032-1447-2*) U of Nebr Pr.

Life Lived Like a Story: Life Stories of Three Yukon Native Elders. Julie Cruikshank. LC 89-49361. (American Indian Lives Ser.). (Illus.). xvi, 404p. 1991. reprint ed. pap. 16.00 (*0-8032-6352-X*, Bison Books) U of Nebr Pr.

Life Log: Promoting a Lifetime of Good Health. Hillary M. Hulce et al. (Illus.). 80p. (Orig.). 1996. 12.95 (*0-9652193-0-5*) Help Yourself.

Life Long League Digest. Rich Havlik. 138p. (Orig.). 1993. pap. 12.95 (*0-9638188-3-X*) R Havlik.

Life-Long Learning Through Vocational Education: The Path of the Snake. Lisa Whatley. 208p. (Orig.). 1997. pap. 12.95 (*1-890994-22-7*) M Chambers.

***Life, Love & Economics.** 296p. (C). 1999. text 42.50 (*0-536-60338-3*) Pearson Custom.

Life, Love & Laughter: A Collection of Stories from the Heart...& a Few from the Funny Bone Too! Frank Barnicle. 276p. 1997. 19.95 (*0-941072-29-0*) Southern Herit.

Life, Love, & Laughter: Gifts of the Spirit. Helen Heightsman Gordon. 30p. 1998. pap. 4.95 (*0-9666192-0-X*, 101) Anacade Intl.

Life, Love & Other Mysteries. Point of Grace Staff et al. 240p. 1997. per. 14.00 (*0-671-56249-5*) PB.

Life, Love & Other Mysteries: Advice & Inspiration from America's #1 Christian Pop Group. Point of Grace Staff & David Seay. (Illus.). 240p. 1996. 23.00 (*0-671-56251-7*) PB.

Life, Love, Laughter: The Spirituality of the Consciousness Examen. Jim Vlaun. 128p. 1999. pap. 7.95 (*1-878718-43-6*, Resurrection Pr) Catholic Bk Pub.

Life, Love, Music & Money. Susie Shellenberger. (Pretty Important Ideas Ser.: No. 4). 144p. (YA). 1996. pap. 7.99 (*1-55661-485-3*) Bethany Hse.

Life Made Real: Characterization in the Novel since Proust & Joyce. Thomas F. Petruso. 232p. (C). 1992. text 42.50 (*0-472-10266-4*, 10266) U of Mich Pr.

Life Magazine Cuts & Illustrations, 1923-1935. Selected by Carol B. Grafton. LC 95-991. (Pictorial Archive Ser.). (Illus.). 128p. 1995. pap. 7.95 (*0-486-28488-3*) Dover.

Life Magazines: Price & Identification Guide. 3rd rev. ed. Denis C. Jackson. 56p. 2000. pap. 7.95 (*1-888687-11-8*) Illust Collectors.

Life Magic. Melrose Cooper. 128p. (J). (gr. 4-7). 1995. 14.95 (*0-8050-4114-1*, B Martin BYR) H Holt & Co.

Life Magic: The Power of Positive Witchcraft. Susan Bowes. LC 98-41095. (Illus.). 176p. 1999. 20.50 (*0-684-85354-X*) S&S Trade.

Life Makeovers: A Practical & Inspiring Way to Improve Your Life One Week at a Time. Cheryl Richardson. 224p. 12.00 (*0-7679-0663-2*) Broadway BDD.

Life Management. Joanas. 1999. 63.13 (*0-13-535527-3*) P-H.

***Life Management.** Prentice-Hall Staff. 1999. text. write for info. (*0-13-536426-4*, Prentice Hall) P-H.

Life Management. 3rd ed. Ann Daluiso. (Annual Ser.). (Illus.). 256p. 1995. pap. text 12.25 (*1-56134-339-0*, Dshkn McG-Hill) McGrw-H Hghr Educ.

Life Management: Individuals, Families & Group. Aspin. 1995. pap. text. write for info. (*0-582-80547-3*, Pub. by Addison-Wesley) Longman.

Life Management: Skills for Busy People. Sandra L. McKee & Brenda Walters. LC 96-18516. 224p. (C). 1996. pap. text 31.20 (*0-13-227539-2*) P-H.

Life Management of Power Plants: Proceedings International Conference on Life Management of Power Plants (1994: Heriot-Watt University, U.K.) (Conference Publications: No. 401). 245p. 1995. pap. 104.00 (*0-85296-627-X*) INSPEC Inc.

Life Management Skills. O'Connor. (OX - Home Economic Ser.). 1987. mass mkt., wbk. ed. 19.95 (*0-538-32130-X*) S-W Pub.

Life Management Skills. Mae Waters. 1997. pap. text 80.54 (*0-8403-8120-4*) Kendall-Hunt.

Life Management Skills: Taking Charge of Your Future. Driggers. LC 98-20900. 320p. (C). 1998. 33.95 (*0-7668-0506-9*) Delmar.

Life Management Skills No. V: Reproducible Activity Handouts Created for Facilitators. Kathy L. Korb-Khalsa & Estelle A. Leutenberg. (Illus.). 128p. 1999. spiral bd. 41.95 (*1-893277-00-3*) Wellness Reprodns.

Life Management Skills I: Reproducible Activity Handouts Created for Facilitators. rev. ed. Kathy L. Korb-Khalsa et al. (Illus.). 112p. 1993. spiral bd. 39.95 (*0-9622022-4-X*) Wellness Reprodns.

Life Management Skills II: Reproducible Activity Handouts Created for Facilitators. rev. ed. Kathy L. Korb-Khalsa et al. (Illus.). 112p. 1993. spiral bd. 39.95 (*0-9622022-5-8*) Wellness Reprodns.

Life Management Skills III: Reproducible Activity Handouts Created for Facilitators. Kathy L. Korb-Khalsa et al. (Illus.). 128p. 1994. spiral bd. 41.95 (*0-9622022-6-6*) Wellness Reprodns.

Life Management Skills IV: Reproducible Activity Handouts Created for Facilitators. rev. ed. Kathy L. Korb-Khalsa & Estelle A. Leutenberg. (Illus.). 128p. 1996. spiral bd. 41.95 (*0-9622022-7-4*) Wellness Reprodns.

Life Management, 1995-96. 1991. pap. 12.74 (*1-56134-053-7*) McGraw.

Life Mapping. John Trent. LC 94-14106. 1994. 15.99 (*1-56179-251-9*) Focus Family.

***Life Mapping: Finding Your Vision for the Future.** Bill Cohen. LC 97-38812. 176p. 1998. pap. 12.95 (*0-688-15573-1*, Wm Morrow) Morrow Avon.

Life Maps: Of the Great Chess Masters. Nathan Divinsky. Ed. by Jonathan Berry. viii, 312p. 1994. 46.95 (*1-879479-17-6*) ICE WA.

Life Mastery: A Self-Esteem Handbook for Adults & Children. Claudia King. Ed. by Elizabeth Rhudy. (Illus.). 210p. (Orig.). 1994. pap. 12.00 (*0-9639401-0-4*) Light Paths.

Life Matters. Dimitri Mihalas. Ed. by Carmen M. Pursifull. 63p. (Orig.). 1995. pap. 5.00 (*1-881900-03-7*) Hawk Prods.

Life Matters. Sam Simons. 112p. 1998. pap. 10.00 (*0-8059-4464-8*) Dorrance.

Life Maximizers. Ron Jenson. 160p. 1997. pap. 6.99 (*1-56292-158-4*) Honor Bks OK.

Life Meditations. Edward J. Lavin. (Illus.). 192p. 1993. 12.99 (*0-517-09374-X*) Random Hse Value.

Life Memories. Illus. by Anne P. Spangler. LC 90-91787. 84p. (Orig.). 1990. pap. 7.95 (*1-878116-01-0*) JVC Bks.

Life Messages, 2. Witness Lee. 669p. 1992. per. 22.25 (*0-87083-659-5*, 07-036-001) Living Stream Ministry.

***Life Messages: Inspiration for the Woman's Soul.** Josephine Carlton. 224p. 2000. 14.95 (*0-7407-0023-5*) Andrews & McMeel.

Life Metaphors: Stories of Ordinary Survival. Catherine S. Norton. LC 88-17549. 256p. (C). 1989. text 31.95 (*0-8093-1427-4*) S Ill U Pr.

Life, Mind & Laughter: A Theory of Laughter. Roy E. Russell. LC 87-91652. (Illus.). 128p. (Orig.). (C). 1987. pap. 8.50 (*0-9619162-0-6*) Russell WV.

Life, Mind & Spirit. Conwy L. Morgan. LC 77-27207. (Gifford Lectures: 1923). reprint ed. 32.50 (*0-404-60473-0*) AMS Pr.

***Life Model: Living from the Heart Jesus Gave You.** James G. Friesen et al. 90p. 1999. pap. 10.00 (*0-9674357-0-6*, 900) Shepherds Hse.

Life Model of Social Work Practice. Carel B. Germain & Alex Gitterman. LC 79-17816. 1980. text 38.50 (*0-231-04152-7*) Col U Pr.

Life Model of Social Work Practice: Advances in Theory & Practice. 2nd ed. Ed. by Carel B. Germain & Alex Gitterman. 1996. pap., teacher ed. write for info. (*0-231-10555-X*) Col U Pr.

Life Model of Social Work Practice: Advances in Theory & Practice. 2nd ed. Ed. by Carel B. Germain & Alex Gitterman. (Illus.). 490p. 1996. 50.00 (*0-231-06416-0*) Col U Pr.

Life More Abundant: An Owner's Manual. Bill O'Hearn. LC 99-42617. 108p. 2000. pap. 12.00 (*1-58151-045-4*, Pub. by BookPartners) Midpt Trade.

Life More Abundant: Spirit-Filled Messages from the Keswick Convention. Ed. by Herbert Stevenson. 128p. 1987. pap. 7.95 (*0-310-20071-7*, 6326P) Zondervan.

***Life More Abundant: The Science of Zhineng Qigong - Principles & Practice.** Xiaoguang Jin. (Illus.). 370p. 1999. pap. 36.95 (*0-7414-0073-1*) Buy Books.

Life Moses: My Bible Sticker Storybook. Carolyn Magner. 24p. (J). (ps-3). 1994. pap. 2.99 (*0-7814-0141-0*) Chariot Victor.

Life Movement in Plants, 2 vols. J. C. Bose. 650p. 1993. pap. 160.00 (*81-7041-172-6*, Pub. by Print Hse) St Mut.

Life Moves Outside: Stories. Barbara Einzig. (Fiction Ser.). 64p. 1987. pap. 7.00 (*0-930901-42-8*) Burning Deck.

Life, Music & Times of Carlos Gardel. Simon Collier. LC 86-4029. (Pitt Latin American Ser.). 358p. 1986. pap. 111.00 (*0-608-05082-2*, 206563600005) Bks Demand.

Life Nature Library, 24 vols. (SPA.). 12.50 (*0-685-73297-5*); 29.95 (*0-685-73298-3*) Fr & Eur.

***Life near Death: Portraits from a Hospice.** Patricia Smith. (Illus.). 32p. 2000. 15.00 (*0-942908-12-0*) Pancake Pr.

Life Near 310 Kelven: Poems & Readings. Greg Keith. LC 98-7611. 112p. 1998. 24.95 incl. cd-rom, audio compact disk (*0-943389-26-7*) Shetland Piper.

Life Near 310 Kelvin: Poems & Readings. Greg Keith. LC 98-7611. 112p. 1998. pap. 14.95 (*0-943389-25-9*, Pub. by Snow Lion-SLG Bks) Bookpeople.

Life Never Dies. Jack E. Addington. 20p. pap. 3.00 (*0-87516-626-1*) DeVorss.

Life Never Ends. Kay Leedy. 141p. pap. 7.95 (*0-942494-41-5*) Coleman Pub.

Life Notes. Patricia Bell-Scott. 432p. 1995. pap. 12.00 (*0-393-31206-2*) Norton.

Life Notes. Anne Waldman. LC 72-86553. 1973. pap. 3.95 (*0-672-51779-5*, Bobbs) Macmillan.

Life of a Bipolar Child: What Every Parent & Professional Needs to Know. Trudy Carlson. 288p. 2000. pap. 18.95 (*0-9642443-7-3*) Benline Pr.

***Life of a Butterfly.** Scholastic Professional Books Staff. (Super Science Readers Ser.). (Illus.). 16p. (J). 2000. pap. 10.95 (*0-439-16782-5*) Scholastic Inc.

Life of a Cell. Andres L. Ruiz. LC 96-37952. (Cycles of Life Ser.). (Illus.). 32p. (J). 1997. 12.95 (*0-8069-9741-9*) Sterling.

Life of a Communist Revolutionary: Bela Kun. Gyorgy Borsanyi. (Atlantic Studies on Society & Change: No. 75). 320p. (C). 1993. text 50.00 (*0-88033-260-3*, 363, Pub. by East Eur Monographs) Col U Pr.

Life of a Cowboy. George Phippen. LC 70-101102. (Illus.). 104p. reprint ed. 32.30 (*0-8357-9622-1*, 201935200011) Bks Demand.

Life of a Duck. (Non-Fiction Ser.). (J). (gr. k-1). 1989. 35.92 (*0-8123-6525-9*); pap. 5.36 (*0-8123-6526-7*) McDougal-Littell.

Life of a Fossil Hunter. Charles H. Sternberg. LC 89-38604. (Illus.). 313p. 1990. 31.95 (*0-253-35549-4*); pap. 13.95 (*0-253-20571-9*, MB-571) Ind U Pr.

***Life of a Geisha.** Eleanor Underwood. LC 99-30457. (Illus.). 64p. 1999. 9.98 (*0-7651-1739-8*) Smithmark.

Life of a Karma Yogi. AVS Staff. (Illus.). 32p. 1973. pap. 4.50 (*0-942401-04-2*) Am Vegan Soc.

Life of a Lab. E. Donnall Thomas, Jr. LC 99-25187. (Illus.). 144p. 1999. 29.50 (*1-57223-265-X*, 265x) Willow Creek Pr.

Life of a Legal Secretary, B. C. (Before Computers) Kathleen C. Steele. (Hindsight Saga Ser.). (Illus.). 22p. 1987. pap. 1.95 (*0-915433-13-3*) Packrat WA.

Life of a Midwife: A Celebration of Midwifery. Midwifery Today Magazine Staff. LC 98-198139. (Illus.). 92p. 1997. pap. 25.00 (*1-890446-05-X*) Midwifery Today.

Life of a Miner. Bobbie Kalman & Kate Calder. LC 99-23488. (Life in the Old West Ser.). (Illus.). 32p. (J). (gr. 3-9). 1999. pap. 7.95 (*0-7787-0109-3*) Crabtree Pub Co.

***Life of a Miner.** Bobbie Kalman & Kate Calder. LC 99-23488. (Life in the Old West Ser.). (Illus.). 32p. (J). (gr. 4-9). 1999. lib. bdg. 19.96 (*0-7787-0077-1*) Crabtree Pub Co.

Life of a Painter: The Autobiography of Gino Severini. Tr. by Jennifer Franchina. LC 95-22065. 356p. 1995. text 31.95 (*0-691-04419-8*, Pub. by Princeton U Pr) Cal Prin Full Svc.

An Asterisk (*) at the beginning of an entry indicates that the title is appearing for the first time.

Life of a Patron: Zhou Lianggong (1612-1672) & the Painters of Seventeenth-Century China. Hongnam Kim. Ed. by Marilyn W. Gleysteen. LC 96-86267. (CHI & ENG., Illus.). 223p. (Orig.). 1996. pap. 40.00 (0-9654270-0-5) China Institute Gallery.

Life of a Photograph: Archival Processing, Matting, Framing & Storage. Laurence E. Keefe, Jr. & Dennis Inch. (Illus.). 331p. 1987. pap. 24.95 (0-240-80005-2, Focal) Buttrwrth-Heinemann.

Life of a Pioneer. James S. Brown. LC 77-17574. reprint ed. 46.50 (0-404-08432-X) AMS Pr.

Life of a Poet: Rainer Maria Rilke. Ralph Freedman. Tr. by Helen Sword. LC 94-24634. 640p. 1996. 35.00 (0-374-18690-1) FS&G.

Life of a Poet: Rainer Maria Rilke. Ralph Freedman. LC 98-5275. (Illus.). 640p. 1998. pap. text 22.95 (0-8101-1543-3) Northwestern U Pr.

Life of a Preacher. 2.95 (0-936672-44-7) Aerial Photo.

***Life of a River.** Andy Russell. (Douglas Gibson Bks.). 192p. 2000. reprint ed. pap. 15.95 (0-7710-7876-5) McCland & Stewart.

Life of a Roman Slave. Don Nardo. LC 97-46715. (Way People Live Ser.). (YA). (gr. 7 up). 1998. lib. bdg. 22.45 (1-56006-388-2) Lucent Bks.

***Life of a Roman Soldier.** Don Nardo. LC 00-9161. (Way People Live Ser.). 2000. write for info. (1-56006-679-2) Lucent Bks.

Life of a Salmon. Arthur Morton. (Illus.). (J). (gr. k-3). 1994. 12.50 (1-57842-052-0) Delmas Creat.

Life of a Salmon. Arthur Morton. Tr. by Suon Thach. (CAM.). (J). (gr. k-3). 1995. 12.50 (1-57842-054-7) Delmas Creat.

Life of a Science: The Development of a New Medicine. Kari Cantell. LC 98-198486. 239p. 1997. text 15.00 (981-02-3148-2) World Scientific Pub.

Life of a Scientist. R. S. Mulliken. (Illus.). 180p. 1989. 86.95 (0-387-50375-7) Spr-Verlag.

Life of a Simple Man. 3rd rev. ed. Emile Guillaumin. Ed. by Eugen Weber. Tr. by Margaret Crosland from FRE. LC 82-40339. 231p. 1982. pap. text 14.95 (0-87451-246-8) U Pr of New Eng.

***Life of a Slave on a Southern Plantation.** Stephan Currie. LC 99-25966. (Way People Live Ser.). (Illus.). 96p. (YA). (gr. 6-9). 2000. lib. bdg. 18.96 (1-56006-539-7) Lucent Bks.

Life of a South African Tribe, 2 vols., Set. Henri Alexandre Junod. (Monographs in Anthropology). (Illus.). 1984. reprint ed. 145.00 (0-404-15860-9) AMS Pr.

***Life of a Style: Beginnings & Endings in the Narrative History of Art.** Jonathan Gilmore. LC 00-9221. 2000. write for info. (0-8014-3695-8) Cornell U Pr.

Life of a Text: Performing the "Ramcaritmanas of Tulsidas" Philip Lutgendorf. (Illus.). 450p. 1990. 55.00 (0-520-06690-1, Pub. by U CA Pr) Cal Prin Full Svc.

Life of a Useless Man. Maxim Gorki. Tr. by Moura Budberg. 240p. 1990. pap. 10.95 (0-88184-647-3) Carroll & Graf.

Life of a Useless Man. Maxim Gorki. 1988. 18.50 (0-8446-6340-9) Peter Smith.

Life of a Young Inventor. Jon S. Frear. 60p. (YA). (gr. 7-12). 1996. mass mkt. 5.95 (1-928793-00-2, 2015-3) Rocky Mtn K C.

Life of Abdul Hamid. Edwin Pears. LC 73-6296. (Middle East Ser.). 1973. reprint ed. 28.95 (0-405-05354-1) Ayer.

Life of Abraham: The Obedience of Faith. F. B. Meyer. Ed. by Lance Wubbels. (Bible Character Ser.). 192p. 1996. pap. 9.99 (1-883002-34-6) Emerald WA.

Life of Abraham Lincoln. Isaac N. Arnold. LC 94-17449. xvi, 471p. 1994. pap. 14.95 (0-8032-5924-7, Bison Books) U of Nebr Pr.

Life of Abraham Lincoln. John L. Scripps. Ed. by Roy P. Basler & Lloyd A. Dunlap. LC 68-56041. (Illus.). 192p. 1969. reprint ed. lib. bdg. 35.00 (0-8371-0650-8, SCAL, Greenwood Pr) Greenwood.

Life of Abraham Lincoln: From His Birth to His Inauguration As President. Ward H. Lamon. LC 99-10195. (Illus.). 592p. 1999. pap. 22.00 (0-8032-7985-X, Bison Books) U of Nebr Pr.

Life of Abu Bakr. S. M. Haq. 1989. pap. 9.95 (1-56744-123-8) Kazi Pubns.

Life of Adam. Giovanni Loredano. LC 67-26617. 108p. 1967. reprint ed. 50.00 (0-8201-1031-0) Schol Facsimiles.

Life of Adam & Eve & Related Literature. Marinus De Jonge & Johannes Tromp. (GAP Ser.: Vol. 4). 104p. 1997. pap. 14.95 (1-85075-764-X, Pub. by Sheffield Acad) CUP Services.

Life of Adam Smith. Ian S. Ross. (Illus.). 524p. 1995. 39.95 (0-19-828821-2, Clarendon Pr) OUP.

Life of Adam Smith. John Rae. LC 63-23522. (Reprints of Economic Classics Ser.). xv, 449p. 1965. reprint ed. 57.50 (0-678-00101-4) Kelley.

Life of Admiral Christopher Columbus by His Son Ferdinand. Fernando Colon. Tr. by Benjamin Keen from ITA. LC 77-27400. (Illus.). 316p. 1978. reprint ed. lib. bdg. 35.00 (0-313-20175-7, COAC, Greenwood Pr) Greenwood.

Life of Admiral De Ruyter. Petrus J. Blok. Tr. by G. J. Renier. LC 74-9393. (Illus.). 338p. 1975. reprint ed. lib. bdg. 55.00 (0-8371-7666-2, BLAR, Greenwood Pr) Greenwood.

Life of Admiral George Dewey & the Dewey Family History. A. M. Dewey et al. (Illus.). 1120p. 1989. reprint ed. pap. 159.00 (0-8328-0475-4); reprint ed. lib. bdg. 167.00 (0-8328-0474-6) Higginson Bk Co.

Life of Ailred of Rievaulx. Walter Daniel. Ed. by Maurice Powicke. 272p. 1979. reprint ed. text 85.00 (0-19-822256-4) OUP.

Life of Albert Gallatin. Henry (Brooks) Adams. (Works of Henry Adams). 1989. reprint ed. lib. bdg. 79.00 (0-7812-1436-X) Rprt Serv.

Life of Albert Pike. Walter L. Brown. LC 97-19116. (Illus.). 800p. 1997. 48.00 (1-55728-469-5) U of Ark Pr.

Life of Alexander H. Stephens. Richard M. Johnston & William H. Browne. (Select Bibliographies Reprint Ser.). 1977. reprint ed. 35.95 (0-8369-6655-4) Ayer.

Life of Alexander in the Thornton Manuscript. Ed. by Mary Hamel. (Medieval Texts Ser.: Vol. 17). 300p. 43.00 (0-8240-3139-3, H1138) Garland.

Life of Alexander Pope. Owen Ruffhead. (Anglistica & Americana Ser.: No. 5). 586p. 1968. 89.70 (0-317-05061-3, 05101959) G Olms Pubs.

Life of Alfred the Great. Reinhold Pauli. Tr. by B. Thorpe. LC 68-57869. (Bohn's Antiquarian Library). reprint ed. 46.00 (0-404-50021-8) AMS Pr.

Life of Algernon Charles Swinburne. Edmund W. Gosse. (BCL1-PR English Literature Ser.). 362p. 1992. reprint ed. lib. bdg. 89.00 (0-7812-7679-9) Rprt Serv.

***Life of Alice Bush.** Fay Hercock. 300p. 1999. pap. 24.95 (1-86940-206-5, Pub. by Auckland Univ) Paul & Co Pubs.

Life of Alimqul: A Native Chronicle of Nineteenth Century Central Asia. Timur Beisembiev. (Illus.). 388p. 1998. 95.00 (0-7007-1114-7, Pub. by Curzon Pr Ltd) Paul & Co Pubs.

Life of Alton Glass. Intro. by Mary E. Glass. 99p. 1966. lib. bdg. 29.50 (1-56475-015-9); fiche. write for info. (1-56475-016-7) U NV Oral Hist.

Life of Ambrose Bierce. Walter C. Neale. LC 77-93773. reprint ed. 20.00 (0-404-04668-1) AMS Pr.

Life of Ambrose Bierce. Walter C. Neale. (BCL1-PS American Literature Ser.). 489p. 1992. reprint ed. lib. bdg. 99.00 (0-7812-6678-5) Rprt Serv.

Life of Amos A. Lawrence. William J. Lawrence. LC 70-154158. (Select Bibliographies Reprint Ser.). 1977. reprint ed. 23.95 (0-8369-5774-1) Ayer.

Life of an American Jew in Racist, Marxist Israel. Jack Berstein. 48p. 1991. reprint ed. pap. 2.98 (0-939482-01-0, 0253, Noontide Pr) Legion Survival.

***Life of an American Soldier.** Diane Yancey. LC 00-8386. (American War Library). 2000. lib. bdg. write for info. (1-56006-676-8) Lucent Bks.

***Life of an American Soldier in Europe (WWII)** John F. Wukovits. LC 99-42767. (American War Library). (Illus.). 144p. (YA). (gr. 6-9). 2000. lib. bdg. 23.70 (1-56006-666-0) Lucent Bks.

Life of an American Workman. Walter P. Chrysler. (American Biography Ser.). 219p. 1991. reprint ed. lib. bdg. 69.00 (0-7812-8069-9) Rprt Serv.

Life of an Amorous Man. Saikaku Ihara. 233p. 1993. pap. 12.95 (0-8048-1069-9) Tuttle Pubng.

Life of an Amorous Woman & Other Writings. Ihara Saikaku. Ed. & Tr. by Ivan Morris from JPN. LC 63-6505. (Illus.). 1969. reprint ed. pap. 13.95 (0-8112-0187-2, NDP270, Pub. by New Directions) Norton.

Life of an Anarchist: The Alexander Berkman Reader. Ed. by Gene Fellner. (Illus.). 288p. 1992. pap. 16.95 (1-888363-17-7) Seven Stories.

***Life of an Astronaut.** Bobbie Kalman. (Eye on the Universe Ser.). (Illus.). 32p. (J). (gr. 2-4). 2000. pap. 5.95 (0-86505-693-5); lib. bdg. 19.96 (0-86505-683-8) Crabtree Pub Co.

Life of an Oak: An Intimate Portrait. Glenn Keator. LC 97-29094. (Illus.). 256p. (Orig.). 1998. pap. 17.95 (0-930588-98-3) Heyday Bks.

Life of an Ordinary Woman. Anne Ellis. (Illus.). 300p. 1999. pap. 14.00 (0-395-95783-4, Mariner Bks) HM.

Life of an Ordinary Woman. Anne Ellis. LC 74-3946. (Women in America Ser.). (Illus.). 330p. 1974. reprint ed. 26.95 (0-405-06092-0) Ayer.

Life of an Ordinary Woman. Anne Ellis. (American Biography Ser.). 301p. 1991. reprint ed. lib. bdg. 79.00 (0-7812-8122-9) Rprt Serv.

Life of Andrew Hamilton, 1676-1741. Burton A. Konkle. LC 72-27. (Select Bibliographies Reprint Ser.). 1977. reprint ed. 19.95 (0-8369-9962-2) Ayer.

Life of Andrew Jackson. Robert V. Remini. (Illus.). 416p. 1990. pap. 14.95 (0-14-013267-8, Penguin Bks) Viking Penguin.

Life of Andrew Jackson. John Reid & John Eaton. Ed. by Frank L. Owsley, Jr. LC 74-2567. (Southern Historical Publications: No. 19). 536p. reprint ed. 166.20 (0-8357-9619-1, 201321500083) Bks Demand.

Life of Andrew Jackson, Major-General in the Service of the United States. John H. Eaton. LC 77-146393. (First American Frontier Ser.). 1971. reprint ed. 28.95 (0-405-02846-6) Ayer.

Life of Andrew Johnson, Seventeenth President of the United States. James S. Jones. LC 70-170824. reprint ed. 55.00 (0-404-04606-1) AMS Pr.

Life of Anne Bronte. Edward Chitham. (Illus.). 232p. 1993. reprint ed. pap. 25.95 (0-631-18944-0) Blackwell Pubs.

Life of Anne Catherine Emmerich, 2 vols., 1. Carl E. Schmoger. 1992. reprint ed. pap. 18.75 (0-89555-059-8) TAN Bks Pubs.

Life of Anne Catherine Emmerich, 2 vols., 2. Carl E. Schmoger. 1992. reprint ed. pap. 18.75 (0-89555-060-1) TAN Bks Pubs.

Life of Anne Catherine Emmerich, 2 vols., Set. Carl E. Schmoger. 1992. reprint ed. pap. 37.50 (0-89555-061-X) TAN Bks Pubs.

Life of Anne of Hanover, Princess Royal. Veronica P. Baker-Smith. (Publications of the Sir Thomas Browne Institute, Leiden, New Ser.). xi, 190p. 1995. 83.00 (90-04-10198-5) Brill Academic Pubs.

Life of Antony. Plutarch. Ed. by Christopher B. R. Pelling. (Illus.). 352p. 1988. text 65.00 (0-521-24066-2); pap. text 24.95 (0-521-28418-X) Cambridge U Pr.

Life of Apollonius of Tyana. Epistles of Apollonius & the Treatise of Eusebius, 2 vols., 1. Flavius Philostratus. (Loeb Classical Library: No. 16-17). 610p. 1912. text 18.95 (0-674-99018-8) HUP.

Life of Apollonius of Tyana. Epistles of Apollonius & the Treatise of Eusebius, 2 vols., 2. Flavius Philostratus. (Loeb Classical Library: No. 16-17). 630p. 1912. text 18.95 (0-674-99019-6) HUP.

Life of Aratus. Plutarch. Ed. by W. R. Connor. LC 78-18593. (Greek Texts & Commentaries Ser.). (Illus.). 1979. reprint ed. lib. bdg. 19.95 (0-405-11434-6) Ayer.

Life of Archbishop John Ireland. James H. Moynihan. LC 76-6358. (Irish Americans Ser.). (Illus.). 1976. reprint ed. 40.95 (0-405-09351-9) Ayer.

Life of Archibald Alexander. J. W. Alexander. 1992. 33.99 (0-87377-931-2) GAM Pubns.

Life of Arseniev: Youth. Ivan A. Bunin. Tr. by Gleb Struve et al from RUS. (Studies in Russian Literature & Theory). 300p. 1994. 54.95 (0-8101-1187-X); pap. 17.95 (0-8101-1172-1) Northwestern U Pr.

Life of Arthur Lee, 2 Vols., Set. Richard H. Lee. LC 69-18528. (Select Bibliographies Reprint Ser.). 1977. 54.95 (0-8369-5010-0) Ayer.

Life of Arthur Schopenhauer. William Wallace. 1971. reprint ed. 59.00 (0-403-00196-X) Scholarly.

Life of Arthur Tappan. Lewis Tappan. LC 75-125718. (American Journalists Ser.). 1971. reprint ed. 23.95 (0-405-01699-9) Ayer.

Life of Arthur Young, 1741-1820. John G. Gazley. LC 72-89402. (American Philosophical Society, Memoirs Ser.: Vol. 97). 745p. reprint ed. pap. 200.00 (0-608-13258-6, 202513300042) Bks Demand.

Life of Bandmaster Richard Willis. George E. Ryan. LC 99-74474. (Illus.). 256p. 2000. 34.95 (0-8158-0540-3) Chris Mass.

Life of Beethoven. David W. Jones. LC 98-3638. (Musical Lives Ser.). (Illus.). 225p. (C). 1999. pap. 14.95 (0-521-56878-1); text 39.95 (0-521-56019-5) Cambridge U Pr.

Life of Bellini. John Rosselli. LC 95-39270. (Musical Lives Ser.). (Illus.). 194p. (C). 1997. pap. 14.95 (0-521-46781-0); text 39.95 (0-521-46227-4) Cambridge U Pr.

Life of Benedict Arnold. Isaac N. Arnold. Ed. by Richard H. Kohn. LC 78-22373. (American Military Experience Ser.). 1980. reprint ed. lib. bdg. 33.95 (0-405-11851-1) Ayer.

Life of Benjamin Banneker: The First African American Man of Science. Silvio A. Bedini. LC 98-22848. Date not set. pap. write for info. (0-938420-63-1) MD Hist.

Life of Benjamin Banneker: The First African-American Man of Science. 2nd rev. expanded ed. Silvio A. Bedini. LC 98-22848. (Illus.). 448p. 1998. 35.00 (0-938420-59-3) MD Hist.

Life of Benjamin Franklin. Mason L. Weems. LC 75-31137. reprint ed. 47.50 (0-404-13611-7) AMS Pr.

Life of Benjamin West. John Galt. LC 60-5041. 448p. 1979. reprint ed. lib. bdg. 75.00 (0-8201-1251-8) Schol Facsimiles.

Life of Benvenuto Cellini. Benvenuto Cellini. Tr. by John A. Symonds. (Arts & Letters Ser.). (Illus.). 496p. (C). 1995. pap. 14.95 (0-7148-3364-9, Pub. by Phaidon Press) Phaidon Pr.

Life of Berlioz. Peter Bloom. LC 98-3050. (Musical Lives Ser.). (Illus.). 208p. (C). 1998. pap. 14.95 (0-521-48548-7) Cambridge U Pr.

Life of Bertrand Russell. Ray Monk. 1996. 35.00 (0-02-921672-9) Free Pr.

Life of Bertrand Russell in Pictures & in His Own Words. Ed. by Christopher Farley & David Hodgson. (Illus.). 97p. (Orig.). 1972. pap. 28.50 (0-685-71540-X, Pub. by Spkesman) Coronet Bks.

Life of "Big Foot" Wallace: The Great Ranger Captain. Andrew J. Sowell. LC 89-4246. (Illus.). 210p. 1989. reprint ed. pap. 12.95 (0-938349-36-8) State House Pr.

Life of "Billy" Dixon: Plainsman, Scout & Pioneer. 2nd ed. Olive K. Dixon. LC 87-42528. (Illus.). 298p. 1987. reprint ed. pap. 16.95 (0-938349-12-0) State House Pr.

Life of Billy Yank: The Common Soldier of the Union. Bell I. Wiley. LC 75-162619. (Illus.). 454p. 1971. 29.95 (0-8071-1908-3); pap. 16.95 (0-8071-0476-0) La State U Pr.

Life of Birds. David Attenborough. LC 98-30705. (Illus.). 320p. 1998. 29.95 (0-691-01633-X, Pub. by Princeton U Pr) Cal Prin Full Svc.

Life of Birds. 4th ed. Carl Welty & Luis Baptista. (Illus.). 600p. (C). 1988. text 84.00 (0-03-068923-6) SCP.

Life of Bishop Machebeuf. rev. ed. W. J. Howlett. Ed. by Thomas J. Steele et al. (Illus.). 462p. 1987. reprint ed. 24.95 (0-944340-01-6); reprint ed. pap. 11.95 (0-944340-02-4) Regis Coll.

Life of Black Hawk. Black Hawk. LC 93-47326. (Illus.). 128p. 1994. reprint ed. pap. 6.95 (0-486-28105-1) Dover.

Life of Black Hawk. Black Hawk. Ed. by J. B. Patterson. LC 93-7289. (Native American Voices Ser.). 1993. reprint ed. 21.99 (0-7835-1770-X) Time-Life.

***Life of Blackstone.** Lewis C. Warden. xiv, 451p. 1999. reprint ed. 140.00 (1-56169-478-9) Gaunt.

***Life of Blessed Francis Xavier Seelos, Redemptorist.** Carl Hoegerl & Alicia Von Stamwitz. 128p. 2000. pap. 6.95 (0-7648-0651-3) Liguori Pubns.

Life of Blessed Margaret of Castello. William R. Bonniwell. LC 83-70524. 113p. (J). (gr. 8). 1993. reprint ed. pap. 7.50 (0-89555-213-2) TAN Bks Pubs.

Life of Bret Harte. Thomas E. Pemberton. LC 74-133530. (Select Bibliographies Reprint Ser.). 1977. reprint ed. 23.95 (0-8369-5562-5) Ayer.

Life of Brian. Monty Python. 124p. (C). 1992. pap. 19.95 (0-7493-0997-0, A0665) Heinemann.

Life of Brian Houghton Hodgson. William W. Hunter. (C). 1991. reprint ed. text 35.00 (81-206-0566-7, Pub. by Asian Educ Servs) S Asia.

Life of Brian Houghton Hudgson: British Resident at the Court of Nepal. W. W. Hunter. (C). 1991. text 60.00 (0-7855-0148-7, Pub. by Ratna Pustak Bhandar) St Mut.

Life of Buddha: According to Pali Canon. Bhikkhu Nanamoli. 400p. 1992. 19.20 (955-24-0063-5, Pub. by Buddhist Pub Soc) Vipassana Res Pubns.

Life of Buddha: According to the Legends of Ancient India. A. Ferdinand Herold. LC 55-12748. 296p. 1954. pap. 12.95 (0-8048-0382-X) Tuttle Pubng.

Life of Buddha: As Legend & History. Edward J. Thomas. 321p. 1992. 38.50 (81-215-0586-0, Pub. by M Manoharial) Coronet Bks.

Life of Buddha: As Legend & History. Edward J. Thomas. (C). 1993. 22.00 (81-208-0984-X, Pub. by Motilal Bnarsidass) S Asia.

Life of Buddha: From Prince Siddhartha to Buddha. George Hulskramer. (Illus.). 72p. 1995. pap. 14.95 (90-74597-17-3, Pub. by Binkey Kok) Weiser.

***Life of Buddha as Legend & History.** Edward J. Thomas. LC 99-88879. 2000. 9.95 (0-486-41132-X) Dover.

Life of Buddha on the Stupa of Barabudur, According to the Lalitavistara-Text. Ed. by Nicolaas J. Krom. LC 78-72460. reprint ed. 30.00 (0-404-17328-4) AMS Pr.

***Life of Buddhism.** Ed. by Frank E. Reynolds & Jason A. Carbine. (Life of Religion Ser.). (Illus.). 247p. 2000. pap. 17.95 (0-520-22337-3) U CA Pr.

***Life of Buddhism.** Ed. by Frank E. Reynolds & Jason A. Carbine. LC 00-30260. (Life of Religion Ser.: Vol. 1). (Illus.). 247p. 2000. 45.00 (0-520-21105-7) U CA Pr.

***Life of Buffalo Bill.** William F. Cody. (Illus.). 365p. 1999. reprint ed. pap. text 17.00 (0-7881-6650-6) DIANE Pub.

Life of Burns. John S. Blackie. LC 75-30844. (English Literature Ser.: No. 33). 1975. lib. bdg. 75.00 (0-8383-2102-X) M S G Haskell Hse.

Life of Caesar. Guglielmo Ferrero. Tr. by Alfred E. Zimmern. LC 77-9520. 525p. 1977. reprint ed. lib. bdg. 38.50 (0-8371-9090-8, FELC, Greenwood Pr) Greenwood.

Life of Canning. Harold W. Temperley. LC 69-14110. 293p. 1970. reprint ed. lib. bdg. 65.00 (0-8371-4105-2, TECA) Greenwood.

Life of Canning. Harold W. Temperley. LC 68-25269. (English Biography Ser.: No. 31). (Illus.). 1969. reprint ed. lib. bdg. 75.00 (0-8383-0247-5) M S G Haskell Hse.

Life of Captain James Cook. John C. Beaglehole. LC 73-87124. (Illus.). xiv, 804p. 1974. pap. 24.95 (0-8047-2009-6) Stanford U Pr.

Life of Captain John Smith, the Founder of Virginia. William Gilmore Simms. LC 75-133533. (Select Bibliographies Reprint Ser.). 1977. 23.95 (0-8369-5565-X) Ayer.

Life of Captain Stephen Palmer Blake: From His Journals. Elizabeth H. Ellwood. LC 95-75248. (Illus.). 576p. 1995. lib. bdg. 33.95 (1-881851-06-0) Genealogy Pub.

Life of Cardinal Innocenzo del Monte, Together with Materials for a History of the House of Ciocchi del Monte: Scandal in Scarlet. Michael L. Doerrer & Francis A. Burkle-Young. LC 97-26519. (Renaissance Studies: Vol. 2). 264p. 1997. text 89.95 (0-7734-8581-3) E Mellen.

Life of Casanova. Mitchell S. Buck. LC 76-51406. (Studies in Italian Literature: No. 46). 1977. lib. bdg. 75.00 (0-8383-2120-8) M S G Haskell Hse.

Life of Cassius Marcellus Clay. Cassius M. Clay. (American Biography Ser.). 535p. 1991. reprint ed. lib. bdg. 99.00 (0-7812-8072-9) Rprt Serv.

Life of Celine. Nicholas Hewitt. LC 98-7229. (Blackwell Critical Biographies Ser.). (Illus.). 416p. 1999. 34.95 (0-631-17615-2) Blackwell Pubs.

Life of Cervantes. Robertson Smith. LC 73-20337. (Studies in Spanish Literature: No. 36). 1974. lib. bdg. 75.00 (0-8383-1812-6) M S G Haskell Hse.

Life of Cesar Moro: A Latinamerican Signer of the Surrealist Manifesto. Andre Coyne. Ed. by Cecilia Bustamante. (Illus.). (C). 1989. write for info. (0-318-66713-4) Extramares Edit.

Life of Character. rev. ed. James R. Miller. 1998. pap. 14.99 (0-89957-239-1) AMG Pubs.

Life of Charlemagne. Einhard. 80p. 1960. pap. text 11.95 (0-472-06035-X, 06035, Ann Arbor Bks) U of Mich Pr.

Life of Charles Brockden Brown. Paul Allen. LC 75-25800. 424p. 1975. lib. bdg. 75.00 (0-8201-1160-0) Schol Facsimiles.

Life of Charles Brockden Brown. William Dunlap. (Notable American Authors Ser.). 1992. reprint ed. lib. bdg. 75.00 (0-7812-2718-6) Rprt Serv.

Life of Charles Brockden Brown. William H. Prescott. (Notable American Authors Ser.). 1999. reprint ed. lib. bdg. 125.00 (0-7812-8767-7) Rprt Serv.

Life of Charles Brockden Brown, Vol. 1. William Dunlap. 1988. reprint ed. lib. bdg. 75.00 (0-7812-0361-9) Rprt Serv.

Life of Charles Dickens, 2 vols. Percy H. Fitzgerald. LC 72-4115. (Studies in Dickens: No. 52). 1972. reprint ed. lib. bdg. 150.00 (0-8383-1607-7) M S G Haskell Hse.

Life of Charles Erskine Scott Wood. Erskine Wood. 192p. 1991. 24.95 (0-9631232-0-3) Rose Wind Pr.

Life of Charles G. Finney. A. M. Hills. 1991. reprint ed. pap. 11.99 (0-88019-282-8) Schmul Pub Co.

Life of Charles Hodge, Professor in the Theological Seminary, Princeton, New Jersey. Archibald A. Hodge. LC 71-83425. (Religion in America, Ser. 1). 1977. reprint ed. 35.95 (0-405-00250-5) Ayer.

***Life of Charles Ives.** Stuart Feder. LC 98-49662. (Musical Lives Ser.). (Illus.). 208p. (C). 1999. 49.95 (0-521-59072-8); pap. 14.95 (0-521-59931-8) Cambridge U Pr.

Life of Charles Lamb, 2 vols. in 1. 5th rev. ed. E. V. Lucas. LC 68-59324. reprint ed. 124.50 (0-404-04059-4) AMS Pr.

Life of Charles Lamb, 2 vols., Set. Edward V. Lucas. (BCL1-PR English Literature Ser.). 1992. reprint ed. lib. bdg. 150.00 (0-7812-7586-5) Rprt Serv.

An Asterisk (*) at the beginning of an entry indicates that the title is appearing for the first time.

Life of Charles Loring Brace: Chiefly Told in His Own Letters. Emma Brace. LC 75-17205. (Social Problems & Social Policy Ser.). (Illus.). 1976. reprint ed. 41.95 (*0-405-07478-6*) Ayer.

Life of Charles M. Doughty. D. G. Hogarth. LC 70-131744. (Illus.). 216p. 1972. reprint ed. 29.00 (*0-403-00631-7*) Scholarly.

Life of Charles Robinson: The First State Governor of Kansas. Frank W. Blackmar. LC 70-169751. (Select Bibliographies Reprint Ser.). 1977. reprint ed. 30.95 (*0-8369-5971-X*) Ayer.

Life of Charles Stewart Parnell, 1846-1891, 2 Vols, Set. Richard O'Brien. LC 68-25256. (English Biography Ser.: No. 31). 1969. reprint ed. lib. bdg. 150.00 (*0-8383-0167-3*) M S G Haskell Hse.

Life of Charlotte Bronte. Elizabeth Gaskell. (Everyman Paperback Classics). 430p. 1997. pap. 8.95 (*0-460-87555-8*, Everyman's Classic Lib) Tuttle Pubng.

***Life of Charlotte Bronte.** Elizabeth Gaskell. (Oxford World Classics Ser.). 624p. 2000. pap. 9.95 (*0-19-283805-9*) OUP.

Life of Charlotte Bronte. Elizabeth Gaskell. Ed. & Intro. by Elisabeth Jay. LC 98-139488. 544p. 1998. pap. 10.95 (*0-14-043493-3*) Viking Penguin.

Life of Charlotte Bronte. large type ed. Elizabeth Gaskell. 768p. 1988. 27.99 (*0-7089-8505-X*, Charnwood) Ulverscroft.

Life of Charlotte Bronte. Augustine Birrell. Ed. by E. S. Robertson. LC 78-148752. reprint ed. 32.50 (*0-404-08726-4*) AMS Pr.

Life of Chekhov. Irene Nemirovsky. LC 74-7101. (Studies in Russian Literature & Life: No. 100). 1974. lib. bdg. 75.00 (*0-8383-1865-7*) M S G Haskell Hse.

Life of Chesed: Chaim Gelb, a Biography. D. Fisher. 1989. 15.99 (*0-89906-566-X*); 12.99 (*0-89906-567-8*) Mesorah Pubns.

Life of Christ. (Explore the Bible Ser.). (Illus.). 692p. 1998. teacher ed. 49.95 (*1-892114-50-X*) Sky Media.

Life of Christ. (Explore the Bible Ser.). (Illus.). 360p. (J). (gr. 3-8). 1998. student ed. 21.95 (*1-892114-52-6*); pap., student ed., wbk. ed. 12.95 (*1-892114-51-8*) Sky Media.

Life of Christ. Frederick W. Farrar. 1994. 19.95 (*0-88494-939-7*) Bookcraft Inc.

***Life of Christ.** Robert C. Girard. Ed. by Larry Richards. LC 99-67256. (God's Word for the Biblically-Inept Ser.: Vol. 1). (Illus.). 352p. 2000. pap. 16.95 (*1-892016-23-0*, Pub. by Starburst) Natl Bk Netwk.

***Life of Christ.** Robert C. Girard. (God's Word for the Biblically-Inept Ser.: Vol. 2). (Illus.). 352p. 2000. pap. 16.95 (*1-892016-39-7*) Starburst.

Life of Christ. Nancy Grubb. LC 96-12915. (Tiny Folio Ser.). (Illus.). 288p. 1996. pap. 11.95 (*0-7892-0144-5*) Abbeville Pr.

Life of Christ. Irving L. Jensen. (Bible Self-Study Guides Ser.). 119p. pap. 6.99 (*0-8024-4462-8*, 456) Moody.

Life of Christ. Nan Pollard. 1998. pap. text 1.49 (*0-7847-0756-1*) Standard Pub.

***Life of Christ.** Ralph M. Riggs. (Discovery Ser.). 2000. pap. text. write for info. (*1-891110-12-8*, ATTS Pubns) Africa Theolog Trng.

Life of Christ. Mark Strauss. Date not set. 26.99 (*0-310-22697-X*) Zondervan.

Life of Christ. abr. ed. Fulton J. Sheen. LC 77-81295. 480p. 1977. pap. 13.95 (*0-385-13220-4*, Image Bks) Doubleday.

***Life of Christ.** unabridged ed. Sheryl Williams. (Illus.). 42p. (J). (gr. 2-6). 1998. pap. 4.50 (*0-89137-069-2*, 70692) Quality Pubns.

Life of Christ: A Stanzaic Life of Christ Compiled from Higden's Polychronicon & the Legenda Aurea. (EETS, OS Ser.: No. 166). 1969. reprint ed. 70.00 (*0-527-00163-5*) Periodicals Srv.

Life of Christ: Behold the Man. Serendipty House Staff. (301 Depth Bible Study Ser.). 1998. pap. text 5.99 (*1-57494-105-4*) Serendipty Hse.

Life of Christ: Bible Study. Raymond Schumacher. 48p. 1996. pap. 37.99 (*0-8100-0594-8*, 22N0953) Northwest Pub.

Life of Christ: Birth & Boyhood of Christ. (Life & Teachings of Christ Ser.: Vol. 1). (SPA.). 1973. 3.95 (*0-89985-263-7*) Christ for the Nations.

Life of Christ: Classic Bible Stories. Lise Caldwell. LC 97-50563. (Illus.). 24p. (J). (ps-1). 1998. pap. 1.99 (*0-7847-0828-2*, 24-04258) Standard Pub.

Life of Christ: Early Ministry of Christ. (Life & Teachings of Christ Ser.: Vol. 2). (SPA.). 1973. 3.95 (*0-89985-264-5*) Christ for the Nations.

Life of Christ: Liar, Lunatic or Lord? Dennis B. Harris. Ed. by Kay Harris. (Illus.). 44p. 1997. 25.95 (*1-890022-46-2*) Lfestyle Min.

Life of Christ: Prophet, Priest, & King. Richard W. Fry. 36p. 1982. wbk. ed. write for info. (*1-892771-04-7*) Prom Life.

Life of Christ - Vida de Cristo: Call & Sending of the Twelve - Llamado y Enviode los Doce. (Life & Teachings of Christ Ser.: Vol. 3). (SPA.). 1973. 3.95 (*0-89985-265-3*) Christ for the Nations.

Life of Christ - Vida de Cristo: Christ Teaches the Apostles - Cristo Ensena a los Apostoles. (Life & Teachings of Christ Ser.: Vol. 5). (SPA.). 1973. 3.95 (*0-89985-267-X*) Christ for the Nations.

Life of Christ - Vida de Cristo: Gathering Storm & Last Great Miracles - Recoguendo Tormenta y los Ultimos Grandes Milagros. (Life & Teachings of Christ Ser.: Vol. 4). (SPA.). 1973. 3.95 (*0-89985-266-1*) Christ for the Nations.

Life of Christ - Vida de Cristo: Last Days & Controversies with the Pharisees - Ultimos Dias y Controversias con los Fariseneś. (Life & Teachings of Christ Ser.: Vol. 6). (SPA.). 1973. 3.95 (*0-89985-270-X*) Christ for the Nations.

Life of Christ - Vida de Cristo: Passion, Death & Resurrection - La Pasion, la Muerte y la Resurrecion. (Life & Teachings of Christ Ser.: Vol. 7). (SPA.). 1973. 3.95 (*0-89985-271-8*) Christ for the Nations.

Life of Christ & the Death of a Loved One: Crafting the Funeral Homily. Barbara G. Schmitz. LC 94-24350. 108p. (Orig.). 1995. pap. 10.95 (*0-7880-0363-1*) CSS OH.

***Life of Christ Series Gift Set.** Charles E. Spurgeon. 2000. pap. 59.94 (*1-883002-53-2*) Emerald WA.

Life of Christina of Markyate: A Twelfth Century Recluse. Ed. & Tr. by C. H. Talbot. (Oxford Medieval Texts Ser.). (Illus.). 210p. 1987. text 59.00 (*0-19-821274-7*) OUP.

Life of Christina of Markyate: A Twelfth Century Recluse. Ed. & Tr. by C. H. Talbot. LC 98-208816. (Medieval Academy Reprints for Teaching Ser.: Vol. 39). 212p. 1998. reprint ed. pap. text 14.95 (*0-8020-8202-5*) U of Toronto Pr.

Life of Christina Rossetti. Mary F. Sandars. (BCL1-PR English Literature Ser.). 291p. 1992. reprint ed. lib. bdg. 79.00 (*0-7812-7625-X*) Rprt Serv.

Life of Christina the Astonishing: English Translation. 2nd ed. Thomas De Cantimpre. Tr. & Intro. by Margot H. King. (Translation Ser.). 57p. 1997. pap. 8.00 (*0-920669-01-8*, Pub. by Peregrina Pubng) Cistercian Pubns.

Life of Cicero, 2 vols. Anthony Trollope. Ed. by N. John Hall. LC 80-1899. (Selected Works of Anthony Trollope). 1981. reprint ed. lib. bdg. 99.95 (*0-405-14186-6*) Ayer.

Life of Clara Barton, 2 vols. William E. Barton. LC 71-86171. reprint ed. 78.50 (*0-404-00730-9*) AMS Pr.

Life of Cola Di Rienzo. Tr. by John Wright from LAT. 166p. 12.00 (*0-88844-267-X*) Brill Academic Pubs.

Life of Collecting: Victor & Sally Ganz. Ed. by Michael Fitzgerald. (Illus.). 244p. 1998. 100.00 (*0-8109-6358-2*, Pub. by Abrams) Time Warner.

Life of Colman Son of Luachan. Ed. by Kuno Meyer. LC 78-72616. (Royal Irish Academy. Todd Lecture Ser.: Vol. 17). reprint ed. 27.50 (*0-404-60577-X*) AMS Pr.

Life of Colombia. Jeremy Horner. (Illus.). 207p. 1998. 60.00 (*958-9138-99-3*, Pub. by Villegas Ed) Rizzoli Intl.

Life of Colonel Davy Crockett. Edward Ellis. (Old West Ser.). 272p. (Orig.). 1999. reprint ed. 18.00 (*1-889128-57-0*) Mantle Ministries.

Life of Colonel Paul Revere, 2 Vols., Set. Elbridge H. Goss. LC 78-157339. (Select Bibliographies Reprint Ser.). 1977. reprint ed. 54.95 (*0-8369-5799-7*) Ayer.

Life of Colonel Paul Revere, 2 vols., Set. Elbridge H. Goss. LC 72-8757. (American Revolutionary Ser.). (Illus.). 768p. reprint ed. lib. bdg. 48.00 (*0-8398-0670-1*) Irvington.

Life of Columba. 2nd ed. Adomnan. Ed. & Tr. by Alan D. Anderson. Tr. by Marjorie O. Anderson. (Oxford Medieval Texts Ser.). (Illus.). 344p. 1991. text 120.00 (*0-19-820215-6*) OUP.

Life of Columba: An Abridged Translation of Adamnan's Vita. Tr. by John Gregory. (Illus.). 64p. 1999. pap. 10.95 (*0-86315-288-0*) Anthroposophic.

Life of Commodore Joshua Barney, U. S. Navy Hero, 1776-1812, Including Interesting Facts & General Material. W. F. Adams. (Illus.). 228p. 1993. reprint ed. pap. 36.00 (*0-8328-1681-7*); reprint ed. lib. bdg. 46.00 (*0-8328-1680-9*) Higginson Bk Co.

Life of Confucius. Qu Chunli. 645p. 1996. pap. 19.95 (*7-119-01863-9*, Pub. by Foreign Lang) China Bks.

Life of Cornish. Crysten Fudge. (C). 1989. 40.00 (*0-907566-20-0*, Pub. by Dyllansow Truran) St Mut.

Life of D. M. Lloyd-Jones: The First Forty Years, 1899-1939. Iain H. Murray. (Illus.). 408p. 1983. 35.99 (*0-85151-353-0*) Banner of Truth.

Life of D. M. Lloyd-Jones Vol. 2: The Fight of Faith, 1939-1981. Iain H. Murray. 862p. 1990. 39.99 (*0-85151-564-9*) Banner of Truth.

Life of D. M. Moody. 1980. 15.95 (*0-87398-508-7*) Sword of Lord.

Life of Daniel Boone. Lyman C. Draper. LC 98-27008. (Illus.). 576p. 1998. 39.95 (*0-8117-0979-5*) Kitch Keepsakes.

Life of Daniel Hale Williams. Judith Kaye. (Pioneers in Health & Medicine Ser.). (Illus.). 88p. (J). (gr. 4-7). 1995. lib. bdg. 13.95 (*0-8050-2302-X*) TFC Bks NY.

Life of Dante Gabriel Rossetti. Joseph Knight. LC 75-38359. (Select Bibliographies Reprint Ser.). 1977. reprint ed. 19.95 (*0-8369-6776-3*) Ayer.

Life of David. Larry Fourman. (Covenant Bible Studies). 40p. 1990. pap. 4.95 (*0-87178-518-8*, 8188) Brethren.

Life of David. Arthur W. Pink. 768p. (YA). (gr. 10). 1998. reprint ed. pap. 24.99 (*0-8010-7061-9*) Baker Bks.

***Life of David: Blueprints for 30 Messages Built upon God's Word.** Steve Jones. Ed. by Jim Eichenberger. (Solid Foundation Sermon Starters Ser.: Vol. 5). 64p. 1999. pap. 5.99 (*0-7847-0935-1*, 23013, Solid Fnd Res) Standard Pub.

Life of David: The Man after God's Own Heart. F. B. Meyer. Ed. by Lance Wubbles. (Bible Character Ser.). 182p. 1995. pap. 9.99 (*1-883002-21-4*) Emerald WA.

Life of David Belasco, 2 vols. William Winter. LC 72-91590. (Illus.). 1972. reprint ed. 58.95 (*0-405-09087-0*) Ayer.

Life of David Belasco. William Winter. (Notable American Authors Ser.). 1999. reprint ed. lib. bdg. 125.00 (*0-7812-7775-2*) Rprt Serv.

Life of David Belasco, 2 Vols., Set. William Winter. LC 72-107837. (Select Bibliographies Reprint Ser.). 1977. 47.95 (*0-8369-5202-2*) Ayer.

Life of David Belasco, 2 vols., Vol. 1. William Winter. LC 72-91590. (Illus.). 1972. reprint ed. 29.95 (*0-405-09088-9*) Ayer.

Life of David Belasco, Vol. 1. William Winter. LC 72-107837. 530p. reprint ed. lib. bdg. 19.00 (*0-8290-0502-1*) Irvington.

Life of David Belasco, 2 vols., Vol. 2. William Winter. LC 72-91590. (Illus.). 1972. reprint ed. 29.95 (*0-405-09089-7*) Ayer.

Life of David Belasco, Vol. 2. William Winter. LC 72-107837. 563p. reprint ed. lib. bdg. 19.00 (*0-8290-0503-X*) Irvington.

Life of David Brainerd: Pioneer Missionary to the American Indians. John Thornbury. 320p. (Orig.). 1996. pap. 14.99 (*0-85234-348-5*, Pub. by Evangelical Pr) P & R Pubng.

Life of David Brainerd: The Works of Jonathan Edwards, Vol. 7. Jonathan Edwards. Ed. by Norman Pettit. LC 83-23445. Vol. 7. (Illus.). 640p. 1984. 80.00 (*0-300-03004-5*) Yale U Pr.

Life of David Dudley Field. Henry M. Field. xviii, 361p. 1995. reprint ed. 47.50 (*0-8377-2140-7*, Rothman) W S Hein.

Life of David Rittenhouse. James Renwick. 1993. reprint ed. lib. bdg. 89.00 (*0-7812-5822-7*) Rprt Serv.

Life of David S. Terry. Ed. by A. E. Wagstaff. LC 75-112407. xxxiii, 526p. 1971. reprint ed. 19.50 (*0-678-04541-0*) Kelley.

Life of David S. Terry. A. E. Wagstaff. 33, 526p. 1971. reprint ed. 45.00 (*0-8377-2725-1*, Rothman) W S Hein.

Life of Death: A Novel. Philip Lewis. 253p. 1993. 18.95 (*0-932511-74-0*); pap. 8.95 (*0-932511-75-9*) Fiction Coll.

Life of Debussy. Roger Nichols. LC 97-25666. (Musical Lives Ser.). (Illus.). 192p. (C). 1998. pap. 14.95 (*0-521-57887-6*); text 39.95 (*0-521-57026-3*) Cambridge U Pr.

Life of Devereux Jarratt, Rector of Bath Parish, Dinwiddee County, Virginia. Devereux Jarratt. LC 79-83427. (Religion in America, Ser. 1). 1975. reprint ed. 21.95 (*0-405-00252-1*) Ayer.

Life of Dick Turpin. P. N. Jackson & E. D. Jackson. 88p. (C). 1989. 80.00 (*0-7223-2259-3*, Pub. by A H S Ltd) St Mut.

Life of Dion. Plutarch. Ed. by W. R. Connor. LC 78-18594. (Greek Texts & Commentaries Ser.). (Illus.). 1979. reprint ed. lib. bdg. 21.95 (*0-405-11435-4*) Ayer.

Life of Dr. Benjamin Franklin. Mason L. Weems. (Notable American Authors Ser.). 1999. reprint ed. lib. bdg. 125.00 (*0-7812-9926-8*) Rprt Serv.

***Life of Dr. Isaac Blowers Ward (1800-1843) & His Wife Ann Vines (1803-1852) With Some Account of Their Near Relatives, Some Brief Genealogies.** fac. ed. Harry Parker Ward. 251p. 1999. reprint ed. 48.00 (*0-8328-9958-5*); reprint ed. pap. 38.00 (*0-8328-9959-3*) Higginson Bk Co.

Life of Dom John de Castro, the Fourth Vice-Roy of India Wherein Are Seen the Portuguese's Voyages to the East Indies, Their Discoveries & Conquest There. Dom J. De Castro. (C). 1994. 68.00 (*81-206-0900-X*, Pub. by Asian Educ Servs) S Asia.

Life of Dorothea Lynde Dix. Francis Tiffany. 392p. 1992. reprint ed. lib. bdg. 42.00 (*0-8328-2271-X*) Higginson Bk Co.

Life of Dorothea Von Montau, a Fourteenth-Century Recluse. Johannes Von Marienwerder. Tr. by Ute Stargardt from GER. LC 97-25135. (Studies in Women & Religion: Vol. 39). 272p. 1997. text 89.95 (*0-7734-8568-6*) E Mellen.

Life of Dr. William F. Carver of California. William F. Carver. (American Biography Ser.). 177p. 1991. reprint ed. lib. bdg. 59.00 (*0-7812-8062-1*) Rprt Serv.

Life of Duke Bernhard of Saxe-Weimar-Eisenach: General of the Infantry of the Royal Dutch Army. R. Starklof. Ed. by C. J. Jeronimus. Tr. by William Jeronimus. LC 96-14739. 592p. (C). 1996. lib. bdg. 64.00 (*0-7618-0351-3*) U Pr of Amer.

Life of Edgar Allan Poe. J. A. Harrison. LC 70-115184. (Studies in Poe: No. 23). 1970. reprint ed. lib. bdg. 75.00 (*0-8383-1008-7*) M S G Haskell Hse.

Life of Edgar Allan Poe, Personal & Literary, 2 Vols. George E. Woodberry. LC 65-23484. 1909. 45.00 (*0-8196-0163-2*) Biblo.

Life of Edgar Allan Poe, Personal & Literary, 2 vols., Set. George E. Woodberry. (BCL1-PS American Literature Ser.). 1992. reprint ed. lib. bdg. 150.00 (*0-7812-6836-2*) Rprt Serv.

Life of Edmund Kean, 2 vols., 1 bk. Frederick W. Hawkins. LC 76-82831. 896p. 1972. 42.95 (*0-405-08603-2*, Pub. by Blom Pubns) Ayer.

Life of Edmund Kean, 2 vols., 1 bk. Bryan W. Procter. LC 70-82840. 560p. 1972. reprint ed. 39.95 (*0-405-08864-7*, Pub. by Blom Pubns) Ayer.

Life of Edvard Benes, 1884-1948: Czechslovakia in Peace & War. Zbynek Zemen & Antonin Klimek. LC 98-135341. (Illus.). 304p. (C). 1997. text 78.00 (*0-19-820583-X*) OUP.

Life of Edward Fitzgerald, 2 vols., Set. Thomas Wright. LC 70-108556. (Illus.). 1971. reprint ed. 59.00 (*0-403-00254-0*) Scholarly.

Life of Edward FitzGerald, 2 vols., Set. Thomas Wright. (BCL1-PR English Literature Ser.). 1992. reprint ed. lib. bdg. 150.00 (*0-7812-7529-6*) Rprt Serv.

Life of Edward Irving: The Fore-Runner of the Charismatic Movement. Arnold A. Dallimore. 179p. (C). 1983. pap. 13.99 (*0-85151-369-7*) Banner of Truth.

Life of Edwin Forest, 2 vols., 1. William R. Alger. LC 76-84505. 1972. 24.95 (*0-405-08199-5*, Pub. by Blom Pubns) Ayer.

Life of Edwin Forest, 2 vols., 2. William R. Alger. LC 76-84505. 1972. 24.95 (*0-405-08200-2*, Pub. by Blom Pubns) Ayer.

Life of Edwin Forest, 2 vols., Set. William R. Alger. LC 76-84505. 1972. 48.95 (*0-405-08198-7*, Pub. by Blom Pubns) Ayer.

Life of Edwin Forrest with Reminiscences & Personal Recollections. James Rees. 524p. 1993. reprint ed. lib. bdg. 99.00 (*0-7812-5285-7*) Rprt Serv.

Life of Einhard. David Ganz. (Recentiores: Later Latin Texts & Contexts Ser.). (Illus.). (C). text. write for info. (*0-472-09639-7*); pap. text. write for info. (*0-472-06639-0*) U of Mich Pr.

Life of Eknath. Justin E. Abbott. reprint ed. 11.00 (*0-8364-0746-6*, Pub. by Motilal Bnarsidass) S Asia.

Life of Elbridge Gerry, 2 vols. James T. Austin. LC 77-99470. (American Public Figures Ser.). 1970. reprint ed. lib. bdg. 89.50 (*0-306-71841-3*) Da Capo.

Life of Eleanora Duse. Emil A. Rheinhardt. LC 73-82841. 292p. 1972. 24.95 (*0-405-08883-3*, Pub. by Blom Pubns) Ayer.

Life of Elie Metchnikoff. Olga Metchnikoff. LC 72-7248. (Select Bibliographies Reprint Ser.). 1977. reprint ed. 24.95 (*0-8369-6949-9*) Ayer.

Life of Elijah. Arthur W. Pink. 313p. 1991. reprint ed. pap. 6.99 (*0-85151-041-8*) Banner of Truth.

Life of Elizabeth I. Alison Weir. LC 98-34917. 512p. 1998. 27.50 (*0-345-40533-1*) Ballantine Pub Grp.

Life of Elizabeth I. Alison Weir. 544p. 1999. pap. 14.95 (*0-345-42550-2*) Ballantine Pub Grp.

Life of Emanuel Swedenborg Together with a Brief Synopsis of His Writings Both Philosophical & Theosophical (1866) William White. 270p. 1998. reprint ed. pap. 19.95 (*0-7661-0306-4*) Kessinger Pub.

Life of Emerson. Richard Garnett. LC 73-21630. (American Biography Ser.: No. 32). 1974. lib. bdg. 75.00 (*0-8383-1775-8*) M S G Haskell Hse.

Life of Emerson. Van Wyck Brooks. LC 80-2528. reprint ed. 37.00 (*0-404-19252-1*) AMS Pr.

Life of Emily Dickinson. Richard B. Sewall. LC 96-129683. (Illus.). 928p. 1994. pap. text 22.95 (*0-674-53080-2*, SEWLIX) HUP.

Life of Emma Thursby. R. McCandless Gipson. LC 79-25093. (Music Reprint Ser.). 1980. reprint ed. lib. bdg. 39.50 (*0-306-76016-9*) Da Capo.

Life of Erwin Schrodinger. Walter Moore. (Canto Book Ser.). (Illus.). 363p. (C). 1994. pap. 12.95 (*0-521-46934-1*) Cambridge U Pr.

Life of Esther De Berdt, Afterwards Esther Reed, of Pennsylvania. Esther Reed. LC 72-140877. (Eyewitness Accounts of the American Revolution Ser.). 1971. reprint ed. 23.95 (*0-405-01208-X*) Ayer.

Life of Evelyn Waugh: A Critical Biography. Douglas L. Patey. LC 97-15469. (Critical Biographies Ser.: Vol. 8). (Illus.). 480p. 1998. 47.95 (*0-631-18933-5*) Blackwell Pubs.

Life of Faith see Living the Drama of Faith: What Faith Is & Where It Leads You

Life of Faith. C. Nuzum. 95p. 1956. pap. 4.50 (*0-88243-539-6*, 02-0539) Gospel Pub.

Life of Faith. A. W. Pink. 8.50 (*1-85792-047-3*, Pub. by Christian Focus) Spring Arbor Dist.

Life of Faith. Ar Pink. 1994. pap. 9.99 (*1-85792-271-9*, Pub. by Christian Focus) Spring Arbor Dist.

Life of Father Hecker. Walter Elliott. LC 75-38446. (Religion in America, Ser. 2). 456p. 1972. reprint ed. 30.95 (*0-405-04065-2*) Ayer.

***Life of Faustina Kowalska: The Authorized Biography.** Sophia Michalenko. LC 99-17574. 1999. pap. 12.99 (*1-56955-153-7*) Servant.

Life of Ferdinand Magellan & the First Circumnavigation of the Globe. Francis H. Guillemard. LC 70-127901. reprint ed. 49.50 (*0-404-02947-7*) AMS Pr.

Life of Forms in Art. Henri Focillon. Tr. by George Kubler from FRE. LC 88-20598. (FRE., Illus.). 190p. 1989. reprint ed. pap. 14.95 (*0-942299-57-4*) Zone Bks.

Life of Fraenkel's Death: A Biographical Inquest. Walter Lowenfels et al. LC 71-11331. (Illus.). 102p. reprint ed. pap. 31.70 (*0-608-18349-0*, 203303000083) Bks Demand.

Life of Francis Bacon. Martin Davy. 120p. 1996. reprint ed. pap. 16.95 (*1-56459-640-0*) Kessinger Pub.

Life of Francis Daniel Pastorius. Marion D. Learned. 1993. reprint ed. lib. bdg. 89.00 (*0-7812-5480-9*) Rprt Serv.

Life of Francis Higginson: First Minister in the Massachusetts Bay Colony. Thomas W. Higginson. (Notable American Authors Ser.). 1992. reprint ed. lib. bdg. 75.00 (*0-7812-3106-X*) Rprt Serv.

Life of Francis Marion. William Gilmore Simms. LC 75-153130. (Select Bibliographies Reprint Ser.). 1977. reprint ed. 25.95 (*0-8369-5740-7*) Ayer.

Life of Francis Parkman. Charles H. Farnham. LC 68-24975. (American Biography Ser.: No. 32). 1969. reprint ed. lib. bdg. 75.00 (*0-8383-0938-0*) M S G Haskell Hse.

Life of Francis Parkman. Charles H. Farnham. LC 71-108480. 1970. reprint ed. 15.00 (*0-403-00208-7*) Scholarly.

Life of Francis Parkman. Charles H. Farnham. (BCL1 - U. S. History Ser.). 394p. 1991. reprint ed. lib. bdg. 89.00 (*0-7812-6024-8*) Rprt Serv.

Life of Francis Thompson. Everard Maynell. 1988. reprint ed. lib. bdg. 75.00 (*0-317-90165-6*) Rprt Serv.

Life of Francis Thompson. Everard Meynell. (BCL1-PR English Literature Ser.). 360p. 1992. reprint ed. lib. bdg. 89.00 (*0-7812-7504-0*) Rprt Serv.

Life of Francis Thompson. Everard Meynell. (Illus.). 1971. reprint ed. 18.00 (*0-403-01107-8*) Scholarly.

Life of Francois Rabelais. Jean Plattard. Tr. by L. D. Roache. 308p. 1968. reprint ed. 35.00 (*0-7146-2077-7*, BHA-02077, Pub. by F Cass Pubs) Intl Spec Bk.

Life of Franklin Pierce. Nathaniel Hawthorne. 1988. reprint ed. lib. bdg. 49.00 (*0-7812-0059-8*) Rprt Serv.

Life of Franklin Pierce. Nathaniel Hawthorne. (Notable American Authors Ser.). 1992. reprint ed. lib. bdg. 75.00 (*0-7812-3047-0*) Rprt Serv.

Life of Franklin Pierce. Nathaniel Hawthorne. LC 72-78731. 1952. reprint ed. 39.00 (*0-403-04146-5*) Somerset Pub.

Life of Franz Schubert. George L. Austin. LC 74-27330. reprint ed. 32.50 (*0-404-12856-4*) AMS Pr.

An Asterisk (*) at the beginning of an entry indicates that the title is appearing for the first time.

Life of Fray Antonio Margil De Jesus. Eduardo E. Rios. (Illus.). 1959. 25.00 (*0-88382-254-7*) AAFH.
Life of Frederick Marryat. D. Hannay. LC 73-6945. (English Biography Ser.: No. 31). 1973. reprint ed. lib. bdg. 75.00 (*0-8383-1695-6*) M S G Haskell Hse.
***Life of Frederick William Von Steuben: Major General, United States Army.** 3rd unabridged ed. Friedrich Kapp. 720p. 1999. reprint ed. pap. 24.95 (*0-87928-132-4*) Corner Hse.
Life of Fredrich Schiller. Thomas Carlyle. 200p. 1994. pap. 25.00 (*0-87556-790-8*) Saifer.
Life of Friedrich Engels, 2 vols. W. O. Henderson. Incl. Vol. 1. Young Revolutionary. 388p. 1974. Vol. 2. Marx's Alter Ego. 488p. 1974. (Illus.). 1974. 85.00 (*0-7146-3065-9*, Pub. by F Cass Pubs) Intl Spec Bk.
Life of Friedrich Schiller see Works of Thomas Carlyle
Life of Galileo. Bertolt Brecht. Ed. & Tr. by John Willett from GER. Ed. by Ralph Manheim. LC 94-4009. 288p. (C). 1994. pap. 10.45 (*1-55970-254-0*, Pub. by Arcade Pub Inc) Time Warner.
Life of Galileo, the Resistible Rise of Arturo Uo, the Caucasian Chalk Circle. Bertolt Brecht. Tr. by John Willett et al from GER. LC 93-24754. 352p. (Orig.). 1994. pap. 12.45 (*1-55970-190-0*, Pub. by Arcade Pub Inc) Time Warner.
Life of Gampopa: The Incomparable Dharma Lord of Tibet. Jampa M. Stewart. LC 94-39646. 200p. 1994. 12.95 (*1-55939-038-7*) Snow Lion Pubns.
Life of Garrick, 2 vols., 1 bk. Arthur Murphy. LC 76-84521. 840p. 1972. 42.95 (*0-405-08811-6*, Pub. by Blom Pubns) Ayer.
Life of Gen. Albert Sidney Johnston: Embracing His Services in the Armies of the United States, the Republic of Texas, & the Confederate States. limited ed. William P. Johnston. LC 97-37453. (Illus.). 781p. 1997. denim 75.00 (*1-880510-49-9*) State House Pr.
Life of Gen. Albert Sidney Johnston: Embracing His Services in the Armies of the United States, the Republic of Texas, & the Confederate States. William P. Johnston. LC 97-8742. (Illus.). 807p. 1997. reprint ed. pap. 19.95 (*0-306-80791-2*) Da Capo.
Life of Gen. Albert Sidney Johnston: Embracing His Services in the Armies of the United States, the Republic of Texas, & the Confederate States. William P. Johnston. LC 97-37453. (Illus.). 781p. 1997. reprint ed. 45.00 (*1-880510-48-0*) State House Pr.
Life of General Ely S. Parker: Last Grand Sachem of the Iroquois & General Grant's Military Secretary. Arthur C. Parker. LC 83-19752. (Buffalo Historical Society, Publication Ser.: 23). (Illus.). 408p. reprint ed. 52.50 (*0-404-15658-4*) AMS Pr.
Life of General Francis Marion. Mason L. Weems. (Notable American Authors Ser.). 1999. reprint ed. lib. bdg. 125.00 (*0-7812-9923-3*) Rprt Serv.
***Life of General Francis Marion: A Celebrated Partisan Officer, in the Revolutionary War, Etc.** P. Horry & M. L. Weems. 254p. 2000. reprint ed. pap. 9.95 (*0-89587-196-3*) Blair.
Life of General Garibaldi: Translated from His Private Papers. Theodore Dwight. (Notable American Authors Ser.). 1992. reprint ed. lib. bdg. 75.00 (*0-7812-2731-3*) Rprt Serv.
Life of General John Sevier. Francis M. Turner. (Illus.). 128p. (YA). 1997. reprint ed. 19.95 (*1-57072-058-4*) Overmountain Pr.
Life of General Lafayette, 2 vols. Bayard Tuckerman. LC 72-177575. reprint ed. 97.50 (*0-404-07187-2*) AMS Pr.
Life of General Nathan Bedford Forrest. John A. Wyeth. 656p. 1996. 12.98 (*0-7858-0705-5*) Bk Sales Inc.
Life of General Nathan Bedford Forrest. John A. Wyeth. 656p. 1996. pap. 17.95 (*0-685-72791-2*, Bellum Edits) R Bemis Pub.
Life of General Philip Schuyler, 1733-1804. Bayard Tuckerman. LC 71-95081. (Select Bibliographies Reprint Ser.). 1977. 31.95 (*0-8369-5031-3*) Ayer.
***Life of General Robert E. Lee.** John Esten Cooke. 252p. 2000. pap. 9.95 (*0-594-00576-0*) Eighth Hundrd.
Life of General Samuel K. Zook: Another Forgotten Union Hero. A. M. Gambone. (Army of the Potomac Ser.). (Illus.). 265p. (C). 1996. 30.00 (*0-935523-53-7*) Butternut & Blue.
Life of General Stonewall Jackson. Mary L. Williamson. Ed. by Michael J. McHugh. (Illus.). 122p. 1997. pap. text 6.00 (*1-930092-21-0*) Christian Liberty.
Life of General Zachary Taylor. Benjamin P. Poore. (Notable American Authors Ser.). 1999. reprint ed. lib. bdg. 125.00 (*0-7812-8760-X*) Rprt Serv.
Life of Genghis-Khan. Boris Vladimirtsov. Tr. by Dimitry S. Mirsky from RUS. LC 76-82003. 1972. reprint ed. 18.95 (*0-405-09048-X*) Ayer.
Life of Geoffrey Chaucer, 4 vols. William Godwin. LC 71-168173. 1974. reprint ed. 145.00 (*0-404-02850-0*) AMS Pr.
Life of Geoffrey Chaucer: A Critical Biography. Derek Pearsall. 336p. 1995. pap. 25.95 (*1-55786-665-1*) Blackwell Pubs.
Life of George Bent: Written from His Letters. George E. Hyde. Ed. by Savoie Lottinville. (Illus.). 389p. 1987. pap. 19.95 (*0-8061-1577-7*) U of Okla Pr.
Life of George Berkeley Bishop of Cloyne: 1949 Edition. Arthur A. Luce. 302p. 1996. reprint ed. 58.00 (*1-85506-128-7*) Bks Intl VA.
Life of George Cabot Lodge. Henry (Brooks) Adams. (Works of Henry Adams). 1989. reprint ed. lib. bdg. 79.00 (*0-7812-1444-0*) Rprt Serv.
Life of George Cabot Lodge. Henry (Brooks) Adams. LC 78-16619. 1978. reprint ed. 50.00 (*0-8201-1316-6*) Schol Facsimiles.
Life of George Dempster, Scottish M. P. of Dunnichen, 1732-1818. Andrew M. Lang. LC 98-4383. 352p. 1998. text 99.95 (*0-7734-8386-1*) E Mellen.
Life of George Henry. George Henry. LC 73-164389. (Black Heritage Library Collection). 1977. reprint ed. 21.95 (*0-8369-8848-5*) Ayer.
Life of George Rogers Clark. James A. James. LC 74-108769. reprint ed. 37.50 (*0-404-03549-3*) AMS Pr.
Life of George Washington, 5 vols. John Marshall. Ed. by B. Washington. LC 69-19159. 495.00 (*0-404-04250-3*) AMS Pr.
Life of George Washington. John Marshall. (Notable American Authors Ser.). 1999. reprint ed. lib. bdg. 125.00 (*0-7812-3948-6*) Rprt Serv.
Life of George Washington. David Ramsay. (Notable American Authors Ser.). 1999. reprint ed. lib. bdg. 125.00 (*0-7812-8776-6*) Rprt Serv.
Life of George Washington. Jared Sparks. LC 75-31134. reprint ed. 37.50 (*0-404-13610-9*) AMS Pr.
***Life of George Washington: Commander in Chief of the Armies of the United States of America Throughout the War Which Established Their Independence & First President of the United States.** annot. anniversary ed. David Ramsay. Ed. & Illus. by John T. Phillips, II. Illus. by Wade C. Snyder. (Compleat George Washington Ser.: Vol. 2). 368p. 2000. reprint ed. lthr. 39.95 (*0-9656758-2-3*) Goose Creek.
***Life of George Washington: Special Edition for Schools.** John Marshall. Ed. by Robert Faulkner & Paul Carrese. (Illus.). 2000. 25.00 (*0-86597-276-1*) Liberty Fund.
***Life of George Washington: Special Edition for Schools.** John Marshall et al. LC 99-462077. (Illus.). 2000. pap. 14.00 (*0-86597-277-X*) Liberty Fund.
Life of George Westinghouse. Henry G. Prout. LC 72-5068. (Technology & Society Ser.). (Illus.). 406p. 1977. reprint ed. 34.95 (*0-405-04719-3*) Ayer.
Life of Gerald Hallock, Thirty-Three Years Editor of the New York Journal of Commerce. William H. Hallock. LC 78-125696. (American Journalists Ser.). 1978. reprint ed. 30.95 (*0-405-01675-1*) Ayer.
Life of Glory. Marianne Dorman. 73p. (C). 1989. pap. text 39.00 (*1-872795-78-1*, Pub. by Pentland Pr) St Mut.
Life of God, As Told by Himself. Franco Ferrucci. Tr. by Raymond Rosenthal. 288p. 1996. 22.00 (*0-226-24495-4*) U Ch Pr.
Life of God, As Told by Himself. Franco Ferrucci. 284p. 1997. pap. 11.95 (*0-226-24496-2*) U Ch Pr.
Life of God in the Soul of Man. Henry Scongal. pap. 2.00 (*0-8358-0158-6*) Upper Room Bks.
Life of God in the Soul of Man. Henry Scougal. 1996. 6.99 (*1-85792-105-4*, Pub. by Christian Focus) Spring Arbor Dist.
Life of God in the Soul of Man. Henry Scougal. 1992. pap. 10.99 (*0-87377-950-9*) GAM Pubns.
Life of Goethe. John R. Williams. Ed. by Claude Rawson. LC 97-32840. (Critical Biographies Ser.). 400p. 1998. 39.95 (*0-631-16376-X*) Blackwell Pubs.
Life of Goethe, 3 vols. Albert Bielschowsky. Tr. by William A. Cooper. LC 73-113555. (BCL Ser. I). (Illus.). reprint ed. 125.00 (*0-404-00870-4*) AMS Pr.
Life of Goethe, 3 Vols. Albert Bielschowsky. LC 70-92935. (Studies in German Literature: No. 13). 1969. reprint ed. lib. bdg. 199.00 (*0-8383-1000-1*) M S G Haskell Hse.
Life of Goethe, 2 Vols, Set. P. Hume Brown. LC 77-163114. (Studies in German Literature: No. 13). 1971. reprint ed. lib. bdg. 150.00 (*0-8383-1307-8*) M S G Haskell Hse.
Life of Goodrich. James C. Lam. LC 87-82702. 160p. 1987. pap. text 5.50 (*0-940043-26-2*) Evangel Lit.
Life of Gotama Buddha (Compiled Exclusively from the Pali Canon) Compiled by Earl H. Brewster. LC 78-72380. reprint ed. 34.50 (*0-404-17229-6*) AMS Pr.
Life of Graham Greene, 1904-1939, Vol. 1. Norman Sherry. (Illus.). 704p. 1990. pap. 18.95 (*0-14-014450-1*, Penguin Bks) Viking Penguin.
Life of Graham Greene, 1939-1955, Vol. 2. Norman Sherry. (Illus.). 592p. 1996. pap. 17.95 (*0-14-024526-X*, Penguin Bks) Viking Penguin.
Life of Greece. Will Durant. (Story of Civilization Ser.: Vol. 2). (Illus.). 758p. 1993. 17.98 (*1-56731-013-3*, MJF Bks) Fine Comms.
Life of Greece. Will Durant & Ariel Durant. (Story of Civilization Ser.: Vol. 2). (Illus.). 768p. 1980. 40.00 (*0-671-41800-9*) S&S Trade.
Life of Gudmund the Good, Bishop of Holar. Tr. by Gabriel Turville-Petre & E. S. Olszewska. LC 77-90461. (Viking Society for Northern Research: Translation Ser.: Vol. 3). reprint ed. 39.50 (*0-404-60013-1*) AMS Pr.
Life of Guido Reni. Carlo C. Malvasia. Tr. by Catherine Enggass & Robert Enggass from ITA. LC 80-11650. (Illus.). 150p. 1981. 28.50 (*0-271-00264-6*) Pa St U Pr.
Life of Gwendolyn Brooks. George E. Kent. 296p. 1990. pap. 18.00 (*0-8131-0827-6*) U Pr of Ky.
Life of Handel. Victor Schoelcher. LC 79-12290. (Music Reprint Ser.). 1979. reprint ed. lib. bdg. 52.50 (*0-306-79572-8*) Da Capo.
Life of Handel: The Kelkel Edition. James C. Hadden. LC 74-24096. reprint ed. 34.50 (*0-404-12941-2*) AMS Pr.
Life of Harman Blennerhassett. William H. Safford. LC 78-39476. (Select Bibliographies Reprint Ser.). 1977. reprint ed. 17.95 (*0-8369-9921-5*) Ayer.
Life of Harold Sellers Colton. Miller. 15.95 (*0-912586-70-2*) Dine College Pr.
Life of Harriet Beecher Stowe: Compiled from Her Letters & Journals. Harriet Beecher Stowe. (American Biography Ser.). 530p. 1991. reprint ed. lib. bdg. 99.00 (*0-7812-8370-1*) Rprt Serv.
Life of Harriot Stuart, Written by Herself. Charlotte Lennox. Ed. & Intro. by Susan Kubica. LC 94-29387. 328p. 1995. 45.00 (*0-8386-3579-2*) Fairleigh Dickinson.
Life of Harrison. Moses Dawson. 1993. reprint ed. lib. bdg. 89.00 (*0-7812-5354-3*) Rprt Serv.
Life of Haydn. Nohl Ludwig. 195p. 1990. reprint ed. lib. bdg. 59.00 (*0-685-35205-6*, 10,068) Rprt Serv.
Life of Haydn. Louis Nohl. 1889. reprint ed. 49.00 (*0-403-00343-1*) Scholarly.
Life of Haydn. 7th ed. Ludwig Nohl. Tr. by George P. Upton. LC 73-173796. reprint ed. 37.50 (*0-404-04786-6*) AMS Pr.
Life of Heber C. Kimball. Orson F. Whitney. (Collector's Edition Ser.). 1992. 12.95 (*0-88494-833-1*) Bookcraft Inc.
Life of Heinrich Conried. Montrose J. Moses. Ed. by Andrew Farkas. LC 76-29959. (Opera Biographies Ser.). (Illus.). 1977. reprint ed. lib. bdg. 35.95 (*0-405-09699-2*) Ayer.
Life of Henry Brulard. Stendhal, pseud. Tr. by Jean Stewart & B. C. Knight. (FRE., Illus.). viii, 348p. 1999. pap. 12.95 (*0-226-77251-9*) U Ch Pr.
Life of Henry Brulard. Stendhal, pseud. Tr. & Intro. by John Sturrock. 1995. pap. 12.95 (*5-600-14044-4*, Penguin Classics) Viking Penguin.
Life of Henry Clay. Carl Schurz. (Notable American Authors Ser.). 1999. reprint ed. lib. bdg. 125.00 (*0-7812-8873-8*) Rprt Serv.
Life of Henry Clay. Glyndon G. Van Deusen. LC 78-23688. 448p. 1979. reprint ed. lib. bdg. 45.50 (*0-313-20717-8*, VAHC, Greenwood Pr) Greenwood.
Life of Henry Cornelius Agrippa: Doctor & Knight, Commonly Known As a Magician. Henry Morley. 342p. 1993. reprint ed. pap. 24.95 (*1-56459-388-6*) Kessinger Pub.
Life of Henry David Thoreau. Henry S. Salt. LC 68-24942. (American Biography Ser.: No. 32). 1969. reprint ed. lib. bdg. 75.00 (*0-8383-0272-6*) M S G Haskell Hse.
Life of Henry David Thoreau. Henry S. Salt. (BCL1-PS American Literature Ser.). 208p. 1992. reprint ed. lib. bdg. 79.00 (*0-7812-6885-0*) Rprt Serv.
***Life of Henry David Thoreau.** Henry S. Salt. Ed. by George Hendrick et al. 192p. 2000. reprint ed. pap. 14.95 (*0-252-06906-4*) U of Ill Pr.
***Life of Henry Fielding.** Ronald Paulson. LC 99-43635. (Critical Biographies Ser.). 368p. 2000. 54.95 (*0-631-19146-1*) Blackwell Pubs.
Life of Henry Irving, 2 vols., 1 bk. Austin Brereton. LC 74-88604. (Illus.). 1972. 36.95 (*0-405-08305-X*, Pub. by Blom Pubns) Ayer.
Life of Henry James. Sheldon M. Novick. write for info. (*0-679-45023-8*) Fodors Travel.
Life of Henry the Fifth. M.H. Publications Staff. 242p. 1990. 95.00 (*1-872680-07-0*, Pub. by M H Pubns) St Mut.
Life of Henry the Fifth. annot. ed. William Shakespeare. LC 97-10059. 170p. 1999. pap. 12.95 (*1-55783-288-9*) Applause Theatre Bk Pubs.
Life of Henry, Third Earl of Southampton, Shakespeare's Patron. Charlotte Stopes. LC 78-130619. reprint ed. 45.00 (*0-404-06286-5*) AMS Pr.
Life of Henry W. Grady, Including His Writings & Speeches. Ed. by Joel Chandler Harris. LC 70-39490. (American Biography Ser.: No. 32). 650p. 1972. reprint ed. lib. bdg. 75.00 (*0-8383-1402-3*) M S G Haskell Hse.
Life of Henry Wadsworth Longfellow. Samuel Longfellow. (Notable American Authors Ser.). 1999. reprint ed. lib. bdg. 125.00 (*0-7812-3851-X*) Rprt Serv.
Life of Henry Wadsworth Longfellow, with Extracts from His Journals & Correspondence, 3 vols., Set. Henry Wadsworth Longfellow. Ed. by Samuel Longfellow. LC 04-17165. 1968. reprint ed. 55.00 (*0-403-00078-5*) Scholarly.
Life of Henry Wadsworth Longfellow, with Extracts from His Journals & Correspondence, 3 vols., Set. Samuel Longfellow. (BCL1-PS American Literature Ser.). 1992. reprint ed. lib. bdg. 225.00 (*0-7812-6781-1*) Rprt Serv.
Life of Her Own: Feminism in Vera Brittain's Theory, Fiction, & Biography. Britta Zangen. Ed. by Uwe Baumann & Herwig Friedl. LC 96-36740. (Dusseldorfer Beitrage aus Anglistik und Amerikanistik Ser.: Vol. 6). 207p. 1996. 44.95 (*3-631-30949-X*) P Lang Pubng.
Life of Her Own: Feminism in Vera Brittain's Theory, Fiction, & Biography. Britta Zangen. (Dusseldorfer Beitrage aus Anglistik und Amerikanistik Ser.: Vol. 6). 207p. 1996. 44.95 (*0-8204-3227-X*) P Lang Pubng.
Life of Her Own: The Transformation of a Countrywoman in 20th-Century France. Emilie Carles. Tr. by Avriel H. Goldberger. (Illus.). 304p. 1992. pap. 14.95 (*0-14-016965-2*, Penguin Bks) Viking Penguin.
Life of Herbert Hoover: Master of Emergencies, 1917-1918, Vol. 3. George H. Nash. (Illus.). 704p. 1996. 45.00 (*0-393-03841-6*) Norton.
Life of Herbert Hoover: The Humanitarian, 1914-1917, Vol. 2. George H. Nash. (Illus.). 1988. 25.00 (*0-393-02550-0*) Norton.
Life of Herman Melville, 1. Hershel Parker. Date not set. write for info. (*0-393-03842-4*) Norton.
Life of High Countess Gritta Ratsinourhouse. Bettine Von Arnim & Giseta Von Arnim Grimm. Tr. by Lisa Ohm from GER. LC 98-47692. (European Women Writers Ser.). 192p. 1999. pap. 15.00 (*0-8032-9620-7*) U of Nebr Pr.
Life of Hilaire Belloc. Robert Speaight. LC 78-136655. (Biography Index Reprint Ser.). 1977. 31.95 (*0-8369-8050-6*) Ayer.
Life of Hildegard of Bingen. Gottfried of Disibodenberg & Theodoric of Echternach. Tr. by Hugh Feiss. (Translation Ser.). 99p. 1996. pap. 11.00 (*0-920669-54-9*, Pub. by Peregrina Pubng) Cistercian Pubns.
Life of Hiuen-Tsiang. Hui Lin & Samuel Beal. LC 98-904952. 218 p. 1998. write for info. (*81-206-1278-7*) Asian Educ Servs.
Life of Hon. William F. Cody. William F. Cody. (American Biography Ser.). 365p. 1991. reprint ed. lib. bdg. 79.00 (*0-7812-8081-8*) Rprt Serv.
Life of Hon. William F. Cody, Known As Buffalo Bill, the Famous Hunter, Scout & Guide. William F. Cody. LC 78-18732. (Illus.). xviii, 365p. 1978. pap. 11.95 (*0-8032-6303-1*, Bison Books) U of Nebr Pr.
Life of Horace Binney. Charles J. Binney. LC 72-2577. (Select Bibliographies Reprint Ser.). 1977. reprint ed. 29.95 (*0-8369-6849-2*) Ayer.
Life of Horace Greeley. James Parton. LC 70-125711. (American Journalists Ser.). 442p. 1977. reprint ed. 35.95 (*0-405-01692-1*) Ayer.
Life of Horace Greeley: Founder of the N. Y. Tribune. Lurton D. Ingersoll. (American Newspapermen 1790-1933 Ser.). (Illus.). 688p. 1974. reprint ed. text 38.95 (*0-8464-0018-9*) Beekman Pubs.
Life of Horace Mann. Mary T. Mann. LC 73-89396. (Black Heritage Library Collection). 1977. 28.95 (*0-8369-8624-5*) Ayer.
Life of Horace Walpole. Stephen L. Gwynn. LC 73-160974. (Select Bibliographies Reprint Ser.). 1977. reprint ed. 23.95 (*0-8369-5842-X*) Ayer.
Life of Horace Walpole. Stephen L. Gwynn. LC 76-160467. (English Biography Ser.: No. 31). 1971. reprint ed. lib. bdg. 75.00 (*0-8383-1302-7*) M S G Haskell Hse.
***Life of Horses.** Jane Holderness-Roddam. 256p. 1999. 34.95 (*1-58245-048-X*) Howell Bks.
Life of Ibn Khaldun & His Work. M. A. Ednan. 1991. 16.50 (*1-56744-124-6*) Kazi Pubns.
Life of Ibsen. Halvdan Koht. Ed. by Einar Haugen & A. E. Santaniello. LC 69-16322. (Illus.). 1972. 36.95 (*0-405-08715-2*) Ayer.
Life of Illness: One Woman's Journey. Carol T. Olson. LC 91-33457. (SUNY Series, The Body in Culture, History, & Religion). 203p. (C). 1992. text 18.50 (*0-7914-1199-0*) State U NY Pr.
Life of Insects. Victor Pelevin. 192p. 1999. pap. 11.95 (*0-14-027972-5*) Viking Penguin.
***Life of Insects.** Victoria Pelevin. 1999. pap. 5.00 (*5-7027-0773-7*) Distribks Inc.
Life of Insects: A Novel. Victor Pelevin. Tr. by Andrew Bromfield from RUS. LC 97-11106. 179p. 1998. 22.00 (*0-374-18625-1*) FS&G.
Life of Integrity: 12 Outstanding Leaders Raise the Standard for Today's Christian Men. Promise Keepers Speakers Staff. Ed. by Howard Hendricks. LC 96-40127. 160p. 1997. 14.99 (*1-57673-136-7*, Multnomah Bks) Multnomah Pubs.
Life of Ira Remsen. Frederick H. Getman. Ed. by I. Bernard Cohen. LC 79-7962. (Three Centuries of Science in America Ser.). (Illus.). 1980. reprint ed. lib. bdg. 18.95 (*0-405-12543-7*) Ayer.
Life of Irony & the Ethics of Belief. David Wisdo. LC 91-38202. (SUNY Series in Philosophy). 163p. (C). 1992. pap. text 19.95 (*0-7914-1222-9*) State U NY Pr.
Life of Isaac Mason As a Slave. Isaac Mason. LC 72-89393. (Black Heritage Library Collection). 1977. 11.95 (*0-8369-8627-X*) Ayer.
Life of Isaac Newton. Richard Westfall. (Canto Book Ser.). (Illus.). 350p. (C). 1994. pap. 13.95 (*0-521-47737-9*) Cambridge U Pr.
Life of Isambard Kingdom Brunel: Civil Engineer (1870) Isambard Brunel. LC 72-850. (Illus.). 568p. 1972. 80.00 (*0-8386-1201-6*) Fairleigh Dickinson.
Life of Isle Royale see Superior Wilderness: Isle Royale National Park
Life of Ismail Ferik Pasha: Novel. Rhea Galanaki. Tr. & Frwd. by Kay Cicellis. LC 96-156091. 166p. 1996. 29.95 (*0-7206-0965-8*, Pub. by P Owen Ltd) Dufour.
Life of Its Own: The Politics & Power of Water. Robert Gottlieb. 350p. 1988. 20.95 (*0-15-195190-X*) Harcourt.
Life of Ivy Compton-Burnett. Elizabeth Sprigge. LC 73-330734. 1973. write for info. (*0-575-00632-3*) V Gollancz.
Life of J. E. B. Stuart. Mary L. Williamson. Ed. by Michael J. McHugh. (Illus.). 132p. (YA). (gr. 7-12). 1997. pap. text 6.00 (*1-930092-22-9*, CLP29910) Christian Liberty.
Life of J. Pierpont Morgan. Carl Hovey. (Select Bibliographies Reprint Ser.). 1977. reprint ed. 23.95 (*0-8369-6692-9*) Ayer.
Life of J. S. Mill: 1888 Edition. W. L. Courtney. 212p. 1996. reprint ed. 58.00 (*1-85506-358-1*) Bks Intl VA.
Life of Jacob Boehme. Franz Hartmann. 1985. pap. 7.95 (*0-916411-97-4*, Sure Fire) Holmes Pub.
Life of Jacob Persinger. Joseph Persinger. 23p. 1983. pap. 4.95 (*0-87770-296-9*) Ye Galleon.
***Life of James Boswell.** Peter Martin. 624p. 2000. 35.00 (*0-300-08489-7*) Yale U Pr.
Life of James Buchanan, 2 vols., Set. George T. Curtis. 1993. reprint ed. lib. bdg. 150.00 (*0-7812-5444-2*) Rprt Serv.
Life of James Buchanan, Fifteenth President of the United States, 2 Vols., Set. George T. Curtis. LC 69-16849. (Select Bibliographies Reprint Ser.). 1977. 48.95 (*0-8369-5004-6*) Ayer.
Life of James Buchanan, Fifteenth President of the United States, 2 Vols., Vol. 2. George T. Curtis. LC 69-16849. (Select Bibliographies Reprint Ser.). 1977. 24.95 (*0-8369-9648-8*); 24.95 (*0-8369-9649-6*) Ayer.
Life of James Dwight, Dana, Scientific Explorer, Mineralogist, Geologist, Zoologist, Professor in Yale University. Daniel C. Gilman. 1977. 21.95 (*0-8369-7138-8*, 7971) Ayer.
Life of James Fisk Jr. Marshall P. Stafford. Ed. by Stuart Bruchey. LC 80-1345. (Railroads Ser.). (Illus.). 1981. reprint ed. lib. bdg. 33.95 (*0-405-13816-4*) Ayer.
Life of James J. Hill, Vol. 2. Joseph G. Pyle. 1990. 14.50 (*0-8446-1369-X*) Peter Smith.
Life of James Mars: A Slave Born & Sold in Connecticut. James Mars. LC 76-89394. (Black Heritage Library Collection). 1977. 9.00 (*0-8369-8626-1*) Ayer.
Life of James McCosh: 1896 Edition. Ed. by William M. Sloane. 294p. 1996. reprint ed. 70.00 (*1-85506-154-6*) Bks Intl VA.

L

Life of James McNeill Whistler, 2 vols. Elizabeth R. Pennell & Joseph Pennell. LC 70-148285. (Illus.). reprint ed. 135.00 (0-404-04988-5) AMS Pr.

Life of James Monroe. George Morgan. LC 76-106979. reprint ed. 74.50 (0-404-00594-2) AMS Pr.

Life of James Otis of Massachusetts. William Tudor. LC 70-118203. (Era of the American Revolution Ser.). 1970. reprint ed. lib. bdg. 55.00 (0-306-71936-3) Da Capo.

Life of James Watt. James P. Muirhead. (Industrial Antiquities Ser.). (Illus.). 608p. 1998. reprint ed. pap. 240.00 (1-85297-016-2, Pub. by Archival Facs) St Mut.

Life of Jane Austen. John Halperin. LC 84-9741. 424p. 1984. reprint ed. pap. 131.50 (0-608-03687-0, 206451300009) Bks Demand.

Life of Jane Austen. John Halperin. 390p. 1996. reprint ed. pap. 16.95 (0-8018-5509-8) Johns Hopkins.

Life of Jedidiah Morse: A Station of Peculiar Exposure. Richard J. Moss. LC 94-28143. (Illus.). 192p. (C). 1995. text 28.00 (0-87049-868-1) U of Tenn Pr.

Life of Jefferson Davis, with a Secret History of the Southern Confederacy, Gathered Behind the Scenes in Richmond. Edward A. Pollard. LC 75-95074. (Select Bibliographies Reprint Ser.). 1977. 36.95 (0-8369-5074-7) Ayer.

Life of Jehoshua. Franz Hartmann. 208p. 1996. reprint ed. spiral bd. 17.00 (0-7873-0379-8) Hlth Research.

Life of Jehoshua, the Prophet of Nazareth: An Occult Study & a Key to the Bible. Franz Hartmann. 208p. 1996. reprint ed. spiral bd. 15.00 (1-885395-65-5) Book Tree.

Life of Jehoshua the Prophet of Nazareth: An Occult Study & a Key to the Bible Containing the History of an Initiate. Franz Hartmann. 200p. 1992. reprint ed. pap. 16.00 (1-56459-184-0) Kessinger Pub.

Life of Jehudi Ashmun. Ralph R. Gurley. LC 73-149867. (Black Heritage Library Collection). 1977. 29.95 (0-8369-8749-7) Ayer.

Life of Jenny Lind. Maude. Ed. by Andrew Farkas & W. R. Moran. LC 76-29953. (Illus.). 222p. 1997. reprint ed. pap. 19.95 (0-88143-201-6) Ayer.

Life of Jenny Lind. Jenny M. Maude. Ed. by Andrew Farkas. LC 76-29953. (Opera Biographies Ser.). (Illus.). 1977. reprint ed. lib. bdg. 21.95 (0-405-09694-1) Ayer.

Life of Jenny Lind: Briefly Told by Her Daughter. Jenny M. Maude. LC 74-24149. (Illus.). reprint ed. 32.50 (0-404-13041-0) AMS Pr.

Life of Jesus see Vida de Jesucristo

Life of Jesus. (HUN.). 1995. pap. 6.99 (1-85792-062-7, Pub. by Christian Focus) Spring Arbor Dist.

Life of Jesus. (Catholic Classics Ser.). (J). 1997. pap. 1.50 (0-88271-458-9) Regina Pr.

Life of Jesus. R. Billington. mass mkt. 11.95 (0-340-69357-6, Pub. by Hodder & Stought Ltd) Trafalgar.

Life of Jesus. Rachel Billington. (Illus.). 144p. 1997. pap. 19.95 (0-340-69356-8, Pub. by Hodder & Stought Ltd) Trafalgar.

*__Life of Jesus.__ David Holdaway. 1999. pap. 14.99 (1-85240-247-4) SOV5.

Life of Jesus. Koch. 1985. pap. 6.95 (0-8159-6110-3) Devin.

Life of Jesus. Rudolph Koch. (Illus.). 56p. 1987. 10.00 (0-8159-6118-9) Devin.

Life of Jesus. Roberta Letwenko & Edward Letwenko. (Jeremy the Bible Bookworm Ser.). (Illus.). 32p. (J). 3.95 (0-614-22062-9) Regina Pr.

Life of Jesus. C. Mackenzie. (Jesus Ser.). 1995. 12.99 (0-906731-89-5, Pub. by Christian Focus); pap. 6.99 (1-85792-061-9, Pub. by Christian Focus) Spring Arbor Dist.

Life of Jesus, 10 vols. Regina Press Staff. 1998. pap. text 9.90 (0-88271-636-0) Regina Pr.

Life of Jesus. Ernest Renan. LC 91-61904. (Great Minds Ser.). 235p. (Orig.). 1991. pap. 11.95 (0-87975-704-3) Prometheus Bks.

Life of Jesus. Louis M. Savary. (Illus.). 43p. (J). (ps-4). 1989. 5.95 (0-88271-099-0) Regina Pr.

Life of Jesus. Isobel Tallach. (Orig.). (J). (ps-3). 1984. pap. 1.75 (0-85151-345-X) Banner of Truth.

Life of Jesus. Shusaku Endo. Tr. by Richard Schuchert from JPN. LC 78-61721. 192p. 1979. reprint ed. pap. 11.95 (0-8091-2319-3) Paulist Pr.

Life of Jesus. Maurice Goguel. Tr. by Olive Wyon. LC 75-41114. reprint ed. 45.00 (0-404-14546-9) AMS Pr.

Life of Jesus. Friedrich Daniel Ernst Schleiermacher. Ed. by Jack C. Verheyden & Leander E. Keck. Tr. by S. MacLean Gilmour from GER. 542p. 1997. reprint ed. pap. 26.00 (1-888961-04-X, 104X) Sigler Pr.

Life of Jesus. unabridged ed. Bruce Babcock. (Illus.). 15p. (J). (ps-6). 1998. pap. 5.95 (1-892161-01-X) Babcock Publ.

Life of Jesus: Adapted from NRSV. Illus. by Dorothee Duntze. LC 93-28776. 105p. (J). 1993. 14.95 (0-8146-2303-4) Liturgical Pr.

*__Life of Jesus: As Seen Through the Eyes of a Shepherd Boy.__ large type ed. Lempi Sample. (Illus.). 67p. 1999. 9.95 (1-55967-234-X) Triune Bib Univ.

Life of Jesus: In Masterpieces of Art. Mary Pope Osborne. LC 98-60316. (Illus.). 48p. (J). (gr. 3-5). 1998. 17.99 (0-670-87313-6, Viking) Viking Penguin.

Life of Jesus: Little Angel. Date not set. 1.95 (0-88271-201-2, 1802) Regina Pr.

Life of Jesus Activity Book. Ed. by Travis Tyre. (Illus.). 48p. (Orig.). (J). (ps-3). 1996. pap. 5.00 (1-887710-42-6, ArtCan Drama) Promise Prodns.

Life of Jesus Christ. Albert J. Nevins. 247p. (Orig.). 1987. pap. 12.95 (0-87973-500-7, 500) Our Sunday Visitor.

Life of Jesus Christ. Regina Press. 1999. 19.95 (0-88271-462-7) Regina Pr.

Life of Jesus Christ, Vol. 1. Leonard Moreno. 108p. (Orig.). 1992. pap. text 7.77 (0-9631137-7-1) Morenos Pub.

Life of Jesus Christ & Biblical Revelations, Set. Anne C. Emmerich. Ed. by Carl E. Schmoger. LC 86-50154. 1994. reprint ed. 60.00 (0-89555-293-0) TAN Bks Pubs.

Life of Jesus Christ & Biblical Revelations, Vol. 1. Anne C. Emmerich. Ed. by Carl E. Schmoger. LC 86-50154. 486p. 1994. reprint ed. 15.00 (0-89555-289-2) TAN Bks Pubs.

Life of Jesus Christ & Biblical Revelations, Vol. 2. Anne C. Emmerich. Ed. by Carl E. Schmoger. LC 86-50154. 481p. 1993. reprint ed. 15.00 (0-89555-290-6) TAN Bks Pubs.

Life of Jesus Christ & Biblical Revelations, Vol. 3. Anne C. Emmerich. Ed. by Carl E. Schmoger. LC 86-50154. 594p. 1993. reprint ed. 15.00 (0-89555-291-4) TAN Bks Pubs.

Life of Jesus Christ & Biblical Revelations, Vol. 4. Anne C. Emmerich. Ed. by Carl E. Schmoger. LC 86-50154. 476p. 1994. reprint ed. 15.00 (0-89555-292-2) TAN Bks Pubs.

*__Life of Jesus Critically Examined, 3 Vol.__ David F. Strauss. Tr. by George Eliot. 1360p. 1998. 295.00 (1-85506-587-8) Thoemmes Pr.

Life of Jesus Critically Examined. David F. Strauss. Ed. by Peter C. Hodgson. Tr. by George Eliot from GER. LC 94-65347. 816p. 1994. reprint ed. pap. 29.00 (0-9623642-6-6) Sigler Pr.

Life of Jesus Critically Examined, 2 vols., Set. David F. Strauss. Tr. by Marian Evans. LC 74-107193. 1970. reprint ed. 79.00 (0-403-00238-9) Scholarly.

Life of Jesus for Children. Savary. (J). 1980. pap. 2.50 (0-88271-154-7) Regina Pr.

Life of Jesus Research: An Annotated Bibliography. Craig A. Evans. xviii, 335p. 1996. 123.00 (90-04-10282-5) Brill Academic Pubs.

Life of Jesus the Christ. Henry W. Beecher. (Works of Henry Ward Beecher). 1989. reprint ed. lib. bdg. 79.00 (0-7812-0919-6) Rprt Serv.

Life of Jesus the Christ: An Edgar Cayce Guide, Vol. 1. Richard H. Drummond. 1996. mass mkt. 5.99 (0-312-96057-3) St Martin.

Life of Jim Baker. Nolie Mumey. 1976. 24.95 (0-8488-0246-2) Amereon Ltd.

Life of Joaquim Nabuco. Carolina Nabuco. Ed. by Ronald Hilton. LC 50-8549. 398p. 1950. reprint ed. pap. 30.00 (0-608-08257-0, 202508400042) Bks Demand.

Life of Johannes Brahms, 2 vols., Set. Florence May. 1976. lib. bdg. 79.00 (0-403-03630-5) Scholarly.

Life of Johannes Brahms, 2 vols., Set. Florence May. 1988. reprint ed. lib. bdg. 99.00 (0-7812-0192-6) Rprt Serv.

Life of John Adams, 2 Vols. Clarks F. Adams & John Q. Adams. LC 68-24969. (American Biography Ser.: No. 32). 1969. reprint ed. lib. bdg. 150.00 (0-8383-0151-7) M S G Haskell Hse.

Life of John Adams, 2 vols., Set. Charles F. Adams. LC 78-108455. 1971. reprint ed. 150.00 (0-403-00470-5) Scholarly.

Life of John Adams, Vol. 1. John Adams. 1988. reprint ed. lib. bdg. 75.00 (0-317-90161-3) Rprt Serv.

Life of John Adams: Begun by John Quincy Adams, 2 vols., 1. rev. ed. Charles F. Adams. (History - United States Ser.). 1992. reprint ed. write for info. (0-7812-0161-6) Rprt Serv.

Life of John Adams: Begun by John Quincy Adams, 2 vols., 2. rev. ed. Charles F. Adams. (History - United States Ser.). 1992. reprint ed. write for info. (0-7812-0162-4) Rprt Serv.

Life of John Adams: Begun by John Quincy Adams, 2 vols., Set. rev. ed. Charles F. Adams. (History - United States Ser.). 1992. reprint ed. lib. bdg. 150.00 (0-7812-6138-4) Rprt Serv.

Life of John Alexander Symington, Bibliographer & Librarian, 1887-1961: A Bookman's Rise & Fall. John Smurthwaite. LC 95-3011. (Illus.). 176p. 1996. text 79.95 (0-7734-9021-3) E Mellen.

*__Life of John Baptist de La Salle, Founder of the Brothers of the Christian Schools: A Biography in Three Books.__ Jean-Baptiste Blain. Ed. by Luke Salm. Tr. by Richard Arnandez from FRE. (Lasallian Resources Ser.: Vol. 2, Bk. 1). Orig. Title: La Vie de Jean-Baptiste de La Salle, Instituteur des Freres des Ecoles Chretiennes. (Illus.). xiv, 158p. 2000. 25.00 (0-944808-33-6); pap. 20.00 (0-944808-34-4) Lasallian Pubns.

Life of John Bright. George M. Trevelyan. LC 72-110873. (Illus.). 480p. 1971. reprint ed. lib. bdg. 75.00 (0-8371-4552-X, TRJB, Greenwood Pr) Greenwood.

*__Life of John Calvin.__ Theodore Bexa. 1999. pap. 10.99 (0-85234-404-X) Evangelical Pr.

Life of John Calvin. Theodore Beza. Ed. by Gary Sanseri. Tr. by Henry Beveridge. LC 96-84651. (Illus.). 150p. 1996. reprint ed. 19.95 (1-880045-16-8) Back Home Indust.

Life of John Calvin: A Study in the Shaping of Western Culture. Alister E. McGrath. (Illus.). 320p. 1993. reprint ed. pap. 28.95 (0-631-18947-5) Blackwell Pubs.

Life of John Clare. Frederick Martin. (BCL1-PR English Literature Ser.). 301p. 1992. reprint ed. lib. bdg. 89.99 (0-7812-7497-4) Rprt Serv.

Life of John Clare. 2nd ed. Frederick Martin. (Illus.). 319p. 1964. 27.50 (0-7146-2070-X, Pub. by F Cass Pubs) Intl Spec Bk.

Life of (John) Conrad Weiser, the German Pioneer. Clement Z. Weiser. 1993. reprint ed. lib. bdg. 89.00 (0-7812-5854-5) Rprt Serv.

Life of John Dryden. fac. ed. Sir Walter Scott. LC 63-8121. 492p. 1963. reprint ed. pap. 152.60 (0-7837-8308-6, 204909400010) Bks Demand.

Life of John Duncan. A. Moody Stuart. 256p. 1992. 16.99 (0-85151-608-4) Banner of Truth.

Life of John Eliot: The Apostle to the Indians. Convers Francis. 1972. reprint ed. lib. bdg. 32.00 (0-8422-8049-9) Irvington.

Life of John Greenleaf Whittier. W. Sloane Kennedy. LC 72-2002. (American Biography Ser.: No. 32). 1972. lib. bdg. 75.00 (0-8383-1452-X) M S G Haskell Hse.

Life of John James Audubon, the Naturalist. John James Audubon. 1993. reprint ed. lib. bdg. 89.00 (0-7812-5422-1) Rprt Serv.

Life of John Jay, 2 Vols., Set. William Jay. (Select Bibliographies Reprint Ser.). 1977. reprint ed. 52.95 (0-8369-6858-1) Ayer.

Life of John Keats. William M. Rossetti. LC 75-122695. reprint ed. 29.50 (0-404-05428-5) AMS Pr.

Life of John Kline. Benjamin Funk. 1974. reprint ed. 9.95 (0-87178-516-1, 8004) Brethren.

Life of John Knox. Thomas McCrie. LC 83-45584. (Illus.). reprint ed. 57.50 (0-404-19902-X) AMS Pr.

Life of John, Lord Campbell: Lord High Chancellor of Great Britain, 2 vols. Ed. by Mary S. Hardcastle. 938p. 1997. reprint ed. 235.00 (1-56169-332-4) Gaunt.

Life of John Marshall, 4 vols. bound in 2. Albert J. Beveridge. LC 90-2613. (Illus.). 2496p. 1990. reprint ed. 150.00 (0-87797-181-1) Cherokee.

Life of John Marshall, 4 vols. Albert J. Beveridge. 1997. reprint ed. 495.00 (1-56169-305-7) Gaunt.

Life of John Marshall, 4 vols., Set. Albert J. Beveridge. (BCL1 - U. S. History Ser.). 1991. reprint ed. lib. bdg. 300.00 (0-7812-6127-9) Rprt Serv.

Life of John Marshall, Vol. 1 & 2. Albert J. Beveridge. LC 90-2613. 1998. 85.00 (0-87797-182-X) Cherokee.

Life of John Marshall, Vol. 3 & 4. Albert J. Beveridge. 1998. 85.00 (0-87797-183-8) Cherokee.

*__Life of John Milton.__ Barbara Lewalski. 2001. 39.95 (0-631-17665-9) Blackwell Pubs.

Life of John Milton. Richard Garnett. LC 77-112638. reprint ed. 22.50 (0-404-02686-9) AMS Pr.

Life of John Milton. 3rd ed. Charles Symmons. LC 71-128979. 1970. reprint ed. 39.50 (0-404-06325-X) AMS Pr.

Life of John Paul Jones. John S. Abbott. xi, 359p. 1985. reprint ed. 49.00 (0-932051-77-4) Rprt Serv.

Life of John Pendleton Kennedy. Henry T. Tuckerman. (Notable American Authors). 1999. reprint ed. lib. bdg. 125.00 (0-7812-9844-X) Rprt Serv.

Life of John Randolph of Roanoke, 2 vols. in 1. Hugh A. Garland. 1981. reprint ed. lib. bdg. 25.00 (0-403-00212-5) Scholarly.

Life of John Randolph of Roanoke. 11th ed. Hugh A. Garland. (History - United States Ser.). 1992. reprint ed. lib. bdg. 89.00 (0-7812-6130-9) Rprt Serv.

Life of John Randolph of Roanoke, 2 Vols, Set. 11th ed. Hugh Garland. LC 68-24977. (American Biography Ser.: No. 32). 1969. reprint ed. lib. bdg. 150.00 (0-8383-0159-2) M S G Haskell Hse.

Life of John Redmond. Denis Gwynn. LC 77-169761. (Select Bibliographies Reprint Ser.). 1977. reprint ed. 54.95 (0-8369-5981-7) Ayer.

Life of John Ruskin, 2 vols. Edward T. Cook. LC 68-24903. (English Biography Ser.: No. 31). 1969. reprint ed. lib. bdg. 150.00 (0-8383-0155-X) M S G Haskell Hse.

Life of John Ruskin, 2 vols., Set. Edward T. Cook. (BCL1-PR English Literature Ser.). 1992. reprint ed. lib. bdg. 150.00 (0-7812-7638-1) Rprt Serv.

Life of John Taylor. B. H. Roberts. 11.95 (0-88494-106-X) Bookcraft Inc.

Life of John Taylor: The Story of a Brilliant Leader in the Early Virginia State Rights School. Henry H. Simms. viii, 234p. 1992. reprint ed. 38.00 (0-8377-2650-6, Rothman) W S Hein.

Life of John Wesley Hardin As Written by Himself. John W. Hardin. LC 61-6493. (Western Frontier Library: No. 16). (Illus.). 1983. reprint ed. pap. 9.95 (0-8061-1051-1) U of Okla Pr.

Life of John Wheatley. John Hannan. 179p. 1988. 42.50 (0-85124-487-4, Pub. by Spkesman) Coronet Bks.

Life of John Wilkes. Owen A. Sherrard. 319p. 1977. 23.95 (0-8369-5910-8) Ayer.

Life of John Wilkes. Owen A. Sherrard. LC 72-177508. 1972. reprint ed. 26.95 (0-405-08967-8, 1386) Ayer.

Life of John William Strutt, Third Baron Rayleigh, O. M., F. R. S. Robert J. Rayleigh. LC 68-16063. 467p. reprint ed. pap. 144.80 (0-608-14658-7, 202372200033) Bks Demand.

Life of Johnny Reb: The Common Soldier of the Confederacy. Bell I. Wiley. LC 71-162618. (Illus.). 444p. 1971. 29.95 (0-8071-1909-1); pap. 14.95 (0-8071-0475-2) La State U Pr.

Life of Johnson. James Boswell. LC 92-52915. 1328p. 1992. 25.00 (0-679-41717-6) Everymns Lib.

Life of Johnson. James Boswell. 2000. 22.00 (0-679-60204-6) Modern Lib NY.

Life of Johnson. James Boswell. (English Library). 384p. 1979. pap. 11.95 (0-14-043116-0, Penguin Classics) Viking Penguin.

*__Life of Johnson: Unabridged.__ James Boswell. Ed. by R. W. Chapman & J. D. Fleeman. (Oxford World's Classics Ser.). 1536p. 1998. pap. 17.95 (0-19-283531-9) OUP.

Life of Jonathan Swift, Dean of St. Patrick's Dublin. Henry Craik. (BCL1-PR English Literature Ser.). 576p. 1992. reprint ed. lib. bdg. 99.00 (0-7812-7412-5) Rprt Serv.

Life of Joseph: Beloved, Hated, & Exalted. F. B. Meyer. Ed. by Lance Wubbels. (Bible Character Ser.). 149p. 1995. pap. 9.99 (1-883002-23-0) Emerald WA.

Life of Joseph Brant: Thayendanegea, Including the Indian Wars of the American Revolution, 2 vols., Set. William L. Stone. LC 75-108544. (American Indian History Ser.). 1970. reprint ed. 27.50 (0-403-00226-5) Scholarly.

Life of Joseph Conrad: A Critical Biography. John Calvin Batchelor. Ed. by Claude Rawson. (Critical Biographies Ser.). (Illus.). 336p. 1996. pap. 25.95 (0-631-19912-8) Blackwell Pubs.

Life of Joseph Hodges Choate: As Gathered Chiefly from His Letters, 2 vols. Edward S. Martin. 1997. reprint ed. 255.00 (1-56169-349-9) Gaunt.

Life of Joseph Smith: An Atlas, Chronological Outline & Documentation Harmony. Duane S. Crowther. 32p. 1989. pap. 4.98 (0-88290-350-0) Horizon Utah.

Life of Joy & Peace: An Exposition of Philippians. D. M. Loyd Jones. 512p. 1999. pap. 19.99 (0-8010-5816-3) Baker Bks.

Life of Juliana of Mont-Cornillon. 2nd rev. ed. Tr. & Intro. by Barbara Newman. (Translations Ser.: Vol. 13). 164p. 1999. pap. 20.00 (0-920669-13-1, Pub. by Peregrina Pubng) Cistercian Pubns.

Life of Katherine Mansfield. Ruth E. Mantz & John M. Murry. LC 75-42109. (English Literature Ser.: No. 33). 1974. lib. bdg. 75.00 (0-8383-1882-7) M S G Haskell Hse.

Life of Keswick. 1997. pap. 8.99 (1-85078-248-2, Pub. by Sheffield Acad) CUP Services.

Life of King Arthur. Wace & Lawman. Ed. by Judy Weiss & Rosamund Allen. (Everyman Paperback Classics). 256p. 1997. pap. 8.95 (0-460-87570-1, Everyman's Classic Lib) Tuttle Pubng.

Life of King Edward Who Rests at Westminster: Attributed to a Monk of St. Bertin. Ed. by Frank Barlow. LC 80-2170. (Norman Conquest Ser.).Tr. of Vita Aedwardi Regis Qui Apud Westmonasterium Requiescit. (ENG & LAT.). 312p. 1984. reprint ed. 37.50 (0-404-18751-X) AMS Pr.

Life of King Edward Who Rests at Westminster: Attributed to a Monk of St. Bertin. 2nd ed. Frank Barlow. (Oxford Medieval Texts Ser.).Tr. of Vita Aedwardi Regis Qui Apud Westmonasterium Requiescit. (Illus.). 254p. 1992. text 85.00 (0-19-820203-2) OUP.

Life of Kit Carson. Edward S. Ellis. LC 97-75727. (Illus.). 364p. (YA). (gr. 4 up). 1998. reprint ed. pap. 14.95 (1-890623-04-0) Lost Classics.

Life of Knut Wicksell. Torsten Gardlund. Tr. by Nancy Adler. LC 95-42420. (Illus.). 376p. (C). 1996. 95.00 (1-85898-404-1) E Elgar.

Life of Krishna in Indian Art. P. Banerjee. (Illus.). 348p. 1978. 94.95 (0-318-36269-4) Asia Bk Corp.

Life of Lamartine, 2 Vols. Henry R. Whitehouse. LC 73-103672. (Select Bibliographies Reprint Ser.). 1977. 68.95 (0-8369-5172-7) Ayer.

Life of Langston Hughes, 1902-1941 Vol. I: I, Too, Sing America. Arnold Rampersad. (Illus.). 448p. (C). 1986. text 39.95 (0-19-504011-2) OUP.

Life of Langston Hughes, 1902-1941 Vol. I: I, Too, Sing America. Arnold Rampersad. (Illus.). 480p. 1988. pap. 17.95 (0-19-505426-1) OUP.

Life of Langston Hughes, Vol. I, 1902-1941: I, Too, Sing America. Arnold Rampersad. (Illus.). 448p. 1986. pap. 9.95 (0-685-13534-9) OUP.

Life of Langston Hughes, Vol. II, 1941-1967: I Dream a World. Arnold Rampersad. (Illus.). 526p. 1988. reprint ed. text 39.95 (0-19-504519-X) OUP.

Life of Langston Hughes, Vol. II, 1941-1967: I Dream a World. Arnold Rampersad. (Illus.). 528p. 1989. reprint ed. pap. 17.95 (0-19-506169-1) OUP.

Life of las Casas: The Apostle of the Indies. Arthur Helps. 1976. lib. bdg. 75.00 (0-8490-2165-0) Gordon Pr.

Life of Latimer: The Christian Martyr, Born 1485, Burned at the Stake 1555. R. Demaus. reprint ed. pap. 40.00 (0-943698-33-2) Papyrus Letterbox.

Life of Lazarillo de Tormes. J. Gerald Markley. LC 55-34585. 80p. (C). 1954. pap. text 7.51 (0-02-376160-1, LLA37, Macmillan Coll) P-H.

*__Life of Lazaros of Mt. Galesion: An Eleventh-Century Pillar Saint.__ Gregory & Richard P. Greenfield. LC 99-30808. (Byzantine Saints' Lives in Translation Ser.). 1999. write for info. (0-88402-272-2) Dumbarton Oaks.

Life of Learning: Haskins Lectures Sponsored by the American Council of Learned Societies. Douglas Greenberg & Stanley Katz. LC 93-37336. 192p. 1994. text 55.00 (0-19-508339-3) OUP.

Life of Leontios, Patriarch of Jerusalem: Text, Translation & Commentary. Tr. & Comment by Dimitris Tsougarakis. LC 93-471. (Medieval Mediterranean Ser.: Vol. 2). (ENG & GRE., Illus.). viii, 252p. 1993. 110.50 (90-04-09827-5) Brill Academic Pubs.

Life of Leopold Bloom: A Novel. Peter Costello. LC 92-61909. 197p. (Orig.). 1993. pap. 9.95 (1-879373-34-3) Roberts Rinehart.

Life of Lidian Jackson Emerson. rev. ed. Ellen T. Emerson. LC 91-29778. 350p. (C). 1991. reprint ed. pap. 16.95 (0-87013-303-9) Mich St U Pr.

Life of Lieutenant-General Hugh Mackay. John Mackay. LC 74-172708. (Bannatyne Club, Edinburgh. Publications: No. 53). reprint ed. 27.50 (0-404-52763-9) AMS Pr.

Life of Light. Leslie Goerner. 68p. (Orig.). 1994. pap. 9.00 (0-944920-14-4) Bellowing Ark Pr.

Life of Lincoln. William H. Herndon. (Quality Paperbacks Ser.). 560p. 1983. pap. 14.95 (0-306-80195-7) Da Capo.

Life of Liza Lehmann. Liza Lehmann. LC 79-25647. (Music Reprint Ser.). (Illus.). 1980. reprint ed. lib. bdg. 29.50 (0-306-76010-X) Da Capo.

Life of Lloyd: First Lord Kenyon, Lord Chief Justice of England, with Portraits. George T. Kenyon. (Illus.). xi, 403p. 1990. reprint ed. 45.00 (0-8377-0778-1, Rothman) W S Hein.

Life of Lope de Vega. Hugo A. Rennert. LC 67-13337. 1972. reprint ed. 30.95 (0-405-08878-7) Ayer.

Life of Lord Byron. Roden B. Noel. LC 72-990. reprint ed. 21.50 (0-404-07436-7) AMS Pr.

Life of Lord Clive, 2 vols., Set. George Forrest. (C). 1986. reprint ed. 105.00 (81-212-0063-6, Pub. by Gian Publng Hse) S Asia.

An Asterisk (*) at the beginning of an entry indicates that the title is appearing for the first time.

Life of Lord Curzon, Being the Authorized Biography of George Nathaniel, Marquess Curzon of Kedleston. Lawrence J. Zetland. 1977. 65.95 (*0-8369-6988-X*, 7865) Ayer.

Life of Lord Darling. Derek Walker-Smith. 330p. 1996. reprint ed. 95.00 (*1-56169-202-6*) Gaunt.

Life of Lord Jeffrey with a Selection from His Correspondence, 2 vols. in 1. Henry T. Cockburn. LC 70-148763. reprint ed. 105.00 (*0-404-07297-6*) AMS Pr.

Life of Lord John Russell, 2 Vols, Set. Spencer Walpole. LC 68-25281. (English Biography Ser.: No. 31). 1969. reprint ed. lib. bdg. 150.00 (*0-8383-0188-6*) M S G Haskell Hse.

Life of Lord Kelvin, 2 vols. 2nd ed. Silvanus P. Thompson. LC 75-45133. (Illus.). 1977. text 49.50 (*0-8284-0292-2*) Chelsea Pub.

Life of Lord Stirling: Collections of the N. J. Historical Society, Vol. II. William A. Duer. (American Revolution Ser.: Vol. 4). (Illus.). 162p. 1997. 11.95 (*1-58057-018-6*, LOLS001B) Digital Antiq.

Life of Lord Timothy Dexter: With Sketches of the Eccentric Characters That Composed His Associates; Including His Own Writings, "Dexter's Pickle for the Knowing Ones," Etc. Samuel L. Knapp. (Illus.). 157p. 1998. reprint ed. lib. bdg. 29.00 (*0-8328-9709-4*) Higginson Bk Co.

Life of Louis Kossuth, Governor of Hungary. Phineas C. Headley. LC 78-154152. (Select Bibliographies Reprint Ser.). 1977. reprint ed. 35.95 (*0-8369-5768-7*) Ayer.

Life of Louis Riel. Peter Charlebois. (Illus.). 256p. 1978. text 24.95 (*0-919601-12-X*, Pub. by NC Ltd) U of Toronto Pr.

Life of Ludwig van Beethoven, 1. Alexander W. Thayer. (Centaur Classics Ser.). (Illus.). 399p. reprint ed. pap. 123.70 (*0-608-11124-4*, 2051321) Bks Demand.

Life of Ludwig van Beethoven, 2. Alexander W. Thayer. LC ML0410.B4T33. (Centaur Classics Ser.). (Illus.). 424p. 1962. reprint ed. pap. 131.50 (*0-608-08259-7*, 205132100002) Bks Demand.

Life of Ludwig van Beethoven, 3. Alexander W. Thayer. LC ML0410.B4T33. (Centaur Classics Ser.). (Illus.). 358p. 1962. reprint ed. pap. 111.00 (*0-608-08260-0*, 205132100003) Bks Demand.

Life of Lutgard of Aywieres. Thomas De Cantempre. Tr. by Margot H. King. (Translation Ser.). 207p. 1991. pap. write for info. (*0-920669-09-3*, Pub. by Peregrina Pubng) Cistercian Pubns.

Life of Luxury: Europe's Oldest Cookery Book. Archestratus et al. (GRE., Illus.). 110p. 1994. pap. 17.00 (*0-907325-53-X*, Pub. by Prospect) Food Words.

Life of Ma-Ka-Tai-Me-She-Kia-Kiak, or Black Hawk. Black Hawk. (American Biography Ser.). 206p. 1991. reprint ed. lib. bdg. 69.00 (*0-7812-8023-0*) Rprt Serv.

Life of Macrina. Gregory of Nyssa. Tr. by Kevin Corrigan. (Translation Ser.). (Illus.). 74p. 1996. pap. 9.00 (*0-920669-12-3*, Pub. by Peregrina Pubng) Cistercian Pubns.

Life of Maharaja Sir Jung Bahadur of Nepal. Padma J. Rana. 1980. 75.00 (*0-7855-0317-X*, Pub. by Ratna Pustak Bhandar) St Mut.

Life of Maharaja Sir Jung Bahadur of Nepal. Pudma J. Rana. 1980. 75.00 (*0-7855-0259-9*, Pub. by Ratna Pustak Bhandar) St Mut.

Life of Maharaja Sir Jung Bahadur of Nepal. Pudma J. Rana. 314p. (C). 1980. 100.00 (*0-89771-064-9*, Pub. by Ratna Pustak Bhandar); 100.00 (*0-89771-112-2*, Pub. by Ratna Pustak Bhandar) St Mut.

Life of Mahatma Gandhi. Louis Fischer. 659p. 1994. pap. 23.00 (*0-934676-79-8*) Greenlf Bks.

Life of Mahler. Peter Franklin. LC 96-25105. (Musical Lives Ser.). (Illus.). 238p. (C). 1997. pap. 14.95 (*0-521-46761-6*) Cambridge U Pr.

Life of Mahomet. H. De Boulainvilliers. 416p. 1983. 250.00 (*1-85077-005-0*, Pub. by Darf Pubs Ltd) St Mut.

Life of Mammals: Their Anatomy & Physiology. 2nd ed. John Z. Young & M. J. Hobbs. (Illus.). 1976. text 39.00 (*0-19-857156-9*) OUP.

Life of Margaret Fuller. Madeleine B. Stern. LC 68-29738. (American Biography Ser.: No. 32). (Illus.). 1969. reprint ed. lib. bdg. 75.00 (*0-8383-0286-6*) M S G Haskell Hse.

Life of Margaret Fuller, 123. 2nd rev. ed. Madeleine B. Stern. LC 90-14001. (Contributions in Women's Studies: No. 123). 432p. 1991. 65.00 (*0-313-27526-2*, SLK/, Greenwood Pr) Greenwood.

Life of Margaret of Ypres. 2nd ed. Thomas De Cantempre. Tr. & Intro. by Margot H. King. LC 97-18324. (Translations Ser.: Vol. 15). (LAT & ENG., Illus.). 91p. 1999. pap. 9.00 (*0-920669-50-6*, Pub. by Peregrina Pubng) Cistercian Pubns.

*__Life of Marie d'Agoult, Alias Daniel Stern.__ Phyllis Stock-Morton. LC 99-47883. .p. 2000. 42.50 (*0-8018-6313-9*) Johns Hopkins.

Life of Marie d'Oignies & Supplement to the Life. 4th ed. Jacques De Vitry & Thomas De Cantempre. Tr. by Hugh Feiss & Margot H. King. (Translations Ser.). 298p. 1998. pap. write for info. (*0-920669-51-4*, Pub. by Peregrina Pubng) Cistercian Pubns.

Life of Mark M. Pomeroy. Mary E. Tucker. LC 77-125721. (American Journalists Ser.). 1971. reprint ed. 15.95 (*0-405-01704-9*) Ayer.

Life of Marlowe. Brooke C. Tucker. (Works & Life of Christopher Marlowe Ser.: Vol. 1). 238p. 1966. reprint ed. 50.00 (*0-87752-194-8*) Gordian.

Life of Marmaduke Rawdon of York. Ed. by Robert Davies. (Camden Society, London. Publications, First Ser.: No. 85). reprint ed. 55.00 (*0-404-50185-0*) AMS Pr.

*__Life of Marpa.__ Shambhala Publications Staff. 1999. pap. write for info. (*1-56957-112-0*, Pub. by Shambhala Pubns) Random.

Life of Marpa the Translator. Chogyam Trungpa. 1995. pap. 16.00 (*1-57062-087-3*, Pub. by Shambhala Pubns) Random.

*__Life of Marshal of the Raf Lord Tedder of Glenguin.__ Vincent Orange. 400p. 2000. text 35.00 (*0-7146-4817-5*) F Cass Pubs.

Life of Martyrs. Georges Duhamel. 1990. lib. bdg. 79.95 (*0-8490-4056-6*) Gordon Pr.

Life of Mary. (Catholic Classics Ser.). (J). 1997. pap. 1.50 (*0-88271-459-7*) Regina Pr.

Life of Mary, 10 Vols. Regina Press Staff. 1998. pap. text 9.90 (*0-88271-637-9*) Regina Pr.

Life of Mary. L. Savory. (J). 1996. 7.95 (*0-88271-128-8*) Regina Pr.

Life of Mary: A Poem-Novella. unabridged ed. Charlotte Mandel. LC 87-28677. (Listen to the Poet Ser.). (Illus.). 72p. 1988. pap. 7.00 (*0-938158-10-4*) Saturday Pr.

Life of Mary: A Poem-Novella. unabridged ed. Charlotte Mandel. LC 87-28677. (Listen to the Poet Ser.). 1993. audio 9.00 (*0-938158-14-7*) Saturday Pr.

Life of Mary & Birth of Jesus: The Ancient Infancy Gospel of James. Ronald F. Hock. Ed. by Ray Riegert. LC 97-28452. (Illus.). 128p. 1997. 16.00 (*1-56975-079-3*) Ulysses Pr.

Life of Mary As Seen by the Mystics. Compiled by Raphael Brown. LC 90-71852. 264p. 1994. reprint ed. pap. 12.50 (*0-89555-436-4*) TAN Bks Pubs.

Life of Mary Baker Eddy. Sibyl Wilbur. (Twentieth Century Biographers Ser.). 406p. 1994. reprint ed. 24.95 (*0-87510-285-9*) Writings of Mary Baker.

Life of Mary Baker G. Eddy & the History of Christian Science. Willa Cather & Georgine Milmine. LC 92-37437. (Illus.). xxvii, 520p. (C). 1993. pap. 14.95 (*0-8032-6349-X*, Bison Books); text 45.00 (*0-8032-1453-7*) U of Nebr Pr.

Life of Mary Baker G. Eddy & the History of Christian Science. Willa Cather & Georgine Milmine. (Collected Works of Willa Cather). 495p. 1998. reprint ed. lib. bdg. 108.00 (*1-58201-568-6*) Classic Bks.

*__Life of Mary Wollstonecraft.__ Gordon. 2000. pap. 18.00 (*0-06-095774-3*) HarpC.

*__Life of Mary Wollstonecraft.__ Lyndall Gordon. 2000. 35.00 (*0-06-019802-8*) HarpC.

Life of Melania the Younger: Introduction, Translation & Commentary. Elizabeth Ann Clark. LC 84-20635. (Studies in Women & Religion: Vol. 14). 305p. 1984. lib. bdg. 99.95 (*0-88946-535-5*) E Mellen.

Life of Menasseh Ben Israel: Rabbi, Printer & Diplomat. Cecil Roth. LC 74-29518. (Modern Jewish Experience Ser.). (Illus.). 1975. reprint ed. 35.95 (*0-405-06743-7*) Ayer.

*__Life of Mendelssohn.__ Peter Mercer-Taylor. LC 99-58441. (Musical Lives Ser.). (Illus.). 200p. (C). 2000. text 49.95 (*0-521-63025-8*); pap. text 17.95 (*0-521-63972-7*) Cambridge U Pr.

Life of Meriasek: A Medieval Cornish Miracle Play. Markham Harris. LC 77-21760. 155p. reprint ed. pap. 48.10 (*0-608-15259-5*, 202952500061) Bks Demand.

Life of Metrical & Free Verse in Twentieth-Century Poetry. Jon Silkin. LC 96-44850. 432p. 1997. text 59.95 (*0-312-17239-7*) St Martin.

Life of Michael Schlatter. Henry Harbaugh. (Notable American Authors Ser.). 1992. reprint ed. lib. bdg. 75.00 (*0-7812-3010-1*) Rprt Serv.

Life of Michelangelo. 2nd ed. Ascanio Condivi & Hellmut Wohl. LC 98-37313. 442p. 1999. 19.00 (*0-271-01853-4*) Pa St U Pr.

Life of Michelangelo, 2 vols., Set. Herman F. Grimm. 45.00 (*0-403-00399-7*) Scholarly.

*__Life of Michelangelo Buonarroti: Based on Studies in the Archives of the Buonarroti Family, 2 vols., Set.__ John Addington Symonds. (Illus.). 2001. pap. write for info. (*0-8122-1761-6*) U of Pa Pr.

Life of Midhat Pasha. Ali H. Midhat. LC 73-6290. (Middle East Ser.). 1973. reprint ed. 24.95 (*0-405-05348-7*) Ayer.

Life of Milarepa: A New Translation from the Tibetan. Lobsang P. Lhalungpa. 256p. 1992. pap. 14.95 (*0-14-019350-2*, Arkana) Viking Penguin.

Life of Milton. William Hayley. LC 78-122485. 366p. 1970. reprint ed. 50.00 (*0-8201-1081-7*) Schol Facsimiles.

Life of Mind. Elijah Jordan. LC 75-3205. reprint ed. 37.50 (*0-404-59203-1*) AMS Pr.

Life of Mind: Introduction to Philosophy. Cole. (Philosophy Ser.). 2000. pap. 36.00 (*0-534-55851-8*) Wadsworth Pub.

Life of Mitzvah: Rabbi Joseph Mayer Jacobson: Boston's Premier Orthodox Jewish Leader. Jack N. Porter. (Illus.). 125p. 1997. pap. 10.00 (*0-932270-15-8*) Spencer Pr.

Life of Mohammad. Sliman B. Ibrahim. 1990. 29.98 (*1-55521-513-0*) Bk Sales Inc.

Life of Mohammad from Original Sources. rev. ed. William Muir. Ed. by Thomas H. Weir. LC 78-180366. reprint ed. 57.50 (*0-404-56306-6*) AMS Pr.

Life of Mohammed. Washington Irving. 250p. 1996. pap. 13.95 (*0-614-21712-1*, 719) Kazi Pubns.

Life of Monsieur de Moliere. Mikhail Afanasevich Bulgakov. Tr. by Mirra Ginsburg from RUS. LC 70-93921. (New Directions Classics Ser.). 272p. 1986. reprint ed. pap. 12.95 (*0-8112-0956-3*, NDP601, Pub. by New Directions) Norton.

*__Life of Moravia.__ Alberto Moravia, pseud & Alain Elkann. Tr. by William Weaver from ITA. (Steerforth Italia Ser.). Orig. Title: Vita di Moravia. (Illus.). 350p. 2000. 27.00 (*1-883642-50-7*, Pub. by Steerforth Pr) Publishers Group.

Life of Moses. (Learn About God Ser.). Date not set. pap. 4.99 (*0-906731-50-X*, Pub. by Christian Focus) Spring Arbor Dist.

*__Life of Moses: Blueprints for Thirty Messages Built upon God's Word.__ David Faust. Ed. by Jim Eichenberger. (Solid Foundation Sermon Starters Ser.). 64p. 2000. pap. 6.99 (*0-7847-1169-0*, 23017) Standard Pub.

Life of Moses: The Man of God. Edmond Fleg & Faith A. Sand. Tr. by Stephen L. Haden-Guest. LC 95-22612. 209p. (J). 1995. pap. 12.95 (*0-932727-82-4*) Hope Pub Hse.

Life of Moses: The Man of God. rev. ed. Edmond Fleg. Ed. by Faith A. Sand. Tr. by Stephen L. Haden-Guest from FRE. LC 95-22612. 210p. (J). 1995. reprint ed. lib. bdg. 19.95 (*0-932727-84-0*) Hope Pub Hse.

Life of Moses: The Servant of God. F. B. Meyer. Ed. by Lance Wubbels. (Bible Character Ser.). 170p. 1996. pap. 9.99 (*1-883002-35-4*) Emerald WA.

Life of Moses: The Yahwist As Historian in Exodus-Numbers. John Van Seters. 448p. 1994. text 39.95 (*0-664-22038-X*) Westminster John Knox.

Life of Mozart. John Rosselli. LC 97-33013. (Musical Lives Ser.). (Illus.). 184p. (C). 1998. pap. 14.95 (*0-521-58744-1*); text 39.95 (*0-521-58317-9*) Cambridge U Pr.

Life of Mozart. Stendhal, pseud. Tr. by Daniel Sloate from FRE. 82p. 1991. pap. 10.00 (*0-920717-59-4*) SPD-Small Pr Dist.

Life of Mozart. Edward Holmes. (Music Reprint Ser.). 1980. reprint ed. lib. bdg. 45.00 (*0-306-79560-4*) Da Capo.

Life of Mozart. Edward Holmes. LC 79-25356. 303p. 1980. reprint ed. lib. bdg. 47.50 (*0-313-22283-5*, HOLM, Greenwood Pr) Greenwood.

Life of Mozart. Franz X. Niemtschek. 1988. reprint ed. lib. bdg. 49.00 (*0-7812-0253-1*) Rprt Serv.

Life of Mozart. Franz X. Niemtschek. LC 74-181224. 87p. 1956. reprint ed. 49.00 (*0-403-01751-3*) Scholarly.

Life of Mozart. Louis Nohl. Tr. by John J. Lalor. LC 82-1593. (Music Reprint Ser.). (GER., Illus.). 236p. 1982. reprint ed. lib. bdg. 29.50 (*0-306-76171-8*) Da Capo.

Life of Mozart: Music Book Index. Edward Holmes. 307p. 1993. reprint ed. lib. bdg. 89.00 (*0-7812-9715-X*) Rprt Serv.

Life of Mr. Richard Savage. Intro. by Timothy Erwin. LC 92-23642. (Augustan Reprints Ser.: No. 247). 1992. reprint ed. 14.50 (*0-404-70247-3*) AMS Pr.

Life of Mr. Thomas Betterton: The Late Eminent Tragedian. Charles Gildon. (Eighteenth Century Shakespeare Ser.: Vol. 4). 279p. 1970. reprint ed. 27.50 (*0-7146-2517-5*, Pub. by F Cass Pubs) Intl Spec Bk.

Life of Mrs. Catherine Clive with an Account of Her Adventures on & off the Stage, a Round of Her Characters, Together with Her Correspondence. Percy H. Fitzgerald. 1972. 19.95 (*0-405-18159-0*, 1719) Ayer.

Life of Mrs. E. G. White, Seventh-Day-Adventist Prophet. D. M. Canright. 190p. 1998. reprint ed. pap. text 12.95 (*0-9664531-0-7*) UT State Installations.

Life of Mrs. Godolphin: Now First Published & Edited by Samuel Lord Bishop of Oxford, Chancellor of the Most Noble Order of the Garter. John Evelyn. LC 72-5552. (Select Bibliographies Reprint Ser.). 1977. reprint ed. 23.95 (*0-8369-6905-7*) Ayer.

Life of Mrs. Mary Fletcher, Consort & Relict of the Rev. John Fletcher. Henry Moore. 295p. 1997. pap. 13.99 (*0-88019-371-9*) Schmul Pub Co.

Life of Muhammad. M. H. Haykal. Tr. by R. I. Faruqi. LC 76-3060. 1976. 12.95 (*0-89259-002-5*) Am Trust Pubns.

Life of Muhammad. Ibn Ishaq. Tr. by Alfred Guillaume. 815p. 1996. 39.95 (*0-614-21086-0*, 720) Kazi Pubns.

Life of Muhammad. Ed. by Uri Rubin. LC 98-6041. (Formation of the Classical Islamic World Ser.: Vol. 4). 1p. 1998. text 129.95 (*0-86078-703-6*, BP75.L53, Pub. by Ashgate Pub) Ashgate Pub Co.

Life of Muhammad. rev. ed. Abdul H. Siddiqui. 1991. 15.50 (*0-934905-21-5*) Kazi Pubns.

Life of Muhammad: A Translation of Isbaq's Sirat Rasul Allah. Tr. & Intro. by A. Guillaume. LC 98-115611. (The Jubilee Ser.).Tr. of Sirat Rasul Allah. 866p. 1998. 85.00 (*0-19-577828-6*) OUP.

Life of Muhammad: Collector's Edition. Sliman B. Ibrahim. 240p. 1996. reprint ed. 49.95 (*0-614-21087-9*, 723) Kazi Pubns.

Life of Muhammad the Earliest Biography. Ibn Ishaq. 600p. (C). 1997. 59.95 (*1-871031-70-2*) Kazi Pubns.

Life of Music in North India: The Organization of an Artistic Tradition. Daniel M. Neuman. LC 89-20604. (Illus.). 302p. 1990. reprint ed. pap. text 25.00 (*0-226-57516-0*) U Ch Pr.

*__Life of Musorgsky.__ Caryl Emerson. LC 98-47948. (Musical Lives Ser.). (Illus.). 216p. (C). 1999. 44.95 (*0-521-48009-4*); pap. 15.95 (*0-521-48507-X*) Cambridge U Pr.

Life of My Own: Daily Meditations on Hope & Acceptance. Karen Casey. 400p. (Orig.). pap. 10.00 (*0-89486-863-2*, 1070A) Hazelden.

Life of Nancy. Sarah Orne Jewett. LC 77-98579. (Short Story Index Reprint Ser.). 322p. 1977. reprint ed. 21.95 (*0-8369-3153-X*) Ayer.

Life of Nancy. Sarah Orne Jewett. (Collected Works of Sarah Orne Jewett). 1988. reprint ed. lib. bdg. 59.00 (*0-7812-1312-6*) Rprt Serv.

Life of Napoleon Bonaparte, 4 vols. William M. Sloane. (Illus.). reprint ed. 300.00 (*0-404-06100-1*) AMS Pr.

Life of Nathanael Greene: Major-General in the Army of the Revolution. George W. Greene. LC 72-5507. (Select Bibliographies Reprint Ser.). 1977. reprint ed. 92.95 (*0-8369-6910-3*) Ayer.

Life of Nathaniel Hawthorne. Moncure D. Conway. LC 68-24935. (Studies in Hawthorne: No. 15). 1969. reprint ed. lib. bdg. 75.00 (*0-8383-0931-3*) M S G Haskell Hse.

Life of Nathaniel Hawthorne. Moncure D. Conway. (Works of Moncure Daniel Conway). 1990. reprint ed. lib. bdg. 79.00 (*0-7812-2341-5*) Rprt Serv.

Life of Nelson. Robert Southey. Ed. by Jack Sweetman. LC 90-6290. (Classics of Naval Literature Ser.). 256p. 1990. 32.95 (*0-87021-301-6*) Naval Inst Pr.

*__Life of Nelson.__ Robert Southey. (Illus.). 360p. 2000. 35.00 (*0-09-479810-9*, Pub. by Constable & Co) Trafalgar.

Life of Nelson. Alfred Thayer Mahan. (Notable American Authors Ser.). 1999. reprint ed. lib. bdg. 125.00 (*0-7812-3920-6*) Rprt Serv.

Life of Nelson: The Embodiment of the Sea Power of Great Britain, 2 vols. in 1. Alfred Thayer Mahan. 1999. 26.00 (*0-403-00076-9*) Scholarly.

*__Life of Nelson: The Embodiment of the Sea Power of Great Britain.__ fac. ed. Alfred Thayer Mahan. (Illus.). 792p. 2000. 84.95 (*0-9674826-2-3*) Regatta Pr.

Life of Nelson: The Embodiment of the Sea Power of Great Britain, 2 Vols. Alfred Thayer Mahan. LC 68-26361. (English Biography Ser.: No. 31). 1969. reprint ed. lib. bdg. 99.95 (*0-8383-0182-7*) M S G Haskell Hse.

Life of Nicholas Lewis, Count Zinzendorf. A. G. Spangenberg. 1993. reprint ed. lib. bdg. 89.00 (*0-7812-5835-9*) Rprt Serv.

Life of Obedience. Kenneth E. Hagin, Jr. 1986. pap. 2.95 (*0-89276-720-0*) Faith Lib Pubns.

Life of Okah Tubbee. Okah Tubbee. Ed. by Daniel R. Littlefield, Jr. LC 88-4758. 203p. 1988. reprint ed. pap. 63.00 (*0-7837-8901-7*, 204961200001) Bks Demand.

*__Life of Olaudah Equiano: or Gustavus Vassa, the African.__ Olaudah Equiano. LC 98-48384. 192p. 1999. pap. text 2.00 (*0-486-40661-X*) Dover.

Life of Ole Bull. Mortimer B. Smith. (Illus.). 220p. 1993. reprint ed. lib. bdg. 29.50 (*0-8328-2897-1*) Higginson Bk Co.

Life of Ole Bull. Mortimer B. Smith. (Music Book Index Ser.). 220p. 1992. reprint ed. lib. bdg. 79.00 (*0-7812-9466-5*) Rprt Serv.

Life of Olive Schreiner. Samuel Cronwright-Schreiner. LC 72-2122. (Studies in Women's Rights: No. 51). (Illus.). 1972. reprint ed. lib. bdg. 75.00 (*0-8383-1461-9*) M S G Haskell Hse.

Life of Oliver Goldsmith. Austin Dobson. LC 72-38350. (Select Bibliographies Reprint Ser.). 1977. reprint ed. 20.95 (*0-8369-6767-4*) Ayer.

Life of Oliver Goldsmith. John Forster. (BCL1-PR English Literature Ser.). 460p. 1992. reprint ed. lib. bdg. 99.00 (*0-7812-7359-5*) Rprt Serv.

Life of Oliver P. Morton, 2 vols. William D. Foulke. LC 77-168129. reprint ed. 115.00 (*0-404-04592-8*) AMS Pr.

*__Life of One's Own.__ Zofia Jaremko-Pytowska. 372p. 2000. pap. 17.95 (*1-58244-054-9*) Rutledge Bks.

Life of One's Own: Individual Rights & the Welfare State. David Kelley. LC 98-37024. 165p. 1998. 18.95 (*1-882577-70-1*, Pub. by Cato Inst); pap. 9.95 (*1-882577-71-X*, Pub. by Cato Inst) Natl Bk Netwk.

Life of Oscar Wilde. Hesketh Pearson. LC 78-6898. (Illus.). 399p. 1978. reprint ed. lib. bdg. 37.50 (*0-313-20491-8*, PEOW, Greenwood Pr) Greenwood.

Life of Other Days. Tim Cramer. 172p. 1991. pap. 14.95 (*0-9516036-6-3*) Dufour.

Life of Our Design: Organization & Related Strategies in Troilus & Cressida. Vernon P. Loggins. 116p. (C). 1992. lib. bdg. 38.00 (*0-8191-8510-8*) U Pr of Amer.

Life of Our Father among the Saints: Moses the Ethiopian. Neketas S. Palassis. (Illus.). 1992. pap. 3.00 (*0-913026-30-1*) St Nectarios.

Life of Our Holy Father Theodosius, Archbishop of Chernigov. 1996. pap. 0.50 (*0-89981-166-3*) Eastern Orthodox.

Life of Our Holy Mother Mary of Egypt. 3rd ed. Ed. & Tr. by Lazarus Moore from GRE. (Illus.). 48p. 1995. reprint ed. pap. 3.50 (*0-913026-31-X*) St Nectarios.

Life of Our Language: Kaqchikel Maya Maintenance, Shift & Revitalization. Susan Garzon et al. LC 97-45751. 248p. 1998. 35.00 (*0-292-72813-1*, GARLIF); pap. 17.95 (*0-292-72814-X*, GARLIP) U of Tex Pr.

Life of Our Lord. Charles Dickens. LC 99-48913. 128p. 1999. 14.95 (*0-684-86537-8*) S&S Trade.

Life of Our Lord. Charles Dickens. LC 86-28079. (Illus.). 128p. 1981. reprint ed. pap. 19.95 (*0-664-25680-5*) Westminster John Knox.

*__Life of Our Times.__ Rajeshwar Dayal. LC 98-907278. 1998. 36.00 (*81-250-1546-9*, Pub. by Orient Longman Ltd) S Asia.

*__Life of P. T. Barnum.__ P. T. Barnum. LC 99-462094. (Illus.). 2000. pap. write for info. (*0-252-06902-1*) U of Ill Pr.

Life of Pachomius: Vita Prima Graeca. Tr. by Apostolos N. Athanassakis. LC 75-37766. (Society of Biblical Literature. Texts & Translations Ser.: No. 7). 213p. reprint ed. pap. 66.10 (*0-7837-5445-0*, 204521000005) Bks Demand.

*__Life of Padre Pio: Between the Altar & the Confessional.__ Gennaro Preziuso. Tr. by Jordan Aumann from ITA. LC 99-40385. (Illus.). x, 241p. 2000. pap. 16.95 (*0-8189-0831-9*) Alba.

Life of Paisij Velyckovs'kyj. Tr. by J. M. Featherstone. LC 89-81727. (Harvard Library of Early Ukrainian Literature: Vol. 4). 208p. 1990. 18.00 (*0-916458-36-9*) Harvard Ukrainian.

Life of Paracelsus, & the Substance of His Teachings. 2nd ed. Franz Hartman. Ed. by R. I. Robb & Helena P. Blavatsky. LC 81-52063. (Secret Doctrine Reference Ser.). 240p. 1997. reprint ed. 16.00 (*0-913510-71-8*) Wizards.

Life of Passmore Edwards. R. S. Best. (C). 1989. text 45.00 (*0-907566-18-9*, Pub. by Dyllansow Truran) St Mut.

Life of Pat F. Garrett. John M. Scanland. (Wild & Woolly West Ser., No. 17). (Illus.). 1970. reprint ed. pap. 4.00 (*0-910584-76-1*) Filter.

L

Life of Patrick Hughes Mell. P. H. Mell. 1995. 17.99 (*0-87377-167-2*) GAM Pubns.

Life of Paul see Vida de San Pablo

Life of Paul: A Servant of Jesus Christ. F. B. Meyer. Ed. by Lance Wubbels. (Bible Character Ser.). 179p. 1995. pap. 9.99 (*1-883002-22-2*) Emerald WA.

Life of Paul Jones. Alexander S. Mackenzie. LC 70-160981. (Select Bibliographies Reprint Ser.). 1977. reprint ed. 23.95 (*0-8369-5849-7*) Ayer.

Life of Percy Bysshe Shelley. Thomas J. Hogg. (BCL1-PR English Literature Ser.). 585p. 1992. reprint ed. lib. bdg. 99.00 (*0-7812-7653-5*) Rprt Serv.

Life of Percy Bysshe Shelley. Thomas J. Hogg. LC 74-145088. 1971. reprint ed. 59.00 (*0-403-00754-2*) Scholarly.

Life of Percy Bysshe Shelley. Thomas Medwin. 1988. reprint ed. lib. bdg. 59.00 (*0-7812-0194-2*) Rprt Serv.

Life of Percy Bysshe Shelley. Thomas Medwin. 1971. reprint ed. 59.00 (*0-403-01100-0*) Scholarly.

Life of Percy Bysshe Shelley, 2 vols., Set. Edward Dowden. (BCL1-PR English Literature Ser.). 1992. reprint ed. lib. bdg. 150.00 (*0-7812-7650-0*) Rprt Serv.

Life of Perfection: Shama'il of Rasulullah. unabridged ed. Abidullah Ghazi. Ed. by Huda Quraishi-Ahmed & Mahlaqa Patel. LC 96-79299. (Illus.). 124p. (J). (gr. 4-6). 1997. pap. text 8.00 (*1-56316-203-2*) Iqra Intl Ed Fdtn.

***Life of Peter: Blueprints for 30 Messages Built upon God's Word.** Sherwood Smith. Ed. by Jim Eichenberger. (Solid Foundation Sermon Starters Ser.: Vol. 7). 64p. 2000. pap. 5.99 (*0-7847-1155-0*, 23015) Standard Pub.

Life of Peter: Fisherman, Disciple, Apostle. F. B. Meyer. Ed. by Lance Wubbels. (Bible Character Ser.). 192p. 1996. pap. 9.99 (*1-883002-36-2*) Emerald WA.

Life of Philip Melanchthon. Francis A. Cox. LC 83-45641. reprint ed. 72.50 (*0-404-19824-4*) AMS Pr.

Life of Philip Melanchthon. Joseph Stump. (Illus.). 272p. 1997. reprint ed. pap. 15.00 (*1-893118-10-X*) J Gerhard Inst.

Life of Picasso, 1881-1906, Vol. 1. John Richardson. (Illus.). 560p. 1996. pap. 30.00 (*0-679-76421-6*) Random.

Life of Pierre Charles l'Enfant. H. Paul Caemmerer. LC 71-87546. (Architecture & Decorative Art Ser.: Vol. 33). 1970. reprint ed. lib. bdg. 65.00 (*0-306-71381-0*) Da Capo.

Life of Plants. E. J. Corner. LC 81-11436. 330p. 1981. pap. text 14.95 (*0-226-11586-0*) U Ch Pr.

Life of Plants. M. Angels Julivert. (Invisible World Ser.). (Illus.). 32p. (J). (gr. 4 up). 1994. lib. bdg. 15.95 (*0-7910-2129-7*) Chelsea Hse.

Life of Plants. Edred J. Corner. LC 81-11436. (Illus.). 367p. reprint ed. pap. 113.80 (*0-608-08818-8*, 206945700004) Bks Demand.

Life of Poetry. Muriel Rukeyser. LC 96-22476. 256p. 1996. pap. 14.95 (*0-9638183-3-3*) Paris Pr MA.

Life of Pope Leo XIII. Francis M. Crawford. (Works of Francis Marion Crawford). 1990. reprint ed. lib. bdg. 79.00 (*0-7812-2568-X*) Rprt Serv.

Life of Porphyry, Bishop of Gaza. Mark The Deacon. 1973. pap. 2.95 (*0-89981-041-1*) Eastern Orthodox.

Life of Prayer. Sun Myung Moon. 142p. 14.95 (*0-910621-59-4*); pap. 9.95 (*0-910621-60-8*) HSA Pubns.

Life of Prayer. Edith Schaeffer. LC 92-20130. 160p. 1992. pap. 10.99 (*0-89107-649-2*) Crossway Bks.

Life of Prayer. A. B. Simpson. pap. 8.99 (*0-87509-620-4*) Chr Pubns.

Life of Prayer: Cultivating the Inner Life of the Christian Leader. Paul A. Cedar. LC 98-15084. (Swindoll Christian Leadership Library). 262p. 1998. 24.99 (*0-8499-1355-1*) Word Pub.

***Life of Prayer: Cultivating the Inner Life of the Christian Leader, Supersaver Edition.** Paul A. Cedar. (Swindoll Leadership Library). 1998. 19.97 (*0-8499-1564-3*) Tommy Nelson.

Life of Prayer: Faith & Passion for God Alone. James M. Houston. (Classics of Faith & Devotion Ser.). 288p. 1999. pap. 9.99 (*1-55661-833-6*) Bethany Hse.

Life of Prayer - A Learners' Workbook, Pt. A. 1996. pap. text 14.95 (*0-87159-992-9*, 2107, Unity Schl Relgs Studies) Unity Bks.

Life of Prayer - Instructors' Course Guide, Pt. A. 1996. ring bd. 17.95 (*0-87159-993-7*, 2106, Unity Schl Relgs Studies) Unity Bks.

Life of Prayer - Instructors' Course Guide, Pt. B. 1998. ring bd. 17.95 (*0-87159-989-9*, 2110, Unity Schl Relgs Studies) Unity Bks.

Life of Prayer - Learners' Workbook, Pt. B. (Unity School for Religious Studies). (Orig.). 1998. pap. text 14.95 (*0-87159-988-0*, 2111, Unity Schl Relgs Studies) Unity Bks.

***Life of Prayer in a World of Science: Protestants, Prayer & American Culture, 1870-1930.** Rick Ostrander. (Religion in America Ser.). 240p. 2000. text 39.95 (*0-19-513610-1*) OUP.

Life of Prince Henry of Portugal. Richard H. Major. 487p. 1967. reprint ed. 49.50 (*0-7146-1045-3*, Pub. by F Cass Pubs) Intl Spec Bk.

Life of Principled Obedience. A. N. Martin. 22p. 1992. pap. 2.00 (*0-85151-634-3*) Banner of Truth.

Life of Proclus & Commentary on the "Dedomena" of Euclid Extant Works. Marinos Of Neapolis. (Ancient Greek & Roman Writers Ser.). xvi, 107p. 1977. pap. 20.00 (*0-89005-218-2*) Ares.

Life of Proclus by Marinus. Thomas Taylor. 1986. reprint ed. pap. 8.95 (*0-916411-57-5*) Holmes Pub.

Life of Prophet Muhammad: Al-sira Al-nabawiyya. Ibn Kathir. (Life of the Prophet Muhammad Ser.). 1999. 95.00 (*1-873938-29-2*) Garnet Publishing Ltd.

Life of Prophet Muhammad-I. A. S. Hashim. (Islamic Books for Children: Bk. 4). (J). 1987. pap. 8.50 (*1-56744-125-4*) Kazi Pubns.

Life of Prophet Muhammad-II. A. S. Hashim. (Islamic Books for Children: Bk. 5). (J). 1994. pap. 10.50 (*1-56744-126-2*) Kazi Pubns.

Life of Propriety: Anne Murray Powell & Her Family, 1755-1849. Katherine M. McKenna. 352p. 1994. 49.95 (*0-7735-1175-X*, Pub. by McG-Queens Univ Pr) CUP Services.

Life of Psychic Storm Wyrt, Vol. I. Storm Wyrt. (Illus.). (Orig.). 1995. pap. 3.95 (*0-9646522-0-X*) Lightening Looks.

Life of Pythagoras. Iamblichus. Tr. by Thomas Taylor. 90p. 1998. reprint ed. pap. 16.95 (*0-7661-0217-3*) Kessinger Pub.

Life of Python: And Now for Something Completely Different. George Perry. (Illus.). 192p. (Orig.). 1984. pap. 12.95 (*0-316-70015-0*) Little.

Life of Python: The History of Something Completely Different. George Perry. (Illus.). 192p. 1995. pap. 16.95 (*1-56138-568-9*) Running Pr.

Life of R. M. M'Cheyne. Andrew A. Bonar. 1978. pap. 5.99 (*0-85151-085-X*) Banner of Truth.

Life of Radclyffe Hall. Una Vincenzo. LC 75-12350. (Homosexuality Ser.). (Illus.). 1975. reprint ed. 15.95 (*0-405-07355-0*) Ayer.

Life of Ramakrishna. Romain Rolland. 310p. 1928. 4.95 (*81-85301-44-1*, Pub. by Advaita Ashrama) Vedanta Pr.

Life of Ranchoddas Bhavan Lotvala. Indulal K. Yajnik. (Great Men of India Ser.). 1980. lib. bdg. 69.95 (*0-8490-3080-3*) Gordon Pr.

Life of Rear-Admiral John Paul Jones, Chevalier of the Military Order of Merit: Compiled from His Original Journals & Correspondence. John P. Jones. (American Biography Ser.). 399p. 1991. reprint ed. lib. bdg. 79.00 (*0-7812-8224-1*) Rprt Serv.

***Life of Reason.** George Santayana. LC 98-15125. (Great Books in Philosophy). (Illus.). 512p. 1998. pap. 9.95 (*1-57392-210-2*) Prometheus Bks.

Life of Reason: Hobbes, Locke, Bolingbroke. David G. James. LC 76-38378. (Biography Index Reprint Ser. - English Augustans: Vol. 1). 1977. reprint ed. 20.95 (*0-8369-8122-7*) Ayer.

***Life of Reilly: Three Decades Under the Blimp: The Best of Sports Illustrated's Rick Reilly.** Rick Reilly. 224p. 2000. 22.95 (*1-892129-88-4*) Total Sprts.

Life of Religion: A Marquette University Symposium on the Nature of Religious Belief. Ed. by Stanley M. Harrison & Richard C. Taylor. 124p. (Orig.). (C). 1986. pap. text 17.50 (*0-8191-5559-4*); lib. bdg. 40.50 (*0-8191-5558-6*) U Pr of Amer.

Life of Rev. Orange Scott. Lucius C. Matlack. LC 70-138343. (Black Heritage Library Collection). 1977. 30.95 (*0-8369-8735-7*) Ayer.

Life of Rev. Orange Scott. Orange Scott. (American Biography Ser.). 307p. 1991. reprint ed. lib. bdg. 79.00 (*0-7812-8347-7*) Rprt Serv.

Life of Richard F. Trevellick, the Labor Orator, or the Harbinger of the Eight-Hour System. Obediah Hicks. LC 73-156418. (American Labor Ser., No. 2). 1977. reprint ed. 23.95 (*0-405-02926-8*) Ayer.

Life of Richard Kane: Britain's First Lieutenant-Governor of Minorca. Bruce Laurie. LC 92-54650. 1994. 42.50 (*0-8386-3501-6*) Fairleigh Dickinson.

Life of Richard Owen, 2 vols. Richard S. Owen. LC 72-1697. (Illus.). reprint ed. 124.50 (*0-404-07995-4*) AMS Pr.

Life of Richard Rolle. Frances M. Comper. 1988. reprint ed. lib. bdg. 59.00 (*0-7812-0348-1*) Rprt Serv.

Life of Richard Steele, 2 vols. G. A. Aitken. LC 68-24893. (English Biography Ser.: No. 31). (Illus.). 1968. reprint ed. lib. bdg. 150.00 (*0-8383-0152-5*) M S G Haskell Hse.

Life of Richard Steele, 2 vols., Set. George A. Aitken. (BCL1-PR English Literature Ser.). 1992. reprint ed. lib. bdg. 150.00 (*0-7812-7407-9*) Rprt Serv.

***Life of Richard Strauss.** Bryan Gilliam. LC 98-47947. (Musical Lives Ser.). (Illus.). 202p. (C). 1999. write for info. (*0-521-57019-0*); pap. 14.95 (*0-521-57895-7*) Cambridge U Pr.

Life of Richard Wagner, 4 vols. Ernest Newman. reprint ed. lib. bdg. 236.00 (*0-685-14824-6*) Rprt Serv.

Life of Richard Wagner, Vol. 1. Ernest Newman. LC 76-22682. reprint ed. pap. 148.00 (*0-608-15758-9*, 2031699) Bks Demand.

Life of Richard Wagner: Being an Authorized English Version of das Leben Richard Wagner, 6 vols., 1. William A. Ellis & Carl F. Glasenapp. (Music Reprint Ser.). 1977. reprint ed. lib. bdg. 52.50 (*0-306-70881-7*) Da Capo.

Life of Richard Wagner: Being an Authorized English Version of das Leben Richard Wagner, 6 vols., 2. William A. Ellis & Carl F. Glasenapp. (Music Reprint Ser.). 1977. reprint ed. lib. bdg. 52.50 (*0-306-70882-5*) Da Capo.

Life of Richard Wagner: Being an Authorized English Version of das Leben Richard Wagner, 6 vols., 3. William A. Ellis & Carl F. Glasenapp. (Music Reprint Ser.). 1977. reprint ed. lib. bdg. 52.50 (*0-306-70883-3*) Da Capo.

Life of Richard Wagner: Being an Authorized English Version of das Leben Richard Wagner, 6 vols., 4. William A. Ellis & Carl F. Glasenapp. (Music Reprint Ser.). 1977. reprint ed. lib. bdg. 52.50 (*0-306-70884-1*) Da Capo.

Life of Richard Wagner: Being an Authorized English Version of das Leben Richard Wagner, 6 vols., 5. William A. Ellis & Carl F. Glasenapp. (Music Reprint Ser.). 1977. reprint ed. lib. bdg. 52.50 (*0-306-70885-X*) Da Capo.

Life of Richard Wagner: Being an Authorized English Version of das Leben Richard Wagner, 6 vols., 6. William A. Ellis & Carl F. Glasenapp. (Music Reprint Ser.). 1977. reprint ed. lib. bdg. 52.50 (*0-306-70886-8*) Da Capo.

Life of Richard Wagner: Being an Authorized English Version of das Leben Richard Wagner, 6 vols., Set. William A. Ellis & Carl F. Glasenapp. (Music Reprint Ser.). 1977. reprint ed. lib. bdg. 315.00 (*0-306-70887-6*) Da Capo.

Life of Riches: Your Own Personal Success Manual. Joseph Chirra. LC 93-81278. 112p. (Orig.). 1994. pap. 13.95 (*0-9639958-7-1*) Mervilla.

Life of Robert Browning. William Sharp. LC 77-165809. (Select Bibliographies Reprint Ser.). 1977. reprint ed. 20.95 (*0-8369-5963-9*) Ayer.

Life of Robert Browning: A Critical Biography. Clyde DiRyals. (Critical Biographies Ser.). (Illus.). 304p. 1996. pap. 25.95 (*0-631-20093-2*) Blackwell Pubs.

Life of Robert Burns. J. Veitch. (C). 1988. pap. 50.00 (*0-907526-19-5*, Pub. by Alloway Pub) St Mut.

Life of Robert Burns. James C. Higgins. LC 73-144513. (Illus.). reprint ed. 45.00 (*0-404-08515-6*) AMS Pr.

Life of Robert Burns. John G. Lockhart. Ed. by William S. Douglas. LC 70-144515. reprint ed. 52.50 (*0-404-08517-2*) AMS Pr.

Life of Robert Burns. John Macintosh. LC 78-144517. (Illus.). reprint ed. 37.50 (*0-404-08519-9*) AMS Pr.

Life of Robert Hall: Indian Fighter & Veteran of Three Great Wars: Also Sketch of Big Foot Wallace. Brazos. LC 92-28058. (Illus.). 160p. 1992. 24.95 (*0-938349-89-9*) State House Pr.

Life of Robert Hall: Indian Fighter & Veteran of Three Great Wars: Also Sketch of Big Foot Wallace. Brazos. LC 92-28058. (Illus.). 160p. 1992. pap. 14.95 (*0-938349-90-2*) State House Pr.

Life of Robert Hall: Indian Fighter & Veteran of Three Great Wars: Also Sketch of Big Foot Wallace. limited ed. Brazos. LC 92-28058. (Illus.). 160p. 1992. 60.00 (*0-938349-91-0*) State House Pr.

Life of Robert Hare: An American Chemist, 1781-1858. Edgar F. Smith. Ed. by I. Bernard Cohen. LC 79-7995. (Three Centuries of Science in America Ser.). (Illus.). 1980. reprint ed. lib. bdg. 48.95 (*0-405-12580-1*) Ayer.

Life of Robert Lewis Dabney. Thomas C. Johnson. 1977. 27.99 (*0-85151-253-4*) Banner of Truth.

Life of Robert Louis Stevenson, 2 vols., Set. Graham Balfour. (BCL1-PR English Literature Ser.). 1992. reprint ed. lib. bdg. 150.00 (*0-7812-7670-5*) Rprt Serv.

Life of Robert Louis Stevenson, 2 vols., Set. Graham Balfour. LC 01-25406. 1968. reprint ed. 29.00 (*0-403-00143-9*) Scholarly.

Life of Robert Owen: With Selections from His Writings & Correspondence, 2 vols. i. Robert Owen. LC 66-21690. 1977. 75.00 (*0-678-00271-1*) Kelley.

Life of Robert Schumann Told in His Letters, 2 vols. Robert Schumann. 1990. reprint ed. lib. bdg. 140.00 (*0-685-35223-4*) Rprt Serv.

Life of Robert Sidney. Millicent V. Hay. LC 82-49311. 256p. 1984. 45.00 (*0-918016-70-3*) Folger Bks.

Life of Robert Watts. Rodgers. 1991. pap. 2.50 (*1-871676-15-0*, Pub. by Christian Focus) Spring Arbor Dist.

Life of Roger Brooke Taney: Chief Justice of the United States Supreme Court. Bernard C. Steiner. 553p. 1997. reprint ed. 120.00 (*1-56169-304-9*) Gaunt.

Life of Roger Brooke Taney, Chief Justice of the United States Supreme Court. Bernard C. Steiner. 1971. reprint ed. lib. bdg. 75.00 (*0-8371-4344-6*, STRT, Greenwood Pr) Greenwood.

Life of Roscoe Pound. Paul Sayre. (Illus.). 412p. 1981. reprint ed. 45.00 (*0-8377-1120-7*, Rothman) W S Hein.

Life of Rossini. Stendhal, pseud. Tr. & Anno. by Richard N. Coe. 600p. 1982. pap. 13.95 (*0-7145-0632-X*) Riverrun NY.

Life of Rossini. Stendhal, pseud. 566p. reprint ed. lib. bdg. 69.00 (*0-685-14796-7*) Rprt Serv.

Life of Rt. Rev. Joseph Rosati, D. M., First Bishop of St. Louis, 1789-1843. Frederick J. Easterly. LC 73-3587. (Catholic University of America. Studies in Romance Languages & Literatures: No. 33). reprint ed. 38.00 (*0-404-57783-0*) AMS Pr.

Life of Rutherford Birchard Hayes, 2 vols. Charles R. Williams. LC 79-87678. (American Scene Ser.). 1971. reprint ed. lib. bdg. 95.00 (*0-306-71714-X*) Da Capo.

Life of Rutherford Birchard Hayes, 2 vols., Set. Charles R. Williams. (History - United States Ser.). 1992. reprint ed. lib. bdg. 150.00 (*0-7812-6207-0*) Rprt Serv.

Life of Rutherford Birchard Hayes, 2 vols., Set. Charles R. Williams. 1993. reprint ed. lib. bdg. 150.00 (*0-7812-5418-3*) Rprt Serv.

Life of S. Satyamurti. P. G. Sundararajan. (C). 1988. 17.50 (*81-7003-090-0*, Pub. by S Asia Pubs) S Asia.

Life of Saint Augustine. Possidius. Ed. by John E. Rotelle. Tr. by Matthew O'Connell from LAT. LC 88-71357. (Augustinian Ser.). (Illus.). 144p. 1988. pap. 7.95 (*0-941491-19-6*) Augustinian Pr.

Life of Saint Birgitta of Sweden. Birger Gregersson & Thomas Gascoigne. Tr. by Julia B. Holloway. (Translation Ser.). 64p. 1991. pap. 10.00 (*0-920669-17-4*, Pub. by Peregrina Pubng) Cistercian Pubns.

Life of St. Columba. William Muir. 1997. pap. 4.95 (*0-89979-095-X*) British Am Bks.

Life of Saint Cuthbert. Tr. by W. Forbes-Leith from LAT. 1986. reprint ed. 8.50 (*0-89981-043-8*) Eastern Orthodox.

Life of Saint Dominic Savio. 3rd ed. St. John Bosco. Tr. by Paul Aronica from ITA.Tr. of St. Vita Del Giovanetto Savio Domenico. 177p. (Orig.). (YA). 1996. pap. 8.00 (*0-89944-375-3*) Salesiana Pubs.

Life of Saint Francis of Assisi. Ariel Books Staff. LC 97-164228. 128p. 1996. 3.95 (*0-8362-1012-3*, Arie Bks) Andrews & McMeel.

Life of Saint George of Choziba & The Miracles of the Holy Mother of God at Choziba. Antony of Choziba. Tr. by Tim Vivian & Apostolos N. Athnassakis from GRE. 130p. 1994. 64.95 (*1-883255-59-7*) Intl Scholars.

Life of Saint George of Choziba & The Miracles of the Holy Mother of God at Choziba. Tr. by Tim Vivian & Apostolos N. Athnassakis from GRE. 130p. 1994. pap. 34.95 (*1-883255-58-9*) Intl Scholars.

Life of Saint Hilarion. Jerome. 1976. pap. 1.95 (*0-89981-047-0*) Eastern Orthodox.

Life of Saint Joseph. Maria Cecilia Baij. 416p. 1997. pap. 10.00 (*1-890137-01-4*) One Hund-One Fnd.

Life of St. Kiaran the Elder of Seir. D. B. Mulcahy. 1998. pap. 3.50 (*0-89979-107-7*) British Am Bks.

Life of St. Margaret Mary Alacoque, 1647-1690. Emile Bougaud. LC 86-80329. (Illus.). 388p. 1994. reprint ed. pap. 13.50 (*0-89555-297-3*) TAN Bks Pubs.

Life of Saint Martin of Tours. Sulpicius Severus. 1992. pap. 3.95 (*0-89981-050-0*) Eastern Orthodox.

Life of Saint Mary Magdalene & of Her Sister Saint Martha. Rhabanus Maurus. Tr. by David Mycoff. (Cistercian Studies: No. 108). 166p. 1989. 31.95 (*0-87907-608-9*); pap. 15.95 (*0-87907-908-8*) Cistercian Pubns.

***Life of Saint Nicholas.** R. O. Blechman. (Illus.). 120p. 2000. reprint ed. text 19.00 (*0-7881-9052-0*) DIANE Pub.

Life of St. Nicholas Vol. 3: A Cloud of Witnesses. Nina S. Seco. (Illus.). (Orig.). (J). (gr. k-3). 1993. pap. 6.00 (*0-913026-36-0*) St Nectarios.

Life of Saint Nicholas of Sion. Ihor Sevcenko & Nancy P. Sevcenko. (Archbishop Iakovos Library of Ecclesiastical & Historical Sources: Vol. 10). (ENG, GEC & GRE., Illus.). 157p. (C). 1984. 9.95 (*0-917653-02-5*); pap. 6.95 (*0-917653-03-3*, Pub. by Hellenic Coll Pr) BookWorld.

Life of Saint Nikon Metanoeite. Denis F. Sullivan. Ed. by Nomikos M. Vaporis. (Archbishop Iakovos Library of Ecclesiastical & Historical Sources: No. 14). (GER.). 1987. 6.95 (*0-917653-29-7*, Pub. by Hellenic Coll Pr); pap. 6.95 (*0-917653-30-0*, Pub. by Hellenic Coll Pr) BookWorld.

Life of St. Nina. Nina S. Seco. (Cloud of Witnesses Ser.). (Illus.). (Orig.). (J). (ps-1). 1991. pap. 6.00 (*0-913026-28-X*) St Nectarios.

Life of St. Oswin, King & Martyr 651 A. D. 1998. pap. 3.95 (*0-89979-109-3*) British Am Bks.

Life of Saint Patrick. John B. Bury. 432p. 1998. pap. 12.95 (*0-486-40037-9*) Dover.

Life of St. Patrick: His Place in History. John B. Bury. LC 79-175691. (Select Bibliographies Reprint Ser.). 1977. reprint ed. 26.95 (*0-8369-6606-6*) Ayer.

Life of St. Paul. James Stalker. 185p. 1998. reprint ed. pap. 17.95 (*0-7661-0655-1*) Kessinger Pub.

***Life of St. Paul the First Hermit: Also Called St. Paul of Thebes.** Saint Jerome. 1999. pap. 2.50 (*0-89981-225-2*) Eastern Orthodox.

Life of St. Sava. rev. ed. Nicholai Velimirovich. Ed. by Lydia W. Kesich. LC 88-24021. 161p. 1989. reprint ed. pap. 11.95 (*0-88141-065-9*) St Vladimirs.

Life of Saint Seraphim of Sarov. 275p. 1992. pap. write for info. (*1-880364-07-7*) New Sarov.

Life of Saint Seraphim Wonderworker of Sarov. Maria Naumenko.Tr. of Zhitie Prepodobnovo Seraphima, Sarovskovo Chudotvortsa. (Illus.). 22p. (Orig.). (J). (gr. 5-10). 1992. pap. 3.00 (*0-88465-049-9*) Holy Trinity.

Life of Saint Seraphim Wonderworker of Sarov: (Zhitie Prepodobnovo Serpahima, Sarovskovo Chudotvortsa) Maria Naumenko. (RUS., Illus.). 22p. (Orig.). (J). (gr. 5-10). 1992. pap. 3.00 (*0-88465-052-9*) Holy Trinity.

Life of Saint Severin & Other Minor Works. Eugippius. Tr. by Ludwig Bisler & Ludmilla Krestan. LC 65-12908. (Fathers of the Church Ser.: Vol. 55). 139p. 1965. 16.95 (*0-8132-0055-5*) Cath U Pr.

Life of St. Simon Stylites. Richard Challoner. 1991. pap. text 1.95 (*0-89981-051-9*) Eastern Orthodox.

Life of St. Teresa of Avila. Elizabeth Hamilton. 200p. 1994. reprint ed. mass mkt. 7.95 (*0-940147-32-7*) Source Bks CA.

Life of Saint Teresa of Avila by Herself. Intro. by John M. Cohen. 320p. 1988. pap. 10.95 (*0-14-044073-9*, Penguin Classics) Viking Penguin.

Life of Saint Wilfrid: Edmer's Vita Sanci Wilfridi. Ed. by Bernard J. Muir & Andrew J. Turner. (Exeter Medieval Texts & Studies). 304p. 1998. text 95.00 (*0-85989-597-1*) Univ Exeter Pr.

Life of Saladin. Beha ed-Din. 1972. lib. bdg. 250.00 (*0-87968-480-1*) Krishna Pr.

Life of Saladin. Beha Ed-Din. 420p. 1985. 29.00 (*1-56744-422-9*) Kazi Pubns.

Life of Sam Houston: The Only Authentic Memoir of Him Ever Published. Charles E. Lester. LC 70-38360. (Select Bibliographies Reprint Ser.). 1977. reprint ed. 25.95 (*0-8369-6777-1*) Ayer.

Life of Samson (Judges 13-16) A Critical-Literary Analysis. Yair Zakovitch. (HEB.). 256p. 1982. text 14.00 (*965-223-411-7*, Pub. by Magnes Pr) Eisenbrauns.

Life of Samuel F. B. Morse, L. L. D: Inventor of the Electro-Magnetic Recording Telegraph. Samuel I. Prime. LC 74-4691. (Telecommunications Ser.). (Illus.). 816p. 1974. reprint ed. 60.95 (*0-405-06054-8*) Ayer.

Life of Samuel Johnson. James Boswell. (Modern Library College Editions). 559p. (C). 1964. pap. 8.44 (*0-07-553645-5*, T62) McGraw.

Life of Samuel Johnson: A Critical Biography. Robert De Maria. LC 92-23302. (Blackwell Critical Biographies Ser.: Vol. 2). 354p. 1994. pap. 25.95 (*1-55786-664-3*) Blackwell Pubs.

An Asterisk (*) at the beginning of an entry indicates that the title is appearing for the first time.

Life of Samuel Johnson with Critical Observations on His Work. 3rd ed. Robert Anderson. 678p. 1973. reprint ed. lib. bdg. 150.00 (*3-487-04534-6*) G Olms Pubs.

Life of Samuel of Kalamun. Anthony Alcock. 1983. pap. 39.95 (*0-85668-219-5*, Pub. by Aris & Phillips) David Brown.

Life of Samuel Taylor Coleridge: A Critical Biography. Rosemary Ashton. Ed. by Claude Rawson. LC 95-2820. (Critical Biographies Ser.: Vol. 7). (Illus.). 480p. (C). 1996. 60.95 (*0-631-18746-4*) Blackwell Pubs.

Life of Samuel Taylor Coleridge: A Critical Biography. Rosemary Ashton. Ed. by Claude Rawson. LC 95-2820. (Critical Biographies Ser.: Vol. 7). (Illus.). 480p. (C). 1997. pap. 26.95 (*0-631-20754-6*) Blackwell Pubs.

Life of Sariputta. Nyanaponika Thera. 112p. 1987. 3.00 (*955-24-0015-5*, Pub. by Buddhist Pub Soc) Vipassana Res Pubns.

***Life of Schubert.** Christopher Gibbs. (Musical Lives Ser.). (Illus.). 225p. (C). 2000. 44.95 (*0-521-59426-X*); pap. 14.95 (*0-521-59512-6*) Cambridge U Pr.

Life of Science: Essays in the History of Civilization. George Sarton. LC 70-167410. (Essay Index Reprint Ser.). 1977. reprint ed. 18.95 (*0-8369-2472-X*) Ayer.

Life of Search. D. Elton Trueblood. LC 96-4142. 122p. 1996. 10.50 (*0-944350-36-4*) Friends United.

***Life of Selina Campbell: A Fellow Soldier in the Cause of Restoration.** Loretta M. Long. 2000. 34.95 (*0-8173-1059-2*) U of Ala Pr.

Life of Service: William Augustus Newell. Lloyd R. Applegate. (Illus.). (Orig.). 1994. pap. 10.00 (*0-941965-08-2*) Ocean Cnty Hist.

Life of Shah Waliyullah. G. N. Jalbani. 92p. (Orig.). 1985. pap. 7.50 (*1-56744-324-9*) Kazi Pubns.

Life of Shinram Shonin: The Journey of Self Acceptance. rev. ed. Alfred Bloom. (Institute of Buddhist Studies). 80p. 1994. pap. 6.95 (*0-940583-00-3*) Inst Buddhst Studies Pr.

Life of Silas Doty, 1800-1876: A Forgotten Autobiography; the Most Noted Thief & Daring Burglar of His Time. Silas Doty. (American Biography Ser.). 288p. 1991. reprint ed. lib. bdg. 69.00 (*0-7812-8109-1*) Rprt Serv.

Life of Silas Talbot. Henry T. Tuckerman. (Notable American Authors). 1999. reprint ed. lib. bdg. 125.00 (*0-7812-9842-3*) Rprt Serv.

Life of Simon Peter. Lester Sumrall. 70p. (Orig.). (C). 1986. pap. text 10.00 (*0-937580-81-3*) Sumrall Pubng.

***Life of Sir Aglovale de Galis.** Clemence Housman. 320p. 2000. pap. 14.95 (*1-928999-08-5*) Green Knight.

Life of Sir Arthur Conan Doyle. John Dickson Carr. 1976. 27.95 (*0-89109-973-5*) Amereon Ltd.

Life of Sir Arthur Conan Doyle. John Dickson Carr. (Illus.). 310p. 1987. pap. 8.95 (*0-88184-372-5*) Carroll & Graf.

Life of Sir Edward Clarke. Derek Walker-Smith & Edward Clarke. LC 79-8083. reprint ed. 32.50 (*0-404-18392-1*) AMS Pr.

Life of Sir Edwin Lutyens. Christopher Hussey. (Illus.). 628p. 1989. 79.50 (*0-907462-59-6*) Antique Collect.

Life of Sir Humphrey Gilbert, England's First Empire Builder. William G. Gosling. LC 76-109737. 1970. reprint ed. lib. bdg. 69.50 (*0-8371-4227-X*, GOHG, Greenwood Pr) Greenwood.

Life of Sir Joseph Banks. Edward Smith. LC 74-26292. (History, Philosophy & Sociology of Science Ser.). (Illus.). 1975. reprint ed. 33.95 (*0-405-06618-X*) Ayer.

Life of Sir Robert Jones. Frederick Watson. Ed. by William R. Phillips & Janet Rosenberg. LC 79-6928. (Physically Handicapped in Society Ser.). (Illus.). 1980. reprint ed. lib. bdg. 31.95 (*0-405-13135-6*) Ayer.

Life of Sir Thomas More. William Roper. (Illus.). 125p. 1983. pap. 9.95 (*0-87243-118-5*) Templegate.

Life of Sir Thomas More. William Roper. write for info. Yale U Pr.

Life of Sir Walter Scott. D. Carswell. LC 70-176490. (English Biography Ser.: No. 31). 1971. lib. bdg. 75.00 (*0-8383-1365-5*) M S G Haskell Hse.

Life of Sir Walter Scott. Stephen L. Gwynn. 1977. 19.95 (*0-8369-6939-1*, 7820) Ayer.

Life of Sir Walter Scott. LeGrys G. Norgate. LC 74-30271. (Sir Walter Scott Ser.: No. 73). 1974. lib. bdg. 75.00 (*0-8383-1927-0*) M S G Haskell Hse.

Life of Sir Walter Scott. S. Wright. LC 70-176493. (English Literature Ser.: No. 33). 1971. lib. bdg. 75.00 (*0-8383-1361-2*) M S G Haskell Hse.

Life of Sir Walter Scott, 10 vols. John G. Lockhart. LC 73-144426. (Illus.). 7536p. 1983. reprint ed. 950.00 (*0-404-07700-5*) AMS Pr.

Life of Sir William Phips. Cotton Mather. LC 75-137260. reprint ed. 31.50 (*0-404-04249-X*) AMS Pr.

Life of Sir William Phips. Cotton Mather. (BCL1 - United States Local History Ser.). 208p. 1991. reprint ed. lib. bdg. 79.00 (*0-7812-6266-6*) Rprt Serv.

Life of Sir William Rowan Hamilton, 3 vols. Robert P. Graves. LC 74-26266. (History, Philosophy & Sociology of Science Ser.). 1975. reprint ed. 173.95 (*0-405-06594-9*) Ayer.

Life of Sister St. Rita of Cascia see St. Rita of Cascia: Saint of the Impossible & Model of Maidens, Wives, Mothers, Widows, & Nuns

***Life of Sitting Bull: History of the Indian War of 1890-91.** W. Fletcher Johnson. (Illus.). 544p. 2000. write for info. (*1-58218-197-7*); write for info. (*1-58218-198-5*) Digital Scanning.

Life of Smith Wigglesworth: One Man, One Holy Passion. Jack Hywell-Davies. 171p. (Orig.). 1988. pap. 9.99 (*0-89283-387-4*, Vine Bks) Servant.

Life of Spirit, Vol. I. Robert R. Leichtman & Carl Japikse. (Illus.). 216p. (Orig.). 1986. pap. 8.95 (*0-89804-132-5*) Ariel GA.

Life of Spirit, Vol. II. Robert R. Leichtman & Carl Japikse. (Illus.). 275p. (Orig.). 1987. pap. 8.95 (*0-89804-133-3*) Ariel GA.

Life of Spirit, Vol. III. Robert R. Leichtman & Carl Japikse. (Illus.). 200p. (Orig.). 1988. pap. 8.95 (*0-89804-134-1*) Ariel GA.

Life of Sri Aurobindo. 4th ed. A. B. Purani. 440p. 1987. pap. 15.00 (*81-7058-080-3*, Pub. by SAA) E-W Cultural Ctr.

Life of Sri Ramakrishna. Compiled by Advaita Ashrama Staff. 472p. 1940. pap. 8.95 (*81-7505-070-5*, Pub. by Advaita Ashrama) Vedanta Pr.

Life of Sri Ramuja. Swami Ramakrisnananda. 1979. pap. 5.95 (*81-7120-433-3*) Vedanta Pr.

Life of St. Alexis, the Man of God. 1985. pap. 1.50 (*0-317-30438-0*) Holy Trinity.

Life of St. Alexius see Adam Davy's Five Dreams about Edward 2nd

Life of St. Andrew the Fool, 2 vols., Set. Ed. by Lennart Ryden. LC 96-164247. (Studia Byzantina Upsaliensia Ser.: No. 4, Nos. 1-2). 741p. 1995. pap. 137.50 (*91-554-3651-X*, Pub. by Uppsala Univ Acta Univ Uppsaliensis) Coronet Bks.

Life of St. Anna of Novgorod. Tr. by Isaac E. Lambertsen from RUS. 16p. (Orig.). 1983. pap. 1.00 (*0-912927-06-2*, X006) St John Kronstadt.

Life of St. Anthony Mary Claret. Fanchon Royer. LC 85-52248. 302p. (Orig.). 1992. reprint ed. pap. 15.00 (*0-89555-288-4*) TAN Bks Pubs.

Life of St. Anthony the Great see Zhitie Prepodobnago Antonija Velikago

Life of St. Anthony the Great. Athanasius. 1991. pap. 3.95 (*0-89981-042-X*) Eastern Orthodox.

Life of St. Benedict. M. Allibert. LC 70-168505. (Black Heritage Library Collection). 1977. reprint ed. 25.95 (*0-8369-8859-0*) Ayer.

Life of St. Benedict: Text & Commentary. Tr. by Hilary Costello & Eoin De-Bhaldraithe. LC 93-420. 186p. 1993. pap. 19.95 (*0-932506-77-1*) St Bedes Pubns.

Life of St. Benedict (480-547) Pope St. Gregory the Great. 71p. 1995. pap. 2.00 (*0-89555-512-3*) TAN Bks Pubs.

Life of St. Claude de la Colombiere: Spiritual Director of St. Margaret Mary Alacoque. rev. ed. Ruth A. LaVigne. 127p. 1992. pap. 7.95 (*0-8198-4467-5*) Pauline Bks.

Life of St. Columba. Richard Sharpe. (Illus.). 462p. 1995. pap. 13.95 (*0-14-044462-9*, Penguin Classics) Viking Penguin.

Life of St. Cyprian. Pontus. 1987. pap. 2.50 (*0-89981-046-2*) Eastern Orthodox.

Life of St. Dominic. Augustus T. Drane. LC 88-50268. 1988. reprint ed. pap. 12.00 (*0-89555-336-8*) TAN Bks Pubs.

Life of St. Edmund by Matthew Paris. Matthew Paris. 1997. pap. text 21.95 (*0-7509-1129-8*, Pub. by Sutton Pub Ltd) Intl Pubs Mktg.

Life of St. Edward the Confessor. Aelred Rievaulx. Tr. by Jerome Bertram. (Illus.). 140p. 1997. pap. 16.95 (*1-901157-75-X*) St Austin.

Life of St. Ephraem the Syrian. 1991. pap. 0.50 (*0-89981-218-X*) Eastern Orthodox.

Life of St. Ethelwold. Wulfstan. Ed. by Michael Lapidge & M. Winterbottom. (Oxford Medieval Texts Ser.). 294p. 1991. text 95.00 (*0-19-822266-1*) OUP.

Life of St. Finan. Tr. by Robert A. Macalister from IRI. 1987. reprint ed. pap. 1.95 (*0-89979-035-6*) British Am Bks.

Life of St. Francis of Assisi. LC 88-50746. 187p. 1988. reprint ed. pap. 10.00 (*0-89555-343-0*) TAN Bks Pubs.

Life of St. Francis of Assisi. E. E. Reynolds. 128p. 1994. reprint ed. mass mkt. 6.95 (*0-940147-28-9*) Source Bks CA.

Life of St. Fursa. Ed. & Tr. by Whitley Stokes from IRI. 1987. pap. 7.50 (*0-89979-034-8*) British Am Bks.

Life of St. George by Alexander Barclay. W. Nelson. (EETS Original Ser.: Vol. 230). 1963. reprint ed. 30.00 (*0-19-722230-7*, Pub. by EETS) Boydell & Brewer.

Life of St. Ignatus of Loyola. S. J. Genelli. LC 88-50847. 398p. 1988. reprint ed. pap. 16.50 (*0-89555-345-7*) TAN Bks Pubs.

Life of St. John the Almsgiver. 1990. pap. 1.25 (*0-89981-048-9*) Eastern Orthodox.

Life of St. Katharine of Alexandria. John Capgrave. Ed. by C. Horstmann. (EETS, OS Ser.: No. 100). 1969. reprint ed. 72.00 (*0-527-00102-3*) Periodicals Srv.

Life of St. Macrina. Gregory. 1974. reprint ed. pap. 2.95 (*0-89981-049-7*) Eastern Orthodox.

Life of St. Mary of Egypt. 2nd ed. Tr. by Mother Katherine & Mother Thekla. (Library of Orthodox Thinking). 39p. 1997. pap. 4.00 (*0-920669-25-5*, Pub. by Peregrina Pubng) Cistercian Pubns.

Life of St. Maximus the Confessor. Ed. by Holy Transfiguration Monastery Staff. Tr. by Christopher Birchall from GRE. LC 82-81455. (Illus.). 73p. (Orig.). 1982. pap. 8.00 (*0-913026-52-2*) St Nectarios.

Life of St. Monica see St. Monica (c. 332-387): Model of Christian Mothers

Life of St. Moses the Black. Palladius. 1990. pap. 1.00 (*0-89981-113-2*) Eastern Orthodox.

Life of St. Nicholas. Sebastian Dabovich. 1990. pap. 0.50 (*0-89981-085-3*) Eastern Orthodox.

Life of St. Norbert by John Capgrave, O. E. S. A. (1393-1464) John Capgrave. Ed. by Cyril L. Smetana. (Illus.). x, 179p. pap. text 24.57 (*0-88844-040-5*) Brill Academic Pubs.

Life of Stanley D. Porteus. Elizabeth D. Porteus. 10.95 (*0-914916-86-6*) Ku Paa.

Life of Stanley Marean, Reclamationist. Intro. by Mary E. Glass. 54p. 1966. lib. bdg. 25.50 (*1-56475-025-6*); fiche. write for info. (*1-56475-026-4*) U NV Oral Hist.

Life of Stefan Banach. Roman Kaluza. Ed. & Tr. by Wojbor Woyczynski & Ann S. Kostant. LC 95-25811. (Illus.). 137p. 1996. 24.50 (*0-8176-3772-9*) Birkhauser.

Life of Stephen F. Austin, Founder of Texas, 1793-1836: A Chapter in the Westward Movement of the Anglo-American People. Eugene C. Barker. LC 70-111473. (BCL Ser. I). reprint ed. 42.50 (*0-404-00653-1*) AMS Pr.

Life of Stephen F. Austin, Founder of Texas, 1793-1836: A Chapter in the Westward Movement of the Anglo-American People. Eugene C. Barker. LC 68-27723. (American Scene Ser.). (Illus.). 1968. reprint ed. 65.00 (*0-306-71153-2*) Da Capo.

Life of Stephen F. Austin, Founder of Texas, 1793-1836: A Chapter in the Westward Movement of the Anglo-American People. Eugene C. Barker. (BCL1 - United States Local History Ser.). 551p. 1991. reprint ed. lib. bdg. 99.00 (*0-7812-6307-7*) Rprt Serv.

Life of Stephen F. Austin, Founder of Texas, 1793-1836: A Chapter in the Westward Movement of the Anglo-American People. Eugene C. Barker. 1993. reprint ed. lib. bdg. 75.00 (*0-7812-5914-2*) Rprt Serv.

***Life of Stephen of Mar Sabas.** J. C. Lamoreaux. (Corpus Scriptorum Christianorum Orientalium Ser.). xii,137p. 1999. 57.00 (*90-429-0691-X*, Pub. by Peeters Pub) Bks Intl VA.

***Life of Stephen of Mar Sabas.** John C. Lamoreaux. LC 99-510754. (Corpus Scriptorum Christianorum Orientalium Ser.). xiv,153p. 1999. write for info. (*90-429-0690-1*, Pub. by Peeters Pub) Bks Intl VA.

Life of Stid. Don Asussen. (Illus.). (Orig.). 1986. pap. 5.95 (*0-937217-02-6*) Fifth Estate.

Life of Stonewall Jackson: From Official Papers, Contemporary Narratives, & Personal Acquaintance. John E. Cooke. LC 76-179511. (Select Bibliographies Reprint Ser.). 1977. reprint ed. 25.95 (*0-8369-6640-6*) Ayer.

Life of Sts. Cyprian & Justina. 1989. pap. 1.00 (*0-89981-213-9*) Eastern Orthodox.

Life of Swami Vivekananda, Vol. 1. rev. ed. Eastern & Western Disciples of Vivekananda Staff. 629p. 1980. 12.95 (*81-7505-043-8*) Vedanta Pr.

Life of Swami Vivekananda, Vol. 2. rev. ed. Eastern & Western Disciples of Vivekananda Staff. 1979. 12.95 (*81-7505-044-6*) Vedanta Pr.

***Life of Tecumseh an His Brother the Prophet: A History of the Shawnee.** Benjamin Drake. LC 99-91264. 236p. 1999. reprint ed. pap. text 19.95 (*1-889037-21-4*) Wennawoods.

Life of Tecumseh & His Brother . . . With an Historical Sketch of the Shawanoe Indians. Benjamin Drake. (Notable American Authors Ser.). 1992. reprint ed. lib. bdg. 75.00 (*0-7812-2686-4*) Rprt Serv.

Life of Tecumseh & of His Brother the Prophet: With a Historical Sketch of the Shawanoe Indians. Benjamin Drake. LC 78-90173. (Mass Violence in America Ser.). 1977. reprint ed. 24.95 (*0-405-01307-8*) Ayer.

Life of Teresa of Jesus. E. Allison Peers. 400p. 1991. pap. 14.95 (*0-385-01109-1*, Image Bks) Doubleday.

Life of Texas Jack: Eight Years a Criminal - 41 Years Trusting in God. Nathanial Reed. (American Biography Ser.). 66p. 1991. reprint ed. lib. bdg. 59.00 (*0-7812-8321-3*) Rprt Serv.

Life of the Academic Professional in America: An Inventory of Tasks, Tensions & Achievements. Gerhard Falk. LC 90-43111. (Studies in Education: Vol. 15). 248p. 1990. lib. bdg. 89.95 (*0-88946-797-8*) E Mellen.

Life of the Admiral Christopher Columbus by His Son Ferdinand. rev. ed. Benjamin Keen. 340p. 1992. reprint ed. 38.00 (*0-8135-1869-5*); reprint ed. pap. 16.95 (*0-8135-1801-6*) Rutgers U Pr.

Life of the Alter & the Tent. Watchman. 14p. 1998. pap. 1.00 (*1-57593-870-7*, 18-063-001) Living Stream Ministry.

Life of the Ancient East - Being Some Chapters of Romance of Modern Excavation. James Baikie. (African Studies). 464p. reprint ed. 60.00 (*0-685-56711-7*) ECA Assoc.

Life of the Ancient Egyptians. Eugen Strouhal. LC 92-54140. (Illus.). 280p. 1992. 45.00 (*0-8061-2475-X*) U of Okla Pr.

Life of the Automobile. Llya Ehrenburg. 176p. 1999. pap. 12.99 (*1-85242-636-5*, Pub. by Serpents Tail) Consort Bk Sales.

***Life of the Average Roman: A Symposium.** Mary R. DeMaine & Rabun M. Taylor. (Illus.). 137p. 1999. pap. 30.00 (*0-9673471-0-6*) PZA Pubng.

Life of the Beloved: Spiritual Living in a Secular World. Henri J. M. Nouwen. 120p. 1992. 14.95 (*0-8245-1184-0*) Crossroad NY.

Life of the Black Prince. Chandos Herald. LC 74-178519. reprint ed. 57.50 (*0-404-56532-8*) AMS Pr.

Life of the Blessed Virgin Mary. A. C. Emmerick. (Roman Catholic Ser.). 1979. lib. bdg. 69.95 (*0-8490-2959-7*) Gordon Pr.

Life of the Blessed Virgin Mary. Anne C. Emmerich. Tr. by Michael Palairet from GER. 1994. reprint ed. pap. 16.50 (*0-89555-048-2*) TAN Bks Pubs.

Life of the Bones to Come. Larry Laurence. 70p. 1999. pap. 11.95 (*0-930773-57-8*, Pub. by Black Heron Pr) Midpt Trade.

Life of the Book. Hellmut Lehmann-Haupt. LC 75-17193. (Illus.). 240p. 1975. reprint ed. lib. bdg. 65.00 (*0-8371-8293-X*, LELB, Greenwood Pr) Greenwood.

Life of the Buddha: Ancient Scriptural & Pictoral Traditions. Patricia E. Karetzky. 320p. (Orig.). (C). 1992. pap. text 31.00 (*0-8191-8791-7*) U Pr of Amer.

Life of the Buddha: Ancient Scriptural & Pictoral Traditions. Patricia E. Karetzky. 320p. (Orig.). (C). 1992. lib. bdg. 58.00 (*0-8191-8790-9*) U Pr of Amer.

Life of the Butterfly. Heiderose Fischer-Nagel & Andreas Fischer-Nagel. Tr. by Noel Simon from GER. (Nature Watch Bks.).Tr. of Bunte Welt der Schmetterlinge das Tagpfauenauge. (Illus.). 48p. (J). (gr. 2-5). 1987. pap. 7.95 (*0-87614-484-9*, Carolrhoda) Lerner Pub.

***Life of the Caterpillar.** J. H. Fabre. 224p. 2000. pap. 16.00 (*1-58776-027-4*, Carrot Sky Pr) Vivisphere.

Life of the Christmas Party. rev. ed. Ed. by David C. Olsen. 160p. (Orig.). (YA). 1996. pap. text 19.95 (*0-89898-645-1*, TMF0182C) Wrner Bros.

Life of the Cosmos. Lee Smolin. LC 96-27912. (Illus.). 368p. 1997. 30.00 (*0-19-510837-X*) OUP.

Life of the Cosmos. Lee Smolin. 368p. 1999. pap. 16.95 (*0-19-512664-5*) OUP.

Life of the Dead in Mexican Folk Art see Dia de los Muertos

Life of the Drama. Eric Bentley. 384p. 1991. reprint ed. pap. 12.95 (*1-55783-110-6*) Applause Theatre Bk Pubs.

Life of the Emperor Napoleon. Henry Lee. (Notable American Authors Ser.). 1999. reprint ed. lib. bdg. 125.00 (*0-7812-3788-2*) Rprt Serv.

Life of the Far North: Subscription Edition. W. A. Fuller & J. C. Holmes. 1972. 4.25 (*0-07-046014-0*) McGraw.

***Life of the Fly.** J. H. Fabre. 224p. 2000. pap. 16.00 (*1-58776-026-6*, Carrot Sky Pr) Vivisphere.

Life of the Flycatcher. Alexander F. Skutch. LC 96-47006. (Animal Natural History Ser.: Vol. 3). (Illus.). 192p. 1997. 40.00 (*0-8061-2919-0*) U of Okla Pr.

Life of the Fool for Christ-Pelagia Ivanovna Serebrennikova see Skazanije o Khrista Radi Jurodivoj - Pelagiji Ivanovna Serebrennikva

Life of the Gallant Pelham. Philip Mercer. (Illus.). 189p. 1995. reprint ed. 25.00 (*1-56837-316-3*) Broadfoot.

Life of the Great Martyr Saint George. Tr. by Georgia Hronas. LC 98-139789. (Illus.). (Orig.). 1997. pap. 5.95 (*1-880971-34-8*) Light&Life Pub Co MN.

Life of the Green Plant. 3rd ed. Arthur W. Galston et al. 1980. 26.67 (*0-13-536326-8*) P-H.

Life of the Green Plant. 3rd ed. Arthur W. Galston et al. (C). 1980. pap. text 46.60 (*0-13-536318-7*) P-H.

Life of the Holy & Great Martyr Barbara. Ed. & Tr. by Georgia Hronas from GRE. (Illus.). (Orig.). 1996. pap. 4.00 (*0-913026-45-X*) St Nectarios.

Life of the Holy Apostle & Evangelist Luke: And the Liturgical Service in His Honor. Tr. by Isaac E. Lambertsen from RUS. (Illus.). 32p. (Orig.). 1989. pap. 2.50 (*0-912927-32-1*, X032) St John Kronstadt.

***Life of the Holy Hierarch & Confessor Glicherie of Romania.** Sorin Comanescu & Gheorghe Balaban. LC 99-61475. 1999. write for info. (*0-911165-38-X*) Ctr Trad Orthodox.

Life of the Holy Hildegard. Gottfried & Theoderic Monks. Tr. by James McGrath. LC 94-23992. 144p. 1995. pap. 11.95 (*0-8146-2244-5*, Liturg Pr Bks) Liturgical Pr.

Life of the Holy Prince Vladimir the Great of Kiev: With Liturgical Service, & Akathist Hymn. Tr. by Isaac E. Lambertsen from SLA. (Illus.). 48p. (Orig.). 1993. pap. 3.00 (*0-912927-55-0*, X046) St John Kronstadt.

Life of the Honeybee. Andreas Fischer-Nagel & Heiderose Fischer-Nagel. (Nature Watch Bks.).Tr. of Im Bienenstock Wunderwelt der Honigbienen. (Illus.). 48p. (J). (gr. 2-5). 1986. pap. 6.95 (*0-87614-470-9*, Carolrhoda) Lerner Pub.

Life of the Honorable Henry Cavendish. George Wilson. LC 74-26308. (History, Philosophy & Sociology of Science Ser.). 1975. reprint ed. 41.95 (*0-405-06631-7*) Ayer.

Life of the Honourable Robert Boyle. Thomas W. Birch. 476p. reprint ed. write for info. (*0-318-71887-1*) G Olms Pubs.

Life of the Hunt. John Barsness. LC 95-60555. (Illus.). 192p. 1995. 29.00 (*1-885106-17-3*) Wild Adven Pr.

***Life of the Jura Fathers: The Life & Rule of the Holy Fathers Romanus, Lupicinus & Eugendus, Abbots of the Monasteries in the Jura Mountains: With Appendices, Avitus of Vienne, Letter XVIIII to Viventiolus-Eucherius of Lyon, the Passion of the Martyrs of Agaune, Saint Maurice & His Companions & in Praise of the Desert.** Tim Vivian et al. LC 99-39501. (Studies Ser.). 1999. pap. write for info. (*0-87907-778-6*) Cistercian Pubns.

Life of the Ladybug. Andreas Fischer-Nagel & Heiderose Fischer-Nagel. LC 85-25467. (Nature Watch Bks.).Tr. of Marienkafer die Wunderbare Verwandlung aus dem Ei. (Illus.). 48p. (J). (gr. 2-5). 1986. lib. bdg. 19.95 (*0-87614-240-4*, Carolrhoda) Lerner Pub.

Life of the Law: Proceedings of the Tenth British Legal History Conference, Oxford, 1991. Ed. by Peter B. H. Birks. LC 93-4567. 256p. 1993. 60.00 (*1-85285-102-3*) Hambledon Press.

Life of the Law: The People & Cases That Have Shaped Our Society, from King Alfred to Rodney King. Alfred H. Knight. 288p. 1998. reprint ed. pap. 14.95 (*0-19-512239-9*) OUP.

***Life of the Lord Jesus as Written & Unwritten.** Lazarus W. Gilles. LC 99-93928. 2000. pap. 35.00 (*0-533-13204-5*) Vantage.

Life of the Lord Keeper North by Roger North. Mary Chan & Roger North. LC 95-2968. (Studies in British History: Vol. 41). (Illus.). 644p. 1995. text 129.95 (*0-7734-8972-X*) E Mellen.

Life of the Mind. Hannah Arendt. LC 80-25403. 300p. 1981. pap. 15.00 (*0-15-651992-5*, Harvest Bks) Harcourt.

Life of the Mind. Jason W. Brown. (Comparative Cognition & Neuroscience Ser.). 440p. 1988. pap. text 45.00 (*0-8058-0422-6*) L Erlbaum Assocs.

Life of the Mind. Jason W. Brown. (Comparative Cognition & Neuroscience Ser.). 440p. 1988. 99.95 (*0-8058-0236-3*) L Erlbaum Assocs.

Life of the Mind. Ornstein. 2001. write for info. (*0-15-100423-4*) Harcourt.

L

An Asterisk (*) at the beginning of an entry indicates that the title is appearing for the first time.

Life of the Mind: The Vision Cry. J. R. Challacombe. LC 95-92533. 262p. (Orig.). (C). 1995. pap. 19.95 (*1-886287-13-9*) Clair Studies.

Life of the Most Reverend John Hughes, First Archbishop of New York. John R. Hassard. LC 74-83423. (Religion in America, Ser. 1). 1980. reprint ed. 39.95 (*0-405-00248-3*) Ayer.

Life of the Novel. David Goldknopf. LC 72-75512. 256p. (C). 1993. pap. text 2.95 (*0-226-30143-5*) U Ch Pr.

***Life of the Parties: A History of American Political Parties.** A. James Reichley. 512p. 2000. pap. 29.95 (*0-7425-0888-9*) Rowman.

Life of the Parties: Activists in Presidential Politics. Ed. by Ronald B. Rapoport et al. LC 85-22510. 256p. 1986. 29.95 (*0-8131-1559-0*) U Pr of Ky.

Life of the Party. Mary Fleener. (Illus.). 152p. (Orig.). 1996. pap. 14.95 (*1-56097-261-0*) Fantagraph Bks.

Life of the Party. Irvin S. Cobb. (Collected Works of Irvin S. Cobb). 66p. 1998. reprint ed. lib. bdg. 88.00 (*1-58201-596-1*) Classic Bks.

Life of the Party: A Guide to Building Your Party Plan Business. Betty Bowes. 1998. pap. text 10.95 (*1-56052-471-5*) Crisp Pubns.

Life of the Party: The Biography of Pamela Digby Churchill Hayward Harriman. Christopher Ogden. 1998. mass mkt. 6.50 (*0-446-78858-9*) Warner Bks.

Life of the Party: The Biography of Pamela Digby Churchill Hayward Harriman. Christopher Ogden. (Illus.). 576p. 1995. reprint ed. mass mkt. 6.50 (*0-446-60264-7*, Pub. by Warner Bks) Little.

Life of the Party Lyric, 10 pts. 320p. (Orig.). 1996. pap. 18.95 (*0-7692-1034-1*, TMF0057C) Wrner Bros.

Life of the Party, 1994. rev. ed. 1994. pap. 19.95 (*0-7692-1035-X*, TMF0056C) Wrner Bros.

Life of the Past. 4th ed. William I. Ausich & N. Gary Lane. LC 98-18770. 321p. 1998. pap. text 48.00 (*0-13-896069-0*) P-H.

Life of the Past: An Introduction to Paleontology. George G. Simpson. LC 52-12078. (Illus.). 210p. reprint ed. pap. 65.10 (*0-8357-8210-7*, 203389000087) Bks Demand.

Life of the Patriarch Tarasios. Ignatios. Tr. by Stephanos Efthymiadis from GEC. LC 98-13095. (Birmingham Byzantine & Ottoman Monographs). 1998. 78.95 (*0-86078-681-1*) Ashgate Pub Co.

Life of the Pigeon. Alexander F. Skutch. LC 90-55753. (Comstock Bk.). (Illus.). 192p. 1991. text 49.95 (*0-8014-2528-X*) Cornell U Pr.

Life of the Pleistocene or Glacial Period. Frank C. Baker. LC 74-80996. (BCL Ser. I). 1969. reprint ed. 49.50 (*0-404-00449-0*) AMS Pr.

Life of the Poet: Beginning & Ending Poetic Careers. Lawrence Lipking. LC 81-1067. (Illus.). (C). 1995. lib. bdg. 26.50 (*0-226-48450-5*) U Ch Pr.

Life of the Poet: Beginning & Ending Poetic Careers. Lawrence Lipking. LC 81-1067. (Illus.). 260p. (C). 1997. pap. text 9.95 (*0-226-48451-3*) U Ch Pr.

Life of the Prophet Muhammad. Leila Azzam & Aisha Gouverneur. (Illus.). 137p. (Orig.). (YA). (gr. 10 up). 1995. pap. 19.95 (*0-946621-02-0*, Pub. by Islamic Texts) Intl Spec Bk.

Life of the Prophet Muhammad, 4. AL-SIRA AL-NABAWIYYA. (Life of the Prophet Muhammad Ser.). 1999. 95.00 (*1-85964-040-0*) Garnet Publishing Ltd.

Life of the Prophet Muhammad, Vol. 3. AL-SIRA AL-NABAWIYYA. 1999. 95.00 (*1-85964-009-5*) Garnet Pubg.

***Life of the Prophet Muhammad: A Brief History.** Marmaduke W. Pickthall. LC 98-35847. 1998. 9.95 (*0-915957-86-8*) amana pubns.

***Life of the Prophet Muhammad Vol. I: Al-Sira al-Nibawiyya.** Ibn Kathir. Tr. by Trevor Le Gassick. (Great Books of Islamic Civilization Ser.). 424p. 2000. pap. 30.00 (*1-85964-142-3*) Garnet Publishing Co.

***Life of the Prophet Muhammad Vol. II: Al-Sira al-Nabawiyya.** Ibn Kathir. Tr. by Trevor Le Gassick. (Great Books of Islamic Civilization Ser.). 412p. 2000. pap. 30.00 (*1-85964-143-1*) Garnet Publishing Co.

Life of the R. Hon. Richard B. Sheridan, 2 vols. Thomas Moore. 1981. reprint ed. lib. bdg. 59.00 (*0-403-01763-7*) Scholarly.

Life of the Renowned Sir Philip Sidney. Fulke Greville. LC 83-4483. 288p. 1984. reprint ed. 50.00 (*0-8201-1390-5*) Schol Facsimiles.

Life of the Rev. George Whitefield, 2 vols. Luke Tyerman. LC 75-31102. reprint ed. 97.50 (*0-404-13540-4*) AMS Pr.

Life of the Reverend Devereux Jarratt in His Letters to Rev. John Coleman. Devereux Jarratt. (American Biography Ser.). 223p. 1991. reprint ed. lib. bdg. 69.00 (*0-7812-8214-4*) Rprt Serv.

Life of the Reverend Mr. George Trosse. George Trosse. Ed. by A. W. Brink. LC 73-79097. 150p. reprint ed. pap. 46.50 (*0-608-12526-1*, 202385300034) Bks Demand.

Life of the Right Honorable Richard Brinsley Sheridan, 2 vols., Set. Thomas Moore. 1826. 59.00 (*0-403-00072-6*) Scholarly.

Life of the Right Honourable Sir Edward Coke, Knt., Lord Chief Justice of the King's Bench. Humphry W. Woolrych. 243p. 1972. reprint ed. 39.00 (*0-8377-2727-8*, Rothman) W S Hein.

Life of the Right Honourable Stratford Canning, Viscount Stratford de Redcliffe, 2 vols. Stanley Lane-Poole. LC 73-171653. reprint ed. 115.00 (*0-404-07387-5*) AMS Pr.

Life of the Right Honourable William Pitt, 4 vols. Philip H. Stanhope. LC 71-108929. reprint ed. 285.00 (*0-404-06250-4*) AMS Pr.

Life of the Snail. Theres Buholzer. Tr. by Noel Simon from GER. (Nature Watch Bks.).Tr. of Schneckenleben. (Illus.). 48p. (J). (gr. 2-5). 1987. lib. bdg. 19.95 (*0-87614-246-3*, Carolrhoda) Lerner Pub.

Life of the Soul. large type ed. Samuel Miller. (Large Print Inspirational Ser.). 208p. 1986. pap. 12.95 (*0-8027-2551-1*) Walker & Co.

Life of the Soul: The Wisdom of Julian of Norwich. Tr. by Edmund Colledge & James Walsh. LC 96-14803. (Spiritual Samplers Ser.). 96p. (Orig.). 1996. pap. 1.95 (*0-8091-3673-2*) Paulist Pr.

Life of the Spirit & the Life of Today. Evelyn Underhill. Ed. by Susan Howatch. LC 94-26943. (Yes: Library of Anglican Spirituality Ser.). 272p. 1995. pap. 13.95 (*0-8192-1632-1*) Morehouse Pub.

Life of the Spirit & the Life of Today. Evelyn Underhill. 252p. 1999. reprint ed. pap. 18.95 (*0-7661-0836-8*) Kessinger Pub.

Life of the Spirit in the Modern English Poets. Vida D. Scudder. LC 78-39074. (Essay Index Reprint Ser.). 1977. reprint ed. 23.95 (*0-8369-2720-6*) Ayer.

Life of the Spirit in Women: A Jungian Approach. Helen M. Luke. LC 79-91960. (C). 1980. pap. 4.00 (*0-87574-230-0*) Pendle Hill.

Life of the Sudanese Mahdi. Haim Shaked. LC 76-7552. (Shiloah Center Ser.). (Illus.). 284p. 1978. 39.95 (*0-87855-132-8*) Transaction Pubs.

Life of the Tanager. Alexander F. Skutch. LC 88-47765. (Comstock Bk.). (Illus.). 152p. 1989. text 42.50 (*0-8014-2226-4*) Cornell U Pr.

Life of the Transcendental Ego: Essays in Honor of William Earle. Ed. by Edward S. Casey & Donald V. Morano. LC 86-5835. 217p. (C). 1986. pap. text 18.95 (*0-88706-170-2*) State U NY Pr.

Life of the Valaam Monk Herman (of Alaska)-Missionary to America see Zhizn' Valaamskago Monakha Germana (Aljaskinskago)-Amerikanskago Missionjera

Life of the Very Noble King of Castile & Leon, Saint Ferdinand III. C. Fernandez De Castro. LC 86-83054. (Illus.). 280p. (Orig.). (J). (gr. 8). 1987. pap. 13.95 (*1-877905-09-7*) Am Soc Defense TFP.

Life of the Virgin Mary, the Theotokos. Holy Apostles Convent Staff. LC 89-81686. (Illus.). 640p. (C). 1989. 35.00 (*0-944359-03-5*) Holy Apostles Convent.

Life of the Woodpecker. Alexander F. Skutch. LC 85-80841. (Illus.). 136p. 1988. reprint ed. 49.95 (*0-934797-00-5*) Cornell U Pr.

Life of the World to Come: Near-Death Experience & Christian Hope: The Albert Cardinal Meyer Lectures. Carol G. Zaleski. (Illus.). 112p. 1996. 25.00 (*0-19-510335-1*) OUP.

Life of the Writer, the Life of the Career: Prolegomena to a Personal Ethics. unabridged ed. Joyce Carol Oates. (Ben Belitt Lectureship Ser.: Vol. 17). (Illus.). 24p. (Orig.). 1995. pap. 5.00 (*0-614-10189-1*) Bennington Coll.

Life of Themistocles: A Critical Survey of the Literary & Archaeological Evidence. Anthony J. Podlecki. LC 73-93001. 272p. reprint ed. pap. 84.40 (*0-7837-1027-5*, 204133800020) Bks Demand.

Life of Theobald Wolfe Tone. rev. ed. Theobald W. Tone. Ed. by Thomas Bartlett. 1056p. 1998. pap. 39.95 (*1-901866-04-1*, Pub. by Lilliput Pr) Irish Bks Media.

Life of Thomas Bailey Aldrich. Ferris Greenslet. (BCL1-PS American Literature Ser.). 303p. 1992. reprint ed. lib. bdg. 89.00 (*0-7812-6669-6*) Rprt Serv.

Life of Thomas Carlyle. Richard Garnett. LC 75-30023. reprint ed. 34.50 (*0-404-14028-9*) AMS Pr.

Life of Thomas Eddy: Comprising an Extensive Correspondence with Many of the Most Distinguished Philosophers & Philanthropists of This & Other Countries. Samuel L. Knapp. LC 75-17229. (Social Problems & Social Policy Ser.). 1976. reprint ed. 33.95 (*0-405-07499-9*) Ayer.

Life of Thomas Hardy. Ernest Brennecke. LC 72-8648. (Studies in Thomas Hardy). 1973. reprint ed. lib. bdg. 75.00 (*0-8383-1672-7*) M S G Haskell Hse.

Life of Thomas Hardy: A Critical Biography. Paul D. Turner. Ed. by Claude Rawson. LC 97-24557. (Critical Biographies Ser.). 300p. (C). 1998. text 47.95 (*0-631-16881-8*) Blackwell Pubs.

Life of Thomas Holcroft, 2 vols., 1 bk. Thomas Holcroft. Ed. by Elbridge Colby. LC 67-31457. 1972. reprint ed. 48.95 (*0-405-08632-6*, Pub. by Blom Pubns) Ayer.

Life of Thomas Holcroft, 2 vols., Vol. 1. Thomas Holcroft. Ed. by Elbridge Colby. LC 67-31457. 1972. reprint ed. 24.95 (*0-405-08633-4*, Pub. by Blom Pubns) Ayer.

Life of Thomas Holcroft, 2 vols., Vol. 2. Thomas Holcroft. Ed. by Elbridge Colby. LC 67-31457. 1972. reprint ed. 24.95 (*0-405-08634-2*, Pub. by Blom Pubns) Ayer.

Life of Thomas Hutchinson. James K. Hosmer. (Notable American Authors Ser.). 1992. reprint ed. lib. bdg. 75.00 (*0-7812-3175-2*) Rprt Serv.

Life of Thomas Jefferson, 3 vols. Henry S. Randall. LC 79-172011. (American Scene Ser.). (Illus.). 1972. reprint ed. lib. bdg. 175.00 (*0-306-70250-9*) Da Capo.

Life of Thomas Jefferson. George Tucker. (Notable American Authors). 1999. reprint ed. lib. bdg. 125.00 (*0-7812-9833-4*) Rprt Serv.

Life of Thomas Jefferson, 3 Vols, Set. Henry S. Randall. LC 72-117890. (Select Bibliographies Reprint Ser.). 1977. 108.95 (*0-8369-5343-6*) Ayer.

***Life of Thomas Moore.** Peter Ackroyd. 480p. 1999. pap. 17.50 (*0-385-49693-1*, Anchor NY) Doubleday.

Life of Thomas Paine. John Cheetham. LC 89-10446. 368p. 1989. 50.00 (*0-8201-1439-1*) Schol Facsimiles.

Life of Thomas Paine. Moncure D. Conway. 1972. 30.95 (*0-405-09114-1*, 1707) Ayer.

Life of Thomas Paine. Moncure D. Conway. (Works of Moncure Daniel Conway). 1990. reprint ed. lib. bdg. 79.00 (*0-7812-2343-1*) Rprt Serv.

Life of Thurlow Weed, 2 vols. Incl. Vol. 1. Autobiography of Thurlow Weed. LC 79-87686. Vol. 2. Memoir of Thurlow Weed. LC 79-87686. LC 79-87686. (American Public Figures Ser). 1970. reprint ed. Set lib. bdg. 115.00 (*0-306-71706-9*) Da Capo.

Life of Thurlow Weed, 2 vols. Thurlow Weed. Ed. by Thurlow W. Barnes & Harriet A. Weed. LC 70-177857. reprint ed. 95.00 (*0-404-04639-8*) AMS Pr.

Life of Thurlow Weed, 2 vols., Set. Thurlow Weed. (American Biography Ser.). 1991. reprint ed. lib. bdg. 148.00 (*0-7812-8406-6*) Rprt Serv.

Life of Tintoretto. Carlo Ridolfi. Tr. by Catherine Enggass & Robert Enggass from ITA. LC 83-23829. 112p. 1984. 28.50 (*0-271-00369-3*) Pa St U Pr.

Life of Titian by Carlo Ridolfi. Ed. by Julia C. Bondanella et al. Tr. by Peter Bondanella. (Illus.). 168p. 1996. pap. 22.50 (*0-271-01627-2*) Pa St U Pr.

Life of Titian by Carlo Ridolfi. Carlo Ridolfi. Ed. by Julia C. Bondanella et al. Tr. by Peter Bondanella. LC 95-38040. (Illus.). 168p. 1996. 45.00 (*0-271-01547-0*) Pa St U Pr.

Life of Tom Horn, Government Scout & Interpreter: Written by Himself: Together with His Letters & Statements by His Friends. Tom Horn. (American Biography Ser.). 328p. 1991. reprint ed. lib. bdg. 79.00 (*0-7812-8192-X*) Rprt Serv.

Life of Tom Horn, Government Scout & Interpreter, Written by Himself, Together with His Letters & Statements by His Friends: A Vindication. Tom Horn. LC 64-20758. (Western Frontier Library: No. 26). 1973. pap. 12.95 (*0-8061-1044-9*) U of Okla Pr.

***Life of Total Prayer: Selected Writings of Catherine of Siena.** Ed. by Stephen S. Wilburn. LC 99-40407. (Spiritual Classics). 95p. 2000. pap. 5.00 (*0-8358-0903-X*) Upper Room Bks.

Life of Toussaint L'Ouverture, the Negro Patriot of Haiti. John R. Beard. LC 75-109316. (Illus.). 335p. 1970. reprint ed. lib. bdg. 35.00 (*0-8371-3572-9*, BTL&) Greenwood.

Life of Toyotomi Hideyoshi. 3rd ed. Walter Dening. LC 79-136391. (BCL Ser. II). reprint ed. 34.50 (*0-404-02078-X*) AMS Pr.

Life of Tukaram. xx, 346p. 1986. 12.50 (*0-317-61122-4*, Pub. by Motilal Bnarsidass) S Asia.

Life of Tukaram. Mahipati. Tr. by Justin E. Abbott from MAR. 346p. 1986. reprint ed. 12.95 (*81-208-0169-5*, Pub. by Motilal Bnarsidass); reprint ed. pap. 9.50 (*81-208-0170-9*, Pub. by Motilal Bnarsidass) S Asia.

Life of Tulasei Devei & Her Care & Worship. Amala-Bhakta Dasa. LC 98-175273. xvii, 100 p. 1997. write for info. (*0-89213-315-5*) BBT Sci Bks.

Life of Ulysses S. Grant. Benjamin P. Poore. (Notable American Authors Ser.). 1999. reprint ed. lib. bdg. 125.00 (*0-7812-8764-2*) Rprt Serv.

Life of Una Marson, 1905-1965. Jarrett. LC 97-4355. (Illus.). 272p. 1998. 39.95 (*0-7190-5284-X*, Pub. by Manchester Univ Pr) St Martin.

Life of Union with OUr Divine Lord see Pocket Retreat for Catholics: Thirty Simple Steps to Holiness - In Just Ten Minute a Day!

Life of Vallie Jo Whitfield: Notebook Life & Records. Vallie J. Whitfield. 100p. 1983. 5.00 (*0-930920-16-3*) Whitfield Bks.

***Life of Verdi.** John Rosselli. LC 99-59952. (Musical Lives Ser.). (Illus.). 220p. (C). 2000. text 49.95 (*0-521-66011-4*); pap. text 17.95 (*0-521-66957-X*) Cambridge U Pr.

Life of Vertebrates. 3rd ed. J. Z. Young. (Illus.). 668p. (C). 1991. pap. text 54.95 (*0-19-857173-9*, 23) OUP.

Life of Villiers de l'Isle-Adam. A. W. Raitt. (Illus.). 470p. 1981. text 64.00 (*0-19-815771-1*) OUP.

Life of Vittoria Colonna. T. Adolphus Trollope. 248p. 1996. reprint ed. pap. text 25.00 (*0-87556-831-9*) Saifer.

Life of Vivekananda: Universal Gospel. Romain Rolland. 382p. pap. 5.95 (*81-85301-00-X*) Vedanta Pr.

Life of Voltaire, 2 Vols. S. G. Tallentyre. LC 72-2504. (Select Bibliographies Reprint Ser.). 1977. reprint ed. 52.95 (*0-8369-6867-0*) Ayer.

***Life of W. B. Yeats: A Critical Biography.** Terence Brown. LC 99-28388. (Critical Biographies Ser.). 384p. (C). 1999. 39.95 (*0-631-18298-5*) Blackwell Pubs.

Life of Walt Whitman. Henry B. Binns. LC 78-92937. (Studies in Whitman). 1969. reprint ed. lib. bdg. 75.00 (*0-8383-1001-X*) M S G Haskell Hse.

Life of Walter Pater, 2 Vols. Thomas Wright. LC 68-24928. (English Biography Ser.: No. 31). 1969. reprint ed. lib. bdg. 150.00 (*0-8383-0178-9*) M S G Haskell Hse.

Life of Walter Pater, 2 vols., Set. Thomas Wright. (BCL1-PR English Literature Ser.). 1992. reprint ed. lib. bdg. 150.00 (*0-7812-7613-6*) Rprt Serv.

Life of Walter Quintin Gresham, 1832-1895, 2 Vols, 1. Matilda Gresham. LC 70-137378. (Select Bibliographies Reprint Ser.). 1977. 38.95 (*0-8369-9657-7*) Ayer.

Life of Walter Quintin Gresham, 1832-1895, 2 Vols, Set. Matilda Gresham. LC 70-137378. (Select Bibliographies Reprint Ser.). 1977. 77.95 (*0-8369-5579-X*) Ayer.

Life of Walter Quintin Gresham, 1832-1895, 2 Vols, Vol. 2. Matilda Gresham. LC 70-137378. (Select Bibliographies Reprint Ser.). 1977. 38.95 (*0-8369-9658-5*) Ayer.

Life of Walter Scott: A Critical Biography. John Sutherland. Ed. by Claude Rawson. LC 95-25769. (Critical Biographies Ser.). (Illus.). 386p. 1998. pap. 26.95 (*0-631-20317-6*) Blackwell Pubs.

Life of Washington. Mason L. Weems. Ed. by Marcus Cunliffe. LC 62-20253. (John Harvard Library). (Illus.). 288p. 1962. pap. 16.00 (*0-674-53251-1*) HUP.

Life of Washington. Mason L. Weems. LC 95-26565. (American History Through Literature Ser.). 220p. (C). (gr. 13). 1996. 66.95 (*1-56324-698-8*); pap. 21.95 (*1-56324-699-6*) M E Sharpe.

Life of Washington. James K. Paulding. (Notable American Authors Ser.). 1999. reprint ed. lib. bdg. 125.00 (*0-7812-8703-0*) Rprt Serv.

Life of Washington, Vol. 3. Josephine Pollard. (Illus.). 136p. (J). 1998. 15.00 (*1-889128-44-9*) Mantle Ministries.

Life of Washington Irving, 2 vols., Set. Stanley T. Williams. 1993. reprint ed. lib. bdg. 150.00 (*0-7812-5291-1*) Rprt Serv.

Life of Webern. Kathryn Bailey. LC 97-25751. (Musical Lives Ser.). (Illus.). 238p. (C). 1998. pap. 14.95 (*0-521-57566-4*) Cambridge U Pr.

Life of Wholeness: Reflections on Abundant Living. rev. ed. Ed. by Ann Raber. LC 93-19617. 160p. 1993. pap. 9.99 (*0-8361-3646-2*) Herald Pr.

Life of William Barnes, Poet & Philologist, by His Daughter. Lucy E. Baxter. (BCL1-PR English Literature Ser.). 358p. 1992. reprint ed. lib. bdg. 89.00 (*0-7812-7429-X*) Rprt Serv.

Life of William Blake. Alexander Gilchrist. LC 97-35392. 533p. 1998. pap. 14.95 (*0-486-40005-0*) Dover.

Life of William Congreve. Edmund W. Gosse. (BCL1-PR English Literature Ser.). 181p. 1992. reprint ed. lib. bdg. 69.00 (*0-7812-7336-6*) Rprt Serv.

Life of William Cowper. Thomas Wright. LC 77-153641. (English Literature Ser.: No. 33). 1971. reprint ed. lib. bdg. 79.95 (*0-8383-1251-9*) M S G Haskell Hse.

Life of William Ewart Gladstone, 3 vols., Set. John Morley. LC 70-145193. 1966p. 1972. reprint ed. 125.00 (*0-403-01117-5*) Scholarly.

Life of William Ewart Gladstone, 3 Vols, Set. John M. Morley. LC 68-57630. (Illus.). 1971. reprint ed. lib. bdg. 125.00 (*0-8371-0576-5*, MOWG) Greenwood.

Life of William Ewart Gladstone, Vol. 1. John M. Morley. LC 68-57630. 1971. lib. bdg. 45.00 (*0-8371-3146-4*, Greenwood Pr) Greenwood.

Life of William Ewart Gladstone, 3 vols., Vol. 1. John M. Morley. LC 68-57630. (Illus.). 1971. reprint ed. lib. bdg. 24.00 (*0-313-21287-2*, MOWA) Greenwood.

Life of William Ewart Gladstone, 3 Vols, Vol. 2. John M. Morley. LC 68-57630. (Illus.). 1971. reprint ed. lib. bdg. 45.00 (*0-8371-0827-6*, MOWB) Greenwood.

Life of William Ewart Gladstone, 3 Vols, Vol. 3. John M. Morley. LC 68-57630. (Illus.). 1971. reprint ed. lib. bdg. 45.00 (*0-8371-0828-4*, MOWC) Greenwood.

Life of William Faulkner. Richard Gray. Ed. by Claude Rawson. (Critical Biographies Ser.: Vol. 5). (Illus.). 448p. (Orig.). 1996. pap. 28.95 (*0-631-20316-8*) Blackwell Pubs.

Life of William Hazlitt. Percival P. Howe. LC 72-7505. (Illus.). 433p. 1972. reprint ed. lib. bdg. 35.00 (*0-8371-6512-1*, HOWH, Greenwood Pr) Greenwood.

Life of William Inge: The Strains of Triumph. Ralph F. Voss. LC 88-33902. (Illus.). xviii, 318p. 1989. pap. 14.95 (*0-7006-0442-1*) U Pr of KS.

Life of William J. Brown, of Providence, R. I. With Personal Recollections of Incidents in Rhode Island. William J. Brown. LC 78-164382. (Black Heritage Library Collection). 1977. reprint ed. 22.95 (*0-8369-8841-8*) Ayer.

Life of William McKinley, 2 vols., Set. Charles S. Olcott. LC 79-128946. (American Statesmen Ser.: Nos. 38, 39). reprint ed. 90.00 (*0-404-50893-6*) AMS Pr.

Life of William Morris. J. W. MacKail. 1996. 26.75 (*0-8446-6878-8*) Peter Smith.

Life of William Morris, 2 vols., 1 bk. John W. MacKall. LC 68-57988. 1972. reprint ed. 36.95 (*0-405-08767-5*, Pub. by Blom Pubns) Ayer.

Life of William Morris. unabridged ed. J. W. Mackail. LC 95-17066. (Illus.). 800p. 1995. reprint ed. pap. text 18.95 (*0-486-28793-9*) Dover.

Life of William Morris, 2 vols., Set. John W. Mackail. LC 79-118180. (English Biography Ser.: No. 31). 1970. reprint ed. lib. bdg. 150.00 (*0-8383-1070-2*) M S G Haskell Hse.

Life of William Penn. Mason L. Weems. (Notable American Authors Ser.). 1999. reprint ed. lib. bdg. 125.00 (*0-7812-9929-2*) Rprt Serv.

Life of William Penn: With Selections from His Correspondence & Autobiography. Samuel M. Janney. LC 74-130555. (Select Bibliographies Reprint Ser.). 1977. reprint ed. 26.95 (*0-8369-5528-5*) Ayer.

Life of William Pinkney. William Pinkney, Jr. LC 75-75276. (Law, Politics & History Ser.). 1969. reprint ed. lib. bdg. 49.50 (*0-306-71307-1*) Da Capo.

Life of William Pitt: Earl of Chatham, 2 vols., Set. Basil Williams. reprint ed. 75.00 (*0-7146-1525-0*, Pub. by F Cass Pubs) Intl Spec Bk.

Life of William Plumer. William Plumer, Jr. LC 77-87384. (American History, Politics & Law Ser.). 1969. reprint ed. lib. bdg. 69.50 (*0-306-71608-9*) Da Capo.

Life of William Shakespeare. James O. Halliwell-Phillipps. LC 73-168223. reprint ed. 50.00 (*0-404-03065-3*) AMS Pr.

Life of William Shakespeare. Sidney Lee. (BCL1-PR English Literature Ser.). 476p. 1992. reprint ed. lib. bdg. 99.00 (*0-7812-7282-3*) Rprt Serv.

Life of William Shakespeare. Sidney Lee. LC 70-145137. (Illus.). 1971. reprint ed. 59.00 (*0-403-01069-1*) Scholarly.

Life of William Shakespeare. William J. Rolfe. LC 70-174961. reprint ed. 57.50 (*0-404-05387-4*) AMS Pr.

Life of William T. Porter. Francis Brinley. LC 79-125680. (American Journalists Ser.). 1978. reprint ed. 23.95 (*0-405-01655-7*) Ayer.

Life of William Wilberforce. Robert I. Wilberforce & Samuel Wilberforce. 1977. 36.95 (*0-405-30201-0*) Ayer.

Life of William Wilberforce. Robert I. Wilberforce & Samuel Wilberforce. 1972. 36.95 (*0-8369-9720-4*) Ayer.

Life of William Wilberforce. Robert I. Wilberforce & Samuel Wilberforce. 1977. 36.95 (*0-8369-9719-0*); 36.95 (*0-8369-9718-2*) Ayer.

An Asterisk (*) at the beginning of an entry indicates that the title is appearing for the first time.

L

Life of William Wilberforce: By His Sons, 5 vols, Set. Robert I. Wilberforce & Samuel Wilberforce. LC 72-5506. (Black Heritage Library Collection). 1977. reprint ed. 183.95 (*0-8369-9151-6*) Ayer.

Life of William Woodbridge. Charles Lanman. (Notable American Authors Ser.). 1999. reprint ed. lib. bdg. 125.00 (*0-7812-3738-6*) Rprt Serv.

Life of Woodrow Wilson, 1856-1924. Josephus Daniels. LC 72-114509. (Illus.). 381p. 1971. reprint ed. lib. bdg. 69.50 (*0-8371-4729-8*, DAWW, Greenwood Pr) Greenwood.

Life of Woodrow Wilson, 1856-1924. Josephus Daniels. (History - United States Ser.). 381p. 1992. reprint ed. lib. bdg. 89.00 (*0-7812-6227-5*) Rprt Serv.

Life of Woodrow Wilson, 1856-1924. Josephus Daniels. LC 70-144965. (Illus.). 1971. reprint ed. 18.00 (*0-403-00934-0*) Scholarly.

Life of Yeasts. 2nd enl. rev. ed. H. J. Phaff et al. (Illus.). 320p. 1978. 44.00 (*0-674-53325-9*) HUP.

Life of Zabolotsky. Nikita Nikolaevich Zabolotskii et al. LC 95-121540. Orig. Title: Zhizn' N.A. Zabolotskogo. (ENG & RUS.). xx, 380p. 1994. write for info. (*0-7083-1262-4*) Univ Wales Pr.

Life of Zoroaster: In the Words of His Own Hymns the "Gathas" Tr. by Kenneth S. Guthrie. LC 73-131036. reprint ed. 39.50 (*0-404-02964-7*) AMS Pr.

Life Offshore. (Rotary Drilling Ser.: Unit V, Lesson 9). (Illus.). 28p. (Orig.). 1978. pap. text 15.00 (*0-88698-076-3*, 2.50910) PETEX.

Life on A Balance Beam: It Helps If You Don't Look Down! : A Guide to Positive Living in A Precarious World. Paula Statman. LC 98-96571. 165 P. ;p. 1998. write for info. (*0-9640042-1-6*) Picollo Pr CA.

Life on a Beanstalk: A Small Collection of Ice Box Poems. Eileen A. Schrottke Loos. LC 86-70612. (Illus.). 116p. (Orig.). 1988. pap. 12.00 (*0-9616160-0-8*) Bench Pr NY.

***Life on a Coral Reef.** Susan Tejada. (All-Star Readers Ser.). (Illus.). 48p. (J). 2001. 3.99 (*1-57584-727-2*, Pub. by Rdrs Digest) S&S Trade.

Life on a Dead Planet. Frank Kuppner. 198p. (Orig.). 1996. pap. 15.95 (*0-7486-6151-4*, Pub. by Polygon) Subterranean Co.

Life on a Farm. Margie Burton et al. Ed. by Susan Evento. (Early Connections Ser.). 16p. (J). (gr. k-2). 1998. pap. 4.25 (*1-892393-55-7*) Benchmark Educ.

Life on a Half Share: Mechanisms of Social Recruitment Among the Mapuche of Southern Chile. Milan Stuchlik. LC 75-6049. (Illus.). 300p. (C). 1976. text 39.95 (*0-312-48440-2*) St Martin.

***Life on a Limb.** Thomas Kunkel. LC 99-34703. 592p. 2000. 26.95 (*0-375-50397-8*) Random Hse Chldrns.

Life on a Little-Known Planet. Howard E. Evans. LC 84-86. (Illus.). (C). 1984. pap. 11.95 (*0-226-22258-6*) U Ch Pr.

Life on a Little Known Planet. Howard E. Evans. LC 93-19877. (Illus.). 320p. 1993. reprint ed. pap. 14.95 (*1-55821-249-3*) Lyons Pr.

Life on a Medieval Barony. William S. Davis. (Illus.). 414p. 1990. pap. 25.00 (*0-8196-2061-0*) Biblo.

Life on a Medieval Pilgrimage. Gail B. Stewart. (Way People Live Ser.). (Illus.). 112p. (YA). (gr. 5-12). 1996. lib. bdg. 22.45 (*1-56006-325-4*) Lucent Bks.

Life on a Mexican Ranche. Margaret M. McKellar. Ed. by Dolores L. Latorre. LC 93-42774. 1994. 38.50 (*0-934223-31-9*) Lehigh Univ Pr.

Life on a Modern Planet: A Manifesto for Progress. Richard D. North. LC 94-28599. 304p. 1995. 35.00 (*0-7190-4566-5*, Pub. by Manchester Univ Pr); pap. write for info. (*0-7190-4567-3*, Pub. by Manchester Univ Pr) St Martin.

Life on a Pig Farm. Judy Wolfman. LC 97-21771. (Illus.). 48p. (J). (gr. 2-8). 1998. 22.60 (*1-57505-237-7*, Carolrhoda) Lerner Pub.

***Life on a Pioneer Homestead.** Sally S. Isaacs. LC 99-89883. (Picture the Past Ser.). 2000. lib. bdg. write for info. (*1-57572-313-1*) Heinemann Lib.

Life on a Plantation see Historic Communities Series

Life on a Plantation. Bobbie Kalman. (Historic Communities Ser.). 1996. 13.15 (*0-606-12757-7*, Pub. by Turtleback) Demco.

***Life on a Southern Plantation.** Sally Senzell Isaacs. LC 00-20644. (Picture the Past Ser.). 2000. write for info. (*1-57572-316-6*) Heinemann Lib.

***Life on a Submarine.** Robert C. Kennedy. LC 00-23358. (High Interest Bks.). (Illus.). 48p. (J). (gr. 4-7). 2000. pap. write for info. (*0-516-23549-4*) Childrens.

***Life on a Submarine.** Gregory Payan. (High Interest Bks.). (Illus.). (YA). 2000. 19.00 (*0-516-23349-1*) Childrens.

***Life on Alcatraz.** Judith J. Presnall. LC 00-8056. (Way People Live Ser.). 2000. write for info. (*1-56006-639-3*) Lucent Bks.

Life on All Fronts: Women in the First World War. Gill Thomas. (Women in History Ser.). (Illus.). 48p. (C). 1989. pap. 13.95 (*0-521-34841-2*) Cambridge U Pr.

Life on an April Canvas: An Afrikan Man's Story of Love, Betrayal, & Struggle. Kiarri T-H. Cheatwood. LC 91-68263. 128p. (Orig.). 1992. 22.98 (*0-9625169-8-8*); pap. 12.98 (*0-9625169-9-6*) Native Sun Pubs.

Life on an Israeli Kibbutz. Linda J. Altman. (Way People Live Ser.). (Illus.). 112p. (J). (gr. 5-12). 1996. lib. bdg. 22.45 (*1-56006-328-9*) Lucent Bks.

***Life on Another Planet.** Eisner Will. (Illus.). 136p. (YA). 2000. pap. 12.95 (*1-56389-677-X*, Pub. by DC Comics) Time Warner.

***Life on Board a Yacht.** 2000. mass mkt. 7.95 (*1-56201-206-1*) Blue Moon Bks.

Life on Commando During the South African War, 1899-1902. Fransjohan Pretorius. 1998. pap. text 39.95 (*0-7981-3806-8*) Human & Rousseau.

Life on Daytime Television: Tuning in American Serial Drama. Mary Cassata & Thomas D. Skill. Ed. by Melvin J. Voigt. LC 84-2853. (Communication & Information Science Ser.). 272p. (C). 1982. text 73.25 (*0-89391-138-0*); pap. text 39.50 (*0-89391-180-1*) Ablx Pub.

Life on Earth. Chinnici et al. 654p. 1997. pap. text, student ed. 26.67 (*0-13-271859-6*) P-H.

Life on Earth. Susan Mayes. (Starting Point Science Ser.). (Illus.). 144p. (J). (gr. 1 up). 1995. pap. 17.95 (*0-7460-1973-4*, Usborne) EDC.

***Life on Earth.** 2nd ed. Audesirk. 1999. suppl. ed. write for info. (*0-13-018815-8*) P-H.

Life on Earth. 2nd ed. S. Audesirk. LC 99-30751. 728p. 1999. pap. text 68.00 incl. audio compact disk (*0-13-915687-9*, Pub. by P-H) S&S Trade.

Life on Earth: Fossils & Human Ancestors see Macmillan Encyclopedia of Science

Life on Earth: Its Origin & Succession. John Phillips. Ed. by Stephen Jay Gould. LC 79-8343. (History of Paleontology Ser.). 1980. reprint ed. lib. bdg. 23.95 (*0-405-12733-2*) Ayer.

Life on Edge Chaos. M. Mitchell Waldrop. 1992. pap. 22.95 (*0-13-529447-9*) P-H.

***Life on Ellis Island.** Renee C. Rebman. LC 99-30876. (Way People Live Ser.). (Illus.). 95p. (YA). (gr. 6-8). 2000. lib. bdg. 18.96 (*1-56006-533-8*) Lucent Bks.

***Life on Fire: Radical Disciplines for Ordinary Living.** Ronnie W. Floyd. 220p. 2000. 17.99 (*0-8499-3748-5*) Word Pub.

Life on Hold. Ida R. Dolphin. LC 92-11891. 1992. 16.95 (*0-87770-506-2*) Ye Galleon.

Life on Homicide: True Cases from the Files of William McCormack. William McCormack. (Illus.). 240p. 1998. 22.95 (*0-7737-3072-9*) Stoddart Publ.

Life on Intertidal Rocks: A Guide to Marine Life of the Rocky North Atlantic Coast. Cherie H. Day. (Illus.). 62p. 1987. pap. 3.00 (*0-912550-15-5*) Nature Study.

Life on Land. Mary K. Hoff & Mary M. Rodgers. (Our Endangered Planet Ser.). (Illus.). 72p. (J). (gr. 4 up). 1992. lib. bdg. 22.60 (*0-8225-2507-0*, Lerner Publctns) Lerner Pub.

Life on Mars. David Getz. LC 95-20504. (J). 1995. 14.95 (*0-8050-3708-X*, Redfeather BYR) H Holt & Co.

Life on Mars. Robert A. Granger. LC 97-69448. (Physical Science Ser.: Vol. 1). (Illus.). xi, 164p. 1997. 59.95 (*0-9659643-0-2*, 6-01-1001); pap. 29.95 (*0-9659643-1-0*, 6-01-1001) Scientif Archives.

Life on Mars. Patrick Moore & Francis Jackson. (Illus.). 1966. 4.50 (*0-393-05225-7*) Norton.

Life on Mars: The Complete Story. Paul Chambers. LC 99-198130. 1999. 22.95 (*0-7137-2747-0*, Pub. by Blandford Pr) Sterling.

Life on Mars for Kids! Carole Marsh. (J). (gr. 2-7). 1997. 24.95 (*0-614-28746-4*); pap. 19.95 (*0-614-28747-2*) Gallopade Intl.

Life on My Breath. David Zeiger. LC 94-69982. 80p. (Orig.). 1995. pap. write for info. (*0-9644763-0-4*) Sarna.

Life on No Creek: Missouri Rural Days. Rex Burress. (Illus.). 128p. (Orig.). 1996. pap. 12.00 (*0-9652079-0-0*) Signs of the Seasons.

Life on Other Worlds: The Twentieth Century Extraterrestrial Life Debate. Steven J. Dick. LC 98-20465. (Illus.). 304p. (C). 1998. 24.95 (*0-521-62012-0*) Cambridge U Pr.

***Life on Other Worlds & How to Find It.** S. Clark. LC 99-58201. (Series in Astronomy & Space Science). 300p. 2000. pap. 32.95 (*1-85233-097-X*, Pub. by Spr-Verlag) Spr-Verlag.

Life on Southern Nigeria: Magic, Beliefs & Customs of the Ibibio Tribe. Percy A. Talbot. (Illus.). 356p. 1967. 47.50 (*0-7146-1726-1*, Pub. by F Cass Pubs) Intl Spec Bk.

***Life on Stage.** Jacob P. Adler. LC 99-31091. 416p. 1999. 30.00 (*0-679-41351-0*) Knopf.

***Life on Sunnyside Farm.** David Motherwell. Ed. by Reta Spears-Stewart & Gina Keckridge. LC 99-95239. (Illus.). 227p. 1999. 19.95 (*1-892477-19-X*); pap. 14.95 (*1-892477-13-0*) Barnabs Pub.

Life on Television: Content Analysis of U. S. TV Drama. Bradley S. Greenberg. LC 80-14478. (Communication & Information Science Ser.). 208p. (C). 1980. pap. 39.50 (*0-89391-062-7*); text 73.25 (*0-89391-039-2*) Ablx Pub.

Life on the African Savannah. Melvin Berger. Ed. by Natalie Lunis. (Ranger Rick Science Spectacular Ser.). 16p. (J). (gr. 2-4). 1995. pap. 16.95 (*1-56784-214-3*) Newbridge Educ.

Life on the African Savannah: Student Book. Melvin Berger. Ed. by Natalie Lunis. (Ranger Rick Science Spectacular Ser.). (Illus.). 16p. (Orig.). (J). (gr. 2-4). 1996. pap. 3.95 (*1-56784-239-9*) Newbridge Educ.

Life on the African Savannah: Theme Pack. Melvin Berger. Ed. by Natalie Lunis. (Ranger Rick Science Spectacular Ser.). (Illus.). (Orig.). (J). (gr. 2-4). 1996. pap. 36.90 (*1-56784-262-3*) Newbridge Educ.

Life on the American Frontier. Stuart A. Kallen. LC 98-19328. (Way People Live Ser.). (Illus.). 108p. (YA). (gr. 5-8). 1998. lib. bdg. 23.70 (*1-56006-366-1*) Lucent Bks.

Life on the Black Rock Desert: A History of Clear Lake, Utah. Venetta Kelsey. Ed. by Michael R. Kelsey. (Illus.). 192p. 1992. pap. 9.95 (*0-944510-03-5*) Kelsey Pub.

Life on the Brick Pile: Answers to Suffering from the Letters of Revelation. James C. Denison. LC 97-36158. 1997. 20.00 (*0-86554-595-2*) Mercer Univ Pr.

***Life on the Causal Plane: A Glimpse of Heaven.** Marian E. Charlton. Ed. by Adam Walker. 231p. 1998. pap. 12.00 (*0-9668638-0-1*, 98-001, Pub. by Kazmar Ent) DeVorss.

***Life on the Circuit with Lincoln: With Sketches of Generals Grant, Sherman & McClellan, Judge Davis, Leonard Swett & Other Contemporaries.** Henry Clay Whitney. LC 00-30968. 2000. write for info. (*1-58477-115-1*) Lawbk Exchange.

Life on the Color Line: The True Story of a White Boy Who Discovered He Was Black. Gregory H. Williams. 288p. 1996. pap. 13.95 (*0-452-27533-4*, Plume) Dutton Plume.

Life on the Color Line: The True Story of a White Boy Who Discovered He Was Black. Gregory H. Willaims. (Illus.). 285p. 1999. reprint ed. text 23.00 (*0-7881-6125-3*) DIANE Pub.

Life on the Cutting Edge. Sal Rachele. 352p. 1994. pap. 14.95 (*0-9640535-0-0*) Liv Awareness.

Life on the Dry Line: Working the Land, 1902-1944. Harry M. Mason. LC 92-53038. 224p. 1992. 19.95 (*1-55591-122-6*) Fulcrum Pub.

Life on the Dry Side: A Nostalgic Journey down the Backroads of the Inland Northwest. Vance Orchard. 192p. 1984. 15.95 (*0-936546-09-3*) Pioneer Pr Bks.

Life on the Edge see Frente a la Vida

Life on the Edge. James Dobson. write for info. (*0-614-24966-X*) Focus Family.

Life on the Edge. James Dobson. 256p. 1995. 19.99 (*0-8499-0927-9*) Word Pub.

Life on the Edge. Judy Horacek. 96p. 1993. pap. 10.95 (*1-875559-11-6*, Pub. by SpiniFex Pr) LPC InBook.

***Life on the Edge: A Young Adult Guide to a Meaningful Future.** gif. ed. James C. Dobson. 124p. 2000. 12.99 (*0-8499-1629-1*) Word Pub.

***Life on the Edge: Amazing Creatures Thriving in Extreme Environments.** Michael Gross. LC 98-4622. Orig. Title: Exzentriker des Lebens. (Illus.). 200p. (C). 1998. 25.95 (*0-306-45786-5*, Plenum Trade) Perseus Pubng.

Life on the Edge: Memoirs of Everest & Beyond. Jim Whittaker. LC 99-6453. (Illus.). 271p. 1999. 26.95 (*0-89886-540-9*) Mountaineers.

***Life on the Edge: Memoirs of Everest & Beyond.** Jim Whittaker. (Illus.). 272p. 2000. reprint ed. pap. 26.95 (*0-89886-754-1*) Mountaineers.

Life on the Edge: Parenting a Child with ADD/ADHD. David Spohn. LC 98-24858. (Illus.). 70p. 1998. pap. 9.95 (*1-56838-206-5*) Hazelden.

***Life on the Edge: Sustaining Agriculture & Continuity Resources in Fragile Environments.** N. S. Jodha. (Studies in Social Ecology & Environmental History). (Illus.). 336p. 2000. text 24.95 (*0-19-565134-0*) OUP.

Life on the Edge of the Slashings. Betsy Lorentzon. LC 93-85761. pap. write for info. (*0-9637996-0-6*) Shinglemill.

Life on the Fiddle. large type ed. Max Jaffa. (Non-Fiction Ser.). (Illus.). 496p. 1992. 27.99 (*0-7089-8662-5*) Ulverscroft.

***Life on the Fringes: A Feminist Journey Toward.** Haviva Ner-David. 2000. 21.95 (*0-9664306-7-0*) JFL Bks.

Life on the Great Lakes: A Wheelsman's Story. Fred Dutton. Ed. by William D. Ellis. LC 90-49241. (Great Lakes Bks.). (Illus.). 176p. 1991. pap. 16.95 (*0-8143-2261-1*, Great Lks Bks); text 29.95 (*0-8143-2260-3*, Great Lks Bks) Wayne St U Pr.

Life on the High Wire: Faith & a Man's Search for Balance. Martin Camp. LC 96-39503. 160p. 1997. pap. 12.00 (*0-687-05239-4*) Dimen for Liv.

Life on the Highest Plane see Como Vivir en el Plano Superior

Life on the Highest Plane: God's Plan for Spiritual Maturity. Ruth Paxson. 512p. 1996. pap. 16.99 (*0-8254-3461-0*) Kregel.

Life on the Homestead: Interviews with the Women of Northwestern Colorado 1890-1950. Julie Jones-Eddy. (Oral History Ser.: No. 7). 248p. 1992. per. 14.95 (*0-8057-9103-5*, Twyne) Mac Lib Ref.

Life on the Hyphen: The Cuban-American Way. Gustavo Perez Firmat. LC 93-33590. (Illus.). 231p. (C). 1994. pap. 15.95 (*0-292-76551-7*) U of Tex Pr.

Life on the Internet. Stull. LC 97-195997. 56p. (C). 1996. pap. 9.33 (*0-13-268616-3*, Macmillan Coll) P-H.

Life on the Internet: Chemistry. Stull. (C). 1996. pap. 8.00 (*0-13-266560-3*, Macmillan Coll) P-H.

Life on the King Ranch. Frank Goodwyn. LC 93-12756. (Centennial Series of the Association of Former Students: Vol. 49). (Illus.). 344p. (C). 1995. reprint ed. pap. 15.95 (*0-89096-569-2*) Tex A&M Univ Pr.

Life on the Land. J. M. Parramon & Maria Rius. (Habitats Ser.).Tr. of La Vida Sobre la Tierra. (Illus.). 32p. (J). (gr. 3-5). 1987. pap. 6.95 (*0-8120-3864-9*) Barron.

Life on the Line: Facing Challenges, Making Choices & Creating Changes. Rory Elder & Vicky Elder. 216p. (Orig.). 1994. pap. 10.95 (*0-87516-661-X*) DeVorss.

Life on the Line: One Woman's Tale of Work, Sweat & Survival. Solange De Santis. LC 98-51974. 288p. 1999. 24.95 (*0-385-48977-3*) Doubleday.

***Life on the Line: One Woman's Tale of Work, Sweat & Survival.** Solange De Santis. 288p. 2000. pap. text 14.00 (*0-385-48978-1*, Anchor NY) Doubleday.

Life on the Line: Selections on Words & Healing. Ed. by Sue B. Walker & Rosaly Roffman. 660p. 1992. pap. write for info. (*0-942544-15-3*); text. write for info. (*0-942544-16-1*) Negative Capability Pr.

***Life on the Line in Contemporary Manufacturing: The Workplace Experience of Lean Production & the "Japanese" Model.** Rick Delbridge. LC 99-86545. 256p. 2000. pap. 24.95 (*0-19-924043-4*) OUP.

Life on the Mississippi. Mark Twain, pseud. 26.95 (*0-8488-0651-4*) Amereon Ltd.

Life on the Mississippi. Mark Twain, pseud. 320p. 1983. mass mkt. 4.95 (*0-553-21349-0*, Bantam Classics) Bantam.

***Life on the Mississippi.** Mark Twain, pseud. 2000. pap. 2.50 (*0-486-41426-4*) Dover.

Life on the Mississippi. Mark Twain, pseud. LC 93-33253. 504p. 1994. 16.50 (*0-679-60095-7*) Modern Lib NY.

Life on the Mississippi. Mark Twain, pseud. Ed. by John Seelye. (World's Classics Ser.). 522p. 1990. pap. 8.95 (*0-19-281848-1*) OUP.

Life on the Mississippi. Mark Twain, pseud. Ed. by shelley F. Fishkin. (Oxford Mark Twain). (Illus.). 720p. 1997. text 30.00 (*0-19-511407-8*) OUP.

Life on the Mississippi. Mark Twain, pseud. (Signet Classics). 1961. 10.05 (*0-606-03793-4*, Pub. by Turtleback) Demco.

Life on the Mississippi. Mark Twain, pseud. (American Library). 450p. 1985. pap. 9.95 (*0-14-039050-2*, Penguin Classics) Viking Penguin.

Life on the Mississippi. Mark Twain, pseud. Ed. by Shelly F. Fishkin. LC 96-17030. (The Oxford Mark Twain Stories Ser.). (Illus.). 720p. 1996. 25.00 (*0-19-510139-1*) OUP.

Life on the Mississippi. large type ed. Mark Twain, pseud. 560p. 1995. lib. bdg. 24.00 (*0-939495-79-1*) North Bks.

***Life On The Mississippi.** large type ed. Mark Twain, pseud. 608p. 2000. pap. 24.00 (*0-06-095567-8*) HarpC.

Life on the Mississippi. Mark Twain, pseud. 345p. 1983. reprint ed. lib. bdg. 25.95 (*0-89966-469-5*) Buccaneer Bks.

Life on the Mississippi. Mark Twain, pseud. 443p. 1998. reprint ed. lib. bdg. 24.00 (*1-58287-045-4*) North Bks.

Life on the Mississippi. Mark Twain, pseud. (Works of Mark Twain). 1988. reprint ed. lib. bdg. 59.00 (*0-7812-1114-X*) Rprt Serv.

Life on the Mississippi: TV Tie-In Edition. Mark Twain, pseud. (Illus.). 1961. mass mkt. 4.95 (*0-451-52172-2*, Sig Classics) NAL.

Life on the New River: A Pictorial History of the New River Gorge. William E. Cox. (Illus.). 66p. 1984. pap. 5.25 (*0-915992-45-0*) Eastern National.

***Life on the New River: A Pictorial History of the New River Gorge.** rev. ed. William E. Cox. (Illus.). 72p. 1999. pap. 9.95 (*1-888213-51-5*) Eastern National.

Life on the Ohio. Captain James Coomer. LC 97-14526. (Ohio River Valley Ser.). (Illus.). 200p. 1997. 24.95 (*0-8131-2000-4*) U Pr of Ky.

Life on the Ohio Frontier: A Collection of Letters from Mary Lott to Deacon John Phillips, 1826-1846. Jacqueline L. Bachar. LC 94-77122. (Illus.). 146p. 1994. 30.00 (*1-886934-00-2*) Intl Forum.

***Life on the Oregon Trail.** Gary L. Blackwood. (Way People Live Ser.). (Illus.). 112p. (YA). (gr. 4-12). 1999. lib. bdg. 23.70 (*1-56006-540-0*) Lucent Bks.

***Life on the Oregon Trail.** Sally Senzell Isaacs. LC 00-20645. (Picture the Past Ser.). (Illus.). 2000. write for info. (*1-57572-317-4*) Heinemann Lib.

***Life on the Other Side: A Psychic's Tour of the Afterlife.** Sylvia Browne & Lindsay Harrison. 304p. 2000. 23.95 (*0-525-94539-3*, Dutt) Dutton Plume.

Life on the Outside: The Tamil Diaspora & Long Distance Nationalism. Oivind Fuglerud. LC 98-42632. (Anthropology, Culture & Society Ser.). 224p. 1999. 59.95 (*0-7453-1438-4*, Pub. by Pluto GBR) Stylus Pub VA.

***Life on the Outside: The Tamil Diaspora & Long Distance Nationalism.** Oivind Fuglerud. 224p. 1999. pap. 25.00 (*0-7453-1433-3*, Pub. by Pluto GBR) Stylus Pub VA.

Life on the Plains & among the Diggings, Being Scenes & Adventures of an Overland Journey to California. Alonzo Delano. LC 72-9440. (Far Western Frontier Ser.). (Illus.). 396p. 1973. reprint ed. 26.95 (*0-405-04970-6*) Ayer.

Life on the Quads: A Centennial View of the Student Experience at the University of Chicago. Ronald J. Kim. LC 91-39938. (Illus.). 1992. pap. 7.00 (*0-943056-16-0*) Univ Chi Lib.

Life on the Ranch see Life in the Old West Series

Life on the Red Rock Ranch, 1904-1965: An Interview with Lawrence A. Dickinson. Ed. by N. J. Broughton. (Illus.). 198p. 1986. lib. bdg. 41.50 (*1-56475-304-2*); fiche. write for info. (*1-56475-305-0*) U NV Oral Hist.

Life on the Red Rock Ranch, 1931-1965: An Interview with Judie Dickinson. Ed. by N. J. Broughton. (Illus.). 243p. 1986. lib. bdg. 45.50 (*1-56475-302-6*); fiche. write for info. (*1-56475-303-4*) U NV Oral Hist.

Life on the Ridge. J. H. Pratt. (Illus.). 170p. 1987. pap. 9.95 (*1-55787-021-7*, NY76064, Empire State Bks) Hrt of the Lakes.

Life on the Road. Charles Kuralt. 352p. 1991. mass mkt. 6.99 (*0-8041-0869-2*) Ivy Books.

Life on the Road: A Beginner's Guide to the Stage Production Industry. William Boswell. 704p. (C). 1989. pap. text 51.00 (*0-536-57489-8*) Pearson Custom.

Life on the Road: A Beginner's Guide to the Stage Production Touring Industry. 3rd rev. ed. Ed. by William R. Boswell. LC 97-140967. 646p. (C). 1996. pap. text 56.00 (*0-536-59800-2*) Pearson Custom.

Life on the Road: The Gospel Basis for a Messianic Lifestyle. Athol Gill. LC 92-15251. 336p. 1992. reprint ed. pap. 14.99 (*0-8361-3588-1*) Herald Pr.

Life on the Road: The Incredible Rock 'n' Roll Adventures of Dinky Dawson. Dinky Dawson & Carter Alan. LC 98-87331. 354p. 1998. pap. 19.95 (*0-8230-8344-6*) Watsn-Guptill.

***Life on the Rocks: The Art of Survival.** Philippa Nikulinsky & Stephen D. Hopper. (Illus.). 184p. 1999. pap. 24.95 (*1-86368-258-9*, Pub. by Fremantle Arts) Intl Spec Bk.

***Life on the Run.** Bill Bradley. LC 99-36343. 295p. 1999. 29.95 (*1-56000-454-1*) Transaction Pubs.

Life on the Run. Bill Bradley. 1995. pap. 12.00 (*0-679-76208-6*) Vin Bks.

Life on the Russian Country Estate: A Social & Cultural History. Priscilla Roosevelt. LC 94-42337. (Illus.). 384p. 1995. 55.00 (*0-300-05595-1*) Yale U Pr.

An Asterisk (*) at the beginning of an entry indicates that the title is appearing for the first time.

L

Life on the Russian Country Estate: A Social & Cultural History. Priscilla Roosevelt. (Illus.). 384p. 1997. pap. 25.00 (0-300-07262-7) Yale U Pr.
Life on the Screen: Identity in the Age of the Internet. Sherry Turkle. LC 95-38428. 347p. 1995. 25.00 (0-684-80353-4) S&S Trade.
Life on the Screen: Identity in the Age of the Internet. Sherry Turkle. 352p. 1997. per. 14.00 (0-684-83348-4, Touchstone) S&S Trade Pap.
Life on the Tanque Verde: The History, Bk. 1. Erni Cabat & Charlotte M. Cardon. (Illus.). 1983. 9.50 (0-913521-00-0) Cabat Studio Pubns.
Life on the Texas Range. J. Evetts Haley. (M. K. Brown Range Life Ser.). (Illus.). 112p. (Orig.). 1994. reprint ed. pap. 19.95 (0-292-77683-7) U of Tex Pr.
Life on the Trail see Life in the Old West Series
***Life on the Underground Railroad.** Stuart A. Kallen. LC 99-37101. (Way People Live Ser.). (Illus.). 112p. (YA). (gr. 6-9). 2000. lib. bdg. 23.70 (1-56006-667-9) Lucent Bks.
***Life on the Vine: Cultivating the Fruit of the Spirit in Christian Community.** Philip Kenneson. LC 99-36493. 1999. pap. 14.99 (0-8308-2219-4) InterVarsity.
Life on the Wing: Adventures with Birds of Prey. David T. Moran. LC 96-71286. (Illus.). xvii, 275p. 1997. 75.00 (0-9655519-0-3) Round Table CO.
Life on the Yukon, 1865-1867. George R. Adams. Ed. by Richard A. Pierce. (Alaska History Ser.: No. 22). (Illus.). 219p. 1982. 24.00 (0-919642-87-X) Limestone Pr.
***Life on Tour with David Bowie: We Can Be Heros.** Sean Mayes. 2000. pap. text 12.95 (1-897783-17-5) Indep Music Pr.
Life on Wheels: For the Active Wheelchair User. Gary Karp. Ed. by Linda Lamb. LC 99-10557. (Medical Ser.). (Illus.). 573p. 1998. pap. 24.95 (1-56592-253-0) OReilly & Assocs.
Life 101. Peter McWilliams. 1997. 12.95 (0-931580-64-1) Prelude Press.
Life 101 Quote Book. Peter McWilliams. 1997. pap. text 7.95 (0-931580-67-6) Prelude Press.
Life 102: What to Do When Your Guru Sues You. Peter McWilliams. 423p. 1994. 19.95 (0-931580-34-X) Prelude Press.
Life One-0-One: Everything We Wish We Had Learned about Life in School But Didn't. unabridged rev. ed. Peter McWilliams. (Life 101 Ser.). 400p. 1994. pap. 22.95 incl. audio (0-931580-78-1) Prelude Press.
Life Online: Researching Real Experience in Virtual Space. Annette Markham. LC 98-25339. 248p. (C). 1998. 62.00 (0-7619-9030-5); pap. 21.95 (0-7619-9031-3) AltaMira Pr.
Life or Biography of Silas Felton, Written by Himself. Ed. by Rena L. Vassar. 37p. 1960. pap. 3.00 (0-912296-27-5) Am Antiquarian.
Life, or Legend of Gaudama: The Buddha of the Burmese, 2 vols., Set. 4th ed. Paul A. Bigandet. LC 77-8749. reprint ed. 75.00 (0-404-16800-0) AMS Pr.
Life Ought to Come with Directions. Jeff Tucker. 120p. (J). 1998. pap. text 7.99 (0-87788-482-X, H Shaw Pubs) Waterbrook Pr.
Life Out of Bounds: Bioinvasion in a Borderless World. Chris Bright. LC 99-163011. (Illus.). 288p. 1998. pap. 13.00 (0-393-31814-1) Norton.
Life Out of Death. Grace Livingston Hill. 17.95 (0-89190-402-6) Amereon Ltd.
Life Out of Death. Jessie Penn-Lewis. 1979. mass mkt. 5.99 (0-87508-950-X) Chr Lit.
Life Out of Focus: Alzheimer's Disease & Dementia. Carol C. Nadelson. LC 98-26537. (Encyclopedia of Psychological Disorders Ser.). 144p. 1999. 24.95 (0-7910-4896-9) Chelsea Hse.
Life Out There: The Truth of-& Search for-Extraterrestrial Life. Michael James Denham White. LC 98-38377. 1998. 24.00 (0-88001-671-X) HarpC.
Life Outdoors: A Curmudgeon Looks at the Natural World. Wayne Hanley. LC 80-21980. (Illus.). 144p. 1980. pap. 5.95 (0-8289-0403-0) Viking Penguin.
Life Outside: The Signorile Report on Gay Men: Sex, Love, Family, & the Passages of Life. Michelangelo Signorile. 368p. 1998. pap. 13.00 (0-06-092904-9, Perennial) HarperTrade.
Life Outside the Law Firm: Non-Traditional Careers. Karen Treffinger. (Paralegal Law Library). 1995. teacher ed. 9.50 (0-8273-7132-2, VNR) Wiley.
Life Outside the Law Firm: Non-Traditional Careers for Paralegals. Karen Treffinger. LC 94-29379. 224p. (C). 1995. mass mkt. 37.95 (0-8273-6718-X) Delmar.
Life, Paint & Passion: Reclaiming the Magic of Spontaneous Expression. Michelle Cassou & Stewart Cubley. (Illus.). 208p. (Orig.). 1996. pap. 16.95 (0-87477-810-7, Tarcher Putnam) Putnam Pub Group.
Life Paints Its Own Span: On the Significance of Spontaneous Paintings by Severly Ill Children. Susan Bach. 213p. 1995. pap. 35.95 (3-85630-516-5) Continuum.
***Life Passages: Writing Exercises for Self-Exploration.** Allan G. Hunter. LC 00-25988. 203p. 2000. 18.95 (1-56072-787-X, Nova Kroshka Bks) Nova Sci Pubs.
Life Passages for Men: Understanding the Stages of a Man's Life. E. James Wilder. 222p. 1997. pap. 18.00 (1-57910-032-5) Wipf & Stock.
Life Patterns: A Relationship Textbook. Loy Young. Ed. by Kathryn Hall. 108p. (Orig.). 1993. pap. 19.95 (1-882888-00-6) Aquarius Hse.
Life Patterns: A Relationship Textbook. 2nd ed. Loy Young & Robert Young. Ed. by Kathryn Hall. 218p. (Orig.). 1994. pap. 14.95 (1-882888-41-3) Aquarius Hse.
Life Patterns: Responding to Life's Questions, Crises, & Challenges. Jerry Schottelndreier. Tr. by Jakob Cornelis. (Biography & Self-Development Ser.). 64p. 1995. pap. 10.95 (1-869890-27-2, Pub. by Hawthorn Press) Anthroposophic.
Life Patterns: Soul Lessons & Forgiveness. 3rd ed. Henry L. Bolduc. Ed. by Majorie Reynolds. LC 94-68926. (Illus.). 300p. 1994. pap. 14.95 (0-9601302-4-1) Adventures Time.
Life Peak: Personal Achievement Method. Rick Heinick & Jay Ackerman. 200p. 1998. pap. write for info. (0-9665840-7-4) Personal Perform SW.
Life Penalty. Joy Fielding. 400p. 1998. mass mkt. 6.99 (0-440-22338-5) Dell.
Life Performance Testing of Flourescent Lamps: LM-40-87. write for info. (0-87995-077-3, LM-40-87) Illum Eng.
Life Personality & Writings of Al-Junayd. Abdel-Kader. (Gibb Collection). 1962. pap. 20.00 (0-7189-0223-8, Pub. by Aris & Phillips) David Brown.
Life Photographers: What They Saw. John Loengard. LC 98-14442. (Illus.). 456p. (gr. 8). 1998. 35.00 (0-8212-2518-9) Little.
Life Plan: Step by Step Guide to Achieving Prosperity Now. David D. Thornburg. (Illus.). 195p. (C). 1987. pap. 12.95 (0-942207-01-7) Starsong CA.
Life Plan - Finding Your Real Self: The Journey Through Life. R. Allen Walls. (Illus.). 303p. 1991. 20.00 (0-9621790-1-9) Inner Search Found.
Life Plan - Finding Your Real Self: The Journey Through Life. R. Allen Walls. (Illus.). 303p. 1992. pap. 9.95 (0-9621790-2-7) Inner Search Found.
Life Planning. Manly P. Hall. pap. 4.95 (0-89314-328-6) Philos Res.
Life Planning Guide for Women. Mary Vander Goot. 128p. 1982. pap. 12.95 (0-88946-512-6) E Mellen.
Life Planning in New Mexico: Your Guide to State Law on Powers of Attorney, Right to Die, Nursing Home Benefits, Wills, Trusts & Probate. 3rd rev. ed. Merri Rudd. LC 92-70603. 238p. 2000. pap. 16.95 (0-9632173-1-3) Abogada Pr.
Life Planning Workbook: A Hands-on Guide to Help Parents Provide for the Future Security & Happiness of Their Child with a Disability after Their Death. L. Mark Russell & Arnold E. Grant. 300p. (Orig.). 1995. pap. text 24.95 (0-9635780-7-3) Amer Pub IL.
Life-Planning Workbook: The Leap of Faith - The Dance of Change. Nicholas F. Rayder & Sandy Fails. 148p. 1995. write for info. (0-9648454-0-7) Paradise CO.
Life Plus Ninety-Nine Years. Nathan F. Leopold, Jr. LC 73-16644. 381p. 1974. reprint ed. lib. bdg. 69.50 (0-8371-7207-1, LELP, Greenwood Pr) Greenwood.
Life Portraits of William Shakespeare. J. Hain Friswell. LC 76-168063. (Illus.). reprint ed. 32.50 (0-404-02624-9) AMS Pr.
Life Power & How to Use It. Elizabeth Towne. 176p. 1996. reprint ed. spiral bd. 13.00 (0-7873-0886-2) Hlth Research.
Life Power & How to Use It (1906) Elizabeth Towne. 176p. 1996. reprint ed. pap. 12.00 (1-56459-958-2) Kessinger Pub.
Life Prayers: From Around the World: 365 Prayers, Blessings, & Affirmations to Celebrate the Human Journey. Ed. by Elizabeth Roberts & Elias L. Amidon. LC 96-385. 464p. 1996. pap. 17.00 (0-06-251377-X, Pub. by Harper SF) HarpC.
Life Prediction Methodologies & Data for Ceramic Materials. Ed. by C. R. Brinkman & S. F. Duffy. LC 93-44605. (ASTM Special Technical Publication Ser.: Vol. 1201). (Illus.). 425p. 1994. text 59.00 (0-8031-1864-3, STP1201) ASTM.
Life Prediction Methodology for Titanium Matrix Composites. Ed. by W. S. Johnson et al. LC 96-10845. (Special Technical Publication Ser.: No. 1253). (Illus.). 630p. 1996. text 169.00 (0-8031-2039-7, STP1253) ASTM.
Life Prediction of Corrodible Structures. Ed. by R. N. Parkins. LC 94-67148. (Illus.). 1670p. 1994. pap. 132.00 (1-877914-60-6) NACE Intl.
Life Prescription. Mauldin. 128p. 1996. text 24.95 (0-7872-2456-1) Kendall-Hunt.
Life Preservers: Staying Afloat in Love & Life. text. write for info. (0-7881-9185-3) DIANE Pub.
Life Preservers: Staying Afloat in Love & Life. Harriet G. Lerner. 335p. 1998. pap. text 13.00 (0-7881-5906-2) DIANE Pub.
Life Preservers: Staying Afloat in Love & Life. Harriet G. Lerner. 368p. 1997. pap. 13.50 (0-06-092835-2, Perennial) HarperTrade.
Life Principles from the Old Testament. Wayne Barber. (Following God Ser.). 1998. pap. text 16.99 (0-89957-300-2) AMG Pubs.
Life Prints. Carol A. Belding. 10p. 1996. pap. 1.98 (1-888923-01-6) Poetic License.
***Life Prints: A Memoir of Healing & Discovery.** unabridged ed. Mary Grimley Mason. LC 99-56912. (Cross-Cultural Memoir Ser.). (Illus.). 224p. 2000. 19.95 (1-55861-237-8, Pub. by Feminist Pr) Consort Bk Sales.
Life Progress Map: Faith Stages Toward Maturity. 2nd rev. ed. Wilberta L. Chinn. (Illus.). 59p. (Orig.). 1997. spiral bd. 7.95 (0-937673-15-3) Peacock Ent LA.
Life Progress Map Leader's Guide: A 12-Session Curriculum to Guide Others Through Six Stages of Faith. Wilberta L. Chinn. 38p. (Orig.). 1997. spiral bd. 7.95 (0-937673-14-5) Peacock Ent LA.
Life Project: Forming Christian Attitudes Toward Death & Dying. Barbara Blackburn. 32p. (J). (gr. k-2). 1995. pap. 2.95 (0-89243-761-8) Liguori Pubns.
Life Project: Forming Christian Attitudes Toward Death & Dying. Barbara Blackburn. 64p. (gr. 3-5). 1995. pap. 3.95 (0-89243-762-6) Liguori Pubns.
Life Project: Forming Christian Attitudes Toward Death & Dying. Barbara Blackburn. 64p. (gr. 6-8). 1995. pap. 3.95 (0-89243-763-4) Liguori Pubns.
***Life, Psychotherapy & Death: The End of Our Exploring.** Ann Orbach. LC 98-32272. 200p. 1999. 29.95 (1-85302-553-4) Taylor & Francis.
Life Pulse. Joseph Pillitteri. 1989. mass mkt. 3.95 (1-55817-280-7, Pinnacle Kensgtn) Kensgtn Pub Corp.
Life Pulse: Episodes from the Story of the Fossil Record. Niles Eldridge. LC 86-4558. (Illus.). 256p. reprint ed. pap. 79.40 (0-7837-5345-4, 204508800005) Bks Demand.
Life Puzzle: Putting the Pieces Together. Ann G. Kramer. 1998. pap. 24.95 (0-9659426-0-0) Good FourU.
Life Quest: A Journey into Self. Ojela Frank. Ed. by Dorian Caruso. 298p. (Orig.). 1991. pap. 11.95 (0-9619010-2-0) Holistic Hlth.
Life Records of John Milton, 1608-1674, 5 Vols, Set. Ed. by J. Milton French. LC 66-20024. 2368p. 1966. reprint ed. 500.00 (0-87752-039-9) Gordian.
Life Recovery. LC 98-41211. 1998. 54.99 (0-8423-3343-6) Tyndale Hse.
***Life Recovery Bible: New Living Translation.** LC 98-41211. 1600p. 1998. pap. 19.99 (0-8423-3341-X) Tyndale Hse.
Life Recovery Guides, 10 vols., Set. Dale Ryan & Juanita Ryan. (Orig.). 1990. pap., wbk. ed. 49.90 (0-8308-1150-8, 1150) InterVarsity.
Life! Reflections on Your Journey see Vivre!: Reflexions sur la Plus Merveilleuse Aventure
Life Reframing in Hypnosis: The Seminars, Workshops & Lectures of Milton H. Erickson, Vol. 2. Milton H. Erickson. Ed. by Ernest L. Rossi & Margaret O. Ryan. (Illus.). 330p. 1985. 19.95 (0-8290-3155-3); digital audio 39.50 (0-8290-1581-7); digital audio 20.00 (0-8290-3160-X) Irvington.
***Life Regained: Diaries, 1970-1972.** Francis Partridge. 1999. pap. 15.95 (0-7538-0754-8) Phoenix Hse.
Life Region: The Social & Cultural Ecology of Sustainable Development. Per G. Raberg. LC 96-32983. 464p. (C). 1997. 95.00 (0-415-15905-9) Routledge.
Life Riddles. Melrose Cooper. 88p. (J). (gr. 5-7). 1995. 14.95 (0-8050-2613-4, Bks Young Read) H Holt & Co.
Life Risk-Based Capital Report Including Overview & Instructions for Companies. 48p. (C). 1994. pap. 25.00 (0-89382-290-6) Nat Assn Insurance.
Life Row: A Case Study of How a Family Can Survive a Medical Crisis. Ed Linz. LC 97-600095. (Illus.). ix, 351p. (Orig.). 1997. pap. 16.00 (0-9656895-0-6, 02-00097) Exchange Pub WA.
Life Safety Code Handbook. Ron Cote. (Illus.). 1997. 89.50 (0-87765-425-5, 101HB97) Natl Fire Prot.
Life Safety in Underground Rail Systems, TR 833: The Australian Effort. R. P. Londregan. 1983. 4.35 (0-685-07672-5, TR83-3) Society Fire Protect.
Life Sagas. Robert D. Judy. (Illus.). (Orig.). 1990. pap. 8.95 (0-9627383-0-1) RDJ Assocs.
Life Savers of Cape Cod. J. W. Dalton. (Illus.). 176p. (YA). 1991. reprint ed. pap. 8.95 (0-940160-49-8) Parnassus Imprints.
Life-Saving Cures: How to Use the Latest & Most Powerful Cures for the 21st Century. Cass Ingram. 300p. 1999. pap. 18.95 (0-911119-99-X) Igram Pr.
Life Savor: How to Turn on Delight. Roz Van Meter. LC 87-82438. (Illus.). 128p. (Orig.). 1987. pap. 8.95 (0-944486-00-2) Hollngswrth TX.
Life Science. William L. Smallwood. (Challenges to Science Ser.). 1972. text 33.52 (0-07-058415-X) McGraw.
Life Science. Keith Taylor. LC 95-9872. 1995. 20.00 (1-882413-15-6) Hanging Loose.
Life Science. Keith Taylor. LC 95-9872. 72p. 1995. pap. 12.00 (1-882413-14-8) Hanging Loose.
Life Science. Watkins. 1994. text, teacher ed. 105.75 (0-03-097527-1) H Holt & Co.
Life Science. Watkins. 1989. pap. text, teacher ed., lab manual ed. 29.00 (0-15-361465-X); pap. text, student ed. 10.00 (0-15-361474-9); pap. text, lab manual ed. 16.25 (0-15-361462-5) Holt R&W.
Life Science. 3rd ed. Wright. (Life Science Ser.). 1993. text. write for info. (0-13-982125-2) P-H.
Life Science: All Creatures Great & Small. Michael Spear. (J). (gr. 7-9). 1991. pap. 15.00 (0-89824-534-6); pap. 5.00 (0-89824-535-4) Trillium Pr.
Life Science: Content & Learning Strategies. M. Christison & Sharron Bassano. (Science Through Active Reading Ser.). 128p. 1992. pap. 16.35 (0-8013-0347-8, 78122) Longman.
Life Science: Outlines & Activities. 3rd ed. (C). 1997. 18.00 (0-8087-9846-4) Pearson Custom.
***Life Science: Outlines & Activities.** 4th ed. (C). 1999. write for info. (0-8087-7588-X) Pearson Custom.
Life Science: Supplement of Principles of Physics. 2nd ed. Serway. 104p. (C). 1997. pap. text, suppl. ed. 17.00 (0-03-020662-6) SCP.
Life Science: Teacher Edition. 1994. write for info. (0-201-25729-7) Addison-Wesley.
Life Science: (Texas) Watkins. 1994. text, teacher ed. 105.75 (0-03-098089-5) H Holt & Co.
Life, Science & Religious Concerns: Their Interrelations & Life's Meaning. Herbert H. Uhlig. 162p. 1988. 14.95 (0-914960-69-5) Academy Bks.
Life Science & Space Research XXV: Natural & Artificial Ecosystems. R. D. Macelroy. (Advances in Space Research Ser.). 466p. 1994. pap. 165.00 (0-08-042488-0, Pergamon Pr) Elsevier.
Life Science & Space Research XX(4) Planetary Biology & Origins of Life. Greenberg. (Advances in Space Research Ser.: No. 15-3). 1994. pap. write for info. (0-614-01941-9, Pergamon Pr) Elsevier.
Life Science for ESL. M. Christison & Sharron Bassano. (Science Through Active Reading Ser.). 128p. 1992. teacher ed. 11.21 (0-685-59058-5, 79278) Longman.
Life Science Labs Lit. Michael Fleming. (Illus.). 280p. 1985. pap. text 29.95 (0-87628-540-X) Ctr Appl Res.
Life Science Lexicon. William N. Marchuk. 224p. (C). 1991. text. write for info. (0-697-12133-X, WCB McGr Hill) McGrw-H Hghr Educ.
Life Science, 1989. Watkins. 1989. 53.75 (0-15-361450-1); teacher ed. 106.76 (0-15-361453-6) H Holt & Co.
Life Science I Curriculum Set. (Macmillan Early Science Activities Ser.). (Illus.). 384p. (J). (ps-2). 1997. pap. text 115.00 (1-56784-648-3) Newbridge Educ.
Life Science T/e. Bassano. 128p. 1989. 17.98 (0-8013-0985-9) S&S Trade.
Life Science II. 2nd ed. Kneeland K. Nesius. 246p. (C). per. 24.95 (0-7872-6610-8) Kendall-Hunt.
Life Science II Curriculum Set. (Macmillan Early Science Activities Ser.). (Illus.). 384p. (J). (ps-2). 1997. pap. text 115.00 (1-56784-649-1) Newbridge Educ.
Life Sciences. National Research Council Staff. (Space in the 21st Century Ser.). 160p. 1988. pap. text 19.95 (0-309-03880-4) Natl Acad Pr.
Life Sciences: Complex Organics in Space. Ed. by F. Raulin & J. Mayo Greenberg. (Advances in Space Research Ser.: Vol. 19, No. 7). 184p. 1997. pap. 108.00 (0-08-043108-9, Pergamon Pr) Elsevier.
Life Sciences: Life Support Systems Studies - I. Ed. by R. M. Wheeler et al. 272p. 1998. pap. 100.50 (0-08-043307-3, Pergamon Pr) Elsevier.
Life Sciences: Space & Mars Recent Results: Proceedings of the F3.1, F3.4, F2.4 & F3.8 Symposia of COSPAR Scientific Commission F Which Were Held During the Thirtieth COSPAR Scientific Assembly, Hamburg, Germany, 11-21 July 1994. Ed. by A. Brack et al. (Advances in Space Research Ser.: Vol. 18). 272p. 1996. pap. 94.50 (0-08-043082-1, Pergamon Pr) Elsevier.
Life Sciences & Health Challenges. Susan Raymond. (Annals of the New York Academy of Science Ser.). 160p. 1999. pap. 19.95 (0-8018-6300-7) Johns Hopkins.
Life Sciences & Health Challenges. Susan Raymond. 160p. 1998. pap. 30.00 (1-57331-148-0) NY Acad Sci.
Life Sciences & Space Research XXV (1) Gravitational Biology: Proceedings of the Topical Meeting of the COSPAR Interdisciplinary Scientific Commission F (Meeting F1) of the COSPAR 29th Plenary Meeting Held in Washington, D. C., U. S. A. 28 August-5 September, 1992. Ed. by A. Cogoli et al. (Advances in Space Research Ser.: Vol. 14). (Illus.). 472p. 1994. pap. 176.00 (0-08-042485-6) Elsevier.
Life Sciences & Space Research XXV (4) Planetary Biology & Origins of Life. Ed. by J. M. Greenberg et al. (Advances in Space Research (RJ) Ser.: Vol. 15, No. 3). 450p. 1994. pap. 165.00 (0-08-042540-2, Pergamon Pr) Elsevier.
Life Sciences & Space Research XXV: Proceedings of the Topical Meeting of the COSPAR Interdisciplinary Scientific Commission F (Meeting 2) of the COSPAR Twenty-ninth Plenary Meeting Held in Washington, DC, USA 28 August - 5 September 1992. Topical Meeting of the COSPAR Interdisciplinary Sc. Ed. by P. Todd et al. (Advances in Space Research Ser.: Vol. 14). (Illus.). 1074p. 1994. pap. 165.00 (0-08-042487-2, Pergamon Pr) Elsevier.
Life Sciences & Space Research XXIV (2) G. Horneck et al. (Advances in Space Research (RJ) Ser.: Vol. 12). 468p. 1992. 337.75 (0-08-041844-9, Pergamon Pr) Elsevier.
Life Sciences & Space Research XXIV (1) R. S. Young et al. (Advances in Space Research (RJ) Ser.: Vol. 12). 416p. 1992. 165.00 (0-08-041843-0, Pergamon Pr) Elsevier.
Life Sciences & Space Research XXIV (4) Natural & Artificial Ecosystems: Proceedings of the Topical Meeting of the COSPAR Interdiscplinary Scientific Commission F (Meetings F10, F11, F1 & F12) of the COSPAR 28th Plenary Meeting Held in The Hague, The Netherlands, 25 June-6 July, 1990. Ed. by R. D. MacElroy et al. (Advances in Space Research Ser.: Vol. 12). 280p. 1992. pap. 165.00 (0-08-041849-X, Pergamon Pr) Elsevier.
Life Sciences & Space Research XXIV (3) Planetary Biology & Origins of Life: Proceedings of the Topical Meeting of the COSPAR Interdisciplinary Scientific Commission F (Meetings F7, F1, F8 & F9) of the COSPAR 28th Plenary Meeting Held in The Hague, The Netherlands, 25 June-6 July, 1990. Ed. by J. Oro et al. (Advances in Space Research Ser.: Vol. 12). 288p. 1992. pap. 165.00 (0-08-041845-7, Pergamon Pr) Elsevier.
Life Sciences & Space Research XXI (1) Proceedings of the Topical Meeting of the COSPAR Interdisciplinary Scientific Commission F (Meetings F4 & F8) of the COSPAR 25th Plenary Meeting held in Graz, Austria 25 June-7 July 1984. Ed. by H. P. Klein & G. Korneck. (Illus.). 300p. 1985. pap. 54.00 (0-08-032746-X, Pub. by PPL) Elsevier.
Life Sciences & Space Research XXI (2) Proceedings of Workshops VII & XI & of the COSPAR Interdisciplinary Scientific Commission F (Meetings F1, F3, F5, F6, F7, & F9) of the COSPAR 25th Plenary Meeting Held in Graz, Austria, 25 June - 7 July 1984. Ed. by R. S. Young et al. (Illus.). 334p. 1985. pap. 54.00 (0-08-032752-4, Pub. by PPL) Elsevier.
Life Sciences & Space Research XXIII (1) Exobiology Science & Primitive Solar System Bodies: Proceedings of Workshop XXII of the COSPAR 27th Plenary Meeting Held is Espoo, Finland, 18-29 July, 1988. Ed. by J. Oro. (Advances in Space Research Ser.: Vol. 9). 125p. 1989. pap. 79.00 (0-08-037381-X, Pergamon Pr) Elsevier.
Life Sciences & Space Research XXIII (5) Gravitational Biology: Proceedings of the Topical Meeting of the COSPAR Interdisciplinary Scientific Commission F (Meetings F1, F3, F4 & F5) & of Workshops XVII & XVIII of the COSPAR 27th Plenary Meeting Held in Espoo, Finaldn, July, 1988. Ed. by Heinz Oser et al. (Advances in Space Research Ser.: Vol. 9). 302p. 1989. pap. 92.75 (0-08-040154-6, 1702; 0201; 020, Pergamon Pr) Elsevier.

An Asterisk (*) at the beginning of an entry indicates that the title is appearing for the first time.

Life Sciences & Space Research XXIII (3) Natural & Artificial Ecosystems: Proceedings of the Topical Meetings of COSPAR Interdisciplinary Scientific Commission F (Meetings F9, F10, F11 & F12) of the COSPAR 27th Plenary Meeting Held in Espoo, Finland, 18-29 July, 1988, No. XXIII. Ed. by R. D. MacElroy et al. (Advances in Space Research Ser.: Vol. 9). (Illus.). 196p. 1989. pap. 92.75 (*0-08-040150-3*, Pergamon Pr) Elsevier.

Life Sciences & Space Research XXIII (2) Planetary Biology & Origins of Life: Proceedings of the Topical Meeting of COSPAR Interdisciplinary Scientific Commission F (Meetings F1, F7 & F8) & of Workshops XX, XXI & XXIII of the COSPAR 27th Plenary Meeting Held in Espoo, Finland, 18-29 July, '88. Ed. by A. W. Schwartz et al. (Advances in Space Research Ser.: Vol. 9). (Illus.). 232p. 1989. reprint ed. pap. 92.75 (*0-08-040146-5*, Pub. by PPL) Elsevier.

Life Sciences in Eighteenth-Century French Thought. Roger Jacques & Keith R. Benson. LC 96-49548. 800p. 1998. 75.00 (*0-8047-2578-0*) Stanford U Pr.

Life Sciences on File. Diagram Group Staff. (Illus.). 304p. 1986. ring bd. 165.00 (*0-8160-1284-9*) Facts on File.

Life Sciences on File. rev. ed. Diagram Group Staff. LC 98-55738. (Illus.). 302p. 1999. ring bd. 165.00 (*0-8160-3872-4*, Checkmark) Facts on File.

Life Sciences Simulation: Then, Now & When. Ed. by John McLeod. 66p. 1990. pap. 32.00 (*0-911801-70-7*, EMC90-2) Soc Computer Sim.

Life Secrets. Henry Foster. Ed. by Hal H. Helms. LC 95-33709. (Living Library Ser.). 239p. 1995. pap. 9.95 (*1-55725-149-5*, 930-040, Pub. by Paraclete MA) BookWorld.

Life Sentence. Charles W. Colson. 320p. 1999. mass mkt. 6.99 (*0-8007-8668-8*, Spire) Revell.

Life Sentence: The Guy's Survival Guide to Getting Engaged & Married. J. D. Smith. LC 98-49356. (Illus.). 143p. (Orig.). 1999. mass mkt. 9.99 (*0-446-67430-3*, Pub. by Warner Bks) Little.

Life Sentence Prisoners. Roger Sapsford. 160p. 1983. pap. 25.00 (*0-335-10413-4*) OpUniv Pr.

Life Sentences. Joe Kirkup. Ed. by Audrey Saly. (Illus.). 112p. 1998. pap. 15.00 (*0-9664751-0-0*) XPress.

Life Sentences. Richard Nelson. 96p. (Orig.). 1993. pap. 8.95 (*0-571-19831-7*) Faber & Faber.

Life Sentences. John R. Reed. 86p. (Orig.). 1996. pap. 15.95 (*0-8143-2629-3*) Wayne St U Pr.

Life Sentences. Wilbert Rideau. 1992. pap. 16.00 (*0-8129-2048-1*, Times Bks) Crown Pub Group.

Life Sentences: Aspects of the Social Role of Language. Ed. by Romano Harre. LC 75-40021. 194p. reprint ed. pap. 60.20 (*0-608-15877-1*, 203075500070) Bks Demand.

Life Sentences: Freeing Black Relationships. Mzee L. Okpara. 85p. 1993. pap. 8.00 (*0-88378-146-8*) Third World.

Life Sentences: Literary Essays. Joseph Epstein. LC 97-6322. 288p. 1997. 25.00 (*0-393-04546-3*) Norton.

Life Sentences: Selected Poems. Nina Cassian. 1991. pap. 8.95 (*0-393-30721-2*) Norton.

Life Sentences: Writers, Artists, & AIDS. Ed. by Thomas Avena. LC 93-38922. (Illus.). 304p. 1994. pap. 14.95 (*1-56279-051-X*) Mercury Hse Inc.

Life Series. Lifetime Guarantee Ministries Staff & Mars Hill Productions Staff. (Illus.). 62p. 1996. student ed., spiral bd. 8.00 (*0-9624056-6-3*) Mars Hill TX.

Life Services Planning: Creating Your Own Program. 80p. 1988. pap. 11.00 (*0-89707-394-0*, 344-0011) Amer Bar Assn.

Life Services Planning: Support Services & Alternatives to Guardianship. 27p. 1988. pap. 7.00 (*0-89707-395-9*, 344-0010) Amer Bar Assn.

Life Services Planning: Training Volunteers & Practitioners. 118p. 1988. pap. 18.00 (*0-89707-393-2*, 344-0012) Amer Bar Assn.

Life, Sex, & Death: Selected Writings. William H. Gillespie. Ed. & Intro. by Michael D. Sinason. LC 94-42274. (New Library of Psychoanalysis Ser.: Vol. 23). (Illus.). 224p. (C). 1995. pap. 25.99 (*0-415-12805-6*) Routledge.

Life, Sex, & Death: Selected Writings. William H. Gillespie. Ed. & Intro. by Michael D. Sinason. LC 94-42274. (New Library of Psychoanalysis Ser.: Vol. 23). (Illus.). 224p. (C). (gr. 13). 1995. 80.00 (*0-415-12804-8*) Routledge.

Life-Shaping Decisions. Larry Cochran. LC 90-35343. (American University Studies: Psychology: Ser. VIII, Vol. 22). 178p. (C). 1991. text 33.95 (*0-8204-1368-2*) P Lang Pubng.

Life-Sharing for a Creative Tomorrow. Mary-Rose Barral. LC 91-18281. (American University Studies: Philosophy: Ser. V, Vol. 119). 175p. (C). 1992. text 39.95 (*0-8204-1541-3*) P Lang Pubng.

Life Significance of French Baroque Poetry. Marlies Kronegger. (American University Studies: Series 2, Vol. 81). XVIII, 160p. 1988. 30.50 (*0-8204-0639-2*) P Lang Pubng.

Life Signs. Jayanta Mahapatra. (Three Crowns Bks.). (Illus.). 1984. pap. 5.95 (*0-19-561585-9*) OUP.

Life Signs: The Biology of Star Trek. Robert Jenkins. 208p. 1998. 22.00 (*0-06-019154-6*) HarpC.

Life Situation. large type ed. Rosemary Friedman. 592p. 1992. 27.99 (*0-7089-2607-X*) Ulverscroft.

Life 60 Years: An Anniversary Celebration. Life Editors. 192p. 1996. 24.95 (*0-8212-2335-6*, Pub. by Bulfinch Pr) Little.

Life-Size. Shute Jenefer. 320p. 1997. reprint ed. mass mkt. 6.99 (*0-380-73021-9*, Avon Bks) Morrow Avon.

Life-Size. Jennifer Shute. 240p. 1993. reprint ed. pap. 10.00 (*0-380-72064-7*, Avon Bks) Morrow Avon.

Life-Size Living. Leonard W. Mann. Ed. by Michael L. Sherer. (Orig.). 1986. pap. 6.55 (*0-89536-820-X*, 6829) CSS OH.

***Life-Sized Pop-Up Alien Book.** David Hawcock & Clare Bampton. (Illus.). 16p. (J). 2000. pap. 14.99 (*0-307-33203-9*, 33203, Goldn Books) Gldn Bks Pub Co.

Life Sketches of Ellen G. White: An Autobiography. Ellen Gould Harmon White. 1943. reprint ed. pap. 12.99 (*0-8163-0103-4*, 12220-0) Pacific Pr Pub Assn.

Life Sketches of Eminent Lawyers: American, English & Canadian, to Which Is Added Thoughts, Facts & Facetiae, 2 vols., Vol. 1. Gilbert J. Clark. (Illus.). xi, 368p. 1983. reprint ed. 95.00 (*0-8377-0447-2*, Rothman) W S Hein.

Life Sketches of Eminent Lawyers, American, English & Canadian, to Which Is Added Thoughts, Facts & Facetiae, 2 vols., Vol. 2. Gilbert J. Clark. (Illus.). xi, 384p. 1983. reprint ed. write for info. (*0-318-57042-4*) W S Hein.

Life Skillbuilders. (Illus.). 96p. 1994. write for info. (*0-945100-26-4*) Parlay Intl.

Life Skills. Katie Fforde. LC 99-39125. 352p. 1999. text 24.95 (*0-312-20951-7*) St Martin.

Life Skills. Myrl Shireman. (Illus.). 64p. (YA). (gr. 5-8). 1995. pap. text 8.95 (*1-58037-029-2*, Pub. by M Twain Media) Carson-Dellos.

Life Skills. Marlis Wesseler. 112p. 1992. pap. 10.95 (*1-55050-040-6*, Pub. by Coteau) Genl Dist Srvs.

***Life Skills: Keys to Effective Living.** Jill Raiguel. 1999. pap. 14.95 (*1-893897-00-1*) Marshall Edu.

Life Skills: Level 1. Elaine Kirn. (ETC Program Ser.). 143p. (C). 1988. pap. 17.81 (*0-07-553745-1*); pap. 15.31 (*0-07-553747-8*) McGraw.

Life Skills: Level 1. Elaine Kirn. (ETC Program Ser.). (C). 1988. pap., teacher ed. 32.19 (*0-07-553749-4*); pap., teacher ed. 32.19 (*0-07-554243-9*) McGraw.

Life Skills: Level 1. Elaine Kirn. (ETC Program Ser.). (C). 1988. pap. 25.94 (*0-07-553751-6*) McGraw.

Life Skills: Readings & Activities. Thomas Farrell. (Power Reading Ser.: Bk. 4). 104p. (C). 1989. 10.50 (*0-89702-084-7*, Irwn McGrw-H) McGrw-H Hghr Educ.

Life Skills: Taking Charge of Your Personal & Professional Growth. Richard J. Leider. 196p. 1996. pap. text 17.95 (*0-89384-230-3*, Pfffr & Co) Jossey-Bass.

Life Skills: Taking Charge of Your Personal & Professional Growth. Richard J. Leider. 196p. (C). 1996. pap. text 17.95 (*0-13-602616-8*) P-H.

Life Skills: Teaching Attitudes & Behaviors for Success in Life. James Cisek & Anthea George. 280p. 1985. teacher ed. 59.95 incl. digital audio (*0-9604510-9-9*) Life Skills.

Life Skills Activities for Secondary Students with Special Needs. Darlene Mannix. LC 95-12270. (Illus.). 510p. 1995. spiral bd. 29.95 (*0-87628-541-8*) Ctr Appl Res.

Life Skills Activities for Special Children. Darlene Mannix. 368p. 1991. pap. text 27.95 (*0-87628-547-7*) Ctr Appl Res.

Life Skills & Leadership for Engineers. David E. Goldberg. LC 94-5262. 320p. (C). 1994. pap. 28.13 (*0-07-023689-5*) McGraw.

Life Skills & Mathematics. (Connections Ser.). 1997. pap., student ed. 12.24 (*0-8114-5602-1*) Raintree Steck-V.

Life Skills & Writing. (Connections Ser.). 1997. pap., student ed. 12.24 (*0-8114-5600-5*) Raintree Steck-V.

Life Skills Counselor. Jack Rudman. (Career Examination Ser.: C-2917). 1994. pap. 29.95 (*0-8373-2917-5*) Nat Learn.

***Life Skills for Girls.** Tim Smith. LC 00-27252. (YA). 2000. 10.99 (*0-7814-3405-X*) Chariot Victor.

***Life Skills for Guys.** Tim Smith. LC 00-27266. (YA). 2000. 10.99 (*0-7814-3406-8*) Chariot Victor.

***Life Skills for Kids: Equipping Your Child for the Real World.** Christine M. Field. LC 99-55081. (J). 2000. pap. 14.99 (*0-87788-472-2*, H Shaw Pubs) Waterbrook Pr.

Life-Skills for Living. Rafique Y. Rasul. LC 97-93058. (Life-Skill Book for You Ser.). 336p. (Orig.). 1997. pap. 14.95 (*0-9656917-5-6*) LifePubns.

Life Skills for Teens. Susanna Palomares & Dianne Schilling. (Illus.). 91p. (Orig.). (YA). (gr. 7-12). 1994. pap. text 26.95 (*1-56499-024-9*, IP9024) Innerchoice Pub.

***Life Skills for the New Millennium.** Paula Sunray. 166p. 1999. pap. 14.95 (*1-892745-22-4*) Petals of Life.

***Life Skills for the University & Beyond.** Earl Ginter & Ann Glauser. 250p. (C). 1999. per. 34.95 (*0-7872-6085-1*, 41608501) Kendall-Hunt.

Life Skills Handbook. Educational Assessment Publishing Company Staff. (SPA., Illus.). 48p. (YA). (gr. 9-12). 1993. 9.95 (*0-7854-0059-1*, 15468); text 6.95 (*0-7854-0058-3*, 15467) Am Guidance.

Life Skills Handbook. Kenneth Newbury. (Illus.). 48p. (YA). (gr. 9-12). 1993. 9.95 (*0-7854-0057-5*, 15168); text 6.95 (*0-7854-0056-7*, 15167) Am Guidance.

Life Skills Instruction for All Students with Special Needs: A Practical Guide for Integrating Real-Life Content into the Curriculum. Mary E. Cronin & James R. Patton. LC 92-40196. 171p. (Orig.). (C). 1993. pap. text 29.00 (*0-89079-586-X*, 4048) PRO-ED.

***Life Skills 101: A Practical Guide to Leaving Home & Living on Your Own.** Tina Pestalozzi. LC 00-133460. 160p. 2000. pap. 12.95 (*0-9701334-4-8*, 004796) Stonewood.

***Life Skills Picture Math.** Janie Haugen. Ed. by Happy Von Dohlen. (Illus.). 150p. 1998. wbk. ed. 54.95 (*1-884074-62-6*, PCI 716) PCI Educ Pubg.

***Life Skills Practice.** Ellen McPeek Glisan. Ed. by Janie Haugen. 200p. 1999. ring bd. 79.95 (*1-884074-76-6*, PCI 916) PCI Educ Pubg.

Life Skills Presentation Guide. Laurie Cope Grand. LC 99-55782. 304p. 2000. pap. text 49.95 incl. disk (*0-471-37445-8*) Wiley.

Life Skills Reading. Carolyn Mullins. 1985. pap. 10.95 (*0-87694-149-8*) Ed Design Inc.

Life Skills Series Educational Board Game Series, 4 pts., Set. Mary J. Haugen. 4p. 1992. text 69.50 (*1-884074-15-4*) PCI Educ Pubg.

Life Skills Series II: Set of 8 Educational Programs, 8 vols., Set. Janie Haugen. (Life Skills Series Educational Board Games). (Illus.). 400p. 1993. text 359.00 (*1-884074-09-X*, LSG 17, 708) PCI Educ Pubg.

Life Skills Training: Promoting Health & Personal Development. Gilbert J. Botvin. (Illus.). 48p. (J). (gr. 6-9). 1998. pap. text, student ed., wbk. ed. 4.00 (*0-933665-05-9*) Princeton Hlth.

Life Skills Training: Promoting Health & Personal Development, 3 vols., Set. Gilbert J. Botvin. (Illus.). 198p. (YA). 1996. pap., teacher ed., ring bd. 85.00 (*0-933665-00-8*); pap., student ed., wbk. ed. 6.00 (*0-933665-01-6*) Princeton Hlth.

Life Skills Training: Promoting Health & Personal Development - Teacher's Manual, Level 2. Gilbert J. Botvin. (Illus.). 155p. 1997. teacher ed., ring bd. 65.00 (*0-933665-02-4*) Princeton Hlth.

Life Skills Training: Promoting Health & Personal Development, Level 2. Gilbert J. Botvin. (Illus.). 60p. (Orig.). (J). (gr. 6-9). 1997. pap., student ed. 5.00 (*0-933665-03-2*) Princeton Hlth.

Life Skills Training Level 3: Promoting Health & Personal Development/Teacher Manual. Gilbert J. Botvin. (Illus.). 112p. 1998. teacher ed., ring bd. 55.00 (*0-933665-04-0*) Princeton Hlth.

Life Smiles Back. Ed. by Philip B. Kunhardt, Jr. (Illus.). 224p. 1988. per. 14.00 (*0-671-67222-3*) S&S Trade.

***Life So Far.** Betty Friedan. 2001. pap. 15.00 (*0-7432-0024-1*, Touchstone) S&S Trade Pap.

***Life So Far: A Memoir.** Betty Friedan. LC 00-23920. (Illus.). 384p. 2000. 26.00 (*0-684-80789-0*) S&S Trade.

Life So Far P8, Vol. 1. Wagner. 1994. 123.60 (*0-7868-7994-7*) DK Pub Inc.

Life Space & Economic Space: Third World Planning in Perspective. John Friedmann. 316p. 1988. 34.95 (*0-88738-201-0*) Transaction Pubs.

Life Space Intervention: Talking with Children & Youth in Crisis. Mary M. Wood & Nicholas J. Long. LC 90-32277. 342p. 1991. pap. text 34.00 (*0-89079-245-3*, 1437) PRO-ED.

Life Span. Alma L. Villanueva. LC 84-80404. 90p. (Orig.). (C). 1984. 35.00 (*0-916908-23-2*); pap. 9.95 (*0-916908-22-4*) Place Herons.

Life-Span Approach to Nursing Care for Individuals with Developmental Disabilities. Ed. by Shirley P. Roth & Joyce S. Morse. 368p. 1994. 49.95 (*1-55766-151-0*, 1510) P H Brookes.

Life-Span Communication: Normative Processes. Ed. by J. F. Nussbaum. (Communication Textbook Ser.). 392p. 1989. 79.95 (*0-8058-0195-2*) L Erlbaum Assocs.

Life-Span Development. Daniel G. Eckstein. 176p. (C). 1995. pap. text, per. 27.95 (*0-7872-0743-8*) Kendall-Hunt.

Life Span Development. 5th ed. Santrock. 1995. text (*0-697-32736-1*, WCB McGr Hill) McGrw-H Hghr Educ.

Life-Span Development. 5th ed. John W. Santrock. 736p. (C). 1994. text. write for info. (*0-697-14503-4*) Brown & Benchmark.

Life-Span Development. 5th ed. John W. Santrock. (C). 1995. text, student ed. 16.25 (*0-697-26759-8*) Brown & Benchmark.

Life-Span Development. 6th ed. Santrock. 1996. (*0-697-36406-2*, WCB McGr Hill) McGrw-H Hghr Educ.

Life-Span Development. 6th ed. John W. Santrock. 736p. (C). 1997. per. write for info. (*0-07-114653-9*) McGraw.

Life-Span Development. 6th ed. John W. Santrock. LC 95-80202. 720p. (C). 1996. text. write for info. (*0-697-23582-3*, WCB McGr Hill) McGrw-H Hghr Educ.

Life Span Development. 6th ed. John W. Santrock. LC 95-80202. 720p. (C). 1996. text. write for info. (*0-697-23583-1*) Brown & Benchmark.

Life-Span Development. 6th ed. John W. Santrock et al. 272p. (C). 1996. text, student ed. 20.62 (*0-697-23585-8*, WCB McGr Hill) McGrw-H Hghr Educ.

Life-Span Development. 7th ed. Santrock. LC 98-12814. 1998. 47.74 (*0-697-36439-9*, Dshkn McG-Hill) McGrw-H Hghr Educ.

Life-Span Development: A Diversity Reader. Richard A. Pierce & Michael H. Black. 368p. (C). 1993. per. 18.95 (*0-8403-8565-X*) Kendall-Hunt.

Life-Span Development: An Introduction. 5th ed. John W. Santrock. LC 93-73056. 736p. (C). 1994. text. write for info. (*0-697-14504-2*) Brown & Benchmark.

Life Span Development: Concepts Theories & Interventions. Leonie Sugarman. (New Essential Psychology Ser.). 198p. (C). 1986. pap. 18.99 (*0-415-05163-0*) Routledge.

Life-Span Development: Student Study Guide. 6th ed. Santrock. 1996. student ed. 59.00 (*0-697-36916-1*) McGrw-H Hghr Educ.

Life-Span Development & Behavior. David L. Featherman et al. Ed. by Paul B. Baltes et al. (Life-Span Development & Psychology Ser.: Vol. 12). 296p. 1994. 69.95 (*0-8058-1507-4*) L Erlbaum Assocs.

Life-Span Development & Behavior, Vol. 7. Ed. by Paul B. Baltes et al. 352p. (C). 1986. text 99.95 (*0-89859-692-0*) L Erlbaum Assocs.

Life-Span Development & Behavior, Vol. 9. Paul B. Baltes et al. Ed. by David L. Featherman et al. 400p. 1988. 99.95 (*0-8058-0272-X*) L Erlbaum Assocs.

Life-Span Development & Behavior, Vol. 10. Paul B. Baltes et al. Ed. by David L. Featherman et al. 384p. 1990. 105.00 (*0-8058-0609-1*) L Erlbaum Assocs.

Life-Span Development & Behavior, Vol. 11. David L. Featherman et al. Ed. by Paul B. Baltes et al. 240p. 1992. 49.95 (*0-8058-0674-1*) L Erlbaum Assocs.

Life-Span Developmental Psychology: A European Perspective. Andreas Demetriou et al. LC 97-23240. 536p. 1998. pap. 54.00 (*0-471-97078-6*) Wiley.

Life-Span Developmental Psychology: Intergenerational Relations. Ed. by Nancy Datan et al. 296p. (C). 1986. text 69.95 (*0-89859-536-3*) L Erlbaum Assocs.

Life-Span Developmental Psychology: Introduction to Research Methods. Paul B. Baltes et al. 280p. 1988. reprint ed. pap. text 34.50 (*0-8058-0235-5*) L Erlbaum Assocs.

Life-Span Developmental Psychology: Perspectives on Stress & Coping. Ed. by M. E. Cummings & Karraker Greene. 352p. (C). 1991. text 69.95 (*0-8058-0371-8*) L Erlbaum Assocs.

Life-Span Effects of Ionizing Radiation in the Beagle Dog. Roy C. Thompson. 328p. 1989. 52.50 (*0-935470-57-3*) Battelle.

Life-Span Human Development. Carol K. Sigelman & David R. Shaffer. LC 89-29685. 720p. (C). 1990. mass mkt. 52.25 (*0-534-12282-5*) Brooks-Cole.

Life-Span Human Development. Carol K. Sigelman & David R. Shaffer. LC 89-29685. 720p. (C). 1990. pap., student ed. 17.95 (*0-534-12284-1*) Brooks-Cole.

Life-Span Human Development. 2nd ed. Carol K. Sigelman & David R. Shaffer. LC 94-6251. 672p. 1994. pap. 53.25 (*0-534-19578-4*) Brooks-Cole.

Life-Span Human Development. 2nd ed. Carol K. Sigelman & David R. Shaffer. 1994. pap., teacher ed. write for info. (*0-534-19580-6*) Brooks-Cole.

Life-Span Human Development: Study Guide. 2nd ed. Carol K. Sigelman. (Psychology Ser.). 1994. pap., student ed. 18.25 (*0-534-19579-2*) Brooks-Cole.

Life-Span Human Development with Infotrac. 3rd ed. Sigelman. (Psychology Ser.). 1998. 52.25 (*0-534-36362-8*) Brooks-Cole.

Life Span Motor Development. 2nd ed. Kathleen M. Haywood. LC 93-18656. (Illus.). 416p. 1993. text 42.00 (*0-87322-483-3*, BHAY0483) Human Kinetics.

Life Span Nutrition. 2nd ed. Sharon Rady Rolfes & Linda DeBruyne. LC 97-36769. (Health Sciences). 540p. 1997. 49.25 (*0-534-53834-7*) Brooks-Cole.

Life-Span Perspectives & Social Psychology. Ed. by Ronald P. Abeles. 200p. 1987. text 39.95 (*0-89859-953-9*) L Erlbaum Assocs.

Life Span Perspectives of Suicide: Time-Lines in the Suicide Process. Ed. by Antoon A. Leenaars. LC 96-2679. (Illus.). 342p. (C). 1991. text 59.50 (*0-306-43620-5*, Kluwer Plenum) Kluwer Academic.

Life-Span Plus. Prevention Magazine Editors. 422p. 1993. 8.98 (*1-56731-025-7*, MJF Bks) Fine Comms.

Life-Span Radiation Effects Studies in Animals: What Can They Tell Us? Ed. by R. C. Thompson & J. A. Mahaffey. 732p. 1986. pap. 57.50 (*0-935470-70-0*) Battelle.

Life Span Research on the Prediction of Psychopathology. Ed. by L. Erlenmeyer-Kimling et al. 328p. (C). 1986. text 65.00 (*0-89859-587-8*) L Erlbaum Assocs.

Life Spans: Coming of Age in the Twentieth Century. James O. Gollub. 1991. 22.07 (*0-201-15788-8*) Addison-Wesley.

Life, Speeches, Labors & Essays of William H. Sylvis: By His Brother, James C. Sylvis. William H. Sylvis. LC 66-21693. (Library of American Labor History). xi, 456p. 1968. reprint ed. 49.50 (*0-678-00384-X*) Kelley.

Life Spirals. Nathan Bergenfeld. Ed. by Louise Jaffe. (Illus.). 48p. 1987. write for info. (*0-9618733-0-2*) N Bergenfeld.

Life Stages of Woman's Heroic Journey: A Study of the Origins of the Great Goddess Archetype. Susan A. Lichtman. LC 91-31494. 112p. 1991. lib. bdg. 59.95 (*0-7734-9699-8*) E Mellen.

Life Starts in the Sea. Andreu Llamas. LC 95-3962. (Development of the Earth Ser.).Tr. of Vida Empieza en el Mar. (ENG & SPA., Illus.). 32p. (J). (gr. 3-12). 1996. lib. bdg. 15.95 (*0-7910-3451-8*) Chelsea Hse.

Life Stinks: A Wry Look at Hopelessness, Despair, & Disaster. Ariel Books Staff. (Illus.). 80p. 1995. 4.95 (*0-8362-3114-7*) Andrews & McMeel.

Life Stories. Jewel. 2001. pap. 5.99 (*0-06-109713-6*) HarpC.

***Life Stories.** Brian Lamb. (Illus.). 496p. 2000. pap. 16.95 (*0-8129-3339-7*, Times Bks) Crown Pub Group.

Life Stories: A Study in Christian Decision Making. John Sumwalt & Jo Perry-Sumwalt. LC 94-35603. 112p. (Orig.). 1995. pap. 10.95 (*0-7880-0330-5*) CSS OH.

Life Stories: Personal Construct Therapy with the Elderly. Linda L. Viney. LC 92-48823. (Series in Psychotherapy & Counselling). 224p. (Orig.). 1996. pap. 110.00 (*0-471-93867-X*) Wiley.

***Life Stories: Profiles from the New Yorker.** Ed. by David Remnick & Susan M. Choi. LC 99-53712. 480p. 2000. 26.95 (*0-375-50355-2*) Random Hse Value.

Life Stories: The Creation of Coherence. Charlotte Linde. LC 92-25763. (Oxford Studies in Sociolinguistics). 256p. 1993. pap. text 21.00 (*0-19-507373-8*) OUP.

***Life Stories: World Renowned Scientists Reflect on Their Lives & the Future of Life on Earth.** Ed. by Heather Newbold. LC 99-54133. (Illus.). 224p. 2000. 45.00 (*0-520-21114-6*, Pub. by U CA Pr); pap. 16.95 (*0-520-21896-5*, Pub. by U CA Pr) Cal Prin Full Svc.

***Life Stories of Stars.** Roy A. Gallant. LC 99-86675. (Story of Science Ser.). (Illus.). 2000. 28.50 (*0-7614-1152-6*) Marshall Cavendish.

Life Stories of the Nicaraguan Revolution. Denis L. Heyck. (Illus.). 368p. (C). 1990. pap. 20.99 (*0-415-90211-8*, A3844) Routledge.

L

An Asterisk (*) at the beginning of an entry indicates that the title is appearing for the first time.

L

Life Stories of Undistinguished Americans. Ed. by Hamilton Holt. 144p. 1989. 35.00 (0-415-90183-9, A3595) Routledge.

Life Stories of Undistinguished Americans. Ed. by Hamilton Holt. 144p. (C). 1989. pap. 17.99 (0-415-90184-7, A3599) Routledge.

***Life Stories of Undistinguished Americans, As Told by Themselves** Hamilton Holt. LC 99-29904. 1999. pap. 18.99 (0-415-92510-X) Routledge.

Life Story, 001. Virginia L. Burton. (Illus.). 80p. (J). (gr. k-3). 1962. 20.00 (0-395-16030-8) HM.

Life Story. Virginia L. Burton. (Illus.). 80p. (J). (gr. k-3). 1989. pap. 9.95 (0-395-52017-7) HM.

Life Story Interview. Robert Atkinson. LC 97-33761. (Qualitative Research Methods Ser.). 1998. write for info. (0-7619-0427-1); pap. write for info. (0-7619-0428-X) Sage.

Life Story of a Manic Depressive. Madeline. 32p. 1998. pap. 7.00 (0-8059-4271-8) Dorrance.

Life Story of Adam & Havah: A New Targum of Genesis 1:26-5:5. Shira Halevi. LC 96-46018. 328p. 1997. 35.00 (0-7657-5962-4) Aronson.

Life Story of Brigham Young. Susa Y. Gates & Leah D. Widtsoe. LC 74-164602. (Select Bibliographies Reprint Ser.). 1977. reprint ed. 26.95 (0-8369-5886-1) Ayer.

Life Story of John Bunyan. J. Ellis. 1990. reprint ed. pap. 3.99 (0-88019-258-5) Schmul Pub Co.

Life Story of John Wesley. John Telford. 67p. 1994. pap. 6.99 (0-88019-320-4) Schmul Pub Co.

***Life Story of Rose Mitchell: A Navajo Woman, C. 1874-1977.** Rose G. Mitchell & Charlotte J. Frisbie. LC 00-9014. 2001. pap. write for info. (0-8263-2203-4) U of NM Pr.

Life Story of the Fish. 2nd ed. Brian Curtis. 1961. pap. 6.95 (0-486-20929-6) Dover.

Life Story of the Flash. Mark Waid & Brian Augustyn. (Illus.). 96p. 1998. pap. text 12.95 (1-56389-389-4, Pub. by DC Comics) Time Warner.

Life Story of TV Star Herman the Worm. George Sroda. (Illus.). 199p. (Orig.). (J). (gr. 3 up). 10.95 (0-9604486-2-4) G Sroda.

Life Story Work. Tony Ryan & Rodger Walker. 68p. 1993. pap. 50.00 (1-873868-10-3) BAAF.

Life Strategies: Doing What Works, Doing What Matters. Phillip C. McGraw. LC 98-44748. 304p. 1999. 21.95 (0-7868-6548-2, Pub. by Hyperion) Time Warner.

Life Strategies: Doing What Works, Doing What Matters. Phillip C. McGraw. 304p. 2000. pap. 11.95 (0-7868-8459-2, Pub. by Hyperion) Time Warner.

Life Strategies: Doing What Works, Doing What Matters. large type ed. Phillip C. McGraw. LC 99-32482. 1999. pap. 30.00 (0-7838-8676-4) Mac Lib Ref.

Life Strategies: For Happy, Healthful Longevity. Edward F. Tarabilda. (Orig.). (C). 1990. pap. 7.95 (1-878423-02-9) Morson Pub.

Life Strategies: Interacting with Society. Edward F. Tarabilda. 192p. (Orig.). 1990. pap. 7.95 (1-878423-03-7) Morson Pub.

***Life Strategies for the Corporate Environment: A Motivational & Inspirational Survival Kit.** Ellen N. Fleming. (Illus.). 70p. 1999. 12.95 (0-9673191-0-2) E N F Pubns.

Life Strategies, Human Evolution, Environmental Design: Toward a Biological Theory of Health, Vol. I. V. Geist. LC 78-10807. (Illus.). 1979. 135.00 (0-387-90363-1) Spr-Verlag.

Life Strategies Workbook: Exercises & Self-Tests to Help You Change Your Life. Phillip C. McGraw. (Illus.). 224p. 2000. pap., wbk. ed. 12.95 (0-7868-8514-9, Pub. by Hyperion) Time Warner.

Life Streams: Journeys into Meditation & Music. Hal A. Lingerman. LC 87-40522. (Illus.). 309p. 1988. pap. 7.95 (0-8356-0629-5, Quest) Theos Pub Hse.

Life Stress & Coping Strength Inventory. Darrell Franken. (Illus.). 95p. 1986. ring bd. incl. disk (0-934957-19-3) Wellness Pubns.

Life Stress & Coronary Heart Disease. Ulf De Faire & Torres Theorell. 130p. 1984. 18.50 (0-87527-201-0) Green.

Life Structure: The Only Planner Designed for Super Achievement. Chris E. Stout. 100p. 1997. ring bd. 14.95 (1-890056-01-4, 1996-56014) Grayson Pub.

Life Struggle: Hugh MacLennan's The Watch That Ends the Night. W. J. Keith. (Canadian Fiction Studies: No. 29). 120p. (C). 1994. pap. text 14.95 (1-55022-178-7, Pub. by ECW) Genl Dist Srvs.

Life Studies. 5th ed. David Cavitch. 1995. pap. text, teacher ed. 22.00 (0-312-10339-5) St Martin.

Life Studies. 6th ed. David Cavitch. LC 97-74957. 525p. 1998. pap. 35.95 (0-312-15714-2); pap. text 23.00 (0-312-17071-8) St Martin.

***Life Studies.** 6th ed. Spark. 80p. 1998. pap. text 5.00 (0-312-18286-4) St Martin.

Life Studies & for the Union Dead. Robert Lowell. 72p. 1967. pap. 12.00 (0-374-50628-0) FS&G.

Life Studies of Comedy Writers. William F. Fry & Melanie Allen. LC 97-48284. 215p. 1998. pap. text 21.95 (1-56000-838-5) Transaction Pubs.

Life Studies Rules. 3rd ed. David Cavitch. 1996. pap. text 30.60 (0-312-14962-X) St Martin.

Life Study, Vol. 9. Lee Wit. 5551p. 1984. boxed set 350.00 (0-87083-126-7, 10-026-901) Living Stream Ministry.

Life-Study: Experiencing Creative Lives by the Intensive Journal Method. Ira Progoff. LC 83-72877. 302p. (Orig.). 1983. pap. text 14.95 (0-87941-012-4) Dialogue Hse.

Life-Study of Acts: Messages 1-18, 1. Witness Lee. 150p. 1985. per. 9.50 (0-87083-184-4, 10-067-001) Living Stream Ministry.

Life-Study of Acts: Messages 19-34, 2. Witness Lee. 144p. 1985. per. 9.25 (0-87083-185-2, 10-068-001) Living Stream Ministry.

Life-Study of Acts: Messages 35-55, 3. Witness Lee. 187p. 1985. per. 10.25 (0-87083-186-0, 10-069-001) Living Stream Ministry.

Life-Study of Acts: Messages 56-72, 4. Witness Lee. 334p. 1985. per. 10.25 (0-87083-187-9, 10-070-001) Living Stream Ministry.

Life-Study of Daniel. Witness Lee. 114p. 1991. per. 8.75 (0-87083-633-1, 10-089-001) Living Stream Ministry.

Life-Study of Deuteronomy. Witness Lee. 214p. 1991. per. 11.25 (0-87083-567-X, 10-071-001) Living Stream Ministry.

Life-Study of Ephesians: Messages 1-28, 1. Witness Lee. 248p. 1991. per. 12.25 (0-87083-147-X, 10-033-001) Living Stream Ministry.

Life-Study of Ephesians: Messages 29-63, 2. Witness Lee. 287p. 1991. per. 13.00 (0-87083-148-8, 10-034-001) Living Stream Ministry.

Life-Study of Ephesians: Messages 64-97, 3. Witness Lee. 286p. 1991. per. 13.00 (0-87083-149-6, 10-035-001) Living Stream Ministry.

Life-Study of 1 & 2 Chronicles, Ezra, Nehemiah, Esther. Witness Lee. 201p. 1995. per. 10.75 (0-87083-873-3, 10-132-001) Living Stream Ministry.

Life-Study of 1 & 2 Kings. Witness Lee. 160p. 1994. per. 10.00 (0-87083-809-1, 10-113-001) Living Stream Ministry.

Life-Study of 1 & 2 Samuel. Witness Lee. 271p. 1994. per. 12.50 (0-87083-805-9, 10-112-001) Living Stream Ministry.

Life-Study of 1 Corinthians: Messages 1-23, 1. Witness Lee. 210p. 1990. per. 11.00 (0-87083-140-2, 10-052-001) Living Stream Ministry.

Life-Study of 1 Corinthians: Messages 24-47, 2. Witness Lee. 215p. 1990. per. 11.25 (0-87083-141-0, 10-053-001) Living Stream Ministry.

Life-Study of 1 Corinthians: Messages 48-69, 3. Witness Lee. 207p. 1990. per. 11.00 (0-87083-142-9, 10-054-001) Living Stream Ministry.

Life-Study of Franz Kafka (1883-1924) Using the Intensive Journal Method of Ira Progoff. Ronald Gestwicki. LC 92-19123. 180p. 1992. text 79.95 (0-7734-9576-2) E Mellen.

Life-Study of Galatians see Estudio-Vida De Galatas

Life-Study of Galatians: Messages 1-24, 1. Witness Lee. 218p. 1990. per. 11.50 (0-87083-145-3, 10-063-001) Living Stream Ministry.

Life-Study of Galatians: Messages 25-46, 2. Witness Lee. 199p. 1990. per. 11.00 (0-87083-146-1, 10-064-001) Living Stream Ministry.

Life-study of Genesis see Estudio-Vida de Ginesis, Mensajes 56-77

Life-study of Genesis see Estudio-Vida de Ginesis, Mensajes 78-91

Life-study of Genesis see Estudio-Vida de Ginesis, Mensajes 92-109

Life-Study of Genesis see Estudio-Vida De Genesis: 1-17

Life-Study of Genesis see Estudio-Vida De Genesis: #18-36

Life-Study of Genesis see Estudio-Vida De Genesis: #37-55

Life-study of Genesis see Estudio-Vida de Ginesis, Mensajes 110-120

Life-Study of Hebrews see Estudio-Vida De Hebreos: Mensajes 1-17

Life-Study of Hebrews see Estudio-Vida De Hebreos: Mensajes 18-33

Life-Study of Hebrews see Estudio-Vida De Hebreos: Mensajes 34-52

Life-Study of Hebrews see Estudio-Vida De Hebreos: Mensajes 53-69

Life-Study of Hebrews: Messages 1-17, 1. Witness Lee. 190p. 1992. per. 10.75 (0-87083-156-9, 10-094-001) Living Stream Ministry.

Life-Study of Hebrews: Messages 18-33, 2. Witness Lee. 190p. 1993. per. 10.75 (0-87083-157-7, 10-095-001) Living Stream Ministry.

Life-Study of Hebrews: Messages 34-52, 3. Witness Lee. 206p. 1993. per. 11.00 (0-87083-158-5, 10-096-001) Living Stream Ministry.

Life-Study of Hebrews: Messages 53-69. Witness Lee. 186p. 1993. per. 10.00 (0-87083-672-2, 10-097-001) Living Stream Ministry.

Life-Study of Isaiah: Messages 1-16, 1. Witness Lee. 110p. 1991. per. 8.75 (0-87083-580-7, 10-065-001) Living Stream Ministry.

Life-Study of Isaiah: Messages 17-32, 2. Witness Lee. 111p. 1991. per. 8.75 (0-87083-596-3, 10-066-001) Living Stream Ministry.

Life-Study of Isaiah Vol. 3: Messages 33-54. Witness Lee. 226p. 1994. per. 11.25 (0-87083-823-7, 10-136-001) Living Stream Ministry.

Life-Study of Jeremiah & Lamentations. Witness Lee. 281p. 1992. per. 13.50 (0-87083-666-8, 10-045-001) Living Stream Ministry.

Life-Study of Job. Witness Lee. 209p. 1993. per. 11.50 (0-87083-699-4, 10-098-001) Living Stream Ministry.

Life-Study of John (4 Volume Set) see Estudio-Vida De Juan

Life-Study of Joshua, Judges & Ruth. Witness Lee. 305p. 1993. per. 11.25 (0-87083-743-5, 10-109-001) Living Stream Ministry.

Life-Study of Leviticus, Pt. 2, Vol. 2. Witness Lee. 127p. 1989. per. 9.00 (0-87083-465-7, 10-024-001) Living Stream Ministry.

Life-Study of Leviticus, Vol. 1, Pt. 1. Witness Lee. 160p. 1989. per. 12.50 (0-87083-489-4, 10-021-001) Living Stream Ministry.

Life-Study of Leviticus, Vol. 1, Pt. 2. Witness Lee. 134p. 1989. per. 9.25 (0-87083-439-8, 10-023-001) Living Stream Ministry.

Life-Study of Leviticus, Vol. 2, Pt. 1. Witness Lee. 149p. 1990. per. 9.75 (0-87083-504-1, 10-022-001) Living Stream Ministry.

Life-Study of Leviticus: Numbers & Deuteronomy, 2. Witness Lee. 1162p. 1991. boxed set 70.00 (0-87083-599-8, 10-080-901) Living Stream Ministry.

Life-study of Matthew: John, Acts, James, Revelation, 8 vols. Witness Lee. 4811p. 1985. boxed set 350.00 (0-7363-0113-5) Living Stream Ministry.

Life-Study of Matthew-John, Acts, James-Revelation, 8. Witness Lee. 4811p. 1985. 350.00 (0-87083-160-7, 10025901) Living Stream Ministry.

Life-Study of Minor Prophets. Witness Lee. 225p. 1993. per. 11.75 (0-87083-691-9, 10-105-001) Living Stream Ministry.

Life-Study of Numbers: Messages 1-15, 1. Witness Lee. 113p. 1990. per. 11.00 (0-87083-513-0, 10-048-001) Living Stream Ministry.

Life-Study of Numbers: Messages 16-28, 2. Witness Lee. 95p. 1990. per. 8.00 (0-87083-514-9, 10-049-001) Living Stream Ministry.

Life-Study of Numbers: Messages 29-41, 3. Witness Lee. 116p. 1990. per. 8.75 (0-87083-538-6, 10-050-001) Living Stream Ministry.

Life-Study of Numbers: Messages 42-53, 4. Witness Lee. 212p. 1990. per. 8.00 (0-87083-549-1, 10-051-001) Living Stream Ministry.

Life-Study of of Genesis & Exodus, 7. Witness Lee. 3495p. 1987. boxed set 240.00 (0-87083-356-1, 10-020-901) Living Stream Ministry.

Life-Study of Pentateuch: Genesis & Deuteronomy, 9. Witness Lee. 4657p. 1991. boxed set 310.00 (0-87083-598-X, 10-081-901) Living Stream Ministry.

Life-Study of Romans: Messages 1-16, 9, 1. Witness Lee. 202p. 1989. per. 11.00 (0-87083-137-2, 10-029-001) Living Stream Ministry.

Life-Study of Romans: Messages 17-31, 9, 2. Witness Lee. 174p. 1989. per. 10.00 (0-87083-138-0, 10-030-001) Living Stream Ministry.

Life-Study of Romans: Messages 32-50, 9, 3. Witness Lee. 162p. 1989. per. 10.00 (0-87083-139-9, 10-031-001) Living Stream Ministry.

Life-Study of Romans: Messages 51-69, 9, 4. Witness Lee. 178p. 1989. per. 10.25 (0-87083-136-4, 10-032-001) Living Stream Ministry.

Life-Study of Romans - Hebrews, 9. Witness Lee. 5551p. 1984. 350.00 (0-87083-128-3, 10026901) Living Stream Ministry.

Life-Study of Romans, Volume 1 see Estudio-Vida De Romanos

Life-Study of 2 Corinthians: Messages 1-29, 1. Witness Lee. 262p. 1990. per. 12.50 (0-87083-143-7, 10-055-001) Living Stream Ministry.

Life-Study of 2 Corinthians: Messages 30-59, 2. Witness Lee. 257p. 1990. per. 12.50 (0-87083-144-5, 10-056-001) Living Stream Ministry.

Life-Study of the Psalms Vol. 1: Messages 1-23. Witness Lee. 284p. 1993. per. 13.00 (0-87083-726-5, 10-101-001) Living Stream Ministry.

Life-Study of The Psalms Vol. 2: Messages 24-45. Witness Lee. 228p. 1993. per. 12.00 (0-87083-727-3, 10-102-001) Living Stream Ministry.

Life-Study of Zechariah. Witness Lee. 97p. 1992. per. 8.25 (0-87083-639-0, 10-090-001) Living Stream Ministry.

Life Style & Criminality. H. Goppinger. xxi, 303p. 1987. 114.95 (0-387-16688-2) Spr-Verlag.

***Life Style & Ecology.** Ed. by Baidyanath Saraswati. LC 98-915260. (Culture & Development Ser.: No. 5). (Illus.). ix, 237p. 1998. 35.00 (81-246-0103-8, Pub. by D K Printwrld) Nataraj Bks.

Life Style & Mortality: A Large-Scale Census-Based Cohort Study in Japan - Contributions to Epidemiology & Biostatistics, Vol. 6. T. Hirayama. (Illus.). viii, 138p. 1990. 169.75 (3-8055-5201-7) S Karger.

Life Style & Psychographics. Ed. by William D. Wells. LC 74-75130. 371p. reprint ed. pap. 115.10 (0-608-16292-2, 202666800051) Bks Demand.

Life Style of the Eunuchs. M. D. Vyas & Y. Shingala. 116p. (C). 1987. 22.95 (81-7041-026-6) Asia Bk Corp.

Life Styled by God: A Woman's Workshop on Spiritual Discipline for Weight Control. Pam Snyder. (Woman's Workshop Ser.). 112p. (Orig.). 1985. pap. 4.25 (0-310-42791-6, 11378P) Zondervan.

Life-Styled Marketing: How to Position for Premium Profits. rev. ed. Mack Hanan. LC 79-54833. 171p. reprint ed. pap. 53.10 (0-608-12829-5, 202356300033) Bks Demand.

Life Styles: An Intermediate American English Series, 3 bks. Incl. LIFE STYLES STDNT BK LV1. 1982. pap. text 12.95 (0-582-79754-3, 75008); LIFE STYLES STDNT BK LV2. 1982. pap. text 12.95 (0-582-79757-8, 75011); T/M 1 LIFE STYLES LEVEL1. 1989. pap. text, teacher ed. 18.95 (0-582-79755-1, 75009); T/M 2 LIFE STYLES LEVL2. 1989. pap. text, teacher ed. 18.95 (0-582-79758-6, 75012); T/M 3 LIFE STYLES LEV3. 1989. pap. text, teacher ed. 18.95 (0-582-79761-6, 75015); (English As a Second Language Bk.). 1982. write for info. (0-318-54109-2) Longman.

Life Styles of the Fittest: Step-by-Step Guide to Living Longer & Healthier. Paige McClinte. LC 94-65055. 320p. (Orig.). 1999. 29.95 (1-884573-21-5); pap. 19.95 (1-884573-20-7) S-By-S Pubns.

Life Styles of Student Book LV1 see Life Styles: An Intermediate American English Series

Life Styles of Student Book LV2 see Life Styles: An Intermediate American English Series

Life Success Manuscripts. Thomas Willhite. (Illus.). iii, 225p. 1998. 24.95 (0-9659994-0-8) PSI Pub.

Life Support. Tess Gerritsen. LC 97-15511. 336p. 1997. 23.00 (0-671-55303-8) PB.

Life Support. Tess Gerritsen. 1998. per. 6.99 (0-671-55304-6) PB.

Life Support. Suzanne Gordon. 352p. 1998. pap. 13.95 (0-316-32963-0) Little.

***Life Support.** Suzanne Gordon. 1998. mass mkt. 13.95 (0-316-19141-8, Back Bay) Little.

Life Support. Simon Gray. 1998. pap. 12.95 (0-571-19343-9) Faber & Faber.

Life Support. large type ed. Tess Gerritsen. LC 98-16825. 1998. 25.95 (1-56895-561-8, Compass) Wheeler Pub.

Life Support: A Family Clinical Guide. Michael P. Hahn. LC 96-13337. (Illus.). 317p. 1996. lib. bdg. 35.00 (0-7864-0153-2) McFarland & Co.

Life Support: Conserving Biological Diversity. John C. Ryan. 70p. (Orig.). 1992. pap. 5.00 (1-878071-09-2) Worldwatch Inst.

Life Support: Three Nurses on the Front Lines. Suzanne Gordon. LC 96-43759. 352p. 1997. 23.95 (0-316-32117-6) Little.

Life Support & Habitability Vol. II: Space Biology & Medicine. Ed. by Frank M. Sulzman & A. M. Genin. (Space Biology & Medicine Ser.). (Illus.). 423p. 1994. 99.95 (1-56347-082-9, 82-9(890)) AIAA.

Life Support System Design Diving & Hyperbaric Application. M. L. Nuchols & Wayne C. Tucker. 308p. (C). 1996. text 43.00 (0-536-59616-6) Pearson Custom.

Life Support Systems in Intensive Care. Ed. by Robert H. Bartlett et al. LC 84-5054. (Illus.). 629p. reprint ed. pap. 195.00 (0-8357-7607-7, 205693000096) Bks Demand.

Life Supported by Natural Law: Lectures by His Holiness Maharishi Mahesh Yogi to the World Assembly on Vedic Science, July 9-17, 1975, Washington, D.C. Maharishi Mahesh Yogi. LC 86-14204. (Illus.). 210p. 1986. pap. 12.00 (0-89186-051-7) Age Enlight Pr.

Life Supports: New & Collected Poems. William Bronk. LC 97-34066. 250p. 1997. 37.95 (1-883689-60-0); pap. 16.95 (1-883689-59-7) Talisman Hse.

Life Surrendered in God: Yoga-Sutras. Roy E. Davis. 1995. 14.95 (0-87707-246-9) CSA Pr.

Life-Sustaining Technologies & the Elderly. 1991. lib. bdg. 76.95 (0-8490-4974-1) Gordon Pr.

Life-Sustaining Technologies & the Elderly. Ed. by Office of Technology Assessment Task Force Staff. LC 65-20241. 450p. 1988. text 39.95 (0-397-53024-2) Lppncott W & W.

***Life Switch.** Linda J. Runstein. 157p. 1999. pap. 13.95 (0-7414-0123-1) Buy Books.

Life Table & Its Applications. Chin Long Chiang. LC 82-20331. 336p. (C). 1983. 46.50 (0-89874-570-5) Krieger.

Life Table Techniques & Their Applications. Ed. by Krishnan Namboodiri & C. M. Suchindran. (Studies in Population). 1987. text 75.00 (0-12-513930-6) Acad Pr.

***Life Talk.** Iris Alphia Blair Barnett. 2000. pap. 8.95 (0-533-13425-0) Vantage.

"Life Tastes Better Than Steak" Cookbook: Heart Healthy Reversal Recipes. Ed. by Gerry Krag & Marie Zimolzak. LC 96-84503. 304p. 1996. pap. 17.95 (0-932212-90-5) Avery Color.

Life Tastes Better Than Steak Eating Plan: A Diet for a Clogged Artery. Gerry Krag. 104p. 1997. pap. 12.95 (0-932212-96-4) Avery Color.

***Life Teachings: Raising a Child.** Jeanie Davis Pullen. 112p. 1999. mass mkt. 12.95 (0-9672660-0-9, Pub. by Yllow House) Bookmen Inc.

Life, Teachings & Works of Johannes Denck, 1495-1924. Frederick L. Weis. LC 83-45634. reprint ed. 34.50 (0-404-19876-7) AMS Pr.

***Life, Tempature & the Earth: The Self-organizing Biosphere.** David Schwartzman. LC 99-25856. (Illus.). 241p. 1999. 50.00 (0-231-10212-7) Col U Pr.

Life Testing of General Lighting Incandescent Filament Lamps: LM-49-94. (Lighting Measurements Ser.). (Illus.). 4p. 1994. pap. 12.00 (0-87995-107-9, LM-49-94) Illum Eng.

Life Testing of High Intensity Discharge (HID) Lamps: LM-47-95. IESNA Staff. (Illus.). 14p. 1995. pap. 15.00 (0-87995-134-6, LM-47-95) Illum Eng.

Life Testing of LPS Lamps: LM-60-91. (Lighting Measurements Ser.). (Illus.). 3p. 1990. pap. 10.00 (0-87995-060-9, LM-60-91) Illum Eng.

Life Testing of Single Ended Compact Fluorescent Lamps. (Lighting Measurements Ser.). (Illus.). 4p. 1991. pap. 15.00 (0-87995-049-8, LM-65-91) Illum Eng.

Life That Mattered. Betty Feezor. 182p. 1979. 7.95 (0-915605-03-1) B Feezor Bks.

Life That Mattered. Wilbur W. Willey. (Illus.). 152p. (Orig.). 1988. pap. 12.50 (0-9645740-0-4) Wldwood W.

***Life That No One Else Could Live But Argentina.** Argentina Sarhan. LC 00-190068. 80p. 2000. pap. 9.95 (1-56167-601-2) Am Literary Pr.

***Life That Really Matters: The Story of the John Wesley Great Experiment.** Ed. by Danny E. Morris. LC 99-64723. 110p. 1999. 12.95 (1-57736-155-5) Providence Hse.

Life That Ruth Built: A Biography. Marshall Smelser. LC 92-39757. (Illus.). xiv, 592p. 1993. reprint ed. pap. 22.00 (0-8032-9218-X, Bison Books) U of Nebr Pr.

Life That Wins see Vida Cristiana Victoriosa

Life that Wins. Watchman Nee. Ed. by Herbert L. Fader. Tr. & Intro. by Stephen Kaung. 157p. (Orig.). 1986. 11.00 (0-935008-65-9); pap. 5.00 (0-935008-66-7) Christian Fellow Pubs.

Life That Wins. Charles Trumbull. (Vital Ser.). 1997. pap. 0.75 (0-87508-511-3) Chr Lit.

Life the Human Quest for an Ideal, Bk. II. anniversary ed. Ed. by Marlies Kronegger. LC 95-44240. (Analecta Husserliana Ser.: Vol. XLIX). 360p. (C). 1996. lib. bdg. 150.00 (0-7923-3826-X) Kluwer Academic.

Life, the Lab, & Everything. Ian Wilkinson. 178p. 1996. pap. 19.95 (0-915274-85-X, 202676) Am Assn Clinical Chem.

An Asterisk (*) at the beginning of an entry indicates that the title is appearing for the first time.

Life the Movie: How Entertainment Conquered Reality. Neal Gabler. LC 98-36699. 320p. 1998. 27.50 (*0-679-41752-4*) Knopf.

Life, the Universe & Everything. Douglas Adams. Vol. 3. 232p. 1995. mass mkt. 6.99 (*0-345-39182-9*) Ballantine Pub Grp.

Life, the Universe & Everything. Douglas Adams. 240p. 1991. per. 5.99 (*0-671-73967-0*) PB.

Life, the Universe & Everything. Douglas Adams. (Hitchhiker's Trilogy Ser.). (J). 1982. 11.09 (*0-606-03137-5*, Pub. by Turtleback) Demco.

***Life These Days: Stories from Lake Wobegon.** abr. ed. Garrison Keillor. 1999. pap., wbk. ed. 18.95 incl. audio Audio Partners.

***Life They Have.** Ed. by John Sommer & John Daly. LC 99-89822. 416p. 2000. pap. 15.00 (*0-385-49889-6*, Anchor) Doubleday.

Life-Threatened Elderly. Margot Tallmer et al. Ed. by Mahlon S. Hale & Ivan K. Goldberg. LC 83-14263. 352p. 1984. text 57.50 (*0-231-04966-8*) Col U Pr.

Life-Threatening Allergic Reactions: Understanding & Coping with Anaphylaxis. Deryk Williams et al. 1998. pap. 12.95 (*0-7499-1700-8*, Pub. by Piatkus Bks) London Brdge.

Life-Threatening Arrhythmias During Ischemia & Infarction. Ed. by David J. Hearse et al. LC 86-42585. 239p. 1987. reprint ed. pap. 74.10 (*0-608-00358-1*, 206107500007) Bks Demand.

Life-Threatening Coagulation Disorders in Critical Care Medicine. V. Hach-Wunderle & P. P. Nawroth. Tr. by T. C. Telger from GER. LC 96-29356. 100p. 1996. pap. 54.50 (*3-540-61475-3*) Spr-Verlag.

***Life Threatening Emergencies in Dentistry.** V. Chilo. (Illus.). 188p. 1999. text 40.00 (*88-299-0264-0*, Pub. by Piccin Nuova) Gordon & Breach.

Life Threatening Emergencies in Dentistry. V. Chilo et al. 188p. 1988. text 40.00 (*1-57235-015-6*) Piccin Nuova.

Life 3. 7th ed. Meyer. 1996. text 74.49 (*0-13-233131-4*) P-H.

Life Through the Ages. Giovanni Caselli. LC 92-52838. (See & Explore Library). (Illus.). 64p. (J). (gr. 3 up). 1992. 11.95 (*1-56458-143-8*) DK Pub Inc.

Life Ties: Cultivating Relationships That Make Life Worth Living. Judith Balswick & Boni Piper. LC 95-40448. 168p. (Orig.). 1995. pap. 9.99 (*0-8308-1614-3*, 1614) InterVarsity.

Life, Time. Jane F. Rittmayer. LC RC0514.R57. 127p. reprint ed. pap. 39.40 (*0-608-12396-X*, 205557200031) Bks Demand.

Life Time Astrology: From Conception to Transcendance. A. Tad Mann. 288p. 1991. pap. 15.95 (*1-85230-234-8*, Pub. by Element MA) Penguin Putnam.

Life-Time Chart. Lois F. Timmins. 1978. 23.95 (*0-931814-00-6*) Comn Studies.

Life Time Eternity. E Dickinson. pap. 10.95 (*0-8027-2601-1*) Walker & Co.

Life Times: The Life Experiences Journal. deluxe ed. Barbara Ray & Norman H. Ray. LC 89-92021. 288p. 1990. 49.95 (*1-877810-34-7*, LT) Rayve Prodns.

Life, Times & Labours of Robert Owen, 2 vols. in 1. Lloyd Jones. LC 77-134406. (Illus.). reprint ed. 55.00 (*0-404-08449-4*) AMS Pr.

Life, Times & Milieu of V. F. Odoyevsky, 1804-1869. Neil Cornwell. LC 88-174597. xiv, 417p. 1986. write for info. (*0-485-11279-5*, Pub. by Athlone Pr) Transaction Pubs.

Life, Times & Poetry of C. B. Rich. C. B. Rich. (Orig.). 1992. pap. 7.95 (*0-9633062-0-0*) Double Arrow.

Life, Times & Treacherous Death of Jesse James. Frank Triplett. LC 73-79820. xxxvii, 344p. 1974. write for info. (*0-88394-001-9*) Promntory Pr.

Life to Come: And Other Stories. E. M. Forster. 1987. pap. 13.95 (*0-393-30442-6*) Norton.

Life to Come: Stories for Children about the Spiritual World. Gretchen L. Keith. (Illus.). 89p. (J). (gr. 3-7). 1990. pap. 6.45 (*0-945003-03-X*) General Church.

Life to Death: Harmonizing the Transition: A Holistic & Meditative Approach for Care-Givers & the Dying. Richard W. Boerstler et al. LC 95-38850. 256p. (Orig.). 1995. pap. 14.95 (*0-89281-329-6*, Heal Arts VT) Inner Tradit.

***Life to Di For: Princess Diana - Past, Present & Future.** Kay Kellam. 248p. 1999. 17.95 (*0-9670577-0-1*) Bernardo Pr.

Life to Share. Ed. by Rachel Reeder. (Liturgy Ser.). 92p. (Orig.). 1990. 10.95 (*0-918208-53-X*) Liturgical Conf.

Life to the Full: The Practical & Powerful Writings of James, Peter, John & Jude. Douglas Jacoby. (Practical Exposition Ser.). 211p. 1995. pap. 12.99 (*1-884553-71-0*) Discipleshp.

Life to the Fullest. Jim Davis. LC PN6728.G28D3929 1999. (Garfield Ser.). (Illus.). 128p. 1999. pap. 6.95 (*0-345-43239-8*) Ballantine Pub Grp.

Life to the Fullest: Stories of People Coping with Diabetes. Dan Brannan. Orig. Title: Diabetes Doesn't Have to Be a Death Sentence. (Illus.). 221p. (Orig.). 1996. pap. 15.95 (*0-9650228-1-1*) D Brannan.

Life to the Limits: From Everyday Losses to New Possibilities. Remi Parent. Tr. by Peter Heinegg from FRE. LC 97-53211. 112p. 1998. reprint ed. pap. 9.00 (*0-7648-0185-6*, Liguori Triumph) Liguori Pubns.

Life to Those Shadows. Noel Burch. Ed. & Tr. by Ben Brewster. LC 90-50406. (Illus.). 317p. 1991. 60.00 (*0-520-07143-3*, Pub. by U CA Pr); pap. 24.95 (*0-520-07144-1*, Pub. by U CA Pr) Cal Prin Full Svc.

Life Together. Dietrich Bonhoeffer. LC 54-6901. 128p. 1976. reprint ed. pap. 7.95 (*0-06-060851-X*, RD292) Harper SF.

Life Together: A Discussion of Christian Fellowship. Dietrich Bonhoeffer. 128p. 1978. pap. 12.00 (*0-06-060852-8*, Pub. by Harper SF) HarpC.

Life Together: The Classic Exploration of Faith in Community. Dietrich Bonhoeffer. Tr. & Intro. by John W. Doberstein. LC 92-54665. 128p. 1993. reprint ed. 16.00 (*0-06-060853-6*, Pub. by Harper SF) HarpC.

Life Together, a Life Apart: A History of Relations Between Europeans & Aborigines. Bain Attwood et al. 232p. 1994. pap. 24.95 (*0-522-84536-3*, Pub. by Melbourne Univ Pr) Paul & Co Pubs.

Life Together & Prayerbook of the Bible. Dietrich Bonhoeffer. Ed. by Geffrey B. Kelly. Tr. by Daniel W. Bloesch & James H. Burtness. (Dietrich Bonhoeffer Works: Vol. 5). 232p. 1996. 32.00 (*0-8006-8305-6*, 1-8305, Fortress Pr) Augsburg Fortress.

Life Training: 250 Life-Changing Devotions That Build Extreme Faith. Joe White. LC 97-47626. 1998. 17.99 (*1-56179-577-1*) Focus Family.

***Life Training 2: Devotions for Parents & Teens.** Joe White. (YA). 2000. 18.99 (*1-56179-675-1*) Focus Family.

Life Transition Trainer's Manual. Steven M. Smith. Ed. by Yolanda L. Salazar. 44p. 1992. 175.00 (*1-877709-24-7*) ADAPT Pub Co.

Life Transition Workbook. Norman I. Sternfeld. Ed. by Yolanda L. Salazar & Emily A. Cullen. 56p. 1992. 9.95 (*1-877709-23-9*) ADAPT Pub Co.

***Life Transitions in the Older Adult: Issues for Nurses & Other Health Professionals.** Ed. by Elizabeth A. Swanson & Toni Tripp-Reimer. (Advances in Gerontological Nursing Ser.). (Illus.). 208p. 1999. text 35.95 (*0-8261-9112-6*) Springer Pub.

Life, Travels & Opinions of Benjamin Lundy. Benjamin Lundy. (American Biography Ser.). 316p. 1991. reprint ed. lib. bdg. 79.00 (*0-7812-8253-5*) Rprt Serv.

Life Travels & Opinions of Benjamin Lundy: Including His Journeys to Texas. Benjamin Lundy. Ed. by Thomas Earle. LC 76-136302. 316p. 1971. reprint ed. lib. bdg. 49.50 (*0-678-00809-4*) Kelley.

Life, Travels & Opinions of Benjamin Lundy, Including His Journeys to Texas & Mexico. Thomas Earle. LC 70-82188. (Anti-Slavery Crusade in America Ser.). 1970. reprint ed. 16.95 (*0-405-00626-8*) Ayer.

Life Trek. Hal W. Smith. LC 81-50680. (Illus.). 128p. (Orig.). 1981. pap. 3.95 (*0-9606116-0-6*) Youth Challenge.

Life, Trial & Execution of Captain John Brown: With a Full Account of the Attempted Insurrection at Harper's Ferry. LC 70-89398. (Black Heritage Library Collection). 1977. 20.95 (*0-8369-8621-0*) Ayer.

Life, Trial & Execution of Captain John Brown, Known As "Old Brown of Ossawatomie" John Brown. LC 69-18827. (Law, Politics & History Ser.). 1969. reprint ed. lib. bdg. 22.50 (*0-306-71250-4*) Da Capo.

Life Tuning with Prima Sounds: The Discovery of Chokra Music. Arnold Keyserling & Ralph Losey. 38p. 1993. 19.95 incl. cd-rom (*1-883185-05-X*) Schl of Wisdom.

Life under a Cloud: American Anxiety about the Atom. Allan M. Winkler. LC 92-20013. 288p. 1993. text 30.00 (*0-19-507821-7*) OUP.

Life under a Cloud: American Anxiety about the Atom. Allan M. Winkler. LC 98-34622. 1999. pap. 16.95 (*0-252-06773-8*) U of Ill Pr.

***Life under a Leaky Roof: Reflections on Home, Tools & Country Living.** David Owen. LC 99-55760. 208p. 2000. pap. 12.95 (*0-86730-799-4*) Lebhar Friedman.

Life under a Rock. Bill Rose. LC 96-14244. 65p. (Orig.). 1996. pap. 15.00 (*1-883302-07-2*) Trning Res.

***Life Under a Stone.** Janet Halfmann. LC 99-23824. (Lifeviews Ser.). 2000. 22.60 (*1-58341-075-9*) Creative Co.

Life under Extreme Conditions: Biochemical Adaptation. Ed. by G. Di Prisco. (Illus.). 160p. 1991. 78.95 (*0-387-53108-4*) Spr-Verlag.

Life under Glass: The Inside Story of Biosphere 2. Abigail Alling & Mark Nelson. (Illus.). 272p. 1993. pap. 16.95 (*1-882428-07-2*) Synerg CA.

Life under Lake Siskiyou: A Way of Life on a Ranch Many Years Ago. Clelia Price. (Illus.). 40p. (J). (gr. k-4). 1997. pap. 8.95 (*0-9628801-2-4*) Coyote Pub.

***Life under the Jim Crow Laws.** Charles George. LC 99-32526. (Way People Live Ser.). (Illus.). 96p. (YA). (gr. 6-9). 2000. lib. bdg. 18.96 (*1-56006-499-4*) Lucent Bks.

***Life under the Son: Counsel from the Book of Ecclesiastes.** Jay E. Adams. 1999. pap. 9.95 (*1-889032-16-6*) Timeless Texts.

Life Under the Sun: The Art of Charles Lovato. Charles Lovato. Ed. by Gerald Hausman. LC 81-23189. (Illus.). 48p. 1982. 35.00 (*0-86534-010-2*) Sunstone Pr.

Life under Water. Richard Greenberg. 1985. pap. 3.25 (*0-8222-0660-9*) Dramatists Play.

Life Underground. J. M. Parramon & Maria Rius. (Habitats Ser.).Tr. of La Vida Bajo la Tierra. (Illus.). 32p. (J). (gr. 3-5). 1987. pap. 6.95 (*0-8120-3862-2*) Barron.

***Life Underground: The Biology of Subterranean Rodents.** Eileen A. Lacey. LC 99-51019. (Illus.). 1999. pap. text 24.00 (*0-226-46728-7*); lib. bdg. 65.00 (*0-226-46727-9*) U Ch Pr.

Life, Unpublished Letters, & Philosophical Regimen of Anthony, Earl of Shaftesbury: 1900 Edition. Ed. by Benjamin Rand. 567p. 1996. reprint ed. 100.00 (*1-85506-129-5*) Bks Intl VA.

"Life Unworthy of Life" Racial Phobia & Mass Murder in Hitler's Germany. James M. Glass. 270p. 1997. pap. 16.50 (*0-465-09846-0*, Pub. by Basic) HarpC.

Life upon the Wicked Stage: A Visit to the American Theatre of the 1860s, 1870s & 1880s As Seen in the Pages of the New York Clipper. Ed. by William L. Slout. LC 96-1562. (Clipper Studies in the Theatre: No. 14). xii, 169p. 1996. pap. 21.00 (*0-89370-463-6*) Millefleurs.

Life Values & Adolescent Mental Health. Patricia Cohen & Jacob Cohen. (Research Monographs in Adolescence). 192p. 1995. text 45.00 (*0-8058-1774-3*) L Erlbaum Assocs.

Life, Wanderings & Labours in Eastern Africa. Charles New. (Illus.). 529p. 1971. reprint ed. 59.50 (*0-7146-1876-4*, BHA-01876, Pub. by F Cass Pubs) Intl Spec Bk.

Life Was Never Meant to Be a Struggle. Stuart Wilde. LC 97-53042. 1998. pap. 5.00 (*1-56170-535-7*) Hay House.

Life Was Never Meant to Be a Struggle. Stuart Wilde. 64p. 1987. pap. 1.95 (*0-930603-04-4*) White Dove NM.

Life We Are Given: A Daily Program for Realizing the Potential of Body, Mind, Heart, & Soul. George Leonard & Michael Murphy. LC 95-8623. (Inner Work Bks.). (Illus.). 288p. 1995. pap. 15.95 (*0-87477-792-5*, Tarcher Putnam) Putnam Pub Group.

Life We Never Dared Hope For. Roger Schutz. 80p. (Orig.). 1984. 3.95 (*0-8164-2322-9*) Harper SF.

Life Weaving: A Practical Integrative Problem Solving Model, Set, Vols. 1-5. Jude LaClaire. (Illus.). 1995. spiral bd. 49.95 (*0-9629385-6-4*) Heartlnd Personal.

Life Weaving Golden Thread: Archaeological Investigations at the Sampson Mill Village, Greenville County, South Carolina. Michael Trinkley et al. LC 93-10212. (Research Ser.: No. 36). (Illus.). viii, 75p. 1993. pap. 15.00 (*1-58317-032-4*) Chicora Found.

***Life Well Lived.** 5th ed. John Ingram Walker. 207p. 1999. reprint ed. pap. 15.00 (*0-9621073-4-4*, Lifeworks Pub) Lynn Grove Pr.

Life Well Lived: Fantasy Coffins of Kane Quaye. Christine M. Kreamer. (Illus.). 32p. (Orig.). 1994. 20.00 (*0-914489-15-1*) Univ Miss-KC Art.

Life Well Lived: Reflections on Emotional, Intellectual & Spiritual Growth. John I. Walker. 192p. 1988. 15.95 (*0-9621073-0-1*) Lynn Grove Pr.

Life What Is It? Cathy Prather. 120p. 1998. write for info. (*0-9666959-1-7*) Cathy Prather.

Life Wild & Perilous: Mountain Men & the Path to the Pacific. Robert Marshall Utley. LC 97-6. 400p. 1995. 27.50 (*0-8050-3304-1*) H Holt & Co.

Life Wild & Perilous: Mountain Men & the Paths to the Pacific. Robert Marshall Utley. (Illus.). 400p. 1998. pap. 14.95 (*0-8050-5989-X*, Owl) H Holt & Co.

Life Wish: Reincarnation, Reality or Hoax? Maurice Rawlings. LC 81-16763. 157 p. 1981. 4.95 (*0-8407-5792-1*) Nelson Comm.

Life with a Channel Surfer. Carole Achterhof. LC 94-70345. (Illus.). 184p. (Orig.). 1994. pap. 9.95 (*0-9625940-2-4*) Bare Bones Bks.

Life with a Leica. H. Thomas Hallowell, Jr. 1985. 30.00 (*962-217-016-1*) H T Hallowell.

Life with a Purpose - Chinese Edition. Jim Durkin. Tr. by Jensen Kuan. (CHI.). 71p. 1987. pap. 5.00 (*1-56582-099-1*) Christ Renew Min.

Life with a Spiritual Teacher. Wahe G. Khalsa. Ed. by Ravi Singh. (Illus.). 115p. (Orig.). 1991. pap. 10.95 (*0-9615707-3-3*) White Lion Pr.

Life with a Star. Jiri Weil. Tr. by Roslyn Schloss. 280p. 1989. text 22.95 (*0-374-18737-1*) FS&G.

Life with a Star: A Novel. Jiri Weil. Tr. by Rita Klimova & Roslyn Schloss. LC 98-31022. 224p. 1998. pap. 15.95 (*0-8101-1685-5*) Northwestern U Pr.

Life with AIDS. Rose Weitz. LC 90-36219. 224p. (C). 1991. text 35.00 (*0-8135-1629-3*); pap. text 16.00 (*0-8135-1630-7*) Rutgers U Pr.

Life with an Alcoholic. Virginia Crider. 94p. (Orig.). 1996. pap. 5.95 (*0-87813-563-4*) Christian Light.

Life with Animals, Jane Goodall see Benchmark Biographies - Group 1

Life with Billy. Brian Vallee. 256p. (J). 1986. mass mkt. 8.99 (*0-7704-2239-X*) Bantam.

Life with Billy. Brian Vallee. 1989. mass mkt. 5.99 (*0-671-66549-9*) PB.

Life with Birds. Ronald Stevens & Henry T. Swain. (Illus.). 156p. 1995. 49.95 (*0-88839-318-0*) Hancock House.

Life with Bob Board Book. William Joyce. LC PZ7.J857Li 1998. (Illus.). 24p. (J). (ps-k). 1998. 6.95 (*0-694-01181-9*) HarpC.

Life with Borzoi. deluxe ed. Phydelma Gillette. 148p. 1995. pap. 25.00 (*0-614-04526-6*) Donald R Hoflin.

Life with Broadbands. Kenan S. Abosch & Janice S. Hand. (Illus.). 1998. pap. 125.00 (*1-57963-059-6*) Am Compensation.

Life with Charlie: How to Cope with an Alzheimer's Spouse or Other Dementia Patient & Still Keep Your Sanity. Carol Heckman-Owen. LC 91-38235. (Illus.). 144p. 1992. pap. 9.95 (*0-934793-41-7*) Pathfinder CA.

Life with Chronic Illness: Social & Psychological Dimensions. Ariela Royer. LC 98-11133. 232p. 1998. 55.00 (*0-275-96123-0*, Praeger Pubs) Greenwood.

Life with Death: Drawings & Stories by Child Holocaust Survivors. Ed. by Tamar Hendel. (Illus.). 34p. 1996. pap. 19.95 (*0-9655235-0-0*) Create Expressive Arts Pr.

Life with Diabetes: A Series of Teaching Outlines. Ed. by American Diabetes Association Staff. LC 97-22986. (Illus.). 683p. 1997. 75.00 (*0-945448-80-5*, 5507-01) Am Diabetes.

***Life with Diabetes: A Series of Teaching Outlines.** 2nd ed. Martha Mitchell Funnell & University of Michigan Staff. LC 00-36213. 2000. write for info. (*1-58040-056-6*) Am Diabetes.

Life with Father see Best Plays of the Modern American Theatre: Second Series, 1939-1946

Life with Father. Clarence Day. 25.95 (*0-88411-527-5*) Amereon Ltd.

Life with Father. Ed. by Life Magazine Editors. LC 94-46902. 96p. (gr. 8). 1995. 15.00 (*0-316-52635-5*) Little.

Life with Father. Howard Lindsay & Russel Crouse. 1948. pap. 5.25 (*0-8222-0661-7*) Dramatists Play.

Life with Father. Clarence Day. 1981. reprint ed. lib. bdg. 25.95 (*0-89966-430-X*) Buccaneer Bks.

Life with Father. Clarence Day. 1993. reprint ed. lib. bdg. 27.95 (*1-56849-156-5*) Buccaneer Bks.

Life with Father: Parenthood & Masculinity in the Nineteenth-Century American North. Stephen M. Frank. LC 97-50105. (Gender Relations in the American Experience Ser.). (Illus.). 256p. 1998. 34.95 (*0-8018-5855-0*) Johns Hopkins.

Life with Father & I Remember Mama & You Can't Take It with You: Curriculum Unit. Center for Learning Network Staff et al. (Drama Ser.). 62p. (YA). (gr. 9-12). 1995. spiral bd. 18.95 (*1-56077-321-9*) Ctr Learning.

L

Life with God: Basics for New Christians. Helen Johns. LC 88-81959. 64p. 1988. pap. 3.95 (*0-916035-23-9*) Evangel Indiana.

Life with God: Being the Church. David L. Zercher. LC 90-82382. 64p. 1990. pap., teacher ed. 5.95 (*0-916035-41-7*); pap., student ed. 3.95 (*0-916035-40-9*) Evangel Indiana.

Life with God: First Steps. Curtis Byers & Helen Johns. LC 96-85027. 64p. 1996. pap. 3.95 (*0-916035-67-0*) Evangel Indiana.

Life with God: Love in Action. Helen Johns. LC 89-84627. 64p. 1989. pap. 3.95 (*0-916035-28-X*) Evangel Indiana.

Life with Grandma. large type ed. Doreen Tovey. 1993. 39.95 (*0-7066-1008-3*, Pub. by Remploy Pr) St Mut.

Life with Granny. Ric Mandes. 144p. 1997. 12.95 (*0-9652800-3-9*) Mandes Pub.

Life with HWM: From Aston to Facel Vega. Fred Hobbs. (Illus.). 250p. 1990. 24.98 (*0-85429-718-9*, Pub. by GT Foulis) Haynes Manuals.

Life with Idiot. Victor Erofeyev. 256p. 2001. 23.95 (*0-670-85484-0*) NAL.

Life with Jeeves. P. G. Wodehouse. 560p. 1983. pap. 15.95 (*0-14-005902-4*, Penguin Bks) Viking Penguin.

Life with Jesus. Robert B. Burnette. 48p. 1988. pap. 2.95 (*1-881202-00-3*) Anointed Pubns.

Life with Labradors. Bette K. Curtis. (Illus.). 152p. 1995. 30.00 (*0-614-04545-2*) Donald R Hoflin.

Life with Love. Randy Daltlin. 108p. 1998. pap. 9.95 (*1-57502-744-5*, PO2067) Morris Pubng.

Life with Mother. Ed. by Life Magazine Editors. LC 94-46898. 96p. (gr. 8). 1995. 14.95 (*0-316-52636-3*) Little.

Life with Mother. Howard Lindsay & Russel Crouse. 1950. pap. 5.25 (*0-8222-0662-5*) Dramatists Play.

Life with Mother Superior. Jane Trahey & Anna H. Reuter. 1974. pap. 5.25 (*0-8222-0663-3*) Dramatists Play.

Life with Noah: Stories & Adventures of Richard Smith with Noah John Rondeau. Richard Smith & William J. O'Hern. LC 97-15663. 1997. 30.00 (*0-925168-61-0*) North Country.

Life with O. J. Marguerite S. Thomas. 1996. pap. 24.00 (*0-517-70619-9*) Random Hse Value.

Life with One Parent: Single Parent Activity Book. Jim Boulden & Joan Boulden. Ed. by Evelyn M. Ward. (Illus.). 16p. (Orig.). (J). (gr. k-2). 1994. pap. 5.95 (*1-878076-35-3*) Boulden Pub.

Life with Pa Pa: The Berenstain Bears. Stan Berenstain & Jan Berenstain. (Comes to Life Bks.). 16p. (J). (ps-2). 1993. write for info. (*1-883366-01-1*) YES Ent.

Life with People: A Story. Diane L. Bauman. LC 89-90777. (Illus.). 64p. (Orig.). 1989. pap. 6.95 (*0-9622356-0-1*) Paw Prints Pr.

Life with Picasso. Francoise Gilot & Carlton Lake. 352p. 1989. pap. 12.95 (*0-385-26186-1*) Doubleday.

Life with Swan. Paul West. LC 98-24614. 304p. 1999. 23.00 (*0-684-84864-3*) Scribner.

Life with the Esquimaux: A Narrative of Arctic Experience in Search of Survivors of Sir John Franklin's Expedition. Charles F. Hall. (American Biography Ser.). 547p. 1991. reprint ed. lib. bdg. 99.00 (*0-7812-8162-8*) Rprt Serv.

Life with the Forty-Ninth Massachusetts Volunteers. Henry T. Johns. (Illus.). 435p. 1998. reprint ed. lib. bdg. 42.50 (*0-8328-7029-3*) Higginson Bk Co.

Life with the Kids: A Year's Supply of Family Funnies. Lisa J. Peck. 128p. 1998. pap. 6.98 (*0-88290-620-8*, 1086) Horizon Utah.

Life with the Little People. Robert J. Perry. (Frank Waters Memorial Ser.: No. 3). 161p. 1998. pap. 14.95 (*0-912678-98-4*) Greenfld Rev Lit.

***Life with the Navy Seals.** Robert C. Kennedy. (High Interest Bks.). (Illus.). (YA). 2000. 19.00 (*0-516-23351-3*) Childrens.

***Life with the Navy Seals.** Robert C. Kennedy. (High Interest Bks.). (Illus.). 48p. (J). (gr. 4-7). 2000. pap. 6.95 (*0-516-23551-6*) Childrens.

Life with the Panic Monster: A Guide for the Terrified. Evelyn B. Stewart. 144p. (Orig.). 1996. pap. 9.95 (*0-9627963-5-2*) T W Rutledge.

Life with the Pneumococcus: Notes from the Bedside, Laboratory & Library. Robert Austrian. LC 85-1001. (Illus.). 160p. 1985. 49.95 (*0-8122-7977-8*) U of Pa Pr.

Life with the Union Pacific: The Autobiography of Edd Bailey. Edd H. Bailey. (Illus.). 180p. 1989. 24.95 (*0-913473-09-X*) Saltillo Pr.

Life with the Zulus of Natal, South Africa. George H. Mason. 232p. 1968. 45.00 (*0-7146-1835-7*, Pub. by F Cass Pubs) Intl Spec Bk.

Life with Two Languages: An Introduction to Bilingualism. Francois Grosjean. (Illus.). 384p. 1984. pap. 19.50 (*0-674-53092-6*) HUP.

Life with Uncle: The Canadian-American Relationship. John W. Holmes. 112p. 1981. pap. text 13.95 (*0-8020-6460-4*) U of Toronto Pr.

***Life with Unkie.** John Ridland. 40p. 1999. pap. 8.00 (*1-890887-12-9*) Mille Grazie.

Life with Wine: A Practical Guide to the Basice. Dick Patton. LC 94-92254. (Illus.). 128p. (Orig.). 1994. pap. 9.95 (*0-9642885-0-8*) R J Patton.

An Asterisk (*) at the beginning of an entry indicates that the title is appearing for the first time.

Life with Wings. Marge Green. 1966. 10.95 (*0-89137-403-5*); pap. 6.95 (*0-89137-402-7*) Quality Pubns.

Life with Your Parents: Encouraging Words for the Adolescent. Herman C. Ahrens, Jr. LC 84-27371. (Looking up Ser.). 24p. 1983. pap. 1.95 (*0-8298-0667-9*) Pilgrim OH.

Life Within: Celebration of a Pregnancy. Jean Hegland. LC 90-46690. 114p. 1991. 17.95 (*0-89603-196-9*) Humana.

Life Within a Life: The Story & Adventures of Libbie Custer, Wife of General George A. Custer. Pat Kines. LC 98-11532. 287p. 1998. lib. bdg. 23.95 (*1-56072-475-7*, Nova Kroshka Bks) Nova Sci Pubs.

***Life Within Hidden Worlds: Psychotherapy in Prisons.** Ed. by Jessica Williams Saunders. 144p. 2000. pap. 24.00 (*1-85575-219-0*, Pub. by H Karnac Bks Ltd) Other Pr LLC.

Life Within Limits. Eleanor S. Roensch. (Illus.). 66p. (Orig.). 1993. pap. 9.00 (*0-941232-14-X*) Los Alamos Hist Soc.

***Life Without a Compass: With Revealing Comments about the Decline of the Douglas Aircraft Company.** James L. Murray. LC 98-73683. (Illus.). 426p. 1998. write for info. (*0-9673924-0-3*) J L Murray.

Life Without a Crutch: An Introduction to Recovery from Addiction. Linda Ingraham et al. Ed. by Katherine Greene. (Information Ser.). 69p. (Orig.). 1991. pap. 5.95 (*1-878436-10-4*) OPEN TX.

Life Without a Crutch Trainer's Manual. Linda M. Ingraham. 116p. 1997. ring bd. 595.00 (*1-878436-18-X*) OPEN TX.

***Life Without Bread: How a Low-Carbohydrate Diet Can Save Your Life.** Wolfgang Lutz. 288p. 2000. pap. 16.95 (*0-658-00170-1*, 001701, Keats Publng) NTC Contemp Pub Co.

Life Without Death. Satprem Staff & Luc Venet.Tr. of La/Vie Sans Mort. 180p. (Orig.). 1988. pap. text 8.95 (*0-938710-23-0*) Inst Evolutionary.

Life Without Debt: Free Yourself from the Burden of Money Worries Once & for All. Bob Hammond. 256p. 1995. pap. 14.99 (*1-56414-190-X*) Career Pr Inc.

***Life without Disease: The Pursuit of Medical Utopia.** William B. Schwartz. LC 97-41639. 190p. 2000. pap. 15.95 (*0-520-22173-7*, Pub. by U CA Pr) Cal Prin Full Svc.

Life Without Disease: The Search for a Medical Utopia. William B. Schwartz. LC 97-41639. 190p. 1998. 22.00 (*0-520-21467-6*, Pub. by U CA Pr) Cal Prin Full Svc.

Life Without End: The Transplant Story. P. J. Houlihan. 192p. (Orig.). 1987. pap. 12.95 (*1-55021-017-3*, Pub. by NC Ltd) U of Toronto Pr.

Life Without Equal see Vida Sin Igual

Life Without Equal: Discover Purpose, Peace & Power for Living. Bill Bright. (Uniqueness of Jesus Ser.: Bk. 2). 128p. 1992. mass mkt. 4.99 (*1-56399-011-3*) NewLife Pubns.

Life Without Father. David Popenoe. 288p. 1996. 24.50 (*0-684-82297-0*, M Kessler Bks) Free Pr.

Life Without Father: Compelling New Evidence That Fatherhood & Marriage Are Indispensable for the Good of Children & Society. David Popenoe. 288p. 1999. 15.95 (*0-674-53260-0*) HUP.

***Life Without Fear.** Mike Fehlauer. 224p. 2000. pap. 12.99 (*0-88419-672-0*) Creation House.

Life Without Fear: Chiropractic Major Philosophical Tenet, Vol. V. deluxe ed. Frederick H. Barge. LC 94-73474. 147p. 1995. pap. 19.95 (*1-885048-10-6*) Barge Chiropract.

Life Without Guilt: Healing Through Past Life Regression. Hazel M. Denning. LC 98-13884. 240p. (Orig.). 1999. pap. 12.95 (*1-56718-219-4*) Llewellyn Pubns.

Life Without Instruction. Sally Clark. LC 96-106350. (Illus.). 168p. 1994. pap. 13.95 (*0-88922-347-5*, Pub. by Talonbks) Genl Dist Srvs.

Life Without Katy. 2nd ed. Ed. by D. H. Howe. (Illus.). 78p. 1993. pap. text 5.95 (*0-19-585294-X*) OUP.

Life Without Landlords. Mike Davidow. 32p. 1973. pap. 0.40 (*0-87898-100-4*) New Outlook.

Life Without Light: A Journey to Earth's Dark Ecosystems. Melissa Stewart. 1999. pap. text 9.95 (*0-531-15972-8*) Watts.

Life Without Light: A Journey to Earth's Final Frontiers & Beyond. Melissa Stewart. LC 97-35341. (Venture Book Ser.). (J). 1999. 25.00 (*0-531-11529-1*) Watts.

Life Without Limits: Ten Easy Steps to Success & Happiness. Robert B. Stone. LC 98-28150. 240p. 1999. pap. 7.95 (*1-56718-698-X*) Llewellyn Pubns.

Life Without Parole: Living in Prison Today. 2nd ed. Victor Hassine et al. Ed. by Thomas J. Bernard et al. LC 98-19440. 180p. 1999. pap. text. write for info. (*1-891487-13-2*) Roxbury Pub Co.

Life Without Principles: Reconciling Theory & Practice. Joseph Margolis. LC 95-36405. 256p. (C). 1996. 64.95 (*0-631-17462-1*) Blackwell Pubs.

Life Without Problems? The Achievements of a Therapeutic Community. Michael Little. 240p. 1995. 64.95 (*1-85742-317-8*, Pub. by Arena); pap. 28.95 (*1-85742-316-X*, Pub. by Arena) Ashgate Pub Co.

Life Without Stress: A Survival Guide. 2nd ed. George H. Green. 198p. (Orig.). 1997. pap. 11.95 (*1-890669-00-8*, LWS-1) Biofeedback Ctr.

Life Without Stress: The Far Eastern Antidote to Tension & Anxiety. Arthur Sokoloff. 141p. 1995. pap. text 11.95 (*0-9645758-0-9*) Coral Pub Ltd.

Life Without Stress: The Far Eastern Antidote to Tension & Anxiety. Arthur Sokoloff. 192p. 1997. reprint ed. pap. 11.00 (*0-7679-0045-6*) Broadway BDD.

Life Without Strife: How God Can Heal & Restore Broken Relationships. Joyce Meyer. 1995. pap. 12.99 (*0-88419-408-6*) Creation House.

***Life Without Strife: How God Can Heal & Restore Troubled Relationships.** Joyce Meyer. 197p. 2000. pap. 12.99 (*0-88419-734-4*) Creation House.

Life Without Water. Nancy Peacock. 224p. 1998. pap. 11.95 (*0-553-37929-1*) Bantam.

Life Without Water. Nancy Peacock. LC 96-76498. 176p. 1996. 16.95 (*1-56352-337-X*) Longstreet.

Life Work. Donald Hall. LC 93-18418. 136p. 1994. pap. 14.00 (*0-8070-7055-6*) Beacon Pr.

***Life-Work: A Career Guide for Idealists.** 2nd ed. William A. Charland. LC 99-51412. 1999. 15.00 (*0-944350-45-3*) Friends United.

Life, Work & Rebellion in the Coal Fields: Southern West Virginia Miners, 1880-1922. David A. Corbin. LC 80-25493. (Working Class in American History Ser.). (Illus.). 328p. 1990. pap. text 15.95 (*0-252-00895-2*) U of Ill Pr.

Life Work of Dr. Elisabeth Kubler-Ross & Its Impact on the Death Awareness Movement. Michele Chaban. LC 98-8630. (Symposium Ser.: Vol. 49). 406p. 1998. text 109.95 (*0-7734-8302-0*) E Mellen.

***Life Work Transitions.Com: Putting Your Spirit Online.** Sandra S. Butzel & Deborah L. Knox. LC 99-31481. 248p. 1999. pap. text 19.95 (*0-7506-7160-2*) Buttrwrth-Heinemann.

***Life Works & Faith Fits: True Stories for Teens.** Lisa-Marie Calderone-Stewart. 112p. (YA). 1999. pap. 9.95 (*0-88489-547-5*) St Marys.

Life-World & Consciousness: Essays for Aron Gurwitsch. Ed. by Lester E. Embree. LC 71-162930. (Northwestern University Studies in Phenomenology & Existential Philosophy). 641p. reprint ed. pap. 198.80 (*0-608-10177-X*, 201026100068) Bks Demand.

Life Worth Living. Walter E. Adams. 100p. 1996. write for info. (*0-937408-77-8*) GMI Pubns Inc.

Life Worth Living. G. Raymond Carlson. LC 75-22607. (Radiant Life Ser.). 128p. 1975. pap. 3.95 (*0-88243-876-X*, 02-0876); pap., teacher ed. 5.50 (*0-88243-160-9*, 32-0160) Gospel Pub.

Life Worth Living. Ernest Sutton. (American Autobiography Ser.). 350p. 1995. reprint ed. lib. bdg. 89.00 (*0-7812-8648-4*) Rprt Serv.

Life Worth Living: Ecclesiastes & Song of Solomon. Stuart J. Olyott. (Welwyn Commentary Ser.). 1983. pap. 8.99 (*0-85234-173-3*, Pub. by Evangelical Pr) P & R Pubng.

Life Worth Living: How Someone You Love Can Still Enjoy Life in a Nursing Home - the Eden Alternative in Action. William H. Thomas. LC 96-60382. Orig. Title: The Eden Alternative: Nature, Hope & Nursing Homes. (Illus.). 232p. (Orig.). 1996. pap. 17.95 (*0-9641089-6-8*) VanderWyk & Burnham.

Life Worth Living: Practical Strategies for Reducing Depression in Older Adults. 2nd ed. Pearl M. Mosher-Ashley & Phyllis W. Barnett. LC 97-1679. 384p. (Orig.). 1997. pap. 31.95 (*1-878812-03-3*) Hlth Prof Pr.

Life Worth Living: Timeless Values for Changing Times. Barrie Greiff. 240p. 2000. pap. 14.00 (*0-06-098753-7*) HarpC.

Life Would Be Easy If It Weren't for Other People. Connie Podesta & Vicki Sanderson. LC 99-6030. (One-Off Ser.). (Illus.). 200p. 1999. 55.95 (*0-8039-6864-7*); pap. 24.95 (*0-8039-6865-5*) Corwin Pr.

***Life Woven with Song.** Nora M. Dauenhauer. LC 99-6845. (Sun Tracks Ser.). 160p. 2000. pap. 16.95 (*0-8165-2006-2*) U of Ariz Pr.

Life Writing. Winifred B. Horner. LC 96-42302. 344p. (C). 1996. pap. text 34.40 (*0-13-079237-3*) P-H.

Life-Writing: A Glossary of Terms in Biography, Autobiography, & Related Forms. 2nd ed. Donald J. Winslow. LC 94-40735. (Biography Monographs). 112p. (C). 1995. pap. text 10.50 (*0-8248-1713-3*) UH Pr.

***Life Writing: Literarische Identitatskonstruktion in Schwarzaustralischen Autobiographien und Lebensgeschichten.** Heinz Schurmann-Zeggel. 268p. 1999. 41.95 (*3-906762-35-1*) P Lang Pubng.

Life, Writings & Character of Edward Robinson. Smith et al. LC 77-70744. (America & the Holy Land Ser.). 1977. reprint ed. lib. bdg. 19.95 (*0-405-10290-9*) Ayer.

Life, Writings & Correspondence of George Borrow (1803-1881), 2 vols., Set. William I. Knapp. (BCL1-PR English Literature Ser.). 1992. reprint ed. lib. bdg. 150.00 (*0-7812-7449-4*) Rprt Serv.

***Life-Writings by British Women, 1660-1815: An Anthology.** Ed. by Carolyn A. Barros & Johanna M. Smith. LC 99-86617. (Illus.). 416p. 2000. text 50.00 (*1-55553-432-5*); pap. text 20.00 (*1-55553-431-7*) NE U Pr.

***Life Writing/Writing Lives.** Ed. by Bette H. Kirschstein. LC 99-88368. (Open Forum Ser.). 2000. pap. text. write for info. (*1-57524-068-8*) Krieger.

***Life Year in Pictures.** Life Magazine Staff. (Illus.). 2000. 24.95 (*1-883013-87-9*) Tme Inc.

Life Year in Pictures, 1998. Life Magazine Staff. (Illus.). 160p. 1999. 29.95 (*1-883013-60-7*) Tme Inc.

***Life You Imagine: 10 Steps to Ultimate Achievement.** Derek Jeter. (Illus.). 224p. 2000. 21.95 (*0-609-60786-3*) Crown Pub Group.

Life! You Wanna Make Something of It? Tom Costa. Ed. by Warren Bayless. LC 88-82324. 176p. (Orig.). 1988. pap. 8.95 (*0-937611-37-9*, 110) Hay House.

***Life You Were Born to Lead.** Dan Millman. 464p. 2000. 9.98 (*1-56731-398-1*, MJF Bks) Fine Comms.

Life You Were Born to Live see Votre Chemin de Vie: Une Methode pour en Decouvrir la But

Life You Were Born to Live: A Guide to Finding Your Life Purpose. Dan Millman. LC 93-77108. 468p. 1995. pap. 14.95 (*0-915811-60-X*) H J Kramer Inc.

Life Your Great Adventure: A Theosophical View. rev. ed. Eunice Layton & Felix Layton. LC 88-40136. Orig. Title: Theosophy: Key to Understanding. 194p. 1988. reprint ed. pap. 7.25 (*0-8356-0635-X*, Quest) Theos Pub Hse.

Life You've Always Wanted: Spiritual Disciplines for Ordinary People. John Ortberg. LC 97-29959. 208p. 1997. 15.99 (*0-310-21214-6*) Zondervan.

LifeAnswers: Making Sense of Your World. Ken Hemphill. 160p. 1993. pap. text 7.95 (*0-8054-9964-4*, LifeWy Press) LifeWay Christian.

***Lifebeat.** deluxe ed. Betty Johns. 84p. 2000. pap. 12.95 (*1-929302-05-3*); pap. 12.95 (*1-929302-06-1*) FnQualPoets Pubg Servs.

Lifebeats. Linda Strangio. Ed. by Carolyn S. Zagury. LC 96-60791. 208p. 1996. pap. 12.95 (*1-880254-39-5*) Vista.

Lifebirds. George Levine. LC 94-41058. (Illus.). 180p. (C). 1995. 24.95 (*0-8135-2202-1*) Rutgers U Pr.

Lifebirds. George Levine. (Illus.). 180p. 1997. pap. 17.00 (*0-8135-2495-4*) Rutgers U Pr.

Lifeblood: A 365 Days-a-Year New Business Plan for Small Agencies. 6th rev. ed. Anthony P. Mikes. (Illus.). 288p. 1998. pap. 59.95 (*0-9626971-4-1*) Second Wind.

Lifeblood of War: Logistics in Armed Conflict. Julian Thompson. (Illus.). 360p. 1998. pap. 19.95 (*0-08-041776-0*, Pub. by Brasseys) Brasseys.

Lifeblood of War: Logistics in Armed Conflict. Julian Thompson. (Illus.). 360p. 1991. text 39.95 (*0-08-040977-6*, Pub. by Brasseys) Brasseys.

Lifeboat! large type ed. Margaret Dickinson. 336p. 1995. 27.99 (*0-7505-0784-5*, Pub. by Mgna Lrg Print) Ulverscroft.

Lifeboat Sailors: Disasters, Rescues & the Perilous Future of the Coast Guard's Small Boat Stations. Dennis L. Noble. 2000. 27.95 (*1-57488-200-7*) Brasseys.

***Lifeboat Strategies: How to Keep Your Career above Water During Tough Times - Or Any Time.** Robert Barner. (Illus.). 192p. 2000. 16.95 (*0-595-00206-4*, toExcel) iUniversecom.

***Lifeboat Strategies: How to Keep Your Career Above Water During Tough Times - Or Any Time.** Robert Barner. 173p. 1999. reprint ed. pap. text 17.00 (*0-7881-6819-3*) DIANE Pub.

Lifeboatman. rev. ed. Ed. by Richard A. Block. (Illus.). 212p. 1997. pap. text 42.50 (*1-879778-63-7*, BK-105-1) Marine Educ.

Lifeboats. Nicholas Leach. (Album Ser.: No. 336). (Illus.). 32p. 1998. pap. 6.25 (*0-7478-0366-8*, Pub. by Shire Pubns) Parkwest Pubns.

Lifeboats: A Ship's Log of the Inner Sea. R. V. Spelleri. 127p. 1998. 34.50 (*1-57529-062-6*) Kabel Pubs.

Lifebook for Relationship Success: 365 (+31!) Daily Necessities. Pamela B. Brewer. 415p. 1997. mass mkt. 12.00 (*0-9655484-1-4*) Twenty-Six by Two.

Lifebuoy Men, Lux Women: Commodification, Consumption, & Cleanliness in Modern Zimbabwe. Timothy Burke. LC 95-44291. (Body, Commodity, Text Ser.). (Illus.). 312p. 1996. text 49.95 (*0-8223-1753-2*); pap. text 17.95 (*0-8223-1762-1*) Duke.

***LifeCare Digest for Employers: Preventing Violence in the Workplace.** DCC Inc. Staff. 4p. 1999. pap. 1.95 (*1-58559-067-3*) DCC Inc.

***LifeCare Digest on Balancing Work & Life.** DCC Inc., Staff. 4p. 1999. pap. 1.95 (*1-58559-060-6*) DCC Inc.

***LifeCare Digest on Birthing Options.** DCC Inc., Staff. 7p. 2000. pap. 2.50 (*1-58559-027-4*) DCC Inc.

***LifeCare Digest on Blended Families.** DCC Inc., Staff. 4p. 1999. pap. 1.95 (*1-58559-040-1*) DCC Inc.

***LifeCare Digest on Breastfeeding - What You Need to Know Before Your Baby Arrives.** DCC Inc. Staff. 4p. 1999. pap. 1.95 (*1-58559-028-2*) DCC Inc.

***LifeCare Digest on Business Etiquette: England.** DCC Inc. Staff. 1999. pap. 1.50 (*1-58559-064-9*) DCC Inc.

***LifeCare Digest on Career Change.** DCC Inc., Staff. 8p. 2000. pap. 2.50 (*1-58559-072-X*) DCC Inc.

***LifeCare Digest on Choosing Your Child's Medical Provider.** DCC Inc., Staff. 8p. 1999. pap. 2.50 (*1-58559-058-4*) DCC Inc.

***LifeCare Digest on Coping after a Tornado.** DCC Inc. Staff. 3p. 1999. pap. 1.75 (*1-58559-065-7*) DCC Inc.

***LifeCare Digest on Coping with Hurricanes.** DCC Inc. Staff. 4p. 1999. pap. 1.95 (*1-58559-061-4*) DCC Inc.

***LifeCare Digest on Coping with Job Loss.** DCC Inc. Staff. 3p. 1999. pap. 1.75 (*1-58559-068-1*) DCC Inc.

***LifeCare Digest on Formula Feeding.** DCC Inc. Staff. 4p. 2000. pap. 1.95 (*1-58559-034-7*) DCC Inc.

LifeCare Digest on Helping Children Adjust to New Caregivers. D C C, Incorporated Staff. 4p. 1999. pap. 1.95 (*1-58559-003-7*) DCC Inc.

***LifeCare Digest on Helping Children Cope with School Violence.** DCC Inc. Staff. 4p. 1999. pap. 1.95 (*1-58559-069-X*) DCC Inc.

***LifeCare Digest on Kinship Care & Stepparent Adoption.** DCC Inc., Staff. 7p. 1999. pap. write for info. (*1-58559-059-2*) DCC Inc.

***LifeCare Digest on Mergers & Acquisitions.** DCC Inc. Staff. 1999. pap. 1.50 (*1-58559-066-5*) DCC Inc.

***LifeCare Digest on Preventing Workplace Violence.** DCC Inc. Staff. 4p. 1999. pap. 1.95 (*1-58559-063-0*) DCC Inc.

***LifeCare Digest on Relocating with Children.** DCC Inc., Staff. 8p. 1999. pap. 2.50 (*1-58559-057-6*) DCC Inc.

***LifeCare Digest on Residential Cleaning Services.** LifeCare.com, Inc. Staff. 4p. 2000. pap. 1.95 (*1-58559-073-8*) DCC Inc.

***LifeCare Digest on Stress Management.** DCC Inc. Staff. 4p. 1999. pap. 1.95 (*1-58559-062-2*) DCC Inc.

LifeCare Digest on Sunburn Protection. D C C, Incorporated Staff. 3p. 1999. pap. 1.75 (*1-58559-001-0*) DCC Inc.

***LifeCare Guide to ADD/ADHD.** DCC Inc., Staff. 16p. 1999. pap. 10.95 (*1-58559-016-9*) DCC Inc.

***LifeCare Guide to Alzheimer's Disease & Related Dementia.** DCC Inc. Staff. 100p. 1999. pap. 14.95 (*1-58559-036-3*) DCC Inc.

LifeCare Guide to Backup Child Care Options. DCC Inc., Staff. 7p. 1999. pap. 3.95 (*1-58559-007-X*) DCC Inc.

LifeCare Guide to Care Options. DCC Inc., Staff. 1999. pap. 14.95 (*1-58559-004-5*) DCC Inc.

LifeCare Guide to Caregiving. D C C, Incorporated Staff. 1999. pap. 14.95 (*1-58559-000-2*) DCC Inc.

LifeCare Guide to Child Care Centers. DCC Inc., Staff. 7p. 1999. pap. 3.95 (*1-58559-008-8*) DCC Inc.

LifeCare Guide to Child Care Options. DCC Inc., Staff. 5p. 1999. pap. 2.95 (*1-58559-009-6*) DCC Inc.

***LifeCare Guide to Child Development: Birth to Three Years.** DCC Inc., Staff. 20p. 1999. pap. 9.95 (*1-58559-026-6*) DCC Inc.

***LifeCare Guide to College Admissions.** DCC Inc. Staff. 76p. 2000. pap. 12.95 (*1-58559-070-3*) DCC Inc.

***LifeCare Guide to College Financial Aid.** DCC Inc. Staff. 52p. 2000. pap. 12.95 (*1-58559-071-1*) DCC Inc.

***LifeCare Guide to Early Intervention.** DCC Inc. Staff. 12p. 1999. pap. 10.95 (*1-58559-015-0*) DCC Inc.

***LifeCare Guide to Elementary & Secondary Education.** DCC Inc. Staff. 78p. 2000. pap. 12.95 (*1-58559-010-X*) DCC Inc.

***LifeCare Guide to Family Child Care.** DCC Inc. Staff. 5p. 2000. pap. 2.95 (*1-58559-038-X*) DCC Inc.

LifeCare Guide to In-Home Care. D C C, Incorporated Staff. 64p. 1999. pap. 12.95 (*1-58559-002-9*) DCC Inc.

***LifeCare Guide to Parenting Your Toddler.** DCC Inc., Staff. 68p. 1999. pap. 11.95 (*1-58559-013-4*) DCC Inc.

***LifeCare Guide to Protecting Your Child.** LifeCare.com, Inc. Staff. 8p. 2000. 2.50 (*1-58559-074-6*) DCC Inc.

LifeCare Guide to Reducing Child Care Costs. DCC Inc., Staff. 5p. 1999. pap. 3.95 (*1-58559-006-1*) DCC Inc.

***LifeCare Guide to Retirement & Estate Planning.** DCC Inc. Staff. 84p. 2000. pap. 15.95 (*1-58559-035-5*) DCC Inc.

***LifeCare Guide to Summer Care.** DCC Inc. Staff. 46p. 2000. pap. 9.95 (*1-58559-037-1*) DCC Inc.

LifeCare Guide to Visiting & Interviewing Potential Providers. DCC Inc., Staff. 20p. 1999. pap. 10.95 (*1-58559-005-3*) DCC Inc.

Lifecareer: How It Can Benefit You. 2nd ed. Anna Miller-Tiedeman. Ed. by Terry Sherf. LC 92-19764. 50p. 1992. pap. 7.95 (*0-9613436-8-0*) Lifecareer Pr.

Lifecareer: The Quantum Leap into a Process Theory of Career. Anna Miller-Tiedeman. 1988. pap. 9.95 (*0-9613436-3-X*) Lifecareer Pr.

***Life/Choice: The Theory of Just Abortion.** Lloyd Steffen. 180p. (Orig.). 1999. pap. 18.00 (*1-57910-256-5*) Wipf & Stock.

Lifeclock: The Huber Method of Timing in the Horoscope. Bruno Huber & Louise Huber. LC 93-46228. (Illus.). 480p. (Orig.). 1994. pap. 22.95 (*0-87728-803-8*) Weiser.

***Lifecraft: The Art of Meaning in the Everyday.** Forrest Church. LC 99-57359. 144p. 2000. 20.00 (*0-8070-7712-7*) Beacon Pr.

Lifecraft . . . Your Personal Guide to Life. Fordson Wilder. (Unlimit Your Life Ser.: Vol. 10). 29.95 (*0-911505-22-9*) Lifecraft.

***Lifecycle: You Can Have What You Want Most.** Sanford Holst. LC 99-71158. 208p. 1999. 18.95 (*1-887263-12-8*, Pub. by Sierra Sunrise Pub) Seven Hills Bk.

Lifecycles: Reincarnation & the Web of Life. Christopher M. Bache. 237p. 1991. 18.95 (*1-55778-350-0*) Paragon Hse.

Lifecycles: Reincarnation & the Web of Life. Christopher M. Bache. 256p. 1993. pap. 14.95 (*1-55778-645-3*) Paragon Hse.

Lifecycles Vol. 1: Jewish Women on Life Passages & Personal Milestones. Ed. by Debra Orenstein. LC 94-14799. 480p. 1994. 24.95 (*1-879045-14-1*) Jewish Lights.

Lifecycles Vol. 1: Jewish Women on Life Passages & Personal Milestones. Ed. by Debra Orenstein. 480p. 1998. pap. 19.95 (*1-58023-018-0*) Jewish Lights.

Lifecycles Vol. 2: Jewish Women on Biblical Themes in Contemporary Life. Ed. by Debra Orenstein & Jane R. Litman. LC 94-14799. 464p. 1997. 24.95 (*1-879045-15-X*) Jewish Lights.

Lifecycles Vol. 2: Jewish Women on Biblical Themes in Contemporary Life. Ed. by Debra Orenstein & Jane R. Litman. Vol. 2. 464p. 1998. pap. 19.95 (*1-58023-019-9*) Jewish Lights.

Lifecycles Vol. 3: Jewish Women on Holy Days & Communal Celebrations. Ed. by Debra Orenstein. LC 94-14799. (Lifecycles Ser.: Vol. 3). 300p. 24.95 (*1-879045-18-4*) Jewish Lights.

Lifecyles, 4, Set. Gerald Legg. 1998. 80.00 (*0-531-19440-X*) Watts.

LifeDesign: A System for Balanced Living Through Personal Accomplishment. Eric R. Cumley & Patrick J. Welton. 250p. 1994. text 24.95 (*0-9643653-0-8*) Place One.

LifeFacts: AIDS. Jane Stangle. (Illus.). 1991. pap., teacher ed. 199.00 (*1-56304-026-3*) J Stanfield.

LifeFacts: Managing Emotions. James Stanfield & Garilynn Stanfield. (Illus.). 1992. pap. text 199.00 incl. sl. (*1-56304-029-8*) J Stanfield.

LifeFit: An Effective Exercise Program for Optimal Health & a Longer Life. Ralph S. Paffenbarger & Eric Olsen. LC 95-49235. 440p. (Orig.). 1996. pap. 16.95 (*0-87322-429-9*, PPAF0429) Human Kinetics.

Lifeforce Maximizer. David Magee. LC 86-81432. (Illus.). 164p. (Orig.). 1986. pap. 39.50 (*0-938811-00-2*) Life Survival Digest.

An Asterisk (*) at the beginning of an entry indicates that the title is appearing for the first time.

Lifegain: The Exciting New Program That Will Change Your Health & Your Life. Robert F. Allen & Shirley Linde. 248p. 1981. 16.95 (*0-941703-02-9*) Healthyculture.

Lifegames. Yvonne Searkle & Isabelle Streng. 1995. 39.95 (*1-85302-333-7*) Taylor & Francis.

Lifegames: Activity-Centered Learning for Early Childhood Education in Economics. S. Barr. 1985. text 18.00 (*0-201-20094-5*) Addison-Wesley.

Lifegiver. unabridged ed. Joan B. Weller. (Illus.). 195p. 1998. pap. 15.00 (*0-9667262-0-0*) J B Weller.

Lifegivers: A Practical Guide to Reaching Youth in a Challenging World. Chip Borgstadt et al. 160p. 1996. ring bd. 24.95 (*0-687-05575-X*) Abingdon.

***Lifegivers: Framing the Birthparent Experience in Open Adoption.** James L. Gritter & Child Welfare League of America Staff. LC 99-45581. 2000. 14.95 (*0-87868-770-X*, CWLA Pr) Child Welfare.

Lifegoals: Setting & Achieving Goals to Chart the Course of Your Life. Amy E. Dean. Ed. by Dan Olmos. LC 90-80051. 256p. (Orig.). 1991. pap. 12.00 (*0-937611-90-5*, 123) Hay House.

Lifeguard. Mary Morris. LC 98-19831. 192p. 1998. pap. 12.00 (*0-312-18694-0*) St Martin.

Lifeguard. Jack Rudman. (Career Examination Ser.: C-2300). 1994. reprint ed. pap. 29.95 (*0-8373-2300-2*) Nat Learn.

Lifeguard Training: Principles & Administration. 2nd rev. ed. Council for National Cooperation in Aquatics Staff. LC 68-9312. (Illus.). 223p. reprint ed. pap. 69.20 (*0-8357-3831-0*, 203655500004) Bks Demand.

Lifeguarding Instructor's Manual. American Red Cross Staff. (Illus.). 656p. 1994. write for info. (*0-8016-7553-7*) Mosby Inc.

Lifeguarding Manual. Royal Life Saving Society-Australia Staff. (Illus.). 228p. (gr. 13). 1994. pap. text. write for info. (*0-8151-7321-0*, 25244) Mosby Inc.

LifeGuide Bible Studies. 1997. 69.95 incl. cd-rom (*1-57264-213-0*) Parsons Tech.

LifeGuide Bible Studies, 73 bks., Set. 1985. pap., wbk. ed. 364.27 (*0-8308-1100-1*, 1100) InterVarsity.

Lifehouse. Spider Robinson. 288p. 1997. per. 5.99 (*0-671-87777-1*) Baen Bks.

Lifehunter: Selected Stories, Poems & Essays. Priscilla S. Randolph. 326p. 1994. text 19.95 (*0-9642113-0-0*) Beecher Pr.

Lifekeeper. A. Moody. 1998. 5.99 (*0-8024-8470-0*) Moody.

Lifekeeper: Large Monthly. A. Moody. 1998. 8.99 (*0-8024-8465-4*) Moody.

Lifekeeper: Monthly/Weekly Wirebound. A. Moody. 1998. 10.99 (*0-8024-8459-X*) Moody.

Lifekeeper Pocket Monthly. A. Moody. 1998. 3.99 (*0-8024-8477-8*) Moody.

Lifekeeper: Small Monthly. A. Moody. 1998. 5.49 (*0-8024-8468-9*); 5.49 (*0-8024-8481-6*) Moody.

Lifekeeper: Small Pocket. A. Moody. 1998. 5.99 (*0-8024-8472-7*) Moody.

Lifekeeper: Weekly Wirebound. A. Moody. 1998. 8.99 (*0-8024-8460-3*); 8.99 (*0-8024-8461-1*); 8.99 (*0-8024-8462-X*); 8.99 (*0-8024-8463-8*) Moody.

Lifekeeper, Monthly/Weekly Wire-Bound. Moody. 1998. 10.99 (*0-8024-8456-5*); 10.99 (*0-8024-8457-3*); 10.99 (*0-8024-8458-1*) Moody.

Lifekeys: Discovering Who You Are, Why You're Here, What You Do Best. Jane Kise. 288p. 1996. pap. 14.99 (*1-55661-871-9*) Bethany Hse.

Lifekeys Discovery Workbook. Constance Anderson et al. 32p. 1998. pap. 6.99 (*0-7642-2081-0*, 212081) Bethany Hse.

***Lifekey's Leadership Resource.** Hirsh et al. 193p. 1998. pap. 59.99 (*0-7642-2174-4*) Bethany Hse.

Lifeline. Gerry Boyle. 368p. 1997. mass mkt. 5.99 (*0-425-15688-5*) Berkley Pub.

Lifeline. Bobbie J. Weiss & David C. Weiss. (Starfleet Academy Ser.). (J). 1997. write for info. (*0-614-29161-5*, Minstrel Bks) PB.

Lifeline. David Cody Weiss. (Star Trek Voyager Starfleet Academy Ser.). 1997. 9.09 (*0-606-13801-3*, Pub. by Turtleback) Demco.

Lifeline: A Two-Act Play about a Harlot Named Rahab & a God Named Jehovah. Kevin Stone. 1995. pap. 8.99 (*0-8341-9270-5*, MP-758) Lillenas.

LifeLine: How One Night Changed Five Lives. Mary Z. Schomaker. LC 95-69342. 320p. 1995. 22.95 (*0-88282-135-0*) New Horizon NJ.

Lifeline: The Action Guide to Adoption Search. Virgil L. Klunder. Ed. by Edith Wagner. LC 90-85769. (Illus.). 410p. (Orig.). 1991. 29.95 (*1-879499-18-5*); pap. 24.95 (*1-879499-17-7*) Caradium Pub.

Lifeline: The Religious Upbringing of Your Children. James B. Stenson. LC 96-44708. 168p. 1997. pap. 9.95 (*0-933932-97-9*) Scepter Pubs.

Lifeline Earthquake Engineering. Ed. by Michael A. Cassaro. LC 91-23493. (Technical Council on Lifeline Earthquake Engineering, Monographs: No. 4). 1192p. 1991. pap. text 82.00 (*0-87262-821-3*) Am Soc Civil Eng.

Lifeline Earthquake Engineering: Performance, Design & Construction: Proceedings of a Symposium Sponsored by the Technical Council on Lifeline Earthquake Engineering. Ed. by James D. Cooper. 260p. 1984. 30.00 (*0-87262-414-5*) Am Soc Civil Eng.

Lifeline Earthquake Engineering: Proceedings of the Fourth U. S. Conference; San Francisco, California, August 10-12, 1995. Ed. by Michael J. O'Rourke. (Monograph Ser.: No. 6). 824p. 1995. 78.00 (*0-7844-0101-2*) Am Soc Civil Eng.

Lifeline Earthquake Engineering: The Current State of Knowledge: Proceedings of a Conference Sponsored by the Technical Council on Lifeline Earthquake Engineering. Ed. by D. J. Smith, Jr. 359p. 1981. 5.00 (*0-87262-274-6*) Am Soc Civil Eng.

Lifeline Earthquake Engineering - Buried Pipelines, Seismic Risk, & Instrumentation: Presented at the Third National Congress on Pressure Vessels & Piping, San Francisco, California, June 25-29, 1979. National Congress on Pressure Vessels & Piping Sta. Ed. by Teoman Ariman et al. LC 79-50126. (PVP Ser.: No. 34). (Illus.). 291p. reprint ed. pap. 90.30 (*0-8357-2870-6*, 203910600011) Bks Demand.

Lifeline Earthquake Engineering in the Central & Eastern U. S. Proceedings of Three Sessions Sponsored by the Technical Council on Lifeline Earthquake Engineering Research at the ASCE National Convention in New York, New York, September 1992. Ed. by Donald B. Ballantyne. LC 92-26364. 200p. 1992. 26.00 (*0-87262-902-3*) Am Soc Civil Eng.

Lifeline for Singles: "Mending Broken People" Marlene Henderson. x, 112p. 1998. pap. 9.99 (*1-892555-00-X*) Brd New Image.

Lifeline of the Confederacy: Blockade Running During the Civil War. Stephen R. Wise. Ed. by William N. Still, Jr. LC 88-20524. (Studies in Maritime History). (Illus.). 414p. 1991. reprint ed. pap. 19.95 (*0-87249-799-2*) U of SC Pr.

Lifeline Sampler. LC 85-60461. 448p. 1985. pap. 9.40 (*0-9609898-2-X*) Overeaters Anym.

Lifeline Seismic Risk Analysis - Case Studies. Ed. by Ronald T. Eguchi. (Sessions Proceedings Ser.). 138p. 1986. 19.00 (*0-87262-523-0*) Am Soc Civil Eng.

Lifeline to Care with Dignity: Caring for the Memory Impaired. Kathie T. Erwin. 192p. 1997. pap. 14.95 (*1-887454-01-2*) Caremore Pubns.

***Lifeline to the Universe.** Neil F. Comins. 240p. 2000. text 22.00 (*0-7382-0127-8*, Pub. by Perseus Pubng) HarpC.

Lifelines. Robert B. Luce. (Illus.). 48p. 1994. 8.95 (*0-8378-6948-X*) Gibson.

Lifelines. Intro. by Sharon Tanenbaum. (Illus.). 1991. ring bd. write for info. (*1-879344-00-9*) Ctrl City Hosp Hse.

Lifelines. Jane Wexford. (Star Trek: No. 1). (J). 1984. per. 1.75 (*0-671-00845-5*) PB.

Lifelines, Vol. 1. S. Rose. 1999. text 25.00 (*0-8050-3538-9*) St Martin.

Lifelines: A Book of Hope: Some Thoughts to Cling to When Life Brings You Tough Times. 2nd ed. Bill Zimmerman. LC 88-82746. (Illus.). 128p. (Orig.). (YA). 1994. pap. 6.95 (*0-935966-04-8*) Guarionex Pr.

Lifelines: A Personal Journal. Illus. by Lexie L. Foster. 92p. (Orig.). 1987. pap. 9.95 (*0-9619806-0-5*) Simpler Life Pr.

***Lifelines: Audio Adrenaline.** CCM Staff. (Lifelines Ser.). 128p. 2000. pap. 8.99 (*0-7369-0430-1*) Harvest Hse.

LifeLines: Australian Women's Letters & Diaries, 1788-1840. Lorraine Hepburn et al. (Illus.). 280p. (Orig.). 1992. pap. text 22.95 (*1-86373-124-5*, Pub. by Allen & Unwin Pty) Paul & Co Pubs.

Lifelines: Biology Beyond Determinism. Steven Rose. LC 97-29738. (Illus.). 352p. 1997. 30.00 (*0-19-512035-3*) OUP.

Lifelines: Clinical Perspectives on Suicide. Ed. by Ellen L. Bassuk et al. LC 82-9105. 250p. 1982. 45.00 (*0-306-40971-2*, Plenum Trade) Perseus Pubng.

***Lifelines: Collected Poems Created at the Jewish Community Center of Wake County, N. C.** Barbara Brotman-Leve & Julia Fleifeld. (Illus.). 92p. 1999. pap. 9.95 (*1-880849-16-X*) Chapel Hill NC.

Lifelines: Coping Skills in English, No.3. 2nd ed. Barbara Foley & Howard Pomann. (Illus.). 112p. 1993. pap. text 13.93 (*0-13-225574-X*) P-H.

Lifelines: Coping Skills In English, Vol 4. 2nd ed. Barbara Foley & Howard Pomann. 112p. 1995. pap. text 13.93 (*0-13-097544-3*) P-H.

Lifelines: Famous Contemporaries from 600 B. C. to 1975. Frank W. Weis. LC 80-23132. (Illus.). 445p. reprint ed. pap. 138.00 (*0-608-18302-4*, 203156100075) Bks Demand.

Lifelines: Grace Through Seasons of Change. Alla R. Bozarth. LC 96-120976. 128p. (Orig.). 1996. pap. 9.95 (*1-55612-704-9*, LL1704) Sheed & Ward WI.

Lifelines: Marian Engel's Writings. Christi Verduyn. LC 96-132218. 288p. 1995. pap. 24.95 (*0-7735-1338-8*, Pub. by McG-Queens Univ Pr) CUP Services.

Lifelines: Marian Engel's Writings. Christl Verduyn. LC 96-132218. 288p. 1995. 65.00 (*0-7735-1337-X*, Pub. by McG-Queens Univ Pr) CUP Services.

***Lifelines: Newsboys.** 128p. 2000. pap. 8.99 (*0-7369-0438-7*) Harvest Hse.

Lifelines: Patterns of Work, Love, & Learning in Adulthood. Sharan B. Merriam & M. Carolyn Clark. LC 91-10280. (Social & Behavioral Science Ser.). 280p. 1991. 34.95 (*1-55542-364-7*) Jossey-Bass.

***Lifelines: Selected Poems, 1950-1999.** Philip Booth. 2000. pap. 18.00 (*0-14-058926-0*) Penguin Putnam.

Lifelines: Sixpence None the Richer. CCM Staff. (Story Behind the Music Ser.). 128p. Date not set. pap. 7.99 (*0-7369-0248-1*) Harvest Hse.

Lifelines: The Case for River Conservation. Tim Palmer. LC 94-8951. 200p. 1994. pap. 19.95 (*1-55963-220-8*) Island Pr.

LifeLines: The Esoteric Work. Joseph E. Puett, Jr. (Illus.). 50p. (Orig.). 1997. pap., spiral bd. 12.00 (*0-9656662-6-3*) LifeLines Pub.

Lifelines: What You Absolutely, Positively Need to Know about Life! Sharon Silver. LC 94-36735. 256p. (Orig.). 1994. pap. 5.95 (*0-942963-55-5*) Distinctive Pub.

Lifelines No. 1: Coping Skills in English. 2nd ed. Barbara Foley & Howard Pomann. 112p. (C). 1992. pap. text 13.93 (*0-13-529538-6*) P-H.

Lifelines No. 2: Coping Skills in English. 2nd rev. ed. Barbara Foley & Howard Pomann. 112p. 1993. pap. text 13.93 (*0-13-529702-8*) P-H.

Lifelines - Training & Conditioning Program. Garry Ross & Barry Ross. Ed. by Barry Wright. (Illus.). 128p. (Orig.). 1989. pap. text 29.95 (*0-931571-04-9*) RP Pubng.

Lifelines & Risks: Pathways of Youth in Our Time. Robert B. Cairns & Beverley D. Cairns. 325p. (C). 1995. text 59.95 (*0-521-48112-0*) Cambridge U Pr.

Lifelines & Risks: Pathways of Youth in Our Time. Robert B. Cairns & Beverley D. Cairns. 300p. (C). 1995. pap. text 19.95 (*0-521-48570-3*) Cambridge U Pr.

Lifelines from Our Past: A New World History. L. S. Stavrianos. Tr. by Kevin Reilly. LC 92-5462. (Sources & Studies in World History). 288p. (C). (gr. 13). 1992. reprint ed. pap. text 32.95 (*1-56324-031-9*) M E Sharpe.

Lifelines from Our Past: A New World History. rev. ed. L. S. Stavrianos. LC 97-12880. (Sources & Studies in World History). 304p. (C). (gr. 13). 1997. pap. text 30.95 (*0-7656-0180-X*) M E Sharpe.

Lifelines 3: Letters from Famous People about Their Favourite Poem. Ralph Croly et al. LC 97-224487. xv, 291 p. 1997. write for info. (*1-86059-049-7*) Town Hse.

Lifelong: A Personal Health & Medical Journal. I. Cohrs. 160p. 1997. ring bd. write for info. (*0-9659954-8-8*) LIHNC Co.

Lifelong & Continuing Education: What Is a Learning Society? Ed. by Paul Oliver. LC 99-71887. (Monitoring Change in Education Ser.). 240p. 1999. text 65.95 (*1-84014-905-1*, Pub. by Ashgate Pub) Ashgate Pub Co.

Lifelong Education. Ed. by Paul Belanger & Ettore Gelpi. LC 95-9153. 220p. (C). 1995. pap. text 26.50 (*0-7923-3510-4*) Kluwer Academic.

Lifelong Education: A Psychological Analysis. A. J. Cropley. LC 77-5702. 1977. 95.00 (*0-08-021814-8*, Pub. by Pergamon Repr) Franklin.

Lifelong Education & Evaluation Practice: A Study on the Development of a Framework for Designing Evaluation Systems at the School in the Perspective of Lifelong Education. R. Skager. LC 78-40003. (Advances in Lifelong Education Ser.). 156p. 1978. pap. 17.50 (*0-317-67670-9*, Pergamon Pr) Elsevier.

Lifelong Education for Adults: An International Handbook. Ed. by Colin J. Titmus. (Advances in Education Ser.: No. 7). (Illus.). 629p. 1989. 160.00 (*0-08-030851-1*, Pergamon Pr) Elsevier.

Lifelong Fitness: How to Look Great at Any Age. Bob Delmonteque & Scott Hays. 192p. (Orig.). 1993. mass mkt. 14.99 (*0-446-39488-2*) Warner Bks.

Lifelong Health. Mary R. Swope. LC 97-49497. Orig. Title: Are You Sick & Tired of Being Sick & Tired?. 200p. 1997. pap. 6.99 (*0-88368-510-8*) Whitaker Hse.

***Lifelong Integrated Education as a Creator of the Future.** Yoshiko Nomura. 222p. 1999. pap. 29.95 (*1-85856-154-X*, Trentham Bks) Stylus Pub VA.

Lifelong Learners - A New Clientele for Higher Education: Current Issues in Higher Education, 1974. Ed. by Dyckman W. Vermilye. LC 74-6738. (Jossey-Bass Higher Education Ser.). 200p. reprint ed. 62.00 (*0-8357-9331-1*, 201392600087) Bks Demand.

***Lifelong Learning.** (C). 2000. 133.33 (*0-13-089074-X*) P-H.

Lifelong Learning. Ed. by F. W. Jessup. 1969. 86.00 (*0-08-013407-6*, Pub. by Pergamon Repr) Franklin.

Lifelong Learning. Norman Longworth & W. Keith Davies. 192p. 1997. pap. 29.95 (*0-7494-1972-5*, Kogan Pg Educ) Stylus Pub VA.

***Lifelong Learning: A Art of Test Making.** (C). 2000. 133.33 (*0-13-089070-7*) P-H.

Lifelong Learning: A Guide to Adult Education in the Church. Augsburg Fortress Staff. Ed. by R. Grothe. LC 97-13011. 1997. pap. 16.99 (*0-8066-2999-1*, 9-2999) Augsburg Fortress.

Lifelong Learning: An Imperative in Today's Society - A Conference. large type ed. Ed. by Alphonse F. Trezza. LC 93-2434. (Professional Librarian Ser.). 144p. 1993. 24.50 (*0-8161-7348-6*, G K Hall Lrg Type) Mac Lib Ref.

***Lifelong Learning: Appreciating the Divine World.** (C). 2000. 133.33 (*0-13-089078-2*) P-H.

***Lifelong Learning: Body Mind & Will.** (C). 2000. 133.33 (*0-13-089073-1*) P-H.

***Lifelong Learning: Conducting Research.** (C). 2000. 133.33 (*0-13-089084-7*) P-H.

***Lifelong Learning: Critical Thinking.** (C). 2000. 133.33 (*0-13-089069-3*) P-H.

***Lifelong Learning: Criticl Reading Skill.** (C). 2000. 133.33 (*0-13-089089-8*) P-H.

***Lifelong Learning: Education Today.** (C). 2000. 100.00 (*0-13-089093-6*) P-H.

***Lifelong Learning: Effective Writing.** (C). 2000. 133.33 (*0-13-089083-9*) P-H.

***Lifelong Learning: Getting Along.** (C). 2000. 133.33 (*0-13-089077-4*) P-H.

***Lifelong Learning: Goals & values.** (C). 2000. 133.33 (*0-13-089091-X*) P-H.

***Lifelong Learning: Learning Styles.** (C). 2000. 100.00 (*0-13-089097-9*) P-H.

***Lifelong Learning: Listening Skills.** (C). 2000. 133.33 (*0-13-089088-X*) P-H.

***Lifelong Learning: Managing Chang Life.** (C). 2000. 133.33 (*0-13-089060-X*) P-H.

***Lifelong Learning: Managing Fut Career.** (C). 2000. 133.33 (*0-13-089072-3*) P-H.

***Lifelong Learning: Money Matters.** (C). 2000. 133.33 (*0-13-089071-5*) P-H.

***Lifelong Learning: Note Taking.** (C). 2000. 133.33 (*0-13-089085-5*) P-H.

***Lifelong Learning: Power of Memory.** (C). 2000. 133.33 (*0-13-089086-3*) P-H.

***Lifelong Learning: Preparing for Test.** (C). 2000. 133.33 (*0-13-089081-2*) P-H.

***Lifelong Learning: Reading Skills.** (C). 2000. 133.33 (*0-13-089080-4*) P-H.

***Lifelong Learning: Self Awareness.** (C). 2000. 133.33 (*0-13-089092-8*) P-H.

***Lifelong Learning: Skill 21st Central Math.** (C). 2000. 133.33 (*0-13-089075-8*) P-H.

***Lifelong Learning: Skill 21st Central Teaching.** (C). 2000. 133.33 (*0-13-089076-6*) P-H.

***Lifelong Learning: Tapping Power Your Mind.** (C). 2000. 133.33 (*0-13-089096-0*) P-H.

Lifelong Learning: The Politics of the New Learning Environment, 1, 44. Geoffrey Elliot. LC 99-170959. (Higher Education Policy Ser.). 1998. pap. text 34.95 (*1-85302-580-1*) Taylor & Francis.

***Lifelong Learning: Time Management.** (C). 2000. 133.33 (*0-13-089094-4*) P-H.

***Lifelong Learning: Writing Process.** (C). 2000. 133.33 (*0-13-089082-0*) P-H.

Lifelong Learning & Environmental Education. Ed. by Walter L. Filho. LC 97-18417. 201p. 1997. pap. 31.95 (*0-8204-3511-2*) P Lang Pubng.

Lifelong Learning & Environmental Education. Ed. by Walter Leal Filho. LC 97-18417. (GER.). 201p. 1997. pap. 31.95 (*3-631-32258-5*) P Lang Pubng.

Lifelong Learning & Higher Education. 2nd ed. Chris Knapper & Arthur Cropley. 224p. 1991. 62.00 (*0-7494-0297-0*, Kogan Pg Educ) Stylus Pub VA.

***Lifelong Learning & the New Educational Order.** John Field. 200p. 2000. 59.95 (*1-85856-198-1*, Trentham Bks); pap. 25.00 (*1-85856-199-X*, Trentham Bks) Stylus Pub VA.

Lifelong Learning & the University: A Post-Dearing Agenda. David Watson. LC 98-158135. 1998. 85.00 (*0-7507-0785-2*, Falmer Pr); pap. 29.95 (*0-7507-0784-4*, Falmer Pr) Taylor & Francis.

***Lifelong Learning at Its Best: Innovative Practices in Adult Credit Programs.** William H. Maehl. LC 99-6469. (Higher & Adult Education Ser.). 384p. 1999. 34.95 (*0-7879-4603-6*) Jossey-Bass.

Lifelong Learning for All: Meeting of the Education Committee at Ministerial Level, 16-17 January 1996. OECD Staff. LC 96-231285. 230p. (Orig.). 1996. pap. 50.00 (*92-64-14815-9*, Pub. by Org for Econ) OECD.

Lifelong Learning in America. Richard E. Peterson et al. LC 79-83576. (Jossey-Bass Series in Higher Education). 552p. reprint ed. pap. 171.20 (*0-7837-2532-9*, 204269100006) Bks Demand.

***Lifelong Learning in Higher Education.** 3rd ed. Chris Knapper & Arthur Cropley. 224p. 1999. pap. 29.95 (*0-7494-2794-9*, Kogan Pg Educ) Stylus Pub VA.

Lifelong Learning Market Report, 1997: Analysis & Forecast. 1997. 1495.00 (*0-614-25712-3*) Simba Info.

Lifelong Learning or Lifelong Schooling: A Tentative View of the Ideas of Ivan Illich. John Ohlinger & Colleen McCarthy. LC 70-164120. (Occasional Papers: No. 24). 1971. text 2.25 (*0-87060-044-3*, OCP 24) Syracuse U Cont Ed.

Lifelong Leisure Skills & Lifestyles for Persons with Developmental Disabilities. Stuart J. Schleien et al. 352p. 1995. pap. 35.00 (*1-55766-147-2*) P H Brookes.

Lifelong Love Affair. Joseph K. Nowinski. 1989. pap. 7.95 (*0-393-30621-6*) Norton.

Lifelong Management of Hypertension. H. Mitchell Perry. (Developments in Cardiovascular Medicine Ser.). 1983. text 176.50 (*0-89838-582-2*) Kluwer Academic.

Lifelong Motor Development. 2nd ed. Carl P. Gabbard. 480p. (C). 1995. text. write for info. (*0-697-23333-2*) Brown & Benchmark.

Lifelong Motor Development. 2nd ed. Carl P. Gabbard. 480p. (C). 1997. text. write for info. (*0-07-114268-1*) McGraw.

***Lifelong Motor Development.** 3rd ed. Gabbard. LC 99-38965. 444p. 1999. 60.00 (*0-205-30889-9*) Allyn.

Lifelong Passion: Nicholas & Alexandra: Their Own Story. Andrei Maylunas & Sergei Mironenko. Tr. by Darya Galy from RUS. (Illus.). 667p. 1999. text 35.00 (*0-7881-6079-6*) DIANE Pub.

Lifelong Quest for Peace: A Dialogue. Linus Pauling & Daisaku Ikeda. 144p. (C). 2000. 30.00 (*0-86720-278-5*) Jones & Bartlett.

***Lifelong Quotes.** Jean-Claude Guilbaud. 88p. 2000. pap. 10.00 (*0-8059-4755-8*) Dorrance.

***Lifelong Reader.** 2000. write for info. (*0-321-04953-5*) Addison-Wesley.

Lifelong Reading, Bk. 2. Kathleen M. Rouhier. (C). 1993. pap. text 6.50 (*0-13-016098-9*) P-H.

Lifelong Reading, Bk. 3. Kathleen M. Rouhier. (C). 1994. pap. text 6.50 (*0-13-016106-3*) P-H.

Lifelong Reading, Bk. 4. Kathleen M. Rouhier. 1994. pap. text 12.67 (*0-13-532292-8*) P-H.

Lifelong Reading No. 1: A Basic Course. Kathleen M. Rouhier. 128p. 1993. pap. text 6.50 (*0-13-016080-6*) P-H.

Lifelong Values. 1993. 6.00 (*0-939418-62-2*) Ferguson-Florissant.

Lifemanship. Stephen Potter. 1993. reprint ed. lib. bdg. 18.95 (*1-56849-093-3*) Buccaneer Bks.

LifeMapping: Workbook Edition. John Trent. 272p. 1998. pap., wbk. ed. 14.95 (*1-57856-146-9*) Waterbrook Pr.

***Lifemaps of People with Learning Disabilities.** Barry Gray. LC 98-49782. (Special Talents, Special Needs Ser.). 1999. 23.95 (*1-85302-690-5*) Jessica Kingsley.

Lifemask. Frances Galleymore. 288p. 1997. pap. 16.95 (*1-85797-794-7*, Pub. by Orion Pubng Grp) Trafalgar.

LifeNotes: Recording YOUR Memories - The Legacy of a Lifetime. Dee Dees. (Illus.). 90p. 1998. spiral bd. 12.95 (*0-9667829-0-9*) Double D Desktop Pubg.

Lifepac Bible Grade 11 Set. (Illus.). (YA). (gr. 11). 1996. teacher ed., student ed., boxed set 45.95 (*0-86717-210-X*, BIB1115) Alpha AZ.

Lifepac Bible Grade 12 Boxed Set. (Illus.). (YA). (gr. 12). 1996. teacher ed., student ed., boxed set 45.95 (*0-86717-211-8*, BS1215) Alpha AZ.

L

An Asterisk (*) at the beginning of an entry indicates that the title is appearing for the first time.

L

Lifepac Elective: Consumer Math Grade 9-12. (Illus.). (YA). (gr. 9-12). 1979. boxed set 44.50 (*0-00-547119-2*, ES2315) Alpha AZ.
Lifepac Elective: Greek I Grade 9-12. (Illus.). (YA). (gr. 9-12). 1979. pap., boxed set 40.95 (*0-00-547120-6*, ES2415) Alpha AZ.
Lifepac Elective: Home Economics Grade 9-12. (Illus.). (YA). (gr. 9-12). 1979. boxed set 45.95 (*0-00-547121-4*, ES2115) Alpha AZ.
Lifepac Elective: Spanish I Grade 9-12. (Illus.). (YA). (gr. 9-12). 1979. boxed set 100.95 (*0-7403-0082-2*, ES2215) Alpha AZ.
Lifepac Gold Bible Grade 8 Boxed Set. (Illus.). (J). (gr. 8). 1996. teacher ed., student ed., boxed set 45.95 (*0-86717-015-8*, BIB0815) Alpha AZ.
Lifepac Gold Bible Grade 5 Boxed Set. (Illus.). (J). (gr. 5). 1996. teacher ed., student ed., boxed set 45.95 (*0-86717-673-3*, BIB0515) Alpha AZ.
Lifepac Gold Bible Grade 4 Boxed Set. (Illus.). (J). (gr. 4). 1996. teacher ed., student ed., boxed set 45.95 (*0-86717-007-7*, BIB0415) Alpha AZ.
Lifepac Gold Bible Grade 9 Boxed Set. (Illus.). (YA). (gr. 9). 1996. teacher ed., student ed., boxed set 45.95 (*0-86717-017-4*, BIB0915) Alpha AZ.
Lifepac Gold Bible Grade 1 Boxed Set. (Illus.). (J). (gr. 1). 1996. teacher ed., student ed., boxed set 65.90 (*0-86717-671-7*, BIB0115) Alpha AZ.
Lifepac Gold Bible Grade 6 Boxed Set. (Illus.). (J). (gr. 6). 1996. teacher ed., student ed., boxed set 45.95 (*0-86717-011-5*, BIB0615) Alpha AZ.
Lifepac Gold Bible Grade 10 Boxed Set. (Illus.). (YA). (gr. 10). 1996. teacher ed., student ed., boxed set 45.95 (*0-86717-209-6*, BIB1015) Alpha AZ.
Lifepac Gold Bible Grade 3 Boxed Set. (Illus.). (J). (gr. 3). 1996. teacher ed., student ed., boxed set 45.95 (*0-86717-672-5*, BIB0315) Alpha AZ.
Lifepac Gold Bible Grade 2 Boxed Set. (Illus.). (J). (gr. 2). 1996. teacher ed., student ed., boxed set 45.95 (*0-86717-003-4*, BIB0215) Alpha AZ.
Lifepac Gold Bible Grade 7 Boxed Set. (Illus.). (J). (gr. 7). 1996. teacher ed., student ed., boxed set 44.95 (*0-86717-013-1*, BIB0715) Alpha AZ.
Lifepac Gold History - Geography Grade 1 Boxed Set. (Illus.). (J). (gr. 1). 1996. teacher ed., student ed., boxed set 65.90 (*0-86717-025-5*, HIS0115) Alpha AZ.
Lifepac Gold History Grade 8 Boxed Set. Teresa Baskey. (Illus.). (J). (gr. 8). 1999. teacher ed., student ed., boxed set 45.95 (*0-7403-0040-7*, HIS0815) Alpha AZ.
Lifepac Gold History Grade 5 Boxed Set. Terry Baskey. (Illus.). (J). (gr. 5). 2000. teacher ed., student ed., boxed set 45.95 (*0-86717-034-4*, HIS0515) Alpha AZ.
Lifepac Gold History Grade 4 Boxed Set. (Illus.). (J). (gr. 4). 1996. teacher ed., student ed., boxed set 45.95 (*1-58095-648-3*, HIS0415) Alpha AZ.
Lifepac Gold History Grade 9 Boxed Set. (Illus.). (YA). (gr. 9). 1996. teacher ed., student ed., boxed set 45.95 (*0-86717-042-5*, HIS0915) Alpha AZ.
Lifepac Gold History Grade 7 Boxed Set. (Illus.). (J). (gr. 7). 1996. teacher ed., student ed., boxed set 45.95 (*1-58095-657-2*, HIS0715) Alpha AZ.
Lifepac Gold History Grade 6 Boxed Set. (Illus.). (J). (gr. 6). 1996. teacher ed., student ed., boxed set 45.95 (*0-86717-036-0*, HIS0615) Alpha AZ.
Lifepac Gold History Grade 10 Boxed Set. (Illus.). (YA). (gr. 10). 1996. teacher ed., student ed., boxed set 45.95 (*0-86717-044-1*, HIS1015) Alpha AZ.
Lifepac Gold History Grade 3 Boxed Set. (Illus.). (J). (gr. 3). 1996. teacher ed., student ed., boxed set 45.95 (*0-86717-030-1*, HIS0315) Alpha AZ.
Lifepac Gold History Grade 2 Boxed Set. (Illus.). (J). (gr. 2). 1996. teacher ed., student ed., boxed set 44.95 (*0-86717-028-X*, HIS0215) Alpha AZ.
Lifepac Gold Language Arts Grade 8 Boxed Set. (Illus.). (J). (gr. 8). 1996. teacher ed., student ed., boxed set 45.95 (*0-86717-064-6*, LAN0815) Alpha AZ.
Lifepac Gold Language Arts Grade 5 Boxed Set. (Illus.). (J). (gr. 5). 1996. teacher ed., student ed., boxed set 45.95 (*0-86717-058-1*, LAN0515) Alpha AZ.
Lifepac Gold Language Arts Grade 4 Boxed Set. (Illus.). (J). (gr. 4). 1996. teacher ed., student ed., boxed set 45.95 (*0-86717-056-5*, LAN0415) Alpha AZ.
Lifepac Gold Language Arts Grade K Boxed Set. (Illus.). (J). (gr. k). 1996. teacher ed., student ed., boxed set 39.95 (*0-86717-833-7*, LAK015) Alpha AZ.
Lifepac Gold Language Arts Grade 9 Boxed Set. (Illus.). (YA). (gr. 9). 1996. teacher ed., student ed., boxed set 56.85 (*0-86717-066-2*, LAN0915) Alpha AZ.
Lifepac Gold Language Arts Grade 1 Boxed Set. (Illus.). (J). (gr. 1). 1996. teacher ed., student ed., boxed set 90.65 (*0-86717-050-6*, LAN0115) Alpha AZ.
Lifepac Gold Language Arts Grade 7 Boxed Set. (Illus.). (J). (gr. 7). 1996. teacher ed., student ed., boxed set 52.90 (*0-86717-062-X*, LAN0715) Alpha AZ.
Lifepac Gold Language Arts Grade 6 Boxed Set. (Illus.). (J). (gr. 6). 1996. teacher ed., student ed., boxed set 45.95 (*0-86717-060-3*, LAN0615) Alpha AZ.
Lifepac Gold Language Arts Grade 3 Boxed Set. (Illus.). (J). (gr. 3). 1996. teacher ed., student ed., boxed set 45.95 (*0-86717-054-9*, LAN0315) Alpha AZ.
Lifepac Gold Language Arts Grade 2 Boxed Set. (Illus.). (J). (gr. 2). 1996. teacher ed., student ed., boxed set 45.95 (*0-86717-052-2*, LAN0215) Alpha AZ.
Lifepac Gold Language Arts Grade 10 Boxed Set. (Illus.). (YA). (gr. 10). 1996. teacher ed., student ed., boxed set 57.90 (*0-86717-221-5*, LAN1015) Alpha AZ.
Lifepac Gold Mathematics Grade 8 Boxed Set. (Illus.). (J). (gr. 8). 1996. teacher ed., student ed., boxed set 50.95 (*0-86717-088-3*, MAT0815) Alpha AZ.
Lifepac Gold Mathematics Grade 5 Boxed Set. (Illus.). (J). (gr. 5). 1996. teacher ed., student ed., boxed set 45.95 (*1-58095-725-0*) Alpha AZ.
Lifepac Gold Mathematics Grade 4 Boxed Set. (Illus.). (J). (gr. 4). 1996. teacher ed., student ed., boxed set 45.95 (*0-86717-080-8*, MAT0415) Alpha AZ.
Lifepac Gold Mathematics Grade K Boxed Set. (Illus.). (J). (gr. k). 1996. teacher ed., student ed., boxed set 39.95 (*0-86717-838-8*, MAK015) Alpha AZ.
Lifepac Gold Mathematics Grade 9 Boxed Set. (Illus.). (YA). (gr. 9). 1996. teacher ed., student ed., boxed set 50.95 (*0-86717-090-5*, MAT0915) Alpha AZ.
Lifepac Gold Mathematics Grade 1 Boxed Set. (Illus.). (J). (gr. 1). 1996. teacher ed., student ed., boxed set 65.90 (*0-86717-074-3*, MAT0115) Alpha AZ.
Lifepac Gold Mathematics Grade 7 Boxed Set. (Illus.). (J). (gr. 7). 1996. teacher ed., student ed., boxed set 50.95 (*0-86717-086-7*) Alpha AZ.
Lifepac Gold Mathematics Grade 6 Boxed Set. (Illus.). (J). (gr. 6). 1996. teacher ed., student ed., boxed set 45.95 (*0-7403-0026-1*, MAT0615) Alpha AZ.
Lifepac Gold Mathematics Grade 3 Boxed Set. (Illus.). (J). (gr. 3). 1996. teacher ed., student ed., boxed set 45.95 (*1-58095-719-6*, MAT0315) Alpha AZ.
Lifepac Gold Mathematics Grade 2 Boxed Set. (Illus.). (J). (gr. 2). 1996. teacher ed., student ed., boxed set 45.95 (*1-58095-716-1*) Alpha AZ.
Lifepac Gold Mathematics Grade 10 Boxed Set. (Illus.). (YA). (gr. 10). 1996. teacher ed., student ed., boxed set 49.95 (*0-86717-233-9*, MAT1015) Alpha AZ.
Lifepac Gold Mathematics Grade 6: Boxed Set Includes Everything for Both Teacher & Student. Alpha Omega Publishing Staff. (Illus.). 1996. boxed set 44.98 (*0-86717-084-0*) Alpha AZ.
Lifepac Gold Science Grade 8 Boxed Set. (Illus.). (J). (gr. 8). 1996. teacher ed., student ed., boxed set 45.95 (*0-86717-661-X*, SCI0815) Alpha AZ.
Lifepac Gold Science Grade 11 Boxed Set. (Illus.). (YA). (gr. 11). 1996. teacher ed., student ed., boxed set 45.95 (*0-86717-246-0*, HS1115) Alpha AZ.
Lifepac Gold Science Grade 5 Boxed Set. (Illus.). (J). (gr. 5). 1996. teacher ed., student ed., boxed set 45.95 (*0-86717-655-5*, SCI0515) Alpha AZ.
Lifepac Gold Science Grade 4 Boxed Set. (Illus.). (J). (gr. 4). 1996. teacher ed., student ed., boxed set 45.95 (*0-86717-653-9*, SCI0415) Alpha AZ.
Lifepac Gold Science Grade 9 Boxed Set. (Illus.). (YA). (gr. 9). 1996. teacher ed., student ed., boxed set 45.95 (*0-86717-663-6*, SCI0915) Alpha AZ.
Lifepac Gold Science Grade 1 Boxed Set. (Illus.). (J). (gr. 1). 1996. teacher ed., student ed., boxed set 65.90 (*0-86717-098-0*, SCI0115) Alpha AZ.
Lifepac Gold Science Grade 7 Boxed Set. (Illus.). (J). (gr. 7). 1996. teacher ed., student ed., boxed set 45.95 (*0-86717-659-8*, SCI0715) Alpha AZ.
Lifepac Gold Science Grade 6 Boxed Set. (Illus.). (J). (gr. 6). 1996. teacher ed., student ed., boxed set 45.95 (*0-86717-657-1*, SCI0615) Alpha AZ.
Lifepac Gold Science Grade 3 Boxed Set. (Illus.). (J). (gr. 3). 1996. teacher ed., student ed., boxed set 45.95 (*0-86717-651-2*, SCI0315) Alpha AZ.
Lifepac Gold Science Grade 12 Boxed Set. (Illus.). (YA). (gr. 12). 1996. teacher ed., student ed., boxed set 45.95 (*0-86717-247-9*, HS1215) Alpha AZ.
Lifepac Gold Science Grade 2 Boxed Set. (Illus.). (J). (gr. 2). 1996. teacher ed., student ed., boxed set 45.95 (*0-86717-100-6*, SCI0215) Alpha AZ.
Lifepac Gold Science Grade 10 Boxed Set. (Illus.). (YA). (gr. 10). 1996. teacher ed., student ed., boxed set 44.95 (*0-86717-245-2*, SCI1015) Alpha AZ.
Lifepac History Grade 11 Boxed Set. (Illus.). (YA). (gr. 11). 1996. teacher ed., student ed., boxed set 45.95 (*0-86717-258-4*, HS1115) Alpha AZ.
Lifepac History Grade 12 Boxed Set. (Illus.). (YA). (gr. 12). 1996. teacher ed., student ed., boxed set 45.95 (*0-86717-259-2*, HS1215) Alpha AZ.
Lifepac Language Arts Grade 11 Boxed Set. (Illus.). (YA). (gr. 11). 1996. teacher ed., student ed., boxed set 55.35 (*0-86717-222-3*, LS1115) Alpha AZ.
Lifepac Language Arts Grade 12 Boxed Set. (Illus.). (YA). (gr. 12). 1996. teacher ed., student ed., boxed set 44.45 (*0-86717-223-1*, LS1215) Alpha AZ.
Lifepac Mathematics Grade 11 Boxed Set. (Illus.). (YA). (gr. 11). 1996. teacher ed., student ed., boxed set 47.95 (*0-86717-234-7*, MS1115) Alpha AZ.
Lifepac Mathematics Grade 12 Boxed Set. (Illus.). (YA). (gr. 12). 1996. teacher ed., student ed., boxed set 47.95 (*0-86717-235-5*, MS1215) Alpha AZ.
Lifepac Select: Astronomy Grade 9-12. (Illus.). (YA). (gr. 9-12). 1997. 23.95 (*0-86717-676-8*, ES3010) Alpha AZ.
Lifepac Select: Christian Perspective Grade 9-12. (Illus.). (YA). (gr. 9-12). 1997. 23.95 (*0-86717-678-4*, ES3011) Alpha AZ.
Lifepac Select: Civics Grade 9-12. (Illus.). (YA). (gr. 9-12). 1997. 23.95 (*0-86717-679-2*, ES3012) Alpha AZ.
Lifepac Select: Composition. (Illus.). (YA). (gr. 9-12). 1997. 23.95 (*0-86717-680-6*, ES3013) Alpha AZ.
Lifepac Select: General Health Grade 9-12. (Illus.). (YA). (gr. 9-12). 1997. 23.95 (*0-86717-681-4*, ES3014) Alpha AZ.
Lifepac Select: Geography. (Illus.). (YA). (gr. 9-12). 1997. 23.95 (*0-86717-682-2*, ES3015) Alpha AZ.
Lifepac Select: Geology. (Illus.). (YA). (gr. 9-12). 1997. 23.95 (*0-86717-683-0*, ES3016) Alpha AZ.
Lifepac Select: Life Science Grade 9-12. (Illus.). (YA). (gr. 9-12). 1997. 23.95 (*0-86717-684-9*, ES3018) Alpha AZ.
Lifepac Select: Mankind - Anthropology & Sociology. (Illus.). (YA). (gr. 9-12). 1997. 23.95 (*0-86717-685-7*, ES3019) Alpha AZ.
Lifepac Select Life of Christ: Includes 5 Lifepacs & a Complete Teachers Guide. (Illus.). (YA). (gr. 9-12). 1997. 23.95 (*0-86717-677-6*, ES3017) Alpha AZ.
Lifeplan: Your Own Master Plan for Maintaining Health & Preventing Illness. rev. ed. Donald M. Vickery. LC 89-52083. 347p. 1990. pap. 8.75 (*0-9625327-0-3*, M14531) Vicktor.
Lifeplanning. Robb E. Dalton. Ed. by Dale Messmer & Vicky Collins. (Illus.). 164p. (Orig.). 1987. pap. 14.95 (*0-9619467-0-9*) Lifeplanning.
Lifeplans. 2nd ed. Thompson. (OX - Home Economics Ser.). 1989. pap. 46.95 (*0-538-60550-2*) S-W Pub.
Lifepoints. Peggy Brusseau & Peter Cox. LC 97-13141. 1997. pap. 6.99 (*0-684-83373-5*) S&S Trade.
Lifepoints. Cox. 1996. mass mkt. write for info. (*0-312-95783-1*) St Martin.
Lifepoints. Peter Cox & Peggy Brusseau. 1997. 23.00 (*0-614-20669-3*) P-H.
LifePrints: Using Lifeprints. 1997. teacher ed. 75.00 (*1-56420-114-7*) New Readers.
LifePrints No. 1: Assessment. 1997. teacher ed. 19.95 (*1-56420-103-1*) New Readers.
LifePrints No. 2: Assessment. 1997. teacher ed. 19.95 (*1-56420-104-X*) New Readers.
LifePrints No. 3: Assessment. 1997. teacher ed. 19.95 (*1-56420-105-8*) New Readers.
LifePrints 1: Level: Low Beginning, High Beginning, Low Intermediate. 1993. teacher ed. 12.00 (*0-88336-044-6*); teacher ed. 60.00 (*0-88336-037-3*); student ed. 11.00 (*0-88336-034-9*); digital audio 11.95 (*0-88336-047-0*) New Readers.
LifePrints 3: Level: Low Beginning, High Beginning, Low Intermediate. 1993. teacher ed. 12.00 (*0-88336-046-2*); student ed. 11.00 (*0-88336-036-5*); digital audio 11.95 (*0-88336-050-0*) New Readers.
LifePrints 3: Level: Low Beginning, High Beginning, Low Intermediate. 1994. teacher ed. 65.00 (*0-88336-042-X*) New Readers.
LifePrints 2: Level: Low Beginning, High Beginning, Low Intermediate. 1993. teacher ed. 12.00 (*0-88336-045-4*); student ed. 11.00 (*0-88336-035-7*); digital audio 11.95 (*0-88336-049-7*) New Readers.
LifePrints 2: Level: Low Beginning, High Beginning, Low Intermediate. 1994. teacher ed. 65.00 (*0-88336-041-1*) New Readers.
***Lifer USMC.** (Illus.). 167p. 1999. text. write for info. (*0-9675499-0-6*) G F Cribb.
Liferails: Holding Fast to God's Promises. Scott Walker. LC 99-17088. 176p. 1999. pap. 12.99 (*0-8066-3728-5*, 9-3728, Augsburg) Augsburg Fortress.
***Life's a Cinch with Just One Inch.** unabridged ed. Mary Olkowski. LC 99-95296. (Illus.). 100p. (YA). (gr. 4 up). 1999. 19.95 (*0-9668781-2-4*, 1003-1004); pap. 14.95 (*0-9668781-3-2*, 1003-1004) Limpid Butterfly.
Life's a Cycle. Thomas-Cochran. (What a Wonderful World Ser.). 1991. pap. text. write for info. (*0-582-90950-3*, Pub. by Addison-Wesley) Longman.
Life's a Dream. adapted ed. Pedro Calderon de la Barca. Ed. by Adrian Mitchell. 1994. pap. 5.50 (*0-87129-295-5*, L77) Dramatic Pub.
Life's a Funny Proposition, Horatio. Barbara G. Polikoff. LC 91-28010. 112p. (J). (gr. 4-7). 1995. 13.95 (*0-8050-1972-3*, Bks Young Read) H Holt & Co.
Life's a Funny Proposition, Horatio. Barbara G. Polikoff. (Illus.). 112p. (J). (gr. 3-7). 1994. pap. 4.99 (*0-14-036644-X*, PuffinBks) Peng Put Young Read.
Life's a Funny Proposition, Horatio. Barbara G. Polikoff. (J). 1994. 10.09 (*0-606-05906-7*, Pub. by Turtleback) Demco.
Life's a Game Show. Gloria Tinsley. LC 96-68045. 80p. (Orig.). 1996. pap. 9.95 (*1-881576-94-9*) Providence Hse.
***Life's a Joke!** S. "Gabby" Gerber. LC 99-93808. 1999. pap. 7.95 (*0-533-13163-4*) Vantage.
Life's a Jubilee. large type ed. Maud Anson. 349p. 1979. 27.99 (*0-7089-0289-8*) Ulverscroft.
Life's a Lark. Grock. LC 73-84515. 286p. 1972. 24.95 (*0-405-08583-4*, Pub. by Blom Pubns) Ayer.
Life's a Tea Party! Linda R. Wexler. Ed. by Howard B. Raff. (Illus.). 48p. (Orig.). 1997. pap. 5.95 (*1-888230-06-1*) Chelsea St Prods.
Life's Absurd! Our Meaningful & Meaningless Life: A Collection of Thoughts, Ideas & Concerns. Trevor McAlmont. 37p. 1997. pap. 8.95 (*0-533-12448-4*) Vantage.
***Life's Adventure: Virtual Risk in a Real World.** Roger Bate. 192p. 2000. pap. 29.95 (*0-7506-4679-9*) Buttrwrth-Heinemann.
***Life's Been Good: The Children of the Great Depression.** Glen McLaren. 272p. 1999. pap. 19.95 (*1-86368-265-1*, Pub. by Fremantle Arts) Intl Spec Bk.
Life's Beginnings: A Study in Biblical Obstetrics, with Modern Application. 398p. 1998. pap. 19.95 (*0-9668657-0-7*) Ark Pubg.
Life's Beginnings: Our Life Before Birth Helps Us Trace Our Roots. W. J. Howard. LC 90-83709. (Illus.). 128p. (Orig.). 1991. pap. 9.95 (*0-9627341-7-9*) Coast Pub OR.
Life's Big Instruction Book: The Almanac of Indispensable Information. Carol O. Madigan & Ann Elmwood. 1995. pap. write for info. (*0-446-67157-6*) Warner Bks.
***Life's Big Issues: 12 Teen - Adult Sessions.** (YA). 2000. 12.95 (*1-56077-613-7*) Ctr Learning.
***Life's Bits & Pieces.** Betty Jones. 2000. write for info. (*1-58235-479-0*) Watermrk Pr.
Life's Bitter Pool. 1984. pap. 2.50 (*1-892283-00-X*, T84) Derek Prince.
Life's Bitter Pool. (ENG & IND.). 1993. pap. write for info. (*0-934920-51-6*, T-84IN) Derek Prince.
Life's Candle Light. Yvonne Schneider. 82p. pap. 5.95 (*0-942494-29-6*) Coleman Pub.
Life's Career; Aging: Cultural Variations on Growing Old. Ed. by Barbara G. Myerhoff & Andrei Simic. (Cross-Cultural Research & Methodology Ser.: Vol. 4). 252p. 1979. pap. 23.95 (*0-8039-6000-X*) Sage.
Life's Changes. Arlene Maguire. LC 91-9353. (Illus.). 32p. (Orig.). (J). (ps-5). 1991. 6.95 (*0-941992-26-8*) Los Arboles Pub.
Life's Changing Scenes. (Words of Comfort Ser.). (Illus.). 64p. 1993. 6.95 (*0-7117-0418-X*, Pub. by JARR UK) Seven Hills Bk.
Life's Choices. Ed. by R. M. Davis & P. D. Buford. 160p. 1994. reprint ed. pap. 5.99 (*1-56722-055-X*) Word Aflame.
Life's Choices: Problems & Solutions. Richard S. Sharf. LC 00-25258. 384p. 2000. 55.95 (*0-534-35933-7*) Thomson Learn.
Life's Cobwebs: Breaking Free from the Entrapments of the World. Mike Root. LC 96-1632. 1996. pap. 9.99 (*0-89900-760-0*) College Pr Pub.
Life's Companion: Journal Writing As a Spiritual Quest. Christina Baldwin. 368p. 1990. pap. 14.95 (*0-553-35202-4*) Bantam.
Life's Connections. Barbara Patten. LC 95-91034. 224p. (Orig.). 1996. pap. 12.95 (*0-9651082-7-9*) Tenton Pr.
Life's Daughter - Death's Bride: Inner Transformations Through the Goddess Demeter-Persephone. Kathie Carlson. LC 97-9007. 1997. 27.50 (*0-87773-903-X*, Pub. by Shambhala Pubns) Random.
***Life's Delicate Balance: A Guide to Causes & Prevention of Breast Cancer.** Janette D. Sherman. LC 99-35503. (Illus.). 300p. 1999. 25.95 (*1-56032-870-3*) Taylor & Francis.
Life's Detours. Percy Avram. Ed. by Vicky Avram. 352p. 1996. pap. 8.95 (*0-9651737-0-4*) Marva Ent.
Life's Detours. Charles L. Paddock. 32p. 1952. pap. 0.99 (*0-8163-0074-7*, 12225-9) Pacific Pr Pub Assn.
Life's Devices: The Physical World of Animals & Plants. Steven Vogel. (Illus.). 384p. 1989. pap. text 26.95 (*0-691-02418-9*, Pub. by Princeton U Pr) Cal Prin Full Svc.
Life's Dominion: An Argument about Abortion, Euthanasia & Individual Freedom. Ronald M. Dworkin. LC 93-42582. 1994. pap. 13.00 (*0-679-73319-1*) Vin Bks.
Life's down to Old Women's Shoes: Poetry & Personal Essays. Margaret B. Vaughn. LC 97-37386. 1997. write for info. (*1-882845-06-4*) Bell Buckle.
***Life's End: Technocratic Dying in an Age of Spiritual Yearning.** David Wendell Moller. LC 99-33740. 195p. 1999. 36.00 (*0-89503-202-3*) Baywood Pub.
Life's Enthusiasms (1906) David S. Jordan. 64p. 1998. reprint ed. pap. 7.95 (*0-7661-0545-8*) Kessinger Pub.
***Life's Evening Hour.** John Dugdale. 2000. 45.00 (*0-9672484-2-6*) AGW Lithographers.
Life's Extras. 2nd ed. Archibald Rutledge. (Illus.). 56p. 1987. reprint ed. 8.95 (*0-87844-080-1*) Sandlapper Pub Co.
Life's Financial Instruction Book. Joseph Bisignano. 1996. pap. 7.95 (*0-614-12593-6*) Pelican Books.
***Life's Forms: Late Aristotelian Conceptions of the Soul.** Dennis Des Chene. 2000. write for info. (*0-8014-3763-6*) Cornell U Pr.
Life's Golden Gleanings. Ruby E. Stover. 94p. pap. 2.50 (*0-686-29127-1*) Faith Pub Hse.
Life's Golden Tree: Studies in German Literature from the Reformation to Rilke. Ed. by Thomas Kerth & George C. Schoolfield. (GERM Ser.). xiv, 282p. 1996. 70.00 (*1-57113-080-2*) Camden Hse.
***Life's Greatest Journey.** Doug McIntosh. LC 00-25756. 2000. pap. 12.99 (*0-8024-6648-6*) Moody.
***Life's Greatest Lessons: Twenty Things I Want My Kids to Know.** 3rd ed. Hal Urban. LC 97-94299. 164p. 2000. pap. 14.95 (*0-9659684-4-8*) Great Lessons.
Life's Greatest Miracle. Lily Cavell. (Illus.). 20p. 1991. spiral bd. 7.95 (*1-885038-02-X*) Uriel Press.
Life's Hidden Meaning. Niles MacFlouer. (Illus.). 763p. 1999. pap. 39.95 (*0-9648483-0-9*) Ageless Wisdom.
Life's Highest Blessings. R. L. Soni. 94p. 1987. 3.00 (*955-24-0020-1*, Pub. by Buddhist Pub Soc) Vipassana Res Pubns.
Life's Highest Delight: Understand the Person & Passion of God. Ron Williams. LC 97-66623. 225p. 1997. pap. 10.99 (*0-87148-535-4*) Pathway Pr.
Life's Highway. Isabella Wehner. 39p. 1999. pap. 9.95 (*1-892896-69-9*) Buy Books.
Life's Imponderables. David Feldman. 816p. 1999. 33.00 (*1-57866-080-7*) Galahad Bks.
Life's Important Things. Ed. by Brigitta Geltrich. (Anthology Ser.). (Illus.). 84p. 1996. pap. text 3.00 (*0-936945-62-1*) Creat with Wds.
Life's Infinite Spiritual Ideas Cannot be Obliterated. Augusta E. Stetson. LC 91-815606. 44p. 1989. reprint ed. pap. 5.00 (*1-879135-03-5*) Emma Pub Soc.
Life's Inspirations. Gracie T. Alden. (Illus.). 40p. 1998. pap. 6.00 (*1-892609-01-0*) Gracie Pub.
Life's Instruction Book for Women. Barbara Gray. 1993. pap. 5.95 (*0-9637784-0-4*) B Gray ProActives.
Life's Instruction Book for Women, Vol. 2. Barbara Gray. 1994. pap. 5.95 (*0-9637784-1-2*) B Gray ProActives.
Life's Instruction Book for Women, Vol. 3. Barbara Gray. 1994. pap. text 5.95 (*0-9637784-2-0*) B Gray ProActives.
Life's Is a Jungle. R. Snell. 1997. mass mkt. 5.95 (*0-929292-85-5*) Hannibal Bks.
Life's Journey. Charlotte Burke. 1997. pap. write for info. (*1-57553-583-1*) Watermrk Pr.
Life's Journey. Lida Pretty. 56p. 1990. 9.95 (*0-910147-90-6*) World Poetry Pr.
***Life's Journey for One Man.** Robert Anderson, 3rd. 32p. 1999. pap. 8.00 (*0-8059-4829-5*) Dorrance.
Life's Journey in China (1920-89) Memoirs of Mei Tan. 2nd rev. ed. Mei Tan. (Illus.). 244p. 1997. pap. 15.00 (*1-892110-00-8*) Offete Ents.
***Life's Journeys, with Ruth Eagle in Poetry.** Ruth Eagle. 1998. 9.95 (*962-8265-01-6*) Access Pubng.

An Asterisk (*) at the beginning of an entry indicates that the title is appearing for the first time.

Life's Lessons. Howard Wight. (Orig.). 1992. pap. write for info. (*0-9633506-1-7*) Wight Finan Concepts.
Life's Lessons: A Mother's Journal. Bea Nettles. (Illus.). 72p. (Orig.). 1990. pap. 15.00 (*0-930810-05-8*) Inky Pr.
Life's Lessons: Cheat Notes from the Classroom of Life. Donna Blaurock. Ed. by Patrick Caton. LC 96-78973. 168p. 1997. pap. 5.95 (*1-56245-286-X*) Great Quotations.
Life's Lessons: Insights & Information for a Richer Life. Rebecca L. Morgan. 1997. pap. 9.95 (*0-9660740-1-7*) Morgan Seminar.
Life's Lessons from Mayberry. Len Oszustowicz & John Oszustowicz. LC 97-4918. 128p. 1997. 9.99 (*1-56530-250-8*, Pub. by Summit TX) BookWorld.
***Life's Little Barry Cookbook: 101 Berry Recipes.** Joan Bestwick. 144p. 2000. pap. 11.95 (*1-892384-05-1*) Avery Color.
Life's Little Book of Reminders for Latter-Day Saints. Jade Hoang. LC 93-43251. 1994. pap. 6.95 (*1-55503-650-3*, 01111531) Covenant Comms.
Life's Little Book of Virtues. Jo Petty. 160p. 1996. 9.99 (*0-88486-148-1*, Inspirational Pr) Arrowood Pr.
Life's Little Deconstruction Book: Self-Help for the Post-Hip. Andrew Boyd. LC 98-34020. 160p. 1998. pap. 7.95 (*0-393-31870-2*, Norton Paperbks) Norton.
Life's Little Destruction Book. Charles S. Dane. 1992. mass mkt. 6.99 (*0-312-92927-7*) St Martin.
Life's Little Fable. Patricia Cornwell. LC 98-3669. (Illus.). 40p. (J). 1999. 16.99 (*0-399-23316-4*) Putnam Pub Group.
Life's Little Financial Instruction Book. Joseph Bisignano. LC 95-48161. 96p. 1996. pap. 7.95 (*1-56554-153-7*) Pelican.
Life's Little Frustration Book. G. Gaynor McTigue. 1994. mass mkt. 6.99 (*0-312-95215-5*) St Martin.
Life's Little Handbook of Wisdom. deluxe ed. Bruce Bickel. 1995. boxed set 9.97 (*1-55748-681-6*) Barbour Pub.
Life's Little Handbook of Wisdom: Graduate's Edition. Stan Jantz & Bruce Bickel. LC 97-174172. 64p. 1996. 5.97 (*1-55748-827-4*) Barbour Pub.
Life's Little Health Book. C. Buckley, Jr. 160p. 1993. pap. 5.95 (*0-9635231-4-7*) CTA Resrch Corp.
Life's Little Health Book for Women. C. Buckley, Jr. 160p. (Orig.). 1993. pap. 5.95 (*0-9635231-5-5*) CTA Resrch Corp.
Life's Little Inspiration, Bk. 2. Margaret F. Powers. 144p. 1996. pap. 8.95 (*0-00-638585-0*, Pub. by Harper SF) HarpC.
Life's Little Inspiration Book - RI. Margaret F. Powers. LC 98-28710. (Footprints Bks.). 144p. 1998. pap. 9.00 (*0-06-251559-4*, Pub. by Harper SF) HarpC.
Life's Little Instruction. Daily Staff. 1999. 10.99 (*0-8362-0644-4*) Andrews & McMeel.
Life's Little Instruction Book see Petit Livre de la Vie: Manuel d'Instructions
Life's Little Instruction Book. H. Jackson Brown, Jr. LC 91-9800. 160p. 1991. pap. 6.95 (*1-55853-102-5*) Rutledge Hill Pr.
Life's Little Instruction Book, Vol. I. H. Jackson Brown. LC 91-9800. 1992. 12.95 (*1-55853-121-1*) Rutledge Hill Pr.
Life's Little Instruction Book, Vol. II. H. Jackson Brown, Jr. LC 91-9800. 160p. 1993. pap. 6.95 (*1-55853-216-1*) Rutledge Hill Pr.
Life's Little Instruction Book, Vol. II. H. Jackson Brown, Jr. LC 91-9800. 160p. 1994. 12.95 (*1-55853-275-7*) Rutledge Hill Pr.
Life's Little Instruction Book, Vol. 2. large type ed. H. Jackson Brown, Jr. 140p. 1994. lib. bdg. 16.95 (*0-8161-5957-2*, G K Hall Lrg Type) Mac Lib Ref.
Life's Little Instruction Book, Vol. III. H. Jackson Brown, Jr. LC 91-9800. 160p. 1995. pap. 6.95 (*1-55853-353-2*) Rutledge Hill Pr.
Life's Little Instruction Book, Vol. III. H. Jackson Brown. LC 91-9800. 160p. 1997. 12.95 (*1-55853-467-9*) Rutledge Hill Pr.
Life's Little Instruction Book: Business Etiquette. Sokolos. 1996. 5.99 (*0-88144-201-1*) Christian Pub.
Life's Little Instruction Book: 511 Reminders for a Happy & Rewarding Life. large type ed. H. Jackson Brown, Jr. LC 92-31115. (General Ser.). 160p. 1993. 17.95 (*0-8161-5644-1*, G K Hall Lrg Type) Mac Lib Ref.
***Life's Little Instruction Book for Incurable Romantics.** H. Jackson Brown, Jr. & Robyn Spizman. 2000. pap. 6.99 (*1-55853-833-X*) Rutledge Hill Pr.
***Life's Little Instruction Book from Mothers to Daughters.** H. Jackson Brown, Jr. & Kim Shea. 2000. pap. 6.99 (*1-55853-832-1*) Rutledge Hill Pr.
***Life's Little Instructions from the Bible.** H. Jackson Brown, Jr. & Rosemary C. Brown. 2000. pap. 6.99 (*1-55853-831-3*) Rutledge Hill Pr.
Life's Little Ironies. Thomas Hardy. Ed. by Alan Manford. (Oxford World's Classics Ser.). (Illus.). 304p. 2000. pap. 8.95 (*0-19-283663-3*) OUP.
***Life's Little Lessons: A Guide Book to Get You Through.** Kathryn Moravec. 200p. 2000. pap. 15.95 (*1-887472-73-8*) Sunstar Pubng.
Life's Little Miseries: Helping Your Child with the Disasters of Everyday Life. Diane Lynch-Fraser. LC 92-12816. 246p. 1992. 20.95 (*0-02-919323-0*) Jossey-Bass.
Life's Little Pleasures. Jeffrey E. Short. 1999. 3.95 (*0-7117-1053-8*) Seven Hills Bk.
Life's Little Prayer Book. Compiled by Gary Lahoda. (Illus.). 192p. 1996. pap. 11.00 (*0-8092-3178-6*, 317860, Contemporary Bks) NTC Contemp Pub Co.
***Life's Little Prayer Book.** Gary Lahoda. 192p. 2000. pap. 7.99 (*0-517-16198-2*) Random Hse Value.
Life's Little Recipe Book. Karyn L. Wynn. LC 98-96564. 112p. 1998. pap. 12.95 (*0-9665903-0-9*) Hard Pressed.
Life's Little Relaxation Book. Steven M. Selzer. LC 95-559. (Illus.). 176p. 1995. pap. 8.00 (*0-517-88483-6*) Crown Pub Group.
***Life's Little Rhubarb Cookbook: 101 Rhubarb Recipes.** Joan Bestwick. 144p. 1999. pap. 11.95 (*1-892384-00-0*) Avery Color.
Life's Little Rule Book: Simple Rules to Bring Joy & Happiness to Your Life. Starburst Staff. 160p. 2000. pap. 6.95 (*1-892016-17-6*) Starburst.
Life's Little Secrets. J. Donald Walters. 68p. (J). (gr. 4-7). 1993. 5.95 (*1-56589-601-7*) Crystal Clarity.
Life's Little Talks: Harold Almon's Guide to: Insightful Things Someone Meant to Tell You When You Think You Have Had It. rev. ed. Ed. by Harold Almon. 55p. 1996. spiral bd. 12.95 (*0-917921-14-3*) Bee At Ease Pr.
Life's Little Temptations: Forty Bite-Sized Desserts to Sweeten Your Day. Beth Allen. LC 94-21796. (Illus.). 96p. 1994. 8.95 (*1-55958-587-0*) Prima Pub.
Life's Little Treasure Book of Christmas Memories. H. Jackson Brown, Jr. (Life's Little Treasure Bks. Ser.). (Illus.). 96p. 1998. 4.95 (*1-55853-687-6*) Rutledge Hill Pr.
Life's Little Treasure Book of Christmas Traditions. H. Jackson Brown et al. (Illus.). 96p. 1996. 4.95 (*1-55853-418-0*) Rutledge Hill Pr.
Life's Little Treasure Book on Fathers. J. Jackson Brown, Jr. LC 98-150049. (Illus.). 96p. 1998. 4.95 (*1-55853-610-8*) Rutledge Hill Pr.
Life's Little Treasure Book on Friendship. H. Jackson Brown, Jr. LC 97-116080. (Life's Little Treasure Bks.). (Illus.). 96p. 1996. 4.95 (*1-55853-420-2*) Rutledge Hill Pr.
Life's Little Treasure Book on Hope. H. Jackson Brown, Jr. (Life's Little Treasure Bks.). (Illus.). 96p. 1996. 4.95 (*1-55853-419-9*) Rutledge Hill Pr.
Life's Little Treasure Book on Joy. H. Jackson Brown, Jr. 96p. 1994. 4.95 (*1-55853-278-1*) Rutledge Hill Pr.
Life's Little Treasure Book on Love. H. Jackson Brown, Jr. (Illus.). 96p. 1995. 4.95 (*1-55853-329-X*) Rutledge Hill Pr.
Life's Little Treasure Book on Marriage. H. Jackson Brown, Jr. (Illus.). 96p. 1994. 4.95 (*1-55853-277-3*) Rutledge Hill Pr.
Life's Little Treasure Book on Mothers. H. Jackson Brown, Jr. LC 98-150064. (Illus.). 96p. 1998. 4.95 (*1-55853-609-4*) Rutledge Hill Pr.
Life's Little Treasure Book on Parenting. H. Jackson Brown, Jr. (Illus.). 96p. 1995. 4.95 (*1-55853-330-3*) Rutledge Hill Pr.
Life's Little Treasure Book on Success. H. Jackson Brown, Jr. (Illus.). 96p. 1994. 4.95 (*1-55853-280-3*) Rutledge Hill Pr.
Life's Little Treasure Book on Wisdom. H. Jackson Brown, Jr. 96p. 1994. 4.95 (*1-55853-279-X*) Rutledge Hill Pr.
***Life's Little Treasures on Simple Pleasures, 1.** H. Jackson Brown, Jr. LC 99-236736. (Life's Little Treasure Bks.). 1999. 4.95 (*1-55853-746-5*) Rutledge Hill Pr.
Life's Little Treasures on Things That Really Matter, 1. H. Jackson Brown, Jr. (Life's Liffle Treasure Bks.). 1999. 4.95 (*1-55853-747-3*) Rutledge Hill Pr.
Life's Little Zucchini Cookbook: 101 Zucchini Recipes. Joan Bestwick. LC 97-70281. 144p. (Orig.). 1997. pap. 11.95 (*0-932212-94-8*) Avery Color.
Life's Living Toward Dying: A Theological & Medical-Ethical Study. Vigen Guroian. LC 96-10808. 135p. 1996. pap. 12.00 (*0-8028-4190-2*) Eerdmans.
Life's Loss's Loved. Kirk W. Bromley. Ed. by Chad Gracia. (Bromley Plays Ser.: No. 3). 95p. 1998. pap. 15.00 (*1-893194-02-7*, 003) Inverse Theater.
Life's Lure. John G. Neihardt. LC 91-21490. (Landmark Edition Ser.). 277p. 1991. text 50.00 (*0-8032-3333-7*) U of Nebr Pr.
Life's Lure. John G. Neihardt. (Collected Works of John G. Neihardt). 277p. 1999. reprint ed. lib. bdg. 98.00 (*1-58201-783-2*) Classic Bks.
***Life's Matrix: A Biography of Water.** Philip Ball. LC 99-59110. (Illus.). 400p. 2000. text 25.00 (*0-374-18628-6*) FS&G.
Life's Meaning. Marguerite Pedersen. LC 89-60446. 112p. (Orig.). 1989. pap. 7.00 (*0-914752-27-8*) Sovereign Pr.
Life's Memories. 3rd ed. Alice A. Zoerb. 1991. 12.95 (*0-9602888-0-5*) Heritage Rec.
Life's Memory Book. Clyde E. Ray. 224p. 1998. 59.50 (*1-889137-06-5*) Genie Pubng.
Life's Morning, 3 vols. in 1. George R. Gissing. LC 76-75985. reprint ed. 30.00 (*0-404-02779-2*) AMS Pr.
Life's Mosaic: The Autobiography of Phyllis Ntantala. LC 92-20587. (Perspectives on Southern Africa Ser.: Vol. 49). 1993. 35.00 (*0-520-08171-4*, Pub. by U CA Pr) Cal Prin Full Svc.
Life's Mysteries Unveiled. John T. Ferrier. 480p. 1923. text 18.00 (*0-900235-07-1*) Order Of The Cross.
Life's Not Always Fair: A Child's Guide to Managing Emotions. Sharon Scott. LC 97-183400. 1996. pap. text 11.95 (*0-87425-399-3*) HRD Press.
Life's Not Fair, but God Is Good. Robert H. Schuller. 272p. 1997. mass mkt. 6.50 (*0-553-56167-7*) Bantam.
Life's Not Fair, but God Is Good. Robert H. Schuller. Tr. by N. Y. Hsu & P. T. Juan. (Family Ser.). 272p. 1995. pap. 11.95 (*1-885216-03-3*) Evan Formosan.
Life's Obstacle Course: A User's Guide: How to Maneuver from the Obstacle Shoulder onto the Success Superhighway of Life! Marsha Wolak. Ed. by Patricia Rockwood. LC 98-96906. 1999. pap. 11.95 (*0-9669134-9-3*, 682-001) Ascend Pubg.
***Life's Other Secret: The New Mathematics of the Living World.** Ian Stewart. LC 97-18152. 285p. 1999. pap. 16.95 (*0-471-29651-1*) Wiley.
Life's other Secret: The New Mathematic's of the Living World. Ian Stewart. LC 97-18152. 304p. 1997. 24.95 (*0-471-15845-3*) Wiley.
***Life's Passages.** Brenda Blue. 1999. pap. write for info. (*1-58235-294-1*) Watermrk Pr.
Life's Path Unfolding. Marie Moslander. 200p. 1994. pap. 12.95 (*1-884954-00-6*) Evergreen WA.
Life's Planner - My Information Resource Manual: How to Take & Maintain Control over Every Aspect of Your Life. large type ed. Patrick L. Kelly & Rosalind D. Kelly. 243p. 1996. ring bd., wbk. ed. 29.95 (*0-9651102-0-6*) Harbor Ent.
Life's Playground: A Celebration of Spirit, 1. Kathy Safranek. 1999. pap. text 9.95 (*1-885003-21-8*) R D Reed Pubs.
***Life's Poems.** Alice Trapp. 150p. 2000. pap. 8.99 (*1-57532-309-5*) Press-Tige Pub.
Lifes Preservative Against Self Killing (1637) John Sym. Ed. by Michael McDonald. (Tavistock Classic Reprints in the History of Psychiatry Ser.). 384p. 1989. 54.00 (*0-415-00639-2*) Routledge.
Life's Priorities. Keith Johnson. 126p. 1990. pap. 6.99 (*0-89274-710-2*, HH710) Harrison Hse.
Life's Priorities. Keith Johnson. LC 79-63739. 1979. pap. 5.95 (*0-89841-000-2*) Zoe Pubns.
Life's Problems, God's Solutions: Answers to 15 of Life's Most Perplexing Problems. J. Dwight Pentecost. LC 96-46398. 192p. 1998. pap. 10.99 (*0-8254-3454-8*) Kregel.
***Life's Real Moments.** Etta Brown. 1999. pap. write for info. (*1-58235-239-9*) Watermrk Pr.
Life's Reflections. Sharon L. Kelley. 1998. pap. write for info. (*1-57553-836-9*) Watermrk Pr.
Life's Reflections: Dreams & Memories. Bette J. Poisson. 64p. (Orig.). 1992. pap. 9.95 (*1-879260-03-4*) Evanston Pub.
Life's Riddle. Nils A. Amneus. LC 98-10510. 264p. 1998. reprint ed. pap. 11.95 (*1-55700-130-8*) Theos U Pr.
Life's Road: The Legacy of David Ah Fong Cup Choy. Robert K. Cup Choy. (Illus.). 74p. Date not set. pap. text. write for info. (*0-9670036-0-1*) R K H Cup Choy.
Life's Rugged Beauty. Evie Branstner. Ed. by Mark Herringshaw & Jill Herringshaw. (Illus.). 320p. (Orig.). 1995. pap. write for info. (*0-9649290-0-7*) A & V Miller.
Life's Seasons. David R. Furford. (Illus.). 58p. (Orig.). 1994. pap. write for info. (*0-9641207-2-0*) D R Furford.
Life's Seasons (And Other Poems) Evelyn Heinz. 12p. (Orig.). 1994. pap. write for info. (*1-885206-09-7*, Iliad Pr) Cader Pubng.
Life's Second Half. Jerome Ellison. 1978. 10.95 (*0-8159-6116-2*) Devin.
Life's Simple Pleasures. Rodney Guge. 168p. (Orig.). 1994. pap. 5.95 (*1-56245-085-9*) Great Quotations.
Lifes Splendid Drama. Peter J. Bowler. 526p. 1998. pap. text 22.00 (*0-226-06922-2*) U Ch Pr.
Life's Splendid Drama: Evolutionary Biology & the Reconstruction of Life's Ancestry, 1860-1940. Peter J. Bowler. LC 95-25394. (Science & its Conceptual Foundations Ser.). (Illus.). 552p. 1996. 37.95 (*0-226-06921-4*) U Ch Pr.
Life's Story & Healings. Nellie Poulos. 160p. pap. 3.00 (*0-686-29128-X*) Faith Pub Hse.
Lifes Strategies: For the Spiritual Quest. Edward F. Tarabilda. 128p. (Orig.). (C). 1990. pap. 7.95 (*1-878423-04-5*) Morson Pub.
Life's Tapestry. Martin Goldsmith. 237p. 1997. reprint ed. mass mkt. 7.99 (*1-85078-273-3*, Pub. by O M Pubng) OM Literature.
Life's Tapestry: A Collection of Poems. Robert A. Meyer. (Illus.). 164p. 1993. 12.95 (*0-931541-14-X*) Mancorp Pub.
Life's Tiers: A Collection of Short Stories. Laverne G. Hazley. (Illus.). 155p. Date not set. pap. 10.95 (*0-615-11262-5*) Harveys Pub.
Life's Too Short. Abraham J. Twerski. 1997. pap. 10.95 (*0-312-15570-0*) St Martin.
Life's Too Short: Pull the Plug on Self-Defeating Behavior & Turn on the Power of Self-Esteem. Abraham J. Twerski. LC 94-46631. 1995. text 15.95 (*0-312-11846-5*) St Martin.
Life's Too Short Not to Live It As a Texan. Peg Hein. Ed. by Peter H. Lewis. (Illus.). (Orig.). 1991. pap. write for info. (*0-9628815-0-3*) Kathryn Designs.
***Life's Trails.** Robert Daniels. 1998. pap. write for info. (*1-57553-973-X*) Watermrk Pr.
***Life's Treasure Book of Christmas Memories.** Brown Jr. 1999. pap. text 7.95 (*1-55853-804-6*) Rutledge Hill Pr.
***Life's Treasure Book on Friendship.** Brown Jr. (Illus.). 96p. 2000. pap. text 7.95 (*1-55853-802-X*) Rutledge Hill Pr.
***Life's Treasure Book on Things That Really Matter.** Brown Jr. (Illus.). 96p. 2000. pap. text 7.95 (*1-55853-803-8*) Rutledge Hill Pr.
Life's Trek. Che'rune Clewley. LC 99-475894. 32p. 1999. pap. 8.00 (*1-886094-96-9*) Chicago Spectrum.
Life's Ultimate Questions. Ronald H. Nash. LC 99-26079. 464p. 1999. 29.99 (*0-310-22364-4*) HarpC.
Life's Wake-Up Calls. Tanny McCarthy Mann. (Illus.). 368p. 1997. pap. 24.95 (*0-9656667-0-0*) Sales Networks.
Life's Winding Roads. Kimberly Reiners. 1998. pap. write for info. (*1-57553-753-2*) Watermrk Pr.
Life's Winning Tips. Dennis Connor. (Illus.). 78p. (Orig.). 1993. pap. 7.95 (*1-56245-066-2*) Great Quotations.
Life's Work of a Minor Poet: Collected Fiction, Journalism, & Poetry of Edmund McGranaghan. Edmund McGranaghan. Ed. & Intro. by Sarah McKinley. LC 83-80303. (Illus.). 254p. (Orig.). 1983. pap. 12.50 (*0-912681-00-4*) Fidelio Pr.
Lifesavers. Lynn Molyneux. (Illus.). 192p. (gr. k-6). 1987. spiral bd. 14.95 (*0-685-29138-3*) Trellis Bks Inc.
Lifesavers: For Financial Freedom. Mack Timberlake & Brenda Timberlake. 160p. (Orig.). 1996. mass mkt. 5.99 (*0-89274-942-3*, HH-942) Harrison Hse.
Lifesavers: For Your Marriage. Mack Timberlake & Brenda Timberlake. LC 96-155422. 160p. (Orig.). 1995. mass mkt. 5.99 (*0-89274-795-1*, HH-795) Harrison Hse.
Lifesavers: Tips for Success & Sanity for Early Childhood Managers. Sue Baldwin. Ed. by Mary S. Whelan. LC 96-35829. (Illus.). 150p. (Orig.). 1996. pap. 14.00 (*0-9654439-0-6*) Insights Trning.
LifeSavers: 20 Quick & Easy-to-Use Bible Lessons for Kids. Susan R. Swan. LC 99-28245. 144p. (J). (ps-8). 1999. pap. 15.00 (*0-8170-1301-6*) Judson.
Lifesavers & Other Poems. Frank Dickerson. (Illus.). 48p. (Orig.). 1997. pap. 6.95 (*0-9657398-1-3*) Pamet River.
Lifesavers for Substitutes. Mary McMillan. (Illus.). 160p. 1992. student ed. 14.99 (*0-86653-678-7*, 1412) Good Apple.
Lifesavers of Cape Cod. J. W. Dalton. 1967. pap. 14.95 (*0-85699-002-7*) Chatham Pr.
Lifesaving. Boy Scouts of America. (Illus.). 80p. (YA). (gr. 6-12). 1980. pap. 2.90 (*0-8395-3297-0*) BSA.
***Lifesaving: A Memoir.** Judith Barrington. LC 99-46447. 192p. 2000. 22.95 (*0-933377-45-2*); pap. 13.95 (*0-933377-44-4*, Pub. by Eighth Mount Pr) Consort Bk Sales.
Lifesaving First Aid for Children: A Quick-Reference Guide. 2nd rev. ed. American Red Cross Staff. Ed. by Dan Preniszni. (Illus.). 1998. write for info. (*0-9665371-1-4*) Laerdal Med Corp.
Lifescenes: Reading & Writing for Comprehension. Calvin Stone et al. 1986. pap. 9.86 (*0-8092-5103-5*) NTC Contemp Pub Co.
LifeScenes, LifeSkills: Developing Consumer Competence. Calvin Stone et al. 1986. pap. 9.86 (*0-8092-5102-7*) NTC Contemp Pub Co.
***LifeScience: Ars Electronica 99.** Ed. by G. Stocker & C. Schopf. (Illus.). 450p. 1999. pap. 49.00 (*3-211-83368-4*) Spr-Verlag.
Lifescripts: What to Say to Get What You Want in 101 of Life's Toughest Situations. Stephen Pollan & Mark Levine. 1996. pap. 19.95 (*0-614-12587-1*) Macmillan.
Lifescripts: What to Say to Get What You Want in 101 of Life's Toughest Situations. Stephen M. Pollan. LC 96-17332. 464p. 1996. per. 21.95 (*0-02-036048-7*, Pub. by Macmillan) S&S Trade.
***Lifescripts for Employees.** Stephen M. Pollan & Roni Beth Tower. Ed. by Mark Levine. LC 98-55974. (Lifescripts Ser.). (Illus.). 172p. 1999. pap. 14.95 (*0-02-862623-0*, Pub. by Macmillan) S&S Trade.
Lifescripts for Managers. Michael Caplan & Mark Levine. LC 98-52415. 162p. 1999. pap. 14.95 (*0-02-862622-2*, Pub. by Macmillan) S&S Trade.
***Lifescripts For the Self Employed.** Mark Levine. LC 98-52419. (Lifescripts Ser.). (Illus.). 161p. 1999. pap. 14.95 (*0-02-862621-4*, Pub. by Macmillan) S&S Trade.
Lifesearch. (Voyage Through the Universe Ser.). (Illus.). 144p. 1989. 17.27 (*0-8094-6866-2*); lib. bdg. 24.60 (*0-8094-6867-0*) Time-Life.
Lifeship. Harry Harrison. 176p. 1997. 24.00 (*0-7278-5245-0*) Severn Hse.
Lifesigns: Intimacy, Fecundity & Ecstasy in Christian Perspective. Henri J. M. Nouwen. 128p. 1989. pap. 9.95 (*0-385-23628-X*) Doubleday.
Lifesize Animal Counting Book see Comptons les Animaux Grandeur Nature
Lifesize Animal Counting Book. LC 93-33786. (Illus.). 32p. (J). (ps-1). 1994. 12.95 (*1-56458-517-4*) DK Pub Inc.
Lifesize Animal Counting Book. Ed. by Scholastic, Inc. Staff. (Illus.). (J). (ps). text 16.95 (*0-590-24270-9*) Scholastic Inc.
Lifesize Animal Opposites Book. Lee Davis. LC 94-14988. (Illus.). 32p. (J). (ps). 1994. 12.95 (*1-56458-720-7*) DK Pub Inc.
Lifesize Animal Opposites Book. Lee Davis. (Illus.). 32p. (J). (ps). text 16.95 (*0-590-24372-1*) Scholastic Inc.
Lifeskills. Rus Eacker & Judy Eacker. (Illus.). (Orig.). 1996. audio 12.50 (*0-614-25236-9*) Vis Bks Intl.
Lifeskills. Rus Eacker & Judy Eacker. (Illus.). 36p. (Orig.). (J). (ps-5). 1996. pap. 5.95 (*1-56550-059-8*) Vis Bks Intl.
Lifeskills. V. Williams. 1999. pap. 12.00 (*0-8129-3196-3*, Times Bks) Crown Pub Group.
Lifeskills: 8 Simple Ways to Build Stronger Relationships, Improve Your Health, Communicate More Clearly. Redford Williams & Virginia Williams. LC 97-28464. (Illus.). 352p. 1998. 24.00 (*0-8129-2424-X*, Times Bks) Crown Pub Group.
Lifeskills Arithmetic File. David Cassell. 1986. pap. 7.95 (*0-906212-50-2*, Pub. by Tarquin Pubns) Parkwest Pubns.
Lifeskills for Adult Children. Janet G. Woititz & Alan Garner. 120p. 1990. pap. 8.95 (*1-55874-070-8*) Health Comm.
***Lifeskills for Basic Interviewing Skills Mastery Workbook.** Robert W. Skarlinski. 12p. 1999. wbk. ed. 4.95 (*1-58532-012-9*) Basic Ed Materials.
***Lifeskills for Basic Job Applications Mastery Workbook, Vol. 1.** Robert W. Skarlinski. 25p. 1999. wbk. ed. 6.95 (*1-58532-006-4*) Basic Ed Materials.
***Lifeskills for Basic Job Applications Mastery Workbook, Vol. 2.** Robert W. Skarlinski. 25p. 1999. wbk. ed. 6.95 (*1-58532-007-2*) Basic Ed Materials.
***Lifeskills for Basic Maps, Globes & Geography Skills.** Robert W. Skarlinski. 26p. 2000. 6.95 (*1-58532-086-2*) Basic Ed Materials.
***Lifeskills for Basic Workplace Communication Skills Mastery Workbook.** Robert W. Skarlinski. 12p. 1999. wbk. ed. 4.95 (*1-58532-013-7*) Basic Ed Materials.
***Lifeskills for Careers & Occupational Exploration, Vol. 1.** Robert W. Skarlinski. Ed. by Courtney Bright. 26p. 2000. 6.95 (*1-58532-088-9*) Basic Ed Materials.
***Lifeskills for Careers & Occupational Exploration, Vol. 2.** Robert W. Skarlinski. Ed. by Courtney Bright. 26p. 2000. 6.95 (*1-58532-089-7*) Basic Ed Materials.

L

An Asterisk (*) at the beginning of an entry indicates that the title is appearing for the first time.

L

***Lifeskills for Good Grooming Habits Skills Workbook.** Robert W. Skarlinski. 12p. 1999. wbk. ed. 4.95 (*1-58532-008-0*) Basic Ed Materials.
***Lifeskills for Good Health Habits Skills Workbook.** Robert W. Skarlinski. 12p. 1999. wbk. ed. 4.95 (*1-58532-009-9*) Basic Ed Materials.
***Lifeskills for Totaling Grocery Lists.** Robert W. Skarlinski. 25p. 2000. 6.95 (*1-58532-087-0*) Basic Ed Materials.
***Lifeskills for Totaling Monthly Expenses.** Robert W. Skarlinski. 25p. 2000. 6.95 (*1-58532-091-9*) Basic Ed Materials.
Lifeskills Helping. Richard Nelson-Jones. (Counseling Ser.). 1993. pap., student ed. 20.95 (*0-534-19675-6*) Brooks-Cole.
Lifeskills Helping: Helping Others Through a Systematic People Approach. Richard Nelson-Jones. 436p. (C). 1993. pap. 31.95 (*0-534-19674-8*) Brooks-Cole.
Lifeskills 1, No. 1. 2nd ed. Judy De Filippo. 112p. 1991. pap. text 11.75 (*0-201-53366-9*) Addison-Wesley.
LifeSkills 101: Higher Core Values Healthy Winners Live By. Darrell Franken. 330p. 2000. pap. (*0-934957-21-5*) Wellness Pubns.
LifeSkills 101: Overhead Projection for Higher Core Values Healthy Winners Live By. Darrell Franken. 250p. 2000. (*0-934957-22-3*) Wellness Pubns.
LifeSkills 101: Raising Spiritual Values & Enjoying Increased Benefits. Darrell Franken. 235p. 1998. pap. (*0-934957-23-1*) Wellness Pubns.
Lifeskills 3, No. 3. 2nd ed. Judy De Filippo. 112p. 1991. pap. text 11.75 (*0-201-53368-5*) Addison-Wesley.
***LifeSkills 303: Healing Help Through Stress Management (Christians)** Darrell Franken. 350p. 2000. pap. 24.95 (*0-934957-29-0*) Wellness Pubns.
Lifeskills 2, No. 2. 2nd ed. Judy De Filippo. 112p. 1991. pap. text 11.75 (*0-201-53367-7*) Addison-Wesley.
***LifeSkills 202: Christian Teacher's Manual for Skills for Optimum Personal Relations.** Darrell Franken. (Illus.). 121p. 1999. pap. (*0-934957-26-6*) Wellness Pubns.
***LifeSkills 202: Skills for Optimum Personal Relations.** Darrell Franken. 350p. 1999. pap. (*0-934957-25-8*) Wellness Pubns.
***Lifeskills Words for Success Wordsearch Puzzles.** Robert W. Skarlinski. 25p. 1999. 7.95 (*1-58532-015-3*) Basic Ed Materials.
Lifespan. Guy R. Lefrancois. 1996. teacher ed. write for info. (*0-534-25485-3*) Brooks-Cole.
Lifespan. Guy R. Lefrancois. (Education Ser.). 1984. pap., student ed. 8.25 (*0-534-02970-1*) Wadsworth Pub.
Lifespan. Guy R. Lefrancois. LC 96-37204. (Illus.). 640p. (C). 1984. pap. write for info. (*0-534-02969-8*) Wadsworth Pub.
Lifespan. 2nd ed. Guy R. Lefrancois. 664p. (C). 1987. pap. write for info. (*0-534-07470-7*) Wadsworth Pub.
Lifespan. 2nd ed. Guy R. Lefrancois. (Education Ser.). 1987. pap., teacher ed. write for info. (*0-534-07472-3*); pap., student ed. 11.00 (*0-534-07471-5*) Wadsworth Pub.
Lifespan. 3rd ed. Guy R. Lefrancois. (Education Ser.). 1990. pap., student ed. 12.75 (*0-534-11755-4*); mass mkt., teacher ed. write for info. (*0-534-11756-2*) Wadsworth Pub.
Lifespan. 3rd ed. Guy R. Lefrancois. 714p. (C). 1990. pap. write for info. (*0-534-11754-6*) Wadsworth Pub.
Lifespan. 4th ed. Guy R. Lefrancois. 739p. (C). 1993. mass mkt. 48.95 (*0-534-17778-6*) Wadsworth Pub.
Lifespan. 4th ed. Guy R. Lefrancois et al. (Education Ser.). 1993. mass mkt., student ed. 13.50 (*0-534-17779-4*) Wadsworth Pub.
Lifespan. 5th ed. Guy R. Lefrancois. LC 95-17026. (C). 1995. 49.25 (*0-534-25482-9*) Wadsworth Pub.
Lifespan. 5th ed. Guy R. Lefrancois. (Education Ser.). 1995. student ed. 17.25 (*0-534-25484-5*) Wadsworth Pub.
Lifespan. 6th ed. Guy R. Lefrancois. LC 98-47232. (Education Ser.). 1998. pap. 75.95 (*0-534-55692-2*) Wadsworth Pub.
Lifespan. 6th ed. Guy R. Lefrancois. (Education Ser.). 1999. pap., student ed. 17.25 (*0-534-55693-0*) Wadsworth Pub.
LifeSpan: An Autobiography. Audrey Withers. LC 95-107779. (Illus.). 216p. 1994. 19.95 (*0-7206-0927-5*, Pub. by P Owen Ltd) Dufour.
Lifespan: Development & Diversity. Ed. by Wozniak. (C). 1997. text. write for info. (*0-673-99006-0*) Addison-Wesley.
Lifespan: Developmental Psychology. (Dantes Subject Standardized Tests Ser.: DANTES-64). 1994. pap. 23.95 (*0-8373-6664-X*) Nat Learn.
Lifespan: New Perspectives on Extending Human Longevity. Thomas J. Moore. 320p. 1994. pap. 12.00 (*0-671-88622-3*, Touchstone) S&S Trade Pap.
Lifespan: What Really Affects Human Longevity. Thomas J. Moore. (Illus.). 352p. 1993. 23.00 (*0-671-72966-7*) S&S Trade.
Lifespan & Factors Affecting It: Aging Theories in Gerontology. Daniel Hershey. (Illus.). 157p. 1998. reprint ed. pap. text 25.00 (*0-916961-04-4*) Basal Books.
Lifespan & Human Development. 6th ed. Anne V. Gormly. (C). 1996. pap. text, teacher ed. write for info. (*0-15-504209-2*) Harcourt Coll Pubs.
Lifespan Developement. 5th ed. Jeffrey S. Turner. (C). 1994. pap. text, teacher ed. 33.75 (*0-15-502422-1*) Harcourt Coll Pubs.
Lifespan Development. (C). 1997. 11.00 (*0-06-500984-3*) Addson-Wesley Educ.
Lifespan Development. Helen L. Bee. LC 93-20091. (C). 1997. pap., student ed. 28.00 (*0-06-500983-5*) Addson-Wesley Educ.
***Lifespan Development.** Cole et al. 2002. pap. text. write for info. (*0-7167-5108-9*) W H Freeman.
Lifespan Development. Janina M. Jolley & Mitchell. 1995. teacher ed. 26.87 (*0-697-14498-4*) McGraw.
Lifespan Development. Keniston. 1998. pap. text 11.97 (*0-395-90741-1*) HM.
Lifespan Development. Rathus. 2000. pap. text 42.00 (*0-534-52776-0*) Thomson Learn.
Lifespan Development. Leonie Sugarman. (New Essential Psychology Ser.). 198p. 1986. pap. 14.95 (*0-416-34390-2*, 1018) Routledge.
Lifespan Development. 2nd ed. 456p. (C). 1997. text 24.00 (*0-321-00447-7*) Addison-Wesley.
Lifespan Development. 2nd ed. 502p. (C). 1997. text 24.00 (*0-321-00448-5*) Addson-Wesley Educ.
***Lifespan Development.** 2nd ed. 1998. text. write for info. (*0-673-98233-5*, GoodYrBooks) Addson-Wesley Educ.
Lifespan Development. 2nd ed. (C). 1997. 67.00 (*0-321-00576-7*) S&S Trade.
Lifespan Development. 2nd ed. Helen L. Bee. (C). 1998. pap. text, student ed. 22.50 (*0-321-00445-0*) Addson-Wesley Educ.
Lifespan Development. 2nd ed. Ed. by Helen L. Bee. LC 97-5362. 640p. (C). 1997. text 82.00 (*0-321-01121-X*) Allyn.
Lifespan Development. 5th ed. Jeffrey S. Turner. (C). 1994. pap. text, student ed. 27.00 (*0-15-502789-1*) Harcourt Coll Pubs.
Lifespan Development. 5th ed. Jeffrey S. Turner & Donald B. Helms. 640p. (C). 1994. text 85.50 (*0-15-500996-6*) Harcourt.
Lifespan Development: A Topical Approach. Janina M. Jolley & Mark L. Mitchell. 640p. (C). 1995. text. write for info. (*0-697-12981-0*) Brown & Benchmark.
Lifespan Development: Test Bank. 5th ed. Jeffrey S. Turner. (C). 1994. pap. text, teacher ed., suppl. ed. 41.50 (*0-15-502682-8*, Pub. by Harcourt Coll Pubs) Harcourt.
Lifespan Development in a Mixed Economy of Care. Open Learning Foundation Staff. 112p. 1996. pap. write for info. (*0-443-05736-2*) Church.
Lifespan Development of Individuals: Behavioral, Neurobiological, & Psychosocial Perspectives: A Synthesis. Ed. by David Magnusson et al. (Illus.). 546p. (C). 1996. text 105.00 (*0-521-47023-4*) Cambridge U Pr.
Lifespan Development of Individuals: Behavioral, Neurobiological & Psychosocial Perspectives: A Synthesis. Ed. by David Magnusson et al. (Illus.). 546p. 1997. pap. text 47.95 (*0-521-62896-2*) Cambridge U Pr.
Lifespan Developmental Psychology. Donald B. Irwin & Janet A. Simons. 592p. (C). 1993. text. write for info. (*0-697-06430-1*) Brown & Benchmark.
Lifespan Developmental Psychology. Irwin & Simons. 1994. 22.50 (*0-697-22457-0*) McGraw.
Lifespan Developmental Psychology. 2nd ed. Donald B. Irwin & Janet A. Simons. 608p. (C). 1997. per. write for info. (*0-697-23545-9*, WCB McGr Hill) McGrw-H Hghr Educ.
Lifespan Health Psychology: Nursing Problems & Interventions. C. R. Paton. 288p. 1992. pap. 43.25 (*1-56593-008-8*, 0249) Thomson Learn.
Lifespan Human Development. Kelvin Seifert. (C). 1997. pap. text, student ed. 20.36 (*0-395-71143-6*) HM.
Lifespan Human Development. 3rd ed. Sigelman. (Psychology Ser.). 1998. pap., student ed. 21.25 (*0-534-35962-0*) Brooks-Cole.
Lifespan Human Development. 3rd ed. Sigelman. LC 98-17446. (Psychology Ser.). (C). 1998. pap. 51.25 (*0-534-35442-4*) Brooks-Cole.
Lifespan Human Development. 6th ed. Anne V. Gormly. LC 96-75657. 784p. (C). 1996. text 65.00 (*0-15-502034-X*, Pub. by Harcourt Coll Pubs) Harcourt.
Lifespan Human Development. 6th ed. Anne V. Gormly. (C). 1998. pap. text 44.50 (*0-15-507936-0*) Harcourt Coll Pubs.
Lifespan Nutrition: Conception Through Aging. Sharon R. Rolfes et al. Ed. by Marshall. 528p. (C). 1990. mass mkt. 43.50 (*0-314-66811-X*) West Pub.
Lifespan Nutrition: Conception Through Life. 2nd ed. Sharon R. Rolfes et al. (C). 1997. text 53.95 (*0-534-53739-1*) Wadsworth Pub.
Lifespan Nutrition with InfoTrac. 2nd ed. Sharon R. Rolfes & Debruyne. (Health Sciences Ser.). 1997. 49.25 (*0-534-53836-3*) Wadsworth Pub.
Lifespan of Human Development. Goldhab. (C). 1986. text. write for info. (*0-15-540380-X*) Harcourt Coll Pubs.
Lifespan of Human Development. Kelvin Seifert. (C). Date not set. pap., teacher ed. 11.96 (*0-395-69179-6*) HM.
Lifespan of Human Development. Kelvin Seifert. LC 96-76960. (C). 1996. text 64.36 (*0-395-69178-8*) HM.
Lifespan of Human Development. 6th ed. Anne V. Gormly. (C). 1996. pap. text, teacher ed. 28.00 (*0-15-503922-9*) Harcourt Coll Pubs.
Lifespan of Human Development. 6th ed. Anne V. Gormly. (C). 1996. pap. text, student ed. 27.00 (*0-15-504016-2*, Pub. by Harcourt Coll Pubs) Harcourt.
Lifespan Perspectives on the Family & Disability. Judy O. Berry & Michael L. Hardman. 48p. (C). 1997. pap. text, teacher ed. write for info. (*0-205-27397-1*, T7397-7) Allyn.
Lifespan Perspectives on the Family & Disability. Judy V. Berry & Michael L. Hardman. LC 97-16309. 288p. 1997. pap. text 56.00 (*0-205-19395-1*) Allyn.
Lifespan Plus: 900 Natural Techniques to Live Longer! Prevention Magazine Editors. 480p. 1996. reprint ed. mass mkt. 6.99 (*0-425-15413-0*) Berkley Pub.
Lifespan Prolongation. Vladimir V. Frolkis & Khachik K. Muradian. (Illus.). 432p. 1991. lib. bdg. 250.00 (*0-8493-6741-7*, QP85) CRC Pr.
Lifestory Re-Play Circle: A Manual of Activities & Techniques. Rosilyn Wilder. LC 97-60789. 90p. 1997. 19.95 (*0-910251-90-8*, LRC94) Venture Pub PA.
Lifestreams: An Introduction to Biosynthesis. David Boadella. 256p. (Orig.). 1987. pap. 13.95 (*0-7102-1145-7*, Routledge Thoemms) Routledge.
***Lifestyle: A Look at the Erotic Rites of Swingers.** Terry Gould. 392p. 2000. pap. 16.95 (*1-55209-482-0*) Firefly Bks Ltd.
Lifestyle: Butte County. Shari Caudron. (Illus.). (Orig.). 1989. pap. 6.50 (*0-685-29406-4*) Busn Ctr Chico.
Lifestyle & Cancer Prevention. Ernest H. Rosenbaum et al. Ed. by Sheila Mahoney & Nancy Wiltsek. (Illus.). 49p. 1985. pap. 2.50 (*0-933161-05-0*) Better H Prog.
Lifestyle Apocalypse: Savage Readings Embarrassing Pranks Negative Reviews, Vol. 10. Tom Frank. 1997. pap. text 6.00 (*1-888984-09-0*) Baffler.
Lifestyle Capsules see Dynamic Living Workbook
Lifestyle Changes: 12 Step Recovery Nutrition & Diet Guide. Marilyn Rollins. LC 91-24619. 128p. (Orig.). pap. 7.95 (*0-934125-23-6*) Hazelden.
***Lifestyle Characteristics of Sporting Goods Consumers, 1998.** 1999. pap. 235.00 (*0-911841-07-5*) Natl Sporting Goods Assn.
Lifestyle Counselor's Guide for Weight Control. Ed. by Brenda L. Wolfe. (Illus.). 470p. 1996. pap. 49.95 (*1-878513-12-5*) Am Hlth Pub.
Lifestyle Discipleship: The Challenge of Following Jesus in Today's World. Jim Petersen. LC 93-39063. 192p. (Orig.). 1994. pap. 12.00 (*0-89109-775-9*) NavPress.
Lifestyle Enhancement Program Survival Guide for the 90's. Terry Brown. (Illus.). 120p. 1992. pap., student ed. 99.95 incl. audio, digital audio (*0-9632607-1-5*) TJs Body Cnslts.
***Lifestyle Evangelism: Learning to Open Your Life to Those Around You.** Joe Aldrich. 252p. 1999. pap. 6.99 (*1-57673-651-2*) Multnomah Pubs.
Lifestyle for Health: Smart Cooking for Busy People. Cheryl Townsley. 398p. (Orig.). 1994. pap. 24.00 (*0-9644566-0-5*) Lifestyle for Hlth.
Lifestyle for Longevity: How to Extend Your Life with Moderation, Joy & Ease. Norman Ford. Ed. by Emily McKeigue & Marah Ren. LC 82-62228. 176p. 1984. pap. 9.95 (*0-914918-63-X*, Whitford) Schiffer.
***Lifestyle Management for Patients with Coronary Heart Disease.** Steven G. Aldana & James George. 416p. (Orig.). (C). 1999. per. 32.95 (*0-7872-5801-6*) Kendall-Hunt.
Lifestyle Management for Patients with Coronary Heart Disease. Nancy H. Miller & Craig B. Taylor. LC 95-177. (Current Issues in Cardiac Rehabilitation Ser.: Monograph No. 2). 144p. (Orig.). 1995. pap. text 24.00 (*0-87322-441-8*, BHOU0441) Human Kinetics.
Lifestyle Market Segmentation. Ronald D. Michman. LC 90-24530. 232p. 1991. 62.95 (*0-275-93159-5*, C3159, Praeger Pubs) Greenwood.
Lifestyle Math Your Financial Planning Portfolio: A Supplemental Mathematics Unit for Career Choices. Mindy Bingham et al. (Illus.). 112p. 1994. pap. 6.95 (*1-878787-07-1*) Acad Innovat.
***Lifestyle Medicine.** James M. Rippe. LC 99-13000. (Illus.). 1999. 125.00 (*0-86542-294-X*) Blackwell Sci.
Lifestyle Modifications: Urban & Rural Survival. CWL. (Security & Survival Ser.). (Illus.). 48p. 1987. pap. 20.00 (*0-939856-73-5*) Tech Group.
***Lifestyle Nutrition.** Johanna Dwyer & James Rippe. (Illus.). 208p. 2000. pap. 32.95 (*0-632-04548-5*) Blackwell Sci.
Lifestyle of Light. James M. Nesbit. LC 96-95031. 333p. 1996. write for info. (*0-9654294-0-7*) J Nesbit.
Lifestyle of Worship: Making Worship a Joyful, Reviving Part of Your Everyday Experience. David Morris. LC 98-40567. 1998. pap. 9.99 (*0-8307-2199-1*, Renew) Gospel Lght.
***Lifestyle Performance Model: Theory & Application.** Gail Fidler & Beth Velde. 200p. (C). 2001. text 34.00 (*1-55642-466-3*) SLACK Inc.
Lifestyle Priorities. John White. (Fisherman Bible Studyguides Ser.). 64p. 1996. pap. text 4.99 (*0-87788-526-5*, H Shaw Pubs) Waterbrook Pr.
Lifestyle Redesign: Implementing the Well Elderly Program. Deborah Mandel et al. LC 99-219954. (Illus.). 1999. pap. 32.00 (*1-56900-120-0*) Am Occup Therapy.
Lifestyle Sculpting: The Key to Permanent, Painless Weight Loss. Kathleen Wells. LC 94-67234. 300p. 1994. pap. 12.95 (*0-9642099-1-8*) SV Pubns.
Lifestyle Shopping: The Subject of Consumption. Ed. by Rob Shields. LC 91-43287. (International Library of Sociology Ser.). 256p. (C). 1992. pap. 24.99 (*0-415-06060-5*, A7557) Routledge.
Lifestyle Stores. PBC International Staff. 1999. pap. 29.95 (*0-688-15537-5*, Wm Morrow) Morrow Avon.
Lifestyle Stores. Martin M. Pegler. LC 96-15789. 176p. 1996. 37.50 (*0-86636-498-6*) PBC Intl Inc.
Lifestyle Stores. Martin M. Pegler. LC 96-15789. (Illus.). 176p. 1998. pap. 29.95 (*0-86636-499-4*) PBC Intl Inc.
Lifestyle Thin. Trenna Daniells & Trenna Sutphen. 32p. 1986. pap. text 29.95 incl. digital audio (*0-918519-13-6*) Trenna Prods.
Lifestyle with Meaning. Sam Crabtree. (Discipleship Ser.). 118p. (Orig.). 1993. pap. 2.75 (*0-89827-118-5*, BKO91) Wesleyan Pub Hse.
Lifestyle Workshops. Martha I. Carey. LC 88-9142. 455p. 1989. reprint ed. pap. 141.10 (*0-608-04293-5*, 206507200012) Bks Demand.
Lifestyles. Jackie Calhoun. 304p. 1990. pap. 10.95 (*0-941483-57-6*) Naiad Pr.
Lifestyles. David Chaney. LC 96-3282. 208p. (C). 1996. 65.00 (*0-415-11718-6*); pap. 16.95 (*0-415-11719-4*) Routledge.
Lifestyles & Consumer Behavior of Older Americans. Howard Schutz et al. LC 79-13212. 276p. 1979. 65.00 (*0-275-90420-2*, C0420, Praeger Pubs) Greenwood.
Lifestyles & Housing of Older Adults: The Florida Experience. Marie E. Cowart. LC 88-32230. (Journal of Housing for the Elderly: Vol. 5, No. 1). (Illus.). 114p. 1989. text 3.95 (*0-86656-872-7*) Haworth Pr.
Lifestyles for the 21st Century. Marcus Wells. 1999. 26.95 (*0-89334-296-3*, Humanics Pub) Humanics Ltd.
Lifestyles for the 21st Century. Marcus Wells. 1999. pap. 17.95 (*0-89334-294-7*, Humanics Pub) Humanics Ltd.
Lifestyles of Christian Women. Dee Brestin. 180p. 1991. pap., student ed. 9.99 (*0-89693-911-1*, 6-1911, Victor Bks) Chariot Victor.
Lifestyles of Colonial America. Ed. by Alan Quincannon. (Learning & Coloring Bks.). (Illus.). 24p. (YA). (gr. k up). 1992. pap. 3.95 (*1-878452-10-X*, Tory Corner) Quincannon.
Lifestyles of Faith Bk. 1: Choosing to Trust God. Marilyn Kunz & Catherine Schell. (Neighborhood Bible Studies). 64p. 1994. pap. 5.99 (*1-880266-10-5*) Neighborhood Bible.
Lifestyles of Faith Bk. 2: Choosing to Obey God. Marilyn Kunz & Catherine Schell. (Neighborhood Bible Studies). 72p. 1994. pap. 5.99 (*1-880266-11-3*) Neighborhood Bible.
Lifestyles of Previous Tenants. Barbara Wels. 1995. pap. 16.95 (*0-7022-2781-1*, Pub. by Univ Queensland Pr) Intl Spec Bk.
Lifestyles of the Elderly: Diversity in Relationships, Health, & Caregiving. Ed. by L. Ade-Ridder & C. B. Hennon. (Illus.). 256p. 1989. 37.00 (*0-89885-447-4*, Kluwer Acad Hman Sci) Kluwer Academic.
***Lifestyles of the Rich & Faithful: A Handbook for Successful Christian Living.** Betty R. Price. 110p. 1999. pap. 7.99 (*1-883798-40-X*) Faith One.
Lifestyles of the Rich & Famous Cookbook: Recipes & Entertaining Secrets from the Most Extraordinary People in the World Robin Leach & Diane Rozas. LC 91-45173. 280 p. 1992. 24.95 (*0-06-708445-1*) HarpC.
Lifestyles of the Rich & Flatulent. Thelma Labacus. (Illus.). 1996. pap. write for info. (*0-9639812-2-6*) Laid Back Ent.
Lifestyles of the Rich in Spirit: Living in a Win-Win World. Alan Cohen. LC 96-30689. 352p. 1996. pap. 12.95 (*1-56170-339-7*, 849) Hay House.
Lifestyles of the Seashells. Beatrice E. Winner. LC 93-72176. (Illus.). 61p. (Orig.). 1994. pap. 7.00 (*0-9632734-3-4*) E B M.
Lifestyles of the Trim & Healthy. Matthew Bennett. (Illus.). 60p. 1994. pap. 5.95 (*0-9629502-9-7*) Conceivable Concepts.
Lifetaker. Bill Shields. LC 97-151002. 120p. (Orig.). 1995. pap. 11.00 (*1-880985-30-6*) Two Thirteen Sixty-one.
Lifetime. Scott Sommer. 1987. pap. 5.95 (*0-685-18029-8*) PB.
Lifetime: Better Time Management in 21 Days. Angela Booth. 152p. (C). 1998. pap. text 19.95 (*0-13-894973-5*) P-H.
Lifetime Aerobics. Mathew McIntosh. 256p. (C). 1989. text. write for info. (*0-697-10562-8*) Brown & Benchmark.
Lifetime Aerobics. 2nd ed. McIntosh. 1999. pap. text 9.00 (*0-697-12653-6*) McGraw.
Lifetime Allocation of Work & Income: Essays in the Economics of Aging. Juanita M. Kreps. LC 74-161355. 176p. 1971. reprint ed. pap. 54.60 (*0-608-12761-2*, 202341500033) Bks Demand.
Lifetime & Testamentary Estate Planning. 9th ed. William Parsons. 228p. 1983. 27.00 (*0-8318-0431-9*, B431) Am Law Inst.
Lifetime & Testamentary Estate Planning. 10th rev. ed. Harrison Tweed & William Parsons. 230p. 1988. text 94.00 (*0-8318-0541-2*, B541) Am Law Inst.
Lifetime at the Bar. Harvey L. Hardy. LC 98-90733. 1999. 17.95 (*0-533-12899-4*) Vantage.
Lifetime Beginner: An Autobiography. Nikkyo Niwano. Tr. by Richard L. Gage from JPN. LC 79-374242. Orig. Title: Shoshin Issho & Niwano Nikkyo Jiden. (Illus.). 300p. 1990. 19.95 (*4-333-00336-9*, Pub. by Kosei Pub Co) Tuttle Pubng.
Lifetime Body Grafs: Men's Edition. Bruce C. Vandre. (Illus.). 24p. (Orig.). 1990. pap. 4.95 (*0-942223-08-X*) VanPress.
Lifetime Body Grafs: Women's Edition. Bruce C. Vandre. (Illus.). 24p. (Orig.). 1990. pap. 4.95 (*0-942223-07-1*) VanPress.
Lifetime Book of Money Management. 3rd ed. Grace W. Weinstein. 625p. 1993. 15.95 (*0-8103-9444-8*, 089137) Visible Ink Pr.
Lifetime Burning. Ellen Douglas. LC 82-40141. (Voices of the South Ser.). 212p. 1995. pap. 10.95 (*0-8071-2007-3*) La State U Pr.
Lifetime Burning in Every Moment: From the Journals of Alfred Kazin. Alfred Kazin. 352p. 1997. pap. 14.00 (*0-06-092832-8*, Perennial) HarperTrade.
Lifetime Conversation Guide. James K. Van Fleet. 320p. (C). 1984. text 32.95 (*0-13-536400-0*, Busn) P-H.
Lifetime Data. 2nd ed. Lawless. text. write for info. (*0-471-37215-3*) Wiley.
Lifetime Data: Models in Reliability & Survival Analysis. Ed. by Nicholas P. Jewell et al. (Diverse Ser.). 424p. (C). 1995. text 176.50 (*0-7923-3783-2*) Kluwer Academic.
Lifetime Employment. Floyd Kemske. LC 92-16716. 231p. 1992. 19.95 (*0-945774-18-4*, PS3561.E4226L54) Catbird Pr.
***Lifetime Encyclopedia Natural Remedies Borders Press.** (C). 1999. 4.99 (*0-13-017910-8*) Addison-Wesley.
Lifetime Encyclopedia of Letters. expanded rev. ed. Harold E. Meyer. 430p. (C). 1996. 49.95 incl. 3.5 hd (*0-13-256801-2*) P-H.
Lifetime Encyclopedia of Letters. rev. expanded ed. Harold E. Meyer. 430p. 1991. text 34.95 (*0-13-529546-7*) P-H.
Lifetime Encyclopedia of Letters. 2nd rev. ed. Harold E. Meyer. 464p. (C). 1997. pap. text 18.95 (*0-13-894874-7*) P-H.
Lifetime Encyclopedia of Letters. 3rd ed. Meyer. LC 98-27538. (C). 1999. text 34.95 (*0-13-921065-2*) P-H.
Lifetime Encyclopedia of Letters. 3rd rev. expanded ed. Harold E. Meyer. LC 98-27538. 496p. 1999. 35.00 (*0-7352-0034-3*) PH Pr.

An Asterisk (*) at the beginning of an entry indicates that the title is appearing for the first time.

Lifetime Factors in Silicon - STP 712. Ed. by R. D. Westbrook. 258p. 1980. 23.50 (*0-8031-0390-5*, STP712) ASTM.

Lifetime Family Legal Guide. Sack. (C). 1998. 35.00 (*0-13-011513-4*) P-H.

***Lifetime Family Legal Guide.** Steven Mitchell Sack. LC 98-29482. 448p. 1998. text 35.00 (*0-7352-0051-3*) S&S Trade.

Lifetime Financial Plan: The Seven Ages of Financial Health. Jack Oliver. 288p. 1998. pap. 57.50 (*0-273-63052-0*, Pub. by Pitman Pub) Trans-Atl Phila.

Lifetime Fitness. 2nd ed. Mark Stanbrough. 182p. (C). 1996. ring bd. 32.95 (*0-7872-2532-0*) Kendall-Hunt.

Lifetime Fitness. 3rd ed. Mark Stanbrough. 210p. (C). 1999. spiral bd. 40.95 (*0-7872-5842-3*, 41584201) Kendall-Hunt.

Lifetime Fitness. 4th ed. H. Larry Brown. 145p. (Orig.). (C). 1995. pap. text 22.00 (*0-13-776618-1*) P-H.

Lifetime Fitness. 4th ed. Williams. 1995. teacher ed. 12.18 (*0-697-25617-0*, WCB McGr Hill) McGrw-H Hghr Educ.

Lifetime Fitness & Wellness. 3rd ed. Williams. 1992. teacher ed. 14.06 (*0-697-12671-4*) McGraw.

Lifetime Fitness & Wellness. 5th ed. Williams. 1998. pap. text 18.00 (*0-697-29581-8*) McGraw.

Lifetime Fitness & Wellness: A Personal Choice. 3rd ed. Melvin H. Williams. 384p. (C). 1992. text. write for info. (*0-697-12670-6*) Brown & Benchmark.

Lifetime Fitness & Wellness: A Personal Choice. 4th ed. Melvin H. Williams. LC 95-76275. 432p. (C). 1995. text 24.50 (*0-697-24673-6*) Brown & Benchmark.

Lifetime Furniture. Ed. by Stephen Gray. (Mission Furniture Catalogues Ser.: No. 2). 112p. 1981. pap. 10.95 (*0-940326-02-7*) Turn of Cent.

Lifetime Golf Book. Gary Henin. 292p. (Orig.). 1990. 19.95 (*0-9630044-0-9*) Lifetime Bks.

Lifetime Guarantee. Bill Gillham. 1993. pap. 9.99 (*1-56507-075-5*) Harvest Hse.

***Lifetime Guarantees: Literacy Lessons from the Manhattan New School.** Shelley Harwayne. LC 99-462253. 400p. 2000. pap. text 25.00 (*0-325-00241-X*) Heinemann.

Lifetime Guide to Business Writing & Speaking. Jack Griffin. 416p. (C). 1996. text 39.95 (*0-13-311606-9*) P-H.

Lifetime Guide to Success with People: Instant Solutions for Every Situation. James K. Van Fleet. LC 95-32620. 256p. (C). 1995. text 29.95 (*0-13-180639-4*) P-H.

Lifetime in Jerusalem. Edwin Samuel. 346p. 1970. boxed set 44.95 (*0-87855-181-6*) Transaction Pubs.

Lifetime Income Distribution & Redistribution in Australia: Applications of a Microsimulation Model. Ann Harding. LC 93-27427. (Contributions to Economic Analysis Ser.: Vol. 221). 434p. 1993. 129.75 (*0-444-89843-3*, North Holland) Elsevier.

Lifetime Investment. Dana Ransom. (Lucky in Love Ser.: No. 27). 288p. 1993. mass mkt. 3.50 (*0-8217-4113-6*, Zebra Kensgtn) Kensgtn Pub Corp.

Lifetime Isn't Long Enough to Love You. 3rd ed. James Kavanaugh. Ed. by Cheryl Pecaut. (Illus.). 96p. (Orig.). 1995. pap. 12.95 (*1-878995-24-3*) S J Nash Pub.

***Lifetime Labor.** Alice H. Cook. 354p. 2000. 15.95 (*1-55861-257-2*) Feminist Pr.

Lifetime Legal Guide. Steven Mitchell Sack. (Illus.). 300p. 1996. 27.95 (*0-9652312-0-8*) Book Month NY.

Lifetime Legal Guide. Steven Mitchell Sack. LC 96-22814. 300p. 1996. 27.95 (*0-7835-4859-1*) Time-Life.

Lifetime Looking. Howard S. Stern & George West. Ed. by Ellen C. Stern. LC 94-35386. 1994. 40.00 (*0-87483-392-2*); pap. 20.00 (*0-87483-393-0*) August Hse.

***Lifetime Loving You.** Mechelle Avey. 272p. 2000. pap. 6.99 (*1-930758-40-5*) Yeva Corp.

Lifetime Memories, 1995-96: Summer Missions Handbook. rev. ed. Ed. by Sharon R. Poelstra. 1995. pap. text 5.00 (*0-9621469-3-5*) Biola Student Missionary.

Lifetime Memories, 1993-94: Summer Missions Handbook. rev. ed. Ed. by Tracy A. Dugan. 1993. pap. text 5.00 (*0-9621469-2-7*) Biola Student Missionary.

***Lifetime Nature Walk: Always a Babe in the Woods.** Andrew Dequasie. LC 99-91803. 2000. 25.00 (*0-7388-1280-3*); pap. 18.00 (*0-7388-1281-1*) Xlibris Corp.

Lifetime of a Durable Good. Gerrit Antonides. (C). 1990. lib. bdg. 160.00 (*0-7923-0574-4*) Kluwer Academic.

Lifetime of a Jew: Throughout the Ages of Jewish History. rev. ed. Hayyim Schauss. (Illus.). 1986. pap. 12.00 (*0-8074-0096-3*, 383473) UAHC.

Lifetime of a Landslide: Investigations in the French Alps. J. D. Niewenhuis. (Illus.). 160p. (C). 1991. text 104.00 (*90-6191-187-7*, Pub. by A A Balkema) Ashgate Pub Co.

Lifetime of Better Golf. Peter Fox et al. (Illus.). 96p. 1999. pap. write for info. (*1-58382-008-6*) Coaches Choice.

Lifetime of Cars. Lorna D. Smith. 160p. 1995. pap. 9.95 (*0-9632467-3-9*) ApronStrings.

Lifetime of Celebrations with Food. Lorna D. Smith. 160p. 1995. pap. 9.95 (*0-9632467-1-2*) ApronStrings.

Lifetime of Chances. Mary C. VanSoyoc. Ed. by Judy Rombold. (Illus.). 1996. pap. 15.95 (*0-9649065-0-3*) Parkwood Pr.

Lifetime of Homes. Lorna D. Smith. 160p. 1995. pap. 9.95 (*0-9632467-2-0*) ApronStrings.

Lifetime of Labor: The Autobiography of Alice H. Cook. Alice H. Cook. LC 98-18433. (Cross Cultural Memoir Ser.). (Illus.). 368p. 1999. 29.95 (*1-55861-189-4*) Feminist Pr.

Lifetime of Love. Julie Otlewis. 168p. (Orig.). 1994. pap. 5.95 (*1-56245-087-5*) Great Quotations.

Lifetime of Love: How to Bring More Depth, Meaning, & Intimacy into Your Relationship. rev. ed. Daphne R. Kingma. LC 97-37658. Orig. Title: Heart & Soul. 160p. (Orig.). 1998. pap. 10.95 (*1-57324-112-1*) Conari Press.

Lifetime of Loving. Kristin Hungenberg. LC 98-96615. 192p. 1998. 18.95 (*0-8034-9326-6*, Avalon Bks) Bouregy.

Lifetime of Memories Vol. 1: Ten Easy Steps to Writing Your Autobiography. David R. Hoffmann. (Illus.). vii, 197p. (Orig.). 1996. pap. 12.00 (*0-9651982-6-X*) Lifetime Collections.

***Lifetime of Memories & Dreams.** Alice Silcox. 1999. pap. write for info. (*1-58235-407-3*) Watermrk Pr.

Lifetime of Notes: The Memoirs of Tomas O Canainn. Tomas O Cannain. 128p. 1996. pap. 13.95 (*1-898256-11-X*, Pub. by Collins Press) Irish Bks Media.

Lifetime of Notes: The Memoirs of Tomas O'Canainn. Tomas O'Canainn. LC 97-116317. 194p. 1996. pap. 16.95 (*1-898256-18-7*) Dufour.

Lifetime of Opportunities. John O. Todd. LC 95-83516. 350p. (Orig.). (C). 1996. pap. text 20.00 (*0-943590-79-5*) Amer College.

Lifetime of Poetry. Elaine C. Meredith. (Illus.). 221p. (Orig.). 1986. pap. 25.00 (*0-9614058-1-3*) Southco.

Lifetime of Rhyme. Jane Boese. 80p. 1995. pap., per. 9.95 (*1-883852-02-1*) Sagest Pr OK.

Lifetime of Riches. Michael J. Ritt. 304p. 1999. pap. 11.95 (*0-452-27478-8*, Plume) Dutton Plume.

Lifetime of Savings 35-Year Budget Book: (Excellent Prime Productive Years Budget) deluxe ed. Michael Greene, Jr. (Illus.). 498p. 1997. vinyl bd. 46.00 (*1-886197-14-8*) Joy Books.

Lifetime of Sex: The Ultimate Manual on Sex, Women, & Relationships for Every Stage of a Man's Life. Stephen C. George et al. LC 97-22722. 1998. pap. 17.95 (*0-87596-425-7*) Rodale Pr Inc.

Lifetime of Teaching: Portraits of Five Veteran High School Teachers. Rosetta M. Cohen. 136p. (C). 1991. text 33.00 (*0-8077-3096-3*); pap. text 16.95 (*0-8077-3095-5*) Tchrs Coll.

Lifetime Personal Fitness. Roberta Stokes et al. (Illus.). 312p. 1997. text, teacher ed. 37.50 (*0-88725-231-1*) Hunter Textbks.

***Lifetime Physical Fitness.** 2nd ed. Politano et al. 200p. (C). 2000. spiral bd. 29.95 (*0-7872-7303-1*) Kendall-Hunt.

Lifetime Physical Fitness & Wellness with Profile Plus IBM Software. 5th ed. Hoeger. 1997. pap. 27.25 (*0-89582-438-8*) Wadsworth Pub.

Lifetime Physical Fitness & Wellness with Profile Plus Mac Software. 5th ed. Hoeger. 1997. pap. 27.25 (*0-89582-445-0*) Wadsworth Pub.

Lifetime Poetic Conclusions & Wishes. Josephine Bozoukoff. (Illus.). 40p. 1998. pap. 8.00 (*0-8059-4315-3*) Dorrance.

Lifetime Possessions. Gary Myers. LC 98-161467. 36p. 1997. 5.00 (*1-890044-07-5*) Riverstone PA.

Lifetime Prediction & Constitutive Modelling for Creep-Fatigue Interaction. Domagoj Rubesa. LC 97-107878. (Materialkundlich-Technische Reihe Ser.: No. 13). (Illus.). 151p. 1996. 37.70 (*3-443-23015-6*, Pub. by Gebruder Borntraeger) Balogh.

Lifetime Reproduction in Birds. Ed. by Ian Newton. (Illus.). 496p. 1992. pap. text 53.00 (*0-12-517371-7*) Acad Pr.

Lifetime Treasury of Home Remedies. Myra Cameron. LC 93-1957. 448p. (C). 1993. pap. text 12.95 (*0-13-535212-6*) P-H.

Lifetime Weight Control: Seven Steps to Achieving & Maintaining a Healthy Weight. Patrick Fanning. 208p. (Orig.). 1994. pap. 13.95 (*0-934986-83-5*) New Harbinger.

Lifetime Weight Control Patient Counseling. 3rd ed. Nancy J. Gustafson. LC 94-60202. (Illus.). 205p. (C). 1993. pap. 49.95 (*1-878025-75-9*) Western Schls.

Lifetime with Mark Twain. Mary Lawton. LC 72-3627. (American Literature Ser.: No. 49). (Illus.). 1972. reprint ed. lib. bdg. 75.00 (*0-8383-1562-3*) M S G Haskell Hse.

Lifetimer Delivers Success: A Powerful Success Program That Actually Works! Al Carter. LC 91-92167. 283p. 1992. pap. 14.95 (*0-9625946-2-8*) Carter-Grove Pub.

Lifetimes. David L. Rice. Ed. by Glenn J. Hovemann. (Illus.). 36p. (YA). (gr. k up). 1997. 16.95 (*1-883220-58-0*) Dawn CA.

Lifetimes. David L. Rice. Ed. by Glenn J. Hovemann. (Illus.). 32p. (YA). (ps up). 1997. pap. 7.95 (*1-883220-59-9*) Dawn CA.

Lifetimes: The Beautiful Way to Explain Death to Children. Bryan Mellonie & Robert R. Ingpen. 40p. 1983. pap. 11.95 (*0-553-34402-1*) Bantam.

Lifetime's Reading: Five Hundred Great Books to Be Enjoyed over 50 Years. Philip Ward. 384p. 1984. 29.95 (*0-900891-73-4*); pap. 19.95 (*0-900891-74-2*) Oleander Pr.

***Lifetime's Reading: Hispanic Essays for Patrick Gallagher.** Ed. by Don W. Cruickshank. 240p. 1999. 59.95 (*1-900621-21-5*, Pub. by Univ Coll Dublin Pr) Dufour.

Lifetraining: Devotions for Parents & Teens. Joe White. 1999. pap. text 12.99 (*1-56179-726-X*) Focus Family.

Lifetrends: Your Future for the Next Thirty Years. Jerry Gerber et al. 288p. 1991. pap. 8.95 (*0-380-71345-4*, Avon Bks) Morrow Avon.

LifeTypes. Sandra K. Hirsh & Jean Kummerow. 304p. (Orig.). 1989. mass mkt. 13.95 (*0-446-38823-8*, Pub. by Warner Bks) Little.

Lifeviews. R. C. Sproul. LC 85-28282. 220p. 1990. pap. 9.99 (*0-8007-5357-7*) Revell.

Lifeway Leap: The Dynamics of Change in America. Luther P. Gerlach & Virginia H. Hine. LC 72-97762. 342p. reprint ed. pap. 106.10 (*0-608-14656-0*, 205587100039) Bks Demand.

***Lifeways, 4 vols.** Raymond Bial. 2000. boxed set 131.14 (*0-7614-0860-6*) M Cavendish.

***Lifeways, No. 3.** Raymond Bial. (Illus.). (J). 2000. 131.14 (*0-7614-0936-X*, Benchmark NY) Marshall Cavendish.

Lifeways: Working with Family Questions. Gudron Davy & Bons Voors. (Lifeways Ser.). (Illus.). 328p. 1990. pap. text 15.95 (*0-9507062-4-8*, 793, Pub. by Hawthorn Press) Anthroposophic.

***Lifeways-Set 2-Lib.** Benchmark Books Staff. 1999. 131.14 (*0-7614-0800-2*, Benchmark NY) Marshall Cavendish.

Lifework: Finding Your Purpose in Life. Rick Sarkisian. LC 97-70812. 1997. pap. text 11.95 (*0-89870-636-X*) Ignatius Pr.

Lifework: Portraits of Iowa Women Artists. Robbie Steinbach. LC 98-75013. 147p. 1998. pap. 24.95 (*0-9668048-0-5*) Lifework Arts Pr.

***Life@Work Book: Sixteen Respected Leaders Talk about Blending Biblical Wisdom & Business Excellence.** Bill Hybels et al. 176p. 2000. pap. 12.99 (*0-8499-4243-8*) Word Pub.

***Lifeworks: Behavioral Health in the Classroom: A Guidebook for Educators, Counselors, School Professions & Families.** unabridged ed. Nancy Dinatale & Hennie Shore. Ed. by Catherine Barr. (Illus.). v, 200p. (YA). (gr. 6-12). 1999. pap. text 19.95 (*0-9676106-0-5*) Fnd Behavioral Hlth.

Lifeworld & Technology. Ed. by Timothy Casey & Lester Embree. LC 89-39437. (Current Continental Research Ser.: No. 009). (Illus.). 326p. (C). 1990. lib. bdg. 50.50 (*0-8191-7626-5*) U Pr of Amer.

***Lifeworld of Leadership: Creating Culture, Community & Personal Meaning in our Schools.** Thomas J. Sergiovanni. LC 99-6485. 256p. 1999. text 27.95 (*0-7879-5028-9*) Jossey-Bass.

Liffey in Dublin. J. W. De Courcy. LC 97-101754. (Illus.). 512p. 1996. 49.95 (*0-7171-2423-1*, Pub. by Gill & MacMill) Irish Bks Media.

Liflade Ant Te Passiun of Seinte Iuliene. Ed. by S. R. d'Ardenne. (EETS Original Ser.: Vol. 248). 1963. reprint ed. 50.00 (*0-19-722248-X*, Pub. by EETS) Boydell & Brewer.

Liflade of St. Juliana Vol. 51: Two Versions with Translations. Ed. by O. Cockayne & E. Brock. 1969. reprint ed. write for info. (*0-318-58478-6*) Periodicals Srv.

Lift: Wanting, Fearing, & Having a Facelift. Joan Kron. LC 98-23436. 264p. 1998. 23.95 (*0-670-87060-9*) Viking Penguin.

Lift a Rock, Find a Bug. Illus. by Christopher Santoro. LC 91-62580. (Chunky Flap Bks. Ser.). 22p. (J). (ps). 1993. 3.99 (*0-679-80904-X*, Pub. by Random Bks Yng Read) Random.

Lift & Separate: Graphic Design & the Quote Unquote Vernacular. Barbara Glauber. (Illus.). 64p. (Orig.). 1993. pap. 21.95 (*1-878271-95-4*) Princeton Arch.

***Lift & Seperate.** Rick Kirkman. (Baby Blues Scrapbook Ser.: Vol. 12). (Illus.). (J). 2000. pap. 9.95 (*0-7407-0455-9*) Andrews & McMeel.

Lift Erection. 1982. 75.00 (*0-7855-2884-9*) St Mut.

Lift Every Heart. Timothy Dudley-Smith. LC 83-83215. 306p. 1984. pap. 19.95 (*0-916642-21-6*, 1037) Hope Pub.

Lift Every Voice: African American Oratory, 1787-1900. Ed. by Philip S. Foner & Robert J. Branham. LC 97-21268. (Studies in Rhetoric & Communication). 912p. 1997. pap. text 24.95 (*0-8173-0906-3*) U of Ala Pr.

Lift Every Voice: African American Oratory, 1787-1900. Ed. by Philip S. Foner & Robert J. Branham. LC 97-21268. (Studies in Rhetoric & Communication). 1998. text 49.95 (*0-8173-0848-2*) U of Ala Pr.

Lift Every Voice: Constructing Christian Theologies from the Underside. Ed. by Susan B. Thistlethwaite & Mary P. Engel. LC 98-27300. 350p. (Orig.). 1998. pap. 20.00 (*1-57075-163-3*) Orbis Bks.

Lift Every Voice: Expecting the Most & Getting the Best from All of God's Children. Walter Turnbull & Howard Manly. (Illus.). 256p. (J). 1995. 19.45 (*0-7868-6164-9*, Pub. by Hyperion) Time Warner.

Lift Every Voice: Expecting the Most & Getting the Best from All of God's Children. Walter Turnbull & Howard Manly. (Illus.). 256p. (J). 1997. pap. 10.45 (*0-7868-8197-6*, Pub. by Hyperion) Time Warner.

Lift Every Voice: Turning a Civil Rights Setback into a New Vision of Social Justice. Lani Guinier. LC 98-11876. 352p. 1998. 24.50 (*0-684-81145-6*) S&S Trade.

Lift Every Voice & Sing. James Weldon Johnson. LC 92-32283. (Illus.). 32p. (J). (gr. 2 up). 1995. 14.95 (*0-590-46982-7*) Scholastic Inc.

Lift Every Voice & Sing. James Weldon Johnson. (Illus.). 36p. (J). 1993. 14.95 (*0-8027-8250-7*); lib. bdg. 15.85 (*0-8027-8251-5*) Walker & Co.

Lift Every Voice & Sing. James Weldon Johnson. (Illus.). 36p. (J). 1995. pap. 6.95 (*0-8027-7442-3*) Walker & Co.

***Lift every Voice & Sing: A Celebration of the Negro National Anthem 100 Years, 100 Voices.** Ed. by Julian Bond & Sondra Kathryn Wilson. 256p. 2000. 29.95 (*0-679-46315-1*) Random.

***Lift Every Voice & Sing: Selected Poems.** James Weldon Johnson & Sondra Kathryn Wilson. (Penguin Classics Ser.). 112p. 2000. pap. 9.95 (*0-14-118387-X*, Penguin Classics) Viking Penguin.

Lift Every Voice & Sing: St. Louis African Americans in the Twentieth Century. Ed. & Intro. by Ann Morris. LC 99-36741. (Illus.). 240p. 2000. pap. 29.95 (*0-8262-1253-0*) U of Mo Pr.

Lift for Life. Robert F. Harrington. 256p. 1984. pap. 7.95 (*0-912444-30-4*) DARE Bks.

Lift for Life, Vol. II. Robert F. Harrington. LC 94-71005. 1994. pap. 9.95 (*1-55673-935-4*, Fairway Pr) CSS OH.

Lift High the Cross. Robert C. Morgan. LC 94-40486. 144p. (Orig.). 1995. pap. 11.95 (*0-687-21851-9*) Abingdon.

Lift High the Cross: The Story of Trinity Episcopal School for Ministry. Janet Leighton. 1995. 19.99 (*0-87788-474-9*, H Shaw Pubs) Waterbrook Pr.

Lift High the Lord: Songs & Sketches for Contemporary Praise. Des. by Joseph Linn. 140p. 1993. 6.99 (*0-8341-9028-1*, MB-678); pap. 7.00 (*0-685-72856-0*, L-9164C); pap. 250.00 (*0-685-72859-5*, OR-9164); audio compact disk 75.00 (*0-685-72858-7*, MU-9164T) Lillenas.

Lift Him Up. Ellen Gould Harmon White. 834p. 1988. 10.99 (*0-8280-0469-2*) Review & Herald.

***Lift Me Up, Pt. II.** (Illus.). 1999. pap. 7.00 (*0-9657419-3-1*) Glo Pub TX.

Lift Me up, Lord. large type ed. write for info. (*0-318-68657-0*, 7260) LBW.

Lift Modernisation Design Guide. Roger E. Howkins. LC 99-185741. (Illus.). 233p. 1998. 79.95 (*1-886536-24-4*) Elevator Wrld.

Lift Off! An Astronaut's Dream. R. Mike Mullane. LC 94-18122. (Illus.). (J). 1994. lib. bdg. 13.95 (*0-382-24663-2*) Silver Burdett Pr.

Lift Off! An Astronaut's Dream. R. Mike Mullane. LC 94-18122. (Illus.). 114p. (J). (gr. 4). 1994. pap. 4.95 (*0-382-24664-0*) Silver Burdett Pr.

***Lift Off! A Space Adventure.** Rosanna Hansen. (All-Star Readers Ser.). (Illus.). 48p. (gr. 2-3). 2000. pap. 3.99 (*1-57584-659-4*, Pub. by Rdrs Digest) S&S Trade.

Lift-off at Satan. large type ed. Richard Butler. 1996. pap. 18.99 (*1-85389-571-7*, Dales) Ulverscroft.

Lift Off! Chemistry: A Problem-Based Learning Approach. Ehrlich Multimedia Inc Staff et al. 24p. 1996. cd-rom 44.95 (*0-471-01805-8*) Wiley.

Lift Practice. 1982. 100.00 (*0-85083-154-7*) St Mut.

Lift Servicing & Maintenance. 1982. 125.00 (*0-7855-2885-7*) St Mut.

***Lift-the-Flap Bible.** Sally Lloyd Jones. (Illus.). 22p. (J). (ps-k). 2000. bds. 9.99 (*0-7847-0965-3*, 03539) Standard Pub.

Lift the Flaps... If You Dare. Alan Benjamin. (Flaptime Bks.). 14p. (J). (ps-1). 1998. 6.99 (*0-307-33301-9*, 33301, Goldn Books) Gldn Bks Pub Co.

Lift the Lid. Pam Adams. (Toilet Training Ser.). (J). 1995. pap. 4.99 (*0-85953-722-6*) Childs Play.

Lift the Lid on Mummies: Unravel the Mysteries of Egyptian Tombs, & Make Your Own Mummy! Jacqueline Dineen. (Lift the Lid Ser.). (Illus.). 24p. (J). 1998. pap. 19.95 (*0-7624-0208-3*) Running Pr.

***Lift the Lid, Use the Potty.** Random House U. K. Ltd. (J). 2001. mass mkt. 7.99 (*0-375-81146-X*, Pub. by Random Bks Yng Read) Random.

Lift the Sky Up see Levantemos el Cielo

Lift the Veil. J. G. McCann. 120p. 1998. pap. 12.00 (*1-57502-841-7*, PO2307) Morris Pubng.

Lift Thine Eyes: Evening Prayers for Every Day of the Year. 4th ed. Christoph F. Blumhardt. Tr. by Plough Publishing House Staff from GER. Orig. Title: Abendgebete fur Alle Tago des Jahres. 240p. 1998. reprint ed. 13.00 (*0-87486-966-8*) Plough.

Lift Thine Eyes to the Mountains: From Elijah a Capella. Felix Mendelssohn. 4p. 1986. pap. 0.95 (*0-7935-5485-3*, 50292660) H Leonard.

Lift up the Cross. 1993. 1.25 (*0-8341-9022-2*) Nazarene.

***Lift up Your Eyes on High: Understanding the Stars.** James Nickel. (Illus.). (YA). (gr. 7-12). 1999. pap., teacher ed. 7.95 (*1-930367-38-4*, CLP 69595); pap. text 9.95 (*1-930367-37-6*, CLP 69595) Christian Liberty.

Lift up Your Eyes to the Mountains: A Guide to the Spiritual Life. rev. ed. David M. Knight. 166p. 1988. reprint ed. pap. 7.00 (*0-942971-12-4*) His Way.

Lift up Your Head, Tom Dooley: The True Story of the Appalachian Murder That Inspired One of America's Most Popular Ballads. John F. West. Ed. by Dot Jackson. LC 93-71246. (Illus.). 134p. 1993. pap. 13.95 (*1-878086-20-0*, Pub. by Down Home NC) Blair.

Lift up Your Heads: He Is Coming Again. Rolf E. Aaseng. 1995. pap. 6.50 (*0-7880-0583-9*) CSS OH.

Lift up Your Heart: A Guide to Spiritual Peace. Fulton J. Sheen. LC 96-41356. (Liguori Classic Ser.). 288p. 1997. pap. 13.00 (*0-7648-0058-2*, Liguori Triumph) Liguori Pubns.

Lift up Your Hearts. Anthony A. Petrusic. 300p. 1989. pap. 13.50 (*0-937739-10-3*) Roman IL.

Lift up Your Hearts. Howard Vanderwall & Norma de Waal Malfeyt. 78p. pap. 59.95 (*1-56212-112-X*) CRC Pubns.

Lift up Your Hearts: Musical Settings for Holy Communion. Todd A. Conscable. 39p. 1998. pap. 10.00 (*0-9664162-0-1*, PSC1015) Paradoxology.

Lift up Your Hearts: Pew Edition. Ed. by Linda White. 175p. 2000. pap. 10.00 (*0-664-50029-3*) Geneva Press.

Lift up Your Hearts: Worship Leader's Edition. Ed. by Linda White. 175p. 2000. spiral bd. 25.00 (*0-664-50030-7*) Geneva Press.

Lift up Your Hearts - Year A: Eucharistic Prayers Based on the Revised Common Lectionary. rev. ed. Michael J. O'Donnell. Ed. by Timothy J. Crouch. 1504p. 1995. spiral bd. 19.95 (*1-878009-23-0*, OSL Pubns) Order St Luke Pubns.

Lift up Your Hearts - Year B: Eucharistic Prayers Based on the Revised Common Lectionary. rev. ed. Michael J. O'Donnell. Ed. by Timothy J. Crouch. 148p. 1993. spiral bd. 19.95 (*1-878009-16-8*, OSL Pubns) Order St Luke Pubns.

Lift up Your Hearts - Year C: Eucharistic Prayers Based on the Revised Common Lectionary. rev. ed. Michael J. O'Donnell. Ed. by Timothy J. Crouch. 148p. 1994. spiral bd. 19.95 (*1-878009-20-6*, OSL Pubns) Order St Luke Pubns.

***Lift up Your Hearts & Sing.** James P. Kelleher. (Illus.). 30p. 1999. spiral bd. 10.00 (*0-9671732-0-5*) Clondrohid.

L

Lift up Your Voice Like a Trumpet: White Clergy & the Civil Rights & Antiwar Movements, 1954-1973. Michael B. Friedland. LC 97-18418. 336p. 1998. pap. 19.95 (0-8078-4646-5); lib. bdg. 49.95 (0-8078-2338-4) U of NC Pr.

Lift Your Sails: The Challenge of Being a Christian. Vincent Dwyer. LC 98-24352. 176p. 1998. reprint ed. pap. 15.95 (0-8264-1139-8) Continuum.

***Lift Your Voice: The Issues Handbook for Middle School Girls.** Marisa Egerstrom. LC 99-68213. (Illus.). 36p. (YA). (gr. 5-12). 2000. pap. 6.50 (1-883477-36-0, Pub. by Lone Oak MN) Maple Tree.

***Lift Your Voice & Sing.** James Johnson. 32p. (J). 2000. 15.99 (0-7868-0626-5, Pub. by Hyperion) Time Warner.

Lifted by Promises. Claire Vomhof. LC 97-62498. 64p. 1998. pap. 10.99 (1-57921-086-4) WinePress Pub.

Lifted Masks & Other Works. Susan Glaspell & Eric S. Rabkin. 350p. (C). 1993. pap. 16.95 (0-472-06509-2, 06509); text 39.50 (0-472-09509-9, 09509) U of Mich Pr.

Lifted Up: The Victoria Tolbert Story. Victoria Tolbert. 192p. 1996. pap. 9.95 (1-886158-12-6) Macalester.

Lifted up by Angels. Lurlene McDaniel. 240p. (Orig.). (YA). (gr. 7 up). 1997. mass mkt. 4.99 (0-553-57112-5) BDD Bks Young Read.

Lifted up by Angels. Lurlene McDaniel. (Orig.). 1997. 10.09 (0-606-13569-3, Pub. by Turtleback) Demco.

Lifted up on Wings of Faith. Melba M. Christie. 56p. 1995. pap. 6.00 (0-9638434-1-9) Heavenly Mess.

Lifted Veil. George Eliot, pseud. 1976. 16.95 (0-8488-0482-1) Amereon Ltd.

Lifted Veil & Brother Jacob. George Eliot, pseud. Ed. by Helen Small. (Oxford World's Classics Ser.). 160p. 1999. pap. 8.95 (0-19-283295-6) OUP.

Lifting. Mark Rich. (Illus.). 58p. 1990. pap. 7.95 (1-877655-02-3) Wordcraft Oregon.

Lifting a Ton of Feathers: A Woman's Guide to Surviving in the Academic World. Paula Caplan. LC 93-93082. 1993. pap. 18.95 (0-8020-7411-1); text 45.00 (0-8020-2903-5) U of Toronto Pr.

Lifting & Conveying Machinery: Possibilities & Ideas. Josef Kogan. LC TJ1350.K6313. (Illus.). 340p. 1985. reprint ed. pap. 105.40 (0-608-00102-3, 206086700006) Bks Demand.

Lifting As They Climb: African-American Women Writers 1910-1940 by Elizabeth Davis. Gates. LC 96-43478. 1996. 30.00 (0-7838-1419-4, Hall Reference) Macmillan.

Lifting As We Climb: Two Hundred Years Black Church History. (Illus.). 161p. 1984. 19.95 (0-9632246-0-3) S J Bk Sales.

Lifting Belly. Gertrude Stein. Ed. by Rebecca Mark. 112p. 1989. pap. 10.95 (0-941483-51-7) Naiad Pr.

***Lifting Every Voice: Pedagogy & Politics of Bilingualism.** Ed. by Zeyhep F. Beykont. 180p. 1999. pap. 18.95 (1-891792-01-6) HEPG.

Lifting Him Up: How You Can Experience Spirit-Led Praise & Worship. Dick Bernal & Ron Kenoly. LC 95-68302. 1995. pap. 8.99 (0-88419-403-5) Creation House.

Lifting in the Fifth Dimension. Tom Foote & Judd Biasiotto. (Illus.). 157p. (Orig.). 1985. pap. 8.00 (0-933079-03-6) World Class Enterprises.

Lifting Points: A Design Guide. (C). 1984. 125.00 (0-7855-6729-1, Pub. by EEMUA) St Mut.

Lifting Points: A Design Guide (1984) EEMUA Staff. 1984. pap. 150.00 (0-85931-037-X, Pub. by EEMUA) St Mut.

Lifting Properties in Skew-Product Flows with Applications to Differential Equations. R. J. Sacker et al. LC 77-8941. (Memoirs Ser.: No. 11/190). 67p. 1977. pap. 21.00 (0-8218-2190-3, MEMO/11/190) Am Math.

Lifting Solutions to Perturbing Problems in C*-Algebras. Terry A. Loring. LC 96-43189. (Fields Institute Monographs Ser.: Vol. 8). 165p. 1996. text 44.00 (0-8218-0602-5, FIM/8) Am Math.

***Lifting the Bull: Overcoming Chronic Back Pain, Fibromyalgia & Environmental Illness.** Diane Dawber. 176p. 1999. pap. write for info. (1-55082-199-7) Quarry Pr.

Lifting the Curse of Menstruation: A Feminine Appraisal of the Influence of Menstruation on Women's Lives. Ed. by Sharon Golub. LC 84-19804. 156p. 1985. pap. text 14.95 (0-918393-06-X, Harrington Park) Haworth Pr.

Lifting the Curse of Menstruation: A Feminist Appraisal of the Influence of Menstruation on Women's Lives. Ed. by Sharon Golub. LC 83-12723. (Women & Health Ser.: Vol. 8, Nos. 2-3). 156p. 1983. text 39.95 (0-86656-242-7); pap. text 2.95 (0-86656-422-5) Haworth Pr.

***Lifting the Fog of War.** William A. Owens & Ed Offley. LC 99-53312. 256p. 2000. text 25.00 (0-374-18627-8) FS&G.

Lifting the Lid. Ursula Barry. (C). 1990. 40.00 (0-946211-25-6) St Mut.

Lifting the Lid: A Guide to Investigative Research. David Northmore. LC 95-32339. 1996. 65.00 (0-304-33109-0) LPC InBook.

Lifting the Lid: A Guide to Investigative Research. David Northmore. LC 95-32339. 1996. pap. 16.95 (0-304-33113-9) LPC InBook.

***Lifting the Lid: The Life of a Pioneering British Filmmaker.** Betty Box. (Illus.). 288p. 2000. 30.00 (1-85776-489-7, Pub. by Book Guild Ltd) Trans-Atl Phila.

***Lifting the Scientific Veil: Science Appreciation for the Nonscientist.** Paul Sukys. LC 99-12159. 592p. 1999. pap. 45.95 (0-8476-9600-6); pap., teacher ed. 60.00 (0-8476-9601-4) Rowman.

Lifting the Taboo: Women, Death & Dying. Sally Cline. LC 96-48520. 1997. text 55.00 (0-8147-1366-1); pap. text 19.50 (0-8147-1406-4) NYU Pr.

***Lifting the Veil.** David Icke & Jon Rappoport. 135p. 1998. mass mkt. 6.95 (0-939040-05-0) Truth Seeker.

Lifting the Veil. Princess Wahletka. 94p. 1996. reprint ed. spiral bd. 11.00 (0-7873-0916-8) Hlth Research.

Lifting the Veil: A Political History of Struggles for Emancipation. Richard A. Couto. LC 93-23842. (Illus.). 368p. (C). 1993. pap. 18.00 (0-87049-808-8); text 40.00 (0-87049-807-X) U of Tenn Pr.

Lifting the Veil: How You Yourself May Acquire Mystic Power & Develop Mind, Body & Spirit. Princess Wahletka. 94p. 1996. reprint ed. pap. 9.95 (1-56459-838-1) Kessinger Pub.

***Lifting the Veil: Mennonite Life in Russia Before the Revolution.** Jacob H. Janzen & Walter Klaassen. 128p. 1998. pap. text 12.50 (0-9683462-1-9) Pandora Pr.

***Lifting the Veil: Practical Kabbalah with Kundalini Yoga.** Gurunam. 183p. 1999. pap. 18.00 (1-885562-01-2) Root Light.

Lifting the Veil of Oil Infections. W. D. Price. (Technical Papers: Vol. P58). (Illus.). 7p. 1926. pap. text 30.00 (1-55589-353-8) AGMA.

Lifting up for the Downcast. William Bridge. (Puritan Paperbacks Ser.). 1979. pap. 7.50 (0-85151-298-4) Banner of Truth.

***Lifting Voices: Voices of the Collective Struggle.** Peggy M. Fisher. LC 97-95095. 112 p. 1999. 11.95 (0-9662551-0-0) Pyramid Collect.

Liftlog: Diary & Guide for Strength Training. Sportslog Staff et al. (SportsLog Ser.). (Illus.). 176p. 1995. spiral bd. 9.95 (1-57028-056-8, 80568H, Mstrs Pr) NTC Contemp Pub Co.

***Lifts in Berlin: 100 Years of History.** Kerstin Englert. LC 99-200924. 1999. 45.00 (3-931321-96-7) JOVI.

Lifts, LB Two to Eighty-Seven. BSRIA Staff. (C). 1987. 60.00 (0-86022-169-5, Pub. by Build Servs Info Assn) St Mut.

Ligament & Tendon Relaxation (Skeletal Disability) Treated by Prolotherapy (Fibro-Osseous Proliferation) 3rd ed. George S. Hackett. (Illus.). 160p. 1958. 30.95 (0-398-05066-X) C C Thomas.

Ligamentous Articular Strain: Osteopathic Manipulative Techniques for the Body. William T. Crow & Conrad Speece. (Illus.). (C). 2000. write for info. (0-939616-31-9) Eastland.

Ligaments & Ligamentoplasties. Ed. by L. H. Yahia. LC 96-17116. (Illus.). 416p. 1996. pap. 185.00 (3-540-61171-1) Spr-Verlag.

Ligaments of the Knee. Ed. by Alfred J. Tria, Jr. LC 95-8982. (Illus.). 1995. text 115.00 (0-443-08954-X) Church.

Ligand-Binder Assays: Labels & Analytical Strategies. Larry J. Kricka. (Clinical & Biochemical Analysis Ser.: Vol. 17). (Illus.). 336p. (C). 1985. text 175.00 (0-8247-7420-5) Dekker.

Ligand Coupling Reactions with Heteroatomic Compounds. Jean-Pierre Finet. LC 98-29167. (Tetrahedron Organic Chemistry Ser.). 1998. 49.50 (0-08-042793-6, Pergamon Pr); 114.50 (0-08-042794-4, Pergamon Pr) Elsevier.

Ligand Exchange Chromatography. Vadim A. Davankov et al. 240p. 1988. 127.00 (0-8493-6775-1, QD79, CRC Reprint) Franklin.

Ligand Field Theory & Its Applications. Figgis & Hitchman. LC 99-28986. (Special Topics in Inorganic Chemistry Ser.). 354p. (C). 1999. 79.95 (0-471-31776-4) Wiley.

Ligand-Receptor Energetics: A Guide for the Perplexed. Irving M. Klotz. LC 96-34518. 170p. 1997. pap. 52.50 (0-471-17626-5) Wiley.

***Ligands & Modifiers in Vitreous Materials: The Spectroscopy of Condensed Systems.** Alfred Margaryan. LC 99-30374. 160p. 1999. 32.00 (981-02-3899-1) WSC Inst MA Studies.

Ligands, Linkage & Auxiliary Materials for Diagnostic Antibodies, Antigens & Gene Probes. 207p. 1992. 2750.00 (0-89336-929-2, C-156) BCC.

Ligands, Receptors, & Signal Transduction in Regulation of Lymphocyte Function. Ed. by John C. Cambier. (Illus.). 440p. 1990. 49.00 (1-55581-021-7) ASM Pr.

Ligature: That Which Binds or Ties Together. Tom Bourne & Jeannette Clift George. Ed. by Peggy N. Dillard & Deborah Eckols. (Illus.). 80p. 1991. pap., student ed. 6.95 (0-9616513-9-3) Manor of Grace.

Lige Langston: Sweet Iron. Linda Hussa. LC 98-39709. (Literature of the American West Ser.). 322p. 1998. 28.95 (0-8061-3109-8) U of Okla Pr.

Ligeia: A Libretto. Robert Creeley. (Illus.). 40p. 1996. 400.00 (1-887123-11-3) Granary Bks.

Light see Science Works!

Light see Luz

Light. (Jump Ser.). (Illus.). 32p. (J). (gr. 2-7). pap. write for info. (1-882210-28-X) Action Pub.

Light. (Smart Science Ser.). (Illus.). 16p. (J). (gr. 2-5). Date not set. pap. 5.95 (1-58273-505-0) Newbridge Educ.

***Light.** (Designer Shufa Ser.). 160p. 2000. 8.95 (1-55156-167-0); (1-55156-185-9) Paperblank.

Light. Melvin Berger. Ed. by Susan Evento. (Early Science Big Bks.). (Illus.). 16p. (Orig.). (J). (ps-2). 1995. pap. 16.95 (1-56784-105-8) Newbridge Educ.

Light. Samantha Berger. LC 98-53310. 1999. pap. 10.01 (0-439-08120-3) Scholastic Inc.

Light. David Burnie. LC 92-7661. (Eyewitness Books). (Illus.). 64p. (J). (gr. 4-7). 1992. 15.95 (1-879431-79-3) DK Pub Inc.

Light. Catherine Chambers. (Illus.). (J). 1997. 24.95 (0-237-51773-6) EVN1 UK.

Light. Bob Cobbing et al. 14p. (Orig.). 1994. pap. 3.00 (1-57141-002-3) Runaway Spoon.

Light. Jason Cooper. LC 92-8808. (Science Secrets Ser.). (J). 1992. 9.50 (0-685-59295-2) Rourke Corp.

Light. Jason Cooper. LC 92-8808. (Science Secrets Discovery Library). 24p. (J). (gr. k-4). 1992. lib. bdg. 10.95 (0-86593-166-6) Rourke Corp.

Light. Malinda E. Cramer. Ed. by Joan C. McCrary. LC 89-50609. (Come Unto Me Ser.: Vol. 1). 103p. (Orig.). 1989. pap. 9.95 (0-9617598-4-4) Divine Sci Fed.

Light. Trevor Day. LC 97-5991. (Science Projects Ser.). (J). 1998. 24.26 (0-8172-4943-5) Raintree Steck-V.

Light. R. W. Ditchburn. 692p. 1991. pap. 16.95 (0-486-66667-0) Dover.

Light. DK Publishing Staff. (Eyewitness Books). 64p. (J). (gr. 4-7). 1999. 15.95 (0-7894-4885-8, D K Ink) DK Pub Inc.

Light. Robert Gardner. (Investigate & Discover Ser.). (Illus.). 136p. (YA). (gr. 7 up). 1990. pap. 9.95 (0-671-69042-6, Julian Messner) Silver Burdett Pr.

***Light.** Claire Hollis. LC 99-96600. 130p. 1999. pap. 11.95 (0-9673122-2-1) Warfare Plus Min.

Light. Yeedi Ignatow. Ed. by Stanley H. Barkan. (Review Women Writers Chapbook Ser.: No. 9). (Illus.). 48p. 1991. 15.00 (0-89304-440-7); 15.00 (0-89304-442-3); pap. 5.00 (0-89304-441-5); pap. write for info. (0-89304-443-1) Cross-Cultrl NY.

Light. Terry Jennings. LC 95-11539. (Making Science Work Ser.). (Illus.). 32p. (J). (gr. 1-4). 1996. lib. bdg. 21.40 (0-8172-3960-X) Raintree Steck-V.

Light. Terry Jennings. (Making Science Work Ser.). 32p. (J). (gr. 2-4). 1996. pap. text 5.95 (0-8172-4253-8) Raintree Steck-V.

Light. Mona Johnian. 72p. (Orig.). 1985. pap. write for info. (0-318-63704-9) Superior Bks.

Light. Ron Marson. (Task Cards Ser.: No. 17). (Illus.). 88p. 1991. teacher ed. 16.00 (0-941008-87-8) Tops Learning.

Light. Jerry Ratch. LC 88-62610. 64p. 1988. 8.00 (0-929022-03-3) O Bks.

Light. Ed. by Scholastic, Inc. Staff. (Discovery Box Ser.). (Illus.). 32p. (J). (gr. 1-5). 1997. 11.95 (0-590-92675-6) Scholastic Inc.

Light. Michael I. Sobel. LC 86-25024. (Illus.). 288p. 1987. 29.95 (0-226-76750-7) U Ch Pr.

Light. Michael I. Sobel. LC 86-25024. (Illus.). x, 274p. 1989. pap. 21.95 (0-226-76751-5) U Ch Pr.

Light. Daniel J. Spero. (Science Mini-Unit Intermediate Ser.: Vol. 3). (Illus.). 16p. (J). (gr. 3-6). 1994. pap. text 5.95 (1-55799-294-0, EMC834) Evan-Moor Edu Pubs.

Light: A New Paradigm for Healing, Set. Jacob Liberman. 142p. 1995. pap. 16.95 incl. audio (1-879323-27-3) Sound Horizons AV.

Light: Brazilian Traction, Light & Power Co. Ltd., 1899-1945. Duncan McDowell. (Illus.). 495p. (C). 1988. text 39.95 (0-8020-5783-7) U of Toronto Pr.

Light: Finding the Way. Nancy Calhoun-Medlock. 67p. 1998. pap. 3.99 (0-9656256-1-3) S M J.

***Light: Hands on Elementary School Science.** 2nd ed. (Illus.). 60p. 2000. teacher ed. 35.00 (1-883410-50-9) L Poore.

Light: Medicine of the Future: How We Can Use It to Heal Ourselves Now. Jacob Liberman. LC 90-748. (Illus.). 288p. (Orig.). 1993. pap. 16.95 (1-879181-01-0) Bear & Co.

Light: Mini Book. Melvin Berger. Ed. by Susan Evento. (Early Science Big Bks.). (Illus.). 16p. (Orig.). (J). (ps-2). 1995. pap. 3.95 (1-56784-130-9) Newbridge Educ.

Light: Poems from Hollywood. Mark Dunster. 24p. 1998. mass mkt. 5.00 (0-89642-391-3) Linden Pubs.

Light: Replacing Three Centuries of Misconceptions. Peter K. Bros. LC 97-123169. (Copernican Ser.: Vol. 6). 332p. (Orig.). 1996. pap. 16.95 (0-9627769-6-3) Fin Bk Partners.

Light: The First Seven Days. Sarah Waldman. LC 92-8767. (Illus.). 32p. (J). (ps-3). 1993. 14.95 (0-15-220870-4) Harcourt.

Light: The Shape of Space: Designing with Space & Light. Lou Michel. (Architecture Ser.). 277p. 1995. 69.95 (0-471-28618-4, VNR) Wiley.

Light Vol. I: Waves, Photons, Atoms. H. Haken. xvi, 354p. 1986. reprint ed. 80.25 (0-444-86020-7, North Holland) Elsevier.

Light - Its Interaction with Art & Antiquities: Its Interaction with Art & Antiquities. T. B. Brill. LC 80-16975. (Illus.). 298p. (C). 1980. text 65.00 (0-306-40416-8, Kluwer Plenum) Kluwer Academic.

Light - Science & Magic: An Introduction to Photographic Lighting. 2nd ed. Fil Hunter & Paul Fuqua. LC 96-48403. 320p. 1997. pap. 29.95 (0-240-80275-6, Focal) Buttrwrth-Heinemann.

Light - The Shape of Space: Designing with Space & Light. Louis Michel. (Illus.). 288p. 1995. text 59.95 (0-442-01804-5, VNR) Wiley.

Light a Candle: A Whimsical & Uplifting Look at Life from the Pen & Brush of Kristin. Kristin Sheldon. (Illus.). 32p. 1996. 10.95 (0-88396-436-8) Blue Mtn Art.

Light a Candle! The Jewish Experience in Children's Books. 8p. 1993. pap. 4.00 (0-87104-721-7, Branch Libraries) NY Pub Lib.

Light a Penny Candle. Maeve Binchy. 592p. 1997. mass mkt. 7.50 (0-451-19202-8, Sig) NAL.

Light a Small Candle. Bernard Palmer & Marjorie Palmer. LC 82-84439. 1982. pap. 8.95 (7-100-07672-2) Free Church Pubns.

Light Absorption by Aerosol Particles. Ed. by Hermann E. Gerber & Edward E. Hindman. LC 82-80728. (Illus.). 420p. (C). 1982. 58.00 (0-937194-00-X) A Deepak Pub.

Light Abstractions. (Illus.). 85p. 1980. 10.00 (0-9601616-2-7) U MO-St Louis.

Light Across the Prairies: An Illustrated History of Northwestern Public Service Company. Bill Beck. (Illus.). 260p. (Orig.). (C). 1989. write for info. (0-318-65405-9) NW Pub Serv.

Light Action! Amazing Experiments with Optics. Vicki Cobb & Joshua Cobb. LC 92-25528. (Illus.). 208p. (J). (gr. 7-11). 1993. lib. bdg. 15.89 (0-06-021437-6) HarpC Child Bks.

***Light Action in the Caribbean: Stories.** Barry Lopez. 176p. 2000. 22.00 (0-679-43455-0) Knopf.

Light-Activated Pest Control. Ed. by James R. Heitz & Kelsey R. Downum. LC 95-43870. (ACS Symposium Ser.: No. 616). (Illus.). 288p. 1995. text 75.00 (0-8412-3334-9, Pub. by Am Chemical) OUP.

Light-Activated Pesticides. Ed. by James R. Heitz & Kelsey R. Downum. LC 87-1342. (Symposium Ser.: No. 339). 355p. 1987. 80.95 (0-8412-1026-8, Pub. by Am Chemical) OUP.

Light-Activated Pesticides. Ed. by James R. Heitz & Kelsey R. Downum. LC 87-1342. (ACS Symposium Ser.: Vol. 339). 352p. 1987. reprint ed. pap. 109.20 (0-608-03532-7, 206425100008) Bks Demand.

Light after Darkness. (Illus.). 101p. pap. 9.95 (0-930061-01-2) Interspace Bks.

***Light after Death.** 2nd ed. Alan Bryson. 2000. pap. 8.50 (81-207-2072-5, Pub. by Sterling Pubs) S Asia.

Light after Life: A Scientific Journey into the Spiritual World. Konstantin Korotkov. Ed. by Leonid Tunik. 183p. 1997. pap. 12.95 (0-9644311-5-7) Backbone Pubng.

***Light after the Dark: Six True Stories of Triumph after All Hope Has Gone...** Alvin Abram. (Illus.). 304p. 1998. pap. 16.95 (1-55013-998-3, Pub. by Key Porter) Firefly Bks Ltd.

***Light Aglowing.** Emmanuel G. Del Rosario. LC 99-64126. 96p. 2000. 7.95 (1-57258-151-4) Teach Servs.

Light Ahead for the Negro. Edward A. Johnson. LC 74-170817. reprint ed. 20.00 (0-404-00074-6) AMS Pr.

Light, Air, & Color: American Impressionist Paintings from the Collection of the Pennsylvania Academy of the Fine Arts. Susan Danly. (Illus.). 91p. (Orig.). 1990. pap. 14.95 (0-943836-13-1) Penn Acad Art.

Light Aircraft Adventure into PNG. Bob Mossel. (C). 1989. pap. text 45.00 (0-89771-019-3, Pub. by Bob Mossel) St Mut.

Light Aircraft Recognition. 3rd ed. Peter R. March. (Illus.). 116p. 1997. pap. 11.95 (1-882663-15-2) Plymouth VT.

Light Airplane Contruction. ed. Ladislao Pazmany. (Illus.). 92p. (YA). (gr. 10 up). 1970. reprint ed. pap. 30.00 (0-9616777-2-4) Pazmany Aircraft.

Light Airplane Design. Ladislao Pazmany. (Illus.). 22.00 (0-614-13171-5, 21-37839) EAA Aviation.

Light Airplane Design. rev. ed. Ladislao Pazmany. (Illus.). 80p. (YA). (gr. 10 up). 1963. pap. 30.00 (0-9616777-1-6) Pazmany Aircraft.

Light Airplane Navigation Essentials. Paul A. Craig. LC 97-819. (Practical Flying Ser.). (Illus.). 256p. 1997. 34.95 (0-07-013454-5); pap. 24.95 (0-07-013456-1) McGraw.

Light All Night. Richard Robinson. 165p. mass mkt. 4.99 (1-55197-015-5) Picasso Publ.

Light All Night. unabridged ed. Richard Robinson. 143p. 1998. pap. 11.95 (1-892896-63-X) Buy Books.

Light Alloys. 3rd ed. write for info. (0-340-63207-0, Pub. by E A) Routldge.

Light Alloys: Metallurgy of the Light Metals. 3rd ed. Ian J. Polmear. LC 95-31388. 362p. 1995. pap. 99.00 (0-470-23565-9) Wiley.

Light Alloys Metallurgy of the Light Metals. I. J. Polmear. 224p. 1981. 110.00 (0-685-05555-8, Pub. by E A) Routldge.

Light & Air: The Photography of Bayard Wootten. Jerry W. Cotten & Bayard M. Wootten. LC 98-3421. (Illus.). 272p. 1998. 37.50 (0-8078-2445-3) U of NC Pr.

Light & Armament see Collected Works of Count Rumford

Light & Biological Rhythms in Man. Ed. by L. Wetterberg. LC 93-21167. (Wenner-Gren International Ser.). 462p. 1994. 185.25 (0-08-042279-9, Pergamon Pr) Elsevier.

Light & Color. Malcolm Dixon & Karen Smith. LC 98-6974. (Young Scientists Ser.). (Illus.). 32p. (J). 1998. lib. bdg. 21.30 (1-887068-70-8) Smart Apple.

Light & Color. Gary Gibson. (Science for Fun Ser.). 1995. 10.15 (0-606-09825-9, Pub. by Turtleback) Demco.

Light & Color. Frank Millson. (Illus.). 24p. (Orig.). (J). (gr. 3-7). 1996. pap. 6.95 (0-8167-4048-8) Troll Communs.

Light & Color. R. Daniel Overheim & David L. Wagner. LC 81-21955. 288p. (C). 1982. text 81.95 (0-471-08348-8) Wiley.

Light & Color. Peter Riley. 1999. pap. text 6.95 (0-531-15371-1) Watts.

Light & Color: With Easy-to-Make Scientific Projects. Gary Gibson. (Science for Fun Ser.). (Illus.). 32p. (J). (gr. 2-4). 1995. lib. bdg. 20.90 (1-56294-616-1, Copper Beech Bks) Millbrook Pr.

Light & Color In Nature & Art. Samuel J. Williamson & Herman Z. Cummins. LC 82-11167. 512p. 1983. text 93.95 (0-471-08374-7) Wiley.

Light & Color in the Outdoors. M. G. Minnaert. 1994. pap. 24.00 (0-387-84413-9) Spr-Verlag.

Light & Color in the Outdoors. M. G. Minnaert. (Illus.). 223p. 1995. 24.95 (0-387-94413-3) Spr-Verlag.

Light & Color in the Outdoors, Vol. XVII. rev. ed. M. G. Minnaert. Tr. by L. Seymour from DUT. LC 92-33748. (Illus.). 417p. 1995. 65.00 (0-387-97935-2) Spr-Verlag.

Light & Colors. Peter D. Riley. LC 98-18804. (Straightforward Science Ser.). (J). 1999. 19.00 (0-531-14505-0) Watts.

Light & Dark. Jack Challoner. LC 95-30023. (Start-up Science Ser.). (Illus.). 32p. (J). (gr. 1-4). 1996. lib. bdg. 21.40 (0-8172-4321-6) Raintree Steck-V.

Light & Dark. Margaret T. Davis. 452p. 1994. pap. 16.95 (1-873631-43-X, Pub. by B&W Pub) Firebird Dist.

Light & Dark. Sally Hewitt. LC 97-34923. (It's Science Ser.). (Illus.). 32p. (J). (gr. k-3). 1998. 20.00 (0-516-20842-X) Childrens.

An Asterisk (*) at the beginning of an entry indicates that the title is appearing for the first time.

L

Light & Dark. Sally Hewitt. (It's Science! Ser.). (Illus.). 32p. (J). (gr. k-3). 1999. pap. text 6.95 (*0-516-26340-4*) Childrens.

***Light & Dark.** Rebecca Hunter. (Discovering Science Ser.). (Illus.). (J). 2000. pap. 8.95 (*0-7398-3017-1*) Raintree Steck-V.

***Light & Dark.** Rebecca M. Hunter. LC 00-28042. (Discovering Science Ser.). (Illus.). 2000. write for info. (*0-7398-2973-4*) Raintree Steck-V.

Light & Dark. Wendy Madgwick. 1999. pap. text 5.95 (*0-8172-5882-5*) Raintree Steck-V.

Light & Dark. Wendy Madgwick. LC 98-7002. (Science Starters Ser.). (J). 1999. 22.83 (*0-8172-5556-7*) Raintree Steck-V.

Light & Dark. Chris Oxlade. LC 99-179636. (Step-by-Step Science Ser.). 32p. (J). (gr. 2-5). 1999. 18.00 (*0-516-20990-6*) Childrens.

***Light & Dark.** Raintree Steck-Vaughn Staff. (Science Starters Ser.). (Illus.). (J). (ps-3). 2000. 22.83 (*0-8172-5331-9*) Raintree Steck-V.

Light & Dark. large type ed. Margaret T. David. 721p. 1994. 27.99 (*0-7505-0612-1*, Pub. by Mgna Lrg Print) Ulverscroft.

Light & Dark: Poems. Barbara Howes. LC 59-12478. (Wesleyan Poetry Ser.). 86p. 1959. pap. 12.95 (*0-8195-1001-7*, Wesleyan Univ Pr) U Pr of New Eng.

Light & Darkness. Natsume Soseki, pseud. 397p. 1971. 33.00 (*0-7206-0400-1*, Pub. by P Owen Ltd) Dufour.

Light & Death: One Doctor's Fascinating Account of Near-Death Experiences. Michael Sabom. LC 98-41357. 208p. 1998. pap. 12.99 (*0-310-21992-2*) Zondervan.

Light & Delicious. Ed. & Illus. by Maria Athanasiou. 66p. 1995. spiral bd. write for info. (*1-57502-020-3*, Cookbks by Morris) Morris Pubng.

***Light & Easy.** Bob Bowersox. (In the Kitchen with Bob Ser.: Vol. 2). (Illus.). 128p. 2000. 24.00 (*1-928998-01-1*) Q V C Pubg.

Light & Easy. Mayflower Culinary Editors. LC 98-134045. (The Everyday Chef Ser.). 64p. 1997. pap. text 5.99 (*1-58029-010-8*, Everywhere) Hambleton-Hill.

***Light & Easy Baking.** Beatrice Ojakangas. (Illus.). 240p. 2000. 9.99 (*0-517-20962-4*) Random Hse Value.

Light & Easy Chicen Recipes. (Favorite All Time Recipes Ser.). (Illus.). 96p. 1994. 7.98 (*0-7853-0312-X*, 2023500) Pubns Intl Ltd.

Light & Easy Chinese with Quick Wok Cooking. (Favorite All Time Recipes Ser.). (Illus.). 96p. 1993. 7.98 (*1-56173-782-8*, 2017400) Pubns Intl Ltd.

Light & Easy Cookbook. Barbara Gibbons. 1980. 13.95 (*0-02-543120-X*) Macmillan.

Light & Easy Diabetes Cuisine. Betty Marks. 256p. 1990. pap. 15.95 (*0-89586-640-4*, HP Books) Berkley Pub.

Light & Easy Italian Cooking. Sheryle Eastwood. 1993. 12.98 (*1-55521-848-2*) Bk Sales Inc.

Light & Electron Microscopic Studies of Ascobolus Stercorarius. II Ascus & Ascospore Ontogeny. Kenneth Wells. LC 78-182553. (University of California Publications in Social Welfare: Vol. 62). (Illus.). 101p. reprint ed. pap. 31.40 (*0-608-17989-2*, 201470500093) Bks Demand.

Light & Electron Microscopy. Elizabeth M. Slayter & Henry S. Slayter. 319p. 1992. pap. text 32.95 (*0-521-33948-0*) Cambridge U Pr.

Light & Electron Microscopy. Elizabeth M. Slayter & Henry S. Slayter. (Illus.). 330p. (C). 1992. text 80.00 (*0-521-32714-8*) Cambridge U Pr.

Light & Electronmicroscopic Neuropathology - Slow Virus Diseases. Ed. by Pawel P. Liberski. 448p. 1992. lib. bdg. 239.00 (*0-8493-6725-5*, QR201) CRC Pr.

Light & Enlightenment: A Study of the Cambridge Platonists & the Dutch Arminans. Rosalie L. Colie. 176p. reprint ed. pap. 50.20 (*0-608-31001-8*, 2050767) Bks Demand.

Light & Healthy Chinese Cooking: The Best of Traditional Chinese Cuisine Made Low in Sodium, Cholesterol & Calories. Daniel N. Jue & Teresa Chew. LC 83-3837. 250p. 1984. 16.95 (*0-672-52776-6*) Macmillan.

Light & Heat: The Puritan View of the Pulpit. R. Bruce Bickel. 180p. 1999. pap. 14.95 (*1-57358-091-0*) Soli Deo Gloria.

Light & Heavy Vehicle Technology. 2nd ed. M. J. Nunney. (Illus.). 528p. 1992. pap. text 59.95 (*0-7506-0477-8*) Buttrwrth-Heinemann.

Light & Heavy Vehicle Technology. 3rd ed. M. J. Nunney. LC 98-232660. (Illus.). 672p. 2000. pap. text 39.95 (*0-7506-3827-3*) Buttrwrth-Heinemann.

Light & Illusion. Michele Claiborne. (DK Action Packs Ser.). (Illus.). 16p. (J). (gr. 3 up). 1995. pap. 19.95 (*1-56458-897-1*, 5-70552) DK Pub Inc.

Light & Illusion: The Hollywood Portraits of Ray Jones. Tom Zimmerman. LC 97-77841. (Illus.). 120p. 1998. pap. 24.95 (*1-890449-00-8*) Balcony Pr.

Light & Lean Cuisine. Anne Sheasby. 1998. 14.99 (*1-85833-873-5*) Quadrillion Pubng.

Light & Life. (Longman Biology Topics Ser.). Date not set. pap. text. write for info. (*0-582-32301-0*, Pub. by Addison-Wesley) Longman.

Light & Life: Proceedings of the Symposium, Johns Hopkins University, 1960. Light & Life Symposium Staff. Ed. by William D. McElroy & Bentley Glass. LC 60-16544. (Johns Hopkins University, McCollum-Pratt Institute, Contribution: No. 302). 938p. reprint ed. pap. 200.00 (*0-608-12100-2*, 202413900035) Bks Demand.

Light & Life: Renewal in Poland. Grazyna Sikorska. LC 89-11650. 156p. reprint ed. pap. 48.40 (*0-7837-0524-7*, 204084800018) Bks Demand.

Light & Life in the Fourth Gospel. Howard Brinton. LC 76-128679. (Orig.). 1971. pap. 4.00 (*0-87574-179-7*) Pendle Hill.

Light & Lively: A Reader. 2nd ed. Mira B. Felder & Anna B. Bromberg. LC 96-20066. 1996. pap. text 20.21 (*0-201-83413-8*) Longman.

Light & Lucious Teatime Treats. Angela Hynes. (Illus.). 96p. 1991. write for info. (*1-879577-00-3*) Bks Two Thousand.

Light & Luscious Cookbook. Oxmoor House Staff. LC 93-87339. 326p. 1994. 29.95 (*0-8487-1150-5*) Oxmoor Hse.

Light & Matter see Encyclopedia of Physics

Light & Matter, Vol. 1. Tr. of Licht und Materie. 1969. text. write for info. (*0-471-89930-5*); pap. text. write for info. (*0-471-89931-3*) Wiley.

Light & Matter , Vol. 2. 1969. pap. text. write for info. (*0-471-89933-X*) Wiley.

Light & Matter, Vol. 2. Tr. of Licht und Materie. 1969. text. write for info. (*0-471-89932-1*) Wiley.

Light & Movement: Incunabula of the Motion Picture, 1420-1896. Laurent Mannoni et al. (Distributed for the British Film Institute Ser.). 400p. 1996. text 95.00 (*88-86155-05-0*, Pub. by British Film Inst) Ind U Pr.

Light & Natural. Allen H. Benton. (Illus.). 184p. (Orig.). 1992. pap. 9.00 (*0-962788-20-6*) Iris Visual.

Light & Nature in Late Nineteenth Century Nordic Art & Literature. Neil Kent. (Illus.). 92p. (Orig.). 1990. pap. 28.50 (*91-554-2952-1*) Coronet Bks.

Light & Optics see Psyched for Science

***Light & Optics.** John Farndon. LC 99-89898. (Science Experiments Ser.). (YA). 2001. lib. bdg. 24.21 (*0-7614-1090-2*) Marshall Cavendish.

Light & Peace see How to Love God & Keep His Commandments

Light & Peace. R. P. Quadrupani. LC 79-67860. 193p. 1980. reprint ed. pap. 7.00 (*0-89555-133-0*) TAN Bks Pubs.

Light & Photosynthesis in Aquatic Ecosystems. 2nd ed. John T. Kirk. LC 93-37395. (Illus.). 525p. (C). 1994. pap. text 42.95 (*0-521-45966-4*) Cambridge U Pr.

Light & Plant Growth. Ed. by J. W. Hart. (Illus.). 192p. 1987. text 60.00 (*0-04-581022-2*) Routledge.

Light & Plant Growth. Ed. by J. W. Hart. (Illus.). 192p. 1987. 54.95 (*0-04-581023-0*) Thomson Learn.

Light & Plant Responses: A Study of Plant Photophysiology & the Natural Environment. T. H. Attridge. 160p. (C). 1992. pap. text 22.95 (*0-521-42748-7*) Cambridge U Pr.

Light & Relativity: A New Hypothesis. Alvin J. Fray. LC 98-51420. 1998. 59.00 (*1-56072-641-5*) Nova Sci Pubs.

Light & Shade. (Pose File Ser.: Vol. 7). (Illus.). 160p. 1995. pap. 49.95 (*4-87199-043-5*, Pub. by Erute-Shuppan) Bks Nippan.

***Light & Shade.** Parramon's Editorial Team Staff. (Art Handbooks). (Illus.). 96p. 2000. pap. 9.95 (*0-7641-5228-9*) Barron.

Light & Shadow. T. Davis Bunn. LC 50-6541. 160p. (Orig.). (YA). (gr. 7-12). 1995. pap. 5.99 (*0-7814-0116-X*) Chariot Victor.

Light & Shadow. Thomas-Cochran. (What a Wonderful World Intro Ser.). 1993. pap. text. write for info. (*0-582-91090-0*, Pub. by Addison-Wesley) Longman.

Light & Shadow. Claire Yaffa. write for info. (*0-89381-829-1*) Aperture.

Light & Shadow: The Photographs of Claire Yaffa. Photos by Claire Yaffa. LC 97-75181. (Illus.). 64p. 1998. 37.95 (*0-89381-779-1*) Aperture.

Light & Shadow Tarot Book & Cards. Brian Williams et al. LC 96-21846. (Illus.). 256p. 1996. pap. 16.95 (*0-89281-503-5*, Destiny Bks) Inner Tradit.

Light & Shadows: A History of Motion Pictures. 3rd ed. Thomas W. Bohn & Richard L. Stromgren. LC 86-61131. xlv, 427p. (C). 1987. pap. text 51.95 (*0-87484-702-8*, 702) Mayfield Pub.

Light & Shadows: Memories of Yemen. Alexandra Skobeleff. (Illus.). 105p. 1994. pap. 11.00 (*0-9642876-0-9*) Mandaville Assocs.

Light & Shadows: Selected Poems & Prose of Juan Ramon Jimenez. Juan Ramon Jimenez. Tr. by James Wright et al from SPA. 70p. 1987. pap. 9.00 (*0-934834-72-5*) White Pine.

***Light & Sight.** Jon Richards. LC 99-29704. (Science Factory Ser.). (Illus.). 32p. (J). (gr. 1-4). 1999. 21.90 (*0-7613-3255-3*, Copper Beech Bks) Millbrook Pr.

Light & Sound. Chris Oxlade. LC 99-12884. (Science Topics Ser.). 1999. write for info. (*1-57572-774-9*) Heinemann Lib.

Light & Sound. David Palmer. (Tell Me about Ser.). (Illus.). (J). 9.95 (*0-563-39625-3*, BBC-Parkwest) Parkwest Pubns.

***Light & Sound.** Steve Parker. (Illus.). (J). 2000. 27.12 (*0-7398-1011-1*) Raintree Steck-V.

Light & Sound. Peter Riley & Robert Snedden. LC 98-49852. (Smart Science Ser.). (Illus.). 32p. (YA). 1999. 21.36 (*1-57572-870-2*) Heinemann Lib.

Light & Substance. Van D. Coke & Thomas Barrow. (Illus.). 63p. 1974. pap. 4.00 (*0-942006-48-8*) U of CA Art.

Light & the Dark. Dennis Gibbons. 134p. 1998. pap. 12.50 (*1-57502-695-3*, PO1969) Morris Pubng.

Light & the Dark. C. P. Snow. LC 76-29285. 1977. 20.00 (*0-684-14841-2*, Scribners Ref) Mac Lib Ref.

Light & the Dark Vol. I: Dualism in the Archaic & Early Classical Periods of Greek History. P. F. M. Fontaine. LC 86-220950. (Cultural History of Dualism Ser.). xvi, 293p. (C). 1986. pap. 57.00 (*90-70265-40-0*, Pub. by Gieben) J Benjamins Pubng Co.

Light & the Dark Vol. II: Dualism in the Political & Social History of Greece in the Fifth & Fourth Century B.C. P. F. M. Fontaine. (Cultural History of Dualism Ser.). xvi, 295p. (C). 1987. pap. 57.00 (*90-5063-004-9*, Pub. by Gieben) J Benjamins Pubng Co.

Light & the Dark Vol. III: A Cultural History of Dualism: Dualism in Greek Literature & Philosophy in the Fifth & Fourth Centuries B.C. P. F. M. Fontaine. (Cultural History of Dualism Ser.). 241p. (C). 1988. pap. 57.00 (*90-5063-020-0*, Pub. by Gieben) J Benjamins Pubng Co.

Light & the Dark Vol. IV: A Cultural History of Dualism: Dualism in the Ancient Middle East. P. F. M. Fontaine. (Cultural History of Dualism Ser.). 356p. 1989. pap. 57.00 (*90-5063-032-4*, Pub. by Gieben) J Benjamins Pubng Co.

Light & the Dark Vol. VI: Dualism in the Hellenistic World. P. F. M. Fontaine. (Dualism in the Hellanistic World Ser.: Vol. VI). 328p. 1991. pap. 60.00 (*90-5063-076-6*, Pub. by Gieben) J Benjamins Pubng Co.

Light & the Dark Vol. VII: Dualism in the Palestinian-Syrian Region During the First Century A.D. until C.A. 140. P. F. M. Fontaine. (Cultural History of Dualism Ser.). 342p. 1992. pap. 57.00 (*90-5063-085-5*, Pub. by Gieben) J Benjamins Pubng Co.

Light & the Dark Vol. VIII: Gnostic Dualism in Asia Minor During the First Centuries A.D.I. P. F. M. Fontaine. (Cultural History of Dualism Ser.). 385p. 1993. pap. 60.00 (*90-5063-093-6*, Pub. by Gieben) J Benjamins Pubng Co.

Light & the Dark Vol. IX: Gnostic Dualism in Asia Minor During the First Centuries A. D. II. P. F. M. Fontaine. (Cultural History of Dualism Ser.). 355p. 1994. pap. 60.00 (*90-5063-346-3*, Pub. by Gieben) J Benjamins Pubng Co.

Light & the Dark Vol. X: Dualism in Roman History: Imperialism Dualism. P. F. M. Fontaine. (Cultural History of Dualism Ser.). 397p. 1995. pap. 60.00 (*90-5063-537-7*, Pub. by Gieben) J Benjamins Pubng Co.

Light & the Dark Vol. XI: Dualism in Roman History II: Dualism in Interior Politics & Social Life. P. F. M. Fontaine. (Cultural History of Dualism Ser.). 408p. 1996. pap. 60.00 (*90-5063-247-5*, Pub. by Gieben) J Benjamins Pubng Co.

Light & the Dark Vol. XII: Dualism in Roman History III: The Christian Church in Conflict with the Roman Empire & with Judaism. P. F. M. Fontaine. (Cultural History of Dualism Ser.). 293p. 1997. pap. 54.00 (*90-5063-357-9*, Pub. by Gieben) J Benjamins Pubng Co.

***Light & the Dark Vol. XIV: Dualism in Roman History V: Enemies of the Roman Order.** P. F. M. Fontaine. 290p. 1999. pap. 55.00 (*90-5063-148-7*, Pub. by Gieben) J Benjamins Pubng Co.

Light & the Dark - A Cultural History of Dualism Vol. 5: Dualism in Ancient Iran, India, & China. P. F. M. Fontaine. (Cultural History of Dualism Ser.). 312p. 1990. pap. 57.00 (*90-5063-051-0*, Pub. by Gieben) J Benjamins Pubng Co.

Light & the Glory: Did God Have a Plan for America? Peter Marshall & David Manuel. LC 77-23352. 384p. (YA). (gr. 10). 1986. 21.99 (*0-8007-0886-5*) Revell.

Light & the Glory: Did God Have a Plan for America? Peter Marshall & David Manuel. LC 77-23352. 384p. (YA). (gr. 10). 1987. pap. 12.99 (*0-8007-5054-3*) Revell.

Light & the Glory Children's Activity Book. Peter Marshall & David Manuel. 72p. (J). (gr. k-7). 1995. pap. 6.99 (*0-8007-5574-X*) Revell.

Light & the Glory for Children: Discovering God's Plan for America from Christopher Columbus to George Washington. Peter Marshall et al. LC 92-11727. (Illus.). 174p. (J). (gr. 7-10). 1992. pap. 9.99 (*0-8007-5448-4*) Revell.

Light & Truth. R. B. Lewis. 400p. 1998. reprint ed. pap. 45.00 (*1-58073-004-3*) BCP Bks.

Light & Truth. R. B. Lewis. 400p. 1998. reprint ed. pap. 45.00 (*0-933121-73-3*) Black Classic.

Light & Uncertain Hold: A History of the 66th Ohio Volunteer Infantry. David T. Thackery. LC 98-31317. (Illus.). 344p. 1999. text 35.00 (*0-87338-609-4*) Kent St U Pr.

Light & Vision: Photographs from the Beginning Classes at the Media Center, Houston 1969. 48p. 1969. pap. 5.00 (*0-939594-41-2*, Menil Collection) Menil Found.

***Light & Water: Plant Design Basics.** David L. Hamilton. (Illus.). 24p. 1998. pap. 6.95 (*1-877809-64-0*) Park Pl Pubns.

Light & Water: Radiative Transfer in Natural Waters. Charles D. Mobley. (Illus.). 592p. 1994. text 89.00 (*0-12-502750-8*) Acad Pr.

Light Angels. Margaret Shipley. LC 88-28730. 80p. (Orig.). 1989. pap. 7.50 (*0-931832-20-9*) Fithian Pr.

Light Around the Dark. Elizabeth D. Gee. (Center for Human Caring Ser.). 168p. (Orig.). 1992. pap. text 15.95 (*0-88737-554-5*, 14-2476) Natl League Nurse.

Light Artist Anthology: Neon & Related Media. Christian Schiess. 139p. 1994. pap. 15.00 (*0-944094-00-7*) ST Pubns.

***Light as an Eagle: Relaxation Exercises for a Healthy Spirit.** Itamar Azoulay. LC 00-39328. 2000. spiral bd. write for info. (*1-58330-418-5*) Feldheim.

Light As an Energy Source & Information Carrier in Plant Physiology: Proceedings of a NATO ASI Held in Volterra, Italy, September 26-October 6, 1994. Ed. by Robert C. Jennings et al. LC 96-25896. (NATO ASI Ser.: Vol. 287). (Illus.). 310p. 1996. 114.00 (*0-306-45383-5*) Plenum.

***Light at Dusk.** Peter Gadol. LC 00-29814. 288p. 2000. text 24.00 (*0-312-20336-5*, Picador USA) St Martin.

Light at Hand: Photographs, 1970-85. Guy Mendes. LC 85-81724. (Illus.). 64p. 1986. 22.50 (*0-917788-30-3*) Gnomon Pr.

Light at Tern Rock. Julia L. Sauer. (Illus.). 64p. (J). (gr. 3-7). 1994. pap. 4.99 (*0-14-036857-4*, PuffinBks) Peng Put Young Read.

Light at Tern Rock. Julia L. Sauer. 1995. 18.50 (*0-8446-6804-4*) Peter Smith.

Light at Tern Rock. Julia L. Sauer. LC 93-36242. (Puffin Newbery Library). 1994. 10.19 (*0-606-06530-X*, Pub. by Turtleback) Demco.

Light at the Edge of the Universe: Dispatches from the Front Lines of Cosmology. Michael D. Lemonick. LC 94-39324. 336p. 1995. pap. text 14.95 (*0-691-00158-8*, Pub. by Princeton U Pr) Cal Prin Full Svc.

Light at the End of the Bog. 2nd ed. John Norton. 48p. reprint ed. pap. 8.50 (*0-685-61094-2*) Black Star.

Light at the End of the Carpal Tunnel Vol. 1: A Guide to Understanding & Relief from the Pain of Nerve Problems. Scott M. Fried. LC 97-94105. (Illus.). xvi, 205p. (Orig.). 1998. 14.95 (*0-9659267-5-3*) Healing Bks.

Light at the End of the Refrigerator. Maureen K. Salaman. 1993. 16.95 (*0-913087-16-5*) MKS Inc.

Light at the End of the Tunnel. 376p. (C). 1999. pap. 20.00 (*0-536-02134-1*) Pearson Custom.

Light at the End of the Tunnel. Ed. by Edwin Su et al. (Magazine Collection - Gospel Ser.: Vol. 4). 162p. 1992. pap. 4.95 (*1-882324-04-8*) Ambssdrs Christ.

Light at the End of the Tunnel: A Vietnam War Anthology. rev. ed. Andrew J. Rotter. LC 98-40989. 576p. 1999. 55.00 (*0-8420-2712-2*); pap. text 22.95 (*0-8420-2713-0*) Scholarly Res Inc.

Light at the End of the Tunnel: Isaiah's Vision of Hope. Karen Wilk. (Prime-Time Bible Studies). 52p. 1995. pap., teacher ed. 8.95 (*1-56212-116-2*, 1210-3008) CRC Pubns.

Light at Your Shoulder: A Reflection of Angels Present. Karen Troiani. LC 96-225980. (Illus.). 36p. 1995. 9.95 (*0-941461-40-8*) Tunnel Press.

Light Baby Book: A Little Bit of Me. Susan Bruyn. (Illus.). 12p. 1992. reprint ed. pap. 7.50 (*1-891817-03-5*) Light Works Pr.

Light Basics Cookbook: The Only Cookbook You'll Ever Need If You Want to Cook Healthy. Martha R. Shulman. Ed. by Pamela Hoenig. LC 98-17817. (Illus.). 320p. 1999. 25.00 (*0-688-15549-9*, Wm Morrow) Morrow Avon.

Light Beam Alignment. Peter Novellino. LC 81-730690. 1982. student ed. 7.00 (*0-8064-0155-9*, 446) Bergwall.

Light Bearer. Donna Gillespie. 1994. pap. 15.00 (*0-425-14368-6*) Berkley Pub.

Light Bearer. Donna Gillespie. 1024p. 1996. mass mkt. 8.50 (*0-515-11966-0*, Jove) Berkley Pub.

Light Beef & Pork. Time-Life Books Editors. LC 97-3465. (Great Taste - Low Fat Ser.). (Illus.). 160p. (gr. 7). 1999. spiral bd. 14.95 (*0-7835-4565-7*) Time-Life.

Light Before Dawn: New Information about Humanity's Future Based on Dreams & Visions. John Schmidt. LC 96-692421. 72p. (Orig.). 1996. pap. 8.00 (*0-9639132-1-2*) Path Pubng.

***Light Behind Every Dark Cloud.** Marie P. Carter. 132p. (YA). 2000. pap. 12.00 (*1-881524-73-6*) Milligan Bks.

Light Beings - Master Essences. Petra Schneider & Gerhard Pieroth. 272p. 1998. pap. 16.95 (*0-910261-18-0*, Arcana Pubng) Lotus Pr.

Light Between the Fields. Christopher Brookhouse. LC 98-19403. (Signature Poets Ser.). 69p. 1998. 18.00 (*0-930095-34-0*) Signal Bks.

Light Between the Leaves. Elsie W. Stockwell. LC 92-43540. 64p. 1993. pap. 14.95 (*0-7734-2804-6*, Mellen Poetry Pr) E Mellen.

Light Beyond. Raymond A. Moody, Jr. 224p. 1989. mass mkt. 6.50 (*0-553-27813-4*) Bantam.

Light Beyond. E. P. Oppenheim. 319p. Date not set. 24.95 (*0-8488-2376-1*) Amereon Ltd.

Light Beyond. Maurice Maeterlinck. Tr. by Alexander T. De Mattos. LC 70-37844. (Essay Index Reprint Ser.). 1977. reprint ed. 20.95 (*0-8369-2607-2*) Ayer.

Light Beyond: Adventure in Hassidic Thought. Aryeh Kaplan. 384p. (C). 1981. 20.00 (*0-940118-33-5*) Moznaim.

Light Beyond: The Wonderworld of Parapsychology. Stanton A. Coblentz. LC 80-69585. (Illus.). 256p. 1982. 14.95 (*0-8453-4712-8*, Cornwall Bks) Assoc Univ Prs.

Light Beyond the Darkness. T. C. Morton. LC 96-93139. 270p. (Orig.). 1997. pap. 12.95 (*0-9657118-0-3*) Solid Rock MN.

***Light Beyond the Darkness: How I Healed My Suicide Son after His Death.** Dore Deverell. (Illus.). 144p. 2000. pap. 16.95 (*1-902636-19-8*, Pub. by Temple Lodge) Anthroposophic.

Light Beyond the Forest: The Quest for the Holy Grail. Rosemary Sutcliff. 144p. (J). (gr. 7 up). 1994. pap. 4.99 (*0-14-037150-8*, PuffinBks) Peng Put Young Read.

Light Beyond the Forest: The Quest for the Holy Grail. Rosemary Sutcliff. 1994. 9.09 (*0-606-07024-9*, Pub. by Turtleback) Demco.

Light Blooms. Michael T. Kelly. 48p. (Orig.). 1993. pap. 5.95 (*0-914370-59-6*) Mothers Hen.

Light Blue. Roger Grove. 16p. (gr. 3-12). 1973. pap. text 5.95 (*0-87487-648-6*) Summy-Birchard.

Light Blue, Jacquard. 80p. 1990. 3.00 (*0-9620519-3-4*) Iris Bks.

Light Body... A Transformation Cooking Guide to Health-Supportive Eating. Marita R. Collins. LC 96-61615. (Illus.). 240p. 1997. pap. 19.95 (*0-9654751-0-7*) Traveling Gourmet.

Light Body Activation: Science, Dialogue & Non-Practices for Interactive Evolution Saul Goodman. LC 98-232538. 275p. 1997. write for info. (*0-940843-02-1*) Infi-Tech Pubns.

***Light Book.** Christoph Geissmar. (Illus.). 256p. 2000. 80.00 (*3-7643-6303-7*) Birkhauser.

An Asterisk (*) at the beginning of an entry indicates that the title is appearing for the first time.

Light Bright: A Bright Idea for Bright Minds in the Primary Grades. Joyce L. Martin. Ed. by Thompson Mackellar. (Illus.). 212p. 1989. teacher ed. 49.95 (0-9621707-0-4) Port Side Pub.

Light Bringers. Eric Nelson. LC 83-50966. (Series Eight). 52p. 1983. pap. 7.00 (0-931846-23-4) Wash Writers Pub.

Light Bulb: Inventions That Changed Our Lives. Shaaron Cosner. LC 83-40398. 64p. (J). (gr. 5 up). 1984. lib. bdg. 10.85 (0-8027-6527-0) Walker & Co.

Light Bulb to Zipper see CDs, Super Glue & Salsa, Vol. 6, How Everyday Products Are Made

Light Bulbs. Norma M. Bracy. (Illus.). 22p. (J). (ps-12). 1984. pap. text 2.50 (0-915783-01-0) Book Binder.

Light Bulbs for Leaders: A Guide Book for Leaders & Teams. Barbara P. Glacel & Emile A. Robert, Jr. 208p. (Orig.). 1994. pap. text 15.95 (0-9645929-0-8) VIMA Intl.

Light Bulbs for Leaders: A Guide Book for Team Learning. Barbara P. Glacel & Emile A. Robert, Jr. LC 95-42462. 176p. 1996. 24.95 (0-471-14663-3) Wiley.

Light Burden: Easier Ways to Shun Evils. John Odhner. 48p. (Orig.). 1987. pap. 1.00 (0-910557-16-0) Acad New Church.

Light, Chemical Change & Life. Ed. by J. D. Coyle et al. 420p. 1982. pap. 38.00 (0-335-16100-6) OpUniv Pr.

***Light Classics.** 96p. 1999. pap. 9.95 (0-634-00294-5) H Leonard.

Light Classics. 160p. (YA). 1993. pap. 12.95 (0-7692-1466-5, WFM00007) Wrner Bros.

Light, Color & Environment. rev. ed. Faber Birren. LC 88-61470. (Illus.). 128p. 1988. pap. 24.95 (0-88740-131-7) Schiffer.

Light, Colors, Tones & Nature's Finer Forces. Ernest J. Stevens. 268p. 1996. reprint ed. pap. 19.95 (1-56459-805-5) Kessinger Pub.

Light Comes. Prabhat Rainjan Sarkar. 248p. (Orig.). 1989. 4.95 (0-88476-017-0) Ananda Marga.

Light Comes Slowly: Short Poems from Kyoto. Edith M. Shiffert. LC 96-79913. (Illus.). 120p. (Orig.). 1997. pap. 14.95 (0-9638551-6-6) Katsura Pr.

***Light Commercial Cost Data 2000.** 19th ed. R. S. Means Company Staff. 1999. pap. 76.95 (0-87629-562-6) R S Means.

Light-Consciousness: Voices & Visions of the Poets & Prophets in the (Newly Released) Dead Sea Scrolls Nag Hammadi Library & the Bible. Dwight K. Kalita. LC 92-97226. 235p. 1993. 19.95 (0-9635194-0-9) Lghthse Pubns.

Light Construction. Terence Riley. LC 95-78626. (Illus.). 160p. 1995. pap. 29.95 (0-8109-6154-7) Abrams.

Light Cooking for Two. Oxmoor House Staff. 240p. 1995. 29.95 (0-8487-1434-2) Oxmoor Hse.

Light Cuisine. Anne Ager. 1987. 10.98 (0-671-09186-7) S&S Trade.

Light Cuisine. Len Torine. Ed. by Marian Levine. 64p. 1988. pap. 3.95 (0-942320-32-8) Am Cooking.

Light Curve Modeling of Eclipsing Binary Stars. E. F. Milone. LC 92-21532. 1992. 89.95 (0-387-97946-8) Spr-Verlag.

Light Curves of Variable Stars: A Pictorial Atlas. Ed. by Christiaan Sterken & C. Jaschek. (Illus.). 249p. (C). 1996. text 80.00 (0-521-39016-8) Cambridge U Pr.

Light Dances: Illuminating Families with Laughter & Love. Shirley K. Trout. (Illus.). 275p. (Orig.). 1997. pap. 16.95 (0-9638346-1-4) Teachable Moments.

Light Detectors, Photoreceptors, & Imaging Systems in Nature. Jerome J. Wolken. (Illus.). 280p. 1995. text 75.00 (0-19-505002-9) OUP.

Light Divisions in Europe: Forces of the Future? Ed. by David Gates. (C). 1990. 35.00 (0-907967-98-1, Pub. by Inst Euro Def & Strat) St Mut.

Light Eating for Survival. Marcia Acciardo. (Illus.). 106p. (Orig.). 1978. pap. text 14.00 (0-933278-05-5) Twen Fir Cent.

Light Element Abundances: Proceedings of an ESO/EIPC Workshop Held in Marciana Marina, Isola d'Elba, 21-26 May 1994. ESO/EIPC Workshop on the Light Element Abundances. Ed. by Philippe Crane. LC 95-7443. (ESO Astrophysics Symposia Ser.). 434p. 1995. 42.95 (3-540-58978-3) Spr-Verlag.

Light Emerging: The Experience of Healing Through the Human Energy Field. Barbara A. Brennan. LC 92-31473. 352p. 1993. pap. 24.95 (0-553-35456-6) Bantam.

Light Emission from Silicon. Aldo Ferrari. (Solid State Phenomena Ser.: Vol. 54). (Illus.). 152p. (C). 1998. text 90.00 (3-908450-24-1, Pub. by Scitec Pubns) Enfield Pubs NH.

***Light Emission from Silicon: Progress Towards Si-Based Optoelectronics of the E-MRS 1998 Spring Conference, Strasbourg, France, June 16-19, 1998.** J. Linnros. LC 99-228690. 546p. 1999. 177.50 (0-08-043604-8) Elsevier.

Light Emitting Devices for Optoelectronic Applications/SOTAPOCS XXVIII. Ed. by H. Q. Hou et al. LC 99-180626. (Proceedings Ser.: Vol. 98-2). (Illus.). 654p. 1998. 72.00 (1-56677-194-3) Electrochem Soc.

Light-Emitting Diodes Vol. 3002: Research, Manufacturing & Applications II. Ed. by E. Fred Schubert. LC 97-200953. 216p. 1997. 69.00 (0-8194-2413-7) SPIE.

***Light-Emitting Diodes Vol. 3279: Research, Manufacturing & Applications II.** Ed. by E. Fred Schubert. LC 98-171721. 198p. 1998. 59.00 (0-8194-2718-7) SPIE.

Light-Emitting Polymers: Technology & Opportunities. 80p. 1996. spiral bd. 1625.00 (1-56217-022-8) Tech Insights.

Light Endless Light. Sri Aurobindo. 96p. 1991. pap. 0.75 (81-7060-004-9, Pub. by SAA) E-W Cultural Ctr.

Light Energy. Frank Schaffer Publications, Inc. Staff. (Science Notes Ser.). (Illus.). 8p. 1996. 2.49 (0-86734-893-3, FS-62030) Schaffer Pubns.

Light-Energy Transduction in Photosynthesis: Higher Plant & Bacterial Models. Ed. by S. Edward Stevens, Jr. & Donald A. Bryant. LC 88-70762. (Illus.). 398p. (Orig.). (C). 1988. pap. text 20.00 (0-943088-13-5) Am Soc of Plan.

***Light Equipment.** (Carpentry Lev 4 Ser.). 2000. teacher ed., ring bd. 12.00 (0-13-031208-8); student ed., ring bd. 12.00 (0-13-031198-7) P-H.

Light Eternal. 2nd rev. ed. John M. Talbot & Phil Perkins. 104p. 1998. pap. 8.00 (1-883803-08-X) Troubadour Lord.

***Light Falls Through You.** Anne Simpson. 96p. 2001. pap. 14.95 (0-7710-8077-8) McCland & Stewart.

Light Fantastic. Terry Pratchett. 1990. mass mkt. 6.99 (0-552-12848-1) Bantam.

***Light Fantastic.** Terry Pratchett. (Illus.). 272p. 2000. mass mkt. 3.99 (0-06-102070-2, Torch) HarpC.

Light Fantastic. Terry Pratchett. LC 86-60218. 218p. 1987. 27.95 (0-86140-203-0, Pub. by Smyth) Dufour.

Light Fantastic. large type ed. Terry Pratchett. 24.95 (1-85695-369-6, Pub. by ISIS Lrg Prnt) Transaction Pubs.

Light Fantastic: Over 225 Fun, Flavorful, & Fat-Reduced Recipes. Millie Snyder & Alyssa Alia. LC 96-705. (Illus.). 272p. 1996. spiral bd. 16.95 (0-7615-0435-4) Prima Pub.

Light Fantastic: The Art & Design of Stage Lighting. Max A. Keller. (Illus.). 232p. 1999. 75.00 (3-7913-2162-5, Pub. by Prestel) te Neues.

Light Fingered Gentry. David C. Phillips. (Collected Works of David G. Phillips). 1988. reprint ed. lib. bdg. 59.00 (0-7812-1334-7) Rprt Serv.

Light-Fingered Gentry. David G. Phillips. (American Author Ser.). 1981. reprint ed. lib. bdg. 69.00 (0-686-71929-8) Scholarly.

Light Flashbacks to a Dark Time. Chas. P. Haggerty. (Illus.). 130p. 1981. pap. 6.95 (0-9609936-0-6) Santiam Bks.

Light Food. Judy Hogan. (Illus.). 100p. 1989. pap. 10.00 (0-941179-24-9) Carolina Wren.

Light Foods: An Assessment of Their Psychological, Sociocultural, Physiological, Nutritional, & Safety Aspects. J. Leathwood. LC 95-75553. (Illus.). 98p. 1995. pap. 22.50 (0-944398-44-8) ILSI.

Light for an Age of Confusion, 2 vols., Set. Moshe Amiel. 1996. 39.95 (0-87306-693-6) Feldheim.

Light for Life, 3 Vol. Set. LC 96-77418. (Illus.). (Orig.). 1995. pap. text. write for info. (1-887158-06-5) God With Us.

Light for Living: Personal Insights for Daily Devotions. Ray K. Hodge. (Illus.). 259p. (Orig.). 1991. pap. text 12.95 (0-9627087-3-9) Mt Olive Coll Pr.

Light for My Love. Alexis Harrington. 384p. (Orig.). 1995. mass mkt. 4.99 (0-451-40501-3, Topaz) NAL.

Light for Others & Other Jewish Tales from Galicia. Leopold Von Sacher-Masoch. LC 94-8580. (Studies in Austrian Literature, Culture, & Thought. Translation Ser.). 350p. 1994. pap. 25.95 (0-929497-93-7) Ariadne CA.

Light for Our World: Essays Commemorating the 150th Anniversary of Concordia Seminary. Ed. by John W. Klotz. (Illus.). vii, 257p. (C). 1989. 11.95 (0-911770-57-7) Concordia Seminary.

Light for Students: Compiled from the Writings of Sri Aurobindo & the Mother. Sri Aurobindo. Ed. by Vijay. 140p. 1998. pap. 5.95 (81-7060-013-8, Pub. by SAA) E-W Cultural Ctr.

Light for the Day. Ed. by Vicki Radford et al. 368p. 1989. spiral bd. 6.50 (0-9624991-0-2) NWestern Prods.

***Light for the Journey: A Fresh Focus on Doctrine.** A. D. Beacham, Jr. 124p. 1998. pap. 5.95 (0-911866-41-8) LifeSprings Res.

***Light for the Last Days: Jesus' End-Time Prophecies Made Plain in the Book of Revelation.** Hans K. LaRondelle. Ed. by David C. James. LC 99-57497. 187p. 2000. pap. 12.99 (0-8163-1758-5) Pacific Pr Pub Assn.

Light for the New Millennium: Rudolf Steiner's Association with Helmuth & Eliza von Moltke: Letters, Documents & After-Death Communications. Rudolf Steiner. Ed. by T. H. Meyer. Tr. by H. Herrmann-Davey et al from GER. (Illus.). 400p. 1998. pap. 39.95 (1-85584-051-0, 3010, Pub. by R Steiner Pr) Anthroposophic.

Light for the Path, Vol. 1. Selwyn Hughes. (Every Day Light Ser.). 1999. 19.99 (0-8054-2143-2) Broadman.

Light for Your Path Series Leader's Guide. Carol J. Ruvolo. LC 98-15493. (Light for Your Path). 32p. 1998. pap., teacher ed. 2.99 (0-87552-628-4) P & R Pubng.

Light Forces & the Future of U. S. Military Strategy. M. Mazarr. (Association of the U. S. Army Book Ser.). (Illus.). 192p. 1990. 34.00 (0-08-040565-7, 3980M) Brasseys.

Light Frame Construction. Frank R. Dagostino. (Construction & Building Trades Ser.). 1997. teacher ed. 13.95 (0-8273-7122-5); text 55.95 (0-8273-7121-7) Delmar.

Light Freights. William W. Jacobs. LC 77-113678. (Short Story Index Reprint Ser.). 1977. 24.95 (0-8369-3407-5) Ayer.

Light from a Nearby Window: Poems of Contemporary Mexico. Ed. by Juvenal Acosta. 208p. (Orig.). 1994. pap. 12.95 (0-87286-281-X) City Lights.

Light from Above: The Life of Alexander Campbell. Bill J. Humble. 1988. pap. 2.99 (0-89225-327-4) Gospel Advocate.

Light from Ancient Africa. Na'im Akbar. LC 94-96248. 85p. (Orig.). 1994. pap. 9.95 (0-935257-02-0) Mind Prods Assocs.

Light from Ancient Africa. Na'im Akbar. 1994. 15.00 (0-935257-03-9) Mind Prods Assocs.

Light from Another Country: Poetry from American Prisons. Ed. by Joseph Bruchac. LC 83-788. 350p. (Orig.). 1984. pap. 9.95 (0-912678-60-7, Greenfld Rev Pr) Greenfld Rev Lit.

Light from Another Room: New & Selected Poems, 1940-1994. Eileen Lomasney. Ed. by Francine Dempsey. 98p. (Orig.). 1994. pap. 10.00 (0-9641725-1-8) Canticle Press.

Light from Arcturus. Mildred Walker. LC 94-41323. xiii, 343p. 1995. pap. 13.95 (0-8032-9769-6, Bison Books) U of Nebr Pr.

Light from Behind the Bars. Carmelo Di Giovanni. 158p. (C). 1990. 39.00 (0-85439-271-8, Pub. by St Paul Pubns) St Mut.

Light from Beyond. Patience Worth. 295p. 1997. reprint ed. 37.00 (0-7873-5000-1) Hlth Research.

Light from Dead Stars. Martin S. Cohen. 368p. (Orig.). 1997. pap. 10.95 (1-55050-102-X, Pub. by Coteau) Genl Dist Srvs.

Light from Heaven: Love in British Romantic Literature. Frederick L. Beaty. LC 70-157649. 288p. 1971. 28.00 (0-87580-028-9) N Ill U Pr.

Light from Light. Jack Perry. 208p. 1987. 11.95 (0-310-23850-1, 11418) Zondervan.

Light from Light: An Anthology of Christian Mysticism. Ed. by Louis Dupre & James A. Wiseman. 256p. 1988. pap. 22.95 (0-8091-2943-4) Paulist Pr.

Light from Many Lamps. Comment by Lillian E. Watson. 352p. 1988. pap. 12.00 (0-671-65250-8, Fireside) S&S Trade Pap.

***Light from Old Times: Protestant Facts & Men.** deluxe ed. J. C. Ryle. (Illus.). 432p. 2000. 29.95 (0-9677603-0-5) C Nolan.

Light from Out of the Darkness: On the Composition of the Stone of the Philosophers. Marc-Antonio Crasselame. Ed. by Patrick Smith. Tr. by Patrick J. Smith from FRE. (Alchemical Studies Ser.: No. 1). (Illus.). (Orig.). 1990. pap. 8.95 (1-55818-356-6, Alchemical) Holmes Pub.

Light from Paris: Cardinal Lustiger on Faith & Contemporary Culture. Gerard Hanratty. 32p. 1994. pap. 6.00 (1-85182-184-8, Pub. by Four Cts Pr) Intl Spec Bk.

Light from the Ancient East. Adolf Deissmann. Tr. by Lionel Strachan. 536p. 1995. reprint ed. 29.95 (1-56563-155-2) Hendrickson MA.

Light from the Ancient Past: The Archeological Background of Judaism & Christianity, 2 vols., Vol. 1. 2nd ed. Jack Finegan. LC 59-11072. (Illus.). 384p. reprint ed. pap. 119.10 (0-8357-2927-3, 203916600001) Bks Demand.

Light from the Ancient Past: The Archeological Background of Judaism & Christianity, 2 vols., Vol. 2. 2nd ed. Jack Finegan. LC 59-11072. (Illus.). 499p. reprint ed. pap. 154.70 (0-8357-2928-1, 203916600002) Bks Demand.

Light from the Angels. Hallie Deering. 229p. (Orig.). 1995. pap. 15.00 (0-929385-72-1) Light Tech Pubng.

Light from the Ashes: Social Science Careers of Young Holocaust Refugees & Survivors. Ed. by Peter Suedfeld. (Illus.). 436p. pap. 24.95 (0-472-06745-1, 06745) U of Mich Pr.

Light from the Ashes: Social Science Careers of Young Holocaust Refugees & Survivors. Ed. by Peter Suedfeld. (Illus.). 436p. (C). text 75.00 (0-472-09745-8, 09745) U of Mich Pr.

Light from the Dark Room: A Celebration of Scottish Photography: A Scottish-Canadian Collaboration. Sara Stevenson et al. (Illus.). 128p. 1995. pap. write for info. (0-903598-58-2, Pub. by Natl Galleries) Antique Collect.

Light from the Darkness: Paintings by Peter Birkhauser. Kaspar Birkhauser. Ed. by Eva Wertenschlag. (ENG & GER., Illus.). 80p. 1991. 34.50 (0-8176-1190-8) Birkhauser.

Light from the Dust: A Photographic Exploration into the Ancient World of the Book of Mormon. Maurine J. Proctor & Scot F. Proctor. LC 93-72676. (Illus.). 208p. 1993. 39.95 (0-87579-680-X) Deseret Bk.

Light from the East. A. Nichols. 1990. pap. 118.00 (0-7220-5080-1) St Mut.

Light from the East. Michael O'Carroll. LC 98-65203. 183p. 1998. pap. 9.95 (1-57918-062-0, 3632) Queenship Pub.

Light from the East: A Central & Eastern Europe Christmas CD. Canto Rum of St Peters Scholar Staff. 1999. cd-rom 16.95 (0-8146-7933-1) Liturgical Pr.

Light from the East: Studies in Japanese Confucianism. Robert C. Armstrong. 1974. lib. bdg. 300.00 (0-87968-134-9) Krishna Pr.

Light from the Fifth Dimension. Helena E. Ruhnau. LC 79-149287. (Illus.). 171p. (Orig.). 1982. pap. 13.95 (0-941036-05-7) Colleasius Pr.

Light from the Forest: How Santeria Heals Through Plants. George Brandon. 20p. 1991. pap. text 4.50 (0-9631900-0-8) Blue Unity Pr.

Light from the Hearth: Central Minnesota Pioneers & Early Architecture. Marilyn S. Brinkman & William T. Morgan. (Illus.). 144p. (Orig.). 1983. pap. 9.95 (0-87839-038-3) North Star.

Light from the Holy Hills. Moody Stewart. 1997. pap. 6.99 (1-898787-04-2) Emerald House Group Inc.

Light from the Lighthouse: The Poetry of God's Word. David E. Welch. (Illus.). 64p. (Orig.). 1996. pap. 5.95 (0-9654391-1-9) CJ Scott Pubng.

***Light from the River: Central Maine Power Company's First Century of Service, 1899-1999.** unabridged ed. Central ME Power Co. Staff. Ed. by Clark Irwin. (Illus.). 80p. 1999. pap. 15.00 (0-9665645-1-0) Ctrl ME Power.

Light from the Sanctuary of the Royal Arch. Charles A. Snodgrass. 245p. 1996. reprint ed. pap. 19.95 (1-56459-629-X) Kessinger Pub.

***Light from the Shadows: A Mythos of Modern Traditional Witchcraft.** Gwyn. (Illus.). 1999. 21.95 (1-86163-061-1) Holmes Pub.

Light from the Yellow Star. Robert O. Fisch. LC 95-125155. 1996. 14.95 (1-885116-00-4) Weisman Art.

Light from the Yellow Star: Lesson of Love from the Holocaust. Robert O. Fisch. 40p. (YA). (gr. 6 up). 1996. pap. 9.95 (0-9644896-0-0) Yellow Star.

Light from Within: Perspective on the Biblical Drama. Margaret Dewey. 206p. 1994. pap. 9.95 (1-85311-072-8, 844, Pub. by Canterbury Press Norwich) Morehouse Pub.

Light-Front Quantization & Non-Perturbative QCD. unabridged ed. Ed. by James Vary & Frank Woelz. LC 97-78172. 304p. (C). 1997. text 40.00 (1-891815-00-8) Intl Inst TAP.

Light Fruit Desserts. (Recipes of the World Ser.). (Illus.). 1998. write for info. (1-886614-82-2) Intl Masters Pub.

Light Fundamentals. Robert W. Wood. LC 97-23975. (Funtastic Science Activities for Kids Ser.). (Illus.). 160p. (YA). (gr. 3 up). 1999. lib. bdg. 22.95 (0-7910-4843-8) Chelsea Hse.

Light Furniture. Johannes Spalt. (Illus.). 104p. 1995. 34.50 (3-7643-5061-X, Pub. by Birkhauser) Princeton Arch.

***Light Garden of the Angel King: Travels in Afghanistan.** Peter Levi. (Illus.). 2000. pap. 18.95 (1-873429-35-5) Pallas Athene.

***Light-Gathering Poems: Poems of Hope & Healing.** Liz Rosenberg. LC 99-49231. 128p. (YA). 2000. pap. text 16.95 (0-8050-6223-8) St Martin.

Light Has Come: An Exposition of the Fourth Gospel. Lesslie Newbigin. 281p. 1987. reprint ed. pap. 16.00 (0-8028-1895-1) Eerdmans.

Light-Haven. Natalie Tawes. 384p. 1997. 22.00 (0-8059-4220-3) Dorrance.

Light-Healthy Processed Foods & Soft Drinks, No. GA-081. 176p. 1993. 2450.00 (1-56965-100-0) BCC.

Light Heart. Gary Lenhart. 1991. 15.00 (0-914610-92-9); pap. 9.00 (0-914610-91-0) Hanging Loose.

Light Heart. Elswyth Thane. 1996. lib. bdg. 29.95 (1-56849-476-9) Buccaneer Bks.

Light Heart. Elswyth Thane. 1974. reprint ed. lib. bdg. 26.95 (0-88411-951-3) Amereon Ltd.

Light Heart Lives Long. Kathy Davis. Ed. by Debbie Hansen. (Illus.). 168p. (Orig.). 1993. pap. 5.95 (1-56245-074-3) Great Quotations.

Light Heart Lives Long - Journal. Kathy Davis. Ed. by Michael Ryan. (Illus.). (Orig.). 1993. pap. 8.50 (1-56245-029-8) Great Quotations.

Light-Hearted Cooking, By George! George Jacobs. (By George! Cookbooks Ser.). (Illus.). 186p. (Orig.). 1991. text 11.95 (0-9618059-5-1) Cromlech Bks.

Light-Hearted Look at the Desert. fac. ed. Chuck Waggin. LC 74-101697. (Illus.). 95p. pap. 30.00 (0-7837-6955-5, 204690500003) Bks Demand.

Light Helicopter Trade-Off Assessments. Monti D. Callero et al. LC 93-19286. 1993. pap. 13.00 (0-8330-1373-4, MR-198-A) Rand Corp.

Light Her Fire: How to Ignite Passion, Joy & Excitement in the Woman You Love. Ellen Kreidman. 272p. 1992. mass mkt. 6.50 (0-440-21249-9) Dell.

Light His Fire. Ellen Kreidman. 224p. 1991. mass mkt. 6.99 (0-440-20753-3) Dell.

Light Holds: Poems. Harvey Shapiro. LC 83-23339. (Wesleyan Poetry Ser.). 87p. 1984. pap. 12.95 (0-8195-6096-0, Wesleyan Univ Pr) U Pr of New Eng.

Light-Horse Harry Lee & the Legacy of the American Revolution. Charles Royster. LC 82-9620. (Illus.). 336p. 1994. pap. 16.95 (0-8071-1910-5) La State U Pr.

***Light House.** William G. Monahan. LC 99-86047. 208p. 2000. 21.95 (1-57322-158-9, Riverhead Books) Putnam Pub Group.

Light Imagery in the "Romancero" Patricia Pogal. 160p. Date not set. 59.50 (0-614-10347-9) Scripta.

Light Imagery in the Spanish Ballad. Patricia Pogal. LC 98-150775. 164p. 1997. pap. 49.95 (1-57309-233-9) Intl Scholars.

Light in Architecture. James Brogan. (Architectural Design Ser.: Vol. 126). (Illus.). 112p. (Orig.). 1997. pap. 29.95 (1-85490-501-5) Academy Ed UK.

Light in August. William Faulkner. 480p. (C). 1965. pap. 8.44 (0-07-553648-X) McGraw.

Light in August: A Study in Black & White. Alwyn Berland. (Masterwork Studies). 136p. 1992. pap. 13.95 (0-8057-8100-5, 95, Twyne) Mac Lib Ref.

Light in August: A Study in Black & White. Alwyn Berland. (Masterwork Studies: No. 95). 136p. 1992. 29.00 (0-8057-8050-5, Twyne) Mac Lib Ref.

Light in August: The Corrected Text. William Faulkner. 1959. 18.10 (0-606-01720-8, Pub. by Turtleback) Demco.

Light in August: The Corrected Text. William Faulkner. LC 90-50268. (Vintage International Ser.). 512p. 1990. pap. 13.00 (0-679-73226-8) Vin Bks.

Light in August Notes. James L. Roberts. (Cliffs Notes Ser.). 72p. 1964. pap. 4.95 (0-8220-0744-4, Cliff) IDG Bks.

Light in Biology & Medicine, Vol. 1. Ed. by R. H. Douglas et al. (Illus.). 474p. 1988. 110.00 (0-306-42918-7, Plenum Trade) Perseus Pubng.

Light in Biology & Medicine, Vol. 2. Ed. by R. H. Douglas et al. (Illus.). 582p. (C). 1991. text 186.00 (0-306-44025-3, Kluwer Plenum) Kluwer Academic.

Light in Britain. Grace Cooke & Ivan Cooke. (Illus.). 128p. 1971. pap. (0-85487-056-3) White Eagle.

Light in Darkness: Women in Prints of Early Showa Japan, 1925-1941. Kendall Brown et al. Ed. by Mary Lenihan. LC 95-61954. (Illus.). 96p. (Orig.). (C). 1996. pap. 20.00 (0-945192-18-5) USC Fisher Gallery.

An Asterisk (*) at the beginning of an entry indicates that the title is appearing for the first time.

Light in Einstein's Universe: The Role of Energy in Cosmology & Relativity. S. J. Prokhovnik. LC 85-14183. 1985. text 138.50 (*90-277-2093-2*) Kluwer Academic.

Light in Exile. Cheryl J. Franklin. 336p. 1990. mass mkt. 3.95 (*0-88677-417-9*, Pub. by DAW Bks) Penguin Putnam.

Light in Flight or the Holodiagram: The Columbi Egg of Optics, PM27. Nils H. Abramson. LC 96-33735. 1996. 80.00 (*0-8194-2107-3*) SPIE.

Light in My Darkest Night. Catherine Marshall. 1990. mass mkt. 4.99 (*0-380-71023-4*, Avon Bks) Morrow Avon.

***Light in My Darkness.** 2nd ed. Helen Keller. Ed. by Ray Silverman. LC 94-33090. (Illus.). 184p. 2000. pap. 13.95 (*0-87785-398-3*) Swedenborg.

***Light in Our Houses.** Al Maginnes. 72p. 2000. pap. 12.00 (*0-8071-2622-5*) La State U Pr.

Light in Rizal's Death Cell. Manolo O. Vano. 79p. (Orig.). 1985. pap. 9.50 (*971-10-0235-3*, Pub. by New Day Pub) Cellar.

Light in Space. Wendy Orr. (Illus.). 124p. (J). (gr. 4-6). 1994. lib. bdg. 14.95 (*1-55037-368-4*, Pub. by Annick) Firefly Bks Ltd.

Light in Space. Wendy Orr. (Illus.). 124p. (J). (gr. 5-7). 1994. pap. 5.95 (*1-55037-975-5*, Pub. by Annick) Firefly Bks Ltd.

Light in the Attic. Shel Silverstein. LC 80-8453. (Illus.). 176p. (J). 1981. 17.95 (*0-06-025673-7*) HarpC Child Bks.

Light in the Attic. Shel Silverstein. LC 80-8453. (Illus.). 176p. (J). (gr. 2 up). 1981. lib. bdg. 17.89 (*0-06-025674-5*) HarpC Child Bks.

Light in the Castle. Robert Elmer. (Young Underground Ser.: No. 6). 176p. (J). (gr. 3-8). 1996. pap. 5.99 (*1-55661-659-7*) Bethany Hse.

Light in the City: Devotions for Advent. Hillary J. Freeman. LC 98-37272. (Illus.). 36p. 1998. pap. 4.50 (*1-886513-20-1*) Kirk Hse Pubs.

***Light in the City: Why Christians Must Advance.** Janet Parshall & Craig Parshall. 264p. 2000. pap. 12.99 (*0-7852-6890-1*) Nelson.

Light in the Crevice Never Seen. 2nd rev. ed. Haunani-Kay Trask. LC 99-44265. 128p. 1999. 26.95 (*0-934971-71-4*, Pub. by Calyx Bks); pap. 11.95 (*0-934971-70-6*, Pub. by Calyx Bks) Consort Bk Sales.

Light in the Crossing. Kent Meyers. LC 99-22069. 1999. text 21.95 (*0-312-20337-3*) St Martin.

***Light in the Crossing: Stories.** Kent Meyers. 240p. 2000. pap. 12.95 (*0-312-26758-4*) St Martin.

Light in the Dark Ages: The Rise & Fall of San Vincenzo al Volturno. Richard Hodges. LC 97-4117. (Illus.). 1996. text 49.95 (*0-8014-3416-5*) Cornell U Pr.

Light in the Dark Belt: The Story of Rosa Young as Told by Herself. Rosa Young. 200p. 1991. reprint ed. lib. bdg. 59.00 (*0-7812-8435-X*) Rprt Serv.

Light in the Darkness. Joan Chittister. LC 97-52355. 160p. 1998. pap. 12.95 (*0-8245-1748-2*, Crsrd) Crossroad NY.

Light in the Darkness. Ellen M. Fisher. 320p. 1998. mass mkt. 5.50 (*0-553-57922-3*) Bantam.

Light in the Darkness. Sergei Fudel. Tr. by Sophie Koulomzin from RUS. LC 89-6283. 138p. (Orig.). 1989. pap. 7.95 (*0-88141-075-6*) St Vladimirs.

Light in the Darkness. Etan Goldman & Brian Stewart. 119p. 1982. 2.25 (*0-942334-00-0*) Reignbow.

Light in the Darkness. Aaron Zevy. (Illus.). 1998. pap. 5.95 (*0-9680678-9-1*) Tumbleweed Pr.

Light in the Darkness: African Americans & the YMCA, 1852-1946. Nina Mjagkij. LC 93-19857. (Illus.). 216p. 1993. 24.95 (*0-8131-1852-2*) U Pr of Ky.

Light in the Darkness: How to Bring Christ to the Souls You Meet Each Day. rev. ed. Elisabeth Leseur. LC 98-12657. Orig. Title: La Vie Spirituelle. 157p. 1998. pap. 12.95 (*0-918477-72-7*) Sophia Inst Pr.

Light in the Darkness: Studies in the Gospel of John. Homer A. Kent, Jr. (Illus.). pap. 10.99 (*0-88469-055-5*) BMH Bks.

Light in the Dunes. Martha Attema. LC 97-65300. 176p. (YA). (gr. 6-9). 1997. pap. 6.95 (*1-55143-085-1*) Orca Bk Pubs.

Light in the East: A. D. 1000 - 1100 see TimeFrame Series

Light in the East, 1000-1100 AD. (Time Frame Ser.). (Illus.). 176p. 1988. lib. bdg. 25.93 (*0-8094-6430-6*) Time-Life.

Light in the Evening Time. L. Joyce Martin. LC 95-19684. 224p. 1995. pap. 8.99 (*1-56722-132-7*) Word Aflame.

Light in the Field: Historic Light Houses, Barns, Mills, & Fishery Buildings of Prince Edward Island. H. M. Smith. LC 98-108545. (Illus.). 120p. 1997. pap. 16.95 (*0-86492-226-4*, Pub. by Goose Ln Edits) Genl Dist Srvs.

***Light in the Forest.** (YA). 1999. 9.95 (*1-56137-466-0*) Novel Units.

Light in the Forest. Cliffs Notes Staff. (Cliffs Notes Ser.). 64p. 1999. 4.95 (*0-7645-8504-5*) IDG Bks.

Light in the Forest. Holt & Company Staff. 1989. pap., student ed. 11.00 (*0-03-023439-5*) Holt R&W.

***Light in the Forest.** Gloria Levine. 40p. (YA). 1999. 11.95 (*1-56137-467-9*) Novel Units.

Light in the Forest. Conrad Richter. 21.95 (*0-89190-333-X*) Amereon Ltd.

Light in the Forest. Conrad Richter. 1991. lib. bdg. 21.95 (*1-56849-064-X*) Buccaneer Bks.

Light in the Forest. Conrad Richter. 144p. (YA). 1994. mass mkt. 4.99 (*0-449-70437-8*) Fawcett.

Light in the Forest. Conrad Richter. 1994. 10.09 (*0-606-06903-8*, Pub. by Turtleback) Demco.

Light in the Forest, Set. abr. ed. Conrad Richter. (J). 1992. audio 15.99 (*0-553-47047-7*, 391070) BDD Aud Pub.

Light in the Forest, Vol. 1. Linda Butler. (The ESOL Companion Guide Ser.). 128p. (C). 1996. pap. 12.19 (*0-07-009428-4*) McGraw.

Light in the Forest: A Unit Plan. Barbara M. Linde. 166p. 1996. teacher ed., ring bd. 26.95 (*1-58337-155-9*) Teachers Pet Pubns.

Light in the Forest - Study Guide. Crystal Norris. Ed. by Joyce Friedland & Rikki Kessler. (Novel-Ties Ser.). (J). (gr. 6-8). 1993. pap. text 15.95 (*0-88122-117-1*) Lrn Links.

Light in the Forest & A Country of Strangers: Curriculum Unit. Center for Learning Network Staff & Conrad Richter. (Novel Ser.). 100p. (YA). (gr. 9-12). 1990. spiral bd. 18.95 (*1-56077-121-6*) Ctr Learning.

Light in the Grotto see Saint Bernadette Soubirous: Light in the Grotto

Light in the Head. Andrew Forster. (Illus.). 80p. 1995. pap. 10.00 (*0-932526-60-8*) Nexus Pr.

Light in the Kitchen Window. Margaret B. Vaughn. (Illus.). 76p. (Orig.). 1991. pap. 9.95 (*0-9624100-5-5*) Bell Buckle.

Light in the Kitchen Window: Poems. Margaret B. Vaughn. LC 94-6751. (Illus.). 1994. write for info. (*0-916078-35-3*) Iris Pr.

Light in the Land of Shadows Cycle B: Sermons for Advent, Christmas & Epiphany, First Lesson Texts. Harold C. Warlick, Jr. LC 96-5304. 110p. (Orig.). 1996. pap. 10.75 (*0-7880-0769-6*) CSS OH.

Light in the Lord: Reflections on Priesthood. Ed. by Basil Hume. 175p. (C). 1990. 65.00 (*0-85439-400-1*, Pub. by St Paul Pubns) St Mut.

Light in the Lord: Reflections on Priesthood. Basil Hume. 175p. (C). 1996. pap. 39.95 (*0-85439-399-4*, Pub. by St Paul Pubns) St Mut.

Light in the Middle of the Tunnel. I. Howat. 6.99 (*1-85792-099-6*, Pub. by Christian Focus) Spring Arbor Dist.

Light in the Midst of Zion: Calvery Missionary Baptist Church & a History of Black Baptists in Utah 1892-1996. France A. Davis. (Illus.). 150p. (Orig.). 1997. pap. 10.00 (*0-9656532-1-8*) University Pub.

Light in the Mill. D. K. Oklahoma. 80p. (YA). (gr. 10 up). 1989. pap. 5.50 (*0-87129-900-3*, L64) Dramatic Pub.

Light in the Mirror: A New Way to Understand Relationships. Barry Vissell & Joyce Vissell. (Illus.). (Orig.). 1996. pap. 13.95 (*0-9612720-5-8*) Ramira Pub.

Light in the Piazza & Other Italian Tales. Elizabeth Spencer. LC 95-39929. 304p. 1995. reprint ed. pap. 16.95 (*0-87805-837-0*); reprint ed. lib. bdg. 42.50 (*0-87805-836-2*) U Pr of Miss.

Light in the Prairie: Temple Emanu-el of Dallas, 1872-1997. Gerry Cristol. LC 97-37503. (Illus.). 296p. 1998. 29.95 (*0-87565-184-4*) Tex Christian.

Light in the Shadows. Barbara Milman. LC 97-14067. 1997. pap. 14.95 (*0-8246-0401-6*) Jonathan David.

***Light In The Shadows: Emerging from the Darkness of Depression.** William Coleman. LC 00-23352. 194p. 2000. pap. 10.99 (*1-56955-151-0*, Vine Bks) Servant.

***Light in the Shadows: Meditations While Living with a Life-Threatening Illness.** Hank Dunn. 52p. 1999. pap. 3.50 (*1-928560-01-6*) A & A Pubs.

Light in the Skull: An Odyssey of Medical Discovery. Ronald Glasser. LC 96-51607. 210p. 1997. 24.95 (*0-571-19916-X*) Faber & Faber.

Light in the Sky. Herbert Clock & Eric Boetzel. Ed. by R. Reginald & Douglas Melville. LC 77-84211. (Lost Race & Adult Fantasy Ser.). 1978. reprint ed. lib. bdg. 29.95 (*0-405-10966-0*) Ayer.

Light in the Sky: A Biography of Warren G. Grimes & a History of Aviation Lighting. Mike Major & Nancy Patzer. (Illus.). 130p. 1996. 35.00 (*0-9641149-8-4*) Main Graphics.

***Light in the Storm: A Novel.** Chris Heimerdinger. LC 00-43054. 2000. write for info. (*1-57734-684-X*) Covenant Comms.

Light in the Storm: The Civil War Diary of Amelia Martin, Fenwick Island, Delaware, 1861. Karen Hesse. LC 98-49204. (Dear America Ser.). (Illus.). 169p. (J). (gr. 4-9). 1999. 10.95 (*0-590-56733-0*, Pub. by Scholastic Inc) Penguin Putnam.

Light in the Valley. large type ed. Mary Mackie. 1991. 27.99 (*0-7089-2464-6*) Ulverscroft.

Light in the Valley: A Pictorial History of the Fort Valley State College since 1895. Donnie D. Bellamy. LC 95-52671. 1996. write for info. (*0-89865-965-5*) Donning Co.

Light in the Window. Grace L. Judson. (Illus.). 96p. Date not set. pap. 35.95 (*0-9660586-0-7*) Aerial Perspect.

Light in the Window. Jan Karon. (Mitford Years Ser.: Vol. 2). (Illus.). 413p. 1995. pap. 11.95 (*0-7459-2803-X*) Lion USA.

Light in the Window. Jan Karon. (Mitford Ser.). 21.95 (*1-57490-255-5*) T T Beeler.

Light in the Window. Jan Karon. LC 95-35717. (Mitford Years Ser.: Vol. 2). 432p. 1996. pap. 12.95 (*0-14-025454-4*, Penguin Bks) Viking Penguin.

Light in the Window. Jan Karon. LC 98-21317. (Mitford Years Ser.: Vol. 2). 352p. 1998. 24.95 (*0-670-88226-7*) Viking Penguin.

Light in the Window. Georgene Pearson. (Orig.). (J). 1996. pap. 10.00 (*0-57502-143-9*) Morris Pubng.

Light in the Window. Mary Roberts Rinehart. 1986. mass mkt. 3.99 (*0-8217-4021-0*, Zebra Kensgtn) Kensgtn Pub Corp.

Light in the Window, 1. Mary Roberts Rinehart. 352p. 1999. text 11.00 (*1-57566-444-5*) Kensgtn Pub Corp.

Light in the Window. large type ed. Jan Karon. LC 96-42060. (The Mitford Years Ser.: Vol. 2). (Illus.). 492p. 1996. lib. bdg. 26.95 (*1-57490-072-2*, Beeler LP Bks) T T Beeler.

***Light in Their Consciences: The Early Quakers in Britain, 1646-1666.** Rosemary A. Moore. LC 99-35185. 2000. pap. 22.50 (*0-271-01989-1*) Pa St U Pr.

***Light in Their Consciences: The Early Quakers in Britain, 1646-1666.** Rosemary A. Moore. 2000. 65.00 (*0-271-01988-3*) Pa St U Pr.

Light in Their Eyes Creating Multicultural Learning Communities. Sonia Nieto. LC 98-51677. 240p. 1999. pap. 22.95 (*0-8077-3782-8*) Tchrs Coll.

Light in Their Eyes: Creating Multicultural Learning Communities, Vol. #5. Sonia Nieto. LC 98-51677. 5. 240p. 1999. 50.00 (*0-8077-3783-6*) Tchrs Coll.

Light in Watercolor. Patricia Monahan. (Illus.). 96p. 1996. 19.95 (*0-289-80123-0*, Pub. by SVista Bks) Sterling.

Light in Watercolor. John Lidsey. (Learn to Paint Ser.). (Illus.). 1999. pap. 15.95 (*0-00-413343-9*, Pub. by HarpC) Trafalgar.

***Light in Watercolour No. 18: Step-by-Step Leisure Arts.** Jacqueline Barras. Vol. 18. 48p. 2001. pap. 10.95 (*0-85532-906-8*, Pub. by Srch Pr) Midpt Trade.

Light in Zion see Luz en Sion: Cronicas IV

Light in Zion. Bodie Thoene. LC 88-4578. (Zion Chronicles Ser.: Bk. 4). 352p. 1988. pap. 10.99 (*0-87123-990-6*) Bethany Hse.

Light in Zion. Bodie Thoene. (Zion Chronicles Ser.: Bk. 4). 368p. 1998. mass mkt. 6.99 (*0-7642-2110-8*, 202110) Bethany Hse.

Light Infantry Battalion: A Reprinting of U. S. Army Field Manual 7-72, March 1987. Ed. by Bruce A. Hanesalo. (Illus.). 140p. 1998. reprint ed. vinyl bd. 15.00 (*1-886848-37-8*) Mil-Info.

Light Infantry Company: A Reprinting of U. S. Army Field Manual 7-71, August 1987. Ed. by Bruce A. Hanesalo. (Illus.). 156p. 1998. reprint ed. vinyl bd. 15.00 (*1-886848-36-X*) Mil-Info.

Light Inside the Dark: A Guide to the Inner Journey of Spirit & Soul. John Tarrant. LC 98-17676. 272p. 1998. 25.00 (*0-06-017219-3*) HarpC.

Light Inside the Dark: Zen, Soul, & the Spiritual Life. John Tarrant. 272p. 1999. pap. 13.00 (*0-06-093111-6*) HarpC.

Light into Dawn - Randy's Miracle see Light into Dawn - Randy's Miracle

Light into Dawn - Randy's Miracle. Bethel Chang. Ed. by Jack Turner. Tr. by Catherine Chang from CHI. Orig. Title: Child of Oriental Face. 200p. 1999. pap. 5.95 (*0-9669393-0-1*) Mimosa.

Light Invisible: The Freemasonry Answer to Darkness Visible. Vindex. 94p. 1996. reprint ed. pap. 19.95 (*1-56459-997-3*) Kessinger Pub.

Light Is a Living Spirit. 2nd rev. ed. Omraam M. Aivanhov. (Izvor Collection: Vol. 212). (Illus.). 146p. 1987. pap. 7.95 (*2-85566-391-1*, Pub. by Prosveta) Prosveta USA.

Light Is Knowledge. Darwin Gross. LC 88-90608. 242p. (Orig.). 1987. pap. 30.00 (*0-931689-08-2*) Be Good To Your Self.

***Light Is Near Falling.** Margaret B. Ingraham. 40p. 2000. pap. write for info. (*0-9701464-0-X*) Windy Run Pr.

***Light Jewish Holiday Desserts.** Penny Eisenberg. LC 99-30745. (Illus.). 336p. 1999. 25.00 (*0-688-15985-0*, Wm Morrow) Morrow Avon.

Light Journey: The Adventures of Personal Witnessing. Mary L. Serratt. Ed. by Becky Nelson. 32p. (YA). (gr. 7-12). 1993. pap. text 4.95 (*1-56309-063-5*, C936103, Wrld Changers Res) Womans Mission Union.

Light Kitchen Choreography: A Collection of Lower Fat Recipes to Benefit Cleveland Ballet. Cleveland Ballet Council, Cookbook Committee Staff. Ed. by Janie McLaughlin. LC 94-71214. (Illus.). 300p. 1994. text 19.95 (*0-9609252-9-5*) Cleve Ballet Coun.

Light, Lasers & Optics. John H. Mauldin. (Illus.). 240p. 1988. 22.95 (*0-8306-9038-7*, 3038); pap. 16.95 (*0-8306-9338-6*, 3038) McGraw-Hill Prof.

Light, Lasers, & Synchrotron Radiation: A Health Risk Assessment. M. Grandolfo et al. LC 90-23013. (NATO ASI Ser.: Vol. 242). (Illus.). 436p. (C). 1991. text 156.00 (*0-306-43733-3*, Kluwer Plenum) Kluwer Academic.

Light, Lean, & Low-Fat Recipes from the Rice Council. (Favorite All Time Recipes Ser.). (Illus.). 96p. 1993. 7.98 (*1-56173-966-9*, 2013102) Pubns Intl Ltd.

Light, Life & Love: Selections from the German Mystics of the Middle Ages. William R. Inge. 285p. 1996. reprint ed. pap. 21.95 (*1-56459-608-7*) Kessinger Pub.

Light, Light, Light: Effective Use of Daylight & Electric Lighting in Residential & Commercial Spaces. 3rd rev. ed. Jane Grosslight. LC 99-158498. (Illus.). 249p. (C). 1998. pap. 44.00 (*0-927412-06-3*) Durwood Pubs.

Light List: Location & Characteristics of the Lights, Fog Signals, Buoys, Daybeacons, Lightships, Radiobeacons, & Loran Stations, Racons in United States Waters, 7 vols. 1997. lib. bdg. 4299.95 (*0-8490-8101-7*) Gordon Pr.

***Light List, 1998, Atlantic & Gulf Coasts, Little River, South Carolina to Econfina River, Florida (Includes Puerto Rico & the United States Virgin Islands), Vol. 3.** 484p. 1998. per. 41.00 (*0-16-054821-7*) USGPO.

***Light List, 1998, Mississippi River System, Vol. 5.** Government Printing Office Staff. 322p. 1998. per. 29.00 (*0-16-054774-1*) USGPO.

***Light List, 1998, Pacific Coast & Pacific Islands, Vol. 6.** 341p. 1998. per. 30.00 (*0-16-054897-7*) USGPO.

***Light List, 1999, Atlantic Coast, St. Croix River, Maine to Shrewsbury River, New Jersey.** Government Printing Office Staff. 390p. 1999. per. 35.00 (*0-16-056918-4*) USGPO.

***Light List, 1999, Atlantic & Gulf Coasts, Little River, South Carolina to Econfina River, Florida (includes Puerto Rico & the United States Virgin Islands)** Government Printing Office Staff. 495p. 1999. per. 44.00 (*0-16-056910-9*) USGPO.

***Light List, 1999, Great Lakes, United States & Canada.** Government Printing Office Staff. 252p. 1999. per. 25.00 (*0-16-056853-6*) USGPO.

***Light List, 1999, Gulf of Mexico, Econfina River, Florida to Rio Grande, Texas, Vol. 4.** Government Printing Office Staff. 400p. 1999. per. 37.00 (*0-16-056884-6*) USGPO.

***Light List, 1999, Pacific Coast & Pacific Islands, Vol. 6.** Government Printing Office Staff. 340p. 1999. per. 31.00 (*0-16-056917-6*) USGPO.

***Light List, 1999, Atlantic Coast, Shrewsbury River, New Jersey to Little River, South Carolina, Vol. 2.** Government Printing Office Staff. 374p. 1999. per. 34.00 (*0-16-056886-2*) USGPO.

Light List, 1997, Great Lakes, United States & Canada, Vol. 7. 247p. 1997. per. 22.00 (*0-16-054576-5*) USGPO.

***Light List, 2000, Great Lakes, United States & Canada, Vol. 7.** 261p. 2000. per. 24.00 (*0-16-059119-8*) USGPO.

Light Literature & Philosophy of East Asia. Don Y. Lee. LC 82-90698. 220p. (C). 1982. 36.50 (*0-939758-03-2*) Eastern Pr.

Light, Love & Life. Edwin A. Burtt. 115p. (Orig.). 1986. pap. write for info. (*0-9616132-1-1*) E A Burtt.

Light Magic: And Other Science Activities about Energy. Trudy L. Rising. (Owlet Bks.). (J). 1994. 15.15 (*0-606-06531-8*, Pub. by Turtleback) Demco.

Light Magic: And Other Science Activities about Energy. Trudy Rising & Peter Williams. (Illus.). 64p. (YA). (gr. 3-7). 1994. 16.95 (*1-895688-15-9*, Pub. by Greey dePencier) Firefly Bks Ltd.

Light Magic: And Other Science Activities about Energy. Peter Williams et al. LC 93-95371. (Illus.). 64p. (YA). (gr. 3-7). 1994. pap. 9.95 (*1-895688-16-7*, Pub. by Owl Bks) Firefly Bks Ltd.

Light Maintainer. Jack Rudman. (Career Examination Ser.: C-444). 1994. pap. 23.95 (*0-8373-0444-X*) Nat Learn.

Light-Makers. Mary O'Donnell. 193p. 1992. pap. 14.95 (*1-85371-259-0*, Pub. by Poolbeg Pr) Dufour.

Light-Makers. Mary O'Donnell. 193p. 1993. 25.00 (*1-85371-177-2*, Pub. by Poolbeg Pr) Dufour.

Light Menus. Ideals Magazine Staff. (Illus.). 64p. 1989. pap. 4.95 (*0-8249-3083-5*) Ideals.

Light Metals: Science & Technology. Ed. by C. Suryanaryana et al. 282p. (C). 1986. text 100.00 (*0-87849-538-X*, Pub. by Trans T Pub) Enfield Pubs NH.

Light Metals Monopoly. Charlotte F. Muller. LC 68-58611. (Columbia University. Studies in the Social Sciences: No. 519). reprint ed. 22.50 (*0-404-51519-3*) AMS Pr.

Light Metals, 1980: Proceedings of Technical Sessions. Metallurgical Society of AIME Staff. Ed. by Curtis J. McMinn. LC 72-623660. (Conference Proceedings - The Metallurgical Society of AIME Ser.). (Illus.). 1041p. reprint ed. pap. 200.00 (*0-8357-5542-8*, 203515600093) Bks Demand.

Light Metals, 1988: Proceedings of the Technical Sessions by the TMS Light Metals Committee at the 117th TMS Annual Meeting, Phoenix, Arizona, January 25-28, 1988. fac. ed. Metallurgical Society of AIME Staff. Ed. by Larry G. Boxall. LC 72-623660. (Illus.). 930p. 1987. reprint ed. pap. 200.00 (*0-7837-8299-3*, 204908500010) Bks Demand.

Light Metals, 1985: Proceedings of the Technical Sessions. Ed. by H. O. Bohner. LC 84-29479. (Illus.). 1543p. reprint ed. pap. 200.00 (*0-608-17838-1*, 203259900080) Bks Demand.

Light Metals, 1989: Proceedings of the Technical Sessions the TMS Light Metals Committee at the 118 TMS Annual Meeting, Las Vegas, Nevada, February 27-March 3, 1989. Minerals, Metals & Materials Society Staff. Ed. by Paul G. Campbell, Jr. LC 72-623660. (Illus.). 1065p. 1988. reprint ed. pap. 200.00 (*0-7837-9131-3*, 204993100004) Bks Demand.

Light Metals, 1981: Proceedings of the Technical Sessions Sponsored by the TMS Light Metals Committee. Metallurgical Society of AIME Staff. Ed. by Gordon M. Bell. LC 72-623660. 1072p. reprint ed. pap. 200.00 (*0-608-13486-4*, 202544800044) Bks Demand.

Light Metals, 1987: Proceedings of the Technical Sessions Sponsored by the TMS Light Metal Committee at the 116th Annual Meeting, Denver, Colorado, February 24-26, 1987. AIME, Metallurgical Society Staff. Ed. by R. D. Zabreznik. LC TN0773.A43. 900p. reprint ed. pap. 200.00 (*0-7837-2210-9*, 205246000004) Bks Demand.

Light Metals, 1986: Proceedings of the Technical Sessions, Vol. 1. Metallurgical Society of AIME Staff. Ed. by R. E. Miller. LC 85-31081. (Illus.). 1211p. reprint ed. pap. 200.00 (*0-8357-8663-3*, 205230600001) Bks Demand.

Light Metals, 1982: Proceedings of Technical Sessions Sponsored by the TMS Light Metals Committee at the 11th AIME Annual Meeting, Dallas, TX, February 14-18, 1982. Metallurgical Society of AIME Staff. Ed. by J. E. Andersen. LC 72-623660. (Illus.). 1182p. reprint ed. pap. 200.00 (*0-8357-6598-9*, 203599600097) Bks Demand.

Light Metals, 1990: Proceedings of the Technical Sessions Presented by the TMS Light Metals Committee at the 119th Annual Meeting, Anaheim, CA, February 18-22, 1990. Minerals, Metals & Materials Society Staff. LC 72-623660. (Illus.). 1063p. 1990. reprint ed. pap. 200.00 (*0-7837-9132-1*, 204993200004) Bks Demand.

Light Metals 1998. Ed. by B. Welch. (Illus.). 1450p. 1998. 196.00 (*0-87339-390-2*, 3902) Minerals Metals.

Light Metals, 1995: Proceedings of the TMS Annual Meeting (124th: 1995: Las Vegas, NV) Ed. by J. W. Evans. LC 94-74384. (Illus.). 1200p. 1995. 176.00 (*0-87339-276-0*, 2760) Minerals Metals.

Light Metals, 1994. Ed. by Ulrich Mannweiler. LC 94-75197. (Illus.). 1100p. 1994. 164.00 (*0-87339-264-7*, 2647) Minerals Metals.

***Light Metals, 1999.** Ed. by C. E. Eckert. (Illus.). 22p. 1999. 210.00 (*0-87339-425-9*, 4259) Minerals Metals.

Light Metals, 1991: Proceedings of the Technical Sessions, Presented by the TMS Light Metals Committee at the 120th TMS Annual Meeting, New Orleans, LA,

February 17-21, 1991. Minerals, Metals & Materials Society Staff. Ed. by Elwin L. Rooy. LC 90-63987. 1260p. 1990. reprint ed. pap. 200.00 (*0-608-00762-5*, 206156000010) Bks Demand.

Light Metals 1997. Ed. by R. Huglen. (Illus.). 1280p. 1997. 184.00 (*0-87339-362-7*, 3627) Minerals Metals.

Light Metals 1996. M. M. Avedesian et al. 1996. 110.00 (*0-919086-69-1*) CIM.

Light Metals, 1996: Proceedings of the Technical Sessions Presented by the TMS Light Metals Committee at the 125th TMS Annual Meeting, Anaheim, California, February 4-8, 1996. Minerals, Metals & Materials Society Staff. Ed. by Wayne E. Haley. LC 95-81873. (Illus.). 1303p. reprint ed. pap. 200.00 (*0-608-20029-8*, 207130000010) Bks Demand.

Light Metals, 1993: Proceedings of the Technical Sessions Presented by the TMS Light Metals Committee at the 122nd TMS Annual Meeting, Denver, Colorado, February 21-25, 1993. Minerals, Metals & Materials Society, Meeting (1993: Denver, CO) Staff. LC 72-623660. (Illus.). 1206p. 1992. reprint ed. pap. 200.00 (*0-608-04984-0*, 206560200004) Bks Demand.

Light Metals, 1992: Proceedings of the Technical Sessions, Presented by the TMS Light Metals Committee at the 121st TMS Annual Meeting, San Diego, CA, March 1-5, 1992. Minerals, Metals & Materials Society Staff. Ed. by Euel R. Cutshall. LC 72-623660. (Illus.). 1427p. 1991. reprint ed. pap. 200.00 (*0-7837-9130-5*, 204993000004) Bks Demand.

Light Metals, 1978 Vol. 1: Proceedings of Sessions 107th AIME Annual Meeting, Denver, Colorado. Metallurgical Society of AIME Staff. Ed. by John J. Miller. LC 78-50868. 407p. reprint ed. pap. 126.20 (*0-608-17990-6*, 205631700001) Bks Demand.

Light Metals 2000. Ed. by Ray D. Peterson. (Illus.). 940p. write for info. (*0-87339-462-3*) Minerals Metals.

Light Microscopic Techniques in Biology & Medicine. J. James. 1976. text 155.50 (*90-247-1900-3*) Kluwer Academic.

Light-Microscopical Resinography, Vol. 47. Theodore G. Rochow. LC 83-61635. (Illus.). 1983. 30.00 (*0-904962-10-5*) Microscope Pubns.

Light Microscopy. Abramoff. Date not set. 1.50 (*0-7167-9082-3*) W H Freeman.

Light Microscopy: Essential Data. C. Rubbi. LC 94-9543. (Essential Data Ser.). 128p. 1994. pap. 43.95 (*0-471-94270-7*) Wiley.

Light Microscopy in Biology: A Practical Approach. 2nd ed. Alan J. Lacey. (The Practical Approach Ser.: No. 195). (Illus.). 474p. 1999. pap. text 60.00 (*0-19-963669-9*) OUP.

***Light Microscopy in Biology: A Practical Approach.** 2nd ed. Alan J. Lacey. LC 99-461881. (The Practical Approach Ser.: No. 195). (Illus.). 474p. 1999. text 120.00 (*0-19-963670-2*) OUP.

Light Microscopy of Carbon & Low Alloy Steels. Leonard E. Samuels. LC 99-14028. 500p. (C). 1998. 178.00 (*0-87170-655-5*, 6656) ASM.

Light Moving in Time: Studies in the Visual Aesthetics of Avant-Garde Film. William C. Wees. 1992. pap. 17.95 (*0-520-07368-1*, Pub. by U CA Pr) Cal Prin Full Svc.

Light Muffins: 60 Recipes for Sweet & Savory Low-Fat Muffins & Spreads. Beatrice A. Ojakangas. LC 94-42664. 96p. 1995. 12.00 (*0-517-70066-2*) C Potter.

Light My Fire. James Dillon. (My Private Eye Ser.). 150p. (Orig.). 1984. pap. 6.95 (*0-915153-08-4*) Gold Star Pr.

Light My Fire: My Life with the Doors. Ray Manzarek. 1999. reprint ed. pap. 14.95 (*0-425-17045-4*) Berkley Pub.

Light 'n Bright Piano Book. 16p. (YA). 1985. pap. 5.00 (*0-7692-0389-2*, SCHBK09964) Wrner Bros.

Light of All Nations Vol. 3: Essays on the Church in New Testament Research. Daniel J. Harrington. 204p. 1989. pap. 24.00 (*0-89453-291-X*, Pub. by Veritas Pubns) St Mut.

Light of All Stars Illuminates the Way. Hua-Ching Ni. (Self-Development Ser.). 56p. (Orig.). 1994. pap. 4.00 (*0-937064-80-7*) SevenStar Comm.

Light of Asia. Edwin Arnold. 1997. pap. 7.95 (*81-7059-136-8*, 7603, Quest) Theos Pub Hse.

Light of Asia. Edwin Arnold. 239p. 1995. reprint ed. pap. 19.95 (*1-56459-496-3*) Kessinger Pub.

***Light of Asia: Being the Life & Teaching of Guatama, Prince of India & founder of Buddhism, 3.** Edwin Arnold. LC 99-80174. 208p. 2000. write for info. (*1-893766-13-6*) Aeon Pub Co.

Light of Asia: The Life & Teaching of Gautama Buddha. Edwin Arnold. xi, 238p. 1977. 6.00 (*0-938998-17-X*) Theosophy.

Light of China: Selections. Lao-tzu. 1972. lib. bdg. 250.00 (*0-87968-534-4*) Krishna Pr.

Light of Christ: Iconography of Gregory Kroug. Andrew Tregubov. 52p. 1990. pap. 24.95 (*0-88141-096-9*) St Vladimirs.

Light of Consciousness: Explorations in Transpersonal Psychology. Richard D. Mann. LC 83-18088. 177p. (C). 1984. pap. text 14.95 (*0-87395-906-X*) State U NY Pr.

Light of Dawn: A Daybook of Verses from the Holy Qur'an. Selected by Camille A. Helminski. LC 98-9900. 256p. 1999. 24.95 (*0-939660-60-1*) Threshold CA.

Light of Day. Eric Ambler. 224p. 1992. pap. 3.95 (*0-88184-836-0*) Carroll & Graf.

Light of Day. Eric Ambler. 215p. reprint ed. lib. bdg. 21.95 (*0-89190-464-6*, Rivercity Pr) Amereon Ltd.

Light of Discovery. Toni Packer. LC 95-23229. 160p. 1995. 17.95 (*0-8048-3063-0*) Tuttle Pubng.

Light of Discovery. Toni Packer. 1999. pap. 12.95 (*0-8048-3196-3*) Tuttle Pubng.

Light of Early Italian Painting. Paul Hills. 168p. (C). 1990. reprint ed. pap. 20.00 (*0-300-04698-7*) Yale U Pr.

Light of Egypt: The Science of the Soul & the Stars, 2 vols. Thomas H. Burgoyne. 114p. 1980. pap. 34.00 (*0-89540-125-8*, SB-125) Sun Pub.

Light of Egypt: or The Science of the Soul & the Stars, 2 vols. Thomas H. Burgoyne. (Illus.). 600p. 1980. pap. 34.00 (*0-89540-064-2*, SB-064, Sun Bks) Sun Pub.

Light of Exploration. R. P. Kaushik. LC 76-39622. 1977. 8.95 (*0-918038-01-4*); pap. 5.95 (*0-918038-00-6*) Journey Pubns.

Light of Faith: The Compendium of Theology. Aquinas, Thomas, Saint. LC 93-6793. 428p. 1998. reprint ed. pap. 22.95 (*0-918477-67-0*) Sophia Inst Pr.

Light of Falling Stars. J. Robert Lennon. LC 97-10972. 307p. 1998. reprint ed. pap. 13.00 (*1-57322-682-3*, Riverhd Trade) Berkley Pub.

Light of Glory: Readings from John Donne for Lent & Easter Week. Christopher Webber. LC 97-34867. 128p. 1998. pap. 9.95 (*0-8192-1725-5*) Morehouse Pub.

Light of His Coming. 1997. pap. 6.99 (*1-85078-204-0*, Pub. by Sheffield Acad) CUP Services.

Light of Home. R. C. Binstock. 176p. 1992. text 19.00 (*0-689-12156-3*) Atheneum Yung Read.

***Light of Ireland.** 2000th ed. Photos by Ron Rosenstock. (Illus.). 64p. 2000. 45.00 (*0-615-11218-8*) Silver Strand.

Light of Kirpal. Kirpal Singh. LC 80-52537. xv, 446p. 1984. pap. 15.00 (*0-89142-033-9*) Sant Bani Ash.

Light of Knowledge: Essays on the Interplay of Knowledge, Time, & Space. Jack Petranker. LC 97-24726. (Perspectives on TSK Ser.). 1997. pap. 16.95 (*0-89800-287-7*) Dharma Pub.

Light of Krishnamurti. Gabriele Blackburn. LC 96-94645. (Illus.). 256p. 1996. pap. 14.00 (*0-9613054-4-4*) Idylwild Bks.

Light of Learning. Robert R. Leichtman. 188p. 1999. pap. text 13.95 (*0-89804-170-8*) Ariel Prods.

Light of Learning No. 62: Selected Essays of Morton W. Bloomfield. Ed. by Elizabeth Walsh & Susie M. Barrett. XVIII, 348p. (C). 1993. text 62.95 (*0-8204-1766-1*) P Lang Pubng.

Light of Liberation: A History of Buddhism in India. Tarthang Tulku. LC 92-16436. (Crystal Mirror Ser.: Vol. 8). (Illus.). 500p. (Orig.). (C). 1992. pap. 25.00 (*0-89800-242-7*) Dharma Pub.

Light of Liberty. Paul H. Dunn. LC 98-25166. 2000. 19.95 (*1-882723-32-5*) Gold Leaf Pr.

Light of Life. Jeff Lahr. LC 97-191592. 48p. 1997. pap. 3.49 (*0-87227-194-3*, RBP5234) Reg Baptist.

Light of Life: The Mastery of Death. Delmar D. Bryant. 165p. 1996. reprint ed. spiral bd. 13.50 (*0-7873-0126-4*) Hlth Research.

Light of Life: The Ohrhachayim on the Torah. C. Richman. (Adaptation of the Ohrhachayim Ser.: Vol. 1). (HEB.). 320p. 1995. 19.95 (*1-888234-00-8*) Rachav Commun.

Light of Life in the Spirit of Man. Charles Capps. (Orig.). 1987. pap. 4.99 (*0-89274-470-7*, HH-470) Harrison Hse.

Light of Life or the Mastery of Death (1911) Delmar D. Bryant. 170p. 1996. reprint ed. pap. 12.95 (*1-56459-921-3*) Kessinger Pub.

***Light of Life's Darkened Steps: The Dysfunctional Family - God's Therapeudic Plan.** Dennis Walter Smith. 75p. 2000. pap. 10.95 (*0-7414-0371-4*) Buy Books.

Light of Love: My Angel Shall Go Before Thee. Patricia Devlin. LC 95-68111. 382p. (Orig.). 1994. pap. 8.75 (*1-882972-53-8*, 3401) Queenship Pub.

Light of Lucinda. Sherry Lazarus Ross. (Illus.). 253p. (J). (gr. 2-6). Date not set. pap. write for info. (*0-615-11146-7*) WellFire Pubns.

Light of Memory. Marcello Fabbri. Tr. by Jeanne R. Bonaca from ITA. 73p. (Orig.). 1994. pap. text 11.95 (*0-9631200-4-2*) OlivePr CT.

Light of My Heart. Kathleen Karr. (Serenade Saga Ser.: No. 9). 192p. (Orig.). 1984. pap. 2.50 (*0-310-46592-3*, 15518P) Zondervan.

***Light of My Life.** Donna Marie Elizabeth Howard. 1999. pap. 12.95 (*1-929937-00-8*) D Howard.

Light of Nature. Ed. by Roche North. 1985. lib. bdg. 247.50 (*90-247-3165-8*) Kluwer Academic.

***Light of Other Days.** Arthur C. Clarke & Stephen Baxter. 320p. 1999. mass mkt. 7.99 (*0-8125-7640-3*) Tor Bks.

***Light of Other Days.** Arthur C. Clarke & Stephen Baxter. LC 99-89761. 320p. 2000. 24.95 (*0-312-87199-6*, Pub. by Tor Bks) St Martin.

Light of Other Days. Caroline C. Lovell. LC 95-20858. 183p. 1995. 25.00 (*0-86554-465-4*, MUP/H366) Mercer Univ Pr.

Light of Other Days: A Dublin Childhood. Pauline Bracken. (Illus.). 144p. 1998. pap. 10.95 (*1-85635-032-0*, Pub. by Mercier Pr) Irish Amer Bk.

Light of Other Days: The First Twenty Years of the Center for Research on Vermont. George B. Bryan. (Occasional Papers: No. 18). (Illus.). 108p. 1995. pap. text 8.50 (*0-944277-33-0*) U VT Ctr Rsch VT.

Light of Qabalah on the Unknown Secret of the Bible. Ruth Borchard-Berendsohn. LC 96-71338. 1997. pap. 20.00 (*0-88400-197-0*, Shengold Bks) Schreiber Pub.

Light of Saxina in Suhranudi's Philosophy of Illusion. Nosrallah Pourjavady. 1998. pap. 4.00 (*1-883058-99-6*) Global Pubns.

Light of Superconsciousness: How to Benefit from Emerging Spiritual Trends. J. Donald Walters. Ed. by Devi Novak. LC 99-36570. 1999. pap. 12.95 (*1-56589-748-X*) Crystal Clarity.

Light of Ten Thousand Suns. Veda Bharati. (Illus.). 160p. 1998. pap. 15.00 (*0-936663-20-0*) Yes Intl.

Light of the Ages Recently Written by Ancient Immortals & the Death Blow to Poverty. Minerva Merrick. 304p. 1998. reprint ed. pap. 24.95 (*0-7661-0639-X*) Kessinger Pub.

Light of the Bhagavata. A. C. Prabhupada. (Illus.). 147p. 1997. reprint ed. 7.95 (*91-7149-267-4*) Bhaktivedanta.

Light of the Bhagawata: A Presentation of the Source of Oriental Philosophy. A. Bhaktivedanta Swami. (Illus.). 154p. 1984. 12.95 (*0-945475-24-1*, 1022C, Pub. by Mandala Pub Grp); pap. 9.95 (*0-945475-38-1*, 1022L, Pub. by Mandala Pub Grp) Words Distrib.

Light of the Dance Is the Music of Eternity: Poems. Hugo Walter. LC 93-13137. 80p. (Orig.). 1993. pap. 8.95 (*1-56474-061-7*) Fithian Pr.

Light of the East: Orientale Lumen. John Paul, II, pseud. 64p. 1995. pap. 3.50 (*0-8198-4478-0*) Pauline Bks.

Light of the East: Orientale Lumen. John Paul, II, pseud. Tr. by Vatican Staff. 54p. 1995. pap. 5.95 (*1-57455-021-7*) US Catholic.

***Light of the Eyes.** Azariah B. Moses de Rossi & Joanna Weinberg. LC 99-55976. (Judaica Ser.: Vol. 31). (Illus.). 640p. 2000. 75.00 (*0-300-07906-0*) Yale U Pr.

Light of the Guru: The Celebration of Guru Purnima. Intro. by Swami Durgananda. 56p. (Orig.). 1994. pap. 4.75 (*0-911307-32-X*) SYDA Found.

Light of the Home. Green. 1984. 12.95 (*0-07-544318-X*) McGraw.

Light of the Home: An Intimate View of the Lives of Women in Victorian America. Harvey Green & Mary E. Perry. LC 82-18867. (Illus.). 256p. 1984. pap. 11.16 (*0-394-71329-X*) Pantheon.

Light of the Human Face. Kyra June. (Illus.). 68p. 1995. 50.00 (*1-880515-54-7*) Schl Mus Fine.

Light of the Light. Brooks Roddan. 10p. 1987. pap. 12.00 (*0-944034-00-4*) Blue Earth.

Light of the Living, Set, Vols. 1 & 2. Wilford H. Moore. 256p. pap. 10.95 (*0-9644872-0-9*) W H Moore.

Light of the Mind: St. Augustine's Theory of Knowledge. Ronald H. Nash. LC 69-19765. 159p. reprint ed. 49.30 (*0-8357-9790-2*, 201609900098) Bks Demand.

Light of the Morning: A Story of Beginning. Elaine Stienon. 240p. (Orig.). 1988. pap. 8.50 (*0-929328-00-0*) Ensign Pub Hse.

Light of the Night see Light of the Night: The Last Eighteen Months in the Life of Therese of Lisieux

Light of the Night: The Eighteen Months in the Life of Therese of Lisieux. Jean-Francois Six. (Illus.). 1997. pap. 26.00 (*0-334-02658-X*) TPI PA.

Light of the Night: The Last Eighteen Months in the Life of Therese of Lisieux. Jean-Francois Six. Tr. by John Bowden. LC 98-9906. Orig. Title: Lumiere de la Nuit les 18 Derniers Mois de Therese de Lisieux. 1998. pap. 18.00 (*0-268-01321-7*) U of Notre Dame Pr.

Light of the Pentecost: A Unique Historical Account of the New Testament Church. David A. Huston. (Illus.). (YA). (gr. 7 up). 1989. pap. 5.95 (*0-932345-03-4*) Antioch Publishes.

Light of the Prophet. Ahmad Nawaz. LC 98-70771. xiv, 105p. 1998. pap. 10.00 (*1-58225-026-X*) Ananta Prakashani.

***Light of the Prophet.** Ahmad Nawaz. LC 00-131824. 105p. 2000. pap. 10.00 (*1-58225-226-2*) Ananta Prakashani.

Light of the Soul. Alice A. Bailey. 1927. 35.00 (*0-85330-012-7*) Lucis.

Light of the Soul. Alice A. Bailey. 1972. pap. 14.00 (*0-85330-112-3*) Lucis.

Light of the Spirit: An Introductory Guide. Mary Bassano. LC 96-13474. 128p. (Orig.). 1996. pap. 9.95 (*0-87728-871-2*) Weiser.

Light of the Spirit: Portraits of Southern Outsider Artists. Robert Peacock. LC 98-6663. (Illus.). 120p. 1998. 60.00 (*1-57806-025-7*); pap. 35.00 (*1-57806-015-X*) U Pr of Miss.

Light of the Star. 1995. pap. 1.30 (*0-8341-9388-4*, AN-3914) Lillenas.

Light of the Star see Collected Works of Hamlin Garland

Light of the Star. Hamlin Garland. (Collected Works of Hamlin Garland). 1988. reprint ed. lib. bdg. 59.00 (*0-7812-1233-2*) Rprt Serv.

Light of the Tittle. G. W. Lewis. LC 99-191429. 285p. 1998. write for info. (*0-9657415-8-3*) Blue Planet Pubns.

Light of the Torah see Or Hatorah Bamidbar Volz

Light of the Vedas. Manly P. Hall. (Adepts Ser.). pap. 9.95 (*0-89314-530-0*) Philos Res.

Light of the Word: Brief Reflections on the Sunday Readings. Hans U. Von Balthasar. LC 93-78538. 360p. 1993. 19.95 (*0-89870-458-8*) Ignatius Pr.

Light of the World. Jan Van Rijckenborgh.Tr. of Met Light der Wereld. 74p. (Orig.). 1986. pap. 9.50 (*90-70196-69-7*) Rosycross Pr.

Light of the World. Serge S. Verhovskoy. LC 82-16963. 163p. 1982. pap. 9.95 (*0-88141-004-7*) St Vladimirs.

Light of the World: Aura of the Lord Jesus Christ. Josephine C. Trust. 48p. 1938. reprint ed. pap. 3.00 (*1-892203-22-7*, 20, Superet Pr) Mother Trust.

Light of the World: The Story of the Nativity, Bk. 2. Gerald McDermott. LC 97-41484. (J). 1999. 17.00 (*0-689-80707-4*) S&S Childrens.

Light of Torah - Bamidbar see Ohr Hatoran Bamidbar

Light of Touch: Select Works on Paper from the Permanent Collection. Estill C. Pennington. (Illus.). 1993. 19.95 (*0-9638753-0-2*) Morris Mus Art.

Light of Truth. D. Saraswati. 733p. 1994. 16.95 (*0-318-37146-4*) Asia Bk Corp.

Light of Truth & Fire of Love: A Theology of the Holy Spirit. Gary D. Badcock. LC 96-53941. 296p. 1997. pap. 25.00 (*0-8028-4288-7*) Eerdmans.

Light of Truth: or An English Translation of the Satyarth Prakash. Swami D. Saraswati. vi, 732p. 1994. 16.00 (*0-614-00505-1*, Pub. by Sarvadeshik Arya) Nataraj Bks.

Light of Western Stars. Zane Grey. 1976. 27.95 (*0-8488-1024-4*) Amereon Ltd.

Light of Western Stars. Zane Grey. 1995. mass mkt. 4.99 (*0-671-52647-2*, Pocket Books) PB.

Light of Yoga. Alice Christensen. (Illus.). 83p. 3.95 (*0-318-14774-2*) Am Yoga Assn.

Light of Yoga Society Beginner's Manual. Alice Christensen & David Rankin. (Illus.). 64p. 1974. pap. 7.95 (*0-671-21831-X*, Fireside) S&S Trade Pap.

Light of Yoga Society Beginners Manual. Alice Christensen & David Rankin. (Illus.). 62p. 1972. pap. 7.95 (*0-317-01148-0*) Am Yoga Assn.

Light og the Soul: Theories of Ideas in Leibniz, Malebranche, & Descartes. Nicholas Jolley. 220p. 1998. reprint ed. pap. text 19.95 (*0-19-823819-3*) OUP.

Light on a Gray Area: American Public Policy on Aging. Stephen Sapp. 256p. (Orig.). 1992. pap. 16.95 (*0-687-38310-2*) Abingdon.

Light on a Mountain. Helena E. Ruhnau. LC 87-8397. (Illus.). 1976. 13.95 (*0-941036-00-6*); pap. 6.95 (*0-941036-01-4*) Colleasius Pr.

Light on Aging & Dying: Wise Words Selected by Helen Nearing. Helen Nearing. LC 97-20613. 1998. pap. 10.00 (*0-15-600496-8*, Harvest Bks) Harcourt.

Light on Aging & Dying: Wise Words Selected by Helen Nearing. large type ed. Ed. by Helen Nearing. LC 97-16327. (Inspirational Ser.). 125p. 1997. lib. bdg. 22.95 (*0-7838-8222-X*, G K Hall Lrg Type) Mac Lib Ref.

Light on Aging & Dying: Wise Words Selected by Helen Nearing. Helen Nearing. 153p. 1998. reprint ed. write for info. (*0-614-30103-3*, Harvest Bks) Harcourt.

Light on Chantry Island. Mary Weeks-Mifflin & Ray Mifflin. (Illus.). 60p. (Orig.). 1991. pap. 9.00 (*0-919783-45-7*, Pub. by Boston Mills) Genl Dist Srvs.

Light on Dark Matter. Ed. by F. P. Israel. 1986. text 248.00 (*90-277-2254-4*) Kluwer Academic.

Light on Dumyat. McOwan. 1996. pap. text 9.00 (*0-7152-0697-4*, Pub. by St Andrew) St Mut.

Light on Dumyat. Rennie McOwan. 152p. (C). 1992. pap. 32.00 (*0-7855-7006-3*, Pub. by St Andrew) St Mut.

Light on Dumyat. Rennie McOwan. 152p. 1993. pap. 22.00 (*0-7152-0544-7*, Pub. by St Andrew) St Mut.

Light on Enlightenment: Revolutionary Teachings on the Inner Life. Christopher Titmuss. LC 99-34790. 240p. 2000. pap. 13.95 (*1-57062-514-X*, Pub. by Shambhala Pubns) Random.

Light on Her Face. Joseph Walker & Juanita Walker. LC 84-72399. 300p. 1984. 19.95 (*0-935578-05-6*) ASC Holding.

Light on Hogback Hill. Cynthia DeFelice. LC 93-3507. 128p. (J). (gr. 3-7). 1993. mass mkt. 14.00 (*0-02-726453-X*, Mac Bks Young Read) S&S Childrens.

Light on Hogback Hill. Cynthia DeFelice. (J). 1995. 9.60 (*0-606-07788-X*) Turtleback.

Light on Hogback Hill. Cynthia DeFelice. 144p. (J). (gr. 3-7). 1995. reprint ed. mass mkt. 4.50 (*0-380-72395-6*, Avon Bks) Morrow Avon.

Light on Illancrone. Sean McMahon. 114p. 1990. pap. 7.95 (*1-85371-083-0*, Pub. by Poolbeg Pr) Dufour.

Light on Life: An Introduction to the Astrology of India. Hart Defouw & Robert Svoboda. LC 96-904741. 480p. 1996. pap. 14.95 (*0-14-019507-6*, Penguin Bks) Viking Penguin.

Light on Life's Difficulties. James Allen. 137p. 1992. pap. 14.00 (*0-89540-217-3*, SB-217) Sun Pub.

Light on Little Mormon Lake. Peter Wild. 32p. (Orig.). 1984. pap. 5.00 (*0-912449-10-1*) Floating Island.

Light on Masonry. David Bernard. 560p. 1993. reprint ed. pap. 33.00 (*1-56459-361-4*) Kessinger Pub.

Light on Meditation. Dhyanyogi M. Shri. (Illus.). 186p. (Orig.). 1978. pap. 9.00 (*1-883879-00-0*) Dhyanyoga Ctr.

Light on Pranayama. B. K. Iyengar. 200p. 1985. pap. text 19.95 (*0-8245-0686-3*) Crossroad NY.

Light on Quest Mountain. M. Kirchoff & J. M. Ward. 1983. 2.00 (*0-394-53584-7*) Random.

***Light on Relationships: The Synastry of Indian Astrology.** Hart De Fouw & Robert Edwin Svoboda. LC 00-29010. (Illus.). 288p. 2000. pap. 18.95 (*1-57863-148-3*) Weiser.

Light on the Ancient Worlds. 2nd ed. Frithjof Schuon. LC 83-51688. (Library of Traditional Wisdom). 144p. 1984. pap. 8.95 (*0-941532-03-8*) Wrld Wisdom Bks.

Light on the Dark Side of God. M. M. Campbell. 120p. (Orig.). 1989. pap. 6.95 (*0-927022-00-1*) CHJ Pub.

Light on the Eternal City: Observations & Discoveries in the Art & Architecture of Rome. Ed. by Hellmut Hager & Susan S. Munshower. LC 86-43122. (Papers in Art History: Vol. II). (Illus.). 340p. (Orig.). 1987. pap. 20.00 (*0-915773-01-5*) Penn St Univ Dept Art Hist.

Light on the Hill: A History of the University of North Carolina at Chapel Hill. William D. Snider. LC 91-50789. (Illus.). xviii, 370p. (C). 1992. 34.95 (*0-8078-2023-7*) U of NC Pr.

Light on the Hill: A Pictorial History of Alderson-Broaddus College. Richard Withers & Martha R. Roy. LC 95-39378. 1996. write for info. (*0-89865-959-0*) Donning Co.

Light on the Hill: Tampa United Methodist Centers in the Modern Era. Harry Rissetto. (Illus.). 152p. 1998. pap. 9.95 (*0-9672198-0-9*) Tampa Untd Meth.

Light on the Hill: The Australian Labor Party, 1891-1991. Ross McMullin. (Illus.). 560p. 1991. 45.00 (*0-19-554966-X*) OUP.

Light on the Horizon: A Deeper View from Inside the Autism Puzzle. Thomas A. McKean. 95p. (Orig.). 1996. pap. 19.95 (*1-885477-26-0*) Fut Horizons.

***Light on the Horizon: The Joy & Challenge of Real Ideas.** Kelly R. Nicholson. 196p. 1999. pap. 19.95 (*0-9668911-0-4*, Pub. by Homeward Bnd) ACCESS Pubs Network.

Light on the Internet. Wendy G. Lehnert. LC 97-34600. 513p. (C). 1997. pap. text 51.00 (*0-201-32553-5*) Addison-Wesley.

***Light on the Internet.** Wendy G. Lehnert. LC 98-52395. (Illus.). 249p. (C). 1999. pap. 25.00 (*0-201-61266-6*) Addison-Wesley.

An Asterisk (*) at the beginning of an entry indicates that the title is appearing for the first time.

Light on the Land. Art Wolfe. Ed. by Art Davidson. LC 91-25747. (Earthsong Collection). (Illus.). 192p. 1991. 75.00 (0-941831-65-5) Beyond Words Pub.

Light on the Land, Author's Ed. Photos by Art Wolfe. (EarthSong Collection). (Illus.). 156p. 1993. 95.00 (0-614-19290-0) Beyond Words Pub.

Light on the Path. Mabel Collins. 1986. 5.95 (81-7059-011-6, 7183, Quest) Theos Pub Hse.

Light on the Path. Osho. (Talks in the Himalayas Ser.). 416p. 1988. 24.95 (3-89338-030-2, Pub. by Rebel Hse) Oshos.

Light on the Path. Mabel Collins. 46p. 1997. reprint ed. pap. 9.95 (0-7661-0068-5) Kessinger Pub.

Light on the Path. Mabel C. Collins. reprint ed. pap. 5.00 (0-911662-13-8) Yoga.

Light on the Path. 3rd ed. Swami Muktananda. LC 98-14242. 112p. 1994. pap. 8.95 (0-911307-70-2) SYDA Found.

Light on the Path. 4th ed. Mabel Collins. 28p. 1993. reprint ed. spiral bd. 8.00 (0-7873-0193-0) Hlth Research.

Light on the Path: And an Essay on Karma. Mabel Collins. 1999. 2.95 (81-7059-194-5) Theos Pub Hse.

Light on the Path: Proverbs for Growing Wise. Linda J. Sattgast. LC 96-150002. (Illus.). 120p. (J). 1996. 9.99 (0-88070-913-8, Gold n Honey) Zondervan.

Light on the Path & Through the Gates of Gold, 2 vols. in 1. Mabel Collins. 1976. 16.95 (0-911500-37-5) Theos U Pr.

Light on the Path & Through the Gates of Gold, 2 vols. in 1. Mabel Collins. 1977. pap. 10.95 (0-911500-38-3) Theos U Pr.

Light on the Seaway. Ethel Williamson. (Great Lakes Marine History Ser.). (Illus.). 132p. pap. 7.95 (0-919549-20-9, Pub. by RivT) Partners Pubs Grp.

Light on the Subject: Stage Lighting for Directors & Actors - & the Rest of Us. David Hays. LC 89-12491. (Illus.). 176p. (Orig.). 1989. pap. 10.95 (0-87910-126-1) Limelight Edns.

Light on the Tent Wall: A Bridging. Mary TallMountain. Ed. by Kenneth Lincoln. LC 90-80994. (Native American Literature Ser.). (Illus.). 95p. (Orig.). 1990. pap. 12.00 (0-935626-34-4) U Cal AISC.

Light on the Water. Keith McLaren. 160p. 1998. 35.00 (1-55054-658-9) DGL.

Light on the Water: Early Photography of Coastal British Columbia. Keith Mclaren. LC 98-25896. (Illus.). 160p. 1998. 35.00 (0-295-97748-5) U of Wash Pr.

Light on Yoga. B. K. Iyengar. 1995. pap. 18.00 (0-8052-1031-8) Schocken.

***Light on Your Path: True Stories & Scriptures.** Mary Ellen Beachy. 237p. (YA). (gr. 2-12). 1999. pap. 10.95 (1-890050-35-0) Carlisle Press.

Light One Candle: A Guidebook for the Bootstrapping. Michael Richards. 140p. 1998. pap. 9.95 (1-891594-00-1) Innovat Press.

Light One Candle: A Survivor's Tale, from Lithuania to Jerusalem. Solly Ganor. Ed. by Philip Turner. 352p. 1995. 25.00 (1-56836-098-3) Kodansha.

Light One Candle: Quotes for Hope & Action. Ed. by Wayne Meisel & Maura Wolf. (Gift Editions Ser.). (Illus.). 64p. 1991. 7.99 (0-88088-357-X) Peter Pauper.

Light over Ancient Angkor. Tr. by Kazuko Scott & Dale Scott. (Illus.). 108p. 1996. pap. 40.00 (0-9653574-0-6) Frnds Without Border.

Light over Ancient Angkor. Tr. by Kazuko Scott & Dale Scott. (ENG & JPN., Illus.). 108p. 1997. 50.00 (0-9653574-2-2) Frnds Without Border.

Light over Ancient Angkor. 2nd ed. Tr. by Kazuko Scott & Dale Scott. (ENG & JPN., Illus.). 108p. 1997. pap. 40.00 (0-9653574-1-4) Frnds Without Border.

Light over the Scaffold & Cell 18: The Prison Letters of Jacques Fesch. Jacques Fesch. Ed. by Augustin-Michel Lemonnier. Tr. by Mary T. Noble. Orig. Title: L. (FRE.). 256p. (Orig.). 1996. pap. 12.95 (0-8189-0750-9) Alba.

Light Pasta Sauces. Maggie Ramsay. (Illus.). 64p. 1999. 17.50 (0-8478-2188-9) Rizzoli Intl.

Light Paths. Howard V. Hendrix. 352p. 1997. mass mkt. 5.99 (0-441-11470-9) Ace Bks.

Light People: A Novel. Gordon Henry, Jr. LC 93-32144. (American Indian Literature & Critical Studies: Vol. 7). 272p. 1995. pap. 13.95 (0-8061-2735-X) U of Okla Pr.

Light Place. Lemieux. (Fairy Lair Ser.: No. 3). (J). 1998. pap. 16.00 (0-689-81874-2) S&S Childrens.

Light Plane Construction. Ladislao Pazmany. (Illus.). 22.00 (0-614-13172-3, 21-37840) EAA Aviation.

Light Pollution, Radio Interference, & Space Debris. Ed. by D. Crawford. (ASP Conference Series Proceedings: Vol. 17). 331p. 1991. 34.00 (0-937707-36-8) Astron Soc Pacific.

Light Possessed: A Novel. Alan Cheuse. LC 98-12774. 336p. 1998. reprint ed. pap. 12.95 (0-87074-430-5) SMU Press.

Light Princess. George MacDonald. LC 86-33636. (Illus.). 44p. (J). (ps up). 1988. 13.95 (0-15-245300-8, Harcourt Child Bks) Harcourt.

Light Princess. George MacDonald. 110p. (J). (gr. 4-5). pap. 5.95 (0-8072-1396-9) Listening Lib.

Light Princess. rev. ed. George MacDonald. LC 69-14981. (Illus.). 120p. (J). (gr. 4-7). 1969. 15.00 (0-374-34455-8) FS&G.

Light Princess. rev. ed. George MacDonald. LC 69-14981. (Illus.). 120p. (J). (gr. 4-7). 1984. pap. 5.95 (0-374-44458-7) FS&G.

Light Princess & Other Fairy Tales. George MacDonald. (George MacDonald Original Works Ser.: Series III). (Illus.). 305p. (YA). (gr. 5 up). 1997. reprint ed. 22.00 (1-881084-16-7) Johannesen.

Light Princess & Other Fantasy Stories. George MacDonald. Ed. by George G. Sadler. 176p. 1980. pap. 7.00 (0-8028-1861-7) Eerdmans.

Light Propagation & Light Shifts in Optical Pumping Experiments see Progress in Quantum Electronics

Light Pulse Compression. W. Rudolph & B. Wilhelmi. Ed. by V. S. Letokhov. (Laser Science & Technology Ser.: Vol. 3). viii, 132p. 1989. pap. text 162.00 (3-7186-4888-1) Gordon & Breach.

Light, Radiation & You: How to Stay Healthy. John N. Ott. LC 81-69951. (Illus.). 175p. 1990. pap. 11.95 (0-8159-6121-9) Devin.

Light Rail in Denver: Taking the Taxpayers for a Ride. Stephen R. Mueller & Dennis Polhill. (Issue Paper #4-97 Ser.). 17p. 1997. pap. text 8.00 (1-57655-156-3) Independ Inst.

Light Rail Transit. (Special Reports: No. 161). 173p. 1975. 8.00 (0-309-02370-X, SR161) Transport Res Bd.

Light Rail Transit: Planning & Technology. (Special Reports: No. 182). 172p. 1978. 12.00 (0-309-02802-7, SR182) Transport Res Bd.

Light Rail Transit: Planning, Design, & Implementation. (Special Reports: No. 195). 175p. 1982. 22.00 (0-309-03403-5, SR195) Transport Res Bd.

Light Rail Transit: Planning, Design, & Operating Experience: Papers Presented at the Sixth National Conference. LC 92-27243. (Transportation Research Record Ser.: No. 1361). 359p. 1992. 54.00 (0-309-05400-1) Transport Res Bd.

Light Rail Transit: System Design for Cost Effectiveness. (State of the Art Reports: No. 02). 240p. 1985. 15.00 (0-309-03917-7) Transport Res Bd.

Light Rail Transit on the West Coast. Harre Demoro & John Harder. 1989. pap. 13.95 (0-915276-49-6) Quadrant Pr.

Light Rays: James Joyce & Modernism. Ed. by Heyward Ehrlich. 1984. 15.95 (0-88282-302-7) New Horizon NJ.

Light Reaction Path of Photosynthesis. Ed. by F. K. Fong. (Molecular Biology, Biochemistry & Biophysics Ser.: Vol. 35). (Illus.). 350p. 1982. 127.95 (0-387-11379-7) Spr-Verlag.

Light Reading from Alaska. Extry Sarff. LC 98-199561. 63p. 1998. write for info. (0-9662515-0-4) Extry R Sarff.

Light Reading of Our Ancestors. Rowland E. Ernle. LC 73-124234. (Select Bibliographies Reprint Ser.). 1977. 19.95 (0-8369-5422-X) Ayer.

Light Reflected: A Four Petal Trillium. Donald Cook. (Illus.). 7p. 1999. ring bd. 54.90 (0-9614887-4-3) DRC Graphics Serv.

Light Reflections. Alma Barkman. (Quiet Time Books for Women). pap. 4.99 (0-8024-4787-2, 412) Moody.

Light Revealing Architecture. Marietta S. Millet. (Architecture Ser.). (Illus.). 272p. 1995. text 59.95 (0-442-01887-8, VNR) Wiley.

Light Revealing Architecture. Marietta S. Millet. (Architecture Ser.). 183p. 1996. 75.00 (0-471-28644-3, VNR) Wiley.

Light Runner. Karen Randlev. (New Alaskan Poets Ser.). 128p. 1987. pap. 5.95 (0-914221-08-6) Fireweed Pr AK.

Light Salads. (Popular Brands Cookbooks Ser.). (Illus.). 24p. 1997. pap. write for info. (0-7666-0089-0, Honey Bear Bks) Modern Pub NYC.

Light Sauces: Delicious Low-Calorie, Low-Fat, Low-Cholesterol Recipes. Barry Bluestein & Kevin Morrissey. 112p. (Orig.). 1991. pap. 9.95 (0-8092-4063-7) NTC Contemp Pub Co.

Light Scattering: Principles & Development. Ed. by Wyn Brown. LC 95-45401. (Monographs on the Physics & Chemistry of Materials). (Illus.). 544p. (C). 1996. text 175.00 (0-19-851783-1, Clarendon Pr) OUP.

Light Scattering & Photon Correlation Spectroscopy: Proceedings of the NATO Advanced Research Workshop, Krakow, Poland, August 26-30, 1996. Ed. by E. R. Pike & J. B. Abbiss. LC 97-33973. (NATO ASI Ser.). 488p. 1997. text 251.00 (0-7923-4736-6) Kluwer Academic.

Light Scattering by Irregularly Shaped Particles. International Workshop on Light Scattering by Irre. Ed. by Donald W. Schuerman. LC 79-27691. (Illus.). 344p. 1980. reprint ed. pap. 106.70 (0-608-05434-8, 206590300006) Bks Demand.

Light Scattering by Liquid Surfaces & Complementary Techniques. Ed. by Langevin. (Surfactant Science Ser.: Vol. 41). (Illus.). 472p. 1991. text 199.00 (0-8247-8607-6) Dekker.

***Light Scattering by Nonspherical Particles.** Ed. by Michael I. Mishchenko et al. LC 99-61962. 690p. 1999. 115.00 (0-12-498660-9) Acad Pr.

Light Scattering by Particles: Computational Methods. P. W. Barber & S. C. Hill. (Advanced Series in Applied Physics: Vol. 2). 276p. 1990. pap. 40.00 (9971-5-0832-X); text 85.00 (9971-5-0813-3) World Scientific Pub.

Light Scattering by Small Particles. H. C. Van de Hulst. (Illus.). x, 470p. (C). 1982. reprint ed. pap. 12.95 (0-486-64228-3) Dover.

Light-Scattering from Dilute Polymer Solutions, Vol. 3. Ed. by Donald McIntyre & F. Gornick. (International Science Review Ser.). (Illus.). xiv, 318p. 1964. text 307.00 (0-677-00510-5) Gordon & Breach.

***Light Scattering from Microstructures: Lectures of the Summer School of Laredo, University of Cantabria, Held at Laredo, Spain, Sept. 11-13, 1998.** Universidad de Cantabria Staff et al. Ed. by Fernando J. Moreno & Francisco Gonzalez. LC 99-88776. (Lecture Notes in Physics Ser.: Vol. 534). (Illus.). xii, 300p. 2000. 82.80 (3-540-66937-X) Spr-Verlag.

Light Scattering Functions of Flow-Oriented Spheroids. Wilfried Heller et al. LC 74-13817. 1124p. reprint ed. pap. 200.00 (0-608-16623-5, 202768000055) Bks Demand.

Light Scattering in Inhomogeneous Atmospheres. Edgard G. Yanovitskij. LC 96-24479. 371p. 1996. 99.50 (3-540-61362-5) Spr-Verlag.

Light Scattering in Liquids & Macromolecular Solutions. Workshop on Quasielastic Light Scattering Studies. Ed. by V. Degiorgio et al. LC 80-20472. (Illus.). 305p. 1980. reprint ed. pap. 94.60 (0-608-05432-1, 206590100006) Bks Demand.

Light Scattering in Magnetic Solids. Michael G. Cottam & David J. Lockwood. 264p. (C). 1986. reprint ed. text 41.95 (0-471-81701-5) Krieger.

Light Scattering in Semiconductor Structures & Superlattices. Ed. by D. J. Lockwood & J. F. Young. (NATO ASI Ser.: Vol. 273). (Illus.). 616p. (C). 1991. text 186.00 (0-306-44036-9, Kluwer Plenum) Kluwer Academic.

Light Scattering in Solids, No. V. Ed. by M. Cardona & G. Guntherodt. (Topics in Applied Physics Ser.: Vol. 66). (Illus.). 345p. 1989. 102.95 (0-387-50400-1) Spr-Verlag.

***Light Scattering in Solids VIII: Fullerenes, Semiconductor Surfaces, Coherent Phonons.** Ed. by M. Cardona & G. Guentherodt. (Topics in Applied Physics Ser.: Vol. 76). (Illus.). 250p. 1999. 89.95 (3-540-66085-2) Spr-Verlag.

Light Scattering in Solids IV: Electronic Scattering, Spin Effects, SERS & Morphic Effects. Ed. by M. Cardona & G. Guntherodt. LC 83-13095. (Topics in Applied Physics Ser.: Vol. 54). (Illus.). 560p. 1984. 97.95 (0-387-11942-6) Spr-Verlag.

Light Scattering in Solids I. 2nd ed. Ed. by M. Cardona. (Topics in Applied Physics Ser.: Vol. 8). (Illus.). 363p. 1982. 69.95 (0-387-11913-2) Spr-Verlag.

***Light Scattering in Solids VII: Crystal-Field & Magnetic Excitations.** Ed. by M. Cardona & G. Guentherodt. (Topics in Applied Physics Ser.: Vol. 75). (Illus.). 250p. 1999. 99.00 (3-540-66075-5) Spr-Verlag.

Light Scattering in Solids VI: Recent Results Including High-TC Superconductivity. Ed. by M. Cardona & G. Guntherodt. (Topics in Applied Physics Ser.: Vol. 68). (Illus.). xiv, 526p. 1991. 135.95 (0-387-53614-0) Spr-Verlag.

Light Scattering in Solids III: Recent Results. Ed. by M. Cardona & G. Guentherodt. (Topics in Applied Physics Ser.: Vol. 51). (Illus.). 305p. 1982. 91.95 (0-387-11513-7) Spr-Verlag.

Light Scattering in Solids II: Basic Concept & Instrumentation. Ed. by M. Cardona & G. Guentherodt. (Topics in Applied Physics Ser.: Vol. 50). (Illus.). 251p. 1982. 91.95 (0-387-11380-0) Spr-Verlag.

Light Science: Physics & the Visual Arts. Thomas D. Rossing & Christopher Chiaverina. LC 99-18390. (Undergraduate Texts in Contemporary Physics Ser.). 300p. 1999. 69.00 (0-387-98827-0) Spr-Verlag.

Light Search: A Healing Journal. Linda H. Keiser. 80p. (Orig.). 1988. pap. 5.00 (0-944135-05-6) Archedigm Pubns.

Light Shadows. Francis Warner. 1980. 13.95 (0-86140-040-2, Pub. by Smyth) Dufour.

Light Shall Set You Free. Norma J. Milanovich & Shirley McCune. Date not set. wbk. ed. write for info. (0-9627417-1-X) Athena NM.

Light Shall Set You Free. Norma J. Milanovich & Shirley McCune. LC 94-78618. 1996. pap. 17.95 (0-9627417-7-9) Athena NM.

***Light Shines in Central Asia: A Journey into the Tibetan Buddhist World.** Thomas Hale. LC 99-44970. 1999. write for info. (0-87808-350-2) William Carey Lib.

Light Shines in the Darkness. Georgianna Summers. (Orig.). 1987. pap. 2.00 (0-89536-888-9, 7874) CSS OH.

Light Shineth in Darkness: Five Studies in Revelation after Christ. Udo Schaefer. Tr. by Helene M. Neri & Oliver Coburn. 208p. 1977. 18.95 (0-85398-091-8); pap. 12.50 (0-85398-072-1) G Ronald Pub.

Light Shining in Buckinghamshire. Caryl Churchill. 80p. (Orig.). 1997. pap. 10.95 (1-55936-130-1) Theatre Comm.

Light Shining Through an Open Window. Dale Ernst. (Illus.). 40p. (Orig.). 1996. pap. 5.00 (1-57502-117-X) Morris Pubng.

Light Shining Through the Mist: A Photobiography of Dian Fossey. Tom L. Matthews. (Illus.). 64p. (YA). (gr. 5). 1998. per. 17.95 (0-7922-7300-1, T07300C, Pub. by Natl Geog) Publishers Group.

Light Shone in the Darkness. Doreen M. Rossman. 256p. 1997. pap. 12.95 (1-57918-044-2, 3681) Queenship Pub.

Light So Bright. Wendy Pfeffer. (J). Date not set. pap. write for info. (0-06-440924-4, HarpTrophy) HarpC Child Bks.

Light So Bright. Wendy Pfeffer. 40p. (J). (ps-1). Date not set. 15.95 (0-06-029121-4); lib. bdg. 15.89 (0-06-029122-2) HarpC Child Bks.

Light Sources & Wave Optics, Course 5. rev. ed. Center for Occupational Research & Development Staff. (Laser-Electro-Optics Technology Ser.). (Illus.). 268p. (C). 1987. pap. text 28.00 (1-55502-023-2) CORD Commns.

Light Spectroscopy. D. A. Harris. (Introduction to Biotechniques Ser.). 160p. 1998. pap. text 35.95 (1-872748-34-1, Pub. by Bios Sci) Bks Intl VA.

***Light Spirit: Poems from Hollywood.** Mark Dunster. 11p. 1999. pap. 5.00 (0-89642-730-7) Linden Pubs.

Light Station on Tillamook Rock. Madeline DeFrees. Ed. by John Wheatcroft. (Bucknell University Fine Editions: Series in Contemporary Poetry). (Illus.). 60p. 1990. 125.00 (0-916375-11-0) Press Alley.

Light Still Enough to Witness. Terrel Hale. 32p. 1991. pap. 4.00 (1-879645-05-X) Garlic MA.

Light Strike: Skyhawks, Hornets & Corsair IIs. Joe Cupido. (Osprey Colour Library). (Illus.). 128p. 1993. 15.95 (1-85532-309-5, Pub. by Ospry) Motorbooks Intl.

Light Structures, Structures of Light: The Art & Engineering of Tensile Architecture. Horst Berger. (Illus.). 208p. 1996. 60.00 (3-7643-5352-X, Pub. by Birkhauser) Princeton Arch.

Light Tackle Fishing Guides of North America. Richard Swan. (Illus.). 436p. (Orig.). 1986. 29.50 (0-9617364-0-2); pap. 14.95 (0-9617364-1-0) Clear Water Pr.

Light Take Five, a Cookbook. Debbye Dabbs. 112p. 1994. pap. 12.00 (0-9645899-1-5) D Dabbs.

Light Team. Jeff McNair. 200p. 1998. pap. 9.95 (1-58169-005-3, JM101, Third Stry Window) Genesis Comm Inc.

Light-Tech: Towards a Light Architecture. Richard Horden. Ed. by Werner Blaser. LC 95-41154. (GER.). 1995. 74.50 (3-7643-5220-5, Pub. by Birkhauser) Princeton Arch.

Light Techniques That Trigger Transformation. Janet McClure. Ed. by Lillian Harben. 147p. (Orig.). 1989. pap. 11.95 (0-929385-00-4) Light Tech Pubng.

Light That Bends When It Passes: And Other Short Stories & Poems. Phoebe Frank. LC 95-73269. (Illus.). 304p. (Orig.). 1996. pap. text 18.00 (0-914615-24-6) I Nathan Pub Co.

Light That Failed. Rudyard Kipling. (Airmont Classics Ser.). (YA). (gr. 8 up). 1969. mass mkt. 1.50 (0-8049-0199-6, CL-199) Airmont.

Light That Failed. Rudyard Kipling. reprint ed. lib. bdg. 21.95 (0-88411-821-5) Amereon Ltd.

Light That Failed. Rudyard Kipling. 1990. reprint ed. lib. bdg. 17.95 (0-89968-535-8) Buccaneer Bks.

Light That Shone into the Dark Abyss. Maggi Lidchi-Grassi. 144p. 1994. pap. 7.95 (81-7058-380-2, Pub. by SAA) E-W Cultural Ctr.

Light the Candle. Nylea L. Butler-Moore. 1.25 (0-687-08194-7) Abingdon.

Light the Candle! Bang the Drum! A Book of Holidays from Around the World. Ann Morris. LC 97-5373. (Illus.). 32p. (J). (gr. k-2). 1997. 15.99 (0-525-45639-2, Dutton Child) Peng Put Young Read.

***Light the Candles: A Hanukkah Lift-the Flap Book.** Joan Holub. (Illus.). 16p. (J). (ps-1). 2000. pap. 6.99 (0-14-056757-7, PuffinBks) Peng Put Young Read.

Light the Fire Within You. Ida Greene. 143p. (YA). (gr. 9 up). 1991. pap. text 10.00 (1-881165-01-9) People Skills.

Light the Lights! A Story about Celebrating Hanukkah & Christmas. Margaret Moorman. (Illus.). 32p. (J). (ps-2). 1994. 12.95 (0-590-47003-5, Cartwheel) Scholastic Inc.

***Light the Lights! A Story about Celebrating Hanukkah & Christmas.** Margaret Moorman. (Illus.). 32p. (J). (gr. k-2). 1999. mass mkt. 5.99 (0-590-48383-8, Cartwheel) Scholastic Inc.

Light, the Mystery of the Universe: History of Light. Khalil Seyrafi. LC 85-80510. 1986. 18.95 (0-936581-00-X) Electro-Optical.

Light the Night. 3rd ed. John Culea. 389p. 1997. reprint ed. pap. 10.00 (0-9671167-0-8) J & P Pubg.

Light the Shade. Robert Lax. (Illus.). 96p. (Orig.). 1989. pap. text 15.00 (3-85842-166-9, Pub. by Pendo-Verlag) Franciscan Inst.

Light the Torch Pass the Flame: Lessons from Our Fathers. Mark Littleton & Jeanette G. Littleton. LC 98-2671. 44p. 1998. pap. 2.99 (0-8341-1710-X) Beacon Hill.

Light, the Tree & the Artist: Inspirational Images. Donald R. Cook. 16p. (Orig.). 1994. pap. 28.95 (0-9614887-2-7) DRC Graphics Serv.

Light the Window. Floyd McClung. 1999. pap. 8.99 (1-57658-150-0) YWAM Pub.

Light Theme Pack. Melvin Berger. Ed. by Susan Evento. (Macmillan Early Science Big Bks.). (Illus.). (J). (ps-2). 1995. pap. 49.95 (1-56784-187-2) Newbridge Educ.

Light Thickens. Ngaio Marsh. 1976. 21.95 (0-8488-0579-8) Amereon Ltd.

***Light Thickens.** Ngaio Marsh. 5.99p. 2000. mass mkt. 5.99 (0-312-97314-4, Minotaur) St Martin.

Light Through an Eastern Window. K. C. Pillai. 1963. pap. 6.95 (0-8315-0057-3) Speller.

Light Through Glass. large type ed. Elizabeth Lemarchand. 288p. 1986. 15.95 (0-7089-1505-1) Ulverscroft.

Light Through the Leaves: Reflections from Our Family Tree. Roxie Kelley. 1999. 14.95 (0-8362-7851-8) Andrews & McMeel.

Light to All Japan: The Story of Susan Dyck. Eugene Neudorf. 30p. 1998. pap. 3.99 (0-87509-775-8) Chr Pubns.

Light to All Japan: The Story of Susan Dyck. Eugene Neudorf. LC 97-77647. Vol. 19. (Illus.). 206p. (gr. 4-7). 1998. pap. 9.99 (0-87509-724-3) Chr Pubns.

Light to India. Dan Wooding & Lillian Doerksen. LC 97-62216. 256p. 1998. pap. 16.99 (1-57921-075-9) WinePress Pub.

Light to Live By (Wedding Edition) Ed. by Herbert Lockyer. 384p. 1980. 10.95 (0-310-28230-6, 10145) Zondervan.

Light to the Gentiles: The Life Story of the Venerable Francis Libermann. Adrian Van Kaam. LC 84-22034. 370p. 1985. reprint ed. pap. text 28.00 (0-8191-3804-5) U Pr of Amer.

Light to the Isles: Missionary Theology in Celtic & Anglo Saxon Britain. Douglas Dales. 190p. 1998. pap. 25.95 (0-7188-2965-4, Lutterworth-Parkwest) Parkwest Pubns.

Light to the Mountains: Morehead State University, 1887-1997. Donald F. Flatt. LC 97-15542. (Illus.). 267p. 1997. 34.95 (0-945084-60-9) J Stuart Found.

Light Too Bright: The Enlightenment Today: An Assessment of the Values of the European Enlightenment & a Search for New Foundations. Paulos M. Gregorios. LC 91-30801. (SUNY Series in Religious Studies). 261p. (C). 1992. text 24.50 (0-7914-1133-8) State U NY Pr.

Light Touch. Sylvia Ashley. LC 95-90621. (Orig.). 1996. pap. 7.95 (0-533-11660-0) Vantage.

L

An Asterisk (*) at the beginning of an entry indicates that the title is appearing for the first time.

Light Touch: Successful Painting in Oils. David Curtis. (Illus.). 128p. 1997. pap. 19.95 (*0-7153-0623-5*, Pub. by D & C Pub) Sterling.

Light Touch Cookbook: All-Time Favorite Recipes Made Healthful & Delicious. Marie Simmons. Ed. by Rux Martin. (Illus.). 288p. 1992. pap. 14.95 (*1-57630-023-4*, Chapters Bks) HM.

Light Touch Cookbook: All-time Favorite Recipes Made Healthful & Delicious. Marie Simmons. LC 92-13996. (Illus.). 240p. (Orig.). 1992. pap. 19.95 (*0-9631591-6-X*, Chapters Bks) HM.

Light Touching Silver: Photographs by Joseph D. Jachna. Intro. by Steven Klindt. 51p. 1980. pap. 5.00 (*0-685-49239-7*) Columbia College Chi.

Light Transit Systems: Proceedings of the Symposium on the Potential of Light Transit Systems in British Cities, Nottingham, England, March 14-15, 1990. Ed. by B. H. North. 282p. 1990. 10.00 (*0-7277-1590-9*) Am Soc Civil Eng.

***Light Traveler: The Adventure Begins : A Novel.** Brent Rowley. LC 98-220290. 185 P. ;p. 1998. write for info. (*1-57734-310-7*) Covenant Comms.

Light Travels. Keith Waldrop & Rosmarie Waldrop. (Poetry Chapbooks). (Orig.). 1993. pap. 5.00 (*0-930901-92-4*) Burning Deck.

Light Triumphant. Esther Lense. 1977. pap. 3.50 (*0-89536-301-1*, 1253) CSS OH.

Light Truck & Van Repair Manual, 1994-1998. Chilton Automotive Editorial Staff. (C). 1998. 59.95 (*0-8019-7924-2*) Thomson Learn.

Light Truck & Van Service Manual, 1992-96. Chilton Automotive Editorial Staff. 2504p. text 100.00 (*0-8019-8725-3*) Nichols Pub.

Light Truck Suspension Systems. 1996. 30.00 (*1-56091-854-3*, SP-1198) Soc Auto Engineers.

Light Trucks: Drivetrains & Powertrains. 1996. 43.00 (*1-56091-856-X*, SP-1200) Soc Auto Engineers.

Light unto My Path. Mary L. Merrill et al. (Illus.). 185p. 1981. reprint ed. 10.00 (*0-686-33180-X*) Pathway Pubns.

Light unto the Nations. Yoel Schwartz. 1997. 7.95 (*1-58330-098-8*) Feldheim.

Light unto the World. David B. Haight. LC 97-28688. xii, 192p. 1997. 16.95 (*1-57345-302-1*) Deseret Bk.

Light up the Cave. Denise Levertov. LC 81-11295. 224p. 1982. 8.95 (*0-8112-0813-3*, Pub. by New Directions) Norton.

Light up the Sky. Moss Hart. 1950. pap. 5.25 (*0-8222-0664-1*) Dramatists Play.

Light up the Sky. 93rd ed. Ed. by Harcourt Brace Staff. (J). (gr. 5). 1993. text 52.00 (*0-15-300425-8*) Harcourt.

Light up Your Haunted House. Sue Sikking. LC 81-66932. 112p. (Orig.). 1981. pap. 4.95 (*0-87516-453-6*) DeVorss.

Light up Your Life. David Phillips. Ed. by Fran Balkwill. (Making Sense of Science Ser.). (Illus.). 32p. (J). 1997. pap. 12.00 (*1-85578-090-9*, Pub. by Portland Pr Ltd) Ashgate Pub Co.

Light up Your Life: Discover Your True Purpose & Potential. Diana Cooper. LC 97-108279. 186p. 1996. pap. text 12.95 (*0-7499-1557-9*, Pub. by Piatkus Bks) London Brdge.

***Light up Your Life: Discover Your True Purpose & Potential.** Diana Cooper. 192p. 2000. pap. 9.95 (*0-7499-1986-8*, Pub. by Piatkus Bks) London Brdge.

Light up Your Mind with Creative Thinking. Gary Grimm & Karen Ihrig. (Illus.). 40p. (Orig.). (J). (gr. 4-8). 1997. pap. text 9.95 (*1-56490-046-0*) G Grimm Assocs.

Light up Your Mind with Language. Gary Grimm & Karen Ihrig. (Illus.). 40p. (Orig.). (J). (gr. 4-8). 1997. pap. text 9.95 (*1-56490-040-1*) G Grimm Assocs.

Light up Your Mind with Math. Gary Grimm & Karen Ihrig. (Illus.). 40p. (Orig.). (J). (gr. 4-8). 1997. pap. text 9.95 (*1-56490-041-X*) G Grimm Assocs.

Light up Your Mind with Science. Gary Grimm & Karen Ihrig. (Illus.). 40p. (Orig.). (J). (gr. 4-8). 1997. pap. text 9.95 (*1-56490-043-6*) G Grimm Assocs.

Light up Your Mind with Self Concepts. Gary Grimm & Karen Ihrig. (Illus.). 40p. (Orig.). (J). (gr. 4-8). 1997. pap. text 9.95 (*1-56490-047-9*) G Grimm Assocs.

Light up Your Mind with Social Studies. Gary Grimm & Karen Ihrig. (Illus.). 40p. (Orig.). (J). (gr. 4-8). 1997. pap. text 9.95 (*1-56490-042-8*) G Grimm Assocs.

Light up Your Mind with the Arts. Gary Grimm & Karen Ihrig. (Illus.). 40p. (Orig.). (J). (gr. 4-8). 1997. pap. text 9.95 (*1-56490-045-2*) G Grimm Assocs.

Light up Your Mind with Word Power. Gary Grimm & Karen Ihrig. (Illus.). 40p. (Orig.). (J). (gr. 4-8). 1997. pap. text 9.95 (*1-56490-044-4*) G Grimm Assocs.

***Light upon a Hill: The University at Chattanooga, 1886-1996.** unabridged ed. John Longwith. (Illus.). 298p. 2000. 24.95 (*0-944897-04-5*) Magic Chef.

Light upon Light: Inspirations from Rumi. Andrew Harvey. LC 95-51790. (Illus.). 247p. 1996. 20.00 (*1-55643-206-2*) North Atlantic.

Light upon Our Path see Lumbrera a Nuestro Camino

Light upon the Mist: A Reflection of Wisdom for the Future Generations of Native Hawaiians. Ed. by Lee Palaliko & Eleanora DeFries. 125p. reprint ed. pap. text 12.95 (*0-9635173-0-9*) Mahina Prods.

Light Utilization & Photoinhibition of Photosynthesis in Marine Phytoplankton. 49p. (Orig.). (C). 1994. pap. text 40.00 (*0-7881-1096-9*) DIANE Pub.

Light Vegetarian Cooking. Rose Reisman. (Illus.). 192p. 1998. pap. text 17.95 (*1-896503-66-7*) R Rose Inc.

Light Vehicle Fitting. 1982. 50.00 (*0-7855-2890-3*) St Mut.

***Light Verb Construction in Japanese: The Role of the Verbal Noun.** Tadao Miyamoto. LC 99-46742. (Linguistik Aktuell/Linguistics Today Ser.: Vol. 29). (ENG & JPN.). xiv, 232p. 2000. 79.00 (*1-55619-913-9*) J Benjamins Pubng Co.

Light Verse from an Island Parish. Patrick S. Clark. (Illus.). 90p. (Orig.). 1996. pap. write for info. (*1-57502-254-0*, P0936) Morris Pubng.

Light Verse from the Floating World: An Anthology of Premodern Japanese Senryu. Compiled by Makoto Ueda. LC 99-20630. 288p. 1999. pap. 17.50 (*0-231-11551-2*) Col U Pr.

***Light Verse from the Floating World: An Anthology of Premodern Japanese Senryu.** Tr. & Compiled by Makoto Ueda. LC 99-20630. 273p. 1999. 49.50 (*0-231-11550-4*) Col U Pr.

Light-Vesture of the New Man. Jan Van Rijckenborgh & Catharose De Petri.Tr. of Het Lichtkleed van de Niewe Mens. 100p. (Orig.). 1989. pap. 9.50 (*90-6732-035-8*) Rosycross Pr.

Light, Visible & Invisible. Eduard Ruechardt. LC 58-5904. (Ann Arbor Science Library). 201p. reprint ed. pap. 62.40 (*0-608-11839-7*, 205564300029) Bks Demand.

***Light, Visible & Invisible & Its Medical Applications.** Angela Newing. 200p. 1999. 28.00 (*1-86094-164-8*) Imperial College.

***Light Vision.** Mohamad Vajad. (Illus.). 104p. 2000. 50.00 (*0-9666915-1-2*) Graphic Ways Pub.

Light Visions: A Collection of Poetry & Prose. Wilsun Coyet. (Illus.). 70p. 1998. pap. text. write for info. (*0-9644611-0-2*) Sonset Prod.

Light-Walled Rectangular Pipe & Tube from Mexico: An International Trade Investigation. (Illus.). 62p. (Orig.). (C). 1995. pap. text 30.00 (*0-7881-2105-7*) DIANE Pub.

***Light Warriors.** Joyce Tenneson. (Illus.). 112p. 2000. 50.00 (*0-8212-2698-3*) Bulfinch Pr.

***Light Warrior's Guide to High Level Energy Healing: Medical Qigong & a Shaman's Healing Vision.** Michael L. Lomax. (Illus.). 180p. 2000. pap. 24.95 (*0-9674742-5-6*) Spirit Way.

Light Water Reactor Nuclear Fuel Cycle. Ed. by Raymond G. Wymer & Benedict L. Vondra, Jr. LC 80-12432. 272p. 1981. 155.00 (*0-8493-5687-3*, TK9360, CRC Reprint) Franklin.

Light Water Reactor Safety: The Development of Advanced Models & Codes for Light Water Reactor Safety Analysis. J. N. Lillington. LC 95-2322. 374p. 1995. 191.50 (*0-444-89741-0*) Elsevier.

Light Water Reactor Severe Accident Evaluation International Meeting, Cambridge, MA, August 28-Sept. 1, 1983. 1124p. 1983. 110.00 (*0-89448-112-6*, 700085) Am Nuclear Soc.

Light Wave X-Treme. Joshua Tsui. (Illus.). 162p. 1999. pap. 34.95 (*0-7392-0087-9*, PO2958) Morris Pubng.

Light We Are. Karl Kempton. LC 85-12676. 1985. pap. 6.00 (*0-914134-08-6*) Konocti Bks.

Light Weapons & Civil Conflict: Controlling the Tools of Violence. Ed. by Jeffrey Boutwell & Michael T. Klare. LC 98-55389. 256p. 1999. 65.00 (*0-8476-9484-4*) Rowman.

Light Weapons & Civil Conflict: Controlling the Tools of Violence. Ed. by Jeffrey Boutwell & Michael T. Klare. LC 98-55389. (Carnegie Commission on Preventing Deadly Conflict Ser.). 256p. 1999. pap. 22.95 (*0-8476-9485-2*) Rowman.

Light Weaver. Thomas Locke. LC 94-19919. (Spectrum Chronicles Ser.). 176p. (YA). 1994. pap. 5.99 (*1-55661-432-2*) Bethany Hse.

Light-Weight Alloys for Aerospace Applications: Proceedings of a Symposium Sponsored by the TMS Nonferrous Metals Committee, Held During the 1989 TMS Annual Meeting, Las Vegas, Nevada, February 28-March 2, 1989. Minerals, Metals & Materials Society Staff. Ed. by Eui W. Lee et al. LC 89-60375. (Illus.). 518p. 1989. reprint ed. pap. 160.60 (*0-608-01696-9*, 206235100002) Bks Demand.

Light-Weight Alloys for Aerospace Applications No. 2: Proceedings of a Symposium Sponsored by the TMS Nonferrous Metals Committee, Held During the 1991 TMS Annual Meeting, New Orleans, Louisiana, February 17-21, 1991. Ed. by Eui W. Lee & Nack J. Kim. LC 91-62555. 516p. 1991. reprint ed. pap. 160.00 (*0-7837-9127-5*, 204992700004) Bks Demand.

Light Weight Alloys for Aerospace Applications III. Ed. by E. W. Lee et al. LC 95-78393. (Illus.). 466p. 1995. 20.00 (*0-87339-302-3*, 3023) Minerals Metals.

Light Weight Alloys for Aerospace Applications IV. Ed. by E. W. Lee et al. LC 97-71552. (Illus.). 491p. 1997. 146.00 (*0-87339-328-7*, 3287) Minerals Metals.

Light-Weight Steel & Aluminium Structures: Fourth International Conference on Steel & Aluminium Structures. International Conference on Steel & Aluminium Structures Staff et al. LC 99-22873. 894p. 1999. 198.00 (*0-08-043014-7*) Elsevier.

Light While There Is Light: An American History. Keith Waldrop. (Sun & Moon Classics Ser.: No. 33). 208p. (Orig.). 1993. pap. 13.95 (*1-55713-136-8*) Sun & Moon CA.

Light, Wind & Structure: The Mystery of the Master Builders. Robert Mark. (C). 1990. text 38.25 (*0-07-040403-8*) McGraw.

***Light Within.** W. Jeffrey Marsh. LC 00-40442. 2000. write for info. (*1-57345-807-4*) Deseret Bk.

Light Within: The Incredible Story of One Solier's Encounter with the Afterlife! Paul Hughes. LC 93-72058. 248p. 1993. pap. 9.99 (*0-88270-660-8*) Bridge-Logos.

Light Within: The Inner Path of Meditation. Laurence Freeman. 118p. 1995. pap. 11.95 (*0-8245-0785-1*, Crsrd) Crossroad NY.

Light Within: The Inner Path of Meditation. Laurence Freeman. 128p. 1998. reprint ed. pap. 10.95 (*0-8264-1126-6*) Continuum.

Light Within Us. Carl Japikse. 336p. (Orig.). 1988. pap. 9.95 (*0-89804-042-6*) Ariel GA.

Light Within Us. Albert Schweitzer. pap. 0.95 (*0-685-19406-X*, 45, Citadel Pr) Carol Pub Group.

Light Without Gravity. John Hemming. 1999. pap. 21.00 (*1-85072-140-8*, Pub. by W Sessions) St Mut.

Light Without Motion. Giorgio Cheisura. 1989. pap. 15.00 (*0-937669-33-4*) Owl Creek Pr.

Light Without Motion. Giorgio Cheisura. 1989. 22.00 (*0-937669-34-2*) Owl Creek Pr.

***Light Words: The Metaphysical & New Age Spirituality Glossary.** S. Lee Brady. (Illus.). 139p. 2000. 12.95 (*0-9671158-3-3*); pap. 8.99 (*0-9671158-4-1*) Sananda Fndt.

Light Work: Photography over the '70s & '80s. Ed. by Janice Giarraco. (Illus.). 80p. (Orig.). 1985. pap. 10.00 (*0-318-18366-8*) Light Work.

Light Writing & Life Writing: Photography in Autobiography. Timothy Dow Adams. LC 99-21544. (Illus.). 368p. 2000. 49.95 (*0-8078-4792-5*); lib. bdg. 49.95 (*0-8078-2513-1*) U of NC Pr.

Light Year 85. Ed. by Robert Wallace. (Illus.). 200p. 1984. 12.95 (*0-933248-03-2*) Bits Pr.

Light Year 84. Ed. by Robert Wallace. (Illus.). 147p. 1983. 12.95 (*0-933248-02-4*) Bits Pr.

Light Year 87. Ed. by Robert Wallace. (Illus.). 267p. 1986. 13.95 (*0-933248-07-5*) Bits Pr.

Light Year 86. Ed. by Robert Wallace. (Illus.). 279p. 1985. 13.95 (*0-933248-04-0*) Bits Pr.

Light Years. Roberta Chester. Ed. by Constance Hunting. 96p. 1983. pap. 5.95 (*0-913006-29-7*) Puckerbrush.

Light Years. Ralph Gibson. LC 97-157765. (Illus.). 200p. 1996. 49.95 (*3-908162-28-9*, Pub. by Edit Stemmle) Dist Art Pubs.

Light Years. Elizabeth J. Howard. Ed. by Bill Grose. 448p. 1995. per. 14.00 (*0-671-52793-2*) PB.

Light Years. Ed. by Pocket Books Staff. 1988. per. 4.50 (*0-671-65875-1*) PB.

Light Years. James Salter. 1995. pap. 13.00 (*0-679-74073-2*) Vin Bks.

Light Years. Elizabeth J. Howard. Ed. by Bill Grose. (Cazalet Chronicles Ser.). 448p. 1991. reprint ed. mass mkt. 5.95 (*0-671-70908-9*) PB.

Light Years: A Memoir. Le Anne Schreiber. LC 97-21370. 160p. 1997. pap. 11.00 (*0-385-48943-9*, Anchor NY) Doubleday.

Light Years: A Memoir. Le Anne Schreiber. LC 96-16370. (Illus.). 160p. 1996. 20.00 (*1-55821-494-1*) Lyons Pr.

Light Years: New & Selected Poems. Dabney Stuart. LC 94-11453. 184p. 1994. pap. 14.95 (*0-8071-1899-0*); text 24.95 (*0-8071-1898-2*) La State U Pr.

Light Years: Selected Early Works, 1969-1972. Merrill Gilfillan. LC 76-58864. (Selected Works Ser.: No. 1). 1977. pap. 7.95 (*0-912652-30-6*) Blue Wind.

Light Years: The Photographs of Morley Baer. Jim Jordan. Ed. by Carol W. Christopher. (Illus.). 130p. 1988. 150.00 (*0-9616515-2-0*) Photog West Graphics.

***Light Years: The Zumtobel Story 1950-2000.** Ed. by Otto Riewoldt. (Illus.). 600p. 2000. pap. 58.00 (*3-7643-6332-0*) Birkhauser.

***Light Years Ahead: The Illustrated Guide to Full Spectrum & Colored Light in Mindbody Healing.** Jacob Lieberman. (Illus.). 424p. 1999. reprint ed. pap. text 20.00 (*0-7881-6777-4*) DIANE Pub.

Light Years Ahead: The Illustrated Guide to Full Spectrum & Colored Light MindBody Healing. Light Years Ahead Productions Staff. Ed. by Brian Breiling & Bethany Argisle. LC 95-20046. (Illus.). 256p. 1995. pap. 19.95 (*0-89087-762-9*) Celestial Arts.

Light Your Candle. Carl Sommer. LC 99-36452. (Another Sommer-Time Story Ser.). (Illus.). 48p. (J). (ps-4). 2000. 9.95 (*1-57537-019-0*) Advance Pub.

Light Your Candle. Carl Sommer. LC 99-36452. (Another Sommer-Time Story Ser.). (Illus.). 48p. (J). (ps-4). 2000. lib. bdg. 14.95 (*1-57537-068-9*) Advance Pub.

Light Your House with Potatoes: And 99 Other Off-the-Wall Solutions to Life's Little Problems. Jay Kaye. 144p. 1992. pap. 7.95 (*0-8065-1376-4*, Citadel Pr) Carol Pub Group.

***Lightbulb.** Joseph Wallace. (Turning Point Inventions Ser.). (Illus.). 80p. (YA). (gr. 7 up). 1999. 17.95 (*0-689-82816-0*) Atheneum Yung Read.

Lightbulb & How It Changed the World. Michael Pollard. LC 94-15226. (Illus.). 48p. 1995. 16.95 (*0-8160-3145-2*) Facts on File.

Lighted Candle in Her Heart. Sallie Robbin. 200p. 1985. 9.95 (*0-930061-15-2*) Interspace Bks.

Lighted Lantern. Harold Bell Wright & John LeBar. 1998. lib. bdg. 48.95 (*1-56723-114-4*) Yestermorrow.

Lighted Path: A Journey of Transformation & Transcendence. Risha Henrique. LC 97-105471. 224p. 1996. pap. 12.00 (*0-425-15456-4*) Berkley Pub.

Lighted Way. unabridged ed. (Children's Heritage Ser.). (Illus.). 82p. (J). (gr. 4-6). 1996. pap. 5.75 (*1-58339-103-7*, D3) Triangle Press.

Lighted Windows. large type ed. Emilie Loring. 1998. 30.00 (*0-7838-0342-7*, G K Hall Lrg Type) Mac Lib Ref.

Lighted Windows. Emilie Loring. reprint ed. lib. bdg. 24.95 (*0-88411-378-7*) Amereon Ltd.

Lighted Windows & Gardens. Bill Blackman. 48p. 1996. pap. 10.50 (*1-56770-355-0*) S Scheewe Pubns.

***Lighted Windows: or The Humanization of the Bureaucrat Julius Zihal.** Heimito Von Doderer. Tr. & Afterword by John S. Barrett. LC 99-36365. (Studies in Austrian Literature, Culture & Thought). 2000. pap. 14.50 (*1-57241-081-7*) Ariadne CA.

Lighten Their Darkness: The Evangelical Mission to Working-Class London, 1828-1860, 19. Donald M. Lewis. LC 86-12104. (Contributions to the Study of Religion Ser.: No. 19). (Illus.). 386p. 1986. 69.50 (*0-313-25577-6*, LLD/, Greenwood Pr) Greenwood.

Lighten Up! Bruce Lansky. LC 98-8788. 1998. 5.95 (*0-88166-324-7*) Meadowbrook.

***Lighten Up!** Bruce Lansky. LC 99-33561. 1999. write for info. (*0-88166-356-5*) Meadowbrook.

Lighten Up! A Practical Guide to Residential Lighting. Randall D. Whitehead. LC 97-160857. (Illus.). 184p. (Orig.). 1996. pap. text 44.00 (*0-9658655-0-9*) Lght Srce Pub.

Lighten Up! Finding Real Joy in Real Life. Chieko N. Okazaki. LC 92-40396. 232p. 1993. 12.95 (*0-87579-668-0*) Deseret Bk.

Lighten-Up! Five-Ingredient Less Fat Recipes. Jackie Gannaway. 280p. 1994. 15.95 (*0-9629408-2-8*) Cookbook Cup.

Lighten Up! Free Yourself from Clutter. Michelle Passoff. LC 97-45040. 208p. 1998. pap. 13.00 (*0-06-095265-2*) HarpC.

Lighten Up! Gourmet Recipes for Lowfat Lifestyles. Tija Petrovich. (Illus.). 211p. 1992. spiral bd. 14.95 (*0-9630679-0-7*) Nutrit Connect.

Lighten Up! Gourmet Recipes for Lowfat Lifestyles. Tija Petrovich. 240p. 1996. spiral bd. 16.95 (*0-7615-0299-8*) Prima Pub.

Lighten Up! Leader's Guide, 2 vols. Jan Johnson. Ed. by Theresa Hayes. 80p. 1999. pap., teacher ed. 12.99 (*0-7847-7068-9*, 09918) Standard Pub.

Lighten Up: Let C. W. Metcalf Show You How to Be More Productive, Resilient, & Stress-Free by Taking Laughter Seriously. C. W. Metcalf. (Illus.). 256p. 1992. 19.95 (*0-201-56779-2*) Addison-Wesley.

Lighten Up! Low-Fat Cooking in 15 Minutes. Ginny Clark. LC 98-34059. (Illus.). 177p. 1999. mass mkt. 10.99 (*0-446-67507-5*, Pub. by Warner Bks) Little.

Lighten Up! Student Book. Mike Shannon & Jan Johnson. Ed. by Theresa Hayes. 160p. 1999. pap., student ed. 6.99 (*0-7847-7069-7*, 00919) Standard Pub.

Lighten Up: Survival Skills for People under Pressure. C. W. Metcalf & Roma Felible. (Illus.). 304p. 1993. pap. 14.00 (*0-201-62239-4*) Addison-Wesley.

Lighten Up: Tasty, Low-Fat, Low-Calorie Vegetarian Cuisine. Louise Hagler. LC 95-21983. 160p. (Orig.). 1995. pap. text 11.95 (*1-57067-011-0*) Book Pub Co.

Lighten Up: The Art of Low Fat Gourmet Cooking. Mary E. Ross. (Illus.). 304p. 1996. pap. 19.95 (*0-9649771-7-6*, Pub. by Lghten Up Ent) Origin Bk Sales.

Lighten Up! With Non Fat-Low Fat Recipes. Amanda Ruby. 215p. pap. text. write for info. (*0-9644820-0-2*) Amegard.

Lighten Up! 101 Funny Little Poems. Ed. by Bruce Lansky. LC 98-8788. 124p. 1998. pap. 12.00 (*0-671-31632-X*) S&S Childrens.

Lighten up & Enjoy Life More: Everyday Ways to De-Stress Your Lifestyle. Margaret A. Houk. 192p. (Orig.). 1996. pap. 14.00 (*0-8170-1240-0*) Judson.

***Lighten up & Live Longer: A Collection of Jokes, Antidotes & Stories Guaranteed to Tickle Your Soul.** Sue Baldwin. Ed. by Mary Steiner-Whelan. (Illus.). 160p. 1999. pap. 12.00 (*0-9654439-1-4*) Insights Trning.

Lighten up for Dieters. pap. 9.95 (*1-879127-08-3*) Lighten Up Enter.

Lighten up, George. large type ed. Art Buchwald. LC 92-36472. (General Ser.). 447p. 1993. 21.95 (*0-8161-5675-1*, G K Hall Lrg Type) Mac Lib Ref.

Lighten up on God. James A. Murray. Ed. by Patricia E. Heyden. 162p. Date not set. write for info. (*0-9631348-3-3*) Stuart MI.

***Lighten Up 2: 101 More Funny Little Poems, Vol. 2.** Bruce Lansky. Vol. 2. 101p. 1999. per. 5.95 (*0-671-31772-5*) S&S Childrens.

Lighten up Your Body - Lighten up Your Life: Beyond Diet & Exercise - The Inner Path to Lasting Change. Lucia Capacchione et al. 92p. 1990. pap. 12.95 (*0-87877-150-6*, 643) Newcastle Pub.

Lighten-Up's Little Lessons: 2 & 3 Ingredient Recipes for Low Fat Cooking. 30p. 1995. pap. 3.95 (*1-885597-11-8*) Cookbook Cup.

Lightening: A Design Source Book. Elizabeth Wilhide. LC 98-17164. 192p. 1998. 40.00 (*1-55670-698-7*) Stewart Tabori & Chang.

Lightening Across the River: The Story of Gen. John Hunt Morgan's Raid on Clermont County, Ohio - U. S. Grant Clermont County's Most Noted Son. Richard Crawford. Ed. by John M. Spafford. (Illus.). 120p. (Orig.). 1997. pap. 15.00 (*1-890538-18-3*) Rhiannon Pubns.

Lightening Bolt Is Hotter Than the Sun: And Other Amazing Facts about Electricity. Helen Taylor. LC 98-28786. (You'd Never Believe It, but... Ser.). (Illus.). 32p. (J). (gr. k-2). 1998. lib. bdg. 20.90 (*0-7613-0862-8*, Copper Beech Bks) Millbrook Pr.

Lighter Look at the "C" Word. Steve Gould. LC 98-135373. (Illus.). 70p. 1997. pap. 12.00 (*0-9655160-0-8*) Mondays.

***Lighter, Quicker, Better: Cooking for the Way We Eat Today.** Richard Sax & Marie Simmons. LC 99-53287. (Illus.). 432p. 2000. reprint ed. pap. 18.00 (*0-688-17761-1*, Wm Morrow) Morrow Avon.

Lighter, Quicker, Better: Food for the Way We Eat Today: A Positive Approach to Delicious Healthier Eating. Richard Sax & Marie Simmons. LC 94-32293. 416p. 1995. 25.00 (*0-688-13871-3*, Wm Morrow) Morrow Avon.

Lighter Rock. pap. 14.95 (*1-57560-067-6*) Cherry Lane.

Lighter Shade of Blue. large type ed. Christopher Foxley-Norris. (Illus.). 416p. 1996. 27.99 (*0-7089-3462-5*) Ulverscroft.

***Lighter Shade of Brown.** Vicki Andrews. 1999. pap. text 8.95 (*1-885478-75-5*, Pub. by Genesis Press) BookWorld.

Lighter Shade of Pink. Selene Vasquez. (J). (gr. 3-7). 1997. 15.95 (*0-614-28880-0*) Pippin Bks.

***Lighter Side of Christmas.** Hal Leonard Publishing Company Staff. 168p. 2000. pap. 14.95 (*0-634-01822-1*) H Leonard.

An Asterisk (*) at the beginning of an entry indicates that the title is appearing for the first time.

Lighter Side of Gravity. Jayant V. Narlikar. LC 81-19496. (Illus.). 194p. (C). 1982. pap. text 11.20 (*0-7167-1344-6*) W H Freeman.

Lighter Side of Gravity. 2nd ed. Jayant V. Narlikar. (Illus.). 229p. (C). 1996. pap. 17.95 (*0-521-56565-0*); text 44.95 (*0-521-55009-2*) Cambridge U Pr.

Lighter Side of Italy: A Collection of Authentic Italian Recipes That Happen to Be Low in Fat & Cholesterol. Nancy Brannon. LC 91-90752. 272p. 1992. 17.95 (*0-9623036-2-3*) ConAmore Pub.

Lighter Side of Mathematics: Proceedings of the Eugene Strens Memorial Conference on Recreational Mathematics & Its History. Ed. by Richard K. Guy & Robert E. Woodrow. LC 90-70790. (Spectrum Ser.). 376p. 1994. pap. text 20.00 (*0-88385-516-X*, LSMA) Math Assn.

Lighter Side of Overweight: A Self-Help Book for Weight Control (with Cartoons) Peter Migaly. (Smokeless Side: No. 2). (Illus.). 100p. (Orig.). Date not set. pap. 15.95 (*0-9647363-1-4*) P Migaly.

Lighter Side of Practicing Law: We, the Lawyers. Ed. by William F. White. (Illus.). 88p. (Orig.). 1993. ring bd. 20.00 (*0-9640450-0-1*) W F White.

Lighter Side of Practicing Law: We, the Lawyers, Vol. I. 4th large type rev. ed. Ed. & Photos by William F. White. (Illus.). 120p. (Orig.). (C). 1997. pap. 25.00 (*0-9640450-5-2*) W F White.

Lighter Side of Practicing Law Vol. 1: We, the Lawyers. annuals 3rd abr. large type ed. Ed. by William F. White. 124p. (Orig.). 1995. pap., per. 25.00 (*0-9640450-3-6*) W F White.

Lighter Side of Stained Glass. Patrick A. Mosley. (Illus.). 90p. 1984. pap. 6.95 (*0-917661-00-1*) P Mosley.

***Lighter Side of Tennis.** Herb Rosenthal. LC 99-71607. (Illus.). 72p. 1999. pap. 12.95 (*0-87212-267-0*) Libra.

Lighter Side of the Battle. John W. Hazard. LC 87-82710. (Illus.). 200p. 1988. 17.50 (*0-915762-17-X*) Patmos Pr.

Lighter Side of the Southwest. Margot G. Ziemer. (Carefree Cook Ser.). (Illus.). 232p. (Orig.). 1994. pap. 8.95 (*0-9646218-0-0*) M Ziemer.

Lighter Tastes of Aspen: Recipes from Aspen/Snowmass' Finest Restaurants & Caterers. Jill Sheeley. 1994. pap. text 19.95 (*0-9609108-2-4*) Courtney Pr.

Lighter Than Air. David Owen. 1999. 17.99 (*0-7858-1045-5*) Bk Sales Inc.

***Lighter Than Air: A New Report on the Aero-Nautical Adventures Now Taking Place...** Ed Leefeldt. LC 00-191013. (Illus.). 312p. 2000. pap. 9.95 (*0-9679535-0-2*) Lighter Than Air.

***Lighter Than Air: Moral Poems.** Hans Magnus Engensberger. Tr. by Reinhold Grimm.Tr. of Leichter als Luft. (GER & ENG.). 260p. 2000. pap. 15.95 (*1-878818-85-6*, Pub. by Sheep Meadow) U Pr of New Eng.

Lighter Than Air: Stories of Unaided Human Flight. Rodney Charles & Anna Jordan. Ed. by Elizabeth Pasco. LC 95-68466. 250p. (Orig.). 1996. pap. text 14.95 (*0-9638502-7-X*) Sunstar Pubng.

Lighter-Than-Night Verse. Carolyn Stoloff. 1977. per. 2.50 (*0-88031-041-3*) Invisible-Red Hill.

Lighters. LC 96-52101. (ITA.). (Orig.). 1997. pap. 12.95 (*0-8118-1869-1*) Chronicle Bks.

Lightest Blues: Great Humor from the Thirties. Jane Van Nimmen. Ed. by Clive Giboire. (Illus.). 239p. (Orig.). 1984. 25.00 (*0-915829-51-7*); pap. 14.95 (*0-915829-52-5*) Chameleon Bks.

Lightfoot Best of Guitar Tab: Guitar Personality Book. 64p. (Orig.). 1988. pap. 12.95 (*0-7692-0565-8*, GF0355) Wrner Bros.

Lightfoot the Deer. Thornton W. Burgess. LC 97-42201. (Children's Thrift Classics Ser.). (Illus.). (J). 1998. pap. 1.00 (*0-486-40100-6*) Dover.

Lightfoot the Deer. Thornton W. Burgess. (Green Forest Ser.). (J). 1986. reprint ed. lib. bdg. 17.95 (*0-89966-526-8*) Buccaneer Bks.

Lightfoot the Historian: The Nature & Role of History in the Life & Thought of J. B. Lightfoot (1828-1889) As Churchman & Scholar. Geoffrey R. Treloar. LC 98-212144. (Wissenshaftliche Untersuchungen zum Neuen Testament Ser.: No. 103). 477p. 1998. pap. 95.00 (*3-16-146866-X*, Pub. by JCB Mohr) Coronet Bks.

***Lighthearted Devotions for Happy Christians: The Spanking Machine & Other Stories from the Good Old Days.** Wayne Taylor. Ed. by B. Russell Holt. LC 99-89986. 95p. 2000. pap. 6.99 (*0-8163-1784-4*) Pacific Pr Pub Assn.

Lighthearted Gourmet: Recipes for Lighter, Healthier Dinners, Romantic Solo Piano Music. Sharon O'Connor. LC 95-77125. (Sharon O'Connor's Menus & Music Ser.). (Illus.). 240p. 1995. 24.95 incl. audio compact disk (*1-883914-09-4*) Menus & Music.

Lightholder of Ireland & America, 2 vols., Set. LC 96-94416. (Illus.). (Orig.). 1997. pap. 60.00 (*0-9624657-2-0*) L L Kmiecik.

Lightholder of Ireland & America, Vol. I. LC 96-94416. (Illus.). (Orig.). 1997. pap. 60.00 (*0-9624657-3-9*) L L Kmiecik.

Lightholder of Ireland & America, Vol. II. LC 96-94416. (Illus.). (Orig.). 1997. pap. 60.00 (*0-9624657-4-7*) L L Kmiecik.

Lightholder of Ireland & America Vols. I & II: Addenda, Errata & Index. Linda L. Kmiecik. LC 96-94416. 60p. 1998. pap. text. write for info. (*0-9624657-5-5*) L L Kmiecik.

***Lighthouse.** Gerard Donovan. 2000. pap. 12.95 (*1-903392-03-9*, Pub. by Salmon Poetry) Dufour.

Lighthouse. Linda Eberhardt. (Our Town Ser.). 272p. 1997. mass mkt. 5.99 (*0-515-12020-0*, Jove) Berkley Pub.

Lighthouse. David Eckelberry. 1998. 13.95 (*0-7869-1216-2*, Pub. by TSR Inc) Random.

Lighthouse. Marcia Muller. pap. 4.50 (*0-7867-0885-9*) Carroll & Graf.

Lighthouse. Marcia Muller & Bill Pronzini. (Mystery Scene Bk.). 304p. 1992. mass mkt. 4.50 (*0-88184-885-9*) Carroll & Graf.

Lighthouse. Eugenia Price. 352p. 1972. mass mkt. 6.99 (*0-553-26910-0*) Bantam.

***Lighthouse.** Peter Sis. 2002. text (*0-374-34460-4*) FS&G.

Lighthouse. large type ed. Eugenia Price. LC 91-30413. 546p. 1992. reprint ed. lib. bdg. 20.95 (*1-56054-185-7*) Thorndike Pr.

***Lighthouse: Eugenia Price Commemorative Edition.** Ed. by Eugenia Price. LC 99-27182. (St. Simons Trilogy Ser.: Vol. 1). 344p. 1999. pap. 14.95 (*1-57736-154-7*) Providence Hse.

Lighthouse: Living in a Great Lakes Lighthouse, 1910 to 1940. Megan O'Hara. 32p. (J). 1998. 21.00 (*0-516-21252-4*) Childrens.

Lighthouse: The Official Strategy Guide. Corey Sandler. LC 96-70077. 192p. 1996. pap., per. 19.99 (*0-7615-0874-0*) Prima Pub.

Lighthouse Activity Book. Elinor DeWire. (Illus.). 88p. (Orig.). (J). (gr. k-8). 1995. pap. 11.95 (*0-9657313-0-8*) Sentinel Pubns.

Lighthouse Adventure, No. 4. Mary Maden. Ed. by Eric Schroeder. LC 95-83720. (Outer Banks Animals Adventure Ser.). (Illus.). 20p. (Orig.). (J). (gr. 1-4). 1996. pap. 5.95 (*0-9646970-3-3*) Dog & Pony Pub.

Lighthouse Adventures: Heroes, Haunts & Havoc on the Great Lakes. Wes Oleszewski. LC 99-72160. 224p. 1999. pap. 16.95 (*1-892384-01-9*) Avery Color.

Lighthouse by the Freeway. Margaret E. Deming. (Orig.). 1996. pap. write for info. (*1-57553-244-1*) Watermrk Pr.

Lighthouse Children. Syd Hoff. LC 92-41172. (I Can Read Bks.). (Illus.). 32p. (J). (ps-2). 1994. lib. bdg. 15.89 (*0-06-022959-4*) HarpC Child Bks.

Lighthouse Children. Syd Hoff. LC 92-41172. (I Can Read Bks.). (Illus.). 32p. (J). (ps-2). 1996. pap. 3.95 (*0-06-444178-4*, HarpTrophy) HarpC Child Bks.

Lighthouse Children. Syd Hoff. (I Can Read Bks.). (J). (ps-1). 1996. 8.95 (*0-606-09555-1*, Pub. by Turtleback) Demco.

Lighthouse Children: A Study Guide. D. Searl. Ed. by J. Friedland & R. Kessler. (Novel-Ties Ser.). (J). (gr. k-2). 1997. pap. text 15.95 (*0-7675-0146-2*) Lrn Links.

Lighthouse Christmas. Barbara Birenbaum. LC 90-7284. (Kindl Adventure Ser.). (Illus.). 48p. (Orig.). (J). (gr. k-5). 1991. pap. 5.95 (*0-935343-25-3*) Peartree.

Lighthouse Christmas. Barbara Birenbaum. LC 90-7284. (Historical Adventure Ser.: No. 8). (Illus.). 48p. (Orig.). (J). (gr. k-5). 1991. 12.95 (*0-935343-26-1*) Peartree.

***Lighthouse Devotional.** Cornell Haan. 2000. 14.99 (*1-57673-743-8*) Multnomah Pubs.

***Lighthouse Dog.** Betty Waterton. LC 97-67366. (Illus.). 32p. (J). (ps-3). 2000. pap. 6.95 (*1-55143-075-4*) Orca Bk Pubs.

***Lighthouse Dog to the Rescue.** Angeli Perrow. (Illus.). 32p. (J). (gr. k-3). 2000. 14.95 (*0-89272-487-0*) Down East.

Lighthouse Families. Cheryl Shelton-Roberts & Bruce Roberts. LC 97-11616. 176p. 1997. 29.95 (*1-57587-052-5*) Crane Hill AL.

***Lighthouse for the Soul.** Chantelle Anne Cooke. 36p. 1999. pap. 8.95 (*1-58535-011-7*) In His Steps.

Lighthouse Ghosts: 13 Bona Fide Apparitions Standing Watch over America's Shores. Norma Elizabeth & Bruce Roberts. (Illus.). 144p. 1998. pap. 12.95 (*1-57587-092-4*) Crane Hill AL.

Lighthouse Handbook on Vision Impairment & Vision Rehabilitation Vols. 2, Vol. 2, set. Ed. by Barbara Silverstone et al. (Illus.). 1248p. 2000. text 250.00 (*0-19-509489-1*) OUP.

Lighthouse Horrors: Tales of Adventure, Suspense, & the Supernatural. Ed. by Charles G. Waugh et al. LC 93-73752. 256p. (Orig.). 1993. pap. 12.95 (*0-89272-340-8*) Down East.

Lighthouse in My Life: The Story of a Maine Lightkeeper's Family. Philmore B. Wass. LC 87-71322. (Illus.). 272p. 1987. pap. 9.95 (*0-89272-236-3*) Down East.

Lighthouse Keeper. Ronda Armitage. (J). Date not set. pap. text. write for info. (*0-05-004387-0*) Addison-Wesley.

***Lighthouse Keeper.** large type ed. James Michael Pratt. LC 00-39867. 2000. write for info. (*1-56895-896-X*) Wheeler Pub.

***Lighthouse Keeper.** James Michael Pratt. 2001. reprint ed. pap. 6.99 (*0-312-97469-8*) St Martin.

***Lighthouse Keeper's Wife.** 2nd ed. Connie S. Small. Ed. by Andrea C. Hawkes. 214p. 1999. 24.95 (*0-89101-099-8*); pap. 14.95 (*0-89101-098-X*) U Maine Pr.

Lighthouse Mermaid. Kathleen Karr. LC 97-37367. (Hyperion Chapters Ser.). (Illus.). 64p. (J). (gr. 2-4). 1998. pap. 3.95 (*0-7868-1232-X*, Pub. by Hyprn Ppbks); lib. bdg. 14.49 (*0-7868-2297-X*, Pub. by Hyprn Ppbks) Little.

***Lighthouse Mermaid.** Kathleen Karr. (Hyperion Chapters Ser.). 1998. 9.05 (*0-606-13570-7*, Pub. by Turtleback) Demco.

***Lighthouse Movement.** Compiled by Cornell Haan. 96p. 1999. pap. 4.99 (*1-57673-633-4*) Multnomah Pubs.

Lighthouse Mysteries of the North Atlantic, No. 7-A. Robert E. Cahill. Ed. by Stacey Scanlon. (Illus.). 104p. 1998. pap. 6.95 (*1-889193-02-X*) Old Salt Box.

Lighthouse Mystery. Gertrude Chandler Warner. LC 63-20354. (Boxcar Children Ser.: No. 8). (Illus.). 128p. (J). (gr. 2-5). 1963. lib. bdg. 13.95 (*0-8075-4545-7*) A Whitman.

Lighthouse Mystery. Gertrude Chandler Warner. LC 63-20354. (Boxcar Children Ser.: No. 8). (Illus.). 128p. (J). (gr. 2-5). 1990. pap. 3.95 (*0-8075-4546-5*) A Whitman.

Lighthouse Mystery. Gertrude Chandler Warner. (Boxcar Children Ser.: No. 8). 147p. (J). (gr. 2-5). pap. 3.95 (*0-8072-1474-4*) Listening Lib.

Lighthouse Mystery. Gertrude Chandler Warner. (Boxcar Children Ser.: No. 8). (J). (gr. 2-5). 1963. 9.05 (*0-606-04467-1*, Pub. by Turtleback) Demco.

Lighthouse on the Hill: Glenville State College, 1872-1997, a Pictorial History. Nelson L. Wells & Charles Holt. LC 96-54618. 1997. write for info. (*0-89865-987-6*) Donning Co.

Lighthouse Point: An Anthology of Santa Cruz Writing. Ed. by Patrice Vecchione & Steve Wiesinger. 200p. (Orig.). 1987. pap. 12.95 (*0-9619004-1-5*) M Press HI.

***Lighthouse Prayer Journal.** Cornell Haan. 144p. 2000. 12.99 (*1-57673-681-4*, Pub. by Multnomah Pubs) GL Services.

Lighthouse Psalms: God's Gift of Hope & Direction. Honor Books Staff. (Gift Edition Ser.). (Illus.). 128p. 1999. 15.99 (*1-56292-805-8*) Honor Bks OK.

Lighthouse Secrets: A Collection of Recipes from the Nation's Oldest City. Junior Leage of St. Augustine Staff. (Illus.). 256p. 1999. 19.95 (*0-9670320-0-8*) Wimmer Bks.

Lighthouse Service: Its History, Activities & Organization. George Weiss. LC 72-3056. (Brookings Institution. Institute for Government Research. Service Monographs of the U. S. Government: No. 40). reprint ed. 37.50 (*0-404-57140-9*) AMS Pr.

Lighthouse Stevensons: The Extraordinary Story of the Building of the Scottish Lighthouses by the Ancestors of Robert Louis Stevenson. Bella Bathurst. LC 99-26174. 304p. 1999. 24.00 (*0-06-019427-8*) HarpC.

Lighthouse Stevensons: The Extraordinary Story of the Building of the Scottish Lighthouses by the Ancestors of Robert Louis Stevenson. Bella Bathurst. 304p. 2000. pap. 14.00 (*0-06-093226-0*, Perennial) HarperTrade.

***Lighthouse Stevensons: The Extraordinary Story of the Building of the Scottish Lighthouses by the Ancestors of Robert Louis Stevenson.** large type ed. Bella Bathurst. LC 99-88111. (Nonfiction Ser.). 2000. 28.95 (*0-7838-8964-X*, G K Hall Lrg Type) Mac Lib Ref.

Lighthouse That Wanted to Stay Lit. Ernest H. Wakefield. (Illus.). 208p. (Orig.). (C). 1992. pap. 14.95 (*0-943465-54-0*) Honors Pr.

***Lighthouse the Cat & the Sea: A Tropical Tale.** Leigh Rutledge. LC 99-25119. 128p. 1999. 17.95 (*0-525-94349-8*, Dutton Child) Peng Put Young Read.

***Lighthouse, the Cat, & the Sea: A Tropical Tale.** large type ed. Leigh W. Rutledge. LC 00-24257. (Americana Series). 2000. 26.95 (*0-7862-2528-9*) Thorndike Pr.

Lighthouses see Faros

***Lighthouses.** Robert Alberg. (Illus.). 48p. 1999. pap. 23.00 (*1-929602-00-6*) Lighthouse Gift.

Lighthouses. Jason Cooper. (Man-Made Wonders Ser.). 24p. (J). (gr. k-4). 1991. lib. bdg. 14.60 (*0-86592-630-1*) Rourke Enter.

Lighthouses. Brenda Z. Guiberson. (Redfeather Bks.). (Illus.). 70p. (J). (gr. 3-6). 1995. 15.95 (*0-8050-3170-7*) H Holt & Co.

***Lighthouses.** Heather Henson. (Illus.). 2000. 4.95 (*0-7624-0780-8*) Running Pr.

***Lighthouses.** Carol Highsmith. 2000. write for info. (*0-517-20449-5*) Random.

***Lighthouses.** Carol M. Highsmith & Ted Landphair. LC 99-37451. 2000. 9.99 (*0-517-20877-6*) Crown Pub Group.

Lighthouses. F. Ross Holland. 120p. 1995. 16.98 (*1-56799-201-3*, MetroBooks) M Friedman Pub Grp Inc.

Lighthouses. Intro. by James Hyland. LC 99-11962. (Illus.). 72p. 1999. 15.00 (*1-56799-770-8*) M Friedman Pub Grp Inc.

***Lighthouses.** Leo Marriott. (Illus.). 128p. 1999. 16.98 (*0-7651-1686-3*) Smithmark.

Lighthouses. Lynn F. Pearson. (Album Ser.: No. 32). (Illus.). 32p. 1995. pap. 6.25 (*0-7478-0275-0*, Pub. by Shire Pubns) Parkwest Pubns.

Lighthouses. Adele Richardson. LC 98-43599. (Let's Investigate Ser.). lib. bdg. 19.95 (*1-58341-006-6*, Creat Educ) Creative Co.

Lighthouses. Julie S. Taff. LC 98-27703. (Illus.). 112p. 1998. 25.95 (*1-56313-925-1*) BrownTrout Pubs Inc.

Lighthouses. 4th ed. Douglas B. Hague & Rosemary Christie. 307p. 1995. reprint ed. pap. 29.95 (*0-8464-4735-5*) Beekman Pubs.

Lighthouses: A Colorful Tour of America's Coastal Treasures. (Orig.). Date not set. pap. text. write for info. (*1-56944-124-3*) Terrell Missouri.

Lighthouses: Beacons of the Sea. National Geographic Society Staff. LC 99-26494. (Cultural & Geographical Exploration Ser.). (Illus.). 144p. 1999. 19.95 (*0-7910-5444-6*) Chelsea Hse.

Lighthouses: The Life & History of America's Waterways Boxed Set. Bruce Roberts. 1999. 239.60 (*0-7910-5482-9*) Chelsea Hse.

Lighthouses: Their Architecture, History & Archaeology. Douglas B. Hague & Rosemary Christie. 307p. (C). 1985. 30.00 (*0-85088-324-5*, Pub. by Gomer Pr) St Mut.

Lighthouses & Harbors, Vol. 1. Ebbe Almquist. 1999. 19.99 (*0-7858-1102-8*) Bk Sales Inc.

Lighthouses & Keepers: The U. S. Lighthouse Service & Its Legacy. Dennis L. Noble. LC 97-20882. (Illus.). 272p. 1997. 34.95 (*1-55750-638-8*) Naval Inst Pr.

Lighthouses & Legends of the Hudson. 3rd ed. Ruth R. Glunt. LC 74-84583. (Illus.). 154p. 1996. 20.00 (*0-912526-14-9*) Lib Res.

Lighthouses & Lifesaving Along the Massachusetts Coast. James W. Claflin. LC 98-88060. (Images of America Ser.). (Illus.). 228p. 1998. pap. 18.99 (*0-7524-1372-4*) Arcadia Publng.

Lighthouses & Lightships of Casco Bay. rev. ed. Peter D. Bachelder. LC 95-12006. Orig. Title: Lighthouses of Casco Bay. 1995. write for info. (*0-931675-01-4*) Prov Pr Maine.

***Lighthouses & Range Lights of Door County, Wisconsin.** Peter Bosman. LC 00-22688. (Illus.). xii, 118p. 2000. pap. 9.00 (*0-940473-38-0*) Wm Caxton.

Lighthouses from Aloft: 51 Scenic New England Lights. Charles Feil. LC 97-24339. (Illus.). 64p. (Orig.). 1997. pap. 14.95 (*0-89272-394-7*) Down East.

Lighthouses, Lightships, & the Gulf of Mexico. David G. Cipra. LC 96-72414. (Illus.). 260p. (Orig.). 1997. pap. 24.95 (*0-9636412-1-2*) Cypress Communs.

L

***Lighthouses of Atlantic Canada: New Brunswick, Nova Scotia, Prince Edward Island, Newfoundland & Labrador: A Pictorial Guide.** Courtney Thompson. LC 99-96228. (Illus.). 128p. 2000. 24.95 (*0-9651786-8-4*, Pub. by Catnap Publns); pap. 19.95 (*0-9651786-7-6*, Pub. by Catnap Publns) Magazines Inc.

Lighthouses of Cape Cod, Nantucket, Martha's Vineyard: Their History & Lore. Admont G. Clark. LC 91-68256. (Illus.). 258p. (Orig.). 1992. 29.95 (*0-940160-54-4*) Parnassus Imprints.

Lighthouses of Casco Bay see Lighthouses & Lightships of Casco Bay

Lighthouses of Delaware Bay: The Lighthouses & Lightships of Delaware Bay & River. Patrick Hornberger & Joy Waldron. (Illus.). 132p. 1998. 29.95 (*1-885457-11-1*) Eastwind MD.

Lighthouses of Hawai'i. Love Dean. LC 90-11214. (Illus.). 224p. 1991. 19.95 (*0-8248-1319-7*) UH Pr.

Lighthouses of Ireland. Kevin M. McCarthy. LC 96-37699. (Illus.). 140p. 1997. 21.95 (*1-56164-131-6*) Pineapple Pr.

Lighthouses of Maine. 5th ed. Wally Welch. (Illus.). 68p. (Orig.). 1995. pap. text 12.95 (*0-9618410-1-X*) Lighthouse FL.

Lighthouses of Maine & New Hampshire. Kathleen E. Finnegan & Timothy E. Harrison. (Illus.). 96p. 1991. 12.95 (*0-9629882-0-0*) Adfax Pubns.

Lighthouses of Massachusetts: A Pictorial Guide to the Lighthouses of Massachusetts. 2nd ed. Ed. by Pam Steiner. (Illus.). 84p. (Orig.). 1989. pap. 12.95 (*0-9618410-2-8*) Lighthouse FL.

Lighthouses of Michigan: Historic Landmarks. John Penrod. LC 99-169794. 72p. 1998. pap. 14.95 (*0-942618-78-5*) Penrod-Hiawatha.

Lighthouses of Rhode Island. 36p. (Orig.). 8.95 (*0-9618410-0-1*) Lighthouse FL.

Lighthouses of the Carolinas: A Short History & Guide. Terrance Zepke. LC 97-45042. (Illus.). 192p. 1998. pap. 12.95 (*1-56164-148-0*) Pineapple Pr.

Lighthouses of the Chesapeake. Robert De Gast. (Illus.). 176p. (C). 1993. reprint ed. pap. 24.95 (*0-8018-4765-6*) Johns Hopkins.

Lighthouses of the Florida Keys. Love Dean. LC 98-20541. (Illus.). 256p. 1998. 24.95 (*1-56164-160-X*); pap. 18.95 (*1-56164-165-0*) Pineapple Pr.

***Lighthouses of the Hawaiian Islands.** (Illus.). 32p. 2000. 10.95 (*0-9677544-0-2*) Lighthouse People.

***Lighthouses of the Mid-Atlantic States.** large type ed. Donna Mishler. (Illus.). 32p. (J). (gr. k-5). 1999. pap. text, student ed. 5.95 (*1-893709-02-7*) Suthernsky.

Lighthouses of the Pacific. James Gibbs. LC 85-63238. (Illus.). 256p. 1986. 29.95 (*0-88740-054-X*) Schiffer.

***Lighthouses of the Pacific Coast: Your Guide to the Lighthouses of California, Oregon, & Washington.** Photos & Text by Randy Leffingwell. LC 00-26342. (Pictorial Discovery Guide Ser.). (Illus.). 176p. 2000. 29.95 (*0-89658-429-1*) Voyageur Pr.

Lighthouses of the United States in 1874. Charles Nordhoff. Ed. & Intro. by William R. Jones. LC 92-18576. (Illus.). 64p. 1981. pap. 6.95 (*0-89646-086-X*) Vistabooks.

Lighthouses of the World. International Association of Lighthouse Author. LC 99-168107. (Illus.). 1998. pap. 24.95 (*0-7627-0387-3*) Globe Pequot.

Lighthouses of Virginia: The Quick & Easy Guide to All Virginia Lighthouses. Jerry A. Zaccaria. (Illus.). 40p. 1998. 24.95 (*0-9660799-5-7*) tr xiv pub.

Lighting. Pritchard. 1985. pap. text. write for info. (*0-582-30529-2*, Pub. by Addison-Wesley) Longman.

Lighting. 5th ed. Pritchard. (C). 1995. pap. text. write for info. (*0-582-23422-0*, Pub. by Addison-Wesley) Longman.

***Lighting: Exteriors & Landscapes.** Wanda Jankowski. (Illus.). 208p. 2000. reprint ed. text 30.00 (*0-7881-9147-0*) DIANE Pub.

Lighting a Slow Fusse: New & Selected Poems, 1. Nicki Jackowska. LC 99-195819. 1999. pap. text 21.00 (*1-900564-11-4*) Enitha Pr.

Lighting & Electricity. (Fix-It-Yourself Ser.). (Illus.). 144p. 1987. 17.27 (*0-8094-6248-6*); lib. bdg. 23.27 (*0-8094-6249-4*) Time-Life.

Lighting & Electricity. Time-Life Books Editors. (How to Fix It Ser.). (Illus.). 144p. (YA). (gr. 11). 1999. pap. 12.95 (*0-7370-0300-6*) T-L Custom Pub.

Lighting & Electricity. Ed. by Time-Life Books Editors. LC 98-39615. (How to Fix It Ser.). 144p. 1998. 16.99 (*0-7835-5653-5*) Time-Life.

Lighting & Sound. rev. ed. Neil Fraser. (Theater Manuals Ser.). (Illus.). 128p. 1995. reprint ed. pap. 14.95 (*0-7148-2514-X*, Pub. by Phaidon Press) Phaidon Pr.

Lighting & the Design Idea. Linda Essig. LC 96-76632. (C). 1996. pap. text 38.00 (*0-15-502069-2*) Harcourt.

Lighting & the Visual Environment for Senior Living: RP-28-98. (Recommended Practices Ser.). (Illus.). 80p. 1996. pap. 40.00 (*0-87995-131-1*, RP-28-96) Illum Eng.

Lighting Art: The Aesthetics of Stage Lighting Design. 2nd ed. Richard H. Palmer. LC 93-225. 251p. 1993. 79.00 (*0-13-501081-0*) P-H.

Lighting Book. Nonie Niesewand. LC 98-41252. (Illus.). 176p. 1999. 35.00 (*0-8230-2775-9*) Watsn-Guptill.

L

Lighting by Design: A Technical Guide. Brian Fitt & Joe Thornley. 336p. 1995. pap. 39.95 (*0-240-51440-8*, Focal) Buttrwrth-Heinemann.
Lighting Candles: Hospital Memories of Vietnam's Montagnards. Hilary Smith. (Illus.). 120p. (Orig.). 1988. pap. 7.95 (*0-9621110-0-7*) H Smith.
Lighting Candles: New & Selected Poems. Ruth Bidgood. 75p. 1982. pap. 9.95 (*0-907476-13-9*) Dufour.
Lighting Candles in the Dark. Ed. by Marnie Clark et al. (Illus.). 215p. (Orig.). (YA). 1992. pap. 9.50 (*0-9620912-3-5*) Friends Genl Conf.
Lighting Cookbook: Foolproof Recipes for Perfect Glamour, Portrait, Still Life & Corporate Photographs. Jenni Bidner. LC 96-51982. (Illus.). 44p. 1997. pap. 24.95 (*0-8174-4196-4*, Amphoto) Watsn-Guptill.
Lighting Design. Mark Karlen. pap. text 44.95 (*0-471-38162-4*, Wiley Heyden) Wiley.
Lighting Design: An Introductory Guide for Professionals. Carl Gardner & Berry Hannaford. (Illus.). 240p. (C). 1993. 96.95 (*0-85072-305-1*, Pub. by Design Council Bks) Ashgate Pub Co.
Lighting Design on Broadway: Designers & Their Credits, 1915-1990, 11. Bobbi Owen. LC 91-24007. (Bibliographies & Indexes in the Performing Arts Ser.: No. 11). 176p. 1991. lib. bdg. 49.95 (*0-313-26533-X*, OLD, Greenwood Pr) Greenwood.
Lighting Design Process: DG-7-94. (Design Guides Ser.). (Illus.). 18p. 1994. pap. 24.00 (*0-87995-108-7*, DG-7-94) Illum Eng.
Lighting Economics No. 150: An Intermediate Approach to Economics As Applied to the Lighting Practice ED-150.9-91. Cheryl R. English. 32p. (C). 1991. pap. text 24.95 (*0-87995-033-1*, ED150.9-91) Illum Eng.
***Lighting Education Fundamentals.** (Illus.). 234p. 2000. 95.00 (*0-87995-161-3*, ED-100-00) Illum Eng.
Lighting Education Fundamentals: ED-100-93. IESNA Staff. (Lighting Education Ser.). (Illus.). 430p. 1993. ring bd. 60.00 (*0-87995-089-7*, ED-100-93) Illum Eng.
Lighting Efficiency Applications. 2nd ed. Albert Thumann. (Illus.). 354p. 1991. 74.00 (*0-88173-137-4*, 0278) Fairmont Pr.
Lighting Fires. Randy Clark. LC 97-20075. 1998. pap. 9.99 (*0-88419-478-7*) Creation House.
Lighting Fires: Deepening Education Through Meditation. Jorgen Smit. Tr. by Simon Blaxland De Lange. 96p. 1995. pap. 14.95 (*1-869890-45-0*, Pub. by Hawthorn Press) Anthroposophic.
***Lighting Fixtures of the Depression Era.** Jo Ann Thomas. (Illus.). 240p. 2000. pap. 24.95 (*1-57432-198-6*) Collector Bks.
Lighting for Automatic Teller Machines: DG-9-97. (Design Guides Ser.). (Illus.). 15p. 1996. pap. 30.00 (*0-87995-122-2*, DG-9-95) Illum Eng.
***Lighting for Exterior Environments: RP-33-99.** IESNA Staff. (Illus.). 50p. 1999. pap. 45.00 (*0-87995-154-0*, RP-33-99) Illum Eng.
Lighting for Film & Electronic Cinematography. Dave Viera. LC 92-14321. 336p. (C). 1992. 42.75 (*0-534-12810-6*) Wadsworth Pub.
Lighting for Glamour Photography: A Complete Guide to Professional Techniques. David Kimber. LC 94-9028. (Illus.). 160p. 1994. pap. 24.95 (*0-8174-4230-8*, Amphoto) Watsn-Guptill.
***Lighting for Health & Safety.** N. A. Smith. LC 99-88581. (Illus.). 2000. pap. 69.95 (*0-7506-4566-0*) Buttrwrth-Heinemann.
Lighting for Industry & Security: A Handbook for Providers & Users of Lighting. Stanley L. Lyons. LC 92-10329. (Illus.). 320p. 1993. 160.00 (*0-7506-1084-0*) Buttrwrth-Heinemann.
Lighting for Occupational Hygienists. N. A. Smith. 115p. (C). 1991. 150.00 (*0-948237-06-6*, Pub. by H&H Sci Cnslts) St Mut.
***Lighting for Parking Facilities: RP-20-98.** rev. ed. (Recommended Practices Ser.). (Illus.). 15p. 1998. pap. 45.00 (*0-87995-149-4*, RP-20-96) Illum Eng.
***Lighting for People Photography.** 2nd ed. Stephen Crain. (Illus.). 128p. 2000. pap. 29.95 (*1-58428-016-6*) Amherst Media.
***Lighting for Television & Film.** 3rd ed. Gerald Millerson. 448p. 1999. pap. text 47.95 (*0-240-51582-X*, Focal) Buttrwrth-Heinemann.
Lighting for Video. 3rd ed. Gerald Millerson. (Media Manuals Ser.). 176p. 1991. pap. 27.95 (*0-240-51303-7*, Focal) Buttrwrth-Heinemann.
***Lighting Grandma's Fire: Mountain Skills & Valley Pastimes.** Bill Cunningham. LC 99-64981. (Illus.). 180p. 1999. pap. 9.95 (*1-890437-33-6*) Western Reflections.
Lighting Historic Buildings. Derek Phillips. LC 96-29853. (Illus.). 224p. 1997. 79.95 (*0-07-049864-4*) McGraw.
Lighting Historic Buildings: A Prospectus. Derek Phillips. LC 96-51636. 216p. 1997. text 69.95 (*0-7506-3342-5*) Buttrwrth-Heinemann.
Lighting in Commercial Buildings. 1995. lib. bdg. 250.00 (*0-8490-6459-7*) Gordon Pr.
Lighting in the Domestic Interior, Renaissance to Art Nouveau. Bourne. 1991. 95.00 (*0-85667-397-8*) Sothebys Pubns.
Lighting Inspector. Jack Rudman. (Career Examination Ser.: C-2134). 1994. reprint ed. pap. 29.95 (*0-8373-2134-4*) Nat Learn.
Lighting Kitchens & Baths. Jane Grosslight. (How-to-Book Interior Designs Ser.). (Illus.). 152p. (Orig.). 1993. pap. 34.00 (*0-927412-02-0*) Durwood Pubs.
Lighting Listings: A Worldwide Guide to Lighting Publications, Research Organizations, Educational Opportunities & Associations. 2nd rev. ed. Ed. by Judith Block. 223p. (Orig.). 1995. spiral bd. 37.00 (*1-885750-01-3*, LL-95) Visions Communs.
Lighting Management Handbook. Craig DiLouie. LC 93-31081. 300p. 1994. 74.00 (*0-88173-169-2*) Fairmont Pr.
Lighting Merchandising Areas: RP-2-85. rev. ed. Office Lighting Committee Staff. (Recommended Practices Ser.). (Illus.). 72p. 1986. pap. 18.00 (*0-87995-021-8*, RP-2-85) Illum Eng.
Lighting Metrics: TM-1-94. write for info. (*0-87995-097-8*, TM-1-94) Illum Eng.
***Lighting Modern Buildings.** Derek Phillips. 216p. 2000. 79.95 (*0-7506-4082-0*, Architectural Pr) Buttrwrth-Heinemann.
Lighting New Fires: Catholic Schooling in America 25 Years after Vatican II. Michael J. Guerra. 33p. (Orig.). 1991. pap. 4.00 (*1-55833-064-X*) Natl Cath Educ.
Lighting of Underground Mines. Donald A. Trotter. (Mining Engineering Ser.: Vol. 2). 220p. 1982. 50.00 (*0-87849-041-8*, Pub. by Trans T Pub) Enfield Pubs NH.
Lighting Out: A Vision of California & the Mountains. Daniel K. Duane. LC 93-34067. 256p. 1994. 14.00 (*1-55597-210-1*) Graywolf.
Lighting Out for the Territory: Reflections on Mark Twain & American Culture. Shelley F. Fishkin. (Illus.). 256p. 1996. 30.00 (*0-19-510531-1*) OUP.
Lighting Out for the Territory: Reflections on Mark Twain & American Culture. Shelley F. Fishkin. (Illus.). 272p. 1998. reprint ed. pap. 13.95 (*0-19-512122-8*) OUP.
Lighting Pattern Book for Homes. Russell P. Leslie & Kathryn M. Conway. LC 93-80008. (Illus.). 232p. 1993. 40.00 (*1-883297-00-1*) RPI Lght Res.
Lighting Pattern Book for Homes. 2nd ed. Lighting Research Center Staff. LC 96-41380. (Illus.). 208p. 1996. 74.95 (*0-07-038079-1*) McGraw.
Lighting Secrets for the Professional Photographer. Alan Brown et al. (Illus.). 134p. 1990. pap. 26.99 (*0-89879-412-9*, Wrtrs Digest Bks) F & W Pubns Inc.
Lighting Style: The Complete Visual Sourcebook for Every Room in Your House. Kevin McCloud. LC 94-13676. 144p. 1995. 25.00 (*0-671-88706-8*) S&S Trade.
***Lighting Styles.** Sian Rees. (Illus.). 2000. pap. 17.95 (*0-600-60093-9*) P HM.
Lighting Techniques for Photographers. Norman Kerr. LC 97-75209. (Illus.). 120p. 1998. pap. 29.95 (*0-936262-66-4*) Amherst Media.
Lighting Techniques for Video Production: The Art of Casting Shadows. Tom LeTourneau. 172p. 1996. reprint ed. pap. 34.95 (*0-240-80248-9*, Focal) Buttrwrth-Heinemann.
Lighting Technology: A Guide for the Entertainment Industry. Brian Fitt & Joe Thornley. 480p. 1997. pap. 62.95 (*0-240-51449-1*, Focal) Buttrwrth-Heinemann.
Lighting the Bay: Tales of Chesapeake Lighthouses. Pat Vojtech. LC 96-31958. (Illus.). 208p. 1996. 34.95 (*0-87033-466-2*, Tidewtr Pubs) Cornell Maritime.
Lighting the Darkness. Joseph B. Lederleitner. 1995. 13.95 (*0-533-11523-X*) Vantage.
Lighting the Electronic Office. Gary R. Steffe. 1995. pap. 44.95 (*0-442-01238-1*, VNR) Wiley.
Lighting the Electronic Office. Gary R. Steffy. (Architecture Ser.). 154p. 1995. pap. 54.95 (*0-471-28507-2*, VNR) Wiley.
***Lighting the Eye of the Dragon: Inner Secrets of Taoist Feng Shui.** Baolin Wu & Jessica Eckstein. LC 99-86054. (Illus.). 256p. 2000. pap. 14.95 (*0-312-25497-0*) St Martin.
Lighting the Fire: Elsie J. Oxenham, the Abbey Girls & the English Folk Dance Revival. Allison Thompson. 80p. 1998. pap. 10.00 (*0-9666563-0-X*) Squirrel Hil Pr.
Lighting the Flame: A Resource Book for Worship. Charles Cammarata. LC 96-38669. 96p. (Orig.). 1997. pap. 10.95 (*0-7880-0870-6*) CSS OH.
Lighting the Liturgy. Viggo B. Rambusch. (Meeting House Essays Ser.: No. 7). 62p. (Orig.). 1994. pap. 6.00 (*1-56854-061-2*, LITLIT) Liturgy Tr Pubns.
Lighting the Night Sky. Kenneth O. Hanson. LC 82-22768. 70p. 1983. pap. 6.95 (*0-932576-15-X*) Breitenbush Bks.
Lighting the Path. abr. ed. Melody Beattie. audio 12.00 (*0-671-73952-2*, Audioworks) S&S Trade.
Lighting the Seventh Fire: The Science, Healing & Spiritual Ways of the Native Americans. F. David Peat. LC 94-16685. (Illus.). 352p. 1994. 19.95 (*1-55972-249-5*, Birch Ln Pr) Carol Pub Group.
Lighting the Shakespearean Stage, 1567-1642. R. B. Graves. LC 99-19002. 274p. 1999. 44.95 (*0-8093-2275-7*) S Ill U Pr.
Lighting the Town: A Study of Management in the North West Gas Industry, 1805-1880. John F. Wilson. 256p. 1991. 45.00 (*1-85396-176-0*, Pub. by P Chapman) Taylor & Francis.
***Lighting the Way.** 128p. 1999. (*0-309-06435-X*) Natl Acad Pr.
***Lighting the Way: A 90-Day Journey in Sharing Your Faith.** Mary L. Marr. 152p. 2000. pap. write for info. (*0-8341-1840-8*) Beacon Hill.
Lighting the Way: The Centennial History of the Queens Borough Public Library, 1896-1996. Jeffrey A. Kroessler & Queens Library Foundation Staff. LC 96-39153. 1996. write for info. (*0-89865-986-8*) Donning Co.
***Lighting the Way Home Family Bible.** Thomas Kinkade. 960p. 2000. 54.99 (*0-7852-5709-8*); 79.99 (*0-7852-5637-7*) Nelson.
***Lighting the Way Home Family Bible.** deluxe ed. Thomas Kinkade. 960p. 2000. 129.99 (*0-7852-5638-5*) Nelson.
Lighting the Way, 1908-1935: The Early Years of Catholic School Superintendency. John J. Augenstein. 149p. (Orig.). 1996. pap. 13.00 (*1-55833-168-9*) Natl Cath Educ.
Lighting the Way to God: Giving People a Context for Understanding the Gospel. James A. Odens. LC 99-90126. 110p. 1999. pap. 8.95 (*0-9627088-1-X*) J A Odens.
Lighting the World see **Iluminando el Mundo, Vol. II, Hechos 9-15**
Lighting the World: A New Look at Acts - God's Training Manual for Every Christian. C. Peter Wagner. (Acts of the Holy Spirit Ser.: Vol. 2). 251p. 1995. pap. 10.99 (*0-8307-1721-8*, Regal Bks) Gospel Lght.
***Lighting Two Thousand.** Tina Skinner. (Illus.). 112p. 2000. pap. 19.95 (*0-7643-1156-5*) Schiffer.
Lighting Up: One Hundred One Tobacco Tales. Laura Hedlund & Kai Lahti. (Illus.). (Orig.). 1986. pap. 5.95 (*0-9614560-0-0*) Impress.
Lighting up the Terrain: The Poetry of Margaret Avison. Ed. by David A. Kent. 220p. (C). 1987. pap. 15.00 (*0-920763-93-6*, Pub. by ECW); text 25.00 (*0-920763-94-4*, Pub. by ECW) Genl Dist Srvs.
Lighting up the Two-Year Old. Benjie Aerenson. LC 99-215186. 1998. pap. 5.25 (*0-8222-1648-5*) Dramatists Play.
Lighting Your Home. R. Beigel. 1994. pap. 9.95 (*1-870948-94-7*) St Mut.
Lighting Your Home Inside & Out: Design, Select, Install. Jane Cornell. Ed. by Margaret Gallos. LC 95-70917. (Illus.). 176p. 1996. pap. 14.95 (*1-880029-67-7*) Creative Homeowner.
Lightkeeper. Susan Wiggs. 1997. per. 5.99 (*1-55166-301-5*, Mira Bks) Harlequin Bks.
Lightland. Donna Cole. 190p. 1996. pap. 13.00 (*1-883721-19-9*) Silver Mtn Pr.
Lightlike Submanifolds of Semi-Riemannian Manifolds & Applications. Krishan L. Duggal & Aurel Bejancu. LC 96-1346. (Mathematics & Its Applications Ser.: Vol. 364). 308p. (C). 1996. text 166.00 (*0-7923-3957-6*) Kluwer Academic.
Lightly on the Land: The SCA Trail Building & Maintenance Manual. Robert C. Birkby & Student Conservation Association Staff. LC 96-17213. (Illus.). 272p. 1996. pap. 19.95 (*0-89886-491-7*) Mountaineers.
Light'n Lively Reads for ESL, Adult, & Teen Readers: A Thematic Bibliography. La-Vergne Rosow. LC 96-7084. 300p. 1996. lib. bdg. 40.00 (*1-56308-365-5*) Libs Unl.
Lightner Witmer: His Life & Times. Paul McReynolds. LC 97-17508. 353p. 1997. 24.95 (*1-55798-444-1*) Am Psychol.
Lightness, Brightness & Transparency. Ed. by Alan Gilchrist. 328p. 1994. text 69.95 (*0-8058-0800-0*) L Erlbaum Assocs.
***Lightness of Being in China: Adaption & Discursive Figuration in Cinema & Theater.** Harry H. Koushu. LC 99-26969. (Asian Thought & Culture Ser.: Vol. 37). 200p. 1999. 46.95 (*0-8204-4543-6*) P Lang Pubng.
Lightnin' Hopkins Blues Guitar Legend. Tr. by Dan Bowden. 96p. 1995. pap. 12.95 (*0-7866-0238-4*, 95344) Mel Bay.
Lightnin' Hopkins "The Ultimate Texas Bluesman" Richard DeVinck. (Illus.). 128p. (Orig.). 1995. pap. 29.95 (*1-56922-068-9*, 07-4051) Creat Cncpts.
***Lightnin' Hopkins/The Gold Star Years: Intermediate Level.** Tr. by Dan Bowden. 120p. 1998. spiral bd. 17.95 (*0-7866-3050-7*, 96594) Mel Bay.
Lightning see **Relampago**
Lightning. Suzanne Harper. LC 96-33299. (First Bks.). (J). 1997. lib. bdg. 22.00 (*0-531-20290-9*) Watts.
Lightning! Lorraine Jean Hopping. LC 98-7656. (Hello Reader! Ser.). (Illus.). 48p. (J). (gr. 2-4). 1999. pap. 3.99 (*0-590-52285-X*) Scholastic Inc.
Lightning. Dean Koontz. 368p. 1989. mass mkt. 7.99 (*0-425-11580-1*) Berkley Pub.
Lightning. Dean Koontz. 1989. 13.09 (*0-606-00938-8*, Pub. by Turtleback) Demco.
Lightning. Stephen Kramer. (Nature in Action Ser.). (Illus.). 48p. (J). (gr. 1-4). 1992. lib. bdg. 19.95 (*0-87614-659-0*, Carolrhoda) Lerner Pub.
Lightning. Stephen Kramer. (Illus.). 48p. (J). (gr. 1-4). 1993. pap. 7.95 (*0-87614-617-5*, Carolrhoda) Lerner Pub.
Lightning. Peter Murray. (Forces of Nature Ser.). (Illus.). 32p. (J). (gr. 2-6). 1996. lib. bdg. 22.79 (*1-56766-215-3*) Childs World.
Lightning. Gail Saunders-Smith. (Weather Ser.). (Illus.). 24p. (J). (ps-2). 1998. 13.25 (*0-516-21332-6*) Childrens.
Lightning. Seymour Simon. LC 96-16962. (Illus.). 32p. (J). (gr. k-4). 1997. 16.00 (*0-688-14638-4*, Wm Morrow) Morrow Avon.
Lightning. Seymour Simon. LC 96-16962. (Illus.). 32p. (J). (gr. k-4). 1997. lab manual ed. 15.93 (*0-688-14639-2*, Wm Morrow) Morrow Avon.
Lightning. Seymour Simon. 32p. (J). 1999. mass mkt. 5.95 (*0-688-16706-3*, Wm Morrow) Morrow Avon.
***Lightning.** Smallwood & Stewart Staff. (Illus.). (J). 2001. pap. 4.95 (*0-7407-1062-1*) Andrews & McMeel.
Lightning. Danielle Steel. LC 94-43651. 408p. 1995. 24.95 (*0-385-31192-3*) Delacorte.
Lightning. Danielle Steel. 464p. 1996. mass mkt. 7.50 (*0-440-22150-1*) Dell.
Lightning. Danielle Steel. 1996. mass mkt. 8.99 (*0-440-22292-3*) Doubleday.
***Lightning.** limited ed. Sebastian Dowd. 78p. 1999. 90.00 (*1-881119-46-7*) Pyncheon Hse.
Lightning. limited ed. Danielle Steel. 408p. 1995. 200.00 (*0-385-31488-4*) Delacorte.
Lightning. Martin A. Uman. (Physics Ser.). 320p. 1984. reprint ed. pap. 8.95 (*0-486-64575-4*) Dover.
***Lightning.** unabridged ed. Sebastian Dowd. 78p. 1999. 60.00 (*1-881119-30-0*) Pyncheon Hse.
Lightning, Set. abr. ed. Dean Koontz. 1988. 17.00 incl. audio (*0-671-65237-0*, 391071, Pub. by S&S Audio) Lndmrk Audiobks.
Lightning: A Fred Carver Mystery. John Lutz. 88p. 1995. 22.50 (*0-8050-4379-9*) H Holt & Co.
Lightning: An 87th Precinct Novel. Ed McBain, pseud. (Eighty-Seventh Precinct Novel Ser.). 304p. 1985. mass mkt. 4.95 (*0-380-69974-5*, Avon Bks) Morrow Avon.
Lightning: BAC Lightning F Mk3-Mk6. Roger Chesneau & Raymond L. Rimell. (Aeroguide Ser.: No. 8). 1984. pap. 5.50 (*0-918805-07-4*) Pac Aero Pr.
Lightning: Poems from Hollywood. 31p. (Orig.). 1997. pap. 5.00 (*0-89642-388-3*) Linden Pubs.
Lightning: The Poetry of Rene Char. Nancy K. Piore. LC 80-22001. (Illus.). 153p. 1981. text 30.00 (*0-930350-08-1*) NE U Pr.
Lightning: The 101st in the Gulf War. Edward M. Flanagan, II. (Association of the U. S. Army Book Ser.). 280p. 1994. 25.00 (*0-02-881095-3*) Brasseys.
Lightning Aces of the ETO - MTO. John Stanaway. (Illus.). 96p. 1998. pap. 17.95 (*1-85532-698-1*, Pub. by Ospry) Motorbooks Intl.
Lightning Aces of the Pacific & CBI. John C. Stanaway. (Aircraft of the Aces Ser.: No. 14). (Illus.). 96p. 1997. pap. 17.95 (*1-85532-633-7*, Pub. by Ospry) Motorbooks Intl.
Lightning & Boats. Michigan Sea Grant Staff. (Illus.). 9p. 1995. pap. 1.00 (*1-885756-00-3*, MICHU-SG89-700) MI Sea Grant.
Lightning & Boats: A Manual of Safety & Prevention. Michael V. Huck, Jr. 1996. pap. text 9.95 (*0-07-029152-7*) McGraw.
Lightning & Boats: A Manual of Safety & Prevention. Michael V. Huck, Jr. LC 95-232. (Illus.). 80p. 1993. pap. 9.95 (*0-9639566-0-4*) Seaworthy WI.
Lightning & Its Spectrum: An Atlas of Photographs. Salanave. LC 80-18882. (Illus.). 136p. 1980. 34.95 (*0-8165-0374-5*) U of Ariz Pr.
Lightning & Lightning Protection. William C. Hart & Edgar W. Malone. Ed. by Donald R. White. LC 79-65691. (Illus.). 181p. 1979. text 39.00 (*0-932263-14-3*) emf-emi Control.
Lightning & Other Wonders of the Sky. Querida L. Pearce. Ed. by Jane Steltenpohl. (Amazing Science Ser.). (Illus.). 64p. (J). (gr. 4-6). 1989. pap. 5.95 (*0-671-68648-8*, Julian Messner) Silver Burdett Pr.
Lightning & Rainbows. Michael Carroll. (J). (gr. 1-5). 1997. write for info. (*1-56476-603-9*, Chariot Bks); 13.99 (*0-7814-3000-3*, Chariot Bks) Chariot Victor.
Lightning & the Storm. Marsha Newman. 229p. 1986. 9.95 (*0-9608658-2-9*) Wellspring Utah.
Lightning, Auroras, Nocturnal Lights & Related Luminous Phenomena. William R. Corliss. LC 82-99902. (Catalog of Geophysical Anomalies Ser.). (Illus.). 248p. 1982. pap. 16.95 (*0-915554-09-7*) Sourcebook.
Lightning Book. Peter E. Viemeister. (Illus.). 316p. 1972. reprint ed. pap. text 13.00 (*0-262-72004-3*) MIT Pr.
Lightning Bug. Donald Harington. 256p. 1987. pap. 6.95 (*0-15-651998-4*, Harvest Bks) Harcourt.
Lightning Bug Thunder. Katie Burke. LC 98-930990. (Illus.). 32p. (J). (ps-4). 1998. 14.95 (*1-55209-271-2*) Firefly Bks Ltd.
Lightning Discharge. Martin A. Uman. (International Geophysics Ser.). 377p. 1987. text 84.00 (*0-12-708350-2*) Acad Pr.
Lightning Electromagnetics. Ed. by Robert L. Gardner. (Electromagnetics Library). 400p. 1990. 120.00 (*0-89116-988-1*) Hemisp Pub.
Lightning Escape: And Other Stories with Take-Away Value. Nancy Speck. LC 97-4651. (Fairfield Friends Devotional Adventure Ser.). 128p. (J). 1997. pap. 6.99 (*1-55661-962-6*) Bethany Hse.
Lightning-Fast Animation Graphics. Len Dorfman. LC 93-50714. 1994. 48.95 (*0-07-017940-9*, Windcrest) TAB Bks.
***Lightning Fast Enlightenment: A Journey to the Secrets of Happiness.** Jordan S. Metzger. LC 98-91635. xii, 430p. 2000. pap. 18.95 (*0-9665922-6-3*) Profound Pr.
Lightning Field: Travels in & Around New Mexico. Robert Eaton. LC 95-19366. 240p. (Orig.). 1995. 23.00 (*1-55566-153-X*) Johnson Bks.
Lightning Field: Travels in & Around New Mexico. Robert A. Eaton. LC 95-19366. 240p. (Orig.). 1995. pap. 14.95 (*1-55566-159-9*) Johnson Bks.
Lightning, God's Turtle. Ladonna Spencer. 32p. 1986. pap. text 4.00 (*0-88144-078-7*) Christian Pub.
***Lightning in a Bottle.** David Baum. LC 99-88245. 2000. pap. 18.95 (*0-7931-3595-8*) Dearborn.
Lightning in a Bottle - The Sox of '67. Herbert F. Crehan & James W. Ryan. (Illus.). 1993. 19.95 (*0-8283-1967-7*); pap. 13.95 (*0-8283-1968-5*) Branden Bks.
Lightning in a Drought Year: A Novel of the Heartland. Michelle Black. LC 99-63575. 260p. 1999. 22.95 (*0-9658014-2-X*) WinterSun Pr.
***Lightning in a Drought Year: A Novel of the Heartland.** Michelle Black. LC 99-63575. 260p. 2000. pap. 13.95 (*1-929705-00-X*) WinterSun Pr.
***Lightning in a Jar: Catching Racing Fever: A Thoroughbred Owner's Guide.** W. Cothran Campbell. 256p. 2000. 29.95 (*1-58150-053-X*, Pub. by Blood-Horse) IPG Chicago.
Lightning in July. Ann L. McLaughlin. LC 88-37410. 180p. (Orig.). 1989. pap. 9.95 (*0-936784-72-5*) J Daniel.
Lightning in the Storm: The 101st Air Assault Division in the Gulf War. Tom Taylor. LC 93-46236. 468p. 1994. 29.50 (*0-7818-0268-7*) Hippocrene Bks.
Lightning Injuries: Electrical, Medical, Legal Aspects. Christopher J. Andrews. 208p. 1991. lib. bdg. 139.00 (*0-8493-5458-7*, RD96) CRC Pr.
***Lightning Inside You: And Other Native American Riddles.** John Bierhorst. (Illus.). 112p. (gr. 4-7). 1999. mass mkt. 5.95 (*0-688-17298-9*, Grenwillow Bks) HarpC Child Bks.

An Asterisk (*) at the beginning of an entry indicates that the title is appearing for the first time.

L

Lightning Inside You: And Other Native American Riddles. Ed. & Tr. by John Bierhorst. LC 91-21744. (Illus.). 112p. (J). (ps-3). 1992. 14.00 (*0-688-09582-8*, Wm Morrow) Morrow Avon.

*__Lightning Keeper.__ Starling R. Lawrence. 2002. text. write for info. (*0-374-18745-2*) FS&G.

Lightning Liz. Larry D. Brimner. LC 97-13835. (Rookie Readers Ser.). (Illus.). 32p. (J). (gr. k-2). 1998. 17.00 (*0-516-20753-9*) Childrens.

Lightning Liz. Larry D. Brimner. Ed. by Dana Rau. (Rookie Readers Ser.). (Illus.). 32p. (J). 1998. pap. 4.95 (*0-516-26360-9*) Childrens.

"Lightning" Master of the Blues. Fred J. Jackson. 78p. 1998. reprint ed. 12.00 (*1-891934-00-7*) Black Rose CA.

*__Lightning Mule Brigade: The 1863 Raid of Abel Streight into Alabama: 73rd, 51st Indiana, 80th Illinois & 3rd Ohio Regiments & 1st Alabama (Union) Cavalry.__ Robert Willett. LC 99-71525. 225p. 1999. 24.95 (*1-57860-074-X*) Guild Pr IN.

*__Lightning Mule Brigade: The 1863 Raid of Abel Streight into Alabama; 73rd, 51st Indiana, 80th Illinois & 3rd Ohio Regiments & 1st Alabama (Union) Cavalry.__ Robert Willett. LC 99-71525. 225p. 1999. pap. 16.95 (*1-57860-025-1*) Guild Pr IN.

Lightning of August. Jorge Ibarguengoitia. 117p. 1986. pap. 3.95 (*0-380-89617-6*, Avon Bks) Morrow Avon.

*__Lightning on the Sun: A Novel.__ Robert Bingham & Stacey D'Erasmo. LC 99-47900. 288p. 2000. 23.95 (*0-385-48856-4*) Doubleday.

Lightning over the Treasury Building: An Expose of Our Banking & Currency Monstrosity. John R. Elsom. 1979. lib. bdg. 59.95 (*0-8490-2960-0*) Gordon Pr.

*__Lightning over Water: Sharpening America's Light Forces for Rapid-Reaction Missions.__ John Matsumura. LC 00-36920. 2000. write for info. (*0-8330-2845-6*) Rand Corp.

Lightning Protection. J. Lawrence Marshall. LC 73-4415. (Illus.). 206p. reprint ed. pap. 63.90 (*0-608-11499-5*, 200631100058) Bks Demand.

Lightning Protection Components, UL 96. 4th ed. (C). 1994. pap. text 35.00 (*1-55989-602-7*) Underwrtrs Labs.

Lightning Protection for People & Property. Marvin M. Frydenlund. LC 92-30334. 1993. text 59.95 (*0-442-01338-8*, VNR) Wiley.

Lightning Protection for Power Systems. M. Darveniza. (High Voltage Power Transmission Ser.). 1999. 90.00 (*0-86380-241-9*) Research Studies Pr Ltd.

Lightning Protection Manual for Rural Electric Systems. Parrish Kvaltine & Associates, Inc. Staff. 1993. pap. text. write for info. (*0-917599-12-8*) Natl Rural.

Lightning Protection of Buildings & Their Contents. M. Johansson. (C). 1994. pap. 50.00 (*0-86022-361-2*, Pub. by Build Servs Info Assn) St Mut.

Lightning Protection of Buildings Sources of Information. 1979. 60.00 (*0-86022-074-5*, Pub. by Build Servs Info Assn) St Mut.

Lightning-Rod Man see Piazza Tales

Lightning Season. Sara Orwig. 320p. 1993. mass mkt. 3.99 (*0-8217-4052-0*, Zebra Kensgtn) Kensgtn Pub Corp.

*__Lightning Should Have Fallen On Ghalib.__ Mirza A. Ghalib. Tr. by Robert Bly & Sunil Dutta from URD. LC 98-49459. 1998. 21.00 (*0-88001-686-8*) HarpC.

Lightning Song. Lewis Nordan. LC 96-54157. 308p. 1997. 18.95 (*1-56512-084-1*, 72084) Algonquin Bks.

Lightning Song. Lewis Nordan. 1998. 10.95 (*1-56512-220-8*) Algonquin Bks.

Lightning Stick: Arrows, Wounds & Indian Legends. H. Henrietta Stockel. LC 94-43926. (Illus.). 176p. 1995. 24.95 (*0-87417-266-7*) U of Nev Pr.

Lightning, Storms, Natural Disasters & Your Golf Facility. unabridged ed. (NGF Info Pacs Ser.). (Illus.). 118p. (Orig.). 1998. pap. 45.00 (*1-57701-010-8*, 99LB023) Natl Golf.

Lightning Strategies for Innovation: How the World's Best Companies Create New Products. Willard I. Zangwill. 225p. 1992. 24.95 (*0-02-935675-X*) Free Pr.

Lightning Strike. Deborah Morris. (Real Kids Real Adventures Ser.: No. 5). 112p. (J). (gr. 3-7). 1997. mass mkt. 3.99 (*0-425-16117-X*) Berkley Pub.

*__Lightning Strikes.__ V. C. Andrews. (Hudson Ser.: Vol. 2). 384p. 2000. 24.95 (*0-671-00768-8*, PB Hardcover); per. 7.99 (*0-671-00769-6*, Pocket Star Bks) PB.

*__Lightning Strikes.__ V. C. Andrews. (Illus.). (J). 2000. 13.34 (*0-606-18830-4*) Turtleback.

Lightning Strikes. Mary L. Baxter. (Thirty-Six Hours Ser.: No. 1). 1997. per. 4.50 (*0-373-65006-X*, 1-65006-8) Harlequin Bks.

Lightning Strikes. Kathleen Korbel. (Intimate Moments Ser.: No. 351). 1990. per. 2.95 (*0-373-07351-8*) Silhouette.

Lightning Strikes: Men & Machines of the 475th Fighter Group, 1943-1945. Ronald W. Yoshino. (Illus.). 166p. 1992. reprint ed. pap. 22.95 (*0-89745-104-X*) Sunflower U Pr.

Lightning Strikes: The Lives & Times of Boxing's Lightweight Heroes. Gerald Suster. LC 95-73116. 186p. 1996. 26.95 (*0-86051-939-2*, Robson-Parkwest) Parkwest Pubns.

Lightning Strikes Once: All-Phase Electric Supply Co.: The First Thirty Years. Ronald F. Kinney. LC 89-81811. (Illus.). 378p. (Orig.). 1989. 16.95 (*0-9625022-0-0*) All-Phase Pub.

Lightning Strikes Once: All-Phase Electric: The First Thirty Years. Ronald F. Kinney. (Illus.). write for info. (*0-318-66445-6*) All-Phase Pub.

Lightning Strikes Twice. pap. 13.95 (*0-340-71006-3*, Pub. by Hodder & Stought Ltd) Trafalgar.

*__Lightning Strikes Twice: Franklin: The Key to the New Millennium.__ Ed. by Peg Campbell. (Illus.). 240p. 1999. pap. 13.95 (*1-891722-03-4*) Am Hist Co.

Lightning Time. Douglas Rees. LC 97-31028. (Illus.). 172p. (J). (gr. 5-9). 1997. 15.95 (*0-7894-2458-4*) DK Pub Inc.

Lightning Time. Douglas Rees. LC 98-28615. 176p. (J). (gr. 5-9). 1999. pap. 4.99 (*0-14-130317-4*, PuffinBks) Peng Put Young Read.

Lightning War on Waste: A Tactical Handbook for Improving Work Processes - Save Time, Money, People & Material. David G. Freymann. LC 95-61173. 96p. (Orig.). 1995. pap. text 9.95 (*0-9646122-3-2*) Zeon Pub.

Lightning Warrior. Max Brand. 272p. 1998. mass mkt. 4.50 (*0-8439-4420-X*, Leisure Bks) Dorchester Pub Co.

Lightning Warrior. large type ed. Max Brand. Date not set. 20.00 (*0-7838-1667-7*, G K Hall Lrg Type) Mac Lib Ref.

Lightning Warrior. Max Brand. 320p. 1998. reprint ed. mass mkt. 4.99 (*0-8439-4355-6*, Leisure Bks) Dorchester Pub Co.

Lightning Warrior: A North-Western Story. Max Brand. LC 96-6302. 230p. 1996. 16.95 (*0-7862-0656-X*) Five Star.

Lightning Wires: The Telegraph & China's Technological Modernization, 1860-1890, 6. Erik Baark. LC 96-24217. (Contributions in Asian Studies: No. 6). 240p. 1997. 69.50 (*0-313-30011-9*, Greenwood Pr) Greenwood.

Lightning Within: An Anthology of Contemporary American Indian Fiction. Ed. & Intro. by Alan R. Velie. LC 90-12658. x, 164p. 1991. pap. 9.95 (*0-8032-9614-2*, Bison Books) U of Nebr Pr.

Lightningbolt. Hyemeyohsts Storm. (Illus.). 544p. 1994. 30.00 (*0-345-36710-3*) One Wrld.

*__Lightning's Tale.__ Hugh Campbell. (Illus.). 38p. (YA). (gr. 3 up). 2000. reprint ed. pap. 12.95 (*1-57188-199-9*) F Amato Pubns.

Lightpaths. Howard V. Hendrix. 352p. 1997. mass mkt. 5.99 (*0-441-00470-9*) Ace Bks.

Lightplane Maintenance: Aircraft Engineer Operating Guide. Belvoir Publications Staff & Kas Thomas. 224p. 1989. pap. 18.95 (*0-07-155358-4*) McGraw.

Lightplane Refurbishing Techniques. Joe Christy. (Illus.). 160p. 1986. 18.95 (*0-8306-0337-9*, NO. 2437) McGraw-Hill Prof.

Lightposts for Living: The Art of Choosing a Joyful Life. Thomas Kinkade. 1999. 19.99 (*0-7852-6974-6*) Nelson.

Lightposts for Living: The Art of Choosing a Joyful Life. Thomas Kinkade. LC 98-41617. (Illus.). 256p. 1999. 20.00 (*0-446-52522-7*, Pub. by Warner Bks) Little.

*__Lightposts for Living: The Art of Choosing a Joyful Life.__ Thomas Kinkade. 256p. 2000. pap. 12.95 (*0-446-67617-9*) Warner Bks.

Lights. Howard Korder. 1994. pap. 5.25 (*0-8222-1403-2*) Dramatists Play.

Lights. Howard Korder. 1997. pap. 13.95 (*0-413-71190-0*, A0801, Methuen Drama) Methn.

Lights: From the Pythagoreans to the Quantum Theory. Frode Grini. 122p. (C). 1997. pap. 21.00 (*82-00-22764-2*, Pub. by Scand Univ Pr) IBD Ltd.

Lights: Revelations of God's Goodness. Jack Wintz. 160p. 1996. pap. text 7.95 (*0-86716-269-4*) St Anthony Mess Pr.

Lights, Action, Land-Ho! Judy Delton. (Pee Wee Scouts Ser.: No. 18). (Illus.). 112p. (J). (gr. 1-4). 1992. pap. 3.99 (*0-440-40732-X*, YB BDD) BDD Bks Young Read.

Lights, Action, Land-Ho! Judy Delton. (Pee Wee Scouts Ser.). (J). 1992. 9.09 (*0-606-05428-6*, Pub. by Turtleback) Demco.

Lights along the Path: Jewish Folklore Through the Grades for Children Age Four to Twelve. Rebecca Schacht. LC 99-90029. (Illus.). 195p. (J). (ps-7). 1999. pap. 16.95 (*0-9668448-0-7*, 1001) Chelsey Pr.

Lights along the Way. Ruth Crenshaw et al. Ed. by Jim Gray. LC 97-69698. (Illus.). 248p. 1997. pap. 12.95 (*0-9652829-2-9*) Creekwood Pr TN.

*__Lights along the Way: Great Stories of American Faith.__ Thomas Fleming. LC 98-40820. 240p. 1998. pap. 17.95 (*0-8192-1742-5*) Morehouse Pub.

Lights along the Way - Mesillas Yesharim: Timeless Lessons for Today. Abraham J. Twerski. 19.99 (*0-89906-338-1*, LIGH); pap. 16.99 (*0-89906-339-X*, LIGP) Mesorah Pubns.

Lights & Candles. (Sense of History Ser.). Date not set. pap. text. write for info. (*0-582-04026-4*, Pub. by Addison-Wesley) Longman.

Lights & Mysteries. Thomas Centolella. LC 95-32542. 84p. 1995. pap. 12.00 (*1-55659-106-3*) Copper Canyon.

*__Lights & Shades in San Francisco.__ B. E. Lloyd. LC 99-41095. (Illus.). 544p. 1999. pap. 45.00 (*1-893163-10-5*) Berkeley Hills.

Lights & Shades of Hill Life: Kulu Kuram. F. S. Gore. (C). 1995. 54.00 (*3-12-060965-X*, Pub. by Asian Educ Servs) S Asia.

Lights & Shadows: From Bull Run to Bentonville. William B. Westervelt. Ed. by George S. Maharary. LC 97-50174. 273p. 1998. 40.00 (*1-57249-115-9*, Burd St Pr) White Mane Pub.

Lights & Shadows of American Life, 3 vols. Ed. by Mary R. Mitford. 1972. reprint ed. lib. bdg. 99.00 (*0-8422-8098-7*) Irvington.

Lights & Shadows of Freemasonry Consisting of Masonic Tales, Songs & Sketches. Rob Morris. 394p. 1997. reprint ed. pap. 29.95 (*0-7661-0018-9*) Kessinger Pub.

Lights & Shadows of Real Life. Timothy S. Arthur. (Works of Timothy Shay Arthur). 1989. reprint ed. lib. bdg. 79.00 (*0-685-44733-2*) Rprt Serv.

Lights & Shadows of Sailor Life. Joseph G. Clark. LC 70-169754. (Select Bibliographies Reprint Ser.). 1977. reprint ed. 24.95 (*0-8369-5974-4*) Ayer.

*__Lights & Shadows of the Mystic Tie (1889)__ Albert G. Mackey & Rob Morris. 634p. 1999. reprint ed. pap. 45.00 (*0-7661-0770-1*) Kessinger Pub.

Lights & Sirens. James Cowan & Lois Cowan. LC 97-48735. (Behind the Scenes Ser.). (Illus.). 272p. 1998. pap. 16.99 (*0-89879-806-X*, Wrtrs Digest Bks) F & W Pubns Inc.

Lights Are on, Is Anybody Home? Education in America. Wallace K. Pond et al. (Illus.). 270p. 1998. pap. text 19.95 (*1-57981-016-0*) Cummngs & Hath.

Lights! Camcorder! Action! Secrets of Creating Unbelievable, Unforgettable, & Imaginative Home Videos! Kimberly E. Kennedy. 96p. 1993. pap. 8.95 (*0-9645647-0-X*) Am Creat Concepts.

Lights, Camera, Action! Ray Garton. (Secret World of Alex Mack Ser.: No. 33). (J). (gr. 3-6). 1998. pap. 3.99 (*0-671-02109-5*, Minstrel Bks) PB.

Lights! Camera! Action! A Guide to Using Video Production in the Classroom. Bruce Limpus. 88p. 1994. pap. text 19.95 (*1-882664-08-6*) Prufrock Pr.

Lights, Camera, Action! Careers in Film, Television, & Video. 2nd rev. ed. Josephine Langham. (Distributed for the British Film Institute Ser.). 230p. 1996. pap. 19.95 (*0-85170-573-1*, Pub. by British Film Inst) Ind U Pr.

Lights, Camera, Action! Making Movies & TV from the Inside Out. Lisa O'Brien. (Illus.). 64p. (YA). (gr. 5 up). 1998. 19.95 (*1-895688-75-2*, Pub. by Greey dePencier); pap. 12.95 (*1-895688-76-0*, Pub. by Greey dePencier) Firefly Bks Ltd.

Lights! Camera! Action Dog! Nancy Butcher. Ed. by Kevin Ryan. LC 98-84944. (Wishbone Mysteries Ser.: Vol. 11). (Illus.). 144p. (J). (gr. 3-7). 1998. mass mkt. 3.99 (*1-57064-289-3*, Big Red) Lyrick Pub.

Lights! Camera! Action Dog! see Wishbone Mysteries

Lights! Camera! Action Dog!, Vol. 11. Lyrick Publishing Staff. Vol. 11. (gr. 4-7). 1999. pap. text 1.99 (*1-57064-762-3*) Lyrick Pub.

Lights! Camera! Action! Film Animation in the Classroom: The Animation in the Classroom. Richard A. Shade. Ed. by Linda H. Smith. (Triad Prototype Ser.). 24p. 1987. pap. 5.00 (*0-936386-45-2*) Creative Learning.

Lights! Camera! Celebrate! Hollywood Birthdays, Bashes & Blowouts. David Marsh. LC 95-32223. (Illus.). 64p. 1995. 16.95 (*1-883318-26-2*) Angel City Pr.

Lights! Camera! Clues! Carolyn Keene. (Nancy Drew Notebooks: No. 29). (J). (gr. 2-4). 1999. pap. 3.99 (*0-671-02463-9*, Minstrel Bks) PB.

Lights, Camera, Die! M. T. Coffin. (Spinetinglers Ser.: Vol. 20). 128p. (J). 1997. pap. 3.99 (*0-380-78805-5*, Avon Bks) Morrow Avon.

Lights, Camera, Die! M T Coffin. (Spinetinglers Ser.). (J). 1997. 9.09 (*0-606-11560-9*, Pub. by Turtleback) Demco.

*__Lights, Camera, Dil!__ Kitty Richards. (Rugrats Ser.: Vol. 5). (Illus.). 16p. (J). (ps-3). 2000. pap. 3.99 (*0-689-83102-1*, Simon Spot) Litle Simon.

Lights! Camera! Love in Action! Ruth Fowler. (Illus.). 64p. (Orig.). (J). (gr. 4-6). 1989. pap. text 3.95 (*0-936625-68-6*, W897109) Womans Mission Union.

Lights, Camera, Poetry! American Poets Write about the Movies. Ed. by Jason Shinder. 208p. 1996. pap. 14.00 (*0-15-600115-2*, Harvest Bks) Harcourt.

Lights! Cameras! Magic! How to Produce & Perform a Magic Show on TV. Dick Williams & Virginia Williams. Ed. by Samuel P. Smith. (Illus.). 160p. (J). 1993. 35.00 (*1-881099-03-2*) SPS Pubns.

Lights, Colors, Tones & Nature's Finer Forces. Ernest J. Stevens. 268p. 1996. reprint ed. spiral bd. 23.00 (*0-7873-0844-7*) Hlth Research.

*__Lights for Gita.__ Rachna Gilmore. (Illus.). 24p. (J). (ps-3). 2000. pap. 7.95 (*0-88448-151-4*) Tilbury Hse.

*__Lights for Minneapolis.__ Susan Martins Miller. LC 99-159193. (American Adventure Ser.: No. 27). (J). (gr. 3-6). 1998. pap. 3.97 (*1-57748-289-1*) Barbour Pub.

Lights for the World: Training Youth Leaders for Peer Ministry. Lisa-Marie Calderone-Stewart. 120p. (YA). (gr. 9 up). 1995. spiral bd. 15.95 (*0-88489-350-2*) St Marys.

Lights Go on Again. Kit Pearson. 224p. (J). 1999. pap. 3.99 (*0-14-036412-9*, Viking) Viking Penguin.

Lights in the Darkness: For Survivors & Healers of Sexual Abuse. Ave Clark. LC 92-82000. 150p. (Orig.). 1993. pap. 8.95 (*1-878718-12-6*, Resurrection Pr) Catholic Bk Pub.

Lights in the Night: Everything You Always Wanted to Know about Things That Glow. Craig Strasshofer. Ed. by Linda L. Yoshizawa. (Learn by Doing Library). (Illus.). 64p. (Orig.). (J). (gr. 4). 1995. pap. 19.95 (*1-886795-04-5*, Creat Pr) Creat for Kids.

Lights in the Sea. (Evergreen Ser.). 1996. 29.99 (*3-8228-8655-6*) Taschen Amer.

Lights in the Sky. Patricia Armentrout. LC 96-2881. (Earthly Oddities Ser.). 1996. 17.27 (*1-57103-155-3*) Rourke Pr.

Light's Manual: Intertidal Invertebrates of the Central California Coast: S. F. Lights Laboratory & Field Text in Invertebrate Zoology. 3rd rev. ed. Ed. by Ralph Smith & James T. Carlton. (Illus.). 716p. 1974. 60.00 (*0-520-02113-4*, Pub. by U CA Pr) Cal Prin Full Svc.

Lights of Asia. rev. unabridged ed. Sirdar Ikbal Ali Shah. LC 98-61227. 320p. 1998. pap. 25.00 (*2-909347-10-9*, Pub. by Tractus Bks) Tractus.

Lights of Bohemia. Ramon Del Valle-Inclan. Ed. by John Lyon. 1993. 59.95 (*0-85668-564-X*, Pub. by Aris & Phillips); pap. 22.00 (*0-85668-565-8*, Pub. by Aris & Phillips) David Brown.

Lights of Earth. Gina Berriault. LC 97-25630. 176p. 1997. pap. 12.50 (*1-887178-53-8*, Pub. by Counterpt DC) HarpC.

Lights of East Anglia. Neville Long. 182p. (C). 1988. 50.00 (*0-86138-028-2*, Pub. by T Dalton) St Mut.

Lights of East Anglia. Neville Long. 182p. (C). 1990. pap. 35.00 (*0-86138-029-0*, Pub. by T Dalton) St Mut.

Lights of Fortitude: Glimpses into the Lives of the Hands of the Cause of God. Barron Harper. (Illus.). 300p. (Orig.). 1997. pap. 29.95 (*0-85398-413-1*) G Ronald Pub.

Lights of Home. Marilyn Pappano. (Family Continuity Program Ser.: No. 17). 1999. per. 4.50 (*0-373-82165-4*, 1-82165-1) Harlequin Bks.

Lights of Lancaster: Letters to Rome. J. Euclide Caza. Tr. by A. Margaret Caza. (Illus.). 160p. pap. 13.95 (*0-9698752-7-4*) Sh1oreline.

Lights of Passage see Rites of Passage: Celebrating Life's Changes

Lights of Passage. Wall. 1995. 22.50 (*0-8050-2004-7*) H Holt & Co.

Lights of Prophecy: Orot Ha-Nevuah. Bezalel Naor. 96p. (Orig.). (C). 1990. pap. 4.95 (*1-879016-00-1*) UOJC Amer.

Lights of the City. Chuck Taylor. 125p. (Orig.). 1984. pap. 6.95 (*0-941720-17-9*); lib. bdg. 12.95 (*0-941720-15-2*) Slough Pr TX.

*__Lights of the Veil.__ Patty Metzer. 2001. pap. 12.99 (*1-57673-627-X*) Multnomah Pubs.

Lights On! The Wild Century-Long Saga of Night Baseball. David Pietrusza. LC 97-7800. (American Sports History Ser.). 288p. 1997. 39.50 (*0-8108-3307-7*) Scarecrow.

*__Lights on Life Problems: Sri Aurobindo'v Views on Important Life-Problems Compiled from His Writings.__ 200p. 1999. 9.95 (*81-7058-058-7*, Pub. by SAA) E-W Cultural Ctr.

Lights On! Lights Off! Angela C. Santomero et al. (Blues Clues Ser.). (Illus.). 18p. (J). 1998. bds. 4.99 (*0-689-81909-9*) S&S Childrens.

Lights on the Hill. Garth St. Omer. (Caribbean Writers Ser.). 120p. (Orig.). (C). 1986. reprint ed. pap. 8.95 (*0-435-98964-2*, 98964) Heinemann.

Lights on the River. Jane Resh Thomas. LC 93-33636. (Illus.). 32p. (J). (ps-3). 1994. 15.95 (*0-7868-0004-6*, Pub. by Hyprn Child); lib. bdg. 15.89 (*0-7868-2003-9*, Pub. by Hyprn Child) Little.

Lights on the River. Jane Resh Thomas. LC 93-33636. (J). 1996. 10.15 (*0-606-10251-5*, Pub. by Turtleback) Demco.

Lights on Yoga. Sri Aurobindo. 1979. pap. 2.95 (*0-89744-916-9*) Auromere.

Lights on Yoga. 9th ed. Sri Aurobindo. 63p. 1996. pap. 2.95 (*81-7058-057-9*, Pub. by SAA) E-W Cultural Ctr.

Lights on Yoga: With the Mother's Comments. Sri Aurobindo & Mother. 161p. (Orig.). 1988. pap. 5.95 (*0-317-99974-5*, Pub. by Sri Aurob Ashram Trust) Acrpls Bks CO.

*__Lights On/Lights Off.__ Havoc Publishing Staff. 1999. pap. 9.00 (*0-7416-1009-4*) Havoc Pub.

Lights Out. Geoff Edgers. LC 97-193234. 1997. spiral bd. 10.95 (*0-201-15144-8*) Addison-Wesley.

Lights Out! John Himmelman. LC 93-33811. (Illus.). 32p. (J). (gr. k-3). 1997. 13.95 (*0-8167-3450-X*) BrdgeWater.

Lights Out! John Himmelman. LC 93-33811. (Illus.). 32p. (J). (gr. k-3). 1996. pap. 5.95 (*0-8167-3451-8*) Troll Communs.

*__Lights Out!__ Lucille R. Penner. LC 99-42678. (Math Matters Ser.). (Illus.). 32p. (J). (gr. k-2). 2000. pap. 4.95 (*1-57565-092-4*) Kane Pr.

*__Lights Out!__ Lucille R. Penner. (Math Matters Ser.). (Illus.). (J). 2000. 10.40 (*0-606-18220-9*) Turtleback.

Lights Out. R. L. Stine, pseud. Ed. by Patricia MacDonald. (Fear Street Ser.: No. 6). 176p. (YA). (gr. 7 up). 1991. mass mkt. 3.99 (*0-671-72482-7*, Archway) PB.

Lights Out. R. L. Stine, pseud. (Fear Street Ser.: No. 6). (YA). (gr. 7 up). 1991. 9.09 (*0-606-04965-7*, Pub. by Turtleback) Demco.

Lights Out! A Nighttime Diary. (Illus.). 144p. 1998. 15.95 (*0-8118-1849-7*) Chronicle Bks.

Lights Out: Great Fights of the Twentieth Century, Reading Level 3-5. Mel Cebulesh. LC 93-6899. 1993. 4.95 (*0-88336-741-6*); digital audio 9.95 (*0-88336-898-6*) New Readers.

*__Lights Out: The Sleeping Diet.__ T. S. Wiley & Brent Formby. LC 99-88658. 368p. 2000. 24.95 (*0-671-03867-2*, PB Hardcover) PB.

Lights Out: The Witch's Revenge. Lynn Gordon. (Illus.). 6p. (J). (ps-3). 1997. 9.99 (*0-689-81679-0*) S&S Childrens.

Lights Out at Camp What-a-Nut. Paul McCusker. (Adventures in Odyssey Ser.: No. 5). 150p. (J). (gr. 3-7). 1993. pap. 5.99 (*1-56179-134-2*) Focus Family.

Lights Out for the Territory: 9 Excursions in the Secret History of London. Iain Sinclair. LC 97-168128. (Illus.). 386p. 1998. pap. 16.95 (*1-86207-009-1*, Pub. by Granta) Midpt Trade.

Lights Out in the Reptile House. Jim Shepard. 288p. 1991. pap. 10.00 (*0-380-71413-2*, Avon Bks) Morrow Avon.

Lights Out Liverpool. Maureen Lee. 416p. 1995. 26.00 (*1-85797-623-1*, Pub. by Orion Pubng Grp) Trafalgar.

*__Lights-Out Putting: A Mind, Body, & Soul Approach to Golf's Game Within the Game.__ Todd Sones. (Illus.). 144p. 2000. 22.95 (*0-8092-2440-2*, 244020, Contemporary Bks) NTC Contemp Pub Co.

Light's Retention Scale, 1998. H. Wayne Light. 80p. 1998. pap. 30.00 (*0-87879-914-1*, 914-1AN); pap. 22.00 (*0-87879-915-X*); pap., student ed. 75.00 (*0-685-71873-5*, 914-1AN) Acad Therapy.

Light's Retention Scale, 1998. H. Wayne Light. 80p. 1998. pap. 20.00 (*0-87879-916-8*) Acad Therapy.

Lights, Sirens & Donuts. Chuck Swanson. LC 98-210111. 64 p. 1997. write for info. (*0-912981-26-1*) Hse BonGiovanni.

*__Lights, Symbols & Angels: Six Worship Resources for Advent/Christmas.__ Cynthia Cowen. LC 99-37622. 100p. 1999. pap. 10.75 (*0-7880-1517-6*) CSS OH.

Light's Vision: The City of Adelaide & Surrounding Districts. Max Colwell & David Colwell. (Illus.). 88p. (C). 1989. 80.00 (*0-9594393-4-X*, Pub. by M Colwell Pubns) St Mut.

Light's Way. Judy Pelikan. (Illus.). 32p. 1997. 5.95 (*0-7892-0138-0*) Abbeville Pr.

Lightsaber Duelling Pack. (Star Wars Ser.). 128p. 1991. 12.00 (*0-87431-088-1*, 40010) West End Games.

Lightsaber Marker Activity Book, 4. Kerry Milliron. (Star Wars). (Illus.). 32p. (J). (ps-3). 1999. pap. 3.99 (*0-375-80017-4*) Random.

Lightsabers. Kevin J. Anderson. (Star Wars: No. 4). (Orig.). (J). (gr. 3-5). 1996. mass mkt. 5.99 (*0-425-16951-0*) Berkley Pub.

Lightsabers. Kevin J. Anderson & Rebecca Moesta. (Star Wars: No. 4). 240p. (Orig.). (J). (gr. 3-5). 1996. mass mkt. 5.99 (*1-57297-091-X*) Blvd Books.

Lightshift 2000: Let's Turn on the Light of the World! Ken Kalb. LC 97-92837. (Illus.). 121p. 1997. pap. 9.95 (*0-9642927-7-7*) Lucky Star Res.

Lightship. Archie Binns. 345p. 1962. 19.95 (*0-8323-0109-4*) Binford Mort.

Lightship Baskets of Nantucket. Martha Lawrence. Ed. by Nancy N. Schiffer. LC 90-60. (Illus.). 120p. (Orig.). 1990. pap. text 24.95 (*0-88740-256-9*) Schiffer.

***Lightship Baskets of Nantucket.** Martha Lawrence. (Illus.). 120p. (Orig.). 2000. pap. 24.95 (*0-7643-0891-2*) Schiffer.

Lightship Baskets of Nantucket: A Continuing Craft. David H. Wood. LC 94-66244. 62p. 1994. pap. 10.00 (*1-882201-01-9*) Nantucket Hist Assn.

Lightships. C. Noelle Yerkes & Noelle Yerkes. 112p. (Orig.). 1995. pap. 14.95 (*1-887256-00-8*) Ray of Lght Pub.

Lightships The collection: Lightships The Book: finding meaning in light of our loss, ISBN 1-887256-00-8, $14.95 Paperback. Lightships The Audio Book: Healing words for a mending heart/with music ISBN 1-887256-01-6 $11.95 45m Lightships: The Journal Workbook:. Your spiritual journal of the healing heart. Inspirational writing made easy. ISBN 1-887256-02-4, $14.95. Each publication in the series offers distinctively different & enriching insights. They are treasures to have, to give, to experience. They are about love that does not end with loss, they are about healing. They are about building your own lightship, which is healing your heart. They are about transcending from darkness into light. They are about moving from feeling hopeless, helpless & useless, into a life with hope, faith & meaning. We find on this journey of our ship of light, this healing journey of love we are not alone. To order or for more information, please contact Connie at Ray of Light Publishing, 54 B. Kent St., Newburyport, MA 01950. Phone 1-800-430-0398. Fax 978-462-4457. Website: www.rayoflight.com.
Publisher Paid Annotation.

Lightships of Cape Cod. Frederic L. Thompson. (Illus.). 120p. 1983. pap. 15.95 (*0-9611320-0-0*) Congress Sq.

Lightstyling. PBC International Staff. 1999. pap. 19.95 (*0-688-16686-5*, Wm Morrow) Morrow Avon.

Lightstyling: Contrasts in Design. Carol S. King. (Illus.). 104p. 2000. pap. 19.95 (*0-86636-736-5*) PBC Intl Inc.

Lightwave Magic: Expert Edition. Phil South. 1997. 59.99 (*1-56830-434-X*) Hayden.

LightWave Power Guide. Dan Ablan. LC 96-228499. 608p. 1996. 44.99 (*1-56205-633-6*) New Riders Pub.

***LightWave 6 Character Animation in Depth.** Doug Kelly. (Illus.). 744p. 2000. pap. 59.99 (*1-57610-380-3*) Coriolis Grp.

***LightWave 6 Effects Magic.** Julian Kain. (Magic Ser.). (Illus.). 2000. pap. 45.00 (*0-7357-0996-3*) New Riders Pub.

LightWave 3D Applied, Version 5.6. Joe Tracy et al. LC 98-74172. (Illus.). 500p. 1998. pap. 49.95 (*0-929870-48-4*, Advanstar Mktg) Advanstar Commns.

Lightwave 3D Book: Tips, Techniques & Ready-to-Use Objects. LightWavePro Magazine Editors. (Illus.). 288p. 1997. pap. 39.95 incl. cd-rom (*0-87930-455-3*) Miller Freeman.

***LightWave 3D Book: Tips, Techniques, & Ready-to-Use Objects.** 2nd ed. Chris Tome. (Illus.). 400p. 2000. pap. 39.95 incl. cd-rom (*0-87930-576-2*, Pub. by Miller Freeman) Publishers Group.

Lightweight Alpine Climbing with Peter Croft. Peter Croft & Steven Boga. LC 96-8909. (Illus.). 96p. 1996. pap. 10.95 (*0-8117-2841-2*) Stackpole.

Lightweight Artificial & Waste Materials for Embankments over Soft Soils (TRR 1422) Ed. by Anna Rigamer. (Transportation Research Record Ser.). (Illus.). 80p. 1994. pap. text 24.00 (*0-309-05569-5*) Natl Res Coun.

***Lightweight Backpacking: The Importance of Good Form.** Kevin D. Hauser. (Illus.). 60p. (YA). 1999. ring bd. 17.95 (*0-9677587-0-X*) Kuffel Creek.

Lightweight Concrete. American Concrete Institute Staff & Daniel P. Jenny. LC 71-162468. (American Concrete Institute Publication: SP-29). (Illus.). 333p. reprint ed. pap. 103.30 (*0-608-11604-1*, 200308000018) Bks Demand.

Lightweight Expeditions. Rob Collister. (Illus.). 144p. 1989. 24.95 (*0-938567-15-2*) Mountaineers.

Lightweight Fighter Program: A Successful Approach to Fighter Technology Transition. Albert C. Piccirillo & David C. Aronstein. 59p. 1997. pap. 30.00 (*1-56347-193-0*) AIAA.

Lightweight Gourmet see Trail Food: Drying & Cooking Food for Backpacking & Paddling

Lightworker's Way: Awakening Your Spiritual Power to Know & Heal. Doreen L. Virtue. LC 97-2799. 256p. 1997. pap. 12.95 (*1-56170-390-7*, 896) Hay House.

Lightworks: Interpreted from the Original Hebrew Book of Isaiah. David Rosenberg. LC 78-3356. 78p. 1978. 15.00 (*0-89366-249-5*) Ultramarine Pub.

Lightyears. Beth Brown. LC 81-82663. 75p. 1982. per. 5.00 (*0-916418-36-7*) Lotus.

***Ligitimacy Deficit in Custom: Towards a Deconstructionist Theory.** Ben Chigara. LC 00-42041. 2000. write for info. (*0-7546-2077-8*, Pub. by Ashgate Pub) Ashgate Pub Co.

Lignans. David C. Ayres & John D. Loike. (Chemistry & Pharmacology of Natural Products Ser.). 422p. (C). 1990. text 125.00 (*0-521-30421-0*) Cambridge U Pr.

Ligne de Force. Pierre Herbart. (FRE.). 160p. 1980. pap. 10.95 (*0-7859-2436-1*, 2070372286) Fr & Eur.

***Ligne Maginot et l'Infanterie de Fortresse.** Combined Publishing Staff. (FRE.). 1999. 39.95 (*2-908182-97-1*) Histoire.

***Ligne Siemens.** Elisabeth Buhlmann. (Illus.). xxxii, 165p. 1999. 32.95 (*3-906763-52-8*, Pub. by P Lang) P Lang Pubng.

Lignes de Conduite pour l'Erradication de la Deficience en Vitamine A Et De la Xerophtalmie. G. Arroyave et al. Tr. by Marc Vincent. (FRE., Illus.). 83p. (Orig.). 1984. pap. text 3.50 (*0-935368-38-8*) ILSI.

Lignicolous Corticioid Fungi (Basidiomycota) of North America: Systematics, Distribution, & Ecology, No. 19. J. H. Ginns & M. N. Lefebvre. LC 93-79367. 247p. 1993. 68.00 (*0-89054-155-8*) Am Phytopathol Soc.

Lignin: Historical, Biological & Materials Perspectives. Wolfgang G. Glasser et al. LC 99-16985. (ACS Symposium Ser.: No. 742). (Illus.). 464p. 1999. text 150.00 (*0-8412-3611-9*, Pub. by Am Chemical) OUP.

Lignin: Properties & Materials. Ed. by Wolfgang G. Glasser & Simo Sarkanen. LC 89-15069. (Symposium Ser.: No. 397). (Illus.). xi, 616p. 1989. 119.95 (*0-8412-1631-2*, Pub. by Am Chemical) OUP.

Lignin: Properties & Materials. Ed. by Wolfgang G. Glasser & Simo Sarkanen. LC 89-15069. (ACS Symposium Ser.: No. 397). (Illus.). 560p. 1989. reprint ed. pap. 173.60 (*0-608-03145-3*, 206359800007) Bks Demand.

Lignin & Lignan Biosynthesis. Ed. by Norman G. Lewis & Simo Sarkanen. LC 98-6367. (Symposium Ser.: No. 697). (Illus.). 448p. 1998. text 130.95 (*0-8412-3566-X*, Pub. by Am Chemical) OUP.

Lignin & Pulping Chemistry: Selected Papers. Ed. by Gunther Stegmann. (Holzforschung Ser.: Supplement Vol. 45). (GER.). 112p. (Orig.). (C). 1991. pap. text 192.35 (*3-11-013259-1*, 267-91) De Gruyter.

Lignin Biodegradation: Microbiology, Chemistry & Potential Applications, 2 vols., Vol. 1. T. Kent Kirk et al. 256p. 1980. 144.00 (*0-8493-5459-5*, TS933, CRC Reprint) Franklin.

Lignin Biodegradation: Microbiology, Chemistry & Potential Applications, 2 vols., Vol. 2. T. Kent Kirk et al. 272p. 1980. 152.00 (*0-8493-5460-9*, CRC Reprint) Franklin.

Lignin Biodegradation & Transformation. Ronald L. Crawford. LC 80-39557. 170p. 1981. 37.50 (*0-471-05743-6*) Krieger.

Lignin Structure & Reactions: A Symposium Sponsored by the Division of Cellulose, Wood, & Fiber Chemistry at the 150th Meeting of the American Chemical Society, Atlantic City, NJ, Sept. 13-14, 1965. American Chemical Society Staff. LC 66-28847. (Advances in Chemistry Ser.: Vol. 59). (Illus.). 283p. 1966. reprint ed. pap. 87.80 (*0-608-06914-0*, 206712200009) Bks Demand.

Lignite Resources in Texas. W. R. Kaiser et al. (Reports of Investigations: RI 104). (Illus.). 52p. 1980. pap. 2.00 (*0-318-03244-9*) Bur Econ Geology.

Lignites for North America. Harold H. Schobert. LC 94-41523. (Coal Science & Technology Ser.: Vol. 23). 714p. 1995. 422.25 (*0-444-89823-9*) Elsevier.

Lignocellulosic Materials. (Advances in Biochemical Engineering-Biotechnology Ser.: Vol. 38). (Illus.). 180p. 1988. 119.95 (*0-387-50163-0*) Spr-Verlag.

Ligonier, Indiana: Memories of the First One Hundred Fifty Years, 1835-1985. Matthew et al. Ed. by Ben Zimmerman. 1985. 25.00 (*0-318-18809-0*) Ligonier Comm.

***Ligonier Sightings.** Clark McKowen. (Illus.). 112p. 2000. 13.95 (*0-9665272-1-6*) Laurel Mount.

L'Iguana see Iguana

Ligue Patriotique des Francaises, 1902-1933: A Feminine Response to the Secularization of French Society. Odile Sarti. LC 91-44135. (Modern European History Ser.). 328p. 1992. text 20.00 (*0-8153-0666-0*) Garland.

Liguistic Diversity & National Unity: Language Ecology in Thailand. William A. Smalley. (Illus.). 452p. 1994. pap. text 24.95 (*0-226-76289-0*); lib. bdg. 56.00 (*0-226-76288-2*) U Ch Pr.

Liguori Guide to Catholic U. S. A. A Treasury of Churches, Schools, Monuments, Shrines, & Monasteries. Jay Copp. LC 98-43555. 336p. 1999. pap. 15.95 (*0-7648-0371-9*) Liguori Pubns.

Liguorian Know-Your-Bible Quiz Collection. Mary K. Mazotti. LC 95-82114. 63 ;p. (Orig.). 1996. pap. 3.95 (*0-89243-911-4*) Liguori Pubns.

***Liguria.** (Heritage Guide Ser.). (Illus.). 2001. pap. 16.95 (*88-365-2114-2*, Pub. by Tour Club Ital) Abbeville Pr.

***Liguus Tree Snails of South Florida.** Henry T. Close. 2000. 49.95 (*0-8130-1814-5*) U Press Fla.

Liholiho & Emma: King Kamehameha IV & His Queen. Elizabeth Waldron. Tr. by Rubellite Johnson. (ENG & HAW., Illus.). 32p. (Orig.). 1986. pap. 2.00 (*0-938851-00-4*) Daughters of HI.

Lij Eyasu & Haile Sellassie: Winnowing Out the Myth. W. A. Semerjibashian. 178p. 59.95 (*1-56902-052-3*) Red Sea Pr.

Lij Eyasu & Haile Sellassie: Winnowing Out the Myth. Waj Semerjibashian. 1997. pap. 18.95 (*1-56902-053-1*) Red Sea Pr.

***Lijiang, Yunnan Province, China, Earthquake, February 3, 1996: Reconnaissance Report.** Lloyd Cluff et al. Ed. by Janet L. Cluff. (Illus.). 34p. 1998. pap. 15.00 (*0-943198-66-6*, 98-01) Earthquake Eng.

Lika Mutal. Photos by David Finn. (Illus.). 188p. 1996. 85.00 (*0-8109-6320-5*, Pub. by Abrams) Time Warner.

Like. Ali Smith. LC 97-36508. 352p. (C). 1998. 24.00 (*0-15-100350-5*) Harcourt.

Like a Bulging Wall. Robert Borrud. LC 91-65104. 192p. 1991. pap. 8.95 (*0-914984-28-4*) Starburst.

***Like a Bullet of Night: The Films of Bob Dylan.** C. P. Lee. 2000. pap. 18.95 (*1-900924-06-4*, Pub. by Helter Skelter) Interlink Pub.

Like a Burning Fire: In the Time of Charlemagne. Irene Brand. LC 96-10341. (Legacies of Faith Ser.). (Illus.). 304p. 1996. pap. 9.99 (*0-8254-2145-4*) Kregel.

Like a Civil War: The United States in the 1960s. Maurice Isserman. LC 99-13711. (Illus.). 368p. 2000. pap. text 21.95 (*0-19-509191-4*) OUP.

Like a Diamond. 2nd ed. Malcolm MacDonald. 384p. 1999. text 23.95 (*0-312-20557-0*) St Martin.

Like a Diamondback in the Trunk of a Witness's Buick. Jan Haagensen. LC 77-87233. (CSU Poetry Ser.: No. V). 55p. 1977. pap. 3.50 (*0-914946-07-2*) Cleveland St Univ Poetry Ctr.

Like a Family: The Making of a Southern Cotton Mill World. Jacquelyn D. Hall et al. LC 87-40135. (Fred W. Morrison Series in Southern Studies). (Illus.). xxxiv, 468p. (C). 1987. 49.95 (*0-8078-1754-6*) U of NC Pr.

***Like a Family: The Making of a Southern Cotton Mill World.** Jacquelyn Dowd Hall et al. LC 99-87862. (Fred W. Morrison Series in Southern Studies). (Illus.). 520p. 2000. pap. 18.95 (*0-8078-4879-4*) U of NC Pr.

Like a Field Riddled by Ants. Myra Sklarew. LC 87-16961. (Lost Roads Ser.: No. 32). 120p. (Orig.). 1987. pap. 7.95 (*0-918786-36-3*) Lost Roads.

Like a Film: Ideological Fantasy on Screen, Camera, & Canvas. Timothy Murray. LC 93-17147. (Illus.). 272p. (C). 1993. pap. 21.99 (*0-415-07734-6*) Routledge.

Like a Fire in My Bones. Clifford Goldstein. LC 97-46831. 1998. 12.99 (*0-8163-1580-9*) Pacific Pr Pub Assn.

***Like a Fish in Water: Yoga for Children.** Isabelle Koch. LC 99-28576. (Illus.). 56p. 1999. pap. 12.95 (*0-89281-773-9*) Inner Tradit.

Like a Fish on a Bike! large type ed. Brahm Piterski & Paul Piterski. LC 97-611122. (Illus.). 32p. (J). (gr. 2-5). 1999. 14.95 (*0-9658435-0-5*) Verdant Pub.

Like a Flame. Kemal Ozer. Ed. by Stanley H. Barkan. Tr. by Talat S. Halman. (Review Turkish Writers Chapbook Ser.: No. 4). (ENG & TUR.). 48p. 1991. 15.00 (*0-89304-280-3*); 15.00 (*0-89304-282-X*); pap. 5.00 (*0-89304-281-1*); pap. 5.00 (*0-89304-283-8*) Cross-Cultrl NY.

Like a Flower Blooming. Richard A. Schrader, Sr. 58p. 1999. write for info. (*0-9622987-9-4*) R A Schrader.

Like a Garden: A Biblical Spirituality of Growth. Sara C. Juengst. LC 95-46684. (Illus.). 128p. (Orig.). 1996. pap. 14.95 (*0-664-25654-1*) Westminster John Knox.

Like a God I Love All Things. Billy Childish. 71p. (Orig.). 1991. pap. 12.95 (*1-871894-46-8*, Pub. by Hangman Bks) AK Pr Dist.

Like a Hind Let Loose. Elaine Warick. (Illus.). 80p. (Orig.). 1992. pap. 9.95 (*1-879260-06-9*) Evanston Pub.

Like a Hole in the Head: A Novel. Jen Banbury. LC 97-16935. 304p. (gr. 8). 1998. 21.95 (*0-316-17110-7*) Little.

Like a Hole in the Head: A Novel. Jen Banbury. LC 98-52920. 296p. 1999. mass mkt. 12.00 (*0-446-67517-2*, Pub. by Warner Bks) Little.

Like a Holy Crusade: Mississippi, 1964 - The Turning of the Civil Rights Movement in America. Nicolaus Mills. 228p. 1992. text 22.50 (*0-929587-96-0*) I R Dee.

Like a Holy Crusade: Mississippi, 1964 - The Turning of the Civil Rights Movement in America. Nicolaus Mills. LC 93-11246. 228p. 1993. reprint ed. pap. 9.95 (*1-56663-026-6*, Elephant Paperbacks) I R Dee.

Like a Hurricane. Paul C. Smith & Robert A. Warrior. 400p. 1997. pap. 14.95 (*1-56584-402-5*, Pub. by New Press NY) Norton.

Like a Hurricane: The Indian Movement from Alcatraz to Wounded Knee. Paul C. Smith & Robert A. Warrior. (Illus.). 400p. 1996. 25.00 (*1-56584-316-9*, Pub. by New Press NY) Norton.

Like a Kiss on the Lips: Devotions from Proverbs for Couples. Les Parrott & Leslie L. Parrott. LC 97-3352. 1997. 12.99 (*0-310-21623-0*) Zondervan.

Like a Knife: Ideology & Genre in Contemporary Chinese Popular Music. Andrew F. Jones. (Cornell East Asia Ser.: No. 57). (Illus.). 192p. (Orig.). (C). 1992. pap. 11.90 (*0-939657-57-0*) Cornell East Asia Pgm.

Like a Lamb to Slaughter. Lawrence Block. 272p. 1996. mass mkt. 5.99 (*0-380-78806-3*, Avon Bks) Morrow Avon.

Like a Lamb to the Slaughter. Ted Gibbons. (Personal Enrichment Ser.). 117p. (Orig.). 1991. pap. write for info. (*0-929985-80-X*) Jackman Pubng.

Like a Large Immovable Rock: A Festschrift. Ed. & Intro. by Colin D. Mallard. LC 95-90814. 204p. (Orig.). 1996. pap. 15.00 (*0-9646040-1-9*) Wild Duck Pubng.

Like a Lasting Storm: Helping with Real-Life Problems. Cooper B. Holmes. LC 94-10224. 78p. 1994. pap. 10.95 (*0-88422-124-5*) Clinical Psych.

Like a Lasting Storm: Helping with Real-Life Problems. Cooper B. Holmes. 78p. 1996. pap. 37.50 (*0-471-16211-6*) Wiley.

Like a Maccabee. Audrey Friedman Marcus & Raymond A. Zwerin. (Illus.). (J). (gr. k-3). 1991. 11.95 (*0-8074-0445-4*, 102564) UAHC.

Like a Mighty Army: A History of the Church of God. 3rd ed. Charles W. Conn. (Illus.). 615p. 1996. 26.99 (*0-87148-533-8*) Pathway Pr.

Like a Mighty River. David Manuel. LC 77-90948. (Illus.). 220p. 1977. 5.95 (*0-932260-02-0*) Rock Harbor.

Like a Mighty Wind see Como un Viento Recio

Like a Mighty Wind. Mel Tari & Cliff Dudley. LC 76-182854. 173p. 1997. reprint ed. pap. 8.95 (*0-89221-123-7*) New Leaf.

Like a Miracle. Ernest C. Wilson. 202p. 1971. 3.48 (*0-87159-088-3*) Unity Bks.

Like a Moth to a Flame: The Jim Reeves Story. Michael Streissguth. LC 98-15921. (Illus.). 256p. 1998. 24.95 (*1-55853-607-8*) Rutledge Hill Pr.

Like a One-Eyed Cat: Photographs by Lee Friedlander, 1956-1987. Intro. by Rod Slemmons. LC 88-27500. (Illus.). 120p. 1989. pap. 29.95 (*0-932216-32-3*) Seattle Art.

***Like a Pebble Tossed: The Legacy of a Prayer.** Jean Lovelace Zeiler & Mayo Mathers. 160p. 1998. pap. 10.00 (*1-892525-03-8*) ACW Press.

Like a Pelican in the Desert: Leadership Redefined: Beyond Awkwardness. Stephen M. Gower. LC 94-78477. 158p. 1994. 20.00 (*1-880150-83-2*) Lectern Pub.

***Like a Pelican in the Wilderness: Reflections on the Sayings of the Desert Fathers.** Stelios Ramfos & Norman Russell. LC 99-59976. 2000. pap. write for info. (*1-885652-40-2*) Holy Cross Orthodox.

Like a Phoenix from the Ashes? The Future of Iraqi Military Power. Michael Eisenstadt. LC 93-34927. (Policy Papers: No. 36). 99p. 1993. pap. 8.00 (*0-944029-54-X*) Wash Inst NEP.

Like a Phoenix I'll Rise: An Illustrated History of African Americans in Prince George's County, Maryland, 1696-1996. Alvin Thornton & Karen Gooden. LC 96-53273. 1997. write for info. (*0-89865-984-1*) Donning Co.

Like a Plague of Locusts: From an Antebellum Town to a New South City, Memphis, Tennessee, 1850-1880. Kathleen Berkeley. LC 91-12700. (Dissertations in Nineteenth-Century American Political & Social History). 400p. 1991. 82.00 (*0-8240-8193-5*) Garland.

Like a Prairie Fire: A History of the Assemblies of God in Oklahoma. Bob Burke. Ed. by Robert C. Cunningham & David A. Womack. (Illus.). 518p. 12.00 (*0-9641325-0-8*) OK Dist Coun.

Like a Raging Fire: A Biography of Maurice N. Eisendrath. Avi M. Schulman. LC 93-33072. 108p. 1993. pap. 10.00 (*0-8074-0525-6*, 386052) UAHC.

Like a River Glorious. Lawana Blackwell. LC 95-14548. (Victorian Serenade: No. 1). 1995. pap. 10.99 (*0-8423-7954-1*) Tyndale Hse.

Like a Rock. Mary Tassin. LC 95-92450. 115p. (Orig.). 1995. pap. 14.95 (*0-9631179-1-2*) Penny Hill Rkshp.

Like a Rock: Becoming a Person of Character. Andy Stanley. LC 96-39920. 1997. 19.99 (*0-7852-7612-2*) Nelson.

***Like a Shoe That Pinches: How I Found Serenity Through the 12-Step Program of Emotions Anonymous.** Carrie Connely. LC 99-63060. 70p. 1999. pap. 5.50 (*1-884778-66-6*) Old Mountain.

Like A Sister: A Novel. Janice Daugharty. LC 99-15621. 208p. 1999. 23.00 (*0-06-019360-3*) HarpC.

***Like A Sister: A Novel.** Janice Daugharty. 208p. 2000. pap. 13.00 (*0-06-093179-5*) HarpC.

Like a Straight Pine Tree: Stories of Reconstruction Days in Alabama & Florida 1855-1971. D. A. Avant. (Illus.). 124p. 1971. 7.95 (*0-914570-03-X*) LAvant Studios.

Like a Summer Peach: Sunbright Poems & Old Southern Recipes. Ed. by Blanche F. Farley & Janice T. Moore. LC 96-72. (Illus.). 64p. 1996. 14.95 (*0-918949-89-0*) Papier-Mache Press.

Like a Tear in the Ocean, 3 vols. Manes Sperber. Tr. by Constantine Fitzgibbon. Incl. Vol. 1. Burned Bramble. LC 87-27545. 432p. 1988. 39.50 (*0-8419-1051-0*); Vol. 2. Abyss. LC 87-28099. 272p. 1988. 29.50 (*0-8419-1052-9*); Vol. 3. Journey Without End. LC 87-28613. 272p. 1988. 29.50 (*0-8419-1053-7*); 1988. 95.00 (*0-8419-1188-6*) Holmes & Meier.

Like a Tidal Wave. large type ed. Rhona Ford. (Linford Romance Library). 224p. 1992. pap. 16.99 (*0-7089-7200-4*, Linford) Ulverscroft.

Like a Tree Planted. Lonna L. Williams. (Illus.). 120p. (YA). 1995. text 24.50 (*0-930329-86-4*) Kabel Pubs.

Like a Tree Planted: An Exploration of the Psalms & Parables Through Metaphor. Barbara Green. LC 97-2323. (Connections Ser.). 168p. (Orig.). 1997. pap. text 14.95 (*0-8146-5869-5*, M Glazier) Liturgical Pr.

Like a TV Hero. Linda Bellingham. 112p. (J). (gr. 3-6). 1991. pap. 5.95 (*0-7736-7315-6*) Stoddart Publ.

Like a Two-Edged Sword: The Word of God in Liturgy & History. Ed. by Martin Dudley. 226p. (Orig.). 1995. pap. 16.95 (*1-85311-115-5*, 845, Pub. by Canterbury Press Norwich) Morehouse Pub.

***Like a Virgin.** Gordon Steel. 88p. 2000. pap. 14.95 (*1-84002-140-3*) Theatre Comm.

Like a Virgin: How You Can Convince Your Child to Abstain from Sex. Carole Marsh. (Smart Sex Stuff Ser.). (Orig.). 1994. pap. 19.95 (*1-55609-223-7*) Gallopade Intl.

Like a Walk Through a Park. Norman Fischer. (Orig.). 1980. pap. 3.50 (*0-931416-02-7*) Open Books.

Like a Woman Scorned. Wensley Clarkson. 1996. mass mkt. 4.99 (*1-85782-003-7*, Pub. by Blake Publng) Seven Hills Bk.

Like Abigail. Millie Barger. Ed. by Renee Hermanson. LC 98-14074. 196p. (Orig.). 1998. pap. 12.95 (*1-880292-58-0*) LangMarc.

Like All the Nations? The Life & Legacy of Judah L. Magnes. Ed. by William M. Brinner & Moses Rischin. LC 86-29992. 256p. (C). 1987. pap. text 14.95 (*0-88706-508-2*) State U NY Pr.
Like an Evening Gone. large type ed. Julie Burrows. 380p. 1989. 27.99 (*0-7089-1954-5*) Ulverscroft.
Like an Ocean Full of Waves. Concha Wilkinson. (Illus.). 16p. 1998. mass mkt. 4.95 (*0-9658241-0-1*) Full Life Pub.
***Like & Unlike God.** John Neary. (AAR Reflection & Theory in the Study of Religion Ser.). 201p. 1999. pap. text 34.95 (*0-7885-0569-6*) OUP.
Like Angels from a Cloud: The English Metaphysical Preachers, 1588-1645. Horton Davies. LC 86-10613. 515p. 1986. reprint ed. pap. 159.70 (*0-608-03169-0*, 206362200007) Bks Demand.
Like As of Fire: Newspapers from the Azusa Street World Wide Revival, 1906-1909. Intro. by E. Myron Noble. 68p. (Orig.). 1994. reprint ed. pap. 16.95 (*1-877971-10-3*) Mid Atl Reg Pr.
Like Beads on a String: A Culture History of the Seminole Indians in Northern Peninsular Florida. Brent R. Weisman. LC 88-5765. (Illus.). 216p. 1989. reprint ed. pap. 67.00 (*0-608-01682-9*, 206233800002) Bks Demand.
Like Being Killed. Ellen Miller. 352p. 1999. pap. 12.95 (*0-452-27929-1*, Plume) Dutton Plume.
Like Being Killed. Ellen Miller. 352p. 1998. 24.95 (*0-525-94372-2*) NAL.
***Like Boogie on Tuesday.** unabridged ed. Linda Dominique Grosvenor. LC 00-190504. vi, 456p. 2000. pap. 14.95 (*0-9700102-1-4*) Ardor Bks.
***Like Bread on the Seder Plate: Jewish Lesbians & the Transformation of Tradition.** Rebecca T. Alpert. (Between Men - Between Women Ser.). 225p. 1998. pap. 16.50 (*0-231-09661-5*) Col U Pr.
Like Bread on the Seder Plate: Lesbian Transformation of Jewish Texts. Rebecca T. Alpert. LC 96-43411. (Between Men - Between Women Ser.). 224p. 1997. 26.00 (*0-231-09660-7*) Col U Pr.
***Like Breathing.** R. Rollins. 258p. 1998. pap. 14.00 (*1-892096-33-1*) Ishai Creat.
Like Bugles Passing By: Collected Columns by Lee Woodward. Lee Woodward. Ed. by Mike Kaylor. LC 95-81865. 192p. (Orig.). 1996. pap. 10.00 (*0-916039-08-0*) Kaylor & Kaylor.
Like Butter on Pan. Jonathan London. 32p. 1998. pap. 5.99 (*0-14-055261-8*) Viking Penguin.
Like Butter on Pancakes. Jonathan London. 1998. 11.19 (*0-606-13571-5*, Pub. by Turtleback) Demco.
Like Cats & Dogs. large type ed. Ed. & Intro. by Kenneth Jernigan. (Kernel Bk.: Vol. 12). (Illus.). 96p. 1997. pap. 3.00 (*1-885218-10-9*) Natl Fed Blind.
Like Chinese Milk. Douglas Thiele. LC 97-208343. (Illus.). 32p. (Orig.). 1997. pap. 3.00 (*1-888431-10-5*) ASGP.
Like Christ. Andrew Murray. 240p. 1981. reprint ed. mass mkt. 5.99 (*0-88368-099-8*) Whitaker Hse.
Like Color to the Blind. Donna Williams. 288p. 1996. pap. 19.95 (*0-385-25595-0*) Doubleday.
***Like Color to the Blind: Soul Searching & Soul Finding.** Donna Williams. 290p. 2000. reprint ed. text 24.00 (*0-7881-6887-8*) DIANE Pub.
Like Dew Your Youth: Growing up with Your Teenager. 2nd rev. ed. Eugene H. Peterson. LC 94-25383. 128p. 1994. pap. 10.00 (*0-8028-0116-1*) Eerdmans.
Like Distant Relatives: Adolescent's Perceptions of Social Work & Social Workers. Ray Jones. 1987. text 78.95 (*0-566-05323-3*, Pub. by Avebry) Ashgate Pub Co.
Like Father, Like Daughter: How Father Shapes the Woman His Daughter Becomes. Suzanne Fields. 1983. 15.95 (*0-316-28169-7*) Little.
Like Father, Like Daughter: Men of Glory. Judith Bowen. (Superromance Ser.: No. 791). 1998. per. 4.25 (*0-373-70791-6*, 1-70791-8) Harlequin Bks.
Like Father, Like Son. Don Atkin. LC 96-113698. 154p. (Orig.). 1995. pap. 9.99 (*1-56043-252-7*, Treasure Hse) Destiny Image.
Like Father Like Son. Elizabeth August. 1992. per. 2.69 (*0-373-08857-4*) Harlequin Bks.
Like Father Like Son. Ken Griffey. 1990. 18.95 (*0-671-70259-9*) S&S Trade.
Like Father, Like Son. Lloyd Mackey. LC 97-168937. (Illus.). 200p. 1997. pap. 16.95 (*1-55022-299-6*, Pub. by ECW) Genl Dist Srvs.
Like Father Like Son. H. H. Marshall. 1981. 35.00 (*0-7223-1374-8*, Pub. by A H S Ltd) St Mut.
Like Father, Like Son. Mollie Molay. (Harlequin American Romance Ser.: No. 638). 1996. per. 3.75 (*0-373-16638-9*, 1-16638-8) Harlequin Bks.
Like Father, Like Son: A Book for Anyone Who Is a Father or Who's Had One. Hunter S. Fulghum. 288p. 1997. reprint ed. pap. 12.00 (*0-425-15619-2*) Berkley Pub.
Like Father, Like Son: What Men Should Know. Ricardo A. Scott. (Ras Cardo Speaks to Humanity Ser.). (Illus.). 75p. (Orig.). 1995. pap. 9.95 (*1-883427-63-0*) Crnerstone GA.
Like Fathers, Like Sons: Portraits of Intimacy & Strain. Thomas J. Cottle. LC 81-2171. (Modern Sociology Ser.). 140p. 1981. pap. 39.50 (*0-89391-087-2*); text 73.25 (*0-89391-054-6*) Ablx Pub.
Like Fire in Dry Stubble: The Life of Barton W. Stone. Bill J. Humble. 1992. pap. 3.99 (*0-89225-412-2*) Gospel Advocate.
Like Fresh Bread: Sunday Homilies in the Parish. Robert P. Waznak. LC 93-2695. 288p. 1993. pap. 14.95 (*0-8091-3378-4*) Paulist Pr.
Like Ghosts of Eagles. Robert Francis. LC 73-93273. 94p. 1974. 20.00 (*0-87023-156-1*); pap. 10.95 (*0-87023-157-X*) U of Mass Pr.
***Like Gold Refined.** Janette Oke. LC 00-8127. (Prairie Legacy Ser.: Vol. 4). 256p. 2000. 15.99 (*0-7642-2162-0*); pap. 10.99 (*0-7642-2161-2*) Bethany Hse.
***Like Gold Refined.** large type ed. Janette Oke. (Prairie Legacy Ser.: Vol. 4). 384p. 2000. 15.99 (*0-7642-2163-9*) Bethany Hse.
Like Grandma Used to Make: A Treasury of Fondly Remembered Dishes. Reader's Digest Editors. 1996. 30.00 (*0-89577-890-4*, Pub. by RD Assn) Penguin Putnam.
Like Hidden Fire: The Plot to Bring down the British Empire. Peter Hopkirk. (Illus.). 384p. 1994. 25.00 (*1-56836-020-7*) Kodansha.
Like Hidden Fire: The Plot to Bring down the British Empire. Peter Hopkirk. 448p. 1997. pap. 16.00 (*1-56836-127-0*, Kodansha Globe) Kodansha.
Like It Is. H. Cosell. Date not set. 2.99 (*0-87223-414-2*) Playboy Ent.
Like It Is: A Teen Sex Guide. E. James Lieberman & Karen L. Troccoli. LC 98-27176. (Illus.). 216p. (YA). (gr. 6 up). 1998. pap. 25.00 (*0-7864-0526-0*) McFarland & Co.
***Like It Was.** James Koller. 192p. 1999. pap. 7.00 (*0-942396-84-7*, Pub. by Blackberry ME) SPD-Small Pr Dist.
Like It Was: A Complete Guide to Writing Oral History. Cynthia S. Brown. (Illus.). 144p. (Orig.). (C). 1988. pap. 13.95 (*0-915924-12-9*) Tchrs & Writers Coll.
Like Jake & Me. Mavis Jukes. LC 83-8380. (Borzoi Sprinters Ser.). (Illus.). 32p. (J). (gr. 1-5). 1987. pap. 7.99 (*0-394-89263-1*, Pub. by Knopf Bks Yng Read) Random.
Like Jake & Me. Mavis Jukes. (J). 1987. 13.19 (*0-606-02359-3*, Pub. by Turtleback) Demco.
Like Lesser Gods. Mari Tomasi. LC 88-29117. 298p. 1988. reprint ed. pap. 16.95 (*0-933050-62-3*) New Eng Pr VT.
Like Life. Lorrie Moore. 192p. 1991. reprint ed. pap. 11.95 (*0-452-26637-8*, Plume) Dutton Plume.
Like Likes Like. Chris Raschka. 32p. 15.95 (*0-7894-4481-X*) DK Pub Inc.
Like Likes Like. Chris Raschka. LC 98-3659. (Illus.). (J). (ps-k). 1999. 15.95 (*0-7894-2564-5*, D K Ink) DK Pub Inc.
Like Love, but Not Exactly: Stories. Francois Camoin. 120p. (C). 1992. 19.95 (*0-8262-0845-2*) U of Mo Pr.
Like Mama Used to Say. Audrianne Norwood. LC 92-96895. (Illus.). 208p. (C). 1992. pap. 9.00 (*1-882338-05-7*) Via God Pub.
Like Mama Used to Say. Audrianne Norwood. LC 92-96895. (Illus.). 208p. (C). 1998. 16.00 (*1-882338-13-8*) Via God Pub.
Like Memory, Caverns: Poems. Elizabeth Dodd. LC 92-32627. 72p. (C). 1992. pap. 12.95 (*0-8147-1855-8*); text 25.00 (*0-8147-1854-X*) NYU Pr.
Like Men of War: Black Troops in the Civil War, 1862-1865. Noah A. Trudeau. LC 97-15380. (Illus.). 576p. (gr. 8). 1998. 29.95 (*0-316-85325-9*) Little.
Like Men of War: Black Troops in the Civil War, 1862-1865. Noah A. Trudeau. (Illus.). 576p. 1999. pap. 18.00 (*0-316-85344-5*) Little.
***Like Minds.** Shannon Friesen. (New Muse Award Ser.). 106p. 1998. pap. 12.00 (*0-921411-81-2*) Genl Dist Srvs.
Like Modern Edens: Wine Growing in Santa Clara Valley & Santa Cruz Mountains. Charles L. Sullivan. (Local History Studies: Vol. 28). 1982. pap. 8.95 (*0-614-14413-2*) CA History Ctr.
Like Mother, Like Daughter. Georgina Brown. (Black Lace Ser.). 1999. mass mkt. 6.95 (*0-352-33422-3*) BLA4.
Like Mother, Like Daughter. Cathy Guisewite. (Illus.). 64p. 1993. 4.95 (*0-8362-3049-3*) Andrews & McMeel.
***Like Mother, Like Daughter: How Women Are Influenced by Their Mothers' Relationship with Food - And How to Break the Pattern.** Debra Waterhouse. 232p. 1999. reprint ed. text 22.00 (*0-7881-6698-0*) DIANE Pub.
Like Mother Like Son, Vol. 1. William Flanagan. 1995. mass mkt. 5.50 (*0-312-95643-6*, Pub. by Tor Bks) St Martin.
***Like Never Before.** Ehud Havaselet. LC 99-16323. 288p. 1999. pap. 12.95 (*0-385-49725-3*, Anchor NY) Doubleday.
Like Never Before. Ehud Havazelet. LC 98-12856. 256p. 1998. 23.00 (*0-374-18762-2*) FS&G.
Like New. Remar Sutton. 1999. text 16.00 (*0-670-81080-0*) Viking Penguin.
Like New Age. Remar Sutton. 1999. pap. write for info. (*0-14-008861-X*, Viking) Viking Penguin.
Like Night & Day: Unionization in a Southern Mill Town. Daniel J. Clark. LC 96-7730. 272p. (C). (gr. 13). 1997. 49.95 (*0-8078-2306-6*); pap. 17.95 (*0-8078-4617-1*) U of NC Pr.
***Like No Other.** Melanie George. 2000. mass mkt. 4.99 (*0-8217-6574-4*, Zebra Kensgtn) Kensgtn Pub Corp.
***Like No Other Store. . . The Bloomingdale's Legend & the Revolution in American Marketing.** Marvin Traub & Tom Teicholz. (Illus.). 428p. 1999. reprint ed. text 25.00 (*0-7881-6691-3*) DIANE Pub.
***Like Normal People.** Karen E. Bender. LC 99-56112. 288p. 2000. 23.00 (*0-395-94515-1*) HM.
Like Nothing at All. Aileen Fisher. LC 60-9159. (Illus.). (J). (ps-3). 1962. lib. bdg. 12.89 (*0-690-49379-7*) HarpC Child Bks.
Like One of the Family: Conversations from a Domestic's Life. Alice Childress. LC 85-73367. (Black Women Writers Ser.). 237p. 1986. reprint ed. pap. 15.00 (*0-8070-0903-2*) Beacon Pr.
Like Only Yesterday: The Memoirs of Donald E. Noble Chief Executive Officer Emeritus Rubbermaid Inc. Donald E. Noble. LC 96-42180. 262p. (Orig.). 1996. pap. 12.95 (*1-888683-15-5*) Wooster Bk.
Like Our Sisters Before Us: Women of Wisconsin Labor. Jamakaya & Wisconsin Labor History Society Staff. LC 99-162552. iii, 93p. 1998. write for info. (*0-9663267-0-9*) WI Labor.
***Like Our Very Own: Adoption & the Changing Culture of Motherhood, 1851-1950.** Julie Berebitsky. 2001. 34.95 (*0-7006-1051-0*) U Pr of KS.
Like People in History. Felice Picano. 528p. 1996. pap. 12.95 (*0-14-024525-1*, Penguin Bks) Viking Penguin.
Like People You See in a Dream: First Contact in Six Papuan Societies. Edward L. Schieffelin & Robert Crittenden. LC 90-41760. (Illus.). 344p. 1991. 47.50 (*0-8047-1662-5*); pap. 16.95 (*0-8047-1899-7*) Stanford U Pr.
Like Pure Gold: The Story of Louis G. Gregory. Anne Breneman. LC 97-9451. (Illus.). (J). Date not set. 14.95 (*0-87743-704-1*) Bahai.
Like Real People. Tom Clark. LC 95-38813. 240p. (Orig.). (C). 1995. 25.00 (*0-87685-985-6*); pap. 13.50 (*0-87685-984-8*) Black Sparrow.
Like Real People, signed ed. deluxe ed. Tom Clark. LC 95-38813. 240p. (Orig.). (C). 1995. 35.00 (*0-87685-986-4*) Black Sparrow.
Like Roads. Laura Moriarty. Ed. by Pat Dienstfrey. LC 89-49484. 64p. (Orig.). (C). 1990. pap. text 8.00 (*0-932716-24-5*) Kelsey St Pr.
Like Salt & Sugar: German-American Ethnicity in Southwestern Illinois. John M. Coggeshall. LC 91-9091. (Immigrant Communities & Ethnic Minorities in the U. S. & Canada Ser.: No. 78). 1991. 69.50 (*0-404-19488-5*) AMS Pr.
***Like Sand, Like Stars: A Fresh Look at Genesis.** John Timmer. LC 99-12795. (Fresh Look Ser.). 118p. 1999. pap. 9.95 (*1-56212-395-5*) CRC Pubns.
Like Sand, Like Stars - Leader: A Fresh Look at Genesis. Joel Kok. (Fresh Look Ser.). (Illus.). 85p. 1999. pap. 11.95 (*1-56212-396-3*, 1315-2090) CRC Pubns.
Like Season 'd Timber: New Essays on George Herbert. Edmund Miller & Robert DiYanni. (Seventeenth-Century Texts & Studies). XVI, 396p. 1988. text 55.95 (*0-8204-0466-7*) P Lang Pubng.
***Like Shaking Hands with God: A Conversation about Writing.** Kurt Vonnegut, Jr. & Lee Stringer. 80p. 2000. 9.95 (*0-7434-1058-0*, WSP) PB.
Like Shaking Hands with God: A Conversation about Writing. Kurt Vonnegut, Jr. & Lee Stringer. (Illus.). 80p. 1999. pap. text 15.00 (*1-58322-002-X*, Pub. by Seven Stories) Publishers Group.
Like Sisters on the Homefront. Rita Williams-Garcia. (J). 1998. 10.09 (*0-606-12980-4*, Pub. by Turtleback) Demco.
Like Sisters on the Homefront. Rita Williams-Garcia. 176p. 1998. pap. 4.99 (*0-14-038561-4*) Viking Penguin.
Like Some Kind of Hero. Jan Marino. 224p. (YA). 1993. pap. 3.50 (*0-380-72010-8*, Avon Bks) Morrow Avon.
Like Stone Soup: The Role of the Professional Development School in the Renewal of Urban Schools. Peter C. Murrell, Jr. 64p. 1998. pap. 24.95 (*0-89333-167-8*) AACTE.
Like Subjects, Love Objects: Essays on Recognition & Sexual Difference. Jessica Benjamin. LC 95-14346. 250p. 1995. 35.00 (*0-300-06419-5*) Yale U Pr.
Like Subjects, Love Objects: Essays on Recognition & Sexual Difference. Jessica Benjamin. 250p. 1998. pap. 16.00 (*0-300-07430-1*) Yale U Pr.
Like Taxes: Marching Through Gaul. David Craig. 1990. 21.50 (*0-916379-65-5*) Scripta.
Like the Air. Joyce Sidman. (New Women's Voices Ser.: Vol. 2). 30p. 1999. pap. 9.00 (*0-9664324-2-8*) Finishng Line.
Like the Book of Acts: The Baptist Convention of New York Story. Keith L. Cogburn. LC 96-70444. 256p. (Orig.). 1996. pap. 14.95 (*1-881576-80-9*) Providence Hse.
Like the Deer That Yearns. Salvatore A. Panimolle. 128p. (C). 1996. pap. 39.95 (*0-85439-319-6*, Pub. by St Paul Pubns) St Mut.
Like the Deer That Yearns: Listening to the Word & Prayer. Ed. by Salvatore A. Panimolle. LC 95-44297. 1998. pap. 12.95 (*1-879007-16-9*) St Bedes Pubns.
. . . Like the Devil: The Kansas Tornadoes of April 26, 1991. Sharon Hamric & Wichita Eagle Staff. (Illus.). 80p. 1991. pap. 4.95 (*1-880652-07-2*) Wichita Eagle.
Like the English Sun: The Official Story of Bush. Jennifer Nine. (Illus.). 1999. pap. 19.95 (*0-7535-0189-9*) London Brdge.
Like the Lion's Tooth. Marjorie B. Kellogg. 1995. 17.75 (*0-8446-6822-2*) Peter Smith.
Like the Moon. Mary Lewis Deans. 179p. (Orig.). 1989. pap. 7.95 (*0-9624388-0-4*) Flatrock Bks.
***Like the Roman: The Life of Enoch Powell.** Simon Heffer. 1999. pap. 24.95 (*0-7538-0820-X*, Pub. by Phoenix Hse) Trafalgar.
***Like the Singing Coming Off the Drums: Love Poems.** Sonia Sanchez. (Blue Streak Ser.). 144p. 1999. pap. 12.50 (*0-8070-6843-8*) Beacon Pr.
Like There's No Tomorrow: Meditations for Women Leaving Patriarchy. Carolyn Gage. 224p. 1997. pap. 14.95 (*1-56751-104-X*) Common Courage.
Like There's No Tomorrow: Meditations for Women Leaving Patriarchy. Carolyn Gage. LC 96-48436. 224p. 1997. lib. bdg. 19.95 (*1-56751-105-8*) Common Courage.
Like This. Leo McKay, Jr. LC 95-190470. 160p. (Orig.). 1996. pap. 13.95 (*0-88784-569-X*, Pub. by Hse of Anansi Pr) Genl Dist Srvs.
Like This. Jalal Al-Din Rumi. Tr. by Coleman Barks. 130p. 1990. pap. 7.50 (*0-9618916-2-9*) Maypop.
Like Trees Walking. Dale Freeman. 89p. 1993. pap. 6.95 (*1-880365-42-1*) Prof Pr NC.
Like Underground Water: Poetry of Mid-20th Century Japan. Tr. by Edward Lueders & Naoshi Koriyama from JPN. LC 95-32541. 350p. (Orig.). 1995. 30.00 (*1-55659-102-0*); pap. 15.00 (*1-55659-103-9*) Copper Canyon.
Like unto Like. Sherwood Bonner. LC 96-51295. 220p. 1997. pap. 14.95 (*1-57003-184-3*) U of SC Pr.
Like unto Moses: The Constituting of an Interruption. James Nohmberg. LC 94-18785. (Indiana Studies in Biblical Literature). 368p. 1995. text 39.95 (*0-253-34090-X*) Ind U Pr.
Like Water for Chocolate: A Novel in Monthly Installments, with Recipes, Romances & Home Remedies. Laura Esquivel.Tr. of Como Agua para Chocolate. 256p. 1992. 23.00 (*0-385-42016-1*) Doubleday.
Like Water for Chocolate: A Novel in Monthly Installments, with Recipes, Romances & Home Remedies. Laura Esquivel.Tr. of Como Agua para Chocolate. 1995. 17.05 (*0-606-09556-X*, Pub. by Turtleback) Demco.
Like Water for Chocolate: A Novel in Monthly Installments, with Recipes, Romances & Home Remedies. Laura Esquivel. Tr. by Carol Christensen & Thomas Christensen from SPA.Tr. of Como Agua para Chocolate. 246p. 1995. reprint ed. pap. 11.95 (*0-385-42017-X*) Doubleday.
***Like Water in a Dry Land.** Bettina Selby. 1998. pap. 14.95 (*0-00-628036-6*, Pub. by HarpC) Trafalgar.
Like Water in a Dry Land. large type ed. Bettina Selby. (Ulverscroft Large Print Ser.). (Illus.). 384p. 1998. 29.99 (*0-7089-3943-0*) Ulverscroft.
Like We Say Back Home. Dick Syatt. 1987. pap. 7.95 (*0-8065-1055-2*, Citadel Pr) Carol Pub Group.
Like Whispers in the Wind. LC TXU 752-982. (Illus.). 225p. (Orig.). 1996. pap. 20.00 (*0-9654503-0-9*) Dysart Divrsfied.
Like Will to Like. Ulpian Fulwell. LC 72-133665. (Tudor Facsimile Texts. Old English Plays Ser.: No. 39). reprint ed. 59.50 (*0-404-53339-6*) AMS Pr.
Likeable Recyclables. Linda Schwartz. LC 92-81436. (Illus.). 128p. (J). (gr. 1-6). 1992. pap. 9.95 (*0-88160-210-8*, LW256) Learning Wks.
Likeable Recyclables: Creative Ideas for Reusing Bags, Boxes, Cans, & Cartons. Linda Schwartz. (J). 1992. 15.05 (*0-606-05430-8*, Pub. by Turtleback) Demco.
Likelihood. rev. ed. A. W. Edwards. LC 92-9859. 296p. (C). 1992. text 45.00 (*0-8018-4445-2*); pap. text 17.95 (*0-8018-4443-6*) Johns Hopkins.
Likelihood-Based Inference in Cointegrated Vector Autoregressive Models. Soren Johansen. (Advanced Texts in Econometrics Ser.). (Illus.). 278p. 1996. pap. text 32.00 (*0-19-877450-8*) OUP.
Likelihood, Bayesian, Inference & Their Application to the Solution of New Structures. Ed. by Gerard Bricogne & Charles W. Carter. (Transactions of the American Crystallographic Association Ser.: Vol. 30). 166p. (C). 1997. pap. text 25.00 (*0-937140-39-2*) Am Crystallographic.
***Likelihood Methods in Statistics.** Thomas A. Severini. Vol. 22. (Illus.). 448p. 2000. text 95.00 (*0-19-850650-3*) OUP.
Likelihood of Confusion in Trademark Law. Richard L. Kirkpatrick. 432p. 1995. ring bd. 135.00 (*0-614-17113-X*, G1-1024) PLI.
Likelihood of Coups. Rosemary H. O'Kane. 160p. 1987. text 72.95 (*0-566-05006-4*) Ashgate Pub Co.
Likelihood of Knowledge. Robert G. Meyers. 187p. (C). 1988. text 106.00 (*90-277-2671-X*, D Reidel) Kluwer Academic.
Likelihood Principle. James O. Berger & Robert L. Wolpert. LC 84-48467. (IMS Lecture Notes - Monographs Ser.: Vol. 6). 206p. 1984. pap. 25.00 (*0-940600-06-4*) Inst Math.
Likelihoodbasierte Marginale Regressionsmodelle Fuer Korrelierte Kategoriale Daten. Christian Heumann. Ed. by Helge Toutenburg. (Anwendungsorientierte Statistik Ser.: Vol. 2), (Illus.). 180p. 1998. pap. 37.95 (*3-631-32671-8*) P Lang Pubng.
Likely. Lisa Coffman. LC 96-11211. (Wick Poetry First Bks.: No. 2). 60p. 1996. 17.00 (*0-87338-554-3*); pap. 9.50 (*0-87338-555-1*) Kent St U Pr.
Likely Place. Paula Fox. LC 87-5542. (Illus.). 80p. (J). 1997. per. 3.99 (*0-689-81402-X*) Atheneum Yung Read.
Likely Place. Paula Fox. LC 96-54896. (Illus.). 80p. (J). 1997. write for info. (*0-689-81401-1*) S&S Bks Yung.
Likely Place. Paula Fox. (J). 1997. 9.19 (*0-606-11561-7*, Pub. by Turtleback) Demco.
Likely Stories: A Collection of Untraditional Fiction. Emilio DeGrazia et al. Ed. by Bruce R. McPherson. LC 82-129270. 224p. 1981. 14.50 (*0-914232-42-8*); pap. 7.95 (*0-914232-41-X*) McPherson & Co.
Likely Stories: Essays on Political Philosophy & Contemporary American Literature. Ethan Fishman. (University of Florida Social Sciences Monographs: No. 75). 128p. 1989. pap. text 17.95 (*0-8130-0934-0*) U Press Fla.
Likely Story. Samuel Bousky. LC 93-24001. (Illus.). 80p. (Orig.). 1993. 13.95 (*0-9634250-7-2*) J & L Pubns.
Likely Story. Mary Lavin & Alison Gault. 56p. 1997. pap. 7.95 (*1-85371-104-7*, Pub. by Poolbeg Pr) Dufour.
Likely Story: One Summer with Lillian Hellman. Rosemary Mahoney. LC 98-22116. 288p. 1998. 23.95 (*0-385-47793-7*) Doubleday.
***Likely Story: One Summer with Lillian Hellman.** Rosemary Mahoney. 288p. 1999. pap. 14.00 (*0-385-47931-X*, Anchor NY) Doubleday.
Likely Story: Probability & Play in Fiction. Robert Newsom. 258p. (Orig.). (C). 1988. text 35.00 (*0-8135-1320-0*); pap. text 17.00 (*0-8135-1357-X*) Rutgers U Pr.

L

Likely Story: The Writing Life. Robert Kroetsch. LC 96-135444. 224p. 1995. pap. 14.95 (*0-88995-103-9*, Pub. by Red Deer) Genl Dist Srvs.

Likely to Die. Linda A. Fairstein. 1997. 24.00 (*0-614-27882-1*, Scribners Ref) Mac Lib Ref.

Likely to Die. Linda A. Fairstein. 418p. 1998. mass mkt. 6.99 (*0-671-01493-5*) PB.

Likely to Die. Linda A. Fairstein. LC 97-10841. 1997. 24.00 (*0-684-81488-9*) S&S Trade.

Likely to This. limited ed. Peter Ganick. 68p. (Orig.). 1992. pap. 18.00 (*0-937013-47-1*) Potes Poets.

Likeness. Maria-Xose Queizan. Tr. by Ana M. Spitzmesser from SPA. LC 98-32075. 119p. (C). 1999. text 32.95 (*0-8204-4177-5*) P Lang Pubng.

Likeness: Portrait Photographs from the Collection. Thomas W. Southall. LC 80-53852. (Illus.). 60p. 1980. pap. 4.00 (*0-913689-20-3*) Spencer Muse Art.

Likeness & Beyond: Portraits from Africa & the World. Jean M. Borgatti & Richard Brilliant. LC 90-1354. (Illus.). 1990. 53.50 (*0-945802-05-6*); pap. 27.50 (*0-945802-06-4*) Museum African.

Likeness & Icon: Selected Studies in Classical & Early Medieval Art. H. P. L'Orange. 344p. (Orig.). 1973. pap. 67.50 (*87-7492-062-6*, Pub. by Odense Universitets Forlag) Coronet Bks.

Likeness & Landscape: Thomas M. Easterly & the Art of the Daguerreotype. Dolores A. Kilgo. LC 94-75212. (Illus.). 250p. 1994. 70.00 (*1-883982-03-0*) MO Hist Soc.

Likeness & Presence: A History of the Image Before the Era of Art. Hans Belting. Tr. by Edmund Jephcott from GER. LC 93-3389.Tr. of Bild und Kult. (Illus.). 676p. 1994. 65.00 (*0-226-04214-6*) U Ch Pr.

Likeness & Presence: A History of the Image Before the Era of Art. Hans Belting. Tr. by Edmund Jephcott.Tr. of Bild und Kult. (Illus.). xxiv, 652p. 1996. pap. text 39.95 (*0-226-04215-4*) U Ch Pr.

Likeness & Unlikeness: Selected Paintings. Qi Baishi. Ed. by Helen Chasin. Tr. by Ouyang Caiwei. (Illus.). 1990. 89.95 (*0-8351-2216-6*) China Bks.

Likeness in Stone. J. Wallis Martin. LC 98-10286. 288p. 1998. text 22.95 (*0-312-18626-6*) St Martin.

Likeness in Stone. Julia Wallis Martin. 1999. mass mkt. 6.50 (*0-312-97077-3*, Minotaur) St Martin.

Likeness in Stone. large type ed. J. Wallis Martin. LC 98-42813. 1999. 30.00 (*0-7862-1684-0*) Thorndike Pr.

Likeness in Stone. large type ed. J. Wallis Martin. (Ulverscroft Large Print Ser.). 448p. 1998. 29.99 (*0-7089-3895-7*) Ulverscroft.

Likeness of Thomas More: An Iconographical Survey of Three Centuries. Stanley Morison. Ed. by Nicolas Barker. LC 64-4266. 134p. reprint ed. pap. 41.60 (*0-7837-5614-3*, 204552100005) Bks Demand.

Likeness to Truth. Graham Oddie. 1986. text 129.50 (*90-277-2238-2*) Kluwer Academic.

Likeness Trade: Portrait Painting in Arkansas, 1780-1900. Swannee Bennett. (Illus.). 20p. (Orig.). 1996. pap. write for info. (*0-9651500-0-3*) AR Territorial.

Likenesses. Suzanne Hawkinson. LC 81-84265. 72p. 1982. pap. 5.50 (*0-941866-00-9*) Solo Press MA.

Likenesses of Truth in Elizabethan & Restoration Drama. Harriet Hawkins. 1972. 24.00 (*0-19-812019-2*) OUP.

***Likes of Me.** Randall Beth Platt. LC 99-33284. 256p. (J). (gr. 4-8). 2000. 15.95 (*0-385-32692-0*) Delacorte.

Likewise. Paul Violi. 1988. 15.00 (*0-914610-56-2*); pap. 7.00 (*0-914610-55-4*) Hanging Loose.

Likhaan Book of Poetry & Fiction, 1995. Ed. by Gemino H. Abad & Cristina P. Hidalgo. LC 96-946561. 376p. 1997. pap. text 27.00 (*971-542-136-9*, Pub. by U of Philippines Pr) UH Pr.

Likhachev's Watermarks: Text; Plates & Indexes, 2, Vols. 1&2. Ed. by J. S. Simmons. (Monumenta Chartae Papyraceae Ser.: 15). (Illus.). 450p. (C). 1994. 445.00 (*90-5356-226-5*, Pub. by Amsterdam U Pr) U of Mich Pr.

Liking, Loving & Relating. Clyde Hendrick & Susan Hendrick. LC 82-14561. (Psychology Ser.). 306p. (C). 1983. pap. 18.00 (*0-534-01263-9*) Brooks-Cole.

Likkut Dinei U'Minnogei Roshchodesh. Chaim Rappoport. (HEB.). 140p. 1990. 8.00 (*0-8266-5210-7*) Kehot Pubn Soc.

Likkutei Amarim Tanya. Schneur Zalman. LC 82-81577. (HEB.). 496p. 1996. 17.00 (*0-8266-4600-X*) Kehot Pubn Soc.

Likkutei Amarim Tanya. Schneur Z. M'Liadi. LC 82-81577. (HEB.). 1010p. 1984. reprint ed. 10.00 (*0-8266-1000-5*) Kehot Pubn Soc.

Likkutei Amarim Tanya: Bi-Lingual Edition. Schneur Z. Baruchovitch. Tr. by J. Immanuel Schochet et al. LC 84-82007. 1006p. 1993. reprint ed. 25.00 (*0-8266-0400-5*) Kehot Pubn Soc.

Likkutei Amarim Tanya: First Versions. Schneur Z. M'Liadi. LC 81-86392. (HEB.). 896p. 1981. 20.00 (*0-8266-5555-6*) Kehot Pubn Soc.

Likkutei Archim B'shas Ub'rambam. Menachem M. Schneerson. (HEB.). 300p. 1992. 15.00 (*0-8266-5769-9*) Kehot Pubn Soc.

Likkutei Dibburim, Vol. 1. Yosef Yitchak Schneersohn Obm. Tr. by Uri Kaploun from YID. 360p. 1987. 20.00 (*0-8266-0444-7*) Kehot Pubn Soc.

Likkutei Dibburim, Vol. 2. Yosef Yitchak Schneersohn Obm. Tr. by Uri Kaploun from YID. 328p. 1988. 20.00 (*0-8266-0445-5*) Kehot Pubn Soc.

Likkutei Dibburim, Vol. 3. Yosef Yitchak Scneersohn Obm. Tr. by Uri Kaploun from YID. 320p. 1990. 20.00 (*0-8266-0446-3*) Kehot Pubn Soc.

Likkutei Diburim, 2 vols. 7th ed. Incl., **2 vols.** 7th ed. Joseph T. Schneersohn. (YID.). 1616p. 1992. reprint ed. 15.00 (*0-8266-5416-9*); Vol. 2. 7th ed. Joseph I. Schneersohn. (YID.). 1992. reprint ed. 15.00 (*0-8266-5417-7*); 30.00 (*0-8266-5415-0*) Kehot Pubn Soc.

Likkutei Levi Yitzchak: Beraishes. Levi Y. Schneerson. (HEB.). 305p. reprint ed. 10.00 (*0-8266-5445-2*) Kehot Pubn Soc.

Likkutei Levi Yitzchak: Chidushim Ubiurim Leshas Mishne Ugemoro. Levi Y. Schneerson. (HEB.). 461p. reprint ed. 10.00 (*0-8266-5448-7*) Kehot Pubn Soc.

Likkutei Levi Yitzchak: Likkutim Al Pesukei Tanach Umaamorei Chazal; Igrois. Levi Y. Schneerson. (HEB.). 452p. reprint ed. 10.00 (*0-8266-5447-9*) Kehot Pubn Soc.

Likkutei Levi Yitzchak: Shemot - Devorim. Levi Y. Schneerson. (HEB.). 477p. reprint ed. 10.00 (*0-8266-5446-0*) Kehot Pubn Soc.

Likkutei Sichos, Vol. 1. Menachem M. Schneerson. (Likkutei Sichos Ser.). (HEB & YID.). 306p. reprint ed. 15.00 (*0-8266-5719-2*) Kehot Pubn Soc.

Likkutei Sichos, Vol. 3. Menachem M. Schneerson. (Likkutei Sichos Ser.). (HEB & YID.). 291p. reprint ed. 15.00 (*0-8266-5721-4*) Kehot Pubn Soc.

Likkutei Sichos, Vol. 4. Menachem M. Schneerson. (Likkutei Sichos Ser.). (HEB & YID.). 438p. reprint ed. 15.00 (*0-8266-5722-2*) Kehot Pubn Soc.

Likkutei Sichos, Vol. 6. Menachem M. Schneerson. (Likkutei Sichos Ser.). (HEB & YID.). 420p. reprint ed. 15.00 (*0-8266-5724-9*) Kehot Pubn Soc.

Likkutei Sichos, Vol. 7. Menachem M. Schneerson. (Likkutei Sichos Ser.). (HEB & YID.). 390p. reprint ed. 15.00 (*0-8266-5725-7*) Kehot Pubn Soc.

Likkutei Sichos, Vol. 8. Menachem M. Schneerson. (Likkutei Sichos Ser.). (HEB & YID.). 384p. reprint ed. 15.00 (*0-8266-5726-5*) Kehot Pubn Soc.

Likkutei Sichos, Vol. 9. Menachem M. Schneerson. (HEB & YID.). 512p. reprint ed. 15.00 (*0-8266-5727-3*) Kehot Pubn Soc.

Likkutei Sichos, Vol. 15. (HEB & YID.). 580p. 15.00 (*0-8266-5733-8*) Kehot Pubn Soc.

Likkutei Sichos, Vol. 20. Menachem M. Schneerson. (Likkutei Sichos Ser.). (HEB & YID.). 665p. Date not set. reprint ed. 15.00 (*0-8266-5738-9*) Kehot Pubn Soc.

Likkutei Sichos, Vol. 21. Menachem M. Schneerson. (Likkutei Sichos Ser.). (HEB & YID.). 521p. Date not set. reprint ed. 15.00 (*0-8266-5739-7*) Kehot Pubn Soc.

Likkutei Sichos: Biumrim B'Likkutei Levi Yitchok Al Iggeres Hates Huva. Menachem M. Schneerson. LC 61-57983. (HEB.). 208p. 1992. 12.00 (*0-8266-5780-X*) Kehot Pubn Soc.

Likkutei Sichos: Breishis, Vol. 35. Menachem M. Schneerson. LC 61-57983. (HEB.). 468p. 1996. 20.00 (*0-8266-5781-8*) Kehot Pubn Soc.

Likkutei Sichos Vol. 1: An Anthology of Talks. Menachem M. Schneerson. Tr. by Jacob I. Schochet from HEB. 256p. 1981. 10.00 (*0-8266-0500-1*) Kehot Pubn Soc.

Likkutei Sichos Vol. 2: An Anthology of Talks. Menachem M. Schneerson. Tr. by Jacob I. Schochet from HEB. 256p. 1983. 10.00 (*0-8266-0501-X*) Kehot Pubn Soc.

Likkutei Sichos Vol. 3: An Anthology of Talks. Menachem M. Schneerson. Tr. by Jacob I. Schochet from HEB. 270p. 1987. 10.00 (*0-8266-0502-8*) Kehot Pubn Soc.

Likkutei Sichos Vol. 4: An Anthology of Talks. Menachem M. Scneerson. Tr. by Jacob I. Schochet from HEB. 292p. 1992. 10.00 (*0-8266-0503-6*) Kehot Pubn Soc.

Likkutei Sichos Vol. 16. Menachem M. Schneerson. (Likkutei Sichos Ser.). (HEB & YID.). 664p. reprint ed. 15.00 (*0-8266-5735-4*) Kehot Pubn Soc.

Likkutei Toran, Vol. 2. Schneur Zalman. LC 87-4240.Tr. of Collection of Torah Discourses. (HEB.). 242p. 1996. 27.50 (*0-8266-5552-1*) Kehot Pubn Soc.

Likkuter Sichos, Vol. 2. Menachem M. Schneerson. (Likkutei Sichos Ser.). (HEB & YID.). 474p. reprint ed. 15.00 (*0-8266-5720-6*) Kehot Pubn Soc.

Likkutie Horoos Minhagim Ubiarim Binyanie Shidduchim Venisuen. Menachem M. Schneerson. (HEB.). 319p. 1991. 14.00 (*0-8266-5221-2*) Kehot Pubn Soc.

Likrat Shabbat. deluxe ed. Sidney Greenberg & Jonathan D. Levine. LC 87-60858. 12.50 (*0-685-04133-6*) Prayer Bk.

Likrat Shabbat. large type ed. Sidney Greenberg & Jonathan D. Levine. LC 87-60858. 16.95 (*0-685-04132-8*) Prayer Bk.

Likrat Shabbat. rev. ed. Sidney Greenberg & Jonathan D. Levine. LC 87-60858. 12.95 (*0-87677-079-0*) Prayer Bk.

Likutei Levi Yitzchok: Haordis L'Sefer Ha'Tanya. 3rd ed. Levi Y. Schneersohn. (HEB.). 64p. (Orig.). 1990. reprint ed. pap. 3.00 (*0-8266-5444-4*) Kehot Pubn Soc.

Likutey Etzot see Advice

Likutey Moharan, Vol. 1. 2nd rev. ed. Rabbi Nachman of Breslov. Ed. & Tr. by Moshe Mykoff from HEB. Tr. by Simchah Bergman from HEB. 390p. 1995. 20.00 (*0-930213-92-0*) Breslov Res Inst.

Likutey Moharan, Vol. 2. 2nd rev. ed. Rabbi Nachman of Breslov. Ed. & Tr. by Moshe Mykoff from HEB. Ed. by Ozer Bergman. 385p. 1993. 20.00 (*0-930213-93-9*) Breslov Res Inst.

Likutey Moharan, Vol. 3. Rabbe Nachman. Ed. & Tr. by Moshe Mykoff from HEB. Ed. by Ozer Bergman. Tr. by Chaim Kramer from HEB. 360p. 1990. 20.00 (*0-930213-78-5*) Breslov Res Inst.

Likutey Moharan, Vol. 5. Rabbi Nachman of Breslov. Ed. by Moshe Mykoff. Ed. & Tr. by Ozer Bergman from HEB. 400p. 1997. 20.00 (*0-930213-80-7*) Breslov Res Inst.

Likutey Moharan Vol. 4: Lessons 23-32. Nachman. Ed. & Tr. by Moshe Mykoff from HEB. Ed. by Ozer Bergman. (Illus.). 520p. 1992. 20.00 (*0-930213-79-3*) Breslov Res Inst.

Likutey Moharan Vol. 10: Lessons 109-194. Nachman. Ed. & Tr. by Moshe Mykoff from HEB. Ed. by Ozer Bergman. (Illus.). 480p. 1992. 20.00 (*0-930213-85-8*) Breslov Res Inst.

Li'l Abner. Ed. by Dave Schreiner. LC 88-12831. (Li'l Abner Dailies Ser.: Vol. II). (Illus.). 160p. 1988. pap. 16.95 (*0-87816-041-8*) Kitchen Sink.

Lil Abner, No. 24. Al Capp. Ed. by N. C. Christopher Couch. (Illus.). 176p. 1997. pap. 18.95 (*0-87816-316-6*) Kitchen Sink.

Lil Abner, No. 24. 2nd ed. Al Capp. Ed. by N. C. Christopher Couch. (Illus.). 176p. 1997. 34.95 (*0-87816-317-4*) Kitchen Sink.

Li'l Abner, No. 26. Al Capp. 184p. 1998. pap. 22.95 (*0-87816-290-9*) Kitchen Sink.

Li'l Abner, No. 27. Al Capp. 176p. 1998. pap. 22.95 (*0-87816-295-X*) Kitchen Sink.

Li'l Abner, No. 27. Al Capp. 1999. write for info. (*0-87816-296-8*) Kitchen Sink.

Li'l Abner, Vol. 17. Al Capp. Ed. by James Vance. (Illus.). 160p. 1993. 34.95 (*0-87816-209-7*) Kitchen Sink.

Li'l Abner, Vol. 19. 2nd ed. Al Capp. Ed. by James Vance. (Illus.). 160p. 1994. 34.95 (*0-87816-249-6*) Kitchen Sink.

Li'l Abner, Vol. 21. 2nd ed. Al Capp. (Illus.). 176p. 1995. 34.95 (*0-87816-263-1*) Kitchen Sink.

Li'l Abner, Vol. 22. Al Capp. (Illus.). 192p. 1995. 40.00 (*0-87816-272-0*) Kitchen Sink.

Li'l Abner, Vol. 23. Al Capp. (Illus.). 176p. 1995. 34.95 (*0-87816-305-0*) Kitchen Sink.

Li'l Abner: A Study of American Satire. Arthur A. Berger. LC 94-17079. (Studies in Popular Culture). (Illus.). 191p. 1994. reprint ed. text 30.00 (*0-87805-712-9*); reprint ed. pap. text 14.95 (*0-87805-713-7*) U Pr of Miss.

Li'l Abner: Li'l Abner Meets the Shmoo, No. 27. Al Capp. (Li'l Abner Dailies Ser.). (Illus.). 180p. 1998. reprint ed. pap. 22.95 (*0-87816-116-3*) Kitchen Sink.

Li'l Abner: Vocal Selections. Ed. by Sy Feldman. (Classic Broadway Shows Ser.). 16p. (Orig.). 1994. pap. 10.95 (*0-89724-263-7*, SF0151) Wrner Bros.

Li'l Abner Dailies. A. Capp. (Li'l Abner Dailies Ser.: Vol. XXI). 1995. pap. 18.95 (*0-87816-262-3*) Kitchen Sink.

Li'l Abner Dailies. A. Capp. (Li'l Abner Dailies Ser.: Vol. XXII). (Illus.). 1995. pap. 20.95 (*0-87816-271-2*) Kitchen Sink.

Li'l Abner Dailies, Vol. 23. Al Capp. (Illus.). 176p. 1996. pap. text 18.95 (*0-87816-304-2*) Kitchen Sink.

Li'l Abner Dailies, 1959. Al Capp. (Li'l Abner Dailies Ser.: Vol. 25). (Illus.). 184p. 1996. 34.95 (*0-87816-279-8*); pap. 18.95 (*0-87816-278-X*) Kitchen Sink.

Li'l Abner Dailies 1940, Vol.VI. Al Capp. Ed. by Dave Schreiner. LC 88-12831. (Li'l Abner Dailies Ser.). (Illus.). 174p. 1989. pap. 16.95 (*0-87816-059-0*) Kitchen Sink.

Li'l Abner Dailies 1945, Vol. 11. Al Capp. Ed. by Dave Schreiner & Madeline Gardner. (Al Capp's Li'l Abner Ser.). (Illus.). 158p. 1991. reprint ed. pap. 18.95 (*0-87816-083-3*) Kitchen Sink.

Li'l Abner Dailies 1944, Vol. 10. Al Capp. Ed. by Dave Schreiner. LC 88-12831. (Li'l Abner Dailies Ser.: Vol. X). (Illus.). 168p. 1990. pap. 18.95 (*0-87816-079-5*) Kitchen Sink.

Li'l Abner Dailies 1949 Vol. 15: Kick in the Kigmies! limited ed. Al Capp. Ed. by Dave Schreiner. (Illus.). 176p. 1993. 34.95 (*0-87816-126-0*) Kitchen Sink.

Li'l Abner Dailies 1941, Vol. VII. Al Capp. Ed. by Dave Schreiner. LC 88-12831. (Li'l Abner Dailies Ser.). (Illus.). 1990. 27.95 (*0-87816-064-7*) Kitchen Sink.

Li'l Abner Dailies 1946, Vol. 12. Al Capp. LC 88-12831. (Illus.). 168p. 1991. pap. 18.95 (*0-87816-092-2*) Kitchen Sink.

Li'l Abner Dailies 1943, Vol. IX. Al Capp. Ed. by Dave Schreiner. LC 88-12831. (Illus.). 1990. 29.95 (*0-87816-073-6*) Kitchen Sink.

Li'l Abner Dailies 1939, Vol. 5. Al Capp. Ed. by Dave Schreiner & Julie C. Cairol. LC 88-12831. (Illus.). 176p. 1989. 27.95 (*0-87816-056-6*) Kitchen Sink.

Li'l Abner Dailies, 1938: Abner in the Orphanage, Strange Gal in the Swamp. Al Capp. Ed. by Dave Schreiner. LC 88-12831. (Li'l Abner Dailies Ser.: Vol. IV). (Illus.). 168p. 1989. 27.95 (*0-87816-051-5*); pap. 16.95 (*0-87816-052-3*) Kitchen Sink.

Li'l Abner Dailies, 1950: In Search of the Perfect Woman. limited ed. Al Capp. Ed. by Dave Schreiner. (Li'l Abner Dailies Ser.: Vol. 16). (Illus.). 184p. 1993. 34.95 (*0-87816-143-0*) Kitchen Sink.

Li'l Abner Daily Strips, 1951. Al Capp. Ed. by Dave Schreiner. (Li'l Abner Dailies Ser.: Vol. 17). (Illus.). 180p. 1993. pap. 18.95 (*0-87816-210-0*) Kitchen Sink.

Li'l Abner, 1952, Vol. 18. Al Capp. Ed. by Dave Schriener. (Illus.). 176p. (YA). (gr. 6 up). 1994. reprint ed. 34.95 (*0-87816-242-9*) Kitchen Sink.

Lil Bertha-Compact Electric Furnace. David J. Gingery. 1984. pap. 8.95 (*0-917914-16-3*) Lindsay Pubns.

Lil' Black Girl Eyes 'n Frozen & Dirtied Brown Leaves. Kenneth Bowens. Ed. by Carolyn James. 187p. 1996. pap. 21.95 (*0-9653447-0-3*) Lil Black Girl.

Li'l' Gal. Paul Laurence Dunbar. LC 75-78992. (Black Heritage Library Collection). (Illus.). 1977. 35.95 (*0-8369-8558-3*) Ayer.

Li'l Gal. Paul Laurence Dunbar. LC 73-164800. (Illus.). reprint ed. 19.50 (*0-404-00034-7*) AMS Pr.

Li'l' Gal. Paul Laurence Dunbar. (Illus.). 1991. reprint ed. pap. 22.95 (*0-88143-131-1*) Ayer.

Lil' Havana Blues. Nilda Cepero. (Illus.). 60p. 1998. pap. 8.00 (*1-890953-03-2*, 98LHB) LS Pr.

***Li'l Mac Baseball Book: Stories for Future Baseball Players, Vol. 1.** large type ed. Joe Dicicco. Tr. by Ruben D. Jimenez. (ENG & SPA., Illus.). iii, 17p. (J). (ps). 1999. 7.95 (*1-929528-00-0*) Booker Lane.

***Li'l Mac Baseball Book: Stories for Future Baseball Players, Vol. 2.** large type ed. Joe Dicicco. Tr. by Ruben D. Jimenez. (ENG & SPA., Illus.). iii, 16p. (J). (ps-3). 1999. 7.95 (*1-929528-01-9*) Booker Lane.

***Li'l Mac Baseball Book: Stories for Future Baseball Players, Vol. 3.** large type ed. Joe Dicicco. Tr. by Ruben D. Jimenez. (ENG & SPA., Illus.). iii, 17p. (J). (ps-3). 1999. 7.95 (*1-929528-02-7*) Booker Lane.

***Li'l Mac Baseball Book: Stories for Future Baseball Players, Vol. 4.** large type ed. Joe Dicicco. Tr. by Ruben D. Jimenez. (ENG & SPA., Illus.). iii, 14p. (J). (ps-3). 1999. 7.95 (*1-929528-03-5*) Booker Lane.

Li'l Mama's Rules. Sheneska Jackson. LC 96-29735. 272p. 1997. 21.50 (*0-684-81842-6*, Scribner Pap Fic) S&S Trade Pap.

Li'l Mama's Rules. Sheneska Jackson. 272p. 1998. per. 12.00 (*0-684-84613-6*) Scribner.

Li'l Miss Fuss Budget. Kate Allen. (Illus.). 21p. (J). (gr. k-6). 1996. 14.95 (*1-887218-02-5*) Kumquat Pr.

Lil' Mowande. Demond Wilson. 1999. write for info. (*1-878898-18-3*) Christian Pub.

Li'l Rascals: Tale of a Fish. Loren F. Haker. (Illus.). 66p. (J). (gr. 1-8). 1984. 7.95 (*0-9609964-2-7*); pap. 4.95 (*0-9609964-3-5*) Haker Books.

Li'l Rascals: Timmy & the Bees. Loren F. Haker. (Illus.). 56p. (J). (gr. 1-8). 1984. 7.95 (*0-9609964-0-0*); pap. 4.95 (*0-9609964-1-9*) Haker Books.

Li'l Rex. Sylvester Island, Jr. (Illus.). (J). (ps-6). 1998. 11.95 (*1-892089-53-X*); pap. 6.95 (*1-892089-50-5*) Our Kids Pubn.

Li'l Rex Says, Let's Have Fun with Shapes. Sylvester Island, Jr. (Illus.). (J). (ps-6). 1998. pap. 3.95 (*1-892089-51-3*) Our Kids Pubn.

Li'l Tom: The Adventures of Tom Sawyer's Son. Thom Sayre. 221p. 1990. 27.50 (*0-9628176-9-4*) T F Sayre.

Li'l Tuffy & His ABC's. Jean Pajot-Smith. (Ebony Jr. Bks.). (Illus.). 64p. (J). (ps-4). pap. 5.00 (*0-87485-063-0*) Johnson Chicago.

Li'l Tuffy & His Friends. Jean Pajot-Smith. (ENG & SPA.). 47p. (J). 1976. 5.00 (*0-87485-077-0*) Johnson Chicago.

Lila: An Inquiry into Morals. Robert M. Pirsig. 480p. 1992. mass mkt. 7.99 (*0-553-29961-1*) Bantam.

Lila Says: A Novel. Chimo. LC 98-15753. 128p. 1999. 20.00 (*0-684-83603-3*) S&S Trade.

LILAC: Lessons for Inclusive Language Activities in the Classroom. Gail Raymond & Aileen C. Lau-Dickinson. 192p. (Orig.). (J). (ps-1). 1996. pap. text 18.95 (*0-937857-71-8*) Speech Bin.

Lilac & Flag. John Berger. LC 92-50076. 1992. pap. 12.00 (*0-679-73719-7*) Vin Bks.

Lilac & Lace. Sharon Fuller. 200p. 1998. pap. text 10.95 (*1-57532-088-6*) Press-Tige Pub.

Lilac Bus. Maeve Binchy. 400p. 1992. mass mkt. 7.50 (*0-440-21302-9*) Dell.

Lilac Bus. large type ed. Maeve Binchy. LC 92-17122. (General Ser.). 480p. 1992. 18.95 (*0-8161-5384-1*, G K Hall Lrg Type) Mac Lib Ref.

Lilac Cigarette in a Wish Cathedral: Poems by Robin Magowan. Robin Magowan. Ed. by Richard Howard. LC 97-45433. (Poetry Ser.). 90p. 1998. pap. 9.95 (*1-57003-270-X*); lib. bdg. 15.95 (*1-57003-269-6*) U of SC Pr.

Lilac Circle. Karen Lockwood. 336p. (Orig.). 1995. mass mkt. 5.50 (*0-515-11769-2*, Jove) Berkley Pub.

Lilac Fairy Book. Ed. by Andrew Lang. 26.95 (*0-89190-084-5*) Amereon Ltd.

Lilac Fairy Book. Ed. by Andrew Lang. (Illus.). 369p. (J). (ps-4). 1968. pap. 7.95 (*0-486-21907-0*) Dover.

Lilac Fairy Book. Ed. by Andrew Lang. (Illus.). (J). (gr. 4-12). 1990. 22.25 (*0-8446-2425-X*) Peter Smith.

Lilac Garland. Nancy Richards-Akers. 224p. (Orig.). 1990. mass mkt. 3.95 (*0-446-34923-2*, Pub. by Warner Bks) Little.

Lilac Garland. large type ed. Nancy R. Akers. LC 90-35647. 276p. 1990. reprint ed. lib. bdg. 18.95 (*1-56054-013-3*) Thorndike Pr.

Lilac House. Carolyn C. Dupuis. Ed. by Guri Duncan. 280p. 1997. 25.00 (*0-9638803-2-2*) Driftwood Pr.

Lilac Planting & Preservation. 1998. 14.95 (*1-58017-115-X*) Storey Bks.

Lilac Rose: A Flower's Lifetime. large type ed. Karla B. Whitsitt. LC 98-94216. (Illus.). 16p. (J). (ps-6). 2000. pap. 5.00 (*1-891452-10-X*, 8) Heart Arbor.

Lilac Scented Memories: A Poetic Memoir. Lila G. Kinney. Ed. by Jeanette K. Cakouros & Ruth K. Flowers. LC 88-71050. (Illus.). 112p. (Orig.). 1989. pap. 7.95 (*0-9620600-0-3*) Maine Rhode Pubs.

Lilac Trace. 1998. pap. 15.99 (*1-892571-06-4*) TDC Pr.

Lilacs in Bloom. Ed. by Bettye T. Spinner. (Illus.). 64p. 1994. write for info. (*2-615-36394-8*); 6.00 (*0-9613989-6-5*) E R Kaltovich.

Lilacs on Lace. Linda Ladd. 1996. pap. 5.99 (*0-614-98096-8*, Topaz) NAL.

Lila's April Fool. Molly Mia Stewart. (Sweet Valley Kids Ser.: No. 48). (J). (gr. 1-3). 1994. 8.70 (*0-606-06033-2*, Pub. by Turtleback) Demco.

Lila's Birthday Bash. Created by Francine Pascal. (Sweet Valley Kids Ser.: No. 58). 96p. (J). (gr. 1-3). 1995. pap. 3.50 (*0-553-48209-2*) Bantam.

Lila's Birthday Bash. Molly Mia Stewart. (Sweet Valley Kids Ser.: No. 58). (J). (gr. 1-3). 1995. 8.70 (*0-606-08232-8*, Pub. by Turtleback) Demco.

Lila's Christmas Angel. Molly Mia Stewart. (Sweet Valley Kids Ser.: No. 63). (J). (gr. 1-3). 1995. 8.60 (*0-606-08630-7*, Pub. by Turtleback) Demco.

Lila's Haunted House Party. Created by Francine Pascal. (Sweet Valley Kids Ser.: No. 23). 80p. (J). (gr. 1-3). 1991. pap. 3.50 (*0-553-15919-4*) Bantam.

Lila's House: A Study of Male Prostitution in Latin America. Jacobo Schifter. LC 98-26319. (Illus.). 133p. 1998. pap. 12.95 (*1-56023-943-3*); lib. bdg. 29.95 (*0-7890-0593-X*) Haworth Pr.

Lila's Little Dinosaur. Wolfram Hanel. Tr. by J. Alison James. LC 94-5065. (Illus.). 64p. (J). (gr. 2-4). 1995. pap. 5.95 (*1-55858-522-2*, Pub. by North-South Bks NYC) Chronicle Bks.

Lila's Little Dinosaur. Wolfram Hanel. 1995. 11.15 (*0-606-08800-8*, Pub. by Turtleback) Demco.

An Asterisk (*) at the beginning of an entry indicates that the title is appearing for the first time.

L

Lila's Music Video. Jamie Suzanne. (Sweet Valley Twins Ser.: No. 73). (J). (gr. 3-7). 1993. 8.60 (*0-606-05653-X*, Pub. by Turtleback) Demco.

Lila's New Flame. Created by Francine Pascal. (Sweet Valley High Ser.: No. 135). 208p. (Orig.). (YA). (gr. 7-12). 1997. mass mkt. 3.99 (*0-553-57069-2*) BDD Bks Young Read.

Lila's Secret. Created by Francine Pascal. (Sweet Valley Kids Ser.: No. 6). (J). (gr. 1-3). 1994. pap. 4.99 (*0-553-54182-X*) BDD Bks Young Read.

Lila's Secret. Molly Mia Stewart. (Sweet Valley Kids Ser.: No. 6). (J). (gr. 1-3). 1990. 8.70 (*0-606-04468-X*, Pub. by Turtleback) Demco.

Lila's Secret Valentine. Jamie Suzanne. (Sweet Valley Twins Super Edition Ser.: No. 5). (J). (gr. 3-7). 1995. 9.09 (*0-606-08246-8*, Pub. by Turtleback) Demco.

Lila's Story. Kate William. (Sweet Valley High Super Star Ser.: No. 1). (YA). (gr. 7 up). 1989. 8.60 (*0-606-01723-2*, Pub. by Turtleback) Demco.

Lilaveles "A Little Tale" Veronica Benes. (Illus.). 30p. (J). (ps-4). 1997. 12.97 (*0-9662368-0-7*) V Benes.

Lilayandopal Tu. Jose Sanchez-Boudy. LC 77-78254. 1978. pap. 7.95 (*0-89729-168-9*) Ediciones.

L'Ile Fantastique: Fantastic Island. Susannah Leigh. Ed. by Kathy Gemmell & Nicole Irving. (FRE., Illus.). 25p. (J). (gr. 2-3). reprint ed. 17.00 (*0-7881-9300-7*) DIANE Pub.

L'Ile Fantastique (Fantastic Island) Kathy Gammell & Susannah Leigh. (First Bilingual Readers Ser.). (FRE., Illus.). 24p. (J). (gr. 2 up). 1999. lib. bdg. 13.95 (*0-88110-823-5*, Usborne) EDC.

***Lili.** Abigail DeWitt. LC 00-8058. 307p. 2000. 26.95 (*0-8101-5100-6*, TriQuart) Northwestern U Pr.

Lili Anne Lamb. Carole S. Ford. (Illus.). 32p. (J). (ps). 1997. pap. 4.95 (*1-891533-01-0*) Calvin Prtnership.

Lili at Ballet. Rachel Isadora. LC 92-8429. (Illus.). 32p. (J). (ps-3). 1993. lib. bdg. 15.95 (*0-399-22423-8*, G P Putnam) Peng Put Young Read.

Lili at Ballet. Rachel Isadora. (J). 1996. 11.15 (*0-606-11562-5*, Pub. by Turtleback) Demco.

Lili Backstage. Rachel Isadora. LC 96-16361. (Illus.). 32p. (J). 1997. 15.95 (*0-399-23025-4*, G P Putnam) Peng Put Young Read.

Lili Backstage. Rachel Isadora. (Illus.). 32p. (ps-3). 1999. pap. 5.99 (*0-698-11793-X*, PuffinBks) Peng Put Young Read.

***Lili Kraus: Hungarian Pianist, Texas Teacher & Personality Extraordinaire.** Steven Henry Roberson. LC 99-46975. (Illus.). 160p. 2000. 21.95 (*0-87565-216-6*, Pub. by Tex Christian) Tex A&M Univ Pr.

Lili on Stage. Rachel Isadora. LC 94-5982. (Illus.). 32p. (J). (ps-3). 1995. 15.95 (*0-399-22637-0*, G P Putnam) Peng Put Young Read.

Lili on Stage. Rachel Isadora. (Illus.). 32p. (J). (ps-3). 1998. pap. 5.99 (*0-698-11651-8*, PapStar) Peng Put Young Read.

Lili Rimbaud: Roman. Jacques Jacob. 397p. 1998. (*2-89077-182-2*) Edns Flammarion.

Lili the Brave. Jennifer Armstrong. LC 97-11219. (Children of America Ser.). (Illus.). 80p. 1997. lib. bdg. 11.99 (*0-679-97286-2*) Random.

Lili the Brave, 2. Jennifer Armstrong. (Children of America Ser.). (J). 1997. 9.19 (*0-606-12655-4*, Pub. by Turtleback) Demco.

***Liliaceae, Orchidaceae, Dioscoreaceae, Amaryllidaceae & Iridaceae.** Ed. by V. I. Grubov. (Plants of Central Asia Ser.: Vol. 7). (Illus.). 2002. text. write for info. (*1-57808-118-1*) Science Pubs.

Lilian. Arnold Bennett. LC 74-5330. (Collected Works of Arnold Bennett: Vol. 45). 1977. reprint ed. 23.95 (*0-518-19126-5*) Ayer.

Lilian Jackson Braun. Lilian Jackson Braun. 1988. pap. 14.00 (*0-515-09901-5*, Jove) Berkley Pub.

Lilian Jackson Braun. Lilian Jackson Braun. 1989. 14.00 (*0-685-32996-8*, Jove) Berkley Pub.

Lilian Jackson Braun, 4 vols. Lilian Jackson Braun. 1991. pap. 15.80 (*0-515-10779-4*, Jove) Berkley Pub.

***Lilian Jackson Braun: A Reader's Checklist & Reference Guide.** CheckerBee Publishing Staff. 1999. pap. text 4.95 (*1-58598-008-0*) CheckerBee.

Lilian Jackson Braun: Three Complete Novels. Lilian Jackson Braun. LC 95-25675. 1996. 12.98 (*0-399-14127-8*, G P Putnam) Peng Put Young Read.

Lilian Jackson Braun: Three Complete Novels. Lilian Jackson Braun. LC 97-18197. 1998. 12.98 (*0-399-14364-5*, G P Putnam) Peng Put Young Read.

Lilian Jackson Braun: Three Complete Novels. unabridged ed. Lilian Jackson Braun. LC 94-10502. 608p. 1994. 11.98 (*0-399-13984-2*, G P Putnam) Peng Put Young Read.

Liliana: A Marriage. R. Pease. (Voyages Ser.: Pt. II). 295p. 1995. per. 12.95 (*0-9637154-5-3*) Flagg Mtn Pr.

Liliana, Bruja Urbana (Liliana, Urban Witch) Carmen Posadas. (SPA., Illus.). 48p. (J). (gr. 2). 1995. pap. 5.99 (*968-16-4680-0*, Pub. by Fondo) Continental Bk.

Liliana's Grandmothers. Leyla Torres. LC 97-37256. 32p. (J). (ps-3). 1998. 16.00 (*0-374-35105-8*) FS&G.

Liliane: Resurrection of the Daughter. Ntozake Shange. LC 95-21740. 304p. 1995. pap. 12.00 (*0-312-13559-9*, Picador USA) St Martin.

Lilian's Story. Kate Grenville. LC 94-27261. 240p. 1994. pap. 10.95 (*0-15-600123-3*, Harvest Bks) Harcourt.

Lilia's Haven. Kay D. Rizzo. LC 99-23956. (Serenity Inn Ser.: No. 4). 256p. 1999. pap. 7.99 (*0-8054-1685-4*) Broadman.

Lilias, Yoga & Your Life. Lilias Folan. (Illus.). 178p. 1981. pap. 18.00 (*0-02-080060-6*) Macmillan.

***Lilies.** Intro. by Scott D. Appell. LC 99-53774. (Illus.). 176p. 2000. 40.00 (*1-56799-936-0*, Friedman-Fairfax) M Friedman Pub Grp Inc.

Lilies. Richard Bird. 1991. 12.98 (*1-55521-706-0*) Bk Sales Inc.

Lilies. Michael Marc Bouchard. (FRE.). 1998. pap. 9.95 (*0-88754-545-9*) Theatre Comm.

Lilies. Michael Jefferson-Brown & Harris Howland. (Gardener's Guide Ser.). (Illus.). 160p. 1999. 29.95 (*0-88192-315-X*) Timber.

Lilies. rev. ed. Gertrude Jekyll. LC 82-16368. (Jekyll Garden Bks.). Orig. Title: Lilies for English Gardens: A Guide. (Illus.). 158p. 1983. reprint ed. 24.95 (*0-88143-003-X*) Ayer.

Lilies: A Guide for Growers & Collectors. Edward Austin-McRae. LC 97-22341. (Illus.). 392p. 1998. 34.95 (*0-88192-410-5*) Timber.

Lilies: New Plant Library. Lorenz Staff. (Illus.). 64p. 1998. 9.95 (*1-85967-634-0*) Anness Pub.

Lilies & Clover. Shelly Johnson-Chong. 1998. pap. 10.95 (*1-57008-398-3*) Bookcraft Inc.

Lilies & Related Flowers. Pierre-Joseph Redoute. LC 81-11021. (Illus.). 240p. 1982. 65.00 (*0-87951-135-4*, Pub. by Overlook Pr) Penguin Putnam.

Lilies & Sesame: The Orient, Inversion, & Artistic Creation in "A la Recherche du Temps Perdu" Anthony Everman. LC 97-21388. (Currents in Comparative Romance Languages & Literatures Ser.: Vol. 61). 205p. (C). 1998. text 44.95 (*0-8204-3810-3*) P Lang Pubng.

Lilies for English Gardens. Gertrude Jekyll. 156p. 1994. 25.00 (*1-85149-213-5*) Antique Collect.

Lilies for English Gardens: A Guide see Lilies

Lilies of the Field. William E. Barrett. 17.95 (*0-8488-0424-4*) Amereon Ltd.

Lilies of the Field. William E. Barrett. 128p. 1988. mass mkt. 5.99 (*0-446-31500-1*, Pub. by Warner Bks) Little.

Lilies of the Field. William Edmund Barrett. 1962. 10.60 (*0-606-00966-3*, Pub. by Turtleback) Demco.

Lilies of the Field. Wang Weifan. Ed. by Philip Wickeri & Janice Wickeri. LC 93-60486. 64p. 1993. pap. 9.00 (*0-8358-0688-X*) Upper Room Bks.

Lilies of the Field. Wang Weifan et al. 1993. pap. 8.95 (*0-687-60652-7*) Abingdon.

Lilies of the Field. adapted ed. William E. Barrett. 1967. pap. 5.25 (*0-8222-0665-X*) Dramatists Play.

Lilies of the Field. William E. Barrett. 1993. reprint ed. lib. bdg. 21.95 (*1-56849-166-2*) Buccaneer Bks.

Lilies of the Field: A Study Guide. Barbara Reeves. Ed. by Joyce Friedland & Rikki Kessler. (Novel-Ties Ser.). (YA). (gr. 9-12). 1991. pap. text 15.95 (*0-88122-585-1*) Lrn Links.

***Lilies of the Field: Marginal People Who Live for the Moment.** Sophie Day et al. LC 98-30158. (Studies in the Ethnographic Imagination). 272p. 1998. text 63.00 (*0-8133-3531-0*, Pub. by Westview) HarpC.

Lilies of the Hearth: The Historical Relationship Between Women & Plants. Jennifer Bennett. (Illus.). 192p. 1991. pap. 14.95 (*0-921820-27-5*) Firefly Bks Ltd.

Lilies, Rabbits, & Painted Eggs. Edna Barth. (J). 1970. 11.15 (*0-606-00508-0*, Pub. by Turtleback) Demco.

Lilies, Rabbits, & Painted Eggs: The Story of the Easter Symbols, 001. Edna Barth. LC 74-79033. (Illus.). 64p. (J). (ps-3). 1981. pap. 6.95 (*0-395-30550-0*, Clarion Bks) HM.

Liliiflorae (Liliaceae, Amaryllidaceae, Dioscoreaceae, Iridaceae/Micorspermae) Tr. by Israel Program for Scientific Translations Staff from RUS. (Flora of the U. S. S. R. (Flora SSSR) Ser.: Vol. 4). (Illus.). xxxiv, 586p. 1985. reprint ed. 240.00 (*3-87429-224-X*, 025082, Pub. by Koeltz Sci Bks) Lubrecht & Cramer.

Lilio de Medicina. Bernardo De Gordonio. Ed. by Cynthia M. Wasick. (Medieval Spanish Medical Texts Ser.: No. 25). (SPA.). 14p. 1989. 10.00 incl. fiche (*0-942260-93-7*) Hispanic Seminary.

Lilio de Medicina. Bernardo Gordonio. Ed. by John Cull & Brian Dutton. (Spanish Ser.: No. 31). (SPA.). xxii, 418p. 1991. 35.00 (*0-940639-64-5*) Hispanic Seminary.

***Liliom.** Ferenc Molnar. LC 99-50315. 68p. 1999. pap. 7.00 (*0-88734-798-3*) Players Pr.

Lilith. Allan Havis. 1991. pap. 6.95 (*0-88145-092-8*) Broadway Play.

Lilith. George MacDonald. 1981. pap. 8.00 (*0-8028-6061-3*) Eerdmans.

***Lilith: A Novel of One Woman's Electrifying Obsession.** J. R. Salamanca. 2000. pap. 15.00 (*1-56649-124-X*) Welcome Rain.

Lilith: The Edge of Forever. Filomena M. Pereira. LC 97-46143. (Woman in History Ser.: Vol. 18). (Illus.). xvi, 215p. 1998. pap. 20.00 (*0-86663-222-0*) Ide Hse.

Lilith Bk. 1: Darkness & Light. D. A. Heeley. LC 96-6272. 256p. 1999. pap. 12.95 (*1-56718-355-7*) Llewellyn Pubns.

Lilith - Adam's First Wife: And Other Dramatic Readings. Meg Bowman. (Dramatic Readings on Feminist Issues Ser.: Vol. IV). (Illus.). 265p. (Orig.). 1996. pap. 14.95 (*0-940483-13-0*) Hot Flash Pr.

Lilith - The First Eve: A Psychological Approach to Dark Aspects of the Feminine. Siegmund Hurwitz. 213p. 1995. pap. 17.95 (*3-85630-522-X*) Continuum.

Lilith A & Lilith, 1896: A Duplex. George MacDonald. (George MacDonald Original Works Ser.: Series IV). 388p. 1998. reprint ed. 24.00 (*1-881084-27-2*) Johannesen.

Lilith, a Metamorphosis. Dagmar Nick. Tr. by Maren Partenheimer & David Partenheimer. LC 95-34503. 50p. 1995. pap. 10.00 (*0-943549-32-9*) Truman St Univ.

Lilith & Her Demons. Enid Dame. Ed. by Stanley H. Barkan. (Review Woman Writers Chapbook Ser.: No. 2). 20p. 1989. reprint ed. 15.00 (*0-89304-405-9*, CCC161); reprint ed. 15.00 (*0-89304-407-5*); reprint ed. pap. 5.00 (*0-89304-406-7*); reprint ed. pap. 5.00 (*0-89304-408-3*) Cross-Cultrl NY.

Lilith Ephemeris. Delphine Jay. LC 83-71862. 209p. 1984. reprint ed. pap. 17.95 (*0-86690-255-4*, J2354-044) Am Fed Astrologers.

***Lilith Fair: A Celebration of Women in Music.** 120p. 1998. otabind 19.95 (*0-7935-9748-X*) H Leonard.

***Lilith Fair: A Celebration of Women in Music.** Leonard, Hal, Corporation Staff. 144p. 1998. otabind 19.95 (*0-7935-9772-2*) H Leonard.

***Lilith Fair: A Celebration of Women in Music, 2 & 3.** 160p. 1999. otabind 22.95 (*0-634-00669-X*) H Leonard.

***Lilith Fair: A Celebration of Women in Music, 2 & 3.** 176p. 1999. otabind 19.95 (*0-634-00668-1*) H Leonard.

Lilith Insight: New Light on the Dark Moon. Mae R. Wilson-Ludlam. 128p. 1979. 18.00 (*0-86690-347-X*, W1536-034) Am Fed Astrologers.

Lilith Summer. Hadley Irwin. LC 78-24379. 128p. (YA). (gr. 4-8). 1979. 8.95 (*0-912670-52-5*) Feminist Pr.

Lilith Variorum, 2 vols., Set. George MacDonald. Ed. by Rolland Hein. 800p. 1996. 48.00 (*1-881084-56-6*) Johannesen.

***Lilith's Brood.** Octavia E. Butler. LC 00-25057. 752p. 2000. mass mkt. 13.95 (*0-446-67610-1*, Aspect) Warner Bks.

***Lilith's Castle.** Gillian Alderman. 1999. mass mkt. 12.95 (*0-00-648272-4*, Pub. by HarpC) Trafalgar.

Lilith's Cave: Jewish Tales of the Supernatural. Ed. by Howard Schwartz. (Illus.). 288p. 1991. pap. 14.95 (*0-19-506726-6*) OUP.

Lilith's Daughters: Women & Religion in Contemporary Fiction. Barbara H. Rigney. LC 81-70012. 133p. reprint ed. pap. 41.30 (*0-608-20471-4*, 207172300002) Bks Demand.

Lili'uokalani. Ruby H. Lowe. (Kamehameha Schools Intermediate Reading Program Ser.). (Illus.). 111p. (Orig.). (J). (gr. 3-7). 1993. pap. 7.95 (*0-87336-018-4*) Kamehameha Schools.

Lili'uokalani. Aldyth Morris. LC 93-3717. (Illus.). 88p. (C). 1993. pap. 9.95 (*0-8248-1543-2*) UH Pr.

Lilla Cabot Perry: An American Impressionist. Meredith Martindale & Nancy M. Mathews. LC 90-61820. (Illus.). 164p. 1991. pap. text 29.95 (*0-940979-14-4*) Natl Museum Women.

Lilla Cabot Perry: An American Impressionist. Meredith Martindale et al. (Illus.). 164p. 1995. pap. 35.00 (*0-7892-0045-7*, Cross Riv Pr) Abbeville Pr.

Lilla Italian/Swedish/Italian Dictionary. (ITA & SWE.). 500p. 1998. 29.95 (*0-320-00653-0*) Fr & Eur.

Lille Agglomeration City Plan. (Grafocarte Maps Ser.). 1995. 8.95 (*2-7416-0017-1*, 80017) Michelin.

Lille & the Dutch Revolt: Urban Stability in an Era of Revolution, 1500-1582. Robert S. DuPlessis. (Studies in Early Modern History). (Illus.). 390p. (C). 1991. text 89.95 (*0-521-39415-5*) Cambridge U Pr.

Lille havfrue see Little Mermaid: Film Fashion

Lille havfrue see Little Mermaid: My Coloring Book

Lille havfrue see Little Mermaid

Lille havfrue see Little Mermaid: Walt Disney Pictures Presents

Lille havfrue see Little Mermaid

Lille pige med svovlstikkerne see Little Match Girl

Lille Villeneuve City Plan. (Grafocarte Maps Ser.). 1991. 8.95 (*2-7416-0016-3*, 80016) Michelin.

Lillelord. Johan Borgen. Tr. by Elizabeth B. Moen & Ronald E. Peterson from NOR. LC 81-14216. 384p. 1982. 16.00 (*0-8112-0826-5*, Pub. by New Directions); pap. 7.95 (*0-8112-0827-3*, NDP531, Pub. by New Directions) Norton.

Lillelord. Johan Borgen. 1994. pap. 11.95 (*0-7145-3879-5*) Riverrun NY.

Lillian. William Luce. 1986. pap. 5.25 (*0-8222-0666-8*) Dramatists Play.

Lillian: A Novel. Carl Brahe. LC 93-84239. 280p. 1994. pap. 9.95 (*0-9615743-4-8*) SunShine CO.

Lillian: The Librarain. Terri Barr. (Illus.). 16p. (J). (ps-2). 1999. pap. 3.75 (*1-880612-86-0*) Seedling Pubns.

Lillian Bassman. Lillian Bassman. 108p. 1997. 50.00 (*0-8212-2376-3*, Pub. by Bulfinch Pr) Little.

Lillian Bloom - A Separation. Judith W. Steinbergh. LC 79-92331. (Wampeter Firsts Ser.: No. 3). (Illus.). (Orig.). 1980. pap. 4.95 (*0-931694-07-8*) Wampeter Pr.

Lillian D. Wald: Progressive Activist. Ed. by Clare Coss. LC 89-32110. 120p. (Orig.). 1989. pap. 7.95 (*1-55861-000-6*) Feminist Pr.

Lillian Fuchs: First Lady of the Viola. Amedee D. Williams. LC 94-3814. (Studies in the History & Interpretation of Music: Vol. 45). (Illus.). 202p. 1994. 89.95 (*0-7734-9086-8*) E Mellen.

***Lillian Gish: A Century of Cinema.** Stuart Oderman. LC 99-28402. (Illus.). 408p. 1999. boxed set 55.00 (*0-7864-0644-5*) McFarland & Co.

Lillian Hellman. Katherine Lederer. (United States Authors Ser.: No. 338). 176p. 1979. 22.95 (*0-8057-7275-8*, Twyne) Mac Lib Ref.

Lillian Hellman: A Research & Production Sourcebook, 15. Barbara Lee Horn. LC 98-21824. (Modern Dramatists Research & Production Sourcebooks: Vol. 15). 192p. 1998. lib. bdg. 59.95 (*0-313-30264-2*, Greenwood Pr) Greenwood.

Lillian Hellman: Rebel Playwright. Ruth Turk. LC 94-27060. (Illus.). 128p. (YA). (gr. 5 up). 1995. lib. bdg. 23.93 (*0-8225-4921-2*, Lerner Publctns) Lerner Pub.

Lillian Hellman Biography. Williams Abrahams. 1995. write for info. (*0-316-00433-2*) Little.

Lillian Hellman Collection at the University of Texas. Ed. by Manfred Triesch. LC 67-64819. (Tower Bibliographical Ser.: No. 3). (Illus.). 1966. 15.00 (*0-87959-044-0*) U of Tex H Ransom Ctr.

Lillian Russell: A Bio-Bibliography, 77. Donald R. Schwartz & Anne A. Bowbeer. LC 97-21825. (Bio-Bibliographies in the Performing Arts Ser.: 77). 328p. 1997. lib. bdg. 72.95 (*0-313-27764-8*, Greenwood Pr) Greenwood.

Lillian Russell: A Biography of "America's Beauty" Armond Fields. LC 98-38736. (Illus.). 245p. 1998. boxed set 42.50 (*0-7864-0509-0*) McFarland & Co.

Lillian Simmons: or The Conflict of Sections. Otis M. Shackelford. LC 73-18607. (Illus.). reprint ed. 34.50 (*0-404-11417-2*) AMS Pr.

Lillian Smith, a Southerner Confronting the South. Anne C. Loveland. LC 86-10641. (Southern Biography Ser.). xii, 298p. 1986. text 42.50 (*0-8071-1343-3*) La State U Pr.

***Lillian Too's Easy-to-Use Feng Shui for Love: 168 Ways to Happiness - Enhance Your Relationships, Energize Your Friendships, Maximize Your Love Potential.** Lillian Too. (Illus.). 160p. 2000. pap. 19.95 (*1-85585-758-8*, Pub. by Collins & Br) Sterling.

Lillian Too's Essential Feng Shui: A Step-by-Step Guide to Enhancing Your Relationships, Health, & Prosperity. Lillian Too. LC 99-90103. (Illus.). 192p. 1999. pap. 13.95 (*0-345-42904-4*, Ballantine) Ballantine Pub Grp.

Lillian Too's Feng Shui Kit: All You Need to Get Started with Feng Shui. Lillian Too. 64p. 1997. 29.95 (*1-86204-150-4*, Pub. by Element MA) Penguin Putnam.

***Lillian Too's Feng Shui Space Clearing Kit: Everything You Need to Purify Your Living Space Using Traditional Methods & Techniques.** Lillian Too. (Illus.). 2000. pap. 29.95 (*1-86204-608-5*, Pub. by Element MA) Penguin Putnam.

Lillian Too's Illustrated Encyclopedia of Feng Shui. Lillian Too. (Illus.). 384p. 1999. text 34.95 (*1-86204-596-8*, Pub. by Element MA) Penguin Putnam.

Lillian Too's Little Book of Feng Shui. Lillian Too. 49.50 (*1-86204-457-0*, Pub. by Element MA) Penguin Putnam.

Lillian Too's Little Book of Feng Shui. Lillian Too. 128p. 1999. pap. 4.95 (*1-86204-514-3*, Pub. by Element MA) Penguin Putnam.

Lillian Too's Little Book of Feng Shui at Work. Lillian Too. 128p. 1999. pap. 4.95 (*1-86204-585-2*, Pub. by Element MA) Penguin Putnam.

***Lillian Too's Practical Feng Shui: Formulas for Success.** Lillian Too. (Illus.). 160p. 2000. pap. 16.95 (*1-86204-563-1*, Pub. by Element MA) Penguin Putnam.

***Lillian Toos Practical Feng Shui: Symbols for Good Fortune.** Lillian Too. (Illus.). 160p. 2000. pap. 16.95 (*1-86204-795-2*, Pub. by Element MA) Penguin Putnam.

Lillian Too's Secrets of Feng Shui Success. Lillian Too. LC 99-494979. 1999. pap. 14.95 (*1-85585-690-5*, Pub. by Collins & Br) Sterling.

Lillian Wald Papers: Guide to the Microfilm Collection, Filmed from the Holdings of the Columbia University Library. 60p. (C). 1993. text 85.00 (*0-89235-148-9*) Primary Srce Media.

Lillian's Fish. James Menk. LC 97-12331. (Illus.). 176p. (J). (gr. 3-4). 1997. 14.95 (*1-56145-158-4*) Peachtree Pubs.

Lillie Seline's Confession. Larry G. Stenzel. (Illus.). 96p. (Orig.). 1982. pap. 5.75 (*0-910021-02-3*) Samuel P Co.

Lillies by the Gate. Elizabeth Kessler. LC 96-216377. 128p. (Orig.). 1996. pap. 10.00 (*1-886094-38-1*) Chicago Spectrum.

Lilliputian. Alice O. Apodaca. Ed. by Linda Johnston. (Illus.). 34p. (Orig.). (J). (gr. 4). 1996. pap. text. write for info. (*0-9630505-1-6*) A O Apodaca.

Lillooet Indians. James A. Teit. LC 73-3520. (Jesup North Pacific Expedition. Publications: No. 2, Pt. 5). reprint ed. 40.00 (*0-404-58121-8*) AMS Pr.

Lillooet Language: Phonology, Morphology, Syntax. Jan Van Eijk. LC 97-228627. 279p. 1997. 75.00 (*0-7748-0625-7*) U of Wash Pr.

L'illusione Tecnocratica see Technocratic Illusion: A Study of Managerial Power in Italy

Lilly: Reminiscences of Lillian Hellman. Peter Feibleman. 1990. pap. 10.95 (*0-380-70893-0*, Avon Bks) Morrow Avon.

Lilly & Peggy. large type ed. Ronald Tomanio. (Illus.). (J). (gr. 3). 1997. pap. 8.95 (*0-85398-420-4*) G Ronald Pub.

Lilly Book & Toy Box Set. Kevin Henkes. 32p. (J). 1998. pap. 24.95 (*0-688-16437-4*, Wm Morrow) Morrow Avon.

Lilly Cullen: Helena, Montana 1894. Ann Cullen. 267p. 1999. pap. 9.95 (*0-9670759-0-4*) Bk Montana.

Lilly Industries, Inc. A History of Success, a Future of Possibilities. Robert S. Bailey. LC 98-87856. (Illus.). 120p. 1998. pap. write for info. (*0-9666504-0-9*) Lilly Indust.

Lilly Library: The First Quarter Century, 1960-1985. Pref. by William R. Cagle. (Illus.). 157p. (Orig.). (C). 1985. pap. 15.00 (*1-879598-04-3*) IN Univ Lilly Library.

Lilly on the Bluestone. William Sanders. LC 89-92755. (Illus.). 150p. (Orig.). 1997. reprint ed. pap. 18.00 (*0-9625273-0-0*) W Sanders.

A historical look at the original settlers from the Lilly & Meador (Meadows) families in what is now West Virginia. The area, near the Bluestone River, became this settlement & is the focus of the revised edition of the original LILLY ON THE BLUESTONE. The first printing was followed by the author's NEW RIVER HERITAGE series; a series of four hardbound, attractive books detailing historical sites, graves, families, stories & tales. Third Printing, 1997 - enlarged. *Publisher Paid Annotation.*

An Asterisk (*) at the beginning of an entry indicates that the title is appearing for the first time.

L

***Lilly Plays Her Part.** Brenda Bellingham. (New First Novels Ser.). 64p. 2000. mass mkt. write for info. (*0-88780-500-0*, Pub. by Formac Publ Co) Formac Dist Ltd.

***Lilly Plays Her Part.** Brenda Bellingham & Elizabeth Owen. 64p. (J). 2000. bds. write for info. (*0-88780-501-9*, Pub. by Formac Publ Co) Formac Dist Ltd.

Lilly Pond Family. Rosie Morris. (Illus.). (J). (gr. 3-6). 2000. pap. 6.95 (*0-533-12309-7*) Vantage.

Lilly Reich: Designer. Matilda McQuaid. LC 95-81466. (Illus.). 64p. (Orig.). 1996. pap. text 18.95 (*0-8109-6159-8*, Pub. by Abrams) Time Warner.

Lilly Reich: Designer. Matilda McQuaid. (Illus.). 64p. (Orig.). 1996. pap. 16.95 (*0-87070-144-4*, 0-8109-6159-8, Pub. by Mus of Modern Art) Abrams.

Lilly to the Rescue. Brenda Bellingham. (First Novels). (Illus.). 64p. (J). 1997. bds. 4.95 (*0-88780-387-3*, Pub. by Formac Publ Co) Formac Dist Ltd.

Lilly to the Rescue. Brenda Bellingham. LC 96-950186. (First Novels). (Illus.). 64p. (J). (gr. 1-4). 1998. mass mkt. 3.99 (*0-88780-386-5*, Pub. by Formac Publ Co) Formac Dist Ltd.

Lilly White. Debbie Davis. 1999. pap. 9.95 (*0-9640801-7-6*, 8017-6) Jireh Pubns.

***Lilly y Su Bolso de Plastico Morado.** Kevin Henkes. 1998. 11.95 (*84-241-3366-8*) Everest SP.

Lilly's Good Deed. Brenda Bellingham. LC 98-95021. (Illus.). 64p. (J). (gr. 1-4). 1998. bds. write for info. (*0-88780-461-6*) FMC.

***Lilly's Good Deed.** Brenda Bellingham. LC 98-95021. (First Novels Ser.). (Illus.). 64p. (J). (gr. 1-4). 1998. text 3.99 (*0-88780-460-8*, Pub. by Formac Publ Co) Orca Bk Pubs.

Lilly's Pond: The Adventure of Silly Willy Caterpillie. Linda L. Lumpkin. (Illus.). 48p. (J). (ps-6). 1997. 17.95 (*1-891543-00-8*, Wide-Eyed Pub) MicroNova.

Lilly's Purple Plastic Purse. Kevin Henkes. LC 95-25085. (Illus.). 32p. (J). (ps-3). 1996. 14.95 (*0-688-12897-1*, Grenwillow Bks); 14.89 (*0-688-12898-X*, Grenwillow Bks) HarpC Child Bks.

Lilly's Secret. Miko Imai. LC 94-1. (Illus.). 32p. (J). (ps-2). 1997. reprint ed. pap. 4.99 (*0-7636-0158-6*) Candlewick Pr.

***Lilly's Sticker & Storybook Fun.** Kevin Henkes. (Illus.). 16p. (YA). (ps-3). 2000. pap. 7.95 (*0-688-17710-7*, Wm Morrow) Morrow Avon.

Lilly's Way. Kim D. Cory. Ed. by Jane Austin. 187p. (J). (gr. 4 up). 1998. pap. 9.99 (*0-88092-363-6*, 3636) Royal Fireworks.

Lilmod Ulelamade: From the Teachings of Our Sages on Judges. Mordechai Katz. (Rothman Foundation Ser.). 1986. 15.95 (*0-87306-207-8*) Feldheim.

Lilmod Ulelamade: From the Teachings of Our Sages on Judges. Mordechai Katz. (Rothman Foundation Ser.). 1986. pap. 13.95 (*1-58330-101-1*) Feldheim.

Lilmod Ulelamade on Joshua. Mordechai Katz. (Rothman Foundation Ser.). 1984. 14.95 (*0-87306-925-0*) Feldheim.

LILRC Handbook of Programs & Services. Ed. by Judith B. Neufeld. 1994. ring bd. 25.00 (*0-938435-34-5*) LI Lib Resources.

Lil's Courage. Lillian A. Foell. Ed. by Bonnie F. Olson. 132p. 1997. pap. 12.95 (*0-911042-46-6*) NDSU Inst Reg.

***Lilts: Poems from Hollywood.** Mark Dunster. 11p. 1999. pap. 5.00 (*0-89642-855-9*) Linden Pubs.

Liluli. Romain Rolland. (FRE.). 218p. 1926. pap. 10.95 (*0-7859-5454-6*) Fr & Eur.

Lily. Cindy Bonner. 350p. 1992. 17.95 (*0-945575-95-5*) Algonquin Bks.

***Lily.** Patricia Gaffney. 448p. 2000. pap. 5.99 (*0-8439-4772-1*, Leisure Bks) Dorchester Pub Co.

Lily. Leigh Greenwood. (Seven Brides Ser.). 400p. (Orig.). 1996. mass mkt. 5.99 (*0-8439-4070-0*, Leisure Bks) Dorchester Pub Co.

Lily. Leigh Greenwood. (Seven Brides Ser.). 400p. (Orig.). 1998. mass mkt. 5.99 (*0-8439-4441-2*, Leisure Bks) Dorchester Pub Co.

Lily. Abigail Thomas. LC 93-14199. (Illus.). (YA). (gr. 5 up). 1995. 14.95 (*0-8050-2690-8*) H Holt & Co.

Lily, Vol. 1. Abigail Thomas. (Illus.). (J). (ps-2). 1997. reprint ed. pap. 5.95 (*0-8050-5480-4*) H Holt & Co.

Lily: A Novel. large type ed. Cindy Bonner. LC 93-3766. 365p. 1993. lib. bdg. 17.95 (*1-56054-743-X*) Thorndike Pr.

Lily: The Year I Turned 16, Vol. 4. Diane Schwemm. (Year I Turned Sixteen Ser.). 192p. (YA). 1999. mass mkt. 4.50 (*0-671-00443-3*, Archway) PB.

Lily among the Thorns. Howard G. Hageman. 1978. write for info. (*0-916466-00-0*) Reformed Church.

Lily among Thorns. large type ed. Catrin Morgan. 1993. 18.95 (*0-7505-0266-5*) Ulverscroft.

Lily & Miss Liberty. Carla Stevens. LC 91-14537. 80p. (J). (gr. 4-7). 1993. pap. 2.99 (*0-590-44920-6*) Scholastic Inc.

Lily & Miss Liberty. Carla Stevens. (J). 1992. 8.19 (*0-606-05907-5*, Pub. by Turtleback) Demco.

Lily & Ted. Lucinda Jacob. 32p. 1998. pap. 7.95 (*1-85371-747-9*, Pub. by Poolbeg Pr) Dufour.

Lily & the Hawk. Marlene Suson. 384p. (Orig.). 1993. mass mkt. 4.50 (*0-380-76960-3*, Avon Bks) Morrow Avon.

Lily & the Lost Boy. Paula Fox. LC 87-5778. 160p. (J). (gr. 6-8). 1987. lib. bdg. 17.99 (*0-531-08320-9*) Orchard Bks Watts.

Lily & the Lost Boy. Paula Fox. LC 87-5778. 160p. (J). (gr. 7-12). 1987. 16.95 (*0-531-05720-8*) Orchard Bks Watts.

Lily & the Major. Linda Lael Miller. Ed. by Linda Marrow. 384p. 1990. mass mkt. 5.50 (*0-671-67636-9*) PB.

Lily & the Wooden Bowl. Alan Schroeder. LC 93-17900. (J). 1997. 11.19 (*0-606-11563-3*, Pub. by Turtleback) Demco.

Lily & Trooper's Fall. Jung-Lee Spetter. LC 98-27972. (Illus.). 32p. (J). (ps-1). 1999. 8.95 (*1-886910-38-3*, Pub. by Front Str) Publishers Group.

Lily & Trooper's Spring. Jung-Hee Spetter. LC 98-27973. (Illus.). 32p. (J). (ps-1). 1999. 8.95 (*1-886910-36-7*, Pub. by Front Str) Publishers Group.

Lily & Trooper's Summer. Jung-Hee Spetter. LC 98-35818. (Illus.). 32p. (J). (ps-1). 1999. 8.95 (*1-886910-37-5*, Pub. by Front Str) Publishers Group.

***Lily & Trooper's Winter.** Jung-Lee Spetter. LC 98-27970. (Illus.), 32p. (J). (ps-1). 1999. 8.95 (*1-886910-39-1*, Pub. by Front Str) Publishers Group.

Lily Beach. Jennie Fields. 304p. 1994. mass mkt. 10.99 (*0-446-67038-3*, Pub. by Warner Bks) Little.

Lily Braun (1865-1916) German Writer, Feminist, Socialist. Ute Lischke-McNab. LC 99-59147. (Studies in German Literature, Linguistics, & Culture). 190p. 2000. 55.00 (*1-57113-169-8*) Camden Hse.

***Lily Brett: Collected Stories.** Lily Brett. (Illus.). 1999. pap. 19.95 (*0-7022-3087-1*, Pub. by Univ Queensland Pr) Intl Spec Bk.

Lily Briscoe: A Self-Portrait. Mary Meigs. 264p. 1981. pap. 16.95 (*0-88922-195-2*, Pub. by Talonbks) Genl Dist Srvs.

Lily Cupboard. Shulamith Levey Oppenheim. (J). 1992. 11.40 (*0-606-07789-8*) Turtleback.

Lily Cupboard. 2nd ed. Shulamith L. Oppenheim. LC 90-38592. (Charlotte Zolotow Bk.). (Illus.). 32p. (J). (ps-3). 1995. pap. 5.95 (*0-06-443393-5*, HarpTrophy) HarpC Child Bks.

Lily Dale. Horton Foote. 1987. pap. 5.25 (*0-8222-0667-6*) Dramatists Play.

Lily Daw & the Three Ladies. Ruth Perry & Eudora Welty. 39p. 1972. pap. 3.50 (*0-87129-692-6*, L22) Dramatic Pub.

***Lily Fair.** Kimberly Cates. 1999. per. 6.50 (*0-671-02822-7*, Sonnet Bks) PB.

Lily Hand & Other Stories. Edith Pargeter & Ellis Peters. 281p. 1996. pap. 13.95 (*0-7472-4697-1*, Pub. by Headline Bk Pub) Trafalgar.

Lily Harmon, Fifty Years of Painting: A Retrospective Exhibition. Howard E. Wooden. LC 82-62680. (Illus.). 56p. 1982. pap. 6.00 (*0-939324-07-5*) Wichita Art Mus.

Lily Loh's Chinese Seafood & Vegetables. Lily Loh. Ed. by Amy Addison-Licameli. (Illus.). 222p. 1991. 22.95 (*0-9630299-0-8*) Solana Pub.

Lily Longtail: The Adventures of Jenny Qand. Bill Kruger. (Illus.). 124p. (Orig.). (J). 1997. pap. 6.50 (*0-9651817-1-5*) Sunwood Mills.

Lily Montagu: Sermons, Addresses, Letters & Prayers. Ellen J. Umansky. LC 85-3053. (Studies in Women & Religion: Vol. 15). (Illus.). 415p. 1985. 109.95 (*0-88946-534-7*) E Mellen.

Lily Montagu & the Advancement of Liberal Judaism: From Vision to Vocation. Ellen M. Umansky. LC 83-22005. (Studies in Women & Religion: Vol. 12). 284p. 1983. lib. bdg. 89.95 (*0-88946-537-1*) E Mellen.

***Lily Nevada.** Cecelia Holland. LC 99-36339. 224p. 1999. 22.95 (*0-312-86670-4*, Pub. by Forge NYC) St Martin.

***Lily Nevada.** Cecelia Holland. 2001. pap. 12.95 (*0-312-87416-2*) St Martin.

Lily of the Valley. Suzanne Strempek Shea. LC 99-25768. 304p. 1999. 22.00 (*0-671-02710-7*, PB Hardcover) PB.

***Lily of the Valley.** Suzanne Strempek Shea. 304p. 2000. 13.95 (*0-671-02711-5*, WSP) PB.

Lily of the Valley. 2nd ed. Honore de Balzac. Tr. by Lucienne Hill. LC 97-17484. 256p. 1997. pap. 11.95 (*0-7867-0471-3*) Carroll & Graf.

Lily of the Valleys. large type ed. Catrin Morgan. 1993. 18.95 (*0-7505-0264-9*) Ulverscroft.

Lily Pond: Four Years with a Family of Beavers. Hope Ryden. LC 96-28176. 256p. 1997. pap. 16.95 (*1-55821-455-0*) Lyons Pr.

Lily Pons: A Centennial Portrait. James A. Drake & Kristin B. Ludecke. LC 98-30582. (Opera Biography Ser.: Vol. 11). (Illus.). 330p. 1999. 29.95 (*1-57467-047-6*, Amadeus Pr) Timber.

***Lily Robbins, M. D. Medical Dabbler.** Nancy Rue. (Young Women of Faith Library). (Illus.). (J). 2000. pap. 4.99 (*0-310-23249-X*, Zonderkidz) Zondervan.

Lily Takes a Walk. Satoshi Kitamura. 32p. (J). (ps-k). 1998. pap. 4.95 (*0-374-44480-3*) FS&G.

***Lily the Lost Puppy.** Jenny Dale. (Puppy Friends Ser.). 64p. (gr. k-3). 2000. per. 3.99 (*0-689-83404-7*) Aladdin.

Lily Theatre. Lulu Wang. 2001. pap. 25.00 (*0-385-48986-2*) Doubleday.

Lily Theatre: A Novel of Modern China. Lulu Wang. 400p. 2000. 25.00 (*0-385-48985-4*) Doubleday.

Lily Trail. Gary Lavetta. 144p. (YA). (gr. 7-12). 1990. pap. 4.95 (*0-9618951-2-8*) Memory Ln Bks.

Lily Vanessa & the Pet Panic, Vol. 11. Elaine L. Schulte. LC 96-45835. (Twelve Candles Club Ser.). 128p. (J). (gr. 3-8). 1997. pap. 5.99 (*1-55661-539-6*) Bethany Hse.

Lily White. large type ed. Susan Isaacs. 656p. 1998. mass mkt. 6.99 (*0-06-109309-2*, Harp PBks) HarpC.

Lily White. large type ed. Susan Isaacs. LC 96-21102. 1996. 27.95 (*0-7862-0828-7*) Thorndike Pr.

Lily White. large type ed. Susan Isaacs. LC 96-21102. 1997. pap. 25.95 (*0-7862-0829-5*) Thorndike Pr.

Lily White: Estabrook,&Christine, Set. abr. ed. Susan Isaacs. 1996. audio 18.00 (*0-694-51699-6*, 394209) HarperAudio.

Lily's Crossing. Patricia Reilly Giff. 192p. (J). (gr. 3-7). 1999. pap. 5.50 (*0-440-41453-9*) BDD Bks Young Read.

Lily's Crossing. Patricia Reilly Giff. LC 96-23021. 192p. (J). (gr. 3-7). 1997. 15.95 (*0-385-32142-2*) Delacorte.

***Lily's Crossing.** Patricia Reilly Giff. LC 00-42610. 2000. write for info. (*0-7862-2771-0*) Thorndike Pr.

***Lily's Crossing.** Patricia Reilly Giff. (Yearling Newbery Ser.). (Illus.). (J). 1999. 10.85 (*0-606-14423-4*) Turtleback.

***Lily's Crossing.** Elizabeth Klar. Ed. by Dawn Michelle Robbins. (J). 2000. 9.95 (*1-58130-644-X*); 11.95 (*1-58130-645-8*) Novel Units.

Lily's Secret. 1990. pap. 4.50 (*0-8216-5076-9*, Univ Books) Carol Pub Group.

***Lily's War.** June Francis. 2000. pap. 8.95 (*0-553-40820-8*, Pub. by Transworld Publishers Ltd) Trafalgar.

Lima - Allen County, Ohio: A Practical History. Marilyn R. Stark. LC 93-6273. 1993. write for info. (*0-89865-881-0*) Donning Co.

***Lima Beans Would be Illegal: Children's Ideas of a Perfect World.** Robert Bender. LC 99-32171. (J). 2000. 12.00 (*0-8037-2532-9*, Dial Yng Read) Peng Put Young Read.

Lima, Ohio Police Department: A Century of Service. Joseph C. Bowsher. LC 94-37248. 1994. write for info. (*0-89865-922-1*) Donning Co.

Lima Rooftops. Jane Radcliffe. 1978. 7.25 (*0-941490-09-2*) Solo Pr.

Lima Route. Scott D. Trostel. (Ohio Railroad Heritage Ser.). (Illus.). 232p. 1997. 44.95 (*0-925436-16-X*) Cam-Tech Pub.

Lima-6: A Marine Company Commander in Vietnam. R. D. Camp. Ed. by Paul McCarthy. 360p. 1990. reprint ed. per. 4.99 (*0-671-70436-2*) PB.

Lima-6: A Marine Company Commander in Vietnam. Richard D. Camp & Eric Hammel. LC 99-19185. (Illus.), 295p. 1999. reprint ed. pap. 19.95 (*0-935553-36-3*) Pacifica Military.

Limagier. Universal Center International Studies Staff. (FRE.). pap. text 13.00 (*2-08-160585-6*) Flammarion.

Limas, Veracruz: Y Otros Asentamientos Prehispanicos de la Region Olmeca. Hernando Gomez Rueda. (SPA., Illus.). 135p. 1996. pap. 15.00 (*968-29-9044-0*, IN98, Pub. by Dir Gen Pubicaiones) UPLAAP.

Limb Amputation. Rosalind Ham & Leonard Cotton. Ed. by Jo Campling. (Therapy in Practice Ser.). 140p. 1990. pap. 23.00 (*0-412-34610-9*, A4413) Chapman & Hall.

Limb Deficient Child. fac. ed. Yoshio Setoguchi & Ruth Rosenfelder. (Illus.). 344p. (C). 1982. 56.95 (*0-398-04656-5*) C C Thomas.

Limb Development & Regeneration, 2 vols. Ed. by John F. Fallon et al. (Progress in Clinical & Biological Research Ser.: Vol. 383A-B). 952p. 1993. 450.00 (*0-471-59795-3*, Wiley-Interscience) Wiley.

Limb Development & Regeneration, 2 vols., Pt. A. Ed. by John F. Fallon et al. (Progress in Clinical & Biological Research Ser.: Vol. 383A-B). 484p. 1993. 1.25 (*0-471-59793-7*, Wiley-Liss) Wiley.

Limb Development & Regeneration, 2 vols., Pt. B. Ed. by John F. Fallon et al. (Progress in Clinical & Biological Research Ser.: Vol. 383A-B). 468p. 1993. 1.25 (*0-471-59794-5*, Wiley-Liss) Wiley.

Limb Malformations. Ed. by Daniel Bergsma. (Symposia Ser.: Vol. 10, No. 5). 1974. 15.00 (*0-686-10019-0*) March of Dimes.

Limb of Snow & the Meeting: Two Short Plays. Anna M. Barlow. 1969. pap. 5.25 (*0-8222-0668-4*) Dramatists Play.

Limb of Your Tree, the Story of an Adoptee's Search see Girl Returns to Her Roots: An Adopted Twin's Search

Limb Prosthetics. 6th ed. A. Bennett Wilson, Jr. (Illus.). 136p. 1989. pap. 24.95 (*0-939957-22-1*) Demos Medical.

Limb Regeneration. Panagiotis A. Tsonis. (Developmental & Cell Biology Ser.: No. 31). (Illus.). 253p. (C). 1996. text 80.00 (*0-521-44149-8*) Cambridge U Pr.

Limb Salvage: Major Reconstruction in Oncologic & Nontumoral Conditions, 5th International Symposium - St. Malo. ISOLS-GETO. Ed. by F. Langlais & B. Tomeno. (Illus.). 880p. 1991. 214.00 (*0-387-52861-X*) Spr-Verlag.

Limb Salvage in Musculoskeletal Oncology, 1987. Ed. by T. Yamamuro. 355p. 1989. 174.00 (*0-387-70030-7*) Spr-Verlag.

Limb to Limb. John A. Russo. mass mkt. 5.99 (*1-55197-505-X*) Picasso Publ.

Limba Stories & Story-Telling. Ruth H. Finnegan. LC 80-25904. (Oxford Library of African Literature). 352p. 1981. reprint ed. lib. bdg. 35.00 (*0-313-22723-3*, FILS, Greenwood Pr) Greenwood.

Limbert Arts & Crafts Furniture: The Complete 1903 Catalog. Limbert, Charles P., & Co. Staff. (Illus.). 80p. 1992. reprint ed. pap. 7.95 (*0-486-27120-X*) Dover.

Limbert Furniture. rev. ed. Stephen Gray. (Mission Furniture Catalogues Ser.: No. 4). (Illus.). 180p. 1990. pap. 20.00 (*0-940326-15-9*) Turn of Cent.

***Limbic Brain.** Andrew Lautin. LC 00-30936. 2000. write for info. (*0-306-46086-6*) Kluwer Academic.

Limbic Motor Circuits & Neuropsychiatry. Ed. by Peter W. Kalivas & Charles D. Barnes. 416p. 1993. boxed set 136.95 (*0-8493-4441-7*, QP383) CRC Pr.

***Limbic Seizures in Children.** G. Avanzini et al. 256p. 2000. 68.00 (*0-86196-595-7*, Pub. by John Libby) Buttrwrth-Heinemann.

Limbic System. 2nd ed. Robert L. Isaacson. LC 82-9077. (Illus.). 342p. 1982. 45.00 (*0-306-40874-0*, Plenum Trade) Perseus Pubng.

Limbo. Norman Dugdale. 60p. 1991. pap. 10.95 (*0-85640-468-3*, Pub. by Blackstaff Pr) Dufour.

Limbo. Vincent McConnor. 288p. 1988. mass mkt. 3.95 (*0-445-40677-1*, Pub. by Mysterious Pr) Little.

Limbo. Dixie Salazar. 206p. (Orig.). 1995. pap. 14.00 (*1-877727-45-8*) White Pine.

Limbo: A Memoir about Life in a Nursing Home by a Survivor. Carobeth Laird. LC 79-10937. 190p. 1979. pap. 12.95 (*0-88316-536-8*) Chandler & Sharp.

Limbo: A One-Act Drama. Jerome McDonough. 28p. (YA). (gr. 7 up). 1984. pap. 3.25 (*0-88680-219-9*) I E Clark.

Limbo & the Talking Umbrella. Rose Widner. (Illus.). 16p. (J). (gr. k-3). 1998. pap. 6.00 (*0-8059-4338-2*) Dorrance.

Limbo Ladies. Margaret Yorke. 192p. 1992. reprint ed. 19.00 (*0-7278-4311-7*) Severn Hse.

***Limbo on the Yalu & Beyond: The Ted Sprouse Story.** Robert J. Berens. 2000. pap. 11.95 (*0-941072-35-5*) Southern Herit.

Limbo River. Rick Hillis. 1991. pap. 4.98 (*0-7710-4098-9*) McCland & Stewart.

Limbo River. Rick Hillis. LC 90-33963. (Drue Heinz Literature Prize Ser.). 142p. 1990. 22.50 (*0-8229-3653-4*) U of Pittsburgh Pr.

Limbo Road. Rubin. Date not set. 22.50 (*0-8050-5665-3*); pap. write for info. (*0-8050-5666-1*, Owl) H Holt & Co.

Limbo Search. Parke Godwin. 320p. (Orig.). 1995. mass mkt. 5.50 (*0-380-77300-7*, Avon Bks) Morrow Avon.

Limbo Tales. Len Jenkin. 1982. pap. 5.25 (*0-8222-0669-2*) Dramatists Play.

Lime. (Metals & Minerals Ser.). 1993. lib. bdg. 250.95 (*0-8490-8995-6*) Gordon Pr.

Lime & Alternative Binders in East Africa. Ed. by Elijah Agevi et al. 167p. 1995. pap. 29.50 (*1-85339-330-4*, Pub. by Intermed Tech) Stylus Pub VA.

Lime & Limestone: Chemistry & Technology, Production & Uses. J. A. M. Oates. 474p. 1998. 298.00 (*3-527-29527-5*) Wiley.

Lime & Other Alternative Cements. Ed. by Neville R. Hill et al. (Illus.). 328p. 1993. pap. 47.50 (*1-85339-178-6*, Pub. by Intermed Tech) Stylus Pub VA.

Lime & Salt, Vol. 1. Carole Stone. LC 97-34345. (Orig.). 1997. pap. 16.00 (*0-939713-07-1*) Carriage House.

Lime Creek Odyssey. Steven J. Meyers. LC 88-32705. (Illus.). 124p. 1989. 14.95 (*1-55591-037-8*) Fulcrum Pub.

Lime 5: Exploited by Choice. Mark Crutcher. 320p. (Orig.). 1996. pap. 19.95 (*0-9648886-0-2*) Life Dynamics.

Lime for Environmental Uses, STP 931. Ed. by Kenneth A. Gutschick. LC 86-32078. (Special Technical Publication Ser.). (Illus.). 160p. 1987. text 29.00 (*0-8031-0499-5*, STP931) ASTM.

Lime in the Coconut. David I. Gutierrez. 282p. mass mkt. 4.99 (*1-55197-270-0*) Picasso Publ.

Lime Orchard Woman: Poems. Alberto Rios. LC 88-18534. 94p. (Orig.). 1988. pap. 12.95 (*0-935296-77-8*, Pub. by Sheep Meadow) U Pr of New Eng.

Lime Pit. Jonathan Valin. (Harry Stoner Mystery Ser.). 208p. 1983. pap. 3.50 (*0-380-55442-9*, Avon Bks) Morrow Avon.

Lime Point to Lawson's Landing: Outdoors in Marin Sixty-One More Places to Visit. Dick Murdock. Ed. & Photos by Jayne Murdock. LC 91-20154. (Illus.). 160p. (Orig.). 1992. pap. 10.95 (*0-932916-15-5*) May-Murdock.

Lime Stabilisation: Proceedings of the Seminar Held at Loughborough University Civil & Building Engineering Department on September 25, 1996. Ed. by C. D. Rogers et al. LC 97-109139. 192p. 1996. 48.00 (*0-7277-2563-7*) Am Soc Civil Eng.

Lime Stabilization. (State of the Art Reports: No. 5). 59p. 1987. 8.60 (*0-309-04118-X*) Transport Res Bd.

Lime Street Lecture. J&R Distributors Staff. LC 98-91410. 466p. 1998. pap. 39.95 (*1-57502-805-0*, PO2221) Morris Pubng.

Lime Twig. John Hawkes. LC 60-14719. 1961. pap. 10.95 (*0-8112-0065-5*, NDP95, Pub. by New Directions) Norton.

Lime Twig: Second Skin. John Hawkes. 300p. 1996. pap. 14.95 (*0-14-018982-3*, Penguin Bks) Viking Penguin.

Lime Works. Thomas Bernhard. Tr. by Sophia Wilkins. LC 86-1287. (Illus.). vi, 248p. 1986. pap. 16.95 (*0-226-04397-5*) U Ch Pr.

***Lime Works.** Naoya Hatakeyama. 1998. pap. text. write for info. (*4-915877-39-6*) Synergy Inc.

Limehouse Nights. Thomas Burke. LC 73-103498. (Short Story Index Reprint Ser.). 1977. 21.95 (*0-8369-3240-4*) Ayer.

Limekilns & Limeburning. Richard Williams. 1989. pap. 6.25 (*0-7478-0037-5*, Pub. by Shire Pubns) St Mut.

Limelight: A Greenwich Village Photography Gallery & Coffeehouse in the Fifties. Helen Gee. LC 96-25382. (Illus.). 303p. 1997. 50.00 (*0-8263-1783-9*); pap. 19.95 (*0-8263-1817-7*) U of NM Pr.

Limelight: Photographs by James Abbe. Terence Pepper. (Illus.). 120p. 1996. pap. 18.95 (*1-85514-176-0*, Pub. by Natl Port Gall) Antique Collect.

Limelight Book of Opera. rev. ed. Arthur Jacobs & Stanley Sadie. LC 85-5777. 564p. 1985. reprint ed. pap. 19.95 (*0-87910-044-3*) Limelight Edns.

Limerick: The Paris Edition. 528p. 1979. pap. 14.95 (*0-8065-0713-6*, Citadel Pr) Carol Pub Group.

Limerick Anthology. Ed. by Jim Kemmy. LC 97-145264. (Illus.). 300p. (Orig.). 1996. pap. 21.95 (*0-7171-2458-4*, Pub. by Gill & MacMill) Irish Bks Media.

Limerick Bible. John M. Scott. 1996. pap. 4.95 (*1-55673-983-4*, Fairway Pr) CSS OH.

Limerick Is . . . Ann Gasser. 124p. (Orig.). 1990. pap. 4.99 (*1-884257-04-6*) AGEE Keyboard.

Limerick Lace: A Social History & a Maker's Manual. Nellie O'Cleirigh & Veronica Rowe. LC 95-233670. 92p. 1995. pap. 17.95 (*0-86140-368-1*, Pub. by Smyth) Dufour.

Limerick, Maine, Early Families Of. Robert L. Taylor. 192p. 1993. 45.00 (*0-929539-84-2*) Picton Pr.

Limerick Omnibus. Marsh. (Reference Library). 464p. 1998. pap. 11.95 (*1-85326-490-3*, 4903WW, Pub. by Wrdsworth Edits) NTC Contemp Pub Co.

An Asterisk (*) at the beginning of an entry indicates that the title is appearing for the first time.

***Limerick 101: A Concise Collegiate Course for Constructing Comic Limericks, with 101 Examples.** William J. Middleton. LC 98-96855. (Illus.). 76 p. 1999. pap. 5.00 (*1-886467-42-0*) WJM Press.
Limerick Rake: Versions from the Irish. Desmond O'Grady. 50p. 1978. pap. 11.95 (*0-902996-68-1*) Dufour.
Limerick Run Laces: An Introduction. Pat Earnshaw. (Illus.). 46p. (C). 1992. pap. 17.00 (*0-9513891-6-5*, Pub. by Gorse) Lacis Pubns.
Limerick Tyme. William J. Middleton. (Orig.). 1996. pap. 3.50 (*1-886467-11-0*) WJM Press.
***Limericks.** Isaac Asimov & John Ciardi. LC 99-58756. 2000. 6.99 (*0-517-20882-2*) Random Hse Value.
Limericks: Too Gross; or Two Dozen Dirty Stanzas. Isaac Asimov & John Ciardi. 101p. 1985. reprint ed. pap. 8.95 (*0-393-04530-7*) Norton.
Limerick's Always a Verse. Perrine. (C). 1989. pap. text 21.00 (*0-15-551003-7*) Harcourt Coll Pubs.
Limericks & Rhymes for Critical Times. C. W. Dalton. (Illus.). 204p. (Orig.). 1994. pap. 9.95 (*0-916969-03-7*) Big Blue Bks.
Limericks, Fables & Poems. Henry G. James. (Orig.). (YA). (gr. 12). 1987. 12.00 (*0-942951-00-X*) Universal Res MA.
Limericks for All Occasions. Linda Marsh. 429p. 1999. 24.95 (*1-56649-028-6*); pap. 12.95 (*1-56649-027-8*) Welcome Rain.
***Limericks for Lechers: Lacivious Lyrics, Rambling Ruminations & Titillating Trivia.** Robert William Birch. (Illus.). 249p. 1999. pap. 17.95 (*1-57074-391-6*, Pub. by PEC) ACCESS Pubs Network.
Limericks, Limericks, Limericks, Limericks. F. Oppel. 1992. 7.98 (*1-55521-783-4*) Bk Sales Inc.
Limericks Naughty & Gay. D. Dimock. 1997. pap. 6.50 (*0-9626531-9-5*) Factor Pr.
Limericks New & Naughty: Over 240 Original Limericks. Al Kracht. LC 97-94117. 158 p. 1997. write for info. (*0-9659808-0-4*) Limerick Ln.
Limericks of Maryland. Robert A. Norman. 31p. (Orig.). 1995. pap. 3.95 (*0-9637802-4-7*) North Shore Pr.
Limericks of Massachusetts. Robert A. Norman. (Illus.). 25p. 1996. pap. 4.95 (*0-9637802-7-1*) North Shore Pr.
Limericks of Michigan. Robert A. Norman. 31p. (Orig.). 1995. pap. 3.95 (*0-9637802-5-5*) North Shore Pr.
Limericks of Ohio. Robert A. Norman. (Illus.). 25p. 1996. pap. 4.95 (*0-9637802-6-3*) North Shore Pr.
***Limerock.** Christopher Fahy. 200p. 1999. pap. 12.95 (*0-9626857-5-5*) Coastwise Pr.
Limestone & Clay. Lesley Glaister. 208p. 1994. 19.00 (*0-689-12199-7*) Atheneum Yung Read.
Limestone & Clay. large type ed. Lesley Glaister. LC 94-20366. 314p. 1994. lib. bdg. 17.95 (*0-7862-0247-5*) Thorndike Pr.
Limestone-Building Algae & Algal Limestones. J. Harlan Johnson. 297p. 1961. 2.70 (*0-918062-11-X*) Colo Sch Mines.
Limestone Cave. Wendy Davis. LC 97-26985. (Habitats Ser.). 1997. 24.00 (*0-516-20742-3*) Childrens.
Limestone Cave. Wendy Davis. (Habitats Ser.). (J). (gr. 2-3). 1998. pap. text 6.95 (*0-516-20371-1*) Childrens.
Limestone Caves. Roy A. Gallant. LC 97-3467. (First Book Ser.). 64p. (J). (gr. 4-7). 1998. 22.00 (*0-531-20293-3*) Watts.
Limestone Caves. Roy A. Gallant. (First Book Ser.). (Illus.). 64p. (J). (gr. 4 up). 1998. pap. 6.95 (*0-531-15910-8*) Watts.
Limestone County, 1890, Texas Census Uniquely Reconstructed & Annotated. Compiled by Mary C. Moody. LC 87-63560. 272p. 1988. pap. 32.50 (*0-9615836-3-0*) Blackstone Pub.
Limestone Legends. Norm Shires & Jim Gilford. (Classics of American Sport Ser.). (Illus.). 192p. 1997. pap. 19.95 (*0-8117-2792-0*) Stackpole.
Limestone Locks & Overgrowth: The Rise & Descent of the Chenango Canal. rev. ed. Michele A. McFee. LC 93-40966. (Illus.). 240p. (Orig.). 1993. pap. 25.00 (*0-935796-44-4*) Purple Mnt Pr.
Limestone Moon see Luna de Cal
Limestone Resources of Texas. L. E. Garner. (Mineral Resource Circular Ser.: No. 84). (Illus.). 1994. pap. 3.00 (*0-614-06198-9*) Bur Econ Geology.
Limewood Sculptors of Renaissance Germany, 1475-1525. Michael Baxandall. LC 79-23258. (Illus.). 1982. pap. 32.50 (*0-300-02829-6*, Y-414) Yale U Pr.
***Liminal Acts: A Critical Overview of Contemporary Performance & Theory** Susan Broadhurst. LC 99-20180. 1999. 26.95 (*0-304-70586-1*) Continuum.
Liminal Garden: Drawings of the Liminal Garden. Jacci D. Hartog. LC 98-60443. (Illus.). 22p. 1998. pap. 5.00 (*0-930495-32-2*) San Fran Art Inst.
Liminal Novel: Studies in the Francophone-African Novel As Bildungsroman. Wangari W. Nyatetu-Waigwa. LC 93-470. (American University Studies XVIII: Vol. 6). 134p. (C). 1997. 32.95 (*0-8204-2168-5*) P Lang Pubng.
Liminal Reality & Transformational Power. Timothy L. Carson. LC 97-17052. 144p. 1997. 49.00 (*0-7618-0799-3*); pap. 27.50 (*0-7618-0800-0*) U Pr of Amer.
Liminal Visions of Nicole Brossard. Alice A. Parker. LC 96-38657. (Francophone Cultures & Literatures Ser.: Vol. 16). X, 287p. (C). 1998. text 53.95 (*0-8204-3065-X*) P Lang Pubng.
Liming Acidic Surface Waters. Harvey Olem. (Illus.). 384p. 1990. lib. bdg. 99.95 (*0-87371-243-9*, L243) Lewis Pubs.
Liming of Acidified Surface Waters: A Swedish Synthesis. Y. W. Brodin & L. Henrikson. 1994. write for info. (*0-387-58505-2*) Spr-Verlag.
Liming of Acidified Surface Waters: A Swedish Synthesis. Y. W. Brodin & L. Henrikson. 1995. 108.95 (*3-540-58505-2*) Spr-Verlag.

Limit Algebras. Powers. 1993. pap. 36.54 (*0-582-08781-3*) Longman.
Limit Analysis & Concrete Plasticity. 2nd ed. M.P. Nielsen. LC 98-23303. (New Directions in Civil Engineering Ser.). 936p. 1998. boxed set 84.95 (*0-8493-9126-1*) CRC Pr.
Limit Analysis in Soil Mechanics. Wai-Fah Chen & X. L. Liu. (Developments in Geotechnical Engineering Ser.: No. 52). xiv,478p. 1990. 226.50 (*0-444-43042-3*) Elsevier.
Limit Analysis of Solids & Structures. J. Kamenjarzh. LC 96-26722. 464p. 1996. boxed set 104.95 (*0-8493-2873-X*) CRC Pr.
Limit Analysis of Structures at Thermal Cycling. D. A. Gokhfeld & O. F. Cherniavsky. (Mechanics of Plastic Solids Ser.: No. 4). 576p. 1980. text 355.00 (*90-286-0455-3*) Kluwer Academic.
Limit Controls, UL 353. 5th ed. (C). 1994. pap. text 95.00 (*1-55989-655-8*) Underwrtrs Labs.
Limit Design for Reinforced Concrete Structures: An Annotated Bibliography. M. Z. Cohn. LC 77-12859. (American Concrete Institute Bibliography Ser.: No. 8). 90p. reprint ed. pap. 30.00 (*0-608-15535-7*, 202971500063) Bks Demand.
Limit for Exposure to "Hot Particles" on the Skin. LC 89-71259. (Report Ser.: No. 106). 54p. (Orig.). 1989. pap. text 25.00 (*0-929600-11-8*) NCRP Pubns.
Limit of Delta Y over Delta X. Richard Cumyn. LC 94-218162. 190p. 1994. pap. 12.95 (*0-86492-176-4*, Pub. by Goose Ln Edits) Genl Dist Srvs.
Limit of Influence: Psychokinesis & the Philosophy of Science. Stephen E. Braude. 256p. 1986. 39.95 (*0-7102-0556-2*, 05562, Routledge Thoemms) Routledge.
Limit of Influence: Psychokinesis & the Philosophy of Science. rev. ed. Stephen E. Braude. LC 96-29553. 322p. 1997. 58.50 (*0-7618-0623-7*); pap. 27.50 (*0-7618-0624-5*) U Pr of Amer.
Limit State Design of Prestressed Concrete Vol. 2: The Design of the Member, V. Y. Guyon. (Illus.). 469p. 1974. 108.00 (*0-85334-601-1*) Elsevier.
Limit State of the Plate Elements of Steel Structures. Jozef Djubek et al. 216p. (C). 1984. 76.00 (*0-8176-1478-8*) Birkhauser.
Limit States Design of Structural Steelwork. 2nd ed. D. A. Nethercot. (Illus.). 274p. (C). (gr. 13). 1991. pap. 45.00 (*0-412-39700-5*) Chapman & Hall.
***Limit States Design of Structural Steelwork.** 3rd ed. D. A. Nethercot. LC 00-55646. (Illus.). 2001. write for info. (*0-419-26090-0*, E & FN Spon) Routledge.
Limit Terms, Expanded Democracy. Mike Kelly. 13p. 1990. pap. text 8.00 (*1-57655-131-8*) Independ Inst.
Limit Theorems for Conditional Distributions. George P. Steck. LC 57-9538. (California University Publications in Statistics: Vol. 2, No. 12). 50p. reprint ed. pap. 30.00 (*0-608-30748-3*, 2021184000022) Bks Demand.
Limit Theorems for Functionals of Ergodic Markov Chains with General State Space Xiao-Ming Chen. LC 99-19209. (Memoirs of the Society Ser.). 1999. write for info. (*0-8218-1060-X*) Am Math.
Limit Theorems for Functionals of Random Walks. A. N. Borodin & I. A. Ibragimov. (Proceedings of the Steklov Institute of Mathematics Ser.: Vol. 195). 259p. 1994. 221.00 (*0-8218-0438-3*, STEKLO/195C) Am Math.
Limit Theorems for Large Deviations. L. Saulis & V. A. Statulevicius. (C). 1991. text 155.50 (*0-7923-1475-1*) Kluwer Academic.
Limit Theorems for Random Fields with Singular Spectrum N. N. Leonenko. LC 99-18120. 1999. write for info. (*0-7923-5635-7*) Kluwer Academic.
Limit Theorems for Stochastic Processes. J. Jacod & A. N. Shiryaev. (Grundlehren Ser.: Vol. 288). 630p. 1987. 172.95 (*0-387-17882-1*) Spr-Verlag.
Limit Theorems for Sums of Exchangeable Random Variables. Robert L. Taylor et al. (Monographs in Probability & Statistics). 160p. 1986. 37.00 (*0-8476-7435-5*) Rowman.
Limit Theorems for the Riemann Zeta-Function. Antanas Laurincikas. (Mathematics & Its Applications Ser.: Vol. 352). 312p. (C). 1995. text 158.50 (*0-7923-3824-3*) Kluwer Academic.
Limit Theorems for Unions of Random Closed Sets. Ilya S. Molchanov. (Lecture Notes in Mathematics Ser.: Vol. 1561). 1993. 35.95 (*0-387-57393-3*) Spr-Verlag.
Limit Theorems in Change-Point Analysis. Miklos Csorgo & L. Horvath. LC 98-110380. (Probability & Mathematical Ser.). 438p. 1997. 165.00 (*0-471-95522-1*) Wiley.
***Limit Theorems of Probability Theory.** V. Bentkus et al. Ed. by Yu V. Prokhorov. Tr. by B. D. Seckler from RUS. 320p. 1999. 104.00 (*3-540-57045-4*) Spr-Verlag.
Limit Theorems of Probability Theory. Valentin V. Petrov. (Oxford Studies in Probability: No. 4). 304p. 1995. text 98.00 (*0-19-853499-X*) OUP.
Limit Theorems on Large Deviations for Markov Stochastic Processes. Alexander D. Wentzell. (C). 1990. text 155.00 (*0-7923-0143-9*) Kluwer Academic.
Limit Theory for Mixing Dependent Random Variables. Cheng-Yen Lin & Chuanrong Lu. LC 96-34057. (Mathematics & Its Applications Ser.). 1997. text 160.50 (*0-7923-4219-4*) Kluwer Academic.
Limita Primitiva a Experientei. Thomas H. Ogden. Ed. & Tr. by F. V. Vladescu. Tr. by D. Bucerzan.Tr. of Primitive Edge of Experience. (RUM.). 168p. 1995. pap. text 19.95 (*1-883881-11-0*, 770) S Freud RT&PF.
Limitation Act. M. Malik. (C). 1990. 50.00 (*0-89771-250-1*) St Mut.
Limitation & Assessment in Radiation Protection. Harald H. Rossi. LC 84-11041. (Taylor Lectures: No. 8). 1984. pap. 20.00 (*0-913392-69-3*) NCRP Pubns.
Limitation of Actions. Richard D. James. 150p. 1993. 60.00 (*0-85459-757-3*, Pub. by Tolley Pubng) St Mut.

Limitation of Actions, 2 vols., 1. Corman. 1991. 165.00 (*0-316-15757-0*) Little.
Limitation of Actions, 2 vols., 2. Corman. 1991. 165.00 (*0-316-15759-7*, Aspen Law & Bus) Aspen Pub.
Limitation of Actions, 2 vols., Set. Corman. 1208p. 1991. 295.00 (*0-316-15761-9*, Aspen Law & Bus) Aspen Pub.
Limitation of Actions: Law Commission Consultation, Paper No. 151. (Law Commission (Gt Britain) Reports (Inc. Ann Rpt): No. 81022805). 1998. 65.00 (*0-11-730236-8*, HM02368, Pub. by Statnry Office) Bernan Associates.
Limitation of Actions Handbook - NSW. G. McGrath & I. Davidson. 372p. 1996. pap. write for info. (*0-409-31115-4*, MICHIE) LEXIS Pub.
Limitation of Actions Handbook - Victoria. K. Rees & M. Chapman. 372p. 1996. pap. write for info. (*0-409-31116-2*, MICHIE) LEXIS Pub.
***Limitation of Armament on the Great Lakes.** John Watson Foster & Carnegie Endowment for International Peace Staff. LC 99-56485. 2000. write for info. (*1-57588-538-7*) W S Hein.
Limitation of Exposure to Ionizing Radiation. Intro. by Charles B. Meinhold. LC 93-7142. (Report Ser.: No. 116). 70p. (Orig.). 1993. pap. text 35.00 (*0-929600-30-4*) NCRP Pubns.
Limitation of Free Bargaining & Sanctity of Contracts with Performing Artists & Composers. Ed. by David Peeperkorn. 122p. 1987. pap. 76.00 (*90-6215-169-8*, Pub. by Maklu Uitgev) Gaunt.
Limitation of Infarct Size. Ed. by H. Schmutzler et al. (Illus.). 270p. 1988. 79.95 (*0-387-19148-8*) Spr-Verlag.
Limitation of Liability: A Handbook for Consulting Engineers, Consultants, Architects, Landscape Architects, & Other Design & Technical Consultants. 45.00 (*0-614-05187-8*, PEC10692.4M) ASFE.
Limitation of Liability for Maritime Claims. P. Griggs & R. Williams. (C). 1986. 315.00 (*0-7855-4099-7*, Pub. by Witherby & Co) St Mut.
Limitation of Liability for Maritime Claims. 2nd ed. Patrick Griggs & Richard Williams. LC 87-100832. 228p. 1991. 105.00 (*1-85044-337-8*) LLP.
Limitation of Liability for Maritime Claims. 3rd ed. Patrick Griggs & Richard Williams. LC 98-227233. xxxiii, 429 p. 1998. write for info. (*1-85978-195-0*) LLP.
Limitation of Naval & Military Expenditure see Arms Limitation: Plans for Europe Before 1914
Limitation Periods, Vol. 1. 2nd ed. Andrew McGee. 1994. 176.00 (*0-421-48560-4*, Pub. by Sweet & Maxwll) Gaunt.
Limitation Periods in Personal Injury Actions. Michael A. Jones. 334p. 1995. pap. 54.00 (*1-85431-286-3*, Pub. by Blackstone Pr) Gaunt.
***Limitations.** Eavan Boland. 8p. 2000. pap. 50.00 (*1-891472-18-6*) Dim Gray.
Limitations & Prospects for Retinal Surgery: Proceedings of the Club Jules Gonin Meeting, 8th, Miami, 1972. Club Jules Gonin Meeting Staff et al. (Modern Problems in Ophthalmology Ser.: Vol. 12). (Illus.). 1974. 152.25 (*3-8055-1629-0*) S Karger.
Limitations of Current Tooth Root Stress Analysis. Raymond J. Drago. (Technical Papers: Vol. P229.20). (Illus.). 20p. 1976. pap. text 30.00 (*1-55589-287-6*) AGMA.
Limitations of English Monarchy in the Later Middle Ages. J. R. Lander. (Joanne Goodman Lectures). (Illus.). 104p. 1989. pap. 15.95 (*0-8020-6724-7*); text 25.00 (*0-8020-5807-8*) U of Toronto Pr.
Limitations of Human Responsibility. Francis Wayland. LC 75-3419. reprint ed. 29.50 (*0-404-59416-6*) AMS Pr.
Limitations of Music: A Study in Aesthetics. Eric Blom. LC 72-80139. 1972. reprint ed. 20.95 (*0-405-08275-4*, Pub. by Blom Pubns) Ayer.
Limitations of Popular Techniques for Preproduction Reserve Estimation in Mining. Marvin W. Barnes. LC 89-92063. (Illus.). 88p. (C). 1989. 15.00 (*0-685-27212-5*); pap. 10.00 (*0-685-27213-3*) M Barnes & Assocs.
Limitations of Survey Research Methods in Assessing the Problem of Minority Student Retention in Higher Education: The Focus-Group Method As One Alternative. Abdul K. Banjura. LC 92-4670. 144p. 1992. lib. bdg. 69.95 (*0-7734-9830-3*) E Mellen.
***Limitations of Test Methods for Plastics.** Ed. by James S. Peraro. LC 99-57208. (Illus.). 225p. 2000. pap. text 45.00 (*0-8031-2850-9*, STP1369) ASTM.
Limitations of the Slow Strain Rate Test for Stress Corrosion Cracking Testing, No. 39. (Illus.). 136p. 1994. pap. 98.00 (*1-877914-53-3*) NACE Intl.
Limitations of Worm & Worm: Gear Surfaces in Order to Avoid Undercutting & Appearance of Envelope of Lines in Contact. V. Kin. (Nineteen Eighty-Eight Fall Technical Meeting Ser.: Vol. 88FTMS1). (Illus.). 17p. 1988. pap. text 30.00 (*1-55589-521-2*) AGMA.
Limitations on the Business of Banking: An Analysis of Expanded Securities, Insurance, & Real Estate Activities. R. Daniel Pace. LC 95-23787. (Financial Sector of the American Economy Ser.). 154p. 1995. text 20.00 (*0-8153-2176-7*) Garland.
Limitations on the Treaty-Making Power under the Constitution of the United States, 1915. Henry S. Tucker. LC 99-31589. 1999. reprint ed. 75.00 (*1-58477-015-5*) Lawbk Exchange.
Limitations to Plant Root Growth. Ed. by J. L. Hatfield & B. A. Stewart. (Advances in Soil Science Ser.: Vol. 19). (Illus.). 248p. 1992. 132.95 (*0-387-97767-8*) Spr-Verlag.
Limited Activity & Occupation Sites: A Collection of Conference Papers. Compiled by Albert E. Ward. (Contributions to Anthropological Studies: No. 1). 1978. 20.00 (*0-932752-00-4*) Ctr Anthrop Studies.
***Limited Adversaries: Post-Cold War Sino-American Mutual Images.** Jianwei Wang. LC 99-33000. 320p. 1999. text 45.00 (*0-19-590609-8*) OUP.

***Limited & Universal Salvation: A Text-Oriented & Hermenutical Study of Two Perspectives in Paul.** Sven Hillert. (Coniectanea Biblica Old Testament Ser.: Vol. 51). 272p. 1999. pap. 48.50 (*91-22-01858-1*, Pub. by Almqvist) Coronet Bks.
Limited Bounty: The United States since World War II. Otis L. Graham, Jr. 320p. (C). 1995. pap. 28.44 (*0-07-023979-7*) McGraw.
Limited Budget: Building Great Designs on a Limited Budget. Lesa Sawahata. (Graphic Idea Resource Ser.). (Illus.). 96p. 1998. pap. 15.99 (*1-56496-515-5*) Rockport Pubs.

L

***Limited by Design: R & D Laboratories in the U. S. National Innovation System.** Michael Crow & Barry Bozeman. LC 98-5204. 384p. 1998. 40.00 (*0-231-10982-2*) Col U Pr.
Limited Choices: The Political Struggle for Socialism in Tanzania. Kate Manzo & Dean E. McHenry, Jr. LC 94-14623. 5253p. 1998. pap. 18.95 (*1-55587-556-4*) L Rienner.
Limited Choices: The Political Struggle for Socialism in Tanzania. Dean E. McHenry, Jr. LC 94-14623. 288p. 1994. lib. bdg. 49.95 (*1-55587-429-0*) L Rienner.
Limited-Dependent & Qualitative Variables in Econometrics. G. S. Maddala. LC 82-9554. (Econometric Society Monographs: No. 3). 401p. 1986. pap. text 29.95 (*0-521-33825-5*) Cambridge U Pr.
Limited Elite: Politics & Government in Two Indian Cities. Donald B. Rosenthal. LC 70-121818. 1994. lib. bdg. 22.50 (*0-226-72810-2*) U Ch Pr.
Limited English Proficiency: A Growing & Costly Educational Challenge Facing Many School Districts. (Illus.). 92p. (C). 1996. reprint ed. pap. text 20.00 (*0-7881-3242-3*) DIANE Pub.
Limited Government, Individual Liberty & the Rule of Law: Selected Works by Arthur Asher Shenfield. Arthur A. Shenfield & Norman P. Barry. LC 97-47518. (John Locke Ser.). 384p. 1998. 100.00 (*1-85898-788-1*) E Elgar.
Limited Inc. Jacques Derrida. Tr. by Samuel Weber & Jeffrey Mehlmann from FRE. 160p. 1988. 29.95 (*0-8101-0787-2*); pap. 14.95 (*0-8101-0788-0*) Northwestern U Pr.
Limited Liability Companies. rev. ed. Francis X. Mellon. 138p. 1996. pap. text 65.00 (*0-7811-0146-8*) Res Inst Am.
Limited Liability Companies: A State-by-State Guide to Law & Practice. J. William Callison & Maureen A. Sullivan. 558p. text. write for info. (*0-314-02422-0*) West Pub.
Limited Liability Companies: A State-by-State Guide to Law & Practice, 1995 Supplement. J. William Callison & Maureen A. Sullivan. 268p. (C). 1995. pap. text. write for info. (*0-314-06536-9*) West Pub.
Limited Liability Companies: A State-by-State Guide to Law & Practice, 1996 Supplement. J. William Callison. Ed. by Maureen A. Sullivan. 338p. 1996. pap. text. write for info. (*0-314-20430-X*) West Pub.
Limited Liability Companies: Complete Planning & Practice Guide. Steven Auderieth. 1994. 195.00 (*0-614-00560-4*); ring bd. 195.00 (*1-55645-021-4*, 500004) Busn Legal Reports.
Limited Liability Companies: Formation, Operation & Conversion, 1. Robert W. Wood Esq. PC. 464p. 1993. boxed set 150.00 (*0-7355-1149-7*) Panel Pubs.
Limited Liability Companies: Laws of the United States. Daniel Sitarz. LC 99-39257. (Quick Reference Law Ser.). 159p. 1999. pap. 16.95 (*0-935755-80-2*) Nova Pub IL.
Limited Liability Companies: Legal Research Guide - Pathfinder. Mary V. Moore. LC 94-16191. (Legal Research Guides Ser.: Vol. 17). 96p. 1994. 40.00 (*0-89941-872-4*, 308250) W S Hein.
Limited Liability Companies: State Statutes & Federal Materials, 1995. J. William Callison & Maureen A. Sullivan. 1000p. (C). 1995. pap. text. write for info. (*0-314-06672-1*) West Pub.
Limited Liability Companies: State Statutes & Federal Materials, 1997 J. William Callison. LC 99-159713. 1744 p. 1997. write for info. (*0-314-22806-3*) West Pub.
Limited Liability Companies: Tax & Business Law. Carter G. Bishop & Daniel S. Kleinberger. 1994. ring bd. 185.00 (*0-685-69541-7*, LIM) Warren Gorham & Lamont.
Limited Liability Companies: Tax & Business Law. Carter G. Bishop & Daniel S. Kleinberger. LC 93-61890. 1072p. 1994. 175.00 (*0-7913-1879-6*) Warren Gorham & Lamont.
Limited Liability Companies: A State-by-State Guide: 1997 Supplement. annuals J. William Callison & Maureen A. Sullivan. (Practice Ser.). 414p. 1997. pap. text, suppl. ed. write for info. (*0-314-21468-2*) West Pub.
Limited Liability Companies Guide: Planning & Compliance for Today's Practitioner. 98th ed. III James C. Thomas. 1999. pap. text 99.00 (*0-15-606086-8*) Harcourt.
***Limited Liability Companies in Kentucky.** 2nd ed. Scott W. Dolson et al. (Illus.). 358p. 2000. pap. 45.00 (*1-58757-031-9*, BM035) Univ of KY.
Limited Liability Company. 2nd ed. William D. Bagley & Philip P. Whynott. 525p. 1994. ring bd. 199.00 (*0-938065-64-5*) James Pub Santa Ana.
***Limited Liability Company: Small Business Start-Up Kit.** Daniel Sitarz. LC 99-27441. 288p. 2000. per. 24.95 incl. cd-rom (*0-935755-76-4*) Nova Pub IL.
Limited Liability Company & Partnership Answer Book. Alson R. Martin. 816p. boxed set 118.00 (*1-56706-313-6*, S288) Panel Pubs.
Limited Liability Company & Partnership Answer Book. annuals Alson R. Martin. 512p. 1995. boxed set 136.00 (*1-56706-177-X*) Panel Pubs.

An Asterisk (*) at the beginning of an entry indicates that the title is appearing for the first time.

Limited Liability Company Kit Do-It-Yourself. 24.95 (*1-880398-20-6*) SJT Enterprises.

Limited Liability Co. Made E-Z. E-Z Legal Staff. (Made E-Z Ser.). 216p. 1999. pap. 17.95 (*1-56382-435-3*) E-Z Legal.

Limited Liability Corporations: 1994 Edition. Jerome P. Friedlander. LC 94-75753. 776p. 1994. text 105.00 (*1-55834-151-X*, 61953-10, MICHIE) LEXIS Pub.

Limited Liability Partnerships: Formation, Operation & Taxation. Robert W. Wood. LC 96-39988. (Business Practice Library Ser.). 384p. 1997. boxed set 150.00 (*0-471-16186-1*) Wiley.

Limited Life, Lasting Love: Siblings Grieve Too. Eileen McGrath. 40p. 1997. pap. 3.95 (*0-7829-0880-2*) T More.

Limited Lifetime Warranty: Stories. Nance Van Winckel. LC 93-43630. 176p. 1994. 19.95 (*0-8262-0922-X*) U of Mo Pr.

Limited Livelihoods: Gender & Class in Nineteenth-Century England. Sonia O. Rose. (Studies on the History of Society & Culture: No. 13). (Illus.). 320p. 1991. 50.00 (*0-520-07478-5*, Pub. by U CA Pr); pap. 16.95 (*0-520-07479-3*, Pub. by U CA Pr) Cal Prin Full Svc.

Limited Master, Mate & Operator License Study Course, Bk. 1. rev. ed. Ed. by Richard A. Block. (Illus.). 630p. 1996. pap. text 67.00 (*1-879778-49-1*, BK-001) Marine Educ.

Limited Master, Mate & Operator License Study Course, Bk. 2. rev. ed. Ed. by Richard A. Block. 672p. 1996. pap. text 66.00 (*1-879778-52-1*, BK-002) Marine Educ.

Limited Master, Mate & Operator License Study Course, Bk. 3. rev. ed. Ed. by Richard A. Block. 620p. 1996. pap. text 65.00 (*1-879778-53-X*, BK-003) Marine Educ.

Limited Master, Mate & Operator License Study Course, Bk. 4. rev. ed. Ed. by Richard A. Block. 450p. 1996. pap. text 48.00 (*1-879778-54-8*, BK-004) Marine Educ.

Limited Master, Mate & Operator License Study Course, Bk. 5. rev. ed. Ed. by Richard A. Block. 296p. 1996. pap. text 36.00 (*1-879778-55-6*, BK-005) Marine Educ.

Limited Options: Women Workers in Rural India. Ed. by A. V. Jose. 259p. 1989. 22.50 (*92-2-106717-3*) Intl Labour Office.

Limited Partnership. Ted DeLong. 90p. 1997. 49.00 (*1-885661-07-X*) Estate Protection.

Limited Partnership: Building a Russian-U. S. Security Community. Ed. by James E. Goodby & Benoit Morel. LC 92-27075. (SIPRI Publication). (Illus.). 334p. 1993. text 55.00 (*0-19-829161-2*) OUP.

Limited Partnership: Europe, the United States, & the Burdens of Alliance. Josef Joffe. LC 87-17837. 256p. 1987. text 29.95 (*0-88730-216-5*, HarpBusn) HarpInfo.

***Limited Partnership: Religion & the Politics of Social Services.** Robert J. Wineburg. 320p. 2000. text 49.00 (*0-231-12084-2*); pap. text 22.50 (*0-231-12085-0*) Col U Pr.

Limited Partnership: Russia-China Relations in a Changing Asia: Report of the Carnegie Endowment Study Group on Russia-China Relations. Carnegie Endowment Study Group Staff. 48p. 1998. pap. 6.95 (*0-87003-133-3*) Carnegie Endow.

Limited Partnership Book. Arnold S. Goldstein. 1998. pap. 29.95 (*1-880539-48-9*) Garrett FL.

Limited Partnership Locator. Jon M. Hale & Bill Rentschler. 140p. 1994. pap. text 200.00 (*0-9643196-0-8*) Prtnership Cnslts.

Limited Partnerships: A Practitioner's Guide under Delaware Law, 2 vols. Martin I. Lubaroff & Paul M. Altman. 1270p. 1992. ring bd. 225.00 (*0-13-110222-2*) Aspen Law.

Limited Partnerships: Legal Aspects of Organization, Operation, & Dissolution. 3rd ed. Craig B. Smith & Anne B. Horgan. (Corporate Practice Ser.: No. 24). 1992. ring bd. 95.00 (*1-55871-276-3*) BNA.

Limited Radiography. Frances E. Campeau & Jeana Phelps. LC 92-49682. (C). 1992. mass mkt. 32.00 (*0-8273-3335-8*) Delmar.

***Limited Radiography.** 2nd ed. Campeau. LC 98-27596. (Allied Health Ser.). 352p. 1998. text 45.95 (*0-7668-0205-1*) Delmar.

Limited Radiography: Instructor's Guide. Frances E. Campeau & M. Jeana Phelps. 50p. 1993. 14.00 (*0-8273-3336-6*) Delmar.

Limited Responsibilities. Tamar Pitch. Tr. by John Lea. 256p. (C). 1995. pap. 25.99 (*0-415-08654-X*, B4217) Routledge.

Limited Slip Differential Pinion Operation & Service. George Chrestionson. LC 79-731072. 1978. student ed. 7.00 (*0-8064-0121-4*, 428) Bergwall.

Limited Space Shortwave Antenna Solutions. Frank P. Hughes. (Illus.). 52p. (Orig.). 1988. pap. 12.95 (*0-936653-13-2*) Tiare Pubns.

Limited Time. Robert Greer. LC 99-29484. 352p. 2000. 23.95 (*0-89296-684-X*, Pub. by Mysterious Pr) Little.

Limited to Everyone: An Invitation to Christian Faith. Robert Jones. 144p. (Orig.). 1984. 7.95 (*0-8164-2381-4*) Harper SF.

Limited Views: Essays on Ideas & Letters. Chung-Shu Chien. Tr. by Ronald C. Egan from CHI. LC 97-37383. (Harvard-Yenching Institute Monograph Ser.). 1998. 45.00 (*0-674-53411-5*) HUP.

***Limited Vision: Reflections of a Teenager.** C. J. Wilson. (Illus.). (YA). 1999. pap. 8.95 (*0-9621408-1-3*) New Dawn Pub.

Limited Wants, Unlimited Means: A Reader on Hunter-Gatherer Economics & the Environment. John Gowdy. LC 97-32425. 300p. 1997. pap. text 27.00 (*1-55963-555-X*) Island Pr.

Limited War: An Essay on the Development of the Theory & an Annotated Bibliography. Morton H. Halperin. LC 76-38761. (Harvard University. Center for International Affairs. Occasional Papers in International Affairs: No. 3). reprint ed. 24.50 (*0-404-54603-X*) AMS Pr.

Limited War: The Challenge to American Strategy. Robert E. Osgood. LC 57-5275. 326p. 1998. lib. bdg. 23.00 (*0-226-63779-4*) U Ch Pr.

Limited War in the Nuclear Age. Morton H. Halperin. LC 77-18193. 191p. 1978. reprint ed. lib. bdg. 35.00 (*0-313-20116-1*, HALW, Greenwood Pr) Greenwood.

Limited War Revisited. Robert E. Osgood. LC 89-13427. (Special Studies). 124p. 1979. pap. text 49.00 (*0-89158-465-X*) Westview.

Limited Warfare in the Nuclear Age, Chpts. 27-31. Robert Doughty et al. 192p. (C). 1996. pap. text 21.16 (*0-669-41682-7*) HM Trade Div.

Limited Wisdom, Vol. I. Zhu Xiao Feng. (Selected Works of Zhu Xiao Feng Ser.: Vol. 4). (CHI.). 466p. 1997. 40.00 (*1-891158-03-1*) Am Int Rare Bks.

Limites Para Nuestros Hijos. Henry Cloud. 1999. 9.99 (*0-8297-1689-0*) Vida Pubs.

Limiting Absorption Principle for Partial Differential Operators. M. Ben-Artzi & A. Devinatz. LC 87-1807. (Memoirs of the American Mathematical Society Ser.: Vol. 66/364). 70p. 1987. pap. 16.00 (*0-8218-2426-0*, MEMO/66/364) Am Math.

Limiting Bias in the Assessment of Bilingual Students. Ed. by Else V. Hamayan & Jack S. Damico. LC 89-28783. (Illus.). 363p. (C). 1991. pap. text 35.00 (*0-89079-411-1*, 1594) PRO-ED.

Limiting Central Bank Credit to the Government: Theory & Practice. Carlo Cottarelli. LC 93-42537. (Occasional Papers: No. 110). 57p. 1993. pap. 15.00 (*1-55775-358-X*) Intl Monetary.

Limiting Conventional Arms Exports to the Middle East. (Illus.). 85p. (Orig.). (C). 1992. pap. text 30.00 (*1-56806-105-6*) DIANE Pub.

***Limiting Dilution Analysis of Cells in the Immune System.** 2nd ed. Ivan Lefkovits & Herman Waldmann. LC 98-50046. (Illus.). 320p. 1999. text 149.50 (*0-19-850128-5*) OUP.

Limiting Donor Exposure in Hemotherapy. Ed. by James P. Aubuchon & Linda A. Issitt. LC 94-32345. (Illus.). 99p. (C). 1994. 40.00 (*1-56395-030-8*) Am Assn Blood.

Limiting Equations for Problems Involving Long Range Memory. Moshe Marcus & Victor Mizel. LC 83-3752. (Memoirs of the American Mathematical Society Ser.: No. 43/278). 64p. 1983. pap. 17.00 (*0-8218-2278-0*, MEMO/43/278) Am Math.

Limiting Equilibrium of Brittle Solids with Fractures. V. V. Panasyuk. LC 75-135093. 325p. 1969. 39.00 (*0-403-04527-4*) Scholarly.

Limiting Exchange Rate Flexibility: The European Monetary System. Francesco Giavazzi & Alberto Giovannini. 320p. 1989. 35.00 (*0-262-07116-9*) MIT Pr.

Limiting God. John Hunter. 208p. 1995. pap. 9.95 (*1-886797-01-3*) Fresh Springs.

Limiting Government: An Introduction to Constitutionalism. Andras Sajo. LC 99-27464. 288p. (C). 1999. 49.95 (*963-9116-25-4*); pap. 24.95 (*963-9116-24-6*) Ctrl Europ Univ.

Limiting Legislative Terms. Gerald Benjamin & Michael J. Malbin. 324p. 1992. pap. 23.95 (*0-87187-740-6*) Congr Quarterly.

Limiting Leviathan. Ed. by Donald P. Racheter et al. LC 99-17052. 288p. 1999. 95.00 (*1-84064-024-3*) E Elgar.

Limiting Nuclear Proliferation. Ed. by Jed C. Snyder & Samuel F. Wells, Jr. LC 85-3967. 408p. 1985. 34.95 (*0-88730-042-1*, HarpBusn) HarpInfo.

Limiting Oil Imports: An Economic History & Analysis. Douglas R Bohi & Milton Russell. LC 77-18881. 356p. 1978. 30.50 (*0-8018-2106-1*) Resources Future.

Limiting Rights: The Dilemma of Judicial Review. Janet L. Hiebert. LC 97-198257. 200p. 1996. pap. 22.95 (*0-7735-1437-6*, Pub. by McG-Queens Univ Pr) CUP Services.

Limiting Rights: The Dilemma of Judicial Review. Janet L. Hiebert. LC 97-198257. 200p. 1996. 60.00 (*0-7735-1431-7*, Pub. by McG-Queens Univ Pr) CUP Services.

Limiting Spur Gear Design. C. H. Loguz. (Technical Papers: Vol. P59). (Illus.). 20p. 1925. pap. text 30.00 (*1-55589-263-9*) AGMA.

Limiting Terms of Office for Members of the U. S. House of Representatives & U. S. Senate: Hearing Before the Subcommittee on the Constitution of the Committee on the Judiciary, House of Representatives, 105th Congress, 1st Session, January 22, 1997. USGPO Staff. LC 98-107146. iii, 67 p. 1997. pap. write for info. (*0-16-055598-1*) USGPO.

Limiting the Burdens of Pro Se Inmate Litigation: A Technical-Assistance Manual for Courts, Correctional Officials & Attorneys General Lynn S. Branham & American Bar Association. LC 97-207654. 240p. 1997. write for info. (*1-57073-512-3*) Amer Bar Assn.

Limiting the Risk & Sharing Losses in the Globalized Capital Market. Barry M. Hager. LC 98-16561. (Special Studies Ser.). 96p. 1998. 12.95 (*0-943875-88-9*) W Wilson Ctr Pr.

Limiting What Students Shall Read: Report of a Nationwide School Library & Administration Survey. 1981. 5.00 (*0-685-07075-1*) AAP.

***Limitless Life: Dogen's World.** Rosan Osamu Yoshida. (Illus.). 96p. 1999. pap. 7.00 (*0-9676798-0-X*) Missouri Zen.

Limitless Love of Christ. Charles H. Spurgeon. 160p. 1996. mass mkt. 5.99 (*0-88368-458-6*) Whitaker Hse.

Limits. Alan F. Beardon. LC 97-20490. (Undergraduate Texts in Mathematics Ser.). 1997. 34.95 (*0-387-98274-4*) Spr-Verlag.

Limits. Buchanan. 1990. pap., teacher ed. 24.72 (*0-395-43045-3*) HM.

Limits: The Role of the Law in Bioethical Decision Making. Roger B. Dworkin. LC 95-50697. (Medical Ethics Ser.). 224p. 1996. text 35.00 (*0-253-33075-0*) Ind U Pr.

***Limits & Lies of Human Genetic Research: Dangers for Social Policy.** Jonathan Michael Kaplan. LC 99-44899. (Reflective Bioethics Ser.). 256p. 2000. pap. 22.99 (*0-415-92638-6*) Routledge.

***Limits & Lies of Human Genetic Research: Dangers for Social Policy.** Jonathan Michael Kaplan. LC 99-44899. (Reflective Bioethics Ser.). 256p. (C). 2000. text 85.00 (*0-415-92637-8*) Routledge.

Limits & Possibilities of Schooling: An Introduction to the Sociology of Education. 3rd ed. Christopher J. Hurn. LC 92-449. 432p. 1992. 73.00 (*0-205-14200-1*) Allyn.

Limits & Possibilities of Schooling: An Introduction to the Sociology of Education. 4th ed. Christopher J. Hurn. (C). 2000. teacher ed. write for info. (*0-205-14991-X*, H4991-9) Allyn.

Limits & Relationships of the Lutjanidae & Associated Families. G. David Johnson. (Bulletin of the Scripps Institute of Oceanography Ser.: Vol. 24). 1981. pap. 19.95 (*0-520-09642-8*, Pub. by U CA Pr) Cal Prin Full Svc.

Limits & Scope of Environmental Law. Miguel A. Santos. (Illus.). 368p. 1995. 68.95 (*0-398-06543-8*); pap. 44.95 (*0-398-06544-6*) C C Thomas.

Limits for Intakes of Radionuclides by Workers, 7 vols. International Commission on Radiological Protectio. Ed. by F. D. Sowby. (International Commission of Radiological Protection Ser.: No. 30). 2500p. 1982. 445.00 (*0-08-028863-4*, Pergamon Pr) Elsevier.

Limits for Intakes of Radionuclides by Workers. Ed. by F. D. Sowby. (ICRP Publication Ser.: No. 30, Pt. 3). 128p. 1982. pap. 36.50 (*0-08-026834-X*, Pergamon Pr) Elsevier.

Limits for Intakes of Radionuclides by Workers, Pt. 2. International Commission of Radiological Protectio. (International Commission of Radiological Protection Ser.). 80p. 1980. pap. 41.00 (*0-08-026832-3*, Pergamon Pr) Elsevier.

Limits for Intakes of Radionuclides by Workers: Index. International Commission of Radiological Protection Staff. (International Commission of Radiological Protection Ser.). 73p. 1982. pap. 15.00 (*0-08-028884-7*, Pergamon Pr) Elsevier.

Limits for Intakes of Radionuclides by Workers: Report Commission 2 ICRP ADPTD 7-78, Supercedes ICRP 2. ICRP Staff. (Radiation Protection Ser.: Vol. 30: PT1S). 1980. 252.00 (*0-08-024941-8*, Pub. by Pergamon Repr) Franklin.

Limits for Intakes of Radionuclides by Workers Pt. 4: An Addendum. ICRP Staff. (ICRP Publication Ser.: No. 30). 172p. 1989. pap. 38.50 (*0-08-036886-7*, Pergamon Pr) Elsevier.

Limits for Intakes of Radionuclides by Workers, Supplements A & B to Pt.3, 2 vols. Ed. by F. D. Sowby. (ICRP Publication Ser.: No. 30). (Illus.). 948p. 1982. 215.00 (*0-08-026835-8*, H999, Pergamon Pr) Elsevier.

Limits in Perception: Essays in Honor of Maarten A. Bouman. Ed. by A. J. Van Doorn et al. 579p. 1984. lib. bdg. 145.00 (*90-6764-034-4*, Pub. by VSP) Coronet Bks.

***Limits of a Limitless Science & Other Essays.** Stanley L. Jaki. LC 99-68034. 260p. (C). 2000. pap. 12.95 (*1-882926-46-3*) ISI Books.

Limits of Absolutism in Ancient Regime France: Collected Essays. Richard Bonney. LC 94-37035. (Collected Studies: No. CS491). 352p. 1995. 109.95 (*0-86078-482-7*, Pub. by Variorum) Ashgate Pub Co.

Limits of Acceptable Change & Related Planning Processes: Progress & Future Directions: Proceedings. Ed. by Stephen F. McCool & David N. Cole. (Illus.). 84p. 1999. reprint ed. pap. text 20.00 (*0-7881-8034-7*) DIANE Pub.

Limits of Adjustment in Africa. 1996. 65.00 (*0-435-08986-2*) Heinemann.

Limits of Administration. Christopher C. Hood. LC 75-37850. 225p. reprint ed. 69.80 (*0-8357-9923-9*, 205175100007) Bks Demand.

Limits of Affluence: Welfare in Ontario, 1920-1970. James Struthers. (Ontario Historical Studies). (Illus.). 404p. 1994. text 55.00 (*0-8020-0622-1*); pap. text 24.95 (*0-8020-7582-7*) U of Toronto Pr.

Limits of Agrarian Radicalism: Western Populism & American Politics. Peter H. Argersinger. LC 94-23556. 312p. 1995. 29.95 (*0-7006-0702-1*) U Pr of KS.

Limits of Air Power: The American Bombing of North Vietnam. Mark Clodfelter. 297p. 1989. 32.95 (*0-02-905990-9*) Free Pr.

Limits of Alliance: NATO Out-of-Area Problems since 1949. Douglas Stuart & William Tow. LC 90-4407. (Perspectives on Security Ser.). 400p. 1990. text 64.00 (*0-8018-3808-8*) Johns Hopkins.

Limits of American Literary Ideology in Pound & Emerson. Cary Wolfe. LC 93-18475. (Cambridge Studies in American Literature & Culture: No. 69). 304p. (C). 1994. text 64.95 (*0-521-44555-8*) Cambridge U Pr.

***Limits of Analysis.** unabridged ed. Stanley Rosen. LC 99-48139. 296p. 2000. reprint ed. pap. 28.00 (*1-890318-36-1*, Pub. by St Augustines Pr) Chicago Distribution Ctr.

Limits of Anarchy: Intervention & State Formation in Chad. Sam C. Nolutshungu. 392p. (C). 1996. text 39.50 (*0-8139-1628-3*) U Pr of Va.

Limits of Ancient Christianity: Essays on Late Antique Thought & Culture in Honor of R. A. Markus. R. A. Markus. Ed. by William E. Klingshim & Mark Vessey. LC 98-51221. (Recentiores Ser.). 376p. 1999. text 54.50 (*0-472-10997-9*, 10997) U of Mich Pr.

Limits of Art. Ed. by Huntington Cairns. 1500p. 1996. 19.98 (*1-56731-162-8*, MJF Bks) Fine Comms.

***Limits of Autobiography: Trauma, Testimony, Theory.** Leigh Gilmore. 2001. 39.95 (*0-8014-3799-7*); pap. 16.95 (*0-8014-8674-2*) Cornell U Pr.

Limits of Biological Treatments for Psychological Distress: Comparisons with Psychotherapy & Placebo. Ed. by Seymour Fisher & Roger Greenberg. 376p. (C). 1989. text 79.95 (*0-8058-0138-3*) L Erlbaum Assocs.

Limits of British Influence: South Asia & the Anglo-American Relationship, 1947-56. Anita I. Singh. LC 93-12372. 300p. (C). 1993. 49.95 (*0-7185-1484-X*) St Martin.

Limits of Change: Essays on Conservative Alternatives in Republican China. Ed. by Charlotte Furth. LC 75-23490. (East Asian Monographs: No. 84). 458p. 1976. 40.50 (*0-674-53423-9*) HUP.

Limits of Citizenship: Migrants & Postnational Membership in Europe. Yasemin N. Soysal. 256p. 1994. pap. text 14.00 (*0-226-76842-2*) U Ch Pr.

Limits of Citizenship: Migrants & Postnational Membership in Europe. Yasemin N. Soysal. 256p. 1998. lib. bdg. 37.50 (*0-226-76841-4*) U Ch Pr.

Limits of Coexistence: Identity Politics in Israel. Rebecca L. Torstrick. (Illus.). 352p. (C). text 54.50 (*0-472-11124-8*, 11124) U of Mich Pr.

Limits of Community: A Critique of Social Radicalism. Helmuth Plessner. Tr. by Andy Wallace from GER. 128p. 1997. 39.95 (*0-391-04071-5*) Humanities.

Limits of Community: A Critique of Social Radicalism. Helmuth Plessner. Tr. by Andrew Wallace. LC 99-29377. 225p. 2000. 49.95 (*1-57392-723-6*, Humanity Bks) Prometheus Bks.

Limits of Competence: Knowledge, Higher Education & Society. Barnett Ronald. LC 94-22170. 160p. 1994. pap. 34.95 (*0-335-19341-2*) OpUniv Pr.

Limits of Computing. Henry M. Walker. (Computer Science-Math Ser.). 224p. (C). 1993. pap. text 35.00 (*0-86720-206-8*) Jones & Bartlett.

Limits of Concept Formation in Natural Science: A Logical Introduction to the Historical Sciences. abr. ed. Heinrich Rickert. Ed. & Tr. by Guy Oakes from GER. (Texts in German Philosophy Ser.). 272p. 1986. pap. text 27.95 (*0-521-31015-6*) Cambridge U Pr.

***Limits of Convergence: Globalization & Organizational Change in Argentina, South Korea & Spain.** Mauro F. Guillen. LC 00-41659. 2001. write for info. (*0-691-05705-2*) Princeton U Pr.

Limits of Corporatism: British Experience in the Twentieth Century. John Sheldrake & Sarah Vickerstaff. 131p. 1989. text 87.95 (*0-566-05493-0*, Pub. by Gower) Ashgate Pub Co.

Limits of Disenchantment: Essays on Psychoanalysis, Deconstruction & Critical Theory. Peter Dews. 224p. (C). 1996. pap. 19.00 (*1-85984-022-1*, Pub. by Verso) Norton.

Limits of Dissent: Clement L. Vallandigham & the Civil War. Frank L. Klement. LC 98-47502. (North's Civil War Ser.: No. 8). (Illus.). xxiii, 351p. 1998. 32.50 (*0-8232-1890-2*); pap. 19.95 (*0-8232-1891-0*) Fordham.

Limits of Dissent: The Constitutional Status of Armed Civilian Militias. Thomas Halpern & Brian Levin. LC 96-1095. (Law & Violence Ser.: No. 3). 160p. (Orig.). 1996. pap. 14.00 (*1-880831-17-1*) Aletheia Pr.

Limits of Econometrics. Adrian C. Darnell & J. Lynne Evans. 192p. 1990. text 90.00 (*1-85278-048-7*) E Elgar.

Limits of Econometrics. Adrian C. Darnell & J. Lynne Evans. 192p. 1991. pap. text 30.00 (*1-85278-517-9*) E Elgar.

Limits of Economic Reform in El Salvador. Wim Pelupessy. LC 96-49057. 256p. 1997. text 69.95 (*0-312-17323-7*) St Martin.

Limits of Economic Science. Richard B. McKenzie. 1982. lib. bdg. 73.50 (*0-89838-116-9*) Kluwer Academic.

Limits of Educational Assessment. Andrew J. Davis. (Journal of Philosophy of Education Ser.: Vol. 32). 224p. 1999. pap. 29.95 (*0-631-21020-2*, Pub. by Blckwll Scitfc UK) Blackwell Pubs.

Limits of Empire: The Roman Army in the East. 2nd rev. ed. Benjamin Isaac. (Illus.). 524p. (C). 1993. pap. text 35.00 (*0-19-814952-2*) OUP.

***Limits of Empire: The United States & Southeast Asia since World War II.** Robert McMahon. LC 98-19525. 26p. 1998. pap. 17.50 (*0-231-10881-8*); lib. bdg. 45.00 (*0-231-10880-X*) Col U Pr.

Limits of Enlightenment: Jews, Germans, & the Eighteenth-Century Study of Scripture. Edward Breuer. (Judaic Monographs: Vol. 7). 295p. 1996. 45.00 (*0-674-53426-3*); pap. 17.50 (*0-674-53427-1*) HUP.

Limits of Enlightenment: Joseph II & the Law. Paul P. Bernard. LC 79-12030. 160p. 1979. text 19.95 (*0-252-00735-2*) U of Ill Pr.

Limits of Eroticism in Post-Petrarchan Narrative: Conditional Pleasure from Spenser to Marvell. Dorothy Stephens. LC 97-52750. (Cambridge Studies in Renaissance Literature & Culture: No. 29). 276p. (C). 1999. text 59.95 (*0-521-63064-9*) Cambridge U Pr.

Limits of European Integration. Paul Taylor. Ed. by John G. Ruggie. LC 82-22023. (Political Economy of International Change Ser.). 320p. 1983. pap. text 26.50 (*0-231-05715-6*) Col U Pr.

Limits of Expanding Liability: Eight Fundamental Cases in a Comparative Perspective. Jaap Spier & Christian Von Bar. LC 98-179541. xiii, 244 p. 1998. 81.00 (*90-411-0581-6*) Kluwer Law Intl.

An Asterisk (*) at the beginning of an entry indicates that the title is appearing for the first time.

L

Limits of Family Influence: Genes, Experience & Behavior. David C. Rowe. LC 93-21876. 232p. 1995. pap. text 21.00 (*0-89862-148-8*, 2148) Guilford Pubns.

Limits of Foreign Policy. enl. ed. Charles B. Marshall. LC 88-94. 162p. (Orig.). (C). 1988. reprint ed. pap. text 18.50 (*0-8191-6815-7*) U Pr of Amer.

Limits of Fraternity: Dreyfus, the Jews, & the French Republic. Robert S. Wistrich. 350p. 1997. text 55.00 (*1-874774-02-1*, Pub. by Littman Lib) Intl Spec Bk.

Limits of Freedom. David Fellman. LC 72-9048. 144p. 1973. reprint ed. lib. bdg. 65.00 (*0-8371-6563-6*, FELF, Greenwood Pr) Greenwood.

Limits of Freedom of Contract. Michael J. Trebilcock. LC 93-18706. (Illus.). 336p. 1993. 43.00 (*0-674-53429-8*) HUP.

Limits of Freedom of Contract. Michael J. Trebilcock. (Illus.). 320p. 1997. pap. text 19.50 (*0-674-53430-1*) HUP.

Limits of Freedom of Speech: Prose Literature & Prose Writers in Egypt under Nasser & Sadat. Marina Stagh. (Stockholm Oriental Studies: No. 14). (Illus.). 374p. (Orig.). 1993. pap. 58.75 (*91-22-01585-X*) Coronet Bks.

Limits of Globalization: Cases & Arguments. Ed. by Alan Scott. LC 98-122031. 376p. (C). 1997. 85.00 (*0-415-10565-X*); pap. 27.99 (*0-415-10566-8*) Routledge.

Limits of Government. Joseph F. Johnston, Jr. LC 82-60662. 1984. 19.95 (*0-89526-653-9*) Regnery Pub.

Limits of Government: On Policy Competence & Economic Growth. Ed. by Gunnar Eliasson & Nils Karlson. LC 99-49820. 298p. 2000. 39.95 (*1-56000-437-1*) Transaction Pubs.

Limits of Grammaticalization. Ed. by Anna G. Ramat & Paul J. Hopper. LC 98-21202. (Typological Studies in Linguistics: Vol. 37). vi, 307p. 1998. 79.00 (*1-55619-649-0*); pap. text 29.95 (*1-55619-650-4*) J Benjamins Pubng Co.

Limits of Hegemony: United States Relations with Argentina & Chile During World War II. Michael J. Francis. LC 77-89754. (International Studies Ser.). 1977. text 29.00 (*0-268-01260-1*) U of Notre Dame Pr.

***Limits of Historiography.** Christina Shuttleworth Kraus. LC 99-31269. (Mnemosyne, Supplements, 190 Ser.). 368p. 1999. 109.00 (*90-04-10670-7*) Brill Academic Pubs.

Limits of Hobbesian Contractarianism. Jody S. Kraus. 348p. (C). 1994. text 69.95 (*0-521-42062-8*) Cambridge U Pr.

Limits of Hope: An Adoptive Mother's Story. Ann K. Loux. LC 96-46372. 280p. 1997. 24.95 (*0-8139-1710-7*) U Pr of Va.

Limits of Hope: Soldier Settlement in Victoria, 1915-1938. Marilyn Lake. (Illus.). 272p. 1987. 39.00 (*0-19-554666-0*) OUP.

***Limits of Idealism: When Good Intentions Go Bad.** Melvyn L. Fein. LC 99-42793. (Clinical Sociology Ser.). 270p. 1999. 64.50 (*0-306-46211-7*, Kluwer Plenum) Kluwer Academic.

Limits of Independence. Adam Watson. LC 98-144540. 168p. (C). 1997. 60.00 (*0-415-15811-7*); pap. 20.99 (*0-415-16907-0*) Routledge.

Limits of Independence: American Women, 1760-1800 see Young Oxford History of Women in the United States

Limits of Independence: American Women 1760-1800, Vol. 3. Marylynn Salmon. (Young Oxford History of Women in the United States Ser.). (Illus.). 144p. (J). 1998. reprint ed. pap. 10.95 (*0-19-512401-4*) OUP.

Limits of Indeterminacy in Measure of T-Means of Subseries of a Trigonometric Series. D. E. Men'Sov. LC 81-14992. (Steklov Institute of Mathematics Ser.: No. 149). 56p. 1981. pap. 34.00 (*0-8218-3043-0*, STEKLO/149) Am Math.

Limits of Interdeterminacy in Measure of Trigonometric & Orthogonal Series: Proceedings. Steklov Institute of Mathematics, Academy of Scien. (Proceedings of the Steklov Institute of Mathematics Ser.: No. 99). 67p. 1968. pap. 34.00 (*0-8218-1899-6*, STEKLO/99) Am Math.

Limits of Interpretation. Umberto Eco. LC 89-45999. (Advances in Semiotics Ser.). (Illus.). 304p. 1991. 35.00 (*0-253-31852-1*) Ind U Pr.

Limits of Interpretation. Umberto Eco. LC 89-45999. (Advances in Semiotics Ser.). (Illus.). 304p. 1994. pap. 15.95 (*0-253-20869-6*) Ind U Pr.

Limits of Interpretation. Peter Lomas. LC 90-282. 168p. 1990. 25.00 (*0-87668-797-4*) Aronson.

Limits of Intervention. Townsend Hoopes. 272p. 1987. reprint ed. pap. 7.95 (*0-393-30427-2*) Norton.

Limits of Judicial Power: The Supreme Court in American Politics. William Lasser. LC 88-40141. xi, 354p. (C). 1988. 39.95 (*0-8078-1810-0*) U of NC Pr.

Limits of Judicial Power: The Supreme Court in American Politics. William Lasser. LC 88-40141. 366p. reprint ed. pap. 113.50 (*0-608-08600-2*, 206912300003) Bks Demand.

Limits of Jurisprudence Defined: Being Part Two of an Introduction to the Principles of Morals & Legislation. Jeremy Bentham. LC 71-100143. (Illus.). 358p. 1970. reprint ed. lib. bdg. 35.00 (*0-8371-3249-5*, BEJU, Greenwood Pr) Greenwood.

***Limits of Justice: A Benjamin Justice Mystery.** John Morgan Wilson. LC 99-54077. 320p. 2000. 22.95 (*0-385-49117-4*) Doubleday.

Limits of Knowing & the Knowing of Limits: Living with Uncertainty. Philip G. Gibson. (Illus.). 137p. (Orig.). 1996. pap. 10.00 (*0-9650553-0-2*, 5302) Design Stage.

Limits of Land Settlement: A Report on Present-Day Possiblities. Ed. by Isaiah Bowman. LC 67-30200. (Essay Index Reprint Ser.). 1977. 26.95 (*0-8369-0233-5*) Ayer.

Limits of Language. Stephen D. Ross. LC 93-17970. xix, 290p. (C). 1993. 35.00 (*0-8232-1518-0*) Fordham.

***Limits of Law: Essays on Democratic Governance.** Peter H. Schuck. LC 99-45395. (New Perspectives on Law, Culture & Society Ser.). 1999. 32.00 (*0-8133-6758-1*) Westview.

Limits of Law: The Public Regulation of Private Pollution. Peter C. Yeager. (Illus.). 383p. (C). 1991. text 64.95 (*0-521-36535-X*) Cambridge U Pr.

Limits of Law: The Public Regulation of Private Pollution. Peter C. Yeager. (Illus.). 383p. (C). 1993. pap. text 20.95 (*0-521-44881-6*) Cambridge U Pr.

Limits of Law-Based School Reform: Vain Hopes & False Promises. Todd A. DeMitchell & Richard Fossey. LC 96-61338. 210p. 1997. 39.95 (*1-56676-482-3*, 764823) Scarecrow.

Limits of Law Enforcement. Hans Zeisel. LC 82-8644. (Illus.). 262p. (C). 1983. 24.00 (*0-226-97901-6*) U Ch Pr.

Limits of Liability: Keeping the Floodgates Shut. Ed. by J. Spier. LC 95-42620. (ENG & FRE.). 1996. 65.50 (*90-411-0169-1*) Kluwer Law Intl.

Limits of Liberalism: The Making of Canadian Sociology. Deborah Harrison. 137p. 1981. 38.99 (*0-919619-21-5*, Pub. by Black Rose); pap. 9.99 (*0-919619-22-3*, Pub. by Black Rose) Consort Bk Sales.

Limits of Liberalization: Regulatory Cooperations & the New Transatlantic Agenda. (American Institute for Contemporary German Studies). 50p. 1997. 7.50 (*1-57181-983-5*) Berghahn Bks.

Limits of Liberty: American History, 1607-1992. 2nd ed. Maldwyn A. Jones. (Short Oxford History of the Modern World Ser.). (Illus.). 744p. (C). 1995. pap. text 31.95 (*0-19-820572-4*); 84.95 (*0-19-820571-6*) OUP.

***Limits of Liberty: Between Anarchy & Leviathan.** James M. Buchanan. LC 99-24059. (Collected Works of James M. Buchanan : Vol. 7). 2000. 20.00 (*0-86597-225-7*) Liberty Fund.

Limits of Liberty: Between Anarchy & Leviathan. James M. Buchanan. LC 74-11616. 222p. 1977. reprint ed. pap. text 16.95 (*0-226-07820-5*, P714) U Ch Pr.

***Limits of Liberty Vol. 7: Between Anarchy & Leviathan.** James M. Buchanan. LC 99-24059. (Collected Works of James M. Buchanan). 2000. pap. 12.00 (*0-86597-226-5*) Liberty Fund.

Limits of Life. Ed. by Cyril Ponnamperuma & Lynn Margulis. 200p. 1980. lib. bdg. 75.00 (*90-277-1155-0*) Kluwer Academic.

Limits of Litigation: The Dalkon Shield Controversy. Ronald J. Bacigal. LC 90-81011. 160p. 1990. 25.00 (*0-89089-391-8*); pap. 12.75 (*0-89089-392-6*) Carolina Acad Pr.

Limits of Liturgical Innovation in Light of Martin Luther's "Exhortation . . . (1525)" James Heiser. 16p. 1998. pap. 2.00 (*1-891469-15-0*) Repristination.

Limits of Lockean Rights in Property. Gopal Sreenivasan. 176p. 1995. text 35.00 (*0-19-509176-0*) OUP.

Limits of Logic: Higher-Order Logic & the Lowenheim-Skolem Theorem. Ed. by Stewart Shapiro. (International Research Library of Philosophy). (Illus.). 540p. 1996. text 194.95 (*1-85521-731-7*, Pub. by Dartmth Pub) Ashgate Pub Co.

Limits of Love: Some Theological Explorations. Gilbert C. Meilaender. LC 87-42548. 156p. 1992. 30.00 (*0-271-00611-0*); pap. text 12.95 (*0-271-00862-8*); pap. text 12.95 (*0-271-00790-7*) Pa St U Pr.

Limits of "Love Devine" W. Stephen Gunter. (Wesleyan/Methodist Studies). 1996. pap. 15.95 (*0-687-21856-X*) Abingdon.

Limits of Mathematics: A Course on Information Theory & the Limits of Formal Reasoning. Gregorg J. Chaitin. LC 97-36103. (Springer Series in Discrete Mathematics & Theoretical Computer Science). (Illus.). 160p. 1998. 32.00 (*981-3083-59-X*, Pub. by Spr-Verlag) Spr-Verlag.

Limits of Medicine: How Science Shapes Our Hope for the Cure. Edward S. Golub. LC 96-45668. 1997. pap. 14.95 (*0-226-30207-5*) U Ch Pr.

Limits of Miracles: Poems about the Loss of Babies. Compiled by Marion Deutsche Cohen. LC 84-16813. 52p. 1984. 16.95 (*0-89789-066-3*, Bergin & Garvey) Greenwood.

Limits of Morality. Shelly Kagan. (Oxford Ethics Ser.). 432p. 1989. 65.00 (*0-19-824913-6*) OUP.

Limits of Morality. Shelly Kagan. (Oxford Ethics Ser.). 428p. 1991. reprint ed. pap. text 26.00 (*0-19-823916-5*) OUP.

Limits of Moralizing: Pathos & Subjectivity in Spenser & Milton. David Mikics. 1994. 42.50 (*0-8387-5285-3*) Bucknell U Pr.

Limits of Multiculturalism: Interrogating the Origins of American Anthropology. Scott Michaelsen. 280p. 1999. pap. 19.95 (*0-8166-3247-2*, Pub. by U of Minn Pr); lib. bdg. 49.95 (*0-8166-3246-4*, Pub. by U of Minn Pr) Chicago Distribution Ctr.

Limits of National Liberation: Economic Management & the Reunification of the Democratic Republic of Vietnam. Adam Forde. LC 87-8977. 192p. 1987. 55.00 (*0-7099-1036-3*, Pub. by C Helm) Routldge.

Limits of Organization. Kenneth Joseph Arrow. (Fels Center of Government Ser.). 86p. (C). 1974. pap. text 9.25 (*0-393-09323-9*) Norton.

Limits of Organizational Change. rev. ed. Herbert Kaufman. LC 94-16492. 144p. (C). 1994. pap. 24.95 (*1-56000-768-0*) Transaction Pubs.

Limits of Participation: Women & the Civic Life in the Greek East in the Hellenistic & Roman Periods. Riet Van Bremen. LC 96-176186. (Dutch Monographs on Ancient History & Archaeology: No. XV). 417p. 1996. lib. bdg. 97.00 (*90-5063-567-9*, Pub. by Gieben) J Benjamins Pubng Co.

Limits of Perception. limited ed. Anselm Stalder.Tr. of Der Umfang des Fassungsvermogens. (ENG & GER., Illus.). 72p. 1984. 55.00 (*0-935875-01-8*) P Blum Edit.

Limits of Perfection: A Conversation with J. Lawrence Burkholder. 2nd ed. Ed. by Rodney J. Sawatsky & Scott Holland. LC 96-36237. 154p. 1996. pap. 10.00 (*0-9698762-2-X*, Pub. by Pandora) Routldge.

Limits of Permissiveness in Art. Herbert E. Read. 50p. 1968. pap. 1.00 (*0-8477-2105-1*) U of PR Pr.

Limits of Persuasion: Germany & the Yugoslav Crisis, 1991-1992. Michael Libal. LC 97-2246. 224p. 1997. 59.95 (*0-275-95798-5*, Praeger Pubs) Greenwood.

Limits of Planning. (Analysis Ser.). 1980. pap. 18.00 (*0-938526-02-2*) Inst Analysis.

Limits of Political Science. Nevil Johnson. 150p. 1989. text 39.95 (*0-19-827341-X*) OUP.

Limits of Politics: Collective Goods & Political Change in Post-Industrial Societies. Roger Benjamin. LC 79-19473. (Illus.). 1982. pap. text 7.95 (*0-226-04234-0*) U Ch Pr.

Limits of Politics: Collective Goods & Political Change in Postindustrial Societies. Roger W. Benjamin. LC 79-19473. (Illus.). 162p. reprint ed. pap. 50.30 (*0-608-09385-8*, 205413000004); reprint ed. pap. 50.00 (*0-608-21008-0*, 205453600003) Bks Demand.

Limits of Power: Great Fires & the Process of City Growth in America. Christine Rosen. 418p. 1986. text 89.95 (*0-521-30319-2*) Cambridge U Pr.

Limits of Power: The Nixon & Ford Administrations. John R. Greene. LC 91-47014. (America Since World War II Ser.). 312p. Date not set. reprint ed. pap. 96.80 (*0-608-20546-X*, 205446000002) Bks Demand.

Limits of Power: The United States in Vietnam. Ed. by Choices for 21st Century Education Project. (Choices for the 21st Century Ser.). 114p. (YA). (gr. 9-12). 1993. pap. text 14.00 (*1-891306-14-6*) Watson Inst Intl.

Limits of Predictability. Ed. by Yurii A. Kravtsov. LC 93-7284. (Synergetics Ser.: Vol. 60). 1993. 88.95 (*0-387-56277-X*) Spr-Verlag.

Limits of Principle: Deciding Who Lives & What Dies. Tom Koch. LC 98-23553. 192p. 1998. 35.00 (*0-275-96407-8*, Praeger Pubs) Greenwood.

***Limits of Privacy.** Amitai Etzioni. 288p. 2000. pap. text 16.00 (*0-465-04090-X*, Pub. by Basic) HarpC.

Limits of Privacy. Amital Etzioni. LC 98-47082. 280p. 1999. 25.00 (*0-465-04089-6*, Pub. by Basic) HarpC.

Limits of Privatization. Paul Starr. 20p. (Orig.). 1987. 10.00 (*0-944826-01-6*) Economic Policy Inst.

Limits of Professional Power: National Health Care in the Federal Republic of Germany. Deborah A. Stone. LC 80-16864. (Illus.). 244p. 1995. 25.50 (*0-226-77553-4*) U Ch Pr.

Limits of Professional Power: National Health Care in the Federal Republic of Germany. Deborah A. Stone. LC 80-16864. 224p. reprint ed. pap. 69.50 (*0-608-09541-9*, 205434300005) Bks Demand.

Limits of Property Rights Libertarianism. Ann Levey. 1998. text 34.95 (*0-8133-2020-8*) Westview.

Limits of Property Rights Libertarianism. Ann Levey. (C). 1999. pap. text 14.95 (*0-8133-2021-6*) Westview.

Limits of Public Choice: A Sociological Critique of the Economic Theory of Politics. Lars Udehn. LC 95-19892. 464p. (C). 1995. 110.00 (*0-415-08273-0*); pap. 32.99 (*0-415-12512-X*) Routledge.

Limits of Racial Domination: Plebeian Society in Colonial Mexico City, 1660-1720. R. Douglas Cope. LC 93-23344. 1994. 50.00 (*0-299-14040-7*); pap. 19.95 (*0-299-14044-X*) U of Wis Pr.

Limits of Rationality. Ed. by Karen S. Cook & Margaret Levi. 432p. 1993. lib. bdg. 49.95 (*0-226-74238-5*) U Ch Pr.

Limits of Rationality. Ed. by Karen S. Cook & Margaret Levi. 438p. 1998. pap. text 23.95 (*0-226-74239-3*) U Ch Pr.

Limits of Rationality: An Essay on the Social & Moral Thought of Max Weber. Rogers Brubaker. LC 83-15152. (Controversies in Sociology Ser.: No. 16). 119p. 1984. text 34.95 (*0-04-301172-1*); pap. text 16.95 (*0-04-301173-X*) Routledge.

Limits of Rawlsian Justice. Roberto Alejandro. LC 97-165585. 248p. 1997. text 39.95 (*0-8018-5678-7*) Johns Hopkins.

Limits of Realism: Chinese Fiction in the Revolutionary Period. Marston Anderson. 1989. 50.00 (*0-520-06436-4*, Pub. by U CA Pr) Cal Prin Full Svc.

Limits of Reason: Indeterminacy in Law, Education, & Morality. John A. Eisenberg. 183p. (C). 1992. 34.95 (*1-56000-017-1*) Transaction Pubs.

Limits of Reason: The German Democratic Press & the Collapse of Weimar Democracy. Modris Eksteins. (Oxford Historical Monographs). (C). 1975. 45.00 (*0-19-821862-1*) OUP.

***Limits of Reductionism in Biology.** Gregory Bock et al. LC 98-2779. (Novartis Foundation Symposium Ser.: Vol. 213). 238p. 1998. 128.00 (*0-471-97770-5*) Wiley.

Limits of Reform: The Ministry of Internal Affairs in Imperial Russia, 1802-1881. Daniel T. Orlovsky. LC 80-18868. (Russian Research Center Studies: No. 81). 311p. 1981. reprint ed. pap. 96.50 (*0-7837-4708-X*, 205906000002) Bks Demand.

Limits of Reform: Women, Capital & Welfare. Jennifer G. Schirmer. 210p. 1982. 22.95 (*0-87073-229-3*); pap. 13.95 (*0-87073-255-2*) Schenkman Bks Inc.

Limits of Reform in the Enlightenment: Attitudes Toward the Education of the Lower Classes in Eighteenth-Century France. Harvey Chisick. LC 80-7512. 341p. 1981. reprint ed. pap. 105.80 (*0-7837-9317-0*, 206005700004) Bks Demand.

Limits of Religious Community: Expulsion from the Religious Community Within the Qumran Sect, Within Rabbinic Judaism, & Within Primitive Christianity. Goran Forkman. (Coniectanea Biblica. New Testament Ser.: No. 5). 257p. (Orig.). 1972. pap. 48.00 (*0-317-65807-7*) Coronet Bks.

Limits of Religious Thought Examined. Henry L. Mansel. LC 72-172840. reprint ed. 45.00 (*0-404-04182-5*) AMS Pr.

Limits of Royal Authority: Resistance & Obedience in Seventeenth-Century Castile. Ruth MacKay. LC 98-38428. (Cambridge Studies in Early Modern History). (Illus.). 200p. (C). 1999. text 59.95 (*0-521-64343-0*) Cambridge U Pr.

***Limits of Sayable.** Anthony Alofsin. 1998. 50.00 (*0-226-01506-8*) U Ch Pr.

***Limits of Science.** Ernest Krausz. LC 99-30286. (WPI Studies: Vol. 19). 192p. 2000. text 46.95 (*0-8204-4537-1*) P Lang Pubng.

Limits of Science. Nicholas Rescher. LC 99-6562. 280p. 1999. pap. 19.95 (*0-8229-5713-2*) U of Pittsburgh Pr.

Limits of Scientific Psychiatry: The Role of Uncertainty in Mental Health. John O. Beahrs. LC 86-11692. 250p. 1986. text 39.95 (*0-87630-420-X*) Brunner-Mazel.

Limits of Scientific Reasoning. David Faust. LC 84-5172. 226p. 1984. pap. 17.95 (*0-8166-1359-1*) U of Minn Pr.

Limits of Scripture: Vivekananda's Reinterpretation of the Authority of the Vedas. Anantanand Rambachan. LC 93-44277. 186p. 1993. text 31.00 (*0-8248-1542-4*) UH Pr.

Limits of Settlement Growth: A Theoretical Outline. Roland Fletcher. (New Studies in Archaeology). (Illus.). 302p. (C). 1995. text 85.00 (*0-521-43085-2*) Cambridge U Pr.

Limits of Sino-Russian Strategic Partnership. Jennifer Anderson. LC U162.A3 no. 315. (Adelphi Papers: No. 315). (Illus.). 96p. 1998. pap. text 28.95 (*0-19-829427-1*) OUP.

Limits of Sisterhood: The Beecher Sisters on Women's Rights & Woman's Sphere. Jeanne Boydston et al. LC 87-19771. (Gender & American Culture Ser.). (Illus.). xxvi, 369p. (C). 1988. pap. 24.95 (*0-8078-4207-9*) U of NC Pr.

***Limits of Social Cohesion: Conflict & Mediation in Pluralist Societies: A Report of the Bertelsmann Foundation to the Club of Rome.** Ed. by Peter L. Berger. 416p. 1999. pap. text 26.00 (*0-8133-6719-0*, Pub. by Westview) HarpC.

Limits of Social Democracy: Investment Politics in Sweden. Jonas Pontusson. LC 92-2694. (Cornell Studies in Political Economy). (Illus.). 272p. 1992. text 39.95 (*0-8014-2652-9*) Cornell U Pr.

Limits of Social Democracy: Investment Politics in Sweden. Jonas Pontusson. LC 92-2694. (Studies in Political Economy). (Illus.). 272p. 1994. pap. text 17.95 (*0-8014-8235-6*) Cornell U Pr.

Limits of Social Policy. Nathan Glazer. LC 88-4029. 240p. 1988. 37.95 (*0-674-53443-3*) HUP.

Limits of Social Policy. Nathan Glazer. (Illus.). 240p. 1998. pap. 16.00 (*0-674-53444-1*) HUP.

Limits of Software: People, Project & Perspectives. Robert Britcher. LC 99-24951. (Illus.). 240p. (C). 1999. pap. text 24.95 (*0-201-43323-0*) Addison-Wesley.

Limits of Soviet Power in the Developing World. Ed. by Edward A. Kolodziej & Roger E. Kanet. LC 88-11716. 551p. reprint ed. pap. 170.90 (*0-608-06072-0*, 206640400008) Bks Demand.

Limits of State Action. Wilhelm von Humboldt. Ed. by J. W. Burrow. LC 92-33512. lxii, 162p. 1993. 19.50 (*0-86597-108-0*); pap. 7.50 (*0-86597-109-9*) Liberty Fund.

Limits of State Autonomy: Post-Revolutionary Mexico. Nora Hamilton. LC 82-47596. 411p. 1982. reprint ed. pap. 127.50 (*0-608-03750-8*, 206457400009) Bks Demand.

Limits of Sympathy: Gabrielle Roy's The Tin Flute. Patrick Coleman. (Canadian Fiction Studies: No. 26). 120p. (C). 1993. pap. text 14.95 (*1-55022-135-3*, Pub. by ECW) Genl Dist Srvs.

Limits of Technocratic Politics. Jeffrey D. Straussman. LC 76-1774. 164p. 1978. 39.95 (*0-87855-173-5*); pap. 24.95 (*0-87855-625-7*) Transaction Pubs.

Limits of the City. 2nd rev. ed. Murray Bookchin. 194p. 1986. 46.99 (*0-920057-34-9*, Pub. by Black Rose); pap. 17.99 (*0-920057-64-0*, Pub. by Black Rose) Consort Bk Sales.

Limits of the Coercive Diplomacy. 2nd ed. Ed. by Alexander L. George. 310p. (C). 1993. pap. 33.00 (*0-8133-1787-8*, Pub. by Westview) HarpC.

Limits of the Criminal Sanction. Herbert L. Packer. LC 68-26780. 397p. reprint ed. pap. 30.00 (*0-608-08907-9*, 2069542) Bks Demand.

Limits of the Global Village: Globalization, Nations & the State. LC 96-183976. (World Development Studies: No. 5). 68p. pap. 12.00 (*952-9520-28-X*) UN.

Limits of the Law of Obligations. Ed. by Daniel Visser. 1998. 52.50 (*0-7021-4131-3*, Pub. by Juta & Co) Gaunt.

Limits of the Novel: Evolutions of a Form from Chauser to Robbe-Grillet. David I. Grossvogel. LC 68-16381. 347p. 1968. 20.00 (*0-8014-0162-3*) Lib Soc Sci.

***Limits of the Rule of Law in China.** Karen G. Turner. LC 99-16512. Vol. 14. 384p. 2000. 65.00 (*0-295-97907-0*) U of Wash Pr.

Limits of the Sensible World. James Sallis. (Illus.). 84p. (Orig.). 1995. pap. text 7.50 (*0-924047-11-9*) Host Pubns.

Limits of Theory. Ed. by Thomas M. Kavanagh. LC 88-24969. 272p. 1989. pap. 14.95 (*0-8047-1710-9*) Stanford U Pr.

Limits of Thought: Discussions Between J. Krishnamurti & David Bohm. J. Krishnamurti & David Bohm. Ed. by Ray McCoy. LC 98-35092. 144p. 1998. pap. 17.99 (*0-415-19398-2*, D6212) Routledge.

An Asterisk (*) at the beginning of an entry indicates that the title is appearing for the first time.

Limits of Thought: Discussions Between J. Krishnamurti & David Bohm. J. Krishnamurti & David Bohm. Ed. by Ray McCoy. LC 98-35092. 144p. (C). (gr. 13). 1998. 60.00 (0-415-19397-4, D6208) Routledge.

Limits of Tolerance: Censorship & Intellectual Freedom in Public Libraries. Anny Curry. LC 96-31670. 272p. 1997. 39.50 (0-8108-3224-0) Scarecrow.

Limits of Tolerance: Freedom of Expression & the Public Debate in Chile. Human Rights Watch Staff. 206p. 1998. pap. 15.00 (1-56432-192-4) Hum Rts Watch.

Limits of Trade Union Militancy: The Lancashire Textile Workers, 1910-1914, 5. Joseph L. White. LC 77-87965. (Contributions in Labor History Ser.: No. 5). (Illus.). 258p. 1978. 59.95 (0-313-20029-7, WLT/, Greenwood Pr) Greenwood.

Limits of Trust: Cryptography, Governments, & Electronic Commerce. Stewart A. Baker & Paul R. Hurst. LC 98-26470. 1998. 125.00 (90-411-0635-9) Kluwer Law Intl.

Limits of Victory: The Ratification of the Panama Canal Treaties. George D. Moffett, III. LC 84-14920. 263p. reprint ed. pap. 81.60 (0-608-20924-4, 207202300003) Bks Demand.

Limits of Vision. Robert Irwin. 120p. 1997. pap. 8.99 (1-873982-10-0, Pub. by Dedalus) Subterranean Co.

Limits of Visual Perception. Cronly-Dillon. 1991. 137.00 (0-8493-7505-3, QP464) CRC Pr.

Limits of Voice. Luiz Costa-Lima. Tr. by Paulo H. Britto. LC 95-36712. 375p. 1996. 49.50 (0-8047-2540-3) Stanford U Pr.

Limits on Liberty: The Experience of Mennonite, Hutterite, & Doukhobor Communities in Canada. William Janzen. 380p. 1990. text 39.95 (0-8020-2731-8) U of Toronto Pr.

Limits to Autocracy: From Sung Neo-Confucianism to a Doctrine of Political Rights. Alan T. Wood. LC 95-9836. 1995. text 36.00 (0-8248-1703-6) UH Pr.

Limits to Bureaucratic Growth. Marshall Meyer et al. (Studies in Organization: No. 3). x, 259p. 1985. 52.95 (3-11-009865-2) De Gruyter.

Limits to Capital. David Harvey. 1999. 60.00 (1-85984-714-5, Pub. by Verso); pap. text 18.00 (1-85984-209-7, Pub. by Verso) Norton.

Limits to Capital. David Harvey. LC 82-40322. (Midway Reprint Ser.). xviii, 478p. 1995. reprint ed. pap. text 30.00 (0-226-31954-7) U Ch Pr.

Limits to Certainty. 2nd rev. ed. Orio Giarini. (International Studies in the Service Economy). 296p. (C). 1993. lib. bdg. 158.50 (0-7923-2167-7) Kluwer Academic.

Limits to Certainty: Facing Risks in the New Service Economy. Orio Giarini & Walter R. Stahel. (C). 1989. lib. bdg. 118.00 (0-7923-0468-3, Pub. by Graham & Trotman) Kluwer Academic.

Limits to Competition. Group of Lisbon Staff. (Illus.). 189p. 1996. 30.00 (0-262-07164-9) MIT Pr.

Limits to Dissent. David Farhi. 4.00 (0-686-26003-1) The Aspen Inst.

Limits to International Indebetedness. Ed. by Armin Gutowski & Manfred Holthus. 250p. 1988. pap. 24.95 (0-88738-678-4) Transaction Pubs.

Limits to Medicine: Medical Nemenis: The Expropriation of Health. Ivan Illich. 312p. 1999. reprint ed. pap. 17.95 (0-7145-2993-1, Pub. by M Boyars Pubs) LPC InBook.

Limits to Parallel Computation: P-Completeness Theory. Raymond Greenlaw et al. (Illus.). 320p. 1995. text 65.00 (0-19-508591-4) OUP.

Limits to Satisfaction: An Essay on the Problem of Needs & Commodities. William Leiss. 184p. (C). 1988. reprint ed. pap. 19.95 (0-7735-0688-8, Pub. by McG-Queens Univ Pr) CUP Services.

Limits to Soviet Power. Ed. by Rajan Menon & Daniel N. Nelson. 230p. 1997. reprint ed. pap. text 15.00 (0-7881-5021-9) DIANE Pub.

Limits to Structural Change: A Comparative Study of Foreign Direct Investments in Liberia & Ghana, 1950-71. Jerker Carlsson. 299p. 1981. write for info. (91-7106-190-8, Pub. by Nordic Africa) Transaction Pubs.

Limits to the Welfare State: An Inquiry into the Realizability of Socio-Economic & Political Desiderata in a Highly Industrialized Society. G. J. Van Driel et al. 1980. lib. bdg. 111.00 (0-89838-026-X) Kluwer Academic.

***Limners: America's Earliest Portrait Painters.** Leonard Everett Fisher. LC 99-33369. (Colonial Craftsmen Ser.). (gr. 4-7). 1999. 21.36 (0-7614-0932-7) Marshall Cavendish.

Limning the Psyche: Explorations in Christian Psychology. Ed. by Robert C. Roberts & Mark R. Talbot. LC 97-14456. 382p. 1997. pap. 24.00 (0-8028-4331-X) Eerdmans.

Limnocharitaceae. Robert R. Haynes & Lauritz Holm-Nielsen. (Flora Neotropica Monographs: No. 56). (Illus.). 34p. 1992. pap. text 16.00 (0-89327-369-4) NY Botanical.

Limnoecology: The Ecology of Lakes & Streams. Winfried Lampert & Ulrich Sommer. Tr. by James G. Haney. (Illus.). 400p. (C). 1997. text 59.95 (0-19-509592-8) OUP.

Limnofauna Europaea: A Checklist of the Animals Inhabiting European Inland Waters, with Accounts of Their Distribution & Ecology (Except Protozoa) Ed. by Joachim Illies. xviii, 532p. 1978. text 236.25 (90-265-0275-3) Swets.

Limnologic Studies in Middle America, with a Chapter on Aztec Limnology. Edward S. Deevey, Jr. (Connecticut Academy of Arts & Sciences Ser., Trans.: Vol. 39). 1957. pap. 69.50 (0-685-22895-9) Elliots Bks.

Limnological Analyses. 2nd ed. Robert G. Wetzel & Gene E. Likens. (Illus.). 391p. 1996. 49.95 (0-387-97331-1) Spr-Verlag.

***Limnological Analysis.** 3rd ed. Robert G. Wetzel & Gene E. Likens. LC 99-42459. 448p. 2000. 49.95 (0-387-98928-5) Spr-Verlag.

Limnological Studies of the Island Area of Western Lake Erie. N. Wilson Britt et al. (Bulletin New Ser.: Vol. 4, No. 3). 1973. pap. text 3.00 (0-86727-062-4) Ohio Bio Survey.

Limnologie: L'Etude des Eaux Continentales. 2nd ed. Bernard Dussart. (FRE., Illus.). 680p. 1992. lib. bdg. 180.00 (2-85004-067-3, Pub. by Editions Boubees) Lubrecht & Cramer.

Limnologie der Donau. (GER.). viii, 648p. 1967. 36.00 (3-510-99052-8, Pub. by E Schweizerbartsche) Balogh.

Limnology. 2nd ed. Alexander J. Horne & Charles R. Goldman. LC 93-38109. 480p. (C). 1994. 88.44 (0-07-023673-9) McGraw.

Limnology. 2nd ed. Robert G. Wetzel. 767p. (C). 1983. text 90.50 (0-03-057913-9, Pub. by SCP) Harcourt.

Limnology. 3rd ed. Horne. 2001. 61.00 (0-07-229717-4) McGraw.

***Limnology.** 3rd ed. Robert G. Wetzel. 700p. 1999. 64.95 (0-12-744760-1) Morgan Kaufmann.

Limnology & Fisheries of Georgian Bay & the North Channel Ecosystems. Ed. by M. Munawar. (Developments in Hydrobiology Ser.). 1988. text 245.00 (90-6193-653-5) Kluwer Academic.

Limnology & Marine Biology in the Sudan. Ed. by H. J. Dumont et al. (Developments in Hydrobiology Ser.). 1984. text 289.00 (90-6193-772-8) Kluwer Academic.

Limnology & Remote Sensing: A Contemporary Approach. Ed. by K. Kondratyev et al. LC 98-52345. (Series in Remote Sensing). 400p. 1999. 139.00 (1-85233-112-7) Spr-Verlag.

Limnology, Climatology & Paleoclimatology of the East African Lakes. Ed. by Thomas C. Johnson & Eric O. Odada. 456p. 1996. text 84.00 (2-88449-234-8) Gordon & Breach.

Limnology in Australia. Ed. by P. De Deckker & W. D. Williams. (Monographiae Biologicae). 1986. text 278.50 (90-6193-578-4) Kluwer Academic.

Limnology in Wisconsin: An Original Anthology. Ed. by Frank N. Egerton, 3rd. LC 77-74203. (History of Ecology Ser.). (Illus.). 1978. lib. bdg. 63.95 (0-405-10373-5) Ayer.

Limnology Now: Paradigm of Planetary Problems. Ed. by Ramon Margalef. LC 94-3431. 572p. 1994. 220.50 (0-444-89826-3) Elsevier.

Limnology of Eifel Maar Lakes. Ed. by Burkhard W. Scharf & Sven Bjork. (Advances in Limnology Ser.: Vol. 38). (GER., Illus.). viii, 348p. 1992. pap. text 88.00 (3-510-47039-7, Pub. by E Schweizerbartsche) Balogh.

***Limnology of Humic Waters.** J. Keskitalo & P. Eloranta. (Illus.). 292p. 1999. 93.00 (90-5782-029-3, Pub. by Backhuys Pubs) Balogh.

Limnology of Mountain Lakes. Ed. by J. Fott. LC 93-44968. (Developments in Hydrobiology Ser.). 196p. (C). 1994. text 169.50 (0-7923-2640-7) Kluwer Academic.

***Limo.** Dan Jenkins. 2000. 19.95 (0-942627-68-7); pap. 12.95 (0-942627-70-9) Woodford Pubng.

***Limoges Boxes: A Complete Guide.** Faye Strumpf. LC 99-67649. (Illus.). 176p. 2000. pap. 29.95 (0-87341-837-9, LIMO) Krause Pubns.

Limoges City Plan. (Gräfocarte Maps Ser.). 1996. 8.95 (2-7416-0018-X, 80018) Michelin.

***Limoges Porcelain Box: From Snuff to Sentiments.** Joanne Furio et al. LC 98-66712. 240p. 1998. write for info. (0-9664817-0-4) Lake Warren Pr.

Limon, Colorado: Hub City of the High Plains, 1888-1952. James E. Fell, Jr. LC 97-72248. (Illus.). 64p. 1997. pap. 9.35 (0-9658428-0-0) Limon.

***Limor Livnat: The Leading Lady in Israeli Politics Speaks Her Mind.** Limor Livnat. LC 99-35018. 135p. 1999. 16.95 (965-229-222-2) Gefen Pub Hse.

Limot Hol: Daily Prayer Book (Kol Haneshamah) Ed. by David A. Teutsch. 300p. 1996. 28.00 (0-935457-47-X) Reconstructionist Pr.

Limousine. N. T. Morley. (Orig.). 1997. mass mkt. 6.95 (1-56333-555-7) Masquerade.

Limousine Seventeen. Sharon Hebl. Ed. by Lisa Hebl. LC 96-68966. (Illus.). 300p. (Orig.). (YA). 1997. pap. 15.00 (0-9638995-1-1) Roller Coaster.

***Limp Bizkit.** Colin Devenish. LC 00-39061. 192p. 2000. pap. 12.95 (0-312-26349-X, St Martin Griffin) St Martin.

Limpiar el Colon (Colon Cleanse) Vena Burnett & Jennifer Weiss. (SPA.). 1985. pap. 3.95 (0-913923-51-6) Woodland UT.

***Limpieza de Sangre.** Arturo Perez-Reverte. (Capitan Alatriste Ser.: Vol. 2). 251p. (YA). 1998. pap. 14.95 (84-204-8359-1) Santillana.

Limpieza Interna. Carlson Wade. 352p. (C). 1997. pap. text 12.95 (0-13-863770-9) P-H.

***Limpieza Interna: Como Librarse de la Contaminacion en los Musculos, las Arterias, y las Articul.** Carlson Wade. (SPA.). 2000. pap. 14.00 (0-7352-0191-9) PH Pr.

Limping Towards the Sunrise. 1996. pap. 11.00 (0-7152-0711-3) St Mut.

Limpy's Homemade Sausage: For the Hunter & the Homemaker. S. G. Pierce. (Illus.). 82p. 1998. pap. 15.95 (1-57188-170-0) F Amato Pubns.

LIMS: Implementation Management. Allen S. Nakagawa. 180p. 1994. 73.00 (0-85186-824-X, R6824) CRC Pr.

Limuria: The Lesser Dependencies of Maritius. Robert Scott. LC 75-3741. (Illus.). 1976. reprint ed. lib. bdg. 69.50 (0-8371-8058-9, SCLIM, Greenwood Pr) Greenwood.

Lin Biao & the Gang of Four: Contra-Confucianism in Historical & Intellectual Perspectives. Tien-Wei Wu. LC 82-10292. (Illus.). 296p. 1983. 31.95 (0-8093-1022-8) S Ill U Pr.

Lin Carter: A Look Behind His Imaginary Worlds. Robert M. Price. LC 93-242547. (Starmont Studies in Literary Criticism: No. 36). vi, 172p. 1991. pap. 21.00 (1-55742-229-X) Millefleurs.

Lin Chun: Grizzly Dancer, 4 bks., Bk. 3. Tom Gilmore. 64p. (Orig.). 1990. pap. 1.98 (1-879352-22-2) Mini-Novel Pub.

Lin Chun: Quest for Identity, 4 bks., Bk. 4. Tom Gilmore. 64p. (Orig.). (C). 1990. pap. 1.98 (1-879352-23-0) Mini-Novel Pub.

Lin Chun: The Cynic of Yangshuo, 4 bks., Bk. 1. Tom Gilmore. 64p. (Orig.). (C). 1990. pap. 1.98 (1-879352-20-6) Mini-Novel Pub.

Lin Chun: Tong War at Chinese Camp, 4 bks., Bk. 2. Tom Gilmore. 64p. (Orig.). (C). 1990. pap. 1.98 (1-879352-21-4) Mini-Novel Pub.

Lin Emery: Borrowing the Forces of Nature. Edward Lucie-Smith. (Illus.). 64p. 1996. pap. 19.95 (0-89494-055-4) New Orleans Mus Art.

Lin Family of Sinapore. M. H. Finlay. (Illus.). 280p. (YA). (gr. 7-10). 1982. 9.75 (0-7399-0133-8, 2308) Rod & Staff.

Lin He-Jing: Recluse Poet of Orphan Mountain. Lin He-Jing. Tr. by Paul Hansen. 44p. 1993. 25.00 (0-918116-73-2) Brooding Heron Pr.

Lin He-Jing's Art of Poetry. Lin He-Jing. Tr. by Paul Hansen from CHI. (Illus.). 28p. 1997. pap. 8.00 (1-890654-03-5) Wood Work.

Lin He-Jing's Art of Poetry. aut. ed. Lin He-Jing. Tr. by Paul Hansen from CHI. (Illus.). 28p. 1997. 25.00 (1-890654-07-8) Wood Work.

Lin McLean. Owen Wister. 1998. mass mkt. 4.99 (0-8125-8044-3, Pub. by Forge NYC) St Martin.

Lin McLean. Owen Wister. LC 76-104600. (Illus.). 292p. reprint ed. lib. bdg. 39.50 (0-8398-2174-3) Irvington.

Lin Piao Affair: Power, Politics & Military Coup. Ed. by Michael Y. Kau. LC 73-92807. 669p. reprint ed. 200.00 (0-8357-9436-9, 201541200093) Bks Demand.

Lina. Martha Bueno. LC 95-83322. (Coleccion Caniqui). (SPA.). 175p. (Orig.). 1996. pap. 15.00 (0-89729-781-4) Ediciones.

Lina: Portrait of a Damascene Girl. Samar Attar. 217p. (Orig.). 1994. pap. 16.00 (0-89410-780-1, Three Contnts) L Rienner.

Lina Bo Bardi. Lina B. Bardi. (Illus.). 336p. 1996. pap. text 55.00 (88-86158-80-7, Pub. by Charta) Dist Art Pubs.

***Linac & Gamma Knife Radiosurgery.** Ed. by Isabelle M. Germano. Orig. Title: Stereotactic Radiosurgery. (Illus.). 1999. write for info. (1-879284-70-7) Am Assn Neuro.

Linac Radiosurgery: A Practical Guide. William A. Friedman & University of Florida Staff. LC 97-7619. 288p. 1997. 89.00 (0-387-94698-5) Spr-Verlag.

Linaceae. C. M. Rogers. LC 84-14891. (North American Flora Ser.: No. 2, Pt. 12). (Illus.). 58p. 1984. 10.75 (0-89327-260-4) NY Botanical.

Linajes y Oficios en Tres Entremeses del Siglo de Uro. Maria C. De Moux. (Iberian Studies: No. 7). (SPA.). 150p. (Orig.). 1996. pap. text 39.95 (1-889431-08-7) Univ Pr South.

Linchpin: French-German Relations, 1950-1990, 154. Julius W. Friend. Ed. by Walter Laqueur. LC 91-28631. (Washington Papers: No. 154). 160p. 1991. 55.00 (0-275-94257-0, C4257, Praeger Pubs); pap. 12.95 (0-275-94256-2, B4256, Praeger Pubs) Greenwood.

Lincoln. Victor Alba. LC 90-156584. (Memoria de La Historia Ser.). 1998. pap. 14.95 (84-320-4520-9) Planeta.

Lincoln. Amy Cohn & Suzy Schmidt. LC 96-48709. (J). 1999. write for info. (0-590-93566-6) Scholastic Inc.

Lincoln. David Herbert Donald. LC 95-4782. (Illus.). 599p. 1995. 35.00 (0-684-80846-3) S&S Trade.

Lincoln. David Herbert Donald. 720p. 1996. per. 17.00 (0-684-82535-X) S&S Trade.

Lincoln. David Herbert Donald. (Reading Group Guides Ser.). 1997. pap. write for info. (0-684-00446-1, Touchstone) S&S Trade Pap.

Lincoln. Jan Morris. 1999. 0.00 (0-375-50159-2) Random.

***Lincoln.** Random House Value Publishing Staff. 1999. pap. 5.00 (0-517-20742-7) Random Hse Value.

Lincoln. George Tice. LC 83-23002. 72p. 1984. 45.00 (0-8135-1045-7) Rutgers U Pr.

Lincoln. abr. ed. David H. Donald. 1995. audio. write for info. (0-671-53681-8, Pub. by S&S Audio) Lndmrk Audiobks.

Lincoln, Vol. 1. large type ed. David Herbert Donald. (Niagara Large Print Ser.). 733p. 1996. 29.50 (0-7089-5841-9) Ulverscroft.

Lincoln, Vol. 2. large type ed. David Herbert Donald. (Niagara Large Print Ser.). 695p. 1996. 29.50 (0-7089-5842-7) Ulverscroft.

***Lincoln: A Foreigner's Quest.** Jan Morris. LC 99-48516. 208p. 2000. 23.00 (0-684-85515-1) S&S Trade.

Lincoln: A Novel. Gore Vidal. 672p. 1985. mass mkt. 6.99 (0-345-31221-X) Ballantine Pub Grp.

***Lincoln: A Novel.** Gore Vidal. (Ace's Exambusters Ser.). 2000. pap. 16.00 (0-375-70876-6) Vin Bks.

Lincoln: A Novel. aut. ed. Gore Vidal. 1998. 21.00 (0-676-54646-3) Random.

Lincoln: A Novel. Gore Vidal. 1995. reprint ed. lib. bdg. 37.95 (1-56849-626-5) Buccaneer Bks.

***Lincoln: A Photobiography.** 2000. 9.95 (1-56137-517-9) Novel Units.

Lincoln: A Photobiography. Russell Freedman. (Illus.). 160p. (J). (gr. 4 up). 1987. 18.00 (0-89919-380-3, Clarion Bks) HM.

Lincoln: A Photobiography. Russell Freedman. (Illus.). 160p. (J). (gr. 4 up). 1989. pap. 7.95 (0-395-51848-2, Clarion Bks) HM.

Lincoln: A Photobiography. Russell Freedman. (Illus.). 1987. 13.05 (0-606-01729-1, Pub. by Turtleback) Demco.

Lincoln: A Pictorial History. Edward Steers, Jr. (Illus.). 135p. (C). 1994. pap. text 12.95 (0-939631-66-0) Thomas Publications.

Lincoln: A Picture Story of His Life. (Illus.). 1981. 14.95 (0-918058-04-X) Authors Edn MA.

Lincoln: An Album of Photographs & Words. (Album Ser.: No. 3). 1976. pap. 7.95 (0-87130-053-2) Eakins.

Lincoln: An Illustrated Biography. Philip B. Kunhardt. (Illus.). 432p. 1994. pap. 30.00 (0-679-75563-2) Knopf.

***Lincoln: An Illustrated Biography.** Philip B. Kunhardt. LC 99-14880. 1999. 24.99 (0-517-20715-X) Random Hse Value.

Lincoln: Authoritarian Savior. Alexander J. Groth. LC 96-110203. 330p. 1995. pap. 12.50 (0-9647759-0-5) Groth Assocs.

Lincoln: Authoritarian Savior. Alexander J. Groth. LC 96-33245. 238p. 1997. pap. text 29.50 (0-7618-0478-1) U Pr of Amer.

Lincoln: In His Own Words. Ed. by Milton Melzer. LC 92-17431. (Illus.). 224p. (J). (gr. 3-7). 1993. 22.95 (0-15-245437-3) Harcourt.

Lincoln: Some Descendants of Stephen Lincoln of Wymondham, England; Edmund Larkin of England; Thomas Oliver of Bristol, England. W. E. Lincoln. 322p. 1993. reprint ed. pap. 49.50 (0-8328-3704-0); reprint ed. lib. bdg. 59.50 (0-8328-3703-2) Higginson Bk Co.

Lincoln: The Ancestry of Abraham Lincoln. J. H. Lea & J. R. Hutchinson. (Illus.). 310p. 1991. reprint ed. pap. 40.00 (0-8328-1819-4); reprint ed. lib. bdg. 50.00 (0-8328-1818-6) Higginson Bk Co.

***Lincoln: The Northeastern Pennsylvania Connection.** Aileen Sallom Freeman. LC 99-95164. (Illus.). 384p. 2000. pap. 14.95 (0-9644199-5-5, FOSI) Freeman Open Syst.

Lincoln: The Prairie Capital. James L. McKee. (Illus.). 123p. 1989. reprint ed. pap. 17.95 (0-934904-07-3) J & L Lee.

Lincoln: The Road to War. Frank Van Der Linden. LC 98-35214. (Illus.). 400p. 1998. 29.95 (1-55591-420-9) Fulcrum Pub.

Lincoln: Twenty Years on the Eastern Prairie. Donald G. Richter. (Illus.). 348p. 1999. 35.00 (0-9654976-2-3) Vermil.

***Lincoln, a Foreigner's Quest.** Jan Morris. LC 00-37745. 2000. pap. write for info. (0-7862-2624-2) Thorndike Pr.

Lincoln & Black Freedom: A Study in Presidential Leadership. LaWanda Cox. LC 84-16445. (Blacks in the New World Ser.). 272p. 1985. reprint ed. pap. 10.95 (0-252-01173-2) U of Ill Pr.

Lincoln & Black Freedom: A Study in Presidential Leadership. rev. ed. LaWanda Cox. LC 93-37859. 270p. (C). 1994. reprint ed. pap. 12.95 (0-87249-997-9) U of SC Pr.

Lincoln & Civil War Politics. Ed. by James A. Rawley. LC 77-8812. (American Problem Studies). 136p. 1977. reprint ed. pap. text 10.50 (0-88275-576-5) Krieger.

Lincoln & His Ancestors. Ida M. Tarbell. LC 97-1527. (Illus.). xxi, 434p. 1997. pap. 20.00 (0-8032-9430-1, Bison Books) U of Nebr Pr.

Lincoln & His Contemporaries. Ed. by Charles Hubbard. LC 98-50768. 176p. 1999. 27.95 (0-86554-627-4) Mercer Univ Pr.

***Lincoln & His Generals.** T. Harry Williams. LC 00-37571. 2000. pap. write for info. (0-517-16237-7) Bell T.

Lincoln & His Generals. T. Harry Williams. (YA). (gr. 9 up). 1967. pap. text 7.95 (0-07-553705-2) McGraw.

Lincoln & His Generals. Clarence E. Macartney. LC 70-124241. (Select Bibliographies Reprint Ser.). (Illus.). 1977. reprint ed. 18.95 (0-8369-5429-7) Ayer.

Lincoln & His Party in the Secession Crisis. David M. Potter. LC 95-23562. 440p. (C). 1995. pap. 19.95 (0-8071-2027-8) La State U Pr.

Lincoln & Liberty: The Emergence of a President. David E. Long. (Illus.). 400p. 1998. 29.95 (0-8117-0971-X) Stackpole.

Lincoln & Seward. Gideon Welles. LC 79-85082. (Select Bibliographies Reprint Ser.). 1977. 26.95 (0-8369-5081-X) Ayer.

Lincoln & Slavery. Peter Burchard. LC 98-12464. (Illus.). 208p. (J). (gr. 7 up). 1999. 17.00 (0-689-81570-0) S&S Childrens.

***Lincoln & the Abolition of Slavery (Civil War)** Russell Roberts. LC 99-23477. (American War Library). (Illus.). 144p. (YA). (gr. 6-9). 2000. lib. bdg. 23.70 (1-56006-580-X) Lucent Bks.

Lincoln & the Black Hawk War. Lloyd H. Efflandt. (Illus.). (Orig.). 1992. pap. text 4.95 (0-9617938-2-1) Rock Isl Arsenal Hist Soc.

Lincoln & the Bluegrass. William H. Townsend. LC 88-36669. (Illus.). 448p. 1990. pap. 19.00 (0-8131-0196-4) U Pr of Ky.

Lincoln & the Bluegrass. William H. Townsend. LC 88-36669. (Illus.). 448p. 1990. text 34.00 (0-8131-1687-2) U Pr of Ky.

Lincoln & the Common Law. Dan W. Bannister. 261p. (Orig.). 1992. pap. 12.95 (0-9623335-1-4) HSP IL.

Lincoln & the Economics of the American Dream. Gabor S. Boritt. LC 94-21005. 416p. 1994. reprint ed. 16.95 (0-252-06445-3) U of Ill Pr.

Lincoln & the First Shot. Richard N. Current. 230p. (C). 1990. reprint ed. pap. text 11.95 (0-88133-498-7) Waveland Pr.

Lincoln & the Illinois Supreme Court. Dan W. Bannister. Ed. by Barbara Hughett. LC 94-96808. (Illus.). 224p. 1995. 23.95 (0-9644649-0-X) D W Bannister.

***Lincoln & the Indians.** David A. Nichols. LC 99-37213. 2000. pap. 15.95 (0-252-06857-2) U of Ill Pr.

Lincoln & the Lady. Ted Gibbons. (Keepsake Bookcards Ser.). 21p. (YA). 1989. pap. text 2.50 (0-929985-11-7) Jackman Pubng.

An Asterisk (*) at the beginning of an entry indicates that the title is appearing for the first time.

Lincoln & the Negro. Benjamin Quarles. (Quality Paperbacks Ser.). (Illus.). 275p. 1991. reprint ed. pap. 13.95 (*0-306-80447-6*) Da Capo.

Lincoln & the Prairie After. Eloise B. Fink. LC 98-61212. (Illus.). 96p. (Orig.). 1999. pap. 7.95 (*0-939395-23-1*) Thorntree Pr.

Lincoln & the Preachers. Edgar D. Jones. (Biography Index Reprint Ser.). 1977. 23.95 (*0-8369-8018-2*) Ayer.

Lincoln & the Radicals. Thomas H. Williams. LC 41-53088. 429p. reprint ed. pap. 133.00 (*0-608-20485-4*, 207173700002) Bks Demand.

Lincoln & the Railroads. John W. Starr, Jr. Ed. by Stuart Bruchey. LC 80-1346. (Railroads Ser.). 1981. reprint ed. lib. bdg. 35.95 (*0-405-13817-2*) Ayer.

Lincoln & the South. James G. Randall. LC 80-22084. (Walter Lynwood Fleming Lectures in Southern History). (Illus.). 161p. 1980. reprint ed. lib. bdg. 55.00 (*0-313-22843-4*, RALS, Greenwood Pr) Greenwood.

Lincoln & the Tools of War. Robert V. Bruce. (Illus.). 400p. (Orig.). 1989. text 32.50 (*0-252-01665-3*); pap. text 15.95 (*0-252-06090-3*) U of Ill Pr.

Lincoln As a Lawyer. John Frank. 208p. 1996. reprint ed. 40.00 (*0-9625290-2-8*); reprint ed. pap. 20.00 (*0-9625290-4-4*) Abraham Lincoln.

Lincoln As a Lawyer: An Annotated Bibliography. Elizabeth W. Matthews. LC 90-39143. 272p. (C). 1991. 31.95 (*0-8093-1644-7*) S Ill U Pr.

Lincoln As I Knew Him: Gossip, Tributes & Revelations from His Best Friends & His Worst Enemies. Ed. & Compiled by Harold Holzer. LC 99-23450. 352p. 1999. 16.95 (*1-56512-166-X*, 72166) Algonquin Bks.

Lincoln Assassination in American History. Robert Somerlott. LC 97-23480. (In American History Ser.). (Illus.). 128p. (YA). (gr. 6 up). 1998. lib. bdg. 20.95 (*0-89490-886-3*) Enslow Pubs.

Lincoln at Gettysburg. William E. Barton. (History - United States Ser.). 263p. 1992. reprint ed. lib. bdg. 79.00 (*0-7812-6168-6*) Rprt Serv.

***Lincoln at Gettysburg: The Words That Remade America.** Garry Wills. LC 99-52704. 2000. 27.95 (*0-7838-8857-0*) Mac Lib Ref.

Lincoln at Gettysburg: The Words That Remade America. Garry Wills. 320p. 1993. per. 13.00 (*0-671-86742-3*) S&S Trade Pap.

***Lincoln at Home: Two Glimpses of Abraham Lincoln's Family Life.** David Herbert Donald. LC 00-41294. (Illus.). 2000. write for info. (*0-7432-0199-X*) S&S Trade.

***Lincoln at War: 1944 - 1966.** Mike Garbett & Brian Goulding. (Illus.). 2000. 34.95 (*0-7110-0847-7*, Pub. by Ian Allan) Combined Pub.

Lincoln Battalion. Edwin Rolfe. LC 74-651. (World History Ser.: No. 48). 1974. lib. bdg. 75.00 (*0-8383-1762-6*) M S G Haskell Hse.

Lincoln Beachey: The Man Who Owned the Sky. Frank Marrero. (Illus.). 208p. (Orig.). 1996. pap. 14.95 (*0-942087-12-7*) Scottwall Assocs.

Lincoln Before Washington: New Perspectives on the Illinois Years. Douglas L. Wilson. LC 96-45798. 208p. 1997. text 26.95 (*0-252-02331-5*) U of Ill Pr.

Lincoln Before Washington: New Perspectives on the Illinois Years. Douglas L. Wilson. 1998. pap. text 15.95 (*0-252-06627-8*) U of Ill Pr.

Lincoln Cent Numisma, 1909-1997. Bruce A. Vogel. (Illus.). 295p. 1998. pap. 50.00 (*1-893055-05-1*) B A Vogel.

Lincoln College Story, 1865-1995. Barbar Hughett. (Illus.). 112p. 1995. pap. 14.95 (*0-9630754-2-X*) Civil War RT.

Lincoln College Story, 1865-1995. Barbara Hughett. (Illus.). 112p. 1995. 24.95 (*0-9630754-1-1*) Civil War RT.

Lincoln Conspiracy. David W. Balsiger & Sellier. 1994. reprint ed. lib. bdg. 29.95 (*1-56849-531-5*) Buccaneer Bks.

Lincoln County, Colorado. Eastern Colorado Plainsman Staff. (Illus.). 233p. 1987. 50.00 (*0-88107-078-5*) Curtis Media.

Lincoln County, Colorado War Book. Alice Potter. (Illus.). 115p. 1993. 35.00 (*0-88107-230-3*) Curtis Media.

Lincoln County, Mississippi: A Pictorial History. Durr Walker. LC 98-18168. 1998. write for info. (*1-57864-035-0*); write for info. (*1-57864-034-2*) Donning Co.

Lincoln County Poems, & Poems from Other Places. Ramona Weeks. LC 73-19892. 1973. 8.00 (*0-914134-00-0*) Konocti Bks.

Lincoln County Trilogy. Fred N. Kimmel. LC 97-61971. 708p. 1998. 67.70 (*0-9661115-0-8*) Zantanon Pr.

Lincoln Day-by-Day: A Chronology, 1809-1865. rev. ed. Earl S. Miers. 1164p. 1988. reprint ed. 45.00 (*0-89029-542-5*) Morningside Bkshop.

Lincoln Douglas: The Text. William H. Bennett. iii,60,xivp. (Orig.). (YA). (gr. 7-12). 1989. pap. text 19.95 (*1-889510-24-6*) Chmpionship Debate.

Lincoln, Douglas, & Slavery: In the Crucible of Public Debate. David Zarefsky. LC 90-30121. 324p. (C). 1993. pap. 14.95 (*0-226-97876-1*) U Ch Pr.

Lincoln, Douglas, & Slavery: In the Crucible of Public Debate. David Zarefsky. LC 90-30121. 324p. 1998. 41.95 (*0-226-97875-3*) U Ch Pr.

Lincoln Douglas Block Encyclopedia Vol. 1: Values. Teresa A. Gonsalves et al. Ed. by Anthony J. Gonsalves. 200p. (Orig.). (YA). (gr. 7-12). 1997. pap. text 47.00 (*1-889510-29-7*) Chmpionship Debate.

Lincoln Douglas Block Encyclopedia Vol. 2: Values. Teresa A. Gonsalves et al. Ed. by Anthony J. Gonsalves. 200p. (Orig.). (YA). (gr. 7-12). 1997. pap. text 47.00 (*1-889510-30-0*) Chmpionship Debate.

Lincoln Douglas Block Encyclopedia Vol. 3: Values. Teresa A. Gonsalves et al. Ed. by Anthony J. Gonsalves. 200p. (Orig.). (YA). (gr. 7-12). 1997. pap. text 47.00 (*1-889510-31-9*) Chmpionship Debate.

Lincoln Douglas Block Encyclopedia Vol. 4: Criteria. Teresa A. Gonsalves et al. Ed. by Anthony J. Gonsalves. 200p. (Orig.). (YA). (gr. 7-12). 1997. pap. text 47.00 (*1-889510-32-7*) Chmpionship Debate.

Lincoln Douglas Block Encyclopedia Vol. 5: Philosophers. Teresa A. Gonsalves et al. Ed. by Anthony J. Gonsalves. 200p. (Orig.). (YA). (gr. 7-12). 1997. pap. text 47.00 (*1-889510-33-5*) Chmpionship Debate.

Lincoln-Douglas Debate. Michael D. Bartanen. LC 92-80478. 200p. 1994. pap. 23.99 (*0-8442-5014-7*) NTC Contemp Pub Co.

***Lincoln-Douglas Debate.** Dana Hensley & Diana Carlin. 1999. pap., teacher ed. 8.00 (*0-931054-63-X*) Clark Pub.

***Lincoln-Douglas Debate.** Jeffery Wiese. 1999. 30.00 (*0-931054-61-3*) Clark Pub.

***Lincoln-Douglas Debate: An Introductory Guide & Reader.** abr. ed. Michael Kim. (Illus.). (YA). (gr. 9-12). 1999. pap. 22.25 (*0-9664003-1-3*) M Kim.

Lincoln-Douglas Debates. Brendan January. LC 97-9302. (Cornerstones to Freedom Ser.). 32p. (J). 1998. 19.50 (*0-516-20844-6*) Childrens.

Lincoln-Douglas Debates. Brendan January. Ed. by Sarah DeCapua. (Cornerstones to Freedom Ser.). 32p. (J). 1998. pap. 5.95 (*0-516-26335-8*) Childrens.

Lincoln-Douglas Debates of 1858. Abraham Lincoln & Stephen Douglas. Ed. by Robert W. Johannsen. 336p. (Orig.). 1965. pap. 21.95 (*0-19-500921-5*) OUP.

Lincoln Encyclopedia: The Spoken & Written Words of A. Lincoln Arranged for Ready Reference. Abraham Lincoln. Ed. by Archer H. Shaw. LC 80-12651. 395p. 1980. reprint ed. lib. bdg. 45.50 (*0-313-22471-4*, SHLE, Greenwood Pr) Greenwood.

Lincoln, England, Marriage Licences: An Abstract of the Allegation Books Preserved by the Registry of the Bishop of Lincoln, 1598-1628. Ed. by A. Gibbons. (Illus.). 163p. 1998. reprint ed. pap. 19.50 (*0-8328-7042-0*) Higginson Bk Co.

Lincoln, English: Lincoln Diocese Documents. (EETS, OS Ser.: No. 149). 1969. reprint ed. 63.00 (*0-527-00145-7*) Periodicals Srv.

Lincoln Fair & Other Poems by Bernard Gilbert. Ed. by Patrick O'Shaughnessy. (Illus.). 72p. (C). 1989. text 40.00 (*0-902662-34-1*, Pub. by R K Pubns); pap. text 30.00 (*0-902662-35-X*, Pub. by R K Pubns) St Mut.

Lincoln Finds a General: A Military Study of the Civil War, Vol. 1. Kenneth P. Williams. LC 85-42531. (Illus.). 464p. 1985. pap. 6.95 (*0-253-20359-7*, MB-359) Ind U Pr.

Lincoln for the Defense: The Only Known Transcript of an Abraham Lincoln Criminal Jury Trial. Ed. by Ross F. Plaetzer. 198p. 1994. pap. 15.95 (*0-9641176-0-6*) High Hse Pr.

Lincoln Forum: Abraham Lincoln, Gettysburg & the Civil War. Ed. by John Y. Simon et al. LC 99-71103. (Illus.). 192p. (C). 1999. 19.95 (*1-882810-37-6*) Savas Pub.

Lincoln Highway. Brian A. Butko. (Pennsylvania Traveler's Guide Ser.). (Illus.). 352p. 1996. pap. 16.95 (*0-8117-2495-6*) Stackpole.

Lincoln Highway: Main Street Across America. expanded ed. Drake Hokanson. LC 98-54125. (Illus.). 256p. 1999. pap. 29.95 (*0-87745-676-3*) U of Iowa Pr.

Lincoln Highway: Nebraska. Gregory M. Franzwa. Ed. by Betty Burnett. (Illus.). 1996. 34.50 (*1-880397-15-3*); lthr. 150.00 (*1-880397-16-1*) Patrice Pr.

Lincoln Highway Vol. 1: Iowa. deluxe ed. Gregory M. Franzwa. Ed. by Betty Burnett. LC 95-12142. (Illus.). 1995. lthr. 150.00 (*1-880397-10-2*) Patrice Pr.

Lincoln Highway Vol. 1: Iowa, Vol. 1. Gregory M. Franzwa. Ed. by Betty Burnett. LC 95-12142. (Illus.). 199p. 1995. 34.50 (*1-880397-09-9*) Patrice Pr.

***Lincoln Highway Vol. 3: Wyoming.** Ed. by Gregory M. Franzwa & Betty Burnett. (Illus.). 191p. 1999. 34.50 (*1-880397-20-X*); lthr. 150.00 (*1-880397-21-8*) Patrice Pr.

Lincoln Images: Augustana College Centennial Essays. Ed. by O. Fritiof Ander. LC 60-12543. (Augustana College Library Publications: No. 29). (Illus.). 161p. 1960. 13.00 (*0-910182-29-9*) Augustana Coll.

Lincoln in American Memory. Merrill D. Peterson. (Illus.). 496p. 1995. pap. 15.95 (*0-19-509645-2*) OUP.

***Lincoln in Bloomington - Normal: A Historical Tour of Lincoln Sites in Bloomington & Normal Illinois.** Donna Reinking. (Illus.). 24p. 1998. pap. 3.50 (*0-943788-18-8*) McLean County.

Lincoln, in His Own Words. limited ed. Ed. by Milton Melzer. LC 92-17431. (Illus.). 240p. (J). 1993. 150.00 (*0-15-245438-1*) Harcourt.

Lincoln in Text & Context: Collected Essays. Don E. Fehrenbacher. LC 86-14346. 376p. 1987. 47.50 (*0-8047-1329-4*); pap. 16.95 (*0-8047-1517-3*) Stanford U Pr.

Lincoln in the Telegraph Office: Recollections of the United States Military Telegraph Corps During the Civil War. David H. Bates. LC 95-10908. (Illus.). xxi, 432p. 1995. pap. 14.95 (*0-8032-6125-X*, Bison Books) U of Nebr Pr.

Lincoln in the Telegraph Office: Recollections of the United States Military Telegraph Corps During the Civil War. large type unabridged ed. David H. Bates. (Illus.). viii, 432p. (C). 1996. reprint ed. 33.95 (*1-889881-09-0*) Old Bks Pub.

Lincoln, Johnson, & Grant. Richard Steins. LC 95-43546. (Complete History of Our Presidents Ser.: Vol. 5). (J). 1996. write for info. (*0-86593-409-6*) Rourke Corp.

Lincoln, Land, & Labor, 1809-60. Olivier Fraysse. Tr. by Sylvia Neely. LC 93-1569. 264p. (C). 1994. text 29.95 (*0-252-01979-2*) U of Ill Pr.

Lincoln Libraries, 1798-1984. John C. MacLean & Margaret M. Martin. (Illus.). 112p. (Orig.). 1984. pap. 15.00 (*0-944856-06-3*) Lincoln Hist Soc.

Lincoln Library of Sports Champions, 14 vols. 6th ed. Frontier Press Company Staff. LC 92-75323. (Illus.). 1792p. (YA). (gr. 4-12). 1993. lib. bdg. 399.00 (*0-912168-14-5*) Frontier Pr Co.

Lincoln Literary Collection. J. P. McCaskey. LC 71-108586. (Granger Index Reprint Ser.). 1977. 29.95 (*0-8369-6114-5*) Ayer.

Lincoln Lived Here: The Lincoln Heritage Trail. Illus. by Walter H. Miller et al. 32p. 1994. 4.95 (*0-9638258-2-8*) Bicast.

Lincoln-Lore: Lincoln in the Popular Mind. Ed. by Ray B. Browne. LC 96-29461. (Illus.). 344p. 1996. 49.95 (*0-87972-719-5*); pap. 19.95 (*0-87972-720-9*) Bowling Green Univ Popular Press.

Lincoln Mailbag: Letters to the President, 1861-1865. Harold Holzer. LC 97-42164. 288p. 1998. 29.95 (*0-8093-2072-X*) S Ill U Pr.

Lincoln Memorial. Carol M. Highsmith. (Anything Book D. C. Ser.). 160p. 1998. 5.99 (*0-517-18880-5*) Random Hse Value.

Lincoln Memorial. Deborah Kent. LC 96-17627. (Cornerstones to Freedom Ser.). 32p. (J). 1996. lib. bdg. 19.50 (*0-516-20006-2*) Childrens.

Lincoln Memorial. Deborah Kent. (Cornerstones to Freedom Ser.). 32p. (J). (gr. 4-6). 1997. pap. 5.95 (*0-516-26070-7*) Childrens.

Lincoln Memorial. Catherine Reef. LC 93-13708. (Places in American History Ser.). (Illus.). 72p. (J). (gr. 4 up). 1994. text 14.95 (*0-87518-624-6*, Dillon Silver Burdett) Silver Burdett Pr.

***Lincoln Memorial: A Great President Remembered.** Frederic Gilmore. LC 99-86280. (Illus.). (J). 2000. write for info. (*1-56766-759-7*) Childs World.

Lincoln Memorial: A Guide to the Lincoln Memorial, District of Columbia. 48p. 1986. pap. 145.00 (*0-16-003532-5*) USGPO.

Lincoln Memorial: A Guide to the Lincoln Memorial, District of Columbia. Paul M. Angle. LC 85-600059. (Official National Park Handbook Ser.: No. 129). (Illus.). 48p. 1986. pap. 3.00 (*0-912627-28-X*, S/N 024-005-00974-4) Natl Park Serv.

***Lincoln Migration from Kentucky to Indiana, 1816.** R. Gerald McMurtry. 46p. 1999. pap. 5.00 (*0-931244-09-9*) Hardin County Historical Society.

***Lincoln Money Martyred.** R. E. Search. 153p. 1998. pap. 8.00 (*0-944379-23-0*) CPA Bk Pub.

Lincoln Money Martyred. unabridged ed. R. E. Search. 153p. 1935. reprint ed. pap. 15.00 (*0-945001-25-8*) GSG & Assocs.

Lincoln Money Martyred: How the Money Power Bankers Killed Lincoln. R. E. Search. 1979. lib. bdg. 69.95 (*0-8490-2961-9*) Gordon Pr.

Lincoln Motor Cars 1946-1960 Photo Archive: Photographs from the Detroit Public Library's National Automotive History Collection. Mark A. Patrick. LC 96-76228. (Photo Archive Ser.). (Illus.). 128p. 1996. pap. 29.95 (*1-882256-58-1*) Iconografix.

Lincoln Motor Cars 1920-1942 Photo Archive: Photographs from the Detroit Public Library's National Automotive History Collection. Ed. by Mark A. Patrick. LC 96-76227. (Photo Archive Ser.). (Illus.). 128p. 1996. pap. 29.95 (*1-882256-57-3*) Iconografix.

Lincoln Murder Conspiracies. William Hanchett. LC 83-1065. (Illus.). 320p. 1983. 15.95 (*0-252-01361-1*) U of Ill Pr.

Lincoln Murder Plot. Karen Zeinert. LC 98-36971. (Illus.). xvii, 113p. (YA). (gr. 6 up). 1999. lib. bdg. 22.50 (*0-208-02451-4*, Linnet Bks) Shoe String.

Lincoln, New Mexico: As It Was One Day. Walt Wiggins. LC 75-7275. 1975. pap. 4.95 (*0-686-24292-0*) Pintores Pr.

Lincoln 1958-1969. James W. Howell. LC 97-19000. (Illus.). 160p. 1997. pap. 24.95 (*0-7603-0059-3*) MBI Pubg.

Lincoln No One Knows: Unsolved Mysteries of the Man Who Ran the Civil War. Webb Garrison. LC 92-32431. 1993. 16.95 (*1-55853-198-X*) Rutledge Hill Pr.

Lincoln Nobody Knows. Richard N. Current. (American Century Ser.). 314p. 1963. pap. 9.95 (*0-8090-0059-8*) Hill & Wang.

Lincoln Nobody Knows. Richard N. Current. LC 80-16138. 314p. 1980. reprint ed. lib. bdg. 69.50 (*0-313-22450-1*, CULN, Greenwood Pr) Greenwood.

Lincoln Observed: The Civil War Dispatches of Noah Brooks. Noah Brooks. Ed. by Michael Burlingame. LC 97-41950. 240p. 1998. 25.95 (*0-8018-5842-9*) Johns Hopkins.

***Lincoln of Kentucky.** Lowell Hayes Harrison. LC 99-48123. (Illus.). 320p. 2000. 22.00 (*0-8131-2156-6*) U Pr of Ky.

Lincoln on Black & White: A Documentary History. Ed. by Arthur Zilversmit. LC 83-6184. 206p. 1983. reprint ed. pap. text 10.50 (*0-89874-633-7*) Krieger.

***Lincoln on Black & White: A Documentary History.** Arthur Zilversmit. 206p. 2000. reprint ed. pap. 13.50 (*1-57524-152-8*) Krieger.

***Lincoln on God & Country.** Gordon Leidner. (Illus.). 241p. 2000. 19.95 (*1-57249-207-4*, WM Books) White Mane Pub.

Lincoln on Leadership: Executive Strategies for Tough Times. Donald T. Phillips. 208p. 1993. reprint ed. mass mkt. 13.95 (*0-446-39459-9*, Pub. by Warner Bks) Little.

***Lincoln on Lincoln.** Paul M. Zall. LC 99-15217. 208p. 1999. 25.00 (*0-8131-2141-8*) U Pr of Ky.

Lincoln on the Eve of '61: A Journalist's Story. Henry Villard. Ed. by Oswald G. Villard. LC 73-16631. 105p. 1974. reprint ed. lib. bdg. 38.50 (*0-8371-7202-0*, VILI, Greenwood Pr) Greenwood.

Lincoln on the Greensprings. Anne E. Foley. (Illus.). 30p. 1985. pap. 3.95 (*0-943388-07-4*) South Oregon.

Lincoln Parish, Louisiana Marriage Records, 1873-1901. Willie H. Farley. 77p. (Orig.). 1987. pap. text 15.00 (*1-57088-007-7*) J&W Ent.

Lincoln Park Cookbook: Recipes from Chicago's Finest Northside Eateries. (Illus.). 80p. 1997. pap. 14.95 (*0-9664694-0-2*) Lincoln Pk.

***Lincoln Park Remembered, 1894-1987.** Ed. by Joseph D. Thomas et al. LC 99-71184. 200p. 1999. 45.00 (*0-932027-50-4*); pap. 25.00 (*0-932027-49-0*) Spinner Pubns.

Lincoln Parks: The Story Behind the Scenery. rev. ed. Larry Waldron. LC 95-76874. (Illus.). 48p. (Orig.). 1995. pap. 7.95 (*0-88714-100-5*) KC Pubns.

Lincoln Persuasion: Remaking American liberalism. David Greenstone. LC 92-40075. (Studies in American Politics: Historical, International, & Comparative Perspectives). 352p. 1993. text 49.50 (*0-691-08790-3*, Pub. by Princeton U Pr) Cal Prin Full Svc.

Lincoln Persuasion: Remaking American Liberalism. J. David Greenstone. (Studies in American Politics: Historical, International, & Comparative Perspectives). 352p. 1993. pap. text 16.95 (*0-691-03764-7*, Pub. by Princeton U Pr) Cal Prin Full Svc.

Lincoln Postcard Catalog. James L. Lowe. LC 73-83549. (Illus.). 144p. 1973. reprint ed. pap. 5.95 (*0-913782-05-X*) Deltiologists Am.

Lincoln Reader. Ed. by Paul M. Angle. 33.95 (*0-89190-866-8*) Amereon Ltd.

Lincoln Reader. Ed. by Paul M. Angle. (Quality Paperbacks Ser.). (Illus.). 608p. 1990. pap. 16.95 (*0-306-80398-4*) Da Capo.

Lincoln Reader. Paul M. Angle. (History - United States Ser.). 564p. 1993. reprint ed. lib. bdg. 99.00 (*0-7812-4897-3*) Rprt Serv.

Lincoln Reading Dictionary. Morris. 1990. pap. 13.25 (*0-15-321129-6*) Harcourt Schl Pubs.

Lincoln Real Wheel Drive, 1970-96. LC 96-78645. (Automobile Repair Manuals Ser.). (Illus.). 1997. pap. 17.95 (*1-56392-240-1*, MBI 124688AM) Haynes Manuals.

Lincoln Reconsidered. David Herbert Donald. 1956. pap. 5.95 (*0-685-02838-0*) Knopf.

Lincoln Reconsidered: Essays on the Civil War Era. David Herbert Donald. 1989. pap. 13.00 (*0-679-72310-2*) Vin Bks.

Lincoln Reconsidered: Essays on the Civil War Era. David Herbert Donald. LC 80-22804. (Illus.). 200p. 1981. reprint ed. lib. bdg. 38.50 (*0-313-22575-3*, DOLR, Greenwood Pr) Greenwood.

***Lincoln Seen & Heard.** Harold Holzer. LC 99-43535. (Illus.). 240p. 2000. text 29.95 (*0-7006-1001-4*) U Pr of KS.

***Lincoln, Slavery & the Civil War.** Johnson. 2001. text. write for info. (*0-312-22763-9*) St Martin.

Lincoln Stories for Leaders. Donald T. Phillips. LC 96-51265. 128p. 1997. pap. 12.99 (*1-56530-242-7*, Pub. by Summit TX) BookWorld.

Lincoln Takes Command. 2nd rev. ed. John S. Tilley. 371p. 1998. reprint ed. pap. 19.95 (*0-931709-12-1*) B Coats.

Lincoln the Lawyer. Frederick T. Hill. xviii, 332p. 1997. reprint ed. 105.00 (*1-56169-254-9*) Gaunt.

Lincoln the Lawyer. Frederick T. Hill. (Illus.). xviii, 332p. 1986. reprint ed. 42.50 (*0-8377-0711-0*, Rothman) W S Hein.

Lincoln the Litigant, 1925. fac. ed. William H. Townsend. LC 99-16499. 2000. 60.00 (*1-58477-021-X*) Lawbk Exchange.

Lincoln the Man. 2nd rev. ed. Edgar Lee Masters. LC 97-40670. (Illus.). 536p. 1997. 29.95 (*0-9623842-6-7*) Fndtn Amer Ed.

Lincoln, the Politician. S. Neal. 1999. text. write for info. (*0-670-80883-0*) Viking Penguin.

Lincoln, the Prairie Capital: An Illustrated History. rev. ed. James L. McKee. (Illus.). 192p. 1984. 24.95 (*0-89781-109-7*) Am Historical Pr.

***Lincoln the President.** J. G. Randall & Richard N. Current. LC 99-39598. 2000. pap. 19.95 (*0-252-06872-6*) U of Ill Pr.

Lincoln the President: Last Full Measure. Richard N. Current & James G. Randall. 440p. 1991. text 39.95 (*0-252-01785-4*) U of Ill Pr.

Lincoln, the South, & Slavery: The Political Dimension. Robert W. Johannsen. LC 90-48474. (Walter Lynwood Fleming Lectures). 128p. 1993. pap. 11.95 (*0-8071-1887-7*) La State U Pr.

Lincoln the Unknown. Dale Carnegie. 256p. 1993. reprint ed. lib. bdg. 29.95 (*0-89968-320-7*, Lghtyr Pr) Buccaneer Bks.

Lincoln Writing Dictionary. Holt & Company Staff. 1989. text 53.00 (*0-03-023378-X*) Holt R&W.

Lincoln Writing Dictionary for Children. (Illus.). 901p. (J). (gr. 2-9). 1988. 17.95 (*0-15-152394-0*) Harcourt.

Lincoln's Abolitionist General: The Biography of David Hunter. Edward A. Miller, Jr. LC 95-50217. (Illus.). 350p. 1997. 29.95 (*1-57003-110-X*) U of SC Pr.

Lincoln's Admiral: The Civil War Campaigns of David Farragut. James P. Duffy. LC 96-34986. 288p. 1997. 27.95 (*0-471-04208-0*) Wiley.

Lincoln's Assassins: A Complete Account of Their Capture, Trial, & Punishment. Roy Z. Chamlee, Jr. LC 89-42708. (Illus.). 634p. 1990. lib. bdg. 60.00 (*0-89950-420-5*) McFarland & Co.

Lincoln's Cavalrymen: A History of the Mounted Forces of the Army of the Potomac. Edward G. Longacre. LC 99-86635. 2000. 34.95 (*0-8117-1049-1*) Kitch Keepsakes.

Lincoln's Commando: The Biography of Commander W. B. Cushing, USN. Ralph J. Roske & Charles Van Doren. LC 95-32381. (Illus.). 328p. 1995. pap. 15.95 (*1-55750-737-6*) Naval Inst Pr.

Lincoln's Critics: The Copperheads of the North. Frank L. Klement. LC 98-46687. 272p. 1998. 40.00 (*1-57249-128-0*, Burd St Pr) White Mane Pub.

L

An Asterisk (*) at the beginning of an entry indicates that the title is appearing for the first time.

Lincoln's Deathbed in Art & Memory: The "Rubber Room" Phenomenon. Harold Holzer & Frank J. Williams. (Illus.). 44p. 1998. pap. 10.00 (*1-57747-028-1*) Thomas Publications.

Lincoln's Devotional. Carl Sandburg. LC 94-39875. 1995. 13.95 (*0-8050-3852-3*) H Holt & Co.

Lincoln's Doctor's Dog: A Collection of Grace Notes. 2nd ed. Photos by Danny Bolin. LC 98-92699. (Illus.). xv, 357p. 1997. reprint ed. pap. 19.95 (*0-9663086-0-3*) G M Brown.

Lincoln's Doctor's Dog & Other Stories. Richard Grayson. LC 81-69117. 187p. 1982. 11.95 (*0-917976-13-4*, White Ewe Pr) Thunder Baas Pr.

Lincolns Dreams. Willis. 1999. text 14.95 (*0-312-94288-5*) St Martin.

Lincoln's Dreams. Connie Willis. (Spectra Ser.). 256p. 1992. mass mkt. 6.50 (*0-553-27025-7*) Bantam.

Lincoln's Favorite Poets. David J. Harkness & R. Gerald McMurtry. LC 59-9718. 108p. 1959. reprint ed. pap. 33.50 (*0-608-14038-4*, 202221500025) Bks Demand.

Lincoln's Foreign Legion: The 39th New York Infantry, the Garibaldi Guard. Michael Bacarella. LC 96-33042. (Illus.). 330p. 1996. 34.95 (*1-57249-016-0*) White Mane Pub.

Lincoln's Generals. Michael Fellman et al. Ed. by Gabor S. Boritt. (Illus.). 272p. 1995. pap. 13.95 (*0-19-510110-3*) OUP.

Lincoln's Herndon. Intro. by David Herbert Donald. (Quality Paperbacks Ser.). (Illus.). 442p. 1989. pap. 13.95 (*0-306-80353-4*) Da Capo.

Lincoln's Inn: Its Ancient & Modern Buildings with an Account of the Library. 2nd ed. William H. Spilsbury. (Illus.). xi, 251p. 1988. reprint ed. 38.50 (*0-8377-2619-0*, Rothman) W S Hein.

Lincoln's Journalist: John Hay's Anonymous Writings for the Press, 1860-1864. John Hay. Ed. by Michael Burlingame. LC 98-22056. 416p. 1999. 49.95 (*0-8093-2205-6*) S Ill U Pr.

Lincoln's Legacy: The Emancipation Proclamation & the Gettysburg Address. Abraham Lincoln. (Illus.). 24p. 1994. pap. 2.95 (*0-87328-149-7*) Huntington Lib.

Lincoln's Letters: The Private Man & the Warrior. unabridged ed. Abraham Lincoln. 1995. lib. bdg. 18.95 incl. audio (*1-883049-51-2*) Sound Room.

Lincoln's Letters: The Private Man & the Warrior, Set. unabridged ed. Abraham Lincoln. 1995. 16.95 incl. audio (*1-883049-50-4*, Pub. by Sound Room) Penton Overseas.

***Lincoln's Little Girl: A True Story.** Fred Trump. LC 93-73695. (Illus.). 184p. (YA). (gr. 4 up). 2000. pap. 8.95 (*1-56397-852-0*) Boyds Mills Pr.

Lincoln's Little War: How His Carefully Crafted Plans Went Astray. Webb Garrison. LC 97-12348. 224p. 1997. pap. 12.95 (*1-55853-460-1*) Rutledge Hill Pr.

Lincoln's Log. Barry Kornhauser. 96p. (YA). (gr. 5-12). 1999. pap. 7.00 (*0-87602-369-3*) Anchorage.

Lincoln's Loyalists: Union Soldiers from the Confederacy. Richard N. Current. 224p. 1992. text 30.00 (*1-55553-124-5*) NE U Pr.

***Lincolns Men: How President Lincoln Became Father to an Army & a Nation.** William C. Davis. 336p. 2000. per. 14.00 (*0-684-86294-8*) S&S Trade.

Lincoln's Men: How President Lincoln Became Father to an Army & a Nation. William C. Davis. LC 98-8069. 352p. 1999. 25.00 (*0-684-83337-9*) Free Pr.

Lincoln's Navy: The Ships, Men & Organization, 1861-65. Don L. Canney. (Illus.). 240p. 1998. 49.95 (*1-55750-519-5*) Naval Inst Pr.

Lincoln's New Salem. rev. ed. Benjamin P. Thomas. LC 87-12988. (Illus.). 183p. 1988. reprint ed. pap. 9.95 (*0-8093-1389-8*) S Ill U Pr.

Lincoln's Own Yarns & Stories. 1980. pap. 8.95 (*0-935650-00-8*) Bengal Pr.

Lincoln's Plan of Reconstruction. William B. Hesseltine. 1990. 16.50 (*0-8446-1236-7*) Peter Smith.

Lincoln's Plan of Reconstruction. Charles H. McCarthy. LC 01-26549. reprint ed. 37.50 (*0-404-04105-1*) AMS Pr.

Lincoln's Preparation for Greatness. Paul Simon. 344p. 1990. 21.95 (*0-252-00203-2*) U of Ill Pr.

Lincoln's Prose: Major Works of a Great American Writer. unabridged ed. Abraham Lincoln. 1995. lib. bdg. 18.95 incl. audio (*1-883049-53-9*) Sound Room.

Lincoln's Prose: Major Works of a Great American Writer, Set. unabridged ed. Abraham Lincoln. 1995. 16.95 incl. audio (*1-883049-52-0*, Pub. by Sound Room) Penton Overseas.

Lincoln's Ransom. Tim Champlin. LC 99-19835. 250p. 1999. 30.00 (*0-7862-1574-7*) Thorndike Pr.

Lincoln's Ransom. large type ed. Tim Champlin. LC 00-24242. (G. K. Hall Western Ser.). 275p. 2000. 24.95 (*0-7838-0313-3*, G K Hall Lrg Type) Mac Lib Ref.

Lincoln's Rise to Power. William Baringer. (Illus.). xi, 373 p. 1971. reprint ed. 59.00 (*0-403-00853-0*) Scholarly.

***Lincoln's Sacred Effort: Defining Religion's Role in American Self-Government.** Lucas E. Morel. LC 99-53362. 272p. 2000. 70.00 (*0-7391-0105-6*); pap. 23.95 (*0-7391-0106-4*) Lxngtn Bks.

Lincoln's Secretary: A Biography of John G. Nicolay. Helen Nicolay. LC 70-138169. (Illus.). 363p. 1971. reprint ed. lib. bdg. 65.00 (*0-8371-5626-2*, NILS, Greenwood Pr) Greenwood.

Lincoln's Supreme Court. David M. Silver. LC 97-32780. 280p. 1998. text 21.95 (*0-252-06719-3*) U of Ill Pr.

Lincoln's Unsung Heroes. Philip R. N. Katcher. (Illus.). 240p. 1997. 29.95 (*1-85409-350-9*, Pub. by Arms & Armour) Sterling.

Lincoln's War Cabinet. Burton J. Hendrick. (History - United States Ser.). 559p. 1993. reprint ed. lib. bdg. 99.00 (*0-7812-4896-5*) Rprt Serv.

Lincoln's Youth: Indiana Years, Seven to Twenty-One, 1816-1830. Louis A. Warren. LC 90-19784. (Illus.). xxii, 298p. 1991. reprint ed. 19.95 (*0-87195-063-4*) Ind Hist Soc.

Lincolnshire. David Kaye. (Country Guide Ser.: No. 2). (Illus.). 128p. pap. 12.50 (*0-7478-0271-8*, Pub. by Shire Pubns) Parkwest Pubns.

Lincolnshire. Henry Thorold. (Pimlico County History Guides Ser.). (Illus.). 142p. 1997. pap. 19.95 (*0-7126-9892-2*, Pub. by Pimlico) Trafalgar.

Lincolnshire Folk. Fred Dobson. (Illus.). (C). 1989. text 30.00 (*0-902662-36-8*, Pub. by R K Pubns) St Mut.

Lincolnshire Potato Railways. Ed. by Stewart E. Squires. (C). 1985. 39.00 (*0-85361-352-4*) St Mut.

Linconville, Northport, Belmont, Morrill, Searsmont & Waldo Town Register, 1907 (Town Histories & Directories) Compiled by Mitchell et al. 175p. 1997. reprint ed. pap. 27.50 (*0-8328-5867-6*) Higginson Bk Co.

Lind Coulee Site (45GR97), 1973 Field Season. fac. ed. Ann M. Irwin & Ula Moody. (Washington Archaeological Research Center Project Reports: No. 36). (Illus.). 71p. (C). 1976. reprint ed. pap. text 8.44 (*1-55567-504-2*) Coyote Press.

Lind Coulee Site (45GR97), 1974 Field Season. fac. ed. Ann M. Irwin & Ula Moody. (Washington Archaeological Research Center Project Reports: No. 53). (Illus.). 113p. (C). 1977. reprint ed. pap. text 12.50 (*1-55567-503-4*) Coyote Press.

Linda Arnold Songbook. (Songs for Kids Ser.). (Illus.). 64p. (Orig.). (J). 1993. pap. 9.95 (*0-7935-2377-X*, 00815002) H Leonard.

Linda Clark's Cookbook. Linda Clark. LC 77-8716. (Illus.). 128p. (Orig.). 1977. pap. 5.95 (*0-89407-009-6*) Strawberry Hill.

Linda Condon. Joseph Hergesheimer. (Collected Works of Joseph Hergesheimer). 304p. 1998. reprint ed. lib. bdg. 98.00 (*1-58201-654-2*) Classic Bks.

Linda Conner: Lux Three. limited ed. Linda Connor. LC 94-61918. (Lux Ser.: Vol. III). (Illus.). 52p. 1998. pap. 19.95 (*0-9630393-3-4*) Ctr for Photo.

Linda Connor: Spiral Journey: Photographs, 1967-1990. Pref. by Denise Miller-Clark. 70p. 1990. pap. 25.00 (*0-932026-21-4*) Columbia College Chi.

Linda Craig: Search for Scorpio. Ann Sheldon. Ed. by Wendy Barish. 160p. (Orig.). (J). (gr. 3 up). 1984. pap. 3.95 (*0-671-53237-5*) S&S Trade.

Linda Craig: The Haunted Valley. Ann Sheldon. Ed. by Wendy Barish. (Linda Craig Ser.: No. 7). 192p. (J). (gr. 3-7). 1982. 8.50 (*0-671-45551-6*) S&S Trade.

Linda Eder - And So Much More. 71p. 1994. pap. 16.95 (*0-89524-877-8*, 02502154, Pub. by Cherry Lane) H Leonard.

Linda Eder (Piano - Vocal) Linda Eder. Ed. by Milton Okun. (Illus.). 52p. (Orig.). pap. text 14.95 (*0-89524-666-X*, Pub. by Cherry Lane) H Leonard.

Linda Goodman's Love Signs: A New Approach to the Human Heart. Linda Goodman. LC 91-55516. (Illus.). 1212p. 1999. reprint ed. pap. 18.00 (*0-06-096896-6*, Perennial) HarperTrade.

Linda Goodman's Relationship Signs. Linda Goodman. 480p. 1999. mass mkt. 7.99 (*0-553-58015-9*) Bantam.

***Linda Goodman's Star Cards.** Crystal Bush. (Illus.). 2000. 24.95 (*1-57174-185-2*) Hampton Roads Pub Co.

Linda Goodman's Star Signs. Linda Goodman. 1993. mass mkt. 7.99 (*0-312-95191-4*) St Martin.

Linda Goodman's Star Signs. Linda Goodman. 535p. 2000. pap. 16.95 (*0-312-19203-7*) St Martin.

Linda Goodman's Sun Signs. Linda Goodman. 512p. 1984. mass mkt. 7.99 (*0-553-27882-7*) Bantam.

Linda Goodman's Sun Signs. Linda Goodman. LC 68-31737. 1968. 29.95 (*0-8008-4900-0*) Taplinger.

Linda Her & the Fairy Garden: Two Related Short Plays. Harry Kondoleon. 1985. pap. 5.25 (*0-8222-0671-4*) Dramatists Play.

Linda Matalon: Sculpture. Laura Cottingham. (Illus.). 8p. (Orig.). 1993. pap. 5.00 (*0-9626731-5-3*) Yoshii Gallery.

***Linda McCartney: A Portrait.** Danny Fields. (Illus.). 272p. 2000. 24.95 (*1-58063-104-5*) Renaissance.

***Linda Mccartney: Wide Prairie.** 104p. 1999. pap. text 17.95 (*0-634-00293-7*) H Leonard.

Linda McCartney on Tour: 200 Meat-Free Dishes from Around the World. Linda McCartney. LC 98-17947. (Illus.). 192p. (gr. 8). 1998. 29.95 (*0-8212-2487-5*) Little.

Linda McCartney's Home Cooking: Quick, Easy & Economical Dishes for Today. Linda McCartney. (Illus.). 176p. 1992. pap. 19.45 (*1-55970-160-9*, Pub. by Arcade Pub Inc) Time Warner.

Linda McCartney's Home Cooking: Quick, Easy, & Economical Vegetarian Dishes for Today. Linda McCartney. (Illus.). 176p. 1990. 27.45 (*1-55970-097-1*, Pub. by Arcade Pub Inc) Time Warner.

Linda McCartney's Sixties: Portrait of an Era. Linda McCartney. (Illus.). 175p. 1992. 60.00 (*0-8212-1959-6*, Pub. by Bulfinch Pr) Little.

Linda McCartney's Sixties: Portrait of an Era, Vol. 1. Linda McCartney. (Illus.). 176p. 1993. pap. 29.95 (*0-8212-2056-X*, Pub. by Bulfinch Pr) Little.

***Linda McCartney's World of Vegetarian Cooking.** Linda McCartney. (Illus.). 192p. 2001. pap. 19.95 (*0-8212-2696-7*) Bulfinch Pr.

Linda Miles Practice Dynamics. Linda Miles. 160p. 1986. 29.95 (*0-87814-301-7*) PennWell Bks.

***Linda Mullin's Teddy Bear & Friends Identification & Price Guide.** Linda Mullins. (Illus.). 160p. 2000. 19.95 (*0-87588-580-2*) Hobby Hse.

***Linda Radke's Promote Like a Pro - Small Budget, Big Show: A Step-by-Step Guide to Promoting Anything from Books to Businesses.** Linda F. Radke. Ed. by Sal Caputo & Sue DeFabis. LC 99-54903. (Illus.). 182p. 2000. pap. 19.95 (*1-877749-36-2*) Five Star AZ.

Linda Raza: Cultural & Artistic Traditions of the Hispanic Southwest. Angel Vigil. LC 97-24290. (Illus.). 256p. 1998. pap. 22.95 (*1-55591-958-8*) Fulcrum Pub.

Linda Ronstadt: Mexican-American Singer. Richard Amdur. (Hispanics of Achievement Ser.). (Illus.). 120p. (YA). (gr. 5 up). 1994. lib. bdg. 19.95 (*0-7910-1781-8*) Chelsea Hse.

Linda Ronstadt - Cry Like a Rainstorm, Howl Like the Wind: Piano - Vocal. Ed. by Milton Okun. (Illus.). 52p. (Orig.). 1990. pap. text 14.95 (*0-89524-501-9*) Cherry Lane.

Linda Ronstadt - Lush Life - What's New. 96p. (Orig.). (C). 1985. pap. text. write for info. (*0-7692-0558-5*, VF1203) Wrner Bros.

Linda Ronstadt - 'Round Midnight: With Nelson Riddle & His Orchestra. Ed. by Carol Cuellar. 292p. (Orig.). (C). 1986. pap. text 22.95 (*0-7692-0489-9*, VF1284) Wrner Bros.

Linda 67: Historia De Un Crimen. 2nd ed. Fernando Del Paso. 1996. pap. 26.95 (*968-11-0163-4*) Plaza.

Linda Tressel, 2 vols. Anthony Trollope. LC 80-1887. (Selected Works of Anthony Trollope). 1982. reprint ed. lib. bdg. 49.95 (*0-405-14152-1*) Ayer.

Linda Tressell: (trollope 1999) Skilton. 40.00 (*1-870587-70-7*) Ashgate Pub Co.

Lindane. (Environmental Health Criteria Ser.: No. 124). (ENG, FRE & SPA.). 208p. 1991. pap. text 37.00 (*92-4-157124-1*, 1160124) World Health.

Lindane (GAMMA-HCH) Health & Safety Guide. (Health & Safety Guides Ser.: No. 54). 41p. 1991. pap. text 5.00 (*92-4-151054-4*, 1860054) World Health.

Linda's Indian Home. Martha F. McKeown. LC 56-8826. (Illus.). 80p. (J). (gr. 3-7). 1969. 7.95 (*0-8323-0151-5*) Binford Mort.

Linda's Kitchen: Simple & Inspiring Meatless Meals. Linda McCartney. 192p. 1997. pap. 19.95 (*0-8212-2393-3*, Pub. by Bulfinch Pr) Little.

Linda's Kitchen: Simple & Inspiring Recipes for Meatless Meals. Linda McCartney. 192p. 1995. 29.95 (*0-8212-2123-X*, Pub. by Bulfinch Pr) Little.

Linda's Song. Genny Waddell & Agnes Smith. 136p. (Orig.). 1985. pap. 6.95 (*0-89265-095-8*) Randall Hse.

Linda's Strange Vacation. Marcus Huttning. 128p. 1998. pap. 12.95 (*1-84068-001-6*) Creation Books.

Lindbergh. A. Scott Berg. (Illus.). 1999. pap. 16.00 (*0-425-17041-1*) Berkley Pub.

***Lindbergh.** A. Scott Berg. LC 98-18548. (Illus.). 628p. 1998. 30.00 (*0-399-14449-8*) Putnam Pub Group.

***Lindbergh: A Biography.** Leonard Mosley. 2000. pap. 12.95 (*0-486-40964-3*) Dover.

Lindbergh: His Story in Pictures. Francis T. Miller. Ed. by James B. Gilbert. LC 79-7286. (Flight: Its First Seventy-Five Years Ser.). (Illus.). 1980. reprint ed. lib. bdg. 36.95 (*0-405-12195-4*) Ayer.

Lindbergh: His Story in Pictures. Francis T. Miller. (Illus.). 318p. 1989. reprint ed. pap. 14.95 (*0-910667-14-4*) USM.

Lindbergh: The Crime. Noel Behn. 512p. 1995. mass mkt. 5.99 (*0-451-40589-7*, Onyx) NAL.

Lindbergh: Triumph & Tragedy. Richard Bak. LC 99-38311. 2000. 32.95 (*0-87833-246-4*) Taylor Pub.

Lindbergh & the Spirit of St. Louis. Bruce LaFontaine. 1999. pap. text 2.95 (*0-486-40567-2*) Dover.

***Lindbergh Baby Kidnapping in American History.** Judith Edwards. LC 99-30815. (In American History Ser.). (Illus.). 128p. (YA). (gr. 5 up). 2000. lib. bdg. 20.95 (*0-7660-1299-9*) Enslow Pubs.

***Lindbergh Baby Kidnapping Trial: A Headline Court Case.** Judy Monroe. LC 99-50666. (Headline Court Cases Ser.). (Illus.). 128p. (gr. 6 up). 2000. lib. bdg. 20.95 (*0-7660-1389-8*) Enslow Pubs.

Lindbergh Case. Jim Fisher. (Illus.). 480p. (C). 1994. reprint ed. pap. 17.95 (*0-8135-2147-5*) Rutgers U Pr.

Lindbergh Half-Century. Robert Lietz. (Poetry Ser.). 75p. (Orig.). (C). 1987. pap. 8.00 (*0-934332-47-9*) LEpervier Pr.

Lindbergh Kidnapping: The Original 1935 "Crime of the Century" Comic Serial. Lou Wedemar. (Illus.). 32p. 1999. pap. 6.95 (*0-9662789-2-5*) Hunterdon Cnty.

L'inde Tamoule. Pierre Suau. LC 98-902762. 248p. 1997. write for info. (*81-206-1192-6*) Asian Educ Servs.

Linden. Lauren Pancurak Yeats. (Images of America Ser.). 128p. 1999. pap. 16.99 (*0-7524-0869-0*) Arcadia Publng.

Linden Girl: A Story of Outlawed Lives. Pamela Rajkowski. LC 95-213632. 304p. (C). 1995. pap. 24.95 (*1-875560-25-4*, Pub. by Univ of West Aust Pr) Intl Spec Bk.

Linden Hills. Gloria Naylor. (Contemporay American Fiction Ser.). 320p. 1986. pap. 12.95 (*0-14-008829-6*, Penguin Bks) Viking Penguin.

Linden on the Saugus Branch. Elliot Paul. (American Autobiography Ser.). 401p. 1995. reprint ed. lib. bdg. 99.00 (*0-7812-8609-3*) Rprt Serv.

***Linden Tree.** large type ed. Anna Barrie. 432p. 1999. 31.99 (*0-7505-1364-0*, Pub. by Mgna Lrg Print) Ulverscroft.

Linden Tree. large type ed. Hester Rowan. 320p. 1985. 27.99 (*0-7089-1331-8*) Ulverscroft.

Lindenmayer Systems: Impacts on Theoretical Computer Science, Computer Graphics, & Developmental Biology. Ed. by Grzegorz Rozenberg & Arto Salomaa. LC 92-14822. ix, 514p. 1992. write for info. (*3-540-55320-7*); 114.95 (*0-387-55320-7*) Spr-Verlag.

Lindenmayer Systems, Fractals, & Plants. P. Prusinkiewicz & Joe J. Hanan. (Lecture Notes in Biomathematics Ser.: Vol. 79). viii, 120p. 1992. 43.95 (*0-387-97092-4*) Spr-Verlag.

Linder Family. Penny Linder & O. D. Linder. LC 90-62412. (Illus.). 220p. 1991. 35.00 (*0-9627513-0-8*) Linder.

Switzerland-Canton of Bern;Meiringen, 1500-1800ds-Brienz, 1600-1900ds/Canada-Alberta,USA-KS, WIS, AK, CA, PA.NY, ILL, MT, WV. Some of the families included are: Heinrich Linder, wife Lucy Buehler, Robert Linder, wife Margaritha Stahi (Stohli), Herminia Linder, husband Edward Fagan, Alfred Linder, wife Rosa Borter, Hermann Linder, wife Marie Berger. Many related families are given the book. *Publisher Paid Annotation.*

***Lindey & Parley on Separation Agreements & Antenuptial Contracts.** 2nd ed. Alexander Lindey & Louis I. Parley. LC 99-48711. 1999. 350.00 (*0-8205-4188-5*) Bender.

Lindey on Entertainment, Publishing & the Arts: Agreements & the Law, 4 vols. 2nd ed. Alexander Lindey & Michael Landau. LC 80-10991. (Entertainment & Communication Law Ser.). 1980. ring bd. 580.00 incl. disk (*0-87632-005-1*) West Group.

Lindgren Three: Ancient Greek Bronze Coins from the Lindgren Collection. Henry C. Lindgren. LC 93-74078. (Illus.). 228p. 1993. 90.00 (*0-9636738-1-5*) Classical Numismatic Grp.

Lindi's Costume Parade. Sarah Albee. (Stickers & Shapes Ser.). (J). 2000. mass mkt. 3.99 (*0-689-81307-4*) S&S Childrens.

Lindisfarne Gospels. Janet Backhouse. (Illus.). 96p. 1990. pap. 14.95 (*0-7148-2461-5*, Pub. by Phaidon Pr) Phaidon Pr.

Lindisfarne Gospels Address Book. British Library Staff. (Illus.). 96p. 1997. pap. 9.95 (*0-7123-4550-7*) U of Toronto Pr.

Lindisfarne Gospels Book of Days. British Library Staff. (Illus.). 96p. 1998. pap. 9.95 (*0-7123-4551-5*) U of Toronto Pr.

Lindisfarne Landscapes. 1996. pap. 13.90 (*0-7152-0713-X*) St Mut.

***Lindisfarne Painting Book.** Aidan Meehan. LC 99-65175. (Illus.). 64p. 2000. pap. 9.95 (*0-500-28184-X*, Pub. by Thames Hudson) Norton.

Lindiwi Finds a Way. Eileen Molver. (Junior African Writers Ser.). (Illus.). 80p. (J). (gr. 3 up). 1992. pap. 4.95 (*0-7910-2915-8*) Chelsea Hse.

Lindley & Banks on Partnerships. 17th ed. Roderick L. Banks. 1994. 232.00 (*0-421-48260-5*, Pub. by Sweet & Maxwll) Gaunt.

Lindley Murray: The Educational Works. Intro. by David Reibel. 5240p. (C). 1996. 1320.00 (*0-415-12307-0*) Routledge.

Lindley Murray (1745-1826) Stephen Allott. 1999. pap. 21.00 (*1-85072-088-6*, Pub. by W Sessions) St Mut.

Lindo: An Optimization Modeling System. 5th ed. Schrage. 1997. 69.75 (*0-7895-0153-8*) Course Tech.

Lindo: Optimization Modeling System. 5th ed. Schrage. (QM - Quantitative Methods Ser.). 1997. pap. 52.25 (*0-7895-0151-1*) S-W Pub.

LINDO, an Optimization & Modeling System: Text & Software. 4th ed. Linus E. Schrage. 370p. (C). 1993. pap. 57.75 (*0-89426-150-9*) Course Tech.

Lindo Don Diego. 5th ed. Agustin M. Cavanna. 152p. 1987. pap. 9.95 (*0-7859-5210-1*) Fr & Eur.

Lindos, Fouilles de l'Acropole, 1902-1914 No. 4, Pt. 2: Excavations & Surveys in Southern Rhodes the Post Mycenaean Periods until Roman Times & the Medieval Period. Lone W. Sorensen & Peter Pentz. Ed. & Intro. by Soren Dietz. (Illus.). 254p. (C). 1992. pap. 40.00 (*87-7288-503-3*, Pub. by Aarhus Univ Pr) David Brown.

Lind's List Camera Price Guide & Master Data Catalog, 1996-1997. Joan C. McKeown et al. (Illus.). 400p. 1996. pap. 44.95 (*0-931838-26-6*) Centennial Photo Serv.

Lindsay. Ed. by Helen Exley. (Tartan Notebks.). 80p. 1997. 9.00 (*1-85015-862-2*) Exley Giftbooks.

Lindsay: A Woman of Courage. Joanne Ryan. LC 97-90084. 179p. (Orig.). 1997. pap. 12.95 (*0-533-12281-3*) Vantage.

***Lindsay Anderson.** Gavin Lambert. LC 99-59305. (Illus.). 320p. 2000. 29.95 (*0-679-44598-6*) Knopf.

Lindsay Anderson: Maverick Film Maker. Erik Hedling. LC 97-4308. 246p. 1998. 74.95 (*0-304-33605-X*); pap. 27.50 (*0-304-33606-8*) Continuum.

Lindsay Bradshaw's One Hour Party Cakes. Lindsay J. Bradshaw. 1994. 19.95 (*1-85391-044-9*) Sterling.

Lindsay Letters, 1828-1838. Lea Leever Oldham. LC 98-92948. 83p. 1998. per. 10.00 (*1-55856-279-6*, 185) Closson Pr.

Lindsey Hits the Club. Susan Uhlig. (Illus.). 96p. (J). (gr. 3-6). 1999. pap. 6.75 (*1-889658-17-0*) New Canaan Pub.

***Lindy Hop, an Open Class with Paulette Brockington.** 2000. write for info. (*0-9678185-0-8*) Artspectrum.

Lindzey Vol 1 Handbook see Handbook of Social Psychology

Lindzey Vol 2 Handbook see Handbook of Social Psychology

Lindzey Vol 3 Handbook see Handbook of Social Psychology

Lindzey Vol 4 Handbook see Handbook of Social Psychology

Line. Bob McGuire. 1996. mass mkt. 6.50 (*0-312-95874-9*) St Martin.

Line. Bob McGuire. 1996. mass mkt. 5.99 (*0-614-20523-9*, St Martins Paperbacks) St Martin.

Line. Foxer Wood. 512p. (Orig.). 1993. pap. 14.95 (*1-879260-11-5*) Evanston Pub.

Line: Essays on Mexican - American Border Literature. Ed. by Harry Polkinhorn et al. (Binational Press Ser.: No. 1). (ENG & SPA.). 192p. 1988. pap. 10.00 (*0-916304-92-2*) SDSU Press.

Line Algebras. Ed. by G. Benkart & J. M. Osborn. (Lecture Notes in Mathematics Ser.: Vol. 1373). v, 145p. 1989. 32.95 (*0-387-51147-4*) Spr-Verlag.

Line & Color Magic for Glass Design. Kay B. Weiner. (Illus.). 84p. (Orig.). (C). 1990. pap. text 15.95 (*0-9625663-1-4*) Eastman Pub.

Line & Wash: Watercolour & Pen Techniques. Wendy Jelbert. (Illus.). 48p. 1997. pap. 11.95 (*0-85532-833-9*, 8339, Pub. by Srch Pr) A Schwartz & Co.

Line By Line: Beginning Text. 2nd ed. Steven J. Molinsky & Bill Bliss. 128p. (C). 1989. pap. text 20.40 (*0-13-536871-5*, Macmillan Coll) P-H.

Line by Line: English Through Grammar Stories, Bk. 1A. Steven J. Molinsky & Bill Bliss. (Illus.). 128p. (C). 1983. pap. text 10.00 (*0-13-537092-2*) P-H.

Line by Line: English Through Grammar Stories, Bk. 2A. Steven J. Molinsky & Bill Bliss. (Illus.). 128p. (C). 1983. pap. text 10.00 (*0-13-537241-0*) P-H.

Line by Line: English Through Grammar Stories, Bk. 2B. Steven J. Molinsky & Bill Bliss. (Illus.). 28p. (C). 1983. pap. text 7.60 (*0-13-537258-5*) P-H.

Line by Line: English Through Grammar Stories, Bk.1B. Steven J. Molinsky & Bill Bliss. (Illus.). 112p. (C). 1983. pap. text 10.00 (*0-13-537175-9*) P-H.

Line by Line: How to Improve Your Own Writing. Claire K. Cook. pap. 8.95 (*0-685-54946-1*, H-01031) HM.

Line by Line: Intermediate Text. 2nd ed. Steven J. Molinsky & Bill Bliss. 112p. (C). 1991. pap. text 20.40 (*0-13-536889-8*) P-H.

Line by Line: The MLA's Guide to Improving Your Writing, 001. Claire K. Cook. Ed. by Reference Division Staff. LC 85-8346. 240p. 1986. pap. 10.00 (*0-395-39391-4*) HM.

Line by Line Beginning Typing. 2nd ed. Molinsky. 1990. text. write for info. (*0-13-536897-9*) P-H.

Line Dances of Central Maryland. W. L. Smith. LC 95-100388. 210p. 1993. pap. 24.95 (*1-886019-00-2*, Swift Feet Dancing) Waltech.

Line Dancing. Paul Bottomer. (Dance Crazy Ser.). (Illus.). 64p. 1996. 12.95 (*1-85967-231-0*, Lorenz Bks) Anness Pub.

Line Dancing. Aine Quinn. 1997. pap. 14.00 (*0-00-472149-7*) Collins.

Line Dancing: Run to the Floor for Country Western . . . Hilton Osborne. (Illus.). 192p. (Orig.). 1994. pap. 19.95 (*1-882180-37-2*) Griffin CA.

Line Dancing Including Line, Circle, Novelty, & Mixers. Earl Atkinson. (Ballroom Dance Ser.). 1986. lib. bdg. 250.00 (*0-8490-3640-2*) Gordon Pr.

Line Diagrams for Logic: Drawing Conclusions - Problems in Contemporary Philosophy. George Englebretsen. LC 98-48177. 120p. 1999. text 59.95 (*0-7734-8190-7*) E Mellen.

***Line Drawings: Defining Women Through Feminist Practice.** Cressida J. Heyes. 2000. pap. text 17.95 (*0-8014-8669-6*) Cornell U Pr.

Line Finder: Rhyming Dictionary (Rhymes "Lines" Not Words) 4th rev. ed. Jim Disney. LC 98-91425. 364p. 1998. 34.95 (*0-9664220-0-7*) JAD Music Grp.

***Line Form Color.** Ellsworth Kelly & Harry Cooper. (Illus.). 110p. 1999. write for info. (*1-891771-06-X*) Harvard Art Mus.

***Line Form Color.** Ellsworth Kelly & Harry Cooper. (Illus.). 108p. 1999. pap. 25.00 (*1-891771-05-1*, Pub. by Harvard Art Mus) U Ch Pr.

***Line Form Color French Language.** Ellsworth Kelly. 1999. pap. text 25.00 (*1-891771-10-8*, Pub. by Harvard Art Mus) U Ch Pr.

Line Forms Here. David Lehman. (Poets on Poetry Ser.). (Illus.). 264p. (C). 1992. pap. 13.95 (*0-472-06483-5*, 06483) U of Mich Pr.

Line Forms Here. David Lehman. (Poets on Poetry Ser.). (Illus.). 264p. (C). 1992. text 39.50 (*0-472-09483-1*, 09483) U of Mich Pr.

Line in Postmodern Poetry. Ed. by Robert Frank & Henry Sayre. LC 87-19206. 272p. (C). 1988. text 27.95 (*0-252-01488-X*) U of Ill Pr.

Line in the Margin: Juan Ramon Jimenez & His Readings in Blake, Shelley, & Yeats. Howard T. Young. LC 79-3963. 319p. 1980. reprint ed. pap. 98.90 (*0-608-01869-4*, 206252100003) Bks Demand.

Line in the Sand. Ron Rendleman. LC 97-66514. 200p. 1997. pap. 11.95 (*0-9650884-1-3*) Sterling Prodns.

***Line in the Sand.** Gerald Seymour. 2000. 25.00 (*0-684-85477-5*) Simon & Schuster.

Line in the Sand. Guillermo Verdecchia & Marcus Youseff. LC 98-110506. 128p. 1997. pap. 11.95 (*0-88922-375-0*, Pub. by Talonbks) Genl Dist Srvs.

***Line in the Sand.** large type ed. Gerald Seymour. 480p. 2000. write for info. (*0-7089-9131-9*) Ulverscroft.

Line in the Sand: The Alamo Diary of Lucinda Lawrence, Gonzales, Texas, 1836. Sherry Garland. LC 97-40638. (Dear America Ser.). (Illus.). 201p. (YA). (gr. 3-9). 1998. 9.95 (*0-590-39466-5*, Pub. by Scholastic Inc) Penguin Putnam.

***Line in the Sand: The Alamo in Blood & Memory.** Randy Roberts & James N. Olson. 1999. write for info. (*0-684-00982-X*) Free Pr.

***Line in the Sand: The Alamo in Blood & Memory.** Randy Roberts & James N. Olson. 352p. 2000. 25.50 (*0-684-83544-4*) Free Pr.

***Line in the Snow: Battle #4 of the Christmas Wars.** Paul A. Lidbert. Ed. by D. B. Lincoln. (Illus.). 24p. (YA). 1999. 5.95 (*1-929332-14-9*, CFE0704) Crunchy Frog.

Line Is Draughon: Political Cartoons. Dennis Draughon. (Illus.). 132p. (Orig.). (C). 1988. pap. 5.95 (*0-929133-00-5*) Barefoot Pr.

Line Isolation Monitors, UL 1022. 4th ed. (C). 1998. pap. text 135.00 (*1-55989-558-6*) Underwrtrs Labs.

Line-Item Veto: A Constitutional Approach. USGPO Staff. LC 96-174379. (S. Hrg. Ser.). iv, 99 p. 1996. write for info. (*0-16-052792-9*) USGPO.

Line Item Veto: Hearing Before the Subcommittee on Legislative & Budget Process of the Committee on Rules, House of Representatives, 105th Congress, 2nd Session, on the Line Item Veto After One Year: The Process & Its Implementation, March 11 & 12, 1998. USGPO Staff. LC 98-192900. iv, 245p. 1998. pap. write for info. (*0-16-057030-1*) USGPO.

Line Letters to Elizabeth. Louis-Ferdinand Celine. Ed. by Alphonse Juilland. (Illus.). 104p. (Orig.). (C). 1990. pap. 24.00 (*1-884868-04-5*) Montparnasse.

Line of Cutting Women. Ed. by Beverly MacFarland et al. LC 98-42510. 256p. (C). 1998. pap. 16.95 (*0-934971-62-5*) Calyx Bks.

***Line of Cutting Women.** Ed. by Beverly MacFarland et al. LC 98-42510. 256p. (C). 1998. 32.00 (*0-934971-63-3*) Calyx Bks.

Line of Duty. Merline Lovelace. 416p. 1996. mass mkt. 5.99 (*0-451-40671-0*, Onyx) NAL.

Line of Duty. Merline Lovelace. 1999. pap. 21.95 (*0-525-94176-2*) NAL.

Line of Duty. Frank Meyer. Ed. by Gwen Costa. LC 90-43991. 1992. pap. 15.95 (*0-87949-332-1*) Ashley Bks.

Line of Duty: Maverick Congressmen & the Development of American Political Culture, 1836-1860, 80. Johanna N. Shields. LC 84-25205. (Contributions in American Studies: No. 80). (Illus.). 297p. 1985. 65.00 (*0-313-24470-7*, SMC/) Greenwood.

Line of Fall. Miles Wilson. LC 89-36788. (John Simmons Short Fiction Award Ser.). 191p. 1989. 10.00 (*0-87745-259-8*) U of Iowa Pr.

Line of Fire. Peter David. (Star Trek Ser.). (J). 1993. 9.09 (*0-606-05622-X*, Pub. by Turtleback) Demco.

Line of Fire. D. A. Hodgman. (Stakeout Ser.). 1995. per. 4.99 (*0-373-63410-2*, 1-63410-4) Harlequin Bks.

Line of Fire: Political Cartoons by Jim Morin. Jim Morin. (Illus.). 264p. 1991. 29.95 (*0-8130-1081-0*); pap. 16.95 (*0-8130-1101-9*) U Press Fla.

Line of Fire: Reading Level 3-4. (Stormy Night Stories Ser.). 16p. 1993. 2.50 (*0-88336-078-0*) New Readers.

Line of Life. John Ford. LC 70-38186. (English Experience Ser.: No. 457). 144p. 1972. reprint ed. 25.00 (*90-221-0457-5*) Walter J Johnson.

Line of Love. James Branch Cabell. (Collected Works of James Branch Cabell). 368p. 1998. reprint ed. lib. bdg. 98.00 (*1-58201-562-7*) Classic Bks.

Line of Love, Dizain des Mariages. James Branch Cabell. LC 79-996077. (Select Bibliographies Reprint Ser.). 1977. 26.95 (*0-8369-5106-9*) Ayer.

Line of Power. A. Strathern. 176p. (Orig.). 1984. pap. text 15.95 (*0-422-78900-3*, 9110, Pub. by Tavistock) Routldge.

***Line of Sight** Kelly Jack. 2001. mass mkt. write for info. (*0-7868-8980-2*) Disney Pr.

***Line of Sight.** Jack Kelly. 352p. 2000. 23.95 (*0-7868-6614-4*, Pub. by Disney Pr); pap. 13.95 (*0-7868-8531-9*, Pub. by Disney Pr) Time Warner.

Line of the Sun: A Novel by Judith Ortiz Cofer. Judith O. Cofer. LC 88-22042. 304p. 1991. reprint ed. pap. 14.95 (*0-8203-1335-1*) U of Ga Pr.

Line Out for a Walk: Familiar Essays. Joseph Epstein. 336p. 1992. pap. 13.95 (*0-393-30854-5*) Norton.

Line Rider's Revenge. Chet Cunningham. 256p. 1994. mass mkt. 3.50 (*1-55817-787-6*, Pinncle Kensgtn) Kensgtn Pub Corp.

Line Rollering Simulation. 4th ed. Clayton. (TA - Typing/Keyboarding Ser.). 1996. mass mkt. 18.95 (*0-538-65094-X*) S-W Pub.

Line Screw: My Twelve Riotous Years Working Behind Bars in Some of Canada's Toughest Jails. J. Michael Yates. 1994. 24.95 (*0-7710-9082-X*) McCland & Stewart.

Line Sophie Drew see Circle Sarah Drew

Line-Up Book. Marisabina Russo. LC 85-24907. (Illus.). 24p. (J). (ps-1). 1986. 15.00 (*0-688-06204-0*, Grenwillow Bks) HarpC Child Bks.

Line Upon Line see Bible Truths for Little Children

Line upon Line. Brooks A. Bryan. LC 98-94863. 1999. write for info. (*0-7392-0058-5*) Morris Pubng.

Line upon Line: Challenging Crossword Classics for Latter-Day Saints. Deanna Moller. 56p. 1993. 8.98 (*0-88290-480-9*, 2061) Horizon Utah.

Line upon Line: Essays on Mormon Doctrine. Ed. by Gary J. Bergera. LC 88-30867. (Essays on Mormonism Ser.: No. 1). 198p. 1989. pap. 14.95 (*0-941214-69-9*) Signature Bks.

Linea - Portrait of a Kaibab Squirrel: With Sketches of Other Wildlife on the North Rim of Grand Canyon. unabridged ed. Joseph G. Hall. (Illus.). iv, 54p. 1998. pap. 9.95 (*0-9662734-0-0*) J G Hall.

Linea del Sol. Judith O. Cofer. 302p. 1996. pap. 12.95 (*0-8477-0249-9*) U of PR Pr.

Linea Longobarda. Luigi Ballerini. (Stanford French & Italian Studies: Vol. 82). (ITA.). 125p. (Orig.). 1996. pap. 56.50 (*0-915838-48-6*) Anma Libri.

Lineage & Other Stories. Bo Lozoff. 120p. (Orig.). 1989. pap. 7.00 (*0-9614444-1-X*) Human Kind Found.

Lineage Book of the British Army: Mounted Corps & Infantry. LC 72-10747. 378p. reprint ed. pap. 117.20 (*0-608-30773-4*, 205531900013) Bks Demand.

Lineage, Life & Labors of Jose Rizal: The Philippine Patriot, a Study of the Growth of Free Ideas in the Transpacific American Territory. Austin Craig. 1977. lib. bdg. 59.95 (*0-8490-2168-5*) Gordon Pr.

Lineage of Diamond Light. rev. ed. Tarthong Tulku. LC 75-642463. (Crystal Mirror Ser.: Vol. 5). 403p. 1991. reprint ed. pap. 22.00 (*0-89800-239-7*) Dharma Pub.

Lineage of Ragpickers, Songpluckers, Elegiasts & Jewelers: Selected Poems of Jewish Family Life, 1973-1995. Albert Goldbarth. LC 96-737. 168p. 1996. 22.95 (*1-56809-021-8*); pap. 14.95 (*1-56809-022-6*) Time Being Bks.

Lineage of the Bowens of Woodstock, Conn. Edward A. Bowen. (Illus.). 251p. 1988. reprint ed. pap. 37.50 (*0-8328-0291-3*); reprint ed. lib. bdg. 45.50 (*0-8328-0290-5*) Higginson Bk Co.

Lineage of the Codes of Light. Jessie E. Ayani. 304p. 1998. pap. 18.00 (*0-9648763-1-0*) Hrt of the Sun.

Lineage of the Polish Arabian Horses: Die Abstammung der Polnischen Araber. Ursula Guttmann & F. B. Klynstra. Tr. by Erika Schiele from ENG. (Illus.). 35p. 1968. boxed set. write for info. (*0-318-71576-7*) G Olms Pubs.

Lineage Principle in Gusii Society. Philip Mayer. LC 79-320820. (International African Institute Ser.: No. 24). 35p. reprint ed. pap. 30.00 (*0-8357-3020-4*, 205710600010) Bks Demand.

Lineages of Members of the National Society of Sons & Daughters of the Pilgrims, 2 vols. 1004p. 1988. reprint ed. 75.00 (*0-8063-1210-6*, 4610) Genealog Pub.

Lineages of the Absolutist State. Perry Anderson. 576p. (C). 1985. pap. 25.00 (*0-86091-710-X*, Pub. by Verso) Norton.

Lineages of the Present. Aijaz Ahmad. (C). 65.00 (*1-85984-877-X*, Pub. by Verso) Norton.

***Lineages of the Present: Ideological & Political Genealogies of Contemporary South Asia.** Aijaz Ahmad. 352p. (C). 2000. 35.00 (*1-85984-765-X*, Pub. by Verso) Norton.

Lineages of the Present: Political Essays. Aijaz Ahmad. 1996. 48.00 (*81-85229-03-1*, Pub. by Manohar) S Asia.

Lineages of the Present: Political Essays. Aijaz Ahmad. 1997. pap. 20.00 (*1-85984-114-7*, Pub. by Verso) Norton.

Lineagics. Hamilton P. Traub. (Illus.). 163p. 1964. 10.00 (*0-930653-04-1*) Intl Bulb Soc.

Lineale. (C). 1989. text. write for info. (*0-201-51071-5*) Addison-Wesley.

Lineaments of Wrath: Race, Violent Crime, & American Culture. James W. Clarke. LC 97-51699. 339p. 1998. 39.95 (*1-56000-358-8*) Transaction Pubs.

Linear Accelerator & Beam Optics Codes. Ed. by Charles Eminhizer. LC 88-46074. (AIP Conference Proceedings Ser.: No. 177). 381p. 1988. lib. bdg. 65.00 (*0-88318-377-3*) Am Inst Physics.

Linear Accelerators for Radiation Therapy. 2nd ed. D. Greene & P. C. Williams. LC 97-28042. (Medical Science Ser.). 1997. 156.00 (*0-7503-0402-2*) IOP Pub.

Linear Accelerators for Radiation Therapy. 2nd ed. D. Greene & P. C. Williams. LC 97-28042. (Medical Science Ser.). 1997. pap. 50.00 (*0-7503-0476-6*) IOP Pub.

Linear Active Circuits: Design & Analysis. William Rynone. LC 85-73317. (Illus.). 613p. 1986. reprint ed. pap. 190.10 (*0-7837-9772-9*, 206050100005) Bks Demand.

Linear Aggregation Theory in Cell Biology. T. L. Hill. (Molecular Biology Ser.). (Illus.). 350p. 1987. 232.00 (*0-387-96490-8*) Spr-Verlag.

Linear Algebra. 1983. 41.00 (*0-387-12477-2*) Spr-Verlag.

Linear Algebra. 300p. 1997. text 33.00 (*981-02-3092-3*) World Scientific Pub.

Linear Algebra. R. B. Allenby. (Modular Mathematics Ser.). 227p. 1995. pap. 17.95 (*0-340-61044-1*, Pub. by E A) Routldge.

Linear Algebra. Stephen Andrilli & David Hecker. (C). 1993. text 77.95 (*0-534-17964-9*) PWS Pubs.

Linear Algebra. Craig Borghesani. (Mathematics Ser.). 1998. student ed., suppl. ed. 28.95 (*0-534-95249-6*) PWS Pubs.

Linear Algebra. David Carlson. Ed. by Heather Bennett. (Electronic Companion Ser.). (Illus.). 300p. (Orig.). (C). 1998. pap. text, wbk. ed. write for info. (*1-888902-54-X*); pap. text, wbk. ed. write for info. incl. cd-rom (*1-888902-76-0*) Cogito Lrning.

Linear Algebra. Harold M. Edwards. LC 94-35356. xiii, 184p. 1995. 43.50 (*0-8176-3731-1*) Birkhauser.

Linear Algebra. George M. Eid. 224p. (C). 1995. text, teacher ed. 16.88 (*0-697-14889-0*, WCB McGr Hill) McGrw-H Hghr Educ.

Linear Algebra. George M. Eid. 592p. (C). 1996. text 58.13 (*0-697-14887-4*, WCB McGr Hill) McGrw-H Hghr Educ.

Linear Algebra. John B. Fraleigh & Raymond A. Beauregard. LC 85-30647. (Illus.). (C). 1987. text. write for info. (*0-201-15459-5*) Addison-Wesley.

Linear Algebra. Jimmie Gilbert. 1995. pap. text 8.00 (*0-12-282791-0*) Acad Pr.

Linear Algebra. Henry Helson. 160p. (Orig.). (C). 1990. pap. text 28.95 (*0-8162-3761-1*) Holden-Day.

Linear Algebra. Hwei P. Hsu. 343p. (C). 1990. pap. text 14.50 (*0-15-601526-9*) Harcourt Coll Pubs.

Linear Algebra. V. A. Ilyin & E. G. Poznyak. 286p. (C). 1986. 43.00 (*0-7855-4985-4*, Pub. by Collets) St Mut.

Linear Algebra. William B. Jacob. 512p. (C). 1990. teacher ed. 9.60 (*0-7167-2177-5*) W H Freeman.

Linear Algebra. Klaus Janich. LC 94-7232. (Undergraduate Texts in Mathematics Ser.). 204p. 1994. 43.95 (*0-387-94128-2*) Spr-Verlag.

Linear Algebra. Burton W. Jones. LC 72-83244. (C). 1973. text 30.00 (*0-8162-4544-4*) Holden-Day.

Linear Algebra. Richard Kaye & Robert Wilson. LC 97-43432. (Illus.). 242p. 1998. pap. text 30.00 (*0-19-850237-0*) OUP.

Linear Algebra. Richard Kaye & Robert Wilson. LC 97-43432. (Illus.). 242p. (C). 1998. text 65.00 (*0-19-850238-9*) OUP.

Linear Algebra. Terry Lawson. LC 95-49808. 432p. 1996. text 92.95 (*0-471-30897-8*) Wiley.

Linear Algebra. Peter Lax. LC 96-36417. (Pure & Applied Mathematics: A Wiley-Interscience Series of Texts, Monographs & Tracts). 272p. 1996. 79.95 (*0-471-11111-2*) Wiley.

Linear Algebra. Nakos. LC 97-47341. (Mathematics Ser.). 666p. 1998. mass mkt. 88.95 (*0-534-95526-6*) PWS Pubs.

Linear Algebra. Nakos. (Mathematics Ser.). 1998. pap., student ed. 28.95 (*0-534-95529-0*) PWS Pubs.

Linear Algebra. Walter Nef. 320p. 1988. pap. 9.95 (*0-486-65772-8*) Dover.

Linear Algebra. Jack Rudman. (Dantes Subject Standardized Tests Ser.: DANTES-27). 1994. pap. 23.95 (*0-8373-6627-5*) Nat Learn.

Linear Algebra. Shores. 1998. pap. 22.19 (*0-07-154167-5*) McGraw.

***Linear Algebra.** Frank Uhling. 450p. 1999. pap. 40.00 (*1-886855-47-1*) Tavenner Pub.

Linear Algebra. Venit. (Mathematics Ser.). 1995. teacher ed. 23.25 (*0-534-95191-0*) Brooks-Cole.

Linear Algebra. Venit. (Adaptable Courseware Ser.). 1996. suppl. ed. 10.50 (*0-534-49714-4*) Brooks-Cole.

Linear Algebra. Venit & Bishop. 1996. 32.00 (*0-534-49713-6*) Thomson Learn.

Linear Algebra. Stewar M. Venit. (Mathematics Ser.). 1995. mass mkt., student ed. 25.50 (*0-534-95194-5*) PWS Pubs.

Linear Algebra. Carroll O. Wilde. LC 87-1313. (Illus.). 448p. 1987. text 38.75 (*0-201-13089-0*) Addison-Wesley.

Linear Algebra. Norman J. Bloch & John G. Michaels. (Illus.). 352p. (C). 1992. reprint ed. text 65.00 (*1-878907-59-X*) TechBooks.

Linear Algebra. Georgi E. Shilov. Tr. by Richard A. Silverman from RUS. LC 77-75267. 387p. (C). 1977. reprint ed. pap. text 11.95 (*0-486-63518-X*) Dover.

Linear Algebra. Michael Stecher. LC 87-17711. 336p. reprint ed. pap. 104.20 (*0-7837-4055-7*, 204388800011) Bks Demand.

Linear Algebra. unabridged ed. W. E. Deskins. LC 95-38346. (Illus.). 640p. 1996. reprint ed. pap. 15.95 (*0-486-68888-7*) Dover.

Linear Algebra. 2nd ed. John B. Fraleigh & Raymond A. Beauregard. (Illus.). 576p. (C). 1990. text 89.00 (*0-201-11949-8*) Addison-Wesley.

Linear Algebra. 2nd ed. Kenneth Hoffman & Ray Kunze. LC 75-142120. (Illus.). 407p. (C). 1971. 93.33 (*0-13-536797-2*) P-H.

Linear Algebra. 2nd ed. David C. Lay. 304p. (C). 1999. pap. text, student ed. write for info. (*0-201-64847-4*) Addison-Wesley.

Linear Algebra. 2nd ed. L. Smith. (Undergraduate Texts in Mathematics Ser.). (Illus.). 415p. 1995. 49.95 (*0-387-96015-5*) Spr-Verlag.

Linear Algebra. 2nd rev. ed. Henry Helson. 226p. (Orig.). (C). 1997. pap. text 20.00 (*0-9655211-0-9*) H Helson.

Linear Algebra. 3rd ed. 400p. (C). 1995. text 24.00 (*0-201-52676-X*) Addison-Wesley.

Linear Algebra. 3rd ed. (C). 1995. text 67.00 (*0-201-53479-7*) Addison-Wesley.

Linear Algebra. 3rd ed. John Fraleigh. 144p. (C). 1995. pap. text, student ed. 26.00 (*0-201-52677-8*) Addison-Wesley.

Linear Algebra. 3rd ed. John B. Fraleigh & Raymond A. Beauregard. LC 93-49722. 608p. (C). 1994. text 89.00 (*0-201-52675-1*) Addison-Wesley.

Linear Algebra. 3rd ed. Stephen H. Friedberg et al. LC 96-26503. 557p. (C). 1996. 93.33 (*0-13-233859-9*) P-H.

Linear Algebra. 3rd ed. Kenneth Hoffman. (C). 1999. 69.33 (*0-13-181496-6*) P-H.

Linear Algebra. 3rd ed. Serge A. Lang. (Undergraduate Texts in Mathematics Ser.). (Illus.). 200p. 1996. 39.95 (*0-387-96412-6*) Spr-Verlag.

Linear Algebra. 3rd ed. Michael O'Nan & Herbert B. Enderton. 461p. (C). 1989. pap. text 20.75 (*0-15-551009-6*) SCP.

Linear Algebra. 3rd ed. L. Smith. LC 97-48884. (Undergraduate Texts in Mathematics Ser.). (Illus.). 464p. (C). 1998. 49.95 (*0-387-98455-0*) Spr-Verlag.

Linear Algebra. 4th rev. ed. W. H. Greub. Ed. by J. H. Ewing et al. (Graduate Texts in Mathematics Ser.: Vol. 23). (Illus.). xvii, 451p. 1995. 65.95 (*0-387-90110-8*) Spr-Verlag.

Linear Algebra. 6th ed. 1996. text 26.00 (*3-540-59223-7*) Spr-Verlag.

Linear Algebra: A First Course with Applications to Differential Equations. Tom M. Apostol. LC 96-37131. (Illus.). 368p. 1997. 84.95 (*0-471-17421-1*) Wiley.

Linear Algebra: A Geometric Approach. Edoardo Sernesi. Tr. by J. Montaldi. (Illus.). 384p. (C). (gr. 13). 1993. ring bd. 47.95 (*0-412-40680-2*, A7012, Chap & Hall CRC) CRC Pr.

Linear Algebra: A Geometric Approach. Edoardo Sernesi. Tr. by J. Montaldi. (Chapman & Hall Mathematics Ser.). (Illus.). 256p. (C). 1992. text 82.50 (*0-412-40670-5*, A7008) Chapman & Hall.

Linear Algebra: A Modern Approach. Poole. (Mathematics Ser.). 2001. mass mkt. 47.00 (*0-534-34174-8*) Brooks-Cole.

Linear Algebra: A Student's Solution Manual. Moore & Adil M. Yaqub. (C). 1992. pap. text 18.00 (*0-673-46288-9*) Addson-Wesley Educ.

Linear Algebra: An Interactive Laboratory Approach with Mathematica. John R. Wicks. LC 96-11294. 384p. 1996. pap. text 100.00 (*0-201-82642-9*) Addison-Wesley.

Linear Algebra: An Interactive Laboratory Approach with Mathematica. John R. Wicks. (C). 1997. write for info. (*0-201-46091-2*) Addison-Wesley.

Linear Algebra: An Introduction. Richard Bronson. (Illus.). 504p. 1995. pap. text 45.00 (*0-12-135245-5*) Acad Pr.

Linear Algebra: An Introduction to Abstract Mathematics. Robert J. Valenza. LC 99-207207. (Undergraduate Texts in Mathematics Ser.). (Illus.). 265p. 1993. write for info. (*3-540-94099-5*) Spr-Verlag.

Linear Algebra: An Introduction to the Theory & Use of Vectors & Matrices. Alan Tucker. (Illus.). 544p. (C). 1993. teacher ed. write for info. (0-318-69562-6) Macmillan.

***Linear Algebra: An Introduction Using Mathematics.** Fred E. Szabo. (Illus.). 662p. 2000. 69.95 (0-12-680135-5) Acad Pr.

Linear Algebra: An Introduction with Concurrent Examples. A. G. Hamilton. 338p. (C). 1990. text 100.00 (0-521-32517-X) Cambridge U Pr.

Linear Algebra: An Introductory Approach. C. W. Curtis. (Undergraduate Texts in Mathematics Ser.). (Illus.). 340p. 1997. 39.95 (0-387-90992-3) Spr-Verlag.

Linear Algebra: Challenging Problems for Students. Fuzhen Zhang. LC 96-12568. (Studies in the Mathematical Sciences). 176p. 1996. text 35.00 (0-8018-5458-X); pap. text 14.95 (0-8018-5459-8) Johns Hopkins.

Linear Algebra: Gateway to Mathematics. Robert Messer. LC 93-21043. 560p. (C). 1997. 100.00 (0-06-501728-5) Addson-Wesley Educ.

Linear Algebra: Ideas & Applications. Richard C. Penney. LC 97-17169. 400p. 1997. text 95.95 (0-471-18179-X) Wiley.

Linear Algebra: Introduction to Abstract Mathematics. Robert J. Valenza. LC 93-26143. (Undergraduate Texts in Mathematics Ser.). (Illus.). 237p. 1995. 39.95 (0-387-94099-5) Spr-Verlag.

Linear Algebra: Maple Labs. Lawson. 112p. 1996. pap. text, suppl. ed. 21.95 (0-471-13594-1) Wiley.

***Linear Algebra: Modules for Interactive Learning Using Maple.** rev. ed. 326p. (C). 1999. pap. text 19.13 (0-201-64846-6) Addison-Wesley.

***Linear Algebra: Modules for Interactive Learning Using Maple, Preliminary Version.** Herman. 1999. pap. text 15.73 (0-201-61838-9) Addison-Wesley.

Linear Algebra: Study Manual. John B. Fraleigh & Raymond A. Beauregard. LC 85-30647. (Illus.). (C). 1987. 12.75 (0-201-15458-7) Addison-Wesley.

Linear Algebra: Theory & Application. Roberts. (C). 1998. text 69.50 (0-03-097169-1) Harcourt Coll Pubs.

Linear Algebra: With Applications Chapter, Set. 7th ed. Howard Anton. 570p. 1994. pap. text 47.50 (0-471-01562-8) Wiley.

Linear Algebra & Application. Bretscher. 1998. pap. text 29.33 (0-13-576273-1) P-H.

Linear Algebra & Applications. David C. Lay. (C). 1994. pap. text. write for info. (0-201-84556-3) Addison-Wesley.

Linear Algebra & Different Equations using Matlab. Martin Golubitsky. (Mathematics Ser.). 1999. mass mkt. 20.00 (0-534-36306-7) Brooks-Cole.

Linear Algebra & Differential Equations. Charles G. Cullen. 1979. mass mkt. 45.00 (0-87150-262-3, PWS 2131) PWS Pubs.

***Linear Algebra & Differential Equations Using Matlab.** Golubitsky. LC 98-44500. (Mathematics Ser.). 1999. 90.95 (0-534-35425-4) Brooks-Cole.

Linear Algebra & Geometry. A. I. Kostrikin & Yu I. Manin. (Algebra, Logica & Applications Ser). ix, 309p. 1997. pap. text 44.00 (90-5699-049-7) Gordon & Breach.

Linear Algebra & Geometry, Vol. 1. Yu I. Manin & Alexei I. Kostrikin. x, 310p. 1989. text 240.00 (2-88124-683-4) Gordon & Breach.

Linear Algebra & Group Representations, 2 vols. Shaw. 1983. 231.00 (0-12-639200-5) Acad Pr.

Linear Algebra & Group Representations: Linear Algebra & Introduction to Group Representations, Vol. 1. Ronald Shaw. 1983. text 116.00 (0-12-639201-3) Acad Pr.

Linear Algebra & Group Representations: Multilinear Algebra & Group Representations, Vol. 11. Ronald Shaw. 1983. text 116.00 (0-12-639202-1) Acad Pr.

Linear Algebra & Group Theory for Physicists. K. N. Srinivasa Rao. 400p. 1996. text 39.95 (0-470-22061-9) Halsted Pr.

Linear Algebra & Its Applications. 2nd ed. 640p. (C). 1996. 74.33 (0-201-82479-5) Addison-Wesley.

Linear Algebra & Its Applications. 2nd ed. David C. Lay. Ed. by Karen Guardino. LC 96-9417. 560p. (C). 1996. 97.00 (0-201-82478-7) Addison-Wesley.

Linear Algebra & Its Applications. 2nd ed. David C. Lay. (C). 1997. pap. text. write for info. (0-201-76717-1) Addison-Wesley.

Linear Algebra & Its Applications. 2nd ed. David C. Lay. 272p. (C). 1997. pap. text, student ed. 15.00 (0-201-82477-9) Addison-Wesley.

Linear Algebra & Its Applications. 3rd ed. Gilbert Strang. 505p. (C). 1988. text 96.50 (0-15-551005-3) SCP.

Linear Algebra & Its Applications. 3rd ed. Gilbert Strang. 505p. (C). 1988. pap. text 20.75 (0-15-551006-1) SCP.

Linear Algebra & Its Applications. 4th ed. Strang. (C). 1998. pap. text, teacher ed. 29.75 (0-03-010568-4) Harcourt Coll Pubs.

Linear Algebra & Its Applications. 4th ed. Gilbert Strang. (C). Date not set. pap. text 79.50 (0-03-010567-6) Harcourt Coll Pubs.

Linear Algebra & Its Applications, Vol. 1. David Griffel. 226p. 1989. text 49.95 (0-470-21242-X) P-H.

***Linear Algebra & Its Applications Updated.** 2nd ed. 640p. (C). 1999. pap. text 74.33 (0-201-64845-8) Addison-Wesley.

Linear Algebra & its Applications Updated. 2nd ed. David C. Lay. LC 99-37547. 576p. (C). 1999. 86.00 incl. cd-rom (0-201-34774-1) S&S Trade.

Linear Algebra & Its Role in Systems Theory. Ed. by Richard A. Brualdi et al. LC 85-18620. (Contemporary Mathematics Ser.: Vol. 47). 506p. 1985. pap. 46.00 (0-8218-5041-5, CONM/47) Am Math.

Linear Algebra & Its Role in Systems Theory: Proceedings of the AMS-IMS-SIAM Joint Summer Research Conference Held on July 29-August 4, 1984, with Support from the National Science Foundation. Ed. by Richard A. Brualdi et al. LC 85-18620. (Contemporary Mathematics Ser.: No. 47). (Illus.). 520p. 1985. reprint ed. pap. 161.20 (0-608-07823-9, 205266800010) Bks Demand.

Linear Algebra & Linear Models. 2nd ed. R. B. Bapat. LC 99-30383. (Universitext Ser.). 184p. 1999. 44.95 (0-387-98871-8) Spr-Verlag.

***Linear Algebra & Linear Operators in Engineering: With Applications in Mathematica.** H. Ted Davis. 522p. 2000. 89.95 (0-12-206349-X) Acad Pr.

Linear Algebra & Matrix Theory. Jimmie Gilbert & Linda Gilbert. (Illus.). 394p. (C). 1995. text 42.00 (0-12-282970-0) Acad Pr.

Linear Algebra & Matrix Theory. 2nd ed. Evar D. Nering. 368p. (C). 1976. text 106.95 (0-471-63178-7) Wiley.

Linear Algebra & Ordinary Differential Equations. Jeffrey. 1136p. 1991. lib. bdg. 49.95 (0-86542-114-5) Blackwell Sci.

Linear Algebra & Ordinary Differential Equations. Alan Jeffrey. 1136p. 1991. boxed set 78.95 (0-86542-113-7) CRC Pr.

Linear Algebra Applications. 7th ed. Howard Anton. 864p. 1994. text 58.00 (0-471-07276-1) Wiley.

Linear Algebra Applications 97. 2nd ed. Lay. 1997. text (0-201-30121-0) Addison-Wesley.

Linear Algebra Done Right. Sheldon Axler. Ed. by F. W. Gehring & P. R. Halmos. LC 95-44889. (Undergraduate Texts in Mathematics Ser.). 248p. (C). 1995. 53.95 (0-387-94595-4); pap. 31.95 (0-387-94596-2) Spr-Verlag.

Linear Algebra Done Right. 2nd ed. Sheldon J. Axler. LC 97-16664. (Undergraduate Texts in Mathematics Ser.). 1997. 59.95 (0-387-98259-0) Spr-Verlag.

Linear Algebra Done Right. 2nd ed. Sheldon J. Axler. LC 97-16664. (Undergraduate Texts in Mathematics Ser.). 251p. 1997. pap. 29.00 (0-387-98258-2) Spr-Verlag.

Linear Algebra Experiments Using the Derive Program. Mary Salter & Lawrence G. Gilligan. (Illus.). 128p. (C). 1992. pap. text 19.95 (0-9626661-4-9) Gilmar Pub.

Linear Algebra for Calculus. 2nd ed. Stewart et al. (Mathematics Ser.). 1995. mass mkt. 22.50 (0-534-25248-6) Brooks-Cole.

Linear Algebra for Control Theory. Ed. by Paul Van Dooren & Bostwick Wyman. LC 94-249. (IMA Volumes in Mathematics & Its Applications Ser.: Vol. 62). (Illus.). xvi, 189p. 1994. 65.95 (0-387-94267-X) Spr-Verlag.

Linear Algebra for Engineer. Cowen. 1999. pap. text 64.95 (0-7167-3207-6) W H Freeman.

Linear Algebra for Engineering & Science: Preliminary Edition. 2nd ed. Carl C. Cowen. (Illus.). viii, 462p. 1997. pap. text 40.00 (0-9650717-4-X) West Pickle.

***Linear Algebra for Engineers & Scientists.** Ed. by Prentice-Hall Staff. 420p. (C). 2000. 77.33 (0-13-906728-0) P-H.

Linear Algebra for John Abbott College. Norman Lay. (C). 1998. pap. text. write for info. (0-201-45673-7) Addison-Wesley.

Linear Algebra for Large-Scale & Real-Time Applications: Proceedings of the NATO Advanced Study Institute, Leuven, Belgium, August 3-14, 1992. Ed. by Marc S. Moonen. (NATO ASI Series E, Applied Sciences). 436p. (C). 1993. text 241.50 (0-7923-2151-0) Kluwer Academic.

***Linear Algebra for Quantum Theory.** Per-Olov Lowdin. LC 97-22362. 458p. 1998. 94.95 (0-471-19958-3, Wiley-Interscience) Wiley.

Linear Algebra for Signal Processing. Ed. by Adam Bojanczyk & George Cybenko. LC 95-2605. (IMA Volumes in Mathematics & Its Applications Ser.: Vol. 69). (Illus.). 200p. 1995. 59.95 (0-387-94491-5) Spr-Verlag.

Linear Algebra, Geodesy & GPS. Gilbert Strang & K. Borre. LC 96-44288. 1997. 68.75 (0-9614088-6-3) Wellesley-Cambridge Pr.

Linear Algebra in Signals, Systems, & Control. Ed. by Biswa N. Datta et al. LC 88-60026. (Proceedings in Applied Mathematics Ser.: No. 32). xiv, 667p. 1988. 65.75 (0-89871-223-8) Soc Indus-Appl Math.

Linear Algebra Labs with Matlab. 2nd ed. David R. Hill & David E. Zitarelli. 320p. (C). 1996. pap. text, lab manual ed. 30.00 (0-13-505439-7) P-H.

Linear Algebra, Markov Chains, & Queueing Models. Ed. by Carl D. Meyer & Richard J. Plemmons. LC 93-2100. (IMA Volumes in Mathematics & Its Applications Ser.: Vol. 48). (Illus.). 1993. 69.95 (0-387-94085-5); write for info. (3-540-94085-5) Spr-Verlag.

Linear Algebra, Mat Labs. Lawson. 83p. 1996. pap., lab manual ed. 23.95 (0-471-14953-5) Wiley.

***Linear Algebra Northern Illinois University.** 582p. (C). 1999. pap. 101.00 (0-201-63647-6) S&S Trade.

Linear Algebra over Commutative Rings. Bernard R. McDonald. (Pure & Applied Mathematics Ser.: Vol. 87). (Illus.). 568p. 1984. text 175.00 (0-8247-7122-2) Dekker.

Linear Algebra Problem Book. Paul R. Halmos. LC 94-79588. 340p. (C). 1995. pap. text 39.95 (0-88385-322-1, DOL-16) Math Assn.

Linear Algebra Problem Solver. rev. ed. Research & Education Association Staff. LC 79-92402. (Illus.). 1022p. 1999. pap. text 29.95 (0-87891-518-4) Res & Educ.

Linear Algebra Projects Using Mathematica. Andrews & Morely. (C). 1993. pap. text 11.74 (0-07-001868-5) McGraw.

Linear Algebra Quick Review. Steven A. Leduc. (Cliffs Quick Reviews Ser.). (Illus.). 101p. (Orig.). 1996. pap. text 9.95 (0-8220-5331-4, Cliff) IDG Bks.

Linear Algebra, Rational Approximation Orthogonal Polynomials. Adhemar Bultheel & Marc Van Barel. LC 97-40610. (Studies in Computational Mathematics: 6). 464p. 1997. 158.00 (0-444-82872-9) Elsevier.

Linear Algebra, Students Solutions Manual. Lawson. 112p. 1996. pap., student ed. 23.95 (0-471-14954-3) Wiley.

Linear Algebra through Geometry. T. F. Banchoff & J. Wermer. (Undergraduate Texts in Mathematics Ser.). (Illus.). 257p. 1983. 32.00 (0-387-90787-4) Spr-Verlag.

Linear Algebra Through Geometry. 2nd ed. T. F. Banchoff & J. Wermer. (Undergraduate Texts in Mathematics Ser.). (Illus.). xii, 305p. 1995. 43.95 (0-387-97586-1) Spr-Verlag.

Linear Algebra to Accompany Calculus with Analytics. Anton. 160p. 1995. pap. text, suppl. ed. 17.95 (0-471-10677-1) Wiley.

Linear Algebra W/applications. 2nd ed. Jeanne Agnew & Robert C. Knapp. LC 82-20752. (Math). 400p. (C). 1983. mass mkt. 33.50 (0-534-01364-3) Brooks-Cole.

***Linear Algebra with Applications** 1998. teacher ed. write for info. (0-13-576265-0) P-H.

Linear Algebra with Applications. Agnew. (Math). 1978. mass mkt. 22.25 (0-8185-0256-8) Brooks-Cole.

Linear Algebra with Applications. Otto Bretscher. LC 96-36942. (Illus.). 587p. (C). 1996. 93.33 (0-13-190729-8) P-H.

Linear Algebra with Applications. Charles G. Cullen. (C). 1997. text 59.33 (0-673-18570-2) Addison-Wesley Educ.

Linear Algebra with Applications. John T. Scheick. LC 96-27488. (International Series in Pure & Applied Mathematics). 464p. (C). 1996. 65.31 (0-07-055184-7) McGraw.

Linear Algebra with Applications. 2nd ed. Gareth Williams. 504p. (C). 1991. text 56.25 (0-697-09738-2, WCB McGr Hill) McGraw-H Hghr Educ.

Linear Algebra with Applications. 2nd ed. Gareth Williams. 504p. (C). 1991. text, student ed. 18.75 (0-697-11368-X, WCB McGr Hill) McGraw-H Hghr Educ.

Linear Algebra with Applications. 2nd ed. Gareth Williams. 52p. (C). 1991. text, student ed. 9.38 (0-697-11375-2, WCB McGr Hill); text, student ed. 9.38 (0-697-11376-0, WCB McGr Hill); text, student ed. 9.38 (0-697-11377-9, WCB McGr Hill); text, student ed. 9.38 (0-697-11378-7, WCB McGr Hill) McGrw-H Hghr Educ.

Linear Algebra with Applications. 3rd ed. Jeanne L. Agnew & Robert C. Knapp. 392p. (C). 1989. text 72.95 (0-534-09456-2) Brooks-Cole.

Linear Algebra with Applications. 3rd ed. Nicholson. (Mathematics Ser.). 1994. mass mkt., student ed. 27.75 (0-534-93668-7) PWS Pubs.

Linear Algebra with Applications. 3rd ed. W. Keith Nicholson. LC 93-28879. 1994. mass mkt. 62.50 (0-534-93666-0) PWS Pubs.

Linear Algebra with Applications. 3rd ed. Gareth Williams. 560p. (C). 1995. text 19.38 (0-697-26851-9, WCB McGr Hill) McGrw-H Hghr Educ.

Linear Algebra with Applications. 3rd ed. Gareth Williams. 576p. (C). 1995. text 58.13 (0-697-26849-7, WCB McGr Hill); text, boxed set 23.13 incl. disk (0-697-26852-7, WCB McGr Hill); text, boxed set 23.13 incl. disk (0-697-26853-5, WCB McGr Hill) McGrw-H Hghr Educ.

Linear Algebra with Applications. 3rd ed. Gareth Williams & Lisa O. Coulter. 80p. (C). 1995. text, student ed. 18.75 (0-697-29714-4, WCB McGr Hill) McGrw-H Hghr Educ.

Linear Algebra with Applications. 3rd ed. Gareth Williams et al. 52p. (C). 1995. student ed. write for info. (0-697-32963-1, WCB McGr Hill) McGrw-H Hghr Educ.

***Linear Algebra with Applications.** 4th ed. Gareth Williams. LC 00-30734. 2000. write for info. (0-7637-1451-8) Jones & Bartlett.

Linear Algebra with Applications. 5th ed. Steven J. Leon. LC 97-31804. 491p. 1997. 93.33 (0-13-849308-1) P-H.

Linear Algebra with Applications: Solutions Manual. 2nd ed. Charles G. Cullen. 192p. (C). 1997. pap. text, student ed. 25.00 (0-673-98317-X) Addison-Wesley.

Linear Algebra, with Applications to Differential Equations. P. G. Kumpel & J. A. Thorpe. LC 82-60630. 353p. (C). 1983. text 77.00 (0-03-060556-3) SCP.

Linear Algebra with Business Applications. 2nd ed. Brown & Donald R. Sherbert. (C). 1993. pap. text 31.00 (0-07-056966-5) McGraw.

***Linear Algebra with MATLAB: Interactive Text with CD.** S. K. Jain et al. 306p. (C). 2000. pap. 54.95 incl. cd-rom (1-930190-16-6) Key Coll.

Linear Algebra with the HP-48G/GX. Donald R. LaTorre. (Illus.). 226p. (C). 1995. pap. 15.95 (1-886801-20-7) Thomson Learn.

Linear Algebraic Groups. 2nd ed. T. A. Springer. LC 98-9333. (Progress in Mathematics Ser.). 1998. write for info. (3-7643-4021-5) Birkhauser.

Linear Algebraic Groups. 2nd ed. Tony A. Springer. LC 98-9333. (Progress in Mathematics Ser.). 350p. 1998. 64.50 (0-8176-4021-5) Birkhauser.

Linear Algebraic Groups. 2nd enl. ed. Armand Borel. Ed. by J. H. Ewing et al. (Graduate Texts in Mathematics Ser.: Vol. 126). 304p. 1997. reprint ed. text 49.95 (0-387-97370-2) Spr-Verlag.

Linear Algebraic Groups, Vol. XVI. rev. ed. J. E. Humphreys. Ed. by J. H. Ewing et al. LC 98-151622. (Graduate Texts in Mathematics Ser.: Vol. 21). 253p. (C). 1995. 54.95 (0-387-90108-6) Spr-Verlag.

Linear Algebraic Groups & Their Representations. Ed. by Richard S. Elman et al. LC 93-5642. (Contemporary Mathematics Ser.: Vol. 153). 200p. 1993. pap. 42.00 (0-8218-5161-6, CONM/153) Am Math.

Linear Alkylbenzene Sulfonates & Related Compounds. (Environmental Health Criteria Ser.: Vol. 169). 328p. (C). 1996. pap. 62.00 (92-4-157169-1, 1160169) World Health.

Linear Analysis. Ralph Henstock. LC 79-1233. 451p. reprint ed. pap. 139.90 (0-608-13233-0, 205579600038) Bks Demand.

***Linear Analysis: An Introductory Course.** 2nd ed. Bela Bollobas. LC 99-11614. 245p. (C). 1999. pap. text 27.95 (0-521-65577-3) Cambridge U Pr.

Linear Analysis & Representation Theory. S. A. Gaal. LC 72-95686. (Grundlehren der Mathematischen Wissenschaften Ser.: Vol. 198). ix, 688p. 1973. 93.95 (0-387-06195-9) Spr-Verlag.

Linear Analysis of Competitive Economies. L. S. Ramaiah. LC 94-31582. (L. S. E. Handbooks in Economics Ser.). 184p. (C). 1995. pap. 42.00 (0-13-342973-3, Pub. by Wheatsheaf Bks) P-H.

Linear & Complex Analysis Problem Book. V. P. Havin et al. (Lecture Notes in Mathematics Ser.: Vol. 1043). xviii, 721p. 1984. 61.95 (0-387-12869-7) Spr-Verlag.

Linear & Complex Analysis Problem Book, No. 3. Ed. by V. P. Havin & N. K. Nikolski. LC 94-9649. (Lecture Notes in Mathematics Ser.: Vol. 1573-1574). 1996. 95.00 (0-387-57870-6) Spr-Verlag.

Linear & Discrete Optimization & Modeling Software: A Resource Handbook. Ramesh Sharda. 1995. 49.95 (0-9629217-5-0) Lionheart Pub.

Linear & Graphical Models: For the Multivariate Complex Normal Distribution. N. Wermuth et al. (Lecture Notes in Statistics Ser.; Vol. 101). (Illus.). x, 184p. 1995. 48.95 (0-387-94521-0) Spr-Verlag.

Linear & Integer Programming: Theory & Practice. Gerard Sierksma. (Monographs & Textbooks in Pure & Applied Mathematics: No. 198). (Illus.). 696p. 1996. text 175.00 incl. cd-rom (0-8247-9695-0) Dekker.

Linear & Multilinear Algebra see Introduction to Vectors & Tensors

***Linear & Non-Linear Aspects of Vortices: The Ginzburg--Landau Model.** Frank Pacard & Tristan Riviere. LC 00-36108. (Progress in Nonlinear Differential Equations & Their Applications Ser.). 2000. write for info. (3-7643-4133-5) Birkhauser.

Linear & Non-Linear Circuits. L. O. Chua et al. 839p. (C). 1987. 104.06 (0-07-010898-6) McGraw.

***Linear & Nonlinear Aspects of Vortices: The Ginzburg-Landau Model.** Frank Pacard & T. Riviere. (Progress in Nonlinear Differential Equations & Their Applications Ser.: Vol. 39). 360p. 2000. 79.95 (0-8176-4133-5) Birkhauser.

Linear & Nonlinear Conjugate Gradient-Related Methods. Ed. by Loyce M. Adams & J. L. Mazareth. LC 96-68754. (Proceedings in Applied Mathematics Ser.: No. 85). xvi, 164p. 1996. pap. 34.00 (0-89871-376-5, PR85) Soc Indus-Appl Math.

***Linear & Nonlinear Crack Growth Using Boundary Elements.** Adrian P. Cisilino. (Topics in Engineering Ser.: Vol. 36). 208p. 1999. 126.00 (1-85312-700-0, 7000, Pub. by WIT Pr) Computational Mech MA.

Linear & Nonlinear Differential Equations. Ian D. Huntley & R. M. Johnson. (Mathematics & Its Applications Ser.). 190p. 1983. pap. text 33.95 (0-470-27420-4) P-H.

Linear & Nonlinear Filtering for Engineers & Scientists. N. U. Ahmed. 250p. 1999. 42.00 (981-02-3609-3) World Scientific Pub.

Linear & Nonlinear Finite Element Analysis in Engineering Practice: Includes Examples with Algor Accupak/VE. Constantine C. Spyrokos & John Raftoyiannis. LC 97-75327. (Illus.). 528p. 1997. text 179.00 (0-9652806-2-4) Algor PA.

Linear & Nonlinear Models for the Analysis of Repeated Measure. Edward F. Vonesh & Vernun M. Chinchilli. LC 96-41105. (Statistics: Textbooks & Monographs: Vol. 154). (Illus.). 576p. 1996. text 85.00 (0-8247-8248-8) Dekker.

Linear & Nonlinear Optical Properties of Molecules: An Overview. George H. Wagniere. LC 93-37111. (Illus.). 195p. (C). 1993. 79.95 (3-527-29045-1, Wiley-VCH) Wiley.

Linear & Nonlinear Parabolic Complex Equations. Guo Chun Wen. LC 99-13750. 250p. 1999. 48.00 (981-02-3856-8) World Scientific Pub.

Linear & Nonlinear Perturbations of the Operator. V. G. Osmolovskii. Tr. by Tamara Rozhkovskaya from RUS. LC 96-40489. (Translations of Mathematical Monographs: Vol. 160). 104p. 1997. text 59.00 (0-8218-0586-X, MMONO/160) Am Math.

Linear & Nonlinear Programming. Stephen G. Nash & Ariela Sofer. (Series in Industrial Engineering & Management Science). (Illus.). 692p. (C). 1995. 90.63 (0-07-046065-5) McGraw.

Linear & Nonlinear Programming. 2nd ed. David G. Kuenberger. (Illus.). 512p. (C). 1984. text 86.00 (0-201-15794-2) Addison-Wesley.

Linear & Nonlinear Programming: An Introduction to Linear Methods in Mathematical Programming. Roger Hartley. (Mathematics & Its Applications Ser.). 1985. pap. text 23.95 (0-470-20179-7) P-H.

Linear & Nonlinear Random Waves. Yu S. Kivshar et al. 300p. 1994. text 46.00 (981-02-1022-1) World Scientific Pub.

Linear & Nonlinear Spin Waves in Magnetic Films & Superlattices. M. G. Cottam. 400p. 1994. text 106.00 (981-02-1006-X) World Scientific Pub.

Linear & Nonlinear Waves. G. B. Whitham. (Pure & Applied Mathematics: A Wiley-Interscience Series of Texts, Monographs & Tracts). 656p. 1974. 195.00 (0-471-94090-9) Wiley.

Linear & Nonlinear Waves. G. B. Whitham. LC 99-28957. (Pure & Applied Mathematics: A Wiley-Interscience Series of Texts, Monographs & Tracts). 638p. 1999. pap. 64.95 (0-471-35942-4) Wiley.

Linear & Quasilinear Equations of Parabolic Type. Olga A. Ladyzhenskaja et al. LC 68-19440. (Translations of Mathematical Monographs: Vol. 23). 648p. 1969. reprint ed. pap. 49.00 (0-8218-1573-3, MMONO/23) Am Math.

An Asterisk (*) at the beginning of an entry indicates that the title is appearing for the first time.

L

Linear & Quasilinear Parabolic Problems Vol. 1: Abstract Linear Theory. Herbert Amann. LC 95-7400. (Monographs in Mathematics: Vol. 89). 376p. 1995. 119.00 (*0-8176-5114-4*) Birkhauser.

Linear & Tensor Algebra. Robert Hermann. (Interdisciplinary Mathematics Ser.: No. 2). 183p. 1973. 25.00 (*0-915692-01-5*, 991600266) Math Sci Pr.

Linear Approximation. Arthur Sard. LC 63-11988. (Mathematical Surveys & Monographs: No. 9). 544p. 1963. reprint ed. pap. 70.00 (*0-8218-1509-1*, SURV/9) Am Math.

Linear Approximations in Convex Metric Spaces. Bela Gyires. 133p. 1993. text 45.00 (*981-02-1483-9*) World Scientific Pub.

Linear Associative Alegebra. Benjamin Peirce. (Notable American Authors Ser.). 1999. reprint ed. lib. bdg. 125.00 (*0-7812-8735-9*) Rprt Serv.

Linear B: An Introduction. T. J. Hooker. (C). 1980. reprint ed. pap. text 33.95 (*0-906515-62-9*, Pub. by Brist Class Pr) Focus Pub-R Pullins.

Linear B & Related Scripts. John Chadwick. (Reading the Past Ser.: Vol. 1). 64p. (Orig.). (C). 1987. pap. 13.95 (*0-520-06019-9*, Pub. by U CA Pr) Cal Prin Full Svc.

Linear Carbohydrates As Chiral Selectors in Capillary Electrophoresis. Annick D'Hulst. (Acta Biomedica Lovaniensia Ser.: No. 135). (Illus.). 141p. (Orig.). 1996. pap. 42.50 (*90-6186-760-6*, Pub. by Leuven Univ) Coronet Bks.

Linear Chumash. Bamidbar. LC 97-3090. (ENG & HEB.). 1997. 16.95 (*0-87306-797-5*) Feldheim.

Linear Chumash. Devarim. 1997. 16.95 (*0-87306-798-3*) Feldheim.

Linear Chumash: Bereishis. Bereishis Genesis. 1987. 16.95 (*0-87306-414-3*) Feldheim.

Linear Chumash: Shemos. 1987. 16.95 (*0-87306-607-3*) Feldheim.

Linear Chumash: Vayikra. 1987. 16.95 (*0-87306-660-X*) Feldheim.

***Linear Circuit Analysis.** (C). 1999. text. write for info. (*0-201-43337-0*) Addison-Wesley.

Linear Circuit Analysis. Davis. LC 97-30067. (Electrical Engineering Ser.). (C). 1998. 101.95 (*0-534-95095-7*) PWS Pubs.

Linear Circuits. rev. ed. Heath Company Staff. (Circuit Files Ser.). (Illus.). 89p. 1981. reprint ed. ring bd. 49.95 (*0-87119-002-8*, EH-801) Heathkit-Zenith Ed.

Linear Circuits, Set. Ronald E. Scott. Incl. Pt. 2. Frequency-Domain Analysis. 1961. 1961. Set text 32.75 (*0-201-06820-6*) Addison-Wesley.

Linear Circuits Vol. 1: Operational Amplifiers Data Book, Vols. A & B. Texas Instruments Engineering Staff. 1424p. 1997. 36.00 (*0-685-62492-7*, SLYD003A) Tex Instr Inc.

Linear Circuits Vol. 2: Data Acquisition & Conversion Data Book. Texas Instruments Engineering Staff. 896p. 1992. 15.00 (*0-685-62493-5*, SLYD004A) Tex Instr Inc.

Linear Circuits Analysis. Swaminathan Madhu. (Illus.). 850p. 1988. text. write for info. (*0-318-62359-5*) P-H.

Linear Circuits, Systems & Signal Processing: Advanced Theory & Applications. Ed. by Nobuo Nagai. (Electrical Engineering & Electronics Ser.: Vol. 62). (Illus.). 456p. 1989. text 160.00 (*0-8247-8185-6*) Dekker.

Linear Collider BB Factory: Proceedings. D. Stork. 464p. (C). 1987. pap. 54.00 (*9971-5-0357-3*); text 144.00 (*9971-5-0356-5*) World Scientific Pub.

Linear Complementarity Problem. Richard W. Cottle et al. (Computer Science & Scientific Computing Ser.). (Illus.). 762p. 1992. text 74.95 (*0-12-192350-9*) Acad Pr.

Linear Control System Analysis & Design: Conventional & Modern. 4th ed. John J. D'Azzo & Constantine H. Houpis. LC 94-25299. (Electrical & Computer Engineering Ser.). 800p. (C). 1995. 98.13 (*0-07-016321-9*) McGraw.

Linear Control System Analysis & Design: Conventional & Modern, Solutions Manual. 4th ed. John D'Azzo & Constantine Houpis. 1995. pap. text. write for info. (*0-07-016322-7*) McGraw.

Linear Control Systems. Rohrs. 1993. student ed. 20.62 (*0-07-041526-9*) McGraw.

Linear Control Systems. Charles E. Rohrs. 672p. (C). 1992. 82.19 (*0-07-041525-0*) McGraw.

Linear Control Systems: A Computer-Aided Approach. Mohammad Jamshidi & M. Malek-Zavarei. 450p. 1986. pap. text 54.00 (*0-08-028702-6*, Pergamon Pr) Elsevier.

Linear Control Systems: A Computer-Aided Approach. Mohammad Jamshidi & Manu Malek-Zavarei. LC 84-6164. (International Series on Systems & Control: No. 7). 636p. 1985. pap. 197.20 (*0-608-04997-2*, 206561500004) Bks Demand.

Linear Control Systems Engineering. Morris Driels. LC 94-11331. (Series in Mechanical Engineering). 628p. (C). 1995. 88.44 (*0-07-017824-0*) McGraw.

Linear Control Systems Management: Solutions Manual. Morris Driels. 1995. text. write for info. (*0-07-017825-9*) McGraw.

Linear Control Theory. Frederick W. Fairman. LC 97-41830. 330p. 1998. 110.00 (*0-471-97489-7*) Wiley.

***Linear Dependence: Theory & Computation.** S. N. Afriat. LC 00-34933. 2000. write for info. (*0-306-46428-4*) Kluwer Academic.

Linear-Derived Harmony. Arthur J. Komar. (Illus.). 225p. (Orig.). (C). 1995. 35.00 (*1-886464-03-0*) Ovenbird Pr.

Linear Design Seminar. Ed. by Walt Kester & James Bryant. (Technical Reference Bks.). (Illus.). 710p. (Orig.). 1995. pap. 25.00 (*0-916550-15-X*) Analog Devices.

Linear Difference Equations with Discrete Transform Methods. Abdul J. Jerri. LC 96-199. (Mathematics & Its Applications Ser.: Vol. 363). 464p. (C). 1996. lib. bdg. 199.00 (*0-7923-3940-1*) Kluwer Academic.

Linear Differential & Difference Equations: A Systems Approach for Mathematicians & Engineers. R. M. Johnson. LC 97-178115. 176p. 1997. pap. 29.95 (*1-898563-12-8*, Pub. by Horwood Pub) Paul & Co Pubs.

Linear Differential Equations & Group Theory from Riemann to Poincare. 2nd ed. J. J. Gray. LC 99-14284. (Illus.). 360p. 1999. 64.50 (*0-8176-3837-7*) Birkhauser.

Linear Differential Equations in Banach Space. S. G. Krein. Tr. by J. Danskin. LC 71-37141. (Translations of Mathematical Monographs: Vol. 29). 390p. 1972. text 70.00 (*0-8218-1579-2*, MMONO/29) Am Math.

Linear Differential Equations in the Complex Domain: Problems of Analytic Continuation. Ed. & Tr. by Yasutaka Sibuya. LC 90-825. (Translations of Mathematical Monographs: No. 82). 267p. 1990. text 81.00 (*0-8218-4535-7*, MMONO/82) Am Math.

Linear Differential Equations of Principal Type. Yu V. Egorov. LC 86-25408. (Contemporary Soviet Mathematics Ser.). (Illus.). 310p. (C). 1987. text 132.00 (*0-306-10992-1*, Kluwer Plenum) Kluwer Academic.

Linear Differential Operators. Cornelius Lanczos. LC 96-14933. (Classics in Applied Mathematics Ser.: No. 18). xviii, 564p. 1996. pap. 53.00 (*0-89871-370-6*, CL18) Soc Indus-Appl Math.

Linear Differential Operators. unabridged ed. Cornelius Lanczos. LC 97-26069. (Illus.). 576p. 1997. reprint ed. pap. 14.95 (*0-486-68035-5*) Dover.

Linear Differential Operators with Constant Coefficients. V. P. Palamodov. Tr. by A. A. Brown. LC 79-104712. (Grundlehren der Mathematischen Wissenschaften Ser.: Vol. 168). 1970. 97.95 (*0-387-04838-3*) Spr-Verlag.

Linear Discrete Systems. Strum. 60p. (C). 2001. pap. 12.00 (*0-13-907395-7*, Macmillan Coll) P-H.

***Linear Elastic Fracture Mechanics for Engineers: Theory & Applications.** L. P. Pook. 176p. (C). 2000. text 95.00 (*1-85312-703-5*, 7035) Computational Mech MA.

Linear Electric Actuators & Generators. I. Boldea & Syed A. Nasar. (Illus.). 247p. (C). 1997. text 64.95 (*0-521-48017-5*) Cambridge U Pr.

Linear Electric Field Effect in Paramagnetic Resonance. W. B. Mims. (Illus.). 1976. 49.50 (*0-19-851944-3*) OUP.

Linear Electronics. Frank Getz. Ed. by Larry Ryan. (Illus.). 216p. 1990. ring bd. write for info. (*0-89704-050-3*) E&L Instru.

Linear Electronics: Integrated & Discrete. 2nd abr. rev. ed. Cox. (Electronics Technology Ser.). 1998. text, teacher ed. 14.00 (*0-8273-6852-6*) Delmar.

Linear Electronics in Control Systems. Robert C. Baker. (Illus.). 240p. 1988. text 49.95 (*0-943876-03-6*) Barks Pubns.

Linear Energy Transfer, No. 16. International Commission on Radiation Units & Meas. LC 72-113962. viii, 51p. 1970. 25.00 (*0-913394-09-2*) Intl Comm Rad Meas.

Linear Equations & Systems of Equations. rev. ed. Mervin L. Keedy & Marvin L. Bittinger. (Algebra, a Modern Introduction Ser.). (gr. 7-9). 1981. pap. text. write for info. (*0-201-03986-9*) Addison-Wesley.

Linear Equations in Banach Spaces. S. G. Krein. 128p. 1982. text 24.50 (*3-7643-3101-1*) Birkhauser.

***Linear Estimation.** Thomas Kailath et al. LC 99-47033. 854p. 2000. 99.00 (*0-13-022464-2*) P-H.

Linear Fingerboard Harmony for Bass. Gary Willis. 72p. 1997. pap. 17.95 (*0-7935-6043-8*) H Leonard.

Linear Fracture Mechanics. Ed. by G. C. Sih et al. LC 75-18287. 324p. 1976. 23.50 (*0-932871-03-8*) Envo Pub Co.

Linear Functional Analysis. W. Orlicz. Tr. by Lee Peng Yee from CHI. (Series in Real Analysis: Vol. 4). 220p. 1992. text 48.00 (*981-02-0853-7*) World Scientific Pub.

Linear Functional Equations: Operator Approach. Anatolij Antonevich. Tr. by Victory Muzafarov & Andrei Iacob from RUS. (Operator Theory, Advances, & Applications Ser.: Vol. 83). 1995. write for info. (*0-8176-2931-9*) Birkhauser.

Linear Functional Equations: Operator Approach. Anatolij Antonevich. Tr. by Victory Muzafarov & Andrei Iacob from RUS. (Operator Theory, Advances, & Applications Ser.: Vol. 83). 192p. 1996. 123.00 (*3-7643-2931-9*) Birkhauser.

Linear Functions & Matrix Theory: An Introduction. Bill Jacob. LC 95-3756. (Textbooks in Mathematical Sciences Ser.). (Illus.). 330p. 1995. 24.95 (*0-387-94451-6*) Spr-Verlag.

Linear Geometry with Computer Graphics. John Loustau & Meighan Dillon. (Pure & Applied Mathematics Ser.: Vol. 170). (Illus.). 458p. 1992. text 69.75 incl. disk (*0-8247-8898-2*) Dekker.

Linear Goal Programming. Marc J. Schniederjans. (Illus.). 50p. 1986. pap., teacher ed. 20.00 (*0-89433-250-3*); text 24.95 (*0-89433-243-0*) Petrocelli.

Linear IC Applications: A Designer's Handbook. Joseph J. Carr. LC 96-42135. (Illus.). 356p. 1996. pap. text 52.95 (*0-7506-3370-0*) Buttrwrth-Heinemann.

Linear IC Handbook. Michael S. Morley. (Illus.). 624p. 1986. 49.50 (*0-8306-0472-3*, NO. 2672) McGraw-Hill Prof.

Linear Images of the Living Figure. Gerry Grout. pap. 18.95 (*0-9642346-0-2*) Thnderbird Art.

Linear Induction Drives. Jacek F. Gieras. (Monographs in Electrical & Electronic Engineering: No. 30). (Illus.). 316p. (C). 1994. text 89.00 (*0-19-859381-3*) OUP.

Linear Inequalities & Related Systems. G. B. Dantzig et al. Ed. by Harold W. Kuhn & A. W. Tucker. LC 56-8385. (Annals of Mathematics Studies: No. 38). 346p. reprint ed. pap. 107.30 (*0-608-06437-8*, 206665000008) Bks Demand.

Linear Infinite Particle Operators. V. A. Malyshev & R. A. Minlos. LC 94-42578. (Translations of Mathematical Monographs: Vol. 143).Tr. of Lineinye Operatory v Beskonechnochastichnykh Sistemakh. (ENG & RUS.). 298p. 1995. text 125.00 (*0-8218-0283-6*, MMONO/143) Am Math.

Linear Integral Equations. Rainer Kress. (Applied Mathematical Sciences Ser.: Vol. 82). (Illus.). 320p. 1989. 65.95 (*0-387-50616-0*) Spr-Verlag.

Linear Integral Equations. Solomon G. Mikhlin. (Russian Monographs & Texts on the Physical Sciences). viii, 224p. 1961. text 195.00 (*0-677-20320-9*) Gordon & Breach.

Linear Integral Equations. 2nd ed. Rainer Kress. Ed. by J. E. Marsden & L. Sirov. LC 98-51753. (Illus.). 384p. 1999. 59.95 (*0-387-98700-2*) Spr-Verlag.

Linear Integral Equations: Theory & Technique. 2nd ed. Ram P. Kanwal. LC 96-43283. 318p. 1996. 78.50 (*0-8176-3940-3*) Birkhauser.

Linear Integral Equations: Theory & Techniques. 2nd ed. Ram P. Kanwal. LC 96-43283. 1996. write for info. (*3-7643-3940-3*) Birkhauser.

Linear Integrated Circuit Applications: Hardware & Software Exercises Using Electronics Workbench. John P. Borris. LC 99-20176. 195p. 1999. pap. text 41.00 (*0-13-280835-8*) P-H.

Linear Integrated Circuits. Joe Carr. LC 95-26394. (Illus.). 352p. 1996. pap. text 46.95 (*0-7506-2591-0*) Buttrwrth-Heinemann.

Linear Integrated Circuits. Paynter. (Electronics Technology Ser.). 1996. teacher ed. 12.00 (*0-8273-6384-2*) Delmar.

Linear Integrated Circuits. Paynter. (Electronics Technology Ser.). 1996. text 52.95 (*0-8273-6383-4*) Delmar.

Linear Integrated Circuits. Paynter. (Electronics Technology Ser.). 2001. pap. 52.50 (*0-7668-1270-7*) Delmar.

Linear Integrated Circuits. Winzer. (C). 1992. pap. text 9.50 (*0-03-032469-6*) Harcourt Coll Pubs.

Linear Integrated Circuits. Winzer. (C). 1993. pap. text, lab manual ed. 34.00 (*0-03-094314-0*, Pub. by Harcourt Coll Pubs) Harcourt.

Linear Integrated Circuits. Jack Winzer. 710p. (C). 1992. text 96.00 (*0-03-032468-8*) SCP.

Linear Integrated Circuits: Experiments. Dungan. (Electronics Technology Ser.). 1984. pap. 27.00 (*0-8273-3840-6*) Delmar.

Linear Integrated Circuits: Operation & Application. Michael McMenamin. (Illus.). 400p. (C). 1985. text 52.00 (*0-13-537333-6*) P-H.

Linear Kinetic Theory & Particle Transport in Stochastic Mixtures. G. C. Pomraning. (Series on Advances in Mathematics for Applied Sciences: Vol. 7). 250p. 1991. text 61.00 (*981-02-0844-8*) World Scientific Pub.

Linear Lattices. 2nd abr. ed. Hidegoreo Nakano. LC 66-24169. 157p. reprint ed. pap. 48.70 (*0-7837-3774-2*, 204359200010) Bks Demand.

Linear Least Squares Computations. R. W. Farebrother. (Statistics: Textbooks & Monographs: Vol. 91). (Illus.). 320p. 1988. text 137.50 (*0-8247-7661-5*) Dekker.

Linear Low Density Polyethylene Materials, Processing, Applications: Regional Technical Conference: Quaker Square Hilton, Akron, Ohio, September 21 & 22, 1982. Society of Plastics Engineers Staff. LC TP1180.P65. 244p. reprint ed. pap. 75.70 (*0-608-14340-5*, 201965300013) Bks Demand.

Linear Mathematics. Newman. 494p. (C). 1991. pap. text 49.00 (*0-536-57952-0*) Pearson Custom.

Linear Mathematics: A Practical Approach. Patricia C. Kenschaft. LC 77-81757. (Illus.). 1978. text 49.95 (*0-87901-084-3*) Worth.

Linear Mathematics & Its Applications. Larry J. Goldstein et al. (C). 1989. pap. text 17.40 (*0-536-05726-5*) Pearson Custom.

Linear Mathematics & Its Applications. 3rd ed. 184p. (C). 1997. text 19.80 (*0-536-00162-6*) Pearson Custom.

Linear Matrix Inequalities in System & Control Theory. Laurent El Ghaoui et al. Ed. by Stephen Boyd et al. LC 94-10477. (Studies in Applied Mathematics: Vol. 15). x, 193p. 1994. 41.50 (*0-89871-334-X*) Soc Indus-Appl Math.

Linear Measures: American Units Basic 9.1. 7th ed. (C). 1995. text 0.66 (*0-201-41091-5*) Addison-Wesley.

Linear Measures: Metric System Basic 9.2. 7th ed. (C). 1995. text 0.66 (*0-201-41092-3*) Addison-Wesley.

Linear Megillas Esther. Pesach Goldberg. LC 97-3088. (ENG & HEB.). 1997. pap. 4.95 (*0-87306-788-6*) Feldheim.

***Linear Mixed Models for Longitudinal Data.** G. Verbeke & G. Molenberghs. (Series in Statistics). 600p. 2000. 79.95 (*0-387-95027-3*) Spr-Verlag.

Linear Mixed Models in Practice: An SAS-Oriented Approach, 126. Geert Verbeke & Geert Molenberghs. LC 97-15705. (Lecture Notes in Statistics Ser.: Vol. 126). 1997. text. write for info. (*0-387-98222-1*) Spr-Verlag.

Linear Model in Statistics. Alvin C. Rencher. LC 99-30176. 578p. 1999. 84.95 (*0-471-31564-8*) Wiley.

Linear Models. S. R. Searle. LC 70-138919. (Wiley Classics Library Editions Ser.). 532p. 1997. pap. 54.95 (*0-471-18499-3*) Wiley.

Linear Models. 2nd ed. C. R. Rao & H. Toutenburg. Ed. by P. Bickel et al. LC 99-14735. (Series in Statistics). (Illus.). 464p. 1999. 69.95 (*0-387-98848-3*) Spr-Verlag.

Linear Models: A Mean Model Approach. Barry K. Moser. LC 96-33930. (Probability & Mathematical Statistics Ser.). (Illus.). 228p. 1996. text 49.95 (*0-12-508465-X*) Acad Pr.

Linear Models: Least Squares & Alternative Methods. Radhakrishna Rao & Helge Toutenburg. LC 95-23947. (Springer Series in Statistics). 352p. 1995. 57.95 (*0-387-94562-8*) Spr-Verlag.

Linear Models for Multivariate, Time Series & Spatial Data. R. Christensen. (Texts in Statistics Ser.). (Illus.). 336p. 1997. 72.95 (*0-387-97413-X*) Spr-Verlag.

Linear Models for the Prediction of Animal Breeding Values. R. A. Mrode. (A CAB International Publication). 200p. 1996. text 75.00 (*0-85198-996-9*) OUP.

Linear Models for Unbalanced Data. Shayle R. Searle. 560p. 1987. 135.00 (*0-471-84096-3*) Wiley.

Linear Models in Social Research. Ed. by Peter V. Marsden. LC 81-9402. (Illus.). 336p. reprint ed. pap. 104.20 (*0-7837-1114-X*, 204164400022) Bks Demand.

Linear Models with Correlated Disturbances. P. Knottnerus. (Lecture Notes in Economics & Mathematical Systems Ser.). viii, 196p. 1991. 38.95 (*0-387-53901-8*) Spr-Verlag.

Linear Multivariable Control. 1991. 86.95 (*0-387-96071-6*) Spr-Verlag.

Linear Multivariable Control: Algebraic Analysis & Synthesis Methods. A. I. Vardulakis. LC 90-12638. 384p. 1991. 320.00 (*0-471-92859-3*) Wiley.

Linear Network Optimization: Algorithms & Codes. Dimitri P. Bertsekas. (Illus.). 275p. 1991. 52.50 (*0-262-02334-2*) MIT Pr.

Linear Network Theory: Analysis, Properties, Design & Synthesis. Theodore A. Bickart & Norman Balabanian. (Illus.). 648p. 1985. 64.95 (*0-916460-10-X*, Matrix Pubs Inc) Weber Systems.

Linear Networks & Systems: Algorithm & CPT-Aided Implementations. 2nd ed. W. K. Chen. (Advanced Series in Electrical & Computer Engineering: Vol. 3). 900p. 1990. text 61.00 (*9971-5-0684-X*) World Scientific Pub.

Linear Networks & Systems: Algorithm & CPT-Aided Implementations, 1. 2nd ed. Wai Kai Chen. (Advanced Series in Electrical & Computer Engineering: Vol. 3). 700p. 1990. pap. text 36.00 (*9971-5-0998-9*) World Scientific Pub.

Linear Networks & Systems: Algorithms. Wai Kai Chen. 500p. 1994. pap. text 48.00 (*981-02-1454-5*) World Scientific Pub.

***Linear Operator Theory in Engineering & Science,** A. W. Naylor & G. R. Sell. (Applied Mathematical Sciences Ser.: 40). (Illus.). 664p. 2000. pap. 39.95 (*0-387-95001-X*) Spr-Verlag.

Linear Operator Theory in Engineering & Science. A. W. Naylor & George R. Sell. (Applied Mathematical Sciences Ser.: Vol. 40). (Illus.). 624p. 1994. 69.95 (*0-387-90748-3*) Spr-Verlag.

Linear Operators Pt. 1: General Theory. Neilson Dunford & Jacob T. Schwartz. (Classics Library). 872p. 1988. pap. 89.95 (*0-471-60848-3*) Wiley.

Linear Operators Pt. 2: Spectral Theory, Vol. 2. Neilson Dunford & Jacob T. Schwartz. (Classics Library). 1088p. 1988. pap. 195.00 (*0-471-60847-5*) Wiley.

Linear Operators Pt. 3: Spectral Operators, Vol. 3. Neilson Dunford & Jacob T. Schwartz. (Classics Library). 688p. 1988. pap. 165.00 (*0-471-60846-7*) Wiley.

Linear Operators & Approximation, 2 vols., Vol. 1. Ed. by Paul L. Butzer et al. (International Series of Numerical Mathematics: Nos. 20 & 25). 506p. 1980. 97.00 (*0-8176-0590-8*) Birkhauser.

Linear Operators & Approximation, 2 vols., Vol. 2. Ed. by Paul L. Butzer et al. (International Series of Numerical Mathematics: Nos. 20 & 25). 608p. 1980. 118.00 (*0-8176-0760-9*) Birkhauser.

Linear Operators & Ill-Posed Problems. M. M. Lavrent'ev & L. Ya Savel'ev. LC 95-22545. (Illus.). 396p. (C). 1995. text 120.00 (*0-306-11035-0*, Kluwer Plenum) Kluwer Academic.

Linear Operators for Quantum Mechanics. Thomas F. Jordan. 156p. (C). 1990. reprint ed. pap. text 11.50 (*0-9602762-0-3*) Krieger.

Linear Operators in Function Spaces: 12th International Conference on Operator Theory, 1988. Grigore Arsene. (Operator Theory Ser.: No. 43). 350p. 1989. 137.00 (*0-8176-2343-4*) Birkhauser.

Linear Operators in Hilbert Space. J. L. Soule. (Notes on Mathematics & Its Applications Ser.). x, 40p. (Orig.). 1968. pap. text 77.00 (*0-677-30175-8*) Gordon & Breach.

Linear Operators in Hilbert Spaces. J. Weidmann. Tr. by J. Szuecs from GER. (Graduate Texts in Mathematics Ser.: Vol 68). 400p. 1997. 55.00 (*0-387-90427-1*) Spr-Verlag.

Linear Optimal Control. Jeffrey B. Burl. LC 98-36516. 432p. (C). 1998. 95.00 (*0-201-80868-4*, Prentice Hall) P-H.

Linear Optimal Control of Bilinear Systems: With Applications to Singular Perturbations & Weak Coupling, Vol. X. Zoran Aganović & Zijad Gajić. Ed. by M. Thoma. (Lecture Notes in Control & Information Sciences: Vol. 206). 133p. 1995. 45.00 (*3-540-19976-4*) Spr-Verlag.

Linear Optimal Control Systems. Huibert Kwakernaak & Raphael Sivan. 608p. 1972. 198.50 (*0-471-51110-2*, Wiley-Interscience) Wiley.

Linear Optimization & Approximation: An Introduction to the Theoretical Analysis & Numerical Treatment of Semi-Infinite Programs. K. Glashoff & S. A. Gustafson. (Applied Mathematical Sciences Ser.: Vol. 45). (Illus.). 197p. 1983. 59.95 (*0-387-90857-9*) Spr-Verlag.

Linear Optimization & Extensions. Manfred Padberg. LC 94-47365. (Algorithms & Combinatorics Ser.: Vol. 12). 1995. 109.95 (*3-540-58734-9*) Spr-Verlag.

L

***Linear Optimization & Extensions.** 2nd expanded rev. ed. M. Padberg. Ed. by R. L. Graham et al. LC 99-23776. (Algorithms & Combinatorics Ser.: Vol. 12). (Illus.). xxi, 501p. 1999. 106.00 (*3-540-65833-5*) Spr-Verlag.

Linear Optimization in Applications. S. L. Lang. 166p. 1999. pap. 23.50 (*962-209-483-X*, Pub. by HK Univ Pr) Coronet Bks.

Linear Order & Generative Theory. Ed. by Martin D. Pam & Jurgen M. Meisel. (Current Issues in Linguistic Theory Ser.: No. 7). ix, 512p. 1979. 94.00 (*90-272-0908-1*) J Benjamins Pubng Co.

Linear Ordinary Differential Equations. Earl A. Coddington & Robert Carlson. LC 96-53262. (Miscellaneous Bks.: No. 57). (Illus.). xii, 341p. 1997. pap. text 59.50 (*0-89871-388-9*, OT0057) Soc Indus-Appl Math.

Linear Panel Analysis: Quantitative Models of Change. Ronald Kessler & David Greenberg. LC 81-3504. (Quantitative Studies in Social Relations). 1981. text 55.00 (*0-12-405750-0*) Acad Pr.

Linear Partial Differential Equations. Francois Treves. (Notes on Mathematics & Its Applications Ser.). x, 120p. 1970. text 195.00 (*0-677-02520-3*) Gordon & Breach.

Linear Partial Differential Equations with Constant Coefficients, Vol. 6. Francois Treves. (Mathematics & Its Applications Ser.). x, 534p. 1966. text 552.00 (*0-677-01190-3*) Gordon & Breach.

Linear Partial Differential Operators in Gevrey Spaces. L. Rodino. 250p. 1993. text 61.00 (*981-02-0845-6*) World Scientific Pub.

Linear Piezoelectric Plate Vibrations: Elements of the Linear Theory of Piezoelectricity & the Vibrations of Piezoelectric Plates. H. F. Tiersten. LC 69-14562. 227p. reprint ed. pap. 70.40 (*0-608-13241-1*, 205579400038) Bks Demand.

Linear Pro-P-Groups of Finite Width, Vol. 167. G. Klaas et al. LC 97-38718. (Lecture Notes in Mathematics Ser.: Vol. 1674). vii, 115p. 1997. pap. 27.00 (*3-540-63643-9*) Spr-Verlag.

Linear Probability, Logit, & Probit Models. John H. Aldrich & Forrest D. Nelson. LC 84-51766. (Quantitative Applications in the Social Sciences Ser.: Vol. 45). 95p. 1984. pap. 10.95 (*0-8039-2133-0*) Sage.

***Linear Processes in Function Spaces: Theory & Applications.** D. Bosq. (Lecture Notes in Statistics Ser.: Vol. 149). 296p. 2000. pap. 59.95 (*0-387-95052-4*) Spr-Verlag.

Linear Programming. James E. Calvert & William L. Voxman. 655p. (C). 1989. text 77.50 (*0-15-551027-4*) SCP.

Linear Programming. James E. Calvert & William L. Voxman. 655p. (C). 1989. pap. text 28.00 (*0-15-551028-2*) SCP.

Linear Programming. James E. Calvert & William L. Voxman. 655p. (C). 1989. 7.00 (*0-15-551029-0*) SCP.

Linear Programming. Vasek Chvatal. LC 82-21132. (Illus.). 478p. (C). 1983. pap. text 47.95 (*0-7167-1587-2*) W H Freeman.

Linear Programming. James P. Ignizio & Tom M. Cavalier. LC 93-22179. 666p. (C). 1993. 70.60 (*0-13-183757-5*) P-H.

Linear Programming. Katta G. Murty. LC 83-7012. 512p. (C). 1983. text 105.95 (*0-471-09725-X*) Wiley.

Linear Programming. Katta G. Murty. 231p. (C). 1984. pap. text, suppl. ed. 20.00 (*0-471-89249-1*) Wiley.

Linear Programming. M. Sakarovitch. (Texts in Electrical Engineering Ser.). (Illus.). 206p. 1983. 75.95 (*0-387-90829-3*) Spr-Verlag.

Linear Programming. 2nd ed. H. Karloff. (Progress in Theoretical Computer Science Ser.). viii, 142p. 1996. 39.95 (*0-8176-3561-0*) Birkhauser.

Linear Programming: A Modern Integrated Analysis, Vol. 1. Romesh Saigal. LC 95-34605. (International Series in Operations Research & Management Science). 360p. (C). 1995. lib. bdg. 127.00 (*0-7923-9622-7*) Kluwer Academic.

Linear Programming: An Introduction. Bruce R. Feiring. (Quantitative Applications in the Social Sciences Ser.: Vol. 60). 96p. (Orig.). (C). 1986. pap. text 10.95 (*0-8039-2850-5*) Sage.

Linear Programming: An Introduction. W. Allen Spivey. LC 63-16407. 192p. reprint ed. pap. 59.60 (*0-608-15174-2*, 205607400046) Bks Demand.

Linear Programming: Foundations & Extensions. Robert J. Vanderbei. LC 96-47149. (International Series in Operations Research & Management Science). 440p. (C). 1996. lib. bdg. 129.95 (*0-7923-9804-1*) Kluwer Academic.

Linear Programming: Foundations & Extensions. Robert J. Vanderbei. (International Series in Operations Research & Management Science: No. 4). 440p. 1998. pap. write for info. (*0-7923-8141-6*) Kluwer Law Intl.

Linear Programming: Introduction. George B. Dantzig & Mukund N. Thapa. LC 96-36411. (Springer Series in Operations Research). (Illus.). 435p. 1997. 54.95 (*0-387-94833-3*) Spr-Verlag.

Linear Programming: Mathematics, Theory & Algorithms. Michael J. Panik. (Applied Optimization Ser.: Vol. 2). 508p. (C). 1996. text 217.50 (*0-7923-3782-4*) Kluwer Academic.

Linear Programming & Applications: A Course Text. Will McLewin. (Illus.). xvi, 216p. 1990. text. write for info. (*0-904870-11-1*, Pub. by Input-Output Pub) UH Pr.

Linear Programming & Associated Techniques: A Comprehensive Bibliography on Linear, Nonlinear & Dynamic Programming. rev. ed. Vera Riley & Saul I. Gass. LC 58-3589. 623p. reprint ed. pap. 193.20 (*0-608-11401-4*, 201040600069) Bks Demand.

Linear Programming & Economic Analysis. Robert Dorfman et al. ix, 525p. 1987. reprint ed. pap. text 14.95 (*0-486-65491-5*) Dover.

Linear Programming & Extensions. George B. Dantzig. (Rand Corporation Research Studies). 642p. 1963. text 95.00 (*0-691-08000-3*, Pub. by Princeton U Pr); pap. text 29.95 (*0-691-05913-6*, Pub. by Princeton U Pr) Cal Prin Full Svc.

Linear Programming & Extensions. Nesa Wu & Richard Coppins. (Industrial Engineering & Management Science Ser.). (Illus.). 480p. (C). 1981. text 115.00 (*0-07-072117-3*) McGraw.

Linear Programming & Its Applications. J. K. Stryer. (Undergraduate Texts in Mathematics Ser.). (Illus.). 272p. 1989. 49.95 (*0-387-96930-6*) Spr-Verlag.

Linear Programming & Network Flows. 2nd ed. Mokhtar S. Bazaraa et al. LC 89-32063. 704p. 1990. text 108.95 (*0-471-63681-9*) Wiley.

Linear Programming Applications to Agriculture. Raymond R. Beneke & Ronald D. Winterboer. LC 72-2298. 252p. 1973. reprint ed. pap. 78.20 (*0-608-00067-1*, 206083300006) Bks Demand.

Linear Programming Duality: An Introduction to Oriented Matroids. Achim Bachem & Walter Kern. LC 92-14021. 1992. 62.95 (*0-387-55417-3*) Spr-Verlag.

Linear Programming for Operations Research. Donald M. Simmons. LC 70-188129. (C). 1972. text 36.00 (*0-8162-7986-1*) Holden-Day.

Linear Programming in Decision Making. Shabir H. Banday. 150p. 1992. 60.00 (*81-7041-582-9*, Pub. by Scientific Pubs) St Mut.

Linear Programming in Industry, Theory & Applications: An Introduction. rev. ed. S. Dano. LC 73-13172. (Illus.). 180p. 1974. 39.95 (*0-387-81189-3*) Spr-Verlag.

Linear Programming in Infinite-Dimensional Spaces: Theory & Applications. fac. ed. Edward J. Anderson & Peter Nash. LC 86-32579. (Wiley-Interscience Series in Discrete Mathematics & Optimization). (Illus.). 184p. 1987. reprint ed. pap. 57.10 (*0-608-00992-X*, 206184900012) Bks Demand.

Linear Programming Methods & Applications. Gass. (GC - Principles of Management Ser.). 1995. pap. 83.95 (*0-7895-0333-6*) S-W Pub.

Linear Programming with Statistical Applications. Vincent A. Sposito. LC 88-13590. (Illus.). 288p. 1989. reprint ed. pap. 89.30 (*0-608-00066-3*, 206083200006) Bks Demand.

Linear Programs & Related Problems. Evar D. Nering & Albert W. Tucker. (Computer Science & Scientific Computing Ser.). 584p. 1992. text 59.00 (*0-12-515440-2*) Acad Pr.

***Linear-Quadratic Control: An Introduction.** Peter Dorato et al. (Illus.). (C). 2000. reprint ed. text. write for info. (*1-57524-156-0*) Krieger.

Linear Quadratic Regulator Design for an Unpowered, Winged Re-Entry Vehicle. E. Mooij. (Series 08 - Astrodynamics & Satellite Systems 03). (Illus.). 150p. 1998. pap. 32.50 (*90-407-1597-1*, Pub. by Delft U Pr) Coronet Bks.

Linear Raman Spectroscopy. Long. text. write for info. (*0-471-49028-8*) Wiley.

Linear Rational Expectations Models: A User's Guide. Charles H. Whiteman. LC 83-1280. 149p. 1983. reprint ed. pap. 46.20 (*0-608-00797-8*, 205934600010) Bks Demand.

Linear Reactivity Model for Nuclear Fuel Management. M. J. Driscoll et al. 256p. 54.00 (*0-89448-035-9*, 350014) Am Nuclear Soc.

Linear Regression Analysis. G. A. Seber. LC 76-40117. (Probability & Mathematical Statistics Ser.). 496p. 1977. 159.95 (*0-471-01967-4*) Wiley.

Linear Regression Analysis - Apple. Thomas F George. Ed. by Mary E. George. (Illus.). 40p. (Orig.). (C). 1989. pap. text 10.95 (*0-929683-12-9*) Servs by George.

Linear Regression Analysis - IBM. Thomas F. George. Ed. by Mary E. George. 40p. (Orig.). (C). 1989. pap. text 10.95 (*0-929683-13-7*) Servs by George.

Linear Regression Model under Test. W. Kramer. (Illus.). x, 200p. 1987. 75.95 (*0-387-91287-8*) Spr-Verlag.

Linear Representation of Groups. Ernst B. Vinberg. (Basler Lehrbucher Ser.: No. 2). 150p. 1989. 42.50 (*0-8176-2288-8*) Birkhauser.

Linear Representations of Finite Groups. 4th ed. Jean-Pierre Serre. Tr. by L. L. Scott from FRE. LC 76-12585. (Graduate Texts in Mathematics Ser.: Vol. 42). x, 170p. 1996. 42.95 (*0-387-90190-6*) Spr-Verlag.

Linear Representations of Finite Groups. 5th ed. Jean Pierre Serre. LC 97-105409. (Graduate Texts in Mathematics Ser.). x, 170 p. 1996. write for info. (*3-540-90190-6*) Spr-Verlag.

Linear Representations of Partially Ordered Sets & Vector Space Categories. Daniel Simson. LC 92-26073. (Algebra, Logic & Applications Ser.: Vol. 4). 516p. 1993. text 114.00 (*2-88124-828-4*) Gordon & Breach.

Linear Representations of the Lorentz Group. A. Swinfen & M. A. Naimark. LC 63-10025. (International Series of Monographs on Pure & Applied Mathematics: Vol. 63). 1964. 200.00 (*0-08-010155-0*, Pub. by Pergamon Repr) Franklin.

Linear Semi-Infinite Optimization. M. A. Goberna & M. A. Cerda. 356p. 1998. 125.00 (*0-471-97040-9*) Wiley.

Linear Simulation of Time Dependent Towing of Ocean Vehicles. Robert Latorre et al. LC VM0521.. (University of Michigan, Dept. of Naval Architecture & Marine Engineering, Report Ser.: No. 268). 82p. reprint ed. pap. 30.00 (*0-608-18656-2*, 202482500038) Bks Demand.

Linear Spaces & Approximation: Proceedings. Ed. by Paul L. Butzer. (International Series of Numerical Mathematics: No. 40). 688p. 1980. 111.00 (*0-8176-0979-2*) Birkhauser.

Linear Spaces with Few Lines. K. Metsch. Ed. by A. Dold et al. (Lecture Notes in Mathematics Ser.: Vol. 1490). xiii, 196p. 1991. 41.95 (*0-387-54720-7*) Spr-Verlag.

Linear Statistical Inference. Ed. by T. Calinski & W. Klonecki. (Lecture Notes in Statistics Ser.: Vol. 35). vi, 318p. 1986. 70.95 (*0-387-96255-7*) Spr-Verlag.

Linear Statistical Inference & Its Applications. Rao. 371p. 1998. pap. text 199.95 (*0-471-13733-2*) Wiley.

Linear Statistical Inference & Its Applications. 2nd ed. C. Radhakrishna Rao. (Probability & Mathematical Statistics Ser.). 656p. 1973. 199.95 (*0-471-70823-2*) Wiley.

Linear Statistical Inference & Its Applications , Vol. 1. 3rd ed. Rao. 640p. write for info. (*0-471-24061-3*) Wiley.

Linear Statistical Models. James H. Stapleton. LC 94-39384. (Series in Probability & Mathematics). 472p. 1995. 89.95 (*0-471-57150-4*) Wiley.

Linear Statistical Models. 2nd ed. Milton. 1998. pap. 53.44 (*0-07-232708-1*) McGraw.

Linear Statistical Models: An Applied Approach. Bruce L. Bowerman & Richard O'Connell. 614p. (C). 1986. pap. 39.00 (*0-87150-904-0*, 36G8200) PWS Pubs.

Linear Statistical Models - Cloth. 2nd ed. Bruce L. Bowerman & Richard T. O'Connell. (Business Statistics). 1024p. (C). 1990. pap. 54.50 (*0-534-92177-9*) Wadsworth Pub.

Linear Stochastic Control Systems. G. R. Chen et al. LC 95-10426. 400p. 1995. boxed set 99.95 (*0-8493-8075-8*, 8075) CRC Pr.

Linear Stochastic Systems. 2nd ed. Davis & Heunis. (Stochastic Modeling Ser.). (Illus.). 256p. (C). (gr. 13). 1997. 54.95 (*0-412-31740-0*) Chapman & Hall.

Linear Stochastic Systems with Constant Coefficients: A Statistical Approach. M. Arato. (Lecture Notes in Control & Information Sciences: Vol. 45). 309p. 1982. 33.95 (*0-387-12090-4*) Spr-Verlag.

Linear Structures. Jan R. Magnus. (Charles Griffin Book). 218p. 1988. text 60.00 (*0-19-520655-X*) OUP.

Linear Synchronous Motors Transportation & Automation System. Jacek F. Gieras. LC 99-38333. 344p. 1999. boxed set 89.95 (*0-8493-1859-9*) CRC Pr.

***Linear Syntax.** Andreas Kathol. 320p. 2000. text 74.00 (*0-19-823734-0*) OUP.

Linear System: Solutions Manual. Szidarovszky. 1997. lib. bdg. write for info. (*0-8493-1105-5*) CRC Pr.

***Linear System Vol. D, Pt. 1: Robust Control.** Ed. by A. Isidori et al. 580p. 1999. pap. 126.00 (*0-08-043215-8*) Elsevier.

***Linear System Vol. D, Pt. 2: Robust Control.** Ed. by A. Isidori & T. Gladman. 568p. 1999. pap. 126.00 (*0-08-043216-6*) Elsevier.

Linear System Analysis. Davis. (Electrical Engineering Ser.). 2001. mass mkt. 74.95 (*0-534-95086-8*) PWS Pubs.

Linear System Fundamentals. Reid. 1983. text, student ed. 28.75 (*0-07-051809-2*) McGraw.

Linear System Fundamentals: Continuous, Discrete & Modern. Gary Reid. (McGraw-Hill Series in Electrical Engineering). (Illus.). 512p. (C). 1983. 99.38 (*0-07-051808-4*) McGraw.

Linear System Theory. F. M. Callier & C. A. Desoer. (Texts in Electrical Engineering Ser.). (Illus.). xiv, 509p. 1994. 79.95 (*0-387-97573-X*) Spr-Verlag.

Linear System Theory. Lofti A. Zadeh & Charles A. Desoer. LC 78-26008. 650p. 1979. reprint ed. lib. bdg. 69.50 (*0-88275-809-8*) Krieger.

Linear System Theory. 2nd ed. Wilson J. Rugh. LC 95-21164. (Information & System Sciences Ser.). 581p. (C). 1995. 105.00 (*0-13-441205-2*) P-H.

Linear System Theory & Design. Chi-Tsong Chen. 662p. (C). 1984. student ed. write for info. (*0-03-071691-8*) SCP.

Linear System Theory & Design. 2nd ed. Chen. 688p. 1995. pap., student ed. 26.00 (*0-19-511595-3*) OUP.

Linear System Theory & Design. 3rd ed. Chi-Tsong Chen. (The Oxford Series in Electrical & Computer Engineering). (Illus.). 352p. 1998. text 88.00 (*0-19-511777-8*) OUP.

Linear Systems. Panos Antsaklis & Anthony Michel. LC 97-3753. 688p. (C). 1997. 100.31 (*0-07-041433-5*) McGraw.

Linear Systems. C. Heij. text. write for info. (*0-471-49139-X*) Wiley.

Linear Systems. Thomas Kailath. (Information & System Sciences Ser.). (Illus.). (C). 1979. text 63.00 (*0-13-536961-4*) P-H.

Linear Systems: Time Domain & Transform Analysis. Michael F. O'Flynn & Gene M. Moriarty. 512p. 1986. text 99.95 (*0-471-60373-2*) Wiley.

***Linear Systems & Exponential Dichotomy Structure of Sets of Hyperbolic Points.** Zhensheng Lin & Yan-Xia Lin. 200p. 2000. 32.00 (*981-02-4283-2*) World Scientific Pub.

Linear Systems & Optimal Control. Charles K. Chui & G. Chen. (Information Sciences Ser.: Vol. 18). (Illus.). 120p. 1988. 75.95 (*0-387-18737-5*) Spr-Verlag.

Linear Systems & Signals. Zoran Gajic. (C). 2000. text 69.00 (*0-201-61854-0*) Addison-Wesley.

Linear Systems & Signals. B. P. Lathi. LC 91-75492. 656p. (C). 1992. 79.95 (*0-941413-34-9*) Berkeley-Cambridge.

Linear Systems Control. Andrew P. Sage. (Illus.). 560p. 1978. 49.95 (*0-916460-19-3*, Matrix Pubs Inc) Weber Systems.

Linear Systems, Fourier Transforms & Optics. Jack D. Gaskill. LC 78-1118. (Pure & Applied Optics Ser.). 576p. 1978. 135.00 (*0-471-29288-5*) Wiley.

Linear Systems over Commutative Rings. James W. Brewer & John W. Bunce. (Lecture Notes in Pure & Applied Mathematics Ser.: Vol. 104). (Illus.). 216p. 1986. pap. text 125.00 (*0-8247-7559-7*) Dekker.

Linear Systems Properties: A Quick Reference. Venkatarama Krishnan. LC 97-48753. 304p. 1998. per. 24.95 (*0-8493-2291-X*) CRC Pr.

Linear Systems Theory. Szidarovszky. 448p. 1992. lib. bdg. 79.95 (*0-8493-8013-8*, QA402) CRC Pr.

Linear Systems Theory. 2nd ed. Ferenc Szidarovszky & Terry Bahill. LC 97-42062. 460p. 1997. lib. bdg. 79.95 (*0-8493-1687-1*) CRC Pr.

Linear Systems Theory & Introductory Algebraic Geometry. Robert Hermann. (Interdisciplinary Mathematics Ser.: No. 8). 282p. 1974. 42.00 (*0-915692-07-4*, 991600207) Math Sci Pr.

Linear Temporal Stability Analysis. P. J. Moeleker. (Series 01 - Aerodynamics: No. 07). (Illus.). 70p. 1998. pap. 14.95 (*90-407-1570-X*, Pub. by Delft U Pr) Coronet Bks.

Linear Theory of Colombeau Generalized Functions. M. Nedeljkov et al. (Pitman Research Notes in Mathematics Ser.: No. 385). 168p. 1998. pap. 42.00 (*0-582-35683-0*, LM5683, Chap & Hall CRC) Addison-Wesley.

Linear Time, Branching Time & Partial Order in Logics & Models for Concurrency. Ed. by J. W. De Bakker et al. (Lecture Notes in Computer Science Ser.: Vol. 354). viii, 713p. 1989. 74.00 (*0-387-51080-X*) Spr-Verlag.

Linear Time Delay Systems. J. M. Dion. LC 98-55500. 222p. 1999. pap. 63.50 (*0-08-043047-3*) Elsevier.

Linear Transformations in Hilbert Space & Their Applications to Analysis. M. H. Stone. LC 33-2746. (Colloquium Publications: Vol. 15). 622p. 1932. reprint ed. pap. 73.00 (*0-8218-1015-4*, COLL/15) Am Math.

Linear Turning Point Theory. Wolfgang Wasow. (Applied Mathematical Sciences Ser.: Vol. 54). (Illus.). 280p. 1985. 79.95 (*0-387-96046-5*) Spr-Verlag.

Linear Vector Spaces & Cartesian Tensors. James K. Knowles. LC 97-8936. (Illus.). 128p. (C). 1997. text 34.00 (*0-19-511254-7*) OUP.

Linear Vibration Theory: Generalized Properties & Numerical Methods. James B. Vernon. LC QA0935.V38. 381p. reprint ed. pap. 118.20 (*0-608-10309-8*, 200740500062) Bks Demand.

Linear Vibrations. P. C. Muller & W. O. Schiehlen. LC 59-1296. 1985. text 233.50 (*90-247-2983-1*) Kluwer Academic.

Lineare Albegra: 11., Uberarbeitete Auflage. Hans-Joachim Kowalsky & Gerhard O. Michler. 1998. pap. 30.00 (*3-11-016185-0*) De Gruyter.

Lineare Algebra: 11., Uberarbeitete Auflage. Hans-Joachim Kowalsky & Gerhard O. Michler. 400p. 1998. 61.00 (*3-11-016186-9*) De Gruyter.

Linearization Method for Constraint Optimization. Boris N. Pshenichny. Tr. by Steven S. Wilson from RUS. LC 94-1938. (Computational Mathematics Ser.: Vol. 22).Tr. of Metod Linearizatsii. viii, 147p. 1994. 103.95 (*0-387-57037-3*) Spr-Verlag.

Linearization Method in Hydrodynamical Stability Theory. V. Yudovich. LC 89-315. (Translations of Mathematical Monographs: Vol. 74). 170p. 1989. text 85.00 (*0-8218-4528-4*, MMONO/74) Am Math.

***Linearized Theory of Elasticity.** William S. Slaughter. 2000. 69.95 (*0-8176-4117-3*) Spr-Verlag.

Linear/Non Linear Circuits. Ayrom. 1987. student ed. 27.50 (*0-07-010899-4*) McGraw.

Linebacker: Overview of the First 120 Days. Melvin F. Porter. 79p. 1993. reprint ed. pap. 12.50 (*0-923135-68-5*) Dalley Bk Service.

Linebacker Operations: September-December, 1972. Calvin R. Johnson. 106p. 1993. reprint ed. pap. 12.50 (*0-923135-67-7*) Dalley Bk Service.

Linebacker Raids: The Bombing of North Vietnam, 1972. John Smith. LC 99-188760. (Illus.). 208p. 1998. 24.95 (*1-85409-450-5*, Pub. by Arms & Armour) Sterling.

***Linebacker Raids: The Bombing of North Vietnam, 1972.** John T. Smith. (Illus.). 2000. pap. 16.95 (*0-304-35295-0*) Continuum.

Linebrook Parish Church Records, 1747-1819. M. V. Perley & Thomas Waters. 135p. (Orig.). 1995. pap. 25.00 (*1-878545-02-7*) ACETO Bookmen.

Lined Fire Hose & Hose Assemblies: UL 19. 11th ed. 1995. write for info. (*1-55989-942-5*, UL 19) Underwrtrs Labs.

Lined Fire Hose for Interior Standpipes, UL 219. 2nd ed. (C). 1993. pap. text 95.00 (*1-55989-399-0*) Underwrtrs Labs.

Lineinye Operatory v Beskonechnochastichnykh Sistemakh see Linear Infinite Particle Operators

Lineland: Mortality & Mercy on the Internet's Pynchon-L@waste.org Discussion List. Jules Siegel & Virginia C. Wexler. Ed. by Dale L. Larson. LC 97-71389. (Illus.). 196p. (Orig.). 1997. pap. 9.95 (*1-885876-04-1*) Intangible Assets.

Lineman. Jack Rudman. (Career Examination Ser.: C-1347). 1994. pap. 23.95 (*0-8373-1347-3*) Nat Learn.

Lineman (Electrical Power) Jack Rudman. (Career Examination Ser.: C-450). 1994. pap. 23.95 (*0-8373-0450-4*) Nat Learn.

Lineman Thiel & Other Stories. Gerhart Hauptmann. LC 88-70553. 96p. 1990. 22.00 (*0-946162-27-1*, Pub. by Angel Bks); pap. 13.95 (*0-946162-28-X*, Pub. by Angel Bks) Dufour.

Lineman's & Cableman's Field Manual. Mack. LC 99-87049. 300p. 2000. pap. 49.95 (*0-07-135470-0*) McGraw-Hill Prof.

Lineman's & Cableman's Handbook. 9th rev. ed. E. B. Kurtz & Thomas M. Shoemaker. LC 97-16556. (Illus.). 1080p. 1997. 89.95 (*0-07-036011-1*) McGraw.

Lineman's Quick Reference on Wood Safety. Philip M. Opsal. LC 95-51663. 1996. 39.95 (*0-87814-474-9*) PennWell Bks.

Linen: Hand Spinning & Weaving. Patricia Baines. (Illus.). 208p. (Orig.). 1990. 21.95 (*0-934026-52-1*) Interweave.

Linen & Cotton: Classic Sewing Techniques for Great Results. Susan Khalje. LC 98-33436. 1999. pap. 21.95 (*1-56158-250-6*) Taunton.

Linen Cupboard. Gloria Nicol. (Illus.). 80p. 1998. 19.95 (*1-57076-115-9*, Trafalgar Sq Pub) Trafalgar.

Linen, Family & Community in Tullylish, County Down, 1690-1914. Marilyn Cohen. LC 98-113382. 320p. 1997. boxed set 60.00 (*1-85182-312-3*, Pub. by Four Cts Pr) Intl Spec Bk.

An Asterisk (*) at the beginning of an entry indicates that the title is appearing for the first time.

***Linen Management Practice: Bridges to Operational Management.** Judy Kehoe et al. LC 98-60557. xii, 91 p. 1998. write for info. (*0-9663708-1-3*) Standard Textile.

Linen Minus. Susan Gevirtz. LC 92-73492. 64p. (Orig.). (C). 1992. pap. text 8.00 (*0-939691-07-8*) Avenue B.

Linen Napkins to Paper Plates. Junior Auxillary of Clarksville. (Illus.). 256p. 1998. 19.95 (*0-9663244-0-4*) Jr Aux.

Linen Threads & Broom Twines Vol. 1: An Irish & American Album & Directory of the People of the Dunbarton Mill, Greenwich, New York, 1879-1952. William T. Ruddock. LC 98-146872. (Illus.). 179p. 1997. pap. text 14.50 (*0-7884-0770-8*, R811) Heritage Bk.

Linen Trade: Ancient & Modern. A. J. Warden. 745p. 1967. reprint ed. 37.50 (*0-7146-1114-X*, Pub. by F Cass Pubs) Intl Spec Bk.

Liner Market: An Analysis of the Major European Operators. 2nd ed. Paul Gardiner. (Lloyd's Business Intelligence Centre Ser.). 153p. 1994. pap. 695.00 (*1-85044-501-X*) LLP.

Liner Notes: George Strait. David Cantwell. 128p. 1996. pap. 7.95 (*1-57297-121-5*) Blvd Books.

Liner Notes: Neil Young. Brian Keizer. 128p. 1996. pap. 7.95 (*1-57297-123-1*) Blvd Books.

Liner Notes: Soul Asylum. Danny Alexander. 128p. 1996. pap. 7.95 (*1-57297-122-3*) Blvd Books.

Liner Shipping Economics. Jan O. Jansson & D. Sheerson. 280p. 1987. 59.95 (*0-412-26310-6*, 1104) Chapman & Hall.

Liners: A Voyage of Discovery. William Miller & Rob McAuley. LC 97-49037. (Illus.). 160p. 1997. 29.95 (*0-7603-0465-3*) MBI Pubg.

Liners in Battledress: Wartime Camouflage & Colour Schemes for Passenger Ships. David Williams. (Illus.). 160p. 1997. 29.95 (*0-920277-50-0*, Pub. by Vanwell Publ) Howell Pr VA.

***Liners to the Sun.** John Maxtone-Graham. LC 99-89712. (Illus.). 512p. 1999. 35.00 (*1-57409-108-5*); pap. 19.95 (*1-57409-107-7*) Sheridan.

Lines: No Fire Could Burn. John Hejduk. LC 99-29211. (Illus.). 127p. 1999. pap. 14.95 (*1-58093-038-7*, Pub. by Monacelli Pr) Penguin Putnam.

Lines: Sight Reading & Sight Singing Exercises. Bruce E. Arnold. 120p. 1999. pap. text 31.50 (*1-890944-09-2*) Muse Eek.

Lines Across Europe: Nature & Extent of Cocaine Use in Barcelona, Rotterdam & Turin. B. Bieleman et al. x, 222p. 1993. pap. 44.00 (*90-265-1347-X*) Swets.

Lines & Circles. Spode Group Staff. 1991. pap. 13.95 (*1-871315-25-5*) Ashgate Pub Co.

Lines & Electromagnetic Fields for Engineers. Gayle F. Miner. (Illus.). 1008p. 1996. text 92.00 (*0-19-510409-9*) OUP.

Lines & Fields in Electronic Technology. William D. Stanley & Richard Harrington. LC 93-48719. 448p. (C). 1994. 106.00 (*0-02-415654-X*, Pub. by P-H) S&S Trade.

Lines & Paper Works: A Selection in English of Name of Things, New Poems, Love in Lima, Discernment, Legend Noa Noa - Poetry Collection. Cecilia Bustamante. Tr. by Maureen Ahern et al from SPA. 56p. (C). 1990. teacher ed. 10.80 (*0-685-33318-3*) Extramares Edit.

Lines & Paper Works: Selected Poetry of Cecilia Bustamante. 1990. write for info. (*0-318-67004-6*) Extramares Edit.

Lines & Segments see Key to Geometry Series - Book 1-8

Lines & Shadows. Joseph Wambaugh. 416p. 1984. mass mkt. 6.99 (*0-553-27148-2*) Bantam.

Lines, Borders & Connections: Challenges & Possibilities in Multicultural America. Otis Scott. LC 97-201499. 240p. (C). 1997. per. 35.95 (*0-7872-4227-6*, 41422701) Kendall-Hunt.

Lines Drawn from Durer. Norbert Krapf. (Illus.). 48p. 1981. pap. 4.95 (*0-915408-26-0*) Ally Pr.

Lines During War: A Collaboration of Word & Image after the Persian Gulf Incident. 1995. pap. 4.95 (*0-9623693-4-9*) Heaven Bone Pr.

Lines from My Life: Poems & Essays. Peg Sherry. 78p. 1992. pap. 10.95 (*0-9634844-0-0*) Wrd Weavers.

Lines from the O. U. Mathematics Letter. Ed. by Josephine P. Andree. Incl. Vol. 1, Number Extensions. 1.00 Vol. 2, Theory of GAmes. 0.75 Vol. 3, Geometric Extensions. 1985. 1.25 write for info. (*0-318-59521-4*) Mu Alpha Theta.

Lines in Her Face. Bonnie I. Tunick. (Illus.). 64p. (Orig.). Date not set. pap. 9.95 (*0-9639894-8-0*) Wild Dove.

***Lines in the Sand: Race & Class in Lowcountry Georgia, 1750-1860.** Timothy James Lockley. LC 00-36461. 2000. write for info. (*0-8203-2228-8*) U of Ga Pr.

Lines in the Sea. Ed. by G. Francalanci & T. Scovazzi. LC 94-14879. 1994. lib. bdg. 168.00 (*0-7923-2846-9*) Kluwer Academic.

Lines, Lofting & Half Models. Walter J. Simmons. (Boatbuilding Ser.). (Illus.). 159p. 1991. pap. 25.00 (*0-924947-06-3*) Duck Trap Pr.

Lines Long & Short. Henry B. Fuller. (Collected Works of Henry B. Fuller). 1988. reprint ed. lib. bdg. 59.00 (*0-7812-1208-1*) Rprt Serv.

Lines Long & Short. Henry B. Fuller. 1984. reprint ed. 29.00 (*0-403-04592-4*) Scholarly.

***Lines of Activity: Performance, Historiography, Hull-House Domesticity.** Shannon Jackson. LC 99-55252. (Illus.). 384p. (C). 2000. text 45.00 (*0-472-11112-4*, 11112) U of Mich Pr.

Lines of Argument. Carol Winkler et al. 240p. (C). 1993. text. write for info. (*0-697-13242-0*) Brown & Benchmark.

Lines of Argument for Policy Debate. Carol Winkler et al. 224p. (C). 1993. text. write for info. (*0-697-13240-4*) Brown & Benchmark.

Lines of Authority: Politics & English Literary Culture, 1649-1689. Steven N. Zwicker. LC 92-33995. 272p. 1993. text 45.00 (*0-8014-2070-9*) Cornell U Pr.

Lines of Authority: Politics & English Literature Culture, 1649-1689. Steven N. Zwicker. 272p. 1996. pap. text 17.95 (*0-8014-8336-0*) Cornell U Pr.

Lines of Communication: Bar Code & Data Collection Technologies for the 90s. Craig K. Harmon. LC 96-149100. (Illus.). 380p. (Orig.). 1994. pap. 39.95 (*0-911261-07-9*) Helmers Pub.

Lines of Country: An Atlas of Railway & Waterway History in Canada. Christopher Andreae. (Illus.). 240p. 1996. 68.00 (*0-614-17726-X*, Pub. by Boston Mills) Genl Dist Srvs.

Lines of Country: An Atlas of Railway & Waterway History in Canada. Christopher Andreae. (Illus.). 240p. 1997. 68.00 (*1-55046-133-8*, Pub. by Boston Mills) Genl Dist Srvs.

Lines of Desire: Reading Gombrowicz's Fiction with Lacan. Hanjo Berressem. LC 97-53227. 340p. 1998. 79.95 (*0-8101-1309-0*) Northwestern U Pr.

Lines of Fate. Mark Kharitonov. Tr. by Helena Goscilo from RUS. 368p. 1996. 25.00 (*1-56584-230-8*, Pub. by New Press NY) Norton.

Lines of Fate. Mark Kharitonov. 1997. pap. 13.00 (*1-56584-371-1*, Pub. by New Press NY) Norton.

Lines of Fire. Tirman. 1997. 25.00 (*0-02-874026-2*) Macmillan.

Lines of Fire: Women Writers of World War II. Margaret Higonnet. (Illus.). 592p. 1999. pap. 19.95 (*0-452-28146-6*, Plume) Dutton Plume.

Lines of Flight: Reading Deleuze with Hardy, Gissing, Conrad, Woolf. John Hughes. 185p. 1997. pap. write for info. (*1-85075-807-7*, Pub. by Sheffield Acad) CUP Services.

Lines of Light. Daniele Del Giudice. 208p. 1988. 19.95 (*0-15-152420-3*) Harcourt.

Lines of Light. John Light. 67p. pap. write for info. (*3-7052-0414-9*, Pub. by Poetry Salzburg) Intl Spec Bk.

Lines of Light: The Sources of Dispersive Spectroscopy, 1800-1930. J. C. Brand. 280p. 1995. text 154.00 (*2-88449-162-7*); pap. text 66.00 (*2-88449-163-5*) Gordon & Breach.

Lines of Light: With Prayers for the Heart. Barbara Rasp. LC 95-60621. (Illus.). 128p. (Orig.). 1995. pap. 9.95 (*0-9643006-6-4*) Equalite Pr.

Lines of My Hand. Robert Frank. 1992. 39.95 (*3-907509-04-8*, Pub. by Parkett Verlag AG) Dist Art Pubs.

***Lines of Narrative: Psychosocial Perspectives.** Molly Andrews. LC 00-42472. 2000. write for info. (*0-415-24233-9*) Routledge.

Lines of Nazca. Ed. by Anthony F. Aveni. LC 89-84667. (Memoirs Ser.: Vol. 183). (Illus.). 230p. (C). 1990. 30.00 (*0-87169-183-3*, M183-AVA) Am Philos.

Lines of Power - Limits of Language. Gunnar Olsson. (Illus.). 144p. (C). 1991. 24.95 (*0-8166-1949-2*) U of Minn Pr.

Lines of the Los Angeles Railway: A Complete History of the Routes Where the Streetcars Ran. Edmund J. Keilty. Ed. by John Heller. (Illus.). 300p. 1999. 75.00 (*0-9664304-2-5*) Elctrc Rlwy Hist.

Lines of Thought. Charles Price. (Illus.). 48p. 1997. pap. 18.00 (*1-880897-17-2*) Lyme Hist.

Lines of Thought: Discourse, Architectonics, & the Origin of Modern Philosophy. Claudia B. Lacour. LC 95-40105. 176p. 1996. text 49.95 (*0-8223-1777-X*); pap. text 16.95 (*0-8223-1774-5*) Duke.

Lines of Thought: Selected Papers of Maurice B. Line. Maurice B. Line. Ed. by L. J. Anthony. LC 88-24376. 354p. 1988. reprint ed. pap. 109.80 (*0-7837-9269-7*, 206000600004) Bks Demand.

***Lines of Torres Verdras: The Cornerstone of Wellington's Strategy in the Peninsula 1809-12.** John R. Grehan. 256p. 2000. 80.00 (*1-86227-080-5*, Pub. by Spellmnt Pubs) St Mut.

Lines on Stone: The Prehistoric Rock Art of India. Erwin Neumayer. (C). 1993. 54.00 (*81-7304-046-X*, Pub. by Manohar) S Asia.

Lines on the Water: A Fisherman's Life on the Miramichi. David Adams Richards. 1998. 29.95 (*0-385-25697-3*) Bantam.

Lines Out. Rosamond Rosenmeier. LC 89-14855. 72p. 1989. pap. 9.95 (*0-914086-88-X*) Alice James Bks.

Lines Shaping America. David Swanberg. LC 97-78462. 275p. 2000. pap. 16.50 (*0-88739-208-3*) Creat Arts Bk.

***Lines That Divide: Historical Archaeologies of Race, Class & Gender.** Ed. by James A. Delle et al. LC 99-50986. (Illus.). 368p. (C). 2000. text 52.00 (*1-57233-086-4*, Pub. by U of Tenn Pr) U Ch Pr.

Lines to a Little Lady from Someone Who Begs to Be Remembered. Harry L. Faggett. (Illus.). 56p. 1993. 10.00 (*0-8059-3390-5*) Dorrance.

Lines to an Old Apple Tree. Luke Faust. LC 87-90973. (Illus.). 64p. 1988. lib. bdg. 5.00 (*0-9619784-0-6*) Township Pub.

Lines to the Mountain Gods: Nazca & the Mysteries of Peru. Evan Hadingham. LC 87-40562. (Illus.). 320p. 1988. reprint ed. pap. 19.95 (*0-8061-2130-0*) U of Okla Pr.

Lines upon Lines: Contemporary Poetry in Traditional Forms. Robert Hughes. LC 98-65046. 1998. write for info. (*0-9662387-0-2*) Lily Peak Pubg.

Lines upon the Water: A Collection of Original Songs. Sheila Douglas. 112p. 1998. pap. 11.95 (*0-946005-89-3*, OS10496, Pub. by Ossian) Music Sales.

Lines, Waves, & Antennas: The Transmission of Electric Energy. 2nd ed. Robert G. Brown et al. LC 92-15562. 486p. (C). 1992. reprint ed. lib. bdg. 72.50 (*0-89464-758-X*) Krieger.

Lines, Wheels, Paints & Remedies. Anthony B. James. (Illus.). 193p. 1995. 39.95 (*1-886338-08-6*) Meta Jrnl Pr.

Lineshaft Driven Line Roller Conveyor No. 406: CEMA 406-1996. (Illus.). 33p. 1996. pap. 15.00 (*1-891171-10-0*) Conveyor Equip Mfrs.

Lines's Eye: Poetic Experience, American Sight. Elisa New. LC 98-23450. 1998. 49.95 (*0-674-53462-X*) HUP.

Lines's Eye: Poetic Experience, American Sight. Elisa New. LC 98-23450. x, 352p. 1999. text 24.95 (*0-674-53463-8*) HUP.

Linford Christie. Duncan Mackay. (Illus.). 96p. 1996. 24.95 (*0-297-83530-0*, Pub. by Weidenfeld & Nicolson) Trafalgar.

Linford Western Library. large type ed. Ben Bridges. (Linford Western Large Pr. Ser.). 1995. pap. 16.99 (*0-7089-7756-1*, Linford) Ulverscroft.

L'Informe: Mode d'Emploi see Formless: A User's Guide

Ling & the Little Devils. Joan Tate. (Illus.). (J). (ps-3). 9.95 (*0-317-61896-2*, Viking Child) Peng Put Young Read.

Ling Chi Shen Suan Man Tan see Encounters with the World of Spirits

Ling Cho & His Three Friends. V. J. Pacilio. LC 97-50210. (Illus.). 32p. (YA). (ps-3). 2000. 16.00 (*0-374-34545-7*) FS&G.

***Ling Ling: The Most Beautiful Giant Panda in the World.** Bernadette Shih. Ed. by Dionysia. (Illus.). 48p. (J). 1999. 16.95 (*1-902587-04-9*, Pub. by Opal Books) Brit Bk Co Inc.

Ling Shu or the Spiritual Pivot. Tr. by Jing-Nuan Wu from CHI. 304p. (C). 1993. text 32.00 (*0-8248-1557-2*) UH Pr.

Lingala-English - English-Lingala Dictionary & Phrasebook. Thomas Antwi-Akowoah. LC 96-17266. 120p. (Orig.). 1996. pap. 11.95 (*0-7818-0456-6*) Hippocrene Bks.

Lingala-English Dictionary. Lumana Pashi & Alan Turnbull. LC 94-71163. 256p. 1994. text 54.00 (*0-931745-86-1*) Dunwoody Pr.

Lingala-Russian Dictionary. I. N. Toporova. (RUS.). 333p. 1983. 35.00 (*0-8288-1620-4*, F47730) Fr & Eur.

Lingard: Bank Security Documents. James R. Lingard. 1993. write for info. (*0-406-00491-9*, LBSD3, MICHIE) LEXIS Pub.

Linger. M. E. Kerr. LC 92-30988. (Trophy Bk.). 224p. (YA). (gr. 7 up). 1995. pap. 4.95 (*0-06-447102-0*, HarpTrophy) HarpC Child Bks.

Linger. M. E. Kerr. (J). 1995. 10.30 (*0-606-07790-1*) Turtleback.

Linger Not at Chebar. Barbara F. Vroman. 282p. 1992. 17.95 (*0-939995-09-3*) Angel Pr WI.

***Lingerie: A History & Celebration of Silks, Satins, Laces, Linens & Other Bare Essentials.** Catherine Bardey. LC 00-24400. (Illus.). 192p. 2000. 10.98 (*1-57912-105-5*, 81105) Blck Dog & Leventhal.

***Lingerie Design on the Stand: Designs for Underwear & Nightwear.** Dawn Cloake. (Illus.). 96p. 2000. pap. 23.95 (*0-7134-8552-3*) B T B.

Lingerie Industry in France: A Strategic Entry Report, 1997. Compiled by Icon Group International Staff. (Illus.). 121p. 1999. ring bd. 1210.00 incl. audio compact disk (*0-7418-0760-2*) Icon Grp.

***Lingerie Secrets: Sew a Perfect Fit for Every Body.** Jan Bones. LC 99-69481. (Illus.). 128p. 2000. pap. 21.95 (*0-87341-852-2*, BLIN) Krause Pubns.

Lingerie Shots: Pro-Lighting. Rotovision S. A. Staff. (Pro-Lighting Ser.). (Illus.). 160p. 1995. pap. 29.95 (*0-8230-6466-2*, Amphoto) Watsn-Guptill.

Lingering Doubt. Warwick Downing. Ed. by Dana Isaacson. 320p. (Orig.). 1993. mass mkt. 4.99 (*0-671-76034-3*) PB.

Lingering Echoes, in the Land of the Cherokee. Rus L. Brown. Ed. by Marilee Smede. LC 94-70999. (Orig.). pap. 10.00 (*0-9633230-1-6*) R L Brown Ent.

Lingering Fever: A World War II Nurse's Memoir. LaVonne T. Camp. LC 96-48855. (Illus.). 184p. 1997. lib. bdg. 25.00 (*0-7864-0322-5*) McFarland & Co.

Lingering in Tahoe's Wild Gardens see Hiking Tahoe's Wildflower Trails

Lingering Melody. large type ed. Patricia Wilson. 1995. 27.99 (*0-7505-0748-9*, Pub. by Mgna Lrg Print) Ulverscroft.

Lingering Memories. Lillian S. Henley. 1997. pap. write for info. (*1-57553-519-X*) Watermrk Pr.

***Lingering Memories: A Scrapbook of Southern Rural Life.** John W. Reynolds. (Illus.). 96p. 1999. pap. 9.95 (*1-886699-23-2*) Five Corners.

Lingering Shadow of Nazism. Max E. Riedlsperger. (East European Monographs: No. 42). 214p. 1978. text 54.50 (*0-914710-35-4*, Pub. by East Eur Monographs) Col U Pr.

Lingering Shadows. Penny Jordan. 1993. per. 5.99 (*0-373-97122-2*, 1-97122-5) Harlequin Bks.

Lingering Shadows. large type ed. Nancy M. Kennedy. (Linford Romance Library). 288p. 1995. pap. 16.99 (*0-7089-7774-X*, Linford) Ulverscroft.

Lingha Purana, Pt. II. Ed. by J. L. Shastri. (Ancient Indian Tradition & Mythology Ser.: Vol. 6). 1982. 26.00 (*0-685-35377-X*, Pub. by Motilal Bnarsidass) S Asia.

Lingo. Tab Julius. 384p. 1996. 45.00 (*1-56205-592-5*) New Riders Pub.

Lingo. Jim Menick. 336p. 1992. pap. 10.95 (*0-88184-812-3*) Carroll & Graf.

Lingo: A Course on Words & How to Use Them, North American Edition. A. Spooner & E. Phinney. LC 95-60099. (Texts Ser.). (Illus.). 158p. (J). (gr. 7-8). 1995. pap. 18.95 (*0-941051-22-6*) Focus Pub-R Pullins.

Lingo: Listening to Australian English. Graham Seal. LC 99-488379. 224p. 1998. pap. 25.00 (*0-86840-680-5*, Pub. by New South Wales Univ Pr) Intl Spec Bk.

Lingo: Teacher's Manual. A. Spooner & E. Phinney. LC 95-60099. (Focus Texts Ser.). (Illus.). 84p. (Orig.). 1995. pap., teacher ed. 12.95 (*0-941051-50-1*, 800-848-7236) Focus Pub-R Pullins.

Lingo No. 4: A Journal of the Arts. (Illus.). 168p. (Orig.). 1995. pap. 12.50 (*1-889097-02-0*) Hard Pr MA.

Lingo No. 6: A Journal of the Arts. Jon Gams. 184p. 1996. pap. text 12.50 (*1-889097-08-X*) Hard Pr MA.

Lingo No. 9: A Journal of the Arts. Gams. 120p. 1998. pap. 12.95 (*1-889097-25-X*) Hard Pr MA.

Lingo & Shockwave Sourcebook. Vineel Shah. LC 96-47551. 512p. 1997. pap. text 39.95 incl. cd-rom (*0-471-16893-9*) Wiley.

Lingo 8: A Journal of the Arts. Jonathan Gams. (Lingo Magazine Ser.). 152p. 1998. pap. text 12.50 (*1-889097-18-7*, Pub. by Hard Pr MA) Consort Bk Sales.

Lingo for Director 5 Authorized. Macromedia, Inc. Staff. LC 97-164748. 288p. 1997. pap. 39.95 incl. cd-rom (*0-201-68830-1*) Peachpit Pr.

Lingo Handbook: The Complete Guide to Marcromedia Director Scripting. Rich Grace. LC 97-26439. 528p. (C). 1997. pap. 39.95 incl. cd-rom (*0-13-287061-4*) P-H.

Lingo in a Nutshell. Bruce A. Epstein. 634p. 1998. pap. 24.95 (*1-56592-493-2*) OReilly & Assocs.

Lingo of Linguistics, 1966. Eugen Rosenstock-Huessy. (Eugen Rosenstock-Huessy Lectures: Vol. 29). 63p. 1997. pap. 23.00 incl. audio (*0-912148-48-9*) Argo Bks.

Lingo 7: A Journal of the Arts. Jon Gams. (Lingo Magazine: Vol. 7). 184p. 1997. pap. text 12.50 (*1-889097-09-8*) Hard Pr MA.

Lingo Sorcery. 2nd ed. Small. LC 98-37545. 590p. 1999. pap. 59.95 (*0-471-98615-1*) Wiley.

Lingthem Revisited. R. R. Gowloog. (C). 1995. 18.50 (*81-241-0275-9*, Pub. by Har-Anand Pubns) S Asia.

Lingua. Thomas Tomkis. LC 73-133747. (Tudor Facsimile Texts. Old English Plays Ser.: No. 116). reprint ed. 59.50 (*0-404-53416-3*) AMS Pr.

***Lingua Ex Machina: Reconciling Darwin & Chomsky with the Human Brain.** William H. Calvin & Derek Bickerton. LC 99-33464. (Illus.). 304p. 2000. 26.95 (*0-262-03273-2*) MIT Pr.

Lingua Facts: Dimes y Directes en Espanol. Myers. 272p. 1998. pap. text 36.95 (*0-536-01694-1*) Pearson Custom.

Lingua Franca: An Anthology of Poetry by Linguists. Ed. by Donna J. Napoli & Emily N. Rando. ii, 157p. (Orig.). 1990. pap. 24.00 (*0-933104-29-4*) Jupiter Pr.

Lingua Franca in the Mediterranean. J. E. Wansbrough. LC 97-162115. 260p. (C). 1995. text 75.00 (*0-7007-0309-8*, Pub. by Curzon Pr Ltd) Paul & Co Pubs.

Lingua Latina: Colloqvia Personarvm. Hans H. Orberg. 96p. 1994. pap. 7.00 (*87-88073-75-0*, Pub. by Mus Tusculanum) Paul & Co Pubs.

Lingua Latina: Exercitia Latina. Hans H. Orberg. 154p. 1994. pap. 9.00 (*87-88073-77-7*, Pub. by Mus Tusculanum) Paul & Co Pubs.

Lingua Latina: Grammatica Latina. Hans H. Orberg. 38p. 1994. pap. 6.00 (*87-88073-07-6*, Pub. by Mus Tusculanum) Paul & Co Pubs.

Lingua Latina Pt. 1: Familia Romana. Hans H. Orberg. 328p. 1994. pap. 34.00 (*87-7289-139-4*, Pub. by Mus Tusculanum) Paul & Co Pubs.

Lingua Latina Pt. II: Roma Aeterna. Hans H. Orberg. 424p. 1994. pap. 55.00 (*87-7289-107-6*, Pub. by Mus Tusculanum) Paul & Co Pubs.

Lingua Latina Mortua Non Est! Latin Is Not Dead. Ed. by Lauren Pearl & Doris F. Kennedy. 22p. 1991. pap. text 3.10 (*0-939507-31-5*, B5) Amer Classical.

Lingua Mentalis: The Semantics of Natural Language. Anna Wierzbicka. 1981. text 79.95 (*0-12-750050-2*) Acad Pr.

Lingua Press Collection One Catalogue, Vol. 1. Lingua Press Staff. Ed. by Kenneth Gaburo. (Illus.). 44p. 1976. 1.50 (*0-939044-00-5*) Lingua Pr.

Lingua Press Collection Three Catalogue, Vol. 3. Lingua Press Staff. Ed. by Kenneth Gaburo. (Illus.). 150p. pap. 8.50 (*0-939044-23-4*) Lingua Pr.

Lingua Press Collection Two Catalogue, Vol. 2. Lingua Press Staff. Ed. by Kenneth Gaburo. (Illus.). 132p. 1978. pap. 3.95 (*0-939044-17-X*) Lingua Pr.

Lingua Three - In the Can: A Dialectic Mix in Three Rounds. Kenneth Gaburo. (Illus.). 220p. 25.98 (*0-939044-18-8*) Lingua Pr.

Lingua Universalis vs. Calculus Ratiocinator: An Ultimate Presupposition of Twentieth-Century Philosophy. Jaakko Hintikka. LC 96-45990. (Jaakko Hintikka Selected Papers HISP: Vol. 2). 288p. (C). 1996. text 117.50 (*0-7923-4246-1*) Kluwer Academic.

LinguaFun! Language Learning Card Games: French. Donald S. Rivera. (Travel Ser.). (ENG & FRE.). (J). 1996. pap. 12.95 incl. audio (*1-56015-603-1*) Penton Overseas.

LinguaFun! Language Learning Card Games: French. unabridged ed. Donald S. Rivera. (Family Ser.). (FRE & ENG.). (J). (gr. 4 up). 1996. pap. 12.95 incl. audio (*1-56015-591-4*) Penton Overseas.

LinguaFun! Language Learning Card Games: German. Donald S. Rivera. (Family Ser.). (ENG & GER.). (J). (gr. 4 up). 1996. pap. 12.95 incl. audio (*1-56015-600-7*) Penton Overseas.

***LinguaFun! Language Learning Card Games: German.** Donald S. Rivera. (Travel Ser.). (ENG & GER.). (J). 1998. pap. 12.95 incl. audio (*1-56015-605-8*) Penton Overseas.

LinguaFun! Language Learning Card Games: Ingles (English for Spanish-speakers) unabridged ed. Donald S. Rivera. (Family Ser.). (SPA & ENG.). (J). 1996. pap. 12.95 incl. audio (*1-56015-592-2*) Penton Overseas.

LinguaFun! Language Learning Card Games: Italian. Donald S. Rivera. (Family Ser.). (ENG, ITA & SPA.). (J). (gr. 4 up). 1996. pap. 12.95 incl. audio (*1-56015-601-5*) Penton Overseas.

***LinguaFun! Language Learning Card Games: Italian.** Donald S. Rivera. (Travel Ser.). (ENG & ITA.). 1998. pap. 12.95 incl. audio (*1-56015-606-6*) Penton Overseas.

L

L

LinguaFun! Language Learning Card Games: Spanish. Donald S. Rivera. (Travel Ser.). (ENG & SPA.). (J). 1996. pap. 12.95 incl. audio (*1-56015-602-3*) Penton Overseas.

LinguaFun! Language Learning Card Games: Spanish. unabridged ed. Donald S. Rivera. (Family Ser.). (SPA & ENG.). (J). 1996. pap. 12.95 incl. audio (*1-56015-590-6*) Penton Overseas.

Lingual & Gastric Lipases: Their Role in Fat Digestion. Ed. by Margit Hamosh. 248p. 1990. 143.00 (*0-8493-6863-4*, QP609, CRC Reprint) Franklin.

Lingual Apparatus of the African Gray Parrot "Psittacus erithacus" Linne (Aves:Psittacidae): Description & Theoretical Mechanical Analysis. D. G. Homberger. (Ornithological Monographs: Vol. 39). (Illus.). 233p. 1986. pap. 30.00 (*0-943610-49-4*) Am Ornithologists.

***Lingual Orthodontics.** Ed. by Rafi Romano. 211p. 1998. boxed set 169.00 incl. cd-rom (*1-55009-040-2*) DEKR.

Linguaphone Afrikaans Course for English Speakers: Beginner's Course. Linguaphone Staff. (AFR & ENG.). 1991. student ed. 250.00 incl. digital audio (*0-8288-4050-4*, F60960) Fr & Eur.

Linguaphone American Course for Japanese Speakers: Beginner's Course. Linguaphone Staff. (ENG & JPN.). 1991. student ed. 395.00 incl. cd-rom (*0-8288-4287-6*) Fr & Eur.

Linguaphone Arabic Course for English Speakers: Beginner's Course. Linguaphone Staff. (ARA & ENG.). 1991. student ed. 295.00 incl. digital audio (*0-8288-4051-2*, F127355) Fr & Eur.

Linguaphone Arabic Course for French Speakers: Beginner's Course. Linguaphone Staff. (ARA & FRE.). 1991. student ed. 295.00 incl. digital audio (*0-8288-4052-0*, F43160) Fr & Eur.

Linguaphone Business English Course for Dutch Speakers: Beginner's Course. Linguaphone Staff. (DUT & ENG.). 1991. student ed. 295.00 incl. digital audio (*0-8288-4053-9*) Fr & Eur.

Linguaphone Business English Course for Finnish Speakers: Beginner's Course. Linguaphone Staff. (ENG & FIN.). 1991. student ed. 250.00 incl. digital audio (*0-8288-4057-1*) Fr & Eur.

Linguaphone Business English Course for French Speakers: Beginner's Course. Linguaphone Staff. (ENG & FRE.). 1991. student ed. 250.00 incl. digital audio (*0-8288-4054-7*) Fr & Eur.

Linguaphone Business English Course for German Speakers: Beginner's Course. Linguaphone Staff. (ENG & GER.). 1991. student ed. 250.00 incl. digital audio (*0-8288-4055-5*) Fr & Eur.

Linguaphone Business English Course for Mandarin-Chinese Speakers: Beginner's Course. Linguaphone Staff. (CHI & ENG.). 1991. student ed. 250.00 incl. digital audio (*0-8288-4056-3*) Fr & Eur.

Linguaphone Continental Spanish Course for Danish Speakers: Beginner's Course. Linguaphone Staff. (DAN & SPA.). 1991. student ed. 295.00 incl. audio, digital audio (*0-8288-4077-6*) Fr & Eur.

Linguaphone Continental Spanish Course for Dutch Speakers: Beginner's Course. Linguaphone Staff. (DUT & SPA.). 1991. student ed. 295.00 incl. digital audio (*0-8288-4078-4*) Fr & Eur.

Linguaphone Continental Spanish Course for Finnish Speakers: Beginner's Course. Linguaphone Staff. (FIN & SPA.). 1991. student ed. 295.00 incl. digital audio (*0-8288-4063-6*) Fr & Eur.

Linguaphone Continental Spanish Course for French Speakers: Beginner's Course. Linguaphone Staff. (FRE & SPA.). 1991. student ed. 295.00 incl. digital audio (*0-8288-4062-8*) Fr & Eur.

Linguaphone Continental Spanish Course for Italian Speakers: Beginner's Course. Linguaphone Staff. (ITA & SPA.). 1991. student ed. 295.00 incl. digital audio (*0-8288-4065-2*) Fr & Eur.

Linguaphone Continental Spanish Course for Japanese Speakers: Beginner's Course. Linguaphone Staff. (JPN & SPA.). 1991. student ed. 295.00 incl. digital audio (*0-8288-4066-0*) Fr & Eur.

Linguaphone Continental Spanish Course for Norwegian Speakers: Beginner's Course. Linguaphone Staff. (NOR & SPA.). 1991. student ed. 295.00 incl. digital audio (*0-8288-4067-9*) Fr & Eur.

Linguaphone Czech Course for English Speakers: Beginner's Course. Linguaphone Staff. (CZE & ENG.). 1991. student ed. 95.00 incl. digital audio (*0-8288-3272-2*) Fr & Eur.

Linguaphone Danish Course for English Speakers: Beginner's Course. Linguaphone Staff. (DAN & ENG.). 1991. student ed. 250.00 incl. digital audio (*0-8288-4068-7*) Fr & Eur.

Linguaphone Danish Course for Icelandic Speaking People: Beginner's Course. Linguaphone Staff. (DAN & ICE.). 1991. student ed. 250.00 incl. digital audio (*0-8288-4069-5*) Fr & Eur.

Linguaphone Dutch Course for English Speakers: Beginner's Course. Linguaphone Staff. (DUT & ENG.). 1991. student ed. 250.00 incl. digital audio (*0-8288-4070-9*) Fr & Eur.

Linguaphone Dutch Course for French Speakers: Beginner's Course. Linguaphone Staff. (DUT & FRE.). 1991. student ed. 295.00 incl. digital audio (*0-8288-3284-6*) Fr & Eur.

Linguaphone English Course for Arabic Speakers: Beginner's Course. Linguaphone Staff. (ARA & ENG.). 1991. student ed. 295.00 incl. digital audio (*0-8288-4074-1*) Fr & Eur.

Linguaphone English Course for Arabic Speakers: Intermediate Course. Linguaphone Staff. (ARA & ENG.). 1991. student ed. 225.00 incl. digital audio (*0-8288-4079-2*) Fr & Eur.

Linguaphone English Course for Cantonese Speakers: Beginner's Course. Linguaphone Staff. (CHI & ENG.). 1991. student ed. 225.00 incl. audio, digital audio (*0-8288-4080-6*); pap., student ed. 395.00 incl. cd-rom (*0-685-52090-0*) Fr & Eur.

Linguaphone English Course for Czech Speakers: Beginner's Course. Linguaphone Staff. (CZE & ENG.). 1991. student ed. 225.00 incl. digital audio (*0-8288-4087-3*) Fr & Eur.

Linguaphone English Course for Danish Speakers: Beginner's Course. Linguaphone Staff. (DAN & ENG.). 1991. student ed. 295.00 incl. audio, digital audio (*0-8288-4088-1*); pap., student ed. 395.00 incl. cd-rom (*0-8288-4089-X*) Fr & Eur.

Linguaphone English Course for Dutch Speakers: Beginner's Course. Linguaphone Staff. (DUT & ENG.). 1991. student ed. 295.00 incl. digital audio (*0-8288-3280-3*) Fr & Eur.

Linguaphone English Course for Dutch Speakers: Intermediate Course. Linguaphone Staff. (DUT & ENG.). 1991. student ed. 225.00 incl. digital audio (*0-8288-4091-1*) Fr & Eur.

Linguaphone English Course for English Speakers: Beginner's Course. Linguaphone Staff. 1991. pap., student ed. 395.00 incl. cd-rom (*0-685-52093-5*) Fr & Eur.

Linguaphone English Course for Finnish Speakers: Beginner's Course. Linguaphone Staff. (ENG & FIN.). 1991. pap., student ed. 395.00 incl. cd-rom (*0-8288-4094-6*) Fr & Eur.

Linguaphone English Course for Finnish Speakers: Intermediate Course. Linguaphone Staff. (ENG & FIN.). 1991. student ed. 225.00 incl. audio, digital audio (*0-8288-4093-8*) Fr & Eur.

Linguaphone English Course for French Speakers: Advanced Course. Linguaphone Staff. (ENG & FRE.). 1991. student ed. 225.00 incl. digital audio (*0-8288-3285-4*) Fr & Eur.

Linguaphone English Course for French Speakers: Beginner's Course. Linguaphone Staff. (ENG & FRE.). 1991. student ed. 295.00 incl. audio, digital audio (*0-8288-4072-5*); pap., student ed. 395.00 incl. cd-rom (*0-8288-4097-0*) Fr & Eur.

Linguaphone English Course for French Speakers: Intermediate Course. Linguaphone Staff. (ENG & FRE.). 1991. student ed. 225.00 incl. digital audio (*0-8288-4073-3*) Fr & Eur.

Linguaphone English Course for German Speakers: Beginner's Course. Linguaphone Staff. (ENG & GER.). 1991. 295.00 incl. audio, digital audio (*0-8288-4098-9*); pap., student ed. 395.00 incl. cd-rom (*0-8288-4100-4*) Fr & Eur.

Linguaphone English Course for German Speakers: Intermediate Course. Linguaphone Staff. (ENG & GER.). 1991. student ed. 225.00 incl. digital audio (*0-8288-4099-7*) Fr & Eur.

Linguaphone English Course for Greek Speakers: Beginner's Course. Linguaphone Staff. (ENG & GRE.). 1991. student ed. 295.00 incl. digital audio (*0-8288-4101-2*) Fr & Eur.

Linguaphone English Course for Greek Speakers: Intermediate Course. Linguaphone Staff. (ENG & GRE.). 1991. student ed. 225.00 incl. digital audio (*0-8288-4102-0*) Fr & Eur.

Linguaphone English Course for Hebrew Speakers: Beginner's Course. Linguaphone Staff. (ENG & HEB.). 1991. student ed. 295.00 incl. digital audio (*0-8288-4103-9*) Fr & Eur.

Linguaphone English Course for Hungarian Speakers: Beginner's Course. Linguaphone Staff. (ENG & HUN.). 1991. student ed. 225.00 incl. digital audio (*0-8288-4105-5*) Fr & Eur.

Linguaphone English Course for Icelandic Speakers: Beginner's Course. Linguaphone Staff. (ENG & ICE.). 1991. student ed. 295.00 incl. digital audio (*0-8288-4104-7*) Fr & Eur.

Linguaphone English Course for Italian Speakers: Beginner's Course. Linguaphone Staff. (ENG & ITA.). 1991. student ed. 295.00 incl. digital audio (*0-8288-4106-3*) Fr & Eur.

Linguaphone English Course for Italian Speakers: Intermediate Course. Linguaphone Staff. (ENG & ITA.). 1991. student ed. 225.00 incl. digital audio (*0-8288-4107-1*) Fr & Eur.

Linguaphone English Course for Japanese Speakers: Intermediate Course. Linguaphone Staff. (ENG & JPN.). 1991. student ed. 295.00 incl. digital audio (*0-8288-4108-X*) Fr & Eur.

Linguaphone English Course for Malay Speakers: Beginner's Course. Linguaphone Staff. (ENG & MAY.). 1991. student ed. 295.00 incl. digital audio (*0-8288-4109-8*) Fr & Eur.

Linguaphone English Course for Mandarin Speakers: Beginner's Course. Linguaphone Staff. (CHI & ENG.). 1991. student ed. 295.00 incl. audio, digital audio (*0-8288-4110-1*); pap., student ed. 395.00 incl. cd-rom (*0-8288-4112-8*) Fr & Eur.

Linguaphone English Course for Mandarin Speakers: Intermediate Course. Linguaphone Staff. (CHI & ENG.). 1991. student ed. 225.00 incl. digital audio (*0-8288-4111-X*) Fr & Eur.

Linguaphone English Course for Norwegian Speakers: Beginner's Course. Linguaphone Staff. (ENG & NOR.). 1991. student ed. 295.00 incl. audio, digital audio (*0-8288-4113-6*); pap., student ed. 395.00 incl. cd-rom (*0-8288-4115-2*) Fr & Eur.

Linguaphone English Course for Norwegian Speakers: Intermediate Course. Linguaphone Staff. (ENG & NOR.). 1991. student ed. 225.00 incl. digital audio (*0-8288-4114-4*) Fr & Eur.

Linguaphone English Course for Persian Speakers: Beginner's Course. Linguaphone Staff. (ENG & PER.). 1991. student ed. 225.00 incl. digital audio (*0-8288-4116-0*) Fr & Eur.

Linguaphone English Course for Polish Speakers: Beginner's Course. Linguaphone Staff. (ENG & POL.). 1991. student ed. 225.00 incl. digital audio (*0-8288-4117-9*, F127355) Fr & Eur.

Linguaphone English Course for Portuguese Speakers: Beginner's Course. Linguaphone Staff. (ENG & POR.). 1991. student ed. 295.00 incl. digital audio (*0-8288-3307-9*) Fr & Eur.

Linguaphone English Course for Portuguese Speakers: Intermediate Course. Linguaphone Staff. (ENG & POR.). 1991. student ed. 225.00 incl. digital audio (*0-8288-3308-7*) Fr & Eur.

Linguaphone English Course for Russian Speakers: Beginner's Course. Linguaphone Staff. (ENG & RUS.). 1991. student ed. 295.00 incl. digital audio (*0-8288-4118-7*, F60960) Fr & Eur.

Linguaphone English Course for Serbian Speakers: Beginner's Course. Linguaphone Staff. (ENG & SER.). 1991. student ed. 295.00 incl. digital audio (*0-8288-4119-5*, F43160) Fr & Eur.

Linguaphone English Course for Serbo-Croatian Speakers: Beginner's Course. Linguaphone Staff. (ENG & SER.). 1991. student ed. 295.00 incl. digital audio (*0-8288-4121-7*) Fr & Eur.

Linguaphone English Course for Slovenian Speakers: Beginner's Course. Linguaphone Staff. (ENG & SLV.). 1991. student ed. 295.00 incl. digital audio (*0-8288-4120-9*) Fr & Eur.

Linguaphone English Course for Spanish Speakers: Beginner's Course. Linguaphone Staff. (ENG & SPA.). 1991. student ed. 295.00 incl. digital audio (*0-8288-4085-7*) Fr & Eur.

Linguaphone English Course for Spanish Speakers: Intermediate Course. Linguaphone Staff. (ENG & SPA.). 1991. student ed. 225.00 incl. digital audio (*0-8288-4086-5*) Fr & Eur.

Linguaphone English Course for Swedish Speakers: Beginner's Course. Linguaphone Staff. (ENG & SWE.). 1991. student ed. 295.00 incl. audio, digital audio (*0-8288-4122-5*); pap., student ed. 395.00 incl. cd-rom (*0-8288-4124-1*) Fr & Eur.

Linguaphone English Course for Swedish Speakers: Intermediate Course. Linguaphone Staff. (ENG & SWE.). 1991. student ed. 225.00 incl. digital audio (*0-8288-4123-3*) Fr & Eur.

Linguaphone English Course for Thai Speakers: Beginner's Course. Linguaphone Staff. (ENG & THA.). 1991. student ed. 295.00 incl. digital audio (*0-8288-4125-X*) Fr & Eur.

Linguaphone English Course for Thai Speakers: Intermediate Course. Linguaphone Staff. (ENG & THA.). 1991. student ed. 225.00 incl. digital audio (*0-8288-4126-8*) Fr & Eur.

Linguaphone English Course for Turkish Speakers: Beginner's Course. Linguaphone Staff. (ENG & TUR.). 1991. student ed. 295.00 incl. digital audio (*0-8288-4127-6*) Fr & Eur.

Linguaphone English Course for Turkish Speakers: Intermediate Course. Linguaphone Staff. (ENG & TUR.). 1991. student ed. 225.00 incl. digital audio (*0-8288-4128-4*) Fr & Eur.

Linguaphone English Course for Vietnamese Speakers: Beginner's Course. Linguaphone Staff. (ENG & VIE.). 1991. student ed. 225.00 incl. digital audio (*0-8288-4129-2*) Fr & Eur.

Linguaphone Finnish Course for English Speakers: Beginner's Course. Linguaphone Staff. (ENG & FIN.). 1991. student ed. 225.00 incl. digital audio (*0-8288-4130-6*) Fr & Eur.

Linguaphone Finnish Course for Swedish Speakers: Beginner's Course. Linguaphone Staff. (FIN & SWE.). 1991. student ed. 225.00 incl. digital audio (*0-8288-4131-4*) Fr & Eur.

Linguaphone French Course for Arabic Speakers: Beginner's Course. Linguaphone Staff. (ARA & FRE.). 1991. student ed. 225.00 incl. digital audio (*0-8288-4132-2*) Fr & Eur.

Linguaphone French Course for Cantonese-Chinese Speakers: Beginner's Course. Linguaphone Staff. (CHI & ENG.). 1991. student ed. 395.00 incl. cd-rom (*0-8288-4260-4*) Fr & Eur.

Linguaphone French Course for Czech Speakers: Beginner's Course. Linguaphone Staff. (CZE & FRE.). 1991. student ed. 225.00 incl. digital audio (*0-8288-4137-3*) Fr & Eur.

Linguaphone French Course for Danish Speakers: Beginner's Course. Linguaphone Staff. (DAN & FRE.). 1991. student ed. 295.00 incl. audio, digital audio (*0-8288-4138-1*); pap., student ed. 395.00 incl. cd-rom (*0-8288-4139-X*) Fr & Eur.

Linguaphone French Course for Dutch Speakers: Beginner's Course. Linguaphone Staff. (DUT & FRE.). 1991. student ed. 295.00 incl. digital audio (*0-8288-3281-1*) Fr & Eur.

Linguaphone French Course for Dutch Speakers: Intermediate Course. Linguaphone Staff. (DUT & FRE.). 1991. student ed. 225.00 incl. digital audio (*0-8288-3282-X*) Fr & Eur.

Linguaphone French Course for English Speakers: Beginner's Course. Linguaphone Staff. (ENG & FRE.). 1991. student ed. 295.00 incl. audio, digital audio (*0-8288-4142-X*); pap., student ed. 395.00 incl. cd-rom (*0-8288-4144-6*) Fr & Eur.

Linguaphone French Course for English Speakers: Intermediate Course. Linguaphone Staff. (ENG & FRE.). 1991. student ed. 225.00 incl. digital audio (*0-8288-4143-8*) Fr & Eur.

Linguaphone French Course for Finnish Speakers: Beginner's Course. Linguaphone Staff. (FIN & FRE.). 1991. student ed. 295.00 incl. audio, digital audio (*0-8288-4145-4*); pap., student ed. 395.00 incl. cd-rom (*0-8288-4147-0*) Fr & Eur.

Linguaphone French Course for Finnish Speakers: Intermediate Course. Linguaphone Staff. (FIN & FRE.). 1991. student ed. 225.00 incl. digital audio (*0-8288-4146-2*) Fr & Eur.

Linguaphone French Course for German Speakers: Beginner's Course. Linguaphone Staff. (FRE & GER.). 1991. student ed. 295.00 incl. audio, digital audio (*0-8288-4148-9*); pap., student ed. 395.00 incl. cd-rom (*0-8288-4149-7*) Fr & Eur.

Linguaphone French Course for German Speakers: Intermediate Course. Linguaphone Staff. (FRE & GER.). 1991. student ed. 225.00 incl. digital audio (*0-8288-4150-0*) Fr & Eur.

Linguaphone French Course for Greek Speakers: Beginner's Course. Linguaphone Staff. (FRE & GRE.). 1991. student ed. 295.00 incl. digital audio (*0-8288-4151-9*) Fr & Eur.

Linguaphone French Course for Greek Speakers: Intermediate Course. Linguaphone Staff. (FRE & GRE.). 1991. student ed. 225.00 incl. digital audio (*0-8288-4152-7*) Fr & Eur.

Linguaphone French Course for Italian Speakers: Beginner's Course. Linguaphone Staff. (FRE & ITA.). 1991. student ed. 295.00 incl. digital audio (*0-8288-4153-5*) Fr & Eur.

Linguaphone French Course for Italian Speakers: Intermediate Course. Linguaphone Staff. (FRE & ITA.). 1991. student ed. 225.00 incl. audio, digital audio (*0-8288-4154-3*) Fr & Eur.

Linguaphone French Course for Japanese Speakers: Beginner's Course. Linguaphone Staff. (FRE & JPN.). 1991. student ed. 295.00 incl. digital audio (*0-8288-4155-1*) Fr & Eur.

Linguaphone French Course for Mandarin-Chinese Speakers: Beginner's Course. Linguaphone Staff. (CHI & ENG.). 1991. student ed. 395.00 incl. cd-rom (*0-8288-4259-0*) Fr & Eur.

Linguaphone French Course for Norwegian Speakers: Beginner's Course. Linguaphone Staff. (FRE & NOR.). 1991. student ed. 295.00 incl. audio, digital audio (*0-8288-3298-6*); pap., student ed. 395.00 incl. cd-rom (*0-8288-4158-6*) Fr & Eur.

Linguaphone French Course for Norwegian Speakers: Intermediate Course. Linguaphone Staff. (FRE & NOR.). 1991. student ed. 225.00 incl. digital audio (*0-8288-3299-4*) Fr & Eur.

Linguaphone French Course for Persian Speakers: Beginner's Course. Linguaphone Staff. (FRE & PER.). 1991. student ed. 225.00 incl. digital audio (*0-8288-4159-4*) Fr & Eur.

Linguaphone French Course for Portuguese Speakers: Beginner's Course. Linguaphone Staff. (FRE & POR.). 1991. student ed. 295.00 incl. digital audio (*0-8288-3303-6*) Fr & Eur.

Linguaphone French Course for Portuguese Speakers: Intermediate Course. Linguaphone Staff. (FRE & POR.). 1991. student ed. 225.00 incl. digital audio (*0-8288-3304-4*) Fr & Eur.

Linguaphone French Course for Serbian Speakers: Beginner's Course. Linguaphone Staff. (FRE & SER.). 1991. student ed. 295.00 incl. digital audio (*0-8288-4160-8*) Fr & Eur.

Linguaphone French Course for Slovenian Speakers: Beginner's Course. Linguaphone Staff. (FRE & SLV.). 1991. student ed. 295.00 incl. digital audio (*0-8288-4161-6*) Fr & Eur.

Linguaphone French Course for Spanish Speakers: Beginner's Course. Linguaphone Staff. (FRE & SPA.). 1991. student ed. 295.00 incl. digital audio (*0-8288-4134-9*) Fr & Eur.

Linguaphone French Course for Spanish Speakers: Intermediate Course. Linguaphone Staff. (FRE & SPA.). 1991. student ed. 225.00 incl. digital audio (*0-8288-3311-7*) Fr & Eur.

Linguaphone French Course for Swedish Speakers: Beginner's Course. Linguaphone Staff. (FRE & SWE.). 1991. student ed. 295.00 incl. audio, digital audio (*0-8288-4163-2*); student ed. 395.00 incl. cd-rom (*0-8288-4164-0*) Fr & Eur.

Linguaphone French Course for Swedish Speakers: Intermediate Course. Linguaphone Staff. (FRE & SWE.). 1991. student ed. 225.00 incl. digital audio (*0-8288-4162-4*) Fr & Eur.

Linguaphone French Course for Turkish Speakers: Beginner's Course. Linguaphone Staff. (FRE & TUR.). 1991. student ed. 295.00 incl. digital audio (*0-8288-4165-9*) Fr & Eur.

Linguaphone German Course for Cantonese Chinese Speakers: Beginner's Course. Linguaphone Staff. (CHI & GER.). 1991. student ed. 395.00 incl. cd-rom (*0-8288-4187-X*) Fr & Eur.

Linguaphone German Course for Chinese-Mandarin Speakers: Beginner's Course. Linguaphone Staff. (CHI & GER.). 1991. student ed. 395.00 incl. cd-rom (*0-8288-4261-2*) Fr & Eur.

Linguaphone German Course for Danish Speakers: Beginner's Course. Linguaphone Staff. (DAN & GER.). 1991. student ed. 295.00 incl. audio, digital audio (*0-8288-3279-X*); student ed. 395.00 incl. cd-rom (*0-8288-4170-5*) Fr & Eur.

Linguaphone German Course for Dutch Speakers: Beginner's Course. Linguaphone Staff. (DUT & GER.). 1991. student ed. 295.00 incl. digital audio (*0-8288-4171-3*) Fr & Eur.

An Asterisk (*) at the beginning of an entry indicates that the title is appearing for the first time.

Linguaphone German Course for Dutch Speakers: Intermediate Course. Linguaphone Staff. (DUT & GER.). 1991. student ed. 225.00 incl. digital audio (*0-8288-4172-1*) Fr & Eur.

Linguaphone German Course for English Speakers: Beginner's Course. Linguaphone Staff. (ENG & GER.). 1991. student ed. 295.00 incl. audio, digital audio (*0-8288-4173-X*); student ed. 395.00 incl. cd-rom (*0-8288-4175-6*) Fr & Eur.

Linguaphone German Course for English Speakers: Intermediate Course. Linguaphone Staff. (ENG & GER.). 1991. student ed. 225.00 incl. digital audio (*0-8288-4174-8*) Fr & Eur.

Linguaphone German Course for Finnish Speakers: Beginner's Course. Linguaphone Staff. (FIN & GER.). 1991. student ed. 295.00 incl. audio, digital audio (*0-8288-4176-4*); student ed. 395.00 incl. cd-rom (*0-8288-4178-0*) Fr & Eur.

Linguaphone German Course for Finnish Speakers: Intermediate Course. Linguaphone Staff. (FIN & GER.). 1991. student ed. 225.00 incl. digital audio (*0-8288-4177-2*) Fr & Eur.

Linguaphone German Course for French Speakers: Beginner's Course. Linguaphone Staff. (FRE & GER.). 1991. student ed. 295.00 incl. audio, digital audio (*0-8288-4179-9*); student ed. 395.00 incl. cd-rom (*0-8288-4181-0*) Fr & Eur.

Linguaphone German Course for French Speakers: Intermediate Course. Linguaphone Staff. (FRE & GER.). 1991. student ed. 225.00 incl. digital audio (*0-8288-4180-2*) Fr & Eur.

Linguaphone German Course for Greek Speakers: Beginner's Course. Linguaphone Staff. (GER & GRE.). 1991. student ed. 295.00 incl. digital audio (*0-8288-4182-9*) Fr & Eur.

Linguaphone German Course for Greek Speakers: Intermediate Course. Linguaphone Staff. (GER & GRE.). 1991. student ed. 225.00 incl. digital audio (*0-8288-4183-7*) Fr & Eur.

Linguaphone German Course for Italian Speakers: Beginner's Course. Linguaphone Staff. (GER & ITA.). 1991. student ed. 295.00 incl. digital audio (*0-8288-4184-5*) Fr & Eur.

Linguaphone German Course for Italian Speakers: Intermediate Course. Linguaphone Staff. (GER & ITA.). 1991. student ed. 225.00 incl. digital audio (*0-8288-4185-3*) Fr & Eur.

Linguaphone German Course for Japanese Speakers: Beginner's Course. Linguaphone Staff. (GER & JPN.). 1991. student ed. 295.00 incl. digital audio (*0-8288-4186-1*) Fr & Eur.

Linguaphone German Course for Mandarin Chinese Speakers: Beginner's Course. Linguaphone Staff. (CHI & GER.). 1991. student ed. 295.00 incl. digital audio (*0-8288-4188-8*) Fr & Eur.

Linguaphone German Course for Norwegian Speakers: Beginner's Course. Linguaphone Staff. (GER & NOR.). 1991. student ed. 395.00 incl. cd-rom (*0-8288-4293-0*) Fr & Eur.

Linguaphone German Course for Portuguese Speakers: Beginner's Course. Linguaphone Staff. (GER & POR.). 1991. student ed. 295.00 incl. digital audio (*0-8288-3305-2*) Fr & Eur.

Linguaphone German Course for Serbian Speakers: Beginner's Course. Linguaphone Staff. (GER & SER.). 1991. student ed. 295.00 incl. digital audio (*0-8288-4189-6*) Fr & Eur.

Linguaphone German Course for Slovenian Speakers: Beginner's Course. Linguaphone Staff. (GER & SLV.). 1991. student ed. 295.00 incl. digital audio (*0-8288-4190-X*) Fr & Eur.

Linguaphone German Course for Spanish Speakers: Beginner's Course. Linguaphone Staff. (GER & SPA.). 1991. student ed. 295.00 incl. digital audio (*0-8288-4167-5*) Fr & Eur.

Linguaphone German Course for Spanish Speakers: Intermediate Course. Linguaphone Staff. (GER & SPA.). 1991. student ed. 225.00 incl. digital audio (*0-8288-4168-3*) Fr & Eur.

Linguaphone German Course for Swedish Speakers: Beginner's Course. Linguaphone Staff. (GER & SWE.). 1991. student ed. 295.00 incl. audio, digital audio (*0-8288-4192-6*); student ed. 395.00 incl. cd-rom (*0-8288-4193-4*) Fr & Eur.

Linguaphone German Course for Swedish Speakers: Intermediate Course. Linguaphone Staff. (GER & SWE.). 1991. student ed. 225.00 incl. digital audio (*0-8288-4191-8*) Fr & Eur.

Linguaphone German Course for Turkish Speakers: Beginner's Course. Linguaphone Staff. (GER & TUR.). 1991. student ed. 295.00 incl. digital audio (*0-8288-4194-2*) Fr & Eur.

Linguaphone Greek Course for English Speakers: Beginner's Course. Linguaphone Staff. (ENG & GRE.). 1991. student ed. 250.00 incl. digital audio (*0-8288-4195-0*) Fr & Eur.

Linguaphone Greek Course for French Speakers: Beginner's Course. Linguaphone Staff. (FRE & GRE.). 1991. student ed. 225.00 incl. digital audio (*0-8288-4196-9*) Fr & Eur.

Linguaphone Greek Course for German Speakers: Beginner's Course. Linguaphone Staff. (GER & GRE.). 1991. student ed. 250.00 incl. digital audio (*0-8288-4197-7*) Fr & Eur.

Linguaphone Hebrew Course for English Speakers: Beginner's Course. Linguaphone Staff. (ENG & HEB.). 1991. student ed. 250.00 incl. digital audio (*0-8288-4198-5*) Fr & Eur.

Linguaphone Hebrew Course for French Speakers: Beginner's Course. Linguaphone Staff. (FRE & HEB.). 1991. student ed. 250.00 incl. digital audio (*0-8288-4199-3*) Fr & Eur.

Linguaphone Hindi Course for English Speakers: Beginner's Course. Linguaphone Staff. (ENG & HIN.). 1991. student ed. 225.00 incl. digital audio (*0-8288-3273-0*) Fr & Eur.

Linguaphone Icelandic Course for English Speakers: Beginner's Course. Linguaphone Staff. (ENG & ICE.). 1991. student ed. 225.00 incl. digital audio (*0-8288-4200-0*) Fr & Eur.

Linguaphone Italian Course for Danish Speakers: Beginner's Course. Linguaphone Staff. (DAN & ITA.). 1991. student ed. 295.00 incl. digital audio (*0-8288-4207-8*) Fr & Eur.

Linguaphone Italian Course for Dutch Speakers: Beginner's Course. Linguaphone Staff. (DUT & ITA.). 1991. student ed. 295.00 incl. audio (*0-8288-3283-8*) Fr & Eur.

Linguaphone Italian Course for Spanish Speakers: Beginner's Course. Linguaphone Staff. (ITA & SPA.). 1991. student ed. 295.00 incl. digital audio (*0-8288-4206-X*) Fr & Eur.

Linguaphone Persian Course for English Speakers: Beginner's Course. Linguaphone Staff. (ENG & PER.). 1991. student ed. 95.00 incl. digital audio (*0-8288-4254-X*) Fr & Eur.

Linguaphone Portuguese Course for Danish Speakers: Beginner's Course. Linguaphone Staff. (DAN & POR.). 1991. student ed. 225.00 incl. digital audio (*0-8288-4059-8*) Fr & Eur.

Linguaphone Portuguese Course for Dutch Speakers: Beginner's Course. Linguaphone Staff. (DUT & POR.). 1991. student ed. 225.00 incl. digital audio (*0-8288-4058-X*) Fr & Eur.

Linguaphone Portuguese Course for French Speakers: Beginner's Course. Linguaphone Staff. (FRE & POR.). 1991. student ed. 250.00 incl. digital audio (*0-8288-4060-1*) Fr & Eur.

Linguaphone Portuguese Course for Norwegian Speakers: Beginner's Course. Linguaphone Staff. (NOR & POR.). 1991. student ed. 225.00 incl. digital audio (*0-8288-4076-8*) Fr & Eur.

Linguarum Vetterum Septentrionalium Thesaurus Grammatico-Criticus et Archaeologicus, 2 vols. in 1. George Hickes. lxxxii, 1038p. 1970. reprint ed. write for info. (*0-318-70759-4*) G Olms Pubs.

Lingue Europeenne de Cooperation Economique, 1946-1981. Michel Dumoulin & Anne-Myriam Dutrieue. 280p. 1993. 40.80 (*3-906750-74-4*) P Lang Pubng.

***Linguistica Tyrrhenica II: The Etruscan Liturgical Calendar from Capua, Addenda et Corrigenda ad Volumen I.** Fred C. Woudhuizen. 221p. 1998. pap. 45.00 (*90-5063-577-6*, Pub. by Gieben) J Benjamins Pubng Co.

Linguistic Action: Some Empirical-Conceptual Studies. Ed. by Jef Verschueren & Roy O. Freedle. LC 86-28904. (Advances in Discourse Processes Ser.: Vol. 23). 176p. (C). 1987. text 78.50 (*0-89391-365-0*) Ablx Pub.

Linguistic Analyses of Aphasic Language. Ed. by Wolfgang U. Dressler & Jack A. Stark. (Neuropsychology Ser.). (Illus.). 365p. 1988. 128.00 (*0-387-96692-7*) Spr-Verlag.

Linguistic Analysis: The Non-Bantu Languages of North-Eastern Africa. Archibald N. Tucker & M. A. Bryan. LC 66-71417. (Handbook of African Languages Ser.: Pt. 3). 670p. reprint ed. pap. 200.00 (*0-8357-6975-5*, 203903500009) Bks Demand.

Linguistic Analysis & Phenomenology. Ed. by S. C. Brown & Wolfe Mays. LC 70-165551. 307p. 1972. 36.50 (*0-8387-1025-5*) Bucknell U Pr.

Linguistic Analysis & Programming for Mechanical Translation. Ed. by Silvio Ceccato. (Illus.). 246p. 1961. text 190.00 (*0-677-00110-X*) Gordon & Breach.

Linguistic Analysis & Text Interpretation: Essays on the Bill of Rights & on Keats, Shakespeare & Dreiser. Juhani Rudanko. LC 97-9489. 144p. 1997. 49.00 (*0-7618-0734-9*); pap. 26.50 (*0-7618-0735-7*) U Pr of Amer.

Linguistic Analysis of Children's Speech: Readings. Ed. by Thomas M. Longhurst. 1974. 32.00 (*0-8422-5173-1*); pap. text 12.95 (*0-8422-0404-0*) Irvington.

Linguistic Analysis of the Rgveda-Padapatha. Vashishtha N. Jha. (Pre-Paninian Grammatical Traditions Ser.: Pt. I). (C). 1992. 24.00 (*81-7030-320-6*) S Asia.

Linguistic & Cultural Influences on Learning Mathematics. Ed. by Rodney R. Cocking & Jose P. Mestre. (Instructional Psychology Ser.). 320p. 1988. text 65.00 (*0-89859-876-1*) L Erlbaum Assocs.

Linguistic & Literary Studies in Honor of Archibald A. Hill: General & Theoretical Linguistics, Vol. 1. Ed. by Mohammad A. Jazayery et al. (Trends in Linguistics, Studies & Monographs: No. 7). 1978. 110.80 (*90-279-7717-8*) Mouton.

Linguistic & Literary Studies in Honor of Archibald A. Hill Vol. 1: General & Theoretical Linguistics. Ed. by Mohammad A. Jazayery et al. 412p. 1976. pap. 71.00 (*90-316-0108-X*, Pub. by B R Gruner) Humanities.

Linguistic & Literary Studies in Honor of Archibald A. Hill Vol. 2: Descriptive Linguistics. Ed. by Mohammad A. Jazayery et al. (Trends in Linguistics, Studies & Monographs: No. 10). 1978. text 96.15 (*90-279-7727-5*) Mouton.

Linguistic & Literary Studies in Honor of Archibald A. Hill Vol. 3: Historical & Comparative Linguistics. Ed. by Mohammad A. Jazayery et al. (Trends in Linguistics, Studies & Monographs: No. 10). 1978. text 96.15 (*90-279-7737-2*) Mouton.

Linguistic & Literary Studies in Honor of Archibald A. Hill Vol. 4: Linguistics & Literature, Sociolinguistics & Applied Linguistics. Ed. by Mohammad A. Jazayery et al. (Trends in Linguistics, Studies & Monographs: No. 10). 1979. text 96.15 (*90-279-7747-X*) Mouton.

Linguistic & Literary Studies in Honor of Helmut A. Hatzfeld. Ed. by Alessandro S. Crisafulli. LC 64-55374. 426p. reprint ed. pap. 132.10 (*0-608-17256-1*, 202950800061) Bks Demand.

Linguistic & Non-Linguistic Aspects of Qur'an Translating to Yoruba. R. 'Deremi Abubakre. (Studien Zur Sprachwissenschaft Ser.: Vol. 3). vi, 104p. 1986. 24.00 (*3-487-07804-X*) G Olms Pubs.

Linguistic & Non-Linguistic Aspects of Qur'an Translating to Yoruba, 10 vols., Set. Wilhelm Ahlwardt. (Handschriften-Verzeichnisse der Koniglichen Bibliothek Zu Berlin Ser.: Vols. VII-IX, XVI-XXII). (Illus.). lvi, 6042p. 1980. reprint ed. 1950.00 (*3-487-06932-6*) G Olms Pubs.

Linguistic Anthropology. Alessandro Duranti. LC 96-44608. (Textbooks in Linguistics). (Illus.). 420p. (C). 1997. text 64.95 (*0-521-44536-1*); pap. text 24.95 (*0-521-44993-6*) Cambridge U Pr.

Linguistic Anthropology. Hickers. 1997. mass mkt. 19.75 (*0-03-006956-4*) H Holt & Co.

Linguistic Anthropology. 2nd ed. Hickerson. (C). 1999. pap. text 23.50 (*0-15-505178-4*) Harcourt.

Linguistic Anthropology of Praxis & Language Shift: Arvanitika (Albanian) & Greek in Contact. Lukas D. Tsitsipis. (Oxford Studies in Language Contact). 176p. 1999. text 72.00 (*0-19-823731-6*) OUP.

Linguistic Approach to Buddhist Thought. Genjun H. Sasaki. x, 194p. (C). 1992. 17.00 (*81-208-0038-9*, Pub. by Motilal Bnarsidass) S Asia.

***Linguistic Approach to Reading & Writing.** Robert James Scholes. LC 99-41481. (Studies in Linguistics & Semiotics: Vol. 3). 162p. 1999. text 79.95 (*0-7734-7919-8*) E Mellen.

Linguistic Approaches to Artificial Intelligence. Ed. by Ulrich Schmitz et al. (Duisburg Papers for Research in Language & Culture: Vol. 6). (Illus.). 564p. 1990. 91.00 (*3-631-40737-8*) P Lang Pubng.

Linguistic Atlas of England. Ed. by Harold Orton & Stewart F. Sanderson. (Illus.). 488p. (C). 1998. 195.00 (*0-415-15129-5*) Routledge.

Linguistic Atlas of Late Mediaeval English, 4 vols., Set. A. McIntosh et al. 2400p. 1987. 670.00 (*0-08-032437-1*, Pub. by Aberdeen U Pr) Macmillan.

Linguistic Atlas of New England, 6 pts. in 3 vols., Set. Ed. by Hans Kurath et al. LC 77-37507. reprint ed. 2550.00 (*0-404-10040-6*) AMS Pr.

Linguistic Atlas of the Middle & South Atlantic States: Fascicles 1 & 2, 1. Raven I. McDavid, Jr. & Raymond K. O'Cain. LC 79-24748. (Illus.). 1994. pap. text 15.00 (*0-226-55742-1*) U Ch Pr.

Linguistic Atlas of the Middle & South Atlantic States: Fascicles 1 & 2, 2. Raven I. McDavid, Jr. & Raymond K. O'Cain. LC 79-24748. (Illus.). 128p. 1980. pap. text 18.00 (*0-226-55744-8*) U Ch Pr.

***Linguistic Attractors: The Cognitive Dynamics of Language Aquisition & Change.** David L. Cooper. LC 99-10761. (Human Cognitive Processing Ser.: Vol. 2). xv, 375p. 1999. 90.00 (*1-55619-202-9*) J Benjamins Pubng Co.

Linguistic Auditing: A Guide to Identifying Foreign Language Communication Needs in Corporations. Nigel Reeves & Colin Wright. LC 95-42195. (Topics in Translation Ser.: No. 9). 130p. 1996. 39.95 (*1-85359-328-1*, Pub. by Multilingual Matters); pap. 24.95 (*1-85359-327-3*, Pub. by Multilingual Matters) Taylor & Francis.

Linguistic Basis of Communication Disorders. Schwartz. 1998. 36.00 (*1-56593-137-8*) Singular Publishing.

Linguistic Behavior. Jonathan Bennett. LC 89-27985. 320p. (C). 1990. reprint ed. pap. 16.95 (*0-87220-092-2*); reprint ed. lib. bdg. 37.95 (*0-87220-093-0*) Hackett Pub.

Linguistic Bibliography for the Year, 1979. J. J. Beylsmit. 1982. 135.00 (*0-686-37163-1*) Kluwer Academic.

Linguistic Bibliography for the Year, 1981. Ed. by J. J. Beylsmit. 911p. 1984. lib. bdg. 450.50 (*90-247-2953-X*) Kluwer Academic.

Linguistic Bibliography for the Year, 1976. Ed. by J. J. Beylsmit & J. C. Rijlaarsdam. xlviii, 736p. 1980. lib. bdg. 306.00 (*90-247-2242-X*) Kluwer Academic.

Linguistic Bibliography for the Year, 1983. Hans Borkent. Ed. by Mark Janse. 1985. text 477.00 (*90-247-3241-7*) Kluwer Academic.

Linguistic Bibliography for the Year, 1990. Ed. by Mark Janse & Sijmen Tol. 1993. text 563.00 (*0-7923-1894-3*) Kluwer Academic.

Linguistic Bibliography for the Year 1994. Ed. by Mark Janse & Sijmen Tol. 1408p. 1998. text 561.00 (*0-7923-4465-0*) Kluwer Academic.

Linguistic Bibliography for the Year, 1978. Ed. by J. J. Beylsmit. 760p. 1981. lib. bdg. 417.00 (*90-247-2509-7*) Kluwer Academic.

Linguistic Categories: Auxiliaries & Related Puzzles, 2 Vols. Frank Heny & Barry Richards. 308p. 1983. lib. bdg. 146.00 (*90-277-1478-9*, D Reidel) Kluwer Academic.

Linguistic Categories Vol. II: Auxiliaries & Related Puzzles: The Scope, Order, & Distribution of English Auxiliary Verbs. Ed. by Frank Henry & B. Richards. (Studies in Linguistics & Philosophy: No. 20). 269p. 1983. lib. bdg. 129.50 (*90-277-1479-7*) Kluwer Academic.

Linguistic Categorization: Proceedings of an International Symposium in Milwaukee, Wisconsin, April 10-11, 1987. Ed. by Roberta L. Corrigan et al. LC 89-15193. (Current Issues in Linguistic Theory Ser.: No. 61). viii, 348p. 1989. 89.00 (*90-272-3558-9*) J Benjamins Pubng Co.

Linguistic Categorization: Prototypes in Linguistic Theory. 2nd ed. John R. Taylor. (Illus.). 328p. 1995. text 59.00 (*0-19-870013-X*); pap. text 21.00 (*0-19-870012-1*) OUP.

Linguistic Change. Edgar H. Sturtevant. LC 63-9732. 1961. pap. text 2.45 (*0-226-77915-7*, P60) U Ch Pr.

Linguistic Change & Reconstruction Methodology. Ed. by Philip Baldi. (Trends in Linguistics, Studies & Monographs: No. 45). (Illus.). xii, 752p. (C). 1990. lib. bdg. 213.85 (*0-89925-546-9*) Mouton.

Linguistic Change in French. Rebecca Posner. LC 97-2027. (Illus.). 530p. (C). 1997. text 125.00 (*0-19-824036-8*) OUP.

Linguistic Change under Contact Conditions. Ed. by Jacek Fisiak. LC 95-10316. (Trends in Linguistics, Studies & Monographs: No. 81). xii, 438p. (C). 1995. lib. bdg. 152.30 (*3-11-013950-2*) Mouton.

Linguistic Choice Across Genres: Variation in Spoken & Written English. Ed. by Antonio Sanchez-Macarro & Ronald Carter. LC 98-6208. (Current Issues in Linguistics Trends Ser.: Vol. 158). viii, 338p. (C). 1998. 79.00 (*1-55619-874-4*) J Benjamins Pubng Co.

Linguistic Comp Tech Mach Trans. Whitelock. (Centre for Computational Linguistics (CCL) Book Ser.). 224p. 1994. 65.00 (*1-85728-216-7*, Pub. by UCL Pr Ltd) Taylor & Francis.

Linguistic Complexity & Text Comprehension: Readability Issues Reconsidered. Ed. by Alice Davison & Georgia Green. 312p. (C). 1988. text 59.95 (*0-89859-541-X*) L Erlbaum Assocs.

Linguistic Concept of Word: Analytic Bibliography. Alphonse Juilland & Alexandra Roceric. (Janua Linguarum, Ser. Minor: No. 130). 118p. 1972. pap. text 50.00 (*90-279-2188-1*) Mouton.

Linguistic Concepts: An Introduction to Tagmemics. Kenneth L. Pike. LC 81-19814. (Illus.). 162p. 1982. reprint ed. pap. 50.30 (*0-7837-6889-3*, 204671900003) Bks Demand.

Linguistic Concepts & Methods in CSCW. John H. Connolly & Lyn Pemberton. LC 96-24165. (Computer Supported Cooperative Work Ser.). (Illus.). 200p. 1996. pap. 59.95 (*3-540-19984-5*) Spr-Verlag.

Linguistic Concordance of Jeremiah: Hebrew Vocabulary & Idiom, Vol. 14. Anderson & Forbes. 1977. 129.95 (*0-935106-06-5*) E Mellen.

Linguistic Concordance of Ruth & Jonah: Hebrew Vocabulary & Idiom. Francis I. Andersen & A. Dean Forbes. (Computer Bible Ser.: Vol. 9). 1976. pap. 89.95 (*0-935106-12-X*) E Mellen.

Linguistic Construction of Reality. George W. Grace. 128p. 1988. lib. bdg. 52.50 (*0-7099-3886-1*, Pub. by C Helm) Routldge.

Linguistic Contributions see American Contributions: Proceedings of the International Congress of Slavists, 6th, 1968

***Linguistic Creativity: Exercises in 'Philosophical Therapy'** Eugen Fischer. 208p. 2000. 90.00 (*0-7923-6124-5*) Kluwer Academic.

Linguistic Criticism. 2nd ed. Roger Fowler. 270p. 1996. pap. text 16.95 (*0-19-289261-4*) OUP.

Linguistic Culture & Language Policy. Harold F. Schiffman. LC 95-14742. (Politics of Language Ser.). 368p. (C). (gr. 13). 1996. 100.00 (*0-415-12875-7*) Routledge.

Linguistic Culture & Language Policy. Harold F. Schiffman. (Politics of Language Ser.). 368p. (C). 1998. pap. 29.99 (*0-415-18406-1*) Routledge.

Linguistic Cultures of the World: A Statistical Reference. Philip M. Parker. LC 96-36681. (Cross-Cultural Statistical Encyclopedia of the World: Vol. 2). 448p. 1997. lib. bdg. 95.00 (*0-313-29769-X*, Greenwood Pr) Greenwood.

Linguistic Databases. Ed. by John Nerbonne. LC 97-15734. (Lecture Notes Ser.: Vol. 77). 243p. (C). 1998. text 64.95 (*1-57586-093-7*); pap. text 24.95 (*1-57586-092-9*) CSLI.

Linguistic Density Plots in Ezekiel: The Computer Bible, Vol. 27, A & B. Van Dyke H. Parunak. Ed. by Arthur J. Baird & David Freedman. 528p. 1984. pap. 89.95 (*0-935106-22-7*) E Mellen.

Linguistic Differences in Speaking & Writing. Rekha Aslam. 1990. 16.00 (*81-85119-86-4*, Pub. by Northern Bk Ctr) S Asia.

Linguistic Disorders & Pathologies: An International Handbook. Ed. by Gerhard Blanken et al. LC 93-34475. (Handbooks of Linguistics & Communication Science: Vol. 8). xiv, 962p. (C). 1993. lib. bdg. 638.50 (*3-11-011324-4*) De Gruyter.

Linguistic Diversity. D. H. Nettleton. LC 98-53373. (Illus.). 180p. 1999. text 65.00 (*0-19-823858-4*); pap. text 19.95 (*0-19-823857-6*) OUP.

Linguistic Diversity in Space & Time. Johanna Nichols. LC 91-43682. (Illus.). 374p. 1992. 42.50 (*0-226-58056-3*) U Ch Pr.

Linguistic Diversity in Space & Time. Johanna Nichols. 1999. pap. text 19.00 (*0-226-58057-1*) U Ch Pr.

Linguistic Dynamics: Discourses, Procedures & Evolution. Ed. by Thomas T. Ballmer. (Research in Text Theory Ser.: Vol. 9). (Illus.). viii, 366p. 1985. 146.15 (*3-11-010115-7*) De Gruyter.

Linguistic Ecology: Language Change & Linguistic Imperialism in the Pacific Rim. 416th ed. Peter Muhlhausler. (Politics of Language Ser.). 416p. (C). 1995. 75.00 (*0-415-05635-7*) Routledge.

Linguistic Entropy in Othello of Shakespeare. N. Narasimha Ramayya. LC 93-910449. 95p. (C). 1998. pap. 63.00 (*81-85880-22-0*, Pub. by Print Hse) St Mut.

Linguistic Evidence: Language, Power & Strategy in the Courtroom. Jean F. O'Barr. (Illus.). 192p. 1995. reprint ed. pap. text 29.95 (*0-12-523521-6*) Acad Pr.

Linguistic Families of California. fac. ed. R. B. Dixon & A. L. Kroeber. (University of California Publications in American Archaeology & Ethnology: Vol. 16: 3). 73p. (C). 1919. reprint ed. pap. text 8.44 (*1-55567-223-X*) Coyote Press.

L

Linguistic Features & Genre Profiles of Scientific English. Rosemarie Claser. LC 95-20842. (Leipziger Fachsprachen-Studien: Bd. 9). (Illus.). XIV, 248p. 1995. 51.95 (*3-631-47870-4*) P Lang Pubng.

Linguistic Framework & Ontology. B. Norton. 1977. 51.55 (*3-10-800283-X*) Mouton.

Linguistic French & Arabic Dictionary: Dictionnaire de Linguistique Francais-Arabe. Bassam Barake. (ARA & FRE.). 298p. 1986. 39.95 (*0-8288-1586-0*, M2310) Fr & Eur.

***Linguistic Genocide in Education or Worldwide Diversity & Human Rights?** Tove Skutnabb-Kangas. LC 99-34376. 544p. 2000. write for info. (*0-8058-3467-2*); pap. write for info. (*0-8058-3468-0*) L Erlbaum Assocs.

Linguistic Guide to English Poetry. Geoffrey N. Leech. (English Language Ser.). 240p. 1973. pap. text 13.95 (*0-582-55013-0*) Longman.

Linguistic Guide to Language Learning. 2nd ed. William G. Moulton. xii, 140p. (Orig.). 1970. pap. 10.00 (*0-87352-027-0*, E3000) Modern Lang.

***Linguistic Historiography: Projects & Prospects.** E. F. K. Koerner. LC 99-39778. (Studies in the History of the Language Sciences: Vol. 92). x, 236p. 1999. 69.00 (*1-55619-607-5*) J Benjamins Pubng.

Linguistic History of Italian. Martin Maiden. LC 93-46832. (Longman Linguistics Library). 1994. write for info. (*0-582-05929-1*, Pub. by Addison-Wesley) Longman.

Linguistic Human Rights: Overcoming Linguistic Discrimination. Ed. by Tove Skutnabb-Kangas et al. LC 94-26525. (Contributions to the Sociology of Language Ser.: No. 67). 484p. (C). 1994. lib. bdg. 167.70 (*3-11-014370-4*) Mouton.

Linguistic Human Rights: Overcoming Linguistic Discrimination. Ed. by Tove Skutnabb-Kangas et al. 1995. pap. 34.95 (*3-11-014878-1*) Mouton.

Linguistic Imperialism. R. Phillipson. (Illus.). 374p. 1992. pap. text 21.95 (*0-19-437146-8*) OUP.

Linguistic Individuals. Almerindo E. Ojeda. LC 92-5935. (Center for the Study of Language & Information-Lecture Notes Ser.: No. 31). 200p. (C). 1993. 54.95 (*0-937073-85-7*); pap. 18.95 (*0-937073-84-9*) CSLI.

Linguistic Influence of Polish on Joseph Conrad's Style. Mary Morzinski. 200p. 1995. 29.50 (*0-88033-309-X*, 412, Pub. by East Eur Monographs) Col U Pr.

Linguistic Inquiry Index. Michiga Kawai & Yasuo Ishii. 1989. pap. 19.95 (*0-262-75035-X*) MIT Pr.

Linguistic Instruments in Requirements Engineering. J. F. Burg. LC 96-79146. 320p. (YA). (gr. 12). 1996. 89.00 (*90-5199-316-1*, 316-1) IOS Press.

Linguistic Interference & Convergent Change. V. Ju. Rozencvejg. (Janua Linguarum, Series Minor: No. 99). (Illus.). 58p. 1976. pap. text 64.60 (*90-279-3414-2*) Mouton.

Linguistic Interrelations in Early Rus' Northmen, Finns & East Slavs (Ninth to Eleventh Centuries) Bohdan Struminski. LC 96-930557. 353p. 1996. pap. 49.95 (*1-895571-16-2*) Ukrainian Acad.

Linguistic Introduction to the History of English. Leonard D. Newmark & Morton W. Bloomfield. LC 79-4563. (Illus.). 414p. 1979. reprint ed. lib. bdg. 52.50 (*0-313-20936-7*, BLLI, Greenwood Pr) Greenwood.

Linguistic Investigation of Aphasic Chinese Speech. Jerome L. Packard. LC 93-28051. (Studies in Theoretical Psycholinguistics: Vol. 18). 344p. (C). 1993. text 179.50 (*0-7923-2466-8*) Kluwer Academic.

Linguistic Investigations of Aphasia. 2nd ed. Lesser. 1989. 64.50 (*1-56593-541-1*, 0045) Singular Publishing.

Linguistic Levels in Aphasiology. Ed. by Evy Visch-Brink & Roelien Bastiaanse. LC 97-52722. (Neurogenic Communication Disorders Ser.). (Illus.). 250p. 1998. pap. 79.95 (*1-56593-860-7*, 1680) Thomson Learn.

Linguistic Material from the Tribes of Southern Texas & Northeastern Mexico. Ed. by John R. Swanton. (Bureau of American Ethnology Bulletins Ser.). 145p. 1995. lib. bdg. 79.00 (*0-7812-4127-8*) Rprt Serv.

Linguistic Meaning, 2 vols., I. Keith Allan. 1986. text 18.50 (*0-7102-0699-2*, Routledge Thoemms) Routledge.

Linguistic Meaning, 2 vols., Vol. I. Keith Allan. 400p. 1986. text 18.50 (*0-7100-9587-2*, Routledge Thoemms) Routledge.

Linguistic Meaning, 2 vols., Vol. II. Keith Allan. 400p. 1986. text 45.00 (*0-7102-0697-6*, Routledge Thoemms) Routledge.

Linguistic Means of Determining the Dates of Old English Literary Texts. Ashley C. Amos. LC 79-89570. (Medieval Academy Bks: No. 90). 1980. 32.00 (*0-910956-70-7*) Medieval Acad.

Linguistic Method: Essays in Honor of Herbert Penzl. Ed. by Irmengard Rauch & Gerald F. Carr. (Janua Linguarum, Series Major: No. 79). 1979. text 142.35 (*90-279-7767-4*) Mouton.

Linguistic Minorities & Literacy: Language Policy Issues in Developing Countries. Ed. by Florian Coulmas. LC 84-14746. (Trends in Linguistics, Studies & Monographs: No. 26). (Illus.). x, 133p. 1984. 40.00 (*3-11-009867-9*) Mouton.

***Linguistic Minorities & Modernity: A Sociolinguistic Ethnography.** Monica Heller. LC 98-30249. (Real Language Ser.). 296p. (C). 1999. pap. text 29.68 (*0-582-27948-8*, Prentice Hall) P-H.

***Linguistic Minorities & Modernity: A Sociolinguistic Ethnography.** Monica Heller. LC 98-30249. (Real Language Ser.). 256p. (C). 1999. text 75.24 (*0-582-27947-X*, Prentice Hall) P-H.

Linguistic Minorities in Central & Eastern Europe. Christina B. Paulston & Donald Peckham. LC 98-6230. (Multilingual Matters Ser.: Vol. 109). 289p. 1998. 59.00 (*1-85359-416-4*) Multilingual Matters.

Linguistic Minorities in Multilingual Settings: Implications for Language Policies. Christina Bratt Paulston. LC 93-44796. (Studies in Bilingualism: No. 4). xi, 136p. 1994. pap. 19.95 (*1-55619-540-0*); lib. bdg. 39.00 (*1-55619-347-5*) J Benjamins Pubng Co.

Linguistic Minorities in Western Europe. Meic Stephens. LC 77-363811. 832p. reprint ed. pap. 200.00 (*0-608-18759-3*, 205640100065) Bks Demand.

Linguistic Minorities of New York City. Suzanne DeCamp. LC 92-195680. 77p. 1991. pap. 9.00 (*0-88156-114-2*) Comm Serv Soc NY.

Linguistic Minorities, Society & Territory. Ed. by Colin H. Williams. (Multilingual Matters Ser.: No. 78). 350p. 1991. 119.00 (*1-85359-132-7*, Pub. by Multilingual Matters); pap. 39.95 (*1-85359-131-9*, Pub. by Multilingual Matters) Taylor & Francis.

Linguistic Moment: From Wordsworth to Stevens. Joseph H. Miller. LC 84-42894. 467p. 1985. reprint ed. pap. 144.80 (*0-608-02504-6*, 206314800004) Bks Demand.

Linguistic Perspective of Literary Style. Ravinder Gargesh. 1990. 24.00 (*0-8364-2628-2*, Pub. by Motilal Bnarsidass) S Asia.

Linguistic Perspectives on Second Language Acquisition. Ed. by Susan M. Gass & Jacquelyn Schachter. (Cambridge Applied Linguistics Ser.). (Illus.). 304p. (C). 1989. pap. text 22.95 (*0-521-37811-7*) Cambridge U Pr.

Linguistic Perspectives on the Romance Languages: Selected Papers from the Linguistic Symposium on Romance Linguistics, Santa Barbara, February 21-24, 1991. Ed. by William J. Ashby et al. LC 93-18384. (Current Issues in Linguistic Theory Ser.: Vol. 103). xxii, 404p. 1993. 100.00 (*1-55619-557-5*) J Benjamins Pubng Co.

Linguistic Perspectives on the Romance Languages: Selected Papers from the 21st Linguistic Symposium on Romance Languages (ISRL XXI), Santa Barbara, California, 21-24 February 1991. Linguistic Symposium on Romance Languages Staff & William J. Ashby. LC 93-18384. xxii, 404 p. 1993. write for info. (*90-272-3605-4*) J Benjamins Pubng Co.

Linguistic Phenomenology: Philosophical Method in J. L. Austin. Joseph J. DiGiovanna. (American University Studies: Philosophy: Ser. V, Vol. 63). XIV, 211p. (C). 1989. text 33.70 (*0-8204-0877-8*) P Lang Pubng.

***Linguistic Philosophy of Language.** Paul Rastall. LC 99-58703. (Studies in Linguistics & Semiotics: Vol. 6). 328p. 2000. text 99.95 (*0-7734-7778-0*) E Mellen.

Linguistic Position of South-Eastern Papua. Arthur Capell. LC 75-32803. reprint ed. 29.50 (*0-404-14107-2*) AMS Pr.

Linguistic Processes in Sociocultural Practice. Gunther Kress. 101p. (C). 1995. pap. 50.00 (*0-7300-0343-4*, ECS806, Pub. by Deakin Univ) St Mut.

Linguistic Reconstruction: An Introduction to Theory & Method. Anthony Fox. (Oxford Textbooks in Linguistics Ser.). (Illus.). 390p. 1995. text 58.00 (*0-19-870000-8*); pap. text 19.95 (*0-19-870001-6*) OUP.

Linguistic Reconstruction: Its Potentials & Limitations in New Perspective. Henrik Birnbaum. (Journal of Indo-European Studies: No.2). 1976. pap. text 20.00 (*0-941694-26-7*) Inst Study Man.

Linguistic Reconstruction & Indo-European Syntax: Proceedings of the Colloquium of the "Indogermanische Gesellschaft", University of Pavia, 6-7 September 1979. Ed. by Paolo Ramat et al. (Current Issues in Linguistic Theory Ser.: No 19). viii, 263p. 1980. 59.00 (*90-272-3512-0*) J Benjamins Pubng Co.

Linguistic Relationship Between Armenian & Greek. James Clackson. LC 94-26076. (Publications of the Philological Society). 276p. (Orig.). (C). 1995. pap. 37.95 (*0-631-19197-6*) Blackwell Pubs.

Linguistic Relativity Principle & Humboldtian Ethnolinguistics. Robert L. Miller. LC 68-13340. (Janua Linguarum, Ser.). 1968. pap. text 44.60 (*90-279-0595-9*) Mouton.

Linguistic Relativity vs. Innate Ideas. Julia M. Penn. LC 77-170003. (Janua Linguarum, Ser. Minor: No. 120). 62p. (Orig.). 1972. pap. text 30.80 (*90-279-2003-6*) Mouton.

Linguistic Representation. J. F. Rosenberg. LC 74-26886. (Philosophical Studies: No. 1). 166p. 1974. lib. bdg. 70.50 (*90-277-0533-X*) Kluwer Academic.

Linguistic Representation. J. F. Rosenberg. LC 74-26886. (Philosophical Studies: No. 1). 166p. 1978. pap. text 39.50 (*90-277-0946-7*) Kluwer Academic.

Linguistic Representation: Structural Analogy & Stratification. John M. Anderson. LC 92-26797. (Trends in Linguistics, Studies & Monographs: Vol. 67). x, 254p. (C). 1992. lib. bdg. 113.85 (*3-11-013531-0*) Mouton.

Linguistic Science & the Teaching of English. Henry L. Smith, Jr. LC 55-11607. (Inglis Lectures: 1954). 71p. 1956. 8.95 (*0-674-53500-6*) HUP.

Linguistic Self-Criticism see Persian Words in English

Linguistic Semantics. William Frawley. 544p. 1992. pap. 55.00 (*0-8058-1075-7*); text 100.00 (*0-8058-1074-9*) L Erlbaum Assocs.

Linguistic Semantics: An Introduction. John Lyons. 394p. (C). 1996. pap. text 20.95 (*0-521-43877-2*) Cambridge U Pr.

Linguistic Sex Roles in Conversation. Bent Preisler. (Contributions to the Sociology of Language Ser.: No. 45). (Illus.). xviii, 350p. 1986. lib. bdg. 115.40 (*0-89925-225-7*) Mouton.

Linguistic Shaping of Accounting. Ahmed Riahi-Belkaoui. LC 95-19470. 192p. 1995. 59.95 (*0-89930-992-5*, Quorum Bks) Greenwood.

Linguistic Shaping of Thought: A Study in the Impact of Language on Thinking in China & the West. Alfred H. Bloom. 128p. 1981. text 29.95 (*0-89859-089-2*) L Erlbaum Assocs.

Linguistic Structure & Change: An Explanation from Language Processing. Thomas Berg. (Illus.). 350p. 1998. text 95.00 (*0-19-823672-7*) OUP.

Linguistic Structure in Language Processing. Ed. by Greg N. Carlson & Michael K. Tanenhaus. (C). 1988. lib. bdg. 167.00 (*1-55608-074-3*) Kluwer Academic.

Linguistic Structures & Linguistic Laws. Ferenc Kovacs. Tr. by Sandor Simon. 398p. 1971. 59.00 (*90-6032-492-7*) J Benjamins Pubng Co.

Linguistic Structures in Poetry. Samuel R. Levin. (Janua Linguarum, Ser. Minor: No. 23). 1973. pap. text 20.00 (*90-279-0678-5*) Mouton.

Linguistic Structures in Scientific Texts. Myrna Gopnik. (Janua Linguarum, Ser. Minor: No. 129). 1972. text 36.95 (*90-279-2295-0*) Mouton.

Linguistic Studies. Jan Safarewicz. (Janua Linguarum, Ser. Major: No. 76). 395p. 1974. text 84.60 (*90-279-3003-1*) Mouton.

Linguistic Studies in Germanic, 5 vols., Set. Chicago University Staff. reprint ed. 105.00 (*0-404-50280-6*) AMS Pr.

Linguistic Studies in Honor of Bohdan Saciuk. unabridged ed. Ed. by Robert M. Hammond & Marguerite D. MacDonald. (ENG & SPA.). xi, 360p. (C). 1997. pap. text. write for info. (*0-9661014-0-5*) Learn Systs.

Linguistic Studies in Medieval Spanish: Dedicated to Dennis P. Seniff. Ed. by Raymond Harris-Northall & Thomas D. Cravens. (SPA.). vi, 208p. 1992. 20.00 (*0-940639-67-X*) Hispanic Seminary.

Linguistic Studies in Romance Languages: Proceedings of the Third Linguistic Symposium on Romance Languages. Linguistic Symposium on Romance Languages Staff. Ed. by R. Joe Campbell et al. LC 74-76135. 271p. reprint ed. pap. 84.10 (*0-7837-6310-7*, 204602500010) Bks Demand.

Linguistic Studies on Latin: Selected Papers from the 6th International Colloquium on Latin Linguistics (Budapest, 23-27 March 1991) Ed. by Jozsef Herman. LC 94-26068. (Studies in Language Companion: No. 28). ix, 421p. 1994. 89.00 (*1-55619-380-7*) J Benjamins Pubng Co.

Linguistic Study of the Development of Scientific Vocabulary in Standard Arabic. Abdul S. Ali. 200p. 1987. text 95.00 (*0-7103-0023-9*) Routledge.

Linguistic Subgrouping & Lexicostatistics. Isidore Dyen. LC 73-82418. (Janua Linguarum, Series Minor: No. 175). (Illus.). 251p. 1975. pap. text 56.95 (*90-279-3054-6*) Mouton.

Linguistic Survey of the Northern Bantu Borderland, 2 vols., Vol. 1. International African Institute Staff. LC 57-2700. 171p. 1956. reprint ed. pap. 53.10 (*0-8357-3229-0*, 205712400001) Bks Demand.

Linguistic Survey of the Northern Bantu Borderland, Vol. 2. Irvine Richardson. LC 57-2700. 98p. reprint ed. pap. 30.40 (*0-8357-6967-4*, 203902700009) Bks Demand.

Linguistic Survey of the Northern Bantu Borderland, 2 vols., Vol. 4. International African Institute Staff. LC 57-2700. 100p. 1957. reprint ed. pap. 31.00 (*0-8357-3230-4*, 205712400004) Bks Demand.

Linguistic Theories in Dante & the Humanists: Studies of Language & Intellectual History in Late Medieval & Early Renaissance Italy. Angelo Mazzocco. LC 93-21469. (Studies in Intellectual History: No. 38). xvi, 270p. 1993. 93.00 (*90-04-09702-3*) Brill Academic Pubs.

Linguistic Theories of Humor. Salvatore Attardo. LC 93-43697. (Humor Research Ser.: No. 1). 426p. 1994. lib. bdg. 144.65 (*3-11-014255-4*) Mouton.

Linguistic Theory. De Beaugrande. 1991. text. write for info. (*0-582-08210-2*, Pub. by Addison-Wesley) Longman.

Linguistic Theory & Grammatical Description: Nine Current Approaches. Ed. by Flip G. Droste & John E. Joseph. LC 91-34226. (Current Issues in Linguistic Theory Ser.: No. 75). viii, 354p. 1991. 112.00 (*1-55619-103-0*) J Benjamins Pubng Co.

Linguistic Theory & Historical Linguistics see Linguistics Across Historical & Geographical Boundaries in Honor of Jacek Fisiak on the Occasion of His Fiftieth Birthday

Linguistic Theory & the Function of Word Order in Dutch. A. Verhagen. (PDA Ser.). xii, 288p. 1986. 98.45 (*90-6765-159-1*) Mouton.

Linguistic Theory & the Romance Languages. Ed. by John C. Smith & Martin Maiden. LC 95-280. (Current Issues in Linguistic Theory Ser.: No. 122). xiii, 240p. 1995. 68.00 (*1-55619-576-1*) J Benjamins Pubng Co.

Linguistic Theory, Language Contact & Modern Hindustani: The Three Sides of a Linguistic Story, Vol. 31. Rajendra Singh. Tr. by Hugh J. McDonald. LC 94-38189. (American University Studies, Linguistics: Ser. XIII). XIII, 154p. (C). 1995. 39.95 (*0-8204-2687-3*) P Lang Pubng.

Linguistic Theory of America. 2nd ed. Frederick J. Newmeyer. (C). 1986. text 89.95 (*0-12-517151-X*); pap. text 49.95 (*0-12-517152-8*) Acad Pr.

Linguistic Thought in England. Ed. by Roy Harris. 212p. 1988. text 45.00 (*0-415-90066-2*) Routledge.

Linguistic Turn: Essays in Philosophic Method. Ed. by Richard McKay Rorty. 416p. 1992. pap. text 19.95 (*0-226-72569-3*) U Ch Pr.

Linguistic Turn: Recent Essays in Philosophic Method. Ed. by Richard McKay Rorty. viii, 402p. 1997. pap. text 19.95 (*0-226-72568-5*, Midway Reprint) U Ch Pr.

Linguistic Turn in Hermeneutic Philosophy. Cristina Lafont. Tr. by Jose Medina from SPA. LC 99-23900. (Studies in Contemporary German Social Thought Ser.). 377p. 1999. 45.00 (*0-262-12217-0*) MIT Pr.

Linguistic Typology. Paolo Ramat. (Empirical Approaches to Language Typology Ser.: No. 1). (Illus.). xii, 244p. (C). 1987. lib. bdg. 89.25 (*0-89925-085-8*) Mouton.

***Linguistic Typology: Morphology & Syntax.** Jae Jung Song. LC 00-42834. (Linguistics Library). 2001. write for info. (*0-582-31221-3*) Longman.

Linguistic Typology, Universality & the Realism of Reconstruction. Frederick W. Schwink. (Journal of Indo-European Studies: NNo.12). 140p. 1994. pap. text 28.00 (*0-941694-43-7*) Inst Study Man.

Linguistic Variables: Towards a Unified Theory of Linguistic Variation. Hans-Heinrich Lieb. LC 93-5760. (Current Issues in Linguistic Theory Ser.: Vol. 108). xiv, 261p. 1993. 68.00 (*1-55619-562-1*) J Benjamins Pubng Co.

Linguistica Aplicada: A la Ensenanza del Espanol a Anglohablantes. Tracy D. Terrell & Maruxa Salgues de Cargill. LC 78-21016. 240p. 1979. pap. 59.95 (*0-471-03946-2*) Wiley.

Linguistica Aplicada a la Terapia Del Lenguaje. Antonio Quilis & C. Hernandez Alonso. (SPA.). 552p. 1993. 125.00 (*84-249-1427-9*) Elliots Bks.

Linguistica Moderna: Terminologia y Bibliografia. W. Welte. (SPA.). 752p. 1993. pap. 175.00 (*84-239-1006-7*) Elliots Bks.

Linguistica Tyrrhenica: A Compendium of Recent Results in Etruscan Linguistics. Fred C. Woudhuizen. 117p. 1992. pap. 34.00 (*90-5063-081-2*, Pub. by Gieben) J Benjamins Pubng Co.

Linguisticae Scientiae Collectanea: Ausgewahlte Schriften. Wolfgang P. Schmid. Ed. by Joachim Becker et al. (GER.). 518p. (C). 1994. lib. bdg. 200.00 (*3-11-013440-3*) De Gruyter.

Linguistically & Culturally Diverse Students Populations: African American & Hmong. Kate Morand. LC 98-163767. 109p. (Orig.). 1997. pap. text 21.00 (*1-57337-049-5*) WI Dept Pub Instruct.

Linguistically Motivated Principles of Knowledge-Based Systems. Hans Weigand. (Functional Grammar Ser.). 220p. 1990. pap. 53.85 (*3-11-013142-0*) Mouton.

Linguistics. Jean Atchison. (Illus.). 240p. 1995. pap. 10.95 (*0-8442-3929-1*, Teach Yrslf) NTC Contemp Pub Co.

Linguistics. David Crystal. 1990. pap. 15.95 (*0-14-013531-6*, Pub. by Pnguin Bks Ltd) Trafalgar.

***Linguistics.** Victoria A. Fromkin. 500p. 1999. 79.95 (*0-631-19709-5*); pap. 39.95 (*0-631-19711-7*) Blackwell Pubs.

Linguistics: A Guide to the Reference Literature. 2nd ed. Anna Demiller. LC 99-16318. (Humanities Ser.). 400p. 1999. 65.00 (*1-56308-619-0*) Libs Unl.

Linguistics: An Introduction. Donna J. Napoli. (Illus.). 592p. (C). 1996. pap. text 44.95 (*0-19-509175-2*) OUP.

Linguistics: An Introduction to Language & Communication. 4th ed. Adrian Akmajian et al. LC 95-11668. 530p. 1995. pap. text 32.00 (*0-262-51086-3*) MIT Pr.

Linguistics: An Introduction to Language & Communication. 4th ed. Adrian Akmajian et al. LC 95-11668. 530p. 1995. 55.00 (*0-262-01150-6*) MIT Pr.

Linguistics: An Outline Guide. 1991. lib. bdg. 256.95 (*0-8490-5095-2*) Gordon Pr.

Linguistics: Linguistic Theory: Extensions & Implications. Ed. by Frederick J. Newmeyer. (Cambridge Survey Ser.: Vol. 2). 328p. (C). 1989. pap. text 23.95 (*0-521-37581-9*) Cambridge U Pr.

Linguistics: Teaching & Interdisciplinary Relations. fac. ed. Georgetown University Round Table on Languages & L. Ed. by Francis P. Dinneen. LC 58-31607. 208p. 1974. reprint ed. pap. 64.50 (*0-7837-8042-7*, 204754700007) Bks Demand.

Linguistics Vol. 3: The Cambridge Survey: Language: Psychological & Biological Aspects. Ed. by Frederick J. Newmeyer. 368p. (C). 1989. pap. text 23.95 (*0-521-37582-7*) Cambridge U Pr.

Linguistics Vol. 3: The Cambridge Survey: Psychological & Biological Aspects. Ed. by Frederick J. Newmeyer. 366p. 1988. text 69.95 (*0-521-30835-6*) Cambridge U Pr.

Linguistics Vol. 4: The Cambridge Survey: Language: The Socio-Cultural Context. Ed. by Frederick J. Newmeyer. 304p. (C). 1989. pap. text 25.95 (*0-521-37583-5*) Cambridge U Pr.

Linguistics Vol. 4: The Cambridge Survey: The Socio-Cultural Context. Ed. by Frederick J. Newmeyer. 304p. 1988. text 69.95 (*0-521-30834-8*) Cambridge U Pr.

Linguistics Across Cultures: Applied Linguistics for Language Teachers. Robert Lado. 160p. 1957. pap. text 19.95 (*0-472-08542-5*, 08542) U of Mich Pr.

Linguistics Across Historical & Geographical Boundaries in Honor of Jacek Fisiak on the Occasion of His Fiftieth Birthday, 2 vols. Ed. by Dieter Kastovsky & Aleksander Szwedek. Incl. Vol. 1. Linguistic Theory & Historical Linguistics. xxiv, 778p. 1986. Vol. II. Descriptive, Contrastive & Applied Linguistics. xiv, 760p. 1986. (Illus.). 1986. 356.70 (*0-89925-180-3*) Mouton.

Linguistics & Adjacent Arts & Sciences see Current Trends in Linguistics

Linguistics & Biblical Hebrew. Ed. by Walter R. Bodine. LC 92-29716. x, 285p. 1992. text 39.50 (*0-931464-55-2*) Eisenbrauns.

Linguistics & Biblical Interpretation. Max Turner & Peter Cotterell. LC 88-32868. 341p. (Orig.). 1989. pap. 22.99 (*0-8308-1751-4*, 1751) InterVarsity.

Linguistics & Communicative Competence: Topics in ESL. Christina B. Paulston. (Multilingual Matters Ser.: No. 85). 160p. 1992. 74.95 (*1-85359-149-1*, Pub. by Multilingual Matters); pap. 29.95 (*1-85359-148-3*, Pub. by Multilingual Matters) Taylor & Francis.

Linguistics & Composition: A Method to Improve Expository Writing Skills. Louis A. Arena. LC 75-34100. 212p. reprint ed. pap. 65.80 (*0-7837-6304-2*, 204601900010) Bks Demand.

An Asterisk (*) at the beginning of an entry indicates that the title is appearing for the first time.

L

Linguistics & Computation. Ed. by Jennifer Green et al. 308p. 1995. 54.95 (*1-881526-82-8*); pap. 22.95 (*1-881526-81-X*) CSLI.

Linguistics & Economics. Ferruccio Rossi-Landi. (Janua Linguarum, Series Major: No. 81). 240p. 1977. pap. text 30.00 (*90-279-3243-3*) Mouton.

Linguistics & English Linguistics. 2nd ed. Compiled by Harold B. Allen. LC 75-42974. (Goldentree Bibliographies Series in Language & Literature). (C). 1977. pap. text 16.95 (*0-88295-558-6*) Harlan Davidson.

Linguistics & Evolutionary Theory: Three Essays. August Schleicher & Wilhelm Bleek. (Amsterdam Classics in Linguistics Ser.: No. 6). xlvi, 84, 78p. 1983. 52.00 (*90-272-0877-8*) J Benjamins Pubng Co.

Linguistics & Formulas in Homer: Scalarity & Description of the Particle Per. Egbert J. Bakker. LC 88-10110. x, 306p. (C). 1988. 65.00 (*1-55619-046-8*) J Benjamins Pubng Co.

Linguistics & Language Teaching: Proceedings of the 6th Joint LSH-HATESL Conference. Ed. by Cynthia Reves et al. (Technical Report Ser.: No. 10). 368p. 1996. pap. text 20.00 (*0-8248-1851-2*) Sec Lang Tching.

Linguistics & Languages in Science Fiction-Fantasy. Myra J. Barnes. LC 74-17864. (Science Fiction Ser.). 208p. 1975. reprint ed. 16.95 (*0-405-06319-9*) Ayer.

Linguistics & Literary Criticism. Giacomo Devoto. Tr. by M. F. Edgerton, Jr. 1963. 20.00 (*0-913298-08-5*) S F Vanni.

Linguistics & Literary Theory. Nigel Fabb. LC 97-9054. (Blackwell Textbooks in Linguistics Ser.: No. 12). 352p. 1997. text 62.95 (*0-631-19242-5*); pap. text 26.95 (*0-631-19243-3*) Blackwell Pubs.

Linguistics & New Testament Interpretation. David A. Black. (Orig.). 1993. pap. 15.99 (*0-8054-1509-2*, 4215-09) Broadman.

Linguistics & Philology in Spanish America: A Survey (1925-1970) Yakov Malkiel. (Janua Linguarum, Ser. Minor: No. 97). 179p. (Orig.). 1972. pap. text 36.95 (*90-279-2313-2*) Mouton.

Linguistics & Philosophy: Festschrift For Rulon S. Wells. Ed. by Adam Makkai & Alan K. Melby. LC 85-20099. (Current Issues in Linguistic Theory Ser.: No. 42). xviii, 472p. 1986. 94.00 (*90-272-3536-8*) J Benjamins Pubng Co.

Linguistics & Philosophy: The Controversial Interface. Ed. by Rom Harre & Roy Harris. LC 92-44812. (Language & Communication Library: Vol. 13). 268p. 1993. text 102.50 (*0-08-041937-2*, Pergamon Pr) Elsevier.

Linguistics & Poetics see American Contributions

Linguistics & Poetics of Latvian Folksongs. Ed. by Vaira Vikis-Freibergs. (Studies in Ethnic History). 396p. (C). 1989. text 65.00 (*0-7735-0661-6*, Pub. by McG-Queens Univ Pr) CUP Services.

Linguistics & Pseudo-Linguistics. Robert A. Hall, Jr. LC 87-21053. (Current Issues in Linguistic Theory Ser.: Vol. 55). vii, 147p. (C). 1987. 33.00 (*90-272-3549-X*) J Benjamins Pubng Co.

Linguistics & Psychoanalysis: Freud, Saussure, Hjelmslev, Lacan & Others. Michel Arrive. LC 92-8213. (Semiotic Crossroads Ser.: No. 4). xvi, 180p. 1992. 56.00 (*1-55619-338-6*) J Benjamins Pubng Co.

Linguistics & Reading. Charles C. Fries. LC 63-14410. (Illus.). 1983. reprint ed. 40.50 (*0-8290-0684-2*); reprint ed. pap. text 14.95 (*0-8290-1682-1*) Irvington.

Linguistics & Second Language Pedagogy: A Theoretical Study. E. Glyn Lewis. LC 73-79891. (Janua Linguarum, Ser. Didactica: No. 10). 137p. (Orig.). 1974. pap. text 32.35 (*90-279-2707-3*) Mouton.

Linguistics & Semiotics in Music. Raymond Monelle. (Contemporary Music Studies). 350p. 1992. text 52.00 (*3-7186-5208-0*, Harwood Acad Pubs); pap. text 25.00 (*3-7186-5209-9*, Harwood Acad Pubs) Gordon & Breach.

***Linguistics & the New Testament: Critical Junctures.** Ed. by Stanley E. Porter & D. A. Carson. LC 99-460563. (Journal for the Study of the New Testament, Supplement Ser.: No. 168). 304p. 1999. 75.00 (*1-85075-991-X*, Pub. by Sheffield Acad) CUP Services.

Linguistics & the Professions. Ed. by Robert J. DiPietro & Roy O. Freedle. LC 81-22905. (Advances in Discourse Processes Ser.: Vol. 8). 288p. (Orig.). (C). 1982. pap. 42.50 (*0-89391-120-8*); text 78.50 (*0-89391-092-9*) Ablx Pub.

Linguistics & the Third Reich: Mother-Tongue Fascism, Race, & the Science of Language. Christopher Hutton. LC 98-13546. 352p. (C). 1998. 110.00 (*0-415-18954-3*) Routledge.

Linguistics & Theology: The Significance of Noam Chomsky for Theological Construction. Irene Lawrence. LC 80-24210. (American Theological Library Association Monograph: No. 16). 214p. 1980. 29.00 (*0-8108-1347-5*) Scarecrow.

Linguistics at the Crossroads. Ed. by Adam Makkai et al. LC 79-312499. viii, 502p. (Orig.). (C). 1977. pap. 48.00 (*0-933104-02-2*) Jupiter Pr.

Linguistics at Work: A Reader of Applications. Dallin D. Oaks. LC 97-70417. 768p. (C). 1997. pap. text 36.50 (*0-15-503532-0*, Pub. by Harcourt Coll Pubs) Harcourt.

Linguistics Dictionary: Linguistisches Woerterbuch, 3 vols., Set. 5th ed. Theodor Lewandoski. (GER.). 1287p. 1985. 150.00 (*0-8288-1977-7*, M15160) Fr & Eur.

Linguistics Encyclopedia. Ed. by Kirsten Malmkjaer. (Illus.). 592p. (C). (gr. 13). 1991. 125.00 (*0-415-02942-2*, A6266) Routledge.

Linguistics Encyclopedia. Ed. by Kirsten Malmkjaer. (Illus.). 592p. (C). (gr. 13). 1995. pap. 29.99 (*0-415-12566-9*, C0435) Routledge.

Linguistics for ESL Teachers. Francine G. Hallcom. 124p. (C). 1995. pap. text, per. 20.95 (*0-7872-0998-8*) Kendall-Hunt.

Linguistics for Machine Translation. Ed. by Frank Van Eynde. 224p. (C). 1993. text 79.00 (*1-85567-024-0*, Pub. by P P Pubs) Cassell & Continuum.

Linguistics for Non Linguistics. 3rd ed. 96p. (C). 2000. pap. write for info. (*0-205-31640-9*) Allyn.

***Linguistics for Non-Linguistics: A Primer with Exercises.** 3rd ed. Ed. by Parker & Riley. LC 99-36109. 341p. (C). 1999. pap. text 41.00 (*0-205-29930-X*) Allyn.

Linguistics for Students of Literature. Elizabeth C. Traugott & Mary L. Pratt. 444p. (C). 1980. pap. text 41.50 (*0-15-551030-4*, Pub. by Harcourt Coll Pubs) Harcourt.

Linguistics for Students of New Testament Greek: A Survey of Basic Concepts & Applications. 2nd ed. David A. Black. LC 95-15091. 222p. 1995. pap. 14.99 (*0-8010-2016-6*) Baker Bks.

***Linguistics for Teachers.** David E. Freeman. 2001. pap. text. write for info. (*0-325-00274-6*) Heinemann.

Linguistics for Teachers. Michael D. Linn & Linda M. Cleary. LC 92-26665. (C). 1992. pap. text 52.50 (*0-07-037946-7*) McGraw.

Linguistics for Writers. Colleen Donnelly. LC 92-36122. 251p. (C). 1994. text 54.50 (*0-7914-1571-6*); pap. text 20.95 (*0-7914-1572-4*) State U NY Pr.

Linguistics in America, 1769-1924: A Critical History. Julie T. Andresen. (History of Linguistic Thought Ser.). 320p. (C). 1996. pap. 25.99 (*0-415-13259-2*) Routledge.

Linguistics in Clinical Practice. 2nd ed. Ed. by Kim Grundy. (Illus.). 410p. (C). 1995. 59.95 (*1-56593-514-4*, 1186) Thomson Learn.

Linguistics in Context: Connecting Observation & Understanding. Ed. by Deborah Tannen & Roy O. Freedle. LC 87-19704. (Advances in Discourse Processes Ser.: Vol. 29). 352p. 1988. pap. 42.50 (*0-89391-455-X*); text 78.50 (*0-89391-454-1*) Ablx Pub.

Linguistics in East Asia & Southeast Asia see Current Trends in Linguistics

Linguistics in North America see Current Trends in Linguistics

Linguistics in Oceania see Current Trends in Linguistics

Linguistics in Remedial English. John C. Fisher. (Janua Linguarum, Ser. Practica: No. 47). (Orig.). 1966. pap. text 21.55 (*90-279-0659-9*) Mouton.

Linguistics in South Asia see Current Trends in Linguistics

Linguistics in South West Asia & North Africa see Current Trends in Linguistics

Linguistics in the Netherlands. Helen De Hoop. Ed. by Jane Coerts. (AVT Publications: Vol. 14). x, 230p. 1997. pap. 55.00 (*1-55619-221-5*) J Benjamins Pubng Co.

Linguistics in the Netherlands, 1989. Hans Bennis & Ans Van Kemenade. (AVT Publications). x, 194p. (Orig.). (C). 1989. pap. 42.90 (*90-6765-420-5*) Mouton.

Linguistics in the Netherlands, 1990. Reineke Bok-Bennema & Peter Coopmans. 164p. 1990. pap. 38.50 (*3-11-013036-X*) Mouton.

Linguistics in the Netherlands, 1974-1976. Ed. by Wim Zonneveld. (AVT Publications). v, 220p. (C). 1978. pap. text 53.85 (*3-11-013320-2*) Mouton.

Linguistics in the Netherlands, 1977-1979. Ed. by Wim Zonneveld & Fred Weerman. (Publications in Language Sciences: No. 1). x, 483p. (C). 1980. pap. text 88.50 (*3-11-013321-0*) Mouton.

Linguistics in Western Europe see Current Trends in Linguistics

Linguistics Inside Out: Roy Harris & His Critics. Roy Harris. Ed. by George Wolf & Nigel Love. LC 96-52209. (Current Issues in Linguistic Theory Ser.: Vol. 148). xxviii, 344p. 1997. lib. bdg. 79.00 (*1-55619-863-9*) J Benjamins Pubng Co.

Linguistics into Interpretation: Speeches of War in Herodotus VII 5 & 8-18. J. M. van Ophuijsen et al. LC 99-23081. (Mnemosyne, Bibliotheca Classica Batava: Supplementum Ser.). 368p. 1999. 126.50 (*90-04-11455-6*) Brill Academic Pubs.

Linguistics, Language & Verbal Art. Ruqaiya Hasan. 124p. (C). 1985. pap. 45.00 (*0-7300-0310-8*, ECS805, Pub. by Deakin Univ) St Mut.

Linguistics, Literary Analysis, & Literary Translation. Henry G. Schogt. 1988. text 35.00 (*0-8020-2649-4*) U of Toronto Pr.

Linguistics of American Sign Language: A Resource Text for ASL Users. Clayton Valli & Ceil Lucas. LC 92-13355. 1992. 45.00 incl. VHS (*1-56368-047-5*, Clerc Bks) Gallaudet Univ Pr.

Linguistics of American Sign Language: An Introduction. 2nd ed. Clayton Valli & Ceil Lucas. LC 95-19664. (Illus.). 460p. 1995. 60.00 (*1-56368-042-4*, Clerc Bks) Gallaudet Univ Pr.

Linguistics of British Sign Language: An Introduction. Rachel Sutton-Spence & Bencie Woll. LC 98-20588. (Illus.). 320p. (C). 1999. text 64.95 (*0-521-63142-4*); pap. text 24.95 (*0-521-63718-X*) Cambridge U Pr.

Linguistics of Giving. Ed. by John Newman. LC 97-39855. (Typological Studies in Language: Vol. 36). (ENG & MUL.). xv, 373p. 1998. pap. 34.95 (*1-55619-648-2*); lib. bdg. 98.00 (*1-55619-647-4*) J Benjamins Pubng Co.

Linguistics of Literacy. Ed. by Pamela Downing et al. LC 92-7341. (Typological Studies in Language: No. 21). xx, 334p. 1992. 97.00 (*1-55619-406-4*); pap. 32.95 (*1-55619-407-2*) J Benjamins Pubng Co.

Linguistics of Punctuation. Geoffrey Nunberg. LC 90-1411. (CSLI Lecture Notes Ser.: No. 18). 160p. (C). 1990. 59.95 (*0-937073-47-4*); pap. 17.95 (*0-937073-46-6*) CSLI.

Linguistics of Writing: Arguments Between Language & Literature. Ed. by Nigel Fabb et al. 384p. 1988. text 45.00 (*0-416-01841-6*); pap. text 15.95 (*0-416-01851-3*) Routledge.

Linguistics, Philosophy, & Montague Grammar. Conference on Montague Grammar, Philosophy, & Linguistics, 1977, State Univ. of NY at Albany, Staff. Ed. by Steven Davis & Marianne Mithun. LC 79-13975. 352p. reprint ed. pap. 109.20 (*0-608-20101-4*, 207137300011) Bks Demand.

Linguistics, Psycholinguistics & the Teaching of Reading: An Annotated Bibliography. 3rd ed. Kenneth S. Goodman & Yetta M. Goodman. LC 80-16364. 83p. reprint ed. pap. 30.00 (*0-608-15283-8*, 202959700061) Bks Demand.

Linguistics Series. Charles-James N. Bailey. (Orig.). (C). 1992. pap. write for info. (*1-881309-02-9*) Orchid Land.

Linguistics Terms & Concepts. Finch. LC 99-15612. 1999. pap. 16.95 (*0-312-22647-0*) St Martin.

Linguistics Wars. Randy A. Harris. LC 92-34789. (Illus.). 368p. (C). 1993. 35.00 (*0-19-507256-1*) OUP.

Linguistics Wars. Randy A. Harris. (Illus.). 368p. 1995. reprint ed. pap. 19.95 (*0-19-509834-X*) OUP.

Linguistics Workbook. 3rd ed. Ann K. Farmer & Richard A. Demers. (Illus.). 304p. (Orig.). (C). 1995. pap. text 17.50 (*0-262-56091-7*) MIT Pr.

Linguistik der Wissenschaftssprache. Ed. by Heinz Kretzenbacher & Harald Weinrich. (Akademie der Wissenschaften zu Berlin Forschungsbericht Ser.: No. 10). (GER.). 413p. (C). 1994. lib. bdg. 126.15 (*3-11-014043-8*) De Gruyter.

Linguistique Generale et Romane: Etudes en Allemand, Anglais, Espagnol et Francais. Bertil Malmberg. (Janua Linguarum, Series Major: No. 66). 1973. 112.35 (*90-279-2429-5*) Mouton.

Linguistique Moderne Appliquee a la Pedagogie: Regards et Reflexions sur les Cas du Francais, de l'Anglais et du Creole Haitien. Intro. by G. Carlo Jean. (FRE., Illus.). 200p. (Orig.). (C). 1988. pap. write for info. (*0-9620460-0-0*) G C Jean.

Linguistique Naturaliste en France. E. Peters. 1998. 57.95 (*90-6831-878-0*, Pub. by Peeters Pub) Bks Intl VA.

Linguistische Beitrage Zur Muntzerforschung. Hans O. Spillmann. (GER.). x, 346p. 1991. write for info. (*3-487-09464-9*) G Olms Pubs.

Linguistische Theorien der Moderne. Winfred P. Lehmann. (Germanistische Lehrbuchsammlung Ser.: Vol. 19). (GER.). 173p. 1981. 9.00 (*3-261-04889-1*) P Lang Pubng.

Linguistische Uebengen Fuer Sprachgestoerte No. 3: Durchgesehene Auflage. 3rd ed. Berthold Simons. (Bad Salzhausener Beitraege Zur Aphasieforschung Ser.: Bd. 2). (GER.). 222p. 1998. 34.95 (*3-631-33019-7*) P Lang Pubng.

***Liniile Directoare Pentru Comunitatile: De Reevaluare Prin Consiliere.** Tr. by Ileana Vajda. Orig. Title: Guidelines for the Re - evaluation Conseling Communities. (RUM.). 38p. 1999. pap. 2.00 (*1-58429-053-6*) Rational Isl.

Lining Systems & Containment Membranes. Richard K. Miller & Marcia E. Rupnow. LC 90-83853. (Survey on Technology & Markets Ser.: No. 148). 50p. 1991. pap. text 200.00 (*1-55865-173-X*) Future Tech Surveys.

***Linings & Screens for Use with Burglar-Alarm Systems, UL 606.** 4th ed. (C). 1999. pap. text 95.00 (*1-55989-670-1*) Underwrtrs Labs.

***Linin's Revolution Ressia, 1917-1921.** David Marples. 144p. 1999. pap. 11.95 (*0-582-31917-X*) Addison-Wesley.

***Link.** Walt Becker. LC 98-24615. 432p. 2000. mass mkt. 6.99 (*0-380-73161-4*, Avon Bks) Morrow Avon.

***Link.** Walt Becker. (Illus.). (J). 2000. 12.34 (*0-606-17976-3*) Turtleback.

***Link: A Critical Journal on the Arts in Baltimore & the World: "This Place Meant/Displacement"** Contrib. by Link Editorial Staff. (Illus.). 176p. 2000. pap. 10.00 (*1-892813-03-3*, Pub. by Link) Bernhard DeBoer Inc.

Link: A Novel. Walt Becker. LC 98-24615. (Illus.). 384p. 1998. 25.00 (*0-688-15822-6*, Wm Morrow) Morrow Avon.

***Link: "... An Exciting Breakthrough Employing the Powerful Connection Between the Mind & Health"** rev. ed. Gerald B. Johnson. Ed. & Illus. by Rick R. Schuster. 256p. 2000. pap. 14.95 (*0-9677875-0-5*) Pennworthie Pr.

Link: Extraordinary Gifts of a Teenage Psychic. Matthew Manning. (Illus.). 176p. 1987. reprint ed. pap. 10.95 (*0-86140-283-9*, Pub. by Smyth) Dufour.

Link: Pocket Book. Melchizedek M. Solis. (Illus.). 295p. (Orig.). 1997. pap. 9.95 (*0-9651680-1-8*) Srmnk Pubs.

LINK No. 1: A Critical Journal on the Arts in Baltimore & the World: Inaugral Issue. LINK Editors. (Illus.). 136p. 1996. pap. 7.00 (*1-892813-00-9*) Link.

LINK No. 2: A Critical Journal on the Arts in Baltimore & the World: "You Are Here" LINK Editors. (Illus.). 186p. 1997. pap. 8.00 (*1-892813-01-7*) Link.

LINK No. 3: A Critical Journal on the Arts in Baltimore & the World: "RE:Visionary Art" LINK Editors. 1998. pap. 10.00 (*1-892813-02-5*) Link.

Link - Age: Composing in the Online Classroom. Joan C. Tornow. LC 96-45822. (Illus.). 264p. (Orig.). 1997. pap. 19.95 (*0-87421-221-9*) Utah St U Pr.

Link Across America: A Story of the Historic Lincoln Highway. Mary E. Anderson. LC 97-65052. (Illus.). 52p. (J). (gr. 1-8). 1997. 14.95 (*1-877810-97-5*, LINK) Rayve Prodns.

Link among the Days: The Life & Times of the Reverend Doctor William Archer Rutherfoord Goodwin. Dennis Montgomery. (Illus.). 344p. 1998. 25.95 (*0-87517-100-1*); pap. 19.95 (*0-87517-094-3*) Dietz.

Link Between ADD & Addiction: Getting the Help You Deserve. Wendy Richardson. LC 97-5122. 315p. (Orig.). 1997. pap. 16.00 (*1-57683-004-7*) Pinon Press.

***Link Between Childhood Trauma & Mental Illness: Effective Interventions for Mental Health Professionals.** Barbara Everett & Ruth Gallop. LC 00-9214. 2000. write for info. (*0-7619-1699-7*) Sage.

Link Between HR & Customer Bonding. K. Mezzacappa. (Financial Times Management Briefings Ser.). 1997. pap. 94.50 (*0-273-63256-6*, Pub. by F T P-H) Trans-Atl Phila.

Link Between Language & Consciousness: A Practical Philosophy. Marlene Carpenter. 120p. (Orig.). (C). 1991. pap. text 19.00 (*0-8191-8090-4*); lib. bdg. 39.50 (*0-8191-8089-0*) U Pr of Amer.

Link Invariants of the Chern-Simons Field Theory: New Developments in Topological Quantum Field Theory. Enore Guadagnini. LC 93-4729. (Expositions in Mathematics Ser.: Vol. 10). (Illus.). xiv, 312p. (C). 1993. lib. bdg. 89.95 (*3-11-014028-4*) De Gruyter.

Link Proceedings 1991, 1992: Selected Papers from Meetings in Moscow, 1991, & Ankara, 1992. Ed. by Bert G. Hickman & Lawrence Robert Klein. LC 98-42904. (Studies in Applied International Economics: Vol. 1). 350p. 1997. 58.00 (*981-02-3234-9*) World Scientific Pub.

Link the Generations with Love: "The Linker" (Director of Training) Laura R. Hess et al. (Wingborne Trilogy: Off the Page into Action Ser.). 49p. 1993. student ed. 4.10 (*0-9629755-3-2*) Wingborne-Diaconal.

Link Theory in Manifolds, Vol. 166. Uwe Kaiser. Ed. by A. Dold & F. Takens. LC 97-34437. (Lecture Notes in Mathematics Ser.: Vol. 1669). xiv, 167p. 1997. pap. 33.00 (*3-540-63435-5*) Spr-Verlag.

Link to Senior Golf: How to Play Better & Have More Fun. Jim Linkin. (Illus.). 150p. 1998. pap. 12.95 (*1-57167-241-9*) Sports Pub.

Link to the Links: The Golfer's Handbook. 112p. 1991. 9.95 (*0-9630417-0-3*) Optima Grp.

Link-Up - A Resource Directory: Interagency Collaborations to Help Children Achieve. Kristen J. Amundson. (NSBA Best Practices Ser.). (Orig.). 1991. pap. 15.00 (*0-88364-150-X*, 04-109) Natl Sch Boards.

Link with Nature & Divine Mediations in Asia. Ed. by Bernard Formoso. 176p. 1997. pap. 15.00 (*1-57181-121-4*) Berghahn Bks.

Link with the River. Desmond Hogan. 326p. 1989. 17.95 (*0-374-18461-5*) FS&G.

Linkage & Developing Countries see Information Processing 1994: Proceedings of the 13th World Computer Congress-IFIP Congress '94, Hamburg, Germany, 28 August - 2 September 1994

Linkage for Peace Through Economic Cooperation: Workshop on Security in the Pacific Rim, Tacoma, Washington, May 12-15, 1985. (Report Ser.: No. 23). 46p. 1985. 10.00 (*0-937722-25-1*) Intl Peace.

***Linkage Inc.'s Best Practices in Leadership Development Handbook: Case Studies, Instruments, Training.** Ed. by David J. Giber et al. LC 99-42894. (Illus.). 432p. 2000. 65.00 (*0-7879-5237-0*, Pfffr & Co) Jossey-Bass.

***Linkage, Inc.'s Best Practices in Organization & Human Resources Development Handbook: Case Studies - Models - Tools - Research.** Marshall Goldsmith et al. LC 99-91848. 607p. 2000. write for info. (*0-9677965-0-4*) Linkage Inc.

Linkage Methods for Environment & Health Analysis: General Guidelines. Ed. by D. Briggs et al. 136p. (Orig.). 1996. pap. text 16.20 (*0-614-17676-X*, 1930089) World Health.

Linkage of Effects to Tissue Residues: Development of a Comprehensive Database for Aquatic Organisms Exposed to Inorganic & Organic Chemicals. Alfred W. Jarvinen & Gerald T. Ankley. LC 98-22670. 15p. 1998. 98.00 (*1-880611-13-9*, SETAC Pr) SETAC.

Linkage of Psychological Components with Vocational Loss/Access - An Assessment/Forensic Tool: Appendix Listing DOT Titles & Temperaments. Michelle A. Rowe. Ed. by Norman Iden. 367p. 1998. pap. 49.95 (*0-9666080-0-3*) Rowe Rehab.

Linkage or Bondage: U. S. Economic Relations with the Asean Region, 91. Hans H. Indorf & Patrick N. Mayerchak. LC 88-29613. (Contributions in Economics & Economic History Ser.: No. 91). 149p. 1989. 47.95 (*0-313-26615-8*, ILB/, Greenwood Pr) Greenwood.

Linkages. Center for Occupational Research & Development Staff. (Mechanical Technology Ser.). (Illus.). 258p. (C). 1983. pap. text 28.00 (*1-55502-153-0*) CORD Commns.

Linkages. Patrice Connerton & Reid. (J). 1993. mass mkt., teacher ed. 9.95 (*0-8384-4205-6*) Heinle & Heinle.

Linkages. Patrice Connerton & Frances Reid. 280p. (J). 1993. mass mkt. 25.95 (*0-8384-3955-1*) Heinle & Heinle.

Linkages. Connerton & Reid. (J). 1993. VHS 114.95 (*0-8384-5090-3*) Heinle & Heinle.

Linkages. Connerton & Reid. (J). 1993. mass mkt. 57.95 (*0-8384-4204-8*) Heinle & Heinle.

Linkages: OECD & Major Developing Economies. LC 95-211977. 185p. (Orig.). 1995. pap. 47.00 (*92-64-14438-2*, Pub. by Org for Econ) OECD.

LinkAges: Planning an Intergenerational Program for Preschool. Merle D. Griff et al. Ed. by Lois Fowkes. (Illus.). 98p. (Orig.). 1995. pap., teacher ed. 11.95 (*0-201-49427-2*) Supplementary Div.

Linkages Between Agriculture & Nutrition: Implications for Policy & Research. Eileen Kennedy & Howarth Bouis. LC 93-26471. 1993. write for info. (*0-89629-328-9*) Intl Food Policy.

***Linkages Between Ecosystems in the South Florida Hydroscape.** James W. Porter & Karen G. Porter. 600p. 1999. 89.95 (*0-8493-2026-7*) CRC Pr.

***Linkages Between Global Vegetation & Climate: An Analysis Based on NOAA Advanced Very High Resolution Radiometer Data.** Sietse Oene Los. 204p. 1998. pap. text 29.00 (*0-16-049527-X*) USGPO.

L

*Linkages Between Government Spending, Growth, & Poverty in Rural India. Shenggen Fan et al. LC 99-47926. 1999. write for info. (0-89629-113-8) Intl Food Policy.
Linkages in Developing Economies: A Philippine Study. Gustav Ranis et al. LC 89-48871. 83p. 1990. pap. 14.95 (1-55815-049-8) ICS Pr.
*Linked Faiths: Essays on Chinese Religions & Traditional Culture in Honor of Kristofer Schipper. Kristofer M. Schipper et al. LC 99-50301. (Sinica Leidensia Ser.). 250p. 1999. 74.50 (90-04-11540-4) Brill Academic Pubs.
Linked Lives: A Tale of Yesterday & Today. Isabella Ingalese. 230p. 1996. reprint ed. spiral bd. 16.50 (0-7873-1259-2) Hlth Research.
Linked National Models: A Tool for International Food Policy Analysis. Gunther Fischer et al. (C). 1988. lib. bdg. 156.00 (90-247-3734-6) Kluwer Academic.
Linked Systems for Resource Sharing. Bernard G. Sloan. (Professional Librarian Ser.). 131p. 1990. 30.00 (0-8161-1865-5, Hall Reference); 25.00 (0-8161-1874-4, Hall Reference) Macmillan.
Linked Systems Project: A Networking Tool for Libraries. Ed. by Beacher Wiggins. (Library, Information, & Computer Science Ser.: No. 6). (Illus.). 152p. (Orig.). 1988. pap. text 13.50 (1-55653-039-0) OCLC Online Comp.
*Linked to Jesus. Cassie Carstens. 1999. pap. text 12.95 (0-86997-768-7) Lux Verbi.
Linked to Someone in Pain. Cheryl Sanfacon & Joyce Moccero. 192p. (Orig.). 1993. pap. 7.99 (1-56476-117-7, 6-3117, Victor Bks) Chariot Victor.
Linked Weekly, Monthly, Quarterly Econometric Models of the U. S. Economy, Vol. 1. Richard G. Zambell. LC 84-3727. (Illus.). 485p. 1984. 34.95 (0-9613048-2-0) M D Weiss Pub.
*Linkers & Loaders. John Levine. LC 99-47127. (Operating Systems Ser.). 400p. 1999. pap. 36.95 (1-55860-496-0, Pub. by Morgan Kaufmann) Harcourt.
Linking: Probability, Statistics & the TI-82. Iris B. Fetta. 58p. (YA). (gr. 9 up). 1995. pap. text 10.95 (1-881641-39-2); pap. text 20.95 incl. disk (1-881641-40-6); pap. text 20.95 incl. disk (1-881641-41-4) Pencil Point.
Linking Alcoholism Treatment Research with Clinical Practice. (Illus.). 56p. (Orig.). (C). 1992. pap. text 25.00 (1-56806-071-8) DIANE Pub.
Linking America's School & Colleges: Guide to Partnerships & National Directory. 2nd rev. ed. Franklin P. Wilbur & Leo M. Lambert. LC 96-122146. 480p. (C). 1995. 55.00 (1-882982-10-X) Anker Pub.
Linking Arms Together: American Indian Treaty Visions of Law & Peace, 1600-1800. Robert A. Williams, Jr. (Illus.). 208p. 1997. text 35.00 (0-19-506591-3) OUP.
*Linking Arms Together: American Indian Treaty Visions of Law & Peace, 1600-1800. Robert A. Williams. LC 99-32374. 1999. pap. 19.99 (0-415-92577-0) Routledge.
Linking Assessment & Early Intervention: An Authentic Curriculum-Based Approach. 3rd ed. Stephen J. Bagnato et al. LC 96-43160. 1996. 44.95 (1-55766-263-0) P H Brookes.
Linking Auditing & Metaevaluation: Enhancing Quality in Applied Research. Thomas A. Schwandt & Edward S. Halpern. (Applied Social Research Methods Ser.: Vol. 11). 152p. (C). 1988. text 42.00 (0-8039-2967-6); pap. text 18.95 (0-8039-2968-4) Sage.
Linking Autocad Concepts to 3DS r3 for Architecture. Daniel Douglas et al. (Onword - CAD Titles Ser.). 224p. (C). 1996. pap. 35.00 (0-8273-7695-2) Delmar.
Linking AutoCAD to 3D Studio V2 for Architecture. Michele Bousquet et al. LC 96-2519. 224p. (C). 1996. pap. 55.95 (0-8273-8081-X) Delmar.
*Linking by Types in the Hierarchical Lexicon. Anthony R. Davis. LC 99-43705. (Studies in Constraint-Based Lexicalism (SCBL): No. 4). 280p. 1999. 64.95 (1-57586-223-9, Pub. by CSLI); pap. 22.95 (1-57586-224-7, Pub. by CSLI) Cambridge U Pr.
Linking Citizens to Government: Interest Group Politics at Common Cause. Lawrence S. Rothenberg. (Illus.). 324p. (C). 1992. text 74.95 (0-521-41560-8); pap. text 20.95 (0-521-42577-8) Cambridge U Pr.
Linking Community & Corrections in Japan. Elmer Hubert Johnson & Carol H. Johnson. LC 99-17489. (Illus.). 336p. 2000. 44.95 (0-8093-2279-X) S Ill U Pr.
Linking Crop Models with a Geographic Information System to Assist Decisionmaking: A Prototype for the Indian Semiarid Tropics. U. Singh et al. LC 93-24979. (Papers: No. P-19). 40p. 1993. pap. text 20.00 (0-88090-103-9) Intl Fertilizer.
Linking Data. Nigel G. Fielding & Jane L. Fielding. (Qualitative Research Methods Ser.: Vol. 4). 96p. 1985. text 24.00 (0-8039-2563-8); pap. text 10.50 (0-8039-2518-2) Sage.
Linking Economic Policy & Foreign Policy. Charles Wolf, Jr. 176p. (C). 1991. 39.95 (0-88738-399-8) Transaction Pubs.
*Linking Employee Satisfaction to Business Results Paula S. Topolosky. LC 99-30495. (Studies on Industrial Productivity). 1999. write for info. (0-8153-3487-7) Garland.
*Linking Employee Share Schemes to Corporate Objectives. E. Hubbick. (Financial Times Management Briefings Ser.). 1998. pap. 94.50 (0-273-63575-1, Pub. by F T P-H) Trans-Atl Phila.
Linking Europe: Transport Policies & Politics in the European Union. John F. Ross. LC 97-21850. 288p. 1998. 59.95 (0-275-95248-7, Praeger Pubs) Greenwood.
Linking Fact & Fiction in the Fur Trade: A Teaching Guide for Traders in Time by Janie Lynn Panagopoulos. Jean Shafer. 32p. 1993. teacher ed. 8.95 (0-938682-25-3) River Rd Pubns.
Linking Fact & Fiction in the Great Lakes Lumbering Past: A Teacher's Guide for "Journey Back to Lumberjack Camp" by Janie Panagopoulos. Jean Shafer. 32p. 1994. pap. 8.95 (0-938682-28-8) River Rd Pubns.
Linking Family Support & Early Childhood Programs: Issues, Experience, Opportunities. Mary Larner. Ed. by Jacqueline Lalley. (Guidelines for Effective Practice Ser.). 40p. (Orig.). 1995. pap. 7.00 (1-885429-09-6) Family Resource.
Linking Federal Programs & Service Learning: A Planning, Implementation & Evaluation Guide. Shelley H. Billig & Nancy P. Kraft. LC 98-89827. 376p. 1999. pap. text 59.95 (1-56676-745-8) Scarecrow.
Linking Flexibility, Uncertainty & Variability in Manufacturing Systems: Managing Un-Planned Change in the Automotive Industry. Henrique L. Correa. 208p. 1994. 66.95 (1-85628-620-7, Pub. by Avebry) Ashgate Pub Co.
Linking for Learning: Developing Telecommunications Technologies & Distance Learning. 1990. 250.00 (0-8490-4029-9) Gordon Pr.
*Linking Genetic Resources & Geography: Emerging Strategies for Conserving & Using Crop Biodiversity. Ed. by Stephanie L. Greene & Luigi Guarino. LC 99-72729. 1999. write for info. (0-89118-548-8) Am Soc Agron.
Linking Health & Mental Health. Ed. by Anthony Broskowski et al. LC 81-8875. (Sage Annual Reviews of Community Mental Health Ser.: No. 2). 296p. reprint ed. pap. 91.80 (0-8357-8480-0, 203474700091) Bks Demand.
Linking Health Care & Social Services: International Perspectives. Ed. by Merl C. Hokenstad, Jr. & Roger A. Ritvo. LC 82-705. (Social Service Delivery Systems Ser.: No. 5). (Illus.). 304p. reprint ed. pap. 94.30 (0-8357-4807-3, 203774400009) Bks Demand.
Linking Home & School: Partnership in Practice in Primary Education. Hugh Waller. LC 98-184572. (Home-School--A Working Alliance Ser.). 120p. 1998. pap. 26.95 (1-85346-482-1, Pub. by David Fulton) Taylor & Francis.
Linking Housing & Community Services: A Housing Primer for Local Officials. 17p. 1997. 3.00 (1-886152-40-3, No. 6301) Natl League Cities.
Linking Housing & Health Services for Older Persons. Frwd. by Daniel M. Fox & Sheldon L. Goldberg. LC 97-160855. 48p. (Orig.). 1997. pap. write for info. (1-887748-09-1) Milbank Memorial.
Linking HRD Programs with Organizational Strategy: Twelve Case Studies from the Real World of Training. Ed. by William J. Rothwell & Jack J. Phillips. LC 98-71679. (In Action Ser.). 221 p. 1998. pap. 50.00 (1-56286-087-9) Am Soc Train & Devel.
Linking Laboratory & In Situ Activation Analysis of Rock-Forming Elements Using a 14 MeV Neutron Source. Jerome Truax. (Illus.). 196p. (Orig.). (C). 1995. pap. 87.50 (90-407-1124-0, Pub. by Delft U Pr) Coronet Bks.
Linking Language: Simple Language & Literacy Activities Throughout the Curriculum. Robert Rockwell et al. LC 99-28325. (Illus.). 256p. (J). 1999. pap. 19.95 (0-87659-202-7, 17561, Pub. by Gryphon Hse) Consort Bk Sales.
Linking LANs. 2nd ed. Stanley Schatt. 352p. 1995. 45.00 (0-07-057063-9) McGraw.
Linking Links: Persons Who Prepare Others for Caregiving: Instructor's Lesson Plans. Whorl et al. Ed. by Wingborne. (Illus.). 50p. (Orig.). 1992. pap. text, student ed. 12.95 (0-9629755-1-6) Wingborne-Diaconal.
Linking Literacies: Perspectives on L2 Reading - Writing Connections. Ed. by Diane D. Belcher & Alan R. Hirvela. (Illus.). 300p. (C). text 44.50 (0-472-09753-9); pap. text 29.95 (0-472-06753-2) U of Mich Pr.
*Linking Literacy & Technology: A Guide for K-8 Classrooms. Ed. by Shelley B. Wepner et al. LC 99-86755. 2000. pap., teacher ed. 24.95 (0-87207-258-4, 258) Intl Reading.
Linking Literature & Comprehension. Shirley Cook. Ed. by Jan Keeling. (Integrating Literature into Basic Skills Programs Ser.). (Illus.). 240p. (Orig.). (J). (gr. k-4). 1992. pap. text 16.95 (0-86530-205-7, IP193-3) Incentive Pubns.
Linking Literature & Writing. Shirley Cook & Kathy Carl. (Illus.). 240p. (J). (gr. 1-4). 1989. pap. text 16.95 (0-86530-064-X, IP 166-5) Incentive Pubns.
Linking Literature with Self-Esteem. Shirley Cook. Ed. by Jan Keeling. (Integrating Literature into Basic Skills Programs Ser.). (Illus.). 160p. (Orig.). (J). (gr. k-4). 1992. pap. text 14.95 (0-86530-196-4, IP194-6) Incentive Pubns.
Linking Macroeconomic & Agricultural Policies for Adjustment with Growth: The Columbian Experience. Vinod Thomas. LC 85-45105. 270p. reprint ed. pap. 83.70 (0-7837-4248-7, 204393800012) Bks Demand.
Linking Marketing & Technology Strategies: December 3-5, 1989. Ed. by Ronald McTavish. LC 90-162. 49p. 1990. reprint ed. pap. 30.00 (0-608-04083-5, 206481500011) Bks Demand.
Linking Mathematics & Language: Practical Classroom Activities. Richard W. McCallum & Robert Whitlow. (The Pippin Teacher's Library Ser.). 140p. 1994. pap. 17.00 (0-88751-038-8, 00765) Heinemann.
Linking Methods in Critical Point Theory Martin Schechter. LC 98-32108. 1998. write for info. (3-7643-4095-9) Birkhauser.
*Linking Methods in Critical Point Theory. Martin Schechter. LC 98-32108. 1998. 59.95 (0-8176-4095-9) Birkhauser.
Linking Objects & Linking Phenomena. Vamik D. Volkan & Harold F. Searles. LC 81-14278. 330p. 1981. 60.00 (0-8236-3030-7) Intl Univs Pr.
Linking or Isolating Economies? A Look at Trucking along the Texas-Mexico Border. David J. Molina & James R. Giermanski. (U. S. - Mexican Policy Reports: No. 6). 100p. 1994. pap. 15.00 (0-89940-322-0) LBJ Sch Pub Aff.
Linking Our Lives: Chinese American Women of Los Angeles. Lucie Cheng et al. LC 84-72431. (Illus.). xvii, 122p. (Orig.). (C). 1993. pap. 10.95 (0-930377-00-1) Chinese Hist CA.
Linking Parents to Play Therapy. Deborah K. McGuire & Donald E. McGuire. LC 98-4117. 1998. 40.00 (0-7657-0169-3) Aronson.
*Linking Parties with People? Party Membership in Sweden, 1960-1997. Anders Widfeldt. LC 98-74934. 334p. 1999. text 70.95 (1-84014-758-X, Pub. by Ashgate Pub) Ashgate Pub Co.
Linking Pay to Performance: An Approach to Designing a Merit Pay Plan. Steven P. Seltz & Robert L. Heneman. (Building Blocks Ser.: Vol. 12). (Illus.). 20p. (Orig.). 1993. pap. 24.95 (1-57963-015-4, A0032) Am Compensation.
Linking People to the Global Networked Society. Charles R. McClure & John C. Bertot. 109p. (Orig.). 1998. pap. 25.00 (0-937597-45-7, IR-105) ERIC Clear.
Linking Public Capital to Economic Performance: Public Capital: The Missing Link Between Investment & Economic Growth. Sharon J. Erenburg. (Public Policy Brief Ser.: No. 14). (Illus.). 58p. (Orig.). 1994. pap. 3.00 (0-941276-02-3) J Levy.
Linking Quality to Profits: Quality Based Cost Management. Hawley Atkinson et al. LC 94-17503. 405p. 1994. 43.00 (0-87389-189-9, H0725) ASQ Qual Pr.
Linking Reading Assessment. Shearer. 1993. pap. text, teacher ed. 0.30 (0-312-04717-7) St Martin.
Linking Reading Assessment to Instruction: An Application Worktext for Elementary Classroom Teachers. Arleen P. Shearer & Susan P. Homan. 272p. 1995. pap. 18.50 (0-8058-8006-2); pap., teacher ed. write for info. (0-8058-8007-0) L Erlbaum Assocs.
Linking Reading Assessment to Instruction: An Application Worktext for Elementary Classroom Teachers. Arleen P. Shearer & Susan P. Homan. 272p. 1993. pap. text 14.00 (0-312-04765-7) St Martin.
Linking Reading Assessment to Instruction: An Application Worktext for Elementary Classroom Teachers. 2nd ed. Arleen S. Mariotti & Susan P. Homan. LC 97-10898. 1997. pap. 23.50 (0-8058-2651-3) L Erlbaum Assocs.
*Linking Research & Marketing Opportunities for Pulses in the 21st Century. R. Knight. LC 98-53212. (Current Plant Science & Biotechnology in Agriculture Ser.). 1999. write for info. (0-7923-5565-2) Kluwer Academic.
Linking Research to Crop Production. Boyce Thompson Institute for Plant Research Confer. Ed. by Richard C. Staples & Ronald J. Kuhr. LC 79-25737. (Illus.). 249p. 1980. reprint ed. pap. 77.20 (0-608-05442-9, 206591100006) Bks Demand.
Linking Roots: Writing by Six Women with Distinct Ethnic Heritages. Ed. by Bryce Milligan. 56p. 1993. pap. 7.00 (0-913983-07-1) M & A Edns.
Linking Rural Housing & Social Services: Case Studies. Housing Assistance Council Staff. 52p. 1998. 5.00 (1-58064-082-6) Housing Assist.
Linking SAPs & EAPs Against Drug, Alcohol, Gambling & Greed Dependencies. rev. ed. Kenneth G. Koym. (Illus.). 189p. 1994. pap. text 28.55 (0-614-00517-5, 8-94-153139) Advocacy Servs Pr.
Linking School & Work: Roles for Standards & Assessment. Ed. by John G. Wirt & Lauren B. Rensick. (Education Ser.). 491p. 1995. text 47.00 (0-7879-0165-2) Jossey-Bass.
Linking Science & Technology to Society's Environmental Goals. National Research Council Staff. LC 96-47176. 544p. 1996. text 69.95 (0-309-05578-4) Natl Acad Pr.
Linking Separate Worlds: Urban Migrants & Rural Lives in Peru. Karsten Paerregaard. LC 97-202655. (Explorations in Anthropology Ser.). (Illus.). 256p. 1997. 55.00 (1-85973-103-1, Pub. by Berg Pubs); pap. 19.50 (1-85973-108-2, Pub. by Berg Pubs) NYU Pr.
Linking Social & Ecological Systems: Management Practices & Social Mechanisms for Building Resilience. Ed. by Fikret Berkes et al. (Illus.). 476p. (C). 1998. text 80.00 (0-521-59140-6) Cambridge U Pr.
*Linking Social & Ecological Systems: Management Practices & Social Mechanisms for Building Resilience. Ed. by Fikret Berkes & Carl Folke. (Illus.). 459p. (C). 2000. pap. 31.95 (0-521-78562-6) Cambridge U Pr.
Linking Social Science Information to Policy-Making. Cheol H. Oh. LC 96-34116. (Political Economy & Public Policy Ser.: Vol. 10). 1996. 78.50 (0-7623-0155-4) Jai Pr.
Linking Social Structure & Personality. Ed. by Glen H. Elder, Jr. LC 73-94131. (Sage Contemporary Social Science Issues Ser.: No. 12). 160p. reprint ed. pap. 49.60 (0-608-10120-6, 202189200026) Bks Demand.
Linking Sustainable Community Activities to Pollution Prevention: A Sourcebook. Beth E. Lachman. LC 97-8330. 86p. 1997. pap. 15.00 (0-8330-2500-7, MR-855-OSTP) Rand Corp.
Linking Teachers' Professional Development to Standards & Assessment. 1995. write for info. (0-614-06033-8) AACTE.
Linking the Export Processing Zone to Local Industry. Ed. by Richard L. Bolin. 174p. (C). 1990. pap. text 40.00 (0-945951-04-3) Flagstaff Inst.
Linking the Gaseous & Condensed Phases of Matter: The Behavior of Slow Electrons. L. G. Christophorou et al. (NATO ASI Ser.: Vol. 326). (Illus.). 606p. (C). 1994. 149.50 (0-306-44800-9, Kluwer Plenum) Kluwer Academic.
Linking the Governors & the Governed. Austin Ranney et al. Ed. by Richard W. Taylor. (Illus.). 238p. 1981. pap. text 9.95 (0-933522-09-6) Kent Popular.
*Linking the National Assessment of Educational Progress (NAEP) & the Third International Mathematics & Science Study (TIMSS) Eighth-Grade Results. Eugene G. Johnson & Gary W. Philips. 100p. (C). 2000. reprint ed. pap. text 25.00 (0-7881-8574-8) DIANE Pub.
Linking the Natural Environment & the Economy: Essays from the Eco-Eco Group. Ed. by Carl Folke & Tomas Kaberger. (Ecology, Economy & Environment Ser.). 320p. 1991. text 193.50 (0-7923-1227-9) Kluwer Academic.
Linking the U. S. National Technical Information Service with Academic & Public Libraries. Charles R. McClure et al. LC 86-8067. 320p. 1986. text 73.25 (0-89391-377-4) Ablx Pub.
*Linking Theory to Practice: Case Studies for Working with College Students. 2nd ed. Michael Dannells & Frances K. Stage. LC 99-57551. (C). 2000. 29.95 (1-56032-865-7) Taylor & Francis.
Linking to the Church. Barbara Brower. (Core Value Ser.). 62p. 1998. pap. 2.95 (1-56212-335-1, 1960-0054) CRC Pubns.
Linking to the Lost. Donna Vander Griend. (Core Value Ser.). 62p. 1998. pap. text, teacher ed. 2.95 (1-56212-085-9) CRC Pubns.
Linking Tourism, the Environment, & Sustainability. Stephen F. McCool & Alan E. Watson. (Illus.). 95p. (C). 1997. reprint ed. pap. text 30.00 (0-7881-3862-6) DIANE Pub.
Linking Trade & Technology Policies: An International Comparison of the Policies of Industrialized Nations. National Academy of Sciences, Committee on Linking. Ed. by Gordon E. Moore & Martha C. Harris. LC 92-29614. (Prospering in a Global Economy Ser.). 176p. (C). 1992. pap. text 26.00 (0-309-04645-9) Natl Acad Pr.
Linking Training Strategy to Corporate Strategy. Jerome M. Rosow & Robert Zager. Ed. by Jill Casner-Lotto. (Training for New Technology Ser.: Part I). 76p. 1985. 95.00 (0-89361-058-5) Work in Amer.
Linking Up! Using Music, Movement, & Language Arts to Promote Caring, Cooperation, & Communication. Sarah Pirtle. Ed. by Laura P. Roerden. (Illus.). 309p. 1998. pap. 29.00 incl. audio compact disk (0-942349-10-5) Eductrs Soc Respons.
*Linking Up, 1999: Planning Your Traffic-Free Bike Ride Between Pittsburgh, PA & Washington, DC. Mary Shaw & Roy Weil. 32p. 1999. pap. 2.95 (0-9646014-4-3) Shaw-Weil Assocs.
*Linking Welfare Recipients to Jobs: The Role of Temporary Help Agencies. Alicia Bugarin. 39p. 1998. pap. write for info. (1-58703-096-9, CRB-98-017) CA St Libry.
Linking with Employers, Options: Expanding Educational Services for Adults. National Center for Research in Vocational Educati. 1987. 39.95 (0-317-03900-8, SP500D) Ctr Educ Trng Employ.
Linking with Farmers: Networking for Low-External-Input & Sustainable Agriculture. Ed. by Carine Alders et al. LC 99-939620. (Illus.). 200p. 1993. pap. 25.00 (1-85339-210-3, Pub. by Intermed Tech) Stylus Pub VA.
Linking Work-Family Issues to the Bottom Line, Report No. 962. Dana E. Friedman. (Report: No. 962). (Illus.). 60p. (Orig.). 1991. pap. text 100.00 (0-8237-0409-2) Conference Bd.
Linking Your Y with the World: An Instructor's Guide for Global Environment & Development. Ed. by Kathleen M. Haskin. (Illus.). 91p. 1993. write for info. (0-9675828-1-4) Frost Valley.
Linkman. large type ed. Charles Burnham. (Linford Western Library). 272p. 1995. pap. 16.99 (0-7089-7748-0, Linford) Ulverscroft.
*Links. Ed. by Sim F. Sutterby, Sr. et al. 1999. pap. 12.95 (1-930293-00-3) PoetWorks Pr.
Links. Robert Hunter. (Illus.). 160p. 1998. reprint ed. 55.00 (1-886947-51-1) Sleepng Bear.
Links: A History of Transport & New Zealand Society. James Watson, Jr. LC 97-151223. (Illus.). 315p. 1996. 39.95 (1-86956-168-6, Pub. by GP Pubns) Accents Pubns.
Links: An Exploration into the Mind, Heart, & Soul of Golf. Lorne Rubenstein. 176p. 1993. pap. 10.95 (1-55958-279-0) Prima Pub.
Links Between Structural Adjustment & Poverty: Causal or Remedial? J. J. Thomas et al. LC 98-204620. 1993. write for info. (92-2-308803-8) Intl Labour Office.
Links Beyond Time: The Book of Esther in Light of the Life of Yosef. Yoel T. Cahn. 279p. 1995. 19.95 (1-56871-074-7, Pub. by Targum Pr); 19.95 (0-568-71074-6) Targum Pr.
Links in a Golden Chain: Essays on the History of the Niadh Nask. Ed. by Count of Clandermond. (Illus.). 225p. 1998. 40.00 (0-9654220-2-X) Gryfons Pubs & Dist.
Links in the Chain: Isolation & Interdependence in Nathaniel Hawthorne's Fictional Characters. Arne Axelsson. (Studia Anglistica Upsaliensia Ser.: No. 17). 190p. (Orig.). 1974. pap. 27.50 (91-554-0124-4, Pub. by Uppsala Univ Acta Univ Upsaliensis) Coronet Bks.
Links in the Chain: Shapers of the Jewish Tradition. Naomi Pasachoff. (Oxford Profiles Ser.). (Illus.). 240p. (YA). (gr. 5 up). 1997. 35.00 (0-19-509939-7) OUP.
Links in the Chain Vol. M13: Greenbelt, Maryland & the New Town Movement in America. Susan L. Klaus. 1987. 5.00 (1-888028-11-4) GWU Ctr WAS.

An Asterisk (*) at the beginning of an entry indicates that the title is appearing for the first time.

Links in the Chassidic Legacy No. 1: Biographical Sketches That First Appeared in the Classical Columns of HaTamim. Tr. by Shimon Neubort from YID. LC 97-141956. 224p. 1997. 18.00 (*1-881400-23-9*) S I E.

Links in the History of Engineering & Technology from Tudor Times. Rhys Jenkins. LC 72-121481. (Essay Index Reprint Ser.). 1977. 23.95 (*0-8369-2167-4*) Ayer.

Links Lore: Dramatic Moments & Forgotten Milestones from Golf's History. Peter F. Stevens. LC 98-8638. 224p. 1998. 24.95 (*1-57488-184-1*) Brasseys.

Links LS 98: Official Strategy Guide. Mike Ferguson. LC 97-67542. 192p. 1997. per. 19.99 (*0-7615-1208-X*) Prima Pub.

Links of Heaven: A Complete Guide to Golf Journeys in Ireland. Richard Phinney & Scott Whitley. LC 95-81020. (Great Golf Journeys Ser.). (Illus.). 306p. (Orig.). 1996. pap. 19.95 (*1-888132-02-7*) Baltray Bks.

Links to Ancestral Ties: George Primm, Sr., Family. Pearlie Ponder. 208p. 1995. text 17.00 (*0-9644034-0-4*) P Ponder.

Links to Architecture: AutoCAD & 3D Studio. Autodeskpress Staff. (Onword - CAD Titles Ser.). 1996. 249.95 (*0-8273-7729-0*) Delmar.

Links to Logic. Betty Brammer. (Illus.). 96p. 1997. pap. 10.95 (*1-880505-53-3*, CLC0204) Pieces of Lrning.

Links to Mechanical Design & Drafting: CAD Design 3D. Autodeskpress Staff. (Onword - CAD Titles Ser.). 1996. 250.00 (*0-8273-7730-4*) Delmar.

***Links to Your Canadian Past Tome 1: Acadia & the Maritimes.** Peter Gagne. 231p. 1999. pap. 22.95 (*1-58211-118-9*) Quintin Pub RI.

***Links to Your Canadian Past Tome 2: Quebec.** Peter Gagne. 264p. 1999. pap. 22.95 (*1-58211-119-7*) Quintin Pub RI.

***Links to Your Canadian Past Tome 3: Ontario, Manitoba, Saskatchewan, Alberta, British Columbia.** Peter Gagne. 278p. 1999. pap. 22.95 (*1-58211-120-0*) Quintin Pub RI.

Linksman Learning Style Preference Assessment & Brain Hemispheric Preference Assessment: Assessment Booklet. Ricki Linksman. 24p. 1993. pap. 10.00 (*1-928997-10-4*) Natl Read Diag.

Linksman Learning Style Preference Assessment & Brain Hemispheric Preference Assessment: Instruction Manual. Ricki Linksman. 1993. pap., teacher ed. 30.00 (*1-928997-09-0*) Natl Read Diag.

Linksman Passage Reading Tests to Diagnose Reading Skills: Grades 1-12. Ricki Linksman. 1993. pap. 20.00 (*1-928997-11-2*) Natl Read Diag.

Linksman Phonics Diagnostic Test. Ricki Linksman. (Illus.). 28p. 1993. pap. 30.00 (*1-928997-08-2*) Natl Read Diag.

Linksman Phonics Diagnostic Test: Instruction Manual. Ricki Linksman. 50p. 1993. pap. 30.00 (*1-928997-07-4*) Natl Read Diag.

Linkups. Barbara Fisher. (Illus.). (Orig.). (J). (ps-3). 1977. boxed set 2.00 (*0-934830-05-3*) Ten Penny.

***Linkword Lang Courses: Spanish.** Gruneberg. 2000. 22.95 (*0-552-00501-0*, Pub. by Transworld Publishers Ltd); pap. 8.95 (*0-552-13055-9*, Pub. by Transworld Publishers Ltd) Trafalgar.

***Linkword Language Courses: French.** Gruneberg. 2000. 22.95 (*0-552-00500-2*, Pub. by Transworld Publishers Ltd); pap. 8.95 (*0-552-13053-2*, Pub. by Transworld Publishers Ltd) Trafalgar.

Linkword Welsh. Michael Gruneburg. 247p. 1995. pap. 17.95 (*0-8464-4747-9*) Beekman Pubs.

Linmill Stories. Robert McLellan. (Classics Ser.). 280p. 1994. pap. 11.95 (*0-86241-282-X*, Pub. by Canongate Books) Interlink Pub.

Linn: Descendants of George Linn. Evangeline L. Halleck. 227p. 1998. reprint ed. pap. 34.00 (*0-8328-9735-3*); reprint ed. lib. bdg. 44.00 (*0-8328-9734-5*) Higginson Bk Co.

Linn: Genealogical History of the Family of William Linn, Who Came from Belfast, Ireland, in 1771. Margarett V. Hull. (Illus.). 146p. 1994. reprint ed. pap. 25.00 (*0-8328-4223-0*); reprint ed. lib. bdg. 35.00 (*0-8328-4222-2*) Higginson Bk Co.

Linn County, Kansas: A History. William A. Mitchell. 404p. 1994. reprint ed. lib. bdg. 40.00 (*0-8328-4001-7*) Higginson Bk Co.

Linn County, Oregon Pioneer Settlers: John McCoy. 115p. write for info. (*0-939509-32-6*); pap. 12.00 (*0-317-58902-4*) L Benton Geneal.

Linn County, Oregon Pioneer Settlers DLC to 1855, Vol. 1. 115p. write for info. (*0-939509-01-6*) L Benton Geneal.

Linn County, Oregon Pioneer Settlers DLC to 1855, Vol. 2. 115p. write for info. (*0-939509-02-4*) L Benton Geneal.

Linn County, Oregon Pioneer Settlers DLC to 1855, Vol. 3. 115p. write for info. (*0-939509-03-2*); pap. 12.00 (*0-317-58888-5*) L Benton Geneal.

Linn County, Oregon Pioneer Settlers DLC to 1855, Vol. 4. 115p. write for info. (*0-939509-04-0*) L Benton Geneal.

Linn County, Oregon Pioneer Settlers DLC to 1855, Vol. 5. 115p. write for info. (*0-939509-05-9*) L Benton Geneal.

Linn County, Oregon Pioneer Settlers DLC to 1855, Vol. 6. 115p. write for info. (*0-939509-06-7*) L Benton Geneal.

Linn County, Oregon Pioneer Settlers DLC to 1855, Vol. 7. 115p. write for info. (*0-939509-07-5*) L Benton Geneal.

Linn County, Oregon Pioneer Settlers DLC to 1855, Vol. 8. 115p. 1987. write for info. (*0-939509-08-3*) L Benton Geneal.

Linn County, Oregon Pioneer Settlers DLC to 1855, Vol. 10. 115p. 1987. write for info. (*0-939509-10-5*) L Benton Geneal.

Linn County, Oregon Pioneer Settlers DLC to 1855 Series, Set. write for info. (*0-939509-00-8*) L Benton Geneal.

Linn County, Oregon Pioneer Settlers Marriage Licenses, Set. (Complete Ser.). write for info. (*0-939509-39-3*) L Benton Geneal.

Linn County, Oregon Pioneer Settlers Marriage Licenses, Vol. 1. 115p. write for info. (*0-939509-40-7*) L Benton Geneal.

Linn County, Oregon Pioneer Settlers Marriage Licenses, Vol. 2. 115p. write for info. (*0-939509-41-5*); pap. 12.00 (*0-685-18249-5*) L Benton Geneal.

Linn County, Oregon Pioneer Settlers Marriage Licenses, Vol. 3. 115p. write for info. (*0-939509-42-3*) L Benton Geneal.

Linn County, Oregon Pioneer Settlers Marriage Licenses, Vol. 4. 115p. write for info. (*0-939509-43-1*); pap. 12.00 (*0-317-58916-4*) L Benton Geneal.

Linn Grove, 1880-1940: A Cultural History of a Small Town in Iowa. Richard D. Peterson, II. LC 98-68557. (Illus.). 410p. 1999. pap. write for info. (*0-941795-03-9*) R D Peterson & Sons.

Linna en el Jardin de Monet. Christina Bjork. 1996. 15.95 (*968-6582-15-0*) Samara Ediciones.

Linnaean Keepsake. Ed. by G. S. Daniels. (ENG & LAT., Illus.). 70p. 1973. 13.00 (*0-913196-15-0*) Hunt Inst Botanical.

Linnaeana. G. A. Rudolph & Evan N. Williams. LC 72-636354. (Libraries Bibliography: No. 7). 1970. pap. 5.00 (*0-686-20815-3*) KSU.

Linnaea's World. Verna E. Pratt. Ed. & Photos by Frank G. Pratt. LC 96-83135. (Illus.). 50p. (Orig.). (J). (gr. 3-6). 1996. 19.95 (*0-9623192-6-0*); pap. 11.95 (*0-9623192-5-2*) Alaskakrafts Pub.

Linnaeus: Nature & Nation. Lisbet Koerner. LC 99-34570. 320p. 1999. 39.95 (*0-674-09745-9*) HUP.

Linnaeus: The Man & His Work. rev. ed. Intro. by Tore Frangsmyr. LC 94-10558. (Upsala Studies in History of Science: Vol. 18). (Illus.). 232p. (C). 1994. reprint ed. pap. text 14.95 (*0-88135-154-7*, Sci Hist); reprint ed. lib. bdg. 19.95 (*0-88135-155-5*, Sci Hist) Watson Pub Intl.

Linnaeus Protist. K. W. Estep & F. Rey. 1995. 42.95 (*3-540-14502-8*); cd-rom 39.00 (*3-540-14503-6*) Spr-Verlag.

Linnea in Monet's Garden. Christina Bjork. Tr. by Joan Sandin from SWE. LC 87-45163. (Illus.). 52p. (J). (gr. 4-7). 1987. 13.00 (*91-29-58314-4*, Pub. by R & S Bks) FS&G.

Linnea's Alamanac. Christina Bjork. Tr. by Joan Sandin. LC 89-83540. (Illus.). 60p. (J). (gr. 2-5). 13.00 (*91-29-59176-7*, Pub. by R & S Bks) FS&G.

Linnea's Windowsill Garden. Christina Bjork. LC 87-15016. (Illus.). 60p. (J). 13.00 (*91-29-59064-7*, Pub. by R & S Bks) FS&G.

Linnea's Windowsill Garden. Storey Publishing Staff. 1997. 13.00 (*0-676-57049-6*) Random.

Linnet's Folly. large type ed. Jacquelyn Aeby. (Linford Mystery Library). 256p. 1993. pap. 16.99 (*0-7089-7426-0*, Linford) Ulverscroft.

Linney's Secret. Lois Moore. 200p. 1998. pap. 10.95 (*1-57532-161-0*) Press-Tige Pub.

Linnie, Your Water's Boiling! Patricia M. Spross. (Illus.). 224p. (Orig.). 1993. pap. 9.95 (*0-923568-35-2*) Wilderness Adventure Bks.

Linn's ABC Book. (Illus.). 28p. (Orig.). (J). (ps). 1993. 9.95 (*0-940403-57-9*) Linns Stamp News.

Linn's Focus on Forgeries: How to Detect Forgeries of Common Stamps. Varro E. Tyler. (Illus.). 168p. (Orig.). 1993. pap. 14.95 (*0-940403-55-2*) Linns Stamp News.

Linn's Guide to Stamp Collecting Software & Collecting on the Internet. William F. Sharpe. (Illus.). 96p. 1997. pap. 14.95 (*0-940403-76-5*) Linns Stamp News.

Linn's History of a Fragment of the Clan Linn & a Genealogy of the Linn & Related Families. George W. Linn. 204p. 1996. reprint ed. pap. 31.00 (*0-8328-5334-8*); reprint ed. lib. bdg. 41.00 (*0-8328-5333-X*) Higginson Bk Co.

Linn's Introduction to the Stamps of Mexico. Dale Pulver. 112p. 1992. 30.00 (*0-940403-49-8*) Linns Stamp News.

Linn's Introduction to the Stamps of Mexico. Dale Pulver. (Illus.). 112p. 1992. pap. 14.95 (*0-940403-48-X*) Linns Stamp News.

Linn's Introduction to U. S. Revenue Stamps. Richard Friedberg. (Handbook Ser.: Vol. 4). (Illus.). 160p. (Orig.). 1994. 30.00 (*0-940403-63-3*); pap. 14.95 (*0-940403-62-5*) Linns Stamp News.

Linn's More Who's Who on U. S. Stamps. Richard L. Thomas. 288p. 1992. 30.00 (*0-940403-51-X*); pap. 14.95 (*0-940403-50-1*) Linns Stamp News.

Linn's Philatelic Gems, No. 4. Donna O'Keefe. (Illus.). 167p. 1989. pap. 9.95 (*0-940403-12-9*) Linns Stamp News.

Linn's Stamp Identifier. Ed. by Donna O'Keefe. LC 93-2693. 144p. (Orig.). 1993. pap. 9.95 (*0-940403-52-8*) Linns Stamp News.

Linn's U. S. Stamp Yearbook, 1998, Vol. 16. George Amick. (Illus.). 504p. 1999. 35.00 (*0-940403-84-6*) Linns Stamp News.

Linn's U. S. Stamp Yearbook, 1988. George Amick. 384p. 1989. 35.00 (*0-940403-15-3*); pap. 22.00 (*0-940403-11-0*) Linns Stamp News.

Linn's U. S. Stamp Yearbook, 1987. Fred Boughner. (Illus.). 240p. (Orig.). 1988. pap. 22.00 (*0-940403-07-2*) Linns Stamp News.

Linn's U. S. Stamp Yearbook, 1983. Fred Boughner. (Illus.). 240p. (Orig.). 1984. pap. 22.00 (*0-940403-31-5*) Linns Stamp News.

Linn's U. S. Stamp Yearbook, 1985. Fred Boughner. 304p. (Orig.). 1985. pap. 22.00 (*0-940403-33-1*) Linns Stamp News.

Linn's U. S. Stamp Yearbook, 1989. George Amick. (Illus.). 300p. 1990. reprint ed. 35.00 (*0-940403-24-2*); reprint ed. pap. 25.00 (*0-940403-23-4*) Linns Stamp News.

Linn's U. S. Stamp Yearbook, 1986. Fred Boughner. (Illus.). 240p. 1987. reprint ed. pap. 25.00 (*0-940403-01-3*) Linns Stamp News.

Linn's U. S. Stamp Yearbook, 1984. Fred Boughner. 288p. 1985. reprint ed. pap. 25.00 (*0-940403-32-3*) Linns Stamp News.

Linn's U. S. Stamp Yearbook, 1994. George Amick. 504p. (Orig.). 1995. 35.00 (*0-940403-65-X*) Linns Stamp News.

Linn's U. S. Stamp Yearbook, 1994. George Amick. 512p. (Orig.). 1995. pap. 22.00 (*0-940403-64-1*) Linns Stamp News.

Linn's U. S. Stamp Yearbook, 1990. George Amick. (Illus.). 300p. (Orig.). 1991. 35.00 (*0-940403-41-2*); pap. 22.00 (*0-940403-40-4*) Linns Stamp News.

Linn's U. S. Stamp Yearbook, 1991. George Amick. (Illus.). 448p. (Orig.). 1992. 35.00 (*0-940403-47-1*); pap. 22.00 (*0-940403-46-3*) Linns Stamp News.

Linn's U. S. Stamp Yearbook, 1992. George Amick. (Illus.). 448p. (Orig.). 1993. 35.00 (*0-940403-54-4*); pap. 22.00 (*0-940403-53-6*) Linns Stamp News.

Linn's U. S. Stamp Yearbook, 1993. George Amick. (Illus.). 408p. (Orig.). 1994. 35.00 (*0-940403-61-7*); pap. 22.00 (*0-940403-60-9*) Linns Stamp News.

Linn's U. S. Stamp Yearbook, 1996. George Amick. (Illus.). 456p. 1997. 35.00 (*0-940403-73-0*); pap. 22.00 (*0-940403-72-2*) Linns Stamp News.

Lino Tagliapietra. Thomas S. Buechner. 1998. 75.00 (*1-902535-01-4*) Antique Collect.

Lino Tagliapietra Glass, 1980-1993. Giovanni Sarpellon. (Illus.). 160p. 1994. 50.00 (*88-7743-149-0*, Pub. by Arsenale Editrice) Antique Collect.

Linocuts of the Machine Age: Claude Flig. limited ed. Coppel. 205p. 1995. 795.00 (*1-85928-179-6*) Ashgate Pub Co.

Linocuts of the Machine Age A Catalogue Raisonne: Claude Flight & His Followers. Stephan Coppel. 205p. 1995. 139.95 (*0-85967-945-4*, Pub. by Scolar Pr) Ashgate Pub Co.

Linoleum, Better Babies, & the Modern Farm Woman, 1890-1930. LC 94-18773. (Illus.). 250p. 1995. 34.95 (*0-8263-1635-2*) U of NM Pr.

Linoleum Block Printing. Francis J. Kafka. (Illus.). 84p. 1972. reprint ed. pap. 6.95 (*0-486-20308-5*) Dover.

L'Inoubliable Fondateur see Man Lowell Remembered: Andre Garin OMI, 1822-1895

LINPACK Users' Guide. Jack J. Dongarra et al. LC 78-78206. (Miscellaneous Bks.: No. 8). viii, 367p. 1979. pap. 40.50 (*0-89871-172-X*) Soc Indus-Appl Math.

Linpar for Windows: Matrix Parameters for Multiconductor Transmission Lines. Antonije R. Djordjevic et al. 234p. 1999. pap. 375.00 (*1-58053-061-3*) Artech Hse.

Lin's Backpack see Mochila de Lin

Linscott's Directory of Immunological & Biological Reagents. 10th rev. ed. William D. Linscott. 377p. 1998. pap. 85.00 (*0-9604920-9-7*) Linscotts Direct.

***L'Inscription de l'Oral et de l'Ecrit Dans le Theatre de Tristan Tzara.** Katherine Papachristos. (Currents in Comparative Romance Languages & Literatures Ser.: Vol. 69). xi, 226p. (C). 1999. text 51.00 (*0-8204-3956-8*) P Lang Pubng.

Linsey Woolsey. Tasha Tudor. (Illus.). 50p. (J). 1998. 6.95 (*0-446-91216-6*) Warner Bks.

Linsey-Woolsey & Pongees: John Hampton Atkinson: A Retrospective 1868-1953. John H. Atkinson. Ed. by Marian Tisdale. LC 86-50281. (Illus.). 176p. 1986. write for info. (*0-9616672-0-6*) Tisdale Pub.

Excerpts from articles & books of a native of rural, southern Ohio, reflecting the life, ideals & values of early settlers of the 19th Century, plus a complete collection of the poems of this dedicated professor of English. ***Publisher Paid Annotation.***

LINSTAT '93: Proceedings of the International Conference on Linear Statistical Inference. Ed. by T. Calinski. LC 94-32306. (Mathematics & Its Applications Ser.: Vol. 306). xviii, 306p. (C). 1994. text 166.50 (*0-7923-3136-2*) Kluwer Academic.

Lint. Mark Dunster. 24p. (Orig.). 1983. pap. 4.00 (*0-89642-100-7*) Linden Pubs.

Lint Testing: A Panel Discussion: Transcription of Panel Discussion on Lint Testing TAPPI Printing & Reporgraphy Conference, Chicago, IL, November 10, 1980. Technical Association of the Pulp & Paper Industry. Ed. by Patrice J. Mangin. LC 84-189656. 35p. reprint ed. pap. 30.00 (*0-608-14577-7*, 202492000040) Bks Demand.

Linton: The Trainer's Resource Directory. 5th rev. ed. Orig. Title: The Linton Register. (Illus.). 600p. 1996. pap. 125.00 (*0-9626607-2-8*) Linton Pub Co.

Linton Register see Linton: The Trainer's Resource Directory

Linton Register, 1990-1991: The Trainer's Resource Directory. Ed. by Thomas Linton. 2000p. (C). 1992. 125.00 (*0-9626607-0-1*) Linton Pub Co.

Linus & Lucy the Pink Panther. 56p. (Orig.). 1994. pap. 9.95 (*0-7692-1036-8*, F3009SMB) Wrner Bros.

Linus Pauling. Ted Goertzel & Ben Goertzel. 384p. 1996. pap. 16.00 (*0-465-00673-6*) HarpC.

***Linus Pauling.** Tom Hager. (Oxford Portraits in Science Ser.). (Illus.). 144p. 2000. pap. 11.95 (*0-19-513972-0*) OUP.

Linus Pauling: And the Chemistry of Life. Tom Hager. LC 97-43403. (Oxford Portraits in Science Ser.). (Illus.). 144p. (J). (gr. 7 up). 1998. 22.00 (*0-19-510853-1*) OUP.

Linus Pauling: Investigating the Magic Within. Victoria Sherrow. LC 96-20311. (Innovative Minds Ser.). 112p. (J). 1997. lib. bdg. 27.11 (*0-8172-4400-X*) Raintree Steck-V.

Linus Pauling: Scientist & Advocate. David E. Newton. LC 93-31719. (Makers of Modern Science Ser.). (Illus.). 144p. (YA). (gr. 7-12). 1994. 19.95 (*0-8160-2959-8*) Facts on File.

Linus Pauling in His Own Words: Selections from Writings Speeches & Interviews. Ed. by Barbara Marinacci. 384p. 1995. 27.50 (*0-684-80749-1*, Touchstone) S&S Trade Pap.

Linus Pauling on Peace: A Scientist Speaks Out on Humanism & World Survival. Linus Pauling. Ed. by Barbara Marinacci & Ramesh Krishnamurthy. LC 98-86622. (Illus.). 296p. 1998. pap. 17.95 (*0-933670-03-6*) Rising Star.

Linus Welch. Toby Amirault. 80p. (Orig.). 1991. pap. 7.95 (*0-9625432-0-9*) Ivy Pr MA.

***Linux.** John Levine. 1999. pap. write for info. (*0-201-35456-X*) Peachpit Pr.

***Linux.** 3rd ed. Richard Petersen. (Unix Tools Ser.). 900p. 1999. pap. 39.99 (*0-07-212161-0*) Osborne-McGraw.

Linux: A Webserver for Your Office. 500p. 1920. 34.99 (*0-672-31833-4*) Sams.

Linux: Configuration & Installation. Patrick Volkerding et al. 552p. 1995. pap. 39.95 incl. cd-rom (*1-55828-426-5*, MIS Pr) IDG Bks.

***Linux! I Didn't Know You Could Do That...** 4th ed. Nicholas Wells. 304p. 1999. pap. text 19.99 (*0-7821-2612-X*) Sybex.

Linux: Installation, Configuration, Use. 2nd ed. Michael Kofler. 800p. (C). 1999. pap. text 44.95 (*0-201-59628-8*) Addison-Wesley.

***Linux: Module 1.** Niit. (CT Course Instructor Training Ser.). 2000. 8.00 (*0-619-02344-9*) Course Tech.

***Linux: Module 2.** Niit. (CT Course Instructor Training Ser.). 2000. 8.00 (*0-619-02345-7*) Course Tech.

Linux: The Complete Reference. Richard Petersen. (Complete Reference Ser.). 816p. 1996. pap. text 39.95 (*0-07-882189-4*) Osborne-McGraw.

Linux: The Complete Reference. 2nd ed. Richard Petersen. LC 98-116323. (Complete Reference Ser.). 1008p. 1997. pap. 49.99 (*0-07-882461-3*) Osborne-McGraw.

***Linux: The Complete Reference.** 3rd ed. Richard Petersen. 929p. 1999. pap. 39.99 (*0-07-212164-5*) Osborne-McGraw.

Linux: The Complete Reference. 7th ed. Ed. by Robert Kiesling. 1631p. 1998. pap. 39.95 (*1-57176-199-3*) Walnut Creek.

***Linux: The Complete Reference.** 7th ed. John Purcell. (Illus.). 2000. pap. text 39.95 (*1-57176-165-9*) Walnut Creek.

***Linux: The Complete Reference Advanced.** 7th ed. John Purcell. (Illus.). 1999. pap. text 39.95 (*1-57176-249-3*) Walnut Creek.

***Linux Vol. 1: AC - Zcat: The Basics.** Dale Scheetz & Mark Williams Company Staff. xix, 602p. 1999. pap. 42.95 (*0-9659575-2-7*) Linux Pr.

***Linux - Guia del Administrador en Espanol: Linux - Administrator's Guide in Spanish.** deluxe ed. Hector Facundo Arena. (Manuales Compumagazine Ser.). (SPA., Illus.). 288p. 2000. pap. 19.90 incl. cd-rom (*987-526-035-5*, Pub. by MP Ediciones) Downtown Bk.

Linux - Unleashing the Workstation in Your PC. 3rd ed. S. Strobel. Tr. by Robert Bach & Aileen Darling. LC 97-10096. (Illus.). 608p. 1997. pap. 29.95 (*0-387-94880-5*) Spr-Verlag.

Linux A to Z. Phil Cornes. LC 96-25462. (C). 1996. pap. 34.95 (*0-13-234709-1*) P-H.

***Linux Administracion: Version 2.0 a 2.2 del Nucleo.** ENI Publishing Ltd. Staff. (Mega Plus Ser.). 2000. pap. text 24.95 (*2-7460-0686-3*) ENI Publng.

***Linux Administration: A Beginner's Guide.** Steve Shah. 1999. pap. 39.99 (*0-07-212229-3*) Osborne-McGraw.

Linux Administration Black Book. Steve Pritchard. (Black Book Ser.). 1999. pap. text 49.99 (*1-57610-419-2*) Coriolis Grp.

***Linux Administration by Example.** Que Corporation Staff. 550p. 2000. 24.99 (*0-7897-2313-1*) Que.

***Linux Administration for Dummies.** Michael Bellomo. (For Dummies). 408p. 1999. pap. 24.99 incl. cd-rom (*0-7645-0589-0*) IDG Bks.

***Linux Administration Kernal Version 2.0 to 2.2.** ENI Publishing Ltd. Staff. (Keeping Ahead Ser.). 1999. pap. 24.95 (*2-7460-0535-2*) ENI Publng.

Linux Administrator's Guide. Ray Mendonsa. 800p. 2000. pap. 49.99 (*0-7615-2157-7*) Prima Pub.

Linux & Unix Shell Programming. David Tansley. 320p. (C). 1999. pap. text 44.95 (*0-201-67472-6*) Addison-Wesley.

Linux & Windows NT: Integration & Migration. Arnold Villeneuve. (UNIX Tools Ser.). 544p. 1999. pap. 39.99 (*0-07-134983-9*) McGraw.

***Linux Apache Web Server Administration.** Charles Aulds. (Illus.). 2000. pap. 39.99 (*0-7821-2734-7*) Sybex.

Linux Application Development. Michael Johnson. LC 97-49039. 576p. (C). 1998. 47.95 (*0-201-30821-5*) Addison-Wesley.

***Linux Assembly Language Programming.** Bob Neveln. 350p. 2000. pap. 44.99 incl. cd-rom (*0-13-087940-1*, Prentice Hall) P-H.

Linux at Work: Building Strategic Applications for Business. Marcus Goncalves. LC 99-10789. (Illus.). 384p. (C). 1999. pap. 39.99 incl. cd-rom (*0-471-33349-2*) Wiley.

***Linux Bible.** Candace Leiden. (Bible Ser.). (Illus.). 1000p. 2000. pap. text 39.99 (*0-7645-4662-7*) IDG Bks.

L

L

Linux Bible: The GNU Testament. Linux Documentation Project Staff & Yggdrasil Computing, Inc. Staff. (Illus.). 764p. 1994. pap. 39.95 (*1-883601-07-X*) Yggdrasil Comput.

Linux Bible: The GNU Testament. 2nd ed. Linux Documentation Project Staff & Yggdrasil Computing, Inc. Staff. (Illus.). 1000p. 1994. pap. 34.95 (*1-883601-11-8*) Yggdrasil Comput.

Linux Bible: The GNU Testament. 3rd ed. 1591p. 1996. 39.95 incl. cd-rom (*1-883601-12-6*, Ibib) Yggdrasil Comput.

Linux Bible: The GNU Testament. 4th ed. Linux Documentation Project Staff. LC 96-25216. (Illus.). 1850p. Date not set. pap. 39.95 incl. cd-rom (*1-883601-20-7*) Yggdrasil Comput.

***Linux by Example.** Bruno Bratti & Ted Brockwood. (Illus.). 450p. 2000. 24.99 (*0-7897-2260-7*) Que.

Linux Clearly Explained. Bryan Pfaffenberger. (Clearly Explained Ser.). 300p. (C). 1999. pap. 44.95 incl. cd-rom (*0-12-553169-9*) Acad Pr.

***Linux Command Instant Reference.** Bryan Pfaffenberger. 2000. pap. 24.99 (*0-7821-2748-7*) Sybex.

***Linux Command Summary.** Clarica Grove & Phil Hughes. 174p. 2000. 8.00 (*1-57831-014-8*) Specialized Sys.

***Linux Complete.** Grant Taylor. 1040p. 1999. 19.99 (*0-7821-2567-0*) Sybex.

Linux Complete Command Reference. John Purcel. LC 97-66202. 1495p. 1997. 49.99 (*0-672-31104-6*) Sams.

Linux Configuration & Installation. 3rd ed. Volkerding et al. 1997. 39.95 incl. audio compact disk (*0-8052-8566-0*, M&T Bks) IDG Bks.

Linux Configuration & Installation. 4th ed. Patrick Volkerding et al. 600p. 1998. 39.99 incl. cd-rom (*0-7645-7005-6*, M&T Bks) IDG Bks.

Linux Core Kernel Commentary. Scott E. Maxwell. LC 99-45422. 575p. 1999. pap. text 39.99 (*1-57610-469-9*) Coriolis Grp.

***Linux Database Bible.** Uche Ogbuji. 650p. 2000. pap. 39.99 (*0-7645-4641-4*) IDG Bks.

Linux Database Design & Development with Postgresql. 504p. 1920. 39.99 (*0-672-31866-0*) Sams.

***Linux Desk Reference.** Scott Hawkins. 600p. 1999. pap. 34.99 (*0-13-016391-0*) P-H.

Linux Device Drivers. Alessandro Rubini. Ed. by Andy Oram. LC 98-134181. 442p. (Orig.). 1998. pap. 29.95 (*1-56592-292-1*) OReilly & Assocs.

***Linux DNS Server Administration.** Craig Hunt. (Illus.). 2000. pap. 39.99 (*0-7821-2736-3*) Sybex.

Linux, DOS, & Windows: A How to Build Yourself a 95/NT, 2000 Microsoft Active Directory Clone Now with NDS Networking! Reginald Burgess. (Illus.). 267p. 1999. pap. 37.95 (*1-891950-03-7*) Amer Group Pub.

Linux, DOS, & Windows . . . How to Build Yourself a 95/NT Clone: Available CD with Linux Operating System, Netscape Browser, Real Audio Player, Caldera 1.3 O/S & 2nd CD with Apps. Reginald Burgess. 160p. 1997. pap. 27.95 incl. cd-rom (*1-891950-02-9*, 98190201) Amer Group Pub.

Linux Encyclopedia. 6th rev. ed. Matt Welsh et al. Ed. by Mark Bolzern. (Linux-Flagship Ser.). (Illus.). 1600p. 1998. pap. 49.00 (*0-9644309-2-4*) WrkGrp Solns.

***Linux Enterprise Administration Certification Handbook.** Caldera Systems Staff. (Open Source Technology Ser.). 520p. 2000. pap. text 44.99 (*0-13-019314-3*) P-H.

***Linux Enterprise Security.** John's Flowers Staff. (Circle Ser.). 400p. 1999. pap. 39.99 (*1-57870-197-X*) New Riders Pub.

***Linux Essential Reference.** Ed Petron. (Essential Reference Ser.). 400p. 1999. pap. 37.95 (*0-7357-0852-5*) New Riders Pub.

***Linux Exam Prep.** Dee-Ann LeBlanc. (Exam Prep Ser.). (Illus.). 695p. 1999. pap. 49.99 (*1-57610-567-9*) Coriolis Grp.

Linux Firewalls. Robert Ziegler. 350p. 1999. 29.99 (*0-7357-0900-9*) New Riders Pub.

Linux for Dummies. 2nd ed. Jon Hall et al. LC 99-60531. (For Dummies Ser.). (Illus.). 384p. 1999. pap. 24.99 incl. cd-rom (*0-7645-0421-5*) IDG Bks.

***Linux for Dummies.** 3rd ed. Jon Hall. (For Dummies Ser.). 384p. 2000. pap. 24.99 incl. cd-rom (*0-7645-0744-3*) IDG Bks.

Linux for Dummies Quick Reference. 2nd ed. Phil Hughes. LC QA76.76.O63H844 1998. (For Dummies). 224p. 1998. spiral bd. 14.99 (*0-7645-0422-3*) IDG Bks.

***Linux for Kids.** Bob Rankin. LC 00-30741. 2000. pap. 24.95 (*1-886411-39-5*) No Starch Pr.

Linux for Scientists. Yamazaki. (C). 1995. pap. text. write for info. (*0-201-42735-4*) Addison-Wesley.

***Linux for the Laptop.** David Williams. 300p. 2000. pap. 29.99 (*0-13-017228-6*) P-H.

Linux for User & System Administrators. Mark F. Komarinski. LC 96-3083. 208p. 1996. pap. text 24.95 (*0-13-231838-5*) P-H.

***Linux for Your Laptop.** Bill Ball. 2000. pap. 39.99 (*0-7615-2816-4*) Prima Pub.

Linux from PC to Workstation: Unleashing the Workstation in Your PC. Stefan Strobel & Thomas Uhl. Tr. by Robert Bach. LC 94-34258. 1994. write for info. (*3-540-58077-8*) Spr-Verlag.

Linux from PC to Workstation: Unleashing the Workstation in Your PC. Thomas Uhl et al. 265p. 1995. pap. 29.00 (*0-387-58077-8*) Spr-Verlag.

Linux from PC to Workstation: Unleashing the Workstation in Your PC. 2nd ed. Thomas Uhl & Stefan Strobel. 446p. 1995. pap. text 32.95 (*0-387-94601-2*) Spr-Verlag.

***Linux Fundamentals: A4, Version 3.07.** Jeremy Teitelbaum. Ed. by Jill McKenna & Susan M. Lane. (Certified Linux Administrator Track A4 Ser.). (Illus.). 1999. pap. write for info. (*1-58143-101-5*) Prosoft I-net.

***Linux Fundamentals: Version 3.07.** Jeremy Teitelbaum. Ed. by Jill McKenna & Susan M. Lane. (Certified Linux Administrator Track Ser.). (Illus.). 1999. pap. write for info. (*1-58143-097-3*) Prosoft I-net.

***Linux GNOME/GTK+ Programming Bible.** Arthur Griffith. (Bible Ser.). 888p. 2000. pap. text 39.99 (*0-7645-4640-6*) IDG Bks.

***Linux Graphics Programming with SVGalib: An Easy to Use Reference for Linux Graphics Programmers.** Jay Link. LC 99-53503. (Illus.). 600p. 2000. pap. 49.99 (*1-57610-524-5*) Coriolis Grp.

***Linux Hardware Handbook: Selecting, Installing, & Configuring the Right Components for Your Linux System.** Roderick Smith. 700p. 2000. 39.99 (*0-672-31918-7*) Sams.

***Linux in a Box for Dummies.** Ed. by IDG Books Staff. (For Dummies Ser.). (Illus.). 128p. 2000. pap. 24.99 incl. cd-rom (*0-7645-0714-1*) IDG Bks.

***Linux in a Nutshell.** 2nd ed. Ellen Siever & O'Reilly & Associates Staff. Ed. by Andy Oram. (In a Nutshell Ser.). (Illus.). 628p. 1999. pap. 29.95 (*1-56592-585-8*) OReilly & Assocs.

***Linux in a Nutshell.** 3rd ed. Ellen Siever. (In a Nutshell Ser.). 2000. pap. 29.95 (*0-596-00025-1*) OReilly & Assocs.

Linux Install & Configuration Little Black Book. Dee-Ann LeBlanc. LC 99-43504. 1999. pap. text 24.99 (*1-57610-489-3*) Coriolis Grp.

***Linux Internals.** Moshe Bar. (Application Development Ser.). (Illus.). 2000. pap. 49.99 (*0-07-212598-5*) Osborne-McGraw.

***Linux Internet Server: Visual Black Book.** Coriolis Group Staff. LC 00-22693. (Illus.). 250p. 1999. pap. write for info. (*1-57610-569-5*) Coriolis Grp.

Linux IP Stacks Commentary. Stephen Satchell & H. B. J. Clifford. LC 99-45280. 1999. pap. text 39.99 (*1-57610-470-2*) Coriolis Grp.

***Linux Journal 94-98 Archive CD-ROM.** (Illus.). 1999. 29.95 (*1-57831-013-X*) Specialized Sys.

Linux Kernel. Rusling. (ITCP-UK Computer Science Ser.). (C). 1998. pap. 34.99 (*1-85032-338-0*, VNR) Wiley.

Linux Kernel Architecture. 600p. 1900. 49.99 (*1-57169-167-7*, Waite Grp Pr) Sams.

Linux Kernel Book Card. pap. text. write for info. (*0-471-49178-0*) Wiley.

Linux Kernel Book. Remy Card & Eric Dumas. LC 98-18121. 548p. 1998. pap. text 49.00 incl. cd-rom (*0-471-98141-9*) Wiley.

Linux Kernel Internals. 2nd ed. Michael Beck et al. LC 98-120732. (Illus.). 496p. 1997. pap. text 49.95 (*0-201-33143-8*) Peachpit Pr.

Linux Man: The Essential Man Pages for Linux. Ed. by John Purcell. 1218p. 1996. 29.95 (*1-885329-07-5*, Iman) Linux Syst.

Linux Mandrake O/S 7.0 Professional Suite Edition. 1900. 149.95 (*1-57595-399-4*) Macmillan Digit.

Linux Mandrake O/S 7.0 Secure Server Edition. 1900. 99.95 (*1-57595-401-X*) Macmillan Digit.

***Linux-Mandrake Six: Unleashed.** 1200p. 2000. 39.99 (*0-672-31811-3*) Sams.

***LINUX Manual de Referencia en Espanol/Spanish con CDROM.** Luis Tomas Wayar. (SPA.). 228p. 1999. pap. 19.90 incl. cd-rom (*987-97441-2-8*, Pub. by MP Ediciones) Am Wholesale.

Linux Multimedia Guide. Jeff Tranter. Ed. by Andy Oram. LC 96-228345. (Illus.). 386p. (Orig.). 1996. pap. 32.95 (*1-56592-219-0*) Thomson Learn.

***Linux Music & Sound.** Dave Phillips. LC 99-42680. (Illus.). 350p. 2000. 39.95 (*1-886411-34-4*) No Starch Pr.

Linux Network. Fred Butzen & Christopher Hilton. 552p. 1998. 39.99 incl. cd-rom (*1-55828-589-X*, M&T Bks) IDG Bks.

***Linux Network Administration Certification Handbook.** Caldera Systems Staff. (Open Source Technology Ser.). 500p. 2000. pap. text 44.99 (*0-13-019315-1*) P-H.

***Linux Network Administration Certification Handbook: Solutions Manual.** 2000. write for info. (*0-13-019383-6*) P-H.

Linux Network Administrator's Guide. Olaf Kirch. Ed. by Andy Oram. (Illus.). 400p. 1995. pap. 29.95 (*1-56592-087-2*) Thomson Learn.

Linux Network Administrator's Guide. 2nd ed. Olaf Kirch & Terry Dawson. Ed. by Andy Oram. (Illus.). 450p. 2000. pap. 34.95 (*1-56592-400-2*) OReilly & Assocs.

***Linux Network Administrator's Interactive Workbook.** Joe Kaplenk. 552p. 1999. pap. text 39.99 incl. audio compact disk (*0-13-020790-X*) P-H.

***Linux Network Management Tools.** Steve Maxwell. (Illus.). 2000. pap. 49.99 (*0-07-212262-5*) McGrw-H Intl.

Linux Network Servers. 3rd ed. Craig Hunt. (24seven Ser.). 672p. 1999. pap. text 34.99 (*0-7821-2506-9*) Sybex.

Linux Network Toolkit. Paul G. Sery. LC 97-75020. (Illus.). 624p. 1998. pap. 49.99 (*0-7645-3146-8*) IDG Bks.

***Linux Networking Clearly Explained.** Bryan Pfaffenberger. (Clearly Explained Ser.). (Illus.). 400p. 2000. pap. text 44.95 (*0-12-533171-1*) Morgan Kaufmann.

***Linux Networking Unleashed.** Matthew Marsh. (Illus.). 1100p. 2000. 49.99 (*0-672-31765-6*) Sams.

Linux Pro - Installation & More: Why Linux? Fall in Love Again. Paul Poduska et al. Ed. by Mark Bolzern. (Illus.). 40p. (Orig.). 1997. pap. 19.95 incl. cd-rom (*1-888894-39-3*) WrkGrp Solns.

Linux Pro Sampler, 5 CD-Roms. Paul R. Poduska. (Illus.). 134p. 1998. pap. 49.00 incl. cd-rom (*1-888894-42-3*) IPG Chicago.

Linux Pro User's Guide. (Illus.). 180p. 1996. pap. 39.00 incl. cd-rom (*0-9644309-9-1*) WrkGrp Solns.

***Linux Problem Solver: What to Do When Linux Won't Print, Fax, Backup, or Connect to the Web.** Brian Ward. LC 99-49513. (Illus.). 300p. 2000. pap. 34.95 incl. cd-rom (*1-886411-35-2*) No Starch Pr.

Linux Programmer's Reference. Richard Petersen. LC 98-216387. 303p. 1998. pap. 16.99 (*0-07-882587-3*) Osborne-McGraw.

***Linux Programmer's Reference.** 2nd ed. Richard Petersen. 443p. 1999. pap. 19.99 (*0-07-212355-9*) McGraw.

Linux Programming. Patrick Volkerding. LC 96-46890. 408p. 1996. pap. 39.95 (*1-55828-507-5*, MIS Pr) IDG Bks.

***Linux Programming Bible.** John Goerzen. 864p. 2000. pap. 39.99 (*0-7645-4657-0*) IDG Bks.

***Linux Programming for Dummies.** Francis Litterio. (For Dummies Ser.). 384p. 2000. pap. 24.99 (*0-7645-0691-9*) IDG Bks.

Linux Programming Unleashed. Kurt Wallace. (Illus.). 1999. pap. text 39.99 (*0-672-31607-2*) Sams.

***Linux Programming White Papers.** Esther Schindler. LC 99-47031. 1999. 24.99 (*1-57610-473-7*) Coriolis Grp.

Linux Quick Reference. Michele Petrovsky. 200p. 1999. pap. 9.99 (*0-7897-2170-8*) Que.

Linux Quick Reference: International Edition. 200p. 9.99 (*0-7897-2188-0*) Que.

***Linux Routers: A Primer for Network Administrators.** Tony Mancil. 350p. 2000. 44.99 (*0-13-086113-8*) P-H.

Linux Sampler. Ed. by Belinda Frazier & Laurie Tucker. 250p. (Orig.). 1994. pap. 18.95 (*0-916151-74-3*) Specialized Sys.

Linux Security. John S. Flowers. 1999. pap. text 29.99 (*0-7357-0035-4*) Que.

***Linux Security Toolkit.** David A. Bandel. 480p. 2000. pap. text 39.99 (*0-7645-4690-2*) IDG Bks.

***Linux Shells by Example.** Ellie Quigley. LC 00-24614. (Illus.). 784p. 2000. pap. text 44.99 incl. cd-rom (*0-13-014711-7*) P-H.

***Linux Socket Programming.** Sean Walton. (Illus.). 400p. 2000. pap. 39.99 incl. cd-rom (*1-57169-173-1*, Waite Grp Pr) Sams.

***Linux Socket Programming.** Sean Walton. 2000. pap. 39.99 (*0-672-31935-7*) Sams.

***Linux Socket Programming: By Example.** Warren W. Gay. LC 99-66454. (Illus.). 576p. 2000. 29.99 (*0-7897-2241-0*) Que.

Linux Start-Up Guide: A Self-Contained Introduction. F. Hantelmann. Tr. by A. Faber & R. Pook from GER. LC 97-30066. (Illus.). 320p. 1997. pap. 29.95 (*3-540-62676-X*) Spr-Verlag.

Linux System Administration. (Professional Ser.). 448p. 1999. 29.99 (*1-56205-934-3*) New Riders Pub.

***Linux System Administration.** (Illus.). 608p. 2000. pap. 39.99 (*0-7821-2735-5*) Sybex.

Linux System Administration. Anne Carasik. LC QA76.76.O63C3729. 480p. 1998. pap. text 39.99 (*0-7645-7008-0*, M&T Bks) IDG Bks.

Linux System Administration. Walker. 1998. 39.95 (*1-55828-600-4*, MIS Pr) IDG Bks.

***Linux System Administration Certification Handbook.** Caldera Systems Staff. (Open Source Technology Ser.). 490p. 2000. pap. text 44.99 (*0-13-019317-8*) P-H.

***Linux System Administration Certification Handbook: Solutions Manual.** 2000. write for info. (*0-13-019384-4*) P-H.

Linux System Administration Handbook. Carey Collet & Mark F. Komarinski. LC 97-52143. 416p. (C). 1998. pap. text 39.95 (*0-13-680596-5*) P-H.

***Linux System Administration White Papers.** Esther Schindler. LC 99-38872. 1999. pap. 24.99 (*1-57610-474-5*) Coriolis Grp.

***Linux System Administrator's Survival Guide.** 2nd ed. Timothy Parker. (Illus.). 1999. pap. 49.99 (*0-672-31793-1*) Sams.

***Linux System & Network Administration: A4, Version 3.07.** Jeremy Teitelbaum. Ed. by Susan M. Lane & Jill McKenna. (Certified Linux Administrator Track A4 Ser.). (Illus.). 1999. pap. write for info. (*1-58143-102-3*) Prosoft I-net.

***Linux System & Network Administration: Version 3.07.** Jeremy Teitelbaum. Ed. by Susan M. Lane & Jill McKenna. (Certified Linux Administrator Track Ser.). (Illus.). 1999. pap. write for info. (*1-58143-098-1*) Prosoft I-net.

***Linux System Commands.** Patrick Volkerding. 480p. 2000. pap. 19.99 (*0-7645-4669-4*) IDG Bks.

***Linux System Security.** 1999. 59.95 (*1-57595-332-3*) Macmillan Digit.

***Linux System Security: The Administrator's Guide to Open Source Security Tools.** Scott Mann. LC 99-59100. 604p. 1999. 48.99 (*0-13-015807-0*) P-H.

Linux Universe: Installation & Configuration. Thomas Uhl & Stefan Strobel. (Illus.). viii, 152p. 1995. pap. 38.95 incl. cd-rom (*0-387-94506-7*) Spr-Verlag.

Linux Universe: Installation & Configuration. 2nd ed. Thomas Uhl & Stefan Strobel. LC 96-124069. 156p. 1996. pap. text 38.95 incl. audio compact disk (*0-387-94600-4*) Spr-Verlag.

Linux Universe: Installation & Configuration. 3rd ed. Stefan Strobel et al. LC 96-53012. (Illus.). 228p. 1997. text 34.95 incl. cd-rom (*0-387-94879-1*) Spr-Verlag.

Linux Unleashed. 3rd ed. Tim Parker. LC 98-85650. 1998. pap. 39.99 (*0-672-31372-3*) Sams.

***Linux Unleashed.** 4th ed. Timothy Parker. (Unleashed Ser.). (Illus.). 1999. pap. 49.99 (*0-672-31688-9*) Sams.

Linux User Manual: The Manual You Should Have Received with Linux. Que Staff. 1998. pap. text 19.99 (*0-7897-1877-4*) Que.

Linux User's Resource: Developer's Resource. James Mohr. LC 97-22733. (Developer's Resource Ser.). 848p. (C). 1997. pap. 49.95 incl. cd-rom (*0-13-842378-4*) P-H.

Linux Web Server Toolkit. Nicholas Wells. LC 98-138213. 528p. 1998. pap. 39.99 (*0-7645-3167-0*) IDG Bks.

Linux Window Managers. 350p. 1999. 34.99 (*1-56205-933-5*) New Riders Pub.

Linux X User's Guide. Ellen Siever. Ed. by Mark Stone. (Illus.). 550p. 2000. pap. 34.95 (*1-56592-652-8*) OReilly & Assocs.

L'invitation au Chateau see Pieces Brillantes: L'invitation au chateau, Colombe, La repetition ou L'amour puni [et] L'ecole des peres

L'invitation au Chateau. Jean Anouilh. 1962. pap. 11.95 (*0-7859-0352-6*, F81877) Fr & Eur.

Linwoods: or "Sixty Years Since" in America, 2 vols. Catharine Maria Sedgwick. LC 78-64095. reprint ed. 75.00 (*0-404-17370-5*) AMS Pr.

Lion. Caroline Arnold. LC 94-23880. (More Animal Favorites ser.). (Illus.). 48p. (J). (gr. 2 up). 1995. lib. bdg. 15.93 (*0-688-12693-6*, Wm Morrow) Morrow Avon.

***Lion.** Illus. by Valerie Guidoux et al. LC 00-22082. (J). 2000. 6.95 (*0-7892-0663-3*, Abbeville Kids) Abbeville Pr.

Lion. Bill Jordan. (Natural World Ser.). 48p. (J). (gr. 4-7). 1999. pap. 7.95 (*0-7398-0948-2*) Raintree Steck-V.

Lion. Joseph Kessel. (Folio Ser.: No. 808). (FRE.). pap. 9.25 (*2-07-036808-4*) Schoenhof.

Lion. Joseph Kessel. (FRE.). 250p. 1976. pap. 10.95 (*0-7859-2371-3*, 2070368084) Fr & Eur.

***Lion.** Donna Jo Napoli. LC 99-89923. (J). 2000. write for info. (*0-689-83589-2*) Atheneum Yung Read.

***Lion: Habitats, Life Cycles, Food Chains, Threats.** Bill Jordan. LC 99-18098. 48p. (J). 2000. lib. bdg. 25.69 (*0-7398-1057-X*) Raintree Steck-V.

Lion: The History of an 1846 Locomotive Engine in Maine. Paul E. Rivard. (Business & Technology Ser.). (Illus.). 64p. 1987. pap. text 6.50 (*0-913764-19-1*) Maine St Mus.

Lion Amongst the Cattle: Reconstruction & Resistance in the Northern Transvaal. Peter Delius. LC 96-41888. (Heinemann Social History of Africa Ser.). 1997. 60.00 (*0-435-07416-4*); pap. 24.95 (*0-435-07415-6*) Heinemann.

Lion & Dragon in Northern China. Reginald F. Johnston. (Illus.). 476p. 1987. text 39.95 (*0-19-583794-0*) OUP.

Lion & Gazelle, Vol. 1. Humphreys. Date not set. pap. text 49.50 (*1-86064-229-2*, Pub. by I B T) St Martin.

Lion & Lamb see Bank Street Ready-to-Read Books: Levels 1, 2 & 3

Lion & Lamb. Cora E. Cypser. (Illus.). 95p. (Orig.). 1992. pap. 7.95 (*0-9625774-4-8*) Kim Pathways.

Lion & Lamb. Brennan Manning. LC 86-15409. 192p. (gr. 10). 1986. pap. 9.99 (*0-8007-9083-9*) Chosen Bks.

Lion & Lamb Step Out see Bank Street Ready-to-Read Books: Levels 1, 2 & 3

***Lion & the Black.** Kirk Graves. 1999. pap. text 12.95 (*1-883697-03-4*) Hara Pub.

Lion & the Boy. Sandy Lyne. (Illus.). 48p. (J). (gr. 4-7). 1988. 12.95 (*0-933905-04-1*); pap. 9.95 (*0-933905-15-7*) Claycomb Pr.

Lion & the Bull: The Gospels of Mark & Luke. Henry Wansbrough. pap. write for info. (*0-232-52162-X*) S Asia.

Lion & the Cricket. Orig. Title: El Leon y el Grillito. (Illus.). 16p. (J). (ps-3). 1972. pap. 1.00 (*0-941270-11-4*) Ancient City Pr.

Lion & the Eagle: Interdisciplinary Essays on German-Spanish Relations over the Centuries. Thomas Wolber. Ed. by Conrad Kent. LC 99-18156. 528p. 2000. 49.95 (*1-57181-131-1*) Berghahn Bks.

Lion & the Giant of My Dreams: An Autobiography. Maxene Hewitt. 176p. 1990. 19.95 (*0-86315-062-4*, 1241, Pub. by Floris Bks) Anthroposophic.

Lion & the Gypsy. Geoffrey Patterson. (J). 1990. 14.95 (*0-385-44521-0*) Doubleday.

Lion & the Hare. Kumuda Reddy & John E. Pruitt. (Illus.). 31p. (J). (gr. 1-6). 1997. 13.67 (*1-929297-09-2*, Pub. by Samhita Prodns) ACCESS Pubs Network.

***Lion & the Jackal.** Adiccabandhu & Padmasri. (Illus.). 32p. (J). 1999. pap. 10.95 (*1-899579-13-3*, Pub. by Windhorse) Weatherhill.

Lion & the Jewel. Wole Soyinka. (Three Crowns Bks.). 70p. 1966. pap. text 10.95 (*0-19-911083-2*) OUP.

***Lion & the Lamb.** John-Marc Grob. (Bible Kingdom Ser.). 2000. pap. 1.99 (*0-8054-0979-3*) Broadman.

Lion & the Lamb. John P. Newport. LC 85-29887. 384p. 1986. 14.99 (*0-8054-1324-3*, 4213-24) Broadman.

Lion & the Lamb. John P. Newport. 1998. pap. text 14.99 (*0-8054-1868-7*) Broadman.

Lion & the Lark. Doreen O. Malek. 1996. mass mkt. 4.99 (*0-8217-5291-X*, Zebra Kensgtn) Kensgtn Pub Corp.

Lion & the Little Red Bird. Elisa Kleven. (J). 1996. 11.19 (*0-606-08561-0*, Pub. by Turtleback) Demco.

Lion & The Mouse see Leonardo el Leon y Ramon el Raton

Lion & the Mouse see Leon y el Raton

***Lion & the Mouse.** Aesop. (Illus.). 32p. (J). (gr. k-3). 2000. 15.95 (*0-7358-1220-9*, Pub. by North-South Bks NYC) Chronicle Bks.

Lion & the Mouse. Aesop. LC 80-28154. (Illus.). 32p. (J). (gr. k-3). 1981. lib. bdg. 15.85 (*0-89375-466-8*) Troll Communs.

Lion & the Mouse. Aesop. (J). 1996. pap. 1.25 (*0-8167-0424-4*) Troll Communs.

Lion & the Mouse. Aesop. LC 80-28154. (Illus.). 32p. (J). (gr. k-3). 1981. pap. 3.95 (*0-89375-467-6*) Troll Communs.

Lion & the Mouse. Aesop. LC 97-220917. (Illus.). 16p. (J). 1998. write for info. (*0-8172-7266-6*) Raintree Steck-V.

Lion & the Mouse. Carol Barnett & Aesop. (Illus.). 64p. (J). (ps-3). 1994. 7.95 (*0-8442-9420-9*, Natl Textbk Co) NTC Contemp Pub Co.

An Asterisk (*) at the beginning of an entry indicates that the title is appearing for the first time.

Lion & the Mouse. Carol Barnett & Aesop. (StoryLand Fables Ser.). (Illus.). 48p. (J). (ps-4). 1995. pap. 8.95 incl. audio (0-8442-9432-2) NTC Contemp Pub Co.

***Lion & the Mouse.** Gail Herman & Aesop. LC 97-38601. (Early Step into Reading Ser.). (Illus.). 32p. (J). (ps-k). 1998. pap. 3.99 (0-679-88674-5, Pub. by Random Bks Yng Read); lib. bdg. 11.99 (0-679-98674-X, Pub. by Random Bks Yng Read) Random.

Lion & the Mouse. Carol Jones & Aesop. LC 97-1524. (J). (ps-3). 1997. 14.00 (0-395-86956-0) HM.

***Lion & the Mouse.** Lauri Posner. (Between the Lions Ser.). (Illus.). (J). 2000. pap. 3.99 (0-307-25214-0, Goldn Books) Gldn Bks Pub Co.

Lion & the Mouse. Jane P. Resnick & Aesop. (Aesop's Fables Ser.). (Illus.). (J). 1992. bds. 3.25 (0-8378-2526-1) Gibson.

Lion & the Mouse, Vol. 1. Carla Dijs & Aesop. (My First Book of Fables Ser.). (Illus.). 10p. (J). (ps-2). 1997. 5.99 (0-689-81480-1) Litle Simon.

***Lion & the Mouse: And Other Aesop's Fables.** Doris Orgel. (Illus.). 40p. (J). (ps-3). 2000. 16.95 (0-7894-2665-X) DK Pub Inc.

Lion & the Mouse: Big Book. large type ed. Cheyenne Cisco. (Little Books & Big Bks.). (Illus.). 16p. (J). (gr. 1-3). 1997. pap. text 29.85 (0-8215-0984-5) Sadlier.

Lion & the Mouse; The Wind & the Sun, 2 bks. in 1. Aesop. (Aesop's Fables - Two in One Tales Ser.). (Illus.). 24p. (Orig.). (J). (gr. 1-4). 1993. pap. 2.50 (1-56144-302-6, Honey Bear Bks) Modern Pub NYC.

Lion & the Ostrich Chicks. Ashley Bryan. (Illus.). 96p. (J). (gr. 2-6). 1996. mass mkt. 6.95 (0-689-80713-9) S&S Childrens.

Lion & the Ostrich Chicks & Other African Folk Tales. Ashley Bryan. LC 86-3349. 1996. 12.05 (0-606-09557-8, Pub. by Turtleback) Demco.

Lion & the Ostrich Chicks & Other African Folk Tales. large type ed. Illus. & Retold by Ashley Bryan. 1993. 25.00 (0-614-09836-X, L-34117-00) Am Printing Hse.

Lion & the Puppy & Other Stories for Children. Leo Tolstoy. Tr. by James Riordan from RUS. LC 87-28653. (Illus.). 80p. (J). (gr. 1 up). 1995. 15.95 (0-8050-0735-0, Bks Young Read) H Holt & Co.

***Lion & The Rat.** Brian Wildsmith. (Illus.). 32p. 2000. pap. 8.95 (0-19-272399-5) OUP.

Lion & the Rose: Songs Included. Mary L. Burkhalter. 160p. 1998. pap. 50.00 (0-934284-06-7) Jolean Pub Co.

Lion & the Star: Gentile-Jewish Relations in Three Hessian Towns, 1919-1945. Jonathan Friedman. LC 97-33201. 292p. (C). 1998. text 36.95 (0-8131-2043-8) U Pr of Ky.

Lion & the Sun. Maurice D. Sassoon. 200p. 1998. pap. 14.95 (1-892896-93-1) Buy Books.

Lion & the Throne: Stories from the Shahnameh of Ferdowsi. Ed. by Ehsan Yarshater. Tr. by Dick Davis from PER. LC 96-44432. (Illus.). 272p. 1998. 75.00 (0-934211-50-7) Mage Pubs Inc.

Lion & the Throne: The Life & Times of Sir Edward Coke (1552-1634) Catherine D. Bowen. 1990. pap. 12.95 (0-685-45399-5) Little.

Lion & the Unicorn. Gary L. Blackwood. LC 82-90758. 291p. (Orig.). 1983. pap. 6.95 (0-910971-00-5) Eagle Bks.

Lion & the Unicorn. Richard H. Davis. LC 71-94715. (Short Story Index Reprint Ser.). 1977. 19.95 (0-8369-3094-0) Ayer.

Lion & the Unicorn. Shirley Hughes. LC 98-6499. 64p. (J). (gr. 2-6). 1999. 17.95 (0-7894-2555-6, D K Ink) DK Pub Inc.

Lion & the Unicorn: Socialism & the English Genius. George Orwell. LC 75-41205. reprint ed. 22.50 (0-404-14691-0) AMS Pr.

Lion & Tiger. Rod Theodorou & Carole Telford. LC 96-7235. (Discover the Difference Ser.). (Illus.). (J). 1998. (1-57572-103-1) Heinemann Lib.

Lion at Bedtime. Debi Glioti. LC 93-51089. (Illus.). 32p. (J). (ps-2). 1994. 12.95 (0-8120-6379-1); pap. 4.95 (0-8120-1680-7) Barron.

Lion at Sea. large type ed. Max Hennessy. 476p. 1981. 27.99 (0-7089-0696-6) Ulverscroft.

Lion at the Door: A Novel. David Attoe. 240p. 1989. 17.95 (0-316-05800-9) Little.

***Lion Attack: I Ain't Gonna Die on My Birthday.** Bill White. (Illus.). 40p. 1999. pap. 5.95 (0-929259-01-7) Converse Pr.

***Lion Attacks.** Patrick J. Fitzgerald. LC 99-54151. (Animal Attacks Ser.). (Illus.). (J). 2000. 19.00 (0-516-23315-7) Childrens.

***Lion Attacks.** Patrick J. Fitzgerald. LC 99-54151. (High Interest Bks.). (Illus.). 48p. (J). (gr. 4-7). 2000. pap. 6.95 (0-516-23515-X) Childrens.

Lion Bat la Campagne. Jacques De Bourbon Busset. (FRE.). 276p. 1986. pap. 11.95 (0-7859-2027-7, 2070377121) Fr & Eur.

Lion Bible Stories see Historias de la Biblia

Lion Bible Stories see Historias de la Biblia: Old Testament

Lion Bible Stories see Historias de la Biblia, Vol. I

Lion Bibles Stories see Historias de la Biblia, Vol. 2, New Testament

Lion Book of First Prayers. 128p. (J). 1997. write for info. (0-7459-3441-2, Lion) Chariot Victor.

Lion Books & the Lion Library: A Checklist. C. P. Stephens. 62p. 1992. pap. 7.95 (0-89366-124-4) Ultramarine Pub.

Lion Bridge: Selected Poems, 1972-1995. Michael Palmer. LC 97-47579. 260p. 1998. pap. 18.95 (0-8112-1383-8, NDP863, Pub. by New Directions) Norton.

Lion by the Mane. large type ed. Eva Dane. 336p. 1986. 27.99 (0-7089-1445-4) Ulverscroft.

Lion Calls a Meeting, the Lion Foiled, the Lion in Love. Pilar Enciso & Lauro Olmo. Ed. by Martha T. Halsey. Tr. by Carys Evans-Corrales. LC 96-86437. (Contemporary Spanish Plays Ser.: Vol. 11). (Illus.). 80p. (Orig.). (J). (gr. 1-8). 1997. pap. 6.00 (1-888463-01-5) Estreno.

Lion Christian Poetry Collection. Mary Batchelor. LC 98-195121. 576 p. 1995. write for info. (0-7459-2746-7) Lion USA.

Lion Club: Pitit Lyon/Le Lionceau. Maude Heurtelou. Ed. by Fequiere Vilsaint. 20p. Date not set. pap. 12.00 (1-881839-70-2) Educa Vision.

Lion Concise Bible Encyclopedia. large type ed. Ed. by Pat Alexander. 716p. 1992. 29.95 (1-55905-103-5, Pub. by Clio Pr) HM.

Lion Concise Book of Christian Thought A. N. Lane. LC 85-174392. 239 p. 1984. pap. write for info. (0-85648-505-5) Lion USA.

Lion Country. Eduard Zingg. Ed. by Bob Italia. LC 93-3687. (J). 1993. lib. bdg. 15.98 (1-56239-218-2) ABDO Pub Co.

Lion Country: Inside Penn State Football: The Triumphs & Glories of Penn State Foorball As Told by Lettermen from Different Eras, 1948-1981. fac. ed. Frank Bilovsky. LC 82-81802. (Illus.). 176p. 1982. reprint ed. pap. 54.60 (0-608-00948-2, 206176200011) Bks Demand.

Lion Cubs see Books for Young Explorers

Lion Cubs & Their World: A National Geographic Pop-Up Book. National Geographic Society Staff. (Pop-Up Bks.). (Illus.). 10p. (YA). (gr. k up). 1991. 16.00 (0-87044-871-4, Pub. by Natl Geog) S&S Trade.

Lion Dancer: Ernie Wan's Chinese New Year. Kate Waters. LC 89-6423. 40p. (J). (ps-2). 1991. pap. 3.95 (0-590-43047-5) Scholastic Inc.

Lion Dancer: Ernie Wan's Chinese New Year. Kate Waters. (Reading Rainbow Bks.). (J). 1990. 9.15 (0-606-04729-8, Pub. by Turtleback) Demco.

Lion-Dog of Buddhist Asia. Elsie P. Mitchell. LC 91-70174. (Illus.). 192p. 1991. 50.00 (0-9628495-0-2); pap. 27.50 (0-9628495-1-0) Fugaisha US.

Lion, Eagle & Swastika: Bavarian Monarchism in Weimar Germany, 1918-1933. Robert S. Garnett, Jr. LC 91-12023. (Modern European History Outstanding Studies & Dissertations). 414p. 1991. text 25.00 (0-8153-0410-2) Garland.

Lion Encyclopedia of the Bible. Ed. by Pat Alexander. 352p. 1978. 29.95 (0-88469-201-9) BMH Bks.

Lion et la Souris - The Lion & the Mouse. Dorothy S. Bishop. (French/English Bilingual Fables Ser.). (ENG & FRE., Illus.). 72p. (J). 1992. pap. 4.95 (0-8442-1084-6, 10846, Natl Textbk Co) NTC Contemp Pub Co.

Lion Family Book. Angelika Hofer. LC 88-15139.Tr. of Lowen Kinder-Busch. (Illus.). 52p. (J). (gr. k up). 1991. pap. 15.95 (0-88708-070-7, Picture Book Studio) S&S Childrens.

Lion Family Book. Angelika Hofer & Gunter Ziesler. Tr. by Patricia Crampton. LC 95-6603.Tr. of Lowen Kinder-Busch. (Illus.). 56p. (J). (gr. 1-5). 1995. pap. 8.95 (1-55858-502-8, Pub. by North-South Bks NYC) Chronicle Bks.

Lion Feuchtwanger: A Bibliographic Handbook, 1. John M. Spalek & Sandra H. Hawrylchak. LC 98-189716. 1998. 117.00 (3-598-11378-1) K G Saur Verlag.

Lion Feuchtwanger's Erfolg: A "Grosstadt" Novel. Judith Wessler. (Studies in Modern German Literature: Vol. 11). 212p. (C). 1988. text 34.50 (0-8204-0449-7) P Lang Pubng.

Lion for Love: A Critical Biography of Stendhal. Robert Alter & Carol Cosman. 304p. 1986. pap. 17.00 (0-674-53575-8) HUP.

***Lion for Michael.** Uri Orlev. (Illus.). 32p. (J). (gr. k-4). 2000. 15.95 (1-58653-172-7) Mondo Pubng.

Lion Handbook: The Library & Information Organizations & Networks Handbook. Sue Broughton. 220p. 1998. 65.00 (1-85604-126-3, LAP1263) Library Association.

Lion Has Roared. Wayne Van Horne. 96p. (Orig.). (C). 1995. pap. 7.95 (1-883893-23-2) WinePress Pub.

Lion Has Wings: The Race to Prepare the RAF for World War II, 1935-1940. L. F. E. Coombs. LC 98-108337. x, 176 p. 1997. write for info. (1-85310-805-7) Airlife Publishing.

***Lion Heart.** Tanya A. Crosby. 352p. 2000. mass mkt. 5.99 (0-380-78575-7, Avon Bks) Morrow Avon.

***Lion House Desserts.** Melba Davis. LC 99-86125. (Illus.). 2000. write for info. (1-57345-550-4) Deseret Bk.

Lion House International Recipes. Melba Davis & Lion House Staff. LC 97-8704. (Illus.). 134p. 1997. 19.95 (1-57345-245-9) Deseret Bk.

Lion House Lite Recipes. Compiled by Melba Davis. LC 95-51135. (Illus.). vii, 160p. 1996. 19.95 (0-87579-904-3) Deseret Bk.

Lion House Recipes. Photos by Craig W. Dimond & Borge B. Andersen. LC 80-19719. (Illus.). 122p. 1984. reprint ed. 21.95 (0-87747-831-7, Shadow Mount) Deseret Bk.

Lion Hunter of South Africa: Five Years Adventures in the Far Interior of South Africa, with Notices of the Native Tribes & Savage Animals. Roualeyn G. Gordon-Cumming. 1977. 22.95 (0-8369-9187-7, 9056) Ayer.

Lion Hunting & Other Mathematical Pursuits: A Collection of Mathematics, Verse & Stories. Ralph P. Boas, Jr. Ed. by Gerald L. Alexanderson & Dale H. Mugler. LC 94-78313. 320p. 1995. pap. text 25.00 (0-88385-323-X, DOL-15) Math Assn.

Lion in the Evening. large type ed. Alan Scholefield. 308p. 1980. 27.99 (0-7089-0515-3) Ulverscroft.

Lion in the Fire. C. W. Moulton. LC 96-86151. 100p. (Orig.). 1996. pap. 12.95 (0-9653938-0-1) Fresno Poets.

Lion in the Lake (Le Lion dans le Lac) A Bilingual Alphabet (Un Abecedaire Bilingue) Sheldon Oberman. (ENG & FRE., Illus.). 56p. (J). (gr. k-3). 1988. text 8.00 (0-920541-36-4) Peguis Pubs Ltd.

Lion in the Meadow. Margaret Mahy. (Illus.). 32p. (J). (ps-3). 1992. 13.95 (0-87951-446-9, Pub. by Overlook Pr) Penguin Putnam.

Lion in the Moon: Two Against the Sahara. Babs S. Harrison & Staefan E. Rada. LC 93-37515. (Illus.). 296p. 1994. pap. 19.95 (1-56825-006-1) Rainbow Books.

***Lion in the Room Next Door.** Merilyn Simonds. LC 99-37416. 272p. (J). 2000. reprint ed. 23.95 (0-399-14591-5, G P Putnam) Peng Put Young Read.

***Lion in the Sand: The British in the Middle East.** Gerald Butt. (Illus.). 215p. 2000. reprint ed. 27.00 (0-7881-9378-3) DIANE Pub.

Lion in the Streets. Judith Thompson. LC 96-931989. 64p. 1997. pap. text 10.95 (0-88754-515-7) Theatre Comm.

***Lion in the Valley.** Elizabeth Peters, pseud. 384p. 1999. mass mkt. 6.99 (0-380-73119-3, Avon Bks) Morrow Avon.

Lion in the Valley. Elizabeth Peters, pseud. (Amelia Peabody Mystery Ser.). 320p. 1990. reprint ed. mass mkt. 4.99 (0-8125-1242-1, Pub. by Tor Bks) St Martin.

Lion in Winter. James Goldman. 18.95 (0-88411-652-2) Amereon Ltd.

Lion in Winter. James Goldman. 128p. 1983. pap. 8.95 (0-14-048174-5, Penguin Bks) Viking Penguin.

Lion Is in the Streets. Adria Langley. lib. bdg. 25.95 (0-8488-1991-8) Amereon Ltd.

Lion King. (Super Coloring Book Ser.). (J). pap. text 2.29 (0-307-03437-2, 03437); pap. text 2.99 (0-307-05588-4, 05588) Gldn Bks Pub Co.

Lion King. 32p. 1994. pap. 2.95 (0-7935-3463-1); per. 16.95 (0-7935-3416-X) H Leonard.

Lion King. Disney Staff. (Illus.). 96p. (J). 1994. 7.98 (1-57082-128-3, Pub. by Mouse Works) Time Warner.

***Lion King.** Disney Staff. (SPA., Illus.). 64p. (ps-2). 1999. pap. text 4.99 (0-7364-0130-X, Pub. by Mouse Works) Time Warner.

Lion King. Disney Studios Staff. (Classics Ser.). (Illus.). 96p. (J). 1994. 7.98 (1-57082-087-2, Pub. by Mouse Works) Little.

Lion King. Adapted by Gina Ingoglia. LC 97-80392. (Wonderful World of Disney Ser.). (Illus.). 64p. (J). (gr. 3-7). 1998. pap. 3.25 (0-7868-4219-9, Pub. by Disney Pr) Time Warner.

Lion King. Mouse Works Staff. (Disney's Read-Aloud Storybooks Ser.). (Illus.). 64p. (J). (ps-2). 1999. 6.99 (0-7364-0123-7, Pub. by Mouse Works) Time Warner.

***Lion King.** Mouseworks Staff. (Seek & See Ser.). (Illus.). 24p. (J). 1998. 3.99 (1-57082-938-1, Pub. by Mouse Works) Time Warner.

Lion King: An Animated Flip Book. Walt Disney's Feature Animation Department Staff. (Illus.). 96p. (J). 1994. pap. 3.95 (0-7868-8009-0, Pub. by Hyperion) Time Warner.

Lion King: Best Friends. Golden Books Staff. (Super Coloring Book Ser.). (Illus.). (J). 1997. pap. text 2.29 (0-307-03442-9, 03442, Goldn Books) Gldn Bks Pub Co.

Lion King: Circle of Life Board Book. Julie Taymor. LC PZ7.D62543772 1998. 14p. (J). 1998. 6.95 (0-7868-3216-9, Pub. by Disney Pr) Time Warner.

Lion King: Illustrated Classic (Mini Edition) Gina Ingoglia. LC 94-80011. (Disney Press Miniature Classics Ser.). (Illus.). 96p. (J). 1996. 5.95 (0-7868-3074-3, Pub. by Disney Pr) Little.

Lion King: Jungle Days. Illus. by Atelier Philippe Harchy. LC 94-67861. (Tiny Changing Pictures Bk.). 10p. (J). (ps-k). 1995. 4.95 (0-7868-3011-5, Pub. by Disney Pr) Little.

Lion King: Just Can't Wait to Be King. Gabrielle Charbonnet. (Disney Chapters Ser.). (Illus.). 64p. (J). (gr. 2-4). 1998. pap. 3.95 (0-7868-4178-8, Pub. by Disney Pr) Time Warner.

Lion King: Little Library. Disney Studios Staff. LC 96-232650. (Illus.). (J). 1994. 5.98 (1-57082-088-0, Pub. by Mouse Works) Little.

Lion King: Morning at Pride Rock. Teddy Slater. LC 93-74741. (Illus.). 32p. (J). 1997. pap. 4.95 (0-7868-4130-3, Pub. by Disney Pr) Time Warner.

Lion King: Mufasa's Little Instruction Book. A. L. Singer. LC 94-70989. (Illus.). 128p. (J). 1994. pap. 5.95 (0-7868-4015-3, Pub. by Disney Pr) Little.

Lion King: Pride Rock on Broadway. Julie Taymor. (Illus.). 160p. (J). 1998. 40.00 (0-7868-6342-0, Pub. by Hyperion) Time Warner.

Lion King: Simba's Hide & Seek. (My First Read-Alongs Ser.). (J). 7.99 incl. audio (1-55723-747-6) W Disney Records.

Lion King: Spanish Read Aloud. Mouseworks Staff. (SPA., Illus.). 64p. (ps-2). 1999. pap. 6.99 (0-7364-0138-5, Pub. by Mouse Works) Time Warner.

Lion King: The Broadway Musical. 112p. 1999. otabind 19.95 (0-7935-9194-5) H Leonard.

Lion King: The Pal Patrol. Disney Enterprises, Inc. Staff. (Disney's "Storytime Treasures" Library: Vol. 1). (Illus.). 44p. (J). (gr. 1-6). 1997. 3.49 (1-885222-97-1) Advance Pubs.

Lion King - Far from the Pridelands. (Disney Read-Alongs Ser.). (J). 7.99 incl. audio (1-55723-673-9) W Disney Records.

Lion King - Film Version. (Disney Read-Alongs Ser.). (J). 7.99 incl. audio (1-55723-591-0) W Disney Records.

Lion King & Pocahontas for Easy Guitar. 56p. 1996. pap. 9.95 (0-7935-6558-8) H Leonard.

***Lion King & the Lion King II.** Golden Book Staff. 2000. pap. text 3.99 (0-307-25252-3) Gldn Bks Pub Co.

***Lion King II; Simba's Pride.** Disney Staff. 48p. 1998. per. 14.95 (0-634-00031-4) H Leonard.

Lion King Look & Find. Publications International, Ltd. Editorial Staff. pap. 6.98 (0-7853-1189-0) Pubns Intl Ltd.

Lion King Mask Book. Gina Ingoglia. LC 94-71012. (Illus.). 26p. (J). (ps-3). 1994. pap. 12.95 (0-7868-4007-2, Pub. by Disney Pr) Little.

***Lion, King of the Beasts.** Christine Denis-Huot & Michel Denis-Huot. LC 99-48027. (Animal Close-Ups Ser.). (Illus.). (J). 2000. pap. 6.95 (1-57091-426-5) Charlesbridge Pub.

L

Lion King Paint with Water Book. (J). (ps-3). 1994. pap. 1.79 (0-307-01479-7, Goldn Books) Gldn Bks Pub Co.

Lion King Puzzle Pop-Up Game Book. Illus. by Atelier Philippe Harchy. LC 94-71801. 12p. (J). (ps-3). 1995. 17.95 (0-7868-3037-9, Pub. by Disney Pr) Little.

Lion King Read-Along; The Brightest Star. 1994. pap. 6.98 incl. audio (1-55723-618-6) W Disney Records.

Lion Let Loose. Nigel Tranter. (Illus.). (J). 1993. mass mkt. 11.95 (0-340-58698-2, Pub. by Hodder & Stought Ltd) Trafalgar.

Lion Let Loose: The Structure & Meaning of St. Mark's Gospel. John Sergeant. 95p. 1992. reprint ed. pap. 8.50 (0-85364-475-6, Pub. by Paternoster Pub) OM Literature.

Lion Lover. Mercedes Kelly. 256p. (Orig.). 1997. mass mkt. 5.95 (0-352-33162-3, Pub. by BLA4) London Brdge.

Lion Mountain: A Novel. Mustapha Tlili. LC 97-52967. 180p. 1998. pap. 15.95 (0-89410-878-6) L Rienner.

Lion Named Shirley Williamson. Bernard Waber. LC 96-11187. (Illus.). 40p. (J). (ps-3). 1996. 15.95 (0-395-80979-7) HM.

***Lion Named Shirley Williamson.** Bernard Waber. LC 96-11187. (Illus.). 40p. (J). (ps-3). 2000. pap. 6.95 (0-618-05580-0) HM.

***Lion Named Shirley Williamson.** Bernard Waber. (Illus.). (J). 2000. 12.34 (0-606-18212-8) Turtleback.

Lion Never Sleeps: Preparing Those You Love for Satan's Attacks. Mike Taliaferro. 96p. 1996. pap. 7.99 (1-884553-78-8) Discipleshp.

Lion of Arles: A Portrait of Mistral & His Circle. Tudor Edwards. LC 63-16396. 225p. reprint ed. pap. 69.80 (0-7837-0445-3, 204076800018) Bks Demand.

Lion of Comarre. Arthur C. Clarke. LC 68-28816. 214p. 1968. 5.75 (0-15-152524-2) Harcourt.

Lion of Comarre: Against the Fall of Night. Arthur C. Clarke. 228p. 1986. pap. 9.95 (0-15-652517-8) Harcourt.

Lion of Egypt: Sultan Baybars & the Near East in the 13th Century. Peter Thorau. LC 91-2403. (C). 1991. pap. text 41.50 (0-582-06823-1) Addison-Wesley.

Lion of Egypt: Sultan Baybars I & the Near East in the Thirteenth Century. Peter Thorau. LC 91-2403. 1992. text. write for info. (0-582-06822-3) Longman.

Lion of Farside. John Dalmas. 448p. 1995. mass mkt. 5.99 (0-671-87674-0) Baen Bks.

Lion of God: A Biography of John G. Mitchell, D. D. Dick Bohrer. LC 94-75841. 480p. (Orig.). 1994. pap. 11.95 (0-9640330-0-3) Multnomah Bible.

Lion of Ireland. Morgan Llywelyn. 1996. mass mkt. 6.99 (0-8125-5399-3, Pub. by Tor Bks) St Martin.

Lion of Islam. Howard L. Oleck. (Orig.). 1980. mass mkt. 1.95 (0-89083-615-9, Zebra Kensgtn) Kensgtn Pub Corp.

***Lion of Janina: or The Last Days of the Janissaries.** Maurus Jokai. 252p. 2000. pap. 9.95 (0-594-01525-1) Eightn Hundrd.

Lion of Judah. Janice L. Dennie. 250p. 1997. pap. 6.99 (0-9643349-0-9) Kente Pubns.

Lion of Judah Hath Prevailed: Being the Biography of His Imperial Majesty Haile Selassie I. Christine Sandford. LC 73-135611. (Illus.). 192p. 1972. reprint ed. lib. bdg. 55.00 (0-8371-5198-8, SLJ&, Greenwood Pr) Greenwood.

Lion of Justice Margaret Butler. LC 75-326959. 280p. (J). 1975. write for info. (0-333-14769-3) Macmillan.

Lion of Justice. Jean Plaidy, pseud. Date not set. lib. bdg. 23.95 (0-8488-2157-2) Amereon Ltd.

***Lion of Saint Mark: A Tale of Venice in the 14th Century.** G. A. Henty. 2000. 19.99 (1-887159-52-5); pap. 13.99 (1-887159-53-3) Preston-Speed.

***Lion of Scotland.** Neil Robinson. (Illus.). 156p. 1999. pap. 13.95 (1-84158-009-0, Pub. by Birlinn Ltd) Dufour.

Lion of the Covenant. M. Grant. 1997. pap. 16.99 (0-85234-395-7, Pub. by Evangelical Pr) P & R Pubng.

Lion of the Fold: James Larkin. Ed. by Donal Nevin. LC 98-231150. (Illus.). 464p. 1998. pap. 19.95 (0-7171-2779-6, Pub. by Gill & MacMill) Irish Bks Media.

Lion of the Forest: James B. Finley, Frontier Reformer. Charles C. Cole, Jr. LC 93-47932. (Ohio River Valley Ser.). 288p. (C). 1994. 34.95 (0-8131-1863-8) U Pr of Ky.

Lion of the Kalahari. Sam B. Hobson & George C. Hobson. 17.95 (0-88411-708-1) Amereon Ltd.

Lion of the Lord: Essays on the Life & Service of Brigham Young. Ed. by Susan E. Black & Larry C. Porter. LC 95-42591. xii, 462p. 1996. 19.95 (1-57345-112-6) Deseret Bk.

Lion of the North. Suzanne Barclay. LC 95-15859. (Historical Ser.). 299p. 1995. per. 4.50 (0-373-28872-7, 1-28872-9) Harlequin Bks.

***Lion of the North: A Tale of the Times of Gustavua Adolphus.** G. A. Henty. 2000. 19.99 (1-887159-42-8); pap. 13.99 (1-887159-43-6) Preston-Speed.

Lion of the North: A Tale of the Times of Gustavus Adolphus & the Wars of Religion. G. A. Henty. (Illus.). 236p. 1996. pap. 5.99 (0-88019-355-7) Schmul Pub Co.

Lion of the North Vol. 2: A Tale of the Times of Gustavus Adolphus & the Wars of Religion. G. A. Henty. (Illus.). 200p. 1997. pap. 5.99 (0-88019-359-X) Schmul Pub Co.

L

Lion of the South: General Thomas C. Hindman. Diane Neal. 1997. pap. text 17.95 (0-86554-556-1, P165) Mercer Univ Pr.
Lion of the Tribe of Judah Shall Prevail. Elizabeth R. Visland. LC 97-194677. 155p. 1994. pap. 9.95 (0-9633106-1-5) E R Visland.
Lion of the Valley: St. Louis, Missouri, 1764-1980. 3rd rev. ed. James N. Primm. LC 98-20315. (Illus.). 621p. 1998. 35.95 (1-883982-24-3, Pub. by MO Hist Soc); pap. 27.95 (1-883982-25-1) MO Hist Soc.
Lion of the West. James K. Paulding. Ed. by Frank Gado. (Masterworks of Literature Ser.). 1994. 12.95 (0-8084-0428-8) NCUP.
Lion of Wall Street: The Two Lives of Jack Dreyfus. Jack J. Dreyfus. LC 95-37523. (Illus.). 352p. 1996. 24.95 (0-89526-461-7) Regnery Pub.
***Lion on the Freeway: A Thematic Introduction to Contemporary South African Literature in English.** 2nd ed. Theodore F. Sheckels, Jr. (Studies of World Literature in English: Vol. 5). XXI, 250p. (C). 1999. reprint ed. pap. text 34.95 (0-8204-4887-7) P Lang Pubng.
Lion Pit, Bk. 6A. Groves. (J). Date not set. pap. text. write for info. (0-582-18797-4, Pub. by Addison-Wesley) Longman.
Lion Rampant: Essays in the Study of British Imperialism. Donald A. Low. (Studies in Commonwealth Politics & History: No. 1). 232p. 1973. 35.00 (0-7146-2986-3, Pub. by F Cass Pubs) Intl Spec Bk.
Lion Returns. John Dalmas. 1999. mass mkt. 6.99 (0-671-57824-3) S&S Trade.
Lion Roars. Jim Boulden & Joan Boulden. Ed. by Kari Kennedy. (Illus.). 24p. (J). (gr. 4-7). 1999. pap. 5.95 (1-892421-09-7, 09-7AB) Boulden Pub.
Lion Roars: Selected Speeches & Letters of Haile Selassie. Lance Seunarine. LC 97-95522. 156p. 1998. pap. 14.95 (0-9662524-2-X) Trican Bks.
Lion Rugs: The Lion in the Art & Culture of Iran. Parviz Tanavoli. (Illus.). 151p. 1985. 19.00 (0-317-43008-4, Pub. by Wepf & Co) H B Fenn Co.
Lion Sneezed: Folktales & Myths of the Cat. Maria Leach. LC 77-3665. (J). (gr. 3-5). 1977. 12.95 (0-690-01364-7) HarpC Child Bks.
Lion Sticker Paper Doll. Cathy Beylon. (Illus.). (J). 1995. pap. 1.00 (0-486-28423-9) Dover.
Lion Storyteller Bible. Bob Hartman. 120p. (J). 1996. 12.99 (0-7459-2921-4) Lion USA.
***Lion Sun: Poems by Pavel Chichikov.** Pavel Chichikov. LC 99-90616. (Illus.). 96p. 1999. pap. 12.95 (0-9671901-0-X) Grey Owl.
Lion Sutra: On Perfect Transcendence of the Primal Act, Which Is the Ego-"I", the Self-Contraction, or Attention Itself & All the Illusions of Separateness, Otherness, Relatedness & Difference. Adi Da Avabhasa. 508p. 1995. pap. 24.95 (1-57097-012-2) Dawn Horse Pr.
Lion Tales. Photos by Tippi Hedren & Bill Dow. (Illus.). 24p. (Orig.). 1991. pap. 20.00 (0-9620574-2-8) MGM Pr.
Lion Tamer. S. J. Revich. 140p. (J). (ps-8). 1990. 12.95 (1-56062-038-2); pap. 9.95 (1-56062-054-4) CIS Comm.
Lion Tamer. E. M. Hull. 1976. reprint ed. lib. bdg. 25.95 (0-89190-732-7, Rivercity Pr) Amereon Ltd.
Lion Tamer's Daughter & Other Stories. Peter Dickinson. (YA). (gr. 7 up). 1997. 15.95 (0-614-28684-0, Delacorte Pr Bks) BDD Bks Young Read.
***Lion Tamer's Daughter & Other Stories.** Peter Dickinson. 1998. 10.09 (0-606-13572-3, Pub. by Turtleback) Demco.
Lion Tamer's Daughter & Other Stories. Peter Dickinson. 304p. (YA). (gr. 7 up). 1998. reprint ed. mass mkt. 4.99 (0-440-22690-2, LLL BDD) BDD Bks Young Read.
Lion, the Eagle, & Upper Canada: A Developing Colonial Ideology. Jane Errington. 290p. 1987. 65.00 (0-7735-0603-9, Pub. by McG-Queens Univ Pr) CUP Services.
Lion, the Eagle, & Upper Canada: A Developing Colonial Ideology. Jane Errington. 286p. (C). 1994. pap. text 22.95 (0-7735-1204-7, Pub. by McG-Queens Univ Pr) CUP Services.
Lion, the Witch & the Wardrobe see Armoire Magique
Lion, the Witch & the Wardrobe. C. S. Lewis. (Chronicles of Narnia Ser.: Bk. 1). (J). (gr. 4-8). 1976. 20.95 (0-8488-0823-1) Amereon Ltd.
Lion, the Witch & the Wardrobe. C. S. Lewis. (Chronicles of Narnia Ser.: Bk. 1). (J). (gr. 4-8). 1989. pap. 5.95 (0-87129-265-3, L62) Dramatic Pub.
Lion, the Witch & the Wardrobe. C. S. Lewis. LC 93-8889. (Chronicles of Narnia Ser.: Bk. 1). (Illus.). 208p. (J). (gr. 4-7). 1994. 16.95 (0-06-023481-4); pap. 4.95 (0-06-447104-7, HarpTrophy); lib. bdg. 16.89 (0-06-023482-2) HarpC Child Bks.
***Lion, the Witch & the Wardrobe.** C. S. Lewis. (Chronicles of Narnia Ser.: Bk. 1). 40p. (J). (gr. 4-8). 1999. 9.95 (1-56137-243-9) Novel Units.
***Lion, the Witch & the Wardrobe.** C. S. Lewis. (Chronicles of Narnia Ser.: Bk. 1). (J). (gr. 4-8). 1999. 11.95 (1-56137-704-X) Novel Units.
Lion, the Witch & the Wardrobe. C. S. Lewis. LC 83-61572. (Chronicles of Narnia Ser.: Bk. 1). (Illus.). 160p. (J). (gr. 4-8). 1988. lib. bdg. 22.95 (0-02-758200-0, Mac Bks Young Read) S&S Childrens.
***Lion, the Witch & the Wardrobe.** C. S. Lewis. 112p. 1999. pap. 10.95 (1-84002-049-0, Pub. by Theatre Comm) Consort Bk Sales.
Lion, the Witch & the Wardrobe. C. S. Lewis. LC 99-57460. (Chronicles of Narnia Ser.: Bk. 1). (Illus.). (J). (gr. 4-8). 1950. 21.95 (0-7862-2232-8) Thorndike Pr.
Lion, the Witch & the Wardrobe. C. S. Lewis. LC 93-8889. (Chronicles of Narnia Ser.: Bk. 1). (J). (gr. 4-8). 1994. 12.05 (0-606-06532-6, Pub. by Turtleback); 10.05 (0-606-06533-4, Pub. by Turtleback) Demco.
Lion, the Witch & the Wardrobe. C. S. Lewis. (Chronicles of Narnia Ser.: Bk. 1). (J). (gr. 4-8). 1995. 16.15 (0-606-07791-X) Turtleback.
***Lion, the Witch & the Wardrobe.** C. S. Lewis et al. LC 99-51480. (Illus.). (J). 2000. lib. bdg. 14.89 (0-06-029013-7) HarpC.
Lion, the Witch & the Wardrobe. abr. ed. C. S. Lewis. LC 93-8889. (Chronicles of Narnia Ser.: Bk. 1). (Illus.). 208p. (J). (gr. 4-7). 1994. pap. 6.95 (0-06-440499-4) HarpC Child Bks.
Lion, the Witch & the Wardrobe. abr. ed. C. S. Lewis. LC 94-13165. (Trophy Picture Bk.). (Illus.). 64p. (J). (gr. 4-7). 1995. pap. 11.95 (0-06-443399-4, HarpTrophy) HarpC Child Bks.
Lion, the Witch & the Wardrobe. anniversary ed. C. S. Lewis & Scholastic, Inc. Staff. (Chronicles of Narnia Ser.: Bk. 1). 16p. (J). (gr. 4-8). 1997. pap. text 3.95 (0-590-36647-5) Scholastic Inc.
Lion, the Witch & the Wardrobe. C. S. Lewis. (Chronicles of Narnia Ser.: Bk. 1). (J). (gr. 4-8). 1986. reprint ed. pap. 7.95 (0-02-044490-7) Macmillan.
Lion, the Witch & the Wardrobe: A Literature Unit. Michael Shepherd & C. S. Lewis. (Literature Units Ser.). (Illus.). 48p. (gr. 3-5). 1992. student ed. 7.95 (1-55734-409-4) Tchr Create Mat.
Lion, the Witch & the Wardrobe: A Study Guide. Beatrice G. Davis. (Novel-Ties Ser.). (J). (gr. 3-5). 1985. pap. text, teacher ed., student ed. 15.95 (0-88122-078-7) Lrn Links.
***Lion, the Witch & the Wardrobe: Bound Complete Narnia Teacher's Guide.** C. S. Lewis. (Chronicles of Narnia Ser.). (J). 2000. pap. write for info. (0-06-449255-9, HarpTrophy) HarpC Child Bks.
***Lion, the Witch & the Wardrobe: (C. Birmingham Edition)** abr. ed. C. S. Lewis. LC 99-51480. (Illus.). 48p. (J). (gr. 1-5). 2000. 15.95 (0-06-029011-0) HarpC Child Bks.
Lion, the Witch & the Wardrobe: (El Lion, la Bruja y el Armario) C. S. Lewis. LC 49-124440. (SPA.). (J). (gr. 4-7). 1995. 11.95 (84-204-4564-9) Santillana.
***Lion, the Witch & the Wardrobe: Full-Color Collector's Edition.** C. S. Lewis. LC 93-8889. (Chronicles of Narnia Ser.: Bk. 1). (Illus.). 208p. (J). (gr. 4-7). 2000. mass mkt. 7.95 (0-06-440942-2, HarpTrophy) HarpC Child Bks.
***Lion, the Witch & the Wardrobe: Teacher's Guide.** C. S. Lewis. (J). 2000. pap., teacher ed. write for info. (0-06-447260-4, HarpTrophy) HarpC Child Bks.
Lion, the Witch & the Wardrobe - One Act - Two Character. C. S. Lewis. 30p. 1989. pap. 5.50 (0-87129-668-3, L54) Dramatic Pub.
Lion, the Witch & the Wardrobe Deluxe Edition: Deluxe Edition. deluxe ed. C. S. Lewis. LC 96-49854. (Chronicles of Narnia Ser.: Bk. 1). (Illus.). 176p. (J). (gr. 3-7). 1994. 24.95 (0-06-027724-6) HarpC.
Lion, the Witch & the Wardrobe Study Guide. Andrew Clausen. 52p. (J). (gr. 4-7). 1993. student ed., ring bd. 12.99 (1-58609-136-0) Progeny Pr WI.
Lion to Guard. Houghton Mifflin Company Staff. (Literature Experience 1991 Ser.). (J). (gr. 5). 1990. pap. 10.24 (0-395-55167-6) HM.
Lion to Guard Us. Clyde R. Bulla. LC 80-2455. (Illus.). 128p. (J). (gr. 2-5). 1981. lib. bdg. 14.89 (0-690-04097-0) HarpC Child Bks.
Lion to Guard Us. Clyde R. Bulla. (J). 1989. 10.05 (0-606-04267-9, Pub. by Turtleback) Demco.
Lion to Guard Us. Clyde Robert Bulla. LC 80-2455. (Trophy Bk.). (Illus.). 128p. (J). (gr. 2-5). 1989. pap. 4.95 (0-06-440333-5, HarpTrophy) HarpC Child Bks.
Lion to Guard Us: A Study Guide. B. Ferraro. Ed. by J. Friedland & R. Kessler. (Novel-Ties Ser.). (J). (gr. 3-5). 1997. pap. text 15.95 (0-7675-0154-3) Lrn Links.
Lion Triumphant. Philippa Carr, pseud. 1976. 26.95 (0-8488-0447-3) Amereon Ltd.
Lion Who Couldn't Roar. Gary Hogg. (Happy Hawk Golden Thought Ser.). (Illus.). 24p. (J). 1994. pap. 4.95 (0-930771-12-5) Buckaroo UT.
Lion Who Had Asthma. Jonathan London. Ed. by Abby Levine. LC 91-16553. (Albert Whitman Concept Bks.). (Illus.). 32p. (J). (ps-2). 1992. lib. bdg. 14.95 (0-8075-4559-7) A Whitman.
Lion Who Had Asthma. Jonathan London. (Illus.). 32p. (J). (ps-1). 1997. reprint ed. pap. 5.95 (0-8075-4560-0) A Whitman.
Lion Who Lost His Roar. Betty Langdon. 51p. 1969. pap. 3.25 (0-87129-980-1, L24) Dramatic Pub.
Lion Who Saw Himself in the Water. Idries Shah. LC 97-5170. (Illus.). 32p. (J). (gr. 4-7). 1998. 17.00 (1-883536-12-X, Hoopoe Books) ISHK.
Lion Who Wanted to Love. Giles Andreae. LC 97-24542. (Illus.). 32p. (J). (ps-2). 1998. 14.95 (1-888444-25-8, 21023) Little Tiger.
Lion with Wings: A Narrative - Critical Approach to Mark's Gospel. Stephen H. Smith. (Biblical Seminar Ser.: No. 38). 258p. 1996. pap. 28.50 (1-85075-784-4, Pub. by Sheffield Acad) CUP Services.
Liona Boyd: A Guitar for Christmas. 48p. 1986. pap. 9.95 (0-7935-2740-6, 00699070) H Leonard.
Liona Boyd: Favorite Solos for Classical Guitar. 72p. 1988. pap. 9.95 (0-7935-2261-7, 00699076) H Leonard.
Liona Lou & the Kitchen Crash. 24p. (J). 1991. write for info. (1-55513-952-3, Chariot Bks) Chariot Victor.
***Lionel: A Century of Classic Toy Trains.** Dan Ponzol. (Illus.). 160p. 2000. 35.00 (1-56799-966-2, Friedman-Fairfax) M Friedman Pub Grp Inc.
***Lionel: America's Favorite Toy Trains.** Gerry Souter & Janet Souter. (Illus.). 160p. 2000. 29.95 (0-7603-0505-6, 130132AP, Pub. by MBI Pubg) Motorbooks Intl.
Lionel & Amelia. Leone Peguero. LC 95-49117. (Illus.). 32p. (J). (gr. 2-6). 1996. pap. 4.95 (1-57255-197-6) Mondo Pubng.
Lionel & His Friends. Stephen Krensky. LC 94-37434. (Illus.). 48p. (J). (ps-3). 1996. 13.99 (0-8037-1750-4, Dial Yng Read) Peng Put Young Read.
Lionel & His Friends. Stephen Krensky. 48p. (J). (gr. 1-4). 1999. pap. 3.99 (0-14-038742-0, PuffinBks) Peng Put Young Read.
***Lionel & His Friends.** Stephen Krensky. (Illus.). (J). 1999. 9.34 (0-606-18418-X) Turtleback.
Lionel & Louise. Stephen Krensky. (Puffin Easy-to-Read Ser.). (J). 1997. 8.70 (0-606-11564-1, Pub. by Turtleback) Demco.
Lionel & Louise. Stephen Krensky. (Illus.). (J). (gr. 1-4). 1997. pap. 3.50 (0-14-038617-3) Viking Penguin.
Lionel at Large. Stephen Krensky. (Dial Easy-to-Read Ser.). (J). 1986. 9.19 (0-606-01661-9, Pub. by Turtleback) Demco.
Lionel at Large Level 3: Yellow. Stephen Krensky. LC 85-15930. (Easy-to-Read Bks.). (Illus.). (J). (ps-3). 1993. pap. 3.99 (0-14-036542-7, PuffinBks) Peng Put Young Read.
***Lionel at School.** Stephen Krensky. LC 99-10695. (Easy-to-Read Bks.). (Illus.). (J). 2000. 20.01 (0-8037-2463-2) Peng Put Young Read.
Lionel Blue. Lionel Blue. Ed. by Gordian Marshall & Daphne Richardson. (Modern Spirituality Ser.). 96p. 1987. pap. 4.95 (0-87243-168-1) Templegate.
Lionel in Spring. Stephen Krensky. (Illus.). 40p. (J). (gr. 1-4). 1997. pap. 3.99 (0-14-038463-4) Viking Penguin.
Lionel in the Fall. Stephen Krensky. (J). 1987. 9.19 (0-606-01748-8, Pub. by Turtleback) Demco.
Lionel in the Fall Level 3: Yellow. Stephen Krensky. LC 93-6554. (Easy-to-Read Bks.). (Illus.). (J). (ps-3). 1993. pap. 3.99 (0-14-036545-1, PuffinBks) Peng Put Young Read.
Lionel in the Spring. Stephen Krensky. (Puffin Easy-to-Read Ser.). (J). 1997. 8.70 (0-606-11565-X, Pub. by Turtleback) Demco.
Lionel in the Summer. Stephen Krensky. LC 97-10218. (Illus.). 48p. (J). (gr. 1-3). 1998. 13.99 (0-8037-2243-5, Dial Yng Read) Peng Put Young Read.
***Lionel in the Summer.** Stephen Krensky. (Puffin Easy-to-Read Program Ser.). (Illus.). 48p. (J). (gr. 1-4). 2000. pap. 3.99 (0-14-130824-9, PuffinBks) Peng Put Young Read.
***Lionel in the Summer.** Stephen Krensky. (Illus.). (J). 2000. 9.44 (0-606-18419-8) Turtleback.
Lionel in the Winter. Stephen Krensky. (Puffin Easy-to-Read Ser.). (J). 1996. 8.70 (0-606-11566-8, Pub. by Turtleback) Demco.
Lionel Inspiration. William J. Brennan. LC 97-70600. (Illus.). 128p. 1997. 49.95 (1-878887-76-9) Morning NJ.
Lionel Lincoln. James Fenimore Cooper. (Works of James Fenimore Cooper). 1990. reprint ed. lib. bdg. 79.00 (0-7812-2373-3) Rprt Serv.
Lionel Lincoln: or The Leaguer of Boston. James Fenimore Cooper. LC 84-8675. (Writings of James Fenimore Cooper). 437p. (C). 1985. text 59.50 (0-87395-416-5); pap. text 24.95 (0-87395-671-0) State U NY Pr.
Lionel Murphy: A Political Biography. Jenny Hocking. LC 97-19622. (Illus.). 376p. (C). 1997. text 64.95 (0-521-58108-7) Cambridge U Pr.
Lionel Richie. Ed. by Milton Okun & Dan Fox. (Illus.). 64p. 1982. pap. 9.95 (0-89524-175-7) Cherry Lane.
Lionel Richie - Can't Slow Down. Ed. by Milton Okun. pap. 9.95 (0-89524-194-3) Cherry Lane.
Lionel Richie - Complete: Piano - Vocal. Ed. by Milton Okun. (Illus.). 264p. (Orig.). 1990. pap. text 24.95 (0-89524-370-9) Cherry Lane.
Lionel Richie - Dancing on the Ceiling: Piano - Vocal. Ed. by Milton Okun. (Illus.). 61p. (Orig.). 1990. pap. text 9.95 (0-89524-324-5) Cherry Lane.
Lionel Richie - Love Ballads. Ed. by Milton Okun. pap. 12.95 (0-89524-355-5) Cherry Lane.
Lionel Richie Greatest Hits: Ez Piano. Ed. by Milton Okun. (Illus.). 72p. (Orig.). 1990. pap. text 10.95 (0-89524-292-3) Cherry Lane.
Lionel Richie Songbook. Lionel Richie. (Illus.). 144p. 24.95 (0-89524-220-6); pap. text 19.95 (0-89524-248-6, 9970) Cherry Lane.
Lionel Sotheby's Great War: Diaries & Letters from the Western Front. Lionel Sotheby. Ed. by Donald C. Richter. LC 96-6568. 168p. 1997. text 27.95 (0-8214-1178-0) Ohio U Pr.
Lionel Standard Gauge Era. Harold H. Carstens. LC 64-56883. (Hobby Bks.). (Illus.). 36p. 1987. pap. 4.00 (0-911868-13-5, C13) Carstens Pubns.
Lionel Trains: Standard of the World, 1900-1943. 2nd ed. National TCA Book Committee Staff et al. (Illus.). 256p. (YA). 1989. reprint ed. 34.95 (0-917896-02-5) TCA PA.
Lionel Trilling. Stephen L. Tanner. (United States Authors Ser.: No. 523). 160p. 1988. 22.95 (0-8057-7503-X, Twyne) Mac Lib Ref.
Lionel Trilling: An Annotated Bibliography. Thomas M. Leitch. LC 92-23192. (Bibliographies of Modern Critics & Critical Schools Ser.: Vol. 19). 672p. 1992. text 40.00 (0-8240-7128-X, H1303) Garland.
Lionel Trilling: The Work of Liberation. Daniel T. O'Hara. LC 87-37178. 332p. (Orig.). (C). 1988. pap. text 19.95 (0-299-11314-0) U of Wis Pr.
Lionel Trilling & the Critics: Opposing Selves. Ed. by John Rodden. LC 98-53491. 407p. 1999. pap. text 29.95 (0-8032-8974-X) U of Nebr Pr.
***Lionel Trilling & the Critics: Opposing Selves.** Ed. by John Rodden. LC 98-53491. 407p. 1999. text 70.00 (0-8032-3922-X) U of Nebr Pr.
Lionel's Model Builder: The Magazine That Shaped the Toy Train Hobby. Roger Carp. Ed. by Terry Thompson. (Illus.). 96p. 1998. pap. 15.95 (0-89778-446-4, 10-8235, Kalmbach Books) Kalmbach.
Lionel's Postwar F3's. Ed. by Joseph P. Algozzini. (Toy Train Reference Ser.: No. 1). (Illus.). 80p. 1995. pap. 16.95 (0-89778-398-0, 10-7950, Greenberg Books) Kalmbach.
Lionel's Postwar Space & Military Trains. Joseph Algozzini. (Toy Train Reference Ser.: No. 2). (Illus.). 80p. (Orig.). 1996. pap. 16.95 (0-89778-429-4, 10-8075, Greenberg Books) Kalmbach.
***Lionel's Word Magic.** Golden Books Staff. (Illus.). (J). 2000. 7.99 (0-307-33236-5, Goldn Books) Gldn Bks Pub Co.
***Lioness.** Nell Brien. 408p. 2000. mass mkt. 5.99 (1-55166-598-0, 1-66598-3, Mira Bks) Harlequin Bks.
Lioness in Bloom: Modern Thai Fiction about Women. Ed. & Tr. by Susan F. Kepner from THA. LC 95-52953. 281p. (C). 1996. 48.00 (0-520-08902-2, Pub. by U CA Pr); pap. 17.95 (0-520-08903-0, Pub. by U CA Pr) Cal Prin Full Svc.
Lioness Rampant. Tamora Pierce. (Song of the Lioness Ser.). (YA). (gr. 5 up). 1997. pap. 4.99 (0-614-28947-5) Random Bks Yng Read.
Lioness Tamer: Man of the Month. Rebecca Brandewyne. (Desire Ser.: No. 1171). 1998. per. 3.75 (0-373-76171-6, 1-76171-7) Harlequin Bks.
Lionhead Lodge. Lloyd Peters. 180p. 1976. 12.00 (0-87770-167-9) Ye Galleon.
Lionheads. Josiah Bunting. LC 78-188356. 214p. 1972. 19.95 (0-8076-0632-4, Pub. by Braziller) Norton.
Lionheart in Hollywood: The Autobiography of Henry Wilcoxon. Henry Wilcoxon & Katherine Orrison. LC 91-36890. (Filmmakers Ser.: No. 27). (Illus.). 384p. 1991. 45.00 (0-8108-2476-0) Scarecrow.
***Lionhearted Queen: Berengaria of Navarre.** Victoria Sauers. 248p. 2000. pap. 14.95 (0-9666294-2-6) Blue Bear Pr.
Lionhearts: Heroes of Israel. Ed. by Michael Bar-Zohar. LC 98-84483. (Illus.). 352p. 1998. 30.00 (0-446-52358-5, Pub. by Warner Bks) Little.
Lionhearts: Heroes of Israel. Ed. by Michael Bar-Zohar. 352p. 1999. pap. write for info. (0-446-67528-8) Warner Bks.
Lionhearts: Richard I, Saladin & the Era of the Third Crusade. Geoffrey Regan. LC 98-53348. (Illus.). 288p. 1999. reprint ed. 25.00 (0-8027-1354-8) Walker & Co.
Lionness Roars: Shrew Stories from Late Imperial China. Tr. by Yenna Wu from CHI. LC 96-142439. (Cornell East Asia Ser.: Vol. 81). (Illus.). 170p. (C). 1995. 18.70 (1-885445-71-7, 81); pap. 11.90 (1-885445-81-4, 81) Cornell East Asia Pgm.
Lions see Zoobooks
Lions see Endangered! - Group 3
Lions. Brian Bertram. LC 98-17626. (Worldlife Library). (Illus.). 72p. (YA). 1998. pap. 16.95 (0-89658-399-6) Voyageur Pr.
***Lions.** Kathy Darling. LC 99-32632. (Nature Watch Ser.). (Illus.). 48p. (J). (gr. 2-5). 2000. 22.60 (1-57505-404-3, Carolrhoda) Lerner Pub.
Lions. Kevin J. Holmes. LC 98-17328. (Animals Ser.). (J). 1998. 14.00 (0-7368-0065-4) Bridgeview.
Lions. Don Middleton. LC 97-32690. (Big Cats Ser.). 24p. (J). (gr. k-4). 1998. 17.27 (0-8239-5208-8) Rosen Group.
Lions. Kate Petty. (Baby Animals Ser.). (Illus.). 24p. (J). (gr. k-3). 1993. pap. 3.95 (0-8120-1490-1) Barron.
Lions. Claire Robinson. LC 97-12310. (In the Wild Ser.). (Illus.). 24p. (J). (ps-2). 1998. 18.59 (1-57572-132-5) Heinemann Lib.
***Lions.** Susan Schafer. LC 00-24362. (Illus.). (J). 2000. write for info. (0-7614-1166-6) Marshall Cavendish.
Lions. Lee Server. (Illus.). 72p. 10.98 (1-57717-079-2) Todtri Prods.
Lions. Lynn M. Stone. (Big Cat Discovery Library). (Illus.). 24p. (J). (gr. k-5). 1989. 8.95 (0-685-58629-4) Rourke Corp.
Lions. Lynn M. Stone. (Big Cat Discovery Library). (Illus.). 24p. (J). (gr. k-4). 1989. lib. bdg. 14.60 (0-86592-501-1) Rourke Enter.
Lions. Anne Welsbacher. LC 98-4554. (Wild Cats Ser.). (Illus.). 24p. (J). 2000. lib. bdg. 18.60 (1-57765-086-7, Checkerboard Library) ABDO Pub Co.
Lions. Wildlife Education, Ltd. Staff et al. (Zoobooks Ser.). (Illus.). 24p. (J). 1993. 13.95 (0-937934-81-X) Wildlife Educ.
Lions. Wildlife Education, Ltd. Staff et al. (Zoobooks Ser.). (Illus.). 24p. (J). 1998. pap. 2.75 (0-937934-42-9) Wildlife Educ.
Lions & Bears! The Story of David the Shepherd Boy. Patricia L. Nederveld. LC 97-32476. (God Loves Me Ser.). (Illus.). 24p. (J). (ps). 1998. pap. 2.45 (1-56212-287-8, 1105-0118) CRC Pubns.
***Lions & Eagles & Bulls: Early American Tavern & Inn Signs from the Connecticut Historical Society.** Ed. by Susan P. Schoelwer. (Illus.). 192p. 2000. 49.50 (0-691-07060-1) Princeton U Pr.
Lions & Lobsters & Foxes & Frogs: Fables from Aesop. Ennis Rees et al. LC 75-155912. 48p. (J). 1971. write for info. (0-201-09246-8) Peachpit Pr.
***Lions & Shadows: An Education in the Twenties.** Christopher Isherwood. LC 99-59205. 2000. 15.95 (0-8166-3604-4) U of Minn Pr.
Lions & Tigers. Joanne Mattern. LC 92-19053. (Illus.). 24p. (J). (gr. 4-7). 1992. pap. 1.95 (0-8167-2956-5) Troll Communs.
Lions & Tigers & Bears. Alicia Williams. (Orig.). 1999. pap. 12.50 (1-889316-02-4) Ecrivez.
Lions & Tigers & Bears: Coping with Evil & Other Meditations for Soul & Mind. David Sugarbaker. 210p. 1997. pap. 15.00 (1-57502-590-6, PO1685) Morris Pubng.
Lions & Tigers & Leopards: The Big Cats, Set. Jennifer C. Urquhart. (Books for Young Explorers: Set 17, No. 3). (Illus.). (J). (gr. k-4). 1994. 8.00 (0-87044-820-X) Natl Geog.

***Lions at Lunchtime.** Mary Pope Osborne. (Magic Tree House Ser.: No. 11). (Illus.). (J). (gr. k-3). 1998. 9.09 (*0-606-12981-2*, Pub. by Turtleback) Demco.

Lions at Lunchtime, No. 11. Mary Pope Osborne. LC 97-19885. (Illus.). (J). (gr. k-3). 1998. pap. 3.99 (*0-679-88340-1*, Pub. by Random Bks Yng Read) Random.

Lions at Lunchtime, No. 11. Mary Pope Osborne. LC 97-19885. (Magic Tree House Ser.: No. 11). (Illus.). (J). (gr. k-3). 1998. lib. bdg. 11.99 (*0-679-98340-6*, Pub. by Random Bks Yng Read) Random.

Lion's Bride. Iris Johansen. 448p. 1996. mass mkt. 6.99 (*0-553-56990-2*, Fanfare) Bantam.

Lion's Bride. Connie Mason. 448p. (Orig.). 1995. pap. text, mass mkt. 5.99 (*0-8439-3884-6*) Dorchester Pub Co.

Lion's Child. Kathy Hooper. (Illus.). 80p. (J). (gr. 5). 1997. pap. 8.00 (*1-57502-622-8*, PO 1775) Morris Pubng.

Lions' Commentary on UNIX: Including Source Code. 6th ed. John Lions. 264p. 1996. pap. 29.95 (*1-57398-013-7*) Annabooks.

Lion's Cub. Richard H. Stoddard. (Notable American Authors Ser.). 1999. reprint ed. lib. bdg. 125.00 (*0-7812-8956-4*) Rprt Serv.

Lion's Daughter. Loretta Chase. 384p. (Orig.). 1992. mass mkt. 5.99 (*0-380-76647-7*, Avon Bks) Morrow Avon.

***Lion's Daughter.** large type ed. Pamela Hill. (G. K. Hall Nightingale Ser.). 2000. pap. 21.95 (*0-7838-8861-9*, G K Hall Lrg Type) Mac Lib Ref.

Lions' Den: Facing Yours. Preston Parrish. 88p. 1992. pap. text 4.95 (*0-9633470-8-X*) Awakenings.

Lions Don't Need to Roar: Using the Leadership Power of Personal Presence to Stand Out, Fit in & Move Ahead. D. A. Benton. 272p. 1993. reprint ed. mass mkt. 13.99 (*0-446-39499-8*, Pub. by Warner Bks) Little.

Lion's Game. Nelson DeMille. LC 99-52476. 528p. 2000. 26.95 (*0-446-52065-9*, Pub. by Warner Bks) Little.

***Lion's Game.** Nelson DeMille. 2001. mass mkt. 7.99 (*0-446-60826-2*, Warner Vision) Warner Bks.

Lion's Game. large type ed. Nelson DeMille. LC 99-88731. 1950. pap. 29.95 (*0-7862-2020-1*) Mac Lib Ref.

***Lion's Game.** large type ed. Nelson DeMille. LC 99-88731. (Basic Ser.). 2000. 31.95 (*0-7862-2019-8*) Thorndike Pr.

***Lions' Gate.** Lilia D'Acres & Donald Luxton. 160p. 2000. 26.95 (*0-88922-416-1*) Talonbks.

Lion's Gate: Selected Poems, 1963-1986. Keith Wilson. LC 87-72809. 96p. (Orig.). 1988. pap. text 8.95 (*0-938317-05-9*) Cinco Puntos.

Lion's Gaze: A Commentary on Tsig Sum Nedek. Palden S. Rinpoche & Tsewang D. Rinpoche. Ed. by Joan Kaye. Tr. by Sara Harding from TIB. (Illus.). 216p. 1998. mass mkt. write for info. (*1-880975-05-X*) Sky Dancer Pr.

Lions Gaze: A Dzogchen Commentary on Three Statements of Garalo Dorje & the Special Teaching of the Wise & Glorious Sovereign by Patrol Rindpoche. Khenchen P. Rinpoche & Khenpo T. Rinpoche. Ed. by Joan Kaye. Tr. by Sarah Harding from TIB. (Dzog-chen - The Clear Light Great Perfection Ser.). (Illus.). 240p. 1998. 90.00 (*1-880975-04-1*) Sky Dancer Pr.

Lion's Heart. Suzanne Barclay. LC 95-7108. (Historical Ser.). 299p. 1995. per. 3.99 (*0-373-28852-2*, 1-28852-1) Harlequin Bks.

Lion's Hunger: Poems of First Love. Ann W. Turner. LC 98-10865. (Illus.). 48p. (YA). (gr. 8-10). 1999. 15.95 (*0-7614-5035-1*) Marshall Cavendish.

Lions in the Path. S. E. White. (Illus.). 352p. 1987. reprint ed. 25.00 (*0-935632-55-7*) Wolfe Pub Co.

Lion's Lady. Julie Garwood. Ed. by Linda Marrow. 1991. per. 6.99 (*0-671-73783-X*) PB.

Lion's Lady. large type ed. Julie Garwood. LC 93-46288. 498p. 1994. pap. 17.95 (*0-8161-5388-4*, G K Hall Lrg Type) Mac Lib Ref.

Lion's Lady: The Sutherland Series. Suzanne Barclay. (Historical Ser.). 1998. per. 4.99 (*0-373-29011-X*, 0-29011-4) Harlequin Bks.

Lion's Legacy. Suzanne Barclay. LC 96-7292. (Historical Ser.). 296p. 1996. per. 4.50 (*0-373-28904-9*, 1-28904-0) Harlequin Bks.

Lions, Lions! The Story of Daniel. Patricia L. Nederveld. LC 97-32484. (God Loves Me Ser.). (Illus.). 24p. (J). (ps). 1998. pap. 2.45 (*1-56212-292-4*, 1105-0123) CRC Pubns.

Lions, Lizards & Ladybugs. Ed. by Kathleen L. Mendel. LC 89-51485. (Illus.). 80p. (J). (gr. k-6). 1989. pap. 9.95 (*0-9624384-2-1*) Telstar MI.

Lion's Mouth, Vol. 1. Caterina Edwards. (Prose Ser.: No. 16). 272p. 1993. pap. 12.00 (*0-920717-67-5*) Guernica Editions.

Lions' Mouths. Alan Brownjohn. LC 67-28704. 1967. 15.95 (*0-8023-1132-6*) Dufour.

Lions of Al-Rassan, The, RI. Guy Gavriel Kay. 554p. 1999. mass mkt. 6.50 (*0-06-105621-9*, HarperPrism) HarpC.

Lions of Flanders: Flemish Volunteers of the Waffen-SS, Eastern Front, 1941-1945. Richard Landwehr. 163p. 1998. pap. 32.00 (*1-899765-03-4*) Intl Spec Bk.

Lions of July: Prelude to War, 1914. William Jannen, Jr. LC 95-9454. (Illus.). 480p. 1997. pap. 18.95 (*0-89141-637-4*) Presidio Pr.

Lions of the Desert. Linda Chaikin. LC 97-27848. 454p. 1997. pap. 9.99 (*1-57673-114-6*, Multnomah Bks) Multnomah Pubs.

Lions of the Desert: Arab Volunteers in the German Army, 1941-1945. 2nd ed. Antonio J. Munoz. (Illus.). 36p. 1994. pap. 18.00 (*1-891227-03-3*, Axis Europa Bks) Axis Europa.

Lions of the Lord, a Tale of the Old West. Harry Leon Wilson. (Collected Works of Harry Leon Wilson). 520p. 1999. reprint ed. lib. bdg. 128.00 (*1-58201-878-2*) Classic Bks.

Lions of the Punjab. Richard G. Fox. 1986. 120.00 (*0-7855-1819-3*, Pub. by Archives Pubs) St Mut.

Lion's Pride: Theodore Roosevelt & His Family in Peace & War. Edward J. Renehan, Jr. LC 98-23998. (Illus.). 320p. 1998. 27.50 (*0-19-512719-6*) OUP.

Lion's Pride: Theodore Roosevelt & His Family in Peace & War. Edward J. Renehan. (Illus.). 320p. 1999. pap. 16.95 (*0-19-513424-9*) OUP.

Lions Raw: A Captain's Story - South Africa, 1997. Martin Johnson & Howard Johnson. (Illus.). 208p. 1998. 35.00 (*1-84018-023-4*, Pub. by Mainstream Pubng) Trafalgar.

Lion's Roar: Actualizing Buddhism in Daily Life & Building the Pure Land in Our Midst. Hsing Yun & Charles Wei. Tr. by Yung Kai & Chen Xin. LC 90-25346. (Asian Thought & Culture Ser.: Vol. 6). XVII, 218p. (C). 1991. text 35.95 (*0-8204-1544-8*) P Lang Pubng.

Lion's Roar: Chinese Luogu Percussion Ensembles. 2nd ed. Kuo-huang Han & Patricia S. Campbell. (Illus.). 69p. 1997. pap. 22.95 incl. audio compact disk (*0-937203-77-7*); pap. 22.95 incl. audio (*0-937203-78-5*) World Music Pr.

Lion's Roar: Chinese Luogu Percussion Ensembles, Incl. slides. Kuo-huang Han & Patricia S. Campbell. (Illus.). 69p. (Orig.). 1992. pap. 35.00 incl. audio (*0-937203-49-1*) World Music Pr.

Lion's Roar: Sihanada Suttas (MN 11 & 12) Tr. by Bhikkhu Nanamoli. 48p. 1993. 3.75 (*955-24-0115-1*, Pub. by Buddhist Pub Soc) Vipassana Res Pubns.

Lions Roar of Queen Srimala. Alex Wayman & Hideko Wayman. 1990. reprint ed. 20.00 (*81-208-0731-6*, Pub. by Motilal Bnarsidass) S Asia.

***Lion's Shadow.** Marthe Arends. (Illus.). 330p. 1999. mass mkt. 6.99 (*1-929613-05-9*) Avid MI.

Lions Shadow. Elizabeth De Guise. 1980. pap. 1.50 (*0-373-58006-1*) Harlequin Bks.

***Lion's Share.** Chris Conover. (Illus.). 40p. (J). 2000. 16.00 (*0-374-39974-3*) FS&G.

Lion's Share. El Gilbert. 24p. (Orig.). 1990. pap. 4.95 (*1-878781-02-2*) Free River Pr.

Lion's Share. Rochelle Ratner. LC 91-24085. 176p. (Orig.). 1991. pap. 10.95 (*0-918273-87-0*) Coffee Hse.

Lion's Share. Arnold Bennett. LC 74-17027. (Collected Works of Arnold Bennett: Vol. 46). 1977. reprint ed. 34.95 (*0-518-19127-3*) Ayer.

Lions Share. 3rd ed. Bernard Porter. LC 95-50463. 464p. (C). 1996. pap. text 23.44 (*0-582-08943-3*, Pub. by Addison-Wesley) Longman.

Lions Share: A Short History of British Imperialism, 1850-1995. 3rd ed. Bernard Porter. 464p. (C). 1996. text 59.06 (*0-582-29294-8*) Addison-Wesley.

Lion's Share: How Three Small-Town Grocers Created America's Fastest-Growing Supermarket Chain & Made Millionaires of Scores of Their North Carolina Friends & Neighbors. Mark Wineka & Jason Lesley. Ed. by Jerry Bledsoe. (Illus.). 265p. 1991. 19.95 (*1-878086-07-3*, Pub. by Down Home NC) Blair.

Lion's Share: The GI's of the Snow Mountains. Donald J. Young. LC 90-81492. 149p. (Orig.). 1990. pap. 7.95 (*0-9625886-0-1*) Avranches Pr.

Lion's Skin: A Historical Novel & a Novel History. John S. Wise. LC 72-2066. (Black Heritage Library Collection). 1977. reprint ed. 35.95 (*0-8369-9073-0*) Ayer.

Lion's Tale: A History of the Wellesley Hospital. Joan Hollobon. 182p. 1987. 24.95 (*0-7725-1220-5*) Genl Dist Srvs.

Lions, Tigers & Leopards: The Big Cats. National Geographic Society Staff. (Kids Want to Know Ser.). (Illus.). 32p. (J). (ps-3). pap. 4.95 (*0-7922-3603-3*, Pub. by Natl Geog) Publishers Group.

***Lions to Lamb.** David E. Preston. LC 99-94919. 2000. pap. 9.95 (*0-533-13222-3*) Vantage.

Lion's Way. Lewis Orde. 1987. mass mkt. 4.50 (*0-8217-2087-2*, Zebra Kensgtn) Kensgtn Pub Corp.

***Lion's Whelp.** Amelia E. Barr. 252p. 2000. pap. 9.95 (*0-594-00426-8*) Eightn Hundrd.

Lion's Whelp. Nigel Tranter. 320p. 1997. 27.00 (*0-340-65998-X*, Pub. by Hodder & Stought Ltd) Trafalgar.

Lion's Whelp. Nigel Tranter. 320p. 1998. pap. 11.95 (*0-340-65999-8*, Pub. by Hodder & Stought Ltd) Trafalgar.

Lion's Whiskers: An Ethiopian Folktale. Nancy R. Day. LC 94-14453. (Illus.). 32p. (J). (gr. k-3). 1995. 14.95 (*0-590-45803-5*) Scholastic Inc.

Lion's Whiskers & Other Ethiopian Tales. rev. ed. Ed. by Brent K. Ashabranner. LC 97-3981. (Illus.). xvi, 96p. (J). (gr. 3 up). 1997. lib. bdg. 19.95 (*0-208-02429-8*, Linnet Bks) Shoe String.

Lios. Ty Heintze. LC 98-92959. (Illus.). (YA). (gr. 3-11). 1998. pap. 9.95 (*0-9665317-0-1*) Btemn Pr.

Lip & the Self-Managed Counter-Revolution. 1975. pap. 1.75 (*0-934868-14-X*) Black & Red.

Lip Flexibilities: For All Brass Instruments. Bai Lin. 40p. 1996. pap. text 14.00 (*0-9630856-6-2*) Balquhidder.

Lip Reading Made Easy. Edward B. Nitchie. 1998. pap. text 10.00 (*0-9666932-8-0*) Breakout Prods Inc.

Lip Service. Robert McRoberts. LC 76-55803. 59p. 1976. 3.50 (*0-87886-078-9*, Greenfld Rev Pr) Greenfld Rev Lit.

***Lip Service.** M. J. Rose. LC 99-35880. 304p. 1999. 18.00 (*0-671-04131-2*, PB Hardcover) PB.

***Lip Service.** M. J. Rose. 320p. 2000. reprint ed. per. 12.95 (*0-671-04132-0*) PB.

Lip Service: Alluring New Lesbian Erotica. Ed. by Jess Wells. LC 99-36468. 272p. 1999. pap. 12.95 (*1-55583-503-1*, Pub. by Alyson Pubns) Consort Bk Sales.

Lip Service vs. Customer Service: Making Customer Cents from Customer Sense. Lynda Jeppesen. 176p. 1996. pap. text, per. 14.95 (*0-7872-1969-X*) Kendall-Hunt.

Lipa's Legacy: Proceedings of the BERS Colloquium, October 19-20, 1995, Graduate School & University Center of CUNY. Ed. by Jozef Dodziuk & Linda Keen. LC 97-25848. (Contemporary Mathematics Ser.: Vol. 211). 488p. 1997. pap. 71.00 (*0-8218-0671-8*) Am Math.

Lipase- & Protease-Catalyzed Transformations with Unnatural Acyl Acceptors. Marian De Zoete. (Illus.). 125p. (Orig.). 1995. pap. 57.50 (*90-407-1135-6*, Pub. by Delft U Pr) Coronet Bks.

Lipase & Phospholipase Protocols. Mark Doolittle & Karen Reue. LC 98-22766. (Methods in Molecular Biology Ser.: Vol. 109). 384p. 1998. 79.50 (*0-89603-546-8*) Humana.

Lipases. B. Borgstrom & H. L. Brockman. 500p. 1984. 318.75 (*0-444-80526-5*, I-208-84) Elsevier.

Lipases: Structure, Mechanisms & Genetic Engineering. Ed. by L. Alberghina et al. (GBF Monographs: Vol:16). (Illus.). 441p. (Orig.). 1991. pap. 131.00 (*3-527-28332-3*, Wiley-VCH) Wiley.

Lipases: Structure, Mechanisms & Genetic Engineering. Ed. by R. D. Schmid et al. (GBF Monographs: Vol. 16). 440p. (Orig.). 1991. pap. 104.00 (*1-56081-165-X*, Wiley-VCH) Wiley.

Lipases: Their Structure, Biochemistry & Application. Ed. by Paul Woolley & Steffen B. Petersen. (Illus.). 377p. (C). 1994. text 74.95 (*0-521-44546-9*) Cambridge U Pr.

Lipases Pt. A: Biotechnology, Pt. A. Ed. by Byron Rubin et al. (Methods in Enzymology Ser.: Vol. 284). (Illus.). 408p. 1997. text 89.95 (*0-12-182185-4*) Morgan Kaufmann.

Lipases Pt. B: Enzyme Characterization & Utilization, Pt. B. Ed. by John N. Abelson et al. (Methods in Enzymology Ser.: Vol. 286). (Illus.). 563p. 1997. text 99.95 (*0-12-182187-0*) Morgan Kaufmann.

Lipatti. Dragos Tanasescu & Grigore Bargauanu. Ed. & Tr. by Carola Grindea. Tr. by Anne Goosens. (Illus.). 256p. 1988. 26.50 (*0-912483-18-0*) Pro-Am Music.

Lipetsk Oblast: Economy, Industry, Government, Business. 2nd rev. ed. Russian Information & Business Center, Inc. Staff. (Russian Regional Business Directories Ser.). (Illus.). 200p. 1997. pap. 99.00 (*1-57751-396-7*) Intl Business Pubns.

***Lipetsk Oblast Regional Investment & Business Guide.** Global Investment & Business Center, Inc. Staff. (Russian Regional Investment & Business Guides Ser.: Vol. 43). (Illus.). 350p. 1999. pap. 99.00 (*0-7397-0847-3*) Intl Business Pubns.

***Lipetsk Oblast Regional Investment & Business Guide.** Contrib. by Global Investment & Business Center, Inc. Staff. (Russian Regional Investment & Business Guides Ser.: Vol. 27). (Illus.). 350p. 2000. pap. 99.95 (*0-7397-2991-8*) Intl Business Pubns.

Lipid Analysis. F. W. Hemming et al. (Introduction to Biotechniques Ser.). 192p. 1996. pap. 37.90 (*1-872748-98-8*, Pub. by Bios Sci) Bks Intl VA.

Lipid Analysis: Isolation, Separation, Identification & Structural Analysis of Lipids. 2nd ed. W. W. Christie. LC 82-491. (Illus.). 224p. 1982. pap. text 42.00 (*0-08-023792-4*, Pergamon Pr) Elsevier.

Lipid & Biopolymer Monolayers at Liquid Interfaces. K. S. Birdi. LC 88-23172. (Illus.). 336p. (C). 1989. text 110.00 (*0-306-42870-9*, Kluwer Plenum) Kluwer Academic.

Lipid & Protein Traffic: Pathways & Molecular Mechanisms. Jos A. Kamp. LC 98-2792. (NATA ASI Ser.: Series H, Vol. 106). (Illus.). x, 364p. 1998. 159.00 (*3-540-64115-7*) Spr-Verlag.

Lipid Binding Proteins Within Molecular & Cellular Biochemistry. David A. Bernlohr & Leonard Banaszak. LC 98-28801. (Developments in Molecular & Cellular Biochemistry Ser.). 1998. write for info. (*0-7923-8223-4*) Kluwer Academic.

Lipid Biochemistry: An Introduction. 3rd ed. M. I. Gurr & A. T. James. 1980. pap. 22.50 (*0-412-22630-8*, 6334) Chapman & Hall.

Lipid Biochemistry: An Introduction. 4th ed. M. I. Gurr & J. L. Harwood. (Illus.). 340p. 1990. text 87.50 (*0-412-26610-5*, A3901) Chapman & Hall.

Lipid Biochemistry of Fungi & Other Organisms. John D. Weete. LC 80-22158. (Illus.). 400p. 1980. reprint ed. pap. 124.00 (*0-608-05399-6*, 206586800006) Bks Demand.

Lipid Chromatographic Analysis. Ed. by Takayuki Shibamoto. (Chromatographic Science Ser.: Vol. 65). (Illus.). 424p. 1993. text 165.00 (*0-8247-8941-5*) Dekker.

Lipid Chromatographic Analysis, Vol. 1. 2nd ed. Ed. by Guido V. Marinetti. LC 75-42515. 351p. reprint ed. pap. 108.90 (*0-7837-0008-3*, 201768900001) Bks Demand.

Lipid Chromatographic Analysis, Vol. 2. 2nd ed. Ed. by Guido V. Marinetti. LC 75-42515. 383p. reprint ed. pap. 118.80 (*0-7837-0009-1*, 201768900002) Bks Demand.

Lipid Chromatographic Analysis, Vol. 3. Ed. by Guido V. Marinetti. LC 75-42515. 300p. reprint ed. pap. 93.00 (*0-8357-9085-1*, 201768900003) Bks Demand.

Lipid Glossary. F. D. Gunstone & B. G. Herslof. (Oily Press Lipid Library: Vol. 3). (Illus.). 120p. 1992. 28.00 (*0-9514171-2-6*, Pub. by Oily Pr) Matreya.

Lipid Handbook. 2nd ed. J. L. Harwood & Frank D. Gunstone. (Illus.). 1312p. (C). (gr. 13). 1997. ring bd. 519.95 (*0-412-43320-6*, Chap & Hall CRC) CRC Pr.

Lipid Homeostasis & the Kidney. Ed. by W. F. Keane & B. L. Kasiske. (Journal: Mineral & Electrolyte Metabolism Ser.: Vol. 19, No. 3, 1993). (Illus.). 96p. 1993. pap. 41.00 (*3-8055-5832-5*) S Karger.

Lipid Hormone-Based Drug Therapies. Lynn Gray. LC 98-120893. (Report Ser.: No. B-116). (Illus.). 191p. 1997. 3150.00 (*1-56965-379-8*, B-116) BCC.

Lipid Lowering Therapy & Progression of Coronary Atherosclerosis. Ed. by A. V. Bruschke. (Developments in Cardiovascular Medicine Ser.). 240p. (C). 1996. text 129.00 (*0-7923-3807-3*) Kluwer Academic.

Lipid Mediators in Allergic Diseases of the Respiratory Tract. Clive Robinson. 268p. 1994. lib. bdg. 225.00 (*0-8493-5416-1*, RC859) CRC Pr.

Lipid Mediators in Eye Inflammation. Ed. by Nicolas G. Bazan. (New Trends in Lipid Mediators Research Ser.: Vol. 5). (Illus.). x, 192p. 1990. 155.00 (*3-8055-5067-7*) S Karger.

Lipid Mediators in Ischemic Brain Damage & Experimental Epilepsy. Ed. by Nicolas G. Bazan. (New Trends in Lipid Mediators Research Ser.: Vol. 4). (Illus.). viii, 262p. 1990. 207.00 (*3-8055-5068-5*) S Karger.

Lipid Mediators in the Immunology of Shock. Ed. by M. Paubert-Braquet et al. LC 87-29239. (NATO ASI Series A, Life Sciences: Vol. 139). (Illus.). 540p. 1988. 135.00 (*0-306-42694-3*, Plenum Trade) Perseus Pubng.

Lipid Metabolism in Mammals, 2 vols. Ed. by Fred Snyder. Incl. Vol. 1. LC 77-913. 420p. 1977. 55.00 (*0-306-35802-6*, Kluwer Plenum); Vol. 2. LC 77-913. 408p. 1977. 55.00 (*0-306-35803-4*, Kluwer Plenum); LC 77-913. (Monographs in Lipid Research). (Illus.). 1977. write for info. (*0-318-55329-5*, Plenum Trade) Perseus Pubng.

Lipid Metabolism in Normoxic & Ischemic Heart. Ed. by Ger J. Van der Vusse. (Developments in Molecular & Cellular BioChemistry Ser.). Orig. Title: Molecular & Cellular Biochemistry. (C). 1989. reprint ed. text 199.50 (*0-7923-0479-9*) Kluwer Academic.

Lipid Metabolism in Plants. Thomas S. Moore, Jr. 672p. 1993. 218.00 (*0-8493-4907-9*, QK898) CRC Pr.

Lipid Metabolism in the Healthy & Diseased Heart: Proceedings of the 3rd International Symposium on Lipid Metabolism in the Normoxic & Ischemic Heart, September 9-10, 1991, Rotterdam, The Netherlands. Ed. by Ger J. Van Der Vusse & Hans Stam. LC 92-23631. 208p. (C). 1992. text 210.50 (*0-7923-1850-1*) Kluwer Academic.

Lipid Metabolism Membrane Functions of the Mammary Gland see Progress in the Chemistry of Fats & Other Lipids

Lipid Modification of Proteins. Milton J. Schlesinger. 208p. 1992. lib. bdg. 189.00 (*0-8493-6740-9*, QP552) CRC Pr.

Lipid Modification of Proteins: A Practical Approach. Ed. by N. M. Hooper & A. J. Turner. (Practical Approach Ser.: Vol. 95). (Illus.). 312p. 1992. 85.00 (*0-19-963274-X*); pap. text 49.95 (*0-19-963273-1*) OUP.

Lipid Modifications of Proteins. Ed. by Patrick J. Casey & Janice E. Buss. (Methods in Enzymology Ser.: Vol. 250). (Illus.). 754p. 1995. text 104.00 (*0-12-182151-X*) Acad Pr.

Lipid Nutrition: Understanding Fats & Oils in Health & Disease. Randy L. Wysong. LC 90-82662. (Illus.). 170p. (Orig.). 1990. 14.95 (*0-918112-04-4*); pap. 12.95 (*0-918112-03-6*) Inquiry Pr.

Lipid Oxidation. unabridged ed. Edwin N. Frankel. (Oily Press Lipid Library: Vol. 10). (Illus.). 300p. 1998. 76.00 (*0-9514171-9-3*) Matreya.

Lipid Oxidation in Food. Ed. by Allen J. St. Angelo. LC 92-19970. (ACS Symposium Ser.: No. 500). (Illus.). 364p. 1992. text 98.00 (*0-8412-2461-7*, Pub. by Am Chemical) OUP.

Lipid Peroxidation in Biological Systems. Ed. by Alex Sevanian. 254p. 1988. 40.00 (*0-935315-18-7*) Am Oil Chemists.

Lipid Peroxidation in Biomembranes. Valerian E. Kagan. 192p. 1988. 112.00 (*0-8493-6923-1*, QP752, CRC Reprint) Franklin.

Lipid Second Messengers. Ed. by Robert M. Bell et al. (Handbook of Lipid Research Ser.: Vol. 8). (Illus.). 330p. 1996. 89.50 (*0-306-45174-3*, Kluwer Plenum) Kluwer Academic.

Lipid Second Messengers. Ronald P. Rubin & Suzanne Laychock. LC 98-50105. (Methods in Life Sciences - Signal Transduction Ser.). 160p. 1998. per. 94.95 (*0-8493-3383-0*) CRC Pr.

Lipid-Soluble Antioxidants: Biochemistry & Clinical Applications. Ed. by A. S. Ong & Lester Packer. LC 92-49649. (Molecular & Cell Biology Updates Ser.). xii, 640p. 1992. 165.00 (*0-8176-2667-0*, Pub. by Birkhauser) Princeton Arch.

Lipid Storage Disorders: Biological & Medical Aspects. Ed. by R. Salvayre et al. (NATO ASI Series A, Life Sciences: Vol. 150). (Illus.). 856p. 1988. 165.00 (*0-306-42928-4*, Plenum Trade) Perseus Pubng.

Lipid Synthesis & Manufacture. Sheffield Academic Press Staff. LC 98-11206. 1998. ring bd. 135.00 (*0-8493-9737-5*) CRC Pr.

Lipid Synthesis & Manufacture: Chemistry & Technology of Oils & Fats. (Sheffield Oils & Fats Ser.: Vol. 1). 352p. 1998. write for info. (*1-85075-931-6*, Pub. by Sheffield Acad) CUP Services.

Lipid Technologies & Applications. Ed. by F. D. Gunstone & Fred B. Padley. LC 97-8301. (Illus.). 848p. 1997. text 225.00 (*0-8247-9838-4*) Dekker.

LIPIDAT: A Cent. Database for Therm Data on Lipid Mesmo Etc. Martin Caffrey. 320p. 1993. lib. bdg. 159.00 (*0-8493-8924-0*, QP751) CRC Pr.

Lipids see Methods in Enzymology

Lipids, Pt. C. Ed. by Sidney P. Colowick et al. (Methods in Enzymology Ser.: Vol. 71). 1981. text 188.00 (*0-12-181971-X*) Acad Pr.

Lipids, Pt. D. Ed. by Sidney P. Colowick et al. (Methods in Enzymology Ser.: Vol. 72). 1981. text 188.00 (*0-12-181972-8*) Acad Pr.

Lipids: Biochemistry, Vol. 1. fac. ed. International Congress for Fat Research Staff. Ed. by Rodolfo Paoletti et al. LC 74-21982. (Illus.). 300p. pap. 93.00 (*0-7837-7140-1*, 204715400001) Bks Demand.

Lipids: Chemistry, Biochemistry & Nutrition. J. F. Mead et al. LC 85-19304. (Illus.). 494p. (C). 1986. text 130.00 (*0-306-41990-4*, Kluwer Plenum) Kluwer Academic.

L

Lipids: Current Perspectives. Ed. by D. John Betteridge. 312p. (C). 1996. text. write for info. (1-85317-231-6) Mosby Inc.

Lipids: Directory of Authors of New Medical & Scientific Reviews with Subject Index. Science & Life Consultants Association Staff. 160p. 1995. 47.50 (0-7883-0594-8); pap. 44.50 (0-7883-0595-6) ABBE Pubs Assn.

Lipids: New Technologies, Applications & Markets. 176p. 1993. 2850.00 (0-89336-957-8, C-165) BCC.

Lipids & Cardiovascular Disease. Ed. by D. J. Galton & G. R. Thompson. (Illus.). 264p. 1990. text 135.00 (0-443-04327-2) Church.

Lipids & Heart Diseases: A Guide for the Primary Care Team. 2nd ed. Madaleine Ball & Jim Mann. (Illus.). 184p. 1995. pap. text 39.50 (0-19-262495-4) OUP.

Lipids & Lipid Disorders. 2nd ed. Feher. 1997. text 15.00 (0-7234-2830-1) Wolfe Pubng AZ.

Lipids & Lipoproteins. Ed. by M. Fondu. (Journal: Nutrition & Metabolism: Vol. 24, Suppl. 1). (Illus.). iv, 212p. 1980. 42.75 (3-8055-1266-X) S Karger.

Lipids & Lipoproteins in Clinical Practice. Neil & McIntyre. 160p. (C). (gr. 13). 1990. text 59.00 (0-7234-0946-3) Mosby Inc.

Lipids & Related Compounds. Ed. by Alan A. Boulton et al. LC 88-8909. (Neuromethods Ser.: Vol. 7). (Illus.). 360p. 1989. 99.50 (0-89603-124-1) Humana.

Lipids & Renal Disease. Ed. by William F. Keane. (Contemporary Issues in Nephrology Ser.: Vol. 24). (Illus.). 216p. 1991. text 73.00 (0-443-08779-2) Church.

Lipids & Syndromes of Insulin Resistance: From Molecular Biology to Clinical Medicine. Ed. by Steven M. Haffner et al. LC 97-18285. (Annals of the New York Academy of Sciences Ser.: No. 827). 582p. 1997. 160.00 (1-57331-070-0) NY Acad Sci.

Lipids & Syndromes of Insulin Resistance: From Molecular Biology to Clinical Medicine. Ed. by Iwar Klimes et al. LC 97-18285. (Annals of the New York Academy of Sciences Ser.: No. 827). 582p. 1997. pap. 160.00 (1-57331-071-9) NY Acad Sci.

Lipids & the Kidney. Ed. by William F. Keane & Bertram L. Kasiske. LC 97-2775. (Contributions to Nephrology Ser.: Vol. 120, 1997). (Illus.). x, 234p. 1997. 199.25 (3-8055-6389-2) S Karger.

Lipids & Tumors. Ed. by K. K. Carroll. (Progress in Biochemical Pharmacology Ser.: Vol. 10). (Illus.). 300p. 1975. 128.75 (3-8055-1708-4) S Karger.

Lipids & Women's Health. Ed. by Geoffrey P. Redmond. (Illus.). 272p. 1990. 89.00 (0-387-97318-4) Spr-Verlag.

Lipids As a Source of Flavor. Ed. by Michael K. Supran. LC 78-9739. (ACS Symposium Ser.: Vol. 75). 131p. 1978. reprint ed. pap. 40.70 (0-608-03933-0, 206438000009) Bks Demand.

Lipids, Health, & Behavior. Ed. by Marc Hillbrand & Reuben T. Spitz. LC 96-41709. 341p. 1996. 29.95 (1-55798-384-4, 431-8530) Am Psychol.

Lipids in Cereal Technology. Ed. by Peter Barnes. (Food Science & Technology Ser.). 1984. text 142.00 (0-12-079020-3) Acad Pr.

Lipids in Food Flavors. Ed. by Chi-Tang Ho & Thomas G. Hartman. LC 94-13923. (ACS Symposium Ser.: Vol. 558). 344p. 1994. text 98.00 (0-8412-2922-8, Pub. by Am Chemical) OUP.

Lipids in Freshwater Ecosystems. M. T. Arts & B. Wainman. (Illus.). 384p. 1998. 69.95 (0-387-98505-0) Spr-Verlag.

***Lipids in Health & Nutrition.** Ed. by J. H. P. Tyman. (Special Publication Ser.: Vol. 244). 180p. 1999. 119.00 (0-85404-798-0) Royal Soc Chem.

Lipids in Infant Nutrition. Ed. by Yung-Sheng Huang & Andrew J. Sinclair. LC 98-14490. (Illus.). 304p. 1998. lib. bdg. 99.00 (0-935315-92-6, PC121) Am Oil Chemists.

Lipids in Modern Nutrition. Ed. by Marc Horisberger & Umberto Bracco. LC 86-43184. (Nestle Nutrition Workshop Ser.: Vol. 13). 264p. 1987. reprint ed. pap. 81.90 (0-608-00335-2, 206105200007) Bks Demand.

Lipids in Photosynthesis: Structure, Function & Genetics. Paul A. Siegenthaler & Norio Murata. LC 98-26188. (Advances in Photosynthesis Ser.). 1998. write for info. (0-7923-5173-8) Kluwer Academic.

Lipids in Plants & Microbes. J. L. Harwood & N. J. Russell. (Illus.). 192p. (C). 1984. pap. text 21.95 (0-04-574022-4) Routledge.

Lipids, Malnutrition & the Developing Brain: A Ciba Foundation. Symposium on Lipids, Malnutrition & the Developing. LC 72-76009. 338p. reprint ed. pap. 104.80 (0-608-16195-0, 201464200094) Bks Demand.

Lipids-Molecular Organization, Physical Function & Technical Applications. Kare Larsson. (Oily Press Lipid Library Ser.). (Illus.). 235p. (C). 1994. 60.00 (0-9514171-4-2, Pub. by Oily Pr) Matreya.

Lipids of Fungi see Progress in the Chemistry of Fats & Other Lipids

Lipids of Human Milk. Robert G. Jensen. 224p. 1988. 129.00 (0-8493-6559-7, QP246, CRC Reprint) Franklin.

Lipids of Pathogenic Fungi. Ed. by R. Prasad & Mahoud A. Ghannoum. LC 96-24683. 304p. 1996. boxed set 189.95 (0-8493-4794-7) CRC Pr.

Lipika. Rabindranath Tagore. 140p. 1977. 24.00 (0-7206-0505-9) Dufour.

Lipika. Rabindranath Tagore. Tr. by Aurobindo Bose. 140p. 1977. 23.00 (0-685-18792-6, Pub. by P Owen Ltd) Dufour.

Lipizzan Spirit. Betsy S. Siino. (Spirit of the Horse Ser.: No. 5). (Illus.). 64p. 2001. pap. 16.95 (1-889540-18-8) Bowtie Press.

Lipizzaner Horse see Learning about Horses Series

Lipizzaner Horse. Charlotte Wilcox. (Learning about Horses Ser.). (Illus.). (J). 1997. 19.00 (0-516-20517-X) Childrens.

Lipizzaner Horses see Magnificent Horses of the World

Lipizzans. Lynn Stone. LC 98-25095. (Horses Ser.). (J). 1998. 55.01 (0-86593-512-2) Rourke Corp.

Liplap's Wish. Jonathan London. LC 93-31007. (Illus.). 32p. (J). (ps-3). 1994. 13.95 (0-8118-0505-0) Chronicle Bks.

Liplap's Wish. Jonathan London. (Illus.). 32p. (J). (ps-3). 1997. pap. 6.95 (0-8118-1810-1) Chronicle Bks.

Lipmann Symposium: Energy, Regulation & Biosynthesis in Molecular Biology. Ed. by Dietmar Richter. 698p. (C). 1974. 138.50 (3-11-004976-7) De Gruyter.

Lipo-Corticotropic Hormones & Cushing's Disease. Ed. by G. Copinschi & P. Jaquet. (Journal: Hormone Research Ser.: Vol. 13, No. 4-5). (Illus.). 152p. 1981. pap. 57.50 (3-8055-3410-8) S Karger.

Lipofuscin & Ceroid Pigments. Ed. by Ernesto Porta. (Advances in Experimental Medicine & Biology Ser.: Vol. 266). (Illus.). 393p. 1989. 110.00 (0-306-43519-5, Plenum Trade) Perseus Pubng.

Lipofuscin & Ceroid Pigments: State of the Art, 1995. Ed. by K. Kitani et al. (Journal Ser.: Vol. 41, No. 2, 1995). (Illus.). x, 330p. 1996. pap., suppl. ed. 50.50 (3-8055-6259-4) S Karger.

Lipoic Acid: The Metabolic Antioxidant. Richard A. Passwater. (Good Health Guides Ser.). 48p. (Orig.). 1996. pap. 3.95 (0-87983-720-9, 37209K, Keats Publng) NTC Contemp Pub Co.

Lipoic Acid in Health & Disease. Ed. by Fuchs et al. LC 97-22478. (Antioxidants in Health & Disease Ser.: Vol. 7). (Illus.). 504p. 1997. text 175.00 (0-8247-0093-7) Dekker.

Lipolysis: The Theory & Practice of Suction Lipectomy. Gregory P. Hetter. 448p. 1984. 125.00 (0-316-35920-3, Little Brwn Med Div) Lppncott W & W.

Lipomatous Tumors: Diagnosis & Primary Treatment. Ed. by I. De Wever & M. Stas. (Illus.). 161p. (Orig.). 1997. pap. 47.50 (90-6186-798-3, Pub. by Leuven Univ) Coronet Bks.

Lipophilicity in Drug Action & Toxicology. Ed. by Bernard Testa et al. (Methods & Principles in Medicinal Chemistry Ser.: Vol. 4). (Illus.). 439p. 1996. 205.00 (3-527-29383-3, Wiley-VCH) Wiley.

Lipoplasty: The Theory & Practice of Blunt Suction Lipectomy. 2nd ed. Gregory P. Hetter. 360p. 1990. text 250.00 (0-316-35918-1, Little Brwn Med Div) Lppncott W & W.

Lipoprotein Analysis: A Practical Approach. Ed. by Carolyn A. Converse & Roy Skinner. (Practical Approach Ser.). (Illus.). 272p. 1992. pap. text 42.00 (0-19-963231-6) OUP.

Lipoprotein Deficiency Syndromes. Ed. by Aubie Angel & Jiri Frohlich. LC 86-16852. (Advances in Experimental Medicine & Biology Ser.: Vol. 201). (Illus.). 314p. 1986. 75.00 (0-306-42380-4, Plenum Trade) Perseus Pubng.

Lipoprotein Metabolism. Ed. by S. Eisenberg. (Progress in Biochemical Pharmacology Ser.: Vol. 15). (Illus.). 1979. 112.25 (3-8055-2985-6) S Karger.

Lipoprotein Precipitation. M. Burstein & P. Legmann. (Monographs on Atherosclerosis: Vol. 11). (Illus.). viii, 132p. 1982. 84.50 (3-8055-3512-0) S Karger.

Lipoprotein Protocols. Jose M. Ordovas. LC 98-228469. (Methods in Molecular Biology Ser.: Vol. 110). (Illus.). 304p. 1998. 79.50 (0-89603-420-8) Humana.

Lipoprotein Subfraction Omega-3 Fatty Acids. Tr. by H. U. Klor. (Recent Developments in Lipid & Lipoprotein Research Ser.). (Illus.). 133p. 1989. 62.95 (0-387-19146-1) Spr-Verlag.

Lipoproteins. Ed. by Edward G. Perkins. 176p. 1993. pap. 35.00 (0-935315-48-9) Am Oil Chemists.

Lipoproteins & Atherosclerosis. Ed. by C. L. Malmendier & P. Alaupovic. LC 87-2345. (Advances in Experimental Medicine & Biology Ser.: Vol. 210). 266p. 1987. 69.50 (0-306-42487-8, Plenum Trade) Perseus Pubng.

Lipoproteins As Carriers of Pharmacological Agents. Ed. by Michael J. Shaw. (Targeted Diagnosis & Therapy Ser.: Vol. 5). (Illus.). 408p. 1991. text 225.00 (0-8247-8505-3) Dekker.

Lipoproteins in Health & Disease. Ed. by John Betteridge & James Shepherd. LC 98-3650. (Arnold Publication Ser.). 1300p. 1998. text 225.00 (0-340-55269-7, Pub. by E A) Routldge.

Liposome Drug Delivery Systems. Guru Betageri et al. LC 93-60519. 140p. 1993. pap. text 84.95 (1-56676-030-5) Technomic.

Liposome Protocols. Ed. by Ashok K. Shukla. (Methods in Molecular Biology Ser.). 1999. 79.50 (0-89603-715-0) Humana.

Liposome Technology, I. 2nd ed. Gregory Gregoriadis. 656p. 1992. lib. bdg. 179.00 (0-8493-6707-7, RS201) CRC Pr.

Liposome Technology, II. 2nd ed. Ed. by Gregory Gregoriadis. 368p. 1992. lib. bdg. 179.00 (0-8493-6708-5, RS201) CRC Pr.

Liposome Technology, III. 2nd ed. Gregory Gregoriadis. 432p. 1992. lib. bdg. 179.00 (0-8493-6709-3, RS201) CRC Pr.

Liposome Technology, Vol. I. Gregory Gregoriadis. 288p. 1984. lib. bdg. 179.00 (0-8493-5316-5, RS201) CRC Pr.

Liposome Technology, Vol. II. Gregory Gregoriadis. 256p. 1984. lib. bdg. 179.00 (0-8493-5317-3) CRC Pr.

Liposome Technology, Vol. III. Gregory Gregoriadis. 312p. 1984. lib. bdg. 179.00 (0-8493-5318-1, RS201) CRC Pr.

Liposomes: From Biophysics to Therapeutics. Ed. by Marc J. Ostro. (Illus.). 418p. 1987. text 225.00 (0-8247-7762-X) Dekker.

Liposomes: From Physics to Applications. Danilo D. Lasic. LC 92-49031. 594p. 1993. 323.50 (0-444-89548-5) Elsevier.

Liposomes: Rational Design. Ed. by Andrew S. Janoff. LC 98-46309. (Illus.). 618p. 1998. text 185.00 (0-8247-0225-5) Dekker.

Liposomes As Tools in Basic Research & Industry. Ed. by Jean R. Philippot & Francis Schuber. 286p. 1994. boxed set 246.95 (0-8493-4569-3, 4569) CRC Pr.

Liposomes in Biological Systems. Ed. by Gregory Gregoriadis & Anthony C. Allison. LC 79-40507. (Illus.). 424p. reprint ed. pap. 131.50 (0-608-17646-X, 203050400069) Bks Demand.

Liposomes in Biomedical Applications. Ed. by Pang N. Shek. (Drug Testing & Delivery Ser). 304p. 1995. text 132.00 (3-7186-5701-5, Harwood Acad Pubs) Gordon & Breach.

Liposomes in Cell Biology & Pharmacology. Patrick Machy & Lee Leserman. (Research in Ser.). 192p. 1987. 51.00 (2-85598-327-4) S M P F Inc.

Liposomes in Drug Delivery. Ed. by G. Gregoriadis et al. (Drug Targeting & Delivery Ser.). 256p. 1993. text 128.00 (3-7186-5265-X) Gordon & Breach.

Liposomes in Drug Delivery. Ed. by Gregory Gregoriadis et al. LC 92-49658. (Drug Targeting & Delivery Ser.: Vol. 2). 1992. write for info. (3-7186-5248-X) Gordon & Breach.

Liposomes in Gene Delivery. Danilo D. Lasic. LC 96-35300. (Illus.). 320p. 1997. spiral bd. 74.95 (0-8493-3109-9) CRC Pr.

Liposuction: New Hope for a New Figure Through the Art of Body Contouring. Leon Tcheupdjian. (Illus.). 244p. (Orig.). 1989. text 29.95 (0-9621284-0-6); pap. text 24.95 (0-9621284-1-4) Liposuction Inst Am.

Liposuction & Aesthetic Surgery. Gerald H. Pitman. LC 92-532. (Illus.). 478p. 1992. 200.00 (0-942219-18-X); 245.00 incl. VHS (1-57626-041-0, QMP) Quality Med Pub.

Lipoxins: Biosynthesis, Chemistry, & Biological Activities. Ed. by P. Y. Wong & C. N. Serhan. LC 88-2544. (Advances in Experimental Medicine & Biology Ser.: Vol. 229). (Illus.). 174p. 1988. 65.00 (0-306-42819-9, Plenum Trade) Perseus Pubng.

Lipoxygenase & Lipoxygenase Pathway Enzymes. Ed. by G. J. Piazza. 248p. 1996. 85.00 (0-935315-74-8) Am Oil Chemists.

Lipoxygenases & their Metabolites: Biological Functions. Ed. by S. Nigam & Cecil R. Pace-Asciak. LC 98-46245. (Advances in Experimental Medicine & Biology Ser.: 447). (Illus.). 230p. (C). 1999. text 95.00 (0-306-46044-0, Kluwer Plenum) Kluwer Academic.

Lipper Directory of Emerging Funds see Lipper International Closed-End Funds Service

Lipper International Closed-End Funds Service, 2 vols., Set. Lipper Analytical Services International Corporati. Ed. by Cherie McKinney. Orig. Title: Lipper Directory of Emerging Funds. 1200p. 1994. 4200.00 (0-9640376-4-5) Lipper Analytical.

Lippincott Manual of Nursing Practice. 6th ed. Lillian S. Brunner. (Illus.). 1,552p. 1996. text 56.95 (0-397-55163-0) Lppncott W & W.

Lippincott Manual of Nursing Practice. 7th ed. Sandra M. Nettina. 1728p. text 58.95 (0-7817-2296-9) Lppncott W & W.

Lippincott Manual of Primary Eye Care. Ed. by Kevin Alexander. (Illus.). 650p. (C). 1994. text 65.00 (0-397-51109-4, Lippnctt) Lppncott W & W.

Lippincott Manual of Primary Eye Care. Ed. by Kevin L. Alexander. LC 94-24472. (Illus.). 576p. reprint ed. pap. 178.60 (0-608-09718-7, 206988400007) Bks Demand.

Lippincott's Cancer Chemotherapy Handbook. Delia C. Baquiran & Jean Gallagher. LC 97-34705. 384p. 1997. pap. text 27.00 (0-397-55470-2) Lppncott W & W.

Lippincott's Computed Tomography Review. Phlipt-Scroggins. 288p. 1995. pap. text 26.95 (0-397-55157-6) Lppncott W & W.

Lippincott's Guide to Behavior Management in Home Care. Nina A. Klebanoff & Nina M. Smith. LC 96-53511. 448p. 1997. pap. text 24.95 (0-397-55432-X) Lppncott W & W.

Lippincott's Handbook of Medical Assisting Procedures. Julie B. Hosley & Elizabeth Molle-Matthews. LC 98-21796. 416p. 1998. spiral bd. 20.95 (0-7817-1458-3) Lppncott W & W.

Lippincott's Home Care Manual Package. Mary Ann Chestnut. 1997. pap. text 127.00 (0-7817-1622-5) Lppncott W & W.

Lippincott's Illustrated Review: Physiology. Harvey. 1993. text. write for info. (0-397-51141-8) Lppncott W & W.

Lippincott's Illustrated Reviews: Biochemistry. Pamela C. Champe & Richard A. Harvey. LC 65-9665. 441p. 1987. text 25.95 (0-397-50801-8, Lippnctt) Lppncott W & W.

Lippincott's Illustrated Reviews: Biochemistry. 2nd ed. Pamela C. Champe & Richard A. Harvey. (Illus.). 440p. 1994. pap. text 29.95 (0-397-51091-8) Lppncott W & W.

Lippincott's Illustrated Reviews Biochemistry. 3rd ed. Pamela C. Champe & Richard A. Harvey. 420p. pap. text. write for info. (0-7817-2265-9) Lppncott W & W.

Lippincott's Illustrated Reviews: Immunology. William Winter. 256p. 1998. pap. text 29.95 (0-397-51761-0) Lppncott W & W.

Lippincott's Imaging Review Series: Ultrasound. Roger C. Sanders & Jann Dolk. 448p. pap. text. write for info. (0-7817-1778-7) Lppncott W & W.

Lippincott's Magnetic Resonance Imaging Review. Shappell. 256p. 1996. pap. text 26.95 (0-397-55156-8) Lppncott W & W.

Lippincott's Manual of Psychiatric Nursing Care Plans. 5th ed. Judith M. Schultz & Sheila L. Dark Videbeck. LC 97-26210. 480p. 1997. pap. text 36.00 (0-397-55417-6) Lppncott W & W.

Lippincott's Need-to-Know: Research Survival Guide. Ann M. Doordan. LC 97-13229. 144p. 1997. pap. text 14.95 (0-7817-1040-5) Lppncott W & W.

Lippincott's Need-to-Know ECG Facts. Mary J. Boyer. 192p. 1997. pap. text 14.95 (0-397-55461-3) Lppncott W & W.

Lippincott's Need-to-Know Psychotropic Drug Facts. Katharine Bailey & Amy M. Karch. LC 97-42713. (Need-to-Know Ser.). 240p. 1997. pap. text 14.95 (0-7817-1039-1) Lppncott W & W.

Lippincott's Need-to-Know Reference Facts. Maryann Foley. LC 97-22695. 288p. 1997. pap. text 14.95 (0-7817-1444-3) Lppncott W & W.

***Lippincott's Nursing Drug Guide.** 4th ed. Amy M. Karch. 1360p. 1998. spiral bd. 24.95 (0-7817-1731-0, Lippnctt) Lppncott W & W.

Lippincott's Nursing Drug Guide, 2000. Lippincott-Raven Staff. 1,456p. pap. text 32.95 (0-7817-1985-2) Lppncott W & W.

Lippincott's Nursing Drug Guide, 2001. 1456p. pap. text 32.95 (0-7817-2556-9) Lppncott W & W.

Lippincott's Pocket Manual of Nursing Practice. Sandra Nettina. LC 96-15107. 976p. 1996. pap. text 25.95 (0-397-55355-2) Lppncott W & W.

Lippincott's Review for NCLEX-PN. 5th ed. Barbara Kuhn Timby & Bennita Vaughans. LC 97-36376. 512p. 1998. pap. text 31.00 (0-397-55471-0) Lppncott W & W.

Lippincott's Review for NCLEX-RN. 6th ed. D. McGovern Billings. LC 97-3490. 720p. 1997. pap. text 29.95 (0-397-55452-4) Lppncott W & W.

Lippincott's Review Series: Maternal-Newborn Nursing. 3rd ed. Barbara R. Stright. 320p. pap. text. write for info. (0-7817-2238-1) Lppncott W & W.

Lippincott's Review Series: Medical-Surgical Nursing. 3rd ed. Ray A. Hargrove-Huttel. pap. text. write for info. (0-7817-1964-X) Lppncott W & W.

Lippincott's Review Series: Mental Health & Psychiatric Nursing. 3rd ed. Ann Isaacs. 320p. pap. text. write for info. (0-7817-2188-1) Lppncott W & W.

Lippincott's Review Series: Pediatric Nursing. 3rd ed. Mary Muscari. 448p. pap. text. write for info. (0-7817-2187-3) Lppncott W & W.

Lippincott's State Board Review for NCLEX-RN. 4th ed. Edwina A. McConnell & LuVerne W. Lewis. 1989. text 24.50 (0-397-54722-6, Lippnctt) Lppncott W & W.

Lippincott's Textbook for Clinical Medical Assisting. Julie B. Hosley & Elizabeth Molle-Matthews. 800p. 52.00 (0-7817-2339-6) Lppncott W & W.

***Lippincott's Textbook of Clinical Medical Assisting.** Julie B. Hosley. LC 98-45295. 1999. 37.95 (0-7817-1457-5) Lppncott W & W.

Lippisch P 13A: The Experimental DM-1. Hans-Peter Dabrowski. Tr. by James Carle. (Illus.). 48p. (Orig.). 1993. pap. 9.95 (0-88740-479-0) Schiffer.

LIPRO 2.0: An Application of a Dynamic Demographic Projection Model to Household Structure in the Netherlands. E. Van Imhoff & Nico W. Keilman. (NIDI-CBGS Publications: Vol. 23). xvi, 248p. 1992. pap. 49.00 (90-265-1241-4) Swets.

Lips Together, Teeth Apart. Terrence McNally. 1992. pap. 5.25 (0-8222-0670-6) Dramatists Play.

Lips Together, Teeth Apart. Terrence McNally. 112p. 1992. pap. 9.95 (0-452-26807-9, Plume) Dutton Plume.

Lipsanothek von Brescia. Johannes Kollwitz. (Studien zur Spaetantiken Kunstgeschichte: Vol. 7). (Illus.). 74p. (C). 1978. reprint ed. 192.30 (3-11-005701-8) De Gruyter.

Lipschitz Algebras. N. Weaver. LC 99-30373. 1999. 55.00 (981-02-3873-8) World Scientific Pub.

***Lipshtick: Life as a Girl.** Gwen Macsai. LC 99-24462. 288p. 2000. 23.00 (0-06-019101-5) HarpC.

***Lipsmackin' Backpackin'** Christine Conners & Tim Conners. LC 99-54507. (Illus.). 256p. 2000. pap. 15.95 (1-56044-881-4) Falcon Pub Inc.

Lipsome Dermatics: Mit 119 Abbildungen und 48 Tabellen. Ed. by O. Braun-Falco et al. LC 92-26372. (Griesbach Conference Ser.). (Illus.). xix, 360p. 1992. write for info. (3-540-55646-X) Spr-Verlag.

Lipstick. Gwen Macsai. Date not set. pap. 13.00 (0-06-093061-6) HarpC.

Lipstick. Jessica Pallingston. LC 98-27749. (Illus.). 228p. 1998. text 17.95 (0-312-19914-7) St Martin.

Lipstick & Lies. L. Adamson. text 35.00 (0-340-71317-8, Pub. by Hodder & Stought Ltd) Trafalgar.

Lipstick on His Collar. Elizabeth Villars. 1990. 18.95 (0-446-51512-4) Warner Bks.

Lipstick on His Collar. Elizabeth Villars. 1991. mass mkt. 4.95 (0-446-36090-2, Pub. by Warner Bks) Little.

Lipstick Proviso: Women, Sex, & Power in the Real World. Karen Lehrman. LC 96-49392. 240p. 1997. 23.95 (0-385-47481-4, Anchor NY) Doubleday.

Lipstick, Sex & Poetry: An Autobiography. Jeremy Reed. 119p. 1991. 30.00 (0-7206-0817-1, Pub. by P Owen Ltd) Dufour.

***Lipstick, Sweat & Sweatrag.** Beth Beckett. 1998. pap. 24.95 (1-875998-37-3, Pub. by Central Queensland) Accents Pubns.

Lipstick Traces: A Secret History of the Twentieth Century. Greil Marcus. LC 88-24678. (Illus.). 512p. 1989. 37.00 (0-674-53580-4) HUP.

Lipstick Traces: A Secret History of the Twentieth Century. Greil Marcus. (Illus.). 512p. 1990. pap. text 19.50 (0-674-53581-2) HUP.

Liptako Speaks: History from Oral Tradition in Africa. Paul B. Irwin. LC 80-7531. (Illus.). 234p. reprint ed. pap. 72.60 (0-8357-3695-4, 203641900003) Bks Demand.

Lipton & Hertzberg's Understanding Company Law in Hong Kong. Krishman Arjunan & Chee Keong. LC 96-207799. 550p. 1996. pap. 80.00 (0-455-21422-0, Pub. by Cavendish Pubng) Gaunt.

Lipton Noodles Alfred Case: A Case for Learning Marketing Research. John F. Tanner. 90p. 1995. pap. text 11.00 (0-314-06149-5) West Pub.

Liptons Noodles. Tanner. Date not set. pap. text, teacher ed. write for info. (0-314-06991-7) West Pub.

An Asterisk (*) at the beginning of an entry indicates that the title is appearing for the first time.

Liptser Festschrift: Statistics & Control of Stochastic Processes Steklov Mathematical Institute, 1995-1996. Ed. by Yu M. Kabanov et al. 350p. 1998. 86.00 (*981-02-3292-6*) World Scientific Pub.

Liquefaction of Cohesive Sediments Caused by Waves. P. J. De Wit. (Studies in Integrated Water Management: Vol. 6). (Illus.). xii, 194p. (Orig.). 1995. pap. 42.50 (*90-407-1139-9*, Pub. by Delft U Pr) Coronet Bks.

***Liquefaction of the Blood of St. Januarius at Naples: An Historical & Critical Examination of the Miracle.** 1998. reprint ed. pap. 7.50 (*0-89979-116-6*) British Am Bks.

Liquefaction Problems in Geotechnical Engineering. 394p. 1976. pap. 5.00 (*0-87262-324-6*) Am Soc Civil Eng.

Liquefied Gas Handling Principles on Ships & in Terminals. SIGTTO Staff. (C). 1986. 250.00 (*0-900886-93-5*, Pub. by Witherby & Co) St Mut.

Liquefied Natural Gas: Developing & Financing International Energy Projects. Ed. by Gerald B. Greenwald. LC 98-29106. (International Energy & Resources Law & Policy Ser.: Vol. 12). 392p. 1998. 150.00 (*90-411-9664-1*) Kluwer Law Intl.

Liquefied Natural Gas & Liquefied Petroleum Gas: Views, Practices, Policy & Safety. U. S. Coast Guard Staff. 42p. 1980. pap. text 6.75 (*1-879778-32-7*, BK-662) Marine Educ.

Liquefied Petroleum Gases: Guide to Properties, Applications & Uses. 2nd expanded ed. A. F. Williams & W. L. Lom. 522p. 1982. text 148.00 (*0-470-27275-9*) P-H.

Liquefield Gas Handling Principles on Ships & in Terminals. SIGTTO Staff. 1996. pap. 150.00 (*1-85609-087-6*, Pub. by Witherby & Co) St Mut.

Liqueurs for Dessert. Sandra Wong. 60p. (Orig.). 1989. pap. 9.95 (*0-88925-884-8*) Gordon Soules Bk.

Liquid: A Source of Meaning & Structure in Claude Simon's "La Bataille de Pharsale" Neal Storrs. (American University Studies: Ser. II, Vol. 4). 151p. (C). 1983. pap. text 16.85 (*0-8204-0021-1*) P Lang Pubng.

Liquid - Liquid Extraction Equipment. Ed. by J. C. Godfrey & M. J. Slater. LC 93-50763. 788p. 1994. 405.00 (*0-471-94156-5*) Wiley.

Liquid Affairs. Mitch Highfill. 1995. pap. 7.00 (*0-935992-02-2*) United Art Bks.

Liquid & Amorphous Metals: Mechanics of Plastic Solids. Ed. by E. Luscher & H. Coufal. (NATO-Advanced Study Institute Ser.). 672p. 1980. text 247.50 (*90-286-0680-7*) Kluwer Academic.

Liquid & Surface-Borne Particle Measurement Handbook. Ed. by Julius Z. Knapp et al. (Illus.). 896p. 1996. text 215.00 (*0-8247-9386-2*) Dekker.

Liquid & Vapor Flows in Porous Bodies: Surface Phenomena. N. V. Churaev. Ed. by A. K. Galwey. 344p. 1999. text 98.00 (*90-5699-149-3*) Gordon & Breach.

***Liquid Assets: A History of New York City's Water System.** Diane Galusha. LC 99-42714. 1999. pap. write for info. (*0-916346-74-9*) Harbor Hill Bks.

***Liquid Assets: A History of New York City's Water System.** Contrib. by Diane Galusha. LC 99-42714. (Illus.). 303p. 1999. lib. bdg. 37.00 (*0-916346-73-0*) Purple Mnt Pr.

Liquid Atomization. Ed. by L. P. Bayvel & Z. Orzechowski. (Combustion: An International Ser.). 420p. 1993. 124.00 (*0-89116-959-8*, Pub. by Tay Francis Ltd) Taylor & Francis.

Liquid Babylon. Susan S. Nash. 55p. pap. 8.00 (*1-884438-07-5*) Epiphany AR.

Liquid Babylon. limited ed. Susan S. Nash. 54p. 1994. 18.00 (*0-937013-50-1*) Potes Poets.

Liquid Chillers in Germany: A Strategic Entry Report, 1997. Compiled by Icon Group International Staff. (Illus.). 96p. 1999. ring bd. 960.00 incl. audio compact disk (*0-7418-0748-3*) Icon Grp.

Liquid Chromatographic Data Compilation - AMD 41. 196p. 1975. pap. 15.00 (*0-8031-0805-2*, 10-041000-39) ASTM.

Liquid Chromatography: Essential Data. D. Patel. LC 96-53627. (Essential Data Ser.). 160p. 1997. pap. 39.95 (*0-471-97270-3*) Wiley.

Liquid Chromatography - Mass Spectrometry: Applications in Agricultural, Pharmaceutical, & Environmental Chemistry. Ed. by Mark A. Brown. LC 89-18611. (ACS Symposium Ser.: No. 420). (Illus.). 280p. 1989. text 75.00 (*0-8412-1740-8*, Pub. by Am Chemical) OUP.

Liquid Chromatography & Mass Spectrometry: Techniques & Applications. A. L. Yergey et al. (Modern Analytical Chemistry Ser.). (Illus.). 316p. (C). 1989. text 79.50 (*0-306-43186-6*, Kluwer Plenum) Kluwer Academic.

Liquid Chromatography Column Theory. Raymond P. Scott. (Separation Science Ser.: No. 1811). 292p. 1991. 360.00 (*0-471-93305-8*) Wiley.

Liquid Chromatography Detectors. Ed. by Thomas M. Vickrey. LC 83-7428. (Chromatographic Science Ser.: Vol. 23). (Illus.). 448p. 1983. text 210.00 (*0-8247-1916-6*) Dekker.

Liquid Chromatography for the Analyst. Raymond P.W. Scott. LC 93-43899. (Chromatographic Science Ser.: Vol. 67). (Illus.). 344p. 1994. text 85.00 (*0-8247-9184-3*) Dekker.

Liquid Chromatography in Clinical Analysis. Ed. by Pokar M. Kabra & Laurence J. Marton. LC 80-84083. (Biological Methods Ser.). 466p. 1981. 125.00 (*0-89603-026-1*) Humana.

Liquid Chromatography in Environmental Analysis. Ed. by James F. Lawrence. LC 83-10711. (Contemporary Instrumentation & Analysis Ser.). 385p. 1984. 99.50 (*0-89603-045-8*) Humana.

Liquid Chromatography in Practice. P. A. Bristow. 28.00 (*0-9504833-1-1*); pap. 20.00 (*0-9504833-0-3*); fiche 10.00 (*0-9504833-2-X*) Lab Data Control.

Liquid Chromatography in the Biomedical Sciences: Invited Papers from the 15th International Symposium Held in Ronneby, Sweden, 18-21 June 1984. Ed. by S. Eksborg et al. 200p. 1985. pap. 28.00 (*0-08-032600-5*, Pergamon Pr) Elsevier.

Liquid Chromatography-Mass Spectrometry. 2nd ed. W. M. Niessen. LC 98-39466. (Chromatographic Science Ser.). (Illus.). 648p. 1998. text 195.00 (*0-8247-1936-0*) Dekker.

Liquid Chromatography of Oligomers. Constantin V. Uglea. LC 96-19179. (Chromatographic Science Ser.: Vol. 72). (Illus.). 360p. 1996. text 165.00 (*0-8247-9720-5*) Dekker.

Liquid Chromatography of Polymers & Related Materials. International Symposium on Liquid Chromatographic. Ed. by Jack Cazes. LC 77-6373. (Chromatographic Science Ser.: No. 8). 192p. reprint ed. pap. 59.60 (*0-7837-4229-0*, 204391700012) Bks Demand.

Liquid Chromatography of Polymers & Related Materials, Part III. J. Cazes. (Chromatographic Science Ser.: Vol. 19). (Illus.). 312p. 1981. text 165.00 (*0-8247-1514-4*) Dekker.

Liquid Chromatography of Polymers & Related Materials, Pt. II. J. Cazes & Delamare. (Chromatographic Science Ser.: Vol. 13). (Illus.). 272p. 1980. text 145.00 (*0-8247-6985-6*) Dekker.

***Liquid City: Houston Writers on Houston.** Marc Atkins & Iain Sinclair. (Illus.). 223p. 1999. pap. 29.95 (*1-86189-037-0*, Pub. by RBL) Consort Bk Sales.

***Liquid Composite Molding.** Richard S. Parnas. LC 00-31931. 2000. write for info. (*1-56990-287-9*) Hanser-Gardner.

Liquid Conspiracy: LSD, JFK, the CIA, Area 51 & UFOs. George Piccard. 256p. 1999. pap. 14.95 (*0-932813-57-7*) Adventures Unltd.

Liquid Cryogens, 2 Vols., Vol. I: Theory & Equipment. Ed. by F. J. Edeskuty & K. D. Williamson, Jr. 224p. 1983. 118.00 (*0-8493-5727-6*, TP482, CRC Reprint) Franklin.

Liquid Cryogens, 2 Vols., Vol. II: Properties & Applications. Ed. by F. J. Edeskuty & K. D. Williamson, Jr. 176p. 1983. 99.00 (*0-8493-5728-4*, CRC Reprint) Franklin.

Liquid Crystal - Applications & Uses. 604p. 1990. lib. bdg. 34.00 (*981-02-2975-5*) World Scientific Pub.

Liquid Crystal - Applications & Uses, 2. 452p. 1991. lib. bdg. 27.00 (*981-02-2951-8*) World Scientific Pub.

Liquid Crystal - Applications & Uses, 3. 428p. 1992. lib. bdg. 27.00 (*981-02-2952-6*) World Scientific Pub.

Liquid Crystal Devices: Physics & Applications. Vladimir G. Chigrinov. LC 99-10564. 380p. 1999. 99.00 (*0-89006-898-4*) Artech Hse.

Liquid Crystal Displays. Birendra Bahadur. (Molecular Crystals & Liquid Crystals Ser.). 100p. 1984. pap. text 142.00 (*0-677-06675-9*) Gordon & Breach.

Liquid Crystal Displays & Devices. Day & Devereux. (Optical & Quantum Electronics Ser.). (Illus.). 400p. 1997. write for info. (*0-412-64440-1*, Chap & Hall NY) Chapman & Hall.

Liquid Crystal Futures: Contemporary Japanese Photography. Shinji Kohmoto et al. (Illus.). 144p. 1995. pap. 39.95 (*0-947912-17-7*) Dist Art Pubs.

Liquid Crystal Materials & Devices Vol. 559: Materials Research Society Symposium Proceedings. Ed. by T. J. Bunning et al. LC 99-37083. 284p. 1999. text 68.00 (*1-55899-466-1*) Materials Res.

Liquid Crystal Materials, Devices & Applications V, Vol. 3015. Ed. by Ranganathan Shashidhar. 214p. 1997. 69.00 (*0-8194-2426-9*) SPIE.

Liquid Crystal Materials, Devices & Applications VI, Vol. 3297. Ed. by Ranganathan Shashidhar. 132p. 1998. 69.00 (*0-8194-2737-3*) SPIE.

***Liquid Crystal Materials, Devices & Applications VII.** Ed. by Ranganathan Shashidhar. 160p. 1999. pap. text 62.00 (*0-8194-3106-0*) SPIE.

Liquid Crystal Polymers. Cox & Wilton. (Rapra Review Reports: Vol. 1). 1992. pap. 115.00 (*0-08-035923-X*, Pergamon Pr) Elsevier.

Liquid-Crystal Polymers. N. A. Plate. (Specialty Polymers Ser.). (Illus.). 448p. (C). 1992. text 120.00 (*0-306-44219-1*, Kluwer Plenum) Kluwer Academic.

Liquid Crystal TV Displays. D. Kaneko. 1987. text 267.50 (*90-277-2362-1*) Kluwer Academic.

Liquid Crystalline & Mesomorphic Polymers. Ed. by Valery Shibaev & Lui Lam. LC 93-10429. (Partially Ordered Systems Ser.). 1994. 149.95 (*0-387-94046-4*) Spr-Verlag.

Liquid-Crystalline Polymer Systems: Technological Advances. American Chemical Society Staff. Ed. by Avraam I. Isayev et al. LC 96-20169. (ACS Symposium Ser.: No. 632). (Illus.). 432p. 1996. text 130.00 (*0-8412-3408-6*, Pub. by Am Chemical) OUP.

Liquid Crystalline Polymers. National Research Council Staff. (Illus.). 122p. (Orig.). (C). 1990. pap. text 17.00 (*0-309-04231-3*) Natl Acad Pr.

Liquid-Crystalline Polymers. Ed. by R. A. Weiss & C. K. Ober. LC 90-41743. (ACS Symposium Ser.: No. 435). (Illus.). 495p. 1990. text 110.00 (*0-8412-1849-8*, Pub. by Am Chemical) OUP.

Liquid Crystalline Polymers: Proceedings of the International Workshop, WLCP 93, Capri, Italy, June 1-4, 1993. Ed. by C. Carfagna. LC 93-43406. 272p. 1994. text 145.25 (*0-08-042149-0*, Pergamon Pr) Elsevier.

Liquid Crystallinity in Polymers: Principles & Fundamental Properties. Ed. by Alberto Ciferri. 438p. 1991. 95.00 (*0-89573-771-X*, Wiley-VCH) Wiley.

Liquid Crystallinity in Polymers: Principles & Fundamental Properties. Ed. by Alberto Ciferri. 438p. 1991. 155.00 (*0-471-18736-4*) Wiley.

Liquid Crystals. 188p. 1990. 2650.00 (*0-89336-700-1*, GB119) BCC.

Liquid Crystals. 1992. 803.95 (*0-387-55503-X*); 1919.95 (*0-387-55504-8*) Spr-Verlag.

Liquid Crystals. Ed. by Iam-Choon Khoo. LC 98-122613. 230p. 1997. 69.00 (*0-8194-2565-6*) SPIE.

Liquid Crystals. L. Pohl et al. (Topics in Physical Chemistry Ser.: Vol. 3). 1994. 51.95 (*0-387-91421-8*) Spr-Verlag.

Liquid Crystals. 2nd ed. S. Chandrasekhar. (Illus.). 476p. (C). 1993. text 145.00 (*0-521-41747-3*); pap. text 49.95 (*0-521-42741-X*) Cambridge U Pr.

Liquid Crystals: Applications & Uses, Vol. 1. Ed. by B. Bahadur. 604p. (C). 1990. text 138.00 (*981-02-0110-9*) World Scientific Pub.

Liquid Crystals: Applications & Uses, Vol. 2. B. Bahadur. 448p. 1991. text 101.00 (*981-02-0111-7*) World Scientific Pub.

Liquid Crystals: Applications & Uses, Vol. 3. B. Bahadur. 325p. 1992. text 102.00 (*981-02-0403-5*) World Scientific Pub.

***Liquid Crystals: Experimental Study of Physical Properties & Phase Transitions.** Ed. by Satyendra Kumar. LC 99-87679. (Illus.). 512p. (C). 2000. text Price not set. (*0-521-46132-4*) Cambridge U Pr.

Liquid Crystals: Nature's Delicate Phase of Matter. Peter J. Collings. (Science Library). (Illus.). 252p. 1991. pap. 15.95 (*0-691-02429-4*, Pub. by Princeton U Pr); text 49.50 (*0-691-08509-9*, Pub. by Princeton U Pr) Cal Prin Full Svc.

Liquid Crystals: Physical Properties & Nonlinear Optical Phenomena. Iam-Choon Khoo. 320p. 1994. 107.95 (*0-471-30362-3*) Wiley.

Liquid Crystals: Proceedings. International Conference on Liquid Crystals (6th:. Ed. by S. Chandrasekhar. LC QD0921.I53. (Illus.). 659p. reprint ed. pap. 200.00 (*0-608-18776-3*, 202979700065) Bks Demand.

Liquid Crystals: The Fourth State of Matter. Ed. by Franklin D. Saeva. LC 79-18501. (Illus.). 503p. 1979. reprint ed. pap. 156.00 (*0-608-00254-2*, 206076900006) Bks Demand.

Liquid Crystals: Their Physics, Chemistry & Applications. Charles Frank. (Series A: Vol. 309). (Illus.). 169p. 1983. text 55.00 (*0-85403-210-X*) Royal Soc London.

Liquid Crystals: Transition Temperatures & Related Properties of Three-Ring Systems Without Bridging Groups, Vol. C. V. Vill. Ed. by J. Thiem. 240p. 1993. 775.95 (*0-387-56136-6*) Spr-Verlag.

Liquid Crystals, Subvol. D, Transition Temperatures & Related Properties of Three-Ring Systems with One Bridging Group see Macroscopic & Technical Properties of Matter: Group IV

Liquid Crystals, Subvol. E, Three-Ring Systems with Two Bridging Systems see Macroscopic & Technical Properties of Matter: Group IV

***Liquid Crystals Vol. 3318: Physics, Technology & Applications.** Ed. by Jolanta Rutowska et al. LC 98-172296. 556p. 1998. 99.00 (*0-8194-2759-4*) SPIE.

Liquid Crystals Vol. 3319: Chemistry & Structure. Ed. by Marzena Tykarska et al. LC 98-171720. 374p. 1998. 80.00 (*0-8194-2760-8*) SPIE.

Liquid Crystals & Ordered Fluids. Ed. by Julian F. Johnson & Roger Porter. Incl. Vol. 1. 494p. 1970. 85.00 (*0-306-30466-X*, Kluwer Plenum); Vol. 2. 784p. 1974. 105.00 (*0-306-35182-X*, Kluwer Plenum); Vol. 3. 560p. 1978. 95.00 (*0-306-35183-8*, Kluwer Plenum); write for info. (*0-318-55330-9*, Plenum Trade) Perseus Pubng.

Liquid Crystals for Advanced Technologies. Ed. by T. J. Bunning et al. (MRS Symposium Proceedings Ser.: Vol. 425). 346p. 1996. 74.00 (*1-55899-328-2*, 425) Materials Res.

Liquid Crystals for Optics. Ed. by Stephen D. Jacobs. 722p. 1992. pap. 50.00 (*0-8194-0847-6*) SPIE.

Liquid Crystals for Optics, Vol. MS46. Ed. by Stephen D. Jacobs. 722p. 1992. 65.00 (*0-8194-0846-8*) SPIE.

Liquid Crystals II, Vol. 3475. Ed. by Iam-Choon Khoo. LC 99-182527. 1998. 59.00 (*0-8194-2930-9*) SPIE.

Liquid Crystals in Complex Geometries Formed by Polymer & Porous Networks. Ed. by Gregory P. Crawford & Slobodan Zumer. 584p. 1996. 110.00 (*0-7484-0464-3*) Taylor & Francis.

Liquid Crystals in the '90s & Beyond. Satyen Kumar. 300p. 1996. text 86.00 (*981-02-2192-4*) World Scientific Pub.

Liquid Crystals of One & Two Dimensional Order: Proceedings. W. Helfreich & G. Heppke. (Chemical Physics Ser.: Vol. 11). (Illus.). 416p. 1980. 48.00 (*0-387-10399-6*) Spr-Verlag.

Liquid Crystals I. Ed. by D. M. Mingos. LC 99-201840. (Structure & Bonding Ser.: Vol. 94). (Illus.). 222p. 1999. 159.00 (*3-540-64936-0*) Spr-Verlag.

Liquid Crystals II. Ed. by D. M. Mingos. (Structure & Bonding Ser.: Vol. 95). (Illus.). 200p. 1999. 199.00 (*3-540-64937-9*) Spr-Verlag.

Liquid Desires: An Urbino Macintyre Mystery. Edward Sklepowich. (Mystery of Venice Ser.). 320p. 1994. reprint ed. mass mkt. 4.99 (*0-380-72150-3*, Avon Bks) Morrow Avon.

Liquid Detergents. Kuo-Yann Lai. LC 96-44787. (Surfactant Science Ser.: Vol. 67). (Illus.). 576p. 1996. text 225.00 (*0-8247-9391-9*) Dekker.

Liquid Dreams of Vampires. Martin V. Riccardo. LC 96-9053. (Illus.). 264p. (Orig.). 1999. pap. 14.95 (*1-56718-571-1*) Llewellyn Pubns.

Liquid Explorations. rev. ed. Leigh Agler. Ed. by Lincoln Bergman et al. (Great Explorations in Math & Science (GEMS) Ser.). (Illus.). 80p. (Orig.). (J). (gr. 1-3). 1993. reprint ed. pap., teacher ed. 10.50 (*0-912511-51-6*, GEMS) Lawrence Science.

Liquid Film Coating: Scientific Principles & Their Technological Implications. Ed. by Stephan F. Kistler & Peter M. Schweizer. LC 96-86101. 796p. 1997. write for info. (*0-412-06481-2*) Kluwer Academic.

Liquid Filtration. 2nd ed. Nicholas P. Cheremisnoff. 512p. 1998. text 75.00 (*0-7506-7047-9*) Buttrwrth-Heinemann.

Liquid Filtration for Process & Pollution Control. Nicholas P. Cheremisinoff & David S. Azbel. (Illus.). 530p. (C). 1989. pap. text 39.95 (*0-925760-00-5*) SciTech Pubs.

Liquid Fire: Transcendental Mysticism in the Romances of Nathaniel Hawthorne. Harvey L. Gable, Jr. (Early American Literature & Culture Through the American Renaissance Ser.: Vol. 2). XXII, 324p. (C). 1998. pap. text 32.95 (*0-8204-3830-8*) P Lang Pubng.

***Liquid Form: 1985-99.** Martin Kemp. (Illus.). 142p. 2000. 60.00 (*1-900829-07-X*, Pub. by M Hue-Williams) Dist Art Pubs.

Liquid Fuel-Burning Heating Appliances for Manufactured Homes & Recreational Vehicles, UL 307A. 7th ed. (C). 1995. pap. text 330.00 (*1-55989-704-X*) Underwrtrs Labs.

Liquid Fuel Developments. Donald L. Wise. 224p. 1983. 128.00 (*0-8493-6094-3*, TP630, CRC Reprint) Franklin.

Liquid Fuel Systems. Ed. by Donald L. Wise. 224p. 1983. 126.00 (*0-8493-6093-5*, TP343, CRC Reprint) Franklin.

Liquid Fuels & Industrial Products from Renewable Resources: Proceedings of the 3rd Liquid Fuel Conference. Ed. by John S. Condiff. LC 96-86289. 375p. 1996. pap. 58.75 (*0-929355-79-2*, P0896) Am Soc Ag Eng.

Liquid Fuels from Renewable Resources: Proceedings Alternative Energy Conference, December 1992. LC 92-74909. 219p. 1992. pap. 62.50 (*0-929355-36-9*, P1292) Am Soc Ag Eng.

Liquid Fuels in Australia: A Social Science Research Perspective. J. Black. 280p. 1983. 42.00 (*0-08-024834-9*, Pergamon Pr); pap. 23.00 (*0-08-024833-0*, Pergamon Pr) Elsevier.

Liquid Fuels, Lubricants & Additives from Biomass. Ed. by Bruce E. Dale. LC 94-71222. 200p. 1994. text 58.75 (*0-929355-49-0*) Am Soc Ag Eng.

Liquid Gas Carrier Register, 1988. 23rd ed. 200p. 1988. 195.00 (*0-8002-4220-3*) Taylor & Francis.

Liquid Hydrogen-Fuel of the Future. W. Peschka. Tr. by E. Wilhelm from GER. (Illus.). 256p. 1992. 147.95 (*0-387-82250-X*) Spr-Verlag.

Liquid Interfaces in Chemistry & Biology. Alexander G. Volkov et al. Tr. by Darrell L. Tanelian. LC 97-6045. 551p. 1997. 99.00 (*0-471-14872-5*) Wiley.

Liquid-Level Gauges & Indicators for Anhydrous Ammonia & LP-Gas, UL 565. 5th ed. (C). 1998. pap. text 95.00 (*1-55989-497-0*) Underwrtrs Labs.

Liquid-Level Indicating Gauges for Oil Burner Fuels, UL 180. 6th ed. (C). 1996. pap. text 135.00 (*0-7629-0001-6*) Underwrtrs Labs.

Liquid Life: Abortion & Buddhism in Japan. William R. Lafkeur. 275p. 1992. pap. text 16.95 (*0-691-02965-2*, Pub. by Princeton U Pr) Cal Prin Full Svc.

Liquid Light of Sex: Kundalini Rising as Mid-Life Crisis. Barbara H. Clow. 1996. pap. text 15.00 (*1-879181-40-1*) Bear & Co.

Liquid-Liquid Equilibrium Data Collection: Ternary & Quaternary Systems, Vol. V, Pt. 3. Reiner Eckermann & W. Arlt. Ed. by D. Behrens & J. M. Sorensen. (Dechema Chemistry Data Ser.). 605p. 1981. lib. bdg. 240.00 (*3-921567-19-X*, Pub. by Dechema) Scholium Intl.

Liquid-Liquid Equilibrium Data Collection: Ternary Systems, Vol. V, Pt. 2. Reiner Eckermann et al. Ed. by D. Behrens. (Dechema Chemistry Data Ser.). 1981. lib. bdg. 240.00 (*3-921567-18-1*, Pub. by Dechema) Scholium Intl.

Liquid-Liquid Equilibrium Data Collection Suppl. 1: Tables, Diagrams & Model Parameters for Binary, Ternary & Quaternary Systems. E. A. Macedo & P. Rasmussen. (Dechema Chemistry Data Ser.: Vol. V, Pt. 4). (Illus.). 340p. 1987. text 260.00 (*3-921567-73-4*, Pub. by Dechema) Scholium Intl.

Liquid-Liquid Interfaces: Theory & Methods. Ed. by Alexander G. Volkov & David W. Deamer. 448p. 1996. boxed set 169.95 (*0-8493-7694-7*) CRC Pr.

Liquid-Liquid Systems. Ed. by N. N. Kulov. 393p. (C). 1996. 175.00 (*1-56072-189-8*) Nova Sci Pubs.

***Liquid Locomotive: Legendary Whitewater River Stories.** John Long. LC 99-36761. (Adventure Ser.). 250p. 1999. pap. 14.95 (*1-56044-856-3*) Falcon Pub Inc.

Liquid Love. Date not set. pap. 9.95 (*1-929383-03-7*) Flaming Heart.

Liquid Manure Application Systems Design Manual, Vol. 89. Mark Dougherty et al. (Illus.). 168p. 1998. pap. text 20.00 (*0-935817-24-7*, NRAES-89) NRAES.

Liquid Membranes: Chemical Applications. Ed. by Takeo Araki. 232p. 1990. lib. bdg. 225.00 (*0-8493-5314-9*, QP562) CRC Pr.

Liquid Membranes: Theory & Applications. Ed. by Richard D. Noble & J. Douglas Way. LC 87-18684. (Symposium Ser.: No. 347). (Illus.). ix, 223p. 1987. 54.95 (*0-8412-1407-7*) Am Chemical.

Liquid Membranes: Theory & Applications. Ed. by Richard D. Noble & J. Douglas Way. LC 87-18684. (ACS Symposium Ser.: Vol. 347). 208p. 1987. reprint ed. pap. 64.50 (*0-608-03870-9*, 206431700008) Bks Demand.

Liquid Metal Atomization: Fundamentals & Practice. Ed. by Khershed P. Cooper et al. (Illus.). 250p. 62.00 (*0-87339-465-8*) Minerals Metals.

Liquid Metal Coolants for Heat Pipes & Power Plants. P. I. Bystrovetal. 1990. 160.00 (*0-89116-303-4*) Hemisp Pub.

L

Liquid Metal Fast Breeder Reactor: An Environmental & Economic Critique. Thomas B. Cochran. LC 73-19349. 287p. reprint ed. pap. 89.00 (*0-7837-3138-8*, 204284900006) Bks Demand.

Liquid-Metal Heat Transfer & Fluid Dynamics: Presented at the Annual Winter Meeting of ASME, New York,N. Y., November 30, 1970. Ed. by John C. Chen & A. A. Bishop. LC 76-141816. 185p. 1970. reprint ed. pap. 57.40 (*0-608-10921-5*, 201689300005) Bks Demand.

Liquid-Metal Heat Transfer Media. 1958th ed. S. S. Kutateladze & V. M. Borishanskii. LC 59-4583. (Soviet Journal of Atomic Energy: No. 2). 157p. reprint ed. pap. 48.70 (*0-608-11846-X*, 202065100018) Bks Demand.

Liquid Metal Magnetohydrodynamics. Ed. by J. Lielpeteris & R. Moreau. (C). 1989. text 234.50 (*0-7923-0344-X*) Kluwer Academic.

***Liquid Metal Processing: Applications to Aluminium Alloy Production.** I. G. Brodova et al. (Advances in Metallic Alloys Ser.: Vol. 1). 288p. 2000. text 110.00 (*90-5699-229-5*, G & B Science) Gordon & Breach.

Liquid Metal Systems: Material Behavior & Physical Chemistry in Liquid Metal Systems, Vol. 2. H. U. Borgstedt. (Illus.). 432p. (C). 1995. text 130.00 (*0-306-45069-0*, Kluwer Plenum) Kluwer Academic.

Liquid Metals: Chemistry & Physics. Ed. by Sylvan Z. Beer. LC 78-157836. (Monographs & Textbooks in Material Science: No. 4). (Illus.). 743p. reprint ed. pap. 200.00 (*0-7837-0830-0*, 204114400019) Bks Demand.

Liquid Metals: Concepts & Theory. Norman H. March. (Cambridge Monographs on Mathematical Physics). 454p. (C). 1990. text 140.00 (*0-521-30279-X*) Cambridge U Pr.

Liquid Mirrors. David Cornberg. (ENG.). 68p. 1986. pap. text 8.00 (*1-57833-022-X*) Todd Commns.

***Liquid Modernity.** Zygmunt Bauman. 240p. 2000. text 59.95 (*0-7456-2409-X*, Pub. by Polity Pr); pap. text 24.95 (*0-7456-2410-3*, Pub. by Polity Pr) Blackwell Pubs.

Liquid Moulding Technologies: Resin Transfer Moulding, Structural Reaction Injection Moulding & Related. C. D. Rudd et al. 464p. 1997. boxed set 170.00 (*1-85573-242-4*, Pub. by Woodhead Pubng) Am Educ Systs.

Liquid Moulding Technologies: Resin Transfer Moulding, Structural Reaction Injection Moulding, & Related Processing Techniques. C. D. Rudd. LC 97-19335. 1997. 75.00 (*0-7680-0016-5*, R-204) Soc Auto Engineers.

Liquid Nourishment: Potable Foods & Stimulating Drinks. Ed. by C. Anne Wilson. (Food & Society in History Today Ser.). (Illus.). 128p. 1993. 50.00 (*0-7486-0424-3*, Pub. by Edinburgh U Pr) Col U Pr.

Liquid Paint Finishing Defects. Robert D. Grear. Ed. by Richard Perich. LC 91-66715. (Illus.). 65p. 1991. pap. 19.00 (*0-87263-413-2*) SME.

Liquid Paper: New & Selected Poems. Peter Meinke. LC 91-50108. (Poetry Ser.). 120p. (C). 1991. pap. 12.95 (*0-8229-5455-9*); text 29.95 (*0-8229-3681-X*) U of Pittsburgh Pr.

Liquid Particle Size Measurement Techniques, Vol. 2. Ed. by E. Dan Hireleman et al. LC 90-821. (Special Technical Publication (STP) Ser.: No. 1083). (Illus.). 270p. 1990. text 71.00 (*0-8031-1459-1*, STP1083) ASTM.

Liquid Particle Size Measurement Techniques - STP 848. ASTM Committee E-29 on Particle Size. Ed. by J. M. Tichkoff et al. LC 83-73515. 200p. 1984. text 37.00 (*0-8031-0227-5*, STP848) ASTM.

Liquid Penetrant Testing Classroom Training Book. 128p. 1977. pap. 12.50 (*0-318-17235-6*, 1608) Am Soc Nondestructive.

Liquid Penetrant Testing Programmed Instruction Book. (Self-Study Instruction Handbook Ser.). 276p. 1977. pap. 20.75 (*0-318-17225-9*, 1502) Am Soc Nondestructive.

Liquid Phase. D. H. Trevena. (Wykeham Science Ser.: No. 37). 122p. pap. 18.00 (*0-85109-031-1*) Taylor & Francis.

Liquid Phase. D. H. Trevena & R. J. Cooke. LC 75-19034. (Wykeham Science Ser.: No. 37). 122p. (C). 1975. 18.00 (*0-8448-1164-5*, Crane Russak) Taylor & Francis.

Liquid-Phase Epitaxial Growth of III-V Compound Semiconductor Materials & Their Device Applications. M. G. Astles. (Illus.). 232p. 1990. 122.00 (*0-7503-0044-2*) IOP Pub.

Liquid Phase High Pressure Chemistry. Neil S. Isaacs. LC 80-40844. (Illus.). 422p. reprint ed. pap. 130.90 (*0-608-17690-7*, 203041000069) Bks Demand.

Liquid Phase Methanol (Lpmeoh) Project: Final Environmental Assessment. Sun W. Chun. (Illus.). 36p. (C). 1999. reprint ed. pap. text 20.00 (*0-7881-7721-4*) DIANE Pub.

Liquid Phase Oxidation see Comprehensive Chemical Kinetics

Liquid-Phase Oxidation of Hydrocarbons. N. M. Emanuel et al. LC 66-12888. 350p. 1967. 39.50 (*0-306-30292-6*, Plenum Trade) Perseus Pubng.

Liquid-Phase Oxidation of Hydrocarbons. N. M. Emanuel et al. LC 66-12888. 364p. reprint ed. pap. 112.90 (*0-608-13244-6*, 205579200038) Bks Demand.

Liquid-Phase Oxidation of Unsaturated Compounds. Ed. by V. L. Rubajlo et al. 227p. 1993. text 145.00 (*1-56072-119-7*) Nova Sci Pubs.

Liquid Phase Oxidations over Chromium & Related Metal-Substituted Molecular Sieve Catalysts. Ji Dong Chen. (Illus.). 163p. (Orig.). 1995. pap. 59.50 (*90-407-1164-X*, Pub. by Delft U Pr) Coronet Bks.

Liquid-Phase Reaction Rate Constants. Evgenii T. Denisov. LC 73-79419. 797p. reprint ed. pap. 200.00 (*0-608-16624-3*, 202630300049) Bks Demand.

Liquid Phase Sintering. Randall M. German. LC 85-25786. (Illus.). 252p. (C). 1985. 90.00 (*0-306-42215-8*, Plenum Trade) Perseus Pubng.

Liquid Pleasures: Social History of Drinks in Modern Britain. John Burnett. LC 98-54588. 1999. pap. 24.99 (*0-415-13182-0*); text. write for info. (*0-415-13181-2*) Routledge.

Liquid Propellant Gun Technology. Gunter Klingenberg et al. LC 98-224250. 592p. 1997. 109.95 (*1-56347-196-5*) AIAA.

Liquid Propellant Rockets. David Altman. LC 60-12048. (Princeton Aeronautical Paperbacks Ser.: No. 1). 197p. reprint ed. pap. 61.10 (*0-8357-6192-4*, 205682300090) Bks Demand.

Liquid Refreshment: Two Thousand Years of Drinks & Drinking Glasses. (Illus.). 16p. (Orig.). 1993. pap. 3.95 (*0-87290-131-9*) Corning.

Liquid Ring Vacuum Pumps & Compressors. EEMUA Staff. 1987. pap. 150.00 (*0-85931-133-3*, Pub. by EEMUA) St Mut.

Liquid Ring Vacuum Pumps & Compressors: Applications & Principles of Operation. W. Hakim Faragallah. LC 87-31506. (Illus.). 224p. 1988. reprint ed. pap. 69.50 (*0-608-07942-1*, 206791500012) Bks Demand.

Liquid Rocket Engine Combustion Instability. Ed. by Vigor Young & William E. Andersen. 1995. 79.95 (*1-56347-183-3*, V-169) AIAA.

Liquid Rocket Propulsion Design Principles. David H. Mohr. Date not set. write for info. (*0-89464-064-X*) Krieger.

Liquid Scintillation Alpha Spectrometry. W. Jack McDowell & Betty L. McDowell. LC 93-8546. 160p. 1993. lib. bdg. 89.95 (*0-8493-5288-6*) CRC Pr.

Liquid Scintillation Counting: Proceedings of a Symposium on Liquid Scintillation Counting, 5th, Bath, England, September 13-16, 1977, Vol. 3. Liquid Scintillation Counting Symposium Staff. Ed. by M. A. Crook & P. Johnson. LC 70-156826. 321p. 1974. reprint ed. pap. 99.60 (*0-608-14248-4*, 2024009) Bks Demand.

Liquid Scintillation Counting: Proceedings of a Symposium on Liquid Scintillation Counting, 5th, Bath, England, September 13-16, 1977, Vol. 4. Liquid Scintillation Counting Symposium Staff. Ed. by M. A. Crook & P. Johnson. LC 70-156826. 279p. 1977. reprint ed. pap. 86.50 (*0-608-14249-2*, 202401000004) Bks Demand.

Liquid Scintillation Counting: Proceedings of a Symposium on Liquid Scintillation Counting, 5th, Bath, England, September 13-16, 1977, Vol. 5. Liquid Scintillation Counting Symposium Staff. Ed. by M. A. Crook & P. Johnson. 232p. 1978. reprint ed. pap. 72.00 (*0-608-14099-6*, 2024011) Bks Demand.

Liquid Scintillation Counting & Organic Scintillators. Ed. by Harley Ross et al. 752p. 1991. lib. bdg. 119.00 (*0-87371-246-3*, L246) Lewis Pubs.

Liquid Scintillation Counting Practice. Alan Dyer. LC 82-100882. (Illus.). 114p. 1980. reprint ed. pap. 35.40 (*0-608-18843-3*, 203049900069) Bks Demand.

Liquid Scintillation Spectrometry, 1994. Ed. by G. T. Cook et al. LC 96-45900. (Illus.). 396p. (C). 1997. text 20.00 (*0-9638314-3-7*) Radiocarbon.

Liquid Scintillation Spectrometry, 1992. Ed. by J. E. Noakes et al. LC 93-36422. 483p. 1993. 10.00 (*0-9638314-0-2*) Radiocarbon.

Liquid Semiconductors. Vasilii M. Glazov. LC 68-31237. (Monographs in Semiconductor Physics: Vol. 2). 374p. reprint ed. pap. 116.00 (*0-608-16632-4*, 202630400049) Bks Demand.

Liquid-Solid Flows, 1994. Ed. by M. C. Roco et al. LC 93-75377. (Fluid Engineering Division Conference Ser.: Vol. 189). 257p. 1994. pap. 45.00 (*0-7918-1372-X*) ASME.

***Liquid State: Applications of Molecular Simulations.** David M. Heyes. LC 97-27622. (Wiley Series in Theoretical Chemistry). 264p. 1998. 185.00 (*0-471-97716-0*) Wiley.

Liquid State & Its Electrical Properties. Ed. by Erich E. Kunhardt et al. (NATO ASI Series B, Physics: Vol. 193). (Illus.). 586p. 1988. 145.00 (*0-306-43145-9*, Plenum Trade) Perseus Pubng.

Liquid Thermal Diffusion. AEC Technical Information Center Staff et al. Ed. by Phillip H. Abelson. (National Nuclear Energy Ser.: Div. IX, Vol. 1). 258p. 1958. 36.50 (*0-87079-259-8*, TID-5229); mic. film 9.00 (*0-87079-260-1*, TID-5229) DOE.

Liquid-Tight Flexible Nonmetallic Conduit, UL 1660. 2nd ed. (C). 1994. pap. text 330.00 (*1-55989-720-1*) Underwrtrs Labs.

Liquid-Tight Flexible Steel Conduit, UL 360. 4th ed. 1996. write for info. (*0-7629-0036-9*) Underwrtrs Labs.

Liquid to Gas & Back. John M. Patten, Jr. LC 95-6214. (Read All about Let's Wonder about Science Ser.). 24p. (J). (gr. 1-4). 1995. lib. bdg. 18.60 (*1-55916-129-9*) Rourke Bk Co.

Liquid-Vapor Phase-Change Phenomena: An Introduction to the Thermophysics of Vaporization & Condensation in Heat Transfer Equipment. Van P. Carey. 700p. 1992. pap. text 66.95 (*1-56032-074-5*) Hemisp Pub.

Liquidated Damages & Extensions of Time in Construction Contracts. B. Eggleston. (Illus.). 320p. 1992. 99.95 (*0-632-03295-2*) Blackwell Sci.

Liquidated Damages & Extensions of Time in Construction Contracts. 2nd ed. Brian Eggleston. LC 97-19448. 1997. 85.00 (*0-632-04213-3*) Blackwell Sci.

Liquidity Analysis & Management. George W. Gallinger & P. Basil Healey. LC 96-6458. (Illus.). 605p. (C). 1987. text 42.36 (*0-201-10518-7*) Addison-Wesley.

Liquidity Analysis & Management. 3rd ed. George W. Gallinger. 1996. text. write for info. (*0-201-56710-5*) Addison-Wesley.

Liquidity Preferences of Commercial Banks. George R. Morrison. LC 66-13882. (Chicago University Economics Research Center Studies). 175p. reprint ed. pap. 54.30 (*0-608-10208-3*, 202013000016) Bks Demand.

***Liquidity Risk Practice & Applications.** Lore & Borodovsky. 2001. 74.95 (*0-7506-5024-9*) Buttrwrth-Heinemann.

Liquidity Structure of Firms & Monetary Economics. William J. Frazer. LC 65-63999. (University of Florida Monographs: Social Sciences: No. 27). 98p. reprint ed. pap. 30.40 (*0-7837-4988-0*, 204465500004) Bks Demand.

Liquidos Exoticos. Leopoldo G. Colin. (Cienciapara Todos Ser.). (SPA.). pap. 6.99 (*968-16-3580-9*, Pub. by Fondo) Continental Bk.

Liquids & Amorphous Materials. Ed. by Arthur Bienenstock. (Transactions of the American Crystallographic Association Ser.: Vol. 10). 84p. 1974. pap. 25.00 (*0-686-60381-8*) Polycrystal Bk Serv.

Liquids & Liquid Mixtures. 2nd ed. J. S. Rowlinson. LC 79-75522. 372p. 1969. 37.50 (*0-306-30694-8*, Plenum Trade) Perseus Pubng.

Liquids & Solids. Michael Sprackling. (Student Physics Ser.). (Illus.). 248p. (Orig.). 1985. pap. 9.95 (*0-7102-0484-1*, Routledge Thoemms) Routledge.

***Liquids & Solids.** 5th ed. James M. Postma et al. 2000. pap. text, lab manual ed. 1.95 (*0-7167-9432-2*) W H Freeman.

Liquids & Solutions: Structure & Dynamics. Peeter Kruus. LC 76-1795. 592p. reprint ed. pap. 183.60 (*0-7837-3364-X*, 204332200008) Bks Demand.

Liquids at Interfaces: Proceedings of the Les Houches Summer School, Course XLVIII, May-June, 1988. Ed. by J. Charvolin et al. (Houches Summer School Proceedings Ser.: Vol. 48). xxxvi, 644p. 1990. 256.50 (*0-444-88450-5*, North Holland) Elsevier.

Liquids for Life. McIntyre. 1998. 25.00 (*0-8050-5246-1*) H Holt & Co.

Liquids, Freezing & the Glass Transition Pts. 1 & 2: Proceedings of the Les Houches Summer School, Course LI, 3-28 July 1989. Ed. by J. P. Hansen et al. (Houches Summer School Proceedings Ser.: No. 51). 1125p. 1991. 223.50 (*0-685-41439-6*, North Holland) Elsevier.

Liquids, Freezing & the Glass Transition Pts. 1 & 2: Proceedings of the Les Houches Summer School, Course LI, 3-28 July 1989. Ed. by J. P. Hansen et al. (Houches Summer School Proceedings Ser.: Vol. 51). xxxiv, 504p. 1991. 173.00 (*0-444-88927-2*, North Holland); 173.00 (*0-444-88928-0*, North Holland) Elsevier.

Liquids into Fibrous Media: Spontaneous & Forced Processes. B. Miller. (Surfactant Science Ser.). Date not set. write for info. (*0-8247-9393-5*) Dekker.

Liquids Processing Equipment in France: A Strategic Entry Report, 1997. Compiled by Icon Group International Staff. (Illus.). 122p. 1999. ring bd. 1220.00 incl. audio compact disk (*0-7418-0842-0*) Icon Grp.

Liquid/Solid Separation Equipment. Richard K. Miller et al. (Market Research Survey Ser.: No. 283). 50p. 1996. 200.00 (*1-55865-306-6*) Future Tech Surveys.

Liquified Gas Handling Principles on Ships & in Terminals. SIGTTO Staff et al. (C). 1986. 250.00 (*0-7855-3920-4*, Pub. by Witherby & Co) St Mut.

***Liquified Natual Gas Equipment in United Arab Emirates: A Strategic Entry Report, 1998.** Compiled by Icon Group International Staff. (Country Industry Report). (Illus.). 101p. 1999. ring bd. 1010.00 incl. audio compact disk (*0-7418-0516-2*) Icon Grp.

Liquified Petroleum Gas Tanker Practice. T. W. Woolcott. (C). 1987. 175.00 (*0-85174-524-5*) St Mut.

Liquified Petroleum Gas Tanker Practice. 2nd ed. T. W. Woolcott. 142p. 1987. text 65.00 (*0-85174-510-5*) Sheridan.

Liquor & Anti-liquor in Virginia, 1619-1919. C. C. Pearson & J. Edwin Hendricks. LC 67-18530. 354p. reprint ed. pap. 109.80 (*0-608-11977-6*, 202343300033) Bks Demand.

Liquor & Labor in Southern Africa. Ed. by Jonathan Crush & Charles Ambler. LC 92-27473. 448p. (C). 1992. text 39.95 (*0-8214-1027-X*) Ohio U Pr.

Liquor & Poverty: Skid Row As a Human Condition. Leonard U. Blumberg et al. LC 76-620080. (Monographs: No. 13). 1978. 12.00 (*0-911290-46-X*) Rutgers Ctr Alcohol.

Liquor Control Act of the State of Delaware: 1999 Edition. The Publisher's Editorial Staff. 126p. pap. 25.00 (*0-327-10232-2*) LEXIS Pub.

Liquor Control Act of the State of Delaware 1998-99 Supplement. 41p. 1999. write for info. (*0-327-07740-9*, 2216910) LEXIS Pub.

Liquor, Guns & Ammo: The Collected Short Fiction & Non-Fiction of Kent Anderson. Kent Anderson. 296p. 1998. 30.00 (*0-939767-29-5*) D McMillan.

Liquor Industry in the U. S. J. Wichert. 600p. 1999. 1195.00 (*0-318-03903-6*) Busn Trend.

***Liquor Liability: A Primer for Winning Your Case.** Ronald S. Beitman et al. LC 99-61271. 344p. 1999. 125.00 (*0-8318-0792-X*, B792) Am Law Inst.

Liquor Liability Law, 2 vols. James F. Mosher. 1987. ring bd. 280.00 (*0-8205-1498-5*) Bender.

Liquor Licenses: A Guide to California Retail Alcoholic Beverage Licensing. David E. McCrory. LC 86-83036. (Illus.). 186p. (Orig.). 1987. pap. 29.95 (*0-9617755-0-5*) Full Ct Pr CA.

Liquor Problem: A Summary of Investigations Conducted by the Committee of Fifty, 1893-1903. Fifty Committee. LC 70-112533. (Rise of Urban America Ser.). 1978. reprint ed. 19.95 (*0-405-02444-4*) Ayer.

Liquor Problem in All Ages. Daniel Dorchester. Ed. by Gerald N. Grob. LC 80-1268. (Addiction in America Ser.). (Illus.). 1981. reprint ed. lib. bdg. 71.95 (*0-405-13582-3*) Ayer.

Liquor to Casket. Regina P. Krummel. (Orig.). 1994. pap. write for info. (*0-943025-48-6*) Cummngs & Hath.

Liquorlicious: Alcohol Beverage Cookbook. Camille Cooper. Ed. by Robert Wittig. (Illus.). (Orig.). 1994. pap. 19.95 (*0-9640349-3-X*) Unorthodox Pr.

Lira - Archivio Tematico Della Lirica Italiana. Giovan B. Marino. (Archivio Tematico Della Lirica Italiana - Atli Ser.: Vol. 1). vii, 488p. 1992. write for info. (*3-487-09526-2*) G Olms Pubs.

Lira Criolla (Decimas Cubanas) Oscar P. Moro & Dario E. Perez. LC 86-83149. (Coleccion Espejo de Paciencia). 85p. (Orig.). 1987. pap. 9.95 (*0-89729-430-0*) Ediciones.

Lira da Braccio. Sterling S. Jones. LC 94-9019. (Publications of the Early Music Institute). (Illus.). 136p. 1995. pap. 22.50 (*0-253-20911-0*) Ind U Pr.

Lirazel. Louise L. Cripps. LC 96-9785. 232p. 1997. 18.95 (*0-8453-4864-7*, Cornwall Bks) Assoc Univ Prs.

Lire avec Plaisir. Barnett. (College French Ser.). (FRE.). (C). 1987. pap., teacher ed. 2.95 (*0-8384-3660-9*) Heinle & Heinle.

Lire avec Plaisir. 2nd ed. Barnett. (C). 1992. pap., teacher ed. write for info. (*0-8384-3662-5*) Heinle & Heinle.

Lire Descartes Aujourd'Hui. E. Peters. 1998. 35.95 (*90-6831-870-5*, Pub. by Peeters Pub) Bks Intl VA.

Lire, Enfin, Robbe-Grillet. Robert R. Brock. LC 90-46510. (American University Studies: Romance Languages & Literature: Ser. II, Vol. 163). 152p. (C). 1991. text 31.95 (*0-8204-1451-4*) P Lang Pubng.

Lire Piaget see Understanding Piaget

Liren' Nikolai Aseev et al. (RUS.). 40p. (C). 1989. reprint ed. pap. 7.00 (*0-933884-70-2*) Berkeley Slavic.

Lirica Personal. Juana I. De la Cruz. (Obras Completas de Sor Juana Ines de la Cruz: Vol. I). (SPA.). 639p. 1994. reprint ed. 22.99 (*968-16-3016-5*, Pub. by Fondo) Continental Bk.

***L'Ironie d'Alberto Savino a la Croisee des Discours.** Thomas Bernet. (Publications Universitaires Europeennes). 246p. 1999. 41.95 (*3-906763-75-7*, Pub. by P Lang) P Lang Pubng.

LIRT Library Instruction Book. Ed. by May Brottman & Mary Loe. 175p. 1990. lib. bdg. 26.50 (*0-87287-664-0*) Libs Unl.

Lis de Mer. Andre Pieyre de Mandiargue. (FRE.). 1972. pap. 8.95 (*0-7859-4051-0*) Fr & Eur.

***Lis Interactive Training Course.** Dell. (C). 1999. pap. 49.33 (*0-13-017619-2*) P-H.

Lisa. Bonnie Bryant. (Saddle Club Ser.). 304p. (J). (gr. 4-6). 1999. pap. 4.50 (*0-553-48676-4*) BDD Bks Young Read.

Lisa. Helen Duncan. 144p. 1998. pap. 6.95 (*0-9652813-4-5*) Dello & Assoc.

Lisa. Ellen James. (Sisters Ser.). 1997. per. 3.99 (*0-373-70738-X*, 1-70738-9) Harlequin Bks.

Lisa. Matthew Lipman. (Philosophy for Children Ser.). 96p. (YA). (gr. 7-10). 1983. pap. 10.50 (*0-916834-21-2*) Inst Advncmnt Philos Child.

Lisa. Betty Shaffer. (Springsong Bks.). 144p. (J). (gr. 7-10). 1994. mass mkt. 4.99 (*1-55661-449-7*) Bethany Hse.

Lisa: A Legacy in Poetry. Camille Fattoross & Lisa Tedesco. (Illus.). 50p. (Orig.). 1989. pap. 8.95 (*0-9618462-0-8*) Capricorn Bks.

Lisa: The Story of an Irish Drug Addict. 205p. 1988. pap. 8.95 (*1-85371-011-3*, Pub. by Poolbeg Pr) Dufour.

***Lisa & Co.** Jilly Cooper. 2000. pap. 8.95 (*0-552-12041-3*, Pub. by Transworld Publishers Ltd) Trafalgar.

Lisa & David/Jordi/Little Ralphie & the Creature. Theodore Isaac Rubin. LC 97-33049. 224p. 1998. 22.95 (*0-312-86372-1*, Pub. by Forge NYC); pap. 11.95 (*0-312-86373-X*, Pub. by Forge NYC) St Martin.

Lisa & Her Soundless World. Edna S. Levine. (Illus.). (J). (gr. 1-5). 1984. 18.95 (*0-87705-104-6*, Kluwer Acad Hman Sci); pap. 10.95 (*0-89885-204-8*, Kluwer Acad Hman Sci) Kluwer Academic.

Lisa & Lottie. Erich Kastner. Tr. by Cyrus Books. (Illus.). 136p. (J). (gr. 3-7). 1982. pap. 2.95 (*0-380-57117-X*, Avon Bks) Morrow Avon.

Lisa & the Raindrops. Anita M. Hamm. (J). (gr. 1-4). 1977. 3.50 (*0-935513-01-9*) Samara Pubns.

***Lisa & the Snowman.** Coby Hol. LC 89-42614. (Illus.). 32p. (J). (ps-1). 1999. pap. 6.95 (*0-7358-1199-7*, Pub. by North-South Bks NYC) Chronicle Bks.

Lisa, Bright & Dark. John Neufeld. LC 75-85002. (YA). (gr. 7-12). 1970. mass mkt. 4.99 (*0-451-16684-1*) NAL.

Lisa, Bright & Dark. John Neufeld. (YA). (gr. 7 up). 1969. 26.95 (*0-87599-153-X*) S G Phillips.

Lisa Bright & Dark. John Neufeld. 1987. 10.09 (*0-606-12396-2*, Pub. by Turtleback) Demco.

Lisa, Bright & Dark: A Novel. John Neufeld. LC 99-25551. (Illus.). 143p. (YA). (gr. 5-9). 1999. pap. 4.99 (*0-14-130434-0*, PuffinBks) Peng Put Young Read.

Lisa, Hedda & Joel. Sam Erlich. 1989. pap. write for info. (*0-318-64761-3*) St Martin.

Lisa in London. Victor. 1983. pap. text. write for info. (*0-582-53347-3*, Drumbeat) Longman.

Lisa in Sugarland, a Child's Book on Nutrition to Be Digested Before Eating. Anita M. Hamm. (J). (gr. 1-4). 1978. 3.50 (*0-935513-02-7*) Samara Pubns.

***Lisa Leslie.** Andrews McMeel Publishing Staff. (Illus.). 2000. pap. 4.95 (*0-7407-0604-7*) Andrews & McMeel.

Lisa Leslie. Terri Dougherty. (Jam Sessions Ser.). 1999. pap. text 6.95 (*1-57765-345-9*) ABDO Pub Co.

***Lisa Leslie.** Terry Dougherty. LC 98-27129. (Jam Sessions Ser.). (J). 1999. 14.95 (*1-57765-313-0*) ABDO Pub Co.

***Lisa Leslie.** Brent Kelley. (Women Who Win Ser.). 2000. 17.95 (*0-7910-5794-1*) Chelsea Hse.

***Lisa Leslie.** Brent Kelley. (Women Who Win Ser.). (Illus.). 2000. pap. 7.95 (*0-7910-6154-X*) Chelsea Hse.

An Asterisk (*) at the beginning of an entry indicates that the title is appearing for the first time.

Lisa Leslie: Queen of the Court. Mark Stewart. LC 96-40435. (Sports Stars Ser.). 48p. (J). 1997. 19.00 (*0-516-20585-4*) Childrens.

Lisa Leslie: Queen of the Court. Mark Stewart. Ed. by Mark Friedman. (Sports Stars Ser.). (Illus.). 48p. (J). 1998. pap. 5.95 (*0-516-26118-5*) Childrens.

***Lisa Lisa: Two Prosays.** Anthony Barnett. 36p. 2000. pap. 15.00 (*0-907954-28-6*, Pub. by Allardyce Barnett) SPD-Small Pr Dist.

Lisa Loeb Firecracker. 88p. 1997. otabind 16.95 (*0-7935-9064-7*) H Leonard.

Lisa Yuskavage. Contrib. by Faye Hirsh & Chuck Close. (Illus.). 40p. 1996. pap. 10.00 (*0-9646426-5-4*, Pub. by Smart Art Pr) RAM Publications.

Lisan al Arab, 5 vols., Set. Ibn Manzur.Tr. of Arabic Language. (ARA & ENG.). 600p. 1979. 295.00 (*0-86685-541-6*, LDL349, Pub. by Librairie du Liban) Intl Bk Ctr.

Lisardo Enamorado. Alonso del Castillo Solorzano. Ed. by Eduardo Julia y Martinez. (SPA.). 333p. 1968. pap. 100.00 (*0-614-00225-7*) Elliots Bks.

Lisa's Boy: A Novel. Joseph Machlis. 416p. 1982. 13.95 (*0-393-01606-4*) Norton.

Lisa's Daddy & Daughter Day. Eloise Greenfield. (Illus.). (J). (gr. k-2). 1993. pap. 8.95 incl. audio (*0-7608-0492-3*); pap. 4.95 (*0-88741-919-4*) Sundance Pub.

Lisa's Daddy & Daughter Day, Big bk. Eloise Greenfield. (Illus.). (J). (gr. k-2). 1993. pap. 17.95 (*0-88741-918-6*) Sundance Pub.

Lisa's down Home Tennessee Country Cookin' Lisa E. Brown & David W. Davis. LC 98-93346. (Illus.). 200p. 1998. pap. 9.95 (*1-892642-48-4*, B6-947) Aalida Pr.

Lisa's Picture Puzzle Books. Tony Tallarico. (Picture Puzzle Bks.). (Illus.). 24p. (J). 1991. 3.98 (*1-56156-007-3*) Kidsbks.

***Lisa's Story.** Tom Batiuk. 2000. pap. 12.95 (*0-399-52666-8*, Perigee Bks) Berkley Pub.

Lisa's Story. Lisa Paxton & Cecil Paxton. Ed. by C. J. McGuire. 30p. pap. Price not set. (*1-881541-19-3*, 404) A Wommack.

Lisbon. 64p. pap. text 9.95 (*88-7009-597-5*, Pub. by Bonechi) Eiron.

Lisbon. pap. 6.95 (*0-528-95197-1*) Rand McNally.

***Lisbon.** Ed. by Berlitz Publishing Staff. (Pocket Guides Ser.). (Illus.). 2001. pap. 8.95 (*2-8315-7697-0*) Berlitz.

Lisbon. Deni Bown. LC 97-16878. (Eyewitness Travel Guides Ser.). 192p. 1997. 22.95 (*0-7894-2253-0*) DK Pub Inc.

Lisbon. Jorge Gaspar & Allan M. Williams. (World Cities Ser.). 224p. 2000. 49.95 (*0-471-94904-3*) Wiley.

Lisbon. Koneman. (Architecture Guides Ser.). (Illus.). 320p. 1998. pap. 5.95 (*3-8290-0473-7*, 520549) Konemann.

Lisbon. Compiled by John Laidlar. LC 98-109802. (World Bibliographical Ser.: Vol. 199). 304p. 1997. lib. bdg. 54.00 (*1-85109-268-4*) ABC-CLIO.

Lisbon. 2nd ed. Insight Guides Staff. (Insight Guides). 1998. pap. text 7.95 (*0-88729-539-8*) Langenscheidt.

***Lisbon, \.** 2nd ed. Insight Guides Staff. (Insight Guides). 1998. pap. text 12.95 (*0-88729-892-3*) Langenscheidt.

***Lisbon.** 2nd ed. Marc Rigole. (Illus.). 2001. pap. 13.95 (*2-89464-233-4*) Ulysses Travel.

Lisbon. 3rd ed. Insight Guides Staff. (Insight Guides). 1998. pap. text 21.95 (*0-88729-701-3*) Langenscheidt.

Lisbon, Rassegna 59. (Illus.). 110p. 1994. pap. 35.00 (*88-85322-17-4*, Pub. by Birkhauser) Princeton Arch.

Lisbon: Cities of the World. Andreas Schafler & Gabriela Wachter. (Illus.). 96p. 1998. 20.00 (*1-85995-370-0*) Parkstone Pr.

Lisbon As a Port Town, the British Seaman, & Other Maritime Themes. Ed. by Stephen Fisher. (Illus.). 152p. 1988. pap. text 15.95 (*0-85989-313-8*, Pub. by Univ Exeter Pr) Northwestern U Pr.

Lisbon for Less. (For Less Compact Guides Ser.). 1999. pap. 9.95 (*1-901811-55-7*) IPG Chicago.

Lisbon in the Renaissance. Damiao De Gois. Tr. & Intro. by Jeffrey S. Ruth. LC 96-25081. (Historical Travel Ser.). (Illus.). 88p. (Orig.). 1996. pap. 14.00 (*0-934977-36-4*) Italica Pr.

Lisbon in Your Pocket Guide. Ed. by Michelin Staff. (In Your Pocket Guide Ser.). 1998. per. 9.95 (*2-06-652301-1*, 6523) Michelin.

Lisbon Massacre of 1506 & the Royal Image in the Shebet Yehudah. Yosef H. Yerushalmi. LC 77-376456. (Hebrew Union College Annual Supplements Ser.: No. 1). 105p. reprint ed. pap. 32.60 (*0-7837-2997-9*, 204294400006) Bks Demand.

Lisbon Pocket Guide 1998. rev. ed. Berlitz Editors. (Pocket Guides Ser.). (Illus.). 144p. 1998. pap. 8.95 (*2-8315-6559-6*) Berlitz.

Lisbon Town Register, 1905 (Town History & Directory) Compiled by Mitchell & Campbell. 117p. 1997. reprint ed. pap. 19.50 (*0-8328-5868-4*) Higginson Bk Co.

Lisbon Traviata. Terrence McNally. 1992. pap. 5.25 (*0-8222-0673-0*) Dramatists Play.

Lisbon/Matzko: 2 Views. Sarah J. Rogers. (Illus.). 48p. 1995. pap. 10.00 (*1-881390-11-X*) OSU Wexner Ctr.

Lisbonne. (FRE.). 1999. 9.95 (*2-06-657301-9*) Michelin.

Lise Meitner: A Life in Physics. Ruth L. Sime. LC 95-35246. (Illus.). 540p. (C). 1996. 40.00 (*0-520-08906-5*, Pub. by U CA Pr) Cal Prin Full Svc.

Lise Meitner: A Life in Physics. Ruth L. Sime. LC 95-35246. (California Studies in the History of Science: Vol. 13). (Illus.). 1997. pap. 18.95 (*0-520-20860-9*, Pub. by U CA Pr) Cal Prin Full Svc.

***Lise Meitner: Discoverer of Nuclear Fission.** Rachel Barron. LC 99-49724. (Great Scientists Ser.). (Illus.). 112p. (YA). (gr. 5 up). 1999. lib. bdg. 19.95 (*1-883846-52-8*) M Reynolds.

Lise Meitner & the Dawn of the Nuclear Age. Patricia Rife. LC 97-52076. (Illus.). 250p. 1997. 39.95 (*0-8176-3732-X*, Pub. by Birkhauser) Spr-Verlag.

Lise Meitner & the Dawn of the Nuclear Age. Patricia Rife & Lise Meitner. LC 97-52076. xviii, 432 p. 1998. 39.95 (*3-7643-3732-X*) Birkhauser.

Lisel's Shawl, Vol. 3. Merilyn Wakefield. 150p. 1997. pap. 7.00 (*0-9657993-2-8*) mwynhad.

Lisette: The Story of a Teen-Age Girl in the French Resistance. Elisabeth Sevier & Robert W. Sevier. 165p. 1996. 25.00 (*0-9652703-0-0*) Wesley Pub Co.

***Lisette Model.** Photos by Lisette Model. 360p. 2000. 85.00 (*0-944092-77-2*) Twin Palms Pub.

Lisette Model. Ann Thomas. (Illus.). 300p. 1993. pap. 39.95 (*0-88884-605-3*, Pub. by Natl Gallery) U Ch Pr.

***Lisette's Angel.** Illus. by Amy Littlesugar & Max Ginsburg. LC 99-87549. 2001. write for info. (*0-8037-2435-7*) Peng Put Young Read.

Lishmor Velaasos: Guide to Basic Principles of Jewish Law & Their Applications in Theory & Practice. Mordechai Katz. (Rothman Foundation Ser.). 159p. 1981. 15.95 (*0-87306-974-9*); pap. 13.95 (*1-58330-158-5*) Feldheim.

Lisi & the Kittens. Krister Green. Tr. by Ramona Coughlin from SWE. (Illus.). 28p. (J). (gr. 3-5). 1990. 12.95 (*0-940607-07-7*) Pictura NJ.

Lisiere. Patrick Grainville. (FRE.). 478p. 1990. pap. 13.95 (*0-7859-2583-X*, 2070382125) Fr & Eur.

Lisle Letters, 6 vols., Set. Ed. by Muriel S. Byrne. LC 80-12019. 3982p. (C). 1981. lib. bdg. 400.00 (*0-226-08801-4*) U Ch Pr.

Lisle Letters: An Abridgement. Ed. by Muriel S. Byrne & Bridget Boland. LC 82-15914. xxvi, 464p. 1983. reprint ed. 35.00 (*0-226-08800-6*) U Ch Pr.

Lisle Letters: An Abridgement. Ed. by Muriel S. Byrne & Bridget Boland. LC 82-15914. xxvi, 436p. 1995. reprint ed. pap. 12.95 (*0-226-08810-3*) U Ch Pr.

***L'isola Del Giorno Prima.** Umberto Eco. 1999. 17.95 (*88-452-2813-4*) Fabbri.

LISP. Patrick H. Winston. (Programming Languages Library). (C). 1996. pap. text. write for info. (*0-201-58040-3*) Addison-Wesley.

LISP. 2nd ed. Patrick H. Winston. (Computer Science Ser.). 1985. pap. 32.25 (*0-201-08372-8*) Addison-Wesley.

LISP. 3rd ed. Patrick H. Winston & Berthold K. Horn. (Computer Science Ser.). (Illus.). 611p. (C). 1989. pap. text 42.19 (*0-201-08319-1*) Addison-Wesley.

LISP in Small Pieces. Christian Queinnec. 534p. (C). 1996. text 64.95 (*0-521-56247-3*) Cambridge U Pr.

LISP LORE: A Guide to Programming the LISP Machine. Hank Bromley. 1986. text 89.00 (*0-89838-220-3*) Kluwer Academic.

LISP LORE: A Guide to Programming the LISP Machine. 2nd rev. ed. Hank Bromley & Richard Lamson. (C). 1987. text 110.50 (*0-89838-228-9*) Kluwer Academic.

LISP, Lore & Logic. W. R. Stark. (Illus.). 320p. 1990. 60.95 (*0-387-97072-X*) Spr-Verlag.

LISP One-Point-Five Programmer's Manual. John McCarthy. 1962. pap. text 11.00 (*0-262-13011-4*) MIT Pr.

LISP Programming for AI: A Common LISP Tutorial. David Steele. (Illus.). 500p. (C). 1989. pap. text 37.33 (*0-201-41653-0*) Addison-Wesley.

LISP Standardization & Evolution: Proceedings of the 1st International Workshop, Paris, France, 1988. Ed. by J. Chailloux & Christian Queinnec. (Frontiers in Artificial Intelligence & Applications Ser.: Vol. 2). 86p. (gr. 12). 1988. pap. 37.00 (*90-5199-008-1*, Pub. by IOS Pr) IOS Press.

LISP-Stat: An Object-Oriented Environment for Statistical Computing & Dynamic Graphics. Luke Tierney. 416p. 1990. 98.95 (*0-471-50916-7*) Wiley.

LISPcraft. Robert Wilensky. 385p. (C). 1984. pap. text 47.25 (*0-393-95442-0*) Norton.

LISPcraft. Robert Wilensky. (C). 1984. pap. text, teacher ed. 6.25 (*0-393-95455-2*) Norton.

Lisrel Approaches to Interaction Effects in Multiple Regression. James Jaccard & Choi K. Wan. LC 95-50187. (Quantitative Applications in the Social Science Ser.: Vol. 114). 96p. (C). 1996. pap. 10.95 (*0-8039-7179-6*) Sage.

LISREL 8: New Statistical Features. Karl G. Joreskog et al. (Illus.). xx, 260p. 1999. pap. 30.00 (*0-89498-045-9*) Sci Ware.

LISREL 8: Structual Equation Modeling with the SIMPLIS Command Language. Karl G. Joreskog & Dag Sorbom. 200p. 1993. text 59.95 (*0-8058-1441-8*); pap. text 35.00 (*0-8058-1442-6*) L Erlbaum Assocs.

LISREL 8: Structural Equation Modeling with the SIMPLIS Command Language. Karl G. Joreskog & Dag Sorbom. 1993. pap. 35.00 (*0-89498-033-5*) Sci Ware.

LISREL Issues, Debates, & Strategies. Leslie A. Hayduk. (Illus.). 280p. (C). 1996. text 39.95 (*0-8018-5336-2*) Johns Hopkins.

LISREL 7: A Guide to the Program & Applications. 2nd ed. Karl G. Joreskog & Dag Sorbum. 368p. 1991. pap. 26.95 (*0-918469-94-5*) SPSS Inc.

Lissa. large type ed. Mira Stables. (Linford Romance Library). 336p. 1997. pap. 16.99 (*0-7089-5181-3*) Ulverscroft.

Lissa Stratton Strikes: Musical Comedy Suggested by Aritophanes' Lysistrata. Charles Avery. (Illus.). 60p. 1986. pap. 4.50 (*0-88680-277-6*) I E Clark.

Lissa's Groom, 1. Jill Henry. (Zebra Splendor Historical Romances Ser.). 352p. 1999. mass mkt. 4.99 (*0-8217-6260-5*) Kensgtn Pub Corp.

Lissauer's Encyclopedia of Popular Music in America: 1888 to the Present. 2nd ed. Robert Lissauer. 1584p. 1996. 185.00 (*0-8160-3238-6*) Facts on File.

Lissitzky. Sophie Lissitzky-Kuppers. (GER., Illus.). 412p. 1992. text 50.00 (*3-364-00226-6*) Gordon & Breach.

Lissitzky. Sophie Lissitzky-Kuppers. LC 79-83561. (Illus.). 410p. 1992. 70.00 (*0-500-23090-0*, Pub. by Thames Hudson) Norton.

***Lissitzky: Beyond the Abstract Cabinet.** Margarita Tupitsyn. (Illus.). 256p. 1999. 65.00 (*0-300-08170-7*) Yale U Pr.

Lissitzky, 1890-1941. Frank Lubbers. 1991. pap. 55.00 (*0-500-97393-8*, Pub. by Thames Hudson) Norton.

List. William W. Cecil. (Illus.). 7.95 (*0-9602766-0-2*) Whitten Pub Co.

List. Lawrence E. Newman. (Orig.). Date not set. pap. 6.99 (*0-9650996-0-1*) Newman & Assocs.

List. Barbara Raskin. 1990. 18.95 (*0-685-33569-0*) Random.

***List.** Robert Whitlow. LC 99-45922. 400p. 2000. 12.99 (*0-8499-1640-2*) Word Pub.

List. abr. ed. Steve Martini. 1997. audio 25.00 (*0-671-53454-8*, 692868) S&S Audio.

List. large type ed. Steve Martini. 451p. 1997. mass mkt. 7.50 (*0-515-12149-5*, Jove) Berkley Pub.

List. large type ed. Steve Martini. LC 96-54263. 650p. 1997. 28.95 (*0-7838-8089-8*, G K Hall Lrg Type); pap. 26.95 (*0-7838-8090-1*, G K Hall Lrg Type) Mac Lib Ref.

List. 2nd ed. Harvey Jackins. LC 97-8536. (Illus.). 1997. 5.00 (*1-885357-48-6*) Rational Isl.

List, Vol. I. Harvey Jackins. (RUM.). 154p. 1999. pap. 50.00 (*1-58429-041-2*) Rational Isl.

L.I.S.T. A Listing of International Schools Today. Jim Paffrath & Karen Cangialosi. Ed. by Colleen Gilbride & Christine Paffrath. (Orig.). 1984. pap. 3.95 (*0-910703-09-4*) JP Pubns CA.

List: Composers: Their Birthdates & Deathdates. Ed. by David J. Askine. 300p. 1993. pap. 49.95 (*0-9643903-0-2*) List Pubng.

List: Composers: Their Birthdates & Deathdates. 2nd ed. Ed. by David J. Askine. 1995. pap. 49.95 (*0-9643903-1-0*) List Pubng.

List: Composers: Their Birthdates & Deathdates. 3rd rev. ed. Ed. by David J. Askine. 350p. 1996. pap. 49.95 (*0-9643903-2-9*) List Pubng.

List: Lots of List for Laughs & Lifts, Vol. I. Derric Johnson. 208p. (Orig.). 1993. reprint ed. pap. 12.95 (*0-9653348-0-5*) Yess Pr.

List: Lots of List for Laughs & Lifts, Vol. II. Derric Johnson. 240p. (Orig.). 1995. reprint ed. pap. 12.95 (*0-9653348-1-3*) Yess Pr.

List & Index to the Proceedings in Star Chamber for the Reign of James I (1603-1625) in the Public Record Office, London: Class STAC8, 3 vols., Set. American Bar Foundation Staff. Ed. by Thomas G. Barnes. LC 75-542. (American Bar Foundation Publication Ser.). 2312p. 1975. 135.00 (*0-910058-68-7*, 304950) W S Hein.

List More, Sell More. Jerry Bresser. 320p. 1983. 33.00 (*0-9611574-0-2*) Bresser Pub.

List of Adrian Messenger. Philip MacDonald. 1976. 20.95 (*0-8488-0570-4*) Amereon Ltd.

List of Adrian Messenger. Philip MacDonald. 1993. reprint ed. lib. bdg. 16.95 (*1-56849-210-3*) Buccaneer Bks.

List of Agricultural Periodicals in the United States & Canada Published During the Century July 1810 to July 1910. Ed. by S. C. Stuntz. LC 72-89093. (Rural America Ser.). 1973. reprint ed. 23.00 (*0-8420-1500-0*) Scholarly Res Inc.

***List of Air Carriers Certificated by Title 14 of the Code of Federal Regulations, April 22, 1998 Part 135.** 103p. 1998. pap. 9.00 (*0-16-062439-8*) USGPO.

List of All Those Who Have Been Members of the First Congregational Church in New London Connecticut. Contrib. by Charles D. Townsend. 78p. 1996. reprint ed. pap. 8.00 (*1-878545-22-1*) ACETO Bookmen.

List of Ancient Irish Authors. Ed. by Whitley Stokes. (IRI.). 1996. pap. 1.50 (*0-89979-091-7*) British Am Bks.

List of Battles & Roster of Regimental Surgeons & Assistant Surgeons During the War of the Rebellion (with a New Index to Names) United States Pension Office Staff. LC 88-60668. (American Civil War Surgery Ser.: No. 11). 386p. 1990. reprint ed. 65.00 (*0-930405-10-2*) Norman SF.

List of Bombay Grasses & Their Uses. Ed. by J. C. Lisboa. 142p. (C). 1979. text 125.00 (*0-89771-579-9*, Pub. by Intl Bk Distr) St Mut.

List of Bombay Grasses & Their Uses. J. C. Lisboa. 142p. 1979. reprint ed. 95.00 (*0-7855-3116-5*, Pub. by Intl Bk Distr) St Mut.

List of Books & of Articles in Periodicals Relating to Interoceanic Canal & Railway Routes. Hugh A. Morrison. 174p. 1988. reprint ed. 15.00 (*0-913129-21-6*) La Tienda.

List of Books, Magazine Articles & Maps Relating to Brazil. Philip L. Phillips. (Brazil Ser.). 1979. lib. bdg. 44.95 (*0-8490-2962-7*) Gordon Pr.

List of Books, Magazine Articles & Maps Relating to Central America. P. Lee Phillips. 109p. 1984. reprint ed. pap. 12.50 (*0-913129-11-9*) La Tienda.

List of Books on Puerto Rico with References to Periodicals. A. F. Griffin. 1976. lib. bdg. 59.95 (*0-8490-2169-3*) Gordon Pr.

List of Books Suitable for a Psychiatric Library. rev. ed. Royal College of Psychiatrists, Education Committe. LC Z 6664.. (Special Publication: No. 3). 68p. reprint ed. pap. 30.00 (*0-7837-0997-8*, 204130300020) Bks Demand.

List of Catalogues of English Book Sales, 1676-1900: Now in the British Museum. Alfred W. Pollard. 539p. 1995. reprint ed. 90.00 (*1-888262-59-1*) Martino Pubng.

***List of Certificated Pilot Schools.** 29p. 1998. pap. 2.75 (*0-16-062441-X*) USGPO.

List of Classes of United States Government Publications Available for Selection by Depository Libraries. Government Printing Office Staff. per. 15.00 (*0-16-011184-6*) USGPO.

List of Components see Aegyptischen Personennamen

List of Conversion Factors for Atomic Impurities to PPM by Weight. Aymbe Cornu & R. Massot. LC 68-20754. 148p. reprint ed. pap. 45.90 (*0-608-14065-1*, 202400300035) Bks Demand.

List of Discussions of the 14th & 15th Amendments with Special Reference to Negro Suffrage. United States Library of Congress, Division of Bib. 1977. text 13.95 (*0-8369-9213-X*, 9069) Ayer.

List of Doctoral Dissertations by Chinese Students in the United States, 1961-1964. Tze-Chung Li. LC 67-30284. 1967. pap. 5.95 (*0-686-24155-X*) Chinese Cult Serv.

List of Documents in Spanish Archives Relating to the History of the United States. J. A. Robertson. (Carnegie Institute Ser.: Vol. 19). 1910. 40.00 (*0-527-00699-8*) Periodicals Srv.

List of Editions of Baroque Music: In His Music in the Baroque Era. Manfred F. Bukofzer. 1993. reprint ed. lib. bdg. 89.00 (*0-7812-9695-1*) Rprt Serv.

***List of Editions of the Holy Scriptures & Parts Thereof Printed in America Previous to 1860.** Edmund Z. O'Callaghan. 415p. 2000. reprint ed. 65.00 (*1-57898-183-2*) Martino Pubng.

***List of Emigrant Ministers to America, 1690-1811.** Gerald Fothergill. 65p. 2000. pap. 12.00 (*0-8063-0149-X*, Pub. by Clearfield Co) ACCESS Pubs Network.

List of English Plays Written Before 1643 & Printed Before 1700. Walter Greg. LC 68-25311. (Studies in Drama: No. 39). 1969. reprint ed. lib. bdg. 75.00 (*0-8383-0950-X*) M S G Haskell Hse.

List of English Plays Written Before 1643 & Printed Before 1700: Printed Before Seventeen Hundred. Walter W. Greg. LC 76-131724. xi, 158p. 1972. reprint ed. 25.00 (*0-403-00611-2*) Scholarly.

List of Ex-Soldiers, Sailors & Marines Living in Iowa. 772p. 1997. reprint ed. lib. bdg. 75.00 (*0-8328-6670-9*) Higginson Bk Co.

List of FAA Certificated Aviation Maintenance Technician Schools & List of Certificated Pilot Schools. 1996. lib. bdg. 250.95 (*0-8490-6065-6*) Gordon Pr.

List of Fellows, 1913. American College of Surgeons Staff. ix, 187p. reprint ed. 39.00 (*0-932051-29-4*) Rprt Serv.

List of Field Officers of the Confederate Army. John M. Carroll. 29.95 (*0-8488-0010-9*, J M C & Co); pap. 19.95 (*0-8488-0044-3*, J M C & Co) Amereon Ltd.

List of Freeholders, Albany, New York, 1720. Orange County Genealogical Society Staff. 1986. pap. text 0.50 (*0-937135-07-0*) Orange County Genealog.

List of Freemen of Massachusetts, 1630-1691. Lucius R. Paige. LC 78-50979. 60p. 1998. reprint ed. pap. 10.95 (*0-8063-0806-0*) Clearfield Co.

List of Geographical Atlases in the Library of Congress, 5 vols. Compiled by Clara Egli Le Gear. 2535p. 1996. reprint ed. 350.00 (*1-888262-94-X*) Martino Pubng.

List of Geographical Atlases in the Library of Congress, 4 vols., Set. Philip L. Phillips. 3673p. 1995. reprint ed. 35.00 (*1-888262-82-6*) Martino Pubng.

List of Inhabitants in Dutchess County, 1714. Orange County Genealogical Society Staff. 1986. pap. text 0.50 (*0-937135-08-9*) Orange County Genealog.

List of Inhabitants of Orange County, 1702. Orange County Genealogical Society Staff. 1986. pap. text 0.50 (*0-937135-09-7*) Orange County Genealog.

List of Linnaean Generic Names & Their Types. C. E. Jarvis. Ed. by W. Greuter. (Regnum Vegetabile Ser.: Vol. 127). 100p. 1993. pap. 34.00 (*3-87429-347-5*, 053045, Pub. by Koeltz Sci Bks) Lubrecht & Cramer.

List of MAK & BAT Values, 1993. 167p. 1993. pap. 30.00 (*3-527-27558-4*, Wiley-VCH) Wiley.

List of MAK & BAT Values, 1994. Deutsche Forschungsgemeinschaft. 181p. 1995. pap. 30.00 (*3-527-27564-9*, Wiley-VCH) Wiley.

List of MAK & BAT Values, 1998 No. 33: Maximum Concentrations & Biological Tolerance Values at the Workplace. Commission for the Investigation of Health of Chemical Compunds in the Work Area Staff. (MAK & BAT Values Ser.). 220p. 1998. pap. 64.95 (*3-527-27585-1*) Wiley.

List of MAK & BAT Values 1995: Maximum Concentrations & Biological Tolerance Values at the Workplace, Report 31. Ed. by Commission for the Investigation of Health Hazards. (Reports: Vol. 31). (Illus.). 193p. 1995. pap. 59.95 (*3-527-27570-3*, Wiley-VCH) Wiley.

List of MAK & BAT Values, 1996 Report No. 32: Maximum Concentrations & Biological Tolerance Values at the Workplace. 203p. 1996. pap. 59.95 (*3-527-27572-X*, Wiley-VCH) Wiley.

List of MAK & BAT Values 1997 Report No. 33: Maximum Concentrations & Biological Tolerance Values at the Workplace. Ed. by Deutsche Forschungsgemeinschaft Staff. 212p. 1997. pap. 84.95 (*3-527-27575-4*, Wiley-VCH) Wiley.

***List of MAK & BAT Values 1999: Maximum Concentrations & Biological Tolerance Values at the Workplace, Report No. 35.** Ed. by Commission for the Investigation of Health of Chemical Compunds in the Work Area Staff. 228p. 1999. 54.95 (*3-527-27590-8*) Wiley.

List of Manuscripts Concerning American History Preserved in European Libraries. D. M. Matteson. (Carnegie Institute Ser.: Vol. 10). 1925. 30.00 (*0-527-00690-4*) Periodicals Srv.

List of Masques, Pageants, Etc. Supplementary to a List of English Plays. Walter Greg. LC 68-25312. (Studies in Drama: No. 39). 1969. reprint ed. lib. bdg. 75.00 (*0-8383-0942-9*) M S G Haskell Hse.

L

L

List of Materials Acceptable for Use on Systems of Rus Electrification Borrowers. Government Printing Office Staff. 1986. ring bd. 38.00 (*0-16-016415-X*, Agriculture Dept) USGPO.

List of Materials Acceptable for Use on Telecommunications Systems of Rus Borrowers. Government Printing Office Staff. 1983. ring bd. 103.00 (*0-16-016417-6*, Agriculture Dept) USGPO.

List of Members. Iau. 1990. pap. text 53.50 (*0-7923-0582-5*) Kluwer Academic.

List of Members - International Society for Soil Mechanics & Foundation Engineering 1993. (Illus.). 278p. (C). 1994. text 91.00 (*90-5410-167-9*, Pub. by A A Balkema) Ashgate Pub Co.

List of Members '89. List. 1990. 91.00 (*90-6191-982-7*) Ashgate Pub Co.

***List of Members '97.** 1998. pap. 91.00 (*90-5410-681-6*) Ashgate Pub Co.

List of Military & Armored Fighting Vehicle Photographs in the World War II Collection of Seized Enemy Records Group Rg-242-Gap in the National Archives. 2nd rev. ed. Ray Price et al. (World War II Monograph: Vol. 14). (Illus.). 44p. 1997. 17.95 (*1-57638-048-3*, M14H) Merriam Pr.

List of Military & Armored Fighting Vehicle Photographs in the World War II Collection of Seized Enemy Records Group Rg-242-Gap in the National Archives: In the World War II Collection of Seized Enemy Records Group RG-242-GAP in the National Archives. 2nd rev. ed. Ray Price et al. (World War II Monograph Ser.: Vol. 14). (Illus.). 35p. 1997. pap. 7.95 (*1-57638-041-6*, M14S) Merriam Pr.

List of Names see Aegyptischen Personennamen

List of Names of Succulent Plants Other Than Cacti from Repertorium Plantarum Succulentarum 1950-1992, Pt. 1. Ed. by U. Eggli & N. P. Taylor. 176p. 1994. pap. 20.00 (*0-947643-63-X*, Pub. by Royal Botnic Grdns) Balogh.

List of Officers of the Navy of the U. S. & of the Marine Corps, 1775-1900. Edward W. Callahan. LC 68-31274. (Genealogy Ser.: No. 43). 1969. reprint ed. lib. bdg. 75.00 (*0-8383-0327-7*) M S G Haskell Hse.

List of Officers of the Navy of the U. S. & the Marine Corps from 1775-1900. Edward W. Callahan. 750p. 1989. reprint ed. 35.00 (*0-942211-74-X*) Olde Soldier Bks.

List of Olympian Victors. Sextus J. Africanus. Ed. by I. Rutgers. 196p. 1980. pap. 20.00 (*0-89005-351-0*) Ares.

List of Orchid Hybrids of Singapore & Malaysia, 1960-1980. V. P. Phang. 92p. (Orig.). 1983. pap. 20.00 (*9971-69-062-4*, Pub. by Sngapore Univ Pr) Coronet Bks.

List of Paintings in the Sterling & Francine Clark Art Institute. LC 92-6127. (Illus.). 124p. 1992. pap. 16.95 (*0-931102-31-6*) S & F Clark Art.

List of Parish Registers & Other Genealogical Works. Ed. by Frederick A. Crisp. xxx, 343p. 1997. reprint ed. pap. 27.00 (*0-7884-0692-2*, C637) Heritage Bk.

List of Parties Excluded from Federal Procurement or Nonprocurement Programs. Government Printing Office Staff. 1983. pap. 99.00 (*0-16-011246-X*) USGPO.

List of Pensioners, Chicago & Cook County, Illinois, January 1, 1883. 43p. 1985. pap. 5.00 (*1-881125-09-2*) Chi Geneal Soc.

List of Pensioners of the War of 1812 (Vermont Claimants) Byron N. Clark. (Illus.). 171p. 1996. reprint ed. pap. 18.00 (*0-8063-0074-4*, 1000) Clearfield Co.

List of Places Included in the 19th Century Virginia Directories. Ray O. Hummel, Jr. LC 60-9519. 153p. 1981. pap. 7.95 (*0-88490-047-9*) Library of VA.

List of Proprietary Substances & Nonfood Compounds, Authorized for Use under USDA Inspection & Grading Programs, Effective As of Jan. 1, 1998. (Miscellaneous Publication Ser.: No. 1419). 478p. 1989. pap. 33.00 (*0-16-036215-6*, 901-007-00000-4) USGPO.

List of Publications of the American Bureau of Ethnology, with Index to Authors & Titles. reprint ed. 19.00 (*0-403-03633-X*) Scholarly.

List of Publications of the Bureau of American Ethnology, with Index to Authors & Titles. (Bureau of American Ethnology Bulletins Ser.). 99p. 1995. lib. bdg. 69.00 (*0-7812-4031-X*); lib. bdg. 89.00 (*0-7812-4036-0*); lib. bdg. 69.00 (*0-7812-4049-2*); lib. bdg. 69.00 (*0-7812-4058-1*) Rprt Serv.

List of Publications with Index. Bureau of American Ethedogy Staff. 1988. reprint ed. lib. bdg. 49.00 (*0-7812-0015-6*) Rprt Serv.

List of Sea State Parameters: International Association for Hydraulic Research. 50p. (C). 1986. text 26.00 (*90-6191-690-9*, Pub. by A A Balkema) Ashgate Pub Co.

List of 7. Mark Frost. 416p. 1994. mass mkt. 5.99 (*0-380-72019-1*, Avon Bks) Morrow Avon.

List of Species & Genera & Indian Planerograms Not Included in Sir J. D. Hooker's Flora of British India. C. C. Calder. (C). 1978. text 250.00 (*0-89771-576-4*, Pub. by Intl Bk Distr) St Mut.

List of Statutory Instruments, 1992. 319p. 1993. pap. 25.00 (*0-11-500362-2*, HM03622, Pub. by Statnry Office) Bernan Associates.

List of Statutory Instruments, 1996. 319p. 1998. pap. 30.00 (*0-11-500540-4*, HM005404, Pub. by Statnry Office) Bernan Associates.

List of Statutory Instruments, 1995. TSO Staff. 319p. 1997. pap. 30.00 (*0-11-500497-1*, HM04971, Pub. by Statnry Office) Bernan Associates.

List of Statutory Instruments 1986. 319p. 1988. pap. 25.00 (*0-11-500131-X*, HM3127) Statnry Office.

List of Statutory Instruments 1985. 319p. 1986. pap. 25.00 (*0-11-500123-9*, HM1958) Statnry Office.

List of the Books, Periodicals & Pamphlets in the Library of the Royal Aeronautical Society: With Which Is Incorporated the Institution of Aeronautical Engineers. Royal Aeronautical Society Staff. Ed. by James B. Gilbert. LC 79-7295. (Flight: Its First Seventy-Five Years Ser.). 1980. reprint ed. lib. bdg. 26.95 (*0-405-12202-0*) Ayer.

List of the Colonial Soldiers of Virginia. Hamilton J. Eckenrode. 91p. 1997. reprint ed. pap. 12.00 (*0-8063-0099-X*, 1570) Clearfield Co.

List of the Early Settlers of Georgia. E. Merton Coulter & Albert B. Saye. LC 83-80998. 111p. 1998. reprint ed. pap. 15.00 (*0-8063-1031-6*) Clearfield Co.

List of the Ferns of Simla & North Western Himalaya. H. F. Blandford. (Illus.). 22p. 1978. reprint ed. 2.00 (*0-88065-065-6*) Scholarly Pubns.

List of the Original Appearances of Dashiell Hammett's Magazine Work. E. H. Mundell. LC 75-97620. (Serif Series: Bibliographies & Checklists: No. 13). 52p. 1968. text 15.00 (*0-87338-033-9*) Boulevard.

List of the Original Appearances of Dashiell Hammett's Magazine Work. Compiled by E. H. Mundell. LC 75-97620. No. 13. 60p. 1997. reprint ed. pap. 25.00 (*0-317-55821-8*, 2029408) Bks Demand.

List of the Principal Officers of Vermont, from 1777 to 1918. Ed. by John M. Comstock. 411p. 1997. reprint ed. lib. bdg. 45.00 (*0-8328-6494-3*) Higginson Bk Co.

List of the Publications of the Bureau of Ethnology: With Index to Authors & Subjects. Frederick W. Hodge. (Bureau of American Ethnology Bulletins Ser.). 99p. 1995. lib. bdg. 69.00 (*0-7812-4024-7*) Rprt Serv.

List of the Writings of Charles Ralph Boxer Published Between 1926 & 1984. S. George West. (Monagrafias A Ser.: Vol. CX). (Illus.). 91p. (Orig.). (C). 1984. 41.00 (*0-7293-0187-7*, Pub. by Tamesis Bks Ltd) Boydell & Brewer.

List of Translations of Foreign Literature on Hydraulics. (ASCE Manual & Report on Engineering Practice Ser.: No. 35). 140p. 1968. pap. 3.00 (*0-87262-212-6*) Am Soc Civil Eng.

List of Treaty Collections/Liste de Recueils de Traites/Lista de Colecciones de Tratados. United Nations Office of Legal Affairs Codification. LC 81-51629. 174p. 1981. reprint ed. 75.00 (*0-918542-01-4*, Pub. by Symposia Pr) Gaunt.

List of Voters for Elections of Burgesses, 1764-1769, Halifax County, Virginia. Marian D. Chiarito. 44p. 1986. 6.00 (*0-945503-11-3*) Clarkton Pr.

List of Words & Phrases in Every-Day Use by the Natives of Hetton-Le-Hole. Ed. by F. M. Palgrave. (English Dialect Society Publications: No. 74). 1969. reprint ed. pap. 25.00 (*0-8115-0492-1*) Periodicals Srv.

List of Words from Tennessee; Report of a Recent Project of Collecting. Gordon R. Wood & Frederic G. Cassidy. (Publications of the American Dialect Society: No. 29). 51p. 1958. pap. text 5.00 (*0-8173-0629-3*) U of Ala Pr.

List Poem: A Guide to Teaching & Writing Catalog Verse. Larry Fagin. 220p. 1991. pap. 15.95 (*0-915924-37-4*) Tchrs & Writers Coll.

List Your Creative Self: Listmaking As the Way to Unleash Your Creativity, 1 vol. Ilene Segalove & Paul B. Velick. 1999. 12.95 (*0-7407-0208-4*) Andrews & McMeel.

List Your Self: Listmaking As the Way to Self-Discovery. Ilene Segalove & Paul B. Velick. LC 96-16181. 288p. 1996. pap. 14.95 (*0-8362-2179-6*) Andrews & McMeel.

***List Your Self For Kids: Listmaking as a Fun Way to Get to Know Yourself, 1 vol.** Ilene Segalove. 1999. 12.95 (*0-7407-0207-6*) Andrews & McMeel.

List Yourself for Parents: Listmaking As the Way to Celebrate & Enrich Parenting. Ilene Segalove. 1999. 12.95 (*0-8362-8180-2*) Andrews & McMeel.

List Yourself for Pregnancy: Listmaking As the Way to Self-Discovery for the Mother-to-Be. Ilene Segalove. 1999. 12.95 (*0-8362-8181-0*) Andrews & McMeel.

***Lista.** Steve Martini. 1999. 29.95 (*84-08-02992-4*) Planeta.

Lista Anotada de los Mamiferos Peruanos. Victor Pacheco et al. (SPA.). 32p. 1994. pap. 7.00 (*1-881173-06-2*) Conser Intl.

Lista Anotada dos Mamiferos do Brasil: Annotated List of Brazilian Mammals. Gustavo A. Da Fonseca et al. (Occasional Papers in Conservation Biology). (ENG & POR., Illus.). 35p. (Orig.). (C). Date not set. pap. text 10.00 (*1-881173-17-8*) Conser Intl.

Lista de Encabezamientos de Materia para Bibliotecas, 3 vols. y Suplementos-1967. (Manuales del Bibliotecario Ser.: No. 6). (SPA.). 1977. write for info. (*0-8270-3125-4*); write for info. (*0-8270-3130-0*) OAS.

Lista de Encabezamientos de Materia para Bibliotecas, 3 vols. y suplementos-1967, I. (Manuales del Bibliotecario Ser.: No. 6). (SPA.). 1977. write for info. (*0-8270-3105-X*) OAS.

Lista de Encabezamientos de Materia para Bibliotecas, 3 vols. y suplementos-1967, Set. (Manuales del Bibliotecario Ser.: No. 6). (SPA.). 1977. 25.00 (*0-686-76837-X*) OAS.

Lista de Encabezamientos de Materia para Bibliotecas, 3 vols. y suplementos-1967, Vol. II. (Manuales del Bibliotecario Ser.: No. 6). (SPA.). 1977. write for info. (*0-8270-3115-7*) OAS.

Lista de Encabezamientos de Materia para Bibliotecas, 3 vols. , Vol. 3. (Manuales del Bibliotecario Ser.: No. 6). (SPA.). 1977. write for info. (*0-318-54736-8*) OAS.

Lista General: Enero-Diciembre de 1959. (Documentos Oficiales Ser.). (SPA.). pap. 1.00 (*0-8270-0010-3*) OAS.

Lista General Vol. 4, No. 1: Enero-Junio, 1963. (Documentos Oficiales Ser). (SPA.). pap. 1.00 (*0-8270-0020-0*) OAS.

Lista General Vol. 4, No. 2: Julio-Diciembre, 1963. (Documentos Oficiales Ser). (SPA.). pap. 1.00 (*0-8270-0025-1*) OAS.

Lista General Vol. 5, No. 1: Enero-Junio, 1964. (Documentos Oficiales Ser). (SPA.). pap. 1.00 (*0-8270-0030-8*) OAS.

Lista General Vol. 5, No. 2: Julio-Diciembre, 1964. (Documentos Oficiales Ser). (SPA.). pap. 1.00 (*0-8270-0035-9*) OAS.

Lista General Vol. 6, No. 1: Enero-Junio, 1965. (Documentos Oficiales Ser). (SPA.). pap. 1.00 (*0-8270-0040-5*) OAS.

Lista General Vol. 6, No. 2: Julio-Diciembre, 1965. (Documentos Oficiales Ser). (SPA.). pap. 1.50 (*0-8270-0045-6*) OAS.

Lista General Vol. 7, No. 1: Enero-Junio, 1966. (Documentos Oficiales Ser). (SPA.). pap. 1.50 (*0-8270-0050-2*) OAS.

Lista General Vol. 11, No. 1: Enero-Julio, 1970. (Documentos Oficiales Ser). (SPA.). pap. 1.50 (*0-8270-0090-1*) OAS.

Lista General Vol. 11, No. 2: Julio-Diciembre, 1970. (Documentos Oficiales Ser). (SPA.). 69p. 1970. pap. 2.00 (*0-8270-0095-2*) OAS.

Lista General Vol. 12: Enero-Diciembre, 1971. (Documentos Oficiales Ser). (SPA.). 190p. 1971. pap. 2.00 (*0-8270-0100-2*) OAS.

Liste Alphabetique Globale see Thesaurus du Cemagref

Liste Chronologique des Oeuvres de William Hazlitt. Jules Douady. LC 78-164776. reprint ed. 31.50 (*0-404-07305-0*) AMS Pr.

Liste der Koptischen Handschriften des Neuen Testaments: I. Die Sahidischen Handschriften der Evangelien, Part 2, Vol. 1. Ed. by Franz-Juergan Schmitz & Gerd Mink. (Arbeiten zur Neutestamentlichen Textforschung Ser.: No. 13). (GER.). x, 449p. (C). 1989. lib. bdg. 111.55 (*3-11-012255-3*) De Gruyter.

Liste der Koptischen Handschriften des Neuen Testaments No. 1: Die Sahidischen Handschriften der Evangelien 2 Teil, 2 Halbband Arbeiten zur Neutestamentlichen Textforschung, Vol. 15. Ed. by Franz-Jurgen Schmitz & Gerd Mink. (GER.). xii, 829p. (C). 1991. lib. bdg. 198.50 (*3-11-013015-7*) De Gruyter.

Liste Thematique see Thesaurus du Cemagref

Listed Companies: Law & Market Practice. Martin K. Earp & Gai M. McGrath. LC 96-147237. 706p. 1996. pap. 95.00 (*0-455-21383-6*, Pub. by Cavendish Pubng) Gaunt.

Listed Stock Options: The Hands-On Study Guide for Investors & Traders. rev. ed. Carl F. Luft & Richard K. Sheiner. 1993. per. 24.95 (*1-55738-520-3*, Irwn Prfssnl) McGraw-Hill Prof.

Listen. Becky Daniel & Nancee McClure. 64p. teacher ed. 8.99 (*0-86653-728-7*, GA1450) Good Apple.

Listen. Claudette C. Mitchell et al. (Visions: African-American Experiences: Vol. 34). (Illus.). 8p. (Orig.). (J). (gr. k-1). 1996. pap. text 3.00 (*1-57518-076-6*) Arborlake.

Listen. Fran Parker. 50p. 1983. pap. 8.00 (*0-686-40982-5*) TarPar.

Listen. 3rd ed. Joseph Kerman. 1980. text 45.95 (*0-87901-127-0*) Worth.

***Listen.** 4th ed. Kerman. 1999. pap. text 46.95 (*1-57259-422-5*); pap. text 53.95 (*1-57259-795-X*) St Martin.

Listen: Brief Edition. Joseph Kerman. 411p. (C). 1987. pap. 32.95 (*0-87901-364-8*) Worth.

Listen: Brief Edition. Joseph Kerman. 411p. (C). 1987. 36.95 (*0-87901-373-7*) Worth.

Listen: Brief Edition. 3rd ed. Joseph Kerman. (Illus.). 450p. (C). 1997. pap. text 33.80 (*1-57259-642-2*) Worth.

Listen: Instructor's Resource Manual. Joseph Kerman & Vivian Kerman. 1996. teacher ed. write for info. (*1-57259-061-0*) Worth.

Listen: Second Brief Edition. 2nd ed. Joseph Kerman. (Illus.). 438p. (C). 1991. text 39.95 (*0-87901-517-9*); pap. text 35.95 (*0-87901-549-7*) Worth.

Listen: Second Brief Edition, 6 cass. 2nd ed. Joseph Kerman. (C). 1992. audio 42.00 (*0-87901-560-8*); audio 24.00 (*0-87901-561-6*) Worth.

Listen: Second Brief Edition. 2nd ed. Joseph Kerman. (Illus.). 438p. (C). 1992. pap. text, student ed. 7.80 (*0-87901-565-9*) Worth.

Listen: Second Brief Edition, 6 CDs, Set. 2nd ed. Joseph Kerman. (C). 1992. cd-rom 63.00 (*0-87901-562-4*); cd-rom 35.00 (*0-87901-563-2*) Worth.

Listen: Second Brief Edition, Set. 2nd ed. Joseph Kerman. (Illus.). 438p. (C). 1992. lp 50.00 (*0-87901-564-0*) Worth.

Listen . . . the Speaking Heart. Doris. LC 79-50254. 1979. pap. 3.75 (*0-87516-361-0*) DeVorss.

Listen . . . What Do You Hear? Nicholas Wood & Jennifer Rye. LC 90-40136. (First Science Ser.). (Illus.). 32p. (J). (gr. k-3). 1991. lib. bdg. 17.25 (*0-8167-2120-3*) Troll Communs.

Listen . . . What Do You Hear? Nicholas Wood & Jennifer Rye. LC 90-40136. (First Science Ser.). (Illus.). 32p. (J). (gr. k-3). 1997. pap. 3.95 (*0-8167-2121-1*) Troll Communs.

Listen - My Children: (So It Can't Happen Again) unabridged ed. Joseph W. Lovoi. LC 96-94410. (Illus.). 200p. 1996. 9.50 (*0-9652646-0-2*) J W Lovoi.

Listen, a Story Comes: Escuchaque, Viene un Cuento. Teresa Pijoan. Ed. & Tr. by Sharon Franco from SPA. LC 96-33039. (ENG & SPA., Illus.). 192p. (Orig.). 1996. pap. 14.95 (*1-878610-59-7*) Red Crane Bks.

Listen, America, You Don't Even Own Your Name. William Joyce. 80p. (Orig.). 1989. pap. 10.00 (*0-685-27229-X*) Wall St Pr.

Listen & Be Listened To, Set. pap. 155.00 incl. audio (*0-7612-0797-X*, 80204); pap., wbk. ed. 30.00 incl. audio (*0-7612-0796-1*, 80205) AMACOM.

Listen & Draw: An Integrated Skills Activity Program. Laura Grey & Michael Groudket. (Illus.). 84p. 1992. 44.00 incl. audio (*0-7616-7744-5*) Commun Skill.

Listen & Enjoy French Poetry. Listen & Enjoy Staff. (Listen & Enjoy Cassettes Ser.). 1991. pap. 9.95 incl. audio (*0-486-99927-0*) Dover.

Listen & Enjoy German Poetry. Listen & Enjoy Staff. (Listen & Enjoy Cassettes Ser.). 1991. pap. 9.95 incl. audio (*0-486-99929-7*) Dover.

Listen & Enjoy Italian Poetry. Listen & Enjoy Staff. (Listen & Enjoy Cassettes Ser.). 1998. pap. 9.95 incl. audio (*0-486-99930-0*) Dover.

Listen & Enjoy Spanish Poetry. Dover Publications Staff. (Listen & Enjoy Cassettes Ser.). 1991. pap. 9.95 incl. audio (*0-486-99928-9*) Dover.

Listen & Learn Beginner's English Reader. Barbara Dogger. 64p. 1995. pap. 42.32 incl. audio (*0-8442-5357-X*, 5357X, Natl Textbk Co) NTC Contemp Pub Co.

Listen & Learn French. (Listen & Learn Ser.). (ENG & FRE.). 1986. pap. 2.50 (*0-486-25274-4*) Dover.

Listen & Learn French. Listen & Learn Staff. 8.95 incl. audio (*0-486-99914-9*) Dover.

Listen & Learn French, Set. Ed. by Brian Hill. (ENG & FRE., Illus.). 1997. pap. 29.95 incl. audio (*0-8442-9571-X*, Passprt Bks) NTC Contemp Pub Co.

Listen & Learn German. Dover Staff. (Listen & Learn Ser.). (ENG & GER.). 1986. pap. 2.50 (*0-486-25275-2*) Dover.

Listen & Learn German. 2nd ed. Ed. by Brian Hill. (Just Listen N Learn Ser.). (GER., Illus.). 240p. 1995. 29.95 incl. audio (*0-8442-9652-X*, Passprt Bks) NTC Contemp Pub Co.

Listen & Learn Italian. Dover Staff. (Listen & Learn Ser.). (ENG & ITA.). 1986. pap. 2.50 (*0-486-25276-0*) Dover.

Listen & Learn Italian. Listen & Learn Staff. 9.95 incl. audio (*0-486-99916-5*) Dover.

Listen & Learn Japanese. (Listen & Learn Ser.). (ENG & JPN.). 1986. pap. 2.50 (*0-486-25277-9*) Dover.

Listen & Learn Japanese. Dover Publications Staff. 14.95 (*0-486-98880-5*) Dover.

Listen & Learn Japanese. Listen & Learn Staff. 9.95 incl. audio (*0-486-99917-3*) Dover.

Listen & Learn Modern Greek. (Listen & Learn Ser.). (ENG & GRE.). 1986. pap. 2.50 (*0-486-25278-7*) Dover.

Listen & Learn Modern Greek. Listen & Learn Staff. 9.95 incl. audio (*0-486-99921-1*) Dover.

Listen & Learn Modern Hebrew. (Listen & Learn Ser.). (ENG & HEB.). 1986. pap. 2.50 (*0-486-25279-5*) Dover.

Listen & Learn Modern Hebrew. Listen & Learn Staff. 9.95 incl. audio (*0-486-99923-8*) Dover.

Listen & Learn 101 Japanese Idioms. Michael L. Maynard & Senko K. Maynard. (JPN.). 224p. 1995. pap. 29.95 incl. audio (*0-8442-8341-X*, 8341X, Passprt Bks) NTC Contemp Pub Co.

Listen & Learn Portuguese. (Listen & Learn Ser.). (ENG & POR.). 1986. pap. 2.50 (*0-486-25280-9*) Dover.

Listen & Learn Portuguese. Listen & Learn Staff. 8.95 incl. audio (*0-486-99919-X*) Dover.

Listen & Learn Russian. (Listen & Learn Ser.). (ENG & RUS.). 1986. pap. 2.50 (*0-486-25281-7*) Dover.

Listen & Learn Russian. Listen & Learn Staff. (Illus.). 9.95 incl. audio (*0-486-99920-3*) Dover.

Listen & Learn Spanish. Dover Staff. (Listen & Learn Ser.). (ENG & SPA.). 1986. pap. 2.50 (*0-486-25282-5*) Dover.

Listen & Learn Spanish. Listen & Learn Staff. 9.95 incl. audio (*0-486-99918-1*) Dover.

Listen & Learn Swedish. Dover Staff. (Listen & Learn Ser.). (ENG & SWE.). 1986. pap. 2.50 (*0-486-25283-3*) Dover.

Listen & Learn Swedish. Listen & Learn Staff. 1986. 9.95 incl. audio (*0-486-99922-X*) Dover.

Listen & Perform see Ecoutez et Representez: The TPR Student Book

Listen & Perform: The Teacher's Guidebook. Stephen M. Silvers. Ed. by James J. Asher. (Illus.). 59p. (Orig.). 1985. pap. text 4.95 (*0-940296-30-6*) Sky Oaks Prodns.

Listen & Perform: TPR Student Notebook (English) 2nd ed. Stephen M. Silvers. Ed. by James J. Asher. (Illus.). 213p. (Orig.). 1994. pap. text 15.95 (*1-56018-496-5*) Sky Oaks Prodns.

Listen & Perform in Spanish: The TPR Student Book. Stephen Mark Silvers. Ed. by James J. Asher. Tr. by Francisco Cabello. (SPA., Illus.). 145p. 1999. pap. text 15.95 (*1-56018-450-7*, 274) Sky Oaks Prodns.

Listen & Play with My Friends & Me Activity Manual. Duane Davis. (My Friends & Me Ser.). (J). (ps). 1988. student ed. 33.95 (*0-88671-331-5*, 4631) Am Guidance.

Listen & Read - Shakespeare's Sonnets. William Shakespeare. 1998. 6.95 incl. audio (*0-486-40131-6*) Dover.

Listen & Read a Child's Garden of Verses. Robert Louis Stevenson. 96p. (Orig.). (J). 1996. pap. text 5.95 incl. audio (*0-486-29305-X*) Dover.

Listen & Read Aladdin & Other Favorite Arabian Nights Stories. Ed. by Philip Smith. Date not set. 5.95 (*0-486-40108-1*) Dover.

Listen & Read Best-Loved Poems. Ed. by Philip Smith. 112p. (Orig.). (J). 1996. pap. text 5.95 incl. audio (*0-486-29302-5*) Dover.

Listen & Read Charles Dickens' a Christmas Carol. Charles Dickens. 96p. (J). 1996. pap. 5.95 incl. audio (*0-486-29103-0*) Dover.

Listen & Read Edgar Allan Poe's The Raven & Other Poems. Edgar Allan Poe. 1998. pap. 6.95 incl. audio (*0-486-40130-8*) Dover.

Listen & Read Edgar Allan Poe's The Tell-Tale Heart & Other Stories. Edgar Allan Poe. (Illus.). 128p. (Orig.). 1996. pap. text 5.95 incl. audio (*0-486-29123-5*) Dover.

Listen & Read Emily Dickinson's Selected Poems. Emily Dickinson. (Illus.). 64p. (Orig.). (YA). 1996. pap. text 5.95 incl. audio (*0-486-29118-9*) Dover.

An Asterisk (*) at the beginning of an entry indicates that the title is appearing for the first time.

Listen & Read Favorite Irish Fairy Tales. Ed. by Philip Smith. 96p. (J). 1997. 5.95 incl. audio (*0-486-29829-9*) Dover.
Listen & Read Favorite North American Indian Legends. Ed. by Philip Smith. 96p. (J). 1997. 5.95 incl. audio (*0-486-29830-2*) Dover.
Listen & Read Great Love Poems. Ed. by Shane Weller. (Illus.). 128p. (Orig.). 1996. pap. text 5.95 incl. audio (*0-486-29307-6*) Dover.
Listen & Read James Joyce's Dubliners. James Joyce. (Illus.). 160p. (Orig.). 1996. pap. text 5.95 incl. audio (*0-486-29121-9*) Dover.
Listen & Read Sherlock Holmes Stories. unabridged ed. Arthur Conan Doyle. 112p. (J). 1997. 6.95 incl. audio (*0-486-29827-2*) Dover.
Listen & Read the Adventures of Peter Cottontail. Thornton W. Burgess. (Illus.). 96p. (Orig.). (J). 1996. pap. text 5.95 incl. audio (*0-486-29101-4*) Dover.
Listen & Read the Tale of Peter Rabbit & Other Favorite Stories. Beatrix Potter. (Illus.). 96p. (Orig.). (J). 1996. pap. text 5.95 incl. audio (*0-486-29299-1*) Dover.
Listen & Read the Ugly Duckling & Other Fairy Tales. Hans Christian Andersen. (Illus.). 96p. (Orig.). (J). 1996. pap. text 5.95 incl. audio (*0-486-29100-6*) Dover.
Listen & Recall: Memory Strategies for Adolescents & Adults. Carrie Van Der Laan. LC 97-198. 1997. pap. 37.00 (*1-888222-00-X*) Thinking Pubns.
Listen & Say It Right in English. Nina Weinstein. 104p. 1994. pap. 29.95 incl. audio (*0-8442-0436-6*, 0436X, Natl Textbk Co) NTC Contemp Pub Co.
Listen & Say It Right in English. Nina Winstein. 104p. pap. 29.95 incl. audio (*0-8325-0436-X*, 0436X, Natl Textbk Co) NTC Contemp Pub Co.
Listen & Say It Right in English. Nina Winstein. 104p. 1991. boxed set 49.20 (*0-8442-0453-6*, Natl Textbk Co) NTC Contemp Pub Co.
Listen & Say It Right in English: When to Use Formal & Everyday English. Nina Weinstein. 1988. pap., teacher ed. 8.41 (*0-8325-0451-3*); pap., teacher ed., student ed. 59.95 incl. audio (*0-8325-0453-X*); pap., student ed. 9.25 (*0-8325-0450-5*) NTC Contemp Pub Co.
Listen & Sing. Damschrod. 1995. pap. write for info. (*0-02-870330-8*) Macmillan.
Listen & Sing. Damschroder. 1997. 40.00 (*0-02-864933-8*) Mac Lib Ref.
Listen & Sing: Lessons in Ear-Training & Sight-Singing. David A. Damschroder. LC 96-182413. 1995. pap., teacher ed. write for info. (*0-02-870667-6*, Schirmer Books) Mac Lib Ref.
Listen & Sing: Lessons in Ear-Training & Sight-Singing. David Damschroder. (Illus.). 492p. (C). 1995. 40.00 (*0-02-870665-X*, Schirmer Books) Mac Lib Ref.
Listen, Brief: Third Brief Edition. 3rd ed. Joseph Kerman. 385p. 1995. pap. text 32.80 (*1-57259-058-0*) Worth.
Listen, Brief: Third Brief Edition. 3rd ed. Joseph Kerman. 385p. 1995. text 37.00 (*1-57259-059-9*) Worth.
Listen, Buddy. Helen Lester. LC 94-33634. (Illus.). 32p. (J). (gr. k-3). 1995. 15.00 (*0-395-72361-2*) HM.
Listen, Buddy. Helen Lester. 32p. 1997. pap. 5.95 (*0-395-85402-4*) HM.
Listen, Buddy. Helen Lester. (J). 1997. pap. text 4.95 (*0-395-72631-X*) HM.
Listen, Buddy. Helen Lester. (J). 1997. 10.15 (*0-606-11567-6*, Pub. by Turtleback) Demco.
Listen Children: An Anthology of Black Literature. Ed. by Dorothy Strickland. (Illus.). 144p. (YA). (gr. 5). 1999. pap. 4.99 (*0-440-41555-1*) BDD Bks Young Read.
Listen Children: An Anthology of Black Literature. Dorothy S. Strickland. 1986. 9.09 (*0-606-00912-4*, Pub. by Turtleback) Demco.
Listen, Communist! The Christo-Judean Faith & the Philosophy of Classless Society. Thomas J. Kuna-Jacob. 96p. 1992. reprint ed. ring bd. 8.95 (*1-878030-03-5*) Assn World Peace.
Listen... Dad's Calling. Betty Bockoras. iv, 126p. 1998. pap. 5.75 (*0-9669213-0-5*) Joy of Life.
Listen First. Jayme Adelson-Goldstein. (Illus.). 96p. 1991. pap. text, student ed. 9.95 (*0-19-434422-3*) OUP.
Listen First. Ann Creighton & Jayme Adelson-Goldstein. (Illus.). 64p. 1991. pap. text, teacher ed. 10.95 (*0-19-434423-1*) OUP.
Listen for a Change. Ed. by Annejet Campbell. LC 86-81348. (Illus.). 116p. 1987. 7.50 (*1-85239-001-8*) Grosvenor USA.
Listen for a Lonesome Drum. Carl Carmer. 381p. 1993. reprint ed. lib. bdg. 89.00 (*0-7812-5119-2*) Rprt Serv.
Listen for a Lonesome Drum: A York State Chronicle. Carl Carmer. LC 94-42361. 450p. 1995. pap. 17.95 (*0-8156-0261-8*) Syracuse U Pr.
Listen for It: Student Book. 2nd ed. Jack C. Richards et al. (Illus.). 96p. 1995. pap. text, student ed. 11.95 (*0-19-434656-0*) OUP.
Listen for It: Teacher's Guide. 2nd ed. Jack C. Richards et al. (Illus.). 108p. 1995. pap. text, teacher ed. 9.50 (*0-19-434657-9*) OUP.
Listen for Rachel. Lou Kassem. 176p. (J). (gr. 5). 1992. mass mkt. 3.99 (*0-380-71231-8*, Avon Bks) Morrow Avon.
Listen for Success: A Guide to Effective Listening. Arthur Robertson. LC 93-14441. 216p. 1993. 19.95 (*1-55623-830-4*, Irwn Prfssnl) McGraw-Hill Prof.
Listen for the Bus: David's Story. Patricia McMahon. LC 94-73316. (Illus.). 48p. (J). (gr. k-5). 1995. 15.95 (*1-56397-368-5*) Boyds Mills Pr.
Listen for the Crickets. Chad E. Gunter. Ed. by Mary H. Stancil. (Illus.). xii, 224p. 1998. pap. 7.95 (*1-892212-01-3*) Love Pubg Co.
Listen for the Rainbird: A Novel. Carol Tipton. LC 91-18674. 192p. (Orig.). 1991. pap. 10.95 (*0-86534-161-3*) Sunstone Pr.
Listen for the Whippoorwill: Harriet Tubman. Dave Jackson & Neta Jackson. (Trailblazer Bks.). 144p. (J). (gr. 3-7). 1993. pap. 5.99 (*1-55661-272-9*) Bethany Hse.
Listen for the Whisperer. Phyllis A. Whitney. 23.95 (*0-8488-1222-0*) Amereon Ltd.
Listen for the Whisperer. Phyllis A. Whitney. 1987. mass mkt. 5.99 (*0-449-21478-8*) Fawcett.
Listen! God Is Speaking to You! God's Word for Seniors. Henry Paustian. LC 92-50172. 205p. (Orig.). 1992. pap. 10.99 (*0-8100-0431-3*, 06N0694) Northwest Pub.
***Listen, God Is Speaking to You: True Stories of His Love & Guidance.** Quin Sherrer. LC 99-14694. 194p. 1999. pap. 10.99 (*1-56955-146-4*, Vine Bks) Servant.
Listen, God May Be Speaking. L. M. Thorne. 32p. 1999. pap. 9.95 (*0-9668657-2-3*) Ark Pubg.
Listen Here. Vernon Duke. 1963. 14.95 (*0-685-06621-5*); pap. 10.95 (*0-8392-5010-X*) Astor-Honor.
Listen Here: Songs by Dave Frishberg. 144p. 1995. otabind 16.95 (*0-7935-4060-7*, 00306016) H Leonard.
Listen, Humanity. 5th rev. ed. Meher Baba. Ed. & Narrated by Don E. Stevens. LC 97-32417. 288p. 1998. 24.95 (*0-8245-1731-8*, Crsrd) Crossroad NY.
Listen In. Gabler. 1995. pap. text, teacher ed. 5.00 (*0-312-11112-6*) St Martin.
Listen In, Bk. 1. David Nunan. 1998. teacher ed. 18.75 (*0-8384-7653-8*) Heinle & Heinle.
Listen In, Bk. 1. David Nunan & Christine A. Wenger. 96p. pap. 20.95 (*0-534-83536-8*, Pub. by Heinle & Heinle) Thomson Learn.
Listen In, Bk. 2. David Nunan. 96p. pap. 20.95 (*0-534-83537-6*, Pub. by Heinle & Heinle) Thomson Learn.
Listen-In' Speaking Listening Attack Strategies for Students of ESL. Burt Gabler & Nadia F. Scholnick. 224p. 1995. pap. 24.95 (*0-312-11110-X*) St Martin.
Listen-In Catalog: A Guide to the Audio Cassette & Compact Disc Service of the North State Cooperative Library System, 1996 Edition. rev. ed. Compiled by North State Cooperative Library System Staff & Tom McElroy. 447p. 1996. ring bd. 52.00 (*1-891367-01-3*) North State Coop.
Listen-In Catalog: A Guide to the Audio Cassette & Compact Disc Service of the North State Cooperative Library System, 1998 Edition. rev. ed. Compiled by North State Cooperative Library System Staff & Tom McElroy. 507p. 1998. ring bd. 60.00 (*1-891367-08-0*) North State Coop.
Listen, Iris! Letters from Croatia 199. Simun S. Coric. Ed. by Ziral Staff & Vinko D. Lasic. Tr. by Z. Crnkovic & B. Tinskamper from GER. (Ziral Bks.: No. 69). (Illus.). 88p. 1995. pap. 16.00 (*1-880829-05-3*) Z I R A L.
Listen, Kids . . . Czech Fairy Tales. Karel J. Erben. Ed. by Lillian Ciuffreda. Tr. by Julius Kalnoky. LC 87-83652. (Illus.). 65p. (J). (gr. 3-8). 1988. 13.95 (*0-9619982-0-2*) Kalnoky Pr.
Listen, Listen - Do You Hear . . . Vol. 1: Voices of the Seasons. Mary A. Loepke. Ed. by Shirley S. Stevens. LC 96-95354. (Illus.). 40p. (Orig.). 1996. pap. 6.00 (*0-9654487-0-3*, 96-625) M A Koepke.
Listen Listen Listen. Louis Gittner. Ed. by Starr Farish. 320p. (Orig.). 1980. pap. 9.95 (*0-9605492-0-X*) Touch Heart.
Listen, Listen, Listen see Curriculum Written for Partners in Parenting Education
Listen, Little Man! Wilhelm Reich. Tr. by Ralph Manheim from GER. Vol. 271. (Illus.). 144p. 1974. pap. 11.00 (*0-374-50401-6*) FS&G.
Listen Look & Think: A Self-Regulation Program for Children. Harvey C. Parker. 8p. (Orig.). 1992. pap., teacher ed. 22.00 (*1-886941-12-2*, 0955) Spec Pr FL.
Listen, Lord: Prayer for Plodders. Joseph McGloin. (Illus.). 115p. (Orig.). 1987. pap. 2.95 (*0-8199-0915-7*, Frncscn Herld) Franciscan Pr.
Listen, Love. Patricia Goedicke. LC 85-72585. 102p. (Orig.). 1987. pap. 7.95 (*0-935306-39-0*) Barnwood Pr.
***Listen, Love & Advocate: A Parent's Story of Living with Attention Deficit Disorder.** Kathryn Anderson. LC 00-34126. 2000. write for info. (*0-936389-80-X*) Tudor Pubs.
Listen, Mother of God! Reflections on the Litany of Loreto. Charles Dollen. LC 89-60266. 227p. (Orig.). 1989. pap. 6.95 (*0-87973-427-2*, 427) Our Sunday Visitor.
***Listen, My Children -- So It Can't Happen Again.** Joseph W. Lovoi. 2000. 17.95 (*0-533-13225-8*) Vantage.
Listen, My Dears. Annabelle H. Haven. LC 94-76775. (Illus.). 120p. (Orig.). 1996. pap. 12.00 (*1-884540-05-8*) Haleys.
***Listen, My Son: St. Benedict for Fathers.** Dwight Longnecker. LC 99-86446. 320p. 2000. pap. 17.95 (*0-8192-1856-1*) Morehouse Pub.
Listen-No Echo. Dion O'Donnol. (Destiny Ser). pap. 5.00 (*0-686-00949-5*) Wagon & Star.
Listen! Our Dying Savior Speaks. Lehman Strauss. LC 86-21460. Orig. Title: The Day God Died. 112p. 1987. reprint ed. pap. 7.99 (*0-87213-828-3*) Loizeaux.
Listen, Read & Learn Spanish. 1996. 12.95 incl. audio (*0-935540-08-3*) Plymouth Pr.
Listen, Read & Learn Spanish. 12th ed. Carol L. Flatto & Edwin Flatto. (ENG & SPA.). 54p. 1997. 12.95 incl. audio (*0-935540-16-4*) Plymouth Pr.
Listen Son: 12 Heart to Heart Talks. 1996. pap. text 4.45 (*0-935952-97-7*) Angelus Pr.
Listen Speak: Pathways to Better Speech. 2nd ed. Joyce Buck & Irene Alterbaum. 512p. 1996. pap. text 35.95 (*0-8403-8016-X*) Kendall-Hunt.
Listen, Speak, Present. Martha Graves Cummings. (J). 1991. mass mkt. 26.95 (*0-8384-3012-0*) Heinle & Heinle.
Listen, Speak, Present. Martha Graves Cummings. (J). 1992. mass mkt., teacher ed. 8.95 (*0-8384-3013-9*) Heinle & Heinle.
Listen, Talk & Read in Preschool: Prepares Preschool or At-Risk Primary Children for Reading. Date not set. write for info. (*1-882183-16-9*) A Page.
Listen, the Lord: Instructions in Spiritual Awareness & Interior Prayer As Given to Seven Listeners. 2nd ed. Ed. by William M. Justice et al. 124p. 1972. pap. 6.00 (*0-9618516-0-0*); boxed set 6.00 (*0-9618516-1-9*) Juniper NM.
***Listen! There's a World Waiting to Be Heard! The Empowerment of Listening.** Carol McCall. LC 99-93677. 2000. 14.95 (*0-533-13115-4*) Vantage.
Listen to a Shadow. fac. ed. Mary Zuverink & Georgette Haskin. LC 76-18758. (Illus.). 34p. 1994. pap. 30.00 (*0-7837-7714-0*, 204747600007) Bks Demand.
Listen to Her Voice: Women of the Hebrew Bible. Miki Raver. LC 97-49312. (Illus.). 176p. 1998. 27.50 (*0-8118-1895-0*) Chronicle Bks.
Listen to Me. Faye Kicknosway. 32p. (Orig.). 1992. pap. text 5.00 (*1-56439-018-7*) Ridgeway.
Listen to Me. Barbara J. Neasi. LC 86-10664. (Rookie Readers Ser.). (Illus.). 32p. (J). (ps-3). 1986. pap. 4.95 (*0-516-42072-0*); lib. bdg. 17.00 (*0-516-02072-2*) Childrens.
Listen to Me: A Book for Women & Men about Father-Son Relationships. Gerald G. Jampolsky & Lee L. Jampolsky. 220p. 1997. pap. 12.95 (*0-89087-850-1*) Celestial Arts.
Listen to Me: A Book for Women & Men about Fathers & Sons. Gerald G. Jampolsky & Lee L. Jampolsky. LC 96-13861. 220p. 1996. 21.95 (*0-89087-810-2*) Celestial Arts.
Listen to Me! Beginning Listening Comprehension. 2nd ed. Barbara H. Foley. LC 93-25538. 160p. (J). 1993. mass mkt. 20.95 (*0-8384-5264-7*) Heinle & Heinle.
Listen to Me: Communicating the Needs of People with Profound & Multiple Disabilities. Pat Fitton. LC 93-33895. 200p. 1994. pap. 24.95 (*1-85302-244-6*) Taylor & Francis.
Listen to Me--Please! A Communication Handbook. Judith K. Schneider et al. (Competent Caregiver Ser.). (Illus.). 52p. (C). 1986. pap., student ed. 10.95 (*0-944454-11-9*) CAPE Center.
Listen to Me--Please! A Communication Handbook. rev. ed. Judith K. Schneider et al. (Competent Caregiver Ser.). (Illus.). 52p. (C). 1986. pap. text 10.95 (*0-944454-02-X*) CAPE Center.
Listen to Me Good: The Life Story of an Alabama Midwife. Margaret C. Smith & Linda J. Holmes. LC 96-15037. (Women & Health Ser.). (Illus.). 178p. 1996. pap. 18.00 (*0-8142-0701-4*) Ohio St U Pr.
Listen to Me, Listen to You: Interpersonal Skills Training Manual & Masters. Anne Kotzman. 1995. 70.00 (*0-86431-167-2*, Pub. by Aust Council Educ Res) St Mut.
Listen to Me, Listen to You: Interpersonal Skills Training Manual & Masters. Anne Kotzman. 1995. pap. 70.00 (*0-86431-168-0*, Pub. by Aust Council Educ Res) Stylus Pub VA.
Listen to Me, Satan! Carlos Annacondia & Gisela Sawin. Tr. by Sylvia Cudich from ENG. LC 98-21052. 1999. pap. 12.99 (*0-88419-524-4*) Dake Pub.
Listen to Mom & Dad. William A. Grable. 90p. (J). (gr. 1-8). 1995. 19.50 (*1-887508-04-X*); pap. 14.95 (*1-887508-03-1*) MGM Sahara.
Listen to Music. 2nd ed. Wright. Date not set. pap. text, teacher ed. write for info. (*0-314-07502-X*) West Pub.
Listen to Music. 2nd ed. Wright. 1996. student ed. 17.25 (*0-314-07500-3*) West Pub.
Listen to My Feelings. Ruth Reardon & Roland Rodegast. (Illus.). (J). 1992. 8.95 (*0-8378-2499-0*) Gibson.
Listen to My Touch. Joanne N. Hoey. LC 81-67487. (Illus.). 56p. 10.00 (*0-940538-01-6*); pap. 5.00 (*0-940538-00-8*) Blackbird Pr Pubns.
Listen to Our Words: Oral Histories of the Jewish Community of Westmoreland County, Pennsylvania. Richard D. Wissolik & Jennifer Campion. LC 97-38772. 1997. 30.00 (*1-885851-10-3*) St Vincent Coll.
Listen to the Action. Judith M. Knowlton. Ed. by Rebecca D. Chaitin. (Illus.). 232p. 1987. text 12.95 (*0-934391-07-6*) Quotidian.
Listen to the Animals. William L. Coleman. LC 79-11312. 128p. (J). (ps-6). 1979. pap. 6.99 (*0-87123-341-X*) Bethany Hse.
Listen to the Children. Jean Benefein et al. LC 86-60493. (Illus.). 55p. 1986. pap. 6.00 (*0-935989-00-5*, NAEYC #304) Natl Assn Child Ed.
Listen to the Children: A Study of the Impact on the Mental Health of Children of a Parent's Catastrophic Illness. Cancer Care, Inc. Staff & National Cancer Foundation, Inc. Staff. LC 77-94376. 1977. 2.50 (*0-9606494-1-7*) Cancer Care.
Listen to the Children: Parents Tell Their Stories. 2nd ed. Annejet Campbell. LC 87-81505. (Yes (with Listen for a Change) Ser.). (Illus.). 112p. 1987. pap. 7.50 (*1-85239-006-9*) Grosvenor USA.
Listen to the City. Rachel Isadora. LC 98-20282. (J). 1999. 15.99 (*0-399-23047-5*) Putnam Pub Group.
Listen to the Crows. Laurence Pringle. LC 75-43535. (Illus.). 40p. (J). (gr. 3-7). 1976. lib. bdg. 12.89 (*0-690-01069-9*) HarpC Child Bks.
Listen to the Desert. Gregory Mayers. 128p. 1997. pap. 35.00 (*0-86012-272-7*, Pub. by Srch Pr) St Mut.
Listen to the Desert: Secrets of Spiritual Maturity from the Desert Fathers & Mothers. Gregory Mayers. LC 96-12888. (Illus.). 160p. (Orig.). 1996. pap. 11.00 (*0-89243-930-0*, Liguori Triumph) Liguori Pubns.
Listen to the Desert - Oye al desierto. Pat Mora. LC 93-31463. (ENG & SPA., Illus.). 32p. (J). (ps-2). 1994. 16.00 (*0-395-67292-9*, Clarion Bks) HM.
***Listen to the Drum: Blackwolf Shares His Medicine.** Blackwolf Jones & Gina Jones. 192p. 2000. pap. 12.95 (*1-56838-567-6*) Hazelden.
Listen to the Echo. 96p. 1996. mass mkt. 10.00 (*0-9664946-1-X*) Indel Etch.
Listen to the Emerging Markets of Southeast Asia: Long Term Strategies for Effective Partnerships. Corrado G. M. Letta. LC 96-22604. 240p. 1999. 189.95 (*0-471-96448-4*) Wiley.
Listen to the Heart: Creating Intimate Families Through the Power of Unconditional Love. Roberta Meyer. LC 88-40603. 208p. 1990. mass mkt. 8.95 (*0-446-39134-4*, Pub. by Warner Bks) Little.
Listen to the Heart: Story Meditations on the Fruits of the Spirit. Bobbie Reed. LC 97-29637. 1997. pap. text 11.99 (*0-8066-2827-8*, Augsburg) Augsburg Fortress.
Listen to the Heron's Words: Reimagining Gender & Kinship in North India. Gloria G. Raheja & Ann G. Gold. LC 93-12586. 1994. 50.00 (*0-520-08370-9*, Pub. by U CA Pr); pap. 19.95 (*0-520-08371-7*, Pub. by U CA Pr) Cal Prin Full Svc.
Listen to the Howl of the Wolf. William E. McCullough. LC 95-4128. 160p. (J). (gr. 6-7). 1996. 14.95 (*1-57168-026-8*, Eakin Pr) Sunbelt Media.
***Listen to the Land.** Larry Stone. (Illus.). 225p. 1999. pap. 17.95 (*0-931209-82-X*) Mid-Prairie Bks.
Listen to the Mermaids. Kate Spohn. 1999. pap. 13.99 (*0-670-85271-6*) Viking Penguin.
Listen to the Mockingbird. Sidney J. Perelman. 18.95 (*0-89190-422-0*) Amereon Ltd.
Listen to the Mockingbird: Satiric Songs to Tunes You Know. Tuli Kupferberg. LC 72-95284. (Illus.). 64p. (Orig.). 1973. pap. 4.25 (*0-87810-025-3*) Times Change.
Listen to the Moon. Whitney Scott. (Illus.). 24p. (Orig.). 1988. pap. 4.00 (*0-9621039-0-X*) Outrider Pr.
Listen to the Moon Pt. 1: Message from Yin. Marion C. Carion. 32p. (Orig.). 1997. pap. 6.00 (*1-890185-01-9*) Half-Moon.
***Listen to the Music: The Life of Hilary Koprowski.** Roger Vaughn. LC 99-24754. (Illus.). 304p. 1999. 35.00 (*0-387-98849-1*) Spr-Verlag.
Listen to the Night: Poems for the Animal Spirits of Mother Earth. Mary TallMountain. Ed. by Ben Clarke. (Illus.). 72p. (Orig.). (C). 1995. pap. 10.95 (*0-9625153-6-1*) Freedom Voices Pubns.
Listen to the Nightingale. Rumer Godden. 208p. (J). (gr. 3-7). 1994. pap. 4.99 (*0-14-036091-3*, PuffinBks) Peng Put Young Read.
Listen to the Nightingale. Rumer Godden. 1994. 9.09 (*0-606-07026-5*, Pub. by Turtleback) Demco.
Listen to the Prophets. Walter E. Adams. Ed. by Candy L. Adams. 48p. (Orig.). 1990. pap. text 3.95 (*0-937408-96-4*) GMI Pubns Inc.
Listen to the Prophets. Walter E. Adams. 100p. (Orig.). write for info. (*0-944938-00-0*) Prophecy Pr.
***Listen to the Quiet: The Gentle Art of Nourishing Your Soul.** Alda Ellis. LC 99-43334. 48p. 2000. 11.99 (*0-7369-0217-1*) Harvest Hse.
Listen to the Rain. Bill Martin, Jr. & John Archambault. LC 88-6502. (Illus.). 32p. (J). (ps-2). 1995. 15.95 (*0-8050-0682-6*, Bks Young Read) H Holt & Co.
Listen to the Shadows. Joan H. Hovey. 1991. mass mkt. 4.50 (*0-8217-3606-X*, Zebra Kensgtn) Kensgtn Pub Corp.
Listen to the Silence. D. Barrett. 1990. pap. 10.75 (*0-89084-749-5*, 047662) Bob Jones Univ.
***Listen to the Silence.** Marcia Muller. LC 99-87734. 304p. 2000. 24.95 (*0-89296-689-0*, Pub. by Mysterious Pr) Little.
Listen to the Silence. Frances J. Roberts. 1964. pap. 3.25 (*0-932814-23-9*) Kings Farspan.
***Listen to the Silence.** large type ed. Marcia Muller. LC 00-39871. 2000. write for info. (*1-56895-908-7*) Wheeler Pub.
Listen to the Silences: Mexican American Interaction in the Composition Classroom & the Community. Kay M. Losey. LC 96-13155. (Second Language Learning Ser.). 238p. 1996. pap. 39.50 (*1-56750-269-5*); text 73.25 (*1-56750-268-7*) Ablx Pub.
Listen to the Snow. Max C. Golightly. 20p. (Orig.). 1995. pap. 3.00 (*1-57514-106-X*, 3044) Encore Perform Pub.
Listen to the Soul. Charim Walder. 1996. 17.95 (*0-87306-780-0*) Feldheim.
***Listen to the Stories: Nat Hentoff on Jazz & Country Music.** Nat Hentoff. 240p. 2000. pap. 16.00 (*0-306-80982-6*, Pub. by Da Capo) HarpC.
Listen to the Storyteller: A Trio of Musical Tales from Around the World. Illus. by Kristen Balouch. LC 97-43615. 32p. (J). 1999. 16.99 (*0-670-88054-X*) Viking Penguin.
Listen to the Sunrise: Hymns & Prayers. Kenneth I. Morse. LC 92-191169. 112p. (Orig.). 1991. reprint ed. pap. 34.80 (*0-608-04179-3*, 206491400011) Bks Demand.
***Listen to the Trees.** Don MacCaskill. 2000. pap. 19.95 (*0-946487-65-0*) Luath Pr Ltd.
Listen to the Trees. Eugene Scherley. LC 96-69091. (Illus.). 112p. (Orig.). 1996. 10.95 (*1-56167-314-5*) Noble Hse MD.
Listen to the Trees. John Sexton. 1994. write for info. (*0-8212-2165-5*) Little.
Listen to the Trees: Jews & the Earth. Molly Cone. (Illus.). (Orig.). (J). (gr. 4-6). 1995. pap. text 14.95 (*0-8074-0536-1*, 104064) UAHC.
Listen to the Trees: Jews & the Earth. Gabriel Goldman. (Illus.). (Orig.). (J). (gr. 4-6). 1995. pap., teacher ed. 10.00 (*0-8074-0559-0*, 208038) UAHC.
Listen to the Trees Vol. 1. John Sexton. (Illus.). 92p. 1994. 55.00 (*0-8212-1952-9*, Pub. by Bulfinch Pr) Little.
Listen to the Voice: Selected Stories. Iain C. Smith. (Classics Ser.). 338p. 1994. pap. 11.95 (*0-86241-434-2*, Pub. by Canongate Books) Interlink Pub.
Listen to the Voice Within. Chrsitopher Perry. 1991. pap. 15.95 (*0-687-85683-3*) Abingdon.

L

An Asterisk (*) at the beginning of an entry indicates that the title is appearing for the first time.

L

Listen to the Voices: Conversations with Contemporary Writers. Jo Brans. LC 87-42939. (Illus.). 284p. 1988. 24.95 (0-87074-265-5); pap. 12.95 (0-87074-266-3) SMU Press.

***Listen to the Voices from the Sea: Writings of the Fallen Japanese Students.** Midori Yamanouchi Rynn. LC 00-37418. 2000. pap. write for info. (0-940866-85-4) U Scranton Pr.

Listen to the Whistle: An Anecdotal History of the Wallkill Valley Railroad in Orange & Ulster Counties, New York. Carleton Mabee. Ed. by John K. Jacobs. LC 95-42950. (Illus.). 168p. 1995. lib. bdg. 29.00 (0-935796-69-X) Purple Mnt Pr.

Listen to the Wind. James Reaney. 208p. 1972. reprint ed. 12.95 (0-88922-002-6, Pub. by Talonbks) Genl Dist Srvs.

Listen to the World: A Book of Sounds. Edith Borroff. (Illus.). 62p. (J). (gr. 4-5). 1998. pap. write for info. (1-888701-14-5) Jarrett Pr.

Listen to These Nouns. Linda G. Richman. (Illus.). 288p. (Orig.). 1994. spiral bd. 29.00 (1-884135-01-3) Mayer-Johnson.

Listen to This. Linda G. Richman. (Illus.). 294p. 1987. spiral bd. 29.00 (0-9609160-2-4) Mayer-Johnson.

Listen to This: Developing an Ear for Expository. Marcia S. Freeman. LC 97-4166. 96p. (Orig.). 1997. pap., teacher ed. 14.95 (0-929895-19-3) Maupin Hse.

Listen to This! Leading Musicians Recommend Their Favorite Artists & Recordings. Alan Reder & John Baxter. LC 99-19504. 512p. 1999. pap. 16.95 (0-7868-8260-3, Pub. by Hyperion) Time Warner.

"Listen to This Voice" Selected Speeches of Governor Zell Miller. Zell Miller. LC 98-33971. 640p. 1998. text 50.00 (0-86554-641-X) Mercer Univ Pr.

Listen to TOEFL. 1987. mass mkt. 13.00 (0-446-73546-9, Pub. by Warner Bks) Little.

Listen to Understand. Helen Clinard. (Illus.). 49p. (Orig.). 1995. pap. 5.00 (0-614-14785-9) Effect Trg Consult.

Listen to Us: The Children's Express Report. Ed. by Dorriet Kavanaul. LC 77-94032. 256p. (YA). (gr. 7 up). 1978. 18.00 (0-89480-018-3, 170); pap. 5.95 (0-89480-017-5) CEF Inc.

Listen to Us, We're Not That Stupid: The People's Prescription for What Really Ails America's Health Care System. John E. Skvarla, III & Frank Elliott. LC 93-38373. 197p. 1994. 16.95 (0-930095-28-6); pap. 12.00 (0-930095-29-4) Signal Bks.

Listen to Verbs Those. Linda G. Richman. (Illus.). 264p. (Orig.). 1994. spiral bd. 29.00 (1-884135-02-1) Mayer-Johnson.

Listen to Women for a Change. Ed. by Isabelle Chester. (Illus.). 65p. 1986. pap. 3.00 (0-686-30399-7) WILPF.

Listen to Women for a Change: Every Woman's Handbook. Lee Byrd & Yvonne Kranz. (Illus.). 250p. (Orig.). 1995. pap. 12.00 (0-9644942-0-5) Uppity Woman.

Listen to Your Angel. Kim Anderson. 1998. 10.00 (0-7852-1731-2) Gibson.

***Listen to Your Angel: Kim Anderson Collection.** Kim Anderson. (Illus.). 2000. 8.99 (0-7667-6653-5) Gibson.

Listen to Your Body. Prevention Magazine Editors et al. 544p. 1994. 9.98 (1-56731-038-9, MJF Bks) Fine Comms.

Listen to Your Body: A Gynecologist Answers Women's Most Intimate Questions. Niels H. Lauersen & Eileen Stukane. (Orig.). pap. 7.99 (0-425-13921-2) Berkley Pub.

Listen to Your Body: A Gynecologist Answers Women's Most Intimate Questions. Niels H. Lauersen & Eileen Stukane. (Orig.). 2000. reprint ed. pap. 16.00 (0-684-85411-2, Fireside) S&S Trade Pap.

***Listen to Your Body: And Add 10-15 Happy Healthy Years to Your Life.** Lyle M. Becker. Ed. by Nancy Marriott. LC 99-98131. 126p. 2000. pap. 9.95 (0-9661143-1-0) Caliana Pub.

***Listen to Your Body: Your Best Friend on Earth, 1.** 3rd ed. Lise Bourbeau. 1999. pap. text 16.95 (2-920932-02-0) E T C.

Listen to Your Child: A Parent's Guide. David Crystal. pap. 15.95 (0-14-011015-1, Pub. by Pnguin Bks Ltd) Trafalgar.

Listen to Your Heart. Kenneth E. Hagin, Jr. 73p. 1992. pap. 4.95 (0-89276-726-X) Faith Lib Pubns.

***Listen to Your Heart.** Fern Michaels. 214p. 2000. 20.00 (1-57566-572-7) Kensgtn Pub Corp.

***Listen to Your Heart.** large type ed. Fern Michaels. 2000. 26.95 (1-56895-876-5) Wheeler Pub.

Listen to Your Inner Self: A Ten-Week Program to Achieve the Healing Power Within You. Rachel Carr. 160p. 1993. pap. 16.95 (0-8048-1827-4) Tuttle Pubng.

***Listen to Your Inner Voice: Harness Your Creativity, Conscience, & Intuition.** Ellen Hall & James Wawro. 2000. 16.95 (1-86204-851-7) Element MA.

***Listen to Your Instincts.** Cynthia MacGregor. LC 97-49227. (Abduction Prevention Library). (J). 1998. 15.93 (0-8239-5249-5, PowerKids) Rosen Group.

Listen to Your Mother. Robert F. Brunner et al. (Illus.). 70p. (Orig.). (J). (ps-3). 1991. teacher ed. write for info. (0-318-68317-2); lib. bdg. write for info. (1-879209-00-4) Saundras Story Bks.

Listen to your Neighbor's Heart: A Book about the Awesome Power of Listening. Steve Powers. LC 96-94690. 215 P. ;p. 1997. write for info. (0-9654075-0-0) Listeners Pr OH.

Listen to Your Pain: The Active Person's Guide to Understanding. Ben E. Benjamin & Gale Borden. LC 82-20066. (Illus.). 1984. pap. 18.95 (0-14-006687-X, Penguin Bks) Viking Penguin.

Listen to Yourself; Think Everything Over, Vol 1. Hsuan Hua. Tr. by Buddhist Text Translation Society Staff from CHI. (Illus.). 153p. 1978. pap. 7.00 (0-917512-24-3) Buddhist Text.

Listen to Yourself; Think Everything Over, Vol. II. Tripitaka Master Hua. Tr. by Buddhist Text Translation Society Staff from CHI. 172p. 1983. pap. 7.00 (0-88139-010-0) Buddhist Text.

Listen Up. Courtney Ross. 1990. mass mkt. write for info. (0-446-11411-1, Pub. by Warner Bks) Little.

Listen Up. unabridged ed. Robert L. Montgomery & Robert Montgomery. (Smart Tapes Ser.). 28p. 1994. pap., pap. text 19.95 incl. audio (1-55678-053-2, 3225) Learn Inc.

Listen Up! Hear What's Really Being Said. Jim Dugger. LC 95-79755. (AMI How-to Ser.). 79p. 1995. per. 12.95 (1-884926-40-1, TAKE) Amer Media.

***Listen Up: How to Improve Relationships, Reduce Stress & Be More Productive by Using the Power.** Larry L. Barker & Kittie W. Watson. (Illus.). 288p. 2000. 25.95 (0-312-24265-4) St Martin.

Listen Up: Learning Activities. Kittie W. Watson & Larry L. Barker. LC 94-69551. 138p. 1995. ring bd. 79.95 (0-88930-467-X, Pfffr & Co) Jossey-Bass.

Listen Up! Spoken Word Poetry. Ed. by Zoe Angelsey. LC PS615.L47 1999. 192p. 1999. pap. 12.50 (0-345-42897-8) Ballantine Pub Grp.

Listen Up!: Teenage Mothers Speak Out see Teen Pregnancy Prevention Library

Listen Up: The Lives of Quincy Jones. Courtney Ross. 1990. pap., mass mkt. 39.95 incl. cd-rom (0-446-39286-3, Pub. by Warner Bks); mass mkt. 34.95 (0-446-39233-2, Pub. by Warner Bks) Little.

Listen Up: Voices from the Next Feminist Generation. Ed. by Barbara Findlen. LC 94-42609. 288p. (Orig.). 1995. pap. 14.95 (1-878067-61-3) Seal Pr WA.

Listen up Girlfriends. Connie Chruch et al. 1996. mass mkt. 5.99 (0-312-95790-4, Pub. by Tor Bks) St Martin.

***Listen up, Girlfriends! Lessons on Life from the Queen of Advice.** Mother Love & Connie Church. (Illus.). 185p. 2000. reprint ed. text. write for info. (0-7881-9047-4) DIANE Pub.

Listen Up! Language Arts: Activities to Improve Language Arts & Listening Skills. Ann R. Fisher & Betsy Fisher. Ed. by Judy Mitchell. (Illus.). 96p. (Orig.). (J). (gr. k-3). 1995. pap. 9.95 (1-57310-022-6) Teachng & Lrning Co.

Listen Up, Lover. Lori Herter. (Yours Truly Ser.). 1995. per. 3.50 (0-373-52002-6, 1-52002-2) Silhouette.

Listen Up! Math: Activities to Improve Math & Listening Skills. Ann R. Fisher. (Illus.). 96p. (J). (gr. k-3). 1994. pap., teacher ed. 9.95 (1-57310-005-6) Teachng & Lrning Co.

Listen Up! Science: Activities to Improve Science & Listening Skills. Ann R. Fisher & Bryce A. Fisher. Ed. by Judy Mitchell. (Illus.). 96p. (Orig.). (J). (gr. k-3). 1995. pap. 9.95 (1-57310-021-8) Teachng & Lrning Co.

Listen up, You Primitive Screwheads!!! Michael Pondsmith & Ross Winn. (Cyberpunk Ser.). (Illus.). 112p. (Orig.). 1994. pap. 10.00 (0-937279-45-5, CP3291) Talsorian.

Listen Very Carefully, I Shall Say This Only Once: An Autobiography. Jeremy Lloyd. (Illus.). 170p. 1995. 21.95 (0-563-36203-0, BBC-Parkwest) Parkwest Pubns.

Listen with Love: Meditations for the Advent Season. Helen R. Ferguson. (Illus.). 56p. (Orig.). 1992. pap. 2.00 (0-88028-132-4, 1174) Forward Movement.

Listen with Mother: Consulting Users of Maternity Services. Rosemary Dodds. 84p. 1996. pap. text 32.00 (1-898507-48-1) Buttrwrth-Heinemann.

***Listen with Your Heart: Seeking the Sacred in Romantic Love.** Eileen Flanagan. LC 98-14922. 210p. 1999. mass mkt. 12.99 (0-446-67448-6, Pub. by Warner Bks) Little.

Listener. Taylor Caldwell. 1984. mass mkt. 3.95 (0-553-24483-3) Bantam.

Listener. Hausam. (J). 2000. mass mkt. 16.00 (0-689-80182-3) S&S Bks Yung.

Listener. Taylor Caldwell. 288p. reprint ed. lib. bdg. 22.95 (0-88411-166-0) Amereon Ltd.

Listener: A Novella & Other Stories. Bo Huston. 176p. 1994. pap. 8.95 (0-312-11313-7, Stonewall Inn) St Martin.

Listener: A Psychoanalyst Examines His Life. Allen Wheelis. LC 99-21607. 304p. 1999. text 25.95 (0-393-04783-0) Norton.

Listener, & Other Stories. Algernon Blackwood. LC 70-150537. (Short Story Index Reprint Ser.). 1977. reprint ed. 19.95 (0-8369-3834-8) Ayer.

Listener Guide to Music. 8th ed. Dallin. 1993. teacher ed. 30.62 (0-697-12510-6) McGraw.

***Listener in the Snow: The Practice & Teaching of Poetry.** Mark Statman. LC 99-54406. 174p. 2000. pap. 14.95 (0-915924-59-5, Pub. by Tchrs & Writers Coll) SPD-Small Pr Dist.

Listeners. Christopher Pike, pseud. 352p. (Orig.). 1995. mass mkt. 5.99 (0-8125-5039-0, Pub. by Tor Bks) St Martin.

Listener's Book on Harmony. Lawrence Abbott. LC 74-27325. reprint ed. 34.50 (0-404-12850-5) AMS Pr.

Listener's Guide to Classical Music: An Introduction to the Great Classical Composers & their Works. Kenneth McLeish & Valerie McLeish. 288p. 1991. 35.00 (0-8161-7369-9, Hall Reference) Macmillan.

Listener's Guide to Classical Music: An Introduction to the Great Classical Composers & their Works. Kenneth McLeish & Valerie McLeish. 288p. 1992. 15.95 (0-8161-7370-2, Hall Reference) Macmillan.

Listeners' Guide to Medieval English: A Discography. Betsy Bowden. LC 88-24325. 164p. 1989. text 10.00 (0-8240-6347-3, 912) Garland.

Listeners Guide to Musical Understanding. 7th ed. Leon Dallin. 416p. (C). 1990. text. write for info. (0-697-12883-0) Brown & Benchmark.

Listener's Guide to Musical Understanding. 8th ed. Leon Dallin. 376p. (C). 1993. text. write for info. (0-697-12509-2) Brown & Benchmark.

Listener's Guide to Musical Understanding. 8th ed. Leon Dallin. 376p. (C). 1993. text, pap. text. write for info. incl. disk (0-697-24597-7); text, ring bd. write for info. incl. audio compact disk (0-697-24598-5); audio. write for info. (0-697-12512-2) Brown & Benchmark.

Listener's History of Music. Percy A. Scholes. 1990. reprint ed. lib. bdg. write for info. (0-318-67044-5, 10025) Rprt Serv.

Listener's Music Book. Olga S. Samaroff-Stokowski. (Music Book Index Ser.). 293p. 1992. reprint ed. lib. bdg. 79.00 (0-7812-9485-1) Rprt Serv.

Listener's Music Book. rev. ed. Olga S. Samaroff-Stokowski. LC 72-164473. 293p. reprint ed. lib. bdg. 15.50 (0-8371-6217-3, STLM, Greenwood Pr) Greenwood.

Listener's Musical Companion. Bernard H. Haggin. 1991. pap. 14.95 (0-685-54062-6) OUP.

Listener's Musical Companion. Bernard H. Haggin. Ed. by Thomas S. Hathaway. 520p. 1991. pap. 14.95 (0-685-46318-4) OUP.

Listening. Anne Anderson & Tony Lynch. Ed. by C. N. Candlin & H. G. Widdowson. (Illus.). 160p. 1988. pap. text 14.95 (0-19-437135-2) OUP.

Listening. Judi Brownell. LC 95-23519. 353p. 1995. pap. text 52.00 (0-13-146937-1) P-H.

Listening. Anne Long. pap. write for info. (0-232-51834-3) S Asia.

Listening. Ed. by Alan Maley. (Illus.). 154p. 1998. pap. text 13.95 (0-19-437216-2) OUP.

Listening. 5th ed. Wolvi & Coakley. 1995. teacher ed. 55.00 (0-697-24665-5, WCB McGr Hill) McGrw-H Hghr Educ.

Listening. 5th ed. Andrew D. Wolvin & Carolyn G. Coakley. 416p. (C). 1995. text. write for info. (0-697-24664-7) Brown & Benchmark.

Listening. 6th ed. Andrew Wolvin & Carolyn Gwynn Coakley. 1999. pap. text 24.75 (0-697-35510-1) McGraw.

Listening, Vol. 1, No. 2. Ed. by J. Kondo. (Contemporary Music Review Ser.). ii, 120p. 1987. pap. text 15.00 (3-7186-0381-0) Gordon & Breach.

***Listening: A Book of Poems.** Frieda Feldman. Ed. by Jepson Wulff. (Illus.). iv, 74p. 1998. pap. 6.95 (0-9666801-0-3) Occasional Ed.

Listening: A Collection of Critical Articles on Radio. Albert N. Williams. LC 68-57345. (Essay Index Reprint Ser.). 1977. 19.95 (0-8369-1000-1) Ayer.

Listening: A Pastoral Style. Frances Moran. LC 98-194769. 160p. (Orig.). 1997. pap. 11.95 (0-85574-318-2, Pub. by E J Dwyer) Morehouse Pub.

Listening: A Program to Build Listening Skills. Susan R. Simms et al. 186p. 1992. 109.95 incl. audio (1-55999-235-2) LinguiSystems.

Listening: A Skill for Everyone. Nan Van Der Merwe. (Illus.). 71p. pap. 17.00 (0-9583083-2-2, Pub. by Juta & Co) Intl Spec Bk.

Listening: An Introduction to the Perception of Auditory Events. Stephen Handel. LC 88-22502. 611p. 1989. 65.00 (0-262-08179-2, Bradford Bks) MIT Pr.

Listening: How to Increase Awareness of Your Inner Guide. Lee Coit. 80p. 1994. pap. 6.95 (0-936475-00-5, 654) Las Brisas.

Listening: How to Increase Awareness of Your Inner Guide. rev. ed. Lee Coit. LC 96-8984. 100p. 1996. pap. 7.95 (1-56170-400-8, 654) Hay House.

Listening: The Basic Connection. Mary Micallef. (Illus.). 96p. (J). (gr. 3-8). 1984. student ed. 11.99 (0-86653-188-2, GA 555) Good Apple.

Listening: The Forgotten Skill & Managing Assertively:How to Improve Your People Skills. 2nd ed. Burley-Allen. 418p. pap. 29.90 (0-471-12376-5) Wiley.

Listening: Ways of Hearing in a Silent World. Hannah Merker. LC 99-46960. 224p. 1999. reprint ed. pap. 12.95 (0-87074-448-8, Pub. by SMU Press) Tex A&M Univ Pr.

Listening . . . Still: How to Increase Your Acceptance of Perfection. Lee Coit. 130p. 1985. pap. 8.95 (0-936475-04-8, 655) Las Brisas.

Listening - The Forgotten Skill: A Self-Teaching Guide. 2nd ed. Madelyn Burley-Allen. (Self-Teaching Guides Ser.). 208p. 1995. pap. 16.95 (0-471-01587-3) Wiley.

Listening--An Inner Journey. Connie Hunt. LC 86-20494. (Illus.). 96p. 1986. pap. 6.95 (0-9609442-2-2) Pulsar Pub.

Listening: A Tool for Caring Parents see Escuchar: Una Herramienta Valiosa

Listening, a Tool for Caring Parents. Patricia Wipfler. 7p. (Orig.). 1989. pap. 1.00 (1-891670-02-6) Parents Ldshp.

Listening Activities for Beginning Readers: Grades 1-2. Lloyd Harnishfeger. 1988. pap. 7.95 (0-89108-176-3, 8808) Love Pub Co.

Listening Activities for Children: Grades 3-4. Lloyd Harnishfeger. 1988. pap. 7.95 (0-89108-177-1, 9-8809) Love Pub Co.

Listening Aids Through the Grades: 232 Listening Activities. enl. ed. David H. Russell & Elizabeth F. Russell. LC 79-607. 191p. 1979. reprint ed. pap. 59.30 (0-608-02758-8, 206382100007) Bks Demand.

Listening & Caring Skills in Ministry: A Guide for Pastors, Counselors & Small Group Leaders. John Savage. 160p. 1996. pap. 13.95 (0-687-01716-5) Abingdon.

Listening & Hearing. Henry A. Pluckrose. LC 97-30963. (Senses Ser.). 1998. 21.40 (0-8172-5226-6) Raintree Steck-V.

Listening & Helping in the Workplace: A Guide for Mangers, Supervisors & Colleagues Who... Frank Parkinson. 272p. 1996. pap. text 14.95 (0-285-63242-6, Pub. by Souvenir Pr Ltd) IPG Chicago.

Listening & Interpreting: The Challenge of the Work of Robert Langs. Ed. by James O. Raney. LC 83-8816. 544p. 1984. 50.00 (0-87668-624-2) Aronson.

Listening & Processing Auditory Directions. Jean G. DeGaetano. 66p. 1995. pap. text 23.00 (1-886143-27-7) Grt Ideas Tching.

Listening & Recall. Franklin I. Bacheller. (Illus.). 192p. (C). 1986. pap. text 30.00 (0-13-537481-2) P-H.

Listening & Remembering Specific Details. Jean G. DeGaetano. (Illus.). 58p. (Orig.). 1997. pap. text 22.00 (1-886143-37-4, G841) Grt Ideas Tching.

Listening & Speaking. 96p. pap. text. write for info. (0-7506-3329-8) Buttrwrth-Heinemann.

Listening & Speaking for Beginning Students of the English Language, Bk. 1. Boyd. 112p. 1996. pap. text 15.73 (0-13-299785-1) P-H.

Listening & Speaking for Job & Personal Use. Masters. (YA - Adult Education Ser.). 1992. pap. 9.95 (0-538-70568-X) S-W Pub.

Listening & Speech Package: LAS-PAC, 2 vols. Frederick S. Berg. Incl. Vol. 2. Speech Workbook. 304p. 1978. text 60.50 (0-8089-1129-5, 790552, W B Saunders Co); 1978. 88.00 (0-685-62780-2, Grune & Strat) Harcrt Hlth Sci Grp.

Listening & Talking: A Guide to Promoting Spoken Language in Hearing-Impaired Children. Elizabeth B. Cole. 201p. (Orig.). (C). 1992. pap. text 25.95 (0-88200-172-8) Alexander Graham.

Listening at Prayer. Benedict J. Groeschel. 80p. (Orig.). 1984. pap. 7.95 (0-8091-2582-X) Paulist Pr.

Listening Back. William D. Barney. LC 92-74619. (Illus.). 61p. (Orig.). 1992. pap. 10.00 (1-878149-16-4) Counterpoint Pub.

Listening Behavior. Larry L. Barker. 154p. (C). 1991. reprint ed. pap. text 18.95 (0-685-27249-4) SPECTRA Inc.

Listening Book: Discovering Your Own Music. W. A. Mathieu. LC 90-53384. 144p. (Orig.). 1991. pap. 14.00 (0-87773-610-3, Pub. by Shambhala Pubns) Random.

Listening by Doing. Kathleen Galvin. 128p. 1985. pap. 16.93 (0-8442-5530-0) NTC Contemp Pub Co.

***Listening Carefully to Jesus.** R. E. O. White. LC 99-86144. 96p. 2000. pap. 12.00 (0-8028-4397-2) Eerdmans.

Listening Chamber: Poems by William Aberg. William Aberg. LC 97-942. (Poetry Award Ser.). 1997. pap. 12.00 (1-55728-463-6) U of Ark Pr.

Listening Chamber: Poems by William Aberg. William Aberg. LC 97-942. (Poetry Award Ser.). 1997. 20.00 (1-55728-464-4) U of Ark Pr.

Listening Child. Ed. by Lucy W. Thacher. LC 79-50851. (Granger Poetry Library). 1979. reprint ed. 35.00 (0-89609-171-6) Roth Pub Inc.

Listening Church: Automony & Communion in African Churches. Elochukwu E. Uzukwu. LC 96-15146. 160p. (Orig.). 1996. pap. 19.00 (1-57075-060-2) Orbis Bks.

Listening Composer. George Perle. 1990. 40.00 (0-520-06991-9, Pub. by U CA Pr) Cal Prin Full Svc.

Listening Composer. George Perle. LC 89-20436. (Ernest Bloch Lectures; Vol. 7). (Illus.). 202p. (C). 1996. pap. 15.95 (0-520-20518-9, Pub. by U CA Pr) Cal Prin Full Svc.

Listening Comprehension Skills for Intermediate & Advanced Students. Marielle Rainbow-Vigourt. 1994. text 24.92 (0-8013-1085-7) Addison-Wesley.

Listening Comprehension Training Program: Manuals A-E. Mary L. Kleman & James A. Kleman. 40p. (J). (gr. 4-8). 1982. student ed. 5.00 (0-938464-01-9) JML Enter MD.

Listening Cycles. John R. Boyd & Mary A. Boyd. 112p. (Orig.). 1985. teacher ed. 1.95 (0-933759-01-0); student ed. 4.50 (0-933759-02-9); pap. text 8.95 (0-933759-00-2); audio 19.95 (0-933759-03-7) Abaca Bks.

Listening Dictation: Understanding English Sentence Structure. Joan Morley. 152p. 1976. pap. text 12.95 (0-472-08667-7, 08667) U of Mich Pr.

Listening Dictation: Understanding English Sentence Structure. Joan Morley. LC 73-31050. (Illus.). 152p. (C). 1984. audio 85.00 U of Mich Pr.

Listening Ear: The Development of Speech As a Creative Influence in Education. Audrey E. McAllen. (Learning Resources Ser.). (Illus.). 162p. 1989. pap. 14.95 (1-869890-18-3, 1477, Pub. by Hawthorn Press) Anthroposophic.

Listening Ebony: Moral Knowledge, Religion, & Power among the Uduk of Sudan. Wendy James. (Illus.). 418p. 1988. text 110.00 (0-19-823403-1) OUP.

Listening Ebony: Moral Knowledge, Religion & Power among the Uduk of Sudan. Wendy James. (Illus.). 416p. 2000. pap. text 35.00 (0-19-823416-3) OUP.

Listening Effectively. John A. Kline. (Illus.). 70p. 1996. pap. 4.25 (1-58566-009-4) Air Univ.

***Listening Effectively to Children.** Patty Wipfler. 1999. pap. 7.00 (1-58429-036-6) Rational Isl.

Listening Experience: Elements, Forms, & Styles in Music. 2nd ed. James P. O'Brien. (C). 1995. pap. 35.00 (0-02-872139-X, Schirmer Books) Mac Lib Ref.

Listening Experience: Elements, Forms, & Styles in Music. 2nd ed. James P. O'Brien. (C). 1997. teacher ed. write for info. (0-02-872134-9, Schirmer Books) Mac Lib Ref.

Listening Eye. Patricia Wentworth. 1990. mass mkt. 4.50 (0-446-34857-0) Warner Bks.

Listening Eye. large type ed. Patricia Wentworth. 1981. 12.00 (0-7089-0661-3) Ulverscroft.

Listening Eye. Patricia Wentworth. 1976. reprint ed. lib. bdg. 23.95 (0-88411-738-3) Amereon Ltd.

Listening Focus. Ellen Kisslinger & Michael A. Rost. (Lingual House Listening Skills Ser.). 1980. audio 55.00 (0-940264-07-2, 78393) Longman.

Listening Focus. Ellen Kisslinger & Michael A. Rost. (Lingual House Listening Skills Ser.). (Illus.). 1989. pap. text 18.60 (0-940264-05-6, 78392) Longman.

An Asterisk (*) at the beginning of an entry indicates that the title is appearing for the first time.

Listening for a God Who Whispers: A Woman's Discovery of Quiet Understanding. Peggy Benson. Date not set. pap. write for info. (0-9677725-1-6) Deeper Life Pr.

Listening for a President: A Citizen's Campaign Methodology. Ruth M. Brennan & Dan F. Hahn. LC 89-29764. 217p. 1990. 55.00 (0-275-93245-1, C3245, Greenwood Pr) Greenwood.

Listening for Articulation All Year Round: A Language Based Articulation Program. Brenda Brumbaugh & Nan Thompson-Trenta. 208p. 1993. spiral bd. 37.95 (1-55999-262-X) LinguiSystems.

Listening for Basic Concepts All Year 'Round: An Active Listening Program for Teaching Basic Concepts. Brenda Brumbaugh & Nan Thompson-Trenta. 186p. 1990. spiral bd. 37.95 (1-55999-108-9) LinguiSystems.

Listening for Cactus. Mary McGinnis. LC 96-30940. 96p. (Orig.). 1996. pap. 14.00 (0-9644196-4-5) Sherman Asher Pub.

***Listening for Coyote: A Walk Across Oregon's Wilderness.** William L. Sullivan. (Illus.). 256p. 2000. pap. 18.95 (0-87071-526-7) Oreg St U Pr.

Listening for Feelings: Helping Children Express Emotions in a Healthy Way. John F. Taylor. LC 95-78004. (Family Power Ser.). (Illus.). 27p. 1992. 4.95 (1-884063-78-0) Mar Co Prods.

***Listening for God.** John Cheever. (Listening for God Ser.). 2000. pap. 11.99 (0-8066-3962-8) Augsburg Fortress.

Listening for God: A Believer's Journey Through Silence & Doubt. Renita J. Weems. LC 98-54817. 224p. 1999. 22.00 (0-684-83323-9) S&S Trade.

***Listening for God: Leader Edition.** John Cheever. (Listening for God Ser.). 2000. pap. 3.99 (0-8066-3963-6) Augsburg Fortress.

Listening for God: Religion & Moral Discernment. Howard Lesnick. LC 98-18062. xiii, 249p. 1998. 29.95 (0-8232-1860-0); pap. 18.95 (0-8232-1861-9) Fordham.

Listening for God: Spiritual Directives for Searching Christians. Ben C. Johnson. LC 97-22781. 96p. (Orig.). 1997. pap. 7.95 (0-8091-3718-6, 3718-6) Paulist Pr.

Listening for God Vol. 1: Contemporary Literature & the Life of Faith. Ed. by Paula J. Carlson & Peter S. Hawkins. 1994. pap., teacher ed. 3.99 (0-8066-2716-6, 10-27166, Augsburg) Augsburg Fortress.

Listening for God Leader's Guide Vol. 2: Contemporary Literature & the Life of Faith. Ed. by Paula J. Carlson & Peter S. Hawkins. 1996. pap., teacher ed. 3.99 (0-8066-2845-6, 10-28456) Augsburg Fortress.

Listening for God Reader Vol. 1: Contemporary Literature & the Life of Faith. Ed. by Paula J. Carlson & Peter S. Hawkins. LC 93-50662. 1994. pap. 12.99 (0-8066-2715-8, 10-27158) Augsburg Fortress.

Listening for God Reader Vol. 2: Contemporary Literature & the Life of Faith. Ed. by Paula J. Carlson & Peter S. Hawkins. 144p. 1996. pap. 12.99 (0-8066-2844-8, 10-28448) Augsburg Fortress.

Listening for Heaven's Sake: Building Healthy Relationships with God, Self & Others. Gary Sweeten et al. (Apples of Gold Ser.: Bk. 1). (Illus.). 209p. (Orig.). 1993. 16.95 (0-9638518-0-2); pap. 15.00 (0-9638518-1-0) Teleios Pubns.

Listening for Language All Year 'Round: An Active Listening Program for Teaching Semantics. Brenda Brumbaugh & Nan Thompson-Trenta. 187p. (gr. 2-6). 1993. spiral bd. 37.95 (1-55999-250-6) LinguiSystems.

Listening for Leroy. Betsy Hearne. LC 98-4495. 224p. (J). (gr. 4-7). 1998. per. 16.00 (0-689-82218-9) McElderry Bks.

Listening for Success: How to Master the Most Important Skill of Network Marketing. Steve Shapiro. (Illus.). 50p. Date not set. pap. 9.95 (0-9623804-2-3) Chica Pubns.

***Listening for the Crack of Dawn: A Master Storyteller Recalls the Appalachia of His Youth.** Donald Davis. 2000. reprint ed. pap. 11.95 (0-87483-605-0) August Hse.

Listening for the Crack of Dawn: A Master Storyteller Recalls the Appalachia of the 1950's & 60's. Donald D. Davis. 220p. 1991. pap. 12.95 (0-87483-130-X) August Hse.

Listening for the Crack of Dawn, a Master Storyteller Recalls the Appalachia of the 1950's & 60's. Donald Davis. 1991. 18.05 (0-606-12397-0, Pub. by Turtleback) Demco.

Listening for the Heartbeat of God: A Celtic Spirituality. J. Philip Newell. LC 97-20783. 128p. 1998. pap. 8.95 (0-8091-3759-3, 3759-3) Paulist Pr.

***Listening for the Night Bird Collection V: The Poetry of Richard Otis Denston.** Richard O. Denston. LC 99-94752. (Illus.). iv, 29p. 1999. pap. 5.00 (1-890770-00-0, Swann Pubns) F Swann Pubns.

***Listening for the Soul: Pastoral Care & Spiritual Direction.** Jean Stairs. LC 00-35465. 2000. write for info. (0-8006-3239-7) Augsburg Fortress.

Listening for the Text: On the Uses of the Past. Brian Stock. LC 96-41321. (Middle Ages Ser.). 208p. 1997. pap. text 16.50 (0-8122-1612-1) U of Pa Pr.

Listening for the Text: On the Uses of the Past. Brian Stock. LC 89-45494. (Parallax Ser.). 208p. 1990. reprint ed. pap. 64.50 (0-608-03694-3, 206451900009) Bks Demand.

Listening for Vocabulary All Year 'Round: An Active Listening Program for Teaching Vocabulary. Brenda Brumbaugh & Nan Thompson-Trenta. 196p. 1992. spiral bd. 37.95 (1-55999-225-5) LinguiSystems.

Listening from the Beginning to the End. Jean G. DeGaetano. 60p. (J). (gr. k). 1998. pap. text 23.00 (1-886143-42-0) Grt Ideas Tching.

Listening Games for Pre-Readers: Grades Preschool-K. Lloyd Harnishfeger. 1988. pap. 7.95 (0-89108-175-5, 8807) Love Pub Co.

Listening Groups: Mass Media in Adult Education. John Ohliger. 1967. 2.50 (0-317-18228-5, REP 119) Syracuse U Cont Ed.

Listening Guide to Psychology. 4th ed. Koch. (Psychology Ser.). Date not set. mass mkt., student ed. 5.25 (0-8185-0227-4) Brooks-Cole.

***Listening Hand: Self-Healing Through the Rubenfeld Synergy Method of Talk & Touch.** Ilana Rubenfeld. LC 00-37842. 320p. 2000. 25.95 (0-553-11144-2) Bantam.

Listening Heart. Rose Otis. 426p. 1993. 14.99 (0-8280-0769-1) Review & Herald.

Listening Heart: Create Your Own Space, Lose the Weight of Your Past, Vol. 1. Mary Butler & Richard Ernest. 1997. mass mkt. 12.50 incl. audio (1-929990-01-4) Listening Heart.

***Listening Heart: Guided Meditations That Help You Take Charge of Your Life.** Mary Butler & Richard Ernest. 11p. 1999. pap. 5.00 (1-929990-00-6) Listening Heart.

***Listening Heart: Relax on the Great Salt Lake, Step into the Spotlight, Vol. 3.** Mary Butler & Richard Ernest. 1998. mass mkt. 12.50 incl. audio (1-929990-03-0) Listening Heart.

***Listening Heart: The Art of Contemplation.** expanded rev. ed. David Steindl-Rast. LC 99-34367. 1999. pap. 13.95 (0-8245-1780-6) Crossroad NY.

Listening Heart Journal. 160p. 1993. 5.99 (0-8280-0779-9) Review & Herald.

Listening Hearts: Discerning Call in Community. rev. ed. Suzanne G. Farnham et al. LC 91-2220. 144p. 1991. reprint ed. pap. 10.95 (0-8192-1563-5) Morehouse Pub.

Listening Hearts: Manual for Discussion Leaders. Suzanne G. Farnham. 36p. (Orig.). 1993. pap. 5.95 (0-8192-1608-9) Morehouse Pub.

Listening Hearts Retreat Designs: With Meditation Exercises & Leader Guidelines. Suzanne G. Farnham. LC 94-8963. (Listening Hearts Ser.). (Illus.). 64p. 1994. pap. 9.95 (0-8192-1621-6) Morehouse Pub.

Listening Hearts Songbook. Ed. by Suzanne G. Farnham. LC 94-28508. (Illus.). 64p. 1994. pap. 9.95 (0-8192-1630-5) Morehouse Pub.

Listening House. Mabel Seeley. 256p. Date not set. 22.95 (0-8488-2618-3) Amereon Ltd.

Listening In. Sorrell Ames. 256p. 1998. mass mkt. 5.99 (0-451-19233-8, Onyx) NAL.

***Listening In.** Susan J. Douglas. 2000. pap. 16.00 (0-8129-3300-1, Times Bks) Crown Pub Group.

Listening In: A Multicultural Readings of the Psalms. Stephen B. Reid. LC 97-42691. 176p. 1997. pap. 19.95 (0-687-01194-9) Abingdon.

Listening In: Children Talk about Books (& Other Things) Thomas Newkirk & Patricia McLure. 176p. (C). 1993. pap. 14.95 (0-435-08713-4, 08713) Heinemann.

Listening In: Dialogues with the Wiser Self. Ellen Meredith. LC 93-77564. 304p. (Orig.). 1993. pap. 14.95 (0-9636073-5-9) Horse Mtn Pr.

Listening In: Intercepting German Trench Communications in World War I. Henry F. Schorreck, Jr. Ed. by Ernest H. Hinricks. LC 95-19515. 148p. 1996. 19.95 (0-942597-78-8) White Mane Pub.

Listening In: Radio & the American Imagination, from Amos 'n' Andy & Edward R. Murrow to Wolfman Jack & Howard Stern. Susan J. Douglas. (Illus.). 496p. 1999. 27.50 (0-8129-2546-7, Times Bks) Crown Pub Group.

Listening In: The First Decade of Canadian Broadcasting, 1922-1932. Mary Vipond. 400p. 1992. 65.00 (0-7735-0917-8, Pub. by McG-Queens Univ Pr) CUP Services.

Listening in Action. Michael A. Rost. 160p. (C). 1991. pap. 24.33 (0-13-538778-7) P-H.

Listening in & Speaking Out: Beginning Book. Charles G. Whitley et al. (Illus.). 138p. (Orig.). 1989. pap. text 11.95 (0-937354-25-2) Delta Systems.

Listening in & Speaking Out: Intermediate. Sharon Bode et al. (Listening in & Speaking Out Ser.). (Illus.). 128p. (Orig.). 1980. pap. text 32.57 (0-582-79736-5, 74992) Longman.

Listening in & Speaking Out Advanced Pack: Book & Cassette. Sharon Bode et al. (English As a Second Language Bk.). 1989. pap. text 43.09 (0-582-79780-2, 75034) Longman.

***Listening in Classrooms.** Mary M. McCaslin & Thomas L. Good. 232p. 2000. pap. text 17.00 (0-7881-9030-X) DIANE Pub.

Listening in Classrooms. Mary M. McCaslin et al. LC 95-41088. (Illus.). 224p. (C). 1997. pap. 43.00 (0-673-46881-X) Addson-Wesley Educ.

Listening In Context. Smith. 2002. 34.00 (0-07-234757-0) McGraw.

Listening in Everyday Life: A Personal & Professional Approach. Ed. by Deborah Borisoff & Michael Purdy. 338p. (C). 1991. pap. text 24.50 (0-8191-8212-5) U Pr of Amer.

Listening in Everyday Life: A Personal & Professional Approach. 2nd ed. Ed. by Michael Purdy & Deborah Borisoff. LC 96-9654. 360p. 1996. pap. text 26.50 (0-7618-0461-7); lib. bdg. 52.00 (0-7618-0460-9) U Pr of Amer.

Listening in Paris: A Cultural History. James H. Johnson. LC 94-6492. (Studies on the History of Society & Culture: Vol. 21). 1994. 45.00 (0-520-08564-7, Pub. by U CA Pr) Cal Prin Full Svc.

Listening in Paris: A Cultural History. James H. Johnson. (Studies on the History of Society & Culture: Vol. 21). (Illus.). 363p. 1996. pap. 17.95 (0-520-20648-7, Pub. by U CA Pr) Cal Prin Full Svc.

Listening in the Dark: The Acoustic Orientation of Bats & Men. Donald R. Griffin. LC 85-48242. (Illus.). 464p. 1986. pap. text 27.50 (0-8014-9367-6) Cornell U Pr.

Listening in the Dusk. large type ed. Celia Fremlin. 416p. 1992. 27.99 (0-7089-2623-1) Ulverscroft.

Listening in the Quality Organization. Andrew D. Wolvin. 54p. 1998. pap. 7.95 (0-9658952-3-8) Finger Lakes.

Listening in the Real World: Clues to English Conversation. Michael A. Rost & Robert K. Stratton. 144p. 1978. pap. text 14.50 (0-685-03056-3, 78390); audio 88.00 (0-685-03057-1, 78391) Longman.

Listening Is a Way of Loving. Terry L. Graham. LC 92-5801. 176p. (J). (ps-3). 1992. lib. bdg. 28.95 (0-89334-235-1) Humanics Ltd.

Listening Ones. Naomi M. Stokes. LC 97-2146. 416p. 1997. text 25.95 (0-312-86108-7) St Martin.

Listening Ones. Naomi M. Stokes. 1999. mass mkt. 6.99 (0-8125-4295-9, Pub. by Tor Bks) St Martin.

Listening Outside, Listening Inside. unabridged ed. Ferida Wolff. 192p. 1999. per. 15.99 (0-9671540-0-6) Universal Vision.

Listening Partnerships for Parents see Asociaciones Co-escucha para Padres

Listening Partnerships for Parents. Patricia Wipfler. (Illus.). 47p. (Orig.). 1991. pap. 3.00 (1-891670-00-X) Parents Ldshp.

Listening, Playing, Creating: Essays on the Power of Sound. Ed. by Carolyn B. Kenny. LC 94-4920. 316p. 1995. text 57.50 (0-7914-2285-2); pap. text 18.95 (0-7914-2286-0) State U NY Pr.

Listening Pleasure, No. 33. 64p. 1985. pap. 4.95 (0-7935-3619-7, 00243436) H Leonard.

Listening Plus. McDowell & Hart. 1992. pap. text. write for info. (0-17-556150-8) Addison-Wesley.

Listening Point. Sigurd F. Olson. LC 97-22180. (Fesler-Lampert Minnesota Heritage Book Ser.). 1997. write for info. (0-8166-2996-X) U of Minn Pr.

Listening Prayer: Learning to Hear God's Voice & Keep a Prayer Journal. Leanne Payne. LC 94-37753. 264p. 1999. pap. 12.99 (0-8010-5916-X) Baker Bks.

Listening Prayer: My Sheep Hear My Voice. unabridged ed. Linda Olson & David Olson. 189p. 1997. 16.95 (1-893498-01-8); pap. 12.95 (1-893498-00-X) Listen Prayer.

Listening Process. Robert J. Langs. LC 78-68010. 688p. 1978. 40.00 (0-87668-341-3) Aronson.

Listening Processes: Attention, Understanding, Evaluation. 2nd ed. (What Research Says to the Teacher Ser.). 1986. pap. 3.95 (0-8106-1071-X) NEA.

Listening, Reading, & Writing: Analysis & Application. Ed. by Barbara H. Wing. (Reports of the Northeast Conference on the Teaching of Foreign Languages). 174p. 1986. pap. 10.95 (0-915432-86-2) NE Conf Teach Foreign.

Listening Self: Personal Growth, Social Change & the Closure of Metaphysics. David M. Levin. 352p. (C). 1989. pap. 26.99 (0-415-02583-4, A3269) Routledge.

Listening Self: Personal Growth, Social Change & the Closure of Metaphysics. David M. Levin. 320p. 1989. 47.00 (0-415-02582-6, A1581) Routledge.

***Listening Skills.** Ian MacKay. 80p. 2000. pap. 17.95 (0-8464-5105-0) Beekman Pubs.

Listening Skills. Masters. (YA - Adult Education Ser.). 1993. pap. 5.95 (0-538-70777-1) S-W Pub.

***Listening Skills.** David Wilson & Ruth A. Wilson. (Illus.). 64p. (YA). (gr. 5). 1998. pap. text 8.95 (1-58037-067-5, Pub. by M Twain Media) Carson-Dellos.

Listening Skills: Are You Hearing the Real Message? rev. ed. American Correctional Association Staff. LC 99-175542. (Illus.). 96p. 1998. pap. 17.95 (1-56991-086-3, 144) Am Correctional.

Listening Skills: Objectives & Criterion Referenced Exercises for Grades K-12. Larry L. Barker. (Illus.). 115p. (Orig.). 1988. pap. text 27.95 (0-685-27247-8) SPECTRA Inc.

Listening Sky. Dorothy Garlock. 416p. (Orig.). 1996. mass mkt. 5.99 (0-446-60252-3, Pub. by Warner Bks) Little.

Listening Sky. Bernice A. Poole. 224p. 1996. mass mkt. 5.99 (0-87067-864-7) Holloway.

Listening Sky. large type ed. Dorothy Garlock. LC 96-11053. (Orig.). 1996. 25.95 (1-56895-317-8) Wheeler Pub.

Listening Subjects: Music, Psychoanalysis, Culture. David Schwarz. LC 96-39870. (Illus.). 248p. 1997. lib. bdg. 49.95 (0-8223-1929-2) Duke.

Listening Subjects: Music, Psychoanalysis, Culture. David Schwarz. LC 96-39870. (Illus.). 211p. 1997. pap. text 17.95 (0-8223-1922-5) Duke.

Listening System. Berman. 1999. 13.00 (0-07-232871-1) McGraw.

Listening Tasks: For Intermediate Students of American English. Sandra Schecter & Sandra R. Schecter. 112p. 1984. pap. text, teacher ed. 14.95 (0-521-27897-X); pap. text 12.95 (0-521-27898-8); audio 17.95 (0-521-26258-5) Cambridge U Pr.

Listening Test: Complete Set. Linda J. Bowers et al. (J). 1992. spiral bd. 89.95 (1-55999-240-9) LinguiSystems.

Listening Test: Examiner's Manual. Linda J. Bowers et al. 1992. spiral bd. 66.00 (1-55999-241-7) LinguiSystems.

Listening, Thinking, Speaking: A College Course. Skip Lowery. 112p. (C). 1997. per. 16.95 (0-7872-3733-7) Kendall-Hunt.

Listening, Thinking, Speaking: A College Course. 2nd ed. Skip Lowery. 110p. (C). 1998. per. 25.95 (0-7872-5244-1, 41524401) Kendall-Hunt.

***Listening Threads: The Formal Cosmology of Emanuel Swedenborg.** Norman Newton. LC 99-59854. 1999. 24.95 (0-915221-70-5) Swedenborg Sci Assn.

Listening to a Teenager. Ruth Reardon. LC 95-184472. (Illus.). 64p. 1995. 8.95 (0-8378-8830-1) Gibson.

Listening to Africa: Developing Africa from the Grassroots. Pierre Pradervand. LC 89-35347. 250p. 1989. 65.00 (0-275-93389-X, C3389, Praeger Pubs) Greenwood.

Listening to Africa: Developing Africa from the Grassroots. Pierre Pradervand. 1990. pap. 14.95 (0-275-93692-9, B3692, Praeger Pubs) Greenwood.

Listening to American Jews. Oppenheim. 1987. 16.95 (1-55774-004-6) Lambda Pubs.

Listening to American Jews. Ed. by Carolyn T. Oppenheim. 210p. 1988. pap. 13.95 (1-55774-002-X) Lambda Pubs.

Listening to Children. Carol R. Lewis. LC 84-11154. 208p. 1992. pap. 35.00 (0-87668-285-9) Aronson.

Listening to Children: Crying. Patricia Wipfler. (Illus.). 15p. (Orig.). 1990. pap. 1.25 (1-891670-07-7) Parents Ldshp.

Listening to Children: Healing Children's Fears. Patricia Wipfler. (Listening to Children's Ser.). 22p. (Orig.). 1990. pap. 1.25 (1-891670-09-3) Parents Ldshp.

Listening to Children: Play Listening. Patricia Wipfler. 18p. (Orig.). 1990. pap. 1.25 (1-891670-06-9) Parents Ldshp.

Listening to Children: Reaching for Your Angry Child. Patricia Wipfler. (Listening to Children Ser.). 16p. 1990. pap. 1.25 (1-891670-11-5) Parents Ldshp.

Listening to Children: Special Time. Patricia Wipfler. (Listening to Children Ser.). 11p. (Orig.). 1988. pap. 1.25 (1-891670-10-7) Parents Ldshp.

Listening to Children: Tantrums & Indignation. Patricia Wipfler. 11p. 1990. pap. 1.25 (1-891670-08-5) Parents Ldshp.

Listening to Children: Crying see Escuchando a los Ninos: El Llanto

Listening to Children: Healing Children's Fears see Escuchando a los Ninos: Para Vencer los Temores de los Ninos

***Listening to Children; Healing Children's Fears.** Patty Wipfler. 1999. pap. 2.00 (1-58429-030-7) Rational Isl.

Listening to Children: Play Listening see Escuchando a los Ninos: Jugemos a Escuchar

Listening to Children: Reaching for Your Angry Child see Escuchando a los Ninos: Para Acercarce a su Nino Enojado

Listening to Children Read Aloud - Grade 4. Gay S. Pinnell et al. (Illus.). 92p. (C). 1997. reprint ed. pap. text 25.00 (0-7881-3796-4) DIANE Pub.

Listening to Children: Special Time see Escuchando a los Ninos: Tiempo Especial

Listening to Children: Tantrums & Indignation see Escuchando a los Ninos: Berrinches e Indignacion

Listening to Communicate in English. Virginia Nelson. 1997. pap. text. write for info. (0-8442-0693-8) NTC Contemp Pub Co.

Listening to Communicate in English, Set. Virginia Nelson. 176p. 1995. student ed. 39.95 incl. audio (0-8442-0692-X, Natl Textbk Co) NTC Contemp Pub Co.

Listening to Communicate in English: 30 Engaging Conversations & Skill-Building Activities with Functional Goals. Virginia Nelson. 1997. pap., teacher ed., wbk. ed. 19.95 (0-8442-0530-3); pap., student ed., wbk. ed. 14.60 (0-8442-0528-1) NTC Contemp Pub Co.

Listening to Conflict: Finding Constructive Solutions to Workplace Disputes. Erik J. Van Slyke. LC 98-31116. (Illus.). 224p. 1999. 22.95 (0-8144-0429-4) AMACOM.

Listening to Crickets: A Story about Rachel Carson. Candice F. Ransom. (Creative Minds Biographies Ser.). (Illus.). (J). (gr. 3-6). 1993. lib. bdg. 19.95 (0-87614-727-9, Carolrhoda) Lerner Pub.

Listening to Crickets: A Story about Rachel Carson. Candice F. Ransom. (Illus.). 56p. (J). (gr. 3-6). 1993. pap. 5.95 (0-87614-615-9, Carolrhoda) Lerner Pub.

Listening to Different Drummers. Ciaran O'Driscoll. 88p. 1993. pap. 11.95 (1-873790-36-8) Dufour.

Listening to English at Home & on the Road. rev. ed. Ed. by Michael F. Sudlow. (Illus.). 124p. 1996. pap. text 12.95 incl. audio (1-877591-35-1) Excellence Education.

Listening to Farmers: Participatory Assessment of Policy Reform in Zambia's Agriculture Sector. Paul A. Francis et al. LC 97-30780. (Technical Paper Ser.: No. 375). 50p. 1997. pap. 22.00 (0-8213-4029-8, 14029) World Bank.

Listening to God, Vol. 9. Colin Dye. (Sword of the Spirit Ser.). 1999. pap. write for info. (1-85240-208-3, Pub. by SOV5) R G Mitchell Bks.

Listening to God: Experience a Deeper Relationship with God by Learning to Hear His Voice. Charles Stanley. LC 97-121371. 120p. 1996. pap. 7.99 (0-7852-7257-7) Nelson.

Listening to God: Lessons from Everyday Places. Janice Kempe. (Orig.). 1985. pap. 1.95 (0-310-34822-6, 12748P) Zondervan.

Listening to God: Using Scripture As a Path to God's Presence. Jan Johnson. LC 99-163459. 1998. pap. 12.00 (1-57683-050-0) NavPress.

Listening to God in Times of Choice: The Art of Discerning God's Will. Gordon T. Smith. LC 96-48377. 168p. (Orig.). 1997. pap. 9.99 (0-8308-1367-5, 1367) InterVarsity.

***Listening to God with Children: The Montessori Method Applied to the Catechesis of Children.** Gianna Gobbi. 2000. pap. 12.95 (1-886510-14-8) Treehaus Bks.

Listening to God's Word - Year A: Activities & Stories. Judy Rothfork & Eileen Drilling. 176p. 1998. pap. 15.00 (1-56854-226-7, LCATA) Liturgy Tr Pubns.

Listening to God's Word - Year A: Adult's Journal. Judy Rothfork & Eileen Drilling. 60p. (Orig.). 1998. pap. 5.00 (1-56854-227-5, AJORNA) Liturgy Tr Pubns.

Listening to God's Word - Year A: Child's Journal. Judy Rothfork & Eileen Drilling. 60p. (Orig.). (J). (gr. 1-4). 1998. pap. 5.00 (1-56854-228-3, CJORNA) Liturgy Tr Pubns.

Listening to God's Word - Year B: Activities & Stories. Judy Rothfork & Eileen Drilling. 176p. 1996. pap. 15.00 (1-56854-177-5, LCATB) Liturgy Tr Pubns.

L

Listening to God's Word - Year B: Adult Journal. Judy Rothfork & Eileen Drilling. 60p. (Orig.). 1996. pap., wbk. ed. 5.00 (*1-56854-206-2*, ADJORN) Liturgy Tr Pubns.

Listening to God's Word - Year B: Child's Journal. Judy Rothfork & Eileen Drilling. 60p. (Orig.). (J). (gr. 1-4). 1996. pap., wbk. ed. 5.00 (*1-56854-207-0*, CHJORN) Liturgy Tr Pubns.

Listening to God's Word - Year C: Activities & Stories. Judy Rothfork & Eileen Drilling. 176p. 1997. pap. 15.00 (*1-56854-209-7*, LCATC) Liturgy Tr Pubns.

Listening to God's Word - Year C: Adult's Journal. Judy Rothfork & Eileen Drilling. 60p. (Orig.). 1997. pap. 5.00 (*1-56854-210-0*, AJORNC) Liturgy Tr Pubns.

Listening to God's Word - Year C: Child's Journal. Judy Rothfork & Eileen Drilling. 60p. (Orig.). (J). (gr. 1-4). 1997. pap. 5.00 (*1-56854-211-9*, CJORNC) Liturgy Tr Pubns.

Listening to Gynaecological Patients' Problems. 2nd ed. D. Jenkins. LC 98-33389. (Illus.). viii, 104p. 1999. pap. 39.00 (*1-85233-109-7*) Spr-Verlag.

Listening to Her Understanding Him. Lam Kam Chuen. LC 99-210829. 1997. pap. 8.99 (*1-56229-112-2*) Pneuma Life Pub.

Listening to History: The Authenticity of Oral Evidence. Trevor Lummis. 175p. 1988. 48.50 (*0-389-20779-9*, N8338) B&N Imports.

Listening to Learn: A Handbook for Parents of a Hearing-Impaired Child. Arlie J. Adam et al. (Centennial Celebration Ser.). 110p. (Orig.). 1990. pap. text 19.95 (*0-88200-166-3*) Alexander Graham.

Listening to Life Stories: A New Approach to Stress Intervention in Health Care. Bruce Rybarczyk & Albert Bellg. 168p. 1997. 36.95 (*0-8261-9570-9*) Springer Pub.

Listening to Life's Messages: Adapted from the Works of the Lubavitcher Rebbe Rabbi Menachem M. Schneerson. Dovid S. Polter. 80p. 1997. pap. 8.00 (*1-881400-25-5*) S I E.

Listening to Midlife: Turning Your Crisis into a Quest. Mark F. Gerzon. LC 95-30767. 336p. 1996. pap. 16.00 (*1-57062-168-3*, Pub. by Shambhala Pubns) Random.

Listening to Movies: Film Lover's Guide to Film Music. Fred Karlin. 400p. 1994. 35.00 (*0-02-873315-0*, Schirmer Books) Mac Lib Ref.

Listening to Mozart. Charles Wyatt. LC 95-4777. (John Simmons Short Fiction Award Ser.). 194p. 1995. 22.95 (*0-87745-524-4*) U of Iowa Pr.

Listening to Music. Wright. 1992. 3.5 hd 60.25 (*0-314-00546-3*) Wadsworth Pub.

Listening to Music. Wright. Date not set. text. write for info. (*0-314-02639-8*) West Pub.

Listening to Music. Wright. 1992. pap., student ed. 18.50 (*0-314-00818-7*) West Pub.

Listening to Music. Craig Wright. Ed. by Baxter. 419p. (C). 1992. mass mkt. 33.25 (*0-314-91106-5*) West Pub.

Listening to Music. Winthrop Sargeant. LC 76-58564. (Illus.). 302p. 1977. reprint ed. lib. bdg. 65.00 (*0-8371-9461-X*, SALM, Greenwood Pr) Greenwood.

Listening To Music. 2nd ed. Craig Wright. LC 95-31764. (Music). 425p. (C). 1996. pap. 51.95 (*0-314-06752-3*) West Pub.

Listening to Music. 2nd ed. Zorn. 1994. pap. text, student ed. 69.00 (*0-13-147950-4*) P-H.

Listening to Music. 2nd ed. Jay D. Zorn. LC 94-30741. 432p. 1994. pap. text 47.00 (*0-13-035916-5*) P-H.

Listening to Music. 3rd ed. Ed. by Prentice-Hall Staff. (C). 1999. text 14.00 (*0-13-040239-7*) P-H.

***Listening to Music.** 3rd ed. Ed. by Prentice-Hall Staff. (C). 1999. text 37.80 (*0-13-040238-9*); pap. text 40.00 (*0-13-907346-9*) P-H.

Listening to Music. 3rd ed. Ed. by Prentice-Hall Staff. (C). 2000. text. write for info. (*0-13-040237-0*); text. write for info. (*0-13-040241-9*); text. write for info. (*0-13-040242-7*) P-H.

Listening to Music. 3rd ed. Wright. LC 99-52933. (Music Ser.). 1999. 37.50 (*0-534-51733-1*) Wadsworth Pub.

Listening to Music. 3rd ed. Ed. by Jay D. Zorn. (C). 1999. text 39.80 (*0-13-040244-3*) P-H.

Listening to Music Introduction. Wright. 1992. mass mkt. 9.50 (*0-314-00777-6*) Wadsworth Pub.

Listening to Music W/cd. 3rd ed. Wright. pap. write for info. (*0-534-71386-6*) Wadsworth Pub.

Listening to Muzac: Trapped in the Great Elevator of Life or Rising above Self-Esteem. Mona Lovejoy. 1997. pap. text 5.95 (*0-9650821-2-1*, Halfway Hse) Lazarus Trust.

Listening to Myself. Alvin Renetzky. LC 78-50943. 1978. pap. 3.95 (*0-930946-02-2*) Newaves Pub.

Listening to Nature. Joseph Cornell. (Illus.). 96p. 1987. pap. 13.95 (*0-916124-35-5*, ES3) Dawn CA.

Listening to Okhudzhava: Twenty Three Aural Comprehension Exercises in Russian. V. Tumanov. (Texts Ser.). (RUS.). (Orig.). 1996. pap. 24.95 incl. audio compact disk (*0-941051-53-6*) Focus Pub-R Pullins.

Listening to Okudzhava: 23 Aural Comprehension Exercises in Russian. V. Tumanov. 1996. pap. 24.95 incl. audio (*0-941051-99-4*) Focus Pub-R Pullins.

***Listening to Old Pete: An Historical Alternative.** Robert W. Taylor. LC 98-91117. 1999. pap. 12.95 (*0-533-13056-5*) Vantage.

Listening to Old Voices: Folklore, Life Stories, & the Elderly. Patrick B. Mullen. (Folklore & Society Ser.). (Illus.). 312p. 1991. text 30.95 (*0-252-01808-7*) U of Ill Pr.

Listening to Others. Huggett. pap. 6.95 (*0-340-72230-4*, Pub. by Hodder & Stought Ltd) Trafalgar.

***Listening to Our Grandmother's Stories: The Bloomfield Academy for Chickasaw Females, 1825-1949.** Amanda J. Cobb. (North American Indian Prose Award Ser.). (Illus.). 192p. 2000. text 27.50 (*0-8032-1509-6*, Bison Books) U of Nebr Pr.

Listening to Ourselves: The Key to Everything That Matters. Dwight O. Nichols. 326p. 1993. 21.95 (*0-9624064-0-6*) New Era Trng.

Listening to Parents: An Approach to the Improvement of Home-School Relations. Janet Atkin et al. 208p. 1988. lib. bdg. 47.50 (*0-7099-5039-X*, Pub. by C Helm) Routldge.

***Listening to Patients: Relearing the art of Healing in Psychotherapy.** Richard G. Druss. 160p. 2000. 19.95 (*0-19-513593-8*) OUP.

Listening to Prozac: A Psychiatrist Explores Antidepressant Drugs & the Remaking of the Self. rev. ed. Peter D. Kramer. LC 92-50733. 448p. 1997. pap. 13.95 (*0-14-026671-2*) Viking Penguin.

Listening to Radio, 1920-1950. Ray Barfield. LC 95-52706. 248p. 1996. 49.95 (*0-275-95492-7*, Praeger Pubs) Greenwood.

Listening to Reading. Stephen Ratcliffe. LC 99-88760. (C). 2000. text 59.50 (*0-7914-4503-8*); pap. text 19.95 (*0-7914-4504-6*) State U NY Pr.

Listening to Salsa: Gender, Latin Popular Music, & Puerto Rican Cultures. Frances R. Aparicio. LC 97-9121. (Music - Culture Ser.). (Illus.). 302p. 1998. pap. 19.95 (*0-8195-6308-0*, Wesleyan Univ Pr) U Pr of New Eng.

Listening to Silence. Michael Hubaut. 96p. 1996. pap. 65.00 (*0-85439-478-8*, Pub. by St Paul Pubns) St Mut.

Listening to Silences: New Essays in Feminist Criticism. Ed. by Shelley F. Fishkin & Elaine Hedges. LC 93-43199. 336p. 1994. pap. text 29.95 (*0-19-507307-X*) OUP.

Listening to Strauss Operas: The Audiences' Multiple Standpoints. D. B. Greene. viii, 188p. 1990. text 26.00 (*2-88124-407-6*) Gordon & Breach.

Listening to the Beatles: An Audiophile's Guide to the Sound of the Fab Four: Singles, Vol. I. David Schwartz. LC 89-92316. (Rock & Roll Reference Ser.: No. 35). (Illus.). 300p. 1990. 37.50 (*1-56075-005-7*) Popular Culture.

Listening to the Bells: Learning to Read Poetry by Writing Poetry. Florence Grossman. LC 90-22440. 133p. (Orig.). (YA). (gr. 7 up). 1991. pap. text 18.50 (*0-86709-274-2*, 0274, Pub. by Boynton Cook Pubs) Heinemann.

Listening to the Candle: A Poem on Impulse. Peter D. Scott. LC 92-4597. 240p. (Orig.). 1992. pap. 13.95 (*0-8112-1214-9*, NDP747, Pub. by New Directions) Norton.

Listening to the Cicadas: A Study of Plato's Phaedrus. G. R. Ferrari. (Cambridge Classical Studies). 306p. (C). 1990. pap. text 22.95 (*0-521-40932-2*) Cambridge U Pr.

***Listening to the Displaced: Action Research to the Conflict Zones of Sri Lanka.** Kerry Demusz. (Working Papers). 80p. 2000. pap. 18.95 (*0-85598-437-6*, Pub. by Oxfam Pub) Stylus Pub VA.

Listening to the Earth. Robert F. Harrington. LC 95-207236. (Illus.). 95p. 1995. pap. 8.95 (*0-88839-367-9*) Hancock House.

Listening to the Enemy: Key Documents on the Role of Communications Intelligence in the War with Japan. Ed. by Ronald H. Spector. LC 87-9478. 285p. 1988. 65.00 (*0-8420-2275-9*) Scholarly Res Inc.

Listening to the Engine. Julie Montgomery. 118p. 1995. 19.95 (*1-886701-03-2*) Lifescapes.

Listening to the Future: The Time of Progressive Rock, 1968-1978. Bill Martin, Jr. LC 97-36495. (Feedback: Vol. 2). 256p. (Orig.). (C). 1997. pap. 19.95 (*0-8126-9368-X*) Open Court.

Listening to the Garden Grow: Finding Miracles in Daily Life. Betty S. Eaton. LC 95-73262. (Illus.). 112p. 1996. 14.95 (*1-883478-14-6*) Stillpoint.

Listening to the Giants: Chinese Edition. Warren W. Wiersbe. Tr. by Wesley K. Shao. (CHI.). 281p. 1997. pap. 14.50 (*1-56582-029-0*) Christ Renew Min.

Listening to the God Who Speaks: Reflections on God's Guidance from Scripture & the Lives of God's People. Klaus Bockmuehl. 176p. (Orig.). 1990. pap. 15.95 (*0-939443-18-X*) Helmers Howard Pub.

Listening to the Grass Grow. Harry C. Bagley. Ed. by Richard H. Bagley. (Illus.). 162p. 1987. 10.00 (*0-9619190-0-0*) R H Bagley.

Listening to the Holy Spirit see **Escuchando al Espiritu Santo**

Listening to the Land: Nature, Culture & Eros. Derrick Jensen. LC 94-35086. 328p. 1995. pap. 15.00 (*0-87156-417-3*, Pub. by Sierra) Random.

Listening to the Law: English Listening Comprehension Cassettes for Lawyers & Other Legal Professionals. John J. Coleman. (Illus.). (C). pap. text. write for info. (*0-472-08425-9*) U of Mich Pr.

Listening to the Learner: An Exploratory Study of Personal Meaning in College Geography Courses. L. Dee Fink. LC 77-15501. (University of Chicago, Department of Geography, Research Paper Ser.: No. 184). 199p. 1977. reprint ed. pap. 61.70 (*0-608-02274-8*, 206291500004) Bks Demand.

Listening to the Least: Doing Theology from the Outside In. Ian A. McFarland. LC 98-36234. 160p. 1998. pap. 15.95 (*0-8298-1283-0*) Pilgrim OH.

Listening to the Leaves Form: Poems. James Grabill. LC 97-16189. 1997. write for info. (*0-89924-097-6*); pap. write for info. (*0-89924-096-8*) Lynx Hse.

***Listening to the Light: How to Bring Quaker Simplicity & Integrity into Our Lives.** Jim Pym. 192p. 2000. pap. 14.95 (*0-7126-7020-3*, Pub. by Rider) Trafalgar.

Listening to the Littlest. Ruth Reardon. (Illus.). 48p. 1984. 8.95 (*0-8378-1749-8*) Gibson.

Listening to the Metropolis. (Illus.). 96p. 1974. 5.00 (*0-318-16372-1*, 123); 3.50 (*0-318-16373-X*) Regional Plan Assn.

Listening to the Oracle. Dianne Skafte. LC 97-17950. 2000. pap. 12.00 (*0-06-251445-8*) HarpC.

Listening to the Oracle: The Ancient Art of Finding Guidance in the Signs & Symbols All Around Us see **When Oracles Speak: Understanding the Signs & Symbols All Around Us**

Listening to the Orchestra. Kitty Barne. LC 72-13098. (Essay Index Reprint Ser.). 1977. reprint ed. 21.95 (*0-8369-8146-4*) Ayer.

Listening to the People's Voice: Erudite & Popular Literature in North East Brazil. Mark Dinneen. LC 95-44325. (Illus.). 280p. 1996. 93.50 (*0-7103-0545-1*, Pub. by Kegan Paul Intl) Col U Pr.

Listening to the River: Family Biography. Malachi McCormick. 60p. 1989. 24.00 (*0-943984-35-1*) Stone St Pr.

Listening to the River: Seasons in the American West. Robert Adams. (Illus.). 112p. 1994. 68.00 (*0-89381-565-9*) Aperture.

Listening to the Sea: The Politics of Improving Environmental Protection. Robert J. Wilder. LC 98-8947. (Illus.). 316p. 1998. pap. 19.95 (*0-8229-5663-2*); text 45.00 (*0-8229-4059-0*) U of Pittsburgh Pr.

Listening to the Spirit: Prayers for All Occasions. John E. Biegert. LC 95-51674. 104p. (Orig.). 1996. pap. 11.95 (*0-8298-1075-7*) Pilgrim OH.

***Listening to the Spirit & the Text.** Gordon D. Fee. 2000. pap. 22.95 (*1-57383-176-X*) Regent College.

***Listening to the Spirit in the Text.** Gordon D. Fee. 160p. 2000. pap. 12.00 (*0-8028-4757-9*) Eerdmans.

Listening to the Text: Oral Patterning in Paul's Letters. John D. Harvey. LC 98-19538. (Evangelical Theological Society Studies). 376p. 1999. pap. 24.99 (*0-8010-2200-2*) Baker Bks.

Listening to the Voice of God: How Your Ministry Can Be Transformed. David L. Goetz. (Pastor's Soul Ser.). 176p. 1998. text 16.99 (*1-55661-972-3*) Bethany Hse.

Listening to the Voice of the Customer. Jon Anton. LC 97-67089. 152p. 1997. pap. 39.95 (*0-915910-43-8*) Customer Srv Grp.

Listening to the Voices: Stories from the Flannery O'Connor Award. Charles East. LC 97-40051. 1998. pap. 15.95 (*0-8203-1994-5*) U of Ga Pr.

Listening to the Word: Studies in Honor of Fred B. Craddock. Ed. by Gail R. O'Day & Thomas G. Long. LC 92-38030. 256p. 1993. pap. 16.95 (*0-687-37062-0*) Abingdon.

Listening to Theatre: The Aural Dimension of Beijing Opera. Elizabeth Wichman. LC 88-38574. (Illus.). 360p. 1991. text 49.00 (*0-8248-1221-2*) UH Pr.

Listening to Their Voices: The Rhetorical Activities of Historical Women. Ed. by Molly M. Wertheimer. LC 97-4866. (Studies in Rhetoric/Communication). 398p. (C). 1997. 49.95 (*1-57003-171-1*); pap. 24.95 (*1-57003-172-X*) U of SC Pr.

Listening to TOEFL. TOEFL Program Staff. (TOEFL Test Kits Ser.). 136p. (C). 1984. student ed. 13.00 (*0-88685-020-7*) Educ Testing Serv.

Listening to TOEFL: Test Kit 2. Educational Testing Service Staff. 1986. pap. 13.00 (*0-446-38487-9*, Pub. by Warner Bks) Little.

***Listening to Urban Kids: School Reform & the Teachers They Want.** Bruce L. Wilson & Dick Corbett. (C). 2001. pap. text 16.95 (*0-7914-4840-1*) State U NY Pr.

***Listening to Urban Kids: School Reform & the Teachers They Want.** Bruce L. Wilson & Dick Corbett. (C). 2001. text 49.50 (*0-7914-4839-8*) State U NY Pr.

Listening to Whales Sing. Faith McNulty. LC 94-40993. (Hello Reader! Ser.: Level 4). (Illus.). 32p. (J). (ps-3). 1996. pap. 3.99 (*0-590-47871-0*, Cartwheel) Scholastic Inc.

Listening to Whales Sing. Faith McNulty. (Hello, Reader! Ser.). 1996. 9.19 (*0-606-09558-6*, Pub. by Turtleback) Demco.

***Listening to Wild Dolphins: Learning Their Secrets for Living with Joy.** Bobbie Sandoz. LC 99-37725. 272p. 1999. pap. 14.95 (*1-58270-019-2*, Pub. by Beyond Words Pub) Publishers Group.

Listening to Winter. Molly Fisk. LC 99-41369. (California Poetry Ser.: Vol. 4). 64p. 1999. pap. 12.50 (*0-9666691-3-4*, Pub. by Heyday Bks) SPD-Small Pr Dist.

Listening to Women Talk about Their Health: Issues & Evidence from India. Ed. by Pertti J. Pelto et al. (C). 1994. text 34.00 (*81-241-0274-0*, Pub. by Har-Anand Pubns) S Asia.

***Listening to Young People in School, Youth Work & Counselling.** Nick Luxmoore. LC 00-41265. (Illus.). 2000. pap. write for info. (*1-85302-909-2*, Pub. by Jessica Kingsley) Taylor & Francis.

***Listening to Your Donors.** Bruce Campbell. 208p. 2000. pap. 27.95 (*0-7879-5037-8*, Pfffr & Co) Jossey-Bass.

Listening to Your Hormones. Gillian Ford. 496p. 1997. per. 18.00 (*0-7615-1002-8*) Prima Pub.

Listening to Your Hormones: From PMS to Menopause Every Woman's Complete Guide. Gillian Ford. LC 95-23405. 496p. 1996. 22.95 (*0-7615-0113-4*) Prima Pub.

Listening to Your Inner Guide. Jon Mundy. 176p. (Orig.). 1995. pap. 13.95 (*0-8245-1498-X*) Crossroad NY.

Listening to Your Inner Voice: Discover the Truth Within You & Let It Guide Your Way. Douglas Bloch. 232p. pap. 9.95 (*1-56838-079-8*) Hazelden.

Listening to Your Life: Meditations with Frederick Buechner. Frederick Buechner. 384p. 1992. pap. 14.00 (*0-06-069864-0*, Pub. by Harper SF) HarpC.

***Listening to Your Soul.** Dick Wilson. 2000. pap. 15.95 (*0-85207-328-3*) C W Daniel.

Listening Voice: An Essay on the Rhetoric of Saint-Amant. John D. Lyons. LC 82-82429. (French Forum Monographs: No. 40). 138p. (Orig.). 1982. pap. 10.95 (*0-917058-39-9*) French Forum.

Listening Walk. Paul Showers. LC 90-30526. (Trophy Picture Bk.). (Illus.). 32p. (J). (ps-3). 1993. pap. 5.95 (*0-06-443322-6*, HarpTrophy) HarpC Child Bks.

Listening Walk. Paul Showers. LC 61-10495. (Let's-Read-&-Find-Out Science Bks.). (Illus.). 40p. (J). (gr. k-3). 1961. 13.89 (*0-690-49663-X*) HarpC Child Bks.

Listening Walk. Paul Showers. 1991. 11.15 (*0-606-02710-6*, Pub. by Turtleback) Demco.

Listening Walk. rev. ed. Paul Showers. LC 90-30526. (Illus.). 32p. (J). (ps-2). 1991. lib. bdg. 15.89 (*0-06-021638-7*) HarpC Child Bks.

Listening Walk . . . & Other Stories. Gene Hill. LC 84-27080. (Illus.). 208p. 1985. 17.95 (*0-8329-0385-X*, Winchester Pr) New Win Pub.

***Listening Walk Big Book.** Showers. 32p. (J). (ps-2). 1999. pap. 19.95 (*0-06-443324-2*) HarpC Child Bks.

Listening Walls. Margaret Millar. 236p. 1986. pap. 5.95 (*0-930330-52-8*) Intl Polygonics.

Listening with Different Ears: Counseling People over Sixty. James Warnick. LC 93-48690. 224p. (Orig.). 1995. 24.95 (*0-936609-31-1*); pap. 19.50 (*0-936609-28-1*) QED Ft Bragg.

Listening with Heart. Heather Whitestone. (Illus.). 224p. 1998. pap. 10.00 (*0-385-48899-8*) Doubleday.

Listening with New Ears. Phyllis Ward. Ed. by Vince Patton. LC 98-7104. (Illus.). 48p. (YA). 1998. 7.95 (*1-57895-054-6*) Bridge Resources.

Listening with the Heart & Other Communication Skills. Sara Bhakti. 60p. (Orig.). 1997. pap. 7.00 (*0-9630514-2-3*) Gaea Pubs.

Listening with the Mind's Inner Ear: The Value of Metaphors in Forming & Developing Belief Systems & Attitudes. E. Gene Rooney. 165p. (Orig.). 1993. student ed. 25.00 (*1-881596-02-8*) L E A D Cnslts.

Listening with the "Third Ear" Reading What Patients Write - a Basic Course. Jimmie R. Rankin. (Literature of Patient Response Ser.). 100p. 1995. pap. 29.95 incl. VHS (*1-883338-21-2*) Dry Bones Pr.

***Listening with Zachary.** (Books to Go Ser.). 1998. pap. write for info. (*0-8136-7880-3*) Modern Curr.

Listening Woman. Tony Hillerman. 336p. 1990. mass mkt. 6.50 (*0-06-100029-9*, Harp PBks) HarpC.

Listening Woman. Tony Hillerman. 1979. pap. 3.95 (*0-380-43554-3*, Avon Bks) Morrow Avon.

Listening Woman. large type ed. Tony Hillerman. LC 92-40633. (General Ser.). 303p. 1994. pap. 18.95 (*0-8161-5435-X*, G K Hall Lrg Type) Mac Lib Ref.

Listening Woman: A Joe Leaphorn mystery. large type ed. Tony Hillerman. LC 92-40633. (General Ser.). 303p. 1993. lib. bdg. 22.95 (*0-8161-5434-1*, G K Hall Lrg Type) Mac Lib Ref.

Lister Hill: Statesman from the South. Virginia Van der Veer Hamilton. LC 87-1863. (Fred W. Morrison Series in Southern Studies). (Illus.). 391p. reprint ed. pap. 121.30 (*0-608-20080-8*, 207135200011) Bks Demand.

Listerdale Mystery. Agatha Christie. Date not set. lib. bdg. 20.95 (*0-8488-1964-0*) Amereon Ltd.

***Listeria, Listeriosis & Food Safety.** 2nd expanded ed. Elliot T. Ryser & Elmer H. Marth. LC 98-50963. (Food Science & Technology Ser.). (Illus.). 1030p. 1999. text 195.00 (*0-8247-0235-2*) Dekker.

Listeriosis Research: Present Situation & Perspective. B. Ralovich. 222p. (C). 1984. 90.00 (*963-05-3657-9*, Pub. by Akade Kiado) St Mut.

Listing of Biotopes in Europe According to Their Significance for Invertebrates. (Nature & Environment Ser.: No. 77). 1996. 18.00 (*92-871-3002-7*, Pub. by Council of Europe) Manhattan Pub Co.

Listing of Companies. 434p. (C). 1992. ring bd. 150.00 (*0-89382-198-5*) Nat Assn Insurance.

Listing of Companies. 430p. (C). 1992. ring bd. 150.00 (*0-89382-220-5*) Nat Assn Insurance.

Listing of Companies. 456p. 1993. ring bd. 150.00 (*0-89382-243-4*) Nat Assn Insurance.

Listing of Companies. 456p. 1993. ring bd. 150.00 (*0-89382-254-X*) Nat Assn Insurance.

Listing of Companies. annuals 547p. (C). 1994. ring bd. 150.00 (*0-89382-274-4*) Nat Assn Insurance.

Listing of Companies. 540p. (C). 1994. ring bd. 150.00 (*0-89382-314-7*) Nat Assn Insurance.

Listing of Companies. (Semiannual Ser.). 567p. (C). 1995. ring bd. 175.00 (*0-89382-350-3*) Nat Assn Insurance.

Listing of Companies. 1000p. (C). 1997. ring bd. write for info. (*0-89382-503-4*, LOC-ZU1298) Nat Assn Insurance.

Listing of Companies. rev. ed. 590p. (C). 1995. ring bd. 175.00 (*0-89382-363-5*, LOC-25) Nat Assn Insurance.

Listing of Companies. rev. ed. 910p. 1999. ring bd. 190.00i (*0-89382-588-3*, LOC-ZM) Nat Assn Insurance.

Listing of Companies. annuals rev. ed. Ed. by Roger Graves. 600p. (Orig.). (C). 1996. ring bd. 190.00 (*0-89382-410-0*, LOC-ZS) Nat Assn Insurance.

Listing of Companies. 20th rev. ed. Ed. by Jean Buckley. 590p. (C). 1996. ring bd. 190.00 (*0-89382-435-6*, LOC-ZS) Nat Assn Insurance.

Listing of Companies. 21st rev. ed. Ed. by Jean Buckley. 806p. 1997. pap. 190.00 (*0-89382-465-8*, LOC-ZS) Nat Assn Insurance.

Listing of ISO 9000 National & International Quality System - 3rd Party Registration Organization: Listing of ISO 9000 Registrars. Gunther B. Gumpp. 54p. (Orig.). 1994. pap. 28.00 (*1-881006-14-X*) Qual Cont Systs Srvs.

Listing of Letters Found in the Wheeling, WV Post Office. Carol A. Scott. 34p. 1990. per. 5.00 (*1-55856-075-0*, 070) Closson Pr.

An Asterisk (*) at the beginning of an entry indicates that the title is appearing for the first time.

Listing Securities in the United States & the United Kingdom: A Comparative Guide to the Regulatory & Accounting Requirements. Kenneth Rayner. 288p. 1991. lib. bdg. 146.00 (*1-85333-565-7*, Pub. by Graham & Trotman) Kluwer Academic.

Listless. Ivan W. Rayworth. 254p. 1997. pap. text, per. 8.95 (*0-9658263-0-9*) I W Rayworth.

Listmaker. Robin Klein. LC 98-200369. 218p. (J). 1997. write for info. (*0-670-87175-3*) Viking Penguin.

ListMan: List Management - Direct Mail & Telemarketing. Advantage International, Inc. Staff. 1992. 99.00 (*1-56756-003-2*, OD500I); 599.00 (*1-56756-023-7*, OD510I); student ed. 35.00 (*1-56756-018-0*) Advant Intl.

Listo Al Trabajo: Job Ready. Scott E. Davis. (SPA.). 36p. (Orig.). 1994. pap. 4.95 (*0-9640932-9-4*) Simsbury Mgmt.

Listo Para Reedificar. T. R. Price.Tr. of Ready to Rebuild. 1997. pap. text 10.99 (*1-56063-514-2*, 498445) Editorial Unilit.

Listos, en Sus Marcas, Adelante! Sharon Peters. (SPA., Illus.). 32p. (J). (gr. k-2). 1995. pap. 2.50 (*0-89375-957-0*) Troll Communs.

Listowel Literary Phenomenon: North Kerry Writers. Ed. by Gabriel Fitzmaurice. LC 94-241722. 152p. pap. 14.95 (*1-874700-87-7*, Pub. by Clo Iar-Chonnachta) Dufour.

Lists. deluxe ed. Jean-Jacques Cory. 64p. (Orig.). 1974. pap. 10.00 (*0-915066-06-8*) Assembling Pr.

Lists & Returns of Connecticut Men in the Revolution, 1775-1783. Connecticut Historical Society Staff. 489p. (Orig.). 1995. pap. 31.00 (*0-7884-0312-5*) Heritage Bk.

Lists, Lists, Lists. Beverly Woolhiser. 1992. pap. text 19.95 (*1-880118-07-6*) MESD Pr.

Lists of Clay. Zoe Maude. 272p. 1998. pap. 16.95 (*1-892745-01-1*) Petals of Life.

Lists of Foreign Protestants & Aliens Resident in England, 1618-1688. Ed. by William D. Cooper. LC 17-1252. (Camden Society, London. Publications, First Ser.: No. 82). reprint ed. 35.00 (*0-404-50182-6*) AMS Pr.

Lists of Germans from the Palatinate Who Came to England in 1709. John Tribbeko & George Ruperti. 44p. 1998. pap. 7.00 (*0-8063-0329-8*, 5840, Pub. by Clearfield Co) ACCESS Pubs Network.

Lists of Inhabitants of Colonial New York. Edmund B. O'Callaghan. LC 79-52062. 351p. 1999. reprint ed. 25.00 (*0-8063-0847-8*) Genealog Pub.

Lists of Londoners. 2nd ed. J. S. W. Gibson & Heather Creaton. 39p. 1997. pap. 7.50 (*0-8063-1563-6*) Genealog Pub.

Lists of Members & the Rules. Bannatyne Club Staff. LC 76-160006. (Bannatyne Club, Edinburgh. Publications: No. 116). reprint ed. 39.50 (*0-404-52874-0*) AMS Pr.

Lists of Officers of the Colonies on the Delaware & the Province of Pennsylvania, 1614-1776. John B. Linn & William H. Egle. 221p. 1992. reprint ed. pap. 25.00 (*0-8063-5000-8*, 9284) Clearfield Co.

Lists of Passengers Arriving at U. S. Ports, Jan. 1880-Dec. 1884. Ed. by Ira A. Glazier & P. William Filby. LC 92-24504. (Italians to America Ser.: Vol. 1). 650p. 1992. 75.00 (*0-8420-2451-4*) Scholarly Res Inc.

Lists of Passengers Arriving at U. S. Ports, Jan. 1885-June 1887. Ed. by Ira A. Glazier & P. William Filby. (Italians to America Ser.: Vol. 2). 650p. 1992. 75.00 (*0-8420-2452-2*) Scholarly Res Inc.

Lists of Passengers Arriving at U. S. Ports, Jan. 1892-Dec. 1892. Ed. by Ira A. Glazier & P. William Filby. (Italians to America Ser.: Vol. 6). 576p. 1997. 75.00 (*0-8420-2456-5*) Scholarly Res Inc.

Lists of Passengers Arriving at U. S. Ports, Jan. 1893-Sept. 1893. Ed. by Ira A. Glazier & P. William Filby. (Italians to America Ser.: Vol. 7). 630p. 1997. 75.00 (*0-8420-2457-3*) Scholarly Res Inc.

Lists of Passengers Arriving at U. S. Ports, July 1887-June 1889. Ed. by Ira A. Glazier & P. William Filby. (Italians to America Ser.: Vol. 3). 650p. 1993. 75.00 (*0-8420-2453-0*) Scholarly Res Inc.

Lists of Passengers Arriving at U. S. Ports, July 1889-Oct. 1890. Ed. by Ira A. Glazier & P. William Filby. (Italians to America Ser.: Vol. 4). 650p. 1993. 75.00 (*0-8420-2454-9*) Scholarly Res Inc.

Lists of Passengers Arriving at U. S. Ports, July 1896-June 1897. Ed. by Ira A. Glazier & P. William Filby. (Italians to America Ser.: Vol. 10). 600p. 1998. 75.00 (*0-8420-2460-3*) Scholarly Res Inc.

***Lists of Passengers Arriving at U. S. Ports, June 16, 1897-May 26, 1898.** Ed. by Ira A. Glazier & P. William Filby. (Italians to America Ser.: Vol. 11). 600p. 2000. 75.00 (*0-8420-2461-1*) Scholarly Res Inc.

Lists of Passengers Arriving at U. S. Ports, June 1895-June 1896. Ed. by Ira A. Glazier & P. William Filby. (Italians to America Ser.: Vol. 9). 600p. 1997. 75.00 (*0-8420-2459-X*) Scholarly Res Inc.

***Lists of Passengers Arriving at U. S. Ports, May 27, 1898-Apr. 30, 1899.** Ed. by Ira A. Glazier & P. William Filby. (Italians to America Ser.: Vol. 12). 600p. 2000. 75.00 (*0-8420-2462-X*) Scholarly Res Inc.

Lists of Passengers Arriving at U. S. Ports, Nov. 1890-Dec. 1891. Ed. by Ira A. Glazier & P. William Filby. LC 92-24504. (Italians to America Ser.: Vol. 5). 670p. 1995. 75.00 (*0-8420-2455-7*) Scholarly Res Inc.

Lists of Passengers Arriving at U. S. Ports, Oct. 1893-May 1895. Ed. by Ira A. Glazier & P. William Filby. (Italians to America Ser.: Vol. 8). 600p. 1997. 75.00 (*0-8420-2458-1*) Scholarly Res Inc.

Lists of Personal Names from the Temple School of Nippur: Lists of Sumerian Personal Names. Edward Chiera. LC 17-5006. (University of Pennsylvania, the University Museum, Publications of the Babylonian Section: Vol. 11, No. 3). 136p. pap. 42.20 (*0-608-13635-2*, 205202700027) Bks Demand.

***Lists to Live By, No. 2.** Alice Gray. 2001. pap. 11.99 (*1-57673-685-7*) Multnomah Pubs.

***Lists to Live by: For Everything That Really Matters.** Compiled by Alice Gray et al. LC 99-12863. 280p. 1999. pap. 11.99 (*1-57673-478-1*) Multnomah Pubs.

Lisu Religion. E. Paul Durrenberger. (Occasional Papers: Vol. 13). 44p. 1989. pap. 9.95 (*1-877979-13-9*) SE Asia.

Lisuride & Other Dopamine Agonists: Basic Mechanisms & Endocrine & Neurological Effects. fac. ed. Ed. by Donald B. Calne et al. LC 82-42592. (Illus.). 575p. pap. 178.30 (*0-7837-7507-5*, 204699900005) Bks Demand.

Liszt. Bryce Morrison. (Illustrated Lives of the Great Composers Ser.). (Illus.). 112p. 1989. pap. 17.95 (*0-7119-1682-9*, OP44999) Omnibus NY.

Liszt. Tutti S. A. Inc. Staff. (TuTTi Ser.: No. 7). 176p. 1996. pap. text 16.95 incl. audio compact disk (*1-57301-021-9*) TuTTi USA.

Liszt. Derek Watson. 404p. 1989. 24.95 (*0-02-872705-3*, Schirmer Books) Mac Lib Ref.

***Liszt.** Derek Watson. (Master Musicians Ser.). (Illus.). 416p. 2000. pap. 19.95 (*0-19-816499-8*) OUP.

Liszt. Klara Hamburger. Tr. by Gyula Gulyas from HUN. (Music Ser.). (Illus.). 243p. 1987. reprint ed. lib. bdg. 35.00 (*0-306-79661-9*) Da Capo.

Liszt: Music Book Index. Ralph Hill. 144p. 1993. reprint ed. lib. bdg. 69.00 (*0-7812-9605-6*) Rprt Serv.

Liszt: My Travelling Circus Life. David I. Allsobrook. LC 91-3578. (Music in Georgian & Victorian Society Ser.). (Illus.). 272p. (C). 1991. 36.95 (*0-8093-1785-0*) S Ill U Pr.

Liszt: Sonata in B Minor. Kenneth Hamilton. (Cambridge Music Handbooks Ser.). 101p. (C). 1996. pap. text 13.95 (*0-521-46963-5*) Cambridge U Pr.

Liszt: Sonata in B Minor. Franz Liszt. Ed. by Kenneth Hamilton. (Cambridge Music Handbks.). 101p. (C). 1996. text 39.95 (*0-521-46570-2*) Cambridge U Pr.

Liszt - Hungarian Rhapsody No. 2. Ed. by Maurice Hinson. 24p. 1987. pap. 5.95 (*0-7390-0565-0*, 897) Alfred Pub.

Liszt & His Country, 1874-1886. Dezso Legany. Tr. by Elizabeth Smith-Csicsery-Ronay from HUN. (Illus.). 331p. 1992. 39.50 (*0-911050-66-3*) Occidental.

Liszt, Carolyne, & the Vatican Documents. Alan Walker. LC 91-24067. (Franz Liszt Ser.: No. 1). (Illus.). 1991. lib. bdg. 56.00 (*0-945193-09-2*) Pendragon NY.

Liszt, Composer, & His Piano Works. Herbert Westerby. LC 72-109874. (Illus.). 336p. 1971. reprint ed. lib. bdg. 35.00 (*0-8371-4365-9*, WELI, Greenwood Pr) Greenwood.

Liszt in Germany, 1840-1845. Michael M. Saffle. (Franz Liszt Ser.: No. 2). (Illus.). 1994. lib. bdg. 54.00 (*0-945193-39-4*) Pendragon NY.

Liszt Very Best for Piano. Ed. by John L. Haag. (Illus.). 144p. (Orig.). 1995. pap. 14.95 (*1-56922-094-8*, 07-2036) Creat Cncpts.

Lisztian Keyboard Energy - Liszt et la Pedagogie du Piano: An Essay on the Pianism of Franz Liszt. Bertrand Ott. Tr. by Donald H. Windham. LC 92-25796. (FRE., Illus.). 308p. 1992. reprint ed. text 99.95 (*0-7734-9589-4*) E Mellen.

Liszt's Complete Piano Transcriptions from Wagner's Operas. Franz Liszt. Ed. by Charles Suttoni. (Illus.). 176p. 1981. pap. 9.95 (*0-486-24126-2*) Dover.

Liszt's Music Manuscripts in the National Szechenyi Library. Maria Eckhardt & Zoltan Falvy. (Studies in Central & Eastern European Music: No. 2). (Illus.). 252p. 1987. lib. bdg. 57.00 (*963-05-4177-7*) Pendragon NY.

Lit. Ron Silliman. 96p. 1987. pap. 7.50 (*0-937013-18-8*) Potes Poets.

***Lit: A Place in the Sun.** 72p. 2000. otabind 19.95 (*0-634-01050-6*) H Leonard.

Lit & Culture in Northern Ireland since 1965. Richard Kirkland. (Studies in Twentieth-Century Literature). 200p. (C). 1996. 74.00 (*0-582-23885-4*) Addison-Wesley.

Lit d'Acajou. Jean Diwo. (Dames Du Fauborg Ser.: Vol. II). (FRE.). 563p. 1989. pap. 16.95 (*0-7859-2120-6*, 2070381498) Fr & Eur.

Lit Defait. Francoise Sagan. (FRE.). 250p. 1985. pap. 10.95 (*0-7859-5570-4*) Fr & Eur.

Lit Ed. Anthony Curtis. LC 99-218128. 356p. 1998. 45.00 (*1-85754-149-9*, Pub. by Carcanet Pr) Paul & Co Pubs.

Lit en Cont Text & Cassette. Luce. 1994. 50.50 (*0-15-501561-3*, Pub. by Harcourt Coll Pubs) Harcourt.

***LIT Environment.** Phillips. 216p. 2001. 74.95 (*0-7506-4889-9*, Architectural Pr) Buttrwrth-Heinemann.

Lit for Today's Young Adults. 3rd ed. Alleen P. Nilsen & Kenneth L. Donelson. (C). 1989. 56.00 (*0-673-38400-4*) Addison-Wesley Educ.

***LIT Interior.** William J. Fielder & Frederick H. Hones. (Illus.). 216p. 2001. pap. 74.95 (*0-7506-4890-2*, Architectural Pr) Buttrwrth-Heinemann.

Lit Window. Michael Umphrey. (CSU Poetry Ser.: Vol. XXII). 83p. (Orig.). 1987. pap. 6.00 (*0-914946-61-7*) Cleveland St Univ Poetry Ctr.

Lita - Lita Ford (Guitar - Vocal) Ed. by Mark Phillips. (Illus.). 51p. (Orig.). 1990. pap. text 19.95 (*0-89524-394-6*) Cherry Lane.

Lita Albuquerque: Reflections. Ed. by Steven Keeva. LC 89-85568. (Illus.). 76p. (Orig.). 1990. pap. 24.00 (*0-911291-17-2*) Fellows Cont Art.

Litanies & Other Prayers for the Revised Common Lectionary: Year A. Everet Tilson & Phyllis Cole. LC 92-12750. 208p. (Orig.). 1992. pap. 13.95 (*0-687-22119-6*) Abingdon.

Litanies & Other Prayers for the Revised Common Lectionary: Year B. Phyllis Cole & Everett Tilson. LC 92-47126. (Orig.). 1993. pap. 13.95 (*0-687-22120-X*) Abingdon.

Litanies & Other Prayers for the Revised Common Lectionary: Year C. Phyllis Cole & Everett Tilson. LC 93-42153. (Orig.). 1994. pap. 13.95 (*0-687-22122-6*) Abingdon.

Litanies for All Occasions. Garth House. 72p. (Orig.). 1989. pap. 11.00 (*0-8170-1144-7*) Judson.

Litany. Elizabeth Eddy. (Morning Coffee Chapbook Ser.). (Illus.). 13p. 1984. pap. 12.00 (*0-915124-97-1*) Coffee Hse.

Litany. Scott Sonders. LC 86-73071. 96p. (Orig.). 1988. pap. 9.95 (*0-912159-11-1*) Center Pr CA.

Litany in Time of Plague. K. D. Miller. LC 95-108751. 160p. 1994. pap. write for info. (*0-88984-145-4*) Porcup Quill.

***Litany of Evil: Crime & Punishment in Scotland.** Sheila Livingstone. (Orig.). 1999. pap. 19.95 (*1-84158-002-3*) Birlinn Ltd.

Litany of Friends: New & Selected Poems. 2nd ed. Dudley Randall. LC 83-82770. 103p. (YA). (gr. 9-12). 1983. per. 6.00 (*0-916418-50-2*) Lotus.

Litany of Saints. Ann Ball. LC 92-61546. 224p. (Orig.). 1993. pap. 8.95 (*0-87973-460-4*, 460) Our Sunday Visitor.

***Litany of the Long Sun.** Gene Wolfe. 544p. 2000. pap. 16.95 (*0-312-87291-7*, Pub. by Tor Bks) St Martin.

Litany of the Tribes. Vol. 1. 20.00 (*1-56504-302-2*) White Wolf.

Litany of the Tribes. Wolf White Wolf Publishing Staff. (Werewolf Ser.: Vol. 2). (Illus.). 1998. reprint ed. pap. 20.00 (*1-56504-303-0*, 3381) White Wolf.

Litany of the Tribes, Vol. 3. Brian Campbell et al. (Werewolf Ser.). (Illus.). 1998. reprint ed. pap. 20.00 (*1-56504-304-9*, 3382) White Wolf.

***Litany of the Tribes, Vol 4.** Bill Bridges. 2000. pap. text 22.95 (*1-56504-305-7*) White Wolf.

Litany of Wings. limited ed. Amber C. Sumrall. (Illus.). 96p. 1998. pap. 13.50 (*0-9652575-3-3*, Pub. by Many Names) Bookpeople.

Litany Sung at Hell's Gate. Bryce Milligan. (Illus.). x, 36p. (Orig.). 1990. pap. 8.00 (*0-913983-08-X*) M & A Edns.

Litauische Marchen, Sprichworte, Ratsel und Lieder, Gesammelt und Ubersetzt. August Schleicher. (GER.). ix, 244p. 1975. reprint ed. write for info. (*3-487-05682-8*) G Olms Pubs.

Litauisches Etymologisches Woerterbuch, Vol. 2. Ernst Fraenkel. (GER & LIT.). 1965. 395.00 (*0-8288-6751-8*, M-7542) Fr & Eur.

Litauisches Etymologisches Woerterbuch Vol. 1: Lithuanian Etymological Dictionary. Ernst Fraenkel. (GER & LIT.). 1960. 395.00 (*0-8288-6841-7*, M-7541) Fr & Eur.

Litchfield: A Strange & Twisted Saga of Murder in the Midwest. William Stage. (Illus.). 272p. (Orig.). 1998. pap. 8.95 (*0-9629124-1-7*) Floppinfish.

Litchfield & Morris Inscriptions. Charles T. Payne. (Illus.). 330p. 1996. reprint ed. pap. 23.00 (*0-7884-0560-8*, P095) Heritage Bk.

Litchfield & Morris Inscriptions: Record of Inscriptions upon the Tombstones in the Towns of Litchfield & Morris, Connecticut. Transcribed by Charles T. Payne. (Illus.). 304p. 1997. reprint ed. lib. bdg. 35.00 (*0-8328-5661-4*) Higginson Bk Co.

Litchfield, Connecticut, Book of Days: A Collation of the Historical, Biographical & Literary Reminiscences of the Town of Litchfield, Connecticut. Ed. by George C. Boswell. (Illus.). 221p. 1992. reprint ed. lib. bdg. 27.50 (*0-8328-2354-6*) Higginson Bk Co.

Litchfield County. CCS Inc. Staff. (Street Directions Without a Map Ser.). 150p. 1992. pap. 14.95 (*1-881638-03-0*) CCS Inc.

Litchfield County Biographical Review: Biographical Sketches of the Leading Citizens of Litchfield, County, Connecticut. (Illus.). 670p. 1997. reprint ed. lib. bdg. 69.00 (*0-8328-5664-9*) Higginson Bk Co.

Litchfield County Sketches. Newell M. Calhoun. 177p. 1997. reprint ed. pap. 22.00 (*0-8328-5660-6*) Higginson Bk Co.

Litchfield Family in America, Pt. 1, Nos. 1-5. W. J. Litchfield. 384p. 1989. reprint ed. pap. 57.00 (*0-8328-0772-9*); reprint ed. lib. bdg. 65.00 (*0-8328-0771-0*) Higginson Bk Co.

Lite & Luscious Cuisine of India: Recipes & Tips for Healthy & Quick Meals. Madhu Gadia. LC 96-92639. (Illus.). 320p. 1997. 19.95 (*0-9653915-0-7*) Piquant Pub.

Lite Delight. (Favorite All Time Recipes Ser.). (Illus.). 96p. 1993. 7.98 (*0-7853-0064-3*, 2014903); spiral bd. 3.50 (*1-56173-546-9*, 2014900) Pubns Intl Ltd.

Lite-er & More Fantastic. Eileen Dardick & Sheila Ferrendelli. 1994. 15.95 (*0-9641615-1-6*) Ideal Image.

Lite Lean & Low Fat. International Publications Staff. (Illus.). 7.98 (*1-56173-263-X*) Pubns Intl Ltd.

Lite Lifestyle. Laura Creavalle. 126p. 1999. pap. 19.95 (*0-9669168-4-0*) Club Creavalle.

Lite Sweet Delites: Sweetened with Sugar Substitutes. Lee M. Cirillo. LC 89-91755. (Illus.). 226p. (Orig.). 1989. pap. 13.50 (*0-9623225-0-4*) SCP Rochester.

Lite Switch: Low Fat Cookbook & Health Guide. 10th ed. June M. Jeter. 400p. (Orig.). 1992. spiral bd. 19.95 (*0-9634783-0-3*) Lite Switch.

Lite up Your Life: A Delicious Variety of Low-Sodium, Low-Cholesterol, Low-Fat Recipes for Everyday Eating. Waynell Harris & Sherry Whitehurst. LC 91-11689. (Illus.). 304p. 1991. ring bd. 14.95 (*0-937552-40-2*) Quail Ridge.

Lite'n Up! A Sensible Approach to Healthy Living & Safe Weight Management. Tom Iselin. Ed. by Jack Ewing. 168p. (Orig.). 1996. pap. 14.95 (*0-9649139-0-9*) Pelican Lake.

Lite'n Up! - Low-Fat Cooking: Healthier Ways to Prepare America's Favorite Foods. Tom Iselin. Ed. by Jack Ewing. 168p. (Orig.). 2000. pap. 14.95 (*0-9649139-1-7*) Pelican Lake.

Lite'n Up! Your Kitchen: 1001 Secrets for Health-Conscious Looks. unabridged ed. Tom Iselin. Ed. by Jack Ewing. 250p. (Orig.). 2000. pap. 16.95 (*0-9649139-4-1*) Pelican Lake.

Lite'n Up! Your Life: 365 Insights & Suggestions on How to Manage Weight & Live Healthfully. unabridged ed. Tom Iselin. Ed. by Jack Ewing. 168p. (Orig.). 2000. pap. 6.95 (*0-9649139-3-3*) Pelican Lake.

Literacies. Priscilla Perkins. LC 97-162631. (C). 1997. pap. text, teacher ed. write for info. (*0-393-97116-3*) Norton.

Literacies. Kem Smith. (C). 1997. pap. write for info. (*0-393-98221-1*) Norton.

Literacies: A Rutgers Reader. 2nd ed. Smith et al. (C). 1994. pap. text 25.50 (*0-07-058982-8*) McGraw.

Literacies: Reading, Writing, Interpretation. Ken Smith. Ed. by Terence Brunk et al. LC 96-17093. (C). 1996. pap. 36.25 (*0-393-97043-4*) Norton.

***Literacies: Reading, Writing, Interpretation.** 2nd ed. Diamond et al. LC 99-48832. 2000. pap. text 26.00 (*0-393-97537-1*) Norton.

***Literacies & Technologies: A Reader for Contemporary Writers.** Robert Yagelski. LC 00-41957. 2000. write for info. (*0-321-05118-1*) Longman.

***Literacies & Technology.** 2000. teacher ed. write for info. (*0-321-07755-5*) Addison-Wesley.

Literacies & the Workplace: A Collection of Original Essays. Deakin University Press Staff. 1996. pap. 59.95 (*0-7300-1923-3*, Pub. by Deakin Univ) St Mut.

Literacies Lost: When Students Move from a Progressive Middle School to a Traditional High School. M. Cyrene Wells. LC 95-30977. 208p. (C). 1995. text 40.00 (*0-8077-3478-0*); pap. text 18.95 (*0-8077-3477-2*) Tchrs Coll.

Literacies of Power: What Americans Are Not Allowed to Know. Donaldo P. Macedo. LC 94-3375. (Edge Ser.). (C). 1994. pap. 24.00 (*0-8133-2253-7*, Pub. by Westview) HarpC.

Literacy. Viv Edwards & David Corson. LC 97-18842. (Encyclopedia of Language & Education Ser.). 1997. lib. bdg. write for info. (*0-7923-4595-9*) Kluwer Academic.

Literacy. Margaret Jackson. (Primary Curriculum Ser.). 192p. 1993. pap. 32.00 (*1-85346-197-0*, Pub. by David Fulton) Taylor & Francis.

Literacy. Johnson. 2000. pap. text 11.97 (*0-395-97210-8*) HM.

Literacy, 2 vols. 2nd ed. Cooper. (C). 1992. pap. text 41.56 (*0-395-64782-7*) HM.

Literacy: A Redefinition. Ed. by Nancy J. Ellsworth et al. 312p. 1994. pap. 36.00 (*0-8058-1455-8*); text 69.95 (*0-8058-1454-X*) L Erlbaum Assocs.

Literacy: An International Handbook. Ed. by Daniel A. Wagner et al. LC 98-45253. 544p. 2000. text 99.00 (*0-8133-9058-3*, Pub. by Westview) HarpC.

Literacy: An Introduction to the Ecology of Language. David Barton. 232p. 1994. pap. 28.95 (*0-631-19091-0*) Blackwell Pubs.

***Literacy: Background & Bibliography.** Ed. by S. N. Colamery. 227p. 2000. lib. bdg. 49.00 (*1-56072-833-7*) Nova Sci Pubs.

Literacy: Helping Children Construct Meaning, 3 vols. J. David Cooper. (C). 1997. text, teacher ed. 11.96 (*0-395-79003-4*) HM.

Literacy: Helping Children Construct Meaning, 3 vols. 3rd ed. J. David Cooper. 608p. (C). 1996. pap. text 41.56 (*0-395-79002-6*) HM.

Literacy: Interdisciplinary Conversations. Deborah Keller-Cohen. Ed. by Marcia Farr. LC 94-2969. (Written Language Ser.). 440p. 1994. text 79.50 (*1-881303-48-9*); pap. text 29.95 (*1-881303-49-7*) Hampton Pr NJ.

Literacy: Reading the Word & the World. Paulo Freire & Donaldo P. Macedo. LC 87-10295. (Critical Studies in Education). 207p. 1987. 49.95 (*0-89789-125-2*, Bergin & Garvey); pap. 19.95 (*0-89789-126-0*, Bergin & Garvey) Greenwood.

Literacy: Signs for Our Times. Ed. by Malcolm P. Douglass. (Claremont Reading Conference Yearbook Ser.). 178p. (Orig.). 1988. pap. 20.00 (*0-941742-06-7*) Claremont Grad.

Literacy: The Growing Influence of Linguistics. 2nd ed. Sarah C. Gudschinsky. (Trends in Linguistics, State-of-the-Art Reports: No. 2). (Orig.). 1982. pap. text 30.80 (*90-279-3064-3*) Mouton.

Literacy: Traditional, Cultural, Technology: Selected Papers from the 23rd Annual Conference of the IASL. Ed. by Donald Adcock. 141p. 1994. pap. 25.00 (*1-890861-16-2*) IASL.

Literacy, Access & Libraries among the Language Minority Community. Rebecca Constantino. LC 97-24393. 264p. 1998. 36.00 (*0-8108-3418-9*) Scarecrow.

Literacy Acquisition & Social Context. Egbert Assink. 304p. (C). 1995. pap. text 38.00 (*0-13-342734-X*) P-H.

Literacy Across Communities. Beverly J. Moss. Ed. by Marcia Farr. LC 94-7395. (Written Language Ser.). 240p. (C). 1994. text 47.50 (*1-881303-61-6*); pap. text 21.95 (*1-881303-62-4*) Hampton Pr NJ.

Literacy Across Languages & Cultures. Ed. by Bernardo M. Ferdman et al. LC 93-750. (SUNY Series, Literacy, Culture, & Learning). 346p. (C). 1994. text 64.50 (*0-7914-1815-4*); pap. text 21.95 (*0-7914-1816-2*) State U NY Pr.

Literacy Across the Curriculum. Ed. by Carolyn N. Hedley et al. LC 92-12459. 336p. 1992. 73.25 (*0-89391-859-8*); pap. 39.50 (*0-89391-915-2*) Ablx Pub.

***Literacy Aesthetics: An Anthology.** Ed. by Alan Singer et al. 288p. 1999. 62.95 (*0-631-20868-2*) Blackwell Pubs.

Literacy Agenda: Issues for the '90s. Ed. by Elaine Furniss & Pamela Green. 175p. (C). 1991. pap. text 21.00 (*0-435-08707-X*, 08707) Heinemann.

***Literacy All Day Long.** Outward Bound, Inc. Staff. 250p. (C). 2000. per. 19.95 (*0-7872-7272-8*) Kendall-Hunt.

L

L

Literacy among Afro-American Youth: Issues in Learning, Teaching & Schooling. Vivian L. Gadsden & Daniel A. Wagner. LC 94-27878. (Literacy Research, Policy & Practice Ser.). 336p. (C). 1995. text 67.50 (*1-881303-27-6*); pap. text 27.50 (*1-881303-28-4*) Hampton Pr NJ.

Literacy & Adult Education in the 104th Congress: A Legislative Guide. 49p. (Orig.). (C). 1995. pap. text 25.00 (*0-7881-2481-1*) DIANE Pub.

Literacy & Basic Education on the Eve of the 21st Century: Report of the 6th European Conference of Directors of Educational Research Institutions, Bled (Yugoslavia), 9-12 October 1991. Ed. by Paul Belanger et al. LC 92-27540. 258p. 1992. 76.00 (*90-265-1264-3*) Swets.

Literacy & Bilingualism: A Handbook for All Teachers. Maria E. Brisk & Margaret M. Harrington. LC 99-31664. 160p. 1999. pap. write for info. (*0-8058-3165-7*) L Erlbaum Assocs.

Literacy & Competencies. Suzanne Mellor. 1996. pap. 35.00 (*0-86431-185-0*, Pub. by Aust Council Educ Res) Stylus Pub VA.

Literacy & Computers: Complicating Our Vision of Teaching & Learning with Technology. Ed. by Cynthia L. Selfe & Susan J. Hilligoss. LC 93-26959. (Research & Scholarship in Composition Ser.: No. 2). iii, 350p. 1994. pap. 19.75 (*0-87352-580-9*, RS02P); lib. bdg. 37.50 (*0-87352-579-5*, RS02C) Modern Lang.

Literacy & Cultural Transmission in the Reading, Writing & Rewriting of Jewish Memorial Books. Rosemary Horowitz. LC 97-3084. 320p. 1997. 74.95 (*1-57292-040-8*) Austin & Winfield.

Literacy & Deafness. Peter V. Paul. LC 97-21431. 358p. 1997. 60.00 (*0-205-17576-7*) P-H.

Literacy & Democracy: Teacher Research & Composition Studies in Pursuit of Habitable Spaces: Further Conversations from the Students of Jay Robinson. Ed. by Cathy Fleischer & David Schaafsma. LC 98-39385. (Illus.). 266p. 1998. pap. 26.95 (*0-8141-2977-3*) NCTE.

Literacy & Education: Essays in Memory of Dina Feitelson. Ed. by Joseph Shimron. 304p. (Orig.). (C). 1996. text 65.00 (*1-57273-032-3*); pap. text 26.50 (*1-57273-033-1*) Hampton Pr NJ.

Literacy & Empowerment. Venkatesh B. Athreya & Sheela R. Chunkath. LC 96-28843. 1996. 38.00 (*0-8039-9337-4*) Sage.

Literacy & Empowerment. Venkatesh B. Athreya et al. LC 96-28843. 290p. (C). 1997. 38.00 (*0-8039-9336-6*, 93366) Sage.

Literacy & Empowerment: The Meaning Makers. Patrick L. Courts. LC 91-2267. (Language & Ideology Ser.). 216p. 1991. 57.95 (*0-89789-260-7*, H260, Bergin & Garvey); pap. 22.95 (*0-89789-261-5*, G261, Bergin & Garvey) Greenwood.

Literacy & Language Analysis. Ed. by Robert J. Scholes. 232p. 1993. text 49.95 (*0-8058-0920-1*) L Erlbaum Assocs.

Literacy & Language Diversity in the United States. Terrence G. Wiley. LC 96-1799. (Language in Education Ser.). 1996. write for info. (*0-937354-86-4*) Delta Systems.

Literacy & Learning in Content. 2nd ed. Randall Ryder & Michael F. Graves. LC 97-22988. 385p. 1997. pap. text 48.00 (*0-13-267774-1*) P-H.

Literacy & Learning in Families & Communities Action-Learning Manual. (Literacy Linkage Series Manuals). 58p. (Orig.). 1996. pap. 6.50 (*0-932288-97-9*) Ctr Intl Ed U of MA.

***Literacy & Learning Through Talk: Strategies for the Primary Classroom** Roy Corden. LC 99-44708. 2000. pap. write for info. (*0-335-20451-1*) OpUniv Pr.

Literacy & Living: The Literate Lives of Three Adults. Lorri Neilsen. LC 88-35973. 150p. (Orig.). (C). 1989. pap. 14.95 (*0-435-08493-3*, 08493) Heinemann.

***Literacy & Motivation: Reading Engagement in Individuals & Groups.** Ed. by Ludo Verhoeven & Catherine E. Snow. 304p. 2000. write for info. (*0-8058-3193-2*); pap. write for info. (*0-8058-3194-0*) L Erlbaum Assocs.

Literacy & Orality. Ed. by David R. Olson & Nancy Torrance. (Illus.). 300p. (C). 1991. text 69.95 (*0-521-39217-9*); pap. text 23.95 (*0-521-39850-9*) Cambridge U Pr.

Literacy & Orality in Ancient Greece. Rosalind Thomas. (Key Themes in Ancient History Ser.). (Illus.). 213p. (C). 1992. text 59.95 (*0-521-37346-8*); pap. text 19.95 (*0-521-37742-0*) Cambridge U Pr.

Literacy & Paideia in Ancient Greece. Kevin Robb. (Illus.). 320p. 1994. text 55.00 (*0-19-505905-0*) OUP.

Literacy & Power in Anglo-Saxon Literature. Seth Lerer. LC 90-40463. (Regents Studies in Medieval Culture). xii, 269p. 1991. text 45.00 (*0-8032-2895-3*) U of Nebr Pr.

Literacy & Power in the Ancient World. Ed. by Alan K. Bowman & Greg Woolf. (Illus.). 259p. 1997. pap. text 19.95 (*0-521-58736-0*) Cambridge U Pr.

Literacy & Praxis: Culture, Language & Pedagogy. Ed. by Catherine Walsh. LC 90-38886. 240p. (C). 1991. pap. 39.50 (*0-89391-717-6*); text 73.25 (*0-89391-648-X*) Ablx Pub.

Literacy & Religion: The Textual Politics & Practice of Seventh-Day Adventism. Cushla Kapitzke. LC 95-17946. (Studies in Written Language & Literacy: No. 2). xxi, 343p. 1995. lib. bdg. 79.00 (*1-55619-318-1*) J Benjamins Pubng Co.

Literacy & Schooling. Ed. by David Bloome. LC 86-20642. 416p. (C). 1987. text 78.50 (*0-89391-331-6*) Ablx Pub.

Literacy & Schooling. Frances Christie & Ray Misson. LC 97-47649. 200p. (C). 1998. 65.00 (*0-415-17017-6*); pap. 20.99 (*0-415-17018-4*) Routledge.

Literacy & Script Reform in Occupation Japan: Reading Between the Lines. J. Marshall Unger. (Illus.). 192p. 1996. text 45.00 (*0-19-510166-9*) OUP.

Literacy & Society. Copenhagen University, Center for Research in the. Ed. by Karen Schousboe & M. T. Larsen. 248p. (Orig.). 1989. pap. 87.50 (*87-500-2784-0*) Coronet Bks.

Literacy & the Arts for the Integrated Classroom. 2nd ed. Nancy L. Cecil. (C). 1998. pap. text. write for info. (*0-8013-1860-2*) Addison-Wesley.

Literacy & the Arts for the Integrated Classroom: Alternative Ways of Knowing. Nancy Lee Cecil & Phyllis Lauritzen. 192p. (C). 1994. pap. text 40.31 (*0-8013-1096-2*, 79549) Longman.

Literacy & the Competencies: Teachers' Perspectives. Suzanne Mellor. 1966. 100.00 (*0-86431-216-4*, Pub. by Aust Council Educ Res) St Mut.

***Literacy & the Politics of Writing.** Albertine Gaur. 224p. 2000. text 44.95 (*1-84150-011-9*, Pub. by Intellect) Intl Spec Bk.

***Literacy & Written Culture in Early Modern Central Europe.** Istvan Gyorgy Toth. 200p. (C). 2000. 41.95 (*963-9116-85-8*) Ctrl Europ Univ.

Literacy as a Moral Imperative: Facing the Challenges of a Pluralistic Society. Rebecca L. Powell. LC 99-15039. 168p. 1999. 55.00 (*0-8476-9458-5*) Rowman.

***Literacy as a Moral Imperative: Facing the Challenges of a Pluralistic Society.** Rebecca L. Powell. LC 99-15039. (Culture & Education Ser.). 168p. 1999. pap. 17.95 (*0-8476-9459-3*) Rowman.

Literacy As Involvement: The Acts of Writers, Readers, & Texts. Deborah Brandt. LC 89-27409. 224p. (C). 1990. text 26.95 (*0-8093-1570-X*) S Ill U Pr.

Literacy As Social Exchange: Intersections of Class, Gender, & Culture. Maureen M. Hourigan. LC 93-43234. (SUNY Series, Literacy, Culture, & Learning: Theory & Practice). 152p. (C). 1994. pap. text 14.95 (*0-7914-2070-1*) State U NY Pr.

Literacy As Social Exchange: Intersections of Class, Gender, & Culture. Maureen M. Hourigan. LC 93-43234. (SUNY Series, Literacy, Culture, & Learning: Theory & Practice). 152p. (C). 1994. text 44.50 (*0-7914-2069-8*) State U NY Pr.

Literacy Assessment: A Handbook of Instruments. Ed. by Lynn K. Rhodes. LC 92-1619. 181p. (C). 1992. pap. text 28.00 (*0-435-08759-2*, 08759) Heinemann.

Literacy Assessment & Intervention. (C). 2002. pap. write for info. (*0-13-016397-X*) P-H.

Literacy Assessment for Bilingual Learners. Sandra R. Hurley & Josefina V. Tinajero. (C). 2000. pap. 27.00 (*0-205-27443-9*, Macmillan Coll) P-H.

Literacy Assessment for Today's Schools. Ed. by Martha D. Collins & Barbara G. Moss. (Monograph Series of the College Reading Association). 234p. (Orig.). (C). 1996. pap. 15.00 (*1-883604-25-7*) Coll Read Assn.

Literacy at the Crossroads: Crucial Talk about Reading, Writing & Other Teaching Dilemmas. Regie Routman. LC 96-12254. 222p. 1996. pap. text 21.00 (*0-435-07210-2*) Heinemann.

Literacy at Work: The Workbook for Program Developers. Jorie Philippi. 1991. mass mkt. 200.00 (*0-13-528837-1*) P-H.

Literacy at Work: The Workplace Basic Education Project Model of Delivery. Jude Newcombe. 1996. pap. 59.95 (*0-7300-1757-5*, Pub. by Deakin Univ) St Mut.

Literacy Before Schooling. Emilia Ferreiro & Ana Teberosky. Tr. by Karen G. Castro. LC 82-15839. 289p. (C). 1985. pap. text 27.50 (*0-435-08220-5*, 08220) Heinemann.

Literacy Begins at Home: Helping Your Child Grow up Reading & Writing. Judith I. Schwartz. (Illus.). 150p. 1991. pap. 20.95 (*0-398-06417-2*) C C Thomas.

Literacy Begins at Home: Helping Your Child Grow up Reading & Writing. Judith I. Schwartz. (Illus.). 150p. (C). 1991. text 35.95 (*0-398-05743-5*) C C Thomas.

Literacy Behind Prison Walls. 1997. lib. bdg. 250.95 (*0-8490-8226-9*) Gordon Pr.

Literacy, Bible Reading & Church Growth Through the Ages. Morris G. Watkins. LC 78-15315. (Illus.). 224p. 1978. pap. 6.95 (*0-87808-325-1*) William Carey Lib.

Literacy Center: Contexts for Reading & Writing. Lesley M. Morrow. (Illus.). 240p. (Orig.). (C). 1997. pap. text 22.50 (*1-57110-022-9*) Stenhse Pubs.

Literacy con Carino: A Story of Migrant Children's Success. Curtis W. Hayes. LC 98-8505. 1998. pap. text 21.00 (*0-325-00007-7*) Heinemann.

Literacy Con Carino: A Story of Migrant Children's Success. Curtis W. Hayes et al. LC 90-24464. (Illus.). 142p. (Orig.). (C). 1991. pap. text 18.50 (*0-435-08551-4*, 08551) Heinemann.

Literacy Connection. Ed. by Alice S. Horning & Ronald A. Sudol. LC 98-55712. 288p. (C). 1998. text 55.00 (*1-57273-216-4*); pap. text 24.95 (*1-57273-217-2*) Hampton Pr NJ.

Literacy Connection: Language & Learning Across the Curriculum (An Anthology) Ed. by Elaine Furniss & Pamela Green. (Illus.). 184p. 1991. pap., teacher ed. 17.00 (*1-875327-09-6*, Pub. by E Curtain) Peguis Pubs Ltd.

Literacy Crisis: False Claims, Real Solutions. Jeff McQuillan. LC 98-17263. 115p. 1998. pap. 16.00 (*0-325-00063-8*) Heinemann.

Literacy, Culture & Identity. Jill S. Bell. LC 96-42924. (American University Studies XIV: Vol. 42). 236p. (C). 1998. text 43.95 (*0-8204-3656-9*) P Lang Pubng.

Literacy Development in a Multilingual Context: Cross-Cultural Perspectives. Ed. by Aydin Durgunoglu & Ludo Verhoeven. LC 97-43202. 250p. 1998. write for info. (*0-8058-2442-1*); pap. write for info. (*0-8058-2443-X*) L Erlbaum Assocs.

Literacy Development in the Early Years. 3rd ed. Lesley M. Morrow. LC 96-10711. 418p. 1996. pap. text 51.00 (*0-205-17442-6*) P-H.

Literacy Development in the Early Years: Helping Children Read & Write. 4th ed. Ed. by Allyn & Bacon Staff. LC 00-20251. 400p. (C). 2000. pap. text 48.00 (*0-205-30589-X*) Allyn.

Literacy Development Through Family Reading. Mina Hassman. Ed. by Gwen Costa. LC 91-666. (Illus.). 1990. 14.95 (*0-87949-341-0*) Ashley Bks.

Literacy Dictionary: The Vocabulary of Reading & Writing. Ed. by Theodore L. Harris & Richard E. Hodges. LC 95-20233. 1995. pap. 35.00 (*0-87207-138-3*) Intl Reading.

Literacy Difficulties: Diagnosis & Instruction. Cathy C. Block. LC 96-76564. 608p. (C). 1996. text 61.50 (*0-15-500364-X*, Pub. by Harcourt Coll Pubs) Harcourt.

Literacy Difficulties: Diagnosis & Instruction. 2nd ed. Cathy C. Block et al. 608p. (C). 1996. text 64.50 (*0-15-502841-3*, Pub. by Harcourt Coll Pubs) Harcourt.

Literacy Disorders: Holistic Diagnosis & Remediation. Anthony V. Manzo & Ula C. Manzo. 512p. (C). 1993. pap. text 4.00 (*0-03-097349-X*, Pub. by Harcourt Coll Pubs); lib. bdg. write for info. (*0-03-072566-6*) Harcourt Coll Pubs.

Literacy, Economy & Society: Results of the 1st International Adult Literacy Survey. LC 96-700247. (ENG & FRE., Illus.). 200p. 1995. pap. 40.00 (*92-64-14655-5*, Pub. by Org for Econ) OECD.

Literacy, Education & Society in New Mexico, 1693-1821. Bernardo P. Gallegos. LC 91-40574. 127p. 1992. reprint ed. pap. 39.40 (*0-608-07281-8*, 206750900009) Bks Demand.

Literacy Education in the 21st Century: A Special Double Issue of the Peabody Journal of Education. Ed. by John W. Miller & Michael C. McKenna. 392p. 1999. pap. 45.00 (*0-8058-9804-2*) L Erlbaum Assocs.

Literacy, Emotion & Authority: Reading & Writing on a Polynesian Atoll. Niko Besnier. (Studies in the Social & Cultural Foundations of Language: No. 16). (Illus.). 254p. (C). 1995. text 59.95 (*0-521-48087-6*); pap. text 20.95 (*0-521-48539-8*) Cambridge U Pr.

Literacy Enhancement for Adults, Options: Expanding Educational Services for Adults. National Center for Research in Vocational Educati. 1987. 9.50 (*0-317-03901-6*, SP500FB) Ctr Educ Trng Employ.

Literacy Evaluation: Issues & Practicalities. Ed. by Chrystine Bouffler. LC 92-40331. 120p. (C). 1993. pap. text 16.50 (*0-435-08791-6*, 08791) Heinemann.

Literacy Events in a Community of Young Writers. Ed. by Yetta W. Goodman & Sandra Wilde. (Language & Literacy Ser.). 264p. (C). 1992. text 42.00 (*0-8077-3212-5*); pap. text 18.95 (*0-8077-3211-7*) Tchrs Coll.

Literacy for a Changing World. Frances Christie. (C). 1990. 60.00 (*0-86431-059-5*, Pub. by Aust Council Educ Res) St Mut.

Literacy for a Diverse Society: Perspectives, Practices, & Policies. Ed. by Elfrieda H. Hiebert. (Language & Literacy Ser.: No. 2). 328p. (C). 1991. text 47.00 (*0-8077-3098-X*) Tchrs Coll.

Literacy for a Diverse Society: Perspectives, Practices & Policies. Ed. by Elfrieda H. Hiebert. (Language & Literacy Ser.: No. 2). 328p. (C). 1991. pap. text 21.95 (*0-8077-3097-1*) Tchrs Coll.

Literacy for a Technological World. Michael J. Dyrenfurth. 37p. 1984. 3.75 (*0-318-22145-4*, IN266) Ctr Educ Trng Employ.

Literacy for All: Issues in Teaching & Learning. Ed. by Jean Osborn & Fran Lehr. LC 98-6175. 353p. 1998. pap. text 25.00 (*1-57230-349-2*, C0349); lib. bdg. 45.00 (*1-57230-348-4*, C0348) Guilford Pubns.

Literacy for All by 2001: Strategies at District Level (Based on 1991 Census Results) K. G. Jolly. (C). 1992. 14.00 (*81-7018-717-6*, Pub. by BR Pub) S Asia.

Literacy for Citizenship: Gender & Grassroots Dynamics in Brazil. Nelly P. Stromquist. LC 96-4548. (SUNY Series, Literacy, Culture, & Learning: Theory & Practice). 248p. (C). 1997. text 62.50 (*0-7914-3165-7*); pap. text 20.95 (*0-7914-3166-5*) State U NY Pr.

Literacy for Life: Adult Learners, New Practices. Hanna A. Fingeret & Cassandra Drennon. LC 97-20388. (Language & Literacy Ser.). 1997. 36.00 (*0-8077-3659-7*); pap. 16.95 (*0-8077-3658-9*) Tchrs Coll.

Literacy for Life: The Demand for Reading & Writing. Ed. by Richard W. Bailey & Robin M. Fosheim. LC 83-8265. x, 272p. 1983. pap. 19.75 (*0-87352-131-5*, J303P); lib. bdg. 37.50 (*0-87352-130-7*, J303C) Modern Lang.

Literacy for Social Change. 1993. 11.95 (*0-88336-557-X*) New Readers.

Literacy for Sustainable Development in the Age of Information. Naz Rassool. LC 98-44259. (Language & Education Library). 250p. 1999. pap. text 34.95 (*1-85359-432-6*) Multilingual Matters.

***Literacy for Sustainable Development in the Age of Information.** Naz Rassool. LC 98-44259. 250p. 1999. 95.00 (*1-85359-433-4*) Multilingual Matters.

Literacy for the 21st Century: A Balanced Approach. Gail E. Tompkins. LC 96-22788. 530p. (C). 1996. pap. 59.00 (*0-02-420651-2*, Macmillan Coll) P-H.

***Literacy for the 21st Century: A Balanced Approach.** 2nd ed. Gail E. Tompkins. LC 00-28375. 2001. write for info. (*0-13-017297-9*) Prntice Hall Bks.

Literacy for the Twenty-First Century: Research, Policy, Practices & the National Adult Literacy Survey. Ed. by M. Cecil Smith. LC 98-9946. 224p. 1998. 59.95 (*0-275-95786-1*, Praeger Pubs) Greenwood.

Literacy for Young Children. 2nd rev. ed. Terry S. Salinger. LC 94-47494. 336p. 1995. pap. text 36.00 (*0-02-405272-8*, Macmillan Coll) P-H.

***Literacy from Home to School: Reading with Alice.** Robin Campbell. 182p. 1999. pap. 19.95 (*1-85856-166-3*, Trentham Bks) Stylus Pub VA.

Literacy, Gender & Work in Families & in School. Judith W. Solsken. LC 92-27534. (Language & Educational Processes Ser.). 256p. 1993. text 73.25 (*0-89391-877-6*) Ablx Pub.

Literacy, Gender & Work in Families & School. Judith W. Solsken. LC 92-27534. (Language & Educational Processes Ser.). 256p. 1993. pap. 39.50 (*0-89391-918-7*) Ablx Pub.

Literacy Goes to School: The Parents' Role in Young Children's Literacy Learning. Jo Weinberger. (One-Off Ser.). (Illus.). 176p. 1996. pap. (*1-85396-292-9*) Corwin Pr.

Literacy, Home, & School: Research & Practice in Teaching Literacy with Parents. Peter Hannon. LC 94-37537. 178p. 1994. 85.00 (*0-7507-0359-8*, Falmer Pr); pap. 27.95 (*0-7507-0360-1*, Falmer Pr) Taylor & Francis.

Literacy Hour & Language Knowledge: Developing Literacy Through Fiction & Poetry. Peta Lloyd. 1999. pap. text 26.95 (*1-85346-578-X*) Taylor & Francis.

Literacy, Ideology, & Dialogue: Towards a Dialogic Pedagogy. Irene Ward. LC 94-4832. (SUNY Series, Teacher Empowerment & School Reform). 225p. (C). 1994. text 49.50 (*0-7914-2197-X*); pap. text 16.95 (*0-7914-2198-8*) State U NY Pr.

Literacy-Illiteracy in the World: A Bibliography, 6. Compiled by John Hladczuk et al. LC 89-27165. (Bibliographies & Indexes in Education Ser.: No. 6). 216p. 1989. lib. bdg. 65.00 (*0-313-26252-7*, ELU/, Greenwood Pr) Greenwood.

Literacy in a Digital World. Kathleen Tyner. LC 98-25290. 300p. 1998. 65.00 (*0-8058-2227-5*); pap. write for info. (*0-8058-2226-7*) L Erlbaum Assocs.

Literacy in Action. David Wray et al. 200p. 1989. 75.00 (*1-85000-604-0*, Falmer Pr); pap. 34.95 (*1-85000-605-9*, Falmer Pr) Taylor & Francis.

***Literacy in African American Communities.** Ed. by Joyce L. Harris et al. LC 99-88717. 288p. 2000. write for info. (*0-8058-3401-X*) L Erlbaum Assocs.

***Literacy in African American Communities.** Joyce L. Harris et al. LC 99-88717. 288p. 2000. pap. write for info. (*0-8058-3402-8*) L Erlbaum Assocs.

Literacy in American Schools: Learning to Read & Write. Ed. by Nancy L. Stein. LC 85-24625. 224p. (C). 1986. pap. text 14.50 (*0-226-77178-4*) U Ch Pr.

Literacy in Colonial New England: An Inquiry into the Social Context of Literacy in the Early Modern West. Kenneth A. Lockridge. (Illus.). 164p. (C). 1974. 9.75 (*0-393-05522-1*) Norton.

Literacy in Colonial New England: An Inquiry into the Social Context of Literacy in the Early Modern West. Kenneth A. Lockridge. (Illus.). 164p. (C). 1975. pap. text 5.50 (*0-393-09263-1*) Norton.

Literacy in Contexts: Australian Perspectives & Issues. Ed. by Allan Luke & Pamela Gilbert. 144p. (Orig.). 1993. pap. text 14.95 (*1-86373-340-X*, Pub. by Allen & Unwin Pty) Paul & Co Pubs.

Literacy in Human Development. Marta K. Oliveira & Jane Valsiner. LC 97-35105. 1998. 73.25 (*1-56750-366-7*); pap. 39.50 (*1-56750-367-5*) Ablx Pub.

Literacy in Lifeskills, Bk. I. Sally Gati. (J). 1992. pap. text 15.95 (*0-8384-3846-6*) Heinle & Heinle.

Literacy in Lifeskills, Bk. II. S. Gati. (J). 1992. pap. text 15.95 (*0-8384-3907-1*) Heinle & Heinle.

Literacy in Medieval Celtic Societies. Contrib. by Huw Pryce et al. LC 97-9721. (Studies in Medieval Literature: No. 33). (Illus.). 314p. (C). 1998. text 64.95 (*0-521-57039-5*) Cambridge U Pr.

Literacy in Multimedia America: Integrating Media Across the Curriculum. Ladislaus Semali. Ed. by Joe Kincheloe & Shirley R. Steinberg. (Critical Education Practice Ser.). 250p. Date not set. text 38.00 (*0-8153-2295-X*); pap. text 18.95 (*0-8153-2293-3*) Garland.

Literacy in Nursery Education. Robin Campbell. 72p. 1996. pap. 9.00 (*1-85856-064-0*, Trentham Bks) Stylus Pub VA.

***Literacy in Perspective.** Rose et al. 2000. pap. text 46.95 (*0-312-25042-8*) St Martin.

Literacy in Process: The Heinemann Reader. Ed. by Brenda M. Power & Ruth Hubbard. LC 90-37651. 352p. (C). 1990. pap. text 29.50 (*0-435-08532-8*, 08532); pap. text, teacher ed. 5.50 (*0-435-08533-6*, 08533) Heinemann.

Literacy in School & Society: Multidisciplinary Perspectives. E. Z. Sonino. (Topics in Language & Literature Ser.). (Illus.). 312p. (C). 1989. 65.00 (*0-306-43166-1*, Plenum Trade) Perseus Pubng.

Literacy in Science, Technology & the Language Arts: An Interdisciplinary Inquiry. Mary Hamm & Dennis Adams. LC 98-3300. 216p. 1998. 59.95 (*0-89789-575-4*, Bergin & Garvey); pap. 18.95 (*0-89789-576-2*, Bergin & Garvey) Greenwood.

***Literacy in the Age of the Internet.** Todd Taylor. LC 98-21549. 200p. 1998. pap. 17.50 (*0-231-11331-5*); lib. bdg. 47.50 (*0-231-11330-7*) Col U Pr.

***Literacy in the Labor Force: Results from the National Adult Literacy Survey.** Andrew Sum. LC 99-490821. 360p. 1999. per. 33.00 (*0-16-050175-X*) USGPO.

Literacy in the Library: Negotiating the Spaces Between Order & Desire. Mark Dressman. LC 97-18571. (Critical Studies in Education & Culture). 216p. 1997. 57.95 (*0-89789-495-2*, Bergin & Garvey) Greenwood.

Literacy in the Open-Access College. Richard C. Richardson et al. LC 83-11999. (Jossey-Bass Higher Education Ser.). 207p. reprint ed. pap. 64.20 (*0-8357-4919-3*, 203784900009) Bks Demand.

An Asterisk (*) at the beginning of an entry indicates that the title is appearing for the first time.

Literacy in the Pre-School. Bronwyn Reynolds. 72p. 1997. pap. 11.95 (*1-85856-075-6*, Trentham Bks) Stylus Pub VA.

Literacy in the Roman World. Mary Beard et al. (JRA Supplementary Ser.: No. 3). (ENG & FRE., Illus.). 198p. 1991. 39.75 (*1-887829-03-2*) Jour Roman Arch.

Literacy in the Television Age. 2nd ed. Susan B. Newman. (Illus.). 232p. 1995. pap. 39.50 (*1-56750-162-1*); text 73.25 (*1-56750-161-3*) Ablx Pub.

Literacy in the United States: Readers & Reading since 1880. Carl F. Kaestle. (Illus.). 352p. (C). 1991. 45.00 (*0-300-04946-3*) Yale U Pr.

Literacy in the United States: Readers & Reading since 1880. Carl F. Kaestle et al. LC 90-46716. 352p. (C). 1993. reprint ed. pap. 20.00 (*0-300-05430-0*) Yale U Pr.

Literacy in Traditional Societies. Ed. by Jack Goody. LC 69-10427. 358p. reprint ed. pap. 102.10 (*0-608-12078-2*, 2024575) Bks Demand.

***Literacy, Inquiry & Teaching.** Gretchen Owocki. 2001. pap. text. write for info. (*0-325-00270-3*) Heinemann.

Literacy Instruction Content Area. Patricia Anders. LC 95-79772. (C). 1995. pap. text 34.00 (*0-15-500820-X*, Pub. by Harcourt Coll Pubs) Harcourt.

Literacy Instruction for Culturally & Linguistically Diverse Students: A Collection of Articles & Commentaries. Michael F. Opitz & International Reading Association Staff. LC 98-27561. 1998. 29.95 (*0-87207-194-4*) Intl Reading.

Literacy Instruction in Half- & Whole-Day Kindergarten: Research to Practice. Lesley M. Morrow et al. LC 98-12319. (Literacy Studies Ser.). 1998. pap. 24.95 (*0-87207-188-X*, 188) Intl Reading.

Literacy Instruction In Multicultural Settings. Kathryn H. Au. 224p. (C). 1993. pap. text 34.00 (*0-03-076847-0*, Pub. by Harcourt Coll Pubs) Harcourt.

Literacy, Intellectual Property, & the Status Quo. Andrea A. Lunsford. Ed. by Lillian Bridwell-Bowles & Kim Donehower. (Technical Reports: Vol. 6). 12p. (Orig.). 1996. pap. 2.00 (*1-881221-12-1*) U Minn Ctr Interdis.

Literacy Intercrossings: East Asia & the West. Ed. by Mabel Lee & A. D. Syrokomia-Stefanowska. (University of Sydney World Literature Ser.: Vol. 2). 226p. (C). 1998. pap. text 27.00 (*0-9586526-5-1*) UH Pr.

Literacy Is Not Enough: Essays on the Importance of Reading. Brian Cox. 208p. 1999. pap. 19.95 (*0-7190-5669-1*) Manchester Univ Pr.

Literacy, Language & Community Publishing: Essays in Adult Education. Ed. by Jane Mace. LC 94-47982. 1995. 84.95 (*1-85359-280-3*, Pub. by Multilingual Matters); pap. 34.95 (*1-85359-279-X*, Pub. by Multilingual Matters) Taylor & Francis.

Literacy, Law, & Social Order. Edward W. Stevens. LC 87-16016. 1988. text 32.00 (*0-87580-131-5*) N Ill U Pr.

Literacy Learning: A Revolution in Progress. David B. Doake. LC 94-27467. (Illus.). 430p. (Orig.). (C). 1995. pap. text 25.95 (*0-7802-2680-1*) Wright Group.

Literacy Learning in the Early Years: Through Children's Eyes. Linda Gibson. (Early Childhood Education Ser.: No. 22). 192p. 1989. pap. text 17.95 (*0-8077-2952-3*) Tchrs Coll.

Literacy Map: Guiding Children to Where They Need to Be. J. Richard Gentry. LC 99-45900. (Illus.). 144p. (gr. k-3). 1999. 21.95 (*1-57255-737-0*) Mondo Pubng.

***Literacy Matters: Writing & Reading the Social Self** Robert Yagelski. LC 99-36582. (Language & Literacy Ser.). 240p. 1999. pap. text 25.95 (*0-8077-3892-1*) Tchrs Coll.

***Literacy Matters: Writing & Reading the Social Self.** Robert Yagelski. LC 99-36582. (Language & Literacy Ser.). 240p. 1999. write for info. (*0-8077-3893-X*) Tchrs Coll.

Literacy Moments to Report Cards. Linda Wasson-Ellam. LC 94-31530. 125p. 1994. pap. text 16.50 (*0-435-08838-6*, 08838) Heinemann.

Literacy Myth: Cultural Integration & Social Structure in the Nineteenth Century. Harvey J. Graff. 352p. (C). 1991. pap. 24.95 (*0-88738-884-1*) Transaction Pubs.

Literacy, Not Labels: Celebrating Students' Strengths Through Whole Language. Kathleen Strickland. LC 94-46635. 162p. 1995. pap. text 21.00 (*0-86709-354-4*, 0354, Pub. by Boynton Cook Pubs) Heinemann.

Literacy of Older Adults in America: Results from the National Adult Literacy Survey. Helen Brown. 203p. (Orig.). 1996. pap. 18.00 (*0-16-048896-6*) USGPO.

Literacy of Older Adults in America: Results from the National Adult Literacy Survey. Helen Brown et al. (Illus.). 187p. (Orig.). (C). 1997. pap. text 40.00 (*0-7881-3998-3*) DIANE Pub.

Literacy Online: The Promise (& Peril) of Reading & Writing with Computers. Ed. by Myron C. Tuman. LC 91-50754. (Series in Composition, Literacy, & Culture). (Illus.). 304p. (C). 1992. pap. 19.95 (*0-8229-5465-6*); text 49.95 (*0-8229-3701-8*) U of Pittsburgh Pr.

***Literacy Partners Books & Hands-On Library, Set.** Irene D. H. Sasman. (Illus.). (J). (gr. k-3). 1998. pap. 99.95 (*1-56831-533-3*) Lrning Connect.

***Literacy Partners Books & Hands-On Library, Set.** Irene D. H. Sasman. (Illus.). (J). (gr. 3-4). 1998. pap. 99.95 (*1-56831-536-8*) Lrning Connect.

***Literacy Partners Books & Hands-On Library, Set.** Irene D. H. Sasman. (Illus.). (J). (ps-1). 1998. pap. 99.95 (*1-56831-532-5*) Lrning Connect.

Literacy Points Workbook. Janet Spiegel-Podnecky. 1990. pap. text, wbk. ed. 7.89 (*0-201-50810-9*) Addison-Wesley.

Literacy, Politics, & Artistic Innovation in the Early Medieval West: Papers Delivered at a Symposium on Early Medieval Culture, Bryn Mawr College, Bryn Mawr, PA. Ed. by Celia M. Chazelle. (Illus.). 146p. (Orig.). (C). 1992. pap. text 19.50 (*0-8191-8563-9*); lib. bdg. 41.50 (*0-8191-8562-0*) U Pr of Amer.

Literacy Portfolios: Using Assessment to Guide Instruction. Roberta B. Wiener & Judith H. Cohen. LC 96-44644. (Illus.). 351p. (C). 1997. pap. 40.00 (*0-02-427472-0*) Macmillan.

Literacy Portfolios in Action. Valencia. LC 97-71347. (C). 1997. pap. text 35.00 (*0-15-505139-3*, Pub. by Harcourt Coll Pubs) Harcourt.

***Literacy, Power & Social Justice.** Adrian Blackledge. 204p. 2000. pap. 24.94 (*1-85856-158-2*, Trentham Bks) Stylus Pub VA.

Literacy Practices. Mike Baynham. LC 93-39308. 1999. text. write for info. (*0-582-08709-0*, Pub. by Addison-Wesley) Longman.

Literacy Programs for Adults with Developmental Disabilities. Gerard Giordano. 360p. 1996. pap. 39.95 (*1-56593-629-9*, 1304) Thomson Learn.

Literacy Schools in a Rural Society: A Study of Yemissrach Dimts Literacy Campaign in Ethiopia. Margareta Sjostrom & Rolf Sjostrom. (Research Report Ser.: No. 39). 130p. 1977. write for info. (*91-7106-109-6*, Pub. by Nordic Africa) Transaction Pubs.

Literacy Shutdown: Language, Arrogance & American Women. Daphne Key. LC 98-34002. (Literacy Studies Ser.). 1998. pap. 19.95 (*0-87207-196-0*, 196) Intl Reading.

Literacy Skills for the Knowledge Society: Further Results from the International Adult Literacy Survey. Nancy Darcovich et al. LC 98-700475. (Illus.). 195p. 1997. 41.75 (*92-64-15624-0*) Org for Econ.

Literacy, Socialization & Employment. Catherine Sterq. 128p. 1993. pap. 24.95 (*1-85302-209-8*) Taylor & Francis.

Literacy, Society, & Schooling. Ed. by Suzanne De Castell et al. (Illus.). 352p. 1986. pap. text 29.95 (*0-521-31340-6*) Cambridge U Pr.

Literacy Student Book. 1997. text 10.55 (*0-673-43786-8*) Addison-Wesley.

Literacy, Technology & Society: Confronting the Issues. Gail E. Hawisher & Cynthia L. Selfe. LC 96-39125. 604p. (C). 1996. pap. text 42.00 (*0-13-227588-0*) P-H.

Literacy Through Literature. Terry D. Johnson & Daphne R. Louis. LC 87-14831. 168p. (Orig.). (C). (ps). 1987. pap. 19.50 (*0-435-08451-8*, 08451) Heinemann.

Literacy Through Play. Gretchen Owocki. LC 98-54827. 126p. 1999. pap. text 17.00 (*0-325-00127-8*) Heinemann.

Literacy Through Symbols: Improving Access for Children & Adults. Tina Detheridge & Mike Detheridge. LC 97-197225. 144p. 1997. pap. 24.95 (*1-85346-483-X*, Pub. by David Fulton) Taylor & Francis.

Literacy Through the Book Arts. Paul Johnson. LC 93-18134. 164p. (C). 1993. pap. 18.95 (*0-435-08766-5*, 08766) Heinemann.

Literacy Through Whole Language. Len Zarry. (Illus.). 216p. (gr. k-3). 1991. pap. 18.00 (*1-895411-33-5*) Peguis Pubs Ltd.

***Literacy Today: Standards Across the Curriculum.** Dennis M. Adams & Mary Hamm. LC 99-53868. (Reference Library of Social Science). 2000. pap. write for info. (*0-8153-3404-4*) Garland.

Literacy with an Attitude: Educating Working-Class Children in Their Own Self-Interest. Patrick J. Finn. LC 99-26086. 288p. (C). 1999. pap. text 16.95 (*0-7914-4286-1*) State U NY Pr.

Literacy with an Attitude: Educating Working-Class Children in Their Own Self-Interest. Patrick J. Finn. LC 99-26086. 288p. (C). 1999. text 49.50 (*0-7914-4285-3*) State U NY Pr.

Literacy Workbook. Steven J. Molinsky. (C). 1998. pap. 13.33 (*0-13-150939-X*) P-H.

Literacy Workshop Photocopy Masters. (Training by Design Ser.). 1994. 40.00 (*1-56420-038-8*, 2038-8) New Readers.

Literacy Workshop Presentations, 2 vols., Vols. 1 & 2. 1994. 125.00 (*1-56420-036-1*, 2036-1) New Readers.

Literacy's Beginnings: Supporting Young Readers & Writers. 3rd ed. Lea M. McGee & Richgels. LC 99-40038. 396p. 1999. pap. text 51.00 (*0-205-29931-8*, Longwood Div) Allyn.

Literae Cantuarienses: The Letter Books of the Monastery of Christ Church, Canterbury, 3 vols. Ed. by J. B. Sheppard. (Rolls Ser.: No. 85). 1969. reprint ed. 210.00 (*0-8115-1158-8*) Periodicals Srv.

Literal Exposition of Job: A Scriptual Commentary Concerning Providence. Aquinas, Thomas, Saint. Tr. by Anthony Damico. LC 88-31855. (American Academy of Religion, Classics in Religious Studies). 496p. 1989. 62.95 (*1-55540-291-7*, 01-05-07); pap. 41.95 (*1-55540-292-5*) OUP.

Literal Figures: Puritan Allegory & the Reformation Crisis in Representation. Thomas H. Luxon. LC 94-30412. 262p. 1995. 28.00 (*0-226-49785-2*) U Ch Pr.

Literal Interpretation of the Bible. Paul L. Tan. LC 78-73220. 1978. pap. text 2.95 (*0-932940-04-8*) Bible Coms.

Literal Lee & His Very Own Self. Jim George. LC 96-5810. (Ha! Ser.). (Illus.). 32p. (Orig.). (J). (ps up). 1996. pap. write for info. (*1-56844-049-9*) Enchante Pub.

Literal Literacy: What Every American Needs to Know First. George Kovacs. LC 93-28139. 184p. 1993. text 79.95 (*0-7734-3042-3*) E Mellen.

Literal Literacy II: What Every American Needs to Know Second. George Kovacs. LC 93-26232. 156p. 1993. text 69.95 (*0-7734-3044-X*) E Mellen.

Literal Madness: Three Novels, My Death My Life by Pier Paulo Pasolini; Kathy Goes to Haiti; Florida. Kathy Acker. LC 87-14860. 352p. 1989. pap. 12.00 (*0-8021-3156-5*, Grove) Grove-Atltic.

Literal Meaning of Genesis. Augustine, Saint. Tr. & Anno. by John H. Taylor. (Ancient Christian Writers Ser.: No. 41, Vol. 1). 292p. 1983. 29.95 (*0-8091-0326-5*) Paulist Pr.

Literal Meaning of Genesis. Augustine, Saint. Tr. & Anno. by John H. Taylor. (Ancient Christian Writers Ser.: No. 42, Vol. 2). 358p. 1983. 22.95 (*0-8091-0327-3*) Paulist Pr.

***Literal Translation Bible.** 2000. 59.95 (*1-878442-75-9*) Sovreign Grace Pubs.

Literal Translation of the Holy Bible. 3rd ed. Jay P. Green. 1995. 49.99 (*1-878442-73-2*) Moravian Ch in Amer.

Literal Truth: Rizzoli Dreams of Eating the Apple of Earthly Delights. Mark Ciabattari. LC 94-70904. 128p. (Orig.). 1994. pap. 12.00 (*0-9630164-7-4*) Canios Edit.

Literal Violence *see* **Paperplay Mini-Books**

Literal Word: Revelation. M. D. Treece. 1997. 29.99 (*1-56043-303-5*, Treasure Hse) Destiny Image.

Literal Word: The Acts. M. D. Treece. 532p. (Orig.). 1993. 29.99 (*1-56043-779-0*, Treasure Hse) Destiny Image.

Literal Word: The Acts I. M. D. Treece. 532p. 1993. 29.99 (*1-56043-533-X*, Treasure Hse) Destiny Image.

Literal Word: The Acts II. M. D. Treece. 444p. 1993. 29.99 (*1-56043-533-X*, Treasure Hse) Destiny Image.

Literal Word: The I Corinthians. M. D. Treece. 460p. (Orig.). 1995. 29.99 (*1-56043-844-4*, Treasure Hse) Destiny Image.

Literal World. unabridged ed. Jean Day. LC 98-137442. 112p. 1998. pap. 12.95 (*1-891190-01-6*, Pub. by Atelos) SPD-Small Pr Dist.

Literally Entitled: A Dictionary of the Origins of the Titles of over 1,300 Major Literary Works of the Nineteenth & Twentieth Century. Adrian Room. LC 95-38299. 255p. 1996. lib. bdg. 48.50 (*0-7864-0110-9*) McFarland & Co.

Literally Horses: Artistic Expressions of the Horse - Collection I. Laurie A. Cerny. Ed. by Renee Puckett. LC 98-94877. (Illus.). 56p. 1999. pap. 8.95 (*0-9644233-3-2*, Pub. by Equestrienne) Amazon Com.

Literarische Einheit des Johannesevangeliums: Der Gegenwartige Stand der Einschlagigen Forschungen: Mit Einem Vorwort von Martin Hengel. Eugen Ruckstuhl. (Novum Testamentum et Orbis Antiquus Ser.: Vol. 5). (GER.). 331p. 1987. text 61.75 (*3-7278-0542-0*, Pub. by Presses Univ Fribourg) Eisenbrauns.

Literarische Formalistische Versuche Zu Seiner Bestimmung. Andras Horn. (C). 1978. 104.60 (*3-11-007600-4*) De Gruyter.

Literarische Handschriften: Einfuhrung in die (Critique Genetique) Almuth Gresillon. 311p. 1999. 34.95 (*3-906760-65-0*) P Lang.

Literarische Keilschrifttexte aus Uruk. Adam Falkenstein. LC 78-72735. (Ancient Mesopotamian Texts & Studies). reprint ed. 27.50 (*0-404-18174-0*) AMS Pr.

Literarische Nachlass, 3 vols., Set. Giorgio Vasari. (Illus.). xli, 1994p. 1982. reprint ed. write for info. (*3-487-07214-9*) G Olms Pubs.

Literarische Portrat der Griechen Im Funften und Vierten Jahrhundert v. Chr. - Die Personlichkeit in der Geschichtsschreibung der Alten, 2 vols. in 1. Ivo Bruns. 715p. 1985. reprint ed. 135.00 (*3-487-00082-2*) G Olms Pubs.

Literarische Praxis von Frauen Um, 1800. Anita Runge. (Germanistische Texte und Studien: Bd. 55). 267p. 1997. 40.00 (*3-487-10259-5*) G Olms Pubs.

Literarische Spurensuche Psychischer und Physischer Konsequenzen der Sudafrikanischen Apartheidspolitik. Ellen Putzki. (Europaische Hochschulschriften, Reihe 14: No. 335). 327p. 1997. 57.95 (*3-631-31302-0*) P Lang Pubng.

Literarische Werk Neil Munros. Hermann Volkel. Ed. by Horst W. Drescher. (Scottish Studies International: Bd. 22). (GER.). 311p. 1996. 57.95 (*3-631-46080-5*) P Lang Pubng.

Literarische Zensur in der BRD Nach, 1945. Silke Buschmann. (GER.). 139p. 1997. 32.95 (*3-631-31923-1*) P Lang Pubng.

Literarischen Beziehungen Zwischen Den Buchern Jeremia und Ezechiel. Dieter Vieweger. (Beitrage zur Erforschung des Alten Testaments & Antiken Judentums Ser.: Bd. 26). (GER.). 220p. 1993. 38.80 (*3-631-40725-4*) P Lang Pubng.

Literarisches Zentralblatt Fur Deutschland, 1850-1945. reprint ed. write for info. (*0-318-71840-5*) G Olms Pubs.

***Literarisierung ALS Aneignung Von Alteritat.** Klaus Maiwald. 425p. 1999. 56.95 (*3-631-34609-3*) P Lang Pubng.

Literarisierungsprozefs der Volksaufklarung des Spaten 18. und Fruhen 19. Jahrhunderts: Dargestellt Anhand der Volksschriften von Schlosser, Rochow, Becker, Salzmann und Hebel Mit Einer Aktualisierten Bibliographie der Volksaufklarungsschriften. Annegret Volpel. (GER.). 1996. 69.95 (*3-631-48802-5*) P Lang Pubng.

Literary Absolute. Philippe Lacoue-Labarthe & Jean-Luc Nancy. Tr. by Philip Barnard & Cheryl Lester from FRE. LC 87-10047. (SUNY Series, Intersections: Philosophy & Critical Theory). 169p. (C). 1988. pap. text 19.95 (*0-88706-661-5*) State U NY Pr.

Literary Absolute: The Theory of Literature in German Romanticism. Philippe Lacoue-Labarthe & Jean-Luc Nancy. Tr. by Philip Barnard & Cheryl Lester from FRE. LC 87-10047. (SUNY Series, Intersections: Philosophy & Critical Theory). 169p. (C). 1988. text 59.50 (*0-88706-660-7*) State U NY Pr.

Literary Admirers of Alfred Stieglitz. F. Richard Thomas. LC 82-10543. (Illus.). 128p. 1983. 21.95 (*0-8093-1097-X*) S Ill U Pr.

***Literary Aesthetics: An Anthology.** Alan Singer. 288p. 1999. pap. 27.95 (*0-631-20869-0*) Blackwell Pubs.

Literary Aftershocks: American Writers, Readers, & the Bomb. Albert E. Stone. (Twayne's Literature & Society Ser.). 225p. 1994. 26.95 (*0-8057-8853-0*, Twyne) Mac Lib Ref.

Literary Agents: A Writer's Guide. Ed. by Adam Begley. LC 83-617350. 192p. 1993. pap. 10.00 (*0-913734-17-9*) Poets & Writers.

Literary Agents: A Writer's Guide. Adam Begley. 96p. 1993. pap. 12.95 (*0-14-017215-7*, Penguin Bks) Viking Penguin.

***Literary Agents: A Writer's Introduction.** John F. Baker. LC 98-50769. 256p. 1999. pap. 14.95 (*0-02-861740-1*, Pub. by Macmillan) S&S Trade.

Literary Agents: The Essential Guide for Writers. Debby Mayer. LC 97-34446. 172p. 1998. pap. 12.95 (*0-14-026873-1*) Viking Penguin.

Literary Agents: What They Do, How They Do It, How to Find & Work with the Right One for You. rev. ed. Michael Larsen. LC 95-53093. 207p. 1996. pap. 15.95 (*0-471-13046-X*) Wiley.

Literary Agent's Guide to Getting Published & Making Money from Your Writing. Bill Adler, Jr. LC 99-21349. 288p. 1999. pap. 14.95 (*1-892025-00-0*, Pub. by Claren Bks) IPG Chicago.

Literary Agents of North America. 3rd ed. Ed. by Arthur Orrmont & Leonie Rosenstiel. 200p. (Orig.). 1988. pap. 19.95 (*0-911085-04-1*) Author Aid.

Literary Agents of North America. 5th rev. ed. Arthur Orrmont & Leonie Rosenstiel. (Orig.). 1993. pap. 33.00 (*0-911085-12-2*) Author Aid.

Literary Agents of North America: 1984-85 Marketplace. Ed. by Author Aid-Research Associates International Staff. 144p. (Orig.). 1984. pap. 16.95 (*0-911085-00-9*, 0082-1) Author Aid.

***Literary Almanac.** 288p. 1999. 7.98 (*1-56731-328-0*, MJF Bks) Fine Comms.

Literary America: A Chronicle of American Writers from 1607-1952. David E. Scherman & Rosemarie Redlich. LC 75-76. (Illus.). 175p. 1978. reprint ed. lib. bdg. 49.75 (*0-8371-8017-1*, SCLA, Greenwood Pr) Greenwood.

Literary America: An Introduction to the Literature of the United States. Sigmund Ro. 310p. (C). 1997. pap. 37.00 (*82-00-21954-2*, Pub. by Scand Univ Pr) IBD Ltd.

Literary America, 1903-1934: The Mary Austin Letters, 5. Ed. by T. M. Pearce. LC 78-67914. (Contributions in Women's Studies: No. 5). (Illus.). 296p. 1979. 55.00 (*0-313-20636-8*, PEL/, Greenwood Pr) Greenwood.

***Literary Analysis of Charlotte Delbo's Concentration Camp Writings.** Nicole Thatcher. LC 99-48755. 224p. 2000. 89.95 (*0-7734-7826-4*) E Mellen.

Literary Anatomies: Women's Bodies & Health in Literature. Delese Wear & Lois L. Nixon. LC 93-26096. (Illus.). 150p. (C). 1994. text 49.50 (*0-7914-1925-8*); pap. text 16.95 (*0-7914-1926-6*) State U NY Pr.

Literary & Art Theories in Japan. Makoto Ueda. LC 91-319. (Michigan Classics in Japanese Studies: No. 6). xiv, 274p. 1991. reprint ed. pap. 12.50 (*0-939512-52-1*) U MI Japan.

Literary & Characteristic Lives: To Which Are Added a Dissertation on Public Spirit; & Three Essays. William Smellie. LC 78-67540. reprint ed. 67.50 (*0-404-17203-2*) AMS Pr.

Literary & Cultural Journeys: Selected Letters to Arturo Torres-Rioseco. 2nd ed. Ed. by Carlota Caulfield et al. Tr. by Rosalie Torres-Rioseco & Rose Passalacqua. (ENG & SPA., Illus.). 231p. (Orig.). 1995. pap. 20.00 (*0-9648938-1-9*) Mills Coll Ctr Bk.

Literary & Cultural Spaces of Restoration London. Cynthia Wall. LC 98-13380. (Illus.). 300p. (C). 1999. 59.95 (*0-521-63013-4*) Cambridge U Pr.

Literary & Educational Effects of the Thought of John Henry Newman. Ed. by Michael Sundermeier & Robert Churchill. LC 94-38965. (Roman Catholic Studies: Vol. 7). 276p. 1995. text 89.95 (*0-7734-8984-3*) E Mellen.

Literary & Educational Writings, 2 vols. Desiderius Erasmus. Ed. by J. Kelley Sowards. (Collected Works of Erasmus: Vols. 25 & 26). 752p. 1985. text 110.00 (*0-8020-5521-4*) U of Toronto Pr.

Literary & Educational Writings, 2 vols., Set, Vols. 5 & 6. Desiderius Erasmus. Ed. & Tr. by A. H. Levi from LAT. (Collected Works of Erasmus: Nos. 27 & 28). 668p. 1986. text 110.00 (*0-8020-5602-4*) U of Toronto Pr.

Literary & Educational Writings, Vol. 7. Desiderius Erasmus. Ed. by Elaine Fantham & Erika Rummel. (Collected Works of Erasmus: No. 29). 608p. 1989. text 110.00 (*0-8020-5818-3*) U of Toronto Pr.

Literary & Educational Writings: Antibarbari, de Copia, de Rationae Studii, Parabolae. Desiderius Erasmus. Ed. by Craig R. Thompson. LC 78-6904. (Collected Works of Erasmus: Vols. 23 & 24). 1978. text 110.00 (*0-8020-5395-5*) U of Toronto Pr.

Literary & Epigraphical Testimonia. R. E. Wycherley. LC 75-517025. (Athenian Agora Ser.: Vol. 3). (Illus.). x, 260p. 1973. reprint ed. 25.00 (*0-87661-203-6*) Am Sch Athens.

Literary & Historical Miscellanies. George Bancroft. 1977. 22.95 (*0-8369-7208-2*, 8007) Ayer.

Literary & Historical Miscellanies. George Bancroft. (Works of George Bancroft). 1989. reprint ed. lib. bdg. 79.00 (*0-685-27846-8*) Rprt Serv.

Literary & Historical Perspectives of the Middle Ages: Proceedings of the 1981 SEMA Conference. Ed. by Patricia W. Cummins. 232p. 1982. pap. 12.00 (*0-937058-15-7*) West Va U Pr.

Literary & Linguistic History of New Brunswick. Reavley Gair. 286p. 1985. 19.95 (*0-86492-052-0*, Pub. by Goose Ln Edits); pap. 11.95 (*0-86492-039-3*, Pub. by Goose Ln Edits) Genl Dist Srvs.

L

An Asterisk (*) at the beginning of an entry indicates that the title is appearing for the first time.

L

Literary & Linguistic Terms: Arabic-Arabic. Magdi Wahba & Muhandes. (ARA & ENG.). 266p. 35.00 (*0-86685-131-3*, LDL1313, Pub. by Librairie du Liban) Intl Bk Ctr.

Literary & Media Texts in Secondary English: New Strategies. Andrew Goodwyn. 160p. 1999. 69.95 (*0-304-70358-3*); pap. 21.50 (*0-304-70359-1*) Continuum.

Literary & Miscellaneous Texts in the Ashmolean Museum. Ed. by Oliver R. Gurney. (Oxford Editions of Cuneiform Texts Ser.: Vol. XI). (Illus.). 88p. 1989. pap. 68.00 (*0-19-815468-2*) OUP.

Literary & Rhetorical Theories in Greek Scholia. Roos Meijering. xi, 327p. (C). 1987. 52.00 (*90-6980-011-X*, Pub. by Egbert Forsten) Hod1der & Stoughton.

Literary Anecdotes of the Eighteenth Century, 9 vols. John Nichols. LC 11-32672. reprint ed. 425.00 (*0-404-04720-3*) AMS Pr.

Literary Anecdotes of the Nineteenth Century, 2 vols. William R. Nicoll & Thomas J. Wise. LC 11-21329. reprint ed. 115.00 (*0-404-04717-3*) AMS Pr.

Literary Angels. Ed. by Harriet S. Chessman. 288p. 1994. pap. 10.00 (*0-449-90774-0*) Fawcett.

Literary Annuals & Gift Books: A Bibliography, 1823-1903. Frederick Faxon. 220p. 1973. 20.00 (*0-900002-62-X*, Pub. by Priv Lib Assn) Oak Knoll.

Literary Anthropology: A New Interdisciplinary Approach to People, Signs & Literature. Ed. by Fernando Poyatos. LC 87-21820. xxiii, 342p. (C). 1988. 97.00 (*90-272-2041-7*); pap. 27.95 (*90-272-2059-X*) J Benjamins Pubng Co.

Literary Antipietism in Germany During the First Half of the Eighteenth Century. William E. Petig. LC 83-49223. (Stanford German Studies: Vol. 22). 236p. (Orig.). (C). 1984. pap. text 22.65 (*0-8204-0087-4*) P Lang Pubng.

Literary Appreciations. George M. Harper. LC 74-117802. (Essay Index Reprint Ser.). 1977. 21.95 (*0-8369-1754-5*) Ayer.

***Literary Appropriations of the Anglo-Saxons from the Thirteenth to the Twentieth Century.** Ed. by Donald G. Scragg & Carole Weinberg. (Cambridge Studies in Anglo-Saxon England: No. 39). (Illus.). 257p. (C). 2000. 69.95 (*0-521-63215-3*) Cambridge U Pr.

Literary Architecture: Essays Toward a Tradition: Walter Pater, Gerard Manley Hopkins, Marcel Proust, Henry James. Ellen E. Frank. (Illus.). 328p. 1979. pap. 15.95 (*0-520-04772-9*, Pub. by U CA Pr) Cal Prin Full Svc.

Literary Art of Eugene Fromentin: A Study in Style & Motif. Arthur R. Evans. LC 64-18123. 168p. 1964. reprint ed. pap. 52.10 (*0-608-05957-9*, 206629400008) Bks Demand.

Literary Art of the Bible: A Commentary. Mario D'Avanzo. 266p. (C). 1988. pap. text 24.95 (*0-89641-172-9*) American Pr.

Literary Artistry in Leviticus. Wilfried Warning. LC 98-30142. (Biblical Interpretation Ser.: Vol. 35). xiv, 256p. 1998. 75.00 (*90-04-11235-9*) Brill Academic Pubs.

Literary Arts, Bk 2. LC 64-19848. write for info. U Ch Pr.

Literary Authority & the Modern Chinese Writer: Ambivalence & Autobiography. Wendy Larson. LC 90-27835. 222p. 1991. text 42.95 (*0-8223-1113-5*) Duke.

Literary Ballad in Early Nineteenth-Century Russian Literature. Michael Katz. (Oxford Modern Languages & Literature Monographs). 1976. 24.95 (*0-19-815528-X*) OUP.

Literary Based Seasonal. Ed. by Scholastic, Inc. Staff. 1991. pap. 12.95 (*0-590-49134-2*) Scholastic Inc.

Literary Begins at Birth see Your Child Learns to Read & Write

Literary Bent: In Search of High Art in Contemporary American Writing. James D. Bloom. LC 96-36882. (Penn Studies in Contemporary American Fiction). 168p. 1997. 34.95 (*0-8122-3375-1*); pap. text 14.95 (*0-8122-1598-2*) U of Pa Pr.

Literary Bible of Thomas Jefferson, His Commonplace Book of Philosophers & Poets. Thomas Jefferson. LC 73-90537. 210p. 1970. reprint ed. lib. bdg. 35.00 (*0-8371-2251-1*, JELB, Greenwood Pr) Greenwood.

Literary Biography: Problems & Solutions. Ed. by Dale Salwak. LC 95-62101. 198p. 1996. text 27.95 (*0-87745-553-8*) U of Iowa Pr.

Literary Blasphemies. Ernest A. Boyd. LC 76-90472. 265p. 1970. reprint ed. lib. bdg. 65.00 (*0-8371-2516-2*, BOLB, Greenwood Pr) Greenwood.

Literary Blasphemies. Ernest A. Boyd. (BCL1-PR English Literature Ser.). 265p. 1992. reprint ed. lib. bdg. 79.00 (*0-7812-7008-1*) Rprt Serv.

Literary Bondage: Slavery in Cuban Narrative. William Luis. LC 89-37603. (Texas Pan American Ser.). 326p. 1990. text 40.00 (*0-292-72463-2*) U of Tex Pr.

***Literary Book of Answers.** Carol Bolt. 704p. 2000. 14.95 (*0-7868-6699-3*, Pub. by Hyperion) Time Warner.

Literary Bookstores: A Cross-Country Guide. rev. ed. Compiled by Poets & Writers, Inc. 1994. pap. 12.50 (*0-913734-27-6*) Norton.

Literary Britain & Ireland. 2nd ed. Ian Ouby. (Blue Guide Ser.). 1990. pap. 19.95 (*0-393-30490-6*) Norton.

Literary By-Paths in Old England. Henry C. Shelley. 25.00 (*0-8196-2715-1*) Biblo.

Literary Bypaths of the Renaissance. Elbert N. Thompson. LC 73-176152. reprint ed. 22.50 (*0-404-06399-3*) AMS Pr.

Literary Bypaths of the Renaissance. Elbert N. Thompson. LC 68-20343. (Essay Index Reprint Ser.). 1977. reprint ed. 18.95 (*0-8369-0933-X*) Ayer.

Literary Byways of Boston & Cambridge. Noelle B. Beatty. LC 90-26071. (Literary Cities Ser.). (Illus.). 80p. (Orig.). 1991. pap. 8.95 (*0-913515-60-4*, Starrhill Press) Black Belt Communs.

Literary Cafes of Paris. Noel R. Fitch. LC 88-32399. (Literary Cities Ser.). (Illus.). 80p. (Orig.). 1989. pap. 8.95 (*0-913515-42-6*, Starrhill Press) Black Belt Communs.

***Literary Cambridge.** Lisa Sargood. 128p. 2000. pap. 16.95 (*0-7509-2288-5*) Sutton Publng.

Literary Canon of Southeast Asia: Literatures of Burma, Cambodia, Indonesia, Laos & Malaysia, Philippines, Thailand, & Vietnam. David Smyth. 304p. 1997. text 69.95 (*1-86064-177-6*) I B T.

Literary Capital & the Late Victorian Novel. Norman N. Feltes. LC 92-35455. 185p. reprint ed. pap. 57.40 (*0-608-09907-4*, 206924500003) Bks Demand.

Literary Career of Charles W. Chesnutt. William L. Andrews. LC 79-25875. (Southern Literary Studies). (Illus.). 308p. reprint ed. pap. 95.50 (*0-608-09820-5*, 206998800007) Bks Demand.

Literary Career of Maurice Thompson. fac. ed. Otis B. Wheeler. LC 64-23151. (Louisiana State University Studies: Vol. 14). 170p. 1965. reprint ed. pap. 52.70 (*0-7837-7758-2*, 204751400007) Bks Demand.

Literary Career of Nathaniel Tucker. Lewis Leary. LC 78-115998. (Duke University. Trinity College Historical Society. Historical Papers: No. 29). 1970. reprint ed. 30.00 (*0-404-51779-X*) AMS Pr.

Literary Character. Ed. by John V. Knapp. LC 92-23599. (Style Ser.: Vol. 24, No. 3). 160p. (C). 1993. lib. bdg. 39.50 (*0-8191-8885-9*) U Pr of Amer.

Literary Charleston: A Lowcountry Reader. Ed. by Curtis Worthington. 432p. 1996. 24.95 (*0-941711-17-X*) Wyrick & Co.

Literary Chinese by the Inductive Method. Herlee G. Creel et al. Incl. Selections from the Lun Yu. 1994. lib. bdg. 14.00 (*0-226-12032-5*); pap. write for info. (*0-318-56056-9*) U Ch Pr.

Literary Chinese by the Inductive Method: The Mencius, Vol. 3. enl. rev. ed. Herrlee G. Creel et al. LC 48-8466. 340p. reprint ed. pap. 105.40 (*0-608-18227-3*, 205663500078) Bks Demand.

Literary Christmas: Great Contemporary Christmas Stories. Ed. by Lilly Golden. LC 92-10703. 336p. 1994. pap. 15.00 (*0-87113-583-3*, Atlntc Mnthly) Grove-Atltic.

***Literary Circles & Cultural Communities in Renaissance England.** Ed. by Claude J. Summers & Ted-Larry Pebworth. 264p. 2000. 39.95 (*0-8262-1317-0*) U of Mo Pr.

Literary Circles of Washington. Edith N. Schafer. LC 93-34514. (Literary Cities Ser.). 1993. pap. 8.95 (*0-913515-92-2*, Starrhill Press) Black Belt Communs.

Literary Classification. Milind S. Malshe. 200p. 1993. text 35.00 (*81-85218-35-8*, Pub. by Prestige) Advent Bks Div.

Literary Companion to Rome. John Varriano. LC 95-5219. 1995. pap. 14.95 (*0-312-13112-7*) St Martin.

Literary Companion to Travel in Greece. Ed. by Richard Stoneman. LC 94-9813. (Illus.). 360p. 1994. pap. 17.95 (*0-89236-298-7*) OUP.

Literary Companion to Venice. 3rd ed. Ian Littlewood. LC 95-5220. 1995. pap. 14.95 (*0-312-13113-5*) St Martin.

Literary Comparison in Jacobean Prose. Douglas S. Mead. (English Literature Ser.: No. 33). 1970. reprint ed. pap. 24.95 (*0-8383-0054-5*) M S G Haskell Hse.

Literary Computing & Literary Criticism: Theoretical & Practical Essays on Theme & Rhetoric. Ed. by Rosanne G. Potter. LC 88-38159. (Illus.). 320p. (C). 1989. text 45.00 (*0-8122-8156-X*) U of Pa Pr.

Literary Contributions see American Contributions: Proceedings of the International Congress of Slavists, 6th, 1968

***Literary Conversation: Thinking, Talking, & Writing about Literature.** Patsy Callaghan & Ann Dobyns. LC 95-34155. 260p. 2005. pap. text 28.00 (*0-205-16897-3*) Allyn.

***Literary Converts: Spiritual Inspiration in an Age of Unbelief.** Joseph Pearce. 465p. 2000. 24.95 (*0-89870-790-0*) Ignatius Pr.

Literary Coptic Manuscripts in the A. S. Pushkin State Fine Arts Museum in Moscow. Ed. by Alla I. Elanskaya. LC 93-42892. (Supplements to Vigiliae Christianae Ser.: Vol. 18). 1994. 202.00 (*90-04-09528-4*) Brill Academic Pubs.

***Literary Copyright Reform in Early Victorian England: The Framing of the 1842 Copyright Act.** Catherine Seville. (Cambridge Studies in English Legal History). (Illus.). 300p. (C). 1999. 64.95 (*0-521-62175-5*) Cambridge U Pr.

Literary-Critical Analysis of the Complete Prose Works of Lytton Strachey (1880-1932) A Re-Assessment of His Achievement & Career. Barry Spurr. LC 94-26361. (Studies in British Literature: Vol. 19). (Illus.). 320p. 1995. text 99.95 (*0-7734-9042-6*) E Mellen.

Literary-Critical Approaches to the Bible: A Bibliograhical Supplement. Mark Minor. LC 96-16495. 310p. (C). 1996. lib. bdg. 40.00 (*0-933951-69-8*) Locust Hill Pr.

Literary Criticism: A Short History, 2 vols. William K. Wimsatt, Jr. & Cleanth Brooks. LC 78-55046. 1993. reprint ed. pap. text 17.95 (*0-226-90175-0*) U Ch Pr.

Literary Criticism: A Short History, 2 vols. William K. Wimsatt, Jr. & Cleanth Brooks. LC 78-55046. 1994. reprint ed. pap. text 19.95 (*0-226-90176-9*) U Ch Pr.

Literary Criticism: An Autopsy. Mark Bauerlein. (Critical Authors & Issues Ser.). 176p. (C). 1997. pap. 16.50 (*0-8122-1625-3*) U of Pa Pr.

Literary Criticism: An Autopsy. Mark Bauerlein. LC 97-14199. (C). (gr. 13). 1997. text 36.50 (*0-8122-3411-1*) U of Pa Pr.

Literary Criticism: An Introduction to Theory & Practice. 2nd ed. Charles E. Bressler. LC 98-33496. 308p. 1998. pap. text 30.80 (*0-13-897422-5*) P-H.

Literary Criticism: Plato Through Johnson. Vernon Hall. LC 76-123515. (Goldentree Bibliographies Series in Language & Literature). (C). 1970. pap. text 6.95 (*0-88295-516-0*) Harlan Davidson.

Literary Criticism: Plato to Dryden. Ed. by Allan H. Gilbert. LC 61-12266. (Waynebooks Ser.: No. 1). 714p. 1962. pap. 19.95 (*0-8143-1160-1*) Wayne St U Pr.

Literary Criticism: Pope to Croce. Ed. by Gay W. Wilson & Harry H. Clark. LC 61-12267. (Waynebooks Ser.: No. 2). 670p. 1962. pap. 18.95 (*0-8143-1158-X*) Wayne St U Pr.

Literary Criticism Vol. 1: Essays, American & English Writers. Henry James. Ed. by Leon Edel & Mark Wilson. LC 91-58224. 1484p. 1984. 45.00 (*0-940450-22-4*, Pub. by Library of America) Penguin Putnam.

Literary Criticism Vol. 2: European Writers & Prefaces. Henry James. Ed. by Leon Edel & Mark Wilson. LC 91-58224. 1408p. 1984. 45.00 (*0-940450-23-2*, Pub. by Library of America) Penguin Putnam.

Literary Criticism & Authors' Biographies: An Annotated Index. Compiled by Alison P. Seidel. LC 78-11857. 215p. 1978. 21.00 (*0-8108-1172-3*) Scarecrow.

Literary Criticism & Biblical Hermeneutics. Lynn M. Poland. (American Academy of Religion Academy Ser.: No. 48). 220p. (C). 1985. pap. 15.95 (*0-89130-836-9*, 01-01-48) OUP.

Literary Criticism & Myth. Ed. & Intro. by Robert A. Segal. LC 95-36269. (Theories of Myth Ser.: Vol. 4). 392p. 1995. text 80.00 (*0-8153-2258-5*) Garland.

Literary Criticism & Myth. Ed. by Joseph P. Strelka. LC 79-15111. (Yearbook of Comparative Criticism Ser.: Vol. 9). 1980. text 30.00 (*0-271-00225-5*) Pa St U Pr.

Literary Criticism & Philosophy. Ed. by Joseph P. Strelka. LC 82-10137. (Yearbook of Comparative Criticism Ser.: Vol. 10). 288p. (C). 1983. text 30.00 (*0-271-00324-3*) Pa St U Pr.

Literary Criticism & Psychology. Ed. by Joseph P. Strelka. LC 75-27285. (Yearbook of Comparative Criticism Ser.: Vol. 7). 240p. 1976. 30.00 (*0-271-01218-8*) Pa St U Pr.

Literary Criticism & Sociology. Ed. by Joseph P. Strelka. LC 72-136963. (Yearbook of Comparative Criticism Ser.: Vol. 5). 307p. 1973. 30.00 (*0-271-01152-1*) Pa St U Pr.

Literary Criticism from 1400 to 1800, Vol. 16. James E. Person, Jr. 500p. 1991. text 150.00 (*0-8103-6115-9*) Gale.

Literary Criticism from 1400 to 1800, Vol. 17. James E. Person, Jr. 500p. 1991. text 150.00 (*0-8103-6116-7*) Gale.

Literary Criticism from 1400 to 1800, Vol. 18. James E. Person, Jr. 500p. 1992. text 150.00 (*0-8103-7960-0*) Gale.

Literary Criticism from 1400 to 1800, Vol. 21. James E. Person, Jr. 500p. 1993. text 150.00 (*0-8103-7963-5*) Gale.

Literary Criticism from 1400 to 1800, Vol. 22. James E. Person, Jr. 500p. 1993. text 150.00 (*0-8103-7964-3*) Gale.

Literary Criticism from 1400 to 1800, Vol. 23. James E. Person, Jr. 500p. 1993. text 150.00 (*0-8103-7965-1*) Gale.

Literary Criticism from 1400 to 1800, Vol. 24. James E. Person, Jr. 500p. 1994. text 150.00 (*0-8103-8462-0*) Gale.

Literary Criticism from 1400 to 1800, Vol. 25. James E. Person, Jr. 500p. 1994. text 150.00 (*0-8103-8463-9*) Gale.

Literary Criticism from 1400 to 1800, Vol. 26. James E. Person, Jr. 500p. 1994. text 150.00 (*0-8103-8464-7*) Gale.

Literary Criticism from 1400 to 1800, Vol. 30. Jennifer Brostrom & Kasinec. 500p. 1995. text 150.00 (*0-8103-9275-5*) Gale.

Literary Criticism from 1400 to 1800, Vol. 31. Brostrom & Kasinec. 500p. 1996. text 150.00 (*0-8103-9276-3*) Gale.

Literary Criticism from 1400 to 1800, Vol. 38. 500p. 1997. text 150.00 (*0-7876-1132-8*, 00156236) Gale.

Literary Criticism from 1400 to 1800, Vol. 39. 500p. 1997. text 150.00 (*0-7876-1248-0*, 00156424) Gale.

***Literary Criticism from 1400 to 1800, Vol. 40.** 500p. 1998. text 150.00 (*0-7876-1249-9*, 00156425) Gale.

***Literary Criticism from 1400 to 1800, Vol. 41.** 500p. 1998. text 150.00 (*0-7876-2410-1*, 00158071) Gale.

Literary Criticism in America. Albert Van Nostrand. 333p. 1977. 22.95 (*0-8369-1632-8*) Ayer.

Literary Criticism in Antiquity Vol. 2: Graeco-Roman. John W. Atkins. (Orig.). 1961. 16.50 (*0-8446-1033-X*) Peter Smith.

Literary Criticism in Medieval Arabic Islamic Culture: The Making of a Tradition. Wen-Chin Ouyang. LC 98-179549. 256p. 1998. 68.00 (*0-7486-0897-4*, Pub. by Edinburgh U Pr) Col U Pr.

Literary Criticism in the Age of Johnson. 2nd rev. ed. Aisso Bosker. LC 79-128185. 335p. (C). 1970. reprint ed. 75.00 (*0-87752-133-6*) Gordian.

Literary Criticism Index. 2nd ed. Alan R. Weiner & Spencer Means. LC 93-16137. 580p. 1993. 70.00 (*0-8108-2665-8*) Scarecrow.

Literary Criticism of Dante Alighieri. Dante Alighieri. Ed. by Robert S. Haller. LC 72-85402. (Regents Critics Ser.). 242p. reprint ed. pap. 75.10 (*0-8357-2745-9*, 203985400013) Bks Demand.

Literary Criticism of George Henry Lewes. George Henry Lewes. Ed. by Alice R. Kaminsky. LC 64-17230. (Regents Critics Ser.). 183p. reprint ed. pap. 56.80 (*0-7837-6014-0*, 204582500008) Bks Demand.

Literary Criticism of James Russell Lowell. James Russell Lowell. Ed. by Herbert F. Smith. LC 69-10408. 290p. reprint ed. pap. 89.90 (*0-7837-6016-7*, 204582800008) Bks Demand.

Literary Criticism of John Dryden. John Dryden. Ed. by Arthur C. Kirsch. LC 66-23019. (Regents Critics Ser.). 192p. reprint ed. 59.60 (*0-8357-9709-0*, 201265800083) Bks Demand.

Literary Criticism of John Ruskin. John Ruskin. Ed. & Selected by Harold Bloom. (Quality Paperbacks Ser.). xxvii, 398p. 1987. pap. 12.95 (*0-306-80294-5*) Da Capo.

Literary Criticism of Oscar Wilde. Oscar Wilde. Ed. by Stanley Weintraub. LC 68-22414. (Regents Critics Ser.). 289p. reprint ed. pap. 89.60 (*0-608-17099-2*, 202729200055) Bks Demand.

Literary Criticism of Sainte-Beuve. Charles-Augustin Sainte-Beuve. LC 75-132560. (Regents Critics Ser.). 188p. reprint ed. pap. 58.30 (*0-8357-3812-4*, 203653900003) Bks Demand.

Literary Criticism of the Old Testament. Norman C. Habel. Ed. by J. Coert Rylaarsdam. LC 78-157548. (Guides to Biblical Scholarship: Old Testament Ser.). 96p. 1971. pap. 12.00 (*0-8006-0176-9*, 1-176, Fortress Pr) Augsburg Fortress.

Literary Criticisms: And Other Papers. Horace B. Wallace. LC 72-1319. (Essay Index Reprint Ser.). 1977. reprint ed. 27.95 (*0-8369-2872-5*) Ayer.

***Literary Criticisms of Law.** Guyora Binder & Robert Weisberg. LC 99-37484. 2000. write for info. (*0-691-00723-3*); pap. text. write for info. (*0-691-00724-1*) Princeton U Pr.

Literary Crowd: Writers, Critics, Scholars, Wits. Kitty Benedict & Karen Covington. LC 98-54938. (Illus.). 80p. (gr. 4-7). 2000. lib. bdg. 28.55 (*0-8172-5732-2*) Raintree Steck-V.

Literary Cryptograms. Louise Moll. LC 97-43672. 128p. 1998. 5.95 (*0-8069-9616-1*) Sterling.

Literary Culture: Read & Write Literary Arguments. Bensel Meyers. 638p. 1998. pap. 34.60 (*0-536-01629-1*) Pearson Custom.

Literary Culture & the Pacific: Nineteenth-Century Textual Encounters. Vanessa Smith. LC 97-7612. (Studies in Nineteenth-Century Literature & Culture: Vol. 13). (Illus.). 322p. (C). 1998. text 59.95 (*0-521-57359-9*) Cambridge U Pr.

***Literary Culture & Us Imperialism: From the Revolution to World War II.** John Carlos Rowe. 368p. 2000. pap. 19.95 (*0-19-513151-7*); text 55.00 (*0-19-513150-9*) OUP.

Literary Culture in Early New England, 1620-1730. Thomas G. Wright. (BCL1 - United States Local History Ser.). 322p. 1991. reprint ed. text 89.00 (*0-7812-6264-X*) Rprt Serv.

Literary Culture in the Holy Roman Empire, 1555-1720. James A. Parente, Jr. et al. LC 90-12891. (Germanic Languages & Literatures Ser.: No. 113). (Illus.). xiv, 292p. (C). 1991. 45.00 (*0-8078-8113-9*) U of NC Pr.

Literary Curiosity: The Pyramid Renga "Open" Bambi Walker & Jane Reichhold. 310p. (Orig.). 1989. pap. 25.00 (*0-944676-18-9*) AHA Bks.

Literary Cyclist: Great Bicycling Scenes in Literature. Ed. by James E. Starrs. (Illus.). 392p. 1997. reprint ed. pap. 16.95 (*1-55821-562-X*, Pub. by Breakaway Bks) Consort Bk Sales.

Literary Debate: Texts & Contexts; Postwar French Thought, Vol. II. Ed. by Denis Hollier et al. LC 99-19036. 1998. 40.00 (*1-56584-289-8*, Pub. by New Press NY) Norton.

Literary Discipline. John Erskine. LC 74-90635. (Essay Index Reprint Ser.). 1977. 20.95 (*0-8369-1257-8*) Ayer.

Literary Discourse: Aspects of Cognitive & Social Psychological Approaches. Ed. by Laszlo Halasz. (Research in Text Theory Ser.: Vol. 11). (Illus.). vi, 242p. 1987. lib. bdg. 100.80 (*3-11-010685-X*) De Gruyter.

Literary Diseases: Theme & Metaphor in the Italian Novel. Gian-Paolo Biasin. LC 74-30345. 188p. reprint ed. pap. 58.30 (*0-8357-7718-9*, 203607500002) Bks Demand.

Literary Disorders: Holistic Diagnosis & Remediation. Ula C. Manzo & Anthony V. Manzo. (Illus.). 515p. (C). 1993. text 81.00 (*0-03-072633-6*, Pub. by Harcourt Coll Pubs) Harcourt.

Literary Disruptions: The Making of a Post-Contemporary American Fiction. 2nd ed. Jerome Klinkowitz. LC 80-1592. 308p. 1980. pap. text 15.95 (*0-252-00810-3*) U of Ill Pr.

Literary Dissent in Communist China. Merle R. Goldman. LC 67-17311. (East Asian Monographs: No. 29). 360p. 1985. 35.00 (*0-674-53625-8*) HUP.

Literary Doctrine in China & Soviet Influence, 1956-1960. D. W. Fokkema. 1965. text 48.00 (*90-279-0994-6*) Mouton.

Literary Dog: Great Contemporary Dog Stories. Jeanne Schinto. LC 90-34831. 384p. 1991. pap. 15.00 (*0-87113-504-3*, Atlntc Mnthly) Grove-Atltic.

Literary Education: A Re-Evaluation. James Gribble. LC 82-23527. 168p. 1983. pap. text 24.95 (*0-521-27308-0*) Cambridge U Pr.

Literary Eidetics. Nicholas Churchill. (Orig.). 1990. pap. 4.44 (*0-913412-32-5*) Brandon Hse.

Literary Endeavors of Joseph L. Vitelli. Joseph L. Vitelli. Ed. & Pref. by Tom Vitelli. (Illus.). 60p. 1995. 25.00 (*1-883696-02-X*) EveryWare Bks.

Literary Englands: Versions of Englishness in Modern Writing. David Gervais. LC 92-47285. 296p. (C). 1993. text 64.95 (*0-521-44338-5*) Cambridge U Pr.

Literary Enterprise in Eighteenth-Century France. Remy G. Saisselin. LC 78-11253. (Illus.). 187p. reprint ed. pap. 58.00 (*0-608-16053-9*, 203318300084) Bks Demand.

Literary Essays. Ernst Bloch. Tr. by Andrew Joron from ENG. LC 98-11401. (Meridian Ser.). 448p. 1998. 65.00 (*0-8047-2706-6*) Stanford U Pr.

An Asterisk (*) at the beginning of an entry indicates that the title is appearing for the first time.

L

Literary Essays. Ernst Bloch. Tr. by Andrew Joron from ENG. LC 98-11401. (Meridian Ser.). (Illus.). 448p. 1998. pap. 22.95 (*0-8047-2707-4*) Stanford U Pr.

Literary Essays. John Heath-Stubbs. Ed. & Intro. by Trevor Tolley. LC 99-207023. 180p. 1998. pap. 29.95 (*1-85754-352-1*, Pub. by Carcanet Pr) Paul & Co Pubs.

***Literary Essays.** William T. Shedd. 378p. 1999. pap. 31.00 (*1-57910-286-7*) Wipf & Stock.

Literary Essays. Ezra Pound. LC 78-13133. 464p. 1978. reprint ed. lib. bdg. 75.00 (*0-313-21167-1*, POLE, Greenwood Pr) Greenwood.

Literary Essays. Ezra Pound. Ed. by T. S. Eliot. LC 54-7905. 1968. reprint ed. pap. 13.95 (*0-8112-0157-0*, NDP250, Pub. by New Directions) Norton.

Literary Essays, 2 vols, Set. James Russell Lowell. LC 72-5803. (Essay Index Reprint Ser.). 1977. reprint ed. 49.95 (*0-8369-2998-5*) Ayer.

Literary Essays: A Selection in English. Johann Wolfgang Von Goethe. Ed. by J. E. Springarn. (Essay Index Reprint Ser.). 1977. 18.95 (*0-8369-0478-8*) Ayer.

Literary Essays & Reviews. John Whitehead. 1995. 39.95 (*0-9520471-0-1*, Pub. by New South Wales Univ Pr) Intl Spec Bk.

Literary Essays of Thomas Merton. Thomas Merton. Ed. by Patrick Hart. LC 84-2056. Vol. 587. 549p. 1985. pap. 18.95 (*0-8112-0931-8*, NDP587, Pub. by New Directions) Norton.

Literary Essays on Language & Meaning in the Poem Called "Beowulf" Beowulfiana Literaria. Raymond P. Tripp, Jr. LC 92-28592. 316p. 1992. text 99.95 (*0-7734-9162-7*) E Mellen.

Literary Exile & Displacement: An Analysis & Biographical Dictionary of a Twentieth-Century Phenomenon. Ed. by Martin Tucker. LC 89-25920. 880p. 1991. lib. bdg. 115.00 (*0-313-23870-7*, TLE/, Greenwood Pr) Greenwood.

Literary Existence of Germain de Stael. Charlotte Hogsett. LC 87-4295. (Ad Feminam: Women & Literature Ser.). 224p. 1987. text 31.95 (*0-8093-1387-1*) S Ill U Pr.

Literary Exorcisms of Stalinism: Russian Writers & the Soviet Past. Margaret Ziolkowski. LC 97-39775. 250p. 1998. 65.00 (*1-57113-179-5*) Camden Hse.

Literary Expressionism in Argentine Literature: The Presentation of Incoherence. Naomi Lindstrom. LC 77-24558. 89p. 1978. pap. 10.00 (*0-87918-038-2*) ASU Lat Am St.

***Literary Faculty of the Native Races of America.** John Reade. (LC History-America-E). 30p. 1999. reprint ed. lib. bdg. 69.00 (*0-7812-4289-4*) Rprt Serv.

Literary Fallacy. Bernard A. De Voto. (BCL1-PS American Literature Ser.). 1993. reprint ed. lib. bdg. write for info. (*0-7812-6580-0*) Rprt Serv.

Literary Fat Ladies: Rhetoric, Gender, Property. Patricia Parker. 320p. 1988. text 47.50 (*0-416-91600-7*); pap. text 15.95 (*0-416-91610-4*) Routledge.

Literary Feast: An Anthology. Ed. by Lilly Golden. LC 93-22856. 288p. 1995. pap. 12.00 (*0-87113-596-5*, Atlntc Mnthly) Grove-Atltic.

Literary Feasts: Recipes from the Classics of Western Literature. Barbara Scrafford. LC 95-47836. (Illus.). 192p. 1996. 18.95 (*1-55972-358-0*, Birch Ln Pr) Carol Pub Group.

Literary Federalism in the Age of Jefferson: Joseph Dennie & the Port-Folio. William C. Dowling. LC 97-45469. 160p. 1999. 24.95 (*1-57003-243-2*) U of SC Pr.

***Literary Feminisms.** Ruth Robbins. LC 99-43176. 2000. pap. 19.95 (*0-312-22808-2*); text 55.00 (*0-312-22807-4*) St Martin.

***Literary Field of Twentieth-Century China.** Michel Hock. LC 99-22714. (Chinese Worlds Ser.). 288p. (C). 1999. pap. 25.95 (*0-8248-2202-1*) UH Pr.

***Literary Field of Twentieth-Century China.** Michel Hockx. LC 99-22714. 288p. 1999. 45.00 (*0-8248-2201-3*) UH Pr.

Literary Figures in French Drama (1784-1834) E. H. Kadler. (International Archives of the History of Ideas Ser.: No. 26). 154p. 1969. lib. bdg. 73.50 (*90-247-0202-X*, Pub. by M Nijhoff) Kluwer Academic.

Literary Folkloristics & the Personal Narrative. Sandra D. Stahl. LC 87-46369. 160p. 1989. 10.95 (*0-253-33515-9*) Ind U Pr.

Literary Food for the American Market: Patrick Byrne's Exports to Mathew Carey. Vincent Kinane. 17p. 1995. pap. 7.00 (*0-944026-64-8*) Am Antiquarian.

Literary Formations: Postcolonialism, Nationalism, Globalism. Anne Brewster. Ed. by Ken Ruthven. LC 96-139398. (Interpretations Ser.). 160p. 1995. pap. 19.95 (*0-522-84534-7*, Pub. by Melbourne Univ Pr) Paul & Co Pubs.

Literary Forms in the New Testament: A Handbook. James L. Bailey & Lyle D. Vander Broek. 224p. (Orig.). 1992. pap. 22.95 (*0-664-25154-4*) Westminster John Knox.

Literary Fortifications: Rousseau, Laclos, Sade. Joan DeJean. LC 84-42593. 368p. 1984. reprint ed. pap. 114.10 (*0-7837-9329-4*, 206007000004) Bks Demand.

Literary France: The Making of a Culture. Priscilla P. Clark. 289p. 1987. 50.00 (*0-520-05703-1*, Pub. by U CA Pr) Cal Prin Full Svc.

Literary France: The Making of a Culture. Priscilla P. Clark. (Illus.). 289p. 1991. pap. 15.95 (*0-520-07397-5*, Pub. by U CA Pr) Cal Prin Full Svc.

Literary Freud: Mechanisms of Defense & the Poetic Will. Ed. by Joseph H. Smith. LC 79-19104. (Psychiatry & the Humanities Ser.: Vol. 4). 390p. 1980. 45.00 (*0-300-02405-3*) Yale U Pr.

Literary Friends & Acquaintances. William Dean Howells. (Notable American Authors Ser.). 1992. reprint ed. lib. bdg. 75.00 (*0-7812-3276-7*) Rprt Serv.

Literary Friends & Acquaintances: A Personal Retrospect of American Authorship, 2 vols., Set. William Dean Howells. (American Biography Ser.). 1991. reprint ed. lib. bdg. 148.00 (*0-7812-8203-9*) Rprt Serv.

Literary Friendship: Correspondence Between Caroline Gordon & Ford Madox Ford. Ed. & Intro. by Brita Lindberg-Seyersted. LC 98-40213. 152p. 1999. 22.50 (*1-57233-046-5*, Pub. by U of Tenn Pr) U Ch Pr.

Literary Friendship: The Correspondence of Ralph Gustafson & W. W. E. Ross. Ralph Gustafson & W. W. Ross. Ed. by Bruce Whiteman. 140p. (C). 1984. pap. text 14.00 (*0-920802-57-5*, Pub. by ECW) Genl Dist Srvs.

Literary Function of Possessions in Luke-Acts. Luke T. Johnson. LC 77-21055. (Society of Biblical Literature. Dissertation Ser.: No. 39). 251p. reprint ed. pap. 77.90 (*0-7837-5426-4*, 204519000005) Bks Demand.

***Literary Garden: Bringing Fiction's Best Gardens to Life.** Ed. & Intro. by Michael Weishan. (Illus.). 2000. pap. 13.95 (*0-425-16874-3*) Berkley Pub.

Literary Gardener. Walter Chandoha. LC 97-28061. (Illus.). 125p. 1997. 19.50 (*1-57223-083-5*, 0835) Willow Creek Pr.

Literary Garveyism: Garvey, Black Arts & the Harlem Renaissance. Tony Martin. LC 83-60952. (New Marcus Garvey Library: No. 1). (Illus.). xii, 204p. 1983. pap. text 9.95 (*0-912469-01-3*) Majority Pr.

Literary Gems: A Reading List of Great Short Books. 2nd rev. ed. John T. Reeves. 46p. 1998. pap. 5.95 (*1-882063-13-9*) Cottage Pr MA.

Literary Generations: A Festschrift in Honor of Edward D. Sullivan by His Friends, Colleagues, & Former Students. Ed. by Alain Toumayan. LC 91-73986. (French Forum Monographs: No. 78). 250p. (Orig.). 1992. pap. 17.95 (*0-917058-82-8*) French Forum.

Literary Genius of the New Testament. Percy C. Sands. LC 74-109837. 214p. 1970. reprint ed. lib. bdg. 59.50 (*0-8371-4328-4*, SANT, Greenwood Pr) Greenwood.

Literary Genres of Edmund Burke: The Political Uses of Literary Form. Frans De Bruyn. 330p. 1996. text 72.00 (*0-19-812182-2*) OUP.

Literary Ghost. Ed. by Larry Dark. LC 91-15052. 384p. 1992. pap. 13.00 (*0-87113-483-7*, Atlntc Mnthly) Grove-Atltic.

Literary Guide & Companion to Middle England. Robert M. Cooper. LC 92-13580. (Illus.). 398p. (C). 1992. text 34.95 (*0-8214-1032-6*) Ohio U Pr.

Literary Guide & Companion to Middle England. Robert M. Cooper. LC 92-13580. (Illus.). 398p. (C). 1993. reprint ed. pap. 16.95 (*0-8214-1033-4*) Ohio U Pr.

Literary Guide & Companion to Northern England. Robert M. Cooper. (Illus.). 398p. 1994. text 34.95 (*0-8214-1095-4*) Ohio U Pr.

Literary Guide & Companion to Northern England. Robert M. Cooper. LC 94-21981. (Illus.). 398p. 1995. pap. 16.95 (*0-8214-1096-2*) Ohio U Pr.

Literary Guide & Companion to Southern England. Robert M. Cooper. LC 97-49201. xxi, 389p. 1998. pap. 19.95 (*0-8214-1226-4*) Ohio U Pr.

Literary Guide & Companion to Southern England. rev. ed. Robert M. Cooper. LC 97-49201. 350p. 1998. reprint ed. text 39.95 (*0-8214-1225-6*) Ohio U Pr.

Literary Guide to Dublin. 1994. pap. 19.95 (*0-413-69120-9*) Methn.

Literary Guide to the Bible. Ed. by Robert Alter & Frank Kermode. 704p. 1990. pap. text 17.95 (*0-674-87531-1*) Belknap Pr.

Literary Guide to the Bible. Ed. by Robert Alter & Frank Kermode. LC 86-32172. (Illus.). 688p. 1987. text 52.95 (*0-674-87530-3*) HUP.

Literary Heritage of Childhood: An Appraisal of Children's Classics in the Western Tradition, 20. Charles H. Frey & John Griffith. LC 87-266. (Contributions to the Study of World Literature Ser.: No. 20). 254p. 1987. 59.95 (*0-313-25681-0*, GLL/) Greenwood.

Literary Heritage of Classical Islam: Arabic & Islamic Studies in Honor of James A. Bellamy. Ed. by Mustansir Mir & Jarl E. Fossum. LC 93-785. (Illus.). 356p. 1993. 35.00 (*0-87850-099-5*) Darwin Pr.

Literary Heritage of Wisconsin, Vol. II, Pt. A. Ed. by Richard Boudreau. 360p. 1995. 35.00 (*1-55780-142-8*); pap. 25.00 (*1-55780-141-X*) Juniper Pr ME.

Literary Heritage of Wisconsin Vol. 1: An Anthology of Wisconsin Literature from Beginnings to 1925. Intro. by Richard Boudreau. (Inland Seas Ser.: No. 4). 440p. (Orig.). 1986. 35.00 (*1-55780-079-0*) Juniper Pr ME.

Literary Heritage of Wisconsin Vol. 1: An Anthology of Wisconsin Literature from Beginnings to 1925. deluxe ed. Intro. by Richard Boudreau. (Inland Seas Ser.: No. 4). 440p. (Orig.). 1986. 50.00 (*1-55780-090-1*) Juniper Pr ME.

Literary Hills of San Francisco. Luree Miller. LC 91-44656. (Literary Cities Ser.). (Illus.). 72p. (Orig.). 1992. pap. 8.95 (*0-913515-76-0*, Starrhill Press) Black Belt Communs.

Literary History & the Challenge of Philology: The Legacy of Erich Auerbach. Ed. by Seth Lerer. LC 95-10992. 308p. 1996. 45.00 (*0-8047-2545-4*) Stanford U Pr.

Literary History in the Wake of Roland Barthes: Re-Defining the Myths of Reading. Roland A. Champagne. LC 83-50516. 158p. 1984. pap. 13.00 (*0-917786-36-X*) Summa Pubns.

Literary History, Modernism & Postmodernism: The Harvard University Erasmus Lectures, Spring 1983. Douwe W. Fokkema. LC 84-23498. (Utrecht Publications in General & Comparative Literature Ser.: 19). vi, 63p. 1984. pap. 13.95 (*90-272-2204-5*) J Benjamins Pubng Co.

Literary History of Alabama: The Nineteenth Century. Benjamin B. Williams. LC 76-50286. 258p. 1979. 35.00 (*0-8386-2054-X*) Fairleigh Dickinson.

Literary History of America. Barrett Wendell. LC 68-24945. (American History & Americana Ser.: No. 47). 1969. reprint ed. lib. bdg. 75.00 (*0-8383-0257-2*) M S G Haskell Hse.

Literary History of America. Barrett Wendell. (BCL1-PS American Literature Ser.). 574p. 1992. reprint ed. lib. bdg. 99.00 (*0-7812-6607-6*) Rprt Serv.

Literary History of Canada. Ed. by W. H. New. 492p. 1990. text 60.00 (*0-8020-5685-7*) U of Toronto Pr.

Literary History of Canada. Ed. by W. H. New. (Literature in English Ser.: Vil. 4). 492p. 1990. pap. 24.95 (*0-8020-6610-0*) U of Toronto Pr.

Literary History of Canada: Canadian Literature in English. Ed. by Carl F. Klinck & Alfred G. Bailey. LC 65-1360. 959p. reprint ed. pap. 200.00 (*0-8357-6362-5*, 203571600096) Bks Demand.

Literary History of Canada: Canadian Literature in English, Vol. 1. 2nd ed. Ed. by Carl F. Klinck et al. LC 76-12353. 564p. reprint ed. pap. 174.90 (*0-8357-3643-1*, 203637100001) Bks Demand.

Literary History of Canada: Canadian Literature in English, Vol. 2. 2nd ed. Ed. by Carl F. Klinck et al. LC 76-12353. 416p. reprint ed. pap. 129.00 (*0-8357-3644-X*, 203637100002) Bks Demand.

Literary History of Early Christianity, 2 vols. Charles T. Cruttwell. LC 76-129369. reprint ed. 95.00 (*0-404-01877-7*) AMS Pr.

Literary History of England. 2nd ed. Ed. by Albert C. Baugh et al. (C). 1967. text, student ed. 105.00 (*0-13-537605-X*) P-H.

Literary History of England in the End of the Eighteenth & Beginning of the Nineteenth Century, 3 vols. Margaret O. Oliphant. LC 76-121021. reprint ed. 45.00 (*0-404-04830-7*) AMS Pr.

Literary History of Hamlet. Kemp Malone. LC 65-15886. (Studies in Shakespeare: No. 24). 1969. reprint ed. lib. bdg. 75.00 (*0-8383-0593-8*) M S G Haskell Hse.

Literary History of India. R. W. Frazer. LC 78-128001. (Studies in Asiatic Literature: No. 57). 1970. reprint ed. lib. bdg. 75.00 (*0-8383-1150-4*) M S G Haskell Hse.

Literary History of Iowa. Clarence A. Andrews. LC 72-76304. 301p. 1972. text 34.95 (*0-87745-032-3*) U of Iowa Pr.

Literary History of Kentucky. William S. Ward. LC 88-1277. (Illus.). 416p. 1988. 45.00 (*0-87049-577-1*); pap. 21.95 (*0-87049-578-X*) U of Tenn Pr.

Literary History of New England. Perry D. Westbrook. LC 87-45767. 368p. 1988. 49.50 (*0-934223-02-5*) Lehigh Univ Pr.

Literary History of Persia, 4 vols., Set. Edward G. Browne. LC 96-44208. (Classics of Iranian Studies: No. 1). (Illus.). 2324p. 1996. lib. bdg. 275.00 (*0-936347-66-X*) IBEX.

Literary History of Persia, 4 vols., Set. E. G. Browne. (Illus.). 2268p. 1996. reprint ed. boxed set 395.00 (*0-7007-0406-X*, Pub. by Curzon Pr Ltd) Paul & Co Pubs.

Literary History of Persia: From the Earliest Times until Firdawsi; From Firdawsi to Sad'i; The Tartar Dominion (1265-1502); Modern Times, 4 vols. E. G. Browne. (C). 1997. 175.00 (*81-215-0753-7*, Pub. by M Manoharial) Coronet Bks.

Literary History of Persia Vol. I: From the Earliest Times until Firdawsi. Edward G. Browne. LC 96-44208. (Classics of Iranian Studies: No. 1). (Illus.). 536p. 1996. lib. bdg. 75.00 (*0-936347-62-7*) IBEX.

Literary History of Persia Vol. II: From Firdawsi to Saadi. Edward G. Browne. LC 96-44208. (Classics of Iranian Studies). (Illus.). 584p. 1996. lib. bdg. 75.00 (*0-936347-63-5*) IBEX.

Literary History of Persia Vol. III: The Tartar Dominion (1265-1502) Edward G. Browne. LC 96-44208. (Classics of Iranian Studies: No. 1). (Illus.). 626p. 1996. lib. bdg. 75.00 (*0-936347-64-3*) IBEX.

Literary History of Persia Vol. IV: Modern Times (1500-1924) Edward G. Browne. LC 96-44208. (Classics of Iranian Studies: No. 1). (Illus.). 578p. 1995. lib. bdg. 75.00 (*0-936347-65-1*) IBEX.

Literary History of Rome in the Silver Age: From Tiberius to Hadrian. 3rd ed. John W. Duff. Ed. by A. M. Duff. LC 79-9906. 607p. 1979. reprint ed. lib. bdg. 47.50 (*0-313-20939-1*, DULH, Greenwood Pr) Greenwood.

Literary History of Sanskrit Buddhism. Gushtaspshah K. Nariman. LC 78-70106. reprint ed. 37.50 (*0-404-17356-X*) AMS Pr.

Literary History of Sanskrit Buddhism: From Winternitz, Sylvain Levi, Huber. J. K. Nariman. (C). 1992. reprint ed. text 16.00 (*81-208-0795-2*, Pub. by Motilal Bnarsidass) S Asia.

Literary History of the American Revolution, 1763-1783. Moses C. Tyler. (Notable American Authors Ser.). 1999. reprint ed. lib. bdg. 125.00 (*0-7812-9856-3*) Rprt Serv.

Literary History of the Arabs. Reynold A. Nicholson. 536p. (C). 1995. pap. 32.50 (*0-7007-0336-5*, Pub. by Curzon Pr Ltd) Paul & Co Pubs.

Literary History of the Arabs. Reynold A. Nicholson. LC 96-41815. (The Kegan Paul Arabia Library). 1997. 110.00 (*0-7103-0566-4*, Pub. by Kegan Paul Intl) Col U Pr.

Literary History of the Arabs. Reynold A. Nicholson. LC 74-401710. 538p. reprint ed. pap. 153.40 (*0-608-13031-1*, 2024502) Bks Demand.

Literary History of the English Jesuits: A Century of Books, 1615-1714. Thomas H. Clancy. LC 93-41584. 284p. 1996. 69.95 (*1-883255-25-2*); 49.95 (*1-883255-24-4*) Intl Scholars.

Literary History of the English People, 3 vols. Jean A. Jusserand. LC 67-29561. 1972. reprint ed. 90.95 (*0-405-08680-6*) Ayer.

Literary History of the English People, 3 vols. 3rd rev. ed. Jean Jusserand. Incl. Vol. 1. From the Origins to the End of the Middle Ages. 3rd ed. LC 68-29336. 1968. reprint ed. (*0-87752-250-2*); Vol. 2. Time of Renaissance. 3rd ed. LC 68-29336. 1968. reprint ed. (*0-87752-251-0*); Vol. 3. Age of Elizabeth. 3rd ed. LC 68-29336. 1968. reprint ed. (*0-87752-252-9*); LC 68-29336. 1735p. 1968. reprint ed. 300.00 (*0-87752-057-7*) Gordian.

Literary History of the English People, 3 vols., 1. Jean A. Jusserand. LC 67-29561. 1972. reprint ed. 30.95 (*0-405-08681-4*) Ayer.

Literary History of the English People, 3 vols., Set. Jean A. Jusserand. (BCL1-PR English Literature Ser.). 1992. reprint ed. lib. bdg. 225.00 (*0-7812-7003-0*) Rprt Serv.

Literary History of the English People, 3 vols., Vol. 2. Jean A. Jusserand. LC 67-29561. 1972. reprint ed. 30.95 (*0-405-08682-2*) Ayer.

Literary History of the English People, 3 vols., Vol. 3. Jean A. Jusserand. LC 67-29561. 1972. reprint ed. 30.95 (*0-405-08683-0*) Ayer.

Literary History of the Popular Ballad. David C. Fowler. LC 68-19917. 360p. reprint ed. pap. 111.60 (*0-608-13863-0*, 202376100033) Bks Demand.

Literary I. Mary Weidman. 45p. (C). Date not set. teacher ed. 30.00 (*0-9618340-8-0*) Prof Educ Dist.

Literary II. Mary Weidman. 45p. (C). Date not set. teacher ed. 30.00 (*0-9618340-9-9*) Prof Educ Dist.

Literary Images of Ontario. W. J. Keith. (Ontario Historical Studies). (Illus.). 288p. 1992. text 45.00 (*0-8020-3470-5*); pap. text 18.95 (*0-8020-3469-1*) U of Toronto Pr.

***Literary Imagination: Ancient & Modern.** Todd Breyfogle. LC 98-50892. 405p. 1999. pap. text 19.00 (*0-226-07425-0*) U Ch Pr.

Literary Imagination: Studies in Dante, Chaucer & Shakespeare. Derek Traversi. LC 81-50650. 272p. 1982. 37.50 (*0-87413-198-7*) U Delaware Pr.

***Literary Imagination, Ancient & Modern: Essays in Honor of David Grene.** Todd Breyfogle. LC 98-50892. 1999. lib. bdg. 50.00 (*0-226-07424-2*) U Ch Pr.

Literary Imagination of the Mariel Generation. Lillian D. Bertot. 105p. (C). 1995. pap. text 14.00 (*1-884619-05-3*) Endowment CAS.

Literary Imagination of Ultra-Orthodox Jewish Women: An Assessment of a Writing Community. Alyse F. Roller. LC 99-25985. (Illus.). 198p. 1999. lib. bdg. 29.95 (*0-7864-0721-2*) McFarland & Co.

Literary Imitation in the Italian Renaissance: The Theory & Practice of Literary Imitation in Italy from Dante to Bembo. Martin L. McLaughlin. (Oxford Modern Languages & Literature Monographs). 322p. 1996. text 75.00 (*0-19-815899-8*) OUP.

Literary Impressionism. Maria E. Kronegger. 1973. pap. 15.95 (*0-8084-0365-6*) NCUP.

Literary Impressionism in Jean Rhys, Ford Madox Ford, Joseph Conrad, & Charlotte Bronte. Ed. by Todd K. Bender. LC 97-10566. (Origins of Modernism Ser.: Vol. 9). (Illus.). 184p. 1997. text 60.00 (*0-8153-1943-6*, H1887) Garland.

Literary Index to American Magazines, 1850-1900, 22. Compiled by Daniel A. Wells. LC 95-26447. (Bibliographies & Indexes in American Literature Ser.: No. 22). 456p. 1996. lib. bdg. 95.00 (*0-313-29840-8*, Greenwood Pr) Greenwood.

Literary India: Comparative Studies in Aesthetics, Colonialism, & Culture. Ed. by Patrick C. Hogan & Lalita Pandit. LC 94-16097. (SUNY Series in Hindu Studies). 289p. (C). 1995. text 59.50 (*0-7914-2395-6*); pap. text 19.95 (*0-7914-2396-4*) State U NY Pr.

Literary Industries. fac. ed. Hubert H. Bancroft. LC 67-29422. (Works of Hubert Howe Bancroft Ser.). 1967. reprint ed. 50.00 (*0-914888-43-9*) Bancroft Pr.

***Literary Industries.** Hubert Howe Bancroft. (Works of Hubert Howe Bancroft: Vol. 39). 814p. 1999. reprint ed. lib. bdg. 90.00 (*0-7812-7832-5*) Rprt Serv.

Literary Influence & African-American Writers. Ed. by Tracy Mishkin. LC 95-19543. (Wellesley Studies in Critical Theory, Literary History & Culture: Vol. 10). (Illus.). 400p. 1995. text 80.00 (*0-8153-1724-7*, H1849) Garland.

Literary Influences of Philip Freneau. Harry H. Clark. 33p. (Orig.). (C). 1925. reprint ed. pap. 39.95 (*0-8383-0014-6*) M S G Haskell Hse.

Literary Inheritance. Roger Sale. LC 84-8757. 240p. 1985. lib. bdg. 30.00 (*0-87023-450-1*) U of Mass Pr.

Literary Integrity & Political Action. Kathleen Farrell. LC 99-47281. (Polemics Ser.). 212p. 1999. text 55.00 (*0-8133-9071-0*) Westview.

Literary Intellectuals & the Dissolution of the State: Professionalism & Conformity in the GDR. Robert Von Hallberg. Tr. by Kenneth J. Northcott from GER. 378p. 1996. pap. 18.95 (*0-226-86498-7*); lib. bdg. 56.00 (*0-226-86497-9*) U Ch Pr.

Literary Inter-Relations: Ireland, Egypt, & the Far East. Ed. by Mary Massoud. (Irish Literary Studies: No. 47). 458p. 1996. text 70.00 (*0-86140-377-0*) OUP.

Literary Interest: The Limits of Anti-Formalism. Steven Knapp. LC 92-44269. 184p. 1993. 36.50 (*0-674-53651-7*) HUP.

Literary Intersections of Masculinity & Race: Contemporary Writing by U.S. Men. John Christopher Cunningham. (Studies in American Popular History & Culture). 200p. 1999. 50.00 (*0-8153-3139-8*) Garland.

***Literary Interview: Rhetoric, Invention, Performance.** John Rodden. 2000. text 70.00 (*0-8032-3939-4*) U of Nebr Pr.

Literary into Cultural Studies. Anthony Easthope. (Illus.). 192p. (C). (gr. 13). 1991. pap. 27.99 (*0-415-06641-7*, A6172) Routledge.

Literary Ireland. Photos by Tom Kelly. (Illus.). 156p. 1997. 35.00 (*1-57098-167-1*) Roberts Rinehart.

Literary Ireland. Photos by Tom Kelly. (Illus.). 156p. 1998. pap. 24.95 (*1-57098-230-9*, R Rinehart Intl) Roberts Rinehart.

Literary Issues see Woman Question: Society & Literature in Britain & America, 1837-1883

Literary Journalism: A Biographical Dictionary of Writers & Editors. Edd Applegate. LC 96-7142. 352p. 1996. lib. bdg. 89.50 (*0-313-29949-8*, Greenwood Pr) Greenwood.

Literary Journalism: A New Collection of the Best American Nonfiction. Ed. by Norman Sims & Mark Kramer. LC 94-96759. 416p. 1995. pap. 12.50 (*0-345-38222-6*) Ballantine Pub Grp.

Literary Journalism in the Twentieth Century. Ed. by Norman Sims. (Illus.). 320p. (C). 1990. pap. text 22.95 (*0-19-505965-4*) OUP.

Literary Journalists. Ed. by Norman Sims. 352p. 1984. pap. 11.00 (*0-345-31081-0*, Ballantine) Ballantine Pub Grp.

Literary Journals in Imperial Russia. Ed. by Deborah A. Martinsen. LC 97-7613. (Studies in Russian Literature). 283p. (C). 1998. text 64.95 (*0-521-57292-4*) Cambridge U Pr.

Literary Knowledge: Humanistic Inquiry & the Philosophy of Science. Paisley Livingston. LC 87-47821. 296p. 1988. pap. 15.95 (*0-8014-9422-2*) Cornell U Pr.

Literary Labyrinth: Contemporary Critical Discourses. Bernard Sharratt. LC 84-16726. 272p. 1984. 50.00 (*0-389-20526-5*, BNB-08088) B&N Imports.

Literary Ladies: A Selection of First Books of Women Writers. Joanna Taylor. 116p. (Orig.). 1981. pap. 8.00 (*0-686-34550-9*) J Taylor Bks.

Literary Landmarks: A Guide to Good Reading for Young People. Mary E. Burt. 1977. lib. bdg. 59.95 (*0-8490-2170-7*) Gordon Pr.

Literary Landmarks of Edinburgh. Laurence Hutton. (Notable American Authors Ser.). 1992. reprint ed. lib. bdg. 75.00 (*0-7812-3311-9*) Rprt Serv.

Literary Landmarks of Florence. Laurence Hutton. (Notable American Authors Ser.). 1992. reprint ed. lib. bdg. 75.00 (*0-7812-3318-6*) Rprt Serv.

Literary Landmarks of Jerusalem. Laurence Hutton. (Notable American Authors Ser.). 1992. reprint ed. lib. bdg. 75.00 (*0-7812-3315-1*) Rprt Serv.

Literary Landmarks of London. Laurence Hutton. (Notable American Authors Ser.). 1992. reprint ed. lib. bdg. 75.00 (*0-7812-3306-2*) Rprt Serv.

Literary Landmarks of Oxford. Laurence Hutton. (Notable American Authors Ser.). 1992. reprint ed. lib. bdg. 75.00 (*0-7812-3320-8*) Rprt Serv.

Literary Landmarks of Rome. Laurence Hutton. (Notable American Authors Ser.). 1992. reprint ed. lib. bdg. 75.00 (*0-7812-3316-X*); reprint ed. lib. bdg. 75.00 (*0-7812-3317-8*) Rprt Serv.

Literary Landmarks of the Scottish Universities. Laurence Hutton. (Notable American Authors Ser.). 1992. reprint ed. lib. bdg. 75.00 (*0-7812-3321-6*) Rprt Serv.

Literary Landscapes: Walking Tours in Great Britain & Ireland. L. N. Franco. LC 98-39502. (Illus.). 151p. 1999. pap. 15.95 (*0-8076-1438-6*) Braziller.

Literary Landscapes of the British Isles: A Narrative Atlas. David Daiches & John Flower. LC 78-11446. 287p. reprint ed. pap. 89.00 (*0-608-16427-5*, 202721700054) Bks Demand.

Literary Language of Shakespeare. S. S. Hussey. LC 81-20889. 214 p. 1982. write for info. (*0-582-49228-9*) Addison-Wesley.

Literary Language of Shakespeare. 2nd ed. S. S. Hussey. 272p. (C). 1992. pap. text 33.25 (*0-582-08770-8*, 79360) Longman.

Literary Language of the Bible: The Collected Essays of Luis Alonso Schokel. Luis A. Schokel. Tr. by Harry Spencer from SPA. LC 99-6540. (Collected Essays Ser.: Vol. 3). (Orig.). 1998. pap. 18.95 (*0-941037-43-6*, BIBAL Press) D & F Scott.

Literary Lapses. Stephen Leacock. LC 70-122728. (Short Story Index Reprint Ser.). 1980. 18.95 (*0-8369-3561-6*) Ayer.

Literary Lapses. Stephen Leacock. 160p. 1996. pap. text 5.95 (*0-7710-9983-5*) McClelland & Stewart.

Literary Las Vegas: The Best Writing about America's Most Fabulous City. Ed. by Mike Tronnes. LC 94-43199. 256p. 1995. 30.00 (*0-8050-3669-5*); pap. 12.95 (*0-8050-3670-9*) H Holt & Co.

Literary Laurels: A Reader's Guide to Award-Winning Fiction. Ed. by Laura Carlson et al. 80p. (Orig.). 1995. pap. 9.95 (*0-9647361-0-1*) Hillyard.

Literary Laurels - Kid's Edition: A Guide to Award-Winning Children's Books. Ed. by Laura Carlson et al. LC 96-180880. 138p. (Orig.). 1996. pap. 11.95 (*0-9647361-1-X*) Hillyard.

Literary Leaders of America. Richard Burton. LC 71-105001. (Essay Index Reprint Ser.). 1977. 21.95 (*0-8369-1455-4*) Ayer.

Literary Legacy of Rebecca West. Carl Rollyson. LC 97-33532. 266p. 1997. pap. 54.95 (*1-57309-181-2*) Intl Scholars.

Literary Legacy of Rebecca West. Carl Rollyson. LC 97-33532. 266p. 1998. 74.95 (*1-57309-182-0*) Intl Scholars.

Literary Lennon: A Comedy of Letters. James Sauceda. LC 83-62327. (Rock & Roll Reference Ser.: No. 9). (Illus.). 232p. 1983. 40.00 (*0-87650-161-7*) Popular Culture.

Literary Levees of New Orleans. Alan Brown. 1998. pap. text 8.95 (*0-913515-44-2*, Starrhill Press) Black Belt Communs.

Literary Leviathan: Thomas Hobbes's Masterpiece of Language. Charles Cantalupo. LC 89-46576. 280p. 1991. 39.50 (*0-8387-5186-5*) Bucknell U Pr.

Literary Life & Correspondence of the Countess of Blessington, 3 vols. Richard R. Madden. reprint ed. 210.00 (*0-404-07720-X*) AMS Pr.

Literary Life in German Expressionism & the Berlin Circles. Roy F. Allen. LC 82-4762. (Studies in the Fine Arts: The Avant-Garde: No. 25). (Illus.). 414p. reprint ed. pap. 128.40 (*0-8357-1315-6*, 207060100005) Bks Demand.

Literary life in Tokyo, 1885-1915: Tayama Katai's memoirs 'Thirty years in Tokyo' Katai Tayama & Kenneth G. Henshall. LC 87-703. 1987. reel tape. write for info. (*90-04-08119-4*) Brill Academic Pubs.

Literary Life of the Early Friends, 1650-1725. Luella M. Wright. LC 32-25426. reprint ed. 31.50 (*0-404-07046-9*) AMS Pr.

Literary Lifelines, 10 vols. LC 97-49180. (Illus.). (YA). (gr. 6). 1998. lib. bdg. 335.00 (*0-7172-9211-8*) Grolier Educ.

Literary Likings. Richard Burton. LC 79-37510. (Essay Index Reprint Ser.). 1977. reprint ed. 25.95 (*0-8369-2538-6*) Ayer.

Literary Lion. (Illus.). 184p. (J). 1997. pap. text. write for info. (*0-940429-18-7*) M B Glass Assocs.

Literary Lion. George. A. Jackson School Staff. (Illus.). 148p. (Orig.). (J). 1992. pap. text 10.00 (*0-940429-10-1*) M B Glass Assocs.

Literary Lion, 1995. Jackson, George. A., School Staff. (Illus.). 162p. (Orig.). (J). 1995. pap. text. write for info. (*0-940429-13-6*) M B Glass Assocs.

Literary Lion, 1994. Jackson, George. A., School Staff. (Illus.). 160p. (Orig.). (J). 1994. pap. text. write for info. (*0-940429-12-8*) M B Glass Assocs.

Literary Lion, 1996. Jackson, George. A., School Staff. (Illus.). 178p. (Orig.). (J). 1996. pap. text. write for info. (*0-940429-15-2*) M B Glass Assocs.

Literary Lion, 1993. George A. Jackson School Students. (Illus.). 164p. (Orig.). (J). 1993. pap. 10.00 (*0-940429-11-X*) M B Glass Assocs.

Literary Lion, 98-99. limited ed. Students of George A. Jackson School. (Illus.). 180p. 1998. pap. text. write for info. (*0-940429-21-7*) M B Glass Assocs.

Literary Lion '97-'98. Students of the George A. Jackson School. (Illus.). 190p. 1998. pap. text. write for info. (*0-940429-19-5*) M B Glass Assocs.

***Literary Lives: Biography & the Search for Understanding.** David Ellis. 2000. 35.00 (*0-415-92880-X*) Routledge.

Literary Lives of Jesus: An International Bibliography. Alice Birney. LC 88-24727. 224p. 1989. text 15.00 (*0-8240-8475-6*) Garland.

Literary Lodgings: Historic Hotels in Britain Where Famous Writers Lived. Elaine Borish. 1996. pap. 17.95 (*0-9524881-0-8*, Pub. by Fidelio Pr) IPG Chicago.

Literary London. Spellmount Ltd. Publishers Staff. (C). 1986. 120.00 (*0-946771-64-2*, Pub. by Spellmnt Pubs) St Mut.

***Literary Lorgnette: Attending Opera in Imperial Russia.** Julie A. Buckler. LC 99-86375. (Illus.). 322p. 2000. 45.00 (*0-8047-3247-7*) Stanford U Pr.

Literary Love Letters & Other Stories see Collected Works of Robert Herrick

Literary Love Letters & Other Stories. Robert Herrick. 1972. reprint ed. lib. bdg. 20.00 (*0-8422-8075-8*) Irvington.

Literary Love Letters & Other Stories. Robert Herrick. (Collected Works of Robert Herrick). 1988. reprint ed. lib. bdg. 59.00 (*0-7812-1261-8*) Rprt Serv.

Literary Lover: Great Contemporary Stories of Passion & Romance. Ed. by Larry Dark. 384p. 1994. pap. 13.95 (*0-14-017164-9*, Penguin Bks) Viking Penguin.

Literary Lovers: The Private & Public Passions of Famous Writers. J. Booth. (Illus.). 180p. 1999. text 19.95 (*0-233-99436-X*, Pub. by Andre Deutsch) Trafalgar.

Literary Luxuries: American Writing at the End of the Millennium. Joe D. Bellamy. LC 95-20790. 248p. (C). 1995. 29.95 (*0-8262-1029-5*) U of Mo Pr.

Literary Machines 93.1. rev. ed. Theodor H. Nelson. (Illus.). 286p. 1992. pap. 25.00 (*0-89347-062-7*) Mindful Pr.

Literary Man: Essays Presented to Donald W. Hannah. Ed. by Karl-Heinz Westarp. (Illus.). 240p. (Orig.). (C). 1996. pap. text 17.95 (*87-7288-540-8*, Pub. by Aarhus Univ Pr) David Brown.

Literary Map of Latin America. Intro. by Molly Maguire. (Literary Maps Ser.). (Illus.). (Orig.). (J). (gr. 6-12). 1988. pap. 4.95 (*0-937609-12-9*) Aaron Blake Pubs.

Literary Map of Los Angeles. Ed. by Aaron Silverman & Molly Maguire. (Literary Maps Ser.). (Illus.). (Orig.). 1987. pap. 4.95 (*0-937609-06-4*) Aaron Blake Pubs.

Literary Map of New York City. Ed. by Aaron Silverman & Molly Maguire. (Literary Maps Ser.). (Illus.). (Orig.). 1988. pap. 4.95 (*0-937609-07-2*) Aaron Blake Pubs.

Literary Map of the American South. Intro. by Molly Maguire. (Literary Maps Ser.). (Illus.). (Orig.). (J). (gr. 6-12). 1988. pap. 4.95 (*0-937609-11-0*) Aaron Blake Pubs.

Literary Maps for Young Adult Literature. Mary E. Snodgrass. (Illus.). xi, 223p. 1995. pap. text 34.50 (*1-56308-164-4*) Libs Unl.

Literary Market Place,1999: The Directory of the American Book Publishing Industry, 2 vols. Ed. by Bowker Staff. 2100p. 1998. 189.95 (*0-8352-4053-3*) Bowker.

***Literary Market Place 2001: The Directory of the American Book Publishing Industry, 2 vols., Set.** annuals 61st ed. Ed. by Bowker Staff. 2100p. 2000. pap. 199.95 (*0-8352-4346-X*) Bowker.

"No well-stocked library can afford to be without this annually updated reference to the publishing industry."--BOOKWATCH. "LMP is a reference without competition. Those needing current data on publishers, their rapidly circulating staff, & support systems must have LMP."--REFERENCE & RESEARCH BOOK NEWS. "(Among) the 10 most frequently thumbed (reference books) by Boston Public Library's humanities reference librarians are...Literary Market Place, Ulrich's International Periodicals Directory, ⊞ Books in Print."--BOSTON GLOBE. This is perhaps the single most essential directory for almost every North American book publisher."--HUENEFELD REPORT. Literary Market Place 2001 is the ultimate insider's guide to the U.S. book publishing industry, covering every conceivable aspect of the business. In two, easy-to-use volumes, it provides: *50 sections organizing everyone & everything in the business - from publishers, agents, & ad agencies to associations, distributors, & events *Over 14,500 listings in all - featuring names, addresses, & numbers...personnel...activities, specialties, & other relevant data...e-mail addresses & Web sites...& more * Some 24,000 decision - makers throughout the industry, listed in a separate "Personnel Yellow Pages" section in each volume. *Thousands of services & suppliers equipped to met every publishing need or requirement *More than 400 new entries to this edition plus thousands of updated listings throughout. LMP 2001 leaves no stone unturned in connecting you with the publishing firm, service, or product you or your patrons need. It's completely revised & updated to help: *Publishers locate other publishers, freelancers, agents, printers, wholesalers, manufacturers, & more *Suppliers find names & numbers of potential publishing customers *Job seekers locate contact names, addresses, & phone numbers throughout the industry *Booksellers get publishers ordering & shipping information *Writers locate publishers for their works *Librarians provide patrons with the reference source they need to find their way through the publishing industry. When it comes to books, you can reach the people who publish, package, review, represent, edit, translate, typeset, illustrate, design, print, bind, promote, publicized, ship, distribute, & export them, all at one world-famous business address: Literary Market Place 2001. ***Publisher Paid Annotation.***

***Literary Market Place 2000: The Directory of the American Book Publishing Industry, 2 vols., Set.** Ed. by Bowker Staff. LC 88-644926. 1999. 189.95 (*0-8352-4218-8*) Bowker.

***Literary Masterpieces.** (Study Guides to Great Literature: Vol. 6). 200p. 2000. 49.95 (*0-7876-4472-2*) Gale.

***Literary Masterpieces: Beloved.** (Study Guides to Great Literature: Vol. 4). 200p. 2000. 49.95 (*0-7876-3968-0*) Gale.

Literary Masterpieces of the Western World. Ed. by Francis H. Horn. 255p. 1977. 19.95 (*0-8369-0547-4*) Ayer.

***Literary Masters.** (Study Guides to Great Literature: Vol. 6). 200p. 2000. 49.95 (*0-7876-4470-6*) Gale.

Literary Mate. Mary L. Burkhalter. 90p. 1998. pap. 150.00 (*0-934284-08-3*) Jolean Pub Co.

Literary Material see Monastery of Epiphanius at Thebes

Literary Meaning. Wendell V. Harris. (C). 1997. pap. text 18.50 (*0-8147-3500-2*) NYU Pr.

Literary Meaning: Reclaiming the Study of Literature. Wendell V. Harris. 256p. (C). 1996. text 45.00 (*0-8147-3525-8*) NYU Pr.

Literary Meaning & Augustan Values. Irvin Ehrenpreis. LC 73-94275. 131p. reprint ed. pap. 40.70 (*0-608-08553-7*, 206907600002) Bks Demand.

Literary Memoirs. Jose Victorino Lastarria. Ed. by Frederick M. Nunn. Tr. by R. Kelly Washbourne from SPA. LC 99-55771. (Library of Latin America). 448p. 2000. 30.00 (*0-19-511685-2*); pap. 19.95 (*0-19-511686-0*) OUP.

Literary Memoirs of the Nineteenth Century. George E. Woodberry. (BCL1-PR English Literature Ser.). 320p. 1992. reprint ed. lib. bdg. 89.00 (*0-7812-7059-6*) Rprt Serv.

Literary Message of Isaiah. Avraham Gileadi. LC 94-76821. 610p. 1994. 25.00 (*0-9626643-1-6*) Hebraeus Press.

Literary Methods & Sociological Theory: Case Studies of Simmel & Weber. Bryan Green. 320p. 1993. lib. bdg. 45.00 (*0-226-30612-7*) U Ch Pr.

Literary Methods & Sociological Theory: Case Studies of Simmel & Weber. Bryan Green. 312p. 1998. pap. text 19.50 (*0-226-30613-5*) U Ch Pr.

Literary Milton: Text, Pretext, Context. Ed. by Diana T. Benet & Michael Lieb. LC 94-11292. (Duquesne Studies: Language & Literature Ser.: Vol. 16). 274p. (C). 1994. 48.00 (*0-8207-0259-5*) Duquesne.

Literary Mind. Mark Turner. LC 95-50366. (Illus.). 208p. 1996. 27.50 (*0-19-510411-0*) OUP.

Literary Mind: Portraits in Pain & Creativity. Leo Schneiderman. 240p. (C). 1988. 42.95 (*0-89885-394-X*, Kluwer Acad Hman Sci); pap. 18.95 (*0-89885-404-0*, Kluwer Acad Hman Sci) Kluwer Academic.

Literary Mind: The Origins of Thought & Language. Mark Turner. (Illus.). 208p. 1998. reprint ed. pap. 13.95 (*0-19-512667-X*) OUP.

Literary Modernism & the Occult Tradition. Ed. by Leon Surette & Demetres P. Tryphonopoulos. 1996. 35.00 (*0-943373-40-9*); pap. 20.00 (*0-943373-41-7*) Natl Poet Foun.

Literary Moment As a Lens on Reality. James R. King. LC 82-17319. 224p. 1983. text 29.95 (*0-8262-0393-0*) U of Mo Pr.

Literary Moments, 180 WPM. Stephen Edmondson. Ed. by Monette Benoit. 1994. pap. 22.95 (*1-881149-04-8*) CRRB.

Literary Monographs, Vol. 1. LC 66-25869. 336p. reprint ed. pap. 104.20 (*0-608-02215-2*, 200204200011) Bks Demand.

Literary Monographs, Vol. 2. Ed. by Eric Rothstein & Richard N. Ringler. LC 66-25869. 261p. reprint ed. pap. 81.00 (*0-608-02216-0*, 200204200002) Bks Demand.

Literary Monographs, Vol. 3. Ed. by Eric Rothstein. LC 66-25869. 233p. reprint ed. pap. 72.30 (*0-608-02217-9*, 200204200003) Bks Demand.

Literary Monographs, Vol. 4. LC 66-25869. 234p. reprint ed. pap. 72.60 (*0-608-02218-7*, 200204200004) Bks Demand.

Literary Monographs, Vol. 5. LC 66-25869. 220p. reprint ed. pap. 68.20 (*0-608-02219-5*, 200204200005) Bks Demand.

Literary Monographs, Vol. 6. LC 66-25869. 192p. reprint ed. pap. 59.60 (*0-608-02220-9*, 200204200006) Bks Demand.

Literary Monographs, Vol. 7. LC 66-25869. 172p. reprint ed. pap. 53.40 (*0-608-02221-7*, 200204200007) Bks Demand.

Literary Monographs, Vol. 8. LC 66-25869. 224p. reprint ed. pap. 69.50 (*0-608-02222-5*, 200204200008) Bks Demand.

Literary Monographs, Vol. 9. LC 66-25869. 168p. reprint ed. pap. 52.10 (*0-608-02223-3*, 200204200009) Bks Demand.

Literary Moscow: Historical-Local Lore Encyclopaedia for Students. Korneliia Starodub. (RUS., Illus.). 368p. (C). 1997. 20.95 (*0-8285-5531-1*) Firebird NY.

Literary Movement in France During the Nineteenth Century. Georges Pellisier. LC 71-150197. 504p. reprint ed. lib. bdg. 28.00 (*0-8290-0508-0*) Irvington.

Literary Movement in France During the Nineteenth Century. Georges Pellissier. LC 71-150197. (Select Bibliographies Reprint Ser.). 1977. reprint ed. 31.95 (*0-8369-5710-5*) Ayer.

Literary Murder. Batya Goor. LC 92-56195. 368p. 1994. pap. 12.00 (*0-06-092548-5*) HarperTrade.

Literary Nashville. Ed. by Patrick Allen. LC 99-37701. 320p. 1999. pap. 16.95 (*1-892514-11-7*) Hill St Pr.

Literary Neighborhoods of New York. Marcia Leisner. LC 88-34870. (Literary Cities Ser.). (Illus.). 72p. (Orig.). 1989. pap. 8.95 (*0-913515-40-X*, Starrhill Press) Black Belt Communs.

Literary New Mexico: Essays from Book Talk. Dwight Myers & Carol Myers. LC 97-38390. 1998. 70.00 (*1-58096-001-4*) Ancient City Pr.

***Literary New Orleans.** Ed. by Judy Long. 288p. 1999. pap. 16.95 (*1-892514-05-2*) Hill St Pr.

Literary New Orleans: Essays & Meditations. Ed. by Richard S. Kennedy. (Southern Literary Studies). (Illus.). 112p. 1998. pap. 9.95 (*0-8071-2273-4*) La State U Pr.

Literary New Orleans in the Modern World. Ed. by Richard S. Kennedy. LC 97-50294. (Southern Literary Studies). (Illus.). 208p. 1998. 26.95 (*0-8071-2208-4*) La State U Pr.

Literary Nominalism & the Theory of Rereading Late Medieval Texts: A New Research Paradigm. Richard J. Utz. LC 95-6070. (Medieval Studies: Vol. 5). 264p. (Orig.). 1995. text 89.95 (*0-7734-8882-0*) E Mellen.

Literary Nonfiction: Theory, Criticism, Pedagogy. Ed. by Chris Anderson. LC 88-18726. 256p. (C). 1989. text 31.95 (*0-8093-1405-3*) S Ill U Pr.

Literary North Carolina. Richard Walser & E. T. Malone, Jr. (Illus.). ix, 182p. 1986. pap. 10.00 (*0-86526-222-5*) NC Archives.

Literary Objects: Flaubert. Philippe Desan & Mark Wolff. LC 96-86470. (Illus.). 64p. (Orig.). 1996. pap. 9.95 (*0-935573-17-8*) D & A Smart Museum.

Literary Objects d'Art: Ekphrasis in Medieval French Romance, 1150-1210. Linda M. Clemente. LC 90-24421. (American University Studies: Romance Languages & Literature: Ser. II, Vol. 166). 157p. (C). 1992. text 35.95 (*0-8204-1506-5*) P Lang Pubng.

Literary Odysseys. Mary K. Ziemer-Kapelinski. (Illus.). 350p. (C). pap. text 21.95 (*0-472-08603-0*, 08603) U of Mich Pr.

Literary Olympians 11. 500p. 1988. 18.95 (*0-9619332-9-1*) Crosscurrents Anthologies.

Literary 100: A Ranking of the Most Influential Novelists, Playwrights & Poets of All Time. Daniel S. Burt. LC 98-13729. (Illus.). 256p. 1998. 29.95 (*0-8065-1956-8*, Citadel Pr) Carol Pub Group.

***Literary 100: A Ranking of the Most Influential Novelists, Playwrights & Poets of All Time.** Daniel S. Burt. (Illus.). 416p. 2001. 35.00 (*0-8160-4382-5*, Checkmark); pap. 19.95 (*0-8160-4383-3*, Checkmark) Facts on File.

Literary Opinion in America Vol. 1: Essays Illustrating the Status, Methods & Problems of Criticism in the United States in the Twentieth Century. Morton D. Zabel. 1981. 16.50 (*0-8446-1487-4*) Peter Smith.

An Asterisk (*) at the beginning of an entry indicates that the title is appearing for the first time.

Literary Origin of the Gospel of John. Howard M. Teeple. LC 73-87487. x, 297p. (Orig.). 1974. pap. 6.00 (*0-914384-00-7*) Relig & Ethics.

Literary Outlaw: The Life & Times of William S. Burroughs. Ted Morgan. (Illus.). 1990. pap. 12.95 (*0-380-70882-5*, Avon Bks) Morrow Avon.

***Literary Oxford.** Nancy Hood. (Illus.). 128p. 2000. pap. 16.95 (*0-7509-2115-3*) Sutton Publng.

Literary Pages. Michael Wilding. LC 99-178131. 1998. pap. 18.95 (*0-7022-3019-7*, Pub. by Univ Queensland Pr) Intl Spec Bk.

Literary Papyri: Poetry see Papyri

Literary Paris. Illus. by Linda Ayriss. (Literary Maps Ser.). (Orig.). (J). (gr. 6-12). 1988. pap. 4.95 (*0-937609-09-9*) Aaron Blake Pubs.

Literary Paris. Jeffrey Kraft. 1999. 18.95 (*0-8174-2830-5*) Watsn-Guptill.

Literary Paris. Jeffrey Kraft. LC 99-10878. (Illus.). 112p. 1999. pap. text 18.95 (*0-8230-2830-5*) Watsn-Guptill.

Literary Patronage in England, 1650-1800. Dustin H. Griffin. (Illus.). 327p. (C). 1996. text 54.95 (*0-521-56085-3*) Cambridge U Pr.

Literary Patronage in Greece & Rome. Barbara K. Gold. LC 86-25044. xiv, 267p. (C). 1987. 32.50 (*0-8078-1739-2*) U of NC Pr.

Literary Patronage in Greece & Rome. Barbara K. Gold. LC 86-25044. 281p. 1987. reprint ed. pap. 87.20 (*0-608-02069-9*, 206272200003) Bks Demand.

Literary Patronage in Late Medieval Japan. Ed. by Steven D. Carter. LC 93-14920. (Michigan Papers in Japanese Studies: No. 23). ix, 175p. (C). 1993. pap. 13.95 (*0-939512-60-2*) U MI Japan.

Literary Patronage in the English Renaissance: The Pembroke Family. Michael Brennan. 224p. 1988. lib. bdg. 59.95 (*0-415-00327-X*) Routledge.

Literary Patterns, Theological Themes & the Genre of Luke-Acts. Charles H. Talbert. LC 74-78620. (Society of Biblical Literature, Ser.: No. 20). 168p. reprint ed. 52.10 (*0-8357-9577-2*, 201750900007) Bks Demand.

Literary Pedagogics after Deconstruction: Scenarios & Perspectives in the Teaching of English Literature. Ed. by Per S. Petersen. (The Dolphin Ser.: No. 22). 112p. (C). 1992. pap. 19.95 (*87-7288-372-3*, Pub. by Aarhus Univ Pr) David Brown.

Literary Percys: Family History, Gender, & the Southern Imagination. Bertram Wyatt-Brown. LC 94-4173. (Mercer University Lamar Memorial Lectures: No. 37). 144p. 1994. 19.95 (*0-8203-1665-2*) U of Ga Pr.

Literary Persona. Robert C. Elliott. LC 81-19656. (Illus.). 1982. 24.00 (*0-226-20502-9*) U Ch Pr.

Literary Persona. Robert C. Elliott. LC 81-19656. 188p. reprint ed. pap. 58.30 (*0-608-09458-7*, 205425800005) Bks Demand.

Literary Perspectives, Vol. I. 2nd ed. Don L. Powell. 1000p. 1998. per. 77.95 (*0-7872-4213-6*, 41421301) Kendall-Hunt.

Literary Perspectives, Vol. II. Don L. Powell. 448p. 1992. pap. text 49.95 (*0-8403-7871-8*) Kendall-Hunt.

Literary Pilgrim in England. Edward Thomas. LC 69-17591. (Essay Index Reprint Ser.). 1977. 21.95 (*0-8369-0094-4*) Ayer.

Literary Pioneers. Orie W. Long. 1975. 250.00 (*0-87968-301-5*) Gordon Pr.

Literary Pioneers: Early American Explorers of European Culture. Orie W. Long. (BCL1-PS American Literature Ser.). 267p. 1993. reprint ed. lib. bdg. 79.00 (*0-7812-6576-2*) Rprt Serv.

Literary Pluralities. Ed. by Christi Verduyn. 340p. 1998. pap. 18.95 (*1-55111-203-5*) Broadview Pr.

Literary Polemics: Bataille, Sartre, Valery, Breton. Suzanne Guerlac. LC 96-2739. 1997. 55.50 (*0-8047-2715-5*) Stanford U Pr.

***Literary Polemics: Bataille, Sartre, Valery, Breton.** Suzanne Guerlac. 2000. pap. text 19.95 (*0-8047-4004-6*) Stanford U Pr.

Literary Politics in America. Richard Kostelanetz. LC 73-9098. 498p. 1981. reprint ed. pap. 75.00 (*0-932360-41-6*) Archae Edns.

Literary Politics in the Soviet Ukraine, 1917-1934. George S. Luckyj. LC 75-165645. (Select Bibliographies Reprint Ser.). 1977. reprint ed. 24.95 (*0-8369-5954-X*) Ayer.

Literary Politics in the Soviet Ukraine, 1917-1934. rev. ed. George S. Luckyj. LC 90-3499. (Studies of the Harriman Institute). 367p. (C). 1990. reprint ed. text 49.95 (*0-8223-1081-3*); reprint ed. pap. text 24.95 (*0-8223-1099-6*) Duke.

Literary Portraits. J. Donnie Snyder. (J). 1991. mass mkt. 23.95 (*0-8384-3334-0*) Heinle & Heinle.

Literary Portraits. Charles Whibley. LC 68-55864. (Essay Index Reprint Ser.). 1977. 20.95 (*0-8369-0988-7*) Ayer.

Literary Portraits in the Novels of Henry Fielding. Sean Shesgreen. LC 72-1389. 206p. 1972. 28.00 (*0-87580-029-7*) N Ill U Pr.

Literary Portrayal of Passion Through the Ages: An Interdisciplinary View. Ed. by Keith Cameron. LC 95-47647. (Illus.). 144p. 1996. 69.95 (*0-7734-8786-7*) E Mellen.

Literary Power & the Criteria of Truth. Laura Quinney. LC 94-42895. 192p. (C). 1995. 49.95 (*0-8130-1345-3*) U Press Fla.

Literary Practice: Esthetic Qualities & Values in Literature; A Humanistic & a Biometric Appraisal, Vol. 1. Dushan Bresky & Miroslav Malik. (American University Studies: General Literature: Ser. XIX, Vol. 1). 215p. (C). 1984. text 25.50 (*0-8204-0199-4*) P Lang Pubng.

Literary Practice Vol. 2: Esthetics of Style. Dushan Bresky. (American University Studies: General Literature: Ser. XIX, Vol. 21). 244p. (C). 1989. text 39.00 (*0-8204-1033-0*) P Lang Pubng.

Literary Precursors to the Book of Twelve. James Nogalski. (Beiheft zur Zeitschrift fuer die Alttestamentliche Wissenschaft Ser.: Vol. 217). x, 301p. (C). 1993. lib. bdg. 106.15 (*3-11-013702-X*) De Gruyter.

Literary Presentations of Divided Germany: The Development of a Central Theme in East German Fiction, 1945-1970. Peter Hutchinson. LC 76-51414. (Anglica Germanica Ser.: No. 2). 212p. reprint ed. pap. 60.50 (*0-608-15741-4*, 2031673) Bks Demand.

Literary Primer. William C. Brown. 97p. (Orig.). 1994. pap. 9.95 (*0-9642156-0-8*) QCorp.

Literary Products of the Lewis Carroll - George MacDonald Friendship. John Docherty. LC 94-45740. 420p. 1995. text 109.95 (*0-7734-9038-8*) E Mellen.

Literary Profection in the Elizabethan Age. Phoebe Sheavyn & Anne Beale. (BCL1-PR English Literature Ser.). 222p. 1992. reprint ed. pap. text 59.00 (*0-685-52132-X*); reprint ed. lib. bdg. 79.00 (*0-7812-7037-5*) Rprt Serv.

Literary Profession in the Elizabethan Age. Phoebe Sheavyn. LC 65-15880. (Studies in Drama: No. 39). 1969. reprint ed. lib. bdg. 75.00 (*0-8383-0621-7*) M S G Haskell Hse.

***Literary Prose of Westminster Magazine (1773-1785) An Annotated Index under Contributors' Names, Pseudonymous Signature & Ascriptions.** Edward W. R. Pitcher. LC 99-53208. (Studies in British & American Magazines). 316p. 2000. 99.95 (*0-7734-7834-5*) E Mellen.

Literary Publishing in America, 1790-1850. William Charvat. LC 92-2663. 104p. (C). 1993. reprint ed. pap. 10.95 (*0-87023-801-9*) U of Mass Pr.

Literary Reader see Collage: An Intermediate French Program

***Literary Reading of John 5: Text as Construction.** Francisco Lozada. (Studies in Biblical Literature: Vol. 20). 152p. (C). 2000. text 40.95 (*0-8204-4533-9*) P Lang Pubng.

Literary Realism & the Ekphrastic Tradition. Mack Smith. 264p. 1998. 40.00 (*0-271-01329-X*) Pa St U Pr.

Literary Recordings: A Checklist of the Archive of Recorded Poetry & Literature in the Library of Congress. 1986. lib. bdg. 79.95 (*0-8490-3540-6*) Gordon Pr.

Literary Recreations. Edward T. Cook. LC 68-54340. (Essay Index Reprint Ser.). 1977. 20.95 (*0-8369-0331-5*) Ayer.

Literary Recreations & Miscellanies. John Greenleaf Whittier. (Notable American Authors Ser.). 1999. reprint ed. lib. bdg. 125.00 (*0-7812-9974-8*) Rprt Serv.

Literary Reflection: A Language Arts Unit for High-Ability Learning. Center for Gifted Education Staff. 346p. (C). 1998. boxed set 65.95 (*0-7872-5287-5*) Kendall-Hunt.

Literary Reflections. James A. Michener. 1995. pap. 4.99 (*0-8125-5052-8*, Pub. by Forge NYC) St Martin.

Literary Reflections: A Shoring of Images, 1960-1993. R. W. B. Lewis. 288p. 1993. text 40.00 (*1-55553-160-1*) NE U Pr.

Literary Reflections: Michener on Michener, Hemingway, Capote, & Others. James A. Michener. LC 93-32356. (Illus.). 224p. 1993. 21.95 (*1-880510-06-5*) State House Pr.

Literary Relations of England & Germany in the 17th Century. Gilbert Waterhouse. LC 68-818. (Studies in Comparative Literature: No. 35). 1969. reprint ed. lib. bdg. 75.00 (*0-8383-0689-6*) M S G Haskell Hse.

Literary Relations of England & Scandinavia in the Seventeenth Century. Ethel Seaton. LC 72-83605. 1972. reprint ed. lib. bdg. 26.95 (*0-405-08943-0*) Ayer.

***Literary Relationship of Lord Byron & Thomas Moore.** Jeffery W. Vail. LC 00-28201. 296p. 2001. 42.50 (*0-8018-6500-X*) Johns Hopkins.

Literary Relativity: An Essay on Twentieth Century Narrative. Betty J. Craige. LC 81-69634. (Illus.). 136p. 1982. 26.50 (*0-8387-5034-6*) Bucknell U Pr.

Literary Remains. Joseph B. Ladd. 1972. reprint ed. lib. bdg. 21.50 (*0-8422-8141-X*) Irvington.

Literary Remains: Consisting of Lectures & Tracts on Political Economy. Richard Jones. LC 64-24344. (Reprints of Economic Classics Ser.). xl, 620p. 1964. reprint ed. 57.50 (*0-678-00063-8*) Kelley.

Literary Remains of Joseph Brown Ladd, M. D. Joseph B. Ladd. (Notable American Authors Ser.). 1999. reprint ed. lib. bdg. 125.00 (*0-7812-3680-0*) Rprt Serv.

Literary Remains of Samuel Taylor Coleridge, 4 vols. Samuel Taylor Coleridge. Ed. by Henry N. Coleridge. reprint ed. 400.00 (*0-404-01710-X*) AMS Pr.

Literary Reputation of Else Lasker-Schueler: Criticism, 1901-1993. Calvin N. Jones. (LCGERM Ser.). xiv, 178p. 1994. 55.00 (*1-879751-83-6*) Camden Hse.

Literary Reputation of Mark Twain from 1910-1950. Roger Asselineau. LC 73-98744. 240p. 1971. reprint ed. lib. bdg. 65.00 (*0-8371-3069-7*, ASLR, Greenwood Pr) Greenwood.

Literary Research Guide. 2nd fac. ed. Margaret C. Patterson. LC 82-20386. 685p. 1984. reprint ed. pap. 200.00 (*0-7837-8032-X*, 204778800008) Bks Demand.

Literary Research Guide: An Annotated Listing of Reference Sources in English Literary Studies. 3rd ed. James L. Harner. LC 98-10028. 900p. 1998. lib. bdg. 45.00 (*0-87352-573-6*, S205C) Modern Lang.

Literary Research Guide: An Annotated Listing of Reference Sources in English Literary Studies. 3rd rev. ed. James L. Harner. LC 98-10028. 900p. 1998. pap. 19.75 (*0-87352-574-4*, S205P) Modern Lang.

Literary Responses to the Holocaust, 1945-1995. Ed. by Yehoshua Gitay. LC 98-12596. 408p. 1997. 70.00 (*1-57309-031-X*, Jewish Scholars); pap. 50.00 (*1-57309-030-1*, Jewish Scholars) Intl Scholars.

Literary Reviewing. Ed. by James O. Hoge. LC 87-8309. 154p. reprint ed. pap. 47.80 (*0-608-10479-5*, 207109700008) Bks Demand.

Literary Reviews & Criticisms. Prosser H. Frye. LC 68-8462. (Essay Index Reprint Ser.). 1977. reprint ed. 20.95 (*0-8369-0465-6*) Ayer.

Literary Reviews & Criticisms. Prosser H. Frye. LC 68-59378. 320p. (C). 1968. reprint ed. 50.00 (*0-87752-040-2*) Gordian.

Literary Reviews & Essays on American, English & French Literature. Henry James. Ed. by Albert Mordell. 1957. pap. 14.95 (*0-8084-0202-1*) NCUP.

Literary Revolution. Stanton A. Coblentz. LC 72-94308. (BCL Ser.: No. I). reprint ed. 20.00 (*0-404-01579-4*) AMS Pr.

Literary Revolution. Stanton A. Coblentz. (BCL1-PR English Literature Ser.). 202p. 1992. reprint ed. lib. bdg. 79.00 (*0-685-52152-4*) Rprt Serv.

Literary Russia: A Guide. Anna Benn & Rosamund Bartlett. LC 98-145251. (Illus.). 495p. 1998. pap. 29.50 (*0-333-71197-1*, Pub. by Papermac) Trans-Atl Phila.

***Literary St. Louis: A Guide.** William H. Gass & Lorin Cuoco. (Illus.). 250p. 2000. pap. 19.95 (*1-883982-35-9*) U of Mo Pr.

Literary Sands of Key West. Patricia Altobello & Deirdre Pierce. (Literary Cities Ser.). (Illus.). 80p. (Orig.). 1996. pap. 8.95 (*1-57359-004-5*, Starrhill Press) Black Belt Communs.

Literary Santa Barbara: Between Great Mountains & a Great Sea. Steven Gilbar & Dean Stewart. LC 97-4976. 1997. write for info. (*0-87461-112-1*) McNally & Loftin.

Literary Savannah. Ed. by Patrick Allen. 296p. 1998. pap. 16.95 (*1-892514-01-X*) Hill St Pr.

Literary Sculptors. Margaret F. Thorp. LC 65-13655. (Illus.). 242p. reprint ed. pap. 75.10 (*0-608-11261-5*, 201793800010) Bks Demand.

***Literary Seductions.** Frances Wilson. 256p. 2000. text 23.95 (*0-312-26193-4*) St Martin.

Literary Selves: Autobiography & Contemporary American Nonfiction, 50. James N. Stull. LC 93-10376. (Contributions to the Study of World Literature Ser.: No. 50). 176p. 1993. 57.95 (*0-313-28825-9*, GM8825, Greenwood Pr) Greenwood.

Literary Sessions. Eric Partridge. LC 70-117904. (Select Bibliographies Reprint Ser.). 1977. reprint ed. 21.95 (*0-8369-5357-6*) Ayer.

Literary Sign Language of German Romanticism. Marianne Thalmann. LC 77-184484. 163p. reprint ed. pap. 50.60 (*0-7837-3810-2*, 204363000010) Bks Demand.

Literary Sources of Secular Music in Italy, 1500. Walter H. Rubsamen. LC 72-4482. (Music Ser.). 82p. 1972. reprint ed. lib. bdg. 21.50 (*0-306-70496-X*) Da Capo.

Literary Speech Act: Don Juan with J. L. Austin, or Seduction in Two Languages. Shoshana Felman. Tr. by Catherine Porter. LC 83-45144. 176p. 1983. 35.00 (*0-8014-1458-X*) Cornell U Pr.

Literary Spotlight. Ed. by John C. Farrar. LC 70-117789. (Essay Index Reprint Ser.). 1977. 23.95 (*0-8369-1874-6*) Ayer.

Literary Standards in Practice. 36p. 1998. pap. text 24.95 (*1-58303-072-7*) Pthways Pubng.

Literary Statesmen: And Others. Norman Hapgood. LC 75-37796. (Essay Index Reprint Ser.). 1977. reprint ed. 18.95 (*0-8369-2593-9*) Ayer.

Literary Structure & Rhetorical Strategies in the Hebrew Bible. Ed. by L. J. De Regt et al. LC 96-9273. x, 270p. 1996. text 42.50 (*1-57506-011-6*) Eisenbrauns.

Literary Structure, Evolution, & Value: Russian Formalism & Czech Structuralism Reconsidered. Jurij Striedter. LC 88-11036. (Studies in Comparative Literature: No. 38). 317p. 1989. 43.50 (*0-674-53653-3*) HUP.

Literary Structure of Scientific Argument: Historical Studies. Ed. by Peter Dear. LC 90-45803. 224p. (C). 1991. text 34.95 (*0-8122-8185-3*) U of Pa Pr.

Literary Structure of the Old Testament: A Commentary on Genesis-Malachi. David A. Dorsey. LC 99-40433. 352p. 1999. 34.99 (*0-8010-2187-1*) Baker Bks.

Literary Studies. Charles Whibley. LC 70-90693. (Essay Index Reprint Ser.). 1977. 23.95 (*0-8369-1238-1*) Ayer.

Literary Studies & Reviews. Richard Aldington. LC 68-16901. (Essay Index Reprint Ser.). 1977. 19.95 (*0-8369-0143-6*) Ayer.

Literary Studies in Action. Alan Durant & Nigel Fabb. LC 89-10465. 256p. (C). 1990. pap. 24.99 (*0-415-02945-7*, A3649) Routledge.

Literary Studies in Luke - Acts. Richard P. Thompson. 1998. pap. 25.00 (*0-86554-631-2*) Mercer Univ Pr.

Literary Studies (Miscellaneous Essays) Walter Bagehot. Ed. by Richard H. Hutton. (Works of Walter Bagehot, 1826-1877). 357p. reprint ed. lib. bdg. 49.00 (*0-7812-0893-9*) Rprt Serv.

Literary Studies with a Prefatory Memoir, 2 vols. Walter Bagehot. Ed. by Richard H. Hutton. LC 72-148745. (BCL Ser.: No. I). reprint ed. 115.00 (*0-404-07235-6*) AMS Pr.

Literary Study & the Scholarly Profession. Hardin Craig. LC 72-84303. (Essay Index Reprint Ser.). 1977. 19.95 (*0-8369-1079-6*) Ayer.

Literary Study of the Bible. Richard G. Moulton. LC 70-4534. 1898. 59.00 (*0-403-00113-7*) Scholarly.

Literary Study of the Bible. Richard G. Moulton. 1988. reprint ed. lib. bdg. 59.00 (*0-7812-0552-2*) Rprt Serv.

Literary Style of the Old Bible & the New. Ed. by D. G. Kehl. LC 72-117334. (Composition & Rhetoric Ser.: No. 21). (Orig.). (C). 1970. pap. write for info. (*0-672-60907-X*, CR21, Bobbs) Macmillan.

Literary Subversions: New American Fiction & the Practice of Criticism. Jerome Klinkowitz. LC 85-1887. (Crosscurrents-Modern Critiques, Third Ser.). 224p. 1985. text 26.95 (*0-8093-1209-3*) S Ill U Pr.

***Literary Sydney: A Walking Guide.** Jill Diamond & Peter Kirkpatrick. 2000. pap. 19.95 (*0-7022-3150-9*, Pub. by Univ Queensland Pr) Intl Spec Bk.

Literary Symbiosis: Science Fiction-Fantasy Mystery, 6. Hazel B. Pierce. LC 83-1710. (Contributions to the Study of Science Fiction & Fantasy Ser.: No. 6). 255p. 1983. 49.95 (*0-313-23065-X*, PLS/, Greenwood Pr) Greenwood.

Literary Systematics. Helmut Bonheim. (Illus.). 392p. (C). 1990. 75.00 (*0-85991-298-1*) Boydell & Brewer.

Literary Taste: How to Form It. Arnold Bennett. LC 74-16487. (Collected Works of Arnold Bennett: Vol. 47). 1977. reprint ed. 22.95 (*0-518-19128-1*) Ayer.

Literary Temper of the English Puritans, 9. Lawrence A. Sasek. LC 78-88936. 131p. 1970. reprint ed. lib. bdg. 35.00 (*0-8371-2333-X*, SAEP, Greenwood Pr) Greenwood.

Literary Terms: A Dictionary. 3rd rev. ed. Karl Beckson & Arthur Ganz. LC 88-34368. 308p. 1989. pap. 11.00 (*0-374-52177-8*) FS&G.

***Literary Terms: A Practical Glossary.** Brian Moon. LC 99-46413. (Chalkface Ser.). (Illus.). 192p. 1999. pap. 21.95 (*0-8141-3008-9*, 30089) NCTE.

Literary Terms & Criticism. Peck. 1997. text 14.95 (*0-333-58887-8*, Pub. by Macmillan) St Martin.

Literary Text in the Digital Age. Ed. by Richard J. Finneran. LC 96-9951. (Editorial Theory & Literary Criticism Ser.). 264p. 1996. text 49.50 (*0-472-10690-2*, 10690) U of Mich Pr.

***Literary Texts & Greek Historian.** C. B. Pelling. LC 99-33324. 336p. 1999. pap. 24.99 (*0-415-07351-0*) Routledge.

***Literary Texts & Greek Historian.** Christopher B. R. Pelling. LC 99-33324. 336p. (C). 2000. text 65.00 (*0-415-07350-2*) Routledge.

Literary Texts & the Roman Historian. David S. Potter. LC 98-8690. (Approaching the Ancient World Ser.). 265p. (C). 1999. pap. 20.99 (*0-415-08896-8*) Routledge.

Literary Texts & the Roman Historian. David S. Potter. LC 98-8690. (Approaching the Ancient World Ser.). (Illus.). 256p. (C). 1999. 60.00 (*0-415-08895-X*) Routledge.

Literary Texts from the Temple of Nabu see Cuneiform Texts from Nimrud

Literary Themes A-I, Vol. 1. Jean-Charles Seigneuret. 1988. lib. bdg. 185.00 (*0-313-26396-5*, SLT01, Greenwood Pr) Greenwood.

Literary Themes J-Z, Vol. 2. Jean-Charles Seigneuret. 1988. lib. bdg. 185.00 (*0-313-26397-3*, SLT02, Greenwood Pr) Greenwood.

Literary Theories: A Case Study in Critical Performance. Ed. by Julian Wolfreys & William Baker. LC 96-8941. 259p. (C). 1996. text 45.00 (*0-8147-1294-0*); pap. text 18.50 (*0-8147-1293-2*) NYU Pr.

***Literary Theories: A Reader & Guide.** Ed. by Julian Wolfreys. 700p. 1999. text 79.50 (*0-8147-9360-6*) NYU Pr.

Literary Theories: A Reader & Guide. Ed. by Julian Wolfreys. LC 99-20887. 672p. 1999. pap. text 29.50 (*0-8147-9361-4*) NYU Pr.

Literary Theories in Praxis. Ed. by Shirley F. Staton. LC 86-24898. 484p. 1987. text 54.95 (*0-8122-8037-7*); pap. text 21.95 (*0-8122-1234-7*) U of Pa Pr.

Literary Theories of August Wilhelm Schlegel. Ralph W. Ewton, Jr. (De Proprietatibus Litterarum, Ser. Practica: No. 47). 120p. (Orig.). 1972. pap. text 16.95 (*3-11-000272-8*) Mouton.

Literary Theories of Daniel Heinsius: A Study of the Development & Background of His Views on Literary Theory & Criticism During the Period from 1602 to 1612. J. H. Meter. LC 84-241833. (Republica Literaria Neerlandica Ser.). 433 p. 1985. 55.00 (*90-232-1892-2*, Pub. by Van Gorcum) Eisenbrauns.

Literary Theory. Jonathan Culler. LC 97-17713. (Very Short Introductions Ser.). (Illus.). 152p. 1998. pap. 8.95 (*0-19-285318-X*) OUP.

Literary Theory. David Dawson. LC 95-5492. (Guides to Theological Inquiry Ser.). 128p. 1995. pap. 14.00 (*0-8006-2693-1*, 1-2693, Fortress Pr) Augsburg Fortress.

Literary Theory: A Practical Introduction. Michael Ryan. LC 98-28722. 512p. 1999. 59.95 (*0-631-17275-0*); pap. 27.95 (*0-631-17276-9*) Blackwell Pubs.

***Literary Theory: A Very Short Introduction.** 160p. 2000. 8.95 (*0-19-285383-X*) OUP.

Literary Theory: An Anthology. Ed. by Julie Rivkin & Michael Ryan. LC 97-20348. (Illus.). 960p. (C). 1998. text 84.95 (*0-631-20028-2*); pap. text 42.95 (*0-631-20029-0*) Blackwell Pubs.

Literary Theory: An Introduction. 2nd rev. ed. Terry Eagleton. 288p. (C). 1996. pap. text 15.95 (*0-8166-1251-X*) U of Minn Pr.

Literary Theory - Renaissance Texts. Ed. by Patricia Parker & David Quint. LC 85-23799. 408p. 1986. reprint ed. pap. 126.50 (*0-608-03741-9*, 206456600009) Bks Demand.

Literary Theory after Davidson. Ed. by Reed W. Dasenbrock. LC 92-14885. 336p. (C). 1993. 50.00 (*0-271-00895-4*); pap. 19.95 (*0-271-00898-9*) Pa St U Pr.

Literary Theory & Children's Literature. Roderick McGillis. 1996. 22.95 (*0-8057-7810-1*, Twyne) Mac Lib Ref.

Literary Theory & Criticism. Edgar Allan Poe. Ed. by Leonard Cassuto. LC 99-36639. 256p. 1998. pap. 11.95 (*0-486-40155-3*) Dover.

Literary Theory & Criticism: A Collection of Essays in Honor of Rene Wellek on the Occasion of His 80th Birthday, 2 vols. 2nd ed. Ed. by Joseph P. Strelka. (Illus.). 1460p. 1984. 83.00 (*0-8204-0178-1*) P Lang Pubng.

L

Literary Theory & English Teaching. Peter Griffin. (English, Language & Education Ser.). 160p. 1987. pap. 40.95 (0-335-15250-3) OpUniv Pr.

Literary Theory & Poetry: Extending the Canon. David Murray. LC 90-114975. 216p. 1989. write for info. (0-7134-5814-3, Pub. by B T B) U of Pa Pr.

Literary Theory & Sanskrit Poetics: Language, Consciousness, & Meaning. William S. Haney, II. LC 93-34118. 200p. 1993. 79.95 (0-7734-9379-4) E Mellen.

Literary Theory & the Claims of History: Postmodernism, Objectivity, Multicultural Politics. Satya P. Mohanty. LC 97-3820. 304p. 1996. text 39.95 (0-8014-2902-1); pap. text 15.95 (0-8014-8135-X) Cornell U Pr.

Literary Theory at Work: Three Texts. Ed. by Douglas Tallack. LC 86-17378. 192p. 1987. 46.00 (0-389-20666-0, N8224) B&N Imports.

***Literary Theory From Plato to Barthes: An Introductory History.** Richard Harland. LC 99-22571. 1999. text 59.95 (0-312-22481-8) St Martin.

***Literary Theory from Plato to Barthes: An Introductory History.** Richard Harland. LC 99-22571. 1999. pap. 19.95 (0-312-22482-6) St Martin.

Literary Theory Today. Ed. by Peter Collier & Helga Geyer-Ryan. LC 90-55166. 280p. 1990. pap. 17.95 (0-8014-9761-2) Cornell U Pr.

Literary Theory Today. Ed. by M. A. Abbas & Tak-Wai Wong. LC 83-127859. 265p. 1981. reprint ed. pap. 82.20 (0-608-01393-5, 206215400002) Bks Demand.

***Literary Theory Toolbox: An Introduction to Theory in Practice.** Jeffrey Nealon. 208p. 2000. 49.95 (0-631-20536-5); pap. 19.95 (0-631-20537-3) Blackwell Pubs.

Literary Theory's Future(s) Ed. by Joseph P. Natoli. LC 88-31742. 352p. 1989. text 34.95 (0-252-01599-1); pap. text 14.95 (0-252-06049-0) U of Ill Pr.

***Literary Topics.** (Study Guides to Great Literature: Vol. 6). 200p. 2000. 49.95 (0-7876-4471-4) Gale.

***Literary Topics: Black Aesthetic Movement.** (Study Guides to Great Literature: Vol. 4). 200p. 2000. 49.95 (0-7876-3969-9) Gale.

***Literary Trail of Greater Boston: A Tour of Sites in Boston, Cambridge & Concord.** Susan Wilson. LC 99-89829. (Illus.). 161p. 2000. pap. 10.00 (0-618-05013-2) HM.

***Literary Trails: British Writers in Their Landscapes.** Christina Hardyment. (Illus.). 256p. 2000. 49.50 (0-8109-6705-7, Pub. by Abrams) Time Warner.

Literary Translation in Russia: A Cultural History. Maurice Friedberg. LC 96-6726. 1997. 42.50 (0-271-01600-0) Pa St U Pr.

Literary Transmission & Authority: Dryden & Other Writers. Jennifer Brady et al. Ed. by Earl Miner. LC 92-29788. (Cambridge Studies in Eighteenth-Century English Literature & Thought: No. 17). 175p. (C). 1993. text 54.95 (0-521-44111-0) Cambridge U Pr.

***Literary Trauma: Sadism, Memory, & Sexual Violence in American Women's Fiction.** Deborah M. Horvitz. LC 99-89796. (C). 2000. pap. text 19.95 (0-7914-4712-X) State U NY Pr.

***Literary Trauma: Sadism, Memory, & Sexual Violence in American Women's Fiction.** Deborah M. Horvitz. LC 99-89796. (C). 2000. text 59.50 (0-7914-4711-1) State U NY Pr.

Literary Travel Log: Integrating Literature & Global Awareness. Candy Ruckdashel. Ed. by Jan Keeling. (Illus.). 64p. (Orig.). (J). (gr. 1-6). 1993. pap. text 8.95 (0-86530-256-1) Incentive Pubns.

Literary Traveler. Larry Dark. 1999. pap. 22.50 (0-670-85333-X) Viking Penguin.

Literary Travelogue: A Comparative Study with Special Relevance to Russian Literature from Fonvizin to Pushkin. Wilson. 148p. 1974. pap. text 65.00 (90-247-1558-X, Pub. by M Nijhoff) Kluwer Academic.

***Literary Trips: Following in the Footsteps of Fame.** Victoria Brooks & Alex Ignatius. 2000. pap. 19.95 (0-9686137-0-5) GE com.

Literary Trivia: Fun & Games for Book Lovers. Richard Lederer. (Illus.). 208p. 1994. pap. 12.00 (0-679-75380-X) Vin Bks.

Literary Underground: Writers & the Totalitarian Experience, 1900-1950. John Hoyles. LC 91-404. 320p. 1991. text 49.95 (0-312-06183-8) St Martin.

Literary Underground of the Old Regime. Robert Darnton. (Illus.). 272p. 1982. pap. text 10.50 (0-674-53657-6) HUP.

Literary Universe of Jack B. Yeats. Nora A. McGuinness. LC 90-2536. 288p. 1992. text 45.95 (0-8132-0737-1) Cath U Pr.

Literary Universe of Jorge Luis Borges: An Index to References & Allusions to Persons, Titles & Places in His Writings, 9. Compiled by Daniel Balderston. LC 86-14947. (Bibliographies & Indexes in World Literature Ser.: No. 9). 306p. 1986. lib. bdg. 75.00 (0-313-25083-9, BWS/) Greenwood.

Literary Values. John Burroughs. (Works of John Burroughs). 1989. reprint ed. lib. bdg. 79.00 (0-7812-2190-0) Rprt Serv.

Literary Values, & Other Papers. John Burroughs. LC 76-156624. (Essay Index Reprint Ser.). 1977. reprint ed. 21.95 (0-8369-2347-2) Ayer.

Literary Villages of London. Luree Miller. LC 88-36889. (Literary Cities Ser.). (Illus.). 80p. (Orig.). 1989. pap. 8.95 (0-913515-41-8, Starrhill Press) Black Belt Communs.

Literary Virtual Reality: Writing Fiction with the Breath of Life. 2nd ed. Regina Emig-Ronk. 120p. 1998. pap. 16.95 (0-9658891-2-2) Sharon Rose.

Literary Vision of Gabrielle Roy. 2nd ed. Paula R. Gilbert. LC 84-50323. 335p. 1993. 33.95 (0-917786-05-X) Summa Pubns.

Literary Visions of Homosexuality. Ed. by Stuart Kellogg. LC 83-4300. (Journal of Homosexuality: Vol. 8, Nos. 3-4). 174p. (C). 1983. text 39.95 (0-86656-183-8); pap. text 3.95 (0-86656-231-1) Haworth Pr.

Literary Vocation of Henry Adams. William M. Decker. LC 89-36157. xii, 324p. (C). 1990. 45.00 (0-8078-1874-7) U of NC Pr.

Literary Voice: The Calling of Jonah. Donald Wesling & Tadeusz Slawek. LC 94-45743. (SUNY Series, The Margins of Literature). 238p. (C). 1995. text 59.50 (0-7914-2627-0); pap. text 19.95 (0-7914-2628-9) State U NY Pr.

Literary Vorticism of Ezra Pound & Wyndham Lewis: Towards the Condition of Painting. Reed W. Dasenbrock. LC 84-20179. 284p. 1985. reprint ed. pap. 88.10 (0-608-03649-8, 206447500009) Bks Demand.

Literary Washington: A Complete Guide to the Literary Life in the Nation's Capital. 2nd ed. David Cutler. 356p. (Orig.). 1991. pap. 12.95 (0-8191-8245-1) Madison Bks UPA.

***Literary Washington, D. C.** Ed. by Patrick Allen. LC 99-88137. 320p. 2000. pap. 16.95 (1-892514-63-X) Hill St Pr.

Literary West: An Anthology of Western American Literature. Ed. by Thomas J. Lyon. LC 99-10579. (Illus.). 464p. 1999. 35.00 (0-19-512460-X); pap. 18.95 (0-19-512461-8) OUP.

***Literary Wit.** Bruce Michelson. 2000. pap. 15.95 (1-55849-274-7) U of Mass Pr.

Literary Women & the French Revolution of 1789. Ed. by Catherine R. Montfort. LC 94-69023. (Illus.). 318p. 1995. lib. bdg. 45.95 (1-883479-07-X) Summa Pubns.

Literary Work of Art: An Investigation of the Borderlines of Ontology, Logic, & the Theory of Language. Roman Ingarden. Tr. by George G. Grabowicz. (Studies in Phenomenology & Existential Philosophy). 415p. 1974. 42.95 (0-8101-0418-0); pap. 22.95 (0-8101-0537-3) Northwestern U Pr.

Literary Works of Jack B. Yeats. John W. Purser. (Princess Grace Irish Library). 220p. (C). 1990. text 75.00 (0-389-20929-5) B&N Imports.

Literary Works of Machiavelli: With Selections from the Private Correspondence. Niccolo Machiavelli. Ed. by John Rigby Hale. LC 79-4216. 202p. 1979. reprint ed. lib. bdg. 35.00 (0-313-21248-1, MALW) Greenwood.

Literary Year, 1. Ronnie Sellers Productions Staff. 1999. 11.95 (1-56906-150-5) R Sellers Prods.

Literary Zodiac. Paul Wright. 240p. (Orig.). 1988. pap. 14.95 (0-916360-40-7) CRCS Pubns CA.

Literate America Emerging: Seventeen New Readers Speak Out. Ed. by Barbara Prete & Gary E. Strong. 128p. (Orig.). 1991. pap. 11.95 (0-929722-45-0) CA State Library Fndtn.

Literate Apprenticeships: The Emergence of Language & Literacy in the Preschool Years. Ed. by Hillel Goelman et al. (Advances in Discourse Processes Ser.: Vol. 56). (Illus.). 174p. 1996. text 78.50 (1-56750-148-6) Ablx Pub.

Literate Apprenticeships: The Emergence of Language & Literacy in the Preschool Years. Hillel Goelman et al. (Advances in Discourse Processes Ser.: Vol. 56). (Illus.). 158p. 1996. pap. 42.50 (1-56750-149-4) Ablx Pub.

Literate Bassist. Fred Paterno. 80p. 1982. pap. 10.95 (0-87166-958-7, 93822) Mel Bay.

Literate Beginnings: Programs for Babies & Toddlers. Debby A. Jeffery. LC 95-10691. (Illus.). 162p. (Orig.). 1995. pap. 30.00 (0-8389-0640-0, 0640-0-2045) ALA.

Literate Cat. Ed. by Marc A. Brown. (Illus.). 112p. 1995. 25.95 (1-56313-740-2) BrownTrout Pubs Inc.

Literate Communist: 150 Years of the "Communist Manifesto" Donald C. Hodges. LC 98-30633. (Major Concepts in Politics & Political Theory Ser.: Vol. 16). VI, 217p. (C). 1999. pap. text 29.95 (0-8204-4187-2) P Lang Pubng.

Literate Community: Common Threads & Unique Patterns in Teaching & Learning. Carole C. Freeman. LC 94-24364. 318p. (C). 1995. lib. bdg. 42.50 (0-8191-9781-5) U Pr of Amer.

Literate Culture: Pope's Rhetorical Art. Ruben Quintero. LC 90-50939. 192p. 1992. 36.50 (0-87413-433-1) U Delaware Pr.

Literate Economist: A Brief History of Economics. 2nd ed. E. Ray Canterbery. 1999. pap. text 28.00 (981-02-3849-5) World Scientific Pub.

***Literate Economist: A Brief History of Economics.** 2nd ed. E.R. Canterbery. 224p. 1999. 52.00 (981-02-3848-7) World Scientific Pub.

Literate Education in the Hellenistic & Roman Worlds. Teresa Morgan. LC 98-13857. (Cambridge Classical Studies). (Illus.). 382p. (C). 1999. text 64.95 (0-521-58466-3) Cambridge U Pr.

***Literate Executive: Learn How to Write Like a Leader.** Laurie N. Rozakis. 304p. 1999. 19.95 (0-07-135288-0) McGraw.

Literate Horse. A. D. Syrokomia-Stefanowska. 1998. 10.99 (0-7631-1369-7) BrownTrout Pubs Inc.

Literate Imagination: Renewing the Secondary English Curriculum. Bernard Harrison. 192p. 1994. pap. 24.95 (1-85346-300-0, Pub. by David Fulton) Taylor & Francis.

Literate Lawyer: Legal Writing & Oral Advocacy. 2nd ed. Robert B. Smith. 200p. 1991. pap. 29.50 (0-88063-746-3, MICHIE) LEXIS Pub.

Literate Life: Exploring Language Arts Standards Within a Cycle of Learning. NCTE Elementary Section Steering Committee & National Council of Teachers of English Staff. LC 97-1785. 56p. pap. 8.95 (0-8141-2976-5) NCTE.

Literate Mode of Cicero's Legal Rhetoric. Richard L. Enos. LC 87-12670. 149p. 1987. text 21.95 (0-8093-1382-0) S Ill U Pr.

Literate Passion: Letters of Anais Nin & Henry Miller, 1932-1953. Henry Miller & Anais Nin. Ed. by Gunther Stuhlmann. 1987. 19.95 (0-15-152729-6) Harcourt.

Literate Passion: Letters of Anais Nin & Henry Miller, 1932-1953. Anais Nin & Henry Miller. 448p. 1989. pap. 16.00 (0-15-652791-X) Harcourt.

Literate Person's Guide to Naming a Cat. Lawrence Jarchow. (Illus.). 96p. (Orig.). 1991. pap. 5.95 (0-939395-15-0) Thorntree Pr.

Literate Programming. Donald E. Knuth. LC 91-39510. (Center for the Study of Language & Information-Lecture Notes Ser.). 368p. (C). 1992. 64.95 (0-937073-81-4); pap. 25.95 (0-937073-80-6) CSLI.

Literate Puzzler. Rita Norr & Audrey Tumbarello. LC 94-19668. (Illus.). 128p. 1994. pap. 5.95 (0-8069-0706-1) Sterling.

Literate Systems & Individual Lives: Perspectives on Literacy & Schooling. Ed. by Edward M. Jennings & Alan C. Purves. LC 90-33715. (SUNY Series, Literacy, Culture, & Learning: Theory & Practice). 222p. (C). 1991. text 21.50 (0-7914-0513-3); pap. text 21.95 (0-7914-0514-1) State U NY Pr.

Literate Typographer. Daniel Margulis & John Schroeder. (Illus.). 240p. 1984. pap. 20.00 (0-938304-03-8) Cornell Daily.

Literate Writer: A Rhetoric with Readings Across Four Genres. David J. Kann. xviii, 830p. (C). 1995. pap. text 42.95 (1-55934-372-9, 1372) Mayfield Pub.

Literate Writer, Instructor's Manual. David J. Kann. (C). 1995. pap. text, teacher ed. write for info. (1-55934-373-7, 1373) Mayfield Pub.

Literati & Self-Representation: Autobiographical Sensibility in the Eighteenth-Century Chinese Novel. Martin W. Huang. LC 94-33002. xiv , 238p. 1995. 35.00 (0-8047-2462-8) Stanford U Pr.

Literati Identity & Its Fictional Representations in Late Imperial China. Stephen Roddy et al. LC 97-40032. 1998. write for info. (0-8047-3131-4) Stanford U Pr.

Literati Purges: Political Conflict in Early Yi Korea. Edward W. Wagner. LC 74-21777. (East Asian Monographs: No. 58). 200p. 1975. 30.00 (0-674-53618-5) HUP.

Literati Tradition in Chinese Thought. Yao-Yu Wu et al. LC 95-60454. (Ethnographics Monographs). 539p. (Orig.). (C). 1995. 25.00 (1-878986-06-6) Ethnographics Pr.

Literatia Macabre. Ed. by Danya D'Arcy. (Illus.). 112p. (Orig.). 1996. pap. 11.95 (0-9651215-0-X) Strait-Jacket.

Literatim Transcription of the Manuscripts of William Butler Yeats's The Speckled Bird. William Butler Yeats. Ed. by William H. O'Donnell. LC 76-6047. 486p. 1976. lib. bdg. 75.00 (0-8201-1171-6) Schol Facsimiles.

Literatur- Und Kunsthistorische Schriften. Gustav Radbruch & Herman Klenner. LC 98-166620. x, 454 p. 1997. write for info. (3-8114-2896-9) C F Mueller.

Literatur als Gegenwelt: Zur Geschichlichkeit Literarischer Komik am Beispiel Fischarts und Lessings. Frank Schlossbauer. (Studies in Modern German Literature: Vol. 80). VI, 297p. (C). 1998. text 52.95 (0-8204-3013-7) P Lang Pubng.

Literatur Als Sprachlehre. Hans Hunfeld. 216p. 1990. 25.50 (3-468-49440-8) Langenscheidt.

Literatur Als Theologieersatz: Heinrich Boll: "Sie Sagt, Ihr Kuba Ist Hier und Auch Ihr Nicaragua" Stephan Gustrau. (Wurzburger Studien Zur Fundamentaltheologie Ser.: Bd. 6). (GER.). III, 113p. 1990. 29.80 (3-631-42897-9) P Lang Pubng.

Literatur der Aegypter see Ancient Egyptian Poetry & Prose

Literatur der Agypter. Adolf Erman. xvi, 389p. 1971. reprint ed. write for info. (0-318-71775-1) G Olms Pubs.

Literatur der DDR see Literatur und Landeskunde

Literatur der Deutschen Ubersetzer der Griechen, 3 vols. Johann F. Degen. write for info. (0-318-71761-1) G Olms Pubs.

Literatur der Deutschen Ubersetzer der Griechen: Altenburg und Erlangen, 1797-1801, 3 vols. Johann F. Degen. (GER.). lxxxii, 1435p. 1999. reprint ed. 475.00 (3-487-10185-8, Pub. by G Olms Verlag) Lubrecht & Cramer.

Literatur der Geschichte. Johann S. Ersch. (Handbuch der Deutschen Literatur Seit der Mitte des 18. Jahrhunderts Bis Auf die Neueste Zeit Ser.: Vols. VII-VIII). 1720p. reprint ed. write for info. (3-487-07252-1) G Olms Pubs.

Literatur der Jurisprudenz. Johann S. Ersch. (Handbuch der Deutschen Literatur Seit der Mitte des 18. Jahrhunderts Bis Auf die Neueste Zeit Ser.: Vol. III). 712p. 1982. reprint ed. write for info. (3-487-07248-3) G Olms Pubs.

Literatur der Mathematik. Johann S. Ersch. (Handbuch der Deutschen Literatur Seit der Mitte des 18. Jahrhunderts Bis Auf die Neueste Zeit Ser.: Vol. VI). 1740p. 1982. reprint ed. write for info. (3-487-07251-3) G Olms Pubs.

Literatur der Medizin. Johann S. Ersch. (Handbuch der Deutschen Literatur Seit der Mitte des 18. Jahrhunderts Bis Auf die Neueste Zeit Ser.: Vol. V). 750p. 1965. reprint ed. write for info. (3-487-07250-5) G Olms Pubs.

Literatur der Philologie: Philosophie und Padagogik. Johann S. Ersch. (Handbuch der Deutschen Literatur Seit der Mitte des 18. Jahrhunderts Bis Auf die Neueste Zeit Ser.: Vol. I). 584p. 1982. reprint ed. write for info. (3-487-07246-7) G Olms Pubs.

Literatur der Schonen Kunste. Johann S. Ersch. (Handbuch der Deutschen Literatur Seit der Mitte des 18. Jahrhunderts Bis Auf die Neueste Zeit Ser.: Vol. IV). 1608p. 1982. reprint ed. write for info. (3-487-07249-1) G Olms Pubs.

Literatur der Technologie. Gottfried E. Rosenthal. (Documenta Technica Ser.: No. 11). 420p. 1972. reprint ed. write for info. (3-487-04206-1) G Olms Pubs.

Literatur der Theologie. Johann S. Ersch. (Handbuch der Deutschen Literatur Seit der Mitte des 18. Jahrhunderts Bis Auf die Neueste Zeit Ser.: Vol. II). 588p. 1982. reprint ed. write for info. (3-487-07247-5) G Olms Pubs.

Literatur der Totentanze. H. F. Massmann. 162p. 1963. reprint ed. write for info. (0-318-71844-8) G Olms Pubs.

Literatur Ebersetzen in der DDR La Traduction Litteraire en RDA: La Traduction Litteraire en RDA. Ed. by Walter Lenschen. (GER., Illus.). 178p. 1998. 27.95 (3-906760-19-7) P Lang Pubng.

***Literatur Im Kontext Robert Musil Litterature dans le Contexte de Robert Musil.** Ed. by Marie-Louise Roth. (Musiliana Ser.: Bd. 6). 366p. 1999. 53.95 (3-906761-93-2, Pub. by P Lang) P Lang Pubng.

Literatur Texte Zur Deutschen Frage Nach, 1945 see Literatur und Landeskunde

***Literatur Und Erziehung: Lehrerbilder Und Schulmodelle in Kulturhistorischer Perspektive.** Albrecht Weber. (Illus.). 1548p. 1999. 96.95 (3-631-34087-7) P Lang Pubng.

Literatur und Landeskunde. Incl. Vol. 1. Literatur Texte Zur Deutschen Frage Nach, 1945. Jerzewski. 64p. 10.50 (3-468-49470-X); Vol. 2. Neue Literatur Von Frauen. Ed. by Inge Bauer-Derber. (GER.). 72p. 10.50 (3-468-49471-8); Vol. 4. Literatur der DDR. Kroker. 104p. 13.00 (3-468-49473-4); write for info. (0-318-60301-2) Langenscheidt.

***Literatur und Medien in Studium und Deutschunterricht.** Bodo Lecke. (Illus.). 373p. 1998. 56.95 (3-631-31742-5) P Lang Pubng.

Literatur und Politik -- Mario Vargas Llosa. Sabine Kollmann. (Perspectivas Hispanicas Ser.). 404p. 54.95 (3-906756-47-5, Pub. by P Lang) P Lang Pubng.

Literatur und Quantentheorie: Die Rezeption der Modernen Physik in Schriften Zur Literatur Und Philosophie Deutschsprachiger Autoren (1925-1970) Elisabeth Emter. (Quellen und Forschungen zur Literatur und Kulturgeschichte: Bd. 2(236)). (GER.). x, 358p. (C). 1995. lib. bdg. 129.25 (3-11-014873-0) De Gruyter.

Literatur und Regionalitat. Ed. by Anselm Maler. (Studien Zur Neuren Literatur: Bd. 4). (Illus.). 228p. 1997. pap. 40.95 (3-631-32067-1) P Lang Pubng.

Literatur Zu Umweltschutz und Umweltforschung. 3rd enl. rev. ed. Roswitha Poll. (GER.). x, 380p. 1984. 31.00 (3-510-65119-7, Pub. by E Schweizerbartsche) Balogh.

Literatur zur Angewandten Statistik see Guide to Statistical Methods & to the Pertinent Literature

Literatur Zur Deutsch-Sprachigen Presse (Literature on German-Language Press), 13 vols. & 3 index vols. Gert Hagelweide. (Dortmunder Beitrage Zur Zeitungsforschung Ser.: Vol. 35). 1985. write for info. (3-598-21305-0) K G Saur Verlag.

Literatur Zur Geschichte der Erdkunde Vom Mittelalter An. Sophus Ruge. 299p. 1979. reprint ed. write for info. (3-487-06730-7) G Olms Pubs.

Literatura. Jose M. Valverde. (SPA.). 118p. 1981. pap. 7.00 (84-85859-43-X, 2112) Ediciones Norte.

Literatura - Paraliteratura: Puig, Borges, Donoso, Cortazar, Vargas Llosa. Myrna Solotorevsky. LC 88-83025. 188p. 1988. 15.00 (0-935318-16-X) Edins Hispamerica.

Literatura Africana de Expressao Portuguesa Vol. 1: Poesia. Mario De Andrade. (B. E. Ser.: No. 31). (POR.). 1967. 35.00 (0-8115-2982-7) Periodicals Srv.

Literatura Africana de Expressao Portuguesa Vol. 2: Prosa. Mario De Andrade. (B. E. Ser.: No. 32). (POR.). 1968. 35.00 (0-8115-2983-5) Periodicals Srv.

Literatura Centroamericana: Visiones y Revisiones. Ed. by Jorge Roman-Lagunas. LC 94-5647. (SPA.). 364p. 1994. text 99.95 (0-7734-9082-5) E Mellen.

Literatura Chicana: Creative & Critical Writings. Compiled by Roberto G. Trujillo. 95p. 1990. 23.00 (0-915745-04-6) Floricanto Pr.

Literatura Chicana, 1965-1995: An Anthology in Spanish, English, & Calo. Ed. by Manuel De Jesus Hernandez-Gutierrez & David Foster. LC 96-24202. 520p. 1997. reprint ed. text 100.00 (0-8153-2077-9); reprint ed. pap. text 27.95 (0-8153-2080-9) Garland.

Literatura de Bonafoux. Luis Bonafoux. Ed. by Socorro Giron. LC 89-38004. (Coleccion Puertorriquena Ser.). 325p. (Orig.). 1990. pap. 10.95 (0-8477-3642-3) U of PR Pr.

Literatura De Dos Mundos: Espana E Hispanoamerica. Ella R. Gomez-Quintero. LC 93-71414. (SPA.). 175p. (Orig.). 1993. pap. 19.00 (0-89729-687-7) Ediciones.

Literatura de Frontera Mexico, Estados Unidos: Mexican & American Border Writing. Ed. by Jose M. Di-Bella et al. 212p. 1987. text 10.00 (0-614-25814-6) SDSU Inst Reg Studies.

Literatura de Hostos: Critica, Vol. I, Tomo III. Eugenio M. De Hostos. (Hosto's Works). (SPA.). 624p. 1995. pap. 8.50 (0-8477-3680-6) U of PR Pr.

Literatura de Hostos: Critica, Vol. 1, Tomo III. Eugenio M. Hostos. (Hosto's Complete Works). (SPA.). 624p. 1995. 12.95 (0-8477-3681-4) U of PR Pr.

Literatura de Hostos: Cuento, Teatro & Poesia, Vol. 1, Tomo II. Eugenio M. De Hostos. (Hostos' Complete Works). 1993. 13.50 (0-8477-3671-7); pap. 8.50 (0-8477-3670-9) U of PR Pr.

Literatura en Periodicos & Revistas de Puerto Rico: Siglo XIX. Otto Olivera. LC 85-1143. (Comunicacion Ser.: No. 74). (SPA.). 410p. 1987. pap. 10.00 (0-8477-0074-7) U of PR Pr.

Literatura en Publicaciones Periodicas de Guatemala: Siglo XIX, Vol. 5. Otto Olivera. 273p. 1974. pap. 7.00 (0-912788-04-6) Tulane Romance Lang.

Literatura Espanola. Julio Torri. (Breviarios Ser.). (SPA.). pap. 10.99 (968-16-0063-0, Pub. by Fondo) Continental Bk.

An Asterisk (*) at the beginning of an entry indicates that the title is appearing for the first time.

Literatura Espanola Tomo 1: Una Antologia: De los Origenes Hasta 1700, Vol. 1. David W. Foster. LC 95-19115. 904p. 1995. pap. text 37.95 (*0-8153-2012-4*) Garland.

Literatura Espanola Tomo 2: Una Antologia: De 1700 Hasta la Actualidad. Ed. by David W. Foster. LC 95-19115. 640p. 1995. text 40.00 (*0-8153-2063-9*) Garland.

Literatura Espanola Vol. 1: Una Antologia: De los Origenes Hasta 1700. David W. Foster. LC 95-19115. (SPA.). 904p. 1995. text 40.00 (*0-8153-1755-7*, H1871) Garland.

Literatura Espanola Vol. 2: Una Antologia: De 1700 Hasta la Actualidad. David W. Foster. LC 95-19115. 640p. 1995. pap. text 32.95 (*0-8153-2064-7*) Garland.

Literatura Espanola del Ultimo Exilio. Antonio Ferres & Jose Otega. LC 75-20183. (SPA.). 176p. (Orig.). (C). 1975. 30.00 (*0-87752-203-0*); pap. 7.95 (*0-685-55211-X*) Gordian.

Literatura Francofona. Lopez Mora. (SPA.). 16.99 (*968-16-4607-X*, Pub. by Fondo) Continental Bk.

Literatura Hispanoamericana: Del Modernismo a Nuestros Dias. Joaquin Marco. (Nueva Austral Ser.: Vol. 17). (SPA.). 1991. pap. text 34.95 (*84-239-1817-3*) Elliots Bks.

Literatura Hispanoamericana - Spanish American Literature: Una Antologia - An Anthology. Ed. by David W. Foster. LC 93-26830. 1216p. 1994. text 125.00 (*0-8153-1538-4*, H1963); pap. text 32.50 (*0-8153-1284-9*, H1693) Garland.

Literatura Hispanoamericana de Protesta Social. Armando Zarate. 500p. (Orig.). (C). 1993. pap. text 39.50 (*0-8191-9234-1*) U Pr of Amer.

Literatura Hispanoamericana de Protesta Social. Armando Zarate. 500p. (Orig.). (C). 1994. lib. bdg. 72.50 (*0-8191-9233-3*) U Pr of Amer.

Literatura Hispanoamericana E Ideologia Liberal: Surgimiento y Crisis. Hernan Vidal. 118p. 1976. 4.00 (*0-935318-01-1*) Edins Hispamerica.

Literatura Moderna Hispanica: An Antholoy. Ed. by J. R. Gonzalez. (SPA.). 320p. 1975. pap. 27.55 (*0-8442-7029-6*) NTC Contemp Pub Co.

Literatura Taxonomica Dipterorum (1758-1930), 2 vols. Neal L. Evenhuis. (Illus.). 426p. 1997. lib. bdg. 200.00 (*90-73348-59-5*, Pub. by Backhuys Pubs) Balogh.

Literatura y Paternalismo en Puerto Rico: Estudio del Canon. Jaun Gelpi. (Caribbean Collection). 1993. pap. 10.50 (*0-8477-0194-8*) U of PR Pr.

Literatura y Periodismo en el Fin de Siglo, 1880-1907. Maria P. Valero. 85.50 (*0-685-69526-3*) Scripta.

Literatura y Politica: El "Libro de los Estados" y el "Libro de las Armas" de Don Juan Manuel. Maria C. Ruiz. 1990. 37.50 (*0-916379-63-9*) Scripta.

Literatura y Testimonio. Ed. by Hernan Vidal & Rene Jara. LC 86-62062. (Monographic Series of the Society for the Study of Contemporary Hispanic & Lusophone Revolutionary Literatures: No. 3). (SPA.). 400p. 1986. pap. 9.95 (*0-910235-13-9*) Prisma Bks.

Literaturas Hispanicas: Introduccion a su Estudio, Vol. I. Evelyn P. Garfield & Ivan A. Schulman. LC 90-38058. (SPA., Illus.). 246p. (C). 1990. pap. text 27.95 (*0-8143-1863-0*) Wayne St U Pr.

Literaturas Hispanicas Vol. II: Espana: Introduccion a Su Estudio. Evelyn P. Garfield & Ivan A. Schulman. LC 90-38058. (Literaturas Hispanicas Ser.). (SPA.). 376p. (C). 1990. pap. text 29.95 (*0-8143-1864-9*) Wayne St U Pr.

Literaturas Hispanicas Vol. III: Hispanoamerica: Introduccion a su Estudio. Evelyn P. Garfield & Ivan A. Schulman. LC 90-38058. (SPA.). 402p. 1990. pap. text 29.95 (*0-8143-1865-7*) Wayne St U Pr.

***Literaturdidaktik Und Asthetik: Eine Didaktik der Asthetischen Umorientierung, Dargestellt an Untersuchungen Zur Dramatischen Form.** Jens Bause. 256p. 1999. 45.95 (*3-631-34030-3*) P Lang Pubng.

Literature, 9 vols. 643.50 (*0-405-06186-2*, 15314) Ayer.

Literature. (College Board SAT II Subject Test Ser.). 1997. pap. 23.95 (*0-8373-6310-1*, SATII-10) Nat Learn.

Literature. Clara Calvo & Jean J. Weber. LC 97-47183. (Illus.). 176p. (C). 1998. wbk. ed. 70.00 (*0-415-16986-0*) Routledge.

Literature. Alan Duff & Alan Maley. (Illus.). 176p. 1990. pap. text 13.95 (*0-19-437094-1*) OUP.

Literature. Barbara Gruber. (Instant Idea Bks.). (Illus.). 64p. 1989. 7.95 (*0-86734-077-0*, FS-8315) Schaffer Pubns.

Literature. Lee A. Jacobus. LC 93-15570. 1934p. 1995. 58.00 (*0-13-282633-X*) P-H.

Literature. Intro. by Roslyn Rosen. LC 98-44004. (Female Firsts in Their Field Ser.). (Illus.). 64p. (YA). (gr. 4-7). 1999. 16.95 (*0-7910-5146-3*) Chelsea Hse.

Literature. Jack Rudman. (Undergraduate Program Field Tests (UPFT) Ser.: Vol. 14). 43.95 (*0-8373-6064-1*) Nat Learn.

Literature. Jack Rudman. (Undergraduate Program Field Tests Ser.: UPFT-14). 1994. pap. 23.95 (*0-8373-6014-5*) Nat Learn.

Literature. Jack Rudman. (Teachers License Examination (TLE) Ser.: Vol. G-3). 1994. pap. 27.95 (*0-8373-8193-2*) Nat Learn.

Literature. Peter Widdowson. LC 98-35341. (New Critical Idiom Ser.). 184p. (C). 1999. 50.00 (*0-415-16913-5*); pap. 12.99 (*0-415-16914-3*) Routledge.

Literature. Herman Grimm. LC 76-37520. (Essay Index Reprint Ser.). 1977. reprint ed. 23.95 (*0-8369-2551-3*) Ayer.

Literature. Harry T. Peck. (Notable American Authors Ser.). 1999. reprint ed. lib. bdg. 125.00 (*0-7812-8724-3*) Rprt Serv.

Literature. 2nd ed. Kirszner. (C). 1993. pap. text, teacher ed. 4.50 (*0-15-501027-1*) Harcourt Coll Pubs.

Literature. 4th ed. Diyanni. 1999. 37.74 (*0-07-234945-X*) McGraw.

Literature. 5th ed. Compiled by James H. Pickering & Jeffrey D. Hoeper. LC 96-7112. 1951p. 1996. pap. text 57.00 (*0-13-226770-5*) P-H.

Literature, Pt. 2, Vol. A & B. (Astronomy & Astrophysics Abstracts Ser.). 1759p. 1994. 352.95 (*0-387-58326-2*) Spr-Verlag.

Literature see Who's Who in the Arts & Literature

Literature: A Contemporary Introduction. James Hurt. LC 93-12570. 1501p. (C). 1993. 57.00 (*0-02-359011-4*, Macmillan Coll) P-H.

Literature: A Crash Course. Leland Howard & Julian Bell. (Crash Course Ser.). (Illus.). 144p. 1999. 14.95 (*0-8230-0980-7*) Watsn-Guptill.

Literature: A Student's Guide to Research & Writing. Robert Skapura & John Marlowe. 46p. (YA). (gr. 7-12). 1988. pap. 10.00 (*0-87287-650-0*) Libs Unl.

Literature: An Embattled Profession. Carl Woodring. LC 98-49583. 224p. 1999. 29.50 (*0-231-11522-9*) Col U Pr.

Literature: An Introduction to Critical Reading. William Vesterman. 1024p. (C). 1993. pap. text 48.50 (*0-03-046914-7*, Pub. by Harcourt Coll Pubs); pap. text, teacher ed. 4.75 (*0-03-046917-1*) Harcourt Coll Pubs.

***Literature: An Introduction to Fiction Poetry & Drama.** 1999. (*0-673-52552-X*, GoodYrBooks) Addson-Wesley Educ.

***Literature: An Introduction to Fiction Poetry & Drama.** 2nd ed. Ed. by Kennedy. 1531p. (C). 1999. pap. 48.00 (*0-321-01555-X*) Addson-Wesley Educ.

Literature: An Introduction to Fiction, Poetry & Drama. 6th ed. Ed. by X. J. Kennedy & Dana Gioia. 1995. text. write for info. (*0-201-34644-3*) Addison-Wesley.

Literature: An Introduction to Fiction, Poetry & Drama. 6th ed. X. J. Kennedy & Dana Gioia. 1920p. (C). 1995. text 46.88 (*0-673-52509-0*) Addson-Wesley Educ.

Literature: An Introduction to Fiction, Poetry & Drama. 7th ed. X. J. Kennedy & Dana Gioia. 448p. 1998. 11.00 (*0-321-02736-1*) Addson-Wesley Educ.

Literature: An Introduction to Fiction, Poetry & Drama. 7th ed. Kennedy et al. LC 98-7902. 1980p. (C). 1998. pap. 60.00 (*0-321-01557-6*) Addison-Wesley.

Literature: An Introduction to Reading & Writing, Compact. Roberts. 1504p. (C). 1998. pap. text 39.20 (*0-13-275926-8*, Prentice Hall) P-H.

***Literature: An Introduction to Reading & Writing with MLA.** rev. ed. Edgar V. Roberts. 1472p. 1998. pap. text 49.33 (*0-13-012123-1*) P-H.

Literature: Aristotle - Fulgentius, Vol. 2. (Bibliographical Guide to Classical Studies). 355p. 1997. write for info. (*3-487-10466-0*) G Olms Pubs.

Literature: CUNY Panel: Rethinking the Disciplines, Vol. 8E. Joan E. Hartman et al. (Women in the Curriculum Ser.). 70p. 1997. pap. 10.00 (*1-885303-13-0*) Towson St Univ.

Literature: Discovering Ourselves Through Great Books. Joris Heise. (English Ser.). 262p. (Orig.). (C). 1995. pap. text 24.95 (*0-89641-232-6*) American Pr.

Literature: Experience & Meaning. Martha McGowan. 1105p. (C). 1988. pap. text 3.00 (*0-15-551085-1*) Harcourt Coll Pubs.

***Literature: Human Experience Shorter.** 7th ed. Abcarian & Klotz. 1999. pap. text 28.95 (*0-312-20691-7*) St Martin.

***Literature: Intro To Reading & Writg Nasta.** 6th ed. (C). 2000. text 59.96 (*0-13-032470-1*) PH School.

***Literature: Introduction to Fictional Poetry & Drama.** 176p. (C). 1998. 12.00 (*0-321-04976-4*) Addison-Wesley.

***Literature: Introduction to Fictional Poetry & Drama.** 2nd ed. 384p. (C). 1999. 26.00 (*0-321-06094-6*) Addison-Wesley.

Literature: Its Opponents & Its Power. Arther Trace. LC 96-43481. 160p. 1996. 37.50 (*0-7618-0589-3*) U Pr of Amer.

Literature: Literature & Interpretive Techniques. Wilfred L. Guerin. 1184p. (C). 1997. pap. text 67.00 (*0-06-042553-9*) Addson-Wesley Educ.

Literature: MLA '98. 5th rev. ed. Roberts & Jacobs. 1998. pap. text 57.00 (*0-13-010076-5*) P-H.

Literature: Options for Reading & Writing. 2nd ed. Donald A. Daiker et al. 1328p. (C). 1997. pap. text 59.00 (*0-06-041483-9*) Addson-Wesley Educ.

Literature: Reading & Responding to Fiction, Poetry, Drama & the Essay. Joel Wingard. (C). 1997. text, teacher ed. 24.00 (*0-06-501736-6*) Addson-Wesley Educ.

Literature: Reading & Writing, the Human Experience. 7th ed. Ed. by Richard Abcarian & Marvin Klotz. LC 97-65206. 1460p. 1997. pap. text 50.95 (*0-312-15311-2*) St Martin.

***Literature: Reading Fiction, Poetry, & Drama.** Robert DiYanni. LC 99-14165. (Illus.). 2000. write for info. (*0-07-229507-4*); write for info. (*0-07-229509-0*); write for info. (*0-07-229510-4*); write for info. (*0-07-229511-2*) McGrw-H Hghr Educ.

Literature: Reading Fiction, Poetry, Drama & the Essay. 4th ed. Robert Diyanni. LC 96-54711. 2064p. (C). 1997. 48.13 (*0-07-017037-1*) McGraw.

Literature: Reading Fiction, Poetry, Drama & the Essay. 4th ed. Robert Diyanni. LC 96-54711. 1997. pap. write for info. (*0-07-017038-X*) McGraw.

Literature: Reading, Reacting. 3rd ed. Laurie G. Kirszner. LC 96-75432. (C). 1996. text 60.50 (*0-15-503622-X*) Harcourt.

Literature: Reading, Reacting, Writing. Laurie G. Kirszner. (C). 1991. pap. text, teacher ed. 34.00 (*0-03-067999-0*) Harcourt Coll Pubs.

***Literature: Reading, Reacting, Writing.** 4th ed. Kirszner. 1999. pap. 50.00 (*0-15-507348-6*) Harcourt.

Literature: Reading, Reacting, Writing (Instructor's Resource Guide) 3rd ed. Laurie G. Kirszner & Stephen R. Mandell. 488p. (C). 1996. pap. text, teacher ed. 28.00 (*0-15-503623-8*) Harcourt Coll Pubs.

Literature: Structure, Sound, & Sense. 6th ed. Laurence Perrine. (C). 1993. pap. text, teacher ed. 30.00 (*0-15-500299-6*) Harcourt Coll Pubs.

Literature: The Evolving Canon. 2nd ed. Sven P. Birkerts. LC 95-19938. 1698p. 1995. 54.00 (*0-205-17515-5*) Allyn.

Literature: The Evolving Canon: Examination Copy. 2nd ed. Sven P. Birkerts. 1728p. (C). 1995. text. write for info. (*0-205-19390-0*, H9390-9) Allyn.

Literature: The Human Experience. 2nd rev. ed. Ed. by Richard Abcarian & Marvin Klotz. 934p. (C). 1984. teacher ed. write for info. (*0-318-57731-3*) St Martin.

Literature: The Human Experience. 7th ed. Abcarian. 1998. pap. text, teacher ed. 10.00 (*0-312-16656-7*) St Martin.

Literature: The Human Experience, Shorter with Essays. 5th ed. Richard Abcarian & Marvin Klotz. LC 90-71627. 960p. (C). 1991. pap. text, teacher ed. 2.66 (*0-312-06740-2*) St Martin.

Literature: The New York Public Library Book of Answers. Melinda Corey & George Ochoa. 256p. (Orig.). 1993. pap. 11.00 (*0-671-78164-2*, Fireside) S&S Trade Pap.

Literature: The Power of Language. Thomas McLaughlin & Frank Lentricchia. 1488p. (C). 1989. teacher ed. 7.00 (*0-15-551093-2*) Harcourt Coll Pubs.

Literature: Thinking, Reading & Writing Critically. 2nd ed. Sylvan Barnet. LC 96-18848. 1800p. (C). 1997. 65.00 (*0-673-52523-6*) Longman.

Literature: Thinking Reading Writing Critical. 2nd ed. (C). 1997. (*0-321-40203-0*) Benjamin-Cummings.

Literature Vol. 66-70: Chinese Children's Stories. Hwa-I Publishing Co., Staff. Ed. by Emily Ching et al. Tr. by Wonder Kids Publications Staff from CHI. (Literature Ser.). (Illus.). 28p. (J). (gr. 3-6). 1991. reprint ed. 39.75 (*1-56162-066-1*) Wonder Kids.

Literature? Why Bother? Anne D. Jordan. (Tall Literary Companion Ser.). (Illus.). 64p. (Orig.). 1997. pap. 9.95 (*1-890429-02-3*) Essmont Pub.

Literature about Language. Valerie Shepherd. LC 93-2062. (Interface Ser.). 192p. (C). 1993. pap. 24.99 (*0-415-06997-1*) Routledge.

Literature Across Culture. 2nd ed. Sheena Gillespie et al. LC 97-11641. 1046p. 1997. pap. text 48.00 (*0-205-27205-3*) P-H.

***Literature Across Cultures.** 3rd ed. 2000. teacher ed. write for info. (*0-205-32698-6*) Allyn.

***Literature Across Cultures.** 3rd ed. 1216p. (C). 2000. write for info. (*0-205-32455-X*); pap. 58.67 (*0-205-31902-5*) Allyn.

Literature Across Cultures: Examination Copy. 2nd ed. Sheena Gillespie et al. 1072p. (C). 1997. pap. text. write for info. (*0-205-27670-9*, T7670-7) Allyn.

Literature Activities for Reluctant Readers: Intermediate. John Carratello & Patty Carratello. (Illus.). 112p. (J). (gr. 3-5). 1991. student ed. 11.95 (*1-55734-354-3*) Tchr Create Mat.

Literature Activities for Reluctant Readers: Primary. John Carratello & Patty Carratello. (Illus.). 112p. (J). (gr. 1-3). 1991. student ed. 11.95 (*1-55734-353-5*) Tchr Create Mat.

Literature Activity Books: An Index to Materials for Whole Language & Shared Literature. Marybeth Green & Beverly Williams. viii, 203p. (Orig.). 1993. pap. text 27.00 (*1-56308-011-7*) Libs Unl.

Literature Against Itself: Literary Ideas in Modern Society. Gerald Graff. 276p. 1995. pap. text 12.95 (*1-56663-097-5*, Elephant Paperbacks) I R Dee.

Literature Against Itself: Literary Ideas in Modern Society. Gerald Graff. LC 78-9879. x, 250p. (C). 1995. pap. text 12.00 (*0-226-30598-8*) U Ch Pr.

Literature Against Philosophy, Plato to Derrida: A Defence of Poetry. Mark Edmundson. 255p. (C). 1995. pap. text 21.95 (*0-521-48532-0*) Cambridge U Pr.

Literature Alive! Teri Gamble & Michael Gamble. LC 92-80505. 472p. 1994. pap. 28.19 (*0-8442-5000-7*) NTC Contemp Pub Co.

Literature Alive! 2nd ed. Teri Gamble. 128p. 1994. pap. 8.40 (*0-8442-5001-5*) NTC Contemp Pub Co.

Literature & Aesthetics. Monroe C. Beardsley. LC 68-57656. 1968. pap. 2.50 (*0-672-60903-7*, Bobbs) Macmillan.

Literature & Aging: An Anthology. Ed. by Martin Kohn et al. LC 92-7855. (Literature & Medicine Ser.: No. 1). (Illus.). 456p. (Orig.). 1992. pap. 29.00 (*0-87338-466-0*) Kent St U Pr.

***Literature & Analysis: Intertextual Readings.** Ruth Parkin-Gounelas. LC 00-33343. (Illus.). 2000. write for info. (*0-312-23740-5*) St Martin.

Literature & Anthropology. Ed. by Philip A. Dennis & Wendell M. Aycock. LC 89-4279. (Studies in Comparative Literature: No. 20). x, 227p. (C). 1989. 24.95 (*0-89672-166-3*) Tex Tech Univ Pr.

Literature & Anthropology. Ed. by Phillip A. Dennis & Wendell M. Aycock. LC 89-4279. (Comparative Literature Ser.: No. 20). 238p. (C). 1998. reprint ed. pap. 12.95 (*0-89672-167-1*) Tex Tech Univ Pr.

Literature & Anthropology. 3rd ed. International Conference on Literary Theory Staff. Ed. by Jonathan Hall & Ackbar Abbas. LC 87-400046. 301p. 1986. reprint ed. pap. 93.40 (*0-608-01384-6*, 206214500002) Bks Demand.

Literature & Artifacts. G. Thomas Tanselle. LC 98-25657. 376p. 1998. 60.00 (*1-883631-06-8*) Biblgraph Soc.

Literature & Belief: Three Spiritual Exercises. Ben Belitt. (Chapbooks in Literature Ser.). (Illus.). 29p. (Orig.). 1985. pap. text 5.00 (*1-878603-02-7*) Bennington Coll.

Literature & Child. 4th ed. Cullinan. (C). 1997. pap. text, teacher ed. write for info. (*0-15-508173-X*) Harcourt Coll Pubs.

Literature & Class. Ed. by Schuster. (Special Topics in English Ser.). 400p. (C). 2000. pap. 47.41 (*0-321-01163-5*) Addson-Wesley Educ.

Literature & Cognition. Jerry R. Hobbs. LC 90-1615. (CSLI Lecture Notes Ser.: No. 21). 180p. (C). 1990. 44.95 (*0-937073-53-9*); pap. 16.95 (*0-937073-52-0*) CSLI.

Literature & Culture in Early Modern London. Lawrence Manley. LC 93-51069. (Illus.). 619p. (C). 1995. text 80.00 (*0-521-46161-8*) Cambridge U Pr.

Literature & Culture in Exile: Collected Essays in the German Speaking Emigration after 1933. Guy Stern. 428p. 1998. pap. 46.00 (*3-931828-05-0*, Pub. by Dresden Univ Pr) Paul & Co Pubs.

Literature & Culture in Modern Britain, Vol. 2. Gary Day. (C). 1997. pap. text 28.00 (*0-582-07550-5*) Addison-Wesley.

***Literature & Culture in Modern Britain, 1956 - 1990: Supplement, Vol. 3.** Clive Bloom & Gary Day. 288p. 2000. 85.95 (*0-582-07553-X*) Longman.

***Literature & Culture in Modern Britain, 1956-1990.** Clive Bloom. 2000. pap. 23.95 (*0-582-07552-1*) Addison-Wesley.

Literature & Culture in Northern Ireland since 1965: Moments of Danger. Richard Kirkland. (Studies in Twentieth Century Literature). 200p. (C). 1996. pap. 28.00 (*0-582-23884-6*) Longman.

Literature & Culture Series. Schuster. (C). 1998. text. write for info. (*0-321-01161-9*) Addson-Wesley Educ.

Literature & Degree in Renaissance England: Nashe, Bourgeois Tragedy, Shakespeare. Peter Holbrook. LC 92-50883. 1994. 34.50 (*0-87413-474-9*) U Delaware Pr.

Literature & Dialectical Materialism. John Strachey. LC 74-6468. (Studies in Comparative Literature: No. 35). (C). 1974. lib. bdg. 49.95 (*0-8383-1938-6*) M S G Haskell Hse.

***Literature & Dictatorship in Africa & Latin America.** Josaphat Bekunuru Kubayanda. LC 99-53996. 1999. write for info. (*0-88258-201-1*) Howard U Pr.

Literature & Dictatorship in Africa & Latin America, 1958-1987. Josaphat B. Kubayanda. LC 97-2789. 1997. write for info. (*0-88258-038-8*) Howard U Pr.

Literature & Dogma: An Essay Towards a Better Apprehension of the Bible. Matthew Arnold. LC 78-126650. 1970. reprint ed. 38.50 (*0-404-00387-7*) AMS Pr.

Literature & Domination: Sex, Knowledge, & Power in Modern Fiction. M. Keith Booker. LC 92-41442. 224p. 1993. 49.95 (*0-8130-1195-7*) U Press Fla.

Literature & Drama. Angela S. Medearis. (J). 1997. lib. bdg. 16.98 (*0-8050-4488-4*) H Holt & Co.

Literature & Education: Encounter & Experience. Edwin Webb. (Falmer Press Library on Aesthetic Education). 224p. 1992. 85.00 (*1-85000-767-5*, Falmer Pr); pap. 29.95 (*1-85000-768-3*, Falmer Pr) Taylor & Francis.

Literature & Ethics: Essays Presented to A.E. Malloch. Ed. by Gary Wihl & David Williams. (Illus.). 184p. (C). 1988. 65.00 (*0-7735-0662-4*, Pub. by McG-Queens Univ Pr) CUP Services.

Literature & Evil. Georges Bataille. Tr. by Alastair Hamilton from FRE. LC 83-25872. 208p. 1986. pap. 14.95 (*0-7145-0346-0*) M Boyars Pubs.

Literature & Existentialism. Jean-Paul Sartre. 1962. pap. 6.95 (*0-8065-0105-7*, Citadel Pr) Carol Pub Group.

***Literature & Expressive Activity.** 2nd ed. (C). 1998. write for info. (*0-8087-1770-7*) Pearson Custom.

Literature & Feminism: An Introduction. Pam Morris. LC 92-41839. 220p. 1993. pap. 26.95 (*0-631-18421-X*) Blackwell Pubs.

Literature & Film. Ed. by Cyndy Hendershot. (Illus.). 188p. 1998. pap. text 15.00 (*1-881604-38-1*) Scopcraeft.

Literature & Film: An Annotated Bibliography, 1978-1988. Jeffrey E. Welch. LC 92-18074. 352p. 1992. text 20.00 (*0-8240-5843-7*, H1114) Garland.

***Literature & Film as Modern Mythology.** William K. Ferrell. LC 99-36018. 224p. 2000. pap. 22.95 (*0-275-96813-8*, Praeger Pubs) Greenwood.

Literature & Film in the Historical Dimension: Selected Papers from the 15th Annual Florida State University Conference on Literature & Film. Ed. by John D. Simons. LC 39-35012. (Florida State University Annual Conference on Literature & Film Ser.). 192p. (C). 1994. pap. 19.95 (*0-8130-1285-6*) U Press Fla.

Literature & Films of other Cultures , Vol 2. (C). 1990. pap. 58.00 (*0-536-57867-2*) Pearson Custom.

Literature & Films other Cultures , Vol 1. 354p. (C). 1990. pap. 58.00 (*0-536-57825-7*) Pearson Custom.

Literature & Folklore see American Contributions

Literature & Folklore after Poststructuralism. Gurbhagat Singh. (C). 1991. 22.50 (*81-202-0300-3*, Pub. by Ajanta) S Asia.

Literature & Gender. Ed. by Lizbeth Goodman. (Approaching Literature Ser.). 424p. (C). 1996. 90.00 (*0-415-13573-7*); pap. 24.99 (*0-415-13574-5*) Routledge.

***Literature & Gender: Thinking Critically Through Fiction, Poetry, & Drama.** Wiegman & Weigman Glasberg. 160p. 1999. 18.00 (*0-321-02742-6*) Addison-Wesley Educ.

***Literature & German Reunification.** Stephen Brockmann. LC 98-53641. (Studies in German). 230p. (C). 1999. 59.95 (*0-521-66054-8*) Cambridge U Pr.

Literature & Gerontology: A Research Guide, 29. Robert E. Yahnke & Richard M. Eastman. LC 95-2462. (Bibliographies & Indexes in Gerontology Ser.: No. 29). 256p. 1995. lib. bdg. 77.95 (*0-313-29349-X*, Greenwood Pr) Greenwood.

Literature & History. Ed. by Harry R. Garvin. LC 77-74403. (Bucknell Review Ser.: Vol. 23, No. 2). 186p. 1978. 22.00 (*0-8387-2139-7*) Bucknell U Pr.

An Asterisk (*) at the beginning of an entry indicates that the title is appearing for the first time.

Literature & History. Ed. by Leonard Schulze & Walter Wetzels. LC 83-6746. 232p. (Orig.). (C). 1983. lib. bdg. 53.00 (*0-8191-3280-2*) U Pr of Amer.

Literature & History: Theoretical Problems & Russian Case Studies. Ed. by Gary S. Morson. LC 85-27843. 352p. 1986. 47.50 (*0-8047-1302-2*) Stanford U Pr.

Literature & History in the Age of Ideas: Essays on the French Enlightenment. Charles G. Williams. LC 74-23240. 434p. reprint ed. pap. 134.60 (*0-608-09898-1*, 206986400006) Bks Demand.

Literature & History of Aviation Series, 35 bks., Set. Ed. by James B. Gilbert. 1972. reprint ed. 953.00 (*0-405-03789-9*) Ayer.

Literature & Humanitarian Reform in the Civil War Era. Gregory Eiselein. LC 95-33576. (Philanthropic Studies). (Illus.). 256p. 1996. text 39.95 (*0-253-33042-4*) Ind U Pr.

Literature & Ideas. 1949. pap. 25.00 (*0-527-01712-4*, YFS NO. 4) Periodicals Srv.

Literature & Ideology. Harry R. Garvin. LC 81-69441. (Bucknell Review Ser.: Vol. 27, No. 1). (Illus.). 192p. 1982. 22.00 (*0-8387-5049-4*) Bucknell U Pr.

Literature & Imperialism. Ed. by Robert Giddings. LC 90-42643. 240p. 1991. text 45.00 (*0-312-05312-6*) St Martin.

Literature & Inner Exile: Authoritarian Spain, 1939-1975. Paul Ilie. LC 80-18281. 207p. reprint ed. pap. 64.20 (*0-8357-6615-2*, 203526000094) Bks Demand.

Literature & Insurgency. John C. Underwood. 1914. 30.00 (*0-8196-0318-X*) Biblo.

Literature & Its Interpretation. Ed. by L. Nyiroe. (De Proprietatibus Litterarum, Ser. Minor: No. 24). 1979. pap. text 40.00 (*90-279-3387-1*) Mouton.

Literature & Its Theorists: A Personal View of Twentieth-Century Criticism. Tzvetan Todorov. Tr. by Catherine Porter. LC 87-47605. 216p. (C). 1987. text 37.50 (*0-8014-1816-X*) Cornell U Pr.

Literature & Its Times: Profiles of 300 Notable Literary Works & the Historical Events That Influenced Them, 5 vols. Joyce Moss & George Wilson. 2500p. 1997. 395.00 (*0-7876-0606-5*, GML00198-109703) Gale.

***Literature & Its Writers.** 2nd ed. Charters. 2000. pap. text. write for info. (*0-312-20979-7*) St Martin.

Literature & Language Bibliographies from the American Yearbook, 1910-1919: The Predecessor of the MLA Bibliography. Compiled by Arnold N. Rzepecki. (Cumulated Bibliography Ser.: No. 1). 1970. 29.50 (*0-87650-013-0*) Pierian.

Literature & Language Teaching. Christopher J. Brumfit & Ronald A. Carter. (Illus.). 304p. 1987. pap. text 15.95 (*0-19-437082-8*) OUP.

Literature & Legal Discourse: Equity & Ethics from Sterne to Conrad. Dieter Polloczek. LC 98-48324. 287p. (C). 1999. 59.95 (*0-521-65251-0*) Cambridge U Pr.

Literature & Legal Problem Solving: Law & Literature as Ethical Discourse. Ed. by Paul J. Heald. LC 97-50391. vii, 191p. 1998. 30.00 (*0-89089-791-3*) Carolina Acad Pr.

Literature & Life. William Dean Howells. (Notable American Authors Ser.). 1992. reprint ed. lib. bdg. 75.00 (*0-7812-3278-3*) Rprt Serv.

Literature & Life. Edwin P. Whipple. LC 72-8540. (Essay Index Reprint Ser.). 1977. reprint ed. 24.95 (*0-8369-7340-2*) Ayer.

Literature & Life: Things Seen, Heard & Read. Edward B. Osborn. LC 68-16963. (Essay Index Reprint Ser.). 1977. reprint ed. 17.95 (*0-8369-0755-8*) Ayer.

Literature & Liminality: Festive Readings in the Hispanic Tradition. Gustavo Perez Firmat. LC 85-13077. xxi, 182p. 1986. text 37.95 (*0-8223-0658-1*) Duke.

***Literature & Literati: The Literary Correspondence & Notebooks of Henry Mackenzie.** Horst W. Drescher. (Scottish Studies International). 287p. (C). 1999. text 52.95 (*0-8204-4360-3*) P Lang Pubng.

***Literature & Literati the Literary Correspondence & Notebooks of Henry MacKenzie: Notebooks, 1763-1824.** Ed. by Horst W. Drescher. (Scottish Studies International: Vol. 2). 287p. 1999. 52.95 (*3-631-46084-8*) P Lang Pubng.

Literature & Madness. Allan Ingram. LC 91-10635. 208p. (C). 1992. 90.00 (*0-415-03190-7*, A6060) Routledge.

Literature & Mass Culture. Leo Lowenthal. (Communication & Society Ser.: Vol. 1). 338p. 1984. 44.95 (*0-87855-489-0*) Transaction Pubs.

***Literature & Material Culture from Balzac to Proust: The Collection & Consumption of Curiosities.** Janell Watson. (Cambridge Studies in French: No. 62). 230p. (C). 2000. 64.95 (*0-521-66156-0*) Cambridge U Pr.

Literature & Moral Understanding: A Philosophical Essay on Ethics, Aesthetics, Education, & Culture. Frank Palmer. LC 92-9977. 272p. 1992. text 75.00 (*0-19-824232-8*) OUP.

Literature & Music: Essays on Form. Ed. by Nancy A. Cluck. LC 81-1070. viii, 258p. 1981. pap. 9.95 (*0-8425-1943-2*, Friends of the Library) Brigham.

***Literature & Nation: Britain & India, 1800-1990.** Harish Trivedi & Richard Allen. LC 00-42205. (Illus.). 2000. write for info. (*0-415-21207-3*) Routledge.

Literature & National Identity: Nineteenth-Century Russian Critical Essays. Ed. by Paul Debreczeny & Jesse Zeldin. LC 77-109598. 214p. reprint ed. pap. 66.40 (*0-8357-6193-2*, 203466600090) Bks Demand.

Literature & Nationalism. Ed. by Vincent Newey & Ann Thompson. 288p. (C). 1991. text 64.00 (*0-389-20954-6*) B&N Imports.

***Literature & Nationalism in Partitioned Poland, 1795-1918.** Stanisaw Eile. LC 99-56329. 2000. 65.00 (*0-312-23159-8*) St Martin.

Literature & Negation. Maire J. Kurrik. LC 79-15949. (Illus.). 1979. text 65.50 (*0-231-04342-2*) Col U Pr.

Literature & Negation. Maire J. Kurrik. LC 79-15949. (Illus.). 1988. pap. text 20.50 (*0-231-04343-0*) Col U Pr.

Literature & Occult Traditions. Denis Saurat. LC 68-759. (Studies in Comparative Literature: No. 35). 1969. reprint ed. lib. bdg. 75.00 (*0-8383-0617-9*) M S G Haskell Hse.

Literature & Ourselves. 2nd ed. Gloria Henderson. 1400p. (C). 1999. pap. text 55.00 (*0-321-05789-9*) Addson-Wesley Educ.

Literature & Ourselves: A Thematic Introduction for Readers & Writers. 2nd ed. (C). 1997. (*0-321-40192-1*) Benjamin-Cummings.

***Literature & Ourselves: Beloved Casebook.** 3rd ed. 2000. write for info. (*0-321-08085-8*) Addison-Wesley.

Literature & Philosophy in Dialogue: Essays in German Literary Theory. Hans-Georg Gadamer. Tr. & Intro. by Robert H. Paslick. LC 93-18448. (SUNY Series in Contemporary Continental Philosophy). 182p. (C). 1993. pap. text 16.95 (*0-7914-1736-0*) State U NY Pr.

Literature & Philosophy in Dialogue: Essays in German Literary Theory. Hans-Georg Gadamer. Tr. & Intro. by Robert H. Paslick. LC 93-18448. (SUNY Series in Contemporary Continental Philosophy). 182p. (C). 1993. text 49.50 (*0-7914-1735-2*) State U NY Pr.

Literature & Photography: Interactions, 1840-1990: A Critical Anthology. Ed. by Jane M. Rabb. LC 95-4369. (Illus.). 634p. 1995. pap. 24.95 (*0-8263-1663-8*) U of NM Pr.

Literature & Political Change: Budapest, 1908-1918. Mario D. Fenyo. LC 86-72880. (Transactions Ser.: Vol. 77, Pt. 6). (Illus.). 160p. (Orig.). (C). 1987. pap. 20.00 (*0-87169-776-9*, T776-FEM) Am Philos.

Literature & Politics: The Colonial Experience in Nine Philippine Novels. Jaime L. An Lim. 182p. (Orig.). 1993. pap. 16.50 (*971-10-0478-X*, Pub. by New Day Pub) Cellar.

Literature & Politics in Central Europe: Studies in Honour of Marketa Goetz-Stankewicz. Ed. by Leslie Miller et al. LC 93-1490. (GERM Ser.). 158p. 1993. 60.00 (*1-879751-68-2*) Camden Hse.

Literature & Politics in the Age of Nero. J. P. Sullivan. LC 84-14278. 224p. (C). 1985. 37.50 (*0-8014-1740-6*) Cornell U Pr.

Literature & Politics in the Age of Nero. John P. Sullivan. LC 84-14278. 219p. reprint ed. pap. 67.90 (*0-608-20951-1*, 207205000003) Bks Demand.

Literature & Politics in the Central American Revolutions. John Beverley & Marc Zimmerman. LC 90-12667. (New Interpretations of Latin America Ser.). 270p. (Orig.). reprint ed. pap. 83.70 (*0-608-20862-0*, 207196100003) Bks Demand.

Literature & Propaganda. A. P. Foulkes. 136p. 1983. pap. 12.95 (*0-416-71720-9*, NO. 6521) Routledge.

Literature & Psychoanalysis: The Question of Reading: Otherwise. Ed. by Shoshana Felman. 512p. 1982. reprint ed. pap. 16.95 (*0-8018-2754-X*) Johns Hopkins.

Literature & Race. Ed. by Schuster. (Special Topics in English Ser.). (C). 1998. text. write for info. (*0-321-01162-7*) Addson-Wesley Educ.

***Literature & Race I/M.** 1999. text. write for info. (*0-321-02743-4*) P-H.

Literature & Rationality: Ideas of Agency in Theory & Fiction. Paisley Livingston. 266p. (C). 1992. text 69.95 (*0-521-40540-8*) Cambridge U Pr.

Literature & Religion: A Study in Conflict. Charles I. Glicksberg. LC 77-23753. 265p. 1977. reprint ed. lib. bdg. 65.00 (*0-8371-9753-8*, GLLR, Greenwood Pr) Greenwood.

Literature & Religion: Pascal, Gryphius, Lessing, Holderlin, Novalis, Kierkegaard, Dostoyevsky, Kafka. Hans Kung & Walter Jens. 308p. (C). 1990. reprint ed. 22.95 (*1-55778-282-2*) Paragon Hse.

Literature & Religion at Rome: Cultures, Contexts, & Beliefs. Denis Feeney. LC 97-6950. (Roman Literature & Its Contexts Ser.). 173p. (C). 1998. text 54.95 (*0-521-55104-8*); pap. text 18.95 (*0-521-55921-9*) Cambridge U Pr.

Literature & Religion in the Later Middle Ages: Philological Studies in Honor of Siegfried Wenzel. Ed. by Richard Newhauser & John A. Alford. (Medieval & Renaissance Texts & Studies: Vol. 118). 432p. 1995. 25.00 (*0-86698-172-1*, MR118) MRTS.

Literature & Renewal Public Speaking. Gallagher. LC 99-33527. 1999. text 55.00 (*0-312-22672-1*) St Martin.

Literature & Research. James D. Lester. (C). 1999. pap. text 7.50 (*0-321-02764-7*) Addson-Wesley Educ.

Literature & Resistance in Guatemala: Textual Modes & Cultural Politics from El Senor Presidente to Rigoberta Menchu, 2 vols. Marc Zimmerman. LC 95-8918. (Monographs in International Studies, Latin America Ser.: No. 22). 822p. (Orig.). (C). 1994. pap. text 50.00 (*0-89680-183-7*) Ohio U Pr.

Literature & Revolution in England, 1640-1660. Nigel Smith. LC 94-11191. (Illus.). 432p. 1994. 50.00 (*0-300-05974-4*) Yale U Pr.

Literature & Revolution in England, 1640-1660. Nigel Smith. (Illus.). 432p. 1997. pap. 20.00 (*0-300-07153-1*) Yale U Pr.

Literature & Revolution in Soviet Russia, 1917-1962. Ed. by Max Hayward & Leopold Labedz. LC 75-38382. 235p. 1976. reprint ed. lib. bdg. 35.00 (*0-8371-8651-X*, HALR, Greenwood Pr) Greenwood.

Literature & Sacrament: The Sacred & the Secular in John Donne. Theresa M. DiPasquale. LC 99-6301. (Medieval & Renaissance Literary Studies). 300p. 1999. text 58.00 (*0-8207-0309-5*) Duquesne.

Literature & Science. Aldous Huxley. LC 90-25714. vi, 118p. 1991. reprint ed. pap. 15.00 (*0-918024-85-4*) Ox Bow.

Literature & Science: Theory & Practice. Ed. by Stuart Peterfreund. 248p. 1999. reprint ed. text 22.00 (*0-7881-6387-6*) DIANE Pub.

Literature & Science in Musil's Man Without Qualties. Thomas Sebastian. (GERM Ser.). 2001. 55.00 (*1-57113-116-7*) Camden Hse.

Literature & Science Theory & Practice. Ed. by Stuart Peterfreund. (Illus.). 248p. 1989. text 47.50 (*1-55553-058-3*) NE U Pr.

Literature & Social Practice. Ed. by Philippe Desan et al. 307p. 1989. pap. text 16.50 (*0-226-14342-2*) U Ch Pr.

Literature & Social Practice. Ed. by Philippe Desan et al. 202p. 1989. lib. bdg. 36.00 (*0-226-14341-4*) U Ch Pr.

Literature & Society. Ed. by Peter Davison et al. LC 77-90613. (Literary Taste, Culture & Mass Communication Ser.: Vol. 5). 281p. 1978. lib. bdg. write for info. (*0-85964-040-X*) Chadwyck-Healey.

Literature & Society. David Daiches. LC 74-95422. (Studies in Comparative Literature: No. 35). 1970. reprint ed. lib. bdg. 75.00 (*0-8383-0970-4*) M S G Haskell Hse.

Literature & Society. English Institute Staff. Ed. by Edward W. Said. LC 79-17484. (Selected Papers from the English Institute; 1982-83, New Ser.: No. 3). 224p. reprint ed. pap. 69.50 (*0-7837-7055-3*, 204686700004) Bks Demand.

Literature & Society. 3rd ed. Pamela J. Annas & Robert C. Rosen. LC 99-29038. 1467p. (C). 1999. pap. text 50.67 (*0-13-012481-8*) P-H.

Literature & Society: Advanced Reader of Modern Chinese. Chih-Ping Chou. 504p. (C). 1999. pap. text 49.50 (*0-691-01044-7*, Pub. by Princeton U Pr) Cal Prin Full Svc.

Literature & Society: Intro to Fiction Poetry Drama. 3rd ed. (C). 2000. pap. text. write for info. (*0-13-025757-5*) P-H.

Literature & Society in Early Virginia, 1608-1840. Richard B. Davis. LC 72-89896. (Southern Literary Studies). 356p. 1973. pap. 110.40 (*0-7837-8510-0*, 204931900011) Bks Demand.

***Literature & Society in Eighteenth-Century Englandture, 1680-1820.** Speck. 232p. (C). 1998. pap. 31.20 (*0-582-26570-3*) Addison-Wesley.

Literature & Society in Imperial Russia, 1800-1914. Ed. by William M. Todd, III. LC 77-76153. x, 306p. 1978. 42.50 (*0-8047-0961-0*) Stanford U Pr.

Literature & Society in Renaissance Crete. Ed. by David Holton. (Illus.). 351p. (C). 1991. text 80.00 (*0-521-32579-X*) Cambridge U Pr.

Literature & Society in the Canadas, 1817-1850. Mary L. MacDonald. LC 92-11215. 368p. 1992. lib. bdg. 99.95 (*0-7734-9524-X*) E Mellen.

Literature & Society in 18th Century England, 1680-1820. Speck. (C). 1998. text 61.95 (*0-582-26518-5*, Pub. by Addison-Wesley); pap. text. write for info. (*0-582-26470-7*, Pub. by Addison-Wesley) Longman.

Literature & Spirit: Essays on Bakhtin & His Contemporaries. David Patterson. LC 88-9743. 176p. 1988. 23.00 (*0-8131-1647-3*) U Pr of Ky.

Literature & Technology. Ed. by Mark L. Greenberg & Lance Schachterle. LC 91-60584. (Research in Technology Studies: Vol. 5). (Illus.). 320p. 1992. 45.00 (*0-934223-20-3*) Lehigh Univ Pr.

Literature & the Aborigine in Australia. 2nd ed. J. J. Healy. (Studies in Australian Literature). 314p. (C). 1989. pap. text 29.95 (*0-7022-2150-3*, Pub. by Univ Queensland Pr) Intl Spec Bk.

Literature & the American College: Essays in Defense of the Humanities. Irving Babbitt. LC 86-62218. 228p. 1986. text 12.00 (*0-932783-01-5*) Natl Human Inst.

Literature & the American College: Essays in Defense of the Humanities. Irving Babbitt. LC 74-138537. viii, 263p. 1972. reprint ed. lib. bdg. 37.50 (*0-678-03561-X*) Kelley.

Literature & the American Tradition. Leon Howard. LC 78-180985. 354p. (C). 1972. reprint ed. 75.00 (*0-87752-156-5*) Gordian.

Literature & the Art of Creation. Ed. by Robert Welch & Suheil B. Bushrui. 280p. 1988. 57.00 (*0-389-20783-7*, N8342) B&N Imports.

Literature & the Arts. rev. ed. (GED Exercise Bks.). (YA). (gr. 8-12). 1997. pap. 7.96 (*0-8114-7368-6*) Raintree Steck-V.

Literature & the Arts in the Reign of Francis I: Essays Presented to C. A. Mayer. Ed. by Pauline M. Smith & I D. McFarlane. LC 84-81850. (French Forum Monographs: No. 56). (Illus.). 264p. (Orig.). 1985. pap. 24.95 (*0-917058-56-9*) French Forum.

Literature & the Arts in Twentieth Century China. Adolphe C. Scott. LC 81-13405. (Illus.). 212p. 1982. reprint ed. lib. bdg. 59.50 (*0-313-23227-X*, SCLT, Greenwood Pr) Greenwood.

Literature & the Body: Essays on Populations & Persons. Ed. by Elaine Scarry. LC 87-46308. (Selected Papers from the English Institute; 1982-83, New Ser.: No. 12). 240p. 1990. reprint ed. pap. text 14.95 (*0-8018-4109-7*) Johns Hopkins.

Literature & the Changing Ireland. Ed. by Peter Connolly. (Irish Literary Studies: Vol. # 9). 230p. 1982. 35.00 (*0-86140-043-7*, Pub. by Smyth) Dufour.

Literature & the Child. 3rd ed. Cullinan. (C). 1993. pap. text, teacher ed. 5.50 (*0-15-501740-3*) Harcourt Coll Pubs.

Literature & the Child. 4th ed. Bernice E. Cullinan & Lee Galda. LC 97-73555. 608p. (C). 1997. text 69.00 (*0-15-503956-3*, Pub. by Harcourt Coll Pubs) Harcourt.

Literature & the Child: Romantic Continuations, Postmodern Contestations. Ed. by James H. McGavran. LC 99-24458. (Illus.). 280p. 1999. text 32.95 (*0-87745-690-9*) U of Iowa Pr.

***Literature & the Contemporary.** Roger Luckhurst & Peter Marks. LC 98-37102. (Studies in Twentieth-Century Literature). (C). 1999. 65.95 (*0-582-31203-5*) Addison-Wesley.

***Literature & the Contemporary: Fictions & Theories of the Present.** Roger Luckhurst & Peter Marks. LC 98-37102. (Studies in Twentieth-Century Literature). 232p. 1999. pap. 29.73 (*0-582-31204-3*) Longman.

Literature & the Continuances of Virtue. Warner Berthoff. LC 86-15103. 306p. reprint ed. pap. 94.90 (*0-608-06425-4*, 206663800008) Bks Demand.

Literature & the Environment. Ed. by Anderson. LC 98-29887. 510p. (C). 1998. pap. 44.00 (*0-321-01149-X*) Addison-Wesley Educ.

Literature & the Environment: A Reader on Nature & Culture. Lorraine Anderson et al. 18.00 (*0-321-02741-8*) Addson-Wesley Educ.

Literature & the Ethical Question. Yale French Studies Staff. Ed. by Claire Nouvet. (French Studies: No. 79). 280p. (C). 1991. pap. 18.00 (*0-300-05000-3*) Yale U Pr.

Literature & the Historical Process. Ed. by David Hershberg. 120p. 1988. pap. 10.00 (*0-8131-0714-8*) U Pr of Ky.

Literature & the Image of Man. Leo Lowenthal. LC 78-134110. (Essay Index Reprint Ser.). 1980. 21.95 (*0-8369-1982-3*) Ayer.

Literature & the Image of Man, Vol. 2. Leo Lowenthal. (Communication & Society Ser.). 224p. (C). 1985. 44.95 (*0-88738-057-3*) Transaction Pubs.

Literature & the Immigrant Community: The Case of Arthur Landfors. Alan Swanson. LC 89-21803. 128p. (C). 1990. 21.95 (*0-8093-1590-4*) S Ill U Pr.

***Literature & the Internet: A Guide for Students, Teachers, & Scholars.** Stephanie Browner et al. LC 99-27760. (Wellesley Studies in Critical Theory, Literary History & Culture). 300p. 1999. pap. 24.95 (*0-8153-3453-2*) Garland.

***Literature & the Land.** Emmanuel N. Roussakis. 2000. 25.00 (*0-86709-568-7*, Pub. by Boynton Cook Pubs) Heinemann.

Literature & The Learner. Goforth. LC 97-13263. (Education). 1997. 50.00 (*0-314-20413-X*) Wadsworth Pub.

***Literature & the Learner.** Frances S. Goforth. 1999. 0.00 (*0-534-53893-2*) Wadsworth Pub.

Literature & the Learner with Infotrac. Goforth. (Education Ser.). 1997. 50.00 incl. cd-rom (*0-534-54097-X*) Wadsworth Pub.

Literature & the Learner (With Infotrac) Instructor's Resource Manual. write for info. (*0-314-20893-3*) West Pub.

Literature & the Marketplace: Romantic Writers & Their Audiences in Great Britain & the United States. William G. Rowland, Jr. LC 96-33836. xv, 232p. 1996. text 50.00 (*0-8032-3918-1*) U of Nebr Pr.

Literature & the Modern World. Constance Rooke. 212p. (C). 1990. pap. 37.40 (*0-536-57833-8*) Pearson Custom.

Literature & the Multiple Intelligences. 64p. 1998. pap. text 29.95 (*1-58303-073-5*) Pthways Pubng.

Literature & the Other Arts. Ed. by David Hershberg. 112p. 1987. pap. 10.00 (*0-8131-0713-X*) U Pr of Ky.

Literature & the Pastoral. Andrew V. Ettin. LC 83-26052. 210p. reprint ed. pap. 65.10 (*0-7837-3295-3*, 205769700006) Bks Demand.

Literature & the Philosophy of Intention. Patrick Swinden. LC 98-40373. 256p. 1999. text 59.95 (*0-312-21963-6*) St Martin.

Literature & the Political Imagination. Ed. by John Horton & Andrea Baumeister. LC 95-35921. 272p. (C). 1996. 85.00 (*0-415-12914-1*); pap. 27.99 (*0-415-12915-X*) Routledge.

Literature & the Relational Self. Barbara A. Schapiro. LC 93-12879. (Literature & Psychoanalysis Ser.: Vol. 3). 201p. (C). 1993. text 50.00 (*0-8147-7969-7*) NYU Pr.

Literature & the Relational Self. Barbara A. Schapiro. (Literature & Psychoanalysis Ser.). 201p. (C). 1995. pap. text 19.50 (*0-8147-8022-9*) NYU Pr.

Literature & the Right in Postwar France: The Story of the "Hussards" Nicholas Hewitt. Ed. by John E. Flowers. (French Studies). 268p. 1996. 47.50 (*1-85973-029-9*) Berg Pubs.

Literature & the Sea. (Illus.). 59p. (Orig.). (C). 1993. pap. text 20.00 (*0-7881-0168-4*) DIANE Pub.

Literature & the Supernatural: Essays for the Maynooth Bicentenary. Ed. by Brian Cosgrove. LC 95-225665. 175p. 1995. pap. 49.95 (*1-85607-143-X*, Pub. by Columba Press) Intl Scholars.

Literature & the Supernatural: Essays for the Maynooth Bicentenary. Ed. by Brian Cosgrove. 175p. 1995. 64.95 (*1-85607-215-0*) Intl Scholars.

Literature & the Visual Arts: A Special Issue of Pequod. Ed. by Mark Rudman. (Illus.). 303p. (Orig.). 1990. pap. 17.95 (*1-878818-01-5*, Pub. by Sheep Meadow) U Pr of New Eng.

***Literature & the Visual Arts in Ancient Greece & Rome.** D. Thomas Benediktson. LC 99-39788. (Series in Classical Culture). 272p. 2000. 37.95 (*0-8061-3207-8*) U of Okla Pr.

Literature & the Visual Arts in Contemporary Society. Ed. by Suzanne Ferguson & Barbara Groseclose. LC 85-13618. (Illus.). 334p. reprint ed. pap. 103.60 (*0-608-09671-7*, 206978600006) Bks Demand.

Literature & the Writing Process. 5th ed. Elizabeth Mcmahan. LC 98-25650. 1188p. (C). 1998. pap. text 50.67 (*0-13-913211-2*) P-H.

Literature & Theater of the States & Regions of the United States: An Historical Bibliography. Ed. by Clarence L. Gohdes. LC 66-30584. 288p. reprint ed. pap. 89.30 (*0-608-12726-4*, 202338600032) Bks Demand.

Literature & Theology in Colonial New England. Kenneth B. Murdock. LC 78-104247. 235p. 1970. reprint ed. lib. bdg. 38.50 (*0-8371-3990-2*, MUCN, Greenwood Pr) Greenwood.

An Asterisk (*) at the beginning of an entry indicates that the title is appearing for the first time.

Literature & Writing Connections. Norris & Evans. (How to Make Books with Children Ser.). (Illus.). 160p. (J). (gr. 1-6). Date not set. pap., teacher ed. 16.95 (1-55799-578-8, 777) Evan-Moor Edu Pubs.

Literature, Arts & Religion. Harry R. Garvin. LC 80-70270. (Bucknell Review Ser.: Vol. 26, No. 2). (Illus.). 192p. 1982. 22.00 (0-8387-5021-4) Bucknell U Pr.

***Literature as a Unifying Cultural Force & A Retrospective.** Dorothy M. Figueira et al. (Review of National Literatures & World Report Ser.: Vol. 2). 132p. 1999. pap. 40.00 (0-918680-78-6) Griffon House.

Literature As a Way of Knowing. Kathy Short. LC 97-33164. (Strategies for Teaching & Learning Ser.). 120p. 1997. pap. text 15.00 (1-57110-063-6) Stenhse Pubs.

***Literature as Communication: The Foundations of Mediating Criticism.** Roger D. Sell. (Pragmatics & Beyond New Ser.: Vol. 78). 280p. 2000. write for info. (1-55619-838-8) J Benjamins Pubng.

Literature As Discourse: Textual Strategies in English & History. Robert I. Hodge. LC 89-77606. (Parallax Ser.). (Illus.). 269p. 1990. reprint ed. pap. 83.40 (0-608-07333-4, 206756100009) Bks Demand.

Literature As Exploration. 5th ed. Louise M. Rosenblatt. LC 95-38208. xx, 321p. 1995. pap. 12.50 (0-87352-568-X, T301P); lib. bdg. 28.00 (0-87352-567-1, T301C) Modern Lang.

Literature As Introspection: Spain Confronts Trafalgar, Vol. 57. Ronald J. Quirk. LC 97-15055. (Currents in Comparative Romance Languages & Literatures Ser.). 89p. (C). 1998. text 36.95 (0-8204-3754-9) P Lang Pubng.

Literature As National Institution: Studies in the Politics of Modern Greek Criticism. Vassilis Lambropoulos. LC 87-32712. 271p. reprint ed. pap. 84.10 (0-608-06399-1, 206676000008) Bks Demand.

Literature As Pulpit: The Christian Social Activism of Nellie L. McClung. Randi R. Warne. 236p. (C). 1993. pap. 19.95 (0-88920-235-4) W Laurier U Pr.

Literature As Sheltering the Human. Frederic Will. LC 93-19292. 212p. 1993. text 89.95 (0-7734-3038-5) E Mellen.

Literature As Social Action: Modernist & Traditionalist Narratives in Germany in the 17th & 18th Centuries. Pamela Currie. (GERM Ser.). x, 258p. 1995. 65.00 (1-57113-022-5) Camden Hse.

Literature As System: Essays Toward the Theory of Literary History. Claudio Guillen. LC 76-132240. (Princeton University Press on Demand Edition Ser.). (Illus.). 537p. reprint ed. pap. 166.50 (0-8357-6194-0, 203429500089) Bks Demand.

***Literature As Writing.** Bartholomae. 2001. pap. write for info. (0-312-18352-6) St Martin.

Literature at the Barricades: Essays on the American Writers in the 1930's. Ed. by Ralph F. Bogardus & Fred Hobson. LC 81-3015. 247p. 1982. pap. 76.60 (0-7837-8364-7, 205917300009) Bks Demand.

***Literature at War, 1914-1940: Representing the Time of Greatness in Germany.** Wolfgang G. Natter. LC 98-39029. (Illus.). 280p. 1999. 35.00 (0-300-05558-7) Yale U Pr.

Literature-Based Art & Music: Children's Books & Activities to Enrich the K-5 Curriculum. Ed. by Mildred K. Laughlin & Terri P. Street. LC 91-33662. 168p. 1991. pap. 29.95 (0-89774-661-9) Oryx Pr.

Literature-Based Bulletin Boards. Elizabeth S. Wollner. 1997. pap. 10.95 (0-590-89640-7) Scholastic Inc.

Literature-Based Composition: Teacher's Manual. 1999. teacher ed. 13.36 (0-02-654100-9) Glencoe.

Literature-Based Geography. Scholastic, Inc. Staff. 112p. (J). (gr. k-4). 1992. pap. 14.95 (0-590-49184-9) Scholastic Inc.

Literature-Based History Activities for Children. Patricia Roberts. LC 96-53228. 236p. (C). 1997. pap. text 29.00 (0-205-27090-5) Allyn.

Literature Based Instruction: Reshaping the Curriculum. Ed. by Taffy E. Raphael & Kathryn H. Au. LC 98-106739. 408p. (J). (gr. k-8). 1998. pap. text, teacher ed. 46.95 (0-926842-70-6) CG Pubs Inc.

Literature-Based Math. Scholastic, Inc. Staff. 112p. (J). (gr. k-4). 1992. pap. 14.95 (0-590-49201-2) Scholastic Inc.

***Literature-Based Mini-Lessons: 15 Engaging Lessons That Use Your Favorite Picture Books to Help Every Student Become a More Fluent Reader.** Susan Lunsford. (Illus.). 160p. (J). 2000. pap. 16.95 (0-439-08682-5) Scholastic Inc.

Literature-Based Moral Education: Children's Books & Activities to Enrich the K-5 Curriculum. Linda L. Lamme et al. LC 92-3190. 160p. 1992. pap. 29.95 (0-89774-723-2) Oryx Pr.

Literature-Based Multicultural Activities. Scholastic, Inc. Staff. 144p. (J). (gr. k-4). 1992. pap. 15.95 (0-590-49185-7) Scholastic Inc.

Literature-Based Reading Activities. 2nd ed. Hallie K. Yopp & Ruth H. Yopp. LC 95-37380. 160p. 1995. pap. 24.00 (0-205-16387-4) Allyn.

***Literature-based Reading Activities.** 3rd ed. Ruth H. Yopp & Hallie K. Yopp. 160p. 2000. pap. 24.33 (0-205-31963-7) Allyn.

Literature-Based Reading Programs at Work. Ed. by Joelie Hancock & Susan Hill. LC 87-33627. 118p. (C). 1988. pap. 15.95 (0-435-08466-6, 08466) Heinemann.

Literature-Based Reading/Language Arts Implementation Guide. 3rd unabridged ed. Clifford Russell et al. (Illus.). 122p. (Orig.). (C). 1997. pap., ring bd. 52.00 (0-9657270-0-9) Germane Pubs.

Literature-Based Science: Children's Books & Activities to Enrich the K-5 Curriculum. Christine R. Hefner & Kathryn R. Lewis. LC 94-44843. 186p. 1995. pap. 27.50 (0-89774-741-0) Oryx Pr.

Literature-Based Science Experiences for Young Children: Integrated Thematic Units to Develop Beginning Skills. Mardi Gork. Ed. by Leslie Britt. LC 94-75265. (Illus.). 96p. (Orig.). (J). (ps). 1994. pap. text 10.95 (0-86530-257-X, 270-4) Incentive Pubns.

Literature-Based Social Studies: Children's Books & Activities to Enrich the K-5 Curriculum. Mildred K. Laughlin & Patricia P. Kardaleff. LC 90-46103. 160p. 1990. pap. 27.50 (0-89774-605-8) Oryx Pr.

Literature Based Spelling. Nancy Polette. 1993. pap. 7.95 (1-880505-74-6) Pieces of Lrning.

Literature-Based Thematic Activities: It's about Color. Veronika Winkler et al. LC 98-10261. 1998. pap. 35.00 (1-888222-14-X) Thinking Pubns.

Literature-Based Thematic Activities: Time & Then Some. Veronika Winkler et al. LC 98-11853. 1998. pap. 35.00 (1-888222-19-0) Thinking Pubns.

Literature Basica de Rotary. David H. Bailey & Louise Gottlieb. Ed. by Willmon L. White & Mark Perlberg. (POR., Illus.). 506p. 1982. 16.75 (0-915062-14-3) Rotary Intl.

Literature Board: A Brief History. Thomas W. Shapcott. 320p. (Orig.). (C). 1988. pap. text 29.95 (0-7022-2125-2, Pub. by Univ Queensland Pr) Intl Spec Bk.

***Literature Celebrations: Catalysts to High-Level Book Responses.** Bertie Kingore. (Illus.). 60p. 1999. pap. 11.95 (0-9657911-7-3) Pro Assocs.

***Literature Circles.** Amy Seely Flint. 76p. 1999. pap., teacher ed. 9.95 (1-57690-480-6, TCM2480) Tchr Create Mat.

Literature Circles: Cooperative Learning for Grades 3-8. Mimi Neamen & Mary Strong. (Illus.). xiv, 103p. 1992. pap. text 18.00 (0-87287-987-9) Teacher Ideas Pr.

Literature Circles: Voice & Choice in the Student-Centered Classroom. Harvey Daniels. LC 94-17107. (Illus.). 216p. 1994. pap. text 20.00 (1-57110-000-8) Stenhse Pubs.

Literature Circles & Response. Ed. by Nancy J. Johnson et al. 260p. 1995. pap. text 34.95 (0-926842-48-X) CG Pubs Inc.

Literature Compact: Reading, Reacting, Writing. 3rd ed. Laurie G. Kirszner & Stephen R. Mandell. 1584p. (C). 1996. pap. text 37.00 (0-15-505322-1) Harcourt Coll Pubs.

***Literature Composition.** 5th ed. 368p. (C). 1999. pap. 26.00 (0-321-05815-1) Addison-Wesley.

Literature Connection. Ed. by Scholastic, Inc. Staff. 1994. pap. 19.95 (0-590-49471-6) Scholastic Inc.

Literature Connection. Betty A. Smallwood. 1991. pap. text 29.95 (0-201-51706-X) Addison-Wesley.

Literature Connection: Using Children's Books in the Classroom, K-Grade 8. Liz C. Rothlein & Anita M. Meinbach. 1990. pap. 24.95 (0-673-38450-0, GoodYrBooks) Addson-Wesley Educ.

Literature Connections to American History, K-6: Resources to Enhance & Entice. Lynda G. Adamson. LC 97-14283. 542p. (gr. 5-6). 1997. lib. bdg. 33.50 (1-56308-502-X) Libs Unl.

Literature Connections to American History, 7-12: Resources to Enhance & Entice. Lynda G. Adamson. LC 97-19560. 624p. (YA). (gr. 7-12). 1997. lib. bdg. 34.50 (1-56308-503-8) Libs Unl.

Literature Connections to World History, K-6: Resources to Enhance & Entice. Lynda G. Adamson. LC 97-35952. 326p. 1998. lib. bdg. 30.00 (1-56308-504-6) Libs Unl.

Literature Connections to World History, 7-12: Resources to Enhance & Entice. Lynda G. Adamson. LC 97-35953. 511p. 1998. lib. bdg. 32.50 (1-56308-505-4) Libs Unl.

Literature, Criticism & the Theory of Signs. Victorino V. Tejera. LC 95-5028. (Semiotic Crossroads Ser.: Vol. 7). x, 168p. 1995. lib. bdg. 49.00 (1-55619-341-6) J Benjamins Pubng Co.

Literature, Criticism & the Universities: Interviews with Leonie Kramer, S. L. Goldberg & Howard Felperin. Richard Freadman. pap. 2.00 (0-909751-81-1, Pub. by Univ of West Austr Pr) Intl Spec Bk.

***Literature Criticism from 1400 - 1800, Vol. 47.** Gale Research Staff. 500p. 1999. text 150.00 (0-7876-2416-0) Gale.

***Literature Criticism from 1400 - 1800, Vol. 49.** Gale Group Staff. 500p. 1999. text 150.00 (0-7876-3264-3) Gale.

***Literature Criticism from 1400-1800, Vol. 56.** 500p. 2000. text 150.00 (0-7876-3271-6, UXL) Gale.

Literature Criticism from 1400 to 1800, Vol. 1. Ed. by James E. Person, Jr. 500p. 1984. text 150.00 (0-8103-6100-0) Gale.

Literature Criticism from 1400 to 1800, Vol. 2. Ed. by James E. Person, Jr. 600p. 1985. text 150.00 (0-8103-6101-9) Gale.

Literature Criticism from 1400 to 1800, Vol. 3. Ed. by James E. Person, Jr. 600p. 1986. text 150.00 (0-8103-6102-7) Gale.

Literature Criticism from 1400 to 1800, Vol. 4. Ed. by James E. Person, Jr. 567p. 1986. text 150.00 (0-8103-6103-5) Gale.

Literature Criticism from 1400 to 1800, Vol. 5. Ed. by James E. Person, Jr. 555p. 1987. text 150.00 (0-8103-6104-3) Gale.

Literature Criticism from 1400 to 1800, Vol. 6. Ed. by James E. Person, Jr. 545p. 1987. text 150.00 (0-8103-6105-1) Gale.

Literature Criticism from 1400 to 1800, Vol. 7. Ed. by James E. Person, Jr. LC 83-20504. 600p. 1988. text 150.00 (0-8103-6106-X) Gale.

Literature Criticism from 1400 to 1800, Vol. 8. Ed. by James E. Person, Jr. 600p. 1988. text 150.00 (0-8103-6107-8) Gale.

Literature Criticism from 1400 to 1800, Vol. 9. Ed. by James E. Person, Jr. 600p. 1988. text 150.00 (0-8103-6108-6) Gale.

Literature Criticism from 1400 to 1800, Vol. 10. Ed. by James E. Person, Jr. 500p. 1989. text 150.00 (0-8103-6109-4) Gale.

Literature Criticism from 1400-1800, Vol. 11. Ed. by James E. Person, Jr. & Sandra L. Williamson. 535p. 1989. text 150.00 (0-8103-6110-8) Gale.

Literature Criticism from 1400-1800, Vol. 12. Ed. by James E. Person, Jr. & James P. Draper. 500p. 1990. text 150.00 (0-8103-6111-6) Gale.

Literature Criticism from 1400 to 1800, Vol. 14. James E. Person, Jr. 500p. 1990. text 150.00 (0-8103-6113-2) Gale.

Literature Criticism from 1400 to 1800, Vol. 15. James E. Person, Jr. 500p. 1991. text 150.00 (0-8103-6114-0) Gale.

Literature Criticism from 1400 to 1800, Vol. 19. James E. Person, Jr. 500p. 1992. text 150.00 (0-8103-7961-9) Gale.

Literature Criticism from 1400 to 1800, Vol. 20. James E. Person, Jr. 500p. 1992. text 150.00 (0-8103-7962-7) Gale.

Literature Criticism from 1400 to 1800, Vol. 27. Ed. by James E. Person. 535p. 1995. text 150.00 (0-8103-8943-6) Gale.

Literature Criticism from 1400 to 1800, Vol. 28. Ed. by James E. Person. 500p. 1995. text 150.00 (0-8103-8944-4, 001412) Gale.

Literature Criticism from 1400 to 1800, Vol. 33. Jennifer Brostrom & Kasinec. 500p. 1996. text 150.00 (0-8103-9975-X, GML00597-001582) Gale.

***Literature Criticism from 1400 to 1800, Vol. 50.** Gale Group Staff. 500p. 1999. text 150.00 (0-7876-3265-1) Gale.

***Literature Criticism from 1400 to 1800, Vol. 51.** Gale Group Staff. 500p. 1999. text 150.00 (0-7876-3266-X) Gale.

Literature Criticism from 1400 to 1800 Vol. 29: 18th Century Scottish Poetry. Ed. by Jennifer Brostrom. 500p. 1995. text 140.00 (0-8103-8945-2, 001413) Gale.

Literature Criticism from 1400 to 1800, Vol. 13. Ed. by James P. Draper & James E. Person, Jr. (Illus.). 541p. 1990. text 150.00 (0-8103-6112-4) Gale.

Literature Criticism from 1400 to 1800, Vol. 34. 500p. 1996. text 150.00 (0-8103-9976-8, GML00597-001583) Gale.

Literature Criticism from 1400 to 1800, Vol. 35. 500p. 1996. text 150.00 (0-8103-9977-6, GML00597-001584) Gale.

Literature Criticism from 1400 to 1800, Vol. 36. 500p. 1997. text 150.00 (0-7876-1130-1, GML00597-110444) Gale.

Literature Criticism from 1400 to 1800, Vol. 37. 500p. 1997. text 150.00 (0-7876-1131-X, GML00597-110445) Gale.

***Literature Criticism from 1400 to 1800, Vol. 42.** 500p. 1998. 140.00 (0-7876-2411-X, GML00198-111935) Visible Ink Pr.

***Literature Criticism from 1400 to 1800, Vol. 43.** 500p. 1998. text 150.00 (0-7876-2412-8) Gale.

***Literature Criticism from 1400 to 1800, Vol. 44.** 500p. 1998. text 150.00 (0-7876-2413-6) Gale.

***Literature Criticism from 1400 to 1800, Vol. 45.** 500p. 1999. text 150.00 (0-7876-2414-4) Gale.

***Literature Criticism from 1400 to 1800, Vol. 46.** 500p. 1999. text 150.00 (0-7876-2415-2) Gale.

***Literature Criticism from 1400 to 1800, Vol. 48.** 500p. 1999. text 150.00 (0-7876-3263-5, GML00299-112867, Gale Res Intl) Gale.

***Literature Criticism from 1400 to 1800, Vol. 53.** Vol. 53. 500p. 2000. text 150.00 (0-7876-3268-6) Gale.

***Literature Criticism from 1400 to 1800, Vol. 54.** Vol. 54. 500p. 2000. text 150.00 (0-7876-3269-4) Gale.

***Literature Criticism from 1400 to 1800, Vol. 55.** Vol. 55. 500p. 2000. text 150.00 (0-7876-3270-8) Gale.

***Literature Criticism from 1400 to 1800, Vol.52.** Vol. 52. 500p. 1999. text 150.00 (0-7876-3267-8) Gale.

***Literature, Culture & Class.** (C). 2000. text (0-321-02744-2) Addison-Wesley.

Literature, Culture & Society. Andrew Milner. LC 96-8253. 224p. (C). 1996. text 50.00 (0-8147-5565-8); pap. text 19.50 (0-8147-5564-X) NYU Pr.

Literature, Education, & Romanticism: Reading As Social Practice, 1780-1832. Alan Richardson. LC 93-49343. (Cambridge Studies in Romanticism: No. 8). (Illus.). 345p. (C). 1995. text 64.95 (0-521-46276-2) Cambridge U Pr.

Literature Eins. 2nd ed. Ed. by Robert Spaethling & Eugen Weber. (Illus.). 226p. (C). 1979. pap. 27.25 (0-393-95041-7) Norton.

Literature England Single Vol Edition. 3rd ed. George K. Anderson & William E. Buckler. 1263p. (C). 1999. 95.00 (0-673-15155-7) Addson-Wesley Educ.

Literature, English & American: A Bibliography of Bibliographies. Theodore Besterman. LC 74-29403. 457p. 1971. write for info. (0-87471-052-9) Rowman.

Literature Express Level 2: Text. Gonzales Lee. 2002. pap. text 30.00 (0-8384-0122-8) Heinle & Heinle.

Literature Express: Text. Gonzales Lee. 2002. pap. text 30.00 (0-8384-0112-0) Heinle & Heinle.

***Literature Express Level 4.** Amato. (C). 2002. text 32.50 (0-8384-0174-0) Heinle & Heinle.

Literature Express Level 4: Assessment. Amato. 2002. pap. 32.50 (0-8384-0169-4) Heinle & Heinle.

Literature Express Level 4: Text. Amato. 2002. pap. text 30.00 (0-8384-0165-1) Heinle & Heinle.

Literature Express Level 4: Workbook. Amato. 2002. pap. 9.50 (0-8384-0168-6) Heinle & Heinle.

Literature Express Level 3: Assessment. Decker. 2002. pap. 32.50 (0-8384-0156-2) Thomson Learn.

Literature Express Level 3: Text. Decker. (C). 2002. pap. text 30.00 (0-8384-0151-1) Heinle & Heinle.

Literature Express Level 3: Workbook. Decker. 2002. pap. 9.50 (0-8384-0155-4) Thomson Learn.

Literature Express Level 2: Assessment. Gonzales Lee. 2002. pap. 32.50 (0-8384-0134-1) Heinle & Heinle.

Literature Express Level 2: Workbook. Gonzales Lee. 2002. pap. 9.50 (0-8384-0124-4) Heinle & Heinle.

Literature Express Level 1: Assessment. Gonzales Lee. 2002. pap. text 32.50 (0-8384-0115-5) Heinle & Heinle.

Literature Express Level 1: Workbook. Gonzales Lee. 2002. pap. text 9.50 (0-8384-0114-7) Heinle & Heinle.

Literature for Adventures in the Human Spirit, Vol. 1. Philip E. Bishop. LC 94-28737. 320p. (C). 1994. pap. text 28.00 (0-13-141251-5) P-H.

Literature for Adventures in the Human Spirit: Literature, Vol. 2. Philip E. Bishop. LC 94-28737. Vol. 2. 320p. (C). 1995. pap. text 28.00 (0-13-141269-8) P-H.

Literature for All: Developing Literature in the Curriculum for Pupils with Special Educational Needs. Nicola Grove. (Entitlement for All Ser.). 1998. pap. 24.95 (1-85346-495-3) Taylor & Francis.

Literature for Children. David L. Russell. 160p. (C). 1991. pap. text 20.95 (0-8013-0673-6, 78660) Longman.

Literature for Children. 3rd ed. David L. Russell. 288p. (J). 1996. pap. 42.00 (0-8013-1773-8) Longman.

***Literature for Children.** 4th ed. Ed. by Longman Staff. 288p. (C). 2000. pap. 42.00 (0-8013-3086-6); pap. 0.00 (0-8013-3087-4) Longman.

Literature for Children: Contemporary Criticism. Peter Hunt. (Critical Approach Ser.). 176p. (C). (gr. 13). 1993. text 69.95 (0-415-06826-6, A7844) Routledge.

Literature for Children about Asians & Asian Americans: Analysis & Annotated Bibliography, with Additional Readings for Adults, 12. Esther C. Jenkins & Mary C. Austin. LC 87-23627. (Bibliographies & Indexes in World Literature Ser.: No. 12). 317p. 1987. lib. bdg. 59.95 (0-313-25970-4, JLC/) Greenwood.

Literature for Children & Young Adults about Oceania: Analysis & Annotated Bibliography with Additional Readings for Adults, 49. Mary C. Austin & Esther C. Jenkins. LC 95-24515. 352p. 1996. lib. bdg. 75.00 (0-313-26643-3, Greenwood Pr) Greenwood.

Literature for Children in England & America from 1646-1774. Ruth K. MacDonald. LC 81-52810. viii, 204p. 1982. 35.00 (0-87875-227-7) Whitston Pub.

***Literature for Composition.** (C). 2000. 39.50 (0-536-61112-2) Pearson Custom.

***Literature for Composition.** Barnet & Berman. 1998. pap. 45.00 (0-201-45651-6) Addison-Wesley.

***Literature For Composition.** 5th ed. (C). 2000. write for info. (0-321-07519-6) Addison-Wesley.

***Literature for Composition.** 5th ed. (C). 2000. 50.00 (0-201-66962-5) Addison-Wesley.

Literature for Composition: Essays, Fiction, Poetry & Drama Sylvan Barnet et al. LC 83-11332. xvii, 774p. 1984. write for info. (0-316-08151-5) Little.

Literature for Composition: Essays, Fiction, Poetry & Drama. 3rd ed. Sylvan Barnet. LC 91-16457. xxiii, 1100 p. 1992. teacher ed., student ed. write for info. (0-673-52180-X, GoodYrBooks) Addson-Wesley Educ.

Literature for Composition: Essays, Fiction, Poetry & Drama. 5th ed. Ed. by Sylvan Barnet et al. LC 99-16379. 1408p. (C). 1999. pap. 53.00 (0-321-02153-3) Addison-Wesley Educ.

Literature for Composition: Essays, Fiction, Poetry & Drama : Includes 1998 MLA Guidelines. 4th ed. Barnet. (C). 1998. pap. text 53.00 (0-321-05787-2) Addison-Wesley Educ.

Literature for Democracy: Reading As a Social Act. Gordon M. Pradl. LC 95-47260. 163p. (Orig.). 1996. pap. text 24.50 (0-86709-380-3, 0380, Pub. by Boynton Cook Pubs) Heinemann.

Literature for Grades 7, 8 & 9. Mary M. Stroh. LC 77-177737. (Columbia University. Teachers College. Contributions to Education Ser.: No. 232). reprint ed. 37.50 (0-404-55232-3) AMS Pr.

Literature for History - Social Science: Kindergarten Through Grade Eight. Zoe Acosta. (Illus.). 128p. (C). 1998. reprint ed. pap. text 35.00 (0-7881-3906-1) DIANE Pub.

Literature for History-Social Science, K-8. rev. ed. California Department of Education Staff. (Illus.). 128p. 1993. pap. 9.00 (0-8011-1107-2) Calif Education.

Literature for Life & Work. 11th ed. Larocco. (CA - Career Development Ser.). (YA). (gr. 9). Date not set. pap. write for info. (0-314-21768-1) S-W Pub.

Literature for Life & Work. 11th ed. Larocco. (EJ - Tech Prep Ser.). (YA). (gr. 10). Date not set. pap. write for info. (0-314-21769-X) S-W Pub.

Literature for Life & Work, Level 9. Johnson & Larocco. (Ej - Tech Prep). 1996. mass mkt. 43.95 (0-538-66713-3) S-W Pub.

Literature for Life & Work, Level 10. Johnson & Larocco. (Ej - Tech Prep). 1996. mass mkt. 34.00 (0-538-66714-1) S-W Pub.

Literature for Our Time. Ed. by Harlow O. Waite & Benjamin P. Atkinson. LC 78-111869. (Play Anthology Reprint Ser.). 1977. 55.95 (0-8369-1731-6) Ayer.

Literature for Science & Mathematics: Kindergarten Through Grade 12. (Illus.). 136p. 1998. reprint ed. pap. text 35.00 (0-7881-4199-6) DIANE Pub.

Literature for Science & Mathematics, K-12. California Department of Education Staff. (Illus.). 152p. 1993. pap. 11.00 (0-8011-1066-1) Calif Education.

Literature for the Journey: World Literature & the Inner Life. Nila J. Webster. 1992. student ed. 23.00 (1-881678-29-6) CSEE.

An Asterisk (*) at the beginning of an entry indicates that the title is appearing for the first time.

L

Literature for the Journey: World Literature & the Inner Life. Nila J. Webster. (YA). (gr. 9-12). 1992. teacher ed. 34.00 (*1-881678-28-8*) CSEE.

Literature for Today's Young Adult. 5th ed. Aleen P. Nilsen & Kenneth L. Donelson. LC 95-26604. 640p. (YA). 1997. pap. 74.00 (*0-673-99737-5*) HarpC.

***Literature for Todays Young Adults.** 6th ed. (C). 2000. pap. text 0.00 (*0-321-03788-X*, Celebration) Addson-Wesley Educ.

***Literature for Todays Young Adults.** 6th ed. (C). 2001. pap. text 0.00 (*0-321-07618-4*, Celebration) Addson-Wesley Educ.

***Literature for Today's Young Adults.** 6th ed. 2000. teacher ed. write for info. (*0-321-08361-X*) Addison-Wesley.

Literature for Visual & Performing Arts: Kindergarten Through Grade Twelve. Diane L. Brooks. 66p. (C). 1998. reprint ed. pap. text 25.00 (*0-7881-3920-7*) DIANE Pub.

Literature for Voice: An Index of Songs in Collections & Source Book for Teachers of Singing. Thomas Goleeke. LC 84-5461. 234p. 1984. 32.00 (*0-8108-1702-0*) Scarecrow.

Literature for Voices in Combination with Electronic & Tape Music: An Annotated Bibliography. J. Michele Edwards. (Music Library Association Index & Bibliography Ser.: No. 17). 194p. 1977. pap. 12.50 (*0-914954-09-1*) Scarecrow.

Literature for Young Children. 4th ed. Joan I. Glazer. LC 99-23476. 330p. 1999. pap. text 37.00 (*0-13-010987-8*) P-H.

Literature for Your People on War & Peace: An Annotated Bibliography, 24. Compiled by Harry E. Eiss. LC 89-17212. (Bibliographies & Indexes in World Literature Ser.: No. 24). 148p. 1989. lib. bdg. 49.95 (*0-313-26068-0*, EYP/, Greenwood Pr) Greenwood.

Literature Frameworks: From Apples to Zoos. Sharron L. McElmeel. LC 96-43888. (Professional Growth Ser.). 278p. 1996. pap. 29.95 (*0-938865-53-6*) Linworth Pub.

Literature Francaise, Vol. I. Berg. (C). 1996. text 64.50 (*0-03-072392-2*) Harcourt Coll Pubs.

Literature Francaise: Histoire et Anthologie. Daniele Nony & Alain Andre. (FRE., Illus.). 464p. (C). 1987. text 19.95 (*2-218-00976-5*, U0976, Pub. by Edns Didier) Hatier Pub.

Literature, General & Comparative: Classified, Alphabetical, & Chronological Listings. Harvard University Library Staff. LC 68-15926. (Widener Library Shelflist: No. 18). 197p. 1968. text 12.50 (*0-674-53650-9*) HUP.

***Literature Guide: Anne Frank.** Anne Frank. (Illus.). 16p. 1999. pap. 3.95 (*0-590-51377-X*) Scholastic Inc.

***Literature Guide: Great Gilly Hopkins.** Katherine Paterson. (Illus.). 16p. 1999. pap. 3.95 (*0-590-04116-9*) Scholastic Inc.

Literature Guide: Guests. Scholastic Professional Books Staff. 16p. 1997. pap. text 3.95 (*0-590-06570-X*) Scholastic Inc.

***Literature Guide: Hatchet.** Gary Paulsen. (Illus.). 16p. 1999. pap. 3.95 (*0-590-38924-6*) Scholastic Inc.

Literature Guide for Beowulf & the Hobbit. Johanna Wrinkle. (ECS Literature Guide Ser.). 128p. (Orig.). 1995. pap. 10.95 (*1-57022-044-1*) ECS Lrn Systs.

Literature Guide for the Identification of Plant Pathogenic Fungi. Amy Y. Rossman et al. LC 87-70764. 252p. 1987. 32.00 (*0-89054-080-2*) Am Phytopathol Soc.

Literature Guide for the Miracle Worker. Pat Watson. (ECS Literature Guide Ser.). 96p. (Orig.). 1995. pap. 10.95 (*1-57022-046-8*) ECS Lrn Systs.

Literature Guide to the GLC of Body Fluids. Austin V. Signeur. LC 82-490. (IFI Data Base Library). 396p. 1982. 110.00 (*0-306-65203-X*, Kluwer Plenum) Kluwer Academic.

Literature Guide to the Hospitality Industry, 10. Compiled by Philip Sawin et al. LC 90-31740. (Bibliographies & Indexes in Economics & Economic History Ser.: No. 10). 112p. 1990. lib. bdg. 49.95 (*0-313-26721-9*, MLH, Greenwood Pr) Greenwood.

Literature Guides: Bridge to Terabithia. Scholastic Professional Books Staff. 16p. 1997. pap. text 3.95 (*0-590-06569-6*) Scholastic Inc.

Literature Guides: Julie of the Wolves. Scholastic Professional Books Staff. (Illus.). 16p. 1997. pap. text 3.95 (*0-590-99615-0*) Scholastic Inc.

Literature Guides: My Side of the Mountain. Scholastic Professional Books Staff. 16p. 1997. pap. text 3.95 (*0-590-06571-8*) Scholastic Inc.

Literature Guides: Sarah, Plain & Tall. Scholastic Professional Books Staff. 16p. 1997. pap. text 3.95 (*0-590-06572-6*) Scholastic Inc.

Literature Guides: The Great Fire. Scholastic Professional Books Staff. 16p. 1997. pap. text 3.95 (*0-590-99616-9*) Scholastic Inc.

Literature in a Changing Age. Ashley H. Thorndike. LC 70-90685. (Essay Index Reprint Ser.). 1977. 23.95 (*0-8369-1234-9*) Ayer.

Literature in Adult Education Reflections on Practice. P. Preston. LC 96-175052. 1995. pap. 40.00 (*1-85041-079-8*, Pub. by Univ Nottingham) St Mut.

Literature in America: An Anthology of Literary Criticism. Philip Rahv. 1993. 18.75 (*0-8446-2776-3*) Peter Smith.

Literature in English. Jack Rudman. (Graduate Record Examination Ser.: GRE-11). 1994. pap. 23.95 (*0-8373-5211-8*) Nat Learn.

Literature in English. Ed. by Harry K. Russell et al. LC 73-132139. (Play Anthology Reprint Ser.). 1977. 51.95 (*0-8369-8218-5*) Ayer.

***Literature in English: A Guide for Librarians in the Digital Age.** Betty H. Day & William A. Wortman. LC 00-24213. (ACRL Publications in Librarianship). 2000. write for info. (*0-8389-8081-3*) Assn Coll & Res Libs.

***Literature in English: African Literature in Novels, Oral Literature, Drama, Short Stories.** Stephen N. Bakuli. 160p. (C). 2000. pap. 29.95 (*1-891016-34-2*) Esparto Pr.

Literature in Exile. Ed. by John Glad. LC 89-20694. 190p. (C). 1990. text 32.95 (*0-8223-0987-4*) Duke.

Literature in Ireland: Studies Irish & Anglo-Irish. Thomas MacDonagh. 209p. 1996. pap. 15.95 (*0-946327-16-5*, Pub. by Relay Pubns) Irish Bks Media.

Literature in Its Place. James N. Britton. LC 92-24089. 136p. (J). 1993. pap. text 17.50 (*0-86709-315-3*, 0315, Pub. by Boynton Cook Pubs) Heinemann.

Literature in Medicine Monograph. Valeria J. Gilchrist & Delese Wear. 265p. 1995. 20.00 (*0-614-07964-0*) Soc Tchrs Fam Med.

Literature in My Time. Compton Mackenzie. LC 67-28758. (Essay Index Reprint Ser.). 1977. 18.95 (*0-8369-0654-3*) Ayer.

Literature in the Adult Class: Tradition & Challenge. Ed. by Peter Preston. 200p. 1994. 24.95 (*1-85041-072-0*, Pub. by U of Nottingham) Paul & Co Pubs.

***Literature in the Greek & Roman Worlds: A New Perspective.** Ed. by Oliver Taplin. LC 99-57693. 512p. 2000. 35.00 (*0-19-210020-3*) OUP.

Literature in the Language Classroom: A Resource Book of Ideas & Activities. Joanne Collie & Stephen Slater. (Cambridge Handbooks for Language Teachers Ser.). 272p. 1988. pap. text 20.95 (*0-521-31224-8*) Cambridge U Pr.

Literature in the Light of the Emblem. 2nd ed. Peter M. Daly. LC 99-180754. 312p. 1999. text 65.00 (*0-8020-0910-7*); pap. text 22.95 (*0-8020-7891-5*) U of Toronto Pr.

Literature in the Light of the Emblem: Structural Parallels Between the Emblem & Literature in the Sixteenth & Seventeenth Centuries. Peter M. Daly. LC 79-11863. 259p. reprint ed. pap. 80.30 (*0-608-15394-X*, 202932700060) Bks Demand.

Literature in the Making, by Some of Its Makers. Joyce Kilmer. (Collected Works of Joyce Kilmer). 318p. 1998. reprint ed. lib. bdg. 98.00 (*1-58201-663-1*) Classic Bks.

Literature in the Marketplace: Nineteenth-Century British Publishing & Reading Practices. Ed. by John O. Jordan & Robert L. Patten. (Studies in Nineteenth-Century Literature & Culture: No. 5). (Illus.). 352p. (C). 1995. text 69.95 (*0-521-45247-3*) Cambridge U Pr.

Literature in the Modern World: Critical Essays & Documents. Ed. by Dennis Walder. 394p. 1991. pap. text 19.95 (*0-19-871037-2*) OUP.

Literature in the Theatre, & Other Essays. William A. Darlington. LC 68-16924. (Essay Index Reprint Ser.). 1977. 19.95 (*0-8369-0362-5*) Ayer.

Literature in the Vedic Age: Brahmanas, Aranyakas, Upanishads & Sutras, Vol. 2. Sukumari Bhattacharji. 400p. 1986. 32.50 (*0-8364-1859-X*, Pub. by KP Bagchi) S Asia.

Literature Instruction: A Focus on Student Response. Judith A. Langer. 211p. 1992. pap. 14.95 (*0-8141-3318-5*) NCTE.

Literature Instruction: Practice & Policy. Ed. by James Flood & Judith A. Langer. LC 93-39342. 1995. 29.95 (*0-590-49756-1*, 15755u5l59) Scholastic Inc.

Literature Journal. C. Welsh-Charrier. Ed. by Shawn Mahshie. (Sharing Ideas). (Illus.). 52p. 1991. reprint ed. pap. text 9.95 (*0-88095-203-2*) Gallaudet U Pre Coll.

Literature, Language & the Media in India. Ed. by Mariola Offredi. (C). 1992. text 30.00 (*81-85425-75-2*, Pub. by Manohar) S Asia.

***Literature Links for Nutrition & Health.** Valerie A. Ubbes & Diana M. Spillman. 227p. 1999. pap. text 31.00 (*0-205-30954-2*) Allyn.

Literature Links to Phonics: A Balanced Approach. Karen M. Durica. 150p. 1996. pap. text 22.00 (*1-56308-353-1*) Teacher Ideas Pr.

Literature, Literacy & Learning: Library Media Specialists, Classroom Teachers & the Literature-Based Curriculum. Eleanor Kullesied & Dorothy Strickland. 72p. 1989. pap. text 18.00 (*0-8389-3376-9*) ALA.

Literature Lost: Social Agendas & the Corruption of the Humanities. John M. Ellis. LC 96-37680. 272p. 1997. 25.00 (*0-300-06920-0*) Yale U Pr.

Literature Lost: Social Agendas & the Corruption of the Humanities. John M. Ellis. 272p. 1999. pap. text 14.95 (*0-300-07579-0*) Yale U Pr.

Literature Lover's Book of Lists. (C). 1997. 24.95 (*0-13-896564-1*, Macmillan Coll) P-H.

***Literature Lovers Book of Lists.** 1998. 25.00 (*0-13-030406-9*) P-H.

***Literature Lover's Book of Lists.** Strouf. 2000. pap. 15.00 (*0-13-019493-X*) P-H.

Literature Lover's Book of Lists: Serious Trivia for the Bibliophile. Ross et al. LC 98-25544. (Illus.). 380p. 1998. text 25.00 (*0-7352-0017-3*) PH Pr.

***Literature, Markets & Media in Germany & Austria Today.** Ed. by Arthur Williams et al. (University of Bradford Studies: Vol. 5). x, 336p. 2000. pap. 47.95 (*0-8204-5059-6*) P Lang Pubng.

Literature, Media, Information Systems. Ed. & Intro. by John Johnston. (Critical Voices Ser.). 208p. 1997. text 23.00 (*90-5701-071-2*); pap. text 18.00 (*90-5701-061-5*) Gordon & Breach.

Literature, Modernism & Myth: Belief & Responsibility in the Twentieth Century. Michael Bell. 268p. 1997. text 59.95 (*0-521-58016-1*) Cambridge U Pr.

Literature, Nature, & Other: Ecofeminist Critiques. Patrick D. Murphy. LC 93-8733. 212p. (C). 1995. text 59.50 (*0-7914-2277-1*); pap. text 19.95 (*0-7914-2278-X*) State U NY Pr.

Literature News: Nine Stories from the Newspaper of the Vietnam Writers Union. Rosemary Nguyen. (Lac Viet Series, Yale Southeast Asia Studies: Vol. 16). (Illus.). 192p. 1997. pap. 18.00 (*0-938692-65-8*) Yale U SE Asia.

Literature, 1988, Pt. 2. (Astronomy & Astrophysics Abstracts Ser.: Vol. 46). 1300p. 1989. 278.95 (*0-387-51164-4*) Spr-Verlag.

Literature, 1988, Pt. 2. Ed. by U. Esser et al. (Astronomy & Astrophysics Abstracts Ser.: Vol. 45). (Illus.). 1300p. 1988. 230.95 (*0-387-50475-3*) Spr-Verlag.

Literature, 1985, Pt. 1. Ed. by S. Bohme et al. (Astronomy & Astrophysics Abstracts Ser.: Vol. 39). 1048p. 1985. 158.95 (*0-387-16032-9*) Spr-Verlag.

Literature, 1985, Pt. 2. Ed. by S. Bohme et al. (Astronomy & Astrophysics Abstracts Ser.: Vol. 40). 1100p. 1986. 158.95 (*0-387-16655-6*) Spr-Verlag.

Literature, 1984, Pt. 2. Ed. by S. Bohme et al. Tr. by G. Zech. (Astronomy & Astrophysics Abstracts Ser.: Vol. 38). 920p. 1985. 151.95 (*0-387-15562-7*) Spr-Verlag.

Literature, 1989, Pt. 1. (Astronomy & Astrophysics Abstracts Ser.: Vol. 49). (Illus.). 1216p. 1990. 318.95 (*0-387-52308-1*) Spr-Verlag.

Literature, 1987, Pt. 1. Ed. by S. Bohme et al. (Astronomy & Astrophysics Abstracts Ser.). 1200p. 1988. 182.95 (*0-387-18640-9*) Spr-Verlag.

Literature, 1987, Pt. 2. Ed. by S. Bohme et al. (Astronomy & Astrophysics Abstracts Ser.: Vol. 44). 1300p. 1988. 206.95 (*0-387-19283-2*) Spr-Verlag.

Literature, 1986, Part 1. Ed. by S. Bohme et al. (Astronomy & Astrophysics Abstracts Ser.: Vol. 41). 1100p. 1986. 158.95 (*0-387-17252-1*) Spr-Verlag.

Literature, 1983, Pt. 1. Ed. by S. Boehme et al. (Astronomy & Astrophysics Abstracts Ser.: Vol. 33). 815p. 1983. 118.95 (*0-387-13017-9*) Spr-Verlag.

Literature, 1983, Pt. 2. Ed. by S. Bohme et al. (Astronomy & Astrophysics Abstracts Ser.: Vol. 34). 960p. 1984. 151.95 (*0-387-13485-9*) Spr-Verlag.

Literature, 1990, Pt. 1. Ed. by G. Burkhardt et al. (Astronomy & Astrophysics Abstracts Ser.: Vol. 51). viii, 1526p. 1991. 358.95 (*0-387-53533-0*) Spr-Verlag.

***Literature, 1998, Pt. 2.** Ed. by Astronomisches Rechen-Institut Heidelberg Staff. (Astronomy & Astrophysics Abstracts Ser.: Vol. 70). xviii, 1931p. 1999. 389.00 (*3-540-66096-8*) Spr-Verlag.

Literature, 1998 Pt. 1: A Publication of the Astronomisches Rechen-Institut Heidelberg Produced in Cooperation with the Fachinformationszentrum Karlsruhe & the Institution of Electrical Engineering, U. K. Ed. by G. Burkhardt et al. (Astronomy & Astrophysics Abstracts Ser.: Vol. 69). xviii, 1931p. 1999. 399.00 (*3-540-65481-X*) Spr-Verlag.

Literature, 1997. Ed. by G. Burkhardt et al. (Astronomy & Astrophysics Abstracts Ser.: Vol. 68). xviii, 1794p. 1998. 375.00 (*3-540-64596-9*) Spr-Verlag.

Literature, 1996, Pt. 1. 1997. 369.00 (*3-540-62554-2*) Spr-Verlag.

Literature, 1993, 2 vols., Vols. A & B, Pt. 1. Ed. by G. Burkhardt et al. (Astronomy & Astrophysics Abstracts Ser.: Vol. 57). x, 1663p. 1994. 325.95 (*0-387-57721-1*) Spr-Verlag.

Literature, 1992, Pt. 2. Ed. by I. Heinrich et al. 1062p. 1993. 295.95 (*0-387-57081-0*) Spr-Verlag.

Literature of Adult Education: A Bibliographic Essay. Cyril O. Houle. LC 92-12659. (Higher & Adult Education Ser.). 464p. 1992. text 45.00 (*1-55542-470-8*) Jossey-Bass.

Literature of Africa. LC 98-31285. (Traditions in World Literature Ser.). 1998. 21.19 (*0-8442-1201-6*) NTC Contemp Pub Co.

Literature of Africa. N T C Contemporary Publishing Company Staff. 1998. pap. 17.44 (*0-8442-1202-4*) NTC Contemp Pub Co.

Literature of Africa & the African Continuum. Ed. by Mildred P. Mortimer et al. LC 84-51450. (African Literature Association Annuals Ser.). 140p. (Orig.). 1988. 22.00 (*0-89410-460-8*); pap. 14.00 (*0-89410-461-6*) Cornell AS&RC.

Literature of Agricultural Engineering. Ed. by Carl W. Hall & Wallace C. Olsen. (Illus.). 432p. 1993. text 69.95 (*0-8014-2812-2*) Cornell U Pr.

***Literature of Al-Andalus.** Ed. by Maria Rosa Menocal et al. (The Cambridge History of Arabic Literature). (Illus.). 600p. (C). 2000. Price not set. (*0-521-47159-1*) Cambridge U Pr.

Literature of American History: A Bibliographical Guide. Ed. by J. N. Larned. 588p. 1995. reprint ed. lib. bdg. 59.95 (*0-8328-4487-X*) Higginson Bk Co.

Literature of American History: A Bibliographical Guide. Ed. by J. N. Larned. 588p. 1995. reprint ed. lib. bdg. 64.50 (*0-8328-4506-X*) Higginson Bk Co.

Literature of American Music III & Checklist of Writings on American Music, 2 vols. Guy A. Marco. 105.00 (*0-8108-3451-0*) Scarecrow.

Literature of American Music in Books & Folk Music Collections: A Fully Annotated Bibliography. David Horn. LC 76-13160. 570p. 1977. 50.00 (*0-8108-0996-6*) Scarecrow.

Literature of American Music in Books & Folk Music Collections: A Fully Annotated Bibliography, Supplement 1. David Horn & Richard Jackson. LC 87-9630. 586p. 1988. 60.00 (*0-8108-1997-X*) Scarecrow.

Literature of American Music in Books & Folk Music Collections, 1983-1993. Guy A. Marco. LC 95-26774. 472p. 1996. 69.50 (*0-8108-3132-5*) Scarecrow.

Literature of Analytical Chemistry: Scientometric Evaluation. T. Braun & E. Bujdoso. LC 86-6842. 272p. 1986. 154.00 (*0-8493-6591-0*, CRC Reprint) Franklin.

Literature of Ancient Egypt: An Anthology of Stories, Instructions, & Poetry. Ed. by William K. Simpson. Tr. by Raymond O. Faulkner et al. LC 73-77814. (Illus.). 345p. 1973. pap. 20.00 (*0-300-01711-1*) Yale U Pr.

Literature of Animal Science & Health. Ed. by Wallace C. Olsen. 400p. 1993. text 79.95 (*0-8014-2886-6*) Cornell U Pr.

Literature of Arabia see Oriental Literature

***Literature of Asia.** Ed. by NTC Contemporary Publishing Staff. LC 98-44317. (Traditions in World Literature Ser.). 1998. write for info. (*0-8442-1157-5*); pap. write for info. (*0-8442-1158-3*) NTC Contemp Pub Co.

Literature of Australian Birds: A History & Bibliography. Herbert M. Whittel. (Illus.). 915p. 1994. 100.00 (*1-888262-68-0*) Martino Pubng.

Literature of Belief. Ed. by Neal E. Lambert. (Monograph Ser.: Vol. 5). 1981. 4.95 (*0-88494-409-3*) Bookcraft Inc.

***Literature of California, Vol. 1.** Ed. by Jack Hicks et al. (Illus.). 870p. 2000. pap. 24.95 (*0-520-22212-1*) U CA Pr.

***Literature of California Vol. 1: Native American Beginnings to 1945.** Ed. by Jack Hicks et al. LC 00-37410. (Illus.). 870p. 2000. 60.00 (*0-520-21524-9*) U CA Pr.

Literature of Chamber Music. Arthur Cohn. 3075p. 1998. 275.00 (*0-937276-16-2*) Hinshaw Mus.

Literature of Chemical Technology: Based on Papers Presented at Two Symposia Sponsored by the Division of Chemical Literature of the American chemical Society at the 143rd Meeting, Cincinnati, OH, Jan. 13-14, 1963, & the 145th Meeting, New York, Sept. 9-13, 1963. American Chemistry Society Staff. LC 68-59481. (Advances in Chemistry Ser.: No. 78). 742p. 1968. reprint ed. pap. 200.00 (*0-608-06810-1*, 206700700009) Bks Demand.

Literature of China see Oriental Literature

Literature of China in the 20th Century. Kam Louie & Bonnie S. McDougall. LC 97-2533. 352p. 1997. 37.00 (*0-231-11084-7*) Col U Pr.

Literature of China in the Twentieth Century. Kam Louie & Bonnie S. McDougall. 320p. 1999. pap. 17.50 (*0-231-11085-5*) Col U Pr.

Literature of Cinema, 48 bks., Set. Ed. by Martin S. Dworkin. (Series One). 1970. 2045.00 (*0-405-01600-X*) Ayer.

Literature of Cinema, 15 bks., Set. Ed. by Martin S. Dworkin. (Series Two). 1972. reprint ed. 353.00 (*0-405-03887-9*) Ayer.

Literature of Commitment. Charles I. Glicksberg. LC 75-5148. 467p. 1976. 50.00 (*0-8387-1685-7*) Bucknell U Pr.

Literature of Communism in America: A Selected Reference Guide. Robert F. Delaney. LC 62-6923. 447p. reprint ed. pap. 138.60 (*0-608-11183-X*, 200537800053) Bks Demand.

Literature of Controversy: Polemical Strategy from Milton to Junius. Ed. by Thomas N. Corns. 1987. 29.50 (*0-7146-3292-9*, Pub. by F Cass Pubs) Intl Spec Bk.

Literature of Crime Detection & Espionage, 2, Vol. 2. Robin W. Winks. (Scribners Writers Ser.). 1296p. 1998. 225.00 (*0-684-80521-9*) S&S Trade.

Literature of Crop Science. Ed. by Wallace C. Olsen. (Literature of the Agricultural Sciences Ser.). (Illus.). 544p. 1995. text 79.95 (*0-8014-3138-7*) Cornell U Pr.

Literature of Delight: A Critical Guide to Humorous Books for Children. Kimberly O. Fakih. 269p. 1993. 40.00 (*0-8352-3027-9*) Bowker.

***Literature of Developing Nations for Students, 2 Vols. Set.** 1000p. 2000. 150.00 (*0-7876-4928-7*, UXL) Gale.

Literature of Egypt & the Soudan to 1885: A Bibliography, 2 vols. Ibrahim-Hilmy. 900p. 1994. reprint ed. 90.00 (*1-888262-48-6*) Martino Pubng.

Literature of Emigration & Exile. James Whitlark & Wendell M. Aycock. 192p. 1992. text 24.95 (*0-89672-263-5*) Tex Tech Univ Pr.

Literature of Exhaustion. deluxe ed. John Barth. 100p. 1982. 75.00 (*0-935716-16-5*) Lord John.

Literature of Fact: Selected Papers from the English Institute. Ed. by Angus Fletcher. LC 76-25582. (Essays of the English Institute Ser.). 172p. 1976. text 49.00 (*0-231-04144-6*) Col U Pr.

Literature of Forestry & Agroforestry. Ed. by Peter McDonald & James P. Lassoie. LC 95-39328. (Literature of the Agricultural Sciences Ser.). (Illus.). 445p. 1996. text 79.95 (*0-8014-3181-6*) Cornell U Pr.

Literature of Formative Judaism: Controversies on the Literature of Formative Judaism. Ed. by Jacob Neusner. LC 92-13897. (Origins of Judaism Ser.: Vol. 13). 400p. 1991. text 20.00 (*0-8240-8184-6*) Garland.

Literature of Formative Judaism: The Midrash Compilations, 2 vols. Jacob Neusner. LC 90-13899. (Origins of Judaism Ser.: Vol. 11). 1072p. 1991. text 45.00 (*0-8240-8182-X*) Garland.

Literature of Formative Judaism: The Mishnah & the Tosefta. LC 90-13901. (Origins of Judaism Ser.: Vol. 9). 328p. 1991. text 20.00 (*0-8240-8180-3*) Garland.

Literature of Formative Judaism: The Talmuds. Ed. by Jacob Neusner. LC 90-13900. (Origins of Judaism Ser.: Vol. 10). 496p. 1991. text 25.00 (*0-8240-8181-1*) Garland.

Literature of Formative Judaism: The Targumim & Other Jewish Writings in Late Antiquity. Ed. by Jacob Neusner. LC 90-13898. (Origins of Judaism Ser.: Vol. 12). 384p. 1991. text 20.00 (*0-8240-8183-8*) Garland.

***Literature of Georgia: A History.** 2nd rev. ed. Donald Rayfield. 288p. 1999. (*0-7007-1163-5*, Pub. by Curzon Pr Ltd) Paul & Co Pubs.

Literature of Greece & Rome. LC 98-31286. (Traditions in World Literature Ser.). 1998. pap. write for info. (*0-8442-1287-3*) NTC Contemp Pub Co.

An Asterisk (*) at the beginning of an entry indicates that the title is appearing for the first time.

Literature of Greece & Rome. N T C Contemporary Publishing Company Staff. 1998. 21.19 (*0-8442-1191-5*) NTC Contemp Pub Co.

Literature of Higher Education, 1971. Lewis B. Mayhew. LC 74-155167. (Higher Education Ser.). 176p. reprint ed. 54.60 (*0-8357-9332-X*, 201381800087) Bks Demand.

Literature of Higher Education, 1972. Lewis B. Mayhew. LC 74-155167. (Jossey-Bass Higher Education Ser.). 198p. reprint ed. 61.40 (*0-8357-9333-8*, 201385900088) Bks Demand.

Literature of Human Experience. 6th ed. Abcarian. 1993. pap. text 5.00 (*0-312-08409-9*) St Martin.

Literature of Images: Narrative Landscape from Julie to Jane Eyre. Doris Y. Kadish. 280p. (C). 1986. text 40.00 (*0-8135-1183-6*) Rutgers U Pr.

Literature of India see Oriental Literature

***Literature of Indian Diaspora: Essays in Criticism.** A. L. McLeod. 2000. 42.00 (*81-207-2248-5*, Pub. by Sterling Pubs) S Asia.

Literature of Isolationism: Non-Interventionist Scholarship, 1930-1972. Justus D. Doenecke. LC 72-80272. 90p. 1972. pap. 1.85 (*0-87926-016-5*) R Myles.

Literature of Japan see Oriental Literature

Literature of Jazz: A Critical Guide. Donald Kennington. LC 74-151831. 156p. reprint ed. pap. 48.40 (*0-608-12798-1*, 202421100035) Bks Demand.

Literature of Journalism: An Annotated Bibliography. Warren C. Price. LC 59-13522. 507p. reprint ed. pap. 157.20 (*0-608-11245-3*, 200100600053) Bks Demand.

Literature of Journalism: Text & Context. R. Thomas Berner. LC 98-21190. 288p. 1999. pap. text 24.95 (*1-891136-00-3*) Strata Pub Co.

Literature of Labor & the Labors of Literature: Allegory in Nineteenth-Century American Fiction. Cindy Weinstein. (Studies in American Literature & Culture: No. 89). 282p. (C). 1995. text 64.95 (*0-521-47054-4*) Cambridge U Pr.

Literature of Memory: Modern Writers of the American South. Richard J. Gray. LC 78-309287. xi, 377 p. 1977. write for info. (*0-7131-5861-1*) E Arnld Pubs.

Literature of Misogyny in Medieval Spain: The "Arcipreste de Talavera" & the "Spill" Michael Solomon. LC 96-44935. (Cambridge Studies in Latin American & Iberian Literature: Vol. 10). 231p. (C). 1997. text 59.95 (*0-521-56390-9*) Cambridge U Pr.

Literature of Modern Arabia: An Anthology. Salma Khadra Jayyusi. 1998. pap. text 42.50 (*0-7103-0263-0*, Pub. by Kegan Paul Intl) Col U Pr.

Literature of Music. James E. Matthew. LC 69-12688. (Music Ser.). 1969. reprint ed. lib. bdg. 37.50 (*0-306-71227-X*) Da Capo.

Literature of Music Bibliography: An Account of the Writings on the History of Music Printing & Publishing. Donald W. Krummel. LC 92-10492. (Reference Books in Music: No. 21). xix, 447p. 1993. 75.00 (*0-914913-21-2*, Fallen Lef Pr) Scarecrow.

Literature of Mystery & Detention, 44 vols. Harry M. Geduld. 1976. 1260.50 (*0-405-07860-9*, 486) Ayer.

Literature of National Music. Carl Engel. LC 74-24076. reprint ed. 27.50 (*0-404-12905-6*) AMS Pr.

Literature of Nationalism: Essays on East European Identity. Ed. by Robert B. Pynsent. 256p. 1996. text 65.00 (*0-312-16008-9*) St Martin.

***Literature of Nature: An International Sourcebook.** Ed. by Patrick D. Murphy. LC 98-233184. 512p. 1998. lib. bdg. 95.00 (*1-57958-010-6*) Fitzroy Dearborn.

Literature of Nature: The British & American Traditions. Robert J. Begiebing & Owen Grumbling. (Illus.). 730p. 1990. 49.00 (*0-937548-16-2*) Plexus Pub.

Literature of Nature: The British & American Traditions. Ed. by Robert J. Begiebing & Owen Grumbling. (Illus.). 730p. 1990. pap. 37.50 (*0-937548-17-0*) Plexus Pub.

Literature of New York: A Selective Bibliography of Colonial & Native New York State Authors. Lewis Turco. 1970. pap. 1.95 (*0-930000-12-9*) NY St Eng Coun.

Literature of Nihilism. Charles I. Glicksberg. 354p. 1975. 45.00 (*0-8387-1520-6*) Bucknell U Pr.

Literature of 1980-1981 see Alcohol Education Materials: Annotated Bibliographies

Literature of 1950-1973 see Alcohol Education Materials: Annotated Bibliographies

Literature of 1978-1979 see Alcohol Education Materials: Annotated Bibliographies

Literature of 1979-1980 see Alcohol Education Materials: Annotated Bibliographies

Literature of 1973-1978 see Alcohol Education Materials: Annotated Bibliographies

Literature of Persia see Oriental Literature

Literature of Photography, 62 bks., Set. Ed. by Peter C. Bunnell & Robert A. Sobieszek. 1973. 1301.50 (*0-405-04889-0*) Ayer.

Literature of Piano. David Dubal. 1992. pap. write for info. (*0-679-41225-5*) McKay.

Literature of Police Corruption: A Selected, Annotated Bibliography, Vol. II. Nina Duchaine. LC 76-30895. 1979. 12.50 (*0-89444-008-X*) John Jay Pr.

Literature of Police Corruption Vol. 1: A Guide to Bibliography & Theory. Antony E. Simpson. LC 76-30895. 1977. lib. bdg. 12.50 (*0-89444-003-9*) John Jay Pr.

Literature of Political Economy: A Classified Catalogue of Select Publications in the Different Departments of the Science, with Historical, Critical & Biographical Notices. John R. McCulloch. LC 86-7486. (Reprints of Economic Classics Ser.). xiii, 407p. 1991. reprint ed. lib. bdg. 57.50 (*0-678-01457-4*) Kelley.

Literature of Political Science: A Guide for Students, Librarians, & Teachers. Clifton Brock. LC 79-79426. 244p. reprint ed. pap. 75.70 (*0-608-11188-0*, 201758600007) Bks Demand.

Literature of Protest: The Franco Years. Margaret C. Gonzalez. LC 98-22790. 144p. (C). 1998. 32.00 (*0-7618-1155-9*) U Pr of Amer.

***Literature of Provence: An Introduction.** Daniel Vitaglione. (Illus.). 192p. 2000. per. 32.00 (*0-7864-0843-X*) McFarland & Co.

Literature of Provence: An Introduction. Daniel Vitaglione. LC 98-8706. 1998. write for info. (*0-7618-1212-1*) U Pr of Amer.

Literature of Quilts: A Resource Guide. Jocelyn Riley. 114p. 1995. 45.00 (*1-877933-09-0*) Her Own Words.

Literature of Renaissance England. Ed. by John Hollander & Frank Kermode. (Anthology of English Literature Ser.). (Illus.). 1114p. 1973. text 31.95 (*0-19-501637-8*) OUP.

Literature of Replenishment. deluxe ed. John Barth. 1982. 125.00 (*0-935716-91-2*) Lord John.

Literature of Rock, 1954-1978. Frank Hoffmann. LC 80-23459. 349p. 1981. 39.50 (*0-8108-1371-8*) Scarecrow.

Literature of Rock III, 1984-1990: With Additional Material for the Period 1954-1983. Frank Hoffmann & B. Lee Cooper. LC 93-36263. 1023p. 1995. 104.50 (*0-8108-2762-X*) Scarecrow.

***Literature of Roguery in Seventeenth & Eighteenth-Century Russia.** Marcia A. Morris. LC 00-8054. (Studies in Russian Literature & Theory). 2000. 79.95 (*0-8101-1753-3*) Northwestern U Pr.

Literature of Satire in the Twelfth Century: A Neglected Mediaeval Genre. Ronald Pepin. (Studies in Medieval Literature: Vol. 2). 150p. 1989. write for info. (*0-88946-316-6*) E Mellen.

Literature of Soil Science. Ed. by Peter McDonald. LC 93-27394. (Literature of the Agricultural Sciences Ser.). (Illus.). 456p. 1994. text 72.50 (*0-8014-2921-8*) Cornell U Pr.

Literature of Spain & the Americas. N T C Contemporary Publishing Company Staff. 1998. 21.99 (*0-8442-1198-2*); pap. 17.44 (*0-8442-1199-0*) NTC Contemp Pub Co.

Literature of Spiritual Values & Catholic Fiction. Michelle Gable. Ed. & Intro. by Nancy Hynes. LC 96-14164. (Illus.). 330p. 1996. lib. bdg. 54.00 (*0-7618-0343-2*) U Pr of Amer.

Literature of Struggle: An Anthology of Chartist Fiction. Ian Haywood. LC 95-667. (Nineteenth Century Ser.). 224p. 1995. 78.95 (*1-85928-032-3*, Pub. by Scolar Pr) Ashgate Pub Co.

Literature of Terrorism: A Selectively Annotated Bibliography. Compiled by Edward F. Mickolus. LC 80-541. 553p. 1980. lib. bdg. 125.00 (*0-313-22265-7*, MLT/, Greenwood Pr) Greenwood.

Literature of the Age of Elizabeth. Edwin P. Whipple. LC 72-8542. (Essay Index Reprint Ser.). 1977. reprint ed. 25.95 (*0-8369-7341-0*) Ayer.

Literature of the Age of Elizabeth. Edwin P. Whipple. (Essay Index Reprint Ser.). 364p. reprint ed. lib. bdg. 22.00 (*0-8290-0465-3*) Irvington.

Literature of the American People. Arthur H. Quinn. 1177p. 1989. reprint ed. text 137.50 (*0-8290-2464-6*) Irvington.

Literature of the Ancient Egyptians see Ancient Egyptian Poetry & Prose

Literature of the Ancient Egyptians. Johann P. Erman. Tr. by Aylward M. Blackman. LC 68-56522. 1972. reprint ed. 23.95 (*0-405-08489-7*, Pub. by Blom Pubns) Ayer.

Literature of the Bahamas, 1724-1992: The March Towards National Identity. Anthony G. Dahl. 236p. (C). 1995. lib. bdg. 42.50 (*0-7618-0092-1*) U Pr of Amer.

Literature of the Combustion of Petroleum: A Collection of Papers Presented at the Symposium on the Literature of the Combustion of Petroleum Held by the Division of Chemical Literature & the Division of Petroleum Chemistry at the 129th National Meeting of the American Chemical Society in Dallas, TX, April 1956. American Chemical Society Staff. LC 59-627. (Advances in Chemistry Ser.: Vol. 20). (Illus.). 299p. 1958. reprint ed. pap. 92.70 (*0-608-06903-5*, 206711100009) Bks Demand.

Literature of the Early Church. Ed. by Everett Ferguson. LC 92-39999. (Studies in Early Christianity: Vol. 2). 368p. 1993. text 72.00 (*0-8153-1062-5*) Garland.

Literature of the Empire: The Art of the Empire see British Empire

***Literature of the French & Occitan Middle Ages: Eleventh to Fifteenth Centuries.** Ed. by Deborah M. Sinnreich-Levi. LC 99-24673. (Dictionary of Literary Biography Ser.). 500p. 1999. text 155.00 (*0-7876-3102-7*) Gale.

Literature of the Great Lakes Region: An Annotated Bibliography. Donald W. Maxwell. LC 91-14663. 502p. 1991. text 20.00 (*0-8240-7027-5*, H1252) Garland.

Literature of the Highlands. Magnus Maclean. LC 70-144492. reprint ed. 32.50 (*0-404-08595-4*) AMS Pr.

Literature of the Holocaust: The Imagination after Auschwitz. Judith Klau. (YA). (gr. 9-12). 1985. 17.50 (*1-881678-20-2*) CSEE.

Literature of the Hundred Flowers, 2 vols. Ed. by Hualing Nieh. LC 80-36748. (Modern Asian Literature Ser.). 1981. text 58.00 (*0-231-05074-7*) Col U Pr.

Literature of the Hundred Flowers, 2 vols., Set. Ed. by Hualing Nieh. LC 80-36748. (Modern Asian Literature Ser.). 1981. text 173.50 (*0-231-05264-2*) Col U Pr.

Literature of the Hundred Flowers, 2 vols., Vol. II: Poetry & Fiction. Ed. by Hualing Nieh. LC 80-36748. (Modern Asian Literature Ser.). 618p. 1981. text 110.50 (*0-231-05076-3*) Col U Pr.

Literature of the Hundred Flowers: Criticism & Polemics, Vol. 1. Ed. by Hua-ling Nieh. LC 80-36748. (Modern Asian Literature Ser.). 338p. reprint ed. pap. 104.80 (*0-8357-4274-1*, 203707200001) Bks Demand.

***Literature of the Law.** Brian Harris. LC 98-182133. xviii, 340p. 1998. pap. 44.00 (*1-85431-733-4*) Gaunt.

Literature of the Life Sciences. David A. Kronick. (Medical Library Association). 219p. 1985. 22.50 (*0-8108-2432-9*) Scarecrow.

Literature of the Lost Home: Kobayashi Hideo-Literary Criticism, 1924-1939. Ed. & Tr. by Hideo Kobayashi from JPN. LC 94-49638. 192p. 1995. 35.00 (*0-8047-2537-3*) Stanford U Pr.

Literature of the Low Countries: A Short History of Dutch Literature in the Netherlands & Belgium. Reinder P. Meijer. 1978. pap. 12.95 (*0-89197-825-9*); text 42.50 (*0-8057-3431-7*) Irvington.

Literature of the Middle Western Frontier, 2 vols. Ralph L. Rusk. (BCL1-PS American Literature Ser.). 1992. reprint ed. lib. bdg. 150.00 (*0-7812-6627-0*) Rprt Serv.

Literature of the Nonprofit Sector: A Bibliography with Abstracts, Vol. 2. Foundation Center Staff. Ed. by Margaret Derrickson & Kevin Kurdylo. 1990. pap. 45.00 (*0-87954-343-4*) Foundation Ctr.

Literature of the Nonprofit Sector: A Bibliography with Abstracts, Vol. 3. Ed. by Mildred Bobrovich & Kevin Kurdylo. 1991. pap. text 45.00 (*0-87954-386-8*) Foundation Ctr.

Literature of the Nonprofit Sector: A Bibliography with Abstracts, Vol. V. 1993. 45.00 (*0-87954-509-7*, INS5) Foundation Ctr.

Literature of the Nonprofit Sector Vol. 1: A Bibliography with Abstracts. Ed. by Margaret Derrickson. (Orig.). 1989. pap. text 55.00 (*0-87954-287-X*) Foundation Ctr.

Literature of the Nonprofit Sector Vol. 4: A Bibliography with Abstracts. Ed. by Kevin Kurdylo. 192p. (Orig.). 1992. pap. 45.00 (*0-87954-447-3*) Foundation Ctr.

Literature of the Nonprofit Sector Vol. 8: A Bibliography with Abstracts. 1996. 45.00 (*0-87954-702-2*) Foundation Ctr.

Literature of the North. D. Hewitt & M. Spiller. 224p. 1983. text 20.00 (*0-08-028453-1*, Pergamon Pr); pap. text 11.00 (*0-08-028468-X*, Pergamon Pr) Elsevier.

Literature of the Old Testament. 3rd ed. Julius A. Bewer & Emil G. Kraeling. LC 62-17061. (Records of Civilization: Sources & Studies: No. 5). 512p. reprint ed. pap. 158.80 (*0-608-12520-2*, 202497500040) Bks Demand.

Literature of the People's Republic of China. Ed. by Kai-yu Hsu & Wang Ting. LC 78-24807. (Chinese Literature in Translation Ser.). 992p. 1980. reprint ed. pap. 200.00 (*0-608-01064-2*, 205937200001) Bks Demand.

***Literature of the Personalists of Early Buddhism.** Bhiksho Thich Thein Chau. 242p. 1999. pap. 150.00 (*81-208-1622-6*, Pub. by Motilal Bnarsidass) St Mut.

***Literature of the Polar Regions.** J. Chavanne. xvi, 336p. 1999. reprint ed. 60.00 (*1-57898-141-7*) Martino Pubng.

Literature of the Political Economy. Samuel Hollander. LC 97-11430. 432p. (C). 1997. 100.00 (*0-415-11429-2*) Routledge.

Literature of the Prairie: A Resource Guide. Jocelyn Riley. 114p. 1995. 45.00 (*1-877933-14-7*) Her Own Words.

Literature of the Rebellion. John R. Bartlett. LC 77-109311. 477p. 1970. reprint ed. lib. bdg. 69.50 (*0-8371-3568-0*, BLR&) Greenwood.

Literature of the Romantic Period: A Bibliographical Guide. Ed. by Michael O'Neill. 418p. 1998. text 79.00 (*0-19-871120-4*) OUP.

Literature of the Romantic Period: A Bibliographical Guide. Ed. by Michael O'Neill. 418p. 1998. pap. text 24.95 (*0-19-871121-2*) OUP.

Literature of the Second Self. Carl F. Keppler. LC 71-163012. 255p. reprint ed. pap. 79.10 (*0-608-15194-7*, 202738300055) Bks Demand.

***Literature of the Western World, 1.** 5th ed. Brian Wilkie & James Hurt. 2384p. 2000. pap. 49.33 (*0-13-018666-X*) P-H.

***Literature of the Western World,, 2.** 5th ed. Brian Wilkie & James Hurt. 2384p. 2000. pap. 49.33 (*0-13-018667-8*) P-H.

Literature of the Western World: Neoclassicism Through the Modern Period, Vol. 2. 4th ed. Brian Wilkie & James Hurt. LC 96-20978. Vol. 2. 2089p. (C). 1996. pap. text 56.00 (*0-13-227562-7*) P-H.

Literature of the Western World: The Ancient World Through the Renaissance, Vol. 1. 4th ed. Brian Wilkie & James Hurt. Vol. 1. (Illus.). 2232p. (C). 1996. pap. text 56.00 (*0-13-220872-5*) P-H.

***Literature of Their Own.** Elaine Showalter. 1999. pap. 18.95 (*0-691-00476-5*, Pub. by Princeton U Pr) Cal Prin Full Svc.

Literature of Tomorrow: An Anthology of Student Fiction, Poetry, & Drama. Donald M. Murray. (C). 1990. teacher ed. write for info. (*0-03-032919-1*) Harcourt Coll Pubs.

Literature of Travel in the Japanese Rediscovery of China, 1862-1945. Joshua A. Fogel. LC 95-448. 375p. 1996. 49.50 (*0-8047-2567-5*) Stanford U Pr.

Literature of Unlikeness. Charles Dahlberg. LC 87-22730. 221p. reprint ed. pap. 68.60 (*0-7837-6203-8*, 204592400009) Bks Demand.

Literature of Wales. Dafydd Johnston. LC 95-227729. (Pocket Guides Ser.). viii, 145p. 1996. reprint ed. pap. write for info. (*0-7083-1265-9*, Pub. by Univ Wales Pr) Paul & Co Pubs.

Literature of Witchcraft. Ed. by Brian P. Levack. LC 92-21029. (Articles on Witchcraft, Magic, & Demonology Ser.: Vol. 4). 352p. 1992. text 68.00 (*0-8153-1026-9*) Garland.

Literature of Work: Short Stories, Essays, & Poems by Men & Women of Business. Ed. by Sheila Murphy et al. LC 91-67284. 314p. 1991. 24.95 (*1-880708-00-0*) U Phoenix Pr.

Literature on the History of Physics in the 20th Century. Compiled by John L. Heilbron & Bruce R. Wheaton. LC 80-51580. (Berkeley Papers in History of Science: No. 5). 485p. (Orig.). 1981. pap. 20.00 (*0-918102-05-7*) U Cal Hist Sci Tech.

Literature on Wildlife Research in the Madrean Archipelago, 1800s-1994. Michael L. Morrison et al. 62p. 1997. reprint ed. 13.20 (*0-89904-614-2*, Wildlife Resrch Grp); reprint ed. pap. 7.20 (*0-89904-615-0*, Wildlife Resrch Grp) Crumb Elbow Pub.

Literature 1 Anthology. 1993. 10.00 (*0-88336-109-4*); teacher ed. 7.50 (*0-88336-110-8*); 31.99 (*0-88336-111-6*) New Readers.

Literature Online: Reading & Internet Activities for Libraries & Schools. Karen Moran. LC 99-21415. 94p. 1999. pap. 16.95 (*1-57950-032-3*, Alleyside) Highsmith Pr.

Literature or Life. Jorge Semprun. 320p. 1998. pap. 13.95 (*0-14-026624-0*) Viking Penguin.

Literature Packet for Persuasion. Center for Gifted Education Staff. 42p. (C). 1998. 65.95 (*0-7872-5342-1*) Kendall-Hunt.

Literature, Painting & Music: An Interdisciplinary Approach to Comparative Literature. P. Egri. (Studies in Modern Philology: Vol. 4). (Illus.). 234p. (C). 1988. pap. 48.00 (*963-05-4629-9*, Pub. by Akade Kiado) St Mut.

Literature Patterns. Linda Milliken. (Illus.). 128p. 1993. pap. 11.95 (*1-56472-007-1*) Edupress Inc.

Literature, Politics & Culture in Postwar Britain, 1997. Alan Sinfield. LC 97-26568. 384p. 1997. pap. 35.00 (*0-485-12132-8*, Pub. by Athlone Pr) Humanities.

Literature, Politics & Theory: Papers from the Essex Conference, 1976-1984. Ed. by Francis Barker et al. (New Accents Ser.). 288p. 1987. 39.95 (*0-416-90020-8*, 9920); pap. 14.95 (*0-416-90030-5*, 9945) Routledge.

Literature, Popular Culture & Society. Leo Lowenthal. LC 61-13532. (Paperbounds Ser.: No. PB-4). xxiv, 169p. 1968. reprint ed. pap. 12.95 (*0-87015-166-5*) Pacific Bks.

Literature, Predecessor of Times Literary Supplement, 9 Vols., Set. LC 74-3197. (Illus.). 1974. reprint ed. 500.00 (*0-685-00511-9*) Ayer.

***Literature, Psychoanalysis & the New Sciences of Mind.** Leonard Jackson. LC 99-43724. 256p. (C). 2000. 79.95 (*0-582-06653-0*) Addison-Wesley.

***Literature, Psychoanalysis & the New Sciences of Mind.** Leonard Jackson. LC 99-43724. 256p. 2000. pap. 28.00 (*0-582-06652-2*) Longman.

Literature Resources for Chemical Process Industries: A Collection of Papers Comprising Five Symposia & Thirteen General Papers Presented Before the Division of Chemical Literature at Several Recent National Meetings of the American Chemical Society. American Chemical Society Staff. LC 54-4626. (Advances in Chemistry Ser.: Vol. 10). (Illus.). 588p. 1954. reprint ed. pap. 182.30 (*0-608-06909-4*, 206711700009) Bks Demand.

Literature Review of Sexual Abuse. Diane DePanfilis. Ed. by Marsha K. Salus. 48p. 1986. write for info. (*0-318-61650-5*) US HHS.

Literature Searching in Science, Technology & Agriculture. rev. ed. Eileen R. Pritchard & Paula Scott. LC 95-39491. 216p. 1996. lib. bdg. 65.00 (*0-313-26212-8*, Greenwood Pr) Greenwood.

Literature, Social Consciousness & Polity. Iqbal Narain. Ed. by L. Lutze. (C). 1987. 17.00 (*81-85054-21-5*, Pub. by Manohar) S Asia.

Literature, Spirituality & the Theater. Peter Malekin. LC 96-44006. 200p. 1997. text 49.95 (*0-312-16015-1*) St Martin.

Literature Study Circles in a Multicultural Classroom. Gail Whang & Katharine D. Samway. LC 95-33304. (Illus.). 168p. (C). 1995. pap. text 18.50 (*1-57110-018-0*) Stenhse Pubs.

Literature Study in the High Schools. 3rd ed. Dwight L. Burton. LC 74-94346. viii, 357p. 1970. write for info. (*0-03-081119-8*) H Holt & Co.

Literature Study Partner. Terry Moss. LC 94-77900. (Final Exam Ser.). 68p. 1994. pap. 5.49 (*1-885962-57-6*) Lincoln Lrning.

Literature Supplement to the Abbey Newsletter: References & Publications Collected, 1992-1997. Ed. by Ellen McCrady. 39p. 1998. spiral bd. write for info. (*0-9622071-5-2*) Abbey Pubns.

Literature Suppressed on Political Grounds, 4 vols. Nicholas J. Karolides. LC 97-31648. (Banned Bks.). 567p. 1998. 35.00 (*0-8160-3304-8*) Facts on File.

Literature Suppressed on Religious Grounds, 4 vols. Margaret Bald. LC 97-43638. (Banned Bks.). 352p. 1998. 35.00 (*0-8160-3306-4*) Facts on File.

Literature Suppressed on Sexual Grounds, 4 vols. Dawn B. Sova. LC 97-40369. (Banned Bks.). 269p. 1998. 35.00 (*0-8160-3305-6*) Facts on File.

Literature Suppressed on Social Grounds, 4 vols. Dawn B. Sova. LC 97-45158. (Banned Bks.). 306p. 1998. 35.00 (*0-8160-3303-X*) Facts on File.

Literature Talk Play. Phyllis Roth. 10p. 1997. teacher ed., spiral bd. 15.00 (*1-892593-03-3*) R & R Creat.

Literature Teacher's Book of Lists. Judie L. Strouf. 416p. 1997. pap. 29.50 (*0-87628-554-X*) Ctr Appl Res.

Literature Teacher's Book of Lists. Judie L. H. Strouf. LC 92-40675. 416p. 1993. spiral bd. 29.50 (*0-87628-548-5*) Ctr Appl Res.

Literature Teaches about the U. S. A. Tanya Lieberman & Annalisa Suid. 48p. (Orig.). (J). (gr. 3-6). 1996. pap. 6.95 (*1-878279-92-0*, MM2021) Monday Morning Bks.

Literature, the Arts & Democracy: Spain in the '80s. Ed. by Samuel Amell. LC 88-46146. 144p. 1990. 32.50 (*0-8386-3373-0*) Fairleigh Dickinson.

Literature, the Arts, & the Holocaust, Vol. III. Ed. by Sanford Pinsker & Jack R. Fischel. (Holocaust Studies Annual). (Illus.). 288p. (C). 1987. lib. bdg. 30.00 (*0-913283-21-5*) Penkevill.

Literature the Leading Educator. Francis P. Donnelly. LC 79-107694. (Essay Index Reprint Ser.). 1977. 21.95 (*0-8369-1497-X*) Ayer.

Literature Through the Eyes of Faith: Christian College Coalition Series. Roger Lundin & Susan Gallagher. LC 88-45684. (Christian College Coalition Ser.). 192p. 1989. pap. 13.00 (*0-06-065318-3*, Pub. by Harper SF) HarpC.

***Literature, Travel, & Colonial Writing in the English Renaissance 1545-1625.** Andrew Hadfield. LC 98-34187. (Illus.). 320p. 1999. text 72.00 (*0-19-818480-8*) OUP.

Literature 2 Anthology. 1993. 10.00 (*0-88336-112-4*); teacher ed. 7.50 (*0-88336-113-2*); 31.99 (*0-88336-114-0*) New Readers.

Literature under Communism. Avrahm Yarmolinsky. LC 72-75515. (Select Bibliographies Reprint Ser.). 1977. 15.95 (*0-8369-5019-4*) Ayer.

Literature under the Microscope: A Christian Case for Reading. Louis Whitworth. 59p. 1984. pap. 2.99 (*0-614-25149-4*) Probe Bks.

Literature vs. Theatre: Textual Problems & Theatrical Realization in the Later Plays of Heiner Muller. David Barnett. LC 98-23149. (British & Irish Studies in German Language & Literature: No. 14). 289p. 1998. pap. text 37.95 (*0-8204-4203-8*) P Lang Pubng.

Literature Workbook. Clara Calvo & Jean J. Weber. LC 97-47183. 176p. (C). 1998. pap. 20.99 (*0-415-16987-9*) Routledge.

Literature y Arte: Intermediate Spanish. 6th ed. John G. Copeland et al. (SPA.). 304p. (C). 1996. pap. text 34.00 (*0-03-017513-5*) Holt R&W.

Literature, 1996, Pt. 2. Ed. by Astronomisches Rechen-Institut Staff. (Astronomy & Astrophysics Abstracts Ser.: Vol. 66). viii, 1904p. 1997. 338.00 (*3-540-63304-9*) Spr-Verlag.

***Literature, 1999, Pt. 1.** Ed. by Astronomisches Rechen-Institut Staff. (Astronomy & Astrophysics Abstracts Ser.: Vol. 71). x, 1967p. 2000. 375.00 (*3-540-67069-6*) Spr-Verlag.

Literatures in Transition: The Many Voices of the Caribbean Area. Desnoes et al. Ed. by Rose S. Minc. LC 82-84104. (ENG & SPA.). 180p. 1983. pap. 13.00 (*0-935318-10-0*) Edins Hispamerica.

Literatures of Asia, Africa & Latin America. Willis Barnstone & Tony Barnstone. LC 95-25423. 2016p. (C). 1998. pap. text 55.00 (*0-02-306065-4*, Macmillan Coll) P-H.

Literatures of India: An Introduction. Edward C. Dimock, Jr. et al. LC 73-87300. 1993. reprint ed. pap. text 6.95 (*0-226-15233-2*, P768) U Ch Pr.

Literatures of the American Indian see Indians of North America

***Literatures of the Diaspora: World Literatures.** 180p. 2000. pap. text 20.00 (*0-9652860-1-0*) Diaspora Pr of Am.

Literatures of the World. Freddy Thomas. 998p. (C). 1992. pap. text 72.00 (*0-536-58286-6*) Pearson Custom.

Literaturlenkung Im "Dritten Reich", Band I. Norbert Hopster & Petra Josting. (GER.). xviii, 500p. 1993. write for info. (*3-487-09686-2*) G Olms Pubs.

Literaturlenkung Im "Dritten Reich" Vol. 1: Eine Bibliographie. Norbert Hopster et al. (GER.). 518p. 1993. write for info. (*3-487-09878-4*) G Olms Pubs.

Literaturlenkung Im "Dritten Reich" Vol. 2: Eine Annotierende Bibliographie Von Bibliographien. Norbert Hopster et al. (GER.). 316p. 1994. write for info. (*0-614-22125-0*) G Olms Pubs.

Literaturnaja Mysl, 3 bde. in 1. (GER.). 905p. 1981. reprint ed. write for info. (*3-487-06975-X*) G Olms Pubs.

Literaturnoe Nasledie Kirilla Turovskogo. Kirill. Ed. by Igor P. Eremin. (Monuments of Early Russian Literature Ser.: Vol. 2). (RUS.). 117p. (Orig.). 1989. pap. 12.00 (*0-933884-76-1*) Berkeley Slavic.

Literaturnye Salony i Kruzki. (GER., Illus.). xxi, 592p. 1984. reprint ed. write for info. (*3-487-07403-6*) G Olms Pubs.

Literaturparodie in Ovids "Ars Amatoria" Marion Steudel. (Altertumswissenschaftliche Texte und Studien: Band 25). (GER.). viii, 228p. 1992. write for info. (*3-487-09671-4*) G Olms Pubs.

Literaturplagiat - Tatbestand und Rechtsfolgen. Florian Fischer. (GER.). XLI, 157p. 1996. 42.95 (*3-631-30289-4*) P Lang Pubng.

Literaturwissenschaft Zwischen Extremen. Armin P. Frank. (Studienbuch Ser.). (C). 1977. 36.95 (*3-11-007025-1*) De Gruyter.

Literaturwissenschaftliches Woerterbuch fur Romanisten. 3rd ed. Rainer Hess. (GER.). 490p. 1989. 55.00 (*0-7859-8508-5*, 3825213730) Fr & Eur.

Literaturwoerterbuch: Dictionary of Literature. W. Ruttkowski & R. Blake. (ENG, FRE & GER.). 68p. 1969. pap. 24.95 (*0-8288-6605-8*, M-7543) Fr & Eur.

Literatuur Als Systeem. E. Peters. 1998. 20.00 (*90-6831-818-7*, Pub. by Peeters Pub) Bks Intl VA.

***Literture of Africa.** N T C Contemporary Publishing Company Staff. 1998. 17.44 (*0-8442-1328-4*) NTC Contemp Pub Co.

***Lites & Camera.** (Rugrats Ser.). (J). (gr. k-3). 2000. per. 3.99 (*0-7434-0802-0*) PB.

Lithic Illustration: Drawing Flaked Stone Artifacts for Publication. Lucile R. Addington. LC 85-8121. (Prehistoric Archeology & Ecology Ser.). (Illus.). xviii, 140p. 1986. lib. bdg. 41.00 (*0-226-00634-4*) U Ch Pr.

Lithic Illustration: Drawing Flaked Stone Artifacts for Publication. Lucile R. Addington. LC 85-8121. (Prehistoric Archeology & Ecology Ser.). (Illus.). 253p. reprint ed. pap. 78.50 (*0-608-09372-6*, 205411700004) Bks Demand.

Lithic Landscapes & Settlement Patterns: A Cultural Resources Survey of Alamo Lake, La Paz County, Arizona. Bruce A. Jones et al. (Statistical Research Technical Ser.: No. 25). (Illus.). 150p. 1990. reprint ed. spiral bd. 13.75 (*1-879442-22-1*) Stats Res.

Lithic Procurement & Manufacturing Sequences at SBA-1542, Vandenberg Air Force Base, California. Teresa P. Rudolph. (Illus.). 111p. (C). 1984. reprint ed. pap. text 12.19 (*1-55567-447-X*) Coyote Press.

Lithic Procurement & Rock Varnish Dating: Investigations at CA-KER-140, a Small Quarry in the Western Mojave Desert. Karen G. Harry. (Statistical Research Technical Ser.: No. 36). (Illus.). 150p. 1992. spiral bd. 15.00 (*1-879442-34-5*) Stats Res.

Lithic Studies among the Contemporary Highland Maya. Ed. by Brian Hayden. LC 86-25093. (Illus.). 387p. 1987. 54.00 (*0-8165-0901-8*) U of Ariz Pr.

Lithics: Macroscopic Approaches to Analysis. William Andrefsky, Jr. LC 97-35227. (Cambridge Manuals in Archaeology). (Illus.). 286p. (C). 1998. text 69.95 (*0-521-57084-0*); pap. text 27.95 (*0-521-57815-9*) Cambridge U Pr.

Lithics after the Stone Age: A Handbook of Stone Tools from the Levant. Steven A. Rosen. LC 96-51250. (Illus.). 184p. 1997. 69.00 (*0-7619-9123-9*); pap. 27.95 (*0-7619-9124-7*) AltaMira Pr.

Lithics & Landscape: Archaeological Discoveries on the Thames Water Pipeline at Gatehampton Farm, Goring, Oxfordshire. T. G. Allen. (Thames Valley Ser.: Vol. 7). (Illus.). 140p. 1995. pap. 32.00 (*0-947816-85-2*, Pub. by Oxford Univ Comm Arch) David Brown.

Lithium. (Metals & Minerals Ser.). 1993. lib. bdg. 261.95 (*0-8490-9019-9*) Gordon Pr.

Lithium. 1927. 265.00 (*0-387-93267-4*) Spr-Verlag.

Lithium: Actions & Mechanisms. Rif S. El-Mallakh. (Progress in Psychiatry Ser.: No. 50). 208p. 1996. text 32.00 (*0-88048-481-0*, 8481) Am Psychiatric.

Lithium: Clinical & Biological Aspects. Ed. by F. A. Freyhan. (International Pharmacopsychiatry Ser.: Vol. 5, No. 2-4). (Illus.). 192p. 1972. pap. 51.50 (*3-8055-1277-5*) S Karger.

Lithium: Current Applications in Science, Medicine & Technology. Ed. by Ricardo Bach. LC 84-22210. 442p. 1985. text 100.00 (*0-471-80073-2*) Krieger.

Lithium: International Strategic Minerals Inventory Summary Report. (Illus.). 28p. (Orig.). (C). 1993. pap. text 20.00 (*1-56806-194-3*) DIANE Pub.

Lithium: What You Should Know see Drug Abuse Prevention Library: Getting Off Dangerous Ground

Lithium & Cell Physiology. Ed. by R. O. Bach & V. S. Gallicchio. (Illus.). 200p. 1990. 125.00 (*0-387-97128-9*) Spr-Verlag.

Lithium & Lithium Crystals. 1991. lib. bdg. 79.75 (*0-8490-4936-9*) Gordon Pr.

Lithium & Lithium Crystals. Haroldine. Ed. by Tom Brown. LC 88-71234. (Illus.). 130p. 1988. spiral bd. 14.95 (*0-945685-02-5*) Borderland Sciences.

Lithium & Manic Depression: A Guide. rev. ed. John T. Bohn & James W. Jefferson. 31p. 1999. pap. 4.95 (*1-890802-18-2*) Madison Inst of Med.

Lithium & the Blood. Ed. by V. S. Gallicchio. (Lithium Therapy Monographs: Vol. 4). (Illus.). x, 150p. 1991. 137.50 (*3-8055-5279-3*) S Karger.

Lithium & the Cell: Pharmacology & Biochemistry. Ed. by Nicholas J. Birch. (Illus.). 351p. 1991. text 104.00 (*0-12-099300-7*) Acad Pr.

Lithium & the Endocrine System. Ed. by F. N. Johnson. (Lithium Therapy Monographs: Vol. 2). (Illus.). xiv, 226p. 1987. 172.25 (*3-8055-4606-8*) S Karger.

Lithium & the Kidney. Ed. by S. Christensen. (Lithium Therapy Monographs: Vol. 3). (Illus.). xii, 188p. 1990. 164.50 (*3-8055-5042-1*) S Karger.

***Lithium Batteries.** Ed. by S. Surampudi & R. Marsh. 576p. 1999. 102.00 (*1-56677-210-9*, PV 98-16) Electrochem Soc.

Lithium Batteries: New Materials, Development & Perspectives. Ed. by G. Pistoia. LC 93-42028. (Industrial Chemistry Library: Vol. 5). 494p. 1993. 295.25 (*0-444-89957-X*) Elsevier.

Lithium Batteries: Proceedings of the Symposium. Symposium on Lithium Batteries Staff. Ed. by H. V. Venkatasetty. LC 81-66184. (Electrochemical Society Proceedings Ser.: No. 81-4). 514p. reprint ed. pap. 159.40 (*0-608-17747-4*, 205224500070) Bks Demand.

Lithium Batteries: Proceedings of the Symposium, San Diego, CA, 1986. Ed. by A. N. Dey. LC 87-80472. (Electrochemical Society Proceedings Ser.: No. 87-1). 568p. reprint ed. pap. 176.10 (*0-7837-1454-8*, 205243000022) Bks Demand.

Lithium Batteries: Proceedings of the Symposium, Washington, DC, 1983. Symposium on Lithium Batteries Staff. Ed. by A. N. Dey. LC 84-80273. (Electrochemical Society, Proceedings Ser.: Vol. 84-1). 458p. 1984. reprint ed. pap. 142.00 (*0-608-04662-0*, 205257900002) Bks Demand.

Lithium Batteries, UL 1642. 3rd ed. (C). 1995. pap. text 330.00 (*1-55989-829-1*) Underwrtrs Labs.

Lithium Chemsitry: A Theoretical & Experimental Overview. Ed. by Anne-Marie Sapse & Paul V. Schleyer. LC 94-20176. 595p. 1995. 120.00 (*0-471-54930-4*) Wiley.

Lithium Combination Treatment. Ed. by F. N. Johnson. (Lithium Therapy Monographs: Vol. 1). (Illus.). xiv, 274p. 1987. 172.25 (*3-8055-4475-8*) S Karger.

Lithium Encyclopedia for Clinical Practice. 2nd ed. James W. Jefferson et al. LC 86-28685. 762p. 1987. reprint ed. pap. 200.00 (*0-608-06669-9*, 206686600009) Bks Demand.

Lithium in Biology & Medicine. Ed. by G. N. Schrauzer & K. F. Klippel. 209p. 1991. 75.00 (*3-527-28203-3*, Wiley-VCH) Wiley.

Lithium in Biology & Medicine: With Subject Analysis & Reference Bibliography. Roy R. Zimmerman. LC 85-48084. 150p. 1987. 47.50 (*0-88164-440-4*); pap. 44.50 (*0-88164-441-2*) ABBE Pubs Assn.

Lithium-Ion Batteries. Masataka Wakihara & Osamu Yamamoto. LC 98-221222. 258p. 1998. 195.00 (*3-527-29569-0*) Wiley.

Lithium Murder: A Gloria Lamerino Mystery. Camille Minichino. LC 98-47505. 240p. 1999. 24.00 (*0-688-16784-5*, Wm Morrow) Morrow Avon.

Lithium Niobate Crystals. Yu S. Kuz'minov. 180p. 1995. pap. 70.00 (*1-898326-30-4*, Pub. by CISP) Balogh.

Lithium Nonaqueous Battery Electrochemistry: Proceedings of the Workshop June 4-6, 1980, Case Western Reserve University, Cleveland, Ohio. Workshop on Lithium Nonaqueous Battery Electrochem. Ed. by Ernest B. Yeager et al. LC 80-70420. (Electrochemical Society Proceedings Ser.: Vol. 80-7). (Illus.). 328p. 1980. pap. 101.70 (*0-7837-9000-7*, 205926500002) Bks Demand.

Lithium Polymer Batteries. Ed. by J. Broadhead & B. Scrosati. LC 97-137472. (Proceedings Ser.: Vol. 96-17). (Illus.). 304p. 1997. 59.00 (*1-56677-167-6*) Electrochem Soc.

Lithium Treatment of Manic-Depressive Illness: A Practical Guide. 5th rev. ed. M. Schou. (Illus.). viii, 56p. 1993. pap. 15.75 (*3-8055-5667-5*) S Karger.

Lithogenetic Stratigraphy of the Triassic Dockum Formation, Palo Duro Basin, Texas. D. A. Johns. (Reports of Investigations: RI 182). (Illus.). 71p. 1989. pap. 4.00 (*0-317-03116-3*) Bur Econ Geology.

***Lithographed Paper Toys Books & Games: Eighteen Eighty to Nineteen fifteen.** Judith Anderson Drawe & Kathleen Bridge Greenstein. (Illus.). 192p. 2000. 49.95 (*0-7643-1124-7*) Schiffer.

Lithographers Manual. 9th rev. ed. Ed. by Thomas M. Destree. LC 93-78999. (Illus.). 426p. (C). 1994. text 75.00 (*0-88362-169-X*, 1407) GATFPress.

Lithographic Offset Press Operating. rev. ed. Charles W. Latham. LC 57-22887. 273p. reprint ed. pap. 84.70 (*0-7837-0365-1*, 204068700018) Bks Demand.

Lithographic Press Operator's Handbook. Pamela Groff et al. LC 87-82358. (Illus.). 80p. (Orig.). (C). 1988. pap. text 40.00 (*0-88362-104-5*, 1524) GATFPress.

Lithographic Pressman. Jack Rudman. (Career Examination Ser.: C-445). 1994. pap. 27.95 (*0-8373-0445-8*) Nat Learn.

Lithographic Presswork. A. S. Porter. LC Z 0252.. 316p. reprint ed. pap. 98.00 (*0-7837-0363-5*, 204068500018) Bks Demand.

Lithographic Technology. Dennis. 96p. 1996. teacher ed. 12.00 (*0-8273-8132-8*) Delmar.

Lithographic Technology. Ervin A. Dennis. LC 96-210. (Graphic Communications Ser.). 640p. (C). 1996. mass mkt. 68.95 (*0-8273-6124-6*) Delmar.

Lithographic Technology. Ervin A. Dennis. LC 79-16756. 1980. write for info. (*0-672-97164-X*); teacher ed. write for info. (*0-672-97165-8*); student ed. write for info. (*0-672-97166-6*) Macmillan.

Lithographic Technology. Dennise. 1986. pap. 9.32 (*0-02-681700-4*) Macmillan.

Lithographs & Etchings of Philip Pearlstein. Richard S. Field. LC 78-52835. (Illus.). (Orig.). 1978. pap. text 12.95 (*0-934306-01-X*) Springfield.

Lithographs of Charles Banks Wilson. David C. Hunt. LC 88-40211. (Illus.). 280p. 1989. 75.00 (*0-8061-2151-3*) U of Okla Pr.

Lithographs of James McNeill Whistler Vols. 1 & 2: A Catalogue Raisonne; Correspondence & Technical Studies, Nesta Spink et al. LC 97-15806. (Illus.). 992p. 1998. boxed set 395.00 (*0-86559-150-4*) Art Inst Chi.

Lithographs of Prentiss Taylor: A Catalogue Raisonne. Ed. by Ingrid Rose & Roderick S. Quiroz. (Illus.). xii, 133p. 1996. 49.95 (*0-8232-1672-1*) Fordham.

Lithographs of Robert Riggs with a Catalogue Raisonne. Ben L. Bassham. (Illus.). 104p. 1987. 40.00 (*0-87982-514-6*) Art Alliance.

Lithographs of Stow Wengenroth, 1931-1972. Ronald Stuckey & Joan Stuckey. (Illus.). 1974. 75.00 (*0-89073-035-0*, 124) Boston Public Lib.

***Lithographs of Thomas Hart Benton.** Creekmore Fath. (Illus.). 246p. 2000. 95.00 (*1-55660-306-1*) A Wofsy Fine Arts.

Lithography at the Wavelength of Light: Co-Sponsored with SPIE. 1998. pap. write for info. (*1-892568-06-3*) Smicndctr Equip.

***Lithography Challenges & Opportunities.** 1999. 185.00 (*1-892568-34-9*) Smicndctr Equip.

***Lithography for Semiconductor Manufacturing.** Ed. by Chris A. Mack & Tom Stevenson. (Europto Ser.: Vol. 3741). 270p. 1999. pap. text 72.00 (*0-8194-3221-0*) SPIE.

Lithography in Microelectronics. Ed. by T. M. Makhviladze. (Proceedings of the Institute of General Physics of the Academy of Sciences of the U. S. S. R. Ser.: Vol. 8). 207p. 1989. text 165.00 (*0-941743-30-6*) Nova Sci Pubs.

Lithography Primer. 2nd ed. Daniel G. Wilson. LC 97-74134. (Illus.). 180p. (C). 1997. pap. text 25.00 (*0-88362-206-8*, 13322) GATFPress.

Lithography Process Control. Harry J. Levinson. LC 98-44433. (Tutorial Texts in Optical Engineering Ser.). 190p. 1999. pap. text 42.00 (*0-8194-3052-8*) SPIE.

Lithology, Microstructures, Fluid Inclusions, & Geochemistry of Rock Salt & of the Cap-Rock Contact in Oakwood Dome, East Texas: Significance for Nuclear Waste Storage. O. R. Dix & M. P. Jackson. (Reports of Investigations: RI 120). (Illus.). 59p. 1982. pap. 3.00 (*0-318-03261-9*) Bur Econ Geology.

Lithops. Desmond T. Cole et al. LC 68-22957. (Illus.). 114p. 1975. 85.00 (*0-8386-6902-6*) Fairleigh Dickinson.

Lithostratigraphy & Hydrostratigraphy of the Floridan Aquifer System in Florida, No. T185. Ed. by Scott. (IGC Field Trip Guidebooks Ser.). 88p. 1989. 21.00 (*0-87590-635-4*) Am Geophysical.

Lithostratigraphy & Paleoenvironments of Upper Paleozoic Continental Red Beds, North-Central Texas: Bowie (New) & Wichita (Revised) Groups. T. F. Hentz. (Reports of Investigations: RI 170). (Illus.). 55p. 1988. pap. 3.00 (*0-317-03109-0*) Bur Econ Geology.

Lithuania see Cultures of the World - Group 14

***Lithuania.** Economic Commission for Europe, Committee on Environmental Policy. (Environmental Performance Reviews Ser.). 190p. 1999. pap. 35.00 (*92-1-116709-4*) UN.

Lithuania. Ed. by Lerner Geography Department Staff. LC 92-9698. (Then & Now Ser.). (Illus.). 64p. (YA). (gr. 6-9). 1992. lib. bdg. 23.93 (*0-8225-2804-5*, Lerner Publctns) Lerner Pub.

Lithuania. unabridged ed. Rupert Brooke. Ed. by William-Alan Landes. LC 97-29922. 55p. (Orig.). 1997. pap. 6.00 (*0-88734-341-4*) Players Pr.

***Lithuania: A Country Study Guide.** Global Investment & Business Center, Inc. Staff. (World Country Study Guides Library: Vol. 100). (Illus.). 350p. 2000. pap. 59.00 (*0-7397-2398-7*) Intl Business Pubns.

Lithuania: An Opportunity for Economic Success. LC 98-23755. (Country Study Ser.). 51p. 1998. pap. 22.00 (*0-8213-4244-4*, 14244) World Bank.

Lithuania: IMF Economic Review. International Monetary Fund Staff. v, 73p. 1992. pap. 10.00 (*1-55775-254-0*) Intl Monetary.

Lithuania: New & Selected Poems. Myra Sklarew. 192p. (C). 1995. pap. 12.95 (*1-885214-02-2*) Azul Edits.

Lithuania: The Bradt Travel Guide. 2nd ed. Gordon McLachlan. LC 99-14550. (Bradt Country Guides Ser.). (Illus.). 256p. 1999. pap. 17.95 (*1-898323-91-7*, Pub. by Bradt Pubns) Globe Pequot.

Lithuania: The Rebirth of a Nation, 1991-1994. Alexandra Ashbourne. LC 99-20819. 256p. 1999. 60.00 (*0-7391-0027-0*) Lxngtn Bks.

Lithuania: Transition to a Market Economy. LC 93-16713. (Country Study Ser.). 428p. 1993. pap. 26.00 (*0-8213-2350-4*, 12350) World Bank.

Lithuania Vol. II: An Opportunity for Economic Success/Analytic Background. LC 98-23755. (Country Study Ser.). 367p. 1998. pap. 35.00 (*0-8213-4327-0*, 14327) World Bank.

Lithuania - A Country Study Guide: Basic Information for Research & Pleasure. Global Investment Center, USA Staff. (World Country Study Guide Library: Vol. 100). (Illus.). 350p. 1999. pap. 59.00 (*0-7397-1497-X*) Intl Business Pubns.

***Lithuania - Independent Again: The Autobiography of Vytautas Landsbergis.** (Illus.). 320p. 1999. 65.00 (*0-7083-1454-6*, Pub. by Intl Bks) Paul & Co Pubs.

Lithuania & the United States: The Establishment of State Relations. Constantine R. Jurgela. LC 85-82066. (Illus.). 264p. 1985. 20.00 (*0-918920-04-3*) Lith Res & Studies.

Lithuania Ascending: A Pagan Empire Within East-Central Europe, 1295-1345. S. C. Rowell. (Cambridge Studies in Medieval Life & Thought: No. 25). (Illus.). 415p. (C). 1994. text 74.95 (*0-521-45011-X*) Cambridge U Pr.

Lithuania Awakening. Alfred E. Senn. LC 90-32503. (Societies & Culture in East-Central Europe Ser.: No. 4). (Illus.). 238p. 1990. 40.00 (*0-520-07170-0*, Pub. by U CA Pr) Cal Prin Full Svc.

Lithuania Business & Investment Opportunities Yearbook-98: Business, Investment, Export-Import. Contrib. by Russian Information & Business Center, Inc. Staff. (Business & Investment Opportunity Library-98). (Illus.). 350p. 1998. pap. 99.00 (*1-57751-936-1*) Intl Business Pubns.

***Lithuania Business Intelligence Report, 190 vols.** Global Investment & Business Center, Inc. Staff. (World Business Intelligence Library: Vol. 100). (Illus.). 350p. 2000. pap. 99.95 (*0-7397-2598-X*) Intl Business Pubns.

***Lithuania Business Law Handbook, 190 vols.** Global Investment & Business Center, Inc. Staff. (Global Business Law Handbooks Library: Vol. 100). (Illus.). 350p. 2000. pap. 99.95 (*0-7397-1997-1*) Intl Business Pubns.

Lithuania Business Law Handbook-98. Russian Information & Business Center, Inc. Staff. (World Business Law Library-98). (Illus.). 350p. 1998. pap. 99.00 (*1-57751-806-3*) Intl Business Pubns.

***Lithuania Business Opportunity Yearbook.** Global Investment & Business Center, Inc. Staff. (Global Business Opportunity Yearbooks Library: Vol. 100). (Illus.). 2000. pap. 99.95 (*0-7397-2198-4*) Intl Business Pubns.

***Lithuania Business Opportunity Yearbook: Export-Import, Investment & Business Opportunities.** International Business Publications, U. S. A. Staff & Global Investment Center, U. S. A. Staff. (Global Business Opportunity Yearbooks Library: Vol. 100). (Illus.). 350p. 1999. pap. 99.95 (*0-7397-1298-5*) Intl Business Pubns.

***Lithuania Country Review 2000.** Robert C. Kelly et al. (Illus.). 60p. 1999. pap. 39.95 (*1-58310-524-7*) CountryWatch.

***Lithuania Export-Import & Business Directory: Ultimate Directory for Conducting Export-Import Operations in the Country. Largest Exporters & Importers, Strategic Government & Business Contacts, Selected Export-Import Regulations & More.** International Business Publications, USA Staff & Global Investment Center, USA Staff. (World Export-Import & Business Library: 20). (Illus.). 250p. 2000. pap. 99.95 (*0-7397-3396-6*) Intl Business Pubns.

***Lithuania Foreign Policy & Government Guide.** Global Investment & Business Center, Inc. Staff. (World Foreign Policy & Government Library: Vol. 96). (Illus.). 350p. 1999. pap. 99.00 (*0-7397-3594-2*) Intl Business Pubns.

***Lithuania Foreign Policy & Government Guide.** Global Investment & Business Center, Inc. Staff. (World Foreign Policy & Government Library: Vol. 96). (Illus.). 350p. 2000. pap. 99.95 (*0-7397-3798-8*) Intl Business Pubns.

***Lithuania, Free at Last: The Autobiography of Vytautas Landsbergis.** Vytautas Landsbergis. Tr. by Anthony Packer & Eimutis Sova. (Illus.). 352p. 2000. 35.00 (*0-295-97959-3*) U of Wash Pr.

***Lithuania Government & Business Contacts Handbook: Strategic Government & Business Contacts for Conducting Succesful Business, Export-Import & Investment Activity, 110.** International Business Publications, USA Staff & Global Investment Center, USA Staff. (World Export-Import & Business Library: 51). (Illus.). 250p. 2000. pap. 99.95 (*0-7397-6090-4*) Intl Business Pubns.

***Lithuania Government & Business Contacts Handbook: Strategic Government & Business Contacts for Conducting Successful Business, Export-Import & Investment Activity.** Contrib. by International Business Publications, USA Staff & Global Investment Center, USA Staff. (World Export-Import & Business Library: Vol. 18). (Illus.). 350p. 2000. pap. 99.95 (*0-7397-6056-4*) Intl Business Pubns.

***Lithuania in European Politics: The Years of The First Republic, 1918-1940.** Alfonsas Eidintas. 1999. pap. 18.95 (*0-312-22458-3*) St Martin.

Lithuania in Twentieth-Century Europe: The Nation & State, 1918-1940. A. Eidintas et al. LC 97-3589. 249p. 1998. text 49.95 (*0-312-17232-X*) St Martin.

***Lithuania Industrial & Business Directory.** Global Investment & Business Center, Inc. Staff. (NIS Industrial & Business Directories Ser.: Vol. 10). (Illus.). 350p. 1999. pap. 99.00 (*0-7397-0709-4*) Intl Business Pubns.

***Lithuania Investment & Business Guide.** Global Investment & Business Center, Inc. Staff. (Global Investment & Business Guide Library: Vol. 100). (Illus.). 2000. pap. 99.95 (*0-7397-1798-7*) Intl Business Pubns.

Lithuania Investment & Business Guide: Economy, Export-Import, Business & Investment Climate, Business Contacts. Contrib. by Russian Information & Business Center, Inc. Staff. (Russia, NIS & Emerging Markets Investment & Business Library-98). (Illus.). 350p. 1998. pap. 99.00 (*1-57751-856-X*) Intl Business Pubns.

***Lithuania Investment & Business Guide: Export-Import, Investment & Business Opportunities.** International Business Publications, USA Staff & Global Investment Center, USA Staff. (World Investment & Business Guide Library-99: Vol. 100). (Illus.). 350p. 1999. pap. 99.95 (*0-7397-0295-5*) Intl Business Pubns.

***Lithuania 2000: Images of Lithuania - Remembering the Past - Looking to the Future.** Algimantas Kezys. LC 99-73281. (Illus.). 150p. 1999. pap. 20.00 (*1-886060-17-7*) Galerija.

Lithuanian - English Dictionary. V. Baravykas. (ENG & LIT.). 39.95 (*0-8288-2486-X*) Fr & Eur.

Lithuanian - English Dictionary. Vilius Peteraitis. 1991. 49.95 (*0-8288-2626-9*, F58440) Fr & Eur.

Lithuanian - English Phrase-Book. B. Svecevicius. 1991. lib. bdg. 19.95 (*0-8288-2633-1*) Fr & Eur.

Lithuanian American Physicians (1884-1984) see Amerikos Lietuviai Gydytojai: Lithuanian American Physicians (1884-1984)

Lithuanian Artists in North America: Exhibitors in DAILE '91, '92 & '93. Algimantas Kezys. LC 93-70282. (Faces of Two Worlds Ser.: Vol. 2). (Illus.). 200p. 1993. pap. 20.00 (*0-9617756-7-X*) Galerija.

Lithuanian Celebrations: Lietuviu Sventes a Collection of Photographs. Lithuanian Photographers Staff. Ed. by Algimantas Kezys. LC 90-84748. (Illus.). 1991. pap. 20.00 (*0-9617756-4-5*) Galerija.

***Lithuanian Children of the Nineties.** Ed. by Algimantas Kezys. LC 99-76120. (LIT., Illus.). 160p. 1999. pap. 20.00 (*1-886060-22-3*) Galerija.

Lithuanian Cookbook. Maria G. De Gorgey. LC 98-8285. 176p. 1998. 24.95 (*0-7818-0610-0*) Hippocrene Bks.

Lithuanian Diaspora: Konigsberg to Chicago. Antanas J. Van Reenan. (Illus.). 356p. (C). 1990. lib. bdg. 53.00 (*0-8191-7867-5*) U Pr of Amer.

Lithuanian Dictionary: English-Lithuanian, Lithuanian-English. Bronius Piesarskas & Bronius Svecevicius. LC 95-18213. (ENG & LIT.). 848p. (C). (gr. 13). 1995. pap. 32.99 (*0-415-12857-9*) Routledge.

Lithuanian-English - English-Lithuanian Concise Dictionary. Victoria Martsinkyavitshute. (Concise Dictionaries Ser.). (ENG & LIT.). 382p. (Orig.). 1993. pap. 14.95 (*0-7818-0151-6*) Hippocrene Bks.

Lithuanian-English Dictionary. Vilius Peteraitis. (ENG & LIT.). 42.50 (*0-87559-037-3*) Shalom.

Lithuanian-English Dictionary. B. Piesarskas. (ENG & LIT.). 511p. 1991. 39.95 (*0-8288-4015-6*, F109070) Fr & Eur.

Lithuanian-English Phrase-Book. B. Svecevicius. (ENG & LIT.). 19.95 (*0-8288-8002-6*, 087052111X) Fr & Eur.

Lithuanian Ethnographic Crafts. Lithuanian Photographers Staff. Ed. by Algimantas Kezys. LC 98-72196. (LIT., Illus.). 180p. 1998. pap. 15.00 (*1-886060-12-6*) Galerija.

Lithuanian Families of Luzerne Co., PA. Joseph A. King. (Illus.). 96p. 1986. pap. text 20.00 (*0-9608500-1-5*) K & K Pubns.

Lithuanian Hasidism. Rabinowicz. 1970. 27.50 (*0-85303-021-9*, Pub. by M Vallentine & Co) Intl Spec Bk.

Lithuanian Institute of Education, 1958-1983. Ed. by Robert A. Vitas. LC 82-83234. Orig. Title: Pedagoginis Lithuanistikos Institutas: 1958-1983. (Illus.). 128p. (Orig.). 1983. pap. 5.00 (*0-936694-49-1*) Lith Inst Educ.

Lithuanian Jewish Communities. Nancy Schoenburg & Stuart Schoenburg. LC 96-24430. (Illus.). 520p. 1997. reprint ed. pap. 45.00 (*1-56821-993-8*) Aronson.

Lithuanian "Living Sober" Alcoholics Anonymous World Services, Inc., Staff. 1993. 8.40 (*0-916856-60-7*) AAWS.

Lithuanian Medley. (LIT.). 60p. pap. 24.95 incl. audio (*1-57970-007-1*, SLT100) Audio-Forum.

***Lithuanian New Testament.** 1999. pap. text 3.95 (*5-550-00762-2*) Nairi.

***Lithuanian Photography '98: A Juxtaposition of Traditional & Computer-Generated Works.** Lithuanian Photographers Staff. Ed. by Algimantas Kezys. LC 99-71655. (ENG & LIT., Illus.). 250p. 1999. pap. 20.00 (*1-886060-15-0*) Galerija.

Lithuanian Physicians Across Six Continents see Lietuviai Gydytojai Sesiuose Kontinentuose

***Lithuanian Publishers Directory.** Lee Burchinal & Dale Lukas. LC 99-13922. 207p. 1999. pap. 49.50 (*1-57387-076-5*) Info Today Inc.

Lithuanian Scouting. 2nd rev. ed. Petra Molis et al. Ed. by Robertas Vitas. (Illus.). 40p. 1983. reprint ed. pap. write for info. (*0-9611488-0-2*) Lith Scouts.

Lithuanian Social Democracy in Perspective, 1893-1914. Leonas Sabaliunas. LC 89-27306. (Duke Press Policy Studies). 210p. (C). 1990. text 38.95 (*0-8223-1015-5*) Duke.

Lithuanian Wedding Celebration Songs: From the Memory of Bronius Krokys. Ed. by Joseph Kasinskas. (Illus.). 47p. 1997. reprint ed. pap. text 30.00 (*0-7881-3770-0*) DIANE Pub.

Lithuanians in the U. S. A. Aspects of Ethnic Identity. David Fainhauz. (Illus.). 246p. 1991. pap. 15.00 (*0-932042-29-5*) Lithuanian Lib.

Lithuania's Accession to the European Union: Successes & Challenges for a Rural Economy in Transition. Ed. by William H. Meyers et al. LC 98-44966. (Illus.). 238p. 1999. text 49.95 (*0-8138-1973-3*) Iowa St U Pr.

Litigating Ada Claims: Forms, Pleadings, & Practical Guidance. Thomas D'Agostino. LC 96-39407. 1996. write for info. (*1-57834-001-2*) LRP Pubns.

Litigating Against the Government: Leveling the Playing Field Robert H. Bork. LC 99-165558. 22p. 1996. pap. write for info. (*0-937299-51-0*) Natl Legal Ctr Pub Interest.

Litigating Against the U. S. Government. Ed. by Law & Business Inc. Staff & Legal Times Seminars Staff. (Seminar Course Handbks.). 1983. pap. 30.00 (*0-686-89357-3*, C00906) Harcourt.

Litigating Against the United States Government (1992) 65p. 1992. pap. text 15.00 (*1-56986-010-6*) Federal Bar.

Litigating Age Discrimination Cases. Andrew J. Ruzicho & Louis A. Jacobs. LC 86-11736. 1992. 140.00 (*0-685-14016-4*) West Group.

Litigating Age Discrimination Cases. annuals Andrew J. Ruzicho & Louis A. Jacobs. 1992. suppl. ed. write for info. (*0-318-60923-1*) West Group.

Litigating Breast Implant Cases: A Satellite Program. (Litigation & Administrative Practice Course Handbook, 1983-84 Ser.: Vol. 451). 470p. 1992. 70.00 (*0-685-65529-6*, H4-5149) PLI.

Litigating Breast Implant Cases: A Satellite Program. (Litigation & Administrative Practice Course Handbook, 1983-84 Ser.: Vol. 451). 470p. 1993. 70.00 (*0-685-65534-2*, H4-5149) PLI.

Litigating Child Restraint Cases. Joseph W. Moch & Arthur Borja. (Illus.). 576p. 1993. 45.00 (*0-88450-094-2*, 0942-N) Lawyers & Judges.

Litigating Copyright, Trademark & Unfair Competition Cases. (Patents, Copyrights, Trademarks, & Literary Property Ser.). 603p. 1991. pap. text 70.00 (*0-685-56906-3*, G4-3875) PLI.

Litigating Copyright, Trademark & Unfair Competition Cases, 1988. (Patents, Copyrights, Trademarks, & Literary Property Ser.). 528p. 1988. 17.50 (*0-685-44529-1*, G4-3824) PLI.

Litigating Copyright, Trademark & Unfair Competition Cases, 1994. (Patents, Copyrights, Trademarks, & Literary Property Ser.). 872p. 1994. pap. 99.00 (*0-685-65514-8*, G4-3925) PLI.

Litigating Copyright, Trademark & Unfair Competition Cases, 1995. (Patents, Copyrights, Trademarks, & Literary Property Course Handbook, 1994-95 Ser.). Date not set. pap. 99.00 (*0-614-17241-1*, G4-3954) PLI.

Litigating Employment Discrimination Cases: How to Win. (Litigation & Administrative Practice Course Handbook, 1983-84 Ser.). 616p. 1994. pap. 99.00 (*0-614-17260-8*, H4-5212) PLI.

Litigating Federalism: The States Before the U. S. Supreme Court, 88. Eric N. Waltenburg & Bill Swinford. LC 98-15331. (Contributions in Legal Studies: Vol. 88). 176p. 1999. 55.00 (*0-313-30607-9*, Greenwood Pr) Greenwood.

Litigating for & Against the FDIC & the RTC, 1992. (Commercial Law & Practice Course Handbook Ser.). 760p. 1992. pap. 70.00 (*0-685-69460-7*) PLI.

Litigating for & Against the FDIC & the RTC, 1993. (Commercial Law & Practice Course Handbook Ser.: Vol. 666). 878p. 1993. 70.00 (*0-685-69715-0*, A4-4429) PLI.

***Litigating in Federal Court: A Guide to the Rules.** Ann E. Woodley. LC 99-65881. 158p. 1999. pap. text 17.95 (*0-89089-970-3*) Carolina Acad Pr.

Litigating in Spain: Considerations for Foreign Practitioners; Including International Judicial Assistance, Enforcement of Foreign Judgments, Bankruptcy, Arbitration & Other Civil Proceedings. Bernardo M. Cremades & E. G. Cabiedes. 580p. 1989. 108.00 (*90-6544-377-0*) Kluwer Law Intl.

Litigating Intelligence: IQ Tests, Special Education, & Social Science in the Courtroom. Rogers Elliott. LC 86-32068. 240p. (C). 1987. 52.95 (*0-86569-156-8*, Auburn Hse) Greenwood.

Litigating International Commercial Disputes. Lawrence W. Newman & David Zaslowsky. LC 96-18073. 410p. (C). 1996. pap. text 50.00 (*0-314-09367-2*) West Pub.

Litigating Libel & Privacy Suits. (Patents, Copyrights, Trademarks, & Literary Property Course Handbook, 1994-95 Ser.). Date not set. pap. 99.00 (*0-614-17246-2*, G4-3963) PLI.

Litigating Morality: American Legal Thought & Its English Roots. Alice F. Bartee & Wayne C. Bartee. LC 91-27816. 168p. 1992. 55.00 (*0-275-94127-2*, C4127, Praeger Pubs) Greenwood.

Litigating National Security Issues. 48p. 1983. pap. 3.00 (*0-685-11007-9*, 355-0002) Amer Bar Assn.

Litigating Neck & Back Injuries. 2nd ed. John A. Tarantino. 436p. 1995. ring bd. 119.00 incl. disk (*0-938065-26-2*) James Pub Santa Ana.

Litigating Private Antitrust Actions. Philip C. Jones. (Federal Publications). 626p. 1984. text 105.00 (*0-07-032789-0*) Shepards.

Litigating Sexual Harassment & Sex Discrimination Cases. Dolores Y. Leal & Elizabeth Hubbard. 500p. 1997. ring bd. 99.00 (*0-938065-99-8*) James Pub Santa Ana.

Litigating the Aviation Case: From Pretrial to Closing Argument. LC 87-70657. viii, 240p. 1987. 69.95 (*0-89707-296-0*, 519-0068) Amer Bar Assn.

Litigating the Aviation Case from Pre-Trial to Closing Argument. 2nd ed. Desmond T. Barry. LC 98-27113. xii, 349p. 1998. 84.95 (*1-57073-595-6*) Amer Bar Assn.

Litigating the Commercial Case. Ed. by Harvey W. Berman & Larry J. Saylor. LC 91-78182. 460p. 1992. 115.00 (*0-685-65663-2*, 92-020) U MI Law CLE.

Litigating the Complex Motor Vehicle Case, 1992: Accident Reconstruction, Biomedical Analysis, & the Seat Belt Defense. (Litigation & Administrative Practice Course Handbook, 1983-84 Ser.: Vol. 450). 507p. 1992. 70.00 (*0-685-65527-X*, H4-5145) PLI.

Litigating the Coverage Claim: Denial of Coverage & Duty to Defend. LC 92-71264. 488p. 1992. pap. 69.95 (*0-89707-779-2*, 519-0212, ABA Tort) Amer Bar Assn.

Litigating the Coverage Claim II: Pretrial Procedures & Strategies for Insurers, Insureds, & Their Counsel. LC 93-70307. 310p. 1993. pap. 79.95 (*0-89707-820-9*, 519-0220, ABA Tort) Amer Bar Assn.

Litigating the Employment Tort Case: A Guide for Plaintiff & Defense Attorneys. LC 95-76128. 168p. 1995. pap. 54.95 (*1-57073-159-4*, 519-0247, ABA Tort) Amer Bar Assn.

Litigating the Legal Malpractice Case. 1997. 99.00 incl. audio PA Bar Inst.

Litigating the Sexual Harassment Case: A Guide for Plaintiff & Defense Attorneys. LC 94-72687. 1994. pap. 69.95 (*1-57073-036-9*, 519-00242, ABA Tort) Amer Bar Assn.

Litigating the Value of Contaminated Property - A Mock Trial. 215p. 1994. pap. 30.00 (*0-614-26710-2*, 1035); pap. 175.00 incl. VHS (*0-614-26711-0*, 30351) NYS Bar.

Litigating Under Nineteen Hundred & Eighty-Three. 1996. 99.00 incl. audio PA Bar Inst.

Litigating Wrongful Discharge Claims, 2 vols., Set. Paul H. Tobias. LC 87-13832. 1992. 350.00 (*0-685-18646-6*) West Group.

Litigation. 260p. (C). 1990. pap. 100.00 (*1-85352-811-0*, Pub. by HLT Pubns) St Mut.

Litigation, 3 vols., Set. 2nd ed. James W. Jeans, Sr. 1992. 225.00 (*0-87473-952-7*, MICHIE) LEXIS Pub.

Litigation: Ten-Year Index. LC 75-652545. 48p. 1985. pap. 7.95 (*0-89707-176-X*, 531-0048-01) Amer Bar Assn.

Litigation & Administrative Practice Series, 1992-1993, 28 vols., Set. 1993. pap. 825.00 (*0-685-69461-5*) PLI.

Litigation & Arbitration in Central & Eastern Europe: IBA 26th Biennial Conference, Berlin, October 20-25, 1996. International Bar Association Staff et al. LC 98-13841. 1998. 124.00 (*90-411-0583-2*) Kluwer Law Intl.

Litigation & Inequality: Federal Diversity Jurisdiction in Industrial America, 1870-1958. Edward A. Purcell. 464p. 1992. text 75.00 (*0-19-507329-0*) OUP.

Litigation & Pleadings. Charles P. Nemeth. (Paralegal Workbook Ser.). 60p. (C). 1996. pap. text 9.95 (*0-87084-614-0*) Anderson Pub Co.

Litigation & Practice under Rule 10B-5, 6 vols. 2nd ed. Arnold S. Jacobs. LC 81-15493. (Securities Law Ser.). 1981. ring bd. 795.00 (*0-87632-093-0*) West Group.

Litigation & Settlement in a Game with Incomplete Information: An Experimental Study. Wolfgang Ryll. LC 96-20401. (Lecture Notes in Economics & Mathematical Systems Ser.). 174p. 1996. pap. 52.00 (*3-540-61304-8*) Spr-Verlag.

Litigation & Trial Practice for the Legal Assistant. 3rd ed. Roderick D. Blanchard. Ed. by Tubb. 509p. (C). 1990. text 57.25 (*0-314-56995-2*) West Pub.

Litigation Assistant: A Guide for the Defendant Physician. American College of Obstetricians & Gynecologists. LC 86-25856. 1986. 12.00 (*0-915473-07-0*) Am Coll Obstetric.

Litigation Assistant: A Guide for the Defendant Physician. 2nd ed. American College of Obstetricians & Gynecologists. LC 98-14138. 1998. 19.00 (*0-915473-45-3*) Am Coll Obstetric.

Litigation Case Management for Legal Assistants - A Satellite Program. (Litigation & Administrative Practice Course Handbook, 1983-84 Ser.). Date not set. pap. 99.00 (*0-614-17268-3*, H4-5224) PLI.

Litigation, Courts, Women Workers. Karen J. Maschke. LC 88-36993. 118p. 1989. 45.00 (*0-275-93065-3*, C3065, Praeger Pubs) Greenwood.

Litigation Economics. Ed. by Patrick A. Gaughan & Robert J. Thornton. LC 93-47538. (Contemporary Studies in Economic & Financial Analysis: Vol. 74). 1994. 78.50 (*1-55938-756-4*) Jai Pr.

Litigation Ethics. Underwood. LC 96-755591. 736p. 1996. boxed set 160.00 (*0-316-88827-3*, Aspen Law & Bus) Aspen Pub.

Litigation-Evidence & Procedure. 4th ed. M. I. Aronson et al. 1988. 83.00 (*0-409-49507-7*, AT, MICHIE); pap. 105.00 (*0-409-49508-5*, AT, MICHIE) LEXIS Pub.

Litigation Guide for Paralegals: Research & Drafting, 2, Vol. 2. 2nd ed. Cynthia M. Osborne. 760p. 1995. boxed set 145.00 (*0-471-01644-6*) Wiley.

Litigation in a Nutshell - Section 1983. Michael G. Collins. LC 97-30637. (Paralegal). 351p. (C). 1997. pap. text 15.00 (*0-314-21190-X*) West Pub.

Litigation Issues in the Distribution of Securities: An International Perspective, Vol. IBAS. Ed. by William G. Horton & Gerhard Wegen. LC 97-32. (International Bar Association Ser.). 1997. 345.00 (*90-411-0950-1*) Kluwer Law Intl.

Litigation Management. Kevin M. Quinley. 221p. (C). 1995. pap. 49.99 (*1-886813-00-0*) Intl Risk Mgt.

Litigation Management & Organization: The Winning Edge. Mark A. Dombroff. 1985. 25.00 (*1-55917-392-0*, 5314); audio 125.00 (*1-55917-390-4*); VHS 395.00 (*1-55917-391-2*) Natl Prac Inst.

***Litigation Manual.** 3rd ed. John G. Koeltl & John S. Kiernan. LC 98-52430. 1999. write for info. (*1-57073-656-1*) Amer Bar Assn.

Litigation Manual: A Primer for Trial Lawyers. John G. Koeltl & John S. Kiernan. LC 98-52430. 1998. write for info. (*1-57073-639-1*) Amer Bar Assn.

Litigation Manual: A Primer for Trial Lawyers. 2nd ed. 1232p. 1989. pap. 85.00 (*0-89707-409-2*, 531-0061-01) Amer Bar Assn.

Litigation, 1998 Supplement, Vols. 1-3. 2nd ed. James W. Jeans, Sr. 42p. 1998. pap. write for info. (*0-327-00850-4*, 6355511) LEXIS Pub.

Litigation, 1992, 3 vols. 2nd ed. James Jeans. 3446p. 1992. text 225.00 (*0-87473-779-6*, 63556-10, MICHIE) LEXIS Pub.

Litigation of Federal Tax Controversies. F. Gerald Burnett & Gerald A. Kafka. 2094p. 1986. pap. text 125.00 (*0-07-009069-6*) Shepards.

Litigation of Federal Tax Controversies: Civil Practice & Procedure. Marvin J. Garbis et al. 1024p. 1991. suppl. ed. 59.75 (*0-7913-0987-8*) Warren Gorham & Lamont.

Litigation of Federal Tax Controversies: Civil Practice & Procedure, 2. Marvin J. Garbis et al. LC 96-61000. 1024p. 1997. 215.00 (*0-7913-2982-8*, FCTC) Warren Gorham & Lamont.

Litigation of International Disputes in U. S. Courts. Ved P. Nanda & David K. Pansius. LC 86-13667. (International Business & Law Ser.). 1986. ring bd. 145.00 (*0-87632-509-6*) West Group.

Litigation of Questioned Settlement Claims: A Bayesian Nash-Equilibrium Approach. Stephen W. Salant & Gregory Rest. LC 84-19943. (Illus.). 1982. pap. text 4.00 (*0-8330-2312-8*, P-6809) Rand Corp.

Litigation Organization & Management, 2 vols. 2nd ed. Mark A. Dombroff. 1338p. 1991. ring bd. 195.00 (*0-13-072489-0*) Aspen Law.

Litigation Organization & Management: Effective Tactics & Techniques. Mark A. Dombroff. LC 84-1257. 1984. 60.00 (*0-15-004369-4*, #H43694) Harcourt.

Litigation Paralegal, 1. 2nd ed. Phillip J. Signey. 472p. 1997. boxed set 78.00 (*0-471-01997-6*) Wiley.

Litigation Paralegal: A Systems Approach. 3rd ed. James W. McCord. (Paralegal Ser.). (C). 1997. pap. 19.25 (*0-314-20702-3*) Brooks-Cole.

Litigation Paralegal: Systems Approach 3E. 3rd ed. LC 97-4930. (Paralegal). 600p. (C). 1997. mass mkt. 85.95 (*0-314-20252-8*) West Pub.

Litigation, Pleadings & Arbitration. 2nd ed. Charles P. Nemeth. LC 97-70034. 668p. (C). 1997. pap. 52.95 (*0-87084-543-8*) Anderson Pub Co.

Litigation Public Relations: Courting Public Opinion. Suzanne A. Roschwalb & Richard A. Stack. LC 95-6541. xix, 240p. 1995. pap. 45.00 (*0-8377-1048-0*, Rothman) W S Hein.

***Litigation Services Handbook: The Role of the Acco Untant As Expert, 1999 Cumulative.** Weil. 207p. 1999. pap., suppl. ed. 80.00 (*0-471-29909-X*) Wiley.

Litigation Services Handbook: The Role of the Accountant As Expert. 2nd ed. Ed. by Roman L. Weil et al. LC 94-46825. 936p. 1995. 165.00 (*0-471-10944-4*) Wiley.

***Litigation Services Handbook: The Role of the Accountant As Expert, January 2000 Supplement.** 2nd ed. Ed. by Roman L. Weil et al. 272p. 2000. pap. 85.00 (*0-471-36136-4*) Wiley.

Litigation Strategy at the International Court. Terry D. Gill. (C). 1989. lib. bdg. 132.50 (*0-7923-0332-6*) Kluwer Academic.

Litigation Support. Harris. (Paralegal Ser.). (C). 1999. mass mkt. 25.50 (*0-7668-0770-3*) Delmar.

Litigation Support: For the Proactive Corporate Information Manager. Peggy A. Reid. (Illus.). 149p. (Orig.). 1990. student ed. 129.95 (*0-9625994-0-9*, TX2 817 405) Independent.

An Asterisk (*) at the beginning of an entry indicates that the title is appearing for the first time.

L

Litigation Support & Financial Assessment of Damages. 2nd ed. Donald R. Chilvers et al. 346p. 1991. boxed set 120.00 (*0-406-00259-2*, UK, MICHIE) LEXIS Pub.

Litigation Support for Scientists & Engineers. V. Steve Reed. (Geraghty & Miller Environmental Science & Engineering Ser.). Date not set. 59.95 (*1-56670-210-0*) Lewis Pubs.

Litigation Support Management: The Winning Edge. Vicky Harris. 190p. 1994. text 54.00 (*1-86287-143-4*, Pub. by Federation Pr) Gaunt.

Litigation Support Systems, 1990. E. Hugh Kinney. LC 80-26267. 98.00 (*0-317-12023-9*) West Group.

Litigation Techniques for Legal Assistants: Becoming a More Effective Member of the Litigation Team. Laurie P. Roselle. 476p. 1991. 70.00 (*0-685-69462-3*); VHS 195.00 (*0-685-69463-1*) PLI.

Litigation Techniques for Legal Assistants: Becoming a More Effective Member of the Litigation Team - a Satellite Program. (Litigation & Administrative Practice Ser.). 476p. 1992. pap. text 70.00 (*0-685-56919-5*, H4-5118) PLI.

Litigation under Florida Probate Code. 3rd ed. Florida Bar Members. LC 96-72410. 272p. 1997. ring bd. 90.00 (*0-945979-94-0*, 204) FL Bar Legal Ed.

Litigation under the Federal Freedom of Information Act & Privacy Act, 1990. 15th ed. Ed. by Allan R. Adler. 494p. 1990. pap. text 45.00 (*0-86566-052-2*); pap. text, student ed. 15.00 (*0-685-11916-5*) ACLU DC.

Litigation under the Federal Open Government Laws. 20th rev. ed. Ed. by Allan R. Adler. 500p. 1997. pap. 45.00 (*0-914031-27-9*) Amer Civil Lib.

Litigation under the Federal Open Government Laws: The Freedom of Information Act, the Privacy Act, the Government in the Sunshine Act, the Federal Advisory Comm. Act. 18th ed. Ed. by Allan R. Adler. 512p. (Orig.). (C). 1993. pap. 45.00 (*0-86566-064-6*) Ctr Natl Security.

Litigation under the Handicapped Children's Protection Act: Case Annotations. 20p. 1988. pap. 3.50 (*0-685-29764-0*, 43,600) NCLS Inc.

Litigation with the Federal Government. 3rd ed. David Schwartz et al. LC 92-71547. 772p. 1994. 76.00 (*0-8318-3701-2*, B701) Am Law Inst.

Litigation/trial Prac F/legal Asst Hc 4e. 4th ed. Roderick D. Blanchard. LC 94-40807. (Paralegal). 692p. (C). 1995. pap. 85.95 (*0-314-04446-9*) West Pub.

Litigious Athenian. Matthew R. Christ. LC 97-52752. (Ancient Society & History Ser.). 264p. 1998. 39.95 (*0-8018-5863-1*) Johns Hopkins.

Litigious Vermonters: Court Records to 1825. P. Jeffrey Potash & Samuel B. Hand. (Occasional Papers: No. 2). (Illus.). 30p. (Orig.). 1979. pap. text 5.00 (*0-944277-03-9*, P67) U VT Ctr Rsch VT.

Litig/trial Prac F/legal Asst Stdy Gde 4e. 4th ed. Blanchard. (Paralegal). (C). 1995. student ed. 16.25 (*0-314-04936-3*) Delmar.

Litle Tot Bible Mazes. Becky Radtke. (Illus.). (J). 1997. pap. text 2.29 (*0-7647-0082-0*) Schaffer Pubns.

Litmus Body. Nadine McInnis. 88p. 1992. pap. 12.95 (*1-55082-037-0*, Pub. by Quarry Pr) LPC InBook.

Litraege Zum Verstaednids der Odyssee. Hartmut Erbse. (Untersuchungen zur Antiken Literatur und Geschichte Ser.: Vol. 13). (C). 1972. 97.70 (*3-11-004045-X*) De Gruyter.

Litso Zhar Ptitsy. 2nd ed. Alla Ktorova. LC 82-84748. (RUS.). 220p. (Orig.). 1984. 8.50 (*0-911971-01-7*) Effect Pub.

Litstart: Literacy Strategies for Adult Reading Tutors. 1993. 12.95 (*0-88336-653-3*) New Readers.

Littell's Political Transactions in & Concerning Kentucky. Ed. by Temple Bodley. LC 70-146375. (First American Frontier Ser.). 322p. 1971. reprint ed. 33.95 (*0-405-02826-1*) Ayer.

Littera et Sensus: Essays on Form & Meaning in Medieval French Literature. Ed. by Trotter. (Illus.). 142p. 1989. text 59.00 (*0-85989-333-2*, Pub. by Univ Exeter Pr) Northwestern U Pr.

Litteratur der Landesvermessung. J. H. Graf. (FRE & GER.). 712p. 1997. reprint ed. 95.00 (*1-57898-053-4*) Martino Pubng.

Litteratur Om Afrika: Annoterad Bibliografi. Anna-Britta Wallenius. 168p. 1973. write for info. (*91-7106-060-X*, Pub. by Nordic Africa) Transaction Pubs.

Litteratur Om Sodra Afrika: Kommenterad Bibliografi, 1989. Tore L. Eriksen. 174p. 1990. write for info. (*91-7106-303-X*, Pub. by Nordic Africa) Transaction Pubs.

Litterature. Jean Giraudoux. (Coll. Idees). (FRE.). 1967. pap. 10.95 (*0-8288-9805-7*, F104140) Fr & Eur.

Litterature: Textes et Methode. Helene Sabbah. (FRE., Illus.). 415p. 1993. pap. text 42.95 (*2-218-00627-8*, Pub. by Ed Hatier) Hatier Pub.

Litterature Americaine. Charles Cestre. (BCL1-PS American Literature Ser.). 218p. 1993. reprint ed. lib. bdg. 79.00 (*0-7812-6565-7*) Rprt Serv.

Litterature Aujourd'hui see Litterature Francaise

***Litterature Belge d'Expression Francaise au Miroir de la Correspondance Albert Mockel - Georges Marlow (1894-1943)** Francesca Bianca Crucitti Ullrich. (Illus.). XLI, 598p. 1998. 86.00 (*3-631-31521-X*) P Lang Pubng.

Litterature Comparee. Louis P. Betz. LC 77-101092. (BCL Ser. I). (FRE.). 1969. reprint ed. 34.00 (*0-404-00793-7*) AMS Pr.

Litterature Comparee. Louis P. Betz. LC 68-25307. (Studies in Comparative Literature: No. 35). 1969. reprint ed. lib. bdg. 75.00 (*0-8383-0911-9*) M S G Haskell Hse.

Litterature Comparee - Litterature Mondiale - Comparative Literature - World Literature Actes du Xleme Congres de l'AILC, Paris, 1985: Proceedings of the XIth Congress of the International Comparative Literature Association, Vol. 5. Ed. by Gerald Gillespie. 254p. 1991. pap. 38.80 (*0-8204-1443-3*) P Lang Pubng.

Litterature D'Oc. Jean Rouquette. (FRE.). 125p. 1968. 9.95 (*0-8288-7417-4*) Fr & Eur.

Litterature Engagee: Essai. Andre Gide. pap. 9.95 (*0-685-34151-8*) Fr & Eur.

Litterature et Architecture: Le Dix-Neuvieme Siecle. Agnes Peysson-Zeiss. LC 98-11247. 168p. 1998. 34.00 (*0-7618-1059-5*) U Pr of Amer.

Litterature et la Hantise du Mal: Lectures de Barbey d'Aurevilly, Huysmans et Baudelaire. Alain Toumayan. LC 87-81917. (French Forum Monographs: No. 69). (FRE.). 127p. (Orig.). 1987. pap. 13.95 (*0-917058-70-4*) French Forum.

Litterature et le Mal. Georges Bataille. (Folio Essais Ser.: No. 148). (FRE.). 1990. pap. 9.95 (*2-07-032607-1*) Schoenhof.

Litterature et Philosophie Melees: Edition Critique, 2 vols. Bernardin J. De Saint-Pierre. (FRE.). 349p. 1984. pap. 11.95 (*0-7859-1180-4*, 2253007293) Fr & Eur.

Litterature et Spectacle. Tadeusz Kowzan. (Approaches to Semiotics Ser.: No. 58). (FRE.). 240p. 1975. text 36.95 (*90-279-3486-X*) Mouton.

Litterature Francaise, 5 tomes. Henri Lemaitre. Incl. Tome I. Du Moyen Age a L'age Baroque. 29.95 Tome II. Des Classiques aux Philosophes. 29.95 Tome III. Evolutions du Dix-Neuvieme Siecle. 29.95 Tome IV. Metamorphoses du Vingtieme Siecle. 29.95 Tome V. Litterature Aujourd'hui. 17.50 write for info. (*0-318-52038-9*) Fr & Eur.

Litterature Francaise, Vol. 1. Berg. (FRE.). (C). 1994. text 64.50 (*0-03-039849-5*) Harcourt Coll Pubs.

Litterature Francaise, 5 tomes, Vol. 1. Ed. by Henri Lemaitre. write for info. (*0-8288-7870-6*, FA104) Fr & Eur.

Litterature Francaise Vol. 1: Le Moyen Age. Editions Arthaud Staff. (FRE.). 1990. pap. 38.95 (*0-7859-3292-5*, 2700304152) Fr & Eur.

Litterature Francaise Vol. 2: De Villon a Ronsard. Editions Arthaud Staff. (FRE.). 1991. pap. 38.95 (*0-7859-3295-X*, 2700305132) Fr & Eur.

Litterature Francaise Vol. 3: De Montaigne a Corneille. Editions Arthaud Staff. (FRE.). 1991. pap. 38.95 (*0-7859-3296-8*, 2700305140) Fr & Eur.

Litterature Francaise Vol. 4: Le Classicisme, 1660-1680. Editions Arthaud Staff. (FRE.). 1990. pap. 38.95 (*0-7859-3294-1*, 2700304799) Fr & Eur.

Litterature Francaise Vol. 5: De Fenelon a Voltaire, 1698-1750. Editions Arthaud Staff. (FRE.). 1990. pap. 38.95 (*0-7859-3293-3*, 2700304381) Fr & Eur.

Litterature Francaise Vol. 7: De Chateaubriand a Baudelaire, 1820-1869. Editions Arthaud Staff. (FRE.). 1990. pap. 38.95 (*0-7859-3297-6*, 2700305159) Fr & Eur.

Litterature Francaise Vol. 8: De Zola a Apollinaire, 1869-1920. Editions Arthaud Staff. (FRE.). 1990. pap. 38.95 (*0-7859-3298-4*, 2700305167) Fr & Eur.

Litterature Francaise au Moyen Age (Eleventh to Fourteenth Centuries) Gaston B. Paris. LC 73-178583. reprint ed. 62.50 (*0-404-56658-8*) AMS Pr.

Litterature Francaise Contemporaine. Joseph-Marie Querard. (FRE.). 3150p. 1965. 1095.00 (*0-7859-5223-3*) Fr & Eur.

Litterature Francaise Contemporaine, 6 tomes, Set. Joseph-Marie Querard. 262.50 (*0-685-35980-8*) Fr & Eur.

Litterature Francaise du Moyen Age. V. L. Saulnier. 136p. 1943. 9.95 (*0-8288-7409-3*) Fr & Eur.

Litterature Francaise du Siecle Classique. V. L. Saulnier. 133p. 1943. 9.95 (*0-8288-7408-5*) Fr & Eur.

Litterature Francaise du Siecle Philosophique. V. L. Saulnier. 136p. 1943. 9.95 (*0-8288-7411-5*) Fr & Eur.

Litterature Francaise du Siecle Romantique. V. L. Saulnier. 1945. 9.95 (*0-8288-7410-7*) Fr & Eur.

Litterature Franco-Americaine Ecrivains et Ecritures: Franco-American Literature Writers & Their Writings. Intro. by Claire Quintal. (ENG & FRE.). 193p. (Orig.). (C). 1992. pap. text 10.95 (*1-880261-00-6*) FI Assump Coll.

Litterature Latine au Moyen-Age, 2 vols. in 1. Joseph De Ghellinck. 383p. 1975. reprint ed. write for info. (*3-487-02339-3*); reprint ed. write for info. (*0-318-71345-4*); reprint ed. write for info. (*0-318-71346-2*) G Olms Pubs.

Litterature Moderne du Monde Francophone: Une Anthologie. Peter S. Thompson. (ACE & FRE.). 160p. (C). pap. 19.95 (*0-8442-1588-0*, VF1588-0) NTC Contemp Pub Co.

Litterature Occitane: Bibliographie Selective et Critique. Robert A. Taylor. LC 77-20895. (Medieval Bibliographies Ser.). 1978. text 32.50 (*0-8020-5407-2*) U of Toronto Pr.

Litterature Personnelle. La. LC PQ3908.L57. (Revue d'Histoire Litteraire du Quebec & du Canada Francais Ser.: Vol. 9). (FRE.). 178p. 1985. reprint ed. pap. 55.20 (*0-608-02208-X*, 206287900004) Bks Demand.

Litteratures du Sahel: Langue(s), Langue(s), Parole(s) dans les Litteratures du Sahel. Christopher Wise et al. (FRE.). 150p. 1998. pap. 10.00 (*0-9655761-6-7*) Kola Tree Pr.

Litteratures Emergentes (Emerging Literatures) Ed. by Jean-Marie Grassin. (Actes du XIe Congres de l'Association Internationale de Litterature Comparee Ser.: Vol. 10). (FRE.). 272p. 1996. 43.95 (*3-906754-35-9*, Pub. by P Lang) P Lang Pubng.

Litteratures En Contexte: Le Monde Francophonr. Luce. (C). 1994. wbk. ed. 36.00 (*0-15-501103-0*) Harcourt Coll Pubs.

Litteratures en Contexte Grammar. Luce. (C). 1994. pap. text 48.50 (*0-15-501102-2*) Harcourt Coll Pubs.

Litteratures Populaires de Toutes les Nations: Conteurs et Poetes de Tous Pays, 53 vols., Set. 695.00 (*0-685-34000-7*) Fr & Eur.

***Litterbox Training: And Other Feline Hygiene Etiquette.** Pam Johnson Bennett. (Laugh Your Way Through... Ser.). 1999. pap. text. write for info. (*1-889540-54-4*) Bowtie Press.

Litterbug on the Loose! Easy Peel Sticker Book. Golden Books Staff. 16p. (ps-3). 1999. pap. text 2.99 (*0-307-28303-8*) Gldn Bks Pub Co.

Litterms: A Tutorial for Understanding Poetry, Fiction, Drama. Richard D. Rust. (C). 1988. student ed. 26.00 incl. disk (*0-15-551090-8*) Harcourt Coll Pubs.

"Littery Man" Mark Twain & Modern Authorship. Richard S. Lowry. (Commonwealth Center Studies in American Culture). 192p. (C). 1996. text 45.00 (*0-19-510212-6*) OUP.

Littest Dinosaurs: Mini-Book. Most. (J). 1995. 4.95 (*0-15-200381-9*, Harcourt Child Bks) Harcourt.

Littig: Descendants of Peter Littig, Godfrey Rogge & Others. M. D. Littig et al. 40p. 1994. reprint ed. pap. 8.00 (*0-8328-4125-0*) Higginson Bk Co.

Litt'l Bits: The Spring Festival. 32p. (J). 1993. pap. 2.95 (*0-8125-2321-0*, Pub. by Tor Bks) St Martin.

Little. David Treuer. LC 95-77949. 224p. 1995. 22.95 (*1-55597-231-4*) Graywolf.

Little. David Treuer. LC 96-31779. 272p. 1996. pap. 12.00 (*0-312-15164-0*) St Martin.

Little: Genealogy of the Little Family: Descendants of George Little, Who Came to Newbury, Massachusetts, in 1640. G. T. Little. (Illus.). 82p. 1993. reprint ed. pap. 16.50 (*0-8328-3366-5*); reprint ed. lib. bdg. 26.50 (*0-8328-3365-7*) Higginson Bk Co.

***Little 'a' Sellers.** (J). 2000. 3.95 (*0-552-52872-2*, Pub. by Transworld Publishers Ltd) Trafalgar.

Little ABC Book. Ed. by Little Simon Staff. (Chubby Board Bks.). 16p. (J). 1980. pap. 3.50 (*0-671-41342-2*) Litle Simon.

Little ABC Book. Bob Staake. (Illus.). 30p. (J). (ps-k). 1998. mass mkt. 6.99 (*0-689-81659-6*) S&S Childrens.

Little ABC Coloring Book. Anna Pomaska. (Illus.). (J). (gr. k-3). 1998. pap. 1.00 (*0-486-25156-X*) Dover.

Little ABC of the Church Interior. Josef Braun. Tr. by Linda M. Maloney from GER. LC 97-197755. 32p. (Orig.). 1997. pap. text 3.95 (*0-8146-2413-8*, Liturg Pr Bks) Liturgical Pr.

***Little ABC Phonics Book.** Carole M. Gallagher. (Illus.). 72p. (J). 2000. text 14.50 (*0-9702197-0-9*) C M Gallagher.

Little ABC's of Balance: How to Live Successfully & Avoid Burnout! Barry Wagner & John Bancom. LC 97-71522. i, 128p. (Orig.). 1997. pap. 9.95 (*0-9653714-1-7*) LA Press.

Little Abner & His Ark: Abner Bartlett's Role in Constructing Largest Hotel in the World, The Waldorf-Astoria Hotel. large type ed. Bruce Campbell Adamson. Ed. by Dennis McDonough. (Illus.). 50p. 1998. 10.00 (*1-892501-13-9*) B C Adamson.

Little Acts of Kindness. (Children's Tiny Treasures Ser.). 1995. 4.99 (*0-310-96340-0*) Zondervan.

Little Address Book of 1000 Stars. Ed. by James Bowman. 1986. pap. 7.50 (*0-934969-01-9*) Bowman Pub Inc.

Little Adsorption Book: A Practical Guide for Engineers & Scientists. Diran Basmadjian. LC 96-32834. (Illus.). 160p. 1996. per. 44.95 (*0-8493-2692-3*) CRC Pr.

Little Adventures in Tokyo: 39 Thrills for the Urban Explorer. 2nd rev. ed. Rick Kennedy. LC 98-14426. (Illus.). 176p. 1998. pap. 12.95 (*1-880656-34-5*) Stone Bridge Pr.

Little African-American Girl. Sylvia Walker. (Little Activity Bks.). (Illus.). (J). 1995. pap. 1.00 (*0-486-28439-5*) Dover.

Little African Girl Paper Dolls. Tom Tierney. (Illus.). (J). (gr. k-3). 1993. pap. 1.00 (*0-486-27441-1*) Dover.

***Little Airline That Could! Eastern Provincial Airways - The First Fifteen Years.** Marsh Jones. 168p. 1998. pap. 9.95 (*1-895387-95-7*) Creative Bk Pub.

Little Airplane Book. Shana Corey. (J). 2000. 4.99 (*0-679-89480-2*) Random.

Little Aliens. Myra Kelly. LC 74-27992. (Modern Jewish Experience Ser.). (Illus.). 1975. reprint ed. 26.95 (*0-405-06719-4*) Ayer.

Little Alphabet. Trina S. Hyman. LC 92-29692. (Books of Wonder). (Illus.). 40p. (J). (ps-3). 1993. reprint ed. mass mkt. 5.95 (*0-688-12034-2*, Wm Morrow) Morrow Avon.

Little Alphabet Follow-the-Dots Book. 70th ed. Anna Pomaska. (Activity Bk.). (J). (ps up). 1988. pap. 1.00 (*0-486-25623-5*) Dover.

Little Altars Everywhere. Rebecca Wells. 224p. 1998. 22.00 (*0-06-019362-X*) HarpC.

Little Altars Everywhere. Rebecca Wells. 240p. 1996. pap. 13.00 (*0-06-097684-5*, Perennial) HarperTrade.

***Little Altars Everywhere.** Rebecca Wells. 224p. 1998. 22.00 (*0-06-019349-2*, Cliff Street) HarperTrade.

***Little Altars Everywhere.** large type ed. Rebecca Wells. 352p. 1999. pap. 20.00 (*0-06-093318-6*) HarpC.

Little Anabo from Boriken. Victor M. Misla. (Illus.). 28p. (Orig.). (YA). (gr. 6-7). 1987. pap. 5.00 (*0-9626870-0-6*) NW Monarch Pr.

Little & Big. Judy Hindley. LC 95-364. (Illus.). (J). (ps-3). 1996. pap. 4.99 (*1-56402-677-9*) Candlewick Pr.

Little Angel. Joyce Thomas. 18p. (J). Date not set. 6.99 (*0-7868-0563-3*) Little.

Little Angel: And Other Stories. Leonid Andreyev. Ed. by Mark Willson. (European Classics). 255p. 1997. reprint ed. pap. 8.95 (*0-946626-42-1*, Pub. by Dedalus) Subterranean Co.

Little Angel, & Other Stories. Leonid N. Andreev. LC 78-167439. (Short Story Index Reprint Ser.). 1977. reprint ed. 32.95 (*0-8369-3965-4*) Ayer.

Little Angel Dancer. Oradel N. Morris. (Illus.). (Orig.). (J). (gr. 1-8). 1999. pap. write for info. (*0-944064-06-X*) Paupieres Pub.

Little Angel Tiffany & the Boy Who Wants a Toy. Ramona C. Moore. (Illus.). 16p. (J). (gr. k-3). 1997. pap. 6.00 (*0-8059-4115-0*) Dorrance.

***Little Angel/Little Rascal.** Havoc Publishing Staff. 1999. 9.00 (*0-7416-1006-X*) Havoc Pub.

Little Angels. Maira Kalman. Ed. by Marla H. Kennedy & Susan Martin. (Picture This Ser.). (Illus.). 96p. (J). 1997. 14.95 (*1-890576-00-X*) Picture This.

Little Angels' Alphabet of Love. Joan W. Anglund. (Illus.). 32p. (J). 1997. per. 4.99 (*0-689-81145-4*) S&S Childrens.

Little Angels & the Fruit of the Spirit. (Coloring Bks.). 16p. (J). (gr. k-5). 1996. pap. 1.49 (*0-7847-0511-9*) Standard Pub.

Little Angels' Book of Christmas. Joan W. Anglund. (Illus.). 32p. (J). 1997. 4.99 (*0-689-81468-2*) S&S Childrens.

Little Angels Coloring & Activity Book: The Special Gift. large type ed. Annie Ruth. (Illus.). 24p. (J). (gr. k-3). 1999. 3.50 (*0-9656306-2-5*) A Ruth Creations.

Little Angels Joyful Christmas. Rock. 1997. pap. 2.95 (*0-7459-3787-X*, Pub. by Lion Pubng) Trafalgar.

***Little Angels Praise Him.** Norma Garris. 1999. pap. 2.49 (*0-7847-0982-3*) Standard Pub.

Little Angels with Topsy Turvy Halos. Merry A. Tague. (Illus.). 47p. (J). 1994. pap. 3.95 (*0-937242-12-8*) Scandia Pubs.

Little Animal ABC Coloring Book. 80th ed. Nina Barbaresi. (Illus.). (J). (gr. k-3). 1998. pap. 1.00 (*0-486-25834-3*) Dover.

Little Animal Activity Book. Nina Barbaresi. (Illus.). (J). (gr. k-3). 1990. pap. 1.00 (*0-486-26272-3*) Dover.

Little Animal Follow-the-Dots Coloring Book. 80th ed. Roberta Collier. (Illus.). (J). (gr. k-3). 1991. pap. 1.00 (*0-486-26666-4*) Dover.

Little Animal Sermons: Six Children's Sermons with Activity Pages. Julia Bland. (Illus.). 28p. 1999. pap. 4.95 (*0-7880-1349-1*) CSS OH.

Little Animals. Debby Slier. (Hello Baby Bks.). 12p. (J). (ps). 1989. 2.95 (*1-56288-147-7*) Checkerboard.

Little Animals Stained Glass Book. T. Menten. 1991. text 1.00 (*0-486-25733-9*) Dover.

Little Annie Fountainhead. Kathy Miskov. 1998. 14.95 (*0-9654436-3-9*) Honey Creek WI.

***Little Annie Fountainhead.** large type ed. Ann Elizabeth. Ed. by Karl Larson. (Illus.). 32p. (J). (gr. k-6). 1999. pap. 8.95 (*0-9654436-5-5*) Honey Creek WI.

Little Annie of Christian Creek. Thomas J. Sanker. (Illus.). 60p. (Orig.). (YA). (gr. 4-8). 1994. pap. 11.95 (*1-880812-16-9*) S Ink WA.

Little Annie's Art Book of Etiquette & Good Manners. Barry Stebbing. Ed. by Saundra Stebbing & Pam Torgersen. (Illus.). 102p. (J). (gr. k-4). 1995. 14.95 (*0-9700405-0-4*) How Great Thou Art.

Little Anodynes from Taliaferro. Ruth Specht. LC 85-81201. (Illus.). 224p. (Orig.). 1985. pap. 10.00 (*0-931889-03-0*) Epistemology Pubs.

Little Ant. Shirleyann Costingan. (ESL Theme Links Ser.). (Illus.). (J). (gr. k-3). 1993. 35.00 (*1-56334-316-9*); audio 10.50 (*1-56334-315-0*) Hampton-Brown.

Little Ant. Michael Walker, Jr. (Amazing English Ser.: Little Bks., Level B). (J). 1995. pap. text 17.64 (*0-201-85363-9*) Addison-Wesley.

Little Ant: Big Book. Shirleyann Costigan. (ESL Theme Links Ser.). (Illus.). 16p. (Orig.). (J). (gr. 1-3). 1992. pap. text 29.95 (*1-56334-066-6*) Hampton-Brown.

Little Ant: Small Book. Shirleyann Costigan. (ESL Theme Links Ser.). (Illus.). 16p. (Orig.). (J). (gr. 1-3). 1992. pap. text 6.00 (*1-56334-072-0*) Hampton-Brown.

Little Ant - La Hormiga Chiquita. Michael R. Ramirez & Linda Sawaya. LC 95-10282.Tr. of La Hormiga Chiquita. (ENG & SPA., Illus.). 32p. (J). 1995. 12.95 (*0-8478-1922-1*, Pub. by Rizzoli Intl) St Martin.

Little Ant Little Book Level B, Level B. Pals. 16p. (J). 1995. ring bd. 4.78 (*0-201-85357-4*) Addison-Wesley.

Little Ant Teacher's Guide. (ESL Theme Links Ser.). (Illus.). 1993. teacher ed. 15.00 (*1-56334-427-0*) Hampton-Brown.

Little Ant Theme Link. Shirleyann Costingan. (ESL Theme Links Ser.). (Illus.). (J). (gr. k-3). 1993. 99.50 (*1-56334-317-7*) Hampton-Brown.

Little Anthology. Vincent Starrett. (Vincent Starrett Memorial Library: Vol. 9). viii, 221p. 1996. 25.00 (*1-896648-00-2*) Battered Silicon.

Little Anthropology. 3rd ed. Dennison Nash. LC 98-30166. 210p. 1998. pap. text 27.20 (*0-13-906736-1*) P-H.

Little Apocalypse. Wendy Battin. LC 97-71487. (Richard Snyder Publication Award Ser.). 83p. (Orig.). 1997. pap. 10.00 (*0-912592-40-0*) Ashland Poetry.

Little Ark. Jan De Hartog. Date not set. lib. bdg. 20.95 (*0-8488-2099-1*) Amereon Ltd.

Little Arliss. Fred Gipson. LC 77-17643. (Illus.). (J). (gr. 4-6). 1978. 12.95 (*0-06-022008-2*) HarpC Child Bks.

Little Artist: A Child's Art Book. Bonnie Sose. 32p. (J). (gr. 3 up). 11.00 (*0-685-65933-X*) Character Builders.

***Little Audio CD Book.** Robert A. Starrett & Joshua McDaniel. 200p. 2000. pap. 19.99 (*0-201-70897-3*) Addison-Wesley.

***Little Auto.** Lois Lenski. (J). 2001. mass mkt. 13.99 (*0-375-91073-5*, Pub. by Random Bks Yng Read); mass mkt. 11.95 (*0-375-81073-0*, Pub. by Random Bks Yng Read) Random.

Little Avant Garde: Piano for Pre-Schoolers. 3rd rev. ed. S. Covello. 40p. 1986. pap. 4.95 (*0-7935-3981-1*) H Leonard.

Little Awards Sticker Book. Nina Barbaresi. (Little Activity Bks.). (Illus.). (J). 1991. pap. 1.00 (*0-486-26388-6*) Dover.

An Asterisk (*) at the beginning of an entry indicates that the title is appearing for the first time.

***Little 'b'** Sellers. (J). 2000. 3.95 (*0-552-52873-0*, Pub. by Transworld Publishers Ltd) Trafalgar.

Little Babies. Debby Slier. (Hello Baby Bks.). 12p. (J). (ps). 1989. 2.95 (*1-56288-148-5*) Checkerboard.

Little Baby Animals Stained Glass Coloring Book. John Green. (Illus.). (J). (gr. k-3). 1992. pap. 1.00 (*0-486-27222-2*) Dover.

Little Baby Bobby. Nancy Van Laan. (Dragonfly Bks.). (Illus.). 32p. (J). 1999. pap. 6.99 (*0-375-80052-2*) Knopf.

Little Baby Bobby. Nancy Van Laan. LC 94-45093. (Illus.). 40p. (J). (ps-3). 1997. lib. bdg. 18.99 (*0-679-94922-4*) Random.

Little Baby Book. (Illus.). 80p. 1992. 4.95 (*0-8362-3001-9*) Andrews & McMeel.

Little Baby Snoogle-Fleejer. Jimmy Carter & Amy Carter. LC 95-41408. (Illus.). 32p. (gr. 2 up). 1995. 17.00 (*0-8129-2731-1*, Times Bks) Crown Pub Group.

Little Baby Steps to Happiness. John Q. Baucom. LC 96-68841. 160p. 1996. pap. 6.95 (*0-914984-87-X*) Starburst.

Little Baby Steps to Success. Vince Lombardi, Jr. & John Q. Baucom. LC 96-72371. 160p. 1997. pap. 6.95 (*0-914984-96-9*) Starburst.

***Little Badger Knitwear: Knitted Projects for Babies & Toddlers.** Rosemary Badger & Elaine Scott. LC 99-86090. (Illus.). 2000. pap. 19.95 (*1-56158-414-2*) Taunton.

***Little Badger, Terror of the Seven Seas.** Eve Bunting. LC 00-8451. (Illus.). (J). 2001. write for info. (*0-15-202395-X*, Harcourt Child Bks) Harcourt.

Little Badness. large type ed. Josephine Cox. 560p. 1997. 27.99 (*0-7089-8888-1*) Ulverscroft.

Little Ballerina. Sally Grindley. LC 99-11610. (Eyewitness Readers). 32p. (J). (gr. 1-3). 1999. pap. 3.95 (*0-7894-4004-0*) DK Pub Inc.

***Little Ballerina.** Sally Grindley. LC 99-11610. (Eyewitness Readers). 32p. (J). (gr. 1-3). 1999. 12.95 (*0-7894-4005-9*) DK Pub Inc.

Little Ballerina. Katharine Ross. LC 92-42093. (J). 1996. pap. 3.25 (*0-679-84915-7*, Pub. by Random Bks Yng Read) Random.

Little Ballerinas. Ann Morris. (All Aboard Reading Ser.). (Illus.). 32p. (Orig.). (J). (ps-3). 1997. pap. 2.99 (*0-448-41607-7*, G & D) Peng Put Young Read.

Little Band. James Sage. LC 90-40089. (Illus.). 32p. (J). (ps-3). 1991. 13.95 (*0-689-50516-7*) McElderry Bks.

***Little Banquets for Ordinary People: Epiphanies of Every Day.** Edward J. Farrell. LC 99-55135. 175p. 2000. pap. 9.95 (*0-8189-0873-4*) Alba.

Little Baron's Christmas Angel. Curt H. Von Dornheim. (Illus.). 64p. Date not set. 12.95 (*0-89404-222-X*) Aztex.

Little Bathroom Book. Claire Richardson. 1998. pap. text 6.95 (*1-84024-048-2*, Pub. by Summers) Seven Hills Bk.

Little Bear see Osito

Little Bear. (I Can Read Bks.). (J). (ps-1). 1999. pap. 1.95 (*0-590-31967-1*) Scholastic Inc.

Little Bear. Else H. Minarik. LC 57-9263. (I Can Read Bks.). (Illus.). 64p. (J). (ps-3). 1957. 15.95 (*0-06-024240-X*); lib. bdg. 15.89 (*0-06-024241-8*) HarpC Child Bks.

Little Bear. Else H. Minarik. (I Can Read Bks.). (Illus.). 64p. (J). (ps-1). 1978. pap. 3.95 (*0-06-444004-4*, HarpTrophy) HarpC Child Bks.

Little Bear. Else H. Minarik. (I Can Read Bks.). (J). (ps-1). 1978. 8.95 (*0-606-01530-2*, Pub. by Turtleback) Demco.

Little Bear. Diane Namm. (My First Reader Ser.). (Illus.). 28p. (J). (ps-2). 1990. pap. 3.95 (*0-516-45356-4*) Childrens.

Little Bear. unabridged ed. Else H. Minarik. LC 57-9263. (I Can Read Bks.). (Illus.). 64p. (J). (gr. k-3). 1990. pap. 8.95 incl. audio (*1-55994-234-7*) HarperAudio.

Little Bear, 3 bks., Set. Else H. Minarik. (I Can Read Bks.). (Illus.). 160p. (J). (ps-3). 1992. pap. 11.25 (*0-06-444197-0*, HarpTrophy) HarpC Child Bks.

Little Bear: A Study Guide. Duncan Searl. Ed. by J. Friedland & R. Kessler. (Novel-Ties Ser.). 1993. pap. text 15.95 (*0-88122-876-1*) Lrn Links.

Little Bear - Osito. Else H. Minarik. (SPA.). (J). 9.95 (*84-204-3044-7*) Santillana.

Little Bear & His Teddy Bear. Doug Renahan. 1989. 6.95 (*0-89137-060-9*) Quality Pubns.

Little Bear & the Big Fight. Jutta Langreuter. LC 97-43157. (Little Bear Ser.). (Illus.). 32p. (J). (ps-k). 1998. pap. 6.95 (*0-7613-0375-8*); lib. bdg. 21.40 (*0-7613-0403-7*) Millbrook Pr.

***Little Bear at the Seaside.** Jane Brett. (Bear Pack Ser.). (Illus.). 12p. (J). (ps-k). 1999. 8.98 (*0-7651-1699-5*) Smithmark.

Little Bear Audio Collection. unabridged ed. Else H. Minarik. (I Can Read Bks.). (J). (ps-3). 1992. pap. 11.95 incl. audio (*1-55994-543-5*) HarperAudio.

Little Bear Book see Libro del Osito

Little Bear Book. Anthony Browne. (Illus.). 24p. (J). (ps). 1989. 4.95 (*0-385-26006-7*) Doubleday.

Little Bear Brushes His Teeth. Jutta Langreuter. LC 96-36469. (Illus.). 32p. (J). (ps-k). 1997. pap. 6.95 (*0-7613-0230-1*); lib. bdg. 21.40 (*0-7613-0190-9*) Millbrook Pr.

Little Bear Goes to Kindergarten. Jutta Langreuter. LC 96-35112. (Illus.). 32p. (J). (ps-k). 1997. pap. 6.95 (*0-7613-0231-X*); lib. bdg. 21.40 (*0-7613-0191-7*) Millbrook Pr.

Little Bear Is a Big Brother. Jutta Langreuter. LC 97-44623. (Little Bear Ser.). (Illus.). 32p. (J). (ps-k). 1998. pap. 6.95 (*0-7613-0376-6*) Millbrook Pr.

Little Bear Lost. Jane Hissey. (Illus.). 30p. (J). (ps). 1994. pap. 9.99 (*1-881445-44-5*) Sandvik Pub.

Little Bear Paints a Picture. (J). 1988. 1.98 (*0-671-09562-5*) S&S Trade.

Little Bear Story: Adventures of a Retarded Gopher Skinner. Richard Wheeler. (Illus.). 234p. 1998. 8.00 (*1-889128-47-3*) Mantle Ministries.

Little Bear Visits His Grandparents. Doug Renahan. (J). 1994. 6.95 (*0-89137-066-8*) Quality Pubns.

***Little Bear Won't Go to Bed.** Jutta Langreuter. LC 99-56178. (Little Bear Collection). (Illus.). (J). 2000. pap. 7.95 (*0-7613-1395-8*) Millbrook Pr.

***Little Bear's Baby Book.** Martin Waddell. (Illus.). 48p. (J). 2000. 12.99 (*0-7636-1117-4*) Candlewick Pr.

Little Bear's Best Birthday. Rocco Rotunno & Betsy Rotunno. (Stamptime Stories Ser.). (Illus.). 12p. (J). (gr. 2-6). 1992. 7.00 (*1-881980-00-6*) Noteworthy.

Little Bear's Big Adventure. Kathleen Allan-Meyer. LC 98-11239. (Illus.). 32p. (J). 1998. 5.49 (*1-57924-060-7*) Bob Jones Univ.

***Little Bear's Christmas.** Jane Brett. (Bear Packs Ser.). (Illus.). 12p. (J). (ps-k). 1999. 8.98 (*0-7651-1700-2*) Smithmark.

Little Bear's Christmas. Norbert Landa. LC 99-25069. (Illus.). 32p. (J). (gr. k-3). 1999. 14.95 (*1-888444-60-6*, Pub. by Little Tiger) Futech Educ Prods.

Little Bear's Friend. Else H. Minarik. LC 60-6370. (I Can Read Bks.). (Illus.). 64p. (J). (ps-3). 1960. lib. bdg. 15.89 (*0-06-024256-6*) HarpC Child Bks.

Little Bear's Friend. Else H. Minarik. LC 60-6370. (I Can Read Bks.). (Illus.). 64p. (J). (ps-3). 1984. mass mkt. 3.95 (*0-06-444051-6*, HarpTrophy) HarpC Child Bks.

Little Bear's Friend. Else H. Minarik. (I Can Read Bks.). (J). (ps-1). 1984. 8.95 (*0-606-03384-X*, Pub. by Turtleback) Demco.

Little Bear's Friend. Maurice Sendak & Else H. Minarik. (I Can Read Bks.). (Illus.). 64p. (J). (ps-1). 1960. 15.95 (*0-06-024255-8*) HarpC Child Bks.

Little Bear's Friend. unabridged ed. Else H. Minarik. LC 60-6370. (I Can Read Bks.). (Illus.). 64p. (J). (gr. k-3). 1990. pap. 8.95 incl. audio (*1-55994-235-5*) HarperAudio.

Little Bear's Friends - Los Amigos de Osito. Else H. Minarik. (SPA.). (J). 7.95 (*84-204-3049-8*) Santillana.

***Little Bear's Outdoor Adventure Guide.** Richard Wheeler. (Illus.). 200p. 2000. pap. 12.00 (*1-889128-61-9*) Mantle Ministries.

***Little Bear's Secret.** Kathleen Allan-Meyer. LC 99-462161. (Illus.). (J). 2000. write for info. (*1-57924-358-4*) Bob Jones Univ.

***Little Bear's Surprise.** Kathleen Allan-Meyer. LC 99-23596. (Illus.). 32p. (J). 1999. 5.49 (*1-57924-066-6*) Bob Jones Univ.

Little Bear's Trousers. Jane Hissey. (Illus.). 32p. (J). (ps-1). 1996. pap. 6.99 (*0-698-11395-0*, PapStar) Peng Put Young Read.

Little Bear's Trousers. Jane Hissey. LC 99-228237. (Illus.). 28p. (ps). 1999. 6.99 (*0-399-23367-9*, Philomel) Peng Put Young Read.

Little Bear's Visit. Else H. Minarik. (I Can Read Bks.). (Illus.). 64p. (J). (ps-1). 1961. lib. bdg. 15.89 (*0-06-024266-3*) HarpC Child Bks.

Little Bear's Visit. Else H. Minarik. LC 61-11451. (I Can Read Bks.). (Illus.). 64p. (J). (ps-3). 1961. 15.95 (*0-06-024265-5*) HarpC Child Bks.

Little Bear's Visit. Else H. Minarik. LC 61-11451. (I Can Read Bks.). (Illus.). 64p. (J). (ps-3). 1979. pap. 3.95 (*0-06-444023-0*, HarpTrophy) HarpC Child Bks.

Little Bear's Visit. Else H. Minarik. (I Can Read Bks.). (Illus.). 64p. (J). (ps-1). 1985. 5.98 incl. audio (*0-694-00032-9*, JC-023, HarpTrophy) HarpC Child Bks.

Little Bear's Visit. Else H. Minarik. (I Can Read Bks.). (J). (ps-1). 1971. 8.95 (*0-606-02159-0*, Pub. by Turtleback) Demco.

Little Bear's Visit. unabridged ed. Else H. Minarik. LC 61-11451. (I Can Read Bks.). (Illus.). 64p. (J). (ps-3). 1990. pap. 8.95 incl. audio (*1-55994-236-3*) HarperAudio.

Little Beaver & the Echo. Amy MacDonald. (CHI & ENG., Illus.). 32p. (J). (ps-2). 1997. write for info. (*1-85430-507-7*, Pub. by MAGI1 UK); write for info. (*1-85430-509-3*, Pub. by MAGI1 UK); write for info. (*1-85430-511-5*, Pub. by MAGI1 UK) Midpt Trade.

Little Beaver & the Echo. Amy MacDonald. (Illus.). 32p. (J). (ps-3). 1990. 15.95 (*0-399-22203-0*, G P Putnam) Peng Put Young Read.

Little Beaver & the Echo. Amy MacDonald. (Illus.). 32p. (J). (ps-3). 1998. pap. 6.99 (*0-698-11628-3*, PapStar) Peng Put Young Read.

Little Beep. Robert Kraus. (Stickers 'n' Shapes Ser.: No. 1). (Illus.). 24p. (J). (ps-2). 1997. mass mkt. 3.99 (*0-689-81103-9*) S&S Childrens.

Little Beep. Robert Kraus. (Stickers 'n' Shapes Ser.: No. 2). (Illus.). 24p. (J). (ps-2). 1997. mass mkt. 3.99 (*0-689-81104-7*) S&S Childrens.

Little Better Than Plumb: The Biography of a House. Mem. of Henry Giles & Janice H. Giles. (Illus.). 280p. 1995. 30.00 (*0-8131-1897-2*); pap. 17.00 (*0-8131-0833-0*) U Pr of Ky.

Little Betty Blue. Le Rap. (Nursery Rhymes Ser.). 15p. (J). (gr. k-2). 1991. pap. text 23.00 (*1-56843-042-6*); pap. text 4.50 (*1-56843-089-2*) EMG Networks.

Little Bible Treasury: Daniel in the Lions' Den; David & Goliath; Jonah & the Whale; Noah's Ark; Joseph's Coat of Many Colors; Prayers & Poems, Set. (Illus.). 24p. (J). 1993. boxed set 9.98 (*0-7853-0236-0*) Pubns Intl Ltd.

Little Big Book (Alcoholics Anonymous) Alcoholics Anonymous World Services, Inc. Staff. 164p. 1993. 4.00 (*0-916856-59-3*) AAWS.

***Little Big Book for Moms.** Ed. by Lena Tabori & Alice Wong. (Illus.). 352p. 2000. 24.95 (*0-941807-41-X*) Stewart Tabori & Chang.

***Little Big Book of Christmas.** Lena Tabori. LC 99-30364. (Illus.). 352p. 1999. 24.95 (*0-688-17414-0*, Wm Morrow) Morrow Avon.

***Little Big Book of Love.** Lena Tabori. LC 99-44175. (Illus.). 352p. 2000. 24.95 (*0-688-17415-9*, Wm Morrow) Morrow Avon.

"Little" BIG Book of Prayer for Families to Share: 310 Rhyming Prayers for Practically Every Holiday, Occasion, Person, & Emotion You Can Think Of. Jay. LC 97-19819. 80p. 1998. vinyl bd. 5.00 (*1-886197-27-X*) Joy Books.

Little Big Ears. Cynthia Moss. LC 96-7404. (Illus.). 40p. (J). (gr. k-5). 1996. per. 17.00 (*0-689-80031-2*) S&S Bks Yung.

Little Big Girl. Althea J. Horner. (Illus.). 32p. (J). (ps-3). 1982. pap. 10.95 (*0-89885-287-0*, Kluwer Acad Hman Sci) Kluwer Academic.

Little Big Horn. Robert Nightengale. LC 96-230437. (Illus.). 318p. (Orig.). 1996. 35.00 (*0-9652889-0-0*) Far West Publng.

Little Big Horn: A Second Battle. James B. Sammons. Ed. by Hilaire R. Kallendorf. LC 94-92119. (Illus.). 275p. (Orig.). pap. 12.95 (*0-9646373-9-1*) J B Sammons.

Little Big Horn: A Second Battle. James B. Sammons. Ed. by Hilaire R. Kallendorf. LC 94-92119. (Illus.). 275p. (Orig.). (C). 18.95 (*0-9646373-4-0*) J B Sammons.

Little Big Horn Battlefield Montana Territory, 1876. Earl B. McElfresh. (American Battlefields Watercolor Map Ser.). (Illus.). 1996. 9.95 (*1-885294-09-3*) McElfresh Map.

Little Big Horn Diary: Chronicle of the 1876 Indian War. 2nd ed. James Willert. LC 82-51072. (Illus.). 520p. 1982. 60.00 (*0-930798-05-8*) J Willert.

Little Big Horn Diary: Chronicle of the 1876 Indian War, May 17-June 28, 1876. James Willert. LC 77-81807. (Custer Trails Ser.: Vol. 6). (Illus.). 480p. 1997. 125.00 (*0-912783-27-3*) Upton & Sons.

Little Big Horn, 1876. Peter Panzieri. (Campaign Ser.). (Illus.). 96p. 1995. pap. 14.95 (*1-85532-458-X*, 9535, Pub. by Ospry) Stackpole.

Little Big Man. Thomas Berger. 30.95 (*0-8488-0429-5*) Amereon Ltd.

Little Big Man. Thomas Berger. 480p. 1989. pap. 13.95 (*0-385-29829-3*, Delta Trade) Dell.

Little Big Men: Bodybuilding Subculture & Gender Construction. Alan M. Klein. LC 92-30816. (SUNY Series on Sport, Culture, & Social Relations). 326p. (C). 1993. pap. text 19.95 (*0-7914-1560-0*) State U NY Pr.

Little Big Men: Bodybuilding Subculture & Gender Construction. Alan M. Klein. LC 92-30816. (SUNY Series on Sport, Culture, & Social Relations). 326p. (C). 1993. text 49.50 (*0-7914-1559-7*) State U NY Pr.

Little Big Mouse. Nurit Karlin. LC 90-36192. (Illus.). 32p. (J). (ps-1). 1991. 13.95 (*0-06-021607-7*) HarpC Child Bks.

Little Big Wolf. Carlton T. Scott. (Illus.). 32p. (J). (gr. k-5). 1999. 9.95 (*0-9636652-8-6*) Ends of the Earth.

Little Bighorn. Randy Krehbiel. LC 97-29420. (Battlefields Across America Ser.). 64p. (YA). (gr. 5 up). 1997. 23.40 (*0-8050-5236-4*) TFC Bks NY.

Little Bighorn. Philip Steele. LC 91-24065. (Great Battles & Sieges Ser.). (Illus.). 32p. (J). (gr. 6 up). 1992. text 21.00 (*0-02-786885-0*, Mac Bks Young Read) S&S Childrens.

***Little Bighorn Battlefield.** Jason Cooper. LC 00-38727. (Historic Landmarks Ser.). (Illus.). (J). 2000. write for info. (*1-55916-325-9*) Rourke Bk Co.

Little Bighorn Battlefield. Robert Marshall Utley. LC 86-600325. (Official National Park Handbook Ser.: No. 132). (Illus.). 112p. 1988. pap. 5.50 (*0-912627-34-4*) Natl Park Serv.

Little Bighorn Battlefield National Monument. Mark Gardner. LC 96-6887. (Illus.). 16p. 1996. pap. 3.95 (*1-877856-61-4*) SW Pks Mnmts.

***Little Bighorn Campaign: March-September, 1876.** Wayne M. Sarf. 1999. pap. 18.95 (*1-58097-025-7*, 970257) Combined Pub.

***Little Bighorn Remembered: The Untold Indian Story of Custer's Last Stand.** Herman J. Viola. LC 99-19919. (Illus.). 224p. 1999. 45.00 (*0-8129-3256-0*, Times Bks) Crown Pub Group.

***Little Bill's Punch-Out Valentines.** Bill Cosby. (Illus.). 16p. (ps-3). 1999. pap. text 2.99 (*0-439-05204-1*) Scholastic Inc.

Little Billy. Carolyn S. Baber. (Illus.). 200p. (J). (gr. 5-9). 1995. lib. bdg. 14.95 (*0-944727-29-8*) Jason & Nordic Pubs.

***Little Bird.** Rod Campbell. (Illus.). 20p. (J). (ps-k). 2000. 10.99 (*1-85292-234-6*) Campbell Bks Ltd.

***Little Bird.** Rod Campbell. (J). 2000. pap. 4.99 (*0-333-63340-7*) Mcm Child Bks.

Little Bird. Cullinan. 1994. text 13.90 (*0-15-302283-3*) Harcourt.

Little Bird. Mary Gallagher. 1984. pap. 5.25 (*0-8222-0672-2*) Dramatists Play.

Little Bird. Barbara Sobel. LC 86-81462. (January Bks.). (Illus.). 32p. (J). (gr. k-2). 1986. pap. 2.95 (*0-87386-014-4*) Jan Prods.

Little Bird. large type ed. Marie Hoover et al. (Illus.). 8p. (J). (gr. k-3). 1999. pap. text 6.00 (*1-58084-163-5*) Lower Kuskokwim.

Little Bird. unabridged ed. Barbara Sobel. LC 86-81462. (Friends & Neighbors Ser.). (Illus.). 32p. (J). (gr. k-2). 1986. lib. bdg. 16.99 incl. audio (*0-87386-018-7*) Jan Prods.

Little Bird & Moon Sandwich. Illus. by Linda Berkowitz. LC 97-24270. 32p. (J). 1998. lib. bdg. 17.99 (*0-517-70962-7*, Pub. by Crown Bks Yng Read) Random.

Little Bird & the Moon Sandwich. Illus. by Linda Berkowitz. LC 97-24270. 32p. (J). 1998. 16.00 (*0-517-70961-9*, Pub. by Crown Bks Yng Read) Random.

Little Bird Told Me So: Birds in Mythology & History. Eleanor H. Stickney. (Illus.). 240p. 1997. pap. 14.95 (*1-887750-67-3*) Rutledge Bks.

Little Birds. Anais Nin. 176p. 1990. per. 5.99 (*0-671-68011-0*) PB.

Little Bird's House see Casita del Pajarito

Little Bird's House. Donna L. Pape. (Whole-Language Big Bks.). (Illus.). 16p. (Orig.). (J). (ps-2). 1994. pap. 16.95 (*1-56784-072-8*) Newbridge Educ.

Little Bit: The Sound of "Short L" Peg Ballard & Cynthia F. Klingel. LC 99-25499. (Wonder Books Ser.). (Illus.). 24p. (J). 1999. lib. bdg. 21.41 (*1-56766-698-1*) Childs World.

Little Bit Dead. Chap Reaver. LC 92-7185. 240p. (YA). (gr. 6 up). 1992. 15.00 (*0-385-30801-9*) Delacorte.

Little Bit Dead. Chap Reaver. LC 92-7185. 1992. 9.09 (*0-606-06534-2*, Pub. by Turtleback) Demco.

Little Bit Dead. large type ed. Chap Reaver. LC 93-42210. (J). 1994. lib. bdg. 15.95 (*0-7862-0139-8*) Thorndike Pr.

***Little Bit for Every Holiday.** Vickey Higley. (Illus.). 60p. 2000. pap. 10.50 (*1-56770-477-8*) S Scheewe Pubns.

Little Bit India, Little Bit U. S. A. Soma Vira. 118p. 1981. 9.95 (*0-318-36910-9*) Asia Bk Corp.

Little Bit India, Little Bit U. S. A. Living in Two Worlds--From India to the U. S. A. rev. ed. Soma Vira. LC 96-71651. 118p. 1997. pap. 12.95 (*0-9646057-7-5*) Space Link Bks.

Little Bit Know Something: Stories in a Language of Anthropology. Robin Ridington. LC 89-48164. (Illus.). 299p. (C). 1990. pap. text 13.95 (*0-87745-286-5*) U of Iowa Pr.

***Little Bit of Anarchy.** R. Christopherson. 184p. 2000. mass mkt. 9.95 (*0-914597-02-7*) Pubs West AZ.

Little Bit of Everything Good. Ed. by Ideal Instructional Fair Staff. 1999. pap. 16.95 (*1-56822-877-5*); pap. 16.95 (*1-56822-878-3*); pap. 16.95 (*1-56822-879-1*); pap. 16.95 (*1-56822-880-5*); pap. 16.95 (*1-56822-881-3*) Instruct Fair.

Little Bit of Everything Good. Watts & Gary Null. 1978. pap. 7.75 (*0-89137-619-4*) Quality Pubns.

Little Bit of Everything-Grade 5. Ed. by Ideal Instructional Fair Staff. 1999. pap. 16.95 (*1-56822-882-1*) Instruct Fair.

Little Bit of Everything-Grade 6. Ed. by Ideal Instructional Fair Staff. (J). 1999. pap. 16.95 (*1-56822-883-X*) Instruct Fair.

Little Bit of God's Wisdom & Wit. 1994. pap. text 5.99 (*0-932081-42-8*) Victory Hse.

Little Bit of God's Wisdom & Wit for Men. 1994. pap. text 5.99 (*0-932081-43-6*) Victory Hse.

Little Bit of Gods Women. Victory House Staff. Date not set. pap. text 5.99 (*0-932081-44-4*) Victory Hse.

Little Bit of History Series Bk. 1: Tribute to G. C. Dude Calvert, Mr. Michigan City. G. C. Calvert. 40p. 1987. 2.00 (*0-935549-10-2*) MI City Hist.

Little Bit of Love: Ada & Ida Stoltzfus in India, Three Years of Relief Work. Marie E. Cutman. (Illus.). xiii, 199p. 1994. 14.95 (*0-9672285-0-6*); pap. 9.95 (*0-9672285-1-4*) MecPublishing.

Little Bit of Rob. Barbara J. Turner. (Illus.). 32p. (J). (gr. 2-5). 1996. lib. bdg. 14.95 (*0-8075-4577-5*) A Whitman.

Little Bit of Thunder: The Strange Inner World of the Kingston Whig-Standard. Douglas Fetherling. 336p. 1993. 24.95 (*0-7737-2706-X*) Genl Dist Srvs.

Little Bit of Winter. Paul Stewart. LC 98-73585. (Illus.). 32p. (J). (ps-2). 1999. 12.95 (*0-06-028278-9*) HarpC Child Bks.

***Little Bit of Winter.** Paul Stewart. 32p. (J). 2000. pap. 5.95 (*0-06-443749-3*, HarpTrophy) HarpC Child Bks.

Little Bit of Wisdom: Conversations with a Nez Perce Elder. Horace Axtell & Margo Aragon. LC 96-85612. 1997. 25.00 (*1-881090-23-X*) Confluence Pr.

***Little Bit of Wisdom: Conversations with a Nez Perce Elder.** Horace Axtell & Margo Aragon. (Illus.). 232p. 2000. pap. 11.95 (*0-8061-3269-8*) U of Okla Pr.

Little Bit Pregnant. Charlotte Maclay. (American Romance Ser.). 1998. per. 3.99 (*0-373-16728-8*, 1-16728-7) Harlequin Bks.

Little Bit Scary. Gill Davies. (Illus.). 48p. (J). (gr. k-4). 1997. 9.00 (*1-85854-527-7*) Brimax Bks.

Little Bit Sideways: One Week Inside Nascar Winston Cup Race Team. Scott Huler. LC 98-46892. 256p. 1999. pap. 14.95 (*0-7603-0455-6*) Motorbooks Intl.

Little Bit(e) of Dried Tomatoes. Karen Q. Cox. (Illus.). 13p. (Orig.). 1991. pap. text 3.00 (*1-886501-01-7*) Tomato Press.

Little Bits: A Special Gift for a Special Mom. Sheila Huffman Dailey. 104p. (Orig.). 1994. pap. 6.95 (*0-9651392-4-7*); pap. text 5.00 (*0-9651392-2-0*) SHD Enter.

Little Bits: A Special Gift for a Special Mom, Master Sheets Set. Sheila Huffman Dailey. (Little Bits Ser.: No. 1). (Illus.). 104p. (Orig.). 1994. pap. 90.00 (*0-9651392-0-4*) SHD Enter.

Little Bits: The Humorous Comments of Jo, Flo, Oxy, Ron & Mo. rev. ed. Curtis Williams. (Illus.). 1997. write for info. (*1-878382-15-2*) Book Gallery.

Little Bits: Un Regalo Especial Para una Mama Especial. Sheila Huffman Dailey. 104p. (Orig.). 1995. pap. 6.95 (*0-9651392-5-5*); pap. text 5.00 (*0-9651392-3-9*) SHD Enter.

Little Bits: Un Regalo Especial Para una Mama Especial, Master Sheets Set. Sheila Huffman Dailey. (Little Bits Ser.: No. 2). (SPA., Illus.). 104p. (Orig.). 1995. pap. 90.00 (*0-9651392-1-2*) SHD Enter.

Little Bits about . . . America Online3 for Macintosh. Paul Rego. (Little Bits Ser.). (Illus.). 209p. 1996. spiral bd. 19.95 (*0-945876-11-4*) Insight Data.

Little Bits about . . . How to Buy a Computer. Paul Rego. Ed. by Sylvia Rego. (Little Bits Ser.). (Illus.). 131p. 1996. spiral bd. 9.95 (*0-945876-09-2*) Insight Data.

Little Bits about . . . Macintosh Resources. Paul Rego. (Little Bits Ser.). 48p. 1996. spiral bd. 2.95 (*0-945876-10-6*) Insight Data.

Little Bits of Whimsy: A Pattern Book. Kathleen R. Brooks. Ed. by Debra Feece. LC 97-22066. (Illus.). 32p. (Orig.). 1997. pap. 12.95 (*1-885588-15-1*) Chitra Pubns.

Little Bits of Wisdom: Tips for Surviving Teenage Years. Abby Shields. Ed. by Yvette B. McCann. LC 96-83444. (Illus.). 112p. (J). (gr. 5-12). 1996. pap. 10.00 (*0-9649914-3-8*) ASC Pubng.

***Little Bits of Wisdom English: Special Book for Special Mom.** (Illus.). 86p. 2000. 6.95 (*1-931023-00-X*) SHD Enter.

***Little Bits of Wisdom Spanish: Special Book for a Special Mom.** (Illus.). 86p. 2000. 6.95 (*1-931023-01-8*) SHD Enter.

Little Bitties, 6 vols. (J). (ps). 1991. boxed set 18.00 (*0-8120-7843-8*) Barron.

Little Bitties ABC. Tessa Krailing. (Little Bitty Ser.). (Illus.). 20p. (J). (ps-k). 1991. bds. 3.50 (*0-8120-6266-3*) Barron.

Little Bitty Bunny. Demi. LC 90-85828. (Mini Soft & Furry Board Bks.). (Illus.). 12p. (J). (ps-3). 1992. bds. 4.95 (*0-448-41089-3*, G & D) Peng Put Young Read.

Little Bitty Snake. Jorma Rodieck. Tr. by Yumiko M. Burnett. LC 82-60393.Tr. of Le Tout P'tit Serpent. (ENG & JPN., Illus.). 24p. (J). (ps-4). 1983. pap. 4.95 (*0-940880-07-5*) Open Hand.

Little Bitty Snake. Jorma Rodieck. Tr. by Moyra Confreras. LC 82-60393.Tr. of Le Tout P'tit Serpent. (ENG & SPA., Illus.). 24p. (J). (ps-4). 1983. pap. 4.95 (*0-940880-03-2*) Open Hand.

Little Bitty Snake. Jorma Rodieck. Tr. by Michele Presse. LC 82-60393.Tr. of Le Tout P'tit Serpent. (ENG & FRE., Illus.). 24p. (J). (ps-4). 1983. pap. 4.95 (*0-940880-05-9*) Open Hand.

***Little Bitz.** Queen Bee. 64p. 2000. pap. 10.00 (*0-9679509-0-2*) Aura Pubng MA.

Little Black & White Book of Film Noir. Peggy Thompson. 1993. per. 4.95 (*0-88978-257-1*, Pub. by Arsenal Pulp) LPC InBook.

***Little Black Book.** Hank H. Hanegraaff. 175p. 2000. 14.99 (*0-8499-1666-6*) Word Pub.

Little Black Book. Eldon Taylor. 1987. lthr. 2.00 (*0-916095-17-7*) R K Bks.

Little Black Book of Budgets & Forecasts. Michael C. Thomsett. 176p. 1988. pap. 14.95 (*0-8144-7692-9*) AMACOM.

Little Black Book of Business Etiquette. Michael C. Thomsett. 200p. 1991. pap. 14.95 (*0-8144-7754-2*, 040551) AMACOM.

Little Black Book of Business Letters. Michael C. Thomsett. LC 88-47710. 160p. 1988. pap. 14.95 (*0-8144-7694-5*) AMACOM.

Little Black Book of Business Meetings. Michael C. Thomsett. LC 89-45458. 192p. 1989. pap. 14.95 (*0-8144-7716-X*) AMACOM.

Little Black Book of Business Reports. Michael Thomsett. LC 88-47712. 176p. 1988. pap. 14.95 (*0-8144-7693-7*) AMACOM.

Little Black Book of Business Statistics. Michael C. Thomsett. LC 90-55214. (Little Black Book Ser.). 200p. (Orig.). 1990. pap. 14.95 (*0-8144-7731-3*) AMACOM.

***Little Black Book of Dermatology.** Stanford I. Lamberg. (Little Black Book Ser.). (Illus.). 300p. 2000. pap. 39.95 (*0-632-04519-1*) Blackwell Sci.

Little Black Book of Geriatrics. Karen Gershman & Dennis M. McCollough. LC 97-37996. (Illus.). 1997. pap. 35.95 (*0-632-04328-8*) Blackwell Sci.

Little Black Book of Home Care Cues. Ed. by Minnie B. Rose. LC 96-31652. (Illus.). 144p. (Orig.). 1996. ring bd. 21.95 (*0-87434-880-3*) Springhouse Corp.

Little Black Book of More Dating Ideas. John Graham & Stuart Ough. Ed. by Buzz Boxx Staff. LC 96-86659. 144p. (Orig.). 1997. pap. 7.95 (*1-885174-03-9*) Andrews & McMeel.

Little Black Book of Neurology: A Manual for Neurological House Officers. 3rd ed. Ed. by Alan J. Lerner. LC 94-22738. (Illus.). 456p. (C). (gr. 13). 1994. pap. text 37.95 (*0-8151-5440-2*, 24022) Mosby Inc.

Little Black Book of Primary Care: Pearls & References. 2nd ed. Daniel K. Onion. 600p. (C). 1995. pap. write for info. (*0-393-71024-6*) Norton.

Little Black Book of Primary Care: Pearls & References. 3rd ed. Daniel K. Onion. LC 98-17781. 700p. 1996. spiral bd. 34.95 (*0-86542-489-6*) Blackwell Sci.

Little Black Book of Primary Care: Pearls & References. 3rd ed. Daniel K. Onion. LC 98-17781. (Little Black Book Ser.). (Illus.). 923p. 1998. pap. 39.95 (*0-632-04345-8*) Blackwell Sci.

Little Black Book of Project Management. Michael C. Thomsett. LC 90-55215. (Little Black Book Ser.). 200p. (Orig.). 1990. pap. 14.95 (*0-8144-7732-1*) AMACOM.

***Little Black Book of Psychiatry.** David P. Moore. LC 99-24497. (Little Black Book Ser.). 1999. pap. 32.95 (*0-86542-562-0*) Blackwell Sci.

Little Black Book of Visual Effects. Ed. by Bernice Kenton-Briggs et al. LC 98-91541. (Illus.). 280p. 1998. pap. 38.00 (*0-9665351-0-3*) PnnyLn Animatn.

Little Black Book on Whitewater. Brian Wilson. 220p. (Orig.). 1996. pap. 12.95 (*0-9651948-7-6*) Myrmidon MD.

Little Black Book Windows 1.0. Education Research Staff. 1995. 69.95 (*0-393-71027-0*) Norton.

Little Black CookBook. Pat Neaves. (Illus.). 140p. 1992. spiral bd. 9.95 (*1-879806-01-0*) From My Heart.

Little Black Dog see Collected Works of Robert Herrick

Little Black Dog. Robert Herrick. (Collected Works of Robert Herrick). 1988. reprint ed. lib. bdg. 59.00 (*0-7812-1282-0*) Rprt Serv.

Little Black Dog Buccaneer. J. B. Spooner. LC 98-21595. (Illus.). 32p. (J). 1998. 15.95 (*1-55970-448-9*, Pub. by Arcade Pub Inc) Time Warner.

Little Black Dress. Amy H. Edelman. LC 97-24635. (Illus.). 160p. 1997. 29.50 (*0-684-82232-6*, S&S Edns) Simon & Schuster.

Little Black Fish: Mahi Siah Kuchulu. Samad Behrangi. Tr. by Hooshang Amuzegar. LC 96-36970. (Classics of Persian Literature Ser.: Vol. 2). (Illus.). 64p. (Orig.). (J). 1997. pap. 8.50 (*0-936347-78-3*) IBEX.

Little Black Fish & Other Modern Persian Stories. 2nd ed. Samad Behrangi. Tr. by Mary Hegland & Eric Hooglund from PER. LC 87-26680. 106p. 1987. reprint ed. pap. 10.00 (*0-89410-621-X*, Three Contnts) L Rienner.

Little Black Leather Book of Rock'n'Roll. Ed. by Divine Laboratories. 96p. 1994. per. 4.95 (*1-55152-003-6*, Pub. by Arsenal Pulp) LPC InBook.

Little Black Sambo Story Book. Helen Bannerman. 64p. 1983. reprint ed. lib. bdg. 25.95 (*0-89966-298-6*) Buccaneer Bks.

Little Black Sheep. Elizabeth Shaw. (Illus.). 64p. 1997. pap. 6.95 (*0-86278-463-8*, Pub. by OBrien Pr) Irish Amer Bk.

Little Black Truck. Gray. LC 92-24413. (Illus.). 32p. (J). (ps-3). 1998. per. 5.99 (*0-689-82135-2*) S&S Childrens.

Little Black Truck. Libba M. Gray. LC 92-24413. (Illus.). 40p. (J). (ps-1). 1994. 15.00 (*0-671-78105-7*) S&S Bks Yung.

***Little Black Working Guide: Cutting Pain & Other Symptoms.** Mary Anne V. Simpson. 96p. 1999. 39.95 (*1-890622-75-3*) Leathers Pub.

Little Blaine Creek is Rising: Memories from Kentucky. Everett J. Ball. 242p. 1991. 35.00 (*0-9628918-0-0*) J R Ball.

Little Blank Book. Betty Sprague. (Illus.). 64p. 1982. pap. 5.95 (*0-942494-24-5*) Coleman Pub.

Little Blaze & the Buffalo Jump. Peter Roop. (Indian Culture Ser.). (Illus.). 28p. (Orig.). (J). (gr. 3-8). 1984. pap. 4.95 (*0-89992-089-6*) Coun India Ed.

Little Blessings: A Child's First Book of Riddles. Sally A. Conan. (Illus.). 32p. (J). (ps-1). 1996. pap. 6.95 (*0-8091-6632-1*, 6632-1) Paulist Pr.

***Little Blessings New Testament & Psalms.** Little Blessings Staff. (Little Blessings Ser.). 2000. 14.99 (*0-8423-3517-X*) Tyndale Hse.

Little Blue & Little Yellow. Leo Lionni. (Illus.). (J). (gr. k-1). 1959. 14.95 (*0-8392-3018-4*) Astor-Honor.

Little Blue & Little Yellow. Leo Lionni. (J). 1995. 10.15 (*0-606-07792-8*, Pub. by Turtleback) Demco.

Little Blue & Little Yellow. Leo Lionni. LC 94-7324. (Illus.). 48p. (J). (ps-3). 1995. reprint ed. mass mkt. 5.95 (*0-688-13285-5*, Wm Morrow) Morrow Avon.

***Little Blue Book: Pocket Guide to Selected Health & Social Services.** Ed. by Carol Southern. 108p. 1999. pap. 11.90 (*0-925133-65-5*) Volt Directory.

Little Blue Book of Fitness & Health. Gary Savage et al. LC 98-8452. 160p. 1998. pap. 6.95 (*1-55853-674-4*) Rutledge Hill Pr.

Little Blue Book of UFOs. Colombo. 96p. 1995. per. 4.95 (*0-88978-256-3*, Pub. by Arsenal Pulp) LPC InBook.

Little Blue Book on Power. John T. Wood. (Orig.). 1990. pap. 9.95 (*1-878964-01-1*) Zen N Ink Pubs.

Little Blue Books: Orginal Anthology. Ed. by David White. LC 74-15744. (Popular Culture in America Ser.). 576p. 1975. reprint ed. 46.95 (*0-405-06379-2*) Ayer.

Little Blue Day Care. Bonnie Worth. (Illus.). 16p. (J). (ps-k). 1996. bds. 4.99 (*0-689-80427-X*) Litle Simon.

Little Blue Hen. large type ed. Phoebe Gilman. (J). (ps-2). 1989. 19.95 (*0-590-73273-0*) Scholastic Inc.

Little Blue School: The Story of a School & Ranching Community in Early-Day Wyoming. 2nd ed. Frances S. Husdale et al. (Illus.). 96p. 1993. pap. 12.50 (*0-9639489-0-3*) Tongue River.

***Little Blue Star Christmas Cantata.** Ray Leland Caley. 37p. 1999. pap. text 14.95 (*0-910987-13-0*) Dragons Lair.

Little Blues Book. Brian Robertson. LC 96-19571. (Illus.). 160p. 1996. pap. 9.95 (*1-56512-137-6*) Algonquin Bks.

***Little Bo: The Story of Bonnie Boadicea.** Julie Andrews. 96p. (J). 1999. 16.99 (*0-7868-0598-6*) Little.

Little Bo: The Story of Bonnie Boadicea. Julie Andrews Edwards. LC 99-24797. (Illus.). 96p. (gr. 3-7). 1999. 17.49 (*0-7868-2449-2*, Pub. by Hyprn Child) Little.

***Little Bo: The Story of Bonnie Boadicea.** Julie Andrews Edwards. LC 99-24797. (Illus.). 88p. (J). (gr. 3-7). 1999. 16.99 (*0-7868-0514-5*, Pub. by Hyprn Child) Time Warner.

***Little Bo Gift Set.** Julie Andrews Edwards. (Illus.). (J). 2000. 29.99 (*0-7868-0677-X*, Pub. by Hyprn Child) Time Warner.

Little Bo-Peep, Incl. 2 puppets. Illus. by Rebecca Archer. LC 97-71902. (Hand Puppet Bks.). 16p. (J). (ps). 1998. 12.95 (*0-448-41742-1*, G & D) Peng Put Young Read.

Little Bo-Peep: Mother Goose. Illus. by Carl Morton. (J). (gr. k-1). 1992. 7.50 (*1-57842-097-0*) Delmas Creat.

Little Bo-Peep & Other Favorite Nursery Rhymes. Illus. by Kay Widdowson. (Nursery Rhyme Fun Ser.). 12p. (J). 1995. boxed set 6.95 (*1-884628-23-0*, Flyng Frog) Allied Pub MD.

Little Bo Peep's Library Book. Cressida Cowell. LC 98-42424. (Illus.). 32p. (J). (ps-2). 1999. 14.95 (*0-531-30179-6*) Orchard Bks Watts.

***Little Bo Sequel.** Julie Andrews Edwards. 96p. (J). 2001. 19.99 (*0-7868-0658-3*, Pub. by Hyperion) Time Warner.

***Little Boat.** Opal Dunn. (Track-Me-Back Board Bks.). 12p. (J). 2000. bds. 5.95 (*0-8050-6416-8*) H Holt & Co.

Little Boat. Kathy Henderson. LC 94-41789. (Illus.). 32p. (J). (ps-3). 1995. 15.95 (*1-56402-420-2*) Candlewick Pr.

Little Boat. Kathy Henderson. LC 94-41789. (Illus.). 32p. (J). (ps-3). 1998. pap. 5.99 (*0-7636-0370-8*) Candlewick Pr.

Little Boat. Kathy Henderson. (J). 1998. 11.19 (*0-606-13573-1*, Pub. by Turtleback) Demco.

Little Boat. Sian Tucker. (Illus.). 10p. (J). (ps). 1993. pap. 2.95 (*0-671-79736-0*) Litle Simon.

Little Boat That Almost Sank: Matthew 14:22-23, Mark 6:45-51. Mary P. Warren & Rada Warren. LC 64-23371. (Arch Bks.). 24p. 1970. pap. 1.99 (*0-570-06010-9*, 59-1111) Concordia.

Little Boats & Big Salmon: Fishing Adventures in Alaska. Erv Jensen. LC 98-90980. (Illus.). 208p. 1999. pap. 11.95 (*0-9668753-0-3*) Three Trees.

Little Bobo. Serena Romanelli. LC 95-20321. (Illus.). 32p. (J). (gr. k-3). 1995. 15.95 (*1-55858-490-0*, Pub. by North-South Bks NYC) Chronicle Bks.

Little Bobo. Serena Romanelli. LC 95-20321. (Illus.). 32p. (J). (gr. k-3). 1999. pap. 6.95 (*0-7358-1097-4*, Pub. by North-South Bks NYC) Chronicle Bks.

Little Bobo Saves the Day see Kleiner Dodo, Lass den Drachen Fliegen!

Little Bobo Saves the Day see Gogo e l'Aquilone Bianco

Little Bodice Construction Book: A Workbook on Period Bodices. Bonnie A. Ambrose. LC 98-114660. (Illus.). 56p. (Orig.). 1995. pap. 7.95 (*0-89676-131-2*, Costume & Fashion Pr) QSMG Ltd.

***Little Boo!** Colin McNaughton. (Illus.). 14p. (J). (ps-k). 2000. 5.95 (*0-15-202671-1*, Harcourt Child Bks) Harcourt.

Little Book: Key to the Bible & Heaven. Ludwig B. Larsen. 280p. 1996. reprint ed. spiral bd. 18.50 (*0-7873-0535-9*) Hlth Research.

Little Book about Baby. Compiled by Gladys Pucillo. 1981. 6.95 (*0-8378-1932-6*) Gibson.

***Little Book for a Friend.** Ed. by Helen Exley. (Minute Mini Ser.). (Illus.). 96p. 1999. 6.50 (*1-86187-132-5*) Exley Giftbooks.

Little Book for a Little Cook. Pillsbury Company Staff. 32p. (J). 1992. 14.95 (*1-55709-172-2*) Applewood.

Little Book for Christmas. Cyrus T. Brady. LC 73-167443. (Short Story Index Reprint Ser.). (Illus.). 1977. reprint ed. 19.95 (*0-8369-3969-7*) Ayer.

Little Book for Lovers. Dana Goodwin. 1996. pap. 11.95 (*1-85230-784-6*, Pub. by Element MA) Penguin Putnam.

Little Book for Mother. Exley Gift Books Staff. 1999. 6.50 (*1-86187-118-X*) Exley Giftbooks.

***Little Book for My Grandma.** Ed. by Helen Exley & Juliette Clarke. (Minute Mini Ser.). (Illus.). 96p. 1999. 6.50 (*1-86187-130-9*) Exley Giftbooks.

Little Book for Preachers: 101 Ideas for Better Sermons. James E. Miller. 112p. 1996. pap. 6.99 (*0-8066-2991-6*, 9-2991, Augsburg) Augsburg Fortress.

Little Book for Small Churches That Want to Grow. Baxter Hood. 88p. 1991. pap. 7.99 (*0-8341-1398-8*) Beacon Hill.

Little Book of a Thousand Eyes. limited ed. Lyn Hejinian. 44p. (Orig.). 1996. 110.00 (*1-887289-99-2*); pap. 40.00 (*1-887289-98-4*) Rodent Pr.

Little Book of Acid. Cam Cloud. LC 99-219950. (Illus.). 128p. 1999. pap. 12.95 (*0-914171-88-7*) Ronin Pub.

***Little Book of Altar Magic.** D. J. Conway. (Little Book Ser.). (Illus.). 2000. pap. 9.95 (*1-58091-052-1*) Crossing Pr.

Little Book of American Humorous Verse. Ed. by T. A. Daly. LC 73-38597. (Granger Index Reprint Ser.). 1977. reprint ed. 18.95 (*0-8369-6329-6*) Ayer.

Little Book of American Poets, 1787-1900. Ed. by Jessie B. Rittenhouse. LC 74-149110. (Granger Index Reprint Ser.). 1977. 29.95 (*0-8369-6235-4*) Ayer.

Little Book of Angel Wisdom. Peter Wilson. (Little Bks.). 48p. 1997. pap. 5.95 (*1-86204-048-6*, Pub. by Element MA) Penguin Putnam.

Little Book of Angels. Ariel Books Staff. (Illus.). 16p. 1995. pap. 4.95 (*0-8362-0365-8*, Arie Bks) Andrews & McMeel.

Little Book of Angels. Peter L. Wilson. (Little Bks.). (Illus.). 48p. 1993. pap. 5.95 (*1-85230-436-7*, Pub. by Element MA) Penguin Putnam.

Little Book of Angels: Delightful Inspirations & Magical Guidance. Dezra-Lehr Guthrie. 380p. 1997. pap. 6.95 (*1-881542-41-6*) Blue Star Prodns.

Little Book of Arthurian Wisdom. J. Matthews. 48p. 1994. pap. 5.95 (*1-85230-565-7*, Pub. by Element MA) Penguin Putnam.

Little Book of Awkward Questions. Igor S. Popovich. 160p. 1995. pap. 5.95 (*0-86417-670-8*, Pub. by Kangaroo Pr) Seven Hills Bk.

Little Book of Baby Animals. Zokeisha. Ed. by Kate Klimo. (Chubby Board Bks.). (Illus.). 16p. (J). 1982. pap. 2.95 (*0-671-44840-4*) Litle Simon.

Little Book of Bad Business Advice. Steve Altes. LC 97-170092. 1997. mass mkt. 6.99 (*0-312-96223-1*) St Martin.

Little Book of Baking. Josephine Bacon. 1994. 4.98 (*1-55521-979-9*) Bk Sales Inc.

Little Book of Barbecues. Jillian Stewart. 1994. 4.98 (*0-7858-0141-3*) Bk Sales Inc.

Little Book of Bear Care. Pauline Cockrill. LC 92-53230. (Little Bear Library). (Illus.). 48p. 1992. 8.95 (*1-56458-081-4*) DK Pub Inc.

Little Book of Bible. John Baldock. (Little Bks.). (Illus.). 48p. 1993. pap. 5.95 (*1-85230-447-2*, Pub. by Element MA) Penguin Putnam.

***Little Book of Big Ideas.** Harold R. McAlindon. LC 99-44288. 256p. 1999. pap. 10.95 (*1-58182-054-2*, Cumberland Hearthside) Cumberland Hse.

Little Book of Big Motivation: One Hundred Eighty Simple Ways to Overcome Obstacles & Realize Your Goals. Eric Jensen. 192p. (Orig.). 1995. pap. 7.50 (*0-449-90946-8*) Fawcett.

Little Book of Big Primes. Paulo Ribenboim. 304p. 1993. 32.95 (*0-387-97508-X*) Spr-Verlag.

Little Book of Big Principles: Values & Virtues for a More Successful Life. rev. ed. Wilbur L. Brower. LC 97-65513. 80p. (Orig.). 1998. 14.95 (*1-887798-07-2*) WriteMore Pubns.

Little Book of Big Profits. Bill Buchsbaum. LC 96-70374. (Illus.). 128p. 1996. 12.95 (*0-02-861283-3*) Macmillan.

Little Book of Big Questions, 1. Dianna Daniels Booher. 1999. 9.99 (*0-8499-5482-7*) Word Pub.

***Little Book of Big Questions.** Jackie French. (Illus.). 128p. (J). (gr. 3-7). 2000. 19.95 (*1-55037-655-1*, Pub. by Annick Pr); per. 9.95 (*1-55037-654-3*, Pub. by Annick Pr) Firefly Bks Ltd.

Little Book of Big Questions: 200 Ways to Explore Your Spiritual Nature. Jonathan Robinson. 120p. (Orig.). 1995. pap. 8.95 (*1-57324-014-1*) Conari Press.

Little Book of Big Workshop Ideas: Introductions, Energizers & Transitional Activities for Facilitators, Teachers & Group Leaders. Katherine J. Ives. Ed. by Kathleen C. Newman. 50p. 1997. pap., spiral bd. 10.00 (*0-9660834-0-7*) KIA Counseling.

Little Book of Birding. George H. Harrison. LC 98-10162. (Illus.). 112p. 1998. 14.95 (*1-57223-142-4*, 1424) Willow Creek Pr.

Little Book of Bread. Josephine Bacon. 1995. 4.98 (*0-7858-0346-7*) Bk Sales Inc.

***Little Book of Breast Cancer: A Breast Cancer Self-Teaching Guide.** Michael A. Hunter. LC 98-92918. 157p. 1998. 14.95 (*0-9663813-0-0*) CancerInfo Pr.

Little Book of Buddhist Wisdom. Richard St. Ruth. LC 97-178505. (Little Bks.). 48p. 1997. pap. 5.95 (*1-86204-055-9*, Pub. by Element MA) Penguin Putnam.

Little Book of Business Math. Michael C. Thomsett. 208p. 1988. pap. 14.95 (*0-8144-7691-0*) AMACOM.

Little Book of Business Wisdom: Practical Insights for Entrepreneurs, Professionals, & Business Owners. Brian Banashak. 160p. 1997. pap. 5.95 (*0-9637311-6-5*) Genesis Comm Inc.

***Little Book of Business Wisdom: Practical Insights for Entrepreneurs, Professionals, & Business Owners.** Brian Banashak. 96p. 2000. pap. 5.95 (*1-58169-041-X*, Evergrn Pr AL) Genesis Comm Inc.

***Little Book of Business Wisdom: Rules of Success from More Than 50 Business Legends.** Peter Krass. 240p. 2000. 18.95 (*0-471-36979-9*) Wiley.

Little Book of Buzzwords. Pleasant Company Staff. 1999. pap. text 1.95 (*1-56247-727-7*) Pleasant Co.

Little Book of Cake Making. Josephine Bacon. 1995. 4.98 (*0-7858-0230-4*) Bk Sales Inc.

Little Book of Calm. Paul Wilson. LC 96-34166. 160p. 1999. pap. 7.95 (*0-452-27793-0*, Plume) Dutton Plume.

Little Book of Campaign Etiquette: For Everyone with a Stake in Politicians & Journalists. Stephen Hess. LC 98-25365. (Illus.). 100p. 1998. 14.95 (*0-8157-3586-3*) Brookings.

***Little Book of Campaign Etiquette 2000: For Everyone with a Stake in Politicians & Journalists.** Stephen Hess. 2000. pap. 12.95 (*0-8157-3577-4*) Brookings.

Little Book of Campfire Songs. Illus. by Brian Denington. 60p. 1995. 7.95 (*0-8118-0821-1*) Chronicle Bks.

***Little Book of Candle Magic.** D. J. Conway. (Little Book Ser.). 130p. 2000. pap. 9.95 (*1-58091-043-2*, Pub. by Crossing Pr) Publishers Group.

Little Book of Canons. Rod L. Ronneberg. Ed. by Prue Renneberg. (Illus.). 67p. (Orig.). 1997. spiral bd., wbk. ed. 15.00 (*1-892573-00-8*, 0001) Camphor Pr.

***Little Book of Cat Names.** Eleanora Walker. 144p. 2000. 6.99 (*1-57866-095-5*) Galahad Bks.

Little Book of Cat Poems. Sara L. Whittier. 160p. 1998. 6.99 (*1-57866-019-X*) Promntory Pr.

Little Book of Cats: Poems & Prose. Robin L. Sommer. 64p. 1995. 4.98 (*0-9636673-2-7*) DoveTail Bks.

Little Book of Celebrity Bears. Pauline Cockrill. LC 92-53229. (Little Bear Library). (Illus.). 48p. 1992. 8.95 (*1-56458-082-2*) DK Pub Inc.

Little Book of Celtic Blessings. C. Matthews. 48p. 1994. pap. 5.95 (*1-85230-564-9*, Pub. by Element MA) Penguin Putnam.

***Little Book of Celtic Lore.** Caitlin Matthews & John Matthews. LC 98-22914. (Illus.). 48p. 1998. 5.95 (*1-86204-229-2*, Pub. by Element MA) Penguin Putnam.

Little Book of Celtic Proverbs (Irish) W. A. Ross. (Illus.). 60p. 1996. 9.95 (*0-86281-572-X*, Pub. by Appletree Pr) Irish Bks Media.

Little Book of Celtic Verse. W. A. Ross. (Illus.). 60p. 1996. 9.95 (*0-86281-603-3*, Pub. by Appletree Pr) Irish Bks Media.

Little Book of Celtic Wisdom. Sean McMahon. (Illus.). 60p. 1995. 9.95 (*0-86281-561-4*, Pub. by Appletree Pr) Irish Bks Media.

Little Book of Celtic Wisdom. Giuletta Wood. LC 97-9023. (Little Bks.). 48p. 1997. pap. 5.95 (*1-86204-049-4*, Pub. by Element MA) Penguin Putnam.

***Little Book of Chaos: Tips to Irritate.** Craig Brown. LC 98-56277. 96p. 1999. pap. 7.95 (*1-57322-759-5*, Riverhead Books) Putnam Pub Group.

Little Book of Cherished Poems: Beautiful Poetry to Treasure Always. Kay Anne Carson. 320p. 1999. 7.99 (*1-57866-060-2*) Galahad Bks.

Little Book of Chicken. Josephine Bacon. 1994. 4.98 (*1-55521-980-2*) Bk Sales Inc.

Little Book of Chinese Cooking. Josephine Bacon. 1994. 4.98 (*1-55521-983-7*) Bk Sales Inc.

Little Book of Chocolate. Laura Potts. 1994. 4.98 (*0-7858-0139-1*) Bk Sales Inc.

Little Book of Christian Character & Manners. William Dedrick & Colleen Dedrick. 128p. 1997. pap. 8.99 (*1-888306-22-X*) Holly Hall.

Little Book of Christian Questions & Responses in Which the Principal Headings of the Christian Religion Are Briefly Set Forth. Theodore Beza. Tr. by Kirk M. Summers from LAT. LC 86-25583. (Princeton Theological Monographs: No. 9).Tr. of Quaestionum et Responsionum Christianarum Libellus. (Orig.). 1986. pap. 8.00 (*0-915138-91-3*) Pickwick.

Little Book of Christmas. John K. Bangs. LC 77-116933. (Short Story Index Reprint Ser.). (Illus.). 1977. 19.95 (*0-8369-3435-0*) Ayer.

An Asterisk (*) at the beginning of an entry indicates that the title is appearing for the first time.

Little Book of Christmas Carols. Ariel Books Staff. (Illus.). 16p. 1993. 4.95 (*0-8362-3041-8*, Arie Bks) Andrews & McMeel.
Little Book of Christmas Joys. H. Jackson Brown, Jr. et al. 160p. 1994. pap. 4.95 (*1-55853-310-9*) Rutledge Hill Pr.
Little Book of Classics. Larry Lukas. 32p. (Orig.). 1997. pap. text 7.95 (*1-889416-07-X*, LS40008) Lukasound.
Little Book of Clever Card Tricks. Jon Tremaine. 1995. 4.98 (*0-7858-0288-6*) Bk Sales Inc.
***Little Book of Coaching: Motivating People to Be Winners.** Kenneth H. Blanchard & Don Shula. LC 00-40884. 2001. write for info. (*0-06-662103-8*) HarperTrade.
Little Book of Cocktail Classics. (Tiny Tomes Ser.). (Illus.). 128p. 1998. 3.95 (*0-8362-6815-6*) Andrews & McMeel.
Little Book of Coffee. Andrews & McMeel Staff. (Tiny Tomes Ser.). 1998. 3.95 (*0-8362-5243-8*) Andrews & McMeel.
Little Book of Collectible Teddy Bears. Nicola Dent. 1995. 4.98 (*0-7858-0237-1*) Bk Sales Inc.
Little Book of Colors. Zokeisha. Ed. by Kate Klimo. (Chubby Board Bks.). (Illus.). 16p. (J). 1982. pap. 2.95 (*0-671-45570-2*) Litle Simon.
Little Book of Comfort. Anthony Guest. 160p. 1995. pap. 10.00 (*0-551-02968-4*, Pub. by HarpC) Harper SF.
Little Book of Confucian Wisdom. Brian Bocking. LC 98-20067. (Little Bks.). (Illus.). 48p. 1998. 5.95 (*1-86204-230-6*, Pub. by Element MA) Penguin Putnam.
Little Book of Cookery for Diabetics. Josephine Bacon. 1995. 4.98 (*0-7858-0289-4*) Bk Sales Inc.
Little Book of Cookies. Josephine Bacon. 1995. 4.98 (*0-7858-0233-9*) Bk Sales Inc.
Little Book of Cooking for 1. Josephine Bacon. 1995. 4.98 (*0-7858-0292-4*) Bk Sales Inc.
Little Book of Cooking for 2. Josephine Bacon. 1995. 4.98 (*0-7858-0291-6*) Bk Sales Inc.
Little Book of Corporate Lies: What They Say - What They Really Mean. Bruce T. Smith et al. Ed. by Cliff Carle. 128p. 1997. pap. 6.95 (*1-57644-024-9*) CCC Pubns.
***Little Book of Cosmic Colour.** Betty Shine. 2000. pap. 5.95 (*0-00-653200-4*, Pub. by HarpC) Trafalgar.
Little Book of Courage. Illus. by Penny Dann. LC 93-6640. (Quotations for Kids Ser.). 32p. (J). (gr. 1-8). 1994. lib. bdg. 18.50 (*1-56766-094-0*) Childs World.
***Little Book of Crafty Cats.** Ed. by Helen Exley. (Minute Mini Ser.). (Illus.). 64p. 1999. 6.50 (*1-86187-136-8*, Pub. by Exley Pubns Ltd) Exley Giftbooks.
Little Book of Creative Cocktails. Nicola Dent. 1995. 4.98 (*0-7858-0344-0*) Bk Sales Inc.
Little Book of Creative Dried & Silk Flowers. Laura Potts. 1995. 4.98 (*0-7858-0239-8*) Bk Sales Inc.
Little Book of Creative Flower Arranging. Laura Potts. 1995. 4.98 (*0-7858-0345-9*) Bk Sales Inc.
Little Book of Creative Magic. Jon Fremaine. 1995. 4.98 (*0-7858-0287-8*) Bk Sales Inc.
Little Book of Creative Origami. Jon Taemaine. 1995. 4.98 (*0-7858-0282-7*) Bk Sales Inc.
Little Book of Creative Papercrafts. C. L. Books. 1995. 4.98 (*0-7858-0283-5*) Bk Sales Inc.
Little Book of Crossword Puzzles. Ed. by Dover Publications Staff. (Little Activity Bks.). (Illus.). (J). 1995. pap. 1.00 (*0-486-28559-6*) Dover.
Little Book of Decorative Napkin Folding. Pamela Westland. 1995. 4.98 (*0-7858-0374-2*) Bk Sales Inc.
Little Book of Dental Hygienists' Rules. Esther M. Wilkins. 128p. 1997. pap. 8.95 (*1-56053-265-3*, 895696) Hanley & Belfus.
Little Book of Desserts. Kate Cranshaw. 1994. 4.98 (*0-7858-0140-5*) Bk Sales Inc.
***Little Book of Detox.** Jane Scrivner. 160p. 2000. pap. 4.95 (*0-7499-1994-9*) Piatkus Bks.
***Little Book of Doctors' Rule No. II: A Compilation.** Clifton K. Meador. LC 99-63780. 80p. (C). 1999. pap. text 9.95 (*1-56053-365-X*, Pub. by Hanley & Belfus) Mosby Inc.
Little Book of Doctors' Rules. Clifton K. Meador. 128p. (Orig.). 1992. pap. text 9.95 (*1-56053-061-8*) Hanley & Belfus.
Little Book of Dreams. LC 95-80739. (Little Bks.). (Illus.). 80p. 1996. 4.95 (*0-8362-1051-4*) Andrews & McMeel.
Little Book of Dried Flowers. Janice Seymour. 1994. 4.98 (*1-55521-991-8*) Bk Sales Inc.
Little Book of Early American Crafts & Trades. Ed. by Peter Stockham. LC 75-46194. (Illus.). 140p. 1976. reprint ed. pap. 4.95 (*0-486-23336-7*) Dover.
Little Book of Egyptian Wisdom. Compiled by Naomi Ozaniec. LC 97-9024. (Little Bks.). (Illus.). 48p. 1997. 5.95 (*1-86204-110-5*, Pub. by Element MA) Penguin Putnam.
Little Book of Embroidered Garden Flowers. Diana Lampe. 1999. 9.95 (*1-86351-226-8*) Sally Milner.
Little Book of English Teas. Rosa Mashiter. (Illus.). 60p. 1995. 7.95 (*0-8118-1011-9*) Chronicle Bks.
Little Book of Fish & Seafood. Josephine Bacon. 1995. 4.98 (*0-7858-0229-0*) Bk Sales Inc.
Little Book of Fishing: An Anthology. Ed. by Will Balliett. LC 93-46760. (Illus.). 160p. 1994. 16.00 (*0-87113-568-X*, Atlntc Mnthly) Grove-Atltic.
Little Book of Flyfishing. Tom Davis & Dale C. Spartas. LC 97-1342. (Illus.). 112p. 1997. 14.95 (*1-57223-106-8*, 1068) Willow Creek Pr.
Little Book of Forgiveness: Challenges & Meditations for Anyone with Something to Forgive. D. Patrick Miller. 90p. 1999. reprint ed. pap. 12.95 (*0-9656809-1-6*) Fearless Bks.
***Little Book of Free Things: Guide to Thousands of Wonderful Free Things.** Linda Kalian & Bob Kalian. 400p. 2000. pap. 6.95 (*0-934968-15-2*, 494-007, Pub. by Roblin Pr) BookWorld.
Little Book of Friendship. Illus. by Penny Dann. LC 93-12918. (Quotations for Kids Ser.). 32p. (J). (gr. 1-8). 1994. lib. bdg. 18.50 (*1-56766-095-9*) Childs World.
Little Book of Friendship. Compiled by Gladys Pucillo. 1981. 5.95 (*0-8378-1931-8*) Gibson.
Little Book of Frogs. Dylan Thomas. (Little Bks.). (Illus.). 56p. 1997. 8.95 (*0-297-83534-3*, Pub. by Weidenfeld & Nicolson) Trafalgar.
Little Book of Gaelic Proverbs (Scottish) W. A. Ross. (Illus.). 60p. 1996. 9.95 (*0-86281-596-7*, Pub. by Appletree Pr) Irish Bks Media.
Little Book of Gargoyles. Mike Harding. (Little Books Of Ser.). 1998. pap. 9.95 (*1-85410-561-2*, Pub. by Aurum Pr) London Brdge.
Little Book of Garlands & Festive Decorations. C. L. Books. 1995. 4.98 (*0-7858-0285-1*) Bk Sales Inc.
***Little Book of God's Love.** Law. (J). 1999. pap. 7.50 (*0-7459-4074-9*, Pub. by Lion Pubng) Trafalgar.
***Little Book of God's Promises.** Law. (J). 1999. pap. 7.50 (*0-7459-4075-7*, Pub. by Lion Pubng) Trafalgar.
Little Book of Golf Slang: From Fried Eggs to Frog Hairs, Words to Help You Pass As a Golfer. Randy Voorhees. LC 97-71630. (Illus.). 144p. (Orig.). 1997. pap. 7.95 (*0-8362-3532-0*) Andrews & McMeel.
Little Book of Golf Slang: From Fried Eggs to Frog Hairs, Words to Help You Pass as a Golfer. Randy Voorhees. 1998. 4.95 (*0-8362-5265-9*) Andrews & McMeel.
Little Book of Hangover Cures. Alex Denady. (Illus.). 60p. 1998. 9.95 (*0-86281-631-9*, Pub. by Appletree Pr) Irish Bks Media.
***Little Book of Hannukah.** Steven Zorn. (Illus.). 2000. 4.95 (*0-7624-0790-5*) Running Pr.
Little Book of Happies. Elizabeth Belew. 128p. (Orig.). 1996. pap. 5.95 (*1-889116-03-3*) Penbrooke Pub.
***Little Book of Happiness: Your Guide to a Better Life.** Patrick Whiteside. 160p. 2000. pap. 4.95 (*0-7407-1031-1*) Andrews & McMeel.
Little Book of Hats: Alternative Headcover for Cancer Survivors. Gwenn Schultze. (Illus.). 44p. 1996. reprint ed. 10.00 (*0-9632739-0-6*) Galatea.
Little Book of Hedgehogs. (Little Bks.). (Illus.). 56p. 1997. 8.95 (*0-297-83533-5*, Pub. by Weidenfeld & Nicolson) Trafalgar.
Little Book of Herbs. Margaret Carter. 1994. 4.98 (*1-55521-988-8*) Bk Sales Inc.
Little Book of Herbs & Spices. Kate Cranshaw. 1994. 4.98 (*0-7858-0144-8*) Bk Sales Inc.
***Little Book of Heroin.** Francis Moraes. (Little Book Ser.). (Illus.). 96p. (Orig.). 2000. pap. 12.95 (*0-914171-98-4*, Pub. by Ronin Pub) Publishers Group.
Little Book of Hindu Wisdom. Compiled by Stephen Cross. LC 97-25236. (Little Bks.). (Illus.). 48p. 1997. 5.95 (*1-86204-109-1*, Pub. by Element MA) Penguin Putnam.
Little Book of History Bk. 6: Bodyville & Eddyville School. Compiled by Ruth Hall. (Illus.). 13p. 1995. pap. 2.00 (*0-614-13851-5*) MI City Hist.
Little Book of Hugs. Steve Weisinger. LC 90-60083. (Chunky Bks. Ser.). (Illus.). 28p. (J). (ps). 1991. 3.99 (*0-679-80755-1*, Pub. by Random Bks Yng Read) Random.
***Little Book of Hugs for Friends: Inspiration for the Heart.** Ed. by Philis Boultinghouse. (Little Book of Hugs Ser.). (Illus.). 80p. 2000. 4.99 (*1-58229-118-7*) Howard Pub LA.
***Little Book of Hugs for Friends: Inspiration for the Heart.** Howard Publishing Staff. 2000. pap. 4.95 (*0-7407-1182-2*) Andrews & McMeel.
***Little Book of Hugs for Mom: Inspiration for the Heart.** Ed. by Philis Boultinghouse. (Little Book of Hugs Ser.). (Illus.). 80p. 2000. 4.99 (*1-58229-119-5*) Howard Pub LA.
***Little Book of Hugs for Mom: Inspiration for the Heart.** Howard Publishing Staff. 2000. pap. 4.95 (*0-7407-1183-0*) Andrews & McMeel.
***Little Book of Hugs for Sisters: Inspiration for the Heart.** Ed. by Philis Boultinghouse. (Little Book of Hugs Ser.). (Illus.). 80p. 2000. 4.99 (*1-58229-123-3*) Howard Pub LA.
***Little Book of Hugs for Sisters: Inspiration for the Heart.** Howard Publishing Staff. 2000. pap. 4.95 (*0-7407-1184-9*) Andrews & McMeel.
***Little Book of Hugs for Teachers: Inspiration for the Heart.** Ed. by Philis Boultinghouse. (Little Book of Hugs Ser.). (Illus.). 80p. 2000. 4.99 (*1-58229-122-5*) Howard Pub LA.
***Little Book of Hugs for Teachers: Inspiration for the Heart.** Howard Publishing Staff. 2000. pap. 4.95 (*0-7407-1185-7*) Andrews & McMeel.
***Little Book of Hugs for Women: Inspiration for the Heart.** Ed. by Philis Boultinghouse. (Little Book of Hugs Ser.). (Illus.). 80p. 2000. 4.99 (*1-58229-121-7*) Howard Pub LA.
***Little Book of Hugs for Women: Inspiration for the Heart.** Howard Publishing Staff. 2000. pap. 4.95 (*0-7407-1186-5*) Andrews & McMeel.
***Little Book of Hugs to Encourage & Inspire: Inspiration for the Heart.** Ed. by Philis Boultinghouse. (Little Book of Hugs Ser.). (Illus.). 80p. 2000. 4.99 (*1-58229-120-9*) Howard Pub LA.
***Little Book of Hugs to Encourage & Inspire: Inspiration for the Heart.** Howard Publishing Staff. 2000. pap. 4.95 (*0-7407-1187-3*) Andrews & McMeel.
Little Book of Humility & Patience see Patience & Humility: A Handbook for Christians
Little Book of Humorous Quotations. Ed. by David Notely. (Little Book Ser.). 1998. 7.00 (*0-7117-0983-1*, Pub. by JARR UK) Seven Hills Bk.
Little Book of Indian Cooking. Josephine Bacon. 1994. 4.98 (*1-55521-984-5*) Bk Sales Inc.
Little Book of Indian Vegetarian Cookery. Jillian Stewart. 1995. 4.98 (*0-7858-0290-8*) Bk Sales Inc.
***Little Book of Inner Space: Your Guide to Finding Personal Peace.** Stafford Whiteaker. 2000. pap. 4.95 (*0-7407-1030-3*) Andrews & McMeel.
Little Book of Inspiration. Jim Beggs. LC 93-36646. (Illus.). 64p. (Orig.). 1994. 6.95 (*0-87573-028-0*) Jain Pub Co.
Little Book of Inspiration. Katina Kefalos. (Illus.). 14p. 1998. pap. 4.95 (*0-9666822-5-4*) Emerald Prodns.
Little Book of Inspiration, Bk. 2. Katina Kefalos. (Illus.). 14p. 1998. pap. 4.95 (*0-9666822-6-2*) Emerald Prodns.
Little Book of Irish Family Cooking. Ruth I. Ross. 1996. 13.95 (*0-614-19384-2*) St Martin.
Little Book of Irish Family Cooking. Ruth I. Ross. LC 96-37351. (Illus.). 112p. 1997. text 13.95 (*0-312-15165-9*) St Martin.
Little Book of Irish Myths. Bob Welch. (Illus.). 60p. 1996. pap. 9.95 (*0-86281-301-8*, Pub. by Appletree Pr); pap. 9.95 (*0-86281-501-0*, Pub. by Appletree Pr) Irish Bks Media.
Little Book of Irish Quotations. Sean McMahon. (Little Irish Book Ser.). (Illus.). 60p. 1995. 9.95 (*0-86281-480-4*, Pub. by Appletree Pr) Irish Bks Media.
Little Book of Irish Recipes. Josephine Bacon. 1995. 4.98 (*0-7858-0293-2*) Bk Sales Inc.
Little Book of Irish Sayings. Illus. by Jon Berkely. (Little Irish Book Ser.). 60p. 1995. 9.95 (*0-86281-517-7*, Pub. by Appletree Pr) Irish Bks Media.
Little Book of Irish Superstitions. Kim Lenaghan. (Little Irish Bookshelf Ser.). (Illus.). 60p. 1995. 9.95 (*0-86281-545-2*, Pub. by Appletree Pr) Irish Bks Media.
Little Book of Irish Verse. National Gallery of Ireland Staff. (Illus.). 60p. 1993. 7.95 (*0-8118-0508-5*) Chronicle Bks.
Little Book of Iron John. Wilhelm K. Grimm & Jacob W. Grimm. (Little Book Ser.). (Illus.). 48p. 1993. pap. 5.95 (*1-85230-451-0*, Pub. by Element MA) Penguin Putnam.
Little Book of Italian Cooking. Josephine Bacon. 1995. 4.98 (*0-7858-0234-7*) Bk Sales Inc.
Little Book of Jewish Wisdom. Martin Horan. (Illus.). 48p. 1995. pap. 5.95 (*1-85230-722-6*, Pub. by Element MA) Penguin Putnam.
Little Book of Joy: An Interactive Journal for Thoughts, Prayers, & Wishes. Bill Zimmerman. (Illus.). 150p. (Orig.). pap. 8.95 (*1-56838-041-0*) Hazelden.
Little Book of Ketamine. Kit Kelly. (Illus.). 96p. 1999. pap. 12.95 (*0-914171-97-6*, Pub. by Ronin Pub) Publishers Group.
***Little Book of Kids' Talk.** Nanette Newman. (Illus.). (J). 2000. pap. 4.95 (*0-7407-0473-7*) Andrews & McMeel.
Little Book of Kisses. Steve Weisinger. LC 90-60082. (Chunky Bks. Ser.). (Illus.). 28p. (J). (ps). 1991. 3.99 (*0-679-80754-3*, Pub. by Random Bks Yng Read) Random.
***Little Book of Knock Knock Jokes.** Kaitlyn Bayne. (Illus.). 120p. 2000. 4.95 (*1-930408-04-8*) Lawrnce Teach.
***Little Book of Knowledge.** Kingfisher Books Staff. LC 99-88381. (Illus.). 320p. (J). 2000. pap. 11.95 (*0-7534-5299-5*, Kingfisher) LKC.
***Little Book of Letting Go: A Revolutionary 30 Day Program to Cleanse Your Mind, Revive Your Soul & Lift Your Spirit.** Hugh Prather. 200p. 2000. pap. 14.95 (*1-57324-503-8*) Conari Press.
Little Book of Lies. Phyllis Hotch. (Illus.). 32p. 1993. pap. text 6.00 (*1-883968-01-1*) Blinking Yellow.
Little Book of Life after Death. Gustav T. Fechner. Ed. by Robert J. Kastenbaum. LC 76-19570. (Death & Dying Ser.). 1977. reprint ed. lib. bdg. 18.95 (*0-405-09565-1*) Ayer.
Little Book of Limericks. Ed. by H. I. Brock. LC 71-84351. (Granger Index Reprint Ser.). 1977. 19.95 (*0-8369-6053-X*) Ayer.
Little Book of Little Quilts. Katharine Guerrier. 144p. 1998. 29.95 (*0-8230-2826-7*) Watsn-Guptill.
***Little Book of Living Green.** Mark Hegarty. (Illus.). 124p. 2000. mass mkt. 4.99 (*1-903222-13-3*, Pub. by Wimbledon Publishing Co) Anthem.
***Little Book of Living on the Edge.** Ashley Pomeroy. (Pocket Oracle Ser.). (Illus.). 124p. 2000. mass mkt. 4.99 (*1-903222-16-8*, Pub. by Wimbledon Publishing Co) Anthem.
***Little Book of Long Life.** Dan Fielder. (Pocket Oracle Ser.). (Illus.). 136p. 2000. mass mkt. 4.99 (*1-903222-15-X*, Pub. by Wimbledon Publishing Co) Anthem.
Little Book of Love. (Illus.). 24p. 1997. 4.95 (*1-85479-982-7*, Pub. by M OMara) Assoc Pubs Grp.
Little Book of Love. Andrews & McMeel Staff. LC 98-194454. (Tiny Tomes Ser.). (Illus.). 128p. (J). 1997. 3.95 (*0-8362-3637-8*) Andrews & McMeel.
Little Book of Love. John Baldock. LC 98-188282. (Little Bks.). (Illus.). 48p. 1997. pap. 5.95 (*1-86204-050-8*, Pub. by Element MA) Penguin Putnam.
Little Book of Love. John Beldock. 1994. pap. 5.95 (*1-85230-471-5*, Pub. by Element MA) Penguin Putnam.
***Little Book of Love.** Exley Giftbooks Editors. 2000. 6.50 (*1-86187-166-X*) Exley Pubns Ltd.
***Little Book of Love.** Havoc Publishing Staff. 1999. 8.00 (*0-7416-1106-6*) Havoc Pub.
Little Book of Love. Fleur Robertson. 1995. 4.98 (*0-7858-0294-0*) Bk Sales Inc.
Little Book of Love: Mini Book. Brownlow. LC 99-237089. 1999. pap. text 5.99 (*1-57051-251-5*) Brownlow Pub Co.
Little Book of Love Letters. Lil Copan. (Shaw Greetings Ser.). 80p. 1998. pap. text 5.99 (*0-87788-471-4*, H Shaw Pubs) Waterbrook Pr.
Little Book of Love Magic. Patricia Telesco. LC 98-49315. 184p. 1999. pap. 9.95 (*0-89594-887-7*) Crossing Pr.
Little Book of Love Poems. Contrib. by Elizabeth Barrett Browning et al. (Illus.). 60p. 1998. 9.95 (*0-86281-454-5*, Pub. by Appletree Pr) Irish Bks Media.
Little Book of Love Spells. Rebecca Sargent. LC 97-71619. (Illus.). 112p. 1997. 9.95 (*0-8362-3261-5*) Andrews & McMeel.
Little Book of Love Tips. Martha B. Beveridge. Ed. by Terrisa Bruce-Phipps. 36p. (Orig.). 1996. pap. 5.95 (*1-889237-00-0*) Options Now.
Little Book of Love Tips, Vol. II. Ed. by Terrisa Bruce-Phipps. 40p. 1997. pap. 5.95 (*1-889237-10-8*) Options Now.
Little Book of Low Calorie Cooking. Josephine Bacon. 1994. 4.98 (*1-55521-978-0*) Bk Sales Inc.
Little Book of Manners. Emilie Barnes. Ed. by Anne C. Buchanan. LC 97-36915. (Illus.). 32p. (J). 1998. 14.99 (*1-56507-678-8*) Harvest Hse.
***Little Book of Manners for Boys: A Game Plan for Getting along with Others.** gif. ed. Bob Barnes & Emilie Barnes. (Illus.). 32p. (J). 2000. 14.99 (*0-7369-0128-0*) Harvest Hse.
Little Book of Meat. Selima Hill. 64p. 1994. pap. 12.95 (*1-85224-243-4*, Pub. by Bloodaxe Bks) Dufour.
Little Book of Mexican Cooking. Josephine Bacon. 1995. 4.98 (*0-7858-0236-3*) Bk Sales Inc.
Little Book of Miracles: Collection of Stories of How Simple Faith Can Change Your Daily Life. Barbara H. Martin. (Illus.). 56p. (Orig.). 1996. pap. 9.95 (*1-884707-22-X*) Lifestyles.
Little Book of Miracles: Quotations from a Course in Miracles. Hebe Taylor. 48p. 1995. pap. 5.95 (*1-85230-618-1*, Pub. by Element MA) Penguin Putnam.
Little Book of Miracles: Testimonies of God's Grace. Annie Davis. 112p. 1998. pap. 6.99 (*1-884369-83-9*) McDougal Pubng.
Little Book of Misericords. Mike Harding. (Little Books Of Ser.). 1998. pap. 9.95 (*1-85410-562-0*, Pub. by Aurum Pr) London Brdge.
Little Book of Missionary Reminders. Mark W. Newman. LC 95-154135. 1996. pap. 7.95 (*1-55503-774-7*, 01111884) Covenant Comms.
Little Book of Modern British Verse. Ed. by Jessie B. Rittenhouse. LC 78-149111. (Granger Index Reprint Ser.). 1977. 21.95 (*0-8369-6236-2*) Ayer.
Little Book of Modern Verse. Ed. by Jessie B. Rittenhouse. LC 71-149112. (Granger Index Reprint Ser.). 1977. 18.95 (*0-8369-6237-0*) Ayer.
Little Book of Money. Ed. by Evelyn Steinberg & Marilyn Williams. 96p. 1995. pap. 4.95 (*1-55152-011-7*) LPC InBook.
Little Book of Native American Wisdom. S. McFadden. 48p. 1994. text 5.95 (*1-85230-566-5*, Pub. by Element MA) Penguin Putnam.
Little Book of Nature. Penny Dann. LC 94-7881. (Quotations for Kids Ser.). 24p. 1998. lib. bdg. 18.50 (*1-56766-152-1*) Childs World.
Little Book of Naughty Quotations. Ed. by David Notley. (Little Book Ser.). 1998. 7.00 (*0-7117-0982-3*, Pub. by JARR UK) Seven Hills Bk.
Little Book of Necessary Nonsense. Ed. by Burges Johnson. LC 72-116408. (Granger Index Reprint Ser.). 1977. 13.95 (*0-8369-6149-8*) Ayer.
Little Book of New Year's Resolutions. Shoo Raynor. (J). 1994. pap. 5.95 (*0-14-036804-3*, Pub. by Pnguin Bks Ltd) Trafalgar.
Little Book of No: Secrets for Success. Susan D. Artof. LC 96-20324. (Psycho Silly Act Bk.). (Orig.). pap. 7.95 (*0-9626888-6-X*) Ctr Pr CA.
***Little Book of Nostradamus: Prophecies for the 21st Century.** Herbie Brennan. 2000. pap. 8.95 (*0-7225-3984-3*, Pub. by Thorsons PA) HarpC.
***Little Book of Notes.** Pleasant Company Staff. 1999. pap. text 1.95 (*1-56247-797-8*) Pleasant Co.
Little Book of Nurses' Rules. Ed. by Rosalie Hammerschmidt & Clifton K. Meador. LC 92-75322. 150p. (Orig.). 1993. pap. text 9.95 (*1-56053-065-0*) Hanley & Belfus.
Little Book of Object-Oriented Programming. Henry Ledgard. LC 95-22671. 224p. (C). 1995. pap. 16.20 (*0-13-396342-X*) P-H.
***Little Book of Office Spells.** Sophia. LC 98-48179. 1999. 9.95 (*0-8362-8182-9*) Andrews & McMeel.
Little Book of Old Roses. Hazel Le Rougetel. (Illus.). 60p. 1998. 9.95 (*0-86281-333-6*, Pub. by Appletree Pr) Irish Bks Media.
Little Book of Online Romance: How to Find It, How to Keep It. Lorilyn Bailey. (Illus.). 128p. Date not set. pap. 6.95 (*0-9641239-6-7*) Lormax Commun.
Little Book of Opera. Ed. by Duncan Bock. LC 96-28051. (Illus.). 176p. 1996. 20.00 (*0-87113-649-X*, Atlntc Mnthly) Grove-Atltic.
***Little Book of Opium.** Francis Moraes. (Little Book Ser.: Vol. 4). (Illus.). 96p. 2000. pap. 12.95 (*1-57951-018-3*, Pub. by Ronin Pub) Publishers Group.
Little Book of Oral Argument. Alan L. Dworsky. LC 91-22872. xii, 77p. 1991. pap. 9.95 (*0-8377-0557-6*, Rothman) W S Hein.
Little Book of Owls. (Little Bks.). (Illus.). 56p. 1997. 8.95 (*0-297-83535-1*, Pub. by Weidenfeld & Nicolson) Trafalgar.
Little Book of Pasta Cooking. Josephine Bacon. 1994. 4.98 (*1-55521-982-9*) Bk Sales Inc.
***Little Book of Planes.** Billy Steers. LC 98-53287. (Jellybean Bks.). (Illus.). 24p. (J). (ps-k). 1999. lib. bdg. 7.99 (*0-375-90219-8*, Pub. by Random Bks Yng Read) Random.
***Little Book of Planes.** Billy Steers. LC 98-53287. (Jellybean Bks.). (Illus.). 24p. (J). (ps-1). 1999. 2.99 (*0-375-80219-3*, Pub. by Random Bks Yng Read) Random.
Little Book of Poems & Prayers. Joan W. Anglund. LC 89-5914. (Illus.). 48p. (J). 1997. mass mkt. 4.99 (*0-689-81448-8*) Atheneum Yung Read.

L

An Asterisk (*) at the beginning of an entry indicates that the title is appearing for the first time.

L

Little Book of Poems & Prayers. Joan Walsh Anglund. LC 89-5914. (Illus.). 48p. (J). (ps-1). 1989. lib. bdg. 13.00 (*0-671-67115-4*) S&S Childrens.

Little Book of Poems & Songs. Faye Horne. 40p. write for info. (*0-9676062-0-9*) F Horne.

Little Book of Poems, Prayers, & Pearls. Caryl W. Krueger. (Illus.). 100p. (Orig.). 1996. pap. 6.00 (*0-938632-06-X*) Belleridge.

Little Book of Potatoes. Josephine Bacon. 1995. 4.98 (*0-7858-0347-5*) Bk Sales Inc.

Little Book of Potpourri. Mary Lawrence. 1994. 4.98 (*1-55521-989-6*) Bk Sales Inc.

Little Book of Prayers. David Schiller. LC 94-31588. (Illus.). 400p. 1996. pap. 6.95 (*0-7611-0453-4*, 10453) Workman Pub.

Little Book of Profitable Tales. Eugene Field. LC 76-98568. (Short Story Index Reprint Ser.). 1977. 20.95 (*0-8369-3142-4*) Ayer.

Little Book of Proverbs. Andrews & McMeel Staff. LC 98-84246. (Little Bks.). (Illus.). 80p. 1999. 4.95 (*0-8362-6803-2*) Andrews & McMeel.

Little Book of Psalms. Andrews & McMeel Staff. LC 98-84247. (Illus.). 80p. 1999. 4.95 (*0-8362-6804-0*) Andrews & McMeel.

Little Book of Puppies. Andrews & McMeel Staff. LC 98-194455. (Tiny Tomes Ser.). (Illus.). 128p. (J). 1997. 3.95 (*0-8362-3639-4*) Andrews & McMeel.

Little Book of Qi-Gong: The Easiest, Most Effective Seated Qi-Gong Exercises for Better Meditation. Stuart Olson. 88p. 1998. pap. 12.95 (*1-889633-15-1*) Jade Forest.

Little Book of Rabbits. (Little Bks.). (Illus.). 56p. 1997. 8.95 (*0-297-83532-7*, Pub. by Weidenfeld & Nicolson) Trafalgar.

Little Book of Relaxation Techniques. Dale Colton. (Illus.). 48p. spiral bd. 18.00 (*0-9640043-0-5*) Mat Possessions.

Little Book of Renoir. Juliet Rodway. 1994. 4.98 (*1-55521-985-3*) Bk Sales Inc.

Little Book of Romantic Lies. Bruce T. Smith & Laura G. Burns. Ed. by Cliff Carle. 144p. (Orig.). 1997. pap. 5.95 (*1-57644-042-7*) CCC Pubns.

Little Book of Roses. Andrews & McMeel Staff. (Little Bks.). 1998. 4.95 (*0-8362-5217-9*) Andrews & McMeel.

Little Book of Rubaiyat of Omar Khayyam. Edward FitzGerald. (Illus.). 48p. 1995. pap. 5.95 (*1-85230-718-8*, Pub. by Element MA) Penguin Putnam.

Little Book of Saints. Ariel Books Staff. LC 95-60371. (Illus.). 80p. 1995. pap. 4.95 (*0-8362-3129-5*, Arie Bks) Andrews & McMeel.

Little Book of Scotch Whiskies. Derek Cooper. (Illus.). 60p. 1992. 7.95 (*0-8118-0253-1*) Chronicle Bks.

Little Book of Scottish Baking. Marion Maxwell & Catherine McWilliams. LC 97-1655. 60p. 1997. 8.95 (*1-56554-290-8*) Pelican.

Little Book of Scottish Castles. Charles Maclean. Ed. by Sheila Maclean. (Little Irish Bookshelf Ser.). (Illus.). 60p. 1995. 9.95 (*0-86281-546-0*, Pub. by Appletree Pr) Irish Bks Media.

Little Book of Scottish Clans. Alexander Fulton. 64p. 1995. 5.98 (*0-7858-0082-4*) Bk Sales Inc.

Little Book of Scottish Heather. Brian Osborne. (Illus.). 60p. 1998. 9.95 (*0-86281-705-6*, Pub. by Appletree Pr) Irish Bks Media.

Little Book of Scottish Quotations. J. D. Sutherland. (Illus.). 60p. 1997. 9.95 (*0-86281-678-5*, Pub. by Appletree Pr) Irish Bks Media.

Little Book of Scottish Sayings. J. D. Sutherland. (Illus.). 60p. 1998. 9.95 (*0-86281-699-8*, Pub. by Appletree Pr) Irish Bks Media.

***Little Book of Secrets: 81 Secrets for Living a Happy, Prosperous & Successful Life.** Chris Prentiss. 163p. 2000. pap. 7.95 (*0-943015-33-2*); pap. 7.95 (*0-943015-34-0*); pap. 7.95 (*0-943015-35-9*); pap. 7.95 (*0-943015-36-7*); pap. write for info. (*0-943015-37-5*) Power Press.

Little Book of Sensual Comfort. Jennifer Louden. LC 93-46348. (Little Book of Wisdom Ser.). 96p. 1994. pap. 8.00 (*0-06-251112-2*, Pub. by Harper SF) HarpC.

***Little Book of Shakespeare.** Kate Harris, pseud & John Mannion. 1999. pap. 3.95 (*0-00-325254-X*, Pub. by HarpC) Trafalgar.

***Little Book of Short Prayers.** Law. 1998. pap. 7.50 (*0-7459-4062-5*, Pub. by Lion Pubng) Trafalgar.

***Little Book of Sign Language: Mini Edition.** Running Press Staff. 2000. pap. 4.95 (*0-7624-0706-9*, Courage) Running Pr.

Little Book of Silk Ribbon Flowers. Helen Dafter. 1999. 9.95 (*1-86351-229-2*) Sally Milner.

Little Book of Soccer: Everyone's Illustrated Guide to the Laws of the Game. Paul Harris. 48p. 1976. pap. 6.95 (*0-916802-00-0*) Soccer for Am.

Little Book of Soups. Josephine Bacon. 1995. 4.98 (*0-7858-0232-0*) Bk Sales Inc.

***Little Book of Spiritual Wisdom.** Law. 1998. pap. 7.50 (*0-7459-4063-3*, Pub. by Lion Pubng) Trafalgar.

Little Book of Spirituality & Counseling. Faiver. (Counseling Ser.). 2000. pap. text 26.00 (*0-534-57582-X*) Brooks-Cole.

Little Book of Stained Glass. Mike Harding. (Little Books Of Ser.). 1998. pap. 9.95 (*1-85410-564-7*, Pub. by Aurum Pr) London Brdge.

Little Book of Stars. Sheila Gilheany. (Illus.). 60p. 1996. text 7.95 (*0-89815-812-5*) Ten Speed Pr.

***Little Book of Stars.** James B. Kaler. (Illus.). 188p. 2000. 20.00 (*0-387-95005-2*) Spr-Verlag.

Little Book of Streamlines. Pozrikidis. LC 98-88662. 162p. (C). 1999. text 49.95 (*0-12-563855-8*) Acad Pr.

Little Book of Stress. Exley Giftbooks Editors. 1998. 6.00 (*1-86187-094-9*) Exley Giftbooks.

***Little Book of Stress: Calm Is for Whimps; Get Real, Get Stressed.** Rohan Candappa. 2000. pap. 4.95 (*0-7407-0474-5*) Andrews & McMeel.

Little Book of Stupid Questions: 300 Hilarious, Bold, Embarrassing, Personal & Basically Pointless Queries. David Borgenicht. 1999. pap. 7.95 (*1-887166-50-5*, Hysteria Pubns) Sourcebks.

Little Book of Sufi Wisdom. John Baldock. LC 95-30359. (Illus.). 48p. 1995. pap. 5.95 (*1-85230-717-X*, Pub. by Element MA) Penguin Putnam.

Little Book of Table Graces. D. S. Baker. (Illus.). 60p. 1998. 9.95 (*0-86281-551-7*, Pub. by Appletree Pr) Irish Bks Media.

Little Book of Tea. Andrews & McMeel Staff. (Little Bks.). 1998. 4.95 (*0-8362-5227-6*) Andrews & McMeel.

Little Book of Thai Cooking. Josephine Bacon. 1995. 4.98 (*0-7858-0231-2*) Bk Sales Inc.

Little Book of the Big Bang. C. Hogan. LC 97-39340. (Illus.). 200p. 1998. text 20.00 (*0-387-98385-6*) Spr-Verlag.

Little Book of the Green Man. Mike Harding. (Little Books Of Ser.). 1998. 9.99 (*1-85410-563-9*, Pub. by Aurum Pr) London Brdge.

Little Book of the Tao Te Ching. John Mabry. (Illus.). 48p. 1995. pap. 5.95 (*1-85230-707-2*, Pub. by Element MA) Penguin Putnam.

Little Book of the Work of Infinite Love. Louise M. De La Touche. LC 79-90490. 1988. reprint ed. pap. 3.00 (*0-89555-130-6*) TAN Bks Pubs.

Little Book of Theatre Games Vol. 1. Jim Custer & Bob Hoose. 1998. pap. 14.99 (*0-8341-9773-1*) Nazarene.

Little Book of Thoughtful Moments. Fleur Robertson. 1994. 4.98 (*1-55521-992-6*) Bk Sales Inc.

Little Book of Tracing Paper. Ed. by Dover Publications Staff. (Illus.). (J). 1990. pap. text 1.00 (*0-486-26394-0*) Dover.

Little Book of Tropical Drinks. Claire Clifton. (Little Cookbooks Ser.). (Illus.). 1993. 6.95 (*0-8118-0362-7*) Chronicle Bks.

Little Book of Tropical Drinks. Claire Clifton. (Illus.). 60p. 1995. 7.95 (*0-8118-1040-2*) Chronicle Bks.

Little Book of Unsuspected Subversion. Edmond Jabes. Tr. by Rosmarie Waldrop. LC 95-38273. 90p. 1996. pap. 12.95 (*0-8047-2684-1*) Stanford U Pr.

Little Book of Unsuspected Subversion. Edmond Jabes. Tr. by Rosmarie Waldrop. 90p. 1996. 29.50 (*0-8047-2683-3*) Stanford U Pr.

Little Book of Useful Poems. Arja Marttinen. LC 96-83414. 64p. 1996. 8.95 (*1-56167-249-1*) Am Literary Pr.

Little Book of Van Gogh. Juliet Rodway. 1994. 4.98 (*1-55521-986-1*) Bk Sales Inc.

Little Book of Vegetarian Cooking. Josephine Bacon. 1994. 4.98 (*1-55521-977-2*) Bk Sales Inc.

Little Book of Venom. Compiled by Jennifer Higgie. LC 98-6777. 176p. 1998. pap. 12.95 (*0-8092-2808-4*, 280840, Contemporary Bks) NTC Contemp Pub Co.

Little Book of Vinegars. Ann Creber. (Illus.). 114p. 1991. 11.95 (*0-685-41000-5*) HarpC.

Little Book of Virtues. Peg Augustine. 48p. 1996. 5.00 (*0-687-01600-2*) Dimen for Liv.

Little Book of Welsh Proverbs. W. A. Ross. (Illus.). 60p. 1996. 9.95 (*0-86281-624-6*, Pub. by Appletree Pr) Irish Bks Media.

Little Book of Welsh Quotations. Meic Stephens. (Illus.). 60p. 1997. 9.95 (*0-86281-684-X*, Pub. by Appletree Pr) Irish Bks Media.

Little Book of Welsh Sayings. Meic Stephens. (Illus.). 60p. 1998. pap. 9.95 (*0-86281-703-X*, Pub. by Appletree Pr) Irish Bks Media.

Little Book of Western Verse. Eugene Field. (Notable American Authors Ser.). (J). 1992. reprint ed. lib. bdg. 75.00 (*0-7812-2642-2*) Rprt Serv.

Little Book of Wildflowers in Silk Ribbon. Jenny Bradford. 1999. 9.95 (*1-86351-227-6*) Sally Milner.

Little Book of Wisdom. Ed. by David Notley. (Little Book Ser.). 1998. 7.00 (*0-7117-0985-8*, Pub. by JARR UK) Seven Hills Bk.

Little Book of Wisdom. Illus. & Compiled by Richard Torregrossa. 384p. (Orig.). 1996. pap. 8.95 (*1-55874-422-3*, 4223) Health Comm.

Little Book of Wit. Ed. by David Notley. (Little Book Ser.). 1998. 7.00 (*0-7117-0984-X*, Pub. by JARR UK) Seven Hills Bk.

Little Book of Wok & Stir Fry. Josephine Bacon. 1995. 4.98 (*0-7858-0235-5*) Bk Sales Inc.

Little Book of Women's Prayer. Rachel Stowe. 114p. 1996. pap. 5.99 (*0-551-03015-1*, Pub. by M Pickering) Harper SF.

***Little Book of Women's Wisdom.** Ed. by Jennifer Howie. (Illus.). 120p. 2000. 4.95 (*1-930408-00-5*) Lawrnce Teach.

***Little Book of Women's Wit: A Bouquet of Quotations.** Ed. by Melissa Lieberman. (Illus.). 126p. 2000. 4.95 (*1-930408-01-3*) Lawrnce Teach.

Little Book of Wool & Silk Embroidery. Jenny Bradford. 1999. 9.95 (*1-86351-228-4*) Sally Milner.

Little Book of Wrinkles. Steinberg. Ed. by Williams. 96p. 1993. per. 4.95 (*0-88978-264-4*, Pub. by Arsenal Pulp) LPC InBook.

***Little Book of Wrong Shui: How to Drastically Improve Your Life by Basically Moving Stuff Around.** Rohan Candappa. 160p. 2000. pap. 4.95 (*0-7407-0475-3*) Andrews & McMeel.

Little Book of Yankee Humor. Clarissa M. Silitch. (Illus.). 288p. 1983. pap. 10.95 (*0-89909-016-8*, 80-950-6) Yankee Bks.

Little Book of Zen. (Tiny Tomes Ser.). (Illus.). 128p. 1998. 3.95 (*0-8362-6814-8*) Andrews & McMeel.

Little Book of Zen Wisdom. John Baldock. 48p. 1994. pap. 5.95 (*1-85230-563-0*, Pub. by Element MA) Penguin Putnam.

Little Book on Forgiving: A Surrender in 7 Steps Toward Peace & Freedom. Rick Kitzman. LC 97-78004. 112p. 1998. pap. 6.95 (*0-87516-714-4*) DeVorss.

Little Book on Legal Writing. 2nd ed. Alan L. Dworsky. LC 92-8448. xvii, 142p. 1992. pap. 11.95 (*0-8377-0560-6*, Rothman) W S Hein.

Little Book on Love. Jacob Needleman. LC 96-1. 1996. 90.00 (*0-385-48289-2*) Doubleday.

***Little Book on Love: A Wise & Inspiring Guide to Discovering the Gift of Love.** Jacob Needleman. 192p. 2000. pap. 9.95 (*0-385-33432-X*, Delta Trade) Dell.

***Little Book on PERL.** Robert W. Sebesta. LC 99-51528. 190p. 2000. pap. 29.00 (*0-13-927955-5*) P-H.

Little Book on the Human Shadow. Robert Bly. Ed. by William C. Booth. LC 87-45687. 96p. 1988. pap. 11.00 (*0-06-254847-6*, PL 4255, Pub. by Harper SF) HarpC.

Little Book Poems & Other Things from the Connecticut Store. Charlie Chase. 24p. 1996. pap. text 5.00 (*1-887012-02-8*) Hanovr Pr.

Little Books, Ages 4-6. Christine E. McCormick & Jana M. Mason. 80p. 1989. pap. 8.95 (*0-673-38878-6*, GoodYrBooks) Addson-Wesley Educ.

Little Books & Big Books Level K, Set 1: Teacher's Resource Guide. (Illus.). 28p. (J). (ps-1). 1998. pap., teacher ed. 3.00 (*0-8215-0881-4*) Sadlier.

Little Books & Big Books Level K, Set 2: Teacher's Resource Guide. (Illus.). 28p. (J). (ps-1). 1998. pap. 3.00 (*0-8215-0882-2*) Sadlier.

Little Books & Big Books Level K, Set 3: Teacher's Resource Guide. (Illus.). 28p. (J). (ps-1). 1998. pap. 3.00 (*0-8215-0883-0*) Sadlier.

Little Books & Big Books Level K, Set 4: Teacher's Resource Guide. (Illus.). 28p. (J). (ps-1). 1998. pap. 3.00 (*0-8215-0884-9*) Sadlier.

Little Books for Cooks Apples. Andrews & McMeel Staff. (Little Books for Cooks). 1998. 4.95 (*0-8362-5228-4*) Andrews & McMeel.

Little Books for Cooks Herbs. Andrews & McMeel Staff. (Little Books for Cooks). 1998. 4.95 (*0-8362-5229-2*) Andrews & McMeel.

Little Books for Cooks Salsas. Andrews & McMeel Staff. LC 97-74527. (Little Books for Cooks). 1998. 4.95 (*0-8362-5230-6*) Andrews & McMeel.

Little Books from A to Z. Christine E. McCormack. 1998. pap. 9.95 (*0-673-57727-9*, GoodYrBooks) Addson-Wesley Educ.

Little Books-Indians. Hannah Weiner. (Roof Bks.). 88p. (Orig.). 1983. pap. text 60.00 (*0-937804-02-9*) Segue NYC.

Little Books 1,2,3. Christine E. McCormack. 1998. pap. text 9.95 (*0-673-58659-6*) Addson-Wesley Educ.

Little Box. Vasko Popa. Tr. by Charles Simic. LC 78-134539. 1973. 7.50 (*0-910350-09-4*) Charioteer.

Little Box. Donna Schwalbe. Ed. by Byron Miller. LC 94-75226. (Illus.). 24p. (Orig.). (J). 1994. pap. 5.95 (*0-9636637-2-0*) Impatience Pubns.

Little Box of Ballet Stories, 3 vols. Illus. by Francesca Crespi. Incl. Coppelia. LC 86-930. (Illus.). 1986. Fire Bird. LC 86-930. (Illus.). 1986. Petrushka. LC 86-930. (Illus.). 1986. LC 86-930. (Illus.). 28p. (J). (ps-3). 1986. 8.95 (*0-8037-0265-5*, Dial Yng Read) Peng Put Young Read.

Little Box of Crayons. Shane Derolf. (J). 1998. pap. 16.99 (*0-679-85460-6*) Knopf Bks Yng Read.

***Little Box of Inner Calm.** Christopher Titmuss. 64p. 1999. pap. text 19.95 (*0-7641-7303-0*) Barron.

Little Boxes. R. Martin Helick. 1982. spiral bd. 17.50 (*0-912710-10-1*) Regent Graphic Serv.

Little Boy Blue. Eddie Bunker. LC 97-16103. 320p. 1997. text 22.95 (*0-312-16907-8*) St Martin.

Little Boy Blue. Edward Bunker. 240p. 1998. pap. 13.95 (*0-312-19504-4*, Pub. by Tor Bks) St Martin.

Little Boy Blue. large type ed. Ed Dee. LC 97-15302. (Wheeler Large Print Book Ser.). 1997. pap. 22.95 (*1-56895-452-2*) Wheeler Pub.

Little Boy Blue. Ed Dee. 320p. 1998. reprint ed. mass mkt. 6.99 (*0-446-60522-0*, Pub. by Warner Bks) Little.

Little Boy Blue: Switched at Birth. Suzannah Davis. (Special Edition Ser.: No. 1149). 1998. per. 3.99 (*0-373-24149-6*, 1-24149-6) Silhouette.

Little Boy Blue & Other Rhymes. Ed. by Iona Opie. LC 97-65085. (My Very First Mother Goose Board Bks.). (Illus.). 16p. (J). (ps). 1997. bds. 6.99 (*0-7636-0354-6*) Candlewick Pr.

Little Boy Book. Paula Yates. (Illus.). 96p. 1995. text 5.95 (*1-85227-481-6*, Pub. by Virgin Bks) London Brdge.

Little Boy Book: A Guide to the First Eight Years. Sheila Moore. LC 97-97007. 320p. 1998. pap. 11.00 (*0-345-42350-X*) Ballantine Pub Grp.

Little Boy Book: A Guide to the First Eight Years. Sheila Moore & Roon Frost. 320p. 1987. mass mkt. 5.99 (*0-345-34466-9*) Ballantine Pub Grp.

Little Boy in Confederate Mobile. Peter Hamilton. (American Autobiography Ser.). 21p. 1995. reprint ed. lib. bdg. 69.00 (*0-7812-8548-8*) Rprt Serv.

***Little Boy Jesus.** Concordia Publishing Staff. LC 99-182962. (Small Big Bks.). (Illus.). 16p. (J). (ps-1). 1998. pap. 2.49 (*0-570-05544-X*, 54-0081GJ) Concordia.

***Little Boy Jesus.** Lynn Moore. (Baby Blessings Ser.). (Illus.). 12p. (J). 2000. 7.99 (*0-7847-1190-9*, 04330) Standard Pub.

***Little Boy Lost.** Adrianne Lee. (Intrigue Ser.). 2000. mass mkt. 4.25 (*0-373-22580-6*, 1-22580-4) Harlequin Bks.

Little Boy Lost. T. M. Wright. 256p. 1995. 4.99 (*0-8125-5069-2*, Pub. by Tor Bks) St Martin.

Little Boy Lost. William Henry Hudson. reprint ed. 64.50 (*0-404-03403-9*) AMS Pr.

Little Boy Named Avram. Dina Rosenfeld. (Little Greats Ser.). (Illus.). 32p. (J). (ps-1). 1989. 9.95 (*0-922613-08-7*); pap. 6.95 (*0-922613-09-5*) Hachai Pubng.

Little Boy with Three Names: Stories of Taos Pueblo. Ann N. Clark. LC 89-81127. (Illus.). 80p. (J). (gr. 3 up). 1990. reprint ed. pap. 8.95 (*0-941270-59-9*) Ancient City Pr.

Little Boy with Three Names & Other Stories. rev. ed. Ann N. Clark. (Illus.). 48p. (J). (gr. k-7). 1999. pap. 6.95 (*1-885772-16-5*) Kiva Pubng.

Little Boy's Anthology. Peter T. Ferrero, 3rd. (Illus.). 128p. (Orig.). 1996. pap. 12.50 (*0-9657096-0-4*) P T Ferrero.

***Little Boys Bible Storybook for Mothers & Sons.** Illus. by Caron Turk. 360p. (gr. 1-4). 1999. 16.99 (*0-8010-4433-2*, New Kids Media) Baker Bks.

***Little Boys Come from the Stars.** Emmanuel Dongala. Tr. by Joel Rejouis et al from FRE. 256p. 2001. 22.00 (*0-374-18496-8*) FS&G.

***Little Boys Lunch, 6 vols.** (Illus.). (J). 1999. pap. 9.00 (*0-87162-835-X*) Warner Pr.

Little Boys' Picnic. Date not set. pap. 5.95 (*0-87162-985-2*) Warner Pr.

***Little Boysu Bible Activity Calendar.** Carolyn Larsen & Vicki Totel. 368p. (J). (ps-8). 2000. spiral bd. 9.99 (*0-8010-4457-X*, New Kids Media) Baker Bks.

***Little Boysu Book of Prayers.** Carolyn Larsen. 192p. (J). (ps-7). 2000. 12.99 (*0-8010-4440-5*, New Kids Media) Baker Bks.

***Little Brave Son.** Alexandra Machover. (J). (gr. 1-3). 2000. 10.95 (*0-533-13474-9*) Vantage.

Little Brazil: An Ethnography of Brazilian Immigrants in New York City. Maxine L. Margolis. LC 93-13699. (Illus.). 328p. 1994. text 55.00 (*0-691-03348-X*, Pub. by Princeton U Pr) Cal Prin Full Svc.

Little Britches. Ralph Moody. (J). 1976. 23.95 (*0-8488-1105-4*) Amereon Ltd.

Little Britches. Ralph Moody. 262p. 1986. reprint ed. lib. bdg. 29.95 (*0-89966-563-2*) Buccaneer Bks.

Little Britches: Father & I Were Ranchers. Ralph Moody. LC 91-4139. (Illus.). 260p. 1991. reprint ed. pap. 10.95 (*0-8032-8178-1*, Bison Books) U of Nebr Pr.

Little Brother. Allan Baillie. LC 91-28797. 1994. 9.09 (*0-606-06535-0*, Pub. by Turtleback) Demco.

Little Brother. Regina Brown. (Illus.). (J). (gr. 3-7). 1962. 8.95 (*0-8392-3019-2*) Astor-Honor.

Little Brother. Bill Eidson. 288p. 1991. mass mkt. 4.50 (*0-8217-3397-4*, Zebra Kensgtn) Kensgtn Pub Corp.

Little Brother. Josiah F. Willard. LC 68-57562. (Muckrakers Ser.). reprint ed. lib. bdg. 22.75 (*0-8398-2170-0*) Irvington.

Little Brother Goes Down: An Erotic Exorcism. Carl D. Birman. LC 95-67314. (Illus.). 80p. (Orig.). 1995. pap. 9.95 (*0-9635181-1-9*) Plutonia Pr.

Little Brother, Little Sister & Out of the Flying Pan: Two Plays. David Campton. 1967. pap. 5.25 (*0-8222-0674-9*) Dramatists Play.

Little Brother Moose. James Kasperson. (Illus.). 32p. (J). (ps-5). 1995. pap. 7.95 (*1-883220-33-5*) Dawn CA.

Little Brother Moose. James Kasperson. 1995. 12.15 (*0-606-08801-6*, Pub. by Turtleback) Demco.

Little Brother of the Rich. Joseph M. Patterson. LC 68-57545. (Muckrakers Ser.). (Illus.). reprint ed. lib. bdg. 22.50 (*0-8398-1553-0*) Irvington.

Little Brother of the Rich. Joseph M. Patterson. (Muckrakers Ser.). (C). 1987. reprint ed. pap. text 7.95 (*0-8290-2377-1*) Irvington.

Little Brother of the Wilderness: The Story of Johnny Appleseed. Meridel Le Sueur. (Illus.). 80p. 1996. pap. text 7.95 (*0-930100-71-9*) Holy Cow.

***Little Brother of War.** large type ed. Gerald B. Mirra. Ed. by Karen Bernardo. (Illus.). 32p. (J). (gr. 3-6). 1999. pap. 6.95 (*0-9655486-2-7*, 103) Signature Pub.

Little Brothers. Rick Hautala. 1988. mass mkt. 4.50 (*0-8217-4020-2*, Zebra Kensgtn) Kensgtn Pub Corp.

Little, Brown & Company Rights Guide: Including Atlantic Monthly Press Books & New York Graphic Society Books. Ed. by Little, Brown & Company Staff. 1984. write for info. (*0-318-57553-1*, Aspen Law & Bus) Aspen Pub.

Little Brown Bear Does Not Want to Eat. Claude Lebrun. LC 95-1134. (Little Brown Bear Ser.). (Illus.). 16p. (J). (gr. k-2). 1996. 3.95 (*0-516-17823-7*) Childrens.

Little Brown Bear in I Won't Take a Nap. Jane Dyer. (Illus.). 32p. (J). 2000. write for info. (*0-316-19764-5*) Little.

Little Brown Bear Is Afraid of the Dark. Claude Lebrun. LC 95-1133. (Little Brown Bear Ser.). (Illus.). 16p. (J). (ps-2). 1995. pap. 3.95 (*0-516-17825-3*) Childrens.

Little Brown Bear Is Sick. Claude Lebrun. LC 95-1138. (Little Brown Bear Ser.). (Illus.). 16p. (J). (ps-2). 1995. pap. 3.95 (*0-516-17821-0*) Childrens.

Little Brown Bear Plays in the Snow. Claude Lebrun. LC 95-26330. (Little Brown Bear Ser.). 16p. (J). 1997. 3.95 (*0-516-17847-4*) Childrens.

Little Brown Bear Says "No" to Everything. Claude Lebrun. LC 95-5732. (Little Brown Bear Ser.). (Illus.). 16p. (J). (ps-2). 1995. 3.95 (*0-516-17828-8*) Childrens.

Little Brown Bear 3, 4 vols., Set. Claude Lebrun. (J). 1996. boxed set 15.80 (*0-516-17804-0*) Childrens.

Little Brown Bear Wants to Be Read To. Claude Lebrun. LC 95-5733. (Little Brown Bear Ser.).Tr. of Petit Ours Brun Vent des Histoires. (Illus.). 16p. (J). (gr. k-3). 1996. 3.95 (*0-516-17829-6*) Childrens.

Little Brown Bear Wants to Go to School. Claude Lebrun. LC 95-5734. (Little Brown Bear Ser.). (Illus.). 16p. (J). (ps-2). 1995. pap. 3.95 (*0-516-17830-X*) Childrens.

Little Brown Book of Restaurant Success. Bob Brown & Bill Still. LC 94-94450. (Illus.). 142p. 1994. pap. 17.95 (*0-9640485-1-5*) Reinhardt & Still.

Little Brown Brother. Leon Wolff. (Illus.). 384p. 1992. pap. text 29.95 (*0-19-588986-X*) OUP.

Little, Brown Compact Handbook. 2nd ed. Jane E. Aaron. (Illus.). 320p. (C). 1997. text 22.66 (*0-673-99408-2*) Addson-Wesley Educ.

An Asterisk (*) at the beginning of an entry indicates that the title is appearing for the first time.

L

Little, Brown Compact Handbook. 2nd ed. Jane E. Aaron. 320p. 1995. spiral bd. 22.95 (*0-8230-5001-7*) Watsn-Guptill.

Little, Brown Compact Handbook. 2nd ed. A. Daedalus. 1997. cd-rom 17.86 (*0-673-97260-7*) Addson-Wesley Educ.

Little Brown Compact Handbook. 3rd ed. (C). 1997. write for info. (*0-321-00243-1*) Addison-Wesley.

***Little, Brown Compact Handbook.** 3rd ed. Jane E. Aaron. 416p. (C). 1998. spiral bd. 29.06 (*0-321-03796-0*) Addson-Wesley Educ.

***Little, Brown Compact Handbook.** 4th ed. Jane E. Aaron. LC 00-31024. 2000. write for info. (*0-321-07509-9*) Addson-Wesley Educ.

Little Brown Donkey. Kathleen C. Dahlquist. Ed. by Alice Drake. LC 94-71676. (Illus.). 64p. (Orig.). (J). (gr. 3). 1994. pap. 7.95 (*0-9634122-8-0*) Feather Fables.

Little Brown Essential Handbook for Business Writers. Aaron. (C). 2000. spiral bd. Price not set. (*0-321-02697-7*) Addison-Wesley.

Little Brown Essential Handbook for Technical Writers. Aaron. (C). 2000. spiral bd. Price not set. (*0-321-02695-0*) Addison-Wesley.

***Little Brown Essential Handbook for Writers.** 3rd ed. 144p. (C). 2000. 9.60 (*0-321-06129-2*) Addison-Wesley.

Little Brown Essential Handbook for Writers. 3rd ed. James Aaron. LC 99-28869. 247p. (C). 1999. spiral bd. 16.00 (*0-321-04970-5*) Addson-Wesley Educ.

Little, Brown Handbook. 5th ed. H. Ramsey Fowler & Jane E. Aaron. (C). 1997. 43.00 (*0-673-52132-X*) Addson-Wesley Educ.

Little, Brown Handbook. 7th ed. Ed. by H. Ramsey Fowler. 600p. (C). 1997. pap. text, wbk. ed. 25.66 (*0-321-01217-8*) Addson-Wesley Educ.

***Little Brown Handbook.** 8th ed. 2000. teacher ed. write for info. (*0-321-07764-4*) Addison-Wesley.

***Little, Brown Handbook.** 8th ed. H. Ramsey Fowler & Jane E. Aaron. LC 00-31332. 2000. write for info. (*0-321-07507-2*) Longman.

***Little Brown Handbook: Documentation Guide.** 8th ed. 2000. write for info. (*0-321-07761-X*) Addison-Wesley.

***Little Brown Handbook: Second Canadian Edition.** 1998. teacher ed. (*0-321-40199-9*) S&S Trade.

***Little, Brown Handbook: With MLA Update.** 7th ed. H. Ramsey Fowler. 912p. (C). 1998. text 34.69 (*0-321-03797-9*) Addson-Wesley Educ.

Little, Brown Handbook: Writer's Workshop Windows. 6th ed. Fowler Companies, Inc. Staff. (C). 1997. text 11.25 (*0-673-52521-X*) Addson-Wesley Educ.

Little Brown Handbook with daedalus. 7th ed. Daedalus. (C). 1999. 39.00 (*0-321-06489-5*) Addison-Wesley.

Little Brown Hen's Shower. Pamela Duncan Edwards. LC 99-28506. 32p. 2000. lib. bdg. 14.49 (*0-7868-2409-3*, Pub. by Hyprn Child) Little.

Little Brown Hen's Shower. Pamela Duncun Edwards. (Illus.). 32p. (J). 2000. 13.99 (*0-7868-0467-X*, Pub. by Hyprn Child) Little.

Little Brown Jay: A Tale from India. Elizabeth Claire. LC 94-14366. (Mondo Folktales ser.). (Illus.). 24p. (Orig.). (J). (gr. k-4). 1994. pap. 4.95 (*1-879531-23-2*); lib. bdg. 9.95 (*1-879531-44-5*) Mondo Pubng.

Little Brown Kitten. large type ed. Pam Jarrell. (Cuddle Bks.). (Illus.). 7p. (J). (ps-k). 1997. pap. text 10.95 (*1-57332-090-0*) HighReach Lrning.

Little Brown Monkey. (Choices & Decisions Ser.). (J). (gr. k-1). 1990. audio 7.92 (*0-8123-6494-5*) McDougal-Littell.

Little Brown Reader. 5th ed. Marcia Stubbs & Sylvan Barnet. (C). 1997. 49.00 (*0-673-39679-7*) Addson-Wesley Educ.

Little, Brown Reader. 7th ed. (C). 1995. pap., teacher ed. write for info. (*0-673-54266-1*) Addson-Wesley Educ.

***Little Brown Reader.** 8th ed. Stubbs. LC 99-36899. 893p. (C). 1999. pap. 42.00 (*0-321-02401-X*) Addson-Wesley Educ.

Little Brown Roadrunner: Who Did It Herself. Leon Wender. LC 92-72166. (Illus.). 24p. (Orig.). (J). (gr. 1-3). 1992. pap. text 4.00 (*0-938513-14-1*) Amador Pubs.

***Little Brown Workbook.** 2000. write for info. (*0-321-07776-8*) Addison-Wesley.

Little, Brown Workbook. 4th ed. Donna Gorrell. (C). 1989. pap. text 24.60 (*0-673-39925-7*) Addson-Wesley Educ.

Little, Brown's Maternal-Newborn Nursing Review. Irene M. Bobak et al. LC 96-9117. 1997. pap. text 22.95 (*0-316-10209-1*) Lppncott W & W.

Little, Brown's Medical-Surgical Nursing Review. Robyn M. Nelson et al. LC 96-23717. 1997. pap. text 22.95 (*0-316-81169-6*) Lppncott W & W.

Little, Brown's NCLEX-RN Examination Review. rev. ed. Irene M. Bobak et al. Ed. by Sally L. Lagerquist. LC 95-49688. (Illus.). 680p. 1996. pap. text 34.95 (*0-316-51279-6*, Little Brwn Med Div) Lppncott W & W.

Little, Brown's Nursing Q&A: Critical-Thinking Exercises. Sally L. Lagerquist. LC 96-10793. (RN NCLEX Review Ser.). 350p. 1996. pap. text 26.95 (*0-316-51298-2*) Lppncott W & W.

Little, Brown's Pediatric Nursing Review. Geraldine C. Colombraro & Sally L. Lagerquist. LC 96-20788. 1997. pap. text 22.95 (*0-316-15137-8*) Lppncott W & W.

Little, Brown's Psychiatric-Mental Health Nursing Review. Sally L. Lagerquist. LC 96-9116. 1997. pap. text 22.95 (*0-316-51299-0*) Lppncott W & W.

Little Budget Book: A Portable Budgeting Guide for Local Government. Len Wood. LC 93-92644. 184p. 1993. 29.95 (*0-9634374-1-0*) Trng Shoppe.

Little Buggers: Insect & Spider Poems. J. Patrick Lewis. LC 94-31900. (Illus.). 32p. (J). (gr. k up). 1998. 15.89 (*0-8037-1770-9*, Dial Yng Read) Peng Put Young Read.

***Little Buggers: Insect & Spider Poems.** J. Patrick Lewis. LC 94-31900. (Illus.). 32p. (J). (gr. 1-4). 1998. 15.99 (*0-8037-1769-5*, Dial Yng Read) Peng Put Young Read.

Little Bugler: The True Story of a Twelve Year Old Boy in the Civil War. William B. Styple. LC 98-72201. (Illus.). 184p. 1998. 21.95 (*1-883926-11-4*) Belle Grv Pub.

Little Bugler: The True Story of a Twelve-Year-Old Boy in the Civil War. William B. Styple. (Civil War Ser.). (Illus.). 184p. 1998. pap. 17.95 (*1-883926-12-2*) Belle Grv Pub.

Little Bulbs: A Tale of Two Gardens. Elizabeth Lawrence. LC 57-6248. 261p. (Orig.). 1986. reprint ed. pap. 16.95 (*0-8223-0739-1*); reprint ed. text 39.95 (*0-8223-0671-9*) Duke.

Little Bull: Growing up in Africa's Elephant Kingdom. Ellen F. James. LC 98-181024. (Illus.). 48p. (J). (gr. 3-7). 1998. 12.95 (*0-8069-2098-X*) Sterling.

Little Bunnies All Through the Year: A Word Picture Book. Ladybird Books Staff. (Little Bunnies Word Books Ser.: No. S9012-2). (J). 1990. pap. 3.95 (*0-7214-5289-2*, Ladybrd) Penguin Putnam.

Little Bunnies Around Town. (Little Bunnies Word Books Ser.: No. S9012-3). (J). 1990. pap. 3.95 (*0-7214-5290-6*, Ladybrd) Penguin Putnam.

Little Bunnies at Home: A Picture Word Book. Ladybird Books Staff. (Little Bunnies Word Books Ser.: No. S9012-1). (J). 1990. pap. 3.95 (*0-7214-5288-4*, Ladybrd) Penguin Putnam.

Little Bunnies on the Move: A Word Picture Book. Ladybird Books Staff. (Little Bunnies Word Books Ser.: No. S9012-4). (J). 1990. pap. 3.95 (*0-7214-5291-4*, Ladybrd) Penguin Putnam.

Little Bunnies on Vacation: A Word Picture Book. Ladybird Books Staff. (Little Bunnies Word Books Ser.: No. S9012-5). (J). 1990. pap. 3.95 (*0-7214-5292-2*, Ladybrd) Penguin Putnam.

Little Bunny. Stephanie Calmenson. (Chubby Shape Bks.). (Illus.). 16p. (J). (ps-k). 1985. pap. 3.50 (*0-671-53110-7*) Litle Simon.

Little Bunny. Stephanie Calmenson. (Illus.). (J). (gr. 2-6). 1986. 4.95 (*0-671-62974-7*) Litle Simon.

Little Bunny - Duck, 2 bks., Set. (J). 1993. pap. 9.90 (*0-590-66845-5*) Scholastic Inc.

Little Bunny - Duck, 2 bks., Set. Ed. by Scholastic, Inc. Staff. (J). 1994. pap. 9.90 (*0-590-66919-2*) Scholastic Inc.

***Little Bunny Adventures.** Emma Satchell. LC 98-183792. (Illus.). 24p. (J). (ps-1). 1998. 7.98 (*0-7651-0691-4*) Smithmark.

Little Bunny Bobkin. James Riordan. LC 98-15771. (Illus.). 32p. (J). (ps-1). 1999. 14.95 (*1-888444-38-X*) Little Tiger.

Little Bunny Follows His Nose. Katherine Howard. LC 98-85958. (Golden Scratch & Sniff Bks.). (Illus.). 32p. (J). (ps-3). 1971. 9.99 (*0-307-13536-5*, Goldn Books) Gldn Bks Pub Co.

Little Bunny on the Move. Peter McCarty. LC 98-29787. 32p. (J). (ps-1). 2000. 14.95 (*0-8050-4620-8*) H Holt & Co.

Little Bunny's Christmas Present. Setsuo Yazaki. Tr. by Diane T. Ooka from JPN. (Illus.). 32p. (J). (ps-8). 1983. 12.95 (*0-89346-225-X*) Heian Intl.

Little Bunny's Cool Tool Set. Maribeth Boelts. LC 96-54862. (Concept Bks.). (Illus.). 32p. (J). (ps-1). 1997. lib. bdg. 14.95 (*0-8075-4584-8*) A Whitman.

Little Bunny's Cool Tool Set. Maribeth Boelts. (Illus.). 32p. (J). (ps-1). 1999. pap. 6.95 (*0-8075-4585-6*) A Whitman.

Little Bunny's Easter Day: Bend n' Snuggle Book. Illus. by Jane Moday. 18p. (J). (ps). 1999. 9.99 (*0-7847-0971-8*, 03541) Standard Pub.

Little Bunny's Easter Egg Surprise. Susan Hood. (Illus.). 24p. (J). (ps-2). 1997. pap. 3.95 (*0-8167-3739-8*, Whistlstop) Troll Communs.

Little Bunny's Easter Surprise, 1 vol. Lucinda McQueen. 1999. 3.50 (*0-590-65029-7*) Scholastic Inc.

***Little Bunny's Easter Surprise.** Jeanne Modesitt. LC 98-28841. (Illus.). 32p. (J). (ps-1). 1999. 12.95 (*0-689-82491-2*) S&S Bks Yung.

Little Bunny's Pacifier Plan. Maribeth Boelts. LC 98-35244. (Illus.). (J). (ps-k). 1999. lib. bdg. 14.95 (*0-8075-4581-3*) A Whitman.

Little Bunny's Preschool Countdown. Maribeth Boelts. (Illus.). 32p. (J). (ps-1). 1996. lib. bdg. 14.95 (*0-8075-4582-1*) A Whitman.

Little Bunny's Preschool Countdown. Maribeth Boelts. (Illus.). 32p. (J). (ps-1). 1999. pap. 6.95 (*0-8075-4583-X*) A Whitman.

Little Bunny's Sleepless Night. Carol Roth. LC 98-41047. (Illus.). (J). (ps-2). 1999. 15.95 (*0-7358-1069-9*, Pub. by North-South Bks NYC); lib. bdg. 15.88 (*0-7358-1070-2*, Pub. by North-South Bks NYC) Chronicle Bks.

Little Business in the American Economy, Volume 42. Joseph D. Phillips. LC 81-4217. (Illinois Studies in the Social Sciences: Vol. 42). (Illus.). 135p. 1981. reprint ed. lib. bdg. 59.50 (*0-313-23055-2*, PHLB, Greenwood Pr) Greenwood.

Little Butch Book. Leslea Newman. LC 98-27367. (Illus.). 64p. 1998. 10.00 (*0-934678-96-0*) New Victoria Pubs.

Little Butterflies Stained Glass Coloring Book. John Green. (Illus.). (J). (gr. k-3). 1993. pap. 1.00 (*0-486-27010-6*) Dover.

Little Butterfly. Sherry Shahan. LC 97-28745. (J). 1998. pap. 3.25 (*0-679-88809-8*, Pub. by Random Bks Yng Read) Random.

Little Butterfly. Sherry Shahan. (J). 1998. 8.35 (*0-606-13964-8*, Pub. by Turtleback) Demco.

Little Butterfly Stickers, Vol. 80. Nina Barbaresi. (Illus.). (J). (gr. k-3). 1993. pap. 1.00 (*0-486-27663-5*) Dover.

Little by Little: Six Decades of Collecting American Decorative Arts. Nina F. Little. LC 97-62560. (Illus.). 308p. 1998. pap. 35.00 (*0-87451-866-0*) U Pr of New Eng.

Little by Little: The Pieces Add Up. Stephen Glick. (Illus.). 392p. 1990. 8.95 (*0-925190-11-X*) Fairview Press.

***Little by Little Art Book.** Edmund F. Benson & Susan Benson. (Illus.). (J). (gr. 3-4). 1999. pap. text 9.99 (*1-58614-002-7*) Arise Found.

Little by Little Manual. Edmund F. Benson & Susan Benson. (Illus.). (J). (gr. 3-4). 1994. pap. text 64.95 (*1-58614-000-0*) Arise Found.

***Little by Little Puppet Plays.** Edmund F. Benson & Susan Benson. (Illus.). (J). (gr. 3-4). 1999. pap. text 7.49 (*1-58614-001-9*) Arise Found.

***Little 'c' Sellers.** (J). 2000. 3.95 (*0-552-52874-9*, Pub. by Transworld Publishers Ltd) Trafalgar.

Little C++ (Made Easy) Ray Leo. (Illus.). 200p. (Orig.). 1996. pap. 14.95 (*0-9654634-1-9*) Leo Pr.

Little Caballero Piano Solo. Stecher & Horo. 4p. 1986. pap. 3.95 (*0-7935-5314-8*, 50452590) H Leonard.

Little Caesar. W. R. Burnett. 156p. 1986. pap. 3.50 (*0-88184-235-4*) Carroll & Graf.

Little Caesar. W. R. Burnett. 316p. 1994. 35.00 (*1-883402-78-6*) S&S Trade.

Little Caesar. W. R. Burnett. 308p. reprint ed. lib. bdg. 20.95 (*0-89190-485-9*, Rivercity Pr) Amereon Ltd.

Little Calf. Kim Lewis. LC 99-28784. 24p. (J). 2000. 9.99 (*0-7636-0899-8*) Candlewick Pr.

Little Calf. Kath Mellentin & Tim Woods. (Farm Babies Ser.). (Illus.). 10p. (J). 1997. bds. 3.50 (*1-884628-58-3*, Flyng Frog) Allied Pub MD.

Little California Cookbook. John Carroll. (Illus.). 60p. 1992. 7.95 (*0-8118-0097-0*) Chronicle Bks.

Little Candle Book. Anness Publications Staff. 1999. 11.95 (*0-7548-0188-8*) Random.

Little Candles: A Collection of Poems & Stories. Margaret H. Clem. LC 95-80768. 64p. (Orig.). 1995. pap. 4.95 (*1-878044-45-1*, Wld Rose) Mayhaven Pub.

Little Capoeira Book. Nestor Capoeira. Tr. by Alex Ladd from POR. LC 95-2216. (Illus.). 150p. (Orig.). (C). 1995. pap. 11.95 (*1-55643-199-6*) North Atlantic.

***Little Car.** Opal Dunn. (Track-Me-Back Board Bks.). 12p. (J). 2000. bds. 5.95 (*0-8050-6417-6*) H Holt & Co.

Little Car. Sian Tucker. (Illus.). 10p. (J). (ps). 1993. pap. 2.95 (*0-671-79737-9*) Litle Simon.

Little Caribbean Cookbook. Jill Hamilton. (Illus.). 60p. 1990. 7.95 (*0-87701-685-2*) Chronicle Bks.

Little Caribbean Girl Paper Doll. Sylvia Walker. (Illus.). (J). (gr. k-3). 1993. pap. 1.00 (*0-486-27442-X*) Dover.

Little Caribou. Sarah Fox-Davies. LC 95-34546. (Illus.). 32p. (J). (gr. k-3). 1996. 15.99 (*1-56402-923-9*) Candlewick Pr.

Little Caribou. Sarah Fox-Davies. 1997. 11.19 (*0-606-13574-X*, Pub. by Turtleback) Demco.

Little Caribou. Sandra Fox-Davies. LC 95-34546. (Illus.). 32p. (J). (gr. k-3). 1997. reprint ed. pap. 5.99 (*0-7636-0350-3*) Candlewick Pr.

Little Carthaginian, Vol. IV. Tr. by P. Nixon. (Loeb Classical Library: No. 260). 15.50 (*0-674-99286-5*) HUP.

Little Cat That Could Not Sleep. Frances M. Fox. LC 72-89335. (Illus.). 32p. (J). (gr. k-4). 1973. 12.95 (*0-87592-030-6*) Scroll Pr.

Little Cat Who Had No Name. Tulsi Reynolds. LC 90-62915. (Illus.). 32p. 1990. pap. 9.25 (*1-877675-04-0*) Midmarch Arts.

Little Catechism of the Cure of Ars. John Vianney. LC 87-50943. (Illus.). 139p. 1994. reprint ed. pap. 6.00 (*0-89555-323-6*) TAN Bks Pubs.

Little Catechism on the Holy Rosary: In Relation to the Image of Our Lade of Guadalupe. Miguel Guadalupe. LC 96-7084. 64p. (Orig.). 1997. pap. text 2.95 (*1-882972-78-3*, 3522) Queenship Pub.

***Little Caterpillar That Finds Jesus (La Oruguita que Encuentra a Jesus) A Parable of the Eucharist (Una Parabola Acerca de la Eucaristia)** Susan A. Brindle et al. Tr. by Carmen A. Emmanuelli Klosterman. (Seven Sacraments Ser.). (ENG & SPA., Illus.). 72p. (gr. k-10). 1999. pap. 9.95 (*1-889733-08-3*, 01011) Precious Life Bks.

Little Cats see Zoobooks

Little Cats see Animals & Critters

Little Cats. Bobbie Kalman. (Crabapples Ser.). 1994. 11.15 (*0-606-07027-3*, Pub. by Turtleback) Demco.

Little Cats. Wildlife Education, Ltd. Staff & John B. Wexo. (Zoobooks Ser.). (Illus.). 24p. (J). 1993. 13.95 (*0-937934-82-8*) Wildlife Educ.

Little Cats. Wildlife Education, Ltd. Staff & John B. Wexo. (Zoobooks Ser.). (Illus.). 200p. (YA). (gr. 5 up). 1998. pap. 2.75 (*0-937934-16-X*) Wildlife Educ.

Little Celebrations Machines. (J). (gr. k). 1997. (*0-673-80568-9*, Scott Frsmn) Addson-Wesley Educ.

Little Celtic Alphabet. Andrew Whitson. (Illus.). 80p. 1997. 13.95 (*0-86281-664-5*, Pub. by Appletree Pr) Irish Bks Media.

***Little Chapters about Mission San Juan Capistrano.** 42nd ed. St. John O'Sullivan. (Special Bks.: Vol. 4). (Illus.). v, 33p. 1998. reprint ed. pap. 9.95 (*1-891030-05-1*) Paragon Agency.

Little Character That's Me, Vol. I. Barbara Schwartz. (Illus.). 65p. (Orig.). (J). (ps-6). 1988. student ed. 11.95 (*0-685-22570-4*); audio 14.95 (*0-685-22571-2*) Little Prodns.

Little Chefs Cook Book. B. B. Stabell. 70p. (J). (gr. 7 up). 1982. pap. 4.75 (*0-9610872-0-X*) B B Stabell.

Little Chick. Stephanie Calmenson. (Chubby Shape Bks.). 16p. (J). (ps-1). 1985. 3.50 (*0-671-53111-5*) Litle Simon.

Little Chick. Stewart Cowley. LC 95-80204. (Fluffy Tales Ser.). (Illus.). 10p. (J). (gr. k-3). 1996. bds. 4.99 (*1-57584-007-3*, Pub. by Rdrs Digest) Random.

Little Chick. Lisa McCue. LC 85-63658. (Board Bks.). (Illus.). 7p. (J). (ps). 1986. 4.99 (*0-394-88017-X*, Pub. by Random Bks Yng Read) Random.

***Little Chick.** Allia Robel-Nolan. (Fluffy Tales Ser.). (Illus.). 10p. (J). (ps-k). 2000. bds. 5.99 (*0-7847-0889-4*, 03699) Standard Pub.

Little Chick Chick. Demi. LC 90-85829. (Mini Soft & Furry Board Bks.). (Illus.). 12p. (J). (ps-3). 1992. bds. 4.95 (*0-448-41090-7*, G & D) Peng Put Young Read.

Little Chicken. Margaret Wise Brown. LC 43-16942. (Illus.). 32p. (J). (ps-3). 1943. 13.00 (*0-06-020739-6*) HarpC Child Bks.

Little Chicken Chicken. David Martin. LC 96-43694. (Illus.). 32p. (J). (ps up). 1997. pap. 5.99 (*0-7636-0121-7*) Candlewick Pr.

Little Chicken Chicken. David Martin. LC 95-43694. (J). 1997. 11.19 (*0-606-11568-4*, Pub. by Turtleback) Demco.

***Little Chick's Big Adventure.** Fowler. (J). 2000. 10.95 (*0-385-40728-9*, Pub. by Transworld Publishers Ltd) Trafalgar.

Little Chick's Big Day. Mary D. Kwitz. LC 80-7905. (I Can Read Bks.). (Illus.). 32p. (J). (ps-3). 1981. 7.89 (*0-06-023667-1*) HarpC Child Bks.

Little Chick's Breakfast. Mary D. Kwitz. LC 82-48259. (I Can Read Bks.). 32p. (J). (ps-3). 1983. 8.95 (*0-06-023674-4*) HarpC Child Bks.

Little Chick's Easter Surprise. Lucinda McQueen. 1999. pap. 3.50 (*0-590-64985-X*) Scholastic Inc.

Little Chick's Easter Surprise. Rock. (J). 1997. pap. 2.95 (*0-7459-3730-6*, Pub. by Lion Pubng) Trafalgar.

Little Chick's Friend, Duckling. Mary D. Kwitz. LC 90-5027. (I Can Read Bks.). (Illus.). 32p. (J). (ps-2). 1995. pap. 3.95 (*0-06-444179-2*) HarpC Child Bks.

Little Chick's Friend, Duckling. Mary D. Kwitz. (I Can Read Bks.). (J). (ps-1). 1995. 8.95 (*0-606-07793-6*) Turtleback.

Little Chief Mischief. Nigel Salter-Mathieson. (Illus.). (J). (gr. 2-7). 1962. 10.95 (*0-8392-3020-6*) Astor-Honor.

Little Child in the Sky. Alexandra Stoll. LC 93-20692. (Illus.). 48p. (Orig.). 1993. pap. 7.95 (*0-9627226-7-7*) Excalibur Pub.

Little Children Suffer. Ed. by Norbette Mette & Maureen Junker-Kenny. (Concilium Ser.). 150p. (Orig.). 1996. pap. 15.00 (*1-57075-071-8*) Orbis Bks.

Little China: The Annamese Lands. Alan H. Brodrick. LC 74-179173. (South & Southeast Asia Studies). reprint ed. 21.50 (*0-404-54803-2*) AMS Pr.

Little Chinese Astrology Book. George R. Siciliano. (Illus.). 50p. (Orig.). 1996. pap. 7.00 (*0-9658860-0-X*) G R Siciliano.

Little Chinese Girl Paper Dolls. Tom Tierney. (Illus.). (J). (gr. k-3). 1993. pap. 1.00 (*0-486-27432-2*) Dover.

Little Choocolate Bunny. Catherine Samuels. (Illus.). 16p. (J). (ps-3). 1998. 3.99 (*0-689-81803-3*) Litle Simon.

Little Christmas Activity Book, Vol. 200. Anna Pomaska. (Activity Bk.). (J). (ps up). 1988. pap. 1.00 (*0-486-25679-0*) Dover.

Little Christmas Angel. Illus. by John Spiers. (Jewel Sticker Stories Ser.). 24p. (Orig.). (J). (ps-2). 1996. pap. 3.95 (*0-448-41484-8*, G & D) Peng Put Young Read.

***Little Christmas Angels.** Jennifer Stewart. (Illus.). 16p. (J). (ps-k). 2000. pap. 1.69 (*0-7847-1191-7*) Standard Pub.

Little Christmas Classics: Jolly Old Santa Claus & The Nutcracker, 2 Bks., Set. rev. ed. Perf. by Sarah Moore et al. (Illus.). 24p. (J). (ps-2). 4.99 incl. audio (*1-57102-083-7*, Ideals Child) Hambleton-Hill.

Little Christmas Classics: The Night Before Christmas & The Story of Christmas for Children, 2 Bks., Set. rev. ed. Perf. by Sarah Moore et al. (Illus.). 24p. (J). (ps-2). 4.99 incl. audio (*1-57102-084-5*, Ideals Child) Hambleton-Hill.

Little Christmas Concertina Book see Pequeno Libro de la Navidad

Little Christmas Cookbook. Ariel Books Staff. (Illus.). 16p. 1993. 4.95 (*0-8362-3039-6*, Arie Bks) Andrews & McMeel.

Little Christmas Elf. Eileen Curran. LC 84-8628. (Giant First Start Reader Ser.). (Illus.). 32p. (J). (gr. k-2). 1985. lib. bdg. 17.25 (*0-8167-0352-3*) Troll Communs.

Little Christmas Elf. Eileen Curran. LC 84-8628. (Giant First Start Reader Ser.). (Illus.). 32p. (J). (gr. k-2). 1997. pap. 3.95 (*0-8167-0432-5*) Troll Communs.

Little Christmas Sticker Book. Anna Pomaska. (Little Activity Bks.). (Illus.). (J). 1989. pap. 1.00 (*0-486-26069-0*) Dover.

Little Christmas Treasure Books: Christmas Joys. Lucy Rigg. (Illus.). (J). (gr. 2 up). 1989. 2.95 (*0-8378-1870-2*) Gibson.

Little Christmas Treasures: The Traditions of Christmas. Claudine Gandolfi. LC 98-140896. (Charming Petites Ser.). (Illus.). 80p. 1997. 4.95 (*0-88088-818-0*) Peter Pauper.

Little Church House by the River. Marla Martin. 1994. 14.95 (*0-87813-552-9*) Christian Light.

Little Church House Takes a Ride. Marla Martin. (Illus.). 104p. (J). (ps-5). 1995. 14.95 (*0-87813-553-7*) Christian Light.

Little Church That Could! Rose Grindheim Sinis. (Illus.). 40p. (Orig.). (J). (gr. k-8). 1975. spiral bd. 10.95 (*1-882415-04-3*) New Life Church.

***Little Church That Could: Raising Small Church Esteem.** Steven E. Burt & Hazel Ann Roper. 128p. (YA). 2000. pap. 14.00 (*0-8170-1370-9*) Judson.

***Little Chute - A Century of Progress - 1899-1999.** Louis J. Van Eperen. LC 99-75774. x, 402p. 2000. 25.00 (*0-9676179-0-1*) G H Van Hoof.

Little Citizens: The Humors of School Life. Myra Kelly. 1990. 16.50 (*0-8446-1259-6*) Peter Smith.

Little Citizens: The Humors of School Life. Myra Kelly. LC 70-163036. (Short Story Index Reprint Ser.). 1977. reprint ed. 26.95 (*0-8369-3950-6*) Ayer.

Little City by the Sea. Harold F. Osborne. (Illus.). 136p. (Orig.). 1990. pap. 10.95 (*0-9627567-0-9*) Apple Tree Pr.

An Asterisk (*) at the beginning of an entry indicates that the title is appearing for the first time.

Little City of Hope. Francis M. Crawford. (Works of Francis Marion Crawford). 1990. reprint ed. lib. bdg. 79.00 (0-7812-2558-2) Rprt Serv.

Little Clam. Lynn Reiser. LC 97-34511. (Illus.). 24p. (J). (ps-3). 1998. 15.00 (0-688-15908-7, Grenwillow Bks) HarpC Child Bks.

*Little Clam. Lynn Reiser. LC 97-34511. (Illus.). 24p. (J). (ps-3). 1998. 14.89 (0-688-15909-5, Grenwillow Bks) HarpC Child Bks.

Little Clancy's New Drum. Tony Kerins. LC 96-7130. (Illus.). 24p. (J). (ps). 1996. 9.99 (0-7636-0061-X) Candlewick Pr.

Little Clancy's New Drum. Tony Kerins. LC 96-7130. (Giggle Club Ser.). (Illus.). 24p. (J). (ps-1). 1997. reprint ed. pap. 3.29 (0-7636-0277-9) Candlewick Pr.

Little Class on Murder. Carolyn G. Hart. 272p. 1989. mass mkt. 5.99 (0-553-28208-5) Bantam.

Little Clay Cart. H. L. Luthra. 1998. pap. 20.00 (81-209-0807-4, Pub. by Pitambar Pub) St Mut.

Little Clay Cart. Ed. by J. A. Van Buitenen. LC 67-25441. 1968. text. write for info. (0-318-51416-8) Col U Pr.

Little Clay Cart: An English Translation of the Mrcchakatika of Sudraka As Adapted for the Stage by A. L. Basham. Ed. by Arvind Sharma. LC 92-46701. (SUNY Series in Hindu Literature). 175p. (C). 1994. text 49.50 (0-7914-1725-5); pap. text 16.95 (0-7914-1726-3) State U NY Pr.

Little Clearing in the Woods. Maria D. Wilkes. LC 97-44602. (Little House). (Illus.). 336p. (J). (gr. 3-7). 1998. 15.95 (0-06-026997-9) HarpC.

Little Clearing in the Woods. Maria D. Wilkes. (Little House). (Illus.). (J). (gr. 3-6). 1998. 10.05 (0-606-13575-8, Pub. by Turtleback) Demco.

Little Clearing in the Woods. adapted ed. Maria D. Wilkes. LC 97-44602. (Little House). (Illus.). 336p. (J). (gr. 3-7). 1998. pap. 4.95 (0-06-440652-0) HarpC.

Little Clearing in the Woods. adapted ed. Maria D. Wilkes. LC PZ7.W648389Lf 1998. (Little House). (Illus.). 336p. (J). (gr. 3-6). 1998. lib. bdg. 15.89 (0-06-026998-7) HarpC.

Little Cliff & the Porch People. Clifton L. Taulbert. Ed. by Cindy Kane. LC 98-5503. (Illus.). 32p. (J). (ps-3). 1999. 15.99 (0-8037-2174-9, Dial Yng Read); 15.89 (0-8037-2175-7, Dial Yng Read) Peng Put Young Read.

*Little Cliff's First Day of School. Clifton L. Taulbert. LC 99-56115. (Illus.). (J). 2001. 16.99 (0-8037-2557-4, Dial Yng Read) Peng Put Young Read.

*Little Clocks Midnight 2000. Christina Goodings. 1999. pap. 2.95 (0-7459-3904-X, Pub. by Lion Pubng) Trafalgar.

Little Cloud. Eric Carle. LC 95-38119. (Illus.). 32p. (J). (gr. k-2). 1996. 15.95 (0-399-23034-3, Philomel) Peng Put Young Read.

Little Cloud. Eric Carle. LC 98-189863. (Illus.). 28p. (J). (ps-1). 1998. bds. 6.99 (0-399-23191-9, Philomel) Peng Put Young Read.

Little Coffee Cookbook. Janet Laurence. (Illus.). 60p. 1995. 7.95 (0-8118-1036-4) Chronicle Bks.

Little Colonel. Annie F. Johnston. LC 96-9808. (Little Colonel Ser.). (Illus.). 192p. (J). (gr. 3-8). 1997. reprint ed. pap. 9.95 (1-55709-315-6) Applewood.

Little Colonel: Maid of Honor. Annie F. Johnston. (YA). (gr. 5 up). 1982. 16.95 (0-89201-034-7) Zenger Pub.

Little Colonel at Boarding School. Annie F. Johnston. (YA). (gr. 5 up). 1982. 16.95 (0-89201-032-0) Zenger Pub.

Little Colonel in Arizona. Annie F. Johnston. (YA). (gr. 5 up). 1982. 16.95 (0-89201-033-9) Zenger Pub.

Little Colonel Stories, First Series. Annie F. Johnston. (YA). (gr. 5 up). 1982. 16.95 (0-89201-070-3) Zenger Pub.

Little Colonel Stories, Second Series. Annie F. Johnston. (YA). (gr. 5 up). 1982. 16.95 (0-89201-071-1) Zenger Pub.

Little Colonel's Christmas Vacation. Annie F. Johnston. (YA). (gr. 5 up). 1982. 16.95 (0-89201-035-5) Zenger Pub.

Little Colonel's Chum: Mary Ware. Annie F. Johnston. (YA). (gr. 5 up). 1982. 16.95 (0-89201-036-3) Zenger Pub.

Little Colonel's Hero. Annie F. Johnston. (YA). (gr. 5 up). 1982. 16.95 (0-89201-037-1) Zenger Pub.

Little Colonel's Holidays. Annie F. Johnston. (YA). (gr. 5 up). 1982. 16.95 (0-89201-038-X) Zenger Pub.

Little Colonel's House Party. Annie F. Johnston. (YA). (gr. 5 up). 1982. 16.95 (0-89201-039-8) Zenger Pub.

Little Colonel's Knight Comes Riding. Annie F. Johnston. (YA). (gr. 5 up). 1982. 18.95 (0-89201-072-X) Zenger Pub.

Little Colonial Girl. Tom Tierney. (Little Activity Bks.). (Illus.). (J). 1995. pap. 1.00 (0-486-28802-1) Dover.

Little Comic Shop of Horrors. R. L. Stine, pseud. (Give Yourself Goosebumps Ser.: No. 17). (J). 1997. pap. text 3.99 (0-590-93483-X, Apple Paperbacks) Scholastic Inc.

Little Comic Shop of Horrors. R. L. Stine, pseud. (Give Yourself Goosebumps Ser.: No. 17). (J). 1997. 9.09 (0-606-11569-2, Pub. by Turtleback) Demco.

Little Commonwealth: Family Life in Plymouth Colony. John P. Demos. 1988. 24.00 (0-8446-6308-5) Peter Smith.

Little Commonwealth: Family Life in Plymouth Colony. 2nd ed. John Demos. LC 99-12551. (Illus.). 240p. 1999. pap. 11.95 (0-19-512890-7) OUP.

Little Community. Robert Redfield. 266p. 1960. pap. text 5.00 (0-226-70664-8, P53) U Ch Pr.

Little Community. Robert Redfield. 1973. lib. bdg. 10.00 (0-226-70649-4) U Ch Pr.

Little Community & Peasant Society & Culture. Robert Redfield. 284p. 1989. pap. text 23.00 (0-226-70670-2, Midway Reprint) U Ch Pr.

Little Compton Families, 2 Vols. 5th ed. Benjamin Franklin Wilbour. (Illus.). 839p. 2000. pap. 70.00 (0-8063-4703-1) Clearfield Co.

Little Computer. Mister Tom. (Illus.). 32p. (J). (gr. 2-4). 1978. write for info. (0-318-57344-X) Oddo.

Little Cookie. Margaret Hillert. (Illus.). (J). (ps). 1981. pap. 5.10 (0-8136-5562-5, TK2325); lib. bdg. 7.95 (0-8136-5062-3, TK2324) Modern Curr.

Little Coquette. Joan Smith. 1998. mass mkt. 4.99 (0-449-00153-9, Crest) Fawcett.

*Little Coquette: Love Is in the Air. large type ed. Joan Smith. LC 98-50795. (G. K. Hall Core Ser.). 1999. 25.95 (0-7838-8501-6, G K Hall Lrg Type) Mac Lib Ref.

Little Corner of Freedom: Russian Nature Protection from Stalin to Gorbachev. Douglas R. Weiner. LC 97-40206. 570p. 1999. 45.00 (0-520-21397-1, Pub. by U CA Pr) Cal Prin Full Svc.

Little Corset Construction Book: A Workbook on Period Underwear. Bonnie A. Ambrose. (Little Costume Workbook Ser.). (Illus.). 52p. (Orig.). 1997. pap. 7.95 (0-89676-130-4, Costume & Fashion Pr) QSMG Ltd.

Little Cottontail. Claude Memling. (Little Golden Storybks.). (Illus.). (J). 1998. 3.99 (0-307-16158-7, 16158, Goldn Books) Gldn Bks Pub Co.

Little Counting. Richard Scarry. (Illus.). 24p. (J). (ps-3). 1998. 1.99 (0-679-89238-9, Pub. by Random Bks Yng Read) Random.

Little Country. Charles De Lint. 608p. 1993. mass mkt. 5.99 (0-8125-2248-6, Pub. by Tor Bks) St Martin.

Little Country. large type ed. Fred Harrison. (Linford Western Library). 272p. 1995. pap. 16.99 (0-7089-7704-9, Linford) Ulverscroft.

Little Country Town. Southwell. LC 99-53628. (Illus.). 32p. (ps-2). 2000. 15.95 (0-8050-5711-0) H Holt & Co.

Little Course in Dreams. Robert Bosnak. 1998. pap. 10.00 (1-57062-386-4, Pub. by Shambhala Pubns) Random.

Little Cow in Valle Grande. Skillman C. Hunter. (Illus.). 28p. (Orig.). (J). (ps-1). 1995. pap. 4.95 (1-882351-01-0) Acrobytes Sftware.

Little Cowboy: Pursuing Dana's Dream. Marion Michaels. viii, 120p. 1998. pap. 12.95 (0-9661615-0-5, 00132545, A Genius) Michaels News.

Little Cowboy & Big . . . Margaret Hillert. (Illus.). (J). (ps). 1981. pap. 5.10 (0-8136-5576-5, TK2327); lib. bdg. 7.95 (0-8136-5076-3, TK2326) Modern Curr.

Little Coyote. Charles J. Keim. 864p. 1996. 25.00 (1-57510-022-3) Pictorial Hist.

Little Coyote Runs Away. Craig K. Strete. LC 95-12604. (Illus.). 32p. 1997. 15.95 (0-399-22921-3, G P Putnam) Peng Put Young Read.

Little Creatures. Donna Jo Napoli. LC 98-49675. (Angelwings Ser.: No. 2). (Illus.). 96p. (J). (gr. 2-4). 1999. per. 3.99 (0-689-82695-8) Aladdin.

*Little Creatures. Donna Jo Napoli. (Illus.). (J). 1999. 9.34 (0-606-17905-4) Turtleback.

*Little Creatures' Crusade (La Cruzada de las Criaturitas) A Story of Confirmation (Un Cuentro Acerca de la Confirmacion) Susan A. Brindle & Miriam A. Lademan. Tr. by Carmen A. Emmanuelli Klosterman. (Seven Sacraments Ser.). (ENG & SPA., Illus.). 56p. (gr. k-10). 1999. pap. 9.95 (1-889733-07-5, 01009) Precious Life Bks.

Little Crescent Moon & the Bright Evening Star. 2nd ed. Walter J. Humann. (Illus.). (J). (ps-5). pap. 9.95 (0-9674864-1-6) W J H Pubg.

*Little Crescent Moon & the Bright Evening Star. 2nd ed. Walter J. Humann. (Illus.). (J). (ps-5). 1999. 14.95 (0-9674864-0-8) W J H Pubg.

Little Criminals. Dennis Foon. (Illus.). 144p. 1998. pap. 14.95 (0-921368-62-3) Blizzard Publ.

Little Critter at Scout Camp. (Look-Look Bks.). (Illus.). (J). (ps-3). 1991. 3.29 (0-307-12629-3, 12629) Gldn Bks Pub Co.

Little Critter Just a Pirate. Mercer Mayer. (Magic Touch Talking Bks.). (Illus.). 22p. (J). (ps-2). 1996. 19.99 (1-888208-12-0) Hasbro.

Little Critter Just Going to the Moon. Mercer Mayer. (Magic Touch Talking Bks.). (Illus.). 22p. (J). (ps-2). 1996. 19.99 (1-888208-11-2) Hasbro.

*Little Critter Sleeps Over. Mercer Mayer. LC 97-80729. (Road to Reading Ser.). (Illus.). 32p. (J). (gr. 1-2). 1999. 10.99 (0-307-46203-X, Goldn Books) Gldn Bks Pub Co.

Little Critter Sleeps Over. Mercer Mayer. LC 97-80729. (Road to Reading Ser.). (Illus.). 32p. (J). 1999. pap. text 3.99 (0-307-26203-0, Goldn Books) Gldn Bks Pub Co.

Little Critters. Jeanne H. Fallier. LC 52-561. (Illus.). 58p. (Orig.). 1984. pap. 8.95 (0-9611554-2-6) Rugging Rm.

Little Critter's Holiday Fun Sticker Book. Mercer Mayer. (Illus.). 16p. (J). (ps-1). 1994. bds. 4.95 (0-590-48640-3, Cartwheel) Scholastic Inc.

Little Critter's Joke Book. Mercer Mayer. (Look-Look Bks.). (Illus.). 24p. (J). (ps-3). 1993. pap. 3.29 (0-307-12790-7, 12790) Gldn Bks Pub Co.

Little Critter's Little Red Riding Hood: Little Critter Chunky Flap Book. Mercer Mayer. LC 94-68286. (Illus.). 1995. 3.99 (0-679-87346-5) Random.

*Little Critters of the Southwest. Sarah Gustafson. LC 99-34986. (Illus.). 16p. (Orig.). (J). (gr. 2-6). 1999. pap. 3.95 (1-877856-99-1, L1070) SW Pks Mnmts.

Little Critter's Read-It-Yourself Storybook: Six Funny Easy-to-Read Stories. Mercer Mayer. (Illus.). 196p. (J). (gr. k-2). 1993. 17.95 (0-307-16840-9, 16840) Gldn Bks Pub Co.

Little Critters Search for the Beautiful Princess. Mercer Mayer. (Illus.). 1995. 12.00 (0-679-87351-1) McKay.

*Little Critter's the Best Present. Mercer Mayer. LC 99-89570. (Road to Reading Ser.). (Illus.). (J). 2000. pap. 3.99 (0-307-26215-4) Gldn Bks Pub Co.

Little Crooked Christmas Tree. Michael Cutting. (Illus.). 24p. (J). (ps-2). 1995. pap. 5.95 (1-895565-76-6) Firefly Bks Ltd.

Little Crow, Spokesman for the Sioux. Gary C. Anderson. LC 86-795. (Illus.). 259p. (Orig.). 1986. pap. 11.95 (0-87351-196-4) Minn Hist.

Little Crumb: Tales of the Back Bay. Joan E. Pizzo. (Illus.). 35p. (Orig.). (J). (gr. k-6). 1980. teacher ed. 8.95 (0-939126-03-6); pap. 7.95 (0-939126-01-X); lib. bdg. 10.95 (0-939126-00-1) Back Bay Bks.

Little Crumb Fun Book. Joan E. Pizzo. (Illus.). 32p. (Orig.). (J). (gr. k-6). 1983. pap. 3.95 (0-939126-04-4) Back Bay Bks.

Little Cup of Tea: Quiet Moments with Friends. (Little Treasures Ser.). (Illus.). 88p. 1994. 4.99 (1-57051-031-8) Brownlow Pub Co.

Little Cyanide Cookbook: Delicious Recipes Rich in Vitamin B17. June De Spain. 192p. 1976. pap. text 12.50 (0-912986-00-X) Am Media.

Little Czech & the Great Czech Nation: National Identity & the Post-Communist Social Transformation. Ladislav Holy. (Cambridge Studies in Social & Cultural Anthropology: No. 103). 236p. (C). 1996. text 64.95 (0-521-55469-1) Cambridge U Pr.

*Little 'd' Sellers. (J). 2000. 3.95 (0-552-52875-7, Pub. by Transworld Publishers Ltd) Trafalgar.

Little Daisy & the Swearing Class. rev. ed. (Character Building Ser.). (Illus.). 95p. (J). (gr. 4-6). 1990. pap. 4.98 (1-58339-054-5, C5) Triangle Press.

Little Daisy Girl & Other Poems. Jacquelyn Hedge-Cheney & Roland J. Cheney. (Illus.). 48p. (Orig.). (J). (gr. 6 up). 1989. pap. write for info. (0-9621283-0-9) Lil Daisy Bks.

Little Daniel & Revelation. C. L. Rockne. 248p. 1996. spiral bd. 14.95 (0-9656048-2-9) Little Garden.

Little Daniel & the Jewish Delicacies. Smadar S. Sidi. (Illus.). (J). (ps-5). 1988. 9.95 (1-55774-028-3) Lambda Pubs.

Little Danny Dinosaur. Janet Craig. LC 87-16228. (Illus.). 32p. (J). (gr. k-2). 1997. pap. 2.50 (0-8167-1230-1) Troll Communs.

Little Danny Dinosaur. Janet Craig. 1999. pap. text 2.50 (0-8167-3286-8) Troll Communs.

Little Danny Dinosaur. enl. ed. Janet Craig. 1999. pap. text 16.95 (0-8167-4091-7) Troll Communs.

Little Dark Cloud. Bridget Fitzgerald. LC 78-189877. (Story & Its Verse Ser.). (Illus.). 44p. (J). (gr. 1-2). 1973. 2.50 (0-87884-012-5) Unicorn Ent.

Little Darlin' Cheryl Reavis. 1998. per. 4.25 (0-373-24177-1, 1-24177-7) Silhouette.

*Little Data Book 2000. 2000. 15.00 (0-8213-4679-2, 14679) World Bank.

*Little David. Jacqueline Klinger. LC 99-68044. 200p. 1999. 18.95 (1-882792-71-8) Proctor Pubns.

Little David & Big Goliath. Tracy Harrast. (Peek-A-Boo Ser.). 1999. 6.99 (0-310-97586-7) Zondervan.

Little David & the Giant. Mary Josephs. (Bible Story Flap Bks.). (Illus.). 22p. (J). (ps). 1994. 3.99 (0-679-86141-6, Pub. by Random Bks Yng Read) Random.

Little David Had No Fear. Judith A. Still. (Illus.). 118p. (Orig.). (J). (gr. 3-8). 1999. pap. 19.95 (1-877873-03-9) Master-Player Lib.

*Little Death. Laura Wilson. 2000. mass mkt. 5.99 (0-553-58281-X) Bantam.

Little Death. Michael Nava. 165p. 1997. reprint ed. pap. 9.95 (1-55583-388-8) Alyson Pubns.

Little Deception among Friends: The Short StOURy (Our Story) Conversations. Derek Van Johnson. Ed. & Photos by Lisa Sherrie Johnson. LC 98-212864. (Illus.). 96p. (Orig.). 1998. pap. 14.95 (0-9663279-0-X) One Fear.

Little Deer of the Florida Keys. rev. ed. Hope Ryden. (Illus.), 64p. (Orig.). (J). (gr. 5 up). 1986. reprint ed. pap. 8.95 (0-912451-14-9) Florida Classics.

Little Deer of the Florida Keys. rev. ed. Hope Ryden. (Illus.). 64p. (Orig.). (YA). (gr. 5 up). 1986. reprint ed. 13.95 (0-912451-13-0) Florida Classics.

*Little Detours: The Letters & Plays of Luise Gottsched (1713-1762) Susanne Kord. LC 99-49774. (Studies in German Literature, Linguistics & Culture). (Illus.). 260p. 2000. 55.00 (1-57113-148-5) Camden Hse.

Little Devils. Ed. by Marla H. Kennedy & Susan Martin. (Picture This Ser.). (Illus.). 96p. (C). 1997. 14.95 (1-890576-01-8, Pub. by Picture This) Dist Art Pubs.

Little Dickens Bird. Sally K. Sharkey. (Illus.). iii, 31p. (Orig.). (J). (gr. k-5). 1996. pap. 9.95 (0-9653032-0-9) Sal Mar Pr.

*Little Dictators. Dan Manning. LC 99-93681. 1999. 21.95 (0-533-13120-0) Vantage.

Little Dictionary French to Khmer. Tep & Gandh Thao. (CAM & FRE.). 1998. 135.00 (0-320-00396-5) Fr & Eur.

Little Dictionary French to Provencal. J. Coupier. (FRE & PRO.). 1998. 69.95 (0-320-00187-3) Fr & Eur.

Little Dinners with the Sphinx, & Other Prose Fancies. Richard Le Gallienne. LC 72-11932. (Short Story Index Reprint Ser.). 1977. reprint ed. 26.95 (0-8369-4239-6) Ayer.

Little Dinosaur. Bob Reese. Ed. by Dan Wasserman. (Ten Word Book Ser.). (Illus.). (J). (gr. k-1). 1979. 9.95 (0-89868-070-0); pap. 3.95 (0-89868-081-6) ARO Pub.

*Little Dinosaur. Mike Thaler. 2000. pap. text 15.95 (0-8050-6213-0) St Martin.

Little Dinosaur ABC Coloring Book. Winky Adam. (Illus.). 64p. (J). 1998. pap. 1.00 (0-486-40301-7) Dover.

Little Dinosaur Activity Book. 80th ed. Anna Pomaska. (J). (ps up). 1987. pap. 1.00 (0-486-25344-9) Dover.

Little Dinosaur Splash! Norman Gorbaty. (Bathtime Bks.). (Illus.). 5p. (J). (ps). 1995. 4.99 (0-679-86563-2, Pub. by Random Bks Yng Read) Random.

Little Dinosaurs. unabridged ed. Bernard Most & Don Freeman. (Illus.). (J). (gr. k-1). 1993. 22.95 incl. audio (0-87499-192-7) Live Oak Media.

Little Disturbances of Man. Grace Paley. LC 84-18951. (Fiction Ser.). 192p. 1985. pap. 16.99 (0-14-007557-7, Penguin Bks) Viking Penguin.

Little Ditties. Dave Schultz. 64p. (Orig.). (YA). pap. 3.00 (0-937393-08-8) Fred Pr.

Little Ditties. 2nd ed. Dave Schultz. (Illus.). 80p. (Orig.). 1999. pap. 5.00 (0-937393-11-8) Fred Pr.

Little Doctor. 1981. 1.95 (0-8351-0931-3) China Bks.

Little Doctor. Frederick W. Herman. LC 78-54149. 128p. 1978. 9.95 (0-915010-21-6) Sutter House.

Little Dog Lost, Vol. 1. Anne L. Kahn. LC 97-91332. (Illus.). 24p. (J). (gr. k-6). 1997. pap. 10.00 (0-9655920-3-0) A H Sutherland.

Little Dog Lost: In Search of Honey. K. Suzanne Moorhouse. (Illus.). 122p. 1997. 20.00 (1-85776-181-2, Pub. by Book Guild Ltd) Trans-Atl Phila.

Little-Dog-of-Iron. 2nd ed. Philip St. Clair. Ed. by Tom Trusky. LC 85-72152. (Ahsahta Press Modern & Contemporary Poets of the West Ser.). 55p. (Orig.). 1985. pap. 6.95 (0-916272-29-X) Ahsahta Pr.

Little Dog Poems. Kristine O'Connel George. LC 97-46678. (Illus.). 40p. (J). (ps-3). 1999. 12.00 (0-395-82266-1, Clarion Bks) HM.

Little Dog Scooter. Sue Pickett. 21p. (J). (gr. 4). 1992. pap. text. write for info. (0-9633197-0-1) Instant Heirloom.

Little Dog Trusty, the Orange Man, & the Cherry Orchard: Being the Tenth Part of Early Lessons. Maria Edgeworth. LC 92-24529. (Augustan Reprints Ser.: Nos. 263-264). 1990. reprint ed. 21.50 (0-404-70263-5, PR4644) AMS Pr.

Little Dog Who Wouldn't Be. Katy D. Oana. LC 77-18351. (Illus.). 32p. (J). (gr. 2-4). 1978. lib. bdg. 9.95 (0-87783-150-5) Oddo.

Little Dogs Say "Rough!" Rick Walton. LC 99-24690. (Illus.). 32p. (J). (ps-2). 2000. 12.99 (0-399-23228-1, G P Putnam) Peng Put Young Read.

Little Donald Lee, Miss Etta G, & the Two Room Schoolhouse. Don L. Madaris. (Illus.). 112p. (Orig.). 1991. pap. 7.95 (0-943487-34-X) Sevgo Pr.

Little Donkey see Burrito de Belen

*Little Donkey. Illus. by Caroline J. Church. (Waggy Tales Ser.). 10p. (J). (ps). 1999. bds. 5.99 (0-7847-1115-1, 03523) Standard Pub.

*Little Donkey. Gerda M. Scheidl. LC 87-73271. (Illus.). 32p. (J). (ps-3). 1998. pap. 6.95 (1-55858-952-X, Pub. by North-South Bks NYC) Chronicle Bks.

Little Donkey Close Your Eyes. Margaret Wise Brown. LC 94-16523. (Illus.). 32p. (J). (ps-3). 1995. 14.95 (0-06-024482-8); lib. bdg. 13.89 (0-06-024483-6) HarpC Child Bks.

Little Donkey Close Your Eyes. Margaret Wise Brown. LC 94-16523. (Illus.). 32p. (J). (ps-3). 1998. pap. 5.95 (0-06-443507-5, HarpTrophy) HarpC Child Bks.

Little Donkey's Day with Jesus. Alice J. Davidson. (J). (ps-3). 1997. 3.99 (0-310-97169-1) Zondervan.

Little Door Slides Back, Vol. 32. Jeff Clark. (New American Poetry Ser.). 120p. 1998. pap. text 10.95 (1-55713-314-X) Sun & Moon CA.

Little Dorrit see Oxford Illustrated Dickens

Little Dorrit. Charles Dickens. LC 92-52919. 1992. 20.00 (0-679-41725-7) Everymns Lib.

Little Dorrit. Charles Dickens. Ed. by Harvey Peter Sucksmith. (Oxford World's Classics Ser.). (Illus.). 750p. 1999. pap. 7.95 (0-19-283566-1) OUP.

Little Dorrit. Charles Dickens. LC 99-462630. 752p. 1998. pap. 8.95 (0-14-043492-5) Viking Penguin.

Little Dorrit. Charles Dickens. (Classics Library). Date not set. pap. 3.95 (1-85326-182-3, 1823WW, Pub. by Wrdsworth Edits) NTC Contemp Pub Co.

Little Dorrit. Charles Dickens. (J). (ps-8). 1990. reprint ed. lib. bdg. 39.95 (0-89966-680-9) Buccaneer Bks.

Little Dorrit's Shadows: Character & Contradiction in Dickens. Brian Rosenberg. 200p. (C). 1995. text 35.95 (0-8262-1058-9) U of Mo Pr.

Little DOS Will Do You. Thomas Benjamin. 144p. 1990. pap. 9.95 (0-931011-29-9) Grapevine Pubns.

Little Dots & Tiny Specks: Drawings by Edmund Bennett. Edmund Bennett. LC 97-69571. (Illus.). ii, 202p. 1997. 59.00 (0-9658481-1-6) S F Reynolds.

Little Dragon. (Toddlers' Storytime Ser.). (Illus.). 96p. (J). (ps). 1999. write for info. (1-85854-777-6) Brimax Bks.

Little Dragon. Heather Amery. (Castle Tales Ser.). (Illus.). 16p. (J). (ps-3). 1996. pap. 4.50 (0-7460-2508-4, Usborne); lib. bdg. 12.95 (0-88110-868-5, Usborne) EDC.

Little Dragons. Michael J. Bugeja. 175p. 1996. pap. text 12.95 (0-942544-21-8) Negative Capability Pr.

Little Dream Maker Keepsake Book see Flavia for Baby

Little Dreaming. Fenton Johnson. 7.00 (0-405-18496-4) Ayer.

*Little Dreams of Happiness. Julia Glynn Smith. 2000. 9.95 (0-7407-0549-0) Andrews & McMeel.

*Little Dreams of Love. Julia Glynn Smith. 2000. 9.95 (0-7407-0550-4) Andrews & McMeel.

Little Drops of Water Little Grains of Sand. Gertrude M. Parker. 32p. (Orig.). 1983. pap. write for info. (0-89279-055-5) G M Parker.

Little Drummer Boy. 12p. (YA). 1994. pap. 2.95 (0-7692-1511-4, 2793LHBX) Wrner Bros.

Little Drummer Boy. (Favorite Christmas Tales Ser.). (Illus.). 24p. (J). 1993. 4.98 (1-56173-714-3) Pubns Intl Ltd.

*Little Drummer Boy. Ezra Jack Keats. LC 00-8665. (Illus.). 32p. (J). (ps-2). 2000. 15.99 (0-670-89226-2, Viking Child) Peng Put Young Read.

*Little Drummer Boy. Ezra Jack Keats. LC 00-8665. (Illus.). 32p. (J). (ps-3). 2000. pap. 6.99 (0-14-056743-7, PuffinBks) Peng Put Young Read.

Little Drummer Boy. Ezra Jack Keats. (Illus.). (J). 1972. 10.15 (0-606-03810-8, Pub. by Turtleback) Demco.

Little Drummer Boy. Illus. by Yoshi Miyake. 32p. (J). (ps-3). 1998. pap. 3.50 (0-8167-4809-8) Troll Communs.

Little Drummer Boy. Illus. by Ezra Jack Keats. LC 87-1476. 32p. (J). (gr. k-3). 1987. reprint ed. mass mkt. 4.95 (0-689-71158-1) Aladdin.

An Asterisk (*) at the beginning of an entry indicates that the title is appearing for the first time.

***Little Drummer Girl.** John Le Carre, pseud. 672p. 2000. reprint ed. per. 7.99 (0-671-04278-5, Pocket Books) PB.

Little Drummer Girls. Illus. by Marcy Dunn Ramsey. (Sweet Valley Kids Ser.: No. 75). 96p. (J). (gr. 1-3). 1998. pap. 3.50 (0-553-48614-4, Sweet Valley) BDD Bks Young Read.

Little Duck see Big Red Box of Books: Five Picture-Book Favorites

***Little Duck.** Beth Cuthand. (Illus.). 28p. (J). (gr. k-3). 1999. pap. 7.95 (0-919441-74-2, Pub. by Theytus Bks) Orca Bk Pubs.

Little Duck. Judy Dunn. LC 75-36467. (Pictureback Ser.). (Illus.). 32p. (J). (ps-1). 1976. pap. 3.25 (0-394-83247-7, Pub. by Random Bks Yng Read) Random.

Little Ducks Don't Fly. (Illus.). 32p. (J). (ps-3). write for info. (0-914082-27-2) Syentek.

Little Duck's Easter Surprise, 1 vol. Lucinda McQueen. 1999. 3.50 (0-590-68130-3) Scholastic Inc.

Little Duke. Joseph D. Ossorio et al. (Under Twenty Writing Society Ser.). (Illus.). 48p. (J). (gr. 3-5). 1994. pap. 6.95 (1-56721-049-X) Twnty-Fifth Cent Pr.

Little Dutch Boy: A Tale of Perseverance. Sarah Toast et al. LC 97-220748. (Illus.). 1997. write for info. (0-7853-2137-3) Pubns Intl Ltd.

***Little 'e' Sellers.** (J). 2000. 3.95 (0-552-52876-5, Pub. by Transworld Publishers Ltd) Trafalgar.

Little Easter. Reed F. Coleman. LC 92-34305. 221p. 1993. 22.00 (1-877946-23-0) Permanent Pr.

Little Ebony Readers: Muffin Goes to School. Linda Waters. (Illus.). 32p. (J). (gr. 1). 1997. 4.50 (0-9630887-7-7) Ethnic Bks.

Little Ed & Golden Bear. Eligio S. Gallegos. 170p. (C). 1993. pap. 12.00 (0-944164-06-4) Moon Bear Pr.

Little Eddy Elephant. Anne T. Perkins. (Big Books - Mini Bks.). (Illus.). 8p. (J). (ps). 1993. 12.00 (1-884204-06-6) Teach Nxt Door.

Little Eden: A Child at War. Eva Figes. 140p. 1988. 14.95 (0-89255-121-6); pap. 8.95 (0-89255-137-2) Persea Bks.

Little Edge of Darkness. Tanya Faludy & Alexander Faludy. 175p. 1996. 17.95 (1-85302-357-4, Pub. by Jessica Kingsley) Taylor & Francis.

Little Ego. Vittorio Giardino. 48p. (Orig.). 1994. pap. 10.95 (1-56163-094-2, Eurotica) NBM.

Little Egypt. Lynn Siefert. 1995. pap. 5.25 (0-8222-1338-9) Dramatists Play.

***Little Egyptian Mazes.** Winky Adam. (Little Activity Bks.). 64p. (J). 1999. pap. 1.00 (0-486-40733-0) Dover.

Little Eight John. Jan Wahl. (J). 1998. 11.19 (0-606-12982-0, Pub. by Turtleback) Demco.

Little Elephant. Miela Ford. LC 93-25208. (Illus.). 24p. (J). 1994. lib. bdg. 14.93 (0-688-13141-7, Grenwillow Bks) HarpC Child Bks.

Little Elephant Thunderfoot. Sally Grindley. LC 97-52591. (Illus.). 32p. (J). (gr. k-2). 1999. 15.95 (1-56145-180-0) Peachtree Pubs.

Little Elephant Who Liked to Play. Naomi Sellers. LC 94-20299. (Illus.). (J). 1995. pap. 3.95 (0-382-24682-9, Silver Pr NJ) Silver Burdett Pr.

***Little Elephant's Song.** Wolfram Hanel. (Illus.). 32p. (J). (gr. k-3). 2000. 15.95 (0-7358-1297-7, Pub. by North-South Bks NYC) Chronicle Bks.

Little Elephant's Walk. Adrienne Kennaway. LC 91-19727. (Willa Perlman Bks.). (Illus.). 32p. (J). (ps-2). 1992. 13.95 (0-06-020377-3) HarpC Child Bks.

Little Elephant's Walk. Adrienne Kennaway. LC 91-19727. (Willa Perlman Bks.). (Illus.). 32p. (J). (ps-2). 1992. lib. bdg. 13.89 (0-06-020378-1) HarpC Child Bks.

***Little Ellie Claus.** James Manos, Jr. 256p. 2000. 15.95 (0-7434-0624-9) PB.

Little Elmo's Book of Colors. Anna Ross. LC 91-23979. (Sesame Street Toddler Bks.). (Illus.). 24p. (J). (ps). 1992. 5.99 (0-679-82238-0, Pub. by Random Bks Yng Read) Random.

***Little Elmo's Toy Box.** Sesame Street Staff. (Toddler Bks.). (Illus.). 12p. (J). (ps). 2000. bds. 2.99 (0-375-80288-6, Pub. by Random Bks Yng Read) Random.

Little Empire of Their Own. Bruce W. Farcau. 352p. 21.95 (0-918339-54-5) Vandamere.

Little Endarkenment, & in My Poetry You Will Find Me. Robert Duncan. 48p. 1997. 7.00 (1-887289-23-2) Rodent Pr.

Little Engine Play-a-Sound. (J). 1995. write for info. (0-7853-1038-X) Pubns Intl Ltd.

Little Engine That Could. Cristina Ong. (Wee Sing Ser.). (Illus.). 12p. (J). 1998. mass mkt. 9.99 incl. audio (0-8431-7837-X) Putnam Pub Group.

Little Engine That Could. Watty Piper. (Illus.). 40p. (J). (ps-k). 1997. 3.97 (1-57748-081-3) Barbour Pub.

Little Engine That Could. Watty Piper. 37p. (J). (gr. k-1). pap. 7.99 (0-8072-1262-8) Listening Lib.

Little Engine That Could. Watty Piper. (Illus.). 48p. (J). 1930. 6.99 (0-448-40520-2, Plat & Munk) Peng Put Young Read.

Little Engine That Could. Watty Piper. LC 99-44044. (Pop-up Bks.). (Illus.). 12p. (J). (ps up). 1984. 10.99 (0-448-18963-1, Philomel) Peng Put Young Read.

Little Engine That Could. Watty Piper. (Illus.). 10p. (J). (ps-3). 1991. 5.99 (0-448-40101-0, Plat & Munk) Peng Put Young Read.

***Little Engine That Could.** Watty Piper. (Illus.). 40p. (J). (ps-3). 1999. pap. 19.99 (0-698-11856-1, PapStar) Peng Put Young Read.

Little Engine That Could. Retold by Watty Piper. (Comes to Life Bks.). 16p. (J). (ps-2). 1993. 18.99 (1-883366-15-1) YES Ent.

Little Engine that Could. Watty Piper. (Illus.). 12p. (J). 1998. pap. 5.99 (0-525-46075-6, Dutton Child) Peng Put Young Read.

Little Engine That Could. Watty Piper. 40p. (J). 1981. reprint ed. lib. bdg. 15.95 (0-89966-366-4); reprint ed. lib. bdg. 10.95 (0-89967-040-7, Harmony Rain) Buccaneer Bks.

Little Engine that Could: A Storybook & Windup Train. Watty Piper. (Illus.). (J). (ps-2). 1998. pap. 18.99 (0-525-46029-2, Dutton Child) Peng Put Young Read.

***Little Engine That Could: Giant Lift-&-Learn Book.** Watty Piper. (Illus.). 12p. (J). (ps-3). 2000. 9.99 (0-448-42400-2, Planet Dexter) Peng Put Young Read.

Little Engine That Could: Miniature Edition. Watty Piper. (Illus.). 48p. (J). 1990. 4.99 (0-448-40071-5, Plat & Munk) Peng Put Young Read.

Little Engine That Could: Sixtieth Anniversary Edition. 60th anniversary ed. Watty Piper. (Illus.). 48p. (J). 1990. 16.99 (0-448-40041-3, Plat & Munk) Peng Put Young Read.

***Little Engine That Could - ABC Time.** Watty Piper. (Illus.). 32p. (J). (ps-3). 2000. pap. 3.49 (0-448-42166-6, G & D) Peng Put Young Read.

Little Engine That Could & the Big Chase. Michaela Muntean. (All Aboard Bks.). (Illus.). 32p. (J). (ps-3). 1988. pap. 2.99 (0-448-19095-8, Plat & Munk) Peng Put Young Read.

Little Engine That Could & the Snowy, Blowy Christmas. Watty Piper. LC 97-47358. (All Aboard Bks.). (Illus.). 24p. (J). (ps-3). 1998. bds. 2.95 (0-448-41850-9, G & D) Peng Put Young Read.

***Little Engine That Could Helps Out, 1 vol.** Cristina Ong. 32p. (ps-1). 1999. pap. text 3.99 (0-448-41973-4) Putnam Pub Group.

Little Engine That Could Let's Count 123. Watty Piper. LC 90-83240. (Illus.). 24p. (J). (ps-1). 1991. 12.95 (0-448-40131-2, Plat & Munk) Peng Put Young Read.

Little Engine That Could Let's Sing ABC. Illus. by Cristina Ong. 24p. (J). (ps). 1993. 12.95 (0-448-40509-1, Plat & Munk) Peng Put Young Read.

Little Engine That Could Pudgy Word Book. Illus. by Cristina Ong. (Pudgy Board Bks.). 18p. (J). (ps up). 1988. bds. 3.99 (0-448-19054-0, Plat & Munk) Peng Put Young Read.

Little Engine That Could Rides Again. Illus. by Cristina Ong. (Sticker Stories Ser.). 16p. (J). (ps-1). 1996. pap. text 4.99 (0-448-41145-8, G & D) Peng Put Young Read.

Little Engine That Laughed. Alf Evers. (J). 1987. pap. text 0.99 (0-8431-4236-7, Price Stern) Peng Put Young Read.

***Little Engines Can Do Big Things.** Random House Staff. (Illus.). 24p. (J). (ps-1). 2000. pap. 3.25 (0-375-80553-2, Pub. by Random Bks Yng Read) Random.

Little English Cookbook. Rosa Mashiter. (Illus.). 60p. 1989. 7.95 (0-87701-631-3) Chronicle Bks.

Little English Handbook. 2nd ed. Bell & Corbett. 288p. (C). 1996. pap. text. write for info. (0-471-79892-4) Wiley.

***Little English Handbook.** 8th ed. Corbett. 273p. 1998. pap. text 23.53 (0-321-04965-9) Addison-Wesley.

Little English Handbook: Choices & Conventions. Edward P. Corbett & Sheryl L. Finkle. LC 97-9865. 1997. write for info. (0-673-98048-0) Addison-Wesley.

Little English Handbook: Choices & Conventions. Edward P. J. Corbett & Sheryl L. Finkle. LC 94-18590. (C). 1995. pap. 10.50 (0-673-99323-X) HarpC.

Little English Handbook: Choices & Conventions. 7th ed. Edward P.J. Corbett & Sheryl L. Finkle. 288p. 1995. pap. 14.95 (0-8230-5002-5) Watsn-Guptill.

Little Enough: Forty-Nine Haiku. Matsu Basho et al. Tr. & Pref. by Cid Corman. LC 91-72695. 80p. (Orig.). 1991. pap. 10.00 (0-917788-48-6) Gnomon Pr.

Little Entente & Europe (1920-1929) M. Adam. 330p. (C). 1993. 120.00 (963-05-6320-7, Pub. by Akade Kiado) St Mut.

Little Entente & Europe (1920-1929) M. Adam. 330p. (C). 1993. 120.00 (963-05-6420-3, Pub. by Akade Kiado) St Mut.

Little Ernie's ABC's. Anna Ross. LC 91-27823. (Sesame Street Toddler Bks.). (Illus.). 24p. (J). (ps). 1992. 5.99 (0-679-82240-2, Pub. by Random Bks Yng Read) Random.

Little Ernie's Animal Friends. Random House Staff. (Board Bks.). (J). 1997. 2.50 (0-679-88884-5, Pub. by Random Bks Yng Read) Random.

Little Essays Drawn from the Writings of George Santayana. George Santayana. Ed. by Logan P. Smith. LC 67-23267. (Essay Index Reprint Ser.). 1977. 23.95 (0-8369-0848-1) Ayer.

Little Essays in Literature & Life. Richard Burton. LC 74-93322. (Essay Index Reprint Ser.). 1977. 23.95 (0-8369-1277-2) Ayer.

Little Essays Toward Truth. rev. ed. Aleister Crowley. LC 91-60059. 96p. 1991. pap. 9.95 (1-56184-000-9) New Falcon Pubns.

Little Exercise for Young Theologians. Helmut Thielicke. (Orig.). 1962. pap. 6.00 (0-8028-1198-1) Eerdmans.

Little Exercise for Young Theologians. Helmut Thielicke. (Biblical Classics Library: Vol. 24). 41p. (Orig.). 1997. reprint ed. mass mkt. 2.99 (0-85364-767-4, Pub. by Paternoster Pub) OM Literature.

Little Eyoif see Master Builder & Other Plays

Little Eyold see Ibsen: Plays Three

***Little 'f' Sellers.** (J). 2000. 3.95 (0-552-52877-3, Pub. by Transworld Publishers Ltd) Trafalgar.

Little Factory. Sarah Weeks & Michael Abbott. LC 98-221668. (Laura Geringer Bks.). (Illus.). 40p. (J). (ps-2). 1998. 19.95 incl. cd-rom (0-06-027429-8) HarpC Child Bks.

Little Faith. John Skoyles. LC 80-70564. (Poetry Ser.). 1981. pap. 11.95 (0-915604-44-2) Carnegie-Mellon.

Little Faith. John Skoyles. LC 80-70564. (Poetry Ser.). 1981. 20.95 (0-915604-43-4) Carnegie-Mellon.

***Little Faith: The Child of the Toy Stall.** O. F. Walton. 2000. pap. 5.99 (1-85792-567-X) Christian Focus.

Little Faith Builders. Judy Shaw. 30p. (Orig.). (J). (gr. 1-3). 1983. pap. 0.99 (0-89274-290-9, HH-290) Harrison Hse.

Little Farm Activity Book. Becky J. Radtke. (Illus.). (J). pap. text 1.00 (0-486-29423-4) Dover.

Little Farm by the Sea. Kay Chorao. LC 97-24431. (Illus.). 32p. (J). (ps-2). 1998. 15.95 (0-8050-5053-1) H Holt & Co.

Little Farm in the Ozarks. Roger L. MacBride. (Little House). (Illus.). 256p. (J). (gr. 3-6). 1994. 15.95 (0-06-024245-0) HarpC Child Bks.

Little Farm in the Ozarks. Roger L. MacBride. LC 93-23688. (Little House). (Illus.). 304p. (J). (gr. 4-7). 1994. pap. 4.95 (0-06-440510-9, HarpTrophy) HarpC Child Bks.

Little Farm in the Ozarks. Roger Lea Macbride. (Little House). (Illus.). (J). (gr. 3-6). 1994. 10.05 (0-606-06537-7, Pub. by Turtleback) Demco.

Little Farmer. Sarah Weeks. 24p. (J). (ps up). 9.95 (0-694-01203-3) HarpC Child Bks.

***Little Farmyard Adventures Carry Case.** Kate Brookes. LC 98-235715. (Illus.). 24p. (J). (ps-1). 1998. 7.98 (0-7651-0700-7) Smithmark.

Little Father. Gelett Burgess. (Sunburst Ser.). (Illus.). 32p. (J). (ps-3). 1987. pap. 3.95 (0-374-44486-2) FS&G.

Little Fawn Little Elk Love Poems. Christine Tarantino. 32p. 1998. spiral bd. 3.95 (1-887480-97-8) Wrds Lght Intl.

Little Fear. Patricia Wrightson. 1986. mass mkt. write for info. (0-09-148450-2) Random.

Little Fears. Emanuel Peluso. 1967. pap. 3.25 (0-8222-0675-7) Dramatists Play.

Little Feelings. Judy S. Barton. LC 97-41720. (Illus.). 67p. (J). 1998. pap. text 9.95 (1-57392-183-1) Prometheus Bks.

Little Feet. 1997. pap. 1.75 (0-8289-1008-1) Viking Penguin.

***Little Feet.** Photos by Marina Drasnin Gilboa. LC 99-33592. (Illus.). 72p. 2000. 9.95 (0-8118-2452-7) Chronicle Bks.

Little Ferry's Christmas. Martha W. Briggs. LC 97-68566. (Illus.). (Orig.). (J). 1997. pap. 6.50 (0-9633240-3-9, LFC-97) Dory Pr.

Little Figure Skater. Barbara Steadman. (Little Activity Bks.). (Illus.). (J). 1995. pap. 1.00 (0-486-28653-3) Dover.

Little Fingerling. Illus. by Brenda Clark. LC 92-85. 32p. (J). (gr. k-3). 1992. 13.95 (0-8249-8553-2, Ideals Child) Hambleton-Hill.

Little Fingerling: A Japanese Folk Tale. Illus. by Brenda Clark. 32p. (J). 1989. pap. 4.95 (1-55074-075-X) Kids Can Pr.

Little Fingers Go to Church, Bk. 1. Contrib. by Jolene Boyd. 40p. 1989. 7.99 (0-8341-9630-1, MB-605) Lillenas.

Little Fingers Go to Church, Bk. 2. 36p. 1989. 7.99 (0-8341-9122-9, MB-606) Lillenas.

Little Fir Tree. Margaret Wise Brown. (Illus.). 32p. (J). (ps-1). Date not set. 15.95 (0-06-028189-8); pap. 5.95 (0-06-443529-6); lib. bdg. 15.89 (0-06-028190-1) HarpC.

Little Fir Tree. Margaret Wise Brown. LC 54-5534. (Illus.). 24p. (J). (gr. k-3). 1979. lib. bdg. 14.89 (0-690-04016-4) HarpC Child Bks.

Little Fir Tree: A Musical for Primary Children Based on a Story by Hans Christian Andersen. Allison Woyiwada. LC 93-50820. 16p. (J). (gr. k-6). 1994. pap. 5.00 (0-88734-428-3) Players Pr.

Little Fir Tree: Music & Lyrics. Allison Woyiwada. 1992. pap. 15.00 (0-88734-033-4) Players Pr.

Little Fir Trees Busy for Xmas Book. Rock. (J). 1996. pap. 5.95 (0-7459-3426-9, Pub. by Lion Pubng) Trafalgar.

***Little Fire Engine.** Lois Lenski. (Illus.). (J). 2000. 13.95 (0-375-81070-6) Random.

***Little Fire Engine.** Lois Lenski. (Illus.). (J). 2000. 15.99 (0-375-91070-0) Random Bks Yng Read.

***Little Fire Truck.** Joy Labrack. (Illus.). (J). 2000. mass mkt. 4.99 (0-375-81041-2) Random.

Little Firefly. Terri Cohlene. (Native American Legends Ser.). (Illus.). 48p. (J). (gr. 4-8). 1990. lib. bdg. 16.95 (0-86593-005-8) Rourke Corp.

Little Firefly: An Algonquian Legend. Terri Cohlene. (Illus.). 48p. (J). (gr. 4-7). 1996. pap. 4.95 (0-8167-2363-X) Troll Communs.

Little Fireman. Margaret Wise Brown. LC 84-43127. (Illus.). 40p. (J). 1952. 11.95 (0-201-09261-1) HarpC Child Bks.

Little Fires. Beth Bentley. LC 98-109798. (Local International Ser.). 128p. 1998. pap. 15.95 (1-885942-04-4) Cune.

Little Fish. Ralph Moisa. Ed. by Susan C. Thies. LC 98-207752. (Illus.). 56p. (J). (gr. 2-4). 1997. 13.55 (0-7807-6691-1); pap. 8.35 (0-7891-2003-8) Perfection Learn.

Little Fish in a Big Pond. Theresa O'Brien. (FRE., Illus.). 32p. (J). 1990. pap. 3.99 (0-85953-465-0) Childs Play.

Little Fish in a Big Pond. Theresa O'Brien. LC 90-46519. (Illus.). 32p. (J). (ps-3). 1990. 7.99 (0-85953-390-5); pap. 3.99 (0-85953-391-3) Childs Play.

Little Fish in a Big Pond. Michael Twinn. (J). 1996. lib. bdg. 11.95 (0-85953-891-5) Childs Play.

***Little Fish in a Big Pond: A Support Guide for Actors.** Lizzie Maxwell. Ed. by Nan T. Dudley et al. 193p. 1999. pap. 14.95 (0-9671273-0-0) DreamLover Pubg.

Little Fish Lost. Nancy Van Laan. LC 96-26344. (Illus.). 32p. (J). (ps-k). 1998. 15.00 (0-689-81331-7) Atheneum Yung Read.

Little Fish Story. Georgene Hartophilis. (J). 1996. pap. 1.25 (0-8167-0391-4) Troll Communs.

Little Fishes. Erik C. Haugaard. (Illus.). 1990. 18.00 (0-8446-6245-3) Peter Smith.

Little Five Hundred: The Making of the World's Greatest College Weekend. John Schwarb. LC 99-22906. 1999. 39.95 (0-253-33573-6) Ind U Pr.

Little Flea. Ralph F. Parkison. Ed. by Marion O. Withrow. (Illus.). 21p. (Orig.). (J). (gr. 2-8). 1988. pap. write for info. (0-318-63995-5) Little Wood Bks.

Little Fling & Other Essays. Sam Pickering. LC 99-6208. 196p. 1999. 26.00 (1-57233-062-7, Pub. by U of Tenn Pr) U Ch Pr.

***Little Flower.** Gloria Rand. 2001. text 15.95 (0-8050-6480-X) H Holt & Co.

Little Flower: A Story for Children. Laura McAndrew. LC 98-46960. (Illus.). (J). 1999. 6.95 (0-87868-714-9, Child-Family Pr) Child Welfare.

Little Flower: The Story of Saint Therese of the Child Jesus. Mary F. Windeatt. LC 90-71829. (Stories of the Saints for Young People Ages 10 to 100 Ser.). Orig. Title: Little Queen: (The Story of) St. Therese of the Child Jesus. (Illus.). 167p. (J). (gr. 5-9). 1994. reprint ed. pap. 8.00 (0-89555-413-5) TAN Bks Pubs.

Little Flower Girl. Linda T. Brandon. LC 96-2559. (Picturebacks Ser.). (Illus.). 24p. (J). (ps-1). 1997. pap. 3.25 (0-679-87695-2) Random.

Little Flower King. Kveta Pacovska. Tr. by Anthea Bell. LC 95-23866. (Illus.). 40p. (J). (gr. k-3). 1996. 15.95 (1-55858-532-X, Pub. by North-South Bks NYC) Chronicle Bks.

Little Flower of St. Francis. Tr. by Raphael Brown. 368p. 1971. pap. 9.95 (0-385-07544-8, Image Bks) Doubleday.

Little Flower's Mother. 2nd ed. Albert H. Dolan. (Illus.). 96p. 1994. pap. 6.95 (1-885553-36-6) Firefly Press.

***Little Flowers New Testament with Psalms, 1.** Nelson Word Publishing Group Staff. 640p. 2000. pap. 4.99 (0-7852-0486-5); pap. 4.99 (0-7852-0493-8); pap. 4.99 (0-7852-0496-2); pap. 4.99 (0-7852-0498-9) W1CL.

Little Flowers of Madame de Montespan. Jane Urquhart. LC 96-106132. (Illus.). 80p. 1995. pap. write for info. (0-88984-165-9) Porcup Quill.

Little Flowers of St. Francis: A Paraphrase. Donald E. Demaray. LC 91-42793. 170p. (Orig.). 1992. pap. 8.95 (0-8189-0618-9) Alba.

Little Flowers of St. Francis of Assisi. St. Francis of Assisi. Ed. by Roger Hudleston. 264p. 1988. pap. 14.95 (0-87243-246-7) Templegate.

Little Flowers of Saint Francis of Assisi. large type ed. Ed. by Louise Bachelder. (Large Print Inspirational Ser.). (Illus.). 112p. 1986. pap. 7.95 (0-8027-2526-0) Walker & Co.

Little Flowers of St. Francis of Assisi, No. 4. John F. Thornton. Tr. by W. Heywood. LC 97-48815. 176p. 1998. pap. 9.95 (0-375-70020-X) Vin Bks.

Little Folded Hands. large type ed. write for info. (0-318-68653-8, 9305) LBW.

Little Folded Hands. rev. ed. Allan H. Jahsmann. LC 59-12074. (Illus.). 48p. (J). (gr. 1-5). 1968. pap. 3.99 (0-570-03416-7, 56-1037) Concordia.

Little Folk: Stories from Around the World. Paul R. Walker. LC 96-2456. (Illus.). 80p. (J). 1997. 17.00 (0-15-200327-4) Harcourt.

Little Folk Lyrics. F. D. Sherman. LC 79-84353. (Granger Index Reprint Ser.). 1977. 18.95 (0-8369-6062-9) Ayer.

Little Follies: The Personal History, Adventure, Experiences & Observations of Peter Leroy (So Far) Eric Kraft. LC 94-46561. 1995. pap. 13.00 (0-312-11928-3) St Martin.

Little Follow the Dots Book. 80th ed. Anna Pomaska. (J). 1986. pap. 1.00 (0-486-25157-8) Dover.

***Little Foot Care Book.** Erika Dillman. LC 00-39898. 2000. write for info. (0-446-67626-8) Warner Bks.

Little Footprints: A Special Babies Memory Book. Dorothy Ferguson. Ed. by Joy Johnson. (Illus.). 24p. 1989. pap. 6.00 (1-56123-008-1, LIFC) Centering Corp.

Little Footprints: A Special Babies Memory Book. Dorothy Ferguson. 1989. 6.00 (1-56123-112-6) Centering Corp.

Little Footsteps. Ted Tally. 1986. pap. 5.25 (0-8222-0676-5) Dramatists Play.

Little Foster & His Friends: A Program to Develop Self Concept & Tolerance. Brenda J. Lewis. (Illus.). 21p. (Orig.). (J). (ps-2). 1993. pap. 6.95 (1-884063-58-6) Mar Co Prods.

Little Foster & Maria: A Program about Abuse. Brenda J. Lewis. LC 93-79189. 32p. (J). (ps-2). 1993. 6.95 (1-884063-04-7) Mar Co Prods.

Little Foster & Miss Mable: A Program about Death & Grief. Brenda J. Lewis. LC 95-78484. (Illus.). 31p. (J). (ps-2). 1995. 6.95 (1-884063-67-5) Mar Co Prods.

Little Foster & Sam: A Program about Drugs. Brenda J. Lewis. LC 93-81084. 24p. (J). (ps-2). 1994. 6.95 (1-884063-18-7) Mar Co Prods.

Little Fox. Marilyn Janovitz. LC 99-17371. (Illus.). 32p. (J). (ps-2). 1999. lib. bdg. 15.88 (0-7358-1161-X, Pub. by North-South Bks NYC) Chronicle Bks.

***Little Fox.** Marilyn Janovitz. LC 99-17371. (Illus.). 32p. (J). (ps-2). 1999. 15.95 (0-7358-1160-1, Pub. by North-South Bks NYC) Chronicle Bks.

Little Fox & the Golden Hawk. Gail Berry. (Illus.). 32p. (J). (gr. 1-9). 1991. 9.50 (0-912411-36-8) Open Horizons.

Little Foxes see Six Modern American Plays

Little Foxes. Lillian Hellman. 1947. pap. 5.25 (0-8222-0677-3) Dramatists Play.

Little Foxes & Another Part of the Forest. Lillian Hellman. 300p. 1998. lib. bdg. 23.95 (1-56723-045-8) Yestermorrow.

Little Foxes That Ruin the Vineyard. Clay Sterrett. 36p. 1994. pap. 2.50 (0-9621713-5-2) CFC Literature.

Little Foxes That Spoil the Vines. W. Barry Miller. LC 96-78091. 104p. (Orig.). 1997. pap. 7.99 (0-8361-9056-4) Herald Pr.

Little Foxes That Spoil Vines see Zorras Pequenas Que Echan A Perder las Vinas

L

An Asterisk (*) at the beginning of an entry indicates that the title is appearing for the first time.

L

Little Fox's Airbrush Stencil Techniques. Dave Perry. (Illus.). 125p. (Orig.). 1982. pap. text 14.95 (*0-9603530-8-9*) US Screen.
Little Fox's Secret: The Mystery of Bent's Fort. Mary P. Finley. LC 98-83091. (Illus.). 68p. (J). (gr. 3-4). 1999. lib. bdg. 15.95 (*0-86541-049-6*) Filter.
***Little fox's Secret: The Mystery of Bent's Fort.** Mary Pearce Finley. LC 98-83091. (Illus.). 60p. (J). (gr. 3-5). 2000. pap. 5.95 (*0-86541-050-X*) Filter.
Little Fragments of Life. Charles Saltzman. (Illus.). 338p. (Orig.). 1993. pap. 12.95 (*0-9639464-0-4*) Saltzman Pubns.
Little Freddie at the Kentucky Derby. Kathryn Cocquyt. (Illus.). 128p. (J). (gr. 4-7). 1995. pap. 9.95 (*1-56554-159-6*) Pelican.
Little Freddie's Legacy. Kathryn Cocquyt. LC 93-5558. (Illus.). 152p. (J). (gr. 3-7). 1994. 13.95 (*1-56554-000-X*) Pelican.
Little French ABC Coloring Book. Anna Pomaska. (FRE., Illus.). (J). 1991. pap. 1.00 (*0-486-26812-8*) Dover.
Little French Cookbook. Janet Laurence. (Illus.). 60p. 1989. 7.95 (*0-87701-642-9*) Chronicle Bks.
Little French Meadow. 4.98 (*0-317-38611-5*) Gick.
Little French Notebook: A Breakthrough in Early Speaking. Charles M. Long. LC 98-68584. (ENG & FRE., Illus.). v, 75p. 2000. 24.95 (*0-9667172-2-8*) Reflective Bks.
Little Friend. Emilio Rojas. (Illus.). 125p. 1992. pap. 16.95 (*1-85230-281-X*, Pub. by Element MA) Penguin Putnam.
Little Friends: In Verse & Photography. Mike Logan. LC 92-70042. (Illus.). 30p. (J). (ps-3). 1992. pap. 9.95 (*1-56044-139-9*) Falcon Pub Inc.
***Little Frog.** Christopher Gunson. (J). 2000. 17.95 (*0-385-40785-8*, Pub. by Transworld Publishers Ltd) Trafalgar.
Little Frog Learns to Sing. L. Le Blanc. LC 68-16394. (Illus.). 32p. (J). (ps-2). 1967. lib. bdg. 9.95 (*0-87783-022-3*); audio 7.94 (*0-87783-191-2*) Oddo.
Little Frog's Song. Alice Schertle. LC 91-10405. (Illus.). 32p. (J). (ps-2). 1992. lib. bdg. 14.89 (*0-06-020060-X*) HarpC Child Bks.
Little Frog's Song. Alice Schertle. LC 91-10405. (Illus.). 32p. (J). (ps-2). 1992. 15.00 (*0-06-020059-6*) HarpC Child Bks.
Little Fugue. Bach & McGinty. 1990. 10.00 (*0-685-32109-6*, 77-189) Hansen Ed Mus.
Little Fur Family. Margaret Wise Brown. LC 51-11657. (Illus.). 32p. (J). (ps-3). 1951. 15.95 (*0-06-020745-0*) HarpC Child Bks.
Little Fur Family Fur Edition. Margaret Wise Brown. LC 51-11657. (Illus.). 16p. (J). (ps-3). 1985. 7.95 (*0-694-00004-3*) HarpC Child Bks.
***Little 'g'** Sellers. (J). 2000. 3.95 (*0-552-52878-1*, Pub. by Transworld Publishers Ltd) Trafalgar.
Little Garage of Love. Al Blair. 4p. 1990. pap. 3.95 (*0-930366-34-4*) Northcountry Pub.
***Little Gardener.** Nancy Akmon & Roni Akmon. 84p. (J). 2000. 18.95 (*1-884807-48-8*, EC748) Blushing Rose.
***Little Gas Station.** Cathy Beylon. (Illus.). (J). 1998. pap. 1.00 (*0-486-40311-4*) Dover.
Little Gate. Nick Butterworth. (Illus.). (J). (ps-3). 1989. 4.99 (*0-310-55970-7*) Zondervan.
Little Gearhead Series Boxed Set, 3 bks. Molly Pearce. (Illus.). (J). 1996. boxed set 8.95 (*1-57098-098-5*) Roberts Rinehart.
Little Gems for Inspirational Leaders, Vol. 1. 64p. 1998. pap. 4.95 (*0-9667316-0-3*) Fine Print Impr.
Little German ABC Coloring Book. Nina Barbaresi. (Illus.). (J). (gr. k-3). 1993. pap. 1.00 (*0-486-27463-2*) Dover.
Little German Cookbook. Gertrud P. Matthes. (Illus.). 60p. 1995. 7.95 (*0-8118-1013-5*) Chronicle Bks.

Little German Notebook: A Breakthrough in Early Speaking. Charles Merlin Long. LC 98-92112. (GER & ENG., Illus.). 75p. 1999. 24.95 (*0-9667172-0-1*) Reflective Bks.
This highly innovative notebook introduces a revolutionary new learning technique that enables speaking of a European language in 12 weeks. Using the technique, a novice can mentally identify English cognate words & mentally transform them (in this case) into correct German words - instantly - without the aid of a dictionary! National think tank consultant & author, Charles Long, uses his recent linguistic discoveries, a patent-pending invention, & the well-proven knowledge transfer technique to forge this early speaking breakthrough. Chapters include "Prerequisites of Early Speaking," "Transfer English Words, Alphabet, Spelling & Pronunciation," "Learn Key Native German Words & Simplified German Grammar," "Multiply German Words with Simple Techniques," "Learn Self-Conceived Sentence Speaking" & "Appendix of 3,000 Transferable English Words." The Notebook has varied applications. It can be an opening 12-week language program for Middle School students, or a study aid for accelerating speaking at higher academic levels, or a self-learning book for international travelers & individuals for seeking career advancement. The Notebook's hardback, coffee-table quality, color-coded text learning aids, 40 colorful German photos, & 75-page brevity make the learning easy, pleasant & permanent. This is the first of "Little (foreign language) Notebooks." ***Publisher Paid Annotation.***

Little Germany: Ethnicity, Religion & Class in New York City, 1845-80. Stanley Nadel. LC 89-20684. (Illus.). 264p. 1990. text 37.50 (*0-252-01677-7*) U of Ill Pr.
Little Germany on the Missouri: The Photographs of Edward J. Kemper, 1895-1920. Ed. by Anna K. Hesse et al. LC 98-23340. (Illus.). 184p. 1998. 29.95 (*0-8262-1205-0*) U of Mo Pr.
Little Ghost. Vivian French. LC 93-29804. (Illus.). 32p. (J). (ps up). 1994. 4.99 (*1-56402-394-X*) Candlewick Pr.
Little Ghost. Fun Works Staff. LC 97-200322. (Illus.). 5p. (J). 1997. 5.98 (*1-57082-716-8*, Pub. by Mouse Works) Time Warner.
Little Ghost Goes to School. Marsha Marquardt. (Illus.). 12p. (Orig.). (J). (gr. 1). 1993. pap. text. write for info. (*1-882225-12-0*) Tott Pubns.
***Little Ghost Who Wouldn't Go Away: A Story for Children.** Joseph J. Ruiz. (SPA & ENG., Illus.). 96p. (J). (gr. 2-8). 2000. pap. 10.95 (*0-86534-303-9*) Sunstone Pr.
Little Ghost's Baby Brother. Marsha Marquardt. (Illus.). 12p. (Orig.). (J). (gr. 1). 1994. pap. text. write for info. (*1-882225-17-1*) Tott Pubns.
Little Ghost's Vacation. Marsha Marquardt. 8p. (J). (gr. 1). 1990. pap. text 2.50 (*1-882225-01-5*) Tott Pubns.
***Little Giant: The Life & Times of Speaker Carl Albert.** Carl Albert. 400p. 1999. pap. 14.95 (*0-8061-3200-0*) U of Okla Pr.
***Little Giant & Jabber-Jabber.** Hiawyn Oram & Ken Brown. (Illus.). 32p. (J). 1998. 19.95 (*0-86264-798-3*, Pub. by Random) Trafalgar.
***Little Giant Book of after School Fun.** Sheila A. Barry. Ed. by Paul Sloane et al. LC 99-45913. (Illus.). 352p. (J). 1999. 6.95 (*0-8069-7122-3*) Sterling.
***Little Giant Book of Card Tricks.** Bob Longe. LC 99-87963. 2000. 6.95 (*0-8069-4471-4*) Sterling.
Little Giant Book of Insults & Putdowns. Charles Keller. LC 98-40408. (J). 1998. 6.95 (*0-8069-0467-4*) Sterling.
Little Giant Book of Jokes. Joseph Rosenbloom. LC 96-28373. (Illus.). 352p. (J). 1996. 6.95 (*0-8069-6101-5*) Sterling.
Little Giant Book of Kid's Games. Vecchione. LC 99-21112. 351p. (J). 1999. pap. 6.95 (*0-8069-6341-7*) Sterling.
Little Giant Book of Knock Knocks. Charles Keller. LC 96-40058. (Illus.). 352p. (J). (gr. 3-7). 1997. pap. 6.95 (*0-8069-8108-3*) Sterling.
Little Giant Book of Optical Illusions. Keith Kay. LC 97-417. (Illus.). 352p. (J). 1997. pap. 6.95 (*0-8069-6174-0*) Sterling.
***Little Giant Book of Optical Tricks.** Keith Kay. LC 99-52193. (Illus.). 2000. 6.95 (*0-8069-4972-4*) Sterling.
Little Giant Book of Riddles. Joseph Rosenbloom. (Illus.). 352p. (J). 1996. pap. 6.95 (*0-8069-6100-7*) Sterling.
Little Giant Book of School Jokes. Charles Keller. (J). Date not set. write for info. (*0-8069-0469-0*) Sterling.
Little Giant Book of Tongue Twisters. Mike Artell. LC 99-21361. 351p. (J). 1999. write for info. (*0-8069-0951-X*) Sterling.
Little Giant Book of True Ghost Stories: 84 Scary Tales. Arthur Myers. LC 98-151818. (Illus.). 352p. (J). 1998. 6.95 (*0-8069-0555-7*) Sterling.
Little Giant Book of Whodunits. Hy Conrad & Matt LaFleur. LC 98-6165. (Illus.). 352p. (J). 1998. pap. 6.95 (*0-8069-0473-9*) Sterling.
***Little Giant Encyclopedia of Aromatherapy.** David Schiller & Carol Schiller. LC 99-33939. (Little Giant Ser.). 512p. 1999. pap. 9.95 (*0-8069-2065-3*) Sterling.
***Little Giant Encyclopedia of Baseball Quizzes.** Idea Logical Company Staff. LC 99-31393. (Little Giant Ser.). 1999. pap. 9.95 (*0-8069-1899-3*) Sterling.
Little Giant Encyclopedia of Card & Magic Tricks. Diagram Group Staff. LC 96-25432. (Illus.). 512p. 1996. pap. 9.95 (*0-8069-9347-2*) Sterling.
Little Giant Encyclopedia of Card Games. Diagram Group Staff. LC 94-45496. (Illus.). 512p. 1995. pap. 9.95 (*0-8069-1330-4*) Sterling.
Little Giant Encyclopedia of Card Games Gift Set. Diagram Group Staff. 1995. pap. text 19.95 (*0-8069-3815-3*) Sterling.
Little Giant Encyclopedia of Dream Symbols. Klausbernd Vollmar. LC 97-27939. (Little Giant Ser.). (Illus.). 510p. (J). 1997. pap. 9.95 (*0-8069-9787-7*) Sterling.
Little Giant Encyclopedia of Fortune Telling. Diagram Group. LC 98-47995. (Little Giant Ser.). 510 p. 1999. pap. 9.95 (*0-8069-4823-X*) Sterling.
Little Giant Encyclopedia of Gambling Games. Diagram Group Staff. LC 96-24655. (Illus.). 512p. 1996. pap. 9.95 (*0-8069-8128-8*) Sterling.
Little Giant Encyclopedia of Games for One or Two. 1998. write for info. (*0-8069-9663-3*) Sterling.
Little Giant Encyclopedia of Games for One or Two. Diagram Group Staff. LC 98-14805. (Illus.). 512p. 1998. 9.95 (*0-8069-0981-1*) Sterling.
***Little Giant Encyclopedia of Handwriting Analysis.** Sterling Publishing Staff & Diagram Group Staff. LC 99-39410. (Little Giant Ser.). 512p. 1999. pap. 9.95 (*0-8069-1831-4*) Sterling.
***Little Giant Encyclopedia of Home Remedies.** Carly Wall. LC 99-12496. (Illus.). 512p. 2000. pap. 9.95 (*0-8069-9815-6*) Sterling.
***Little Giant Encyclopedia of IQ Tests.** Philip J. Carter & Kenneth A. Russell. LC 00-28502. 2000. pap. 9.95 (*0-8069-2889-1*) Sterling.
Little Giant Encyclopedia of Magic. Longe. LC 99-30553. (Little Giant Ser.). 1999. pap. 9.95 (*0-8069-2058-0*) Sterling.
Little Giant Encyclopedia of Mazes. Diagram Group Staff. 1995. pap. text. write for info. (*0-8069-3808-0*) Sterling.
Little Giant Encyclopedia of Mazes. Diagram Group Staff. LC 98-141286. (Illus.). 512p. (J). 1997. 9.95 (*0-8069-9724-9*) Sterling.
***Little Giant Encyclopedia of Meditations & Blessings.** Nathaniel Altman. LC 99-44618. (Illus.). 512p. 2000. pap. 9.95 (*0-8069-6517-7*) Sterling.
Little Giant Encyclopedia of Names. Nathaniel Altman. 512p. (J). 1999. 9.95 (*0-8069-9840-7*) Sterling.
Little Giant Encyclopedia of Names. Sterling Publishing Staff. LC 99-42989. (Little Giant Ser.). 1999. pap. 9.95 (*0-8069-6509-6*) Sterling.
Little Giant Encyclopedia of Natural Healing. Diagram Group Staff. LC 99-21691. (Little Giant Ser.). 512p. 1999. pap. 9.95 (*0-8069-3948-6*) Sterling.
Little Giant Encyclopedia of One-Liners. Gene Perret & Terry Martin. LC 99-31374. (Little Giant Ser.). 512p. 1999. pap. 9.95 (*0-8069-1905-1*) Sterling.
Little Giant Encyclopedia of Palmistry. rev. ed. Nathaniel Altman. LC 98-44562. (Little Giant Ser.). (Illus.). 1999. pap. 9.95 (*0-8069-6161-9*) Sterling.
Little Giant Encyclopedia of Puzzles. Diagram Group Staff. LC 95-43151. (Illus.). 512p. 1996. 9.95 (*0-8069-4258-4*) Sterling.
***Little Giant Encyclopedia of Runes.** Sirona Knight. 2000. pap. 9.95 (*0-8069-4994-5*) Sterling.
***Little Giant Encyclopedia of Spells & Magic.** Diagram Group Staff. LC 99-36257. (Little Giant Ser.). 512p. 1999. pap. 9.95 (*0-8069-1833-0*) Sterling.
Little Giant Encyclopedia of Superstitions. Diagram Group Staff. LC 99-22531. (Little Giant Ser.). 1999. pap. 9.95 (*0-8069-6913-X*) Sterling.
Little Giant Encyclopedia of the Zodiac. Diagram Group Staff. LC 96-48341. (Illus.). 512p. 1997. 9.95 (*0-8069-9529-7*) Sterling.
Little Giant Encyclopedia of Toasts & Quotes. Diagram Group Staff. (Illus.). 512p. 1998. pap. 9.95 (*0-8069-6337-9*) Sterling.
Little Giant Encyclopedia of Travel & Holiday Games. Diagram Group Staff. LC 96-48345. (Illus.). 512p. 1997. 9.95 (*0-8069-9531-9*) Sterling.
***Little Giant Encyclopedia of UFOs.** Jenny Randles. (Illus.). 512p. 2000. pap. 9.95 (*0-8069-1891-8*) Sterling.
***Little Giant Encyclopedia of Wedding Toasts.** Katherine Young. 2000. pap. 9.95 (*0-8069-4175-8*, Chapelle) Sterling.
Little Giant Encyclopedia of Word Puzzles. Ricky Kane. LC 99-220412. 512p. 1998. 9.95 (*0-8069-1759-8*) Sterling.
Little Giants: U. S. Escort Carriers Against Japan. William T. Y'Blood. (Illus.). 448p. 1987. 31.95 (*0-87021-275-3*) Naval Inst Pr.
***Little Giants: U.S. Escort Carriers Against Japan.** William T. Y'Blood. 1999. pap. 21.95 (*1-55750-980-8*) Naval Inst Pr.
Little Gift Book of Oregon. Whitecap Books Staff. (Illus.). 96p. 1993. 12.95 (*1-55110-056-8*) Gr Arts Ctr Pub.
Little Gift Book of Washington. Whitecap Books Staff. (Illus.). 96p. 1992. 12.95 (*1-895099-37-4*) Gr Arts Ctr Pub.
Little Girl & the Inchworm. Ralph F. Parkison. Ed. by Marion O. Withrow. (Illus.). 75p. (Orig.). (J). (gr. 2-8). 1988. pap. write for info. (*0-318-63996-3*) Little Wood Bks.
Little Girl Book. David Laskin & Kathleen O. Laskin. 304p. (Orig.). 1992. pap. 11.00 (*0-345-36802-9*) Ballantine Pub Grp.
Little Girl Book. Paula Yates. (Illus.). 96p. 1995. text 5.95 (*1-85227-476-X*, Pub. by Virgin Bks) London Brdge.
Little Girl Book: Everything You Need to Know to Raise a Daughter Today. David Laskin & Kathleen O'Neill. 1996. mass mkt. 5.99 (*0-345-38678-7*) Ballantine Pub Grp.
Little Girl Fly Away: A Shattering True Story of Psychological Terror. Gene Stone. Ed. by Julie Rubenstein. 320p. 1995. mass mkt. 5.99 (*0-671-51952-2*, Pocket Star Bks) PB.
Little Girl Fly Away: Haunted by the Demons Within Her: One Woman's True Story. Gene Stone. 1994. 22.00 (*0-671-78085-9*) S&S Trade.
***Little Girl Found: Lovers Under Cover.** 2000. mass mkt. 4.25 (*0-373-22568-7*) Harlequin Bks.
Little Girl in the Woods. Phyllis J. Peterson. Ed. by Allen D. Peterson. LC 98-92383. (Illus.). 1998. pap. 10.00 (*0-9646503-2-0*) A D Peterson.
Little Girl Is Something to Love. (Little Remembrance Gift Editions Ser.). (J). 6.95 (*0-87741-002-X*) Makepeace Colony.
Little Girl Lost. Leisha Joseph. 240p. 1999. pap. 11.95 (*0-385-49240-5*) Doubleday.
Little Girl Lost. Adrianne Lee. 1997. per. 3.75 (*0-373-22438-9*, 1-22438-5) Harlequin Bks.
Little Girl Lost. Joan Merriam. 1998. mass mkt. 5.99 (*0-7860-0487-8*, Pinncle Kensgtn) Kensgtn Pub Corp.
Little Girl Lost. Isabel Sinclair. 134p. mass mkt. 4.99 (*1-55197-040-6*) Picasso Publ.
Little Girl Lost. Drew Barrymore & Todd Gold. Ed. by Jane Chelius. 303p. 1991. reprint ed. per. 6.99 (*0-671-68923-1*, Pocket Star Bks) PB.
Little Girl Lost: One Woman's Journey Beyond Rape. Leisha Joseph & Deb Mendenhall. LC 98-17683. 224p. 1998. 19.95 (*0-385-49239-1*) Doubleday.
Little Girl Lost: The Troubled Childhood of Princess Diana by the Woman Who Raised Her. Mary Clarke. (Illus.). 256p. 1996. 19.95 (*1-55972-330-0*, Birch Ln Pr) Carol Pub Group.
Little Girl Named Miriam. Dina Rosenfeld. (Little Greats Ser.). (Illus.). (J). (ps-1). Date not set. 9.95 (*0-922613-79-6*) Hachai Pubng.
Little Girl, the Lillipop, & the Green Bird, Bk. 1. Ralph F. Parkison. Ed. by Marion O. Withrow. (Illus.). 31p. (Orig.). (J). (gr. 2-6). 1988. pap. 4.25 (*0-929949-00-5*) Little Wood Bks.
Little Girl Who Lived down the Lane. Laird Koenig. LC 98-115341. 1997. pap. 5.25 (*0-8222-1571-3*) Dramatists Play.
***Little Girls Bible Activity Calendar.** Carolyn Larsen & Vicki Totel. 368p. (J). (ps-8). 2000. spiral bd. 9.99 (*0-8010-4456-1*, New Kids Media) Baker Bks.
***Little Girls Bible Christmas Storybook.** Carolyn Larson. 32p. (ps-2). 1999. 7.99 (*0-8010-4431-6*, New Kids Media) Baker Bks.
Little Girls Bible Easter Storybook. Carolyn Larsen. (Illus.). 32p. (ps-2). 1999. 7.99 (*0-8010-4421-9*, New Kids Media) Baker Bks.
***Little Girls Bible Storybook Coloring Book.** Ed. by Jennifer Stewart. (Illus.). 48p. (J). (ps-2). 1999. pap. 2.49 (*0-7847-0986-6*, 22056) Standard Pub.
***Little Girls Bible Storybook On Cd Rom: Includes Storybook Music Room Cookbook Fashion Center My.** Standard Publishing Staff. 1999. 29.99 (*5-559-71174-8*) Standard Pub.
***Little Girls Bible Storybook Sticker Book.** Ed. by Jennifer Stewart. (Illus.). 24p. (J). (ps-2). 1999. pap. 2.99 (*0-7847-1094-5*, 20078) Standard Pub.
Little Girls Book of Prayers. Carolyn Larson. (Illus.). 192p. (ps-2). 1999. 12.99 (*0-8010-4422-7*, New Kids Media) Baker Bks.
***Little Girls Devotional Storybook.** Carolyn Larsen. 192p. (J). (ps-7). 2000. 16.99 (*0-8010-4446-4*, New Kids Media) Baker Bks.
Little Girl's Dream? A JonBenet Ramsey Story. Eleanor Von Duyke & Dwight Wallington. LC 98-60173. 280p. 1998. pap. 11.95 (*1-881636-44-5*) Windsor Hse Pub Grp.
Little Girls Have to Sleep. Jim Muir. LC 92-37456. (Illus.). (J). 1993. pap. 16.00 incl. audio (*1-881320-03-0*, Black Belt) Black Belt Communs.
Little Girls in Church. Kathleen Norris. LC 94-44508. (Poetry Ser.). 80p. 1995. text 24.95 (*0-8229-3875-8*) U of Pittsburgh Pr.
Little Girls in Church. Kathleen Norris. 80p. 1995. pap. 10.95 (*0-8229-5556-3*) U of Pittsburgh Pr.
***Little Girls in Pretty Boxes: The Making & Breaking of Elite Gymnasts & Figure Skaters.** Joan Ryan. 2000. pap. write for info. (*0-446-67682-9*) Warner Bks.
Little Girls in Pretty Boxes: The Making & Breaking of Elite Gymnasts & Figure Skaters. rev. ed. Joan Ryan. 228p. 1996. mass mkt. 12.99 (*0-446-67250-5*, Pub. by Warner Bks) Little.
Little Girl's Treasury. unabridged ed. (Children's Heritage Ser.). (Illus.). 156p. (J). (gr. 4-6). 1996. pap. 7.50 (*1-58339-125-8*, D25) Triangle Press.
Little Goat: Story Pak. Jean de La Fontaine. (Graphic Learning Literature Program Series: Folk Tales). (ENG & SPA., Illus.). (J). 1992. 45.00 (*0-87746-243-7*) Graphic Learning.
Little Goat on the Roof. Jody Littler. (Illus.). 32p. (J). (ps-3). 1998. pap. 8.95 (*1-57534-029-1*) Skandisk.
Little God: The Twilight of Patriarchy in a Southern African Chiefdom. Diana Wylie. LC 89-49462. (Illus.). 293p. reprint ed. pap. 90.90 (*0-608-09098-0*, 206973200005) Bks Demand.
Little Gold-Mine. Arthur Berry. 1990. 45.00 (*0-9511427-7-1*, Pub. by Bullfinch Pubns) St Mut.
Little Gold Ring & Other Stories. Cosmo Hamilton. LC 70-121557. (Short Story Index Reprint Ser.). 1977. 24.95 (*0-8369-3514-4*) Ayer.
Little Gold Star: A Spanish American Cinderella Story. Robert D. San Souci. LC 99-50290. 32p. (J). (gr. k up). 2000. 15.89 (*0-688-14781-X*, Wm Morrow) Morrow Avon.
Little Gold Star: A Spanish American Cinderella Tale. Robert D. San Souci. LC 99-50290. 32p. (J). (gr. k up). 2000. 15.95 (*0-688-14780-1*, Wm Morrow) Morrow Avon.
***Little Gold Star (Estrellita de Oro) A Cinderella Cuento.** Joe Hayes. LC 99-57104. (SPA & ENG., Illus.). 32p. (J). (ps-3). 2000. 15.95 (*0-938317-49-0*) Cinco Puntos.
Little Golden America. Ilya Ilf & Eugene Petrov. Tr. by Charles Malmouth. LC 73-13139. (Foreign Travelers in America, 1810-1935 Ser.). 400p. 1974. reprint ed. 29.95 (*0-405-05461-0*) Ayer.
Little Golden Book - Bible Set. Western Publishing Co., Inc. Staff. (Illus.). (J). (gr. k-4). 1994. pap. 10.00 (*1-882954-12-2*) Aspen Press.
***Little Golden Lamb.** Ellin Greene. LC 99-36025. (Illus.). 32p. (J). 2000. 15.00 (*0-395-71526-1*, Clarion Bks) HM.
Little Golf Treasury. Ed. by Jane P. Resnick. 400p. 1966. 8.98 (*1-884822-50-9*) Blck Dog & Leventhal.
Little Goo-Roo: Lessons from Your Baby. Jan Kirschner & Tracy Kirschner. LC 97-93617. (Illus.). 144p. 1998. 16.95 (*0-9657960-1-9*) Atlas Press.
Little Gorilla see Gorilita
Little Gorilla. Ruth Borenstein. (Carry-Along Book & Cassette Favorites Ser.). (Illus.). (J). (ps-1). 1995. pap. 9.95 incl. audio (*0-395-72091-5*, 111771, Clarion Bks) Ticknor & Flds Bks Yng Read.
Little Gorilla, 001. Ruth Bornstein. LC 75-25508. (Illus.). 32p. (J). (ps-2). 1979. 15.00 (*0-395-28773-1*, Clarion Bks) HM.
***Little Gorilla.** Ruth Bornstein. (Illus.). 28p. (J). (ps-k). 2000. 4.95 (*0-618-05158-9*, Clarion Bks) HM.
Little Gorilla. Ruth Bornstein. (Carry Along Book & Cassette Favorites Ser.). (J). 1986. 11.15 (*0-606-12398-9*, Pub. by Turtleback) Demco.
Little Gorilla. Ruth L. Bornstein. LC 75-25508. (Illus.). 32p. (J). (ps-2). 1986. pap. 5.95 (*0-89919-421-4*, Clarion Bks) HM.

An Asterisk (*) at the beginning of an entry indicates that the title is appearing for the first time.

Little Gospel. Leo Tolstoy. Tr. by Sasha Newborn from RUS. LC 86-72787. (Humanist Classics Ser.). 129p. 1987. pap. text 11.00 (*0-942208-02-1*) Bandanna Bks.

Little Gourmet Shopping List. 6.95 (*0-89480-660-2*) Workman Pub.

Little Grammar Book: Ten Minutes a Day to Better Speech & Writing. Frank E. Cooke. 100p. 1999. pap. 12.95 (*0-940076-10-1*, GB99FC) Fiesta City.

Little Grandmother of the Russian Revolution. Ekaterina Breshko-Breshkovskaia. (American Biography Ser.). 348p. 1991. reprint ed. lib. bdg. 79.00 (*0-7812-8038-9*) Rprt Serv.

Little Gray Cloud. Ron Curran. (Oracle of Delphi Chronicles). 1997. 20.00 (*0-9656372-0-4*) Venture Bks CA.

Little Gray Men: Roswell & the Rise of a Popular Culture. Toby Smith. LC 99-27120. 208p. 2000. 24.95 (*0-8263-2121-6*) U of NM Pr.

Little Greatness. Joe Noland. LC 98-73190. 223p. 1998. pap. 6.00 (*0-9657601-4-6*, Crest Books) SANP.

Little Greek Cookbook. Rena Salaman. (Little Bks.). (Illus.). 60p. 1990. 7.95 (*0-87701-795-6*) Chronicle Bks.

Little Green Book: Questions for Radiology Conference & Examination Preparation. Eric P. Tamm. 480p. pap. text 45.00 (*0-683-30635-9*) Lppncott W & W.

Little Green Book: Quotations on the Environment. Oline Luinenberg & Stephen Osborne. 96p. 1995. per. 3.95 (*0-88978-225-3*, Pub. by Arsenal Pulp) LPC InBook.

Little Green Book of Investment Wisdom. Kenneth S. Janke, Sr. 1997. write for info. (*0-8129-2685-4*, Times Bks) Crown Pub Group.

Little Green Book of the Last Lost Dinosaurs. Angie Sage. (Illus.). 64p. (J). (gr. 3-6). 1995. pap. 7.95 (*0-14-036875-2*, Pub. by Pnguin Bks Ltd) Trafalgar.

Little Green Dragon Steps Out. Klaus Baumgart. LC 92-5120. (Little Green Dragon Ser.). (Illus.). 32p. (J). (ps-3). 1992. 12.95 (*1-56282-254-3*, Pub. by Hyprn Child) Little.

Little Green Fingers: A Kid's Guide to Growing Things. Clare Chandler. (Illus.). 28p. (J). (gr. 1-4). 5.95 (*1-55110-258-7*) Whitecap Bks.

Little Green Friend. Lynn M. List. (Illus.). 36p. (J). (gr. k-5). 1998. 14.95 (*0-9662900-0-3*) Skinny Lamb Publ.

Little Green Frog, Vol. 3622. Rozanne L. Williams. (Emergent Reader Bks.). 8p. 1994. pap. 1.75 (*0-916119-50-5*) Creat Teach Pr.

Little Green Frog, Vol. 3679. Rozanne L. Williams. (Emergent Reader Big Bks.). (Illus.). 8p. (J). (gr. k-2). 1995. pap. 8.98 (*1-57471-062-1*) Creat Teach Pr.

Little Green Frog & Other Poems. Joan B. Barsotti. LC 98-93135. (Illus.). 32p. (J). (ps-4). 1999. 14.95 (*0-9642112-6-2*); pap. 6.95 (*0-9642112-5-4*) Barsotti Bks.

Little Green Goose. Adele Sansone. LC 98-48759. (Illus.). (J). (ps-2). 1999. lib. bdg. 15.88 (*0-7358-1072-9*, Pub. by North-South Bks NYC) Chronicle Bks.

Little Green Goose. Adele Sansone. LC 98-48759. (Illus.). 32p. (J). (ps-2). 1999. 15.95 (*0-7358-1071-0*, Pub. by North-South Bks NYC) Chronicle Bks.

Little Green Guys from Mars. M. Friedman & E. Weiss. (Illus.). (J). 1997. pap. write for info. (*0-679-87665-0*); lib. bdg. write for info. (*0-679-97665-5*, Bullseye Bks) Random Bks Yng Read.

Little Green Hummingbird. James R. Linn. Ed. by Dwayne L. Huston. LC 92-75969. (Illus.). 44p. (J). (gr. 3). 1993. pap. 7.98 (*1-882798-01-5*) Erth & Sky Pub.

Little Green Man in Ireland: A Mystery. Mary Branham. Ed. by James C. Smith. LC 96-12084. 160p. 1997. 24.95 (*0-86534-248-2*) Sunstone Pr.

Little Green Man Visits a Farm, Vol. 4352. Kimberlee Graves. (Fun & Fantasy Ser.). (Illus.). 16p. (J). (ps-1). 1997. pap. 2.75 (*1-57471-249-7*, 4352) Creat Teach Pr.

Little Green Man Visits Pine Cone Grove, Vol. 2915. Margaret Allen. Ed. by Joel Kupperstein. (Dr. Maggie's Phonics Readers Ser.). (Illus.). 16p. (J). (ps-2). 1999. pap. 2.99 (*1-57471-590-9*) Creat Teach Pr.

Little Green Men. Christopher Buckley. LC 98-36418. 300p. 1999. 24.95 (*0-679-45293-1*) Random.

***Little Green Men: A Novel.** Christopher Buckley. LC 99-55682. 320p. 2000. pap. 13.00 (*0-06-095557-0*, Perennial) HarperTrade.

Little Green Mobile. Wilson-Max. 1997. pap. write for info. (*0-590-10284-2*) Scholastic Inc.

Little Green Monsters: Story Book in Young Children in Sign Language. Sue Johnson. (Talking Fingers Bks.). (Illus.). 36p. (J). (ps-6). 1985. pap. 4.50 (*0-916708-15-2*) Modern Signs.

Little Green Mountain Fire. Lee D. Cowan. LC 98-86879. 192p. 1999. pap. 12.95 (*1-56167-506-7*, Five Star Spec Ed) Am Literary Pr.

Little Green Thumbs. Mary A. Van Hage. LC 95-45497. (Illus.). 32p. (J). (gr. 2-4). 1996. lib. bdg. 21.40 (*1-56294-270-0*) Millbrook Pr.

Little Green Tow Truck. Ken Wilson-Max. (Illus.). 14p. (J). 1997. pap. 14.95 (*0-590-89802-7*) Scholastic Inc.

***Little Green Tow Truck: Mini Edition.** Illus. by Ken Wilson-Max. 14p. (J). (ps-k). 2000. 7.95 (*0-439-13654-7*, Cartwheel) Scholastic Inc.

Little Green Tree. Helen Masters. (Illus.). 24p. (J). (gr. k-6). 1999. pap. 7.00 (*0-8059-4636-5*) Dorrance.

Little Greenish-Brown Book of Slugs. Corbel. 96p. 1993. per. 4.95 (*0-88978-267-9*, Pub. by Arsenal Pulp) LPC InBook.

Little Grey Flannel Book: Quotations on Men. Oline Luinenberg & Stephen Osborne. 108p. 1995. per. 3.95 (*0-88978-239-3*, Pub. by Arsenal Pulp) LPC InBook.

Little Grey Partridge: The Diary of Ishobel Ross, Serbia, 1916-1917. Jess Dixon. (Illus.). 100p. 1988. pap. 14.00 (*0-08-036419-5*, Pub. by Aberdeen U Pr) Macmillan.

Little Grey Sparrows of the Anglican Diocese of Bunbury, Western Australia. Merle Bignell. vii, 207 p. 1992. 39.95 (*1-875560-16-5*, Pub. by Univ of West Aust Pr) Intl Spec Bk.

***Little Groundhog's Shadow.** Janet Craig. LC 98-122860. (First Start Easy Reader Ser.). 1998. pap. text 2.95 (*0-8167-4519-6*) Troll Communs.

Little Grounding Book. Judith Poole. (Illus.). 40p. 1993. spiral bd. 9.95 (*0-9674257-0-0*) Pooled Res.

Little Grown-Ups. Photos by Tom Arma. (Illus.). 18p. (J). (ps up). 1995. bds. 4.95 (*0-448-40093-6*, G & D) Peng Put Young Read.

Little Grunt & the Big Egg. Tomie De Paola. (Illus.). (J). (ps-3). 1990. reprint ed. pap. 6.95 (*0-8234-1027-7*) Holiday.

Little Grunt & the Big Egg: A Prehistoric Fairy Tale. Tomie De Paola. LC 88-17009. (Illus.). 32p. (J). (ps-3). 1990. lib. bdg. 16.95 (*0-8234-0730-6*) Holiday.

***Little Guide to Babies.** Macmillan Children's Book Staff. (Illus.). (J). 2000. 3.99 (*0-333-73422-X*) Mcm Child Bks.

***Little Guide to Dads.** Macmillan Children's Book Staff. (Illus.). (J). 2000. 3.99 (*0-333-73420-3*) Mcm Child Bks.

***Little Guide to Mums.** Macmillan Children's Book Staff. (Illus.). (J). 2000. 3.99 (*0-333-73419-X*) Mcm Child Bks.

***Little Guide to Pets.** Macmillan Children's Book Staff. (Illus.). (J). 2000. 3.99 (*0-333-73421-1*) Mcm Child Bks.

Little Gumbo Book: Twenty-Seven Carefully Created Recipes That Will Enable Everyone to Enjoy the Special Experience of Gumbo. Gwen McKee. LC 94-5662. (Illus.). 64p. (Orig.). 1986. 8.95 (*0-937552-17-8*) Quail Ridge.

Little Gus's Big Boo-Boo: Paint Box Book. Golden Books Staff. 32p. (J). 1998. pap. 3.99 (*0-307-09217-8*, 09217, Goldn Books) Gldn Bks Pub Co.

Little Guy's Business Success. 2nd ed. Albert C. Smith. Ed. by Laura T. Smith. LC 96-97052. (Little Guy's Investment Ser.). 100p. 1997. pap. 5.95 (*0-933086-13-X*) Cromwell-Smith.

Little Guy's Sailboat Success. 2nd ed. Albert C. Smith, Jr. LC 96-96010. (Little Guy's Investment Ser.). Orig. Title: Little Guy's Sailboat Success Guide. (Illus.). 80p. 1996. pap. 4.95 (*0-933086-12-1*) Cromwell-Smith.

Little Guy's Sailboat Success Guide see Little Guy's Sailboat Success

Little Guy's Stock Market Future Effectiveness. Albert C. Smith, Jr. LC 94-92092. (Little Guy's Investment Ser.). (Illus.). 140p. (Orig.). 1994. pap. 8.95 (*0-933086-10-5*) Cromwell-Smith.

***Little Guy's Tax Survival Guide.** 2nd rev. ed. Albert C. Smith, Jr. LC 98-90283. (Little Guy's Investment Ser.). (Illus.). 112p. 1998. pap. 5.95 (*0-933086-16-4*, 933086) Cromwell-Smith.

***Little 'h' Sellers.** (J). 2000. 3.95 (*0-552-52879-X*, Pub. by Transworld Publishers Ltd) Trafalgar.

***Little Ha-Ha.** Christopher Boyce. (J). (gr. 2-5). 2000. pap. 5.95 (*0-533-13264-9*) Vantage.

Little Halloween Activity Book. A. Pomaska. (Little Activity Bks.). (J). 1993. pap. 1.00 (*0-486-27601-5*) Dover.

Little Halloween Stained Glass. T. Menten. (J). 1991. pap. 1.00 (*0-486-25736-3*) Dover.

Little Halloween Sticker Book. Nina Barbaresi. (Little Activity Bks.). (Illus.). (J). 1991. pap. 1.00 (*0-486-26390-8*) Dover.

Little Handbook of Office Humors. Claudette V. Copney. (Illus.). 48p. 1998. pap. 8.95 (*1-56167-453-2*) Am Literary Pr.

Little Handbook on Having a Soul. David Hansen. LC 97-12920. 168p. 1997. pap. 9.99 (*0-8308-1679-8*, 1679) InterVarsity.

Little Hands Art Book: Exploring Arts & Crafts with 2-to-6 Year Olds. Judy Press. LC 94-13910. 1994. 18.05 (*0-606-10252-3*, Pub. by Turtleback) Demco.

Little Hands Art Book: Exploring Arts & Crafts with 2-to-6 Year Olds. Judy Press. LC 94-1391. (Little Hands Bks.: No. 1). (Illus.). 160p. (J). (ps-1). 1994. pap. 12.95 (*0-913589-86-1*) Williamson Pub Co.

Little Hands Big Fun Craft Book: Creative Fun for 2- to 6-Year-Olds. Judy Press. LC 95-17574. (Little Hands Bks.: Vol. 2). (Illus.). 144p. (J). (ps-1). 1996. pap. 12.95 (*0-913589-96-9*) Williamson Pub Co.

Little Hands Nature Book: Earth, Sky, Critters & More. Nancy F. Castaldo. Ed. by Susan Williamson. LC 97-13774. (Little Hands Ser.: Vol. 7). Orig. Title: Sunny Days & Starry Nights, a Little Hands Nature Book. (Illus.). 144p. (Orig.). (J). (ps-1). 1997. pap. 12.95 (*1-885593-16-3*) Williamson Pub Co.

***Little Hands Playtime! Book: 50 Activities to Encourage Cooperation & Sharing.** Regina Curtis. LC 99-88073. (Illus.). 144p. (J). (ps-1). 2000. pap. 12.95 (*1-885593-42-2*) Williamson Pub Co.

***Little Hands Story Bible.** Carine MacKenzie. (Illus.). (J). 1999. 9.99 (*1-85792-342-1*) Christian Focus.

Little Hands with First Drawing Practice. Henry J. Filson. (Draw-Sketch Practice Ser.). (Illus.). 28p. (J). (gr. 10 up). 1978. 2.75 (*0-918554-01-2*) Old Violin.

Little Harbor. Christopher Bursk. (QRL Poetry Bks.: Vol. XXIII). 1982. 20.00 (*0-614-06400-7*) Quarterly Rev.

Little Hatmaking Book: A Workbook on Turn-of-the-Century Hats, Vol. 1. Bonnie A. Ambrose. LC 94-50778. 1994. pap. 7.95 (*0-89676-126-6*, Costume & Fashion Pr) QSMG Ltd.

Little Havana Blues: A Cuban-American Literature Anthology. Ed. by Virgil Suarez & Delia Poey. LC 96-14242. 448p. 1996. pap. 19.95 (*1-55885-160-7*) Arte Publico.

Little Hawk's New Name. Don Bolognese. LC 93-40723. (Hello Reader! Ser.). (Illus.). 48p. (J). (ps-3). 1995. 3.99 (*0-590-48292-0*, Cartwheel) Scholastic Inc.

Little Hawk's New Name. Don Bolognese. (Hello Reader! Level 4 Ser.). (J). 1995. 9.19 (*0-606-07795-2*, Pub. by Turtleback) Demco.

***Little Heaven Below: Worship at Early Methodist Quarterly Meetings.** Lester Ruth. 256p. 2000. pap. 25.00 (*0-687-09024-5*) Abingdon.

Little Hebrew Alphabet Coloring Book. 81st ed. Jill Dubin. (HEB., Illus.). (J). 1992. pap. 1.00 (*0-486-27018-1*) Dover.

Little Hen see Gallinita Roja

Little Henry: The Stolen Child. Timothy Flint. LC 73-104452. (J). reprint ed. lib. bdg. 40.00 (*0-8398-0558-6*) Irvington.

***Little Henry & the Phantom Dream.** Henry Defraites. (Illus.). 32p. (J). (gr. 1-7). 1999. 7.95 (*0-9676825-0-9*) Abound Inc.

Little Herb Encyclopedia. Jack Ritchason. 126p. 1984. pap. 5.95 (*0-913923-18-4*) Woodland UT.

Little Herb Encyclopedia. 2nd ed. Jack Ritchason. 126p. 1994. pap. 9.95 (*0-913923-89-3*) Woodland UT.

Little Herb Gardens. Storey Publishing Staff. 1997. pap. 12.95 (*0-676-57003-8*) Random.

Little Herb Gardens: Simple Solutions for Great Gardens - Indoors & Out. Georgeanne Brennan & Mimi Luebbermann. LC 92-25637. (Illus.). 96p. 1993. pap. 12.95 (*0-8118-0249-3*) Chronicle Bks.

Little Herball of the Properties of the Herbes. Anthony Askham. LC 77-6848. (English Experience Ser.: No. 843). 1977. reprint ed. lib. bdg. 20.00 (*90-221-0843-0*) Walter J Johnson.

Little Herder in Autumn. Ann N. Clark. Ed. by John P. Harrington. Tr. by Robert W. Young. LC 88-70848. (ENG & NAV., Illus.). 96p. (J). (gr. 3 up). 1988. reprint ed. pap. 9.95 (*0-941270-46-7*) Ancient City Pr.

Little Heroes. Arthur Dobrin. (Ethical Humanist Society Monograph: No. 1). (Illus.). 1977. pap. 5.00 (*0-89304-200-5*, CCC111) Cross-Cultrl NY.

Little Hex Book for Women. Rebecca Sargent. LC 97-71620. (Illus.). 112p. 1997. 9.95 (*0-8362-3260-7*) Andrews & McMeel.

Little Hippo & the New Baby. Harriet Ziefert & Emilie Boon. LC 97-27435. (Illus.). (J). 1997. write for info. (*0-7894-2191-7*) DK Pub Inc.

Little Hippo's New Friend. Harriet Ziefert. LC 98-10189. (Illus.). (J). 1998. write for info. (*0-7894-3409-1*) DK Pub Inc.

Little Hippo's New Friend. Harriet Ziefert & Emilie Boon. (Little Hippo Ser.). (Illus.). (J). (ps). 1998. write for info. (*0-7894-3105-X*) DK Pub Inc.

Little Hippo's New House. Harriet Ziefert. LC 97-27434. (Illus.). (J). 1997. write for info. (*0-7894-2192-5*) DK Pub Inc.

Little Hippo's New School. Harriet Ziefert. LC 98-10190. (Illus.). (J). 1998. write for info. (*0-7894-3408-3*) DK Pub Inc.

Little Hippo's New School. Harriet Ziefert & Emilie Boon. (Little Hippo Ser.). (Illus.). (J). (ps). 1998. write for info. (*0-7894-3106-8*) DK Pub Inc.

Little History of Australia. Mark Peel. (Illus.). 96p. 1997. 9.95 (*0-522-84757-9*, Pub. by Melbourne Univ Pr) Paul & Co Pubs.

Little History of Bothell, Washington. Jack R. Evans. (Little History Ser.). (Illus.). 44p. (Orig.). 1989. pap. 3.95 (*1-877882-00-3*) SCW Pubns.

Little History of Gig Harbor, Washington. Jack R. Evans. (Little History Ser.). (Illus.). 32p. (Orig.). 1988. pap. 3.95 (*1-877882-01-1*) SCW Pubns.

Little History of Golf. Kim Leneghan. (Illus.). 60p. 1996. 7.95 (*0-8118-1266-9*) Chronicle Bks.

Little History of Ireland. Martin Wallace. (Illus.). 60p. 1995. 7.95 (*0-8118-0818-1*) Chronicle Bks.

Little History of Ireland. Martin Wallace & Ian McCullough. (Illus.). 60p. 1994. 9.95 (*0-86281-455-3*, Pub. by Appletree Pr) Irish Bks Media.

Little History of North Bend - Snoqualmie, Washington. Jack R. Evans. (Little History Ser.). (Illus.). 61p. (Orig.). 1990. pap. 4.95 (*1-877882-03-8*) SCW Pubns.

Little History of Pike Place Market: Seattle, Washington. Jack R. Evans. Ed. by Barbara Evans. (Little History Ser.). (Illus.). 81p. (Orig.). 1991. pap. 6.95 (*1-877882-04-6*) SCW Pubns.

Little History of Renton, Washington. Jack R. Evans & Paul Rowe. (Little History Ser.). (Illus.). 24p. (Orig.). 1987. pap. 2.25 (*1-877882-02-X*) SCW Pubns.

Little Hobbin. Theodor Storm. Tr. by Anthea Bell. LC 95-11691. (Illus.). 24p. (J). (gr. k-3). 1995. 15.95 (*1-55858-460-9*, Pub. by North-South Bks NYC); lib. bdg. 15.88 (*1-55858-461-7*, Pub. by North-South Bks NYC) Chronicle Bks.

Little Hobo. Melba M. Ashburn. (Illus.). 130p. (Orig.). (J). (gr. 3 up). 1997. pap. 15.95 (*0-9656829-4-3*) Syringa.

Little Hobo. Dave Sargent. LC 96-33908. (Illus.). 135p. (J). (gr. 2-8). 1993. pap. 5.45 (*1-56763-051-0*); lib. bdg. 16.95 (*1-56763-050-2*) Ozark Pub.

Little Holiday Shop. Christopher Carrie. (Coloring Storybook Ser.). (Illus.). 32p. (Orig.). (J). (gr. 2-5). 1989. pap. 1.99 (*0-86696-241-7*) Binney & Smith.

Little Hoot. Louise Woelber. LC 97-94890. 1996. write for info. (*1-891614-00-2*) Hopscotch CO.

Little Hopper: Catches a Cold. (Dr. Wellbook Collection). (Illus.). 24p. (J). (ps-3). 1996. reprint ed. pap. 7.95 (*1-879874-27-X*) T Peters & Co.

Little Horn of the Book of Daniel. Bob L. Ross. 1983. mass mkt. 3.00 (*1-56186-511-7*) Pilgrim Pubns.

***Little Horse.** Betsy C. Byars. 2000. text, pap. text 15.95 (*0-8050-6413-3*) St Martin.

Little Horse. Frank Mindgue. LC 98-19145. (Illus.). 80p. (J). (gr. 3-12). 1999. pap. 9.95 (*0-932991-59-9*, Different Bks) Place in the Woods.

Little Horses Stained Glass Coloring Book, Vol. 200. John Green. (Illus.). (J). (gr. k-3). 1992. pap. 1.00 (*0-486-27224-9*) Dover.

Little Horsey Little Lessons: A Young Girl & Her Special Horse Help Teach Skills for Life. Patricia DeMeyer. LC 98-86663. (Illus.). 40p. (J). (gr. 1-6). 1998. pap. 9.95 (*0-9666433-0-5*) Saddle Tree.

Little Hotel: A Novel. Christina Stead. LC 92-18898. 192p. 1995. pap. 12.95 (*0-8050-2412-3*, Owl) H Holt & Co.

Little Hotel on the Prairie: The "Missing Link" Years: a Story of the Charles Ingalls Family in Burr Oak, Winneshick County, Iowa. John A. Bass. (Ingalls-Wilder-Lane Signature Ser.: Bk. 8). (Illus.). 100p. 1998. pap. 10.00 (*1-891453-08-4*) Ingalls-Wilder.

Little House, 001. Virginia L. Burton. (Illus.). 44p. (J). (gr. k-3). 1978. 14.95 (*0-395-18156-9*) HM.

Little House, 001. Virginia L. Burton. LC 88-176374. (Illus.). 44p. (J). (ps-3). 1978. pap. 5.95 (*0-395-25938-X*) HM.

Little House. Virginia L. Burton. (J). 1969. 11.15 (*0-606-01531-0*, Pub. by Turtleback) Demco.

***Little House.** Itzik Kipnis. Tr. by Curt Leviant from YID. (Illus.). 24p. (J). (ps-3). 1999. pap. 7.95 (*1-894303-21-0*) RRP.

Little House. MQ Publications Staff. (Little Brown Notebooks Ser.). 1998. 9.99 (*1-84072-064-6*, Pub. by M Q Pubns) Watsn-Guptill.

Little House. large type ed. Philippa Gregory. LC 97-3567. 1997. pap. 23.95 (*1-56895-422-0*) Wheeler Pub.

Little House: A Story of the Charles Ingalls Family in Rutland Township, Montgomery County, Kansas. John A. Bass. (Ingalls-Wilder-Lane Signature Ser.: Bk. 6). (Illus.). 100p. 1998. pap. 10.00 (*1-891453-06-8*) Ingalls-Wilder.

Little House: An Architectural Seduction. Jean-Francois De Bastide. Tr. by Rodolfe El-Khoury from FRE. (Illus.). 112p. (Orig.). 1996. pap. 14.95 (*1-56898-017-5*) Princeton Arch.

Little House Baby Book. Laura Ingalls Wilder. (Illus.). 64p. (J). (ps-1). 1996. 14.95 (*0-694-00746-3*, HarpFestival) HarpC Child Bks.

Little House Birthday. Laura Ingalls Wilder. LC 96-41512. (My First Little House Bks.). (Illus.). 40p. (J). (ps-3). 1997. 12.95 (*0-06-025928-0*) HarpC.

Little House Birthday. Laura Ingalls Wilder. LC 96-41512. (My First Little House Bks.). (Illus.). 32p. (J). (ps-3). 1998. pap. 5.95 (*0-06-443494-X*) HarpC.

Little House Books, 9 vols. Laura Ingalls Wilder. Incl. By the Shores of Silver Lake. LC 52-7529. (Illus.). 304p. (J). (gr. 3-7). 1953. pap. 4.95 (*0-06-440005-0*, HarpTrophy); Farmer Boy. LC 52-7527. (Illus.). 384p. (J). (gr. 3-7). 1953. pap. 4.95 (*0-06-440003-4*, HarpTrophy); First Four Years. Intro. by Roger Lea Macbride. LC 76-135774. (Illus.). 160p. (J). (gr. 3-7). 1953. pap. 4.95 (*0-06-440031-X*, HarpTrophy); Little House in the Big Woods. LC 52-7525. (Illus.). 256p. (J). (gr. 4-7). 1953. pap. 4.95 (*0-06-440001-8*, HarpTrophy); Little House on the Prairie. LC 52-7526. (Illus.). 352p. (J). (gr. 4-7). 1953. pap. 4.95 (*0-06-440002-6*, HarpTrophy); Little Town on the Prairie. LC 52-7531. (Illus.). 320p. (J). (gr. 3-7). 1953. pap. 4.95 (*0-06-440007-7*, HarpTrophy); Long Winter. LC 52-7530. (Illus.). 352p. (J). (gr. 3-7). 1953. pap. 4.95 (*0-06-440006-9*, HarpTrophy); LC 52-7525. (Illus.). (J). (gr. 3-7). 1973. reprint ed. Set pap. 44.55 (*0-06-440040-9*, HarpTrophy) HarpC Child Bks.

Little House by Boston Bay. Melissa Wiley. LC 99-11748. (Little House). (Illus.). 208p. (J). (gr. 3-7). 1999. 15.95 (*0-06-027011-X*); pap. 4.95 (*0-06-440737-3*); lib. bdg. 15.89 (*0-06-028201-0*) HarpC Child Bks.

Little House Chapter Book, No. 25. Melissa Wiley. (J). pap. write for info. (*0-06-442111-2*, HarpTrophy) HarpC Child Bks.

Little House Chapter Book, No. 26. Melissa Wiley. (J). lib. bdg. write for info. (*0-06-028557-5*) HarpC Child Bks.

***Little House Chapter Book, No. 26.** Melissa Wiley. (J). 2001. pap. write for info. (*0-06-442112-0*, HarpTrophy) HarpC Child Bks.

***Little House Chapter Book, No. 29.** Melissa Wiley. (J). 2002. pap. write for info. (*0-06-442139-2*, HarpTrophy); lib. bdg. write for info. (*0-06-029175-3*) HarpC Child Bks.

***Little House Chapter Book, No. 30.** Melissa Wiley. (J). 2002. pap. write for info. (*0-06-442140-6*, HarpTrophy); lib. bdg. write for info. (*0-06-029176-1*) HarpC Child Bks.

***Little House Chapter Book, No. 31.** Maria D. Wilkes. (J). 2002. pap. write for info. (*0-06-442141-4*, HarpTrophy); lib. bdg. write for info. (*0-06-029177-X*) HarpC Child Bks.

***Little House Chapter Book, No. 32.** Roger Lea Macbride. 2002. lib. bdg. write for info. (*0-06-029178-8*) HarpC Child Bks.

***Little House Chapter Book, No. 32.** Roger Lea Macbride. (J). 2002. pap. write for info. (*0-06-442142-2*, HarpTrophy) HarpC Child Bks.

Little House Christmas: Holiday Stories from the Little House Books. Laura Ingalls Wilder. (Little House). (Illus.). 96p. (J). (gr. 3-6). 1995. pap. 9.95 (*0-06-440615-6*, HarpTrophy) HarpC Child Bks.

Little House Christmas: Holiday Stories from the Little House Books. Laura Ingalls Wilder. (Little House). (Illus.). (J). (gr. 3-6). 1995. 15.15 (*0-606-12983-9*, Pub. by Turtleback) Demco.

Little House Christmas: Holiday Stories from the Little House Books, No. 2. Laura Ingalls Wilder. (Little House). (Illus.). 112p. (J). (gr. 3-6). 1997. lib. bdg. 19.89 (*0-06-027490-5*) HarpC Child Bks.

Little House Christmas: Holiday Stories from the Little House Books, Vol. 2. 2nd ed. Laura Ingalls Wilder. (Little House). (Illus.). 112p. (J). (gr. 3-6). 1997. 19.95 (*0-06-027489-1*) HarpC Child Bks.

L

L

Little House Cookbook: Frontier Foods from Laura Ingalls Wilder's Classic Stories. Barbara M. Walker. LC 76-58733. (Illus.). 256p. (YA). (gr. 3 up). 1979. 16.95 (0-06-026418-7); lib. bdg. 15.89 (0-06-026419-5) HarpC Child Bks.

Little House Cookbook: Frontier Foods from Laura Ingalls Wilder's Classic Stories. Barbara M. Walker. LC 76-58733. (Trophy Bk.). (Illus.). 256p. (YA). (gr. 3 up). 1989. pap. 9.95 (0-06-446090-8, HarpTrophy) HarpC Child Bks.

Little House Cookbook: Frontier Foods from Laura Ingalls Wilder's Classic Stories. Barbara M. Walker. 1979. 12.05 (0-606-04268-7, Pub. by Turtleback) Demco.

Little House Diecut Standee. Harper Collins Staff. 1999. pap. text 0.00 (0-06-028429-3) HarpC.

***Little House Farm Days.** Illus. by Renee Graef. (Little House Chapter Bks.: No. 7). (J). (gr. k-2). 1998. 9.15 (0-606-13576-6, Pub. by Turtleback) Demco.

Little House Farm Days. adapted ed. Illus. by Renee Graef. LC 97-34350. (Little House Chapter Bks.: No. 7). 80p. (J). (gr. 2-5). 1998. lib. bdg. 13.89 (0-06-027793-9, HarpTrophy) HarpC Child Bks.

Little House Farm Days. adapted ed. Illus. by Renee Graef. LC 97-34350. (Little House Chapter Bks.: No. 7). 80p. (J). (gr. 2-5). 2000. pap. 4.25 (0-06-442078-7, HarpTrophy) HarpC Child Bks.

Little House Friends. Illus. by Renee Graef. LC 97-39280. (Little House Chapter Bks.: No. 9). 80p. (J). (gr. 2-5). 1998. lib. bdg. 14.89 (0-06-027894-3) HarpC.

Little House Friends. Illus. by Renee Graef. LC PZ7.L7347 1998. (Little House Chapter Bks.: No. 9). 80p. (J). (gr. k-2). 2000. pap. 4.25 (0-06-442080-9, HarpTrophy) HarpC Child Bks.

Little House Guidebook. William Anderson. (Illus.). 96p. (J). (gr. 3 up). 1996. pap. 9.95 (0-06-446177-7, HarpTrophy) HarpC Child Bks.

Little House Guidebook. William Anderson. 1996. 14.15 (0-606-12984-7, Pub. by Turtleback) Demco.

***Little House "History Comes to Life" Event Kit.** Laura Ingalls Wilder. (J). 2000. write for info. (0-06-028839-6) HarpC Child Bks.

Little House in Brookfield. Maria D. Wilkes. (Little House). (Illus.). 320p. (J). (gr. 3-6). 1996. 15.95 (0-06-026459-4); pap. 4.95 (0-06-440610-5, HarpTrophy) HarpC Child Bks.

Little House in Brookfield. Maria D. Wilkes. (Little House). (Illus.). (J). (gr. 3-6). 1996. 10.05 (0-606-09559-4, Pub. by Turtleback) Demco.

Little House in Louisiana: The Complete Story of the Wilder Family in Louisiana. John A. Bass. (Ingalls-Wilder-Lane Signature Ser.: Bk. 13). (Illus.). 100p. 1998. pap. 10.00 (1-891453-13-0) Ingalls-Wilder.

Little House in Rothville: A Story of the Charles Ingalls Family in Rothville, Chariton County, Missouri: Little House: the Untold Story-the Other "Missing Link" John A. Bass. (Ingalls-Wilder-Lane Signature Ser.: Bk. 5). (Illus.). 100p. 1997. pap. 10.00 (1-891453-05-X) Ingalls-Wilder.

Little House in the Big Woods see Little House Books

Little House in the Big Woods. Rebecca Gilleland. 58p. (J). (gr. 3-6). 1994. student ed., ring bd. 12.99 (1-58609-131-X) Progeny Pr WI.

***Little House in the Big Woods.** Jean Jamieson. 44p. (J). (gr. 3-6). 1999. 11.95 (1-56137-705-8) Novel Units.

***Little House in the Big Woods.** Laura Ingalls Wilder. (J). (gr. 3-6). 1999. 9.95 (1-56137-030-4) Novel Units.

Little House in the Big Woods. Laura Ingalls Wilder. (Little House). (J). (gr. 3-6). 1971. 10.05 (0-606-03811-6, Pub. by Turtleback) Demco.

Little House in the Big Woods. rev. ed. Laura Ingalls Wilder. (Little House). (Illus.). 256p. (J). (gr. 3-6). 1953. 16.95 (0-06-026430-6); lib. bdg. 16.89 (0-06-026431-4) HarpC Child Bks.

Little House in the Big Woods: A Study Guide. Estelle Kleinman. Ed. by J. Friedland & R. Kessler. (Novel-Ties Ser.). (J). (gr. 3-5). 1996. pap. text 15.95 (1-56982-623-4) Lrn Links.

Little House in the Big Woods: Curriculum Unit. Center for Learning Network Staff. (Novel Ser.). 96p. 1994. teacher ed., spiral bd. 18.95 (1-56077-291-3) Ctr Learning.

Little House in the Big Woods: Literature Unit. Laurie Swinwood. (Illus.). 1994. 7.95 (1-55734-522-8) Tchr Create Mat.

Little House in the Classroom. Christine Hackett. (Illus.). 112p. (J). (gr. 3-5). 1989. student ed. 12.99 (0-86653-444-X, GA1052) Good Apple.

Little House in the Highlands. Melissa Wiley. LC PZ7.W64814Li 1999. (Little House). 288p. (J). (gr. 3-6). 1999. lib. bdg. 15.89 (0-06-028202-9) HarpC Child Bks.

Little House in the Highlands. Melissa Wiley. LC 98-34910. (Little House). (Illus.). 288p. (J). (gr. 3-7). 1999. pap. 4.95 (0-06-440712-8, HarpTrophy) HarpC Child Bks.

Little House in the Highlands. Melissa Wiley et al. LC 98-34910. (Little House). (Illus.). 288p. (J). (gr. 3-7). 1999. 15.95 (0-06-027983-4) HarpC Child Bks.

Little House in the Ozarks. Laura Ingalls Wilder. 320p. (J). (gr. 4-7). 1996. 9.98 (0-88365-968-9) Galahad Bks.

Little House in Westville: A Story of the Ingalls & Wilder Families in Westville, Holmes County, Florida. John A. Bass. (Ingalls-Wilder-Lane Signature Ser.: Bk. 11). (Illus.). 100p. 1998. pap. 10.00 (1-891453-11-4) Ingalls-Wilder.

***Little House Life Magazine, Vol. 2.** (J). 2000. pap. write for info. (0-06-449279-6, HarpTrophy) HarpC Child Bks.

***Little House Life Magazine Vol. 2: With Hardware.** (J). 2000. pap. write for info. (0-06-449258-3, HarpTrophy) HarpC Child Bks.

Little House Literature Mini-Unit. Janet Lovelady. (Illus.). 32p. (J). (gr. 2-4). 1989. student ed. 4.95 (1-56096-000-0) Mari.

***Little House Magazine, No. 1.** (J). 2000. write for info. (0-06-028850-7) HarpC Child Bks.

Little House of Horrors. Keith Faulkner. LC 96-6214. (Illus.). 24p. (J). (ps-2). 1997. boxed set 9.95 (0-8120-8468-3) Barron.

***Little House of My Own: 47 Grand Designs for 47 Tiny Houses.** Lester Walker. 224p. 2000. 19.98 (1-57912-151-9) Blck Dog & Leventhal.

Little House on Rocky Ridge. Roger L. MacBride. LC 92-39132. (Little House). (Illus.). 368p. (J). (gr. 3-7). 1993. pap. 4.95 (0-06-440478-1, HarpTrophy) HarpC Child Bks.

Little House on Rocky Ridge. Roger L. MacBride. (Little House). (Illus.). (J). (gr. 3-6). 1993. 10.05 (0-606-05432-4, Pub. by Turtleback) Demco.

Little House on Rocky Ridge. 305th ed. Roger L. MacBride. LC 92-39132. (Little House). (Illus.). 368p. (J). (gr. 4-7). 1993. 16.95 (0-06-020842-2) HarpC Child Bks.

Little House on the Freeway: Help for the Hurried Home. rev. ed. Tim Kimmel. 224p. 1994. pap. 12.99 (0-88070-628-7, Multnomah Bks) Multnomah Pubs.

Little House on the Prairie see Little House Books

***Little House on the Prairie.** Phyllis A. Green. 36p. 1999. 9.95 (1-56137-031-2) Novel Units.

Little House on the Prairie. Linda L. Maifair. (Literature Unit Ser.). (Illus.). 48p. 1995. pap., teacher ed. 7.95 (1-55734-539-2) Tchr Create Mat.

Little House on the Prairie. Laura Ingalls Wilder. (Illus.). (J). (gr. 4-7). 1989. pap. 2.95 (0-317-53651-6) HarpC.

Little House on the Prairie. Laura Ingalls Wilder. LC 98-54782. (Little House). (Illus.). 320p. (J). (gr. 3-6). 1999. 29.95 (0-06-028244-4) HarpC Child Bks.

***Little House on the Prairie.** Laura Ingalls Wilder. (J). 1999. 11.95 (1-56137-834-8) Novel Units.

Little House on the Prairie. Laura Ingalls Wilder. (Little House). (J). (gr. 3-6). 1981. 10.05 (0-606-03812-4, Pub. by Turtleback) Demco.

Casa del la Pradera - Little House on the Prairie. Laura Ingalls Wilder. 1996. pap. text 7.95 (84-279-3195-6) Lectorum Pubns.

Little House on the Prairie Pb. Laura Ingalls Wilder. (J). 1990. pap. 3.50 (0-06-107006-8, Harp PBks) HarpC.

Little House on the Prairie. Wolf. LC 96-31197. (Twayne's masterworks studies). xvi, 168 p. 1996. per. 14.95 (0-8057-8821-2, Twyne) Mac Lib Ref.

Little House on the Prairie. Virginia L. Wolf. LC 96-31197. 1996. 29.00 (0-8057-8820-4, Twyne) Mac Lib Ref.

Little House on the Prairie. deluxe ed. Laura Ingalls Wilder. LC 52-7526. (Little House). (Illus.). 352p. (J). (gr. 3-7). 1997. 24.95 (0-06-027723-8) HarpC Child Bks.

Little House on the Prairie. large type ed. Laura Ingalls Wilder. (Little House). (Illus.). 420p. (J). (gr. 3-6). 1999. lib. bdg. 35.95 (1-58118-051-9, 22771) LRS.

Little House on the Prairie. Laura Ingalls Wilder. (Little House). 250p. (J). (gr. 3-6). 1991. reprint ed. lib. bdg. 19.95 (0-89966-868-2) Buccaneer Bks.

Little House on the Prairie. rev. ed. Laura Ingalls Wilder. LC 52-7526. (Little House). (Illus.). 352p. (J). (gr. 4-7). 1953. 16.95 (0-06-026445-4); lib. bdg. 16.89 (0-06-026446-2) HarpC Child Bks.

Little House on the Prairie: A Study Guide. James H. Macon. (Novel-Ties Ser.). (J). (gr. 3-5). 1989. pap. text, teacher ed., student ed. 15.95 (0-88122-051-5) Lrn Links.

***Little House Parties.** Illus. by Renee Graef. LC 98-41707. (Little House Chapter Bks.: No. 14). 80p. (J). (gr. 2-5). 1999. lib. bdg. 13.89 (0-06-027951-6) HarpC Child Bks.

***Little House Parties.** Illus. by Renee Graef. LC PZ7.L73463 1999. (Little House Chapter Bks.: No. 14). 80p. (J). (gr. k-2). 2000. pap. 4.25 (0-06-442085-X, HarpTrophy) HarpC Child Bks.

Little House Pioneer Girls. Maria D. Wilkes et al. (J). (gr. 3-7). 1998. pap., boxed set 14.85 (0-06-440709-8, HarpTrophy) HarpC Child Bks.

Little House Reader: A Collection of Writings. Laura Ingalls Wilder & William Anderson. LC 97-2767. (Illus.). 208p. (J). (gr. 3-7). 1998. 16.95 (0-06-026358-X) HarpC.

***Little House Readers Club.** 2000. write for info. (0-06-028855-8) HarpC Child Bks.

Little House Sampler. Laura Ingalls Wilder & Rose W. Lane. Ed. by William T. Anderson. LC 89-45118. (Illus.). 256p. (gr. 2 up). 1995. reprint ed. pap. 12.50 (0-06-097240-8, Perennial) HarperTrade.

Little House Sisters: Collected Stories from the Little House Books. Laura Ingalls Wilder. LC 96-34742. (Little House). (Illus.). 96p. (J). (gr. 3-7). 1997. 19.95 (0-06-027587-1) HarpC Child Bks.

Little House Treasury. Laura Ingalls Wilder. 640p. 5.00 (0-06-028238-X) HarpC.

Little House Trivia Book. Laura Ingalls Wilder. LC PS3545.I342Z765 1996. (Illus.). 150p. (J). (gr. 3-7). 1996. pap. 7.95 (0-694-00834-6, HarpFestival) HarpC Child Bks.

Little House with the Slanted Roof. Gloria L. Smith. 24p. (J). (gr. 2-5). 1979. pap. text 5.00 (1-929655-09-6) Trailstones Heritage.

Little "Hu" (Illus.). 150p. 1997. pap. write for info. (0-9658738-1-1) LA Polit.

***Little Hummingbird.** Pat Clark. (Illus.). 36p. (J). 2000. pap. 22.95 (1-57532-289-7) Press-Tige Pub.

Little Humpback Horse. Lowell Swortzell. (J). (gr. 1 up). 1984. pap. 6.50 (0-87602-244-1) Anchorage.

Little Humpbacked Horse: A Russian Tale. Illus. by Alexander Koshkin. LC 95-43994. 32p. (J). (gr. 1-5). 1997. 14.95 (0-395-65361-4, Clarion Bks) HM.

Little Hungarian Pornography. Peter Esterhazy. Tr. by Judith Sollosy from HUN. LC 95-25048. 224p. (C). 1995. 24.95 (0-8101-1340-6, Hydra Bks) Northwestern U Pr.

Little Hungarian Pornography. Peter Esterhazy. Tr. by Judith Sollosy. 216p. 1997. pap. 15.95 (0-8101-1577-8, Hydra Bks) Northwestern U Pr.

Little Hut: Manuscript Edition. Nancy Mitford & Andre Roussin. 1957. pap. 13.00 (0-8222-0678-1) Dramatists Play.

***Little 'i'** Sellers. (J). 2000. 3.95 (0-552-52880-3, Pub. by Transworld Publishers Ltd) Trafalgar.

***Little "i"** Sellers. (J). 2000. 3.95 (0-552-52883-8, Pub. by Transworld Publishers Ltd) Trafalgar.

***Little i Book Book.** John Tollett & Robin Williams. 200p. 1999. pap. text 18.99 (0-201-70093-X) Peachpit Pr.

Little I Saw of Cuba. Burr McIntosh. 1976. lib. bdg. 59.95 (0-8490-2174-X) Gordon Pr.

***Little Ice Age.** Fagan. 2000. 26.00 (0-465-02271-5, Pub. by Basic); pap. 15.00 (0-465-02272-3, Pub. by Basic) HarpC.

Little Ice Age. Jean M. Grove. 500p. 1988. text 144.00 (0-416-31540-2) Routledge.

Little Ice Age. 2nd ed. Jean M. Grove. 496p. (C). 1999. write for info. (0-415-09948-X); pap. write for info. (0-415-09949-8) Routledge.

Little Icicle. Lois Szymanski. 96p. (Orig.). (J). (gr. 4-7). 1995. mass mkt. 3.99 (0-380-77567-0, Avon Bks) Morrow Avon.

Little Icicle. Lois Szymanski. (Orig.). (J). 1995. 9.19 (0-606-07796-0) Turtleback.

Little Ike Templin: And Other Stories. Richard M. Johnston. LC 72-3343. (Short Story Index Reprint Ser.). 1977. reprint ed. 21.95 (0-8369-4151-9) Ayer.

Little iMac Book. Robin Williams. LC 99-184714. (Illus.). 160p. (C). 1998. pap. text 17.99 (0-201-35421-7, Pub. by Peachpit Pr) Addison-Wesley.

***Little iMac Book.** 2nd ed. Robin Williams. (Illus.). 224p. 2000. pap. text 17.99 (0-201-70446-3) Addison-Wesley.

***Little Inchkin.** Fiona French. 32p. (J). (ps-3). 2000. 7.99 (0-7112-0917-0, Pub. by F Lincoln) Antique Collect.

***Little Indian & Whiney Gator.** Kay S. Manning. 36p. (J). 2001. 22.95 (1-57532-291-9) Press-Tige Pub.

Little Indian Girl. Tom Tierney. (Little Activity Bks.). (Illus.). (J). 1993. pap. 1.00 (0-486-27004-1) Dover.

Little Indians' ABC. Faustina H. Lucero. LC 73-87800. (Illus.). 32p. (J). (gr. k-2). 1974. lib. bdg. 9.95 (0-87783-129-7) Oddo.

Little Indians' ABC. deluxe ed. Faustina H. Lucero. LC 73-87800. (Illus.). 32p. (J). (gr. k-2). 1974. pap. 3.94 (0-87783-130-0) Oddo.

Little Innocent Lamb: Negro Spiritual a Capella. 16p. 1986. pap. 1.25 (0-7935-5488-8, 50304530) H Leonard.

Little Instruction Book of Business Etiquette: A Valuable "Briefcase" of Good Manners for Every Business Professional! Valerie Sokolosky. 160p. 1996. pap. text, per. 6.99 (1-57757-201-7) Trade Life.

Little Inventions That Made Big Money. Illus. by George A. Brewster. 155p. (Orig.). 1983. pap. text. write for info. (1-877782-11-4) MGM & Assocs.

Little Irish Baking Book. Marion Maxwell. (Little Irish Book Ser.). (Illus.). 60p. 1995. 9.95 (0-86281-534-7, Pub. by Appletree Pr) Irish Bks Media.

Little Irish Banking Book. Ruth I. Ross. (Illus.). 112p. 1996. text 12.95 (0-312-14005-3) St Martin.

Little Irish Birthday Book. Marian Clark. (Illus.). 125p. 1994. 13.95 (0-86281-458-8, Pub. by Appletree Pr) Irish Bks Media.

Little Irish Book of Days. (Illus.). 128p. 1992. 11.95 (0-86281-289-5, Pub. by Appletree Pr) Irish Bks Media.

Little Irish Cookbook. John Murphy. (Little Bks.). (Illus.). 60p. 1996. 7.95 (0-8118-1085-2) Chronicle Bks.

Little Irish Songbook: Words & Music to 27 Classic Irish Songs. Illus. by Ian McCullough. 60p. 1992. 7.95 (0-8118-0187-X) Chronicle Bks.

Little Ironies: Stories of Singapore. Catherine Lim. (Writing in Asia Ser.). 106p. (C). 1978. pap. 5.00 (0-435-00224-4, 00244) Heinemann.

Little Is Big: Jesus Feeds the Crowd. Claudia Courtney. (Phonetic Bible Stories). (Illus.). 16p. (J). (ps-1). 1998. pap. 2.59 (0-570-05094-4) Concordia.

Little Island. Margaret Wise Brown. (Dell Picture Yearling Ser.). (J). 1973. 11.19 (0-606-05908-3, Pub. by Turtleback) Demco.

Little Island. G. Macdonald. (Illus.). 48p. (J). 1993. pap. 5.99 (0-440-40830-X) Dell.

Little Island: A Study Guide. Garrett Christopher. Ed. by Joyce Friedland & Rikki Kessler. (Little Novel-Ties Ser.). (J). (gr. k-2). 1991. pap. text 14.95 (0-88122-592-4) Lrn Links.

Little Italian Cookbook. Anna Del Conte. (Illus.). 60p. 1990. 7.95 (0-87701-754-9) Chronicle Bks.

Little Italian Cookbook. Anna Del Conte. 60p. 1996. 7.95 (0-8118-1287-1) Chronicle Bks.

Little Italian Cookbook. Jennie Sacco. (Illus.). (Orig.). 1988. pap. write for info. (0-318-62576-8) J Sacco.

Little Italian Girl. Sylvia Walker. (Little Activity Bks.). (Illus.). (J). 1993. pap. 1.00 (0-486-26996-5) Dover.

Little Italy Cookbook. David Ruggerio. LC 97-15261. (Illus.). 232p. 1997. 29.95 (1-885183-54-2) Artisan.

Little Italy Cookbook: Recipes from North American's Italian Communities. Maria Pace & Louisa Scaini-Jojic. (Illus.). 220p. (Orig.). 1996. pap. 16.95 (1-895629-72-1) Warwick Publ.

***Little 'j'** Sellers. (J). 2000. 3.95 (0-552-52881-1, Pub. by Transworld Publishers Ltd) Trafalgar.

Little Jack Horner. S & J Products Int., Inc. Staff. (Mother Goose & Then Some Ser.). (Illus.). 12p. (Orig.). (J). (ps). 1995. pap. 5.45 (1-884851-16-9) S&J Prods.

Little Japanese Cookbook. Emi Kazuko. (Little Bks.). (Illus.). 60p. 1991. 7.95 (0-8118-0029-6) Chronicle Bks.

Little Jar of Oil: The Story of Elisha & the Widow. Patricia L. Nederveld. LC 97-32478. (God Loves Me Ser.). (Illus.). 24p. (J). (ps). 1998. pap. 2.45 (1-56212-289-4, 1105-0120) CRC Pubns.

Little Java, a Few Patterns. Matthias Felleisen & Daniel P. Friedman. LC 97-40548. (Language, Speech & Communication Ser.). (Illus.). 240p. 1997. pap. text 20.00 (0-262-56115-8, Bradford Bks) MIT Pr.

Little Jay Learns Karate. Chris Thomas. LC 96-96949. (Illus.). 48p. (J). (gr. k-5). 1997. pap. 9.95 (1-889267-01-5) G Dillman Karate.

Little Jeannie. Barbara Steadman. (Little Activity Bks.). (Illus.). (J). 1994. pap. 1.00 (0-486-28265-1) Dover.

Little Jeff: The Jeff Davis Legion, Cavalry, Army of Northern Virginia. Donald A. Hopkins. LC 99-33601. (Illus.). 339p. 1999. 40.00 (1-57249-172-8) White Mane Pub.

Little Jemima Puddle Duck Stickers. Anna Pomaska. (Illus.). (J). (gr. k-3). 1993. pap. 1.00 (0-486-27637-6) Dover.

Little Jesus, Little Me. Doris Rikkers. 12p. 2000. 5.99 (0-310-23205-8, Zonderkidz) Zondervan.

***Little Jesus of Sicily.** Fortunato Pasqualino. Tr. by Louise Rozier from ITA. LC 99-38364. (Illus.). 96p. 1999. 22.00 (1-55728-572-1); pap. 14.00 (1-55728-573-X) U of Ark Pr.

Little Jewel: The Key to Successful Telemarketing. Edward D. Curry. Ed. by Letha S. Curry. (Orig.). (C). 1994. text 39.95 (0-9633590-1-0) Target Mktg-Mgmt.

Little Jewel Bird. Lucy Conley. (Jewel Book Ser.: Set 1). (Illus.). 32p. (J). (ps-2). 1986. pap. 2.55 (0-7399-0028-5, 2311) Rod & Staff.

Little Jewish Cookbook. Barbara Bloch. (Illus.). 60p. 1995. 7.95 (0-8118-1016-X) Chronicle Bks.

Little Jimmie by James "Jim Larkin" Toler. Gloria M. Houston. 1993. 10.05 (0-606-12402-0, Pub. by Turtleback) Demco.

Little Jimmie by James "Jim Larkin" Toler. Jim Toler. Ed. & Photos by Amy Weems. (Illus.). 184p. 1997. write for info. (0-9659453-0-8) Baby Best.

Little Jinx. Abram Tertz, pseud. Tr. by Larry P. Joseph & Rachel May from RUS. (Studies in Russian Literature & Theory). 100p. 1992. 24.95 (0-8101-1016-4); pap. 10.95 (0-8101-1041-5) Northwestern U Pr.

Little Joanna. Elizabeth W. Bellamy. (Works of Elizabeth Whitfield Bellamy). 1989. reprint ed. lib. bdg. 79.00 (0-7812-1947-7) Rprt Serv.

Little Joe, a Hopi Indian Boy, Learns a Hopi Indian Secret. Terry Latterman. Ed. by Mary E. Hawkins. LC 85-61836. (Illus.). 32p. (J). (gr. 4-12). 1985. 12.95 (0-934739-01-3) Pussywillow Pub.

Little Joe Monaghan. Barbara Lebow. 1995. pap. 5.25 (0-8222-1414-8) Dramatists Play.

Little Joe Otter. Thornton W. Burgess. (J). 18.95 (0-8488-0398-1) Amereon Ltd.

Little Joe Otter. Thornton W. Burgess. 103p. (J). 1981. reprint ed. lib. bdg. 17.95 (0-89966-353-2); reprint ed. lib. bdg. 17.95 (0-89967-027-X, Harmony Rain) Buccaneer Bks.

Little Joe, Superstar: The Films of Joe Dallesandro. 2nd ed. Michael Ferguson. LC 98-70584. (Illus.). 216p. 1998. pap. 18.95 (1-889138-09-6) Companion Press.

***Little John - The Webb City Kid.** John D. Gassett. (Illus.). 125p. (J). (gr. 1-8). 1999. pap. write for info. (0-9671895-0-0) J D Gassett.

Little John Challenge Walk - 28 Miles. 32p. 1987. 29.00 (0-907496-46-6, Pub. by JNM Pubns) St Mut.

Little Johnny Buttermilk: After an Old English Folktale. Jan Wahl. LC 99-13121. (Illus.). 32p. (J). (ps-1). 1999. 15.95 (0-87483-559-3) August Hse.

Little Johnny Raindrop. James A. Chappell. LC 88-2173. (Illus.). 32p. (J). (ps-3). 1988. 12.95 (0-938349-28-7) State House Pr.

Little Jollys Find a Home. Valerie Hannah. Ed. by George H. Herrick. (Illus.). 36p. (Orig.). (J). (gr. k-3). 1991. pap. 5.95 (0-941281-79-5) V H Pub.

Little Jordan. Marly Youmans. 112p. 1995. 18.95 (1-56792-029-2) Godine.

Little Jordan. Marly Youmans. LC 95-17092. 112p. (YA). (gr. 7-12). 1999. mass mkt. 6.99 (0-380-73136-3, Avon Bks) Morrow Avon.

Little Journey in the World. Charles D. Warner. LC 67-29283. (Americans in Fiction Ser.). reprint ed. pap. 7.95 (0-89197-826-7); reprint ed. lib. bdg. 22.75 (0-8398-2154-9) Irvington.

Little Journey in the World. Charles D. Warner. (BCL1-PS American Literature Ser.). 396p. 1992. reprint ed. lib. bdg. 89.00 (0-7812-6892-3) Rprt Serv.

Little Journey in the World. Charles D. Warner. (Notable American Authors Ser.). 1999. reprint ed. lib. bdg. 125.00 (0-7812-9906-3) Rprt Serv.

Little Journeys: A Photo Tour Guide Through Historic Macon County. Hildegard Sandhusen. (Illus.). 56p. 1996. pap. 10.95 (0-9638930-2-5) Teresita Pr.

Little Journeys into Storyland. Reynold. 235p. 1992. pap. 6.95 (1-881545-06-7) Angelas Bkshelf.

Little Journeys to the Homes of Great Musicians Series. write for info. (0-89904-727-0, Silhouette Imprints) Crumb Elbow Pub.

Little Journeys to the Homes of the Good Men & Great, Vol. 1. Elbert Hubbard. 378p. 1998. reprint ed. pap. 30.00 (0-7661-0398-6) Kessinger Pub.

Little Journeys to the Homes of the Great American Statesmen, Vol. 3. Elbert Hubbard. 344p. 1998. reprint ed. pap. 30.00 (0-7661-0401-X) Kessinger Pub.

Little Journeys to the Homes of the Great Businessmen, Vol. 11. Elbert Hubbard. 460p. 1998. reprint ed. pap. 30.00 (0-7661-0399-4) Kessinger Pub.

Little Journeys to the Homes of the Great Eminent Artists, Vol. 6. Elbert Hubbard. 380p. 1998. reprint ed. pap. 30.00 (0-7661-0403-6) Kessinger Pub.

An Asterisk (*) at the beginning of an entry indicates that the title is appearing for the first time.

L

Little Journeys to the Homes of the Great Eminent Orators, Vol. 7. Elbert Hubbard. 444p. 1998. reprint ed. pap. 30.00 (*0-7661-0409-5*) Kessinger Pub.

Little Journeys to the Homes of the Great Eminent Painters, Vol. 4. Elbert Hubbard. 378p. 1998. reprint ed. pap. 30.00 (*0-7661-0406-0*) Kessinger Pub.

Little Journeys to the Homes of the Great English Authors, Vol. 5. Elbert Hubbard. 372p. 1998. reprint ed. pap. 30.00 (*0-7661-0407-9*) Kessinger Pub.

Little Journeys to the Homes of the Great Famous Women, Vol. 2. Elbert Hubbard. 334p. 1998. reprint ed. pap. 30.00 (*0-7661-0404-4*) Kessinger Pub.

Little Journeys to the Homes of the Great Lovers, Vol. 13. Elbert Hubbard. 466p. 1998. reprint ed. pap. 30.00 (*0-7661-0400-1*) Kessinger Pub.

Little Journeys to the Homes of the Great Musicians, Vol. 14. Elbert Hubbard. 436p. 1998. reprint ed. pap. 30.00 (*0-7661-0429-X*) Kessinger Pub.

Little Journeys to the Homes of the Great Philosophers, Vol. 8. Elbert Hubbard. 454p. 1998. reprint ed. pap. 30.00 (*0-7661-0402-8*) Kessinger Pub.

Little Journeys to the Homes of the Great Reformers, Vol. 9. Elbert Hubbard. 420p. 1998. reprint ed. pap. 30.00 (*0-7661-0405-2*) Kessinger Pub.

Little Journeys to the Homes of the Great Scientists, Vol. 12. Elbert Hubbard. 440p. 1998. reprint ed. pap. 30.00 (*0-7661-0395-1*) Kessinger Pub.

Little Journeys to the Homes of the Great Teachers, Vol. 10. Elbert Hubbard. 400p. 1998. reprint ed. pap. 30.00 (*0-7661-0396-X*) Kessinger Pub.

Little Juan Learns a Lesson: A Story for Children. Joseph J. Ruiz. Tr. by Samuel Adelo. LC 97-28150. (ENG & SPA., Illus.). 64p. (Orig.). (J). (gr. 3-8). 1997. pap. 8.95 (*0-86534-267-9*) Sunstone Pr.

*__Little 'k'__ Sellers. (J). 2000. 3.95 (*0-552-52882-X*, Pub. by Transworld Publishers Ltd) Trafalgar.

Little Karoo. large type ed. Pauline Smith. LC 97-22980. 144p. 1997. text 19.95 (*1-56000-540-8*) Transaction Pubs.

Little Katja's Evening Prayer. Tia Salingre-Williams. (Illus.). 30p. 1997. pap. 6.95 (*0-9657030-0-2*) Lapponia Prodns.

Little Keyboard Book: Eight Tunes of Colonial Virginia Set for Piano or Harpsichord. J. S. Darling. LC 71-165364. 16p. 1972. pap. 4.95 (*0-910412-93-6*) Colonial Williamsburg.

*__Little Kids Adventure Bible.__ Zondervan Bible Publishers Staff. (Illus.). (J). 2000. 17.99 (*0-310-92142-2*) Zondervan.

Little Kids Can Write Books Too! Making Classroom Books with Young Children. Diane Bonica. (Illus.). 112p. 1994. 12.99 (*0-86653-784-8*, GA1478) Good Apple.

Little-Kids' Olympics. Karen O'Connor. (Illus.). 80p. (J). (ps-3). 1994. pap. 4.99 (*0-570-04770-6*, 56-1789) Concordia.

Little Kid's Safety Center. Florence Weiner. (Illus.). 25p. (Orig.). (J). (ps-1). 1998. pap. 19.95 (*1-888241-04-7*) Safety Ctr.

Little Kim's Doll. Kim Yaroshevskaya. (FRE., Illus.). 32p. (ps-1). 1999. 15.95 (*0-88899-353-6*, Pub. by Gro1undwood-Douglas) Publishers Group.

Little Kinder Than Necessary: A Collection of Character-Building Secrets. Beth Strong Taber. LC 98-6503. (Illus.). 96p. (J). 1998. pap. 9.95 (*0-9637077-4-4*) Nicolin Flds.

Little Kingdoms. Steven Millhauser. 1993. 21.00 (*0-671-86890-X*) S&S Trade.

Little Kingdoms: A Novel. John H. Irsfeld. LC 89-42898. (Southwest Life & Letters Ser.). 216p. 1989. reprint ed. pap. 10.95 (*0-87074-294-9*) SMU Press.

*__Little Kingdoms: A Travel Adventure.__ Vikram Sundarji. LC 99-932618. x 223p. 1998. 20.00 (*0-14-026987-8*, Penguin Classics) Viking Penguin.

Little Kingdoms: The Counties of Kentucky, 1850-1891. Robert M. Ireland. LC 76-24341. 196p. reprint ed. pap. 60.80 (*0-7837-5784-0*, 204545000006) Bks Demand.

Little Kingdoms: Three Novellas. Steven Millhauser. LC 97-34396. 1998. pap. 12.00 (*0-375-70143-5*) Vin Bks.

*__Little Kippers: Meow!__ Mick Inkpen. LC 99-50736. (Little Kippers Ser.). 2000. pap. 4.95 (*0-15-202666-5*, Harcourt Child Bks) Harcourt.

Little Kitten. Judy Dunn. LC 82-16711. (Pictureback Ser.). (Illus.). 32p. (J). (ps-4). 1983. pap. 3.25 (*0-394-85818-2*, Pub. by Random Bks Yng Read) Random.

Little Kittens Dress-Up. Ladybird Books Staff. (Kitten Tales Ser.). (Illus.). 28p. (J). (ps-2). 1992. 3.95 (*0-7214-5312-0*, S915-5, Ladybrd) Penguin Putnam.

Little Know-How Book: Everything You Need to Know to Get by in Life from Changing a Tire to Figuring a Tip to Tying Your Shoes. Robert Scher. LC 94-9666. (Illus.). 224p. 1995. pap. 9.00 (*0-517-88031-8*, Crown) Crown Pub Group.

Little Knowledge Is a Dangerous Thing: Understanding Our Global Knowledge of Economy. Dale Neef. LC 98-36796. 1998. 19.95 (*0-7506-7061-4*) Buttrwrth-Heinemann.

Little Known Evidences of the Book of Mormon. Brenton Yorgason. 50p. 1991. pap. 3.95 (*1-55503-128-5*, 0111686) Covenant Comms.

*__Little Known Facts about India.__ S. Khandpur. 1998. pap. 28.00 (*81-86982-20-5*, Pub. by Business Pubns) St Mut.

Little Known History of Newark Delaware, & Its Environments. Francis A. Cooch. (Illus.). 297p. 1997. reprint ed. lib. bdg. 35.00 (*0-8328-7055-2*) Higginson Bk Co.

Little-Known Museums in & Around Berlin. Rachel Kaplan. LC 98-30701. (Illus.). 216p. 1999. 19.95 (*0-8109-2903-1*, Pub. by Abrams) Time Warner.

Little-Known Museums in & Around London. Rachel Kaplan. LC 96-52596. (Illus.). 216p. 1997. pap. 19.95 (*0-8109-2699-7*, Pub. by Abrams) Time Warner.

Little-Known Museums in & Around Paris. Rachel Kaplan. LC 95-52781. (Illus.). 216p. 1996. pap. 19.95 (*0-8109-2676-8*, Pub. by Abrams) Time Warner.

*__Little-Known Museums in & Around Rome.__ Rachel Kaplan. LC 00-20535. 216p. 2000. pap. 19.95 (*0-8109-2914-7*, Pub. by Abrams) Time Warner.

Little-Known Mysteries of New England: True Crime Stories from the Past. Curt Norris. Ed. by Doris M. Johnson. LC 92-70661. (Illus.). 160p. (Orig.). 1992. pap. 10.00 (*0-9628738-1-0*) Jones Riv Pr.

Little Known, Seldom Told Secrets of Book Distribution for Authors & Small Presses. Carole Marsh. (Lifewrite Ser.). (Illus.). 1994. 29.95 (*0-7933-2849-7*); pap. text 19.95 (*0-7933-2850-0*); disk 29.95 (*0-7933-2851-9*) Gallopade Intl.

Little-Known Small House Ruins in the Coconino Forest. M. R. Colton & H. S. Colton. LC 19-15014. (American Anthropological Association Memoirs Ser.: No. 24). 1918. pap. 25.00 (*0-527-00523-1*) Periodicals Srv.

Little-Known Sports. Vern Rutsala. LC 93-34630. 72p. 1994. pap. 9.95 (*0-87023-918-X*); lib. bdg. 20.00 (*0-87023-917-1*) U of Mass Pr.

Little Known Tales from Oregon History, Vol. 1. Ed. by Geoff Hill. LC 88-90788. (Illus.). 92p. (Orig.). 1988. pap. 11.95 (*0-929084-00-4*) Sun Publishing.

Little Known Tales from Oregon History, Vol. II. LC 88-90788. (Illus.). 92p. (Orig.). 1991. pap. 11.95 (*1-882084-00-4*) Sun Publishing.

Little Known Tales in California History. 2nd rev. ed. Alton Pryor. (Illus.). 200p. 1997. reprint ed. pap. 9.95 (*0-9660053-1-7*) Stagecoach Pub.

Little Known Treasures of Northeastern Ohio: The Ethnic & the Elegant. Peter A. Gail. (Illus.). 60p. 1990. pap. 7.50 (*1-879863-63-4*) Goosefoot Acres.

Little Koala Finds a Friend. Margaret Roc. (Illus.). 32p. (J). 1998. 16.00 (*0-207-19121-2*) HarpC.

*__Little Labels - Big Sound.__ Rick Kennedy & Randy McNutt. LC 98-49455. (Illus.). 183p. 1999. text 24.95 (*0-253-33548-5*) Ind U Pr.

Little Lady. LC 96-85845. (Illus.). 16p. (Orig.). (J). (ps-6). 1996. pap. 7.95 (*0-9653017-1-0*) Bywater Bks.

Little Lady of the Big House. Jack London. lib. bdg. 27.95 (*0-8488-1997-7*) Amereon Ltd.

*__Little Lady of the Big House.__ Jack London. (Collected Works of Jack London). 392p. 1998. reprint ed. lib. bdg. 98.00 (*1-58201-723-9*) Classic Bks.

Little Lady Star. Nicholas Augustine & Victoria C. Augustine. (Illus.). 32p. (J). 1991. pap. write for info. (*1-879783-01-0*) Staccato Prodns.

Little Lama of Tibet. Lois Raimondo. LC 93-13627. (Illus.). 40p. (J). (ps-4). 1994. 15.95 (*0-590-46167-2*) Scholastic Inc.

Little Lamb see Big Red Box of Books: Five Picture-Book Favorites

Little Lamb. Judy Dunn. LC 76-24167. (Pictureback Library Editions). (Illus.). (J). (ps-2). 1977. pap. 3.25 (*0-394-83455-0*, Pub. by Random Bks Yng Read) Random.

Little Lamb. Kim Lewis. LC 99-28786. 24p. (J). 2000. 9.99 (*0-7636-0900-5*) Candlewick Pr.

Little Lamb. Kath Mellentin & Tim Woods. (Farm Babies Ser.). (Illus.). 10p. (J). 1997. bds. 3.50 (*1-884628-59-1*, Flyng Frog) Allied Pub MD.

*__Little Lamb.__ Anne H. Thorburgh & Publications International, Ltd. Editorial Staff. LC 98-130684. (Wonder Window Ser.). (Illus.). 1998. write for info. (*0-7853-2686-3*) Pubns Intl Ltd.

Little Lamb & Good Shepherd. Alice J. Davidson. (J). (ps-3). 1997. 3.99 (*0-310-97170-5*) Zondervan.

Little Lamb Who Made Thee. Walter Wangerin, Jr. 2000. 4.99 (*0-310-21483-1*) Zondervan.

Little Lamb, Who Made Thee? A Book about Children & Parents. Walter Wangerin, Jr. 224p. 1993. 15.99 (*0-310-40550-5*) Zondervan.

Little Lamb/Chick, 2 bks., Set. (J). 1993. pap. 9.90 (*0-590-66844-7*) Scholastic Inc.

Little Lamb/Chick, 2 bks., Set. Ed. by Scholastic, Inc. Staff. (J). 1994. pap. 9.90 (*0-590-66918-4*) Scholastic Inc.

Little Lamb's Big Question: Includes Plush Toy. Muff Singer. (Little Hugs Bks.: Vol. 3). (Illus.). 18p. (J). (gr. k-3). 1997. bds. 10.99 (*0-88705-985-6*) Rdrs Digest.

Little Lamb's Easter Surprise, 1 vol. Lucinda McQueen. 1999. 3.50 (*0-590-41968-4*) Scholastic Inc.

Little Lame Prince. Craik. 1997. pap. 2.95 (*0-89375-710-1*) Troll Communs.

Little Lame Prince. Miss Mulock. (Illus.). 116p. 1991. reprint ed. lib. bdg. 14.95 (*0-89966-762-7*) Buccaneer Bks.

Little Lame Prince, Adventures of a Brownie. Dinah M. Mulock. (J). 1976. 20.95 (*0-8488-1109-7*) Amereon Ltd.

Little Lame Prince & the Adventures of a Brownie. Maria M. Craik. Date not set. lib. bdg. 25.95 (*0-8488-2095-9*) Amereon Ltd.

Little Latter-Day Saint Busy Book, Vol. 2. Karen Finch & Jason Finch. (Illus.). 32p. (Orig.). (J). (ps-5). 1994. 2.95 (*1-885476-04-3*) Finch Fmly Games.

Little Lavender Book: Quotations on Gays & Lesbians. Saejo Usukawa. 96p. 1994. per. 4.95 (*1-55152-004-4*, Pub. by Arsenal Pulp) LPC InBook.

Little Leaf. Chana Sharfstein. Ed. by Dina Rosenfeld. LC 94-109804. (Illus.). 32p. (J). (ps-1). 1989. 8.95 (*0-922613-18-4*); pap. 6.95 (*0-922613-19-2*) Hachai Pubng.

*__Little League Confidential.__ Bill Geist. 1999. pap. 12.95 (*0-440-50877-0*) Dell.

Little League Confidential. William Geist. LC 97-224657. 1997. 17.50 (*0-684-84198-3*) S&S Trade.

Little League Drills & Strategies. Ned McIntosh. (Illus.). 160p. (Orig.). 1987. pap. 11.95 (*0-8092-4789-5*, 478950, Contemporary Bks) NTC Contemp Pub Co.

Little League Guide to Tee Ball. Ned McIntosh. LC 92-45097. 160p. 1993. pap. 6.95 (*0-8092-3791-1*, 379110, Contemporary Bks) NTC Contemp Pub Co.

*__Little League Legend Logbook.__ 2nd ed. Glenn Murray. (Illus.). ii, 75p. 1999. 79.95 (*1-58527-010-5*) Legend Pubns NY.

*__Little League Lessons for Parents & Coaches.__ Jeffrey W. Beckman. LC 99-93306. (Little League Tips Ser.: No. 1). 50p. 1999. pap. 7.50 (*0-9672268-0-5*) Christ Dev Res.

Little League's Off. Peter A. Kreutzer. 1996. pap. 14.95 (*0-385-42732-8*) Doubleday.

Little League's Official How-to-Play Baseball Handbook. Peter Kruetzer. 224p. (J). 1990. pap. 11.95 (*0-385-24700-1*) Doubleday.

Little Learning Is a Dangerous Thing: Six Hundred Wise & Witty Observations for Students, Teachers & Other Survivors of Higher Education. Ed. by James Charlton. (Illus.). 128p. 1994. text 14.95 (*0-312-11021-9*) St Martin.

Little Learning Is a Dangerous Thing: 600 Wise & Witty Observations for Students, Teachers & Other Survivors of Higher Education. Ed. by James Charlton. 116p. 1998. text 13.00 (*0-7881-5976-3*) DIANE Pub.

*__Little Lee Lee Goes Fishing.__ Molly Dingles. (Little Lee Lee Ser.). (Illus.). 32p. (J). (ps-1). 2000. 9.99 (*1-891997-13-0*) Dingles & Co.

*__Little Lee Lee's Birthday Band.__ Molly Dingles. (Little Lee Lee Ser.). (Illus.). 32p. (J). (ps-1). 2000. 9.99 (*1-891997-12-2*) Dingles & Co.

*__Little Left of Center: An Editor Reflects on His Mennonite Experience.__ Daniel Hertzler. 176p. 2000. pap. 13.95 (*0-9665021-7-5*; DreamSeeker) Pandora PA.

Little Lefty. Matt Christopher. (J). 1993. 9.05 (*0-606-05718-8*, Pub. by Turtleback) Demco.

Little Legislatures: Committees of Congress. George Goodwin, Jr. LC 75-103477. 304p. 1970. 35.00 (*0-87023-060-3*); pap. 18.95 (*0-87023-073-5*) U of Mass Pr.

Little Lemon: Activities for Developing Motivation & Memory Skills. Betsy Blizzard Lee. (Illus.). 32p. (J). (gr. k-3). 1997. pap., wbk. ed. 8.99 (*0-9658853-2-1*) Learning Abil.

Little Lessons for Little Learners: Angels. Patti Mattozzi. 32p. (J). (gr. 2 up). 1989. pap. 4.50 (*0-8378-1843-5*) Gibson.

Little Lessons for Little Learners: Birthdays Are Special. Patricia R. Mattozzi. 1993. 4.50 (*0-8378-5315-X*) Gibson.

Little Lessons for Little Learners: Heaven. Patti Mattozzi. (J). (gr. 3 up). 1991. 4.50 (*0-8378-1986-5*) Gibson.

Little Lessons for Little Learners: Prayer. Patti Mattozzi. 32p. (J). (gr. 1 up). 1989. 4.50 (*0-8378-1844-3*) Gibson.

Little Lessons for Little Lerners: The New Baby. Patricia R. Mattozzi. (Illus.). 24p. 1994. 4.50 (*0-8378-7689-3*) Gibson.

Little Lessons for Teachers. Mary K. Shanley. 80p. (Orig.). 1995. pap. 5.95 (*1-882835-31-X*) STA-Kris.

*__Little Lessons from Life: My Professors & My Jewish Mother.__ Paul B. Lowney. 1999. pap. 4.95 (*0-9609946-5-3*) C & L Pubs.

*__Little Lesson's from the Hundred-Acre Wood.__ (Illus.). 24p. (J). 2000. 16.99 (*0-7868-3284-3*, Pub. by Disney Pr) Time Warner.

Little Lessons of Love. Elizabeth Heller. (Illus.). 160p. (Orig.). 1995. pap. 8.95 (*0-943233-73-9*) Conari Press.

Little Lieu: And Other Waifs. Del Reitz. LC 97-166101. 20p. 1997. 8.95 (*0-917835-02-6*) Newsletter Inago.

Little Life of Jesus. Lois Rock. 346p. (J). (gr. k-2). 1997. pap. 9.99 (*0-7459-3796-9*, Lion) Chariot Victor.

Little Life Stories. Harry H. Johnston. LC 79-122725. (Short Story Index Reprint Ser.). 1977. 17.95 (*0-8369-3558-6*) Ayer.

Little Light on Angels. Diana Cooper. (Illus.). 128p. (Orig.). 1996. pap. 10.95 (*1-899171-51-7*, Pub. by Findhorn Pr) Words Distrib.

Little Light on Ascension. Diana Cooper. (A Little Light On...Ser.). (Orig.). 1997. pap. 10.95 (*1-899171-81-9*, Pub. by Findhorn Pr) Words Distrib.

Little Light Reading. Mario V. Farina. 304p. 1999. 18.00 (*0-9671440-0-0*) Pippie Pr.

*__Little Light Reading.__ Mario V. Farina. 304p. 1999. pap. 12.00 (*0-9671440-1-9*) Pippie Pr.

*__Little Light Weeding__ Richard Briers. LC 99-169967. 256p. 1998. write for info. (*0-86051-883-3*, Robson-Parkwest) Parkwest Pubns.

Little Light Weeding: Evergreen Reading for the Perennial Gardener. Richard Briers. LC 99-169967. (Illus.). 256p. 1995. pap. 12.95 (*0-86051-936-8*, Robson-Parkwest) Parkwest Pubns.

Little Light Weeding: Gardening Tips. large type ed. Richard Briers. 23.95 (*1-85695-047-6*, Pub. by ISIS Lrg Prnt); pap. 19.95 (*1-85695-038-7*, Pub. by ISIS Lrg Prnt) Transaction Pubs.

Little Lil & the Swing-Singing Sax. Libba M. Gray. LC 95-362. (Illus.). 32p. (J). (gr. k-2). 1996. 16.00 (*0-689-80681-7*) S&S Bks Yung.

Little Lines about Felines. Adele Hackenson. 1998. pap. write for info. (*1-57553-829-6*) Watermrk Pr.

Little Lion. Robert Newcome & Zita Newcome. (Illus.). 32p. (J). (ps-1). 1993. 17.95 (*1-85681-181-6*, Pub. by Julia MacRae) Trafalgar.

Little Lion of the Southwest: A Life of Manuel Antonio Chaves. Marc Simmons. LC 73-1500. (Illus.). 276p. 1997. pap. 14.95 (*0-8040-0633-4*) Swallow.

Little Lions. Jim Arnosky. LC 96-49837. (Illus.). 32p. (J). 1998. 15.99 (*0-399-22944-2*, G P Putnam) Peng Put Young Read.

Little Lisa-Sticker Paper Doll. Robbie Stillerman. (Illus.). (J). 1995. pap. 1.00 (*0-486-26994-9*) Dover.

*__Little Lit: Folklore & Fairy Tale Funnies.__ Art Spiegelman. LC 99-51484. 64p. (J). 2000. 19.95 (*0-06-028624-5*) HarpC Child Bks.

Little Lit Book, No. 2. Art Spiegelman. (J). Date not set. write for info. (*0-06-028626-1*) HarpC Child Bks.

*__Little Lit Book, No. 3.__ Art Spiegelman. 64p. (J). (ps up). 2001. 20.00 (*0-06-028628-8*) HarpC Child Bks.

Little Lit Book, No. 4. Art Spiegelman. (J). Date not set. write for info. (*0-06-028630-X*) HarpC Child Bks.

Little Little PB. M. E. Kerr. LC 80-8454. (Trophy Keypoint Bk.). 192p. (YA). (gr. 7 up). 1991. mass mkt. 3.95 (*0-06-447061-X*, HarpTrophy) HarpC Child Bks.

Little Little LB. M. E. Kerr. LC 80-8454. 160p. (YA). (gr. 7 up). 1981. lib. bdg. 14.89 (*0-06-023185-8*) HarpC Child Bks.

Little, Little Sister. Jane L. Curry. LC 88-13079. (Illus.). 32p. (J). (ps-3). 1989. text 12.95 (*0-689-50459-4*) McElderry Bks.

Little Lives of the Great Saints. John O. Murray. LC 82-50593. 495p. 1991. reprint ed. pap. 18.00 (*0-89555-190-X*) TAN Bks Pubs.

Little Lizard Classic: Easy I Ching for Our Times. Willard L. Johnson. (Illus.). 100p. 1984. pap. 6.95 (*0-317-03342-5*) W Anglia Pubns.

Little Local Murder. Robert Barnard. 192p. 1995. pap. 7.95 (*0-88150-325-8*, Foul Play) Norton.

Little Locksmith. Katharine B. Hathaway. Ed. by William R. Phillips & Janet Rosenberg. LC 79-6904. (Physically Handicapped in Society Ser.). 1980. reprint ed. lib. bdg. 25.95 (*0-405-13113-5*) Ayer.

*__Little Locksmith: A Memoir.__ Katharine Butler Hathaway. 272p. 2000. 35.00 (*1-55861-238-6*, Pub. by Feminist Pr) Consort Bk Sales.

*__Little Locksmith: A Memoir.__ unabridged ed. Katharine Butler Hathaway. LC 00-20345. 272p. 2000. pap. 14.95 (*1-55861-239-4*, Pub. by Feminist Pr) Consort Bk Sales.

Little Long-Nose. Wilhelm Hauff. LC 96-29534. (Candlewick Treasures Ser.). (Illus.). 128p. (J). (gr. 3-9). 1997. 11.99 (*0-7636-0327-9*) Candlewick Pr.

Little Lord Fauntleroy. Frances Hodgson Burnett. (J). 21.95 (*0-8488-0792-8*) Amereon Ltd.

Little Lord Fauntleroy. Frances Hodgson Burnett. (Illus.). 160p. (YA). (gr. 5 up). 1993. 18.95 (*0-87923-958-1*) Godine.

Little Lord Fauntleroy. Frances Hodgson Burnett. LC 95-15325. (Everyman's Library of Children's Classics). (Illus.). (J). 1995. 13.95 (*0-679-44474-2*, Evrymans Lib Childs) Knopf.

Little Lord Fauntleroy. Frances Hodgson Burnett. (Illus.). 256p. (YA). (gr. 5 up). 1996. pap. 4.99 (*0-14-036753-5*, PuffinBks) Peng Put Young Read.

Little Lord Fauntleroy. Frances Hodgson Burnett. (Illus.). (J). 21.95 (*0-590-74607-3*) Scholastic Inc.

Little Lord Fauntleroy. Frances Hodgson Burnett. (J). 1997. pap. 2.95 (*0-8167-1465-7*) Troll Communs.

Little Lord Fauntleroy. Frances Hodgson Burnett. (Puffin Classics). (J). 1994. 9.09 (*0-606-09560-8*, Pub. by Turtleback) Demco.

Little Lord Fauntleroy. Frances Hodgson Burnett. (Children's Library). 1998. pap. 3.95 (*1-85326-130-0*, 1300WW, Pub. by Wrdsworth Edits) NTC Contemp Pub Co.

Little Lord Fauntleroy. large type ed. Frances Hodgson Burnett. (Large Print Heritage Ser.). 272p. (YA). (gr. 7-12). 1997. lib. bdg. 28.95 (*1-58118-002-0*, 21965) LRS.

Little Lord Fauntleroy. Frances Hodgson Burnett. (Illus.). 252p. (J). 1981. reprint ed. lib. bdg. 21.95 (*0-89966-288-9*) Buccaneer Bks.

Little Lord Fauntleroy, Homework Set. unabridged ed. Frances Hodgson Burnett. (J). (gr. 5). 1997. boxed set 56.24 incl. audio (*0-7887-1840-1*, 40620) Recorded Bks.

Little Lord Fauntleroy: A Musical. Gail Erwin. 39p. (J). 1995. pap. 3.50 (*1-57514-148-5*, 0038) Encore Perform Pub.

Little Lords of the Desert. Conrad J. Storad. (Illus.). 32p. (J). (gr. 1-6). 1998. pap. 8.95 (*0-9660293-2-1*) D Atwood.

Little Lost Angel. Michael Quinlan. Ed. by Claire Zion. 320p. (Orig.). 1995. per. 6.99 (*0-671-88468-9*) PB.

Little Lost Duck: A Baby Buddy Book. Dawn Bentley. LC 98-233142. (Baby Buddy Bks.). (Illus.). 12p. (J). (ps up). 1998. bds. 4.95 (*1-888443-72-3*, Piggy Toes Pr) Intervisual Bks.

Little Lost Lamb. Geri Berger. 1981. pap. 2.50 (*0-8198-4415-2*) Pauline Bks.

Little Lost Lamb. Brown. 40p. (J). (ps-3). Date not set. 14.95 (*0-06-027290-2*); lib. bdg. 14.89 (*0-06-027291-0*) HarpC Child Bks.

Little Lost Lamb. Margaret W. Brown. 32p. (J). (ps-1). 2000. lib. bdg. 15.49 (*0-7868-2322-4*, Pub. by Hyprn Child) Little.

Little Lost Lamb. Margaret W. Brown. 32p. (J). (ps-1). Date not set. pap. 5.70 (*0-7868-1258-3*, Pub. by Hyprn Ppbks) Little.

Little Lost Lamb. Margaret W. Brown. 32p. (J). (ps-1). 2000. 14.95 (*0-7868-0372-X*) Hysolli Prod.

Little Lost Lamb. Howard Goldthwaite. (Illus.). 6p. (J). 1994. 5.99 (*1-56476-171-1*, 6-3171, Victor Bks) Chariot Victor.

Little Lost Lamb. Good Little Books for Good Little Children Staff. 12p. (J). (ps). 1986. 3.25 (*0-8378-5206-4*) Gibson.

Little Lost Marion & Other Mercies. Sheldon Vanauken. LC 96-84158. (Illus.). 272p. (Orig.). 1996. pap. 12.95 (*0-940535-88-2*, UP188) Franciscan U Pr.

Little Lost Sheep. Marilyn L. Lindsey. (Happy Day Bks.). (Illus.). 24p. (J). (ps). 1995. 1.99 (*0-7847-0352-3*, 04232) Standard Pub.

Little Lou. Jean Claverie. (Illus.). 48p. (YA). (gr. 3 up). 1990. 22.60 (*0-88682-329-3*, Creative Eds) Creative Co.

An Asterisk (*) at the beginning of an entry indicates that the title is appearing for the first time.

Little Louie the Baby Bloomer. Robert Kraus. LC 96-42434. (Illus.). 32p. (J). (ps-3). 1998. 15.95 (*0-06-026293-1*); lib. bdg. 15.89 (*0-06-026294-X*) HarpC.

***Little Louie the Baby Bloomer.** Robert Kraus. LC 96-42434. (Illus.). 32p. (J). (ps-3). 2000. pap. 5.95 (*0-06-443656-X*, HarpTrophy) HarpC Child Bks.

***Little Louie the Baby Bloomer.** Robert Kraus. (Illus.). (J). 2000. 11.40 (*0-606-18702-2*) Turtleback.

Little Love. Virginia Hamilton. 1985. mass mkt. 2.50 (*0-425-08424-8*) Berkley Pub.

***Little Love.** C. C. Medina. LC 99-51757. 368p. 2000. 18.95 (*0-446-52448-4*, Pub. by Warner Bks) Little.

Little Love, a Little Learning. Nina Bawden. 21.95 (*0-88411-122-9*) Amereon Ltd.

***Little Love, a Little Learning.** large type unabridged ed. Nina Bawden. 296p. 1999. 26.95 (*0-7531-5584-2*, 155842, Pub. by ISIS Lrg Prnt); pap. 19.95 (*0-7531-5863-9*, 158639, Pub. by ISIS Lrg Prnt) ISIS Pub.

Little Love in Big Manhattan: Two Yiddish Poets. Ruth R. Wisse. LC 87-29036. (Illus.). 288p. 1988. 38.50 (*0-674-53659-2*) HUP.

***Little Love Notes.** (Illus.). 96p. 2000. pap. 5.95 (*1-57071-548-3*) Sourcebks.

***Little Love Notes.** Susan Diamond. 2000. 4.99 (*1-56245-405-6*) Great Quotations.

Little Love Notes: A Poet's Heart Beat. Glenn S. Diamond. Ed. by Jeanne B. Ewing. 155p. (Orig.). 1995. pap. 24.95 (*1-884690-09-2*) Owl Press.

Little Love Story. Fernando Krahn. LC 76-12427. (Illus.). (J). (ps-3). 1976. 11.95 (*0-397-31700-X*) HarpC Child Bks.

Little Love's Color Corner: Color Me Book. MaryLou Samaha. (Illus.). 16p. (J). (ps-2). 1988. write for info. (*0-9619988-0-6*) Ronmar Ent.

Little Lower Than the Angels. Virginia Sorensen. LC 97-39403. (Mormon Classics: No. 1). 468p. 1998. reprint ed. pap. 14.95 (*1-56085-103-1*) Signature Bks.

Little Lucky Ducky. Demi. LC 91-77464. (Mini Soft & Furry Board Bks.). (Illus.). 12p. (J). (ps-k). 1993. bds. 4.95 (*0-448-40581-4*, G & D) Peng Put Young Read.

Little Luminous Boy: The Secret Oral Tradition from the Land of Zhang-Zhung Depicted on Two Tibetan Paintings. Samten G. Karmay. (Illus.). 132p. 1999. pap. 29.00 (*974-8299-07-4*) White Orchid.

Little Lumpty. Miko Imai. LC 93-22358. (Illus.). 32p. (J). (ps-3). 1996. pap. 5.99 (*1-56402-829-1*) Candlewick Pr.

Little Lumpty. Miko Imai. LC 93-22358. 1996. 11.19 (*0-606-09561-6*, Pub. by Turtleback) Demco.

Little Lunch: The Story of Jesus & the Hungry Crowd. Patricia L. Nederveld. LC 97-53315. (God Loves Me Ser.). (Illus.). 24p. (J). (ps). 1998. pap. 2.45 (*1-56212-303-3*, 1105-0134) CRC Pubns.

***Little 'm' Sellers.** (J). 2000. 3.95 (*0-552-52884-6*, Pub. by Transworld Publishers Ltd) Trafalgar.

***Little Mac: Demise of an American Hero.** James M. Ridgeway, Jr. LC 99-91008. 1999. pap. 18.00 (*0-7388-0579-3*) Xlibris Corp.

***Little Mac: Demise of an American Hero.** James M. Ridgway, Jr. LC 99-91008. 1999. 25.00 (*0-7388-0578-5*) Xlibris Corp.

Little Mac Book. 5th ed. Robin Williams. LC 98-147138. 384p. (C). 1997. pap. 19.95 (*0-201-69673-8*, Pub. by Peachpit Pr) Addison-Wesley.

***Little Mac Book.** 6th ed. Robin Williams. LC 99-461836. (Illus.). 400p. (C). 1999. pap. text 19.99 (*0-201-35433-0*) Peachpit Pr.

Little Mac Word Book. Helmut Kobler. (Illus.). 240p. 1995. pap. text 15.95 (*0-938151-87-8*) Peachpit Pr.

Little Magazine & Contemporary Literature: A Symposium Held at the Library of Congress, 2 & 3 April, 1965. Modern Language Association Staff. LC 72-3239. 127p. 1966. pap. 39.40 (*0-608-05587-5*, 206604700006) Bks Demand.

Little Magazine Profiles: The Little Magazines in Great Britain, 1939-1993. Wolfgang Gortschacher. 751p. 1993. pap. 29.95 (*3-7052-0608-7*, Pub. by Poetry Salzburg) Intl Spec Bk.

Little Magazines. Reed Whittemore. LC 63-64004. (University of Minnesota Pamphlets on American Writers Ser.: No. 32). 47p. (Orig.). reprint ed. pap. 30.00 (*0-7837-2854-9*, 205760100006) Bks Demand.

Little Magic Shop of Horrors, Vol. 6. A. G. Cascone. (Deadtime Stories Ser.). 1996. pap. 3.50 (*0-8167-4193-X*) Troll Communs.

Little Magothy & Other Stories. Bruce L. Wilson. (Illus.). 208p. (Orig.). 1996. pap. 12.95 (*0-9654651-0-1*) IM Press.

Little Maid of Maryland. Alice T. Curtis. LC 95-49353. (Little Maid Ser.). (Illus.). 192p. (J). (gr. 3-8). 1996. reprint ed. pap. 9.95 (*1-55709-327-X*) Applewood.

Little Maid of Massachusetts Bay Colony. Alice T. Curtis. LC 96-28380. (Little Maid Ser.). (Illus.). 192p. (J). (gr. 3-8). 1996. reprint ed. pap. 9.95 (*1-55709-329-6*) Applewood.

Little Maid of Mohawk Valley. Alice Turner Curtis. LC 98-55146. 192p. 1999. pap. text 9.95 (*1-55709-337-7*, Pub. by Applewood) Consort Bk Sales.

Little Maid of Narragansett Bay. Alice T. Curtis. LC 97-53230. (Little Maid Ser.). 210p. (J). (gr. 3-8). 1998. reprint ed. pap. 9.95 (*1-55709-334-2*) Applewood.

Little Maid of Old Connecticut. Alice T. Curtis. LC 96-28381. (Little Maid Ser.). (Illus.). 192p. (J). (gr. 3-8). 1998. reprint ed. pap. 9.95 (*1-55709-328-8*) Applewood.

***Little Maid of Old Maine.** Alice Turner Curtis. LC 99-42220. 228p. (gr. 4-7). 1999. pap. 9.95 (*1-55709-336-9*, Pub. by Applewood) Consort Bk Sales.

Little Maid of Old New York. Alice T. Curtis. (Little Maid Ser.). (Illus.). 192p. (J). (gr. 3-8). 1996. reprint ed. pap. 9.95 (*1-55709-326-1*) Applewood.

Little Maid of Old Philadelphia. Alice T. Curtis. (Little Maid Ser.). (Illus.). 192p. (J). (gr. 3-8). 1998. reprint ed. pap. 9.95 (*1-55709-325-3*) Applewood.

Little Maid of Provincetown. Alice T. Curtis. LC 97-3987. (Little Maid Ser.). (Illus.). 224p. (J). (gr. 3-8). 1997. reprint ed. pap. 9.95 (*1-55709-331-8*) Applewood.

Little Maid of Ticonderoga. Alice T. Curtis. LC 96-28379. (Little Maid Ser.). (Illus.). 192p. (J). (gr. 3-8). 1996. reprint ed. pap. 9.95 (*1-55709-330-X*) Applewood.

Little Maid of Virginia. Alice T. Curtis. LC 97-53240. (Little Maid Ser.). (Illus.). 192p. (J). (gr. 3-8). 1998. reprint ed. pap. 9.95 (*1-55709-333-4*) Applewood.

Little Maine Cookbook. Barbara Karoff. (Illus.). 60p. 1995. 7.95 (*0-8118-0929-3*) Chronicle Bks.

Little Makana. Helen M. Dano. LC 94-77956. (Illus.). 32p. (J). (gr. k-3). 1994. 8.95 (*1-880188-93-7*) Bess Pr.

Little Man. Graham Jeffrey. (Duckling Ser.). (Illus.). 32p. (J). (ps). 1993. 14.95 (*0-460-88068-3*, Pub. by J M Dent & Sons) Trafalgar.

Little Man. rev. ed. Dorothy B. Davis. (Illus.). 52p. (J). (ps-4). 1966. 2.50 (*0-87178-530-7*, 8307) Brethren.

Little Man: A Farcial Morality in Three Scenes. John Galsworthy & William-Alan Landes. LC 97-19914. 1997. pap. 6.00 (*0-88734-396-1*) Player Pr.

Little Man: Meyer Lansky & the Gangster Life. Robert Lacey. (Illus.). 704p. 1992. mass mkt. 5.99 (*0-316-51163-3*) Little.

Little Man: Short Strips, 1979-1994. Chester Brown. 1998. pap. text 14.95 (*1-896597-13-0*, Pub. by Drawn & Quarterly) LPC InBook.

Little Man & the Little Oyster. Humphrey Nelson. LC 89-21489. 1990. 9.95 (*0-87770-479-1*) Ye Galleon.

Little Man in England. Shauwn Traynor. 112p. (J). 1989. pap. 6.95 (*1-85371-032-6*, Pub. by Poolbeg Pr) Dufour.

Little Man, What Now? Hans Fallada. 384p. 1992. reprint ed. pap. 14.95 (*0-89733-086-2*) Academy Chi Pubs.

Little Man with the Long Shadow: The Life & Times of Frederick M. Hubbell. George S. Mills. LC 88-13117. (Iowa Heritage Collection). (Illus.). 272p. 1988. reprint ed. pap. 10.95 (*0-8138-0242-3*) Iowa St U Pr.

Little Man's Big Friend: James E. Folsom in Alabama Politics, 1946-1958. George E. Sims. LC 84-24057. (Illus.). 288p. 1985. 34.95 (*0-8173-0239-5*) U of Ala Pr.

Little Man's Family. rev. ed. J. B. Enochs. (Illus.). 48p. (J). (gr. k-5). 1999. pap. 6.95 (*1-885772-14-9*) Kiva Pubng.

Little Manual of Calligraphy. Charles Pearce. 32p. 1981. pap. 3.95 (*0-8008-4923-X*) Taplinger.

Little Market Well at Springhill & Dauphin, Mobile, Alabama. Gregory A. Waselkov et al. (Archaeological Monograph Ser.: Vol. 2). (Illus.). iii, 22p. 1996. pap. 8.00 (*1-893955-01-X*) Univ S AL Ctr Archa.

Little Martin Coloring Book. large type ed. Jacquelyn S. Caffey. Ed. by Ron Scarbough & Lenora Houston. (Illus.). 32p. (Orig.). (J). (gr. 1-5). 1983. pap. 5.00 (*1-888587-01-6*) Write to Teach.

Little Martins Learn to Love. Ada Nighswander. (Illus.). 187p. (J). (gr. 3-6). 1982. 8.05 (*0-7399-0085-4*, 2310) Rod & Staff.

Little Mary. Maureen Fischer. Ed. by Patrick Haley & Irene Haley. LC 85-82197. 106p. (YA). (gr. 7-12). 1986. 14.00 (*0-9605738-3-6*); pap. 6.00 (*0-9605738-4-4*) East Eagle.

Little Mary. unabridged ed. (Children's Heritage Ser.). (Illus.). 127p. (J). (gr. 4-6). 1996. pap. 6.98 (*1-58339-123-1*, D23) Triangle Press.

Little Masonic Library, 5 vols., Set. Silas H. Shepherd et al. 1995. reprint ed. 65.00 (*0-88053-005-7*, M-5) Macoy Pub.

Little Master. John T. Trowbridge. (Notable American Authors). 1999. reprint ed. lib. bdg. 125.00 (*0-7812-9804-0*) Rprt Serv.

Little Match Girl see Petite Fille Aux Allumettes

Little Match Girl. Hans Christian Andersen. (Illus.). 32p. (J). (ps-3). 1992. 6.95 (*0-8362-4931-3*) Andrews & McMeel.

Little Match Girl. Hans Christian Andersen. LC 94-79160. (Illus.). 32p. (J). (gr. k-4). 1995. 14.95 (*1-56397-470-3*) Boyds Mills Pr.

Little Match Girl. Hans Christian Andersen. (Scheherezade Children's Stories Ser.). (Illus.). 16p. (J). 1997. 4.95 (*1-873938-89-6*, Pub. by Garnet-Ithaca) LPC InBook.

Little Match Girl. Hans Christian Andersen. LC 68-28050. (Illus.). (J). (gr. k-3). 1975. pap. 1.95 (*0-685-02294-3*) HM.

Little Match Girl. Hans Christian Andersen. LC 85-30082. 1996. 11.15 (*0-606-10253-1*, Pub. by Turtleback) Demco.

Little Match Girl. Hans Christian Andersen.Tr. of Lille pige med svovlstikkerne. (Illus.). 32p. (J). (ps-3). 1987. 15.95 (*0-399-21336-8*, G P Putnam) Peng Put Young Read.

Little Match Girl. Ed. by Phyllis J. Fogelman. LC 99-13814. (Illus.). 32p. (J). (ps-3). 1999. 16.99 (*0-8037-2314-8*, Dial Yng Read) Peng Put Young Read.

***Little Match Girl.** Illus. by Annabel Malak. (Pocketaudio Ser.). (J). (ps-2). 2000. 9.95 incl. audio (*2-921997-88-6*, Pub. by Coffragants) Penton Overseas.

Little Match Girl. Adapted by Jack Neary. 44p. 1996. pap. 5.00 (*0-87440-025-2*) Bakers Plays.

Little Match Girl: A Musical. Hans Christian Andersen. 20p. (Orig.). (J). (gr. 1-8). 1992. pap. 3.50 (*1-57514-221-X*, 0047) Encore Perform Pub.

Little Match Girl: One-Act Dramatization. Hermann Ammann. (Illus.). 36p. (J). (gr. k up). 1970. pap. 3.25 (*0-88680-111-7*) I E Clark.

Little Match Girl: One-Act Dramatization - Director's Script. Hermann Ammann. (Illus.). 36p. (J). (gr. k up). 1970. pap. 7.50 (*0-88680-112-5*) I E Clark.

Little Match Girl: The Musical. Sidney L. Berger. (Illus.). 32p. (Orig.). (J). (gr. 4 up). 1985. pap. 4.00 (*0-88680-230-X*) I E Clark.

Little Matchmaker. Muriel Jensen. (Harlequin Super Romance Ser.). 1997. per. 3.99 (*0-373-70764-9*, Harlequin) Harlequin Bks.

Little Math with Your Business. 8th ed. Boone. (C). 1995. pap. text 11.50 (*0-03-017807-X*) Harcourt Coll Pubs.

Little Matt Mattix. Bobby L. Jackson & Julienne Jones. LC 94-72884. (Illus.). 24p. (Orig.). (J). (ps-k). 1995. pap. 9.95 (*1-884242-95-2*); lib. bdg. 16.95 (*1-884242-96-0*) Multicult Pubns.

Little Matter of Genocide: Holocaust & Denial in the Americas 1492 to the Present. Ward Churchill. 260p. 1997. 37.50 (*0-87286-343-3*); pap. 19.95 (*0-87286-323-9*) City Lights.

Little Matter of We. Max C. Golightly. 27p. (Orig.). 1979. pap. 2.50 (*1-57514-251-1*, 3004) Encore Perform Pub.

Little Me, 3 vols. (Great Me Ser.). 1957. 14.95 (*0-934538-25-5*) Partnership Foundation.

Little Me. Patrick Dennis. 1993. reprint ed. lib. bdg. 29.95 (*1-56849-103-4*) Buccaneer Bks.

Little Me: Vocal Selections. Ed. by Carol Cuellar. 48p. (Orig.). (C). 1993. pap. text 10.95 (*0-7692-0701-4*, VF1941) Wrner Bros.

Little Me - Great Me: Parents & Teachers Manual, Vol. 1. Lou Austin. (J). (ps-5). 1985. pap., teacher ed. 1.25 (*0-934538-06-9*) Partnership Foundation.

Little Me & the Great Me, Vol. 1. Lou Austin. (J). (ps-5). 1985. 6.95 (*0-934538-26-3*) Partnership Foundation.

Little Meals: A Great New Way to Eat & Cook. Rozanne Gold. LC 99-234826. (Illus.). 272p. 1999. pap. 15.00 (*0-316-31013-1*) Little.

Little Medicine Carrier. rev. ed. (Character Building Ser.). (Illus.). 65p. (J). (gr. 4-6). 1990. pap. 4.98 (*1-58339-052-9*, C3) Triangle Press.

Little Memoirs of the Nineteenth Century. Emily M. Symonds. LC 70-86787. (Essay Index Reprint Ser.). 1977. 23.95 (*0-8369-1197-0*) Ayer.

Little Men. Kevin Killian. LC 96-48388. 128p. 1996. pap. text 12.95 (*1-889097-01-2*) Hard Pr MA.

Little Men: Life at Plumfield with Jo's Boys. Louisa May Alcott. Date not set. 20.95 (*0-8488-1476-2*) Amereon Ltd.

Little Men: Life at Plumfield with Jo's Boys. Louisa May Alcott. LC 94-17448. 288p. (J). (gr. 4-6). 1994. pap. 8.95 (*0-316-03104-6*) Little.

Little Men: Life at Plumfield with Jo's Boys. Louisa May Alcott. LC 94-17448. (J). (Orig.). (gr. 7-10). 1994. 16.95 (*0-316-03108-9*) Little.

Little Men: Life at Plumfield with Jo's Boys. Louisa May Alcott. 1986. mass mkt. 4.95 (*0-451-52275-3*, Sig Classics) NAL.

Little Men: Life at Plumfield with Jo's Boys. Louisa May Alcott. (Classics for Young Readers Ser.). (Illus.). 608p. (YA). (gr. 5 up). 1995. pap. 4.99 (*0-14-036713-6*, PuffinBks) Peng Put Young Read.

Little Men: Life at Plumfield with Jo's Boys. Louisa May Alcott. 384p. (J). (gr. 4-7). 1987. pap. 3.99 (*0-590-41279-5*, Apple Paperbacks) Scholastic Inc.

Little Men: Life at Plumfield with Jo's Boys. Louisa May Alcott. (J). 1997. pap. 2.95 (*0-8167-1471-1*) Troll Communs.

Little Men: Life at Plumfield with Jo's Boys. Louisa May Alcott. (Puffin Classics). (J). 1994. 9.09 (*0-606-07797-9*, Pub. by Turtleback) Demco.

Little Men: Life at Plumfield with Jo's Boys. Louisa May Alcott & Robert Blaisdell. LC 97-11716. (Children's Thrift Classics Ser.). (Illus.). (J). 1997. pap. 1.00 (*0-486-29805-1*) Dover.

Little Men: Life at Plumfield with Jo's Boys. large type ed. Louisa May Alcott. LC 95-33070. 460p. (J). 1995. 23.95 (*0-7838-1468-2*, G K Hall Lrg Type) Mac Lib Ref.

Little Men: Life at Plumfield with Jo's Boys. Louisa May Alcott. (J). 1983. reprint ed. lib. bdg. 18.95 (*0-89966-409-1*) Buccaneer Bks.

Little Men: Life at Plumfield with Jo's Boys. Louisa May Alcott. (Works of Louisa May Alcott). (J). 1989. reprint ed. lib. bdg. 79.00 (*0-7812-1629-X*) Rprt Serv.

Little Menorah Who Forgot Chanukah. Jerry Sperling. (Illus.). (J). (gr. k-3). 1993. pap. 12.95 incl. audio (*0-8074-0508-6*, 101971) UAHC.

Little Mermaid see Petite Sirene

***Little Mermaid.** (Penguin Young Reader Ser.). (C). 2000. 6.67 (*0-582-42866-1*) Pearson Educ.

Little Mermaid. Hans Christian Andersen. (Illus.). 32p. (J). (ps-3). 1992. 6.95 (*0-8362-4918-6*) Andrews & McMeel.

Little Mermaid. Hans Christian Andersen. (J). 1980. pap. 2.95 (*0-88388-039-3*) Bellerophon Bks.

Little Mermaid. Hans Christian Andersen. (Hans Christian Andersen's Tales Ser.). 36p. (J). 24.95 (*0-915035-39-1*) Dawn Sign.

Little Mermaid. Hans Christian Andersen. 1994. 3.95 (*0-87129-435-4*, L79) Dramatic Pub.

Little Mermaid. Hans Christian Andersen. LC 92-29807. (Illus.). (J). 1995. 16.95 (*0-8050-1010-6*, Bks Young Read) H Holt & Co.

Little Mermaid. Hans Christian Andersen. LC 89-31602. (Illus.). 42p. (J). (gr. k-3). 1989. 15.95 (*0-15-246320-8*) Harcourt.

Little Mermaid. Hans Christian Andersen. (J). 1997. pap. 6.00 (*0-15-201561-2*, Harcourt Child Bks) Harcourt.

Little Mermaid. Hans Christian Andersen. LC 97-8819. (Illus.). 64p. (J). (gr. 4-7). 1997. 11.45 (*0-7868-0383-5*, Pub. by Hyperion) Little.

Little Mermaid. Hans Christian Andersen. LC 97-8819. (Illus.). 64p. (J). 1997. lib. bdg. 11.89 (*0-7868-2331-3*, Pub. by Hypm Child) Little.

Little Mermaid. Hans Christian Andersen. (Fun-to-Read Fairy Tales Ser.). (Illus.). 24p. (J). 1992. pap. 2.50 (*1-56144-093-0*) Modern Pub NYC.

Little Mermaid. Hans Christian Andersen. (Classics Ser.). (Illus.). 96p. (J). 1994. 7.98 (*1-57082-042-2*, Pub. by Mouse Works) Little.

Little Mermaid. Hans Christian Andersen. (J). 1997. 7.98 (*1-57082-727-3*, Pub. by Mouse Works) Time Warner.

Little Mermaid. Hans Christian Andersen. (Disney's Look & Find Ser.). (Illus.). 24p. (J). 1993. write for info. (*0-7853-0106-2*); 12.98 (*0-7853-0133-X*) Pubns Intl Ltd.

Little Mermaid. Hans Christian Andersen. LC 91-6632. (Step into Reading Ser.: A Step 3 Book). (Illus.). 48p. (J). (gr. 2-3). 1991. pap. 3.99 (*0-679-82241-0*, Pub. by Random Bks Yng Read) Random.

Little Mermaid. Hans Christian Andersen. (Disney Read-Alongs Ser.). (J). 7.99 incl. audio (*0-7634-0286-9*) Walt Disney.

Little Mermaid. Hans Christian Andersen. Tr. by Petra Michel. LC 96-21504. (Illus.). 32p. (J). 1996. 18.95 (*1-885394-17-9*) Bluestar Communs.

Little Mermaid. Hans Christian Andersen. LC 97-4979. Orig. Title: Lille havfrue. (Illus.). (J). 1997. 18.00 (*0-679-88757-1*, Pub. by Random Bks Yng Read) Random.

***Little Mermaid.** Hans Christian Andersen. (Illus.). (J). 2000. 12.44 (*0-606-18420-1*) Turtleback.

***Little Mermaid.** Hans Christian Andersen & Rachel Isadora. (Picture Puffin Ser.). (Illus.). 32p. (J). (ps-3). 2000. pap. 6.99 (*0-698-11829-4*, PuffinBks) Peng Put Young Read.

Little Mermaid. Audrey Daly. (Favorite Tales Ser.). (Illus.). 28p. (J). 1994. 2.99 (*0-7214-5447-X*, Ladybrd) Penguin Putnam.

Little Mermaid. Linda Daugherty. (J). 1995. 6.00 (*0-87602-330-8*) Anchorage.

***Little Mermaid.** Amy Edgar. 64p. (J). 2000. 6.99 (*0-7364-0161-X*, Pub. by Mouse Works) Time Warner.

Little Mermaid. Golden Books Staff.Tr. of Lille havfrue. 24p. 1999. 3.99 (*0-307-16234-6*) Gldn Bks Pub Co.

Little Mermaid. Margaret Maloney. (Illus.). 32p. (J). (gr. k-3). 1983. write for info. (*0-458-95110-2*) Stoddart Publ.

Little Mermaid. Mouseworks Staff. (Spanish Classics Ser.).Tr. of Lille havfrue. (Illus.). (J). 1997. write for info. (*1-57082-872-5*) Mouse Works.

Little Mermaid. Illus. by Andre Pijet. (Classic Stories Ser.). 48p. (J). 9.95 incl. audio (*2-89517-048-7*, Pub. by Coffragants) Penton Overseas.

Little Mermaid. A. L. Singer. LC 92-74260. (Illus.). 96p. (J). (gr. 3-7). 1997. pap. 3.50 (*0-7868-4202-4*, Pub. by Disney Pr) Time Warner.

Little Mermaid. Walt Disney Company Staff. (FRE.). 96p. (J). (gr. k-5). pap. 9.95 (*0-7859-8846-7*) Fr & Eur.

Little Mermaid, 4 vols. Walt Disney Staff. LC 98-104632. (Little Library). 5p. (J). 1997. 5.98 (*1-57082-072-4*, Pub. by Mouse Works) Little.

Little Mermaid, Incl. toy. Walt Disney Press Staff. (Illus.). (J). 1997. pap. 16.95 (*0-7868-4201-6*, Pub. by Disney Pr) Time Warner.

Little Mermaid: A Picture Book. Walt Disney Press Staff. LC 96-65273. (Illus.). 32p. (J). 1997. pap. 4.95 (*0-7868-4175-3*, Pub. by Disney Pr) Time Warner.

Little Mermaid: An under the Sea Christmas: A Holiday Songbook. Hans Christian Andersen. LC 93-70939. (Little Mermaid Novels Ser.). (Illus.). 48p. (J). 1993. pap. 9.95 (*1-56282-504-6*, Pub. by Disney Pr) Time Warner.

Little Mermaid: Director's Script. Rosemary Nursey-Bray. (Illus.). 56p. 1982. pap. 15.00 (*0-88680-114-1*) I E Clark.

***Little Mermaid: Film Fashion.** Golden Books Staff. LC 83-80022. (Disney's the Little Mermaid Ser.).Tr. of Lille havfrue. 12p. (J). 1999. pap. text 3.29 (*0-307-02016-9*, 02016) Gldn Bks Pub Co.

Little Mermaid: Flounder to the Rescue. Bettina Ling. LC PZ7.L66245Dl 1997. (Disney Chapters Ser.). (Illus.). 64p. (J). (gr. 2-4). 1997. pap. 3.50 (*0-7868-4139-7*, Pub. by Disney Pr) Time Warner.

Little Mermaid: Flounder's Gift. Rebecca Bondor. LC 93-78806. (Golden Little Super Shape Bks.). (Illus.). 24p. (J). (ps-3). 1994. 1.79 (*0-307-10560-1*, 10560, Goldn Books) Gldn Bks Pub Co.

Little Mermaid: Full-Color Sturdy Book. Retold by Sheilah Beckett. LC 95-18749. (Little Activity Bks.). (Illus.). 16p. (Orig.). (J). 1995. pap. text 1.00 (*0-486-28825-0*) Dover.

Little Mermaid: Makes a Splash Bath Book. Walter Elias Disney. (Illus.). (J). (ps). 1993. 5.98 (*0-453-03172-2*, Pub. by Mouse Works) Little.

Little Mermaid: My Coloring Book. Hans Christian Andersen.Tr. of Lille havfrue. (J). pap. text 1.09 (*0-307-08630-5*, 08630) Gldn Bks Pub Co.

Little Mermaid: Seek & See. Mouse Works Staff. LC 98-206168. 24p. (J). 1998. 3.98 (*1-57082-936-5*, Pub. by Mouse Works) Time Warner.

Little Mermaid: The Whole Story. (Little Golden Bks.). (J). 2.29 (*0-307-98275-0*, 98275) Gldn Bks Pub Co.

Little Mermaid: Treasures of Old. Disney Enterprises, Inc. Staff. (Disney's "Storytime Treasures" Library: Vol. 7). (Illus.). 44p. (J). (gr. 1-6). 1997. 3.49 (*1-57973-003-5*) Advance Pubs.

Little Mermaid: U. K. English. Adapted by Sarah Harris. (Comes to Life Bks.). 16p. (J). (ps-2). 1995. write for info. (*1-57234-026-6*) YES Ent.

Little Mermaid: Walt Disney Pictures Presents. Illus. by Franc Mateu et al. LC 98-134669. (Golden Super Shape Bks.). Orig. Title: Lille havfrue. 24p. (J). (ps). 1991. pap. 3.29 (*0-307-10027-8*, 10027) Gldn Bks Pub Co.

Little Mermaid: 2-Act Dramatization. Rosemary Nursey-Bray. (Illus.). 56p. 1982. pap. 4.00 (*0-88680-113-3*) I E Clark.

Little Mermaid & Other Fairy Tales. Hans Christian Andersen. Tr. by Neil Philip. LC 98-60069. 144p. (J). 1998. text 21.99 (*0-670-87840-5*) Viking Penguin.

Little Mermaid & Other Fairy Tales. Hans Christian Andersen. LC 93-14418. (Children's Thrift Classics Ser.). (Illus.). 96p. (J). 1993. reprint ed. pap. 1.00 (*0-486-27816-6*) Dover.

An Asterisk (*) at the beginning of an entry indicates that the title is appearing for the first time.

Little Mermaid & Other Hans Christian Andersen Stories. Hans Christian Andersen. 1999. 6.99 (0-517-20733-8) Random Hse Value.

Little Mermaid & Other Stories. Andersen. (Illus.). 96p. (J). 1997. pap. 5.95 incl. audio (0-486-29616-4, 29616-4) Dover.

Little Mermaid & Other Tales. Hans Christian Andersen. (Library of Folklore). (Illus.). 508p. (J). (gr. 3-4). 1998. 19.95 (0-7818-0720-4) Hippocrene Bks.

Little Mermaid Coloring Book. Hans Christian Andersen. (J). 1992. pap. 2.95 (0-486-27130-7) Dover.

Little Mermaid Disney Little Libraries. Walt Disney Staff. (Illus.). (J). (ps-3). 1992. 5.98 (0-453-03076-9, Viking Child) Peng Put Young Read.

Little Mermaid Hunts for Treasure. Hans Christian Andersen. LC 91-73811. (Surprise Lift-the-Flap Bk.). (Illus.). 18p. (J). (ps-1). 1992. 8.95 (1-56282-146-6, Pub. by Disney Pr) Time Warner.

Little Mermaid Novels, 4 bks., Set. Hans Christian Andersen & Suzanne J. Weghorst. (Little Mermaid Novels Ser.). (Illus.). (J). (gr. 1-4). 1993. pap., boxed set 11.80 (1-56282-562-3, Pub. by Disney Pr) Little.

Little Mermaid Piano Fun! Walt Disney Staff. (Music Fun Ser.). 272p. (J). (gr. 3). 1997. pap. 19.95 (0-7935-8158-3, HL00824126) H Leonard.

Little Mermaid Stained Glass Coloring Book. Marty Noble. (Illus.). (J). pap. 1.00 (0-486-29341-6) Dover.

Little Mermaid Treasury Exclusive for AMS. Hans Christian Andersen. 176p. (J). (ps-2). 1997. pap. 17.95 (0-7868-3182-0, Pub. by Disney Pr) Time Warner.

***Little Mermaid II.** Golden Books Staff. (Illus.). (J). 2000. pap. 2.99 (0-307-28319-4, Goldn Books) Gldn Bks Pub Co.

***Little Mermaid II: A Princess in Two Worlds.** Golden Books Staff. (Illus.). (J). 2000. pap. 2.99 (0-307-25734-7, Goldn Books) Gldn Bks Pub Co.

***Little Mermaid II: Return to the Sea.** Catherine McCafferty. (Illus.). (J). 2000. pap. 3.29 (0-307-13260-9, Goldn Books) Gldn Bks Pub Co.

***Little Mermaid 2 (Super Chapter Book)** Amy E. Sklansky. (Illus.). 64p. (J). 2000. 4.99 (0-7868-4431-0, Pub. by Disney Pr) Time Warner.

***Little Messages form God: And Stories That Will Warm Your Heart.** Victory House Staff. 1999. pap. 5.99 (0-932081-68-1) Victory Hse.

Little Mexican Cookbook. Carolyn Dehnel. (Traditional Little Cookbooks of the World Ser.). (Illus.). 60p. 1991. 7.95 (0-87701-860-X) Chronicle Bks.

Little Mexican Girl. Sylvia Walker. (Little Activity Bks.). (Illus.). (J). 1993. pap. 1.00 (0-486-27005-X) Dover.

***Little Mexico.** Cathie John et al. 258p. 2000. pap. 12.95 (0-9634183-7-8, Jrny Bk Pr) CC Comics.

Little Michael's Guide to Raising Good Parents: A Seven Year Old's View. Michael J. Riso. (Illus.). 93p. 1999. pap. 9.95 (0-9668103-0-9) Continuous Lrning Pubs.

Little Mikey. Barbara Steadman. (Little Activity Bks.). (Illus.). (J). 1994. pap. 1.00 (0-486-27934-0) Dover.

Little Minister. J. M. Barrie. 381p. Date not set. 26.95 (0-8488-2205-6) Amereon Ltd.

Little Minister. J. M. Barrie. 300p. (J). 1980. reprint ed. lib. bdg. 18.95 (0-89967-007-5, Harmony Rain) Buccaneer Bks.

Little Minister. J. M. Barrie. 232p. (J). 1981. reprint ed. lib. bdg. 18.95 (0-89966-329-X) Buccaneer Bks.

Little Minister see Works of J. M. Barrie: Peter Pan Edition

Little Miracle: A Hanukah Story. Terry Fox. LC 85-51615. (Illus.). 52p. (Orig.). (J). (ps up). 1985. pap. 5.95 (0-9615397-0-4) Tenderfoot Pr.

Little Miracles: Cherished Messages of Hope, Joy, Love, Kindness & Courage. Dan Zadra. 128p. 1996. 12.95 (1-888387-04-1) Compendium Inc.

***Little Miracles Coupons.** (Illus.). 96p. 2000. pap. 5.95 (1-57071-543-2) Sourcebks.

Little Miss Atlas. Janet Lambert. 20.95 (0-8488-0129-6) Amereon Ltd.

Little Miss Bossy. Roger Hargreaves. (Mr. Men & Little Miss Ser.). (Illus.). 32p. (J). (gr. k up). 1998. pap. 2.99 (0-8431-7423-4) Putnam Pub Group.

Little Miss Busy. Roger Hargreaves. (Mr. Men & Little Miss Ser.). (Illus.). 32p. (J). (gr. k-3). 1997. pap. 2.99 (0-8431-7812-4, Price Stern) Peng Put Young Read.

Little Miss Contrary. Roger Hargreaves. pap. 2.99 (0-8431-7619-9, Price Stern) Peng Put Young Read.

Little Miss Curious. Roger Hargreaves. (Mr. Men & Little Miss Ser.). (Illus.). 32p. (J). 1997. pap. 2.99 (0-8431-7813-2, Price Stern) Peng Put Young Read.

***Little Miss Evil: A Nick Hoffman Mystery.** Lev Raphael. LC 99-88139. 256p. 2000. 23.95 (0-8027-3342-5) Walker & Co.

Little Miss Innocent. Lori Foster. 1999. per. 3.75 (0-373-76200-3, Harlequin) Harlequin Bks.

Little Miss Late. Roger Hargreaves. (Mr. Men & Little Miss Ser.). (Illus.). 32p. (J). (gr. k up). 1998. pap. 2.50 (0-8431-7424-2) Putnam Pub Group.

Little Miss Magi. John Sampson. (Illus.). 195p. 1997. 7.95 (0-9613075-6-0) Thornfield Pr.

***Little Miss Magic.** Roger Hargreaves. (Illus.). 32p. (J). (gr. k-3). 2000. pap. 2.99 (0-8431-7565-6, Price Stern) Peng Put Young Read.

Little Miss Marker. Damon Runyon. reprint ed. lib. bdg. 19.95 (0-89190-436-0, Rivercity Pr) Amereon Ltd.

***Little Miss Muffet.** (Illus.). 12p. (J). 2001. bds. 2.99 (0-307-30153-2, 30153, Goldn Books) Gldn Bks Pub Co.

Little Miss Muffet. Lucy Cousins. LC 97-150996. (J). 1997. pap. 5.99 (0-525-45749-6) NAL.

***Little Miss Muffet.** Illus. by Mary Morgan-Vanroyen & Publications International, Ltd. Editorial Staff. LC 98-176778. (J). 1998. write for info. (0-7853-2633-2) Pubns Intl Ltd.

Little Miss Muffet. Scholastic, Inc. Staff. (Illus.). 22p. (J). (ps-k). 1999. bds. 3.99 (0-590-56601-6) Scholastic.

Little Miss Muffet's Count-Along Surprise. Emma C. Clark. LC 97-204886. (Illus.). 32p. (J). (ps-1). 1997. 15.95 (0-385-32517-7, DD Bks Yng Read) BDD Bks Young Read.

***Little Miss Muffet's Count-Along Surprise.** Emma Chichester Clark. (Illus.). 32p. (J). (ps-1). 2000. pap. 6.99 (0-440-41414-8, Yearling) BDD Bks Young Read.

***Little Miss Muffet's Count-Along Surprise.** Emma Chichester Clark. (Illus.). (J). 2000. 12.44 (0-606-18000-1) Turtleback.

Little Miss Perfect. Megan LeBoutillier. 140p. (Orig.). 1987. pap. 8.95 (0-910223-10-6) MAC Pub.

***Little Miss Priss: Flying Kites & Kisses Not for the Misses.** large type ed. Kitchener L. Harding. 10p. (J). (gr. 1-5). 1999. spiral bd. 4.95 (1-930503-00-8) Office Max.

Little Miss Scatterbrain. Roger Hargreaves. (Mr. Men & Little Miss Ser.). (Illus.). 32p. (J). (gr. k-3). 1998. pap. 2.50 (0-8431-7845-0, Price Stern) Peng Put Young Read.

Little Miss Shy. Roger Hargreaves. (Mr. Men & Little Miss Ser.). (Illus.). 32p. (J). (gr. k-3). 1998. pap. 2.50 (0-8431-7425-0) Putnam Pub Group.

Little Miss Spider. David Kirk. (Miss Spider Ser.). (J). (ps-2). 1999. 155.40 (0-439-11737-2) Scholastic Inc.

***Little Miss Spider.** David Kirk. LC 98-49270. (Miss Spider Ser.). (Illus.). 32p. (J). (ps-2). 1999. 12.95 (0-439-08389-3, Pub. by Scholastic Inc) Penguin Putnam.

***Little Miss Spider at Sunnypatch School.** David Kirk. LC 99-56671. (Miss Spider Ser.:). (Illus.). 32p. (J). (ps-2). 2000. 12.95 (0-439-08727-9) Scholastic Inc.

Little Miss Stoneybrook & Dawn. Ann M. Martin. (Baby-Sitters Club Ser.: No. 15). 192p. (J). (gr. 4-6). 1988. pap. 3.50 (0-590-43717-8) Scholastic Inc.

Little Miss Stoneybrook & Dawn. Ann M. Martin. (Baby-Sitters Club Ser.: No. 15). 1996. pap. text 3.99 (0-590-25170-8) Scholastic Inc.

Little Miss Strange. Joanna Rose. LC 98-11366. 384p. 1998. pap. 12.00 (0-684-84741-8) S&S Trade.

Little Miss Strange: A Novel. Joanna Rose. LC 96-46817. 384p. 1997. 20.95 (1-56512-154-6, 72154) Algonquin Bks.

Little Miss Trouble. Roger Hargreaves. (Mr. Men & Little Miss Ser.). (Illus.). 32p. (J). (gr. k-3). 1998. pap. 2.50 (0-8431-7426-9) Putnam Pub Group.

***Little Miss Twins.** Roger Hargreaves. (Mr. Men & Little Miss Ser.). (Illus.). 32p. (J). (ps-3). 2000. pap. 2.99 (0-8431-7602-4, Price Stern) Peng Put Young Read.

Little Miss Wise. Roger Hargreaves. (Mr. Men & Little Miss Ser.). (Illus.). 32p. (J). (gr. k-3). 1997. pap. 2.99 (0-8431-7817-5, Price Stern) Peng Put Young Read.

Little Miss Wise: A Short Story about Innocence & the Misunderstood. (Illus.). 75p. Date not set. 5.95 (0-9653570-4-X) N J Cipriani.

Little Missionaries & Other Stories. Mary R. Zook. (Illus.). 180p. (J). (gr. 3-6). 1979. 8.05 (0-7399-0087-0, 2315) Rod & Staff.

Little Misunderstandings of No Importance. Antonio Tabucchi. Tr. by Frances Frenaye from ITA. LC 87-1578. 144p. 1987. 16.95 (0-8112-1029-4, Pub. by New Directions) Norton.

Little Misunderstandings of No Importance. Antonio Tabucchi. Tr. by Frances Frenaye from ITA. LC 87-1578. 144p. 1989. pap. 8.95 (0-8112-1111-8, NDP681, Pub. by New Directions) Norton.

Little Mixer. Lillian N. Shearon. 60p. 1987. reprint ed. lib. bdg. 17.95 (0-89966-603-5) Buccaneer Bks.

Little MLer. Matthias Felleisen & Daniel P. Friedman. LC 97-40550. (Illus.). 200p. 1997. pap. text 25.00 (0-262-56114-X) MIT Pr.

Little Mo. Martin Waddell. LC 92-54410. (Illus.). 32p. (J). (ps-2). 1993. 14.95 (1-56402-211-0) Candlewick Pr.

Little Mo. Martin Waddell. LC 92-54410. (Illus.). (J). (ps up). 1995. pap. 5.99 (1-56402-514-4) Candlewick Pr.

Little Mo. Martin Waddell. 1995. 11.19 (0-606-08802-4, Pub. by Turtleback) Demco.

Little Moments of Happiness. Elisabeth Brami. 1997. 140.95 (1-55670-685-5) Stewart Tabori & Chang.

Little Moments of Happiness. Elisabeth Brami. LC 97-16337. (Illus.). 180p. 1997. 14.95 (1-55670-649-9) Stewart Tabori & Chang.

Little Moments to Cherish. Kelly J. Watkins. 260p. 1994. pap. 6.00 (0-9644982-0-0) Express Concepts.

Little Money Bible: The Ten Laws of Abundance. Stuart Wilde. LC 98-15929. 128p. 1998. 12.95 (1-56170-393-1, 895) Hay House.

Little Monk. Harry Farra. LC 94-14506. 288p. 1994. pap. 7.95 (0-8091-3356-3) Paulist Pr.

Little Monk Meditates . . . John C. Huntington. LC 94-45802. (Meditation Techniques Ser.: No. 2). (Illus.). 32p. 1995. pap. 6.95 (0-8348-0329-1) Weatherhill.

Little Monster. Frank Daniel. (Little Activity Bks.). (Illus.). (J). 1995. pap. 1.00 (0-486-28416-6) Dover.

Little Monster at School. 1995. cd-rom 119.95 (1-57135-043-8) Living Bks.

Little Monster at School. 1995. 39.95 (1-57135-042-X) Living Bks.

Little Monster Did. Helen Cooper. 32p. (J). 1996. pap. 17.95 (0-385-40620-7) Doubleday.

Little Monster Did It! Helen Cooper. (J). 1999. pap. 5.99 (0-14-055883-7, PuffinBks) Peng Put Young Read.

Little Monster Goes to School. Alison Inches. LC 97-218839. (Illus.). 16p. (J). (ps-k). 1997. pap. 5.99 (0-14-056224-9) Viking Penguin.

Little Monsters. Jan Pienkowski. (Pienkowski Mini Pop-Up Ser.). (Illus.). 10p. (J). (ps up). 1991. 6.99 (0-8431-2964-6, Price Stern) Peng Put Young Read.

Little Monster's Moving Day. Mercer Mayer. (Little Monster Sticker Bks.). (Illus.). 24p. (J). (ps-1). 1995. bds. 4.95 (0-590-48643-8, Cartwheel) Scholastic Inc.

Little Monster's Sports Fun. Mercer Mayer. (Little Monster Sticker Bks.). (Illus.). 24p. (Orig.). (J). (ps-1). 1995. bds. 4.95 (0-590-48644-6, Cartwheel) Scholastic Inc.

Little More About Me. Pam Houston. LC 99-25336. 224p. 1999. 23.95 (0-393-04805-5) Norton.

***Little More about Me.** Pam Houston. 304p. 2000. 13.95 (0-7434-0633-8, WSP) PB.

Little More Than Kin. Ernest Hebert. LC 81-24135. 224p. 1982. 25.00 (0-89366-139-2) Ultramarine Pub.

Little Mother Goose Coloring Book. 81st ed. Anna Pomaska. (Illus.). (J). (gr. k-3). 1986. pap. 1.00 (0-486-25158-6) Dover.

Little Moule History: 1890's-1937. William R. Moule. LC 90-22041. (Illus.). 624p. 1990. 24.95 (0-931892-61-9) B Dolphin Pub.

Little Mountain. Elias Khoury. Tr. by Maia Tabet from ARA. (Emergent Literatures Ser.). 124p. 1989. pap. 12.95 (0-8166-1770-8) U of Minn Pr.

Little Mountain Bean Bible Cookbook. Wiley J. Smith. (Illus.). 404p. (Orig.). 1993. pap. 12.95 (0-9637763-0-4) BJB.

Little Mouse. John Cast. 1999. 6.99 (0-85953-694-7) Childs Play.

***Little Mouse.** Rebecca Spence. (Illus.). (J). 2000. pap. write for info. (0-9702406-0-0) Little Iris.

Little Mouse. Alana Willoughby. Ed. by Alton Jordan. (Illus.). (J). (gr. k-3). 1984. 7.95 (0-89868-007-7, Read Res); pap. 3.95 (0-89868-040-9, Read Res) ARO Pub.

Little Mouse: The Mouse Who Lived with Henry David Thoreau at Walden Pond. Bill Montague. Ed. by Christopher Roof. LC 93-73231. (Illus.). 56p. (Orig.). (J). (gr. 2-4). 1993. pap. text 7.95 (0-9638644-0-8) Concord MouseTrap.

Little Mouse & Elephant: A Tale from Turkey. Illus. by John Segal. (J). (ps-2). 1995. write for info. (0-614-32087-9) S&S Bks Yung.

***Little Mouse Has a Busy Day.** Steve Lavis. (Ready Readers Ser.). (Illus.). 24p. (J). (ps-1). 2000. 6.95 (1-929927-10-X) Ragged Bears NY.

***Little Mouse Has a Friend.** Steve Lavis. (Ready Readers Ser.). (Illus.). 24p. (J). (ps-1). 2000. 6.95 (1-929927-12-6) Ragged Bears NY.

***Little Mouse Has a Party.** Steve Lavis. (Ready Readers Ser.). (Illus.). 24p. (J). (ps-1). 2000. 6.95 (1-929927-11-8) Ragged Bears NY.

***Little Mouse Has an Adventure.** Steve Lavis. (Ready Readers Ser.). (Illus.). 24p. (J). (ps-1). 2000. 6.95 (1-929927-09-6) Ragged Bears NY.

Little Mouse Learns the ABCs: Book & Toy Set. Elizabeth Worsley. (Illus.). 18p. (J). (ps-3). 1995. 9.95 (0-8050-4096-X) H Holt & Co.

Little Mouse Library, 6 bks., Set. Barbara Davoll. LC 96-205260. (Illus.). 60p. (J). 1996. bds. 10.99 (1-56476-568-7, 6-3568, Victor Bks) Chariot Victor.

Little Mouse Meets the Easter Bunny. Harriet Ziefert. (Lift-the-Flap Bk.). (Illus.). 16p. (J). (ps). 1995. 5.95 (0-694-00660-2, HarpFestival) HarpC Child Bks.

Little Mouse Named Herman. Jerri Hente. (Illus.). (Orig.). (J). (gr. 3-6). 1996. pap. 6.95 (0-533-11942-1) Vantage.

***Little Mouse on the Prairie.** Stephen Cosgrove. (Serendipity Bks.). (Illus.). 32p. (J). (ps-3). 2000. pap. 4.99 (0-8431-7632-6, Price Stern) Peng Put Young Read.

Little Mouse on the Prairie. Stephen Cosgrove. (Serendipity Bks.). (J). 1978. 9.15 (0-606-02404-2, Pub. by Turtleback) Demco.

Little Mouse, the Red Ripe Strawberry & the Big Hungry Bear. Audrey Wood & Don Wood. (Illus.). 24p. (J). (ps-1). 1998. bds. 5.99 (0-85953-659-9) Childs Play.

Little Mouse, the Red Ripe Strawberry & the Big Hungry Bear. Don Wood. LC 90-46414. 32p. (J). (ps-3). 1990. 13.99 (0-85953-182-1); pap. 6.99 (0-85953-012-4) Childs Play.

Little Mouse, the Red Ripe Strawberry & the Big Hungry Bear. Don Wood. 1984. 11.15 (0-606-00871-3, Pub. by Turtleback) Demco.

Little Mouse Was a Grouch. Glenna C. Smith. Ed. by Alton Jordan. (Buppet Bks.). (Illus.). (J). (gr. 1-4). 1980. 9.95 (0-89868-095-6, Read Res); pap. 3.95 (0-89868-106-5, Read Res) ARO Pub.

Little Mouses Big Valent. Thacher Hurd. LC 89-34515. (Illus.). 32p. (J). (ps-1). 1990. 13.95 (0-06-026192-7) HarpC Child Bks.

Little Mouse's Big Valentine. Thacher Hurd. LC 89-34515. (Trophy Picture Bk.). (Illus.). 32p. (J). (ps-1). 1992. pap. 5.95 (0-06-443281-5, HarpTrophy) HarpC Child Bks.

Little Mouse's Big Valentine. Thacher Hurd. (J). 1992. 9.90 (0-606-00564-1, Pub. by Turtleback) Demco.

Little Mouse's Learn-&-Play, 4 bks. Anael Dena. Incl. Colors. LC 97-20901. (Illus.). 48p. (J). (ps up). 1997. lib. bdg. 22.60 (0-8368-1984-5); Letters. LC 97-14783. (Illus.). 48p. (J). (ps up). 1997. lib. bdg. 22.60 (0-8368-1985-3); Numbers. Tr. by Janet Neis from FRE. LC 97-20904. (Illus.). 48p. (J). (ps up). 1997. lib. bdg. 22.60 (0-8368-1986-1); Opposites. LC 97-14784. (Illus.). 48p. (J). (ps up). 1997. lib. bdg. 22.60 (0-8368-1987-X); (Illus.). (J). 1997. Set lib. bdg. 90.40 (0-8368-1983-7) Gareth Stevens Inc.

Little Mouse's Painting. Diane Wolkstein. LC 91-16017. (Illus.). 32p. (J). (ps up). 1992. 16.00 (0-688-07609-2, Wm Morrow) Morrow Avon.

Little Mouse's Trail Tale. JoAnn Vandine. LC 94-30181. (Illus.). 24p. (Orig.). (J). (ps-2). 1994. pap. 4.95 (1-879531-59-3) Mondo Pubng.

Little Movies. Maria Gitin. LC 75-302547. 59p. 1975. 3.50 (0-87886-051-7, Greenfld Rev Pr) Greenfld Rev Lit.

Little Muddy Waters: A Gullah Folk Tale. Ronald H. Daise. Ed. by Carol E. Tuynman. LC 97-80693. (Illus.). 32p. (J). (gr. 2-6). 1998. 14.95 (1-891503-01-4, CP101) G O G Enter.

Little Muffin Cookbook. Steven Stellingwerf. (Illus.). 60p. 1998. 9.95 (0-86281-330-1, Pub. by Appletree Pr) Irish Bks Media.

Little Murders. Jules Feiffer. 1995. reprint ed. lib. bdg. 24.95 (1-56849-667-2) Buccaneer Bks.

Little Museums: Over 1,000 Small & Not-So-Small American Showplaces. Lynne Arany & Archie Hobson. LC 97-9406. (Illus.). 464p. 1998. pap. text 17.95 (0-8050-4823-5, Owl) H Holt & Co.

Little Mushrooms Coloring Book, No. 50. Cathy Prather. (Illus.). 50p. (J). (ps-6). 1998. pap. 2.99 (0-9666959-2-5) Cathy Prather.

Little Mystic Magic Picture Book. Daniel Stoltzius. 231p. 1992. reprint ed. pap. 15.95 (1-56459-027-5) Kessinger Pub.

Little Myth Marker. Robert L. Asprin. (Myth Ser.). 1987. mass mkt. 5.99 (0-441-48499-9) Ace Bks.

Little Myths & Destinies. Albert Steffen. Tr. by Percy MacKaye et al. (Illus.). 80p. (Orig.). 1988. pap. text 8.50 (0-932776-15-9) Adonis Pr.

***Little 'n' Sellers.** (J). 2000. 3.95 (0-552-52885-4, Pub. by Transworld Publishers Ltd) Trafalgar.

Little Ned Stories, Bk. 1. Edward A. Faine. LC 98-52047. (Illus.). 128p. (J). (gr. k-3). 1999. pap. 9.99 (0-9654651-5-2) IM Press.

Little Neighborhood Murder. large type ed. A. J. Orde. (Linford Mystery Library). 448p. 1992. pap. 16.99 (0-7089-7163-6, Linford) Ulverscroft.

***Little Nel - The Nellie Fox Story: An Up-Close & Personal Look at Baseball's "Mighty Mite"** David Gough & Jim Bard. (Illus.). 325p. 2000. pap. 17.95 (0-9660506-1-4) D L Megbec.

***Little Nemo in Slumberland: Birthday Book.** Illus. by Winsor McCay. 50p. 2000. reprint ed. text 18.00 (0-7881-9048-2) DIANE Pub.

Little Nemo in the Palace of Ice, & Further Adventures. Winsor McCay. LC 75-19834. (Illus.). 32p. (Orig.). 1976. pap. 8.95 (0-486-23234-4) Dover.

***Little Nemo, 1905-1914.** Winsor McCay. (Illus.). 2000. 39.99 (3-8228-6300-9) Taschen Amer.

Little Network Book for Windows & Macintosh. Lon Poole & John Rizzo. (Illus.). 280p. (C). 1999. pap. text 19.99 (0-201-35378-4) Peachpit Pr.

Little New England Cookbook. Barbara Bloch. (Traditional Little Cookbooks of the World Ser.). (Illus.). 60p. 1991. 7.95 (0-87701-879-0) Chronicle Bks.

Little New Orleans Cookbook. Norma MacMillan. (Illus.). 60p. 1995. 7.95 (0-8118-0906-4) Chronicle Bks.

Little New Orleans Cookbook: Fifty-Seven Classic Creole Recipes That Will Enable Everyone to Enjoy the Special Cuisine of New Orleans. Gwen McKee. (Illus.). 80p. (Orig.). 1991. 8.95 (0-937552-42-9) Quail Ridge.

Little New York Cookbook. Barbara Bloch. (Traditional Little Cookbooks of the World Ser.). (Illus.). 60p. 1991. 7.95 (0-87701-876-6) Chronicle Bks.

Little Night Music. Hugh Wheeler. (Musical Library). (Illus.). 256p. 1990. 19.95 (1-55783-069-X) Applause Theatre Bk Pubs.

Little Night Music. Hugh Wheeler. (Musical Library). (Illus.). 256p. 1999. pap. 12.95 (1-55783-070-3) Applause Theatre Bk Pubs.

Little Night-Music. Gerald W. Johnson. LC 70-108844. (Illus.). 125p. 1970. reprint ed. lib. bdg. 49.50 (0-8371-3733-0, JONM, Greenwood Pr) Greenwood.

Little Night Music - Vocal Score. 198p. (YA). 1997. reprint ed. pap. 75.00 (0-7692-0049-4) Wrner Bros.

Little Night Music - Vocal Selection. 48p. (YA). 1997. pap. 12.95 (0-7692-1538-6) Wrner Bros.

***Little Night Rainbow.** Susan Aylworth. LC 98-96844. 192p. 1999. lib. bdg. 18.95 (0-8034-9333-9, Avalon Bks) Bouregy.

Little Nightmares, Little Dreams. Rachel Simon. 192p. 1990. 18.95 (0-685-36289-2, Seymour Lawrence) HM.

Little Nightmares, Little Dreams. Rachel Simon. 1990. 18.95 (0-89919-953-4) Ticknor & Fields.

Little Nineveh. Dexter Petley. 232p. (Orig.). 1995. pap. 14.95 (0-7486-6190-5, Pub. by Polygon) Subterranean Co.

Little Nino's Pizzeria. Karen Barbour. LC 86-32006. (Illus.). 32p. (J). (ps-3). 1990. pap. 6.00 (0-15-246321-6, Voyager Bks) Harcourt.

Little Nino's Pizzeria. Karen Barbour. LC 86-32006. (Big Bks.). (Illus.). 32p. (J). (ps-3). 1991. pap. 19.95 (0-15-246322-4, Harcourt Child Bks) Harcourt.

Little Nonsense: Collections of Works by Poets in Delaware, Maryland, Pennsylvania, Virginia, & the District of Columbia. Ed. & Compiled by Joseph D. Adams. (Poet's Domain Ser.: Vol. 14). 144p. (Orig.). 1997. pap. 10.00 (1-880016-25-7) Road Pubs.

Little Norsk see Collected Works of Hamlin Garland

Little Norsk. Hamlin Garland. (Collected Works of Hamlin Garland). 1988. reprint ed. lib. bdg. 59.00 (0-7812-1218-9) Rprt Serv.

Little Northwest Cookbook. Kathleen D. Stang. (Little Cookbooks Ser.). (Illus.). 60p. 1993. 7.95 (0-8118-0356-2) Chronicle Bks.

Little Notes from the Office: Some Do's, Don'ts & Basic Observations That Have Made a Difference. Frank A. Little. LC 94-94159. (Illus.). (Orig.). 1994. pap. 5.95 (0-9641206-3-1) E W Franklin.

Little Novels. Arthur Schnitzler. Tr. by Eric Sutton. LC 77-175574. reprint ed. 37.50 (0-404-08277-7) AMS Pr.

***Little Novels of Sicily.** 3rd ed. Giovanni Verga. Tr. by D. H. Lawrence from ITA. LC 99-43311. (Steerforth Italia). 200p. 2000. pap. 12.00 (1-883642-54-X) Steerforth Pr.

Little Number Book. Bob Staake. (Illus.). 30p. (J). (ps-k). 1998. mass mkt. 6.99 (0-689-81660-X) S&S Childrens.

Little Number Stories Vol. 3736: Addition. Rozanne L. Williams. (Emergent Reader Bks.). (Illus.). 16p. (J). (gr. k-2). 1995. pap. 2.75 (1-57471-007-9) Creat Teach Pr.

L

An Asterisk (*) at the beginning of an entry indicates that the title is appearing for the first time.

L

Little Number Stories Vol. 3737: Subtraction. Rozanne L. Williams. (Emergent Reader Bks.). (Illus.). 16p. (J). (gr. k-2). 1995. pap. text 2.75 (*1-57471-008-7*) Creat Teach Pr.

Little Number Stories Vol. 3979: Addition. Rozanne L. Williams. (Emergent Reader Big Bks.). (Illus.). 16p. (J). (gr. k-2). 1996. pap. 12.98 (*1-57471-117-2*) Creat Teach Pr.

Little Number Stories Vol. 3980: Subtraction. Rozanne L. Williams. (Emergent Reader Big Bks.). (Illus.). 16p. (J). (gr. k-2). 1996. pap. 12.98 (*1-57471-118-0*) Creat Teach Pr.

Little Number Stories: Addition see Cuentitos con Numeros: Suma

Little Number Stories: Subtraction see Cuentitos con Numeros: Sustraccion

Little Numbers Coloring Book. Anna Pomaska. (Illus.). (J). (gr. k-3). 1989. pap. 1.00 (*0-486-25345-7*) Dover.

***Little 'O'** Sellers. (J). 2000. 3.95 (*0-552-52886-2*, Pub. by Transworld Publishers Ltd) Trafalgar.

Little Obie & the Flood. Martin Waddell. LC 91-58741. (Illus.). 80p. (J). (gr. 3-6). 1992. 13.95 (*1-56402-106-8*) Candlewick Pr.

Little Obie & the Flood. Martin Waddell. LC 91-58741. 1996. 10.19 (*0-606-09562-4*, Pub. by Turtleback) Demco.

Little Obie & the Kidnap. Martin Waddell. LC 93-45959. (Illus.). 80p. (J). (gr. 3-6). 1994. 14.95 (*1-56402-352-4*) Candlewick Pr.

Little of Dis & Some of Dat. Walter F. Weiss. Date not set. 22.95 (*1-58244-005-0*) Rutledge Bks.

***Little of This & a Pinch of That.** Fran Stephenson. 292p. 1999. pap. 15.95 (*0-938711-60-1*) Tecolote Pubns.

Little Off the Top at the Barber Shop. William G. Bissell. x, 300p. (Orig.). 1999. pap. 12.00 (*0-9673223-0-8*) William Bissell.

Little Office of the Blessed Virgin. 1997. reprint ed. pap. 3.50 (*0-8199-0896-7*, 38396, Frncscn Herld) Franciscan Pr.

Little Office of the Blessed Virgin Mary. large type rev. ed. Ed. by John E. Rotelle. 192p. 1988. 9.50 (*0-89942-450-3*, 450/10) Catholic Bk Pub.

***Little Office Romance.** Michele Dunaway. (American Romance Ser.: Bk. 848). 2000. mass mkt. 4.25 (*0-373-16848-9*, 1-16848-3) Harlequin Bks.

Little Oh. Laura Krauss Melmed. LC 95-25427. (Illus.). (J). (ps-3). 1997. lib. bdg. 15.93 (*0-688-14209-5*) Lothrop.

Little Oh. Laura Krauss Melmed. LC 95-25427. (Illus.). (J). (ps up). 1997. 16.00 (*0-688-14208-7*) Lothrop.

Little Old Ladies in Tennis Shoes. Sandra Fenichel Asher. 80p. 1989. pap. 5.50 (*1-58342-006-1*, L63) Dramatic Pub.

Little Old Lady Who Couldn't Fall Asleep. Yaffa Ganz. (ArtScroll Middas Ser.). (Illus.). 32p. (J). (gr. k-6). 1989. 7.99 (*0-89906-501-5*) Mesorah Pubns.

Little Old Lady Who Was Not Afraid of Anything. Linda Williams. LC 85-48250. (Illus.). 32p. (J). (ps-3). 1986. 15.95 (*0-690-04584-0*); lib. bdg. 15.89 (*0-690-04586-7*) HarpC Child Bks.

Little Old Lady Who Was Not Afraid of Anything. Linda Williams. LC 85-48250. (Trophy Picture Bk.). (Illus.). 32p. (J). (ps-2). 1988. pap. 5.95 (*0-06-443183-5*, HarpTrophy) HarpC Child Bks.

Little Old Lady Who Was Not Afraid of Anything. Linda Williams. LC 85-48250. 1986. 10.15 (*0-606-09563-2*, Pub. by Turtleback) Demco.

Little Old Lady Who Was Not Afraid of Anything Book & Tape. unabridged ed. Linda Williams. LC 85-48250. (Trophy Picture Bk.). (Illus.). 32p. (J). (gr. 2). 1995. pap. 7.95 incl. audio (*0-694-70015-0*) HarpC Child Bks.

Little Old Lady Who Was Not Afraid of Anything, The (Spanish edition) La viejecita que no le tenia miedo a nada. Linda Williams. Tr. by Yolanda Noda from SPA. LC 95-23887. (Trophy Picture Bk.). (SPA., Illus.). 32p. (J). (ps-3). 1996. pap. 6.95 (*0-06-443420-6*, HpArco Iris) HarpC Child Bks.

Little Old MacDonald's Farm Coloring Book, Vol. 180. Anna Pomaska. (Illus.). (J). (gr. k-3). 1986. pap. 1.00 (*0-486-25159-4*) Dover.

Little Old Man & His Dreams. Lillian Ross. LC 89-34511. (Charlotte Zolotow Bk.). (Illus.). 32p. (J). (gr. k-3). 1990. 14.95 (*0-06-025094-1*) HarpC Child Bks.

Little Old Man Cut Short. Donal O'Donovan. LC 98-167475. 240p. 1998. pap. 19.95 (*1-900505-90-8*, Pub. by Kestrel Bks) Irish Bks Media.

Little Old Mrs. Pepperpot. Alf Proysen. (J). (gr. 1-4). 1960. 12.95 (*0-8392-3021-4*) Astor-Honor.

***Little One.** RACHEL HURST. 1999. pap. text 9.99 (*1-897809-61-1*) Silver Moon.

Little One Free Forever. P. Lynn Mitchell. LC 97-90555. 1999. pap. 11.95 (*0-533-12427-1*) Vantage.

Little One-Inch & Other Japanese Children's Favorite Stories. Florence Sakade. (Illus.). 60p. (J). (gr. 1-5). 1958. pap. 9.95 (*0-8048-0384-6*) Tuttle Pubng.

Little Ones. Jane Weinberger. LC 86-50874. (ENG & FRE., Illus.). 54p. (Orig.). (J). (ps-4). 1987. pap. 3.95 (*0-932433-29-4*) Windswept Hse.

***Little Ones: French & German All-Bisque Dolls.** Florence Theriault. (Illus.). 88p. 1999. 49.00 (*0-912823-92-5*, BT-186, Pub. by Gold Horse) Dollmasters.

***Little One's Bible with "Talkabouts" & Prayers.** Eira Reeves. (Illus.). 384p. (J). (ps-1). 2000. 9.99 (*1-57748-846-6*, Promise Pr) Barbour Pub.

Little One's Draw a Story Drawing Book. Salle W. Vaughn. (Illus.). 120p. (J). (ps-5). 1990. student ed. 35.00 (*0-9625832-0-0*) Crystal TX.

Little Ones Need Jesus. Dykgraaf & Bolt. 57p. 1996. pap. 2.95 (*1-56212-162-6*) CRC Pubns.

Little Ones Praise. Martha Mellinger. 1981. pap. 4.35 (*0-87813-518-9*) Christian Light.

Little Online Book: A Gentle Introduction to Modems, Online Services, Electronic Bulletin Boards, & the Internet. Alfred Glossbrenner. 426p. (C). 1995. pap. text 17.95 (*1-56609-130-6*) Peachpit Pr.

Little Organ Book for Beginners in Organ Playing. Flor Peeters. 114p. (Orig.). (gr. 3-12). 1957. pap. text 14.95 (*0-87487-600-1*) Summy-Birchard.

Little Organ Lexicon. C. W. Lindow & Homer D. Blanchard. (Little Organ Book Ser.: No. 2). 40p. 1981. pap. 7.50 (*0-930112-04-0*) Organ Lit.

Little Original Sin: The Life & Work of Jane Bowles. Millicent Dillon. LC 97-33074. 476p. 1998. pap. 17.95 (*0-520-21193-6*, Pub. by U CA Pr) Cal Prin Full Svc.

Little Orphan Anagram. Charles Bernstein. (Illus.). 40p. 1997. 1500.00 (*1-887123-14-8*) Granary Bks.

Little Orphan Annie & Other Poems. James Whitcomb Riley. 80p. 1994. pap. text 1.00 (*0-486-28260-0*) Dover.

Little Oscar. Carmen A. Fiore. LC 88-10219. 202p. (Orig.). 1988. pap. 7.95 (*0-939219-04-2*) Townhouse Pub.

Little Ouseburn Barrow, 1958. P. Rahtz. 127p. 1989. 13.95 (*0-614-21851-9*, Pub. by U York Dept Archaeol) David Brown.

Little Out of the Ordinary: Daily Reflections for Ordinary Time. John J. McIlhon. LC 93-40564. 216p. (Orig.). 1994. pap. 11.95 (*0-8146-2274-7*) Liturgical Pr.

Little Oxford Bible. 1184p. 1997. 59.99 (*0-19-110148-6*) OUP.

Little Oxford Bible. 1184p. 1999. 24.99 (*0-19-112475-3*); 24.99 (*0-19-112477-X*) OUP.

Little Oxford Bible. Little Oxford Staff. 1184p. 1997. 59.99 (*0-19-110147-8*) OUP.

***Little Oxford Bible.** Little Oxford Staff. 1999. 24.99 (*0-19-112476-1*) OUP.

Little Oxford Dictionary. Maurice Waite. LC 99-201157. 800p. 1999. 13.95 (*0-19-860205-7*) OUP.

Little Oxford Dictionary. 6th large type ed. 1987. 31.99 (*0-7089-1679-1*) Ulverscroft.

Little Oxford Dictionary of English Grammar. Ed. by Sylvia Chalker. (Illus.). 282p. (C). 1995. 12.95 (*0-19-861315-6*) OUP.

***Little Oxford Dictionary of English Grammar.** 2nd ed. Sylvia Chalker. (Illus.). 304p. 1998. pap. 7.95 (*0-19-860210-3*) OUP.

Little Oxford Dictionary of Quotations. Ed. by Susan Ratcliffe. 496p. 1995. 13.95 (*0-19-866207-6*) OUP.

Little Oxford Guide to English Usage. Andrew Delahunty & Edmund S. Weiner. 256p. 1995. 13.95 (*0-19-861301-6*) OUP.

Little Oxford Thesaurus, 1 vol. 2nd rev. ed. Alan Spooner. 622p. 1999. 13.95 (*0-19-860206-5*, Clarendon Pr) OUP.

***Little 'p'** Sellers. (J). 2000. 3.95 (*0-552-52887-0*, Pub. by Transworld Publishers Ltd) Trafalgar.

Little Package: Pages on Literature & Landscape from a Traveling Bookman's Life. Lawrence C. Powell. LC 73-156705. (Essay Index Reprint Ser.). 1977. reprint ed. 20.95 (*0-8369-2422-3*) Ayer.

Little Painter of Sabana Grande. Patricia M. Markun. LC 91-35230. (Illus.). 32p. (J). (ps-2). 1993. text 14.95 (*0-02-762205-3*, Bradbury S&S) S&S Childrens.

***Little Palm Book: A Gentle Guide to Palm III, IIIx, V & VII Devices.** Corbin Collins. (Little Book Ser.). (Illus.). 288p. 1999. pap. text 17.99 (*0-201-69954-0*) Peachpit Pr.

Little Panda. A. L. Singer. 216p. (YA). (gr. 4-7). 1995. pap. 3.50 (*0-590-55206-6*) Scholastic Inc.

Little Panda. Todd Strasser. 144p. (J). (gr. 3-7). 1995. pap. 3.50 (*0-590-55205-8*) Scholastic Inc.

Little Panda: Picture Book. Gail Herman. (Illus.). 32p. (J). (gr. k-2). 1995. pap. 2.95 (*0-590-55207-4*) Scholastic Inc.

Little Panda Bear. Koichi Ono. (Shaggies Ser.). (Illus.). 12p. (J). (ps-2). 1982. 4.95 (*0-671-42549-8*) Litle Simon.

Little Pardner, & Other Stories. Eleanor H. Porter. LC 70-142273. (Short Story Index Reprint Ser.). 1977. 20.95 (*0-8369-3757-0*) Ayer.

Little Paw: The Anthropomorphic Pin-Up of Terrie Smith. Terrie Smith. (Illus.). 112p. 1996. pap. 8.95 (*1-883847-20-6*) MU Press.

***Little Paw 4.** Terrie Smith. 112p. 2000. pap. 9.95 (*1-883847-37-0*) MU Press.

Little Paw II: Another Terrie Smith Pin-Up Anthology! Terrie Smith. (Illus.). 112p. 1997. pap. 8.95 (*1-883847-28-1*) MU Press.

Little Paw 3. Terrie Smith. 112p. 1999. pap. 9.95 (*1-883847-35-4*) MU Press.

***Little PC Book.** 3rd ed. Lawrence J. Magid. LC 99-204285. 380p. (C). 1998. pap. text 19.99 (*0-201-35366-0*, Pub. by Peachpit Pr) Addison-Wesley.

Little Peace & Quiet. Rick Charette & Laurie Bean. (Illus.). 8p. (J). (gr. k-4). 1994. pap. 9.98 incl. audio (*1-884210-06-6*, PPC-006) Energeia Pub.

Little Pear. Eleanor F. Lattimore. Ed. by Diane D'Andrade. LC 90-45526. (Odyssey Ser.). (Illus.). 144p. (J). (gr. 2-5). 1991. pap. 6.00 (*0-15-246685-1*, Harcourt Child Bks) Harcourt.

Little Pear. Eleanor F. Lattimore. (Illus.). (J). 1992. reprint ed. lib. bdg. 14.95 (*0-89966-917-4*) Buccaneer Bks.

Little Pear. Eleanor F. Lattimore. LC 31-22069. (Illus.). (J). (gr. 2-5). 1968. reprint ed. pap. 3.95 (*0-15-652799-5*, Voyager Bks) Harcourt.

Little Pear & His Friends. Eleanor F. Lattimore. LC 90-45519. (Odyssey Ser.). (Illus.). 144p. (J). (gr. 3-7). 1991. pap. 4.95 (*0-15-246863-3*, Harcourt Child Bks) Harcourt.

Little Pearls of Wisdom Book: For the Successful Dental Team. Henry Robinson. LC 95-1025. 1995. 19.95 (*0-87814-442-0*) PennWell Bks.

Little Pee-Wee Christmas Tree. Preston L. Penn. LC 98-92074. (Illus.). 24p. (J). (ps-6). 1998. text 14.95 incl. cd-rom (*0-9667210-0-4*) Little Pee-Wee.

Little Peepers for Little People. Geri Wissinger. (Illus.). 24p. (J). (ps-6). 1998. bds. 6.95 (*0-9667710-0-1*) Spent Wing Pubg.

***Little Peg: A Novel.** Kevin McIlvoy. 256p. 2000. pap. 13.00 (*0-380-81476-5*, Perennial) HarperTrade.

***Little Pelican Alphabet Book.** Gladys E. Dorfman. LC 99-95315. (Illus.). (J). (ps-2). 1999. 14.95 (*0-9671111-1-0*) Hannah Mae Ent.

Little Penguin - Fairy Penguins in Australia. Colin Stahel & Rosemary Gales. (Illus.). 117p. 1987. pap. 22.95 (*0-86840-290-7*, Pub. by New South Wales Univ Pr) Intl Spec Bk.

***Little Penguins, 6 vols.** Kimberly Joan Williams & Erik Daniel Stoops. (Young Explorer Series II). 32p. (J). (gr. 3-7). 2000. lib. bdg. 18.60 (*1-890475-22-X*) Faulkners Pub.

Little Penguin's Tale. Audrey Wood. LC 88-15715. (Illus.). 40p. (J). (ps-1). 1989. 13.95 (*0-15-246475-1*) Harcourt.

Little Penguin's Tale. Audrey Wood. LC 88-15715. (Illus.). 40p. (J). (ps-1). 1993. reprint ed. pap. 6.00 (*0-15-247476-5*, Voyager Bks) Harcourt.

Little People see Gente Pequenita

Little People. Mildred McDowell. LC 72-133255. (Story & Its Verse Ser.). (Illus.). 44p. (J). (gr. 1-2). 1971. 2.50 (*0-87884-002-8*) Unicorn Ent.

Little People. Christopher Pike, pseud. (Spooksville Ser.). 128p. (J). (gr. 4-6). 1996. per. 3.99 (*0-671-55067-5*, Minstrel Bks) PB.

Little People. Christopher Pike, pseud. (Spooksville Ser.). (J). (gr. 4-6). 1996. 9.09 (*0-606-09887-9*, Pub. by Turtleback) Demco.

Little People. Albert Halper. LC 74-26110. (Labor Movement in Fiction & Non-Fiction Ser.). reprint ed. 42.50 (*0-404-58435-7*) AMS Pr.

Little People: Guidelines for Common Sense Child Rearing. 3rd ed. Edward R. Christophersen. LC 88-20789. (Illus.). 216p. 1988. pap. 12.95 (*0-933701-32-2*) Westport Pubs.

Little People: Guidelines for Common Sense Child Rearing. 4th rev. ed. Edward Christophersen. (Illus.). 198p. 1997. pap. 12.95 (*0-930851-05-6*) Overland Pr.

Little People at Home. (Fisher-Price Little People Toddler Skills Workbooks Ser.: Vol. 4). (Illus.). (J). 1998. pap. write for info. (*0-7666-0185-4*, Honey Bear Bks) Modern Pub NYC.

Little People at Work. (Fisher-Price Little People Toddler Skills Workbooks Ser.: Vol. 3). (Illus.). (J). 1998. pap. write for info. (*0-7666-0184-6*, Honey Bear Bks) Modern Pub NYC.

Little People Big Book about Imagination. (Illus.). 64p. (J). (ps-1). 1999. 14.95 (*0-8094-7479-4*) Time-Life.

Little People, Big God. Woodrow Kroll. 1999. pap. text 12.99 (*0-8474-1472-8*) Back to Bible.

Little People Go to Town. (Fisher-Price Little People Toddler Skills Workbooks Ser.: Vol. 1). (Illus.). (J). 1998. pap. write for info. (*0-7666-0182-X*, Honey Bear Bks) Modern Pub NYC.

Little People in America: The Social Dimensions of Dwarfism. Joan Ablon. LC 84-15910. 194p. 1984. 55.00 (*0-275-91109-8*, C1109, Praeger Pubs) Greenwood.

Little People in Tough Spots: Bible Answers for Young Children. V. Gilbert Beers & Ronald A. Beers. (Illus.). 154p. (J). (ps-3). 1992. 7.99 (*0-8407-9157-7*) Nelson.

Little People of the Earth: Ceramic Figures from Ancient America. Gillett G. Griffin & Robert Stroessner. Ed. by Marlene Chambers. LC 90-81361. (Illus.). 52p. (Orig.). 1990. pap. text 16.95 (*0-914738-40-2*) Denver Art Mus.

Little People of the Lost Coast. Ernest Herndon. LC 97-1622. (Eric Sterling, Secret Agent Ser.: Bk. 8). 128p. (J). (gr. 3-7). 1997. pap. 5.99 (*0-310-20733-9*) Zondervan.

Little People on Vacation. (Fisher-Price Little People Toddler Skills Workbooks Ser.: Vol. 2). (Illus.). (J). 1998. pap. write for info. (*0-7666-0183-8*, Honey Bear Bks) Modern Pub NYC.

Little Peoples' Beginning on Michigan. Lois Parker & David McConnell. (Illus.). 32p. (Orig.). (J). (gr. 1-2). 1981. pap. 5.50 (*0-910726-06-X*) Hillsdale Educ.

Little People's Bible. Eugenio Sotillos. Ed. by Eileen Heffernan & Maria Pascual. Tr. by Nathalie Brock & Marianne L'Trouve from SPA.Tr. of Biblia de los Ninos. (Illus.). 164p. (J). (gr. 2-6). 1995. 18.95 (*0-8198-4477-2*) Pauline Bks.

Little People's Dialogues. Clara J. Denton. LC 70-98080. (Granger Index Reprint Ser.). 1977. 15.95 (*0-8369-6075-0*) Ayer.

Little People's Guide to the Big World, Vol. 1. Trevor Romain. (Illus.). 48p. (J). (ps-5). 1993. 13.95 (*1-880092-04-2*) Bright Bks TX.

Little People's Guide to the Big World, Vol. 2. Trevor Romain. LC 94-71144. (Illus.). 32p. (J). (ps-5). 1994. 13.95 (*1-880092-16-6*) Bright Bks TX.

Little People's Speaker. J. W. Shoemaker. LC 72-98086. (Granger Index Reprint Ser.). 1977. 16.95 (*0-8369-6089-0*) Ayer.

Little Person. Patrick Haley. LC 81-65114. (Illus.). 64p. (J). (gr. 2-3). 1981. lib. bdg. 9.00 (*0-9605738-0-1*) East Eagle.

Little Pet Shop of Horrors. Betsy Haynes. (Bone Chillers Ser.: No. 2). (J). (gr. 4-8). 1994. 9.09 (*0-606-07307-8*, Pub. by Turtleback) Demco.

Little Pet Werewolf. Tom B. Stone. (Graveyard School Ser.: No. 4). (J). (gr. 3-7). 1995. 8.70 (*0-606-07593-3*, Pub. by Turtleback) Demco.

Little Petey & Big. Tim Mahurin. 1999. 14.99 (*0-525-45447-0*) NAL.

Little Philip. Leo Tolstoy. 12.95 (*0-86315-188-4*, 1785, Pub. by Floris Bks) Anthroposophic.

***Little Phoenix.** Wang Ling-chi. 2000. pap. 13.95 (*0-533-13296-7*) Vantage.

Little Pianist Opus 823: Complete for the Piano. Carl Czerny. 64p. 1986. pap. 5.95 (*0-7935-2597-7*) H Leonard.

***Little Pickpocket.** Avner Katz.Tr. of Kayas Ha-Katan. (Illus.). 27p. (J). (ps-2). 1999. reprint ed. text 15.00 (*0-7881-6596-8*) DIANE Pub.

***Little Piece of Sky.** Nicole L. Bailey-Williams. 128p. (YA). (gr. 9-12). 2000. pap. 8.95 (*0-9700186-0-6*) Sugarenes.

Little Pieces of Light: Darkness & Personal Growth. Joyce Rupp. LC 94-30803. (Illumination Bks.). 80p. 1994. pap. 5.95 (*0-8091-3512-4*) Paulist Pr.

Little Pig. Cullinan. 1994. text 13.90 (*0-15-302314-7*) Harcourt.

Little Pig. Judy Dunn. LC 86-42956. (Pictureback Ser.). (Illus.). 32p. (J). (ps-3). 1987. pap. 2.25 (*0-394-88774-3*) Random Bks Yng Read.

Little Pig, Bigger Trouble. Eve Tharlet. Tr. by Andrew Clements. LC 91-40637. (Illus.). 28p. (J). (gr. k up). 1992. pap. 14.95 (*0-88708-237-8*, Picture Book Studio) S&S Childrens.

Little Pig Goes a Long Way. George Miller & Chris Noonan. LC 98-30342. (Babe Ser.). 48p. (J). (gr. k-3). 1999. lib. bdg. 11.99 (*0-375-90110-8*) Random.

Little Pigeon Toad. Fred Gwynne. LC 88-11501. (Illus.). 48p. (J). (ps up). 1990. pap. 6.99 (*0-671-69444-8*) S&S Bks Yung.

Little Piggy. Kath Mellentin & Tim Wood. (Farm Babies Ser.). (Illus.). 10p. (J). 1997. bds. 3.50 (*1-884628-60-5*, Flyng Frog) Allied Pub MD.

Little Pig's Bouncy Ball. Alan Baron. LC 95-35347. (Illus.). 24p. (J). (ps). 1997. reprint ed. pap. 3.29 (*0-7636-0126-8*) Candlewick Pr.

Little Pilgrim Girl. Tom Tierney. (Little Activity Bks.). (Illus.). (J). 1994. pap. 1.00 (*0-486-27945-6*) Dover.

Little Pilgrimages among Old New England Inns: Being an Account of Little Journeys to Various Quaint Inns & Hotelries of Colonial New England. Mary C. Crawford. (Illus.). 381p. 1998. reprint ed. pap. 30.00 (*0-7884-0873-9*, C608) Heritage Bk.

Little Pilgrims Progress see Joven Peregrino

Little Pilgrim's Progress. Helen L. Taylor. (J). (gr. 2-7). pap. 7.99 (*0-8024-4926-3*, 551) Moody.

Little Pillows: Good-Night Thoughts for the Little Ones. Frances R. Havergal. (Illus.). 104p. (Orig.). 1978. pap. 3.50 (*1-880960-04-4*) Script Memory Fl.

Little Pine Tree's Christmas Dream. Clarence Thomson. LC 93-5301. (Illus.). 32p. (Orig.). (J). (gr. 1-6). 1993. pap. 4.95 (*0-8091-6614-3*) Paulist Pr.

Little Pink Book: Quotations on Women's Issues. Oline Luinenburg & Stephen Osborne. 96p. 1995. per. 4.95 (*0-88978-226-1*, Pub. by Arsenal Pulp) LPC InBook.

Little Pink Pig. Pat Hutchins. LC 93-18176. (Illus.). 32p. (J). (ps-3). 1994. 16.00 (*0-688-12014-8*, Grenwillow Bks) HarpC Child Bks.

Little Pink Pig. Pat Hutchins. LC 93-18176. (Illus.). 32p. (J). (ps up). 1994. lib. bdg. 15.93 (*0-688-12015-6*, Grenwillow Bks) HarpC Child Bks.

***Little Pink Pig.** Pat Hutchins. LC 93-18176. (Illus.). 32p. (YA). (ps up). 2000. pap. 5.95 (*0-688-17516-3*, Wm Morrow) Morrow Avon.

***Little Pink Pig.** Pat Hutchins. (Illus.). (J). 2000. 11.40 (*0-606-18703-0*) Turtleback.

Little Pioneer Girl Paper Doll. Barbara Steadman. (Illus.). (J). 1997. pap. 1.00 (*0-486-29519-2*) Dover.

Little Pischna: Forty-Eight Preparatory Exercises for Piano. B. Wolff. (Carl Fischer Music Library: No. 475). (ENG & GER.). (J). 1907. pap. 4.00 (*0-8258-0122-2*, L 475) Fischer Inc NY.

Little Pischna: 48 Practice Pieces for the Piano. J. Pischna. 40p. 1986. pap. 3.95 (*0-7935-5312-1*) H Leonard.

Little Plains Indian Girl. Kathy Allert. (Little Activity Bks.). (Illus.). (J). 1995. pap. 1.00 (*0-486-28427-1*) Dover.

***Little Plane.** Opal Dunn. (Track-Me-Back Board Bks.). 12p. (J). 2000. bds. 5.95 (*0-8050-6418-4*) H Holt & Co.

Little Plane. Sian Tucker. (Illus.). 10p. (J). (ps). 1993. 2.95 (*0-671-79735-2*) Little Simon.

Little Planet & the Magic Hats. Bill Crain. Ed. by T. J. Zark. (Little Planet Literacy Ser.). (Illus.). 48p. (Orig.). (J). (gr. k-5). 1995. pap. write for info. (*0-9644866-4-4*) App Learn Tech.

Little Platoons: Local Governments in Modern History. George W. Liebmann. LC 95-5308. 192p. 1995. 57.95 (*0-275-95178-2*, Praeger Pubs) Greenwood.

Little Plays for Little People: Theatre, Games & Activities. Chari R. Greenberg. LC 95-44205. xi, 135p. 1996. pap. text 19.00 (*1-56308-372-8*) Teacher Ideas Pr.

Little Pleasures. Elisabeth Brami. (Illus.). 68p. 1996. 12.95 (*0-7892-0046-5*) Abbeville Pr.

Little Poems for Little People. Harry Bornstein et al. (Signed English Ser.). (Illus.). 56p. (J). (ps-3). 1974. pap. 6.50 (*0-913580-31-7*, Pub. by K Green Pubns) Gallaudet Univ Pr.

Little Poems in Prose. rev. ed. Charles Baudelaire. Ed. by Martin P. Starr. Tr. & Illus. by Aleister Crowley. LC 93-34882. 144p. 1995. 29.95 (*0-933429-08-8*) Teitan Pr.

Little Point Guard, the Greg Brown Story (a Mother's Perspective) Mary Brown. (Illus.). 124p. (Orig.). 1994. 24.95 (*1-880047-20-9*); pap. text 12.95 (*1-880047-16-0*) Creative Des.

Little Polar Bear see Kleiner Eisbar, Wohin Fahrst Du?

Little Polar Bear see Voyage de Plume

Little Polar Bear. Hans De Beer. LC 86-33208. (Illus.). 32p. (J). (gr. k-3). 1987. 15.95 (*1-55858-024-7*, Pub. by North-South Bks NYC) Chronicle Bks.

Little Polar Bear. Hans De Beer. LC 86-33208. (Illus.). 32p. (J). (gr. k-3). 1994. pap. 6.95 (*1-55858-358-0*, Pub. by North-South Bks NYC) Chronicle Bks.

Little Polar Bear. Hans De Beer. (JPN., Illus.). 32p. (J). (gr. k-3). 1997. 15.95 (*4-924684-43-0*, Pub. by North-South Bks NYC) Chronicle Bks.

An Asterisk (*) at the beginning of an entry indicates that the title is appearing for the first time.

Little Polar Bear. Hans De Beer. (Illus.). 14p. (J). (ps). 1999. bds. 6.95 (*0-7358-1080-X*, Pub. by North-South Bks NYC) Chronicle Bks.

Little Polar Bear. Hans De Beer. 1994. 12.15 (*0-606-08803-2*, Pub. by Turtleback) Demco.

Little Polar Bear: A Pop-Up Book. Hans De Beer. (Illus.). 32p. (J). (gr. k-3). 1993. 15.95 (*1-55858-226-6*, Pub. by North-South Bks NYC) Chronicle Bks.

***Little Polar Bear: Mini Book & Audio Package.** Hans De Beer. (Illus.). (J). (gr. k-3). 2000. 11.95 incl. audio (*0-7358-1275-6*, Pub. by North-South Bks NYC) Chronicle Bks.

Little Polar Bear: Mini Pop-Up Book. Hans De Beer. (Illus.). 16p. (J). (ps-2). 1997. 7.95 (*1-55858-711-X*, Pub. by North-South Bks NYC) Chronicle Bks.

Little Polar Bear Address Book. Hans De Beer. (Illus.). 120p. (J). 1990. 7.95 (*1-55858-080-8*, Pub. by North-South Bks NYC) Chronicle Bks.

Little Polar Bear & the Brave Little Hare see Piuma E il Coniglietto Fifone

Little Polar Bear & the Brave Little Hare see Kleine Eisbar und der Angsthase

Little Polar Bear & the Brave Little Hare see Plume et la Station Polaire

Little Polar Bear & the Brave Little Hare. Hans De Beer. LC 92-9803. (Illus.). 48p. (J). (gr. 1-3). 1994. pap. 5.95 (*1-55858-357-2*, Pub. by North-South Bks NYC) Chronicle Bks.

Little Polar Bear & the Brave Little Hare. Hans De Beer. LC 98-17134. (Illus.). 32p. (J). (gr. k-3). 1998. 15.95 (*0-7358-1011-7*, Pub. by North-South Bks NYC); lib. bdg. 15.88 (*0-7358-1012-5*, Pub. by North-South Bks NYC) Chronicle Bks.

***Little Polar Bear & the Brave Little Hare.** Hans De Beer. (Illus.). 32p. (gr. k-3). 2000. pap. 6.95 (*0-7358-1332-9*) North-South Bks NYC.

Little Polar Bear & the Husky Pup see Kleiner Eisbar, Lass Mich Nicht Allein!

Little Polar Bear & the Husky Pup see Plume et le Chien de Traineau

Little Polar Bear & the Husky Pup see Pluma e il Cucciolo di Husky

Little Polar Bear & the Husky Pup. Hans De Beer. LC 99-17369. (Illus.). 32p. (J). (ps-3). 1999. lib. bdg. 15.88 (*0-7358-1155-5*, Pub. by North-South Bks NYC) Chronicle Bks.

***Little Polar Bear & the Husky Pup.** Hans De Beer. LC 99-17369. (Illus.). 32p. (J). (ps-3). 1999. 15.95 (*0-7358-1154-7*, Pub. by North-South Bks NYC) Chronicle Bks.

Little Polar Bear Big Bear see Osito Polar Libro Grande

***Little Polar Bear Big Book.** Hans De Beer. (Illus.). 32p. (J). (gr. k-3). 1999. pap. 19.95 (*0-7358-1216-0*, Pub. by North-South Bks NYC) Chronicle Bks.

Little Polar Bear Birthday Book. Hans De Beer. (Illus.). 120p. (J). 1990. 7.95 (*1-55858-081-6*, Pub. by North-South Bks NYC) Chronicle Bks.

Little Polar Bear Finds a Friend see Kleiner Eisbar, Nimm Mich Mit!

Little Polar Bear Finds a Friend see Plume S'Echappe

Little Polar Bear Finds a Friend. Hans De Beer. LC 89-43727. (Illus.). 32p. (J). (gr. k-3). 1990. 15.95 (*1-55858-092-1*, Pub. by North-South Bks NYC) Chronicle Bks.

Little Polar Bear Finds a Friend. Hans De Beer. LC 89-43727. (Illus.). 32p. (J). (gr. k-3). 1996. pap. 6.95 (*1-55858-607-5*, Pub. by North-South Bks NYC) Chronicle Bks.

Little Polar Bear Finds a Friend. Hans De Beer. (JPN., Illus.). 32p. (J). (gr. k-3). 1997. 15.95 (*4-924684-56-2*, Pub. by North-South Bks NYC) Chronicle Bks.

Little Polar Bear Journal. North-South Books Staff. (J). 1998. 8.95 (*1-55858-909-0*, Pub. by North-South Bks NYC) Chronicle Bks.

Little Polar Bear Mini Book. Hans De Beer. LC 86-33208. (Illus.). 32p. (J). (gr. k-3). 1989. pap. 6.95 (*1-55858-030-1*, Pub. by North-South Bks NYC) Chronicle Bks.

Little Polar Bear, Take Me Home! see Kleiner Eisbar, Kennst du Den Weg?

Little Polar Bear, Take Me Home! see Plume au Pays des Tigres

Little Polar Bear, Take Me Home! see Piuma Nel Paese delle Tigri

Little Polar Bear, Take Me Home! Hans De Beer. LC 96-25525. (Illus.). 32p. (J). (gr. k-3). 1996. 15.95 (*1-55858-630-X*, Pub. by North-South Bks NYC); lib. bdg. 15.88 (*1-55858-631-8*, Pub. by North-South Bks NYC) Chronicle Bks.

***Little Polar Bear with Doll.** Hans De Beer. (Illus.). (ps-k). 2000. bds. 12.95 (*0-7358-1237-3*) North-South Bks NYC.

Little Polish Cookbook. Mary Pininska. (Illus.). 60p. 1992. 7.95 (*0-8118-0262-0*) Chronicle Bks.

Little Pony. Kath Mellentin & Tim Wood. (Farm Babies Ser.). (Illus.). 10p. (J). 1997. bds. 3.50 (*1-884628-57-5*, Flyng Frog) Allied Pub MD.

Little Porcupine's Winter Den. Susan Thompson-Hoffman. (Smithsonian Wild Heritage Collection). (J). 1992. 10.15 (*0-606-07798-7*, Pub. by Turtleback) Demco.

Little Poss & Horrible Hound see Bank Street Ready-to-Read Books: Levels 1, 2 & 3

Little Potted Gardens: Simple Secrets for Glorious Gardens, Indoors & Out. Mimi Luebbermann. LC 97-30800. 1998. pap. text 14.95 (*0-8118-1603-6*) Chronicle Bks.

Little PoTweet. Jim George. LC 96-5808. (Ha! Ser.). (Illus.). 32p. (Orig.). (J). (ps). 1996. pap. write for info. (*1-56844-046-4*) Enchante Pub.

Little Prairie House. Laura Ingalls Wilder. (My First Little House Bks.). (Illus.). 32p. (J). (ps-1). 1999. pap. 5.95 (*0-06-443526-1*) HarpC Child Bks.

Little Prairie House. adapted ed. Laura Ingalls Wilder. LC 96-24060. (My First Little House Bks.). (Illus.). 40p. (J). (ps-3). 1998. 12.95 (*0-06-025907-8*); lib. bdg. 12.89 (*0-06-025908-6*) HarpC.

***Little Prayers & Graces: A Shinging Bright Book.** Illus. by Anne Kennedy. (Baby Blessings Ser.). 12p. (J). 2000. bds. 6.99 (*0-7847-1139-9*, 04319) Standard Pub.

Little Prayers for Little Ones. Zondervan Publishing Staff. (Little Ones Bk.). (J). (ps-3). 5.99 (*0-310-97173-X*) Zondervan.

Little Preacher. Elizabeth Prentiss & George Prentiss. 175p. (Orig.). 1993. pap. 8.95 (*1-879737-10-8*) Calvary Press.

Little Pregnant: Our Memoir of Fertility, Infertility & a Marriage. Linda Carbone & Ed Decker. LC 99-19217. 240p. 1999. 23.00 (*0-87113-751-8*, Pub. by Grove-Atltic) Publishers Group.

Little Pretender. Barbara Cartland. 286p. 1999. 10.95 (*1-885478-72-0*, Pub. by Genesis Press) BookWorld.

Little Prince. James E. Higgins. 1996. 29.00 (*0-8057-8372-5*, Twyne); per. 14.95 (*0-8057-8585-X*, Twyne) Mac Lib Ref.

Little Prince. Antoine de Saint-Exupery. 17.95 (*0-89190-331-3*) Amereon Ltd.

Little Prince. Antoine de Saint-Exupery. Tr. by Katherine Woods. LC 67-1144. (Illus.). 97p. (J). (gr. 4-7). 1943. 16.00 (*0-15-246503-0*, Harcourt Child Bks) Harcourt.

Little Prince. Antoine de Saint-Exupery. Tr. by Katherine Woods. LC 67-1144. (Illus.). 128p. (J). (gr. 3 up). 1968. pap. 6.00 (*0-15-652820-7*) Harcourt.

***Little Prince.** Antoine de Saint-Exupery. Tr. by Richard Howard from FRE. (Illus.). 96p. (J). 2000. 18.00 (*0-15-202398-4*); pap. 12.00 (*0-15-601207-3*); pap. 8.00 (*0-15-601219-7*) Harcourt.

Little Prince. Antoine de Saint-Exupery. (J). 1971. 11.10 (*0-606-03815-9*, Pub. by Turtleback) Demco.

Little Prince. Antoine de Saint-Exupery. (J). 1998. pap. 3.95 NTC Contemp Pub Co.

***Little Prince.** Antoine de Saint-Exupery. (Illus.). (J). 2000. 17.45 (*0-606-18806-1*) Turtleback.

Little Prince. large type ed. Antoine de Saint-Exupery. 125p. 1995. 19.95 (*0-7838-1548-4*, G K Hall Lrg Type) Mac Lib Ref.

Little Prince. Antoine de Saint-Exupery. (J). 1992. reprint ed. lib. bdg. 18.95 (*0-89968-299-5*, Lghtyr Pr) Buccaneer Bks.

Little Prince, Large-Format, Color Edition. Antoine de Saint-Exupery. Tr. by Katherine Woods. LC 67-1144. (Illus.). 97p. (J). (gr. 4-7). 1982. pap. 7.00 (*0-15-646511-6*, Harvest Bks) Harcourt.

Little Prince: A Study Guide. Nicholas Aversa. Ed. by J. Friedland & R. Kessler. (Novel-Ties Ser.). (J). (gr. 6-8). 1987. pap. text, student ed. 15.95 (*0-88122-118-X*) Lrn Links.

***Little Prince - Str., Large Cast.** Rick Cummins & John Scoullar. 89p. 2000. pap. 5.60 (*1-58342-005-3*, LA3) Dramatic Pub.

Little Prince & the Great Treasure Hunt. Peter Kavanagh. LC 96-84984. (Illus.). 32p. (J). (ps-2). 1997. pap. text 4.95 (*0-7641-0001-7*) Barron.

Little Prince Know-It-All. Sheila K. Welch. LC 98-5795. (Road to Reading Ser.). (Illus.). 48p. (J). 1998. pap. 3.99 (*0-307-26301-0*, 26301) Gldn Bks Pub Co.

Little Princes in the Tower. William W. Lace. LC 96-21509. (Mysterious Deaths Ser.). (Illus.). (YA). 1996. lib. bdg. 22.45 (*1-56006-262-2*) Lucent Bks.

Little Princess see Princesita

Little Princess. Carol M. Adorjan. (Troll Illustrated Classics). (Illus.). (J). 1988. 10.15 (*0-606-03607-5*, Pub. by Turtleback) Demco.

Little Princess. Frances Hodgson Burnett. (J). 16.95 (*0-8488-1253-0*) Amereon Ltd.

Little Princess. Frances Hodgson Burnett. 300p. (J). 1977. lib. bdg. 15.95 (*0-89967-005-9*, Harmony Rain) Buccaneer Bks.

***Little Princess.** Frances Hodgson Burnett. LC 00-31778. (Juvenile Classics). (Illus.). 2000. pap. write for info. (*0-486-41446-9*) Dover.

Little Princess. Frances Hodgson Burnett. LC 63-15435. (Illus.). 336p. (J). (gr. 4-7). 1999. 16.95 (*0-397-30693-8*) HarpC Child Bks.

Little Princess. Frances Hodgson Burnett. LC 99-27022. (Illus.). 40p. (J). (ps-3). 2000. 16.95 (*0-06-027891-9*) HarpC Child Bks.

***Little Princess.** Frances Hodgson Burnett. LC 97-43631. (Illus.). 40p. (J). (ps-3). 2000. lib. bdg. 16.89 (*0-06-029010-2*) HarpC Child Bks.

***Little Princess.** Frances Hodgson Burnett. (Illus.). 44p. 1998. pap. 5.25 (*0-19-422875-4*) OUP.

Little Princess. Frances Hodgson Burnett. LC 94-43353. (Illustrated Junior Library). (Illus.). 288p. (J). (gr. 4-7). 1995. 14.95 (*0-448-40949-6*, G & D) Peng Put Young Read.

Little Princess. Frances Hodgson Burnett. (Illus.). 304p. (YA). (gr. 4-7). 1995. pap. 4.99 (*0-14-036688-1*, PuffinBks) Peng Put Young Read.

Little Princess. Frances Hodgson Burnett. LC 93-14000. (Step into Classics Ser.). 107p. (J). (gr. 2-6). 1994. pap. 3.99 (*0-679-85090-2*) Random.

Little Princess. Frances Hodgson Burnett. (Bullseye Step into Classics Ser.). 108p. (J). (gr. 2-6). 1994. pap. 2.99 (*0-685-71036-X*) Random Bks Yng Read.

***Little Princess.** Frances Hodgson Burnett. (Unabridged Classics Ser.). 224p. (YA). 2000. pap. 5.98 (*0-7624-0548-1*, Courage) Running Pr.

Little Princess. Frances Hodgson Burnett. (Illus.). (J). 22.95 (*0-590-24079-X*) Scholastic Inc.

Little Princess. Frances Hodgson Burnett. 256p. (J). (gr. 4-7). 1995. pap. 3.99 (*0-590-54307-5*, Apple Classics) Scholastic Inc.

***Little Princess.** Frances Hodgson Burnett. (Illus.). 272p. (gr. 4-7). 2000. pap. 4.99 (*0-439-10137-9*) Scholastic Inc.

Little Princess. Frances Hodgson Burnett. LC 87-15485. (Illus.). 48p. (J). (gr. 3-6). 1988. lib. bdg. 19.95 (*0-8167-1201-8*) Troll Communs.

Little Princess. Frances Hodgson Burnett. (J). 1997. pap. 2.95 (*0-89375-500-1*) Troll Communs.

Little Princess. Frances Hodgson Burnett. LC 87-15485. (Illus.). 48p. (J). (ps-3). 1998. pap. 5.95 (*0-8167-1202-6*) Troll Communs.

Little Princess. Frances Hodgson Burnett. (Children's Library). (J). Date not set. pap. 3.95 (*1-85326-136-X*, 136XWW, Pub. by Wrdsworth Edits) NTC Contemp Pub Co.

Little Princess. Frances Hodgson Burnett. 1997. pap. text 12.95 (*0-14-086079-7*, PuffinBks) Peng Put Young Read.

Little Princess. Illus. by Natalie Carabetta. LC 96-22426. (All Aboard Reading Ser.: Level 3). 48p. (J). (gr. 2-3). 1996. pap. 3.95 (*0-448-41327-2*, G & D); lib. bdg. 13.99 (*0-448-41329-9*, G & D) Peng Put Young Read.

***Little Princess.** Lucy Coats et al. LC 00-24162. (Young Classics Ser.). (Illus.). (J). 2000. pap. write for info. (*0-7894-6679-1*) DK Pub Inc.

Little Princess. Cathy East Dubowski. LC 93-14000. (Bullseye Step into Classics Ser.). 1994. 9.09 (*0-606-09564-0*, Pub. by Turtleback) Demco.

Little Princess. Deborah Hautzig. (All Aboard Reading Ser.). (J). 1996. 9.15 (*0-606-11570-6*, Pub. by Turtleback) Demco.

Little Princess. Roderick McGillis. 1996. 29.00 (*0-8057-8818-2*, Twyne) Mac Lib Ref.

Little Princess. Roderick McGillis. (Illus.). 144p. 1996. pap. 18.00 (*0-8057-8819-0*, Twyne) Mac Lib Ref.

Little Princess. June W. Rogers. 1978. pap. 3.75 (*0-87129-197-5*, L40) Dramatic Pub.

Little Princess. abr. ed. Frances Hodgson Burnett. (Children's Thrift Classics Ser.). (Illus.). 96p. (J). (gr. 1). 1996. pap. 1.00 (*0-486-29171-5*) Dover.

Little Princess. deluxe ed. Adapted by M. J. Carr. LC 95-196150. 48p. (J). (gr. 4-7). 1995. pap. 12.95 (*0-590-48627-6*) Scholastic Inc.

Little Princess. large type ed. Frances Hodgson Burnett. (Large Print Heritage Ser.). 324p. (YA). 1998. lib. bdg. 31.95 (*1-58118-021-7*, 21998) LRS.

Little Princess. Frances Hodgson Burnett. 232p. (J). 1981. reprint ed. lib. bdg. 15.95 (*0-89966-327-3*) Buccaneer Bks.

Little Princess. Frances Hodgson Burnett. LC 88-46102. (Illus.). 192p. (YA). (gr. 5 up). 2000. reprint ed. 18.95 (*0-87923-784-8*) Godine.

Little Princess. Frances Hodgson Burnett. LC 63-15435. (Trophy Bk.). (Illus.). 336p. (J). (gr. 4-7). 1987. reprint ed. pap. 4.95 (*0-06-440187-1*, HarpTrophy) HarpC Child Bks.

Little Princess, Set. unabridged ed. Frances Hodgson Burnett. (YA). (gr. 3 up). 1995. 24.95 incl. audio (*0-945353-94-4*, H90394, Pub. by Audio Partners) Publishers Group.

Little Princess: Keepsake Book & 8 Notebooks. (Keepsake Collection Bks.). (J). 1998. boxed set 3.99 (*1-57145-074-2*, Thunder Bay) Advantage Pubs.

Little Princess: Picture Book. Frances Hodgson Burnett. (Illus.). 32p. (J). (gr. k-2). 1995. pap. 2.95 (*0-590-55204-X*) Scholastic Inc.

Little Princess Book & Charm. Frances Hodgson Burnett. (Charming Classic Bks.). (Illus.). 336p. (YA). (gr. 4-7). 1999. 5.95 (*0-694-01236-X*, HarpFestival) HarpC Child Bks.

***Little Princess Coloring Book.** Frances Hodgson Burnett. (Illus.). 48p. (J). 1999. pap. 2.95 (*0-486-40561-3*) Dover.

Little Princess Paper Dolls. Frances Hodgson Burnett. (J). (ps-3). 1999. pap. 7.95 (*0-694-00970-9*, HarpFestival) HarpC Child Bks.

Little Princess Picture Book. McClintock. LC 97-43631. (Illus.). 40p. (J). (ps-3). pap. 4.95 (*0-06-443539-3*) HarpC Child Bks.

Little Princess, Sara Crewe. Nancy Seale. (J). 1982. 6.50 (*0-87602-231-X*) Anchorage.

Little Princess's Musical Adventures. Vera Sharp. Orig. Title: Little Princess's Symphony. (Illus.). 76p. (J). boxed set, vinyl bd. Price not set. incl. audio (*0-9616987-0-5*) V Sharp.

Little Princess's Symphony see Little Princess's Musical Adventures

***Little Princess/The Secret Garden.** Frances Hodgson Burnett. 480p. 1999. reprint ed. 8.98 (*0-7624-0564-3*) Running Pr.

Little Prissy & T. C. Colene Copeland. LC 88-81916. (Priscilla Ser.: No. 2). (Illus.). 114p. (Orig.). (J). (gr. 2 up). 1988. 8.95 (*0-939810-07-7*); pap. 3.95 (*0-939810-08-5*) Jordan Valley.

Little Puddles. Magus Magnus. (Poetry I Ser.). (Illus.). 96p. (Orig.). 1994. pap. 10.00 (*0-9638061-0-6*) M DeLeon Bksmith.

Little Puff. Margaret Hillert. (Illus.). (J). (ps-2). 1973. pap. 5.10 (*0-8136-5514-5*); lib. bdg. 7.95 (*0-8136-5014-3*) Modern Curr.

Little Pumpkin Book. Katharine Ross. LC 91-67669. (Chunky Shape Bks.). (Illus.). 22p. (J). (ps). 1992. 3.99 (*0-679-83384-6*, Pub. by Random Bks Yng Read) Random.

***Little Pumpkin Book.** Katharine Ross. (Jellybean Bks.). (Illus.). 24p. (J). (ps-k). 1999. 1.99 (*0-375-80106-5*, Pub. by Random Bks Yng Read); lib. bdg. 7.99 (*0-375-90106-X*, Pub. by Random Bks Yng Read) Random.

Little Pupfish of Salt Creek: Death Valley National Park (Endangered Species) large type ed. Patricia S. Brandt. LC 96-160951. (Illus.). 38p. (Orig.). (J). (gr. k-5). 1995. pap. 5.95 (*0-9649493-0-X*) P S Brandt.

Little Puppy. Judy Dunn. LC 84-2031. (Pictureback Ser.). (Illus.). 32p. (J). (ps-3). 1984. pap. 3.25 (*0-394-86595-2*, Pub. by Random Bks Yng Read) Random.

***Little Puppy.** Kim Lewis. LC 99-34817. (Illus.). 24p. (J). 2000. 9.99 (*0-7636-0901-3*) Candlewick Pr.

***Little Puppy Adventures.** Jenny Millington. LC 98-183779. (Illus.). 10p. (J). (ps-1). 1998. 7.98 (*0-7651-0693-0*) Smithmark.

Little Puppy That Lost Its Tail. Bernadine Cook. LC 94-90799. (Illus.). 16p. (J). (ps-3). 1995. pap. 4.00 (*0-9604726-7-3*) Enterprise Pr.

L

Little Purple Cow of Murphysboro. Illus. by Juanita Merrifield. 18p. (Orig.). (J). (ps-6). 1995. pap. 6.00 (*0-9656822-0-X*) Purple Cow.

***Little 'q'** Sellers. (J). 2000. 3.95 (*0-552-52888-9*, Pub. by Transworld Publishers Ltd) Trafalgar.

Little Quack. Betty Gibson & Kady M. Denton.Tr. of Couac, la Petite Cane. (FRE., Illus.). (J). pap. 13.99 incl. audio (*0-590-73930-1*) Scholastic Inc.

Little Quack. Margaret Hillert. (Illus.). (J). (ps-2). 1961. pap. 5.10 (*0-8136-5544-7*); lib. bdg. 7.95 (*0-8136-5044-5*) Modern Curr.

Little Quaker Sociology Book with Glossary. Lyn Cope-Robinson. (Illus.). 165p. (Orig.). (C). 1995. pap. 14.99 (*1-887774-01-7*) Canmore Pr.

Little Queen: (The Story of) St. Therese of the Child Jesus see Little Flower: The Story of Saint Therese of the Child Jesus

Little Quiet Book. Katharine Ross. LC 88-62101. (Chunky Bks. Ser.). (Illus.). 28p. (J). (ps). 1989. 3.99 (*0-394-82899-2*, Pub. by Random Bks Yng Read) Random.

Little Quilts All Through the House. Alice Berg et al. Ed. by Ursula G. Reikes. LC 93-2611. (Illus.). 80p. 1993. pap. 21.95 (*1-56477-033-8*, B163) Martingale & Co.

***Little 'r'** Sellers. (J). 2000. 3.95 (*0-552-52889-7*, Pub. by Transworld Publishers Ltd) Trafalgar.

Little Rabbit. Sanduik Bokforlag. (Illus.). 9p. (J). (ps). 1994. 19.99 (*1-881445-38-0*) Sandvik Pub.

Little Rabbit. Judy Dunn. LC 79-5241. (Pictureback Ser.). (Illus.). 32p. (J). (ps). 1980. pap. 3.25 (*0-394-84377-0*, Pub. by Random Bks Yng Read) Random.

Little Rabbit. Judy Dunn. 1980. 8.45 (*0-606-12399-7*, Pub. by Turtleback) Demco.

Little Rabbit & the Sea see Conejito y el Mar

Little Rabbit & the Sea. Gavin Bishop. LC 97-16444. (Illus.). 32p. (J). (ps-1). 1997. 15.95 (*1-55858-809-4*, Pub. by North-South Bks NYC); lib. bdg. 15.88 (*1-55858-810-8*, Pub. by North-South Bks NYC) Chronicle Bks.

***Little Rabbit & the Sea.** Gavin Bishop. LC 97-16444. (Illus.). 32p. (J). (ps-1). 2000. pap. 6.95 (*0-7358-1312-4*, Pub. by North-South Bks NYC) Chronicle Bks.

***Little Rabbit & the Sea.** Gavin Bishop. (Illus.). (J). 2000. 12.40 (*0-606-18322-1*) Turtleback.

Little Rabbit Foo Foo. Michael J. Rosen. LC 90-9598. (Illus.). 32p. (J). (ps-1). 1993. pap. 5.99 (*0-671-79604-6*) Litle Simon.

Little Rabbit Foo Foo. Michael J. Rosen. LC 90-9598. (Illus.). 32p. (J). (ps-1). 1990. pap. 15.00 (*0-671-70968-2*) S&S Bks Yung.

Little Rabbit Goes to Sleep. Tony Johnston. LC 92-8543. (Trophy Picture Bk.). (Illus.). 32p. (J). (ps-k). 1995. pap. 4.95 (*0-06-443388-9*) HarpC Child Bks.

Little Rabbit Goes to Sleep. Tony Johnston. (J). 1994. 10.15 (*0-606-07799-5*) Turtleback.

Little Rabbit Is Sad. large type ed. Deborah Williams. (Illus.). 12p. (Orig.). (J). (gr. k-2). 1997. pap. 4.25 (*1-879835-99-1*) Kaeden Corp.

Little Rabbit Who Wanted Red Wings. Carolyn S. Bailey. (All Aboard Bks.). (Illus.). 32p. (J). (ps-1). 1988. pap. 2.99 (*0-448-19089-3*, G & D) Peng Put Young Read.

***Little Rabbit Who Wanted Red Wings.** Carolyn Sherwin Bailey. (Picture Puzzle Board Bks.). (Illus.). 12p. (J). (ps-3). 2000. bds. 6.99 (*0-8431-7567-2*, Price Stern) Peng Put Young Read.

Little Rabbit's Bedtime. Alan Baker. (Illus.). 12p. (J). (ps up). 1998. 10.95 (*0-7534-5143-3*, Kingfisher) LKC.

Little Rabbit's First Number Book. Alan Baker. LC 98-12836. (Little Rabbit Bks.). (J). (gr. 2 up). 1998. 11.95 (*0-7534-5167-0*, Kingfisher) LKC.

***Little Rabbit's First Number Book.** Kate Petty. (Illus.). 30p. (J). 1998. pap. 12.98 (*1-58048-054-3*) Sandvik Pub.

Little Rabbit's First Time Book. Alan Baker. LC 99-11823. (YA). (ps up). 1999. 11.95 (*0-7534-5220-0*) LKC.

Little Rabbit's First Word Book. Alan Baker. (Illus.). 40p. (J). (ps up). 1995. 11.95 (*0-7534-5020-8*) LKC.

Little Rabbit's Loose Tooth. Lucy Bate. LC 75-6833. (Illus.). 32p. (J). (gr. k-3). 1988. pap. 5.99 (*0-517-55122-5*, Pub. by Crown Bks Yng Read) Random.

Little Rabbit's Loose Tooth. Lucy Bate. (J). 1975. 11.19 (*0-606-02965-6*, Pub. by Turtleback) Demco.

Little Rabbit's New Tail. A. J. Wood. LC 98-133296. (Illus.). 16p. (J). (ps). 1998. 12.95 (*0-7613-0292-1*) Millbrook Pr.

Little Rabbit's Snacktime. Alan Baker. LC 97-39697. (Little Rabbit Bks.). (Illus.). 20p. (J). (ps-k). 1998. 10.95 (*0-7534-5144-1*, Kingfisher) LKC.

Little Raccoon Catches a Cold. Susan Canizares. LC 97-49177. (Side-by-Side Ser.). (Illus.). (J). 1997. write for info. (*0-590-10969-3*); pap. 3.50 (*0-590-02601-1*) Scholastic Inc.

Little Rain Forest Activity Book. Suzanne Ross. (Illus.). (J). 1995. pap. 1.00 (*0-486-28569-3*) Dover.

Little Rainman. Karen Sicoli. Ed. by R. Wayne Gilpin. (Illus.). 60p. (Orig.). 1996. pap. 16.95 (*1-885477-29-5*) Fut Horizons.

Little Rascals: The Life & Times of Our Gang. enl. ed. Leonard Maltin & Richard W. Bann. LC 92-16724. 1992. pap. 20.00 (*0-517-58325-9*, Crown) Crown Pub Group.

An Asterisk (*) at the beginning of an entry indicates that the title is appearing for the first time.

Little Readers for Little Readers, Vol. I. Cheryl C. McLean & Linda M. Smiley. (Illus.). 229p. (J). (gr. k-1). 1996. teacher ed., spiral bd. 50.00 (*1-929459-00-9*, Pub. by Lttle Readers) Poor Richards.

Little Readers for Little Readers: Spanish Supplement. Cheryl C. McLean & Linda M. Smiley. (ENG & SPA., Illus.). 110p. (J). (gr. k-1). 1997. teacher ed. 25.00 (*1-929459-01-7*, Pub. by Lttle Readers) Poor Richards.

***Little Readers for Little Readers, with Pointers, 2 vols., Vol. II.** Cheryl C. McLean & Linda M. Smiley. (Illus.). 116p. (J). (gr. k-1). 1998. teacher ed., spiral bd. 35.00 (*1-929459-02-5*, Pub. by Lttle Readers) Poor Richards.

Little Rebel Becomes a Saint. rev. ed. (Character Building Ser.). (Illus.). 113p. (J). (gr. 4-6). 1990. pap. 6.50 (*1-58339-056-1*, C7) Triangle Press.

Little Rebellion. Bridget Moran. 164p. 1994. per. 12.95 (*0-88978-252-0*, Pub. by Arsenal Pulp) LPC InBook.

Little Red & the Wolf: A Puppet Play. Courtaney Brooks. (Illus.). (J). (gr. k up). 1983. pap. text 2.50 (*0-941274-04-7*) Belnice Bks.

Little Red Ant & the Big Crumb. Illus. by Francisco X. Mora. LC 94-27073. 40p. (J). (ps-3). 1999. 16.00 (*0-395-70732-3*, Clarion Bks) HM.

Little Red Ant & the Great Big Crumb. S. Climo. (ps-3). 1999. pap. 5.95 (*0-395-72097-4*, Clarion Bks) HM.

Little Red Barn. Mallory Loehr. (Illus.). (J). 1995. 4.50 (*0-679-86006-1*) Random.

***Little Red Barn Baking Book: Small Treats with Big Flavor.** Adriana Rabinovich. LC 00-21583. (Illus.). 144p. 2000. pap. 22.50 (*0-609-80630-0*) C Potter.

Little Red Blanket. Mary Waters. LC 93-61157. (Illus.). 40p. (J). (ps-3). 1993. lib. bdg. 6.95 (*0-9638123-0-0*) WAI Pubng.

Little Red Book. LC 95-167309. 164p. pap. 7.00 (*0-89486-985-X*, 1034 A) Hazelden.

Little Red Book. James Jennings. 153p. 10.00 (*0-89486-004-6*, 1030A) Hazelden.

Little Red Book. anniversary ed. 9.95 (*1-56838-149-2*, 1029 A) Hazelden.

***Little Red Book: Lessongs & Teachings from a Lifetime in Golf.** Harvey Penick & Bud Shrake. LC 92-202. 176p. 1999. per. 10.00 (*0-684-85924-6*) S&S Trade.

Little Red Book: Study Guide. Bill P. 130p. 1998. student ed., wbk. ed. 12.95 (*1-56838-283-9*) Hazelden.

Little Red Book of Stairs. Stefana Young. (Illus.). 200p. (Orig.). 1996. pap. 12.95 (*0-9655418-7-8*) Coobus Pr.

Little Red Book of Stuff That Works: Advice, Instructions, Ideas, Thoughts & Other Great Stuff That Works! Larry Winget. 220p. 1994. pap. 7.95 (*1-881342-04-2*) Win Pubns OK.

Little Red Box. Ernest L. Norman. (Illus.). 138p. 1968. 7.00 (*0-932642-16-0*); pap. 5.00 (*0-932642-47-0*) Unarius Acad Sci.

Little Red Buckets: A Story of Family & Giving. Lynda M. Nelson. LC 97-6696. 128p. (J). 1997. pap. 13.00 (*0-399-52357-X*, Perigee Bks) Berkley Pub.

Little Red Caboose. Illus. by Jill Dubin. LC 98-24330. (My First Hello Reader Ser.). (J). 1998. 3.99 (*0-590-63598-0*) Scholastic Inc.

Little Red Cap. Grimm. 37p. (J). (gr. k-2). pap. 5.95 (*0-8072-1285-7*) Listening Lib.

Little Red Cap. Jacob W. Grimm & Wilhelm K. Grimm. LC 94-32154. (Illus.). 32p. (J). (gr. k-3). 1995. 14.95 (*1-55858-382-3*, Pub. by North-South Bks NYC); pap. 5.95 (*1-55858-430-7*, Pub. by North-South Bks NYC) Chronicle Bks.

Little Red Cap. Lisbeth Zwerger. 1995. 11.15 (*0-606-08804-0*, Pub. by Turtleback) Demco.

Little Red Car. Ed. by Ladybird Books Staff. (Little Vehicle Stories Ser.). 32p. (J). 1998. text 2.50 (*0-7214-1931-3*, Ladybrd) Penguin Putnam.

***Little Red Car.** K. K. Ross. (Jellybean Bks.). (Illus.). 24p. (J). (ps-k). 1999. lib. bdg. 7.99 (*0-375-90142-6*, Pub. by Random Bks Yng Read) Random.

Little Red Car. K. K. Ross. (Jellybean Bks.). (Illus.). 24p. (J). (ps-k). 2000. 2.99 (*0-375-80142-1*, Pub. by Random Bks Yng Read) Random.

***Little Red Car Has an Accident.** Mathew Price & Steve Augarde. LC 00-35523. (Illus.). 2000. write for info. (*0-7892-0673-0*) Abbeville Pr.

***Little Red Car in the Snow.** Mathew Price. LC 00-29744. (Illus.). (J). 2000. 0.00 (*0-7892-0674-9*, Abbeville Kids) Abbeville Pr.

***Little Red Car Plays Taxi.** Mathew Price & Steve Augarde. LC 00-29997. (Illus.). (J). 2000. write for info. (*0-7892-0675-7*) Abbeville Pr.

Little Red Cowboy Hat. Susan Lowell. LC 96-31201. (Illus.). (J). 1995. 14.95 (*0-8050-3508-7*) H Holt & Co.

***Little Red Cowboy Hat.** Susan Lowell. (Illus.). 32p. (J). (ps-3). 2000. pap. 6.95 (*0-8050-6483-4*) H Holt & Co.

Little Red Hen see Gallinita Roja

Little Red Hen. (J). 2000. 16.00 (*0-689-82581-1*) Atheneum Yung Read.

Little Red Hen. (Stepping into English Ser.: Level 5). 1990. pap. 19.95 incl. audio (*1-57970-008-X*, AFE445) Audio-Forum.

Little Red Hen. (Read Along with Me Ser.). 24p. (J). (ps-3). 1988. pap. 2.25 (*1-56288-152-3*) Checkerboard.

Little Red Hen. 1996. pap. 8.95 (*0-937306-11-8*) Creat Res NC.

Little Red Hen. (Ladybird Bks.). (ARA., Illus.). 52p. 4.95 (*0-86685-203-4*, LDL158, Pub. by Librairie du Liban); 14.95 incl. audio (*0-86685-211-5*, LDL122C, Pub. by Librairie du Liban) Intl Bk Ctr.

Little Red Hen. (Illus.). (J). (ps). 1991. pap. 5.10 (*0-8136-5545-5*, TK2333); lib. bdg. 7.95 (*0-8136-5045-3*, TK2332) Modern Curr.

Little Red Hen. (Story Activity Bks.: No. S909-1). (J). 1991. pap. 1.95 (*0-7214-5278-7*, Ladybrd) Penguin Putnam.

***Little Red Hen.** (First Favourite Tales Ser.). 32p. (J). 1999. text 4.95 (*0-7214-9739-X*, Ladybrd) Penguin Putnam.

Little Red Hen. Carol Barnett. (Illus.). 64p. (J). (ps-3). 1994. 7.95 (*0-8442-9418-7*, Natl Textbk Co) NTC Contemp Pub Co.

Little Red Hen. Carol Barnett. (StoryLand Fables Ser.). (Illus.). 48p. (J). (ps-4). 1995. pap. 8.95 incl. audio (*0-8442-9430-6*) NTC Contemp Pub Co.

Little Red Hen. Illus. & Retold by Byron Barton. LC 91-4051. 32p. (J). (ps-1). 1993. 15.95 (*0-06-021675-1*); lib. bdg. 15.89 (*0-06-021676-X*) HarpC Child Bks.

Little Red Hen. Beverly C. Burgess. LC 86-140407. (Illus.). 32p. (J). (gr. 1-3). 1984. pap. 4.98 (*0-89274-312-3*, HH-312) Harrison Hse.

***Little Red Hen.** Arlene Capriola & Rigmor Swenson. Ed. by Cherisse Mastry. (Once upon a Time Ser.). (Illus.). (J). (gr. k-2). 1998. pap., wbk. ed. Price not set. incl. audio (*1-57022-175-8*) ECS Lrn Systs.

Little Red Hen, 001. Paul Galdone. LC 72-97770. (Illus.). 32p. (J). (ps-2). 1979. 15.00 (*0-395-28803-7*, Clarion Bks) HM.

Little Red Hen. Paul Galdone. LC 84-4311. (Illus.). 48p. (J). (ps-3). 1985. pap. 5.95 (*0-89919-349-8*, Clarion Bks) HM.

***Little Red Hen.** Paul Galdone. (Illus.). (J). (ps-3). 1998. pap. 9.95 incl. audio (*0-395-89902-8*, Clarion Bks) HM.

Little Red Hen. Paul Galdone. (J). 1987. 8.95 incl. audio (*0-89919-684-5*) Ticknor & Flds Bks Yng Read.

Little Red Hen. Paul Galdone. 1973. 11.15 (*0-606-00824-1*, Pub. by Turtleback) Demco.

Little Red Hen. Illus. by Berta Hader & Elmer Hader. LC 93-33702. (Little Activity Bks.). 32p. (J). (gr. 2 up). 1994. pap. 1.00 (*0-486-27977-4*) Dover.

Little Red Hen. Ladybird Books Staff. (Square Format Fairy Tales Ser.: No. S874-1). (Illus.). 28p. (J). (ps up). 1987. 3.95 (*0-7214-5028-8*, Ladybrd) Penguin Putnam.

Little Red Hen. Tammie Lyon. LC 97-221420. (Illus.). 1997. write for info. (*0-7853-2297-3*) Pubns Intl Ltd.

Little Red Hen. Carrie Mapes & Judith Gold. (Folktale Theme Ser.: Vol. 5). (Illus.). 64p. (J). (gr. k-2). 1995. pap. text, teacher ed. 6.95 (*1-55799-376-9*, EMC 528) Evan-Moor Edu Pubs.

Little Red Hen. Lucinda McQueen. (FRE., Illus.). (Orig.). (J). pap. 6.99 (*0-590-71720-0*); pap. 13.99 incl. audio (*0-590-73915-8*) Scholastic Inc.

Little Red Hen. Illus. by Lucinda McQueen. (Easy-to-Read Folktales Ser.). 32p. (Orig.). (J). (ps-3). 1985. pap. 2.99 (*0-590-41145-4*) Scholastic Inc.

Little Red Hen. Illus. by Norman Messenger. LC 96-44203. (Nursery Classics Ser.). 32p. (J). (ps-k). 1997. 8.95 (*0-7894-1171-7*) DK Pub Inc.

Little Red Hen. Ronne P. Randall. (Favorite Tales Ser.). (Illus.). 28p. (J). 1994. 2.99 (*0-7214-5394-5*, Ladybrd) Penguin Putnam.

Little Red Hen. Illus. by Camille Semelet. LC 98-36158. (Little Pebbles Ser.). 32p. (J). (ps-1). 1999. 6.95 (*0-7892-0514-9*, Abbeville Kids) Abbeville Pr.

Little Red Hen. Harriet Ziefert. (Illus.). 1999. pap. write for info. (*0-14-055542-0*) NAL.

Little Red Hen. unabridged ed. Brad Caudle & Melissa Caudle. (Rock 'N Read Ser.). (Illus.). 20p. (J). (gr. 1 up). 1996. pap. 7.95 incl. audio (*1-878489-69-0*, RL969) Rock N Learn.

Little Red Hen, Big bk. Illus. by Lucinda McQueen. (Easy-to-Read Folktales Ser.). 32p. (Orig.). (J). (ps-3). 1985. 19.95 (*0-590-71718-9*) Scholastic Inc.

Little Red Hen, Level 2, Red. Illus. by Emily Bolam. LC 95-11149. (Easy-to-Read Bks.). 32p. (J). (ps-k). 1995. pap. 3.99 (*0-14-037817-0*, PuffinBks) Peng Put Young Read.

Little Red Hen, Set. (ARA., Illus.). (J). (gr. 1-3). 1987. audio 12.95 (*0-86685-632-3*) Intl Bk Ctr.

Little Red Hen, Vol. 2. Carla Dijs. (My First Book of Fables Ser.). (Illus.). 10p. (J). (ps-2). 1997. 5.99 (*0-689-81481-X*) Litle Simon.

Little Red Hen: An Old Story. Margot Zemach. LC 83-14159. (Illus.). 32p. (J). (ps-3). 1983. 14.00 (*0-374-34621-6*) FS&G.

Little Red Hen: An Old Story. Margot Zemach. 32p. (J). (ps-3). 1993. pap. 4.95 (*0-374-44511-7*, Sunburst Bks) FS&G.

Little Red Hen: Easy Readers Tales & Rhymes. Emily Clark. (Easy Readers Ser.). 16p. (J). (ps-1). 1997. pap. 2.49 (*1-57690-286-2*) Tchr Create Mat.

Little Red Hen & the Ear of Wheat. Mary Finch. (Illus.). 32p. (J). (ps-1). 1999. 15.95 (*1-902283-47-3*) Barefoot Bks NY.

Little Red Hen Big Book. Addison-Wesley Publishing Staff. (ESL Ser.). (Illus.). 16p. (J). (gr. k-2). 1989. 23.30 (*0-201-19323-X*) Addison-Wesley.

Little Red Hen Big Book. Illus. & Retold by Byron Barton. LC 91-4051. (Trophy Picture Bk.). 32p. (J). (ps-1). 1994. pap. 21.95 (*0-06-443379-X*, HarpTrophy) HarpC Child Bks.

Little Red Hen Board Book. Byron Barton. (Illus.). 32p. (J). (ps up). 1997. 7.95 (*0-694-00999-7*, HarpFestival) HarpC Child Bks.

Little Red Hen Goes to Washington. Clarence G. Straws. (Illus.). 28p. 1995. 8.95 (*0-9647411-0-5*) Lil Red Hen OK.

Little Red Hen (La Gallina Paulina) Fernando Alonso. (Illus.). 26p. (J). (gr. k-2). 1989. 6.95 (*0-88272-468-1*) Santillana.

Little Red Hen Little Book. Addison-Wesley Publishing Staff. (ESOL Elementary Supplement Ser.). (Illus.). 16p. (J). (gr. k-3). 1989. pap. 4.78 (*0-201-19364-7*) Addison-Wesley.

Little Red Hen Story Book. (C). 1995. write for info. (*0-201-59196-0*) Addison-Wesley.

Little Red Hiding Wolf. Janet M. Holbrook. (Illus.). 35p. (J). (gr. k-12). 1992. pap. 8.95 (*0-9636203-0-4*) Holbrook Dogwoods.

Little Red Lighthouse & the Great Gray Bridge. Hildegarde H. Swift. (J). 1988. 12.20 (*0-606-12400-4*, Pub. by Turtleback) Demco.

Little Red Lighthouse & the Great Gray Bridge. Hildegarde H. Swift & Lynd Ward. LC 42-36286. (Illus.). 51p. (J). (ps-3). 1942. 17.00 (*0-15-247040-9*, Harcourt Child Bks) Harcourt.

Little Red Lighthouse & the Great Gray Bridge. Hildegarde H. Swift & Lynd Ward. LC 73-12861. (Illus.). 52p. (J). (ps-3). 1974. reprint ed. pap. 8.00 (*0-15-652840-1*, Voyager Bks) Harcourt.

Little Red Lighthouse & the Great Gray Bridge. unabridged ed. Hildegarde H. Swift. (Illus.). (J). (gr. k-3). 1992. 24.95 incl. audio (*0-87499-260-5*); pap. 15.95 incl. audio (*0-87499-259-1*) Live Oak Media.

Little Red Lighthouse & the Great Gray Bridge, 4 bks., Set. unabridged ed. Hildegarde H. Swift. (Illus.). (J). (gr. k-3). 1992. pap., teacher ed. 41.95 incl. audio (*0-87499-261-3*) Live Oak Media.

Little Red Plane. Ken Wilson-Max. (Illus.). 14p. (J). (ps-2). 1995. bds. 14.95 (*0-590-43008-4*, Cartwheel) Scholastic Inc.

***Little Red Plane: Mini Edition.** Illus. by Ken Wilson-Max. 14p. (J). (ps-k). 2000. 7.95 (*0-439-13653-9*, Cartwheel) Scholastic Inc.

Little Red-Riding-Hood see Petit Chaperon Rouge

Little Red Riding Hood see Petit Chaperon Rouge

Little Red Riding Hood. 1999. pap. text 5.95 (*1-874735-28-X*) B Small Publishing.

***Little Red Riding Hood.** (Pocketaudio Ser.). (Illus.). (J). (ps-2). 2000. 9.95 incl. audio (*2-921997-83-5*) Coffragants.

Little Red Riding Hood. (FRE & SPA.). (J). (gr. k-3). 4.95 (*0-685-28451-4*); 4.95 (*0-685-28450-6*) Fr & Eur.

Little Red Riding Hood. (ARA., Illus.). (J). (gr. 3-5). 1987. 4.95 (*0-86685-204-2*, LDL186, Pub. by Librairie du Liban) Intl Bk Ctr.

Little Red Riding Hood. (J). Date not set. 4.99 (*0-7214-5405-4*) Nickel Pr.

***Little Red Riding Hood.** (First Favourite Tales Ser.). (Illus.). 32p. (J). (gr. k-3). 1999. text 4.95 (*0-7214-9734-9*, Ladybrd) Penguin Putnam.

Little Red Riding Hood. (Favorite Fairy Tales Ser.). (Illus.). 24p. (J). 1993. 4.98 (*1-56173-916-2*) Pubns Intl Ltd.

Little Red Riding Hood. (J). 1996. pap. 1.25 (*0-8167-1514-9*) Troll Communs.

Little Red Riding Hood. Berthe Amoss. (Illus.). 10p. (J). (ps-7). 1989. pap. 2.95 (*0-922589-11-9*) More Than a Card.

Little Red Riding Hood. Ed. by Janet L. Bolinske. LC 87-61673. (Children's Classics Ser.). (Illus.). 32p. (Orig.). (J). (gr. 1-3). 1987. pap. text 4.95 (*0-88335-573-6*) Milliken Pub Co.

Little Red Riding Hood. Beverly C. Burgess. LC 86-140386. (Illus.). 32p. (Orig.). (J). (gr. 1-3). 1983. pap. 4.98 (*0-89274-289-5*, HH-289) Harrison Hse.

Little Red Riding Hood. Moria Butterfield. LC 97-27965. (Playtales Ser.). (J). 1998. 19.92 (*1-57572-650-5*) Heinemann Lib.

***Little Red Riding Hood.** Arlene Capriola & Rigmor Swenson. Ed. by Cherisse Mastry. (Once upon a Time Ser.). (Illus.). (J). (gr. k-2). 1998. pap., wbk. ed. Price not set. incl. audio (*1-57022-176-6*) ECS Lrn Systs.

Little Red Riding Hood. Charlotte B. Chorpenning. 47p. (J). 1946. 6.00 (*0-87602-149-6*) Anchorage.

Little Red Riding Hood. Illus. by Jane Dyer. LC 85-70289. (Pudgy Pal Board Bks.). 18p. (J). (ps). 1985. bds. 3.95 (*0-448-10227-7*, G & D) Peng Put Young Read.

Little Red Riding Hood. Lisa Campbell Ernst. LC 94-45723. (Illus.). 40p. (J). (gr. k-5). 1995. per. 16.00 (*0-689-80145-9*, Mac Bks Young Read) S&S Childrens.

***Little Red Riding Hood.** Illus. by Kuniro Fukazawa. (Origami Fairy Tale Ser.: Vol. 3). 16p. (J). (gr. k-12). 1999. pap. 4.95 (*0-89346-912-2*) Heian Intl.

Little Red Riding Hood. Jacob W. Grimm & Wilhelm K. Grimm. (Illus.). 32p. (J). (ps-3). 1992. 6.95 (*0-8362-4901-1*) Andrews & McMeel.

Little Red Riding Hood. Jacob W. Grimm & Wilhelm K. Grimm. LC 82-7700. (Illus.). 32p. (J). (gr. k-3). 1983. lib. bdg. 16.95 (*0-8234-0470-6*) Holiday.

Little Red Riding Hood. Jacob W. Grimm & Wilhelm K. Grimm. LC 82-7700. (Illus.). 32p. (J). (gr. k-3). 1987. pap. 6.95 (*0-8234-0653-9*) Holiday.

Little Red Riding Hood. Jacob W. Grimm & Wilhelm K. Grimm. (Easy-to-Read Folktales Ser.). (Illus.). 32p. (J). (gr. k-2). 1986. pap. 2.99 (*0-590-41881-5*) Scholastic Inc.

Little Red Riding Hood. Jacob W. Grimm & Wilhelm K. Grimm. LC 80-27684. (Illus.). 32p. (J). (gr. k-3). 1996. pap. 3.95 (*0-89375-489-7*) Troll Communs.

Little Red Riding Hood. Gill Guile. (Once upon a Time Ser.). (Illus.). 24p. (J). (ps-1). 1996. 3.98 (*1-85854-413-0*) Brimax Bks.

Little Red Riding Hood. M. Hillert. (Illus.). (J). 6.00 (*0-87895-680-8*) Modern Curr.

Little Red Riding Hood. Margaret Hillert. (Illus.). (J). (ps). 1982. pap. 5.10 (*0-8136-5595-1*, TK2171); lib. bdg. 7.95 (*0-8136-5095-X*, TK2170) Modern Curr.

Little Red Riding Hood. Jonathan Langley. (Nursery Pop-Up Bks.). (Illus.). 10p. (J). 1996. 4.95 (*0-8120-6570-0*) Barron.

Little Red Riding Hood. Carrie Mapes & Judith Gold. (Folktale Theme Ser.: Vol. 4). (Illus.). 64p. (J). (gr. k-2). 1995. pap. text, teacher ed. 6.95 (*1-55799-375-0*, EMC 527) Evan-Moor Edu Pubs.

Little Red Riding Hood. Illus. by Jean-Francois Martin. LC 97-23045. (Little Pebbles Ser.). 32p. (J). (ps-1). 1999. 6.95 (*0-7892-0421-5*, Abbeville Kids) Abbeville Pr.

Little Red Riding Hood. McClanahan Staff. (I Can Learn Ser.). (Illus.). 24p. (J). (ps-2). 1994. 1.95 (*1-56293-513-5*, McClanahan Book) Learn Horizon.

Little Red Riding Hood. David McPhail. LC 93-43990. (David McPhail's Favorite Tales Ser.). (Illus.). 32p. (J). (ps-k). 1995. bds. 4.95 (*0-590-48116-9*) Scholastic Inc.

Little Red Riding Hood. Tracey Moroney. (J). 1999. 7.99 (*1-56799-898-4*) M Friedman Pub Grp Inc.

Little Red Riding Hood. Carme Peris. (Fairy Tale Theater Ser.). (Illus.). 32p. (J). (gr. k-3). 1998. pap. 8.95 (*0-7641-5114-2*); pap. 8.95 (*0-7641-5146-0*) Barron.

***Little Red Riding Hood.** Charles Perrault. LC 99-32221. (Illus.). 32p. (YA). (gr. 5 up). 2000. lib. bdg. 13.95 (*1-56846-131-3*, Creat Educ) Creative Co.

Little Red Riding Hood. Charlotte Roederer. (Little Puppet Theaters Ser.). 1998. 19.95 (*1-57178-075-0*) Coun Oak Bks.

Little Red Riding Hood. Yevgeny Schwartz. Tr. by George Shail from RUS. (J). (gr. 4 up). 1992. pap. 3.50 (*0-87129-196-7*, L25) Dramatic Pub.

Little Red Riding Hood. Illus. by Susan Spellman & Sam Thiewes. (Favorite Fairy Tales Ser.). 24p. (J). (gr. 2-4). 1993. lib. bdg. 11.95 (*1-56674-065-7*, HTS Bks) Forest Hse.

Little Red Riding Hood. Swan. Date not set. pap. text. write for info. (*0-582-02570-2*, Pub. by Addison-Wesley) Longman.

Little Red Riding Hood. William Wegman. LC 92-54874. (Fay's Fairy Tales Ser.). (Illus.). 40p. (J). 1993. 16.95 (*1-56282-416-3*, Pub. by Hyprn Child); lib. bdg. 16.89 (*1-56282-417-1*, Pub. by Hyprn Child) Little.

***Little Red Riding Hood.** Harriet Ziefert. LC 99-23210. (Viking Easy-to-Read Ser.). (Illus.). (J). 2000. 13.89 (*0-670-88389-1*, Viking Child) Peng Put Young Read.

***Little Red Riding Hood.** Harriet Ziefert. LC 99-23210. (Puffin Easy-to-Read Program Ser.). (Illus.). 32p. (J). (ps-2). 2000. pap. 3.99 (*0-14-056529-9*, PuffinBks) Peng Put Young Read.

***Little Red Riding Hood.** Harriet Ziefert. (Viking Easy-To-Read Ser.). (Illus.). (J). 2000. 9.44 (*0-606-18421-X*) Turtleback.

Little Red Riding Hood. Jacob W. Grimm & Wilhelm K. Grimm. Ed. by Harriet Pincus. LC 68-11505. (Illus.). 32p. (J). (ps-3). 1989. reprint ed. pap. 10.95 (*0-15-652850-9*, AVB75, Voyager Bks) Harcourt.

Little Red Riding Hood. unabridged ed. Naomi Fox. (Illus.). 24p. (J). (ps-1). 1993. 9.95 incl. audio (*1-882179-14-5*) Confetti Ent.

Little Red Riding Hood, Vol. 520. rev. ed. Alfred Lipton. Ed. & Illus. by Janice Caban. (Once upon a Tale Ser.). 10p. (J). (gr. k). 1989. pap. 2.00 (*1-878501-05-4*) Ntrl Science Indus.

Little Red Riding Hood: A Musical. Sidney Berger & Rob Landes. 1996. pap. 3.50 (*1-57514-197-3*, 0097) Encore Perform Pub.

***Little Red Riding Hood: A Newfangled Prairie Tale.** Lisa Campbell Ernst. LC 94-45723. (Illus.). 40p. (J). (ps-3). 1998. reprint ed. per. 5.99 (*0-689-82191-3*) Aladdin.

Little Red Riding Hood: Can You Tell If the Big Bad Wolf Is Lying? Suzanne Larson. (Distinguished Faculty Lecture Ser.). 16p. 1993. pap. text. write for info. (*0-935615-09-1*) S Utah U Pr.

Little Red Riding Hood: Fairytale Friends. Melissa Tyrrell. (Illus.). 12p. (J). (ps up). 1998. bds. 5.95 (*1-58117-016-5*) Intervisual Bks.

Little Red Riding Hood: Finger Puppet Theater. Peter Stevenson. (Illus.). 16p. (J). 1997. 14.95 (*0-590-05962-9*) Scholastic Inc.

Little Red Riding Hood: Full-Color Sturdy Book. Sheilah Beckett. LC 95-53008. (Illus.). 16p. (J). 1996. pap. 1.00 (*0-486-29168-5*) Dover.

***Little Red Riding Hood: Gift Size Edition.** gif. ed. William Wegman. LC 92-54874. (Illus.). 40p. (ps-3). 1999. pap. text 9.99 (*0-7868-0549-8*, Pub. by Hyprn Child) Time Warner.

Little Red Riding Hood: Interactive Storybook. (Illus.). 8p. (J). (ps-6). 1997. 12.50 (*1-890647-00-4*) Lrning Curve.

Little Red Riding Hood: The Wolf's Tale. Della Rowland. LC 93-42781. (Upside Down Tales Ser.). (Illus.). (J). 1994. pap. 8.95 (*0-8065-1526-0*, Citadel Pr) Carol Pub Group.

Little Red Riding Hood: Told in Signed English. Harry Bornstein & Karen L. Saulnier. (Awareness & Caring Ser.). (Illus.). 48p. (J). (ps-3). 1990. lib. bdg. 16.95 (*1-878363-26-3*) Forest Hse.

Little Red Riding Hood: Told in Signed English. Harry Bornstein & Karen L. Saulnier. LC 90-3477. (Signed English Ser.). (Illus.). 48p. (J). (ps-2). 1990. 14.95 (*0-930323-63-7*, Pub. by K Green Pubns) Gallaudet Univ Pr.

Little Red Riding Hood & the Three Little Pigs. Moses Goldberg. (J). (gr. k-6). 1996. pap. 6.00 (*0-87602-346-4*) Anchorage.

Little Red Riding Hood & the Wolf's Tale. Della Rowland. (J). (ps-3). 1991. 13.95 (*1-55972-072-7*, Birch Ln Pr) Carol Pub Group.

Little Red Riding Hood in the Red Light District. Manlio Argueta. Tr. by Edward W. Hood from SPA. LC 99-86170. 238p. 1998. pap. 14.95 (*1-880684-32-2*) Curbstone.

Little Red Riding Hood Pillow. (J). 1990. pap. 19.95 (*1-55923-044-4*) Wicklow Ltd.

Little Red Riding Hood "Puzzle 'n Book" Z. Tailor. (Illus.). 8p. (J). (gr. k up). 1989. lib. bdg. write for info. (*0-318-64775-3*) ABC Child Bks.

Little Red Riding Hood Sticker Storybook. Marty Noble. (Illus.). (J). 1997. pap. 1.00 (*0-486-29908-2*) Dover.

***Little Red Riding Hood Uncloaked.** Orenstein. 2000. 25.00 (*0-465-04125-6*, Pub. by Basic) HarpC.

Little Red Riding Hood/Capercuita Roja: A Bilingual Book. Jacob W. Grimm & Wilhelm K. Grimm. Tr. by James Surges. LC 99-21354. (Illus.). 32p. (J). (gr. k-2). 1999. pap. 6.95 (*0-8118-2562-0*) Chronicle Bks.

Little Red Riding Hood/Caperucita Roja: A Bilingual Book. Jacob W. Grimm & Wilhelm K. Grimm. Tr. by James Surges. LC 99-21354. 32p. (J). (gr. k-2). 1999. 12.95 (*0-8118-2561-2*) Chronicle Bks.

Little Red Riding Wolf. Laurence Anholt. (J). (gr. 4-6). 2000. pap. 3.95 (*0-689-83293-1*) S&S Childrens.

Little Red Riding Wolf: A 3-Act Play. R. Eugene Jackson. 40p. 1973. pap. 3.50 (*0-88680-115-X*) I E Clark.

Little Red Riding Wolf: Director's Script. R. Eugene Jackson. 40p. 1973. pap. 10.00 (*0-88680-116-8*) I E Clark.

Little Red Ronnika. large type ed. Bobby L. Jackson. LC 98-65052. (Illus.). 32p. (J). (gr. 1-4). 1998. lib. bdg. 16.95 (*1-884242-80-4*) Multicult Pubns.

Little Red Songbook: Songs to Fan the Flames of Discontent. 36th ed. (Illus.). 104p. (Orig.). 1995. pap. 10.00 (*0-917124-08-1*) Indus Workers World.

Little Red Train. Carl Sommer. LC 99-35277. (Another Sommer-Time Story Ser.). (Illus.). 48p. (J). (ps-4). 1999. 9.95 (*1-57537-014-X*) Advance Pub.

Little Red Train. Carl Sommer. (Another Sommer-Time Story Ser.). (Illus.). 48p. (J). (ps-4). 2000. lib. bdg. 14.95 (*1-57537-061-1*) Advance Pub.

Little Red Wagon Painted Blue. Robert Hershon. LC 74-134747. (Illus.). 48p. 1972. pap. 10.00 (*0-87775-039-4*) Unicorn Pr.

Little Red, White & Blue Book. World Almanac Publications Staff. 1987. mass mkt. 4.95 (*0-345-34558-4*) Ballantine Pub Grp.

Little Red Writing Book: A Practical Guide to Writing Your Own Life Story. Lonnie Burstein Hewitt. LC 98-90740. vi, 94p. 1998. pap. 12.95 (*0-9666731-0-7*) TellTale Prods.

Little Red Writing Book 1. Lori Mammen. Ed. by Nancy S. Day. (Illus.). 114p. (J). (gr. 1-2). 1997. pap., wbk. ed. 8.95 (*1-57022-107-3*, ECS1073) ECS Lrn Systs.

Little Red Writing Book 3. Lori Mammen. Ed. by Nancy S. Day. (Illus.). 114p. (J). (gr. 5-7). 1997. pap., wbk. ed. 8.95 (*1-57022-109-X*, ECS109X) ECS Lrn Systs.

Little Red Writing Book 2. Lori Mammen. Ed. by Nancy S. Day. (Illus.). 114p. 1997. pap., wbk. ed. 8.95 (*1-57022-108-1*, ECS1081) ECS Lrn Systs.

Little Red Writing Books, 3 vols. Lori Mammen. Ed. by Nancy Day. (Illus.). (J). (gr. 1-7). pap., wbk. ed. 26.85 (*1-57022-130-8*, ECS-LRWB-SET-03) ECS Lrn Systs.

Little Regiment: And Other Episodes of the American Civil War. Stephen Crane. LC 70-150471. (Short Story Index Reprint Ser.). 1977. reprint ed. 15.95 (*0-8369-3811-9*) Ayer.

Little Regiment" & Other Civil War Stories. Stephen Crane. LC 96-43701. (Thrift Editions Ser.). (Illus.). 80p. (Orig.). 1997. pap. 1.00 (*0-486-29557-5*) Dover.

Little Regiment & Other Episodes of the Civil War. Stephen Crane. (Works of Stephen Crane). 1990. reprint ed. lib. bdg. 79.00 (*0-685-44796-0*) Rprt Serv.

Little Reindeer. Michael Foreman. LC 96-27128. (Illus.). 32p. (J). (ps-3). 1997. 15.99 (*0-8037-2184-6*, Dial Yng Read) Peng Put Young Read.

Little Reindeer: A Little Foil Book. Melissa Tyrrell. (Merry Little Foil Bks.). (Illus.). 10p. (J). (ps up). 1998. 2.95 (*1-58117-010-6*, Piggy Toes Pr) Intervisual Bks.

Little Restaurants of Los Angeles. (Illus.). 1985. pap. 4.95 (*0-913290-01-7*) Camaro Pub.

Little Restaurants of San Francisco. Camaro Editors. LC 73-85631. (Illus.). 1985. 4.95 (*0-913290-06-8*) Camaro Pub.

Little Rhetoric & Handbook. 2nd ed. Edward P. Corbett. LC 81-43604. 637p. 1982. reprint ed. pap. 197.50 (*0-7837-8337-X*, 204912400010) Bks Demand.

Little Rhiny: He Wanted to See the Tourists. Viola E. Iverson. (Illus.). 22p. (Orig.). (J). 1995. pap. 5.95 (*0-9644483-0-0*) Viola Iverson.

***Little Rich Man.** Christian Focus Publishing Staff. 2000. 3.99 (*1-85792-345-6*) Christian Focus.

Little Ricky Rabbit. unabridged ed. Mae O. Ra'Oof & Jum Ra'Oof. (Five Friends of Rainbow Forest Ser.). (Illus.). 61p. (Orig.). (J). (gr. 3-5). 1995. pap. 8.95 (*1-888527-06-4*) New Wrld Ent.

Little Ricky Rabbit. unabridged ed. Mae O. Ra'Oof & Jum Ra'Oof. (Five Friends of Rainbow Forest Ser.). (Illus.). 50p. (Orig.). (J). (ps-2). 1995. pap. 7.95 (*1-888527-00-5*) New Wrld Ent.

Little Riders. Margaretha Shemin. (J). 1993. 10.15 (*0-606-05433-2*, Pub. by Turtleback) Demco.

Little Riders. Margaretha Shemin. LC 92-33065. (Illus.). 80p. (J). (gr. 4 up). 1993. reprint ed. mass mkt. 4.95 (*0-688-12499-2*, Wm Morrow) Morrow Avon.

***Little River: New & Selected Poems.** Linda McCarriston. 2000. pap. 13.95 (*1-903392-01-2*, Pub. by Salmon Poetry) Dufour.

Little Rivers: Tales of a Woman Angler. Margot Page. (Illus.). 144p. 1995. 16.95 (*1-55821-367-8*) Lyons Pr.

Little Robin Redbreast: A Mother Goose Rhyme. Illus. by Shari Halpern. LC 93-38760. 32p. (J). (ps-1). 1994. 14.95 (*1-55858-247-9*, Pub. by North-South Bks NYC); lib. bdg. 14.88 (*1-55858-248-7*, Pub. by North-South Bks NYC) Chronicle Bks.

Little Robin Redbreast: A Mother Goose Rhyme. Illus. by Shari Halpern. LC 93-38760. 32p. (J). (ps-1). 1996. pap. 6.95 (*1-55858-551-6*, Pub. by North-South Bks NYC) Chronicle Bks.

Little Robin's Christmas. Jan Fearnley. LC 98-6895. (Illus.). 32p. (J). (ps-2). 1998. 14.95 (*1-888444-40-1*) Little Tiger.

***Little Robots.** Mike Brownlow. 32p. (J). 2000. 12.95 (*1-929927-05-3*) Ragged Bears NY.

Little Rock: A Postcard History. Ray Hanley & Stephen G. Hanley. LC 98-85861. (Images of America Ser.). (Illus.). 128p. 1998. pap. 16.99 (*0-7524-0988-3*) Arcadia Publng.

Little Rock: And Other Stories. Jack Hasling. LC 96-79026. (Illus.). 32p. (Orig.). (J). (gr. 1-6). 1997. pap. 9.95 (*1-878044-51-6*, Wld Rose) Mayhaven Pub.

Little Rock: One from the Heart. William B. Worthen & Kelley Bass. LC 96-34244. (Urban Tapestry Ser.). 144p. 1996. 44.95 (*1-881096-29-7*) Towery Pub.

Little Rock: The Desegregation of Central High. Laurie A. O'Neill. LC 93-29057. (Spotlight on American History Ser.). (Illus.). 64p. (J). (gr. 4-6). 1994. lib. bdg. 21.90 (*1-56294-354-5*) Millbrook Pr.

Little Rock, AR. (Streetfinder Ser.). (Illus.). 1995. pap. 15.95 (*0-528-91356-5*) Rand McNally.

Little Rock Arkansas, 1. Rand McNally Staff. (Rand McNally Streetfinder Ser.). 1999. pap. text 17.95 (*0-528-97883-7*) Rand McNally.

Little Rock, Arkansas, National Cemetery Burial Roster. Ed. by Desmond W. Allen. 214p. (Orig.). 1997. pap. 28.00 (*1-56546-102-9*) Arkansas Res.

Little Rock Crisis: A Constitutional Interpretation, 30. Tony A. Freyer. LC 83-26663. (Contributions in Legal Studies: No. 30). 186p. 1984. 45.00 (*0-313-24416-2*, FRL/, Greenwood Pr) Greenwood.

***Little Rock Entertainment, 2000.** (Illus.). 406p. 1999. pap. 25.00 (*1-880248-37-9*, 00U6) Enter Pubns.

Little Rock Handbook. James W. Bell. (Illus.). iv, 88p. (Orig.). 1980. pap. 9.95 (*0-939130-00-9*) J W Bell.

Little Rock Photograph Album of the 1890's: The Mary E. Parker Collection. Emelou M. Hamilton. (Illus.). 1981. pap. 10.95 (*0-939130-02-5*) J W Bell.

***Little Rocket's Special Star.** Julie Sykes. (Illus.). 32p. (J). (ps-1). 2000. 15.99 (*0-525-46494-8*, Dutton Child) Peng Put Young Read.

Little Rogue, & Other Stories Vol. 10: Collected Novels & Stories. Guy de Maupassant. Ed. by Ernest A. Boyd. Tr. by Storm Jameson from FRE. LC 73-157788. (Short Story Index Reprint Ser.). 1977. reprint ed. 18.95 (*0-8369-3900-X*) Ayer.

Little Room. Guy N. Pocock. LC 68-55854. (Essay Index Reprint Ser.). 1977. 20.95 (*0-8369-0794-9*) Ayer.

Little Room of Poems. Bob Hickey. 1997. pap. 10.00 (*0-9603432-5-3*) STP.

Little Runaway. Margaret Hillert. (Illus.). (J). (ps). 1966. pap. 5.10 (*0-8136-5552-8*, TK2335); lib. bdg. 7.95 (*0-8136-5052-6*, TK2334) Modern Curr.

Little Runner of the Longhouse. Betty Baker. LC 62-8040. (I Can Read Bks.). (Illus.). 64p. (J). (ps-3). 1962. lib. bdg. 15.89 (*0-06-020341-2*) HarpC Child Bks.

Little Runner of the Longhouse. Betty Baker. LC 62-8040. (I Can Read Bks.). (Illus.). 64p. (J). (ps-3). 1989. pap. 3.95 (*0-06-444122-9*, HarpTrophy) HarpC Child Bks.

Little Runner of the Longhouse. Betty Baker. (I Can Read Bks.). (J). (gr. 1-3). 1989. 8.95 (*0-606-12401-2*, Pub. by Turtleback) Demco.

Little Russian Classics. Ivan Sergeevich Turgenev et al. Ed. & Tr. by Rebecca Scott from RUS. LC 93-26085. 72p. (C). 1993. pap. 9.00 (*1-881119-91-2*) Pyncheon Hse.

Little Russian Cookbook. Tania Alexander. 1997. 7.95 (*0-8118-1652-4*) Chronicle Bks.

Little Russian Cookbook. Tania Alexander & Vera Konova-Stone. (Little Bks.). (Illus.). 60p. 1990. 7.95 (*0-87701-794-8*) Chronicle Bks.

Little Russian-German Polytechnical Dictionary: Kleines Polytechnisches Woerterbuch Russisch-Deutsch. 4th ed. Horst Gorner. (GER & RUS.). 384p. 1990. 49.95 (*0-8288-2137-2*, M6920) Fr & Eur.

Little Russian Philokalia Vol. I: St. Seraphim of Sarov. Seraphim Rose. LC 90-64253. (Illus.). 158p. 1990. reprint ed. pap. 10.00 (*0-938635-30-1*) St Herman Pr.

Little Russian Philokalia Vol. II: Abbot Nazarius of Valaam. Seraphim Rose. (Illus.). 143p. 1983. reprint ed. pap. 10.00 (*0-938635-31-X*) St Herman Pr.

Little Russian Philokalia Vol. III: Treasury of St. Herman's Spirituality. St. Herman of Alaska Brotherhood Staff. Ed. by Abbot Herman. LC 88-63601. (Illus.). 200p. (Orig.). 1989. pap. 10.00 (*0-938635-32-8*) St Herman Pr.

Little Russian Philokalia Vol. IV: St. Paisius Velichkovsky. LC 93-83656. (RUS., Illus.). 151p. 1994. pap. 10.00 (*0-938635-33-6*) St Herman Pr.

Little Ruthie. Rose C. Edelen. (Illus.). 1992. 9.95 (*0-9629758-1-8*) Wordsmith Pr.

***Little 's' Sellers.** (J). 2000. 3.95 (*0-552-52890-0*, Pub. by Transworld Publishers Ltd) Trafalgar.

Little Sable Point Light Station. Thomas A. Tag. (Illus.). 52p. 1996. pap. 9.95 (*0-9649980-1-7*) Data Image.

***Little Saint.** Hannah Green. LC 99-23023. (Illus.). 352p. (J). 2000. 25.95 (*0-394-56595-9*) Random.

Little San Francisco Cookbook. Charlotte Walker. (Illus.). 60p. 1990. 7.95 (*0-87701-619-4*) Chronicle Bks.

Little Sanctuaries: Mikdash Me'at (Hebrew) Ed. by Jerusalem Center for Biblical Studies & Research Staff. (Illus.). 78p. 1988. 4.00 (*1-888235-09-8*) AMI-Jerusalem.

Little Sanctuaries: Miqdash Me'at. 3rd rev. ed. Jerusalem Center for Biblical Studies & Research Staff. (Illus.). 80p. 1998. pap. 5.00 (*1-888235-24-1*) AMI-Jerusalem.

Little SAS Book: A Primer. Lora D. Delwiche & Susan J. Slaughter. 240p. (C). 1998. pap. 24.95 (*1-55544-215-3*, BR55200) SAS Publ.

***Little SAS Book: A Primer.** 2nd ed. Lora D. Delwiche & Susan J. Slaughter. 300p. 1999. pap. 27.95 (*1-58025-239-7*) SAS Publ.

***Little Scandal.** Patricia Cabot. 352p. 2000. mass mkt. 5.99 (*0-312-97413-2*, St Martins Paperbacks) St Martin.

Little Scarecrow Boy. Margaret W. Brown. LC 97-32558. (Illus.). 40p. (J). (ps-2). 1998. 15.95 (*0-06-026284-2*); lib. bdg. 15.89 (*0-06-026290-7*) HarpC.

Little Schemer. 4th rev. ed. Daniel P. Friedman & Matthias Felleisen. LC 95-39853. (Illus.). 216p. 1995. pap. text 19.50 (*0-262-56099-2*) MIT Pr.

Little School: Tales of Disappearance & Survival 2nd Edition. 2nd ed. Alicia Partnoy. Tr. by Lois Athey et al. (Illus.). 200p. (Orig.). (C). 1998. reprint ed. pap. 14.95 (*1-57344-029-9*) Cleis Pr.

Little School of Horrors. Tom B. Stone. (Graveyard School Ser.: No. 26). 112p. (J). (gr. 3-7). 1998. pap. 2.99 (*0-553-48544-X*, Skylark BDD) BDD Bks Young Read.

Little School of Velocity for Piano. Louis Koehler. (Carl Fischer Music Library: No. 480). (Illus.). 1907. pap. 4.50 (*0-8258-0123-0*, L480) Fischer Inc NY.

Little Scientist: An Activity Lab. Jean Stangl. 128p. 1993. pap. 9.95 (*0-07-060764-8*) McGraw.

Little Scientist: An Activity Lab. Jean Stangl. (Illus.). 128p. (J). (ps-1). 1992. 17.95 (*0-8306-4101-7*, 4218); pap. 9.95 (*0-8306-4102-5*, 4218) McGraw-Hill Prof.

***Little Scientists: Exploring the World.** Menucha Fuchs. Tr. by Zelda Goldfield from HEB. (Illus.). 48p. (J). (gr. k-3). 1999. pap. 4.95 (*1-880582-45-7*) Judaica Pr.

Little Scottish Birthday Book. Marian Clark. (Illus.). 124p. 1998. 13.95 (*0-86281-704-8*, Pub. by Appletree Pr) Irish Bks Media.

Little Scottish Cookbook. Paul Harris. (Illus.). 60p. 1988. 7.95 (*0-87701-560-0*) Chronicle Bks.

Little Scottish Cookbook. Paul Harris. 1997. 7.95 (*0-8118-1655-9*) Chronicle Bks.

Little Scottish Girl Paper Doll. Tom Tierney. (Illus.). (J). (gr. k-3). 1993. pap. 1.00 (*0-486-27433-0*) Dover.

Little Scottish Songbook. Clare Hewitt. (Little Irish Bookshelf Ser.). (Illus.). 60p. 1994. 9.95 (*0-86281-482-0*, Pub. by Appletree Pr) Irish Bks Media.

Little Sea Pony. Helen Cresswell. (Chapter Bks.). (Illus.). 304p. (J). (gr. 3-7). 1997. pap. 3.95 (*0-614-19173-4*, HarpTrophy) HarpC Child Bks.

Little Sea Pony. Helen Cresswell. (Trophy Picture Bk.). (Illus.). 80p. (J). (gr. 2-5). 1997. pap. 3.95 (*0-06-442059-0*, HarpTrophy) HarpC Child Bks.

Little Search: A Word Puzzle. Nina Barbaresi. (Illus.). (J). 1990. pap. 1.00 (*0-486-26455-6*) Dover.

Little Seashore Activity Book, Vol. 181. Anna Pomaska. (Activity Bk.). (Illus.). (J). (ps up). 1988. pap. 1.00 (*0-486-25608-1*) Dover.

***Little Secret for Dealing with Teens: One Mom's Revolutionary Approach to the Parent/Teen Relationship.** Jennie Hernandez Hanks. 100p. 2000. pap. 8.95 (*1-55874-757-5*, Simcha Press) Health Comm.

Little Secrets of Friendship. J. Donald Walters. 68p. (J). (gr. 4-7). 1993. 5.95 (*1-56589-602-5*) Crystal Clarity.

Little Secrets of Happiness. J. Donald Walters. (J). (gr. 4-7). 1993. 5.95 (*1-56589-604-1*) Crystal Clarity.

Little Secrets of Success. J. Donald Walters. 68p. (J). (gr. 4-7). 1993. 5.95 (*1-56589-603-3*) Crystal Clarity.

Little Seed. Sandy Ray. Ed. by Cheryle Sytsma. LC 90-63623. (Illus.). 30p. (Orig.). (J). (gr. k-5). 1991. pap. write for info. (*1-879068-01-X*) Ray-Ma Natsal.

Little Seed. Sherry Shahan. (J). 1999. pap. 3.25 (*0-679-89131-5*) Random Bks Yng Read.

Little Seeds. Charles Gallagher. (Celebrate Love Ser.). 58p. (Orig.). 1992. pap. text 3.95 (*0-911905-49-9*) Past & Mat Rene Ctr.

Little Sermons of the Big Joy. James Broughton. 25p. (Orig.). 1994. pap. 7.00 (*1-882827-05-8*) Insight to Riot.

Little Servant. Grace Livingston Hill. 1976. 18.95 (*0-8488-0817-7*) Amereon Ltd.

Little Shepherd. Don J. Black. 1991. pap. 3.95 (*1-55503-191-9*, 0111783) Covenant Comms.

Little Shepherd. Photos by Heidi Bratton. LC 98-43547. (Walking with God II Ser.). (Illus.). 16p. (J). (ps-k). 2000. 5.95 (*0-8091-6660-7*) Paulist Pr.

Little Shepherd. Bijou Le Tord. 1992. 14.95 (*0-385-30707-1*) Doubleday.

Little Shepherd: The 23rd Psalm. Illus. by Bijou Le Tord. 32p. (J). (gr. 1 up). 1995. pap. 4.99 (*0-440-40961-6*, Yearling) BDD Bks Young Read.

Little Shepherd: The 23rd Psalm. Bijou Le Tord. (J). 1995. 10.44 (*0-606-07800-2*) Turtleback.

Little Shepherd of Kingdom Come. John Fox. 1976. 23.95 (*0-8488-1327-8*) Amereon Ltd.

Little Shepherd of Kingdom Come. John Fox. 1976. lib. bdg. 29.95 (*0-89968-039-9*, Lghtyr Pr) Buccaneer Bks.

Little Shepherd of Kingdom Come. John Fox, Jr. LC 87-11882. 336p. 1987. reprint ed. pap. 18.00 (*0-8131-0172-7*) U Pr of Ky.

Little Shiner. Peg Randall. (Illus.). 32p. 1995. 13.95 (*0-9644372-0-1*) Elder Magic.

***Little Ship, Big War: The Saga of DE343.** Edward P. Stafford. LC 99-57720. (Bluejacket Bks.). (Illus.). 336p. 2000. pap. 17.95 (*1-55750-890-9*) Naval Inst Pr.

Little Ship under Full Sail. Janie L. Panagopoulos. LC 97-9604. 146p. (J). 1997. 15.95 (*0-938682-46-6*) River Rd Pubns.

Little Ships: The Heroic Rescue at Dunkirk in World War II. Louise Borden. LC 95-52557. (Illus.). 32p. (J). (gr. 4-7). 1997. 15.00 (*0-689-80827-5*) S&S Childrens.

Little Ships of Dunkirk. Collectors Books Ltd. Staff. (C). 1989. 110.00 (*0-7855-4940-4*, Pub. by Fuel Metallurgical Jrnl) St Mut.

Little Shooter of Birds & the Great Sun. Rochester Folk Art Guild Staff. (J). (ps-7). 1981. 9.50 (*0-686-33125-7*) Rochester Folk Art.

Little Shopping. Cynthia Rylant. LC 97-20996. (Cobble Street Cousins Ser.: Vol. 2). (Illus.). 55p. (J). (gr. 2-5). 2000. per. 4.50 (*0-689-81709-6*) Aladdin.

Little Sia & the Sacred Cloud. large type ed. Nilene O. Foxworth. (Illus.). 21p. (J). (gr. 1-6). 1997. pap. text 12.95 (*0-9644137-5-2*) NOA Intl.

Little Sibu: An Orangutan Tale. Sally Grindley. LC 98-39038. (Illus.). 32p. (J). (ps-3). 1999. 15.95 (*1-56145-196-7*, 51967) Peachtree Pubs.

Little Silver. Karen L. Schnitzspahn. LC 96-231045. (Images of America Ser.). 1996. pap. 16.99 (*0-7524-0284-6*) Arcadia Publng.

Little Silver, Vol. II. Karen L. Schnitzpahn. (Images of America Ser.). (Illus.). 128p. 1998. pap. 16.99 (*0-7524-1217-5*) Arcadia Publng.

Little Silver House. Jennie D. Lindquist. (Illus.). (J). (gr. 2-6). 1990. 16.00 (*0-8446-6190-2*) Peter Smith.

***Little Sip of Chicken Soup for the Golfer's Soul.** Jack Canfield. 2000. pap. 4.95 (*0-7407-1140-7*) Andrews & McMeel.

Little Sip of Chicken Soup for the Soul: Inspiring Stories of Self-Affirmation. Andrews & McMeel Staff. LC 98-125547. (Chicken Soup for the Soul Ser.). 80p. 1997. 4.95 (*0-8362-5087-7*) Andrews & McMeel.

Little Sister. Raymond Chandler. 256p. 1994. 35.00 (*1-883402-79-4*) S&S Trade.

Little Sister. Raymond Chandler. LC 87-45918. (Crime Ser.). 352p. 1988. pap. 10.00 (*0-394-75767-X*) Vin Bks.

Little Sister. Julie Checkoway. 1999. pap. 9.95 (*0-14-017654-3*) Viking Penguin.

Little Sister. Kara Dalkey. LC 96-2556. (Jane Yolen Bks.). 208p. (J). 1996. 17.00 (*0-15-201392-X*) Harcourt.

Little Sister. Kara Dalkey. LC 97-28231. 208p. 1998. pap. 4.99 (*0-14-038631-9*) Viking Penguin.

Little Sister & the Month Brothers. Beatrice S. De Regniers. LC 75-4594. (Illus.). 48p. (J). (ps-3). 1976. 8.95 (*0-8164-3147-7*, Clarion Bks) HM.

Little Sister & the Month Brothers. Beatrice Shenk De Regniers. LC 93-44053. 1994. 10.15 (*0-606-06539-3*) Turtleback.

Little Sister, Big Sister. Pat Brisson. LC 98-33905. (Illus.). (J). (gr. 1-3). 1999. 15.95 (*0-8050-5887-7*) H Holt & Co.

Little Sister Jacket & Vest Book. Barbara B. Doriss. (Illus.). 32p. 1985. pap. 8.00 (*0-932946-17-8*) Burdett CA.

Little Sister: The Story of Blessed Imelda Lambertini, Patroness of First Communicants see Patron Saint of First Communicants: The Story of Blessed Imelda Lambertini

Little Sisters. Stephen Axelsen & Jenny Axelsen. LC 92-34261. (Voyages Ser.). (Illus.). (J). 1993. 4.25 (*0-383-03637-2*) SRA McGraw.

Little Sisters: The Last but Not the Least. Carolyn Lieberg. LC 98-29819. 224p. 1998. pap. 13.95 (*1-885171-24-2*) PageMill Pr.

Little Skaters. Ann Morris. LC 97-18136. (All Aboard Bks.). (Illus.). 32p. (J). (ps-3). 1997. pap. text 2.95 (*0-448-41734-0*, G & D) Peng Put Young Read.

Little Skaters. Ann Morris. 1997. 8.15 (*0-606-12758-5*, Pub. by Turtleback) Demco.

***Little Skratch Pad, Assorted Guatemalan Fabrics.** Tr. by Joshua Gerak. 100p. 1999. 2.99 (*1-892985-00-4*) Adventure Imports.

***Little Skratch Pad, Hemp Fabric.** Photos by Joshua Gerak. 100p. 1999. 3.99 (*1-892985-04-7*) Adventure Imports.

Little Skunk. Susan B. Banks. (Illus.). 40p. (J). (ps-7). 1995. 10.99 (*0-89228-120-0*) Impact Christian.

Little Slaves of the Harp: Italian Child Street Musicians in Nineteenth-Century Paris, London & New York. John E. Zucchi. (Illus.). 240p. 1992. 65.00 (*0-7735-0890-2*, Pub. by McG-Queens Univ Pr) CUP Services.

Little Slaves of the Harp: Italian Child Street Musicians in Nineteenth-Century Paris, London & New York. John E. Zucchi. (Illus.). 248p. 1998. pap. text 19.95 (*0-7735-1755-3*, Pub. by McG-Queens Univ Pr) CUP Services.

Little Sleepy Eyes. Ed. by J. Aaron Brown. (Illus.). 8p. (Orig.). (J). (ps). 1994. 12.95 incl. audio compact disk (*0-927945-08-8*) Someday Baby.

Little Sleepy Eyes. Ed. by J. Aaron Brown. (Illus.). 8p. (Orig.). (J). (ps). 1995. 15.95 incl. audio compact disk (*0-927945-12-6*) Someday Baby.

***Little Snail That Lives Near a Pail.** Al Wingfield. LC 99-68758. (Illus.). 14p. (J). (ps-3). 1999. pap. 7.95 (*1-930260-00-8*) C T S Family.

Little Snow Bear. large type ed. Lisa W. Gilbert & Flavia M. Weedn. LC 94-11278. (Flavia's Dream Maker Stories Ser.). (Illus.). 48p. (J). (ps-3). 1995. 10.95 (*0-7868-0044-5*, Pub. by Hyprn Child) Time Warner.

Little Snow Bear. Flavia Weedn & Lisa Weedn. (Illus.). 40p. (J). 1998. reprint ed. pap. 12.95 (*0-7683-2055-0*) CEDCO Pub.

Little Snow Girl. Nellie McCaslin. 33p. 1963. pap. 3.50 (*0-87129-070-7*, L66) Dramatic Pub.

Little Snowgirl. Carolyn Croll. (Illus.). 32p. (J). (ps-3). 1996. pap. 5.95 (*0-698-11424-8*, PapStar) Peng Put Young Read.

Little Snowgirl, An Old Russian Tale. Carolyn Croll. LC 88-30667. 1996. 11.15 (*0-606-10254-X*, Pub. by Turtleback) Demco.

Little Softies: Farm & Toys. Gerald Hawksley. (Illus.). 12p. (J). (ps up). 1995. pap. 4.95 (*0-689-80133-5*) Little Simon.

Little Something. LC 87-83678. (Illus.). 47p. 1987. 7.00 (*0-9620375-0-8*) Faith Unlimited.

Little Something. Susan Epstein. LC 98-4705. 160p. 1998. pap. 15.00 (*0-688-15572-3*, Quil) HarperTrade.

***Little Something.** Sarah Hartt-Snowbell. (Illus.). 40p. 1998. pap. 7.95 (*0-929141-60-1*) Napoleon Publ.

Little Something Extra. Pam McCutcheon. LC 96-3369. (American Romance Ser.). 248p. 1996. per. 3.50 (*0-373-16614-1*, 1-16614-9) Harlequin Bks.

Little Songs: A Collection of Sonnets & Villanelles. William J. Middleton. LC 96-90477. (Illus.). 52p. (Orig.). 1996. pap. 5.00 (*1-886467-08-0*) WJM Press.

Little Songs for Little Ones. (Children's Tiny Treasures Ser.). 1995. 4.99 (*0-310-96339-7*) Zondervan.

***Little Songs in the Shade of Tamara: Translated from the Arabic by Lisa White with Afterword by Naguib Mafhouz, Nobel Prize Winning Author of Midaq Alley.** Mohammed Afifi. Tr. by Lisa White from ARA. (Arabic Translation Award Ser.). Orig. Title: Taraniim Fii Dhil Tamaara. 112p. 2000. reprint ed. pap. 16.00 (*1-55728-614-0*) U of Ark Pr.

***Little Songs of the Geisba.** Liza Crihfield Dalby. 2000. pap. 12.95 (*0-8048-3250-1*) Tuttle Pubng.

L

An Asterisk (*) at the beginning of an entry indicates that the title is appearing for the first time.

Little Soul & the Sun. Neale Donald Walsch. LC 98-71734. (Illus.). 32p. (J). (gr. 1-6). 1998. 17.95 (*1-57174-087-2*) Hampton Roads Pub Co.

Little Soup's Hayride: A Study Guide. Laurie Diamond. Ed. by J. Friedland & R. Kessler. (Novel-Ties Ser.). 20p. (J). (gr. 2-4). 1992. pap. text 15.95 (*0-88122-699-8*) Lrn Links.

Little Southern Belle. Barbara Steadman. (Little Activity Bks.). (Illus.). (J). 1997. pap. 1.00 (*0-486-29520-6*) Dover.

Little Southwest Cookbook. Barbara Karoff. (Little Cookbooks Ser.). (Illus.). 60p. 1993. 7.95 (*0-8118-0381-3*) Chronicle Bks.

Little Southwest Indian Girl Paper Doll. 80th ed. Kathy Allert. (Illus.). (J). (gr. k-3). 1994. pap. 1.00 (*0-486-27927-8*) Dover.

Little Space: Poems Selected & New, 1968-1998. Alicia S. Ostriker. LC 98-25458. (Pitt Poetry Ser.). 264p. 1998. pap. 16.95 (*0-8229-5680-2*); text 30.00 (*0-8229-4080-9*) U of Pittsburgh Pr.

Little Spanish ABC Coloring Book. 81st ed. Anna Pomaska. (SPA., Illus.). (J). 1988. pap. 1.00 (*0-486-25614-6*) Dover.

Little Spanish Girl Paper Doll. Tom Tierney. (Illus.). (J). (gr. k-3). 1993. pap. 1.00 (*0-486-27677-5*) Dover.

Little Spanish Notebook: A Breakthrough in Early Speaking. Charles M. Long. LC 98-68585. (ENG & SPA., Illus.). v, 75p. 1999. 24.95 (*0-9667172-1-X*) Reflective Bks.

Little Sparrow: A Portrait of Sophia Kovalevsky. Don H. Kennedy. LC 82-12405. (Illus.). 350p. 1982. pap. 19.95 (*0-8214-0703-1*) Ohio U Pr.

Little Sparta: Portrait of a Garden. Ian H. Finlay & Alec H. Finlay. (Illus.). 64p. 1998. 70.00 (*0-903598-85-X*) Natl Galleries.

Little Speech Guide. Gaiz & Kassoway. (C). 1995. pap. text 8.74 (*0-07-034179-6*) McGraw.

Little Speedy Jo: The Antelope Fawn. Ken Ruff. Ed. by Anne M. Martin. LC 98-94880. (Illus.). 88p. (J). 1998. pap. write for info. (*1-57579-141-2*) Pine Hill Pr.

Little Spider see Arana Pequenita, Vol. 11, Pasitos Spanish Language Development Books

***Little Spokane.** Tom I. Davis. 64p. 2000. pap. 10.00 (*0-9668612-7-2*) Lost Horse.

Little Spooner Who Wouldn't Spoon. Deitz. 1994. pap. 6.95 (*0-938985-11-6*) Mntn Memories Bks.

***Little Spoonful of Chicken Soup for the Couple's Soul Gift Book.** Jack Canfield & Mark V. Hansen. 64p. 1999. 6.99 (*1-58375-544-6*) Garborgs.

***Little Spoonful of Chicken Soup for the Kid's Soul Gift Book.** Jack Canfield & Mark V. Hansen. 64p. 1999. 6.99 (*1-58375-545-4*) Garborgs.

Little Spoonful of Chicken Soup for the Soul: Just for friends Gift Book. Jack Canfield & Mark V. Hansen. 64p. 1998. 6.99 (*1-58375-436-9*) Garborgs.

Little Spoonful of Chicken Soup for the Soul Gift Book. Jack Canfield & Mark V. Hansen. 64p. 1998. 6.99 (*1-58375-435-0*) Garborgs.

***Little Spoonful of Chicken Soup for the Soul Gift Book.** Jack Canfield & Mark V. Hansen. 64p. 1998. 6.99 (*1-58375-434-2*); 6.99 (*1-58375-433-4*) Garborgs.

***Little Spoonful of Chicken Soup for the Woman's Soul Gift Book.** Jack Canfield & Mark V. Hansen. 64p. 1999. 6.99 (*1-58375-546-2*) Garborgs.

Little Spot of Color. Kathy Zoefeld & Bill Joyce. (Illus.). 18p. (J). 2000. bds. 5.99 (*0-7364-0172-5*, Pub. by Mouse Works) Time Warner.

Little Spotted Calf. Sanduik Bokforlag. (Illus.). 10p. (J). 1992. pap. 5.25 (*1-881445-05-4*) Sandvik Pub.

Little Spotted Moo. Larry K. Sims. (Illus.). 24p. (Orig.). (J). 1991. pap. text 3.95 (*1-880706-00-8*) Goldrock Bks.

***Little Squeegy Bug.** Bill Martin, Jr. et al. LC 00-32085. (Illus.). 2001. write for info. (*1-890817-90-2*) Winslow Pr.

Little Squire of Flanders. Nellie McCaslin. 55p. (Orig.). 1996. pap. 5.00 (*0-88734-476-3*) Players Pr.

Little Squirrel Went Passing By see Short Story Longs

Little St. Simons Island on the Coast of Georgia. Junius Rochester. LC 93-44483. 1994. 30.00 (*0-913720-90-9*) Beil.

***Little Star.** Gail Herman. (Fairy School Ser.). 80p. (J). 2000. pap. 3.99 (*0-553-48708-6*, Skylark BDD) BDD Bks Young Read.

Little Star. Mary Packard. (J). 1995. 12.95 (*0-590-54425-X*) Scholastic Inc.

Little Stars & Straw Breasts. Anthony Barnett. (Illus.). 52p. (Orig.). 1993. pap. write for info. (*0-907954-20-0*, Pub. by Allardyce Barnett) SPD-Small Pr Dist.

Little Star's Journey. Natalie Hale. (Illus.). 49p. (Orig.). 1994. pap. text 12.00 (*0-938837-18-4*) Behav Sci Ctr Pubs.

Little Steel. Upton Sinclair. LC 74-26122. (Labor Movement in Fiction & Non-Fiction Ser.). reprint ed. 37.50 (*0-404-58470-5*) AMS Pr.

***Little Stevie Wonder.** Shane Evans. (Illus.). 32p. (J). 2003. 15.99 (*0-7868-0682-6*, Pub. by Disney Pr) Time Warner.

Little Stinky Skunk. unabridged ed. Mae O. Ra'Oof & Jum Ra'Oof. (Five Friends of Rainbow Forest Ser.). (Illus.). 69p. (Orig.). (J). (gr. 3-5). 1995. pap. 8.95 (*1-888527-09-9*) New Wrld Ent.

Little Stinky Skunk. unabridged ed. Mae O. Ra'Oof & Jum Ra'Oof. (Five Friends of Rainbow Forest Ser.). (Illus.). 58p. (Orig.). (J). (ps-2). 1995. pap. 7.95 (*1-888527-03-X*) New Wrld Ent.

Little Stitch. Margaret B. Edwards. (Illus.). 24p. (J). (ps-8). 1986. 7.95 (*0-920806-69-4*, Pub. by Penumbra Pr) U of Toronto Pr.

Little Stone: Your Friend for Life. James Wanless. LC 99-19458. (Illus.). 93p. 1999. 10.95 (*1-86204-537-2*, Pub. by Element MA) Penguin Putnam.

Little Stories. Eloise Franco. (Illus.). (J). (gr. k-5). 1979. pap. 4.50 (*0-87516-384-X*) DeVorss.

Little Stories. Silas W. Mitchell. LC 76-85691. (Short Story Index Reprint Ser.). 1977. 17.95 (*0-8369-3034-7*) Ayer.

Little Stories: Clever Little Fairy. Price not set. incl. audio (*0-7214-7374-1*, Ladybrd) Penguin Putnam.

Little Stories for Little Children: A Worship Resource. Donna McKee Rhodes. LC 94-38280. 128p. (J). (ps-6). 1995. pap. 7.99 (*0-8361-9000-9*) Herald Pr.

Little Stories of Courtship. Mary S. Cutting. LC 79-98566. (Short Story Index Reprint Ser.). 1977. 19.95 (*0-8369-3140-8*) Ayer.

Little Stories of Married Life. Mary S. Cutting. LC 70-152968. (Short Story Index Reprint Ser.). 1977. reprint ed. 19.95 (*0-8369-3796-1*) Ayer.

Little Story about a Big Turnip. Tatiana Zunshine. (Illus.). 32p. (J). 1995. write for info. (*0-9646010-0-1*) Pumpkin House.

Little Stowaway. Theresa Tomlinson & Jane Browne. (Illus.). 32p. (J). (gr. k-2). 1998. 19.95 (*1-85681-691-5*, Pub. by Julia MacRae) Trafalgar.

Little Stream. Barry Ellsworth. (Illus.). 48p. Date not set. 9.95 (*1-56684-082-1*) Evans Bk Dist.

Little Striker. Russell G. Moore. LC 81-80507. (Illus.). 128p. (Orig.). 1981. pap. 5.00 (*0-936972-03-3*) Lower Cape.

***Little Suddenly!** Colin McNaughton. (Illus.). 14p. (J). (ps-k). 2000. 5.95 (*0-15-202531-6*, Harcourt Child Bks) Harcourt.

Little Sure Shot: The Story of Annie Oakley. Stephanie Spinner. LC 92-17014. (Step into Reading Ser.: A Step 3 Book). (Illus.). 48p. (J). (gr. 2-3). 1993. pap. 3.99 (*0-679-83432-X*, Pub. by Random Bks Yng Read) Random.

Little Susan. Slightly Off-Center Writers Group Staff. (Spark of Life Ser.). (Illus.). 48p. (J). (gr. 3-5). 1994. pap. 6.95 (*1-56721-079-1*) Twenty-Fifth Cent Pr.

***Little Susy Stories.** Elizabeth Prentiss. (J). 1999. pap. 7.99 (*1-881545-70-9*) Angelas Bkshelf.

Little Swan. Adele Geras. LC 94-35024. (Illus.). (J). 1995. pap. 3.99 (*0-679-87000-8*) Random.

Little Swan. Adele Geras. LC 94-35024. (Illus.). (J). 1995. lib. bdg. 11.99 (*0-679-97000-2*) Random.

Little Swan. Adele Geras. 1995. 9.19 (*0-606-07801-0*, Pub. by Turtleback) Demco.

Little Swedish Girl Paper Doll. Tom Tierney. (Illus.). (J). (gr. k-3). 1993. pap. 1.00 (*0-486-27661-9*) Dover.

Little Swineherd. Paula Fox. (J). 1999. pap. 4.99 (*0-14-037584-8*, Viking) Viking Penguin.

Little System 7.1-7.5 Book. 3rd ed. Kay Yarborough Nelson. 208p. (C). 1995. pap. text 13.95 (*1-56609-151-9*) Peachpit Pr.

***Little 't' Sellers.** (J). 2000. 3.95 (*0-552-52891-9*, Pub. by Transworld Publishers Ltd) Trafalgar.

Little Tale of Benjamin Bunny. Beatrix Potter & Haster. 1990. pap. text 1.00 (*0-486-26239-1*) Dover.

Little Tale of Mr. Jeremy Fisher Coloring Book. Beatrix Potter. (Illus.). (J). (gr. k-3). 1992. pap. 1.00 (*0-486-27291-5*) Dover.

Little Tale of Two Bad Mice Coloring Book. Beatrix Potter. (Illus.). (J). (gr. k-3). 1994. pap. 1.00 (*0-486-27868-9*) Dover.

***Little Tales of Family & War, 1990-1999.** Martha King. LC 00-25118. 2000. pap. write for info. (*1-881471-47-0*) S Duyvil.

Little Tales of Misogyny. Patricia Highsmith. 160p. 1986. 15.45 (*0-89296-244-5*, Pub. by Mysterious Pr) Little.

Little Tales of Misogyny. Patricia Highsmith. 160p. 1987. 45.00 (*0-89296-156-2*, Pub. by Mysterious Pr) Little.

Little Tales of Misogyny. Patricia Highsmith. 160p. 1987. reprint ed. 8.95 (*0-89296-917-2*) Mysterious Pr.

Little Talks for Little People. Susan Luke. 1994. pap. 7.95 (*1-55503-654-6*, 01111507) Covenant Comms.

Little Talks with Jesus. Joan Irland. 256p. (J). 1997. 10.99 (*0-8280-0279-7*) Review & Herald.

Little Tattoo Bug Book. Sharon Shi & Francisco Garofalo. (Illus.). (J). (gr. k-2). 1998. write for info. (*1-892800-02-0*) Temp Tattoo.

***Little Tattoo Bug Book.** rev. ed. Sharon Shi. (Illus.). 24p. (J). (gr. k-2). 2000. mass mkt. 4.99 (*0-9678636-6-X*, B007, Tattootles Bks) Tattoo Manuf.

Little Team That Could: The Incredible Often Wacky Story of the Two Time Little League World Champs. Tom Hennessy & Jeff Burroughs. LC 94-70385. (Illus.). 260p. 1994. 19.95 (*1-56625-008-0*) Bonus Books.

Little Teardrop. Pamela S. Ostwinkle. (Illus.). 27p. (J). (ps-4). 1999. 15.99 (*1-889406-16-3*) Prell Pub.

Little Teddy Bear's Happy Face Sad Face. Lynn Offerman. 12p. (J). (ps-k). 1999. 9.95 (*0-7613-0983-7*, Copper Beech Bks) Millbrook Pr.

***Little Teddy Bear's Happy Face Sad Face.** Lynn Offerman. 4p. (J). 1998. bds. 12.98 (*1-58048-035-7*) Sandvik Pub.

***Little Tenement on the Volga.** C. S. Walton. 130p. 2000. pap. 15.95 (*1-891053-78-7*) Garrett Cty Pr.

Little Terror: First Six Weeks. Charlotte Preston & Trevor Dunton. LC 99-36707. (Baby Tips Ser.: Vol. 1). (Illus.). 144p. 1999. pap. 6.95 (*1-55561-199-0*) Fisher Bks.

Little Terror: Good Behavior Guide. Charlotte Preston & Trevor Dunton. LC 99-38812. (Baby Tips Ser.: Vol. 4). (Illus.). 144p. 1999. pap. 6.95 (*1-55561-202-4*) Fisher Bks.

Little Terror: Good Feeding Guide. Charlotte Preston & Trevor Dunton. LC 99-36707. (Baby Tips Ser.: Vol. 2). (Illus.). 144p. 1999. pap. 6.95 (*1-55561-200-8*) Fisher Bks.

Little Terror: Good Sleeping Guide. Charlotte Preston & Trevor Dunton. LC 99-37067. (Baby Tips Ser.: Vol. 3). (Illus.). 144p. 1999. pap. 6.95 (*1-55561-201-6*) Fisher Bks.

Little Texas. 288p. 1996. pap., per. 12.98 (*0-9658239-1-1*) Chinquapin.

Little Texas - Greatest Hits. Ed. by Carol Cuellar. 64p. (Orig.). (C). 1995. pap. text 16.95 (*0-7692-0693-X*, PF9549) Wrner Bros.

Little Texas Cookbook. Carolyn Dehnel. (Illus.). 60p. 1992. 7.95 (*0-8118-0114-4*) Chronicle Bks.

Little Texas Two-Step. Peggy Moreland. 1997. per. 3.50 (*0-373-76090-6*, 1-76090-9) Silhouette.

Little Thanksgiving Sticker Book. Anna Pomaska. (Little Activity Bks.). (Illus.). (J). 1989. pap. 1.00 (*0-486-26070-4*) Dover.

Little Theater That Could: And the Story of Key Biscayne. Carol-Ann Rudy. LC 96-85492. (Hometown Heritage Ser.: Vol. 1). (Illus.). 32p. (Orig.). (J). (gr. 3-4). 1996. pap. 3.50 (*1-889300-00-4*) Dormouse Prods.

***Little Theatre on the Square: Four Decades of a Small-Town Equity Theatre.** Beth Conway Shervey. LC 00-36543. 2000. pap. write for info. (*0-8093-2355-9*) S Ill U Pr.

Little Things Long Remembered: Making Your Children Feel Special Every Day. Susan Newman. LC 92-42897. 1993. 14.00 (*0-517-59302-5*, Crown) Crown Pub Group.

Little Things Mean A Lot: Creating Happy Memories with Your Granchildren. Susan Newman. 128p. 1996. 14.00 (*0-517-70463-3*, Crown) Crown Pub Group.

Little Things Mean a Lot: Minute Meditations. Marie McIntyre. (Greeting Book Line Ser.). (Illus.). 32p. 1982. pap. 1.95 (*0-89622-155-5*) Twenty-Third.

Little Things Shared: Lasting Connections Between Family & Friends. Susan Newman. LC 97-28721. 1998. 14.00 (*0-517-70821-3*) Crown Pub Group.

Little Thoughts with Love. Anne Geddes. LC 99-199899. (Illus.). 124p. 1998. 29.95 (*0-7683-2020-8*) CEDCO Pub.

***Little Thoughts with Love.** Anne Geddes. 2000. 14.95 (*0-7683-2204-9*) CEDCO Pub.

***Little Thoughts with Love Address Book (Peony Rose Angel)** gif. ed. Anne Geddes. (Illus.). 96p. 1999. 17.95 (*0-7683-2075-5*) CEDCO Pub.

***Little Thoughts with Love Address Book (Wrapped in Blanket)** gif. ed. Anne Geddes. (Illus.). 96p. 1999. spiral bd. 17.95 (*0-7683-2076-3*) CEDCO Pub.

***Little Thumb.** Illus. by Wanda Dionne & Jana Dillon. LC 99-56098. (J). 2000. write for info. (*1-56554-754-3*) Pelican.

Little Tiger Goes Shopping. Vivian French. LC 92-43771. (Illus.). 24p. (J). (ps up). 1994. pap. 3.99 (*1-56402-263-3*) Candlewick Pr.

***Little Tiger Goes to School.** (Illus.). 8p. (J). 1999. 9.99 (*1-58048-083-7*) Sandvik Pub.

Little Tiger Goes to School: Giant Board Book. Julie Sykes. (Illus.). (J). (ps-2). 1998. bds. 11.95 (*1-888444-49-5*) Little Tiger.

Little Tiger in the Chinese Night: An Autobiography in Art. Song Nan Zhang. LC 93-60336. (Illus.). 48p. (J). (gr. 6-9). 1993. 19.95 (*0-88776-320-0*) Tundra Bks.

Little Tiger in the Chinese Night: An Autobiography in Art. Song Nan Zhang. (Illus.). 48p. (J). (gr. 2-6). 1995. pap. 8.95 (*0-88776-356-1*) Tundra Bks.

Little Tiger in the Chinese Night: An Autobiography in Art. Song Nan Zhang. 1993. 15.15 (*0-606-08805-9*, Pub. by Turtleback) Demco.

***Little Tiger's Big Surprise.** (Illus.). 28p. (J). 1999. 9.99 (*1-58048-082-9*) Sandvik Pub.

***Little Tiger's Big Surprise!** Julie Sykes. LC 99-17870. (Illus.). 32p. (J). (ps-k). 1999. 14.95 (*1-888444-52-5*, Pub. by Little Tiger) Futech Educ Prods.

Little Tigress: Tales Out of the Dust of Mexico. Wallace Smith. LC 74-144173. (Short Story Index Reprint Ser.). (Illus.). 1977. reprint ed. 19.95 (*0-8369-3788-0*) Ayer.

***Little Tim & the Brave Sea Captain.** Edward Ardizzone. LC 99-33894. 48p. (YA). 2000. 16.00 (*0-688-17678-X*) Morrow Avon.

Little Time in Texas. Joan Johnston. (Desire Ser.: No. 710). 1992. pap. 2.89 (*0-373-05710-5*, 5-05710-4) Harlequin Bks.

***Little Time in Texas.** Joan Johnston. 2000. mass mkt. 5.99 (*1-55166-629-4*, 1-66629-6, Mira Bks) Harlequin Bks.

***Little Toby & the Big Hair.** Eugenie Fernandes. (Illus.). 32p. (J). (gr. k-2). 1998. 14.95 (*1-55209-273-9*) Firefly Bks Ltd.

Little Toby & the Big Hair. Kim Fernandes. 32p. (J). 1997. text 16.95 (*0-385-25633-7*) Doubleday.

Little Toby & the Big Hair. Kim Fernandes & E. Fernandes. (J). 1998. pap. 12.95 (*0-385-25679-5*) Doubleday.

Little Toby & the Big Hair. Kim Fernandes & Eugenie Fernandes. (Illus.). 32p. (J). (gr. k-2). 1998. pap. 5.95 (*1-55209-257-7*) Firefly Bks Ltd.

Little Toby & the Big Hair. Sheree Fitch. (Illus.). 32p. 1998. pap. 8.95 (*0-385-25678-7*) Doubleday.

Little Tom & Fats. Alvan Mitchell. Ed. by Veneta B. Arrington. LC 83-81560. (Illus.). 272p. 1987. reprint ed. 14.95 (*0-9615098-2-1*) Prairie Imp.

Little Tom Kitten Stickers. Anna Pomaska. (Illus.). (J). (gr. k-3). 1993. pap. 1.00 (*0-486-27640-6*) Dover.

***Little Tom Meets Mr Jonah.** Philip D. Smith & Pat Day-Bivins. LC 99-95496. (Illus.). 32p. (J). (gr. k-5). 2000. 15.95 (*1-886864-16-0*) Goldn Anchor Pr.

Little Tommy & the Basketball. Adrienne V. Sealy. (Illus.). (J). (gr. 2-6). 1980. 3.50 (*0-9602670-4-2*) Assn Family Living.

Little Tommy Parker Celebrated Colored Minstrel Show. Carlyle Brown. 1992. pap. 5.25 (*0-8222-0679-X*) Dramatists Play.

Little Tommy Tinkler. Muriel Valet. (Illus.). 16p. (J). (gr. k-4). 1996. pap. 11.95 (*1-56606-041-9*) Bradley Mann.

Little Too Close to God: The Thrills & Panic of a Life in Modern Israel. David Horovitz. 320p. 2000. 26.00 (*0-375-40381-7*) Knopf.

Little Too Much Is Enough. Kathleen Tyau. LC 95-60673. 228p. 1995. 18.00 (*0-374-18950-1*) FS&G.

Little Too Much Is Enough. Kathleen Tyau. 240p. 1996. pap. 12.00 (*0-393-31559-2*) Norton.

Little Too-Tall. Jane Belk Moncure. LC 87-11632. (Magic Castle Readers Ser.). (Illus.). 32p. (J). (ps-2). 1988. lib. bdg. 21.36 (*0-89565-374-5*) Childs World.

Little Tools of Knowledge. Ed. by Peter Becker & William Clark. (Social History, Popular Culture & Politics in Germany Ser.). (Illus.). 424p. (C). text 52.50 (*0-472-11108-6*, 11108) U of Mich Pr.

Little Toot. Hardie Gramatky. (Illus.). 80p. (J). (ps-3). 1939. 16.95 (*0-399-22419-X*, G P Putnam) Peng Put Young Read.

Little Toot. Hardie Gramatky. (Illus.). 12p. (J). (ps). 1993. bds. 4.99 (*0-448-40585-7*, G & D) Peng Put Young Read.

Little Toot. Hardie Gramatky. LC 97-224327. (Illus.). 96p. (J). (ps-1). 1997. pap. 6.99 (*0-698-11576-7*, PapStar) Peng Put Young Read.

Little Toot. Hardie Gramatky. LC 99-36541. 48p. 1999. write for info. (*0-448-42072-4*, G & D) Peng Put Young Read.

***Little Toot.** Hardie Gramatky. (Illus.). 32p. (J). (ps-3). 2000. pap. 3.49 (*0-448-42297-2*, Planet Dexter) Peng Put Young Read.

Little Toot. Hardie Gramatky. (J). 1978. 11.19 (*0-606-02351-8*, Pub. by Turtleback) Demco.

***Little Toot & the Lighthouse.** Linda Gramatky-Smith. LC 99-23220. (All Aboard Bks.). (Illus.). 32p. (J). 1999. 2.99 (*0-448-42070-8*, G & D) Peng Put Young Read.

Little Toot's Busy World. Hardie Gramatky. 16p. 1999. pap. 4.99 (*0-448-42060-0*, G & D) Peng Put Young Read.

Little Tot Bible Coloring Book. Frank Schaffer Publications, Incorporated Staff. (Illus.). (J). 1997. pap. text 2.29 (*0-7647-0083-9*) Schaffer Pubns.

Little Tot Dot-to-Dot: Activity Book. Becky Radtke. (Illus.). (J). 1997. pap. text 2.29 (*0-7647-0081-2*) Schaffer Pubns.

Little Tot Hidden Pictures. Becky Radtke. (Illus.). (J). 1997. pap. text 2.29 (*0-7647-0084-7*) Schaffer Pubns.

Little Touch of Grace. Curtis Grace. LC 92-60504. (Illus.). 96p. 1992. pap. 6.95 (*0-913383-23-6*) McClanahan Pub.

Little Touch of Heaven for Men: 52 Heartwarming Devotions to Draw You Nearer to God. Robert Strand. LC 97-65166. 144p. 1997. boxed set 12.95 (*0-89221-344-2*) New Leaf.

Little Touch of Heaven for Women: 52 Heartwarming Devotions to Draw You Nearer to God. Robert Strand. LC 97-65167. 144p. 1997. boxed set 12.95 (*0-89221-345-0*) New Leaf.

Little Touch of Monster. Emily Lampert. LC 85-26847. (Illus.). 32p. (J). (ps-3). 1986. lib. bdg. 12.95 (*0-316-51287-7*, 512877, Joy St Bks) Little.

Little Tour in America. S. Reynolds Hole. LC 70-148885. (Select Bibliographies Reprint Ser.). 1977. reprint ed. 28.95 (*0-8369-5652-4*) Ayer.

Little Tour in France see Works of Henry James Jr.: Collected Works

***Little Tow-Watcher's Guide: To Towboats & Barges on the Upper Mississippi River.** 3rd rev. ed. Pamela Eyden. (Illus.). 64p. 1999. pap. 8.50 (*0-9653950-3-0*) Riverwise.

Little Tow-Watcher's Guide - 1997 Edition: To Towboats & Barges on the Upper Mississippi River. unabridged ed. Pamela Eyden. 64p. (Orig.). 1997. pap. 7.95 (*0-9653950-2-2*, BR-14) Big Riv MN.

Little Town: Especially in Its Rural Relationships. Harlan P. Douglass. LC 75-112553. (Rise of Urban America Ser.). (Illus.). 1970. reprint ed. 24.95 (*0-405-02448-7*) Ayer.

Little Town: Especially in Its Rural Relationships. Harlan P. Douglass. (Select Bibliographies Reprint Ser.). 1977. reprint ed. 24.95 (*0-8369-6643-0*) Ayer.

Little Town at the Crossroads. Maria D. Wilkes. LC 96-48096. (Little House). (Illus.). 368p. (J). (gr. 3-7). 1997. 16.95 (*0-06-026995-2*); pap. 4.95 (*0-06-440651-2*, HarpTrophy); lib. bdg. 15.89 (*0-06-026996-0*) HarpC Child Bks.

Little Town at the Crossroads. Maria D. Wilkes. (Little House). (Illus.). (J). (gr. 3-6). 1997. 10.05 (*0-606-11571-4*, Pub. by Turtleback) Demco.

Little Town in a Big Woods. rev. ed. Marilyn Robinson. 1996. 14.95 (*0-923889-20-5*) Inquisitors Pub.

Little Town in the Ozarks. Roger L. MacBride. (Little House). (Illus.). (J). (gr. 3-6). 1996. 15.95 (*0-06-024977-3*) HarpC Child Bks.

Little Town in the Ozarks. Roger L. MacBride. LC 95-47590. (Little House). (Illus.). 352p. (J). (gr. 4-7). 1996. pap. 4.95 (*0-06-440580-X*, HarpTrophy); lib. bdg. 15.89 (*0-06-024970-6*) HarpC Child Bks.

Little Town in the Ozarks. Roger Lea McBride. (Little House). (Illus.). (J). (gr. 3-6). 1996. 10.05 (*0-606-09565-9*, Pub. by Turtleback) Demco.

Little Town on the Prairie see Little House Books

***Little Town on the Prairie.** Laura Ingalls Wilder. (Little House). (J). (gr. 3-6). 2000. pap. 9.90 (*0-06-449101-3*, HarpTrophy) HarpC Child Bks.

Little Town on the Prairie. Laura Ingalls Wilder. (Little House). (J). (gr. 3-6). 1981. 10.05 (*0-606-03820-5*, Pub. by Turtleback) Demco.

Little Town on the Prairie. rev. ed. Laura Ingalls Wilder. LC 52-7531. (Little House). (Illus.). 320p. (J). (gr. 4-7). 1953. 16.95 (*0-06-026450-0*); lib. bdg. 16.89 (*0-06-026451-9*) HarpC Child Bks.

***Little Traditional Quilts.** Jayne Turner. Ed. by Debbie Hearn. Tr. by Guy Cali Van Zandbergen. (Illus.). 32p. 2000. pap. 12.95 (*1-885588-30-5*) Chitra Pubns.

***Little Tragedies.** Aleksandr Pushkin & Nancy K. Anderson. LC 99-46416. (Russian Literature & Thought Ser.). (Illus.). 160p. 2000. 13.00 (*0-300-08027-1*) Yale U Pr.

***Little Train.** Opal Dunn. (Track-Me-Back Board Bks.). 12p. (J). 2000. bds. 5.95 (*0-8050-6419-2*) H Holt & Co.

***Little Train.** Lois Lenski. (Illus.). (J). 2000. 13.95 (*0-375-81071-4*) Random.

An Asterisk (*) at the beginning of an entry indicates that the title is appearing for the first time.

***Little Train.** Lois Lenski. (Illus.). (J). 2000. 15.99 (*0-375-91071-9*) Random Bks Yng Read.

Little Trapshooting Book. Frank Little. (Illus.). 168p. Date not set. pap. 19.95 (*0-925012-02-5*) Shotgun Sports.

***Little Traveling Music, Please.** Margaret Moseley. 2000. mass mkt. 6.50 (*0-425-17551-0*, Prime Crime) Berkley Pub.

Little Treasures. Glenn Ridless. (Charming Petites Ser.). (Illus.). 80p. 1991. 4.95 (*0-88088-733-8*) Peter Pauper.

Little Treasures for Little People. Elizabeth Zerlin. (Illus.). 72p. (J). (gr. k-6). 1999. pap. 8.00 (*0-8059-4621-7*) Dorrance.

Little Treasury of Flintstones. (J). 1989. 5.95 (*0-318-41671-9*) Random Hse Value.

Little Treasury of Gold: Poems of Love & Faith. Kay A. Carson. 1992. 7.98 (*0-88486-062-0*) Arrowood Pr.

***Little Treasury of Prayers.** Walter C. Sutton. 50p. 2000. pap. 7.50 (*0-664-50112-5*, Pub. by Geneva Press) Presbyterian Pub.

Little Treasury of Walt Disney. (J). 1986. 5.98 (*0-685-16883-2*, 616300) Random Hse Value.

***Little Treatise on the Teeth.** Bartolomeo Eustachi et al. Ed. by David A. Chernin & Gerald Shklar. LC 99-39639. (Dental Classics in Perspective). 1999. 59.95 (*0-88135-259-4*) Watson Pub Intl.

Little Tree. Date not set. write for info. (*0-517-80134-5*) Random Hse Value.

Little Tree. Janie S. Gill. (Illus.). 23p. (J). 1999. 5.95 (*0-89868-489-7*); pap. 3.95 (*0-89868-488-9*); lib. bdg. 10.95 (*0-89868-487-0*) ARO Pub.

***Little Tree.** Illus. by Mary C. Smith. 24p. (YA). (ps up). 1999. text 16.95 (*1-902618-55-6*, Pub. by Element Childrns) Penguin Putnam.

Little Tree. Louise Stiles. (Illus.). 32p. (J). (gr. 3 up). 1987. pap. 5.95 (*0-88144-051-5*) Christian Pub.

Little Tree: A Story for Children with Serious Medical Problems. Joyce C. Mills. LC 92-19654. (Illus.). 32p. (J). 1992. 16.95 (*0-945354-52-5*) Am Psychol.

Little Tree: A Story for Children with Serious Medical Problems. Joyce C. Mills. LC 92-19654. (Illus.). 32p. (J). (ps-3). 1992. pap. 8.95 (*0-945354-51-7*) Am Psychol.

***Little Tree Without a Name.** Dennis Mosher. 2000. 10.95 (*0-533-13250-9*) Vantage.

Little Trials of Childhood & Children's Strategies for Dealing with Them. Frances C. Waksler. (World of Childhood & Adolescence Ser.). 240p. 1996. 85.00 (*0-7507-0453-5*, Falmer Pr); pap. 27.95 (*0-7507-0454-3*, Falmer Pr) Taylor & Francis.

Little Tricker the Squirrel Meets Big Double the Bear. Ken Kesey. (J). 1988. write for info. (*0-318-63679-4*, Viking Child) Peng Put Young Read.

Little Trilogy. Henryk Sienkiewicz. Tr. by Miroslaw Lipinsky from POL. 267p. 1994. 19.95 (*0-7818-0293-8*) Hippocrene Bks.

Little Trip to Heaven: Ireland, 1994. Jeffrey Bartlett. 206p. 1997. pap. 10.95 (*1-889883-02-6*) Provine Pr.

Little Troll. Thomas Berger. Tr. by Polly Lawson. (GER., Illus.). 32p. (J). (gr. k-3). 1992. 14.95 (*0-86315-112-4*, Pub. by Floris Bks) Gryphon Hse.

Little Troll Without a Soul: A Search for Happiness in One-Act. Herman Ammann. (Illus.). 27p. (J). (gr. 4-9). 1976. pap. 3.25 (*0-88680-117-6*) I E Clark.

***Little Troll's Big Adventure.** Virginia Ripley. (Illus.). 32p. (J). (gr. k-2). 1999. pap. 12.00 (*0-9674612-0-0*) Strike Pubng.

Little Tropical Fish Coloring Book. Ellen J. McHenry. (Illus.). (J). (gr. k-3). 1994. pap. 1.00 (*0-486-27951-0*) Dover.

Little Trucker Books, Series One, 3 vols. Stephen Reece. (Illus.). 40p. (J). (ps-3). 1998. pap. 7.95 (*1-892388-03-0*) Lttle Trucker.

Little Trucker Books, Series Two, 3 vols. Stephen Reece. (Illus.). 40p. (J). (ps-5). 1998. pap. 7.95 (*1-892388-04-9*) Lttle Trucker.

Little Trucker Counting Book. Stephen Reece. 16p. (J). (ps-3). 1998. pap. 3.65 (*1-892388-01-4*) Lttle Trucker.

***Little Turtle & the Song of the Sea.** Sheridan Cain. LC 99-53456. (Illus.). (J). (gr. k-3). 2000. 15.95 (*1-56656-355-0*, Pub. by Interlink Pub) Kane-Miller Bk.

Little Turtle Got Lost see Tortuguita Se Perdio

Little Turtledove Finds His Mate (El Tortolito Encuentra su Companera) Miriam A. Lademan & Susan A. Brindle. Tr. by Carmen A. Emmanuelli Klosterman. (Seven Sacraments Ser.). (ENG & SPA., Illus.). 56p. (gr. k-10). 1997. pap. 9.95 (*1-889733-06-7*, 01008) Precious Life Bks.

Little Twirly Things. Vincent Farnsworth. Ed. by Edward Mycue. (Took Modern Poetry in English Ser.: No. 9). (Illus.). 28p. (Orig.). 1991. pap. 3.00 (*1-879457-06-7*) Norton Coker Pr.

Little Tyke: The True Story of a Gentle Vegetarian Lioness. rev. ed. Georges Westbeau. LC 85-40772. (Illus.). 162p. 1986. pap. 5.95 (*0-8356-0605-8*, Quest) Theos Pub Hse.

***Little 'u' Sellers.** (J). 2000. 3.95 (*0-552-52892-7*, Pub. by Transworld Publishers Ltd) Trafalgar.

Little Union Scout. Joel Chandler Harris. LC 72-2998. (Black Heritage Library Collection). (Illus.). 1977. reprint ed. 20.95 (*0-8369-9075-7*) Ayer.

***Little 'v' Sellers.** (J). 2000. 3.95 (*0-552-52893-5*, Pub. by Transworld Publishers Ltd) Trafalgar.

Little Vampire & the Midnight Bear. Mary Deball Kwitz. (Puffin Easy-to-Read Program Ser.). (J). (gr. 1-4). 1998. pap. 3.99 (*0-14-130233-X*, PuffinBks) Peng Put Young Read.

Little Venice & Other Stories. Grace D. Litchfield. LC 72-98583. (Short Story Index Reprint Ser.). 1977. 20.95 (*0-8369-3157-2*) Ayer.

Little Venice Makes a Good Drink: or The Family That Stays Together... Leonard Melfi. LC 96-37912. 80p. Date not set. pap. 6.95 (*1-55783-258-7*) Applause Theatre Bk Pubs.

Little Victorian Girl. Tom Tierney. (Little Activity Bks.). (Illus.). (J). 1994. pap. 1.00 (*0-486-27935-9*) Dover.

Little Victories. Lavonne Mueller. 1984. pap. 5.25 (*0-8222-0680-3*) Dramatists Play.

Little Victories Vol. 1: Tales from a World Without End. Webster K. Howell. Ed. by Jane Warth. 146p. (Orig.). 1995. pap. 14.95 (*0-9651851-0-9*) Mountain Pubns.

Little Vine. James R. Rhodes. (Lewiston Poetry Ser.: Vol. 12). (Illus.). 84p. 1986. lib. bdg. 24.95 (*0-88946-049-3*) E Mellen.

Little Virtues. Natalia Ginzburg. Tr. by Dick David from ITA. LC 86-13488. (ITA.). 110p. 1985. 13.95 (*0-8050-0077-1*) Seaver Bks.

Little Virtues. Natalia Ginzburg. Tr. by Dick Davis from ITA. 120p. 1999. reprint ed. 10.95 (*1-55970-028-9*, Pub. by Arcade Pub Inc) Time Warner.

Little Visits Every Day. Mary M. Simon. LC 95-11353. (Little Visits Library: Vol. 3). (Illus.). (ps-2). 1995. 10.00 (*0-570-05807-4*, 06-1205) Concordia.

Little Visits Every Day. Mary M. Simon. (ps-2). 1997. 10.00 (*0-570-05808-2*, 06-1305) Concordia.

Little Visits for Families. Mary M. Simon & Allan Jahsmann. (ps-2). 1997. pap. text 10.00 (*0-570-05810-4*) Concordia.

Little Visits for Families. Allan H. Jahsmann & Martin P. Simon. LC 95-20234. (Little Visits Library: Vol. 5). Orig. Title: More Little Visits with God. (Illus.). 304p. 1995. reprint ed. 12.99 (*0-570-05803-1*, 06-1203) Concordia.

Little Visits for Toddlers. rev. ed. Mary M. Simon. LC 95-20235. (Little Visits Library: Vol. 1). Orig. Title: Little Visits 1-2-3. (Illus.). 304p. 1995. 12.99 (*0-570-05805-8*, 06-1201) Concordia.

Little Visits on the Go. Mary M. Simon. (Little Visits Library). (Illus.). 64p. (J). (ps-7). 1992. pap. 13.99 (*0-570-03084-6*, 06-1199) Concordia.

Little Visits Toddlers. Mary M. Simon. 1997. pap. text 10.00 (*0-570-05806-6*) Concordia.

Little Visits with God. Mary M. Simon et al. (gr. 2-5). 1997. pap. text 10.00 (*0-570-05809-0*) Concordia.

Little Visits with God. rev. ed. Allan H. Jahsmann & Martin P. Simon. (Little Visits Library: Vol. 4). (Illus.). 304p. (J). 1995. 12.99 (*0-570-05801-5*, 06-1204) Concordia.

Little Visits with Great Americans, 2 vols. Orison S. Marden. Incl. Vol. I. 352p. 1997. pap. 35.00 (*0-89540-372-2*); Vol. II. 389p. 1997. pap. 35.00 (*0-89540-373-0*); 742p. 50.00 (*0-89540-374-9*) Sun Pub.

Little Visits with Jesus. rev. ed. Mary M. Simon. (Little Visits Library: Vol. 2). (Illus.). 304p. (J). 1995. 12.99 (*0-570-05804-X*, 06-1202) Concordia.

Little Visits 1-2-3 see Little Visits for Toddlers

Little Voodoo Kit. Jean P. Poupette. LC 97-12810. 1997. text 11.95 (*0-312-15415-1*) St Martin.

***Little 'w' Sellers.** (J). 2000. 3.95 (*0-552-52894-3*, Pub. by Transworld Publishers Ltd) Trafalgar.

Little Walrus Warning. Carol Young. (Smithsonian Oceanic Collection). (Illus.). 32p. (J). (ps-2). 1996. 15.95 incl. audio (*1-56899-271-8*, B4009) Soundprints.

Little Walrus Warning. Carol Young. (Smithsonian Oceanic Collection). (Illus.). 32p. (J). (ps-2). 1996. 19.95 incl. audio (*1-56899-275-0*, BC4009) Soundprints.

Little Walrus Warning, Incl. large toy. Carol Young. (Smithsonian Oceanic Collection). (Illus.). 32p. (J). (ps-2). 1996. 29.95 (*1-56899-273-4*) Soundprints.

Little Walrus Warning, Micro bk. Carol Young. (Illus.). 32p. (J). (ps-2). 1996. 4.95 (*1-56899-272-6*) Soundprints.

Little Walrus Warning, Micro bk., incl. small toy. Carol Young. (Smithsonian Oceanic Collection). (Illus.). 32p. (J). (ps-2). 1996. 9.95 (*1-56899-274-2*) Soundprints.

Little War of Destiny. John C. Jackson. 205p. 1996. 24.95 (*0-87770-564-X*); pap. 14.95 (*0-87770-565-8*) Ye Galleon.

Little War of Private Post: The Spanish-American War Seen up Close. Charles J. Post. LC 99-10211. (Illus.). xviii, 340p. 1999. pap. 15.00 (*0-8032-8757-7*) U of Nebr Pr.

Little Wars. H. G. Wells. LC 77-23580. (Quality Paperbacks Ser.). 1977. reprint ed. pap. 4.95 (*0-306-80075-6*) Da Capo.

Little Water & the Gift of the Animals: A Seneca Legend. C. J. Taylor. LC 92-8413. (Illus.). 24p. (J). (gr. 1-5). 1992. 13.95 (*0-88776-285-9*) Tundra Bks.

Little Water & the Gift of the Animals: A Seneca Legend. C.J. Taylor. LC 97-930059. (Native Legends Ser.). (Illus.). 24p. (J). 1997. pap. 6.95 (*0-88776-400-2*) Tundra Bks.

Little Way: Counsels & Reminiscences of the Little Flower. St. Therese of Lisieux. 96p. 1998. pap. 7.95 (*1-887548-15-7*) St Michael NC.

Little Way of Saint Theresa of Lisieux: Readings for Prayer & Meditation. Compiled by John Nelson. LC 97-32384. 160p. 1998. pap. 9.00 (*0-7648-0199-6*) Liguori Pubns.

Little Way of the Infant Jesus: How the Christ Child Leads You to God. rev. ed. Caryll Houselander. LC 95-31351. Orig. Title: Wood of the Cradle, Wood of the Cross. 176p. 2000. pap. 14.95 (*0-918477-33-6*) Sophia Inst Pr.

Little Ways to Give God Praise. Photos by Heidi Bratton. LC 98-32046. (Walking with God II Ser.). (Illus.). 16p. (J). 2000. 5.95 (*0-8091-6661-5*) Paulist Pr.

Little Ways to Say "I Love You" Marjabelle Y. Stewart. 176p. (Orig.). 1992. pap. 8.95 (*0-312-07237-6*) St Martin.

Little Weaver of Thai-Yen Village. rev. ed. Tran-Khanh-Tuyet. LC 86-17186. (ENG & VIE., Illus.). 24p. (YA). (gr. 4-7). 1987. 15.95 (*0-89239-030-1*) Childrens Book Pr.

Little Web Book: A Gentle Introduction to the World Wide Web. Alfred Glossbrenner & Emily Glossbrenner. (Illus.). 256p. (C). 1996. pap. text 14.95 (*0-201-88367-8*) Peachpit Pr.

***Little Web Cam Book.** Elisabeth Parker. 250p. 1999. pap. text 18.99 (*0-201-35420-9*, Pub. by Peachpit Pr) Addison-Wesley.

Little Western Girl. Tom Tierney. (Little Activity Bks.). (Illus.). (J). 1995. pap. 1.00 (*0-486-28803-X*) Dover.

***Little Whistle.** Illus. by Cynthia Rylant & Tim Bowers. LC 99-12650. 2000. 20.01 (*0-15-201087-4*) Harcourt.

Little Whistle's Dinner Party. Illus. by Cynthia Rylant & Tim Bowers. LC 99-12383. 2001. 20.01 (*0-15-201079-3*) Harcourt.

Little White Bird see Works of J. M. Barrie: Peter Pan Edition

Little White Bird: or Adventures in Kensington Gardens. J. M. Barrie. 1991. reprint ed. lib. bdg. 21.95 (*1-56849-045-3*) Buccaneer Bks.

Little White Cabin. Marian Schooland. (Illus.). 163p. (YA). (gr. 7-10). 1993. pap. 6.20 (*0-7399-0104-4*, 2120) Rod & Staff.

Little White Dog. Laura Godwin. LC 97-21261. (Illus.). 32p. (J). (ps-k). 1998. 14.95 (*0-7868-0297-9*, Pub. by Hyprn Child); lib. bdg. 15.49 (*0-7868-2256-2*, Pub. by Hyprn Child) Little.

***Little White Dog.** Laura Godwin. (Illus.). 32p. (J). (ps-k). 2000. pap. 5.99 (*0-7868-1515-9*) Hyprn Ppbks.

***Little White Dogs Can't Jump.** Bruce Whatley. 32p. (J). (ps-2). 2001. 12.95 (*0-06-028013-1*) HarpC Child Bks.

Little White Dragon. Lyndell Ludwig. (Illus.). 23p. (YA). (gr. 5 up). 1989. pap. 4.95 (*0-9621782-0-9*) Star Dust Bks.

Little White Duck. Zaritzky Whippo. LC 99-13661. (Illus.). 32p. (J). (ps-3). 2000. 13.95 (*0-316-03227-1*) Little.

Little White Father: Redick McKee on the California Frontier. Ray Raphael. LC 93-8515. 1993. pap. 15.95 (*1-883254-00-0*) Humboldt Cnty.

***Little White Hen Called "RolyPoly"** Hazel Hallmark. (Illus.). 15p. (J). 1999. pap. 8.00 (*1-930002-01-7*) I&L Pubs.

Little White Horse. Elizabeth Goudge. 1976. 24.95 (*0-8488-1416-9*) Amereon Ltd.

Little White Horse. Elizabeth Goudge. (J). 1976. 35.95 (*0-89966-474-1*) Buccaneer Bks.

Little White Lie: Institutional Divisions of Labor & Life. Robert E. Agger. LC 78-15884. 207p. reprint ed. pap. 64.20 (*0-608-16310-4*, 202626000049) Bks Demand.

***Little White Lies.** Ron Benrey & Janet Benrey. 2001. pap. 12.99 (*0-8054-2371-0*) Broadman.

***Little White Lies.** Judy Gill. (Bouquet Ser.: Vol. 38). 2000. mass mkt. 3.99 (*0-8217-6532-9*, Zebra Kensgtn) Kensgtn Pub Corp.

Little White Lies. large type unabridged ed. Marjorie Lewty. (Harlequin Ser.). 1994. pap. 19.95 (*0-263-13589-6*) Mac Lib Ref.

Little White Lies, Bk. 10. Beverly Lewis. LC 95-30920. (Holly's Heart Ser.: Vol. 10). 160p. (J). (gr. 5-9). 1995. pap. 6.99 (*0-310-20194-2*) Zondervan.

Little White Schoolhouse. Ellis F. Hartford. LC 76-46028. (Kentucky Bicentennial Bookshelf Ser.). (Illus.). 128p. 1977. 15.00 (*0-8131-0231-6*) U Pr of Ky.

Little Wide Mouth Gecko. David M. Alexander. (Illus.). (J). (ps-3). 1996. pap. 10.00 (*1-892455-00-5*) Desk Top KS.

Little Wild: Poems & Woodcuts. Julia Older. (Illus.). 40p. 1987. 28.00 (*0-930126-19-X*) Typographeum.

Little Wildflowers Stained Glass Coloring Book. John Green. (Illus.). (J). (gr. k-3). 1993. pap. 1.00 (*0-486-27225-7*) Dover.

Little Windows Book, 3.1 Edition. Kay Yarborough Nelson. (Illus.). 144p. 1995. pap. text 12.95 (*0-938151-81-9*) Peachpit Pr.

Little Windows 98 Book. Alan Simpson. LC 99-169229. 408p. (C). 1998. pap. 16.95 (*0-201-35364-4*, Pub. by Peachpit Pr) Addison-Wesley.

Little Windows 95 Book. 3rd ed. Kay Yarborough Nelson. 144p. (C). 1995. pap. text 12.95 (*1-56609-181-0*, Pub. by Peachpit Pr) Addison-Wesley.

Little Wings. C. David Hay. Ed. by Ginny L. Ballor & Carrie Neumann. 40p. (Orig.). (C). 1996. pap. 3.00 (*1-882294-17-3*) Green Gate.

Little Witch. Anna E. Bennett. LC 52-1374. (Illus.). (J). (gr. 3-5). 1953. lib. bdg. 12.89 (*0-397-30261-4*) HarpC Child Bks.

Little Witch. Leanne Mebust & Regina Gismoruli. LC 97-216261. (Illus.). (J). 1997. write for info. (*0-7853-2360-0*) Pubns Intl Ltd.

Little Witch Goes to School. Deborah Hautzig. LC 97-31365. (Step into Reading Ser.: A Step 2 Book: Vol. 3). (Illus.). 48p. (J). (gr. k-3). 1998. pap. 3.99 (*0-679-88738-5*, Pub. by Random Bks Yng Read); lib. bdg. 11.99 (*0-679-98738-X*, Pub. by Random Bks Yng Read) Random.

Little Witch Magic. Robert Bender. (J). (gr. 3). 1995. pap. 5.95 (*0-8050-3549-4*) H Holt & Co.

Little Witch Magic. Robert Bender. LC 92-4054. (Illus.). 32p. (J). (ps-3). 1995. 14.95 (*0-8050-2126-4*, Bks Young Read) H Holt & Co.

Little Witch's Bad Dream. Deborah Hautzig. LC 99-20135. (Step into Reading Ser.). (Illus.). 48p. (J). (gr. k-3). 2000. pap. 3.99 (*0-679-87342-2*, Pub. by Random Bks Yng Read); lib. bdg. 11.99 (*0-679-97342-7*, Pub. by Random Bks Yng Read) Random.

***Little Witch's Bad Dream.** Deborah Hautzig. (Illus.). (J). 2000. 9.44 (*0-606-18855-X*) Turtleback.

Little Witch's Big Night. Deborah Hautzig. LC 84-3309. (Step into Reading Ser.: A Step 2 Book). (Illus.). 48p. (J). (ps-3). 1984. pap. 3.99 (*0-394-86587-1*, Pub. by Random Bks Yng Read) Random.

Little Wives. Barbara Cole. 35p. 1998. 7.00 (*0-937013-82-X*) Potes Poets.

***Little Wizard of Oz Activity Book.** Victoria Fremont & Pat Stewart. (Little Activity Bks.). 64p. (J). 1999. pap. 1.00 (*0-486-40735-7*) Dover.

Little Wizard Stories of Oz. L. Frank Baum. LC 93-77316. (Books of Wonder). (Illus.). 192p. (J). (gr. 2 up). 1994. 20.00 (*0-688-12126-8*, Wm Morrow) Morrow Avon.

***Little Wok Cookbook.** Anness Publications Staff. 1999. 12.95 (*1-84038-400-X*, Pub. by Hermes Hse) Random.

***Little Wok Cookbook.** Ed. by Smithmark Publishing Staff. (Illus.). 64p. 2000. 11.95 (*0-7548-0496-8*, Lorenz Bks) Anness Pub.

Little Wolf & the Giant. Sue Porter. (J). (ps-1). 1990. pap. 13.95 (*0-671-70363-3*) S&S Bks Yung.

Little Wolf at Leyte: Story of the Heroic Men of the USS Samuel B. Roberts in the Battle of Leyte Gulf. Henry Doscher, Jr. (Illus.). 158p. 1996. 18.95 (*1-57168-082-9*, Eakin Pr) Sunbelt Media.

***Little Wolf, Big Wolf.** Matt Novak. LC PZ7.N867Li 2000. (I Can Read Bks.). (Illus.). 48p. (J). (gr. 1-3). 2000. 14.95 (*0-06-027486-7*); lib. bdg. 14.89 (*0-06-027487-5*) HarpC.

***Little Wolf, Big Wolf.** Matt Novak. (I Can Read Bks.). (J). (gr. 1-3). 2001. pap. write for info. (*0-06-444230-6*, HarpTrophy) HarpC Child Bks.

Little Wolf's Birthday. Demco, Inc. Staff & Jane De Broux. (Little Wolf Ser.). 20p. (J). (gr. k-2). 1994. student ed. 1.99 (*1-885360-02-9*) Demco WI.

Little Wolf's Book of Badness. Ian Whybrow. LC 99-30596. (Middle Grade Fiction Ser.). (Illus.). 132p. (J). (gr. 4-7). 1999. 12.95 (*1-57505-410-8*, Carolrhoda) Lerner Pub.

***Little Wolf's Diary of Daring Deeds.** Ian Whybrow. LC 99-53204. (Middle Grade Fiction Ser.). (Illus.). 132p. (J). (gr. 3-6). 2000. lib. bdg. 12.95 (*1-57505-411-6*, Carolrhoda) Lerner Pub.

***Little Wolf's Haunted Hall for Small Horrors.** Ian Whybrow. LC 00-25290. (Middle Grade Fiction Ser.). (Illus.). 132p. (J). (gr. 3-7). 2000. 12.95 (*1-57505-412-4*, Carolrhoda) Lerner Pub.

Little Wolf's School Day. Demco, Inc. Staff & Jane De Broux. (Little Wolf Ser.). 20p. (J). (gr. k-2). 1994. student ed. 1.99 (*1-885360-00-2*) Demco WI.

Little Wolf's Seasons. Demco, Inc. Staff & Jane De Broux. (Little Wolf Ser.). 20p. (J). (gr. k-2). 1994. student ed. 1.99 (*1-885360-01-0*) Demco WI.

Little Woman. Anderson. 32p. (J). Date not set. pap. 5.95 (*0-06-443574-1*) HarpC Child Bks.

Little Woman. William Anderson. 32p. (J). (gr. 2-5). 2001. 15.95 (*0-06-028402-1*) HarpC Child Bks.

***Little Woman.** William Anderson. 32p. (J). (gr. 2-5). 2001. lib. bdg. 15.89 (*0-06-028403-X*) HarpC Child Bks.

Little Woman in China see Pequena Gran Mujer en la China

***Little Women.** (Penguin Readers Ser.: Level 1). (C). 2000. 7.00 (*0-582-41668-X*) Pearson Educ.

***Little Women.** (Pacemaker Classics Ser.). 1998. write for info. (*0-8359-3588-4*) Globe Fearon.

Little Women. Louisa May Alcott. (Keepsake Collection Bks.). (J). 1998. boxed set 3.99 (*1-57145-101-3*, Thunder Bay) Advantage Pubs.

***Little Women.** Louisa May Alcott. (Classics Ser.). 704p. (J). (gr. 4-7). 2000. pap. 5.99 (*0-689-83531-0*) Aladdin.

Little Women. Louisa May Alcott. Date not set. lib. bdg. 19.95 (*0-614-25286-5*) Amereon Ltd.

Little Women. Louisa May Alcott. (Andre Deutsch Classics). 264p. (J). (gr. 5-8). 1996. 9.95 (*0-233-99040-2*, Pub. by Andre Deutsch) Trafalgar.

Little Women. Louisa May Alcott. (Read-Along Ser.). (YA). 1994. pap., student ed. 34.95 incl. audio (*0-88432-965-8*, S23935) Audio-Forum.

Little Women. Louisa May Alcott. 480p. (YA). 1983. mass mkt. 3.95 (*0-553-21275-3*, Bantam Classics) Bantam.

Little Women. Louisa May Alcott. (Young Reader's Christian Library). (Illus.). 192p. (J). (gr. 3-7). 1998. pap. 1.39 (*1-57748-229-8*) Barbour Pub.

***Little Women.** Louisa May Alcott. Ed. by Jane E. Gerver. LC 99-14752. (Eyewitness Classics Ser.). 64p. (gr. 2). 1999. 14.95 (*0-7894-4767-3*) DK Pub Inc.

***Little Women.** Louisa May Alcott. LC 99-48534. (Juvenile Classics). (Illus.). 608p. (J). 2000. pap. 3.00 (*0-486-41023-4*) Dover.

Little Women. Louisa May Alcott. 93p. 1941. pap. 5.50 (*0-87129-320-X*, L27) Dramatic Pub.

Little Women. Louisa May Alcott. 1997. pap. 4.50 (*1-57514-326-7*, 1051) Encore Perform Pub.

Little Women. Louisa May Alcott. (Classic Collection). 1997. 15.99 (*1-56179-552-6*) Focus Family.

Little Women. Louisa May Alcott. (Illus.). 192p. (J). 2.98 (*1-56156-371-4*) Kidsbks.

Little Women. Louisa May Alcott. (Illus.). 524p. (YA). (gr. 7 up). 1968. 19.95 (*0-316-03095-3*) Little.

Little Women. Louisa May Alcott. (Illus.). (J). (gr. 3-7). 1968. 19.95 (*0-685-47121-7*) Little.

Little Women. Louisa May Alcott. (English As a Second Language Bk.). 1981. pap. text 4.46 (*0-582-53489-5*) Longman.

Little Women. Louisa May Alcott. (Modern Library College Editions). 603p. (C). 1983. pap. 8.44 (*0-07-554389-3*) McGraw.

Little Women. Louisa May Alcott. (J). 1981. pap. 6.00 (*0-685-06605-3*) Modern Lib NY.

Little Women. Louisa May Alcott. (Little Brown Notebooks). 1998. 9.99 (*1-897954-77-8*, Pub. by Mus Quilts Pub) Sterling.

Little Women. Louisa May Alcott. write for info. (*0-614-22111-0*, Sig Classics) NAL.

L

Little Women. Louisa May Alcott. 480p. (J). (gr. 3 up). 1983. mass mkt. 3.95 (*0-451-52341-5*, Sig Classics) NAL.

Little Women, 4 vols. Louisa May Alcott. 40.00 (*0-614-30531-4*) NAVH.

Little Women. Louisa May Alcott. Ed. by Jennifer Bassett. (Illus.). 78p. 1995. pap. text 5.95 (*0-19-422756-1*) OUP.

Little Women. Louisa May Alcott. Ed. & Intro. by Valerie Alderson. (Oxford World's Classics Ser.). 526p. 1998. pap. 6.95 (*0-19-283434-7*) OUP.

Little Women. Louisa May Alcott. 1994. mass mkt. 5.99 (*0-671-51764-3*) PB.

***Little Women.** Louisa May Alcott. 1998. pap. 7.00 (*0-582-40194-1*) Pearson Educ.

Little Women. Louisa May Alcott. 32p. (J). (ps-3). 1994. pap. 2.95 (*0-590-22537-5*, PuffinBks) Peng Put Young Read.

Little Women. Louisa May Alcott. (Puffin Classics Ser.). (Illus.). 669p. (J). (gr. 5-9). 1997. pap. 6.99 (*0-14-038022-1*, PuffinBks) Peng Put Young Read.

Little Women. Louisa May Alcott. Ed. by Malvina Vogel. (Great Illustrated Classics Ser.: Vol. 4). (Illus.). 240p. (J). (gr. 3-6). 1989. 9.95 (*0-86611-955-8*) Playmore Inc.

Little Women. Louisa May Alcott. LC 93-38237. (Step into Classics Ser.). 108p. (J). (gr. 4-7). 1994. pap. 3.99 (*0-679-86175-0*, Pub. by Random Bks Yng Read) Random.

Little Women. Louisa May Alcott. 510p. (J). (gr. 4-7). 1994. pap. 3.95 (*0-590-20350-9*) Random Hse Value.

Little Women. Louisa May Alcott. (Classics Ser.). 368p. (YA). (gr. 5 up). 1995. pap. 3.99 (*0-14-036668-7*) Random Hse Value.

Little Women. Louisa May Alcott. 400p. (J). 1998. 5.99 (*0-517-18954-2*) Random Hse Value.

***Little Women.** Louisa May Alcott. (Giant Classics). 688p. (YA). 2000. 8.98 (*0-7624-0565-1*, Courage) Running Pr.

Little Women. Louisa May Alcott. (Illustrated Classics Ser.). (J). 1988. 2.98 (*0-671-09222-7*) S&S Trade.

Little Women. Louisa May Alcott. (YA). 1996. 37.50 (*0-87557-135-2*) Saphrograph.

***Little Women.** Louisa May Alcott. 608p. (gr. 4-7). 2000. pap. 6.99 (*0-439-10136-0*) Scholastic Inc.

Little Women. Louisa May Alcott. (Little Brown Notebook Ser.). (Illus.). 256p. 1995. 6.95 (*0-8069-3975-3*) Sterling.

Little Women. Louisa May Alcott. 480p. 1994. pap. 2.50 (*0-8125-2333-4*, Pub. by Tor Bks) St Martin.

Little Women. Louisa May Alcott. 1997. pap. 4.95 (*0-89375-707-1*) Troll Communs.

Little Women. Louisa May Alcott. 1962. 10.10 (*0-606-00974-4*, Pub. by Turtleback) Demco.

Little Women. Louisa May Alcott. LC 93-38237. (Bullseye Step into Classics Ser.). 1994. 9.09 (*0-606-09566-7*, Pub. by Turtleback) Demco.

Little Women. Louisa May Alcott. Ed. & Intro. by Elaine Showalter. 608p. (J). 1989. pap. 7.95 (*0-14-039069-3*, Penguin Classics) Viking Penguin.

Little Women. Louisa May Alcott. (Children's Library). 1998. pap. 3.95 (*1-85326-116-5*, 1165WW, Pub. by Wrdsworth Edits) NTC Contemp Pub Co.

Little Women. Louisa May Alcott. (J). 1940. 6.00 (*0-87602-150-X*) Anchorage.

Little Women. Louisa May Alcott. (YA). 1994. pap. 3.99 (*0-671-51902-6*, Minstrel Bks) PB.

Little Women. Louisa May Alcott & Jenny Thorne. LC 78-2919. (Illustrated Classics). (J). 1978. write for info. (*0-8393-6210-2*) Raintree Steck-V.

***Little Women.** Stacie Champlin Dreibrodt. (YA). 2000. 9.95 (*1-58130-630-X*); 11.95 (*1-58130-631-8*) Novel Units.

Little Women. Elizabeth Lennox Keyser & Louisa May Alcott. 1997. pap. 13.95 (*0-8057-3896-7*, Twyne) Mac Lib Ref.

Little Women. Elizabeth Lennox Keyser & Louisa May Alcott. 1998. 23.95 (*0-8057-3897-5*, Twyne) Mac Lib Ref.

Little Women. abr. ed. Louisa May Alcott. 256p. (J). (gr. 4-7). 1986. pap. 4.50 (*0-590-43797-6*, Apple Classics) Scholastic Inc.

Little Women. abr. large type ed. Louisa May Alcott. (Illus.). 32p. (J). (gr. k up). 1995. pap. 14.95 (*1-886201-05-6*) Nana Banana.

Little Women. adapted ed. Louisa May Alcott. (Living Classics Ser.). (Illus.). 32p. (J). (gr. 3-7). 1997. 14.95 (*0-7641-7047-3*) Barron.

Little Women. deluxe ed. Louisa May Alcott. (Illus.). 656p. (J). (gr. 4 up). 1947. 18.99 (*0-448-06019-1*, G & D) Peng Put Young Read.

Little Women. deluxe ed. Louisa May Alcott. LC 97-60825. (Illus.). 288p. (J). 1997. pap. 16.99 (*0-670-87706-9*, Viking Child) Peng Put Young Read.

Little Women. large type ed. Louisa May Alcott. 665p. 1998. lib. bdg. 25.00 (*0-939495-51-1*) North Bks.

Little Women. large type ed. Louisa May Alcott. 336p. (J). 1987. 27.99 (*0-7089-8384-7*, Charnwood) Ulverscroft.

Little Women. Louisa May Alcott. (YA). (gr. 6 up). 1983. reprint ed. lib. bdg. 18.95 (*0-89966-408-3*) Buccaneer Bks.

Little Women. Louisa May Alcott. LC 96-39462. (Children's Thrift Classics Ser.). (Illus.). 96p. (J). 1997. reprint ed. pap. text 1.00 (*0-486-29634-2*) Dover.

Little Women. Louisa May Alcott. (Illus.). 352p. (J). 1993. reprint ed. 25.00 (*0-88363-203-9*) H L Levin.

Little Women. Louisa May Alcott. 559p. (J). 1998. reprint ed. lib. bdg. 24.00 (*1-58287-046-2*) North Bks.

Little Women. Louisa May Alcott. (Works of Louisa May Alcott). (J). 1989. reprint ed. lib. bdg. 79.00 (*0-7812-1627-3*) Rprt Serv.

***Little Women.** unabridged ed. Louisa May Alcott. (Wordsworth Classics). (YA). (gr. 6-12). 1998. 5.27 (*0-89061-116-5*, R1165WW, Jamestwn Pub) NTC Contemp Pub Co.

Little Women. 2nd ed. Louisa May Alcott. (Illus.). 62p. 1993. pap. text 5.95 (*0-19-585271-0*) OUP.

Little Women: Adapted for the Stage. Louisa May Alcott. (Illus.). 95p. 1995. pap. 4.00 (*0-88680-412-4*, 412-4) I E Clark.

Little Women: Book & Charm Keepsake. Louisa May Alcott. 48p. (J). (gr. 4-7). 1994. 12.95 (*0-590-22538-3*) Scholastic Inc.

Little Women: Meg, Joe, Beth, & Amy. Louisa May Alcott. (Great Stories Ser.). (Illus.). 526p. (J). 1999. pap. 9.99 (*1-56179-744-8*) Focus Family.

Little Women: Or Meg, Jo, Beth & Amy. Louisa May Alcott. LC 93-18943. (Little Classics Ser.). (Illus.). 308p. (J). (gr. 4-8). 1995. 15.95 (*0-8050-2767-X*, Bks Young Read) H Holt & Co.

Little Women: Or Meg, Jo, Beth & Amy. Louisa May Alcott. LC 94-5865. (Everyman's Library of Children's Classics). 384p. (J). 1994. 14.95 (*0-679-43642-1*, Evrymans Lib Childs) Knopf.

Little Women: Or Meg, Jo, Beth & Amy. Louisa May Alcott. LC 94-17444. 502p. (J). (gr. 4-6). 1994. 18.95 (*0-316-03107-0*) Little.

Little Women: Or Meg, Jo, Beth, & Amy. Louisa May Alcott. LC 94-17444. 502p. (J). (gr. 7-10). 1994. pap. 9.95 (*0-316-03105-4*) Little.

Little Women: The Children's Picture Book. Based on a movie by Robin Swicord. LC 94-37412. (Illus.). 96p. (J). 1994. 15.95 (*1-55704-216-0*, Pub. by Newmarket) Norton.

Little Women & Good Wives. Louisa May Alcott. 464p. 1994. reprint ed. pap. text 5.95 (*0-460-87141-2*, Everyman's Classic Lib) Tuttle Pubng.

Little Women & Little Men. Louisa May Alcott. 1995. 29.95 (*0-679-44610-9*, Evrymans Lib Childs) Knopf.

Little Women & the Feminist Imagination: Criticism, Controversy, Personal Essays. Ed. by Beverly L. Clark et al. LC 98-26670. (Children's Literature & Culture Ser.: Vol. 6). 496p. 1998. reprint ed. 75.00 (*0-8153-2049-3*, H1974) Garland.

***Little Women Book & Charm.** Louisa May Alcott. (J). 2001. write for info. (*0-694-01527-X*, HarpFestival) HarpC Child Bks.

***Little Women by Louisa May Alcott: Curriculum Unit.** Center for Learning Network Staff. (Novel - Drama Ser.). 53p. (YA). (gr. 6-9). 1998. teacher ed., spiral bd. 18.95 (*1-56077-557-2*) Ctr Learning.

Little Women; Little Men; Jo's Boys. Louisa May Alcott. (J). (gr. 4-6). 1994. pap. text, boxed set 25.85 (*0-316-03106-2*) Little.

***Little Women Next Door.** Sheila Solomon Klass. 160p. (J). (gr. 3-7). 2000. 15.95 (*0-8234-1472-8*) Holiday.

Little Women of Orchard House. Louisa May Alcott & David Longest. 116p. 1998. pap. 5.50 (*0-87129-857-0*, L95) Dramatic Pub.

Little Women Paper Dolls. Tom Tierney & Louisa May Alcott. (Illus.). (J). 1994. pap. 3.95 (*0-486-28102-7*) Dover.

Little Wonders: Animal Babies & Their Families. Marilyn Baillie. (Amazing Things Animals Do Ser.). (Illus.). 32p. (YA). (ps up). 1995. 14.95 (*1-895688-37-X*, Pub. by Owl Bks) Firefly Bks Ltd.

Little Wonders: Animal Babies & Their Families. Marilyn Baillie. (Amazing Things Animals Do Ser.). (Illus.). 32p. (YA). (ps up). 1996. pap. 5.95 (*1-895688-31-0*, Pub. by Owl Bks) Firefly Bks Ltd.

Little Wonders: Animal Babies & Their Families. Marilyn Baillie. 1995. 11.15 (*0-606-09567-5*, Pub. by Turtleback) Demco.

Little Wood Duck. Brian Wildsmith. (Illus.). 32p. (J). (gr. 1-3). 1987. pap. 9.50 (*0-19-272101-1*) OUP.

***Little Wood Duck.** Brian Wildsmith. (Illus.). 32p. 2000. pap. 8.95 (*0-19-272401-0*) OUP.

Little Wooden Doll. Bianco. (Illus.). 32p. (J). Date not set. 15.95 (*0-06-028277-0*); pap. 4.95 (*0-06-443548-2*) HarpC.

Little Wooden Table. Bryna Notrog. LC 97-201489. (Illus.). 48p. (J). 1997. lib. bdg. 14.95 (*0-9652479-0-2*) Zipper Pr.

Little Woodlands Indian Girl. Kathy Allert. (Little Activity Bks.). (Illus.). (J). 1994. pap. 1.00 (*0-486-28165-5*) Dover.

Little Woolly Lamb. Sanduik Bokforlag. (Illus.). 10p. (J). 1992. 5.25 (*1-881445-04-6*) Sandvik Pub.

Little Words That Grew: A Guide to Using Proverbs in the Therapeutic Process. Gary Beaulieu. LC 98-17909. 1998. pap. 18.00 (*1-882883-37-3*) Idyll Arbor.

Little World of Don Camillo. Giovanni Guareschi. 19.95 (*0-89190-215-5*) Amereon Ltd.

Little Worlds. Peter Guthrie & Mary Paige. 1985. teacher ed. 6.96 (*0-88334-184-0*, 76150); student ed. 9.99 (*0-8013-0087-8*, 75751) Longman.

Little Worlds: A Collection of Short Stories for the Middle School. Ed. by Peter Guthrie & Mary Page. 274p. (J). (gr. 7-9). 1985. reprint ed. pap. text 13.33 (*1-877653-52-7*) Wayside Pub.

Little Writers. Linda L. Dollard. 48p. (J). (gr. k-1). 1996. 6.99 (*1-56417-859-5*, FE7859) Fearon Teacher Aids.

Little Writing Book: The Cases for Rhetorical Expression. Richard C. Veit. 128p. (C). 1982. pap. text 18.50 (*0-13-538041-3*) P-H.

Little Wynne's Giggly Thing. Laurel D. Gugler. (Illus.). 24p. (J). (ps-2). 1995. pap. 5.95 (*1-55037-406-0*, Pub. by Annick); lib. bdg. 16.95 (*1-55037-407-9*, Pub. by Annick) Firefly Bks Ltd.

***Little 'x'** Sellers. (J). 2000. 3.95 (*0-552-52895-1*, Pub. by Transworld Publishers Ltd) Trafalgar.

***Little 'y'** Sellers. (J). 2000. 3.95 (*0-552-52896-X*, Pub. by Transworld Publishers Ltd) Trafalgar.

Little Years. John Mighton. LC 97-124269. 72p. 1997. pap. text 11.95 (*0-88754-548-3*) Theatre Comm.

Little Yellow Book. Cicely M. Barker. (Flower Fairies Collection). (Illus.). 64p. (J). 1995. 2.99 (*0-7232-4216-X*, F Warne) Peng Put Young Read.

Little Yellow Dog: An Easy Rawlins Mystery. Walter Mosley. LC 96-4231. 300p. 1996. 23.00 (*0-393-03924-2*) Norton.

Little Yellow Dog: An Easy Rawlins Mystery. Walter Mosley. 1997. per. 6.50 (*0-671-88429-8*) PB.

Little Yellow Dog: An Easy Rawlins Mystery. Walter Mosley. 1997. per. 14.00 (*0-671-01986-4*, PB Trade Paper) PB.

Little Yellow Dog: An Easy Rawlins Mystery. large type ed. Walter Mosley. LC 96-24353. 1996. 26.95 (*0-7862-0810-4*) Thorndike Pr.

Little Yellow Dog: An Easy Rawlins Mystery. limited ed. Walter Mosley. 100.00 (*0-393-03978-1*) Norton.

Little Yellow Taxi & His Friends. Ruth Ainsworth. 1997. 12.95 (*0-7188-2554-3*, Lutterworth-Parkwest) Parkwest Pubns.

Little Yoga Book. Erika Dillman. LC 98-21254. (Illus.). 189p. 1999. mass mkt. 9.99 (*0-446-67392-7*, Pub. by Warner Bks) Little.

Little Yuletide Murder. Jessica Fletcher & Donald Bain. (Murder She Wrote Ser.). 299p. 1998. mass mkt. 5.99 (*0-451-19475-6*, Sig) NAL.

***Little Yuletide Murder: A Murder, She Wrote, Mystery.** large type ed. Donald Bain. LC 00-39521. 2000. write for info. (*0-7838-9101-6*, G K Hall & Co) Mac Lib Ref.

***Little 'z'** Sellers. (J). 2000. 3.95 (*0-552-52897-8*, Pub. by Transworld Publishers Ltd) Trafalgar.

Little Zen Companion. 1998. pap. 9.95 (*0-7611-1144-1*) Workman Pub.

Little Zen Companion. David Schiller. LC 92-50936. (Illus.). 400p. 1994. pap. 6.95 (*1-56305-467-1*, 3467) Workman Pub.

Little Zengis ABC's. Chris A. Hall. (ps-3). 1992. 4.95 (*1-881316-32-7*) A&B Bks.

Little Zoo Activity Book. Becky J. Radtke. (Illus.). 1998. pap. text 1.00 (*0-486-28845-5*) Dover.

Little Zoo Animals Coloring Book. Roberta Collier. (Illus.). (J). 1990. pap. text 1.00 (*0-486-26403-3*) Dover.

Littledoobiddles & Doobetterdees. Michael Daniel. (Illus.). 40p. (J). 1995. pap. write for info. (*1-55673-998-2*, Fairway Pr) CSS OH.

Littlegreyman. Scott Morse. (Illus.). 96p. (Orig.). 1997. pap. 6.95 (*1-887279-55-5*) Image Comics.

Littlejim. Gloria M. Houston. LC 92-43775. (Illus.). 176p. (J). (gr. 5 up). 1993. mass mkt. 4.95 (*0-688-12112-8*, Wm Morrow) Morrow Avon.

Littlejim. Gloria M. Houston. (Illus.). 176p. (J). (gr. 3-6). 1990. 14.95 (*0-399-22220-0*, Philomel) Peng Put Young Read.

Littlejim's Dream. Gloria M. Houston. LC 96-46338. (Illus.). 240p. (J). 1997. 16.00 (*0-15-201509-4*) Harcourt.

Littlejim's Gift: An Appalachian Christmas Story. Gloria M. Houston. (Illus.). 32p. (J). (ps-3). 1998. pap. 5.99 (*0-698-11656-9*, PapStar) Peng Put Young Read.

Littlejim's Gift: An Appalachian Christmas Story. Gloria M. Houston. LC 93-41736. (Illus.). 32p. (J). (gr. 1-5). 1994. 15.95 (*0-399-22696-6*, Philomel) Peng Put Young Read.

Littlejohn. large type ed. Howard Owen. LC 92-45722. (Americana Series). 306p. 1993. reprint ed. lib. bdg. 20.95 (*1-56054-658-1*) Thorndike Pr.

Littlejohn's Half Century at the Bench & Bar (1936-1986) Bruce Littlejohn. (Illus.). 232p. 1987. 25.00 (*0-318-23731-8*) SC Bar Found.

Littlejohn's Political Memoirs, 1934-1988. Bruce Littlejohn, (Illus.). 244p. 1989. 1.95 (*0-9625077-0-9*) B Littlejohn.

Littlejohn's Political Memoirs, 1934-1988. Bruce Littlejohn. 256p. (C). 1990. 19.95 (*0-685-30008-0*) B Littlejohn.

***Littleriver's Yesteryears, 1853-1965.** Irene M. Macdonald. Tr. by Emery Escola. LC 99-95194. (Illus.). 220p. 1999. pap. 20.00 (*0-9672398-3-4*) Mendocino Graph.

***Littles.** (J). 1999. 9.95 (*1-56137-284-6*) Novel Units.

Littles. John Peterson. (Littles Ser.). (Illus.). 80p. (J). (gr. 1-5). 1993. pap. 2.99 (*0-590-46225-3*) Scholastic Inc.

Littles. John Peterson. (Littles Ser.). (Illus.). (J). (gr. 1-5). 1967. 8.70 (*0-606-01054-8*, Pub. by Turtleback) Demco.

Littles: A Study Guide. Charlene Forsten. Ed. by Joyce Friedland & Rikki Kessler. (Novel-Ties Ser.). 21p. (YA). (gr. 9-12). 1990. pap. text 15.95 (*0-88122-412-X*) Lrn Links.

Littles & the Great Halloween Scare. John Peterson. (Littles Ser.). (Illus.). (J). (gr. 1-5). 1975. 8.70 (*0-606-06541-5*, Pub. by Turtleback) Demco.

Littles & the Lost Children. John Peterson. (Littles Ser.). (Illus.). 112p. (J). (gr. 1-5). 1991. pap. 3.50 (*0-590-43026-2*) Scholastic Inc.

Littles & the Lost Children. John Peterson. (Littles Ser.). (Illus.). (J). (gr. 1-5). 1991. 8.60 (*0-606-04731-X*, Pub. by Turtleback) Demco.

Littles & the Trash Tinies. John Peterson. (Littles Ser.). (Illus.). 80p. (J). (gr. 4-7). 1993. pap. 2.99 (*0-590-46595-3*) Scholastic Inc.

Littles & the Trash Tinies. John Peterson. (Littles Ser.). (Illus.). (J). (gr. 1-5). 1977. 8.70 (*0-606-02713-0*, Pub. by Turtleback) Demco.

Littles & Their Amazing New Friend. John Peterson. (Littles Ser.). (Illus.). (J). (gr. 1-5). 1999. pap. 3.99 (*0-590-87612-0*) Scholastic Inc.

Littles Give a Party. John Peterson. (Littles Ser.). (Illus.). 96p. (J). (gr. 4-7). 1993. pap. 3.50 (*0-590-46597-X*) Scholastic Inc.

Littles Give a Party. John Peterson. (Littles Ser.). (Illus.). (J). (gr. 1-5). 1972. 8.70 (*0-606-05435-9*, Pub. by Turtleback) Demco.

Littles Go Exploring. John Peterson. (Littles Ser.). (Illus.). 96p. (J). (gr. 1-5). 1993. pap. 3.50 (*0-590-46596-1*) Scholastic Inc.

Littles Go Exploring. John Peterson. (Littles Ser.). (Illus.). (J). (gr. 1-5). 1978. 8.60 (*0-606-05436-7*, Pub. by Turtleback) Demco.

Littles Go to School. John Peterson. (Littles Ser.). (Illus.). 72p. (J). (gr. 4-7). 1994. pap. 2.99 (*0-590-42129-8*) Scholastic Inc.

Littles Go to School. John Peterson. (Littles Ser.). (Illus.). (J). (gr. 1-5). 1983. 8.70 (*0-606-05909-1*, Pub. by Turtleback) Demco.

Littles Have a Wedding. John Peterson. (Littles Ser.). (Illus.). 96p. (J). (gr. 1-5). 1993. pap. 2.99 (*0-590-46224-5*) Scholastic Inc.

Littles Have a Wedding. John Peterson. (Littles Ser.). (Illus.). (J). (gr. 1-5). 1971. 8.60 (*0-606-05437-5*, Pub. by Turtleback) Demco.

Littles Take a Trip. John Peterson. (Littles Ser.). (Illus.). 96p. (J). (gr. 4-7). 1993. pap. 3.50 (*0-590-46222-9*) Scholastic Inc.

Littles Take a Trip. John Peterson. (Littles Ser.). (Illus.). (J). (gr. 1-5). 1993. 8.60 (*0-606-12403-9*, Pub. by Turtleback) Demco.

Littles to the Rescue. John Peterson. (Littles Ser.). (Illus.). 96p. (J). (gr. 1-5). 1993. pap. 3.50 (*0-590-46223-7*) Scholastic Inc.

Littles to the Rescue. John Peterson. (Littles Ser.). (J). 1968. 9.19 (*0-606-02715-7*, Pub. by Turtleback) Demco.

Littlest Aggie. Shelia Henderson & Bonnie S. George. Ed. by S. C. Darr. (Illus.). 56p. (J). 1990. 18.95 (*0-9623171-2-8*); ring bd. 4.95 (*0-9623171-3-6*) LBCo Pub.

Littlest Angel. Charlotte Maclay. 1996. per. 3.75 (*0-373-16657-5*, 1-16657-8) Harlequin Bks.

Littlest Angel. Charles Tazewell. 1998. pap. 7.95 (*0-516-26192-4*) Childrens.

Littlest Angel. Charles Tazewell. LC 97-10833. (Illus.). (J). (gr. 1-3). 1998. lib. bdg. 25.00 (*0-516-20433-5*) Childrens.

Littlest Angel. Charles Tazewell. LC 91-2442. (Illus.). 32p. (J). 1991. 16.95 (*0-8249-8516-8*, Ideals Child) Hambleton-Hill.

Littlest Angel. deluxe ed. Charles Tazewell. LC 91-2442. (Illus.). 32p. (J). 1995. lthr. 39.95 (*1-57102-062-4*, Ideals Child) Hambleton-Hill.

Littlest Angel. Charles Tazewell. (Illus.). 32p. (J). 1962. reprint ed. 6.95 (*0-89542-923-3*, Ideals Child) Hambleton-Hill.

Littlest Angel: And Baby Makes Three: The Next Generation. Sherryl Woods. (Special Edition Ser.: No. 1142). 1997. per. 3.99 (*0-373-24142-9*, 1-24142-1) Harlequin Bks.

Littlest Angel - Musical. Charles Tazewell et al. 1994. 5.95 (*0-87129-504-0*, L02) Dramatic Pub.

Littlest Angel - Str. Charles Tazewell. LC 91-2442. 1964. pap. 5.50 (*0-87129-361-7*, L26) Dramatic Pub.

Littlest Angels. (Look & Find Ser.). (Illus.). 24p. (J). 1993. 7.98 (*0-7853-0328-6*) Pubns Intl Ltd.

Littlest Ballerina. Andrea Ross. (Illus.). 23p. (J). (gr. k-3). 1996. 7.95 (*1-887683-13-5*) Strybook Pr.

Littlest Bible. Billy Flanagan. 72p. 1993. 4.95 (*1-883575-00-1*) Flanagan Pub.

***Littlest Cat Book.** Ed. by Helen Exley. (Minute Mini Ser.). (Illus.). 96p. 1999. 6.50 (*1-86187-122-8*) Exley Giftbooks.

***Littlest Christmas Tree: A Children's Christmas Play.** Willard Rabert, Jr. et al. 8p. 1999. pap. 3.50 (*0-7880-1515-X*) CSS OH.

Littlest Christmas Tree: A Tale of Growing & Becoming. Janie Jasin. LC 97-155118. (Illus.). 32p. 1996. 12.95 (*0-916773-75-2*) Book Peddlers.

Littlest Christmas Tree: A Tale of Growing & Becoming. Janie Jasin. (Illus.). 32p. 1998. 19.95 incl. audio compact disk (*0-916773-82-5*) Book Peddlers.

Littlest Cowboy. Maggie B. Shayne. (Intimate Moments Ser.). 1996. per. 3.99 (*0-373-07716-5*, 1-07716-3) Silhouette.

Littlest Cowboy. large type ed. Maggie Shayne. 1999. 21.95 (*0-373-59508-5*) Harlequin Bks.

Littlest Detective. Kathy Marks. (Harlequin Temptation Ser.: No. 596). 1996. per. 3.50 (*0-373-25696-5*, 1-25696-5) Harlequin Bks.

Littlest Dinosaur Finds a Friend. Sara James. (Illus.). 24p. (Orig.). (J). 1992. pap. 2.50 (*1-56156-110-X*) Kidsbks.

Littlest Dinosaurs. Bernard Most. LC 88-30063. (Illus.). 32p. (J). (ps-2). 1993. pap. 5.95 (*0-15-248126-5*) Harcourt.

Littlest Dinosaurs, 4 bks., Set. Bernard Most. (Illus.). (J). (gr. 1-6). 1993. pap., teacher ed. 33.95 incl. audio (*0-87499-193-5*) Live Oak Media.

Littlest Dinosaurs, Set. unabridged ed. Bernard Most. (Illus.). (J). (gr. 1-6). 1993. pap. 15.95 incl. audio (*0-87499-191-9*) Live Oak Media.

Littlest Duckling. Gail Herman. (J). 1998. 10.19 (*0-606-12985-5*, Pub. by Turtleback) Demco.

***Littlest Gardening Giftbook.** Helen Exley. (Minute Mini Ser.). (Illus.). 96p. 1999. 6.50 (*1-86187-121-X*) Exley Giftbooks.

Littlest Lighthouse. Ruth Sargent. LC 81-66268. (Illus.). 28p. (Orig.). (J). (gr. k-2). 1981. pap. 5.95 (*0-89272-119-7*) Down East.

Littlest Logger: A Christmas Story. J. B. Strasser. 1993. pap. write for info. (*1-883578-00-0*) Red Print.

Littlest Longhorn: The Saga of Bevo. Sheila Henderson. Ed. by Judy Spurgin. (Illus.). 56p. 1989. write for info. (*0-318-65221-8*) LBCo Pub.

Littlest Marine. Maureen Child. (Desire Ser.). 1998. per. 3.75 (*0-373-76167-8*, 1-76167-5) Silhouette.

An Asterisk (*) at the beginning of an entry indicates that the title is appearing for the first time.

Littlest Matchmaker: Under the Mistletoe. Carla Cassidy. (Romance Ser.). 1993. per. 2.75 (*0-373-08978-3*, 5-08978-4) Silhouette.

Littlest Matryoshka. Corinne D. Bliss. LC 98-36156. (Illus.). 32p. (J). (ps-3). 1999. lib. bdg. 16.49 (*0-7868-2125-6*, Pub. by Hyperion) Little.

Littlest Matryoshka. Corinne D. Bliss. LC 98-36156. (Illus.). 32p. (J). (ps-2). 1999. 15.99 (*0-7868-0153-0*, Pub. by Hyprn Child) Time Warner.

Littlest Mermaid. Illus. by Jerry Smath. (Jewel Sticker Stories Ser.). 24p. (Orig.). (J). (ps-2). 1997. pap. 3.95 (*0-448-41596-8*, G & D) Peng Put Young Read.

Littlest Mule. John Barrett. Ed. by Silver Dollar City, Inc. Staff. (City Stories Ser.). (Illus.). (J). (ps-5). 1977. 2.99 (*0-686-19125-0*) Silver Dollar.

Littlest Piggy. Tony Jerris. (Illus.). 20p. (Orig.). (J). (ps up). 1992. pap. 9.95 incl. audio (*0-9630107-2-7*) Little Spruce.

Littlest Red Horse. Charles Tazewell. LC 99-37289. (Illus.). 32p. (J). 1999. 16.95 (*1-57102-157-4*) Hambleton-Hill.

Littlest Reindeer. Muff Singer. (Little Hugs Ser.: Vol. 5). (Illus.). 18p. (J). (gr. k-3). 1998. bds. 10.99 (*1-57584-090-1*, Pub. by Rdrs Digest) Random.

Littlest Spruce. Tony Jerris. (Illus.). 20p. (Orig.). (J). (ps up). 1991. pap. 9.95 incl. audio (*0-9630107-1-9*) Little Spruce.

Littlest Star: A Parable. David K. Tanner. 64p. 1994. pap. 6.95 (*0-9642798-0-0*) Star Right Pub.

Littlest Stowaway: Bachelors & Babies. Gina Wilkins. (Temptation Ser.: No. 749). 1999. per. 3.75 (*0-373-25849-6*, 1-25849-0) Harlequin Bks.

Littlest Tall Fellow. Barry Rudner. Ed. by J. M. Carraro. (Illus.). 32p. (J). (gr. k-6). 1989. pap. 5.95 (*0-925928-00-3*) Tiny Thought.

Littlest Teddy Bear Book. Exley Giftbooks Editors. 1998. 6.50 (*1-86187-103-1*) Exley Giftbooks.

Littlest Tree. Charles Tazewell. LC 97-5873. (Illus.). 32p. (J). 1997. 16.95 (*1-57102-121-3*, Ideals Child) Hambleton-Hill.

Littlest Uninvited One. Charles Tazewell. LC 98-16588. (Illus.). (J). 1998. 16.95 (*1-57102-131-0*, Ideals Child) Hambleton-Hill.

Littlest Vaquero: A Story of the First Texas Cowboys, Longhorns, & the American Revolution. Maurine W. Liles. LC 96-24043. (Illus.). 120p. (J). (gr. 4-6). 1996. 14.95 (*1-57168-103-5*, Eakin Pr) Sunbelt Media.

***Littlest Volcano.** Daniel L. Dulin. (Illus.). 16p. (J). (ps-2). 2000. pap. write for info. (*0-9677274-1-3*) BlacKat Pubng.

***Littlest Witness: (Gallagher Justice)** Amanda Stevens. (Intrigue Ser.: No. 549). 2000. per. 4.25 (*0-373-22549-0*, 1-22549-9, Harlequin) Harlequin Bks.

Littleton. Arthur F. March, Jr. (Images of America Ser.). 1995. pap. 16.99 (*0-7524-0222-6*) Arcadia Publng.

Littleton: Crossroads of Northern New Hampshire. Ed. by John H. Colby. LC 84-4941. 702p. 1984. 34.95 (*0-914659-03-0*) Phoenix Pub.

Littleton Scrapbook: River Barons, Lawyers & Royalty. Ed. by Calvert W. Tazewell. LC 90-80406. (Tazewell & Allied Families Scrapbooks Ser.: Vol. 8). 92p. (Orig.). 1991. pap. 12.00 (*1-878515-08-X*) W S Dawson.

Littleton Waller Tazewell. Norma L. Peterson. LC 83-3501. 225p. reprint ed. pap. 69.80 (*0-7837-4371-8*, 204408100012) Bks Demand.

Littleton's Tenures in English. Ed. by Eugene Wambaugh & Thomas Littleton. (Legal Classic Ser.). lxxxiv, 341p. 1985. reprint ed. 48.00 (*0-8377-0818-4*, Rothman) W S Hein.

Littlewood-Paley Theory & the Study of Function Spaces. Michael Frazier et al. LC 91-11230. (CBMS Regional Conference Series in Mathematics: No. 79). 132p. 1991. pap. 42.00 (*0-8218-0731-5*, CBMS/79) Am Math.

Littlewood-Paley Theory on Spaces of Homogeneous Type & the Classical Function Spaces. Y. S. Han & E. T. Sawyer. LC 94-13336. (Memoirs of the American Mathematical Society Ser.: No. 530). 126p. 1994. pap. 34.00 (*0-8218-2592-5*, MEMO/110/530) Am Math.

Littlewood's Miscellany. Bela Bollobas. 208p. 1986. pap. text 22.95 (*0-521-33702-X*) Cambridge U Pr.

Littlewoods Organisation PLC & Freemans PLC (A Subsidiary of Sears PLC) A Rep Monopolies & Mergers Commission Report, Command Paper 3761. (Command Papers (All) Ser.: No. 81011068). 1997. 45.00 (*0-10-137612-X*, HM7612X, Pub. by Statnry Office) Bernan Associates.

Lituma en Los Andes see Death in the Andes

***Lituma En Los Andes.** Mario Vargas Llosa. (SPA.). 1999. pap. text 14.95 (*84-08-02002-1*) Planeta.

Liturature of Greece & Rome. N T C Contemporary Publishing Company Staff. 1998. pap. 17.44 (*0-8442-1192-3*) NTC Contemp Pub Co.

Liturgia de Difuntos: The Funeral Rite. 49p. 1993. pap. 1.95 (*0-8146-6107-6*) Liturgical Pr.

Liturgical & Mystical Theology of Nicolas Cabasilas. 3rd ed. Constantine N. Tsirpanlis. 103p. 1986. pap. 22.95 (*0-317-36317-4*) EO Pr.

Liturgical Art. Meinrad Craighead. LC 88-61723. (Illus.). 34p. 1988. pap. 24.95 (*1-55612-069-9*, LL1069) Sheed & Ward WI.

Liturgical Calenders, Saints, & Services in Medieval England. Richard W. Pfaff. LC 98-71752. (Variorum Collected Studies Ser.: Vol. 610). 320p. 1998. text 89.95 (*0-86078-677-3*, Pub. by Variorum) Ashgate Pub Co.

Liturgical Chant of the Russian Orthodox Church; History see Bogosluzhebnoje Penije Russkoj Pravoslavnoj Tserkvi: Istorija

Liturgical Context of Early European Drama. Salvatore Paterno. 1990. 33.50 (*0-916379-62-0*) Scripta.

Liturgical Dictionary of Eastern Christianity. Peter Day. 344p. 1994. 82.50 (*0-86012-216-6*, Pub. by Srch Pr) St Mut.

Liturgical Element in the Earliest Forms of Medieval Drama. Paul E. Kretzmann. LC 68-54169. (Studies in Drama: No. 39). 1969. reprint ed. lib. bdg. 75.00 (*0-8383-0578-4*) M S G Haskell Hse.

Liturgical Environment: What the Documents Say. Mark G. Boyer. 176p. (Orig.). 1991. pap. 9.95 (*0-8146-1963-0*) Liturgical Pr.

Liturgical Hermeneutics: Interpreting Liturgical Rites in Performance. Bridget Nichols. LC 96-4312. 318p. 1996. pap. 57.95 (*0-8204-2987-2*, BX5145) P Lang Pubng.

Liturgical Inculturation: Sacramentals, Religiosity, & Catechesis. Anschar J. Chupungo. 176p. (Orig.). 1992. pap. 14.95 (*0-8146-6120-3*, Pueblo Bks) Liturgical Pr.

Liturgical Index to the Hymnal, 1982. Marion J. Hatchett. (Hymnal Studies: No. 5). 343p. 1986. pap. 16.95 (*0-89869-131-1*) Church Pub Inc.

Liturgical Language: Keeping It Metaphoric, Making It Inclusive. Gail Ramshaw. LC 95-33193. (American Essays in Liturgy Ser.). 64p. (Orig.). 1996. pap. 5.95 (*0-8146-2408-1*, Liturg Pr Bks) Liturgical Pr.

Liturgical Law Today: New Style, New Spirit. Thomas Richstatter. LC 77-3008. 271p. reprint ed. pap. 84.10 (*0-608-13632-8*, 201910400011) Bks Demand.

Liturgical Ministry: A Practical Guide to Spirituality. Donna Cole. LC 96-8153. 96p. (Orig.). 1996. pap. 8.95 (*0-89390-372-8*) Resource Pubns.

Liturgical Ministry of Deacons. Michael Kwatera. (Ministry Ser.). 96p. 1985. pap. 1.95 (*0-8146-1386-1*) Liturgical Pr.

***Liturgical Music Answer Book.** Peggy Lovrien. LC 99-27873. (101 Most-Asked Questions Ser.). 160p. 1999. 14.95 (*0-89390-454-6*) Resource Pubns.

***Liturgical Music as Ritual Symbol: A Case Study of Jacques Berthier's Taize Music.** J. M. Kubicki. xv, 207p. 1999. 34.00 (*90-429-0740-1*, Pub. by Peeters Pub) Bks Intl VA.

Liturgical Nestorianism & the Regulative Principle: A Critical Review of Worship in the Presence of God. James B. Jordan. 92p. (Orig.). 1994. pap. 7.00 (*1-883690-03-X*) Transfig Pr.

Liturgical Objects in the Walters Art Gallery: A Picture Book. LC 67-9432. (Illus.). 1967. pap. 1.25 (*0-911886-12-5*) Walters Art.

Liturgical Organist, Vol. 7. Prod. by Zobeida Perez. 122p. (Orig.). 1985. pap. 16.95 (*0-7692-1433-9*, FE08910) Wrner Bros.

Liturgical Question Box. Petter J. Elliott. LC 97-76854. 1998. pap. text 12.95 (*0-89870-677-7*) Ignatius Pr.

Liturgical Revolution: Prayer Book Revision & Associated Parishes : A Generation of Change in the Episcopal Church. Michael Moriarty. LC 96-71102. 1996. write for info. (*0-89869-203-2*) Church Pub Inc.

Liturgical Revolution Vol. 2: Pope John's Council. 2nd ed. Michael Davies. 331p. 1992. reprint ed. pap. text 10.95 (*0-935952-04-7*) Angelus Pr.

Liturgical Revolution Vol. 3: Pope Paul's New Mass. 3rd ed. Michael Davies. 673p. 1992. reprint ed. pap. text 19.95 (*0-935952-02-0*) Angelus Pr.

Liturgical Shipwreck - 25 Years of the New Mass. Michael Davies. 42p. 1995. pap. 1.50 (*0-89555-535-2*) TAN Bks Pubs.

Liturgical Spirituality. Philip H. Pfatteicher. LC 97-7376. 302p. (Orig.). 1997. pap. 22.00 (*1-56338-194-X*) TPI PA.

Liturgical Spirituality & the Rite of Christian Initiation of Adults. Shawn Madigan. LC 97-22387. (Forum Essays Ser.: No. 5). 120p. 1997. pap. 6.00 (*0-929650-80-8*, LITSPI) Liturgy Tr Pubns.

Liturgical Terms for Music Students: A Dictionary. Dom A. Hughes. 1988. reprint ed. lib. bdg. 49.00 (*0-685-55952-1*) Rprt Serv.

Liturgical Terms for Music Students: A Dictionary. Compiled by Dom A. Hughes. LC 70-166236. 1972. reprint ed. 49.00 (*0-403-01363-1*) Scholarly.

Liturgical Theology: A Primer. Kevin W. Irwin. (American Essays in Liturgy Ser.). 80p. 1991. pap. 6.95 (*0-8146-1977-0*) Liturgical Pr.

Liturgical Witness of the New Testament: 14 Worship Services Drawn from the New Testament. Charles M. Mountain. LC 95-41228. 266p. (Orig.). 1996. pap. 18.50 (*0-7880-0714-9*) CSS OH.

Liturgical Year. (Supplemental Liturgical Resource Ser.: No. 7). 256p. (Orig.). 1992. pap. 19.95 (*0-664-25350-4*) Westminster John Knox.

Liturgical Year, 4 vols., Set. Adrian Nocent. 1977. pap. 40.00 (*0-8146-0971-6*) Liturgical Pr.

Liturgical Year, Vol. 1. Leonard Soroka. 127p. 1987. 16.95 (*1-878997-12-2*) St Tikhons Pr.

Liturgical Year: Its History & Its Meaning after the Reform of the Liturgy. Adolf Adam. 308p. 1992. pap. 19.95 (*0-8146-6047-9*, Pueblo Bks) Liturgical Pr.

Liturgical Year Vol. 1: Advent, Christmas, Epiphany, Sundays 2-8 in Ordinary Time. Adrian Nocent. 446p. 1977. pap. 10.00 (*0-8146-0962-7*) Liturgical Pr.

Liturgical Year Vol. 2: Lent & Holy Week. Adrian Nocent. 251p. (C). 1977. pap. 10.00 (*0-8146-0963-5*) Liturgical Pr.

Liturgical Year Vol. 3: Paschal Triduum, Easter Season, & Solemnities of the Lord. Adrian Nocent. 326p. (C). 1977. pap. 10.00 (*0-8146-0964-3*) Liturgical Pr.

Liturgical Year Vol. 4: Sundays Nine to Thirty-Four in Ordinary Time. Adrian Nocent. 406p. (C). 1977. pap. 10.00 (*0-8146-0965-1*) Liturgical Pr.

Liturgies of Lament. J. Frank Henderson. LC 94-27599. 92p. (Orig.). 1994. pap. 11.95 (*0-929650-78-6*, LAMENT) Liturgy Tr Pubns.

Liturgies of Saints Mark, James, Clement, Chrysostom, & the Church of Malabar. Orthodox Eastern Church Staff. LC 76-83374. reprint ed. 42.00 (*0-404-04658-4*) AMS Pr.

Liturgies of Saints Mark, James, Clement, Chrysostom, Basil. Orthodox Eastern Church Staff. LC 79-80721. 1969. reprint ed. 42.00 (*0-404-04657-6*) AMS Pr.

Liturgies of the Earth. Richard Kuykendall. 56p. 1992. pap. 8.95 (*1-877871-38-9*, 3575) Ed Ministries.

Liturgies of the Future: The Process & Methods of Inculturation. Anscar J. Chupungco. 1989. pap. 9.95 (*0-8091-3095-5*) Paulist Pr.

Liturgies of the Western Church. Ed. by Bard Thompson. LC 80-8044. 434p. 1980. reprint ed. pap. 23.00 (*0-8006-1428-3*, 1-1428, Fortress Pr) Augsburg Fortress.

Liturgies on the Holocaust. Ed. by Marcia S. Littell. LC 86-23507. 208p. 1986. lib. bdg. 89.95 (*0-88946-030-2*) E Mellen.

Liturgies on the Holocaust: An Interfaith Anthology. Ed. by Marcia S. Littell & Sharon W. Gutman. LC 96-1862. 216p. 1996. pap. 20.00 (*1-56338-138-9*) TPI PA.

Liturgikon: The Book of Divine Services for the Priest & Deacon. Ed. by Basil Essey. LC 89-27744. 528p. 1989. 65.00 (*0-9624190-0-1*) Antakya Pr.

Liturgikon: The Book of Divine Services for the Priest & Deacon. Ed. & Tr. by Basil Essey from ARA. xvi, 528p. (C). 1989. write for info. (*0-318-65829-1*) Antakya Pr.

Liturgische Bibliographie des XV: Jahrhunderts. Hanns Bohatta. 79p. 1960. reprint ed. 25.00 (*0-318-71744-1*) G Olms Pubs.

Liturgische Gerate, Kreuze & Reliquiare der Christlichen Kirchen - Objects Liturgiques, Croix et Reliquaires des Eglises Chretiennes see Glossarium Artis, a Specialized & Systematic Dictionary

Liturgische Tropen. (Munchener Beitrage zur Mediavistik und Renaissance-Forschung Ser.: Bd. 36). (GER.). xii, 222p. 1985. 65.00 (*3-615-00167-2*) G Olms Pubs.

Liturgisches Woerterbuch. deluxe ed. Wolfgang Jung. (GER.). 1964. 27.95 (*0-8288-6778-X*, M-7544) Fr & Eur.

Liturgist's Guide to Inclusive Language. Ronald D. Witherup. 120p. (Orig.). 1996. pap. 8.95 (*0-8146-2257-7*, Liturg Pr Bks) Liturgical Pr.

Liturgy: Celebrating Marriage, Vol. 4, No. 2. Ed. by Rachel Reeder. (Illus.). 80p. 1984. pap. text 8.95 (*0-918208-34-3*) Liturgical Conf.

Liturgy: Central Symbols. Ed. by Rachel Reeder. (Quarterly Journal of The Liturgical Conference: Vol. 7, No. 1). (Illus.). 96p. (Orig.). 1988. pap. text 8.95 (*0-918208-45-9*) Liturgical Conf.

Liturgy: Covenant with the World. Ed. by Rachel Reeder. (Quarterly Journal of The Liturgical Conference: Vol. 6, No. 4). 112p. 1987. pap. 8.95 (*0-918208-44-0*) Liturgical Conf.

Liturgy: Diakonia. Ed. by Rachel Reeder. (Journals of The Liturgical Conference: Vol. 2, No. 4). (Illus.). 84p. (Orig.). 1982. pap. 8.95 (*0-918208-28-9*) Liturgical Conf.

Liturgy: Ethics & Justice. Ed. by Rachel Reeder. (Quarterly Journal of The Liturgical Conference: Vol. 7, No. 4). (Illus.). 111p. (Orig.). 1989. pap. text 8.95 (*0-918208-48-3*) Liturgical Conf.

Liturgy: Feasts & Fasting. Ed. by Rachel Reeder. (Quarterly Journal of The Liturgical Conference: Vol. 2, No. 1). (Illus.). 80p. (Orig.). 1981. pap. text 8.95 (*0-918208-25-4*) Liturgical Conf.

Liturgy: Holy Places. Rachel Reeder. (Quarterly Journal of The Liturgical Conference: Vol. 3, No. 4). (Illus.). 96p. (Orig.). 1983. pap. text 8.95 (*0-918208-32-7*) Liturgical Conf.

Liturgy: In Daily Life. R. Grimes et al. (Liturgy Ser.: Vol. 7, No. 3). (Illus.). 105p. (Orig.). 1988. pap. 8.95 (*0-918208-47-5*) Liturgical Conf.

Liturgy: In Spirit & Truth. Ed. by Rachel Reeder. (Quarterly Journal of The Liturgical Conference: Vol. 5, No. 3). (Illus.). 96p. (Orig.). 1986. pap. text 8.95 (*0-918208-39-4*) Liturgical Conf.

Liturgy: Ministries to the Sick. Ed. by Rachel Reeder. (Quarterly Journal of The Liturgical Conference: Vol. 2, No. 2 of Liturgy). (Illus.). 80p. 1982. 8.95 (*0-918208-26-2*) Liturgical Conf.

Liturgy: One Church, Many Churches. Ed. by Rachel Reeder. (Quarterly Journal of The Liturgical Conference: Vol. 3, No. 2). (Illus.). 96p. (Orig.). 1983. pap. text 8.95 (*0-918208-30-0*) Liturgical Conf.

***Liturgy: Praying in the Home, Vol. 15, Pt. 2.** Ed. by Samuel Torvend. (Illus.). 52p. 1999. pap. 10.95 (*0-918208-82-3*) Liturgical Conf.

Liturgy: Putting on Christ, Vol. 4, No. 1. Ed. by Rachel Reeder. (Illus.). 80p. 1983. pap. text 8.95 (*0-918208-33-5*) Liturgical Conf.

Liturgy: Scripture & the Assembly. Ed. by Rachel Reeder. (Quarterly Journal of The Liturgical Conference: Vol. 2, No. 3 of Liturgy). (Illus.). 80p. 1982. 8.95 (*0-918208-27-0*) Liturgical Conf.

Liturgy: Teaching Prayer. Ed. by Rachel Reeder. (Quarterly Journal of The Liturgical Conference: Vol. 5, No. 1). (Illus.). 96p. (Orig.). 1985. pap. text 8.95 (*0-918208-37-8*) Liturgical Conf.

Liturgy: The Calendar. Ed. by Rachel Reeder. (Liturgy, the Quarterly Journal of the Liturgical Conference: Vol. 1, No. 2). (Illus.). 92p. 1980. pap. 8.95 (*0-918208-01-7*) Liturgical Conf.

Liturgy: The Healing Word. Ed. by Rachel Reeder. (Quarterly Journal of The Liturgical Conference: Vol. 7, No. 2). (Illus.). 104p. (Orig.). 1988. pap. text 8.95 (*0-318-41831-2*) Liturgical Conf.

Liturgy: The Holy Cross. Ed. by Rachel Reeder. (Liturgy, the Quarterly Journal of the Liturgical Conference: Vol. 1, No. 1). (Illus.). 76p. 1980. pap. 8.95 (*0-918208-00-9*) Liturgical Conf.

Liturgy: The Lord's Day. E. Glenn Hinson et al. (Liturgy Ser.: Vol. 8, No. 1). (Illus.). 103p. (Orig.). 1989. pap. 8.95 (*0-918208-49-1*) Liturgical Conf.

Liturgy: The Power That Unites, Vol. 6, No. 2. Ed. by Rachel Reeder. (Illus.). 96p. (Orig.). 1986. pap. 8.95 (*0-918208-42-4*) Liturgical Conf.

Liturgy: The Song of All Creation. Ed. by Rachel Reeder. (Quarterly Journal of The Liturgical Conference: Vol. 6 No. 3). (Illus.). 88p. (Orig.). 1987. pap. 8.95 (*0-918208-43-2*) Liturgical Conf.

Liturgy: With All the Saints. Ed. by Rachel Reeder. (Quarterly Journal of The Liturgical Conference: Vol. 5, No. 2). (Illus.). 112p. (Orig.). 1985. pap. text 8.95 (*0-918208-38-6*) Liturgical Conf.

Liturgy: With Lyre & Harp. Ed. by Rachel Reeder. (Quarterly Journal of The Liturgical Conference: Vol. 3, No. 3). (Illus.). 88p. (Orig.). 1983. pap. text 8.95 (*0-918208-31-9*) Liturgical Conf.

Liturgy According to the Use of the Liberal Catholic Church, Prepared for the Use of English-Speaking Congregations. 3rd ed. General Episcopal Synod Staff. 421p. 1987. reprint ed. 9.00 (*0-935461-11-6*) St Alban Pr CA.

Liturgy & Anthropology: A Monastic Death Ritual of the Eleventh Century, Vol. II. Frederick S. Paxton. LC 93-1787. (Chalice of Repose Project: Studies in Music-Thanatology: Vol. 2). 20p. 1993. pap. text 0.95 (*1-882878-87-6*) Saint Dunstans.

Liturgy & Communication. John Rodgers. (C). 1988. 45.00 (*0-85439-113-4*, Pub. by St Paul Pubns) St Mut.

Liturgy & Ecology in Dialogue. Lawrence E. Mick. LC 97-956. 104p. 1997. pap. 8.95 (*0-8146-2447-2*) Liturgical Pr.

Liturgy & Hermaneutics. Joyce A. Zimmerman. LC 98-52226. (American Essays in Liturgy Ser.). 109p. 1999. pap. 9.95 (*0-8146-2497-9*) Liturgical Pr.

Liturgy & Learning Through the Life Cycle. rev. ed. John H. Westerhoff & William H. Willimon. Ed. by Timothy J. Crouch. (Illus.). 168p. (Orig.). 1994. pap. text 14.95 (*1-878009-21-4*, OSL Pubns) Order St Luke Pubns.

Liturgy & Music: Lifetime Learning. Robin A. Leaver & Joyce A. Zimmerman. LC 98-12229. 464p. 1998. pap. 34.95 (*0-8146-2501-0*) Liturgical Pr.

Liturgy & Ritual: The Liturgy of the Holy Apostles Adai & Mari. Nestorian Church Staff. LC 79-131032. reprint ed. 29.50 (*0-404-03997-9*) AMS Pr.

Liturgy & Ritual of the Ante-Nicene Church. 2nd rev. ed. Frederick E. Warren. LC 78-177851. reprint ed. 47.50 (*0-404-06847-2*) AMS Pr.

Liturgy & Ritual of the Celtic Church. Frederick E. Warren. 1990. reprint ed. pap. 12.50 (*0-89981-110-8*) Eastern Orthodox.

Liturgy & the Arts. Albert Rouet. Tr. by Paul Philibert from FRE. LC 96-41896. (FRE & ENG.). 192p. (Orig.). 1997. pap. text 19.95 (*0-8146-2393-X*, Liturg Pr Bks) Liturgical Pr.

Liturgy & the Arts in the Middle Ages: Studies in Honour of C. Clifford Flanigan. Ed. by Eva L. Lille & Nils H. Petersen. LC 97-162436. (Illus.). 304p. 1996. 56.00 (*87-7289-361-3*) Paul & Co Pubs.

Liturgy & the Body. Ed. by Louis-Marie Chauvet & Francois K. Lumbala. 150p. (Orig.). 1995. pap. 15.00 (*0-88344-884-X*) Orbis Bks.

Liturgy & the Ecclesiastical History of Late Anglo-Saxon England: Four Studies. David N. Dumville. LC 92-34651. (Studies in Anglo-Saxon History: Vol. 5). 204p. (C). 1992. 75.00 (*0-85115-331-3*, Boydell Pr) Boydell & Brewer.

Liturgy & the Moral Self: Humanity at Full Stretch Before God. E. Byron Anderson & Bruce Morrill. LC 97-52051. xii, 231 p. 1998. pap. 27.95 (*0-8146-6168-8*) Liturgical Pr.

Liturgy & the Social Sciences. Nathan Mitchell. LC 98-34981. (American Essays in Liturgy Ser.). 1999. 10.95 (*0-8146-2511-8*) Liturgical Pr.

Liturgy & Tradition: Theological Reflections of Alexander Schmemann. Ed. by Thomas Fisch. LC 90-36280. 138p. 1990. pap. 9.95 (*0-88141-082-9*) St Vladimirs.

Liturgy & Worship: A Course on Prayer & Sacraments: Keystone Parish Edition. Thomas Richstatter. (Faith & Witness Program Ser.). (Illus.). 128p. (J). (gr. 7-9). 1999. pap. text 7.50 (*0-8215-5655-X*) Sadlier.

Liturgy & Worship: A Course on Prayer & Sacraments, Parish Annotated Guide: Keystone Parish Edition. Isabel F. Blevins & Thomas Richstatter. (Faith & Witness Program Ser.). (Illus.). (J). (gr. 7-9). 1998. pap. 15.00 (*0-8215-5665-7*) Sadlier.

Liturgy & Worship - A Course on Prayer & Sacraments: Keystone School Edition. Thomas Richstatter. (Faith & Witness Program Ser.). (Illus.). 192p. (J). (gr. 7-9). 1998. pap. text 11.40 (*0-8215-5604-5*) Sadlier.

Liturgy & Worship - A Course on Prayer & Sacraments, Journal: Keystone Edition. Helen Hemmer. (Faith & Witness Program Ser.). (Illus.). 64p. (J). (gr. 7-9). 1999. pap., student ed. 4.50 (*0-8215-5634-7*) Sadlier.

Liturgy & Worship - A Course on Prayer & Sacraments, School Guide: Keystone School Edition. annot. ed. Isabel F. Blevins & Thomas Richstatter. (Faith & Witness Program Ser.). (Illus.). 272p. 1998. pap., teacher ed. 21.90 (*0-8215-5614-2*) Sadlier.

Liturgy As Language of Faith: A Liturgical Methodology in the Mode of Paul Ricoeur's Textual Hermeneutics. Joyce A. Zimmerman. LC 88-2797. 284p. (C). 1988. lib. bdg. 43.00 (*0-8191-6908-0*) U Pr of Amer.

***Liturgy Betrayed.** Denis Crouan. 125p. 2000. pap. 11.95 (*0-89870-799-4*, Pub. by Ignatius Pr) Midpt Trade.

***Liturgy Book.** GIA Publishing Company Staff. 1999. 24.95 (*5-550-71945-2*) Nairi.

Liturgy Committee Handbook. Thomas Baker & Frank Fefrrone. 112p. (Orig.). 1998. pap. 14.95 (*0-89622-955-6*) Twenty-Third.

Liturgy Documentary Series 5: General Instruction of the Liturgy of the Hours. National Conference of Catholic Bishops. 78p. (Orig.). (C). 1983. pap. 5.95 (*1-55586-898-3*) US Catholic.

L

An Asterisk (*) at the beginning of an entry indicates that the title is appearing for the first time.

Liturgy Documents, Vol. 2. Ed. by David Lysik. 395p. 1999. pap. 15.00 (*1-56854-245-3*, LDOCZ) Liturgy Tr Pubns.

Liturgy Documents Vol. I: A Parish Resource. 3rd ed. Ed. by Elizabeth Hoffman. 395p. (C). 1991. pap. 15.00 (*0-929650-46-8*, LDOC/R) Liturgy Tr Pubns.

Liturgy Explained. Thomas Howard. (Illus.). 48p. 1981. pap. 6.95 (*0-8192-1285-7*) Morehouse Pub.

Liturgy for Christian Congregations of the Lutheran Faith. Wilhelm Loehe et al. Tr. by F. C. Longaker from GER. 171p. 1997. reprint ed. 25.00 (*1-891469-12-6*) Repristination.

Liturgy for Christian Congregations of the Lutheran Faith. 3rd ed. Wilhelm Loehe. 157p. 1997. reprint ed. 25.00 (*1-893118-01-0*) J Gerhard Inst.

Liturgy for Living. Charles P. Price & Louis Weil. (Church's Teaching Ser.: Vol. 5). 1984. 5.95 (*0-8164-0422-4*) Harper SF.

***Liturgy for Living.** Ed. by Louis Weil. 240p. 2000. pap. 21.00 (*0-8192-1862-6*) Morehouse Pub.

***Liturgy for the New Millennium: A Commentary on the Revised Sacramentary, Essays in Honor of Anscar Chapungco.** Mark R. Francis et al. LC 99-27733. 192p. 2000. 19.95 (*0-8146-6174-2*) Liturgical Pr.

***Liturgy for the People of God: A Trilogy, 3 vols.** Charles E. Miller. (Liturey For the People of God). (YA). 2000. pap. 36.95 (*0-8189-0881-5*, Saint Pauls) Alba.

Liturgy for the Use of the General Church of the New Jerusalem. rev. ed. 1995. 10.00 (*0-945003-08-0*) General Church.

Liturgy in Byzantium & Beyond. Robert F. Taft. LC 95-3347. (Collected Studies: Vol. 493). 1995. 113.95 (*0-86078-483-5*, Pub. by Variorum) Ashgate Pub Co.

Liturgy in Dialogue: Essays in Memory of Ronald Jasper. Ed. by Bryan D. Spinks & Paul F. Bradshaw. 248p. (Orig.). 1995. pap. text 19.95 (*0-8146-6149-1*, Pueblo Bks) Liturgical Pr.

Liturgy Made Simple. Mark Searle. LC 81-4807. 96p. 1981. pap. 5.95 (*0-8146-1221-0*) Liturgical Pr.

Liturgy Models. Center for Learning Network Staff. (Parish Ministry Manuals Ser.). 127p. 1991. spiral bd. 15.95 (*1-56077-032-5*) Ctr Learning.

Liturgy of Funerary Offerings: The Egyptian Texts with English Translations. E. A. Wallis Budge. LC 72-83744. (Illus.). 1972. reprint ed. 24.95 (*0-405-08322-X*, Pub. by Blom Pubns) Ayer.

Liturgy of Funerary Offerings: The Egyptian Texts with English Translations. E. A. Wallis Budge. LC 94-17824. (Illus.). 288p. 1994. reprint ed. pap. text 7.95 (*0-486-28335-6*) Dover.

Liturgy of Holy Week. large type ed. 160p. 1992. pap. 4.95 (*0-8146-2110-4*) Liturgical Pr.

Liturgy of Hours Supplmt. Catholic. 1990. pap. 2.50 (*0-89942-405-8*, 405) Catholic Bk Pub.

Liturgy of St. Basil the Great & the Liturgy of Presanctified Gifts. Ed. by St. Tikhon's Seminary Press Staff. (Service Books of the Orthodox Church: Vol. 2). 209p. 1984. 8.00 (*1-878997-21-1*); 12.00 (*1-878997-22-X*) St Tikhons Pr.

Liturgy of St. John Chrysostom. Ed. by St. Tihon's Seminary Press Staff. (Service Books of the Orthodox Church). 222p. 1984. write for info. (*1-878997-28-9*) St Tikhons Pr.

Liturgy of St. John Chrysostom. Ed. by St. Tihon's Seminary Press Staff. (Service Books of the Orthodox Church: Vol. 1). 222p. 1984. 8.00 (*0-685-54797-3*); 12.00 (*1-878997-20-3*); write for info. (*1-878997-19-X*) St Tikhons Pr.

Liturgy of the Ancient & Accepted Scottish Rite of Freemasonry. Albert Pike. 680p. 1993. reprint ed. pap. 45.00 (*1-56459-310-X*) Kessinger Pub.

Liturgy of the Blue Degrees of the Ancient & Accepted Scottish Rite of Freemasonry for the Southern Jurisdiction. Albert Pike. 227p. 1993. reprint ed. pap. 24.95 (*1-56459-323-1*) Kessinger Pub.

Liturgy of the Hours: Advent & Christmas, Lent & Easter, Ordinary Time-Weeks 1 to 17 & Ordinary Time-Weeks 18 to 34, 4 vols. deluxe ed. 1975. lthr. 155.00 (*0-89942-411-2*, 409/13) Catholic Bk Pub.

Liturgy of the Hours: Your Guide to Praying at Home & in Your Parish Community. Ed. by Nancy Benvenga. (RVC Liturgical Ser.). 48p. (Orig.). 1990. pap. 3.95 (*0-9623410-7-X*, Resurrection Pr) Catholic Bk Pub.

Liturgy of the Hours Annual Guide, 2000 Edition. Catholic Book Staff. 1.75 (*0-89942-429-5*, 400-G) Catholic Bk Pub.

Liturgy of the Hours in East & West. 2nd rev. ed. Robert Taft. 440p. 1986. pap. 24.95 (*0-8146-1405-1*) Liturgical Pr.

Liturgy of the Neighbor: Emmanuel Levinas & the Religion of Responsibility. Jeffrey Bloechl. LC 99-6670. 325p. 2000. text 55.00 (*0-8207-0311-7*) Duquesne.

Liturgy of the Order of Buddhist Contemplatives for the Laity. rev. ed. Compiled by P. T. Jiyu-Kennett. 409p. 1990. pap. 11.00 (*0-930066-12-X*) Shasta Abbey.

Liturgy of the Presanctified Gifts. Ed. by David Drillock & John H. Erickson. 264p. 1990. 40.00 (*0-88141-097-7*); pap. 20.00 (*0-88141-095-0*) St Vladimirs.

Liturgy of the Word for Children. Alison Travers. 72p. (C). 1988. 35.00 (*0-85597-387-0*, Pub. by McCrimmon Pub) St Mut.

Liturgy of the World: Karl Rahner's Theology of Worship. Michael Skelley. 176p. (Orig.). 1991. pap. text 11.95 (*0-8146-6009-6*) Liturgical Pr.

Liturgy: or Order of Christian Worship for the German Reformed Church. Philip Schaff. (Notable American Authors Ser.). 1999. reprint ed. lib. bdg. 125.00 (*0-7812-8863-0*) Rprt Serv.

Liturgy Order & the Law. Rupert D. Bursell. 362p. 1996. text 80.00 (*0-19-826250-7*); pap. text 28.00 (*0-19-826249-3*) OUP.

Liturgy Planning Guide. LC 75-14546. (Illus.). 54p. 1974. pap. 2.95 (*0-915866-05-6*) Am Cath Pr.

Liturgy, Politics & Salvation: The Catholic League in Paris & the Nature of Catholic Reform, 1540-1630. Ann W. Ramsey. LC 99-17827. (Illus.). 512p. 1999. 99.00 (*1-58046-031-3*, Pub. by Univ Rochester Pr) Boydell & Brewer.

Liturgy, Sanctity & History in Tridentine Italy: Pietro Maria Campi & the Preservation of the Particular. Simon Ditchfield. (Cambridge Studies in Italian History & Culture). (Illus.). 413p. (C). 1995. text 80.00 (*0-521-46220-7*) Cambridge U Pr.

Liturgy Trap: The Bible vs. Mere Tradition in Worship. James B. Jordan. 82p. (Orig.). 1994. pap. 7.00 (*1-883690-04-8*) Transfig Pr.

Liturgy with Style & Grace. 3rd rev. ed. Gabe Huck & Gerald Chinchar. LC 98-86330. ix, 133 p. 1998. pap. 12.00 (*1-56854-186-4*) Liturgy Tr Pubns.

***Litvaks: A Short History of the Jews in Lithuania.** Dov Levin. 300p. 2000. 39.95 (*965-308-084-9*, Pub. by Yad Vashem Pubns) Berghahn Bks.

***Litvaks: A Short History of the Jews of Lithuania.** Dov Levin. LC 00-37841. 2001. write for info. (*1-57181-264-4*) Berghahn Bks.

Litwak's Multimedia Producer's Handbook: A Legal & Distribution Guide. Mark Litwak. LC 97-29963. xix, 334p. 1998. pap. text 29.95 (*1-879505-35-5*) Silman James Pr.

Liu Fracture Mechanics Tough. 1982. text 171.00 (*90-247-2536-4*) Kluwer Academic.

Liu Shaoqi & the Chinese Cultural Revolution. rev. ed. Lowell Dittmer. LC 97-41292. 400p. (YA). 1998. text 76.95 (*1-56324-951-0*, East Gate Bk) M E Sharpe.

Liu Shaoqi & the Chinese Cultural Revolution. rev. ed. Lowell Dittmer. LC 97-41292. (Illus.). 400p. (C). (gr. 13). 1998. pap. text 25.95 (*1-56324-952-9*, East Gate Bk) M E Sharpe.

Liu Tsung-Yuan. W. H. Nienhauser. (Twayne's World Authors Ser.). (C). 1971. lib. bdg. 20.95 (*0-8057-2538-5*) Irvington.

Liu Tsung-yuan & Intellectual Change in T'ang China, 773-819. Jo-Shui Chen. (Studies in Chinese History, Literature & Institutions). (Illus.). 235p. (C). 1992. text 80.00 (*0-521-41964-6*) Cambridge U Pr.

Liubov Popova. Magdalena Dabrowski. (Illus.). 136p. 1991. 39.95 (*0-8109-6090-7*, Pub. by Abrams) Time Warner.

Liubov Popova. Magdalena Dabrowski. (Illus.). 136p. 1991. 39.95 (*0-87070-567-9*, 0-8109-6090-7) Mus of Modern Art.

Liubvi Bezumnoe Tomlen'e: Rasskazy I Povesti Russkikh Pisateli XIX Veka. Aleksandr Pushkin et al. Ed. by Igor Efimov. LC 94-47189. (Klassiki Russkoi Literatury (Russian Classics) Ser.). (RUS.). 290p. (Orig.). 1995. pap. 12.00 (*1-55779-081-7*) Hermitage Pubs.

Liudi i Lozhi: Russkie Masony XX Stoletiia. Nina Berberova. LC 85-61638. (RUS.). 300p. (Orig.). 1987. 48.50 (*0-89830-098-3*) Russica Pubs.

Liudmila Kondakova. Catalogue Raisonne Staff. (Illus.). 32p. Date not set. pap. write for info. (*0-9648085-1-X*) Jenkintwn Pr.

Liutprand of Cremona, Mission to Constantinople, 968 A. D. Lynn H. Nelson & Melanie Shirk. 62p. 1972. pap. 5.00 (*0-87291-039-3*) Coronado Pr.

Liuzza (trans.) Beowulf. 24.95 (*1-55111-315-5*) Broadview Pr.

***Liv.** Morgan Yasbincek. 2000. pap. 19.95 (*1-86368-284-8*, Pub. by Fremantle Arts) Intl Spec Bk.

Liv Och Lek i Afrika. Ed. by Karin Himmelstrand & Berit Hard. 184p. 1979. write for info. (*91-7106-162-2*, Pub. by Nordic Africa) Transaction Pubs.

Liv Och Lek i Indien. Rami Chhabra & Willy Petterson. 92p. 1980. write for info. (*91-7106-168-1*, Pub. by Nordic Africa) Transaction Pubs.

***Liv Tyler.** Sue Boulais. (Real-Life Reader Biography Ser.). (Illus.). 32p. (J). (gr. 3-8). 2000. lib. bdg. 15.95 (*1-58415-041-6*) M Lane Pubs.

Livable Cities Almanac: How over 100 Metropolitan Areas Compare in Economic Health, Air Quality, Water Quality, Crime Rate, Life Expectancy, Health Services, Recreational Opportunities, & More. John T. Marlin. 384p. 1992. pap. 14.00 (*0-685-52542-2*, Harper Ref) HarpC.

Livable Cities for the 21st Century. LC 96-222165. (Directions in Development Ser.). 56p. 1996. pap. 22.00 (*0-8213-3812-9*, 13812) World Bank.

Livable Cities for the 21st Century. (SPA.). 64p. 1997. pap. 22.00 (*0-8213-3844-7*, 13844) World Bank.

Livable Cities Observed: A Source Book of Images & Ideas. Suzanne H. Lennard & Henry L. Lennard. (Illus.). 272p. (Orig.). 1995. 38.00 (*0-935824-05-7*); pap. 33.00 (*0-935824-06-5*) Gondolier.

***Livable City: Revitilizing Urban Communities.** Partners for Livable Communities. LC 00-35164. (Illus.). 224p. 2000. pap. text 49.95 (*0-07-135913-3*) McGraw-Hill Prof.

Livable Landscape Design. John F. Collins & Marvin Adleman. (Information Bulletin Ser.). (Illus.). 64p. (Orig.). 1988. pap. 14.00 (*1-57753-029-2*, 1411B211) Corn Coop Ext.

Live: Throwing Copper. 88p. 1996. otabind 19.95 (*0-7935-5093-9*, 00690070) H Leonard.

Live Authentic Guitar-Tab Edition: The Distance to Here. Warner Brothers Publications Staff. 19.95 (*0-7692-9258-5*) Warner Bros.

Live . . . from Golgotha: A One-Act Drama. Jesse Lee. 20p. 1987. pap. 3.25 (*0-88680-272-5*) I E Clark.

Live a Little. Colin Neenan. LC 95-53259. 264p. 1996. pap. 6.00 (*0-15-201243-5*) Harcourt.

Live a Little. Colin Neenan. LC 95-53259. 264p. (J). 1996. 12.00 (*0-15-201242-7*) Harcourt.

Live a Praying Life: Open Your Life to God's Power & Provision. Jennifer Kennedy Dean. 1999. pap. 16.99 (*0-9667125-0-1*) Masters Pub Hse.

Live above This Crazy World. Vernon Howard. 1983. pap. 2.00 (*0-911203-17-6*) New Life.

Live Action Adventures. (Star Wars). 15.00 (*0-87431-286-8*, 40152) West End Games.

Live Action English. Seely & Elizabeth Romijn. 68p. 1979. pap. text 6.25 (*0-88084-025-0*); audio 19.00 (*0-88084-221-0*) Alemany Pr.

Live Action English. 3rd ed. Elizabeth Romijn & Contee Seely. (Live Action Ser.). (Illus.). 96p. 1997. pap. text 9.95 (*0-929724-16-X*, 16-x) Command Performance.

Live Action French! see Vive L'Action!

Live Action Italian! see Viva L'Azione!

Live Action Roleplaying Game. (Star Wars). 20.00 (*0-87431-283-3*, 40130) West End Games.

Live Action Spanish! see Viva la Accion!

Live Again Our Mission Past. enl. ed. 1992. 14.92 (*0-685-56505-X*) Arts Pubns.

Live Again Our Mission Past: California Missions Through Children's Eyes. Ed. by Barbara B. Linse & George Kuska. (Story of Spanish California through the Missions Ser.). (Illus.). 200p. (YA). (gr. 7-12). 1984. pap. 13.95 (*0-9607458-1-5*) Arts Pubns.

***Live Again Our Mission Past for Kids.** Barbara B. Linse. (California Mission Ser.). (SPA.). 108p. (J). (gr. 4-6). 2000. pap. write for info. (*1-878079-26-3*) Arts Pubns.

Live Albom, No. I. Mitch Albom. 1996. mass mkt. 6.95 (*0-937247-06-5*) Detroit Pr.

Live Albom, No. II. Mitch Albom. 1996. pap. 9.95 (*0-937247-54-5*) Detroit Pr.

Live Albom, No. III. Mitch Albom. 1996. pap. 9.95 (*0-937247-71-5*) Detroit Pr.

Live Albom, No. IV. Mitch Albom. 1996. pap. 12.95 (*0-937247-66-9*) Detroit Pr.

Live & Be Well see Folk Remedies That Work

Live & Be Well. Harry R. Litchfield. LC 72-76583. 300p. 1972. 12.95 (*0-87212-022-8*) Libra.

***Live & Be Well: A Celebration of Yiddish Culture in America.** Richard F. Shepard & Vicki Gold Levi. LC 99-48492. (Illus.). 192p. (C). 2000. 28.00 (*0-8135-2812-7*) Rutgers U Pr.

Live & Be Well: A Celebration of Yiddish Culture in America from the First Immigrants to the Second World War. Richard F. Shepard et al. 1982. pap. 9.95 (*0-345-29435-1*) Ballantine Pub Grp.

Live & Be Well: A Celebration of Yiddish Culture in America from the First Immigrants to the Second World War. Richard F. Shepard et al. (Illus.). 192p. 1982. 20.00 (*0-345-30752-6*) Ballantine Pub Grp.

Live & Grow Young (1921) Arthur E. Stilwell. 120p. 1998. reprint ed. pap. 12.95 (*0-7661-0635-7*) Kessinger Pub.

***Live & Kicking: The Rock Concert Industry in the Nineties.** Mark E. Cunningham. 1999. pap. text 19.95 (*1-86074-217-3*) Sanctuary Pr.

Live & Learn. Alma Heaton. pap. 10.95 (*1-55517-357-8*) CFI Dist.

Live & Learn. Stanley Middleton. LC 96-166464. 248p. 1997. 26.00 (*0-09-179220-7*, Pub. by Hutchnson) Trafalgar.

Live & Learn: An Introduction to the Psychology of Growth & Change in Everyday Life. Guy Claxton. 288p. 1984. pap. 34.95 (*0-335-09809-6*) OpUniv Pr.

Live & Learn & Pass It On. H. Jackson Brown, Jr. LC 91-32132. 1992. pap. 6.95 (*1-55853-156-4*) Rutledge Hill Pr.

Live & Learn & Pass It On. H. Jackson Brown, Jr. LC 91-32132. (Illus.). 160p. 1993. 12.95 (*1-55853-149-1*) Rutledge Hill Pr.

Live & Learn & Pass It On, Vol. 2. H. Jackson Brown. LC 91-32132. 160p. 1996. 12.95 (*1-55853-394-X*) Rutledge Hill Pr.

Live & Learn & Pass It On, Vol. III. H. Jackson Brown, Jr. LC 91-32132. (Illus.). 160p. 1997. pap. 6.95 (*1-55853-472-5*) Rutledge Hill Pr.

Live & Learn & Pass It On: People Ages 5 to 95 Share What They've Discovered about Life, Love, & Other Good Stuff, Vol. 2. H. Jackson Brown, Jr. (Live & Learn & Pass It on Ser.). 160p. 1995. pap. 5.95 (*1-55853-331-1*) Rutledge Hill Pr.

Live & Learn for Better Health about the Fountain of Youth. Paul Noth. (Illus.). 40p. 1999. pap. 7.50 (*0-8059-4712-4*) Dorrance.

Live & Learn, Jennifer Parker. Annette P. Bowen. LC 95-5208. 180p. (Orig.). (YA). (gr. 9-12). 1995. pap. 9.95 (*0-87579-879-9*) Deseret Bk.

Live & Let Die. Ian Fleming. (FRE & SPA.). 9.95 (*0-685-11295-0*); pap. 9.95 (*0-685-11296-9*) Fr & Eur.

Live & Let Die. Ian Fleming. 1995. reprint ed. lib. bdg. 24.95 (*1-56849-656-7*) Buccaneer Bks.

Live & Let Die. Ian Fleming. (James Bond Ser.). 218p. 1995. reprint ed. 9.98 (*1-56731-057-5*, MJF Bks) Fine Comms.

Live & Let Live: The Tale of Bossy Bertha. Margaret Hopkins. LC 96-21340. (One Day at a Time Ser.). (Illus.). (J). 1997. write for info. (*0-590-26596-2*) Scholastic Inc.

Live & Let Spy. Elizabeth Cage. (Spy Girls Ser.: No. 2). (YA). (gr. 7 up). 1998. mass mkt. write for info. (*0-671-02287-3*, Minstrel Bks) PB.

Live & Remember. Valentin Rasputin. Tr. by Antonina W. Bouis from RUS. 225p. 1992. reprint ed. pap. 15.95 (*0-8101-1053-9*) Northwestern U Pr.

Live & Work in Australia & New Zealand. Fiona McGregor & Charlotte Denny. (Live & Work Abroad Guides Ser.). 336p. (Orig.). 1997. pap. 16.95 (*1-85458-115-5*, Pub. by Vac Wrk Pubns) Seven Hills Bk.

Live & Work in Australia & New Zealand. 2nd ed. Fiona McGregor & Charlotte Denny. (Live & Work Ser.). 356p. (Orig.). 1999. pap. 19.95 (*1-85458-213-5*, Pub. by Vac Wrk Pubns) Seven Hills Bk.

Live & Work in Belgium, The Netherlands & Luxembourg. Andre De Vries & Greg Adams. (Live & Work Abroad Guides Ser.). 272p. (Orig.). 1997. pap. 16.95 (*1-85458-076-0*, Pub. by Vac Wrk Pubns) Seven Hills Bk.

Live & Work in Belgium, The Netherlands & Luxembourg. 2nd ed. Andre De Vries. (Live & Work Abroad Guides Ser.). 288p. (Orig.). 1998. pap. 17.95 (*1-85458-188-0*, Pub. by Vac Wrk Pubns) Seven Hills Bk.

Live & Work in France. 2nd ed. Victoria Pybus. (Live & Work Abroad Guides Ser.). 248p. 1997. pap. 16.95 (*1-85458-111-2*, Pub. by Vac Wrk Pubns) Seven Hills Bk.

Live & Work in France. 3rd ed. Victoria Pybus. (Live & Work Abroad Guides Ser.). 288p. 1998. pap. 17.95 (*1-85458-180-5*, Pub. by Vac Wrk Pubns) Seven Hills Bk.

Live & Work in Germany. Victoria Pybus. (Live & Work Abroad Guides Ser.). 200p. (Orig.). 1997. pap. 16.95 (*1-85458-071-X*, Pub. by Vac Wrk Pubns) Seven Hills Bk.

Live & Work in Germany. 2nd ed. Victoria Pybus. (Live & Work Abroad Guides Ser.). 256p. (Orig.). 1998. pap. 17.95 (*1-85458-184-8*, Pub. by Vac Wrk Pubns) Seven Hills Bk.

Live & Work in Italy. Victoria Pybus & Richard Robinson. (Live & Work Abroad Guides Ser.). 168p. (Orig.). 1997. pap. 15.95 (*1-85458-067-1*, Pub. by Vac Wrk Pubns) Seven Hills Bk.

Live & Work in Italy. 2nd ed. Victoria Pybus. (Live & Work Abroad Guides Ser.). 224p. (Orig.). 1998. pap. 17.95 (*1-85458-182-1*, Pub. by Vac Wrk Pubns) Seven Hills Bk.

Live & Work in Japan. Victoria Pybus. (Live & Work Ser.). 256p. 1999. pap. 19.95 (*1-85458-209-7*, Pub. by Vac Wrk Pubns) Seven Hills Bk.

Live & Work in Russia & Eastern Europe. (Live & Work Ser.). 300p. pap. 19.95 (*1-85458-190-2*, Pub. by Vac Wrk Pubns) Seven Hills Bk.

Live & Work in Scandinavia. Victoria Pybus & Susan Dunne. (Live & Work Abroad Guides Ser.). 320p. (Orig.). 1997. pap. 16.95 (*1-85458-121-X*, Pub. by Vac Wrk Pubns) Seven Hills Bk.

Live & Work in Spain & Portugal. Rachael Robinson & Victoria Pyrus. (Live & Work Abroad Guides Ser.). 256p. (Orig.). 1997. pap. 16.95 (*1-85458-061-2*, Pub. by Vac Wrk Pubns) Seven Hills Bk.

Live & Work in Spain & Portugal. 2nd ed. Jonathan Packer. (Live & Work Abroad Guides Ser.). 288p. 1998. pap. 17.95 (*1-85458-186-4*, Pub. by Vac Wrk Pubns) Seven Hills Bk.

Live & Work in the U. S. A. & Canada. Adam Lechmere & Susan Catto. (Live & Work Ser.). 288p. 1999. pap. 19.95 (*1-85458-211-9*, Pub. by Vac Wrk Pubns) Seven Hills Bk.

Live & Work in the U. S. A. & Canada. Adam Lechunere & Susan Catto. (Live & Work Abroad Guides Ser.). 272p. (Orig.). 1997. pap. 16.95 (*1-85458-119-8*, Pub. by Vac Wrk Pubns) Seven Hills Bk.

Live Animal Carcass Evaluation & Selection Manual. 4th ed. Donald L. Boggs & Robert A. Merkel. 256p. 1995. per. 31.95 (*0-8403-7609-X*) Kendall-Hunt.

Live Arrival Guaranteed: A Sandhill Memoir. Hazel Grange. LC 95-41960. 384p. 1996. 23.95 (*1-883755-08-5*) Lost Riv Pr.

Live at Five. David Haynes. LC 97-22027. 288p. (C). 1997. pap. 12.00 (*0-15-600503-4*, Harvest Bks) Harcourt.

Live at Five. David Haynes. LC 95-38452. 280p. 1996. 21.95 (*1-57131-009-6*) Milkweed Ed.

Live at Karla's: 13 New Hope Poets. Ed. by Robert Salup & Rosalind Salup. LC 96-94316. (Illus.). 327p. (Orig.). 1996. pap. 19.95 (*1-887213-09-0*) Blck Oak Pr.

Live at the Church. Lewis M. Adams. 7.00 (*0-686-20820-X*); pap. 3.50 (*0-686-20821-8*) Kulchur Foun.

Live at the Ear. Ed. by Charles Bernstein. Date not set. write for info. (*0-614-30092-4*) DILLON ELEMENOPE.

Live at the Ear. Ed. by Charles Bernstein. 32p. (C). 1994. 15.95 incl. audio compact disk (*1-885905-36-X*, 5-7777-2) DILLON ELEMENOPE.

***Live at the Fillmore East: A Photographic Memoir.** Amalie R. Rothschild & Ruth Ellen Gruber. (Illus.). 2000. reprint ed. pap. 24.95 (*1-56025-279-0*, Thunders Mouth) Avalon NY.

Live at the Silver Dollar. Dave Ener. 80p. 1985. pap. 5.95 (*0-933180-74-8*) Spoon Riv Poetry.

Live at the Village Vanguard. Max Gordon. LC 81-22149. (Quality Paperbacks Ser.). (Illus.). 146p. 1982. reprint ed. pap. 10.95 (*0-306-80160-4*) Da Capo.

Live-Away Dads: Staying a Part of Your Children's Lives When They Aren't a Part of Your Home. William C. Klatte. LC 98-11684. 220p. 1999. pap. 12.95 (*0-14-027280-1*) Viking Penguin.

Live Bait. large type ed. Bill Knox. (Linford Mystery Library). 368p. 1993. pap. 16.99 (*0-7089-7345-0*, Linford) Ulverscroft.

Live Bait. large type ed. Bill Walsh. (Mystery Ser.). 1994. pap. 16.99 (*0-7089-7627-1*, Linford) Ulverscroft.

Live Bait Tactics. Louis Bignami. LC 93-83706. (Complete Angler's Library). 250p. 1993. write for info. (*0-914697-55-2*) N Amer Outdoor Grp.

Live Better - Live Longer Resourcebook: Make the Second Half of Your Life the Better Half, Vol. 1. Richard A. Herman. LC 93-73514. 180p. (Orig.). 1994. pap. 12.95 (*1-884258-06-9*) AltaMira Pr.

An Asterisk (*) at the beginning of an entry indicates that the title is appearing for the first time.

Live Better - Live Longer Resourcebook: Make the Second Half of Your Life the Better Half, Vol. 2. Richard A. Herman. LC 93-73514. 180p. (Orig.). 1994. pap. 12.95 (*1-884258-07-7*) AltaMira Pr.
Live Better - Live Longer Resourcebook: Make the Second Half of Your Life the Better Half, Vol. 3. Richard A. Herman. LC 93-73514. 180p. (Orig.). 1994. pap. 12.95 (*1-884258-08-5*) AltaMira Pr.
Live Better & Longer/Healthy Eating. Max. 50p. 1997. pap. 32.00 (*0-922070-35-0*) M Tecton Pub.
Live Better (Creative Science) rev. ed. Hilton Hotema. 151p. 1996. reprint ed. spiral bd. 14.00 (*0-7873-0422-0*) Hlth Research.
Live Better Longer: The Parcells Center 7-Step Plan for Health & Longevity. Joseph Dispenza. LC 96-39224. 240p. 1997. 22.00 (*0-06-251422-9*, Pub. by Harper SF) HarpC.
***Live Better South of the Border in Mexico: Practical Advice for Living & Working.** Mike Nelson. 168p. 2000. pap. 16.95 (*1-55591-394-6*) Fulcrum Pub.
***Live Bodies.** Maurice Gee. LC 98-221790. 1998. write for info. (*0-14-027380-8*) Penguin Books.
Live by the Gun. large type ed. Wayne Barton & Stan Williams. 331p. 1992. pap. 14.95 (*0-8161-5465-1*, G K Hall Lrg Type) Mac Lib Ref.
Live by the Sword: How the Kennedy's Secret War Against Castro Triggered JFK's Assassination & America's Longest Coverup. Gus Russo. LC 98-72307. (Illus.). 617p. 1998. 26.95 (*1-890862-01-0*) Bancroft MD.
Live Chickens Don't Do Backflips. Joyce E. Edie. (Illus.). 96p. 1994. pap. 7.95 (*1-887308-00-8*) Book em Pub.
Live Coal in the Sea. Madeleine L'Engle. 352p. 1996. 24.00 (*0-374-18989-7*) FS&G.
Live Coal In The Sea. Madeleine L'Engle. LC 96-4909. 336p. 1997. pap. 14.00 (*0-06-065286-1*, Pub. by Harper SF) HarpC.
Live Company: Psychoanalytic Therapy with Autistic, Abused & Borderline Psychotic Children. Anne Alvarez. LC 91-40447. 264p. (C). 1992. pap. 24.99 (*0-415-06097-4*, Pub. by Tavistock) Routldge.
Live Data Structures in Logic Programs. Anne Mulkers. LC 93-19196. (Lecture Notes in Computer Science Ser.: Vol. 675). 1993. 39.95 (*0-387-56694-5*) Spr-Verlag.
Live Debt Free. Ted Carroll. 180p. 1991. pap. 7.95 (*1-55850-044-8*) Adams Media.
Live, Direct & Biased? Making Television News in the Satellite Age. Brent Macgregor. LC 96-37949. 1997. text 60.00 (*0-340-66224-7*, Pub. by E A) St Martin.
Live, Direct & Biased? Making Television News in the Satellite Age. Brent MacGregor. LC 96-37949. 248p. 1997. text 19.95 (*0-340-66225-5*, Pub. by E A) OUP.
Live, Don't Diet! The Low-Fat Cookbook That Can Change Your Life! Vicki Park. LC 95-35775. 252p. 1996. mass mkt. 16.99 (*0-446-67229-7*, Pub. by Warner Bks) Little.
Live Each New Day. Bill Rentschler. 1991. pap. 8.95 (*0-913617-14-8*) Highlander Pr.
Live Electronics. Stephen Montague. (Contemporary Music Review Ser.). 237p. 1991. text 23.00 (*3-7186-5116-5*, Harwood Acad Pubs) Gordon & Breach.
Live Events Promotional Graphics. Jim Cowen. (Illus.). 160p. 1994. 34.99 (*1-56496-082-X*) Rockport Pubs.
***Live Feed.** Moses Znaimer. 2001. write for info. (*0-679-31038-X*) Random.
Live Fire Testing of the F-22. National Research Council Staff. 142p. (Orig.). (C). 1995. pap. text 35.00 (*0-309-05333-1*) Natl Acad Pr.
Live Firing Classic Weapons: Powder & Ball Small Arms. Martin Pegler. 1998. 39.95 (*1-85915-069-1*, Pub. by W & G) Motorbooks Intl.
Live 5: My Perfect Theatre. David Tushingham. (Nick Hern Bks.). 80p. 1998. pap. 14.95 (*1-85459-328-5*) Theatre Comm.
Live Flesh. Ruth Rendell. 1987. mass mkt. 5.99 (*0-345-34485-5*) Ballantine Pub Grp.
***Live Food in Aquaculture: Live Food & Marine Larviculture Symposium, 1996, Nagasaki-Shi, Japan.** A. Hagiwara. LC 97-51758. (Developments in Hydrobiology Ser.: Vol. 124). 328p. 1998. 171.00 (*0-7923-4970-9*) Kluwer Academic.
Live Foods. W. Volkart. (Illus.). 160p. 1998. 22.95 (*0-7938-0137-0*, LR-112) TFH Pubns.
Live 4: A Polemic Review of the Performing Arts. Ed. by David Tushingham. 80p. (Orig.). 1996. pap. 14.95 (*1-85459-380-3*, Pub. by N Hern Bks) Theatre Comm.
Live Free. Tom C. McKenney. LC 84-91415. (Illus.). 317p. 1985. 12.95 (*0-934527-04-0*); pap. 8.95 (*0-934527-06-7*) Words Living Minis.
Live Free, Don't Become a Corporate Mule. Robert J. Lytle. (Illus.). 200p. (Orig.). 1990. pap. text 15.95 (*0-9626082-0-3*) Tana Starr Pub.
Live Free Forever, Guaranteed (by New Law) & Save up to 25on Home Purchase: All Because of Jim Anderson's New Home Buyer Law. Jim Anderson. 1996. pap. 20.00 incl. VHS (*0-932574-11-4*) Brun Pr.
Live Free Forever, Guaranteed (by New Law) & Save up to 25on Home Purchase: All Because of Jim Anderson's New Home Buyer Law. 12th enl. rev. ed. Jim Anderson. LC 78-113752. (Illus.). 650p. 1991. reprint ed. 40.00 (*0-932574-10-6*) Brun Pr.
Live Free or Die. Ernest Hebert. 1999. pap. 9.00 (*0-14-012978-2*, Viking) Viking Penguin.
Live Free or Die. Ernest Hebert. LC 94-44581. (Hardscrabble Bks.). 429p. 1995. reprint ed. pap. 15.95 (*0-87451-699-4*) U Pr of New Eng.
Live from Atlantic City: The History of the Miss America Pageant Before, After & in Spite of Television. A. R. Riverol. LC 92-81612. (Illus.). (C). 1992. 24.95 (*0-87972-557-5*); pap. 12.95 (*0-87972-558-3*) Bowling Green Univ Popular Press.
Live from Capitol Hill! Studies of Congress & the Media. Stephen Hess. 178p. 1991. 31.95 (*0-8157-3628-2*); pap. 12.95 (*0-8157-3627-4*) Brookings.
Live from Cedar Hills!, 4. Michael Rose Ramirez. (Chana! Ser.). (J). 1998. 9.09 (*0-606-13263-5*, Pub. by Turtleback) Demco.
Live from Death Row. Mumia Abu-Jamal. 258p. 1995. 20.00 (*0-201-48319-X*) Addison-Wesley.
Live from Death Row. Mumia Abu-Jamal. 208p. 1996. pap. 12.50 (*0-380-72766-8*, Avon Bks) Morrow Avon.
Live, from Feminism: Memoirs of Women's Liberation. Ed. by Ann Snitow & Rachel Blau DuPlessis. LC 98-5660. 464p. 1998. pap. 20.00 (*0-609-80384-0*) C Potter.
Live from Golgotha: The Gospel According to Gore Vidal. Gore Vidal. 240p. 1993. pap. 12.95 (*0-14-023119-6*, Penguin Bks) Viking Penguin.
Live from New York. Alan Gelb. 208p. (J). 1991. mass mkt. 2.95 (*0-380-75745-1*, Avon Bks) Morrow Avon.
***Live from the Gates of Hell: An Insider's Look at the Anti-Abortion Underground.** Jerry Reiter. 280p. 2000. 26.00 (*1-57392-840-2*) Prometheus Bks.
***Live from the Hong Kong Nile Club: Poems, 1975-1990.** August Kleinzahler. 88p. 2000. pap. 13.00 (*0-374-52701-6*) FS&G.
***Live from the Hong Kong Nile Club: Poems, 1975-1990.** August Kleinzahler. LC 99-36986. 2001. text. write for info. (*0-374-18983-8*) FS&G.
Live from the Trenches: The Changing Role of the Television News Correspondent. Joe S. Foote & Garrick Utley. LC 98-18376. (Illus.). 192p. 1998. 22.95 (*0-8093-2232-3*) S Ill U Pr.
Live from the Tundra! Lew Freedman. (ENG.). 191p. 1993. pap. text 14.00 (*1-878100-92-0*) Todd Commns.
Live Girls. Beth Nugent. 1997. pap. 12.00 (*0-679-74424-X*) Vin Bks.
Live Goat. Cecil Dawkins. LC 75-138781. 1971. 25.00 (*0-06-010998-X*) Ultramarine Pub.
Live Hands: A Key to Better Golf. E. M. Prain. LC 94-69413. (Illus.). 128p. 1994. 16.95 (*1-885198-02-7*) Sports Log Pubs.
Live Hands: A Key to Better Golf. E. M. Prain. 1998. text 16.95 (*1-886346-50-X*) Warde Pubs.
Live Healthier, Live Longer. large type ed. Henry Carlen. 195p. 1997. pap. 12.95 (*0-9654810-0-X*) Nutri-fit Pubns.
Live-in Kitchens. Ellen M. Plante. LC 99-18452. (For Your Home Ser.). 1999. pap. text 12.95 (*1-56799-719-8*, Friedman-Fairfax) M Friedman Pub Grp Inc.
Live-In Mom. Laurie Paige. 1997. per. 3.99 (*0-373-24077-5*, 1-24077-9) Silhouette.
***Live In Mum.** large type ed. Laurie Paige. (Silhouette Romance Ser.). 1999. 21.95 (*0-373-59599-9*) Harlequin Bks.
***Live in the Balance: The Ground-Breaking East-West Nutrition Program.** Linda Prout. (Illus.). 304p. 2000. pap. 16.95 (*1-56924-615-7*) Marlowe & Co.
Live in the Beautiful Islands of Hawaii. Glenn P. Chapman. LC 92-81419. 84p. 1992. pap. 15.00 (*0-9632989-0-9*) Opport Hawaii.
Live-Ins. Deborah Cox-Stubblefield. Date not set. pap. write for info. (*1-930183-03-8*, DR-0003-99) Anyanwu.
Live It! Dan Vander Ark. 99p. pap. 20.10 (*0-930265-69-6*) CRC Pubns.
Live It! Dan Vander Ark. (Illus.). 111p. pap., student ed. 11.25 (*0-930265-68-8*) CRC Pubns.
Live It: A Daily Devotional for Students. Becky Tirabassi. 192p. (YA). 1991. pap. 11.99 (*0-310-53751-7*) Zondervan.
Live It Now: New Testament. 1998. pap. 5.99 (*0-8423-3499-8*) Tyndale Hse.
Live It Up: Eternal Perspective. Kevin Scoleri. (Inter Acta Ser.). (Illus.). 6p. (C). 1994. teacher ed., ring bd. 1.25 (*1-885702-42-6*, 741-020t, Inter Acta); student ed., ring bd. 3.25 (*1-885702-41-8*, 741-020s, Inter Acta) WSN Pr.
Live It Up! How to Create a Life You Can Love. rev. ed. Tom Sine. LC 93-32174. (Illus.). 232p. 1994. pap. 14.99 (*0-8361-3629-2*) Herald Pr.
***Live Jesus! Wisdom from Saints Francis de Sales & Jane de Chantal.** Francis et al. LC 00-40412. 2000. write for info. (*0-932085-42-3*) Word Among Us.
Live, Laugh, Love. Ada Steward. 1993. per. 3.39 (*0-373-09808-1*, 5-09808-2) Silhouette.
Live Life First Class! How to Be Happier, Healthier & More Prosperous. 2nd ed. Kenneth T. Hurst. LC 85-3230. 122p. 1990. reprint ed. pap. 6.95 (*0-943914-45-0*) Larson Pubns.
Live Like a King: Developing a Royal Lifestyle from the Beatitudes. Warren W. Wiersbe. LC 94-37814. 176p. 1995. pap. 10.99 (*0-8254-3996-5*) Kregel.
Live Like a King - Chinese Edition. Warren W. Wiersbe. Tr. by Daniel Chen. (CHI.). 242p. 1991. pap. 5.50 (*1-56582-098-3*) Christ Renew Min.
Live Like a Prince in Florida: A History of Woodridge & the Surrounding Community. Doris G. Taylor. (Illus.). 26p. 1995. pap. text 4.95 (*1-879043-02-5*) Taylor Commns.
Live Like You Really Mean It! Finding the Miracle in Your Moments. Lisa Bell. (Illus.). 1999. pap. write for info. (*1-893569-00-4*) Accolade Pub Co.
Live Locomotor Systems. William Hunter. 40p. 1985. 4.00 (*0-8187-0059-9*) Harlo Press.
***Live Long & Die Laughing.** Mark Lowry. 204p. 2000. pap. 12.99 (*0-8499-4204-7*) Word Pub.
Live Long & Prosper. Etta M Ladson. (Illus.). 33p. 1992. teacher ed. 11.95 (*0-9630574-2-1*) Jewelgate.
Live Long & Prosper. Price. 210p. (C). 1998. pap. text 12.00 (*0-536-01444-2*) Pearson Custom.
Live Long, Die Fast: Playing the Aging Game to Win. John H. Bland. LC 96-9430. (Illus.). 240p. (Orig.). 1997. pap. 14.95 (*1-57749-012-6*) Fairview Press.
Live Longer. 2nd ed. Hilton Hotema. 84p. (Orig.). 1996. reprint ed. spiral bd. 11.00 (*0-7873-0436-0*) Hlth Research.
Live Longer & Love It. Gordon R. Heath. LC 80-81595. (Illus.). 78p. (Orig.). 1980. pap. 5.95 (*0-937092-00-2*) Methuselah Bks.
Live Longer Better: Dr. Anderson's Complete Antiaging Health Program. James W. Anderson & Maury M. Breecher. LC 97-31746. 288p. 1997. pap. 12.95 (*0-7867-0472-1*) Carroll & Graf.
***Live Longer, Look Younger! I Can't Believe It's Yoga for the Ageless.** Lisa Trivell. (I Can't Believe It's Yoga! Ser.). (Illus.). 160p. 2000. pap. 14.95 (*1-57826-059-0*, Pub. by Hatherleigh) Norton.
Live Machines: Hired Foreigners & Meiji Japan. H. J. Jones. 226p. 1987. 95.00 (*0-904404-38-2*, Pub. by P Norbury Pubns Ltd) St Mut.
***Live Motion F/X & Design.** Dan Gray. (Illus.). 500p. 2000. pap. 49.99 (*1-57610-676-4*) Coriolis Grp.
Live Now! 66p. 1987. 2.25 (*955-24-0028-7*, Pub. by Buddhist Pub Soc) Vipassana Res Pubns.
Live Now: Inspiring Accounts of Overcoming Adversity. George Klein. Tr. by Clas Von Sydow. LC 97-11796. 311p. 1997. 28.95 (*1-57392-154-8*) Prometheus Bks.
***Live Now, Age Later: Proven Ways to Slow down the Clock.** Isadore Rosenfeld. 480p. 2000. mass mkt. 7.99 (*0-446-60910-2*, Warner Vision) Warner Bks.
***Live Now, Age Later: Proven Ways to Slow down the Clock.** Isadore Rosenfeld. 400p. 2000. pap. 13.95 (*0-446-67602-0*) Warner Bks.
***Live Now, Age Later: Proven Ways to Slow down the Clock, Vol. 1.** large type ed. Isadore Rosenfeld. LC 99-37437. 1999. 28.95 (*0-7838-8741-8*, G K Hall Lrg Type) Mac Lib Ref.
Live Now, Age Later: Proven Ways to Turn Back the Clock. Isadore Rosenfeld. LC 98-50859. 384p. 1999. 24.00 (*0-446-52060-8*, Pub. by Warner Bks) Little.
Live Nude Girls. Danko. LC 98-11780. 160p. 1998. pap. 14.95 (*0-312-18741-6*) St Martin.
Live Oak Splendor. N. Odenwald. 1992. 35.00 (*0-614-30802-X*, OLIVEO) Claitors.
Live Oaking: Southern Timber for Tall Ships. Virginia S. Wood. 1996. text 36.95 (*0-07-071835-0*) McGraw.
Live Oaking: Southern Timber for Tall Ships. Virginia S. Wood. LC 94-45595. (Illus.). 224p. 1995. 38.95 (*1-55750-933-6*) Naval Inst Pr.
Live Oaks. Bubber Jenkinson. 168p. 1996. 22.95 (*0-9638639-6-7*) Nimrod Hse.
Live Oaks Also Die. Roy Gilligan. LC 90-91654. (Pat Riordan Mystery Ser.). 184p. (Orig.). 1990. pap. 8.95 (*0-9626136-0-6*) Brendan Bks.
Live off the Land in the City & Country. Ragnar Benson. (Illus.). 272p. 1981. 29.95 (*0-87364-200-7*) Paladin Pr.
Live on Stage! Performing Arts for Middle School. Carla Blank & Jody Roberts. Ed. by Catherine Anderson et al. (Illus.). (Orig.). (YA). (gr. 6-8). 1996. pap., teacher ed. 35.00 (*1-57232-209-8*, 31500); pap., wbk. ed. 24.95 (*1-57232-374-4*, 31414) Seymour Pubns.
Live 1: Food for the Soul. David Tushingham. 128p. 1995. pap. 19.95 (*0-413-68790-2*) Heinemann.
Live 120 Healthy Happy Years. Bob Swatash. LC 98-44309. 116p. 1999. 18.95 (*1-56072-619-9*) Nova Sci Pubs.
Live Only Love. Bill O'Hearn. Ed. by Thorn Bacon. 140p. (Orig.). 1998. pap. 12.95 (*0-9626161-3-3*) Entheos Pub.
Live or Die see Heart of Anne Sexton's Poetry
Live Performance, Vol. 1. William S. Burroughs. Ed. by Kathelin Hoffman. (Illus.). (C). 12.95 incl. audio (*0-929856-00-7*) Caravan Dreams Prodns.
Live Picture Revealed. Josh Karson. LC 95-81210. 368p. 1996. 40.00 (*1-56830-263-0*) Hayden.
Live Questions: Including Our Penal Machinery & Its Victims. John P. Altgeld. LC 79-156003. (Foundations of Criminal Justice Ser.). reprint ed. 31.50 (*0-404-09103-2*) AMS Pr.
***Live Rich, Vol. 1.** Stephen M. Pollan. 2000. pap. 14.00 (*0-88730-934-8*, HarpBusn) HarpInfo.
Live Rich: An Eighteen Step Guide to a Rewarding Lifestyle, 2 cass. abr. ed. Barry Kaye. 1996. audio. write for info. (*0-7871-1047-7*, Dove Audio) NewStar Media.
Live Rich: Everything You Need to Know to Be Your Own Boss, Whoever You Work For. Stephen M. Pollan & Mark Levine. LC 98-39060. 320p. 1998. 25.00 (*0-88730-935-6*, HarpBusn) HarpInfo.
***Live Rich: Everything You Need to Know to Be Your Own Boss, Whoever You Work For, Set.** Stephen M. Pollan. 1998. audio 18.00 (*0-694-52052-7*) HarperAudio.
***Live Right 4 Your Type.** Peter D'Adamo. 416p. 2001. 24.95 (*0-399-14673-3*) Putnam Pub Group.
Live Robots. Rudy Rucker. LC 93-90822. 368p. 1994. mass mkt. 5.99 (*0-380-77543-3*, Avon Bks) Morrow Avon.
***Live Sand Secrets: Dialogue on Living Sand Filtration.** Bob Goemans. (Illus.). 24p. 1998. pap. 8.99 (*0-9664549-0-1*) M Weiss Cos.
***Live Sand Secrets: Dialogue on Living Sand Filtration.** 2nd rev. ed. Bob Goemans. (Illus.). 1999. pap. 8.99 (*0-9664549-2-8*) M Weiss Cos.
Live Secret Samadhi. 88p. 1997. otabind 19.95 (*0-7935-8062-5*) H Leonard.
Live Sex Acts: Women Performing Erotic Labor. Wendy Chapkis. LC 96-34633. (Illus.). 248p. (C). 1996. pap. 17.99 (*0-415-91288-1*) Routledge.
Live Sex Acts: Women Performing Erotic Labor. Wendy Chapkis. LC 96-34633. (Illus.). 248p. (C). 1997. 70.00 (*0-415-91287-3*) Routledge.
***Live Shot.** Charles Jaco. 1999. 6.99 (*0-345-42186-8*) Ballantine Pub Grp.
Live Sound: PA for Performing Musicians. Peter Buick. (Illus.). 200p. 1997. pap. 18.95 (*1-870775-44-9*, XC8028, Pub. by PC Pubg) Cimino Pub Grp.
Live Sound for Musicians. Rudy Trubitt & David Trubitt. 152p. 1997. otabind 19.95 (*0-7935-6852-8*, HL00330249) H Leonard.
***Live Sound for the Performing Musician.** Paul White. 287p. 1998. pap. 19.95 (*1-86074-210-6*, Pub. by Sanctuary Pubng) Music Sales.
***Live Sound Recording.** Betty Cantor-Jackson. 180p. 2001. pap. 29.95 (*0-87288-755-3*) Intertec Pub.
Live Sound Reinforcement. Scott H. Stark. LC 96-76543. 320p. 1996. pap. 29.95 (*0-918371-07-4*, MixBooks) Intertec Pub.
Live Spelled Backwards. Jerome Lawrence. 1970. pap. 3.25 (*0-8222-0681-1*) Dramatists Play.
***Live Steam: Paddlewheel Steamboats on the Mississippi System.** Jon Kral. 150p. 2000. 55.00 (*1-892695-00-6*, 648-010, Pub. by Long Wind Pub) BookWorld.
Live Television Generation of Hollywood Film Directors: Interviews with Seven Directors. Gorham Kindem. LC 94-3549. (Illus.). 238p. 1994. lib. bdg. 34.50 (*0-89950-986-X*) McFarland & Co.
***Live 10 Healthy Years Longer.** Jan W. Kuzma. LC 99-45953. 200p. 2000. pap. text. write for info. (*0-8499-3770-1*) J Countryman.
***Live the Evil: A Psychological Thriller about Overcoming Destructive Relationships.** Suzanne Leiphart. LC 99-91487. 218p. 2000. pap. 18.00 (*0-7388-0827-X*) Xlibris Corp.
Live the Good Life. Thomas S. Monson. LC 88-71770. 135p. 1988. 12.95 (*0-87579-192-1*) Deseret Bk.
Live the Good Life: World Traveling Harley Man. Ace Martin. (Illus.). 257p. (Orig.). 1991. pap. 19.95 (*0-9631337-0-5*) A Martin Rd Ink.
***Live the Life!** Zondervan Publishing Staff. 1998. pap. 6.99 (*0-310-22582-5*) Zondervan.
***Live the Life! Leaders' Guide.** 1998. pap., teacher ed. 8.99 (*0-310-22578-7*) Zondervan.
Live the Life You Love: In Ten Easy Step-by-Step Lessons. Barbara Sher. 256p. 1997. pap. 9.95 (*0-440-50756-1*, Dell Trade Pbks) Dell.
***Live the Moment: And You See & Recognize Yourself.** 2nd rev. ed. Gabriele Staff. 68p. 1999. pap. 4.99 (*1-890841-13-7*, s315en) Dalrymple Bks.
Live the Story: Short Simple Plays for Church Groups. Compiled by Cheryl Perry. (Whole People of God Library). 144p. Date not set. pap. 15.95 (*1-55145-245-6*, Pub. by Wood Lake Bks) Logos Prods.
Live Theatre: Four Plays for Young People. C. P. Taylor. (Methuen New Theatrescripts Ser.). 128p. (YA). 1988. pap. write for info. (*0-413-51790-X*, A0152, Methuen Drama) Methn.
Live Theatre & Dramatic Literature in the Medieval Arabic World. Shmuel Moreh. (Eastern Civilization Ser.). 240p. (C). 1992. text 45.00 (*0-8147-5481-3*) NYU Pr.
Live Them Again. Time-Life Books Editors. 1953. 1.00 (*0-671-42700-8*) S&S Trade.
Live This Book: Abbie Hoffman's Philosophy for a Free & Green America. Theodore Becker & Anthony Dodson. LC 90-63430. 120p. (Orig.). 1991. pap. 8.95 (*0-9622683-9-9*) Noble Pr.
Live 3: Critical Mass. David Tushingham. 1996. pap. 19.95 (*0-413-69780-0*, Methuen Drama) Methn.
Live to Be 100 Plus: Healthy Choices for Maximizing Your Life. Richard G. Deeb. LC 94-43940. 225p. 1995. 11.95 (*1-885003-07-2*) R D Reed Pubs.
Live to Become a Sophomore. Larry Zessin. 48p. (Orig.). (C). 1984. pap. 1.75 (*0-8100-0195-0*, 12N1728) Northwest Pub.
Live to Ninety & Stay Young. Andrew Stewart. 187p. 17.95 (*0-8464-4246-9*) Beekman Pubs.
Live to Ninety & Stay Young. Andrew Stewart. 184p. 1968. pap. 17.95 (*0-8464-1029-X*) Beekman Pubs.
Live to Regret. Terence Faherty. LC 95-21498. 251p. 1995. per. 3.99 (*0-373-26180-2*, 1-26180-9) Harlequin Bks.
Live 2: Not What I Am. Ed. by David Tushingham. (Methuen Anthologies Ser.). 1996. pap. 11.95 (*0-413-69010-5*) Heinemann.
Live Vigorously - Have Fun: Do It or Diet. Russ Harrison. (Illus.). 150p. (Orig.). 1996. pap. 15.95 (*0-9651425-0-7*) Visionry Pub.
Live Water. Thomas McGuane. LC 96-159320. (Illus.). 133p. 1996. 50.00 (*1-886967-02-4*) Meadow Run Pr.
Live Well, Die Holy: The Art of Being a Saint, Now & Forever. rev. ed. Robert Bellarmine. Tr. by John Dalton from LAT. LC 98-5912. Orig. Title: De Arte Bene Moriendi (Rome, 1620). 150p. 1998. pap. 12.95 (*0-918477-71-9*) Sophia Inst Pr.
Live Well in Honduras: How to Relocate, Retire, & Increase Your Standard of Living. Frank Ford. LC 97-44102. (Illus.). 272p. 1998. 15.95 (*1-56261-339-1*) Avalon Travel.
Live Well in Ireland: How to Relocate, Retire & Increase Your Standard of Living. Steenie Harvey. (Illus.). 240p. 1999. pap. 15.95 (*1-56261-427-4*) Avalon Travel.
Live Well in Mexico: How to Relocate, Retire & Increase Your Standard of Living. Ken Luboff. LC 99-24014. (Illus.). 256p. 1999. pap. 15.95 (*1-56261-432-0*) Avalon Travel.
***Live Well, Live Wisely! Technology for Sustainable Development.** 36p. 2000. pap. 18.00 (*1-85339-512-9*, Pub. by Intermed Tech) Stylus Pub VA.
Live Well with Chiles: The La Cazuela Restaurant Cookbook. Roe Schmidt & Barry Steeves. (Illus.). 139p. (Orig.). 1996. pap. 14.25 (*0-9653957-0-7*) Earthenware Pr.
Live With It. Moore. LC 94-163018. 641p. 1994. pap. 10.95 (*0-921368-39-9*) Blizzard Publ.
Live with Jesus. Alexander Campbell & Gerry Haff. 90p. (Orig.). (J). (gr. 1-6). 1984. pap. 12.95 (*0-940754-20-7*) Ed Ministries.

L

An Asterisk (*) at the beginning of an entry indicates that the title is appearing for the first time.

L

Live with Moses. Alexander Campbell & Gerry Haff. 90p. (Orig.). (J). (gr. 1-6). 1982. pap. 12.95 (*0-940754-13-4*) Ed Ministries.

***Live Work & Play Around the World.** Sharyn McCullum. 160p. 2000. per. 9.00 (*0-7432-0068-3*) Simon & Schuster.

Live, Work & Play in Australia. Sharyn McCullum. 144p. pap. 10.95 (*0-86417-773-9*, Pub. by Kangaroo Pr) Seven Hills Bk.

Live Writing: Breathing Life into Your Words. Ralph Fletcher. LC 98-93659. 144p. (J). (gr. 5-7). 1999. mass mkt. 4.99 (*0-380-79701-1*, Avon Bks) Morrow Avon.

Live Your Dream: Discover & Achieve Your Life Purpose. Joyce Chapman. 190p. 1990. pap. 14.95 (*0-87877-149-2*) Newcastle Pub.

Live Your Dream Workbook: Discover & Live the Life of Your Dreams. Joyce Chapman. 224p. 1994. pap. 12.95 (*0-87877-195-6*) Newcastle Pub.

Live Your Dreams. Les Brown. 272p. 1994. reprint ed. pap. 12.00 (*0-380-72374-3*, Avon Bks) Morrow Avon.

Live Your Dreams: A Fascinating True Love Story. Bernard M. Kane. LC 97-75129. (Illus.). 288p. 1998. 22.95 (*1-878398-40-7*, Blue Note Bks) Blue Note Pubns.

Live Your Dreams: Brown,&Les, Set. abr. ed. Les Brown. 1993. audio 18.00 (*1-55994-750-0*, CPN 2361) HarperAudio.

Live Your Health: The Art & Practice of Holistic Healing. Reuben Halpern & Joshua Halpern. (Healing Arts Ser.). 196p. 1980. pap. 9.95 (*0-89496-020-2*) Ross Bks.

Live Your Health: The Art & Practice of Holistic Healing. Reuben Halpern & Joshua Halpern. (Healing Arts Ser.). 220p. 1980. 12.95 (*0-89496-028-8*) Ross Bks.

Liveable City: The Architecture & Neighbourhoods of Toronto. Photos by S. R. Gage. (Illus.). 160p. 1994. 19.95 (*0-88962-167-5*) Mosaic.

Liveaboard Report: A Boat Dweller's Guide to What Works & What Doesn't. Charlie Wing. LC 93-17644. 1993. pap. 15.95 (*0-87742-378-4*) Intl Marine.

Liveaboard Report: A Boat Dweller's Guide to What Works & What Doesn't. Charlie Wing. 160p. 1993. pap. 15.95 (*0-07-071091-0*) McGraw.

Livebait Cookbook. Kyriakou & Campio. (Illus.). text 40.00 (*0-340-71564-2*, Pub. by Hodder & Stought Ltd) Trafalgar.

Livebait Cookbook: Rambunctious Seafood Cooking. Theodore Kyriakou & Charles Campion. LC 98-27870. (Illus.). 208p. 1998. 30.00 (*1-57959-027-6*, SOMA) BB&T Inc.

Livebearers. Wilfred L. Whitern. (Illus.). 93p. 1979. 9.95 (*0-87666-518-0*, KW-049) TFH Pubns.

Lived Body: Sociological Themes, Embodied Issues. Simon J. Williams & Gillian Bendelow. LC 98-16734. (Illus.). 272p. (C). 1998. 85.00 (*0-415-19425-3*); pap. 25.99 (*0-415-19426-1*) Routledge.

Lived Experience of South Asian Immigrant Women in Atlantic Canada: The Interconnections of Race, Class & Gender. Helen Ralston. LC 96-46146. (Women's Studies: Vol. 14). 194p. 1997. text 79.95 (*0-7734-8761-1*) E Mellen.

Lived Horizon of My Being: The Substantiation of the Self & the Discourse of Resistance in Rigoberta Menchu, MM. Bakhtin & Victor Montejo. Judith Thorn. LC 96-28276. (Special Studies: No. 29). 136p. 1996. pap. 20.00 (*0-87918-084-6*) ASU Lat Am St.

Lived-in Architecture: Le Corbusier's Pessac Revisited. Philippe Boudon. LC 72-169842. (ENG.). 200p. 1972. write for info. (*0-85331-313-X*) Lund Humphries.

Lived-in Architecture: Le Corbusier's Pessac Revisited. Philippe Boudon. LC 70-155321. (ENG.). 200p. 1972. write for info. (*0-262-02083-1*) MIT Pr.

Lived Religion in America: Towards a History of Practice. Ed. by David D. Hall. LC 97-9421. 280p. 1997. text 49.50 (*0-691-01674-7*, Pub. by Princeton U Pr) Cal Prin Full Svc.

Lived Religion in America: Towards a History of Practice. David D. Hall. LC 97-9421. 280p. 1997. pap. text 14.95 (*0-691-01673-9*, Pub. by Princeton U Pr) Cal Prin Full Svc.

Livelihood & Resistance: Peasants & the Politics of Land in Peru. Gavin Smith. (Illus.). 293p. 1991. reprint ed. pap. 17.95 (*0-520-07662-1*, Pub. by U CA Pr) Cal Prin Full Svc.

Livelihood from Fishing: Globalization & Sustainable Fisheries Policies. Alain Le Sann. 112p. 1998. pap. 17.50 (*1-85339-398-3*, Pub. by Intermed Tech) Stylus Pub VA.

Livelihood of Kin: Making Ends Meet "The Kentucky Way" Rhoda H. Halperin. (Illus.). 199p. (Orig.). 1991. pap. 14.95 (*0-292-74670-9*); text 25.00 (*0-292-74669-5*) U of Tex Pr.

Livello Soglia (The Threshold Level for Italian) Council of Europe Staff. (ITA.). 1982. 25.00 (*92-871-0000-4*, Pub. by Council of Europe) Manhattan Pub Co.

Livelong Day: Working in the World. Roger Rosen. Ed. by Patra McSharry. (Icarus World Issues Ser.). (Illus.). (YA). (gr. 7-12). 1992. lib. bdg. 16.95 (*0-8239-1361-9*) Rosen Group.

Livelong Day: Working in the World. Ed. by Roger Rosen & Patra McSharry. (Icarus World Issues Ser.). (Illus.). (YA). (gr. 7-12). 1992. pap. 8.95 (*0-8239-1362-7*) Rosen Group.

Lively Advertising Cuts of the Twenties & Thirties: 1102 Illustrations. Leslie E. Cabarga. (Illus.). 112p. 1990. pap. 7.95 (*0-486-26418-1*) Dover.

Lively Anatomy of God. Nancy Willard. LC 68-24021. 95p. 1968. 30.00 (*0-87130-021-4*) Eakins.

Lively Art: Twenty Years of the American Repertory Theatre. Ed. by Arthur Holmberg. LC 99-19564. (Illus.). 320p. 1999. 28.95 (*1-56663-244-7*, Pub. by I R Dee) Natl Bk Netwk.

Lively Art of Writing. Lucille V. Payne. 1969. mass mkt. 6.99 (*0-451-62712-1*, Ment) NAL.

Lively Arts: Gilbert Seldes & the Transformation of Cultural Criticism in the United States. Michael G. Kammen. (Illus.). 512p. (C). 1996. 35.00 (*0-19-509868-4*) OUP.

Lively Bible Lessons for Grade K-3: 20 Easy-to-Use Programs. Ed. by Cindy S. Hansen. (Illus.). 85p. (J). (gr. k-3). 1991. pap. 16.99 (*1-55945-074-6*, Group Bks) Group Pub.

Lively Bible Lessons for Preschoolers: 20 Easy-to-Use Programs. Ed. by Cindy S. Hansen. (Illus.). 98p. (J). (ps). 1991. pap. 16.99 (*1-55945-067-3*, Group Bks) Group Pub.

Lively Discussions! rev. ed. Russ Korth & Ron Wormser, Jr. 105p. 1988. pap. text 8.00 (*0-934396-43-4*) Churches Alive.

Lively Discussions! Fostering Engaged Reading. Ed. by Linda B. Gambrell & Janice F. Almasi. LC 96-17614. 230p. 1996. pap. 24.95 (*0-87207-147-2*) Intl Reading.

Lively Experiment Continued: Essays in Honor of Sidney E. Mead. Sidney Mead. Ed. by Jerald C. Brauer. LC 87-2752. 288p. 1987. pap. 18.95 (*0-86554-290-2*, P049) Mercer Univ Pr.

Lively Form of Death. large type ed. Kay Mitchell. (General Ser.). 336p. 1993. 27.99 (*0-7089-2864-1*) Ulverscroft.

Lively Garden Prayer Book: Prayers of Backyard Creation from A to Z. William Cleary. LC 97-13947. (Illus.). 111p. 1997. pap. 11.95 (*0-939516-35-7*) Forest Peace.

Lively Ghosts. Susan Crites. (Illus.). 43p. pap. 5.00 (*0-681-87306-X*) Butternut Pubns.

Lively Hope. Richard N. Holzapfel. 1998. 19.95 (*1-57008-562-5*) Bookcraft Inc.

Lively Ideas for Life Skills Teachers. Neil Wilson. (C). 1988. 100.00 (*0-7157-2725-7*) St Mut.

Lively Lady: A Chronicle of Arundel, of Privateering, & of the Circular Prison on Dartmoor. Kenneth Lewis Roberts. 282p. Date not set. 23.95 (*0-8488-2591-8*) Amereon Ltd.

Lively Lady: A Chronicle of Arundel, of Privateering, & of the Circular Prison on Dartmoor. large type ed. Kenneth Lewis Roberts. 1994. write for info. (*0-318-72724-2*, G K Hall Lrg Type); lib. bdg. 20.95 (*0-8161-5996-3*, G K Hall Lrg Type) Mac Lib Ref.

Lively Lady: A Chronicle of Arundel, of Privateering, & of the Circular Prison on Dartmoor. Kenneth Lewis Roberts. LC 97-24404. 288p. 1997. reprint ed. pap. 15.95 (*0-89272-425-0*) Down East.

Lively Language Lessons for Ladies & Gents. John R. Terry. 200p. 1990. pap. 9.50 (*0-933704-84-4*) Dawn Pr.

Lively Legacy: Essays in Honor of Robert Preus. Ed. by Kurt E. Marquart et al. 224p. (Orig.). 1985. 13.95 (*0-9615927-0-2*); pap. 11.95 (*0-9615927-1-0*) Concordia Theo Sem.

Lively Legends - Jewish Values: An Early Childhood Teaching Guide. Miriam P. Feinberg & Rena Rotenberg. LC 93-70474. 244p. 1993. pap. text 26.50 (*0-86705-030-6*) A R E Pub.

***Lively Lessons: Lessons for Classroom Use for Grades 2-5.** Rosanne Sheritz Sartori. (J). (gr. 2-5). 2000. pap. 19.95 (*1-57543-087-8*) Mar Co Prods.

Lively Listening. Beverly Armstrong. (Skill Builder Ser.). (Illus.). 32p. (J). (gr. 4-6). 1981. pap., student ed. 4.95 (*0-88160-080-6*, LW 813) Learning Wks.

Lively Little Logs. Donna McConnell. Ed. by Ursula G. Reikes. LC 93-8014. (Illus.). 72p. 1993. pap. 17.95 (*1-56477-027-3*, B157) Martingale & Co.

***Lively Little Quilt Blocks: 26 Step-by-Step Patterns.** Joyce Libal. Ed. by Debbie Hearn. (Illus.). 32p. 2000. pap. 14.95 (*1-885588-33-X*) Chitra Pubns.

Lively Oracle: A Centennial Celebration of P. L. Travers, Original Creator of Mary Poppins. Ed. by Ellen D. Draper & Jenny Koralek. (Illus.). 224p. 1999. pap. 15.95 (*0-943914-94-9*) Larson Pubns.

Lively Oracles. Ann R. Colton. LC 67-9752. 151p. 1962. 12.95 (*0-917187-13-X*) A R Colton Fnd.

Lively People: Methodism in Nottingham, 1740-1979. R. C. Swift. (C). 1983. text 35.00 (*0-7855-3208-0*, Pub. by Univ Nottingham) St Mut.

Lively People: Methodism in Nottingham 1740-1979. R. C. Swift. 1982. pap. 28.00 (*0-902031-78-3*, Pub. by Continuing Education Pr) St Mut.

Lively Plays for Young Actors. Christina Hamlett. LC 98-14359. (J). (gr. 11-12). 1998. pap. 13.95 (*0-8238-0308-2*) Kalmbach.

Lively Stones: History of Galveston First Presbyterian Church. Retta L. Weber & Gayle W. Strange. (Illus.). 360p. 1993. 40.00 (*1-881576-16-7*) Providence Hse.

Lively Times & Exciting Events: The Drawings of Bill Traylor. Montgomery Museum of Fine Arts Staff. LC 93-29034. (Illus.). 40p. 1993. pap. 12.50 (*0-89280-032-1*) Montgomery Mus.

Lively Years, 1920-1973. Brooks Atkinson & Al Hirschfeld. (Quality Paperbacks Ser.). (Illus.). 312p. 1985. reprint ed. pap. 9.95 (*0-306-80234-1*) Da Capo.

***LiveMotion.** Elaine Weinmann. (Visual QuickStart Guides Ser.). (Illus.). 304p. 2000. pap. 18.99 (*0-201-70473-0*) Peachpit Pr.

Liveness: Performance in a Mediatized Culture. Philip Auslander. LC 98-43440. 1999. 65.00 (*0-415-19689-2*); pap. 19.99 (*0-415-19690-6*) Routledge.

Liver. Charles H. Webb. LC 99-6457. (Felix Pollak Prize in Poetry Ser.: Vol. 6). 80p. (Orig.). 1999. pap. text 11.95 (*0-299-16574-4*) U of Wis Pr.

Liver. Charles Harper Webb. LC 99-6457. (Felix Pollack Prize in Poetry Ser.: Vol. 6). 80p. 1999. text 18.95 (*0-299-16570-1*) U of Wis Pr.

Liver: An Atlas & Text of Ultrastructural Pathology. M. James Phillips. LC 87-43075. (Illus.). 600p. 1987. reprint ed. pap. 186.00 (*0-608-05874-2*, 205984100007) Bks Demand.

Liver: Biology & Pathobiology. 3rd ed. Ed. by Irwin M. Arias et al. LC 93-23602. 1664p. 1994. text 289.00 (*0-7817-0133-3*) Lppncott W & W.

Liver: Normal & Abnormal Functions, 2 pts., Pt. 1. Ed. by Frederick F. Becker. LC 74-77112. (Biochemistry of Disease Ser.: No. 5). (Illus.). 590p. reprint ed. pap. 182.90 (*0-7837-0894-7*, 204120000001) Bks Demand.

Liver: Normal & Abnormal Functions, 2 pts., Pt. 2. Ed. by Frederick F. Becker. LC 74-77112. (Biochemistry of Disease Ser.: No. 5). (Illus.). 465p. reprint ed. pap. 144.20 (*0-7837-0895-5*, 204120000002) Bks Demand.

Liver Vol. 1. Mark Feldman. Ed. by Willis C. Maddrey. LC 95-22343. (Gastroenterology & Hepatology Ser.: Vol. 1). (Illus.). 312p. 1995. text 85.00 (*1-878132-78-4*) Current Med.

Liver & Biliary Diseases. Neil Kaplowitz. (Illus.). 752p. 1992. 115.00 (*0-683-04528-8*) Lppncott W & W.

Liver & Biliary Diseases. 2nd ed. Neil Kaplowitz. LC 95-25736. (Illus.). 736p. 1996. 139.00 (*0-683-04545-8*) Lppncott W & W.

Liver & Biliary Tract Disease in Children. Daniel Alagille & Michel Odievre. LC 79-12254. 375p. reprint ed. pap. 116.30 (*0-608-13286-1*, 205575900037) Bks Demand.

Liver & Its Complaints. Herbert M. Shelton et al. 39p. 1996. reprint ed. spiral bd. 11.00 (*0-7873-1018-2*) Hlth Research.

Liver & Nervous Systems. Ed. by D. Haussinger & K. Jungermann. (Falk Symposium Ser.). 416p. 1998. 210.00 (*0-7923-8742-2*) Kluwer Academic.

Liver & Pancreas: Guides to Clinical Aspiration Biopsy. Denise Frias-Hidvegi. LC 87-4177. (Illus.). 352p. 1988. 95.00 (*0-89640-146-4*) Igaku-Shoin.

Liver & Systemic Disease. Norman Gitlin. LC 97-3036. 1997. text 105.00 (*0-443-05546-7*) Church.

Liver, Biliary Tract & Exocrine Pancreas. 3rd ed. Ed. by W. S. Symmers & D. G. Wight. LC 93-13798. (Systemic Pathology Ser.: No. 11). (Illus.). 450p. 1993. text 189.00 (*0-443-03098-7*) Church.

Liver Biopsy Diagnoses & Reports. J. Ludwig. (Illus.). x, 158p. 1984. 50.50 (*3-8055-3841-3*) S Karger.

Liver Biopsy Evaluation: Histologic Diagnoses with Clinical Correlations. (Illus.). 220p. Date not set. text. write for info. (*0-7216-7692-8*, W B Saunders Co) Harcrt Hlth Sci Grp.

Liver Biopsy Interpretation. 5th ed. Paul J. Scheuer. 1994. text 86.00 (*0-7020-1594-6*, W B Saunders Co) Harcrt Hlth Sci Grp.

***Liver Book: The Patients Guide to Diagnosis, Treatment & Recovery.** Sanjiv Chopra. 2001. 25.95 (*0-7434-0584-6*, PB Hardcover) PB.

Liver Cancer. Ed. by Joseph C. Bottino et al. (Developments in Oncology Ser.). 1985. text 219.00 (*0-89838-713-2*) Kluwer Academic.

Liver Cancer. Okuda. 1997. text 150.00 (*0-443-05481-9*, W B Saunders Co) Harcrt Hlth Sci Grp.

Liver Cancer: Proceedings of a Working Conference Held at the Chester Beatty Research Institute, London, England, 30 June to 3 July 1969. International Agency for Research on Cancer Staff. LC RC0280.L5L58. (IARC Scientific Publications: No. 1). (Illus.). 178p. reprint ed. pap. 55.20 (*0-8357-6446-X*, 203581700097) Bks Demand.

Liver Carcinogenesis: The Molecular Pathays. Ed. by George G. Skouteris. LC 94-31130. (NATO ASI Ser.: 88). 1994. 262.95 (*3-540-58371-8*) Spr-Verlag.

Liver Carcinogenesis: The Molecular Pathways. Ed. by George G. SKouteris. (NATO ASI Series H: Cell Biology: Vol. 88). 512p. 1994. 214.00 (*0-387-58371-8*) Spr-Verlag.

Liver Causes Heart Attacks. W. P. Neufeld. 159p. (Orig.). 1991. pap. 14.95 (*0-88925-816-3*) Gordon Soules Bk.

Liver Cell Carcinoma. Ed. by P. Bannasch et al. (Falk Symposium Ser.). (C). 1989. lib. bdg. 242.00 (*0-7462-0111-7*) Kluwer Academic.

Liver Cirrhosis. Ed. by J. L. Boyer & L. Bianchi. (Falk Ser.: No. 44). 1987. text 206.50 (*0-85200-993-3*) Kluwer Academic.

Liver Cirrhosis. Ed. by Paolo Gentilini & M. U. Dianzani. (Frontiers of Gastrointestinal Research Ser.: Vol. 8). (Illus.). vii, 280p. 1984. 129.75 (*3-8055-3724-7*) S Karger.

Liver Cleansing Diet: Love Your Liver & Live Longer. 2nd rev. ed. Sandra Cabot. (Illus.). 192p. (Orig.). 1997. pap. 19.95 (*0-646-27789-8*, Pub. by SCB Intl) Ten Speed Pr.

Liver Cookies. Dian Curtis Regan. 160p. (J). (gr. 4-6). 1991. pap. 2.75 (*0-590-44337-2*) Scholastic Inc.

Liver Disease & Gallstones: The Facts. 2nd ed. Alan G. Johnson & David R. Triger. LC 92-14362. (Facts Ser.). (Illus.). 136p. 1992. text 27.50 (*0-19-262305-2*) OUP.

Liver Disease in Children: An Atlas of Angiography & Cholangiography. Francis Brunelle et al. (Illus.). 290p. 1994. 165.00 (*3-540-19674-9*) Spr-Verlag.

Liver Disease in Children: An Atlas of Angiography & Cholangiography. Francis Brunelle et al. LC 93-33451. (Illus.). 290p. 1994. 181.00 (*0-387-19674-9*) Spr-Verlag.

Liver Diseases: Targeted Diagnosis & Therapy Using Specific Receptors & Ligands. Ed. by George Y. Wu & Catherine H. Wu. (Targeted Diagnosis & Therapy Ser.: Vol. 4). (Illus.). 376p. 1991. text 175.00 (*0-8247-8486-3*) Dekker.

Liver Diseases & Hepatic Sinusoidal Cells. Ed. by K. Tanikawa. LC 98-45747. (Illus.). 348p. 1998. 149.00 (*4-431-70237-7*) Spr-Verlag.

Liver Diseases in Children. 2nd ed. Frederick J. Suchy. 800p. text 139.00 (*0-7817-2098-2*) Lppncott W & W.

Liver Disorders in Childhood. Mowat. 508p. 1998. pap. text 100.00 (*0-7506-4200-9*) Buttrwrth-Heinemann.

Liver Disorders in Childhood. 3rd ed. Alex P. Mowat. (Illus.). 496p. 1994. 160.00 (*0-7506-1039-5*) Buttrwrth-Heinemann.

***Liver Disorders Sourcebook.** Ed. by Joyce B. Shannon. LC 99-51574. (Health Reference Ser.). (Illus.). 600p. 1999. lib. bdg. 78.00 (*0-7808-0383-3*) Omnigraphics Inc.

Liver Disorders Sourcebook. Howard Worman. LC 99-24103. 352p. 1999. pap. 17.95 (*0-7373-0090-6*) Lowell Hse.

Liver Drugs: From Experimental Pharmacology to Therapeutic Application. Ed. by D. Perrissoud & B. Testa. 288p. 1988. 218.00 (*0-8493-6734-4*, RC846) CRC Pr.

Liver Function Vol. 3: Measurement in Medicine. Ed. by Derek Cramp & Ewart R. Carson. 300p. 1990. 74.95 (*0-412-33950-1*, A4470) Chapman & Hall.

***Liver Growth & Repair.** Ed. by A. J. Strain & A. M. Diehl. (Illus.). 688p. 1998. pap. write for info. (*0-412-71260-1*) Kluwer Academic.

Liver in Systemic Disease. Vinod K. Rustgi. Ed. by David H. Van Thiel. LC 92-48978. (Illus.). 397p. 1993. reprint ed. pap. 123.10 (*0-608-05763-0*, 205972700007) Bks Demand.

Liver Innervation & the Neural Control of Hepatic Function. Shimazu. 484p. 105.00 (*0-86196-535-3*, Pub. by J Libbey Med) Bks Intl VA.

Liver Malignancies: Diagnostic & Interventional Radiology. Ed. by C. Bartolozzi & R. Lencioni. LC 99-23562. (Medical Radiology Ser.). (Illus.). 450p. 1999. 299.00 (*3-540-64756-2*) Spr-Verlag.

Liver Metastasis. Ed. by J. H. Van de Velde et al. (Developments in Oncology Ser.). 1984. text 211.50 (*0-89838-684-5*) Kluwer Academic.

Liver Metastasis: Biology, Diagnosis & Treatment. Ed. by O. J. Garden et al. LC 97-52056. (Illus.). x, 214p. 1998. 79.00 (*3-540-76075-X*) Spr-Verlag.

Liver Microcirculation & Hepatobiliary Function. Ed. by K. Messmer & Michael D. Menger. (Progress in Applied Microcirculation Ser.: Vol. 19). (Illus.). viii, 172p. 1993. 161.75 (*3-8055-5701-9*) S Karger.

Liver, Nutrition, & Bile Acids. Ed. by G. Galli & E. Bosisio. (NATO ASI Series A, Life Sciences: Vol. 90). 270p. 1985. 69.50 (*0-306-42011-2*, Plenum Trade) Perseus Pubng.

Liver Pathology & Alcohol: Drug & Alcohol Abuse Reviews. Ed. by Ronald R. Watson. LC 91-20879. (Drug & Alcohol Abuse Reviews Ser.: No. 2). (Illus.). 620p. 1991. 115.00 (*0-89603-206-X*) Humana.

Liver Pathophysiology: Proceedings of the Annual Meeting of the Italian National Programme on Liver Cirrhosis & Viral Hepatitis, Held at San Miniato, Italy, 13-14 January, 1994. Italian National Programme on Liver Cirrhosis & Vi. Ed. by Mario U. Dianzani & Paolo Gentilini. LC 94-6966. (International Congress Ser.: No. 1060). 306p. 1994. 212.50 (*0-444-81637-2*, Excerpta Medica) Elsevier.

Liver Stem Cells: Special Edition. Stewart Sell & Zoran Illic. LC 96-29706. 335p. 1997. 99.00 (*1-57059-426-0*) Landes Bioscience.

Liver Surgery Approached Through the Mitochondria. K. Ozawa. (Illus.). 222p. 1993. 132.25 (*3-8055-5716-7*) S Karger.

Liver Transplant. JoAnn Cirillo. LC 94-70677. 1994. pap. 9.95 (*1-55673-930-3*, Fairway Pr) CSS OH.

Liver Transplantation. Williams. 1995. text 117.00 (*0-443-04969-6*, W B Saunders Co) Harcrt Hlth Sci Grp.

Liver Transplantation. 2nd ed. Ed. by Roy Y. Calne. 576p. 1987. text 115.00 (*0-8089-1858-3*, 790768, Grune & Strat) Harcrt Hlth Sci Grp.

Liver Transplantation: Practice & Management. Ed. by James Neuberger & Michael Lucey. 420p. 1994. pap. text 59.00 (*0-7279-0787-5*, Pub. by BMJ Pub) Login Brothers Bk Co.

Liver Transplantation & the Alcoholic Patient. Ed. by M. R. Lucey et al. (Illus.). 144p. (C). 1994. text 57.95 (*0-521-43332-0*) Cambridge U Pr.

Liver Transplantation, from Laboratory to Clinic. Franco Filipponi et al. (Illus.). 125p. 1998. text 75.00 (*1-928649-04-1*) Idelson Gnocchi Pub.

Liver Tumors: Multidisciplinary Management. W. John Hodgson. (Illus.). 340p. 1988. 47.50 (*0-87527-351-3*) Green.

Livermore Family of America. W. E. Twing. (Illus.). 479p. 1989. reprint ed. pap. 72.00 (*0-8328-0776-1*); reprint ed. lib. bdg. 80.00 (*0-8328-0775-3*) Higginson Bk Co.

Liverpool. C. Rothwell. LC 97-131013. (Best of Britain in Old Photographs Ser.). (Illus.). 128p. 1998. pap. 15.95 (*0-7509-1276-6*, Pub. by Sutton Pub Ltd) Intl Pubs Mktg.

Liverpool: City of the Sea. Tony Lane. LC 96-130581. 151p. 1997. 34.95 (*0-85323-780-8*, Pub. by Liverpool Univ Pr) Intl Spec Bk.

Liverpool Academy & Other Exhibitions of Contemporary Art in Liverpool, 1774-1867: A History & Index of Artists & Works Exhibited. Edward Morris & Emma Roberts. LC 98-188913. 600p. 1997. 124.95 (*0-85323-672-0*, Pub. by Liverpool Univ Pr) Intl Spec Bk.

Liverpool Accents: Seven Poets & a City. Ed. by Peter Robinson. 224p. 1997. pap. 14.95 (*0-85323-671-2*, Pub. by Liverpool Univ Pr) Intl Spec Bk.

Liverpool & Merseyside: Essays in the Economic & Social History of the Port & Its Hinterland. Ed. by John R. Harris. 287p. 1969. 32.00 (*0-7146-1314-2*, Pub. by F Cass Pubs) Intl Spec Bk.

Liverpool & the Battle of the Atlantic. 1989. pap. 35.00 (*0-907771-55-6*, Pub. by Maritime Bks) St Mut.

***Liverpool Annie.** Maureen Lee. 1999. pap. 13.95 (*0-7528-1698-5*, Pub. by Orion Pubng Grp) Trafalgar.

Liverpool Basque. large type ed. Helen Forrester. 1994. 27.99 (*0-7089-8789-3*) Ulverscroft.

Liverpool Dockers Struggle & the Fight for a New Socialist Party. Socialist Equality Party Staff. 57p. (Orig.). 1996. pap. 2.50 (*1-873045-37-9*, Pub. by Mehring Bks) Mehring Bks.

Liverpool Friends Service Centre, 1942-1949. Joyce Millington. 1999. pap. 21.00 (*1-85072-123-8*, Pub. by W Sessions) St Mut.

Liverpool from the Inside. Stan Liversedge. (Illus.). 224p. 1996. 34.95 (*1-85158-758-6*, Pub. by Mainstream Pubng) Trafalgar.

***Liverpool Lou.** Andrews. (J). 2000. pap. 8.95 (*0-552-13718-9*, Pub. by Transworld Publishers Ltd) Trafalgar.

Liverpool Oratorio: Vocal Score. Paul McCartney. 1992. 19.95 (*0-7935-5369-5*) H Leonard.

Liverpool Park Estates: Their Legal Basis, Creation & Early Management. Susan George. 176p. 1998. pap. 23.95 (*0-85323-409-4*, Pub. by Liverpool Univ Pr) Intl Spec Bk.

Liverpool Porcelain of the Eighteenth Century. Bernard M. Watney. (Illus.). 164p. 1997. 90.00 (*0-903685-51-5*, Pub. by R Dennis) Antique Collect.

Liverpool Printed Tiles. Anthony Ray. (Illus.). 72p. 1994. 69.95 (*0-9512140-7-1*, Pub. by J Horne) Antique Collect.

Liverpool Scene. Edward Lucie-Smith. (Illus.). 1990. 15.50 (*0-8446-2495-0*) Peter Smith.

Liverpool Songbird. large type ed. Lyn Andrews. (Magna Large Print Ser.). 571p. 1997. 27.50 (*0-7505-1124-9*) Thorndike Pr.

Liverpool Studies in Spanish Literature, 4 vols. Ed. by E. Allison Peers. reprint ed. write for info. (*0-404-15030-6*) AMS Pr.

Liverpool-Tomkinson River Systems & Nungbulgarri Creek see Survey of Tidal River Systems in the Northern Territory & Their Crocodile Populations: Monographs

Liverpool Tractate. Catherine Strateman. LC 38-6233. (Columbia University. Studies in the Social Sciences: No. 430). 1937. 20.00 (*0-404-51430-8*) AMS Pr.

Liverworts of New Zealand. K. W. Allison & John Child. 304p. 1996. 29.95 (*0-908569-05-X*, Pub. by Univ Otago Pr) Intl Spec Bk.

Liverwurst Is Missing. Mercer Mayer. LC 90-5435. (Illus.). 32p. (J). (gr. k up). 1990. 16.00 (*0-688-09657-3*, Wm Morrow) Morrow Avon.

Liverwurst Is Missing. Mercer Mayer. (J). 1981. 10.95 (*0-590-07793-7*) Scholastic Inc.

Livery Companies of the City of London. William C. Hazlitt. LC 68-56529. (Illus.). 706p. 1972. reprint ed. 42.95 (*0-405-08504-4*, Pub. by Blom Pubns) Ayer.

Lives. Dan Stryk. Ed. by Patricia Schultz. LC 90-36261. (Mellen Poetry Ser.: Vol. 6). (Illus.). 72p. 1990. pap. text 12.95 (*0-88946-890-7*) E Mellen.

Lives: An Anthropological Approach to Biography. Robert B. Edgerton. LC 81-15460. (Chandler & Sharp Publications in Anthropology Ser.). 232p. (Orig.). (C). 1981. pap. 14.95 (*0-88316-542-2*) Chandler & Sharp.

Lives: Chinese Working Women. Ed. by Mary Sheridan & Janet W. Salaff. LC 83-48401. 272p. reprint ed. pap. 84.40 (*0-8357-6683-7*, 205686200094) Bks Demand.

Lives: Poems about Famous Americans. Lee B. Hopkins. LC 98-29851. (Illus.). 40p. (J). (gr. 3-6). 1999. 15.95 (*0-06-027767-X*) HarpC Child Bks.

Lives: Poems about Famous Americans. Lee B. Hopkins. LC 98-29851. (Illus.). 40p. (J). (gr. 3-6). 1999. lib. bdg. 15.89 (*0-06-027768-8*) HarpC Child Bks.

Lives: 113 Great Irishwomen & Irishmen. Art Byrne & Sean McMahon. (Illus.). 220p. (Orig.). (YA). (gr. 9-12). 1990. pap. 15.95 (*1-85371-094-6*, Pub. by Poolbeg Pr) Dufour.

Lives . . . Get One. Mary Engelbreit. (Illus.). 80p. 1997. 4.95 (*0-8362-2778-6*) Andrews & McMeel.

Lives Across Cultures: Cross-Cultural Human Development. Harry W. Gardiner et al. LC 97-17766. 330p. 1997. pap. text 38.00 (*0-205-19182-7*) P-H.

Lives & Characters of the English Dramatic Poets. Gerard Langbaine. LC 70-144618. reprint ed. 49.50 (*0-404-02769-5*) AMS Pr.

Lives & Criminal Trials of Celebrated Men. 1993. reprint ed. 52.50 (*0-8377-2414-7*, Rothman) W S Hein.

***Lives & Deaths: Selections from the Works of Edwin S. Shneidman.** Edwin S. Shneidman & Antoon A. Leenaars. LC 99-18296. (Series in Death, Dying, & Bereavement). 448p. 1999. pap. text 34.95 (*1-58391-011-5*) Brunner-Mazel.

Lives & Dollars. John D. Ratcliff. LC 70-111859. (Essay Index Reprint Ser.). 1977. 21.95 (*0-8369-2022-8*) Ayer.

Lives & Legends of Buffalo Bill. Donald B. Russell. LC 60-13470. (Illus.). 1979. pap. 22.95 (*0-8061-1537-8*) U of Okla Pr.

Lives & Legends of Flamenco: A Biographical History. rev. ed. D. E. Pohren. (Society of Spanish Studies). (Illus.). 329p. 1988. reprint ed. 29.95 (*0-933224-12-5*, I026, Pub. by Soc Sp Studies) Bold Strummer Ltd.

Lives & Legends of the Georgian Saints. Ed. by David M. Lang. 179p. 1976. pap. 8.95 (*0-913836-29-X*) St Vladimirs.

Lives & Legends of the Saints: With Paintings from the Great Art Museums of the World. Carole Armstrong. LC 94-43009. (Illus.). 45p. (YA). (gr. 5 up). 1995. 17.00 (*0-689-80277-3*) S&S Bks Yung.

Lives & Letters: A. R. Orage; Beatrice Hastings; Katherine Mansfield; John Middleton Murray; S. S. Koteliansky. John Carswell. LC 77-15986. (Illus.). 1978. 15.00 (*0-8112-0681-5*, Pub. by New Directions) Norton.

Lives & Letters of an Immigrant Family: The Van Dreveldts' Experiences along the Missouri, 1844-1866. Kenneth Kronenberg et al. LC 98-19559. (Illus.). xii, 224p. 1998. text 50.00 (*0-8032-2741-8*) U of Nebr Pr.

Lives & Letters of the Sylvesters & Nicholsons. Maureen S. Bryson & Kerry W. Bate. (Illus.). vii, 710p. 1997. 50.00 (*0-9664088-0-2*) M S Bryson.

Lives & Liberation of Princess Mandarava: The Indian Consort of Padmasambhava. Tr. by Sangye Khandro & Lama Chonam from TIB. LC 98-17766. 227p. 1998. pap. 16.95 (*0-86171-144-0*) Wisdom MA.

Lives & Loves of New Kids on the Block. Jill Matthews. 1990. pap. 3.95 (*0-685-33337-X*) PB.

Lives & Moments: An Introduction to Short Fiction. Hans A. Ostrom. 900p. (C). 1991. pap. text 48.00 (*0-03-030374-5*, Pub. by Harcourt Coll Pubs); pap. text 34.00 (*0-03-030377-X*) Harcourt Coll Pubs.

Lives & Paintings of Alfred Partridge Klots & His Son, Trafford Partridge Klots. Alfred P. Klots & Stiles T. Colwill. (Illus.). 136p. 1979. 16.95 (*0-938420-36-4*) MD Hist.

***Lives & Teachings of the Sikh Gurus.** Harish Dhillon. 1998. pap. 16.00 (*81-7476-173-X*, Pub. by UBS Pubs) S Asia.

Lives & Times. Meade Minnigerode. LC 76-121490. (Essay Index Reprint Ser.). 1977. 20.95 (*0-8369-1765-0*) Ayer.

Lives & Times: A World History Reader, Vol. 1. Jiu-Hwa Upshur & Jim Holoka. Ed. by Baxter. LC 95-143802. 150p. (C). 1995. mass mkt. 37.95 (*0-314-04579-1*) West Pub.

Lives & Times: A World History Reader, Vol. 2. Jim Holoka & Jiu-Hwa Upshur. LC 95-143802. 1995. mass mkt. 37.95 (*0-314-05945-8*) West Pub.

Lives & Times of Bonnie & Clyde. E. R. Milner. LC 95-4305. (Illus.). 194p. (C). 1996. 24.95 (*0-8093-1977-2*) S Ill U Pr.

Lives & Times of Ebenezer Scrooge. Paul Davis. 296p. (C). 1990. 40.00 (*0-300-04664-2*) Yale U Pr.

Lives & Times of the Chief Justices of the Supreme Court of the United States, 2 vols., Set. Henry Flanders. LC 70-114030. (Classics in Legal History Reprint Ser.: Vols. 7-8). 1997. 165.00 (*1-57588-323-6*, 308860) W S Hein.

Lives & Works: Young Adult Authors. Grolier Educational Staff. LC 98-4339. (YA). 1999. lib. bdg. 265.00 (*0-7172-9227-4*) Grolier Educ.

Lives & Works Vol. 2: Talks with Women Artists. Beryl Smith et al. 280p. 1996. 58.00 (*0-8108-3153-8*) Scarecrow.

***Lives & Works Vol. II: Talks with Women Artists.** Beryl Smith et al. 288p. 1998. reprint ed. pap. 32.00 (*0-8108-3590-8*) Scarecrow.

Lives & Works in the Arts: From the Renaissance to the 20th Century, 9 vols., Set. LC 96-13236. (Illus.). 1216p. (C). (gr. 13). 1996. text 450.00 (*1-56324-817-4*, Sharpe Ref) M E Sharpe.

Lives & Works of the Apostles. Russell A. Stultz. LC 94-167550. 138p. (Orig.). 1993. pap. 8.95 (*1-55622-039-1*, Seaside Pr) Wordware Pub.

Lives & Works of William & Philip Hayes. rev. ed. Simon Heighes. LC 95-40956. (Outstanding Dissertations in Music from British Universities Ser.). (Illus.). 405p. 1995. text 105.00 (*0-8153-2357-3*) Garland.

Lives at Risk. Hilary Ryglewicz & Bert Pepper. 256p. 1996. 29.95 (*0-684-82807-3*) Free Pr.

Lives at Risk: Hostages & Victims in American Foreign Policy. Russell D. Buhite. LC 95-5688. (Illus.). 268p. 1995. 45.00 (*0-8420-2552-9*); pap. 17.95 (*0-8420-2553-7*) Scholarly Res Inc.

Lives at Risk: Public Health in Nineteenth-Century Egypt. LaVerne Kuhnke. 1990. 50.00 (*0-520-06364-3*, Pub. by U CA Pr) Cal Prin Full Svc.

Lives Behind the Lines: 20 Years of for Better of for Worse, 20th ed. Lynn Johnston. 1999. pap. 14.95 (*0-7407-0199-1*) Andrews & McMeel.

Lives Between Cultures: A Study of Human Nature, Identity & Culture. Richard M. Swiderski. LC 90-49515. (Illus.). 289p. (Orig.). 1991. pap. 25.00 (*0-938737-24-4*) Denali Press.

Lives Beyond Life. Nicholas Basbanes. Date not set. write for info. (*0-8050-5015-9*) H Holt & Co.

Lives Charmed: Intimate Conversations with Extraordinary People. Compiled by Linda Sivertsen. LC 98-28715. 350p. 1998. pap. 12.95 (*1-55874-593-9*) Health Comm.

Lives, Events & Other Players: Studies in Psychobiography. Ed. by Joseph T. Coltrera. LC 79-51911. (Downstate Psychoanalytic Institute Twenty-Fifth Anniversary Ser.: Vol. IV). 1979. 40.00 (*0-87668-369-3*) Aronson.

***Lives in Between: The Experience of Marginality in a Century of Assimilation.** Leo Spitzer. (Illus.). 264p. 1999. pap. 13.00 (*0-8090-1626-5*) Hill & Wang.

Lives in Distress: The Paths of the Elderly to the Psychiatric Ward. Marjorie F. Lowenthal. Ed. by Leon Stein. LC 79-8675. (Growing Old Ser.). 1980. reprint ed. lib. bdg. 28.95 (*0-405-12791-X*) Ayer.

Lives in Education. Smith. 1993. pap. text, teacher ed. 0.33 (*0-312-04699-5*) St Martin.

Lives in Education: A Narrative of People & Ideas. Smith. 48p. 1995. pap., teacher ed. write for info. (*0-8058-8009-7*) L Erlbaum Assocs.

Lives in Education: A Narrative of People & Ideas. 2nd ed. L. Glenn Smith & Joan K. Smith. 472p. 1995. pap. 36.00 (*0-8058-8008-9*) L Erlbaum Assocs.

Lives in Education: A Narrative of People & Ideas. 2nd ed. L. Glenn Smith & Joan K. Smith. 496p. 1993. pap. text 21.00 (*0-312-04698-7*) St Martin.

Lives in Focus: Profiles of Struggle & Strength. Intro. by Dick Myhre. 112p. (Orig.). 1988. pap. 2.95 (*0-939159-15-5*) Cityhill Pub.

Lives in Letters Princess Zinaida Volkonskaya & Her Correspondence. Bayara Aroutunova. (ENG & FRE., Illus.). 224p. 1994. 24.95 (*0-89357-251-9*) Slavica.

Lives in Process: Mildly Retarded Adults in a Large City. Ed. by Robert B. Edgerton. LC 84-2869. (Monographs of the American Association on Mental Retardation: No. 6). 192p. 1984. text 8.00 (*0-940898-13-6*) Am Assn Mental.

Lives in Progress. 3rd ed. White. (C). 1997. pap. text 44.50 (*0-15-504421-4*) Harcourt.

***Lives in Progress: Case Stories in Early Intervention.** P. McWilliam. LC 99-31077. 1999. pap. text 32.00 (*1-55766-365-3*) P H Brookes.

Lives in Science. Capstone Press Staff. 1998. 48.00 (*0-531-19407-8*) Watts.

Lives in Stress: Women & Depression. Ed. by Deborah Belle. LC 81-18379. (Sage Focus Editions Ser.: No. 45). (Illus.). 246p. reprint ed. pap. 76.30 (*0-8357-4737-9*, 203765400009) Bks Demand.

Lives in the Balance: Age-27 Benefit-Cost Analysis of the High Scope Perry Preschool Program. W. Steven Barnett. LC 96-21849. (Monographs of the High/Scope Educational Research Foundation). 120p. 1996. 19.95 (*1-57379-007-9*, R1056) High-Scope.

Lives in the Balance: Perspectives on Global Injustice & Inequality. Pat Lauderdale & Randall Amster. LC 97-16211. (International Studies in Sociology & Social Anthropology). viii, 154p. 1997. 54.50 (*90-04-10875-0*) Brill Academic Pubs.

Lives in the Balance: Youth, Poverty, & Education in Watts. Ann C. Diver-Stamnes. LC 94-46295. (SUNY Series, Urban Voices, Urban Visions). 172p. (C). 1995. pap. text 18.95 (*0-7914-2668-8*) State U NY Pr.

Lives in the Making: The Story of a Manufacturing Family. Kuniyasu Sakai. LC 92-22761. (ICG Pocketbusiness Bks.). 160p. 1992. 9.95 (*1-881267-04-0*) Intercultural.

Lives in Time & Place: The Problems & Promises of Developmental Science. Richard A. Settersten, Jr. LC 99-25384. (Society & Aging Ser.). 310p. 1999. 48.95 (*0-89503-200-7*) Baywood Pub.

Lives in Transit: A Collection of Recent Russian Women's Writing. Intro. by Helena Goscilo. (RUS.). 327p. 1995. 39.95 (*0-87501-100-4*) Ardis Pubs.

Lives in Translation: An Anthology of Contemporary Franco-American Writings. Intro. by Denis Ledoux. 144p. (Orig.). 1990. pap. 12.95 (*0-9619373-1-9*) Soleil Pr.

Lives in Two Languages: Identity & the Multicultural Experience. Linda Watkins-Goffman. (Illus.). 160p. (C). pap. text 24.95 (*0-472-08624-3*, 08624) U of Mich Pr.

Lives Intertwined: Relationships Between Plants & Animals. Allen M. Young. LC 96-4923. (First Books-Biology). (Illus.). 64p. (J). (gr. 4-6). 1996. lib. bdg. 22.00 (*0-531-20251-8*) Watts.

Lives, Lies & the Iran-Contra Affair. Ann Wroe. (Illus.). 349p. 1992. pap. 19.95 (*1-85043-558-8*, Pub. by I B T) St Martin.

Lives, Loves & Art of Arthur B. Davies. Bennard B. Perlman. LC 98-5205. (Illus.). 512p. (C). 1999. pap. text 29.95 (*0-7914-3836-8*) State U NY Pr.

Lives of a Cell: Notes of a Biology Watcher. Lewis Thomas. 160p. 1978. pap. 11.95 (*0-14-004743-3*, Penguin Bks) Viking Penguin.

Lives of a Spirit. Fanny Howe. (Illus.). 80p. 1987. 10.95 (*0-940650-95-9*) Sun & Moon CA.

Lives of a Spirit. deluxe ed. Fanny Howe. (Illus.). 80p. 1987. 30.00 (*0-940650-96-7*) Sun & Moon CA.

Lives of Alchemistical Philosophers: With a Catalogue of Books in Occult Chemistry & a Selection of the Most Celebrated Treatises on the Theory & Practice of the Hermetic Art. 400p. 1993. reprint ed. pap. 27.00 (*1-56459-352-5*) Kessinger Pub.

Lives of Alcyone, 2 vols., Set. Annie W. Besant & C. W. Leadbeater. 737p. 1998. reprint ed. pap. 48.50 (*0-7873-0107-8*) Hlth Research.

Lives of American Merchants, 2 vols. Ed. by Freeman Hunt. LC 66-21679. (Library of Early American Business & Industry: No. 3). 1969. reprint ed. 95.00 (*0-678-00294-0*) Kelley.

Lives of American Women: A History with Documents. Joyce D. Goodfriend & Claudia M. Christie. (Illus.). 368p. (C). 1988. reprint ed. pap. text 31.00 (*0-8191-7017-8*) U Pr of Amer.

Lives of an Architect. J. West. (Illus.). 128p. 1988. 36.00 (*0-929464-00-1*) Fauve Pub.

***Lives of Animals.** J. M. Coetzee & Amu Gutmann. LC 98-39591. (University Center for Human Values Ser.). 1999. 19.95 (*0-691-00443-9*, Pub. by Princeton U Pr) Cal Prin Full Svc.

Lives of Annibale & Agostino Carracci. Giovanni P. Bellori. LC 67-16194. 1968. 28.50 (*0-271-73128-1*) Pa St U Pr.

Lives of Authors. George S. Gordon. LC 76-117796. (Essay Index Reprint Ser.). 1977. 20.95 (*0-8369-1750-2*) Ayer.

Lives of Beryl Markham. Errol Trzebinski. 1995. pap. 12.00 (*0-393-31252-6*) Norton.

Lives of Birds: Birds of the World & Their Behavior. Lester L. Short. 1995. pap. 14.95 (*0-8050-3593-1*) H Holt & Co.

***Lives of Birds: Birds of the World & Their Behavior.** Lester L. Short. (Illus.). 256p. 2000. reprint ed. 25.00 (*0-7881-9249-3*) DIANE Pub.

Lives of Birds: Birds of the World & Their Behavior, from the American Museum of Natural History. Lester L. Short. (Illus.). 288p. 1995. 25.00 (*0-8050-1952-9*) H Holt & Co.

***Lives of Celebrated American Indians.** Samuel G. Goodrich. (LC History-America-E). 315p. 1999. reprint ed. lib. bdg. 89.00 (*0-7812-4255-X*) Rprt Serv.

Lives of Children. George Dennison. 1990. pap. 10.95 (*0-685-47600-6*) Addison-Wesley.

Lives of Children: The Story of the First Street School. George Dennison. LC 99-218648. 320p. 1999. pap. text 15.95 (*0-86709-483-4*) Heinemann.

***Lives of Christopher Chant.** Diana Wynne Jones. (J). (gr. 4-8). 2000. 19.75 (*0-8446-7145-2*) Peter Smith.

***Lives of Christopher Chant.** Diane W. Jones. LC 87-24540. 240p. (YA). (gr. 5-9). 1998. reprint ed. mass mkt. 5.95 (*0-688-16365-3*, Wm Morrow) Morrow Avon.

Lives of Cleopatra & Octavia. Sarah Fielding. Ed. by Christopher D. Johnson. LC 93-56610. 1994. reprint ed. 36.50 (*0-8387-5257-8*) Bucknell U Pr.

Lives of Courage: Women for a New South Africa. Diana E. Russell et al. LC 89-42525. (Illus.). 409p. reprint ed. pap. 126.80 (*0-608-09162-6*, AU0050100005) Bks Demand.

Lives of Dalhousie University: 1818-1925, Lord Dalhousie's College, Vol. I. P. B. Waite. (Illus.). 352p. 1994. 44.95 (*0-7735-1166-0*, Pub. by McG-Queens Univ Pr) CUP Services.

Lives of Dalhousie University: 1925-1980, the Old College Transformed. P. B. Waite. (Illus.). 504p. 1997. text 44.95 (*0-7735-1644-1*, Pub. by McG-Queens Univ Pr) CUP Services.

Lives of Danielle Steel. Vickie Bane et al. 1995. mass mkt. 5.99 (*0-312-95575-8*, Pub. by Tor Bks) St Martin.

***Lives of Dax.** Ed. by Marco Palmieri. (Star Trek Ser.). 1999. per. 14.00 (*0-7434-0081-X*, Star Trek); per. 14.00 (*0-671-02840-5*, Star Trek) PB.

Lives of Edgar Cayce. rev. ed. W. H. Church. Ed. by Joe Dunn. LC 95-16827. 289p. 1995. pap. 12.95 (*0-87604-350-3*, 461) ARE Pr.

Lives of Edward the Confessor. Ed. by Henry R. Luard. (Rolls Ser.: No. 3). 1969. reprint ed. 70.00 (*0-8115-1003-4*) Periodicals Srv.

Lives of Eighteen from Princeton. Ed. by Willard Thorp. LC 68-57341. (Essay Index Reprint Ser.). 1977. 23.95 (*0-8369-0941-0*) Ayer.

Lives of Eminent British Lawyers. Henry Roscoe. 428p. 1982. reprint ed. 46.50 (*0-8377-1037-5*, Rothman) W S Hein.

Lives of Eminent Korean Monks: The Haedong Kosung Chon. Kakhun. Tr. by Peter H. Lee. LC 69-18037. (Harvard-Yenching Institute Studies: No. 25). 132p. 1969. pap. 7.00 (*0-674-53662-2*) HUP.

Lives of Eminent Persons see Works of Samuel Johnson

Lives of Eminent Philosophers, 2 vols., 1. Diogenes Laertius. Tr. by R. D. Hicks. (Loeb Classical Library: No. 184-185). 586p. 1925. 19.95 (*0-674-99203-2*) HUP.

Lives of Eminent Philosophers, 2 vols., 2. Diogenes Laertius. Tr. by R. D. Hicks. (Loeb Classical Library: No. 184-185). 710p. 1925. 19.95 (*0-674-99204-0*) HUP.

Lives of English Laymen: Lord Falkland, Izaak Walton, Robert Nelson. William H. Teale. LC 72-3363. (Essay Index Reprint Ser.). 1977. reprint ed. 23.95 (*0-8369-2930-6*) Ayer.

Lives of Ethnic Americans: Text & Student Guide Value Pak. 2nd ed. Juan L. Gonzales. LC 94-230805. 320p. (C). write for info. (*0-8403-9607-4*); pap. text, student ed. write for info. (*0-8403-9608-2*) Kendall-Hunt.

Lives of Ethnic Americans: Text & Student Guide Value Pak. 2nd ed. Juan L. Gonzales. LC 94-230805. 384p. (C). 1994. 38.69 (*0-8403-9609-0*) Kendall-Hunt.

***Lives of Extraordinary Women.** Kathleen Krull. (Lives of the... Ser.). 2000. 29.97 (*0-7398-3074-0*) Raintree Steck-V.

***Lives of Extraordinary Women: Rulers, Rebels & What the Neighbors Thought.** Kathleen Krull & Kathryn Hewitt. LC 99-6840. (Illus.). 96p. (gr. 4-7). 2000. 20.00 (*0-15-200807-1*, Harcourt Child Bks) Harcourt.

Lives of Famous Poets. William M. Rossetti. LC 77-148292. reprint ed. 42.50 (*0-404-05425-0*) AMS Pr.

Lives of Famous Romans. Olivia Coolidge. LC 91-40360. (Illus.). 248p. (YA). (gr. 8-12). 1992. reprint ed. lib. bdg. 25.00 (*0-208-02333-X*, Linnet Bks) Shoe String.

Lives of Game Animals, 4 vols., Set. Ernest Thompson Seton. 1993. reprint ed. lib. bdg. 300.00 (*0-7812-5151-6*) Rprt Serv.

Lives of Great Composers. 3rd ed. Harold C. Schonberg. (C). 1998. pap. write for info. (*0-393-96680-1*, Norton Paperbks) Norton.

Lives of Great English Writers from Chaucer to Browning. Walter S. Hinchman & Francis B. Gummere. LC 74-106409. (Essay Index Reprint Ser.). 1977. 36.95 (*0-8369-1930-0*) Ayer.

Lives of Great Poisoners. Caryl Churchill. 171p. (C). 1993. write for info. (*0-413-67070-8*, A0669, Methuen Drama) Methn.

Lives of Great 20th Century Artists. Edward Lucie-Smith. LC 98-75076. (Illus.). 352p. 1999. 45.00 (*0-500-23739-5*, Pub. by Thames Hudson) Norton.

Lives of Henry Fielding & Samuel Johnson, with Essays from Gray's Inn Journal, 1752-1792. Arthur Murphy. LC 68-24212. 496p. 1968. 95.00 (*0-8201-1035-3*) Schol Facsimiles.

Lives of Holy Women. Bokenham's. (EETS, OS Ser.: No. 206). 1969. reprint ed. 63.00 (*0-527-00206-2*) Periodicals Srv.

Lives of Hope: Women's & Men's Paths to Success & Fulfillment. Douglas H. Heath. 312p. 1994. pap. 24.00 (*0-9641727-0-4*) Conrow Pubng.

Lives of Illustrious & Distinguished Irishmen, 6 vols. Ed. by James Wills. (Biographical Dictionaries Ser.). 2880p. 1997. reprint ed. 825.00 (*1-85506-515-0*) Thoemmes Pr.

Lives of Illustrious Shoemakers. William E. Winks. 1977. text 18.95 (*0-8369-8181-2*, 8319) Ayer.

***Lives of Indian Images.** Richard H. Davis. 331p. 1999. pap. 150.00 (*81-208-1692-7*, Pub. by Motilal Bnarsidass) St Mut.

Lives of Indian Images. Richard H. Davis. LC 96-22196. 350p. 1997. text 39.50 (*0-691-02622-X*, Pub. by Princeton U Pr) Cal Prin Full Svc.

***Lives Of Indian Images.** Richard H. Davis. 1999. pap. text 18.95 (*0-691-00520-6*, Pub. by Princeton U Pr) Cal Prin Full Svc.

L

*Lives of Insects. Lynn M. Stone. LC 00-36924. (Six Legged World Ser.). (Illus.). 2000. write for info. (1-55916-313-5) Rourke Bk Co.
Lives of Irish Saints, 2 vols. Ed. by Charles Plummer. 1969. 49.50 (0-19-821389-1) OUP.
Lives of Italian Americans: Fifty Biographies. Adolph Caso. (Illus.). 1979. 19.95 (0-8283-1699-6) Branden Bks.
Lives of Jean Toomer: A Hunger for Wholeness. Cynthia E. Kerman & Richard Eldridge. LC 86-27622. (Illus.). 448p. 1989. pap. 16.95 (0-8071-1548-7) La State U Pr.
Lives of Labor: Work in a Maturing Industrial Society. Peter N. Stearns. LC 74-28298. 424p. 1975. 45.00 (0-8419-0192-9) Holmes & Meier.
Lives of Lawyers: Journeys in the Organizations of Practice. Michael J. Kelly. 272p. (Orig.). 1996. pap. text 20.95 (0-472-08385-6, 08385) U of Mich Pr.
Lives of Lee Miller. 2nd ed. Antony Penrose. LC 88-51525. (Illus.). 216p. 1999. reprint ed. pap. 24.95 (0-500-27509-2, Pub. by Thames Hudson) Norton.
Lives of Lesbians, Gays & Bisexuals: Children to Adults. Ed. by Ritch C. Savin-Williams & Kenneth M. Cohen. 528p. (C). 1995. text 44.50 (0-15-501497-8, Pub. by Harcourt Coll Pubs) Harcourt.
Lives of Lesions: Chronology in Dermatopathology. A. Bernard Ackerman & Raqaz. (Illus.). 266p. 1984. text 94.50 (0-8121-1215-6) Lppncott W & W.
Lives of Man. Imam A. Al-Haddad. 98p. 1996. pap. 9.95 (0-614-21182-4, 728) Kazi Pubns.
Lives of Man: A Guide to the Human States: Before Life, in the World, & after Death. Imam A. Al-Haddad. Ed. by Abdal-Hakim Murad. Tr. by Mostafa Al-Badani. 97p. 1998. pap. 11.95 (1-887752-14-5) Fons Vitae.
Lives of Mississippi Authors, 1817-1967. Ed. by James G. Lloyd. LC 81-2515. 513p. reprint ed. pap. 159.10 (0-8357-4346-2, 203714900007) Bks Demand.
Lives of Modern Poets. Ian Hamilton. 464p. 1999. text 24.95 (0-670-84909-X) Viking Penguin.
*Lives of Moral Leadership. Robert Coles. 272p. 2000. 23.95 (0-375-50108-8) Random.
Lives of North American Birds. Kenn Kaufman. (Illus.). 624p. 1996. 35.00 (0-395-77017-3) HM.
Lives of North American Birds: A Natural History Handbook. Kenn Kaufman. 1996. 29.95 (0-614-20696-0); pap. 19.95 (0-614-20697-9) HM.
Lives of Notable Asian Americans: Arts, Entertainment & Sports. Ronald Takaki. LC 94-26812. (Asian American Experience Ser.). (Illus.). 120p. (YA). (gr. 5 up). 1995. lib. bdg. 19.95 (0-7910-2188-2) Chelsea Hse.
Lives of Notable Asian Americans: Business, Politics & Science. Ronald Takaki. LC 94-37528. (Asian American Experience Ser.). (Illus.). 120p. (YA). (gr. 5 up). 1995. lib. bdg. 18.95 (0-7910-2189-0) Chelsea Hse.
Lives of Notable Asian Americans: Literature & Education. Ronald Takaki. (Asian American Experience Ser.). (Illus.). 120p. (YA). (gr. 5 up). 1995. lib. bdg. 19.95 (0-7910-2182-3) Chelsea Hse.
Lives of Our Own. Lorri Hewett. LC 97-42984. 214p. (J). (gr. 7-12). 1998. 15.99 (0-525-45959-6) NAL.
*Lives of Our Own. Lorri Hewett. (Illus.). 224p. (YA). (gr. 7-12). 2000. reprint ed. pap. 5.99 (0-14-130589-4, PuffinBks) Peng Put Young Read.
*Lives of Passion. (In Classical Mood Ser.: Vol. 49). (Illus.). 30p. 1999. write for info. (1-892207-02-8) Intl Masters Pub.
Lives of Robert & James Haldane. Alexander Haldane. 706p. 1991. 34.99 (0-85151-567-3) Banner of Truth.
Lives of St. Augustine & St. Gilbert of Sempringham. John Capgrave. (EETS, OS Ser.: No. 140). 1969. reprint ed. 45.00 (0-527-00137-6) Periodicals Srv.
Lives of St. Eugenia & St. Antipas. 1981. pap. 1.00 (0-317-30436-4) Holy Trinity.
Lives of Saint Mary Magdalene & Saint Martha. Ed. by John R. Smith. (Exeter Hispanic Text Ser.: No. 48). 122p. Date not set. pap. text 17.95 (0-85989-324-3, Pub. by Univ Exeter Pr) Northwestern U Pr.
Lives of Saints. Ed. by William H. Stokes. (Anecdota Oxoniensia Ser.: No. 5). 1988. reprint ed. 97.50 (0-404-63955-0) AMS Pr.
Lives of Saints for Young People: Twelve Saints. Lazar Puhalo. 28p. (YA). (gr. 7-12). Date not set. pap. 4.50 (1-879038-34-X, 9002) Synaxis Pr.
Lives of Saints for Young People: Twelve Saints, Vol. 1. Lazar Puhalo. 28p. (YA). (gr. 7-12). Date not set. pap. 4.50 (1-879038-33-1, 9001) Synaxis Pr.
Lives of Saints for Young People: Twelve Saints, Vol. 3. Lazar Puhalo. 32p. (YA). (gr. 7-12). Date not set. pap. 4.50 (1-879038-35-8, 9003) Synaxis Pr.
Lives of Saints for Young People: Twelve Saints, Vol. 4. Lazar Puhalo. 42p. (YA). (gr. 7-12). Date not set. pap. 4.50 (1-879038-36-6, 9004) Synaxis Pr.
Lives of Saints for Young People: Twelve Saints, Vol. 5. Lazar Puhalo. 32p. (YA). (gr. 7-12). Date not set. pap. 4.50 (1-879038-37-4, 9005) Synaxis Pr.
Lives of Saints for Young People: Twelve Saints, Vol. 6. Lazar Puhalo. 28p. (YA). (gr. 7-12). Date not set. pap. 4.50 (1-879038-38-2, 9006) Synaxis Pr.
Lives of Saints for Young People: Twelve Saints, Vol. 7. Lazar Puhalo. 78p. (YA). (gr. 7-12). Date not set. pap. 6.50 (1-879038-39-0, 9007) Synaxis Pr.
Lives of Saints for Young People: Twelve Saints, Vol. 8. Lazar Puhalo. 32p. (YA). (gr. 7-12). Date not set. pap. write for info. (1-879038-40-4, 9008) Synaxis Pr.
Lives of Saints for Young People: Twelve Saints, Vol. 9. Lazar Puhalo. 28p. (YA). (gr. 7-12). Date not set. pap. 4.50 (1-879038-41-2, 9009) Synaxis Pr.
Lives of Saints for Young People: Twelve Saints, Vol. 10. Lazar Puhalo. 28p. (YA). (gr. 7-12). Date not set. pap. write for info. (1-879038-42-0, 9010) Synaxis Pr.
Lives of Saints, 1623. Alonso de Villegas. Tr. & Compiled by Edward Kinesman. LC 77-378233. (English Recusant Literature, 1558-1640 Ser.). 1977. write for info. (0-85967-423-1) Scolar Pr.
Lives of Service: Obeying God's Call. Desmond T. Smith. (Illus.). 126p. (Orig.). 1996. pap. 9.95 (0-934942-95-1) White Wing Pub.
Lives of Short Duration. David Adams Richards. 1996. pap. 7.95 (0-7710-9886-3) McCland & Stewart.
*Lives of Stardom. Rae Silver. LC 00-190405. 2000. 25.00 (0-7388-1651-5); pap. 18.00 (0-7388-1652-3) Xlibris Corp.
Lives of Teacher Educators. Edward R. Ducharme. 144p. (C). 1993. text 22.00 (0-8077-3257-5) Tchrs Coll.
Lives of Teachers. Michael Huberman et al. Tr. by Jonathan Neufeld. LC 93-30856. 320p. 1993. text 44.00 (0-8077-3322-9); pap. text 21.95 (0-8077-3321-0) Tchrs Coll.
*Lives of The.... Raintree Steck-Vaughn Publishing Staff. 1999. 104.90 (0-7398-0666-1) Raintree Steck-V.
Lives of the Artist (Scholastic) Kathleen Krull. 1996. 19.00 (0-15-200968-X) Harcourt Coll Pubs.
Lives of the Artists, Vol. 1. Giorgio Vasari. Ed. & Tr. by George Bull. 480p. 1988. pap. 11.95 (0-14-044500-5, 732, Penguin Classics) Viking Penguin.
Lives of the Artists, Vol. 2. Giorgio Vasari. Ed. & Tr. by George Bull. 376p. 1988. pap. 11.95 (0-14-044460-2, Penguin Classics) Viking Penguin.
Lives of the Artists, Vols. 1 & 2. Giorgio Vasari. 1993. 46.00 (0-8446-6678-5) Peter Smith.
Lives of the Artists: Masterpieces, Messes (& What the Neighbors Thought) Kathleen Krull. LC 94-35357. (Illus.). 96p. (J). (gr. 3-7). 1995. 20.00 (0-15-200103-4, Harcourt Child Bks) Harcourt.
Lives of the Artists Oxford World's Classics. Giorgio Vasari. Tr. by Julia Conway Bondanella et al from ITA. Intro. by Peter Bondanella. LC 98-195471. (Oxford World's Classics Ser.). 622p. 1998. pap. 11.95 (0-19-283410-X) OUP.
Lives of the Athletes: Thrills, Spills (& What the Neighbors Thought) Kathleen Krull. LC 95-50702. (Illus.). 96p. (J). (gr. 3-6). 1997. 20.00 (0-15-200806-3) Harcourt.
Lives of the Athletes: Thrills, Spills (And What the Neighbors Thought) Kathleen Krull. (Illus.). 96p. (YA). (gr. 6-8). 1998. lib. bdg. 29.98 (0-8172-4191-4) Raintree Steck-V.
Lives of the Bigamists: Marriage, Family, & Community in Colonial Mexico. Richard Boyer. 341p. 1995. 24.95 (0-8263-1571-2) U of NM Pr.
Lives of the Buddha in the Art & Literature of Asia. Mary Cummings. LC 80-67341. (Michigan Papers on South & Southeast Asia: No. 20). (Illus.). xiii, 225p. (C). 1982. pap. 16.95 (0-89148-023-4) Ctr S&SE Asian.
*Lives of the Caesars. Suetonius. Ed. by Catharine Edwards. (Oxford World's Classics Ser.). (Illus.). 352p. 2001. pap. 11.95 (0-19-283271-9) OUP.
Lives of the Caesars, 2 vols., 1. Tr. by J. C. Rolfe. (Loeb Classical Library: No. 31, 38). 532p. 1914. 18.95 (0-674-99035-8) HUP.
Lives of the Caesars, 2 vols., 2. Suetonius. (Loeb Classical Library: No. 31, 38). 564p. 1914. 19.95 (0-674-99042-0) HUP.
Lives of the Chief Justices of England: From the Norman Conquest till the Death of Lord Mansfield, 2 vols. John L. Campbell. 1997. reprint ed. 245.00 (1-56169-312-X) Gaunt.
Lives of the Chief Justices of England: From the Norman Conquest till the Death of Lord Tenterden, 3 Vols., Set. John L. Campbell. LC 70-152976. (Select Bibliographies Reprint Ser.). 1977. reprint ed. 114.95 (0-8369-5728-8) Ayer.
Lives of the Desert Fathers: The Historia Monachorum in Aegypto. Tr. by Benedicta Ward & Norman Russell from GRE. (Cistercian Studies: No. 34). 178p. 1981. pap. 10.95 (0-87907-934-7) Cistercian Pubns.
Lives of the Early Medici As Told in Their Correspondence. Janet Ross. 1977. lib. bdg. 59.95 (0-8490-2175-8) Gordon Pr.
Lives of the English Poets, 3 vols., Set. Samuel Johnson. Ed. by George B. Hill. (Anglistica & Americana Ser.: No. 113). 1968. reprint ed. 226.20 (0-685-66484-8, 05101955) G Olms Pubs.
Lives of the English Poets, 3 vols., Set. Samuel Johnson. (BCL1-PR English Literature Ser.). 1992. reprint ed. lib. bdg. 225.00 (0-7812-7089-8) Rprt Serv.
Lives of the Fathers. Steven Schwartz. (Illinois Short Fiction Ser.). 168p. 1991. 16.95 (0-252-01815-X) U of Ill Pr.
Lives of the Gods. Alberto Savinio. Tr. by James Brook & Susan Etlinger from ITA. 144p. (Orig.). 1992. pap. 12.99 (0-947757-28-7) Serpents Tail.
Lives of the Governors of Pennsylvania with the . . . William Armor. 500p. 1985. reprint ed. lib. bdg. 69.00 (0-932051-37-5) Rprt Serv.
Lives of the Great Composers. Ed. by Alfred L. Bacharach. LC 72-276. (Essay Index Reprint Ser.). 1977. reprint ed. 33.95 (0-8369-2783-4) Ayer.
Lives of the Great Composers. 3rd ed. Harold C. Schonberg. LC 96-13308. (Illus.). 672p. (C). 1997. 35.00 (0-393-03857-2) Norton.
Lives of the Great Romantics: Shelley, Byron & Wordsworth by Their Contemporaries, 3 vols., Set. John Mullan et al. LC 95-21350. 1250p. 1996. text 320.00 (1-85196-270-0, Pub. by Pickering & Chatto) Ashgate Pub Co.
Lives of the Great Romantics II: By Their Contemporaries. John Mullan et al. LC 97-1345. 1997. pap. write for info. (1-85196-371-5, Pub. by Pickering & Chatto) Ashgate Pub Co.
Lives of the Great Romantics II: By Their Contemporaries, 3 vols., Vol. 3. John Mullan et al. LC 97-1345. 1997. write for info. (1-85196-372-3, Pub. by Pickering & Chatto) Ashgate Pub Co.
Lives of the Great Romantics III: Godwin, Wollstonecraft, & Mary Shelley by Their Contemporaries. Pamela Clemit et al. LC 98-56142. 1999. 360.00 (1-85196-373-1, Pub. by Pickering & Chatto) Ashgate Pub Co.
Lives of the Great Romantics III: Godwin, Wollstonecraft & Mary Shelley by Their Contemporaries, 3 vols. Ed. by Pamela Clemit et al. LC 98-56142. 1050p. 1999. 360.00 (1-85196-512-2, Pub. by Pickering & Chatto) Ashgate Pub Co.
Lives of the Heart: Poems. Jane Hirshfield. LC 97-2750. 128p. 1997. pap. 13.00 (0-06-095169-9, Perennial) HarperTrade.
Lives of the Hierarchs: Basil the Great, Gregory the Theologian, & John Chrysostom. unabridged ed. Holy Apostles Convent Staff. LC 97-78151. (Lives of the Saints Ser.: Vol. 1).Tr. of Mega Synaxaristes. (Illus.). 320p. (C). 1998. 21.00 (0-944359-11-6) Holy Apostles Convent.
Lives of the Holy Apostles. Holy Apostles Convent Staff & Issac E. Lambertsen. LC 88-80846. (Illus.). 300p. 1988. 21.00 (0-944359-00-0) Holy Apostles Convent.
Lives of the Holy Elders of the Optina Desert: Zhitia Prepodobnikh Startsev Optinoy Pustini. (RUS., Illus.). 416p. (Orig.). 1992. pap. 20.00 (0-88465-048-0) Holy Trinity.
Lives of the Holy Prophets: The Major & Minor Prophets. unabridged ed. Holy Apostles Convent Staff. LC 98-92985. (Illus.). (C). 1998. 39.50 (0-944359-12-4) Holy Apostles Convent.
Lives of the Holy Women Martyrs: An Orthodox Martyrologion of Spiritual Heroines. Holy Apostles Convent Staff. LC 91-92355. (Illus.). 588p. (C). 1991. 30.00 (0-944359-08-6) Holy Apostles Convent.
Lives of the Hunted. Ernest Thompson Seton. (Illus.). 360p. (YA). 1994. pap. 18.95 (1-885529-12-0) Stevens Pub.
Lives of the Hunted. rev. ed. Ernest Thompson Seton. LC 87-71145. (Illus.). 368p. 1987. reprint ed. pap. 9.95 (0-88739-054-4) Creat Arts Bk.
*Lives of the Indian Princes. S. Allen. 1998. pap. 163.00 (81-86982-05-1, Pub. by Business Pubns) St Mut.
Lives of the Jain Elders. Ed. by Richard Fynes. (Oxford World's Classics Ser.). 322p. 1998. pap. 11.95 (0-19-283227-1) OUP.
Lives of the Judges of Upper Canada & Ontario: From 1791 to the Present Time, Vol. 1. David B. Read. 486p. 1995. reprint ed. 122.00 (1-56169-110-0) Gaunt.
*Lives of the Kings & Queens of England. Antonia Fraser. 384p. 2000. pap. text 27.50 (0-520-22460-4, Pub. by U CA Pr) Cal Prin Full Svc.
Lives of the Kings & Queens of England. Ed. by Antonia Fraser. LC 95-11132. (Illus.). 363p. 1995. reprint ed. pap. 22.00 (0-520-20409-3, Pub. by U CA Pr) Cal Prin Full Svc.
Lives of the Kings & Queens of England. rev. ed. Antonia Fraser. LC 99-169506. 408p. 1998. 39.95 (0-520-21938-4, Pub. by U CA Pr) Cal Prin Full Svc.
Lives of the Later Caesars. Tr. & Intro. by Anthony R. Birley. (Classics Ser.). 336p. (C). 1976. pap. 12.95 (0-14-044308-8, Penguin Classics) Viking Penguin.
Lives of the Laureates: Thirteen Nobel Economists. 3rd ed. Ed. by William Breit & Roger W. Spencer. LC 95-16632. 287p. 1995. 30.00 (0-262-02391-1) MIT Pr.
Lives of the Laureates: Thirteen Nobel Economists. 3rd ed. Ed. by William Breit & Roger W. Spencer. (Illus.). 288p. 1997. reprint ed. pap. text 14.95 (0-262-52238-1) MIT Pr.
Lives of the Liners. Frank O. Braynard. LC 48-304. (Illus.). 220p. 1947. reprint ed. pap. 68.20 (0-608-02462-7, 206310600004) Bks Demand.
Lives of the Literati, 9 vols. Ed. by Richard B. Sher. (Scottish Thought & Culture 1750-1800 Ser.). 3166p. 1997. reprint ed. 995.00 (1-85506-511-8) Thoemmes Pr.
Lives of the Lord Chancellors & Keepers of the Great Seal of England, 10 vols. 5th ed. John C. Campbell. LC 74-39877. reprint ed. 765.00 (0-404-01380-5) AMS Pr.
Lives of the Lord Chancellors & Keepers of the Great Seal of Ireland, 2 vols. J. Roderick O'Flanagan. 1971. reprint ed. 65.00 (0-8377-2500-3, Rothman) W S Hein.
Lives of the Lord Chancellors, 1940-1970, Vol. II. R. F. Heuston. LC 86-28496. (Illus.). 270p. 1987. text 54.00 (0-19-820074-9) OUP.
Lives of the Master: The Rest of the Jesus Story. Glenn Sanderfur. 238p. 1988. pap. 13.95 (0-87604-216-7, 242) ARE Pr.
Lives of the Modern Poets. rev. ed. William H. Pritchard. LC 96-15041. 334p. 1997. reprint ed. pap. text 19.95 (0-87451-787-7) U Pr of New Eng.
Lives of the Monastery Builders: St. Dionysius of Mt. Olympus, St. Nicanor of Mt. Callistratus & St. Paul of Mt. Latros. Holy Apostles Convent Staff & Leo Papadopulos. LC 88-90979. (Holy Apostles Convent Pamphlet Ser.: No. 1). (Illus.). 72p. (C). 1988. pap. 6.00 (0-944359-02-7) Holy Apostles Convent.
Lives of the Monastery Builders of Meteora: Saints Athanasios & Ioasaph, Builders of the Great Meteoron Monastery & Saints Nectarios & Theophanes, Builders of the Varlaam Monastery. Holy Apostles Convent Staff. LC 91-77844. (Holy Apostles Convent Pamphlet Ser.: No. 3). (Illus.). 86p. (C). 1991. pap. 7.00 (0-944359-07-8) Holy Apostles Convent.
Lives of the Monastery Builders of Soumela: Saints Barnabas & Sophronios of Athens & Saint Christopher of Trebizond, Builders of the Mt. Mela Monastery. Holy Apostles Convent Staff. LC 91-77845. (Holy Apostles Convent Pamphlet Ser.: No. 2). (Illus.). 96p. (C). 1991. pap. 7.00 (0-944359-06-X) Holy Apostles Convent.
Lives of the Monastery Builders of the Great Cave (Mega Spelaion) Holy Apostles Convent Staff. LC 92-90642. (Holy Apostles Convent Pamphlet Ser.: No. 4). (Illus.). 104p. (C). 1992. pap. 7.00 (0-944359-09-4) Holy Apostles Convent.
Lives of the Monastery Builders of the Holy Mountain Athos. Holy Apostles Convent Staff. LC 92-90643. (Holy Apostles Convent Pamphlet Ser.: No. 5). (Illus.). 272p. (C). 1992. pap. 15.00 (0-944359-10-8) Holy Apostles Convent.
Lives of the Monster Dogs. Kirsten Bakis. LC 96-25017. 320p. 1997. 23.00 (0-374-18987-0) FS&G.
*Lives of the Monster Dogs. Kirsten Bakis. LC 97-48550. 304p. 1998. mass mkt. 12.99 (0-446-67416-8, Pub. by Warner Bks) Little.
Lives of the Most Eminent Painters, Sculptors & Architects, 10 vols. Giorgio Vasari. LC 71-153610. Orig. Title: Le Vite De' Piu Eccellenti Pittori. (Illus.). reprint ed. 885.00 (0-404-09730-8) AMS Pr.
Lives of the Most Famous English Poets. William Winstanley. LC 63-7095. 256p. 1963. reprint ed. 50.00 (0-8201-1051-5) Schol Facsimiles.
Lives of the Musicians. Kathleen Krull. (Lives of the... Ser.). (Illus.). 96p. (YA). 1998. lib. bdg. 29.98 (0-8172-9233-0) Raintree Steck-V.
Lives of the Musicians: Good Times, Bad Times (& What the Neighbors Thought) Kathleen Krull. LC 91-33497. (Illus.). 96p. (J). (gr. 3-7). 1993. 20.00 (0-15-248010-2) Harcourt.
Lives of the Necromancers. William Godwin. 1975. lib. bdg. 250.00 (0-87968-281-7) Gordon Pr.
Lives of the Neutron Stars: Proceedings of the NATO Advanced Study Institute on the Lives of the Neutron Stars (1993: Kemer, Turkey) NATO Advanced Study Institute Staff. Ed. by Jan Van Paradijs et al. LC 94-40636. (NATO ASI Ser.: Vol. 450). 576p. (C). 1994. text 357.00 (0-7923-3246-6) Kluwer Academic.
Lives of the Ninth-Century Popes: Liber Pontificalis. Tr. by Raymond Davis. 360p. (Orig.). 1996. pap. text 20.95 (0-85323-479-5) U of Pa Pr.
Lives of the Noble Grecians & Romans, 2 vols., Vol. 1. Arthur H. Clough. Tr. by John Dryden. LC 92-50223. 800p. 1992. 20.00 (0-679-60008-6) Modern Lib NY.
Lives of the Noble Grecians & Romans, 2 vols., Vol. 2. Ed. by Arthur H. Clough. Tr. by John Dryden. LC 92-50223. 736p. 1992. 20.00 (0-679-60009-4) Modern Lib NY.
Lives of the Novelists. Sir Walter Scott. reprint ed. lib. bdg. 79.00 (0-7812-0292-2) Rprt Serv.
Lives of the Novelists. Sir Walter Scott. reprint ed. 39.00 (0-403-04158-9) Somerset Pub.
Lives of the Nuns: Biographies of Chinese Buddhist Nuns from the Fourth to Sixth Centuries. Tr. by Kathryn A. Tsai from CHI. 216p. 1994. text 29.00 (0-8248-1541-6) UH Pr.
Lives of the Painters, 4 vols. John E. Canaday. LC 67-17666. (Illus.). (C). 1969. 83.50 (0-393-04231-6) Norton.
Lives of the Painters. John Canady. (C). 1969. 22.25 (0-393-02418-0) Norton.
Lives of the Painters, Sculptors & Architects, 2 vols., Vol. 1,2. Giorgio Vasari. Tr. by Gaston du C. (Illus.). 1996. 60.00 (0-679-45101-3) Knopf.
Lives of the Pillars of Orthodoxy: Saint Photios, Patriarch of Constantinople; Saint Gregory Palamas, Archbishop of Thessalonica; Saint Mark, Metropolitan of Ephesus. Holy Apostles Convent Staff. Ed. & Illus. by Dormition Skete. LC 90-82540. 640p. (C). 1990. 32.00 (0-944359-04-3) Holy Apostles Convent.
Lives of the Poet: The First Century of Keats Biography. William H. Marquess. LC 84-43064. 224p. 1985. 28.50 (0-271-00390-1) Pa St U Pr.
Lives of the Poets. Steve Abbott. 1987. pap. 5.00 (0-9607630-2-3) Black Star.
Lives of the Poets. Doctorow. 1984. 75.00 (0-394-54131-6) Random.
Lives of the Poets. Richard O'Connell. 1990. pap. 6.00 (0-685-38406-3) Atlantis Edns.
*Lives of the Poets. Michael Schmidt. LC 98-51913. 992p. 1999. 35.00 (0-375-40624-7) Knopf.
*Lives of the Poets. Michael Schmidt. LC 98-51913. 2000. pap. 20.00 (0-375-70604-6) Knopf.
Lives of the Poets. E. L. Doctorow. LC 97-12746. 160p. 1997. reprint ed. pap. 10.95 (0-452-27879-1, Plume) Dutton Plume.
Lives of the Poets see Works of Samuel Johnson
Lives of the Poets: Six Stories & a Novella. E. L. Doctorow. 1986. mass mkt. 4.95 (0-380-69996-6, Avon Bks) Morrow Avon.
Lives of the Poets: The Story of One Thousand Years of English & American Poetry by Louis Untermeyer. Louis Untermeyer. 770p. 1999. reprint ed. 44.95 (0-7351-0092-6) Replica Bks.
Lives of the Poets & Other Pieces see Works of Samuel Johnson
Lives of the Poets of Great Britain & Ireland to the Time of Dean Swift, 5 vols., Set. Theophilus Cibber. 1770p. 1968. reprint ed. 320.00 (0-317-05065-6, 05102038) G Olms Pubs.
Lives of the Popes: The Pontiffs from St. Peter to John Paul II. Richard P. McBrien. LC 97-21897. 528p. 2000. pap. 18.00 (0-06-065304-3) HarpC.
Lives of The Popes: The Pontiffs from St. Peter to John Paul II. Richard P. McBrien. LC 97-21897. (Illus.). 528p. 1997. 29.50 (0-06-065303-5) HarpC.

An Asterisk (*) at the beginning of an entry indicates that the title is appearing for the first time.

Lives of the Presidents: Fame, Shame & What the Neighbors Thought. Kathleen Krull. LC 97-33069. (Illus.). 96p. (J). (gr. 4-8). 1998. 20.00 (*0-15-200808-X*) Harcourt.

Lives of the Presidents: Fame, Shame & What the Neighbors Thought. Kathleen Krull. (Illus.). 96p. (J). (gr. 6). 1998. lib. bdg. 29.98 (*0-8172-4049-7*) Raintree Steck-V.

Lives of the Principal Reformers: Both Englishmen & Foreigners. Richard Rolt. (Illus.). 202p. 1997. reprint ed. 39.95 (*1-882542-17-7*) Fndtns NC.

***Lives of the Psychics: The Shared Worlds of Science & Mysticism.** Fred M. Frohock. LC 99-54663. (Illus.). 264p. 1999. 27.50 (*0-226-26586-2*) U Ch Pr.

Lives of the Puritans, 3 vols. Benjamin Brook. 1543p. 1994. reprint ed. 105.00 (*1-877611-79-4*) Soli Deo Gloria.

Lives of the Puritans, 3, Vol. 1. Benjamin Brooks. 480p. 1994. 35.00 (*1-877611-80-8*) Soli Deo Gloria.

Lives of the Puritans, Vol. 2. Benjamin Brook. 507p. 1994. 35.00 (*1-877611-81-6*) Soli Deo Gloria.

Lives of the Puritans, Vol. 3. Benjamin Brook. 556p. 1994. 35.00 (*1-877611-82-4*) Soli Deo Gloria.

Lives of the Russian Saints see Zhitija Russkikh Svatikh, v 2 tom

Lives of the Saints see Zhitija Svjatikh V 12 Tomov

Lives of the Saints. Edward Berridge. 160p. 1995. pap. 14.95 (*0-7022-2749-8*, Pub. by Univ Queensland Pr) Intl Spec Bk.

Lives of the Saints. Alban Butler. 428p. 1995. pap. 18.00 (*0-89555-530-1*) TAN Bks Pubs.

Lives of the Saints. David Ives. Date not set. pap. 5.95 (*0-8222-1746-5*) Dramatists Play.

Lives of the Saints. Augustine Kalberer. 495p. 1976. pap. 18.00 (*0-8199-0539-9*, Frncscn Herld) Franciscan Pr.

***Lives of the Saints.** Amy Lane. 20p. 1999. pap. 2.95 (*1-886383-91-X*) Pride & Imprints.

Lives of the Saints. Nancy Lemann. (Voices of the South Ser.). 160p. 1997. pap. 13.95 (*0-8071-2162-2*) La State U Pr.

Lives of the Saints, 4 vols., Set. Thurston & Donald Attwater. LC 56-5353. 1981. 149.95 (*0-87061-045-7*, 6902); pap. 109.95 (*0-87061-137-2*, 6905) Chr Classics.

Lives of the Saints, Vol. I. Ed. by Charles Plummer. (Celtic Studies). 390p. 1997. 65.00 (*1-85182-223-2*, Pub. by Four Cts Pr); 65.00 (*1-85182-224-0*, Pub. by Four Cts Pr) Intl Spec Bk.

Lives of the Saints, Vol. 1. large type ed. Hugo Hoever. (Illus.). 1990. 7.50 (*0-89942-870-3*, 870/22) Catholic Bk Pub.

Lives of the Saints: A Novel. Nino Ricci. LC 95-21022. 1995. pap. 11.00 (*0-312-13441-X*, Picador USA) St Martin.

Lives of the Saints: Boys Edition. (Catholic Classics Ser.). (J). 1997. pap. 1.50 (*0-88271-460-0*) Regina Pr.

Lives of the Saints: Girls Edition. (Catholic Classics Ser.). (J). 1996. pap. 1.50 (*0-88271-461-9*) Regina Pr.

Lives of the Saints & Everything. Susan Firer. LC 93-71915. (CSU Poetry Ser.: No. 41). 82p. (Orig.). 1993. pap. 10.00 (*1-880834-05-7*) Cleveland St Univ Poetry Ctr.

Lives of the Saints & Everything. Susan Firer. LC 93-71915. (CSU Poetry Ser.: Vol. XLI). 82p. (Orig.). 1993. 15.00 (*1-880834-04-9*) Cleveland St Univ Poetry Ctr.

Lives of the Saints Boxed Set. large type ed. Lawrence G. Lovasik. (Illus.). 1992. boxed set 16.95 (*0-89942-876-2*, 876/GS) Catholic Bk Pub.

Lives of the Saints of the Holy Land & the Sinai Desert. Holy Apostles Convent Staff & Leo Papadopulos. LC 88-90978. (Illus.). 588p. (C). 1988. 25.00 (*0-944359-01-9*) Holy Apostles Convent.

Lives of the Saints II, Vol. 2. large type ed. Catholic Book Staff & Thomas J. Donaghy. (Illus.). 528p. 1993. 7.95 (*0-89942-875-4*, 875/22) Catholic Bk Pub.

Lives of the Saints You Should Know. Margaret R. Bunson & Matthew E. Bunson. LC 94-67356. (Illus.). 150p. (Orig.). 1994. pap. 8.95 (*0-87973-576-7*, 576) Our Sunday Visitor.

Lives of the Saints You Should Know, Vol. 2. Margaret R. Bunson & Matthew E. Bunson. LC 94-67356. (Illus.). 160p. (Orig.). (YA). (gr. 5 up). 1996. pap. 8.95 (*0-87973-753-0*) Our Sunday Visitor.

Lives of the Serbian Saints. Voyeslav Yanich. (Illus.). 1973. 4.95 (*0-89981-053-5*) Eastern Orthodox.

Lives of the Signers of the Declaration of Independence. Charles A. Goodrich. (Notable American Authors Ser.). 1992. reprint ed. lib. bdg. 75.00 (*0-7812-2933-2*) Rprt Serv.

Lives of the Signers of the Declaration of Independence. Benson J. Lossing. (Illus.). 392p. (YA). (gr. 7-12). 1995. reprint ed. pap. 9.95 (*0-925279-45-5*) Wallbuilders.

Lives of the Sophists. Flavius Philostratus. (Loeb Classical Library: No. 134). 19.95 (*0-674-99149-4*) HUP.

Lives of the Spiritual Mothers: An Orthodox Materikon of Women Monastics & Ascetics. Holy Apostles Convent Staff. LC 91-70245. (Illus.). (C). 1991. 32.00 (*0-944359-05-1*) Holy Apostles Convent.

Lives of the Three Mrs. Judsons see Three Mrs. Judsons

Lives of the Twelve Ceasars. Suetonius. (Classics of World Literature Ser.). 1997. pap. 5.95 (*1-85326-475-X*, 475XWW, Pub. by Wrdsworth Edits) NTC Contemp Pub Co.

Lives of the Twins. Rosamond Smith, pseud. 208p. 1989. pap. 3.95 (*0-380-70656-3*, Avon Bks) Morrow Avon.

***Lives of the Two-Headed Baseball Siren.** Frank Van Zant. Ed. by Ruth M. Kempher. (Illus.). 100p. 2000. pap. 13.00 (*1-888832-15-0*) Kings Estate.

Lives of the Virgins 2000 AD. 100.00 (*0-9604252-5-X*) Parpaglion.

Lives of the Visigothic Fathers. Ed. & Tr. by A. T. Fear. (Translated Texts for Historians Ser.). 208p. (C). 1997. pap. 17.95 (*0-85323-582-1*, Pub. by Liverpool Univ Pr) U of Pa Pr.

Lives of the Warriors of the Civil Wars of France & England: Warriors of the Seventeenth Century, 2 vols. Edward Cust. LC 76-38737. (Essay Index Reprint Ser.). 1977. reprint ed. 44.95 (*0-8369-2642-0*) Ayer.

Lives of the Warriors of the Thirty Years' War: Warriors of the Seventeenth Century, 2 vols. Edward Cust. LC 75-38742. (Essay Index Reprint Ser.). 1977. reprint ed. 39.95 (*0-8369-2643-9*) Ayer.

Lives of the Women Poets. April Bernard. Date not set. write for info. (*0-393-03840-8*) Norton.

Lives of the Writers. Kathleen Krull. 1995. 19.00 (*0-15-201032-7*) Harcourt.

Lives of the Writers. Kathleen Krull. (Lives of the... Ser.). (Illus.). 96p. (YA). 1998. lib. bdg. 29.98 (*0-8172-5739-X*) Raintree Steck-V.

Lives of the Writers: Comedies, Tragedies (& What the Neighbors Thought) Kathleen Krull. LC 93-32436. (Illus.). 96p. (J). (gr. 3-7). 1994. 20.00 (*0-15-248009-9*, Harcourt Child Bks) Harcourt.

Lives of Their Own: Blacks, Italians, & Poles in Pittsburgh, 1900-1960. John Bodnar et al. LC 81-3382. (Working Class in American History Ser.). (Illus.). 302p. 1981. text 29.95 (*0-252-00880-4*) U of Ill Pr.

Lives of Their Own: Blacks, Italians, & Poles in Pittsburgh, 1900-1960. John Bodnar et al. LC 81-3382. (Working Class in American History Ser.). (Illus.). 302p. 1983. pap. text 15.95 (*0-252-01063-9*) U of Ill Pr.

Lives of Their Own: Rhetorical Dimensions in Autobiographies of Women Activists. Martha Watson. Ed. by Thomas W. Benson. LC 97-45361. (Studies in Rhetoric/Communication). x, 149 p. 1999. lib. bdg. 24.95 (*1-57003-200-9*) U of SC Pr.

Lives of Thomas: Episodes & Prayers. John High. (Five Fingers Book Ser.: No. 3). (Illus.). 80p. (Orig.). 1991. pap. 7.95 (*0-9618409-6-X*) Five Fingers.

Lives of Thomas - Episodes & Prayers. John High. 89p. 1998. pap. 7.95 (*1-893032-08-6*) Jensen Daniels.

Lives of Those Eminent Antiquaries Elias Ashmole & Mr. William Lilly. Ashmole et al. 410p. 1998. reprint ed. pap. 45.00 (*0-7661-0475-3*) Kessinger Pub.

Lives of Three English Saints. Aelfric. Ed. by G. I. Needham. (Old English Ser.). 1966. pap. text 9.95 (*0-89197-564-0*) Irvington.

Lives of Translation. large type ed. Patricia Wendorf. 496p. 1995. 27.99 (*0-7089-3250-9*) Ulverscroft.

Lives of Two Sainted Christian Families: Christian Families in the Early Church. Georgia Hronas & Helen Hronas. 95p. 1995. pap. 7.95 (*1-880971-07-0*) Light&Life Pub Co MN.

Lives of University Hospitals of Cleveland: The 125-Year Evolution of an Academic Medical Center. Mark Gottlieb. LC 91-66654. (Illus.). 352p. 1991. 21.95 (*0-940601-06-0*, Wilson St Press) Octavia Ohio.

Lives of Value. Sharleen C. Cohen. 576p. 1993. mass mkt. 5.99 (*0-446-36389-8*, Pub. by Warner Bks) Little.

Lives of Vizcaya: Annals of a Great House. Kathryn C. Harwood. (Illus.). xx, 316p. 1985. pap. 17.95 (*0-916224-99-6*) Banyan Bks.

Lives of Whales & Dolphins: From the American Museum of Natural History. Richard C. Connor. 1995. 25.00 (*0-8050-1950-2*) H Holt & Co.

Lives of Whales & Dolphins: From the American Museum of Natural History. Richard C. Connor & Dawn Micklethwaite Peterson. (Illus.). 288p. 1995. pap. 15.95 (*0-8050-4565-1*, Owl) H Holt & Co.

Lives of William Benton. Sidney Hyman. LC 72-88231. 659p. reprint ed. pap. 200.00 (*0-608-15115-7*, 202579500046) Bks Demand.

Lives of Wives. Laura Riding Jackson. (Sun & Moon Classics Ser.: No. 71). 326p. (Orig.). 1995. pap. 13.95 (*1-55713-182-1*) Sun & Moon CA.

***Lives of Wolves.** Lynn M. Stone. LC 00-20870. (Wolves Discovery Library Ser.). (Illus.). (J). 2000. write for info. (*1-55916-239-2*) Rourke Bk Co.

Lives of Women Public Schoolteachers: Scenes from American Educational History. Madelyn Holmes & Beverly J. Weiss. LC 95-3112. (Women's History & Culture; Garland Reference Library of Social Science: Vols. 8 & 833). (Illus.). 264p. (Orig.). 1995. text 25.00 (*0-8153-0838-8*, SS833) Garland.

***Lives of Young Koreans in Japan.** Yasunori Fukuoka. 260p. 1998. 110.00 (*0-7103-0623-7*, Pub. by Kegan Paul Intl) Col U Pr.

Lives on Line. Brewis. LC 95-76341. (C). 1995. pap. text 23.50 (*0-15-501969-4*) Harcourt Coll Pubs.

Lives on Post. Adams. 1997. write for info. (*0-8212-2485-9*) Little.

Lives on the Boundary: A Moving Account of the Struggles & Achievements of America's Educational Underclass. Mike Rose. LC 89-38513. 256p. (C). 1998. pap. text 12.95 (*0-14-012403-9*) Addson-Wesley Educ.

Lives on the Boundary: The Struggles & Achievements of America's Underprepared. Mike Rose. 288p. 1989. 29.95 (*0-02-926821-4*) Free Pr.

Lives on the Edge: Single Mothers & Their Children in the Other America. Valerie Polakow. LC 92-21977. (Illus.). 232p. (C). 1993. 22.50 (*0-226-67183-6*) U Ch Pr.

Lives on the Edge: Single Mothers & Their Children in the Other America. Valerie Polakow. x, 232p. (C). 1994. pap. 10.95 (*0-226-67184-4*) U Ch Pr.

Lives on the Line. student ed. 3.29 (*0-8066-0240-6*) Augsburg Fortress.

***Lives on the Line: American Families & the Struggle to Make Ends Meet.** Martha Shirk. 2000. pap. 17.00 (*0-8133-3820-4*) Westview.

Lives on the Line: American Families & the Struggle to Make Ends Meet. Martha Shirk et al. LC 99-23948. 304p. 1999. 24.00 (*0-8133-6653-4*, Pub. by Westview) HarpC.

***Lives on the Line: Dispatches from the U. S. - Mexican Border.** Miriam Davidson. LC 00-8566. 200p. 2000. 35.00 (*0-8165-1997-8*) U of Ariz Pr.

***Lives on the Line: Dispatches from the U. S. - Mexican Border.** Miriam Davidson. LC 00-8566. (Illus.). 200p. 2000. pap. 17.95 (*0-8165-1998-6*) U of Ariz Pr.

Lives on the Mind Slaves. Matt Cohen. LC 95-109993. 192p. 1994. pap. write for info. (*0-88984-139-X*) Porcup Quill.

Lives Passed: Biographical Sketches from Central New York. Carol Kammen. LC 84-15775. (Illus.). 172p. 1984. pap. 7.50 (*0-932334-69-5*, NY75034); lib. bdg. 15.00 (*0-932334-68-7*, NY65035) Hrt of the Lakes.

Lives Plucked from a Discarded Address Book, 1965-1995. Terry W. Berger. 200p. 1996. 15.00 (*0-9652366-0-9*) TWB.

***Lives Through Literature.** 3rd ed. Helene L. Keating & Walter Levy. 1360p. 2000. pap. 46.67 (*0-13-017006-2*) P-H.

Lives Through Literature: A Thematic Anthology. 2nd ed. Ed. by Helene L. Keating & Walter J. Levy. LC 94-43607. (Illus.). 1408p. (C). 1995. pap. text 56.00 (*0-02-362301-2*, Macmillan Coll) P-H.

Lives Through Time. Jack Block. 313p. 1971. 24.95 (*0-685-53570-3*) Bancroft Bks.

Lives Through Time. Jack Block. 312p. 1971. text 59.95 (*0-9600332-0-3*) L Erlbaum Assocs.

Lives to Come. Philip Kitcher. LC 97-17314. 384p. 1997. per. 14.00 (*0-684-82705-0*) S&S Trade Pap.

Lives to Come: The Genetic Revolution & Human Possibilities. Philip Kitcher. LC 95-41523. 384p. 1996. 25.00 (*0-684-80055-1*) S&S Trade.

Lives to Remember: An Original Anthology. Ed. by Leon Stein & Annette K. Baxter. LC 74-3984. (Women in America Ser.). (Illus.). 1977. reprint ed. 34.95 (*0-405-06109-9*) Ayer.

Lives Together - Worlds Apart: Mothers & Daughters in Popular Culture. Suzanna D. Walters. 1992. 40.00 (*0-520-07851-9*, Pub. by U CA Pr) Cal Prin Full Svc.

Lives Together - Worlds Apart: Mothers & Daughters in Popular Culture. Suzanna D. Walters. (Illus.). 295p. (C). 1994. pap. 16.95 (*0-520-08656-2*, Pub. by U CA Pr) Cal Prin Full Svc.

Lives Together - Worlds Apart: Quechua Colonization in Jungle & City. Sarah L. Skar. 300p. 1994. 18.00 (*82-00-21957-7*) Scandnvan Univ Pr.

Lives Touched by Faith: Second Presbyterian Church 150 Years. George W. Geib. (Illus.). 240p. 1988. 10.00 (*0-9619351-0-3*) Secnd Presby IN.

Lives Turned Upside Down: Homeless Children in Their Own Words & Photographs. Jim Hubbard. (Illus.). 40p. (J). (gr. 3-7). 1996. mass mkt. 17.00 (*0-689-80649-3*) S&S Bks Yung.

***Lives Well Lived: I Remember Baubie & Zadie.** Diane Halperin. (Illus.). 148p. 2001. pap. 15.00 (*1-58151-060-8*, Pub. by BookPartners) Midpt Trade.

Lives Well Spent: Westchester County Obituaries & Death Notices in the Eastern State Journal, May 1845-April 1875. Elizabeth G. Fuller. 320p. (Orig.). 1994. pap. 35.00 (*0-915585-04-9*) West Cnty Hist Soc.

Lives, Wives & Loves of the Great Composers. Fritz Spiegl. 272p. 1996. 35.00 (*0-7145-2917-6*) M Boyars Pubs.

Lives Worth Living: Women's Experience of Chronic Illness. Veronica Marris. 256p. 1996. pap. 14.00 (*0-04-440938-9*, Pub. by Rivers Oram) NYU Pr.

Lives Written in Sand: Addiction Awareness & Recovery Strategies. Thomas Byrd. (Illus.). 354p. (Orig.). 1997. pap. text, per. 33.00 (*0-9653658-0-8*) Hallum Pub.

Lives You Live As Revealed in the Heavens. Ted George. LC 77-73594. 206p. 1977. 21.00 (*0-932782-00-0*, G1143-034) Arthur Pubns.

Livestock. National Research Council Staff. (Managing Global Genetic Resources Ser.). 296p. (C). 1993. text 34.95 (*0-309-04394-8*) Natl Acad Pr.

Livestock & Carcasses Evaluation. 5th ed. Boggs et al. 256p. 1998. per. 37.95 (*0-7872-4569-0*, 41456901) Kendall-Hunt.

Livestock & Equality in East Africa: The Economic Basis for Social Structure. Harold K. Schneider. LC 78-20400. (Illus.). 303p. reprint ed. pap. 94.00 (*0-608-18471-3*, 205671700081) Bks Demand.

Livestock & Land-Use Surveys in Sub-Saharan Africa. William Wint & David Bourne. (Research Discussion Papers). 36p. (C). 1994. pap. 9.95 (*0-85598-284-5*, Pub. by Oxfam Pub) Stylus Pub VA.

Livestock & Meat Market see Agricultural Review for Europe, 1983 & 1984

Livestock & Meat Market, 1992-1993, Vol. 3. (Agricultural Review for Europe: No. 36). 80p. 35.00 (*92-1-116588-1*) UN.

Livestock & Meat Marketing. 3rd ed. J. H. McCoy & M. E. Sarhan. (Illus.). 688p. 1988. text 99.95 (*0-442-20488-4*, VNR) Wiley.

Livestock & Poultry Production see Modern Livestock & Poultry Production

Livestock & Poultry Production. 4th ed. Clarence E. Bundy et al. 1975. text 31.52 (*0-13-538579-2*) P-H.

Livestock & Wildlife Management During Drought. Ed. & Pref. by Robert D. Brown. (Illus.). 66p. (Orig.). 1986. pap. text 5.00 (*0-912229-11-X*) CK Wildlife Res.

***Livestock Behavior Guide.** Keith E. Gilster. 138p. 2000. write for info. (*1-58692-026-X*) Copyright Mgmt.

Livestock Development & Policy in East Africa. Philip Raikes. (Centre for Development Research Publications: No. 6). 254p. 1981. 18.95 (*91-7106-182-7*, Pub. by Nordic Africa) Transaction Pubs.

Livestock Entomology. R. E. Williams et al. LC 84-22208. 352p. 1985. 175.00 (*0-471-81064-9*) Wiley.

Livestock Entomology. 2nd ed. Bob Barker. 216p. (C). 1999. pap. text, lab manual ed. 38.95 (*0-7872-5463-0*, 41546301) Kendall-Hunt.

Livestock Environment: Proceedings of the 5th International Symposium. Ed. by Robert W. Bottcher & Steven J. Hoff. LC 97-71782. 1116p. 1997. pap. 79.00 (*0-929355-84-9*, P0197) Am Soc Ag Eng.

Livestock Environment IV. LC 93-71585. 1274p. 1993. 76.75 (*0-929355-41-5*, P0393) Am Soc Ag Eng.

Livestock Environment III: Third International Livestock Symposium Proceedings. International Livestock Environment Symposium. LC 88-70514. 476p. 1988. pap. 54.25 (*0-916150-92-5*) Am Soc Ag Eng.

***Livestock, Ethics & Quality of Life.** Ed. by J. Hodges & I. K. Hann. LC 99-33192. (CABI Publishing Ser.). 250p. 2000. text 90.00 (*0-85199-362-1*) OUP.

Livestock Extension Policy. J. Morton & R. Matthewman. 1998. pap. 60.00 (*0-85954-484-2*, Pub. by Nat Res Inst) St Mut.

***Livestock Farming Systems: More Than Food Production.** J. T. Sorensen. (Illus.). 1998. pap. 96.00 (*90-74134-49-1*) Wageningen Pers.

Livestock Feeds & Feeding. 4th ed. Richard O. Kellems & David C. Church. LC 96-46382. 573p. 1997. 100.00 (*0-13-241795-2*) P-H.

Livestock for a Small Earth: The Role of Animals in a Just & Sustainable World. Ed. by Jerry Aaker. LC 94-10382. (Illus.). 128p. 1994. pap. 18.95 (*0-929765-28-1*) Seven Locks Pr.

Livestock Handling & Transport. Ed. by T. Grandin. (Illus.). 336p. 1993. text 100.00 (*0-85198-855-5*) OUP.

***Livestock Handling & Transport.** 2nd ed. Temple Grandin. LC 99-58044. 384p. 2000. write for info. (*0-85199-409-1*) OUP.

Livestock Housing: Environmental & Climatic Aspects. Ed. by D. Charles & C. Wathes. LC 95-106794. 448p. 1994. text 120.00 (*0-85198-774-5*) OUP.

Livestock Judging & Evaluation Manual. Harland D. Ritchie. (Illus.). x, 205p. 1983. reprint ed. pap. 8.50 (*0-87013-152-4*) Mich St U Pr.

Livestock Judging Manual. Date not set. write for info. (*1-56918-676-6*) Visual EP.

***Livestock Judging, Selection & Evaluation.** 5th ed. Roger E. Hunsley. 2001. teacher ed. 14.95 (*0-8134-3164-6*) Interstate.

***Livestock Judging, Selection & Evaluation.** 5th ed. Roger E. Hunsley. (Illus.). xviii, 438p. 2001. 62.50 (*0-8134-3163-8*) Interstate.

***Livestock Management in the American Southwest: Ecology, Society & Economics.** Roy Jemison & Carol Raish. LC 00-37554. (Developments in Animal & Veterinary Science Ser.). 2000. pap. write for info. (*0-444-50313-7*) Elsevier.

Livestock Nutrition. Leslie D. Kamstra. (Illus.). 223p. (C). 1982. pap. text 13.95 (*0-89641-081-1*) American Pr.

Livestock Nutrition. Richard Warner. 1999. 29.95 (*0-8493-8763-9*) CRC Pr.

Livestock Production Extension: Issues, Case Studies & Policy Options. J. Morton et al. 1997. pap. 60.00 (*0-85954-480-X*, Pub. by Nat Res Inst) St Mut.

***Livestock Production, Selection & Reasoning: A Text Intended for Competitive Livestock & Equine Judging.** Mark A. Kaufman & Justin L. Schaneman. 250p. (C). 1999. pap. text 59.95 (*0-9674050-0-9*) K S Pubg.

Livestock Productivity Enhancers: An Economic Assessment. Ed. by Martin Bent. (Illus.). 176p. 1993. text 65.00 (*0-85198-800-8*) OUP.

Livestock Protection Dogs: Selection, Care & Training. David E. Sims & Orysia Dawydiak. LC 90-38781. (Illus.). 128p. (Orig.). 1990. pap. 9.95 (*0-940269-05-8*) OTR Pubns.

Livestock Response Functions. Ed. by Earl O. Heady & Shashanka Bhide. LC 83-18547. (Illus.). 339p. 1984. reprint ed. pap. 105.10 (*0-608-00180-5*, 206096200006) Bks Demand.

Livestock Showman's Handbook: A Guide for Raising Animals for Junior Livestock Shows. 2nd ed. Roger Pond. LC 96-70178. (Illus.). 214p. (J). (gr. 4-12). 1997. pap. 17.95 (*0-9617766-3-3*) Pine Forest Pub.

Livestock Waste Facilities Handbook. 3rd ed. Midwest Plan Service Engineers Staff. Ed. by Glenn A. Church, II. LC 93-7384. (Illus.). 112p. 1993. pap. 8.00 (*0-89373-089-0*, MWPS-18) MidWest Plan Serv.

Livestock Waste Management, 2 vols., I. Michael R. Overcash et al. 512p. 1983. 144.00 (*0-8493-5595-8*, TD930) CRC Pr.

Livestock Waste Management, 2 vols., II. Michael R. Overcash et al. 512p. 1983. 146.00 (*0-8493-5596-6*, TD930, CRC Reprint) Franklin.

Livestock Waste Management, 2 vols., Set. Michael R. Overcash et al. 512p. 1983. write for info. (*0-318-57538-8*, TD930) CRC Pr.

Livet Min: My Life. Casper H. Hegdal. LC 97-69855. (Illus.). viii, 98p. (Orig.). 1997. pap. 12.95 (*0-9660848-0-2*) Odyssey Pubns.

Livewire Guide to Going, Being & Staying Veggie! Juliet Gellatley. (Livewire Ser.). 190p. (YA). (gr. 7-11). 1997. pap. 7.95 (*0-7043-4939-6*, Pub. by Womens Press) Trafalgar.

Livi, Titi, Libri XXVI & XXVII. Ed. by Walsh. (LAT.). 1989. 21.95 (*3-322-00734-0*, T1496, Pub. by B G Teubner) U of Mich Pr.

Livi, Titi, Libri XXXI-XL. Ed. by Weissenborn & M. Muller. (LAT.). 1981. reprint ed. 29.95 (*3-519-01488-2*, T1488, Pub. by B G Teubner) U of Mich Pr.

Livi, Titi, Libri XLI-XLV. Ed. by Briscoe. (LAT.). 1986. 95.00 (*3-519-01491-2*, T1491, Pub. by B G Teubner) U of Mich Pr.

L

L

Livi, Titi: Ab Urbe Condita, Libri XXI & XXII. Ed. by Dorey. (LAT.). 1971. 21.95 (*3-322-00159-8*, T1494, Pub. by B G Teubner) U of Mich Pr.

Livi, Titi Libri XLI-XLV: Periochae. Ed. by Weissenborn & M. Muller. (LAT.). 1981. reprint ed. 24.95 (*3-519-01489-0*, T1489, Pub. by B G Teubner) U of Mich Pr.

Livi, Titi Tom. I, Libri XXXI-XXXV: Libri XXXI-XL. Ed. by Briscoe. (LAT.). 1991. 89.50 (*3-519-01492-0*, T1492, Pub. by B G Teubner) U of Mich Pr.

Livi, Titi Tom. II, Libri XXXVI-XL: Libri XXXI-XL. Ed. by Briscoe. (LAT.). 1991. 110.00 (*3-519-01493-9*, T1493, Pub. by B G Teubner) U of Mich Pr.

Livietta e Tracollo: La Contadina Astuta: Intermezzi. Ed. by Gordana Lazaravich. LC 85-753856. (Complete Works of Pergolesi: No. 2, Vol. VI). (Illus.). 132p. 1991. lib. bdg. 112.00 (*0-918728-45-2*) Pendragon NY.

Livin' de Life. Ed Graczyk. (J). 1970. 6.00 (*0-87602-151-8*) Anchorage.

***Livin' la Vida Loca & Other Hits Recorded by Ricky Martin.** Ricky Martin. 1998. pap. 14.95 (*0-7692-9074-4*) Wrner Bros.

Livin' Large. Yinka Adebayo. (J). 1998. mass mkt. 5.99 (*1-874509-34-4*, Pub. by X Pr) LPC InBook.

***Livin' on Country: The Alan Jackson Story.** Scott Gray. 224p. 2000. mass mkt. 5.99 (*0-345-43873-6*, Ballantine) Ballantine Pub Grp.

Livin' on the Net, Vol. 1. Perf. by Howard Rheingold. 1996. 9.99 (*0-941188-55-8*) M Wiese.

Livin' on the Net, Vol. 2. Perf. by Howard Rheingold. 1996. 9.95 (*0-941188-56-6*) M Wiese.

Livin' the Blues: Memoirs of a Black Journalist & Poet. Frank M. Davis. Ed. & Intro. by John E. Tidwell. LC 92-50248. (Studies in American Autobiography). (Illus.). 408p. 1993. 19.95 (*0-299-13500-4*) U of Wis Pr.

Living. Evelyn Carswell & Judy Bisignano. (Illus.). 64p. (J). (gr. 3-8). 1985. student ed. 8.99 (*0-86653-332-X*, GA 679) Good Apple.

Living. Rem Koolhaas & Bruce Mau. (Illus.). 256p. 1998. 45.00 (*1-58093-002-6*) Monacelli Pr.

***Living.** Donnell Linthecome. 1999. pap. write for info. (*1-58235-401-4*) Watermrk Pr.

Living. Paula Toney-Brooks. Ed. by Robert L. Booker & Jacqueline L. Booker. 78p. 1998. 24.95 (*0-9670669-0-5*) Booker Group.

Living. Henry Green, pseud. 1988. reprint ed. lib. bdg. 59.00 (*0-7812-0037-7*) Rprt Serv.

Living. Henry Green, pseud. 1971. reprint ed. 49.00 (*0-403-01001-2*) Scholarly.

Living!, Vol. 3. David A. Clemens. LC 79-55503. (Steps to Maturity Ser.). 1980. teacher ed. 17.95 (*0-86508-006-2*) BCM Pubn.

Living!, Vol. 3. David A. Clemens. LC 79-55503. (Steps to Maturity Ser.). 1980. student ed. 15.95 (*0-86508-005-4*) BCM Pubn.

Living: A Novel. Annie Dillard. LC 91-58376. 464p. 1999. pap. 14.00 (*0-06-092411-X*, Perennial) HarperTrade.

Living: A Novel. large type ed. Annie Dillard. LC 92-19488. 693p. 1992. 23.95 (*1-56054-500-3*) Thorndike Pr.

Living: A Novel. large type ed. Annie Dillard. LC 92-19488. 693p. 1993. pap. 15.95 (*1-56054-925-4*) Thorndike Pr.

Living a Balanced Life: Applying Timeless Spiritual Teachings to Your Everyday Life. Elliott James. LC 89-29546. 144p. (Orig.). 1990. pap. 9.95 (*0-945050-22-4*) Dhamma Bks.

***Living a Balanced Life in an Unbalanced World.** Anthony M. Coniaris. 105p. 2000. pap. 10.95 (*1-880971-62-3*) Light&Life Pub Co MN.

Living a Beautiful Life: 500 Ways to Add Elegance, Order, Beauty & Joy to Every Day of Your... Alexandra Stoddard. 1996. 21.95 (*0-679-45623-6*) Random.

Living a Caring-Based Program. Ed. by Anne Boykin. LC 94-171951. 188p. 1993. 20.95 (*0-88737-591-X*, 14-2536, NLN Pr) Natl League Nurse.

Living a Christian Life Vol. II: Way of the Lord Jesus. Germain Grisez. LC 83-1508. 950p. 1993. 35.00 (*0-8199-0961-0*) Franciscan Pr.

Living a Countersign: From Iona to Basic Christian Communities. Ian Fraser. (C). 1990. text 32.00 (*0-947988-39-4*, Pub. by Wild Goose Pubns) St Mut.

Living a Gentle, Passionate Life: Stories to Warm & Educate the Heart. Robert J. Wicks. LC 98-23205. 144p. 1998. 14.95 (*0-8091-0499-7*) Paulist Pr.

***Living a Gentle, Passionate Life: Stories to Warm & Educate the Heart.** Robert J. Wicks. 2000. pap. 9.95 (*0-8091-3944-8*) Paulist Pr.

***Living a Godly Life.** Michael Eaton. (Theology for Beginners Ser.). 128p. 1998. reprint ed. pap. 11.99 (*1-85078-315-2*, Pub. by O M Pubng) OM Literature.

Living a Good Life. Tr. by Thomas Cleary. LC 96-44398. 80p. 1997. pap. 6.95 (*1-57062-274-4*, Pub. by Shambhala Pubns) Random.

***Living a Good Life in Spite of Evil.** Marcel Sarot. (Contributions to Philosophical Theology Ser.: Vol. 3). 167p. 1999. pap. 29.95 (*3-631-35332-4*) P Lang Pubng.

***Living a Good Life in Spite of Evil.** Marcel Sarot. LC 99-38504. (Contributions to Philosophical Theology Ser.: Vol. 3). 167p. (C). 1999. pap. 29.95 (*0-8204-4374-3*) P Lang Pubng.

***Living a Healthy Life with Chronic Conditions: Self-Management of Heart Disease, Arthritis, Diabetes, Asthma, Bronchitis, Emphysema & Others.** 2nd rev. ed. Kate Lorig et al. (Illus.). 320p. 2000. pap. 18.95 (*0-923521-53-4*, Pub. by Bull Pub) Publishers Group.

Living a Healthy Life with Chronic Conditions: Self-Management of Heart Disease, Arthritis, Strokes, Diabetes, Asthma, Bronchitis, Emphysema & Others. Kate Lorig et al. 280p. 1994. pap. 18.95 (*0-923521-28-3*) Bull Pub.

Living a Jewish Life: Jewish Traditions, Customs & Values for Today's Families. Anita Diamant & Howard Cooper. LC 96-18370. 352p. 1996. pap. 15.00 (*0-06-273443-1*) HarpC.

Living a Joyous Life: Practical Spirituality. Elizabeth Joy. (Illus.). 106p. (Orig.). 1989. pap. 9.95 (*0-944881-04-1*) E Joy Prodns.

Living a Legacy: Making the Most of Every Moment You Share. Deena Lee Wilson. LC 99-37843. 176p. 1999. 12.99 (*0-8307-2386-2*) Gospel Lght.

Living a Lie. large type ed. Josephine Cox. (Charnwood Large Print Ser.). 528p. 1997. 27.99 (*0-7089-8905-5*, Charnwood) Ulverscroft.

Living a Life According to the High Peak of God's Revelation. Witness Lee. 41p. 1994. pap. 4.00 (*0-87083-791-5*, 04-032-001) Living Stream Ministry.

Living a Life According to the Peak of God's Elevation see Vida Conforme a la Cumbre de la Revelacion de Dios

Living a Life in the Spirit. Dennis F. Holt. iii, 66p. 1998. pap., spiral bd. 14.00 (*1-892031-00-0*) Cornelius Hse.

Living a Life of Joy. John R. Price. LC 97-21724. 256p. 1997. pap. 12.00 (*0-449-91138-1*) Fawcett.

Living a Life That Counts. Melvin L. Cheatham & Mark Cutshell. 224p. 1995. pap. 14.99 (*0-7852-7724-2*) Nelson.

Living a Moral Life: Gifted & Growing, Teacher's Annotated Edition. rev. ed. Loretta Pastva. (Light of the World Ser.). 1999. pap. write for info. (*0-02-655825-4*, Benzger Pub) Glencoe.

Living a Pedagogy of Love: Paulo Freire in Practice. Darder. (Cultural Studies Ser.). 128p. 1999. text 60.00 (*0-8133-9105-9*) Westview.

Living a Predicament: Young People Surviving Unemployment. Stephen Hutchens. 224p. 1994. pap. 66.95 (*1-85628-641-X*, Pub. by Avebry) Ashgate Pub Co.

Living a Purpose-Full Life: What Happens When You Say Yes to God. Jan Johnson. LC 98-50854. 240p. 1999. pap. 11.95 (*1-57856-048-9*) Waterbrook Pr.

Living a Sacred Life: 365 Meditations & Celebrations. Robin Heernes Lysne. 240p. 1999. pap. 13.95 (*1-57324-185-7*) Conari Press.

Living a Spiritual Year: Seasonal Festivals in Northern & Southern Hemispheres: an Esoteric Study. Adrian Anderson. LC 92-34742. (Illus.). 336p. (Orig.). 1993. pap. 19.95 (*0-88010-365-5*) Anthroposophic.

***Living A Watercolour Wash.** Frank E. Halliday. 2000. pap. text 10.95 (*0-85532-902-5*) Srch Pr.

Living a Worthy Life. Nancy Ferguson. 208p. 1999. pap. 9.99 (*0-89225-379-7*) Gospel Advocate.

***Living Aboard.** Janet Groene & Gordon Groene. (Illus.). 246p. 2000. spiral bd. 24.95 (*1-892216-27-2*, 272) Bristol Fash.

Living Aboard Your RV. 2nd ed. Gordon Groene. 256p. 1993. pap. 16.95 (*0-07-024901-6*) McGraw.

Living Aboard Your RV: A Guide to the Fulltime Life on Wheels. 2nd ed. Janet Groene & Gordon Groene. LC 92-46578. (Illus.). 256p. 1993. pap. 16.95 (*0-87742-340-7*) Intl Marine.

Living above - Level - Mediocrity see Como Vivir Sobre - Nivel - La Medi

Living above Pain: Experiencing Joy in the Midst of Suffering. Alma Welch. LC 98-60796. (Illus.). 192p. (C). 1998. pap. 12.99 (*1-57921-125-9*, Pub. by WinePress Pub) BookWorld.

Living above Scandal. Randy Bunch. (Book Sermon Ser.). 48p. (Orig.). 1993. pap. 3.95 (*0-940487-11-X*) Jubilee CA.

Living above the Level of Mediocrity. Charles R. Swindoll. 299p. 1989. pap. 10.99 (*0-8499-3177-0*) Word Pub.

Living above the Level of Mediocrity: A Commitement to Excellence. Charles R. Swindoll. 182p. 1997. reprint ed. pap., student ed. 5.95 (*1-57972-089-7*) Insight Living.

Living above Your Circumstances: Real Victory over Disappointment, Depression & Stress. Bob George. 256p. (Orig.). 1996. pap. 7.99 (*1-56507-415-7*) Harvest Hse.

Living Abroad: Personal Adjustment & Personnel Policy in the Overseas Setting. Ingemar Torbiorn. LC 81-14755. (Wiley Series on Studies in Occupational Stress). 199p. reprint ed. pap. 61.70 (*0-7837-0127-6*, 204041000016) Bks Demand.

Living Abundantly. WORD PUBLISHING GROUP NELSON. 1999. pap. 2.99 (*0-7852-0057-6*) Nelson.

Living Abundantly Through Inner Guidance. John McIntosch. 198p. 1998. pap. 16.95 (*1-55212-215-8*, 98-0033, Pub. by Tra3fford) Trafford Pub.

Living Advent: A Daily Companion to the Lectionary, Cycle A. Julia Dugger. LC 94-76026. 64p. 1995. pap. 3.95 (*0-89243-696-4*) Liguori Pubns.

Living Advent: A Daily Companion to the Lectionary, Cycle B. Julia Dugger. LC 94-76025. 64p. 1995. pap. 2.95 (*0-89243-697-2*) Liguori Pubns.

Living Advent (Cycle C) A Daily Companion to the Lectionary. Julia Dugger. LC 94-76238. 64p. (Orig.). 1994. pap. 2.95 (*0-89243-698-0*) Liguori Pubns.

Living Adventures in Science. Henry Thomas & Dana L. Thomas. LC 77-167428. (Essay Index Reprint Ser.). 1977. reprint ed. 23.95 (*0-8369-2573-4*) Ayer.

***Living Adventurously.** Ilee Karger. 1999. pap. 23.00 (*1-85072-159-9*, Pub. by W Sessions) St Mut.

Living after a Death: A Guidebook for the Journey of Bereavement. Mary P. Walsh. 176p. (Orig.). 1995. pap. 12.95 (*1-85607-136-7*, Pub. by Columba Press) Whitecap Bks.

Living after Midnight: A Novella & Stories. Lee K. Abbott. LC 97-51224. 239p. 1998. pap. 16.95 (*0-8142-0792-8*, ABBLIX) Ohio St U Pr.

Living after the Holocaust: Reflections by the Post-War Generation in America. Lucy Y. Steinitz. Ed. by David M. Szonyi. LC 76-8322. (Illus.). 1976. 10.95 (*0-8197-0101-7*) Bloch.

Living Again. George Keithley. (Illus.). 40p. (Orig.). 1997. pap. 7.00 (*0-9657177-0-4*) Bear Star.

Living Again: A Personal Journey for Surviving Spouses. William Wallace. LC 97-51905. 144p. 1998. pap. 12.95 (*1-886110-49-2*) Addax Pubng.

Living Aikido: Form, Training, Essence. Bruce Klickstein. (Illus.). 256p. (Orig.). 1986. pap. 16.95 (*0-938190-85-7*) North Atlantic.

Living Allergy Free: How to Create & Maintain an Allergen- & Irritant-Free Environment. M. Eric Gershwin & Edwin L. Klingelhofer. LC 91-45417. (Illus.). 294p. 1992. 29.50 (*0-89603-225-6*) Humana.

Living Aloft: Human Requirements for Extended Spaceflight, 2 vols., Set. 1994. lib. bdg. 608.75 (*0-8490-6412-0*) Gordon Pr.

Living Alone. Herbert Anderson & Freda Gardner. LC 96-36563. (Family Living in Pastoral Perspective Ser.). 152p. 1997. pap. 14.00 (*0-664-25123-4*) Westminster John Knox.

Living Alone. Robley Wilson, Jr. LC 78-50966. 126p. 1978. pap. 5.00 (*0-931362-00-8*) SDSU Press.

Living Alone. large type ed. Herbert Anderson. LC 98-6247. 1998. 23.95 (*0-7862-1449-X*) Thorndike Pr.

Living Alone & Liking It! Lynn Shahan. 224p. 1988. mass mkt. 4.95 (*0-446-35542-9*, Pub. by Warner Bks) Little.

Living American Poets. Talat S. Halman. (ENG & TUR.). 96p. 1991. 25.00 (*0-89304-073-8*); pap. 10.00 (*0-89304-074-6*) Cross-Cultrl NY.

Living among Cannibals. Thomas H. Harrisson. LC 75-35117. (Illus.). reprint ed. 31.50 (*0-404-14134-X*) AMS Pr.

Living among the Swiss. Michael Wells Glueck. 174p. 1998. write for info. (*0-7541-0489-3*, Pub. by Minerva Pr) Unity Dist.

Living an Idea: Empowerment & the Evolution of an Alternative High School. Edison J. Trickett. (Community & School Psychology Ser.). 238p. 1990. pap. text 17.95 (*0-914797-68-9*) Brookline Bks.

Living Anatomy. Metcalf & Metcalf. 1991. write for info. (*0-8151-5894-7*) Mosby Inc.

Living Anatomy. 2nd ed. Joseph E. Donnelly. LC 89-26982. (Illus.). 248p. (C). 1990. spiral bd. 28.00 (*0-87322-290-3*, BDON0290) Human Kinetics.

Living Anatomy: A Workbook Using Computed Tomography, Magnetic Resonance, & Angiography. Squire & Robert A. Novelline. 1986. 35.00 (*0-8016-4746-0*) Mosby Inc.

Living Anatomy: A Working Atlas Using Computed Tomography, Magnetic Resonance & Angiography Images. Robert A. Novelline & Lucy F. Squire. LC 86-80893. (Illus.). 117p. (Orig.). 1986. pap. text 39.95 (*0-932883-03-6*) Hanley & Belfus.

Living & Active Word: A Way to Preach from the Bible Today. O. C. Edwards. 166p. 1984. 8.20 (*0-8164-0265-5*) Harper SF.

Living & Active Word of God: Studies in Honor of Samuel J. Schultz. Ed. by Morris A. Inch & Ronald Youngblood. LC 82-9376. xiv, 355p. (C). 1983. 39.50 (*0-931464-11-0*) Eisenbrauns.

Living & Believing, 4 bks. Gerald O'Mahony. (C). 1988. write for info. (*0-7855-2582-3*, Pub. by St Paul Pubns) St Mut.

Living & Believing, 4 bks., Bk. 1. Gerald O'Mahony. (C). 1988. 60.00 (*0-85439-163-0*, Pub. by St Paul Pubns) St Mut.

Living & Believing, 4 bks., Bk. 2. Gerald O'Mahony. (C). 1988. 50.00 (*0-85439-174-6*, Pub. by St Paul Pubns) St Mut.

Living & Believing, 4 bks., Bk. 3. Gerald O'Mahony. (C). 1988. 50.00 (*0-85439-175-4*, Pub. by St Paul Pubns) St Mut.

Living & Believing, 4 bks., Bk. 4. Gerald O'Mahony. (C). 1988. 50.00 (*0-85439-176-2*, Pub. by St Paul Pubns) St Mut.

Living & Celebrating the Advent-Christmas Seasons. rev. ed. Edie Staf & Mary Lewis. LC 87-32905. 131p. 1988. spiral bd. 7.95 (*0-8198-4419-5*) Pauline Bks.

Living & Dining in Medieval Paris: The Household of a Fourteenth-Century Knight. Nicole Crossley-Holland. LC 97-156005. (Illus.). 224p. 1997. 55.00 (*0-7083-1368-X*, Pub. by Univ Wales Pr) Paul & Co Pubs.

Living & Dying at Murray Manor. Jaber F. Gubrium. LC 97-23621. (Age Studies). 221p. 1997. pap. text 16.00 (*0-8139-1777-8*) U Pr of Va.

Living (& Dying) in Avalanche Country. John Marshall & Jerry Roberts. (Illus.). 200p. 1998. reprint ed. 29.95 (*0-9632028-0-4*) Simpler Way.

Living & Dying in England, 1100-1540: The Monastic Experience. Barbara F. Harvey. LC 92-21141. (Illus.). 310p. 1995. pap. text 24.00 (*0-19-820431-0*, Clarendon Pr) OUP.

Living & Dying in the U. S. A. Behavioral, Health, & Social Differentials of Adult Mortality. Richard G. Rogers et al. LC 99-61537. (Illus.). 368p. 1999. 69.95 (*0-12-593130-1*) Acad Pr.

Living & Dying Well. Lewis Petrinovich. (Critical Issues in Social Justice Ser.). (Illus.). 374p. 1996. 54.50 (*0-306-45171-9*, Kluwer Plenum) Kluwer Academic.

Living & Dying Well. Lewis Petrinovich. LC 98-29299. (Illus.). 374p. 1998. pap. text 20.00 (*0-262-66142-X*, Bradford Bks) MIT Pr.

Living & Dying with AIDS. P. I. Ahmed. (Illus.). 296p. (C). 1991. 47.50 (*0-306-43851-8*, Plenum Trade) Perseus Pubng.

Living & Dying with Cancer. Ed. by Paul I. Ahmed. LC 80-27582. 343p. reprint ed. pap. 106.40 (*0-608-16261-2*, 205610000049) Bks Demand.

Living & Dying with Grace. Ali I. Talib. 108p. 1996. pap. 16.00 (*0-614-21304-5*, 1457) Kazi Pubns.

Living & Dying with Your IRA & Other Retirement Plans: Estate Planning for People with Large Retirement Plans (After the Taxpayer Relief Act of 1997) Bill S. Wolfkiel. LC 98-72744. (Illus.). vii, 280p. 1998. pap. 79.95 (*0-9665320-0-7*) Guild Pubng CO.

Living & Fighting with the Texas 6th Cavalry. Newton A. Keen. 100p. (Orig.). 1986. 18.50 (*0-942211-87-1*) Olde Soldier Bks.

Living & Fossil Sponges: Notes for a Short Course. W. D. Hartman et al. (Sedimenta Ser.: Vol. VIII). (Illus.). 274p. 1980. 15.00 (*0-932981-07-0*) Univ Miami CSL.

Living & Growing in Later Years. Lloyd H. Ahlem. 112p. (Orig.). 1992. pap. write for info. (*0-9626063-1-6*) Covenant Benevolent Inst.

Living & Growing in the Spirit. Ernest L. Green. 27p. 1978. 1.00 (*0-89814-400-4*) Grace Publns.

Living & Investing in the New Cuba: A Guide to Inexpensive Living & Making Money in the Carribean's Most Beautiful Country. Christopher Howard. LC 99-184820. (Illus.). 260p. 1999. reprint ed. pap. 24.95 (*1-881233-00-6*) Costa Rica Bks.

***Living & Investing in the New Panama: A Guide to Living & Investing in the Panama of the New Millennium.** Christopher Howard. 200p. 1999. pap. 24.95 (*1-881233-12-X*) Costa Rica Bks.

Living & Lasting on Shaky Ground: Earthquake Preparedness for People with Disabilities. rev. ed. Ed. by June I. Kailes. 137p. (C). 1999. pap. text 25.00 (*0-7881-7391-X*) DIANE Pub.

Living & Learning. Gerald Corey et al. LC 96-21357. (Freshman Orientation Ser.). 384p. (C). 1996. 37.95 (*0-534-50500-7*) Wadsworth Pub.

Living & Learning: Essays in Honour of J. F. C. Harrison. Ed. by Malcolm Chase & Ian Dyck. 288p. 1996. 86.95 (*1-85928-110-9*, Pub. by Scolar Pr) Ashgate Pub Co.

Living & Learning for International Interchange: A Sourcebook for Housing Personnel. Richard F. Reiff. 28p. 1986. pap. text 12.00 (*0-912207-13-2*) NAFSA Washington.

Living & Learning Mathematics: Stories & Strategies for Supporting Mathematical Literacy. David J. Whitin et al. LC 89-39556. (Illus.). 176p. (Orig.). (C). (gr. k). 1991. pap. text 19.00 (*0-435-08303-1*, 08303) Heinemann.

Living & Learning with Blind Children: A Guide for Parents & Teachers of Visually Impaired Children. Felicity Harrison & Mary Crow. LC 92-95308. 266p. 1993. text 45.00 (*0-8020-2826-8*); pap. text 17.95 (*0-8020-7700-5*) U of Toronto Pr.

Living & Learning with Nursery Children. Joy Latham. 128p. 1975. pap. 7.99 (*0-8341-0383-4*) Beacon Hill.

Living (And Loving) the Low-Carb Life! Linda Rayburn. 170p. 1999. pap. 21.95 (*0-9670780-0-8*) Darlin Pubns.

Living & Making Money in Costa Rica see Living Overseas Costa Rica

Living & Making Money in Mexico. 2nd rev. ed. Robert Johnston & Christine Pratt. (Living & Making Money Ser.). (Illus.). 253p. 1998. pap. 15.00 (*0-9662421-0-6*) Living Overseas.

Living & Partly Living. Moteane Melamu. 146p. 1999. pap. 12.95 (*0-86543-677-0*) Africa World.

Living & Practical Way to Enjoy Christ see Manera Viva y Practica de Disfrutar a Cristo

Living & Practical Way to Enjoy Christ. Witness Lee. 59p. 1994. pap. 3.75 (*0-87083-775-3*, 07-040-001) Living Stream Ministry.

Living & Praying in Jesus Name see Como Vivir y Orar en el Nombre de Jesus

Living & Praying in Jesus' Name. Dick Eastman & Jack W. Hayford. 240p. 1988. pap. 8.99 (*0-8423-2667-7*) Tyndale Hse.

Living & Praying in Jesus' Name. Jack Hayford & Dick Eastman. 203p. 1999. pap. 8.99 (*0-916847-29-2*) Living Way.

Living & Relating: An Introduction to Phenomenology. Carol S. Becker. (Illus.). 224p. 1992. 48.00 (*0-8039-3902-7*); pap. 23.50 (*0-8039-3903-5*) Sage.

Living & the Dead. Thomas Narcejac. Ed. by Pierre Boileau. 20.95 (*0-8488-0175-X*) Amereon Ltd.

Living & the Dead: A Study of the Symbolic Life of Americans, Vol. 5-- William L. Warner. LC 75-11495. (Yankee City Ser.: Vol. 5). 528p. 1975. reprint ed. lib. bdg. 35.00 (*0-8371-8194-1*, WALD, Greenwood Pr) Greenwood.

Living & the Dead: Robert McNamara & Five Lives of a Lost War. Paul Hendrickson. (Illus.). 427p. 1996. 30.00 (*0-614-20670-7*) Knopf.

Living & the Dead: Robert McNamara & Five Lives of a Lost War. Paul Hendrickson. 448p. 1997. pap. 15.00 (*0-679-78117-X*) Knopf.

Living & the Dead: Robert McNamara & Five Lives of a Lost War. Paul Hendrickson. LC 96-7445. 432p. 1996. 27.50 (*0-679-42761-9*) McKay.

Living & the Dead: The Rise & Fall of the Cult of World War II in Russia. Nina Tumarkin. 256p. 1995. pap. 15.00 (*0-465-04144-2*, Pub. by Basic) HarpC.

Living & Traveling in Mexico. Henry A. Harris. Ed. by Sandra Chatfield. 128p. (Orig.). pap. 12.95 (*1-886084-10-6*) Last Pubng.

Living & Working in America: How to Gain Entry & How to Settle When You Are There. 5th ed. Steve Mills. (Living & Working Abroad Ser.). 272p. 2000. pap. 14.95 (*1-85703-377-9*, Pub. by How To Bks) Midpt Trade.

Living & Working in America: How to Obtain Entry & Settle in Successfully. 4th ed. Steve Mills. (Living & Working Abroad Ser.). 238p. 1997. pap. 19.95 (*1-85703-454-6*, Pub. by How To Bks) Trans-Atl Phila.

An Asterisk (*) at the beginning of an entry indicates that the title is appearing for the first time.

Living & Working in Australia: A Survival Handbook. David Hampshire. (Living & Working Guides Ser.). 512p. 1998. pap. 21.95 (*1-901130-00-2*, Pub. by Survival Books) Seven Hills Bk.

***Living & Working in Australia: Everything You Need to Know for Building a New Life.** 2nd ed. Linda Veltman. 144p. 2000. pap. 14.95 (*1-85703-670-0*, Pub. by How To Bks) Midpt Trade.

Living & Working in Australia: How to Prepare for a Successful Short or Long-Term Stay. 6th ed. Laura Veltman. 250p. 2000. pap. 14.95 (*1-85703-257-8*, Pub. by How To Bks) Midpt Trade.

Living & Working in Britain. 3rd ed. David Hampshire. (Living & Working Guides Ser.). 544p. 1999. pap. 21.95 (*1-901130-50-9*, Pub. by Survival Books) Seven Hills Bk.

Living & Working in Britain: How to Obtain Entry & Settle in Successfully. Christine Hall. (Living & Working Abroad Ser.). 160p. 1996. pap. 19.95 (*1-85703-196-2*, Pub. by How To Bks) Trans-Atl Phila.

Living & Working in Canada. David Hampshire & Janet MacDonald. 500p. 1999. pap. 21.95 (*1-901130-20-7*, Pub. by Survival Books) Seven Hills Bk.

***Living & Working in Canada: A New Life in Canada - All You Need to Know.** Benjamin A. Kranc & Roman. 144p. 2000. pap. 14.95 (*1-85703-553-4*, Pub. by How To Bks) Midpt Trade.

Living & Working in China: How to Obtain Entry & Plan a Successful Stay. Christine Hall. (Living & Working Abroad Ser.). 160p. 1996. pap. 19.95 (*1-85703-419-8*, Pub. by How To Bks) Trans-Atl Phila.

Living & Working in Europe. Anne Fox. 256p. 1996. pap. 32.50 (*0-7487-2582-2*, Pub. by S Thornes Pubs) Trans-Atl Phila.

Living & Working in France. 3rd ed. David Hampshire. 500p. 1999. pap. text 21.95 (*1-901130-55-X*, Amber Books) Survival Books.

Living & Working in France: How to Prepare for a Successful Visit, Be It Short, Long-Term or Forever. Alan Hart. 208p. 2000. pap. 14.95 (*1-85703-439-2*, Pub. by How To Bks) Midpt Trade.

Living & Working in Hong Kong: How to Plan for a Successful Short or Long-Term Stay. Jeremy Gough. (Living & Working Abroad Ser.). 127p. 1996. pap. 19.95 (*1-85703-141-5*, Pub. by How To Bks) Trans-Atl Phila.

Living & Working in Israel: How to Prepare for a Successful Longterm Stay. Ahron Bregman. (Living & Working Abroad Ser.). 128p. 1996. pap. 22.50 (*1-85703-221-7*, Pub. by How To Bks) Trans-Atl Phila.

Living & Working in Italy: Staying in Italy - All You Need to Know. 2nd ed. Amanda Hinton. (Living & Working Abroad Ser.). 160p. 2000. pap. 14.95 (*1-85703-500-3*, Pub. by How To Bks) Midpt Trade.

Living & Working in London. rev. ed. Janet MacDonald. 256p. 1999. pap. 21.95 (*1-901130-11-8*, Pub. by Survival Books) Seven Hills Bk.

***Living & Working in London: All You Need to Know to Enjoy This Capital City.** Joanna Minett. (Living & Working Abroad Ser.). (Illus.). 144p. 2000. pap. 19.95 (*1-85703-556-9*, Pub. by How To Bks) Midpt Trade.

Living & Working in New York: An Introduction to the City for the New Comers. Alsa Chang. 1998. pap. 10.00 (*0-9659141-1-9*) United Pros.

***Living & Working in Portugal: Staying in Portugal - All You Need to Know.** 2nd ed. Sue Tyson-Ward. (Living & Working Abroad Ser.). 144p. 2000. pap. 14.95 (*1-85703-546-1*, Pub. by How To Bks) Midpt Trade.

Living & Working in Saudi Arabia: How to Prepare for a Successful Short or Longterm Stay. Rosalie Rayburn & Kathleen Bush. (Living & Working Abroad Ser.). 158p. 1997. pap. 28.50 (*1-85703-152-0*, Pub. by How To Bks) Trans-Atl Phila.

***Living & Working in South Africa: Survive & Thrive in the New South Africa.** Matthew Seal. 172p. 2000. pap. 14.95 (*1-85703-555-0*, Pub. by How To Bks) Midpt Trade.

Living & Working in Space. Ray Spangenburg & Diane K. Moser. LC 89-1213. (Space Exploration Ser.). 134p. 1989. reprint ed. pap. 41.60 (*0-608-02813-4*, 206388000007) Bks Demand.

Living & Working in Space: A History of Skylab, 2 vols., Set. 1994. lib. bdg. 605.95 (*0-8490-6413-9*) Gordon Pr.

Living & Working in Spain: A Survival Handbook. 2nd ed. David Hampshire. (Living & Working Guides Ser.). 458p. (Orig.). 1998. pap. 21.95 (*0-9519804-2-4*, Pub. by Survival Books) Seven Hills Bk.

Living & Working in Spain: How to Prepare for a Successful Stay, Be It Short, Long-Term, or Forever. 2nd ed. Robert A. Richards. 144p. 2000. pap. 14.95 (*1-85703-278-0*, Pub. by How To Bks) Midpt Trade.

***Living & Working in Switzerland.** 7th ed. David Hampshire. (Living & Working in Ser.). 1999. pap. 21.95 (*1-901130-16-9*) Seven Hills Bk.

Living & Working in Switzerland: A Survival Handbook. 6th ed. David Hampshire. (Living & Working Guides Ser.). 400p. 1998. pap. 21.95 (*0-9519804-8-3*, Pub. by Survival Books) Seven Hills Bk.

Living & Working in the Community. Ed. by Steven J. Friedman & Kenneth G. Terkelsen. (Issues in Community Mental Health Ser.). (C). 1990. pap. text 6.95 (*0-88135-055-9*, Prodist) Watson Pub Intl.

Living & Working in the 21st Century: Exciting Concepts for Making It in the Marketplace of the 21st Century. George Polley. 96p. 1998. pap. 10.95 (*1-893901-01-7*) T & H Pubns.

Living & Working with Bereavement: Guide for Widowed Men & Women. Elsie Palmer & Jill Watt. 129p. (Orig.). 1987. pap. 10.95 (*0-920490-69-7*) Temeron Bks.

***Living & Working with New Biomedical Technologies: Intersections of Inquiry.** Margaret Lock. Ed. by Allan Young & Alberto Cambrosio. (Cambridge Studies in Medical Anthropology: No. 8). (Illus.). 314p. (C). 2000. pap. 22.95 (*0-521-65568-4*) Cambridge U Pr.

***Living & Working with New Biomedical Technologies: Intersections of Inquiry.** Ed. by Margaret Lock et al. (Cambridge Studies in Medical Anthropology: No. 8). (Illus.). 314p. (C). 2000. 59.95 (*0-521-65210-3*) Cambridge U Pr.

Living & Working with Schizophrenia. J. J. Jeffries et al. 164p. 1990. pap. text 13.95 (*0-8020-6781-6*) U of Toronto Pr.

Living & Working with Schizophrenia. Mary V. Seeman. LC 82-246336. 160p. reprint ed. pap. 49.60 (*0-8357-4734-4*, 203765100009) Bks Demand.

Living & Working with the Gods: Studies of Evidence for Private Religion & Its Material Environment in the City of Ostia (100-500 AD) J. T. Bakker. LC 94-132791. 383p. 1992. 100.00 (*90-5063-056-1*, DMAHA, Pub. by Gieben) J Benjamins Pubng Co.

Living Anytime: Prose Poems. Judith W. Steinbergh. LC 87-51334. (Illus.). 95p. 1988. pap. 9.95 (*0-944941-00-1*) Talking Stone Pr.

Living Apart: South Africa under Apartheid. Ian Berry. LC 96-173007. 288p. 1996. 69.95 (*0-7148-3523-4*, Pub. by Phaidon Press) Phaidon Pr.

Living Architecture. Kenneth Bayes. (Rudolf Steiner's Ideas in Practice Ser.). (Illus.). 128p. (Orig.). 1994. pap. 9.95 (*0-88010-380-9*) Anthroposophic.

Living Architecture: A Biography of H. H. Richardson. James F. Ogorman. LC 97-20534. (Illus.). 176p. 1997. 50.00 (*0-684-83618-1*) Simon & Schuster.

***Living Architecture: Frank Lloyd Wright & Taliesin Architects.** John Rattenbury. LC 00-37315. (Illus.). 296p. 2000. boxed set 70.00 (*0-7649-1366-2*, A571) Pomegranate Calif.

Living Arctic: Hunters of the Canadian North. Hugh Brody. LC 90-32419. (Illus.). 270p. 1990. pap. 16.95 (*0-295-97002-2*) U of Wash Pr.

Living Around the World see Cultures of the World

Living Arrangements: Frances Butler, Diane Neumaier, Anton van Dalen. Frances Butler et al. (Illus.). 32p. 1989. pap. 5.00 (*0-930495-07-1*) San Fran Art Inst.

Living Arrangements & Social Networks of Older Adults. Ed. by C. P. Knipscheer et al. 206p. 1996. pap. 22.00 (*90-5383-404-4*, Pub. by VUB Univ Pr) Paul & Co Pubs.

Living Arrangements of Older Persons in Canada: Effects on their Socio-economic Conditions. 116p. 27.00 (*92-1-100779-8*) UN.

Living Arrangements of Women & Their Children in Developing Countries: A Demographic Profile. LC 96-128533. 115p. 25.00 (*92-1-151302-2*) UN.

Living Art of Bonsai: Principles & Techniques of Cultivation & Propagation. Amy Liang. (Illus.). 288p. 1995. pap. 24.95 (*0-8069-8781-2*) Sterling.

Living As a Catholic Today. Francis Colborn. (Catholic Home Library). 128p. 1989. 4.95 (*1-55944-003-1*) Franciscan Comns.

Living As a Lesbian. Cheryl Clarke. LC 86-4648. 96p. (Orig.). 1986. pap. 7.95 (*0-932379-12-5*); lib. bdg. 16.95 (*0-932379-13-3*) Firebrand Bks.

Living As a Trustworthy Woman of God. Priscilla D. Fritz. LC 96-83793. 176p. (Orig.). 1996. pap. 14.95 (*0-9651886-0-4*) Crowne Emerald.

Living As a Winner. Richard H. Stadler. Ed. by William E. Fischer. (Bible Class Course for Young Adults Ser.). (Illus.). 64p. (J). (gr. 9-12). 1985. pap., teacher ed. 7.50 (*0-938272-23-3*, 22-2173) WELS Board.

Living As Equals. Ed. by Paul Barker. (Illus.). 172p. (C). 1997. text 24.95 (*0-19-829205-8*) OUP.

Living as Equals. Ed. by Paul Barker. (Illus.). 176p. 1999. pap. text 16.95 (*0-19-829518-9*) OUP.

Living As God's Beloved: Meeting the Secular & Surviving. Walter H. Krebs. 56p. 1995. pap. 7.95 (*0-7880-0656-8*, Fairway Pr) CSS OH.

Living As God's Chosen People: Colossians. Helmut Harder. LC 86-80675. (Faith & Life Bible Studies). 64p. 1986. pap. 1.95 (*0-87303-107-5*) Faith & Life.

***Living As If Your Life Depended on It! Twelve Gateways to a Life That Works.** Cia Ricco. LC 00-190093. 184p. 2000. pap. 19.95 (*0-9678849-1-8*) Life Cre.

Living at Home. Anthony Giardina. 1990. pap. 5.25 (*0-8222-0682-X*) Dramatists Play.

Living-at-Home Program: Innovations in Service Access & Case Management. Morton D. Bogdonoff et al. LC 91-3870. 328p. 1991. 44.95 (*0-8261-7640-2*) Springer Pub.

***Living at Nature's Pace: Farming & the American Dream.** Gene Logsdon. LC 99-57305. 224p. 2000. pap. 16.95 (*1-890132-56-X*) Chelsea Green Pub.

Living at Night. Mariana Romo-Carmona. LC 97-26929. 300p. (Orig.). 1997. pap. 10.95 (*1-883523-22-2*) Spinsters Ink.

Living at the Boundary: The Collected Works of Laura Perls. Laura P. Perls. 240p. 1991. text 35.00 (*0-939266-15-6*) Gestalt Journal.

Living at the Edge: Explorers, Exploiters & Settlers of the Grand Canyon Region. Michael F. Anderson. Ed. by Sandra Scott & L. Greer Price. LC 97-78140. (Illus.). 184p. 1998. pap. 18.95 (*0-938216-55-4*) GCA.

Living at the Edge of Chaos: Culture, Complexity, Healing & Synchronicity in Postmodern Psychology. Helene Shulman. 256p. 1997. pap. 19.95 (*3-85630-561-0*) Continuum.

Living at the End of the Ages: Apocalyptic Expectation in the Radical Reformation. Walter Klaassen. 162p. (Orig.). (C). 1992. pap. text 24.50 (*0-8191-8507-8*); lib. bdg. 48.00 (*0-8191-8506-X*) U Pr of Amer.

Living at the End of the World. Marina Benjamin. LC 99-221970. (Illus.). 300p. 1998. 29.50 (*0-330-34203-7*, Pub. by Picador) Trans-Atl Phila.

***Living at the End of the World: A Teenager's Survival in the Tunnels of Grand Central Station.** Tina S. Bolnick & Jamie Pastor Bolnick. 288p. 2000. 24.95 (*0-312-20047-1*) St Martin.

***Living at the End of the World: Humanity's Obsession with Its Own Ultimate Demise.** Marina Benjamin. 305p. 1999. pap. 17.95 (*0-330-34204-5*, Pub. by Picador) Trans-Atl Phila.

Living at the Epicenter: The 1995 Morse Poetry Prize. Allison Funk. LC 95-32437. 64p. (Orig.). 1995. pap. text 11.95 (*1-55553-247-0*) NE U Pr.

Living at the Lake: A Complete Guide to Lakefront Living. Mark V. Hoyer et al. (Illus.). 192p. 1998. pap. text. write for info. (*0-916287-29-7*, SP247) Univ Fla Food.

Living at the Movies. Jim Carroll. 100p. 1981. pap. 13.95 (*0-14-042290-0*, Penguin Bks) Viking Penguin.

Living at the Next Level. John C. Maxwell. 128p. 1996. 12.99 (*0-7852-7267-4*, J Thoma Bks) Nelson.

***Living at the Summit: A Life Plan.** Tom Hill et al. 144p. 1999. pap. 19.99 (*0-9671138-4-9*) Images IL.

Living at the Summit: A Novel Approach to an Exceptional Life. Tom Hill et al. 256p. 1999. pap. 11.95 (*0-9667821-3-5*) Goal Coach Pubg.

Living Atlanta: An Oral History of the City, 1914-1948. Clifford M. Kuhn et al. (Illus.). 406p. 1999. reprint ed. text 30.00 (*0-7881-5952-6*) DIANE Pub.

Living Backwards: A Transatlantic Memoir. Carl Dawson. 224p. (C). 1995. 24.95 (*0-8139-1633-X*) U Pr of Va.

Living Banaras: Hindu Religion in Cultural Context. Ed. by Bradley R. Hertel & Cynthia A. Humes. 1998. 36.00 (*81-7304-258-6*) Manohar.

Living Banaras: Hindu Religion in Cultural Context. Ed. by Bradley R. Hertel & Cynthia A. Humes. LC 92-10803. (SUNY Series in Hindu Studies). 320p. (C). 1993. pap. text 21.95 (*0-7914-1332-2*) State U NY Pr.

Living Banaras: Hindu Religion in Cultural Context. Ed. by Bradley R. Hertel & Cynthia A. Humes. LC 92-10803. (SUNY Series in Hindu Studies). 320p. (C). 1993. text 64.50 (*0-7914-1331-4*) State U NY Pr.

***Living Bay: The Underwater World of Monterey Bay.** Lovell Langstroth & Libby Langstroth. LC 00-22014. (Monterey Bay Aquarium Series in Marine Conservation: Vol. 2). (Illus.). 315p. 2000. 60.00 (*0-520-21686-5*) U CA Pr.

***Living Bay: The Underwater World of Monterey Bay.** Lovell Langstroth et al. LC 00-22014. (Monterey Bay Aquarium Series in Marine Conservation : Vol. 2). (Illus.). 315p. 2000. pap. 29.95 (*0-520-22149-4*, Pub. by U CA Pr) Cal Prin Full Svc.

Living Beautiful Life. Alexandra Stoddard. LC 86-3846. (Illus.). 192p. 1988. pap. 14.00 (*0-380-70511-7*, Avon Bks) Morrow Avon.

Living Beautifully Toget. Alexandra Stoddard. 1991. pap. 14.00 (*0-380-70908-2*, Avon Bks) Morrow Avon.

***Living Beauty Detox Program: The Revolutionary Diet for Each Age & Stage of a Woman's Life : Eat Right to Cleanse Yourself of Toxins, Manage Your Hormones, & Bring Out Your Best Looks.** Ann Louise Gittleman & Ann Castro. LC 99-43044. 2000. write for info. (*0-06-251628-0*) Harper SF.

Living Beauty Detox Program: The Revolutionary Diet for Each & Every Season of a Woman's Life. Ann Louise Gittleman. LC 99-43044. 256p. 2000. 24.00 (*0-06-251627-2*) HarpC.

***Living Before God: Deepening Our Sense of the Divine Presence.** Ben Campbell Johnson. LC 99-49159. 150p. 2000. pap. 15.00 (*0-8028-4652-1*) Eerdmans.

Living Behind Bad Memories see Dejando Atras Recuerdos Dolorosos

Living Being "Anthroposophia" Rudolf Grosse. 81p. 1990. pap. 12.95 (*0-919924-28-X*, 1152, Pub. by Steiner Book Centre) Anthroposophic.

Living Beneath Our Dreams. W. Arthur. Ed. by William A. French. 100p. (Orig.). 1988. pap. 5.95 (*0-317-89767-5*) Circadian Pr.

Living Beneath Your Privilege. Darryl P. Griffin. LC 96-110915. 80p. (Orig.). 1995. pap. 7.99 (*1-56043-837-1*, Treasure Hse) Destiny Image.

***Living Better: Every Patient's Guide to Living with Illness.** Carol J. Langenfeld & Douglas E. Langenfeld. 2001. 14.95 (*0-9701545-1-8*) Patient Pr.

Living Better with Arthritis. Arthritis Foundation Staff. (Illus.). (Orig.). 1996. write for info. (*0-912423-11-0*) Arthritis Found.

Living Better with Fibromyalgia. Arthritis Foundation Staff. (Illus.). (Orig.). 1996. pap. write for info. (*0-912423-10-2*) Arthritis Found.

Living Between Danger & Love: The Limits of Choice. Kathleen B. Jones. LC 99-26783. (Illus.). 240p. 2000. 26.00 (*0-8135-2744-9*) Rutgers U Pr.

Living Between Estrogen & Death. large type ed. Barbara Johnson. (Illus.). 259p. 1999. pap. 14.99 (*0-8499-3727-2*) Word Pub.

***Living Between Heaven & Earth: And Other Everyday Miracles.** Jeanne Bohnet. Ed. by Martha Carnahan. (Illus.). 99p. 1999. pap. 18.00 (*0-9665926-0-3*, 1001, Pub. by Rising Phoenix) ACCESS Pubs Network.

Living Between Jobs: Meditations When You're Looking for Work. Harriet E. Crosby. LC 96-22559. 128p. 1996. pap. 9.99 (*0-8066-2753-0*, 9-2753, Augsburg) Augsburg Fortress.

Living Between the Lines. Lucy M. Calkins. LC 90-43146. (Illus.). 315p. (Orig.). (C). 1990. pap. text 26.00 (*0-435-08538-7*, 08538) Heinemann.

Living Between Two Worlds. Joel S. Goldsmith. Ed. by Lorraine Sinkler. LC 96-7937. 140p. 1996. reprint ed. 14.95 (*1-889051-00-4*, I Lvl) Acrpls Bks CO.

Living Between Worlds: Place & Journey in Celtic Spirituality. Philip Sheldrake. 114p. 1995. pap. 9.95 (*1-56101-103-7*) Cowley Pubns.

***Living Beyond Belief: 13 Bible Studies to Help Teenagers Experience God.** Tim Baker & Amy Simpson. LC 99-30359. 1999. 16.99 (*0-7644-2099-2*) Group Pub.

Living Beyond Breast Cancer: A Survivor's Guide for When Treatment Ends & the Rest of Your Life Begins. Marisa Weiss. 1998. pap. 16.00 (*0-8129-3066-5*, Times Bks) Crown Pub Group.

***Living Beyond Breast Cancer: A Survivor's Guide for When Treatment Ends & the Rest of Your Life Begins.** Marisa C. Weiss & Ellen Weiss. 506p. 2000. reprint ed. text 27.00 (*0-7881-9069-5*) DIANE Pub.

Living Beyond Food. Gregory L. Jantz. (Orig.). 1991. pap. 12.95 (*0-9628408-0-7*) Ctr Counsel Hlth Resc.

Living Beyond Loss: Death in the Family. Ed. by Froma Walsh & Monica McGoldrick. 320p. 1995. pap. 21.00 (*0-393-70203-0*, Norton Paperbks) Norton.

***Living Beyond Multiple Sclerosis: A Woman's Guide.** Judith Lynn Nichols. 256p. 2000. pap. 14.95 (*0-89793-293-5*) Hunter Hse.

Living Beyond Our Means: The Coming Economic Catastrophe & What You Can Do about It. 1992. lib. bdg. 96.00 (*0-8490-5388-9*) Gordon Pr.

Living Beyond Our Means: The Extravagance of Biblical Stewardship. Carol Duerksen. (Generation Why: Vol. 2:3). 36p. (YA). (gr. 9-12). 1996. pap. 12.95 (*0-87303-267-5*) Faith & Life.

Living Beyond Success: Balancing the Secular & Spiritual Aspects of Life. George Bockl. 160p. (Orig.). 1993. pap. 10.95 (*0-87516-662-8*) DeVorss.

***Living Beyond the Cycle of Defeat: How to Overcome Self Centeredness.** Don Robbins. LC 99-231254. 252p. 1998. pap. 12.99 (*1-884369-76-6*) McDougal Pubng.

Living Beyond the Daily Grind. Charles R. Swindoll. 1994. 11.99 (*0-88486-095-7*) Arrowood Pr.

Living Beyond the Ordinary, Discovering the Keys to an Abundant Life: A Study of John. William D. Watkins. Ed. by Jack W. Hayford. LC 93-1420. (Spirit-Filled Life Bible Discovery Guide Ser.). 1993. pap. 6.99 (*0-8407-8349-3*) Nelson.

Living Beyond the Ordinary: John see Vida Mas Alla de Lo Ordinario

***Living Beyond Your Lifetime: How to Be Intentional about the Legacy You Leave.** Mike Huckabee. 224p. 2000. 17.99 (*0-8054-2336-2*) Broadman.

Living Beyond Your Losses: The Healing Journey Through Grief. N. Patrick Murray. LC 97-29970. 108p. 1997. pap. 10.95 (*0-8192-1716-6*) Morehouse Pub.

***Living Beyond Yourself: Exploring the Fruit of the Spirit.** Beth Moore. 224p. 1998. pap. text 12.95 (*0-7673-9275-2*, LifeWy Press) LifeWay Christian.

***Living Beyound the Limits.** Franklin Graham. LC 98-11788. 256p. 1998. 19.99 incl. audio (*0-7852-7184-8*) Nelson.

Living Bible. William C. Bower. 229p. 1977. 22.95 (*0-8369-1394-9*) Ayer.

Living Bible: Blessing or Curse. David W. Cloud. 30p. 1991. pap. 3.00 (*1-58318-011-7*, WOL321B) Way of Life.

Living Bible Story Book see Historias de la Biblia Al Dia

Living Bible Storybook see Historias de la Biblia

Living Binge Free: A Personal Guide to Victory over Compulsive Eating. Jane E. Latimer. LC 88-15899. 1991. pap. 11.95 (*1-882109-00-7*) LivingQuest.

Living Biochemistry: Solutions Manual. Ed. by Hall. (C). 1998. pap. text, teacher ed. write for info. (*0-321-40573-0*) Addson-Wesley Educ.

Living Biochemistry: Student's Solutions Manual. Ed. by Hall. (C). 1998. text, student ed. write for info. (*0-321-01524-X*) Addson-Wesley Educ.

Living Biographies of American Statesmen. Henry T. Schnittkind & Thomas D. Schnittkind. LC 78-167412. (Essay Index Reprint Ser.). 1977. reprint ed. 26.95 (*0-8369-2473-8*) Ayer.

Living Biographies of Famous Americans. Henry Thomas & Dana L. Thomas. (Illus.). 307p. 1977. 24.95 (*0-8369-2624-2*) Ayer.

Living Biographies of Famous Rulers. Henry T. Schnittkind & Thomas D. Schnittkind. LC 72-38752. (Essay Index Reprint Ser.). (Illus.). 1977. reprint ed. 26.95 (*0-8369-2671-4*) Ayer.

Living Biographies of Great Philosophers. Henry Thomas & Dana L. Thomas. (Illus.). 335p. 1977. 25.95 (*0-8369-2625-0*) Ayer.

Living Biographies of Great Poets. Henry T. Schnittkind & Thomas D. Schnittkind. LC 79-167415. (Essay Index Reprint Ser.). 1977. reprint ed. 25.95 (*0-8369-2626-9*) Ayer.

Living Boas. Jerry Walls. 288p. 1998. 35.95 (*0-7938-0470-1*) TFH Pubns.

Living Book of Nature. 2nd rev. ed. Omraam M. Aivanhov. (Izvor Collection: Vol. 216). (Illus.). 224p. 1987. pap. 7.95 (*2-85566-396-2*, Pub. by Prosveta) Prosveta USA.

Living Books Library #1: Contains Complete Programs for Little Monster At School, Ruff's Bone. Living Books Staff. 1997. pap. write for info. (*1-57135-332-1*) Rand McNally.

Living Books Library #2: Contains Complete Programs for Harry & the Haunted House, Just Grandma. Living Books, Inc., Staff. 1997. pap. write for info. (*1-57135-334-8*) Rand McNally.

Living Bread. Thomas Merton. 124p. 1994. pap. 45.00 (*0-86012-025-2*, Pub. by Srch Pr) St Mut.

Living Bread: Deeper Healing & Conversion from Visiting with Jesus. 2nd ed. Thomas R. Hyatt. 33p. 1997. reprint ed. pap. 5.00 (*0-9637789-1-9*, 002) T R Hyatt.

Living Bread: Reflections for Eucharistic Prayer. Bernard Camire. 88p. 1998. pap. 4.50 (*0-8198-4485-3*) Pauline Bks.

L

Living Bread, Saving Cup: Readings on the Eucharist. 1987th rev. ed. Ed. by R. Kevin Seasoltz. LC 81-20813. 328p. 1982. pap. 14.95 (*0-8146-1257-1*) Liturgical Pr.

Living Bridges: Memories of an Educator. Alexander M. Dushkin. 320p. 1975. boxed set 39.95 (*0-87855-179-4*) Transaction Pubs.

Living Bridges: The Inhabited Bridge: Past, Present & Future. Ed. by Peter Murray & MaryAnne Stevens. LC 97-170710. (Illus.). 160p. 1997. 55.00 (*3-7913-1734-2*, Pub. by Prestel) te Neues.

Living Buddha: A Comparative Study of Buddha & Yoga. Edmond B. Szekely. (Illus.). 70p. 1977. pap. 5.95 (*0-89564-059-7*) IBS Intl.

Living Buddha: An Interpretive Biography. Daisaku Ikeda. 160p. 1995. pap. text 12.95 (*0-8348-0322-4*) Weatherhill.

Living Buddha, Living Christ. Thich Nhat Hanh. 240p. 1997. pap. 12.00 (*1-57322-568-1*, Riverhd Trade) Berkley Pub.

Living Buddha, Living Christ. Thich Nhat Hanh. 208p. 1995. 20.00 (*1-57322-018-3*, Riverhead Books) Putnam Pub Group.

Living Buddha, Living Christ. Thich Nhat Hahn. 1996. audio 16.00 (*0-671-56256-8*) S&S Audio.

Living Buddha Zen. Lex Hixon. 256p. 1995. pap. 15.95 (*0-943914-75-2*) Larson Pubns.

Living Buddhism. Andrew Powell. LC 95-19685. (Illus.). 200p. 1995. pap. 27.50 (*0-520-20410-7*, Pub. by U CA Pr) Cal Prin Full Svc.

Living Buddhist Masters. Jack Kornfield. 320p. (Orig.). (C). 1993. 18.00 (*955-24-0042-2*, Pub. by Buddhist Pub Soc) Vipassana Res Pubns.

Living Building: Vernacular Environments of South China. Chinese University of Hong Kong, Department of Arc. 1997. pap. text 18.95 (*0-472-50064-3*, Pub. by Chinese Univ) U of Mich Pr.

Living by a Code. (Shorewood Art Programs for Education Ser.). 12p. 1974. teacher ed. 107.00 (*0-88185-051-9*); 143.00 (*0-685-07226-6*) Shorewood Fine Art.

Living by Chance or by Choice: Replacing Choices You Can't Change with Decisions Only You Can Make. Neva Coyle & Zane Anderson. LC 94-38360. 224p. 1995. pap. 8.99 (*1-55661-486-1*) Bethany Hse.

Living by Design: Leslie Cheek & the Arts. Parke Rouse, Jr. LC 85-73016. (Illus.). 197p. 1985. 29.95 (*0-9615670-0-7*) Soc Alu Wm.

Living by Faith. Al Jennings. 12p. (Orig.). 1994. pap. 0.75 (*1-884900-00-3*) Summit City Christian.

Living by Faith. N. Oloniyo. 204p. 1993. pap. 5.95 (*0-88172-201-4*) Believers Bkshelf.

Living by Faith. Stuart Y. Blanch. LC 84-10182. 156p. reprint ed. 48.40 (*0-608-16652-9*, 202753600055) Bks Demand.

Living by Faith: The Lifestyle of the Believer. Keith Hershey. (Christian Life Ser.). 30p. (Orig.). 1992. pap. 1.95 (*0-940487-06-3*) Jubilee CA.

***Living by Fiction.** Annie Dillard. LC 81-47882. 192p. 2000. pap. 12.00 (*0-06-091544-7*, Perennial) HarperTrade.

***Living by Rational Faith: A Freethinker's Choice.** Mohammed Abu-Bakr. LC 99-96361. 92p. 2000. pap. 12.00 (*0-9676815-0-2*) Intl Essay.

***Living by the Book.** Howard G. Hendricks. 2000. pap. 14.99 (*0-8024-9532-X*) Moody.

***Living by the Book, 2 vols.** Howard G. Hendricks. 2000. pap. 24.99 (*0-8024-9539-7*) Moody.

Living by the Book. Howard G. Hendricks & William D. Hendricks. pap. 15.99 (*0-8024-0816-8*, 206) Moody.

Living by the Book: The Joy of Loving & Trusting God's Word. James M. Boice. LC 96-47820. 176p. (Orig.). 1997. pap. 11.99 (*0-8010-5758-2*) Baker Bks.

Living by the Fruit of the Spirit. Don Aycock. LC 99-19009. 1999. pap. 9.99 (*0-8254-2003-2*) Kregel.

Living by the Gospel: Christian Roots of Confidence & Purpose. Klaus E. Bockmuehl. LC 86-27124. 120p. (C). 1986. 17.95 (*0-939443-01-5*) Helmers Howard Pub.

Living by the Moon: A Practical Guide for Choosing the Right Time. Ute York. Tr. by Athene Bengston & Edith Zorn from GER. LC 96-9337. (Illus.). 320p. (Orig.). 1997. pap. 14.95 (*1-885394-15-2*, 94152) Bluestar Communs.

***Living by the Numbers.** George Shaffner. 224p. 2001. pap. 10.95 (*0-345-42645-2*, Ballantine) Ballantine Pub Grp.

Living by the Pen. Cheryl Turner. 224p. (C). 1994. pap. 25.99 (*0-415-11196-X*, B3812) Routledge.

Living by the Pen: Early British Women Writers. Ed. by Dale Spender. (Athene Ser.). 272p. (C). 1992. pap. text 17.95 (*0-8077-6259-8*) Tchrs Coll.

Living by the Pen: Early British Women Writers. Ed. by Dale Spender. (Athene Ser.). 272p. (C). 1992. text 39.00 (*0-8077-6260-1*) Tchrs Coll.

Living by the Power of Faith. Gene R. Cook. 110p. 1991. reprint ed. pap. 8.95 (*0-87579-526-9*) Deseret Bk.

Living by the Rules of the Sea. David M. Bush et al. LC 95-50855. (Living with the Shore Ser.). (Illus.). 208p. 1996. pap. 17.95 (*0-8223-1796-6*); text 49.95 (*0-8223-1801-6*) Duke.

Living by the Spirit. Lorraine Mastrorio. 96p. 1998. pap. 9.95 (*0-88243-223-0*) Gospel Pub.

Living by the Spirit. Marlene Nathan. LC 99-173518. 96p. 1998. pap. 6.50 (*1-57683-084-5*) NavPress.

Living by the Spirit: Study Guide. Lorraine Mastrorio. 93p. 1997. pap., student ed. 4.95 (*0-88243-123-4*) Gospel Pub.

Living by the Sword. Stephen Green. 279p. (Orig.). 1988. 19.95 (*0-915597-60-8*) Amana Bks.

Living by the Word: Selected Writings, 1973-1987. Alice Walker. LC 87-29615. xxi, 196p. 1988. 15.95 (*0-15-152900-0*) Harcourt.

Living by the Word: Selected Writings, 1973-1987. Alice Walker. LC 87-29615. xxi, 196p. 1989. pap. 9.00 (*0-15-652865-7*) Harcourt.

***Living by Water: New Stories of Nature, Animals & Spirit.** 2nd ed. Brenda Peterson. (Illus.). 2000. pap. 13.95 (*0-939165-39-2*) NewSage Press.

Living by Wonder: The Imaginative Life of Childhood. Richard Lewis. LC 97-52573. x, 150 p. 1998. 18.95 (*0-930407-38-5*) Parabola Bks.

Living by Zen. D. T. Suzuki. LC 94-18311. 192p. 1972. pap. 12.95 (*0-87728-194-7*) Weiser.

Living Can Be Hazardous to Your Health. Florian Raymond. 1996. 10.95 (*0-943873-43-6*) Elder Bks.

Living Capsule. Arthur S. Withanage. 176p. (C). 1988. 35.00 (*0-7212-0719-7*, Pub. by Regency Pr GBR) St Mut.

Living Cell. H. Hillman & P. Sartory. 112p. (C). 1991. text 100.00 (*0-906527-01-5*, Pub. by Surrey Beatty & Sons) St Mut.

Living Cell in Four Dimensions. Ed. by Guy Paillotin. LC 91-55209. (AIP Conference Proceedings Ser.: No. 226). 608p. 1991. 105.00 (*0-88318-794-9*) Am Inst Physics.

Living Cells: Structure, Diversity, & Evolution. Jeremy D. Pickett-Heaps & Julianne Pickett-Heaps. (Illus.). 1994. pap., teacher ed. write for info. (*0-87893-653-X*) Sinauer Assocs.

Living Centre of Australia: A Complete Field Guide to the Area. 2nd ed. Alec M. Blombery. (Illus.). 80p. reprint ed. pap. 14.95 (*0-86417-234-6*, Pub. by Kangaroo Pr) Seven Hills Bk.

Living Cheap: The Survival Guide for the 'Nineties. Larry Roth. LC 90-91568. (Illus.). 130p. (Orig.). 1990. pap. 14.95 (*0-9625228-1-3*) Living Cheap.

Living Cheap News: The First Two Years. Larry Roth. LC 93-81070. 104p. (Orig.). 1994. pap. 11.95 (*0-9625228-2-1*) Living Cheap.

***Living Cheaply with Style.** 2nd rev. ed. Ernest Callenbach. 196p. 2000. pap. 11.95 (*1-57951-014-0*, Pub. by Ronin Pub) Publishers Group.

Living Chemistry. 2nd ed. David Ucko. (C). 1986. pap. text, teacher ed. 34.00 (*0-12-705968-7*) Acad Pr.

Living Christ: The Christic Teachings. R. Swinburne Clymer. 58p. 1979. reprint ed. pap. 2.95 (*0-932785-27-1*) Philos Pub.

Living Christianity. Martin E. Palmer. 1993. pap. 11.95 (*1-85230-327-1*, Pub. by Element MA) Penguin Putnam.

Living Christmas Card. Eleanor T. Privette. 32p. 1990. pap. 4.25 (*0-687-22288-5*) Abingdon.

Living Church: A Guide for Revitalization. Donald J. MacNair. (Illus.). 167p. (Orig.). 1980. pap. 5.95 (*0-934688-00-1*) Great Comm Pubns.

Living Churches: A Reconsideration of Their Basis of Life & Leadership. John Williams. 144p. 1975. reprint ed. pap. 5.95 (*0-85364-122-6*) Attic Pr.

Living Cities: Report of the Twentieth Century Fund Task Force on Urban Preservation Policies. 118p. (Orig.). (C). 1985. pap. text 10.00 (*0-87078-167-7*) Century Foundation.

Living City: How America's Cities Are Being Revitalized by Thinking Small in a Big Way. Roberta B. Gratz. LC 94-21414. 448p. (C). 1995. pap. 24.95 (*0-471-14425-8*) Wiley.

Living Classroom: Writing, Reading, & Beyond. David Armington. LC 97-69846. (Illus.). 233p. 1997. pap. 9.00 (*0-935989-83-8*) Natl Assn Child Ed.

***Living Clay.** Priscilla Hoback. LC 00-25215. (Illus.). 104p. 2000. pap. 55.00 (*1-890932-14-0*, Pub. by Sherman Asher Pub) Partners-West.

Living Close to God: Finding His Power in Your Everyday Life. Charles Stanley. 272p. 1999. pap. 35.88 (*0-88486-239-9*, Inspirational Pr) Arrowood Pr.

Living Color: A Writer Paints Her World. Natalie Goldberg. LC 96-43008. 176p. 1997. pap. 16.95 (*0-553-35489-2*) Bantam.

Living Color: Master Lin Yun's Guide to Feng Shui & the Art of Color. Sarah Rossbach. LC 94-10152. (Illus.). 208p. 1994. pap. 18.00 (*1-56836-014-2*) Kodansha.

Living Color: Race & Television in the United States. Ed. by Sasha Torres. LC 97-31459. (Console-ing Passions Ser.). 1998. pap. 17.95 (*0-8223-2195-5*) Duke.

Living Color: Race & Television in the United States. Ed. by Sasha Torres. LC 97-31459. (Console-ing Passions Ser.). (Illus.). 312p. 1998. 49.95 (*0-8223-2178-5*) Duke.

Living Colors: A Designer's Guide to 80 Essential Palettes from Ancient to Modern Times. Margaret Walch & Augustine Hope. LC 94-45289. (Illus.). 160p. 1995. 35.00 (*0-8118-0558-1*) Chronicle Bks.

***Living Community.** Kathleen O'Connell Chesto. LC 99-71458. (F. I. R. E. Ser.). 144p. 1999. pap. 19.95 (*0-7648-0475-8*, Liguori Lifespan) Liguori Pubns.

Living Community: A Permaculture Case Study at Sol y Sombra. Ben Haggard. 160p. (Orig.). 1993. pap. 12.95 (*0-9639546-0-1*) Ctr Study Community.

Living Company. Arie De Geus. LC 96-48384. 224p. 1997. 24.95 (*0-87584-782-X*) Harvard Busn.

***Living Conditions of the Indigenous Populations in American Countries.** Victor G. Garces. (LC History-America-E). 27p. 1999. reprint ed. lib. bdg. 69.00 (*0-7812-4288-6*) Rprt Serv.

Living Consciously: Collected Essays. Jorge Waxemberg. (Illus.). 150p. 1996. pap. 10.95 (*0-9609102-2-0*) CAFH Found Inc.

Living Consciously: The Science of Self. John M. Dorsey & Walter H. Seegers. LC 59-12400. (Illus.). 187p. reprint ed. pap. 58.00 (*0-608-10584-8*, 207120500009) Bks Demand.

Living Consistently: When Life Goes up & Down. J. Allen Blair. LC 94-38138. 112p. 1995. pap. 7.99 (*0-8254-2187-X*) Kregel.

Living Consitution, 1787, 1987, 2187. Ed. by Virginia Geiger & Jeanne M. Stevenson. LC 88-27636. 54p. (Orig.). (C). 1989. pap. text 13.00 (*0-8191-7206-5*) U Pr of Amer.

Living Constitution. annot. ed. Date not set. teacher ed. write for info. (*0-02-822471-X*) Glencoe.

Living Constitution of Fundamental Law? American Constitutionalism in Historical Perspective. Herman Belz. LC 98-11843. 288p. 1998. 58.00 (*0-8476-8642-6*) Rowman.

Living Constitution or Fundamental Law? American Constitutionalism in Historical Perspective. Herman Belz. LC 98-11843. 288p. 1998. pap. 22.95 (*0-8476-8643-4*) Rowman.

Living Contact. Gloria Copeland. LC 97-170884. 131p. (Orig.). 1997. pap. 8.95 (*1-57562-149-5*, 30-0533) K Copeland Pubns.

Living Control Systems: Selected Papers of William T. Powers. William T. Powers. (Illus.). 300p. (Orig.). (C). 1989. reprint ed. pap. text 19.95 (*0-9647121-3-X*) Benchmark CT.

Living Control Systems II: Selected Papers of William T. Powers. William T. Powers. (C). 1992. reprint ed. pap. text 19.95 (*0-9647121-4-8*) Benchmark CT.

***Living Country Blues.** 2000. 29.95 (*0-02-865345-9*, Schirmer Books) Mac Lib Ref.

Living Covenant: The Innovative Spirit in Traditional Judaism. David Hartman. LC 98-10649. 368p. 1998. reprint ed. pap. 18.95 (*1-58023-011-3*) Jewish Lights.

Living Crafts. George B. Hughes. LC 70-156660. (Essay Index Reprints). 1977. reprint ed. 30.95 (*0-8369-2509-2*) Ayer.

Living Creation. Francis Warner. 1985. 13.95 (*0-86140-227-8*, Pub. by Smyth) Dufour.

Living Creatively: How to Discover Your Sources of Originality & Self-Motivation. Adrian Van Kaam. 190p. 1985. reprint ed. pap. text 17.50 (*0-8191-4450-9*) U Pr of Amer.

Living Creatively with Chronic Illness: Transcending the Loss, Pain & Frustration. Eugenie G. Wheeler & Joyce Dace-Lombard. Ed. by Eugene D. Wheeler. LC 89-9250. 240p. (Orig.). 1989. pap. 11.95 (*0-934793-17-4*) Pathfinder CA.

Living Culture in Durham. Ed. by Judy Hogan. (Illus.). 1987. 15.00 (*0-932112-24-2*) Carolina Wren.

Living Dangerously. large type ed. Ranulph Fiennes. 1990. 27.99 (*0-7089-8546-7*, Charnwood) Ulverscroft.

Living Dangerously. large type ed. Katie Forde. 640p. 1996. 27.99 (*0-7089-3498-6*) Ulverscroft.

Living Dangerously. large type ed. Elizabeth Oldfield. 255p. 1992. 11.50 (*0-7505-0317-3*, Pub. by Mgna Lrg Print) Ulverscroft.

Living Dangerously: Multiculturalism & the Politics of Difference. Henry A. Giroux. LC 93-20107. (Counterpoints: Studies in the Postmodern Theory of Education: Vol. 1). XII, 187p. (Orig.). (C). 1993. pap. text 19.95 (*0-8204-1832-3*) P Lang Pubng.

***Living Dangerously: Navigating the Risks of Everyday Life.** John F. Ross. 208p. 2000. pap. text 14.00 (*0-7382-0321-1*) Perseus Pubng.

Living Dangerously: The Earth, Its Resources & the Environment. Heinrich D. Holland & Ulrich Petersen. LC 95-12429. 600p. 1995. pap. text 49.50 (*0-691-03266-1*, Pub. by Princeton U Pr) Cal Prin Full Svc.

Living Dangerously with the Horn. David Kaslow. Ed. by Viola Roth. 160p. 1996. pap. 12.00 (*0-929309-04-9*) Birdalone Bks.

Living Dead. Christopher Pike, pseud. (Spooksville Ser.). (J). (gr. 4-6). 1998. per. 3.99 (*0-671-00269-4*) PB.

Living Dead. Christopher Pike, pseud. (Spooksville Ser.). (J). (gr. 4-6). 1998. 9.09 (*0-606-13797-1*, Pub. by Turtleback) Demco.

Living Dead: A Study of the Vampire in Romantic Literature. James B. Twitchell. LC 79-54290. (Illus.). 232p. (Orig.). (C). 1981. pap. text 16.95 (*0-8223-0789-8*) Duke.

Living Decently: Material Well-Being in Australia. Peter Travers & Susan Richardson. (Illus.). 256p. 1994. pap. text 24.00 (*0-19-553360-7*) OUP.

***Living Deeply Our New Life in Christ: A Wesleyan Spirituality for Today.** Jerry L. Mercer. LC 98-88822. 120p. 2000. pap. 16.95 (*0-88177-275-5*, DR275) Discipleship Res.

Living Deliberately: Experiments in Practical Spirituality. John H. McMurphy. 180p. (Orig.). 1993. pap. 13.95 (*0-9635487-8-6*) Amaranth Pub.

Living Deliberately: The Discovery & Development of Avatar. Harry Palmer. (Illus.). 127p. 1994. text 15.00 (*0-9626874-3-X*) Stars Edge.

Living Democracy in Denmark. Peter Manniche. LC 73-98779. 237p. 1970. reprint ed. lib. bdg. 65.00 (*0-8371-3985-6*, MADD, Greenwood Pr) Greenwood.

Living Desert. Guy Spencer. LC 87-3488. (Let's Take a Trip Ser.). (Illus.). 32p. (J). (gr. 3-6). 1988. lib. bdg. 15.35 (*0-8167-1169-0*) Troll Communs.

Living Desert. Guy Spencer. LC 87-3488. (Let's Take a Trip Ser.). (Illus.). 32p. (J). (gr. 3-6). 1997. pap. 3.95 (*0-8167-1170-4*) Troll Communs.

Living Design: The Daoist Way of Building. C. Thomas Mitchell & Jiangmei Wu. LC 97-39997. (Illus.). 256p. 1998. 49.95 (*0-07-042975-8*) McGraw.

Living Dharma: Teachings of Twelve Buddhist Masters. Jack Kornfield. (Illus.). 336p. 1995. pap. 19.95 (*1-57062-138-1*, Pub. by Shambhala Pubns) Random.

Living "Difference" Lesbian Perspectives on Work & Family Life. Ed. by Gillian A. Dunne. LC 98-38652. 1998. pap. 14.95 (*1-56023-115-7*, Harrington Park) Haworth Pr.

Living "Difference" Lesbian Perspectives on Work & Family Life. Ed. by Gillian A. Dunne. LC 98-38652. 167p. 1998. 39.95 (*0-7890-0537-9*, Harrington Park) Haworth Pr.

Living Dinosaur? In Search of Mokele-mbembe. unabridged ed. Roy P. Mackal. (Illus.). 340p. (YA). (gr. 5 up). 1987. 29.95 (*90-04-08543-2*) Brill Academic Pubs.

Living Discipleship Principles. O. T. Gibson. 136p. (Orig.). 1995. pap. 9.95 (*1-884838-03-0*) Walterick Pubs.

Living Doll. Jane Bradley. LC 94-11244. 202p. 1995. 22.00 (*1-877946-54-0*) Permanent Pr.

Living Doll. Laura A. Shamas. 1990. pap. 3.50 (*0-87129-018-9*, L67) Dramatic Pub.

Living Doubt: Essays Concerning the Epistemology of Charles Sanders Pierce. Guy Debrock. Ed. by Menno Hulswit. LC 94-12528. (Synthese Library: Vol. 243). 336p. (C). 1994. lib. bdg. 140.00 (*0-7923-2898-1*, Pub. by Kluwer Academic) Kluwer Academic.

Living Down the Past: How Europe Can Help Africa Grow. Paul Collier. (Studies in Trade & Development: Vol. 2). 39p. 1998. pap. 13.95 (*0-255-36466-0*) Inst Economic Affairs.

Living Downstream: A Scientist's Personal Investigation of Cancer & the Environment. Sandra Steingraber. LC 98-21955. 384p. 1998. pap. 14.00 (*0-375-70099-4*) Vin Bks.

Living Downstream: An Ecologist Looks at Cancer & the Environment. Sandra Steingraber. LC 97-8164. 1997. 24.00 (*0-201-48303-3*) Addison-Wesley.

Living Downstream: An Ecologist Looks at Cancer & the Environment. Sandra Steingraber. 1997. 24.00 (*0-614-28200-4*) Addison-Wesley.

Living Downtown: The History of Residential Hotels in the United States. Paul Groth. LC 93-39896. 423p. 1994. 45.00 (*0-520-06876-9*, Pub. by U CA Pr) Cal Prin Full Svc.

***Living Downtown: The History of Residential Hotels in the United States.** Paul Groth. 400p. 1999. pap. 22.50 (*0-520-21954-6*, Pub. by U CA Pr) Cal Prin Full Svc.

Living Dragons: A Natural History of the World's Monitor Lizards. Rodney Steel. LC 96-84557. (Illus.). 160p. 1996. 39.50 (*0-88359-040-9*, RCB-0409H, Pub. by R Curtis Pubng) Chelsea Green Pub.

Living Dramatists: Pinero, Ibsen & D'annunzio. Oscar Herrmann. 1977. lib. bdg. 59.95 (*0-8490-2176-6*) Gordon Pr.

Living Dreamer: The Art of Doing It. B. Angelson. Ed. by Carol Lindahl. LC 96-78124. (Illus.). 184p. (Orig.). 1996. pap. 17.95 (*0-9651590-3-5*) Infnty Pub.

Living Each Day. Abraham J. Twerski. (ArtScroll Ser.). 410p. 1988. 21.99 (*0-89906-560-0*); pap. 17.99 (*0-89906-561-9*) Mesorah Pubns.

Living Each Day by the Power of Faith: Thirty Meditations to Deepen Your Trust in God. rev. ed. Barbara S. Ryan. 144p. 1997. pap. 8.95 (*1-878718-39-8*, Resurrection Pr) Catholic Bk Pub.

Living Each Day with Jesus. Nelson Word Publishing Group Staff. 1999. pap. 0.99 (*0-7852-0056-8*) Nelson.

Living Each Week. Abraham J. Twerski. 1992. 21.99 (*0-89906-577-5*) Mesorah Pubns.

Living Each Week. Abraham J. Twrski. 1992. pap. 17.99 (*0-89906-578-3*) Mesorah Pubns.

Living Earth. Eleonore Schmid. LC 94-17263. (Illus.). 32p. (J). (gr. k-3). 1994. 15.95 (*1-55858-298-3*, Pub. by North-South Bks NYC); lib. bdg. 14.88 (*1-55858-299-1*, Pub. by North-South Bks NYC) Chronicle Bks.

***Living Earth.** Eleonore Schmid. LC 94-17263. (Illus.). 32p. (J). (gr. k-3). 2000. pap. 6.95 (*0-7358-1315-9*, Pub. by North-South Bks NYC) Chronicle Bks.

Living Earth: A Chronology of Structural & Life Development on Planet Earth from Precambrian to Cenozoic Eras. Hughes Henshaw Publications Staff. 1998. 20.00 (*0-9617223-6-3*) Hughes Henshaw Pubs.

Living Earth: A Short History of Life & Its Home. Evan G. Nisbet. (Illus.). 238p. (C). 1992. pap. text 25.00 (*0-04-445856-8*, A8183) Routledge.

Living Earth: The Coevolution of the Planet & Life. Jonathon S. Erickson. (Discovering Earth Science Ser.). (Illus.). 212p. 1989. 22.95 (*0-8306-8942-7*, 3142); pap. 14.95 (*0-8306-3142-9*, 3142) McGraw-Hill Prof.

Living Easy in Mexico: A New Guide to Traveling & Living in Marvelous Mexico. rev. ed. Hayes C. Schlundt. (Illus.). 224p. 1996. reprint ed. pap. 12.95 (*0-914924-4-9*) United Res CA.

Living Echoes: Meditations by Retired Lutheran Pastors. Ed. by Howard J. Sortland. LC 97-75651. (Illus.). 250p. 1997. pap. 12.95 (*1-891428-50-0*) Lutheran Bible.

Living Economy. Ed. by Paul Ekins. 400p. (C). 1986. pap. 27.99 (*0-415-03937-1*) Routledge.

Living Economy: A New Economics in the Making. Paul Ekins. 320p. 1987. pap. 17.95 (*0-7102-0946-0*, 09460, Routledge Thoemms) Routledge.

Living Education: Essays in Honor of John Tomlinson. Ed. by Peter Mortimore & Viv Little. 288p. 1997. pap. 49.95 (*1-85396-348-8*, Pub. by P Chapman) Taylor & Francis.

Living End. Stanley Elkin. 160p. 1996. pap. 12.00 (*0-380-72897-4*, Avon Bks) Morrow Avon.

***Living Energy Universe: A Fundament Discovery Transforms Science & Medicine.** Gary E.R. Schwartz. 320p. 1999. 21.95 (*1-57174-170-4*) Hampton Roads Pub Co.

Living English for Spanish Speakers: Conversational Manual. rev. ed. Kathleen Ossip. (Complete Living Language Course Ser.). (ENG & SPA.). 1993. pap. 6.00 (*0-517-59046-8*) Liv Lang.

Living Ethically, Acting Politically. Melissa A. Orlie. LC 97-14935. 248p. 1997. pap. 16.95 (*0-8014-8472-3*); text 39.95 (*0-8014-3355-X*) Cornell U Pr.

Living Ethically in Christ: Is Christian Ethics Unique? Mark C. Miller. LC 93-48502. (American University Studies: Series VII, Vol. 173). VIII, 311p. (C). 1999. text 51.95 (*0-8204-2386-6*) P Lang Pubng.

Living Ethics: Developing Values in Mass Communication. Michael J. Bugeja. (C). 1995. pap. text, teacher ed. write for info. (*0-205-18436-7*, H8436-1) Allyn.

An Asterisk (*) at the beginning of an entry indicates that the title is appearing for the first time.

Living Ethics: Developing Values in Mass Communication. Michael J. Bugeja. LC 95-11987. 503p. 1995. pap. text 41.00 (*0-205-17323-3*) Allyn.
Living Europe: Exploring the Continent's Natural Boundaries. Nick Upton. 1998. 32.50 (*0-7522-1100-5*) Boxtree.
Living Every Day of Your Life: A Psychiatrists's Treasury of Wise Quotes. Richard A. Gardner. 1994. pap. 7.50 (*0-933812-35-3*) Creative Therapeutics.
***Living Every Single Moment.** Angela Payne. LC 99-50937. 2000. 9.99 (*1-56309-765-6*, New Hope) Womans Mission Union.
Living Evil. Ruby J. Jensen. 480p. 1993. mass mkt. 4.50 (*0-8217-4261-2*, Zebra Kensgtn) Kensgtn Pub Corp.
Living Eye. Jean Starobinski. Tr. by Arthur Goldhammer from FRE. LC 88-29398. (Studies in Comparative Literature: No. 40). (Illus.). 264p. 1989. 43.50 (*0-674-53664-9*) HUP.
Living Faith. Jimmy Carter. 1996. 23.00 (*0-8129-2736-2*, Times Bks) Crown Pub Group.
Living Faith. Jimmy Carter. LC 99-204724. 1998. pap. 13.00 (*0-8129-3034-7*, Times Bks) Crown Pub Group.
Living Faith. large type ed. Jimmy Carter. 1996. pap. 24.00 (*0-679-75902-6*) Random Hse Lrg Prnt.
Living Faith: A Study in the Book of James. R. A. Desbonnes. 70p. (Orig.). 1996. pap. write for info. (*1-57502-155-2*) Morris Pubng.
Living Faith: An Historical Study of Quaker Beliefs. Wilmer Cooper. LC 89-28708. 217p. 1990. pap. 14.00 (*0-944350-12-7*) Friends United.
Living Faith: An Introduction to Theology. 2nd ed. Eileen P. Flynn & Gloria B. Thomas. LC 88-62589. 440p. (Orig.). (C). 1995. pap. 18.95 (*1-55612-217-9*) Sheed & Ward WI.
Living Faith: Studies in James. David Rinden. 75p. (Orig.). 1993. pap. 4.95 (*0-943167-25-6*) Faith & Fellowship Pr.
***Living Faith Bible.** Faith Living Staff. 2000. 44.99 (*0-8423-5219-8*) Tyndale Hse.
***Living Faith Bible.** Living Faith Staff. 2000. 26.99 (*0-8423-7358-6*); 44.99 (*0-8423-7359-4*); pap. 19.99 (*0-8423-7357-8*) Tyndale Hse.
***Living Faith Day by Day: How the Sacred Rules of Monastic Traditions Can Help You Live Spiritually in the Modern World.** Debra K. Farrington. LC 00-36719. 288p. 2000. pap. 12.00 (*0-399-52620-X*, Perigee Bks) Berkley Pub.
***Living Faithfully in a Fragmented World: Lessons the the Church from MacIntyre's "After Vir"** Jonathan R. Wilson. LC 97-32871. 96p. 1998. pap. 9.00 (*1-56338-240-7*) TPI PA.
Living Faiths in South Africa. Ed. by Martin Prozesky & John De Gruchy. LC 95-16661. 256p. 1995. text 45.00 (*0-312-12776-6*) St Martin.
Living Fear Free: Overcoming Agoraphobia - The Anxiety & Panic Syndrome. Melvin D. Green. LC 85-80401. 173p. 1985. text 16.95 (*0-939637-00-6*) Fear Free.
Living Fellowship. Richard C. Halverson. 195p. 1986. pap. 5.95 (*0-310-25781-6*, 6873P) Zondervan.
Living Female Writers of the South. Ed. by Mary T. Tardy. 1979. reprint ed. 88.00 (*1-55888-183-2*) Omnigraphics Inc.
Living Feminism: The Impact of the Women's Movement on Three Generations of Australian Women. Chilla Bulbeck. LC 97-26347. (Reshaping Australian Institutions Ser.: Vol. 5). 284p. 1997. pap. text 24.95 (*0-521-46596-6*) Cambridge U Pr.
Living Feminism: The Impact of the Women's Movement on Three Generations of Australian Women. Chilla Bulbeck. LC 97-26347. (Reshaping Australian Institutions Ser.: Vol. 5). (Illus.). 303p. (C). 1997. text 69.95 (*0-521-46042-5*) Cambridge U Pr.
Living Fences. Storey Publishing Staff. 1997. pap. 19.95 (*0-676-57068-2*) Random.
Living Fences: A Gardener's Guide to Hedges, Vines & Espaliers. Ogden Tanner. (Illus.). 128p. 1995. pap. 19.95 (*1-881527-68-9*, Chapters Bks) HM.
Living Fields: Our Agricultural Heritage. Jack R. Harlan. (Illus.). 287p. (C). 1995. text 54.95 (*0-521-40112-7*) Cambridge U Pr.
Living Fields: Our Agricultural Heritage. Jack R. Harlan. (Illus.). 287p. (C). 1998. pap. text 19.95 (*0-521-64992-7*) Cambridge U Pr.
Living Fire: Selected Poetry of Leo E. O'Neil, 1973-1997. Leo E. O'Neil. Ed. by Ray Gamachi. (Illus.). 240p. 1998. pap. 14.95 (*0-9646061-2-7*) Wayfarer Pr.
Living Fire & God's Law of Life. Hilton Hotema. 121p. 1993. reprint ed. spiral bd. 13.00 (*0-7873-0444-1*) Hlth Research.
Living Fit. Francis J. Nagle et al. 300p. (C). 1988. pap. text 23.75 (*0-8053-8180-5*) Benjamin-Cummings.
Living Flame. Barbara Harned Dorsett. Ed. by Imani Kenyatta. LC 98-66322. 168p. 1998. 13.95 (*1-886580-75-8*) Pinnacle-Syatt.
Living Foods for Optimum Health: A Highly Effective Program to Remove Toxins & Restore Your Body to Vibrant Health. Theresa F. DiGeronimo & Brian R. Clement. (Illus.). 288p. 1996. boxed set 22.95 (*0-7615-0258-0*) Prima Pub.
Living Foods for Optimum Health: Staying Healthy in an Unhealthy World. Brian Clement & Theresa Foy Digeronimo. LC 98-28347. (Illus.). 288p. 1998. per. 15.95 (*0-7615-1448-1*) Prima Pub.
Living for Change: An Autobiography. Grace L. Boggs. LC 97-27296. 1998. pap. 18.95 (*0-8166-2955-2*) U of Minn Pr.
Living for Change: An Autobiography. Grace L. Boggs. LC 97-27296. 1998. 47.95 (*0-8166-2954-4*) U of Minn Pr.
Living for Christ. rev. ed. William A. Kramer. LC 72-96585. 94p. 1973. 3.99 (*0-570-03157-5*, 12-2542) Concordia.
***Living for Christ in the End Times.** David R. Reagan. 2000. pap. 10.99 (*0-89221-499-6*) New Leaf.
Living for Christ (One & Two Peter) Michael Bentley. 1990. pap. 11.99 (*0-85234-279-9*, Pub. by Evangelical Pr) P & R Pubng.
Living for Eternity. Bennie Bristow & Gwen Bristow. 1991. pap. 7.75 (*0-89137-451-5*) Quality Pubns.
Living for God. (Precious Moments Ser.). (J). 11.99 (*1-55976-181-4*) CEF Press.
***Living for God.** Charles Grandison Finney. LC 99-88902. Orig. Title: You Can Be Holy. 2000. pap. 9.99 (*0-88368-592-2*) Whitaker Hse.
Living for God. J. Grant. 1996. pap. 9.99 (*0-946351-43-0*, Pub. by John Ritchie) Loizeaux.
Living for God: Daily Bread. (Illus.). (J). (gr. k-4). 1977. pap. 6.99 (*1-55976-325-6*) CEF Press.
Living for the City. Jervey Tervalon. 190p. 1998. pap. 13.00 (*1-888277-08-4*) Incommcdo San Diego.
Living for Tomorrow: A Positive Approach to the Treatment of Cervical Cancer. Margaret Wilson. 272p. (Orig.). 1994. pap. 18.95 (*0-85572-227-4*, Pub. by Hill Content Pubng) Seven Hills Bk.
Living Forest. Reader's Digest Editors. LC 99-10119. (Earth, Its Wonders, Its Secrets Ser.). 1998. write for info. (*0-7621-0137-7*) RD Assn.
***Living Forgiven: An In-Depth Study of Forgiveness.** Craig A. Nelson. 2000. pap. 11.99 (*0-939513-23-4*) Joy Pub SJC.
Living Fossil: The Story of the Coelacanth. Keith S. Thomson. 256p. 1992. pap. 9.95 (*0-393-30868-5*) Norton.
Living Fossils. Ed. by Niles Eldridge & S. M. Stanley. (Casebooks in Earth Sciences Ser.). (Illus.). 305p. 1984. 119.95 (*0-387-90957-5*) Spr-Verlag.
Living Fossils. Joyce Pope. LC 91-13998. (Curious Creatures Ser.). (Illus.). 48p. (J). 1992. lib. bdg. 5.00 (*0-8114-3151-7*) Raintree Steck-V.
Living Free see **In Their Shoes**
Living Free. Neva Coyle. LC 81-3811. 128p. 1981. pap. 6.99 (*0-87123-346-0*) Bethany Hse.
Living Free: A Guide to Forming & Conducting a Recovery Ministry. Ron Halvorson & Valerie Deilgat. (Illus.). 83p. (Orig.). 1992. pap. 5.95 (*0-941405-16-8*) RPI Pubng.
***Living Free: Discovering God's Path to Freedom.** Jimmy Ray Lee & Dan Strickland. 90p. 1999. pap., wbk. ed. 12.99 (*1-58119-043-3*); teacher ed. 299.95 incl. VHS (*1-58119-041-7*) T P Min.
***Living Free: Discovering God's Path to Freedom.** Jimmy Ray Lee & Dan Strickland. 98p. 1999. pap. 15.99 (*1-58119-042-5*) T P Min.
Living Free in Christ see **Viviendo Libre en Cristo**
Living Freight. Dayle C. Gaetz. LC 98-179748. 172p. (YA). (gr. 5 up). 1998. pap. 6.95 (*1-896184-32-4*) Roussan Pubs.
Living Freshwater Protozoa. David J. Patterson. 1992. 88.00 (*0-8493-7735-8*, QL366) CRC Pr.
Living from Lobsters. Robert Stewart. 1978. 55.00 (*0-7855-6935-9*) St Mut.
***Living from the Center: Spirituality in an Age of Consumerism.** Jay McDaniel. 2000. pap. 24.99 (*0-8272-2130-4*) Chalice Pr.
Living from the Heart: Heart Rhythm Meditation for Energy, Clarity, Peace, Joy & Inner Power. Puran Khan Bair. LC 97-49858. 304p. 1998. pap. 14.00 (*0-609-80313-1*) Crown.
Living from Your Soul. Karen Katafiasz. LC 97-72947. (Illus.). 88p. 1997. pap. 4.95 (*0-87029-303-6*, 20146) Abbey.
Living Function of Sleep, Life & Aging. Betty J. Y. Ho. LC 79-13810. (System of Government in the Living Body Ser.). (Illus.). 56p. 1967. pap. 12.00 (*0-9600148-0-2*) Juvenescent.
Living Gita: The Complete Bhagavad Gita. Sri S. Satchidananda. 352p. 1995. pap. 13.95 (*0-8050-1400-4*, Owl) H Holt & Co.
Living Gita: The Complete Bhagavad Gita - A Commentary for Modern Readers. Sri Swami Satchidananda. LC 84-27861. 352p. (Orig.). 1997. reprint ed. pap. 14.95 (*0-932040-27-6*) Integral Yoga Pubns.
Living, Glimmering, Lying. Botho Strauss. Tr. by Roslyn Theobald from GER. LC 99-26414. 176p. 1999. 26.95 (*0-8101-1283-3*, Hydra Bks) Northwestern U Pr.
Living God see **Living God**
Living God. Romano Guardini. LC 96-50905. Orig. Title: Vom Lebendigen Gott. 160p. (Orig.). 1997. reprint ed. pap. 11.95 (*0-918477-49-2*) Sophia Inst Pr.
Living God: A Catechism for the Christian Faith, 2 vols. M. Olivier Clement. Tr. by Olga Dunlap from FRE. LC 89-6291. Tr. of Dieu est Vivant. 445p. (Orig.). 1989. pap. 26.95 (*0-88141-040-3*) St Vladimirs.
Living God: Basal Forms of Personal Religion. Nathan Soderblom. LC 77-27196. (Gifford Lectures: 1931). reprint ed. 49.50 (*0-404-60485-4*) AMS Pr.
Living God: Readings in Christian Theology. Ed. by Millard Erickson. 513p. (C). 1995. reprint ed. ring bd. 25.95 (*1-57383-050-X*) Regent College.
***Living God: Readings in Christian Theology, Vol. 1.** Millard J. Erickson. 512p. 1999. pap. 40.00 (*1-57910-272-7*) Wipf & Stock.
Living God: Schleiermacher's Theological Appropriation of Spinoza. Julia A. Lamm. 1996. 42.50 (*0-271-01540-3*) Pa St U Pr.
Living God Vol. 1: Systematic Theology. Thomas C. Oden. LC 85-45720. 448p. 1992. reprint ed. pap. 26.00 (*0-06-066363-4*, Pub. by Harper SF) HarpC.
Living God Blues. Lee Lozowick. 168p. 1984. pap. 9.95 (*0-934252-09-2*, Pub. by Hohm Pr) SCB Distributors.
Living Goddess: Reclaiming the Tradition of the Mother of the Universe. Linda Johnson. LC 98-54147. 185p. 1999. 20.00 (*0-936663-23-5*) Yes Intl.
Living Goddesses. Marija Gimbutas & Miriam R. Dexter. LC 98-46634. 306p. 1999. 35.00 (*0-520-21393-9*, Pub. by U CA Pr) Cal Prin Full Svc.
Living God's Love: Being a Source of Refreshment in a Dry World. Douglas Cooper. 158p. 1995. pap. 5.97 (*0-8163-1260-5*) Pacific Pr Pub Assn.
Living God's Way. Jessie Schutt. 191p. pap. 16.45 (*1-56212-061-1*) CRC Pubns.
Living God's Way: Nourishment for New Believers. Arthur Wallis. 111p. (Orig.). 1988. reprint ed. pap. 5.95 (*0-939159-07-4*) Cityhill Pub.
Living God's Word. Edwin A. Jiede. 64p. 1968. pap., wbk. ed. 3.25 (*0-570-03505-8*, 14-1262) Concordia.
Living God's Word: Practical Lessons for Applying Scripture to Life. Waylon B. Moore. 96p. 1997. pap. text 7.95 (*0-7673-2604-0*, LifeWy Press) LifeWay Christian.
Living God's Word: Reflections on the Weekly Gospels - Year A. David Knight. 288p. 1998. pap. 10.95 (*0-86716-306-2*) St Anthony Mess Pr.
Living God's Word: Reflections on the Weekly Gospels - Year B. David Knight. 288p. 1999. pap. text 14.95 (*0-86716-307-0*) St Anthony Mess Pr.
***Living God's Word: Reflections on the Weekly Gospels - Year C.** David Knight. 2000. pap. 14.95 (*0-86716-308-9*) St Anthony Mess Pr.
Living Great: Style Expert & Television Star Linda Dano Shows You How to Bring Style Home with Her Easy, Affordable Decorating Ideas & Techniques. Linda Dano & Anne Kyle. 224p. 1999. pap. 16.95 (*0-399-52484-3*, Perigee Bks) Berkley Pub.
Living Greek Theatre: A Handbook of Classical Performance & Modern Production. J. Michael Walton. LC 87-267. 445p. 1987. lib. bdg. 75.00 (*0-313-24597-5*, WLG/, Greenwood Pr) Greenwood.
***Living Greyhawk Gazetteer.** Erik Mona. 2000. pap. text 26.95 (*0-7869-1743-1*) Wizards Coast.
Living Guide Book. Alfred Henry. 608p. (Orig.). 1990. pap. 14.75 (*0-685-33552-6*) Forum Hall.
Living Guidebook. Alfred Henry. 608p. (Orig.). 1990. pap. 14.75 (*0-9626594-0-1*) Forum Hall.
Living Gut. W. N. Ewing & D. J. Cole. 220p. 1999. pap. 100.00 (*1-899043-00-4*, Pub. by FiveM Enterprises) St Mut.
Living Happily Ever After: Couples Talk about Lasting Love. Laurie Wagner & David Collier. (Illus.). 160p. 1996. pap. 19.95 (*0-8118-0889-0*) Chronicle Bks.
Living Happily Ever After: Couples Talk about Lasting Love. Laurie Wagner et al. 1996. 35.00 (*0-8118-0865-3*) Chronicle Bks.
Living Happily Ever Laughter: A Guide to Thinking Funny in a Fast Paced World. Kathy Brown. Ed. by Milton E. Adams. LC 99-60409. (Illus.). 128p. 1997. pap. 7.95 (*1-890676-00-4*) Beavers Pond.
Living Healthy in a Toxic World: Simple Steps to Protect You & Your Family from Everyday Chemicals, Poisons & Pollution. David Steinman & Michael Wisner. LC 95-43241. 208p. (Orig.). 1996. pap. 12.00 (*0-399-52206-9*, Perigee Bks) Berkley Pub.
***Living Healthy W/ Hepatitis C.** Harriet A. Washington. 288p. 2000. mass mkt. 6.50 (*0-440-23608-8*) Dell.
Living Heart Cookbook. Antonio M. Gotto, Jr. 352p. 1994. pap. 14.00 (*0-671-88388-7*, Fireside) S&S Trade Pap.
Living Heart Diet. Michael E. DeBakey et al. LC 83-10933. (Illus.). 423p. reprint ed. pap. 131.20 (*0-608-09740-3*, 206990300007) Bks Demand.
Living Heart Diet: Professional Edition. Michael E. DeBakey et al. 424p. 1984. text 33.50 (*0-89004-672-7*) Lppncott W & W.
Living High: An Unconventional Autobiography. June Burn. LC 92-70139. (Illus.). 292p. 1992. pap. 15.95 (*0-9634562-0-2*) Griffin Bay Bk.
Living High: Daily Marijuana Use among Adults. Herbert Hendin et al. LC 86-27634. 183p. 1987. 34.95 (*0-89885-329-X*, Kluwer Acad Hman Sci) Kluwer Academic.
Living High & Letting Die: Our Illusion of Innocence. Peter Unger. (Illus.). 200p. 1996. pap. 16.95 (*0-19-510859-0*); text 45.00 (*0-19-507589-7*) OUP.
Living Himalayas, Vol. 1. R. K. Gupta. 400p. 1983. 69.95 (*0-318-37004-2*) Asia Bk Corp.
Living Himalayas: Aspects of Environment & Resource Ecology of Garhwal, Vol. 1. R. K. Gupta. 379p. 1983. 59.00 (*1-55528-033-1*, Pub. by Today Tomorrow) Scholarly Pubns.
Living Himalayas Vol. 2: Aspects of Plant Explorations & Phytogeography. R. K. Gupta. (Illus.). 1989. 135.00 (*1-55528-169-9*, Pub. by Today Tomorrow) Scholarly Pubns.
Living Hints to Health. Daniel G. Lipman. LC 97-5733. 96p. 1997. pap. 10.95 (*965-229-170-6*) Gefen Bks.
Living Hirschian Legacy: A Tribute to the Legacy of Samson Raphael Hirsch on the 100th Anniversary of His Passing. 1989. 19.95 (*0-87306-980-3*) Feldheim.
Living History, 4 Vols. Megan O'Hara. 1999. 84.00 (*1-56065-823-1*) Capstone Pr.
Living History: A Memoir. Chaim Herzog. LC 96-14358. 464p. 1996. 30.00 (*0-679-43478-X*) Pantheon.
Living History: Drawing on the Past. Cathy Johnson. (Illus.). 150p. (Orig.). 1994. pap. 11.95 (*0-9638158-0-6*) Graphics-Fine Art.
Living History in the Classroom: Integrative Arts Activities for Making Social Studies Meaningful. Douglas Selwyn. LC 93-8674. 240p. 1993. 32.00 (*0-913705-90-X*) Zephyr Pr AZ.
Living History of the Ozarks. Phyllis Rossiter. LC 92-5309. (Illus.). 488p. 1992. pap. 19.95 (*0-88289-801-9*) Pelican.
Living History Reader Vol. 1: Museums. Ed. by Jay Anderson. LC 91-14576. (American Association for State & Local History Book Ser.). (Illus.). 240p. 1991. reprint ed. pap. 25.95 (*0-942063-13-9*) AltaMira Pr.
Living Homes: Thomas J. Elpel's Field Guide to Integrated Design & Construction. Thomas J. Elpel. (Illus.). 85p. 1998. 14.00 (*1-892784-03-3*) HOPS Pr.
***Living Homes: Thomas J. Elpel's Field Guides to Integrated Design & Construction.** 2nd rev. ed. Thomas J. Elpel. (Illus.). 117p. 1999. spiral bd. 15.00 (*1-892784-06-8*) HOPS Pr.
Living Hope: A Study of the New Testament Theme of Birth from Above. William Orr & William Guy. LC 88-34841. 208p. (Orig.). 1989. pap. 10.95 (*0-86534-132-X*) Sunstone Pr.
Living Hope: Baptism & the Cost of Christian Witness. Robin Maas. LC 97-69412. 96p. 1999. pap. 15.95 (*0-88177-238-0*, DR238) Discipleship Res.
Living Hope: The Comfort & Assurance That Come From Knowing God Cares For You. David Haney. LC 98-44038. (Illus.). 240p. 1999. pap. 11.99 (*1-58134-040-0*) Crossway Bks.
Living Hothouse. Marion Halligan. 283p. (Orig.). 1989. pap. 16.95 (*0-7022-2140-6*, Pub. by Univ Queensland Pr) Intl Spec Bk.
Living House. Nigel Hester. LC 90-32531. (Watching Nature Ser.). (Illus.). 32p. (J). (gr. 5-7). 1991. lib. bdg. 20.00 (*0-531-14120-9*) Watts.
Living House: An Anthropology of Architecture in South-East Asia. Roxana Waterson. 1998. pap. text 35.00 (*0-8230-2835-6*) Watsn-Guptill.
***Living Human Display.** Jim Drobnick. 1999. pap. text 25.00 (*0-226-16475-6*); lib. bdg. 70.00 (*0-226-16474-8*) U Ch Pr.
Living Human Document: Re-Visioning Pastoral Counseling in a Hermeneutical Mode. Charles V. Gerkin. LC 83-14972. 224p. 1984. pap. 15.95 (*0-687-22372-5*) Abingdon.
Living Hymn Stories. rev. ed. Wilbur S. Konkel. 120p. 1994. reprint ed. pap. 6.99 (*0-88019-313-1*) Schmul Pub Co.
Living Ice: Understanding Glaciers & Glaciation. Robert P. Sharp. (Illus.). 248p. (C). 1991. pap. 8.95 (*0-685-47340-6*) Cambridge U Pr.
Living Idioms in Hindustani Music: A Dictionary of Terms & Terminology. Panbdit Amarnath. (C). 1995. 18.00 (*81-7223-104-0*, Pub. by Indus Pub) S Asia.
Living Illustrations. A. B. Earle. 1988. pap. 7.99 (*0-88019-229-1*) Schmul Pub Co.
Living Image. Coral Polge & Kay Hunter. 192p. 1984. 40.00 (*0-7212-0634-4*, Pub. by Regency Pr GBR) St Mut.
Living in a Democracy. Benjamin R. Barber. 24p. 2000. pap. 16.00 (*0-87117-324-7*) Comm Coll Pr Am Assn Comm Coll.
***Living in a Desert.** Allan Fowler. (Rookie Read-About Geography Ser.). (Illus.). 32p. (J). (gr. 1-2). 2000. pap. 5.95 (*0-516-27049-4*) Childrens.
***Living in a Desert.** Jan Kottke. (Welcome Bks.). (Illus.). (J). 2000. 13.50 (*0-516-23300-9*) Childrens.
Living in a Larger World: The Life of Murray S. Kenworthy. Leonard S. Kenworthy. LC 86-31987. (Illus.). 120p. (Orig.). 1987. pap. 9.00 (*0-913408-93-X*) Friends United.
Living in a Lean-To: Philippine Negrito Foragers in Transition. Navin K. Rai. LC 89-12557. (Anthropological Papers Ser.: No. 80). xi, 184p. (Orig.). 1990. pap. 12.00 (*0-915703-17-3*) U Mich Mus Anthro.
Living in a Learning Society: Life-Histories, Identities, & Education. Ari Antikainen et al. (Knowledge, Identity & School Life Ser.: No. 4). 125p. 1996. 85.00 (*0-7507-0497-7*, Falmer Pr); 27.95 (*0-7507-0498-5*, Falmer Pr) Taylor & Francis.
Living in a Lions' Den Without Being Eaten. William C. Peel. LC 94-11890. 252p. (Orig.). 1994. pap. 12.00 (*0-89109-794-5*) NavPress.
Living In A Media World. Hanson. 2001. 44.25 (*0-07-234177-7*) McGraw.
Living in A Medieval Castle. Renzo Rossi. Tr. by Erika Paoli from ITA. LC 99-10948. (Places of Life Ser.). 1999. 23.50 (*0-382-42237-6*, Dillon Silver Burdett) Silver Burdett Pr.
Living in A Medieval Monastery. Renzo Rossi. Tr. by Erika Paoli from ITA. LC 99-10944. (The Places of Life Ser.). 1999. 23.00 (*0-382-42238-4*, Dillon Silver Burdett) Silver Burdett Pr.
Living in a Motor Home. Laura Wolfe. LC 84-50997. (Illus.). 128p. (Orig.). 1984. pap. 5.95 (*0-912661-02-X*) Woodsong Graph.
Living in A Native American Village. Renzo Rossi. LC 99-18243. (The Places of Life Ser.). 1999. 23.00 (*0-382-42240-6*, Dillon Silver Burdett) Silver Burdett Pr.
Living in a Psychic's World: A True-Life Experience. Kevin Quattrin. LC 95-131073. 170p. (Orig.). 1994. pap. 9.95 (*1-878901-94-X*) Hampton Roads Pub Co.
***Living in a Rain Forest.** Allan Fowler. (Rookie Read-About Geography Ser.). (Illus.). 32p. (J). (gr. 1-2). 2000. pap. 5.95 (*0-516-27050-8*) Childrens.
***Living in a Rain Forest.** Joanne Winne. (Welcome Bks.). (Illus.). (J). 2000. 13.50 (*0-516-23301-7*) Childrens.
***Living in a Rain Forest.** Joanne Winne. (Communities Ser.). (Illus.). 24p. (J). (ps-2). 2000. pap. 4.95 (*0-516-23501-X*) Childrens.
Living in A Roman Villa. Renzo Rossi. LC 99-21163. 1999. 23.00 (*0-382-42239-2*, Dillon Silver Burdett) Silver Burdett Pr.
***Living in a Small Space.** Susanne Tamborini. (GER & ENG., Illus.). 160p. 2000. 68.00 (*3-932565-01-0*) Edition A Menges.
Living in a State of Orgasm. Millicent Linden. LC 62-22285. (Illus.). (Orig.). 1967. pap. 5.00 (*0-912628-01-4*) M Linden NY.
Living in a Stepfamily. 2nd ed. Ruth Weber. 110p. 1996. pap. 39.00 (*0-86431-145-1*, Pub. by Aust Council Educ Res) St Mut.

An Asterisk (*) at the beginning of an entry indicates that the title is appearing for the first time.

L

Living in a Stepfamily Without Getting Stepped On. Kevin Leman. LC 94-3565. 1994. 19.99 (0-8407-3492-1) Nelson.
Living in a Technological Culture: Human Tools & Human Issues. Mary Tiles & Hans Oberdiek. LC 95-14746. (Philosophical Issues in Science Ser.). 224p. (C). 1995. pap. 22.99 (0-415-07101-1) Routledge.
Living in a World with AIDS. Anna Forbes. LC 96-5531. (AIDS Awareness Library). (Illus.). 24p. (J). (gr. k-4). 1996. lib. bdg. 15.93 (0-8239-2367-3, PowerKids) Rosen Group.
Living in Africa, Southern Asia & the Pacific Realm. Burton F. Beers. (J). (gr. k-12). 1997. text. write for info. (1-885647-28-X) NCSU Hum Ext.
Living in Alaska. Wilma Barr & Lucille Frey. 100p. (J). 1995. pap. 12.95 (1-878051-44-X) Circumpolar Pr.
Living in Alaska. Wilma Barr & Lucille Frey. (Illus.). 100p. (J). (gr. 2-5). 1995. pap. 9.95 (1-878051-43-1) Circumpolar Pr.
Living in Alaska: Poems of the Last Frontier. Carrie P. Wininger. 70p. 1998. pap. 8.99 (0-9665210-0-5) C Wininger.
Living in America. Alan Poon. 114p. 1996. pap. text 6.00 (1-888065-08-7) New Wrld Poetry.
Living in America. James Snydal. (Illus.). (Orig.). 1997. pap. write for info. (0-614-29881-4) New Thght Jour Pr.
Living in America: A Popular Culture Reader. Ed. by Patricia Y. Murray & Scott F. Covell. LC 97-29734. xxiii, 578p. (C). 1997. pap. text 32.95 (1-55934-977-8, 1977) Mayfield Pub.
Living in America by James Snydal. Photos by Kathryn MacDonald. (Illus.). 36p. 1997. pap. 4.95 (0-9648133-7-8) New Thght Jour Pr.
Living in an Insane World. J. Krishnamurti. 82p. 1989. per. 6.95 (1-888004-15-0) Krishnamurti.
Living in Ancient Rome. Odile Bombarde & Claude Moatti. Tr. by Sarah Matthews from FRE. LC 87-37113. (Illus.). 38p. (J). (gr. k-5). 1988. 5.95 (0-944589-08-1, 081) Young Discovery Lib.
Living in & with the Divine Trinity. Witness Lee. 138p. 1990. per. 6.50 (0-87083-560-2, 05-003-001) Living Stream Ministry.
Living in Arcadia: Ocean Pines, Maryland. E. A. Rogner. (Illus.). 80p. (Orig.). 1990. pap. text 9.95 (0-935045-07-4) D-OR Pr.
Living in Atholl, 1685-1785. Leah Leneman. 200p. 1986. 30.00 (0-85224-507-6, Pub. by Edinburgh U Pr) Col U Pr.
Living in Balance: A Dynamic Approach for Creating Harmony & Wholeness in a Chaotic World. Joel Levey & Michelle Levey. LC 97-31200. (Illus.). 333p. (Orig.). 1998. pap. 17.95 (1-57324-032-X) Conari Press.
Living in Balance: The Universe of the Hope, Zuni, Navajo & Apache. Dorothy K. Washburn. LC 95-10148. (Illus.). 92p. 1995. pap. 12.95 (0-924171-36-7) U Museum Pubns.
Living in Beauty. Joseph Kurian. (Illus.). 263p. 1999. pap. 13.95 (1-893279-00-6) EMC Publishing.
Living in Both Words: Wisdom from Spirit. unabridged ed. Jay F. Sheridan. (Living in Both Worlds Ser.: Vol. 2). 136p. 1998. pap., per. 16.95 (0-9657037-2-X) Paewood Ent.
Living in Both Worlds Vol. 1: A Healer & Her Journey with Spirit. unabridged ed. Julie Rae Paetow & Toni Lynn Wood. LC 97-222612. (Illus.). 312p. (Orig.). 1997. pap., per. 18.95 (0-9657037-0-3) Paewood Ent.
Living in Both Worlds Vol. 3: Piercing the Veil. Toni L. Wood. (Illus.). 1999. write for info. (0-9657037-3-8) Paewood Ent.
Living in Britain: Preliminary Results from the 1996 General Household Survey : a Survey Carried Out. Great Britain. Office for National Statistics. Social Survey Division. LC 98-133816. (Illus.). 1997. write for info. (0-11-620946-1) Statnry Office.
Living in Britain: Results from the 1995 General Household Survey. LC 98-123276. 266 p. 1997. 65.00 (0-11-691550-1, Pub. by Statnry Office) Bernan Associates.
***Living in Britain: Tradition & Design.** Konemann Inc. Staff. (Illus.). 2000. 29.95 (3-8290-4851-3) Konemann.
Living in but Not of the World. Sharlene W. Hawkes. LC 97-25702. xviii, 246p. 1997. 16.95 (1-57345-203-3) Deseret Bk.
Living in Chaos Walking in Peace: A Matter of Ascension. Barbara Knudson. 100p. 1998. pap. 9.95 (1-887747-20-6) Legendary Pub.
Living in China. Andrew Watson. (Illus.). 192p. 1975. 7.95 (0-8226-0327-6) Rowman.
Living in China: A Guide to Teaching & Studying in China, Including Taiwan & Hong Kong. expanded ed. Rebecca Weiner et al. LC 97-66307. 300p. 1997. pap. 19.95 (0-8351-2582-3) China Bks.
***Living in Christ: Essays on the Christian Life by an Orthodox Nun.** Raphaela. LC 99-88452. 2000. write for info. (0-88141-199-X) St Vladimirs.
***Living in Christian Community.** Arthur G. Gish. 382p. 1998. pap. 29.00 (1-57910-159-3) Wipf & Stock.
Living in Christ's Church. Edmund P. Clowney. 1986. teacher ed. 3.95 (0-934688-24-9); pap. text 5.95 (0-934688-22-2) Great Comm Pubns.
Living in Cincinnati. Kevin Walzer. 64p. (Orig.). 1995. pap. 7.95 (0-9633551-1-2) Cinc Writers Proj.
Living in Color. Renae Knapp. LC 98-22594. (Illus.). 112p. 1998. pap. 21.95 (0-910019-75-4, Pub. by Lghthse Pub Gp) Origin Bk Sales.
Living in Crisis. Ernest H. Wilkins. LC 67-22067. (Essay Index Reprint Ser.). 1977. 16.95 (0-8369-0997-6) Ayer.
Living in Disquise. E. A. Markham. 118p. 1986. 24.95 (0-85646-172-5, Pub. by Anvil Press); pap. 14.95 (0-85646-173-3, Pub. by Anvil Press) Dufour.
Living in Dread. Penny Kline. 224p. 1998. 24.00 (0-7278-5372-4) Severn Hse.
***Living in Dread.** large type ed. Penny Kline. 400p. 1999. 31.99 (0-7505-1390-X, Pub. by Mgna Lrg Print) Ulverscroft.
Living in English. Betsy J. Blosser. (Illus.). 160p. 1994. pap. 15.95 (0-8442-7437-2, 74372, Natl Textbk Co) NTC Contemp Pub Co.
Living in English, 2 cass. Betsy J. Blosser. 160p. 1992. pap. 39.95 incl. audio (0-8442-7378-3, 73783, Natl Textbk Co) NTC Contemp Pub Co.
Living in English: Basic Skills for the Adult Learner. (Essential Life Skills Ser.). 1989. pap., teacher ed. 5.57 (0-8442-7438-0) NTC Contemp Pub Co.
Living in Environment. Miller. (Biology Ser.). 1975. pap., student ed. 1.00 (0-534-00454-7) Wadsworth Pub.
Living in Eternity: Channeled Wisdom on Life, the Hereafter, & the Reality of It All. Sylvia A. Murray-Graham. 225p. (Orig.). pap. write for info. (0-9643806-0-9) CandleLght TX.
Living in Fear: The History of Horror in the Mass Media. Les Daniels. LC 82-25261. (Quality Paperbacks Ser.). (Illus.). 256p. 1983. reprint ed. pap. 12.95 (0-306-80193-0) Da Capo.
Living in France. Annie Hawkinson. Ed. by Alvino E. Fantini. (Intercultural Exchange Ser.). 42p. (Orig.). (YA). 1986. pap. 2.50 (0-936141-12-3) Experiment Pr.
Living in France. 4th ed. Ani Hawkinson. 1997. pap. 8.95 (0-86647-111-1) Pro Lingua.
Living in France: A Brief Introduction or Review of the Culture & Language of France for Visitors, Students & Business Travelers. 3rd ed. Annie Hawkinson & Patrick R. Moran. Ed. by Arthur A. Burrows. (Living in Ser.). (Illus.). 58p. 1994. pap. text 4.50 (0-86647-085-9) Pro Lingua.
Living in Freedom: The Exhilaration & Anguish of Prague's Second Spring. Mark Sommer. LC 91-32914. 288p. 1992. 21.95 (1-56279-025-0) Mercury Hse Inc.
Living in Freedom: The New Prague. rev. ed. Mark Sommer. LC 93-12725. 288p. 1994. reprint ed. pap. 11.95 (1-56279-054-4) Mercury Hse Inc.
***Living in Girlfriend's House: Real Woman Survival Tips.** Princess Ivori. 112p. 2000. pap. 10.95 (0-615-11871-2) Linden & Farmer.
Living in God: Daily Reflections. Roy E. Davis. 1997. 7.95 (0-87707-276-0) CSA Pr.
***Living in God: 366 Themes for Daily Meditative Contemplation & Spiritual Enrichment (With Life Enhancing Affirmations & Inspirational Quotations)** Roy Eugene Davis. 159p. 1998. 100.00 (81-208-1543-2, Pub. by Motilal Bnarsidass); pap. 50.00 (81-208-1544-0, Pub. by Motilal Bnarsidass) St Mut.
Living in God's Abundance. William M. Bakkeby, Jr. 120p. 1999. pap. 7.00 (0-9661069-1-1) Word of Grace.
Living in God's Abundance. Billy J. Daugherty. 126p. 1999. pap. 6.95 (1-56267-184-7) Victory Ctr OK.
***Living in God's Embrace: The Practice of Spiritual Intimacy.** Michael Fonseca. LC 00-8399. 240p. 2000. pap. 12.95 (0-87793-939-X) Ave Maria.
Living in God's Grace: Apostles' Creed - Sacraments. Allen J. Foss. Ed. by David Rinden. 266p. (YA). (gr. 6-8). 1989. reprint ed. pap. 5.95 (0-943167-06-X) Faith & Fellowship Pr.
***Living in God's Household: Lessons for a Healthy Church.** Bob Buller. Ed. by Jim Eichenberger. (Solid Foundation Bible Studies: Vol. 8). 64p. 2000. pap. 9.99 (0-7847-1178-X, 41108) Standard Pub.
Living in God's Time: A Primer for Nurturing the Spiritual Life of Children Throughout the Christian Year. Margaret Persky. Ed. by JoAnn Miller. LC 98-55212. 176p. 1999. pap. 10.00 (0-8358-0875-0) Upper Room Bks.
Living in Greece: How to Feel at Home, Make Friends & Enjoy Everyday Life. Lyn Waldie. (Living in Ser.). 1998. pap. text 9.95 (0-86647-102-2) Pro Lingua.
Living in Groups. (Longman Biology Topics Ser.). Date not set. pap. text. write for info. (0-582-32302-9, Pub. by Addison-Wesley) Longman.
Living in Harmony. Kathy A. Long. (Illus.). 32p. (Orig.). (J). (gr. k-4). 1995. pap. text 5.00 (0-9642063-1-5) Best Frnds.
Living in Harmony: Nature Writing by Women in Canada. Ed. by Andrea Lebowitz. 240p. (Orig.). 1996. pap. 15.95 (1-55143-060-6) Orca Bk Pubs.
Living in Harmony with Animals. Carla Bennett. LC 99-58048. 160p. 2000. pap. text 9.95 (1-57067-085-4) Book Pub Co.
Living in Heaven's Blessings Now, 10. Gloria Copeland. 48p. 1999. pap. text 15.00 (1-57794-161-6) Harrison Hse.
Living in Hell: The Dilemma of African-American Survival. Ed. by Mose Pleasure, Jr. & Fred C. Lofton. LC 95-12479. 224p. 1995. pap. 12.99 (0-310-49781-7) Zondervan.
***Living in His Sufficiency.** Charles Stanley. LC 99-229425. (In Touch Study Ser.). 123p. 1999. pap. 7.99 (0-7852-7286-0) Nelson.
***Living in History.** Luca Leoncini. 1999. pap. 55.00 (88-422-0841-8) Dist Art Pubs.
Living in Hope & History: Notes from Our Century. Nadine Gordimer. LC 99-14741. 224p. 1999. text 23.00 (0-374-18991-9) FS&G.
***Living in Hope & History: Notes from Our Century.** Nadine Gordimer. 256p. 2000. pap. 14.00 (0-374-52752-0) FS&G.
Living in India. Anne Singh. Tr. by Sarah Matthews from FRE. LC 87-31803. (Illus.). 38p. (J). (gr. k-5). 1988. 5.95 (0-944589-14-6, 146) Young Discovery Lib.
Living in Integrity: A Global Ethic to Restore a Fragmented Earth. Laura Westra. LC 97-37219. (Studies in Social, Political, & Legal Philosophy). 288p. 1997. pap. 23.95 (0-8476-8927-1) Rowman.
Living in Integrity: A Global Ethic to Restore a Fragmented Earth. Laura Westra. LC 97-37219. (Studies in Social, Political, & Legal Philosophy). 288p. 1998. 63.00 (0-8476-8926-3) Rowman.
Living in Ireland. Walter Pfeiffer. (Illus.). 96p. 1997. 14.95 (2-08-013585-6, Pub. by Flammarion) Abbeville Pr.
Living in Istanbul. Photos by Jerome Darblay. (Illus.). 256p. 1994. 45.00 (2-08-013563-5, Pub. by Flammarion) Abbeville Pr.
Living in Italy. 2nd ed. Alvino E. Fantini. 1997. pap. text 8.95 (0-86647-103-0) Pro Lingua.
***Living in Italy.** 3rd ed. Alvino E. Fantini. (Illus.). 2000. pap. 9.95 (0-86647-126-X) Pro Lingua.
Living in Italy: The Essential Guide for Property Purchasers & Residents. 5th ed. Yve Menzies. (Illus.). 224p. 1999. pap. 16.95 (0-7090-6311-3) Seven Hills Bk.
Living in Japan. Ed. by Japan Travel Bureau Staff. (JTB's Illustrated Japan in Your Pocket Ser.). (Illus.). 192p. 1987. pap. 17.95 (4-533-01350-3, Pub. by Japan Trvl Bur) Bks Nippan.
Living in Japan. Craig Sower. (Illus.). 80p. 1997. pap. 8.95 (0-86647-106-5) Pro Lingua.
Living in Japan: Intermediate Conversational Japanese. Mieko S. Han. (ENG & JPN.). 190p. (Orig.). (C). 1996. pap. text 21.00 (1-878463-04-7) Inst Inter Studies Pr.
Living in Limbo: The Boat Refugees of Hong Kong & Macao. U. S. Committee for Refugees. 19p. 1986. write for info. (0-318-60962-2) US Comm Refugees.
Living in, Living Out: African American Domestics & the Great Migration. Elizabeth Clark-Lewis. Ed. by Deborah Baker. (Illus.). 256p. 1996. pap. 15.00 (1-56836-124-6, Kodansha Globe) Kodansha.
Living in, Living Out: African American Domestics in Washington, D. C., 1910-1940. Elizabeth Clark-Lewis. LC 94-14415. (Illus.). 192p. 1994. text 29.95 (1-56098-362-0) Smithsonian.
Living in London. Photos by Simon Upton. (Illus.). 1999. 50.00 (2-08-013661-5, Pub. by Flammarion) Abbeville Pr.
Living in Love. Alexandra Stoddard. 1997. 22.00 (0-614-20428-3, Wm Morrow); 22.00 (0-688-14338-5, Wm Morrow) Morrow Avon.
Living in Love. Alexandra Stoddard. 272p. 1998. pap. 12.50 (0-380-72621-1, Avon Bks) Morrow Avon.
Living in Love: About Christian Ethics. Rhonda D. Chervin. LC 88-18485. 136p. (C). 1989. pap. 6.95 (0-8198-4452-7) Pauline Bks.
Living in Love: Connecting with the Power of Love Within. Christine A. Adams. LC 93-24748. 200p. 1993. pap. 9.95 (1-55874-278-6) Health Comm.
Living in Love: Real Values for a Relevant Faith. Wayne F. Monbleau. 158p. (Orig.). 1987. pap. 7.00 (0-944648-00-2) Loving Grace Pubns.
Living in Love with Yourself. rev. ed. Barry A. Ellsworth. Ed. by Leonard C. Hawes & Marion McCardell. LC 88-92409. 224p. 1989. pap. 9.95 (0-929175-01-8) Brkthrough Pub UT.
Living in Mexico: A Complete Guide. Michael J. Zamba. LC 98-38553. 144p. 1990. pap. 9.95 (0-8442-9546-9, Passprt Bks) NTC Contemp Pub Co.
Living in Mexico: How to Feel at Home, Make Friends & Enjoy Everyday Life. rev. ed. Alvino E. Fantini & Beatriz C. Fantini. 1993. pap. 7.95 (0-86647-079-4) Pro Lingua.
Living in Mexico: How to Feel at Home, Make Friends & Enjoy Everyday Life. 4th ed. Alvino E. Fantini. (Living in Ser.). (Illus.). 80p. 1998. pap. text 9.95 (0-86647-105-7) Pro Lingua.
Living in My Family. Linda K. Sibley. LC 97-204442. (Confident Kids). (Illus.). 416p. 1997. teacher ed. 39.99 (0-7847-0642-5, 42052) Standard Pub.
Living in Mystery. R. Burrows. 1990. pap. 28.00 (0-7220-5095-X) St Mut.
***Living in New England.** Elaine Louie. (Illus.). 192p. 2000. 34.50 (0-7432-0375-5) S&S Trade.
Living in North Carolina (Living in Our World) Burton F. Beers. (J). (gr. k-12). 1997. text. write for info. (1-885647-27-1) NCSU Hum Ext.
Living in Norway. Elisabeth Holte. (Illus.). 232p. 1994. 45.00 (2-08-013545-7, Pub. by Flammarion) Abbeville Pr.
Living in Our Environment: Proceedings of the 17th Annual Technical Meeting of the Institute of Environmental Sciences, Los Angeles. LC 62-38584. (Illus.). 1971. pap. text 75.00 (0-915414-11-2) IEST.
Living in Paris. Jose Alvarez et al. LC 96-37994. (Illus.). 256p. 1997. 50.00 (2-08-013621-6, Pub. by Flammarion) Abbeville Pr.
***Living in Poetry.** Guillevic. Ed. & Tr. by Denise Levertov & Maureen Smith from FRE. 160p. 1999. pap. 15.95 (1-901233-40-5, Pub. by Dedalus) Dufour.
Living in Portugal. Anne De Stoop. (Illus.). 256p. 1995. 50.00 (2-08-013567-8, Pub. by Flammarion) Abbeville Pr.
Living in Poverty: Coping on the Welfare Grant. Patricia Simpson. LC 92-195651. 150p. (Orig.). 1990. pap. 15.00 (0-88156-108-8) Comm Serv Soc NY.
Living in Prayer: A Practical Guide. Sandra S. Garant. 64p. pap. 1.95 (0-8198-4469-1) Pauline Bks.
Living in Prison: The Ecology of Survival. rev. ed. Hans Toch. LC 92-30700. 403p. 1992. reprint ed. pap. text 19.95 (1-55798-176-0) Am Psychol.
Living in Process: Basic Truths for Living the Path of the Soul. Anne Wilson Schaef. 384p. 1999. pap. 12.95 (0-345-43567-2) Ballantine Pub Grp.
Living in Retirement: And Helping Your Parents Enjoy Retirement. Joy Elaine Canfield. 209p. 1995. pap. 9.95 (0-9639607-1-7) Image Cascade.
***Living in Rome.** Bruno Racine. (Illus.). 216p. 2000. text 50.00 (2-08-013675-5, Pub. by Flammarion) Abbeville Pr.
Living in Rural Wales. Noragh Jones. 357p. 1993. pap. 37.95 (0-8464-4641-3) Beekman Pubs.
Living in Rural Wales. Noragh Jones. 357p. 1993. pap. 40.00 (0-86383-971-1, Pub. by Gomer Pr) St Mut.
Living in St. Lucia. Vincent Bunce & Wendy Morgan. LC 96-229119. (Cambridge Primary Geography Ser.). 48p. (C). 1996. pap. 9.95 (0-521-55658-9) Cambridge U Pr.
Living in Scotland. Lesley Astaire & Roddy Martine. LC 96-61190. (Illus.). 240p. 1997. pap. 29.95 (0-500-27934-9, Pub. by Thames Hudson) Norton.
Living in Sin. Lisa Bragg. LC 97-76654. 112p. 1997. pap. 9.95 (0-9612974-1-7) Patten Pr Inc.
Living in Sin: A Bishop Rethinks Human Sexuality. John S. Spong. LC 87-33654. 256p. 1990. pap. 16.00 (0-06-067507-1, Pub. by Harper SF) HarpC.
***Living in Small Spaces.** Lorrie Mack. 1999. pap. 14.95 (1-85029-800-9) Conran Octopus.
Living in South America. Chantal Henry-Biabaud. Tr. by Vicki Bogard from FRE. LC 90-50773. (Young Discovery Library). (Illus.). 38p. (J). (gr. k-5). 1991. 5.95 (0-944589-28-6, 286) Young Discovery Lib.
Living in Space. David Baker. (Today's World in Space Bks.: Set 11). (Illus.). 48p. (J). (gr. 3-8). 1989. 13.95 (0-685-58639-1) Rourke Corp.
Living in Space. David Baker. (Today's World in Space Bks.: Set 11). (Illus.). 48p. (J). (gr. 3-8). 1989. lib. bdg. 21.27 (0-86592-401-5) Rourke Enter.
Living in Space. Don Berliner. LC 92-24847. (Space & Aviation Ser.). (Illus.). 72p. (YA). (gr. 6-9). 1993. lib. bdg. 22.60 (0-8225-1599-7, Lerner Publctns) Lerner Pub.
Living in Space. Jerry Kay. (Science in Action Learning Ser.). (Illus.). 22p. (Orig.). (J). (gr. 3-7). 1988. 9.95 (0-929201-06-X) Kay Productions.
Living in Space. Larry Kettelkamp. LC 92-35118. (Illus.). 128p. (J). (gr. 3 up). 1993. 14.00 (0-688-10018-X, Wm Morrow) Morrow Avon.
Living in Space. Kathryn Penz & Claire Wandersee. (Illus.). 48p. (J). 1997. pap. 8.00 (0-8059-4077-4) Dorrance.
Living in Space. G. Harry Stine. LC 97-14880. (Illus.). 256p. 1997. 21.95 (0-87131-841-5) M Evans.
***Living in Space.** Felicity Trotman. 2000. 12.95 (0-7641-5305-6) Barron.
***Living in Space: From Science Fiction to the International Space Station.** Giovanni Caprara. (Illus.). 216p. 2000. pap. 29.95 (1-55209-549-5) Firefly Bks Ltd.
Living in Spain. 5th ed. John Ready-Smith. (Illus.). 223p. 1990. 33.50 (0-7090-4100-4) Trans-Atl Phila.
Living in Spain: A Brief Introduction or Review of the Culture & Language of France for Visitors, Students & Business Travelers. Alvino E. Fantini & Cristina Enriquez. Ed. by Arthur A. Burrows. (Living in Ser.). (Illus.). 58p. (Orig.). 1993. pap. text 4.50 (0-86647-058-1) Pro Lingua.
Living in Step. Ruth Roosevelt & Jeannette Lofas. (Paperbacks Ser.). 1977. reprint ed. mass mkt. 10.95 (0-07-053596-5) McGraw.
***Living in Style Without Losing Your Mind.** Marco Pasanella. LC 00-21408. (Illus.). 200p. 2000. 30.00 (0-684-85047-8) S&S Trade.
Living in the Aftermath. Linda B. Milstein. Ed. by Shirley Warren. 36p. 1995. pap. 5.50 (1-877801-27-5) Still Waters.
***Living in the Arctic.** Allan Fowler. LC 99-38877. (Rookie Read-About Geography Ser.). (J). 2000. 19.00 (0-516-21561-2) Childrens.
Living in the Balance of Grace & Faith. 2nd rev. ed. Andrew Wommack. Ed. by Albury Publishing Staff. LC 97-220812. 80p. 1997. pap. 6.99 (1-57778-022-1, AP-022, Pub. by Albury Pub) Appalach Bk Dist.
Living in the Biosphere: Production, Pattern, Population, & Diversity. Dwight Brown. (Active Learning Modules on the Human Dimensions of Global Change Ser.). (Illus.). 158p. (C). 1997. pap., teacher ed. 20.00 (0-89291-231-6); pap., student ed., wbk. ed. 8.75 (0-89291-232-4) Assn Am Geographers.
Living in the Boneyard. John O. Simon. 1974. 1.00 (0-916866-10-6) Cats Pajamas.
***Living in the Breath of the Spirit: Reflections on Prayer.** Joan D. Chittister. 64p. 1999. pap. 5.00 (1-890890-08-1) Benetvision.
Living in the Cave of the Mouth. Douglas B. Smith. 6.00 (0-920635-03-2) Genl Dist Srvs.
Living in the Children of God. David E. Van Zandt. LC 91-10453. (Illus.). 234p. 1991. reprint ed. pap. 72.60 (0-608-02525-9, 206316900004) Bks Demand.
Living in the Combat Zone. Rick Renner. 256p. 1996. pap. 10.99 (1-880089-02-5, Pub. by Albury Pub) Appalach Bk Dist.
Living in the Comfort Zone: The Gift of Boundaries in Relationships. Rokelle Lerner. 200p. 1995. pap. 9.95 (1-55874-370-7, 3707) Health Comm.
Living in the Community with Disability: Service Needs, Use, & Systems. Ed. by Susan Allen & Vincent Mor. LC 97-47018. (Illus.). 352p. 1998. 58.95 (0-8261-1168-8) Springer Pub.
Living in the Depot: The Two-Story Railroad Station. H. Roger Grant. LC 92-37446. (American Land & Life Ser.). (Illus.). 147p. 1997. reprint ed. pap. 15.95 (0-87745-588-0) U of Iowa Pr.
***Living in the Desert.** Jan Kottke. LC 00-24621. (Communities Ser.). (Illus.). 24p. (J). (ps-2). 2000. pap. 4.95 (0-516-23500-1) Childrens.
Living in the Environment. G. Tyler Miller, Jr. (Biology Ser.). 1975. pap. 14.75 (0-534-00347-8) Wadsworth Pub.
Living in the Environment. 2nd ed. G. Tyler Miller, Jr. (Biology Ser.). 1979. pap. 20.75 (0-534-00684-1) Wadsworth Pub.
Living in the Environment. 4th ed. G. Tyler Miller, Jr. (Biology Ser.). Date not set. pap., teacher ed. write for info. (0-534-04334-8) Wadsworth Pub.

An Asterisk (*) at the beginning of an entry indicates that the title is appearing for the first time.

Living in the Environment. 4th ed. G. Tyler Miller, Jr. & Janiskee. 1984. student ed. 8.75 (*0-534-04333-X*) Brooks-Cole.

Living in the Environment. 5th ed. G. Tyler Miller, Jr. (Biology). 1987. pap., teacher ed. write for info. (*0-534-08053-7*) Wadsworth Pub.

Living in the Environment. 6th ed. G. Tyler Miller, Jr. (Biology Ser.). 1990. mass mkt., teacher ed. write for info. (*0-534-12223-X*) Wadsworth Pub.

Living in the Environment. 7th ed. G. Tyler Miller. (Biology Ser.). 1992. pap. write for info. (*0-534-16561-3*) Wadsworth Pub.

Living in the Environment. 8th ed. G. Tyler Miller. (Biology Ser.). Date not set. 39.40 (*0-534-33085-1*) Wadsworth Pub.

Living in the Environment. 8th ed. G. Tyler Miller. (Biology Ser.). 1993. pap., teacher ed. 37.75 (*0-534-19952-6*) Wadsworth Pub.

Living in the Environment. 9th ed. G. Tyler Miller. (Biology Ser.). 1995. pap. text, teacher ed. 57.00 (*0-534-23901-3*) Wadsworth Pub.

***Living in the Environment.** 11th ed. G. Tyler Miller. LC 99-17666. (Biology Ser.). 1999. 59.75 (*0-534-56268-X*) Wadsworth Pub.

***Living in the Environment.** 11th ed. G. Tyler Miller, Jr. (Biology Ser.). 2000. text 19.00 (*0-534-37753-X*) Brooks-Cole.

***Living in the Environment.** 11th ed. G. Tyler Miller, Jr. 1999. pap. 56.00 (*0-534-37608-8*) Thomson Learn.

***Living in the Environment.** 12th ed. G. Tyler Miller, Jr. 2001. pap. 62.00 (*0-534-37697-5*) Thomson Learn.

Living in the Environment: An Introduction to Environmental Science. 4th ed. G. Tyler Miller, Jr. 460p. (C). 1984. pap. 34.50 (*0-534-04332-1*) Wadsworth Pub.

Living in the Environment: An Introduction to Environmental Science. 5th ed. G. Tyler Miller, Jr. 603p. (C). 1987. pap. 35.50 (*0-534-08052-9*) Wadsworth Pub.

Living in the Environment: An Introduction to Environmental Science. 6th ed. G. Tyler Miller, Jr. 620p. (C). 1989. pap. 43.25 (*0-534-12222-1*) Wadsworth Pub.

Living in the Environment: An Introduction to Environmental Science. 7th ed. G. Tyler Miller, Jr. 705p. (C). 1991. pap. 55.95 (*0-534-16560-5*) Wadsworth Pub.

Living in the Environment: Principles, Connections, & Solutions. 8th ed. G. Tyler Miller, Jr. 701p. (C). 1993. pap. 49.25 (*0-534-19950-X*) Wadsworth Pub.

Living in the Environmt, 3rd. 3rd ed. Miller. (Biology Ser.). 1981. pap. write for info. (*0-534-02015-1*) Wadsworth Pub.

Living in the Face of Death: The Tibetan Tradition. Glenn H. Mullin. LC 98-14199. 238p. 1999. pap. 16.95 (*1-55939-100-6*) Snow Lion Pubns.

Living in the Fad Lane: How to Turn Trends into Fortunes Without Getting Left in the Dust. Stu Taylor & Tom Biracree. LC 92-39830. 1993. 18.95 (*1-55972-171-5*, Birch Ln Pr) Carol Pub Group.

Living in the Fire Nest. Linda N. Foster. 140p. (Orig.). 1996. pap. 15.00 (*1-56439-060-8*) Ridgeway.

Living in the Gap Between Promise & Reality: The Gospel According to Abraham. Ian M. Duguid. LC 99-28877. (Gospel According to the Old Testament Ser.). 192p. 1999. pap. 12.99 (*0-87552-652-7*) P & R Pubng.

Living in the Global Society. Roberto Papini et al. 304p. 1997. text 74.95 (*1-85972-575-9*, Pub. by Ashgate Pub) Ashgate Pub Co.

Living in the Heart: The Affinity Process & the Path of Unconditional Love & Acceptance. Paul Ferrini. 144p. 1998. pap. 10.95 (*1-879159-36-8*) Heartways Pr.

Living in the Heart of Africa. Chantal Henry-Biabaud. Tr. by Vicki Bogard from FRE. LC 90-50774. (Young Discovery Library). (Illus.). 38p. (J). (gr. k-5). 1991. 5.95 (*0-944589-29-4*, 294) Young Discovery Lib.

***Living in the Highlands.** Lesley Astaire & Roddy Martine. LC 99-69291. (Illus.). 168p. 2000. 40.00 (*0-500-01986-X*, Pub. by Thames Hudson) Norton.

Living in the Image of God: Jewish Teachings to Perfect the World. Shalom Freedman & Irving Greenberg. LC 97-27108. 368p. 1998. 40.00 (*0-7657-9980-4*) Aronson.

Living in the Joy of Faith: Heidelberg Catechism. Clarence Stam. 353p. 1991. pap. 35.90 (*0-921100-27-2*) Inhtce Pubns.

Living in the Labyrinth. large type ed. Diana F. McGowin. 1994. 36.95 (*0-7862-9976-2*, G K Hall Lrg Type) Mac Lib Ref.

Living in the Labyrinth: A Personal Journey Through the Maze of Alzheimer's. large type ed. Diana F. McGowin. LC 93-33820. 247p. 1994. lib. bdg. 20.95 (*0-7862-0066-9*) Thorndike Pr.

Living in the Labyrinth: A Personal Journey Through the Maze of Alzheimer's. large type ed. Diana F. McGowin. LC 93-33820. 247p. 1995. lib. bdg. 13.95 (*0-7862-0067-7*) Thorndike Pr.

Living in the Labyrinth: A Personal Journey Through the Maze of Alzheimer's. rev. ed. Diana F. McGowin. 176p. 1994. pap. 11.95 (*0-385-31318-7*, Delta Trade) Dell.

Living in the Landscape: Toward an Aesthetics of Environment. Arnold Berleant. LC 96-29328. 176p. 1997. 25.00 (*0-7006-0811-7*) U Pr of KS.

Living in the Lap of the Goddess: The Feminist Spirituality Movement in America. Cynthia Eller. LC 95-16968. 288p. (C). 1995. pap. 16.00 (*0-8070-6507-2*) Beacon Pr.

Living in the Light see Viviendo en la Luz: Una Quia para la Transformacion Personal y Planetaria

Living in the Light. Blackwell North America Staff. 15.95 (*1-882591-01-1*) Nataraj Pub.

Living in the Light: A Guide to Personal & Planetary Transformation. Shakti Gawain. 208p. 1993. mass mkt. 6.50 (*0-553-56104-9*) Bantam.

Living in the Light: A Guide to Personal & Planetary Transformation. 2nd rev. ed. Shakti Gawain. Ed. by Laurel King. LC 98-38364. 256p. 1998. pap. 12.95 (*1-57731-046-2*) New Wrld Lib.

Living in the Light: Daily Reflections, Prayers, & Practices for Lent. Warren J. Savage & Mary A. McSweeney. LC 97-74321. 80p. 1998. pap. 3.95 (*0-7648-0148-1*) Liguori Pubns.

***Living in the Light: Freeing Your Child from the Dark Ages.** Anne R. Stone. LC 99-59339. iv, 154p. 2000. pap. 12.00 (*1-57884-908-X*, 5588) Am Atheist.

Living in the Light: Leading Youth to Deeper Spirituality. Walt Marcum. LC 94-12860. (Essentials for Christian Youth Ser.). 112p. (Orig.). 1994. pap. 13.95 (*0-687-39235-7*) Abingdon.

***Living in the Light of Death: On the Art of Being Truly Alive.** Larry Rosenberg & David Guy. LC 99-58716. 192p. 2000. 22.95 (*1-57062-425-9*, Pub. by Shambhala Pubns) Random.

***Living in the Light of Eternity: Your Life Can Make a Difference.** K. P. Yohannan. 1999. audio 15.99 (*1-56599-989-4*) Yahshua Pub.

Living in the Light of Eternity: Your Life Can Make a Difference. K. P. Yohannan. LC 95-20992. 208p. (gr. 11). 1995. reprint ed. pap. 11.99 (*0-8007-9235-1*) Chosen Bks.

Living in the Light of the Lords Return: Pass on the Torch of Truth to Each Generation until the Lord Jesus Christ Appears Again. Walter Beachy et al. (Biblical Heritage Ser.: No. 6). 72p. (Orig.). 1995. pap. 3.99 (*0-940883-06-6*) Calvary Pubns.

Living in the Light Workbook: A Guide to Personal & Planetary Transformation. 2nd rev. ed. Shakti Gawain. Ed. by Laurel King. 168p. 1998. pap., wbk. ed. 14.00 (*1-57731-047-0*) New Wrld Lib.

Living in the Lightning: A Cancer Journal. Natalie Robins. LC 98-37622. 120p. 1999. pap. 14.00 (*0-8135-2665-5*); text 31.00 (*0-8135-2664-7*) Rutgers U Pr.

Living in the Maniototo. Janet Frame. LC 79-2358. 1980. pap. 12.50 (*0-8076-0958-7*) Braziller.

Living in the Margins: Racism, Sexism & Feminism in Australia. Jan Pettman. 220p. (Orig.). 1992. pap. text 19.95 (*1-86373-005-2*, Pub. by Allen & Unwin Pty) Paul & Co Pubs.

Living in the Margins: The Interpretive Edge of Intentional Christian Communities. Terry A. Veling. LC 95-51044. 264p. 1995. pap. 19.95 (*0-8245-1573-0*) Crossroad NY.

Living in the Maybe: A Steward Confronts the Spirit of Fundamentalism. Christopher Levan. LC 97-48603. (Faith's Horizons Ser.: Vol. 4). 160p. 1998. pap. 18.00 (*0-8028-4347-6*) Eerdmans.

Living in the Meantime: Nine-Tenths of the 20th Century. G. Avery Lee. 192p. 1993. 19.00 (*1-880837-38-2*); pap. 14.00 (*1-880837-39-0*) Smyth & Helwys.

Living in the Middle: Sherpas of the Mid-Range Himalayas. Donna Sherpa. LC 94-175070. (Illus.). 148p. (Orig.). (C). 1994. pap. text 10.50 (*0-88133-745-5*) Waveland Pr.

***Living in the Millennium** Jack Van Impe. LC 99-38050. 1999. 12.99 (*0-8499-4072-9*) Word Pub.

***Living in the Mountains.** Allan Fowler. LC 99-30441. (Rookie Read-About Geography Ser.). (J). 2000. 19.00 (*0-516-21563-9*) Childrens.

***Living in the Mountains.** Allan Fowler. (Rookie Read-About Geography Ser.). (Illus.). 32p. (J). (gr. 1-2). 2000. pap. 5.95 (*0-516-27051-6*) Childrens.

***Living in the Number One Country: Reflections from a Critic of American Empire.** Herbert I. Schiller. 224p. 2000. 25.00 (*1-58322-028-3*) Seven Stories.

Living in the Past: Studies in Archaism of the Egyptian Twenty-Sixth Dynasty. Peter Der Manuelian. LC 92-26097. (Studies in Egyptology). (Illus.). 488p. 1994. 144.50 (*0-7103-0461-7*) Routledge.

Living in the Post-Mastectomy Body: Learning to Live in & Love Your Body Again. Rebecca Zuckweiler. LC 98-18466. (Illus.). 282p. 1998. pap. 19.95 (*0-88179-152-0*) Hartley & Marks.

Living in the Presence: Spiritual Exercises to Open Our Lives to the Awareness of God. Tilden H. Edwards. LC 94-24965. 176p. (gr. 7). 1995. pap. 13.00 (*0-06-062127-3*, Pub. by Harper SF) HarpC.

Living in the Presence of God: Love's Simple Path. John Allan. LC 94-72771. (Illus.). 200p. (Orig.). 1995. pap. 12.00 (*0-9643840-7-8*) Morning S P.

Living in the Presence of God: The Everyday Spirituality of Brother Lawrence. John Kirvan. LC 96-39879. (Thirty Days with a Great Spiritual Teacher Ser.). 216p. (Orig.). 1997. pap. 7.95 (*0-87793-601-3*) Ave Maria.

Living in the Present: An Anthology of Philosophy & Poetry. Jorn K. Bramann. 130p. (Orig.). (C). 1982. per. 7.50 (*0-941452-03-4*) Acheron Pr.

Living in the Question: An Exploration of Formlessness, Change, & Healing. Michael J. Maley. (Illus.). (Orig.). 1995. pap. 13.95 (*0-9649741-0-X*) Bodysmart Pubns.

***Living in the Question: Meditations in the Style of the Lectio Divina.** M. Basil Pennington. LC 99-34434. 1999. pap. 14.95 (*0-8264-1206-8*) Continuum.

Living in the Raw: Recipes for a Healthy Lifestyle. Rose L. Calabro. 192p. 1999. pap. 17.95 (*0-9666816-0-6*, LTR7101) Rose Pubg.

Living in the Reader's World, 4 bks., Bk. 1. Ed. by Dennis Mendyk. (Adult Reading Ser.: Levels 2-6). (Illus.). 160p. 1988. pap. text 6.30 (*0-8428-9514-0*) Cambridge Bk.

Living in the Reader's World, 4 bks., Bk. 2. Ed. by Dennis Mendyk. (Adult Reading Ser.: Levels 2-6). (Illus.). 160p. 1988. pap. text 6.00 (*0-8428-9515-9*) Cambridge Bk.

Living in the Reader's World, 4 bks., Bk. 4. Ed. by Dennis Mendyk. (Adult Reading Ser.: Levels 2-6). (Illus.). 160p. 1988. pap. text 6.00 (*0-8428-9517-5*) Cambridge Bk.

Living in the Real Church: A Fresh Look at How Christians Treat One Another. Randy Moody. LC 97-47608. 1998. pap. 12.99 (*0-89900-801-1*) College Pr Pub.

Living in the Real World Vol. III: Participants Manual - From the "A Path to Responsibility" Treatment Program. G. Richard Kishur. 189p. 1994. student ed., spiral bd. 19.95 (*1-885473-03-6*) Wood N Barnes.

Living in the Realm of the Spirit. Frederick K. Price. 41p. (Orig.). 1995. pap. 2.99 (*1-883798-07-8*) Faith One.

Living in the Realm of the Spirit. Frederick K. Price. 50p. (Orig.). 1989. pap. 4.99 (*0-89274-569-X*) Harrison Hse.

Living in the Resurrection. T. Crunk. LC 95-12681. (Series of Younger Poets: Vol. 90). 1995. 16.00 (*0-300-06525-6*); pap. 10.00 (*0-300-06526-4*) Yale U Pr.

Living in the Rock 'n Roll Mystery: Reading Context, Self, & Others As Clues. H. L. Goodall, Jr. 451p. (C). 1991. 31.95 (*0-8093-1610-2*) S Ill U Pr.

***Living in the Runaway West: Partisan Views from Writers on the Range.** Ed. by High Country News Editors. 256p. 2000. pap. 16.95 (*1-55591-048-3*) Fulcrum Pub.

Living in the Shadow of the Second Coming: American Premillennialism, 1875-1982. enl. rev. ed. Timothy P. Weber. xiv, 306p. 1993. reprint ed. pap. text 12.95 (*0-226-87732-9*) U Ch Pr.

***Living in the Sixth Dimension.** 100p. (J). (gr. 3-8). 1999. pap. 9.95 (*0-9648757-1-3*, Pub. by Pince Nez Pr) Sunbelt Pubns.

Living in the Solution: Understanding & Using the Wisdom of the Rooms of Alcoholics Anonymous. John W & James A. 288p. 1998. pap. 14.00 (*0-7871-1361-1*, NewStar Pr) NewStar Media.

Living in the Spirit. Rachel Hosmer & Alan Jones. (Church's Teaching Ser.: Vol. 7). 272p. 1985. 1.50 (*0-8164-2227-3*) Harper SF.

Living in the Spirit. R. Hollis Gause. 136p. 1996. reprint ed. pap. 9.99 (*0-87148-515-X*) Pathway Pr.

Living in the Spirit of the Beatitudes: Reflections for Lent. Robert R. Gillogly. 116p. (Orig.). 1995. pap. text 5.00 (*0-9634870-3-5*) Asterisk Pubns.

***Living in the State of Stuck: How Assistive Technology Impacts the Lives of People with Disabilities.** 3rd ed. Marcia J. Scherer. LC 00-23702. (Illus.). 2000. pap. write for info. (*1-57129-079-6*) Brookline Bks.

Living in the State of Stuck: How Technology Impacts the Lives of Persons with Disabilities. 2nd ed. Marcia J. Scherer. 256p. 1996. pap. 17.95 (*1-57129-027-3*) Brookline Bks.

Living in the Supernatural. Kathie Walters. LC 93-71666. 64p. (Orig.). 1993. reprint ed. pap. 4.99 (*1-888081-50-3*) Good News Min.

Living in the Tenth Century: Mentalities & Social Orders. Heinrich Fichtenau. Tr. by Patrick J. Geary. LC 90-11134. xxii, 494p. (C). 1993. pap. text 18.95 (*0-226-24621-3*) U Ch Pr.

Living in the Tenth Century: Mentalities & Social Orders. Heinrich Fichtenau. Tr. by Patrick J. Geary. LC 90-11134. 494p. 1998. 60.00 (*0-226-24620-5*) U Ch Pr.

Living in the Third Millennium: Forecasts to Master Your Future. Konrad Kressley. LC 98-206527. (Illus.). 214p. 1998. per. 12.95 (*1-887650-12-1*, Pub. by Factor Pr) BookWorld.

Living in the U. S. A. Judy Burghart. 160p. 1990. pap. 10.55 (*0-8442-7694-4*) NTC Contemp Pub Co.

Living in the U. S. A. 2nd ed. Judy Burghart. 160p. 1990. pap. 10.55 (*0-8442-7695-2*) NTC Contemp Pub Co.

Living in the U. S. A. 5th ed. Alison R. Lanier. LC 95-53161. 240p. 1996. pap. text 15.95 (*1-877864-40-4*, 304R) Intercult Pr.

Living in the U. S. A., Bk. 3. Burkhold. 160p. 1990. pap. 10.55 (*0-8442-7696-0*) NTC Contemp Pub Co.

Living in the U. S. A., Bks. 1, 2 & 3. Burkhold. 1990. pap., teacher ed. 14.05 (*0-8442-7697-9*) NTC Contemp Pub Co.

***Living in the United States: How to Feel at Home, Make Friends & Enjoy Everyday Life: A Brief Introduction to the Culture for Visitors, Students & Business Travelers.** Raymond C. Clark. 1999. pap. 9.95 (*0-86647-114-6*) Pro Lingua.

Living in the United States: How to Feel at Home, Make Friends & Enjoy Everyday Life: A Brief Introduction to the Culture for Visitors, Students & Business Travelers. 4th rev. ed. Annie Hawkinson & Raymond C. Clark. Ed. by Arthur A. Burrows. (Living in Ser.). (Illus.). 60p. 1996. pap. text 4.50 (*0-86647-097-2*) Pro Lingua.

Living in the Wilderness: A Guide. 1991. lib. bdg. 75.00 (*0-8490-4685-8*) Gordon Pr.

Living in the World. Carolyn Nystrom. (Christian Character Bible Studies). 64p. (Orig.). 1992. pap., wbk. ed. 4.99 (*0-8308-1144-3*, 1144) InterVarsity.

Living in the World. Alexandra Parsons. LC 96-11877. (Life Education Ser.). 1997. lib. bdg. 19.00 (*0-531-14430-5*) Watts.

Living in the Zoo & Loving It! Gene Williams. LC 95-31167. 128p. 1995. pap. 8.99 (*0-8341-1601-4*) Beacon Hill.

Living in Time. Rachel Hadas. LC 90-32546. 225p. (Orig.). (C). 1990. text 34.00 (*0-8135-1592-0*) Rutgers U Pr.

Living in Time. Rachel Hadas. LC 90-32546. 225p. (Orig.). (C). 1990. pap. 12.95 (*0-8135-1593-9*) Rutgers U Pr.

Living in Time: The Poetry of C. Day Lewis. Albert Gelpi. LC 96-45410. (Illus.). 256p. 1998. text 55.00 (*0-19-509863-3*) OUP.

Living in Today's World: A Guide for Achievement. Joe C. Harmon. (Hand Program Ser.: No. 1). 60p. Date not set. pap. text 9.95 (*1-928803-00-8*) Access Grp Inc.

Living in Touch with God. Lawrence O. Richards. 128p. (Orig.). 1988. pap. 6.95 (*0-310-39141-5*, 18302P) Zondervan.

Living in Troubled Lands: Beating the Terrorist Threat Overseas. Patrick Collins. 192p. 1991. 20.00 (*0-87364-198-1*) Paladin Pr.

Living in Two Cities: Augustinian Trajectories in Politics. Eugene Te Selle. LC 98-27284. 220p. 1997. 24.95 (*0-940866-68-4*); pap. 18.95 (*0-940866-69-2*) U Scranton Pr.

Living in Two Worlds. John G. Bennett. (Orig.). 1989. pap. 10.95 (*0-934254-31-1*) Claymont Comm.

Living in Two Worlds. Kosof. 1996. write for info. (*0-8050-5276-3*) H Holt & Co.

Living in Two Worlds. Carol Lovejoy. Ed. by Sandy Oakes. 180p. (Orig.). 1992. pap. 12.95 (*0-9633137-6-2*) Golden Globe.

Living in Two Worlds: The Autobiography of Ursula Roberts. Ursula Roberts. Ed. by Regency Press, Ltd. Staff. 200p. 1984. 39.00 (*0-7212-0629-8*, Pub. by Regency Pr GBR) St Mut.

Living in Two Worlds - The Immigrant Children's Experience see Single Titles Series

***Living in Venice.** Frederic Vitoux. 2000. 50.00 (*2-08-013688-7*, Pub. by Flammarion) Abbeville Pr.

Living in Water. (Longman Biology Topics Ser.). Date not set. pap. text. write for info. (*0-582-32304-5*, Pub. by Addison-Wesley) Longman.

Living in Water: An Aquatic Science Curriculum for Grades 5-7. 3rd ed. National Aquarium Staff. LC 98-129711. 420p. (C). 1997. per. 23.95 (*0-7872-4366-3*) Kendall-Hunt.

Living in Westchester. Rasma Koch. 112p. (C). 1996. pap. text, per. 18.95 (*0-7872-2300-X*, 41230001) Kendall-Hunt.

Living in Words: Interviews from the Bloomsbury Review 1981-1988. Ed. by Gregory McNamee. LC 88-12132. 178p. 1988. 19.95 (*0-932576-62-1*); pap. 8.95 (*0-932576-63-X*) Breitenbush Bks.

Living in Wyoming Settling for More: Pioneer Trails Edition. 2nd rev. ed. Susan Anderson. LC 97-69636. (Illus.). 172p. 1997. 39.95 (*0-9660022-0-2*) Rockridge Pr.

Living India. Savel Zimand. LC 72-19. (Select Bibliographies Reprint Ser.). 1977. reprint ed. 22.95 (*0-8369-9974-6*) Ayer.

Living Information: Subconscious Mind & Power. Robert Rison. (Illus.). 61p. (Orig.). (C). 1988. pap. 7.95 (*0-9625706-0-5*) ECLAT Bks.

Living Inside Our Hope: A Steadfast Radical's Thoughts on Rebuilding the Movement. Staughton Lynd. LC 96-39270. (ILR Press Book). (Illus.). 1996. text 39.95 (*0-8014-3363-0*); pap. text 15.95 (*0-8014-8402-2*) Cornell U Pr.

Living Inside Our Hope: A Steadfast Radical's Thoughts on Rebuilding the Movement. Staughton Lynd. 1997. 37.50 (*0-614-27584-9*); pap. 14.95 (*0-614-27583-0*) Cornell U Pr.

Living Inside Out: Learning How to Pray the Serenity Prayer. Jan G. Linn. LC 94-12023. 176p. (Orig.). 1994. pap. 9.99 (*0-8272-2123-1*) Chalice Pr.

Living Inside Out: Saying Yes to the Inner Voice. Ellen F. Solart. Ed. by Tama White. LC 98-94794. 238p. 1999. pap. 14.00 (*0-9663043-1-4*) Desert Sage.

Living Inside Prison Walls: Adjustment Behavior. Victoria R. Derosia. LC 98-15659. 224p. 1998. 55.00 (*0-275-95895-7*, Praeger Pubs) Greenwood.

Living Insights Study Bible. Ed. by Charles R. Swindoll. 1996. 66.99 (*0-614-19770-8*); pap. 19.99 (*0-614-19769-4*) Zondervan.

Living Inspirations. Raja. 1994. pap. 11.95 (*1-85230-557-6*, Pub. by Element MA) Penguin Putnam.

Living Inspired. Akiva Tatz. 216p. 1993. 19.95 (*1-56871-026-7*, Pub. by Targum Pr) Feldheim.

Living Instead. William Bronk. 98p. 1996. 16.95 (*1-883689-40-6*) Talisman Hse.

Living InSync: Creating Your Life with Balance & Purpose. Susan Pilgrim. 320p. (Orig.). 1995. pap. 9.95 (*1-55874-340-5*, 3405) Health Comm.

***Living Intentionally.** Andrew Eschenfelder. LC 98-88568. 368p. 1999. pap. 16.99 (*1-57921-162-3*, Pub. by WinePress Pub) BookWorld.

Living Intentionally & Making Life Happen. rev. ed. John J. Schmidt. LC 93-73272. 160p. (Orig.). 1994. pap. 9.95 (*0-9626185-4-3*) Brookcliff Pubs.

Living Intuitively: Reaping Life's Rich Benefits. Bruce Way. LC 97-38928. 176p. 1997. pap. 9.95 (*0-89087-845-5*) Celestial Arts.

Living Invertebrates. Mildred Buchsbaum et al. LC 86-10790. (Illus.). 848p. (C). 1987. text 54.95 (*0-86542-312-1*) Boxwood.

Living Is Easy. Dorothy West. LC 81-22062. 376p. 1995. pap. 14.95 (*1-55861-147-9*) Feminist Pr.

Living Is Easy. Dorothy West. LC 71-94139. (American Negro: His History & Literature. Series 2). 1970. reprint ed. 45.11 (*0-405-01942-4*) Ayer.

Living Is Forever. J. Edwin Carter. 408p. 1992. pap. 12.95 (*1-878901-42-7*) Hampton Roads Pub Co.

Living Is What I Wanted: Last Poems. David Ignatow. (American Poets Continuum Ser.: Vol. 55). 70p. 1999. 21.95 (*1-880238-77-2*, Pub. by BOA Edns); pap. 12.50 (*1-880238-78-0*, Pub. by BOA Edns) Consort Bk Sales.

Living Islam: From Samarkand to Stornoway. Akbar S. Ahmed. LC 93-38378. (Illus.). 224p. 1994. 24.95 (*0-8160-3103-7*) Facts on File.

***Living Islam: From Samarkand to Stornoway.** Akbar S. Ahmed. (Illus.). 224p. 1999. 31.95 (*0-7351-0210-4*) Replica Bks.

***Living Islam: Women Politics & Religion in Turkey.** Ayse Saktanber. 2000. text 59.50 (*1-86064-178-4*, Pub. by I B T) St Martin.

L

L

Living Islam East & West. Shaykh F. Haeri. 1993. pap. 15.95 (*1-85230-065-5*, Pub. by Element MA) Penguin Putnam.

Living Issues in Ethics. Richard T. Nolan & Frank G. Kirkpatrick. 388p. (C). 1982. 34.50 (*0-534-01140-3*) Wadsworth Pub.

Living Issues in Philosophy. 7th ed. Titus. (Philosophy Ser.). 1979. pap. 23.00 (*0-534-25822-0*) Wadsworth Pub.

Living Issues in Philosophy. 8th ed. Harold H. Titus et al. 529p. (C). 1986. pap. 36.25 (*0-534-05376-9*) Wadsworth Pub.

Living Issues in Philosophy. 8th ed. Titus & Smith. (Philosophy Ser.). 1986. mass mkt., teacher ed. write for info. (*0-534-05377-7*) West Pub.

Living Issues in Philosophy. 9th ed. Marilyn S. Smith et al. LC 94-5625. 480p. 1994. 75.95 (*0-534-24708-3*) Wadsworth Pub.

Living Issues in Religious Thought: From George Fox to Bertrand Russell. Herbert G. Wood. LC 67-22128. (Essay Index Reprint Ser.). 1977. 17.95 (*0-8369-1007-9*) Ayer.

Living Issues in Religious Thought: From George Fox to Bertrand Russell. Herbert G. Wood. LC 67-22128. (Essay Index Reprint Ser.). 187p. 1967. reprint ed. lib. bdg. 16.50 (*0-8290-0489-0*) Irvington.

Living It Up. Karen Finley. 1996. 18.00 (*0-517-70289-4*) Random Hse Value.

Living It Up: Meditations for "Seasoned Saints" Leona Choy. 300p. 1998. pap. 16.95 (*1-889283-14-2*) Golden Morning.

Living It up down Under: or How Much Can a Koala Bear, Vol. I. Robert D. Thomas. (Illus.). 120p. (Orig.). 1985. pap. 7.95 (*0-935865-01-2*) SFX Pr.

***Living It up on the Way Out.** Jim Bloom. 1999. pap. 10.00 (*0-7880-1402-1*) CSS.

Living Jesus: Learning the Heart of the Gospel. Luke T. Johnson. LC 98-22647. 224p. 1999. 22.00 (*0-06-064282-3*, Pub. by Harper SF) HarpC.

Living Jesus: Learning the Heart of the Gospel. Luke T. Johnson. LC 98-22647. 224p. 2000. pap. 15.00 (*0-06-064283-1*, Pub. by Harper SF) HarpC.

Living Jesus: The Words of Jesus of Nazareth. Frederick A. Wiggin. 211p. 1993. reprint ed. spiral bd. 16.50 (*0-7873-0968-0*) Hlth Research.

Living Jewel: A Beginners Guide to Saltwater Aquariums. Robert L. Fuqua. LC 95-70184. (Illus.). 206p. (Orig.). 1995. pap. 10.00 (*0-9640621-0-0*) Dragonfly.

Living Joyfully with Children. Win Sweet & Bill Sweet. LC 97-23182. 1997. pap. 13.95 (*1-889051-17-9*) Acrpls Bks CO.

Living Judaism: The Complete Guide to Jewish Belief, Tradition, & Practice. Wayne Dosick. LC 95-22260. (Illus.). 400p. 1995. 27.50 (*0-06-062119-2*, Pub. by Harper SF) HarpC.

Living Judaism: The Complete Guide to Jewish Belief, Tradition & Practice. Wayne D. Dosick. LC 95-22260. (Illus.). 400p. 1998. pap. 20.00 (*0-06-062179-6*, Pub. by Harper SF) HarpC.

Living Judaism Around the World. Leonard Nadler & Zeace Nadler. LC 97-65959. 264p. (Orig.). 1997. pap. 15.95 (*1-57197-065-7*) Pentland Pr.

Living Juicy: Daily Morsels for Your Creative Soul. Sark, pseud. LC 94-29508. (Illus.). 1994. pap. 15.95 (*0-89087-703-3*) Celestial Arts.

Living Juicy: Daily Morsels for Your Creative Soul. Sark, pseud. (Illus.). 380p. 1995. 22.95 (*0-89087-717-3*) Celestial Arts.

Living Jung: The Good & the Better. Daryl Sharp. (Studies in Jungian Psychology by Jungian Analysts: No. 72). (Illus.). 128p. 1996. pap. 16.00 (*0-919123-73-2*, Pub. by Inner City Bks) BookWorld.

***Living Justice: Catholic Social Teaching in Action.** Thomas Massaro. (Come & See Ser.: Vol. 3). 280p. 2000. pap. 11.95 (*1-58051-046-9*) Sheed & Ward WI.

Living Laboratories: Women & Reproductive Technology. Robyn Rowland. LC 92-13199. 384p. 1992. 37.95 (*0-253-34999-0*); pap. 6.95 (*0-253-20760-6*, MB-760) Ind U Pr.

Living Labyrinth: Exploring Universal Themes in Myth, Dreams & the Symbolism of Working Life. Jeremy Taylor. LC 97-40490. 320p. 1998. pap. 22.95 (*0-8091-3766-6*) Paulist Pr.

Living Land Sourcebook. (Torg Ser.). 128p. 18.00 (*0-87431-304-X*, 20505) West End Games.

Living Landscape. George A. Steiner. 388p. (C). 1991. 77.19 (*0-07-061133-5*) McGraw.

***Living Landscape: An Ecological Approach to Landscape Planning.** 2nd ed. Frederick R. Steiner. LC 99-49557. (Illus.). 477p. 2000. 59.95 (*0-07-079398-0*) McGraw.

Living Landscapes of Kansas. Photos by Steve Mulligan. LC 95-4636. (Illus.). 166p. (C). 1995. 29.95 (*0-7006-0727-7*) U Pr of KS.

Living Language: Conversational German. rev. ed. Crown Publishing Staff. (Living Language Ser.). (GER.). 1998. pap. 7.00 (*0-609-80300-X*) Crown Pub Group.

Living Language: Conversational Italian. rev. ed. Crown Publishing Staff. (Living Language Ser.). 1998. pap. 7.00 (*0-609-80294-1*) Crown Pub Group.

Living Language: Conversational Portuguese. rev. ed. Crown Publishing Staff. (Living Language Ser.). 1998. pap. 7.00 (*0-609-80293-3*) Crown Pub Group.

Living Language: Conversational Russian. rev. ed. Crown Publishing Staff. 1998. pap. 7.00 (*0-609-80291-7*) Crown Pub Group.

Living Language: Conversational Spanish. rev. ed. Crown Publishing Staff. (Living Language Ser.). 1998. pap. 7.00 (*0-609-80288-7*) Crown Pub Group.

Living Language: French 2 All the Way. Annie Heminway. (FRE.). 1995. pap. 65.00 incl. audio (*0-517-70269-X*) Crown Pub Group.

Living Language: German 2 All the Way. Birgit Nielsen. (GER.). 1995. 85.00 incl. cd-rom (*0-517-70216-9*) Crown Pub Group.

Living Language: Reading, Thinking & Writing. Nilsen. LC 98-30375. 490p. 1998. pap. text 37.00 (*0-205-27091-3*) Allyn.

Living Language: Spanish All the Way 2: Conversation, Grammar, Culture, Reading, Writing, Business. Daniel Holodyk. Ed. by Ana Suffredini & Helga Schier. LC 95-1317. (Living Language Ser.). 1995. pap. 15.00 (*0-517-88289-2*, Crown) Crown Pub Group.

Living Language: USA Culture Capsules for ESL Students: Dialogs on Life in the United States. Jerrilou Johnson. 1979. 8.95 (*0-88377-152-7*, Newbury) Heinle & Heinle.

Living Language All the Way Japanese. Crown Staff. (Living Language Ser.). (JPN.). 1998. write for info. (*0-517-70236-3*) Liv Lang.

Living Language Basic Course: French Dictionary. rev. ed. 1993. pap. 5.00 (*0-517-59075-1*) Liv Lang.

Living Language Basic Course: French Manual. rev. ed. 1993. pap. 6.00 (*0-517-59074-3*) Liv Lang.

Living Language Basic Course: German Dictionary. rev. ed. Walter Kleinnland. 1993. pap. 5.00 (*0-517-59044-1*) Liv Lang.

Living Language Basic Course: Japanese Manual. rev. ed. 1993. pap. 6.00 (*0-517-59066-2*) Liv Lang.

Living Language Basic Course: Spanish Dictionary. rev. ed. Irvin Stern. 1993. pap. 5.00 (*0-517-59051-4*) Liv Lang.

Living Language Chinese: Basic-Intermediate: Mandarin. Living Language Staff. LC 99-22778. (Living Language Ser.). (C). 2000. pap. 75.00 incl. audio (*0-517-70877-9*) Liv Lang.

Living Language Complete Course: French. Living Language. (Living Language Ser.). (ENG & FRE.). 1998. 30.00 incl. cd-rom (*0-609-60275-6*, 903601) Liv Lang.

Living Language Complete Course: French. Ralph Weiman. (Living Language Ser.). (ENG & FRE.). 22.50 incl. audio (*0-609-60274-8*, 903593) Liv Lang.

Living Language Complete Course: German. Living Language. (Living Language Ser.). (ENG & GER.). 1998. 30.00 incl. cd-rom, audio compact disk (*0-609-60277-2*, 903603) Liv Lang.

Living Language Complete Course: German. Genevieve A. Martin. (The Living Language Ser.). (GER.). 1998. 22.50 incl. audio (*0-609-60276-4*, 903596) Crown Pub Group.

Living Language Complete Course: Ingles, Level 1. rev. ed. Martin A. Genevieve. (ENG & SPA.). 22.50 incl. audio (*0-609-60273-X*, 903609) Liv Lang.

Living Language Complete Course: Italian. Living Language. (ENG & ITA.). 1998. 30.00 incl. cd-rom, audio compact disk (*0-609-60272-1*, 903604) Liv Lang.

Living Language Complete Course: Italian. Genevieve A. Martin. (ITA.). 1998. 22.50 incl. audio (*0-609-60271-3*, 903598) Crown Pub Group.

Living Language Complete Course: Japanese. Living Language. (ENG & JPN.). 1998. 30.00 incl. cd-rom, audio compact disk (*0-609-60279-9*, 903607) Liv Lang.

Living Language Complete Course: Japanese. Ichiro Shirato. (Living Language Ser.). 1998. 22.50 incl. audio (*0-609-60278-0*, 903599) Crown Pub Group.

Living Language Complete Course: Portuguese (Brazillian) Crown Publishing Staff. (Living Language Ser.). 1998. 22.50 incl. audio (*0-609-60269-1*, 903610) Crown Pub Group.

Living Language Complete Course: Portuguese (Continental) Crown Publishing Staff. (Living Language Ser.). 1998. 22.50 incl. audio (*0-609-60270-5*, 903611) Crown Pub Group.

Living Language Complete Course: Russian. Aron Pressman. (Living Language Ser.). (RUS.). 1998. 22.50 incl. audio (*0-609-60268-3*, 903612) Crown Pub Group.

Living Language Complete Course: Spanish. Living Language. (ENG & SPA.). 30.00 incl. cd-rom, audio compact disk (*0-609-60267-5*, 903608) Liv Lang.

Living Language Complete Course: Spanish. rev. ed. Ralph Weiman & Living Language. (Living Language Ser.). (SPA.). audio 22.50 (*0-609-60266-7*, 903600) Liv Lang.

Living Language Conversational Japanese. rev. ed. Crown Publishing Staff. 1998. pap. 7.00 (*0-609-80302-6*) Crown Pub Group.

Living Language English for Spanish Speaker: Dictionary. rev. ed. Kathleen Ossip. (Complete Living Language Course Ser.). (ENG & SPA.). 1993. pap. 5.00 (*0-517-59047-6*) Liv Lang.

Living Language English for the Real World Russian. Living Language Staff. 1999. 29.95 incl. audio (*0-609-60510-0*, Crown) Crown.

Living Language Fast & Easy: French. Fast N Easy Staff & Carolyn B. Mitchell. 1991. 10.00 incl. audio (*0-517-58576-6*) Liv Lang.

Living Language Fast & Easy: German. Fast N Easy Staff & Carolyn B. Mitchell. 1991. 10.00 incl. audio (*0-517-58577-4*) Liv Lang.

Living Language Fast & Easy: Italian. Fast N Easy Staff & Carolyn B. Mitchelly. 1991. 10.00 incl. audio (*0-517-58580-4*) Liv Lang.

Living Language Fast & Easy Arabic. Living Language Staff. (ENG.). 1998. 9.95 incl. audio (*0-609-60350-7*) Liv Lang.

Living Language Fast & Easy Arabic: The 60-Minute Survival Guide. Crown Living Language Staff. (ARA.). 1992. 10.00 incl. audio (*0-517-58875-7*) Liv Lang.

Living Language Fast & Easy Czech. Living Language Staff. (ENG.). 1998. 9.95 incl. audio (*0-609-60349-3*) Liv Lang.

Living Language Fast & Easy Czech: The 60-Minute Survival Program. Fast N Easy Staff & Carolyn B. Mitchell. 1992. 10.00 incl. audio (*0-517-58748-3*) Liv Lang.

Living Language Fast & Easy French. Living Language Staff. (FRE & ENG.). 1998. 9.95 incl. audio (*0-609-60348-5*) Liv Lang.

Living Language Fast & Easy German. Living Language Staff. (GER & ENG.). 1998. 9.95 incl. audio (*0-609-60347-7*) Liv Lang.

Living Language Fast & Easy Hebrew. Living Language Staff. (ENG.). 1998. 9.95 incl. audio (*0-609-60346-9*) Liv Lang.

Living Language Fast & Easy Hungarian. Living Language Staff. (ENG.). 1998. 9.95 incl. audio (*0-609-60345-0*) Liv Lang.

Living Language Fast & Easy Hungarian: The 60-Minute Survival Guide. Fast N Easy Staff & Carolyn B. Mitchell. 1992. 10.00 incl. audio (*0-517-58818-8*) Liv Lang.

Living Language Fast & Easy Ingles para Hispanohablantes: 60 Minutos de Ingles Basico. Crown Living Language Staff. (SPA & ENG.). 1992. 10.00 incl. audio (*0-517-58792-0*) Liv Lang.

Living Language Fast & Easy Italian. Living Language Staff. (ITA & ENG.). 1998. 9.95 incl. audio (*0-609-60343-4*) Liv Lang.

Living Language Fast & Easy Japanese. Living Language Staff. (JPN & ENG.). 1998. 9.95 incl. audio (*0-609-60342-6*) Liv Lang.

Living Language Fast & Easy Korean. Living Language Staff. (KOR & ENG.). 1998. 9.95 incl. audio (*0-609-60344-2*) Liv Lang.

Living Language Fast & Easy Korean: The 60-Minute Survival Program. Fast N Easy Staff & Carolyn B. Mitchell. 1992. 10.00 incl. audio (*0-517-58749-1*) Liv Lang.

Living Language Fast & Easy Mandarin. Living Language Staff. (CHI & ENG.). 1998. 9.95 incl. audio (*0-609-60341-8*) Liv Lang.

Living Language Fast & Easy Mandarin: The 60-Minute Survival Guide. Crown Living Language Staff. 1992. 10.00 incl. audio (*0-517-58754-8*) Liv Lang.

Living Language Fast & Easy Polish. Living Language Staff. (POL & ENG.). 1998. 9.95 incl. audio (*0-609-60340-X*) Liv Lang.

Living Language Fast & Easy Polish: The 60-Minute Survival Guide. Crown Living Language Staff. (POL.). 1992. 10.00 incl. audio (*0-517-58794-7*) Liv Lang.

Living Language Fast & Easy Portuguese. Living Language Staff. (POR & ENG.). 1998. 9.95 incl. audio (*0-609-60339-6*) Liv Lang.

Living Language Fast & Easy Russian. Living Language Staff. (RUS & ENG.). 1998. 9.95 incl. audio (*0-609-60338-8*) Liv Lang.

Living Language French All the Way: Learn at Home & on the Go. Annie Heminway. LC 93-9000. (ENG & FRE.). 1994. 60.00 incl. audio (*0-517-58368-2*, Crown) Crown Pub Group.

Living Language French on a Rainy Day. Crown. LC 99-13172. (ANG, APA & FRE.). 1999. 14.95 (*0-609-60209-8*) Liv Lang.

Living Language German All the Way Cassette/Book: Learn at Home & on the Go. Ingeborg Lasting & Heidi Singer. LC 93-22955. (ENG & GER.). 1994. 60.00 incl. audio (*0-517-58378-X*, Crown) Crown Pub Group.

Living Language German All the Way Manual: Learn at Home & on the Go. Ingeborg Lasting & Heidi Singer. LC 93-22955. (ENG & GER.). 1994. pap. 16.00 (*0-517-58379-8*, Crown) Crown Pub Group.

Living Language German All the Way 2: Conversation, Grammar, Culture, Reading, Writing, Business. Birgit Nielsen. Ed. by Helga Schier & Ana Suffrendini. LC 95-5241. (Living Language Ser.). 1995. pap. 15.00 (*0-517-88291-4*, Crown) Crown Pub Group.

Living Language German Conversational Manuel: German Manual. rev. ed. 1993. pap. 6.00 (*0-517-59043-3*) Liv Lang.

Living Language German '99: Daily Phrase Book. 1999. pap. 0.00 (*0-609-80328-X*) Liv Lang.

***Living Language Hable Ingles.** Language Living Staff. 1999. 15.95 (*0-609-60533-X*) Crown Bks Yng Read.

Living Language Italian All the Way Cassette/Book: Learn at Home & on the Go. Salvatore Bancheri & Michael Lettieri. LC 93-8975. 1994. 60.00 (*0-517-58375-5*) Crown Pub Group.

Living Language Italian All the Way Manual: Learn at Home & on the Go. Salvatore Bancheri & Michael Lettieri. LC 93-8975. 1994. pap. 16.00 (*0-517-58376-3*) Crown Pub Group.

Living Language Italian Conversational Manual. rev. ed. 1993. pap. 6.00 (*0-517-59039-5*) Liv Lang.

Living Language Italian Dictionary. rev. ed. 1993. pap. 5.00 (*0-517-59040-9*) Liv Lang.

Living Language Italian on a Rainy Day. Crown. LC 99-13163. (ITA.). 1999. 14.95 (*0-609-60211-X*) Liv Lang.

Living Language Italian '99: Daily Phrase Book. 1999. pap. 0.00 (*0-609-80327-1*) Liv Lang.

Living Language Japanese Dictionary: Japanese Dictionary. rev. ed. Hiroko Storm. 1993. pap. 5.00 (*0-517-59067-0*) Liv Lang.

Living Language Russian Conversational Manuel. rev. ed. Nadya Peterson. (RUS.). 1993. pap. 6.00 (*0-517-59054-9*) Liv Lang.

Living Language Russian Dictionary. Crown Publishing Group Staff. (Living Language Ser.). (ENG & RUS.). 1998. pap. 5.00 (*0-609-80290-9*) Liv Lang.

Living Language Russian Dictionary: Dictionary. rev. ed. Nadya Peterson. (Complete Living Language Course Ser.). (ENG & RUS.). 1993. pap. 5.00 (*0-517-59055-7*) Liv Lang.

Living Language Spanish Conversational Manuel: Spanish Manual. rev. ed. 1993. pap. 6.00 (*0-517-59050-6*) Liv Lang.

Living Language Spanish Dictionary. Crown Publishing Group Staff. 1998. pap. 5.00 (*0-609-80289-5*) Liv Lang.

Living Language Spanish on a Rainy Day. Crown. LC 99-19112. (SPA.). 1999. 14.95 (*0-609-60210-1*) Liv Lang.

Living Language Ultimate French Advantage. Crown Staff. LC 97-45798. 1998. pap. 18.00 (*0-609-80251-8*) Crown Pub Group.

Living Language Ultimate German Advantage. Crown Staff. LC 97-45801. 1998. pap. 18.00 (*0-609-80252-6*) Liv Lang.

***Living Language Ultimate Portuguese: Basic-Intermediate.** Living Language Staff. (ENG & POR.). 2000. pap. 75.00 incl. audio (*0-609-60422-8*) Liv Lang.

Living Language Ultimate Russian: Basic. Crown Publihing Group Staff. LC 97-726. 1998. pap. 18.00 (*0-517-88284-1*) Liv Lang.

Living Language Ultimate Spanish Advantage. Crown Staff. LC 97-43608. 1998. pap. 18.00 (*0-609-80253-4*) Crown Pub Group.

***Living Languages.** 1999. write for info. (*0-13-003219-0*) P-H.

Living Languages: Contexts for Reading & Writing. Nancy Buffington et al. LC 96-45326. 462p. (C). 1997. pap. text 37.80 (*0-13-668963-9*) P-H.

Living Languages of the Americas: Combined Volume. Summer Institute of Linguistics Staff. 456p. 1995. pap. 30.00 (*1-55671-023-2*) S I L Intl.

***Living Large: How to Live Well--Even on a Little.** J. Raymond Albrektson. LC 99-44168. 208p. 2000. pap. 10.95 (*1-57856-227-9*) Waterbrook Pr.

Living Latin, Bk. 1. Clara W. Ashley et al. (ENG & LAT., Illus.). 128p. Date not set. pap. 28.20 (*0-8442-8600-1*, E8600-1) NTC Contemp Pub Co.

Living Latin, Bk. 2. Clara W. Ashley et al. (LAT., Illus.). 128p. (C). Date not set. 28.20 (*0-8442-8602-8*, E8602-8) NTC Contemp Pub Co.

Living Latin, Includ. Answer Key. Clara W. Ashley et al. (Illus.). Date not set. wbk. ed. 4.25 (*0-8442-8610-9*, E8610-9); pap., wbk. ed. 4.25 (*0-8442-8609-5*, E8609-5) NTC Contemp Pub Co.

Living, Laughing & Loving Life. Dan Miller. LC 97-60589. 128p. 1997. pap. 9.95 (*1-57921-020-1*, Pub. by WinePress Pub) BookWorld.

Living Law of Democratic Society. Jerome Hall. 146p. 1982. reprint ed. 35.00 (*0-8377-0641-6*, Rothman) W S Hein.

Living Leadership. Ed. by Kenneth F. Hall. 1991. pap. 2.99 (*0-87162-993-3*, D4201) Warner Pr.

Living Lean: How to Lose up to 5 Lbs. Each Week Permanently & Naturally. 2nd rev. ed. John Farley. (Illus.). 87p. 1995. pap. 17.95 (*0-9674252-0-4*) Optml Perform.

Living Lean: The Larry North Program. Larry North. LC 96-46973. (Illus.). 259p. 1997. pap. 12.95 (*0-684-83700-5*, Fireside) S&S Trade Pap.

Living Lean by Choosing More. Cheryl Jennings-Sauer. LC 88-24823. (Illus.). 200p. (Orig.). 1989. pap. 14.95 (*0-87833-604-4*) Taylor Pub.

Living Lean off the Fat of the Land. June Fritchman & Karey Solomon. LC 82-14932. (Illus.). 224p. (Orig.). 1983. pap. 4.95 (*0-943914-03-5*) Larson Pubns.

Living, Learning & Loving: God Hears My Prayers, Let's Love One Another, Living the Golden Rule, 3 bks., Set. Bessie Dean. 1994. pap. 12.98 (*0-88290-479-5*) Horizon Utah.

***Living Legacies: How to Write, Illustrate & Share Your Life Stories.** Duane Elgin. 2001. 18.95 (*1-57324-552-6*) Conari Press.

Living Legacy: How Nineteen Sixty-Four Changed America. Joseph J. Mangano. LC 93-26725. 228p. (Orig.). (C). 1993. pap. text 24.50 (*0-8191-9270-8*) U Pr of Amer.

Living Legacy: Thirty-Seven Architectural Tours. Mark A. Wilson. (Illus.). 335p. 1987. pap. 19.95 (*0-938530-38-0*) Lexikos.

Living Legacy of Fritz & Laura Perls: Contemporary Case Studies. Ed. by Bud Feder & Ruth Ronall. (Illus.). 298p. 1997. pap. 24.00 (*0-9663109-0-X*) B Feder.

Living Legacy of Marx Durkheim & Weber: Applications & Analyses of Classical Sociological Theory by Modern Social Scientists. Ed. by Richard Altschuler. LC 97-78374. (Living Legacy Ser.: Vol. 1). 624p. 1998. pap. text 39.95 (*1-884092-54-3*) R Altschuler.

Living Legend of Saint Patrick. Alannah Hopkin. (Illus.). 192p. 1990. 15.95 (*0-312-03859-3*) St Martin.

Living Legends: Six Stories about Successful Deaf People. Darlene Toole. (Illus.). 64p. (Orig.). 1996. pap. text 7.95 (*1-884362-13-3*) Butte Pubns.

Living Legends: Stories of Early New Mexico. Alice Bullock. LC 72-90383. (Illus.). 1978. pap. 6.95 (*0-913270-06-7*) Sunstone Pr.

Living Legends-The Everly Brothers: The History of the Everly Brothers on Record an Illustrated Discography. John Hosum. LC 84-90525. (Illus.). 64p. (Orig.). 1985. pap. 9.95 (*0-9614221-2-2*) Foreverly.

***Living Legends III: Six Stories about Incredible Deaf People.** Darlene Toole. 64p. (J). (gr. 3-8). 2000. pap. 7.95 (*1-884362-40-0*) Butte Pubns.

Living Legends II: Six Stories about Incredible Deaf People. Darlene Toole. 64p. (YA). (gr. 7-12). 1998. pap., student ed. 7.95 (*1-884362-32-X*) Butte Pubns.

Living Lent. Marianne Dorman. 138p. (C). 1989. text 55.00 (*1-872795-79-X*, Pub. by Pentland Pr) St Mut.

An Asterisk (*) at the beginning of an entry indicates that the title is appearing for the first time.

***Living Lent: Meditations for These Forty Days.** Barbara C. Crafton. 112p. 1998. pap. 8.95 (*0-8192-1756-5*) Morehouse Pub.

Living Letters. Sashi Friedman. LC 98-4446. (Illus.). (J). (gr. 1). 1996. 12.00 (*0-8266-0369-6*, Merkos LInyonei Chinuch) Kehot Pubn Soc.

Living Letters of the Law: Ideas of the Jew in Medieval Christianity. Jeremy Cohen. LC 99-20634. 461p. 1999. 60.00 (*0-520-21680-6*, Pub. by U CA Pr) Cal Prin Full Svc.

***Living Letters of the Law: Ideas of the Jews in Medieval Christianity.** Jeremy Cohen. LC 99-20634. 461p. 1999. pap. text 24.95 (*0-520-21870-1*, Pub. by U CA Pr) Cal Prin Full Svc.

Living Liberation in Hindu Thought. Ed. by Andrew O. Fort & Patricia Y. Mumme. LC 95-3018. 278p. (C). 1996. text 59.50 (*0-7914-2705-6*); pap. text 19.95 (*0-7914-2706-4*) State U NY Pr.

Living Life As a Living Target. Judy Gordon. Ed. by Marquetta Herring. (Illus.). 47p. (Orig.). 1987. pap. 3.50 (*0-942186-02-8*) Paperbacks Plus.

Living Life by God's Law. Gordon K. Reed. 124p. (Orig.). 1984. pap. 6.00 (*0-317-03221-6*) Word Ministries Inc.

***Living Life Free from Pain: Treating Arthritis, Joint Pain, Muscle Pain, & Fibromyalgia with Maharishi Vedic Medicine.** Kumuda Reddy & Cynthia Lane. (Illus.). 300p. 2000. pap. 18.95 (*1-929297-17-3*) Samhita Prodns.

Living Life from the Soul: How a Man Unleashes God's Power from the Inside Out. Robert C. Crosby. LC 97-21009. 192p. 1997. pap. 9.99 (*1-55661-954-5*) Bethany Hse.

Living Life in Harmony: A New Beginning for the Religious Casualty. Phillip L. Stewart. LC 94-61490. 215p. (Orig.). 1994. pap. 14.95 (*0-9643717-0-7*) Eden Publng.

Living Life Intentionally. Richard W. Luecke. (Illus.). xviii, 270p. 1996. 24.00 (*1-889774-02-2*) Lucky Lning.

***Living Life Knowing Why.** Fred Willis. (Illus.). 136p. 2000. pap. 14.95 (*0-9613673-9-3*) V Dumond.

***Living Life on Purpose.** Lysa TerKeurst. 2000. pap. 12.99 (*0-8024-4195-5*) Moody.

Living Life on Purpose: A Guide to Creating a Life of Success & Significance. Greg Anderson. LC 96-32302. 1999. pap. 12.00 (*0-06-060232-5*) HarpC.

Living Life to Live It Longer. Herbert M. Shelton. 139p. 1996. reprint ed. spiral bd. 14.00 (*0-7873-0779-3*) Hlth Research.

Living Life Well: New Strategies for Hard Times. Patricia Robinson. (Illus.). 109p. (Orig.). 1996. pap., wbk. ed. 19.95 (*1-878978-27-6*) Context Pr.

Living Life's Circle: Mescalero Apache Cosmovision. Claire R. Farrer. LC 91-23668. 274p. 1994. pap. 15.95 (*0-8263-1560-7*) U of NM Pr.

Living Life's Emergencies: Text for Total Emergency Preparedness. rev. ed. Patrick Lavalla & Robert C. Stoffel. (Illus.). (C). 1992. pap. 35.00 (*0-913724-40-8*) Emerg Response Inst.

Living Light, Vol. 32, No. 1. Raymond F. Collins et al. 88p. (Orig.). 1995. pap. 8.95 (*1-55586-062-1*) US Catholic.

Living Light: Special Feature: Jesus Christ, the One Savior of the World, Yesterday, Today, & Forever. Michael D. Whalen et al. Ed. by Berard L. Marthaler. 96p. 1996. pap. 8.95 (*1-57455-095-0*) US Catholic.

***Living Light: Special Report - 1997 International Catechetical Congress.** Berard L. Marthaler et al. 96p. (C). 1998. pap. 8.95 (*1-57455-155-8*) US Catholic.

Living Light Vol. 31, No. 4: Summer 1995. Mark O'Keefe et al. Ed. by Berard L. Marthaler. 93p. (Orig.). 1995. pap. 8.95 (*1-55586-060-5*) US Catholic.

Living Light Vol. 32, No. 2: Special Feature - Interreligious Dialogue. John Borelli et al. Ed. by Berard L. Marthaler. (Quarterly Journal). 96p. (Orig.). (C). 1995. pap. 8.95 (*1-55586-064-8*) US Catholic.

Living Light Vol. 32, No. 4: Return to Virtue. Ed. by Berard L. Marthaler. 96p. (C). 1996. pap. 8.95 (*1-55586-071-0*) US Catholic.

Living Light Vol. 33, No. 2, Winter 1996: Curriculum & Content in Catechesis. Janaan Manternach et al. 96p. (Orig.). (C). 1996. pap. 8.95 (*1-57455-096-9*) US Catholic.

Living Light Vol. 33, No. 3: Ministry to Young Adults. William D. Dinges et al. 96p. (Orig.). (C). 1997. pap. 8.95 (*1-57455-097-7*) US Catholic.

Living Light Vol. 33, No. 4: Technology & Catechesis. Kathy Gallo et al. 96p. (C). 1998. pap. 8.95 (*1-57455-098-5*) US Catholic.

Living Light Vol. 34, No. 1: Countdown to the Millennium: The Holy Spirit. Richard E. McCarron et al. Ed. by Berard Marthaler. 96p. (C). 1997. pap. 8.95 (*1-57455-154-X*) US Catholic.

Living Light Vol. 34, No. 4: Special Feature: Death, Burial, & Bereavement. Charles Meyer et al. Ed. by Berard Marthaler. 96p. (C). 1998. pap. 8.95 (*1-57455-157-4*) US Catholic.

Living Light Vol. 35, No. 1: Fall, 1998 - Special Feature - Countdown to the Third Millennium - God the Father. George T. Montague et al. Ed. by Berard L. Marthaler. 104p. 1998. pap. 8.95 (*1-57455-274-0*) US Catholic.

Living Light Vol. 35, No. 2: Special Feature, The Communion of Saints. Gabriel O'Donnell et al. Ed. by Berard Marthaler. 96p. (C). 1999. pap. 8.95 (*1-57455-276-7*) US Catholic.

Living Light 34:3 (Spring 1998) Mission & Missions. Ed. by Berard L. Marthaler. 96p. 1998. pap. 8.95 (*1-57455-156-6*) US Catholic.

***Living Lightly: Travels in Post-Consumer Society.** Walter Schwarz & Dorothy Schwarz. (Illus.). 400p. 1999. pap. 27.95 (*1-897766-44-0*, Pub. by Jon Carpenter) Paul & Co Pubs.

Living Lights, Shining Stars: Ten Secrets to Becoming the Light of the World. M. Norvel Young & Mary Hollingsworth. LC 97-25096. 240p. 1997. 15.99 (*1-878990-76-4*) Howard Pub LA.

Living Like a King's Kid. 2nd rev. ed. Jan Van Dyke. (Illus.). 54p. 1989. reprint ed. pap. text 20.00 (*1-58302-042-X*, BTU-04) One Way St.

Living Like a King's Kin. Dale R. Starks. 96p. (Orig.). 1997. pap. 6.95 (*0-9630790-3-4*) D R Starks.

***Living Like Christ, in Christ.** Sister M. Eugene et al. (Our Holy Faith Ser.: Vol. V). (Illus.). 264p. (J). (gr. 5-6). 1998. reprint ed. text 18.00 (*0-911845-81-X*) Neumann Pr.

Living Like Indians: A Treasury of North American Indian Crafts, Games & Activities. unabridged ed. Allan A. Macfarlan. LC 99-25168. (Illus.). 320p. 1999. pap. text 7.95 (*0-486-40671-7*) Dover.

Living like Jesus: 11 for Growing a Genuine Faith. Ronald J. Sider. LC 98-30976. 192p. (C). (gr. 13). 1998. pap. 9.99 (*0-8010-5843-0*) Baker Bks.

Living Like the Saints: A Novel of Nicaragua. Liston Pope, Jr. LC 95-80678. (Works Ser.: II). 300p. 1997. 24.95 (*0-9638900-1-8*) N A Gilbert.

Living Liqueurs. James A. Duke. LC 85-62813. (Bioactive Plants Ser.: Vol. IV). (Orig.). 1987. pap. 15.00 (*0-88000-143-7*) Quarterman.

Living Literature: The Classics & You, Teleclass Study Guide. Zaborowski. 128p. (C). 1995. pap. text, spiral bd. 30.95 (*0-7872-1799-9*, 41177901) Kendall-Hunt.

Living Liturgy: Elementary Reflections. Sofia Cavalletti. LC 98-65273. 96p. 1998. pap. 10.00 (*1-56854-241-0*) Liturgy Tr Pubns.

***Living Liturgy: Spirituality, Celebration, & Catechesis for Sundays & Solemnities, Year A (2002)** Ed. by Joyce Ann Zimmerman et al. 2001. pap. 14.95 (*0-8146-2569-X*) Liturgical Pr.

Living Liturgy: Spirituality, Celebration & Catechesis for Sundays & Solemnities: Year B 2000. Ed. by Joyce Ann Zimmerman et al. LC 99-28091. 304p. 1999. pap. 14.95 (*0-8146-2567-3*) Liturgical Pr.

Living Liturgy: Spirituality, Celebration & Catechesis for Sundays & Solemnities: Year C 2001. Ed. by Joyce Ann Zimmerman et al. 304p. 2000. pap. 14.95 (*0-8146-2568-1*) Liturgical Pr.

Living Lively Preaching. Jackman. 1997. pap. 13.99 (*1-85792-312-X*, Pub. by Christian Focus) Spring Arbor Dist.

Living Logos. Ed. by David E. Carter. LC 92-74314. (Illus.). 160p. 1993. text 22.95 (*0-88108-107-8*); pap. text 17.50 (*0-88108-108-6*) Art Dir.

Living Logos International Bible Course, 6 vols. Dale R. Starks. 791p. 1997. spiral bd. 105.00 (*0-9630790-4-2*) D R Starks.

Living Long Ago (B - U) H. Edom & F. Brooks. (Explainers Ser.). (Illus.). 96p. (J). (gr. 2-4). 1993. pap. 12.95 (*0-7460-1109-1*) EDC.

Living Long & Loving It! large type rev. ed. Stephen Lang & Adelaide Teninga. (Friendship Ser.). (Illus.). 48p. (Orig.). 1995. pap. 0.70 (*1-882536-11-8*, A100-0035) Bible League.

Living Longer & Better. Harold Elrick. 1978. pap. 5.95 (*0-02-499950-4*, Macmillan Coll) P-H.

Living Longer & Better: Guide to Optimal Health. Harold Elrick et al. LC 78-366. (Illus.). 300p. 1978. pap. 5.95 (*0-89037-125-3*) Anderson World.

Living Longer (& Better) with Health Problems. Springhouse Publishing Company Staff. 528p. 1995. 21.95 (*0-87434-826-9*) Springhouse Corp.

***Living Longer & Livelier: Guidelines for Older Adults.** James H. Humphrey. LC 99-52429. (Illus.). 1999. write for info. (*1-56072-745-4*, Nova Kroshka Bks) Nova Sci Pubs.

Living Longer & Other Sobering Possibilities. Tom Mullen. LC 96-14674. 118p. 1996. 10.00 (*0-944350-39-9*) Friends United.

Living Longer & Stronger: The Six-Week Plan to Enhance & Extend Your Years Over Forty. Ellington Darden. LC 94-26838. 224p. (Orig.). 1995. pap. 13.95 (*0-399-51900-9*, Perigee Bks) Berkley Pub.

Living Longer, Feeling Better: 399 Ways to Defeat Old Age. Janice M. Failes & Frank W. Cawood. 256p. 1998. pap. 6.97 (*1-57748-201-8*) Barbour Pub.

***Living Longer, Growing Stronger: The Vital Role of Geriatric Medicine: Congressional Hearing.** Ed. by Charles E. Grassley. 125p. (C). 2000. reprint ed. pap. text 25.00 (*0-7881-8694-9*) DIANE Pub.

Living Longer, Growing Stronger, the Vital Role of Geriatric Medicine: Forum Before the Special Committee on Aging, United States Senate, One Hundred Fifth Congress, Second Session, Washington, Dc, May 20, 1998. United States. LC 98-215142. 125 p. 1998. write for info. (*0-16-057500-1*) USGPO.

Living Longer in the Boomer Age: Combining Alternative & Conventional Medicine for Maximum Health & Vitality. John L. Zenk. LC 98-73258. 160p. 1998. per. 9.95 (*1-889462-03-9*) Advanced Research Pr.

Living Longer, Living Better, Slowing Aging with the Longevity Factor see Longevity Factor: Chromium Picolinate

Living Longer, Living Stronger. Normal Wall. 200p. 1997. pap. 14.95 (*0-9639683-1-9*) Vitaliity Corp.

***Living Longer, Retiring Earlier: Rethinking the Social Security Retirement Age: Congressional Hearing.** Ed. by Charles Grassley. (Illus.). 142p. (C). 2000. reprint ed. pap. text 25.00 (*0-7881-8686-8*) DIANE Pub.

Living Longer Than Hate: A Story of Survival & Success. C. S. Ragsdale. (Illus.). 1997. lib. bdg. 25.00 (*0-9659781-0-9*) Holcaust Mus.

Living Longer with Heart Disease: The Noninvasive Approach That Will Save Your Life. Howard H. Wayne. LC 98-14179. 260p. 1998. 22.95 (*1-885987-12-9*, Health Info Pr) Practice Mgmt Info.

***Living Love.** Debbie Alsdorf. LC 00-27251. 2000. 7.99 (*0-7814-3383-5*) Cook Communs Minist.

Living Love. J. A. Ferrara. (Illus.). 142p. 1961. 9.45 (*0-933961-04-9*) Mystic Jhamom.

Living Love: A Journey of Loving Yourself. Karen L. Miyares. 110p. 1998. spiral bd. 13.00 (*0-9668365-0-2*) Living Love.

Living Love: The Key to Soul Evolution. Jacqueline Shuler. LC 92-60945. (Illus.). 128p. (Orig.). 1992. pap. 6.95 (*0-913319-20-1*) Sunstone Pubns.

Living Love: What Can Happen When We Learn to Love God's Way. Stuart Briscoe & Jill Briscoe. 220p. (Orig.). 1993. pap. 9.99 (*0-87788-488-9*, H Shaw Pubs) Waterbrook Pr.

Living, Loving & Aging: Sexual & Personal Relationships in Later Life. Wendy Greengross & Sally Greengross. (C). 1989. 40.00 (*0-86242-070-9*, Pub. by Age Concern Eng) St Mut.

Living, Loving & Enduring: A Journey to Love. Juliette Mosteller. 80p. (Orig.). 1996. pap. 9.95 (*1-887798-04-8*) WriteMore Pubns.

Living, Loving & Laughing: A Guide to Self-Awareness. Anthony Andrews-Speed. 160p. (Orig.). 1993. pap. 14.95 (*0-9638880-0-5*) Osmyrrah Pub.

Living, Loving, & Laughing with Pain. Jacqueline J. Pliskin. 272p. 1995. pap. 19.95 (*0-9647480-0-2*) Words & Pict.

Living, Loving & Learning. Leo Buscaglia. 1995. 16.00 incl. audio (*0-671-52062-8*) S&S Trade.

Living, Loving & Learning. Leo F. Buscaglia. 288p. 1985. pap. 10.00 (*0-449-90181-5*, Columbine) Fawcett.

Living, Loving & Learning. Leo F. Buscaglia. LC 81-824284. 264p. 1982. 13.50 (*0-913590-88-6*) SLACK Inc.

Living, Loving, & Loathing: Modern Rhymes & Limericks for the Romantically Inclined & Humorously Correct. Michael Craig Daniels. LC 97-94240. (Illus.). 96p. 1997. 12.95 (*0-9659946-2-7*) Good Knight Bks.

Living, Loving & Lying Awake at Night. Sindiwe Magona. LC 94-4357. (Emerging Voices: New International Fiction Ser.). 208p. 1994. 24.95 (*1-56656-147-7*); pap. 11.95 (*1-56656-141-8*) Interlink Pub.

Living Low-Carb: The Complete Guide to Long-Term Low-Carb Dieting. Fran McCullough. LC 99-57132. 384p. (gr. 8). 2000. 25.95 (*0-316-55768-4*) Little.

Living Lutheran Christianity. J. H. Levang. 129p. (Orig.). 1991. pap. 8.95 (*0-943167-14-0*) Faith & Fellowship Pr.

Living Machines: Bauhaus Architecture As Sexual Ideology. E. Michael Jones. LC 94-76952. 128p. 1995. pap. 11.95 (*0-89870-464-2*) Ignatius Pr.

Living Magically: A New Vision of Reality. Gill Edwards. 224p. 1995. pap. 12.95 (*0-7499-1074-7*, Pub. by Piatkus Bks) London Brdge.

Living Marine Resources of Kuwait, Eastern Saudi Arabia, Bahrain, Gatar, & the FAO Species Identification Field Guide for Fishery Pruposes. FAO Staff. LC 98-126841. (FAO Species Ser.). (Illus.). 293p. 1997. pap. 53.00 (*92-5-103741-8*, F37418, Pub. by FAO) Bernan Associates.

Living Marine Resources of Somalia. C. Sommer et al. (Species Identification Field Guide for Fishery). 400p. 1996. pap. 70.00 (*92-5-103742-6*, F37426, Pub. by FAO) Bernan Associates.

Living Martyrs: Individuals & Revolution in Nepal. James F. Fisher. (Illus.). 334p. 1997. text 27.00 (*0-19-564000-4*) OUP.

***Living Martyrs: Individuals & Revolution in Nepal.** James F. Fisher. (Illus.). 336p. 2000. pap. text 12.95 (*0-19-564544-8*) OUP.

Living Martyrs: Individuals & Revolution in Nepal. James F. Fisher. 1997. pap. 96.00 (*0-7855-7427-1*, Pub. by Ratna Pustak Bhandar) St Mut.

Living Masters: The Paintings of Zhu Qizhan. Asian Art Museum Staff. (Illus.). 24p. (C). 1995. pap. 5.00 (*0-939117-07-X*) Asian Art Mus.

Living Materia Medica, Vol. 1. George Vithoulkas. 350p. 1989. 75.00 (*0-685-44897-5*) Hlth & Habitat.

Living Materials: A Sculptor's Handbook. Oliver Andrews. LC 77-71057. (Illus.). 348p. 1983. pap. 34.95 (*0-520-06452-6*, Pub. by U CA Pr) Cal Prin Full Svc.

Living Matter. Alexander Stojkovic. Ed. by Linda T. Hall. (Illus.). 48p. 1977. 5.75 (*0-918612-00-4*); pap. 2.25 (*0-918612-01-2*) Maxima.

Living Maya. Photos by Jeffrey J. Foxx. (Illus.). 224p. 1987. 49.50 (*0-8109-1298-8*, Pub. by Abrams) Time Warner.

***Living Maya.** Photos by Jeffry Jay Foxx. 224p. 2000. 24.95 (*0-8109-2745-4*, Pub. by Abrams) Time Warner.

***Living Meaningfully, Dying Joyfully: The Profound Practice of Transference of Consciousness.** Geshe Kelsang Gyatso. 1999. 19.95 (*0-948006-64-1*); pap. 15.95 (*0-948006-63-3*) Tharpa Pubns.

Living Meditation: From Principle to Practice. C. Alexander Simpkins. LC 97-4165. 1997. pap. text 16.95 (*0-8048-3114-9*) Tuttle Pubng.

Living Memories. Robert C. Anderson. Ed. by Paula Drieci. 300p. 1999. pap. 19.95 (*1-57635-053-3*) WeWrite.

Living Messages in Sermon Outlines. unabridged ed. John A. Clement. 139p. 1996. reprint ed. pap. 9.99 (*0-88019-349-2*) Schmul Pub Co.

Living Messages of the Books of the New Testament. Ed. by Thomas B. Warren & Garland Elkins. 1976. 14.00 (*0-934916-35-7*) Natl Christian Pr.

Living Metaphors: Stories & Related Experiential Exercises. Jaclyn Gerstein. LC 97-70604. 144p. 1997. per. 23.50 (*0-7872-3567-9*) Kendall-Hunt.

Living Minstrelsy: The Poetry & Music of Sidney Lanier. Jane S. Gabin. LC 85-5015. viii, 182p. 1985. text 18.95 (*0-86554-155-8*, MUP/H145) Mercer Univ Pr.

***Living Miracles: Stories of Hope from Parents of Premature Babies.** Kimberly Powell. Ed. by Kim Wilson. LC 99-89725. (Illus.). 320p. 2000. text 24.95 (*0-312-24550-5*) St Martin.

Living Mission: Challenges in Evangelization Today. James H. Kroeger. LC 94-2788. 160p. (Orig.). 1994. pap. 18.00 (*0-88344-921-8*) Orbis Bks.

Living Monument: The Story of Grace Covenant Presbyterian Church. Jack Abernathy. LC 89-81284. (Illus.). 168p. (Orig.). 1989. 100.00 (*0-9624718-0-1*); pap. 10.00 (*0-9624718-1-X*) Grace Covenant Presbyterian Church.

Living Monuments: Confederate Soldiers' Homes in the New South. R. B. Rosenburg. LC 93-12465. (Illus.). xvi, 240p. (C). 1993. 45.00 (*0-8078-2109-8*) U of NC Pr.

Living Morally: A Psychology of Moral Character. Lawrence Thomas. 278p. 1990. pap. 22.95 (*0-87722-778-0*) Temple U Pr.

Living More with Less. Doris Longacre. LC 80-15461. 304p. 1980. pap. 12.99 (*0-8361-1930-4*) Herald Pr.

***Living More with Less Study/Action Guide.** 2nd rev. ed. Delores H. Friesen. LC 99-72262. 128p. 1999. mass mkt. 10.00 (*0-914966-12-X*, LMWLSAG) Alternatives.

Living Morphogenesis of the Heart. M. V. De la Cruz & R. R. Markwald. LC 99-158844. (Cardiovascular Molecular Morphogenesis Ser.). (Illus.). 232p. 1998. 95.00 (*0-8176-4037-1*) Birkhauser.

Living Morphogenesis of the Heart. Maria Victoria De la Cruz & Roger R. Markwald. LC 99-158844. (Cardiovascular Molecular Morphogenesis Ser.). xviii, 233 p. 1998. write for info. (*3-7643-4037-1*) Birkhauser.

Living Mountain. Rob Carson. (Illus.). 72p. (Orig.). (J). (gr. k-8). 1992. pap. 10.95 (*0-9623072-9-7*) S Ink WA.

Living Mummy. Ambrose Pratt. LC 87-60464. (Illus.). 313p. 1988. reprint ed. pap. 15.95 (*0-915431-02-5*) N American Archives.

Living Museum. Jessica Yu. 2000. 32.00 (*1-57500-035-0*) TV Bks.

Living My Life. Emma Goldman. LC 71-111090. reprint ed. 32.50 (*0-404-02860-8*) AMS Pr.

Living My Life, 2 vols. Emma Goldman. LC 73-109546. (Civil Liberties in American History Ser.). 1976. reprint ed. lib. bdg. 95.00 (*0-306-71900-2*) Da Capo.

Living My Life, 1. Emma Goldman. (Illus.). 1930. reprint ed. pap. 10.95 (*0-486-22543-7*) Dover.

Living My Life, 2. Emma Goldman. (Illus.). 1930. reprint ed. pap. 10.95 (*0-486-22544-5*) Dover.

Living My Life, 2 vols., Set. Emma Goldman. (American Biography Ser.). 1991. reprint ed. lib. bdg. 148.00 (*0-7812-8147-4*) Rprt Serv.

***Living My Life with God.** Joyce Loeck et al. (Illus.). 2000. pap. write for info. (*0-9679793-0-7*) Jesus Cares.

Living Myths: How Myth Gives Meaning to Human Experience. J. F. Bierlein. LC 98-38533. 1999. pap. 14.95 (*0-345-42207-4*) Ball Well.

Living Nach Vol. 1: Joshua, Judges, Kings. Ed. & Tr. by Yaakov Elman from HEB. (Illus.). (C). 1994. 24.00 (*0-940118-29-7*) Moznaim.

Living Nach - Sacred Writings, Vol. III. Ed. by M. H. Mykoff et al. Tr. by Gaviel Rubin et al. (Living Nach Ser.). (Illus.). 943p. 1999. 38.00 (*1-885220-22-7*) Moznaim.

Living Nach-Later Prophets. (The Living Nach Ser.: Vol. 2). (Illus.). 845p. 1995. 30.00 (*1-885220-07-3*) Moznaim.

Living National Treasures: A Celebration of British Craftsmanship Through the Eyes of Country Life. Country Life Magazine Staff. (Illus.). 144p. 1998. 75.00 (*1-86205-032-5*, Pub. by Pavilion Bks Ltd) Trafalgar.

Living Nativity: The Story of St. Francis & the Christmas Manger. David Haidle & Helen Haidle. 32p. 1998. 12.99 (*1-56292-537-7*) Honor Bks OK.

***Living Near a River.** Allan Fowler. LC 99-14943. (Rookie Read-About Geography Ser.). (J). 2000. 19.00 (*0-516-21556-6*) Childrens.

***Living Near a River.** Allan Fowler. (Rookie Read-About Geography Ser.). (Illus.). 32p. (J). (gr. 1-2). 2000. pap. 5.95 (*0-516-27052-4*) Childrens.

***Living Near a River.** Joanne Winne. (Welcome Bks.). (Illus.). (J). 2000. 13.50 (*0-516-23302-5*) Childrens.

***Living near a River.** Joanne Winne. (Communities Ser.). (Illus.). 24p. (J). (ps-2). 2000. pap. 4.95 (*0-516-23502-8*) Childrens.

***Living Near the Sea** Allan Fowler. LC 99-14942. (Rookie Read-About Geography Ser.). (J). 2000. 19.00 (*0-516-21562-0*) Childrens.

***Living Near the Sea.** Allan Fowler. (Rookie Read-About Geography Ser.). 32p. (J). (gr. 1-2). 2000. pap. 5.95 (*0-516-27053-2*) Childrens.

Living Near to Nature's Heart: The History of the Pelican Lake Outing Club. Marjorie W. Richison. 213p. 1992. 29.95 (*1-880458-00-4*) Kingswood.

Living Needed for Building up the Small Group Meetings see Vivir Necesario Para La Edificacion De Las Reuniones De Grupos Pequenos

Living Needed for Building up the Small Group Meetings. Witness Lee. 114p. 1986. per. 6.00 (*0-87083-222-0*, 12-010-001) Living Stream Ministry.

Living New Testament. Tr. by Kenneth N. Taylor. Incl. 1973. 3.95 (*0-8423-2810-6*); 1973. Set kivar 5.95 (*0-8423-2800-9*) Tyndale Hse.

Living New World Monkeys (Platyrrhini) With an Introduction to Primates, Vol. 1. Philip Hershkovitz. LC 75-9059. (Illus.). 1132p. 1978. lib. bdg. 132.00 (*0-226-32788-4*) U Ch Pr.

Living Next Door to Alex. large type ed. Catherine George. (Harlequin Romance Ser.). 1997. 20.95 (*0-263-15065-8*) Thorndike Pr.

L

An Asterisk (*) at the beginning of an entry indicates that the title is appearing for the first time.

L

Living No Longer for Ourselves: Liturgy & Justice for the Nineties. Ed. by Mark R. Francis & Kathleen Hughes. 208p. (Orig.). 1991. pap. text 12.95 (*0-8146-2035-3*) Liturgical Pr.

Living Non-Christian Religions. 160p. 1985. pap. 10.50 (*0-311-72940-1*) Casa Bautista.

Living Non Violence. Arya B. Bhardwaj. xii, 82p. 1986. 9.00 (*1-55528-075-7*, Pub. by Today Tomorrow) Scholarly Pubns.

Living Now. Joel S. Goldsmith. Ed. by Lorraine Sinkler. 192p. 1984. pap. 7.95 (*0-8065-0911-2*, Citadel Pr) Carol Pub Group.

Living Now: Strategies for Success & Fulfillment. Roger L. Miller & Lavina L. Miller. LC 96-268. 1996. pap. 47.50 (*0-314-04919-3*) West Pub.

***Living Now: Strategies for Success & Fulfillment.** 2nd ed. Miller. 1999. pap. text 45.50 (*0-538-42954-2*) Thomson Learn.

Living Now: Strategies for Success & Fulfillment. 2nd ed. Lavina Leed Miller & Roger Leroy Miller. 1999. pap. 189.00 (*0-538-43010-9*) Thomson Learn.

Living Now: Strategies, Success & Fulfillment. Miller. 1996. 12.00 (*0-314-20313-3*, Pub. by West Pub) Thomson Learn.

Living Now Academics. Miller. (Skills Life & Living Now Ser.). 1996. mass mkt. write for info. (*0-314-09793-7*) West Pub.

Living Now Action Book. Miller. (Skills Life & Living Now Ser.). 1996. mass mkt. 24.00 (*0-314-09794-5*) West Pub.

Living Now Careers. Miller. (Skills Life & Living Now Ser.). 1996. mass mkt. write for info. (*0-314-09792-9*) West Pub.

Living Now Student. Miller. 1996. mass mkt., wbk. ed. write for info. (*0-314-09735-X*) West Pub.

Living Now Work & Family. Miller. (Skills Life & Living Now Ser.). 1996. mass mkt. 24.00 (*0-314-09797-X*) West Pub.

Living Ocean. Elizabeth Collins. LC 93-26205. (Earth at Risk Ser.). (Illus.). 128p. (YA). (gr. 5 up). 1994. lib. bdg. 19.95 (*0-7910-1586-6*) Chelsea Hse.

Living Ocean: Understanding & Protecting Marine Biodiversity. 2nd ed. Boyce Thorne-Miller. LC 98-42545. (Illus.). 200p. 1999. pap. 17.95 (*1-55963-678-5*); text 29.95 (*1-55963-677-7*) Island Pr.

Living of Charlotte Perkins Gilman: An Autobiography. Charlotte Perkins Gilman. LC 90-50199. (Studies in American Autobiography). 384p. (C). 1991. pap. 17.95 (*0-299-12744-3*) U of Wis Pr.

Living of Charlotte Perkins Gilman: An Autobiography. Charlotte Perkins Gilman. LC 72-2604. (American Women Ser.: Images & Realities). (Illus.). 386p. 1975. reprint ed. 29.95 (*0-405-04459-3*) Ayer.

Living of Charlotte Perkins Gilman: An Autobiography. Charlotte Perkins Gilman. (American Biography Ser.). 341p. 1991. reprint ed. lib. bdg. 79.00 (*0-7812-8146-6*) Rprt Serv.

Living of Maisie Ward. Dana K. Greene. LC 96-30396. 248p. 1997. text 25.00 (*0-268-01311-X*) U of Notre Dame Pr.

Living of Words: American Women in Print Culture. Ed. by Susan Albertine. LC 94-19670. (Illus.). 272p. (C). 1995. text 38.00 (*0-87049-867-3*) U of Tenn Pr.

***Living off Crime.** Kenneth D. Tunnell. LC 99-41877. .p. 2000. write for info. (*0-8304-1566-1*) Burnham Inc.

Living off the Country see How to Stay Alive in the Woods

Living off the Country: Essays on Poetry & Place. John Haines. (Poets on Poetry Ser.). 200p. 1981. pap. 17.95 (*0-472-06333-2*, 06333) U of Mich Pr.

Living off the Country: For Fun & Profit. John L. Parker. Ed. by B. Lever. (Fun & Profit Ser.). (Illus.). 1978. 7.95 (*0-916302-23-7*); pap. 4.95 (*0-916302-24-5*) Bookworm Pub.

Living off the Earnings of a Hooker: The Seafood Recipes of Jack Nerenberg, PhD. unabridged ed. Jack Nerenberg. (Illus.). 95p. 1997. mass mkt. 15.95 (*0-9661559-0-4*) Aunt Chelada.

***Living off the Land.** Richard Emanuel. 2000. pap. 21.95 (*1-56661-050-8*) Alaska Geog Soc.

***Living off the Land: A Gathering of Writings from the Warrensburg Writers Circle.** Ed. by Robert C. Jones. 140p. 1999. pap. 10.00 (*0-910479-09-7*) Mid-America Pr.

Living off the Land: Space Age Homesteading - 1989. 3rd ed. Marian Van Atta. LC 74-15408. (Illus.). 64p. 1983. pap. 5.95 (*0-938524-00-3*) Geraventure.

Living off the Sea. Charlie White. 1996. pap. text 7.95 (*0-07-069866-X*) McGraw.

***Living Off the Sea.** Charlie White. (Illus.). 128p. 1998. pap. 11.95 (*1-895811-47-3*) Heritage Hse.

Living on a Dream: A Marriage Tale. Patt Blue. LC 97-39452. (Illus.). 200p. 1998. 28.00 (*1-57806-057-5*) U Pr of Miss.

***Living on a Farm** Allan Fowler. LC 99-38878. (Rookie Read-About Geography Ser.). 2000. 19.00 (*0-516-21564-7*) Childrens.

***Living on a Mountain.** Joanne Winne. (Welcome Bks.). (Illus.). (J). 2000. 13.50 (*0-516-23303-3*) Childrens.

***Living on a Mountain.** Joanne Winne. (Communities Ser.). (Illus.). 24p. (J). (ps-2). 2000. pap. 4.95 (*0-516-23503-6*) Childrens.

***Living on a Plain.** Joanne Winne. (Welcome Bks.). (Illus.). (J). 2000. 13.50 (*0-516-23304-1*) Childrens.

***Living on a Plain.** Joanne Winne. LC 00-23362. (Communities Ser.). (Illus.). 24p. (J). (ps-2). 2000. pap. write for info. (*0-516-23504-4*) Childrens.

Living on a Restless Earth: The Challenge of Earthquake Science. National Research Council Staff. (Illus.). 276p. 1998. text 49.95 (*0-309-06562-3*) Natl Acad Pr.

Living on a Tightrope: A Survival Handbook for Principals. 216p. (C). 1995. pap. text 18.95 (*0-9647437-8-7*) RFT Pubng.

Living on a Tropical Island. Bernard Planche. Tr. by Sarah Matthews from FRE. LC 87-34592. (Illus.). 38p. (J). (gr. k-5). 1988. 5.95 (*0-944589-13-8*, 138) Young Discovery Lib.

Living on Air. Nina Zivancevic. Ed. by Ken Jordan. 160p. 1998. 22.95 (*1-887276-08-4*); pap. 12.95 (*1-887276-09-2*) Cool Grove Pub.

***Living on an Island.** Joanne Winne. (Welcome Bks.). (Illus.). (J). 2000. 13.50 (*0-516-23305-X*) Childrens.

***Living on an Island.** Joanne Winne. LC 00-23361. (Communities Ser.). (Illus.). 24p. (J). (ps-2). 2000. pap. write for info. (*0-516-23505-2*) Childrens.

Living on Fire: A Collection of Poems. Virginia Adair. LC 99-52858. 176p. 2000. 22.00 (*0-375-50289-0*) Random.

Living on Flood Plains & Wetlands: A Homeowner's High Water Handbook. Maureen Gilmer. LC 94-42174. 184p. 1995. pap. 12.95 (*0-87833-887-X*) Taylor Pub.

Living on God's Family Plan see O Plano de Deus para a Familia

***Living on Holson Creek: A Choctaw Journal.** Neal White. (Illus.). 176p. 1999. pap. 14.95 (*0-938041-47-9*) Arc Pr AR.

Living on Lassen. Ed. by LoVerne Brown. LC 90-71932. 152p. (Orig.). 1991. pap. 8.95 (*0-938711-09-1*) Tecolote Pubns.

Living on Less. Mother Earth News Editors. (Illus.). (Orig.). 1984. pap. 14.95 (*0-938432-07-9*) Mother Earth.

Living on Less: An Authoritive Guide to Affordable Food, Fuel, & Shelter. Mother Earth News Staff. Ed. by John Vivian. (Illus.). 287p. 1998. pap. 19.95 (*0-9660494-0-3*, Pub. by Sussex Pubs) Chelsea Green Pub.

Living on Less & Liking It More. Maxine Hancock. 180p. (Orig.). 1994. pap. 9.99 (*1-56476-330-7*, 6-3330, Victor Bks) Chariot Victor.

Living on Light: A Source of Nutrition for the New Millennium, 1. Jasmuheen. 1998. pap. 19.95 (*3-929512-35-1*) K Halbig.

Living on Luck: Selected Letters 1960's-1970's, Vol. 2. Charles Bukowski. LC 95-39244. (Illus.). 283p. (C). 1998. pap. 16.00 (*0-87685-981-3*) Black Sparrow.

Living on Luck Vol. 2: Selected Letters 1960's-1970's, Vol. 2. Charles Bukowski. LC 95-39244. (Illus.). 283p. (Orig.). (C). 1998. 25.00 (*0-87685-982-1*) Black Sparrow.

Living on Mangetti: 'Bushman' Autonomy & Namibian Independence. Thomas Widlok. (Oxford Studies in Social & Cultural Anthropology). (Illus.). 312p. 2000. 80.00 (*0-19-823389-2*) OUP.

Living on Mars: Mission to the Red Planet. Michael D. Cole. LC 98-13125. (Countdown to Space Ser.). 48p. (J). (gr. 4-10). 1999. lib. bdg. 18.95 (*0-7660-1121-6*) Enslow Pubs.

***Living on Nothing Atoll, Vol. 1.** Theresa Kelly. LC 99-21167. (Aloha Cove Ser.). 160p. 1999. pap. 5.99 (*0-570-05483-4*) Concordia.

***Living on Purpose: Straight Answers to Universal Questions.** Dan Millman. 140p. 2000. pap. 14.00 (*1-57731-132-9*, Pub. by New Wrld Lib) Publishers Group.

Living on Salt & Stone: Poems from Straight Bay. Alan Brooks & Nancy L. Nielsen. (Illus.). 24p. (Orig.). 1984. pap. 5.00 (*0-914473-00-X*) Stone Man Pr.

Living on the Boott: Historical Archaeology at the Boott Mills Boardinghouses of Lowell, Massachusetts. Stephen A. Mrozowski et al. LC 95-52177. (Illus.). 112p. 1996. 40.00 (*1-55849-034-5*); pap. 13.95 (*1-55849-035-3*) U of Mass Pr.

Living on the Border of Disorder. Dan O'Neill & Cherry B. O'Neill. 28p. (Orig.). 1992. pap. 8.99 (*1-55661-262-1*) Bethany Hse.

Living on the Border of the Holy: Renewing the Priesthood of All. L. William Countryman. LC 98-42777. 224p. 1999. pap. 17.95 (*0-8192-1773-5*) Morehouse Pub.

Living on the Cusp. Andrea H. Budy. Ed. by M. Hettich & Colleen Ahern. 35p. 1980. 3.00 (*0-686-38059-2*) MoonsQuilt Pr.

Living on the Cutting Edge. Christian Harfouche. 54p. (Orig.). 1992. pap. text 6.00 (*0-9634451-0-3*) Power House Pub.

Living on the Devil's Doorstep: A Family's Trail of Compassion from Kabul to Amsterdam. Floyd McClung. (International Adventures Ser.). 196p. 1988. pap. 8.99 (*0-927545-45-4*) YWAM Pub.

Living on the Dry Side of Oregon: Comments from the Cosmic Cowboy. Keith F. May. LC 98-118984. (Illus.). 90p. 1997. pap. 8.95 (*1-57502-648-1*, PO1835) Morris Pubng.

***Living on the Earth.** Alicia Bay Laurel. LC 99-49096. 224p. 2000. pap. 16.95 (*0-375-70881-2*) Villard Books.

Living on the Earth. Ed. by David F. Robinson. 320p. 1988. 29.95 (*0-87044-734-3*); 41.95 (*0-87044-735-1*); lib. bdg. 31.95 (*0-87044-736-X*) Natl Geog.

Living on the Earth: Eclectic Essays for a Sustainable & Joyful Future. 2nd ed. Bill Duesing. 222p. 1997. reprint ed. pap. 11.95 (*0-9659277-0-9*) Solar Farm.

Living on the Edge. David Adamson. (Changing Wales Ser.). 46p. 1996. pap. 11.95 (*0-8464-4620-0*) Beekman Pubs.

Living on the Edge: Breaking Through Instead of Breaking Down. Elizabeth W. McCormick. LC 97-7503. 160p. 1997. pap. 15.95 (*1-85230-966-0*, Pub. by Element MA) Penguin Putnam.

Living on the Edge: Fiction by Peace Corps Writers. Ed. by John Coyne. LC 98-17464. 320p. 1999. pap. 17.95 (*1-880684-57-8*, Pub. by Curbstone) SPD-Small Pr Dist.

Living on the Edge: Legends of the Loveless Logo. Al Williams. Ed. & Illus. by Jim Weyer. 128p. 1992. write for info. (*0-9613834-5-3*) Weyer Intl Bk Div.

Living on the Edge: Spiritual Help for the Soul under attack. Michael S. Pitts. 57p. (Orig.). 1994. reprint ed. pap. 7.00 (*0-9633583-2-4*) Present Trth.

Living on the Edge: The Realities of Welfare in America. Mark R. Rank. LC 93-22818. 266p. 1994. 35.00 (*0-231-08424-2*) Col U Pr.

Living on the Edge: The Realities of Welfare in America. Mark R. Rank. LC 93-22818. 266p. 1995. pap. 20.00 (*0-231-08425-0*) Col U Pr.

Living on the Edge Essays on the Chittagong Hill Tracts. Ray Chaudhury. 1997. pap. 43.00 (*0-7855-7428-X*, Pub. by Ratna Pustak Bhandar) St Mut.

Living on the Edge of America: At Home on the Texas-Mexico Border. Robert L. Maril. LC 91-46457. (Wardlaw Book Ser.). 200p. 1992. 25.95 (*0-89096-505-6*) Tex A&M Univ Pr.

***Living on the Edge of the Rim: Excavations & Analysis of the Silver Creek Archaeological Resea.** Barbara J. Mills. 1999. pap. 29.95 (*1-889747-70-X*) Ariz St Mus.

Living on the Fault Line. Geoffrey Moore. Date not set. pap. 15.00 (*0-88730-971-2*, HarpBusn) HarpInfo.

***Living on the Fault Line: Managing for Shareholder Value in the Age of the Internet.** Geoffrey A. Moore. LC 00-26312. 288p. 2000. 27.00 (*0-88730-888-0*, Hrpr Busn) HarpCollins.

Living on the Fringe: The Archaeology & History of the Negev, Sinai & Neighbouring Regions in the Bronze & Iron Ages. Israel Finkelstein. (Monographs in Mediterranean Archaeology: No. 6). 197p. 1995. 75.00 (*1-85075-555-8*, Pub. by Sheffield Acad) CUP Services.

Living on the Frontline. Susan Pickard. 334p. 1995. 79.95 (*1-85972-168-0*, Pub. by Avebry) Ashgate Pub Co.

Living on the Land: Change among the Inuit of Northern Baffin Island. John Matthiasson. 180p. 1992. pap. text 14.95 (*0-921149-93-X*) Broadview Pr.

Living on the Land: Eleven Thousand Years of Human Adaptation in Southeastern New Mexico. Lynne Sebastian & Signa Larralde. (Cultural Resources Ser.: No. 6). (Illus.). 180p. (Orig.). 1989. pap. write for info. (*1-878178-07-5*) Bureau of Land Mgmt NM.

Living on the Margins: Women Writers on Breast Cancer. Ed. by Hilda Raz. LC 99-32917. 304p. 1999. 25.95 (*0-89255-244-1*, Pub. by Persea Bks) Norton.

Living on the Moon. David Baker. (Today's World in Space Bks.: Set 11). (Illus.). 48p. (J). (gr. 3-8). 1989. 13.95 (*0-685-58642-1*) Rourke Corp.

Living on the Move: Bhotiyas of the Kumaon Himalaya. Vineeta Hoon. (Livelihood & Environment Ser.: Vol. 4). (Illus.). 250p. 1996. 34.00 (*81-7036-560-0*) Sage.

Living on the Move: Bhotiyas of the Kumaon Himalaya. Vineeta Hoon. LC 96-19372. (Livelihood & Environment Ser.: Vol. 4). (Illus.). 254p. 1996. 45.00 (*0-8039-9325-0*) Sage.

Living on the Other Side of Fear: A Spiritual Passion for Life, Vol. 1. Hilda Villaverde. 1999. pap. write for info. (*0-9669607-0-X*) Pluma Pubg.

***Living on the Plains.** Allan Fowler. LC 99-30440. (Rookie Read-About Geography Ser.). (J). 2000. 19.00 (*0-516-21565-5*) Childrens.

***Living on the Plains.** Allan Fowler. (Rookie Read-About Geography Ser.). (Illus.). 32p. (J). (gr. 1-2). 2000. pap. 5.95 (*0-516-27054-0*) Childrens.

Living on the Ragged Edge. Charles R. Swindoll. 1990. pap. 10.99 (*0-8499-3216-5*) Word Pub.

Living on the Spine: A Woman's Life in the Sangre de Cristo Mountains. Christina Nealson. LC 96-53697. (Illus.). 144p. (Orig.). 1997. pap. 12.95 (*1-57601-003-1*) Papier-Mache Press.

Living on the Stem of Hope: An Uplifting Personal Account of One Person's Quest for Wellness Filled with Faith, Humor & Encouragement. large type ed. Jane M. Main. (Illus.). 56p. (Orig.). 1997. pap. 9.95 (*0-9656720-0-X*) J M Main.

Living on the Surface: New & Selected Poems. Miller Williams. LC 89-33078. xvi, 152p. 1989. pap. 14.95 (*0-8071-1574-6*); text 24.95 (*0-8071-1573-8*) La State U Pr.

Living on the Water. Elizabeth McMillan. LC 98-65890. (Illus.). 208p. 1998. 50.00 (*0-8478-2115-3*, Pub. by Rizzoli Intl) St Martin.

Living on the Wind: Across the Hemisphere with Migratory Birds. Scott Weidensaul. LC 99-11693. (Illus.). 432p. 2000. 26.00 (*0-86547-543-1*) N Point Pr.

***Living on the Wind: Across the Hemisphere with Migratory Birds.** Scott Weidensaul. (Illus.). 432p. 2000. pap. 15.00 (*0-86547-591-1*) N Point Pr.

Living on 12 Volts, 1998: With Ample Power. rev. ed. David Smead & Ruth Ishihara. (Illus.). 351p. 1998. pap. text 25.00 (*0-945415-05-2*) Rides Pub.

Living on Two Wheels: The Complete Guide to Buying, Commuting & Touring. Dennis L. Coello. 1982. pap. 9.95 (*0-89496-034-2*) Ross Bks.

Living on Your Own. Kathleen Kole. pap. 4.95 (*1-55105-018-8*) Lone Pine.

Living on Your Own. Stuart B. Schwartz. (Life Skills Ser.). (J). 1998. 19.00 (*0-516-21294-X*) Childrens.

Living on Your Own. Stuart B. Schwartz & Conley. LC 97-51297. (Life Skills Ser.). (YA). (gr. 3 up). 1998. 19.00 (*1-56065-719-7*, Bridgestone Bks) Capstone Pr.

Living One Day at a Time. Compiled by John Cook. LC 97-31317. (Pocket Positives Ser.). 256p. 1997. pap. 8.95 (*1-57749-058-4*) Fairview Press.

***Living or Dying by the Sword.** Rose & Kathi Rose. 1999. pap. text 9.95 (*0-9666819-3-2*) Winners Success Netwrk.

Living Organization: Systems of Behavior. Tracy Lane. LC 88-39746. 229p. 1989. 59.95 (*0-275-93084-X*, C3084, Praeger Pubs) Greenwood.

Living Organization - Spirituality in the Workplace. 2nd ed. William A. Guillory & Rob Johnson. (Illus.). 257p. 1997. reprint ed. 22.95 (*0-933241-15-1*); reprint ed. pap. 14.95 (*0-933241-14-3*) Innovations UT.

***Living Orthodoxy: In the Modern World.** Andrew Walker & Costa Carras. LC 99-88819. 2000. write for info. (*0-88141-212-0*) St Vladimirs.

Living Other Lives. Susanna Jackson. 352p. 1997. pap. 17.95 (*0-7528-0138-4*, Pub. by Orion Pubng Grp) Trafalgar.

Living Our Beliefs: The United Methodist Way. Kenneth L. Carder. LC 96-84123. 144p. 1996. pap. 15.95 (*0-88177-169-4*, DR169) Discipleship Res.

Living Our Dying: A Way to the Sacred in Everyday Life. Joseph Sharp. 256p. (J). 1996. 19.45 (*0-7868-6230-0*, Pub. by Hyperion) Time Warner.

Living Our Dying: A Way to the Sacred in Everyday Life. Joseph Sharp. 256p. (J). 1997. pap. 10.45 (*0-7868-8239-5*, Pub. by Hyperion) Time Warner.

Living Our Life Story: Spiritual Transformation in a Turbulent World. John P. Moran. Ed. by R. Patrick Neary & Michele St. George. LC 94-76730. (Illus.). 208p. 1994. pap. 9.95 (*0-9640806-9-9*) Lightsmith Multimed.

Living Our Own Lives. Veronica Ray. (A Moment to Reflect Ser.). pap. 2.50 (*0-89486-571-4*) Hazelden.

Living Our Stories, Telling Our Truths: Autobiography & the Making of the African-American Intellectual Tradition. Vincent P. Franklin. LC 96-22441. (Illus.). 464p. (C). 1996. pap. 16.95 (*0-19-510373-4*) OUP.

Living Our Stories, Telling Our Truths: The Autobiography & the Making of the African-American Intellectual Tradition. V. P. Franklin. (Illus.). 464p. 1995. 30.00 (*0-689-12192-X*) Atheneum Yung Read.

Living Out Christ's Love: Selected Writings of Toyohiko Kagawa. Ed. by Timothy Jones. LC 97-35464. (Upper Room Spiritual Classics). 72p. 1998. pap. 5.00 (*0-8358-0836-X*, UR836) Upper Room Bks.

Living Out Loud. Anna Quindlen. 272p. 1994. pap. 12.00 (*0-449-90912-3*, Columbine) Fawcett.

Living Out Loud. Anna Quindlen. 272p. 1989. mass mkt. 5.99 (*0-8041-0527-8*) Ivy Books.

Living Out of the Moment: 100 Ways to Obtain Happiness Through Total Denial. Babaloo R. Dust. 80p. 1995. pap. 6.95 (*0-8048-3073-8*) Tuttle Pubng.

Living Outside Inside: A Disabled Woman's Experience Towards a Social & Political Perspective. Susan Hannaford. LC 85-62733. 135p. (Orig.). 1985. pap. 6.95 (*0-933753-02-0*) Canterbury.

Living Outside the Nursing Home: A Care Giver's Guide to Giving Nursing Home Care at Home. Linda Faber-Czingula. (Illus.). 183p. 1996. ring bd. 12.95 (*1-890118-05-2*, QualityCare Pub) Convalescnt Cnslts.

Living over the Abyss: Margaret Atwood's Life Before Man. Carol Beran. (Canadian Fiction Studies: Vol. 23). (Illus.). 99p. (C). 1993. pap. 14.95 (*1-55022-125-6*, Pub. by ECW) Genl Dist Srvs.

Living over the Limit: A Credit Card Survival Kit. Terry Porlier & Linda K. Porlier. 140p. 1989. student ed. write for info. (*0-9623584-1-X*); pap. text 29.95 (*0-9623584-0-1*) Emerald West.

Living over the Limit: How to Get Out & Stay Out of the Credit Trap - the Credit Card Survival Kit. Terry Porlier & Linda K. Porlier. 130p. (Orig.). 1989. 49.95 incl. audio (*0-9623584-2-8*) Emerald West.

Living Overseas: A Book of Preparations. Ted Ward. 352p. 1984. pap. 19.95 (*0-02-933940-5*) Free Pr.

Living Overseas: What You Need to Know. Robert Johnston. 2000. pap. 14.95 (*0-9662421-2-2*, Pub. by Living Overseas) Bookpeople.

***Living Overseas Costa Rica.** 6th rev. ed. Bob Johnston & Christine Prah. (Living Overseas Ser.). Orig. Title: Living & Making Money in Costa Rica. (Illus.). 232p. 1998. pap. 15.00 (*0-9662421-1-4*, Pub. by Living Overseas) Bookpeople.

***Living Overseas Costa Rica.** 7th rev. ed. Robert Johnston. (Illus.). 288p. 2000. 16.95 (*0-9662421-4-9*, Pub. by Living Overseas) Bookpeople.

Living Overseas Mexico. 2nd ed. Robert Johnston. 254p. 1999. pap. 16.95 (*0-9662421-3-0*, Pub. by Living Overseas) Bookpeople.

Living Parables. Kevin O'Sullivan. 120p. 1979. 7.50 (*0-8199-0780-4*, Frncscn Herld) Franciscan Pr.

Living Parables: Illustrated the Message with Drama. Timothy W. Ayers. LC 97-29589. 106p. 1998. pap. 10.25 (*0-7880-1171-5*) CSS OH.

Living Past of Montreal. 3rd ed. Illus. by R. D. Wilson. 128p. 1993. pap. 12.95 (*0-7735-0981-X*, Pub. by McG-Queens Univ Pr) CUP Services.

Living Patiently: When God Seems Far Away. J. Allen Blair. LC 93-41450. 384p. 1994. pap. 13.99 (*0-8254-2185-3*) Kregel.

Living Peacefully: When the World Won't Leave You Alone. J. Allen Blair. LC 93-41447. 256p. 1994. pap. 11.99 (*0-8254-2183-7*) Kregel.

***Living Peacefully in a Stressful World.** Ron Hutchcraft. 256p. (ps up). 2000. pap. 11.99 (*1-57293-059-4*) Discovery Hse Pubs.

Living Perfect Love Vol. 1: Women's Self-Empowerment Alpha Rituals. Angelo A. Zaffuto. Ed. by Michael Bono. (Illus.). 1996p. 1996. pap. 11.95 (*0-9652851-0-3*); lib. bdg. 11.95 (*0-9652851-1-1*) Humantics Multi Media.

Living Philosophies. Albert Einstein et al. LC 75-3009. reprint ed. 49.50 (*0-404-59128-0*) AMS Pr.

Living Philosophy: An Introduction to Applied Ethics. Ray Billington. 288p. 1988. text 15.50 (*0-7102-1303-4*, Routledge Thoemms) Routledge.

Living Philosophy: An Introduction to Moral Thought. 2nd rev. ed. Ray Billington. LC 93-19012. 352p. (C). 1993. pap. 22.99 (*0-415-10028-3*, B2595) Routledge.

Living Pictures: The Origins of the Movies. Deac Rossell. LC 94-27561. (SUNY Series in Cultural Studies in Cinema/Video). (Illus.). 192p. (C). 1998. text 59.50 (*0-7914-3767-1*); pap. text 19.95 (*0-7914-3768-X*) State U NY Pr.

An Asterisk (*) at the beginning of an entry indicates that the title is appearing for the first time.

Living Pictures: Their History, Photo-Production & Practical Working. Henry V. Hopwood. LC 78-124010. (Literature of Cinema, Ser. 1). 1970. reprint ed. 21.95 (*0-405-01616-6*) Ayer.

Living Pictures of the New York Stage. Jack W. McCullough. LC 83-16754. (Theater & Dramatic Studies: No. 13). (Illus.). 212p. reprint ed. pap. 65.80 (*0-8357-1479-9*, 207056100001) Bks Demand.

Living Places: Archaeology, Continuity & Change at Historic Monuments in Northern Ireland. Colm J. Donnelly & Donnelly. LC 98-230937. xiv, 146 p. 1997. write for info. (*0-85389-475-2*) Queens U Belfast.

*__Living Places in Russia.__ Dyranda Prevost & Natalia Dushkina. (Illus.). 108p. 2000. pap. text 29.95 (*1-86470-087-4*, Pub. by Images) Antique Collect.

Living Planet: Preserving Edens of the Earth. World Wildlife Fund Staff. LC 99-12720. 250p. 1999. 40.00 (*0-609-60466-X*) Crown.

*__Living Planet in Crisis: Biodiversity Science & Policy.__ Joel Cracraft. LC 98-31465. 1999. 60.00 (*0-231-10864-8*); pap. text 25.00 (*0-231-10865-6*) Col U Pr.

Living Poetically: Kierkegaard's Existential Aesthetics. Sylvia Walsh. (Literature & Philosophy Ser.). 308p. (C). 1994. 42.50 (*0-271-01328-1*) Pa St U Pr.

Living Polymers & Mechanisms of Anionic Polymerization. Michael Szwarc. (Advances in Polymer Science Ser.: Vol. 49). (Illus.). 187p. 1983. 78.00 (*0-387-12047-5*) Spr-Verlag.

Living Pond. Nigel Hester. LC 90-12129. (Watching Nature Ser.). (Illus.). 32p. (J). (gr. 5-7). 1990. lib. bdg. 20.00 (*0-531-14006-7*) Watts.

Living Pond. Nathalie Tordjman. Tr. by Vicki Bogard from FRE. LC 90-50780. (Young Discovery Library). (Illus.). 38p. (J). (gr. k-5). 1991. 5.95 (*0-944589-38-3*, 383) Young Discovery Lib.

Living Pond: Water Gardens with Fish & Other Creatures. Helen Nash. (Illus.). 2000. 24.95 (*0-8069-0705-3*) Sterling.

Living Poor: A Peace Corps Chronicle. Moritz Thomsen. (Illus.). 280p. 1990. reprint ed. pap. 18.95 (*0-295-96928-8*) U of Wash Pr.

Living Portraits of the Church. Charles R. Swindoll. 1998. pap., student ed. 5.95 (*1-57972-186-9*) Insight Living.

Living Portraits of the Church. rev. ed. Charles R. Swindoll. 64p. 1995. pap. 4.99 (*0-8499-8642-7*) Word Pub.

Living Portuguese: Conversational Manual. rev. ed. Jura Oliveira. (Complete Living Language Course Ser.). (ENG & POR.). 1993. pap. 6.00 (*0-517-59035-2*) Liv Lang.

Living Portuguese: Dictionary. Jura Oliveira. (Complete Living Language Course Ser.). (ENG & POR.). 1993. pap. 5.00 (*0-517-59036-0*) Liv Lang.

Living Positively: A Guide for Parents & Careers of Children Affected by HIV. Christine Hogg. 41p. 1997. pap. 17.50 (*1-874579-97-0*, Pub. by Natl Childrens Bur) Paul & Co Pubs.

Living Positively in a World with HIV-AIDS. Mark De Solla Price. LC 94-16832. 176p. (Orig.). 1995. pap. 10.00 (*0-380-77623-5*, Avon Bks) Morrow Avon.

Living Positively One Day at a Time. Robert H. Schuller. 400p. 1986. mass mkt. 6.99 (*0-515-09608-3*, Jove) Berkley Pub.

Living Positively One Day at a Time. Robert H. Schuller. 366p. 1991. 12.95 (*1-879989-04-2*) New Hope Pub.

Living Power of God's Word. Dennis M. Mulder & Mark Cutshall. 192p. 1996. pap. 14.99 (*0-8054-6080-2*, 4260-80) Broadman.

Living Powers: The Arts in Education. Ed. by Peter Abbs. 250p. 1987. pap. 32.95 (*1-85000-168-5*, Falmer Pr) Taylor & Francis.

Living Prayer. Robert Benson. LC 98-15290. 224p. 1998. 21.95 (*0-87477-920-0*, Tarcher Putnam) Putnam Pub Group.

Living Prayer. Metropolitan A. Bloom. LC 68-16522. 126p. 1968. pap. 9.95 (*0-87243-054-5*) Templegate.

Living Prayer. Robert Benson. LC 99-20278. 224p. 1999. reprint ed. pap. 12.00 (*0-87477-967-7*, Tarcher Putnam) Putnam Pub Group.

Living Prayer. annuals 20th ed. 1994. pap., wbk. ed. 8.95 (*0-687-61376-0*) Abingdon.

Living Prayers. Basil Senger. 1990. im. lthr. 4.95 (*0-89942-915-7*, 915/04) Catholic Bk Pub.

Living Presence: A Sufi Way to Mindfulness & the Essential Self. Kabir E. Helminski. 180p. 1996. pap. 11.95 (*0-614-21305-3*, 1456) Kazi Pubns.

Living Presence: The Sufi Way to Mindfulness & the Unfolding of the Essential Self. Kabir E. Helminski. LC 92-4974. 180p. 1992. pap. 12.95 (*0-87477-699-6*, Tarcher Putnam) Putnam Pub Group.

Living Priesthood. Michael Hollings. 268p. 1993. pap. 35.00 (*0-85597-110-X*) St Mut.

Living Principle: "English" As a Discipline of Thought. F. R. Leavis. LC 97-17238. 266p. 1998. pap. 16.95 (*1-56663-172-6*, Elephant Paperbacks) I R Dee.

Living Proof. John Harvey. 1995. 22.50 (*0-8050-2045-4*) H Holt & Co.

Living Proof. Clebe McClary & Diane Barker. 230p. 1978. pap. 12.95 (*0-9649666-2-X*) C McClary Evang.

Living Proof. Edmund Skellings. LC 86-1923. 64p. 1987. 13.95 (*0-8130-0857-3*) U Press Fla.

Living Proof, Bk. 8. J. Oldfield. (Illus.). (J). mass mkt. 7.95 (*0-340-70874-3*, Pub. by Hodder & Stought Ltd) Trafalgar.

Living Proof: Courage in the Face of AIDS. Carolyn Jones. (Illus.). 88p. 1997. 9.98 (*0-89660-079-3*, Artabras) Abbeville Pr.

Living Proof: Is There Life after Death? Ken Quine. 131p. 1996. pap. 16.50 (*1-85776-064-6*, Pub. by Book Guild Ltd) Trans-Atl Phila.

Living Proof: Sharing the Gospel Naturally. rev. ed. Jim Petersen. LC 88-63874. 252p. 1989. pap. 12.00 (*0-89109-561-6*) NavPress.

Living Proof: Views of a World Living with HIV & AIDs. Nicholas Lowe & M. McMillan. 167p. 1992. pap. 21.00 (*0-9509797-2-4*, Pub. by Bloodaxe Bks) Dufour.

Living Prophet. Dean R. Zimmerman. 1974. pap. 2.95 (*0-89036-041-3*) Liahona Pub Trust.

Living Psalms. Claus Westermann. 1995. pap. 29.95 (*0-567-29156-1*, Pub. by T & T Clark) Bks Intl VA.

Living Psalms. fac. ed. Claus Westermann. Tr. by J. R. Porter. LC 89-1588. 316p. 1989. reprint ed. pap. 98.00 (*0-7837-7979-8*, 204773500008) Bks Demand.

Living Psalms 2001. Abrams. 1997. pap. 9.99 (*0-8423-8869-9*) Tyndale Hse.

Living Psychology: A Lifespan Approach. 4th ed. James O. Lugo. 628p. (C). 1991. pap. text 44.89 (*1-56226-039-1*) CAT Pub.

Living Psychology: An Introduction. 3rd ed. Lugenia Dixon & James Lugo. 462p. (C). 1996. pap. text 50.50 (*1-56226-279-3*) CAT Pub.

Living Psychology Handbook. James Lugo. 156p. (C). 1990. pap. text 15.78 (*0-929655-98-2*) CAT Pub.

Living Psychology Handbook: An Introduction. Lugenia Dixon & James Lugo. 142p. (C). 1996. pap. text 21.35 (*1-56226-301-3*) CAT Pub.

Living Psychology Instructor's Manual. James Lugo. 118p. (C). 1990. pap. text. write for info. (*1-56226-025-1*) CAT Pub.

Living Pythons: A Complete Guide to the Pythons of the World. Jerry Walls. 1998. 49.95 (*0-7938-0467-1*) TFH Pubns.

Living Qigong: The Chinese Way to Good Health & Long Life. John Alton. LC 96-47018. (Illus.). 192p. 1997. pap. 19.95 (*1-57062-106-3*, Pub. by Shambhala Pubns) Random.

Living Rainbows. Gabriel H. Bain. 120p. (Orig.). 1993. pap. 14.95 (*0-929385-42-X*) Light Tech Pubng.

Living Reality in an Unreal World: An Overview of 1 Timothy, 2 Timothy, & Titus. Jack Hayford et al. (Bible Book-a-Month Ser.: Vol. 7). (Illus.). 71p. 1997. pap. 3.95 (*0-916847-24-1*) Living Way.

Living Recovery: Inspirational Moments for 12 Step Living by Men & Women in Anonymous Programs. Hazelden Editors. (Hazelden Recovery Bks.: Bk. 4). 208p. 1990. mass mkt. 5.99 (*0-345-36785-5*) Ballantine Pub Grp.

Living Reed. Pearl Synderstricker Buck. 478p. 1990. pap. 14.95 (*1-55921-022-2*) Moyer Bell.

Living Reiki: Takata's Teachings. Fran Brown. 116p. 1992. pap. 12.95 (*0-940795-10-8*) LifeRhythm.

Living Related Donor Liver Transplantation: Assessment of Graft Viability Based on the Redox Theory. K. Ozawa. (Illus.). xii, 212p. 1994. 195.00 (*3-8055-5800-7*) S Karger.

*__Living Religions.__ 4th ed. Ed. by Prentice-Hall Staff. (Illus.). 485p. (C). 1999. pap. text 44.00 (*0-13-011994-6*) P-H.

Living Religions & a World Faith. William E. Hocking. LC 75-3187. (Hibbert Lectures). reprint ed. 37.50 (*0-404-59189-2*) AMS Pr.

Living Religions of the World: Our Search for Meaning. Carl H. Voss. LC 77-82018. (Library of Liberal Religion). 192p. 1977. pap. 11.95 (*0-87975-215-7*) Prometheus Bks.

Living Religious Vows: A Personal Pilgrimage. Joseph Rayes. 69p. (Orig.). 1987. pap. 5.95 (*0-86716-063-2*) St Anthony Mess Pr.

Living Reminder, The - Reissue: Service & Prayer in Memory of Jesus Christ. Henri J. M. Nouwen. LC BV4011.6.N68 1998. 80p. 1998. reprint ed. pap. 10.00 (*0-86683-915-1*, Pub. by Harper SF) HarpC.

Living Responsibly in an Age of Excuses: Whatever Happened to Moral Responsibility? Anthony M. Coniaris. 105p. 1999. pap. 8.95 (*1-880971-43-7*) Light&Life Pub Co MN.

Living Responsibly in Community: Essays in Honor of E. Clinton Gardner. Ed. by Frederick E. Glennon et al. 286p. 1997. 46.50 (*0-7618-0638-5*) U Pr of Amer.

Living Rhetoric & Composition: Stories of the Discipline. Ed. by Duane H. Roen et al. LC 98-43355. 248p. 1998. 55.00 (*0-8058-2372-7*) L Erlbaum Assocs.

*__Living Rhetoric & Composition Stories of the Discipline.__ Duane H. Roen. LC 98-43355. 1998. write for info. (*0-8058-2373-5*) L Erlbaum Assocs.

Living Rich Lives: Indiana Extension Homemakers Association volume see Memories of Hoosier Homemakers

Living Rich Lives: Indiana Extension Homemakers Association Volume see Memories of Hoosier Homemakers

Living Richly. Gene H. Wise. 180p. 1993. pap. 5.95 (*0-929292-33-2*) Hannibal Bks.

*__Living Rite: Rituals of Christian Affirmation for Daily Life.__ Linda Henke. 160p. 2001. pap. 16.95 (*0-8192-1859-6*) Morehouse Pub.

Living River. Nigel Hester. LC 90-32526. (Watching Nature Ser.). (Illus.). 32p. (J). (gr. 5-7). 1991. lib. bdg. 20.00 (*0-531-14121-7*) Watts.

Living Rock: The Story of Metals since Earliest Times & Their Impact on Civilization. Arthur Wilson. 272p. 1996. pap. 49.95 (*1-85573-301-3*, Pub. by Woodhead Pubng) Am Educ Systs.

*__Living Roman Fort.__ Jacqueline Morley. (Magnifications Ser.). 48p. (YA). (gr. 3 up). 2000. 18.95 (*0-87226-650-8*, P Bedrick Books) NTC Contemp Pub Co.

Living Room. June Jordan. 136p. 1985. pap. 8.95 (*0-938410-26-1*, Thunders Mouth) Avalon NY.

Living Room. Ed. by Elaine Palmer. (Illus.). 128p. (Orig.). 1997. pap. text 14.95 (*1-899571-02-7*, Pub. by Pulp Faction) AK Pr Dist.

Living Room. Nick Waplington. (Illus.). 72p. 1991. 53.00 (*0-89381-481-4*) Aperture.

*__Living Room: A Visitor's Guide to Hell & Heaven.__ Julie Marlin. (Illus.). 208p. 2000. pap. 14.95 (*0-9700813-7-5*) Wild Grace.

Living Room: Twelve Step-by-Step Projects for the Woodworker. Traditional Woodworking Staff. 1998. pap. text 14.95 (*0-8230-5402-0*) Watsn-Guptill.

Living Room Country Furniture for the Home: Timeless Traditional Woodworking Projects. George Buchanan. 1999. pap. text 19.95 (*0-304-34244-0*) Continuum.

Living Room Lectures: The Fifties Family in Film & Television. Nina C. Leibman. LC 94-36606. (Texas Film Studies). (Illus.). 384p. 1995. pap. 18.95 (*0-292-74684-9*); text 45.00 (*0-292-74683-0*) U of Tex Pr.

Living Room Mysteries. Graham Jackson. (Studies in Jungian Psychology by Jungian Analysts). (Illus.). 144p. 1995. pap. 16.00 (*0-919123-61-9*, Pub. by Inner City Bks) BookWorld.

Living Room Retreat. Helen C. Swift. LC 93-39417. 96p. 1994. pap. 4.95 (*0-8189-0687-1*) Alba.

Living Room War. Michael J. Arlen. Ed. by Robert J. Thompson. LC 97-3070. (Television Ser.). xii, 242p. 1997. reprint ed. pap. 17.95 (*0-8156-0466-1*) Syracuse U Pr.

Living Room Wars. Ien Ang. LC 95-16943. 224p. (C). 1995. pap. 22.99 (*0-415-12801-3*) Routledge.

Living Room Wars. Ien Ang. LC 95-16943. 224p. (C). (gr. 13). 1995. 80.00 (*0-415-12800-5*) Routledge.

Living Rooms. Amanda Evans. (Library of Interiors). (Illus.). 96p. 1998. pap. 13.95 (*1-85793-938-7*, Pub. by Pavilion Bks Ltd) Trafalgar.

Living Rooms. Diane D. Saeks. LC 96-35988. (California Design Library). 1997. pap. 16.95 (*0-8118-1309-6*) Chronicle Bks.

Living Rooms: Interior Design Library. Alison Aves. 80p. 1996. pap. text 14.95 (*1-56496-239-3*) Rockport Pubs.

Living Rooms & Home Offices. Norman Smith. (Design Ideas for Small Spaces Ser.). (Illus.). 44p. 1996. pap. 9.99 (*1-56496-304-7*) Rockport Pubs.

Living Rooms As Factories: Class, Gender, & the Satellite Factory System in Taiwan. Ping-Chun Hsiung. (Illus.). (Orig.). (C). 1996. pap. text 22.95 (*1-56639-390-6*); lib. bdg. 69.95 (*1-56639-389-2*) Temple U Pr.

Living Rooms As Symbols of Status: A Study in Social Judgment. James A. Davis. LC 90-42478. (Harvard Studies in Sociology). 250p. 1991. text 30.00 (*0-8240-4324-3*) Garland.

*__Living Root: A Memoir.__ Michael Heller. LC 99-89096. 2000. 18.50 (*0-7914-4633-6*) State U NY Pr.

*__Living Root: A Memoir.__ Michael Heller. LC 99-89096. (C). 2001. pap. text 14.95 (*0-7914-4634-4*) State U NY Pr.

Living Sacrifice. Watchman Nee. Tr. by Stephen Kaung. (Basic Lesson Ser.: Vol. 1). 115p. 1972. 6.00 (*0-935008-07-1*); pap. 4.00 (*0-935008-08-X*) Christian Fellow Pubs.

Living Sacrifice. Bessie Patterson. 1985. pap. 6.95 (*0-89137-436-1*) Quality Pubns.

*__Living Safe in an Unsafe World: The Complete Guide to Family Preparedness.__ Kate Kelly. 2000. mass mkt. 14.95 (*0-451-40932-9*, Sig) NAL.

Living Safely in a Dangerous World: Keys to Abiding in the Secret Place. Mac Hammond. 21p. 1994. pap. 1.25 (*1-57399-002-7*) Mac Hammond.

Living Science, 18 bks. Incl. Science of Air. Sarah Dann. LC 99-55990. (Illus.). 32p. (J). (gr. 2 up). 1999. lib. bdg. 19.93 (*0-8368-2569-1*); Science of Animals. Lauri Seidlitz. LC 99-25571. (J). (gr. 2 up). 1999. lib. bdg. 19.93 (*0-8368-2464-4*); Science of Birds. Janice Parker. LC 99-28912. (Illus.). 32p. (J). (gr. 2 up). 1999. lib. bdg. 19.93 (*0-8368-2465-2*); Science of Energy. Sarah Dann. LC 99-54600. (Illus.). 32p. (J). (gr. 2 up). 1999. lib. bdg. 19.93 (*0-8368-2571-3*); Science of Fire. Rennay Craats. LC 00-28529. (Illus.). 32p. (J). (gr. 2 up). 2000. lib. bdg. (*0-8368-2680-9*); Science of Insects. Janice Parker. LC 99-26933. (Illus.). 32p. (J). (gr. 2 up). 1999. lib. bdg. 19.93 (*0-8368-2466-0*); Science of Light & Color. Patricia Miller-Schroeder. LC 00-28528. (Illus.). 32p. (J). (gr. 2 up). 2000. lib. bdg. 19.93 (*0-8368-2679-5*); Science of Magnets. Jonathan Bockneck. LC 99-52589. 32p. (J). (gr. 2 up). 1999. lib. bdg. 19.93 (*0-8368-2572-1*); Science of Plants. Jonathan Bocknek. LC 99-25570. (Illus.). 32p. (J). (gr. 2 up). 1999. lib. bdg. 19.93 (*0-8368-2467-9*); Science of Reptiles. Janice Parker. LC 00-28527. (Illus.). 32p. (J). (gr. 2 up). 2000. lib. bdg. 19.93 (*0-8368-2681-7*); Science of Senses. Patricia Miller-Schroeder. (Illus.). 32p. (J). (gr. 2 up). 1999. lib. bdg. 19.93 (*0-8368-2573-X*); Science of Soil. Jonathan Bocknek. LC 99-26929. (Illus.). 32p. (J). (gr. 2 up). 1999. lib. bdg. 19.93 (*0-8368-2468-7*); Science of Sound. Rennay Craats. LC 00-28532. (Illus.). 32p. (J). (gr. 2 up). 2000. lib. bdg. 19.93 (*0-8368-2682-5*); Science of the Human Body. Lauri Seidlitz. LC 99-54599. (Illus.). 32p. (J). (gr. 2 up). 1999. lib. bdg. 19.93 (*0-8368-2570-5*); Science of the Sky. Jonathan Bockneck. LC 99-52601. (Illus.). 32p. (J). (gr. 2 up). 1999. lib. bdg. 19.93 (*0-8368-2574-8*); Science of Underwater Life. Patricia Miller-Schroeder. LC 00-28531. (Illus.). 32p. (J). (gr. 2 up). 2000. lib. bdg. 19.93 (*0-8368-2683-3*); Science of Water. Janice Parker. LC 99-28909. (Illus.). 32p. (J). (gr. 2 up). 1999. lib. bdg. 19.93 (*0-8368-2469-5*); Science of Weather. Janice Parker. LC 00-28530. (Illus.). 32p. (J). (gr. 2 up). 2000. lib. bdg. 19.93 (*0-8368-2684-1*); (J). (gr. 2 up). Set lib. bdg. 358.74 (*0-8368-2743-0*) Gareth Stevens Inc.

*__Living Science, 12 bks., Set.__ (Illus.). (J). (gr. 2 up). 1999. lib. bdg. 239.16 (*0-8368-2656-6*) Gareth Stevens Inc.

*__Living Science: Incl. The Science of Air, The Science of the Human Body, The Science of Energy, The Science of Magnets, The Science of Senses & The Science of the Sky, 6 bks.__ (J). (gr. 2 up). 1999. lib. bdg. 119.58 (*0-8368-2568-3*) Gareth Stevens Inc.

Living Science: Includes the Science of Birds, Insects, Soil, Water, Animals, Plants, 6 bks., Set. (Illus.). (J). (gr. 2 up). lib. bdg. 119.60 (*0-8368-2463-6*) Gareth Stevens Inc.

*__Living Science: The Science of Fire; The Science of Light & Color; The Science of Reptiles; The Science of Sound; The Science of Underwater Life, 6 bks.__ (Illus.). (J). (gr. 2 up). 2000. lib. bdg. 119.58 (*0-8368-2678-7*) Gareth Stevens Inc.

Living Scripture: Reproducible Lectionary-Based Reflections on Sunday Scriptures, Cycle C. Mitch Finley. (Illus.). 60p. (Orig.). 1992. pap. 39.95 (*1-55612-572-0*, LL1572) Sheed & Ward WI.

Living Scripture: Reproducible Lectionary-Based Reflections on Sunday Scriptures. Mitch Finley. 54p. (Orig.). 1991. pap. 39.95 (*1-55612-416-3*, LL1416) Sheed & Ward WI.

Living Scripture: Reproducible Lectionary-Based Reflections on Sunday Scriptures, Cycle B. Mitch Finley. 60p. (Orig.). 1990. pap. 39.95 (*1-55612-405-8*) Sheed & Ward WI.

Living Seashore. Nigel Hester. LC 91-30656. (Watching Nature Ser.). (Illus.). 32p. (J). (gr. 5-7). 1992. lib. bdg. 20.00 (*0-531-14190-X*) Watts.

Living Seasonally: The Kitchen Garden & the Table at North Hill. Joe Eck & Wayne Winterrowd. LC 98-35334. (Illus.). 224p. 1999. 40.00 (*0-8050-4786-7*) H Holt & Co.

Living Shrines: Home Alters of New Mexico. Marie R. Cash. LC 98-26816. (Illus.). 124p. 1998. 45.00 (*0-89013-369-7*); pap. 24.95 (*0-89013-370-0*) Museum NM Pr.

Living Simply: An Examination of Christian Lifestyles. Ed. by David Crean et al. 128p. (Orig.). 1984. 5.95 (*0-8164-2340-7*) Harper SF.

Living Simply: How to Live Fully Using the Least Possible Resources. 1991. lib. bdg. 69.95 (*0-8490-4680-7*) Gordon Pr.

Living Simply: Timeless Thoughts for a Balanced Life. Sara Orem & Larry Demarest. LC 94-23548. (Illus.). 200p. (Orig.). 1994. pap. 9.95 (*1-55874-321-9*, 3219) Health Comm.

Living Simply in an Anxious World. Robert J. Wicks. LC 97-35334. (Illumination Bks.). 96p. 1998. reprint ed. pap. 5.95 (*0-8091-3767-4*) Paulist Pr.

Living Simply in God's Abundance: Strength & Comfort for the Seasons of a Woman's Life. Suzanne D. Ezell. LC 97-49903. 256p. 1998. 16.99 (*0-7852-7063-9*) Nelson.

Living Simply, Simply Living. Delia Halverson. 128p. (Orig.). 1996. pap. 8.95 (*0-687-00777-1*) Abingdon.

Living Simply Through the Day: Spiritual Survival in a Complex Age. rev. ed. Tilden Edwards. LC 98-23517. 256p. 1998. pap. 14.95 (*0-8091-3817-4*) Paulist Pr.

Living Single in a Double World: The Joys of Living Alone. Marjorie Barton Wilderman. 1999. pap. 17.95 (*1-58501-004-9*) CeShore Pubg.

Living Skills for the Brain Injured Child & Adolescent: A Rehabilitation Workbook. Julie M. Buxton & Kelly B. Godfrey. 400p. 1999. wbk. ed. 39.95 (*0-937857-80-7*, 1350) Speech Bin.

Living Skills Recovery Workbook. Precin. LC 99-225255. 224p. 1999. pap. text 35.00 (*0-7506-7118-1*) Buttrwrth-Heinemann.

Living Snakes of the World in Color. John M. Mehrtens. LC 87-9932. (Illus.). 480p. 1987. 65.00 (*0-8069-6460-X*) Sterling.

Living Sober see Viviendo Sobrio

Living Sober. 87p. 1975. pap. 1.20 (*0-916856-04-6*) AAWS.

Living Sober. (POL.). 170p. 1986. pap. 2.75 (*0-916856-20-8*) AAWS.

Living Sober. (RUS.). 1990. pap. 1.35 (*0-916856-27-5*) AAWS.

Living Sober. (TUR.). 1994. write for info. (*0-916856-65-8*); write for info. (*0-916856-66-6*) AAWS.

Living Sober Client Workbook. Dennis C. Daley. 27p. 1994. pap. text, wbk. ed. 3.95 (*1-56215-074-X*) GTR Inc.

Living Sober Counseling Manual. Dennis C. Daley. 82p. 1994. pap. text, teacher ed. 8.95 (*1-56215-073-1*) GTR Inc.

Living Sober II Client Workbook. Dennis C. Daley. 27p. 1996. pap. text, wbk. ed. 3.95 (*1-56215-078-2*) GTR Inc.

Living Sober II Counselor Manual. Dennis C. Daley. 43p. 1996. pap. text, teacher ed. 8.95 (*1-56215-077-4*) GTR Inc.

Living Sociology. (C). 1997. write for info. (*0-205-27910-4*, Macmillan Coll) P-H.

Living Sociology. 128p. (C). 1998. write for info. (*0-205-28717-4*, Macmillan Coll) P-H.

Living Sociology. Claire M. Renzetti & Daniel J. Curran. LC 97-44354. 736p. 1997. 70.00 (*0-205-15144-2*) P-H.

Living Sociology. Thompson. 1998. pap. text, student ed. 20.00 (*0-205-27283-5*) Allyn.

Living Sociology. 2nd ed. (C). 1999. pap. 19.00 (*0-205-31641-7*) Allyn.

*__Living Sociology.__ 2nd ed. (C). 1999. write for info. (*0-205-31717-0*) Allyn.

Living Sociology. 2nd ed. 672p. (C). 1999. write for info. (*0-205-31113-X*) S&S Trade.

Living Sociology. 2nd ed. Renzetti & Curran. LC 99-45958. 645p. 1999. 70.00 incl. cd-rom (*0-205-30910-0*) Allyn.

Living Sociology Interactive Edition. abr. ed. Daniel J. Curran. 1998. 66.75 (*0-205-28785-9*) PH Diversified.

Living Sociology & Study Guide, 2 bks. Renzetti. 1998. text, student ed. 77.00 (*0-205-28841-3*) Allyn.

*__Living Sociology with I/a Companion Cdrom.__ 2nd ed. 1999. teacher ed. write for info. (*0-205-31757-X*) Allyn.

*__Living Sociology with Interactive Companion Cd-rom.__ 2nd ed. Renzetti. 1999. pap., suppl. ed. 19.00 (*0-205-31765-0*) Allyn.

L

L

Living Solo. Adrienne Salinger. LC 98-14365. (Illus.). 120p. 1998. pap. 6.95 (*0-8362-6753-2*) Andrews & McMeel.

Living Somewhere Between Estrogen & Death see Cuando Se Vive Entre el Estrogeno y la Muerte

Living Somewhere Between Estrogen & Death. Barbara Johnson. LC 97-1635. 192p. 1997. pap. 10.99 (*0-8499-3653-5*) Word Pub.

Living Somewhere Between Estrogen & Death. Barbara Johnson. 1998. mass mkt. 6.99 (*0-8499-5452-5*) Word Pub.

Living Soul. P. C. Jersild. Tr. by Rika Lesser from SWE. LC 88-63185. 192p. (Orig.). 1988. pap. 19.95 (*1-870041-09-7*, Pub. by Norvik Pr) Dufour.

Living Soul. John Wilson. 180p. 2001. 20.00 (*1-55725-232-7*, Pub. by Paraclete MA) Spring Arbor Dist.

Living Sounds: A Music Appreciation Anthology. Stephen Schultz. 416p. (C). 1993. per. 36.95 (*0-8403-8708-3*) Kendall-Hunt.

Living Space. Ron Schreiber. 64p. 1972. pap. 5.00 (*0-914610-01-5*) Hanging Loose.

Living Space: In Fact & Fiction. Philippa Tristram. (Illus.). 300p. 1989. 55.00 (*0-415-01279-1*) Routledge.

Living Space: Poems of the Dutch "Fiftiers" Ed. by Peter Glassgold. LC 79-15580. 1980. 7.95 (*0-8112-0746-3*, Pub. by New Directions); pap. 3.95 (*0-8112-0747-1*, NDP493, Pub. by New Directions) Norton.

Living Space in Fact & Fiction. Philippa Tristram. LC 89-15801. (Illus.). 320p. reprint ed. pap. 99.20 (*0-608-20393-9*, 207164600002) Bks Demand.

Living Spaces. Thomas Schmitz-Guenther. (Art & Architecture Ser.). 500p. 1999. 39.95 (*3-89508-925-7*, 520349) Konemann.

***Living Spaces.** Stewart Walton. (Illus.). 2000. pap. 12.95 (*0-7548-0310-4*, Lorenz Bks) Anness Pub.

Living Spaces, 6 bks., Reading Level 4. Gail Stewart. (Illus.). 192p. (J). (gr. 3-8). 1990. 71.70 (*0-685-58770-3*) Rourke Corp.

Living Spaces, 6 bks., Set. Gail Stewart. (Illus.). 192p. (J). (gr. 3-8). 1990. lib. bdg. 127.60 (*0-86592-105-9*) Rourke Enter.

Living Spring: Collected True Stories & Messages. Felix Liu & EFC Los Angeles Staff. 238p. 1996. pap. 9.95 (*1-885216-08-4*) Evan Formosan.

Living Staircase. Eisen & Westmoreland. 228p. (C). 1998. per. 28.95 (*0-7872-4904-1*, 41490401) Kendall-Hunt.

Living Standards & the Determinants of Poverty & Income Distribution in Mozambique. David E. Sahn & Carlo Del Ninno. (Working Papers: No. 56). 76p. (C). 1994. pap. 7.00 (*1-56401-156-9*) Cornell Food.

Living Standards of Filipino Families on an Hawaiian Sugar Plantation: Summarizing a Detailed Study. Edna L. Wentworth. LC 75-30088. (Institute of Pacific Relations Ser.). reprint ed. 34.50 (*0-404-59570-7*) AMS Pr.

Living State & Cancer. Albert Szent-Gyorgyi. LC 78-15106. (Illus.). 96p. reprint ed. pap. 30.00 (*0-7837-0678-2*, 204101200019) Bks Demand.

Living State II. Ed. by R. K. Mishra. 712p. 1985. 121.00 (*9971-978-26-1*) World Scientific Pub.

***Living Stone.** Jane Orcutt. 352p. 2000. pap. 10.95 (*1-57856-292-9*) Waterbrook Pr.

Living Stones: St. James Church, Kingston, 1845-1995: From Stuartville to Queen's Campus. David Lyon. (Illus.). 196p. 1995. pap. 19.95 (*1-55082-160-1*, Pub. by Quarry Pr) LPC InBook.

Living Stones: The History & Structure of Catholic Spiritual Life in the United States. Joseph P. Chinnici. 282p. (Orig.). 1996. pap. 16.00 (*1-57075-092-0*) Orbis Bks.

Living Stones of the Himalayas: Adventures of an American Couple in Nepal. Thomas Hale. LC 93-18398. 256p. 1993. pap. 10.99 (*0-310-38511-3*) Zondervan.

Living Stones Pilgrimage: With the Christians of the Holy Land. Betty Bailey & Alison Hilliard. 128p. 1998. pap. 16.50 (*0-304-70466-0*) Continuum.

Living Stones Pilgrimage: With the Christians of the Holy Land. Alison Hilliard. LC 98-44824. xii, 132p. 1999. pap. text 15.00 (*0-268-01322-5*, Pub. by U of Notre Dame Pr) Chicago Distribution Ctr.

Living Stories: Pastoral Counseling in Congregational Context. Donald Capps. LC 98-9235. 1998. pap. text 16.00 (*0-8006-3073-4*, 1-3073, Fortress Pr) Augsburg Fortress.

Living Stories of Famous Hymns. Ernest K. Emurian. LC 55-9054. (Hymns & Their Stories Ser.). 144p. (YA). (gr. 10). 1978. pap. 9.99 (*0-8010-3260-1*) Baker Bks.

Living Stories of the Cherokee. Barbara R. Duncan & Davey Arch. LC 97-35037. (Illus.). 272p. 1998. 29.95 (*0-8078-2411-9*); pap. 15.95 (*0-8078-4719-4*) U of NC Pr.

Living Stories, Telling Lives: Women & the Novel in Contemporary Experience. Joanne S. Frye. (Women & Culture Ser.). 264p. 1986. pap. text 18.95 (*0-472-08065-2*, 08065) U of Mich Pr.

***Living Strategy: Putting People at the Heart of Corporate Purpose.** Lynda Gratton. (Illus.). 256p. 2000. 28.00 (*0-273-65015-7*, Pub. by F T P-H) Trans-Atl Phila.

Living Stream: Holy Wells in Historical Context. James Rattue. (Illus.). 191p. 1995. 55.00 (*0-85115-601-0*) Boydell & Brewer.

Living Stream: Literature & Revisionism in Ireland. Edna Longley. 302p. 1994. pap. 25.00 (*1-85224-217-5*, Pub. by Bloodaxe Bks) Dufour.

Living Stream: Literature & Revisionism in Ireland. Edna Longley. 302p. 1995. 55.00 (*1-85224-216-7*, Pub. by Bloodaxe Bks) Dufour.

Living Strings: An Introduction to Biblical Spirituality. Michael Whelan. 189p. 1995. pap. 11.95 (*0-85574-373-5*, Pub. by E J Dwyer) Morehouse Pub.

Living, Studying & Working in France: Everything You Need to Know to Fulfill Your Dreams of Living Abroad. Saskia Reilly & Lorin Kalisky. LC 99-11623. 272p. 1999. pap. 16.00 (*0-8050-5947-4*, Owl) H Holt & Co.

Living, Studying & Working in Italy: Everything You Need to Know to Fulfill YOur Dreams of Living Abroad. Travis Neighbor & Monica Larner. LC 97-30702. 288p. 1998. pap. 14.95 (*0-8050-5102-3*) H Holt & Co.

***Living Supernaturally in Christ.** Ed. by Bill Bright. 256p. 2000. 19.99 (*1-56399-145-4*) New Life AZ.

Living Sword: A Fencer's Autobiography. Aldo Nadi. Ed. by Lance C. Lobo. LC 94-77796. (Illus.). 416p. 1995. pap. 17.95 (*1-884528-20-1*) Laureate Pr.

Living Sword: Letting the Holy Spirit Interpret God's Word. Harold R. Eberle. Ed. by Barbara Milligan. 135p. 1991. pap. 8.45 (*1-882523-01-6*) Winepress Pubng.

Living Symbol: A Case Study in the Process of Individuation. Gerhard Adler. LC 61-9310. (Bollingen Ser.: No. 63). 491p. reprint ed. pap. 152.30 (*0-7837-0240-X*, 204054800017) Bks Demand.

Living Synergistically. 9th ed. Thomas D. Willhite. 80p. 1999. reprint ed. pap. 14.95 (*0-9659994-2-4*) PSI Pub.

Living Systems. James G. Miller. (Illus.). 1152p. (C). 1992. pap. text 49.95 (*0-87081-363-3*) Univ Pr Colo.

Living Tao: Meditations on the Tao Te Ching to Empower Your Life. Stephen F. Kaufman. LC 98-18498. 128p. 1998. 14.95 (*0-8048-3143-2*) Tuttle Pubng.

Living Tarot. Ann Walker. 1994. pap. 17.95 (*1-898307-27-X*) Holmes Pub.

***Living Terrors: What America Needs to Know to Survive the Coming Bio-Terror Catastrophe.** Michael T. Osterholm. 2000. write for info. (*0-385-33480-X*) Delacorte.

Living Testbook: Using the Newspaper in the Classroom. Knowledge Unlimited Staff. (Illus.). 64p. 1998. teacher ed. 29.95 (*1-55933-233-6*, 4030GD) Know Unltd.

Living Testify. Ed. by Moshe Davis & Meir Hovav. Tr. by Moshe Kohn. (Illus.). 120p. (Orig.). 1994. pap. text 16.95 (*965-229-105-6*, Pub. by Gefen Pub Hse) Gefen Bks.

Living Text of the Gospels. D. C. Parker. 240p. (C). 1997. text 59.95 (*0-521-59062-0*); pap. text 18.95 (*0-521-59951-2*) Cambridge U Pr.

***Living Texts: Interpreting Milton.** Kristin A. Pruitt & Charles Durham. LC 00-34442. (Illus.). 2001. 47.50 (*1-57591-042-X*) Susquehanna U Pr.

***Living Textures: A Creative Guide to Combining Colors & Textures in the Home.** Katherine Sorrell. LC 00-30319. (Illus.). 2001. 24.95 (*0-8118-2950-2*) Chronicle Bks.

Living the American Dream: Pentair, Inc. - The First Twenty-Five Years. Murray J. Harpole. 252p. 1992. 19.95 (*0-9624229-5-9*) St Thomas Tech.

Living the Articles of Faith. Bessie Dean. (Illus.). 88p. (J). (gr. k-4). 1988. pap. 7.98 (*0-88290-336-5*) Horizon Utah.

Living the Authentic Life. David A. Scott. LC 98-65295. 108p. 1999. per. 14.95 (*1-879899-07-8*) Newjoy Pr.

Living the Beatitudes. Abe Bergen. (Fast Lane Bible Studies Ser.). (Illus.). 76p. (J). (gr. 7-9). 1994. pap. 12.95 (*0-87303-211-X*) Faith & Life.

Living the Beatitudes Today: Happily Ever after Begins Here & Now. Bill Dodds & Michael J. Dodds. LC 97-12467. (Seeker Ser.). 1997. pap. 10.95 (*0-8294-0970-X*) Loyola Pr.

Living the Bill of Rights: How to Be an Authentic American. Nat Hentoff. LC 98-18017. 256p. 1998. 25.00 (*0-06-019010-8*) HarpC.

Living the Bill of Rights: How to Be An Authentic American. Nat Hentoff. LC 99-13196. 253p. 1999. pap. 14.95 (*0-520-21981-3*, Pub. by U CA Pr) Cal Prin Full Svc.

Living the Catechism of the Catholic Church Vol. 1: The Creed. Christoph Schonborn. LC 95-75670. 162p. (Orig.). 1995. pap. 9.95 (*0-89870-560-6*) Ignatius Pr.

Living the Christ Life. James Stalker. Ed. by William J. Petersen. LC 81-81097. (Illus.). 172p. 1988. pap. 5.95 (*0-8254-5321-6*) Kregel.

Living the Christian Life. A. N. Martin. 32p. 1986. pap. 2.00 (*0-85151-493-6*) Banner of Truth.

Living the Christian Life: A Guide to Reformed Spirituality. Robert H. Ramey, Jr. & Ben C. Johnson. 208p. (Orig.). 1992. pap. 17.95 (*0-664-25286-9*) Westminster John Knox.

***Living the Christian Story: The Good News in Worship & Daily Life.** Mary Jean Manninen. LC BV4501.2.M3375 2000. 128p. 2000. pap. 12.00 (*0-8028-4706-4*) Eerdmans.

Living the Crucified Life. Ralph V. Reynolds. 118p. (Orig.). (C). 1987. pap. 5.50 (*1-877917-02-8*) Alpha Bible Pubns.

Living the Days of Advent & the Christmas Season 1998. Stephanie Collins. LC 98-218010. (Illus.). 48p. 1998. pap. text 3.95 (*0-8091-3825-5*) Paulist Pr.

***Living the Days of Advent & the Christmas Season 2000.** Stephanie Collins. 48p. 2000. pap. 3.95 (*0-8091-3969-3*) Paulist Pr.

Living the Days of Advent & the Christmas Season,1999. Stephanie Collins. (Illus.). 48p. 1999. pap. 3.95 (*0-8091-3884-0*) Paulist Pr.

Living the Days of Lent 2000. Ed. by Anita M. Constance. 54p. 2000. pap. 3.95 (*0-8091-3917-0*) Paulist Pr.

***Living the Death of God: A Theological Memoir.** Thomas J. J. Altizer. 220p. 2000. 22.00 (*1-58177-067-7*) Barrytown Ltd.

Living the Drama of Faith: What Faith Is & Where It Leads You. rev. ed. Guardimi Romano. LC 98-23177. Orig. Title: The Life of Faith. 158p. 1998. pap. 11.95 (*0-918477-77-8*) Sophia Inst Pr.

Living the Dream. Dot Richardson. 192p. 1998. pap. 12.95 (*1-57566-277-9*, Knsington) Kensgtn Pub Corp.

Living the Dream. Dot Richardson & Don Yaeger. LC 97-71967. 256p. 1997. 19.95 (*1-57566-203-5*) Kensgtn Pub Corp.

***Living the Dream: David Robinson, 100.** Good News Publishing Company Staff. 1999. pap. 8.50 (*5-550-09550-5*) Nairi.

Living the Dream: It's Time: A Chronicle of the Gathering of Equals. Mark Conrad & Keith Varnum. LC 97-75697. (Illus.). 256p. 1998. 22.95 (*1-891569-19-8*, 0001197) Pura Vida.

Living the Easter Faith: Sermons for the Easter Season. Donald W. Dotterer. LC 93-30842. 68p. 1993. pap. 7.50 (*1-55673-522-7*) CSS OH.

Living the Enlightenment: Freemasonry & Politics in 18th-Century Europe. Margaret C. Jacob. (Illus.). 320p. (C). 1991. pap. text 24.95 (*0-19-507051-8*) OUP.

Living the Eternal Way: Spiritual Meaning & Practice for Daily Life. Ellen G. O'Brian. Ed. by Anne Cawley. LC 97-75320. (Illus.). 192p. 1997. pap. 22.95 (*0-9660518-0-7*) Ctr for Spirit.

Living the Ethnographic Life. Dan Rose. (Qualitative Research Methods Ser.: Vol. 23). 64p. (C). 1990. text 24.00 (*0-8039-3998-1*); pap. text 10.50 (*0-8039-3999-X*) Sage.

Living the Faith: The Praxis of Eastern Orthodox Ethics. Stanley S. Harakas. 1993. pap. 19.95 (*0-937032-92-1*) Light&Life Pub Co MN.

Living the Faith You Share: Ten Ecumenical Guidelines for Couples in Roman Catholic - Protestant Marriages. Massachusetts Commission on Christian Unity Staff. 1990. 1.50 (*0-9627112-1-7*) Divinitas Pr.

Living the Global City. Ed. by John Eade. LC 96-7921. 208p. (C). 1996. 80.00 (*0-415-13886-8*); pap. 22.99 (*0-415-13887-6*) Routledge.

Living the Golden Path. Ruth Ryden. 186p. (Orig.). 1994. pap. 11.95 (*0-929385-65-9*) Light Tech Pubng.

Living the Golden Rule: A Storybook to Color. Bessie Dean. 24p. 1979. pap. 4.98 (*0-88290-113-3*) Horizon Utah.

Living the Good Life. Kenneth T. Hurst. 112p. (Orig.). 1990. pap. 6.95 (*0-943914-53-1*) Larson Pubns.

***Living the Good Life: An Astrologer's On-Reaching Message.** 383p. 1999. pap. text 19.95 (*0-86690-491-3*) Am Fed Astrologers.

Living the Good Life: An Introduction to Moral Philosophy. Gordon Graham. (Issues in Philosophy Ser.). 140p. (C). 1990. pap. text 16.95 (*1-55778-235-0*) Paragon Hse.

Living the Good Life in Puerto Rico: Why People Live to a Ripe Old Age in Puerto Rico & How You Can Do It Too. Raoul Gordon. 1978. lib. bdg. 250.00 (*0-8490-2177-4*) Gordon Pr.

Living the Gospel with the Mother. Tr. by Bertha Gonzales from SPA. LC 88-84013. Orig. Title: Viviendo el Evangelio. 704p. 1989. 20.00 (*0-936707-01-1*) Action Life Pubns.

Living the "High" Life: God's Way? Man's Way? Vernelle B. Allen. 226p. 1994. pap. write for info. (*1-885984-09-X*) Wings of Healing.

***Living the Hospitality of God.** Lucien Richard. 2001. pap. 14.95 (*0-8091-3998-7*) Paulist Pr.

Living the Incarnation: Praying with Francis & Clare of Assisi. Frances Teresa. LC 96-14460. (Illus.). 1996. reprint ed. 12.95 (*0-8199-0971-8*) Franciscan Pr.

Living the Infinite Way. Joel S. Goldsmith. LC 92-53895. 128p. 1993. pap. 12.00 (*0-06-250317-0*, Pub. by Harper SF) HarpC.

Living the Intersection: Womanism & Afrocentrism in Theology. Ed. by Cheryl J. Sanders. LC 94-33746. 176p. 1995. pap. 17.00 (*0-8006-2852-7*, 1-2852, Fortress Pr) Augsburg Fortress.

Living the Intifada. Andrew Rigby. 240p. (C). 1991. text 62.50 (*1-85649-039-4*, Pub. by Zed Books); text 22.50 (*1-85649-040-8*, Pub. by Zed Books) St Martin.

***Living the Jazz Life: Conversations with Forty Musicians about Their Careers in Jazz.** W. Royal Stokes. (Illus.). 304p. 2000. 25.00 (*0-19-508108-0*) OUP.

Living the Jesus Prayer. Irma Zaleski. LC 97-50155. 64p. 1998. pap. 8.95 (*0-8264-1090-1*) Continuum.

Living the Kabbalah: A Guide to the Sabbath & the Festivals in the Teachings of Rabbi Moshe Luria. Simcha H. Benyosef. LC 99-11840. 240p. 1999. 29.95 (*0-8264-1149-5*) Continuum.

***Living the Labyrinth.** Jill K. Hartwell Geoffrion. LC 99-54633. 2000. pap. 16.95 (*0-8298-1372-1*) Pilgrim OH.

Living the Legacy: Favorite Talks from Especially for Youth, Boys World of Adventure & Academy for Girls. LC 96-84075. 240p. (Orig.). 1996. pap. 9.95 (*1-57345-160-6*) Deseret Bk.

Living the Life. 52p. 1984. pap. 4.00 (*0-900125-17-9*) Bahai.

Living the Life of a Fabric-aholic. Sandy Gervais. (Illus.). 26p. 1995. reprint ed. 14.95 (*0-9673534-0-8*) Midlife Printing.

Living the Life of Enoch. Ellen Gould Harmon White. LC 95-62230. 96p. 1996. per. 7.95 (*1-57258-072-0*) Teach Servs.

Living the Life of the Lifegiver: Making Simple the Parables & Teachings of Jesus. Ellen Gould Harmon White. (Life-Giving Secrets: Vol. 3). 320p. (Orig.). (C). 1995. pap. 9.95 (*1-883012-67-8*) Remnant Pubns.

***Living the Life You Want: Your Personal Key to True Abundance & the Richness of Everyday Experience.** Sylvia Clare & David Hughes. 208p. 2000. pap. 15.95 (*1-85703-595-X*, Pub. by How To Bks) Midpt Trade.

Living the Life You Were Meant to Live. Tom Peterson. LC 97-53278. 256p. 1998. 19.99 (*0-7852-7195-3*) Nelson.

Living the Little Way: Therese of Lisieux. John Nelson. LC 99-50280. (Christian Living Ser.). 160p. 1999. pap. 10.95 (*1-56548-133-X*) New City.

Living the Liturgy. Stanley S. Harakas. 1974. pap. 8.95 (*0-937032-17-4*) Light&Life Pub Co MN.

Living the Liturgy: The Mass As Personal Growth. Marilyn N. Gustin. LC 93-79676. 96p. 1993. pap. 5.95 (*0-89243-579-8*) Liguori Pubns.

Living the Lord's Prayer. Michelle Gritter-Dykstra. 47p. 1995. pap., student ed. 5.25 (*1-56212-122-7*) CRC Pubns.

Living the Magic: A Life Changing Journey. James M. Rankin. (Method Selling Ser.: Vol. II). 128p. 1998. pap. 8.95 (*0-9641729-1-7*) eDreampubng.

Living the Martial Way: A Manual for the Way a Modern Warrior Should Think. Forrest E. Morgan. LC 92-16969. 320p. 1992. pap. 16.95 (*0-942637-76-3*) Barricade Bks.

Living the Message: Daily Reflections with Eugene H. Peterson. Eugene H. Peterson. 400p. 1996. pap. 13.00 (*0-06-066432-0*, Pub. by Harper SF) HarpC.

Living the Message of the New Testament. Michael F. Pennock. LC 91-77474. (Friendship in the Lord Ser.). (Illus.). 184p. (YA). (gr. 11-12). 1992. pap., teacher ed. 16.95 (*0-87793-468-1*); pap. text, student ed. 12.95 (*0-87793-469-X*) Ave Maria.

Living the Mindful Life. Charles T. Tart. LC 94-6192. 288p. 1994. pap. 14.00 (*1-57062-003-2*, Pub. by Shambhala Pubns) Random.

Living the Moment. Albert Krassner. (Orig.). 1987. pap. 4.95 (*0-912061-12-X*) Veridon Edns.

Living the Mystery: Affirming Catholicism & the Future of Anglicanism. Jeffrey John. pap. write for info. (*0-232-52071-2*) S Asia.

Living the New Life see Exciting New Life

Living the Nightmare: Escape from Kuwait. Karen Huffman. Ed. by Linda J. Dageforde. LC 98-47559. 300p. 1999. pap. 21.95 (*1-886225-34-6*, 2000) Dageforde Pub.

Living the Promises of God: 365 Readings for Recovery from Grief or Loss. Paul F. Keller. LC 88-7405. 376p. 1988. kivar 19.99 (*0-8066-2368-3*, 10-4031, Augsburg) Augsburg Fortress.

Living the Psalms. Maxie Dunham. 1990. pap. 12.95 (*0-687-60683-7*) Abingdon.

Living the Psalms. John Sheridan. 320p. (Orig.). 1996. pap. 14.95 (*0-8198-4481-0*) Pauline Bks.

Living the Psalms: A Confidence for All Seasons. Maxie Dunnam. LC 90-83523. 160p. 1990. pap. 10.00 (*0-8358-0622-7*) Upper Room Bks.

***Living the Questions.** Carolyn Arends. 200p. 2000. pap. 9.99 (*0-7369-0226-0*) Harvest Hse.

Living The Questions: A Guide for Teacher-Researchers. Ruth Hubbard. LC 98-50353. 328p. 1999. 27.50 (*1-57110-081-4*) Stenhse Pubs.

Living the Responsible Life. Cecil A. Ray. Ed. by G. A. Hogg. 160p. 1983. pap. text 12.50 (*0-311-72371-3*) Casa Bautista.

Living the Sacraments. 2nd ed. David M. Knight. 111p. 1989. reprint ed. pap. 6.50 (*0-942971-13-2*) His Way.

Living the Science of Mind. Ernest Holmes. Ed. by Arthur Vergara. LC 90-84240. 444p. 1991. pap. 17.95 (*0-87516-627-X*) DeVorss.

***Living the 7 Habits.** 1998. write for info. (*0-684-84682-9*) S&S Trade.

***Living the 7 Habits.** 2000. per. 14.00 (*0-7432-0292-9*) S&S Trade.

Living the 7 Habits. abr. ed. Stephen R. Covey. audio 12.00 (*0-671-51994-8*, 390132, Pub. by S&S Audio) Lndmrk Audiobks.

***Living the Seven Habits: Applications & Insights.** Stephen R. Covey. 368p. 1999. 12.00 incl. audio (*0-671-04567-9*) S&S Audio.

***Living the Seven Habits: Stories of Courage & Inspiration.** 336p. 1999. 16.00 (*0-684-86981-0*) S&S Trade.

***Living the 7 Habits: Stories of Courage & Inspiration.** Stephen R. Covey. 336p. 2000. per. 14.00 (*0-684-85716-2*, Fireside) S&S Trade Pap.

Living the 7 Habits: Understanding, Using, Succeeding. Stephen R. Covey. LC 99-28061. 336p. 1999. 26.00 (*0-684-84664-0*) S&S Trade.

Living the Simple Life: A Guide to Scaling Down & Enjoying More. Elaine St. James. (Illus.). 350p. (J). 1998. reprint ed. pap. 9.95 (*0-7868-8242-5*, Pub. by Hyperion) Time Warner.

***Living the Simple Life: A Little Treasury.** Elaine St. James. (Illus.). 80p. 2000. 4.95 (*0-7407-0526-1*) Andrews & McMeel.

Living the Sky: The Cosmos of the American Indian. Ray A. Williamson. LC 86-30712. (Illus.). 404p. 1987. pap. 19.95 (*0-8061-2034-7*) U of Okla Pr.

Living the Spirit-Filled Life see Dia a Dia en la Plenitud del Espiritu

Living the Spirit Filled Life. M. Hayford. 1992. pap. 9.99 (*0-8407-8353-1*) Nelson.

Living the Spirit-Led Life. Larry Keefauver. LC 97-37538. 64p. 1997. pap., student ed. 6.99 (*0-88419-471-X*) Creation House.

Living the Spiritually Balanced Life. Ray S. Anderson. LC 98-8101. 192p. 1998. pap. 12.99 (*0-8010-5803-1*) Baker Bks.

Living the Steps to Vibrancy: An Intensive Path to Wholeness & the Life You Ought to Be Living. Richard J. Sandore. x, 230p. 1999. pap. 14.95 (*0-9671522-1-6*) Soaring IL.

Living the Sunday Liturgy. Johnny Doherty. 288p. (Orig.). 1995. pap. 16.95 (*1-85607-137-5*, Pub. by Columba Press) Whitecap Bks.

Living the Tarot. Amber Jayanti. LC 92-39340. (Illus.). 368p. 1999. pap. 15.95 (*0-87542-373-6*) Llewellyn Pubns.

An Asterisk (*) at the beginning of an entry indicates that the title is appearing for the first time.

Living the Ten Commandments: Adult Bible Study Kit. Ted Schroeder. 1996. pap. 149.99 incl. VHS (*0-570-09707-X*, 87-0731) Concordia.

Living the Ten Commandments: Leader's Guide. Ted Schroeder. 80p. 1996. pap. 6.99 (*0-570-09708-8*, 87-0732) Concordia.

Living the Ten Commandments: Participant Guide. Ted Schroeder. 80p. 1996. pap. 2.00 (*0-570-09709-6*, 87-0733) Concordia.

Living the Truth. Josef Pieper. Tr. by Lothar Krauth & Stella Lange from GER. LC 89-84891.Tr. of Reality of the Good. 190p. (Orig.). 1989. reprint ed. pap. text 14.95 (*0-89870-261-5*) Ignatius Pr.

Living the Truth in Love: A Biblical Introduction to Moral Theology. Benedict M. Ashley. LC 96-10967. 572p. (Orig.). 1996. pap. 24.95 (*0-8189-0756-8*) Alba.

Living the Vision: Evangelism & Peace. Eleanor Snyder & David Rogalsky. (Living the Vision Ser.). 62p. 1998. pap. 5.95 (*0-87303-323-X*) Faith & Life.

Living the Vision: Leadership & Community. Ken Hawkley & April Yamasaki. (Living the Vision Ser.). 56p. 1997. pap. 5.95 (*0-87303-317-5*) Faith & Life.

Living the Vision: Spirituality & Stewardship. Eleanor Snyder & Ken Hawkley. (Living the Vision Ser.). 60p. 1997. pap. 5.95 (*0-87303-312-4*) Faith & Life.

Living the Wheel: Working with Emotion, Terror & Bliss Through Imagery. Annabelle Nelson. LC 93-16810. (Illus.). 202p. (Orig.). 1993. pap. 10.95 (*0-87728-782-1*) Weiser.

Living the Word: Reflections on the Gospels of the Three-Year Cycle. Tom Clancy. 224p. (Orig.). 1996. pap. 14.95 (*1-85607-156-1*, Pub. by Columba Press) Whitecap Bks.

Living the Word: Reflections on the Revised Common Lectionary. Ed. by Sojourners Editors. (Illus.). 146p. 1996. pap. 10.00 (*0-9641109-4-6*) Sojrners.

Living the Word of Wisdom: A Guide for Young Latter-Day Saints (A Storybook to Color) Jan Clawson. LC 89-85210. 32p. 1989. pap. 4.98 (*0-88290-354-3*) Horizon Utah.

Living the Writer's Life: A Complete Self-Made Guide. Eric Maisel. LC 99-41976. 192p. 1999. pap. 16.95 (*0-8230-8848-0*) Watsn-Guptill.

Living Theater: A History. 2nd ed. Edwin Wilson & Alvin Goldfarb. LC 93-43475. (C). 1994. text 43.74 (*0-07-070733-2*) McGraw.

Living Theater: A History. 3rd ed. Edwin Wilson. LC 99-26756. 608p. 1999. pap. 50.00 (*0-07-038469-X*) McGraw.

Living Theater: Art, Exile, & Outrage. John Tytell. 448p. 1997. reprint ed. pap. 15.00 (*0-8021-3486-6*, Grove) Grove-Atltic.

Living Theory: The Application of Classical Social Theory to Contemporary Life. Hurst. LC 99-19228. 161p. (C). 1999. pap. text 24.00 (*0-205-27775-6*, Macmillan Coll) P-H.

Living Things. Paul Bennett. 1975. pap. 6.00 (*0-686-18089-5*) Orchard.

Living Things. David Evans & Claudette Williams. (Let's Explore Science Ser.). (Illus.). (J). 12.95 (*0-590-74945-5*) Scholastic Inc.

Living Things. Wendy Madgwick. LC 98-30065. (Science Starters Ser.). 1999. 5.95 (*0-8172-5883-3*) Raintree Steck-V.

***Living Things.** Wendy Madgwick. (J). 1999. 22.83 (*0-8172-5332-7*) Raintree Steck-V.

***Living Things.** Adrienne Mason. (Starting with Science Ser.). 32p. (J). (gr. k-4). 2000. pap. 6.95 (*1-55074-393-7*, Pub. by Kids Can Pr) Genl Dist Srvs.

Living Things. John Russo. 288p. 1988. mass mkt. 3.95 (*0-445-20666-7*, Mysterious Paperbk) Warner Bks.

Living Things. Rebecca Steoff. (Illus.). 32p. (YA). (gr. 1 up). lib. bdg. 45.37 (*0-7614-0448-1*) Marshall Cavendish.

Living Things. unabridged ed. Adrienne Mason & Deborah Hodge. LC 96-931707. (Starting with Science Ser.). (Illus.). 32p. (J). (gr. k-4). 1998. 14.95 (*1-55074-343-0*, Pub. by Kids Can Pr) Genl Dist Srvs.

Living Things. 2nd ed. A. M. Winchester et al. (Pictured Key Nature Ser.). 184p. (C). 1981. text. write for info. (*0-697-04780-6*, WCB McGr Hill) McGrw-H Hghr Educ.

Living Things - Group 1, 6 bks. Rebecca Stefoff. Incl. Chameleon. LC 96-1132. (Illus.). 32p. (J). (gr. 1 up). 1996. lib. bdg. 22.79 (*0-7614-0118-0*, Benchmark NY); Giant Turtle. LC 96-18483. (Illus.). 32p. (YA). (gr. 1 up). 1996. lib. bdg. 22.79 (*0-7614-0121-0*, Benchmark NY); Octopus. LC 96-1131. (Illus.). 32p. (J). (gr. 1 up). 1996. lib. bdg. 22.79 (*0-7614-0119-9*); Praying Mantis. LC 96-18482. (Illus.). 32p. (J). (gr. 1 up). 1996. lib. bdg. 22.79 (*0-7614-0120-2*, Benchmark NY); Sea Horse. LC 96-6212. (Illus.). 32p. (YA). (gr. 1 up). 1996. lib. bdg. 22.79 (*0-7614-0116-4*, Benchmark NY); Starfish. LC 96-2080. (Illus.). 32p. (J). (gr. 1 up). 1996. lib. bdg. 22.79 (*0-7614-0117-2*, Benchmark NY); (YA). (gr. 1 up). 136.71 (*0-7614-0115-6*, Benchmark NY) Marshall Cavendish.

Living Things - Group 2, 6 bks. Incl. Beetle. R. Stefoff. LC 96-37592. (Illus.). 32p. (J). (gr. 1-3). 1997. lib. bdg. 22.79 (*0-7614-0410-4*, Benchmark NY); Butterfly. R. Stefoff. LC 96-46137. (Illus.). 32p. (J). (gr. 1-3). 1997. lib. bdg. 22.79 (*0-7614-0413-9*, Benchmark NY); Frog. Rebecca Stefoff. LC 96-39105. (Illus.). 32p. (J). (gr. 1 up). 1997. lib. bdg. 22.79 (*0-7614-0414-7*, Benchmark NY); Hummingbird. R. Stefoff. LC 96-44018. (Illus.). 32p. (J). (gr. 1 up). 1997. lib. bdg. 22.79 (*0-7614-0415-5*, Benchmark NY); Jellyfish. Rebecca Stefoff. LC 96-39107. (Illus.). 32p. (J). (gr. 1-3). 1997. lib. bdg. 22.79 (*0-7614-0411-2*, Benchmark NY); Snake. Rebecca Stefoff. LC 96-39106. (Illus.). 32p. (J). (gr. 1 up). 1997. lib. bdg. 22.79 (*0-7614-0412-0*, Benchmark NY); (J). 136.71 (*0-7614-0409-0*, Benchmark NY) Marshall Cavendish.

Living Things - Group 3, 4 bks. Incl. Ant. Rebecca Stefoff. LC 97-9132. (Illus.). 32p. (J). (gr. 1 up). 1997. lib. bdg. 22.79 (*0-7614-0447-3*, Benchmark NY); Crab. R. Stefoff. LC 97-9130. (Illus.). 32p. (J). (gr. 1 up). 1997. lib. bdg. 22.79 (*0-7614-0444-9*, Benchmark NY); Owl. Rebecca Stefoff. LC 97-9148. (Illus.). 32p. (J). (gr. 1 up). 1997. lib. bdg. 22.79 (*0-7614-0443-0*, Benchmark NY); Penguin. Rebecca Stefoff. LC 97-8940. (Illus.). 32p. (J). (gr. 4-7). 1997. lib. bdg. 22.79 (*0-7614-0446-5*, Benchmark NY); (J). 91.14 (*0-7614-0441-4*, Benchmark NY) Marshall Cavendish.

***Living Thin/Living Young: An Attitude-Not a Diet/An Attitude-Not an Age.** Sylvia M. Goldman. Ed. by James A. Keene. LC 00-100347. (Illus.). 2000. 21.95 (*0-944435-49-1*) Glenbridge Pub.

Living Thoughts. Ernest Miner. (Book of Inspirational Thoughts). (Illus.). 84p. 1985. 7.95 (*0-935087-00-1*) Wright Pub Co.

***Living Thoughts of Gotama the Buddha.** Ananda Coomaraswamy & I. B. Horner. 2000. pap. 8.95 (*0-486-41439-6*) Dover.

Living Thoughts of Gotama, the Buddha. Ananda K. Coomaraswamy & I. B. Horner. LC 78-72397. reprint ed. 34.50 (*0-404-17256-3*) AMS Pr.

Living Thoughts of Kierkegaard. Soren Kierkegaard. Ed. by W. H. Auden. LC 99-14567. 280p. 1999. reprint ed. pap. 12.95 (*0-940322-13-7*, Pub. by NY Rev Bks) Midpt Trade.

Living Thoughts of Machiavelli. Niccolo Machiavelli. Ed. by Carlo Sforza. LC 74-28758. (Illus.). 161p. 1975. reprint ed. lib. bdg. 35.00 (*0-8371-7923-8*, MALIT, Greenwood Pr) Greenwood.

Living Thoughts of Mazzini Presented by Ignazio Silone. Giuseppe Mazzini. LC 79-138163. (Illus.). 130p. 1972. reprint ed. lib. bdg. 49.50 (*0-8371-5620-3*, MALI, Greenwood Pr) Greenwood.

Living Thoughts of the Prophet Muhammad. Maulana M. Ali. 156p. (Orig.). 1992. pap. 5.95 (*0-913321-19-2*) Ahmadiyya Anjuman.

Living Through a Personal Crisis. Ann K. Stearns. 1985. mass mkt. 5.99 (*0-345-32293-2*) Ballantine Pub Grp.

Living Through Divorce: A Developmental Approach to Divorce Therapy. Joy K. Rice & David G. Rice. LC 85-27173. (Family Therapy Ser.). 303p. 1985. lib. bdg. 42.00 (*0-89862-061-9*) Guilford Pubns.

Living Through Dying: The Spiritual Experience of Saint Paul. Douglas Dales. 100p. 1999. 28.95 (*0-7188-2898-4*, Lutterworth-Parkwest) Parkwest Pubns.

***Living Through Fifty Years of Economic Progress with Ten Presidents: The Most Productive Generation in History, 1946-1996.** David F. Linowes. LC 00-29643. (Industrial Development & the Social Fabric Ser.). (Illus.). 2000. write for info. (*0-7623-0590-8*) Jai Pr.

Living Through Florida History. Miriam B. Lowry. Ed. by Anne Frost. (Illus.). 150p. 1996. 12.95 (*0-9614624-9-3*) Frost Pub.

Living Through Loss: A Manual for Those Working with Issues of Terminal Illness & Bereavement. Fay W. Jacobsen et al. 200p. 1996. pap. 49.95 (*1-85302-395-7*, Pub. by Jessica Kingsley) Taylor & Francis.

Living Through Mourning: Finding Comfort & Hope When a Loved One Has Died. Harriet S. Schiff. 304p. 1987. pap. 13.95 (*0-14-010309-0*, Penguin Bks) Viking Penguin.

***Living Through Pop.** Andrew Blake. LC 99-34829. 192p. 1999. pap. write for info. (*0-415-16199-1*) Routledge.

***Living Through Pop.** Ed. by Andrew Blake. LC 99-34829. 192p. (C). 1999. text 75.00 (*0-415-16198-3*) Routledge.

Living Through the Older Years. Ed. by Clark Tibbitts & Robert J. Kastenbaum. LC 78-22221. (Aging & Old Age Ser.). 1979. reprint ed. lib. bdg. 19.95 (*0-405-11834-1*) Ayer.

Living Tibet: The Dalai Lama in Dharamsala. Bill Warren & Nanci H. Rose. (Illus.). 136p. 1995. pap. 26.95 (*1-55939-042-5*) Snow Lion Pubns.

Living Time. Brian Swann. (QRL Poetry Bks.: Vol. XX). 1978. 20.00 (*0-614-06368-X*) Quarterly Rev.

Living to Be 100: Life Lessons from the Landmark Harvard Medical School Study. Thomas Perls et al. (Illus.). 31p. 2000. 25.00 (*0-465-04142-6*, Pub. by Basic) HarpC.

***Living to 100: Lessons in Living to Your Maximum Potential at Any Age.** Thomas T. Perls. 2000. pap. 14.00 (*0-465-04143-4*, Pub. by Basic) HarpC.

***Living to 100: Lessons in Living to Your Maximum Potential at Any Age.** large type ed. Thomas T. Perls et al. LC 99-45855. 1999. 26.95 (*0-7862-2221-2*), Thorndike Pr.

Living to 102: Natural Health Methods, Testimonials, Personal Experiences, Documentation of Human Longevity. Tymme M. Mitchell. LC 98-68427. xii, 124 p. 1998. write for info. (*1-892681-00-5*) TM Mind Body.

Living to Please God. D. Haag. 8.50 (*0-906731-91-7*, Pub. by Christian Focus) Spring Arbor Dist.

Living to Prowl. Sam Pickering. LC 97-18691. 192p. 1998. 24.95 (*0-8203-1940-6*) U of Ga Pr.

***Living To Tell.** Antonya Nelson. LC 99-88529. 320p. 2000. 23.50 (*0-684-83933-2*) Scribner.

Living to Tell about It: Young Black Men in America Speak. Darrell Dawsey. 368p. 1997. pap. 12.95 (*0-385-47314-1*, Anchor NY) Doubleday.

Living to Tell the Tale: A Guide to Writing Memoir. Jane McDonnell. LC 97-34341. 164p. 1998. pap. 12.95 (*0-14-026530-9*) Viking Penguin.

Living Together. Edgar Bowers. 84p. 1988. 15.00 (*0-936576-12-X*); pap. 5.00 (*0-936576-13-8*) Symposium Pr.

***Living Together.** Created by Francine Pascal. (Sweet Valley University Ser.: No. 51). 240p. (YA). (gr. 7 up). 1999. mass mkt. 4.50 (*0-553-49271-3*) Bantam.

Living Together. Michael Wilding. (Paperbacks Ser.). 224p. 1985. pap. 14.95 (*0-7022-0896-5*, Pub. by Univ Queensland Pr) Intl Spec Bk.

Living Together: A Guide to the Law. Anne Barlow. 259p. (C). 1992. 110.00 (*1-85190-151-5*, Pub. by Tolley Pubng) St Mut.

Living Together: First Grade Student Book see Philosophy for Young Thinkers Program

Living Together: Rationality, Sociality, & Obligation. Margaret Gilbert. 432p. (C). 1996. pap. text 24.95 (*0-8476-8151-3*); lib. bdg. 71.50 (*0-8476-8150-5*) Rowman.

Living Together: The Biology of Animal Parasitism. W. Trager. LC 86-15097. (Illus.). 480p. (C). 1986. text 110.00 (*0-306-42310-3*, Kluwer Plenum) Kluwer Academic.

Living Together: Therapeutic & Social Aspects see Proceedings

Living Together . . . And Loving Every (Other) Minute of It: A Guide to Successful Cohabitation. Hal Greenfader. LC 84-60764. (Illus.). 184p. 1986. pap. 12.95 (*0-915677-21-0*) Roundtable Pub.

Living Together Contract: The Canadian Marriage Contract Kit. 6th ed. Heather Fayers. (Legal Ser.). 64p. 1997. pap. 15.95 (*1-55180-069-1*) Self-Counsel Pr.

Living Together in a Jesuit Community. Carlos G. Valles. LC 84-81259. (Studies on Jesuit Topics IV: No. 10). viii, 119p. 1984. pap. 2.00 (*0-912422-66-1*) Inst Jesuit.

Living Together in Harmony: Economic Viability of Co-Operative Communities. Cecelia A. Winters. (Illus.). 400p. (Orig.). 1997. pap. 19.95 (*1-885610-06-8*) European Amer.

Living Together in Knowledge: What Husbands & Wives Can Learn about Marriage from Each Other. Don McWhorter & Jane McWhorter. 172p. 1988. pap. text 5.95 (*0-929540-00-X*) Pup Designs.

Living Together Kit: A Legal Guide for Unmarried Couples. 9th ed. Toni L. Ihara & Ralph E. Warner. LC 98-25264. 240p. 1999. 24.95 (*0-87337-490-8*) Nolo com.

***Living Together Kit: A Legal Guide for Unmarried Couples.** 10th ed. Toni Lynne Ihara et al. LC 99-39291. 1999. 34.95 (*0-87337-562-9*) Nolo com.

Living Together, Loving Together: A Spiritual Guide to Marriage. Lisa Bellecci-St. Romain & Philip St. Romain. LC 94-73020. 160p. 1995. pap. 6.95 (*0-89243-788-X*) Liguori Pubns.

Living Together on God's Earth. rev. ed. John D. Martin. (Christian Day School Ser.). (J). (gr. 3). 1996. 14.95 (*0-87813-928-1*) Christian Light.

Living Together on God's Earth: Teacher's Guidebook. John D. Martin. (Christian Day School Ser.). (J). (gr. 3). 1975. teacher ed. 15.75 (*0-87813-910-9*) Christian Light.

Living Together Precedents. Jill Bowler et al. (Waterlow Publications). 80p. 1989. pap. 99.00 (*0-08-040119-8*, Pergamon Pr) Elsevier.

Living Together Separately: Arabs & Jews in Contemporary Jerusalem. Michael Romann & Alex Weingrod. LC 90-9073. (Princeton Studies on the Near East). 272p. 1991. reprint ed. pap. 84.40 (*0-608-02572-0*, 206321700004) Bks Demand.

Living Together Trap: Everything Women & Men Should Know. Rosanne Rosen. LC 92-63124. 176p. 1993. pap. 13.95 (*0-88282-075-3*) New Horizon NJ.

Living Together Without Marriage: The Law in New Zealand. W. R. Atkin. 240p. 1991. pap. 81.00 (*0-409-70221-8*, NZ, MICHIE) LEXIS Pub.

***Living Tomb.** Jacqueline Morley. (Magnifications Ser.). (Illus.). (YA). 2000. 18.95 (*0-87226-651-6*, P Bedrick Books) NTC Contemp Pub Co.

Living Tomorrow's Company. Mark Goyder. LC 97-31503. 224p. 1998. pap. 43.95 (*0-566-08020-6*, Pub. by Gower) Ashgate Pub Co.

Living Torah: English Only. Aryeh Kaplan. (Illus.). 647p. (J). (gr. 2-5). 1981. 24.00 (*0-940118-35-1*) Moznaim.

Living Torah: Russian Edition. Aryeh Kaplan. Tr. by Gedalya Spinadel. (RUS., Illus.). 726p. 1999. 24.00 (*1-885220-25-1*) Moznaim.

Living Torah - Hebrew-English Edition (with Haftarot, Bibliography & Index) Aryeh Kaplan. 1428p. 1981. 33.00 (*0-940118-72-6*) Moznaim.

Living Torah Hebrew English Edition (with Haftarot, Bibliography, & Index), 5 vols., Set. Aryeh Kaplan. 1428p. 1981. 50.00 (*0-940118-73-4*) Moznaim.

Living Torah in America. Maurice Lamm. Ed. by William Cutter. (Illus.). 182p. (YA). (gr. 8-10). 1993. 30.00 (*0-87441-513-6*) Behrman.

Living Torch. Ed. by M. Gibbon. LC 72-111862. (Essay Index Reprint Ser.). 1977. 23.95 (*0-8369-1625-5*) Ayer.

Living Toward a Vision: Biblical Reflections on Shalom. Walter Brueggemann. LC 76-22172. 208p. 1982. pap. 11.95 (*0-8298-0613-X*) Pilgrim OH.

Living Town. Nigel Hester. LC 91-34488. (Watching Nature Ser.). (Illus.). 32p. (J). (gr. 5-7). 1992. lib. bdg. 20.00 (*0-531-14202-7*) Watts.

Living Tradition. John Meyendorff. LC 78-2031. 202p. 1970. pap. 9.95 (*0-913836-48-6*) St Vladimirs.

Living Tradition: A Changing Life in Solomon Islands. Michael Kwa'ioloa. Ed. by Ben Burt. LC 97-2097. (Illus.). 192p. 1997. pap. text 23.00 (*0-8248-1960-8*) UH Pr.

Living Tradition: Art, Music & Ideas in the Western World. 2nd ed. Henry Vyverberg. (Illus.). 544p. (C). 1988. pap. text 60.50 (*0-15-551119-X*, Pub. by Harcourt Coll Pubs) Harcourt.

Living Tradition: Art, Music & Ideas in the Western World. 2nd ed. Henry Vyverberg. (Illus.). 544p. (C). 1988. pap. text 5.00 (*0-15-551120-3*) Harcourt Coll Pubs.

Living Tradition of Maria Martinez. rev. ed. Susan Peterson. LC 77-75373. (Illus.). 300p. 1992. pap. 45.00 (*0-87011-497-2*) Kodansha.

Living Tradition of Yupik Mask: Agayuliyararput, Our Way of Making Prayer. Ann Fienup-Riordan. LC 95-23296.Tr. of Our Way of Making Prayer. (Illus.). 320p. 1996. 75.00 (*0-295-97501-6*) U of Wash Pr.

Living Traditions: Mexican Popular Arts. Contrib. by Annie O'Neill. LC 92-62384. (Illus.). 88p. (Orig.). Date not set. pap. 40.00 (*0-910763-07-0*) U Albany Art Mus.

Living Traditions: Studies in the Ethnoarchaeology of South Asia. Ed. by Bridget Allchin. LC 94-907183. (Illus.). 391p. 1995. 49.50 (*81-204-0901-9*, Pub. by Oxbow Bks) David Brown.

Living Traditions of Old Kyoto. Diane Durston. LC 94-15413. (Illus.). 112p. 1995. 28.00 (*4-7700-1870-3*) Kodansha.

Living Traditions of Russian Faith: Books & Manuscripts of the Old Believers: Exhibition at the Library of Congress, May 31-June 29, 1990. Abby Smith & Vladimir Budaragin. LC 90-20114. 51p. 1990. 12.50 (*0-8444-0710-0*) Lib Congress.

Living Traditions of the Bible: Scripture in Jewish, Christian & Muslim Practice. Ed. by James E. Bowley. LC 99-29735. 224p. 1999. pap. 19.99 (*0-8272-2127-4*, 985685, Pub. by Chalice Pr) Abingdon.

Living Treasures: A Celebration of the Human Spirit. Karen N. Brandt & Sharon Niederman. (Illus.). 216p. 1997. pap. text 32.50 (*1-889921-00-9*) Western Edge Pr.

Living Treasures of the Hawaiian Islands: The Story of Hawaii's Native Plants & Animals. Stacey S. Kaopuiki. Ed. by Cindy R. Kaopuiki & Scott Stone. LC 94-75646. (Peter Panini Adventure Ser.). (Illus.). 48p. (J). (gr. k-7). 1994. 14.95 (*1-878498-04-5*) Hawaiian Isl Concepts.

Living Tree. Nigel Hester. (Watching Nature Ser.). (Illus.). 32p. (J). (gr. 5-7). 1990. lib. bdg. 20.00 (*0-531-14007-5*) Watts.

Living Tree: The Changing Meaning of Being Chinese Today. Tu Wei-Ming. xvi , 295p. (C). 1994. 45.00 (*0-8047-2191-2*) Stanford U Pr.

Living Tree: The Changing Meaning of Being Chinese Today. Tu Wei-Ming. xvi , 295p. (C). 1995. pap. 14.95 (*0-8047-2137-8*) Stanford U Pr.

Living Tree: The Roots & Growth of Jewish Law. Elliot N. Dorff & Arthur Rossett. LC 86-14581. 680p. (C). 1987. pap. text 23.95 (*0-88706-460-4*) State U NY Pr.

***Living Tropical Greenhouse: Creating a Haven for Butterflies.** John Tampion. 160p. 1999. pap. text 19.95 (*1-86108-123-5*) Guild Master.

Living Trust. rev. ed. Henry W. Abts, III. 368p. 1993. pap. 24.95 (*0-8092-3918-3*) NTC Contemp Pub Co.

Living Trust. rev. ed. Henry W. Abts, III. LC 97-18356. (Illus.). 320p. 1997. pap. 24.95 (*0-8092-3031-3*, 303130, Contemporary Bks) NTC Contemp Pub Co.

Living Trust: A Private Will That Does Not Have to Be Probated. William L. Papke. (Illus.). 144p. (Orig.). 1987. pap. 14.95 (*0-9619568-0-1*) Wm L Papke.

Living Trust Agreement Kit, Do It Yourself Revocable: Valid in All 50 States. Timothy J. Smith. 1991. 14.95 (*0-9625456-6-X*) SJT Enterprises.

Living Trust Alternative: End Probate Worries for Your Family. Louis Austin. pap. 18.95 incl. audio (*0-9625528-3-6*) Hudspeth Pub.

Living Trust Handbook. David E. Miller. 216p. 1991. pap. 20.00 (*0-9627178-0-0*) D E Miller Law.

Living Trust Kit. Arnold S. Goldstein. 56p. 1991. student ed. 21.95 (*1-56382-142-7*) E-Z Legal.

Living Trust, Living Hell: Why You Should Avoid Living Trusts. John Huggard. LC 98-65265. 144p. 1998. per. 26.00 (*0-7872-4774-X*) Kendall-Hunt.

Living Trust Made E-Z. V. Goldstein. (Made E-Z Ser.). 156p. 1999. pap. 17.95 (*1-56382-425-6*) E-Z Legal.

Living Trust Maker: Version 2.0. 384p. 1998. 79.95 incl. cd-rom (*0-87337-459-2*) Nolo com.

Living Trust Workbook: How You & Your Legal Advisors Can Design, Fund & Maintain Your Living Trust Plan. Robert A. Esperti & Renno L. Peterson. LC 94-18250. 352p. 1995. pap. 19.95 (*0-14-024097-7*, Penguin Bks) Viking Penguin.

Living Trusts: After the 1997 Taxpayer Relief Act. 2nd ed. Doug H. Moy. LC 98-17438. 425p. 1998. pap. text 39.95 incl. disk (*0-471-29027-0*) Wiley.

Living Trusts: Forms & Practice. Dwight F. Bickel. LC 93-16368. 1993. 145.00 (*0-8205-1081-5*) Bender.

Living Trusts & Avoiding Probate, Illinois Edition: The Pros & Cons of the Living Trust & Other Alternatives to Probate. Robert S. Hunter. (Klear-E-Lex Ser.). 140p. (Orig.). 1994. pap. 14.95 (*1-884177-08-5*) Justice IL.

Living Trusts & Simple Ways to Avoid Probate. 2nd ed. Karen A. Rolcik. LC 97-45084. (Legal Survival Guides Ser.). 176p. 1998. pap. 19.95 (*1-57071-336-7*) Sourcebks.

Living Truth. Jean Klein. Ed. by Emma Edwards. LC 94-61608. 160p. (Orig.). 1994. pap. 14.95 (*1-877769-24-X*) Third Millennium.

Living U. S. Constitution. 3rd rev. ed. Saul K. Padover. 416p. (C). 1995. pap. 14.95 (*0-452-01147-7*) NAL.

Living UJA History. Irving Bernstein. LC 97-37382. 1997. 34.95 (*0-8276-0648-6*) JPS Phila.

Living under Apartheid: Aspects of Urbanization & Social Change in South Africa. Ed. by David M. Smith. (London Research Series in Geography: No. 2). 256p. 1986. pap. text 18.95 (*0-04-309112-1*) Routledge.

Living under Contract: Contract Farming & Agrarian Transformation in Sub-Saharan Africa. Ed. by Peter D. Little & Michael Watts. LC 93-6315. 288p. 1994. 68.95 (*0-299-14060-1*); pap. 27.95 (*0-299-14064-4*) U of Wis Pr.

Living Underground. David Kempe. (Illus.). 256p. 1989. 35.00 (*0-906969-86-7*, NAB) I R Dee.

An Asterisk (*) at the beginning of an entry indicates that the title is appearing for the first time.

Living Underground Vol. 3: The Prose Anthology. Ed. by Hugh Fox. LC 87-50378. 416p. 2000. 48.50 (*0-87875-342-7*) Whitston Pub.

Living Unplugged: Young Adults, Faith & the Uncommon Life. Pam Peters-Pries. LC 95-83909. 144p. (C). 1996. pap. 10.95 (*0-87303-251-9*) Faith & Life.

Living up the Street: Narrative Recollections. Gary Soto. 176p. (Orig.). (YA). 1992. mass mkt. 4.99 (*0-440-21170-0*) Dell.

Living Up the Street: Narrative Recollections. Gary Soto. 1985. 9.60 (*0-606-00950-7*, Pub. by Turtleback) Demco.

Living Values: A Guidebook. Gayatri Naraine & Anthony Strano. (Illus.). 110p. (Orig.). (C). 1995. pap. text. write for info. (*1-886872-09-0*) Brahma Kumaris.

Living Values Statements. Gayatri Naraine & Anthony Strano. Ed. by Carol Gill-Kozul. (Illus.). 85p. 1995. pap. text. write for info. (*1-886872-01-5*) Brahma Kumaris.

***Living Vertically: Gospel Sermons for Lent/Easter, Cycle C.** John N. Brittain. LC 00-35799. 2000. disk 10.95 (*0-7880-1732-2*) CSS OH.

***Living Vertically: Gospel Sermons for Lent/Easter, Cycle C.** John Neal Brittain. LC 00-35799. 110p. 2000. pap. 10.95 (*0-7880-1731-4*) CSS OH.

Living Victoriously: When Winning It All Isn't Enough. J. Allen Blair. LC 93-41448. 128p. 1994. pap. 7.99 (*0-8254-2184-5*) Kregel.

Living Virtuously: Moral Decisions & Spiritual Growth. John W. Crossin. LC 98-38275. 160p. 1998. pap. 9.95 (*0-8091-3834-4*) Paulist Pr.

Living-Vivre-Leben. Rem Koolhaas. LC 99-10764. 1998. pap. 35.00 (*3-7643-5638-3*) Birkhauser.

Living Voices: Proceedings of Common Ground: A Conference on Progressive Education. Peter B. Corcoran & Margaret T. Pennock. (Illus.). 212p. (Orig.). 1993. pap. 7.50 (*0-9635242-0-8*) Schl Rose Valley.

Living Volutes. Clifton S. Weaver & John E. DuPont. 390p. 1970. 60.00 (*0-913176-01-X*, Delaware Estuary) Weidner & Sons.

Living Wage: American Workers & the Making of Consumer Society. Lawrence B. Glickman. LC 97-19264. 232p. 1997. 35.00 (*0-8014-3357-6*) Cornell U Pr.

Living Wage: American Workers & the Making of Consumer Society. Lawrence B. Glickman. 1999. pap. text 15.95 (*0-8014-8614-9*) Cornell U Pr.

Living Wage: Building a Fair Economy. Robert Pollin & Stephanie Luce. LC 98-11110. 288p. 1998. 22.50 (*1-56584-409-2*, Pub. by New Press NY) Norton.

***Living Wage: Building a Fair Economy.** Robert Pollin & Stephanie Luce. 272p. 2000. pap. 15.95 (*1-56584-588-9*, Pub. by New Press NY) Norton.

Living Wage: Its Ethical & Economic Aspects. John A. Ryan. LC 72-156422. (American Labor Ser., No. 2). 1971. reprint ed. 24.95 (*0-405-02939-X*) Ayer.

Living Wage for the Forgotten Man: The Quest for Fair Labor Standards, 1933-1941. George E. Paulsen. LC 96-17806. 232p. 1996. 37.00 (*0-945636-91-1*) Susquehanna U Pr.

Living Wage of Women Workers: Study of Incomes & Expenditures of 450 Women in the City of Boston. Louise M. Bosworth. LC 75-16459. (Social Problems & Social Policy Ser.). 1976. reprint ed. 13.95 (*0-405-07477-8*) Ayer.

Living W/Art F Ringgold Vid. Gilbert. 1992. VHS 382.50 (*0-07-023574-0*) McGraw.

Living Water. Frances J. Roberts. 1965. pap. 3.25 (*0-932814-20-4*) Kings Farspan.

***Living Water: A Guide to Baptism for Presbyterians.** James E. Davison. LC 00-37626. 50p. 2000. pap. 5.95 (*0-664-50145-1*, Pub. by Geneva Press) Presbyterian Pub.

Living Water: An Anthology of Letters of Direction. Robin Baird-Smith. LC 88-22096. 204p. reprint ed. pap. 63.30 (*0-7837-0510-7*, 204083400018) Bks Demand.

Living Water: Biography of J. Hudson Taylor. Rod Thomson. 144p. 1999. mass mkt. 5.99 (*0-87508-666-7*, 666) Chr Lit.

Living Water: True Experiences from the Missionary Field. Cyrus Dawsey, Jr. Ed. by James M. Dawsey. 200p. (Orig.). Date not set. pap. 11.95 (*0-89896-160-2*) Larksdale.

Living Water: Viktor Schauberger & the Secrets of Natural Energy. 6th ed. Olof Alexandersson. (Illus.). 160p. 1990. reprint ed. pap. write for info. (*0-946551-57-X*) ACCESS Pubs Network.

Living Water: Vodka & Russian Society on the Eve of Emancipation. David Christian. (Illus.). 458p. 1990. text 95.00 (*0-19-822286-6*) OUP.

***Living Water Bible.** Living Water Anglicized Staff. 2000. 20.99 (*0-8423-4027-0*); pap. 14.99 (*0-8423-4026-2*) Tyndale Hse.

***Living Water Bible.** Living Waters Pubns. Staff. 2000. 19.99 (*0-8423-4029-7*); 39.99 (*0-8423-4033-5*); 39.99 (*0-8423-4034-3*); pap. 14.99 (*0-8423-4031-9*) Tyndale Hse.

Living Water: Bilingual New Testament see Agua Viva - El Nuevo Testamento: Living Water - Bilingual New Testament

***Living Water-Faith Crossings.** Larry Paul Jones. 2000. pap. text 5.99 (*0-8272-9042-X*) Chalice Pr.

***Living Water for Those Who Thrist.** Tyndale House Publishers Staff. 2000. mass mkt. 2.99 (*0-8423-4237-0*) Tyndale Hse.

Living Water, Sealing Spirit: Readings on Christian Initiation. Ed. by Maxwell E. Johnson. 448p. 1995. pap. text 39.95 (*0-8146-6140-8*, Pueblo Bks) Liturgical Pr.

Living Waters. Mosie Lister. 132p. 1988. spiral bd. 7.99 (*0-8341-9282-9*, MB-600) Lillenas.

Living Waters: How to Save Your Local Stream. Owen Owens. LC 93-7641. (Illus.). 220p. (C). 1993. pap. 14.95 (*0-8135-1998-5*); text 35.00 (*0-8135-1997-7*) Rutgers U Pr.

***Living Waters for a Parched Land: The Psalms in Our Lives: Refreshing Reflections on the Psalms for Everyday Living.** Colette D. Jonopulos. 2000. 12.95 (*1-880971-52-6*) Light&Life Pub Co MN.

Living Waters for Your Parched Prayers. Rob Frost. LC 98-48290. 216p. 1999. 12.99 (*1-56476-712-4*) Chariot Victor.

Living Way. Lillian De Waters. 20p. 1996. reprint ed. spiral bd. 8.00 (*0-7873-0276-7*) Hlth Research.

***Living Way: Stories of Kurozumi Munetada, a Shinto Fouder.** Willis Stoesz. Tr. by Sumio Kamiya from JPN. (Sacred Literature Ser.). 272p. 2000. 62.00 (*0-7425-0341-0*) AltaMira Pr.

Living Way: Stories of Kurozumi Munetada, a Shinto Founder. Ed. by Willis Stoesz. Tr. by Sumio Kamiya. (Sacred Literature Ser.: Vol. 6). 272p. 2000. 24.95 (*0-7619-9097-6*) AltaMira Pr.

***Living Way: Stories of Kurozumi Munetada, a Shinto Founder.** Willis Stoesz. Tr. by Sumio Kamiya. (Sacred Literature Ser.). 272p. 2000. 62.00 (*0-7425-9097-6*); pap. 17.95 (*0-7425-9098-4*) AltaMira Pr.

***Living Way: Stories of Kurozumi Munetada, a Shinto Founder.** Ed. by Willis Stoesz. Tr. by Sumio Kamiya. (Sacred Literature Ser.). 272p. 2000. pap. 17.95 (*0-7425-0342-9*) AltaMira Pr.

Living Well. Cu Byer & Shainberg. (C). 1991. pap. text 48.00 (*0-673-39885-4*) Addson-Wesley Educ.

Living Well. Hanawalt-Squire. 1997. 18.50 (*0-697-37749-0*, WCB McGr Hill) McGrw-H Highr Educ.

Living Well. 3rd ed. Fries. 320p. 1999. pap. text 18.00 (*0-7382-0059-X*, Pub. by Perseus Pubng) HarpC.

Living Well. 3rd ed. James Fries. 352p. 1998. pap. 18.00 (*0-201-33994-3*) Addison-Wesley.

Living Well: Answers to Life's Practical Mysteries. Teresa Herring. 1991. pap. 12.95 (*0-87877-165-4*) Newcastle Pub.

***Living Well: Introductory Readings in Ethics.** Steven Luper. LC 98-88277. 592p. (C). 1999. text 40.00 (*0-15-508459-3*) Harcourt Coll Pubs.

***Living Well: Scriptural Reflections for Every Day.** Joan Chittister. 160p. 2000. pap. 14.00 (*1-57075-320-2*) Orbis Bks.

Living Well: Taking Care of Your Health in the Middle & Later Years. 2nd ed. James F. Fries. (Illus.). 352p. 1993. pap. 17.95 (*0-201-62615-2*) Addison-Wesley.

Living Well: The Gay Man's Essential Health Guide. Peter Shalit. LC 98-39946. 336p. 1998. pap. 17.95 (*1-55583-444-2*, Pub. by Alyson Pubns) Consort Bk Sales.

Living Well-Blue Cross Blue Shield of New Jersey. 2nd ed. Fries. 1994. pap. write for info. (*0-201-44220-5*) Addison-Wesley.

Living Well Is the Best Revenge. Calvin Tomkins. LC 98-21090. 1998. 15.95 (*0-679-60308-5*) Modern Lib NY.

***Living Well on a Shoestring: 1,821 Ways to Live Frugally, Efficiently & Masterfully.** Ed. by Yankee Magazine Editors. (Illus.). 400p. 2000. 27.95 (*0-89909-380-9*) Rodale Pr Inc.

Living Well on Practically Nothing. Edward H. Romney. (Illus.). 160p. 1992. pap. 21.95 (*0-87364-694-0*) Paladin Pr.

Living Well on Wheat: How to Cook, Eat, Survive on the Golden Grain. Geri Guidetti. 34p. 1997. spiral bd. 9.95 (*0-938928-02-3*) Ark Inst.

Living Well, Staying Well: The Ultimate Guide to Help Prevent Heart Disease & Cancer. American Heart Association Staff. 336p. 1998. pap. 14.00 (*0-8129-3067-3*, Times Bks) Crown Pub Group.

Living Well-Walter Reed. 2nd ed. Fries. 1994. pap. write for info. (*0-201-62614-4*) Addison-Wesley.

Living Well with a Hidden Disability: Transcending Doubt & Shame & Reclaiming Your Life. Stacy Taylor & Robert Epstein. LC 98-68747. 272p. 1999. pap. 15.95 (*1-57224-132-2*) New Harbinger.

Living Well with a Thorn in the Flesh: Brain Priming for Healthy Life. Sung H. Bae. LC 97-90297. (Illus.). 141p. (Orig.). 1997. pap. 12.95 (*0-533-12348-8*) Vantage.

Living Well with Asthma. Michael R. Freedman et al. LC 97-48747. 213p. 1998. pap. text 15.95 (*1-57230-051-5*, C0051); lib. bdg. 34.95 (*1-57230-318-2*, C0318) Guilford Pubns.

Living Well with Chronic Conditions. (Illus.). 96p. 1998. write for info. (*0-945100-88-4*) Parlay Intl.

Living Well with Chronic Illness. Gayle Heiss. 16p. 1992. pap. 2.00 (*0-936609-10-9*) QED Ft Bragg.

Living Well with Chronic Illness. Marcia Van't Land. 280p. 1994. pap. 9.99 (*0-87788-761-6*, H Shaw Pubs) Waterbrook Pr.

Living Well with Epilepsy. 2nd ed. Robert J. Gumnit. LC 97-31340. 176p. 1997. pap. 19.95 (*1-888799-11-0*) Demos Medical.

Living Well with Hearing Loss: A Guide for the Hearing Impaired & Their Families. Debbie Huning. LC 91-39471. 192p. 1992. pap. 12.95 (*0-471-54522-8*) Wiley.

Living Well with Heart Disease. Fairview Health Services Staff. LC 99-47418. (Illus.). 192p. 2000. pap. 14.95 (*1-57749-089-4*, Pub. by Fairview Press) Natl Bk Netwk.

Living Well with HIV & AIDS. Allen Gifford. 296p. 1996. pap. text 18.95 (*0-923521-35-6*) Bull Pub.

***Living Well with HIV & AIDS.** 2nd rev. ed. Allen Gifford et al. 288p. 2000. pap. write for info. (*0-923521-52-6*, Pub. by Bull Pub) Publishers Group.

***Living Well with Hypothyroidism: What Your Doctor Doesn't Tell You... That You Need to Know.** Mary J. Shomon. LC 99-52974. 352p. 2000. pap. 13.50 (*0-380-80898-6*) Morrow Avon.

***Living Well with Lactose Intolerance.** Healthy Living Editors. 272p. 1999. mass mkt. 5.99 (*0-380-80642-8*, Avon Bks) Morrow Avon.

Living Well with Multiple Sclerosis: A Guide for Patient, Caregiver, & Family. David L. Carroll & Jon Dorman. LC 92-53396. 272p. (Orig.). 1993. pap. 13.00 (*0-06-096980-6*, Perennial) HarperTrade.

Living Well with Parkinsons. Glenna W. Atwood. LC 90-42200. 208p. 1991. pap. 15.95 (*0-471-52539-1*) Wiley.

Living Well with Seated Massage & Chi Kung. Benny K. Lee & Elena Facciola. LC 97-93911. (Illus.). v, 96p. 1997. pap. text 13.95 (*0-9658485-0-7*) Lees Acupressure.

Living Well with Stress: Self-Management Guide. Francine Boucher & Andre Binette. Tr. by Blanche Hodder. (Illus.). 189p. 1999. reprint ed. pap. text 15.00 (*0-7881-6212-8*) DIANE Pub.

Living Well Workbook: Health in Your Hands. 2nd ed. Byer et al. (Health Science Ser.). (C). 1997. pap. text, student ed. 15.00 (*0-673-52396-9*) Jones & Bartlett.

Living Wellness: Directory & Journal of Holistic Practices & Providers Los Angeles 1998-1999, 1. Living Wellness Staff. (Illus.). 127p. 1998. pap. 4.95 (*0-9666402-0-9*) Liv Wellness.

Living West of Australia. Jan Taylor. (Illus.). 112p. 1993. 24.95 (*0-86417-434-9*, Pub. by Kangaroo Pr) Seven Hills Bk.

***Living What You Believe.** Kenneth Boa & William Kruidenier. 2000. pap. 8.00 (*1-57683-198-1*) NavPress.

Living When a Loved One Has Died. 3rd ed. Earl A. Grollman. LC 94-44346. 1995. pap. 10.00 (*0-8070-2719-7*) Beacon Pr.

Living When a Loved One Has Died: Gift Edition. Earl A. Grollman. LC 97-16129. 112p. 1997. 17.00 (*0-8070-2724-3*) Beacon Pr.

Living When a Young Friend Commits Suicide: Or Even Starts Talking about It. Earl A. Grollman & Max Malikow. LC 99-14820. 112p. (YA). 1999. 24.00 (*0-8070-2502-X*); pap. 12.00 (*0-8070-2503-8*) Beacon Pr.

***Living White House.** Lonnelle Aikman. (Illus.). 151p. (C). 1998. pap., pap. text 25.00 (*0-7881-7408-8*) DIANE Pub.

Living White House. 9th ed. Lonelle Aikman. 152p. 1996. 6.50 (*0-912308-55-9*) White House Hist.

Living White House. 9th ed. Lonnelle Aikman & National Geographic Society Editorial Staff. 152p. 1996. pap. 5.00 (*0-912308-54-0*) White House Hist.

Living Whole: Lose Excess Weight . . . Never to Find It Again. Cheryl Townsley & D. J. Tschetter. 250p. 1998. pap. 24.95 (*0-9644566-7-2*) Lifestyle for Hlth.

***Living Whole Without a Better Half.** Wendy Widder. 2000. pap. 9.99 (*0-8254-4111-0*) Kregel.

Living Wicca: A Further Guide for the Solitary Practitioner. Scott Cunningham. LC 93-24673. (Illus.). 208p. 1999. reprint ed. pap. 12.95 (*0-87542-184-9*) Llewellyn Pubns.

***Living Wild.** Art Wolfe. Ed. by Michelle A. Gilders. LC 00-26050. 2000. 55.00 (*0-9675918-0-5*) Wildlands.

Living Will: A Study of Tennyson & 19th Century Subjectivism. William R. Brashear. (Studies in English Literature: No. 52). (Orig.). 1969. text 23.10 (*3-11-000275-2*) Mouton.

Living Will: Power of Attorney for Health Care. LawPak Staff. (Illus.). 198p. (Orig.). 1994. pap. 18.95 (*1-879421-07-0*) LawPak.

Living Will & Power of Attorney for Healthcare Kit. Arnold S. Goldstein. 52p. 1991. teacher ed. 23.95 (*1-56382-139-7*) E-Z Legal.

Living Will & the Durable Power of Attorney for Health Care Book, with Forms. rev. ed. Phillip Williams. LC 90-15715. (Current Issues in Medicine & Law Ser.: Vol. 1). 288p. 1991. pap. 19.95 (*0-936284-23-4*) P Gaines Co.

Living Will Kit, Do It Yourself: Valid in All 50 States. Timothy J. Smith. 1991. 9.95 (*1-880398-00-1*) SJT Enterprises.

***Living Will Made E-Z.** E-Z Legal Staff. (Made E-Z Ser.). 248p. 1999. pap. 17.95 (*1-56382-426-4*) E-Z Legal.

Living Wills: New & Selected Poems. Cynthia Macdonald. LC 90-52737. 160p. 1992. pap. 12.00 (*0-679-74278-6*) Knopf.

***Living Wills & Medical Powers of Attorney: An Interdisciplinary Approach.** 1998. 59.00 incl. audio PA Bar Inst.

Living Wisdom: Growing in the Life of Prayer. Nicholas Turner. 128p. 1995. pap. 10.95 (*0-687-00618-2*) Abingdon.

Living Wisdom: Revisioning the Philosophic Quest. Anthony Damiani. LC 96-78529. (Illus.). 240p. (Orig.). 1996. pap. 15.95 (*0-943914-69-8*) Larson Pubns.

Living Wisdom: Vedanta in the West. Intro. by Pravrajika Vrajaprana. LC 93-43745. 299p. (Orig.). 1994. pap. 14.95 (*0-87481-055-8*) Vedanta Pr.

Living Wisdom for Every Day. Bennet Kelley. (Spiritual Life Ser.). 1991. pap. 6.25 (*0-89942-182-2*, 182/09) Catholic Bk Pub.

Living Wisely in a Foolish World: A Contemporary Look at the Wisdom of Proverbs. H. Wayne House & Kenneth M. Durham. LC 96-52008. 224p. 1997. reprint ed. pap. 12.99 (*0-8254-2877-7*) Kregel.

Living Witchcraft: A Contemporary American Coven. Allen Scarboro. LC 94-1142. 232p. 1994. 57.95 (*0-275-94688-6*, Praeger Pubs) Greenwood.

***Living with... Complete 4-Book Set.** 32p. (gr. 2-4). 1999. pap. 63.92 (*0-8172-5579-6*) Raintree Steck-V.

***Living with a Brain Tumor.** 3rd rev. ed. Deneen Hesser & Gary Hill. Orig. Title: Coping with a Brain Tumor. (Illus.). 40p. 2000. pap. 2.00 (*0-944093-54-X*) Am Brain Tumor.

Living with a Broken String. Mary C. Greene. LC 87-92172. 221p. 1988. 12.95 (*0-9619979-0-7*) M C Greene.

Living with a Brother or Sister with Special Needs: A Book for Sibs. 2nd expanded rev. ed. Donald J. Meyer. LC 96-7020. (Illus.). 144p. (ps up). 1996. pap. 14.95 (*0-295-97547-4*) U of Wash Pr.

Living with a Deaf Dog. Susan C. Becker. (Illus.). viii, 84p. 1997. pap. 15.95 (*0-9660058-0-5*) S C Becker.

***Living with a German Shepherd.** Ed. by Angela Ibbotson. (Living with a Pet Ser.). (Illus.). 128p. 2000. 14.95 (*0-7641-5258-0*) Barron.

***Living with a Golden Retriever.** Ed. by Sally Stewart. (Living with a Pet Ser.). (Illus.). 128p. 2000. 14.95 (*0-7641-5259-9*) Barron.

Living With a Hearing Problem: Coping Strategies & Devices for the Hearing Impaired. Fred M. Roberts. (Illus.). 184p. 1990. pap. 16.95 (*0-912746-10-6*) F M Roberts.

***Living with a Jack Russell Terrier.** Ed. by Rani Morningstar. (Living with a Pet Ser.). (Illus.). 128p. 2000. 14.95 (*0-7641-5261-0*) Barron.

***Living with a Labrador Retriever.** Ed. by Jo Coulson. (Living with a Pet Ser.). (Illus.). 128p. 2000. 14.95 (*0-7641-5260-2*) Barron.

Living with a Learning Disability. rev. ed. Barbara Cordoni. 1991. pap. 17.95 (*0-8093-1668-4*) S Ill U Pr.

Living with a Negative Person. 4.95 (*0-686-40913-2*, SR19) Transitions.

Living with a New Family: Nadia & Rashid's Story. BAAF Staff. 1997. pap. 33.00 (*1-873868-44-8*, Pub. by BAAF) St Mut.

Living with a Sick Child in Hospital. Philip Darbyshire. 225p. 1994. pap. 36.95 (*0-412-61050-7*) Chapman & Hall.

Living with a Sick Child in Hospital: The Experiences of Parents & Nurses. P. Darbyshire. 240p. 1994. 54.25 (*1-56593-374-5*, 0721) Singular Publishing.

Living with a Single Parent. Maxine B. Rosenberg. LC 92-3883. (Illus.). 128p. (J). (gr. 4 up). 1992. text 14.95 (*0-02-777915-7*, Bradbury S&S) S&S Childrens.

Living with a Work in Progress: A Parent's Guide to Surviving Adolescence. Carol G. Freeman. LC 96-36304. 1996. pap. write for info. (*1-56090-113-6*) Natl Middle Schl.

Living with Adam. Jeff Allan. 1995. pap. 8.95 (*1-875243-16-X*) LPC InBook.

Living with ADD: A Workbook for Adults with Attention Deficit Disorder. M. Susan Roberts & Gerard J. Jansen. LC 96-71152. 176p. (Orig.). 1997. pap., wbk. ed. 17.95 (*1-57224-063-6*) New Harbinger.

Living with ADHD: A Practical Guide to Coping with Attention Deficit Hyperactivity Disorder. Rebecca Kajander. (Illus.). 72p. (Orig.). 1995. pap. text 9.95 (*1-884153-08-9*) Prk Nicollet.

Living with ADHD Children: A Handbook for Parents, 2 cass. unabridged ed. Peter H. Buntman. 80p. 1998. pap. 19.95 incl. audio (*0-9623986-3-2*) Ctr Fam Life.

Living with Africa: Reminiscences & Historiography. Jan Vansina. LC 94-588. 328p. 1994. 40.00 (*0-299-14320-1*); pap. 19.95 (*0-299-14324-4*) U of Wis Pr.

Living with AIDS. Ed. by Stephen R. Graubard. 462p. 1990. pap. text 23.00 (*0-262-57079-3*) MIT Pr.

Living with AIDS: A Photographic Journal. Sal Lopes. (Illus.). 133p. 1997. reprint ed. text 15.00 (*0-7881-5077-4*) DIANE Pub.

Living with AIDS: A Survival Guide. rev. ed. Christina Dye. 1999. pap. 0.50 (*0-89230-235-6*) Do It Now.

Living with AIDS: Experiencing Ethical Problems. Miriam Cameron. (Illus.). 256p. (C). 1993. text 48.00 (*0-8039-4778-X*); pap. text 19.95 (*0-8039-4779-8*) Sage.

Living with AIDS in the Community: A Book to Help People Make the Best of Life. (ENG & FRE.). v, 57p. 1993. pap. text 5.40 (*0-614-08017-7*, 1930035) World Health.

Living with Albinism. Elaine Landau. LC 97-1771. (First Book Ser.). (Illus.). 64p. (J). (gr. 5-8). 1997. 21.00 (*0-531-20296-8*) Watts.

Living with Aliens. John DeChancie. 192p. (Orig.). 1995. mass mkt. 4.99 (*0-441-00204-8*) Ace Bks.

***Living with Alzheimer's.** Tom Smith. 2000. pap. 12.95 (*0-85969-832-7*, Pub. by Sheldon Pr) Intl Pubs Mktg.

Living with Alzheimer's: Ruth's Story. Art Danforth. LC 86-21052. Orig. Title: The Book of Ruth. 224p. (Orig.). 1986. 15.95 (*0-939533-02-2*); pap. 9.95 (*0-939533-01-4*) Howarth Pr.

***Living with Alzheimer's Disease: One Couple's Journey.** Frances Siegel. (Illus.). 65p. 2000. pap. 9.95 (*1-889059-81-1*) Regent Pr.

Living with America, 1946-1996. Ed. by Christina Giorcelli & Rob Kroes. LC 98-125617. 330p. 1998. pap. 47.50 (*90-5383-548-2*, Pub. by VU Univ Pr) Paul & Co Pubs.

***Living with an Angel: Guide for a More Enriching Daily Life.** 80p. 1998. 12.95 (*0-9678918-0-9*) M B Neidert.

Living with an Empty Chair: A Guide Through Grief. 2nd ed. Roberta Temes. LC 83-12894. (Illus.). 110p. 1984. 12.95 (*0-8290-1473-X*) Irvington.

Living with an Empty Chair: A Guide Through Grief. 2nd ed. Roberta Temes. LC 83-12894. (Illus.). 110p. 1991. pap. 9.95 (*0-8290-0184-0*) Irvington.

Living with an Empty Chair: A Guide Through Grief. 2nd ed. Roberta Temes. LC 83-12894. 110p. 1992. reprint ed. pap. 9.95 (*0-8290-1773-9*) Irvington.

Living with an Empty Chair: A Guide Through Grief. 6th enl. rev. ed. Roberta Temes. 1992. 15.95 (*0-88282-110-5*) New Horizon NJ.

***Living with Angels.** Joseph Fryman & Paul Lippman. 174p. (Orig.). 1999. pap. 12.95 (*0-7392-0415-7*, PO3666) Morris Pubng.

Living with Angina. Tom Smith. LC 96-71156. 128p. (Orig.). 1997. pap. 12.95 (*1-57224-067-9*) New Harbinger.

An Asterisk (*) at the beginning of an entry indicates that the title is appearing for the first time.

Living with Anorexia & Bulimia. James Moorey. (Living with Ser.). 176p. (C). 1993. text 17.95 (*0-7190-3369-1*, Pub. by Manchester Univ Pr) St Martin.

Living with Aphasia: Psychosocial Issues. D. Lafond et al. LC 92-49888.Tr. of L'Aphasie. (Illus.). 308p. (Orig.). (C). 1992. pap. text 49.95 (*1-56593-067-3*, 0372) Thomson Learn.

***Living with Art.** Karen Wheeler. (Illus.). 2000. 29.95 (*1-84222-068-3*) Carlton Bks Ltd.

Living with Art. 4th ed. Rita Gilbert. 1994. pap. text 48.00 (*0-07-024021-3*) McGraw.

Living with Art. 5th ed. Rita Gilbert. LC 97-11565. 576p. 1997. pap. 55.63 (*0-07-913212-X*) McGraw.

Living with Art. 6th ed. Gilbert. 2001. 42.50 (*0-07-231726-4*) McGraw.

Living with Art, Set. 4th ed. Rita Gilbert. 1994. text. write for info. incl. trans. (*0-07-911749-X*) McGraw.

Living with Art, Set. 4th ed. Rita Gilbert. 576p. (C). 1994. pap. 62.50 (*0-07-911794-5*) McGraw.

Living with Art: The Collection of Ellyn & Saul Dennison. Lisa Dennison. LC 93-79003. 96p. 1993. 9.00 (*0-9613046-3-4*) Morris Mus.

Living with Art Glass. Yvonne Barlog. (Illus.). 48p. 1998. pap. 18.95 (*0-935133-66-6*, 20133666) CKE Pubns.

Living with Art Set 4. Gilbert. 1995. 21.00 (*0-07-912179-9*) McGrw-H Hghr Educ.

Living with Art Three: The Collection of Walter & Dawn Clark Netsch. Walter Netsch. LC 91-60799. 40p. (Orig.). 1991. 12.00 (*0-940784-14-9*) Miami Univ Art.

Living with Art Two. Ed. by James M. Langley. LC 83-62194. (Illus.). 134p. (Orig.). 1983. pap. 15.00 (*0-940784-05-X*) Miami Univ Art.

***Living with Asthma.** Peta Bee. (Living with... Ser.). 32p. 1999. lib. bdg. 22.83 (*0-8172-5576-1*) Raintree Steck-V.

Living with Asthma. Peta Bee. LC 98-18852. 32 p. (J). 2000. write for info. (*0-8172-5568-0*) Raintree Steck-V.

Living with Asthma. Margaret O. Hyde & Elizabeth Forsyth. LC 94-41884. 112p. (J). (gr. 3-7). 1995. 14.95 (*0-8027-8286-8*) Walker & Co.

Living with Asthma. Margaret O. Hyde & Elizabeth Forsythe. LC 94-41884. 112p. (J). (gr. 3-7). 1995. lib. bdg. 15.85 (*0-8027-8287-6*) Walker & Co.

***Living with Asthma: A Guide for Parents & Children.** Margaret O. Hyde & Elizabeth Fosyth. (Illus.). 112p. (J). 2000. pap. 8.95 (*0-8027-7585-3*) Walker & Co.

Living with Ataxia: An Information & Resource Guide. Martha A. Nance. LC 96-72598. Date not set. pap. text 10.00 (*0-943218-09-8*) Natl Ataxia Found.

Living with Attention-Deficit/Hyperactivity Disorder: Sometimes I Get All Scribbly. 2nd ed. Maureen B. Neuville. LC 94-41588. 159p. (C). 1995. pap. text 16.00 (*0-89079-667-X*, 6976) PRO-ED.

Living with Autism: The Parents' Stories. Kathleen M. Dillon. (Illus.). 265p. 1995. pap. 19.95 (*0-9635752-7-9*) Pkway Pubs.

Living with Big Cats: The Story of Jungle Larry, Safari Jane, & David Tetzlaff. Sharon Rendell. LC 94-31632. (Illus.). 222p. 1995. pap. 11.95 (*0-9642604-0-9*) Intl Zool Soc.

Living with Blind Dogs: A Resource Book & Training Guide for the Owners of Blind & Low-Vision Dogs. unabridged ed. Caroline D. Levin. (Illus.). 181p. 1998. pap. 29.95 (*0-9672253-0-2*) Lantern Pubns.

***Living with Blindness.** Patsy Westcott. LC 98-32230. 32p. 1999. lib. bdg. 22.83 (*0-8172-5741-1*) Raintree Steck-V.

Living with Books. Alan Powers. LC 99-11690. (Illus.). 144p. 1999. 35.00 (*1-57959-024-1*, SOMA) BB&T Inc.

Living with Brain Injury: A Guide for Families. 2nd rev. ed. Richard C. Senelick & Cathy E. Ryan. LC 97-77008. (Illus.). 126p. 1998. pap. 8.95 (*1-891525-00-X*, HealthSouth Pr) HealthSouth.

Living with Brain Injury: A Guide for Families & Caregivers. Ed. by Sonia Acorn & Penny Offer. LC 99-181017. (Illus.). 160p. 1998. text 40.00 (*0-8020-4265-1*); pap. text 18.95 (*0-8020-8103-7*) U of Toronto Pr.

***Living with Breast Cancer.** Stacie Zoe Berg. 400p. 1999. pap. 15.95 (*0-02-863491-8*) Macmillan.

Living with Breast Cancer: 39 Women & One Man Speak Candidly about Surviving Breast Cancer. Perry Colmore. (Illus.). 84p. (Orig.). 1997. pap. 24.95 (*0-9655817-0-5*) Andover Townsman.

***Living with Cannibals & Other Women's Adventures.** Michele B. Slung. (Illus.). 256p. 2000. 22.00 (*0-7922-7686-8*); write for info. (*0-7922-7684-1*) Natl Geog.

Living with Cats. Gale B. Nemec. (Illus.). 224p. 1997. reprint ed. pap. text 8.00 (*0-7881-5118-5*) DIANE Pub.

***Living with Ceramics.** Annabel Freyberg. (Illus.). 224p. 2000. 50.00 (*0-8478-2201-X*, Pub. by Rizzoli Intl) St Martin.

***Living with Cerebral Palsy.** Paul Pimm. LC 99-27202. 32p. 1999. lib. bdg. 22.83 (*0-8172-5744-6*) Raintree Steck-V.

Living with Change. Concordia Publishing Staff. (Master's Touch Bible Study Ser.). 1994. pap. 4.50 (*0-570-09439-6*, 20-2460) Concordia.

Living with Change & Choice in Health: Proceedings of the 1st Sigma Theta Tau, Alpha Rho Chapter, National Research Conference. Ed. by Janet F. Wang et al. (Illus.). 374p. 1986. write for info. (*0-930284-25-9*) Morgantown Print & Bind.

Living with Children: New Methods for Parents & Teachers. rev. ed. Gerald R. Patterson. LC 76-23974. 132p. 1976. pap. text 9.95 (*0-87822-130-1*, 0003) Res Press.

Living with China: U. S.-China Relations in the Twenty-First Century. Ed. by Ezra F. Vogel. LC 97-2333. 352p. 1997. 25.00 (*0-393-04540-4*); pap. 18.00 (*0-393-31734-X*) Norton.

Living with Christ. Harold L. Phillips. (Eagle Bible Ser.). 1989. pap. 0.99 (*0-87162-500-8*, D9152) Warner Pr.

Living with Chronic Fatigue: New Strategies for Coping with & Conquering CFS. Susan Conant. LC 89-77048. 148p. 1990. pap. 9.95 (*0-87833-709-1*) Taylor Pub.

Living with Chronic Fatigue Syndrome: A Personal Story of the Struggle for Recovery. Timothy Kenny. 226p. 1994. pap. 12.95 (*1-56025-075-5*, Thunders Mouth) Avalon NY.

Living with Chronic Illness. Pamela L. Robison. 1988. pap. 1.00 (*0-8309-0507-3*) Herald Pub Hse.

Living with Chronic Pain. Concordia Publishing Staff. (Master's Touch Bible Study Ser.). 1994. pap. 4.50 (*0-570-09435-6*, 20-2456) Concordia.

Living with Chronic Pain: One Day at a Time - Daily Meditations. Mark A. Zabawa. (Illus.). 380p. 1993. 8.95 (*0-9637353-0-6*) FE Chronic Pain.

Living with Communism. Anthony Sylvester. LC 67-15648. 1967. 18.95 (*0-370-00375-6*) Dufour.

Living with Complexity: The Lincoln Hill Experience. Compiled by Trustee Renewal Project Staff. (Nonprofit Governance Ser., No. 61: Stories from the Board: Vol. II). 48p. (Orig.). (C). 1994. pap. text 18.00 (*0-925299-36-7*) Natl Ctr Nonprofit.

Living with Compulsive Behaviors. Concordia Publishing Staff. (Master's Touch Bible Study Ser.). 1994. pap. 4.50 (*0-570-09436-4*, 20-2457) Concordia.

Living with Computers. 5th ed. Patrick G. McKeown. LC 93-74844. 720p. (C). 1994. pap. text 74.00 (*0-03-002069-7*) Dryden Pr.

Living with Computers. 5th ed. Patrick G. McKeown. 200p. (C). 1995. pap. text, student ed. 29.50 (*0-03-015354-9*) Harcourt Coll Pubs.

Living with Computers: Commercial Software Version. Patrick G. McKeown. 672p. (C). 1987. teacher ed. write for info. incl. trans. (*0-318-61978-4*); write for info. (*0-318-61977-6*) Dryden Pr.

Living with Contemporary Art. Harry Philbrick. 66p. 1995. pap. 12.00 (*1-888332-00-X*) Aldrich Mus.

***Living with Contradiction: An Introduction to Benedictine Spirituality.** Esther De Waal. LC 97-48801. 176p. 1998. pap. 10.95 (*0-8192-1754-9*) Morehouse Pub.

Living with Contradictions. Lynne Tillman. (Illus.). 44p. (Orig.). 1982. pap. 3.00 (*0-917061-10-1*) Top Stories.

Living with Contradictions: Controversies in Feminist Social Ethics. Ed. by Alison M. Jaggar. LC 93-29466. 698p. (C). 1994. pap. 39.00 (*0-8133-1776-2*, Pub. by Westview) HarpC.

Living with Cows. Bob Artley. (Illus.). 104p. (Orig.). 1996. pap. 14.95 (*0-8138-2648-9*) Iowa St U Pr.

Living with Cross-Stitch. Ondori Publishing Company Staff. (Illus.). 96p. (Orig.). 1988. pap. 11.95 (*0-87040-760-0*) Japan Pubns USA.

Living with Deaf-Blindness: Nine Profiles. Carol Yoken. LC 79-52740. 183p. reprint ed. pap. 56.80 (*0-7837-1853-5*, 204205300001) Bks Demand.

Living with Deafness. Emma Haughton. LC 98-32231. 32p. 1999. lib. bdg. 22.83 (*0-8172-5742-X*) Raintree Steck-V.

Living with Death. Ellis G. Woods. 96p. 1996. 18.95 (*1-888321-00-8*) Semco Bks.

Living with Death. Helmut Thielicke. LC 82-18221. 220p. reprint ed. pap. 68.20 (*0-608-14514-9*, 202534600043) Bks Demand.

Living with Death - Middle School. Judith Bisnignano. 64p. (J). (gr. 5-9). 1991. 8.99 (*0-86653-584-5*, GA1317) Good Apple.

Living with Death - Primary. Mary J. Cera. 64p. (J). (gr. 1-4). 1991. 7.99 (*0-86653-588-8*, GA1316) Good Apple.

Living with Death & Dying. Elisabeth Kubler-Ross. 1997. per. 9.00 (*0-684-83936-9*, Touchstone) S&S Trade Pap.

Living with Decorative Textiles. Nicholas Barnard. LC 94-61397. (Illus.). 192p. 1995. pap. 24.95 (*0-500-27821-0*, Pub. by Thames Hudson) Norton.

Living with Defined Contribution Pensions: Remaking Responsibility for Retirement. Olivia Mitchell. LC 98-13584. (Pension Research Council Publications). (Illus.). 296p. 1998. 47.50 (*0-8122-3439-1*) U of Pa Pr.

***Living with Diabetes.** Jenny Bryan. LC 98-20105. (Living with... Ser.). (Illus.). 32p. (J). (gr. 1-5). 1999. lib. bdg. 22.83 (*0-8172-5575-3*) Raintree Steck-V.

Living with Diabetes. Heather Maclean & Barbara Oram. xii, 154p. 1988. pap. 11.95 (*0-8020-6693-3*) U of Toronto Pr.

Living with Diabetes Disabilities. Sandy Weinrauch & Dana Clark. 256p. 1999. pap. 19.95 (*0-945448-99-6*) Am Diabetes.

Living with Diabetes I: The British Diabetic Association Guide for those Treated with Insulin. John Day. LC 98-23733. 240p. 1998. pap. 38.50 (*0-471-97274-6*) Wiley.

Living with Difference: Families with Dwarf Children. Joan Ablon. LC 87-32790. 204p. 1988. 55.00 (*0-275-92901-9*, C2901, Praeger Pubs) Greenwood.

Living with Dinosaurs. Patricia Lauber. LC 90-43265. (Illus.). 48p. (J). (gr. 1-5). 1991. text 16.95 (*0-02-754521-0*, Bradbury S&S) S&S Childrens.

Living with Dinosaurs. Patricia Lauber. LC 90-43265. (Illus.). 48p. (gr. 1-5). 1999. per. 6.99 (*0-689-82686-9*, 076714007994) S&S Childrens.

Living with Dinosaurs: One Act Plays. Anthony Minghella. (C). 1995. pap. write for info. (*0-413-64240-2*, A0504) Heinemann.

Living with Disabilities: Basic Manuals for Friends of the Disabled, 6 vols. in 1. 2nd ed. Hannah Carlson & Dale Carlson. LC 96-79850. (Illus.). 352p. (Orig.). 1997. pap. 59.70 (*1-884158-15-3*, Pub. by Bick Pub Hse) BookWorld.

Six introductory handbooks about disabilities & special needs, under the direction of Hannah Carlson, M.Ed., CRC, provide basic information for friends, families, teachers, employers & anyone concerned about people with disabilities. Covered are: medical conditions & causes; behaviors, feelings, rehabilitation, resources, ADA rights, funds, adaptive technology, life stories of child & adult models in all fields. "Excellent introductory handbooks offer professional information in an easy-to-use style for the general audience."--Kathleen Laundy, Psy.D., M.S.W., Yale School of Medicine. The series is endorsed by rehabilitation facilities, doctors, therapists. Included are appendices of national & local organizations that serve each disability, technological resources, adaptive devices information, lists of national & regional support centers, who to call for referrals, help & advice. The illustrated series includes: I HAVE A FRIEND WHO IS BLIND, 64 p. $9.95, (1-884158-07-2); I HAVE A FRIEND WHO IS DEAF, 64 p. $9.95 (1-884158-08-0); I HAVE A FRIEND WITH LEARNING DISABILITIES, 64 p. $9.95 (1-884158-12-9); I HAVE A FRIEND WITH MENTAL ILLNESS, 64 p. $9.95 (1-884158-13-7); I HAVE A FRIEND WITH MENTAL RETARDATION, 64 p. $9.95 (1-884158-10-2); I HAVE A FRIEND IN A WHEELCHAIR, 64 p. $9.95 (1-884158-09-9). Sep. vol. set of 6 (1-884158-11-0). Available at: BookWorld Services, Ingram, Baker & Taylor Book Company. To order: Bick Publishing House, 307 Neck Road, Madison, CT 06443. 203-245-0073. Distributed by: BookWorld Services, Inc. *Publisher Paid Annotation.*

***Living with Discernment in the End Times.** Kay Arthur et al. (International Inductive Study Ser.). 128p. 2000. pap. 5.99 (*0-7369-0446-8*) Harvest Hse.

Living with Disfigurement: Psychological Implications of Being Born with a Cleft Palate. Poppy Nash. (CEDR Ser.). 304p. 1995. 79.95 (*1-85628-967-2*, Pub. by Avebry) Ashgate Pub Co.

Living with Distance. Ralph J. Mills. (American Poets Continuum Ser.: No. 3). 71p. 1979. pap. 10.00 (*0-918526-18-3*) BOA Edns.

Living with Divorce - Middle School. Elizabeth Garigan & Michael Urbanski. 64p. (J). (gr. 5-9). 1991. 7.99 (*0-86653-596-9*, GA1315) Good Apple.

Living with Divorce - Primary. Elizabeth Garigan & Michael Urbanski. 64p. (J). (gr. 1-4). 1991. 8.99 (*0-86653-595-0*, GA1314) Good Apple.

Living with Dogs. Larry Sheehan & K. G. Precourt. LC 98-27192. 240p. 1999. 50.00 (*0-517-70875-2*) C Potter.

Living with Dogs: Tales of Love, Commitment, & Enduring Friendship. Henry Korman & Mary Ellen Korman. LC 97-27230. 199p. (Orig.). 1997. pap. 13.95 (*1-885171-19-6*) Wldcat Canyon.

Living with Dolls: Tips & Advice from the Professionals, Vol. I. Marlene Alperin-Hochman. Ed. by Laurie Resnick-Gallo. Date not set. pap. write for info. (*0-9611774-7-0*) Ultimate Coll.

Living with Down Syndrome. Jenny Bryan. LC 98-29145. 32 p. 1999. write for info. (*0-8172-5569-9*) Raintree Steck-V.

***Living with Down Syndrome.** Jenny Bryan. (Living with... Ser.). 32p. (J). 1999. lib. bdg. 22.83 (*0-8172-5577-X*) Raintree Steck-V.

Living with Dragons: Australia Comes to Terms with Asia. Ed. by Greg Sheridan. 256p. 1995. pap. 19.95 (*1-86373-880-0*) Paul & Co Pubs.

Living with Drink: The Biographies of Women Who Live with Problem Drinkers. Richard Vellman. LC 98-20267. 1986. pap. text 21.95 (*0-582-29887-3*) Addson-Wesley Educ.

***Living with Drought: Drought Mitigation for Sustainable Livelihoods, Pal Version Edition.** Astrid Von Kotze & Ailsa Holloway. 206p. 1999. pap. 35.00 (*1-85339-470-X*, Pub. by Intermed Tech) Stylus Pub VA.

***Living with Drought: Drought Mitigation for Sustainable Livelihoods, Pal Version Edition.** Astrid Von Kotze & Ailsa Holloway. 206p. 1999. pap. 35.00 (*1-85339-481-5*, Pub. by Intermed Tech) Stylus Pub VA.

Living with Drugs. 4th ed. Michael Gossop. 239p. 1996. pap. 20.95 (*1-85742-216-3*, Pub. by Arena) Ashgate Pub Co.

***Living with Drugs.** 5th ed. Michael Gossop. 192p. 2000. text 61.95 (*1-84014-935-3*, Pub. by Ashgate Pub); pap. text 21.95 (*1-84014-939-6*, Pub. by Ashgate Pub) Ashgate Pub Co.

Living with Dying. rev. ed. David Carroll. 389p. 1994. pap. 12.95 (*1-56924-998-9*) Marlowe & Co.

Living with Dying: A Guide to Palliative Care. 3rd ed. Cicely M. Saunders et al. (Illus.). 76p. 1995. pap. text 23.95 (*0-19-262514-4*) OUP.

Living with Dying: A Personal Journey. Linda P. Mukai & Janis F. Chan. 225p. (Orig.). 1996. pap. 12.95 (*0-9650961-0-6*) Butterfld Pr CA.

Living with Dyslexia. Barbara Riddick. 248p. (C). 1996. pap. 24.99 (*0-415-12501-4*) Routledge.

Living with Earthquakes in the Pacific Northwest. Robert S. Yeats. LC 98-23913. (Illus.). 304p. 1998. pap. 21.95 (*0-87071-437-6*) Oreg St U Pr.

Living with Enthusiasm. L. Tom Perry. LC 96-580. viii, 136p. 1996. 14.95 (*1-57345-136-3*) Deseret Bk.

Living with Epilepsy. Mark A. Mentzer & David C. Ziegler. LC 81-71463. (Illus.). 144p. (Orig.). 1981. pap. 7.95 (*0-9607240-0-1*) Bubba Pr.

Living with Epilepsy. Patsy Westcott. LC 98-29144. 32 p. 1999. write for info. (*0-8172-5570-2*) Raintree Steck-V.

***Living with Epilepsy.** Patsy Westcott. (Living with... Ser.). 32p. (J). 1999. lib. bdg. 22.83 (*0-8172-5578-8*) Raintree Steck-V.

Living with Flowers. Jane Packer. LC 96-61471. (Illus.). 160p. 1997. 29.95 (*1-57076-079-9*, Trafalgar Sq Pub) Trafalgar.

Living with Flowers. Storey Publishing Staff. 1997. 29.95 (*0-676-57227-8*) Random.

***Living with Flowers.** rev. ed. J. Barry Ferguson. (Illus.). 176p. 2000. text 45.00 (*0-8478-2239-7*) Rizzoli Intl.

Living with Flowers: History of the California Flower Market. Gary Kawaguchi. (C). 1993. 30.00 (*0-614-00189-7*) CA Flower Mkt.

Living with Folk Art: Ethnic Styles from Around the World. Nicholas Barnard. LC 93-113284. (Illus.). 192p. 1998. pap. 24.95 (*0-500-28021-5*, Pub. by Thames Hudson) Norton.

***Living with Folk Art: Ethnic Styles from Around the World.** Country Living Staff. (Illus.). 160p. 2000. pap. 22.00 (*0-688-17769-7*) Morrow Avon.

Living with Food Allergies. Betty Wedman-St. Louis. LC 99-11432. 256p. 1999. pap. 14.95 (*0-8092-2858-0*, 285800, Contemporary Bks) NTC Contemp Pub Co.

Living with Genetic Disorder: The Impact of Neurofibromatosis 1. Joan Ablon. LC 99-11894. 216p. 1999. 59.95 (*0-86569-287-4*, T287, Auburn Hse) Greenwood.

Living with Ghosts: Eleven Extraordinary Tales, Vol. 2. Tr. by Anthony Roberts. (Illus.). 192p. 1996. 25.00 (*0-393-03952-8*) Norton.

Living with Ghosts: True Tales of the Paranormal. Dorothy B. Fiedel. (Illus.). 94p. 1999. per. 6.99 (*0-9640254-3-4*) D B Fiedel.

LIVING WITH GHOSTS: TRUE TALES OF THE PARANORMAL is a fascinating collection of true stories about hauntings, ghosts & other paranormal events. Is there life after death? Can ghosts be photographed? From Lancaster County, PA, Amish Country to Washington State - to the haunted Tower of London in Great Britain, strange tales of the paranormal fill this very entertaining book. From the same author that brought you Haunted Lancaster County, Pennsylvania in 1994, True Ghost Stories of Lancaster County, Pennsylvania, in 1995, & Ghosts & Other Mysteries in 1997, LIVING WITH GHOSTS is sure to fascinate the most discriminate of readers. A most personal & awe-inspiring account of the last moments of life, LIVING WITH GHOSTS was the fulfillment of a promise the author made to her dying husband. He insisted she start writing immediately after his death...little did she realize, he would keep his promise to "provide her with material." Read about a haunted house in Seattle, Washington; the strange presence of a Vietnam soldier; & other paranormal events. Full color cover, 94 pages, perfect bound, photo illustrated, for more information contact: Fiedel Publishers/Dorothy B. Fiedel, 717 Kinderhook Road, Columbia, PA 17512. Phone: 717-684-4251, FAX: 717-684-4175 or e-mail: kinderhook@desupernet.net. *Publisher Paid Annotation.*

Living with God. E. Peters. 1998. 34.95 (*90-6831-966-3*, Pub. by Peeters Pub) Bks Intl VA.

Living with God: Devotions to Strengthen Your Christian Walk. Bill Henegar et al. LC 97-11406. 220p. (Orig.). 1997. 17.99 (*0-89900-781-3*) College Pr Pub.

Living with God: In Good Times & Bad. John Carmody. LC 95-43605. 168p. (Orig.). 1996. pap. 13.95 (*0-8245-1541-2*) Crossroad NY.

Living with God's Kids. Kay Kuzma. LC 83-61552. 1983. pap. 5.95 (*0-910529-03-5*) Family Mtrs.

Living with Grandma. Lucy Arundell. (C). 1989. text 35.00 (*0-948929-06-5*) St Mut.

Living with Green Power: A Gourmet Collection of Living Food Recipes. Elysa Markowitz. LC 97-910032. (Illus.). 176p. 1997. 24.95 (*0-920470-11-4*) Alive Bks.

Living with Grief. Stephen J. Carter. (Master's Touch Bible Study Ser.). 1996. pap. 4.50 (*0-570-09555-7*, 20-2596) Concordia.

Living with Grief: After Sudden Loss: Suicide, Homicide, Accident, Heart Attack, Stroke. Ed. by Kenneth J. Doka. 261p. 1996. pap. text 19.95 (*1-56032-578-X*) Taylor & Francis.

***Living with Grief: At Work, at School, at Worship.** Kenneth J. Doka. 320p. 1999. pap. text 18.95 (*1-58391-006-9*) Brunner-Mazel.

***Living with Grief: Children, Adolescents & Loss.** Charles Corr et al. Ed. by Kenneth A. Doka. 288p. (Orig.). 2000. pap. 16.95 (*1-893349-01-2*, Pub. by Hospice Fndt Amer) Brunner-Mazel.

Living with Grief: Who We Are, How We Grieve. Kenneth J. Doka. LC 98-152429. 1998. pap. text 16.95 (*0-87630-898-1*) Brunner-Mazel.

Living with Grief & Mourning. James Moorey. LC 94-40872. (Living With Ser.). 1995. text 17.95 (*0-7190-3945-2*, Pub. by Manchester Univ Pr) St Martin.

Living with Grief When Illness Is Prolonged. Kenneth J. Doka. LC 97-6211. 1997. write for info. (*1-56032-703-0*) Hemisp Pub.

L

Living with Haemophilia. 4th ed. Peter Jones. (Illus.). 418p. 1995. 49.95 (0-19-263030-X) OUP.
Living with Haemophilia. 4th ed. Peter Jones. (Illus.). 416p. 1998. pap. text 34.50 (0-19-262961-1) OUP.
*__Living with Hazards, Dealing with Disasters: An Introduction to Emergency Management.__ William L. Waugh, Jr. LC 99-41194. (Illus.). 240p. 1999. text 49.95 (0-7656-0195-8) M E Sharpe.
*__Living with Hazards, Dealing with Disasters: An Introduction to Emergency Management.__ William L. Waugh, Jr. (Illus.). 240p. 2000. reprint ed. pap. text 22.95 (0-7656-0196-6) M E Sharpe.
*__Living with Hearing Loss: The Sourcebook for Deafness & Hearing Disorders.__ Carol Turkington & Allen E. Sussman. (Illus.). 256p. 2000. pap. 16.95 (0-8160-4140-7, Checkmark) Facts on File.
Living with Heart Disease. Robert Werman & Gerald M. Phillips. LC 95-10085. 256p. (Orig.). 1995. pap. 16.95 (1-881303-70-5) Hampton Pr NJ.
Living with Heart Disease. rev. ed. Marie R. Squillace & Kathy Delaney. (Illus.). 304p. 1999. pap. 16.95 (0-7373-0082-5) NTC Contemp Pub Co.
Living with Heart Disease: Is It Heart Failure? 24p. 1994. pap. 22.00 (0-16-045049-7) USGPO.
Living with Hepatitis C: A Survivor's Guide. 2nd rev. ed. Gregory T. Everson & Hedy Weinberg. LC 99-24644. 280p. (Orig.). 1999. pap. 14.95 (1-57826-034-5, Pub. by Hatherleigh) Norton.
Living with Herbs: A Treasury of Useful Plants for the Home & Garden. Jo Ann Gardner. LC 96-2828. (Illus.). 256p. 1997. pap. 17.00 (0-88150-359-2, Pub. by Countryman) Norton.
Living with Heroin: The Impact of a Drugs 'Epidemic" on an English Community. Howard Parker et al. 192p. 1988. 113.00 (0-335-15565-0); pap. 36.95 (0-335-15564-2) OpUniv Pr.
Living with High Blood Pressure. Creative Street, Inc. Staff. 1988. 34.95 incl. VHS (0-929079-01-9) Creative Street.
Living with History. Fredrica Harris Thompsett. LC 98-47077. (New Church's Teaching Ser.). 1999. pap. text 11.95 (1-56101-160-6) Cowley Pubns.
Living with History: A Guide to the Preservation Standards for Historically Designed... Paul Jakubovich. 116p. 1997. pap. write for info. (0-9677354-2-4) Cty Milwaukee Devel.
Living with HIV: Experiment in Courage. Mary E. O'Brien. LC 91-44130. 248p. 1992. 57.95 (0-86569-040-5, T040, Auburn Hse); pap. 22.95 (0-86569-203-3, R203, Auburn Hse) Greenwood.
Living with Horsepower! Personally Empowering Life Lessons Learned from the Horse. Rebekah F. Witter. LC 98-29194. (Illus.). 288p. 1998. 24.95 (1-57076-121-3, Trafalgar Sq Pub) Trafalgar.
Living with Huntington's Disease: A Book for Patients & Families. Dennis H. Phillips. LC 81-16492. 251p. reprint ed. pap. 77.90 (0-7837-2645-7, 204299900006) Bks Demand.
Living with Impaired Vision: An Introduction. Anne Yeadon et al. LC 79-18408. 77p. (Orig.). reprint ed. pap. 30.00 (0-7837-0143-8, 204043200016) Bks Demand.
Living with Infertility. Concordia Publishing Staff. (Master's Touch Bible Study Ser.). 1994. pap. 4.50 (0-570-09520-4, 20-2461) Concordia.
Living with Interdependence: The Decades Ahead in America. Abraham M. Sirkin. 22p. 1976. pap. text 12.00 (0-8191-5860-7) U Pr of Amer.
Living with It. Marjorie Power. 60p. 1983. 5.95 (0-931694-24-8) Wampeter Pr.
*__Living with It: A Survivor's Guide to Panic Attacks.__ Bev Aisbett. 1999. pap. 8.95 (0-207-18040-7, Pub. by Colns) Consort Bk Sales.
Living with Jazz: An Appreciation. Frank P. Tirro. (C). 1995. pap. text 47.50 (0-15-500318-6, Pub. by Harcourt Coll Pubs) Harcourt.
Living with Jesus & the Book of Job During Lent. Elaine M. Ward. 106p. 1995. pap. 10.95 (1-877871-94-X, 6226) Ed Ministries.
Living with Joy: Keys to Personal Power & Spiritual Transformation. Sanaya Roman. Ed. by Elaine Ratner. LC 86-80207. (Earth Life Ser.: Bk. I). 216p. (Orig.). 1986. pap. 12.95 (0-915811-03-0) H J Kramer Inc.
*__Living with Juvenile Diabetes: A Family Guide.__ rev. ed. Victoria Peurrung. (Illus.). 264p. 2000. pap. 14.95 (1-57826-057-4, Pub. by Hatherleigh) Norton.
Living with Kids in Los Angeles & Orange County: A Comprehensive Family Resource Guide from Conception to College Planning. Catherine C. Dancer. 288p. (Orig.). 1993. pap. 18.00 (0-938737-29-5) Denali Press.
Living with Kilims. Alastair Hull & Nicholas Barnard. (Illus.). 192p. 1995. pap. 24.95 (0-500-27822-9, Pub. by Thames Hudson) Norton.
Living with Killer Bees: The Story of the Africanized Bee Invasion. Greg Flakus. 144p. 1993. pap. 12.95 (0-932551-12-2) Quick Am Pub.
Living with Kundalini: The Autobiography of Gopi Krishna. Gopi Krishna. Ed. & Intro. by Leslie Shepard. LC 93-21829. (Dragon Editions Ser.). 352p. (Orig.). 1993. pap. 25.00 (0-87773-947-1, Pub. by Shambhala Pubns) Random.
Living with Lace. Bo Niles. LC 90-34556. (Illus.). 176p. 1990. 35.00 (1-55670-156-X) Stewart Tabori & Chang.
Living with Lace. rev. ed. Bo Niles. (Illus.). 176p. 1999. pap. text 20.00 (1-55670-447-X) Stewart Tabori & Chang.
*__Living with Landmines: From International Treaty to Reality.__ Bill Purves. (Illus.). 208p. 2000. pap. 19.99 (1-55164-174-7) Black Rose.
Living with Learning Disabilities: A Guide for Students. David E. Hall. LC 92-46600. (J). (gr. 4-8). 1993. lib. bdg. 19.93 (0-8225-0036-1, Lerner Publctns) Lerner Pub.
Living with Learning Disabilities: A Guide for Students. David E. Hall. (Illus.). 64p. (YA). (gr. 4 up). 1996. pap. 6.95 (0-8225-9723-3) Lerner Pub.
Living with Leviathan: Americans Coming to Terms with Big Government. Linda L. Bennett & Stephen E. Bennett. LC 90-39015. (Studies in Government & Public Policy). xvii, 192p. 1990. 29.95 (0-7006-0432-4); pap. 14.95 (0-7006-0433-2) U Pr of KS.
Living with Life-Threatening Illness: A Guide for Patients, Their Families & Caregivers. Kenneth J. Doka. LC 97-35541. 294p. 1998. pap. 26.95 (0-7879-4048-8) Jossey-Bass.
Living with Limits: Theological Musings for the 21st Century. Harold C. Warlick, Jr. LC 96-10699. 142p. (Orig.). 1996. pap. 12.95 (0-7880-0845-5) CSS OH.
Living with Lincoln: Life & Art in the Heartland. Dan Guillory. 126p. (Orig.). 1989. pap. 11.95 (0-935153-11-X) Stormline Pr.
Living with Liszt: From the Diary of Carl Lachmund, an American Pupil of Liszt, 1882-1884. rev. ed. Carl Lachmund. Ed. & Anno. by Alan Walker. LC 98-3048. (Franz Liszt Studies: Vol. 4). 1998. 54.00 (0-945193-56-4) Pendragon NY.
Living with Little Quilts. Alice Berg et al. Ed. by Janet White. LC 97-16865. (Illus.). 64p. 1997. 16.95 (1-56477-192-X, B306) Martingale & Co.
Living with Llamas: Tales from Juniper Ridge. 4th rev. ed. Rosana Hart. LC 96-215009. (Illus.). 192p. 1996. pap. 14.95 (0-916289-23-0, Juniper Ridge) Hartworks.
Living with Long Island's South Shore. Larry McCormick et al. LC 83-20670. (Living with the Shore Ser.). (Illus.). 167p. (C). 1984. pap. 16.95 (0-8223-0502-X); text 39.95 (0-8223-0501-1) Duke.
*__Living with Loss.__ Carrie Lyn Goldstein. 2000. pap. 8.95 (0-533-13422-6) Vantage.
Living with Loss: A Pastor's Memoir. Ernest Veal. LC 98-67680. 128p. 1998. pap. 11.95 (1-57736-116-4) Providence Hse.
*__Living with Loss, Healing with Hope: A Jewish Perspective.__ Earl A. Grollman. LC 00-8484. 2000. 18.00 (0-8070-2812-6) Beacon Pr.
Living with Low Vision: A Resource Guide for People with Sight Loss. 5th large type ed. Resources for Rehabilitation Staff. 1998. pap. 44.95 (0-929718-20-8) Resc Rehab.
Living with Low Vision: Independence, Driving, & Low Vision Solutions. Daniel Gottlieb et al. (Illus.). 260p. (Orig.). 1996. pap., wbk. ed. 45.00 (1-887617-52-3) St Bart Pr Ltd.
Living with Lung Cancer. Ann G. Fettner. Date not set. pap. 15.00 (0-465-04152-3) Basic.
Living with Lung Cancer: A Guide for Patients & Their Families. 4th rev. ed. Barbara G. Cox et al. LC 97-50581. 144p. 1998. pap. 14.95 (0-937404-53-5) Triad Pub FL.
Living with Lupus: A Comprehensive Guide to Understanding & Controlling Lupus While Enjoying Your Life. Mark Horowitz & Marietta Abrams-Brill. LC 93-21066. (Illus.). 1994. pap. 12.95 (0-452-27056-1, Plume) Dutton Plume.
Living with Lupus: All the Knowledge You Need to Help Yourself. Sheldon P. Blau. (Illus.). 224p. 1993. pap. 12.00 (0-201-60809-X) Addison-Wesley.
Living with Marginal Aggregates - STP 597. 113p. 1982. pap. 5.50 (0-8031-0391-3, STP597) ASTM.
Living with Math: Making Healthy Decisions for Yourself & the Earth. Ira Nirenberg. LC 96-85805. 208p. 1997. pap. 12.95 (1-57706-676-6) Burlington Natl.
*__Living with Me.__ Charles Shepherd. 1999. pap. 19.95 (0-09-181679-3, Pub. by Random) Trafalgar.
Living with Medicine: A Family Guide. Mary E. Smith. 262p. 1987. pap. 9.95 (0-89042-504-3, 2504) Am Psychiatric.
Living with Michigan's Wetlands: A Landowner's Guide. Wilfred Cwikiel & Thomas W. Ford. LC 98-165323. viii, 132 p. 1997. write for info. (1-889313-00-9) Tip of Mitt.
*__Living with Modern Classics: The Chair.__ Elizabeth Wilhide. (Illus.). 80p. 2000. write for info. (0-8230-3109-8) Watsn-Guptill.
*__Living with Modern Classics: The Light.__ Elizabeth Wilhide. (Illus.). 80p. 2000. 19.95 (0-8230-3110-1) Watsn-Guptill.
Living with Modern Sculpture: The John P. Putnam, Jr. Memorial Collection at Princeton. Patrick J. Kelleher. LC 81-80639. (Illus.). 144p. 1981. text 24.00 (0-691-03897-X, Pub. by Princeton U Pr) Cal Prin Full Svc.
*__Living with Moshiach: An Anthology of Brief Homilies & Insights on the Weekly Torah Readings & the Festivals.__ Jacob Immanuel Schochet & Menahem Mendel Schneersohn. LC 99-10268. 171p. 1999. 12.00 (0-8266-0468-4) Kehot Pubn Soc.
Living with Mt. St. Helens: Human Adjustment to Volcano Hazards. Ronald W. Perry & Michael K. Lindell. LC 90-59721. (Illus.). x, 220p. 1990. pap. text 9.95 (0-87422-053-X) Wash St U Pr.
*__Living with Multiple Chemical Sensitivity: Narratives of Coping.__ Gail J. McCormick. 256p. 2000. pap. 35.00 (0-7864-0887-1) McFarland & Co.
Living with Multiple Sclerosis: A Handbook for Families. rev. ed. Robert Shuman & Janice Schwartz. 256p. 1994. reprint ed. per. 12.95 (0-02-082026-7) Macmillan.
*__Living with Multiple Sclerosis: A Wellness Approach.__ 2nd rev. ed. George H. Kraft & Marci Catanzaro. 128p. 2000. pap. 18.95 (1-888799-26-9, Pub. by Demos Medical) SCB Distributors.
Living with Multiple Sclerosis: Personal Accounts of Coping & Adaptation. Sarah Perry. (Developments in Nursing & Health Care Ser.). 272p. 1994. 72.95 (1-85628-893-5, Pub. by Avebry) Ashgate Pub Co.
Living with My Family. Wendy Deaton & Kendall Johnson. 32p. (J). (gr. 4-6). 1991. pap., student ed. 9.95 (0-89793-084-3); 17.95 (0-89793-086-X) Hunter Hse.
Living with My Father. Sherlie Rowe. 1986. pap. 6.35 (0-89137-814-6) Quality Pubns.
Living with My Heart Wide Open. C. S. Krotke. LC 98-61278. '58p. 1998. 10.00 (1-890306-14-2) Warwick Hse.
Living with My Stepfather Is Like Living with a Moose. Lynea Bowdish. LC 96-21313. (Illus.). 64p. (J). (gr. 2-4). 1997. 14.00 (0-374-34630-5) FS&G.
Living with Native Plants: An Illustrated Planting Handbook for the Inland Pacific Northwest. Bev Keating. (Illus.). 200p. (Orig.). 1997. pap. 15.00 (0-9653619-2-6, 1003) Advent Trail.
Living with Nature: Environmental Politics & Cultural Discourse. Ed. by Frank Fischer & Maarten A. Hajer. LC 99-12990. 288p. 1999. text 72.00 (0-19-829226-0) OUP.
Living with Nature: Environmental Politics as Cultural Discourse. Ed. by Frank Fischer & Maarten A. Hajer. LC 99-12990. 284p. 1999. pap. text 27.50 (0-19-829509-X) OUP.
Living with Nuclear Weapons. Harvard Nuclear Study Group Staff. 288p. 1990. 31.00 (0-674-53665-7) HUP.
Living with Old Houses. rev. ed. Greater Portland Landmarks, Inc. Advisory Service. LC 75-28985. (Illus.). 109p. 1985. reprint ed. ring bd. 10.50 (0-9600612-4-X) Greater Portland.
Living with One's Past: Personal Fates & Moral Pain. Norman S. Care. 248p. 1996. pap. text 24.95 (0-8476-8237-4); lib. bdg. 60.50 (0-8476-8236-6) Rowman.
Living with Osteogenesis Imperfecta: A Guidebook for Families. Ed. by Heidi C. Glauser. (Illus.). 287p. (Orig.). 1994. pap. text 19.95 (0-9642189-0-9) Osteogenesis Imper.
Living with Other People: Directions in Christian Ethics from Bernard Lonergan. Kenneth R. Melchin. 120p. 1998. pap. 17.95 (0-8146-5940-3) Liturgical Pr.
Living with Our Genes. Dean Hamer & Peter F. Copeland. 368p. 1999. pap. 14.95 (0-385-48584-0, Anchor NY) Doubleday.
*__Living with P. C. O. S. Polycystic Ovarian Syndrome.__ Angela Boss et al. 165p. 2000. pap. 14.95 (1-886039-49-6, Pub. by Addicus Bks) LPC Group.
Living with Pain: A Story of Encouragement. Samuel C. Gipp. 81p. (Orig.). 1996. pap. 6.00 (1-890120-02-2) DayStar Pub.
Living with Paradox: An Introduction to Jungian Psychology. Anne S. Harris. LC 95-22936. (Counseling Ser.). 250p. 1995. pap. 35.95 (0-534-21643-9) Brooks-Cole.
Living with Paradox: Religious Leadership & the Genius of Double Vision. H. Newton Malony. LC 97-48677. (Religion in Practice Ser.). 160p. 1998. 22.00 (0-7879-4057-7) Jossey-Bass.
Living with Parkinson's Disease. Kathleen E. Biziere & Matthias C. Kurth. LC 96-46633. 160p. 1996. pap. 24.95 (1-888799-10-2) Demos Medical.
Living with Parkinson's Disease: Don't Rush Me! I'm Coping As Fast As I Can. Jon R. Pierce. LC 89-63189. 176p. (Orig.). 1989. pap. text. write for info. (0-9630559-0-9) J R Pierce.
Living with Peril: Eisenhower, Kennedy, & Nuclear Weapons. Andreas Wenger. LC 97-2430. 448p. (Orig.). 1996. pap. 28.95 (0-8476-8515-2); text 73.00 (0-8476-8514-4) Rowman.
*__Living with Plants.__ George Carter. (Illus.). 2000. 29.95 (1-84000-181-X) Mitchell Beazley.
Living with Plants: A Guide to the Practical Application of Botany. Donna N. Schumann. (Illus.). 328p. 1980. pap. text 24.95 (0-916422-20-8) Mad River.
Living with Prostate Cancer. Audrey C. Newton. (Illus.). 192p. 1997. pap. 14.95 (0-7710-6779-8) McCland & Stewart.
Living with Purpose When the Gods Are Gone. Robert P. Crosby. LC 91-18681. (Illus.). 64p. (Orig.). 1991. pap. 5.95 (0-87810-038-5) Times Change.
Living with Racism: The Black Middle-Class Experience. Joe R. Feagin & Melvin P. Sikes. 416p. 1995. pap. 15.00 (0-8070-0925-3) Beacon Pr.
Living with Radiation: The Risk, the Promise. Henry N. Wagner, Jr. & Linda E. Ketchum. LC 88-46063. (Illus.). 206p. reprint ed. pap. 63.90 (0-608-06162-X, 206649500008) Bks Demand.
Living with Rheumatoid Arthritis. Tammi L. Shlotzhauer & James L. McGuire. (Health Bks.). (Illus.). 280p. 1995. reprint ed. pap. 15.95 (0-8018-5185-8) Johns Hopkins.
Living with Scarves. Lorraine E. Hammett. (Illus.). 132p. 1999. reprint ed. pap. text 15.00 (0-7881-6217-9) DIANE Pub.
Living with Schizophrenia. Stuart Emmons et al. LC 97-19055. Vol. 2. 200p. 1997. pap. write for info. (1-56032-556-9) Hemisp Pub.
Living with Seabirds. Bryan Nelson. (Island Biology Ser.: Vol. 2). (Illus.). 240p. 1987. 35.00 (0-85224-523-8, Pub. by Edinburgh U Pr) Col U Pr.
Living with Seizures. Heather Tuttle. LC 95-90999. (Illus.). 20p. (Orig.). (J). (gr. k-12). 1995. pap. 7.95 (0-9649713-0-5) Tuttle Pr.
Living with Shingles: The Chronic Condition of the Reactivated Herpes Zoster Virus. Mary-Ellen Siegel & William Gray, Jr. 224p. 1998. 19.95 (0-87131-828-8) M Evans.
Living with Small & Toy Dogs. Terry Jester. LC 95-36609. (Illus.). 200p. 1996. pap. 16.95 (0-931866-79-0) Alpine Pubns.
Living with Snakes. Daniel Curley. LC 84-22773. (Flannery O'Connor Award for Short Fiction Ser.). 144p. 1985. 19.95 (0-8203-0767-X) U of Ga Pr.
*__Living with Snakes.__ Lynn M. Stone. LC 00-25031. (Eye to Eye with Snakes Ser.). (Illus.). 2000. write for info. (1-55916-264-3) Rourke Bk Co.
Living with Sobriety: Another Beginning. Al-Anon Family Group Headquarters, Inc. Staff. 144p. 1993. pap. 2.50 (0-910034-58-3) Al-Anon.
Living with Spina Bifida: A Guide for Families & Professionals. Adrian Sandler. LC 96-47697. 296p. (gr. 13). 1997. 49.95 (0-8078-2352-X); pap. 19.95 (0-8078-4657-0) U of NC Pr.
*__Living with Spinal Cord Injury.__ Richard J. Boyle. LC 99-93938. 2000. pap. 7.95 (0-533-13199-5) Vantage.
*__Living with Spirit: Conversations on Life in the New Age.__ Jurella d'Esprit. Ed. by Kathleen M. Sewalk. Tr. by Catherine Blake. 96p. 1999. pap. 8.00 (0-941461-11-4) Tunnel Press.
Living with Strangers in the U. S. A. Communicating Beyond Culture. Carol Archer. 128p. (C). 1990. pap. text 28.60 (0-13-538620-9) P-H.
Living with Stress. Brett & Carol Younger. (Extensions Adult Elective Bible Study Ser.). 59p. pap. 9.00 (1-880837-43-9) Smyth & Helwys.
Living with Stress: Biblical Truths to Manage Your Life. Charles R. Gerber. 120p. 1999. pap. 7.99 (0-89900-852-6) College Pr Pub.
Living with Stress - Middle School. Sandra M. Sylvester. 64p. (J). (gr. 5-9). 1991. 8.99 (0-86653-594-2, GA1313) Good Apple.
Living with Stress - Primary. Sandra M. Sylvester. 64p. (J). (gr. 1-4). 1991. 7.99 (0-86653-593-4, GA1312) Good Apple.
Living with Stroke. Richard C. Senelick et al. LC 99-13895. 272p. (Orig.). 1999. pap. 14.95 (0-8092-2607-3, 260730, Contemporary Bks) NTC Contemp Pub Co.
Living with Stroke: A Guide for Families - Help & Hope for All Those Touched by Stroke. Richard C. Senelick et al. LC 99-13880. (Getting People Back/Rehabilitation Ser.). 1998. write for info. (1-891525-02-6, HealthSouth Pr) HealthSouth.
Living with Stroke: A Guide for Families - Help & Hope for All Those Touched by Stroke. Richard C. Senelick et al. LC 94-2480. 256p. 1994. pap. 14.95 (0-8092-3696-6) NTC Contemp Pub Co.
Living with Technology. Michael Hacker. (Tech & Industrial Education Ser.). 1988. pap., teacher ed. 15.00 (0-8273-3249-1); text 36.95 (0-8273-3248-3) Delmar.
Living with Technology. 2nd ed. Michael Hacker & Robert Barden. 1992. pap., teacher ed. 54.95 (0-8273-4909-2) S-W Pub.
Living with Technology. 2nd ed. Michael Hacker & Robert Barden. (J). 1992. text 38.95 (0-8273-4907-6) S-W Pub.
Living with Technology. 3rd ed. Michael Hacker. (TP - Technology Education Ser.). (J). (gr. k-12). 1998. pap., wbk. ed. 24.95 (0-538-65831-2); text 38.95 (0-538-65829-0); text, teacher ed. 47.95 (0-538-65830-4) S-W Pub.
Living with Technology, Testbank. 2nd ed. Michael Hacker & Robert Barden. 1992. pap. 115.95 (0-8273-5303-0) S-W Pub.
Living with Teenagers. Jean Rosenbaum & Veryl Rosenbaum. LC 79-3711. 192p. (C). 1982. pap. 7.95 (0-8128-6144-2, Scrbrough Hse) Madison Bks UPA.
Living with Teenagers: A Survival Manual for Adults. John Reid. LC 81-70265. 268p. (Orig.). 1983. pap. 7.95 (0-9607234-0-4) Ampersand Pub.
Living with Teens & Enjoying Them Too! Specific & Practical Suggestions for Coping with Parent-Teen Issues. Blossom M. Turk. Ed. by Jean Terra. LC 90-60627. (Illus.). (Orig.). 1990. pap. 9.95 (0-9625040-1-7, 297-231-X) Legendary Pub.
Living with Terminal Illness. Nancy Hill. (Master's Touch Bible Study Ser.). 1996. pap. 4.50 (0-570-09556-5, 20-2597) Concordia.
Living with the Active Alert Child: Groundbreaking Strategies for Parents. rev. ed. Linda S. Budd. LC 93-83146. 272p. 1993. reprint ed. pap. 12.95 (0-943990-88-2) Parenting Pr.
Living with the Adirondack Forest: Local Perspectives on Land-Use Conflicts. Catherine H. Knott. LC 97-35390. (Illus.). 314p. 1997. 45.00 (0-8014-3122-0); pap. text 18.95 (0-8014-8500-2) Cornell U Pr.
Living with the Alabama-Mississippi Shore. Wayne F. Canis et al. LC 84-24679. (Living with the Shore Ser.). 232p. 1985. text 39.95 (0-8223-0510-0); pap. text 17.95 (0-8223-0511-9) Duke.
Living with the Ancestors: Kinship & Kingship in Ancient Maya Society. Patricia A. McAnany. LC 94-5469. (Illus.). 248p. (C). 1995. text 30.00 (0-292-75165-6) U of Tex Pr.
*__Living with the Ancestors: Kinship & Kingship in Ancient Maya Society.__ Patricia A. McAnany. (Illus.). 229p. 2000. pap. 16.95 (0-292-75236-9) U of Tex Pr.
*__Living with the Angels.__ large type ed. Joseph A. Fryman. 182p. 1999. pap. 12.95 (0-9676151-0-0) J A Fryman.
Living with the Atom. Ritchie Calder. LC 62-13562. (Illus.). 284p. reprint ed. pap. 88.10 (0-608-09276-2, 205415000004) Bks Demand.
Living with the Bomb: American & Japanese Cultural Conflicts in the Nuclear Age. Ed. by Laura Hein & Mark Selden. LC 96-38664. (Japan in the Modern World Ser.). 310p. (gr. 13). 1997. text 74.95 (1-56324-966-9, East Gate Bk) M E Sharpe.
Living with the Bomb: American & Japanese Cultural Conflicts in the Nuclear Age. Ed. by Laura Hein & Mark Selden. LC 96-38664. (Japan in the Modern World Ser.). (Illus.). 310p. (gr. 13). 1997. pap. text 24.95 (1-56324-967-7, East Gate Bk) M E Sharpe.

An Asterisk (*) at the beginning of an entry indicates that the title is appearing for the first time.

Living with the California Coast. Ed. by Gary B. Griggs & Lauret E. Savoy. LC 84-28814. (Living with the Shore Ser.). (Illus.). 415p. (C). 1985. text 39.95 (0-8223-0632-8); pap. text 19.95 (0-8223-0633-6) Duke.

Living with the Changed World Climate. Walter O. Roberts & Edward J. Friedman. 38p. (Orig.). 1982. pap. text 10.50 (0-8191-5884-4) U Pr of Amer.

Living with the Chesapeake Bay & Virginia's Ocean Shores. Larry G. Ward et al. LC 88-21738. (Living with the Shore Ser.). 250p. 1989. pap. 17.95 (0-8223-0889-4); text 39.95 (0-8223-0868-1) Duke.

Living with the Coast of Alaska. Owen Mason et al. LC 97-15156. (Living with the Shore Ser.). 368p. 1998. lib. bdg. 54.95 (0-8223-2009-6) Duke.

Living with the Coast of Alaska. Owen Mason et al. LC 97-15156. (Living with the Shore Ser.). xix, 348p. 1998. pap. 19.95 (0-8223-2019-3) Duke.

Living with the Coast of Maine. Joseph T. Kelley et al. LC 88-10845. (Living with the Shore Ser.). (Illus.). 185p. 1988. pap. 16.95 (0-8223-0885-1); text 39.95 (0-8223-0864-9) Duke.

Living with the Dead: The Grateful Dead Story. Rich Scully & David Dalton. 1996. 24.95 (0-614-15504-5) Little.

Living with the Dead in the Middle Ages. Patrick J. Geary. (Illus.). 288p. 1994. text 45.00 (0-8014-2856-4); pap. text 16.95 (0-8014-8098-1) Cornell U Pr.

Living with the Earth: Concepts in Environmental Health S Cience : A Web-enhanced Book. Gary S. Moore. LC 99-10845. 672p. 1999. boxed set 79.95 (1-56670-357-3) Lewis Pubs.

Living with the East Florida Shore. Orrin H. Pilkey et al. LC 84-10297. (Living with the Shore Ser.). 275p. 1984. pap. 17.95 (0-8223-0515-1); text 49.95 (0-8223-0514-3) Duke.

Living with the End in Mind: A Practical Checklist for Living Life to the Fullest by Embracing Your Mortality. Erin T. Kramp et al. LC 98-27575. 206p. 1998. pap. 12.00 (0-609-80381-6, Three Riv Pr) Crown Pub Group.

Living with the Enemy. Donna Ferrato. (Illus.). 176p. 1991. 60.00 (0-89381-489-X) Aperture.

Living with the Enemy. Donna Ferrato. (Illus.). 176p. 1992. pap. 37.95 (0-89381-480-6) Aperture.

Living with the Enemy. Laura Martin. 1999. pap. 3.50 (0-373-17420-9, 1-17420-0, Harlequin) Harlequin Bks.

Living with the Environment. L. E. Cram & D. D. Millar. (Illus.). 210p. 1991. pap. text 22.00 (0-08-041574-1) Elsevier.

Living with the Eskimos. Bernard Planche. Tr. by Sarah Matthews from FRE. LC 87-31805. (Illus.). 38p. (J). (gr. k-5). 1988. 5.95 (0-944589-12-X, 12X) Young Discovery Lib.

Living with the European Union: The Northern Ireland Experience. Dennis Kennedy. LC 99-25940. 224p. 1999. text 72.00 (0-312-22545-8) St Martin.

Living with the Georgia Shore. Tonya D. Clayton et al. LC 91-41261. (Living with the Shore Ser.). (Illus.). 296p. 1992. text 49.95 (0-8223-1215-8); pap. text 18.95 (0-8223-1219-0) Duke.

Living with the Giants: The Lives of Great Men of the Faith. Warren W. Wiersbe. 288p. (gr. 10). 1998. pap. 14.99 (0-8010-9721-5) Baker Bks.

Living with the Gods. Jacqueline Dineen. Ed. by Philip Wilkinson. (Illus.). 96p. (YA). (gr. 5 up). 1999. lib. bdg. 19.95 (0-7910-5135-8) Chelsea Hse.

Living with the Himalayan Masters. rev. ed. Swami Rama. LC 80-82974. (Illus.). 486p. 1999. pap. 18.95 (0-89389-156-8) Himalayan Inst.

Living with the Hyenas. Robert Flynn. LC 95-8082. 210p. 1995. 22.50 (0-87565-144-5) Tex Christian.

Living with the Laboratory Standard: A Guide for Chemical Hygiene Officers. Warren K. Kingsley et al. LC 98-36277. 1998. write for info. (0-8412-3626-7) Am Chemical.

Living with the Lake Erie Shore. Charles H. Carter et al. LC 87-5398. (Living with the Shore Ser.). (Illus.). 276p. 1987. pap. 18.95 (0-8223-0741-3) Duke.

Living with the Land: Communities Restoring the Earth. Christine Meyer & Faith Moosang. (New Catalyst Bioregional Ser.). 144p. 1992. pap. 9.95 (0-86571-251-4) New Soc Pubs.

Living with the Land: Deserts, Rain Forests, Arctic & Plains Regions. Mary Shanley-Gates. (Illus.). 1998. pap. 11.95 (0-673-36397-X, GoodYrBooks) Addson-Wesley Educ.

Living with the Lectionary: Preaching the Revised Common Lectionary. Eugene L. Lowry. 128p. (Orig.). 1992. pap. 5.18 (0-687-17921-1) Abingdon.

***Living with the Living God.** J. Owen. 1998. pap. text 4.99 (0-946462-53-4) Grace Pubns Trust.

Living with the Louisiana Shore. Joseph T. Kelley et al. LC 84-4131. (Illus.). 177p. 1984. text 39.95 (0-8223-0518-6) Duke.

Living with the Louisiana Shore. Joseph Kelley et al. LC 84-4131. (Living with the Shore Ser.). (Illus.). 177p. 1984. pap. 16.95 (0-8223-0519-4) Duke.

Living with the New Jersey Shore. Karl Nordstrom et al. LC 85-25251. (Living with the Shore Ser.). (Illus.). 208p. (Orig.). 1986. pap. 17.95 (0-8223-0698-0); text 39.95 (0-8223-0543-7) Duke.

Living with the Parables: Jesus & the Reign of God. J. Edward Carothers. LC BT0738.. 145p. (Orig.). 1984. reprint ed. pap. 45.00 (0-608-00244-5, 206074600006) Bks Demand.

Living with the Passive-Aggressive Man. Scott Wetzler. 1992. 20.00 (0-685-61043-8) S&S Audio.

Living with the Passive-Aggressive Man. Scott Wetzler. LC 92-14598. 1992. pap. 20.00 (0-671-76791-7) S&S Trade.

Living with the Passive-Agressive Man. Scott Wetzler. 208p. 1993. pap. 11.00 (0-671-87074-2, Fireside) S&S Trade Pap.

Living with the Past. Henry Sandon. mass mkt. 15.95 (0-340-69469-6, Pub. by Hodder & Stought Ltd) Trafalgar.

Living with the Past: An International Collection of Literature, Philosophy, & Poetry Specially Selected for Book Discussion Groups by the Great Books Foundation. Ed. & Intro. by Great Bks. Foundation Staff. (Fiftieth Anniversary Ser.). 464p. (Orig.). 1997. pap. 14.95 (1-880323-77-X) Great Bks Found.

Living with the Patriarchs. Richard Gunze. 40p. 1977. pap., student ed. 4.00 (0-8100-0093-8, 22N0772) Northwest Pub.

Living with the Patriarchs. Richard Gunze. 48p. (YA). 1977. pap., teacher ed. 7.50 (0-8100-0092-X, 22N0772) Northwest Pub.

Living with the Puerto Rico Shore. David M. Bush et al. Ed. by Orrin H. Pilkey, Jr. LC 94-42437. (Living with the Shore Ser.). (Illus.). 216p. 1995. pap. 17.95 (0-8223-1590-4); text 49.95 (0-8223-1575-0) Duke.

Living with the Puerto Rico Shore. Bush et al. (Living with the Shore Ser.). (Illus.). 216p. 1995. pap. 17.95 (0-8477-0239-1) U of PR Pr.

Living with the Queen: Behind the Scenes at Buckingham Palace. Malcolm J. Barker & Timothy C. Sobey. LC 92-11345. 1992. 18.95 (0-942637-75-5) Barricade Bks.

Living with the Sages: Rashi & the Tosafists, Vol. I. David Castle. 1996. 19.95 (0-87306-762-2) Feldheim.

Living with the Shore of Puget Sound & the Georgia Strait. Thomas A. Terich. LC 86-29174. (Living with the Shore Ser.). (Illus.). 182p. 1987. pap. 17.95 (0-8223-0745-6); text 39.95 (0-8223-0689-1) Duke.

Living with the South Carolina Coast. Gered Lennon et al. LC 96-17857. (Living with the Shore Ser.). (Illus.). 264p. 1996. pap. 18.95 (0-8223-1815-6); text 49.95 (0-8223-1809-1) Duke.

Living with the Texas Shore. Robert Morton et al. LC 83-1753. (Living with the Shore Ser.). (Illus.). xii, 180p. (C). 1983. pap. 16.95 (0-8223-0500-3) Duke.

***Living with the Unexpected: Linking Disaster Recovery to Sustainable Development in Montserrat.** A. K. Possekel. Tr. by I. Adams from GER. LC 99-16184. (Illus.). 305p. 1999. 109.00 (3-540-65709-6) Spr-Verlag.

Living with the Wall: West Berlin, 1961-1985. Ed. by Richard L. Merritt & Anna J. Merritt. LC 85-10234. (Duke Press Policy Studies). (Illus.). xiv, 242p. 1985. 37.00 (0-8223-0657-3) Duke.

Living with the West Florida Shore. Larry R. Doyle et al. LC 84-13611. (Living with the Shore Ser.). 240p. 1985. pap. 16.95 (0-8223-0517-8); text 39.95 (0-8223-0516-X) Duke.

Living with Too Little Time. Concordia Publishing Staff. (Master's Touch Bible Study Ser.). 1996. pap. 4.50 (0-570-09549-2, 20-2590) Concordia.

Living with Torah. 1992. pap. 3.95 (0-87306-626-X) Feldheim.

Living with Tourette's Syndrome. Elaine F. Shimberg. LC 95-20038. 256p. 1995. per. 12.00 (0-684-81160-X) S&S Trade Pap.

Living with Uncertainty. School Mathematics Project Staff. (Mathematics Series: Ages 16-19). (Illus.). 136p. (C). 1993. pap. text 11.95 (0-521-38846-5) Cambridge U Pr.

Living with Uncertainty: My Bout with Inoperable Cancer. John Wimber. 48p. (Orig.). 1996. pap. 4.99 (0-9651509-0-9) Vineyard Minist.

Living with Uncertainty: New Directions in Pastoral Development in Africa. Ed. by Ian Scoones. 208p. 1994. pap. 18.95 (1-85339-235-9, Pub. by Intermed Tech) Stylus Pub VA.

Living with Vision: Reclaiming the Power of the Heart. Linda Marks. (Orig.). 1991. pap. 15.95 (0-904575-53-5) Sigo Pr.

***Living with Wildlife.** Marilyn Leys. LC 00-101580. (Illus.). 232p. 2000. pap. 16.95 (0-87341-857-3, WILD) Krause Pubns.

Living with Wildlife: How to Enjoy, Cope with & Protect North America's Wild Creatures Around Your Home & Theirs. California Center for Wildlife Staff et al. LC 93-33982. (Illus.). 352p. (Orig.). 1994. pap. 15.00 (0-87156-547-1, Pub. by Sierra) Random.

Living with Wisdom: A Life of Thomas Merton. rev. ed. Jim Forest. LC 91-21922. 100p. 1991. reprint ed. pap. 15.00 (0-88344-755-X) Orbis Bks.

Living with Wolfdogs: An Everyday Guide to a Lifetime Companionship. Nicole Wilde. LC 99-188708. (Illus.). 104p. 1998. pap. 15.95 (0-9667726-0-1) Phantom Pub CA.

Living with Workaholism. Roger Sonnenberg. LC 96-173159. (Master's Touch Bible Study Ser.). 1996. pap. 4.50 (0-570-09553-0, 20-2594) Concordia.

Living with Your Body. Walther Buhler. Tr. by L. Maloney from GER.Tr. of Der/Leib als Instrument der Seele. 117p. (Orig.). 1979. pap. 10.95 (0-85440-345-0, Pub. by R Steiner Pr) Anthroposophic.

Living with Your Hot Tub. Chris Small et al. (Illus.). 148p. (Orig.). 1983. pap. 12.95 (0-941904-04-0); ring bd. 16.95 (0-941904-12-1) Hot Water Pubs.

***Living with Your Husband's Secret Wars.** Marsha Means. LC 99-41564. 224p. 1999. pap. 10.99 (0-8007-5710-6) Revell.

Living with Your Living Trust: A Complete Guide to Funding & Managing Your Living Trust. Thomas P. Roberts. LC 96-85010. 175p. (Orig.). 1996. ring bd. 39.95 (0-9652592-1-8) Daybreaker.

Living with Your Passions. 1983. write for info. (0-88207-838-0, Victor Bks) Chariot Victor.

Living with Your Passions. Erwin W. Lutzer. 156p. 1983. 9.99 (0-88207-294-3, 6-2294, Victor Bks) Chariot Victor.

Living with Your Pool. Chris Small et al. (Illus.). 148p. (Orig.). 1983. pap. 12.95 (0-941904-06-7); ring bd. 16.95 (0-941904-14-8) Hot Water Pubs.

Living with Your Selves: A Survival Manual for People with Multiple Personalities. Sandra J. Hocking et al. LC 92-16514. 90p. (Orig.). 1992. pap. 9.95 (1-877872-06-7) Launch Pr.

Living with Your Spa. Chris Small et al. (Illus.). 148p. (Orig.). 1983. pap. 12.95 (0-941904-05-9); ring bd. 16.95 (0-941904-13-X) Hot Water Pubs.

***Living with Zen.** Ou Baholydin. 2000. 40.00 (0-8048-3266-8) Tuttle Pubng.

***Living Within: The Yoga Approach to Psychological Health & Growth.** Sri Aurobindo. Ed. by A. S. Dalal. 179p. 1998. pap. 7.95 (81-7058-051-X, Pub. by SAA) E-W Cultural Ctr.

Living Within Limits: Ecology, Economics & Population Taboos. Garrett Hardin. LC 92-24250. (Illus.). 352p. 1993. text 35.00 (0-19-507811-X) OUP.

Living Within Limits: Ecology, Economics & Populations Taboos. Garrett Hardin. (Illus.). 352p. 1995. pap. 15.95 (0-19-509385-2) OUP.

Living Within (Yoga Approach to Psychological Health & Growth) Sri Aurobindo & The Mother. Ed. by A. S. Dalal. LC 85-82639. 179p. (Orig.). (C). 1987. pap. 8.95 (0-941524-22-1) Lotus Pr.

Living Without a Constitution: Civil Rights in Israel. Daphna Sharfman. LC 92-31397. 200p. (gr. 13). 1993. text 44.95 (1-56324-145-5) M E Sharpe.

Living Without a Project: Psychoanalysis & the Postmodern Society. Nestor J. Carlisky et al. Tr. by Dora C. Pozzi. LC 97-23742. 112p. 1997. 38.50 (0-7618-0830-2); pap. 19.50 (0-7618-0831-0) U Pr of Amer.

***Living Without Death: The Experience of Physical Immortality.** Bernadeane Brown & James R. Strole. 164p. 1999. pap. 14.95 (0-9673813-0-4) People Unlimit.

Living Without Depression & Manic Depression: A Workbook for Maintaining Mood Stability. Mary E. Copeland. LC 94-67047. 288p. (Orig.). 1994. pap. 18.95 (1-879237-74-1) New Harbinger.

Living Without Dieting. John P. Foreyt & G. Ken Goodrick. 224p. 1994. mass mkt. 10.99 (0-446-38269-8, Pub. by Warner Bks) Little.

***Living Without Electricity.** Stephen Scott & Kenneth Pellman. (People's Place Ser.: No. 9). (Illus.). 128p. 1999. 14.95 (1-56148-291-9) Good Bks PA.

Living Without Fatigue. Richard Ribner. 160p. (Orig.). pap. 9.95 (0-8159-6117-0) Devin.

Living Without Guilt & or Blame: Conscience, Superego & Psychotherapy. 2nd ed. Ben N. Ard, Jr. LC 89-35194. (American University Studies: Psychology: Ser. VIII, Vol. 19). 143p. 1989. text 30.50 (0-8204-1124-8) P Lang Pubng.

Living Without Law. Anthony Bradney & Fiona Cownie. 69.95 (1-85521-555-1) Ashgate Pub Co.

Living Without Oxygen: Closed & Open Systems in Hypoxia Tolerance. Peter W. Hochachka. LC 79-20221. (Illus.). 192p. 1980. 33.95 (0-674-53670-3) HUP.

Living Without Philosophy: On Narrative, Rhetoric, & Morality. Peter Levine. LC 98-7524. 352p. (C). 1998. text 68.50 (0-7914-3897-X); pap. text 22.95 (0-7914-3898-8) State U NY Pr.

Living Without Procrastination. Roberts. 152p. 1999. 6.98 (1-56731-307-8, MJF Bks) Fine Comms.

Living Without Procrastination: How to Stop Postponing Your Life. M. Susan Roberts. LC 95-69484. 168p. 1995. pap. 12.95 (1-57224-026-1) New Harbinger.

Living Without Religion: Eupraxophy. Paul Kurtz. LC 88-64167. 159p. (C). 1994. pap. 10.95 (0-87975-929-1) Prometheus Bks.

Living Without Silver: The Monetary History of Early Medieval North India. John S. Deyell. (Illus.). 392p. 1990. text 35.00 (0-19-562216-2) OUP.

Living Without Slaveries. Waldo Werning. LC 97-214075. 1997. pap. 13.95 (0-7880-0946-X, Fairway Pr) CSS OH.

Living Without Strain. Joseph Murphy. 157p. 1973. pap. 7.50 (0-87516-187-1) DeVorss.

Living Without Violence. 3rd ed. Jody M. Shearer. LC 92-14081. (Fast Lane Bible Studies Ser.). (Illus.). 56p. (J). (gr. 7-9). 1993. 9.95 (0-89303-222-0) Faith & Life.

Living Without Your Twin. Betty J. Case. 89p. (Orig.). 1994. pap. text 9.95 (0-9629948-1-2) Tibbutt Pub.

Living Witness of John Woolman. Phillips P. Moulton. LC 72-94969. 36p. (Orig.). 1973. 4.00 (0-87574-187-8) Pendle Hill.

Living Witness of the Holy Mountain: Contemporary Voices from Mount Athos. Tr. & Intro. by Alexander Golitzin. LC 95-6817. 1995. write for info. (1-878997-48-3) St Tikhons Pr.

Living Word. 2nd ed. Eileen Caddy. 112p. 1991. pap. 6.95 (0-905249-69-0, Pub. by Findhorn Pr) Words Distrib.

Living Word, Bk. 1. Harold Klemp. 269p. (Orig.). 1998. pap. 12.00 (1-57043-022-5) Eckankar.

Living Word: A Collection of Sermons for the Liturgical Year, Vols. 1 & 2. Ed. by Bishop Herman. 1988. 29.90 (1-878997-05-X); 14.95 (1-878997-03-3); 14.95 (1-878997-04-1) St Tikhons Pr.

Living Word: Reading the Scriptures in Public. Audrey Williamson. 188p. 1987. 11.99 (0-8341-1206-X) Beacon Hill.

Living Word of St. John. White Eagle Staff. 208p. 1979. reprint ed. (0-85487-044-X) White Eagle.

***Living Words: Best High Holiday Sermons of 5759.** Susan Berrin. 1999. pap. 14.95 (0-9664306-1-1) JFL Bks.

Living Words: Language, Lexicography & the Knowledge Revolution. Tom McArthur. 304p. 1999. 80.00 (0-85989-611-0, Pub. by Univ Exeter Pr); pap. 29.95 (0-85989-620-X, Pub. by Univ Exeter Pr) Northwestern U Pr.

Living Words: The Postcard Book. Bart Ehmann. LC 93-91026. 68p. (Orig.). 1993. pap. 10.00 (0-9642453-0-2) Ehmann Pubng.

Living Words in First Corinthians. Wayne Detzler. 1983. pap. 8.99 (0-85234-177-6, Pub. by Evangelical Pr) P & R Pubng.

Living Words in First Peter. Wayne Detzler. 1982. pap. 8.99 (0-85234-165-2, Pub. by Evangelical Pr) P & R Pubng.

Living Words in Philippians. Wayne Detzler. 1984. pap. 8.99 (0-85234-183-0, Pub. by Evangelical Pr) P & R Pubng.

Living Words of Jesus. Contrib. by Mark Norton. LC 97-215931. 1997. pap. 2.99 (0-8423-3249-9) Tyndale Hse.

Living World see Record Breakers

Living World. Roger Cleeve. Ed. by Jane Steltenpohl. (Science up Close Ser.). (Illus.). 32p. (J). (gr. 3-5). 1990. pap. 4.95 (0-671-68630-5, Julian Messner) Silver Burdett Pr.

Living World. Ed. by Ben Dupre. (Illus.). 160p. (J). (gr. 3-9). 1993. 40.00 (0-19-910142-6) OUP.

***Living World.** Teresa Farino. 1999. 29.99 (0-86283-775-8) Quadrillion Pubng.

***Living World.** Ann Fullick. LC 98-11593. (Science Topics Ser.). (Illus.). 32p. (J). 1999. write for info. (1-57572-768-4) Heinemann Lib.

Living World. Holman. (UK - Science Ser.). 1991. pap. 31.95 (0-17-438407-6) S-W Pub.

Living World. George B. Johnson & Thomas C. Emmel. LC 96-221029. 672p. (C). 1996. text. write for info. (0-697-22225-X, WCB McGr Hill) McGrw-H Hghr Educ.

Living World. George Johnson & Thomas C. Emmel. 288p. (C). 1997. text, student ed. 17.50 (0-697-22231-4, WCB McGr Hill) McGrw-H Hghr Educ.

Living World. George Johnson & Thomas C. Emmel. 672p. (C). 1997. per. write for info. (0-07-114403-X, WCB McGr Hill) McGrw-H Hghr Educ.

Living World. Brian Williams. LC 92-41309. (Visual Factfinders Ser.). (Illus.). 96p. (J). (gr. 5 up). 1993. 15.90 (1-85697-846-X, Kingfisher) LKC.

Living World. large type ed. Michael Bright. 367p. 1990. 20.95 (1-85089-360-8, Pub. by ISIS Lrg Prnt) Transaction Pubs.

Living World. 2nd ed. Johnson & Emmel. LC 99-29631. 1999. pap. text 39.00 (0-697-36061-X) Harcourt Religion.

Living World. 2nd ed. Johnson & Emmel. 224p. 1999. pap., student ed. 20.00 (0-697-36063-6) McGraw.

Living World. 3rd ed. Johnson. 2002. 58.00 (0-07-234720-1) McGraw.

Living World Encyclopedia. Leslie Colvin. 128p. (gr. 4-7). 1999. 22.95 (1-58086-171-7) EDC.

Living World Encyclopedia. Ed. by Leslie Colvin & Emma Speare. (Encyclopedias Ser.). (Illus.). 128p. (J). (gr. 3-7). 1999. pap. 14.95 (0-7460-3051-7, Usborne) EDC.

Living World Encyclopedia. Leslie Colvin & Corinne Stockley. (Encyclopedias Ser.). (Illus.). 128p. (J). (gr. 5-7). 1992. lib. bdg. 22.95 (0-88110-434-5, Usborne) EDC.

***Living World of Faery.** R. J. Stewart. (Illus.). 244p. 1999. reprint ed. pap. 16.95 (1-892137-09-7, Pub. by Mercury NC) Bookpeople.

Living World of the Old Testament. Anderson. 1988. pap. text. write for info. (0-582-02561-3, Pub. by Addison-Wesley) Longman.

Living World of the Plants: A Book for Children & Students of Nature. Gerbert Grobmann. Ed. by David Mitchell. Tr. by Virginia Freld Birdsad. (Illus.). 114p. 1999. pap. 12.00 (1-888365-12-9) Assn Waldorf Schls.

Living World TA. Johnson. 1993. write for info. (0-8016-6596-5) Mosby Inc.

Living Wreath. Teddy Colbert. (Illus.). 128p. 1996. pap. 19.95 (0-87905-700-9) Gibbs Smith Pub.

Living Wreath. Storey Publishing Staff. 1997. pap. 19.95 (0-676-57050-X) Random.

Living Years. Edgar A. Guest. 192p. 1981. reprint ed. lib. bdg. 18.95 (0-89968-221-9, Lghtyr Pr) Buccaneer Bks.

Living Yoga: A Comprehensive Guide for Daily Life. Ed. by Yoga Journal Staff et al. LC 92-35692. (Illus.). 304p. (Orig.). 1993. pap. 16.95 (0-87477-729-1, Tarcher Putnam) Putnam Pub Group.

Living Younger: A Physicians Formula. Murdock Head. LC 88-7513. 248p. (C). 1989. 19.95 (0-910155-12-7) Bartleby Pr.

***Living Your Christian Values.** Ralph Neighbour. 128p. 1999. pap. text 4.95 (0-7673-9337-6, LifeWy Press) LifeWay Christian.

Living Your Destiny. Hal A. Lingerman. LC 92-7903. 224p. (Orig.). 1992. pap. 10.95 (0-87728-746-5) Weiser.

Living Your Dream. unabridged ed. Elisabeth Haug. Ed. by Lars Perner. LC 98-91385. (Illus.). 380p. 1998. pap. 18.75 (0-9662715-4-8) Pthfndr Pub.

***Living Your Dreams: Daily Encouragement as Close as Your Heart, New King James Version.** Nelson Word Publishing Staff. (Jesus in My Pocket Ser.). 2000. pap. 2.99 (0-7852-0018-5) W1CL.

Living Your Dreams: The Classic Bestseller on Becoming Your Own Dream Expert. Gayle Delaney. LC 96-14653. 400p. 1996. pap. 15.00 (0-06-251446-6, Pub. by Harper SF) HarpC.

Living Your Dying. Stanley Keleman. 166p. 1985. reprint ed. pap. 10.95 (0-934320-09-8) Center Pr.

Living Your Faith: Closing the Gap Between Mind & Heart. Terry L. Miethe. 185p. (Orig.). (C). 1993. pap. 9.99 (0-89900-620-5) College Pr Pub.

Living Your New Life. Stuart Henrich. 1988. pap. 4.00 (0-937396-81-8) Walterick Pubs.

***Living Your Purpose: God Gave You a Dream, Reality Is Changeless, Humility.** Helen Gordon. 12p. 1998. pap. 3.00 (1-930520-03-4) H Gordon.

***Living Your Yoga: Finding the Spiritual in Everyday Life.** Judith Lasater. LC 99-75818. (Illus.). 192p. 2000. pap. 12.95 (0-9627138-8-0, Pub. by Rodmell Pr) SCB Distributors.

L

L

Living Zen. Robert Linssen. Tr. by Diana Abrahams-Curiel from FRE. LC 60-198. 352p. 1988. pap. 14.00 (*0-8021-3136-0*, Grove) Grove-Atltic.

***Living Zen.** Michael Paul. (Illus.). 160p. 2000. 30.00 (*0-7892-0681-1*) Abbeville Pr.

Livingdying. Cid Corman. LC 77-103369. 1970. 5.00 (*0-8112-0261-5*, Pub. by New Directions) Norton.

Livingdying. aut. deluxe limited ed. Cid Corman. LC 77-103369. 1970. 25.00 (*0-8112-0508-8*, Pub. by New Directions) Norton.

***Livings: Play One.** Henry Livings. (Oberon Bks.). 2000. pap. 20.95 (*1-84002-044-X*) Theatre Comm.

***Livingston.** Barry Evenchick. (Images of America Ser.). (Illus.). (Orig.). 1999. pap. 18.99 (*0-7385-0023-2*) Arcadia Publng.

Livingston: The Pedigreed Pooch of Padre Island. P. J. Meltabarger. Ed. by Arnold Samuelson & Billie Samuelson. (Illus.). 150p. (YA). (gr. 7-10). 1988. 19.95 (*0-923133-02-X*) JM Pub.

Livingston: The Story of a Community. WPA Staff. (Illus.). 166p. 1997. reprint ed. pap. 19.00 (*0-8328-6877-9*); reprint ed. lib. bdg. 29.00 (*0-8328-6876-0*) Higginson Bk Co.

Livingston & the Tomato. A. W. Livingston. LC 98-4410. (Illus.). 273p. 1998. pap. text 18.95 (*0-8142-5009-2*, LIVLIX) Ohio St U Pr.

Livingston Codes & the Guatemalan Crisis of 1837-1838 see Applied Enlightenment: Nineteenth Century Liberalism, 1800-1839

Livingston Genealogical Register: A Sequel to the 1986 "Genealogy" for the Friends of Clermont. Ed. by Howland Davis & Arthur C. Kelly. LC 97-113871. 720p. 1995. lib. bdg. 55.00 (*1-56012-136-X*, 135) Kinship Rhinebeck.

Livingston Hall Papers. Livingston Hall et al. LC 90-956107. (American Legal Manuscripts from the Harvard). 40p. 1987. write for info. (*0-89093-806-7*) U Pubns Amer.

Livingstone. Tim Jeal. (Illus.). 425p. 1994. 19.95 (*0-7126-5638-3*, Pub. by Pimlico) Trafalgar.

Livingstone. Reginald J. Campbell. LC 77-138212. (Illus.). 295p. (C). 1972. reprint ed. lib. bdg. 55.00 (*0-8371-5567-3*, CALI, Greenwood Pr) Greenwood.

Livingstone Mouse. Pamela D. Edwards. LC 95-19981. (Illus.). 32p. (J). (ps-2). 1996. 15.95 (*0-06-025869-1*) HarpC Child Bks.

Livingstone Mouse. Pamela D. Edwards. LC 95-19981. (Illus.). 32p. (J). (ps-3). 1996. lib. bdg. 15.89 (*0-06-025870-5*) HarpC Child Bks.

***Livingstone Mouse.** Pamela D. Edwards. LC 95-19981. (Illus.). 32p. (J). (ps-2). 1998. pap. 5.95 (*0-06-443508-3*, HarpTrophy) HarpC Child Bks.

Livingstone Mouse II. Pamela Duncan Edwards. 32p. (J). Date not set. pap. write for info. (*0-7868-1171-4*) Hyprn Child.

Livingstone Mouse II. Pamela Duncan Edwards. 32p. (J). 2000. 15.99 (*0-7868-0307-X*, Pub. by Hyprn Child); lib. bdg. 15.49 (*0-7868-2247-3*, Pub. by Hyprn Child) Little.

Livingstone Mouse II. Pamela Duncan Edwards. 1998. 11.15 (*0-606-13577-4*, Pub. by Turtleback) Demco.

Livingstone's Africa. David Livingstone. LC 70-138340. (Black Heritage Library Collection). 1977. 52.95 (*0-8369-8732-2*) Ayer.

Livingstone's Labour: A Programme for the Nineties. Ken Livingstone. 299p. 1990. text 24.95 (*0-04-440346-1*) Routledge.

Livingstones of Livingston Manor, Being the History of the Branch Which Settled in the Province of New York with an Account of Robert Livingston & Albany & His Principal Descendants. E. B. Livingston. (Illus.). 623p. 1989. reprint ed. pap. 93.50 (*0-8328-0778-8*); reprint ed. lib. bdg. 101.50 (*0-8328-0777-X*) Higginson Bk Co.

Livingston's Complete Music Business Reference, Vol. I. Robert A. Livingston. 260p. 1996. pap. 69.95 (*0-932303-14-5*) GLGLC Music.

Livingston's Complete Music Business Reference, Vol. II. Robert A. Livingston. 255p. 1996. pap. 69.95 (*0-932303-16-1*) GLGLC Music.

Livingstons of Livingston Manor: Being a History of That Branch of the Scottish House of Callendar... 2nd ed. Edwin B. Livingston. LC 98-74849. (Illus.). xxxiii, 590p. 1999. reprint ed. 30.00 (*0-9669674-0-2*) Curtis Hse.

Livingwell: A New Life of Well-Being, Opportunity, & Accomplishment. Gayle S. Wisner. (Illus.). 135p. 1996. ring bd., wbk. ed. 40.00 (*0-9655763-0-2*) Livingwell.

Livingwise Livingwell. T. Huffman Harris. LC 91-73586. 1992. 15.95 (*0-8158-0450-4*) Chris Mass.

Leviticus 1-16, Vol. 3. Jacob Milgrom. 1184p. 1998. 55.00 (*0-385-11434-6*) Doubleday.

Livius, Band. 2, Buch 3: 9 & Buch 4 und 5: 9. Ed. by Wilhelm Weissenborn & Hermann Joseph Muller. (GER.). viii, 455p. 1970. write for info. (*3-296-14402-1*) G Olms Pubs.

Livius, Band. 3, Buch 6-8: 10 & Buch 9 und 10: 9. Ed. by Wilhelm Weissenborn & Hermann Joseph Muller. (GER.). 560p. 1980. write for info. (*3-296-14403-X*) G Olms Pubs.

Livius, Band. 4, Buch 21: 14 & Buch 22: 13. Ed. by Wilhelm Weissenborn & Hermann Joseph Muller. (GER.). 304p. 1970. write for info. (*3-296-14404-8*) G Olms Pubs.

Livius, Band. 5, Buch 24 und 25: 9 & Buch 26: 9. Ed. by Wilhelm Weissenborn & Hermann Joseph Muller. (GER.). 395p. 1976. write for info. (*3-296-14405-6*) G Olms Pubs.

Livius, Band. 6, Buch 27 u. 28: 7 & Buch 29 u. 30: 8. Ed. by Wilhelm Weissenborn & Hermann Joseph Muller. (GER.). 528p. 1975. write for info. (*3-296-14406-4*) G Olms Pubs.

Livius, Band. 7, Buch 31 u. 32: 7 & Buch 33 u. 34: 7. Ed. by Wilhelm Weissenborn & Hermann Joseph Muller. (GER.). 392p. 1960. write for info. (*3-296-14407-2*) G Olms Pubs.

Livius, Band. 8, Buch 35 u. 36: 6 & Buch 37 u. 38: 6. Ed. by Wilhelm Weissenborn & Hermann Joseph Muller. (GER.). 496p. 1973. write for info. (*3-296-14408-0*) G Olms Pubs.

Livius, Bd. 1, Buch 1 und 2. Ed. by Wilhelm Weissenborn & Hermann Joseph Muller. (GER.). viii, 464p. 1969. write for info. (*3-296-14401-3*) G Olms Pubs.

Livius, Bd. 9, Buch 39-42. Ed. by Wilhelm Weissenborn & Hermann Joseph Muller. (GER.). 503p. 1965. write for info. (*3-296-14409-9*); write for info. (*0-318-71164-8*) G Olms Pubs.

Livius, Bd. 10, Buch 43-45. Ed. by Wilhelm Weissenborn & Hermann Joseph Muller. (GER.). 403p. 1966. write for info. (*3-296-14411-0*) G Olms Pubs.

Livius Andronicus - Lexicon Livianum et Naevianum. Ed. by Albertina Cavazza & Anna R. Barrile. (Alpha-Omega, Reihe A Ser.: Bd. XIII). 201p. 1981. 55.00 (*3-487-07077-4*) G Olms Pubs.

Livius Andronicus, Naevius, Pacuvius, Accius see Remains of Old Latin

Livng Beyond Limits. David Spiegel. 336p. 1994. reprint ed. pap. 12.50 (*0-449-90940-9*) Fawcett.

Livonian Rhymed Chronicle. Tr. by Jerry C. Smith & William L. Urban. LC 77-78928. (Uralic & Altaic Ser.: No. 128). 1977. pap. text 10.00 (*0-87750-213-7*) Curzon Pr Ltd.

Livre a Venir. Maurice Blanchot. (FRE.). 1986. pap. 17.95 (*0-7859-2803-0*) Fr & Eur.

Livre a Venir. Maurice Blanchot. (Folio Essais Ser.: No. 48). (FRE.). 340p. 1959. pap. 14.95 (*2-07-032397-8*) Schoenhof.

Livre Anime de Voyage de Babar. Jean de Brunhoff & Tor Lokvig. (J). (gr. k-5). 1991. pap. 39.95 (*0-7859-8795-9*) Fr & Eur.

Livre au Temps de Joseph II & de Leopold II Vol. 2: Code des Lois de Censure du Livre pour les Pays Austro-Bohemiens. Jean-Pierre Lavandier. (FRE.). 388p. 1995. 55.95 (*3-906753-73-5*) P Lang Pubng.

Livre au Temps de Marie-Therese Vol. 1: Code des Lois de Censure du Livre pour les Pays Austro-Bohemiens (1740-1780) Jean-Pierre Lavandier. (FRE.). 168p. 1993. 27.80 (*3-906750-34-5*) P Lang Pubng.

Livre Blanc: The White Book. Jean Cocteau. Tr. by Margaret Crosland from FRE. LC 90-7205. 104p. 1989. pap. 5.95 (*0-87286-238-0*) City Lights.

Livre Brule see Burnt Book: Reading the Talmud

Livre d'Artiste. G. G. Barber. (Illus.). 96p. 1995. pap. 15.00 (*0-907849-54-7*, 547, Pub. by Ashmolean Mus) A Schwartz & Co.

Livre de Chevet. Georges Barbarin. 180p. 1984. 18.50 (*2-920083-05-8*) Edns Roseau.

Livre de Christophe Colomb. Paul Claudel. (FRE.). 252p. 1932. 10.95 (*0-7859-1109-X*, 2070214931) Fr & Eur.

Livre de Dibawaihi, Traite de Grammaire Arabe, 2 vols., Set. Sibawaihi. xlviii, 956p. 1970. reprint ed. write for info. (*0-318-71565-1*) G Olms Pubs.

Livre de Jeremie, No. Betl 54. E. Peters. 1998. 56.95 (*90-6831-941-8*, Pub. by Peeters Pub) Bks Intl VA.

Livre de la Jungle. Rudyard Kipling. (Folio - Junior Ser.: No. 456). (FRE., Illus.). 254p. (J). (gr. 5-10). 1987. pap. 10.95 (*2-07-033456-2*) Schoenhof.

Livre de la Jungle (Jungle Book) Adapted by Sarah Harris. (Comes to Life Bks.). (ENG & FRE.). 16p. (J). (ps-2). 1995. write for info. (*1-57234-039-8*) YES Ent.

Livre de la Langue Francaise. Agnes Rosenstiehl. (Gallimard - Decouverte Cadet Ser.: No. 24). (FRE., Illus.). 93p. (J). (gr. 4-9). 1985. 16.95 (*2-07-039524-3*) Schoenhof.

Livre de la Nuit: Une Composition Egyptienne de l'Au-Dela: I Partie: Traduction et Commentaire. Gilles Roulin. (Orbis Biblicus et Orientalis Ser.: Vol. 147/1). (FRE.). 409p. 1996. text 126.00 (*3-7278-1054-8*, Pub. by Presses Univ Fribourg) Eisenbrauns.

Livre De la Pitie et De la Mort. Ed. by Pierre P. Loti-Viaud & Michel Desbrueres. (Around 1900 Collection). (FRE., Illus.). 248p. 1995. pap. 69.95 (*0-614-14013-7*) Intl Scholars.

Livre de la Tour Eiffel. Musee en Herbe Staff. (Gallimard - Decouverte Cadet Ser.: No. 2). (FRE.). 96p. (J). (gr. 4-9). 1983. 14.95 (*2-07-039502-2*) Schoenhof.

Livre de la Vertu du Sacrement de Mariage. Philippe De Mezieres. Ed. by Joan B. Williamson. LC 92-15499. (FRE.). 442p. 1993. text 59.95 (*0-8132-0767-3*) Cath U Pr.

Livre de l'Automne. Laurence Ottenheimer. (Gallimard - Decouverte Cadet Ser.: No. 6). (FRE., Illus.). 90p. (J). (gr. 4-9). 1983. 8.95 (*2-07-039506-5*) Schoenhof.

Livre de L'Emeraude. Andre Suares. Ed. & Pref. by Bernard Duchatelet. (FRE., Illus.). 320p. 1995. pap. 74.95 (*0-86808-057-8*) Intl Scholars.

Livre de l'Ete. Laurence Ottenheimer. (Gallimard - Decouverte Cadet Ser.: No. 8). (FRE., Illus.). 88p. (J). (gr. 4-9). 1983. 15.95 (*2-07-039508-1*) Schoenhof.

Livre de l'Histoire de France. Jean-Louis Besson. (Gallimard - Decouverte Cadet Ser.: No. 25). (FRE.). 124p. (J). (gr. 4-9). 1986. 18.95 (*2-07-039525-1*) Schoenhof.

Livre de L'Hiver. Laurence Ottenheimer. (Gallimard - Decouverte Cadet Ser.: No. 5). (FRE., Illus.). 93p. (J). (gr. 4-9). 1983. 15.95 (*2-07-039505-7*) Schoenhof.

Livre de l'Orgue Francais (1589-1789), 2 tomes, Set. Dufourcq. 218.75 (*0-685-35984-0*) Fr & Eur.

Livre de Ma Mere. Albert Cohen. (Folio Ser.: No. 561). (FRE.). pap. 6.95 (*2-07-036561-1*) Schoenhof.

Livre de Ma Mere. Albert Cohen. (FRE.). 192p. 1954. pap. 10.95 (*0-7859-1908-2*, 2070365611) Fr & Eur.

Livre de Manuel. Julio Cortazar. (FRE.). 416p. 1987. pap. 13.95 (*0-7859-2059-5*, 2070378128) Fr & Eur.

Livre de Mon Ami. text 7.95 (*0-88436-289-2*) EMC-Paradigm.

Livre de Mon Ami. Anatole France, pseud. (FRE.). 261p. 1956. 10.95 (*0-8288-9758-1*, F101261) Fr & Eur.

Livre de Mon Ami. Anatole France, pseud. LC 75-41102. reprint ed. 27.50 (*0-404-14542-6*) AMS Pr.

Livre de Mon Bord, Notes (1930-1936) Pierre Reverdy. (FRE.). 272p. 1989. pap. 18.95 (*0-686-54724-1*, 271521572X) Fr & Eur.

Livre de Nattes. Pef. (Folio - Cadet Bleu Ser.: No. 240). (FRE.). 78p. (J). (gr. 1-5). 1990. pap. 7.95 (*2-07-031240-2*) Schoenhof.

Livre de Prefaces Suivi d'Essai d'Autobiographique. Jorge Luis Borges. (FRE.). 337p. 1987. pap. 11.95 (*0-7859-2057-9*, 2070377946) Fr & Eur.

Livre de Rire et de l'Oubli. Milan Kundera. (FRE.). 1987. pap. 11.95 (*0-8288-3699-X*) Fr & Eur.

Livre de Sable. Jorge Luis Borges. (FRE.). 1983. pap. 10.95 (*0-7859-1973-2*, 2070374610) Fr & Eur.

Livre de Scenarios Sociaux. Ed. by Carol Gray. (FRE.). 221p. 1997. pap. 44.95 (*1-885477-41-4*) Fut Horizons.

Livre de Sibawaihi, Traite de Grammaire Arabe, 2 vols., Set. Sibawaihi. xlviii, 956p. 1970. reprint ed. write for info. (*0-318-71435-3*) G Olms Pubs.

Livre de Tous les Francais. Olivier Tissot. (Gallimard - Decouverte Cadet Ser.: No. 26). (FRE., Illus.). 92p. (J). (gr. 4-9). 1989. 15.95 (*2-07-039526-X*) Schoenhof.

Livre de Tous les Jours. Jacque Charpentreau & E. Borchers. (Gallimard - Decouverte Cadet Ser.: No. 14). (FRE.). (J). (gr. 4-9). 1980. 17.95 (*2-07-039514-6*) Schoenhof.

Livre des Actes (The Book of Acts) Le Souffle de L'Esprit. Stanley Horton. (FRE., Illus.). 262p. 1998. pap. write for info. (*0-7361-0026-1*) Life Pubs Intl.

Livre des As et des Heros: Histoire de l'Aviation, No. 2. James Prunier. (Gallimard - Decouverte Cadet Ser.: No. 48). (FRE.). 77p. (J). (gr. 4-9). 1988. 13.95 (*2-07-039548-0*) Schoenhof.

Livre des Chansons de France. Roland Sabatier. (Gallimard - Decouverte Cadet Ser.: No. 16). (FRE.). 157p. (J). (gr. 4-9). 1991. 18.95 (*2-07-039516-2*) Schoenhof.

Livre des Chansons de France: Deuxieme Livre. C. Sabatier & Roland Sabatier. (Gallimard - Decouverte Cadet Ser.: No. 29). (FRE.). 163p. (J). (gr. 4-9). 1990. 18.95 (*2-07-039529-4*) Schoenhof.

Livre des Chansons de France: Troisieme Livre. C. Sabatier & Roland Sabatier. (Gallimard - Decouverte Cadet Ser.: No. 35). (FRE.). 165p. (J). (gr. 4-9). 1990. 18.95 (*2-07-039535-9*) Schoenhof.

Livre des Fuites. J. M. Le Clezio. (FRE.). 1989. pap. 16.95 (*0-7859-2941-X*, 2070718204) Fr & Eur.

Livre des Fuites. J. M. Le Clezio. (Imaginaire Ser.). (FRE.). 1990. pap. 13.95 (*2-07-071820-4*) Schoenhof.

***Livre des Haltes--Kitcab Al-Mawcaqif.** Michel Lagarde. LC 00-21146. (FRE.). 2000. write for info. (*90-04-11568-4*) Brill Academic Pubs.

***Livre des Haltes, Kitab Al-Mawaqif, Tome I.** Michel Lagarde. (FRE.). 650p. 2000. text 193.00 (*90-04-11567-6*) Brill Academic Pubs.

Livre des Leurres. E. M. Cioran. (FRE.). 1992. pap. 23.95 (*0-7859-2955-X*, 2070728013) Fr & Eur.

Livre des Nuits. Sylvie Germain. (FRE.). 352p. 1987. pap. 11.95 (*0-7859-2531-7*, 2070378063) Fr & Eur.

Livre des Questions, Tome 1. Edmond Jabes. (Imaginaire Ser.). (FRE.). 437p. 1988. pap. 19.95 (*2-07-071194-3*) Schoenhof.

Livre des Questions, Tome 2. Edmond Jabes. (Imaginaire Ser.). (FRE.). pap. 22.95 (*2-07-071526-4*) Schoenhof.

Livre des Religions. (Gallimard - Decouverte Cadet Ser.). (FRE.). 261p. (J). (gr. 4-9). 1989. 29.95 (*2-07-039556-1*) Schoenhof.

Livre des Routes & des Provinces par Ibn-Khordadbeh. Khurdadbeh. Tr. by C. Barbier De Meynard. (FRE.). 278p. (C). lib. bdg. 60.00 (*0-89241-223-2*) Caratzas.

Livre des Saints. Lovasik. (SPA., Illus.). 124p. (J). 1996. 8.95 (*0-89942-237-3*, 237/5) Catholic Bk Pub.

Livre des Signes et Temoignages: Kabbale et Meditation. Paul F. Case. (FRE., Illus.). 203p. Date not set. pap. 16.00 (*2-907941-02-X*) Builders of Adytum.

Livre des Trains. James Prunier. (Gallimard - Decouverte Cadet Ser.: No. 27). (FRE.). 93p. (J). (gr. 4-9). 1986. 15.95 (*2-07-039527-8*) Schoenhof.

Livre d'Images Universel de la Naissance. Fran P. Hosken. (Childbirth Picture Bks.).Tr. of Universal Childbirth Picture Book. (FRE., Illus.). 76p. (Orig.). 1982. pap. 7.00 (*0-942096-04-5*) WINNEWS.

Livre du Centenaire. Alphonse D. Lamartine. (FRE.). 380p. 1971. pap. 49.95 (*0-686-54277-0*, 2082103161) Fr & Eur.

Livre du Ciel. Jean-Pierre Verdet. (Gallimard - Decouverte Cadet Ser.: No. 12). (FRE.). 89p. (J). (gr. 4-9). 1990. 13.95 (*2-07-039512-X*) Schoenhof.

Livre du Ciel et du Monde. Nicole Oresme. Ed. & Tr. by Albert D. Menut. Ed. by Alexander J. Denomy. LC 67-11061. (University of Wisconsin Publications in Medieval Science). (ENG & FRE., Illus.). 792p. 1968. reprint ed. pap. 200.00 (*0-7837-9787-7*, 206051600005) Bks Demand.

Livre du Jungle. Rudyard Kipling. (FRE.). 215p. 1976. pap. 10.95 (*0-7859-2369-1*, 2070367835) Fr & Eur.

Livre du Printemps. Laurence Ottenheimer. (Gallimard - Decouverte Cadet Ser.: No. 7). (FRE.). 96p. (J). (gr. 4-9). 1983. 15.95 (*2-07-039507-3*) Schoenhof.

Livre D'Urantia. Ed. by Amadon Corporation Staff. (FRE.). 1783p. 1961. 52.00 (*0-942430-00-X*) Amadon.

Livre D'Urantia. Ed. by Urantia Foundation Staff. (FRE.). 2097p. 1994. 65.00 (*0-911560-05-X*) Urantia Foun.

Livre D'Urantia. Ed. by Urantia Foundation Staff. 1998. pap. 30.00 (*0-911560-53-X*) Urantia Foun.

Livre Mondial de la Famille Patronyme. Numa Research Department Staff. 95p. 1994. 52.00 (*1-885808-07-0*); pap. text 46.00 (*1-885808-08-9*) Numa Corp.

Livre Monidal de la Famille Patronyme (Belgium) Noma Research Department Staff. (FRE., Illus.). 95p. 1998. text 45.00 (*1-885808-17-8*); pap. text 40.00 (*1-885808-18-6*) Numa Corp.

Livre Ouvert, 1938-1944. Paul Eluard. (Poesie Ser.). (FRE.). 240p. 1947. 9.95 (*2-07-032132-0*) Schoenhof.

Livre Tout Nu (The Bare Naked Book) Kathy Stinson. (FRE., Illus.). 32p. (J). (ps-1). 1996. pap. 4.95 (*0-920303-96-X*, Pub. by Les Editions) Firefly Bks Ltd.

Livres a Figures Venitiens: Etudes Sur l'Art de la Gravure Sur Lois a Venice, 6 vols. Andre P. Messena Essling. (FRE., Illus.). 2107p. 1995. reprint ed. 550.00 (*1-57898-026-7*) Martino Pubng.

Livres Africains Disponibles see African Books in Print

Livres de l'Annee. annuals (Cercle de la librairie). 1967. 55.00 (*0-685-35968-9*) Fr & Eur.

Livres de l'Annee. annuals (Cercle de la librairie). 1968. 57.50 (*0-685-35969-7*) Fr & Eur.

Livres de l'Annee. annuals (Cercle de la librairie). 1970. 61.00 (*0-685-35970-0*); 75.00 (*0-685-35971-9*) Fr & Eur.

Livres de l'Enfance du Quinzieme au Dix-Neuvieme Siecle. Gumuchian & Cie. (Illus.). 1979. reprint ed. 175.00 (*0-87556-117-9*) Saifer.

Livres de l'Enfrance: A Catalogue of 15th to 19th Century Nursery Books. Gumuchian. 800p. (C). 1988. 750.00 (*0-7855-4039-3*) St Mut.

Livres Disponibles 1993: French Books in Print, 1993, 6 vols. Editions du Cercle Staff. 1993. pap. 995.00 (*0-7859-3903-2*) Fr & Eur.

Livres Disponibles 1995: French Books in Print - Authors & Titles, 4. (FRE.). 1995. 1295.00 (*0-7859-9888-8*) Fr & Eur.

Livres Disponibles 1995: French Books in Print - Authors, Titles, Subjects, 6 vols. (FRE.). 1995. 1595.00 (*0-7859-9889-6*) Fr & Eur.

Livres du Bonheur. Georges Duhamel. (FRE.). 256p. 1957. pap. 15.95 (*0-7859-5562-3*) Fr & Eur.

Livres Saisis a Paris Entre 1678 & 1701: D'Apres une Etude Preliminaire de Motoko Ninomiya. Ann Sauvy. (International Archives of the History of Ideas Ser.: No. 50). 235p. 1973. lib. bdg. 191.50 (*90-247-1347-1*) Kluwer Academic.

Livret de Famille. Patrick Modiano. (FRE.). 1981. pap. 10.95 (*0-7859-2897-9*) Fr & Eur.

Livret de Famille. Patrick Modiano. (Folio Ser.: No. 1293). (FRE.). 1981. pap. 8.95 (*2-07-037293-6*) Schoenhof.

Livret Phonetique (l'Arabe Sans Peine 2) Seul: Phonetic Pamphlet in Arabic for French Speakers. Assimil Staff. (ARA & FRE.). 14.95 (*0-8288-4357-0*) Fr & Eur.

Livrets of Jean-Baptiste Lully's Tragedies Lyriques: A Catalogue Raisonne. Jean-Baptiste Lully. LC 95-203910. 1998. lib. bdg. 150.00 (*0-943930-50-2*) Performers Edit.

***Livy.** Julia Haig Gaisser & T. Davina McClain. 153p. 2000. pap. 7.00 (*0-929524-93-4*) Bryn Mawr Commentaries.

Livy, Bk. 1. H. Gould & J. Whiteley Gould. (Latin Texts Ser.). (LAT.). 1993. pap. 20.95 (*0-86292-296-8*, Pub. by Brist Class Pr) Focus Pub-R Pullins.

Livy, Bk. 2. J. Whiteley. (Latin Texts Ser.). (LAT.). 1995. pap. 22.95 (*1-85399-465-0*, Pub. by Brist Class Pr) Focus Pub-R Pullins.

Livy, Bk. 5. Ed. by R. Ross. (Latin Texts Ser.). (LAT.). 112p. 1996. pap. 22.95 (*1-85399-442-1*, Pub. by Brist Class Pr) Focus Pub-R Pullins.

Livy, Bk. 21. Ed. by P. Walsh. (Bristol Latin Texts Ser.). 272p. 1991. pap. 20.95 (*0-86292-178-3*, Pub. by Brist Class Pr) Focus Pub-R Pullins.

Livy, Bk. 22. Ed. by J. Thompson & F. G. Plaistowe. (Bristol Latin Texts Ser.). 150p. 1988. pap. 18.95 (*1-85399-059-0*, Pub. by Brist Class Pr) Focus Pub-R Pullins.

Livy, Bk. XXXVI. Livy. Ed. by P. G. Walsh. (Classical Texts Ser.). 144p. (C). 1991. 59.99 (*0-85668-523-2*, Pub. by Aris & Phillips) David Brown.

Livy, Bk. 37. Ed. by Walsh. 1992. 59.99 (*0-85668-573-9*, Pub. by Aris & Phillips) David Brown.

Livy: Book XL, Bk. XL. Livy. Ed. & Tr. by P. G. Walsh from LAT. (Classical Texts Ser.). 196p. 1996. 59.99 (*0-85668-672-7*, Pub. by Aris & Phillips); pap. 28.00 (*0-85668-673-5*, Pub. by Aris & Phillips) David Brown.

Livy: Book XXXVI. Livy. Ed. by P. G. Walsh. (Classical Texts Ser.). 144p. (C). 1991. pap. 22.00 (*0-85668-524-0*, Pub. by Aris & Phillips) David Brown.

Livy: Book XXXVII, Bk. 37. Ed. by Walsh. 1992. pap. 28.00 (*0-85668-574-7*, Pub. by Aris & Phillips) David Brown.

Livy: Hannibal the Scourge of Rome: Selections from Book X. Ed. by E. Lake & F. Porter. (Bristol Latin Texts Ser.). (LAT.). 103p. 1976. reprint ed. 16.95 (*0-86292-131-7*, Pub. by Brist Class Pr) Focus Pub-R Pullins.

Livy: Hannibal Victor: Adapted Selections from Book XXI & XXII. Ed. by W. M. Wilson. (Bristol Latin Texts Ser.). (LAT.). 144p. 1985. 16.95 (*0-86292-011-6*, Pub. by Brist Class Pr) Focus Pub-R Pullins.

Livy: His Historical Aims & Methods. P. G. Walsh. 312p. 1996. pap. 29.95 (*1-85399-130-9*, Pub. by Brist Class Pr) Focus Pub-R Pullins.

Livy: His Historical Aims & Methods. Patrick G. Walsh. LC 61-474. 313p. reprint ed. pap. 89.30 (*0-608-17003-8*, 2027271) Bks Demand.

Livy: Reconstructing Early Rome. Gary B. Miles. 256p. 1995. text 39.95 (*0-8014-3060-7*) Cornell U Pr.

Livy: Reconstructing Early Rome. Gary B. Miles. 264p. 1996. pap. 15.95 (*0-8014-8426-X*) Cornell U Pr.

Livy: The Composition of His History. Torrey J. Luce. LC 77-72126. 351p. reprint ed. pap. 108.90 (*0-608-18438-1*, 203263400080) Bks Demand.

Livy Book, No. XXXIX. Gary Forsythe. 96p. (Orig.). (C). 1994. pap. text 6.00 (*0-929524-82-9*) Bryn Mawr Commentaries.

An Asterisk (*) at the beginning of an entry indicates that the title is appearing for the first time.

L

***Livy's Exemplary History.** Jane D. Chaplin. 280p. 2000. text 65.00 (0-19-815274-4) OUP.
Livy's Written Rome. Mary Jaeger. LC 97-21070. 224p. (C). 1997. text 42.50 (0-472-10789-5, 10789) U of Mich Pr.
Liz: An Intimate Biography of Elizabeth Taylor. C. David Heymann. (Illus.). 432p. 1995. 24.95 (1-55972-267-3, Birch Ln Pr) Carol Pub Group.
Liz: An Intimate Biography of Elizabeth Taylor. large type ed. C. David Heymann. LC 95-35145. (Large Print Bks.). 1995. 24.95 (1-56895-250-3, Compass) Wheeler Pub.
Liz: An Intimate Biography of Elizabeth Taylor. rev. ed. C. David Heymann. (Citadel Stars Ser.). (Illus.). 544p. 1996. mass mkt. 6.99 (0-8065-8002-X, Citadel Pr) Carol Pub Group.
***Liz: The Pictorial Biography of Elizabeth Taylor.** Larissa Branin. (Illus.). 2000. 19.98 (0-7624-0774-3) Running Pr.
Liz & Beth Bk. 1: A Good Licking. G. Levis. Ed. by Tom Verre. Tr. by Gil Jordan. (Eros Graphic Novel Ser.: No. 8). (Illus.). 88p. 1993. pap. 13.95 (1-56097-205-X) Fantagraph Bks.
Liz & Beth Bk. 2: Coffee, Tea, or Me? G. Levis. (Eros Graphic Novel Ser.: No. 12). 112p. 1994. pap. 12.95 (1-56097-210-6) Fantagraph Bks.
Liz & Beth Bk. 3: Tit for Twat. G. Levis. (Eros Graphic Novel Ser.: No. 20). 104p. 1995. pap. 12.95 (1-56097-218-1) Fantagraph Bks.
Liz Busca un Hogar. Joanna Cole. (Magic School Bus:). Orig. Title: Liz Looks for a Home. (SPA., Illus.). 24p. (J). (ps-1). 1999. pap. 3.50 (0-590-68935-5) Scholastic Inc.
Liz Carpenter: Girl from Salado. Betty W. Cox. 144p. (J). (gr. 7-8). 1994. 14.95 (0-89015-940-8) Sunbelt Media.
Liz Dearly's Silly Glasses. Donna L. Pape. LC 68-56824. (Sound Ser.). (Illus.). 48p. (J). (gr. 2-5). 1968. lib. bdg. 10.95 (0-87783-023-1) Oddo.
***Liz Druitt's Guide to Little Roses.** Liz Druitt. 2001. 24.95 (0-87833-193-X) Taylor Pub.
Liz Finds a Friend. Tracey West. (Magic School Bus:). (Illus.). 24p. (J). (ps-1). 1999. 3.50 (0-439-08208-0) Scholastic Inc.
Liz Looks for a Home see Liz Busca un Hogar
Liz Looks for a Home. Joanna Cole. LC PZ7.W51937Li 1998. (Magic School Bus:). (Illus.). 24p. (J). (ps-1). 1998. pap. 2.99 (0-590-81839-2, Pub. by Scholastic Inc) Penguin Putnam.
Liz Makes a Rainbow. Tracey West. (Magic School Bus:). (Illus.). 32p. (J). (ps-1). 1999. pap. 3.50 (0-590-66232-5) Scholastic Inc.
Liz on the Move. Tracey West. (Magic School Bus:). (Illus.). 32p. (J). (ps-1). 1999. pap. 3.50 (0-590-66236-8) Scholastic Inc.
Liz Pone Orden. Joanna Cole. (Magic School Bus:).Tr. of Liz Sorts It Out. (SPA.). (J). (ps-1). 1999. pap. 3.50 (0-439-05869-4) Scholastic Inc.
Liz Sorts It Out see Liz Pone Orden
Liz Sorts It Out. Joanna Cole. LC QA248.W47 1998. (Magic School Bus:). (Illus.). 24p. (J). (ps-1). 1998. pap. 2.99 (0-590-81838-4, Pub. by Scholastic Inc) Penguin Putnam.
Liz Story-The Standards. Ed. by Aaron Stang. 64p. (C). 1997. pap. text 19.95 (0-7692-0099-0, PF9723) Wrner Bros.
Liz Takes Flight. Tracey West. (Magic School Bus:). (Illus.). 24p. (J). (ps-1). 1999. 3.50 (0-439-08207-2) Scholastic Inc.
Liza & the Riddling Cave. John Urquhart. 54p. (J). 1999. pap. 7.00 (0-87602-367-7) Anchorage.
Liza Lou. Marcia Tucker & Peter Schjeldahl. (Illus.). 64p. 1998. pap. 20.00 (1-889195-12-X) Smart Art Pr.
Liza Lou & the Yeller Belly Swamp. Mercer Mayer. LC 80-16605. (Illus.). 48p. (J). (gr. k-3). 1997. per. 5.99 (0-689-81505-0) Aladdin.
Liza Lou & the Yeller Belly Swamp. Mercer Mayer. LC 80-16605. (J). 1997. 11.19 (0-606-11572-2, Pub. by Turtleback) Demco.
Liza Minnelli. large type ed. Peter Carrick. (Illus.). 416p. 1995. 27.99 (0-7089-3254-1) Ulverscroft.
Liza of Lambeth. W. Somerset Maugham. 126p. 1992. pap. 10.95 (0-14-018593-3, Penguin Classics) Viking Penguin.
Lizard. Dennis Covington. 208p. (YA). 1993. mass mkt. 4.50 (0-440-21490-4) Dell.
Lizard. Dennis Covington. (J). 1991. 9.09 (0-606-02725-4, Pub. by Turtleback) Demco.
Lizard. Banana Yoshimoto.Tr. of Tokage. 1995. mass mkt. 6.50 (0-671-53650-8) PB.
Lizard. Banana Yoshimoto. Ed. by Donna Ng. Tr. by Ann Sherif from JPN. LC 95-38086.Tr. of Tokage. 192p. 1996. reprint ed. per. 12.00 (0-671-53276-6, WSP) PB.
Lizard: An Owner's Guide to a Happy Healthy Pet. Steve Grenard. LC 97-39712. 126p. 1997. 12.95 (0-87605-429-7) Howell Bks.
Lizard & Other Distractions: Stories. Philip Ward. 1968. 5.95 (0-902675-52-4) Oleander Pr.
Lizard & the Fly. Robert Levin. 320p. 1998. pap. 13.95 (0-9665127-0-7) Voyage Bks.
***Lizard & the Sun: La Lagartija y el Sol.** Alma F. Ada. 48p. (J). (gr. k-3). 1999. pap. 6.99 (0-440-41531-4) BDD Bks Young Read.
Lizard & the Sun/La Lagartija y el Sol: An Old Mexican Folk-Tale. Alma F. Ada. Tr. by Rosa Zubizarreta. LC 95-53283. (ENG & SPA., Illus.). 48p. (J). (gr. k-3). 1997. 16.95 (0-385-32121-X, DD Bks Yng Read) BDD Bks Young Read.
***Lizard Cage.** Karen Connelly. 2001. write for info. (0-679-31022-3) Random.
Lizard Care from A-To-Z. R. D. Bartlett. LC 96-44418. 1997. pap. text 9.95 (0-8120-9810-2) Barron.
Lizard Club. Steve Abbott. 159p. Date not set. 7.00 (0-936756-71-3) Autonomedia.
Lizard Ecology: Historical & Experimental Perspectives. Ed. by Laurie J. Vitt & Eric R. Pianka. LC 93-46274. 416p. 1994. text 47.50 (0-691-03649-7, Pub. by Princeton U Pr) Cal Prin Full Svc.
Lizard Ecology: Studies of a Model Organism. Ed. by Raymond B. Huey et al. (Illus.). 512p. 1983. 49.45 (0-674-53673-8) HUP.
Lizard Fever. unabridged ed. Eugene Walter. LC 94-75463. (Illus.). 94p. (Orig.). 1994. 23.95 (0-942979-17-6, 942979); pap. 10.95 (0-942979-18-4, 942979) Livingston U Pr.
Lizard Flanagan, Supermodel. Gorman. LC 97-49317. (Illus.). 224p. (J). (gr. 3-7). 1999. pap. 4.95 (0-06-440825-6) HarpC Child Bks.
Lizard Flanagan, Supermodel. Carol Gorman. 160p. (J). (gr. 3-7). lib. bdg. 14.89 (0-06-024869-6) HarpC Child Bks.
Lizard Flanagan, Supermodel. Carol Gorman. LC 97-49317. 224p. (J). (gr. 3-7). 1998. 14.95 (0-06-024868-8) HarpC Child Bks.
Lizard in the Grass. John Mills. 256p. (C). 1980. pap. text 3.00 (0-920802-26-5, Pub. by ECW) Genl Dist Srvs.
Lizard in the Sun. Joanne Ryder. LC 89-33886. (Illus.). 32p. (J). (ps up). 1994. mass mkt. 4.95 (0-688-13081-X, Wm Morrow) Morrow Avon.
Lizard in the Sun. Joanne Ryder. LC 89-33866. (Just for a Day Bks.). 1994. 10.15 (0-606-06543-1, Pub. by Turtleback) Demco.
Lizard Keeper's Handbook. Philippe De Vosjoli. (Herpetocultural Library). (Illus.). 176p. (Orig.). 1994. pap. 12.00 (1-882770-25-0) Adv Vivarium.
Lizard King: The Essential Jim Morrison. Jerry Hopkins. LC 93-19987. 224p. 1993. pap. 10.00 (0-02-033286-6) Macmillan.
Lizard King: The Essential Jim Morrison. Jerry Hopkins. 1995. per. 12.00 (0-684-81866-3) S&S Trade.
Lizard Light: Poems from the Earth. Penny Harter. LC 98-5432. 96p. 1998. pap. 14.00 (1-890932-02-7) Sherman Asher Pub.
Lizard Man of Crabtree County. Lucy A. Nolan. LC 98-47938. (Illus.). 32p. (J). (gr. k-3). 1999. 15.95 (0-7614-5049-1, Cav Child Bks) Marshall Cavendish.
Lizard Man Speaks. Eric R. Pianka. LC 93-38067. (Corrie Herring Hooks Ser.: No. 26). (Illus.). 224p. (C). 1994. 24.95 (0-292-76552-5) U of Tex Pr.
***Lizard Meets Ivana the Terrible.** C. Anne Scott. LC 99-19142. (Illus.). 117p. (J). (gr. 2-5). 1999. 15.95 (0-8050-6093-6) H Holt & Co.
Lizard Music. D. Manus Pinkwater. 144p. (J). 1996. pap. 4.50 (0-440-41319-2) Dell.
Lizard Music. Daniel Manus Pinkwater. LC 76-12508. (J). 1996. 9.09 (0-606-03850-7, Pub. by Turtleback) Demco.
Lizard of Oz. Richard W. Seltzer, Jr. LC 74-20172. (Illus.). 128p. (Orig.). (YA). (gr. 7 up). 1974. pap. 10.00 (0-915232-02-8) B & R Samizdat.
Lizard of Oz Playscript. Kathy Smith & Richard W. Seltzer. (J). (gr. 4-9). 1977. 5.00 (0-915232-04-9) B & R Samizdat.
Lizard on the Loose. Mary Small. 1999. pap. 3.95 (0-207-19109-3) HarpC.
Lizard People. M. T. Coffin. (Spinetinglers Ser.: No. 27). 128p. (J). (gr. 3-7). 1997. pap. 3.99 (0-380-79162-5, Avon Bks) Morrow Avon.
Lizard People. M. T. Coffin. (Spinetinglers Ser.). 1997. 9.09 (0-606-12759-3, Pub. by Turtleback) Demco.
Lizard Sanction. Diane Duane E. (Spider-Man Ser.). 1996. mass mkt. 6.50 (1-57297-148-7) Blvd Books.
Lizard Sees the World. Susan Tews. LC 95-9640. (Illus.). 32p. (J). (gr. k-3). 1997. 15.00 (0-395-72662-X, Clarion Bks) HM.
***Lizard Shoppe.** Neal Barrett, Jr. 2000. mass mkt. 6.50 (0-553-58195-3) Bantam.
Lizard Speaks: Essays on the Writings of Frederick Manfred. Nancy O. Nelson. LC 98-23330. (Prairie Plains Ser.: Vol. 6). 250p. 1998. pap. 15.95 (0-931170-67-2) Ctr Western Studies.
Lizard War. John Dalmas. 1989. mass mkt. 4.99 (0-671-69651-6) Baen Bks.
Lizard Watching Guide: To the Common Lizards of Southern California's Mojave & Colorado Deserts. Sherburn R. Sanborn. LC 94-195330. 40p. 1994. pap. 5.95 (0-9638997-0-8) S Sanborn Nature.
Lizard Who Followed Me Home. Kate Allen. (Illus.). 32p. (J). (ps-4). 1995. 14.95 (1-887218-01-7) Kumquat Pr.
Lizard Woman. Frank Waters. Orig. Title: Fever Pitch. 146p. 1995. pap. 14.95 (0-8040-0987-2) Swallow.
Lizard Woman. Frank Waters. LC 85-2624. Orig. Title: Fever Pitch. 1985. 18.00 (0-914476-99-8) Thorp Springs.
Lizard Zen. Vaughn Bode. 1998. pap. 9.95 (1-56097-309-9) Fantagraph Bks.
Lizardmen. Mayfair Games Staff. 1991. 12.00 (0-923763-26-0) Mayfair Games.
Lizards. (Eyes on Nature Ser.). 32p. (J). (gr. 1). pap. write for info. (1-882210-60-3) Action Pub.
Lizards. John Coborn. LC 98-22377. (Basic Domestic Reptile & Amphibian Library). (Illus.). 90p. (YA). (gr. 3 up). 1999. lib. bdg. 17.95 (0-7910-5084-X) Chelsea Hse.
Lizards. James E. Gerholdt. LC 94-6355. (Remarkable Reptiles Ser.). (Illus.). (J). (gr. 3-9). 1994. lib. bdg. 14.98 (1-56239-306-5) ABDO Pub Co.
***Lizards.** Harald Jes. LC 99-89584. (Complete Pet Owner's Manual Ser.). (Illus.). 2000. 6.95 (0-7641-1449-2) Barron.
Lizards. Louise Martin. (Reptile Discovery Library). (Illus.). 24p. (J). (gr. k-5). 1989. 8.95 (0-685-58605-7) Rourke Corp.
Lizards. Louise Martin. (Reptile Discovery Library). (Illus.). 24p. (J). (gr. k-5). 1989. lib. bdg. 14.60 (0-86592-577-1) Rourke Enter.
Lizards. Mattison. (Of the World Ser.). (Illus.). 224p. 1998. pap. 17.95 (0-7137-2357-2, Pub. by Blandford Pr) Sterling.
Lizards. David Moenich. (Illus.). 128p. 1990. 9.95 (0-86622-823-3, KW196) TFH Pubns.
Lizards, 2 vols. Manfred Rogner. Tr. by John Hackworth. Incl. Vol. 2. Lizards 2. LC 95-31852. (Illus.). 318p. 1997. 54.50 (0-89464-968-X); Vol. 1. LC 95-31852. (Illus.). 328p. 1997. 59.50 (0-89464-939-6); LC 95-31852. 97.50 (0-89464-972-8) Krieger.
***Lizards.** Susan Schafer. Ed. by Peter Mavrikis. LC 99-58088. (Perfect Pets Ser.). (Illus.). 32p. (J). (gr. 1-4). 2001. lib. bdg. 22.79 (0-7614-1103-8, Benchmark NY) Marshall Cavendish.
Lizards. Claudia Schnieper. (Nature Watch Bks.). (Illus.). 48p. (J). (gr. 2-5). 1990. lib. bdg. 19.95 (0-87614-405-9, Carolrhoda) Lerner Pub.
Lizards: Includes Anoles, Chameleons, Geckos & Iguanas see Animals & the Environment
Lizards: Keeping & Breeding Them in Captivity. John Coborn. (Illus.). 64p. 1997. pap. text 6.95 (0-7938-2021-9, RE165) TFH Pubns.
Lizards - Los Padres. Bettianne S. Sien. 112p. (Orig.). 1989. pap. 7.00 (0-939821-32-X) HerBooks.
Lizards Again. David Jewell. 48p. (Orig.). 1986. pap. 7.00 (0-916397-01-7) Manic D Pr.
Lizards & Turtles of South Central Texas. Thomas G. Vermersch. (Illus.). 224p. 1992. 24.95 (0-89015-842-8) Sunbelt Media.
Lizards As a New Pet. John Coborn. (Illus.). 64p. 1992. pap. 6.95 (0-86622-536-6, TU-025) TFH Pubns.
Lizards Deadly. (J). 1996. 6.98 (1-57082-395-2, Pub. by Mouse Works) Time Warner.
Lizards for Lunch: A Roadrunner Tale. Conrad J. Storad. (Sonoran Desert Tails Ser.). (Illus.). 32p. (J). (gr. k-4). 1999. per. 6.95 (1-891795-00-7) Resort Gifts.
***Lizards for Lunch: A Roadrunners Tale.** Conrad J. Storad. 32p. (J). (gr. k-4). 1999. 15.95 (1-891795-02-3) Resort Gifts.
***Lizards, Frogs & Pollywogs: Poems & Paintings.** Douglas Florian. LC 99-50830. 2000. write for info. (0-15-202591-X) Harcourt.
Lizard's Home. George Shannon. LC 98-41055. (Illus.). 32p. (J). (ps-3). 1999. 16.00 (0-688-16002-6, Grenwillow Bks) HarpC Child Bks.
***Lizard's Home.** George Shannon. LC 98-41055. (Illus.). 32p. (J). (ps-3). 1999. 15.89 (0-688-16003-4, Grenwillow Bks) HarpC Child Bks.
Lizards in Captivity. Richard H. Wynne. (Illus.). 192p. 1981. 11.95 (0-86622-083-6, PS-769) TFH Pubns.
Lizards in Sturgis. Beth Jacobs. Ed. by Winter C. Neil. 1997. pap. 5.95 (0-9653145-1-0, 97-02, Autumn Bks) Pontalba Pr.
Lizards in the Terrarium. Harald Jes. LC 87-26911. (Illus.). 72p. 1987. pap. 6.95 (0-8120-3925-4) Barron.
Lizards of Australia & New Zealand. Gray & Gunther. 1995. write for info. (0-916984-34-6) SSAR.
***Lizards of Iran.** Steven C. Anderson. LC 99-70849. 1999. write for info. (0-916984-49-4) SSAR.
Lizards of the British Isles. Peter Stafford. (Natural History Ser.: No. 46). (Illus.). 24p. 1989. pap. 5.25 (0-7478-0028-6, Pub. by Shire Pubns) Parkwest Pubns.
Lizards of the Genus Emoia (Scincidae) with Observations on Their Evolution & Biogeography. Walter C. Brown. Ed. by Tomio Iwamoto. (Memoirs of the California Academy of Sciences Ser.: No. 15). 94p. 1990. 25.00 (0-940228-24-6) Calif Acad Sci.
Lizards of the Orient, a Checklist. Kenneth R. Welch et al. LC 89-34220. 168p. 1990. 23.50 (0-89464-327-4) Krieger.
Lizards of the World. Chris Mattison. (Of the World Ser.). (Illus.). 192p. (J). 1989. 29.95 (0-8160-1900-2) Facts on File.
Lizards on the Mantel, Burros at the Door: A Big Bend Memoir. Etta Koch. LC 98-47018. 214p. 1999. 35.00 (0-292-74338-6) U of Tex Pr.
Lizards on the Mantel, Burros at the Door: A Big Bend Memoir. Etta Koch & June C. Price. LC 98-47018. 214p. 1999. pap. 16.95 (0-292-74339-4) U of Tex Pr.
Lizard's Rage. Neal Barrett. (Spider-Man Super-Thriller Ser.: No.8). 144p. 1997. per. 4.99 (0-671-00798-X) PB.
Lizard's Smile. Ribeiro. 320p. 1994. text 21.00 (0-689-12125-3) Atheneum Yung Read.
Lizard's Song see Cancion del Lagarto
Lizard's Song. George Shannon. LC 80-21432. (Illus.). 32p. (J). (ps-3). 1992. mass mkt. 5.95 (0-688-11516-0, Wm Morrow) Morrow Avon.
Lizard's Song. George Shannon. (J). 1992. 10.60 (0-606-01327-X, Pub. by Turtleback) Demco.
Lizard's Tail. Luisa Valenzuela. Tr. by Gregory Rabassa from SPA. 288p. 1992. reprint ed. pap. 14.99 (1-85242-112-6) Serpents Tail.
Lizard's Trail. Carl E. Person. LC 74-22755. (Labor Movement in Fiction & Non-Fiction Ser.). reprint ed. 38.50 (0-404-58508-6) AMS Pr.
Lizards 2 see Lizards
Lizards's Song (Spanish edition) La cancion del lagarto. Tr. by Aida E. Marcuse from ENG. LC 80-21432. (Books in Spanish). (SPA., Illus.). 32p. (J). (ps-3). 1994. reprint ed. mass mkt. 5.95 (0-688-13201-4, Wm Morrow) Morrow Avon.
Liza's Blue Moon. Diane Stevens. LC 94-4111. 192p. (YA). (gr. 7 up). 1995. 15.00 (0-688-13542-0, Grenwillow Bks) HarpC Child Bks.
Liza's Lucky Break. Suzanne Weyn. LC 89-77117. (Sitting Pretty Ser.). 128p. (J). (gr. 4-8). 1997. pap. 2.95 (0-8167-2008-8) Troll Communs.
Liza's Monday & Other Poems. Bettie Sellers. LC 86-13984. 48p. (Orig.). 1986. pap. 5.95 (0-913239-43-7) Appalach Consortium.
Liza's Star Wish. Diane Stevens. LC 96-46256. 192p. (YA). (gr. 5 up). 1997. 15.00 (0-688-15310-0, Grenwillow Bks) HarpC Child Bks.
Lizzie. Dorothy Shawhan. LC 95-77241. 352p. 1995. 20.00 (1-56352-227-6) Longstreet.
***Lizzie.** large type ed. Louise Brindley. 384p. 1999. 31.99 (0-7505-1396-9, Pub. by Mgna Lrg Print) Ulverscroft.
Lizzie: Lethal Innocence. J. Robert Whittle. 213p. 1998. pap. 14.27 (1-55212-225-5, 98-0044) Trafford Pub.
Lizzie - Queen of the Cattle Trails. Ann F. Crawford. (Texas Pioneers Ser.). (Illus.). 64p. (J). (gr. 4-7). 1990. lib. bdg. 12.95 (0-87443-091-7) Benson.
***Lizzie at Last.** C. Mills. 2000. text. write for info. (0-374-34632-1) FS&G.
Lizzie Borden. Elizabeth Engstrom. 352p. 1997. text 14.95 (0-312-86154-0) St Martin.
***Lizzie Borden: Past & Present.** Leonard Rebello. LC 99-94628. (Illus.). xxii, 642p. 1999. 49.95 (0-9670739-0-1) ALZach Pr.
Lizzie Borden & the Mysterious Axe. Robert A. Flynn. LC 92-72996. (Illus.). 30p. 1992. pap. 12.00 (0-9614811-4-5) King Philip Pub.
***Lizzie Borden "Axe Murder" Trial: A Headline Court Case.** Joan Axelrod-Contrada. (Headline Court Cases Ser.). (Illus.). 104p. (YA). (gr. 6 up). 2000. lib. bdg. 20.95 (0-7660-1422-3) Enslow Pubs.
Lizzie Borden Sourcebook. Pref. by David Kent. (Illus.). 360p. 1992. 29.95 (0-8283-1950-2) Branden Bks.
Lizzie Bordon. Historical Briefs, Inc. Staff. Ed. by Thomas Antonucci & Michael Antonucci. 176p. 1991. pap. 19.95 (0-89677-037-0) Hist Briefs.
***Lizzie Didn't Do It.** William L. Masterton. Ed. by Adolph Caso. LC 99-88574. 242p. 2000. pap. 19.95 (0-8283-2052-7) Branden Bks.
Lizzie Learns about Lying. Gary Hogg. (Happy Hawk Golden Thought Ser.). (Illus.). 24p. (J). 1994. pap. 4.95 (0-930771-08-7) Buckaroo UT.
Lizzie Leigh & Other Tales. Elizabeth Gaskell. LC 71-37543. (Short Story Index Reprint Ser.). 1977. reprint ed. 18.95 (0-8369-4102-0) Ayer.
Lizzie Logan Gets Married. Spinelli. LC 96-19025. 96p. (J). (gr. 2-5). 1998. per. 3.99 (0-689-82071-2) S&S Childrens.
Lizzie Logan Gets Married. Eileen Spinelli. LC 96-19025. 96p. (J). (gr. 2-5). 1997. per. 15.00 (0-689-81066-0) S&S Childrens.
***Lizzie Logan, Second Banana.** Eileen Spinelli. 96p. 2000. per. 3.99 (0-689-83048-3) Aladdin.
Lizzie Logan, Second Banana. Eileen Spinelli. LC 97-23905. 96p. (J). (gr. 4-6). 1998. per. 15.00 (0-689-81510-7) Atheneum Yung Read.
Lizzie Logan Wears Purple Sunglasses. Eileen Spinelli. LC 93-29104. (Illus.). 128p. (J). (gr. 2-5). 1995. 14.00 (0-671-74685-5) S&S Bks Yung.
Lizzie Logan Wears Purple Sunglasses. Eileen Spinelli. 128p. (J). (gr. 2-5). 1998. per. 3.99 (0-689-81848-3) S&S Childrens.
Lizzie Logan Wears Purple Sunglasses. Eileen Spinelli. (J). 1998. 9.09 (0-606-12986-3, Pub. by Turtleback) Demco.
Lizzie's Last-Chance Fiance: Wedding Party. Julie Kistler. (American Romance Ser.: Bk. 782). 1999. per. 3.99 (0-373-16782-2, 1-16782-4) Harlequin Bks.
Lizzie's List. Maggie Harrison. LC 92-54580. (Illus.). 112p. (J). (gr. 3-6). 1993. 14.95 (1-56402-197-1) Candlewick Pr.
Lizzie's Soccer Showdown. John Danakas. 124p. (J). (gr. 3-8). 1995. pap. 8.95 (1-55028-464-9); bds. 16.95 (1-55028-465-7) Formac Dist Ltd.
Lizzy Gets a New Liver. unabridged ed. Lizzy Ribal. Ed. by Beth Basham. LC 97-17815. (Illus.). 40p. (Orig.). (J). (gr. 6 up). 1997. pap. 14.95 (1-57895-019-8, Bridge Res) Curriculm Presbytrn KY.
Lizzy Lou Can Color Too! Jim Henson's Staff. (J). 1998. pap. 1.99 (0-679-89171-4, Pub. by Random Bks Yng Read) Random.
Lizzy the Architect Vol. 1: Career Girls & Company. Lucinda C. Klee. (Illus.). 40p. (J). (gr. 2-6). 1997. pap. 5.95 (1-891040-01-4) LCK Pr.
Lizzy the Architect Gift Set. Lucinda C. Klee. (Career Girls & Company Ser.: No. 2A). (Illus.). 40p. (J). (gr. 2-6). 1997. pap. 19.95 (1-891040-03-0) LCK Pr.
Lizzy's Lion. Dennis Lee. (Illus.). 32p. (J). (gr. k-3). 1993. pap. write for info. (0-614-17732-4) Stoddart Publ.
Lizzy's Lion. unabridged ed. Dennis Lee. (Illus.). 32p. (J). (ps-3). 1985. 7.95 (0-7737-0078-1) STDK.
Lizzy's Lion. 2nd unabridged ed. Dennis Lee & Marie-Louise Gay. (Illus.). 32p. (J). (gr. k up). 1984. pap. 5.50 (0-7736-7397-0) STDK.
***Ljadov: Complete Piano Works I.** Ljadov. 1999. pap. 7.95 (963-9155-40-3) Kone Music.
***Ljadov: Complete Piano Works II.** Ljadov. 1999. pap. 7.95 (963-9155-41-1) Kone Music.
***Ljadov: Complete Piano Works III.** Ljadov. 1999. pap. 7.95 (963-9155-42-X) Kone Music.
Ljestvitsa. St. John Climacus.Tr. of Ladder. (RUS.). 266p. (Orig.). 1963. 18.00 (0-88465-033-2); pap. 13.00 (0-317-38080-X) Holy Trinity.
***L.L. Bean Saltwater Fly-Fishing Handbook.** Lefty Kreh. (Illus.). 2001. pap. 18.95 (1-58574-151-5) Lyons Pr.
Llama. Gail LaBonte. LC 88-16407. (Remarkable Animals Ser.). (Illus.). 60p. (J). (gr. 3 up). 1988. text 13.95 (0-87518-393-X, Dillon Silver Burdett) Silver Burdett Pr.
Llama Babies: Up, Dry, & Nursing. Barbara N. Anderson. LC 96-86675. (Illus.). 192p. 1996. pap. 14.95 (0-9654791-0-2) A Plus Llamas.
LLama de Amor ViVa see John of the Cross, the Living Flame of Love: Versions A & B

L

Llama de Amor Vivita Jarchas. Carlos A. Rodriguez-Matos. LC 88-80881. (Arte y Poesia Ser.). (SPA., Illus.). 50p. (Orig.). 1988. pap. 6.00 (*0-685-20049-3*) Ichali.

Llama Handling & Training: The Team Approach. Marty McGee & Linda Tellington-Jones. LC 92-60582. (Illus.). 200p. (Orig.). 1992. pap. text 24.75 (*0-9633002-0-2*) Zephyr Farm.

***Llama Hiking with Katie.** Ruth Bent. 28p. (J). (gr. 1-3). 2000. pap. 8.00 (*0-615-11191-2*) Sijama.

Llama in The Family. Johanna Hurwitz. LC 94-13612. (Illus.). 112p. (J). (gr. 3-7). 1994. 16.00 (*0-688-13388-6*, Wm Morrow) Morrow Avon.

Llama in the Family. Johanna Hurwitz. (Illus.). (J). (gr. 3-7). 1996. pap. text 3.50 (*0-590-54424-1*) Scholastic Inc.

Llama in the Family. Johanna Hurwitz. LC 94-13612. (J). 1996. 8.60 (*0-606-09568-3*, Pub. by Turtleback) Demco.

Llama in the Library. Johanna Hurwitz. LC 98-34374. (Illus.). 144p. (J). (gr. 2-5). 1999. 15.00 (*0-688-16138-3*, Wm Morrow) Morrow Avon.

Llama Pajamas. Susan Clymer. (J). (gr. 4-7). 1996. pap. text 2.99 (*0-590-60510-0*) Scholastic Inc.

Llama Pajamas. Susan Clymer. 1996. 8.09 (*0-606-09569-1*, Pub. by Turtleback) Demco.

***Llama Violeta: Para Sanar Cuerpo, Mente y Alma.** Elizabeth Clare Prophet. (SPA.). 2000. pap. 4.95 (*968-19-0565-2*) Aguilar.

Llama Who Had No Pajama: 100 Favorite Poems. Mary A. Hoberman. LC 95-18491. (Illus.). 68p. (J). (gr. k-4). 1998. 20.00 (*0-15-200111-5*) Harcourt.

Llama Who Wished for Wings. (Illus.). 19p. (J). (ps-6). 1999. pap. 7.00 (*0-9669355-0-0*) L Chiappini.

***Llamada a la Pureza: El Sexo, el Matrimonio y Dios.** Johann Christoph Arnold. (SPA.). 2000. pap. 12.00 (*0-87486-994-3*) Plough.

Llamada de Lo Salvaje. Jack London. 1992. 12.05 (*0-606-10477-1*, Pub. by Turtleback) Demco.

Llamado a la Conciencia - A Call to My Conscience. Fernandez. (SPA.). 127p. 1995. write for info. (*1-56063-880-X*) Editorial Unilit.

Llamado a Siquir a Cristo. Kay Arthur. (International Inductive Study Ser.).Tr. of Call to Follow Jesus. (SPA.). 80p. 1995. pap. 5.99 (*0-8297-1502-9*) Vida Pubs.

***Llamado Al Crecimiento: Discipulo.** Billie Hanks.Tr. of A Call to Growth. (SPA.). 272p. (YA). 1999. pap. 8.50 (*0-311-13867-5*, Edit Mundo) Casa Bautista.

***Llamado al Crecimiento - Maestro.** Billie Hanks.Tr. of Call to Growth - Discipler's Guide. (SPA.). 96p. 1999. pap. 6.50 (*0-311-13868-3*, Edit Mundo) Casa Bautista.

Llamado de Dios Al Adulto Soltero. M. Cavanaugh.Tr. of God's Call to the Single Adult. (SPA.). 128p. 1992. pap. 4.99 (*0-8297-0336-5*) Vida Pubs.

Llamado de la Selva see Serie Illustrada, "Now Age"

Llamado Supremo. Larry Lea.Tr. of Highest Calling. (SPA.). 1992. pap. 8.99 (*0-88113-105-9*) Caribe Betania.

Llamados a Escribir. Robert Reekie.Tr. of Calle to Write. (SPA.). 115p. 1992. pap. 3.99 (*1-56063-108-2*, 498421) Editorial Unilit.

Llamados a Peregrinar. Robert Delaney. (Vivamos las Sagradas Escrituras Ser.). (SPA., Illus.). 64p. 1992. pap. text 2.50 (*1-55944-030-9*) Franciscan Comns.

Llamados 7 Dotados para el Tercer Milenio. U. S. Catholic Bishops Staff. Tr. by Marina Herrera. (SPA.). 28p. (Orig.). (C). 1996. pap. 2.95 (*1-57455-003-9*) US Catholic.

Llaman A La Puerta. Pat Hutchins. 1994. 10.15 (*0-606-06544-X*, Pub. by Turtleback) Demco.

Llaman a la Puerta. unabridged ed. Pat Hutchins.Tr. of Doorbell Rang. (SPA., Illus.). (J). (ps-2). 1996. 24.95 incl. audio (*0-87499-371-7*); pap. 15.95 incl. audio (*0-87499-370-9*) Live Oak Media.

Llaman a la Puerta, 4 bks., Set. unabridged ed. Pat Hutchins.Tr. of Doorbell Rang. (SPA., Illus.). (J). (ps-2). 1996. pap., teacher ed. 31.95 incl. audio (*0-87499-372-5*) Live Oak Media.

Llaman America. Luis J. Rodriguez. Tr. by Tino Villanueva. LC 96-24508. (SPA., Illus.). 32p. 1998. 15.95 (*1-880684-41-1*) Curbstone.

Llamas. Helen Kienlen & Lois Sandercock. (Illus.). 16p. (Orig.). (J). (gr. k-4). 1989. pap. text 4.00 (*0-9626864-0-9*) Holistic Learning.

Llamas. Emilie U. Lepthien. (True Bk.). 48p. 1996. lib. bdg. 21.00 (*0-516-20160-3*) Childrens.

Llamas. Emilie U. Lepthien. (True Bks.). 48p. (J). (gr. 3-4). 1997. pap. 6.95 (*0-516-26108-8*) Childrens.

Llamas: An Introduction to Ownership, Care & Handling. Sandi Burt. LC 90-26083. (Illus.). 208p. 1991. pap. 16.95 (*0-931866-49-9*) Alpine Pubns.

Llamas & Alpacas. Aaron Frisch. LC 98-43886. (Kings of the Mountain Ser.). 24p. 2002. lib. bdg. 14.95 (*1-58340-018-4*) Smart Apple.

Llamas Are the Ultimate: Training, Feeding, Packing, Hunting, Fishing & Care. Doyle Markham. LC 90-92191. (Illus.). 292p. (Orig.). 1990. pap. 14.95 (*0-9628326-0-X*) Snake Riv Llamas.

Llamas for Love & Money. 2nd ed. Rosana Hart. LC 94-156797. (Illus.). 176p. (Orig.). 1994. pap. 14.95 (*0-916289-19-2*, Juniper Ridge) Hartworks.

Llamas on the Loose. Jeri Massi. 140p. (J). 1988. pap. 6.49 (*0-89084-452-6*, 034629) Bob Jones Univ.

Llama's Secret: A Peruvian Legend. Argentina Palacios. LC 92-21436. (Legends of the World Ser.). (Illus.). 32p. (J). (gr. 2-5). 1996. pap. 4.95 (*0-8167-3050-4*) Troll Communs.

Llama's Secret: A Peruvian Legend. Argentina Palacios. LC 92-21436. (Legends of the World Ser.). (Illus.). 32p. (J). (gr. 2-5). 1997. lib. bdg. 18.60 (*0-8167-3049-0*) Troll Communs.

Llama's Secret: A Peruvian Legend. Argentina Palacios. (Legends of the World Ser.). 1993. 9.15 (*0-606-05438-3*, Pub. by Turtleback) Demco.

Llamas, Weavings & Organic Chocolate: Multicultural Grassroots Development in the Andes & Amazon of Bolivia. Kevin Healy. (From the Helen Kellogg Institute for International Studies). 385p. 2000. pap. 30.00 (*0-268-01326-8*, Pub. by U of Notre Dame Pr) Chicago Distribution Ctr.

Llambrec Material. deluxe limited ed. Shuzo Takiguchi. (Ediciones Especiales y de Bibliofilo Ser.). (CAT, ENG, FRE & JPN., Illus.). 106p. 1993. 4750.00 (*84-343-3777-0*) Elliots Bks.

***Llame al Cielo y No Me Oyo.** Planeta Editorial Staff. (SPA.). 1999. pap. 9.95 (*84-239-7063-9*) Espasa Calpe.

***Llamgollen Ladies.** Mary Gordon. (Illus.). 279p. 1999. pap. 23.95 (*0-8464-4958-7*) Beekman Pubs.

Llandysul Yesterday. 96p. 1992. pap. 18.00 (*0-8464-4685-5*) Beekman Pubs.

Llanelli: Postcards of Yesteryear. Brian Cripps. 105p. 1994. pap. 21.00 (*1-85902-193-X*, Pub. by Gomer Pr) St Mut.

Llanfear Pattern. Francis Biddle. 1993. reprint ed. lib. bdg. 89.00 (*0-7812-5426-4*) Rprt Serv.

***Llangollen Ladies: The Story of Lady Eleanor Butler & Miss Sarah Ponsonby, Known As the Ladies of Llangollen.** Mary Gordon. 280p. 2000. pap. 15.95 (*1-871083-91-5*, Pub. by J Jones Pub) Dufour.

Llangollen Vale. Anna Seward. LC 93-46498. (Revolution & Romanticism, 1789-1834 Ser.). 1994. 65.00 (*1-85477-171-X*) Continuum.

Llano en Llamas. Juan Rulfo. 1999. pap. 10.95 (*0-14-025581-8*, Viking) Viking Penguin.

Llano en Llamas. Juan Rulfo. LC 88-190446. (Coleccion Popular Ser.). (SPA.). 1992. pap. 9.99 (*968-16-0207-2*) Fondo.

Llano en Llamas. Juan Rulfo. (SPA.). 1989. 5.50 (*0-8288-2574-2*) Fr & Eur.

Llano en Llamas. 4th ed. Juan R. Vizcaino. 184p. 1988. pap. 10.95 (*0-7859-5224-1*) Fr & Eur.

Llano Estacado: Exploration & Imagination on the High Plains of Texas & New Mexico, 1536-1860. John M. Morris. LC 96-40185. 400p. 1997. 39.95 (*0-87611-154-1*) Tex St Hist Assn.

***Llano River.** large type ed. Elmer Kelton. LC 00-28620. 251p. 2000. write for info. (*0-7862-2585-8*) Thorndike Pr.

Llanos Frontier in Colombian History, 1830-1930. Jane M. Rausch. LC 92-480. (Illus.). 413p. 1993. reprint ed. pap. 128.10 (*0-608-04126-2*, 206485900011) Bks Demand.

Llanstephan, Ms. 6 see Reprints of Welsh Manuscripts

Llantarnam: A Novel. Muriel Maddox. Ed. by James C. Smith, Jr. LC 91-38366. 416p. (Orig.). 1992. pap. 16.95 (*0-86534-173-7*) Sunstone Pr.

Llanto Por un Lobo Muerto. Ernesto Mendez Luengo. (Nueva Austral Ser.: Vol. 49). (SPA.). 1991. pap. text 24.95 (*84-239-1849-1*) Elliots Bks.

***Llave a Sion.** Bodie Thoene.Tr. of Key to Zion. (SPA.). 2000. 9.99 (*1-56063-684-X*, 494584) Editorial Unilit.

Llave a Sion, Cronicas V. Bodie Thoene.Tr. of Key to Zion. (SPA.). 334p. 1994. pap. write for info. (*0-614-27072-3*) Editorial Unilit.

Llave a Sion - Key to Zion: Cronicas V. Bodie Thoene. (SPA.). 334p. 1994. write for info. (*0-614-24376-9*) Editorial Unilit.

Llave al Corazon de tu Hijo. Gary Smalley.Tr. of Key to Your Child's Heart. (SPA.). 160p. (Orig.). 1991. pap. 8.99 (*0-88113-052-4*) Caribe Betania.

Llave de Modulacion y Antiguedades de la Musica. fac. ed. Antonio Soler. (Monuments of Music & Music Literature in Facsimile Ser., Series II: Vol. 42). (Illus.). 1967. lib. bdg. 45.00 (*0-8450-2242-3*) Broude.

Llave Magica. Lynne Reid Banks. 1995. 15.05 (*0-606-10440-2*, Pub. by Turtleback) Demco.

Llave Magica: The Indian in the Cupboard. Lynne Reid Banks. (ENG & SPA.). (J). 1996. pap. 8.95 (*84-241-3266-1*) Lectorum Pubns.

Llave para la Renovacion Carismatica. Vincent M. Walsh. LC 74-82238. 171p. 1989. pap. 5.00 (*0-943374-11-1*) Key of David.

Llaves de la Salud Emocional. S. Omartian. (Actualidades Ser.).Tr. of Keys to Emotional Health. (SPA.). 1986. 2.29 (*1-56063-161-9*, 498123); pap. write for info. (*0-614-27073-1*) Editorial Unilit.

LLBA Linguistics & Language Behavior Abstracts: User's Reference Manual. 3rd ed. Michelle Blackman & Miriam Chall. 82p. 1987. ring bd. 47.50 (*0-930710-05-3*) Soc Abstracts.

LLC Maker: Form Your Own Limited Liability Company. Anthony Mancuso. LC 97-38253. 1997. write for info. (*0-87337-387-1*) Nolo com.

LLC Revolution: LLCs vs. S Corporations. Brent R. Armstrong. 144p. 1995. pap. write for info. (*0-9645073-0-7*) Hamilton Sq Pr.

***LLCS & LLPS: A Wisconsin Handbook.** rev. ed. Joseph W. Boucher et al. LC 99-19741. 1999. ring bd. 165.00 incl. disk (*1-57862-026-0*) State Bar WI.

Lle d'Arturo. Elsa Morante. (FRE.). 606p. 1979. pap. 15.95 (*0-7859-4110-X*, 2070370763) Fr & Eur.

Lledo Toys. Edward Force. LC 96-69940. (Illus.). 160p. 1996. pap. 19.95 (*0-7643-0013-X*) Schiffer.

Llega el Zorro. Jacques Van Hauten. 1996. pap. text 12.95 (*84-372-2192-7*) Santillana.

Llegada: Conica Con "Ficcion" Jose L. Gonzalez. LC 97-60203. 158p. 1997. pap. 11.95 (*0-929157-46-X*) Ediciones Huracan.

Llegamos a Creer - Came to Believe. Alcoholics Anonymous World Services, Inc., Staff. (SPA.). 1987. 2.50 (*0-916856-21-6*) AAWS.

Llegando a Cristo: Por Que Hago Lo Que Hago? Ed. by Dorothy Davis et al. (Happy Heart Ser.: No. 1-882283-09-0). (SPA., Illus.). 48p. (Orig.). pap. 3.00 (*1-882283-03-1*) D M Eichler.

Llegando Al Hogar: Invitacion... Compilado. (Serie Enfoque a la Familia - Focus on the Family Ser.).Tr. of Coming Home: Invitation.... (SPA.). 24p. 1991. 1.99 (*1-56063-052-3*, 497411) Editorial Unilit.

Llegando Al Hogar (Coming Home) Invitacion (Invitation)/Join God's Family. (SPA.). 1.79 (*0-685-74949-5*, 497411) Editorial Unilit.

Llenate de Luz, No de Miedo. Neil Anderson & Rich Miller.Tr. of Know Light, No Fear. (SPA.). 240p. (YA). 1996. 9.99 (*0-88113-432-5*, B052-4325) Caribe Betania.

Lleno del Espiritu! J. Hayford.Tr. of Spirit-Filled!. 4.99 (*0-7899-0309-1*, 497471) Editorial Unilit.

Leonard, the Llama That Lied. Susan Cameron. 32p. (Orig.). (J). (ps-1). 1997. pap. 6.95 (*0-8091-6636-4*) Paulist Pr.

Llewellyn Practical Guide to Astral Projection: The Out-of-Body Experience. 2nd ed. Melita Denning & Osborne Phillips. LC 79-88141. (Practical Guide to Personal Power Ser.). (Illus.). 252p. 1979. reprint ed. pap. 9.95 (*0-87542-181-4*) Llewellyn Pubns.

Llewellyn Practical Guide to Psychic Self-Defense & Well-Being. 2nd enl. ed. Melita Denning & Osborne Phillips. LC 83-80169. (Practical Guide to Personal Power Ser.). (Illus.). 308p. 1999. pap. 9.95 (*0-87542-190-3*) Llewellyn Pubns.

Llewellyn Practical Guide to the Development of Psychic Powers. 3rd ed. Melita Denning & Osborne Phillips. LC 86-20856. (Illus.). 272p. 2000. pap. 9.95 (*0-87542-191-1*) Llewellyn Pubns.

Llewellyn Practical Guide to the Magick of Sex: The Book of Creative Loving. Melita Denning & Osborne Phillips. 312p. 1982. 6.95 (*0-87542-192-X*) Llewellyn Pubns.

Llewellyn's Astrological Pocket Planner: Daily Ephemeris & Aspectarian 2000-2001. John Planner. 176p. 1999. pap. 6.95 (*1-56718-956-3*) Llewellyn Pubns.

Llewellyn's Magical Almanac 1994. Patricia Telesco. (Illus.). 304p. 1993. pap. 6.95 (*0-87542-915-7*) Llewellyn Pubns.

Llewellyn's Moon Sign Book, 1994: And Lunar Planning Guide. (Illus.). 480p. 1993. pap. 4.95 (*0-87542-910-6*) Llewellyn Pubns.

Llewellyn's 1998 Daily Planetary Guide. Ed. by Cynthia Ahlquist. 216p. (Orig.). 1997. spiral bd. 9.95 (*1-56718-934-2*) Llewellyn Pubns.

Llewellyn's 1998 Magical Almanac. Llewellyn Staff. Ed. by Cynthia Ahlquist. (Illus.). 384p. (Orig.). 1997. pap. 6.95 (*1-56718-935-0*) Llewellyn Pubns.

Llewellyn's 1998 Moon Sign Book. Gloria Star. Ed. by Cynthia Ahlquist. (Illus.). 468p. (Orig.). 1997. pap. 6.95 (*1-56718-933-4*) Llewellyn Pubns.

Llewellyn's 1998 Pocket Planner. Ed. by Roxanna Rejali. (Illus.). 208p. (Orig.). 1997. otabind 7.95 (*1-56718-936-9*) Llewellyn Pubns.

Llewellyn's 1998 Sun Sign Book. Gloria Star. Ed. by Roxanna Rejali. (Illus.). 480p. (Orig.). 1997. pap. 6.95 (*1-56718-932-6*) Llewellyn Pubns.

Llewellyn's 1999 Astrological Pocket Planner: Daily Ephemeris & Aspectarian, 1999-2000. Ed. by Roxanna Rejali. 176p. 1999. 7.95 (*1-56718-944-X*) Llewellyn Pubns.

Llewellyn's 1999 Magical Almanac. annuals Ed. by Cynthia Ahlquist. (Illus.). 345p. 1999. pap. 6.95 (*1-56718-940-7*) Llewellyn Pubns.

Llewellyn's Moon Sign Book & Gardening Almanac: 1999 Edition. annuals Cynthia Ahlquist. (Llewellyn's Moon Sign Book Ser.). (Illus.). 448p. 1998. pap. 6.95 (*1-56718-941-5*) Llewellyn Pubns.

Llewellyn's 1999 Sun Sign Book: Horoscopes for Everyone. annuals Gloria Star. Ed. by Corinne Kenner. (Illus.). 480p. 1999. pap. 6.95 (*1-56718-942-3*) Llewellyn Pubns.

Llewellyn's 1999 Witches' Datebook. Ed. by Cynthia Ahlquist. (Illus.). 144p. 1999. spiral bd. 9.95 (*1-56718-949-0*) Llewellyn Pubns.

Llewellyn's 1997 Astrological Pocket Planner: Daily Ephemeris & Aspectarian, 1996-1998. Llewellyn Staff. 208p. 1996. pap. text 7.95 (*1-56718-927-X*) Llewellyn Pubns.

Llewellyn's 1996 Astrological Pocket Planner: Daily Ephemeris & Aspectarian, 1995-1997. 208p. 1995. otabind 7.95 (*1-56718-920-2*) Llewellyn Pubns.

Llewellyn's 1996 Magical Almanac. Edain McCoy et al. (Illus.). 368p. (Orig.). 1995. pap. text 6.95 (*1-56718-914-8*) Llewellyn Pubns.

Llewellyn's 1996 Moon Sign Book & Lunar Planning Guide. (Illus.). 480p. 1995. pap. text 6.95 (*1-56718-912-1*) Llewellyn Pubns.

Llewellyn's 1996 Organic Gardening Almanac: Gardening by the Moon. (Illus.). 352p. 1995. pap. text 6.95 (*1-56718-915-6*) Llewellyn Pubns.

Llewellyn's 1996 Daily Planetary Guide: The Astrologer's Datebook. (Illus.). 288p. 1995. spiral bd. 9.95 (*1-56718-910-5*) Llewellyn Pubns.

Llewellyn's Sun Sign Book, 1995. Gloria Star. (Illus.). 448p. 1994. pap. 4.99 (*1-56718-901-6*) Llewellyn Pubns.

Llewellyn's Sun Sign Book 1994: Horoscopes for Every Sign. Gloria Star. (Illus.). 400p. 1993. pap. 4.95 (*0-87542-911-4*) Llewellyn Pubns.

Llewellyn's 2000 Herbal Almanac. annuals Contrib. by Gretchen Lawlor et al. (Illus.). 336p. 1999. pap. 6.95 (*1-56718-961-X*) Llewellyn Pubns.

Llewellyn's 2000 Magical Almanac. annuals Contrib. by Raymond Buckland et al. (Illus.). 384p. 1999. pap. 6.95 (*1-56718-950-4*) Llewellyn Pubns.

Llewellyn's 2000 Moon Sign Book: And Gardening Almanac. annuals Contrib. by Gloria Star et al. LC 87-2140. (Illus.). 480p. 1999. pap. 6.95 (*1-56718-953-9*) Llewellyn Pubns.

***Moon Sign Book 2001.** (Illus.). 480p. 2000. pap. 7.95 (*1-56718-964-4*) Llewellyn Pubns.

Llewellyn's 2000 Sun Sign Book: Horoscopes for Everyone. annuals Contrib. by Alice DeVille et al. (Illus.). 480p. 1999. pap. 6.95 (*1-56718-954-7*, K-954-7) Llewellyn Pubns.

Llewellyn's Witches' Datebook 2000. Ed. by Cynthia Ahlquist. 144p. 1999. pap. 9.95 (*1-56718-952-0*) Llewellyn Pubns.

Llewelyn, Maskelyne, Talbot: A Family Circle Sun Pictures Catalogue Two. Text by Larry J. Schaaf. (Illus.). 80p. 1986. pap. 30.00 (*1-892535-02-5*) H P Kraus Jr.

Llf Mngrl Accntg, 2e. 2nd ed. Cecily A. Raiborn. (SWC-Accounting). 1995. ring bd. 46.50 (*0-314-07591-7*) West Pub.

LLLI Leader's Handbook. rev. ed. Ed. by Dor Sachetti. LC 98-65508. 308p. 1998. spiral bd. 20.00 (*0-912500-49-2*) La Leche.

***Llora, Alegria.** Cuca Canals. 1999. 21.95 (*84-08-02947-9*) Planeta Edit.

Llorens Artigas: Catalogo de Obra. Francesc Miralles. (Grandes Monografias). (ENG & SPA., Illus.). 432p. 1993. 600.00 (*84-343-0701-4*) Elliots Bks.

Lloro por la Tierra. Mildred D. Taylor. 1992. 14.05 (*0-606-10478-X*, Pub. by Turtleback) Demco.

Llorona. Carmen Toscano. (SPA.). 5.99 (*968-16-1883-1*, Pub. by Fondo) Continental Bk.

Llorona: The Weeping Woman. Joe Hayes. 32p. (J). 1986. pap. 8.95 incl. audio (*0-938317-04-0*) Cinco Puntos.

Llorona: The Weeping Woman. Joe Hayes. (Illus.). 32p. (J). (gr. 1-9). 1998. pap. 5.95 (*0-938317-02-4*) Cinco Puntos.

Llorona Llora. Silvia Gonzalez. 19p. (YA). (gr. 9 up). 1996. pap. 3.50 (*0-87129-552-0*, L82) Dramatic Pub.

Llovizna de Palabras. Kidship Associates Staff. (SPA., Illus.). 114p. pap. text 2.50 (*1-878742-03-5*) Kidship Assoc.

Lloyd: Genealogical Notes Relating to the Families of Lloyd, Pemberton, Hutchinson, Hudson & Parke. J. P. Parke & T. Ward. Ed. by T. A. Glenn. 89p. 1992. reprint ed. pap. 18.00 (*0-8328-2679-0*); reprint ed. lib. bdg. 28.00 (*0-8328-2678-2*) Higginson Bk Co.

Lloyd: What Happened. Stanley Bing. 432p. 1999. pap. 15.00 (*0-375-70564-3*) Vin Bks.

Lloyd Alexander. Jill P. May. (Twayne's United States Authors Ser.: No. 576). 200p. 1991. 21.95 (*0-8057-7622-2*, Twyne) Mac Lib Ref.

Lloyd Alexander. Jill C. Wheeler. LC 97-10223. (Tribute to the Young at Heart Ser.). (Illus.). 32p. (J). 1997. lib. bdg. 14.95 (*1-56239-789-3*) ABDO Pub Co.

Lloyd Alexander: A Bio-Bibliography, 1. James S. Jacobs & Michael O. Tunnell. LC 90-24515. (Bio-Bibliographies in American Literature Ser.: No. 1). 160p. 1991. lib. bdg. 49.95 (*0-313-26586-0*, JLL/, Greenwood Pr) Greenwood.

Lloyd Foltz (1897-1990) - A Retrospective: An Exhibition of Prints, Drawings & Paintings by Prairie Print Maker Lloyd Foltz. Novelene G. Ross. (Illus.). 6p. (Orig.). 1992. pap. write for info. (*0-939324-45-8*) Wichita Art Mus.

Lloyd George. M. Gilbert. 1968. 8.95 (*0-13-535961-X*, Spectrum IN) Macmillan Gen Ref.

Lloyd George. M. Gilbert. 1968. pap. 1.95 (*0-685-03920-X*) P-H.

Lloyd George. Ian Packer. LC 98-21674. 144p. 1998. text 55.00 (*0-312-21707-2*) St Martin.

Lloyd George. Martin Pugh. 1989. text 46.25 (*0-582-02387-4*, Pub. by Addison-Wesley) Longman.

Lloyd George. Martin Pugh. (Illus.). 206p. (C). 1988. pap. text 23.95 (*0-582-55268-0*, 79762) Longman.

Lloyd George. Chris Wrigley. LC 91-44031. (Historical Association Studies). 170p. 1992. pap. 15.95 (*0-631-16608-4*) Blackwell Pubs.

Lloyd George: Backbencher. W. R. George. 484p. (C). 1983. pap. 20.00 (*0-85088-719-4*, Pub. by Gomer Pr) St Mut.

Lloyd George: Twelve Essays. Taylor. 416p. 1994. 75.95 (*0-7512-0137-5*) Ashgate Pub Co.

Lloyd George & Churchill: How Friendship Changed Politics. Marvin Rintala. LC 94-27342. 1994. 27.95 (*1-56833-031-6*) Madison Bks UPA.

Lloyd George & Foreign Policy Vol. 1: The Education of a Statesman, 1890-1916. Michael G. Fry. LC 77-377211. 330p. reprint ed. pap. 102.30 (*0-7837-1148-4*, 204167700001) Bks Demand.

Lloyd George & the Generals. David R. Woodward. LC 81-72060. (Illus.). 368p. 1983. 45.00 (*0-87413-211-8*) U Delaware Pr.

Lloyd George: The Goat in the Wilderness. Campbell. 408p. 1993. 69.95 (*0-7512-0138-3*) Ashgate Pub Co.

Lloyd George Was My Father. Olwen C. Evans & Mary Garner. 173p. (C). 1985. 20.00 (*0-86383-112-5*, Pub. by Gomer Pr) St Mut.

Lloyd Hamrol: Works, Projects, Proposals. Henry Hopkins. LC 85-82589. (Illus.). 56p. (Orig.). 1986. pap. 5.00 (*0-936429-02-X*) LA Municipal Art.

Lloyd (Loyd) Family of Putnam County, Missouri. unabridged ed. Gary G. Lloyd. LC 96-75998. (Illus.). 285p. (Orig.). 1996. pap. 23.00 (*0-9622972-4-0*) G G Lloyd.

Lloyd Purves on Closing Sales. Lloyd Purves. 1978. 4.95 (*0-13-539130-X*, Parker Publishing Co) P-H.

Lloyd Rees: An Artist Remembers. Lloyd Rees. (Illus.). 160p. 1987. text 30.00 (*0-947131-08-6*) Gordon & Breach.

Lloyd Rees: The Last Twenty Years. R. Free. (Illus.). 176p. 1990. text 30.00 (*0-947131-34-5*) Gordon & Breach.

Lloyd Shaw Foundation Recreational Dance Program. Don Armstrong. 133p. (C). 1985. pap. text 20.00 (*0-915213-01-X*) L Shaw Found.

Lloyd Tyler: Folk Artist, Decoy Maker. Henry H. Stansbury. LC 95-70930. (Illus.). 112p. 1995. 40.00 (*0-9631815-5-6*) Decoy Mag.

An Asterisk (*) at the beginning of an entry indicates that the title is appearing for the first time.

Lloyd Ullberg: A Structuralist's Overview, Catalogue. Ed. by Robert Koch Gallery, Inc. Staff. (Illus.). 16p. 1988. 10.00 (*0-929196-00-7*) R Koch Gallery.
Lloyd Wright: The Architecture of Frank Lloyd Wright, Jr. Lloyd Wright. LC 98-25052. (Illus.). 276p. 1998. 75.00 (*0-8109-3996-7*, Pub. by Abrams) Time Warner.
Lloyd Wright Architect: 20th Century Architecture in an Organic Exhibition. David Gebhard & Harriette Von Breton. LC 98-12697. (California Architects & Architecture Ser.). 101p. 1998. pap. 27.50 (*0-940512-10-6*) Hennessey.
Lloyd's Acts, Byelaws & Regulations. ring bd. 450.00 (*1-85044-400-5*) LLP.
Lloyd's & the London Insurance Market, 1994. (Commercial Law & Practice Course Handbook Ser.). 312p. 1994. pap. 99.00 (*0-614-17141-5*, A4-4459) PLI.
Lloyd's & the London Insurance Market, 1996: How Recent Developments Will Affect Your Clients. (Commercial Law & Practice Course Handbook Ser.). Date not set. pap. 99.00 (*0-614-17153-9*, A4-4483) PLI.
Lloyd's at Home. Vanessa Harding & Priscilla Metcalf. (Illus.). 1986. 60.00 (*1-85044-114-6*) LLP.
Lloyd's Bank Annual Review: Privatization & Ownership. Ed. by Christopher Johnson. 200p. 1988. text 42.50 (*0-86187-974-0*) St Martin.
Lloyd's Bank Annual Review: The Market on Trial, Vol. II. Ed. by Christopher Johnson. 200p. 1989. text 45.00 (*0-86187-704-7*) St Martin.
Lloyds Bank Annual Review Vol. 5: Why Inflation? Ed. by Patrick Foley. 224p. 1992. text 59.00 (*1-85567-011-9*) St Martin.
Lloyds Bank, 1918-1969. J. R. Winton. (Illus.). 1982. 37.50 (*0-19-920125-0*) OUP.
Lloyd's Broker. Gordon W. Shaw. 400p. 1995. 140.00 (*1-85044-586-9*) LLP.
Lloyd's Building: London 1986, Richard Rogers Partnership. Kenneth Powell. LC 95-150971. (Architecture in Detail Ser.). (Illus.). 60p. (C). 1994. pap. 29.95 (*0-7148-3006-2*, Pub. by Phaidon Press) Phaidon Pr.
Lloyd's Church Musicians Directory. Ed. by Frederick E. Lloyd. LC 72-1733. reprint ed. 37.50 (*0-404-08319-6*) AMS Pr.
Lloyd's Cruise Industry Direct 1996. Lloyd's of London Press Staff. (Illus.). 104p. 1996. pap. 90.00 (*1-85044-478-1*) LLP.
Lloyd's Introduction to Jurisprudence. 6th ed. Lloyd & M. C. Freeman. 1994. pap. text 55.00 (*0-421-45680-9*, Pub. by Sweet & Maxwll) Gaunt.
Lloyd's Introductory Test Textbook. Andrea H. Bondi & Colin A. Hudson. 104p. 1986. 110.00 (*0-948691-05-0*, Pub. by Witherby & Co) St Mut.
Lloyd's Law Reports Citator & Subject Index, 1987-1994: Including the Supplement to Lloyd's Law Reports Consolidated Subject Index, Vols. 1-8. 1995. pap. 60.00 (*1-85044-469-2*) LLP.
Lloyd's Law Reports Citator, 1919-1986. Lloyd's of London Press Staff. 1988. 300.00 (*1-85044-170-7*) LLP.
Lloyd's Law Reports Subject Index, 1919-1986. Lloyd's of London Press Staff. 1988. 445.00 (*1-85044-171-5*) LLP.
Lloyd's Maritime & Commercial Law Quarterly: Consolidated Contents & Index, 1974-1992. 1992. 95.00 (*1-85044-335-1*) LLP.
Lloyd's Maritime & Commercial Law Quarterly Index, 1974-1994. Francis Rose. 1995. 180.00 (*1-85044-804-3*) LLP.
Lloyd's Maritime Atlas. 18th ed. 1995. 90.00 (*1-85044-226-6*) LLP.
LLoyd's Maritime Atlas. 18th rev. ed. (Illus.). 1995. 90.00 (*1-85978-004-0*) LLP.
Lloyd's Maritime Law Newsletter Index & Bound Volume. 1696p. 1994. write for info. (*1-85044-809-4*) LLP.
Lloyd's Market Handbook. ring bd. 415.00 (*1-85044-878-7*) LLP.
Lloyd's Market Practice. Robert H. Brown & John Wormell. 110p. (C). 1992. 110.00 (*1-85609-023-X*, Pub. by Witherby & Co) St Mut.
Lloyd's Market Results & Prospects 1998. Association of Lloyd's Members. 467p. 1998. pap. 225.00 (*0-9533282-0-1*, Pub. by Woodhead Pubng) Am Educ Systs.
Lloyd's Market Yearbook, 1994-1995. (DYP Textbook Ser.). 600p. 250.00 (*1-870255-12-7*) LLP.
Lloyd's Nautical Year Book 1996. Lloyd's of London Press Staff. 1995. 90.00 (*1-85044-421-8*) LLP.
Lloyd's of London. Joanne Doroshow & Adrian J. Wilkes. 154p. 1988. 10.00 (*0-936758-22-8*) Ctr Responsive Law.
Lloyd's of London: A Study in Individualism. D. E. Gibb. 1957. 50.00 (*1-85044-156-1*) LLP.
Lloyd's of London: An Illustrated History. 3rd rev. ed. R. Flower & M. Wynn Jones. (Illus.). 1987. 50.00 (*0-904093-96-4*) LLP.
Lloyd's Ports of the World 1995. Lloyd's of London Press, Inc. Staff. 1995. 310.00 (*1-85044-325-4*) LLP.
Lloyd's Ports of the World 1995: Directory. (Illus.). 305.00 (*1-85044-559-1*) LLP.
Lloyd's Shipping Connections 1996. Lloyd's of London Press Staff. 1995. 60.00 (*1-85044-493-5*) LLP.
Lloyd's Shipping Connections 1996: Directory. pap. 65.00 (*1-85978-001-6*) LLP.
***Lloyd's Steamboat Directory & Disasters on the Western Waters.** James T. Lloyd. Ed. by Gregory G. Poole. (Illus.). 360p. 2000. reprint ed. pap. 22.00 (*0-9650513-4-X*) Land Yacht Pr.
Lloyd's Survey Handbook. 6th ed. Lloyd's of London Press, Inc. Staff. 337p. 1991. 89.00 (*1-85044-395-5*) LLP.
Lloyd's War Losses - The First World War, 1919-1918. Lloyd's of London Press Staff. 1990. 170.00 (*1-85044-314-9*) LLP.
Lloyd's War Losses - The Second World War, 1939-1945. Lloyd's of London Press Staff. 1989. 170.00 (*1-85044-217-7*) LLP.
Lloyd's War Losses - the Second World War, 1939-1945 Vol. II: Statistics; Vessels Disappeared - Without Trace, Badly Damages; Naval Losses; British, Allied & Neutral Warship Losses; Vessels Sunk by Mines after the War. 1991. 150.00 (*1-85044-412-9*) LLP.
LLRW Disposal Facility Siting: Success & Failure in Six Countries. Anna Vari et al. LC 94-1456. (Technology, Risk & Society Ser.). 328p. 1994. text 145.50 (*0-7923-2743-8*) Kluwer Academic.
Llueve! Llueve! - Rain! Rain! Mills. (Libros Ventanitas - Windows Bks.). (SPA.). (J). 1995. write for info. (*1-56063-832-X*) Editorial Unilit.
Lluis Domenech I. Montaner: Palsu de la Musica Catalana, Barcelona. Manfred Sack. (Opus Ser.: Vol. 8). (ENG & GER.). 1995. 42.00 (*3-930698-08-0*, Pub. by E J Wasmuth) Dist Art Pubs.
Lluvia de Oro: Rain of Gold. Victor Villasenor. 608p. 1996. pap. 14.95 (*0-385-31516-3*, Delta Trade) Dell.
Lluvia de Palabras. Kidship Associates Staff. (SPA., Illus.). 109p. (J). (gr. 1-3). 1988. pap. text 2.00 (*1-878742-00-0*) Kidship Assoc.
Lluvia de Palabras. rev. ed. Kidship Associates Staff. (SPA., Illus.). 110p. (J). (gr. 2-3). 1988. pap. text 3.00 (*1-878742-07-8*) Kidship Assoc.
***Lluvia en el desierto (Rain in the Desert)** Marjorie Agosin. Tr. by Celeste Kostopulos-Cooperman. (SPA & ENG.). 112p. 1999. pap. 15.00 (*1-890932-09-4*) Sherman Asher Pub.
Llyn Foulkes: Between a Rock & a Hard Place. Lynn Foulkes & Rosetta Brooks. Ed. by Sue Hanger. LC 95-30718. (Illus.). 112p. 1995. pap. 26.00 (*0-911291-24-5*, Pub. by Fellows Cont Art) RAM Publications.
Llyr Brwtnn see Armorica: The National Epic of America
***Llywelyn Ap Gruffudd: Prince of Wales.** J. Beverley Smith. LC 99-203186. 664p. 1999. 55.00 (*0-7083-1474-0*, Pub. by Univ Wales Pr) Paul & Co Pubs.
L/M Basic Conversational French. 8th ed. Harris. (C). 1987. pap. text, lab manual ed. 40.00 (*0-03-004364-6*) Harcourt Coll Pubs.
***L.M. Universe: Origins & Evolution.** 2nd ed. Brownsberger Snow. 2001. pap. 23.00 (*0-534-37302-X*) Thomson Learn.
LMB Author's Guide. Roy G. Biv. (Illus.). 57p. 1998. 5.95 (*1-57914-028-9*) Campbell-Smith.
***LMDS - Local Multipoint Distribution Service.** Clint Smith. (Professional Telecom Ser.). 2000. pap. text 59.95 (*0-07-136254-1*) McGraw.
LME Metals Trading Manual. P. D. Crabbe. 288p. 1998. 120.00 (*1-85573-347-1*, Pub. by Woodhead Pubng) Am Educ Systs.
Lmno P. James Bernhard. 95p. (Orig.). 1995. pap. 10.00 (*0-944920-20-9*) Bellowing Ark Pr.
***LMNOP: And All the Letters A to Z.** Howard Schrager. (Illus.). (J). (gr. k-4). 1999. 19.95 (*0-9644846-0-9*) LemonTree Pr.
LMTO Method. H. L. Skriver. (Solid-State Sciences Ser.: Vol. 41). (Illus.). 295p. 1983. 78.95 (*0-387-11519-6*) Spr-Verlag.
LNG Information Book, 1973. 91p. pap. 7.00 (*0-318-12647-8*, X00673) Am Gas Assn.
LNG Plant Design & Construction Guide. 124p. 1979. 6.00 (*0-318-12648-6*, X00479) Am Gas Assn.
***LNG Receiving & Regasification Terminals: An Overview of Design, Operation & Project Development.** Ram R. Tarakad. (Illus.). x, 102p. 2000. pap. 1950.00 (*0-615-11567-5*) Zeus Devel.
Lnu & Indians We're Called: Poems of Rita Joe. Rita Joe. 72p. 1994. pap. 9.95 (*0-921556-22-5*, Pub. by Gynergy-Ragweed) U of Toronto Pr.
***Lo Afro y la Plurinacionalidad: El Caso Ecuatoriano Visto Desde su Literatura.** (Romance Monographs: No. 54). 214p. 1999. pap. 29.00 (*1-889441-04-X*) Romance.
Lo Afronegroide en el Cuento Puertorriqueno. Rafael Falcon. LC 93-72430. (Coleccion Ebano y Canela). (SPA.). 82p. (Orig.). 1993. pap. 12.00 (*0-89729-691-5*) Ediciones.
Lo Americano en el Teatro de Sor Juana Ines de la Cruz. Maria E. Perez. 1975. 14.00 (*0-88303-020-9*); pap. 11.00 (*0-685-73221-5*) E Torres & Sons.
***Lo & Behold: Poems from Hollywood.** Mark Dunster. 11p. 1999. pap. 5.00 (*0-89642-942-3*) Linden Pubs.
Lo Chino en el Habla Cubana. Beatriz Varela. LC 79-54025. (SPA., Illus.). 64p. (Orig.). 1980. pap. 6.95 (*0-89729-233-2*) Ediciones.
Lo Comun Hecho Santo. N. Anderson.Tr. of Common Made Holy. (SPA.). 13.99 (*0-7899-0276-1*, 497393) Editorial Unilit.
Lo del Corazon: A Survey Exhibition. Tr. of Heartbeat of a Culture. 24p. 1986. 10.00 (*0-9605194-1-6*) Mexican Museum.
Lo Efimero y lo Eterno. Ratibor-Ray M. Jurjevich. 1997. pap. 2.95 (*950-724-464-6*) Lumen ARG.
***Lo Esencial en Anatomia.** Phillip Ameerally. (C). 1998. text 14.09 (*84-8174-363-1*) Mosby Inc.
***Lo Esencial en Aparato Digesti.** Cheshire. (C). 1998. text 14.09 (*84-8174-365-8*) Mosby Inc.
Lo Esencial en el Combate de Incendios. 444p. Date not set. 80.00 (*0-614-11242-7*) Inter-Am Safety.
***Lo Esencial en Sistema Nervios.** Daniel Lasserson. (C). 1998. text 14.09 (*84-8174-367-4*) Mosby Inc.
***Lo Hice Bien!** Susan F. Tierno. Tr. by Ana M. Alvarado. (Think-Kids Book Collection).Tr. of I Did My Best Ser.. (SPA., Illus.). 16p. (J). 2000. pap. 2.95 (*1-58237-040-0*) Creat Think.
***Lo Irracional En la Literatura: Prologo Luis A. Acosta.** Manuel M. Aleman. Ed. by Eva P. Membrives. (SPA.). 252p. 1999. 39.95 (*3-906762-29-7*) P Lang Pubng.
***Lo Mein.** Robert Eringer. LC 99-68979. 192p. 2000. 19.95 (*1-929175-14-0*, Corinthian Bks); pap. 14.95 (*1-929175-22-1*, Corinthian Bks) Cote Lit Grp.
Lo Mejor de la Cocina Mexicana. Mexicanos Editores Staff. (SPA.). 1997. pap. text 5.98 (*968-15-0844-0*) Ed Mex.
Lo Mejor de la Literatura Para Ninos (The Best of Literature for Children) Norma G. Castro & Cecilia A. Soberon. (Illus.). 312p. (J). 1998. pap. 16.95 (*970-03-0823-5*) Hispanic Bk Dist.
Lo Mejor de la Vida Sexual de la Pareja. Frank Calderon.Tr. of Best of the Sexual Life of Couples. (SPA.). 192p. 1998. pap. 5.95 (*0-939193-27-2*) Edit Concepts.
***Lo Mejor Que Hago.** Karen Rogers. Tr. by Ana M. Alvarado. (Think-Kids Book Collection).Tr. of What I Do Best!. (SPA., Illus.). 16p. (J). 2000. pap. 2.95 (*1-58237-052-4*) Creat Think.
Lo, Michael. Grace Livingston Hill. 369p. 1975. reprint ed. lib. bdg. 26.95 (*0-89190-014-4*, Rivercity Pr) Amereon Ltd.
Lo, Michael. Grace Livingston Hill. 1990. reprint ed. lib. bdg. 22.95 (*0-89968-526-9*) Buccaneer Bks.
Lo Michael, No. 74. Grace Livingston Hill. (Grace Livingston Hill Ser.: Vol. 74). 328p. 1994. mass mkt. 5.99 (*0-8423-2066-0*) Tyndale Hse.
Lo Primero. Francisco Palafox.Tr. of First One. (SPA.). 64p. 1995. 6.99 (*0-88113-345-0*, B088-3450) Caribe Betania.
Lo Que Creen los Cristianos. Blanchi.Tr. of What Christians Believe?. (SPA.). 1994. pap. write for info. (*0-614-27075-8*) Editorial Unilit.
Lo Que Creen los Cristianos. John Blanchi. (Serie Guia - Bible Manuals Ser.).Tr. of What Christians Believe. (SPA.). 128p. 1986. pap. 5.99 (*0-8423-6269-X*, 490201) Editorial Unilit.
Lo Que Deseo Mis Padres Sepan de Sexualidad. Josh McDowell.Tr. of What I Wish Parents Knew about Sexuality. (SPA.). 1994. pap. 5.99 (*0-8423-6523-0*, 498401) Editorial Unilit.
Lo Que Deseo Que Mis Padres Sepan Acerca de Mi Sexualidad: Los Jovenes Hablan. Josh McDowell. Tr. by Dardo Bruchez from ENG. (SPA.). 210p. (Orig.). 1988. pap. 4.95 (*0-945792-03-4*) Editorial Unilit.
Lo Que Dicen de los Adolescentes de Drogas y el Alcohol. Chris Lutes.Tr. of What Teenagers Are Saying about Drugs & Alcohol. (SPA.). 250p. 1995. pap. 7.99 (*1-56063-088-4*, 490236) Editorial Unilit.
Lo Que Dices, Recibes. D. Gossett.Tr. of What You Say Is What You Get. (SPA.). 208p. 1978. pap. 5.99 (*0-8297-0808-1*) Vida Pubs.
Lo Que Dios Junto. K. Silva.Tr. of What God Has Joined Together. (SPA.). 100. pap. 5.99 (*1-56063-475-8*, 550118) Editorial Unilit.
Lo Que el Diablo No Quiere Que Sepas. R. Comfort.Tr. of Hell's Best Kept Secret. (SPA.). 224p. 1993. pap. 6.99 (*0-8297-0307-1*) Vida Pubs.
Lo Que el Trabajo Requiere de Las Escuelas: Informe de la Comision Scans para America 2000. Government Printing Office Staff. 72p. 1992. pap. 3.50 (*0-16-038243-2*) USGPO.
Lo Que el Varon Debe Ser y Como Debe Amar. Leon.Tr. of What a Man Should Be & How He Should Love. (SPA.). 44p. 1995. 2.29 (*1-56063-687-4*, 496222) Editorial Unilit.
Lo Que Hace Dios Cuando Hombre. William C. Peel. (SPA.). 1998. pap. 5.99 (*0-8297-0469-8*) Vida Pubs.
Lo Que le Paso al Espantapajaro. LC 88-81086. (Coleccion Caniqui). (SPA.). 63p. (Orig.). 1988. pap. 7.95 (*0-89729-487-4*) Ediciones.
Lo Que los Jovenes Deben Saber Acerca de las Drogas: What Youth Should Know about Drugs. Guillermo H. Perez. 80p. 1977. reprint ed. pap. 3.99 (*0-311-46070-4*) Casa Bautista.
Lo Que Los Padres Ignoran. Laurie John. Tr. by Maruja Del Pozo. (Sweet Valley University Ser.: No. 3).Tr. of What Your Parents Don't Know.... (YA). (gr. 7 up). 1994. 15.60 (*0-606-10531-X*, Pub. by Turtleback) Demco.
Lo Que No Se Ha Dicho. Jesus J. Barquet et al. Ed. & Intro. by Pedro R. Monge-Rafuls. LC 94-67316. (Literature/Conversation Ser.: Vol. IV). (ENG & SPA.). 341p. 1994. pap. 20.00 (*0-9625127-3-7*) Ollantay Pr.
Lo Que Nos Dice la Biblica. Henrietta C. Mears.Tr. of What the Bible Is All About. (SPA.). 624p. 1980. 14.99 (*0-8297-0485-X*) Vida Pubs.
***Lo Que Nos Susura el Viento.** XOKONOSCHTLTL. (SPA.). 1998. pap. text 8.95 (*84-01-01142-6*) Plaza.
***Lo Que Nos Susurra el Viento: La Sabiduria de los Aztecas.** (SPA.). 130p. 1998. 17.95 (*84-01-01144-2*, Pub. by Plaza) Lectorum Pubns.
Lo Que Toda Madre Necesita. E. Morgan.Tr. of What Every Mom Needs. (SPA.). 1996. pap. 9.99 (*0-8297-0616-X*) Vida Pubs.
***Lo Que Todo Catolico Debe Preguntar.** James G. McCarthy. (SPA.). 2000. pap. 3.99 (*0-88113-561-5*) Caribe Betania.
Lo Que Usted Debe Saber Sobre el Catecismo de la Iglesia Catolica. Charlene Altemose. LC 94-78007. (SPA.). 64p. (Orig.). 1994. pap. 1.95 (*0-89243-695-6*) Liguori Pubns.
Lo Que Usted Debe Saber Sobre los Sacramentos. Charlene Altemose. LC 95-80150. (SPA.). 64p. 1995. pap. 3.95 (*0-89243-857-6*) Liguori Pubns.
Lo Que Usted Necesita Saber Sobre la Nueva Era. Cesar Manzanares. (Serie Guia de Bolsillo - Pocket Guides Ser.).Tr. of What You Need to Know about the New Age. (SPA.). 101p. 1991. pap. 2.79 (*1-56063-163-5*, 498071) Editorial Unilit.
Lo Scettro di Ottokar. Herge. (ITA., Illus.). 62p. (J). pap. 19.95 (*0-8288-5061-5*) Fr & Eur.
Lo Siento. (Serie Pensamientos de Vida - Thoughts of Life Ser.: Vol. 3).Tr. of Sorry to Hear. (SPA.). 24p. 1986. pap. 1.25 (*0-8423-6298-3*, 497114) Editorial Unilit.
Lo Siento. Gordon Stowell. (Serie Pescaditos - Fish Book Ser.).Tr. of I'm Sorry. (SPA.). 16p. 1987. pap. write for info. (*0-614-27074-X*) Editorial Unilit.
Lo Stivale Sua Ling 2e. 2nd ed. SOTTILE. 1994. 46.00 (*0-07-059783-9*) McGraw.
Lo Symbolique et le Monde Medivol see Symbolism & the Medieval World
Lo! the Bridegroom. Peter C. Krey. LC 66-20393. 1966. 3.95 (*0-686-05043-6*) St Thomas.
Lo T'Kallel Cheresh V'Lifnay Iver lo Titen Michshol see Mitzvah of the Month
Lo-to Hsiang Tzu see Rickshaw: The Novel Lo-t'o hsiang Tzu
Lo Zigarelli 1995 Vocabulario Della Ligua Italiana. 12th ed. Nicola Zingarelli. (ITA.). 2144p. 1994. lib. bdg. 195.00 (*0-8288-3335-4*, F9070) Fr & Eur.
Lo Zingarelli: Vocabolario della Lingua Italiana. Ed. by Nicola Zingarelli. 2145p. 2000. 128.00 (*88-08-02908-5*) S F Vanni.
Lo Zingarelli 1994: Vocabolario Della Lingua Italiana de Nicola Zingarelli. 12th ed. Ed. by Miro Dogliotti & Luigi Rosiello. (Illus.). 2144p. 1994. 85.00 (*88-08-12600-5*) OUP.
Loa-Tzu's Treatise on the Response of the Tao. Li Ying-Chang. 1994. pap. 19.95 (*0-7619-8998-6*) Sage.
Loach on Loach. Ken Loach. Ed. by Graham Fuller. (Illus.). 160p. 1999. 16.00 (*0-571-17918-5*) Faber & Faber.
Load & Resistance Factor Design: Manual for Engineered Wood Construction, 10 vols. (Illus.). 700p. 1996. pap. 99.00 (*0-935018-97-2*, T80) Forest Prod.
Load & Resistance Factor Design of W-Shapes Encased in Concrete. Lawrence G. Griffis. 312p. 1992. 20.00 (*0-685-66657-3*, D806) Am Inst Steel Construct.
Load & Speed Conditions of Wormgear Drives. E. Dukes. (Technical Papers: Vol. P60). (Illus.). 16p. 1929. pap. text 30.00 (*1-55589-419-4*) AGMA.
Load & Speed Conditions of Wormgear Drives, Pt. 2. E. Dukes. (Technical Papers: Vol. P61). (Illus.). 16p. 1930. pap. text 30.00 (*1-55589-420-8*) AGMA.
Load Balancing: An Automated Learning Approach. Pankaj Mehra & Benjamin W. Wah. LC 94-46515. 152p. 1995. text 28.00 (*981-02-2135-5*) World Scientific Pub.
Load Balancing in Parallel Computers: Theory & Practice. Chengzhong Xu. (Kluwer International Series in Engineering & Computer Science). 232p. (C). 1996. text 112.00 (*0-7923-9819-X*) Kluwer Academic.
Load-Bearing Composite Materials. Michael R. Piggott. 1980. text 134.00 (*0-08-024230-8*, Pub. by Pergamon Repr) Franklin.
Load Capacity Evaluation of Existing Bridges. (National Cooperative Highway Research Program Report Ser.: No. 301). 104p. 1987. 11.60 (*0-309-04570-3*, NR301) Transport Res Bd.
Load Carrying Capacity of Bath Nitrided (Tufftrided) Gears. D. Roempler. (Technical Papers: Vol. P109.18). (Illus.). 39p. 1966. pap. text 30.00 (*1-55589-182-9*) AGMA.
Load Carrying Capacity of Bevel Gears According to DIN Standard. Hans Winter & M. Paul. (1985 Fall Technical Meeting Ser.: Vol. 85FTM1). 13p. 1985. pap. text 30.00 (*1-55589-094-6*) AGMA.
Load Carrying Capacity of Nitrided Gears. L. Albertin et al. (Nineteen Ninety-Four Fall Technical Meeting Ser.: Vol. 94FTM4). (Illus.). 10p. 1994. pap. text 30.00 (*1-55589-638-3*) AGMA.
Load Cell Terminology & Test Procedure Recommendations. 20p. 1985. 4.00 (*0-317-01358-0*) Scale Mfrs.
Load Characteristics Research Manual. rev. ed. 139p. 1977. pap. 10.00 (*0-318-12649-4*, F01077) Am Gas Assn.
Load Classification & Service Factors for Flexible Couplings. AGMA Technical Committee. (AGMA Standard Ser.: Vol. 922-A96). (Illus.). 6p. 1996. pap. text 38.00 (*1-55589-680-4*) AGMA.
Load Distribution & Connection Design for Precast Stemmed Multibeam Bridge Superstructures. (National Cooperative Highway Research Program Report Ser.: No. 287). 137p. 1987. 11.80 (*0-309-04021-3*, NR287) Transport Res Bd.
Load Distribution Factor As Applied to High Speed & Wide Face Helical Gears. F. A. Thoma. (Technical Papers: Vol. P229.10). (Illus.). 9p. 1965. pap. text 30.00 (*1-55589-277-9*) AGMA.
Load Distribution Factors in Proposed AGMA & ISO Rating Procedures. G. C. Mudd & E. J. Myers. (Technical Papers: Vol. P219.14). (Illus.). 21p. 1981. pap. text 30.00 (*1-55589-257-4*) AGMA.
Load Distribution Test on Precast Hollow Core Slabs with Openings. (PCI Journal Reprints Ser.). 13p. 1985. pap. 12.00 (*0-318-19745-6*, JR120) P-PCI.
***Load 'em up Trucks.** Debora Pearson. (Mighty Wheels Ser.). (Illus.). 24p. (J). (ps-k). 1999. lib. bdg. 15.95 (*1-55037-593-8*, Pub. by Annick Pr) Firefly Bks Ltd.
Load 'em up Trucks. Debora Pearson. (Mighty Wheels Ser.). (Illus.). 24p. (J). (ps-3). 1999. pap. 5.95 (*1-55037-592-X*, Pub. by Annick Pr) Firefly Bks Ltd.
Load Frequency Control & Operation. (Principles of Steam Generation Ser.: Module 19). (Illus.). 60p. 1982. spiral bd. 20.00 (*0-87683-269-9*) GP Courseware.
Load Leveling: Proceedings of the Symposium. Symposium on Load Leveling Staff. Ed. by N. P. Yao & J. Robert Selman. LC 77-79772. (Electrochemical Society Proceedings Ser.: Vol. 77-4). (Illus.). 409p. 1977. pap. 126.80 (*0-7837-8994-7*, 205925900002) Bks Demand.
Load Leveling & Energy Conservation in Industrial Processes: Proceedings of the Symposium Held 1986, Boston, MA. Symposium on Load Leveling & Energy

L

An Asterisk (*) at the beginning of an entry indicates that the title is appearing for the first time.

L

Conservation i. Ed. by Der-Tau Chin. LC 86-82341. (Electrochemical Society Ser.: No. 86-10). (Illus.). 328p. 1986. reprint ed. pap. 101.70 (0-608-05719-3, 205261100007) Bks Demand.

*Load Line: Instructions for the Guidance of Surveyors. Maritime & Coastguard Agency Staff. 94p. 1999. ring bd. 50.00 (0-11-551999-8, Pub. by Statnry Office) Balogh.

Load of Trouble. 24p. (J). (ps-2). 1997. pap. write for info. (0-7814-3026-7, Chariot Bks) Chariot Victor.

Load of Trouble. Barbara Davoll. (Christopher Churchmouse Classics Ser.). (Illus.). 24p. (J). (ps-2). 1988. pap. 8.99 (0-89693-407-1, 6-1407, Victor Bks) Chariot Victor.

Load of Trouble. Barbara Davoll. (Christopher Churchmouse Classics Ser.). (Illus.). 24p. (J). (ps-3). 1999. 7.99 (0-8024-4932-8) Moody.

Load of Trouble. Barbara Davoll & Dennis Hockerman. (Christopher Churchmouse Ser.). (Illus.). 24p. (J). (gr. 4-7). 1988. 11.99 incl. audio (0-89693-618-X, 3-1618, Victor Bks) Chariot Victor.

Load-Oriented Manufacturing Control. H. P. Wiendahl. LC 92-39850. 1994. 118.95 (0-387-19764-8) Spr-Verlag.

Load-Oriented Manufacturing Control. Hans-Petyer Wiendahl. LC 92-39850. 1993. write for info. (3-540-19764-8) Spr-Verlag.

Load Shape Development. Derek Schrock. LC 97-2312. 1997. 84.95 (0-87814-536-2) PennWell Bks.

Loaded Fictions: Social Critique in the Twentieth-Century Western. Scott Emmert. LC 96-18607. 212p. 1996. text 24.95 (0-89301-194-0) U of Idaho Pr.

Loaded Guns. Larry Scott. 201p. (Orig.). 1991. pap. text 19.95 (0-9631479-0-0) L Scott & Assocs.

Loaded Pen. Linda Boileau. LC 95-17768. (Editorial Cartoonists Ser.). (Illus.). 160p. 1995. pap. 8.95 (1-56554-115-4) Pelican.

Loaded Table: Representations of Food in Roman Literature. Emily Gowers. 346p. 1997. reprint ed. pap. text 26.00 (0-19-815082-2) OUP.

Loaded Vehicles: Studies in African Literary Media. Bernth Lindfors. LC 96-16371. 224p. 1996. 59.95 (0-86543-542-1); pap. 18.95 (0-86543-543-X) Africa World.

Loading Cartridges for the Original .45-70 Springfield Rifle & Carbine. 2nd rev. ed. Pat Wolf. LC 96-90345. (Illus.). 188p. 1996. pap. write for info. (1-57579-019-X) Pine Hill Pr.

Loading the Black Powder Rifle Cartridge. Paul Matthews. 1993. 22.50 (1-879356-20-1) Wolfe Pub Co.

Loading the Dice. Badaracco. 1985. 24.95 (0-07-103206-1) McGraw.

Loading the Scales: Is the Balance Between the Right to Strike & the Right to Operate in Need of Reform? Daniel V. Yager. (Illus.). 188p. (Orig.). 1993. pap. 25.00 (0-916559-41-6) EPF.

Loading Zone. (Kake Ser.: No. 17). 1997. pap. 11.00 (1-879055-31-7) Tom Finland.

Loads & Stresses: Snip 2.01.07-89. Russia's Minstroy Staff. (Snip Building Codes of Russia Ser.). (Illus.). iv, 66p. (Orig.). 1996. ring bd. 1999.95 (1-57937-028-4) Snip Register.

Loads of Codes. Joseph Malkevitch & G. Froelich. (Hi Map Ser.: No. 22). 208p. pap. text 11.99 (0-614-05307-2, HM 5622) COMAP Inc.

Loadstar Bulk Handling Directory, 1992. 1991. 850.00 (0-9510103-1-X) St Mut.

Loaf & Ladle Cookbook. 2nd ed. Joan Harlow. LC 83-72158. 228p. 1983. pap. 12.95 (0-89272-181-2, 523) Down East.

Loaf of Bread. Gail Duff. 1998. 14.99 (0-7858-1012-9) Bk Sales Inc.

Loaf That Became a Legend: A History of St. John's Bread. Kenneth M. Jones & Diane V. Jones. (Illus.). 1997. pap. 14.95 (0-87839-121-5) North Star.

Loafing Around. Sherry B. Inabinet & Ginger M. Inabinet. (Loafing Around Ser.). 263p. 1991. pap. 10.00 (1-887405-00-3) Happleing Hse.

Loafing Around with Pound Cakes & Coffee Cakes. Sherry B. Inabinet & Ginger M. Inabinet. (Loafing Around Ser.). 175p. 1998. pap. 9.50 (1-887405-02-X) Happleing Hse.

Loafing Around with Quick Breads. Sherry B. Inabinet & Ginger M. Inabinet. (Loafing Around Ser.). 245p. 1999. pap. 10.00 (1-887405-01-1) Happleing Hse.

Loafing down Long Island. Charles H. Towne. 212p. 1993. reprint ed. lib. bdg. 79.00 (0-7812-5136-2) Rprt Serv.

Loan Administration in the 90s Vol. 1: Looking Ahead. Charlene Nichols & Darlene Wright. LC 95-152830. 1994. text 65.00 (1-880999-21-8); text 65.00 (1-880999-29-3); text 65.00 (1-880999-20-X); text 585.00 (1-880999-30-7) Loan Admin.

Loan Administration in the 90s Vol. 2: Looking Ahead. Charlene Nichols & Darlene Wright. 1994. text 65.00 (1-880999-22-6) Loan Admin.

Loan Administration in the 90s Vol. 3: Looking Ahead. Charlene Nichols & Darlene Wright. 1994. text 65.00 (1-880999-23-4) Loan Admin.

Loan Administration in the 90s Vol. 4: Looking Ahead. Charlene Nichols & Darlene Wright. 1994. text 65.00 (1-880999-24-2) Loan Admin.

Loan Administration in the 90s Vol. 5: Looking Ahead. Charlene Nichols & Darlene Wright. 1994. text 65.00 (1-880999-25-0) Loan Admin.

Loan Administration in the 90s Vol. 6: Looking Ahead. Charlene Nichols & Darlene Wright. 1994. text 65.00 (1-880999-26-9) Loan Admin.

Loan Administration in the 90s Vol. 7: Looking Ahead. Charlene Nichols & Darlene Wright. 1994. text 65.00 (1-880999-27-7) Loan Admin.

Loan Administration in the 90s Vol. 8: Looking Ahead. Charlene Nichols & Darlene Wright. 1994. text 65.00 (1-880999-28-5) Loan Admin.

Loan Advisor. Jack Rudman. (Career Examination Ser.: C-1321). 1994. pap. 27.95 (0-8373-1321-X) Nat Learn.

Loan Agreements. Sidney Goldstein. Vol. G4. text 82.00 (0-8205-2419-0) Bender.

Loan, Assignments & Participations: A Documentation Handbook. 3rd ed. T. Gooch & L. Klein. 1996. 250.00 (1-85564-458-4, Pub. by Euromoney) Am Educ Systs.

Loan Book. Jedehiah Clauss. 19.95 (0-8488-0121-0) Amereon Ltd.

Loan Book: Complete Step by Step Guide to Getting a Personal or Business Loan. Orlando Antonini & Casey Collay. (Small Business Ser.). 185p. (Orig.). 1990. pap. 19.95 (0-318-50011-6) El Dorado Pr.

Loan Broker Manual. rev. ed. Jae K. Shim & Norman Henreleff. 250p. 1999. student ed., ring bd. 70.00 (1-882312-44-9) Delta Pub CA.

Loan Closing: A Workbook on Executing the Docuements & Transferring the Funds. Robin Chandlee & Sara Sautter. Ed. by Gary Askerooth & Kathryn Fisher. (Training Institute Community Revitalization Ser.). 80p. (Orig.). 1993. pap., student ed. 10.00 (1-884356-02-8) Neighborhd Reinvest.

Loan Collector's Training. Karen Sistare. 100p. 1995. wbk. ed. 53.00 (0-89982-433-1) Am Bankers.

Loan Data - Qualifier: A Program for the HP 17BII Financial Calculator. Edric Cane. 48p. (Orig.). 1991. pap. 14.95 incl. disk (0-916785-12-2) E Cane Sem.

Loan Documentation for Lawyers. John E. Moye. 129p. 1993. pap. 125.00 (0-943380-88-X) PEG MN.

*Loan Documentation Manual. John E. Moye. 1999. write for info. (1-58012-053-9) James Pub Santa Ana.

Loan Exhibition of Paintings by the Wyeth Family. Intro. by Nicholas Wyeth. (Illus.). 10p. (Orig.). (C). 1966. pap. 1.00 (0-943526-44-2) Parrish Art.

*Loan Liquidation & Acquired Property. Jane Palsgrove Butler. 154p. 1998. pap. 14.00 (0-16-061941-6) USGPO.

Loan-Loss Provisions & Third-World Debt. Graham Bird. LC 89-28013. (Essays in International Finance Ser.: No. 176). 34p. 1989. pap. text 10.00 (0-88165-083-8) Princeton U Int Finan Econ.

Loan of the Quick: Poems. James Owens. 40p. 1998. pap. 7.00 (1-885912-18-8) Sows Ear Pr.

Loan Officer Complete Handbook. Don W Coker. (C). 1992. pap. 69.95 (0-13-554288-X) P-H.

Loan Officer's Complete Guide to Marketing & Selling Mortgage Services. David L. Hershman. (Illus.). 260p. 1992. pap. 50.00 (0-945359-12-8) Mortgage Bankers.

Loan Origination: A Workbook on Gathering & Verifying the Information. Robin Chandlee & Sara Sautter. Ed. by Gary Askerooth & Kathryn Fisher. (Training Institute Community Revitalization Ser.). 60p. (Orig.). 1993. pap., student ed. 10.00 (1-884356-00-1) Neighborhd Reinvest.

Loan Phonology & the Two Transfer Types in Language Contact. F. Van Coetsem. (Publications in Language Sciences). xvi, 196p. 1988. pap. 52.35 (90-6765-300-4) Mouton.

Loan Policy Manual for Credit Unions. A. Rex Johnson. 130p. (Orig.). 1991. pap. 89.00 (1-889394-29-7) Credit Union Execs.

Loan Portfolio Management. Ed. by Joan H. Behr. LC 88-29760. (Special Collection from the Journal of Commercial Bank Lending). 108p. (Orig.). 1988. pap. 45.00 (0-936742-58-5, 36037) Robt Morris Assocs.

Loan Pricing: A Special Collection from the Journal of Commercial Bank Lending. Ed. by Joan H. Behr. LC 89-12259. (Illus.). 100p. 1989. pap. 45.00 (0-936742-66-6, 36039) Robt Morris Assocs.

Loan Pushers: The Role of Commercial Banks in the International Debt Crisis. William A. Darity, Jr. & Bobbie L. Horn. 224p. 1988. text 34.95 (0-88730-067-7, HarpBusn) HarpInfo.

Loan Review: A Special Collection from the Journal. LC 84-25573. (Illus.). 128p. (Orig.). 1984. pap. text 45.00 (0-936742-21-6) Robt Morris Assocs.

Loan Review: Starting up & Staying Strong. James C. Harlan. Ed. by Joan H. Behr. LC 91-30820. (Illus.). 64p. (Orig.). 1991. pap. text 44.00 (0-936742-84-4, 32576) Robt Morris Assocs.

Loan Review Deskbook: How to Establish, Maintain & Regulate an Effective Program. S. Wayne Linder. 276p. 1989. ring bd. 135.00 (1-55520-203-9, Irwn Prfssnl) McGraw-Hill Prof.

Loan Risk Management: Strategies & Analytical Techniques for Commercial Bankers. Morton Glantz. LC 94-172527. 1993. text 70.00 (1-55738-384-7, Irwn Prfssnl) McGraw-Hill Prof.

Loan Syntax in Turkic & Iranian: The Verb System of Tajik, Uzbek, & Qasgay. John D. Soper. (Eurasian Language Archives Ser.). 1997. 24.00 (0-931922-58-5) Eurolingua.

Loan Training: A Special Collection from the Journal of Commercial Bank Lending. Ed. by Joan H. Behr. LC 90-32862. (Illus.). 104p. 1990. pap. 45.00 (0-936742-73-9, 36041) Robt Morris Assocs.

Loan Underwriting: A Workbook on Analyzing & Committing to Lend. Robin Chandlee et al. Ed. by Gary Askerooth & Kathryn Fisher. (Training Institute Community Revitalization Ser.). 64p. (Orig.). 1993. pap., student ed. 10.00 (1-884356-01-X) Neighborhd Reinvest.

Loan Verbs in Maltese: A Descriptive & Comparative Study. Manwel Mifsud. LC 94-43608. (Studies in Semitic Languages & Linguistics: Vol. 21). xvii, 339p. 1994. 124.00 (90-04-10091-1) Brill Academic Pubs.

Loan Words in Early Irish from Old Norse, Anglo-Saxon, Early English, Latin & Early French. Kuno Meyer. 1996. pap. 10.00 (0-89979-080-1) British Am Bks.

*Loans & Grants from Uncle Sam. 7th ed. Anna J. Leider. 1999. pap. 6.00 (1-57509-044-9) Octameron Assocs.

Loans & Legitimacy: The Evolution of Soviet-American Relations, 1919-1933. Katherine A. Siegel. LC 95-26338. 240p. 1996. 39.95 (0-8131-1962-6) U Pr of Ky.

Loans by Phone Broker Success Kit. 9th ed. Tyler Gregory Hicks. 176p. 1998. pap. 100.00 (1-56150-222-7) Intl Wealth.

Loans by Phone Broker Success Kit. 10th ed. Tyler Gregory Hicks. 176p. 1999. pap. 100.00 (1-56150-273-1) Intl Wealth.

*Loans by Phone Broker Success Kit. 11th ed. Tyler G. Hicks. 176p. 2000. pap. 100.00 (1-56150-333-9) Intl Wealth.

Loans by Phone Broker Success Kit, 2 bks., Set. 8th ed. Tyler Gregory Hicks. 176p. 1996. pap. 100.00 (1-56150-172-7) Intl Wealth.

Loanwords Dictionary. 2nd ed. Urdang Staff. 1905. 94.00 (0-8103-5476-4) Gale.

Loar Genealogy, with Cognate Branches, 1774-1947. Emma L. Gaddis. (Illus.). 387p. 1993. reprint ed. pap. 59.50 (0-8328-3611-7); reprint ed. lib. bdg. 69.50 (0-8328-3610-9) Higginson Bk Co.

Loathsome Couple. Edward Gorey. LC 76-13353. (Illus.). 64p. 1986. reprint ed. 11.95 (0-926637-10-X) P Weed Bks.

Loathsome Jews & Engulfing Women: Metaphors of Projection in the Works of Wyndham Lewis, Charles Williams & Graham Greene. Andrea F. Loewenstein. LC 93-16362. (Literature & Psychoanalysis Ser.: Vol. 2). 412p. (C). 1993. text 47.50 (0-8147-5063-X) NYU Pr.

Loathsome Jews & Engulfing Women: Metaphors of Projection in the Works of Wyndham Lewis, Charles Williams & Graham Greene. Andrea F. Loewenstein. LC 93-16362. 412p. (C). 1995. pap. text 19.50 (0-8147-5096-6) NYU Pr.

Loaves & Fishes. (Book of Indiana Women Poets Ser.). 44p. 1983. pap. 3.00 (1-880649-12-8) Writ Ctr Pr.

Loaves & Fishes. Ed. by Heather Amery. (Bible Tales Readers Ser.). (Illus.). 16p. (J). (ps-k). 1999. pap. 4.50 (0-7460-2967-5, Usborne) EDC.

*Loaves & Fishes. Ed. by Heather Amery. (Bible Tales Readers Ser.). (Illus.). 16p. (J). (ps-k). 1999. lib. bdg. 12.95 (1-58086-160-1, Usborne) EDC.

Loaves & Fishes. Helen Caswell. LC 93-25308. 24p. (J). 1993. 11.95 (0-687-22526-4) Abingdon.

Loaves & Fishes. Linda Hunt et al. LC 80-12165. (Illus.). 176p. (J). (gr. 2-5). 1980. spiral bd. 10.99 (0-8361-1922-3) Herald Pr.

Loaves & Fishes. John M. Kirkpatrick. LC 95-67131. 1995. 7.95 (0-8158-0513-6) Chris Mass.

Loaves & Fishes. Dorothy Day. LC 97-23637. 221p. 1997. reprint ed. pap. 13.00 (1-57075-156-0) Orbis Bks.

Loaves & Fishes, Vol. 10010. Lou E. Smith. (Illus.). (J). (gr. 1-8). 1996. 8.00 (1-888535-03-2) Firefly Prods.

Loaves & Fishes: A Study of the Miracles, of the Resurrection, & of the Future Life in the Light of Modern Psychic Knowledge (1935) Hereward Carrington. 260p. 1998. reprint ed. pap. 24.95 (0-7661-0315-3) Kessinger Pub.

Loaves & Fishes: From Faith Experience to Empowered Community. Virginia A. Blass. LC 95-30887. 128p. (Orig.). 1996. pap. 11.95 (0-8091-3614-7) Paulist Pr.

*Loaves & Hyacinths: Tea Rooms in London & East Anglia. unabridged ed. Gladys S. Lewis. LC 99-94360. (Illus.). 206p. 1999. 36.00 (0-9669682-0-4) Greystone.

Loaves of Fun: A History of Bread with Activities & Recipes from Around the World. Elizabeth M. Harbison. LC 96-47311. (Illus.). 106p. (Orig.). (J). (gr. 3-6). 1997. pap. 12.95 (1-55652-311-4) Chicago Review.

Loaves of Love. rev. ed. Patricia B. Mitchell. 1991. pap. 4.00 (0-925117-52-8) Mitchells.

Lob to Win: When to Lob. 2nd ed. Jay Burchett. (Illus.). 57p. (Orig.). (C). 1991. pap. 7.95 (1-882013-02-6) Newport Pub Hse.

Loba. Diana Di Prima. LC 97-41144. 325p. 1998. pap. 14.95 (0-14-058752-7) NAL.

Lobar Cerebral Palsy. Snowden. 1996. text 90.00 (0-443-04765-0, W B Saunders Co) Harcrt Hlth Sci Grp.

Lobate Species of Symphyogyna. Alexander W. Evans. (Connecticut Academy of Arts & Sciences Ser., Trans.: Vol. 27). 1925. pap. 49.50 (0-685-22819-3) Elliots Bks.

Lobby Cards: The Classic Comedies. Kathryn L. Scott. (Illus.). 1988. 35.00 (0-938817-13-2) Pomegranate Pr.

Lobby Cards: The Classic Comedies: Portfolio Edition. Kathryn L. Scott. (Illus.). 1988. 45.00 (0-938817-14-0) Pomegranate Pr.

Lobby Cards: The Classic Films. Kathryn L. Scott. LC 87-61592. (Illus.). 1987. 29.95 (0-938817-11-6) Pomegranate Pr.

Lobby Cards: The Classic Films: Portfolio Edition. Kathryn L. Scott. LC 87-61592. (Illus.). 1987. 45.00 (0-938817-12-4) Pomegranate Pr.

Lobby for Your Library: Knowing What Works. Lisa F. Kinney. LC 92-9142. 190p. (C). 1992. pap. text 20.00 (0-8389-3410-2) ALA.

Lobbying. Cass R. Sandak. (Inside Government Ser.). (Illus.). 64p. (J). (gr. 5-8). 1995. lib. bdg. 18.90 (0-8050-3424-2) TFC Bks NY.

Lobbying, Vol. 1. Sandak. (J). 1995. 14.98 (0-8050-4351-9) H Holt & Co.

Lobbying, Advocacy, & Nonprofit Boards. John D. Sparks. 24p. 1997. pap. text 16.00 (0-925299-76-6) Natl Ctr Nonprofit.

Lobbying & Government Relations: A Guide for Executives. Charles S. Mack. LC 88-35730. 244p. 1989. 65.00 (0-89930-390-0, MGV/, Quorum Bks) Greenwood.

Lobbying Congress: How the System Works. 2nd ed. Bruce C. Wolpe & Bertram J. Levine. LC 96-24721. 206p. (YA). (gr. 11). 1996. pap. text 28.95 (1-56802-225-5) Congr Quarterly.

Lobbying for Higher Education: How Colleges & Universities Influence Federal Policy. Constance E. Cook. LC 98-8885. (Issues in Higher Education Ser.). (Illus.). 272p. (C). 1998. 45.00 (0-8265-1316-6); pap. 19.95 (0-8265-1317-4) Vanderbilt U Pr.

Lobbying for Social Change. Willard C. Richan. (Social Administration Ser.). 255p. (C). 1990. pap. text 19.95 (1-56024-074-1) Haworth Pr.

Lobbying for Social Change. Willard C. Richan. (Social Administration Ser.). 255p. (C). 1991. text 39.95 (1-56024-079-2) Haworth Pr.

Lobbying for Social Change. 2nd ed. Willard C. Richan. LC 95-35019. 362p. (C). 1996. 49.95 (0-7890-6002-7); pap. 19.95 (0-7890-6003-5) Haworth Pr.

Lobbying for the People: The Political Behavior of Public Interest Groups. Jeffrey M. Berry. LC 77-71973. 344p. reprint ed. pap. 106.70 (0-608-06428-9, 206664100008) Bks Demand.

Lobbying from Below: Civil Liberty. Ryan. 208p. 1996. 59.95 (1-85728-255-8, Pub. by UCL Pr Ltd); pap. 19.95 (1-85728-256-6, Pub. by UCL Pr Ltd) Taylor & Francis.

Lobbying Handbook. John L. Zorack. 1118p. 1990. lib. bdg. 144.00 (0-933833-19-9) Beacham Pub Corp.

Lobbying in the European Community. Ed. by Sonia Mazey & Jeremy J. Richardson. (Nuffield European Studies, New Ser.). (Illus.). 278p. 1993. text 55.00 (0-19-827789-X) OUP.

Lobbying in the European Union: Companies, Trade Associations & Issue Groups. Ed. by Robin Pedler & M. VanSchendelen. 328p. 1994. 77.95 (1-85521-609-4) Ashgate Pub Co.

Lobbying Manual. 2nd ed. William V. Luneburg & American Bar Association Staff. LC 98-14636. 1998. pap. 89.95 (1-57073-551-4) Amer Bar Assn.

Lobbying Manual: A Compliance Guide for Lawyers & Lobbyists. LC 92-74831. 287p. 1993. pap. 89.95 (0-89707-836-5, 501-0021) Amer Bar Assn.

*Lobbying PACS, & Campaign Finance, 50 State Handbook. Christianson et al. 1184p. 1998. pap. text 65.00 (0-314-22868-3) West Pub.

Lobbying Together: Interest Group Coalitions in Legislative Politics. Kevin W. Hula. LC 98-44648. (American Governance & Public Policy Ser.). 180p. 1999. pap. 23.95 (0-87840-721-9); text 55.00 (0-87840-720-0) Georgetown U Pr.

Lobbyists: How Influence Peddlers Work Their Way in Washington. Jeffrey H. Birnbaum. 1993. pap. 15.00 (0-8129-2314-6, Times Bks) Crown Pub Group.

Lobbyists for Hire. Kevin Moloney. LC 96-1352. (Illus.). 200p. 1996. 77.95 (1-85521-794-5, Pub. by Dartmth Pub) Ashgate Pub Co.

Lobdell Genealogy & Family History a Sequel. Oma L. Rose. LC 95-72999. (Illus.). 736p. 1996. write for info. (0-89725-253-5, 1723, Penobscot Pr) Picton Pr.

Lobedu. Patricia Davison. LC 96-45308. (Heritage Library of African Peoples: Set 4). (Illus.). 64p. (YA). (gr. 7-12). 1996. lib. bdg. 16.95 (0-8239-1989-7, D1989-7) Rosen Group.

Lobello Angela Dyer & Peter Lobello. LC 99-196429. 92p. 1997. write for info. (0-06-237790-6, E Burlingame Bks) HarpC.

L'Oblate see Oblate of St. Benedict

Loblolly Pine: Its Use, Ecology, Regeneration, Protection, Growth, & Management. William G. Wahlenberg. LC 61-1949. (Illus.). 627p. reprint ed. pap. 194.40 (0-7837-6034-5, 204584700008) Bks Demand.

Loblolly Pine (pinus Taeda L.) The Ecology & Culture of Loblolly Pine. Robert P. Schultz. 510p. 1998. boxed set 44.00 (0-16-049279-3) USGPO.

Lobo: Fragtastic Voyage. Alan Grant. LC 98-163782. 1997. 5.95 (1-56389-354-1) DC Comics.

Lobo: The Last Czarnian. Keith Giffen & A. Grant. Ed. by Michael Hill. 112p. 1993. mass mkt. 9.95 (0-930289-99-4, Pub. by DC Comics) Time Warner.

Lobo - Judge Dredd: Psycho Bikers vs. Mutants from Hell. Alan Grant. Ed. by Dan Raspler. (Illus.). 48p. 1995. pap. 4.95 (1-56389-239-1) DC Comics.

*Lobo Case. Winifred B. Senior. 216p. 2000. pap. 16.00 (0-8059-4816-3) Dorrance.

Lobo Estepario. Hermann Hesse. (SPA.). 1997. pap. 5.98 (968-15-0095-4) Edit Diana.

Lobo One. James N. Pruitt. 240p. (Orig.). 1992. mass mkt. 4.50 (0-380-76616-7, Avon Bks) Morrow Avon.

*Lobo Outback Funeral Home. Dave Foreman. 200p. 2000. 24.95 (0-87081-602-0) Univ Pr Colo.

Lobo, The Wolf: King of Currumpaw. rev. ed. Ernest Thompson Seton & Mark Steilen. (Illus.). 72p. (J). (gr. 3-8). 1991. reprint ed. pap. 10.95 (0-9623072-4-6) S Ink WA.

Lobos. Lynn M. Stone. (Animales Norteamericanos Ser.).Tr. of Wolves. 24p. (J). (gr. k-4). 1991. lib. bdg. 14.60 (0-86592-834-7) Rourke Enter.

Lobo's Back's Back. Keith Giffen & A. Grant. Ed. by Bob Kahan. (Illus.). 112p. 1993. pap. 9.95 (1-56389-103-4) DC Comics.

Lobo's Greatest Hits. Ed. by Dan Raspler & Michael C. Hill. (Illus.). 176p. 1992. pap. 12.95 (1-56389-013-5) DC Comics.

*Lobotomy: Surviving the Ramones. Dee Dee Ramone et al. LC 99-42130. Orig. Title: Poison Heart: Surviving the Ramones. 256p. 2000. pap. 14.95 (1-56025-252-9, Thunders Mouth) Avalon NY.

Lobscouse & Spotted Dog. Anne C. Grossman & Lisa G. Thomas. LC 97-17676. 416p. 1997. 29.95 (0-393-04559-5) Norton.

*Lobscouse & Spotted Dog: Which It's a Gastronomic Companion to the Aubrey/Maturin Novels. Anne Chotzinoff Grossman & Lisa Grossman Thomas. 336p. 2000. reprint ed. pap. 16.95 (0-393-32094-4) Norton.

Lobstah: A Board Game. 3rd ed. Franz Anderson. 60p. (C). 1998. 35.95 (0-7872-5460-6) Kendall-Hunt.

An Asterisk (*) at the beginning of an entry indicates that the title is appearing for the first time.

Lobster. Sterling Publishing Company, Inc. Staff. (The Magnet Gourmet Ser.). 10p. 1997. pap. text 5.95 (*0-8069-0634-0*) Sterling.

Lobster & Other Shellfish. Elaine Elliot & Virginia Lee. (Maritime Flavours Ser.). (Illus.). 64p. 1997. pap. 9.95 (*0-88780-354-7*, Pub. by Formac Publ Co) Formac Dist Ltd.

Lobster & Shellfish Friends. 2nd rev. ed. Sherri Eldridge. (Illus.). 32p. 1997. pap. 2.95 (*1-886862-20-6*, MN LOB) Harv Hill ME.

Lobster & the Sea. Esther Chiu. LC 97-10221. (Illus.). 32p. (J). (gr. 1-4). 1998. 14.95 (*1-879965-14-3*) Polychrome Pub.

Lobster at Home. Jasper White. LC 98-10238. (Illus.). 256p. 1998. 29.50 (*0-684-80077-2*) Scribner.

Lobster Boat. Brenda Z. Guiberson. LC 92-4055. (Illus.). 32p. (J). (ps-3). 1995. 14.95 (*0-8050-1756-9*, Bks Young Read) H Holt & Co.

Lobster Boy. Fred Rosen. LC 95-182794. (Illus.). 331p. 1995. mass mkt. 4.99 (*0-7860-0133-X*, Pinncle Kensgtn) Kensgtn Pub Corp.

Lobster for Lunch. Bob Hartman. LC 91-77671. (Illus.). 32p. (J). (gr. k-3). 1992. 14.95 (*0-89272-302-5*) Down East.

Lobster Gangs of Maine. James M. Acheson. LC 87-40506. (Library of New England). (Illus.). 197p. 1988. pap. 14.95 (*0-87451-451-7*) U Pr of New Eng.

Lobster in Every Pot. 1990. pap. 10.95 (*0-89909-216-0*, 80-151-5) Yankee Bks.

***Lobster Kids' Guide to Exploring Vancouver: 12 Months of Fun.** Ed. by Jeni Wright. (Lobster Kids' City Explorers Ser.). (Illus.). 248p. (J). (gr. k-7). 2000. pap. 14.95 (*1-894222-05-9*) LOB4.

Lobster King. E. A. Olsen. LC 68-16400. (Oceanography Ser.). (Illus.). 48p. (J). (gr. 3 up). 1970. lib. bdg. 10.95 (*0-87783-024-X*); audio 10.60 (*0-87783-192-0*) Oddo.

Lobster King. deluxe ed. E. A. Olsen. LC 68-16400. (Oceanography Ser.). (Illus.). 48p. (J). (gr. 3 up). 1970. pap. 3.94 (*0-87783-099-1*) Oddo.

Lobster Lore. Gary Hertz. 24p. 1993. pap. 7.95 (*0-9637327-0-6*) GCH Pub.

Lobster Lover's Cookbook. 2nd rev. ed. Brian M. Coffey. 192p. (Orig.). 1996. pap. 9.95 (*0-924771-87-9*, Covered Brdge Pr) Douglas Charles Ltd.

Lobster Tales. Laura Lobster. LC 96-75799. (Illus.). 70p. (YA). (gr. 5 up). 1996. pap. 10.00 (*0-9652028-0-1*) Infinite Possibilities.

Lobster Tales: Recipes & Recitations Featuring the Maine Attraction. Brooks MacDonald & Martha Griffin. (Orig.). 1995. pap. 14.95 (*0-9649367-0-4*) Lobster Tales.

Lobster Tales: Recipes & Recitations Featuring the Maine Attraction. Martha Griffin & Brooks MacDonald. (Illus.). 96p. (Orig.). 1996. reprint ed. pap. 14.95 (*0-89272-395-5*) Down East.

Lobster Tales: The Adventures of Lobby the Lobster. S. N. Guy. (Illus.). (J). (ps-k). 1995. 7.95 (*0-533-10947-7*) Vantage.

Lobstering & the Maine Coast. Kenneth R. Martin & Nathan R. Lipfert. LC 85-61988. (Illus.). 143p. 1985. pap. 16.50 (*0-937410-04-7*) ME Maritime Mus.

Lobsterman. Dahlov Ipcar. (Illus.). 36p. (J). (ps-3). 1977. reprint ed. pap. 9.95 (*0-89272-032-8*) Down East.

Lobsters. Jason Cooper. LC 95-26010. (Animals Without Bones Discovery Library). (Illus.). 24p. (J). (gr. k-4). 1996. lib. bdg. 15.93 (*0-86625-572-9*) Rourke Pubns.

Lobsters: Florida, Bahamas, & the Caribbean. Martin A. Moe, Jr. LC 91-23948. (Illus.). 512p. (Orig.). 1991. pap. 22.95 (*0-939960-06-0*) Green Turtle Pubns.

Lobsters: Gangsters of the Sea. Mary M. Cerullo. LC 93-1288. (Illus.). 64p. (J). (gr. 4 up). 1994. 16.99 (*0-525-65153-5*, Dutton Child) Peng Put Young Read.

Lobsters & Other Shellfish. Elaine Elliot & Virginia Lee. 1997. pap. 9.95 (*0-614-28087-7*) Formac Dist Ltd.

Lobsters, Crabs & Jellyfish - Oh, My! Grandpa Groveland. (Illus.). 32p. (J). (gr. k up). 1990. pap. 5.95 (*0-924771-22-4*, Covered Brdge Pr) Douglas Charles Ltd.

Lobsters Inside Out: A Lobster Workbook / 3rd ed. Robert C. Bayer & Juanita Bayer. LC 98-66215. 32p. 1998. write for info. (*0-7872-3273-4*) Kendall-Hunt.

Lobsters of the World. L. B. Holthuis. 1995. 79.00 (*3-540-14198-7*) Spr-Verlag.

Lobsters of the World. L. B. Holthuis. 1996. cd-rom 79.00 (*3-540-14197-9*) Spr-Verlag.

Lobster's Secret. Kathleen M. Hollenbeck. LC 95-45886. (Smithsonian Oceanic Collection). (Illus.). 32p. (J). (ps-2). 1996. 15.95 (*1-56899-278-5*) Soundprints.

Lobster's Secret. Kathleen M. Hollenbeck. (Smithsonian Oceanic Collection). (Illus.). 32p. (J). (ps-2). 1996. 19.95 incl. audio (*1-56899-282-3*, BC4010) Soundprints.

Lobster's Secret, Incl. large toy. Kathleen M. Hollenbeck. LC 95-45886. (Smithsonian Oceanic Collection). (Illus.). 32p. (J). (ps-2). 1996. 29.95 (*1-56899-280-7*) Soundprints.

Lobster's Secret, Incl. Sm. & Lg. Plush Toy. Kathleen M. Hollenbeck. LC 96-45886. (Smithsonian Oceanic Collection). (Illus.). 32p. (J). (ps-2). 1996. 38.95 incl. audio (*1-56899-652-7*) Soundprints.

Lobster's Secret, Micro bk. Kathleen M. Hollenbeck. LC 95-45886. (Illus.). 32p. (J). (ps-2). 1996. 4.95 (*1-56899-279-3*) Soundprints.

Lobster's Secret, Micro bk., incl. small toy. Kathleen M. Hollenbeck. LC 95-45886. (Smithsonian Oceanic Collection). (Illus.). 32p. (J). (ps-2). 1996. 9.95 (*1-56899-281-5*) Soundprints.

Loc Clinical Neurology, No. 2. 2nd ed. Paul W. Brazis. 1990. 84.95 (*0-316-10743-3*, Little Brwn Med Div) Lppncott W & W.

Loca. Ian Walker. 250p. mass mkt. 4.99 (*1-896329-80-2*) Picasso Publ.

***Loca Pasion.** Mary Lyons. (Bianca Ser.: No. 181).Tr. of Crazy Passion. (SPA.). 1999. per. 3.50 (*0-373-33531-8*, 1-33531-4) Harlequin Bks.

Loca Sancta. Peter Thomsen. (GER.). xvi, 143p. 1966. reprint ed. write for info. (*0-318-70584-2*) G Olms Pubs.

Loca Viuda: A New Mythology of Mexico City. Ruth M. Kempher. (Illus.). 45p. (Orig.). (C). 1992. pap. 6.95 (*0-934536-50-3*) Rose Shell Pr.

Locadio's Apprentice. Chelsea Quinn Yarbro. LC 84-47632. 224p. (YA). (gr. 7 up). 1984. 13.95 (*0-06-026636-8*) HarpC Child Bks.

Local Acts Creating & Providing for North Carolina City School Administrative Units. Robert E. Phay & Robert M. Ward. 423p. (Orig.). (C). 1972. pap. text 4.50 (*1-56011-173-9*, 72.15) Institute Government.

Local Agenda Setting Processes. fac. ed. Ed. by E. Blaine Liner. LC JF1525.D4L63. (Lincoln Institute of Land Policy Monograph: No. 85-10). 61p. 1985. reprint ed. pap. 30.00 (*0-7837-7827-9*, 204758300007) Bks Demand.

Local Agenda 21 Planning Guide: An Introduction to Sustainable Development Plan. LC 96-204750. 225p. 1996. pap. 30.00 (*0-88936-801-5*, Pub. by IDRC Bks) Stylus Pub VA.

Local Agrarian Societies in Colonial India: Japanese Perspectives. Ed. by Peter Robb et al. (SOAS Collected Papers on South Asia: No. 11). 416p. (C). 1996. text 55.00 (*0-7007-0471-X*, Pub. by Curzon Pr Ltd) UH Pr.

Local Agrarian Societies in Colonial India: Japanese Perspectives. Sugihara & Yanagisqwa. LC 97-906061. (C). 1997. 40.00 (*81-7304-186-5*, Pub. by Manohar) S Asia.

Local Aid to Railroads in Missouri. Edwin L. Lopata. Ed. by Stuart Bruchey. LC 80-1327. (Railroads Ser.). (Illus.). 1981. reprint ed. lib. bdg. 18.95 (*0-405-13801-6*) Ayer.

***Local Algebra - Multiplicities.** J. P. Serre. (Monographs in Mathematics). 110p. 2000. (*3-540-66641-9*) Spr-Verlag.

***Local Anaesthesia in Dentistry.** Fraser McDonald et al. (Illus.). 128p. 2000. pap. text 32.00 (*0-7236-1063-0*, Pub. by John Wright) Buttrwrth-Heinemann.

Local Anaesthetic. Gunter Grass. Tr. by Ralph Manheim from GER. LC 89-38472.Tr. of Ortlich Betaubt. 288p. (C). 1989. pap. 13.00 (*0-15-652940-8*) Harcourt.

Local Analysis, Pts. A & B. C. H. Schriba. 1994. text. write for info. (*3-05-501675-0*) Wiley.

Local Analysis Pt. A: Foundations & Differential Calculus. Carl Heinz-Scriba. 1994. text 68.20 (*3-05-501447-2*, Pub. by Akademie Verlag) Wiley.

Local Analysis Pt. B: First Order Differential Equation. Carl-Heinz Scriba. LC 94-22855. 1994. 70.00 (*3-05-501645-9*, Pub. by Akademie Verlag) Wiley.

Local Analysis for the Odd Order Theorem. Helmut Bender & George Glauberman. (London Mathematical Society Lecture Note Ser.: No. 188). 186p. (C). 1995. pap. text 32.95 (*0-521-45716-5*) Cambridge U Pr.

Local Analysis, Pts. A & B. C. H. Schriba. 591p. 1996. 165.00 (*3-527-40063-X*) Wiley.

Local & Federal Rules. annot. ed. 1999. write for info. (*0-327-08383-2*, 49349-15) LEXIS Pub.

Local & Global Interpretation of Moving Images. Guy L. Scott. (Research Notes in Artificial Intelligence Ser.). (Illus.). 120p. (Orig.). 1988. pap. text 33.95 (*0-934613-62-1*) Morgan Kaufmann.

Local & Global Methods of Nonlinear Dynamics. Ed. by A. W. Saenz et al. (Lecture Notes in Physics Ser.: Vol. 252). vii, 263p. 1986. 35.00 (*0-387-16485-5*) Spr-Verlag.

***Local & Metropolitan Area Networks.** 46p. 2000. teacher ed. write for info. (*0-13-018653-8*) P-H.

***Local & Metropolitan Area Networks.** 5th ed. 1998. teacher ed. write for info. (*0-02-415474-1*, Macmillan Coll) P-H.

Local & Metropolitan Area Networks. 5th ed. William Stallings. LC 95-49213. 752p. (C). 1996. text 78.00 (*0-13-190737-9*) P-H.

***Local & Metropolitan Area Networks.** 6th ed. 2000. teacher ed. write for info. (*0-13-019095-0*) P-H.

***Local & Metropolitan Area Networks.** 6th ed. William Stallings. 478p. 2000. 82.00 (*0-13-012939-9*) P-H.

Local & Parliamentary Politics in Liverpool from 1800 to 1911. Ed. by D. Ben Rees. LC 99-26393. (Studies in British History: Vol. 55). 162p. 1999. text 79.95 (*0-7734-7990-2*) E Mellen.

Local & Public Authorities 1989. Waterlow Staff. (Waterlow Local & Public Authorities Ser.). 224p. 1989. pap. 23.00 (*0-08-036899-9*, Pergamon Pr) Elsevier.

Local & Regional Anesthesia from Birth to Adulthood. Bernard J. Dalens. LC 95-3775.Tr. of Anesthesie Locoregionale de la Naissance a L'age Adulte. (Illus.). 480p. 1995. 105.00 (*0-683-09653-2*) Lppncott W & W.

Local & Regional Authorities & HIV/AIDS. (Congress of Local & Regional Authorities of Europe Ser.: No. 30). 1993. 12.00 (*92-871-2306-3*, Pub. by Council of Europe) Manhattan Pub Co.

Local & Regional Authorities & the Challenge of Unemployment: Action of the CLRAE, 1983-88. Council of Europe Staff. (Congress of Local & Regional Authorities of Europe Ser.: No. 10). 1988. 12.00 (*92-871-1640-7*, Pub. by Council of Europe) Manhattan Pub Co.

Local & Regional Development under the 1990's Transition in Eastern Europe. Ed. by Markku Tykkylainen. LC 95-79585. 169p. 1995. text 72.95 (*1-85972-118-4*, Pub. by Avebry) Ashgate Pub Co.

***Local & Regional Governance in Europe: Evidence from Nordic Regions.** Ed. by Janerik Gidlund & Magnus Jerneck. LC 99-88519. 304p. 2000. 100.00 (*1-84064-368-4*) E Elgar.

Local & Regional Response to Global Pressure: The Case of Italy & Its Industrial Districts. F. Cossentino et al. LC 97-120558. (Research Ser.: Vol. 103). x,206p. 1996. pap. 22.50 (*92-9014-568-4*) Intl Labour Office.

Local & Regional Systems of Innovation. John De La Mothe & Gilles Paquet. LC 98-39380. (Economics of Science, Technology, & Innovation Ser.). 1998. 120.00 (*0-7923-8287-0*) Kluwer Academic.

Local & State Political Campaign Management. Scott Wilcox. 117p. (C). 1996. lib. bdg. 75.00 (*1-56072-306-8*) Nova Sci Pubs.

Local & the Global: Management of Cities in the Information Age. Jordi Borja & Manuel Castells. LC 97-222100. 320p. 1997. pap. 40.00 (*1-85383-441-6*, Pub. by Escan Pubns) Island Pr.

Local & Traditional Costumes in the Victoria & Albert Museum. Victoria & Albert Museum Staff. 1989. 1205.00 (*0-8161-1758-6*, G K Hall & Co) Mac Lib Ref.

Local Anesthesia. Markus D. Lipp. (Illus.). 166p. 1993. text 198.00 incl. VHS (*0-86715-273-7*) Quint Pub Co.

Local Anesthesia. Markus D. Lipp et al. Tr. by Mark Coldwell et al from GER. LC 93-12264. (Illus.). 166p. 1993. text 60.00 (*0-86715-263-X*) Quint Pub Co.

Local Anesthesia. Gary R. Strichartz. 400p. 1997. text. write for info. (*0-397-51430-1*) Lppncott W & W.

Local Anesthesia for Dermatologic Surgery. Michael J. Auletta & Roy C. Grekin. (Practical Manuals in Dermatologic Surgery Ser.). (Illus.). 99p. 1990. pap. text 41.00 (*0-443-08704-0*) Church.

Local Anesthesia of the Oral Cavity. J. Theodore Jastak et al. LC 94-8370. (Illus.). 296p. 1994. pap. text. write for info. (*0-7216-2357-3*, W B Saunders Co) Harcrt Hlth Sci Grp.

Local Anesthetics. (Medical Ser.). 1986. lib. bdg. 79.95 (*0-8490-3802-2*) Gordon Pr.

Local Anesthetics, Vol. 81. Ed. by Gary R. Strichartz. (Handbook of Experimental Pharmacology Ser.). (Illus.). 335p. 1986. 243.00 (*0-387-16361-1*) Spr-Verlag.

Local Applications in the Ecology of Human-Machine Systems. Ed. by Peter A. Hancock et al. LC 94-47100. 488p. 1995. pap. 49.95 (*0-8058-1380-2*); text 99.95 (*0-8058-1379-9*) L Erlbaum Assocs.

Local Approach to Cleavage Fracture: Concepts & Applications. C. S. Wiesner. 70p. 1996. pap. 130.00 (*1-85573-261-0*, Pub. by Woodhead Pubng) Am Educ Systs.

Local Area High Speed Networks. 700p. 2000. 50.00 (*1-57870-113-9*) Macmillan Tech.

Local Area Network Cable Cross Connects Outlets Concentrators & Hubs: Markets Technologies, & Opportunities, 1990-1995 Analysis. Amadee Bender & Frank Murawski. (Illus.). 200p. 1990. pap. text 1800.00 (*1-878218-10-7*) World Info Tech.

Local Area Network Equipment in Taiwan: A Strategic Entry Report, 1997. Compiled by Icon Group International Staff. (Illus.). 117p. 1999. ring bd. 1170.00 incl. audio compact disk (*0-7418-0793-9*) Icon Grp.

***Local Area Network Handbook.** 6th ed. John P. Slone. LC 99-36703. 696p. 1999. boxed set 95.00 (*0-8493-9838-X*) CRC Pr.

Local Area Network Interconnection. R. O. Onvural & A. Nilsson. LC 93-6370. (Illus.). 368p. (C). 1993. 110.00 (*0-306-44630-8*, Plenum Trade) Perseus Pubng.

Local Area Network Interconnection: Forecasts of Markets & Technologies. Bruce R. Kravitz & Lawrence K. Vanston. 116p. 1992. pap. 45.00 (*0-614-18107-0*) Tech Futures.

***Local Area Network Performance.** 3rd ed. Held. LC 99-35766. 366p. 2000. 110.00 (*0-471-98836-7*) Wiley.

Local Area Network Security. Ed. by T. A. Berson & T. Beth. (Lecture Notes in Computer Science Ser.: Vol. 396). x, 152p. 1989. pap. 31.00 (*0-387-51754-5*) Spr-Verlag.

Local Area Network Security, Auditing & Controls (MAP-30) MASP Professional Consulting Staff. (Security, Audit & Control Ser.). (Illus.). 200p. 1996. student ed., ring bd. 250.00 (*0-940706-51-2*) Management Advisory Pubns.

Local Area Networking. Matthew G. Naugle. 400p. 1991. 39.00 (*0-07-046455-3*) McGraw.

Local Area Networking for the Small Library: A How-to-Do-It Manual. 2nd rev. ed. Norman Howden. LC 96-29331. (How-to-Do-It Manuals Ser.). 147p. 1997. pap. 45.00 (*1-55570-285-6*) Neal-Schuman.

Local Area Networking with Novell Software. 2nd ed. Alvin L. Rains & Michael J. Palmer. 392p. (C). 1994. mass mkt., teacher ed. 49.95 (*0-87709-042-4*) Course Tech.

Local Area Networks. Ciampa. (Management Information Systems Ser.). 1996. pap. 34.95 (*0-7895-0585-1*) Course Tech.

Local Area Networks. Ciampa. (Management Information Systems Ser.). 1996. pap. 37.95 (*0-534-20712-X*) S-W Pub.

Local Area Networks. A. Hopper & D. Wheeler. (International Computer Science Ser.). 256p. (C). 1986. pap. text 23.75 (*0-201-13797-6*) Addison-Wesley.

Local Area Networks. Gerd E. Keiser. (Electrical Engineering Ser.). (Illus.). 448p. (C). 1988. text, teacher ed. 27.50 (*0-07-033562-1*) McGraw.

Local Area Networks. Gerd E. Keiser. (Electrical Engineering Ser.). (Illus.). 448p. (C). 1989. text 75.74 (*0-07-033561-3*) McGraw.

Local Area Networks. Thompson. LC 99-20147. (Illus.). 324p. 1999. 87.00 (*0-13-921222-1*) P-H.

***Local Area Networks.** 2nd ed. Goldman. 928p. (C). 2000. pap. 89.95 (*0-471-33047-7*) Wiley.

***Local Area Networks.** 2nd ed. Keiser. 2001. 76.00 (*0-07-239343-2*) McGraw.

Local Area Networks. 2nd ed. David A. Stamper. LC 97-15945. (Illus.). 480p. (C). 1997. pap. 68.00 (*0-8053-7729-8*, Prentice Hall) P-H.

***Local Area Networks.** 3rd ed. David A. Stamper. 448p. 2000. pap. 69.33 (*0-13-018377-6*) P-H.

Local Area Networks: A Client-Server Approach. James E. Goldman. LC 96-31290. 780p. 1996. pap. 86.95 (*0-471-14162-3*) Wiley.

Local Area Networks: A Guide for Midrange Decision Makers. Teresa Elms et al. (Market Intelligence Report). 160p. 1991. pap. 149.00 (*1-880738-00-7*) Elms Info Servs.

Local Area Networks: An Advanced Course. Ed. by D. Hutchison et al. (Lecture Notes in Computer Science Ser.: Vol. 184). viii, 497p. 1988. 54.00 (*0-387-15191-5*) Spr-Verlag.

Local Area Networks: An Introduction to the Technology. John McNamara. 191p. 1996. pap. 32.95 (*1-55558-149-8*, Digital DEC) Buttrwrth-Heinemann.

Local Area Networks: Architectures & Implementations. 2nd ed. James Martin et al. LC 93-37562. (Illus.). 586p. 1993. 85.00 (*0-13-533035-1*, Pub. by P-H) S&S Trade.

Local Area Networks: Making the Right Choices. Philip Hunter. LC 93-19723. 340p. (C). 1993. pap. 34.95 (*0-201-62763-9*) Addison-Wesley.

Local Area Networks: New Technologies, Emerging Standards. 3rd ed. Thomas W. Madron. 400p. 1994. pap. 29.95 (*0-471-00959-8*) Wiley.

Local-Area Networks & Their Architectures. Eduard A. Yakubaitis. Tr. by Martin Morell from RUS. (Illus.). vi, 338p. 1986. 58.50 (*0-89864-018-0*) Allerton Pr.

Local Area Networks Basics with Hands-On Netware Version 3.11/3.12. Patricia Harris. 300p. 1995. pap. 34.38 (*0-07-026915-7*) McGraw.

Local Area Networks in Information Management, 18. Harry M. Kibrige. LC 88-7689. (New Directions in Information Management Ser.). 189p. 1989. 55.00 (*0-313-26191-1*, KLR, Greenwood Pr) Greenwood.

Local Area Networks (LANs) Introduction. Computer Confidence Staff. (Illus.). xiv, 114p. 1995. spiral bd. 29.00 (*1-57533-086-5*, 08030) Comput Confidence.

Local Area Networks '90, Munich, Germany. 1990. 145.00 (*0-614-26517-7*, E90LPR) Info Gatekeepers.

Local Area Networks with Novell. H. Rene Baca et al. 304p. 1994. mass mkt. 34.95 (*0-534-21516-5*) Course Tech.

Local Area Networks with Novell. H. Rene Baca et al. 273p. 1995. 30.00 (*0-534-21510-6*) Course Tech.

Local Assays: On Contemporary American Poetry. Dave Smith. LC 84-150. 272p. 1985. text 27.50 (*0-252-01134-1*) U of Ill Pr.

Local Atomic Arrangements Studied by X-ray Diffraction, Chicago, Illionis, Feruary 15, 1965. Ed. by J. B. Cohen & J. E. Hilliard. LC 66-28062. (Metallurgical Society Conference Ser.: Vol. 36). 393p. reprint ed. pap. 121.90 (*0-608-11325-5*, 200152500079) Bks Demand.

Local Attachments: The Making of an American Urban Neighborhood, 1850-1920. Alexander Von Hoffman. (Creating the North American Landscape Ser.). 1994. text 39.95 (*0-8018-4710-9*) Johns Hopkins.

Local Attachments: The Making of an American Urban Neighborhood, 1850-1920. Alexander Von Hoffman. (Creating the North American Landscape Ser.). (Illus.). 368p. (C). 1996. reprint ed. pap. text 17.95 (*0-8018-5393-1*) Johns Hopkins.

Local Authorities & the Attraction of Industry see Progress in Planning

Local Authorities & the Creation of Employment. J. A. Chandler & Paul Lawless. 300p. 1985. text 77.95 (*0-566-00765-7*) Ashgate Pub Co.

Local Authorities' Budgetary Deficits & Excessive Indebtedness. (Local & Regional Authorities in Europe Ser.: No. 58). 1996. 21.00 (*92-871-3024-8*, Pub. by Council of Europe) Manhattan Pub Co.

Local Authority Access to E. E. C. Aid. J. Glasson. (C). 1984. 35.00 (*0-7855-3839-9*, Pub. by Oxford Polytechnic) St Mut.

Local Authority Accounting Methods: Problems & Solutions, 1909-1934. Richard Brief. LC 90-25398. (New Works in Accounting History). 384p. 1992. text 10.00 (*0-8153-0685-7*) Garland.

Local Authority Accounting Methods: The Early Debate, 1884-1908. Hugh J. Coombs & John Edwards. LC 90-25398. (New Works in Accounting History). 336p. 1991. text 10.00 (*0-8153-0003-4*) Garland.

Local Authority & New Technologies: The European Dimension. Ed. by Kenneth H. Dyson. 192p. 1988. lib. bdg. 52.50 (*0-7099-4570-1*, Pub. by C Helm) Routldge.

Local Authority Property Management: Initiatives, Strategies, Re-Organisation & Reform. Ed. by Mark Deakin. 302p. 1999. text 69.95 (*1-84014-834-9*, Pub. by Ashgate Pub) Ashgate Pub Co.

Local Authority Social Services: An Introduction. Michael Hill & Frank Tolan. 256p. 1999. 69.95 (*0-631-20946-8*) Blackwell Pubs.

Local Authority Social Services: An Introduction. Michael Hill & Frank Tolan. 256p. 2000. pap. 34.95 (*0-631-20947-6*) Blackwell Pubs.

Local Baptists, Local Politics: Churches & Communities in the Middle & Uplands South. Clifford A. Grammich. LC 98-40212. (Illus.). 264p. 1999. text 30.00 (*1-57233-045-7*) U of Tenn Pr.

Local Birds of Los Angeles County: Pocket Size. Local Birds, Inc. Editors. (Illus.). 1995. 7.95 (*1-886403-06-6*) Local Birds.

Local Birds of Marin County: Pocket Size. Local Birds, Inc. Editors. (Illus.). 1995. 7.95 (*1-886403-02-3*) Local Birds.

Local Birds of Orange County: Pocket Size. Local Birds, Inc. Editors. (Illus.). 1995. 7.95 (*1-886403-14-7*) Local Birds.

Local Birds of San Diego County: Pocket Size. Local Birds Editors. (Illus.). 1995. 7.95 (*1-886403-07-4*) Local Birds.

Local Birds of Santa Barbara: Pocket Size. Local Birds, Inc. Editors. (Illus.). 1996. 7.95 (*1-886403-00-7*) Local Birds.

L

An Asterisk (*) at the beginning of an entry indicates that the title is appearing for the first time.

L

Local Birds of the Monterey Pennisula: Pocket Size. Local Birds, Inc. Editors. (Illus.). 1995. 7.95 (*1-886403-11-2*) Local Birds.
Local Birds of the Salton Sea: Pocket Size. Local Birds Editors. (Illus.). 1997. 7.95 (*1-886403-33-3*) Local Birds.
Local Birds of the San Francisco Bay Area: Pocket Size. Local Birds, Inc. Editors. (Illus.). 1995. 7.95 (*1-886403-01-5*) Local Birds.
Local Boy Makes Good. John Gray. 208p. 1987. pap. 16.95 (*0-88922-248-7*, Pub. by Talonbks) Genl Dist Srvs.
Local Bubble & Beyond: Proceedings of the IAU Colloquium No. 166 Held in Garching, Germany, 21-25 April 1997. Ed. by D. Breitschwerdt et al. LC 98-7473. (Lecture Notes in Physics Ser.: Vol. 506). xviii, 603p. 1998. 109.00 (*3-540-64306-0*) Spr-Verlag.
Local Burglar Alarm Units & Systems, UL 609. 11th ed. (C). 1996. pap. text 95.00 (*0-7629-0039-3*) Underwrtrs Labs.
Local Bus Market: A Case Study of Regulatory Change. Peter Mackie & John Preston. LC 96-83233. 248p. 1996. 72.95 (*1-85628-267-8*, Pub. by Avebry) Ashgate Pub Co.
Local Business Taxes in Britain & Germany. Ed. by Robert J. Bennett & Gunter Krebs. 348p. 1988. 79.00 (*3-7890-1536-9*, Pub. by Nomos Verlags) Intl Bk Import.
Local Businesses: Exploring Their History. K. Austin Kerr et al. LC 90-944. (Nearby History Ser.). (Illus.). 128p. 1990. reprint ed. pap. 17.95 (*0-942063-09-0*) AltaMira Pr.
Local Census Listings, 1522-1930: Holdings in the British Isles. 3rd ed. J. S. W. Gibson & Mervyn Medlycott. LC 98-72245. 52p. 1997. pap. 8.50 (*0-8063-1570-9*) Genealog Pub.
Local Chips & Splinters: Medina County Gazette, 1889. Sharon L. Kraynek. 49p. 1993. pap. 5.00 (*1-55856-149-8*, 420) Closson Pr.
Local Chips & Splinters, Medina County Gazette, 1886-88. Sharon L. Kraynek. 140p. 1995. per. 12.00 (*1-55856-195-1*, 419) Closson Pr.
Local Church. Larry Kreiger. (Biblical Foundation Ser.: Vol. 8). (Illus.). 48p. 1997. pap. 2.95 (*1-886973-07-5*) Dove Chr Fel.
Local Church & Mission. Theodore Williams. 1986. pap. 1.25 (*9971-972-43-3*) OMF Bks.
Local Church & the Missions see Iglesia Local y las Misiones
Local Church Evangelism: Patterns & Approaches. D. F. Wright & Alastair Gray. 176p. (C). 1988. pap. text 26.00 (*0-7152-0611-7*) St Mut.
***Local Church in a Global Era: Reflections for a New Century.** Max L. Stackhouse et al. LC 00-32151. 2000. pap. write for info. (*0-8028-4710-2*) Eerdmans.
Local Church, Its Pastor, Officers & Their Ministries. Marshall Gilmore. LC 95-80335. (Reader Resource Ser.). 80p. (Orig.). 1995. pap. text 6.00 (*1-883667-13-5*) Christian Meth.
Local Church Practice. Ed. by Evangelical Press Staff. 1994. pap. 7.99 (*0-85479-681-9*, Pub. by Evangelical Pr) P & R Pubng.
Local Church Says "Hell No" Earl Paulk. 190p. (Orig.). 1991. pap. 9.95 (*0-917595-40-8*) Kingdom Pubs.
Local Code: Constitution of a City at 42 Degrees North Latitude. Michael Sorkin. LC 93-37243. 128p. (Orig.). 1993. pap. 14.95 (*1-878271-79-2*) Princeton Arch.
***Local Coefficients of Friction in Worm Gear Contacts.** K. Steingrover & B. R. Hohn. (Technical Papers: Vol. 98FTM10). 8p. 1998. pap. 30.00 (*1-55589-728-2*) AGMA.
Local Cohomology: An Algebraic Introduction with Geometric Applications. M. P. Brodmann & R. Y. Sharp. LC 97-29059. (Studies in Advanced Mathematics: No. 60). (Illus.). 432p. (C). 1998. text 69.95 (*0-521-37286-0*) Cambridge U Pr.
Local Color. Jon Davis. 32p. 1994. pap. 5.00 (*1-889806-08-0*) Devils Millhopper.
Local Color. Irvin S. Cobb. (Collected Works of Irvin S. Cobb). 460p. 1998. reprint ed. lib. bdg. 108.00 (*1-58201-597-X*) Classic Bks.
Local Color: The di Rosa Collection of Contemporary California Art. Rene Di Rosa. LC 98-38931. (Illus.). 190p. 1999. 60.00 (*0-8118-2376-8*); pap. 35.00 (*0-8118-2377-6*) Chronicle Bks.
Local Colorist. Annie T. Slosson. LC 70-144172. (Short Story Index Reprint Ser.). 1977. reprint ed. 16.95 (*0-8369-3787-2*) Ayer.
Local Colorists: American Short Stories. Claude M. Simpson. (BCL1-PS American Literature Ser.). 340p. 1992. reprint ed. lib. bdg. 89.00 (*0-7812-6657-2*) Rprt Serv.
Local Colors. Wren & Maile. (Keiki's First Bks.). (ENG & HAW., Illus.). 10p. (J). (ps). 1992. bds. 4.95 (*1-880188-02-3*) Bess Pr.
Local Colour. William Plomer. 14p. 1999. 85.00 (*1-893450-02-3*) Elysium Pr.
Local Commons & Global Interdependence: Heterogeneity & Cooperation in Two Domains. Robert O. Keohane & Elinor Ostrom. 256p. 1995. text 75.00 (*0-8039-7962-2*); pap. text 26.95 (*0-8039-7963-0*) Sage.
Local Communities & Mega-Project Development. Beazley et al. 59.95 (*1-85972-520-1*) Ashgate Pub Co.
Local Communities & the Israeli Polity: Conflict of Values & Interests. Ed. by Efraim Ben-Zadok. LC 92-40893. (SUNY Series in Israeli Studies). 285p. (C). 1993. pap. text 21.95 (*0-7914-1562-7*) State U NY Pr.
Local Communities & the Israeli Polity: Conflict of Values & Interests. Ed. by Efraim Ben-Zadok. LC 92-40893. (SUNY Series in Israeli Studies). 285p. (C). 1993. text 64.50 (*0-7914-1561-9*) State U NY Pr.
Local Community Leadership. Linton C. Freeman et al. 1960. 2.50 (*0-87060-083-4*, PUC 15) Syracuse U Cont Ed.
Local Computer Networks. 2nd ed. Joseph L. Hammond. (C). 1995. text. write for info. (*0-201-54341-9*) Addison-Wesley.
***Local Computer Networks: 24th Conference Lowell, MA, 1999.** 263p. 1999. 145.00 (*0-7695-0309-8*) IEEE Comp Soc.
Local Computer Networks, 21st Conference On: LCN 96. LC 07-421303. 512p. 1996. pap. 100.00 (*0-8186-7617-5*) IEEE Comp Soc.
Local Computer Networks, 22nd Conference. 560p. 1997. pap. 140.00 (*0-8186-8141-1*) IEEE Comp Soc.
Local Constraints vs. Economy. David Johnson & Shalom Lappin. LC 98-55973. (Stanford Monographs in Linguistics). 152p. (C). 1999. text 54.95 (*1-57586-183-6*); pap. text 18.95 (*1-57586-182-8*) CSLI.
Local Control & Accountability: How to Get It, Keep It, & Improve School Performance. Richard Sagor. LC 96-10082. (Illus.). 136p. 1996. 45.95 (*0-8039-6411-0*); pap. 19.95 (*0-8039-6412-9*) Corwin Pr.
Local Control of Sertoli Cell Function: Paracrine Factors Produced by Peritubular Myoid Cells & Cytokines. Eva Hoeben. (Acta Biomedica Lovaniensia Ser.: Vol. 161). (Illus.). 166p. 1998. pap. 57.50 (*90-6186-854-8*, Pub. by Leuven Univ) Coronet Bks.
Local Cortical Circuits: An Electrophysiological Study. M. Abeles. (Studies of Brain Function: Vol. 6). (Illus.). 110p. 1982. 38.95 (*0-387-11034-8*) Spr-Verlag.
Local Council Administration. 4th ed. Charles Arnold-Baker. 1994. write for info. (*0-406-04821-5*, U.K., MICHIE) LEXIS Pub.
Local Courts & Municipal Gazette (Toronto), 1865-1872 Vols. 1-8, Set. 1976. 275.00 (*1-57588-324-4*, 104930) W S Hein.
Local Cults in Etruria. Lily R. Taylor. LC 24-2723. (American Academy in Rome, Papers & Monographs: Vol. 2). 274p. reprint ed. pap. 85.00 (*0-608-16453-4*, 202671700051) Bks Demand.
Local Deities. Agnes Bushell. LC 88-43569. 306p. (Orig.). 1990. pap. 11.95 (*0-915306-82-4*) Curbstone.
Local Democracies: A Study. Bowman & Hampton. Date not set. pap. text. write for info. (*0-582-71220-3*, Pub. by Addison-Wesley) Longman.
Local Democracy: A Civic Project. (Congress of Local & Regional Authorities of Europe Ser.: No. 43). 1996. 21.00 (*92-871-3126-0*, Pub. by Council of Europe) Manhattan Pub Co.
Local Democracy in Practice: The Role & Working Environment of Councillors in Scotland. Clive Martlew. 184p. 1988. text 72.95 (*0-566-05508-2*, Pub. by Dartmth Pub) Ashgate Pub Co.
Local Density Theory of Polarization. G. D. Mahan & K. R. Subbaswamy. LC 90-42552. (Physics of Solids & Liquids Ser.). (Illus.). 260p. (C). 1990. 75.00 (*0-306-43685-X*, Kluwer Plenum) Kluwer Academic.
Local Development: Restructuring, Locality & Economic Initiative in Portugal. Stephen Syrett. 372p. 1995. pap. 82.95 (*1-85628-484-0*, Pub. by Avebry) Ashgate Pub Co.
***Local Development: The Simularia Integrated Rural Development Case.** Richard Vengroff. 24p. 1998. pap. 9.95 (*1-56549-086-X*) Kumarian Pr.
Local Development in the Global Economy: The Case of Pakistan. Pervaiz Nazir. 219p. 1991. text 82.95 (*1-85628-106-X*, Pub. by Avebry) Ashgate Pub Co.
Local Disturbance Decoupling with Stability for Nonlinear Systems. L. L. Van der Wegen. Ed. by M. Thoma & A. Wyner. (Lecture Notes in Control & Information Sciences: Vol. 166). (Illus.). 140p. 1991. 31.95 (*0-387-54543-3*) Spr-Verlag.
Local Drug Delivery/Molecular. Edelman. 1995. text 63.00 (*0-7020-1910-0*, W B Saunders Co) Harcrt Hlth Sci Grp.
***Local Dynamics in an Era of Globalization.** Ed. by Shahid Yusuf et al. 2000. pap. text 25.00 (*0-19-521597-4*) OUP.
Local Economic Development: A Geographical Comparison of Rural Community Restructuring. Ed. by Cecily Neil & Markku Tykkylainen. LC 98-40088. 368p. 1998. pap. 24.95 (*92-808-0998-9*, Pub. by UN Univ Pr) Brookings.
Local Economic Development: Analysis & Practice. John P. Blair. LC 95-3023. 330p. 1995. 45.00 (*0-8039-5376-3*) Sage.
Local Economic Development: Strategies & Techniques for Local Government Initiatives. Ed. by Sherman M. Wyman & Robert R. Weaver. 116p. 1987. pap. text 4.00 (*0-936440-73-2*) U TX SUPA.
Local Economic Development: Strategies for a Changing Economy. Ed. by R. Scott Fosler. (Practical Management Ser.). (Illus.). 1991. 23.95 (*0-87326-085-6*) Intl City-Cnty Mgt.
Local Economic Development in Europe & the Americas. Ed. by Christophe Demaziere & Patricia A. Wilson. LC 95-18499. 256p. 1995. 110.00 (*0-7201-2269-4*) Continuum.
Local Economic Development in Texas. Robert R. Weaver. (Illus.). 100p. 1986. pap. text 4.00 (*0-936440-71-6*) U TX SUPA.
Local Economic Development Policy: Strategies & Finance Issues. Robert Wilson & Norman J. Glickman. (Policy Research Project Report Ser.: No. 80). 400p. 1988. pap. 14.00 (*0-89940-684-X*) LBJ Sch Pub Aff.
Local Economic Development Policy: The United States & Canada. Laura A. Reese & Urban Center Staff. Ed. by Richard D. Bingham. LC 96-47040. (Contemporary Urban Affairs Ser.). (Illus.). 176p. 1997. text 37.00 (*0-8153-2383-2*, SS1109) Garland.
Local Economies: The U. S. Common Market of Economic Regions. 37p. 1994. 20.00 (*0-933729-97-9*, No. 5530) Natl League Cities.
***Local Economies in Turmoil.** Arni Sverrisson. LC 99-87607. 2000. text 69.95 (*0-312-23147-4*) St Martin.
Local Economy. Chris Collins. LC 96-8711. (Linguistic Inquiry Monographs: No. 29). (Illus.). 160p. 1996. pap. text 17.50 (*0-262-53144-5*) MIT Pr.
Local Education: Community, Conversation, Praxis. Mark K. Smith. LC 94-14186. 208p. 1994. 118.95 (*0-335-19275-0*); pap. 31.95 (*0-335-19274-2*) OpUniv Pr.
***Local Education Order: Ethnomethodological Studies of Knowledge in Action.** Ed. by Stephen K. Hester & David Francis. LC 99-462313. (Pragmatics & Beyond New Ser.: Vol. 73). viii, 323p. 2000. 79.00 (*1-55619-920-1*) J Benjamins Pubng Co.
Local Emergency Planning Committee Guidebook: Understanding the EBI Risk Management Program Rule. R. J. Walters. 174p. 1998. pap. 59.00 (*0-8169-0749-8*, G-54) Am Inst Chem Eng.
Local Employment Policy in a High-Growth Economy: Matching Training & Jobs in Austin, Texas. Robert W. Glover. (Policy Research Project Report Ser.: No. 49). 33p. 1982. pap. 5.50 (*0-89940-652-1*) LBJ Sch Pub Aff.
Local Empower & Business Service: Britain's Experiment with Training & Enterprise Councils. Bennett et al. 352p. 1994. 95.00 (*1-85728-144-6*, Pub. by UCL Pr Ltd) Taylor & Francis.
Local Energy Centres. N. J. Lucas. (Illus.). 261p. 1978. 63.00 (*0-85334-782-4*) Elsevier.
***Local Enterprise on the North Atlantic Margin: Selected Contributions to the Fourteenth International Seminar on Marginal Regions.** Ed. by Reginald Byron & John Hutson. LC 99-72974. 380p. 1999. text 78.95 (*1-84014-932-9*, Pub. by Ashgate Pub) Ashgate Pub Co.
Local Entrepreneurship in Singapore: Private & State. Lee T. Yuan & Linda Low. 264p. 1990. pap. 22.50 (*981-00-1553-4*, Pub. by Times Academic); boxed set 28.50 (*981-00-1707-3*, Pub. by Times Academic) Intl Spec Bk.
Local Environmental Struggles: Citizen Activism in the Treadmill of Production. Kenneth A. Gould et al. (Illus.). 254p. (C). 1996. text 59.95 (*0-521-55519-1*) Cambridge U Pr.
Local Environmental Struggles: Citizen Activism in the Treadmill of Production. Kenneth A. Gould et al. (Illus.). 254p. (C). 1996. pap. text 18.95 (*0-521-55521-3*) Cambridge U Pr.
Local Equilibrium in Strong Interaction Physics: Proceedings of the First International Workshop, F R Germany. Ed. by D. K. Scott & R. M. Weiner. 480p. 1985. 100.00 (*9971-978-06-7*) World Scientific Pub.
Local Exchange & Early State Development in Southwestern Iran. Gregory A. Johnson. LC 73-623150. (University of Michigan, Museum of Anthropology, Anthropological Papers: No. 51). (Illus.). 244p. reprint ed. pap. 75.70 (*0-608-15520-9*, 202970000063) Bks Demand.
Local Farmlands Protection in California: Studies of Problems, Programs, & Politics in Seven Counties. Ed. by Eleanor M. Cohen. (California Farmlands Project Working Papers: No. 2). 56p. (Orig.). 1983. pap. 10.00 (*0-912102-63-2*) Cal Inst Public.
Local Fields. J. W. Cassels. (London Mathematical Society Student Texts Ser.: No. 4). 360p. 1986. pap. text 31.95 (*0-521-31525-5*) Cambridge U Pr.
Local Fields. Jean-Pierre Serre. Tr. by M. J. Greenberg from FRE. LC 79-12643. (Graduate Texts in Mathematics Ser.: Vol. 67). (Illus.). 241p. 1995. 54.95 (*0-387-90424-7*) Spr-Verlag.
Local Fields & Their Extensions: A Constructive Approach. I. B. Fesenko & S. V. Vostokov. Ed. by Simeon Ivanov. LC 93-14840. (Translations of Mathematical Monographs: Vol. 121). 283p. 1993. pap. 49.00 (*0-8218-4613-2*, MMONO/121) Am Math.
Local Fields at Impurity Atoms in Single Crystals & Epitaxial Layers: The Physics of Ultra-Thin Magnetic Structures. Michael E. Semple. (Uppsala Dissertations from the Faculty of Science Ser.: Vol. 11). (Illus.). 127p. 1996. pap. 39.50 (*91-554-3705-2*) Coronet Bks.
Local Fiscal Effects of Illegal Immigration: Report of a Workshop. National Research Council Staff. Ed. by Barry Edmonston & Ronald Lee. LC 97-102935. 40p. (C). 1996. pap. text 10.00 (*0-309-05592-X*) Natl Acad Pr.
Local Flaps in Facial Reconstruction. Ed. by Shan R. Baker & Neil A. Swanson. (Illus.). 656p. (C). (gr. 13). 1994. text 196.00 (*0-8016-6925-1*, 06925) Mosby Inc.
Local Flavor: Favorite Recipes from Philadelphia-Area Chefs. Connie C. Fisher. 320p. 1998. pap. 15.95 (*0-9661200-0-0*) Small Potatoes.
Local Food: What to Eat in Hawai'i. Joan Clarke. LC 97-67940. (Illus.). 80p. 1997. pap. 4.95 (*0-9643359-1-3*) Namkoong Pubng.
Local Geographies of Unemployment: Long Term Unemployment in Areas of Local Deprivation. Graham Haughton et al. 208p. 1993. 67.95 (*1-85628-459-X*, Pub. by Avebry) Ashgate Pub Co.
***Local Girls.** Alice Hoffman. 208p. 2000. pap. 12.95 (*0-425-17434-4*) Berkley Pub.
Local Girls. Alice Hoffman. LC 98-50632. 197p. 1999. 22.95 (*0-399-14507-9*, G P Putnam) Peng Put Young Read.
***Local Girls.** large type ed. Alice Hoffman. LC 99-27472. 208p. 1999. pap. 26.95 (*0-7862-2010-4*) Mac Lib Ref.
Local Girls. large type ed. Alice Hoffman. LC 99-27472. 1999. 28.95 (*0-7862-2009-0*) Thorndike Pr.
Local Governance & Rural Development in Thailand. Marcus Ingle. (Special Series on Rural Local Government: No. 16). 106p. 1974. pap. 3.50 (*0-86731-102-9*) Cornell CIS RDC.
Local Governance Around the World. Ed. by Henry Teune. LC 94-68310. (Annals of the American Academy of Political & Social Science Ser.: Vol. 540). 1995. 28.00 (*0-8039-7120-6*); pap. 18.00 (*0-8039-7121-4*) Am Acad Pol Soc Sci.
Local Governance of Crime: Appeals to Community & Partnerships. Adam Crawford. LC 97-5572. (Clarendon Studies in Criminology). (Illus.). 384p. 1997. text 69.00 (*0-19-826253-1*, Clarendon Pr) OUP.
Local Governance of Crime: Appeals to Community & Partnerships. Adam Crawford. (Illus.). 384p. 1999. pap. text 29.95 (*0-19-829845-5*) OUP.
Local Government. J. Gillsepie. (Reviews of U. K. Statistical Sources Ser.). 356p. (gr. 13). 1988. text 140.50 (*0-412-31680-3*) Chapman & Hall.
Local Government. Pub. Services COI Staff. LC 97-135863. (Aspects of Britain Ser.). (Illus.). 97p. 1996. pap. 12.00 (*0-11-702037-0*, HM020370, Pub. by Statnry Office) Bernan Associates.
Local Government see Burns Indiana Statutes Annotated 1999 Cumulative Supplement Set: Pocket Part
Local Government: Adaptable to Courses Utilizing Valente & McCarthy's Casebook on Local Government Law. Casenotes Publishing Co., Inc. Staff. Ed. by Norman S. Goldenberg & Peter Tenen. (Legal Briefs Ser.). 1992. pap. write for info. (*0-87457-105-7*, 1590) Casenotes Pub.
Local Government: Is It Manageable? Gordon Bayley. 1979. 58.00 (*0-08-024279-0*, Pub. by Pergamon Repr) Franklin.
Local Government Act, 1993: An Annotated Act. P. Stein. 504p. 1996. pap. write for info. (*0-409-31066-2*, MICHIE) LEXIS Pub.
Local Government & Environmental Control in New South Wales. Ed. by Zada Lipman. 160p. 1991. pap. 35.00 (*1-86287-074-8*, Pub. by Federation Pr) Gaunt.
Local Government & 1992. Bongers. 1990. pap. text. write for info. (*0-582-07570-X*, Pub. by Addison-Wesley) Longman.
Local Government & Politics in New Zealand. 2nd ed. Graham Bush. 336p. 1996. pap. 29.95 (*1-86940-126-3*, Pub. by Allen & Unwin Pty) Paul & Co Pubs.
Local Government & Politics in Uganda. Fred G. Burke. LC 64-16919. 286p. reprint ed. pap. 88.70 (*0-608-15215-3*, 202740900055) Bks Demand.
Local Government & Rural Development in the Philippines. Santiago S. Simpas et al. (Special Series on Rural Local Government: No. 12). 188p. (Orig.). 1974. pap. 3.50 (*0-317-56356-4*) Cornell CIS RDC.
Local Government & Rural Development in Yugoslavia. Zdravji Milinar. (Special Series on Rural Local Government: No. 18). 136p. pap. 3.50 (*0-86731-104-5*) Cornell CIS RDC.
Local Government & Strategic Choice: An Operational Research Approach to the Processes of Public Planning. 2nd ed. John K. Friend & William N. Jessop. 1977. 144.00 (*0-08-021176-3*, Pub. by Pergamon Repr) Franklin.
Local Government & the Regional Policy of the European Communities: Overview. P. Tristan McGee. (C). 1982. 29.00 (*0-7855-3851-8*, Pub. by Oxford Polytechnic) St Mut.
Local Government & Urban Affairs in International Perspective. Ed. by Joachim J. Hesse. 623p. 1991. 161.00 (*3-7890-1835-X*, Pub. by Nomos Verlags) Intl Bk Import.
Local Government at a Crossroads: Choices for South Dakota. Russell L. Smith. 1986. pap. 5.00 (*1-55614-119-X*) U of SD Gov Res Bur.
Local Government Audit & Accounting Manual As of March 1, 1990. American Institute of Certified Public Accountants et al. Ed. by Susan Cornwall. LC HJ9777.. (Nonauthoritative Practice Aid Ser.). 432p. reprint ed. pap. 134.00 (*0-7837-1381-9*, 204155300021) Bks Demand.
Local Government Audit & Accounting Manual As of March 1, 1991. American Institute of Certified Public Accountants. Ed. by Susan Cornwall et al. LC HJ9777.A3L63. (Nonauthoritative Practice Aid Ser.). 432p. reprint ed. pap. 134.00 (*0-7837-3733-5*, 204339900009) Bks Demand.
***Local Government Audits Electronic Workpapers & Reference Guide, 2000** Rhett D. Harrell. 1998. pap. text 137.00 (*0-15-606869-9*, Pub. by Harcourt Coll Pubs) Harcourt.
Local Government Budget & Fiscal Control Act. 3rd ed. David M. Lawrence. 31p. 1988. pap. 6.00 (*1-56011-098-8*) Institute Government.
Local Government Budgeting: A Managerial Approach. Gerasimos A. Gianakis & Clifford P. McCue. LC 98-24563. 208p. 1999. 65.00 (*1-56720-006-0*, Quorum Bks); pap. 22.95 (*0-275-95272-X*, Praeger Pubs) Greenwood.
***Local Government Democratisation & Decentralisation: A Review of the Southern African Experience.** P. S. Reddy. 304p. 1999. pap. 27.95 (*0-7021-4979-9*, Pub. by Juta & Co) Intl Spec Bk.
Local Government Dollars & Sense: 225 Financial Tips for Guarding the Public Checkbook. Len Wood. LC 97-90605. (Illus.). 358p. 1998. 34.95 (*0-9634374-3-7*); pap. 24.95 (*0-9634374-4-5*) Trng Shoppe.
Local Government Election Practices: A Handbook for Public Officials & Citizens. Roger L. Kemp. LC 98-20820. 503p. 1998. lib. bdg. 65.00 (*0-7864-0567-8*) McFarland & Co.
Local Government Election Systems. Terrell Blodgett & Barbara Jordan. LC 84-81908. (Policy Research Project Report: No. 62). 174p. 1984. pap. 8.95 (*0-89940-664-5*) LBJ Sch Pub Aff.

An Asterisk (*) at the beginning of an entry indicates that the title is appearing for the first time.

Local Government Engineering Conference, 7th National, 1993: Effective Use of Technology. (National Conference Publication Ser.: No. 93-5). (Illus.). 398p. (Orig.). 1993. pap. 81.50 (*0-85825-575-8*, Pub. by Inst Engrs Aust-EA Bks) Accents Pubns.

***Local Government Engineering in Australia.** Malcolm J. Jones & Robert French. LC 99-487898. 366p. 1999. pap. 53.95 (*1-86287-309-7*, Pub. by Federation Pr) Gaunt.

***Local Government Ethics Ordinances in California.** Charlene Wear Simmons et al. 68p. 1998. pap. write for info. (*1-58703-080-2*, CRB-98-002) CA St Libry.

Local Government Finance: An International Comparison. Ed. by S. J. Bailey & Ronan Paddison. 208p. 1988. lib. bdg. 59.50 (*0-415-00529-9*) Routledge.

Local Government Finance: International Perspectives. Ed. by Ronan Paddison & Stephen Bailey. LC 89-113801. 277p. reprint ed. pap. 85.90 (*0-608-20311-4*, 207156400002) Bks Demand.

Local Government Finance in Developing Countries: The Case of Kenya. Paul Smoke. (Illus.). 224p. 1994. pap. text 21.00 (*0-19-572787-8*) OUP.

Local Government Finance in North Carolina. rev. ed. David M. Lawrence. 323p. (C). 1990. pap. text 12.00 (*1-56011-099-6*) Institute Government.

Local Government Finance in the Third World. Roy W. Bahl. 1983. 52.95 (*0-275-90939-5*, C0939, Praeger Pubs) Greenwood.

Local Government Finances since Proposition 13: An Historical Primer. Helen C. Paik. 32p. 1995. pap. write for info. (*1-58703-042-X*, CRB-95-007) CA St Libry.

Local Government Guide to Imaging Systems: Planning & Implementation. Tod Newcombe. LC 95-175668. (Special Reports). (Illus.). 120p. 1995. pap. 70.00 (*0-87326-097-X*) Intl City-Cnty Mgt.

Local Government in Ancient India. R. K. Mookerji, 1989. reprint ed. 11.50 (*81-85395-01-2*, Pub. by Low Price) S Asia.

Local Government in Britain. Ed. by Martin Minogue. LC 76-43105. (Documents on Contemporary British Government Ser.: No. 2). 482p. reprint ed. pap. 137.40 (*0-608-15755-4*, 2031694) Bks Demand.

Local Government in China under the Ch'ing. T'ung-tsu Ch'u. (East Asian Monographs: No. 143). 374p. 1989. reprint ed. pap. text 16.00 (*0-674-53678-9*) Coun East Asian Stud.

Local Government in Connecticut. Frank B. Connolly. Ed. by David Pesci & Edward C. Sembor. (Illus.). 76p. (Orig.). 1992. pap. text 10.00 (*1-881866-00-9*) U CT Inst Pub Serv.

Local Government in Eastern Europe: Establishing Democracy at the Grassroots. Ed. by Andrew Coulson. (Studies of Communism in Transition). 304p. 1995. 95.00 (*1-85278-798-8*) E Elgar.

Local Government in Egypt. James B. Mayfield. LC 96-960426. 432p. 1996. 49.00 (*977-424-373-0*, Pub. by Am Univ Cairo Pr) Col U Pr.

***Local Government in European Overseas Empires, 1450-1800.** Ed. by A. J. R. Russell-Woods. LC 99-28798. (An Expanding World Ser.: 23). 832p. 1999. text 240.95 (*0-86078-529-7*, Pub. by Ashgate Pub) Ashgate Pub Co.

Local Government in Georgia. 2nd ed. Mary A. Hepburn. 240p. (YA). (gr. 8-12). 1991. text 13.75 (*0-89854-148-4*) U of GA Inst Govt.

Local Government in Illinois. Albert Shaw. LC 78-63732. (Johns Hopkins University. Studies in the Social Sciences. Thirtieth Ser. 1912: 3). reprint ed. 11.50 (*0-404-61003-X*) AMS Pr.

Local Government in Israel. Ed. by Daniel J. Elazar & Chaim Kalchheim. LC 88-1601. (Illus.). 460p. (Orig.). (C). 1988. lib. bdg. 63.00 (*0-8191-6939-0*, Pub. by Jerusalem Ctr Public) U Pr of Amer.

Local Government in Japan. Kurt Steiner. xii, 564p. 1965. 62.50 (*0-8047-0217-9*) Stanford U Pr.

Local Government in Latin America. R. Andrew Nickson. LC 94-43541. 250p. 1995. pap. text 55.00 (*1-55587-366-9*) L Rienner.

Local Government in Liberal Democracies: An Introductory Survey. Ed. by J. A. Chandler. LC 92-13197. 240p. 1992. pap. 17.95 (*0-415-08875-5*) Routledge.

Local Government in Liberal Democracies: An X International Survey. Ed. by J. A. Chandler. 240p. 1986. 47.50 (*0-7099-3476-9*, Pub. by C Helm) Routldge.

Local Government in North Carolina/Lesson Plans. Margaret C. Henderson & Laura M. Clougherty. (Illus.). 62p. (J). (gr. 3-5). 1997. teacher ed., ring bd. 10.00 (*0-9655694-0-3*) NC City & Cnty.

Local Government in Ohio. Carl M. Broberg. LC 95-79975. (Illus.). 220p. (Orig.). (J). (gr. 8). 1995. pap. text 24.95 (*0-9647908-0-7*) Amer Legal Pubng.

Local Government in Peninsular Malaysia. M. W. Norris. 132p. 1980. text 43.95 (*0-566-00283-3*) Ashgate Pub Co.

Local Government in South Carolina: Problems & Perspectives, Vol. II. Charlie B. Tyer. Ed. by Cole B. Graham, Jr. (Government in South Carolina Ser.). 211p. (Orig.). 1984. pap. 10.00 (*0-917069-03-X*) Univ SC Inst Pub Affairs.

Local Government in South Carolina: The Governmental Landscape, Vol. I. Ed. by Charlie B. Tyer & Cole B. Graham. (Government in South Carolina Ser.). 230p. (Orig.). 1984. pap. 10.00 (*0-917069-02-1*) Univ SC Inst Pub Affairs.

Local Government in the German Federal System. Arthur B. Gunlicks. LC 86-6350. (Duke Press Policy Studies). (Illus.). xii, 247p. 1986. text 53.00 (*0-8223-0674-3*) Duke.

Local Government in the South & Southwest. Edward W. Bemis et al. LC 78-63824. (Johns Hopkins University. Studies in the Social Sciences. Thirtieth Ser. 1912: 11). reprint ed. 11.50 (*0-404-61085-4*) AMS Pr.

Local Government in the Soviet Union: Problems of Implementation & Control. Cameron Ross. LC 86-29861. 240p. 1987. text 45.00 (*0-312-00545-8*) St Martin.

Local Government in the Third World: The Experience of Tropical Africa. Ed. by Philip Mawhood. LC 82-11176. (Wiley Series on Public Administration in Developing Countries). (Illus.). 275p. reprint ed. pap. 85.30 (*0-8357-2954-0*, 203921000011) Bks Demand.

Local Government in West Africa. Laing G. Cowan. LC 75-110429. (BCL Ser. I). reprint ed. 36.00 (*0-404-00144-0*) AMS Pr.

Local Government Information & Training Needs in the 21st Century. Jack P. DeSario et al. LC 93-30989. 160p. 1994. 52.95 (*0-89930-697-7*, Quorum Bks) Greenwood.

Local Government Infrastructure Management. Ed. by Robert E. Baumgardner. (Sessions Proceedings Ser.). 33p. 1986. 3.00 (*0-87262-533-8*) Am Soc Civil Eng.

***Local Government Innovation: Issues & Trends in Privatization & Managed Competition.** Ed. by Robin A. Johnson & Norman Walzer. LC 00-28001. 288p. 2000. 67.00 (*1-56720-382-5*, Q382, Quorum Bks) Greenwood.

Local Government Labor Relations: A Guide for Public Administrators. Joan E. Pynes & Joan M. Lafferty. LC 92-34943. 256p. 1993. 65.00 (*0-89930-783-3*, PLG, Quorum Bks) Greenwood.

Local Government Law. Keith Davies. 350p. 1983. pap. 50.00 (*0-406-25267-X*, UK, MICHIE) LEXIS Pub.

Local Government Law. Clayton P. Gillette. LC 93-86408. 1008p. 1994. 54.00 (*0-316-31461-7*, Aspen Law & Bus) Aspen Pub.

Local Government Law, 6 vols. 2nd ed. Chester James Antieau. LC 97-29353. 1997. ring bd. 1040.00 (*0-8205-1020-3*) Bender.

Local Government Law. 2nd ed. Gerald E. Frug. (American Casebook Ser.). 89p. 1994. pap. text, teacher ed. write for info. (*0-314-05330-1*) West Pub.

Local Government Law. 2nd ed. Gerald E. Frug. (American Casebook Ser.). 924p. (C). 1994. 62.50 (*0-314-04219-9*) West Pub.

Local Government Law, Set. Peter J. Loughlin. (New Hampshire Practice Ser.: Vols. 13 & 14). 1500p. 1994. boxed set 140.00 (*0-614-05922-4*, MICHIE) LEXIS Pub.

Local Government Law: Cases & Materials. Clayton P. Gillette. 1008p. 1994. teacher ed. write for info. (*0-316-35069-9*, 50699) Aspen Law.

Local Government Law: Cases & Materials. 2nd ed. Clayton P. Gillette & Lynn A. Baker. LC 98-47280. 913p. 1999. boxed set 62.00 (*0-7355-0212-9*) Panel Pubs.

Local Government Law: Teacher's Manual, Cases & Materials On. 4th ed. William D. Valente & David J. McCarthy, Jr. (American Casebook Ser.). 94p. 1991. pap. text. write for info. (*0-314-00414-9*) West Pub.

Local Government Law - Cases & Materials. 4th ed. William D. Valente & David J. McCarthy. (American Casebook Ser.). 1158p. (C). 1991. 65.00 (*0-314-90897-8*) West Pub.

Local Government Law - Cases & Materials: 1995 Supplement. 4th ed. William D. Valente & David J. McCarthy Jr. (American Casebook Ser.). 1158p. (C). 1995. pap. text 13.50 (*0-314-06407-9*) West Pub.

Local Government, Law & Order in a Pre-Reform English Parish, 1790-1834. Shirley B. Black. LC 92-45202. (Illus.). 448p. 1993. text 109.95 (*0-7734-9239-9*) E Mellen.

Local Government Law in a Nutshell. 3rd ed. David J. McCarthy, Jr. (Nutshell Ser.). 435p. 1990. pap. text 17.50 (*0-314-74486-X*) West Pub.

Local Government Law in a Nutshell. 4th ed. David J. Marcarthy. (Nutshell Ser.). 472p. (C). 1995. pap. 22.95 (*0-314-07025-7*) West Pub.

Local Government Law in New South Wales. Linda Pearson. 352p. 1994. pap. 49.00 (*1-86287-127-2*, Pub. by Federation Pr) Gaunt.

Local Government Law in New Zealand. 2nd ed. K. A. Palmer. 1993. write for info. (*0-455-21180-9*, Pub. by LawBk Co); pap. write for info. (*0-455-21181-7*, Pub. by LawBk Co) Gaunt.

Local Government Law, Legal & Related Materials, 1986. Jefferson B. Fordham. LC 85-29286. (University Casebook Ser.). 976p. 1986. text 41.95 (*0-88277-318-6*) Foundation Pr.

Local Government Law, 1981-1992, 4 Vols. C. Sands & Michael Libonati. LC 81-10259. 500.00 (*0-685-09235-6*) West Group.

Local Government Law, 1996: Pocket Part. Osborne M. Reynolds, Jr. (Handbook Edition). 190p. 1996. write for info. (*0-314-09763-5*) West Pub.

Local Government Law, 1993: Pocket Part. Osborne M. Reynolds, Jr. (Hornbook Ser.). 200p. 1993. pap. text 12.50 (*0-314-02256-2*) West Pub.

Local Government Major Projects in Japan: A Strategic Entry Report, 1996. Compiled by Icon Group International Staff. (Country Industry Report). (Illus.). 172p. 1999. ring bd. 1720.00 incl. audio compact disk (*0-7418-0589-8*) Icon Grp.

Local Government Network Regional Workshop Meeting Summary. Ed. by Barry Leonard. (Illus.). 71p. 1998. pap. text 20.00 (*0-7881-7022-8*) DIANE Pub.

***Local Government On-Line: Putting the Internet to Work.** John O'Looney. LC 00-21451. 2000. write for info. (*0-87326-170-4*) Intl City-Cnty Mgt.

Local Government Police Management. 3rd ed. Ed. by William A. Geller. (Municipal Management Ser.). (Illus.). 587p. 1991. 41.95 (*0-87326-084-8*) Intl City-Cnty Mgt.

Local Government Police Management Study Guide. 2nd ed. Ralph E. Hendel. 175p. (Orig.). 1978. pap. 28.95 (*1-56325-007-1*, DS024) Davis Pub Law.

Local Government Police Management Study Guide. 3rd ed. Ralph E. Hendel. 198p. (Orig.). 1995. pap. 28.95 (*1-56325-058-6*, DS024) Davis Pub Law.

Local Government Policy-Making & Management: A Crossnational Perspective. Ed. by Nahum Ben-Elia. (Orig.). 1993. pap. 15.00 (*0-944285-32-5*) Pol Studies.

Local Government Property Transactions in North Carolina. David M. Lawrence. 124p. (Orig.). (C). 1987. pap. text 9.00 (*1-56011-100-3*, 87.13) Institute Government.

***Local Government Property Transactions in North Carolina.** 2nd ed. David M. Lawrence. (Orig.). (C). 2000. pap. write for info. (*1-56011-366-9*) Institute Government.

Local Government Reorganisation: The Review & Its Aftermath. Ed. by Steve Leach. LC 97-29368. 160p. 1998. 39.50 (*0-7146-4859-0*, Pub. by F Cass Pubs) Intl Spec Bk.

Local Government Responsibilities in Health Care. (Illus.). 24p. (Orig.). (C). 1994. pap. text 20.00 (*0-7881-1515-4*) DIANE Pub.

Local Government Revenue & Expenditures since Proposition 13: A Historical Primer. Roger Dunstan. 31p. 1993. pap. write for info. (*1-58703-012-8*, CRB-93-006) CA St Libry.

Local Government since 1945. Nirmala Rao & Ken Young. LC 97-10418. (Making Contemporary Britain Ser.). 336p. (C). 1997. pap. text 23.95 (*0-631-19582-3*) Blackwell Pubs.

Local Government since 1945. Ken Young & Nirmala Rao. LC 97-10418. (Making Contemporary Britain Ser.). 336p. (C). 1998. text 68.95 (*0-631-19581-5*) Blackwell Pubs.

Local Government Tax & Land Use Policies in the United States: Understanding the Links. Helen F. Ladd. LC 97-27158. (Studies in Fiscal Federalism & State-Local Finance). 288p. (C). 1998. 90.00 (*1-85898-657-5*) E Elgar.

Local Government Tax Authority & Use. 156p. 1987. 15.00 (*0-933729-23-5*) Natl League Cities.

Local Government Today. 2nd ed. J. A. Chandler. LC 95-26493. 280p. (C). 1996. text 19.95 (*0-7190-4735-8*, Pub. by Manchester Univ Pr) St Martin.

Local Government Women's Committees. Julia Edwards. 208p. (C). 1995. text 66.95 (*1-85628-956-7*, Pub. by Avebry) Ashgate Pub Co.

Local Governmental Accounting Trends & Techniques, 1988. American Institute of Certified Public Accountants. Ed. by Susan Cornwall. LC 88-26313. 236p. reprint ed. pap. 73.20 (*0-8357-4117-6*, 203689900005) Bks Demand.

Local Governmental Audit & Accounting Manual As of March 1, 1992. American Institute of Certified Public Accountants. Ed. by Susan Cornwall. LC HJ9777.A3L63. (Nonauthoritative Practice Aids Ser.). 521p. reprint ed. pap. 161.60 (*0-7837-6628-9*, 204621500011) Bks Demand.

Local Governments. Barbara Silberdick-Feinberg. LC 92-27366. (First Bks.). 64p. (J). 1993. lib. bdg. 22.00 (*0-531-20153-8*) Watts.

Local Governments' Decisions & the Local Tax Base: Proceedings of a Conference, February 9 & 10, 1979, U. S. C. Law Center, Los Angeles. Conference on Local Governments' Decisions & the L. Ed. by George Lefcoe. LC HJ9204.C66. (Lincoln Institute Monograph: No. 79-8). 280p. reprint ed. pap. 86.80 (*0-7837-2169-2*, 204249100004) Bks Demand.

Local Government's Role in International Economic Development. Ed. by Sherman M. Wyman & Michelle M. Wyman. (Texas Local Economic Development Ser.). 124p. 1992. pap. 6.25 (*0-936440-85-6*) U TX SUPA.

Local Habitation: Essays on Poetry. John F. Nims. (Poets on Poetry Ser.). 320p. 1985. pap. 13.95 (*0-472-06356-1*, 06356) U of Mich Pr.

Local Habitations: Regionalism in the Early Novels of George Eliot. Henry Auster. LC 74-116734. 244p. 1970. reprint ed. pap. 75.70 (*0-7837-2218-4*, 205730800004) Bks Demand.

Local Happenings of Chippewa Lake: Correspondence to Medina County, Ohio Gazette. Sharon L. Kraynek. LC 95-143323. 55p. 1994. per. 5.00 (*1-55856-172-2*, 414) Closson Pr.

Local Health Departments: Fifteen Case Studies. Ed. by C. Arden Miller & Merry K. Moos. LC 81-68703. 528p. 1981. 12.00 (*0-87553-094-X*, 061) Am Pub Health.

Local Health Policy in Action: The Municipal Health Services Program. Eli Ginzberg et al. (Conservation of Human Resources Ser.: Vol. 24). 152p. 1985. 50.00 (*0-8476-7425-8*) Rowman.

Local Health Units for the Nation. Haven Emerson & Martha Luginbuhl. Ed. by Barbara G. Rosenkrantz. LC 76-25661. (Public Health in America Ser.). (Illus.). 1977. reprint ed. lib. bdg. 31.95 (*0-405-09816-2*) Ayer.

Local Hero. Nora Roberts. (NR Flowers Ser.: No. 48). 1994. per. 3.59 (*0-373-51048-9*, 1-51048-6) Silhouette.

Local Heroes. William Berkowitz. LC 86-46364. 350p. 1987. pap. 16.95 (*0-669-15830-5*) Lxngtn Bks.

Local Heroes. Adam Hart-Davis & Paul Bader. (Hands on History Ser.). (Illus.). 160p. 1998. pap. 24.95 (*0-7509-1797-0*) Sutton Pub Ltd.

***Local Heroes: Architects of the Sunshine Coast.** Peter Hyatt. (Illus.). 180p. 2000. text 75.00 (*90-5703-402-6*) Gordon & Breach.

Local Heroes: Book of British Ingenuity. Adam Hart-Davis & Paul Bader. (Illus.). 160p. 1997. pap. 22.95 (*0-7509-1473-4*, Pub. by Sutton Pub Ltd) Intl Pubs Mktg.

***Local Heroes: Paintings & Sculpture by Sam Doyle.** Lynne E. Spriggs. LC N6537.D66. (Illus.). 48p. 2000. pap. write for info. (*0-939802-92-9*) High Mus Art.

Local Heroes: The Political Economy of Russian Regional Governance. Kathryn Stoner-Weiss. LC 97-7355. 250p. 1997. text 37.50 (*0-691-01195-8*, Pub. by Princeton U Pr) Cal Prin Full Svc.

***Local Heroes Changing America.** Tom Rankin & Trudy W. Stack. (Illus.). 292p. 2000. 29.95 incl. cd-rom (*0-393-05028-9*) Norton.

Local Historians Glossary & Vade Mecum. J. Bristow. (C). 1989. 100.00 (*0-7855-6424-1*, Pub. by Univ Nottingham) St Mut.

Local Historian's Glossary & Vade Mecum. Compiled by Joy Bristow. 288p. 1998. pap. 36.00 (*1-85041-069-0*, Pub. by U of Nottingham) St Mut.

Local Historians of Attica. Lionel Pearson. LC 81-16556. (American Philological Association Philological Monographs). 167p. 1981. reprint ed. pap. 19.50 (*0-89130-540-8*, 40 00 11) OUP.

***Local Histories/Global Designs: Coloniality, Subaltern Knowledges, & Border Thinking.** Walter D. Mignolo. LC 99-32342. 296p. 2000. 55.00 (*0-691-00139-1*, Pub. by Princeton U Pr); pap. 18.95 (*0-691-00140-5*, Pub. by Princeton U Pr) Cal Prin Full Svc.

Local History. Erica Hunt. LC 93-86358. (Roof Bks.). 73p. (Orig.). 1993. pap. 9.95 (*0-937804-53-3*) Segue NYC.

Local History: How to Gather It, Write It, & Publish It. Donald D. Parker. LC 78-11873. 186p. 1979. reprint ed. lib. bdg. 59.50 (*0-313-21100-0*, PLAH, Greenwood Pr) Greenwood.

Local History: How to Gather It, Write It, & Publish It. Donald D. Parker. (History - United States Ser.). 186p. 1993. reprint ed. lib. bdg. 69.00 (*0-7812-4842-6*) Rprt Serv.

Local History & Genealogical Abstracts from Jonesboro & Gas City, Indiana Newspapers, 1889-1920. Ralph D. Kirkpatrick. vi, 247p. (Orig.). 1996. pap. 21.50 (*0-7884-0574-8*, K365) Heritage Bk.

Local History & Genealogical Abstracts from the Fairmount News, 1901-1905. Ralph D. Kirkpatrick. 175p. 1998. pap. 16.00 (*0-7884-0860-7*, K364) Heritage Bk.

***Local History & Genealogical Abstracts from Upland, Indiana, Newspapers, 1891-1901.** Ralph D. Kirkpatrick. 217p. 1999. 21.00 (*0-7884-1407-0*, K369) Heritage Bk.

Local History & Genealogy Resources of the California State Library. rev. ed. Ed. by Gary E. Strong. 118p. 1991. pap. text 9.95 (*0-929722-25-6*) CA State Library Fndtn.

Local History & Genealogy Abstracts from "Fairmount News" Fairmount, Indiana, 1888-1900. Ralph D. Kirkpatrick. LC 97-184224. iv, 158p. 1997. pap. 16.00 (*0-7884-0653-1*, K367) Heritage Bk.

Local History & Wildlife: Coloring Book. Klamath County Museum Staff. (Illus.). 1989. pap. 3.95 (*0-9619719-1-6*) Klamath Cnty Mus.

Local History Collections in Libraries. Faye Phillips. xii, 164p. 1995. lib. bdg. 34.00 (*1-56308-141-5*) Libs Unl.

Local History in the Public Library: Starting & Building a Collection of Resources; Developing a Local History Collection: A Case Study. Karin E. Ford & Beth Hilbert. 18p. (Orig.). 1985. pap. 1.50 (*0-931406-07-2*) Idaho State Soc.

Local Hospitals in Ancient Rigime France: Rationalization, Resistance, Renewal, 1530-1789. Daniel Hickey. LC 98-123958. (McGill-queen's Hannah Institute Studies in the History of Medicine, Health, & Society Ser.). (Illus.). 296p. 1997. 49.95 (*0-7735-1540-2*, Pub. by McG-Queens Univ Pr) CUP Services.

Local Housing Statistics No. 127: June Quarter 1998. TSO Staff. 201p. 1999. pap. 35.00 (*0-11-753492-7*, HM534927, Pub. by Statnry Office) Bernan Associates.

Local Immune Responses of the GUT. Ed. by T. J. Newby & C. R. Stokes. LC 83-26321. 264p. 1984. 129.00 (*0-8493-5534-6*, QR186, CRC Reprint) Franklin.

Local Immunity in Reproductive Tract Tissues: Proceedings of a Symposium on Local Immunity in Reproductive Tract Issues Convened by the World Health. Ed. by P. D. Griffin & P. M. Johnson. (Scientific Basis of Fertility Regulation Ser.). (Illus.). 614p. (C). 1993. text 120.00 (*0-19-563148-X*) OUP.

Local Immunosuppression of Organ Transplants. Scott A. Gruber. (Medical Intelligence Unit Ser.). 258p. 1996. 99.00 (*1-57059-352-3*) Landes Bioscience.

Local Income Taxes: One Solution to Fiscal Dilemmas Facing Local Governments Today. Robbi R. Dietrich. (Discussion Papers: No. 106). 1976. pap. 10.00 (*1-55869-069-7*) Regional Sci Res Inst.

Local Induction. Ed. by Radu J. Bogdan. LC 75-34922. (Synthese Library: No. 93). 354p. 1975. text 184.00 (*90-277-0649-2*, D Reidel) Kluwer Academic.

Local Institutional Development: An Analytical Sourcebook with Cases. fac. ed. Norman T. Uphoff. LC 86-15288. (Kumarian Press Library of Management for Development). 437p. 1994. pap. 135.50 (*0-7837-7578-4*, 204733100007) Bks Demand.

Local Institutional Development for Agriculture. Norman Uphoff & Katy VanDusen. (Special Series on Local Institutional Development: No. 5). 102p. (C). 1985. pap. text 7.50 (*0-86731-112-6*) Cornell CIS RDC.

Local Institutional Development for Natural Resource Management. Peter Doan et al. (Special Series on Local Institutional Development: No. 2). 66p. (Orig.). (C). 1985. pap. 6.50 (*0-86731-109-6*) Cornell CIS RDC.

Local Institutional Development for Non-Agricultural Enterprise. Johanna Looye & Norman Uphoff. (Special Series on Local Institutional Development: No. 6). 46p. (Orig.). (C). 1985. pap. text 7.50 (*0-86731-113-4*) Cornell CIS RDC.

L

L

Local Institutional Development for Rural Infrastructure. Gregory Schmidt & Norman Uphoff. (Special Series on Local Institutional Development: No. 3). 54p. (C). 1985. pap. text 6.25 (*0-86731-110-X*) Cornell CIS RDC.

Local Institutions & People's Participation in Rural Public Works in Nepal. Prachanda P. Pradhan. (Special Series on Rural Local Organization: No. 4). 103p. (Orig.). (C). 1980. pap. text 5.80 (*0-86731-031-6*) Cornell CIS RDC.

Local Invasion & Spread of Cancer. Ed. by Kenneth W. Brunson. (Cancer Growth & Progression Ser.). (C). 1989. text 207.50 (*0-89838-996-8*) Kluwer Academic.

***Local Ireland Almanac & Yearbook of Facts, 2000.** Helen Curley. 494p. 2000. pap. 14.95 (*0-9536537-0-6*, Pub. by Local Ireland) Dufour.

Local Jet Bundle Formulation of Backlund Transformations. Felix A. Pirani et al. (Mathematical Physics Studies: No. 1). 1979. pap. text 70.50 (*90-277-1036-8*) Kluwer Academic.

Local Justice. Jon Elster. LC 91-39717. 288p. 1992. 32.50 (*0-87154-231-5*) Russell Sage.

Local Justice: How Institutions Allocate Scarce Goods & Necessary Burdens. Jon Elster. 288p. 1993. reprint ed. pap. 14.95 (*0-87154-232-3*) Russell Sage.

Local Justice in America. Ed. by Jon Elster. (Illus.). 384p. 1995. 39.95 (*0-87154-233-1*) Russell Sage.

Local Knowledge. Conor Daly. 1996. pap. 4.99 (*1-57566-036-9*) Kensgtn Pub Corp.

Local Knowledge. Conor Daly. 1997. pap. 9.95 (*1-57566-153-5*) Kensgtn Pub Corp.

Local Knowledge. B. H. Fairchild. (QRL Poetry Bks.: Vol. XXX). 1991. 20.00 (*0-614-06438-4*) Quarterly Rev.

Local Knowledge: Further Essays in Interpretive Anthology. Clifford Geertz. 256p. 2000. pap. 18.00 (*0-465-04162-0*, Pub. by Basic) HarpC.

Local Knowledge & Rural Development in the Philippines. Virginia D. Nazarea-Sandoval. (Food Systems & Agrarian Change Ser.). (Illus.). 264p. 1995. 49.95 (*0-8014-2801-7*) Cornell U Pr.

***Local Knowledge & Wisdom in Higher Education.** G. R. Teasdale & Zane Ma Rhea. LC 99-49933. (Issues in Higher Education Ser.). 2000. write for info. (*0-08-043453-3*) Elsevier.

Local Labour Markets: Problems & Policies. Mike Campbell & Katherine Duffy. LC 93-162543. ix, 202p. 1992. pap. 20.00 (*0-582-09103-9*) Longman.

Local Land Charges. J. F. Garner. 1987. 100.00 (*0-7219-0125-5*, Pub. by Scientific) St Mut.

Local Landscape Ordinances. Gary O. Robinette. (Community Landscape Development Ser.). 348p. 1992. pap. text 24.95 (*1-882240-00-6*) Agora Comms.

Local Law in Massachusetts & Connecticut. William C. Fowler. LC 70-161259. (Black Heritage Library Collection). 1977. reprint ed. 20.95 (*0-8369-8818-3*) Ayer.

Local Laws Affecting County Commissioners in Georgia: A Legal Reference. 4th ed. Paul T. Hardy. LC 94-44986. 94p. 1995. pap. 7.95 (*0-89854-178-6*) U of GA Inst Govt.

***Local Laws Affecting County Commissioners in Georgia: A Legal Reference.** 5th ed. Paul T. Hardy. LC 00-39219. 2000. write for info. (*0-89854-197-2*) U of GA Inst Govt.

Local Leadership for Science Education Reform. NSSA (Roy) Staff & NSELA Staff. 208p. 1995. pap. text, per. 13.95 (*0-8403-9947-2*) Kendall-Hunt.

Local Level Planning & Rural Development: An Analytical Study. A. K. Pandy. 1990. 21.50 (*81-7099-189-7*, Pub. by Mittal Pubs Dist) S Asia.

Local Literacies: Reading & Writing in One Community. David Barton & Mary Hamilton. LC 97-39774. (Illus.). 320p. (C). 1998. 90.00 (*0-415-17149-0*); pap. 27.99 (*0-415-17150-4*) Routledge.

***Local Literacies: Theory & Practice.** Glenys Waters. LC 96-72066. xii, 425p. 1998. pap. 39.00 (*1-55671-038-0*) S I L Intl.

Local Loop: Access Technologies, Services, & Business Issues. IEC Staff. (Illus.). 400p. 1997. pap. 490.00 (*0-933217-34-X*) Prof Educ Intl.

Local Magistrates of Roman Spain. Leonard A. Curchin. (Phoenix Supplementary Volumes Ser.). 276p. 1990. text 65.00 (*0-8020-5841-8*) U of Toronto Pr.

Local Management for More Effective Employment Policies. Sylvain Giguere & Jean-Pierre Pellegrin. 108p. 1998. pap. 20.00 (*92-64-16051-5*, 04 98 02 1 P, Pub. by Org for Econ) OECD.

Local Management in School. Knight. 1989. pap. text. write for info. (*0-582-05318-8*, Pub. by Addison-Wesley) Longman.

Local Management of Schools: Analysis & Practice. Rosalind Levacic. LC 95-5855. 240p. 1995. 124.95 (*0-335-19376-5*) OpUniv Pr.

Local Management of Schools: Analysis & Practice. Rosalind Levacic. LC 95-5855. 240p. 1995. pap. 37.95 (*0-335-19375-7*) OpUniv Pr.

Local Management of Schools: At Work in the Primary School. Derek Nightingale. (School Development & the Management of Change Ser.). 224p. 1990. 59.95 (*1-85000-648-2*, Falmer Pr); pap. 34.95 (*1-85000-649-0*, Falmer Pr) Taylor & Francis.

Local Management of Schools: Research & Experience. Ed. by Gwen Wallace. (BERA Dialogues Ser.: No. 6). 170p. 1992. 74.95 (*1-85359-153-X*, Pub. by Multilingual Matters); pap. 29.95 (*1-85359-152-1*, Pub. by Multilingual Matters) Taylor & Francis.

Local Markets & Regional Trade in Medieval Exeter. Maryanne Kowaleski. (Illus.). 458p. (C). 1995. text 74.95 (*0-521-33371-7*) Cambridge U Pr.

Local Mechanics Concepts for Composite Material Systems: IUTAM Symposium, Blacksburg, VA, 1991. Ed. by J. N. Reddy & K. L. Reifsnyder. LC 92-17944. (International Union of Theoretical & Applied Mechanics Symposia Ser.). xi, 412p. 1992. 181.95 (*0-387-55547-1*) Spr-Verlag.

Local Men & Domains: Two Books of Poetry. James Whitehead. LC 87-5096. 128p. 1987. 9.95 (*0-252-01443-X*) U of Ill Pr.

Local Merchants & the Chinese Bureaucracy, 1750-1950. Susan Mann. LC 86-14403. (Illus.). 296p. 1987. 42.50 (*0-8047-1341-3*) Stanford U Pr.

Local Merchants of Prato: Small Entrepreneurs in the Late Medieval Economy. Richard K. Marshall. LC 98-43545. Vol. 117. 191p. 1999. 42.50 (*0-8018-6057-1*) Johns Hopkins.

Local Methods in Nonlinear Differential Equations. A. D. Bruno. (Illus.). 370p. 1989. 158.95 (*0-387-18926-2*) Spr-Verlag.

***Local Ministry Today.** Andrew Bowden. 2000. pap. 21.95 (*0-304-70625-6*) Continuum.

Local Needs & New Dwellings. Martin Elson & Paul McNamara. (C). 1982. 29.00 (*0-7855-3853-4*, Pub. by Oxford Polytechnic) St Mut.

Local Networks: Strategy & Systems. 536p. 1983. 112.00 (*0-685-09403-0*) Taylor & Francis.

Local News. Gary Soto. LC 92-37905. 144p. (J). (gr. 3-7). 1993. 14.00 (*0-15-248117-6*) Harcourt.

Local News. Gary Soto. LC 92-37905. 160p. (YA). (gr. 7 up). 1994. pap. 3.99 (*0-590-48446-X*) Scholastic Inc.

Local News. Gary Soto. LC 92-37905. (Point Signature Ser.). 1993. 9.05 (*0-606-06545-8*, Pub. by Turtleback) Demco.

Local News: Tabloid Pictures from The Los Angeles Herald Express 1928-1959. Diane Keaton. (Illus.). 144p. 1999. 35.00 (*1-891024-13-2*) Dist Art Pubs.

Local Newspapers, 1750-1920 in England & Wales, Channel Islands, Isle of Man: A Select Location List. Jeremy S. Gibson. (Illus.). 64p. 1989. pap. 8.50 (*0-8063-1242-4*, 2186) Genealog Pub.

Local Officals Guide to Family Day Care Zoning. 77p. 1989. 20.00 (*0-933729-54-5*, No. 8002) Natl League Cities.

Local Officials Guide: Achieving World Class Local Economies. 36p. 1996. 15.00 (*1-886152-32-2*, No. 3534) Natl League Cities.

Local Officials Guide to Community Traffic Safety Programs. 35p. 1990. 20.00 (*0-933729-57-X*, No. 7103) Natl League Cities.

Local Officials Guide to Defense Economic Adjustment. 162p. 1992. 60.00 (*0-933729-82-0*, No. 3019) Natl League Cities.

Local Officials Guide to Drunk Driving Prevention. 104p. 1993. 30.00 (*0-933729-83-9*, No. 7104) Natl League Cities.

Local Officials Guide to Dynamic City Commercial Centers. 40p. 1990. 20.00 (*0-933729-60-X*, No. 3014) Natl League Cities.

Local Officials Guide to Public Real Estate Asset Management. 90p. 1990. 10.00 (*0-933729-59-6*, No. 3015) Natl League Cities.

Local Officials Guide to Small Business Partnerships. 82p. 1989. 20.00 (*0-933729-49-9*, No. 3013) Natl League Cities.

Local Officials Guide to the Community Reinvestment Act. 100p. 1991. 30.00 (*0-933729-64-2*, No. 3016) Natl League Cities.

Local Officials Guide to Transit Financial Planning. 62p. 1989. 20.00 (*0-933729-50-2*, No. 5522) Natl League Cities.

Local Order in Condensed Matter Physics. Ed. by S. D. Mahanti & P. Jena. (Illus.). 287p. (C). 1995. lib. bdg. 165.00 (*1-56072-220-7*) Nova Sci Pubs.

Local Order in Condensed Matter Physics: Proceedings of the International Symposium. P. Jena. 1994. text 86.00 (*981-02-1311-5*) World Scientific Pub.

Local Ordinances: A User's Guide. 83p. (Orig.). 1995. pap. 14.95 (*1-880686-13-9*) Terrene Inst.

Local Organisation, Cultural Identity & National Integration in the North Atlantic. Ed. by Susanne Dybbroe & Poul B. Moller. (North Atlantic Studies: No. 3, Pt. 1). (Illus.). 68p. (Orig.). (C). 1991. pap. 19.95 (*87-983424-8-7*, Pub. by Aarhus Univ Pr) David Brown.

Local Organization Dimensions of Rural Development in Turkey: Socio-Economic Stratification Orientations toward Participation, & Attitudinal Modernity. Halil Copur. (Special Series on Rural Local Organization: No. 5). 77p. 1980. pap. 7.50 (*0-86731-032-4*) Cornell CIS RDC.

Local Organization for Rural Development: Analysis of Asian Experience. Norman Uphoff & Milton J. Esman. (Special Series on Rural Local Government: No. 19). 117p. 1974. pap. 5.00 (*0-86731-105-3*) Cornell CIS RDC.

Local Organizations: Intermediaries in Rural Development. Milton J. Esman & Norman T. Uphoff. LC 83-45932. 392p. 1984. pap. text 19.95 (*0-8014-9508-3*) Cornell U Pr.

Local Organizations for Rural Health in Panama: Community Participation, Bureaucratic Reorientation, & Political Will. Gerard M. LaForgia. (Special Series on Rural Local Organization: No. 8). 153p. 1985. 7.50 (*0-86731-035-9*) Cornell CIS RDC.

Local Parties in Political & Organizational Perspective. Martin Saiz & Hans Geser. LC 98-52839. (Urban Policy Challenges Ser.). 352p. 1999. 75.00 (*0-8133-6687-9*, Pub. by Westview) HarpC.

Local Parties in Political & Organizational Perspective. Martin Saiz & Hans Geser. (Urban Policy Challenges Ser.). 400p. 2000. pap. text 35.00 (*0-8133-6688-7*) Westview.

Local People: The Struggle for Civil Rights in Mississippi. John Dittmer. LC 93-39632. (Blacks in the New World Ser.). (Illus.). 560p. 1994. 29.95 (*0-252-02102-9*) U of Ill Pr.

Local People: The Struggle for Civil Rights in Mississippi. John Dittmer. (Blacks in the New World Ser.). (Illus.). 560p. (C). 1995. pap. text 16.95 (*0-252-06507-7*) U of Ill Pr.

***Local People in Logged Forests: Perspectives on Sustainability & Human Well-Being.** Carol J. Pierce. 2000. 50.00 (*1-891853-05-8*); pap. 25.95 (*1-891853-06-6*) Resources Future.

Local Places: In the Age of the Global City. Ed. by Roger Keil et al. LC 95-79358. 272p. 1996. 48.99 (*1-55164-047-3*, Pub. by Black Rose); pap. 19.99 (*1-55164-046-5*, Pub. by Black Rose) Consort Bk Sales.

Local Plan Inquiry: The Role in Local Plan Preparation, Vol. 19/2. Ed. by G. E. Marsh. (Illus.). 80p. 1983. pap. 22.00 (*0-08-030442-7*, Pergamon Pr) Elsevier.

Local Planning in the Netherlands & England: A Comparison of the Requirements & Procedures of the Two Systems. Ed. by John Minett. (C). 1979. 29.00 (*0-7855-3875-5*, Pub. by Oxford Polytechnic) St Mut.

Local Planning Research. Ed. by P. Healey & C. Lambert. (C). 1986. 29.00 (*0-7855-3831-3*, Pub. by Oxford Polytechnic) St Mut.

Local Police Departments (1993) Brian A. Reaves. 22p. (Orig.). (C). 1996. pap. text 20.00 (*0-7881-3007-2*) DIANE Pub.

Local Politics: Governing at the Grassroots. Terry Christensen. LC 94-15912. 382p. (C). 1994. pap. text 35.50 (*0-534-13332-0*) Harcourt.

Local Politics: The Law of the Fishes: Development Through Political Change in Medak District, Andhra Pradesh (South India) Marguerite S. Robinson. 364p. 1989. 18.95 (*0-19-561992-7*) OUP.

Local Politics & Indian Nationalism: Midnapur, 1919-1944. Bidyut Chakrabarty. (C). 1997. 30.00 (*81-7304-158-X*, Pub. by Manohar) S Asia.

Local Politics & Participation in France & Britain. Ed. by Albert Mabileau et al. (Illus.). 284p. (C). 1990. text 69.95 (*0-521-34576-6*) Cambridge U Pr.

Local Politics in Communist Countries. Ed. by Daniel N. Nelson. LC 78-58121. 240p. 1980. 24.00 (*0-8131-1398-9*) U Pr of Ky.

Local Politics of Kyoto. Teruo Gotoda. LC 84-62677. (Japan Research Monographs: No. 7). 161p. 1985. pap. 15.00 (*0-912966-74-2*) IEAS.

Local Politics of Rural Development: Peasant & Party State in Zambia. Michael Bratton. LC 79-56775. (Illus.). 348p. reprint ed. pap. 107.90 (*0-8357-6509-1*, 203588000097) Bks Demand.

Local Polynomial Modelling & Its Applications. Jinqing Fan. 344p. (gr. 13). 1996. ring bd. 62.95 (*0-412-98321-4*, Chap & Hall CRC) CRC Pr.

Local Power & Post-Soviet Politics. Ed. by Theodore H. Friedgut & Jeffrey W. Hahn. LC 94-10151. (Contemporary Soviet/Post-Soviet Politics Ser.). (Illus.). 308p. (gr. 13). 1994. text 77.95 (*1-56324-403-9*); pap. text 36.95 (*1-56324-404-7*) M E Sharpe.

Local Power in the Japanese State. Michio Muramatsu. Tr. by Betsey Scheiner & James White from JPN. LC 96-41515. (Contemporary Japanese Politics Ser.). 206p. 1997. 45.00 (*0-520-07275-8*, Pub. by U CA Pr); pap. 16.00 (*0-520-07276-6*, Pub. by U CA Pr) Cal Prin Full Svc.

Local Properties of Distributions of Stochastic Functionals. I. A. Davydov et al. Tr. by V. E. Nazaikinski & M. S. Shishkova from RUS. LC 97-44426. (Translations of Mathematical Monographs Ser.). 184p. 1997. text 75.00 (*0-8218-0584-3*) Am Math.

Local Prosecution of Environmental Crime. (Illus.). 124p. 1993. pap. text 35.00 (*1-57979-193-X*) DIANE Pub.

Local Prosecution of Environmental Crime. Theodore M. Hammett & Joel Epstein. (Illus.). 111p. (Orig.). (C). 1994. pap. text 40.00 (*0-7881-0582-5*) DIANE Pub.

Local Prostatic Carcinoma. Ed. by J. J. Rambeaud & F. Vincent. (Contributions to Oncology Ser.: Vol. 47). (Illus.). viii, 146p. 1995. 121.75 (*3-8055-5973-9*) S Karger.

Local Quantum Physics: Fields, Particles, Algebras. Rudolf Haag. Ed. by W. Beiglbock et al. LC 92-45286. (Texts & Monographs in Physics). 384p. (C). 1993. 59.00 (*0-387-53610-8*) Spr-Verlag.

Local Quantum Physics: Fields, Particles, Algebras. 2nd ed. Rudolf Haag. LC 96-18937. (Texts & Monographs in Physics). 295p. 1996. 79.95 (*3-540-61451-6*); pap. 39.95 (*3-540-61049-9*) Spr-Verlag.

Local Radio Journalism. Paul Chantler & Sim Harris. LC 97-179363. (Illus.). 144p. 1992. 26.95 (*0-240-51308-8*, Focal) Buttrwrth-Heinemann.

Local Radio Journalism. 2nd ed. Paul Chantler & Sim Harris. 192p. 1997. pap. 32.95 (*0-240-51422-X*, Focal) Buttrwrth-Heinemann.

Local Referendums. (Local & Regional Authorities in Europe Ser.: No. 52). 1993. 12.00 (*92-871-2396-9*, Pub. by Council of Europe) Manhattan Pub Co.

Local Regression & Likelihood. C. Loader. Ed. by J. Chambers et al. LC 99-14732. (Statistics & Computing Ser.). (Illus.). 304p. 1999. 54.95 (*0-387-98775-4*) Spr-Verlag.

Local Regulation of Ovarian Function. Ed. by N. O. Sjoberg et al. (Illus.). 331p. (C). 1992. text 78.00 (*1-85070-394-9*) Prthnon Pub.

Local Regulators in the Ovary - Paracrine & Autocrine Control. Ed. by H. Mori & Y. Yoshimura. (Journal: Hormone Research Ser.: Vol. 41, Suppl. 1, 1994). (Illus.). iv, 68p. 1994. pap. 31.50 (*3-8055-5994-1*) S Karger.

Local Remedies in International Law. 438p. 1993. text 100.00 (*0-521-46317-3*) Cambridge U Pr.

Local Remedies in International Law. C. F. Amerasinghe. 438p. (C). 1990. 230.00 (*0-949009-79-2*, Pub. by Grotius Pubns Ltd) St Mut.

Local Reporting, 1947-1987: From a Country Vote Fraud to a Corrupt City Council. Heinz-Dietrich Fischer & Erika J. Fischer. (Pulitzer Prize Archive: Vol. 3). 388p. 1989. lib. bdg. 82.00 (*3-598-30173-1*) K G Saur Verlag.

Local Representation: Changing Realities, Emerging Theories. Florence Adams. 200p. 1999. 50.00 (*0-8153-3370-6*) Garland.

Local Representation Theory: Modular Representations As an Introduction to the Local Representation Theory of Finite Groups. J. L. Alperin. (Cambridge Studies in Advanced Mathematics: No. 11). 188p. (C). 1993. pap. text 26.95 (*0-521-44926-X*) Cambridge U Pr.

Local Responses English Reform. Whiting. LC 97-31637. 272p. 1998. text 49.95 (*0-312-21185-6*) St Martin.

***Local Responses to Global Integration.** Ed. by Charalambos Kasimis & Apostolos G. Papadopoulos. 274p. 1999. text 69.95 (*1-84014-844-6*) Ashgate Pub Co.

Local Responses to Global Problems: A Key to Meeting Basic Human Needs. Bruce Stokes. 1978. pap. write for info. (*0-916468-16-X*) Worldwatch Inst.

Local Rules. Jay Brandon. 1996. mass mkt. 5.99 (*0-671-88409-3*, PB Trade Paper) PB.

Local Rules. large type ed. Jay Brandon. LC 95-2921. 532p. 1995. 24.95 (*0-7862-0490-7*) Thorndike Pr.

Local Rules of the Bankruptcy Courts--8th Circuit. text 54.00 (*0-8205-3026-3*) Bender.

Local Rules of the Bankruptcy Courts--1st Circuit. text 54.00 (*0-8205-3019-0*) Bender.

Local Rules of the Bankruptcy Courts--5th Circuit. text 54.00 (*0-8205-3023-9*) Bender.

Local Rules of the Bankruptcy Courts--4th Circuit & D.C. Circuit. text 55.00 (*0-8205-3022-0*) Bender.

Local Rules of the Bankruptcy Courts--2nd Circuit. text 54.00 (*0-8205-3020-4*) Bender.

Local Rules of the Bankruptcy Courts--7th Circuit. text 54.00 (*0-8205-3025-5*) Bender.

Local Rules of the Bankruptcy Courts--6th Circuit. text 54.00 (*0-8205-3024-7*) Bender.

Local Rules of the Bankruptcy Courts--3rd Circuit. text 54.00 (*0-8205-3021-2*) Bender.

Local Rules of the Bankruptcy Courts--10th Circuit. text 54.00 (*0-8205-3042-5*) Bender.

Local Rules of the Bankruptcy Courts--11th Circuit. text 54.00 (*0-8205-3043-3*) Bender.

Local Rules of the Bankruptcy Courts--9th Circuit, 2 vols. text 54.00 (*0-8205-3041-7*) Bender.

Local Rules of the District Courts in Texas, 2 vols. 2nd ed. Sterling W. Steves. Ed. by Richard Robins. Date not set. ring bd. 160.00 (*0-327-01043-6*, 82668-10, MICHIE) LEXIS Pub.

Local Rules of the District Courts in Texas, Issue 5. Sterling W. Steves & Jennifer Nosler Mellett. 301p. 1998. ring bd. write for info. (*0-327-00742-7*, 8267216) LEXIS Pub.

***Local Rules of the District Courts in Texas, Issue 6.** Richard C. Robins. 600p. 1999. ring bd. write for info. (*0-327-01387-7*, 8267217) LEXIS Pub.

Local Rules of the Superior Court: Washington State, 2 vols. Michie Editorial Staff. 1981. ring bd. 95.00 (*0-327-00954-3*, 82823, MICHIE) LEXIS Pub.

Local Rules of the Superior Court, 1981-1993: Washington State, 2 vols., Set. Michie Editorial Staff. 1100p. Date not set. ring bd. 95.00 (*0-409-20200-2*, 82823-10, MICHIE) LEXIS Pub.

Local Rules of the Superior Court, Washinngton State, No. 62. Ed. by LLP Staff. 101p. 1998. ring bd. write for info. (*0-327-00676-5*, 8282720) LEXIS Pub.

Local School Councils . . . Where We Stand. American Association of School Administrators Staf. 12p. 1994. pap. 2.50 (*0-87652-209-6*, 21-00441) Am Assn Sch Admin.

Local Schools: Exploring Their History. Ronald E. Butchart. LC 86-22276. (Nearby History Ser.). (Illus.). 124p. 1986. reprint ed. pap. 17.95 (*0-910050-82-1*) AltaMira Pr.

Local Schools of Thought: A Search for Purpose in Rural Education. R. Wayne Shute et al. LC 95-45043. 77p. 1996. pap. 12.00 (*1-880785-14-5*) ERIC-CRESS.

Local Scripts of Archaic Greece: A Study of the Origin of the Greek Alphabet & Its Development from the Eighth to the Fifth Centuries B.C. 2nd ed. L. H. Jeffery & A. Johnston. (Oxford Monographs on Classical Archaeology). (Illus.). 502p. 1990. text 155.00 (*0-19-814061-4*) OUP.

Local Search in Combinatorial Optimization. Ed. by Emile L. Aarts & Jan K. Lenstra. LC 96-36111. (Wiley-Interscience Series in Discrete Mathematics & Optimization). 522p. 1997. 159.95 (*0-471-94822-5*) Wiley.

Local Self-Government, Territorial Integrity & Protection of Minorities: (Proceedings, Lausanne, 25-27 April, 1996) (Science & Technique of Democracy Ser.: No. 16). 1996. 25.00 (*92-871-3173-2*, Pub. by Council of Europe) Manhattan Pub Co.

Local Service Airline Experiment. George C. Eads. LC 72-141. (Brookings Institution Studies in the Regulations of Economic Activity). 237p. reprint ed. pap. 73.50 (*0-608-12184-3*, 202537400043) Bks Demand.

Local Spectral Theory for Closed Operators. Ivan N. Erdelyi & Wang Shengwang. (London Mathematical Society Lecture Note Ser.: No. 105). 192p. 1985. pap. text 44.95 (*0-521-31314-7*) Cambridge U Pr.

Local Spiritual Assembly Handbook. 3rd ed. NSA of Australia Staff. LC 98-104111. 451p. 1996. pap. 24.95 (*0-909991-78-2*) Bahai.

An Asterisk (*) at the beginning of an entry indicates that the title is appearing for the first time.

Local Stabilizability of Nonlinear Control System. A. Bacciotti. 200p. (C). 1991. text 39.00 (*981-02-0713-1*) World Scientific Pub.

Local State: Public Money & American Cities. Eric H. Monkkonen. LC 95-1074. (Stanford Studies in the New Political History). 214p. 1995. 39.50 (*0-8047-2412-1*) Stanford U Pr.

Local, State & Federal Taxes Affecting Real Estate Transactions. 1995. 99.00 incl. audio 99.00 incl. audio PA Bar Inst.

Local Stereology. LC 97-51328. 247p. 1997. text 54.00 (*981-02-2454-0*) World Scientific Pub.

***Local Strain & Temperature Measurements in Non-Uniform Fields at Elevated Temperatures.** Ed. by J. Ziebs et al. 340p. 1999. pap. 260.00 (*1-85573-424-9*) Am Educ Systs.

Local Strategies for the Reduction of Urban Insecurity in Europe (Barcelona, 1987) Council of Europe Staff. (Urban Renaissance in Europe Ser.: No. 35). 1989. 42.00 (*92-871-1691-1*, Pub. by Council of Europe) Manhattan Pub Co.

***Local Structure from Diffraction: Proceedings of a Conference Held in Traverse City, Michigan, August 10-13, 1997.** Ed. by S. J. Billinge & M. F. Thorpe. LC 98-4348. (Fundamental Materials Research Ser.). (Illus.). 412p. (C). 1998. 120.00 (*0-306-45827-6*, Plenum Trade) Perseus Pubng.

Local Structure of Finite Groups of Characteristic 2 Type. Daniel Gorenstein & Richard Lyons. LC 82-24354. (Memoirs of the American Mathematical Society Ser.: No. 42/276). 731p. 1983. pap. 71.00 (*0-8218-2276-4*, MEMO/42/276) Am Math.

Local Studies Collections, Vol. 1. Michael Dewe. 1987. text 96.95 (*0-566-03522-7*, Pub. by Gower) Ashgate Pub Co.

Local Studies Collections Vol. 2: A Manual. Michael Dewe. 528p. 1991. text 96.95 (*0-566-03631-2*, Pub. by Gower) Ashgate Pub Co.

Local Studies Libraries: Library Association Guidelines for Local Studies Provision in Public Libraries. Library Association Staff. LC 91-105680. 31p. 1990. 14.00 (*1-85604-005-4*, Pub. by Library Association) Bernan Associates.

Local Superior Capstone of Formation: Proceedings & Communications of Regional Meetings of the Sister-Formation Conferences, 1967. Sister Formation Conferences Staff. Ed. by Mary H. Valentine. LC 58-10465. (Sister Formation Ser.). 252p. reprint ed. pap. 78.20 (*0-7837-0475-5*, 204079800018) Bks Demand.

Local Suppliers of Credit in the Third World, 1750-1945. Ed. by Kaoru Sugihara & Gareth Austin. LC 92-19655. 1993. text 65.00 (*0-312-08559-1*) St Martin.

Local Surgery & the Exact Sequence of a Localization for Wall Groups. William Pardon. LC 77-11963. (Memoirs Ser.: No. 12/196). 171p. 1977. pap. 22.00 (*0-8218-2196-2*, MEMO/12/196) Am Math.

Local Talent. Marlene F. Shyer. LC 73-22655. 192p. 1974. 6.95 (*0-672-51980-1*, Bobbs) Macmillan.

Local Touch. Intro. by Harold E. Whittemore. 100p. (Orig.). 1992. pap. 9.95 (*0-9628664-2-3*) Steffen Pr.

***Local Vertical.** Anne M. Lindbergh. Ed. by Noel Perrin & Reeve Lindbergh. 96p. 2000. pap. 15.95 (*1-56792-125-6*) Godine.

***Local Voices, National Issues: The Impact of Local Initiative in Japanese Policy-Making/Edited by Sheila A. Smith.** Sheila A. Smith. LC 99-462352. (Monograph Series in Japanese Studies). xi, 136p. 2000. 32.95 (*0-939512-04-1*, 52093, Pub. by U MI Japan) U of Mich Pr.

Local Warning System Definition. B. D. Miller. LC 70-141214. 147p. 1970. 19.50 (*0-403-04519-3*) Scholarly.

Local Water Supply & Climate Extremes. Brent M. Yarnal. 56.95 (*0-7546-1023-3*) Ashgate Pub Co.

Locale. Jessica Grim. LC 95-134044. 86p. 1995. pap. 10.00 (*0-937013-56-0*) Potes Poets.

Localisation & Bifurcation Theory for Soils & Rocks: Proceedings of the 3rd Workshop, Grenoble, France, 6-9 September 1993. Ed. by R. Chambon et al. (Illus.). 288p. (C). 1994. text 116.00 (*90-5410-511-9*, Pub. by A A Balkema) Ashgate Pub Co.

Localisation & Bifurcation Theory for Soils & Rocks: Proceedings of the 4th International Workshop, Gifu, Japan, 28 September-2 October, 1997. Ed. by Toshihisa Adachi et al. (Illus.). 370p. (C). 1998. text 88.00 (*90-5809-004-3*) Ashgate Pub Co.

Localisation & Interaction in Disordered Metals & Doped Semiconductors. Ed. by D. M. Finlayson. (Scottish Universities Summer School in Physics, a NATO Advanced Study Institute Ser.: No. 31). (Illus.). 394p. 1986. 189.00 (*0-905945-14-X*) IOP Pub.

Localised Prostate Cancer: Recent Advances in Diagnosis & Treatment. Fernand Labrie et al. 319p. (Orig.). 1997. pap. text 65.00 (*1-898099-11-1*) Blackwell Sci.

Localism & Centralism in Europe: The Political & Legal Bases of Local Self-Government. Edward C. Page. (Comparative Politics Ser.). 200p. 1992. 59.00 (*0-19-827727-X*) OUP.

Localist Connectionist Approaches to Human Cognition. Ed. by Jonathan Grainger & Arthur M. Jacobs. LC 97-52267. (Scientific Psychology Ser.). 375p. 1998. write for info. (*0-8058-2556-8*) L Erlbaum Assocs.

Localities: Changing Face of Urban Britain. Ed. by Philip Cooke. LC 88-26991. 334p. (C). 1989. pap. 27.99 (*0-04-445300-0*) Routledge.

Localities: The Changing Face of Urban Britain. Ed. by Phil Cooke. 320p. 1989. text 60.00 (*0-04-445502-X*) Routledge.

Localities of Fossil Vertebrates Obtained from the Niobrara Formation (Cretaceous) of Kansas. David Bardack. (Museum Ser.: Vol. 17,No. 1). 14p. 1965. 1.00 (*0-317-04783-3*) U KS Nat Hist Mus.

Locality: A Theory & Some of Its Empirical Consequences. Maria R. Manzini. (Linguistic Inquiry Monographs: No. 19). (Illus.). 255p. 1992. 40.00 (*0-262-13279-6*); pap. text 20.00 (*0-262-63140-7*) MIT Pr.

Locality & Belonging. Ed. by Nadia Lovell. LC 98-24886. (European Association of Social Anthropologists Ser.). 240p. (C). (gr. 13). 1998. 85.00 (*0-415-18281-6*, D6213) Routledge.

Locality & Belonging. Ed. by Nadia Lovell. LC 98-24886. (European Association of Social Anthropologists Ser.). 240p. (C). (gr. 13). 1998. pap. 25.99 (*0-415-18282-4*, D6217) Routledge.

Locality & Identity: Environmental Issues in Law & Society. Jane Holder. LC 98-49092. (Issues in Law & Society Ser.). 264p. 1999. pap. 25.95 (*1-85521-981-6*) Ashgate Pub Co.

***Locality & Identity: Environmental Issues in Law & Society.** Jane Holder. LC 98-49092. (Issues in Law & Society Ser.). 264p. 1999. 68.95 (*1-85521-976-X*) Ashgate Pub Co.

Locality & Inequality: Farm & Industry Structure & Socioeconomic Conditions. Linda M. Lobao. LC 90-30748. (SUNY Series, the New Inequalities). 291p. (C). 1990. pap. text 21.95 (*0-7914-0476-5*) State U NY Pr.

Locality & Polity: A Study of Warwickshire Landed Society, 1401-1499. Christine Carpenter. 811p. (C). 1992. text 135.00 (*0-521-37016-7*) Cambridge U Pr.

Locality & Practical Judgement: Charity & Sacrifice. Stephen D. Ross. LC 93-47206. x, 345p. 1994. 35.00 (*0-8232-1556-3*) Fordham.

Locality in WH Quantification: Questions & Relative Clauses in Hindi. Veneeta Dayal. LC 96-17891. (Studies in Linguistics & Philosophy). 264p. 1996. text 104.00 (*0-7923-4099-X*) Kluwer Academic.

Locality Principle: Stage Properties for a Farewell Performance. Keith Waldrop. 96p. (Orig.). 1995. pap. text 9.95 (*1-880713-03-9*) AVEC Bks.

Localiza la Diferencia, Parabolas Que Jesus Conto. Hudson.Tr. of Spot the Difference. (SPA.). (J). 1995. write for info. (*0-614-27076-6*) Editorial Unilit.

Localiza la Diferencia, Parabolas Que Jesus Conto (Spot the Difference) Hudson. (SPA.). (J). 1995. write for info. (*0-614-24377-7*) Editorial Unilit.

Localizability & Space in Quantum Physics. H. Barry. (Lecture Notes in Physics Ser.: Vol. 308). vii, 81p. 1988. 29.95 (*0-387-50052-9*) Spr-Verlag.

Localization, Vol. 51, No. 3. Ed. by C. R. Catlow & Mackrodt. 1985. 42.00 (*0-85066-973-1*) Taylor & Francis.

Localization & Confinement of Electrons in Semiconductors: Proceedings of the Sixth International Winter School, Mauterndorf, Austria, February 19-23, 1990. Ed. by F. Kuchar et al. (Solid-State Sciences Ser.: Vol. 97). (Illus.). 352p. 1990. 97.95 (*0-387-53055-X*) Spr-Verlag.

Localization & Delocalization in Quantum Chemistry: Atoms & Molecules in the Ground State, Vol. 1. Ed. by O. Chalvet et al. LC 75-2437. vii, 350p. 1975. text 211.50 (*90-277-0559-3*) Kluwer Academic.

Localization & Delocalization in Quantum Chemistry: Ionized & Excited States: Proceedings, Vol.2. Ed. by O. Chalvet. 1976. text 199.50 (*90-277-0661-1*) Kluwer Academic.

Localization & Fracture Phenomena in Inelastic Solids. Ed. by P. Perzyna. (CISM International Centre for Mechanical Sciences Ser.: Suppl. 386). (Illus.). vii, 468p. 1998. pap. 84.95 (*3-211-82918-0*) Spr-Verlag.

Localization & Iteration of Axiomatic Set Theory. Arthur H. Kruse. LC 68-29739. 226p. reprint ed. pap. 70.10 (*0-7837-3779-3*, 204359800010) Bks Demand.

Localization & Metal-Insulator Transitions. Ed. by Hellmut Fritzche & David A. Adler. LC 85-12161. (Institute for Amorphous Studies). 548p. 1985. 135.00 (*0-306-42077-5*, Plenum Trade) Perseus Pubng.

Localization & Neuroimaging in Neuropsychology. Ed. by Andrew Kertesz. (Foundations of Neuropsychology Ser.). (Illus.). 662p. 1994. text 99.95 (*0-12-405045-X*) Acad Pr.

Localization & Ontogeny of Peptidergic Neurons in Birds: Comparative Studies on the Releasing & Inhibiting Hormones in Birds & Mammals. Bela J. Rita-Mess & R. Jozsa. 95p. 1993. pap. 295.00 (*963-05-6608-7*, Pub. by Akade Kiado) St Mut.

Localization & Sheaves: A Relative Point of View. Pascual Jara. 1995. lib. bdg. 62.95 (*0-582-27372-2*, Pub. by Addison-Wesley) Longman.

***Localization & Solitary Waves in Solid Mechanics.** Ed. by A. R. Champneys et al. (Advanced Series in Nonlinear Dynamics). 320p. 1999. 56.00 (*981-02-3915-7*) World Scientific Pub.

***Localization in China: Best Practice.** Asia Law & Practice Staff. 1999. 225.00 (*962-936-067-5*, Pub. by Asia Law & Practice) Am Educ Systs.

Localization in Clinical Neurology. Paul W. Brazis et al. 429p. 1985. 45.00 (*0-316-10721-2*, Little Brwn Med Div) Lppncott W & W.

Localization in Clinical Neurology. 3rd ed. Paul W. Brazis et al. 384p. 1996. text 105.00 (*0-316-09992-9*) Lppncott W & W.

Localization in Disordered Systems. Ed. by Wolfgang Weller & Paul Ziesche. (Teubner Physics Texts Ser.: Vol 16). 232p. 1988. pap. 35.00 (*3-322-00512-7*, Wiley-VCH) Wiley.

Localization of Brain Lesions & Developmental Functions. Daria Riva & Arthur Benton. 168p. 68.00 (*0-86196-599-X*, Pub. by John Libby) Buttrwrth-Heinemann.

Localization of Deformation in Rocks & Metals. Ed. by Alison Ord et al. LC 92-22431. (PAGEOPH Reprint from Pure & Applied Geophysics Ser.: Vol. 137). v, 150p. 1992. 58.00 (*3-7643-2772-3*, Pub. by Birkhauser); 20.50 (*0-8176-2772-3*, Pub. by Birkhauser) Princeton Arch.

Localization of Genetic Factors for Nonspecific & Syndromic X-Linked Mental Retardation. Stephan Claes. (Acta Biomedica Lovaniensia Ser.: No. 160). (Illus.). 100p. 1997. pap. 34.50 (*90-6186-853-X*, Pub. by Leuven Univ) Coronet Bks.

Localization of Noncommutative Rings. Jonathan S. Golan. (Pure & Applied Mathematics Ser.: Vol. 30). (Illus.). 352p. 1975. text 155.00 (*0-8247-6198-7*) Dekker.

Localization of One-Dimensional Random Walks in Random Environment, Vol. 8. A. V. Letchikov. (SSR SEC Mathematical Physics Review Ser.: Vol. 8, No. 3). ii, 52p. 1989. pap. text 106.00 (*3-7186-4866-0*) Gordon & Breach.

Localization of Putative Steroid Receptors, 2 vols., Vol. I: Experimental Systems. Ed. by Louis P. Pertschuk & Sin H. Lee. 200p. 1985. 116.00 (*0-8493-6048-X*, RC268, CRC Reprint) Franklin.

Localization of Putative Steroid Receptors, 2 vols., Vol. II: Clinically Oriented Studies. Ed. by Louis P. Perschuk & Sin H. Lee. 184p. 1985. 106.00 (*0-8493-6049-8*, CRC Reprint) Franklin.

Localized Corrosion No. 3: NACE Reference Book. Ed. by R. W. Staeble et al. LC 74-83276. (Illus.). 746p. 1974. pap. 46.00 (*0-915567-83-0*) NACE Intl.

***Localized Corrosion & Reliability of Electronic Materials & Devices.** Ed. by R. B. Comizzoli et al. 292p. 2000. 62.00 (*1-56677-252-4*, PV 99-29) Electrochem Soc.

Localized Corrosion-Cause of Metal Failure - STP 516. 322p. 1981. 22.50 (*0-8031-0110-4*, STP516) ASTM.

Localized Corrosion in Halides Other Than Chlorides. Gerhardus H. Koch. LC 95-67421. (MTI Publication: No. 41). 124p. 1995. pap. 90.00 (*1-877914-77-0*) NACE Intl.

Localized Damage, Computer-Aided Assessment & Control: First International Conference, 26-28 June 1990, Portsmouth, U. K., 3 vols., Set. Ed. by M. H. Aliabadi et al. (Illus.). ix, 1307p. 1990. 526.95 (*0-387-52717-6*) Spr-Verlag.

Localized Damage, Computer-Aided Assessment & Control Vol. 1: Fatigue & Fracture Mechanics: First International Conference, 26-28 June 1990, Portsmouth, U. K. Ed. by M. H. Aliabadi et al. (Illus.). ix, 418p. 1990. 182.95 (*0-387-52713-3*) Spr-Verlag.

Localized Damage, Computer-Aided Assessment & Control Vol. 2: Non-Linear Behavior, Dynamics, Composite Materials & Industrial Applications: First International Conference, 26-28 June 1990, Portsmouth, U. K. Ed. by M. H. Aliabadi et al. (Illus.). ix, 371p. 1990. 182.95 (*0-387-52714-1*) Spr-Verlag.

Localized Damage, Computer-Aided Assessment & Control Vol. 3: Advanced Computational Methods: First International Conference, 26-28 June 1990, Portsmouth, U. K. M. H. Aliabaci et al. Ed. by Carlos A. Brebbia & D. J. Cartwright. (Illus.). ix, 518p. 1990. 182.95 (*0-387-52716-8*) Spr-Verlag.

Localized Damage IV: Computer Aided Assessment & Control. Ed. by N. Nisitani et al. 965p. 1996. teacher ed., suppl. ed. 357.00 (*1-85312-397-8*, 3978) Computational Mech MA.

Localized Damage III: Computer Aided Assessment & Control. Ed. by M. H. Aliabadi et al. LC 94-70409. (Localized Damage Ser.: Vol. 3). 752p. 1994. 316.00 (*1-56252-186-1*, 2629) Computational Mech MA.

Localized Damage II: Computer Aided Assessment & Control, 2 vols., Set. Ed. by M. H. Aliabadi et al. LC 92-70434. (Localized Damage Ser.: Vol. 2). 1354p. 1992. 459.00 (*1-56252-100-4*, 1711) Computational Mech MA.

Localized Prostatic Cancer: Heinrich Warner Stiftung. Ed. by H. Huland. (Journal Ser.: Vol. 27, Suppl. 2, 1995). (Illus.). 48p. 1995. pap. 21.75 (*3-8055-6126-1*) S Karger.

Localized RNAs. Howard D. Lipshitz. LC 95-16554. (Molecular Biology Intelligence Unit Ser.). 318p. 1995. 99.00 (*1-57059-276-4*) Landes Bioscience.

Localized RNAs Howard D. Lipshitz. LC 95-16554. (Molecular Biology Intelligence Unit Ser.). 322p. 1995. write for info. (*3-540-60005-1*) Spr-Verlag.

Localizing Global Production: Know-How Transfer in International Manufacturing. Klaus North. LC 97-181070. (Management Development Ser.: Vol. 33). 191p. 1997. pap. 27.00 (*92-2-109512-6*) Intl Labour Office.

Locally Compact Transformation Groups & C*-Algebra. Edward G. Effros & Frank Hahn. LC 52-42839. (American Mathematical Society Ser.: No. 75). 101p. reprint ed. pap. 31.40 (*0-608-09176-6*, 205268000002) Bks Demand.

Locally Compact Transformation Groups & C-Algebras. Edward G. Effros & Frank Hahn. LC 52-42839. (Memoirs Ser.: No. 1/75). 92p. 1985. reprint ed. pap. 16.00 (*0-8218-1275-0*, MEMO/1/75) Am Math.

Locally Conformal Kahler Geometry. Sorin Dragomir & Liviu Ornea. LC 97-27397. (Progress in Mathematics Ser.). 1997. write for info. (*3-7643-4020-7*) Birkhauser.

Locally Conformal Kahler Geometry. Sorin Dragomir & Liviu Ornea. LC 97-27397. (Progress in Mathematics Ser.). 400p. 1997. write for info. (*0-8176-4020-7*) Birkhauser.

Locally Convex Spaces. Kelly McKennon & Jack M. Robertson. LC 75-40934. (Lecture Notes in Pure & Applied Mathematics Ser.: Vol. 15). 77p. reprint ed. pap. 30.00 (*0-608-08961-3*, 206959600005) Bks Demand.

Locally Convex Spaces & Linear Partial Differential Equations. Francois Treves. LC 67-25286. (Grundlehren der Mathematischen Wissenschaften Ser.: Vol. 146). 1967. 54.00 (*0-387-03833-7*) Spr-Verlag.

Locally Finite, Planar, Edge-Transitive Graphs. Jack E. Graver & Mark E. Watkins. LC 96-37447. (Memoirs of the American Mathematical Society Ser.: Vol. 126/601). vi, 75p. 1997. pap. 36.00 (*0-8218-0556-8*, MEMO/126/601) Am Math.

L

Locally Interacting Systems & Their Application in Biology: Proceedings of the School - Seminar on Markov Interaction Processes in Biology, Held in Pushchino, Moscow Region, March, 1976. Ed. by R. L. Dobryshin et al. (Lecture Notes in Mathematics Ser.: Vol. 653). 1978. 27.95 (*0-387-08450-9*) Spr-Verlag.

Locally Multiplicatively-Convex Topological Algebras. E. A. Michael. LC 52-42839. (Memoirs Ser.: No. 1/11). 82p. 1971. reprint ed. pap. 16.00 (*0-8218-1211-4*, MEMO/1/11) Am Math.

Locally Presentable & Accessible Categories. Jiri Adamek & J. Rosicky. (London Mathematical Society Lecture Note Ser.: No. 184). (Illus.). 329p. (C). 1994. pap. text 49.95 (*0-521-42261-2*) Cambridge U Pr.

Locally Semialgebraic Spaces. H. Delfs & M. Knebusch. (Lecture Notes in Mathematics Ser.: Vol. 1173). xvi, 329p. 1986. 46.95 (*0-387-16060-4*) Spr-Verlag.

Locally Unpopular Land Uses (LULUs) 1996. 99.00 incl. audio PA Bar Inst.

Locals & Cosmopolitans: Patterns of Spatial Mobility During the Transition from Youth to Early Adulthood. Donald C. Dahmann. LC 82-2721. (University of Chicago, Department of Geography, Research Paper Ser.: No. 204). 163p. 1982. reprint ed. pap. 50.60 (*0-608-02243-8*, 206288400004) Bks Demand.

***Local's Guide to the Best Kept Dining Secrets.** Brian Katonak & Lynne Katonak. LC 98-29727. 1999. 12.95 (*0-87844-146-8*) Sandlapper Pub Co.

Locals Only. Marshall Lefavor. 64p. 1993. pap. 4.95 (*1-880365-51-0*) Prof Pr NC.

***Locals Only, A Small County in the Sea.** Steven C. Brandt. 70p. 2000. pap. write for info. (*1-888925-22-1*) Archiplgo Pub.

Locandiera. Carlo Goldoni. Ed. by Vincent Luciani. (ITA & ENG.). (C). 1991. pap. 8.95 (*0-913298-18-2*) S F Vanni.

Locas: A Novel. Yxta M. Murray. 256p. 1998. reprint ed. pap. 12.00 (*0-8021-3564-1*, Grove) Grove-Atltic.

Locataire. Georges Simenon. (FRE.). 1978. pap. 10.95 (*0-7859-4091-X*, 2070369986) Fr & Eur.

Locataire. Georges Simenon. (Folio Ser.: No. 998). (FRE.). 181p. 1934. pap. 6.95 (*2-07-036998-6*) Schoenhof.

Locataire, les Suicides, les Pitard. Georges Simenon. (FRE.). 990p. 1992. 49.95 (*0-7859-0491-3*, 2258035244) Fr & Eur.

Locating Alexandra. Margaret Rodgers. LC 95-234501. (Illus.). 175p. 1995. pap. 20.00 (*1-55022-248-1*, Pub. by ECW) Genl Dist Srvs.

Locating Ambulance Dispatch Centers in an Urban Region: A Man-Computer Interactive Problem-Solving Approach. Jerry B. Schneider & John B. Symons, Jr. (Discussion Papers: No. 49). 1971. pap. 10.00 (*1-55869-070-0*) Regional Sci Res Inst.

Locating American Studies: The Evolution of a Discipline. Lucy Maddox. LC 98-18959. (Illus.). 456p. 1998. 19.95 (*0-8018-6056-3*) Johns Hopkins.

Locating & Correcting Reading Difficulties. 7th ed. James L. Shanker & Eldon E. Ekwall. LC 97-33467. 522p. (C). 1997. pap. 40.00 (*0-13-862962-5*) P-H.

Locating & Evaluating Information on the Internet. Art Wolinsky. LC 99-20378. (Internet Library). (Illus.). 64p. (YA). (gr. 4 up). 1999. lib. bdg. 17.95 (*0-7660-1259-X*) Enslow Pubs.

***Locating & Evaluating Information on the Internet.** Art Wolinsky, LC 99-20378. (Internet Library). (Illus.). 64p. (YA). (gr. 4 up). 1999. pap. 9.95 (*0-7660-1745-1*) Enslow Pubs.

Locating & Preserving Your Church's Records. Pat Brown. Ed. by Charles W. Deweese. (Resource Kit for Your Church's History Ser.). 8p. 1984. 0.60 (*0-939804-15-8*) Hist Comm S Baptist.

Locating Australia's Past: A Practical Guide to Writing Local History. Local History Coordination Project Staff. 1989. pap. 22.95 (*0-86840-211-7*, Pub. by New South Wales Univ Pr) Intl Spec Bk.

Locating Consciousness. Valerie G. Hardcastle. LC 95-31971. (Advances in Consciousness Research Ser.: No. 4). xviii, 266p. 1995. pap. 34.95 (*1-55619-184-7*) J Benjamins Pubng Co.

Locating Consensus for Democracy: A Ten-Year U. S. Experiment. unabridged ed. Alan F. Kay. Ed. by Charles Dorris. LC 98-93563. (Illus.). 432p. 1998. pap. 29.95 (*0-9650589-1-3*) Amer Talk Issues.

***Locating Cultural Creativity.** John Liep. LC 00-9108. (Anthropology, Culture & Society Ser.). 2000. write for info. (*0-7453-1703-0*) Stylus Pub VA.

***Locating Filipino Americans: Ethnicity & Cultural Politics of Space.** Rick Bonus. (Asian American History & Culture Ser.). (Illus.). 248p. 2000. 69.50 (*1-56639-778-2*); pap. 19.95 (*1-56639-779-0*) Temple U Pr.

Locating Financial Branch Facilities: A Guide to Techniques & Literature. Douglas O. Love & Jerome A. Deichert. (Nebraska Economic & Business Reports: No. 34). 1983. 10.00 (*0-318-02060-2*) Bur Busn Res U Nebr.

Locating Fire Alarm Sounders for Audibility. H. Butler et al. (C). 1981. pap. 95.00 (*0-86022-100-8*, Pub. by Build Servs Info Assn) St Mut.

L

Locating Gender: Occupational Segregation, Wages, & Domestic Responsibility. Siltanen. LC 94-8047. (Cambridge Studies in Work & Social Inequality: Vol. 1). 224p. 1994. 65.00 (*1-85728-253-1*, Pub. by UCL Pr Ltd); pap. 24.95 (*1-85728-254-X*, Pub. by UCL Pr Ltd) Taylor & Francis.

Locating Health: Sociological & Historical Explorations. Ed. by Sue Scott et al. 288p. 1993. 77.95 (*1-85628-367-4*, Pub. by Avebry) Ashgate Pub Co.

*__Locating Hidden Meaning.__ D. Cushenbery & Meyer. 2000. pap. 4.95 (*0-13-030394-1*) P-H.

Locating Information Fast: Reading & Writing Skills. Jo Ellen Moore. Ed. by Joy Evans. (Illus.). 32p. (J). (gr. 4-6). 1995. pap., wbk. ed. 2.50 (*1-58610-039-4*, Learn on the Go) Learn Horizon.

Locating Learning: Ethnographic Perspectives on Classroom Research. Catherine Emihovich. LC 88-35142. 348p. (C). 1989. pap. 39.50 (*0-89391-577-7*); text 73.25 (*0-89391-505-X*) Ablx Pub.

Locating Lines & Hyperplanes: Theory & Algorithms. Anita Schhobel. LC 98-52905. (Applied Optimization Ser.). 1999. write for info. (*0-7923-5559-8*) Kluwer Academic.

Locating Lost Family Members & Friends. Kathleen W. Hinckley. LC 99-27408. 176p. 1999. pap. 18.99 (*1-55870-503-1*, Betrwy Bks) F & W Pubns Inc.

*__Locating Potential Export Sales Representatives, 2000.__ annuals John R. Jagoe. Ed. by Agnes Brown. (Illus.). 55p. 2000. pap. 40.00 (*0-943677-40-8*) Export USA.

Locating Resources for Healthy People. 1995. lib. bdg. 250.95 (*0-8490-7578-5*) Gordon Pr.

Locating Swift: Essays on the 250th Anniversary of the Death of Jonathan Swift, 1667-1745. Patrick Kelly. Ed. by Aileen Doyle & Ian C. Ross. LC 98-166981. 208p. 1998. boxed set 55.00 (*1-85182-317-4*, Pub. by Four Cts Pr) Intl Spec Bk.

Locating the Business Module, PACE Level 1: A Program for Acquiring Competence in Entrepreneurship, 3 levels. rev. ed. National Center for Research in Vocational Educati. 1983. 2.50 (*0-318-67175-1*, RD240AB7) Ctr Educ Trng Employ.

Locating the Business Module, PACE Level I: A Program for Acquiring Competence in Entrepreneurship, 3 levels. rev. ed. National Center for Research in Vocational Educati. 1983. write for info. (*0-318-67176-X*, RD240AB7) Ctr Educ Trng Employ.

Locating the Business Module, PACE Level 2: A Program for Acquiring Competence in Entrepreneurship, 3 levels. rev. ed. National Center for Research in Vocational Educati. 1983. 2.50 (*0-317-06056-2*, RD240BB7) Ctr Educ Trng Employ.

Locating the Business Module, PACE Level 3: A Program for Acquiring Competence in Entrepreneurship, 3 levels. rev. ed. National Center for Research in Vocational Educati. 1983. 2.50 (*0-317-06057-0*, RD240CB7) Ctr Educ Trng Employ.

Locating the Romantic Subject: Novalis with Winnicott. Gail M. Newman. LC 96-30787. (Kritik: German Literary Theory & Cultural Studies Ser.). 264p. 1997. text 34.95 (*0-8143-2650-1*) Wayne St U Pr.

Locating the Shakers. Ed. by Gidley & Bowles. 168p. 1990. pap. text 16.95 (*0-85989-351-0*, Pub. by Univ Exeter Pr) Northwestern U Pr.

Locating the Transference: Actuality & Illusion in the Psychoanalytic Encounter. Ed. by Reed & Levine. (Psychoanalytic Inquiry Ser.: Vol. 13, No. 4). 1993. 20.00 (*0-88163-941-9*) Analytic Pr.

Locating Trophy Whitetail. David Morris. Ed. by Craig Boddington. (Whitetail Secrets Ser.: No. 8). (Illus.). 151p. 1996. 19.95 (*1-56416-158-7*) Derrydale Pr.

Locating United States Government Information: A Guide to Sources. 2nd ed. Edward Herman. LC 96-51490. xiv, 228p. 1997. 68.00 (*1-57588-203-5*, 310920) W S Hein.

Locating United States Government Information: A Guide to Sources 1999 Internet Supplement. Edward Herman. LC 99-190216. xiv, 228p. 1999. pap. 35.00 (*1-57588-498-4*, 310925) W S Hein.

Locating United States Government Information: A Workbook Guide. Edward Herman. LC 82-83991. ix, 250p. 1983. lib. bdg. 40.00 (*0-89941-182-7*, 302230) W S Hein.

Locating Your Ancestors in Cuban Cities: Methods & Resources. Peter E. Carr. (Illus.). 65p. (Orig.). 1995. pap. 14.95 (*0-9631209-5-6*) TCI Gene Res.

Location Analysis for Multiregional Modeling. B. H. Stevens & George I. Treyz. (Discussion Papers: No. 113). 1979. pap. 10.00 (*1-55869-071-9*) Regional Sci Res Inst.

Location & Change: Perspectives on Economic Geography. Michael Healey & Brian W. Ilbery. (Illus.). 398p. 1991. pap. text 45.00 (*0-19-874155-3*) OUP.

*__Location & Design of Bus Transfer Facilities: An Information Report.__ ITE Technical council Commiteee 5C-1A. LC 99-49634. 1999. write for info. (*0-935403-38-8*) Inst Trans Eng.

Location & Dislocation in Contemporary Irish Society: Perspectives on Irish Emigration & Irish Identities in a Global Context. Jim MacLaughlin. LC 97-27245. 1997. pap. 24.00 (*0-268-01317-9*) U of Notre Dame Pr.

Location & Dislocation in Contemporary Irish Society: Perspectives on Irish Emmigration & Irish Identities in a Global Context. Ed. by Jim MacLaughlin. 256p. 1997. 69.95 (*1-85918-054-X*, Pub. by Cork Univ); pap. 27.95 (*1-85918-055-8*, Pub. by Cork Univ) Intl Spec Bk.

Location & Land Use: Toward a General Theory of Land Rent. William Alonso. LC 63-17193. (Publications of the Joint Center for Urban Studies of the Massachusetts Institute of Technology & Harvard University). 219p. reprint ed. pap. 67.90 (*0-7837-2215-X*, 205730500004) Bks Demand.

Location & Layout Planning. W. Domschke & A. Drexl. (Lecture Notes in Economics & Mathematical Systems Ser.: Vol. 238). iv, 134p. 1985. 29.50 (*0-387-13908-7*) Spr-Verlag.

Location & Movement Review Book. 32p. 1995. pap. text 22.95 (*0-521-43951-5*) Cambridge U Pr.

Location & Racial Composition of Public Housing in the U. S. An Analysis of the Racial Occupancy & Location of Public Housing Developments. John M. Goering et al. (Illus.). 106p. (Orig.). (C). 1995. pap. text 30.00 (*0-7881-1971-0*) DIANE Pub.

Location & Space Economy: A General Theory Relating to Industrial Location, Market Areas, Land Use, Trade & Urban Structures. Isard Walter et al. (Regional Science Reprint Ser.: No. 1). (Illus.). (C). 1979. reprint ed. pap. text 8.00 (*0-943019-00-1*) Cornell CRPP.

Location & Trade Theory: Industrial Location, Comparative Advantage, & the Geographic Pattern of Production in the United States. Joseph T. Johnson. LC 81-11558. (University of Chicago, Department of Geography, Research Paper Ser.: No. 198). 123p. 1981. reprint ed. pap. 38.20 (*0-608-02242-X*, 206288300004) Bks Demand.

Location Criteria for High Schools: Student Transportation & Racial Integration. Fred L. Hall. LC 73-86443. (University of Chicago, Department of Geography, Research Paper Ser.: No. 150). 170p. 1973. reprint ed. pap. 52.70 (*0-608-02257-8*, 206289800004) Bks Demand.

Location Economics: Theoretical Underpinnings & Applications. Melvin L. Greenhut. LC 95-7197. (Economists of the Twentieth Century Ser.). 496p. 1995. 120.00 (*1-85898-138-7*) E Elgar.

Location Guide to the Manuscripts of Supreme Court Justices. rev. ed. Adrienne De Vergie & Mary K. Kell. (Legal Bibliography Ser.: No. 24). 146p. 1981. 15.00 (*0-935630-07-4*) U of Tex Tarlton Law Lib.

Location in Space: Theoretical Perspectives in Economic Geography. 3rd ed. Peter Dicken & Peter E. Lloyd. 431p. (C). 1997. 115.00 (*0-06-041677-7*) Addson-Wesley Educ.

Location in the Upper Peninsula: Poems, Stories, Essays. Jane Piirto. (Illus.). 234p. (Orig.). 1994. pap. text 13.95 (*0-9632975-4-6*) Sampo Pub.

Location Learning: The Field Study Trip. 2nd rev. ed. Lucille Sheets & Fevrel Pratt. (Illus.). 248p. (C). 1989. pap. text 25.00 (*0-9623295-0-9*) Location Lrn Assn.

Location Location Location: How to Select the Best Site for Your Business. Luigi Salvaneschi. Ed. by Camille Akin. LC 96-32255. (Successful Business Library). (Illus.). 280p. 1996. pap. 19.95 (*1-55571-376-9*, Oasis Pr) PSI Resch.

Location Modeling in Practice: Applications (Site Location, Oil Field Generators, Emergency Facilities, Postal Boxes), Theory, & History. Ed. by H. A. Eiselt. LC 92-73996. (Series in Mathematical & Management Sciences: Vol. 31). (Illus.). 94p. 1992. 195.00 (*0-935950-33-8*) Am Sciences Pr.

Location of Acupoints. Compiled by China Academy of Traditional Chinese Medicine, Institute of Acupuncture & Moxibustion Staff. LC 93-242403. 276p. 1990. write for info. (*7-119-01368-8*) Foreign Lang.

Location of Acupoints. Delta Staff. (Illus.). 184p. 1995. 25.00 (*983-9808-32-X*, Pub. by Delta Edits) Weatherhill.

Location of British Army Records. (C). 1987. 30.00 (*0-7855-2125-9*, Pub. by Birmingham Midland Soc) St Mut.

Location of Critical Points of Analytic & Harmonic Functions. Joseph L. Walsh. LC 50-12177. (Colloquium Publications: Vol. 34). 384p. 1950. pap. 52.00 (*0-8218-1034-0*, COLL-34) Am Math.

Location of Critical Points of Analytic & Harmonic Functions. Joseph L. Walsh. LC 50-12177. (Colloquium Publications: No. 34). 396p. reprint ed. pap. 122.80 (*0-7837-3397-6*, 204335600008) Bks Demand.

Location of Culture. Homi K. Bhadha. LC 93-10757. 288p. (C). (gr. 13). 1994. pap. 22.99 (*0-415-05406-0*, A4760) Routledge.

*__Location of Economic Activity in the Eu: Monitoring European Integration.__ 10th ed. Pontus Braunerhjelm et al. (Monitoring European Integration Ser.). 150p. 2000. pap. text 37.50 (*1-898128-46-4*) Ctr Econ Policy Res.

Location of Foreign Direct Investment: Geographic & Business Approaches. Ed. by Milford B. Green & Rod B. McNaughton. 288p. 1995. 77.95 (*1-85972-067-6*, Pub. by Avebry) Ashgate Pub Co.

Location of Immigrant Industry Within a U. K. Assisted Area: The Scottish Experience. Henderson. (Progress in Planning Ser.: Vol. 14, Part 2). (Illus.). 121p. 1980. pap. 16.25 (*0-08-026807-2*, Pergamon Pr) Elsevier.

Location of Jobs in a Developing Metropolis: Patterns of Growth in Bogota & Cali, Colombia. Kyu S. Lee. (World Bank Research Publications Ser.). (Illus.). 192p. 1989. text 24.95 (*0-19-520786-6*) OUP.

Location of Marginal Production for Value-added & Intermediate Goods: Optimal Policies & Trade Volumes. Frank Fuller. LC 97-77345. (Illus.). 1997. write for info. (*0-936911-09-3*) Ctr Agri & Rural Dev.

Location of Responsibility for Product Policy Decisions of United States-Based Multinational Firms Manufacturing Consumer Goods. Cyril M. Logar. Ed. by Stuart Bruchey. LC 80-581. (Multinational Corporations Ser.). (Illus.). 1980. lib. bdg. 25.95 (*0-405-13373-1*) Ayer.

Location of the Monuments, Markers, & Tablets on Gettysburg Battlefield. Kathleen G. Harrison. (Illus.). 46p. (C). 1993. pap. text 4.95 (*0-939631-64-4*) Thomas Publications.

Location of the United States Steel Industry, 1879-1919. Ann K. Harper. Ed. by Stuart Bruchey. LC 76-39829. (Nineteen Seventy-Seven Dissertations Ser.). (Illus.). 1977. lib. bdg. 26.95 (*0-405-09909-6*) Ayer.

Location of Yamatai: A Case Study in Japanese Historiography, 720-1945. John Young. LC 78-64228. (Johns Hopkins University. Studies in the Social Sciences. Thirtieth Ser. 1912: 2). reprint ed. 37.50 (*0-404-61333-0*) AMS Pr.

Location Photographer's Handbook: The Complete Guide for the Out-of-Studio Shoot. Ken Haas. (Illus.). 429p. 1989. pap. 24.95 (*0-471-29087-4*, VNR) Wiley.

*__Location Photography.__ Mark Galer. (Essential Skills Ser.). (Illus.). 192p. 1999. pap. 29.95 (*0-240-51548-X*) Buttrwrth-Heinemann.

Location Portraiture: The Story Behind the Art. William S. McIntosh. (Illus.). 223p. 1996. pap. 49.95 (*1-883403-37-5*, H 883, Silver Pixel Pr) Saunders Photo.

Location Portraiture of Families & Executives. Van W. Frazier & Pam C. Frazier. (Illus.). 86p. 1992. pap. 29.50 (*0-934420-12-2*, 1276) Studio Pr NE.

Location Register of English Literary Manuscripts & Letters: 18th & 19th Centuries, 2 vols., Set. Ed. by David Sutton. 1200p. 1995. 280.00 (*0-7123-0388-X*) U of Toronto Pr.

Location Register of Twentieth Century English Literary Manuscripts & Letters: A Union List of Papers of Modern English, Irish, Scottish & Welsh Authors in the British Isles. British Library Staff. 1200p. (C). 1988. 190.00 (*0-8161-8981-1*, Hall Reference) Macmillan.

Location, Scheduling, Design & Integer Programming. Manfred W. Radberg & Minendra P. Rijal. (International Series in Operations Research & Management Science: Vol. 3). 232p. (C). 1996. lib. bdg. 115.00 (*0-7923-9715-0*) Kluwer Academic.

Location Scouting & Management Handbook: Television, Film & Still Photography. Robert Maier. (Illus.). 192p. 1994. pap. 29.95 (*0-240-80152-0*, Focal) Buttrwrth-Heinemann.

Location Theory. Jean J. Gabszewicz & Jacques-Francois Thisse. (Fundamentals of Pure & Applied Economics Ser.: Vol. 5). viii, 190p. 1986. pap. text 77.00 (*3-7186-0297-0*) Gordon & Breach.

Location Theory, 2 vols. Ed. by Jacques-Francois Thisse et al. LC 96-27871. (Modern Classics in Regional Science Ser.: No. 1). 1144p. 1996. 400.00 (*1-85898-108-5*) E Elgar.

Location Theory & Programming Models: The Von Thunen Case. Benjamin H. Stevens. (Discussion Papers: No. 19). 1967. pap. 10.00 (*1-55869-072-7*) Regional Sci Res Inst.

Locational Analysis for Manufacturing: A Selection of Readings. Ed. by Gerald J. Karaska & David F. Bramhall. (Regional Science Studies Ser.: No. 7). 1969. 38.50 (*0-262-11026-1*) MIT Pr.

Locational Behavior in Manufacturing Industries. William R. Latham. (Studies in Applied Regional Science: No. 4). 1976. pap. text 48.00 (*90-207-0638-1*) Kluwer Academic.

Locational Competition in the World Economy. Ed. by Horst Siebert. (Illus.). 262p. (C). 1996. text 76.50 (*3-16-146519-9*) JCB Mohr.

Locational Competition in the World Economy: Symposium 1994. Horst Siebert. (C). 1996. 76.50 (*0-472-10761-5*) U of Mich Pr.

Locational Conflict: Community Capital & the State. Robert W. Lake. 208p. (C). 1999. 70.00 (*0-415-11571-X*) Routledge.

Locational Developments & Urban Planning. F. J. Van Lierop & Peter Nijkamp. (NATO Advanced Study, Behavioral & Social Sciences Ser.: No. 5). 549p. 1981. lib. bdg. 171.00 (*90-286-2651-4*) Kluwer Academic.

Locational Dynamics of Manufacturing Activity. Ed. by Lyndhurst Collins & David F. Walker. LC 73-21939. 412p. reprint ed. pap. 127.80 (*0-608-15627-2*, 203175600076) Bks Demand.

Locational Factors & Locational Developments in the Soviet Chemical Industry. Leslie Dienes. LC 68-18023. (University of Chicago, Department of Geography, Research Paper Ser.: No. 119). 275p. reprint ed. pap. 85.30 (*0-7837-0396-1*, 204071700018) Bks Demand.

Locations. 1999. write for info. (*0-316-23670-5*) Little.

Locations Locations Locations: Ideal Settings for Your Special Event on the Monterey Peninsula. Janice Block. 168p. (Orig.). 1995. pap. 12.95 (*0-9632181-1-5*) Crits Choice.

Locations, Locations, Locations: Ideal Settings for Your Special Event on the Monterey Peninsula. 2nd rev. ed. Janice Block & David Rankine. Ed. by Shirley Coe. 196p. 1999. pap. 15.95 (*0-9632181-2-3*) Crits Choice.

Locations of Desire. Terry Suhre. 42p. 1990. pap. 5.00 (*0-89792-126-7*) Ill St Museum.

*__Locations of Modernism: Region & Nation in British & American Modernist Poetry.__ Ed. by Alex Davis & Lee M. Jenkins. 309p. (C). 2000. text Price not set. (*0-521-78032-2*) Cambridge U Pr.

Locations of the Sacred: Essays on Religion, Literature & Canadian Culture. William C. James. LC 97-932473. 288p. 1998. 39.95 (*0-88920-293-1*, PR9185) W Laurier U Pr.

Locative Alternation in German: Its Structure & Acquisition. Ursula Brinkmann. LC 97-26692. (Language Acquisition & Language Disorders (LALD) Ser.: Vol. 15). x, 289p. 1997. lib. bdg. 79.00 (*1-55619-778-0*) J Benjamins Pubng Co.

*__Locative Class in Shengologa (Kgalagadi)__ Sabine Neumann. (Research in African Studies). 240p. 1999. 45.95 (*3-631-34938-6*) P Lang Pubng.

*__Locative Class in Shengologa (Kgalagadi)__ Sabine Neumann. LC 99-37953. (Schriften zur Afrikanistik - Research in African Studies: Vol. 2). (Illus.). 240p. (C). 1999. pap. text 45.95 (*0-8204-4347-6*) P Lang Pubng.

Locator: A Step-by-Step Guide to Finding Lost Families, Friends & Loved One Any Where Any Time. Troy Dunn. LC 99-37144. 336p. 2000. pap. 17.95 (*0-385-49452-1*) Doubleday.

Locator: The Complete Guide to Finding Family, Friends & Loved Ones. large type ed. Troy Dunn & Virgil Klunder. Ed. by Arliene Dunn. (Illus.). 720p. 1992. ring bd., lthr. 199.00 (*1-879499-06-1*) Caradium Pub.

Locator II Reference Manual. William Blinn et al. 82p. 1992. 50.00 (*1-880933-00-4*) Mgmt Comp Srvs.

Locators of Health. E. S. Vel'Khover et al. LC 90-44825. 1990. write for info. (*1-56032-008-7*) Hemisp Pub.

Loch. Paul Zindel. LC 94-11252. 224p. (J). (gr. 6-10). 1994. lib. bdg. 15.89 (*0-06-024543-3*) HarpC Child Bks.

Loch. Paul Zindel. LC 94-11252. (Illus.). 224p. (J). (gr. 6-10). 1994. 15.95 (*0-06-024542-5*) HarpC Child Bks.

Loch. Paul Zindel. LC 95-8884. (Illus.). 224p. (J). (gr. 6-10). 1995. pap. 4.95 (*0-7868-1099-8*, Pub. by Hyprn Ppbks) Little.

Loch. Paul Zindel. (J). 1995. 10.05 (*0-606-08806-7*, Pub. by Turtleback) Demco.

Loch: A Year in the Life of a Scottish Loch. Roy Dennis. (Illus.). 192p. 1995. 28.95 (*0-563-36940-X*, BBC-Parkwest) Parkwest Pubns.

Loch Fleet: Post-Mining Catchment Responses. Ed. by Gwyneth Howells. 120p. 1995. pap. text 473.00 (*2-88449-056-6*) Gordon & Breach.

*__Loch Lomond & the Trossachs.__ Robert D. Campbell. (Illus.). 208p. 1999. 19.95 (*1-84018-189-3*, Pub. by Mainstream Pubng) Trafalgar.

Loch Lomond & Trossachs Walks. (Ordnance Survey Pathfinder Guides Ser.). (Illus.). 80p. 1993. pap. 14.95 (*0-7117-0572-0*) Seven Hills Bk.

Loch Ness. Daniel N. Jason. (Illus.). 155p. 1997. pap. 10.00 (*0-9659470-0-9*) Time Dancer Pr.

Loch Ness Conspiracy. John M. Bateman. 240p. 1988. 14.95 (*0-8315-0192-8*) Speller.

Loch Ness Leap. Sandy Schofield. (Quantum Leap Ser.: No. XIV). 256p. 1997. mass mkt. 5.99 (*1-57297-231-9*) Blvd Books.

Loch Ness Monster. Harriette S. Abels. LC 87-9027. (Mystery of...Ser.). (Illus.). 48p. (J). (gr. 5-6). 1987. text 12.95 (*0-89686-343-3*, Crstwood Hse) Silver Burdett Pr.

Loch Ness Monster. Tim Dinsdale. 1982. pap. 7.95 (*0-7100-9022-6*, Routledge Thoemms) Routledge.

Loch Ness Monster. Elaine Landau. LC 92-35145. (Mysteries of Science Ser.). (Illus.). 48p. (J). (gr. 3-6). 1993. lib. bdg. 20.90 (*1-56294-347-2*) Millbrook Pr.

Loch Ness Monster. 4th ed. Tim Dinsdale. (Illus.). 230p. 1982. pap. 14.95 (*0-415-04550-9*) Routledge.

Loch Ness Monster: The Evidence. Stewart Campbell. LC 97-36148. (Illus.). 128p. 1997. pap. text 14.95 (*1-57392-178-5*) Prometheus Bks.

Loch Ness Monster: The Evidence. rev. ed. Steuart Campbell. (Illus.). 128p. 1991. reprint ed. pap. 11.90 (*0-08-041197-5*, Pub. by Aberdeen U Pr) Macmillan.

*__Loch Ness Mystery.__ Willy Vandersteen. (Greatest Adventures of Spike & Suzy Ser.: Vol. 5). (Illus.). 36p. (J). (gr. 2-9). 1999. 11.95 (*0-9533178-5-4*, Pub. by Intes Intl) Diamond Comic Distributors Inc.

Loch Ness Mystery Solved. Ronald Binns. LC 84-43103. (Science & the Paranormal Ser.). (Illus.). 240p. 1984. 19.95 (*0-87975-278-5*); pap. 19.95 (*0-87975-291-2*) Prometheus Bks.

Loch Ness Story. large type ed. Nicholas Witchell. 282p. 1993. 23.95 (*1-85695-066-2*, Pub. by ISIS Lrg Prnt) Transaction Pubs.

Loch Olabhat Project, 1989. Ian Armit. 40p. 1990. pap. 7.50 (*0-614-21847-0*) David Brown.

Lochaber Narrow Gauge Railway. Picton Publishing Staff. (Illus.). (C). 1987. 30.00 (*0-7855-2194-1*, Pub. by Picton) St Mut.

Lochiel of the '45: The Jacobite Chief & the Prince. John Gibson. LC 95-127914. 208p. 1995. pap. 25.00 (*0-7486-0507-X*, Pub. by Edinburgh U Pr) Col U Pr.

*__Lochner Court, Myth & Reality: Substantive Due Process from the 1890s to the 1930s.__ Michael J. Phillips. LC 00-29848. 264p. 2000. 64.00 (*0-275-96930-4*, Praeger Pubs) Greenwood.

Lochner vs. New York: Economic Regulation on Trial. Paul Kens. LC 98-23809. (Landmark Law Cases & American Society Ser.). 192p. 1998. 29.95 (*0-7006-0918-0*); pap. 12.95 (*0-7006-0919-9*) U Pr of KS.

Lochness Monster. Jarrold Staff. (Illus.). 32p. 1993. pap. 3.95 (*0-7117-0229-2*) Seven Hills Bk.

Lochs & Glens of Scotland. Paul Ramsay. (Illus.). 160p. 1994. 29.95 (*1-55859-867-7*) Abbeville Pr.

Lochsa: The Story of a Ranger District & Its People in Clearwater National Forest. Louis F. Hartig. Ed. by Shirley T. Moore. (Illus.). 207p. (Orig.). 1989. pap. text 9.95 (*0-8403-5343-X*) NW Interpretive.

Lochsa Road: A Pilgrim in the West. Kim R. Stafford. LC 91-71651. (Illus.). 110p. (Orig.). 1991. 20.00 (*0-917652-92-4*); pap. 10.00 (*0-917652-93-2*) Confluence Pr.

Lochsa Story: Land Ethics in the Bitterroot Mountains. Bud Moore. LC 96-27228. (Illus.). 476p. 1996. pap. 20.00 (*0-87842-333-8*) Mountain Pr.

Lochsa Story: Land Ethics in the Bitterroot Mountains. Bud Moore. LC 96-27228. (Illus.). 450p. 1996. 36.00 (*0-87842-341-9*) Mountain Pr.

Loci Communes of Philip Melanchthon. Philip Melanchthon. Tr. by Charles L. Hill. LC 83-45649. reprint ed. 32.50 (*0-404-19858-9*) AMS Pr.

Loci, Memory-Minute: How to Improve Your Memory Fast. David L. Riley, Sr. LC 87-90689. (Illus.). 75p. (Orig.). 1987. pap. 10.00 (*0-9618976-0-0*) D L Riley.

An Asterisk (*) at the beginning of an entry indicates that the title is appearing for the first time.

Lock & Key Library: Classic Mystery & Detective Stories. Julian Hawthorne. 1977. 23.95 (*0-8369-4149-7*) Ayer.

Lock-and-Key Principle: The State of the Art--100 Years On, Vol. 1, The State of the Art--100 Years On. Ed. by Jean-Paul Behr. 336p. 1995. 260.00 (*0-471-93902-1*) Wiley.

Lock & the Key. large type ed. Frank Gruber. (Linford Mystery Library). 336p. 1994. pap. 16.99 (*0-7089-7486-4*, Linford) Ulverscroft.

Lock Block Logic. John Messerly. (Illus.). 90p. (J). (gr. 2-6). 1993. pap. text 15.95 (*0-9643700-0-X*) Elmwood Pr.

Lock Box Murders. Dick Beyer. LC 94-60771. 304p. 1994. pap. 5.95 (*0-9635404-0-8*) TwoForYou Bks.

Lock Bypass Methods. LC 98-87336. 127 p. 1998. write for info. (*0-9666087-0-4*) Level Four.

***Lock N Load.** 3rd rev. ed. (Illus.). 2000. reprint ed. pap. text. write for info. (*0-9679400-9-5*) SSDC.

Lock On: A-6E, KA-6D Intruder EA-6B Prowler. Ed. by Francois Verlinden. (Lock On: Vol. 20). (Illus.). 36p. 1993. 14.95 (*1-930607-17-2*, VPI 0798) Verlinden Prod.

Lock On: AH-64A Apache Attack Helicopter. Ed. by Francois Verlinden. (Lock On: Vol. 13). (Illus.). 36p. 1991. 14.95 (*1-930607-10-5*, VPI 0670) Verlinden Prod.

Lock On: Boeing B-17G Flying Fortress. Ed. by Francois Verlinden. (Lock On: Vol. 24). (Illus.). 36p. 1994. 16.95 (*1-930607-21-0*, VPI 0897) Verlinden Prod.

Lock On: F-15E Strike Eagle. Ed. by Francois Verlinden. (Lock On: Vol. 22). (Illus.). 36p. 1993. 15.95 (*1-930607-19-9*, VPI 0856) Verlinden Prod.

Lock On: FIA 18 AK & CF-18C. Ed. by Francois Verlinden. (Lock On: Vol. 15). (Illus.). 36p. 1992. write for info. (*1-930607-12-1*, VPI 0692) Verlinden Prod.

Lock On: Grumman F-14A/B Tomcat. Ed. by Francois Verlinden. (Lock On: Vol. 18). (Illus.). 36p. 1993. 14.95 (*1-930607-15-6*, VPI 0761) Verlinden Prod.

Lock On: Hawker Hurricane Mk XII. Ed. by Francois Verlinden. (Lock On: Vol. 25). (Illus.). 24p. 1994. 16.95 (*1-930607-22-9*, VPI 0898) Verlinden Prod.

Lock On: Lockheed S-3B Viking. Ed. by Francois Verlinden. (Lock On: Vol. 23). (Illus.). 36p. 1994. 16.95 (*1-930607-20-2*, VPI 0896) Verlinden Prod.

Lock On: Memerschmitt Bf-109G-2. Ed. by Francois Verlinden. (Lock On: Vol. 28). (Illus.). 48p. 1997. 15.95 (*1-930607-25-3*, VPI 1030) Verlinden Prod.

Lock On: Mi-24W Hind E Gunship. Ed. by Francois Verlinden. (Lock On: Vol. 16). (Illus.). 36p. 1992. 14.95 (*1-930607-13-X*, VPI 0733) Verlinden Prod.

Lock On: Mikoyan Mig 21 MF Fishbed. Ed. by Francois Verlinden. (Lock On: Vol. 21). (Illus.). 36p. 1993. 14.95 (*1-930607-18-0*, VPI 0799) Verlinden Prod.

Lock On: Mikoyan Mig 29 A/C Fulcrum. Ed. by Francois Verlinden. (Lock On: Vol. 19). (Illus.). 36p. 1993. 14.95 (*1-930607-16-4*, VPI 0762) Verlinden Prod.

Lock On: Northrop F-5E/F Tiger II. Ed. by Francois Verlinden. (Lock On: Vol. 26). (Illus.). 36p. 1994. 16.95 (*1-930607-23-7*, VPI 0928) Verlinden Prod.

Lock On: SU-27 'Sukhoi" Ed. by Francois Verlinden. (Lock On: Vol. 17). (Illus.). 36p. 1992. 14.95 (*1-930607-14-8*, VPI 0734) Verlinden Prod.

***Lock On: Sukhoi Su-22 M3.** Ed. by Francois Verlinden. (Lock On: Vol. 27). (Illus.). 36p. 1998. 17.95 (*1-930607-24-5*, VPI 0938) Verlinden Prod.

Lock On: USS Forrestal. Ed. by Francois Verlinden. (Lock On: Vol. 14). (Illus.). 48p. 1991. 17.95 (*1-930607-11-3*, VPI 0671) Verlinden Prod.

Lock Out - Tag Out Pocket Guide. John V. Conforti. Ed. by Robert A. Roy. (Illus.). 64p. (Orig.). 1993. pap. text 41.80 (*0-931690-59-5*) Genium Pub.

Lock Ridge Furnace. Jean C. Stoneback & Eric Newbauer. Date not set. 10.00 (*0-614-13979-1*) Stoneback Pub.

Lock, Stock, & Barrel. deluxe limited ed. C. Adams & R. Braden. (Illus.). 198p. 1996. boxed set 60.00 (*1-57157-033-0*) Safari Pr.

Lock, Stock & Barrel. R. H. McCrory. 1992. reprint ed. 8.95 (*0-913150-68-1*) Pioneer Pr.

Lock, Stock & Barrel. 2nd ed. Cyril E. Adams. 1996. 24.95 (*1-57157-020-9*) Safari Pr.

***Lock, Stock & Two Smoking Barrels.** Guy Ritchie. (Illus.). 148p. 1999. mass mkt. 10.00 (*0-7472-6205-5*, Pub. by Headline Bk Pub) Trafalgar.

***Lock, Stock & Two Smoking Barrels - The Novel.** Andrew Donkin. 2000. pap. 7.95 (*1-85782-415-6*, Pub. by Blake Publng) Seven Hills Bk.

Lock This Man Up. David L. Rice. LC 77-91707. 67p. 1978. per. 5.00 (*0-916418-14-6*) Lotus.

Lock up the Wolves. 1991. 19.95 (*0-7935-0304-3*, 00660175) H Leonard.

***Lockdown America: Police & Prisons in the Age of Crisis.** Christian Parenti. LC 99-37182. 256p. 1999. 25.00 (*1-85984-718-8*, Pub. by Verso) Norton.

***Lockdown America: Police & Prisons in the Age of Crisis.** Christian Parenti. 320p. 2000. pap. 15.00 (*1-85984-303-4*, Pub. by Verso) Norton.

Locke. Michael Ayers. LC 93-15180. (Arguments of the Philosophers Ser.). 704p. (C). 1993. pap. 29.99 (*0-415-10030-5*, B2455) Routledge.

Locke. Ed. by Vere Chappell. LC 98-2536. (Oxford Readings in Philosophy Ser.). 336p. 1998. pap. text 19.95 (*0-19-875197-4*) OUP.

Locke. Ed. by Vere Chappell. LC 98-2536. (Oxford Readings in Philosophy Ser.). 336p. 1998. text 65.00 (*0-19-875196-6*) OUP.

Locke. Woolhouse. 208p. 1994. 51.95 (*0-7512-0281-9*) Ashgate Pub Co.

Locke. Thomas Fowler. Ed. by John Morley. LC 68-58378. (English Men of Letters Ser.). 1968. reprint ed. lib. bdg. 27.50 (*0-404-51710-2*) AMS Pr.

Locke see Aquinas

***Locke: Great Philosophers, 8.** Michael Ayers. LC 99-22647. Vol. 8. 64p. 1999. pap. 6.00 (*0-415-92383-2*) Routledge.

Locke: His Philosophical Thought. Nicholas Jolley. LC 98-35123. 233p. 1999. pap. 19.95 (*0-19-875200-8*) OUP.

Locke: His Philosophical Thought. Nicholas Jolley. LC 98-35123. 244p. 1999. text 55.00 (*0-19-875201-6*) OUP.

Locke: 1908 Edition. Samuel Alexander. (Key Texts Ser.). 102p. 1996. reprint ed. pap. 19.95 (*1-85506-181-3*) Bks Intl VA.

Locke - Berkeley - Hume: Macintosh. John Locke et al. (Past Masters Ser.). (C). write for info. incl. cd-rom (*1-57085-025-9*) Intelex.

Locke - Berkeley - Hume: Windows. John Locke et al. (Past Masters Ser.). (C). write for info. incl. cd-rom (*1-57085-100-X*) Intelex.

Locke & Blake: A Conversation Across the Eighteenth Century. Wayne Glausser. LC 97-40248. 208p. 1998. 49.95 (*0-8130-1570-7*) U Press Fla.

Locke & French Materialism. John W. Yolton. 248p. 1991. text 65.00 (*0-19-824274-3*) OUP.

Locke & the Way of Ideas: 1956 Edition. John W. Yolton. (Key Texts Ser.). 248p. 1990. reprint ed. pap. 25.00 (*1-85506-226-7*) Bks Intl VA.

Locke Art Glass: A Guide for Collectors with Photographic Illustrations of 190 Examples. Joseph H. Locke & Jane T. Locke. 64p. (Orig.). 1987. pap. 9.95 (*0-486-25400-3*) Dover.

Locke, Berkeley, Hume. Charles R. Morris. LC 79-17847. 174p. 1979. reprint ed. lib. bdg. 38.50 (*0-313-22091-3*, MOLO, Greenwood Pr) Greenwood.

Locke, Berkeley, Hume: Central Themes. Jonathan Bennett. 372p. 1971. pap. text 26.00 (*0-19-875016-1*) OUP.

Locke Genealogy Supplement, Vol. 1. Donald P. Hayes, Jr. (Illus.). 336p. 1997. reprint ed. pap. 25.00 (*0-7884-0642-6*, H096) Heritage Bk.

Locke in America: The Moral Philosophy of the Founding Era. Jerome Huyler. LC 94-26227. (American Political Thought Ser.). 370p. 1995. 40.00 (*0-7006-0642-4*) U Pr of KS.

Locke in 90 Minutes. Paul Strathern. LC 99-34484. (Philosophers in 90 Minutes Ser.). 96p. 1999. pap. 6.95 (*1-56663-262-5*, Pub. by I R Dee); lib. bdg. 14.95 (*1-56663-261-7*, Pub. by I R Dee) Natl Bk Netwk.

Locke, Literary Criticism, & Philosophy. William Walker. (Cambridge Studies in Eighteenth-Century English Literature & Thought: No. 22). 247p. (C). 1995. text 64.95 (*0-521-45105-1*) Cambridge U Pr.

Locke Miscellany. Ed. by Jean S. Yolton. 392p. 1990. 48.00 (*1-85506-009-4*) Bks Intl VA.

Locke on Freedom: An Incisive Study of the Thought of John Locke. Merwyn S. Johnson. LC 77-94130. 1978. pap. 8.75 (*0-9601590-5-3*) M S Johnson.

Locke on Government. David L. Thomas. LC 95-5514. (Philosophy Guidebooks Ser.). 152p. (C). (gr. 13). 1995. pap. 12.99 (*0-415-09533-6*) Routledge.

Locke on Human Understanding. E. J. Lowe. LC 94-43131. (Philosophical Guidebooks Ser.). 224p. (C). (gr. 13). 1995. pap. 12.99 (*0-415-10091-7*, B7020) Routledge.

Locke on Money, 2 vols., Vol. 1. John Locke. Ed. by Patrick H. Kelly. (Clarendon Edition of the Works of John Locke Ser.). (Illus.). 358p. 1991. text 130.00 (*0-19-824546-7*) OUP.

Locke on Money, 2 vols., Vol. 2. John Locke. Ed. by Patrick H. Kelly. (Clarendon Edition of the Works of John Locke Ser.). (Illus.). 330p. 1991. text 110.00 (*0-19-824837-7*) OUP.

Locke Out: The Collected Writings of Richard Locke. Richard Locke. (Illus.). 192p. (Orig.). 1993. pap. 12.95 (*0-943383-06-4*) FirstHand Ltd.

Locke, Rousseau, & the Idea of Consent: An Inquiry into the Liberal-Democratic Theory of Political Obligation, 6. Jules Steinberg. LC 77-91094. (Contributions in Political Science Ser.: No. 6). 155p. 1978. 47.95 (*0-313-20052-1*, SLR/, Greenwood Pr) Greenwood.

Locke, Wesley & the Method of English Romanticism. Richard E. Brantley. LC 83-26026. 311p. 1984. 49.95 (*0-8130-0783-6*) U Press Fla.

Lockean Theory of Rights. A. John Simmons. (Studies in Moral, Political, & Legal Philosophy). 384p. 1992. text 52.50 (*0-691-08630-3*, Pub. by Princeton U Pr) Cal Prin Full Svc.

Lockean Theory of Rights. Alan J. Simmons. LC 91-36773. (Studies in Moral, Political, & Legal Philosophy). 397p. reprint ed. pap. 123.10 (*0-608-20141-3*, 207141300011) Bks Demand.

Locked Down: A Woman's Life in Prison. Idella Serna. LC 92-35499. 192p. (Orig.). 1992. pap. 8.95 (*0-934678-40-5*) New Victoria Pubs.

Locked from the Outside. Susan Timmons. 64p. 1990. pap. 5.95 (*0-916328-19-8*) Yellow Pr.

Locked In. Gerald Locklin. 1973. 5.00 (*0-917554-18-3*) Maelstrom.

***Locked in a Violent Embrace: Understanding & Intervening in Domestic Violence.** Zvi Eisikovitz & Eli Buchbinder. LC 00-8366. (Series on Violence Against Women). 2000. pap. write for info. (*0-7619-0539-1*) Sage.

***Locked in Paradise: Enrique Chagoya.** Steven S. High et al. Tr. by Juan F. Velasco. (SPA., Illus.). 80p. 2000. 20.00 (*0-9658115-5-7*) NV Museum Art.

Locked in the Attic. Paul Hutchens. (Sugar Creek Gang Ser.: No. 35). (J). 1999. pap. 4.99 (*0-8024-7039-4*) Moody.

Locked in the Attic. Kris Jamsa. (Happy & Max Ser.). 64p. 1998. 18.95 incl. cd-rom (*1-884133-85-1*, Jamsa Press) Gulf Pub.

Locked in the Cabinet. Robert B. Reich. 338p. 1997. 3.99 (*0-375-40064-8*) Knopf.

Locked in the Cabinet. Robert B. Reich. LC 97-35525. 1998. pap. 13.00 (*0-375-70061-7*) Vin Bks.

Locked in the Cabinet. large type ed. Robert B. Reich. LC 97-27595. (Americana Series). 668p. 1997. pap. 25.95 (*0-7862-1216-0*) Thorndike Pr.

***Locked In The Library.** Marc A. Brown. (Illus.). (J). 1999. pap. 11.05 (*0-613-07017-8*) Econo-Clad Bks.

Locked in the Library. Marc Tolon Brown. (Arthur Chapter Book Ser.: No. 6). 58p. (J). (gr. 3-6). pap. 3.95 (*0-8072-1300-4*) Listening Lib.

Locked in the Library. Marc Tolon Brown. LC 97-75973. (Arthur Chapter Book Ser.: No. 6). (Illus.). 64p. (J). (gr. 2-4). 1998. 12.95 (*0-316-11557-6*); pap. 3.95 (*0-316-11558-4*) Little.

Locked in the Library. unabridged ed. Marc Tolon Brown. (Arthur Chapter Book Ser.). (J). (gr. 3-6). 1998. pap. 15.98 incl. audio (*0-8072-0388-2*, FTR192SP) Listening Lib.

Locked in the Poorhouse: Cities, Race & Poverty in the United States. Milton S. Eisenhower Foundation Staff. Ed. by Fred R. Harris & Lynn A. Curtis. LC 98-29542. (Illus.). 192p. 1999. 24.95 (*0-8476-9135-7*) Rowman.

Locked in Time. Lois Duncan. 224p. (YA). (gr. 7-12). 1986. mass mkt. 4.99 (*0-440-94942-4*, LLL BDD) BDD Bks Young Read.

Locked in Time. Lois Duncan. (J). 1985. 9.60 (*0-606-03022-0*, Pub. by Turtleback) Demco.

***Locked Inside.** Nancy Werlin. LC 99-16577. 240p. 2000. 15.95 (*0-385-32700-5*) Delacorte.

Locked Out: A Novel. Margaret Yang. LC 95-43016. 128p. (J). (gr. 6-9). 1996. 17.95 (*0-936389-40-0*) Tudor Pubs.

***Locked Out: And Other Tales.** Sherman L. Burson. Ed. by Valerie Burson. 2000. write for info. (*0-9667916-3-0*) Queensbury Pr.

Locked Room: The Locked Room. Ed. by Bernard Hartley & Peter Viney. (Illus.). 20p. 1996. pap. text 4.95 (*0-19-421930-5*) OUP.

Locked Room: The Story of a Crime. Maj Sjowall & Per Wahloo. Tr. by Paul B. Austin from SWE. LC 92-50006. (Crime - Black Lizard Ser.). 1992. pap. 12.00 (*0-679-74222-0*) Vin Bks.

Locked Room Murders. Robert Adey. 411p. 1994. 45.00 (*0-9628870-0-5*) Crossover Pr.

Locked Rooms & Open Doors: Diaries & Letters of Anne Morrow Lindbergh, 1933-1935. Anne M. Lindbergh. (Illus.). 380p. 1993. pap. 12.95 (*0-15-652956-4*) Harcourt.

Locked up, Freed, Busted. Matthew McLean. LC 98-84696. 116p. 1998. pap. 8.95 (*1-56167-426-5*) Am Literary Pr.

Locker. Richie Tankersley-Cusick. (YA). (gr. 7 up). 1994. mass mkt. 3.99 (*0-671-79404-3*, Archway) PB.

Locker Room Mirror: How Sports Reflect Society. Nathan Aaseng. LC 92-34582. (Illus.). 144p. (J). (gr. 5 up). 1993. 14.95 (*0-8027-8217-5*); lib. bdg. 15.85 (*0-8027-8218-3*) Walker & Co.

***Locker Room Mojo: True Tales of Superstitions in Sports.** Nick Newton & Bill Minutaglio. LC 99-61075. 114p. (YA). 1999. 32.95 (*0-9670466-4-5*) Middlefork Pr.

Lockerbie: The Inside Story. Rodney Wallis. LC 98-53392. 192p. 2000. 55.00 (*0-275-96493-0*, Praeger Pubs) Greenwood.

***Lockers: Scenes, Monologues & Short Plays for Young People.** Jeremy Kruse. 72p. (YA). 1999. pap. 5.50 (*0-87129-943-7*, L99) Dramatic Pub.

Lockers, Lunch Lines, Chemistry & Cliques . . . Susie Shellenberger & Greg Johnson. LC 94-49218. 144p. (YA). (gr. 9-12). 1995. pap. 7.99 (*1-55661-483-7*) Bethany Hse.

***Locke's Education for Liberty.** Nathan Tarcov. LC 83-17991. 288p. 1999. pap. 24.95 (*0-7391-0085-8*) Lxngtn Bks.

Locke's Education for Liberty. Nathan Tarcov. LC 83-17991. 280p. (C). 1997. pap. text 16.00 (*0-226-78974-8*) U Ch Pr.

Locke's Enlightenment: Aspects of the Origin, Nature & Impact of His Philosophy. John Rogers. Ed. by Jean Ecole & Robert Theis. (Studien und Texte zur Geschichte der Europaischen Ideen: No. 1, Vol. 3). 208p. 1998. write for info. (*3-487-10529-2*) G Olms Pubs.

Locke's Moral, Political & Legal Philosophy. Ed. & Contrib. by J. R. Milton. (International Library of Critical Essays in the History of Philosophy). 540p. 1999. text 166.95 (*1-84014-413-0*, Pub. by Ashgate Pub) Ashgate Pub Co.

Locke's Philosophy: Content & Context. Ed. by G. A. Rogers. 272p. 1994. 55.00 (*0-19-824076-7*) OUP.

Locke's Philosophy: Content & Context. Ed. by G. A. Rogers. 270p. 1997. reprint ed. pap. text 24.00 (*0-19-823684-0*) OUP.

Lockes Philosophy of Science & Knowledge. Woolhouse. 216p. 1994. 57.95 (*0-7512-0282-7*) Ashgate Pub Co.

Locke's Two Treatises on Government. Richard Ashcraft. 256p. 1989. pap. text 19.95 (*0-04-445338-8*) Routledge.

Locket. Richard Paul Evans. 240p. 1998. 15.95 (*0-684-00786-X*) S&S Trade.

***Locket.** Richard Paul Evans. 368p. 1998. 17.95 (*0-684-83473-1*) Simon & Schuster.

Locket. Brenna Todd. LC 97-10657. 298p. 1994. per. 3.50 (*0-373-70621-9*, 1-70621-7) Harlequin Bks.

***Locket.** large type ed. Richard P. Evans. LC 00-25622. 2000. pap. 10.95 (*1-56895-970-2*) Wheeler Pub.

Locket. large type ed. Richard Paul Evans. LC 99-19121. 1999. 26.95 (*1-56895-702-5*) Wheeler Pub.

***Locket.** Richard Paul Evans. 448p. 2000. reprint ed. per. 6.50 (*0-671-00423-9*, Pocket Star Bks) PB.

***Locket for Maggie.** Carole Gift Page. (Heartland Memories Ser.: Vol. 6). 2000. pap. write for info. (*0-7852-7673-4*) Nelson.

Locket of Dreams: A Modern African American Fairy Tale. Donna L. Clovis. LC 99-72744. (Illus.). 24p. (J). (gr. 3-8). 1999. pap. text 9.95 (*1-58521-001-3*) Bks Black Chldn.

***Lockhart Family in America.** rev. ed. Ann C. Gregath. (Illus.). 1998. lib. bdg. 55.00 (*0-944619-01-0*) Gregath Pub Co.

***Lockhart's Nightmare.** Wayne Barton. 352p. 2000. mass mkt. 6.99 (*0-8125-7196-7*) Forge NYC.

Lockharts Nightmare. Wayne Barton & Stan Williams. LC 98-2878. 384p. 1998. text 24.95 (*0-312-86142-7*) St Martin.

Lockheed. Martin W. Bowman. (Transport Ser.). 128p. 1999. pap. 16.99 (*0-7524-1536-0*) Arcadia Publng.

Lockheed: A Report on the Company's Environmental Policies & Practices. (Illus.). 32p. (C). 1994. reprint ed. pap. text 40.00 (*0-7881-0904-9*, Coun on Econ) DIANE Pub.

***Lockheed AH-56A Cheyenne.** Dennis R. Jenkins & Tony Landis. (WarbirdTech Ser.: Vol. 27). (Illus.). 100p. 2000. pap. 16.95 (*1-58007-027-2*, Pub. by Specialty Pr) Voyageur Pr.

Lockheed Aircraft Cutaways. Mike Badrocke & Bill Bunston. (Illus.). 144p. 1998. 29.95 (*1-85532-775-9*, 126595AE, Pub. by Ospry) Motorbooks Intl.

Lockheed C-130 Hercules. Martin Bowman. LC 99-488320. (Illus.). 200p. 1999. 52.95 (*1-86126-205-1*, 128161AE) Motorbooks Intl.

Lockheed C-121 Constellation. Steven J. Ginter. (Naval Fighters Ser.: No. 8). (Illus.). 78p. (Orig.). 1983. pap. 14.95 (*0-942612-08-6*) Naval Fighters.

Lockheed C-130 Hercules & Its Variants. Chris Reed. LC 98-87296. (Illus.). 136p. (Orig.). 1999. pap. 29.95 (*0-7643-0722-3*) Schiffer.

Lockheed Chronicles. Jerry Hall. (Illus.). 304p. 1996. 22.95 (*0-9652837-0-4*) Lockheed Employ.

Lockheed Constellation: Pictorial History. Curtis K. Stringfellow & Peter M. Bowers. (Illus.). 144p. 1992. pap. 24.95 (*0-87938-379-8*) MBI Pubg.

Lockheed Constellation & Super Constellation: Airlinertech. Scott E. Germain. 1998. pap. text 16.95 (*1-58007-000-0*) Specialty Pr.

***Lockheed Constellation-Super Constellation: Production Line to Flightline 1.** Michael O'Leary. (Illus.). 144p. 1999. pap. 24.95 (*1-85532-928-X*, 129054AE) Ospry.

Lockheed F-94 Starfire: A Photo Chronicle. David R. McLaren & Marty J. Isham. LC 92-62387. (Illus.). 127p. (Orig.). 1993. pap. 19.95 (*0-88740-451-0*) Schiffer.

Lockheed F-117 Nighthawk: An Illustrated History of the Stealth Fighter. Bill Holder & Mike Wallace. LC 96-67855. (Illus.). 64p. 1996. pap. 19.95 (*0-7643-0067-9*) Schiffer.

***Lockheed L-188 Electra.** Jim Upton. (AirlinerTech Ser.: Vol. 5). (Illus.). 100p. 2000. pap. 16.95 (*1-58007-025-6*, Pub. by Specialty Pr) Voyageur Pr.

Lockheed L-1011: Tristar. Philip Birtles. LC 98-42469. (Airliners In Color Ser.). 128p. 1998. pap. 24.95 (*0-7603-0582-X*) MBI Pubg.

***Lockheed Martin F-117 Nighthawk.** Dennis R. Jenkins. (WarbirdTech Ser.: Vol. 25). (Illus.). 100p. 2000. pap. 16.95 (*1-58007-020-5*, Pub. by Specialty Pr) Voyageur Pr.

Lockheed-Martin F-22 Raptor: An Illustrated History. Mike Wallace & Bill Holder. LC 98-84030. (Illus.). 72p. 1998. pap. 19.95 (*0-7643-0558-1*) Schiffer.

Lockheed Martin's Skunk Works: The Official History. rev. ed. Jay Miller. (Illus.). 216p. 1995. pap. 29.95 (*1-85780-037-0*, Pub. by Midland Pubng) Specialty Pr.

Lockheed P-80/F-80: A Photo Chronicle. David R. McLaren. LC 95-72398. (Illus.). 184p. (YA). (gr. 10-13). 1996. pap. 24.95 (*0-88740-907-5*) Schiffer.

Lockheed P-38 Lightning. Steve Pace. (Illus.). 120p. (YA). 1996. pap. 14.98 (*0-7603-0151-4*) MBI Pubg.

Lockheed P-38 Lightning. Frederick A. Johnson. (Warbird Tech Ser.: Vol. 2). (Illus.). 100p. (Orig.). 1996. pap. 16.95 (*0-933424-65-5*) Specialty Pr.

Lockheed P-38 Lightning. Michael O'Leary. (Production Line to Frontline Ser.: Vol. 3). (Illus.). 144p. 1999. pap. 19.95 (*1-85532-749-X*, 128256AE, Pub. by Ospry) Motorbooks Intl.

Lockheed P2V Neptune: An Illustrated History. Wayne Mutza. (Illus.). 176p. 1996. 49.95 (*0-7643-0151-9*) Schiffer.

Lockheed SR-71: The Mach 3 Blackbird. Paul F. Crickmore. (Color Classics Ser.). (Illus.). 128p. 1997. pap. 10.95 (*1-85532-712-0*, Pub. by Ospry) Stackpole.

***Lockheed SR-71: The Secret Missions Exposed.** Paul Crickmore. (Illus.). 262p. 2000. pap. 26.95 (*1-84176-098-6*, 130578AE, Pub. by Ospry) Motorbooks Intl.

Lockheed SR-71 the Secret Missions Exposed. rev. ed. Paul Crickmore. (Illus.). 280p. 1997. 34.95 (*1-85532-681-7*, Pub. by Ospry) Motorbooks Intl.

Lockheed SR-71/YF-12 Blackbirds. Dennis R. Jenkins. (Warbird Tech Ser.). 1997. pap. 16.95 (*0-933424-75-2*) Specialty Pr.

Lockheed T-33: A Photo Chronicle. David McLaren. LC 98-85940. (Illus.). 128p. (Orig.). 1999. pap. 24.95 (*0-7643-0646-4*) Schiffer.

Lockheed T2V-1/T-IA Seastar. Steve Ginter. (Naval Fighters Ser.: No. 42). (Illus.). 72p. 1999. pap. 15.95 (*0-942612-42-6*, NF42) Naval Fighters.

Lockheed U-2 Dragon Lady. Dennis Jenkins. (Warbird Tech Ser.: Vol. 16). (Illus.). 100p. 1998. pap. 16.95 (*1-58007-009-4*) Specialty Pr.

Lockheed XFV-1 VTOL Fighter. Steve Ginter. (Naval Fighters Ser.: Vol. 32). (Illus.). 33p. (Orig.). 1996. pap. 7.95 (*0-942612-32-9*) Naval Fighters.

Lockheed 188 Electra. David G. Powers. Ed. by Jon Proctor. (Great Airliners Ser.: Vol. 5). (Illus.). 128p. 1999. pap. 27.95 (*1-892437-01-5*, 128565AE, Pub. by World Transport) Motorbooks Intl.

An Asterisk (*) at the beginning of an entry indicates that the title is appearing for the first time.

L

***Lockheed's Blackworld Skunkworks: U2, SR-71, F-117.** Paul Crickmore. (Aviation Pioneers Ser.: Vol. 4). (Illus.). 112p. 2000. pap. 16.95 (*1-84176-059-5*, 130580AE, Pub. by Osprey) Motorbooks Intl.

Lockheeds Constellation. Steve Pace. LC 97-45037. (Illus.). 96p. 1998. pap. 13.95 (*0-7603-0303-7*) MBI Pubg.

Lockhorns, No. 2. Bill Hoest. 128p. (Orig.). 1987. reprint ed. pap. 2.50 (*0-8125-7266-1*, Pub. by Tor Bks) St Martin.

Lockhorns: Dessert! We Made It to the Home Stretch. Bill Hoest. 128p. 1989. pap. 2.95 (*0-8125-7256-4*, Pub. by Tor Bks) St Martin.

Lockhorns: I'm Sticking to My Story. Bill Hoest. 128p. 1988. pap. 1.95 (*0-8125-7268-8*, Pub. by Tor Bks) St Martin.

Lockhorns: I'm Trying to Improve My Marriage but I Can't Get Her to Leave. Bill Hoest. 1990. pap. 2.95 (*0-8125-0989-7*, Pub. by Tor Bks) St Martin.

Lockhorns: It's a Letter Inviting Mother to Come Visit Us...I'll Mail It Myself. Bill Hoest. 1990. pap. 2.95 (*0-8125-1020-8*, Pub. by Tor Bks) St Martin.

Lockhorns: Leroy Is Very Proud. Bill Hoest. 1989. pap. 2.95 (*0-8125-0601-4*, Pub. by Tor Bks) St Martin.

Lockie & Dadge. Frank Murphy. 192p. (YA). 1997. pap. 6.95 (*0-86278-424-7*, Pub. by OBrien Pr) Irish Amer Bk.

Lockie Leonard, Human Torpedo. Tim Winton. (J). (gr. 5 up). 1992. 13.95 (*0-316-94753-9*) Little.

Lockie Leonard, Scumbuster. Tim Winton. LC 98-19081. 144p. (YA). (gr. 5-9). 1999. per. 16.00 (*0-689-82247-2*) McElderry Bks.

***Locking Arms for the Harvest: The Power of Partnership.** 2nd ed. Mark Brazee. 46p. 1999. pap. 1.20 (*0-934445-09-5*) Eternal Word.

Locking Out & Tagging Out Accidents: A Compliance Program for OSHA Standard 29 CFR 1910.147. Ennis, Lumsden, Boylston & Associates Staff. 150p. 1992. lib. bdg., ring bd. 385.00 (*0-87371-934-4*, L934) Lewis Pubs.

Lockout: A Norah Mulcahaney Mystery. large type ed. Lillian O'Donnell. LC 94-25459. (Cloak & Dagger Ser.). 353p. 1994. lib. bdg. 21.95 (*0-7862-0294-7*) Thorndike Pr.

Lockout - Tagout: The Process of Controlling Hazardous Energy. 429p. 1993. 69.95 (*0-87912-189-0*, 12175-0100) Natl Safety Coun.

Lockout - Tagout Program. Mark M. Moran. (OSHA Written Compliance Programs Ser.: No. 18). (Illus.). 34p. 1992. ring bd. 169.00 (*1-890966-13-4*) Moran Assocs.

***Lockport.** John M. Lamb. (Images of America Ser.). 1999. pap. 18.99 (*0-7524-1281-7*) Arcadia Publng.

***Lockport Boy: A Memoir of a Magical Time & Place.** Frank Bredell. LC 99-96410. 210p. 1999. pap. 12.00 (*0-9674846-0-X*, Andiamo Pr) Frank Bredell.

Lockport Legacy: Themes in the Historical Geography of an Illinois Canal Town. fac. ed. Ed. by Michael P. Conzen & Adam R. Daniel. LC 90-1711. (Studies on the Illinois & Michigan Canal Corridor: No. 4). (Illus.). 174p. 1990. reprint ed. pap. 54.00 (*0-7837-7835-X*, 204759200007) Bks Demand.

***Locks & Fittings in Mexico: A Strategic Entry Report, 1997.** Compiled by Icon Group International Staff. (Illus.). 141p. 1999. ring bd. 1410.00 incl. audio compact disk (*0-7418-1081-6*) Icon Grp.

Locks & Keys. Gail Gibbons. (J). 1980. 12.95 (*0-690-04058-X*) HarpC Child Bks.

Locks & Lockmaking. Francis J. Butter. (Illus.). 142p. 1985. pap. 15.00 (*0-87556-724-X*) Saifer.

Locks & Lockmaking. F. Edward Butterworth. (Illus.). 135p. 1926. 20.00 (*0-87556-392-9*) Saifer.

Locks & Lockpicking: A Basic Guide for Law Enforcement, Security, Military. J. D. James. LC 87-16585. (Illus.). 1987. pap. 10.00 (*0-942667-23-9*) R & R Pub.

Locks & Lockpicking: The Complete Guide for Law Enforcement Security, Military. J. D. James. (Illus.). pap. write for info. (*0-942667-54-9*) R & R Pub.

Locks, Crocs, & Skeeters: The Story of the Panama Canal. Nancy Winslow Parker. (Illus.). 32p. (J). (gr. 3 up). 1996. 16.00 (*0-688-12241-8*, Grenwillow Bks) HarpC Child Bks.

Locks, Picks & Clicks. (Illus.). 70p. 1976. pap. 12.00 (*0-87364-040-3*) Paladin Pr.

***Locks, Safes & Security: An International Police Reference.** 2nd ed. Marc Weber Tobias. LC 00-29952. 2000. write for info. (*0-398-07079-2*) C C Thomas.

Locksley Nightclub, Bar, & Restaurant Security Handbook. Robert A. McManus & Sean M. O'Toole. 320p. 1995. pap. 49.95 (*0-9647209-0-6*) Locksley Pub.

Locksmith. Jack Rudman. (Career Examination Ser.: C-1348). 1994. pap. 23.95 (*0-8373-1348-1*) Nat Learn.

Locksmithing. Phillips. LC 99-34586. 544p. 1999. pap. 34.95 (*0-07-134436-5*) McGraw.

Locksmithing. F. A. Steed. (Illus.). 182p. 1982. 13.95 (*0-8306-0073-6*) McGraw-Hill Prof.

Locksmithing: From Apprentice to Master. Joseph E. Rathjen. 309p. 1994. pap. 24.95 (*0-07-051645-6*) McGraw.

Lockwood. large type ed. Lauran Paine. 1999. 20.00 (*0-7838-1669-3*, G K Hall Lrg Type) Mac Lib Ref.

Lockwood: A Western Story. Lauran Paine. LC 96-6300. 230p. 1996. 16.95 (*0-7862-0658-6*) Five Star.

Lockwood: A Western Story. large type ed. Lauran Paine. LC 97-18661. 299p. 1997. 18.95 (*0-7862-1121-0*) Thorndike Pr.

Loco. large type ed. Lee Hoffman. (Sagebrush Large Print Westerns Ser.). 172p. 1995. lib. bdg. 17.95 (*1-57490-009-9*) T T Beeler.

***Loco & the Wolf.** large type ed. Todhunter Ballard. LC 99-46304. 215p. 1999. 21.95 (*0-7838-8793-0*) Mac Lib Ref.

***Loco for Lizards.** James Cherry. LC 00-37972. (Illus.). 2000. pap. 7.95 (*0-87358-763-4*) Northland AZ.

Locoland. Chris Morris. LC 97-68996. 176p. 1998. pap. 13.50 (*0-88739-163-X*) Creat Arts Bk.

Locomotion of Tissue Cells. CIBA Foundation Staff. LC 73-80386. (CIBA Foundation Symposium: New Ser.: No. 14). 389p. reprint ed. pap. 120.60 (*0-608-13502-X*, 202214500024) Bks Demand.

Locomotive: Building an Eight-Wheeler. David Weitzman. LC 99-10815. (Illus.). 40p. (J). (gr. 4-6). 1999. 16.00 (*0-395-69687-9*) HM.

Locomotive & Rolling Stock Forecasts. Mary Webb. (Transportation - Related Special Reports). 1997. 695.00 (*0-7106-1424-1*) Janes Info Group.

Locomotive Designers in the Age of Steam. J. N. Westwood. LC 77-90502. 285p. 1978. 25.00 (*0-8386-2220-8*) Fairleigh Dickinson.

Locomotive Engineering Guide to Fuel Conservation: If Trains Are So Efficient, Why Does It Take So Much Fuel to Run Them? Paul E. Rhine. LC 96-69154. (Illus.). 76p. 1996. pap. 19.95 (*0-911382-17-8*) Simmons-Boardman.

***Locomotive Gyrating Warning Lights.** 2nd ed. Stephen L. King. LC 00-130067. (Illus.). 800p. 2000. 155.00 (*0-9676765-1-7*) S L King.

Locomotives of Australia, 1850s-1990s. 3rd ed. Leon Oberg. (Illus.). 368p. 1997. 42.95 (*0-86417-779-8*, Pub. by Kangaroo Pr) Seven Hills Bk.

Locomotives of D. Earle Marsh, 1905-1911. Ed. by Charles Fryer. 1999. pap. 21.00 (*1-85072-151-3*, Pub. by W Sessions) St Mut.

***Locomotives of the World.** Anness Publishing Staff. 2000. pap. 10.95 (*0-7548-0513-1*) Anness Pub.

Locomotor Morphology of the Vampire Bat, Desmodus Rotundus. J. Scott Altenbach. (ASM Special Publications: No. 6). (Illus.). vi, 137p. 1979. 12.00 (*0-943612-05-5*) Am Soc Mammalogists.

Locomotor System of the Domestic Mammals. Ed. by R. Nickel et al. (Anatomy of the Domestic Animals Ser.: Vol. 1). (Illus.). 520p. 1985. 117.95 (*0-387-91259-2*) Spr-Verlag.

Locoregional High-Frequency Hyperthermia & Temperature Measurement: Recent Results in Cancer Research, Vol. 101. M. Wannenmacher. Ed. by G. Bruggmoser et al. (Illus.). 150p. 1985. 89.00 (*0-387-15501-5*) Spr-Verlag.

Locos: A Comedy of Gestures. Felipe Alfau. LC 88-14975. 224p. 1997. reprint ed. pap. 12.95 (*1-56478-171-2*) Dalkey Arch.

Locos: A Comedy of Gestures. rev. ed. Felipe Alfau. LC 88-14975. 206p. 1989. 19.95 (*0-916583-30-9*) Dalkey Arch.

Locrine. Ed. by Tudor Facsimile Texts Editing Staff. LC 78-133696. (Tudor Facsimile Texts. Old English Plays Ser.: No. 75). reprint ed. 49.50 (*0-404-53375-2*) AMS Pr.

Locum Lover. large type ed. Judith Worthy. 331p. 1993. 27.99 (*0-7505-0577-X*, Pub. by Mgna Lrg Print) Ulverscroft.

Locura de Fidel Castro. Gustavo A. Marin. LC 96-83521. (Coleccion Cuba y sus Jueces). (SPA., Illus.). 217p. (Orig.). 1996. pap. 16.00 (*0-89729-795-4*) Ediciones.

Locura de la Cruz. Francisco M. Paoli. (SPA.). 108p. 1997. lib. bdg. 8.00 (*1-881708-16-0*) Edcnes Mairena.

Locus. Jeremy Gilbert-Rolfe et al. Ed. by Mirra Painter. Tr. by Aviva Idan from HEB. LC 92-71271. (Illus.). 68p. (Orig.). (C). 1993. pap. text 20.00 (*0-945192-12-6*) USC Fisher Gallery.

Locus Distributed System Architecture. Gerald J. Popek. (MIT Press Series in Computer Systems). (Illus.). 176p. 1986. 30.00 (*0-262-16102-8*) MIT Pr.

Locus of Care: Families, Communities, Institutions & the Provision of Welfare Since Antiquity. Peregrine Horden & Richard Smith. LC 97-15177. (Social Studies in the History of Medicine). 256p. (C). 1998. write for info. (*0-415-11216-8*) Routledge.

Locus of Control: Current Trends in Theory & Research. 2nd ed. Herbert M. Lefcourt. 288p. (C). 1982. text 55.00 (*0-89859-222-4*) L Erlbaum Assocs.

Locus of Meaning: Six Hyperdimensional Fictions. Herbert Smith. (Theory - Culture Ser.). 176p. 1993. text 50.00 (*0-8020-5711-X*) U of Toronto Pr.

Locus Select. 7th ed. Cheryl Filsinger. 166p. 1992. pap. 49.00 (*0-916754-17-0*) Filsinger & Co.

Locust & Wild Honey. Lawrence Dawson. 252p. (Orig.). 1990. pap. 9.95 (*0-941995-08-9*) Paradigm.

Locust Neurobiology: A Bibliography, 1871-1991. C. H. Rowell. LC 92-11025. 250p. 1992. 70.00 (*0-8176-2747-2*, Pub. by Birkhauser); 70.00 (*0-8176-2748-0*, Pub. by Birkhauser) Princeton Arch.

Locust Site (33Mu160) The 1983 Test Excavation of a Multicomponent Workshop in East Central Ohio. Mark F. Seeman. LC 85-9963. (Kent State Research Papers in Archaeology: No. 7). 119p. reprint ed. pap. 36.90 (*0-7837-1345-2*, 204149300020) Bks Demand.

Locust Story. Illus. by Marla Martin & Miriam Martinez. 62p. (J). (ps-2). 1977. pap. 3.35 (*0-7399-0068-4*, 2320) Rod & Staff.

Locusts. Emmanuel Obiechina. 1976. 2.00 (*0-912678-23-2*, Greenfld Rev Pr) Greenfld Rev Lit.

Locusts & Wild Honey. John Burroughs. (Works of John Burroughs). 1989. reprint ed. lib. bdg. 79.00 (*0-7812-2181-1*) Rprt Serv.

Locusts at the Edge of Summer: New & Selected Poems. John Balaban. 150p. 1997. pap. 15.00 (*1-55659-123-3*) Copper Canyon.

Locusts Have No King. Dawn Powell. LC 95-46742. 286p. 1996. pap. 14.00 (*1-883642-42-6*) Steerforth Pr.

Locutions Francaises. Pierre Guiraud. (FRE.). 122p. 1967. 9.95 (*0-8288-7459-X*) Fr & Eur.

Locutions, Lexikon der Franzoesischen Redewendungen: French-German. Ursula Kosters-Roth. (FRE & GER.). 510p. 1990. 29.95 (*0-7859-8563-8*, 3927117455) Fr & Eur.

Lodes: Poems from Hollywood. Mark Dunster. 11p. 1998. pap. 5.00 (*0-89642-438-3*) Linden Pubs.

***Lodestar: The New Novel of the Future-History Epic of the Space Age.** Michael Flynn. 368p. 2000. 24.95 (*0-312-86137-0*, Pub. by Tor Bks) St Martin.

***Lodestar Vol. III: From the Chronicles of Fiarah.** K. L. Morgan. LC 99-90036. (Illus.). 618p. 2000. pap. 17.95 (*1-58308-177-1*, 81771) TriQuest.

Lodestar & Other Night Lights: Poems. Nagueyalti Warren. LC 92-24883. 68p. 1992. pap. 14.95 (*0-7734-9573-8*, Mellen Poetry Pr) E Mellen.

Lodestone. Russell J. Smith. LC 92-43035. 240p. (Orig.). 1993. pap. 9.95 (*0-910155-26-7*) Bartleby Pr.

Lodge. rev. ed. L. James Rongstad. LC 95-23063. (How to Respond Ser.). 64p. 1995. 3.99 (*0-570-04670-X*, 12-6003) Concordia.

Lodge & the Craft. Rollin C. Blackmer. viii, 295p. 1994. reprint ed. pap. 12.95 (*0-88053-043-X*, M 092) Macoy Pub.

Lodge at Lake Annabel. Herbert Arenson. 88p. 1998. 14.95 (*1-890622-22-2*) Leathers Pub.

Lodge Goat (1909) James P. Pettibone. 602p. 1999. reprint ed. pap. 39.00 (*0-7661-0750-7*) Kessinger Pub.

Lodge in Vietnam: A Patriot Abroad. Anne E. Blair. LC 94-38192. 200p. 1995. 32.00 (*0-300-06226-5*) Yale U Pr.

Lodge, Jacksonville Masonic Fraternities: Warren Masonic Lodge No. 10 A. F. & A. M.; Oregon Chapter No. 4 Royal Arch Masons; Adarel Chapter No. 3 Order of Eastern Star; Warren Assembly No. 84 International Order of Rainbow for Girls. Henry H. Halvorsen. Ed. by Marguerite Black. LC 90-24972. (Illus.). (Orig.). 1991. pap. 18.95 (*1-878815-02-4*) Reflected Images.

Lodge of Sorrows. pap. 3.50 (*0-911164-17-0*) Powner.

Lodge of the Double-Headed Eagle: Two Centuries of Scottish Rite Freemasonry in America's Southern Jurisdiction. William L. Fox. LC 97-14064. 608p. 1997. 46.00 (*1-55728-477-6*) U of Ark Pr.

Lodge of the Lynx. Katherine Kurtz & Deborah T. Harris. (Adept Ser.: No. 2). 1992. mass mkt. 6.50 (*0-441-00344-3*) Ace Bks.

Lodge Presents Chef John Folse's Cast Iron Cooking: An Historical Collection from America's Culinary Regions. John D. Folse. 104p. 1996. 15.95 (*0-9625152-5-6*) Chef John Folse.

Lodgepole Pine in North America. Peter Koch. 1100p. 1996. pap. 95.00 (*0-935018-78-6*, 7297) Forest Prod.

Lodger. Nick Dear. 112p. 1994. pap. 11.95 (*0-413-68620-5*, A0707, Methuen Drama) Methn.

Lodger. Belloc Lowndes. 1976. 24.95 (*0-8488-0180-6*) Amereon Ltd.

Lodger. large type ed. Mary Jane Staples. 508p. 1995. 27.99 (*0-7505-0708-X*, Pub. by Mgna Lrg Print) Ulverscroft.

Lodger. Marie B. Lowndes. 224p. 1986. reprint ed. pap. 5.95 (*0-89733-299-7*) Academy Chi Pubs.

Lodger Overhead, & Others. Charles B. Davis. LC 71-121533. (Short Story Index Reprint Ser.). (Illus.). 1977. 24.95 (*0-8369-3489-X*) Ayer.

Lodgers in London. Adelaide E. Phillpotts. LC 74-150483. (Short Story Index Reprint Ser.). 1977. reprint ed. 20.95 (*0-8369-3824-0*) Ayer.

Lodges Examined by the Bible. J. Rice. 1988. pap. 1.95 (*0-87398-510-9*) Sword of Lord.

Lodging & Food Service Industry. 4th rev. ed. Gerald W. Lattin et al. LC 98-6590. (Illus.). 395p. (C). 1998. pap. 60.95 (*0-86612-169-2*) Educ Inst Am Hotel.

Lodging for Travelers: Upper Midwest. Boyd Brue. (Orig.). 1993. pap. 11.95 (*0-927290-01-4*) Lodging Unlimited.

Lodging in the Hills. Madonna Kimball & Jennifer Hinnenkamp. 22p. 1995. pap. 2.00 (*0-9649407-0-1*) Sun Cntry Pubns.

Lodi a Vintage Valley Town. Christi Kennedy. Ed. by Merlyn Holmes. 112p. 1994. 19.95 (*0-9643583-0-1*) Lodi District.

Lodi alla Madonna see Sing the Joys of Mary

Lodon Harness Horse Parade. Keith Chivers. 1997. 49.00 (*0-85131-690-5*, Pub. by J A Allen) Trafalgar.

Lodore. Mary Wollstonecraft Shelley. Ed. by Lisa Vargo. LC 96-932543. (Literary Texts Ser.). 555p. (C). 1997. pap. 16.95 (*1-55111-077-6*) Broadview Pr.

Lodore, 3 vols., 1 bk. Mary Wollstonecraft Shelley. LC 79-8197. reprint ed. 44.50 (*0-404-62118-X*) AMS Pr.

Lodovico Antonio Muratori und Deutschland: Studien Zur Kultur- und Geistesgeschichte der Fruhaufklarung Unter Mitwirkung Von Christian Weyers. Fabio Marri & Maria Lieber. (GER.). 213p. 1997. 32.95 (*3-631-30551-6*) P Lang Pubng.

Lodovico Dolce: Renaissance Man of Letters. Ronnie H. Terpening. (Toronto Italian Studies). 256p. 1997. text 55.00 (*0-8020-4159-0*) U of Toronto Pr.

Lodovico Gritti in Hungary (1529-1534) A Historical Insight into the Beginnings of Turco-Habsburgian Rivalry. Ferenc Szakaly. LC 94-39768. (Studia Historica; Academiae Scientiarum Hungaricae: No. 197). 144p. 1995. pap. 70.00 (*963-05-6815-2*, Pub. by Akade Kiado) St Mut.

***Lodovico Grossi Da Viadana: Salmi a Quattro Chori.** Lodovico G. Da Viadana. Ed. by Gerhard Wielakker. (Recent Researches in the Music of the Baroque Era Ser.: Vol. RRB86). (Illus.). xxiii, 179p. 1998. pap. 65.00 (*0-89579-398-9*) A-R Eds.

Lodovico Viadana: Sinfonie Musicali a Otto Voci . . . Commod Per Concertare Con O i Sorte Di Stromen . . . Opera XVIII (Venice, 1610), Pt. 1 & 2. Ed. by James Ladewig. LC 93-29317. (Italian Instrumental Music of the Sixteenth & Early Seventeenth Centuries Ser.: Vol. 21). (Illus.). 504p. 1994. text 182.00 (*0-8240-4520-3*) Garland.

Lodown: Graphic Engineering. Thomas Marecki. 192p. 1999. pap. text 39.99 (*3-931126-16-1*, Pub. by Die Gestalten) Consort Bk Sales.

Lodu's Escape: And Other Stories from Africa. Ed. by Phoebe Mugo. (Illus.). 64p. (Orig.). (J). (gr. 3-5). 1994. pap. 6.95 (*0-377-00269-0*) Friendship Pr.

Lodz Ghetto: Inside a Community under Siege. (Illus.). 526p. 1989. text 29.95 (*0-9660440-1-0*, Jewish Herit Bks) Jewish Heritage.

Lodz Ghetto: Inside a Community under Siege - Educational Package. Ed. by Alan Adelson & Robert Lapides. (Illus.). 526p. 1989. text 59.95 (*0-9660440-2-9*, Jewish Herit Bks) Jewish Heritage.

Loeb's Money Guide 1991. Marshall Loeb. 1990. pap. 14.95 (*0-316-53071-9*) Little.

Loess: Its Distribution, Geology & Soils: Proceedings of an International Symposium, New Zealand, 13-21 February, 1987. Ed. by D. N. Eden & R. J. Furkert. (Illus.). 245p. (C). 1988. text 110.00 (*90-6191-851-0*, Pub. by A A Balkema) Ashgate Pub Co.

Loess & the Quaternary: Chinese & Hungarian Case Studies. Marton Pecsi. (Studies in Geography in Hungary: No. 18). 125p. (C). 1985. 42.00 (*963-05-4227-7*, Pub. by Akade Kiado) St Mut.

Loess, Environment & Global Change. Ed. by Liu Tungsheng. 288p. 1996. 20.00 (*7-03-002660-8*, Pub. by Sci Pr) Lubrecht & Cramer.

Loess Valley & Other Korean Short Stories. Kim Tong-ni & O Yong-su. Ed. by Korean National Commission for UNCESCO. Tr. by J. F. Holstein et al from KOR. (Modern Korean Short Stories Ser.: No. 1). viii, 256p. 1983. 20.00 (*0-89209-202-5*) Pace Grp Intl.

***L'Oeuvre de Dieu, la Part du Diable.** John Irving. (FRE.). 1999. pap. 17.95 (*2-02-025780-7*) Editions Seuil.

LOEX of the West: Collaboration & Instructional Design in a Virtual Environment. Anderson et al. LC 99-12397. (Foundations in Library & Information Science: Vol. 43). 1999. 78.50 (*0-7623-0549-5*) Jai Pr.

LOF Ninety & the New Salvage Convention. Gerald Darling & Christopher Smith. 256p. 1991. 110.00 (*1-85044-376-9*) LLP.

Loft. Mayer Rus. LC 98-37001. (Illus.). 240p. 1998. 55.00 (*1-58093-013-1*, Pub. by Monacelli Pr) Penguin Putnam.

Loft Living. Peggy Vance. (Illus.). 160p. 1999. 40.00 (*0-7063-7763-X*, Pub. by WrLock) Sterling.

Loft Living: Culture & Capital in Urban Change. Sharon Zukin. LC 88-21799. (Illus.). 247p. (C). 1989. pap. text 17.00 (*0-8135-1389-8*) Rutgers U Pr.

Loft Living: Culture & Capital in Urban Change. Sharon Zukin. LC 81-20830. (Johns Hopkins Studies in Urban Affairs). 224p. reprint ed. pap. 69.50 (*0-7837-6428-6*, 204642600012) Bks Demand.

Loftier Flight: The Life & Accomplishments of Charles-Louis Didelot, Balletmaster. Mary G. Swift. LC 73-15007. 240p. reprint ed. pap. 74.40 (*0-608-17826-8*, 203249400079) Bks Demand.

Loftier Way see Tales from the Book of Morman

Loftin Component, 23SN42. Ed. by Robert T. Bray. LC 44-14121. (Missouri Archaeologist Ser.: Vol. 44). (Illus.). 134p. (Orig.). 1983. pap. 7.00 (*0-943414-24-5*) MO Arch Soc.

Lofting. Allan H. Vaitses. LC 99-33076. (Illus.). 150p. 1999. spiral bd. 19.95 (*0-937822-55-8*) WoodenBoat Pubns.

Lofts. Atrium. 1999. 37.50 (*0-688-16831-0*, Wm Morrow) Morrow Avon.

Lofts. Marcus Field & Mark Irving. (Illus.). 208p. 1998. pap. 40.00 (*3-927258-83-0*) Gingko Press.

Lofts: Living & Working Spaces. Francisco Asensio Cerver. 1999. pap. text 35.00 (*0-8230-6632-0*) Watsn-Guptill.

Lofts: Living in Space. Orianna Banks & Rebecca Tanqueray. 192p. 1999. pap. 29.95 (*0-7893-0361-2*, Pub. by Universe) St Martin.

***Lofts: New Designs for Urban Living.** Felicia E. Molnar. 160p. 1999. 35.00 (*1-56496-579-1*, Pub. by Rockport Pubs) F & W Pubns Inc.

***Lofts & Apartments in New York.** Ed. by LArchivolto Editors. (Illus.). 240p. 1999. 79.95 (*88-7685-104-6*, Pub. by LArchivolto) Bks Nippan.

Lofts for Pigeons & Doves. J. A. Fancier. (Lofts & Aviaries Ser.: Vol. 1). (Illus.). 250p. 1990. write for info. (*0-9622998-2-0*) WFancier Pubns.

Lofts in Italy. Paola Gallo & LArchivolto Editors. 1997. 79.95 (*88-7685-099-6*) LArchivolto.

Lofts in Italy. LArchivolto Editors. 1998. 79.95 (*1-56970-530-5*) Bks Nippan.

***Lofty Dreams.** Eunice R. Moore. (Illus.). 200p. (J). (gr. 3-8). 2000. pap. 7.99 (*1-57532-295-1*, Pub. by Press-Tige Pub) Barnes & Noble Inc.

Log. Michael E. Weddington. (Illus.). 85p. (Orig.). 1994. pap. 9.95 (*0-9644542-0-3*) Big Pict Pr.

***Log: A Dwarfer's Guide to Everything.** Craig Charles. 128p. 1998. pap. 13.95 (*0-14-026862-6*, Pub. by Pnguin Bks Ltd) Trafalgar.

Log Analysis Handbook. E. R. Crain. 684p. 1986. 35.00 (*0-87814-298-3*, P4407) PennWell Bks.

Log Blood Glucose Levels. Charles E. Hugenberger. 12p. 1992. pap. 3.95 (*1-885057-08-3*) C E Hugenberger.

Log Book: A Pilot's Life. Ed. by Crocker Snow. LC 97-49925. (Illus.). 296p. 1998. pap. 29.95 (*1-57488-175-2*) Brasseys.

Log Book: Selected Poems. Sophia D. Breyner. 144p. 1998. pap. 17.95 (*1-85754-364-5*, Pub. by Carcanet Pr) Paul & Co Pubs.

Log Book for Cruising under Sail. John Mellor. 96p. (C). 1990. text 59.00 (*0-906754-62-3*, Pub. by Fernhurst Bks) St Mut.

An Asterisk (*) at the beginning of an entry indicates that the title is appearing for the first time.

Log Book of a Young Immigrant. Laurence M. Larson. 318p. 1939. 15.00 (*0-87732-021-7*) Norwegian-Am Hist Assn.

Log Buildings of Southern Indiana. Warren E. Roberts. LC 85-51209. (Illus.). 231p. (Orig.). 1984. pap. 10.00 (*0-915305-00-3*) Trickster Pr.

Log Buildings of Southern Indiana. rev. ed. Warren E. Roberts. (Illus.). 228p. (Orig.). 1996. pap. 14.95 (*0-915305-06-2*) Trickster Pr.

Log by Log. Wendy Etzel. 64p. 1998. pap. 19.95 (*1-889825-02-6*) R C W Publng.

Log Cabin. Laura Nownes. LC 90-41882. (Classic Quilt Ser.). (Illus.). 20p. 1990. pap. 6.95 (*0-8442-2612-2*, Quilt Dgst Pr) NTC Contemp Pub Co.

Log Cabin. Rodale Press Staff. (Classic American Quilt Collection Ser.). (Illus.). 138p. 1997. pap. text 14.95 (*0-87596-972-0*) Rodale Pr Inc.

Log Cabin: The Basics: A Workbook for Weavers. Gloria B. Skovronsky. (Illus.). 37p. 1993. pap. 9.95 (*0-9639588-0-1*) Gloriosky Art.

Log-Cabin Campaign. Robert G. Gunderson. LC 76-49604. (Illus.). 292p. 1977. reprint ed. lib. bdg. 65.00 (*0-8371-9395-8*, GULC, Greenwood Pr) Greenwood.

Log Cabin Campfire Cookin, Vol. 5. Colleen Sloan. Ed. by Lori Oakason. (Illus.). 120p. 1997. spiral bd. 8.95 (*0-9630279-5-6*) Log Cabin.

***Log Cabin Christmas.** Illus. by Ellen Howard & Ronald Himler. LC 99-40855. 32p. (J). (ps-3). 2000. 16.95 (*0-8234-1381-0*) Holiday.

Log Cabin Christmas Tree Wallhanging. Eleanor Burns. (Illus.). 16p. 1986. 6.95 (*0-922705-29-1*) Quilt Day.

Log Cabin Christmas Wreath Wallhanging. Eleanor Burns. (Illus.). 16p. 1986. 6.95 (*0-922705-28-3*) Quilt Day.

Log Cabin Cooking: Pioneer Recipes & Food Lore. Barbara Swell. (Illus.). 64p. (Orig.). 1996. pap. 5.95 (*1-883206-25-1*, NGB-800) Native Ground.

Log Cabin Days: Folk Tales of the Adirondacks. 3rd ed. Helen E. Tyler. (Illus.). 112p. 1993. reprint ed. pap. 6.95 (*1-892404-01-X*) Tyler-John Assocs.

Log Cabin Dutch Oven-Black Pot Cookin at Its Best. rev. ed. Colleen Sloan. 112p. 1999. spiral bd. 8.95 (*0-9630279-2-1*) Log Cabin.

Log Cabin Grub: Authentic Pioneer Recipes. Colleen Sloan. 112p. 1990. spiral bd. 8.95 (*0-9630279-0-5*) Log Cabin.

Log Cabin Grub Leftovers: What to Do with Leftover Food. Colleen Sloan. 100p. 1993. spiral bd. 8.95 (*0-9630279-1-3*) Log Cabin.

Log Cabin Holidays: Traditions & Recipes. Colleen Sloan. 230p. 1993. spiral bd. 10.95 (*0-9630279-3-X*) Log Cabin.

Log Cabin Home: Pioneers in the Wilderness. Catherine E. Chambers. LC 83-18277. (Adventures in Frontier America Ser.). (Illus.). 32p. (J). (gr. 4-8). 1984. pap. text 3.50 (*0-8167-0042-7*) Troll Communs.

Log Cabin Home: Pioneers in the Wilderness. Catherine E. Chambers. (Adventures in Frontier America Ser.). (Illus.). 32p. (J). (gr. 4-8). 1998. pap. 3.95 (*0-8167-4889-6*) Troll Communs.

Log Cabin Home: Pioneers in the Wilderness Unit. Troll Books Staff. (J). (gr. 4-8). 1999. pap. text 24.95 (*0-8167-5443-8*) Troll Communs.

Log Cabin Living: Simply Log. Dan Mack. LC 99-30624. (Illus.). 160p. 1999. 39.95 (*0-87905-920-6*) Gibbs Smith Pub.

Log Cabin Logic: Creating Success Where You Are with What You Have. Susan Luke. 150p. 1995. pap. 12.50 (*0-9646034-0-3*) Luke Communs.

Log Cabin Notebook. large type ed. Mary E. Hopkins. Ed. & Illus. by John Shimp. 64p. (Orig.). 1991. pap. 20.00 (*0-929950-06-2*) ME Pubns.

Log Cabin Package, 4 bks., Set. Colleen Sloan. (Illus.). 1994. spiral bd. 35.00 (*0-9630279-4-8*) Log Cabin.

Log Cabin Quilt. Ellen Howard. (Illus.). 32p. (J). (gr. k-3). 1996. lib. bdg. 16.95 (*0-8234-1247-4*) Holiday.

Log Cabin Quilt. Ellen Howard. (Illus.). 32p. (J). (gr. k-3). 1997. reprint ed. pap. 6.95 (*0-8234-1336-5*) Holiday.

Log Cabin Quilt Thank You Notes. 4.48 (*1-56148-282-X*) Good Bks PA.

Log Cabin Quilts. Bonnie Leman & Judy Martin. 36p. 1980. pap. 5.95 (*0-9602970-1-4*) Leman Pubns.

Log Cabin with a Twist. Barbara Kaempfer. 112p. 1995. 18.95 (*0-89145-855-7*, 4545, Am Quilters Soc) Collector Bks.

***Log Cabins.** Janice Brewster. LC 99-12756. (Architecture & Design Library Ser.). (Illus.). 96p. 1999. text 17.95 (*1-56799-723-6*) M Friedman Pub Grp Inc.

Log Cabins: New Techniques for Traditional Quilts. Janet Kime. (Illus.). 160p. 1992. pap. text 24.95 (*0-945169-11-6*) Doheny Pubns.

Log Cabins & Cottages: How to Build & Furnish Them. William S. Wicks. LC 93-81205. (Illus.). 96p. 1994. pap. 12.95 (*0-943972-28-0*) Homestead WY.

Log Cabins & Cottages: How to Build & Furnish Them. William S. Wick. LC 99-29013. (Illus.). 136p. 1999. reprint ed. 12.95 (*0-87905-930-3*) Gibbs Smith Pub.

Log Cabins for Everyone. Ed. by Sandra L. Hatch. LC 96-75670. (Illus.). 160p. 1996. 19.95 (*1-882138-18-X*) Hse White Birches.

Log Cabins of Alaska. Harry M. Walker. Ed. by Victoria Sturgis. (Illus.). 64p. 1999. 16.95 (*0-945397-71-2*) Epicenter Pr.

Log Camp Nurse. large type ed. Arlene J. Fitzgerald. (General Ser.). 352p. 1993. 27.99 (*0-7089-2821-8*) Ulverscroft.

Log Construction in the Ohio Country, 1750-1850. Donald A. Hutslar. (Illus.). 271p. (C). 1992. pap. 19.95 (*0-8214-1035-0*) Ohio U Pr.

Log Data Acquisition & Quality Control. Philippe P. Theys. 352p. (C). 1990. 295.00 (*0-685-40837-X*, Pub. by Edits Technip) Enfield Pubs NH.

Log Data Acquisition & Quality Control. Philippe P. Theys. 352p. 1991. 465.00 (*0-7855-2695-1*, Pub. by Edits Technip) Enfield Pubs NH.

***Log Data Acquisition & Quality Control.** 2nd ed. Philippe P. Theys. 453p. 1999. 89.00 (*2-7108-0748-3*) Edits Technip.

Log Driver's Waltz/Black Fly. 12p. (Orig.). 1990. pap. 4.95 (*0-7692-1037-6*, CCC115) Wrner Bros.

Log Evaluation of Shaly Sandstones: A Practical Guide. George B. Asquith. (Continuing Education Course Note Ser.: No. 31). (Illus.). 59p. (Orig.). 1990. pap. 20.00 (*0-89181-179-6*, 900) AAPG.

Log from the Sea of Cortez. John Steinbeck. LC 95-14802. 288p. 1995. pap. 13.95 (*0-14-018744-8*, Penguin Classics) Viking Penguin.

***Log Garfish.** R. Hugh Rice. (Books for Young Learners). (Illus.). 16p. (J). (gr. k-2). 1999. pap. text 5.00 (*1-57274-267-4*, A2754) R Owen Pubs.

Log Home Appraisal Training Guide. Marshall & Swift Staff. 1998. pap. 10.00 (*1-56842-070-6*) Marshall & Swift.

Log Home Book: Design, Past & Present. Cindy Teipner-Thiede & Arthur Thiede. (Illus.). 224p. 1995. pap. 29.95 (*0-87905-671-1*) Gibbs Smith Pub.

Log Home Plan Book: Favorite Plans, Decor & Advice. Cindy Thiede & Heather Mehra-Pederson. LC 99-28963. (Illus.). 128p. 1999. pap. 24.95 (*0-87905-922-2*) Gibbs Smith Pub.

***Log Homes Built Better.** Douglas P. Short. (Illus.). 132p. 1999. pap. 17.95 (*0-9675789-0-6*) Logs Pubng.

***Log Homes Made Easy.** 2nd ed. Jim Cooper. LC 00-39492. (Illus.). 2000. write for info. (*0-8117-2847-1*) Stackpole.

Log Homes Made Easy: Contracting & Building Your Own Log Home. Jim Cooper. LC 92-32751. (Illus.). 256p. (Orig.). 1993. pap. 14.95 (*0-8117-2422-0*) Stackpole.

Log Hotel. Anne Schreiber. 1994. pap. 2.95 (*0-590-27389-2*) Scholastic Inc.

Log House in America: And the History & Preservation of the Lewis Anderson Homestead. 2nd rev. ed. Dale L. Anderson. (Illus.). 60p. 1999. 19.95 (*1-887188-06-1*); pap. 15.00 (*1-887188-05-3*) Silesia Cos.

Log House in East Tennessee. John Morgan. LC 90-11912. 192p. 1990. pap. text 15.00 (*0-87049-653-0*) U of Tenn Pr.

Log House Plans. rev. ed. B. Allan Mackie. (Illus.). 200p. 1997. pap. 24.95 (*1-55209-103-1*) Firefly Bks Ltd.

Log Houses. Richard Skinulis & Peter Christopher. LC 96-118739. (Illus.). 120p. 1995. 40.00 (*1-55046-099-4*, Pub. by Boston Mills) Genl Dist Srvs.

***Log ID, BGW, Dresden.** Dieter Schemp & Martin Krampen. (Opus Ser.: Vol. 30). (ENG & GER., Illus.). 96p. 1998. 62.00 (*3-930698-30-7*) Edition A Menges.

Log-Linear Models. R. Christensen. (Texts in Statistics Ser.). (Illus.). 424p. 1994. 59.95 (*0-387-97398-2*) Spr-Verlag.

Log-Linear Models. David Knoke & Peter J. Burke. LC 80-17031. (Quantitative Applications in the Social Sciences Ser.: Vol. 20). (Illus.). 80p. 1980. pap. 10.95 (*0-8039-1492-X*) Sage.

Log-Linear Models & Logistic Regression. 2nd ed. Ronald Christensen. LC 97-12465. (Springer Texts in Statistics Ser.). 1997. 64.95 (*0-387-98247-7*) Spr-Verlag.

Log-Linear Models for Event Histories. Jeroen K. Vermunt. LC 97-4805. (Advanced Quantitative Techniques in the Social Sciences Ser.: Vol. 8). 256p. 1997. 45.00 (*0-7619-0937-0*) Sage.

Log of a Cowboy. Andy Adams. 22.95 (*0-88411-929-7*) Amereon Ltd.

Log of a Cowboy. Andy Adams. (Illus.). 416p. 1997. 7.98 (*1-56731-174-1*, MJF Bks) Fine Comms.

Log of a Cowboy. Andy Adams. 387p. 1975. reprint ed. 26.95 (*0-87928-067-0*) Corner Hse.

Log of a Cowboy. Andy Adams. 1993. reprint ed. lib. bdg. 75.00 (*0-7812-5861-8*) Rprt Serv.

Log of a Cowboy, Set. abr. ed. Andy Adams. 1996. text 17.95 incl. audio (*1-57453-058-5*) Audio Lit.

***Log of a Cowboy: A Narrative of the Old Trail Days.** Andy Adams. (Illus.). 384p. 2000. pap. 10.00 (*0-618-08348-0*) HM.

Log of a Cowboy: A Narrative of the Old Trail Days. Andy Adams. LC 03-12817. (Illus.). x, 397p. 1964. pap. 10.95 (*0-8032-5000-2*, Bison Books) U of Nebr Pr.

***Log of a Cowboy: A Narrative of the Old Trail Days.** Andy Adams. 387p. 1999. reprint ed. text 20.00 (*0-7881-6379-5*) DIANE Pub.

Log of Air Navigation. Norris B. Harbold. 125p. (Orig.). 1970. pap. 12.00 (*0-89126-085-4*) MA-AH Pub.

Log of Christopher Columbus' First Voyage to America: In the Year 1492, As Copied Out in Brief by Bartholomew Las Casas. Bartholomew Las Casas. LC 88-32567. (Illus.). 84p. (J). (gr. 3 up). 1989. reprint ed. lib. bdg. 17.00 (*0-208-02247-3*, Linnet Bks) Shoe String.

Log of Christopher Columbus' First Voyage to America in the Year 1492 as Copied Out in Brief by Bartholomew Las Casas One of His Companions see First Voyage to America: From the Log of the "Santa Maria"

Log of Commodore Rollingpin: His Adventures Afloat & Ashore. John H. Carter. LC 74-166690. (Illus.). 1971. reprint ed. 29.00 (*0-403-01452-2*) Scholarly.

Log of Deadwood: A Postmodern Epic of the South Dakota Gold Rush. Gary David. LC 93-6715. 148p. 1993. 9.95 (*1-55643-156-2*) North Atlantic.

Log of H. M. S. Mentor, 1780-1781: A New Account of the British Navy at Pensacola. Ed. by James A. Servies & Robert R. Rea. LC 80-28006. (Illus.). xiv, 206p. 1982. 29.95 (*0-8130-0704-6*) U Press Fla.

Log of Rowing at the University of California Berkeley, 1870-1987. Jim Lemmon. LC 88-33945. (Western Heritage Bks.). (Illus.). 160p. 1989. 35.00 (*0-9621956-0-X*) Wstrn Heritage.

Log of the Ark. Kenneth Walker. 21.95 (*0-8488-1214-X*) Amereon Ltd.

Log of the Cutty Sark. Basil Lubbock. (C). 1987. 145.00 (*0-85174-115-0*) St Mut.

***Log of the "Gloria Scott"** Robert Brodie & Warren Randall. LC 99-234417. (Sherlockian Scholarship Ser.). 1998. 36.00 (*1-55246-057-6*) Battered Silicon.

Log of the Mahina. John Neal. LC 76-150419. (Illus.). 284p. 1995. pap. 16.95 (*0-918074-02-9*) Pacific Intl.

Log of the Near Infrared Photographic Sky Survey. Eric R. Craine. (Astronomy & Astrophysics Ser.). (Illus.). 168p. 1988. pap. 40.00 (*0-934525-04-8*); disk 50.00 (*0-934525-09-9*) West Research.

Log of the Peep O'Day: Summer Cruises in West Florida Waters, 1912-1915. F. F. Bingham. Ed. by Brian R. Rucker & Nathan F. Woolsey. (Illus.). 203p. (Orig.). 1991. pap. 9.95 (*1-882695-03-8*) Patagonia Pr.

Log of the S. S. the Mrs. Unguentine. Stanley Crawford. 110p. 1988. pap. 9.95 (*0-945953-02-X*) Living Batch Bks.

Log of the "Scotia" William S. Bruce. Ed. by Peter Speak. 256p. 1992. text 145.00 (*0-7486-0293-3*, Pub. by Edinburgh U Pr) Col U Pr.

Log of the Sea Angler. C. E. Holder. (Blue Water Classics Ser.). 400p. lthr. 65.00 (*1-56416-143-9*) Derrydale Pr.

Log of the Skipper's Wife. Ed. by James W. Balano. LC 79-52446. (Illus.). 160p. 1979. pap. 10.95 (*0-89272-062-X*) Down East.

Log of the Sloop Advance. Doris R. Adler. 1997. 15.00 (*1-886706-13-1*) Hickory Hse.

Log of the Snack. Charmian K. London. 440p. 1998. pap. 16.95 (*1-885031-03-3*, Capstan Pr) Merritt Communs.

Log of the Union: John Boit's Remarkable Voyage to the Northwest Coast & Around the World 1794-1976. John Boit. Ed. by Edmund Hayes, Sr. LC 80-83181. (North Pacific Studies: No. 6). (Illus.). 176p. 1981. pap. 12.95 (*0-87595-089-2*) Oregon Hist.

Log of the Whaler Helena. Claus Hoie. 48p. 1994. 59.95 (*1-881907-15-5*); pap. 24.95 (*1-881907-16-3*) Two Bytes Pub.

Log of the Whaler Helena. limited ed. Claus Hoie. 48p. 1994. 195.00 (*1-881907-08-2*) Two Bytes Pub.

***Log on to Computers Series, 4 bks.** Jim Drake. 32p. 1999. 85.44 (*1-57572-788-9*) Heinemann Lib.

Log Rhythms. Charles Bernstein. (Illus.). 24p. 1998. pap. 35.00 (*1-887123-25-3*) Granary Bks.

Log Rhythms. David Wann. 64p. 1983. pap. 4.95 (*0-938190-19-9*) North Atlantic.

Log Scale Construction. Arthur A. Merrill. 29p. 1966. pap. 4.00 (*0-911894-31-4*) Analysis.

Log Span Tables: For Floor Joists, Beams & Roof Supports. 3rd rev. ed. B. Allan Mackie et al. (Illus.). 117p. (C). 1993. pap. 15.00 (*0-9636902-0-5*) CN Log Builders.

***Log Spirit.** Linda White. LC 99-57471. (Illus.). 96p. 2000. 21.95 (*0-87905-925-7*) Gibbs Smith Pub.

Logan. Hunce Voelcker. (Illus.). 3.00 (*0-917996-02-X*) Panjandrum.

Logan: A Directory of the Descendants of Andrew & Lydia Logan of Albany, NY & Abbeville, SC. Richard K. Logan. 329p. (Orig.). 1994. pap. text 25.00 (*1-55613-993-4*) Heritage Bk.

Logan, a Family History, 2 vols. John Neal. LC 78-64085. reprint ed. 75.00 (*0-404-17330-6*) AMS Pr.

Logan & the Duck Patrol. Micki Nellis. LC 95-79218. (Illus.). 32p. (J). (gr. k-2). 1996. 14.95 (*1-885534-04-3*) Buffalo Creek.

Logan, Andrew: An Artistic Adventure. Museum of Modern Art Oxford Staff. 1991. pap. 24.00 (*0-905836-73-1*, Pub. by Museum Modern Art) St Mut.

Logan Bruno, Boy Baby-Sitter. Ann M. Martin. (Baby-Sitters Club Special Edition Ser.). 160p. (J). (gr. 3-7). 1993. pap. 3.50 (*0-590-47118-X*) Scholastic Inc.

Logan Bruno, Boy Baby-Sitter. Ann M. Martin. (Baby-Sitters Club Special Edition Ser.). (J). 1993. 8.60 (*0-606-05145-7*, Pub. by Turtleback) Demco.

Logan County, Arkansas Marriage Records, the First Fifty Years. Bobbie J. McLane & Bill Hanks. 219p. (Orig.). 1991. pap. 28.00 (*0-929604-68-7*) Arkansas Ancestors.

Logan County, Colorado, War Book. Florence Rizzolo. (Illus.). 128p. 1992. 35.00 (*0-88107-213-3*) Curtis Media.

Logan County Tax Book 1890: (Reconstructed 1890 Census) Bobbie J. McLane & Bill Hanks. 118p. (Orig.). 1987. pap. 15.00 (*0-929604-42-3*) Arkansas Ancestors.

Logan File. large type ed. Philip McCutchan. (Magna Large Print Ser.). 336p. 1996. 27.99 (*0-7505-1051-X*, Pub. by Mgna Lrg Print) Ulverscroft.

Logan in Overtime. Tom Quarrington. 224p. 1990. pap. 14.95 (*0-385-25152-1*) Doubleday.

Logan Likes Mary Anne! Ann M. Martin. (Baby-Sitters Club Ser.: No. 10). 160p. (J). (gr. 4-6). 1988. pap. 2.75 (*0-590-41124-1*, Apple Paperbacks); pap. 3.50 (*0-590-43387-3*) Scholastic Inc.

Logan Likes Mary Anne! Ann M. Martin. (Baby-Sitters Club Ser.: No. 10). (J). (gr. 3-7). 1996. pap. text 3.99 (*0-590-25165-1*) Scholastic Inc.

Logan Likes Mary Anne! Ann M. Martin. (Baby-Sitters Club Ser.: No. 10). (J). 1988. 9.09 (*0-606-03546-X*, Pub. by Turtleback) Demco.

Logan Pass: Alpine Splendor in Glacier National Park. Jerry DeSanto. LC 95-9692. (Illus.). 64p. (Orig.). 1995. pap. 8.95 (*1-56044-158-5*) Falcon Pub Inc.

Logan Place: A Misty Greene/Barrie Bufford Story. Leslie M. Farrell. (Illus.). 48p. 1998. pap. 8.00 (*0-8059-4356-0*) Dorrance.

Logan Workplace Exposure Evaluation System. Des. by E. I. du Pont de Nemours & Co. Inc. Staff. 99p. 1990. 275.00 incl. disk (*0-932627-42-0*) Am Indus Hygiene.

Logan's Alley: Amador County Yesterdays in Picture & Prose, Vol. 3. Larry Cenotto. (Illus.). 280p. 1999. pap. 29.95 (*0-938121-13-8*) Cenotto Pubns.

Logan's Bride. Elizabeth August. (Intimate Moments Ser.: No. 950). 1999. per. 4.25 (*0-373-07950-8*, 1-07950-8) Silhouette.

Logan's Bride (Holiday Elopement, the Whitaker Brides) Christine Flynn. 1995. per. 3.75 (*0-373-09995-9*, 1-09995-1) Silhouette.

Logan's Child. Lonora Worth. 1998. per. 4.50 (*0-373-87026-4*, Harlequin) Harlequin Bks.

Logan's Choice. Frank Bonham. 128p. 1989. pap. 2.95 (*0-380-70851-5*, Avon Bks) Morrow Avon.

Logan's Run. William F. Nolan. Ed. by Amereon Ltd. Staff. 1985. 18.95 (*0-8488-0103-2*) Amereon Ltd.

Logan's Run. William F. Nolan & George C. Johnson. 1976. 18.95 (*0-8488-0102-4*) Amereon Ltd.

Logan's Run. William F. Nolan & George C. Johnson. 160p. 1992. reprint ed. lib. bdg. 25.95 (*0-89966-896-8*) Buccaneer Bks.

Logan's Story. Ann M. Martin. (Baby-Sitters Club Special Edition Ser.: Vol. 1). 160p. (J). (gr. 3-7). 1992. pap. 3.25 (*0-590-45575-3*, Apple Paperbacks) Scholastic Inc.

Logan's Story. Ann M. Martin. (Baby-Sitters Club Special Edition Ser.). (J). 1992. 8.35 (*0-606-01894-8*, Pub. by Turtleback) Demco.

Logan's Way. Lisa A. Verge. (Temptation Ser.: No. 730). 1999. per. 3.75 (*0-373-25830-5*, 1-25830-0) Harlequin Bks.

Logantown Looters. large type ed. Marshall Grover. (Linford Western Library). 300p. 1989. pap. 16.99 (*0-7089-6669-1*, Linford) Ulverscroft.

Logarithmic Descriptions of Whitehead Groups & Class Groups for P-Groups. R. Oliver & L. Taylor. LC 88-22226. (Memoirs Ser.: No. 76/392). 97p. 1988. pap. 16.00 (*0-8218-2455-4*, MEMO/76/392) Am Math.

Logarithmic Integral, Vol. 2. Paul J. Koosis. (Cambridge Studies in Advanced Mathematics: No. 21). (Illus.). 600p. (C). 1992. text 165.00 (*0-521-30907-7*) Cambridge U Pr.

***Logarithmic Integral Equations in Electromagnetics.** Yu V. Shestopalov et al. (Illus.). 130p. 2000. 106.00 (*90-6764-322-X*, Pub. by Uppsala Universitet) Coronet Bks.

Logarithmic Integral I. Paul J. Koosis. LC 99-198676. (Cambridge Studies in Advanced Mathematics: No. 12). (Illus.). 624p. (C). 1999. pap. text 47.95 (*0-521-59672-6*) Cambridge U Pr.

Logarithmic Potential, 3 vols. in 1. 2nd ed. Gilbert A. Bliss. Incl. Fundamental Existence Theorems. reprint ed. 25.00 (*0-8284-0305-8*) Chelsea Pub.

Logarithmic Potentials with External Fields, Vol. 316. E. B. Saff & V. Totik. LC 97-28048. (Grundlehren der Mathematischen Wissenschaften Ser.). viii, 525p. 1997. write for info. (*3-540-57078-0*) Spr-Verlag.

Logarithmic Trigonometrical Tables to 8 Decimal Places or Numbers 1-200,000 & Trigon: Functions for Sexagesmil Second of the Quadrant, 2vols. 3rd ed. J. Bauschinger & J. Peters. 1971. 175.00 (*0-934454-57-4*) Lubrecht & Cramer.

Logarithmic Video Amplifiers. Richard S. Hughes. LC 70-178294. 190p. reprint ed. pap. 58.90 (*0-608-13084-2*, 202505700041) Bks Demand.

Logarithms & Antilogarithms: An Algebraic Analysis Approach. Danuta Przeworska-Rolewicz. LC 98-10806. (Mathematics & Its Applications Ser.). 348p. 1998. 159.00 (*0-7923-4974-1*) Kluwer Academic.

Logarithms Without a Calculator. Jeff Chadwick. 123p. 1995. pap. text 12.95 (*0-9646272-0-5*) Alpine Pub OR.

Logboats of Scotland. Robert J. Mowat. (Oxbow Monographs in Archaeology: No. 68). (Illus.). 166p. 1996. pap. 40.00 (*1-900188-11-2*, Pub. by Oxbow Bks) David Brown.

***Logbook for Cruising under Sail.** Mellor. 96p. 2000. pap. 14.95 (*1-898660-35-2*, Pub. by Fernhurst Bks) Motorbooks Intl.

Logbook for Speech-Language Pathologists. Sharon G. Webber. (Illus.). 392p. 1995. spiral bd. 19.95 (*1-58650-011-2*, BK-201) Super Duper.

Logbook of the Farallones. Michael Whitt. (Illus.). 120p. 1998. pap. 20.00 (*0-9665110-0-X*) La Ventana.

Logbook of the Farallowes. Michael Whitt. (Illus.). 120p. 1998. 45.00 (*0-9665110-1-8*) La Ventana.

Logbuch des Lukas: Das Antike Schiff in Fahrt und Vor Anker 2., Uberarbeitete und Erweiterte Auflage. 2nd ed. Gunter Kettenbach. (Europaische Hochschulschriften Ser.: Reihe 23, Bd. 276). (GER.). 244p. 1996. 44.95 (*3-631-31238-5*) P Lang Pubng.

Logeuse. Jacques Audiberti. 14.95 (*0-686-54491-9*) Fr & Eur.

Loggerhead Turtle: In the Eastern Gulf of Mexico. Charles R. LeBuff, Jr. LC 89-81763. (Illus.). 236p. 1990. 24.95 (*0-9625013-0-1*, Pub. by Amber Pubng FL) Chelsea Green Pub.

Loggers. Rick Steber. (Tales of the Wild West Ser.: Vol. 7). (Illus.). 60p. 1989. pap. 4.95 (*0-945134-07-X*); lib. bdg. 14.95 (*0-945134-85-1*) Bonanza Pub.

Loggers & Lunches. Alan M. Hofmeister et al. (Reading for All Learners Ser.). (Illus.). (J). pap. write for info. (*1-56861-168-4*) Swift Lrn Res.

Loggers & Railroad Workers. Mimi Winslow. LC 94-39903. (Settling the West Ser.). (Illus.). 96p. (J). (gr. 5-8). 1995. lib. bdg. 20.40 (*0-8050-2997-4*) TFC Bks NY.

Loggers, Monks, Students, & Entrepreneurs: Four Essays on Thailand. Bryan Hunsaker et al. (Occasional Papers: No. 18). 143p. (C). 1997. pap. 14.95 (*1-877979-18-X*) SE Asia.

Loggers of Warner. Roy Morrison. (Poetry Ser.). (Illus.). 96p. 1999. pap. 9.95 (*0-9658903-1-7*) Writers Pubg Coop.

L

Logging & Pulpwood Production. 2nd ed. George Stenzel et al. LC 84-25745. 368p. 1985. 140.00 (*0-471-86822-1*) Wiley.

Logging & Sawmill Operations. 1995. lib. bdg. 260.95 (*0-8490-6605-0*) Gordon Pr.

Logging Burma's Frontier Forests: Resources & the Regime. Jake Brunner et al. LC 98-86983. (Illus.). 56p. 1998. pap. 20.00 (*1-56973-266-3*) World Resources Inst.

Logging Business Management Handbook. Ronald R. Macklin. LC 82-83344. (Forest Industries Book). (Illus.). 176p. 1983. pap. 42.00 (*0-87930-146-5*) Miller Freeman.

Logging in the Maine Woods: The Paintings of Alden Grant. Ed. by Margaret R. Yocom & Stephen A. Richard. (Illus.). 80p. (Orig.). 1994. pap. 15.00 (*0-9642328-0-4*) Rangeley Lks Region.

Logging Modeler's Plan Book. Ken Schmelzer. (Illus.). 135p. 1995. spiral bd. 61.95 (*1-888291-02-8*) Pac Coast Logging.

***Logging on to Courage.Com.** Christine Wood. 2000. 8.99 (*1-57921-181-X*, Pub. by WinePress Pub) BookWorld.

Logging Railroads of Alabama. Thomas Lawson, Jr. LC 96-92823. (Illus.). 296p. 1997. 59.95 (*0-9666247-0-X*) Cabbage Stack Pub.

Logging Railroads of South Carolina. Thomas Fetters. LC 89-84488. (Illus.). 264p. 1990. 42.95 (*0-911581-09-X*) Heimburger Hse Pub.

***Logging Railroads of the Florida Panhandle.** Thomas Lawson, Jr. (Illus.). x, 175p. 2000. 50.00 (*0-9666247-2-6*) Cabbage Stack Pub.

Logging Railroads of the White Mountains. rev. ed. C. Francis Belcher. (Illus.). 256p. 1980. pap. 14.95 (*0-910146-32-2*) AMC Books.

Logging the Globe. M. Patricia Marchak. LC 96-154371. (Illus.). 440p. 1995. 65.00 (*0-7735-1345-0*, Pub. by McG-Queens Univ Pr); pap. 22.95 (*0-7735-1346-9*, Pub. by McG-Queens Univ Pr) CUP Services.

Logging the Redwoods. Lynwood Carranco & John T. Labbe. LC 72-80989. (Illus.). 144p. 1975. pap. 29.95 (*0-87004-236-X*) Caxton.

Logging the Rockies: The Langendorf Olson Story. large type ed. Patricia Langendorf. (Illus.). 249p. (Orig.). 1992. pap. 22.50 (*0-9625714-9-0*); lib. bdg. 40.00 (*0-9625714-8-2*) Spruce Gulch Pr.

Logging the Rogue Valley. Barbara M. Hegne. (Illus.). 110p. 1991. spiral bd. 13.95 (*0-9623847-7-1*) B Hegne.

Logging to the Salt Chuck: Over 100 Years of Railroad Logging in Mason County Washington. John T. Labbe & Peter J. Replinger. Ed. by F. Raoul Martin. (Logging Railroads of Washington State Ser.). (Illus.). 186p. (Orig.). 1989. pap. 36.95 (*0-915370-09-3*) NW Short Line.

Logging Tool Catalog. Wireline Staff. 1900. lib. bdg. 49.00 (*0-86010-537-7*) Kluwer Academic.

Logging Trucks 1915-1970 Photo Archive. Donald F. Wood. LC 96-76230. (Photo Archive Ser.). (Illus.). 128p. 1996. pap. 29.95 (*1-882256-59-X*) Iconografix.

Logging vs. Fisheries & Tourism in Palawan: An Environmental & Economic Analysis. Gregor Hodgson & John A. Dixon. LC 88-170934. (East-West Environment & Policy Institute, Occasional Paper Ser.: Vol. 7). 107p. 1988. reprint ed. pap. 33.20 (*0-608-03574-2*, 206439700009) Bks Demand.

Loggins & Messina. Aaron Stang. (Guitar Anthology Ser.). (Orig.). (C). 1997. pap. text 22.95 (*1-57623-968-3*, PG9710) Wrner Bros.

Logia Iesou: Sayings of Our Lord from an Early Greek Papyrus (1897) Bernard P. Grenfell. 50p. 1996. reprint ed. pap. 8.95 (*1-56459-574-9*) Kessinger Pub.

Logia Masonica. John Ankerberg & John Weldon. (Hechos Acerca de...Ser.).Tr. of Masonic Lodge. (SPA.). 66p. 1994. pap. 3.29 (*1-56063-774-9*, 498430); pap. 3.29 (*0-614-27053-7*) Editorial Unilit.

Logia of Yeshua. Tr. by Gay Davenport & Benjamin Urrutia. 96p. 1998. pap. 10.00 (*1-887178-70-8*, Pub. by Counterpt DC) HarpC.

Logia or Sayings of the Master. John T. Ferrier. 430p. 1916. text 17.00 (*0-900235-06-3*) Order Of The Cross.

Logic see Computatio Sive Logica

Logic see Logique

Logic. (Quick Study Academic Ser.). 4p. pap. 3.95 (*1-57222-084-8*) Barcharts.

Logic. Immanuel Kant. Tr. by Robert S. Hartman & Wolfgang Schwarz. LC 72-10560. (Library of Liberal Arts). 279p. 1974. 5.50 (*0-672-61228-3*, Bobbs) Macmillan.

***Logic.** Graham Priest. (Very Short Introductions Ser.). (Illus.). 114p. 2000. pap. 8.95 (*0-19-289320-3*) OUP.

Logic. Immanuel Kant. 288p. 1988. reprint ed. pap. 8.95 (*0-486-25650-2*) Dover.

Logic. 2nd ed. John Nolt et al. LC 98-28482. (Schaum's Outline Ser.). (Illus.). 280p. 1998. pap. 15.95 (*0-07-046649-1*) McGraw.

Logic. 2nd ed. Russell. 1998. pap. text 26.00 (*0-471-32102-8*) Wiley.

***Logic.** 3rd ed. Steven Roman. (Illus.). 54p. (C). 1999. pap. text. write for info. (*1-878015-19-2*) Innov Textbooks.

Logic. 3rd rev. ed. Gordon H. Clark. Ed. & Frwd. by John W. Robbins. 160p. 1998. text 16.95 (*0-940931-81-8*); pap. text 10.95 (*0-940931-80-X*) Trinity Found.

Logic. 4th ed. Baum. (C). 1995. 110.50 (*0-15-503404-9*) Harcourt.

Logic. 4th ed. Baum. (C). 1995. pap. text, teacher ed. 42.00 (*0-15-503399-9*) Harcourt Coll Pubs.

Logic. 4th ed. Baum. (C). 1996. pap. text, student ed. 22.50 (*0-15-503400-6*, Pub. by Harcourt Coll Pubs) Harcourt.

Logic. 4th ed. Robert Baum. LC 95-77198. 708p. (C). 1995. text 65.00 (*0-15-501617-2*, Pub. by Harcourt Coll Pubs) Harcourt.

Logic: A Dialogue. Arthur K. Bierman. LC 64-16572. (Illus.). 433p. reprint ed. pap. 134.30 (*0-608-30657-6*, 201628600005) Bks Demand.

Logic: A "Hands On" Approach to Teaching . . . Linda-Sue Brisby et al. (Illus.). 180p. 1989. teacher ed. 17.95 (*0-927726-02-5*) Hands On CA.

Logic: An Aristotelian Approach. rev. ed. Mary M. Spangler. LC 92-38172. 284p. (Orig.). (C). 1993. pap. text 29.50 (*0-8191-8967-7*) U Pr of Amer.

Logic: An Introduction. 3rd ed. Churchill. (Philosophy Ser.). 1919. pap. 42.00 (*0-534-50931-2*) Wadsworth Pub.

Logic: An Introduction. 3rd ed. Churchill & Fleishman. (Philosophy Ser.). 1919. mass mkt., student ed. 13.00 (*0-534-50937-1*) Wadsworth Pub.

Logic: An Orthodox Christian Approach. Apostolos Makrakis. Ed. by Orthodox Christian Educational Society Staff. Tr. by Denver Cummings. (Logos & Holy Spirit in the Unity of Christian Thought Ser.: Vol. 3). 200p. 1977. reprint ed. pap. 6.95 (*0-938366-04-1*) Orthodox Chr.

Logic: Deductive, Inductive & Informal Reasoning. Richard L. Wilson. 128p. (C). 1993. spiral bd. 15.95 (*0-8403-8966-3*) Kendall-Hunt.

Logic: Deductive, Inductive & Informal Reasoning (Pak) Richard Wilson. 264p. (C). 1996. 37.95 (*0-7872-1852-9*) Kendall-Hunt.

Logic: From Foundations to Applications: European Logic Colloquium. Ed. by W. A. Hodges et al. LC 97-110319. (Illus.). 550p. (C). 1996. text 135.00 (*0-19-853862-6*) OUP.

Logic: Or the Right Use of Reason. 2nd ed. Isaac Watts. LC 97-162086. 352p. 1996. reprint ed. 29.95 (*1-57358-055-4*) Soli Deo Gloria.

Logic: Techniques of Formal Reasoning. 2nd ed. Donald Kalish et al. 520p. (C). 1980. text 63.50 (*0-15-551181-5*, Pub. by Harcourt Coll Pubs) Harcourt.

Logic: The Art of Defining & Reasoning. 2nd ed. John A. Oesterle. 1963. pap. text 36.00 (*0-13-539999-8*) P-H.

Logic: The Morphology of Knowledge, 2 vols. in 1. Bernard Bosanquet. 663p. 1994. reprint ed. pap. 36.95 (*1-57171-003-5*) Lincoln-Rembrandt.

Logic: Theory of Inquiry. John Dewey. 1982. reprint ed. 49.50 (*0-89197-831-3*) Irvington.

Logic: Undergraduate. 3rd ed. Kreyche. 1997. text 71.00 (*0-03-078095-0*, Pub. by Harcourt Coll Pubs) Harcourt.

Logic - the Worksheet: A Study Guide for Chapters 1, 3, 8, 9 of Copi's Introduction to Logic (7th) 2nd ed. Ronald J. Loo. 114p. (C). 1986. student ed. 11.00 (*1-885332-03-3*) P Nahenahe.

Logic Abelard. Beonio-Brocchiery Fumagalli. Tr. by Simon Pleasance from ITA. (Synthese Library: No. 1). 110p. 1969. text 113.00 (*90-277-0068-0*, D Reidel) Kluwer Academic.

Logic, Action & Cognition: Essays in Philosophical Logic. Ed. by Eva Ejerhed. LC 97-14345. 256p. 1997. text 124.00 (*0-7923-4560-6*) Kluwer Academic.

Logic, Action, Information: Essays on Logic in Philosophy & Artificial Intelligence. Ed. by Andre Fuhrmann & Hans Rott. x, 476p. (C). 1995. lib. bdg. 190.80 (*3-11-013994-4*) De Gruyter.

Logic, Algebra, & Computation. Ed. by F. L. Bauer. (NATO ASI Series F: Computer & Systems Sciences, Special Programme AET: Vol. 79). vii, 485p. 1991. 130.95 (*0-387-54315-5*) Spr-Verlag.

Logic, Algebra & Database. Peter M. Gray. LC 84-12854. (Computers & Their Applications Ser.). 294p. 1985. pap. text 36.95 (*0-470-20259-9*) P-H.

Logic Algebra Problems. Wade H. Sherard, III. (Illus.). 64p. 1997. 10.50 (*0-86651-536-4*) Seymour Pubns.

Logic & Algebra. Ed. by Aldo Ursini & Paolo Agliano. LC 96-13087. (Lecture Notes in Pure & Applied Mathematics Ser.: Vol. 180). (Illus.). 728p. 1996. pap. text 195.00 (*0-8247-9606-3*) Dekker.

Logic & Algebra of Specification. Ed. by F. L. Bauer et al. (NATO ASI Series F: Computer & Systems Sciences, Special Programme AET: Vol. 94). vii, 444p. 1993. 119.95 (*0-387-55813-6*) Spr-Verlag.

Logic & Argumentation. Ed. by J. Van Benthem et al. LC 97-153720. (Verhandelingen der Koninklijke Nederlandse Akademie van Wetenschappen, Afd. Letterkunde, Nieuwe Reeks Ser.: Vol. 70). 260p. pap. 47.00 (*0-444-85814-8*) Elsevier.

Logic & Arguments Custom Education. Finkenbinder. 278p. 1998. pap. text 31.00 (*0-536-01808-1*) Pearson Custom.

Logic & Art: Essays in Honor of Nelson Goodman. Ed. by Richard S. Rudner & Israel Scheffler. LC 76-140799. x, 332p. (C). 1972. lib. bdg. 20.00 (*0-672-51639-X*) Ridgeview.

Logic & Combinatorics. S. Simpson. LC 86-30217. (Contemporary Mathematics Ser.: Vol. 65). 394p. 1987. reprint ed. pap. 46.00 (*0-8218-5052-0*, CONM/65) Am Math.

Logic & Computation: Interactive Proof with Cambridge LCF. L. C. Paulson. (Tracts in Theoretical Computer Science Ser.: No. 2). 320p. 1987. text 69.95 (*0-521-34632-0*) Cambridge U Pr.

Logic & Computation: Interactive Proof with Cambridge LCF. L. C. Paulson. (Tracts in Theoretical Computer Science Ser.: No. 2). 316p. (C). 1990. pap. text 31.95 (*0-521-39560-7*) Cambridge U Pr.

Logic & Computation: (Proceedings of the Workshop) W. Sieg. LC 90-40. (Contemporary Mathematics Ser.: Vol. 106). 297p. 1990. pap. 41.00 (*0-8218-5110-1*, CONM/106) Am Math.

Logic & Computational Complexity: International Workshop, LCC '94, Bloomington, IN, October 13-16, 1994, Vol. VIII. Ed. by Daniel Leivant et al. LC 95-37560. (Lecture Notes in Computer Science Ser.: Vol. 960). 514p. 1995. 81.00 (*3-540-60178-3*) Spr-Verlag.

***Logic & Computer Design Fundamentals.** 2nd ed. Morris M. Mano. LC 99-48790. (Illus.). 652p. 1999. 100.00 incl. cd-rom (*0-13-012468-0*) P-H.

***Logic & Computer Design Fundamentals Solutions Manual.** 2nd ed. 2000. write for info. (*0-13-016661-8*) P-H.

Logic & Computer Science. Ed. by Piergiorgio Odifreddi. (APIC Studies in Data Processing). 430p. 1990. text 78.00 (*0-12-524220-4*) Acad Pr.

Logic & Computer Science: Lectures Given at the First Session of the Centro Internazionale Matematico Estivo (C.I.M.E.) Held at Montecatini Terme, Italy, June 20-18, 1988. Andrej Scedrov et al. Ed. by A. Dold et al. (Lecture Notes in Mathematics Ser.: Vol. 1429). v, 162p. 1990. 34.95 (*0-387-52734-6*) Spr-Verlag.

Logic & Contemporary Rhetoric. Howard Kahane & Cavender. (Adaptable Courseware-Softside Ser). 1998. mass mkt. 16.00 (*0-534-56584-0*) Wadsworth Pub.

Logic & Contemporary Rhetoric. 6th ed. Howard Kahane. (Philosophy Ser.). 1992. mass mkt., teacher ed. write for info. (*0-534-16897-3*) West Pub.

***Logic & Contemporary Rhetoric: Activity Manual.** 8th ed. Howard Kahane. 1998. pap. 14.50 (*0-534-52472-9*) Thomson Learn.

Logic & Contemporary Rhetoric: The Use of Reason in Everyday Life. 4th ed. Howard Kahane. 321p. (C). 1984. pap. write for info. (*0-534-03188-9*) Wadsworth Pub.

Logic & Contemporary Rhetoric: The Use of Reason in Everyday Life. 5th ed. Howard Kahane. 346p. (C). 1987. pap. write for info. (*0-534-09018-4*) Wadsworth Pub.

Logic & Contemporary Rhetoric: The Use of Reason in Everyday Life. 6th ed. Howard Kahane. 350p. (C). 1991. pap. 26.25 (*0-534-16896-5*) Wadsworth Pub.

Logic & Contemporary Rhetoric: The Use of Reason in Everyday Life. 7th ed. Howard Kahane. LC 94-23375. 350p. 1994. mass mkt. 38.95 (*0-534-25464-0*) Wadsworth Pub.

Logic & Contemporary Rhetoric: The Use of Reason in Everyday Life. 8th ed. Howard Kahane & Nancy Cavender. LC 97-19988. (Philosophy Ser.). 365p. (C). 1997. pap. 52.95 (*0-534-52470-2*) Wadsworth Pub.

Logic & Contemporary Rhetoric: Use Of Reason Everyday Life. 9th ed. Howard Kahane. (Philosophy). 2001. pap. 32.25 (*0-534-53578-X*) Wadsworth Pub.

Logic & Data Bases. Ed. by Herve Gallaire & Jack Minker. LC 78-14032. 466p. 1978. 85.00 (*0-306-40060-X*, Plenum Trade) Perseus Pubng.

Logic & Debate Tradition of India, Tibet & Mongolia: History, Reader & Sources. Compiled by Debate Study Group & Sermey G. Tharchin. 281p. (Orig.). 1979. pap. 9.50 (*0-918753-00-7*) Mahayana.

***Logic & Declarative Language.** Michael Downward. 1998. pap. text 49.95 (*0-7484-0802-9*) Tay Francis Ltd.

***Logic & Declarative Language, 1 vol.** Michael Downward. LC 98-179219. 1998. 85.00 (*0-7484-0803-7*) Taylor & Francis.

Logic & Design: The Syntax of Art, Art & Mathematics. Krome Barratt. (Illus.). 328p. 1980. 25.00 (*0-89860-033-2*) Eastview.

Logic & Design in Art, Science, & Mathematics. Krome Barratt. 326p. 1993. pap. 21.95 (*1-55821-268-X*) Lyons Pr.

Logic & Discrete Mathematics: A Computer Science Perspectives. Winfried K. Grassman & Jean-Paul Tremblay. LC 95-38351. 750p. (C). 1995. 85.00 (*0-13-501206-6*) P-H.

Logic & Ethics. Ed. by Peter T. Geach & Jacek Holowka. 326p. (C). 1991. lib. bdg. 186.00 (*0-7923-1044-6*, Pub. by Kluwer Academic) Kluwer Academic.

Logic & Existence. Jean Hyppolite. Tr. by Leonard Lawlor & Amit Sen from FRE. LC 96-13009. (SUNY Series in Contemporary Continental Philosophy). 212p. (C). 1997. text 59.50 (*0-7914-3231-9*); pap. text 19.95 (*0-7914-3232-7*) State U NY Pr.

Logic & Experience: The Origin of Modern American Legal Education. William P. LaPiana. 264p. 1994. text 55.00 (*0-19-507935-3*) OUP.

Logic & Foundations of Mathematics in Frege's Philosophy. Ed. by Hans Sluga. LC 92-39779. (Philosophy of Frege Ser.: Vol. 2). 424p. 1993. text 79.00 (*0-8153-1038-2*) Garland.

Logic & Foundations of Science: Proceedings of the E. W. Beth Memorial Colloquium, Paris, 1964. Beth Memorial Colloquium Staff. Ed. by J. L. Destouches. 137p. 1967. text 120.00 (*90-277-0076-1*) Kluwer Academic.

Logic & General Semantics: Writings of Oliver L. Reiser & Others. Ed. by Sanford I. Berman. LC 88-83271. 1989. 42.95 (*0-685-54382-X*); pap. 19.95 (*0-918970-36-9*) Intl Gen Semantics.

Logic & Grammar see Metaphor

Logic & Information. Keith J. Devlin. 320p. (C). 1991. text 47.95 (*0-521-41030-4*) Cambridge U Pr.

Logic & Information. Keith J. Devlin. 324p. (C). 1995. pap. text 21.95 (*0-521-49971-2*) Cambridge U Pr.

Logic & Information Flow. Ed. by Jan Van Eijck & Albert Visser. (Foundations of Computing Ser.). (Illus.). 200p. 1994. 42.50 (*0-262-22047-4*) MIT Pr.

Logic & Its Applications. Edmund Burke & Eric Foxley. 380p. 1996. pap. 59.00 (*0-13-030263-5*) P-H.

Logic & Its Limits. 2nd ed. Patrick Shaw. LC 97-7419. (Illus.). 272p. (Orig.). 1997. pap. 15.95 (*0-19-289280-0*) OUP.

Logic & Knowledge. Ed. by Bertrand Russell & Robert C. Marsh. 400p. (C). 1988. pap. 25.99 (*0-415-09074-1*) Routledge.

Logic & Knowledge: Essays, 1901 to 1950. Bertrand Russell. Ed. by Robert C. Marsh. 392p. 1988. pap. text 21.95 (*0-04-440260-0*) Routledge.

Logic & Language: Proceedings of the '87 Debrecen Symposium Held from August 25 to 28, 1987. I. Ruzsa & A. Szabolcsi. 252p. (C). 1987. 40.00 (*963-462-238-0*, Pub. by Akade Kiado) St Mut.

Logic & Language: Studies Dedicated to Professor Rudolf Carnap on the Occasion of His 70th Birthday. Ed. by B. H. Kazemier & D. Vusje. (Synthese Library: No. 5). 252p. 1962. text 85.50 (*90-277-0019-2*, D Reidel) Kluwer Academic.

***Logic & Language in Wittgenstein's Tractatus.** Ian Proops. LC 00-26427. (Studies in Philosophy). 2000. pap. write for info. (*0-8153-3793-0*) Garland.

Logic & Lexicon: The Semantics of the Indefinite. Manfred Pinkal. LC 95-3466. (Studies in Linguistics & Philosophy: Vol. 56). 380p. (C). 1995. lib. bdg. 129.00 (*0-7923-3387-X*, Pub. by Kluwer Academic) Kluwer Academic.

Logic & Limits of Bankruptcy Law. Thomas H. Jackson. LC 86-7685. 336p. 1986. 37.00 (*0-674-53745-9*) HUP.

Logic & Logical Thinking: A Modular Approach. Peter A. Facione & Donald Scherer. LC 83-24173. (C). 1984. reprint ed. text 24.95 (*0-918024-33-1*) Ox Bow.

Logic & Logos: Essays on Science, Religion & Philosophy. William S. Hatcher. 160p. (Orig.). 1990. pap. 11.50 (*0-85398-298-8*) G Ronald Pub.

Logic & Machines-Decision Problems & Complexity: Proceedings of the Symposium "Rekursive Kombinatorik" Held from May 23-28, 1983 at the Institut fur Mathematische Logik und Grundlagenfroschung der Universitat Munster-Westfalen. Ed. by E. Borger et al. (Lecture Notes in Computer Science Ser.: Vol. 171). vi, 456p. 1984. pap. 27.50 (*0-685-08952-5*, 13331-3) Spr-Verlag.

Logic & Method of Macro Sociology: An Input-Output Approach to Organizational Networks. Krishnan Namboodiri & Ronald G. Corwin. LC 93-20302. 192p. 1993. 62.95 (*0-275-94529-4*, C4529, Praeger Pubs) Greenwood.

Logic & Methodology of Science in Early Modern Thought: Seven Studies. Fred Wilson. (Illus.). 656p. 1999. text 95.00 (*0-8020-4356-9*) U of Toronto Pr.

Logic & Mr. Limbaugh. Ray Perkins, Jr. 200p. 1995. pap. 14.95 (*0-8126-9294-2*) Open Court.

Logic & Ontology in Heidegger. David A. White. LC 85-15300. 259p. reprint ed. pap. 80.30 (*0-608-09897-3*, 206986300006) Bks Demand.

Logic & Other Nonsense: The Case of Anselm & His God. Ermanno Bencivenga. LC 93-18278. 160p. 1993. text 29.95 (*0-691-07427-5*, Pub. by Princeton U Pr) Cal Prin Full Svc.

Logic & Philosophy. Ed. by George H. Von Wright. (International Institute of Philosophy Ser.). 96p. 1980. text 106.00 (*90-247-2271-3*) Kluwer Academic.

Logic & Philosophy. 3rd ed. Howard Kahane. (Philosophy Ser.). Date not set. pap., teacher ed. write for info. (*0-534-02390-8*) Wadsworth Pub.

Logic & Philosophy. 4th ed. Howard Kahane. (Philosophy Ser.). 1982. pap., teacher ed. write for info. (*0-534-02391-6*); pap., student ed. 7.25 (*0-534-01250-7*) Wadsworth Pub.

Logic & Philosophy. 5th ed. Howard Kahane. (Philosophy Ser.). 1986. pap., student ed. 10.00 (*0-534-05653-9*) Wadsworth Pub.

Logic & Philosophy. 5th ed. Howard Kahane. (Philosophy Ser.). 1986. pap., teacher ed. write for info. (*0-534-05654-7*) Wadsworth Pub.

Logic & Philosophy. 6th ed. Howard Kahane. (Philosophy Ser.). 1990. mass mkt., teacher ed. write for info. (*0-534-12332-5*) Wadsworth Pub.

Logic & Philosophy. 7th ed. Howard Kahane. (Philosophy Ser.). 1995. student ed. 15.25 (*0-534-17761-1*) Wadsworth Pub.

Logic & Philosophy: A Modern Introduction. 5th ed. Howard Kahane. 502p. (C). 1985. mass mkt. 28.00 (*0-534-05652-0*) Wadsworth Pub.

Logic & Philosophy: A Modern Introduction. 6th ed. Howard Kahane. 525p. (C). 1989. pap. 41.95 (*0-534-12330-9*) Wadsworth Pub.

Logic & Philosophy: A Modern Introduction. 6th ed. Howard Kahane. 525p. (C). 1990. mass mkt., student ed. 13.95 (*0-534-12331-7*) Wadsworth Pub.

Logic & Philosophy: A Modern Introduction. 7th ed. Howard Kahane & Paul Tidman. LC 94-34801. 473p. 1994. pap. 44.75 (*0-534-17760-3*) Wadsworth Pub.

Logic & Philosophy: A Modern Introduction. 8th ed. Paul Tidman & Howard Kahane. LC 98-13674. (C). 1998. pap. 67.95 (*0-534-52614-4*) Wadsworth Pub.

***Logic & Philosophy: A Modern Introduction.** 9th ed. Paul Tidman & Howard Kahane. (Philosophy Ser.). (C). 2001. text 48.25 (*0-534-56172-1*) Wadsworth Pub.

Logic & Philosophy: An Integrated Introduction. William H. Brenner. LC 92-56865. (C). 1993. text 34.50 (*0-268-01302-0*); pap. text 18.50 (*0-268-01299-7*) U of Notre Dame Pr.

Logic & Philosophy in the Lvov-Warsaw School. Jan Wolenski. 378p. (C). 1988. lib. bdg. 211.50 (*90-277-2749-X*, Pub. by Kluwer Academic) Kluwer Academic.

Logic & Philosophy of Science in Uppsala: Papers from the 9th International Congress of Logic, Methodology & Philosophy of Science. Ed. by Dag Prawitz & Dag Westerstahl. LC 93-50753. (Synthese Library: Vol. 236). 620p. (C). 1994. lib. bdg. 251.00 (*0-7923-2702-0*, Pub. by Kluwer Academic) Kluwer Academic.

Logic & Philsophy. 8th ed. Howard Kahane. 1999. pap., student ed. 15.25 (*0-534-52615-2*) Brooks-Cole.

Logic & Political Culture: Proceedings of the Colloquium on Logic & Politics, Amsterdam, the Netherlands, 19-22 February 1990. Ed. by E. M. Barth & E. C. W. Krabbe. (Verhandelingen der Koninklijke Nederlandse Akademie van Wetenschappen, Afd. Letterkunde, Nieuwe Reeks Ser.: No. 149). 176p. pap. 49.50 (*0-444-85743-5*) Elsevier.

Logic & Politics: Hegel's Philosophy of Right. Peter J. Steinberger. 1988. 37.50 (*0-300-03982-4*) Yale U Pr.

An Asterisk (*) at the beginning of an entry indicates that the title is appearing for the first time.

Logic & Probability in Quantum Mechanics. Ed. by Patrick C. Suppes. (Synthese Library: No. 78). 556p. 1981. pap. text 62.50 (*90-277-1200-X*) Kluwer Academic.

Logic & Proof. Norman & Sherwood. 206p. (C). 1991. pap. text 45.00 (*0-536-58089-8*) Pearson Custom.

*Logic & Proof for College Algebra.** James Edmondson. 50p. (C). 2000. per. 10.95 (*0-7872-7286-8*) Kendall-Hunt.

Logic & Random Structures: DIMACS Workshop, November 5-7, 1995. NSF Science & Technology Center in Discrete Mathem & DIMACS Staff. Ed. by Ravi B. Boppana & James F. Lynch. LC 97-10666. (DIMACS: Series in Descrete Mathematics & Theoretical Computer Science: Vol. 33). 130p. 1997. text 29.00 (*0-8218-0578-9*) Am Math.

Logic & Reading Review for the GRE, GMAT, LSAT, MCAT. Peterson's Guides Staff. LC 99-28088. 288p. 1999. pap. 16.95 (*0-7689-0229-0*) Petersons.

Logic & Reality. Gustav Bergmann. LC 64-10261. 365p. reprint ed. pap. 113.20 (*0-608-10119-2*, 200423400039) Bks Demand.

Logic & Reality: Essays on the Legacy of Arthur Prior. Ed. by Jack Copeland. LC 97-164768. (Illus.). 556p. 1997. text 112.00 (*0-19-824060-0*) OUP.

Logic & Reality in the Philosophy of John Stuart Mill. Geoffrey F. Scarre. 250p. (C). 1988. lib. bdg. 211.50 (*90-277-2739-2*, Pub. by Kluwer Academic) Kluwer Academic.

Logic & Representation. Robert Moore. LC 94-40413. (CSLI Lecture Notes Ser.: No. 39). 210p. 1995. 49.95 (*1-881526-16-X*); pap. 20.95 (*1-881526-15-1*) CSLI.

Logic & Rhetoric of Constitutional Law. Thomas R. Powell. (Reprint Series in Social Sciences). (C). 1993. reprint ed. pap. text 5.00 (*0-8290-3097-2*, PS-230) Irvington.

Logic & Scientific Methods: An Introductory Course. 3rd ed. Herbert L. Searles. LC 68-13474. (Illus.). 374p. reprint ed. 116.00 (*0-8357-9924-7*, 201340800086) Bks Demand.

Logic & Sexual Morality. Wilson. 1993. 63.95 (*0-7512-0101-4*) Ashgate Pub Co.

Logic & Sin in the Writings of Ludwig Wittgenstein. Philip R. Shields. LC 92-16651. 158p. 1992. 27.50 (*0-226-75301-8*) U Ch Pr.

Logic & Sin in the Writings of Ludwig Wittgenstein. Philip R. Shields. xii, 146p. 1997. pap. text 14.95 (*0-226-75302-6*) U Ch Pr.

Logic & Society: Contradictions & Possible Worlds. Jon Elster. LC 77-9550. 243p. reprint ed. pap. 75.40 (*0-608-13904-1*, 202042900017) Bks Demand.

Logic & Software Engineering: International Workshop Honouring Professor C. S. Tang on the Occasion of His 70th Birthday. LC 97-129099. 300p. 1996. lib. bdg. 51.00 (*981-02-2804-X*) World Scientific Pub.

Logic & Specifiction: Extending VDM-SL for Advanced Formal Specification. Cornelis A. Middelburg. LC 92-38105. 1993. pap. 61.95 (*0-412-48680-6*) Chapman & Hall.

Logic & Structure. 2nd ed. D. Van Dalen. 225p. 1989. pap. 29.00 (*0-387-12831-X*) Spr-Verlag.

Logic & Structure. 3rd ed. Dirk van Dalen. 1997. 38.95 (*0-387-57839-0*) Spr-Verlag.

Logic & Structure. 3rd ed. D. Van Dalen. LC 97-11571. 215p. 1994. pap. 34.95 (*3-540-57839-0*) Spr-Verlag.

Logic & Structured Design for Computer Programmers. 2nd ed. Harold J. Rood. 304p. (C). 1992. mass mkt. 48.95 (*0-534-92966-4*) PWS Pubs.

*Logic & Structured Design for Computer Programmers.** 3rd ed. Rood. (C). 2000. pap. 45.00 (*0-534-37386-0*) Thomson Learn.

Logic & Switching Circuits. Stan Fulton. 127p. (C). 1994. 27.78 (*1-56870-150-0*) RonJon Pub.

Logic & the Basis of Ethics. Arthur N. Prior. 124p. 1949. text 17.95 (*0-19-824157-7*) OUP.

Logic & the Bible. Thomas B. Warren. 1983. pap. 8.00 (*0-934916-01-2*) Natl Christian Pr.

Logic & the Imperial Stoa. Jonathan Barnes. LC 97-10322. (Philosophia Antiqua Ser.: No. 75). 184p. 1997. 66.00 (*90-04-10828-9*) Brill Academic Pubs.

Logic & the Workings of the Mind: The Logic of Ideas & Faculty Psychology in Early Modern Philosophy. Ed. by Patricia A. Easton. (North American Kant Society Studies in Philosophy: Vol. 5). xvi, 345p. 1997. pap. text 27.00 (*0-924922-27-3*); lib. bdg. 49.00 (*0-924922-77-X*) Ridgeview.

Logic & Time: An Essay on Husserl's Theory of Meaning. Krzysztof Michalski. Tr. by Adam Czerniawski from POL. LC 96-19684. (Boston Studies in the Philosophy of Science: NO. 185). 176p. (C). 1996. text 100.50 (*0-7923-4082-5*) Kluwer Academic.

Logic & Transcendence. Frithjof Schuon. 280p. 1996. pap. 22.50 (*0-614-21231-6*, 732) Kazi Pubns.

Logic & Transcendence. Frithjof Schuon. Tr. by Peter N. Townsend from FRE. 273p. 1984. pap. 19.95 (*0-900588-26-8*) S Perennis.

Logic & Visual Information. Eric M. Hammer. (Studies in Logic, Language & Information: No. 3). 136p. (C). 1995. 59.95 (*1-881526-87-9*); pap. 19.95 (*1-881526-99-2*) CSLI.

Logic, Anyone? One Hundred Sixty-Five Brain-Stretching Problems. Beverly Post & Sandra Eads. (Makemaster Bk.). (J). (gr. 5-12). 1982. student ed. 5.99 (*0-8224-4327-9*); pap. 13.99 (*0-8224-4326-0*) Fearon Teacher Aids.

Logic As Algebra. Paul Halmos & Steven Givant. LC 97-80864. (Dolciani Mathematical Expositions Ser.: Vol. 21). 152p. (C). 1998. pap. text, suppl. ed. 27.00 (*0-88385-327-2*, DOL-21) Math Assn.

Logic As Grammar: An Approach to Meaning in Natural Language. Norbert Hornstein. 190p. 1986. pap. text 13.50 (*0-262-58082-9*, Bradford Bks) MIT Pr.

Logic at Botik Eighty-Nine. Ed. by A. R. Meyer & M. A. Taitslin. (Lecture Notes in Computer Science Ser.: Vol. 363). x, 289p. 1989. 37.00 (*0-387-51237-3*) Spr-Verlag.

Logic at Work: Essays Dedicated to the Memory of Helena Rasiowa. Ed. by E. Orlowska. LC 98-48580. (Illus.). 694p. 1999. 139.00 (*3-7908-1164-5*) Spr-Verlag.

Logic-Based Knowledge Representation. Peter Jackson et al. 300p. 1989. 42.50 (*0-262-10038-X*) MIT Pr.

*Logic-Based Methods for Optimization.** John Hooker. LC 99-88732. 464p. 2000. text 89.95 (*0-471-38521-2*) Wiley.

Logic-Based O-1 Constraint Programming. Peter Barth. (Operations Research - Computer Science Interface Ser.: Vol. 5). 272p. (C). 1995. lib. bdg. 119.50 (*0-7923-9663-4*) Kluwer Academic.

*Logic-Based Program Synthesis & Transformation: Selected Papers of the 9th International Workshop, LOPSTR '99, Venice, Italy, September 1999.** Annalisa Bossi. Ed. by International Workshop on Logic Program Synthesis & Transformation Staff. LC 00-41921. (Lecture Notes in Computer Science). 2000. pap. write for info. (*3-540-67628-7*) Spr-Verlag.

Logic-Based Program Synthesis & Transformation: 8th International Workshop, LOPSTR '98, Manchester, U. K. June 15-19, 1998, Selected Papers. Ed. by P. Flener et al. LC 99-14668. (Lecture Notes in Computer Science Ser.: Vol. 1559). x, 331p. 1999. pap. 56.00 (*3-540-65765-7*) Spr-Verlag.

Logic Beneath the Caution: An Analysis of the Buddha's Responses to Questions about the Self. Douglas W. Shrader. 19p. 1992. 3.00 (*0-9633277-3-9*, Oneonta Philosophy) Global Pubns.

Logic, Bivalence & Denotation. rev. ed. Ermanno Bencivenga et al. 260p. 1991. pap. text 24.00 (*0-924922-04-4*) Ridgeview.

Logic, Bivalence & Denotation. 2nd rev. ed. Ermanno Bencivenga et al. 260p. 1991. lib. bdg. 35.00 (*0-924922-54-0*) Ridgeview.

Logic Bomb: Transmissions from the Edge of Style Culture. Steve Beard. LC 98-86427. (Illus.). 224p. 1999. pap. 16.00 (*1-85242-596-2*, Pub. by Serpents Tail) Consort Bk Sales.

Logic Book. Johnson. (Philosophy Ser.). 1986. pap., teacher ed. write for info. (*0-534-06853-7*) Wadsworth Pub.

Logic Book. Robert M. Johnson. 271p. (C). 1986. pap. write for info. (*0-534-06852-9*) Wadsworth Pub.

Logic Book. 2nd ed. Merrie Bergmann et al. 480p. (C). 1990. text 49.00 (*0-07-909524-0*) McGraw.

Logic Book. 2nd ed. Robert M. Johnson. 382p. (C). 1991. pap. 33.25 (*0-534-16500-1*) Wadsworth Pub.

Logic Book. 3rd ed. Merrie Bergmann et al. LC 96-22699. 1996. text. write for info. (*0-07-006059-2*) McGraw.

*Logic Book.** 4th ed. Johnson. (Philosophy Ser.). 2001. 37.50 (*0-534-56108-X*) Wadsworth Pub.

Logic Book: Fundamentals of Reasoning. 3rd ed. Johnson. LC 98-8170. (Philosophy Ser.). 1998. pap. 52.95 (*0-534-54338-3*) Wadsworth Pub.

Logic Brain Boosters. Becky Daniel. (Illus.). 64p. (J). (gr. 1-4). 1992. 8.99 (*0-86653-652-3*, GA1347) Good Apple.

*Logic, Cause & Action: Essays in Honour of Elizabeth Anscombe.** Ed. by Roger Teichmann. LC 99-89258. (Royal Institute of Philosophy Supplements Ser.: No. 46). 240p. (C). 2000. pap. 24.95 (*0-521-78510-3*) Cambridge U Pr.

Logic Circuit Design. Alan W. Shaw. (Illus.). 734p. 1993. text 88.00 (*0-03-050793-6*) OUP.

Logic Colloquium: Proceedings of the Symposium, Boston, 1972-73. Logic Symposium Staff. Ed. by R. Parikh. (Lecture Notes in Mathematics Ser.: Vol. 453). iv, 251p. (Orig.). 1975. 29.95 (*0-387-07155-5*) Spr-Verlag.

Logic Colloquium, 1990: ASL Summer Meeting in Helsinki. Ed. by J. Oikkonen & J. Vaananen. (Lecture Notes in Logic Ser.: Vol. 2). (Illus.). vii, 305p. 1994. 62.95 (*0-387-57094-2*) Spr-Verlag.

Logic Colloquium 1992: SiLLI & CSLI Co-Publications. Ed. by Laszlo Csirmaz et al. (Studies in Logic, Language & Information: No. 1). 334p. 1995. 64.95 (*1-881526-97-6*) CSLI.

Logic Colloquium 1992: SiLLI & CSLI Co-Publications. Ed. by Laszlo Csirmaz et al. (Studies in Logic, Language & Information). (Illus.). 334p. 1995. pap. 22.95 (*1-881526-98-4*) CSLI.

*Logic Colloquium '98.** Ed. by Sam Buss et al. LC 99-51335. (Lecture Notes in Logic Ser.: No. 13). (Illus.). 550p. 2000. 85.00 (*1-56881-113-6*); pap. 40.00 (*1-56881-114-4*) AK Peters.

Logic Colloquium '95: Proceedings of the Annual European Summer Meeting of the Association of Symbolic Logic, Held in Haifa, Israel, August 9-18, 1995. Association of Symbolic Logic Staff. Ed. by Johanna A. Makowsky et al. LC 97-51322. (Lecture Notes in Logic: Vol. 11). xvi, 348p. 1998. pap. 84.95 (*3-540-63994-2*) Spr-Verlag.

Logic Colloquium '96: Proceedings of the Colloquium Held in San Sebastian, Spain, July 9-15, 1996. Ed. by J. M. Larrazabal et al. (Lecture Notes in Logic Ser.: Vol. 12). vii, 261p. 1998. pap. 115.00 (*3-540-64668-X*) Spr-Verlag.

Logic Counts. Ed. by Ewa Zarnecka-Bialy. (Reason & Argument Ser.). 244p. 1990. text 155.00 (*0-7923-0942-1*) Kluwer Academic.

Logic Course. Steven Dehaven. 1995. pap. text 19.95 (*1-55111-062-8*); 3.5 hd 19.95 (*1-55111-060-1*) Broadview Pr.

Logic Course. Steven DeHaven. 245p. (C). 1995. pap., wbk. ed. 12.95 (*1-55111-064-4*) Broadview Pr.

Logic Course. 2nd ed. Steven DeHaven. (Illus.). 247p. (C). 1998. text, wbk. ed. 18.95 (*1-55111-207-8*) Broadview Pr.

Logic Course. 2nd expanded rev. ed. Steven DeHaven. LC 99-169776. (Illus.). 292p. (C). 1998. pap. 27.95 (*1-55111-204-3*) Broadview Pr.

Logic Decimal Problems. Wade H. Sherard, III. (gr. 4-7). 1999. pap. text 10.95 (*0-7690-0082-7*) Seymour Pubns.

Logic Design: An Introduction to Digital Logic. Mike Wharton. (Maplin Ser.). (Illus.). 148p. 1995. pap. text 29.95 (*0-7506-2122-2*) Buttrwrth-Heinemann.

Logic Design & Computer Organization. Morton H. Lewin. LC 81-20636. 478p. 1983. text 38.36 (*0-201-04144-8*) Addison-Wesley.

Logic Design & Switching Theory. Saburo Muroga. 636p. (C). 1990. reprint ed. 69.50 (*0-89464-463-7*) Krieger.

Logic Design for Array-Based Circuits: A Structured Design Methodology. D. E. White. (Illus.). 342p. 1992. text 54.00 (*0-12-746660-6*) Acad Pr.

Logic Design with Integrated Circuits. William E. Wickes. LC 68-21185. 262p. reprint ed. pap. 81.30 (*0-608-13333-7*, 205572100032) Bks Demand.

Logic Designer's Handbook: Circuits & Systems. 2nd ed. Andrew Parr. LC 92-31023. (Illus.). 488p. 1993. pap. text 69.95 (*0-7506-0535-9*) Buttrwrth-Heinemann.

Logic Diagrams. (Fossil Power Plant Startup Training Ser.: Module 5). (Illus.). 147p. 1984. spiral bd. 42.50 (*0-87683-362-8*) GP Courseware.

Logic for Applications. Anil Nerode & Richard Shore. LC 93-27846. (Texts & Monographs in Computer Science). (Illus.). 365p. 1993. 48.95 (*0-387-94129-0*) Spr-Verlag.

Logic for Applications. 2nd ed. Anil Nerode & Richard Shore. LC 96-43297. (Graduate Texts in Computer Science Ser.). (Illus.). 456p. 1997. 49.95 (*0-387-94893-7*) Spr-Verlag.

Logic for Artificial Intelligence. Raymond W. Turner. LC 84-19810. (Artificial Intelligence Ser.). 160p. 1984. text 34.95 (*0-470-20123-1*) P-H.

Logic for Computer Science. Denenberg. (C). 1990. 91.00 (*0-673-39970-2*) Addison-Wesley.

Logic for Computer Science. Nimal Nissanke. 1997. pap. text 14.95 (*3-540-76072-5*) Spr-Verlag.

Logic for Computer Science: Foundations of Automatic Theorem Proving. Jean H. Gallier. LC 85-14071. 526p. reprint ed. pap. 163.10 (*0-7837-2828-X*, 205764400006) Bks Demand.

Logic for Computer Scientists. Uwe Schoning. (Progress in Computer Science & Applied Logic Ser.: No. 8). (Illus.). ix, 166p. 1994. 35.00 (*0-8176-3453-3*) Birkhauser.

Logic for Information Technology. fac. ed. Antony Galton. LC 90-12446. 304p. pap. 94.30 (*0-7837-7374-9*, 204718400005) Bks Demand.

Logic for Lawyers. 3rd ed. Ruggero J. Aldisert. LC 97-215508. 268p. 1997. pap. 37.95 (*1-55681-538-7*) Natl Inst Trial Ad.

Logic for Lawyers: A Guide to Clear Legal Thinking, 1992. Ruggero J. Aldisert. LC 89-31818. 1992. pap. 29.95 (*0-87632-743-9*) West Group.

Logic for Math & Computer Science. Stanley Burris. LC 97-15438. 420p. 1997. 78.67 (*0-13-285974-2*) P-H.

Logic for Mathematicians. rev. ed. A. G. Hamilton. 236p. 1988. pap. text 32.95 (*0-521-36865-0*) Cambridge U Pr.

Logic for Problem Solving. R. A. Kowalski. (Artificial Intelligence Ser.: Vol. 7). 295p. 1979. pap. 24.50 (*0-444-00368-1*) P-H.

Logic for Space Age Kids. Lyn M. Butrick. Ed. by William H. Cooper. LC 84-50892. (My Read & Think Ser.: Vol. II). (Illus.). 32p. (J). (gr. 3-6). 1984. pap. 5.27 (*0-914127-16-0*) Univ Class.

Logic for Strategy. Edwin M. Hartman et al. 216p. 1988. pap. text 17.95 (*0-88730-222-X*, HarpBusn) HarpInfo.

Logic for Strategy. Edwin M. Hartman et al. 216p. 1989. text 32.00 (*0-88730-205-X*, HarpBusn) HarpInfo.

Logic for Use: An Introduction to the Voluntarist Theory of Knowledge. Ferdinand C. Schiller. LC 75-3346. (Philosophy America Ser.). reprint ed. 65.00 (*0-404-59345-3*) AMS Pr.

Logic from a Rhetorical Point of View. Witold Marciszewski. LC 93-45843. (Grundlagen der Kommunikation & Kognition (Foundations of Communication & Cognition) Ser.). xv, 312p. (C). 1993. lib. bdg. 118.50 (*3-11-013683-X*) De Gruyter.

*Logic From A to Z: The Routledge Encyclopedia of Philosophy Glossary of Logical & Mathematical.** JOHN B BACON. 1999. pap. 16.99 (*0-415-21375-4*) Routledge.

Logic from Computer Science: Proceedings of a Workshop Held November 13-17, 1989. Ed. by Shiing-Shen Chern et al. (Mathematical Sciences Research Institute Publications: Vol. 21). (Illus.). 624p. 1991. 89.95 (*0-387-97667-1*) Spr-Verlag.

Logic, God & Metaphysics. Ed. by James F. Harris. 160p. (C). 1992. lib. bdg. 127.50 (*0-7923-1454-9*, Pub. by Kluwer Academic) Kluwer Academic.

Logic Grammars. Harvey Abramson & V. Dahl. (Symbolic Computation - Artificial Intelligence Ser.). (Illus.). 240p. 1989. 58.95 (*0-387-96961-6*) Spr-Verlag.

Logic in Artificial Intelligence, 838. Ed. by D. Pearce et al. LC 94-228872. (Lecture Notes in Artificial Intelligence Ser.). 413p. 1994. 61.95 (*0-387-58332-7*) Spr-Verlag.

*Logic in Computer Science: Proceedings: Symposium on Logic in Computer Science (14th, 1999: Trento, Italy)** 478p. 1999. pap. 140.00 (*0-7695-0158-3*) IEEE Comp Soc.

Logic in Computer Science, 11th Symposium on (LICS 96) LC 10-436871. 536p. 1996. pap. 100.00 (*0-8186-7463-6*) IEEE Comp Soc.

*Logic in Computer Science (LICS '98)** Ed. by IEEE Computer Society Staff. 1998. pap. 140.00 (*0-8186-8506-9*, IEEE Inst Elec) IEEE Comp Soc.

Logic in Computer Science, 10th Symposium on (LICS '95) 528p. 1995. 100.00 (*0-8186-7050-9*, PR07050) IEEE Comp Soc.

Logic in Computer Science, 12th Symposium. LC 10-436871. 500p. 1997. pap. 135.00 (*0-8186-7925-5*) IEEE Comp Soc.

*Logic in Computer Sciences: Modelling & Reasoning about Computer Systems.** M. Huth & M. Ryan. LC 99-15233. (Illus.). 500p. (C). 2000. 99.95 (*0-521-65200-6*); pap. 37.95 (*0-521-65602-8*) Cambridge U Pr.

Logic in Databases: International Workshop LID 96, San Miniato, Italy, July 1996: Proceedings. Dino Pedreschi & Carlo Zaniolo. LC 96-41820. (Lecture Notes in Computer Science Ser.: Vol. 1154). 497p. 1996. text 81.00 (*3-540-61814-7*) Spr-Verlag.

L

Logic in Everyday Life. Seech. (Philosophy Ser.). 1988. pap., teacher ed. write for info. (*0-534-08197-5*) Wadsworth Pub.

Logic in Everyday Life: Practical Reasoning Skills. Zachary Seech. 303p. (C). 1987. pap. write for info. (*0-534-08196-7*) Wadsworth Pub.

Logic in Linguistics. Ed. by J. Allwood et al. LC 76-46855. (Cambridge Textbooks in Linguistics Ser.). (Illus.). 200p. 1977. pap. text 20.95 (*0-521-29174-7*) Cambridge U Pr.

Logic in the Husserlian Context. Johanna Tito. (Studies in Phenomenology & Existential Philosophy). 250p. 1990. 39.95 (*0-8101-0966-2*) Northwestern U Pr.

Logic in the Round. Sandra Eads & Beverly Post. (J). (gr. 5 up). 1989. pap. 8.99 (*0-8224-4206-X*) Fearon Teacher Aids.

Logic, Inductive & Deductive. William Minto. 1977. 19.95 (*0-8369-6997-9*, 7814) Ayer.

Logic International Relation: 8th Edition. 8th ed. Walter S. Jones. LC 96-18900. (C). 1997. pap. 54.35 (*0-673-52478-7*, Harp PBks) HarpC.

Logic, Language & Computation. Seiki Akama. LC 96-52738. (Applied Logic Ser.: APLS Vol. 5). 260p. (C). 1997. text 97.50 (*0-7923-4376-X*) Kluwer Academic.

*Logic, Language & Computation.** Patrick Blackburn et al. (Lecture Notes Ser.: No. 111). 350p. (C). 2000. pap. text. write for info. (*1-57586-268-9*, Pub. by CSLI) Cambridge U Pr.

Logic, Language & Computation. Ed. by Jerry Seligman & Dag Westerstahl. (CSLI Lecture Notes Ser.). 590p. (C). 1996. 49.95 (*1-881526-90-9*); pap. 29.95 (*1-881526-89-5*) CSLI.

Logic, Language & Computation, Vol. 2. Ed. by Lawrence S. Moss et al. (Lecture Notes Ser.: Vol. 91). 440p. (C). 1999. text 64.95 (*1-57586-181-X*); pap. text 26.95 (*1-57586-180-1*) CSLI.

*Logic, Language & Computation, Vol. 3.** Patrick Blackburn et al. (Lecture Notes Ser.: No. 111). 350p. (C). 2000. text. write for info. (*1-57586-267-0*, Pub. by CSLI) Cambridge U Pr.

Logic, Language, & Computation: Festschrift in Honor of Satoru Takasu. Ed. by Neil D. Jones et al. LC 94-10102. (Lecture Notes in Computer Science Ser.). 1994. 44.95 (*0-387-57935-4*); write for info. (*3-540-57935-4*) Spr-Verlag.

Logic, Language, & Meaning Vol. 1: Introduction to Logic. L. T. Gamut. Tr. by Michael Morreau & Babette Greiner. LC 90-10912. (Illus.). 304p. 1990. pap. text 24.00 (*0-226-28085-3*); lib. bdg. 66.00 (*0-226-28084-5*) U Ch Pr.

Logic, Language, & Meaning Vol. 2: Intensional Logic & Logic Grammar. L. T. Gamut. Tr. by Michael Morreau & Babette Greiner. (Illus.). 368p. 1990. pap. text 27.50 (*0-226-28088-8*); lib. bdg. 72.00 (*0-226-28086-1*) U Ch Pr.

Logic, Language & Probability: Proceedings of the International Congress for Logic, Methodology & Philosophy of Science, 4th Bucharest, Sept., 1971. International Congress for Logic, Methodology, & P. Ed. by Radu J. Bogdan & I. Niiniluoto. LC 72-95892. (Synthese Library: No. 51). 333p. 1973. text 177.50 (*90-277-0312-4*, D Reidel) Kluwer Academic.

Logic, Language & Reality: An Introduction to Indian Philosophical Studies. Bimal K. Matilal. 447p. 1985. 29.50 (*81-208-0008-7*, Pub. by Motilal Bnarsidass) S Asia.

Logic, Language & Reasoning: Essays in Honour of Dov Gabbay. Ed. by Dov M. Gabbay et al. LC 99-20301. (Trends in Logic Ser.). 429p. 1999. 204.00 (*0-7923-5687-X*) Kluwer Academic.

Logic, Language, & the Structure of Scientific Theories. Ed. by Wesley Charles Salmon & Gereon Wolters. (Pittsburgh-Konstanz Series in Philosophy & History of Science). 376p. 1994. text 59.95 (*0-8229-3740-9*) U of Pittsburgh Pr.

Logic, Language, Formalism, Informalism. Daniel Richardson. (Illus.). 320p. 1995. mass mkt. 34.95 (*1-85032-127-2*) ITCP.

*Logic, Law & Ethics.** R. J. Chambers & G. W. Dean. LC 00-26480. (Chambers on Accounting Ser.). 2000. write for info. (*0-8153-3786-8*) Garland.

Logic, Laws & Life: Some Philosophical Complications. Ed. by Robert G. Colodny & Leonard J. Savage. LC 76-50886. (University of Pittsburgh Series in the Philosophy of Science: No. 6). (Illus.). 272p. reprint ed. pap. 84.40 (*0-8357-8211-5*, 203395600087) Bks Demand.

Logic, Logic, & Logic. George Boolos. 448p. 1999. pap. 22.95 (*0-674-53767-X*) HUP.

Logic, Logic, & Logic. George Boolos & John P. Burgess. Ed. by Richard C. Jeffrey. LC 97-37668. 448p. 1999. text 45.00 (*0-674-53766-1*) HUP.

Logic Machines & Diagrams. 2nd ed. Martin Gardner. LC 82-11157. xiv, 162p. (C). 1983. pap. 5.95 (*0-226-28244-9*) U Ch Pr.

Logic Made Easy. R. H. Warring. LC 85-12578. (Illus.). 112p. 1985. pap. 9.95 (*0-8306-1853-8*, 1853P) McGraw-Hill Prof.

Logica Magna, Fascicule 8 Pt. 1: Tractatus de Necessititate et Contingentia Futurorum. Paul of Venice. Ed. by C. J. Williams. (Classical & Medieval Logic Texts Ser.: No. VIII). 288p. 1991. pap. 45.00 (*0-19-726101-9*) OUP.

*__Logic, Meaning & Conversation: Semantical Underdeterminacy, Implicature & Their Interface.__ Jay David Atlas. (Illus.). 400p. 2000. text 55.00 (*0-19-513300-5*) OUP.

Logic, Methodology & Philosophy of Science, Vol. 6. Ed. by J. L. Cohen et al. (Studies in Logic & the Foundations of Mathematics: Vol. 104). 104p. 1983. 246.50 (*0-444-85423-1*, North Holland) Elsevier.

Logic, Methodology & Philosophy of Science: Proceedings of the 8th International Congress, Moscow, U. S. S. R., 17-22 Aug., 1987. Ed. by Jens E. Fenstad et al. (Studies in Logic & the Foundations of Mathematics: No. 126). xviii,702p. 1989. 347.00 (*0-444-70520-1*, North Holland) Elsevier.

Logic, Methodology & Philosophy of Science IX: Proceedings: International Congress of Logic, Methodology, & Philosophy of Science (9th: 1991: Uppsala, Sweden) Ed. by Dag Prawitz et al. LC 94-39279. (Studies in Logic & the Foundations of Mathematics: Vol. 134). 1004p. 1995. 269.00 (*0-444-89341-5*) Elsevier.

Logic Minimization Algorithms for VLSI Synthesis. Robert K. Brayton et al. (Kluwer International Series in Engineering & Computer Science). 1984. reprint ed. text 98.50 (*0-89838-164-9*) Kluwer Academic.

Logic Multiparty System. Isee & Manfred J. Holler. 1987. lib. bdg. 184.00 (*90-247-3515-7*, Pub. by M Nijhoff) Kluwer Academic.

Logic Mysteries. Jane Molnar. 1999. pap. text 12.95 (*0-7690-0001-0*) Seymour Pubns.

Logic Number Problems. Wade Sherard. 1997. pap. text 10.50 (*0-86651-425-2*) Seymour Pubns.

*__Logic Number Problems.__ Wade H. Sherard, III. (Illus.). 64p. (J). (gr. 4-8). 1998. pap. 10.95 (*0-7690-0000-2*) Seymour Pubns.

Logic Object-Oriented Concurrent Robot Programming & Performance Aspects. Alfried Pollmann. LC 96-31349. (Programming Complex Systems Ser.). 280p. 1996. 94.95 (*3-11-015072-7*) De Gruyter.

Logic of Accidental Nuclear War. Bruce G. Blair. 364p. 1993. 49.95 (*0-8157-0984-6*); pap. 22.95 (*0-8157-0983-8*) Brookings.

Logic of Action One: Method, Money & the Austrian School. Murray N. Rothbard. LC 96-37189. (Economists of the Twentieth Century Ser.). 480p. 1997. 90.00 (*1-85898-015-1*) E Elgar.

Logic of Action Two: Applications & Criticism from the Austrian School. Murray N. Rothbard. LC 96-37189. (Economists of the Twentieth Century Ser.). 432p. 1997. 85.00 (*1-85898-570-6*) E Elgar.

Logic of Affect Paul Redding. LC 98-55361. 1999. 35.00 (*0-8014-3591-9*) Cornell U Pr.

*__Logic of American Politics.__ Samuel Kernell & Gary C. Jacobson. LC 99-38744. (Illus.). 573p. 1999. pap. 49.95 (*1-56802-395-2*) CQ Pr.

Logic of Analogy: An Interpretation of St. Thomas. Ralph McInerny. 194p. 1971. pap. text 50.50 (*90-247-0104-X*, Pub. by M Nijhoff) Kluwer Academic.

Logic of Anarchy: Neorealism to Structural Realism. Barry G. Buzan et al. LC 92-31656. (New Directions in World Politics Ser.). (Illus.). 256p. (C). 1993. pap. 20.50 (*0-231-08041-7*) Col U Pr.

Logic of Architecture: Design, Computation, & Cognition. William J. Mitchell. (Illus.). 304p. (Orig.). 1990. pap. text 21.95 (*0-262-63116-4*) MIT Pr.

*__Logic of Arithmetic.__ (Lectures on Mathematical Logic Ser.: Vol. 3). 312p. 2000. text 58.00 (*90-5699-268-6*, G & B Science) Gordon & Breach.

Logic of Aspect: An Axiomatic Approach. Antony Galton. (Illus.). 168p. 1984. text 39.95 (*0-19-824430-4*) OUP.

Logic of Being. Ed. by Simo Knuuttila & Jaakko Hintikka. 316p. 1985. lib. bdg. 146.00 (*90-277-2019-3*, D Reidel) Kluwer Academic.

Logic of Being Completely Logical. Harvey Jackins. 1965. pap. 2.00 (*0-911214-12-7*) Rational Isl.

Logic of Biochemical Sequencing. David Blackman. LC 93-12778. 192p. 1993. lib. bdg. 54.95 (*0-8493-4497-2*, QP551) CRC Pr.

Logic of Black Urban Rebellions: Challenging the Dynamics of White Domination in Miami. Daryl B. Harris. LC 98-23569. 160p. 1999. 55.00 (*0-275-95945-7*) Greenwood.

Logic of Business Decision Making. Harvard Business Review Staff. (Help for the General Manager Ser.). 94p. 1991. pap. 19.95 (*0-87584-287-9*) Harvard Busn.

Logic of Business Decision Making. Harvard Business Review Staff. 100p. 1991. pap. 19.95 (*0-07-103347-5*) McGraw.

Logic of Business Strategy. Bruce D. Henderson. LC 84-11119. 128p. 1985. pap. 16.95 (*0-88730-061-8*, HarpBusn) HarpInfo.

Logic of Categories. Gyorgy Tamas. Ed. by Robert S. Cohen. 536p. 1987. text 234.00 (*90-277-1742-7*, D Reidel) Kluwer Academic.

Logic of Causal Order. James A. Davis. LC 85-62371. (Quantitative Applications in the Social Sciences Ser.: Vol. 55). 96p. (Orig.). 1985. pap. text 10.95 (*0-8039-2553-0*) Sage.

*__Logic of Charity.__ Marco H. van Leeuwen. LC 99-40411. 260p. 1999. text 69.95 (*0-312-22853-8*) St Martin.

Logic of Chemical Synthesis. Elias James Corey & Xue-Min Cheng. LC 89-5335. 464p. 1995. pap. 32.95 (*0-471-11594-0*) Wiley.

Logic of Chemistry Synthesis. Elias James Corey & Xue-Min Cheng. LC 89-5335. 436p. 1989. 59.95 (*0-471-50979-5*) Wiley.

Logic of Choice & Economic Theory. S. N. Afriat. 592p. 1987. 105.00 (*0-19-828461-6*) OUP.

Logic of Collective Action: Public Goods & the Theory of Groups. Mancur Olson, Jr. (Economic Studies: Vol. No. 124). 186p. (C). 1965. pap. 15.50 (*0-674-53751-3*) HUP.

Logic of Collective Action: Public Goods & the Theory of Groups. rev. ed. Mancur Olson, Jr. LC 65-19826. (Economic Studies: No. 24). 1965. pap. 6.95 (*0-674-03751-0*) HUP.

Logic of Common Nouns: An Investigation in Quantified Modal Logic. Anil Gupta. LC 79-19684. 196p. 1980. 45.00 (*0-300-02346-4*) Yale U Pr.

Logic of Comparative Social Inquiry. Adam Przeworski & Henry Teune. LC 81-19332. 168p. 1982. reprint ed. lib. bdg. 23.50 (*0-89874-462-8*) Krieger.

Logic of Computation. Ed. by Helmut Schwichtenberg. LC 97-17154. (NATO ASI Series. Series F: No. 157). vii, 396p. 1997. 99.00 (*3-540-62963-7*) Spr-Verlag.

Logic of Conditionals: An Application of Probability to Deductive Logic. E. Adams. LC 75-20306. (Synthese Library: No. 86). 169p. 1975. text 132.00 (*90-277-0631-X*, D Reidel) Kluwer Academic.

Logic of Conflict: Making War & Peace in the Middle East. Steven Greffenius. LC 92-39193. 224p. (gr. 13). 1993. text 70.95 (*1-56324-073-4*) M E Sharpe.

Logic of Congressional Action. R. Douglas Arnold. 293p. (C). 1992. reprint ed. pap. 20.00 (*0-300-05659-1*) Yale U Pr.

Logic of Culture: Advances in Structural Theory & Method. Ed. by Ino Rossi. LC 81-29. 304p. 1982. 42.95 (*0-89789-015-9*, Bergin & Garvey) Greenwood.

Logic of Decision. 2nd ed. Richard C. Jeffrey. LC 82-13465. (C). 1983. lib. bdg. 22.00 (*0-226-39581-2*) U Ch Pr.

Logic of Decision. 2nd ed. Richard C. Jeffrey. LC 82-13465. xiv, 234p. 1990. pap. text 17.95 (*0-226-39582-0*) U Ch Pr.

Logic of Decision & Action. Nicholas Rescher. LC 67-18272. 236p. reprint ed. pap. 73.20 (*0-608-30824-2*, 201049500068) Bks Demand.

Logic of Decision Making: An Introduction to Critical Thinking. Janevive J. Mechanic. (American University Studies: Philosophy: Ser. V, Vol. 39). X, 205p. 1988. text 35.50 (*0-8204-0484-5*) P Lang Pubng.

Logic of Delegation: Congressional Parties & the Appropriations Process. D. Roderick Kiewiet & Mathew D. McCubbins. (American Politics & Political Economy Ser.). (Illus.). 300p. 1991. pap. text 15.95 (*0-226-43531-8*); lib. bdg. 41.00 (*0-226-43529-6*) U Ch Pr.

Logic of Deterrence. Anthony Kenny. LC 85-13944. x, 114p. 1996. pap. text 12.00 (*0-226-43156-8*) U Ch Pr.

Logic of Disclosures. Elizabeth Beirne. 144p. (Orig.). (C). 1996. pap. write for info. (*1-57502-250-8*) Morris Pubng.

Logic of Discovery. Richard D. Carmichael. LC 74-26255. (History, Philosophy & Sociology of Science Ser.). 1975. reprint ed. 24.95 (*0-405-06583-3*) Ayer.

Logic of Discovery: A Theory of the Rationality of Scientific Research. Scott A. Kleiner. LC 93-22798. (Synthese Library: Vol. 231). 352p. 1993. lib. bdg. 155.50 (*0-7923-2371-8*, Pub. by Kluwer Academic) Kluwer Academic.

Logic of Discovery: An Interrogative Approach to Scientific Inquiry, Vol. 168. Sangmo Jung. LC 94-30670. (American University Studies: Ser. V). IX, 211p. (C). 1996. 48.95 (*0-8204-2653-9*) P Lang Pubng.

Logic of Discovery & Logic of Discourse. Ed. by Jaakko Hintikka & Fernand Vandamme. (Illus.). 288p. (C). 1986. 102.00 (*0-306-42157-7*, Plenum Trade) Perseus Pubng.

Logic of Domains. G. Q. Zhang. (Progress in Theoretical Computer Science Ser.). ix, 259p. 1991. 60.50 (*0-8176-3570-X*) Birkhauser.

*__Logic of Economic Reform in Russia.__ Jerry F. Hough. 2000. pap. 18.95 (*0-8157-3753-X*) Brookings.

Logic of Ecstasy: Canadian Mystical Painting, 1920-1940. Ann Davis. (Illus.). 216p. 1992. text 60.00 (*0-8020-5916-3*) U of Toronto Pr.

Logic of Ecstasy: Canadian Mystical Painting, 1920-1940. Ann Davis. (Illus.). 216p. 1992. pap. text 24.95 (*0-8020-6861-8*) U of Toronto Pr.

Logic of Epistemology & the Epistemology of Logic. Jaakko Hintikka & Merrill B. Hintikka. 266p. (C). 1989. pap. text 66.50 (*0-7923-0041-6*, Pub. by Kluwer Academic); lib. bdg. 106.00 (*0-7923-0040-8*, Pub. by Kluwer Academic) Kluwer Academic.

Logic of Essentialism: An Interpretation of Aristotle's Modal Syllogistic. Paul Thom. LC 96-6792. (New Synthese Historical Library: No. 43). 396p. (C). 1996. text 173.50 (*0-7923-3987-8*) Kluwer Academic.

Logic of Evaluation. 2nd ed. Michael Scriven. 125p. 1980. pap. text 8.00 (*0-918528-17-8*) Edgepress.

Logic of Evangelism. William J. Abraham. 208p. (Orig.). (C). 1989. pap. 16.00 (*0-8028-0433-0*) Eerdmans.

Logic of Evil: The Social Origins of the Nazi Party, 1925 to 1933. William Brustein. LC 95-47263. (Illus.). 256p. 1996. 35.00 (*0-300-06533-7*) Yale U Pr.

Logic of Evil: The Social Origins of the Nazi Party, 1925-1933. William Brustein. 256p. 1998. pap. 16.00 (*0-300-07432-8*) Yale U Pr.

*__Logic of Expressive Choice.__ Alexander Schuessler. LC 99-87372. (Illus.). 196p. 2000. 49.50 (*0-691-00661-X*) Princeton U Pr.

*__Logic of Expressive Choice.__ Alexander A. Schuessler. (Illus.). 196p. 2000. pap. 16.95 (*0-691-00662-8*) Princeton U Pr.

Logic of Failure. Dietrich Dorner. Tr. by Rita Kimber & Robert Kimber. LC 97-20511. 240p. 1997. pap. 15.00 (*0-201-47948-6*) Addison-Wesley.

Logic of Failure: Why Things Go Wrong & What We Can Do to Make Them Right. Dietrich Dorner. Tr. by Robert Kimber & Rita Kimber. 288p. 1995. 25.00 (*0-8050-4160-5*) H Holt & Co.

Logic of Fantasy: H. G. Wells & Science Fiction. John Huntington. LC 82-4593. 192p. 1982. text 55.50 (*0-231-05378-9*) Col U Pr.

Logic of Fiction. John Woods. LC 73-92089. (De Proprietatibus Litterarum, Ser. Minor: No. 16). 152p. 1974. pap. text 44.65 (*90-279-3113-5*) Mouton.

Logic of Force: The Dilemma of Limited War in American Foreign Policy. Christopher Gacek. LC 93-44798. 1994. 57.00 (*0-231-09656-9*); pap. 20.50 (*0-231-09657-7*) Col U Pr.

Logic of Gersonides: A Translation of Sefer Ha-Heqqesh Ha-Yashar (The Book of the Correct Syllogism) of Rabbi Levi ben Gershom with Introduction, Commentary, & Analytical Glossary. Charles H. Manekin. (New Synthese Historical Library). 364p. (C). 1991. lib. bdg. 175.00 (*0-7923-1513-8*, Pub. by Kluwer Academic) Kluwer Academic.

Logic of God: Theology & Verification. Malcolm L. Diamond & Thomas V. Litzenburg, Jr. LC 74-32235. 562p. 1975. 17.95 (*0-672-60792-1*, Bobbs) Macmillan.

Logic of Historical Explanation. Clayton Roberts. 328p. 1995. 55.00 (*0-271-01442-3*); pap. 19.95 (*0-271-01443-1*) Pa St U Pr.

Logic of History. Charles Moraze. Tr. by Wilson Clough. (New Babylon Ser.: No. 11). 260p. 1976. text 64.65 (*90-279-7781-X*) Mouton.

Logic of Holocaust & Genocide. (Analysis Ser.: No. 21). 12.50 (*0-686-45490-1*) Inst Analysis.

Logic of Human Personality: An Onto-logical Account Mary L. O'Hara. LC 99-10400. 1999. write for info. (*1-57392-671-X*, Humanity Bks) Prometheus Bks.

Logic of Human Personality: An Ontological Account. Mary L. O'Hara. LC 96-39586. 176p. (C). 1997. text 45.00 (*0-391-04022-7*) Humanities.

Logic of Images in International Relations. Robert Jervis. (Morningside Bk.). 281p. 1989. text 69.00 (*0-231-06932-4*); pap. text 19.50 (*0-231-06933-2*) Col U Pr.

Logic of Imaginative Education: Research Understanding. Dick McCleary. (Advances in Contemporary Educational Thought Ser.). 192p. (C). 1993. text 43.00 (*0-8077-3302-4*); pap. text 18.95 (*0-8077-3301-6*) Tchrs Coll.

Logic of Imperialism. Albert Szymanski. LC 81-5124. 598p. 1981. 65.00 (*0-275-90728-7*, C0728, Praeger Pubs) Greenwood.

Logic of Incest: A Structuralist Analysis of Hebrew Mythology. Seth D. Kunin. LC 95-165102. (Journal for the Study of the Old Testament Supplement Ser.: Vol. 185). 297p. 1995. 85.00 (*1-85075-509-4*, Pub. by Sheffield Acad) CUP Services.

Logic of Induction. Halina Mortimer et al. 168p. 1988. text 41.95 (*0-470-21234-9*) P-H.

Logic of Information Structures. Heinrich T. Wansing. LC 93-29015. (Lecture Notes in Artificial Intelligence Ser.: Vol. 681). x, 163p. 1993. 35.00 (*0-387-56734-8*) Spr-Verlag.

Logic of International Objects: A Meinongian Version of Classical Logic. Jacek Pasniczek. LC 97-32487. (Synthese Library Ser.). 220p. 1998. text 124.00 (*0-7923-4880-X*) Kluwer Academic.

Logic of International Restructuring: The Management of Dependencies in Rival Industrial Complexes. Winfried Ruigrok & Rob Van Tulder. LC 95-20711. (Illus.). 360p. (C). 1996. 90.00 (*0-415-12238-4*) Routledge.

Logic of International Restructuring: The Management of Dependencies in Rival Industrial Complexes. Winfried Ruigrok & Rob Van Tulder. LC 95-20711. (Illus.). 360p. (C). 1996. pap. 27.99 (*0-415-12239-2*) Routledge.

Logic of Internationalism: Coercion & Accommodation. Kjell Goldmann. LC 93-46047. 256p. (C). 1994. pap. 27.99 (*0-415-09599-9*) Routledge.

Logic of Intuitive Decision Making: A Research-Based Approach for Top Management. Weston H. Agor. LC 86-8119. (Illus.). 200p. 1986. 57.95 (*0-89930-177-0*, ALI/, Quorum Bks) Greenwood.

Logic of Japanese Politics: Leaders, Institutions, & the Limits of Change. Gerald L. Curtis. LC 99-19910. 336p. 1999. 27.95 (*0-231-10842-7*) Col U Pr.

*__Logic of Japanese Politics: Leaders, Institutions & the Limits of Change.__ Gerald L. Curtis. LC 99-19910. 2000. pap. 17.50 (*0-231-10843-5*) Col U Pr.

Logic of Knowledge Base. Keshab C. Dash. (C). 1992. 12.00 (*81-7030-346-X*) S Asia.

*__Logic of Knowledge Bases.__ Hector J. Levesque & Gerhard Lakemeyer. LC 00-25413. (Illus.). 583p. 2000. 45.00 (*0-262-12232-4*) MIT Pr.

Logic of Language Development in Early Childhood. Ed. by M. Miller. Tr. by R. T. King from GER. (Language & Communication Ser.: Vol. 3). (Illus.). 1979. 39.95 (*0-387-09606-X*) Spr-Verlag.

Logic of Lawmaking: A Spatial Theory Approach. Gerald S. Strom. LC 89-46209. (Interpreting American Politics Ser.). (Illus.). 168p. 1990. pap. text 14.95 (*0-8018-3994-7*) Johns Hopkins.

Logic of Liberty, 30. G. B. Madison. LC 85-27278. (Contributions in Philosophy Ser.: No. 30). 307p. 1986. 55.00 (*0-313-25018-9*, MLG/, Greenwood Pr) Greenwood.

Logic of Liberty: Reflections & Rejoinders. Michael Polanyi. LC 98-5301. 1998. 16.00 (*0-86597-182-X*); pap. 9.00 (*0-86597-183-8*) Liberty Fund.

Logic of Liberty: Reflections & Rejoinders. Michael Polanyi. LC 51-8809. (Midway Reprint Ser.). 1980. pap. text 12.95 (*0-226-67296-4*) U Ch Pr.

Logic of Life: A History of Heredity. Francois Jacob. Tr. by Betty E. Spillman. LC 92-35369. (Science Library). (Illus.). 358p. 1993. reprint ed. pap. 16.95 (*0-691-00042-5*, Pub. by Princeton U Pr) Cal Prin Full Svc.

Logic of Literature. rev. ed. Kate Hamburger. Tr. by Marilynn J. Rose. LC 92-42553. 400p. 1993. pap. 15.95 (*0-253-20828-9*) Ind U Pr.

Logic of Literature. 2nd rev. ed. Kate Hamburger. Tr. by Marilynn J. Rose. LC 92-42553. 400p. 1993. 36.95 (*0-253-32692-3*) Ind U Pr.

Logic of Logistics: Theory, Algorithms, & Applications for Logistics Management. Julien Bramel & David Simchi-Levi. LC 96-37582. (Springer Series in Operations Research). 312p. 1997. 49.95 (*0-387-94921-6*) Spr-Verlag.

*__Logic of Love.__ Halbert Katzen. 1999. pap. text 14.95 (*1-929749-03-1*) Archstone.

*__Logic of Love: Finding Faith Through the Heart-Mind Connection.__ Halbert Katzen. LC 99-95212. (Illus.). 160p. 1999. pap. 14.95 (*0-9672949-7-5*, Pub. by Insights Out) Blessingway Bks.

Logic of Machines & Structures. Paul Sandori. LC 81-19743. 192p. 1985. reprint ed. 37.95 (*0-471-86397-1*); reprint ed. pap. 25.50 (*0-471-86193-6*) Krieger.

Logic of Markedness. Edwin L. Battistella. 192p. 1996. text 49.95 (*0-19-510394-7*) OUP.

Logic of Marx's Capital: Replies to Hegelian Criticisms. Tony Smith. LC 89-21839. (SUNY Series in the Philosophy of the Social Sciences). 271p. 1990. text 21.50 (*0-7914-0267-3*) State U NY Pr.

Logic of Mathematics: A Modern Course of Classical Logic. Zofia Adamowicz & Pawel Zbierski. LC 95-20818. (Pure & Applied Mathematics: A Wiley-Interscience Series of Texts, Monographs & Tracts). 272p. 1997. 74.95 (*0-471-06026-7*) Wiley.

Logic of Medicine, Vol. 2. 2nd ed. Edmond A. Murphy. LC 96-20279. 516p. 1997. text 55.00 (*0-8018-5415-6*); pap. text 25.95 (*0-8018-5538-1*) Johns Hopkins.

*__Logic of Microspace: Technology & Management of Minimum-Cost Space Missions.__ Rick Fleeter. 460p. 2000. 158.00 (*0-7923-6028-1*, Kluwer Plenum) Kluwer Academic.

Logic of Millennial Thought: Eighteenth-Century New England. James W. Davidson. LC 75-43315. (Yale Historical Publications: Miscellany: No. 112). 320p. reprint ed. pap. 99.20 (*0-8357-8734-6*, 203370300087) Bks Demand.

Logic of Mind. R. J. Nelson. 1982. lib. bdg. 171.00 (*90-277-1399-5*) Kluwer Academic.

Logic of Mind. enl. rev. ed. R. J. Nelson. 410p. (C). 1989. pap. text 59.50 (*90-277-2822-4*, Pub. by Kluwer Academic) Kluwer Academic.

Logic of Mind. 2nd enl. rev. ed. R. J. Nelson. 410p. (C). 1989. lib. bdg. 171.50 (*90-277-2819-4*, Pub. by Kluwer Academic) Kluwer Academic.

Logic of Modern Physics. Percy Williams Bridgman. Ed. by I. Bernard Cohen. LC 79-3117. (Three Centuries of Science in America Ser.). 1980. reprint ed. lib. bdg. 29.95 (*0-405-12594-1*) Ayer.

Logic of Modern Science. J. R. Kantor. 1953. 15.00 (*0-911188-40-1*) Principia Pr.

Logic of New Zealand Business: Strategy, Structure, & Performance. R. T. Hamilton & G. S. Shergill. (Illus.). 182p. 1994. text 42.00 (*0-19-558282-9*) OUP.

Logic of "Normalization" Fred Eidlin. (East European Monographs: No. 74). 278p. 1980. text 61.00 (*0-914710-68-0*, Pub. by East Eur Monographs) Col U Pr.

Logic of Nuclear Terror. Ed. by Roman Kolkowicz. 336p. 1987. text 44.95 (*0-04-497031-5*); pap. text 15.95 (*0-04-497032-3*) Routledge.

Logic of Opposites. Alane Rollings. LC 98-5806. 96p. 1998. text 35.00 (*0-8101-5081-6*); pap. text 14.95 (*0-8101-5082-4*, TriQuart) Northwestern U Pr.

Logic of Organization. Alfred Kuhn & Robert D. Beam. LC 82-48059. (Jossey-Bass Social & Behavioral Science Ser.). (Illus.). 537p. reprint ed. pap. 166.50 (*0-8357-4898-7*, 203782800009) Bks Demand.

Logic of Organizational Disorder. Ed. by Massimo Warglien & Michael Masuch. LC 95-22780. (Studies in Organization: No. 66). ix, 205p. (C). 1995. lib. bdg. 54.95 (*3-11-013707-0*) De Gruyter.

Logic of Organizations. Bengt Abrahamsson. LC 92-33509. (Illus.). 200p. (C). 1993. text 42.00 (*0-8039-5038-1*); pap. text 22.95 (*0-8039-5039-X*) Sage.

Logic of Partial Information. Areski N. Abdallah. LC 93-49421. (EATCS Monographs on Theoretical Computer Science). xxv, 715p. 1995. 98.00 (*0-387-56583-3*) Spr-Verlag.

Logic of Passion: The Literary Criticism of William Hazlitt. rev. ed. John L. Mahoney. LC 81-67501. 135p. reprint ed. pap. 41.90 (*0-7837-5879-0*, 204559900006) Bks Demand.

Logic of Peace. (Analysis Ser.: No. 22). 12.50 (*0-686-45491-X*) Inst Analysis.

*__Logic of Philosophy & the Doctrine of Categories.__ Emil Lask. Tr. by Christian Braun. 400p. 1999. 55.00 (*1-85343-474-4*, Pub. by Free Assoc Bks); pap. 25.00 (*1-85343-475-2*, Pub. by Free Assoc Bks) Intl Spec Bk.

Logic of Planned Economy: The Seeds of the Collapse. Pawe Dembinski. Tr. by Kevin Cook. 264p. 1991. 75.00 (*0-19-828686-4*) OUP.

Logic of Political Belief: A Philosophical Analysis of Ideology. Ian S. Adams. 224p. (C). 1989. text 61.00 (*0-389-20886-8*) B&N Imports.

Logic of Practice. Pierre Bourdieu. Tr. by Richard Nice from FRE. LC 88-63435. 337p. 1990. 47.50 (*0-8047-1727-3*); pap. 16.95 (*0-8047-2011-8*) Stanford U Pr.

Logic of Priorities. Thomas L. Saaty & Luis G. Vargas. 299p. 1991. pap. 50.00 (*0-9620317-3-9*) RWS Pubns.

An Asterisk (*) at the beginning of an entry indicates that the title is appearing for the first time.

Logic of Privatization: The Case of Telecommunications in the Southern Cone of Latin America, 182. Walter T. Molano. LC 96-18230. (Contributions in Economics & Economic History Ser.). 152p. 1997. 57.95 (*0-313-30055-0*) Greenwood.

Logic of Programming & Calculi of Discrete Design. Ed. by Manfred Broy. (NATO Asi Series F: Vol. 36). vii, 415p. 1987. 107.95 (*0-387-18003-6*) Spr-Verlag.

Logic of Programs Workshop Zuerich, 1979: Proceedings. Ed. by Erwin Engeler. (Lecture Notes in Computer Science Ser.: Vol. 125). 245p. 1981. 25.00 (*0-387-11160-3*) Spr-Verlag.

Logic of Provability. George Boolos. 314p. 1995. pap. text 25.95 (*0-521-48325-5*) Cambridge U Pr.

Logic of Racism. E. Ellis Cashmore. 288p. 1986. pap. text 16.95 (*0-04-301256-6*) Routledge.

Logic of Rational Theism: Exploratory Essays. Ed. by William L. Craig & Mark S. McLeod. LC 90-39313. (Problems in Contemporary Philosophy Ser.: Vol. 24). 260p. 1990. lib. bdg. 89.95 (*0-88946-369-7*) E Mellen.

Logic of Real Arguments. Alec Fisher. (Illus.). 208p. 1988. pap. text 16.95 (*0-521-31341-4*) Cambridge U Pr.

Logic of Reflection: German Philosophy in the Twentieth Century. Julian Roberts. 256p. (C). 1992. 37.50 (*0-300-05207-3*) Yale U Pr.

Logic of Regional Integration: Europe & Beyond. Walter Mattli. LC 98-11655. (Illus.). 214p. (C). 1999. text 54.95 (*0-521-63227-7*) Cambridge U Pr.

***Logic of Regional Integration: Europe & Beyond.** Walter Mattli. LC 98-11655. (Cambridge Studies in Comparative Politics). (Illus.). 240p. (C). 1999. pap. text 18.95 (*0-521-63536-5*) Cambridge U Pr.

Logic of Reliable Inquiry. Kevin T. Kelly. (Logic & Computation in Philosophy Ser.). (Illus.). 448p. 1996. text 70.00 (*0-19-509195-7*) OUP.

Logic of Religious Persuasion. John H. Whittaker. LC 89-27218. (American University Studies: Theology & Religion: Ser. VII, Vol. 71). 127p. 1989. text 28.95 (*0-8204-1211-2*) P Lang Pubng.

Logic of Saint Anselm. Henry. 1993. 63.95 (*0-7512-0130-8*) Ashgate Pub Co.

Logic of Science in Psychoanalysis. Benjamin B. Wolman. LC 84-1891. 332p. 1984. text 69.50 (*0-231-05744-X*) Col U Pr.

Logic of Science in Sociology. Walter L. Wallace. LC 71-149845. 139p. 1971. pap. text 23.95 (*0-202-30194-X*) Aldine de Gruyter.

Logic of Scientific Discovery. Gary J. Jason. (American University Studies: Philosophy: Ser. V, Vol. 46). XII, 360p. (C). 1988. text 43.95 (*0-8204-0569-8*) P Lang Pubng.

Logic of Scientific Discovery. 14th ed. Karl R. Popper. 480p. (C). 1992. pap. 34.99 (*0-415-07892-X*) Routledge.

Logic of Sense. Gilles Deleuze. Tr. by Mark Lester & Charles Stivale from FRE. (European Perspectives Ser.). 393p. (C). 1990. text 57.50 (*0-231-05982-5*) Col U Pr.

Logic of Sense. Gilles Deleuze. Tr. by Mark Lester & Charles Stivale from FRE. (European Perspectives Ser.). 393p. (C). 1993. pap. 19.00 (*0-231-05983-3*) Col U Pr.

Logic of Social Control. A. V. Horwitz. (Illus.). 310p. (C). 1990. 49.50 (*0-306-43475-X*, Plenum Trade) Perseus Pubng.

Logic of Social Inquiry. Scott Greer. 252p. 1989. pap. 24.95 (*0-88738-779-9*) Transaction Pubs.

Logic of Social Systems: A Unified, Deductive, System-Based Approach to Social Science. Alfred Kuhn. LC 73-20965. (Jossey-Bass Behavioral Science Ser.). 568p. reprint ed. pap. 176.10 (*0-8357-4990-8*, 203792300009) Bks Demand.

Logic of Solidarity: Commentaries on Pope John Paul II's Encyclical on Social Concern. Ed. by Gregory Baum & Robert Ellsberg. LC 89-27941. 248p. 1989. reprint ed. pap. 76.90 (*0-7837-9836-9*, 206056500005) Bks Demand.

Logic of Special Relativity. S. J. Prokhovnik. LC 67-13854. 142p. reprint ed. pap. 40.50 (*0-608-30418-2*, 2050785) Bks Demand.

Logic of Strategy. Ed. by Cristina Bicchieri et al. LC 98-50190. (Illus.). 208p. 1999. text 45.00 (*0-19-511715-8*) OUP.

Logic of Subchapter K: A Conceptual Approach to the Taxation of Partnership. Noel Cunningham & Laura Cunningham. LC 96-23920. 236p. (C). 1996. 21.00 (*0-314-20017-7*) West Pub.

Logic of Tax. Joseph M. Dodge. (Miscellaneous Ser.). 343p. (C). 1989. pap. 27.00 (*0-314-55868-3*) West Pub.

Logic of the Articles in Traditional Philosophy: A Contribution to the Study of Conceptual Structures. E. M. Barth. Tr. by P. Potts from DUT. LC 73-94452. (Synthese Historical Library: No. 10).Tr. of De Logica Van De Lidwoorden in De Traditionele Filosophy. 560p. 1974. lib. bdg. 211.50 (*90-277-0350-7*) Kluwer Academic.

Logic of the Articles in Traditional Philosophy: A Contribution to the Study of Conceptual Structures. E. M. Barth. Tr. by T. C. Potts. (Synthese Historical Library: No. 10).Tr. of De Logica Van De Lidwoorden in De Traditionele Filosophy. 560p. 1981. pap. text 51.50 (*90-277-1187-9*) Kluwer Academic.

Logic of the Believing Mind. Russell F. Aldwinckle. LC 94-40520. ii, 638p. 1995. write for info. (*0-7734-9068-X*) E Mellen.

***Logic of the Cultural Sciences: Five Studies.** Ernst Cassirer. Tr. & Intro. by S. G. Lofts. LC 00-25024. 208p. 2000. 30.00 (*0-300-08114-6*) Yale U Pr.

***Logic of the Cultural Sciences: Five Studies.** Ernst Cassirer & Steve G. Lofts. LC 00-25024. 208p. 2000. pap. 15.00 (*0-300-08115-4*) Yale U Pr.

Logic of the Gift. Ed. by Alan D. Schrift. LC 96-41607. 352p. (C). 1997. pap. 20.99 (*0-415-91099-4*) Routledge.

Logic of the Gift: Toward an Ethic of Generosity. Alan D. Schrift. LC 96-41607. 352p. (C). 1997. 75.00 (*0-415-91098-6*) Routledge.

Logic of the History of Ideas. Mark Bevir. LC 98-38079. 360p. (C). 1999. text 59.95 (*0-521-64034-2*) Cambridge U Pr.

Logic of the Latifundio: The Large Estates of Northwestern Costa Rica since the Late Nineteenth Century. Marc Edelman. (Illus.). 496p. (C). 1993. 57.50 (*0-8047-2044-4*) Stanford U Pr.

Logic of the Law. Gordon Tullock. 296p. (C). 1987. reprint ed. pap. text 30.50 (*0-8026-0018-2*) Univ Pub Assocs.

Logic of the Living Brain. Gerd Sommerhoff. LC 73-8198. (Illus.). 423p. reprint ed. pap. 131.20 (*0-608-17656-7*, 203051500069) Bks Demand.

Logic of the Living Present: Experience, Ordering, Onto-Poiesis of Culture Oriental-Occidental Phenomenology Dialogue. Ed. by Anna-Teresa Tymieniecka. LC 94-17872. (Analecta Husserliana Ser.: Vol. 46). 320p. (C). 1995. lib. bdg. 156.00 (*0-7923-2930-9*, Pub. by Kluwer Academic) Kluwer Academic.

Logic of the Sciences & the Humanities. F. S. Northrop. LC 83-60576. xiv, 402p. 1983. reprint ed. pap. 17.00 (*0-918024-31-5*) Ox Bow.

Logic of the Sciences & the Humanities. Filmer S. Northrop. LC 78-21524. 402p. 1979. reprint ed. lib. bdg. 35.00 (*0-313-21161-2*, NOLS, Greenwood Pr) Greenwood.

Logic of the Spirit: Human Development in Theological Perspective. James E. Loder. LC 98-29681. (Religion in Practice Ser.). 362p. 1998. pap. 27.95 (*0-7879-0919-X*) Jossey-Bass.

Logic of Theory Change: Proceedings of the Workshop, Konstanz, FRG, October 13-15. Ed. by A. Fuhrmann & Michael Morreau. (Lecture Notes in Artificial Intelligence Ser.: Vol. 465). x, 334p. 1991. 40.00 (*0-387-53567-5*) Spr-Verlag.

Logic of Time. J. V. Benthem. 1982. text 135.00 (*90-277-1421-5*) Kluwer Academic.

Logic of Time: A Model-Theoretic Investigation into the Varieties of Temporal Ontology & Temporal Discourse. 2nd rev. ed. John Van Bentham. 300p. (C). 1991. lib. bdg. 121.50 (*0-7923-1081-0*, Pub. by Kluwer Academic) Kluwer Academic.

Logic of Typed Feature Structures: With Applications to Unification Grammars, Logic Programs & Constraint Resolution. Robert L. Carpenter. (Cambridge Tracts in Theoretical Computer Science Ser.: No. 32). (Illus.). 280p. (C). 1992. text 39.95 (*0-521-41932-8*) Cambridge U Pr.

Logic of U. S. Nuclear Weapons Policy: A Philosophical Analysis. Corbin Fowler. LC 86-31196. (Problems in Contemporary Philosophy Ser.: Vol. 4). 272p. 1987. lib. bdg. 89.95 (*0-88946-330-1*) E Mellen.

Logic of Unity: The Discovery of Zero & Emptiness in Prajnaparamita Thought. Hosaku Matsuo. Tr. by Kenneth K. Inada. LC 86-5916. (SUNY Series in Buddhist Studies). 148p. (C). 1987. text 21.50 (*0-88706-391-8*) State U NY Pr.

Logic of Women on Trial: Case Studies of Popular American Trials. Janice Schuetz. LC 93-10125. 272p. (C). 1994. 36.95 (*0-8093-1869-5*); pap. 18.95 (*0-8093-1926-8*) S Ill U Pr.

Logic of Writing & the Organization of Society. Jack Goody. (Studies in Literacy, Family, Culture & the State). 232p. 1987. text 54.95 (*0-521-32745-8*); pap. text 17.95 (*0-521-33962-6*) Cambridge U Pr.

Logic on the Track of Social Change. David Braybrooke et al. (Clarendon Library of Logic & Philosophy). 292p. 1996. text 65.00 (*0-19-823530-5*) OUP.

Logic, Ontology & Language: Essays on Truth & Reality. Herbert Hochberg. (Analytica Ser.). 448p. 1984. lib. bdg. 119.00 (*3-88405-030-3*) Philosophia Pr.

Logic: or The Morphology of Knowledge. Bernard Bosanquet. 1986. reprint ed. lib. bdg. 53.95 (*0-935005-21-8*) Lincoln-Rembrandt.

Logic Posters, Problems & Puzzles: 4 Big Posters & Dozens of Brain Boosting Reproducibles. Honi Bamberger. (J). 1999. pap. 12.95 (*0-590-64273-1*) Scholastic Inc.

Logic Primer. Colin Allen et al. LC 92-11314. 171p. (C). 1992. pap. text 15.00 (*0-262-51065-0*, Bradford Bks) MIT Pr.

Logic Primer for Undergraduates. J. Daniel Brown. 165p. (C). 1991. pap. text. write for info. (*0-9629643-0-1*) J Daniel Brown.

Logic Primer for Undergraduates Solutions to Exercises. J. Daniel Brown. 36p. (C). 1991. teacher ed. write for info. (*0-9629643-1-X*) J Daniel Brown.

Logic, Probability, & Epistemology: The Power of Semantics. Sahotra Sarkar. LC 95-51785. (Science & Philosophy in the Twentieth Century Ser.: Vol. 3). 424p. 1996. reprint ed. text 85.00 (*0-8153-2264-X*) Garland.

Logic, Probability, & Presumptions in Legal Reasoning. Ed. by Scott Brewer & Robert Nozick. LC 98-5169. (Philosophy of Legal Reasoning Ser.: No. 1). 416p. 1998. reprint ed. text 75.00 (*0-8153-2655-6*) Garland.

Logic Program Synthesis & Transformation: Proceedings of International Workshop on Logic Program Synthesis & Transformation, Louvain-la-Neuve, Belgium, 7-9 July 1993. Ed. by Yves Deville. LC 93-45325. (Workshops in Computing Ser.). 1994. 71.95 (*0-387-19864-4*) Spr-Verlag.

Logic Program Synthesis & Transformation: Proceedings of LOPSTR 91, International Workshop on Logic Program Synthesis & Transformation University of Manchester, 4-5 July 1991. Ed. by Tim P. Clement et al. (Workshops in Computing Ser.). x, 337p. 1992. 59.00 (*0-387-19742-7*) Spr-Verlag.

Logic Program Synthesis & Transformation: Proceedings of LOPSTR '92, International Workshop on Logic Program Synthesis & Trasformation, University of Manchester, 2-3 July, 1992. Ed. by Kung-Kiu Lau & Tim P. Clement. LC 92-43296. (Workshops in Computing Ser.). 1993. 69.00 (*0-387-19806-7*) Spr-Verlag.

Logic Program Synthesis & Transformation: 5th International Workshop, LOPSTR'95, Utrecht, the Netherlands, September 20-22, 1995: Proceedings. Ed. by Maurizio Proietti. LC 96-10638. (Lecture Notes in Computer Science Ser.: Vol. 1048). x, 267p. 1996. pap. 49.00 (*3-540-60939-3*) Spr-Verlag.

Logic Program Synthesis & Transformation: 6th International Workshop, LOPSTR'96, Stockholm, Sweden, August 28-30, 1996, Proceedings. Ed. by J. Gallagher et al. (Lecture Notes in Computer Science Ser.: Vol. 1207). vii, 325p. 1997. pap. 55.00 (*3-540-62718-9*) Spr-Verlag.

Logic Program Synthesis & Transformation: 7th International Workshop, LOPSTR '97, Leuven, Belgium, July, 1997, Vol. 146. Norbert Fuchs. LC 98-42183. (Lecture Notes in Computer Science Ser.). 1998. pap. 59.00 (*3-540-65074-1*) Spr-Verlag.

Logic Program Synthesis & Transformation--Meta-Programming in Logic: Proceedings of the Fourth International Workshop, LOPSTR '94 & META '94, Held at Pisa, Italy, June 1994. International Workshop on Logic Program Synthesis. LC 94-43960. (Lecture Notes in Computer Science Ser.: Vol. 883). 451p. 1994. 62.00 (*0-387-58792-6*) Spr-Verlag.

Logic Program Synthesis from Incomplete Information. Pierre Flener. (International Series in Engineering & Computer Science, Natural Language Processing & Machine Translation). 264p. (C). 1994. text 120.00 (*0-7923-9532-8*) Kluwer Academic.

Logic Program Synthesis Transfer. 1994. 65.95 (*3-540-58792-6*) Spr-Verlag.

Logic Programming. Compiled by I. Balbin & K. Lecot. 1985. pap. text 98.50 (*0-908069-15-4*) Kluwer Academic.

Logic Programming: First Russian Conference on Logic Programming, Irkutsk, Russia, September 14-18, 1990: Second Russian Conference on Logic Programming, St. Petersburg, Russia, September 11-16, 1991 Proceedings. Ed. by A. Voronkov & Joerg H. Siekmann. LC 92-16288. (Lecture Notes in Computer Science, Lecture Notes in Artificial Intelligence Ser.: Vol. 592). ix, 514p. 1992. 76.95 (*0-387-55460-2*) Spr-Verlag.

Logic Programming: Formal Methods & Practical Applications. Ed. by Christoph Beierle & Lutz Plumer. LC 94-40114. (Studies in Computer Science & Artificial Intelligence). 418p. 1994. 158.50 (*0-444-82092-2*) Elsevier.

Logic Programming: Operational Semantics & Proof Theory. J. Andrews. (Distinguished Dissertations in Computer Science Ser.: No. 4). (Illus.). 116p. (C). 1993. text 49.95 (*0-521-43219-7*) Cambridge U Pr.

Logic Programming: Proceedings of the Fourteenth International Conference. Ed. by Lee Naish. (Logic Programming Ser.). (Illus.). 448p. (Orig.). 1997. pap. text 85.00 (*0-262-64035-X*) MIT Pr.

Logic Programming: Proceedings of the Seventh International Conference, 2 vols. Ed. by David H. Warren. (Research Reports & Notes). 750p. 1990. pap. text 60.00 (*0-262-73090-1*) MIT Pr.

Logic Programming: Proceedings of the Tenth International Conference on Logic Programming June 21-24 Budapest, Hungary. Ed. by David S. Warren. (Logic Programming Ser.). (Illus.). 880p. 1993. pap. text 75.00 (*0-262-73105-3*) MIT Pr.

Logic Programming: Proceedings of the 12th International Conference on Logic Programming. Ed. by Leon S. Sterling. (Logic Programming Series Research Reports & Notes). 854p. 1995. pap. text 88.00 (*0-262-69177-9*) MIT Pr.

Logic Programming: Proceedings of the 13th 1996 Joint International Conference & Symposium on Logic Programming, September 2-6, 1996, Bonn, Germany. Ed. by Michael Maher. (Logic Programming Ser.). (Illus.). 576p. 1996. pap. text 85.00 (*0-262-63173-3*) MIT Pr.

Logic Programming: Proceedings of the 1995 International Symposium, Dec. 4-7, Portland, Oregon. Ed. by John Lloyd. (Logic Programming Ser.). (Illus.). 800p. (C). 1995. pap. text 75.00 (*0-262-62099-5*) MIT Pr.

Logic Programming: Proceedings of the 1997 International Symposium. Ed. by Jan Maluszynski. (Logic Programming/Research Reports & Notes Ser.). (Illus.). 443p. 1997. pap. text 85.00 (*0-262-63180-6*) MIT Pr.

Logic Programming: Proceedings of the 1998 Joint International Conference & Symposium on Logic Programming. Ed. by Joxan Jaffar. 381p. 1998. pap. text 85.00 (*0-262-60031-5*) MIT Pr.

***Logic Programming: Proceedings of the 1999 International Conference on Logic Programming.** Ed. by Danny De Schreye. (Illus.). 450p. 1999. pap. 85.00 (*0-262-54104-1*) MIT Pr.

Logic Programming: Proceedings of the '93 International Symposium, Vancouver, British Columbia, October 26-29, 1993, Reports & Notes. Ed. by Dale Miller. (Logic Programming Ser.). (Illus.). 708p. 1993. pap. text 82.50 (*0-262-63152-0*) MIT Pr.

Logic Programming: Proceedings of 11th International Conference, June 13-16, 1994, Santa Margherita Ligure, Italy. Ed. by Pascal Van Hentenryck. (Logic Programming - Research Reports & Notes). 772p. 1994. pap. text 82.50 (*0-262-72022-1*) MIT Pr.

Logic Programming: Prolog & Stream Parallel Languages. Jan Newmarch. 288p. 1991. boxed set 35.00 (*0-13-539842-8*) P-H.

Logic Programming - New Frontiers. Ed. by D. R. Brough. (Diverse Ser.). 300p. (C). 1992. text 141.50 (*0-7923-1546-4*) Kluwer Academic.

Logic Programming & Automated Reasoning: Fifth International Conference, LPAR '94, Kiev, Uraine, July 16-22, 1994. Ed. by Frank Pfenning. LC 94-21152. (Lecture Notes in Computer Science; Lecture Notes in Artificial Intelligence Ser.). 1994. 55.95 (*0-387-58216-9*) Spr-Verlag.

Logic Programming & Automated Reasoning: Proceedings, International Conference, St. Petersburg, Russia, July 15-22, 1992. Ed. by A. Voronkov. LC 92-21886. 1992. write for info. (*3-540-55727-X*); 74.00 (*0-387-55727-X*) Spr-Verlag.

Logic Programming & Automated Reasoning: Proceedings of the Fourth International Conference, LPAR 93, St. Petersburg, Russia, July 13-20, 1993. Ed. by A. Voronkov. (Lecture Notes in Artificial Intelligence Ser.: Vol. 698). xiii, 386p. 1993. 55.95 (*0-387-56944-8*) Spr-Verlag.

***Logic Programming & Automated Reasoning: 6th International Conference, LPAR'99, Tbilisi, Georgia, September 6-10, 1999, Proceedings.** Ed. by H. Ganzinger et al. LC QA76.63.L73 1999. (Lecture Notes in Artificial Intelligence Ser.: Vol. 1705). xii, 397p. 1999. pap. 69.00 (*3-540-66492-0*) Spr-Verlag.

Logic Programming & Databases. S. Ceri et al. (Surveys in Computer Science Ser.). (Illus.). 368p. 1990. 56.95 (*0-387-51728-6*) Spr-Verlag.

Logic Programming & Knowledge Representation: Third International Workshop, LPKR'97, Port Jefferson, New York, USA, October 17, 1997, Selected Papers, Vol. 147. J. Van Leeuwen et al. Ed. by J. Dix et al. LC 98-38787. (Lecture Notes in Computer Science Ser.: Vol. 1471). ix, 246p. 1998. pap. 49.00 (*3-540-64958-1*) Spr-Verlag.

Logic Programming & Non-Monotonic Reasoning: Proceedings of the Second International Workshop. Ed. by Luis M. Pereira & Anil Nerode. (Illus.). 500p. 1993. pap. text 38.50 (*0-262-66083-0*) MIT Pr.

Logic Programming & Non-Monotonic Reasoning: Third International Conference, LPNMR '95, Lexington, KY, USA, June 24-26, 1995: Proceedings. Ed. by Wiktor Marek et al. (Lecture Notes in Computer Science Ser.: No. 928). 1995. write for info. (*0-387-59487-6*) Spr-Verlag.

Logic Programming & Non-Monotonic Reasoning: Third International Conference, LPNMR '95, Lexington, KY, USA, June 24-26, 1995: Proceedings. Ed. by Wiktor Marek et al. (Lecture Notes in Computer Science Ser.: No. 928). 415p. 1995. 68.00 (*3-540-59487-6*) Spr-Verlag.

Logic Programming & Nonmonotonic Reasoning: Proceedings, Fourth International Conference, LPNMR'97, Dagstuhl Castle, Germany, July 28-31, 1997. Ed. by J. Dix et al. LC 97-27551. (Lecture Notes in Artificial Intelligence: Vol. 1265). x, 453p. pap. write for info. (*3-540-63255-7*) Spr-Verlag.

***Logic Programming & Nonmonotonic Reasoning: Proceedings of the 5th International Conference, LPNMR '99, El Paso, Texas, U. S. A., December 2-4, 1999.** Ed. by M. Gelfond et al. LC 99-57419. (Lecture Notes in Artificial Intelligence Ser.: Vol. 1730). xi, 391p. 1999. pap. 69.00 (*3-540-66749-0*) Spr-Verlag.

Logic Programming in Action: Proceedings of Second International Logic Programming Summer School, Zurich, Switzerland, September 7-11, 1992. Ed. by G. Comyn et al. LC 92-28844. x, 324p. 1992. 52.00 (*0-387-55930-2*); pap. write for info. (*3-540-55930-2*) Spr-Verlag.

Logic Programming Languages: Constraints, Functions, & Objects. Ed. by K. R. Apt et al. LC 92-46899. (Logic Programming Ser.). (Illus.). 225p. 1993. 35.00 (*0-262-01134-4*) MIT Pr.

Logic Programming, 1988. Ed. by Koichi Furukawa et al. (Lecture Notes in Artificial Intelligence Ser.: Vol. 383). ix, 251p. 1989. 37.00 (*0-387-51564-X*) Spr-Verlag.

Logic Programming 1985. Ed. by E. Wada. (Lecture Notes in Computer Science Ser.: Vol 221). ix, 311p. 1986. 39.00 (*0-387-16479-0*) Spr-Verlag.

Logic Programming, 1989: Proceedings of the 8th Conference Tokyo, Japan, July 12-14, 1989. Ed. by Koichi Furukawa et al. ix, 183p. 1991. 25.95 (*0-387-53919-0*) Spr-Verlag.

Logic Programming 1986. Ed. by E. Wada. (Lecture Notes in Computer Science Ser.: Vol. 246). vi, 364p. 1987. 30.00 (*0-387-18024-9*) Spr-Verlag.

Logic Programming over Polymorphically Order-Sorted Types. G. Smolka. (Tracts in Theoretical Computer Science Ser.: No. 13). 250p. (C). 1999. text 29.95 (*0-521-39197-0*) Cambridge U Pr.

Logic Programming Paradigm: A 25-year Perspective. Ed. by Krzysztof R. Apt et al. LC 99-18481. (Artificial Intelligence Ser.). xiv, 457p. 1999. 62.00 (*3-540-65463-1*) Spr-Verlag.

Logic Programming Tutor. Jocelyn Paine. 320p. 1992. text 95.00 (*0-7923-1448-4*) Kluwer Academic.

Logic Programming Tutor. Joclyn Paine. 366p. 1992. pap. text 37.95 (*1-871516-09-9*, Pub. by Intellect) Cromland.

Logic, Proof, & Sets. 2nd ed. Marvin L. Bittinger. LC 81-14913. 144p. 1982. pap. text. write for info. (*0-201-10384-2*) Addison-Wesley.

Logic Puzzles. M. Fowler. (Superpuzzles Ser.). (Illus.). 48p. (J). (gr. 7-12). 1994. pap. 7.95 (*0-7460-0733-7*, Usborne) EDC.

Logic Puzzles. M. Fowler. (Superpuzzles Ser.). (Illus.). 48p. (J). (gr. 7 up). 1994. lib. bdg. 15.95 (*0-88110-527-9*, Usborne) EDC.

An Asterisk (*) at the beginning of an entry indicates that the title is appearing for the first time.

L

Logic Puzzles Decoded see Increase Your Puzzle IQ: Tips & Tricks to Increase Your Logic Power

Logic Questions & Answers. Harrison. Date not set. pap. text. write for info. (*0-314-00054-2*) West Pub.

Logic, Science, & Dialectic: Collected Papers in Greek Philosophy. G. E. Owen. LC 85-17479. 394p. pap. text 27.50 (*0-8014-9359-5*) Cornell U Pr.

Logic, Science & Dialectic In Greek Collected Papers G. E. Owen. 394p. 1986. text 57.50 (*0-8014-1726-0*) Cornell U Div Nutrit Scis.

Logic, Semantics, Metamathematics. 2nd ed. Alfred Tarski. Ed. by John Corcoran. Tr. by J. H. Woodger. LC 83-10850. 520p. (C). 1983. reprint ed. pap. text 29.95 (*0-915144-76-X*); reprint ed. lib. bdg. 50.00 (*0-915144-75-1*) Hackett Pub.

Logic, Semiotics & Methodology: Logik, Semiotik, Methodologie. E. Albrecht. (GER & RUS.). 290p. 1983. 39.95 (*0-8288-2276-X*, M15207) Fr & Eur.

Logic Set, 3 bks., Set. Mark Schoenfield & Jeanette Rosenblatt. (J). (gr. 5-7). 25.99 (*1-56417-742-4*, FE7424) Fearon Teacher Aids.

***Logic, Sets & Functions.** Daniel Bonevac et al. 296p. (C). 1999. per. 56.95 (*0-7872-6355-9*, 41635501) Kendall-Hunt.

Logic, Sets & Numbers. 2nd ed. Roethel. (Math). 1976. 23.25 (*0-534-00491-1*) Brooks-Cole.

Logic, Sets, & Recursion. Robert L. Causey. LC 93-6375. 416p. 1994. 57.50 (*0-86720-463-X*) Jones & Bartlett.

Logic Supplement. Scott Surgent. 1997. pap. text 4.95 (*0-7167-3267-X*) W H Freeman.

Logic Synthesis. Srinivas Devadas et al. LC 93-41524. 448p. 1993. 55.00 (*0-07-016500-9*) McGraw.

Logic Synthesis & Optimization. Tsutomou Sasao. LC 92-35290. (International Series in Engineering & Computer Science, VLSI, Computer Architecture, & Digital Screen Processing: Vol. 212). 392p. (C). 1993. text 149.50 (*0-7923-9308-2*) Kluwer Academic.

Logic Synthesis & Verification Algorithms. Gary D. Hachtel & Fabio Somenzi. LC 96-21769. 600p. (C). 1996. text 114.00 (*0-7923-9746-0*) Kluwer Academic.

Logic Synthesis for Control Automata. Samary Baranov. LC 94-12288. 408p. (C). 1994. text 173.50 (*0-7923-9458-5*) Kluwer Academic.

Logic Synthesis for Field-Programmable Gate Arrays. Rajeev Murgai. (Kluwer International Series in Engineering & Computer Science). 448p. (C). 1995. text 126.50 (*0-7923-9596-4*) Kluwer Academic.

Logic Synthesis for Integrated Circuit Design, Selected Papers On. A. R. Newton. 144p. 1987. pap. 39.95 (*0-87942-236-X*, PP02261) Inst Electrical.

Logic Synthesis for Low Power VLSI Designs. Sasan Iman & Massoud Pedram. LC 97-42097. 256p. 1997. text 115.50 (*0-7923-8076-2*, D Reidel) Kluwer Academic.

Logic Synthesis Using Synopsys. Pran Kurup & Taher Abbasi. LC 95-17186. 328p. (C). 1995. text 139.00 (*0-7923-9582-4*) Kluwer Academic.

Logic Synthesis Using Synopsys. 2nd ed. Pran Kurup & Taher Abbasi. LC 96-38284. 344p. (C). 1996. text 120.00 (*0-7923-9786-X*) Kluwer Academic.

Logic, Theory of Sets & Quantum Mechanics see Collected Works

Logic Thinker Sheets. Becky Daniel. 64p. (J). (gr. 4-8). 1989. 8.99 (*0-86653-505-5*, GA1099) Good Apple.

Logic Tools for Programming. Philip Pace & Larry Pace. 320p. (C). 1987. pap. 31.95 (*0-8273-2582-7*) Delmar.

Logic Tools for Programming. Philip Pace & Larry Pace. 320p. (C). 1987. teacher ed. 10.00 (*0-8273-2583-5*) Delmar.

***Logic, Truth & the Modalities: From a Phenomenological Perspective** Jitendranath Mohanty. LC 98-33160. (Synthese Library). 1999. write for info. (*0-7923-5550-4*) Kluwer Academic.

Logic, Values, & Ethical Analysis. 2nd ed. Richard Wilson. 220p. (C). 1996. pap. text, per. 30.95 (*0-7872-3322-6*, 41332201) Kendall-Hunt.

Logic with Symlog. Arthur Portoraro. LC 93-14976. 512p. (C). 1993. 79.00 (*0-13-327628-7*) P-H.

Logic with Trees: An Introduction to Symbolic Logic. Colin Howson. LC 96-7315. 224p. (C). 1997. 75.00 (*0-415-13341-6*); pap. 23.99 (*0-415-13342-4*) Routledge.

Logic Workbook. Elihu Carranza. Ed. & Intro. by John W. Robbins. 140p. 1992. pap., student ed. 11.95 (*0-940931-34-6*) Trinity Found.

Logic-Works 4: Interactive Circuit Design Software. 421p. (C). 1998. pap. text 84.00 incl. cd-rom, audio compact disk (*0-201-32682-5*, Prentice Hall) P-H.

Logica de la Emocion y del Esponsor. Paolo Girone & Beppe Zigoni. (SPA.). 385p. 1993. pap. 29.00 (*84-7978-097-5*, Pub. by Ediciones Diaz) IBD Ltd.

Logica Demonstrativa. Hieronymus Saccherius. (GER.). iv, 309p. 1980. reprint ed. write for info. (*3-487-07012-X*) G Olms Pubs.

Logica et Philosophia Algazelis Arabis & Philosophie Als Denken der Welt Gemass Dem Princip des Kleinsten Kraftmasses. Abu H. Gazali & Richard Avenarius. xiii, 82p. reprint ed. write for info. (*0-318-71510-4*) G Olms Pubs.

Logica in Usum Auditorii Sui Ordine Scientifico. Christian Wolff & Andreas Bohm. (Gesammelte Werke Ser.: Series II, Bd. 41). (GER.). 244p. 1997. write for info. (*3-487-10496-2*) G Olms Pubs.

Logica Magna, Fascicule 5 Pt. 2: Capitula de Conditionali et de Rationali. Paul-of-Venice. Ed. by G. E. Hughes. (Classical & Midieval Logic Texts Ser.: Vol. VI). 592p. 1990. pap. 59.00 (*0-19-726094-2*) OUP.

Logica Magna, Fascicule 3 Pt. 2: Tractatus de Hypotheticis. Paul of Venice. Ed. by Alexander Broadie. (Classical & Medieval Logic Texts Ser.: Vol. VII). 420p. 1990. pap. 59.00 (*0-19-726095-0*) OUP.

Logica Post-Moderna. John Roscoe. LC 93-37303. (Revisioning Philosophy Ser.: Vol. 16). 1994. write for info. (*0-8204-2352-1*) P Lang Pubng.

Logica (Seu Summulae) Paulus Venetus. 230p. 1973. reprint ed. write for info. (*0-318-71286-5*) G Olms Pubs.

Logical Allies. Warriner. 2000. pap. text. write for info. (*0-312-18307-0*) St Martin.

Logical Alternatives: Studies in the Philosophy of Logic & Existence. John Bryant. write for info. (*0-9617444-6-4*) Socratic Pr.

Logical Analysis. (C). 1981. 28.00 (*0-8087-2988-8*) Pearson Custom.

Logical Analysis & Contemporary Theism. John Donnelly. LC 77-168693. 351p. reprint ed. pap. 108.90 (*0-7837-0443-7*, 204076600018) Bks Demand.

Logical & Legal Bases of the Conflict of Laws. Walter W. Cook. LC 43-268. (Harvard Studies in the Conflict of Laws: Vol. 5). xx, 473p. 1978. reprint ed. lib. bdg. 50.00 (*0-89941-130-4*, 300170) W S Hein.

Logical & Logico-Mathematical Calculi, 2: Proceedings. Ed. by V. P. Orevkov. LC 74-8854. 183p. 1974. pap. 66.00 (*0-8218-3021-X*, STEKLO/121) Am Math.

Logical & Mathematical Methods for the IBM Microcomputers. Julio Sanchez. (Illus.). 462p. 1991. per. 74.95 (*0-8493-4288-0*, QA76) CRC Pr.

Logical & Philosophical Papers, 1909-1913. Bertrand Russell. Ed. by John G. Slater & Bernd Frohmann. LC 92-2380. (Collected Papers of Bertrand Russell: Vol. 6). (Illus.). 682p. (C). (gr. 13). 1992. 175.00 (*0-415-08446-6*, A9414) Routledge.

Logical Approach to Chess. Max Euwe et al. (Chess Ser.). (Illus.). 224p. 1982. reprint ed. pap. 6.95 (*0-486-24353-2*) Dover.

Logical Approach to Discrete Math. David Gries & Fred B. Schneider. LC 93-27848. (Texts & Monographs in Computer Science). (Illus.). 497p. 1997. 44.95 (*0-387-94115-0*) Spr-Verlag.

Logical Approach to Discrete Math 3rd ed. David Gries & Fred B. Schneider. LC 95-200128. (Texts & Monographs in Computer Science Ser.). xvi, 497p. 1995. write for info. (*3-540-94115-0*) Spr-Verlag.

***Logical Approach to God.** Cinda L. Smaagaard. LC 99-96893. 2000. 16.95 (*0-533-13359-9*) Vantage.

Logical Approach to Syntax: Foundations, Specifications & Implementations of Theories of Government & Binding. Edward P. Stabler, Jr. (Illus.). 452p. 1993. 49.50 (*0-262-19315-9*) MIT Pr.

Logical Approach to Systems Theory. Shingo Takahaski & Yasuhiko Takahara. Ed. by M. Thoma. LC 95-10722. (Lecture Notes in Control & Information Sciences: Vol. 204). (Illus.). 185p. 1995. 43.00 (*3-540-19956-X*) Spr-Verlag.

Logical Argument in the Research Paper. Russ Ward. LC 96-76274. 318p. (C). 1996. pap. text 19.50 (*0-15-502648-8*, Pub. by Harcourt Coll Pubs) Harcourt.

Logical Aspects of Computational Linguistics: Second International Conference, LACL '97, Nancy, France, September 22-24, 1997, Selected Papers. Ed. by A. Lecomte et al. LC 99-14930. (Lecture Notes in Computer Science Ser.: Vol. 1582). xi, 251p. 1999. pap. 52.00 (*3-540-65751-7*) Spr-Verlag.

Logical Aspects of Computational Linguistics: Selected Papers, 1st International Conference, LACL '96, Nancy, France, April 23-25, 1996. Ed. by Christian Retore. LC 97-43015. (Lecture Notes in Artificial Intelligence Ser.: Vol. 1328). viii, 435p. 1997. pap. 67.00 (*3-540-63700-1*) Spr-Verlag.

Logical Basis for Computer Programming: Combined Volume. Zohar Manna & Richard Waldinger. (Computer Science Ser.). (Illus.). 736p. (C). 1999. 55.95 (*0-201-54886-0*) Addison-Wesley.

Logical Basis for Computer Programming Vol. I: Informal Reasoning. Zohar Manna & Richard Waldinger. 632p. (C). 1985. 49.95 (*0-201-18260-2*) Addison-Wesley.

Logical Basis of Metaphysics. Michael Dummett. LC 90-39999. (William James Lectures). 376p. 1991. 49.50 (*0-674-53785-8*, DUMLOG) HUP.

Logical Basis of Metaphysics. Michael Dummett. (William James Lectures). 376p. (C). 1993. pap. 23.95 (*0-674-53786-6*) HUP.

Logical Basis of Teaching. A. E. Hickey & J. M. Newton. 86p. 1974. reprint ed. pap. text 15.00 (*0-87567-104-7*) Entelek.

Logical Bridge Play. Hugh Kelsey. 192p. 1995. pap. 15.95 (*0-575-05941-9*, Pub. by V Gollancz) Trafalgar.

Logical Business Engineering Analysis. Brian Dickinson. (Business Engineering Ser.). (Illus.). 250p. 1999. pap. text 29.95 (*0-9629276-5-1*) LCI Pr.

Logical Choice: How Political Commercials Use Logic to Win Votes. Elizabeth M. Hughes. 182p. (Orig.). (C). 1994. pap. text 27.50 (*0-8191-9724-6*); lib. bdg. 46.00 (*0-8191-9723-8*) U Pr of Amer.

Logical Criticisms of Textual Criticism. Gordon H. Clark. (Trinity Papers: No. 16). 60p. 1986. pap. 3.25 (*0-940931-16-8*) Trinity Found.

Logical Criticisms of Textual Criticism. 2nd ed. Gordon H. Clark. Ed. & Intro. by John W. Robbins. 60p. 1990. pap. 3.25 (*0-940931-93-1*) Trinity Found.

Logical Data Base Design. 2nd ed. Paul E. Jones & Robert W. Curtice. LC 88-11385. 275p. reprint ed. pap. 85.30 (*0-7837-5889-8*, 204561200006) Bks Demand.

Logical Derivation of Computer Programs. Thomas G. Windeknecht. 240p. 1999. 34.95 (*1-871516-98-6*, Pub. by Intellect) Intl Spec Bk.

Logical Design of Automation System. Sander B. Friedman. 208p. 1989. boxed set 40.00 (*0-685-27162-5*) P-H.

Logical Design of Digital Computers. Montgomery Phister, Jr. LC 58-6082. 424p. reprint ed. pap. 131.50 (*0-608-10265-2*, 201648200004) Bks Demand.

Logical Design of Multiple Microprocessor Systems. B. A. Bowen & Behr. (Illus.). 272p. 1980. text 48.00 (*0-13-539908-4*) P-H.

Logical Dilemmas: The Life & Work of Kurt Godel. John Dawson. LC 96-50001. (Illus.). 376p. 1996. 49.95 (*1-56881-025-3*) AK Peters.

Logical Effort: Designing Fast CMOS Circuits. Ivan E. Sutherland et al. LC 98-53860. 250p. 1999. pap. text 42.95 (*1-55860-557-6*, Pub. by Morgan Kaufmann) Harcourt.

Logical Empiricism & the Special Sciences: Reichenbach, Feigl, & Nagel. Sahotra Sarkar. LC 95-48265. (Science & Philosophy in the Twentieth Century Ser.: Vol. 4). 376p. 1996. reprint ed. text 83.00 (*0-8153-2265-8*) Garland.

Logical Empiricism at Its Peak: Schlick, Carnap, & Neurath. Maria Neurath et al. LC 96-26649. (Science & Philosophy in the Twentieth Century Ser.: Vol. 2). 424p. 1996. reprint ed. text 80.00 (*0-8153-2263-1*) Garland.

Logical Enterprise. Ed. by Alan R. Anderson et al. LC 74-20084. 271p. reprint ed. pap. 84.10 (*0-8357-8735-4*, 203366000087) Bks Demand.

Logical Environments. Ed. by Gerard Huet & G. Plotkin. (Illus.). 352p. (C). 1993. text 69.95 (*0-521-43312-6*) Cambridge U Pr.

Logical Form: From GB to Minimalism. Norbert Hornstein. (Gererative Syntax Ser.). 288p. (C). 1995. pap., per. 29.95 (*0-631-18942-4*) Blackwell Pubs.

Logical Form: Its Structure & Derivation. Robert May. 280p. 1985. pap. text 21.00 (*0-262-63102-4*) MIT Pr.

Logical Form in Natural Language. William G. Lycan. 360p. 1984. 39.50 (*0-262-12108-5*, Bradford Bks) MIT Pr.

Logical Form in Natural Language. William G. Lycan. 360p. 1986. pap. text 12.50 (*0-262-62053-7*, Bradford Bks) MIT Pr.

Logical Form of Negation: A Study of Operator-Variable Structures in Syntax. Paolo Acquaviva. LC 97-12392. (Outstanding Dissertations in Linguistics Ser.). 336p. 1997. text 74.00 (*0-8153-2845-1*) Garland.

***Logical Foundations for Cognitive Agents: Contributions in Honor of Ray Reiter.** Ed. by H. J. Levesque et al. LC 99-23785. (Artificial Intelligence Ser.). 400p. 1999. 56.00 (*3-540-66012-7*) Spr-Verlag.

Logical Foundations of Artificial Intelligence. Nils J. Nilsson & Michael Genesereth. LC 87-5461. (Illus.). 406p. 1980. text 63.95 (*0-934613-31-1*) Morgan Kaufmann.

Logical Foundations of Computer Science: Proceedings of the Third International Symposoium, LFCS '94, St. Petersburg, Russia, July 11-14, 1994. Ed. by Anil Nerode & Y. V. Matiyasevich. LC 94-19257. 1994. 61.95 (*0-387-58140-5*) Spr-Verlag.

Logical Foundations of Computer Science: 4th International Symposium, LFCS '97, Yaroslavl, Russia, July, 6-12, 1997, Proceedings. Ed. by S. I. Adian et al. LC 97-20865. (Lecture Notes in Computer Science Ser.: No. 1234). ix, 431p. 1997. pap. 67.00 (*3-540-63045-7*) Spr-Verlag.

Logical Foundations of Computer Science - Tver '92: Second International Symposium, Tver, Russia, July 20-24, 1992, Proceedings. Ed. by Anil Nerode et al. LC 92-18642. (Lecture Notes in Computer Science Ser.: Vol. 620). ix, 514p. 1992. 76.95 (*0-387-55707-5*) Spr-Verlag.

***Logical Foundations of Constitutional Liberty.** James M. Buchanan. LC 98-45534. (Collected Works of James M. Buchanan : Vol. I). 1999. 20.00 (*0-86597-213-3*); pap. 12.00 (*0-86597-214-1*) Liberty Fund.

Logical Foundations of Mathematics. William S. Hatcher. LC 80-41253. (Foundations & Philosophy of Science & Technology Ser.). 400p. 1982. 144.00 (*0-08-025800-X*, Pub. by Pergamon Repr) Franklin.

Logical Foundations of Statistical Inference. Henry E. Kyburg, Jr. LC 72-92530. (Synthese Library: No. 65). 436p. 1974. pap. text 73.50 (*90-277-0430-9*, D Reidel) Kluwer Academic.

Logical Foundations of Statistical Inference. Henry E. Kyburg, Jr. LC 72-92530. (Synthese Library: No. 65). 436p. 1974. lib. bdg. 152.00 (*90-277-0330-2*, D Reidel) Kluwer Academic.

Logical Foundations of the Marxian Theory of Value. Adolfo Garcia De La Sienra. LC 92-14028. (Synthese Library: Vol. 223). 240p. (C). 1992. lib. bdg. 123.00 (*0-7923-1778-5*, Pub. by Kluwer Academic) Kluwer Academic.

Logical Frameworks. Ed. by Gedeon Huet & G. Plotkin. 415p. (C). 1991. text 85.00 (*0-521-41300-1*) Cambridge U Pr.

Logical Frameworks for Truth & Abstraction: An Axiomatic Study. Andrea Cantini. LC 96-4681. (Studies in Logic & the Foundations of Mathematics Ser.: Vol. 135). 474p. 1996. text 143.50 (*0-444-82306-9*, North Holland) Elsevier.

Logical Geometries. Peter Ganick. 28p. (Orig.). 1993. pap. 5.00 (*0-926935-83-6*) Runaway Spoon.

Logical Influence of Hegel on Marx. Rebecca Cooper. 1974. lib. bdg. 250.00 (*0-8490-0550-7*) Gordon Pr.

Logical Introduction to Databases. John Grant. (Illus.). 480p. (C). 1995. text 52.95 (*0-15-551175-0*) OUP.

***Logical Investigations.** J. N. Findlay & Edmund Husserl. 913p. 2000. pap. 89.95 (*1-57392-866-6*) Prometheus Bks.

Logical Investigations, 2 vols., Set. Edmund Husserl. Tr. by J. N. Findlay. (International Library of Philosophy & Scientific Method). (C). 1970. reprint ed. text 150.00 (*0-391-00053-5*) Humanities.

Logical Issues in Language Acquisition. Ed. by Iggy M. Roca. (Linguistic Models Ser.: No. 15). xxiii, 298p. (Orig.). (C). 1990. pap. text 92.35 (*3-11-013373-3*) Mouton.

***Logical Japanese, 1.** 2nd ed. (C). 1998. 18.40 (*0-8087-9637-2*) Pearson Custom.

Logical Japanese, 2. (C). 1996. write for info. (*0-8087-3073-8*) Pearson Custom.

Logical Japanese, 3. (C). 1997. 16.40 (*0-8087-9625-9*) Pearson Custom.

Logical Journey from Godel to Philosophy. Hao Wang. LC 96-32568. 405p. 1997. 45.00 (*0-262-23189-1*, Bradford Bks) MIT Pr.

Logical Learning Theory: A Human Teleology & Its Empirical Support. Joseph F. Rychlak. LC 93-49664. xix, 387p. 1994. text 45.00 (*0-8032-3904-1*) U of Nebr Pr.

Logical Logic. Barbara Gregorich. (Enrichment & Gifted Ser.). (Illus.). 48p. (J). (gr. 5-8). 1986. pap. 6.95 (*0-88160-123-3*, LW 1003) Learning Wks.

***"Logical" Luther Lee & the Methodist War Against Slavery.** Paul L. Kaufman. Ed. by Donald W. Dayton & Kenneth E. Rowe. LC 99-41934. (Studies in Evangelicalism: No. 17). 304p. 2000. 59.50 (*0-8108-3710-2*) Scarecrow.

Logical Magician. Robert Weinberg. 240p. (Orig.). 1994. mass mkt. 4.99 (*0-441-00059-2*) Ace Bks.

Logical Methods: A Text-Workbook for a General Education Course in Logic. 3rd ed. Elizabeth R. Eames et al. 236p. 1993. pap. text 15.80 (*0-87563-463-X*) Stipes.

Logical Methods: In Honor of Anil Nerode's Sixtieth Birthday. Ed. by John N. Crossley et al. LC 93-21451. (Progress in Computer Science & Applied Logic Ser.: Vol. 12). 1993. 115.00 (*0-8176-3690-0*) Birkhauser.

Logical Models of Legal Argumentation. Giovanni Sartor. Ed. by Henry Prakken. LC 96-53465. 216p. (C). 1997. lib. bdg. 99.50 (*0-7923-4413-8*) Kluwer Academic.

Logical Number Theory: An Introduction, No. I. C. Smorynski. (Illus.). 408p. 1991. 61.95 (*0-387-52236-0*) Spr-Verlag.

Logical Nursing Mathematics. Bruce L. Wilson. 128p. (C). 1987. pap. 23.00 (*0-8273-2934-2*) Delmar.

Logical Nursing Mathematics. Bruce L. Wilson. 128p. (C). 1987. teacher ed. 12.95 (*0-8273-2935-0*); disk 36.75 (*0-8273-2936-9*) Delmar.

Logical Physics. A. A. Zinoviev. 304p. 1983. text 191.50 (*90-277-0734-0*, D Reidel) Kluwer Academic.

Logical Physics on the Uncertainty Principle Is a Cop-Out: A Comprehensive Theory of Atomic Structure & Behavior from Physics to Astronomy. Cecil Ross. LC 97-65061. 217p. 1997. pap. 23.50 (*0-9649888-1-X*) RIE.

Logical Positivism. A. J. Ayer. 1966. pap. 18.95 (*0-02-901130-2*) Free Pr.

Logical Positivism. Alfred Jules Ayer. LC 78-6321. 455p. 1978. reprint ed. lib. bdg. 89.50 (*0-313-20462-4*, AYLP, Greenwood Pr) Greenwood.

Logical Positivism & Analysis. L. Susan Stebbing. 1974. lib. bdg. 35.00 (*0-8490-2180-4*) Gordon Pr.

Logical Positivism, Pragmatism & Scientific Empiricism. Charles W. Morris. LC 75-3285. reprint ed. 29.50 (*0-404-59273-2*) AMS Pr.

Logical Propaedeutic: Pre-School of Reasonable Discourse. Wilhelm Kamlah & Paul Lorenzen. Tr. by Hoke Robinson from GER. Orig. Title: Logische Propadeutik. 220p. (Orig.). 1984. lib. bdg. 46.00 (*0-8191-3638-7*) U Pr of Amer.

Logical Rational Solutions. Harrison. Date not set. pap. text. write for info. (*0-314-82965-2*) West Pub.

Logical Reasoning. Jack Rudman. (General Aptitude & Abilities Ser.: Vol. CS-47). 1994. pap. 27.95 (*0-8373-6747-6*) Nat Learn.

Logical Reasoning with Diagrams. Ed. by Gerard Allwein & Jon Barwise. (Studies in Logic & Computation: No. 6). (Illus.). 288p. 1996. text 55.00 (*0-19-510427-7*) OUP.

Logical Relations in Chinese & the Theory of Grammar. C. T. Huang. LC 98-39398. (Outstanding Dissertations in Linguistics Ser.). 456p. 1998. 89.00 (*0-8153-3136-3*) Garland.

Logical Self Defense. Ralph Johnson & Anthony Blair. 384p. (C). 1994. 35.00 (*0-07-032666-5*) McGraw.

Logical Self-Defense. 3rd ed. Johnson. 1994. teacher ed. 25.00 (*0-07-032698-3*) McGraw.

Logical Semiotics & Mereology. Richard M. Martin. LC 91-41368. (Foundations of Semiotics Ser.: No. 16). xiii, 282p. 1992. 89.00 (*90-272-3288-1*) J Benjamins Pubng Co.

Logical Space. James Reineking. LC 74-82737. (Illus.). 90p. 1975. 25.00 (*0-8150-0703-5*) Oolp Pr.

Logical Status of Diagrams. Sun-Joo Shin. LC 94-8822. (Illus.). 209p. (C). 1995. text 44.95 (*0-521-46157-X*) Cambridge U Pr.

Logical Structure & Linguistic Structure: Cross-Linguistic Perspectives. Ed. by C. T. Huang & Robert May. (Studies in Linguistics & Philosophy). 296p. 1991. lib. bdg. 108.50 (*0-7923-0914-6*) Kluwer Academic.

Logical Structure & Linguistic Structure: Cross-Linguistic Perspectives. C. T. Huang & Robert May. (Studies in Linguistics & Philosophy). 312p. (C). 1992. pap. text 39.00 (*0-7923-1636-3*) Kluwer Academic.

Logical Structure of Linguistic Theory. Noam Chomsky. LC 84-16211. 592p. 1985. pap. text 17.50 (*0-226-10436-2*) U Ch Pr.

Logical Structure of Mathematical Physics. 2nd rev. ed. Joseph D. Sneed. (Synthese Library, 35 - Pallas Paperbacks, 14). 345p. 1979. pap. text 52.00 (*90-277-1059-7*, D Reidel) Kluwer Academic.

Logical Structure of Psychological Common Sense. Jan Smedslund. LC 97-23186. 125p. 1997. write for info. (*0-8058-2903-2*) L Erlbaum Assocs.

Logical Structures for Representation of Knowledge & Uncertainty. Ellen Hisdal. Ed. by J. Kacprzyk. LC 97-39316. (Studies in Fuzziness & Soft Computing: Vol. 14). (Illus.). xxiv, 419p. 1998. 109.00 (*3-7908-1056-8*) Spr-Verlag.

An Asterisk (*) at the beginning of an entry indicates that the title is appearing for the first time.

Logical Studies in Early Analytic Philosophy. Nino B. Cocchiarella. LC 87-1584. 309p. reprint ed. pap. 95.80 (*0-608-09663-6*, 206977800006) Bks Demand.

Logical Theory & Semantic Analysis: Essays Dedicated to Stig Kanger on His Fiftieth Birthday. Soren Stenlund et al. Ed. by Ann-Mari Henshen-Dahlquist. LC 73-94456. (Synthese Library: No. 63). 221p. 1974. text 121.50 (*90-277-0438-4*, D Reidel) Kluwer Academic.

Logical Theory of Teaching: Erotetics & Intentionality. C. J. MacMillan & James W. Garrison. (Philosophy & Education Ser.: No. 1). 254p. (C). 1988. text 137.50 (*90-277-2813-5*) Kluwer Academic.

Logical Thinking. Richard L. Purtill. 174p. (C). 1992. reprint ed. pap. text 19.50 (*0-8191-8493-4*) U Pr of Amer.

Logical Thinking: An Introduction to Logic. 2nd ed. James Stuart. (C). 1997. pap. 24.69 (*0-07-289622-1*) McGrw-H Hghr Educ.

Logical Thinking about a Future Society see Pensando Logicamente Sobre una Sociedad Futura

Logical Thinking about a Future Society. Harvey Jackins. 1990. pap. 3.00 (*0-913937-41-X*) Rational Isl.

Logical Thinking Reader. Howard Snyder. 68p. (C). 1996. pap. text, per. 37.95 (*0-7872-2240-2*, 41224001) Kendall-Hunt.

Logical Thoughts at Four O'Clock A. M. S. Weiner & G. K. McMillan. 118p. 1991. pap. 20.00 (*1-55617-332-6*) ISA.

Logical Tools for Modelling Legal Argument: A Study of Defeasible Reasoning in Law. Henry Prakken. LC 97-31600. (Law & Philosophy Library). 328p. 1997. lib. bdg. 147.00 (*0-7923-4776-5*) Kluwer Academic.

Logical Understanding of Mathematics. (J). (gr. 4-6). 1996. text 50.00 (*0-9655937-0-3*) Logical Connect.

Logical Universe: The Real Universe. Noel Curran. (Avebury Series in Philosophy). 176p. 1994. 66.95 (*1-85628-863-3*, Pub. by Avebry) Ashgate Pub Co.

Logical Way of Doing Things. Karel Lambert. LC 69-15450. 338p. reprint ed. pap. 104.80 (*0-608-30820-X*, 201318400086) Bks Demand.

Logical Works, 2 vols. George Boole. Incl. Vol. 1. Studies in Logic & Probability. 500p. 1952. 29.95 (*0-87548-038-1*); Vol. 2. Laws of Thought. 464p. 1952. 31.95 (*0-87548-039-X*); 1952. write for info. (*0-318-54786-4*) Open Court.

Logical Writings. Jacques Herbrand. Ed. by Warren D. Golfarb. LC 74-146963. 322p. 1971. 35.00 (*0-674-53835-8*) HUP.

Logical Writings. Jacques Herbrand. Ed. by Warren D. Goldfarb. LC 74-146963. 312p. 1971. text 126.50 (*90-277-0176-8*, D Reidel) Kluwer Academic.

Logiciels pour l'Analyse Bioeconomique des Pecheries Beam 3: Simulation Bioeconomique Analytique de Pecheries de Crevettes Tropicales avec Recrutement Fixe ou Aleatoire. (FRE.). 63p. 1990. 12.00 (*92-5-202945-1*, FF9451, Pub. by FAO) Bernan Associates.

Logico-Algebraic Approach to Quantum Mechanics Vol. II: Contemporary Consolidation. Ed. by C. A. Hooker. (University of Western Ontario Series in Phylosophy of Science: No. 5b). 486p. 1979. pap. text 76.00 (*90-277-0709-X*); lib. bdg. 194.00 (*90-277-0707-3*) Kluwer Academic.

Logico-Linguistic Papers. R. M. Martin. (Publications in Language Sciences). xii, 202p. 1981. 67.70 (*90-70176-39-4*); pap. 50.00 (*90-70176-93-9*) Mouton.

Logico-Philosophical Studies. Ed. by A. Menne. Tr. by Horace S. Glover. 145p. 1962. text 68.50 (*90-277-0082-6*, D Reidel) Kluwer Academic.

Logics. John E. Nolt. LC 96-32646. (Philosophy Ser.). (Illus.). 480p. (C). 1996. 69.95 (*0-534-50640-2*) Wadsworth Pub.

Logics: A Sociobiological Approach to Social & Other Logics, No. 2. James H. Parker. LC 92-23596. 104p. (Orig.). (C). 1993. pap. text 17.50 (*0-8191-8882-4*); lib. bdg. 38.50 (*0-8191-8881-6*) U Pr of Amer.

Logics Dictionary German-English-French. A. Bannour. (ENG, FRE & GER.). 231p. 1995. 65.00 (*2-85319-260-1*, Pub. by Conseil Intl Lang) IBD Ltd.

Logics for Concurrency: Structure vs. Automata. Faron Moller & Graham Birtwistle. LC 96-5558. (Lecture Notes in Computer Science Ser.: Vol. 1043). xi, 266p. 1996. pap. 49.00 (*3-540-60915-6*) Spr-Verlag.

Logics for Databases & Information Systems, Vol. 436. Jan Chomicki & Gunter Saake. LC 98-2579. (Engineering & Computer Science Ser.). 430p. 1998. 148.00 (*0-7923-8129-7*) Kluwer Academic.

Logics in AI: European Workshop JELIA '92, Berlin, Germany, September 7-10, 1992, Proceedings. Ed. by D. Pearce & G. Wagner. LC 92-26468. (Lecture Notes in Computer Science Ser.: Vol. 633). viii, 410p. 1992. 63.00 (*0-387-55887-X*) Spr-Verlag.

Logics in AI: Proceedings of the European Workshop JELIA '90 Amsterdam, The Netherlands, September 10-14, 1990. Ed. by Jan Van Eijck. (Lecture Notes in Artificial Intelligence: Vol. 478). ix, 562p. 1991. 59.00 (*0-387-53686-8*) Spr-Verlag.

Logics in Artificial Intelligence. Ed. by J. Dix et al. LC 98-46038. (Lecture Notes in Artificial Intelligence Ser.: Vol. 1489). ix, 391p. 1998. 67.00 (*3-540-65141-1*) Spr-Verlag.

Logics in Artificial Intelligence: European Workshop, Jelia '96, Evora, Portugal, September 30-October 3, 1996, Proceedings. Jose J. Alferes et al. LC 96-33379. (Lecture Notes in Computer Science Ser.: Vol. 1126). 417p. 1996. 68.00 (*3-540-61630-6*) Spr-Verlag.

Logics of Dislocation: Models, Metaphors & Meanings of Economic Space. Trevor J. Barnes. LC 95-42463. (Mappings: Society-Theory-Space Ser.). 292p. 1995. lib. bdg. 44.50 (*1-57230-033-7*, 0033) Guilford Pubns.

Logics of Dislocation: Models, Metaphors & Meanings of Economic Space. Trevor J. Barnes. LC 95-42463. (Mappings). (Illus.). 292p. 1995. pap. text 21.95 (*1-57230-039-6*, 0039) Guilford Pubns.

Logics of Failed Revolt: French Theory after May '68. Peter Starr. LC 94-46160. 288p. 1995. 45.00 (*0-8047-2445-8*); pap. 14.95 (*0-8047-2446-6*) Stanford U Pr.

Logics of Party Formation: Ecological Politics in Belgium & West Germany. Herbert Kitschelt. LC 88-31871. 416p. 1989. 49.95 (*0-8014-2252-3*) Cornell U Pr.

Logics of Preference: A Study of Prohairetic Logics in Twentieth Century Philosophy. NIcholas J. Moutafakis. 296p. (C). 1987. text 139.00 (*90-277-2591-8*, D Reidel) Kluwer Academic.

Logics of Programs. Ed. by R. Parikh. (Lecture Notes in Computer Science Ser.: Vol. 193). vi, 424p. 1985. 42.00 (*0-387-15648-8*) Spr-Verlag.

Logics of Resistance: Globalization & Telephone Unionism in Mexico & British Columbia. Steve Dubb. LC 99-19513. 400p. 1999. 70.00 (*0-8153-3373-0*) Garland.

Logics of Social Structure. Kyriakos M. Kontopoulos. (Structural Analysis in the Social Sciences Ser.: No. 6). (Illus.). 493p. (C). 1993. text 52.95 (*0-521-41779-1*) Cambridge U Pr.

Logics of Television: Essays in Cultural Criticism. Ed. by Patricia Mellencamp. LC 89-46004. (Theories of Contemporary Culture Ser.). 318p. 1990. pap. 15.95 (*0-253-20582-4*, MB-582) Ind U Pr.

Logics of Time & Computation. rev. ed. Robert Goldblatt. LC 92-12978. (Center for the Study of Language & Information-Lecture Notes Ser.: No. 7). 190p. 1992. pap. 17.95 (*0-937073-94-6*) CSLI.

Logics of Time & Computation. 2nd rev. ed. Robert Goldblatt. LC 92-12978. (Center for the Study of Language & Information-Lecture Notes Ser.: No. 7). 190p. 1992. 49.95 (*0-937073-93-8*) CSLI.

LogicWorks. Herrick. (C). 1994. pap. text, student ed. 9.75 (*0-15-502005-6*) Harcourt Coll Pubs.

LogicWorks. Joel Rudinow. (C). 1994. pap. text, student ed. 17.00 (*0-15-501942-2*) Harcourt Coll Pubs.

Logicworks: Interactive Circuit Design Software/ MacTinosh Version/Book & Disk. LC 93-27595. 232p. (C). 1994. pap. text 43.95 (*0-8053-1312-5*) Benjamin-Cummings.

Logicworks 4. Capilano Computing Systems, Ltd., Staff. LC 98-36517. 448p. (C). 1998. pap. text, teacher ed. write for info. (*0-201-44488-7*) Addison-Wesley.

LogicWorks Interactv IBM. (C). 1994. pap. text 21.33 (*0-8053-1315-X*) Benjamin-Cummings.

LogicWorks Verilog Modeler: Interactive Circuit Simulation Software for Windows & Macintosh; Version 3. Capilano Computing Systems, Ltd., Staff. 102p. (C). 1996. 32.00 incl. audio compact disk (*0-201-49885-5*) Addison-Wesley.

LogicWorks Verilog Modeler Manual. Capilano Computing Systems, Ltd., Staff. LC 96-25111. 112p. (C). 1996. pap. text. write for info. (*0-201-89585-4*) Addison-Wesley.

Logicworks 3: Interactive Circuit Design Software for Windows & Macintosh with 3.5 Disk. 2nd ed. Capilano Computing Systems, Ltd., Staff. (C). 1996. pap. text 52.95 (*0-8053-1316-8*) Benjamin-Cummings.

LOGIDATA: Deductive Databases with Complex Objects. Ed. by Paolo Atzeni. LC 93-11824. (Lecture Notes in Computer Science Ser.: Vol. 701). 1993. 44.95 (*0-387-56974-X*) Spr-Verlag.

Logik, Bedeutung und Mathematik: Die Konstruktion Einer Fundamentalsprache der Wissenschaften. D. Marsal. viii, 152p. 1987. 29.00 (*3-510-65131-6*, Pub. by E Schweizerbartsche) Balogh.

Logik, Dedeutung & Mathematik: Die Konstruktion Einer Fundamentalsprache der Wissenschaften. D. Marsal. (GER.). 152p. 1987. pap. 33.60 (*0-685-33223-3*) Lubrecht & Cramer.

Logik der Fragen: Grundlegung einer Interrogative Logik. Juergen Walther. (Grundlagen der Kommunikation-Bibliotheksausgabe Ser.). (GER.). viii, 334p. 1985. 93.85 (*3-11-010550-0*) De Gruyter.

Logik der Reitkunst. Peter Spohr. (Illus.). vl, 571p. 1979. write for info. (*3-487-08187-3*) G Olms Pubs.

Logik und Allgemeine Wissenschaftstheorie: Vorlesungen 1917/18, mit Ergan Zenden Texten aus der Ersten Fassung 1910/11. Edmund Husserl. (Husserliana Collected Works). 448p. (C). 1996. text 209.50 (*0-7923-3731-X*) Kluwer Academic.

Logik und Mathematik: Frege-Kolloquium, 1993. Ed. by Ingolf Max & Werner Stelzner. (Perspektiven der Analytischen Philosophie - Perspectives in Analytical Philosophy Ser.: Bd. 5). (GER.). xi, 553p. (C). 1995. lib. bdg. 207.70 (*3-11-014545-6*) De Gruyter.

Logik und Semiotik in der Philosophie von Leibniz. Hans Burkhardt. (Analytica Ser.). 488p. 1980. lib. bdg. 132.00 (*3-88405-001-X*) Philosophia Pr.

Logik und Zeit in der Phanomenologischen Philosophie Martin Heideggers (1925-1928) Vladimir Vukicevic. (Philosophische Texte und Studien: Vol. 18). (GER.). x, 262p. 1988. write for info. (*3-487-09064-3*) G Olms Pubs.

Logique. Etienne Bonnot de Condillac. Tr. by W. R. Albury. (Janus Ser.).Tr. of Logic. 354p. 1980. lib. bdg. 25.00 (*0-913870-38-2*) Abaris Bks.

Logique & Connaissance Scientifique. Jean Piaget. (Methodique Ser.). 1360p. 55.95 (*0-686-56429-4*) Fr & Eur.

Logique de Leibniz. Louis Couturat. xiv, 608p. 1985. reprint ed. 120.00 (*3-487-00098-9*); reprint ed. pap. 65.00 (*3-487-02381-4*) G Olms Pubs.

Logique des Propositions & des Predicats, Deduction Naturelle see Logique Moderne

Logique des Propositions & des Predicats, Tables de Verite & Axiomatisation see Logique Moderne

***Logique, Discours et Pensee.** Contrib. by Jean-Blaise Grize & Christiane Tripet. (Sciences pour la Communication Ser.: ol. 52). 444p. 1999. 53.95 (*3-906763-24-2*, Pub. by P Lang) P Lang Pubng.

Logique et Connaissance Scientifique. Jean Piaget. (FRE.). 1364p. 1973. lib. bdg. 130.00 (*0-7859-3776-5*, 2070104133) Fr & Eur.

Logique Mathematique see Mathematical Logic

Logique Moderne. Incl. Fascicule I. Logique des Propositions & des Predicats, Deduction Naturelle. Jean-B. Grize. 1969. pap. (*90-279-6320-7*); Fascicule II. Logique des Propositions & des Predicats, Tables de Verite & Axiomatisation. Jean-B. Grize. 1971. pap. 9.35 Fascicule III. Implications-Modalites, Logiques Polyvalentes, Logique Combinatoire, Ontologie & Mereologie de Lesniewski. Jean-Blaise Grize. 1973. pap. 12.70 (*90-279-7286-9*); (Mathematiques et Sciences de l'Homme Ser.). pap. write for info. (*0-318-54404-0*) Mouton.

Logique ou l'Art de Penser. Antoine Arnauld & Pierre Nicole. 389p. 1970. reprint ed. 95.00 (*0-318-71313-6*) G Olms Pubs.

Logiques. Phillipe Sollers. (FRE.). 1968. pap. 39.95 (*0-7859-1236-3*, 2020019426) Fr & Eur.

Logisch-Philosophische Untersuchungen Zu Philosophie-Historischen Themen: Von Platon und Aristoteles Zu Wittgenstein und Popper. Paul Weingartner. (GER.). 350p. 1996. 57.95 (*3-631-49414-9*) P Lang Pubng.

Logisch-Philosophische Untersuchungen Zu Werten und Normen: Werte und Normen in Wissenschaft und Forschung. Paul Weingartner. (GER.). 217p. 1996. 38.95 (*3-631-49415-7*) P Lang Pubng.

Logische Propadeutik see Logical Propaedeutic: Pre-School of Reasonable Discourse

Logische Schriften: Grosses Logikfragment, Grundgesetze des Sollens. E. Mally. LC 73-135106. (Synthese Historical Library: No. 3). (GER.). 357p. 1971. text 141.50 (*90-277-0174-1*, D Reidel) Kluwer Academic.

Logische Untersuchungen, 3 Vols, Set. Edmund Husserl. (GER.). 1968. reprint ed. 73.00 (*3-484-70118-8*) Adlers Foreign Bks.

Logische Untersuchungen: Erster Band. Edmund Husserl. (Husserliana Collected Works: No. 18). 342p. 1975. lib. bdg. 121.50 (*90-247-1722-1*, Pub. by M Nijhoff) Kluwer Academic.

Logische Untersuchungen: Zweiter Band. Edmund Husserl. Ed. by Ursula Panzer. 1024p. 1984. lib. bdg. 579.50 (*90-247-2517-8*, Pub. by M Nijhoff) Kluwer Academic.

Logisches Philosophieren - Festschrift Fuer Albert Menne Zum 60. Ed. by I. M. Bochenski. (GER.). xii, 208p. 1988. write for info. (*3-487-07421-4*) G Olms Pubs.

Logistic Engineering & Management. 5th ed. Benjamin S. Blanchard. LC 98-9446. 526p. (C). 1998. 99.00 (*0-13-905316-6*, Prentice Hall) P-H.

***Logistic Regression: A Primer.** Fred C. Pampel. LC 00-8060. (Quantitative Applications in the Social Sciences Ser.). 2000. pap. write for info. (*0-7619-2010-2*) Sage.

Logistic Regression: A Self-Learning Text. David G. Kleinbaum. LC 93-27484. (Series in Statistics in the Health Sciences). 312p. 1996. 54.95 (*0-387-94142-8*) Spr-Verlag.

Logistic Regression Examples Using the SAS System. 176p. (C). 1998. pap. 24.95 (*1-55544-674-4*, BR55201) SAS Publ.

Logistic Regression with Missing Values in the Covariates. Werner Vach. LC 94-247. (Lecture Notes in Statistics Ser.: Vol. 86). (Illus.). xi, 139p. 1994. 39.95 (*0-387-94263-7*) Spr-Verlag.

Logistic Strategy. Shapiro. Date not set. pap. text, teacher ed. write for info. (*0-314-87076-8*) West Pub.

Logistic Support of a Manned Underwater Production Complex. Michael E. Jones. 1983. lib. bdg. 92.00 (*0-86010-450-8*) G & T Inc.

Logistica en Europa, una Nueva Estrategia-Cliente. Claude Fiore. (SPA.). 214p. 1992. 29.00 (*84-7978-019-3*, Pub. by Ediciones Diaz) IBD Ltd.

Logistical Management: The Integrated Supply Chain Process. Donald J. Bowersox & David J. Closs. LC 95-42252. (Series in Marketing). (Illus.). xix, 730 p. (C). 1996. text 65.74 (*0-07-006883-6*) McGraw.

Logistical Managements: The Integrated Supply Chain Process, Loga: Simulation Software. Donald J. Bowersox & David J. Closs. 1996. pap. text. write for info. (*0-07-841322-2*) McGraw.

Logistics. Langford. 1998. pap. 65.00 (*0-07-134529-9*) McGraw.

Logistics: Change & Synthesis. Ed. by Patrick Gallagher. 288p. 1984. pap. 15.45 (*0-317-06629-3*) Leaseway Trans Corp.

Logistics: Concepts & Applications. John H. Campbell. Ed. by Masao Nishi & William J. O'Neill, Jr. LC 82-84389. 328p. (Orig.). 1982. pap. 15.45 (*0-9610146-0-1*) Leaseway Trans Corp.

Logistics: Contribution & Control. Ed. by Patrick Gallagher. 282p. 1983. pap. 15.45 (*0-9610146-1-X*) Leaseway Trans Corp.

Logistics: International Issues. 1985. write for info. (*0-9610146-3-6*) Leaseway Trans Corp.

Logistics: Issues for the Eighties. John H. Campbell. Ed. by Masao Nishi. LC 81-86565. 211p. 1981. pap. 15.45 (*0-685-07934-1*) Leaseway Trans Corp.

Logistics & Distribution Planning: Strategies for Management. Ed. by J. Cooper. (C). 1990. 305.00 (*0-7855-5726-1*, Pub. by Inst Pur & Supply) St Mut.

Logistics & Distribution Planning: Strategies for Management. James Cooper. (C). 1988. 145.00 (*0-7855-3770-8*, Pub. by Inst Pur & Supply) St Mut.

***Logistics & Retail Management: Insights into Current Practice & Trends from Leading Experts.** John Fernie. LC 99-72247. (Illus.). 1999. 59.95 (*0-8493-4084-5*) CRC Pr.

Logistics & Supply Chain Management: Strategies for Reducing Cost & Improving Service. 2nd ed. Christopher Martin. (Financial Times Ser.). (Illus.). 294p. 1998. 34.95 (*0-273-63049-0*, Pub. by F T P H) Natl Bk Netwk.

***Logistics & the Extended Enterprise: Benchmarks & Best Practices for the Manufacturing Professional.** Sandor Boyson et al. LC 98-33306. (Operations Management Series for Professionals). 230p. 1999. 48.50 (*0-471-31430-7*) Wiley.

Logistics Dictionary, German/English-English/German. Jens Kiesel. (ENG & GER.). 209p. 1997. 125.00 (*0-7859-9515-3*) Fr & Eur.

Logistics for Hazardous Materials Transportation: Scheduling, Routing & Siting. 1997. lib. bdg. 250.95 (*0-8490-7647-1*) Gordon Pr.

Logistics Handbook. Ed. by William C. Copacino & James F. Robeson. 1000p. 1994. 100.00 (*0-02-926595-9*) Free Pr.

Logistics in the National Defense. Henry E. Eccles. LC 81-4920. (Illus.). 347p. 1981. reprint ed. lib. bdg. 77.50 (*0-313-22716-0*, ECLO, Greenwood Pr) Greenwood.

Logistics in World War II. 1996. lib. bdg. 258.99 (*0-8490-6917-3*) Gordon Pr.

Logistics in World War II: Bibliography. 1994. lib. bdg. 250.00 (*0-8490-5710-8*) Gordon Pr.

Logistics in World War 2: Final Report of the Army Service Forces. 296p. 1993. per. 19.00 (*0-16-061302-7*) USGPO.

Logistics Management. Paul Fawcett. 304p. (Orig.). 1992. pap. 39.50 (*0-273-63413-5*, Pub. by Pitman Pub) Trans-Atl Phila.

Logistics Management & U. S. - Mexico Transportation Systems: A Preliminary Investigation. Leigh B. Boske & Robert Harrison. LC 94-78764. (Policy Research Project Report: No. 109). 92p. 1994. pap. 10.50 (*0-89940-717-X*) LBJ Sch Pub Aff.

Logistics of a Distribution System. Peter Attwood & Nigel Attwood. 279p. 1992. 74.95 (*0-566-09098-8*, Pub. by Gower) Ashgate Pub Co.

Logistics of Liberty: American Services of Supply in the Revolutionary War & After. James A. Huston. LC 89-40416. (Illus.). 1991. 49.50 (*0-87413-381-5*) U Delaware Pr.

Logistics of Production & Inventory. Ed. by S. C. Graves et al. LC 92-34645. (Handbooks in Operations Research & Management Science Ser.: Vol. 4). 772p. 1993. 165.00 (*0-444-87472-0*, North Holland) Elsevier.

Logistics of the Roman Army at War (264 B. C.-A. D. 235) Jonathan Roth. LC 98-42368. (Columbia Studies in the Classical Tradition). 1998. 123.50 (*90-04-11271-5*) Brill Academic Pubs.

Logistics Reprints. American Production & Inventory Control Society St. 207p. 1993. 23.00 (*1-55822-031-3*) Am Prod & Inventory.

Logistics Strategy: Cases & Concepts. Roy D. Shapiro & James L. Heskett. (Illus.). 602p. (C). 1984. text 65.75 (*0-314-85297-2*) West Pub.

Logistics Support Analysis Management. Richard E. Biedenbender. 574p. 1992. 60.00 (*0-07-005220-4*) McGraw.

Logistics Systems Analysis. Carlos F. Daganzo. (Lecture Notes in Economics & Mathematical Systems Ser.: Vol. 361). (Illus.). x, 321p. 1991. pap. 40.00 (*0-387-54069-5*) Spr-Verlag.

Logistics Systems Analysis. 2nd enl. rev. ed. Carlos F. Daganzo. LC 95-52401. (Illus.). 324p. 1996. 98.00 incl. 5.25 hd (*3-540-60639-4*) Spr-Verlag.

***Logistics Systems Analysis.** 3rd ed. Carlos F. Daganzo. LC 99-233285. (Illus.). xiv, 242p. 1999. 89.95 (*3-540-65533-6*) Spr-Verlag.

Logit Model: An Introduction for Economists. J. S. Cramer. (Illus.). 120p. 1991. text 39.95 (*0-340-54111-3*, A6423, Pub. by E A) Routldge.

Logit Modeling: Practical Applications. Alfred DeMaris. LC 92-9657. (Quantitative Applications in the Social Sciences Ser.: Vol. 86). 96p. (C). 1992. pap. text 10.95 (*0-8039-4377-6*) Sage.

LOGITDATA Plus: Deductive Databases with Complex Objects. Ed. by Paolo Atzeni. (Lecture Notes in Computer Science Ser.: Vol. 701). vii, 273p. 1993. pap. write for info. (*3-540-56974-X*) Spr-Verlag.

LOGLAN, 1988. A. Kreczmar & Andrzej Salwicki. (Lecture Notes in Computer Science Ser.: Vol. 414). x, 133p. 1990. 24.50 (*0-387-52325-1*) Spr-Verlag.

Loglan 1: A Logical Language. 4th ed. James C. Brown. ("Loglan N" Ser.). 599p. (C). 1989. pap. 21.50 (*1-877665-00-2*) Loglan Inst.

Loglinear Models with Latent Variables. Jacques A. Hagenaars. (Quantitative Applications in the Social Sciences Ser.: Vol. 94). (Illus.). 96p. (C). 1993. pap. text 10.95 (*0-8039-4310-5*) Sage.

Lognormal Distribution: With Special References to Its Uses in Economics. John Aitchison & J. A. Brown. LC 58-1106. (University of Cambridge, Dept. of Applied Economics, Occasional Papers: No. 5). (Illus.). 194p. reprint ed. pap. 55.30 (*0-608-18268-0*, 2032993) Bks Demand.

Lognormal Distributions: Theory & Applications. Edwin L. Crow. Ed. by Kunio Shimizu. (Statistics: Textbooks & Monographs: Vol. 88). (Illus.). 408p. 1987. text 137.00 (*0-8247-7803-0*) Dekker.

Logo. Alan Cooper. (C). 1989. 35.00 (*0-7223-2348-4*, Pub. by A H S Ltd) St Mut.

Logo: A Retrospective. Ed. by Cleborne D. Maddux & D. LaMont Johnson. LC 97-32264. 212p. 1997. 49.95 (*0-7890-0374-0*) Haworth Pr.

L

LOGO: Methods & Curriculum for Teachers. Ed. by D. LaMont Johnson. LC 88-9449. (Computers in the Schools Ser.: Supp. 3). 221p. 1989. text 49.95 (*0-86656-748-8*) Haworth Pr.
Logo: Mit Logo for the Apple. Richard Billstein et al. LC 84-24229. 415p. (C). 1985. pap. text, teacher ed. 41.00 (*0-8053-0860-1*) Addison-Wesley.
LOGO As a Programming Language: The Hitchhikers Guide to Logo. Peter Evans. (C). 1986. 30.00 (*0-7300-0445-7*, Pub. by Deakin Univ) St Mut.
LOGO As an Educational Culture. Peter Evans. (C). 1986. 30.00 (*0-7300-0447-3*, Pub. by Deakin Univ) St Mut.
LOGO for IBM Personal Computers. David Myers & PC World Editors. 1985. pap. 16.95 (*0-671-49284-5*) S&S Trade.
LOGO for Teachers: A Hands-On Approach. Patrick Scott et al. 1986. spiral bd. 12.95 (*0-673-18291-6*, Scott Frsmn) Addson-Wesley Educ.
LOGO for the Apple IIc: The Magic Turtle. Jonathan Price. write for info. (*0-318-58181-7*) P-H.
LOGO for the Macintosh: An Introduction Through Object Logo. Harold Abelson & Amanda Abelson. (Illus.). 400p. 1993. pap. 55.00 incl. disk (*0-262-51070-7*) MIT Pr.
LOGO in the Schools. Ed. by Cleborne D. Maddux. LC 85-8411. (Computers in the Schools Ser.: Vol. 2, Nos. 2-3). 305p. 1985. text 9.95 (*0-86656-424-1*); pap. text 24.95 (*0-86656-425-X*) Haworth Pr.
LOGO International One. Ed. by David E. Carter. LC 84-71451. 260p. 1984. 32.50 (*0-88108-012-8*) Art Dir.
LOGO International Three. Ed. by David E. Carter. LC 84-71451. 192p. 1990. 49.50 (*0-88108-060-8*) Art Dir.
LOGO International Two. David E. Carter. (Illus.). 260p. 1986. 32.50 (*0-88108-033-0*) Art Dir.
LOGO Language: Learning Mathematics Through Programming. Wallace Feurzeig et al. 188p. 1977. pap. text 22.95 (*0-87567-105-5*) Entelek.
LOGO Mathematics in the Classroom. Celia Hoyles & Rosamund Sutherland. 200p. 1989. 55.00 (*0-685-25040-7*) Routledge.
LOGO Programming As Professional Development, 15 bks., Set. Peter Evans. 168p. (C). 1990. 240.00 (*0-7300-0726-X*, Pub. by Deakin Univ) St Mut.
Logo Some Curriculum Perspectives. Chris Bigum. (C). 1986. 30.00 (*0-7300-0442-2*, Pub. by Deakin Univ) St Mut.
Logomachia: The Conflict of the Faculties Today. Ed. by Richard Rand. LC 92-6977. xii, 219p. 1992. pap. text 15.00 (*0-8032-8940-5*, Bison Books) U of Nebr Pr.
Logopower: Creating World-Class Logos & Effective Identities. David E. Carter. 1998. pap. text 39.95 (*0-8230-6603-7*) Watsn-Guptill.
Logos. Steven Skaggs. Ed. by Kay Keppler. LC 92-54358. 128p. (Orig.). 1994. pap. text 12.95 (*1-56052-189-9*) Crisp Pubns.
Logos: Festschrift fuer Luise Abramowski zum 8, Juli 1993. Ed. by Christof Brennecke et al. (Beiheft zur Zeitschrift fuer die Neuetestamentliche Wissenschaft Ser.: Vol. 67). (GER.). xiii, 658p. (C). 1993. lib. bdg. 165.30 (*3-11-013985-5*) De Gruyter.
Logos: Grand Dictionnaire de la Langue Francaise, 3 vols., Set. Jean Girodet. (FRE.). 275.00 (*0-8288-7767-X*, M8805) Fr & Eur.
Logos: LOGO, Identity, Brand, Culture. Conway L. Morgan. (Pro-Graphics Ser.). (Illus.). 160p. 1998. pap. 35.00 (*2-88046-328-9*, Rotovision) Watsn-Guptill.
Logos & Eidos: The Concept in Phenomenology. Ronald Bruzina. LC 70-129299. (Janua Linguarum, Ser. Minor: No. 93). (Orig.). 1971. pap. text 60.00 (*90-279-1542-3*) Mouton.
Logos & Ergon in Thucydides. rev. ed. Adam M. Parry. Ed. by W. R. Connor. LC 80-2660. (Monographs in Classical Studies). 223p. 1981. lib. bdg. 29.95 (*0-405-14045-2*) Ayer.
Logos & Existence: The Relationship of Philosophy & Theology in the Thought of Paul Tillich. Donald R. Ferrell. LC 90-23371. (American University Studies: Theology & Religion: Ser. VII, Vol. 98). 489p. (C). 1992. text 66.95 (*0-8204-1469-7*) P Lang Pubng.
Logos & Language in the Philosophy of Plotinus. John H. Heiser. LC 89-27514. (Studies in the History of Philosophy: Vol. 15). 108p. 1991. lib. bdg. 59.95 (*0-88946-288-7*) E Mellen.
Logos & Life: Creative Experience & the Critique of Reason. Anna-Teresa Tymieniecka. 640p. (C). 1988. pap. text 88.00 (*90-277-2540-3*, D Reidel); lib. bdg. 203.00 (*90-277-2539-X*, D Reidel) Kluwer Academic.
Logos & Life: The Three Movements of the Soul; the Spontaneous & the Creative in Man's Self-Interpretation-in-the-Sacred. Anna-Teresa Tymieniecka. 256p. (C). 1988. pap. text 66.50 (*90-277-2557-8*, D Reidel); lib. bdg. 130.00 (*90-277-2556-X*, D Reidel) Kluwer Academic.
Logos & Mystical Theology in Philo of Alexandria. David Winston. LC 85-13957. 81p. reprint ed. pap. 30.00 (*0-608-09071-9*, 206970500006); reprint ed. pap. 30.00 (*0-608-20516-8*, 207176800002) Bks Demand.
Logos & the Word. Stephanie Merrim. LC 83-47648. (Utah Studies in Literature & Linguistics: Vol. 23). 106p. 1983. pap. 13.70 (*0-8204-0003-3*) P Lang Pubng.
Logos Bible Software: Catholic Scholar's Pack. cd-rom 499.95 (*1-57799-190-7*) Logos Res Sys.
Logos, Doulos & Logos II. OM Staff. 1995. 4.99 (*1-85985-035-9*) O M Lit.
Logos Go Digital. Carter. 1997. 35.00 (*0-688-15701-7*, Wm Morrow) Morrow Avon.
Logos Go Digital. Ed. by David E. Carter. (Illus.). 176p. 1997. pap. 35.00 (*0-8230-6598-7*) Watsn-Guptill.
Logos in Mythos: Ideas & Early French Narrative. Clifton Cherpack. LC 83-80663. (French Forum Monographs: No. 46). 212p. (Orig.). 1983. pap. 14.95 (*0-917058-46-1*) French Forum.
Logos Islamikos: Studia Islamica in Honorem Georgii Michaelis. Ed. by Roger M. Savory & Dionisius A. Agius. (Illus.). x, 351p. pap. text 40.00 (*0-88844-806-6*) Brill Academic Pubs.
Logos lehre des Heiligen Athanasius. Leonhard Atzberger. vii, 246p. 1975. reprint ed. 50.00 (*3-487-05618-6*) G Olms Pubs.
Logos, Mottoes & Abbreviations of International Organizations, 3 vols. Ed. by Union of International Associations Staff. 1997. 675.00 (*3-598-11345-5*) K G Saur Verlag.
Logos of American Restaurants. David E. Carter. (Illus.). 176p. 1997. pap. text 35.00 (*0-8230-4541-2*) Watsn-Guptill.
Logos of America's Fastest Growing Corporations. Ed. by David E. Carter. LC 91-76054. (Illus.). 192p. 1992. text 39.50 (*0-88108-096-9*) Art Dir.
Logos of America's Largest Corporations. Ed. by David E. Carter. LC 88-71637. 180p. 1988. text 39.50 (*0-88108-059-4*) Art Dir.
***Logos of Bars & Restaurants.** David E. Carter. (Illus.). 184p. 2000. pap. 35.00 (*0-8230-7351-3*) Watsn-Guptill.
Logos of Major World Corporations. Ed. by David E. Carter. LC 89-85962. 160p. 1989. text 39.50 (*0-88108-071-3*) Art Dir.
Logos Spermaticos. Edmund Spiess. lxiii, 505p. 1976. reprint ed. write for info. (*3-487-06048-5*) G Olms Pubs.
Logos Story see Barco Llamado Logos
Logos Story. rev. ed. Elaine Rhoton. (Illus.). 192p. 1992. reprint ed. pap. text 5.99 (*0-9630908-4-4*) O M Lit.
Logos-Structure of the World: Language As Model of Reality. Georg Kuhlewind. Tr. by Friedemann Schwarzkopf from GER. (Anomalies: Alternatives to Contemporary Orthodoxies Ser.). 160p. (Orig.). 1992. pap. 14.95 (*0-940262-48-7*, Lindisfarne) Anthroposophic.
Logos, Ursprung und Wesen der Begriffe. Ludwig Noire. (Documenta Semiotica Ser.: Bd. 1). (GER.). 362p. 1989. reprint ed. write for info. (*3-487-09259-X*) G Olms Pubs.
Logostics: Where Ends Have to Meet: Proceedings of the Shell Conference on Logistics, Apeldoorn, the Netherlands, November 2-3, 1988. C. F. Van Rijn. LC 89-16173. (Illus.). 24p. 1989. 118.00 (*0-08-037405-0*, Pub. by Pergamon Repr) Franklin.
Logotherapy: New Help for Problem Drinkers. James C. Crumbaugh et al. LC 79-18635. 176p. 1981. text 27.95 (*0-88229-421-0*) Burnham Inc.
Logotherapy for the Helping Professional: Meaningful Social Work. David L. Guttmann. 264p. 1996. 44.95 (*0-8261-9020-0*) Springer Pub.
***Logoware.** Carter. 1998. 35.00 (*0-688-15348-8*, Wm Morrow) Morrow Avon.
Logoware: The 35 Best Programs for Creating Digital Logos. David E. Carter. 1998. pap. text 35.00 (*0-8230-6602-9*) Watsn-Guptill.
Logrando Excelencia en Manufactura. Robert W. Hall. Tr. by Luis A. Arroyo from ENG. (SPA., Illus.). 320p. (Orig.). (C). 1988. text 21.95 (*0-685-23092-9*) MRP Assistance.
Logs: Quetico by Canoe, 1970 & Bewitched by the BWCA, 1987. 3rd rev. ed. Conrad Gassman. Ed. by Richard Lowenstein. 350p. 1999. 25.00 (*0-9628183-3-X*) Rampage Pr.
Logs & Lumber: The Development of Lumbering in Michigan's Lower Peninsula, 1837-1870. Barbara E. Benson. (Illus.). 1989. 25.00 (*0-916699-14-5*) CMU Clarke Hist Lib.
***Logs & Moonshine: Tales of Buffalo City, N. C.** Suzanne Tate. LC 00-91043. (Illus.). 48p. 2000. pap. 4.95 (*1-878405-29-2*) Nags Head Art.
Logs for Capital: The Timber Industry & Capitalist Enterprise in the 19th Century, 138. Sing C. Chew. LC 92-3033. (Contributions in Economics & Economic History Ser.: No. 138). 208p. 1992. 55.00 (*0-313-28497-0*, CLJ/, Greenwood Pr) Greenwood.
Log's Life. Wendy Pfeffer. LC 95-30020. (Illus.). 32p. (J). (ps-3). 1997. per. 16.00 (*0-689-80636-1*) S&S Childrens.
Logs of the Conquest of Canada, Vol. 4. Ed. by William C. Wood. LC 68-28599. 335p. 1969. reprint ed. lib. bdg. 65.00 (*0-8371-5043-4*, WOLC, Greenwood Pr) Greenwood.
***Logs of the Dead Pirates Society: A Schooner Adventure Around Buzzards Bay.** Randall Peffer. LC 99-86721. 256p. 2000. 23.95 (*1-57409-095-X*) Sheridan.
Lohengrin. Composed by Richard Wagner. 1998. pap. 7.95 (*963-8303-16-6*) Konemann.
Lohengrin. Richard Wagner. Ed. by Nicholas John. (English National Opera Guide Series: Bilingual Libretto, Articles: No. 47). (Illus.). 128p. 1994. pap. 9.95 (*0-7145-3852-3*) Riverrun NY.
Lohengrin in Full Score. Richard Wagner. (Music Scores & Music to Play Ser.). 295p. 1982. reprint ed. pap. 19.95 (*0-486-24335-4*) Dover.
Lohf Years: An Exhibition of Selected Rare Books & Manuscripts Acquired by the Rare Book & Manuscript Library While Kenneth A. Lohf Served As Its Librarian, 1967-1992. Compiled by Rudolph Ellenbogen. (Illus.). 72p. (Orig.). 1992. pap. 10.00 (*0-9607862-4-4*) Columbia U Libs.
Lohia the Rebel Gandhian. Ajay S. Almust. LC 98-901558. xiii, 256p. 1998. 27.00 (*81-7099-633-3*, Pub. by Mittal Pubs Dist) Nataraj Bks.
Lohman Guide to Calling & Decoying Waterfowl. LC 94-240076. 1994. pap. 5.25 (*1-879206-19-6*) Outdoor World Pr.
Lohman Guide to Calling & Rattling Whitetail Bucks. 1993. pap. 5.25 (*1-879206-17-X*) Outdoor World Pr.
Lohman Guide to Successful Turkey Calling. 1994. pap. 5.25 (*1-879206-18-8*) Outdoor World Pr.
Lohnflexibilitat auf Regionalen Arbeitsmarkten in Deutschland und Europa: Aur Curchfuhrbarkeit der Tarifpolitischen Strategie Regionaler Lohnflexibilitat unter Besonderer Berucksichtigung Neuerer Ansatze der Lohntheorie und Politokonomischer Aspekte. Christian Molitor. (Europaische Hochschulschriften: Reihe 5: Bd. 2031). (GER., Illus.). 341p. 1996. pap. 51.95 (*3-631-31141-9*) P Lang Pubng.
Lohnmetaphorik und Arbeitswelt in Mt 20, 1-16: Das Gleichnis von Den Arbeitern Im Weinberg Im Rahmen Rabbinischer Lohngleichnisse. Catherine Hezser. (Novum Testamentum et Orbis Antiquus Ser.: Vol. 15). (GER.). 356p. 1990. text 68.75 (*3-7278-0699-0*, Pub. by Presses Univ Fribourg) Eisenbrauns.
Loie Fuller: Goddess of Light. Richard N. Current & Marcia E. Current. LC 96-52659. (Illus.). 400p. 1997. text 29.95 (*1-55553-309-4*) NE U Pr.
Loimographia: An Account of the Great Plague of London in 1665. William Boghurst. Ed. by J. F. Payne. LC 75-23686. reprint ed. 44.50 (*0-404-13239-1*) AMS Pr.
Loimologia: or An Historical Account of the Plague in London in 1665. Nathaniel Hodges. LC 75-23722. reprint ed. 49.50 (*0-404-13280-4*) AMS Pr.
Loin de Rueil. Raymond Queneau. (FRE.). 1976. pap. 10.95 (*0-8288-3772-4*, F107610) Fr & Eur.
Loin de Rueil. Raymond Queneau. (Folio Ser.: No. 849). (FRE.). 211p. 1976. 8.95 (*2-07-036849-1*) Schoenhof.
Loing du Soleil: Architectural Practice in Quebec City During the French Regime. Marc Grignon. 320p. 1997. 49.95 (*0-614-30265-X*) P Lang Pubng.
Loing du Soleil: Architectural Practice in Quebec City During the French Regime. Marc Grignon. LC 94-14488. (American University Studies IX: Vol. 165). (Illus.). XIII, 295p. (C). 1997. 49.95 (*0-8204-2515-X*) P Lang Pubng.
Loire. Hubrecht Duijker. (Wine Lover's Touring Guides Ser.). (Illus.). 144p. (Orig.). 1995. pap. 15.95 (*1-85365-331-4*, Pub. by Spectrum) Seven Hills Bk.
Loire: A Wine Lover's Touring Guide. Hubrecht Duijker. (Illus.). 143p. 1998. pap. text 17.00 (*0-7881-5968-2*) DIANE Pub.
Loire: Walks, Motor Tours, Gazetteer, Where to Stay, Where to Eat, What to See, Plus Large-Scale IGN Maps. Institute Geographic Nationale Staff. (IGN Touring & Leisure Guides to France Ser.). (Illus.). 144p. (Orig.). 1991. pap. 19.95 (*1-85365-238-5*, Pub. by McCarta) Seven Hills Bk.
Loire Valley. Kathy Arnold & Paul Wade. (Thomas Cook Illustrated Guides Ser.). (Illus.). 192p. (Orig.). 1996. pap. 12.95 (*0-8442-9102-1*, 91021, Passprt Bks) NTC Contemp Pub Co.
Loire Valley. Deni Bown. LC 95-4501. (Eyewitness Travel Guides Ser.). 264p. 1996. pap. 22.95 (*0-7894-0426-5*) DK Pub Inc.
Loire Valley. Arthur Eperon. 1992. pap. 16.95 (*0-8442-9935-9*, Passprt Bks) NTC Contemp Pub Co.
Loire Valley. Shelley Wagner. (Knopf Guide Ser.). (Illus.). 392p. 1996. 25.00 (*0-614-15949-0*) Knopf.
Loire Valley. John McNeill. (Blue Guide Ser.). (Illus.). 256p. 1995. reprint ed. pap. 15.95 (*0-393-31414-6*, Norton Paperbks) Norton.
Loire Valley. 2nd ed. Arthur Eperon & Barbara Eperon. (Regional Guides of France Ser.). (Illus.). 216p. 1994. pap. 17.95 (*0-8442-9088-2*, 90882, Passprt Bks) NTC Contemp Pub Co.
Loire Valley. 2nd ed. Insight Guides Staff. (Insight Guides). 1998. pap. text 22.95 (*0-88729-702-1*) Langenscheidt.
***Loire Valley, \.** 3rd ed. Insight Guides Staff. (Insight Guides). 1998. pap. text 12.95 (*0-88729-893-1*) Langenscheidt.
Loire Valley in Your Pocket Guide. (In Your Pocket Guide Ser.). 1997. per. 9.95 (*2-06-630701-7*, 6307) Michelin.
Lois. Phillipe Sollers. (FRE.). 144p. 1972. pap. 18.95 (*0-7859-1238-X*, 2020019604) Fr & Eur.
Lois: Swiss Roots in Willard Soil. Lois L. De Water. (Illus.). 132p. (Orig.). 1987. pap. 14.95 (*0-9618510-0-7*) Wilderness Valley Pub.
Lois & Clark: A Superman Novel. C. J. Cherryh. 288p. 1997. per. 12.00 (*0-7615-1169-5*) Prima Pub.
Lois & Clark: The New Adventures of Superman. Dan Jurgens et al. Ed. by Bob Kahan. LC 94-234385. (Illus.). 192p. 1994. pap. 9.95 (*1-56389-128-X*) DC Comics.
Lois & the Sleepover. Created by Francine Pascal. (Sweet Valley Kids Ser.: No. 51). 80p. (J). (gr. 1-3). 1994. pap. 3.50 (*0-553-48099-5*) Bantam.
Lois & the Sleepover. Molly Mia Stewart. (Sweet Valley Kids Ser.: No. 51). (J). (gr. 1-3). 1994. 8.70 (*0-606-06784-1*, Pub. by Turtleback) Demco.
Lois de Composition Interne: Poemes Avec Des . . . Problemes! Florentin Smarandache. Ed. by Xiquan Publishing House Staff. Tr. by Chantal Signoret from RUM. (FRE.). 120p. (Orig.). (C). 1993. pap. 11.99 (*1-879585-10-3*) Erhus Univ Pr.
Lois de l'Esprit. Dan Millman.Tr. of Laws of Spirit. (FRE.). 1996. 19.95 (*2-920083-99-6*) Edns Roseau.
Lois Electorales d'Afrique Francophone. Guy Des Aulniers. Ed. by International Foundation Election Systems Staff. (FRE.). xi, 663p. 1998. pap. text 24.00 (*1-879720-51-5*) Intl Fndt Elect.
Lois Graham: A Decade in Review. Matthew Kangas. LC 85-71532. 1985. pap. 9.95 (*0-942342-05-4*) Bellevue Art.
Lois Green Carr: The Chesapeake & Beyond - A Celebration. 228p. 1992. pap. 18.00 (*1-878399-59-4*) Div Hist Cult Progs.
Lois Hole's Bedding Plant Favorites, Vol. 1. Lois Hole & Jill Fallis. (Lois Hole's Gardening Ser.: Vol. 2). (Illus.). 272p. (Orig.). 1996. pap. 15.95 (*1-55105-074-9*) Lone Pine.
Lois Hole's Favorite Trees & Shrubs. Lois Hole & Jill Fallis. LC 96-910897. (Illus.). 368p. (Orig.). 1997. pap. 15.95 (*1-55105-081-1*) Lone Pine.
Lois Hole's Perennial Favorites, Vol. 1. Lois Hole & Jill Fallis. (Lois Hole's Gardening Ser.: Vol. 3). (Illus.). 352p. (Orig.). 1995. pap. 15.95 (*1-55105-076-5*, 1-55105) Lone Pine.
Lois Hole's Rose Favorites: 148 Roses for Scent & Splendor. Lois Hole & Jill Fallis. LC 96-910892. (Illus.). 256p. (Orig.). 1997. pap. 15.95 (*1-55105-079-X*) Lone Pine.
Lois Hole's Tomato Favorites, Vol. 1. Lois Hole & Jill Fallis. (Lois Hole's Gardening Ser.: Vol. 4). (Illus.). 176p. (Orig.). 1996. pap. 12.95 (*1-55105-068-4*, 1-55105) Lone Pine.
Lois Hole's Vegetable Favorites. Lois Hole. (Lois Hole's Gardening Ser.: Vol. 1). (Illus.). 160p. 1993. pap. 11.95 (*1-55105-072-2*, 1-55105) Lone Pine.
Lois Lenski's Christmas Stories. Lois Lenski. LC 68-24417. (Illus.). 160p. (J). (gr. 4-6). 1968. 12.95 (*0-397-31031-5*) HarpC Child Bks.
Lois Lowry. Chaston. LC 97-8271. 1997. 32.00 (*0-8057-4034-1*, Twyne) Mac Lib Ref.
Lois Lowry. Lois Markham. Ed. by Kimberly Clark. (Meet the Author Ser.). 128p. (J). (gr. 5-8). 1995. pap. 6.95 (*0-88160-278-7*, LW348) Learning Wks.
Lois' Luscious Low-Fat Creations: A Collection of Recipes by Lois Paul. Lois Paul. 111p. (Orig.). 1998. spiral bd. 14.95 (*0-9661869-0-7*) Nutritional Consult.
Lois Remembers. Lois W. LC 79-6975. (Illus.). 1979. pap. 9.50 (*0-910034-23-0*) Al-Anon.
Lois Smith's Machine Quiltmaking. Lois T. Smith. LC 97-6202. 1997. 19.95 (*0-89145-796-8*, 4897, Am Quilters Soc) Collector Bks.
Lois Tarlow: A Retrospective. Brockton Art Museum Staff & Patricia Hills. (Illus.). 14p. (Orig.). 1986. pap. 5.00 (*0-934358-16-8*) Fuller Mus Art.
Lois Weber: The Director Who Lost Her Way in History, 54. Anthony Slide. LC 96-159. (Contributions to the Study of Popular Culture Ser.: No. 54). 192p. 1996. 49.95 (*0-313-29945-5*, Greenwood Pr) Greenwood.
***Loisiane.** 2nd ed. Richard Bizier. (Travel Guide (French Guides) Ser.). 1998. pap. text 29.95 (*2-89464-069-2*) Ulysses Travel.
Loisirs de Philothee. Nicolas Mavrocordatos. LC 90-189048. (FRE & GRE., Illus.). 253p. reprint ed. pap. 78.50 (*0-7837-6949-0*, 204677800003) Bks Demand.
Loiterature. Ross Chambers. LC 98-33653. (Stages Ser.). 312p. 1999. text 70.00 (*0-8032-1467-7*, Bison Books); pap. text 25.00 (*0-8032-6392-9*, Bison Books) U of Nebr Pr.
Loiterer's Harvest. Edward V. Lucas. LC 77-142658. (Essay Index Reprint Ser.). 1977. 20.95 (*0-8369-2059-7*) Ayer.
Loitering in the Lakes. D. W. Ball. 1987. 42.00 (*0-7223-2174-0*, Pub. by A H S Ltd) St Mut.
Loitering with Intent. Muriel Spark. 160p. 1990. pap. 9.00 (*0-380-70935-X*, Avon Bks) Morrow Avon.
Loitering with Intent. large type ed. Peter O'Toole. 237p. 1995. 25.95 (*1-85695-051-4*, Pub. by ISIS Lrg Prnt) Transaction Pubs.
***Loitering with Intent: Catholic Evangelization.** Vincent Cacace. 176p. 1999. pap. write for info. (*1-883520-18-5*) Jeremiah Pr.
Loitering with Intent: The Apprentice. Peter O'Toole. (Illus.). 448p. (J). 1997. 24.45 (*0-7868-6065-0*, Pub. by Hyperion) Time Warner.
Loitering with Intent: The Child. Peter O'Toole. (Illus.). 224p. (J). 1997. pap. 12.45 (*0-7868-8196-8*, Pub. by Hyperion) Time Warner.
Loitering with Intent Vol. 2: The Apprentice. Peter O'Toole. (Illus.). 256p. (Orig.). 1997. pap. 19.95 (*0-330-35208-3*, Pub. by Pan) Trans-Atl Phila.
Loizeaux's Plan Book see Classic Houses of the Twenties
Lojor's Letters: A Space-Age Story about a Boy & a Gnome & Learning Italic Handwriting. Jacqueline Svaren. LC 78-60185. (Illus.). 72p. (Orig.). (J). (gr. 1 up). 1981. pap. 10.00 (*0-931474-04-3*) TBW Bks.
Lok Sabha Elections, 1989: Indian Politics in 1990's. Ed. by Mahendra P. Singh. (Illus.). 227p. 1992. 20.00 (*81-85163-31-6*, Pub. by Kalinga) Nataraj Bks.
Lokale Abbreviationen des Decretum Gratiani. Alfred Beyer. 477p. 1998. 67.95 (*3-631-33430-3*) P Lang Pubng.
Lokale Neze. Andreas Zenk. (GER.). (C). 1991. text. write for info. (*0-201-55952-8*) Addison-Wesley.
Lokalkolorit und Zeitgeschichte in den Evangelien: Ein Beitrag zur Geschichte der Synoptischen Tradition. G. Theissen. (Novum Testamentum et Orbis Antiquus Ser.). (GER.). 1989. text 66.00 (*3-7278-0605-2*, Pub. by Presses Univ Fribourg) Eisenbrauns.
Lokapala. Anne Waldman. 32p. 1991. pap. 4.00 (*0-685-56997-7*) Rocky Ledge.
Lokayata-Critical Study. Shubhada A. Joshi & Joshi. (C). 1995. 34.00 (*81-7030-410-5*, Pub. by Sri Satguru Pubns) S Asia.
Loki. Dumezil. 1990. lib. bdg. 34.95 (*0-226-16977-4*) U Ch Pr.
Loki Project: A Novel. Benjamin King. LC 98-55982. 320p. 1999. 22.00 (*1-56554-283-5*) Pelican.
Lokis. Prosper Merimee. 164p. 19.95 (*0-686-54757-8*) Fr & Eur.
LOL: The Humor of the Internet. Ed. by Steve Marshall & Patty Miller-Marshall. LC 99-90710. vii, 157p. Date not set. pap. 12.95 (*0-9673087-0-4*) S Marshall Prodns.
***LOL Humorous Adventures from Cyberspace.** Doug Corwin et al. (Illus.). 228p. 1999. pap. 14.95 (*0-9676980-0-6*) Ross Pubns CA.
Lola. Tim McLaurin. LC 97-69229. 119p. 1997. 14.95 (*1-878086-62-6*, Pub. by Down Home NC) Blair.
***Lola.** John Starkey. (Illus.). 176p. 2000. 59.95 (*1-901295-00-1*, 130694AE, Pub. by Vloce Pub) Motorbooks Intl.
Lola: Can Am & Endurance Race Cars. Dave Friedman. LC 98-34964. (Illus.). 160p. 1998. 39.95 (*0-7603-0646-X*) MBI Pubg.

An Asterisk (*) at the beginning of an entry indicates that the title is appearing for the first time.

Lola Alvarez Bravo: In Her Own Light. Olivier Debroise. Tr. by James Oles from SPA. (Illus.). 88p. 1994. pap. 17.00 (0-938262-24-6) Ctr Creat Photog.
Lola & Miss Kitty see Favorite Friends Set
Lola Casanova. Francisco Rojas. (SPA.). pap. 7.99 (968-16-1559-X, Pub. by Fondo) Continental Bk.
Lola History, 1957-1977, Vol. 1. John Starkey. (Illus.). 192p. 1997. 49.95 (1-874105-86-3, Pub. by Vloce Pub) Motorbooks Intl.
Lola, l'Amour Fou? 31 Images. limited ed. Photos by Ergee. (Illus.). 1994. 7.00 (1-884185-08-8) O Zone.
Lola Montez: A Life. Bruce Seymour. LC 95-36465. (Illus.). 480p. 1996. 40.00 (0-300-06347-4) Yale U Pr.
Lola Montez: A Life. Bruce Seymour. (Illus.). 480p. 1998. pap. 16.00 (0-300-07439-5) Yale U Pr.
Lola Montez: The California Adventures of Europe's Notorious Courtesan. James F. Varley. LC 95-22922. (Illus.). 262p. 1996. 29.50 (0-87062-243-9) A H Clark.
Lola Race Cars, 1962-1990 Photo Album. Norman Hayes. LC 97-70641. (Photo Album Ser.). (Illus.). 112p. 1997. pap. 19.95 (1-882256-73-5) Iconografix.
Lola T70 - The Racing History & Individual Chassis Record. John Starkey. (Illus.). 176p. 1997. 49.95 (1-874105-89-8) Vloce Pub.
Lola y Lalo (Lilly & Billy) Martha Alexander. Tr. by Francisco Segovia. (SPA., Illus.). (J). 1993. 5.99 (968-16-4201-5, Pub. by Fondo) Continental Bk.
Lolita see Major Literary Characters
Lolita. Richard Corliss. (BFI Film Classics Ser.). (Illus.). 72p. 1995. pap. 10.95 (0-85170-368-2) Ind U Pr.
Lolita. Vladimir Nabokov. LC 92-52931. 368p. 1993. 17.00 (0-679-41043-0) Everymns Lib.
Lolita. Vladimir Nabokov. (FRE.). 1973. pap. 13.95 (0-7859-4075-8) Fr & Eur.
Lolita. Vladimir Nabokov. (International Ser.). 336p. 1989. pap. 13.00 (0-679-72316-1) Vin Bks.
Lolita. Vladimir Nabokov. 1996. pap. text 12.00 (0-676-51419-7) Vin Bks.
Lolita. adapted ed. Vladimir Nabokov. 1983. pap. 5.25 (0-8222-0683-8) Dramatists Play.
Lolita. large type ed. Vladimir Nabokov. 483p. 1997. 24.95 (0-7838-8080-4, G K Hall Lrg Type) Mac Lib Ref.
Lolita. Vladimir Nabokov. 300p. 1991. reprint ed. lib. bdg. 22.95 (0-89966-860-7) Buccaneer Bks.
Lolita, No. 3. Belore. (Illus.). 64p. 1997. pap. 9.95 (1-56163-177-9, Eurotica) NBM.
Lolita, Vol. 1. Belore. 64p. 1994. pap. 9.95 (1-56163-116-7, Eurotica) NBM.
Lolita, Vol. 2. Belore. (SPA.). 64p. 1995. pap. 9.95 (1-56163-133-7, Eurotica) NBM.
Lolita: A Janus Text. Lance Olsen. LC 94-24562. (Twayne's Masterwork Studies: Vol. 153). 1995. pap. 18.00 (0-8057-8593-0, Twyne) Mac Lib Ref.
Lolita: A Janus Text. Lance Olsen. LC 94-24562. (Twayne's Masterwork Studies: Vol. 153). 1995. 29.00 (0-8057-8355-5, Twyne) Mac Lib Ref.
Lolita: A Screenplay. Vladimir Nabokov. LC 96-30305. 1997. pap. 12.00 (0-679-77255-3) McKay.
***Lolita: Mason,&James.** abr. ed. Vladimir Nabokov. 1998. audio 12.00 (0-694-52015-2, Caedmon) HarperAudio.
Lolita: The Book of the Film. Stephen Schiff. 200p. 1998. pap. 15.95 (1-55783-354-0) Applause Theatre Bk Pubs.
Lolita in Peyton Place: Highbrow, Middlebrow, & Lowbrow Novels of the 1950's. Ruth P. Wood. LC 95-22338. (Garland Studies in American Popular History & Culture). 192p. 1995. text 58.00 (0-8153-2061-2) Garland.
Lolita Man. Bill James. LC 90-27391. (Detective Colin Harpur Novel Ser.). 158p. 1991. 17.95 (0-88150-198-0, Foul Play) Norton.
Lolita Man. Bill James. (Harpur & Iles Mystery Ser.). 160p. 1998. pap. 10.00 (0-393-31782-X) Norton.
Lollapalooza. Julia Meek. 204p. 1996. 22.95 (0-9638639-5-9) Nimrod Hse.
Lollard Bible & Other Medieval Biblical Versions. Margaret Deanesly. LC 77-84722. reprint ed. 49.50 (0-404-16125-1) AMS Pr.
Lollard Sermons: Edited from British Library MS Additional 41321; Bodleian Library MS Rawlinson C. 751; Manchester, John Rylands Library MS English 412. Ed. by Gloria Cigman. (OS 294 Ser.: No. 294). 416p. 1989. 69.00 (0-19-722296-X) OUP.
Lollard Themes in Reformation Theology of William Tyndale. Donald Smeeton. (Sixteenth Century Essays & Studies: Vol. VI). (Illus.). 240p. 1986. 40.00 (0-940474-06-9, SCJP) Truman St Univ.
Lollards & Protestants in the Diocese of York. A. G. Dickens. 280p. (C). 1983. 50.00 (0-907628-05-2); pap. 18.00 (0-907628-06-0) Hambledon Press.
Lollards & Reformers: Images & Literacy in Late Medieval Religion. Margaret Aston. 405p. 1984. 60.00 (0-907628-03-6); pap. 22.00 (0-907628-18-4) Hambledon Press.
Lollards & Their Books. Anne Hudson. 280p. 1985. 55.00 (0-907628-60-5) Hambledon Press.
Lollards of the Chiltern Hills. William H. Summers. LC 80-12770. (Heresies of the Early Christian & Medieval Era Ser.: Second Ser.). reprint ed. 47.50 (0-404-16245-2) AMS Pr.
Lollardy & the Gentry in the Later Middle Ages. Margaret Aston & Colin Richmond. LC 96-53219. 290p. 1997. text 65.00 (0-312-17388-1) St Martin.
Lollipop. Wendy Watson. LC 75-26642. (Illus.). 28p. (J). (ps-2). 1976. lib. bdg. 10.89 (0-690-00768-X) HarpC Child Bks.
Lollipop Grapes & Clothespin Critters: Quick on the Spot Remedies for Restless Children. Robyn F. Spizman. (J). pap. 89.50 (0-201-57753-4) Addison-Wesley.
Lollipop Lunch. Patricia E. Hoon. LC 95-178070. (Illus.). 1994. 19.95 (0-937857-54-8, 1480) Speech Bin.
Lollipop Model Course. 160p. 1970. 75.00 (0-318-16875-8) World Modeling.
Lollipop Test Manual: A Diagnostic Screening Test for School Readiness. rev. ed. Alexander L. Chew. 32p. (J). (ps-k). 1989. pap., student ed. 15.95 (0-89334-101-0) Humanics Ltd.
Lollipop Trollops & Other Poems. Alexander Theroux. LC 92-12510. 192p. 1992. 19.95 (1-56478-007-4); pap. 10.95 (1-56478-006-6) Dalkey Arch.
Lollipops & Sugarplums. Laura E. Clayton. (Illus.). 28p. (Orig.). (J). (ps-5). 1997. pap. write for info. (1-889732-07-9, Key-A-Teese Prod) Word-For-Word.
Lolls: Poems from Hollywood. Mark Dunster. 11p. 1999. pap. 5.00 (0-89642-645-9) Linden Pubs.
Lolly Willowes. Sylvia T. Warner. 3.95 (0-7043-3824-6, Pub. by Quartet) Charles River Bks.
Lolly Willowes: Or the Loving Huntsman. Sylvia T. Warner. 262p. 1999. reprint ed. pap. 11.95 (0-915864-91-6) Academy Chi Pubs.
Lolly Willowes: or The Loving Huntsman. Sylvia Townsend-Warner. LC 99-14569. 230p. 1999. reprint ed. pap. 12.95 (0-940322-16-1, Pub. by NY Rev Bks) Midpt Trade.
Lolo & Red-Legs. Kirk Reeve. LC 97-49969. 100p. (J). (gr. 5 up). 1998. lib. bdg. 12.95 (0-87358-683-2) Northland AZ.
Lolo & Red Legs. Kirk Reeve. LC 97-49969. (Illus.). 100p. (J). (gr. 3-6). 1998. pap. 6.95 (0-87358-684-0, Rising Moon Bks) Northland AZ.
***Lolo Creek Reflections.** Lolo Woman's Club Staff. (Illus.). 115p. 1999. reprint ed. pap. 13.95 (0-912299-82-7) Stoneydale Pr Pub.
Loma del Angel. Reinaldo Arenas. LC 95-60528. (Coleccion Caniqui). (SPA.). 140p. (Orig.). 1995. reprint ed. pap. 16.00 (0-89729-519-6) Ediciones.
LOMA Handbook of Insurance Policy Forms: Reference. Harriet E. Jones. (C). pap. text 24.95 (1-57974-045-6, Pub. by Life Office) PBD Inc.
Loma Prieta. Francisco X. Alarcon. Ed. by Christopher Funkhouser. (ENG & SPA., Illus.). 32p. (Orig.). 1990. pap. 3.00 (0-9627192-1-8) We Pr.
Loma Prieta, California, Earthquake of October 17, 1989 - Marina District. Ed. by Thomas D. O'Rourke. (Illus.). 215p. (Orig.). (C). 1993. pap. text 45.00 (0-7881-0175-7) DIANE Pub.
Loma Prieta, California, Earthquake of October 17, 1989. LC 92-32287. (U. S. Geological Survey Professional Paper Ser.). 1992. write for info. (0-607-90631-6) USGPO.
Loma Prieta, California, Earthquake of October 17, 1989: Loss Estimation & Procedures. Ed. by Susan K. Tubbesing. (Illus.). 77p. (Orig.). 1996. pap. text 25.00 (0-7881-2959-7) DIANE Pub.
Loma Prieta Earthquake: Studies of Short-Term Impacts. Ed. by Robert Bolin. (Monograph: No. 50). 116p. (Orig.). 1990. pap. 20.00 (1-877943-02-9) Natural Hazards.
Loma Prieta Earthquake of October 17, 1989, Reconnaissance Report. Ed. by Lee Benuska. (Illus.). 450p. 1990. pap. 30.00 (0-943198-71-2, 90-01) Earthquake Eng.
Loma Prieta Quake: What One City Learned. Richard Wilson. (Illus.). 64p. 1991. pap. 18.95 (0-87326-083-X) Intl City-Cnty Mgt.
Loman Family Picnic. rev. ed. Donald Margulies. 1994. pap. 5.25 (0-8222-0684-6) Dramatists Play.
Loma's Glossary of Insurance Terms. 3rd ed. Ed. by Nicholas L. Desoutter & Kenneth Huggins. 190p. pap. text 16.00 (1-57974-004-9, Pub. by Life Office) PBD Inc.
Lomawood: The Evolution of a Village. Grace S. Steiner. 100p. 1995. pap. 15.00 (0-9647567-0-6) G S Steiner.
Lombard Communes. William F. Butler. LC 68-25226. (World History Ser.: No. 48). 1969. lib. bdg. 75.00 (0-8383-0923-2) M S G Haskell Hse.
Lombard Laws. Katherine F. Drew. LC 72-80381. (Middle Ages Ser.). 302p. 1973. pap. 18.95 (0-8122-1055-7) U of Pa Pr.
Lombard Street. Walter Bagehot. Ed. by Mira Wilkins. LC 78-3895. (International Finance Ser.). 1979. reprint ed. lib. bdg. 33.95 (0-405-11201-7) Ayer.
***Lombard Street: A Description of the Money Market.** Walter Bagehot. LC 98-51463. (Investment Classics Ser.). 359p. 1999. 34.95 (0-471-34499-0) Wiley.
Lombard Street: A Description of the Money Market; with "The Currency Monopoly" Walter Bagehot. 218p. 1991. reprint ed. pap. 14.95 (0-87991-252-9) Porcupine Pr.
Lombard Street in War & Reconstruction. Benjamin H. Higgins. (Occasional Papers: No. 28). 123p. 1949. reprint ed. 32.00 (0-87014-343-3) Natl Bur Econ Res.
***Lombard Street P.** Walter Bagehot. LC 98-51463. (Investment Classics Ser.). 359p. 1999. pap. 19.95 (0-471-34536-9) Wiley.
Lombardi. Ed. by John Wiebusch. (Illus.). 216p. 1997. 35.00 (1-57243-028-1) Triumph Bks.
Lombardi: His Life & Times. 2nd ed. Robert W. Wells. LC 97-40008. (Prairie Classics Ser.: No. 5). (Illus.). 208p. 1997. pap. 12.95 (1-879483-43-2) Prairie Oak Pr.
Lombardo's Law. Ellen Wittlinger. LC 92-28916. 144p. (J). 1993. 14.95 (0-395-65969-8) HM.
Lombardo's Law. Ellen Wittlinger. 1995. 10.05 (0-606-07802-9, Pub. by Turtleback) Demco.
Lombardo's Law. Ellen Wittlinger. LC 94-25856. (Illus.). 144p. (YA). (gr. 5 up). 1995. reprint ed. pap. 4.95 (0-688-05294-0, Wm Morrow) Morrow Avon.
Lombards. Neil Christie. LC 95-155447. 320p. 1995. 62.95 (0-631-18238-1) Blackwell Pubs.
Lombards. Neil Christie. (Peoples of Europe Ser.). (Illus.). 264p. 1998. reprint ed. pap. 24.95 (0-631-21197-7) Blackwell Pubs.
Lombardy Milan & the Italian Lakes. 3rd ed. Dana Facaros. 1999. pap. text 17.95 (1-86011-907-7) Cadgn Bks.
L'Ombre de Z see Shadow of Z: Spirou & Fantasio
Lombrices. Arthur Morton. Tr. by Angelita L. Aguilar. (SPA., Illus.). (J). (gr. k-3). 1995. 12.50 (1-57842-037-7) Delmas Creat.
Lombton: An Illustrated History of the County. Glen C. Phillips. (Illus.). 128p. 1999. pap. 22.95 (0-921818-20-3) I G Pub.
Lome Conventions & Development: An Empirical Assessment. Olufemi A. Barbarinde. LC 94-1145. 1994. 77.95 (1-85628-678-9, Pub. by Avebry) Ashgate Pub Co.
Lomen: Genealogies of the Lomen (Ringstad), Brandt & Joys Families. G. J. Lomen. (Illus.). 361p. 1992. reprint ed. pap. 55.50 (0-8328-2322-8); reprint ed. lib. bdg. 65.50 (0-8328-2321-X) Higginson Bk Co.
Lon. D. H. Potts. 183p. 1993. 12.00 (0-911521-36-4) Tafnews.
Lon Chaney: The Man Behind the Thousand Faces. Michael F. Blake. LC 93-20212. (Illus.). 408p. 1994. pap. 19.95 (1-879511-09-6, Vestal Pr) Madison Bks UPA.
Lon Chaney, Jr. Horror Film Star, 1906-1993. Don G. Smith. LC 95-39762. (Illus.). 248p. 1995. lib. bdg. 37.50 (0-7864-0120-6) McFarland & Co.
Lon L. Fuller. Robert S. Summers. LC 83-42834. (Jurists: Profiles in Legal Theory Ser.). 192p. 1984. 32.50 (0-8047-1210-7) Stanford U Pr.
***Lon of New York: American Photography of the Male Nude 1940-1970, Vol 2.** Verlag Janssen. 1998. 44.95 (3-925443-61-4) Janssen.
Lon Po Po: A Red-Riding Hood Story from China. Ed Young. LC 88-1522. (Illus.). 32p. (J). (gr. k-4). 1989. 15.95 (0-399-21619-7, Philomel) Peng Put Young Read.
Lon Po Po: A Red-Riding Hood Story from China. Ed Young. LC 88-15222. (Illus.). 32p. (J). (ps-3). 1996. pap. 6.99 (0-698-11382-9, PapStar) Peng Put Young Read.
Lon Po Po: A Red-Riding Hood Story from China. Ed Young. LC 88-15222. (J). 1996. 11.15 (0-606-09570-5, Pub. by Turtleback) Demco.
Lona Pilgrimage: One Man's Experience. John Kellet. 1987. 25.00 (0-947988-13-0, Pub. by Wild Goose Pubns) St Mut.
Londa Tarot. Londa Marks. 1993. pap. 15.00 (0-88079-664-2, LD78) US Games Syst.
Londagin. Robert H. Redding. LC 97-93463. 192p. 1997. lib. bdg. 18.95 (0-8034-9241-3, Avalon Bks) Bouregy.
Londinium: Architecture & the Crafts. William R. Lethaby. LC 72-83273. (Illus.). 1972. reprint ed. 18.95 (0-405-08743-8) Ayer.
London see International Hydrogeological Map of Europe: Explanatory Notes
London see World Cities
***London.** 208p. 2000. spiral bd. 16.95 (1-56251-329-X, Pub. by AAA) S&S Trade.
London. (J). 1998. pap. 6.95 (0-7894-3800-3) DK Pub Inc.
***London.** (DK Eyewitness City Maps Ser.). 1999. 7.95 (0-7894-4856-4) DK Pub Inc.
London. (Citypacks Ser.). 1996. 10.00 (0-614-12779-3) Fodors Travel.
London. (Arte & Arquitectura Ser.). (Illus.). 360p. 1999. 19.95 (3-8290-2601-3, 540555) Konemann.
***London.** 496p. 1999. pap. 15.95 (0-02-863096-3) Macmillan.
London. (Baedeker's Ser.). (Illus.). 1991. pap. 17.00 (0-13-094764-4, P-H Travel) Prntice Hall Bks.
***London.** (J). (gr. 4-6). 2000. per. 14.95 (0-7922-7694-9) S&S Trade.
London. Sean Callery. (Illus.). 24p. 1996. pap. text 6.95 (0-19-422801-0) OUP.
London. Thomas Cook. (Passport's Illustrated Travel Guides from Thomas Cook Ser.). (Illus.). 192p. 1994. pap. 12.95 (0-8442-9040-8, Passprt Bks) NTC Contemp Pub Co.
London. Compiled by Heather Creaton. LC 96-223555. (World Bibliographical Ser.: Vol. 189). 200p. 1996. lib. bdg. 67.00 (1-85109-248-X, DA679) ABC-CLIO.
London. DK Publishing Staff. LC 92-53470. (Eyewitness Travel Guides Ser.). 432p. 1999. 40.00 (0-7894-4975-7, D K Ink) DK Pub Inc.
***London.** Dorling Kindersley Publishing Inc., Staff. LC 99-55203. (Kids' Travel Guides Ser.). (Illus.). 64p. (J). (gr. 4-7). 2000. pap. 7.95 (0-7894-5249-9, D K Ink) DK Pub Inc.
London. Dunkling. 1984. pap. text. write for info. (0-582-74905-0, Pub. by Addison-Wesley) Longman.
London. Griffin Trade Paperbacks Publishing Staff. (Illus.). 336p. 1999. pap. 16.99 (0-312-24474-6, St Martin Griffin) St Martin.
London. Hallawell. Date not set. pap. text, wbk. ed. write for info. (0-582-02575-3, Pub. by Addison-Wesley) Longman.
***London.** Samantha Hardingham. 2000. pap. 12.00 (1-899858-92-X, Pub. by Ellipsis) Norton.
London. Samantha Hardingham. (Architecture Guides Ser.). (Illus.). 320p. 1997. pap. 5.95 (3-89508-281-3, 520197) Konemann.
London. Burton Holmes. Ed. by Arthur Meier Schlesinger, Jr. LC 97-33419. (World 100 Years Ago Ser.). (Illus.). 144p. (YA). (gr. 5 up). 1999. 29.95 (0-7910-4660-5) Chelsea Hse.
London. Rod Humphries. 256p. 1999. pap. 9.95 (1-85828-581-X, Pub. by Rough Guides) Penguin Putnam.
London. Ed. by Fred L. Israel & Arthur Meier Schlesinger, Jr. LC 97-33419. (World 100 Years Ago Ser.). (Illus.). 144p. (YA). (gr. 5 up). 1999. pap. 19.95 (0-7910-4661-3) Chelsea Hse.
***London.** James Kavanagh. (Pocket Traveller City Ser.). (Illus.). 2000. 5.95 (1-58355-019-4, Pub. by Waterford WA) Falcon Pub Inc.
***London.** Konemann Inc. Staff. (Illus.). 2000. 14.95 (3-8290-4836-X) Konemann.
London. Michael Kronenwetter. LC 91-30306. (Cities at War Ser.). (Illus.). 96p. (J). (gr. 6 up). 1992. text 18.00 (0-02-751050-6, Mac Bks Young Read) S&S Childrens.
London. Michael Leapman. LC 92-53470. (Eyewitness Travel Guides Ser.). (Illus.). 432p. 1993. pap. 24.95 (1-56458-183-7) DK Pub Inc.
London. Dan Levine. (Frommer's Walking Tours Ser.). (Illus.). 176p. 1993. pap. 12.00 (0-671-79836-7, P-H Travel) Prntice Hall Bks.
London. Chiara Libero. (Places & History Ser.). 272p. 1998. 24.95 (1-55670-692-8) Stewart Tabori & Chang.
***London.** Sampson Lloyd. 160p. 1999. 35.00 (1-85585-676-X) Collins & Br.
London. Ian Montgomery. (C). 1988. 45.00 (1-85368-028-1, Pub. by New5 Holland) St Mut.
London. Louise Nicholson. 1989. 16.95 (0-370-31032-2) Random.
London. NTC Publishing Staff. (Passport Essential Guide Ser.). (Illus.). 128p. 1999. pap. 8.95 (0-8442-0089-1, 00891, Passprt Bks) NTC Contemp Pub Co.
London. Pevensey Heritage Guides Staff. (Illus.). 112p. 1994. pap. 9.95 (0-907115-78-0, Pub. by D & C Pub) Sterling.
London. Roy Porter. write for info. (0-393-03762-2) Norton.
London. Ed. by Kenneth Powell. (World Cities Ser.: No. 1). (Illus.). 417p. 1993. 95.00 (1-85490-188-5, Pub. by Wiley) Wiley.
London. Rand McNally Staff. 1998. pap. 5.95 (0-528-94651-X) Rand McNally.
London. Rand McNally Staff. pap. 6.95 (0-528-95955-7) Rand McNally.
***London.** Random House Value Publishing Staff. (Illus.). 128p. 2000. 12.99 (0-517-16174-5) Random Hse Value.
London. John Russell. LC 94-1528. (Illus.). 256p. 1994. 49.50 (0-8109-3570-8) Abrams.
London. Edward Rutherfurd. LC 97-10176. (YA). 1997. 25.95 (0-517-59181-2) Crown Pub Group.
London. Edward Rutherfurd. 1998. mass mkt. 7.99 (0-449-00263-2, Crest) Fawcett.
London. R. Conrad Stein. (Cities of the World Ser.). 64p. (J). 1997. pap. 9.95 (0-516-26122-3) Childrens.
London. Fiona Templeton. LC 84-50328. (Illus.). 56p. (Orig.). 1984. pap. 5.95 (0-940650-34-7) Sun & Moon CA.
***London.** Ed. by Thomas Cook Publishing Staff. (Must-See Guides Ser.). (Illus.). 2000. pap. 14.95 (1-84157-072-9) Thomas Cook Pub.
London. Ed. by Tripbuilder Staff. 1997. pap. 59.50 (1-56621-029-1) TripBuilder.
London. Nick Yapp. (Illus.). 360p. 1999. pap. 19.95 (3-8290-0484-2, 520555) Konemann.
***London.** Ed. by Zagat Surveying Staff. (Illus.). 2000. pap. 21.95 (1-57006-223-4) Zagat.
London. rev. ed. DK Publishing Staff. (Eyewitness Travel Guides Ser.). 432p. 1999. pap. 24.95 (0-7894-4890-4) DK Pub Inc.
***London.** rev. ed. Let's Go Staff. (Let's Go 2001 Ser.). (Illus.). 336p. 2000. pap. 16.99 (0-312-24682-X, St Martin Griffin) St Martin.
London. 2nd ed. Kathy Arnold. LC 94-67812. (Illustrated Travel Guides from Thomas Cook Ser.). (Illus.). 192p. 1994. pap. 12.95 (0-8442-9047-5, Passprt Bks) NTC Contemp Pub Co.
***London.** 2nd ed. Steve Fallon & Pat Yale. (Illus.). 368p. 2000. pap. 15.95 (0-86442-793-X) Lonely Planet.
London. 2nd ed. Insight Guides Staff. (Insight Guides). 1998. pap. text 7.95 (0-88729-540-1) Langenscheidt.
London. 3rd ed. Thomas Cook. (Passport's Illustrated Travel Guides Ser.). (Illus.). 192p. 1998. pap. 14.95 (0-8442-4823-1, 48231, Passprt Bks) NTC Contemp Pub Co.
***London.** 3rd ed. Ed. by Fodors Travel Publications, Inc. Staff. 96p. 2000. pap. 12.00 (0-679-00482-3) Fodors Travel.
***London.** 3rd ed. Andrew Gumbel. (Cadogan City Guides Ser.). 512p. 2000. pap. text 18.95 (1-86011-971-9) Cadgn Bks.
***London.** 3rd ed. Insight Guides Staff. (Insight Guides). 1998. pap. text 12.95 (0-88729-894-X) Langenscheidt.
***London.** 4th ed. Kathy Arnold. (Illustrated Travel Guides Ser.). (Illus.). 2000. pap. 14.95 (0-658-01074-3, Passprt Bks) NTC Contemp Pub Co.
London. 6th ed. Insight Guides Staff. (Insight Guides). 1998. pap. text 21.95 (0-88729-480-4) Langenscheidt.
***London.** 7th ed. Penguin Books Staff. 352p. 1999. pap. 14.95 (0-14-027449-9) Viking Penguin.
London. 16th ed. Ylva French. (Blue Guide Ser.). (Illus.). 448p. 1998. pap. 25.95 (0-393-31747-1) Norton.
London: A City Revealed. Contemporary Books Staff. LC 98-39198. (Illus.). 176p. 1998. 60.00 (0-8092-2802-5, 280250, Contemporary Bks) NTC Contemp Pub Co.
London: A History. Francis Sheppard. LC 98-7999. (Illus.). 496p. 1999. 35.00 (0-19-822922-4) OUP.
***London: A History.** Francis Sheppard. (Illus.). 496p. 2000. pap. 16.95 (0-19-285369-4) OUP.
***London: A Journey Through the Ages.** Konemann Inc. Staff. (Illus.). 2000. 19.95 (3-8290-5034-8) Konemann.
London: A Literary Companion. Peper Vansittart. (Illus.). 311p. 1993. pap. 24.95 (0-7195-5208-7, Pub. by John Murray) Trafalgar.
London: A Literary Companion. Peter Vansittart. (Illus.). 311p. 1993. 39.95 (0-7195-5014-9, Pub. by John Murray) Trafalgar.

L

An Asterisk (*) at the beginning of an entry indicates that the title is appearing for the first time.

L

London: A New Metropolitan Geography. Ed. by Keith Hoggart & David Green. LC 92-16581. (Illus.). 272p. 1993. pap. 25.00 (*0-340-58213-8*, A9890, Pub. by E A) Routldge.

London: A Pilgrimage. Gustave Dore & Blanchard Jerrold. LC 68-56513. (Illus.). 205p. 1978. reprint ed. 48.95 (*0-405-08460-9*, Pub. by Blom Pubns) Ayer.

London: A Pilgrimage. Gustave Dore & Blanchard Jerrold. (Illus.). 191p. 1970. reprint ed. pap. 14.95 (*0-486-22306-X*) Dover.

London: A Social History. Roy Porter. Date not set. 29.95 (*0-614-32353-3*) HUP.

London: A Social History. Roy Porter. LC 94-33025. (Illus.). 448p. 1995. 33.00 (*0-674-53838-2*, PORLON) HUP.

London: A Social History. Roy Porter. 448p. 1999. pap. 19.95 (*0-674-53839-0*) HUP.

London: City on a River. David Paterson. (Illus.). 144p. 1997. pap. 27.50 (*0-9521908-3-4*, Pub. by Peak Pubg Ltd) Trans-Atl Phila.

London: Exploring Museums. Simon Olding. xiii, 110p. 1986. 16.00 (*0-11-290465-3*, Pub. by Statnry Office) Balogh.

London: Globetrotter Travel Guide. Globetrotter Staff. (Illus.). 128p. 1997. pap. text 17.95 (*1-85368-712-X*, Pub. by New5 Holland) Globe Pequot.

***London: Kit & Robin.** Rachel Hawthorne. (Love Stories Ser.). 192p. (YA). (gr. 7-12). 2000. mass mkt. 4.50 (*0-553-49326-4*) Bantam.

***London: More by Fortune Than Design.** Michael Hebbert. LC 97-46063. (World Cities Ser.). 254p. 1998. pap. 59.95 (*0-471-98237-7*) Wiley.

***London: Portrait of a City.** Matthew Weinreb. (Illus.). 240p. 1999. pap. 9.95 (*0-7148-3859-4*) Phaidon Pr.

London: Problems of Change. Ed. by Hugh D. Clout & Peter A. Wood. Date not set. pap. text. write for info. (*0-582-35491-9*, Pub. by Addison-Wesley) Longman.

London: Sight Unseen. Snowdon. 1999. 27.95 (*0-297-82490-2*) Weidenfeld & Nicolson.

London: The Forest City: An Illustrated History of London, Canada. Frederick H. Armstrong. LC 86-23434. 336p. 1986. 29.95 (*0-89781-180-1*) Am Historical Pr.

London: The Hub of the Industrial Revolution. Barnett. 224p. 2000. text 59.50 (*1-86064-196-2*, Pub. by I B T) St Martin.

London: The Promised Land? Anne J. Kershen. (Studies in Migration). 174p. 1997. text 64.95 (*1-85972-630-5*, Pub. by Avebry) Ashgate Pub Co.

London: The Travel Notebook. Pascale Loiseau. 104p. 1997. 14.95 (*2-911141-01-6*, Pub. by Les Edtns Pascale) Assoc Pubs Grp.

London: Underground. pap. 16.95 (*0-528-94976-4*) Rand McNally.

London: Urban Patterns, Problems, & Policies. Ed. by David V. Donnison & David Eversley. LC 73-80440. (Centre for Environmental Studies Ser.: Vol. 2). 464p. reprint ed. pap. 143.90 (*0-608-14193-3*, 202188800026) Bks Demand.

***London: With Day Trips to Bath, Brighton, Cambridge, Oxford, Windsor & Other Popular Destinations.** Corey Sandler. (Econoguides Ser.). (Illus.). 2000. pap. 17.95 (*0-8092-2637-5*, Contemporary Bks) NTC Contemp Pub Co.

London: With Day Trips to Bath, Brighton, Oxford & Other Popular Destinations. Corey Sandler. LC 98-8726. (Econoguide '99 Ser.). (Illus.). xiv, 338 p. 1999. pap. 16.95 (*0-8092-2896-3*, Contemporary Bks) NTC Contemp Pub Co.

London: Yesterday. 96p. 1998. pap. 19.95 (*3-927258-68-7*) Gingko Press.

London - A Modern Project. Rut Blees Luxemburg. (Illus.). 64p. 1997. pap. 19.95 (*1-901033-50-3*, Pub. by Black Dog Pubg) RAM Publications.

***London - Brussels.** Andrew Gumbel & Antony Mason. 2000. pap. 14.95 (*1-86011-939-5*, Pub. by Cadgn Bks) Globe Pequot.

London - World City into the Twenty-First Century. 268p. 1991. pap. 50.00 (*0-11-701558-X*, HM585X, Pub. by Statnry Office) Bernan Associates.

***London A-Z.** (Illus.). 288p. 2000. pap. 14.95 (*0-85039-490-2*, Pub. by Geographers A-Z) Hunter NJ.

London A-Z: Colour Edition. (Illus.). 288p. 1988. pap. 14.95 (*0-85039-195-4*) Hunter NJ.

London Access. Richard S. Wurman. (Access Travel Guides Ser.). (Illus.). 182p. (Orig.). pap. 14.95 (*0-318-39986-5*, Access Trvl) HarpInfo.

London after Dark. Robert Cowan. (Illus.). 128p. (C). 1993. text 35.00 (*0-7148-2870-X*, Pub. by Phaidon Press) Phaidon Pr.

London after Midnight, Pt. 1. large type ed. Ed. by Peter Haining. 1996. pap. 20.95 (*0-7862-0790-6*) Thorndike Pr.

London after Midnight, Pt. 2. large type ed. Ed. by Peter Haining. 1996. pap. 20.95 (*0-7862-0791-4*) Thorndike Pr.

***London After Midnight: Reconstruction of the Lost Classic Silent Film.** 2nd rev. ed. Ed. by John Conforti. (Lost Film Ser.: Vol. 1). (Illus.). 2000. pap. 24.95 (*1-882127-08-0*) Magicimage Filmbooks.

London after the Bomb: What a Nuclear Attack Really Means. Owne Greene et al. (Illus.). 1983. pap. 4.95 (*0-19-285123-3*) OUP.

***London-Amsterdam: City-Centre to City-Centre Less Than an Hour Away.** Andrew Gumbel. (City Guides Ser.). (Illus.). 2000. pap. 14.95 (*1-86011-985-9*) Cadgn Bks.

London & Back: A Book of Personal Drawings. Milton N. Kemnitz. (Illus.). 120p. 1977. 12.50 (*0-89824-009-3*) Trillium Pr.

London & Beyond. Ed. by Peter Titchmarsh. (Ordnance Survey Pathfinder Guides Ser.). (Illus.). 208p. 1993. pap. 15.95 (*0-319-00084-2*) Seven Hills Bk.

London & Its Environs in the 19th Century. Thomas H. Shepherd & James Elmes. LC 67-13341. (Illus.). 1972. reprint ed. 27.95 (*0-405-08962-7*) Ayer.

London & the Civil War. Ed. by Stephen Porter. 240p. 1996. text 65.00 (*0-312-15844-0*) St Martin.

London & the Countrey Carbonadoed & Quartered into Several Characters. Donald Lupton. LC 77-7413. (English Experience Ser.: No. 879). 1977. reprint ed. lib. bdg. 20.00 (*90-221-0879-1*) Walter J Johnson.

London & the English Economy, 1500-1700. F. J. Fisher. 220p. 1990. 55.00 (*1-85285-023-X*) Hambledon Press.

London & the Life of Literature in Late Victorian England: The Diary of George Gissing, Novelist. Ed. by Pierre Coustillas. LC 77-72970. 617p. 1978. 85.00 (*0-8387-2145-1*) Bucknell U Pr.

London & the Middle East: Money, Power, & War, 1902-1922. Roger Adelson. LC 94-36262. (Illus.). 320p. 1995. 42.50 (*0-300-06094-7*) Yale U Pr.

London & the National Government, 1721-1742: A Study of City Politics & the Walpole Administration. Alfred J. Henderson. LC 75-29086. (Perspectives in European History Ser.: No. 7). (Illus.). x, 242p. 1975. reprint ed. lib. bdg. 37.50 (*0-87991-609-5*) Porcupine Pr.

London & the South East. David Jensen. (Radio Times Around Britain Guides Ser.). (Illus.). 96p. 1994. 8.95 (*0-563-36951-5*, Pub. by BBC) Parkwest Pubns.

London Architecture: Features & Facades. Ben Weinreb. (Illus.). 240p. (C). 1993. text 55.00 (*0-7148-2890-4*, Pub. by Phaidon Press) Phaidon Pr.

London As an International Business Centre. Ed. by Roderick Millar. 256p. 1998. pap. 35.00 (*0-7494-2543-1*) Kogan Page Ltd.

London As It Might Have Been. Felix Barker & Ralph Hyde. (Illus.). 224p. 1996. pap. 29.95 (*0-7195-5557-4*, Pub. by John Murray) Trafalgar.

London Assurance. Dion Boucicault. Ed. by James L. Smith. (New Mermaid Ser.). 137p. (C). 1984. pap. text 9.75 (*0-393-90050-9*) Norton.

London at Its Best. Robert S. Kane. (World at Its Best Travel Ser.). (Illus.). 232p. 1989. pap. 9.95 (*0-8442-9562-0*, Passprt Bks) NTC Contemp Pub Co.

London Bibliography of the Social Sciences Vol. 32: Ninth Supplement, 1974. Compiled by British Library of Political & Economic Science St. 461p. 1975. 180.00 (*0-7201-0524-2*) Continuum.

London Bibliography of the Social Sciences Vol. 33: Tenth Supplement, 1975. Compiled by British Library of Political & Economic Science St. 418p. 1976. 180.00 (*0-7201-0634-6*) Continuum.

London Bibliography of the Social Sciences Vol. 34: Eleventh Supplement, 1976. Compiled by British Library of Political & Economic Science St. LC 31-9970. 458p. 1977. lib. bdg. 180.00 (*0-7201-0721-0*) Continuum.

London Bibliography of the Social Sciences Vol. 36: Thirteenth Supplement, 1978. Compiled by British Library of Political & Economic Science St. 416p. 1979. lib. bdg. 180.00 (*0-7201-0929-9*) Continuum.

London Bibliography of the Social Sciences Vol. 41: Eighteenth Supplement, 1983. Compiled by British Library of Political & Economic Science St. 928p. 1984. text 160.00 (*0-7201-1695-3*) Continuum.

London Bibliography of the Social Sciences Vol. 42: Nineteenth Supplement, 1984. Compiled by British Library of Political & Economic Science St. 1056p. 1985. 160.00 (*0-7201-1726-7*) Continuum.

London Bibliography of the Social Sciences Vol. 43: Twentieth Supplement, 1985. Compiled by British Library of Political & Economic Science St. 976p. 1986. text 200.00 (*0-7201-1771-2*) Continuum.

London Bibliography of the Social Sciences Vol. 45: Twenty-Second Supplement, 1987. Compiled by British Library of Political & Economic Science St. 1128p. 1988. text 220.00 (*0-7201-1958-8*) Continuum.

London Bibliography of the Social Sciences Vol. 47: Twenty-Fourth Supplement, 1989. Compiled by British Library of Political & Economic Science St. 1024p. 1990. text 250.00 (*0-7201-2034-9*) Continuum.

London Bibliography of the Social Sciences Vols. 29-31: Eighth Supplement, 1972-1973, Set. D. A. Clarke. 1768p. 1975. text 260.00 (*0-7201-0454-8*) Continuum.

London Blood: Further Adventures of the American Agent Abroad: A Benjamin Franklin Mystery. Robert L. Hall. LC 97-18813. 256p. 1997. 21.95 (*0-312-16908-6*, Thomas Dunne) St Martin.

London Blue Plaque Guide. Robert Nicholas Rennison. 2000. pap. text 16.95 (*0-7509-2091-2*) Sutton Pub Ltd.

London Blues. Anthony Frewin. 304p. 1999. pap. 10.95 (*1-56858-146-7*) FWEW.

London Book Window. James Milne. LC 68-16957. (Essay Index Reprint Ser.). 1977. reprint ed. 18.95 (*0-8369-0709-4*) Ayer.

London Bookshop, Pt. 2. Richard Brown & Stanley Brett. (Illus.). 75p. 1977. 20.00 (*0-900002-23-9*, 1267, Pub. by Priv Lib Assn) Oak Knoll.

***London Bridge.** Louis-Ferdinand Celine. Tr. by Dominic Di Bernardi from FRE. LC 94-25168. 390p. 1999. reprint ed. pap. 14.50 (*1-56478-175-5*, Pub. by Dalkey Arch) SPD-Small Pr Dist.

London Bridge: Guignol's Band II. Louis-Ferdinand Celine. Tr. by Dominic Di Bernardi from FRE. LC 94-25168. 449p. 1995. 23.95 (*1-56478-071-6*) Dalkey Arch.

London, British Library, MS Add., No. 30491. Ed. by Alexander Silbiger. (Seventeenth-Century Keyboard Music Ser.: Vol. 11). 125p. 1987. text 20.00 (*0-8240-8010-6*) Garland.

London, British Library, MS Add (Attributed to Frescobaldi), No. 40080. Ed. by Alexander Silbiger. (Seventeenth-Century Keyboard Music Ser.: Vol. 2). 125p. 1987. text 20.00 (*0-8240-8001-7*) Garland.

London, British Library, MS Add. 31501. Ed. by Alexander Silbiger. LC 88-752439. (Seventeenth-Century Keyboard Music Ser.: Vol. 8). 196p. 1989. text 25.00 (*0-8240-8007-6*) Garland.

London, British Library, MS Royal 8 G. VII. Ed. by Howard Mayer Brown. (Renaissance Music in Facsimile Ser.). 160p. 1987. text 30.00 (*0-8240-1458-8*) Garland.

London, British Library, Royal 20. A. XVI. Ed. by Howard Mayer Brown. (Renaissance Music in Facsimile Ser.: Vol. 10). 96p. 1987. text 30.00 (*0-8240-1459-6*) Garland.

London Bulletin, 1938 to 1940, 2 vols., Set. Ed. by E. L. Mesens & Roland Penrose. LC 77-96917. (Contemporary Art Ser.). (Illus.). 1970. reprint ed. 60.95 (*0-405-00733-7*) Ayer.

London Business School Sourceguide to Central & East European Company Information. London Business School Staff. Ed. by Julie Scott. (London Business School Sourceguide Ser.). 1994. 108.00 (*1-873477-70-8*) Gale.

London Calling see **Thick As Thieves**

London Calling. Natalie J. Prior. LC 97-207107. 200p. (YA). 1997. pap. 12.95 (*0-7022-2948-2*, Pub. by Univ Queensland Pr) Intl Spec Bk.

London Cemeteries: An Illustrated Guide & Gazetteer. 3rd ed. Hugh Meller. (Illus.). 368p. 1994. pap. 43.95 (*0-85967-997-7*, Pub. by Scolar Pr) Ashgate Pub Co.

London Church Courts & Society on the Eve of the Reformation. Richard M. Wunderli. LC 79-89571. 1981. 20.00 (*0-910956-81-2*, SAM7); pap. 12.00 (*0-910956-71-5*) Medieval Acad.

London Classification of Business Studies. Ken D. C. Vernon et al. LC 78-520041. 132 p. 1970. write for info. (*0-902583-00-X*) London Bus Schl.

London Coliseum. Victor Glasstone. (Theatre in Focus Ser.). (Illus.). 120p. 1980. pap. text. write for info. incl. sl. (*0-85964-065-5*) Chadwyck-Healey.

London Conferences: Anglo-American Relations & Cold War Strategy, January-June 1950. Roger Bullen. (Documents on British Policy Overseas Ser.: Vol. 2). xxxiii, 406p. 1987. 90.00 (*0-11-591693-8*, Pub. by Statnry Office) Balogh.

London Confidential. 2nd ed. Neil Saunders. 200p. 1991. 12.95 (*0-945332-27-0*) Agora Inc MD.

London Cookbook. Liz Trigg. (Illus.). 320p. 1996. pap. 24.95 (*1-85626-188-3*, Pub. by Cathie Kyle) Trafalgar.

***London Cuckolds.** Terry Johnson. 1998. pap. 10.95 (*0-413-72950-8*) Methn.

London Cycle Guide. Nicky Crowther. (Illus.). 144p. 1998. pap. 14.95 (*1-85960-320-3*, Pub. by J H Haynes & Co) Motorbooks Intl.

London Deception. Franklin W. Dixon. (Hardy Boys Mystery Stories Ser.: No. 158). 160p. (J). (gr. 4-7). 1999. pap. 3.99 (*0-671-03496-0*) PB.

London Dialect of the Late Fourteenth Century: A Transformational Analysis in Historical Linguistics. Rodolfo Jacobson. LC 73-104465. (Janua Linguarum, Ser.: No. 97). (Illus.). (Orig.). 1970. pap. text 50.00 (*90-279-0739-0*) Mouton.

London Diaries of William Nicolson, Bishop of Carlisle, 1702-1718. William Nicolson. Ed. by Geoffrey Holmes & Clyve Jones. (Illus.). 1985. 115.00 (*0-19-822404-4*) OUP.

London Diary, 1717-1721 & Other Writings. William Byrd. Ed. by Louis B. Wright & Marion Tinglin. LC 77-141208. (Research Library of Colonial Americana). (Illus.). 1972. reprint ed. 42.95 (*0-405-03305-2*) Ayer.

***London Diplomatic List: Incorporating Directory of International Organisations.** Foreign & Commonwealth Office Staff. 101p. 2000. pap. 16.00 (*0-11-591767-5*, Pub. by Statnry Office) Balogh.

London Diplomatic List, December 1998. 95p. 1999. pap. 18.00 (*0-11-591763-2*, HM17632, Pub. by Statnry Office) Bernan Associates.

London Diplomatic List, December 1996. TSO Staff. 95p. 1997. pap. 13.00 (*0-11-591754-3*, HM17543, Pub. by Statnry Office) Bernan Associates.

London Docks, 1800-1980: A Civil Engineering History. Ivan S. Greeves. 167p. 1980. 33.00 (*0-7277-0114-2*, Pub. by T Telford) RCH.

London Dumping Convention: The First Decade & Beyond. International Maritime Organization Staff. 1991. text 280.00 (*0-89771-955-7*, Pub. by Intl Maritime Org) St Mut.

***London Eats Out, 1500-2000: 500 Years of Capital Dining.** Edwina Ehrman et al. (Illus.). 112p. 2000. 37.50 (*0-85667-516-4*) P Wilson.

***London-Edinburgh: Two Historic Capitals Only a Train Journey Apart.** Andrew Gumbel. (City Guides Ser.). (Illus.). 2000. pap. 14.95 (*1-86011-944-1*) Cadgn Bks.

London, 1893: Black & White Masters Tournament. Leopold Hoffer. Ed. by Dale Brandreth. (Tournament Bk.). (Illus.). 17p. 1992. pap. 6.50 (*0-939433-14-1*) Caissa Edit.

London Employment Problem. Nick Buck et al. (Inner City in Context Ser.). (Illus.). 214p. 1986. pap. 19.95 (*0-19-823263-2*) OUP.

London Encyclopedia: The Most Comprehensive Book on London Ever Published. 2nd ed. Ed. by Ben Weinreb & Christopher Hibbert. (Illus.). 1060p. (Orig.). 1993. pap. 67.50 (*0-333-57688-8*, Pub. by Papermac) Trans-Atl Phila.

London, England: A Day Tripper's Travelogue from the Coolest City in the World. Derek Hammond. LC 99-494963. 224p. 1998. pap. 15.95 (*1-85158-989-9*, Pub. by Mainstream Pubng) Trafalgar.

London, England: Cooking with Betty Evans. Betty Evans. LC 87-61698. (Illus.). 120p. 1989. pap. 6.95 (*0-931104-26-2*) SunInk Pubn.

London, England & Wales. 2nd ed. (Nelles Guides Ser.). (Illus.). 256p. 1999. pap. 15.95 (*3-88618-419-6*) Hunter NJ.

London, England & Wales: Nelles Guides. (Illus.). 256p. (Orig.). 1996. pap. 14.95 (*3-88618-413-7*, Pub. by Nelles Verlag) Seven Hills Bk.

London Essays in Economics in Honor of Edwin Cannan. Theodor E. Gregory et al. LC 67-23241. (Essay Index Reprint Ser.). 1977. 21.95 (*0-8369-0624-1*) Ayer.

London Essays in Geography. Laurence D. Stamp & Sidney W. Wooldridge. LC 76-80399. (Essay Index Reprint Ser.). 1977. 26.95 (*0-8369-1050-8*) Ayer.

London Experience of Secondary Education. Margaret E. Bryant. LC 85-22987. (Illus.). 540p. (C). 1986. text 39.95 (*0-485-11302-3*, Pub. by Athlone Pr) Humanities.

London Fields. Martin Amis. LC 90-50471. 480p. 1991. pap. 14.00 (*0-679-73034-6*) Vin Bks.

***London Fitness Guide: The Only Guide You Need to Sports & Fitness Facilities in London, 2000.** Lydia Campbell. 512p. 2000. pap. text 24.95 (*1-84000-210-7*) Mitchell Beazley.

***London Flirtation.** Valerie King. (Zebra Regency Romance Ser.). 2000. mass mkt. 5.99 (*0-8217-6535-3*, Zebra Kensgtn) Kensgtn Pub Corp.

London for Beginners. 2nd ed. Nita Clarke. 1999. pap. text 11.00 (*0-86316-274-6*) Writers & Readers.

London for Dickens Lovers. William Kent. LC 72-2106. (Studies in Dickens: No. 52). 1972. reprint ed. lib. bdg. 75.00 (*0-8383-1480-5*) M S G Haskell Hse.

***London for Dummies.** Donald Olson. (For Dummies Ser.). 384p. 2000. pap. 15.99 (*0-7645-6194-4*) IDG Bks.

***London for Families.** 2nd ed. Larry Lain. (Illus.). 2000. pap. 14.95 (*1-56656-337-2*) Interlink Pub.

London for Free: Hundreds of Free Things to Do in London. 3rd rev. ed. Brian Butler. LC 96-49222. (Illus.). 128p. 1997. pap. 9.95 (*0-914457-86-1*) Mustang Pub.

London for Less. (For Less Compact Guides Ser.). 1999. pap. 9.95 (*1-901811-75-1*) IPG Chicago.

London for Less. Ben Webster. (Illus.). 288p. 1997. pap. 19.95 (*0-9525437-3-7*, Pub. by Metropolis International) IPG Chicago.

London for Less: 2nd Ed. 2nd ed. Ben Webster. 1999. pap. text 19.95 (*1-901811-45-X*) Metropolis International.

London for Lovers. Larry Lain & Barb Lain. LC 99-41374. 272p. 2000. pap. 15.00 (*1-56656-345-3*) Interlink Pub.

London for the Independent Traveler: On Your Own, See the London You Want to See, a Step-by-Step Guide. 4th rev. ed. Ruth Humleker. LC 99-10633. (Illus.). 256p. 1999. pap. 14.95 (*0-943400-99-6*) Marlor Pr.

London Gazette Supplement - New Years Honors: Nos. 54993, 54994, 54996, 54997, 54998, 54999, 55000, 55001, 55002. 17p. 1998. pap. 25.00 (*0-11-664993-3*, HM49933, Pub. by Statnry Office) Bernan Associates.

London "General" Motor Buses. D. E. Brewster. (C). 1985. 39.00 (*0-85361-305-2*) St Mut.

London Gestern (London Yesterday) Leben in Den 20er und 30er Jahren. (GER., Illus.). 96p. (C). 1996. 41.00 (*3-8170-2516-5*, Pub. by Knstvrlag Weingrtn) Intl Bk Import.

London Girls. Gerald Gray. 1997. mass mkt. 6.50 (*1-56333-531-X*) Masquerade.

London Green Guide. Michelin Staff. 1997. pap. 19.95 (*0-7859-9127-1*) Fr & Eur.

London Group: The Artists & Their Works. Denys J. Wilcox. 262p. 1995. 78.95 (*1-85928-048-X*, Pub. by Scolar Pr) Ashgate Pub Co.

London Guide. 2nd ed. Meg Rossoff. 312p. 1998. pap. text 14.95 (*1-883323-79-7*) Open Rd Pub.

London Guide Book: A 1920s Guide to London. Lucia Sachnowsici & Gary O'Connell. Ed. by Lynn Willis. (Call of Cthulhu Roleplaying Game Ser.). (Illus.). 96p. (Orig.). 1996. pap. 14.95 (*1-56882-027-5*, 2347) Chaosium.

London Hanged: Crime & Civil Society in the Eighteenth Century. Peter Linebaugh. (Illus.). 512p. (C). 1992. text 64.95 (*0-521-41842-9*) Cambridge U Pr.

London Hanged: Crime & Civil Society in the Eighteenth Century. Peter Linebaugh. (Illus.). 511p. (C). 1993. pap. 21.95 (*0-521-45758-0*) Cambridge U Pr.

London Higher: The Establishment of Higher Education in London. Ed. by Roderick Floud & Sean Glynn. LC 97-47007. 240p. 1998. 90.00 (*0-485-11524-7*, Pub. by Athlone Pr) Humanities.

London Holiday. Richard Peck. 1999. pap. 12.95 (*0-14-027857-5*) Viking Penguin.

London Holiday. large type ed. Richard Peck. LC 98-36372. 1998. 26.95 (*0-7862-1635-2*) Thorndike Pr.

London Hotel & Restaurant Guide, 1996. Michelin Staff. 1996. 11.95 (*0-7859-9874-8*) Fr & Eur.

London Hotel & Restaurant Guide 1998. Michelin. (ENG, FRE, GER & ITA.). 1998. 11.95 (*0-7859-9611-7*) Fr & Eur.

***London Hotels & Restaurants: 2000 Edition.** 100th ed. Michelin Staff. (Red Guide London Ser.). (Illus.). 1999. pap. text. write for info. (*2-06-966026-5*) Michelin.

London in Old Photographs, 1897-1914. Felix Barker. (Illus.). 208p. 1995. 35.00 (*0-8212-2230-9*, Pub. by Bulfinch Pr) Little.

London in the Age of Chaucer. A. R. Myers. LC 73-177342. (Centers of Civilization Ser.: Vol. 31). (Illus.). 256p. 1988. reprint ed. pap. 9.95 (*0-8061-2111-4*) U of Okla Pr.

London in the Age of Industrialisation: Entrepreneurs, Labour Force & Living Conditions, 1700-1850. L. D. Schwarz. (Studies in Population, Economy & Society in Past Time: No. 19). (Illus.). 304p. (C). 1992. text 59.95 (*0-521-40365-0*) Cambridge U Pr.

London in the Age of Shakespeare. Lawrence Manley. LC 86-20476. 372p. 1986. 35.00 (*0-271-00445-2*) Pa St U Pr.

An Asterisk (*) at the beginning of an entry indicates that the title is appearing for the first time.

London in the Age of Shakespeare: An Anthology Lawrence Manley. LC 88-672399. 372p. 1986. write for info. (*0-7099-3560-9*, Pub. by C Helm) Routldge.

London in Your Pocket Guide. (In Your Pocket Guide Ser.). 1997. per. 9.95 (*2-06-651101-3*, 6511) Michelin.

London Inn Signs. Dominic Rotheroe. (Album Ser.: No. 257). (Illus.). 32p. 1989. pap. 6.25 (*0-7478-0088-X*, Pub. by Shire Pubns) Parkwest Pubns.

*__London Interiors.__ Jane Edwards. Ed. by Angelika Taschen. 2000. 39.99 (*3-8228-6218-5*) Taschen Amer.

*__London Interiors: From the Archives of Country Life.__ Ed. by John Cornforth. (Illus.). 192p. 2000. 60.00 (*1-85410-668-6*, Pub. by Aurum Pr) London Brdge.

London, Jack, Short Stories Of. Jack London. (Airmont Classics Ser.). (YA). (gr. 9 up). 1969. mass mkt. 2.50 (*0-8049-0198-8*, CL-198) Airmont.

London Jamaican: A Case Study in Language Contact. Mark Sebba. LC 92-42560. (Real Language Ser.). 1993. pap. text. write for info. (*0-582-08095-9*) Longman.

London Jamaican: A Case Study in Language Contact. Mark Sebba. LC 92-42560. (Real Language Ser.). 1993. write for info. (*0-582-08096-7*) Longman.

London Jewry & London Politics, 1889-1986. Geoffrey Alderman. 192p. 1989. 49.95 (*0-415-02204-5*) Routledge.

London Jews & British Communism, 1935-1945. Henry F. Srebrnik. LC 93-34043. 1994. 39.50 (*0-85303-238-6*, Pub. by M Vallentine & Co) Intl Spec Bk.

London Journal. Flora Tristan. 1989. pap. 9.95 (*0-318-41761-8*) Random.

London, KY. Carl Keith Greene. LC 97-149510. (Images of America Ser.). (Illus.). 128p. 1996. pap. 16.99 (*0-7524-0529-2*) Arcadia Publng.

London Labour & the London Poor, 4 vols., 2. Henry Mayhew. (Illus.). 1982. pap. 9.95 (*0-486-21935-6*) Dover.

London Labour & the London Poor, 4 vols., 3. Henry Mayhew. (Illus.). 1982. pap. 9.95 (*0-486-21936-4*) Dover.

London Ladies. Lucy Stebbins. LC 52-6272. reprint ed. 20.00 (*0-404-06226-1*) AMS Pr.

London Landmarks from the Air. Photos by Jason Hawkes. (Illus.). 96p. 1997. pap. 16.95 (*0-09-182034-0*, Pub. by Ebury Pr) Trafalgar.

London-Leningrad Championship Games: Rematch Championship Games. Garry Kasparov. 1987. 16.51 (*0-08-032053-8*, Pergamon Pr) Elsevier.

London Life see Works of Henry James Jr.: Collected Works

London Life. Incl. Liar. LC 73-312. Mrs. Temperly. Henry James. LC 73-312. Pataqonia. Henry James. LC 73-312. LC 73-312. (Short Story Index Reprint Ser.). 1977. reprint ed. 27.95 (*0-8369-4247-7*) Ayer.

London Life. Arnold Bennett. LC 74-16480. (Collected Works of Arnold Bennett: Vol. 48). 1977. reprint ed. 22.95 (*0-518-19129-X*) Ayer.

London Life. Henry James. 160p. 1992. reprint ed. lib. bdg. 16.95 (*0-89966-933-6*) Buccaneer Bks.

London Life in the Brazen Age: Francis Langley, 1548-1602. William Ingram. LC 77-28573. 349p. reprint ed. pap. 108.20 (*0-7837-2277-X*, 205736500004) Bks Demand.

London Life in the Eighteenth Century. 2nd ed. M. Dorothy George. LC 99-10241. 457p. (C). 1999. reprint ed. pap. 15.95 (*0-89733-147-8*) Academy Chi Pubs.

London Life in the Eighteenth Century: London School of Economics. M. Dorothy George. (LSE Scarce Tracts in Economics Ser.). 468p. (C). 1997. 105.00 (*0-415-14394-2*) Routledge.

London Linnet. large type ed. Tania Langley. 416p. 1986. 27.99 (*0-7089-1543-4*) Ulverscroft.

London Live: From the Yardbirds to Pink Floyd to the Sex Pistols. Tony Bacon. (Illus.). 192p. 1999. pap. 19.95 (*0-87930-572-X*) Miller Freeman.

London Living. Lisa Lovatt-Smith. LC 97-61390. 216p. 1998. 35.00 (*0-8230-2836-4*) Watsn-Guptill.

London Lodgings: The Quentin Quartet 1. large type ed. Claire Rayner. (Charnwood Large Print Ser.). 512p. 1995. 27.99 (*0-7089-8847-4*, Charnwood) Ulverscroft.

London Lovers. Barbara Hardy. 208p. 1996. 29.95 (*0-7206-0964-X*, Pub. by P Owen Ltd) Dufour.

London Lovers. Barbara Hardy. 208p. 1997. pap. 19.95 (*0-7206-1023-0*, Pub. by P Owen Ltd) Dufour.

London Magazine: The Romantics in Context, 10 vols., Set. 13142p. (C). (gr. 13). 1994. text, boxed set 1640.00 (*0-415-12069-1*, C0400) Routledge.

London Man. Francis B. Chichester. 1988. mass mkt. 8.95 (*0-446-38740-1*, Pub. by Warner Bks) Little.

London Market Yearbook, 1994-1995. (DYP Directory Ser.). 400p. 250.00 (*1-870255-27-5*) LLP.

*__London Markets.__ 2nd ed. Phil Harris. 1999. pap. text 12.95 (*1-86011-903-4*) CDG Bks.

London Merchant. George Lillo. Ed. by William H. McBurney. LC 65-11521. (Regents Restoration Drama Ser.). xxvi, 106p. 1965. pap. text 7.95 (*0-8032-5365-6*) U of Nebr Pr.

London Merchant. Lucy S. Sutherland. 164p. 1962. 28.50 (*0-7146-1515-3*, Pub. by F Cass Pubs) Intl Spec Bk.

London Merchant: The History of George Barnwell. George Lillo. Ed. & Frwd. by William-Alan Landes. 52p. 1995. pap. 7.00 (*0-88734-285-X*) Players Pr.

London Minimum. Herbert Ypma. LC 95-72933. (Illus.). 160p. 1996. pap. 27.50 (*1-55670-478-X*) Stewart Tabori & Chang.

*__London Missionary Society in Southern Africa, 1799-1999: Historical Essays in Celebration of the Bicentenary of the LMS in Southern Africa.__ rev. ed. London Missionary Society Staff. Ed. by John W. De Gruchy. LC 00-36683. 240p. (C). 2000. pap. text 24.95 (*0-8214-1349-X*) Ohio U Pr.

London Missionary Society's Report of the Proceedings Against the Late Rev. J. Smith of Demerara, Who Was Tried Under Martial Law & Condemned to Death, on a Charge of Aiding & Assisting in a Rebellion of Negro Slaves. London Missionary Society Staff. LC 78-79809. 204p. 1970. reprint ed. lib. bdg. 49.50 (*0-8371-1506-X*, LMS&) Greenwood.

*__London Monster: A Sanguinary Tale.__ Jan Bondeson. 2000. 29.95 (*0-8122-3576-2*) U of Pa Pr.

London Motor Bus, 1896 to 1979. R. W. Kidner. (C). 1985. 50.00 (*0-85361-182-3*) St Mut.

London Museums & Galleries Guide. Nicholson. (Illus.). pap. 12.95 (*0-7028-1752-X*) Brtholomew.

London Neighborhoods. Andrew Duncan. LC 97-188747. (Illus.). 208p. 1997. pap. 15.95 (*0-8442-9478-0*, 94780) NTC Contemp Pub Co.

London Newspapers in the Age of Walpole. Michael Harris. LC 86-45934. (Illus.). 256p. 1987. 42.50 (*0-8386-3273-4*) Fairleigh Dickinson.

London, 1980: Phillips & Drew Kings Chess Tournament. William R. Hartston & S. Reuben. (Chess Ser.). (Illus.). 222p. 1981. 25.95 (*0-08-024141-7*, Pergamon Pr); pap. 13.95 (*0-08-024140-9*, Pergamon Pr) Elsevier.

London, 1985. Edmund Antrobus. Ed. by Robert C. Fisher. (Fisher Annotated Travel Guides Ser.). 128p. 1984. pap. 8.95 (*0-8116-0018-1*) NAL.

*__London 1900: The Imperial Metropolis.__ Jonathan Schneer. LC 99-20050. (Illus.). 416p. 1999. 29.95 (*0-300-07625-8*) Yale U Pr.

London, 1968 see Chemistry of Natural Products: Proceedings

London Noir. Ed. by Maxim Jakubowski. LC 93-87448. (Mask Noir Ser.). 256p. 1995. pap. 11.99 (*1-85242-308-0*) Serpents Tail.

London North West. Nikolaus S. Pevsner. (Illus.). 768p. text 65.00 (*0-14-071048-5*, Pub. by Pnguin Bks Ltd) Trafalgar.

London North Western Railway. Compiled by M. Sharman. (Portfolio Ser.: Vol. 1). 95p. (C). 1985. 39.00 (*0-85361-315-X*) St Mut.

London Notes & Lectures. Walter C. Lanyon. 214p. 1983. reprint ed. pap. 10.00 (*1-889870-02-1*) Union Life.

London Notes & Lectures. 2nd ed. Walter C. Lanyon. 213p. 1996. reprint ed. spiral bd. 16.50 (*0-7873-0534-0*) Hlth Research.

*__London off Season & On.__ Doris Lehman et al. LC 99-36165. 272p. 1999. pap. 16.95 (*0-312-20447-7*) St Martin.

London on One Thousand Pounds a Day (Before Lunch) Ferne Kadish & Shelley Clark. LC 90-63163. 464p. 1991. 29.95 (*0-8442-9532-9*, Passprt Bks) NTC Contemp Pub Co.

London on One Thousand Pounds a Day (Before Lunch) Ferne Kadish & Shelley Clark. LC 90-63163. 464p. 1994. pap. 14.95 (*0-8442-9533-7*, Passprt Bks) NTC Contemp Pub Co.

London, 1066-1914, 3 vols. Ed. by Xavier Baron. (Helm Informationliterary Sources And Documents). 1600p. (C). 1997. 425.00 (*1-873403-43-7*) Routledge.

London Ontario Can. WWII. Historical Briefs, Inc. Staff. Ed. by Thomas Antonucci & Michael Antonucci. 176p. 1994. pap. 19.95 (*0-89677-074-5*) Hist Briefs.

London-Paris. Dana Facaros. 1999. pap. text 14.95 (*1-86011-919-0*) Cadgn Bks.

London Parks & Gardens. Pevensey Pr. Staff. (C). 1987. text 60.00 (*0-907115-30-6*, Pub. by Pevensey) St Mut.

London Pass Book. Cecil Woodward. 60p. 1998. pap. 23.00 (*0-7487-2435-4*) St Mut.

London, Past & Present: A Dictionary of Its History Associations & Traditions, 3 vols., Set. Henry B. Wheatley. 1968. 115.00 (*1-55888-184-0*) Omnigraphics Inc.

*__London Perceived.__ V. S. Pritchett. (Illus.). 2001. pap. 19.95 (*1-56792-148-5*) Godine.

London Philharmonic Discography, 69. Philip Stuart. LC 96-32997. (Discographies Ser.). 544p. 1997. lib. bdg. 110.00 (*0-313-29136-5*) Greenwood.

*__London Pocket Guide.__ Berlitz Editors. (Illus.). 144p. 2000. pap. 8.95 (*2-8315-7698-9*) Berlitz.

London Pocket Guide: Spanish ed. 1999. pap. text 8.95 (*2-8315-6564-2*) Berlitz.

London Poets & the American Revolution. James C. Gaston. LC 78-56499. x, 257p. 1979. 39.00 (*0-87875-162-9*) Whitston Pub.

London Prodigal. Ed. by Tudor Facsimile Texts Editing Staff. LC 75-133698. (Tudor Facsimile Texts. Old English Plays Ser.: No. 110). reprint ed. 49.50 (*0-404-53410-4*) AMS Pr.

London Rambles with Charles Dickens. R. Allbut. LC 74-1229. (Studies in Dickens: No. 52). 1974. lib. bdg. 75.00 (*0-8383-1779-0*) M S G Haskell Hse.

London Rediscovered. Louise Nicholson. LC 99-227412. (Illus.). 208p. 1999. 45.00 (*0-7892-0488-6*) Abbeville Pr.

*__London Restaurant Guide 2000.__ Nicholas Foulkes. (Illus.). 240p. 2000. per. 15.00 (*0-684-82367-5*) S&S Trade.

London Restaurants: 1999 Edition. Harden's Guides Staff. (Harden's Guides Ser.). 224p. 1999. pap. text 12.95 (*1-873721-20-X*, Pub. by Hrdens Guides) Seven Hills Bk.

London Review of Books. Alan Bennett. LC 96-48616. 1996. pap. 18.00 (*1-85984-121-X*) Norton.

*__London Rich: The Creation of a Great City, 1666 to the Present.__ Peter Thorold. 2000. 30.00 (*0-312-26616-2*) St Martin.

*__London Rooms: Portfolios from 40 European Interior Designers.__ Stafford Cliff. (Illus.). 2000. 45.00 (*1-56496-498-1*) Rockport Pubs.

London Scene 1997. Gay Men's Press Staff. 256p. 1996. pap. 11.95 (*0-85449-229-1*, Pub. by Gay Mens Pr) LPC InBook.

London School of Economics: Scarce Tracts in Economics, 12 vols. 2788p. (C). 1997. 815.00 (*0-415-14384-5*) Routledge.

*__London Scottish in the Great War.__ Leslie McDonnell. 2000. 34.95 (*0-85052-713-9*, Pub. by Pen & Sword Bks Ltd) Combined Pub.

London Season. Patricia Bray. 208p. 1997. mass mkt. 4.99 (*0-8217-5768-7*, Zebra Kensgtn) Kensgtn Pub Corp.

London Specialist Postgraduate Hospitals. Frank Wellman & Paul Palmer. (King Edward's Hospital Fund Ser.). 1975. pap. 19.00 (*0-8464-0577-6*) Beekman Pubs.

London Stage, 1890-1899: A Calendar of Plays & Players, 2 vols. J. P. Wearing. LC 76-1825. 1242p. 1976. 90.00 (*0-8108-0910-9*) Scarecrow.

London Stage, 1950-1959: A Calendar of Plays & Players, 2 vols. J. P. Wearing. 1807p. 1993. 140.00 (*0-8108-2690-9*) Scarecrow.

London Stage, 1900-1909: A Calendar of Plays & Players, 2 vols. J. P. Wearing. LC 80-28353. 1202p. 1981. 90.00 (*0-8108-1403-X*) Scarecrow.

London Stage, 1910-1919: A Calendar of Plays & Players, 2 Vols. J. P. Wearing. LC 82-19190. 1388p. 1982. 110.00 (*0-8108-1596-6*) Scarecrow.

London Stage, 1930-1939: A Calendar of Plays & Players, 3 vols. J. P. Wearing. LC 90-8883. 1999p. 1990. 150.00 (*0-8108-2349-7*) Scarecrow.

London Stage, 1920-1929: A Calendar of Plays & Players, 3 vols. J. P. Wearing. LC 84-10665. 1808p. 1984. 140.00 (*0-8108-1715-2*) Scarecrow.

London Stage, 1747-1776: A Critical Introduction. George W. Stone, Jr. LC 60-6539. (Arcturus Books Paperbacks). (Illus.). 224p. 1968. pap. 9.95 (*0-8093-0339-6*) S Ill U Pr.

London Stage, 1700-1729: A Critical Introduction, Pt. 2. Emmett L. Avery. LC 60-6539. (Arcturus Books Paperbacks). (Illus.). 199p. 1968. pap. 9.95 (*0-8093-0337-X*) S Ill U Pr.

London Stage, 1776-1800: A Critical Introduction. Charles B. Hogan. LC 60-6539. (Arcturus Books Paperbacks). (Illus.). 230p. 1968. pap. 9.95 (*0-8093-0340-X*) S Ill U Pr.

London Stage, 1660-1800, 3 vols., Set, Pt. 5: 1776-1800. Ed. by Charles B. Hogan. LC 60-6539. (London Stage Ser.). (Illus.). 2838p. 1970. 125.00 (*0-8093-0437-6*) S Ill U Pr.

London Statues & Monuments. Margaret Baker. (Illus.). 128p. pap. 12.50 (*0-7478-0284-X*, Pub. by Shire Pubns) Parkwest Pubns.

London Statues & Monuments. Margaret Baker. 128p. 1989. pap. 30.00 (*0-7478-0162-2*, Pub. by Shire Pubns) St Mut.

London Step by Step. 3rd ed. Christopher Turner. 304p. 1996. pap. 9.95 (*0-312-13667-6*) St Martin.

*__London Stock Exchange: A History.__ Ranald C. Michie. LC 99-25367. (Illus.). 688p. 2000. text 110.00 (*0-19-829508-1*) OUP.

London Suburbs. Andrew Saint. 240p. 1999. 49.95 (*1-85894-077-X*) Merrell Holberton.

London Symphony in Full Score. Ralph Vaughan William. 208p. 1996. pap. 12.95 (*0-486-29263-0*) Dover.

London Taxi. Malcom Bobbit. (Illus.). 160p. 1998. 24.95 (*1-874105-99-5*, Pub. by Vloce Pub) Motorbooks Intl.

London 1075-1187. Ed. by Falko Neininger. (English Episcopal Acta Ser.: No. 15). (Illus.). 296p. 2000. text 49.95 (*0-19-726179-5*) OUP.

London Theatre Walks: Thirteen Walking Tours to London Theatre Sites Past & Present. Jim De Young & John Miller. (Illus.). 224p. 1998. pap. text 14.95 (*1-55783-280-3*) Applause Theatre Bk Pubs.

London Theatres & Concert Halls. Ed. by Debra Shipley & Mary Peplow. 1989. pap. 25.00 (*0-85263-900-7*, Pub. by Shire Pubns) St Mut.

London Through the Ages. H. Bagust. (C). 1988. 39.00 (*0-904110-99-0*, Pub. by Thornhill Pr) St Mut.

London Tilbury & Southend Railway. H. D. Welch. (C). 1985. 45.00 (*0-85361-215-3*) St Mut.

London to Cambridge by Train, 1845-1938. Reginald B. Fellows. (Cambridge Town, Gown & County Ser.: Vol. 4). (Illus.). 40p. 1976. reprint ed. pap. 5.95 (*0-902675-65-6*) Oleander Pr.

London Traffic Monitoring Report for 1995. 58p. 1995. pap. text 25.00 (*0-11-551718-9*, HM17189, Pub. by Statnry Office) Bernan Associates.

London Transformed: Images of the City in the Eighteenth Century. Max Byrd. LC 77-11875. 212p. reprint ed. pap. 65.80 (*0-8357-8736-2*, 203368900087) Bks Demand.

London Transports. Maeve Binchy. 376p. 1995. mass mkt. 7.50 (*0-440-21235-9*) Dell.

London Transports. large type ed. Maeve Binchy. LC 95-16438. (Large Print Bks.). 1995. pap. 22.95 (*1-56895-226-0*) Wheeler Pub.

London 2000. Fodors Travel Publications, Inc. Staff. (2000 Ser.). (Illus.). 1999. pap. 15.00 (*0-679-00318-5*) Fodors Travel.

*__London 2001.__ Fodor's Staff. 2000. pap. 15.00 (*0-679-00545-5*) Fodors Travel.

London under London: A Subterranean Guide. Richard C. Trench & Ellis Hillman. (Illus.). 240p. 1994. pap. 24.95 (*0-7195-5288-5*, Pub. by John Murray) Trafalgar.

London Underground, Rassegna 66. Brandolini. 1996. pap. 35.00 (*88-85322-24-7*, Pub. by Birkhauser) Princeton Arch.

London up Close: District to District, Street to Street. Fiona Duncan et al. (Illus.). 176p. 1994. pap. 12.95 (*0-8442-9451-9*, 94519, Passprt Bks) NTC Contemp Pub Co.

London Venture. Michael J. Arlen. Ed. by Herbert Van Thal. 1968. pap. 4.95 (*0-304-92614-0*) Dufour.

London Villages. John Wittich. (Illus.). 112p. 1989. pap. 12.50 (*0-7478-0181-9*, Pub. by Shire Pubns) Parkwest Pubns.

London Virgin Guide. Globe Pequot Press Staff. (Illus.). 176p. 1999. pap. 16.95 (*0-7627-0565-5*) Globe Pequot.

London Walking Guide: Where to Go - Where to Eat - What to Do. Jeanne Oelerich. (Illus.). 16p. 1998. pap. 6.95 (*1-882546-10-5*) Just Marvelous.

*__London Walks.__ Time Out Magazine Staff. (Time-Out Book of... Ser.). 256p. 2000. pap. 14.95 (*0-14-027897-4*, Penguin Bks) Viking Penguin.

London with Day Trips to Bath, Brighton, Oxford & Other Popular Destinations: 2000 Edition. Corey Sandler. (Econoguides Ser.). (Illus.). 352p. 1999. pap. 16.95 (*0-8092-2895-5*, 289550, Contemporary Bks) NTC Contemp Pub Co.

London Woman. Francis B. Chichester. 1988. mass mkt. 8.95 (*0-446-38742-8*, Pub. by Warner Bks) Little.

London 1958-1959. Mike Seaborne. LC 99-231654. (Illus.). 64p. 1998. pap. 24.95 (*1-899235-71-X*, Pub. by Dewi Lewis) Dist Art Pubs.

*__London 2001.__ Fodors Travel Publications, Inc. Staff. (Pocket Guides Ser.). 2000. pap. 10.00 (*0-679-00571-4*, Pub. by Fodors Travel) Random House.

London 2001. P. Hall. 240p. 1989. pap. 19.95 (*0-04-445556-9*, A8317) Routledge.

Londonderry Plantation, 1609-1914: The History, Architecture & Planning of the Estates of the City of London & Its Livery Companies in Ulster. James Stevens Curl. LC 89-205110. xxiii, 503 p. 1986. write for info. (*0-85033-577-9*) Phillimore & Co.

Londonderry Willey's Book of Nutfield: History of the Part of New Hampshire Comprised Within the Limits of the Old Township of Londonderry, from Its Settlement in 1719 to the Present Time: Biographical, Genealogical, Political, Anecdotal. George F. Willey. 414p. 1997. reprint ed. lib. bdg. 45.00 (*0-8328-6005-0*) Higginson Bk Co.

*__Londoners.__ Margaret A. Pemberton. 2000. pap. 8.95 (*0-552-14123-2*, Pub. by Transworld Publishers Ltd) Trafalgar.

Londoners. large type ed. Margaret A. Pemberton. (Magna Large Print Ser.). 675p. 1996. 27.99 (*0-7505-0907-4*, Pub. by Mgna Lrg Print) Ulverscroft.

London's Art & Artists. Spellmount Ltd. Publishers Staff. (C). 1986. 125.00 (*0-946771-36-7*, Pub. by Spellmnt Pubs) St Mut.

London's Burning: Life, Death & Art in the Second World War. Peter Stansky. xiii, 201p. 1994. 32.50 (*0-8047-2340-0*) Stanford U Pr.

London's City: A Guide Through the Historic Square Mile. Sidney Laurens. LC 94-75991. (Illus.). 344p. (Orig.). 1994. pap. 15.95 (*0-9641263-0-3*) Marmot Pubng.

London's Country House Collections. Julius Bryant. (Illus.). 144p. 1993. 30.00 (*1-85759-013-9*) Scala Books.

London's Country House Collections: Kenwood, Chiswick, Marble Hill, Ranger's House. Julius Bryant. (Illus.). 144p. 1997. pap. 30.00 (*1-85759-012-0*) Scala Books.

London's Daughter. Philip Boast. 608p. 1994. mass mkt. 13.95 (*0-7472-4023-X*, Pub. by Headline Bk Pub) Trafalgar.

London's East End (Life & Traditions) Jane Cox. LC 98-195964. (Illus.). 160p. 1998. pap. (*1-85799-956-8*) Phoenix Hse.

London's Good Coffee Shops. Shaun Beary. (Illus.). 76p. (Orig.). 1997. pap. 5.95 (*0-9528322-0-8*, Pub. by Portfolio) Seven Hills Bk.

London's Lost Route to Basingstoke: The Story of the Basingstoke Canal. Paul A. Vine. LC 68-23819. (Illus.). 1968. 24.95 (*0-678-05641-2*) Kelley.

London's Lost Route to Basingstoke: The Story of the Basingstoke Canal. Paul A. Vine. (Illus.). 256p. 1993. 30.95 (*0-7509-0359-7*, Pub. by Sutton Pub Ltd) Intl Pubs Mktg.

London's Lost Theatres of the Nineteenth Century. Erroll Sherson. LC 70-81200. (Illus.). 1972. 30.95 (*0-405-08969-4*) Ayer.

*__London's Markets for Collectors: A Guide to Finding Antiques, Bric-a-brac & Collectibles.__ Cadogan Books Staff. 64p. 1999. text 12.95 (*1-86011-702-3*) Cadgn Bks.

London's Millionaire. Philip Boast. 496p. 1995. mass mkt. 11.95 (*0-7472-4216-X*, Pub. by Headline Bk Pub) Trafalgar.

London's Most Interesting Pubs: A Selection of London Perceived. David Gammell. Ed. by N. Shepperd. (Illus.). 128p. (Orig.). 1992. reprint ed. pap. 9.95 (*1-873203-16-0*) Sterling Woodfld.

London's Newcomers: The West Indian Migrants. Ruth Glass & Harold Pollins. LC 61-16042. (Illus.). 291p. 1961. 34.95 (*0-674-53850-1*) HUP.

Londons Riverside Panorama. Waldermar. Date not set. pap. text. write for info. (*0-471-87162-1*) Wiley.

London's Rock Routes John A. Platt. LC 86-136225. 180 p. 1985. write for info. (*0-947795-70-7*) Fourth Estate.

London's Top 500 Days Out: Millennium 99/2000 Ed. Best Guides Staff. 1999. pap. text 7.95 (*1-901258-33-5*) Best Guides.

London's Waterway Guide. 2nd rev. ed. Chris Cove-Smith. (Illus.). 200p. (C). 1986. pap. 125.00 (*0-85288-104-5*, Pub. by Laurie Norie & Wilson Ltd) St Mut.

London's Women Teachers: Gender, Class & Feminism 1870-1930. Dina Copelman. LC 95-32403. 312p. (C). 1996. 75.00 (*0-415-01312-7*) Routledge.

Londonwalks. rev. ed. Anton Powell. 258p. 1995. pap. 12.95 (*0-8050-1300-8*, Owl) H Holt & Co.

Londres. (FRE.). 1999. 9.95 (*2-06-656101-0*) Michelin.

Londres Green Guide. Ed. by Michelin Staff. (SPA.). 1998. per. 18.00 (*2-06-459001-3*, 4590) Michelin.

Londres (London) 1999. pap. 9.95 (*2-06-660801-7*) Michelin.

Lone Angler. Herb Curtis. 292p. 1993. pap. 12.95 (*0-86492-162-4*, Pub. by Goose Ln Edits) Genl Dist Srvs.

L

An Asterisk (*) at the beginning of an entry indicates that the title is appearing for the first time.

Lone Bandits. Louise Elliott. (YA). 1995. 12.95 (*0-7022-2706-4*, Pub. by Univ Queensland Pr) Intl Spec Bk.

***Lone Black Gull.** Michael Andrews. 148p. 2000. pap. 14.00 (*0-941017-62-1*) Bombshelter Pr.

Lone Cowboy: My Life Story. Will James. 1993. reprint ed. lib. bdg. 27.95 (*1-56849-239-1*) Buccaneer Bks.

Lone Cowboy: My Life Story. Will James. LC 96-31972. (Illus.). 427p. 1997. reprint ed. 30.00 (*0-87842-357-5*); reprint ed. pap. 16.00 (*0-87842-358-3*) Mountain Pr.

Lone Deputy - Desperate Man. Wayne D. Overholser. 384p. 1995. pap. text, mass mkt. 4.99 (*0-8439-3782-3*) Dorchester Pub Co.

Lone Dog's Winter Count. Diane H. Glancy. (Illus.). 80p. (Orig.). 1991. pap. text 9.95 (*0-931122-64-3*) West End.

Lone Eagle. Cassie Edwards. (Historical Romance Ser.). 1998. mass mkt. 6.99 (*0-451-40862-4*, Topaz) NAL.

Lone Fathers & Masculinities. Richard W. Barker. 304p. 1994. 72.95 (*1-85628-522-7*, Pub. by Avebry) Ashgate Pub Co.

Lone Gunners for Jesus: Letters to Paul J. Hill. Gary North. LC 94-37301. 47p. 1994. pap. 3.95 (*0-930464-73-7*) Inst Christian.

Lone Hand: Frontier Stories. large type ed. T.V. Olsen. LC 96-53929. 262p. 1997. 17.95 (*0-7862-0738-8*) Thorndike Pr.

Lone Hand: Frontier Stories. large type ed. T.V. Olsen. LC 98-5429. 1998. 19.95 (*0-7862-0761-2*) Thorndike Pr.

Lone Heretic. Margaret Rudd. LC 75-31688. 370p. 1976. reprint ed. 75.00 (*0-87752-181-6*) Gordian.

Lone Hunter & the Cheyennes. Donald Worcester. LC 85-4746. (Chaparral Bks.). (Illus.). 78p. (J). (gr. 4 up). 1985. reprint ed. 10.95 (*0-87565-018-X*) Tex Christian.

Lone Hunter's Gray Pony. Donald Worcester. LC 84-16157. (Chaparral Bks.). (Illus.). 70p. (J). (gr. 4 up). 1985. 10.95 (*0-87565-001-5*) Tex Christian.

Lone Hunter's Gray Pony & Lone Hunter & the Cheyennes & War Pony, Set. Donald E. Worcester. (YA). 1992. boxed set 29.95 (*0-87565-109-7*) Tex Christian.

Lone Man. Bernardo Atxaga. 336p. 1998. mass mkt. 11.00 (*1-86046-340-1*) Harvill Press.

Lone Motherhood in Twentieth-Century Britain: From Footnote to Front Page. Kathleen Kiernan et al. (Illus.). 346p. 1998. text 75.00 (*0-19-829070-5*) OUP.

Lone Motherhood in Twentieth-Century Britain: From Footnote to Front Page. Jane Lewis. (Illus.). 346p. 1998. pap. text (*0-19-829069-1*) OUP.

Lone Mothers. A. Leeming et al. (DSS Research Report Ser.). 1994. 35.00 (*0-11-762228-1*, Pub. by Statnry Office) Bernan Associates.

Lone Mothers, Paid Work & Gender. Duncan. LC 99-21783. 1999. text 65.00 (*0-312-22432-X*) St Martin.

Lone Mothers in European Welfare Regimes: Shifting Policy Logics. Ed. by Jane Lewis. LC 97-206164. 224p. 1997. 69.95 (*1-85302-448-1*, Pub. by Jessica Kingsley); pap. 26.95 (*1-85302-461-9*, Pub. by Jessica Kingsley) Taylor & Francis.

Lone Mothers, Social Security & the Family in Hong Kong. Lai-Ching Leung. LC 97-77889. (Illus.). 239p. 1998. text 59.95 (*1-84014-320-7*, Pub. by Ashgate Pub) Ashgate Pub Co.

Lone Parent Lives. 1998. pap. 75.00 (*0-11-762598-1*, HM25981, Pub. by Statnry Office) Bernan Associates.

Lone Parenthood: An Economic Analysis. John F. Ermisch. (Illus.). 210p. (C). 1991. text 69.95 (*0-521-41243-9*) Cambridge U Pr.

Lone Parenthood: Coping with Constraints & Making Opportunities in Single-Parent Families. Ed. by Michael Hardey & Graham Crow. 208p. (Orig.). 1992. text 60.00 (*0-8020-2824-1*); pap. text 19.95 (*0-8020-7694-7*) U of Toronto Pr.

Lone Parents & Work. Stephen McKay & Alan Marsh. (DSS Research Report Ser.: No. 25). 82p. 1994. pap. 25.00 (*0-11-762148-X*, HM2148X, Pub. by Statnry Office) Bernan Associates.

Lone Parents, Work & Benefits. A. Marsh et al. (DSS Research Report Ser.). 1997. write for info. (*0-11-762450-0*, Pub. by Statnry Office) Bernan Associates.

Lone Pilgrim: A Book of Short Stories. Laurie Colwin. LC 89-45642. 224p. 1990. reprint ed. pap. 11.00 (*0-06-097270-X*, Perennial) HarperTrade.

Lone Pine Picnic Guide to British Columbia. Nancy Gibson & John Wittaker. 1989. pap. 9.95 (*0-919433-59-6*) Lone Pine.

Lone Pine Picnic Guide to Ontario. Nancy Gibson & John Wittaker. Ed. by Phillip Kennedy. 1991. pap. 9.95 (*0-919433-69-3*) Lone Pine.

***Lone Point.** large type ed. Grace Livingston Hill. LC 99-43736. (Thorndike Romance Ser.). 1999. 25.95 (*0-7862-2230-1*) Thorndike Pr.

Lone Point. Grace Livingston Hill. reprint ed. lib. bdg. 24.95 (*0-89190-041-1*) Amereon Ltd.

Lone Ranger. Sharon De Vita. 1997. per. 3.99 (*0-373-24078-3*, 1-24078-7) Silhouette.

Lone Ranger. Lee Filbinger. LC 98-140090. (Illus.). 144p. 1997. pap. 18.95 (*1-57432-022-X*, 4950) Collector Bks.

Lone Ranger & the Mystery Ranch. Fran Striker. 1976. reprint ed. lib. bdg. 22.95 (*0-89190-501-4*, Rivercity Pr) Amereon Ltd.

Lone Ranger & the Silver Bullet. Fran Striker. 1976. reprint ed. lib. bdg. 21.95 (*0-89190-503-0*, Rivercity Pr) Amereon Ltd.

Lone Ranger & Tonto. Fran Striker. 21.95 (*0-89190-505-7*) Amereon Ltd.

Lone Ranger & Tonto Fistfight in Heaven. Sherman Alexie. LC 94-12378. 240p. 1998. pap. 13.00 (*0-06-097624-1*, Perennial) HarperTrade.

Lone Ranger in Wild Horse Canyon. Fran Striker. 1976. reprint ed. lib. bdg. 22.95 (*0-89190-504-9*, Rivercity Pr) Amereon Ltd.

Lone Ranger in Wild Horse Canyon. Fran Striker. 1994. reprint ed. lib. bdg. 24.95 (*1-56849-342-8*) Buccaneer Bks.

***Lone Ranger Legacy.** Sharon L. Spinner Reddy. 1998. disk 4.50 (*1-58338-019-1*) CrossrdsPub.

Lone Ranger on Red Butte Trail. Fran Striker. 1976. reprint ed. lib. bdg. 19.95 (*0-89190-502-2*, Rivercity Pr) Amereon Ltd.

Lone Ranger on Red Butte Trail. Fran Striker. 1994. reprint ed. lib. bdg. 24.95 (*1-56849-343-6*) Buccaneer Bks.

Lone Ranger Pictorial Scrapbook. 2nd ed. Lee J. Felbinger. (Illus.). 260p. 1988. pap. 24.95 (*0-9633235-0-4*) Cntryside Ad.

Lone Ranger Traps Smugglers. Fran Striker. (J). 21.95 (*0-8488-1183-6*) Amereon Ltd.

Lone Ranger's Code of the West: Action-Packed Adventure in Values & Ethics. Jim Lichtman. LC 95-92728. 280p. 1996. pap. 15.00 (*0-9648591-0-6*) Scrblrs Ink.

Lone Red Apple: A Novel. Aurelia Smeltz. LC 98-96215. (Illus.). 234p. Date not set. pap. 19.95 (*1-892430-00-2*) Greek America Pr.

Lone Rider. Edwin W. Gibson. Ed. by Leticia Lozano. 125p. 1999. pap. 11.95 (*1-891601-16-4*) Ladies Caliber.

***Lone Rider.** Lee Phillips. 280p. 2000. 18.99 (*0-7089-5685-8*) Ulverscroft.

Lone Rider Takes a Bride: The Rulebreakers. Leanne Banks. (Desire Ser.: No. 1172). 1998. per. 3.75 (*0-373-76172-4*, 1-76172-5) Harlequin Bks.

***Lone Riders: Coral Pink Sand Dunes.** (Illus.). 40p. 1998. pap. 9.95 (*1-878261-50-9*) Outback Pubns.

Lone Rifle. large type ed. Gordon D. Shirreffs. 352p. 1992. pap. 16.99 (*0-7089-7147-4*, Linford) Ulverscroft.

Lone Sailor. large type ed. John T. Sanders. (Illus.). 416p. 1987. 27.99 (*0-7089-1670-8*) Ulverscroft.

Lone Soldier/David Grier. David Grier. 64p. 1997. 14.95 (*0-7866-2895-2*, 96664); pap. 29.95 incl. audio compact disk (*0-7866-2897-9*, 96664CDP) Mel Bay.

***Lone Stallion's Lady.** Lisa Jackson. (Montana Mavericks Ser.: Bk. 1). 256p. 2000. per. 4.50 (*0-373-65046-9*, 1-65046-4) Harlequin Bks.

Lone Star. Katherine Kudlinski. (Once Upon America Ser.). (Illus.). (J). (gr. 2-6). pap. 3.99 (*0-614-15703-X*, PuffinBks) Peng Put Young Read.

Lone Star. James McLure. 1980. pap. 3.25 (*0-8222-0685-4*) Dramatists Play.

Lone Star, 1. Evelyn Rogers. (Texas Empires Ser.). 400p. 1999. mass mkt. 5.99 (*0-8439-4533-8*) Dorchester Pub Co.

Lone Star. Kevin Siembieda et al. Ed. by James Osten. (Rifts Worldbook Ser.: Vol. 13). (Illus.). 176p. (Orig.). (YA). (gr. 8 up). 1997. pap. 16.95 (*1-57457-000-5*, 825) Palladium Bks.

***Lone Star: A History of Texas & the Texans.** T. R. Fehrenbach. 780p. 1999. 39.95 (*0-7351-0167-1*) Replica Bks.

***Lone Star: A History of Texas & the Texans.** rev. ed. T. R. Fehrenbach. 792p. 2000. pap. text 22.00 (*0-306-80942-7*, Pub. by Da Capo) HarpC.

Lone Star: A Story of the Texas Rangers. Kathleen V. Kudlinski. LC 93-23048. (Once upon America Ser.). 1996. 9.19 (*0-606-09571-3*, Pub. by Turtleback) Demco.

Lone Star: The Republic of Texas. Ed. by Mary D. Wade. (Perspectives on History Ser.: Vol. 27). (Illus.). 64p. 1998. pap. 6.95 (*1-878668-63-3*) Disc Enter Ltd.

Lone Star & Deep Water Princess. Wesley Ellis. (Lone Star Ser.: No. 116). 192p. 1992. mass mkt. 3.50 (*0-515-10833-2*, Jove) Berkley Pub.

Lone Star & Double Eagle: Civil War Letters of a German-Texas Family. Ed. by Minetta A. Goyne. LC 82-5491. 276p. 1982. pap. 15.00 (*0-912646-68-3*) Tex Christian.

Lone Star & the Aztec Treasure. Wesley Ellis. (Lone Star Ser.: No. 123). 192p. (Orig.). 1992. mass mkt. 3.99 (*0-515-10981-9*, Jove) Berkley Pub.

Lone Star & the Bellwether Kid. Wesley Ellis. (Lone Star Ser.: No. 133). 192p. (Orig.). 1993. mass mkt. 3.99 (*0-515-11195-3*, Jove) Berkley Pub.

Lone Star & the Black Bandana Gang. Wesley Ellis. (Lone Star Ser.: No. 117). 1992. mass mkt. 3.50 (*0-515-10850-2*, Jove) Berkley Pub.

Lone Star & the Bogus Banker. Wesley Ellis. (Lone Star Ser.: No. 152). 192p. (Orig.). 1995. mass mkt. 3.99 (*0-515-11592-4*, Jove) Berkley Pub.

Lone Star & the Brutus Gang. Wesley Ellis. (Lone Star Ser.: No. 127). 192p. (Orig.). 1993. mass mkt. 3.99 (*0-515-11062-0*, Jove) Berkley Pub.

Lone Star & the Buccaneers. Wesley Ellis. (Lone Star Ser.: No. 122). 192p. (Orig.). 1992. mass mkt. 3.99 (*0-515-10956-8*, Jove) Berkley Pub.

Lone Star & the Cheyenne Showdown. Wesley Ellis. (Lone Star Ser.: No. 100). 192p. 1990. mass mkt. 3.50 (*0-515-10473-6*, Jove) Berkley Pub.

Lone Star & the Chicago Showdown. Wesley Ellis. (Lone Star Ser.: No. 126). 192p. (Orig.). 1993. mass mkt. 3.99 (*0-515-11044-2*, Jove) Berkley Pub.

Lone Star & the Deadly Vixens. Wesley Ellis. (Lone Star Ser.: No. 142). 192p. (Orig.). 1994. mass mkt. 3.99 (*0-515-11376-X*, Jove) Berkley Pub.

Lone Star & the Death Chase. Wesley Ellis. LC 94-137959. (Lone Star Ser.: No. 138). 192p. (Orig.). 1994. mass mkt. 3.99 (*0-515-11314-X*, Jove) Berkley Pub.

Lone Star & the Death Mine, No. 136. Wesley Ellis. 192p. (Orig.). 1993. mass mkt. 3.99 (*0-515-11256-9*, Jove) Berkley Pub.

Lone Star & the Galvanized Yankees. Wesley Ellis. (Lone Star Ser.: No. 150). 192p. (Orig.). 1995. mass mkt. 3.99 (*0-515-11552-5*, Jove) Berkley Pub.

Lone Star & the Gold Mine. Wesley Ellis. (Lone Star Ser.: No 128). 192p. (Orig.). 1993. mass mkt. 3.99 (*0-515-11083-3*, Jove) Berkley Pub.

Lone Star & the Great Pilgrim Heist. Wesley Ellis. (Lone Star Ser.: No. 134). 1993. mass mkt. 3.99 (*0-515-11217-8*, Jove) Berkley Pub.

Lone Star & the Gunrunners. Wesley Ellis. (Lone Star Ser.: No. 121). 192p. (Orig.). 1992. mass mkt. 3.99 (*0-515-10930-4*, Jove) Berkley Pub.

Lone Star & the Hellbound Pilgrims. Wesley Ellis. (Lone Star Ser.: No. 113). 192p. 1992. mass mkt. 3.50 (*0-515-10754-9*, Jove) Berkley Pub.

Lone Star & the Mexican Muskets. Wesley Ellis. (Lone Star Ser.: No. 119). 192p. (Orig.). 1992. mass mkt. 3.50 (*0-515-10881-2*, Jove) Berkley Pub.

Lone Star & the Montana Marauders. Wesley Ellis. (Lone Star Ser.: No. 140). 192p. (Orig.). 1994. mass mkt. 3.99 (*0-515-11357-3*, Jove) Berkley Pub.

Lone Star & the Mountain of Fire. Wesley Ellis. (Lone Star Ser.: No. 153). 192p. (Orig.). 1995. mass mkt. 3.99 (*0-515-11613-0*, Jove) Berkley Pub.

Lone Star & the Nevada Gold. Wesley Ellis. (Lone Star Ser.: No. 147). 192p. (Orig.). 1994. mass mkt. 3.99 (*0-515-11494-4*, Jove) Berkley Pub.

Lone Star & the Redemption Massacre, No. 137. Wesley Ellis. 192p. (Orig.). 1994. mass mkt. 3.99 (*0-515-11284-4*, Jove) Berkley Pub.

Lone Star & the River of No Return. Wesley Ellis. (Lone Star Ser.: No. 135). 1993. pap. 3.99 (*0-515-11239-9*, Jove) Berkley Pub.

Lone Star & the Santa Fe Showdown. Wesley Ellis. (Lone Star Ser.: No. 120). 192p. (Orig.). 1992. mass mkt. 3.99 (*0-515-10902-9*, Jove) Berkley Pub.

Lone Star & the Sierra Sabotage. Wesley Ellis. (Lone Star Ser.: No. 101). 1991. mass mkt. 2.95 (*0-515-10495-7*, Jove) Berkley Pub.

Lone Star & the Slaughter Showdown. Wesley Ellis. (Lone Star Ser.: No. 139). 192p. (Orig.). 1994. mass mkt. 3.99 (*0-515-11339-5*, Jove) Berkley Pub.

Lone Star & the Steel Rail No. 132. Wesley Ellis. (Lone Star Ser.: No. 132). 192p. (Orig.). 1993. mass mkt. 3.99 (*0-515-11167-8*, Jove) Berkley Pub.

***Lone Star & the Swastika: Prisoners of War in Texas.** Richard P. Walker. LC 99-23794. 2000. write for info. (*1-57168-341-0*, Eakin Pr) Sunbelt Media.

Lone Star & the Temperance Army. Wesley Ellis. (Lone Star Ser.: No. 149). 192p. (Orig.). 1995. mass mkt. 3.99 (*0-515-11529-0*, Jove) Berkley Pub.

Lone Star & the Trail of Blood. Wesley Ellis. (Lone Star Ser.: No. 141). 192p. (Orig.). 1994. mass mkt. 3.99 (*0-515-11392-1*, Jove) Berkley Pub.

Lone Star & the Trail to Abilene. Wesley Ellis. (Lone Star Ser.: No. 114). 192p. 1992. mass mkt. 3.50 (*0-515-10791-3*, Jove) Berkley Pub.

Lone Star Baby. Debbie Macomber. (Harlequin Ser.). 1998. per. 4.50 (*0-373-83347-4*) Harlequin Bks.

***Lone Star Baby.** large type ed. Debbie Macomber. 288p. 1999. 25.99 (*0-263-16208-7*, Pub. by Mills & Boon) Ulverscroft.

Lone Star Baby: A Consumer Guide for Expectant & New Parents. Tamra-Shae Oatman. Ed. by Mary Van Pilney. (Orig.). 1988. pap. 8.95 (*0-9620141-0-9*) Oatman-Pilney.

Lone Star Bishops: The Roman Catholic Hierarchy in Texas. Franklin C. Williams, Jr. LC 97-90535. xi, 621p. 1998. 25.00 (*0-87244-101-6*) Texian.

Lone Star Blue & Gray: Essays on Texas in the Civil War. Ed. & Intro. by Ralph A. Wooster. (Fred H. & Ella Mae Moore Texas History Reprint Ser.). (Illus.). 360p. 1995. pap. 16.95 (*0-87611-152-5*) Tex St Hist Assn.

Lone Star Bride: Three Weddings & a Family. Linda Varner. 1998. per. 3.50 (*0-373-19335-1*, 1-19335-8) Silhouette.

Lone Star Christmas. Diana Palmer & Joan Johnson. 1997. per. 7.99 (*0-373-48353-8*) Harlequin Bks.

***Lone Star Christmas . . . And Other Gifts.** Diana Palmer & Joan Johnston. (Promo Ser.). 1999. per. 6.99 (*0-373-48386-4*, 1-48386-6) Harlequin Bks.

Lone Star Cowboy. Leslie Scott. 1998. 17.50 (*0-7540-8034-X*) Chivers N Amer.

Lone Star Defenders: A Chronicle of the Third Texas Cavalry Regiment in the Civil War. Samuel B. Barron. 1983. reprint ed. 27.95 (*0-89201-103-3*) Zenger Pub.

Lone Star Dinosaurs. Louis Jacobs. LC 95-4034. (Louise Lindsey Merrick Natural Environment Ser.: No. 22). (Illus.). 176p. (C). 1995. 27.95 (*0-89096-662-1*) Tex A&M Univ Pr.

Lone Star Dinosaurs. Louis Jacobs. (Illus.). 1999. pap. 14.95 (*0-89096-674-5*) Tex A&M Univ Pr.

***Lone Star Generals in Gray.** Ralph A. Wooster. LC 99-23919. 2000. 24.95 (*1-57168-325-9*) Sunbelt Media.

Lone Star Guitar: Texas Blues & Beyond. Warner Brothers Staff. Ed. by Aaron Stang. 158p. (Orig.). 1996. pap. text 19.95 (*1-57623-289-1*, GF9601) Wrner Bros.

Lone Star Heat. Mary L. Baxter. 1999. mass mkt. 5.99 (*1-55166-289-2*, 0-66289-0, Mira Bks) Harlequin Bks.

Lone Star Heritage: Loyal Sons & Daughters, Trail Herds & Wagon Trains. James W. Guest. 299p. (Orig.). 1996. pap. 12.00 (*1-887301-01-1*) Palmetto Bookworks.

Lone Star in the Sierra Diablos, No. 144. Wesley Ellis. (Lone Star Ser.). 192p. (Orig.). 1994. mass mkt. 3.99 (*0-515-11436-7*, Jove) Berkley Pub.

***Lone Star, Jr. The Autobiography of Racing Legend Johnny Rutherford.** Johnny Rutherford. LC 00-36422. (Illus.). 300p. 2000. 24.95 (*1-57243-353-1*) Triumph Bks.

Lone Star Justice: A Biography of Justice Tom C. Clark. Evan A. Young. LC 98-16575. (Illus.). 160p. (YA). (gr. 7 up). 1998. 17.95 (*1-885777-11-6*) Hendrick-Long.

Lone Star Justice: A Comprehensive Overview of the Texas Criminal Justice System. David M. Horton & Ryan K. Turner. 384p. 1999. pap. 21.95 (*1-57168-226-0*, Eakin Pr) Sunbelt Media.

Lone Star Justice: A Comprehensive Overview of the Texas Criminal Justice System. David M. Horton & Ryan K. Turner. LC 98-28970. 384p. 1999. 29.95 (*1-57168-268-6*, Eakin Pr) Sunbelt Media.

Lone Star Kind of Man. Peggy Moreland. 1997. per. 3.50 (*0-373-76096-5*, 1-76096-6) Silhouette.

Lone-Star Lawman. Kay David. 1998. per. 4.25 (*0-373-07845-5*, 1-07845-0) Silhouette.

Lone Star Lawman (The Cowboy Code) Joanna Wayne. (Intrigue Ser.: No. 505). 1999. per. 3.99 (*0-373-22505-9*, 1-22505-1) Harlequin Bks.

Lone Star Legacies. Patrick M. Reynolds. (Texas Lore Ser.: Vol. 8). (Illus.). 56p. (Orig.). 1990. pap. 3.75 (*0-932514-23-5*) Red Rose Studio.

Lone Star Legacy: A Texas Cookbook. Austin Junior Forum, Inc. Staff. LC 81-69340. (Illus.). 368p. 1981. spiral bd. 17.95 (*0-9607152-0-7*) Austin Junior.

***Lone Star Legacy: The Birth of Group Hospitalization & the Story of Blue Cross & Blue Shield of Texas.** Sam Schaal. (Illus.). 208p. 1999. pap. 14.95 (*1-884363-17-2*) Odenwald Pr.

Lone Star Legacy II: A Texas Cookbook. Austin Junior Forum, Inc. Staff. LC 85-72515. (Illus.). 368p. 1985. spiral bd. 17.95 (*0-9607152-1-5*) Austin Junior.

Lone Star Lover. Gail Link. 1997. per. 3.99 (*0-373-24121-6*, 1-24121-5) Silhouette.

Lone Star Lovin' Debbie Macomber. (Romance Ser.). 1993. mass mkt. 2.99 (*0-373-03271-4*, 1-03271-3) Harlequin Bks.

Lone Star Man. Dorsey Kelley. (Romance Ser.: No. 863). 1992. per. 2.69 (*0-373-08863-9*, 5-08863-8) Silhouette.

***Lone Star Menagerie: True Tales of Texas Wildlife.** Jim Harris. LC 99-51354. 1999. pap. 18.95 (*1-55622-692-6*) Wordware Pub.

Lone Star Millionaire. Susan Mallery. (World's Most Eligible Ser.: No. 10). 1999. per. 4.50 (*0-373-65027-2*, 1-65027-4, Harlequin) Harlequin Bks.

Lone Star on the Hangman's Tale. Wesley Ellis. (Lone Star Ser.: No. 131). 192p. (Orig.). 1993. mass mkt. 3.99 (*0-515-11137-6*, Jove) Berkley Pub.

Lone Star On Treachery Trail. Wesley Ellis. (Lone Star Ser.: No. 1). 192p. 1986. mass mkt. 3.99 (*0-515-08708-4*, Jove) Berkley Pub.

Lone Star Politics. Paul Benson et al. 144p. (C). 1997. pap. text, student ed. 19.50 (*0-15-503544-4*) Harcourt Coll Pubs.

Lone Star Preacher. John W. Thomason, Jr. LC 92-5965. (Texas Tradition Ser.: No. 19). (Illus.). 306p. 1992. reprint ed. 29.95 (*0-87565-106-2*) Tex Christian.

Lone Star Preacher: Being a Chronicle of the Acts of Praxiteles Swan, M. E. Church South, Sometime Captain, 5th Texas Regiment, Confederate States Provisional Army. John W. Thomason, Jr. 1985. 27.95 (*0-8488-0159-8*, J M C & C O) Amereon Ltd.

***Lone Star Prince: The Texas Cattleman's Club.** Cindy Gerard. (Desire Ser.). 1999. mass mkt. 3.75 (*0-373-76256-9*) Silhouette.

Lone Star Rancher. Leanna Wilson. (Romance Ser.: No. 1231). 1997. per. 3.25 (*0-373-19231-2*, 1-19231-9) Silhouette.

Lone Star Ranger. Zane Grey. LC 97-9310. 309p. 1997. lib. bdg. 17.95 (*0-7862-0748-5*) Five Star.

Lone Star Ranger. Zane Grey. Ed. by Doug Grad. 256p. 1984. mass mkt. 3.99 (*0-671-50991-8*) PB.

Lone Star Ranger. Zane Grey. 1995. mass mkt. 4.99 (*0-671-52663-4*) PB.

Lone Star Ranger. large type ed. Zane Grey. LC 98-24417. 1999. 21.95 (*0-7862-0771-X*) Thorndike Pr.

Lone Star Ranger. Zane Grey. 376p. reprint ed. lib. bdg. 26.95 (*0-89190-764-5*, Rivercity Pr) Amereon Ltd.

Lone Star Rising: Lyndon Johnson & His Times, 1908-1960. Robert Dallek. (Illus.). 736p. 1991. text 35.00 (*0-19-505435-0*) OUP.

Lone Star Rising: Lyndon Johnson & His Times, 1908-1960. Robert Dallek. (Illus.). 754p. 1992. pap. 16.95 (*0-19-507904-3*) OUP.

Lone Star State Divided: Texans & the Civil War. Merle Durham. LC 94-1984. (Illus.). 136p. (J). (gr. 4 up). 1994. lib. bdg. 14.95 (*0-937460-97-4*) Hendrick-Long.

Lone Star State of Mind. Bethany Campbell. LC 95-4585. (Crystal Creek Ser.). 299p. 1995. mass mkt. 3.99 (*0-373-82536-6*, 1-82536-3) Harlequin Bks.

Lone Star Surrender. Carol Finch, pseud. 512p. 1988. mass mkt. 3.95 (*0-8217-2479-7*, Zebra Kensgtn) Kensgtn Pub Corp.

Lone Star Swing. Duncan McLean. LC 98-179517. 312p. 1998. pap. 14.00 (*0-393-31756-0*) Norton.

Lone Star Time Machine: Game & Activity Workbook for Texas History Students. Sharline Lavender. (Illus.). 37p. 1986. pap. 7.95 (*0-937460-22-2*) Hendrick-Long.

***Lone Star Wedding.** Sandra Steffen. (Fortunes of Texas Ser.: Vol. 9). 249p. 2000. per. 4.50 (*0-373-65038-8*) Silhouette.

Lone Star Zodiac. David Westheimer. LC 94-44998. (Illus.). 32p. 1995. pap. 5.95 (*0-88415-452-1*, 5452) Gulf Pub.

Lone Stars. Sophia Healy. LC 88-8070. 1990. pap. 8.95 (*0-87113-366-0*, Atlntc Mnthly) Grove-Atltic.

Lone Stars Vol. I: A Legacy of Texas Quilts, 1836-1936. Karoline P. Bresenhan & Nancy O. Puentes. (Illus.). 156p. 1986. pap. 27.95 (*0-292-74649-0*) U of Tex Pr.

Lone Stars Vol. II: A Legacy of Texas Quilts, 1936-1986. Karoline P. Bresenhan & Nancy O. Puentes. (Illus.). 195p. 1990. 39.95 (*0-292-74658-X*); pap. 27.95 (*0-292-74671-7*) U of Tex Pr.

Lone Stars & State Gazettes: Texas Newspapers Before the Civil War. Marilyn M. Sibley. LC 82-45898. (Illus.). 408p. 1983. 31.95 (*0-89096-149-2*) Tex A&M Univ Pr.

Lone Sun. Daniel Maximin. LC 89-30992. (CARAF Bks.). 352p. 1989. text 35.00 (*0-8139-1224-5*) U Pr of Va.

An Asterisk (*) at the beginning of an entry indicates that the title is appearing for the first time.

Lone Survivor: A Diary of the Lukacze Ghetto & Svyniukhy. Michael Diment. Tr. by Shmuel D. Yahalom. 226p. 1992. pap. 13.95 (*0-89604-152-2*, Holocaust Library) US Holocaust.

Lone Survivor: Judge, Jury, & Executioner. Louis B. Antoine. 1998. pap. 12.95 (*0-533-12846-3*) Vantage.

Lone Texan. Lass Small. (Desire Ser.). 1998. per. 3.75 (*0-373-76165-1*, 1-76165-9) Silhouette.

Lone Texas Rider. Owen G. Irons. 1991. mass mkt. 3.50 (*1-55817-514-8*, Pinncle Kensgtn) Kensgtn Pub Corp.

Lone Trainer. Mike Saunders & Keith Holdaway. 136p. 1993. write for info. (*0-7494-0798-0*, Kogan Pg Educ) Stylus Pub VA.

***Lone Traveller.** Susan B. Kelly. 320p. 2000. 26.95 (*0-7490-0462-2*, Pub. by Allison & Busby) Intl Pubs Mktg.

Lone Twin. Joan Woodward. LC 98-168205. 1997. 50.00 (*1-85343-378-0*, Pub. by Free Assoc Bks); pap. 19.50 (*1-85343-374-8*, Pub. by Free Assoc Bks) NYU Pr.

***Lone Voyager: The Extraordinary Adventures of Howard Blackburn, Hero Fisherman of Gloucester.** Joseph E. Garland. 336p. 2000. pap. 13.00 (*0-684-87263-3*, Touchstone) S&S Trade Pap.

Lone Voyagers: Academic Women in Coeducational Universities, 1870-1937. Ed. by Geraldine J. Clifford. LC 89-31878. 336p. (C). 1989. 35.00 (*0-935312-84-6*); pap. 12.95 (*0-935312-85-4*) Feminist Pr.

Lone Wolf. Frederic Bean. 256p. 1997. mass mkt. 4.99 (*0-7860-0359-6*, Pinncle Kensgtn) Kensgtn Pub Corp.

Lone Wolf. Robert E. Boyle. 345p. 1998. pap. 17.95 (*1-892896-96-6*) Buy Books.

Lone Wolf. Kristine L. Franklin. LC 96-33287. (J). (gr. 4-8). 1997. 16.99 (*1-56402-935-2*) Candlewick Pr.

Lone Wolf. Kristine L. Franklin. LC 96-33287. 224p. (J). (gr. 3-7). 1998. pap. 4.99 (*0-7636-0480-1*) Candlewick Pr.

Lone Wolf. Kristine L. Franklin. (J). 1998. 10.09 (*0-606-13578-2*, Pub. by Turtleback) Demco.

Lone Wolf. Gilbert Morris. LC 95-7541. (Reno Western Saga Ser.: Vol. 6). 236p. 1995. pap. 7.99 (*0-8423-1997-2*) Tyndale Hse.

Lone Wolf. Ellen Rogers. (Stolen Moments Ser.). 1993. pap. 1.99 (*0-373-83287-7*, 1-83287-2) Harlequin Bks.

Lone Wolf. large type ed. Bennett Foster. LC 99-30784. 1999. write for info. (*1-57490-199-0*, Sagebrush LP West) T T Beeler.

Lone Wolf: A Biography of Vladimir Ze'ev Jabotinsky, 2 vols. Shmuel Katz. LC 95-15883.Tr. of Z'Abo. (Illus.). 912p. 1996. 100.00 (*1-56980-042-1*) Barricade Bks.

Lone Wolf: Mail Order Men. Sandy Steen. (Temptation Ser.: Vol. 691). 1998. per. 3.75 (*0-373-25791-0*, 1-25791-4) Harlequin Bks.

Lone Wolf: The Life & Death of U-Boat Ace Werner Henke. Timothy P. Mulligan. LC 93-20128. 288p. 1993. 39.95 (*0-275-93677-5*, C3677, Praeger Pubs) Greenwood.

***Lone Wolf: True Stories of Spree Killers.** Pan Pantziarka. (Illus.). 304p. 2000. mass mkt. 7.95 (*0-7535-0437-5*, Pub. by Virgin Bks) London Brdge.

Lone Wolf: Wolf's Bane, No. 19. Joe Dever. 224p. (Orig.). 1995. mass mkt. 4.50 (*0-425-14976-5*) Berkley Pub.

Lone Wolf No. 1: Flight from the Dark. Joe Dever & Gary Chalk. 192p. 1985. mass mkt. 4.50 (*0-425-08436-1*) Berkley Pub.

Lone Wolf No. 10: The Dungeons of Torgar. Joe Dever & Gary Chalk. 1988. mass mkt. 4.50 (*0-425-10930-5*) Berkley Pub.

Lone Wolf No. 12: The Masters of Darkness. Joe Dever. (Lone Wolf Ser.: No. 12). 1989. mass mkt. 4.50 (*0-425-11718-9*) Berkley Pub.

Lone Wolf No. 18: Dawn of the Dragons. Joe Dever. 208p. (Orig.). 1995. pap. text 3.99 (*0-425-14568-9*) Berkley Pub.

Lone Wolf Clan. Bonnie J. Hunt & Lawrence J. Hunt. (Lone Wolf Clan Bks.: No. I). (Illus.). iv, 231p. 1998. pap. 15.00 (*1-928800-00-9*) Mad Bear Pr.

"Lone Wolf" Gonzaullas, Texas Ranger. Brownson Malsch. LC 98-6495. (Illus.). 240p. 1998. pap. 13.95 (*0-8061-3016-4*) U of Okla Pr.

Lone Wolf of Drygulch Trail & More Passion Than Gold. Harry S. Drago. 1990. pap. 3.50 (*0-8125-0542-5*, Pub. by Tor Bks) St Martin.

Lone Wolf vs. Hitchcock: Treaty Rights & Indian Law at the End of the Nineteenth Century. Blue Clark. LC 94-7735. (Law in the American West Ser.: Vol. 5). (Illus.). 198p. 1994. text 45.00 (*0-8032-1466-9*) U of Nebr Pr.

Lone Wolf vs. Hitchcock: Treaty Rights & Indian Law at the End of the Nineteenth Century. Blue Clark. LC 94-7735. (Law in the American West Ser.). (Illus.). 198p. 1999. pap. text 15.00 (*0-8032-6401-1*) U of Nebr Pr.

***Lone Wolf's Child: Sons of Silver Springs.** Patricia Rosemoor. 2000. per. 4.25 (*0-373-22563-6*) Harlequin Bks.

Lone Wolf's Lady. Beverly Barton. (Intimate Moments Ser.). 1998. per. 4.25 (*0-373-07877-3*, 1-07877-3) Silhouette.

***Lone Woman.** Bernardo Atxaga. Tr. by Margaret J. Costa from BAQ. 160p. 1998. 22.00 (*1-86046-421-1*, Pub. by Harvill Press) FS&G.

Lone Woman. Dorey Schmidt. 44p. 1995. pap. 8.95 (*0-945199-02-3*) Double SS Pr.

Lone Woman of Ghalas-Hat. Rice D. Oliver. (Illus.). 32p. (J). (gr. 4-8). 1993. pap. 6.00 (*0-936778-51-2*); lib. bdg. 13.00 (*0-936778-52-0*) Calif Weekly.

Lone Writer & Blazing Bonzo: Tall Universal Tales. Kevin J. Shay. LC 93-93626. (Illus.). 52p. (YA). (gr. 6-10). 1993. pap. 3.95 (*1-881365-71-9*) Shay Pubns.

***Lonelier Than God: Robert Penn Warren & the Southern Exile.** Randy Hendricks. LC 99-40179. (Illus.). 256p. 2000. 40.00 (*0-8203-2178-8*) U of Ga Pr.

Loneliest Campaign: The Truman Victory of 1948. Irwin Ross. LC 75-22761. 304p. 1977. reprint ed. lib. bdg. 35.00 (*0-8371-8353-7*, ROLCT, Greenwood Pr) Greenwood.

Loneliest Cowboy. Pamela Macaluso. 1997. per. 3.50 (*0-373-76048-5*, 1-76048-7) Silhouette.

Loneliest Grief. Karen Holford. 96p. 1995. pap. 7.99 (*1-873796-27-7*) Review & Herald.

Loneliest Journey. Sheila Cassidy. pap. write for info. (*0-232-52120-4*) S Asia.

Loneliest Magician. Irene Radford. 352p. 1996. pap. 5.99 (*0-88677-709-7*, Pub. by DAW Bks) Penguin Putnam.

Loneliest Road in America: Stories. Roy Parvin. LC 96-41761. 192p. 1997. pap. 11.95 (*0-8118-1435-1*) Chronicle Bks.

Loneliest Woman in Africa: Christina Forsyth of Fingoland. W. P. Livingstone. Orig. Title: Christina Forsyth of Fingoland. 160p. 1994. pap. 10.99 (*0-88019-318-2*) Schmul Pub Co.

Loneliness see IVP Booklets

Loneliness see Soledad: El Remedio Supremo

Loneliness. (Pocket Power Ser.). 16p. (Orig.). 1986. pap. 1.25 (*0-89486-369-X*, 5363B) Hazelden.

Loneliness. Ginny W. Ashmore & Paul A. Mickey. (Lifesearch Ser.). 64p. 1996. pap. 4.95 (*0-687-01500-6*) Abingdon.

Loneliness. Laurie Beckelman. LC 93-5625. (Hot Line Ser.). 48p. (J). 1994. pap. 5.95 (*0-382-24745-0*); text 13.95 (*0-89686-843-5*, Crstwood Hse) Silver Burdett Pr.

Loneliness. Laurie Beckelman. LC 93-5625. (Hotline Ser.). 1994. 11.15 (*0-606-10218-3*, Pub. by Turtleback) Demco.

Loneliness. Adam Bittleston. 94p. 1990. 17.50 (*0-86315-056-X*, 1244, Pub. by Floris Bks) Anthroposophic.

Loneliness. Leroy S. Rouner. LC 97-45632. (Boston University Studies in Philosophy & Religion: No. 19). 301p. 1998. 35.00 (*0-268-01318-7*) U of Notre Dame Pr.

Loneliness. Tom Varney. (Institute of Biblical Counseling Discussion Guides Ser.). 64p. (Orig.). 1992. pap. 5.00 (*0-89109-693-0*) NavPress.

Loneliness, 3 bks., Set. Sherwood et al. (Emotional Literacy Ser.). 1995. 19.95 (*1-56844-022-7*) Enchante Pub.

Loneliness: A Sourcebook of Current Theory, Research, & Therapy. Ed. by Letitia A. Peplau & Daniel Perlman. LC 81-16272. (Wiley Series on Personality Processes). 447p. reprint ed. pap. 138.60 (*0-7837-2807-7*, 205766500006) Bks Demand.

Loneliness: How to Overcome It. Ed. by Val Marriott & Terry Timblick. (C). 1989. 35.00 (*0-86242-077-6*, Pub. by Age Concern Eng) St Mut.

Loneliness - The Killer. Frank Marzullo. 32p. 1998. pap. write for info. (*1-892363-25-9*) Christian Covenant.

Loneliness among Children with Special Needs: Theory, Research, Coping, & Intervention. Malka Margalit. LC 93-32707. 1993. 102.00 (*0-387-94158-4*) Spr-Verlag.

Loneliness & Spiritual Growth. Samuel M. Natale. LC 86-10012. 171p. (Orig.). 1986. pap. 16.95 (*0-89135-055-1*) Religious Educ.

***Loneliness in Childhood & Adolescence.** Ed. by Ken J. Rotenberg & Shelley Hymel. LC 98-45621. (Illus.). 432p. (C). 1999. 59.95 (*0-521-56135-3*) Cambridge U Pr.

***Loneliness in Later Life.** H. B. Gibson. LC 00-42238. 2000. write for info. (*0-333-92017-1*) St Martin.

Loneliness of Being Human. Joseph J. DeLuca. Date not set. write for info. (*0-9678892-0-0*) Ind Pubs Soc.

Loneliness of Blizzards: Poems. Jamie Parsley. LC 94-13799. 64p. 1995. pap. 14.95 (*0-7734-0011-7*, Mellen Poetry Pr) E Mellen.

Loneliness of Old Men: Anthropoems. Mando Sevillano. 100p. 1992. pap. 8.95 (*1-879027-01-1*) Eagle Red Bluff.

Loneliness of the Comparative Lawyer & Other Essays in Foreign & Comparative Law. John H. Merryman. LC 99-27523. 1999. 168.00 (*90-411-1215-4*) Kluwer Law Intl.

Loneliness of the Long-Distance Runner. Alan Sillitoe. LC 92-53548. 192p. 1992. reprint ed. pap. 10.95 (*0-452-26908-3*, Plume) Dutton Plume.

Loneliness of the Long Distance Writer: The Works of Love & the Huge Season. Wright Morris. LC 95-47580. 575p. (Orig.). (C). 1996. 30.00 (*0-87685-991-0*); pap. 17.50 (*0-87685-990-2*) Black Sparrow.

Loneliness of the Long Distance Writer: The Works of Love & the Huge Season, signed ed. deluxe ed. Wright Morris. LC 95-47580. 575p. (Orig.). (C). 1996. 40.00 (*0-87685-992-9*) Black Sparrow.

Loneliness of the Palm. Peter L. McNamara. 88p. (Orig.). 1993. pap. 8.95 (*1-879934-11-6*) St Andrews NC.

Loneliness, Solitude, & Companionship. Robert E. Neale. LC 83-26065. 131p. (Orig.). reprint ed. pap. 40.70 (*0-7837-2631-7*, 204298100006) Bks Demand.

***Loneliness Workbook: A Guide to Developing & Maintaining Lasting Connections.** Mary Ellen Copeland. (Illus.). 170p. 2000. pap. 14.95 (*1-57224-203-5*) New Harbinger.

Lonely: A Masai Tale. Illus. by Yumi Heo. LC 94-48449. (J). 1996. lib. bdg. 18.99 (*0-679-96934-9*, Pub. by Knopf Bks Yng Read) Random.

Lonely All the Time: Recognizing, Understanding & Overcoming Sex Addiction, for Addicts & Co-Dependents. 2nd ed. Ralph H. Earle & Gregory Crowe. 352p. 1998. reprint ed. pap. 15.00 (*0-9652879-1-2*, Pub. by Bradt Pubns) St Mut.

Lonely Ameba. Joshua P. Warren. (Illus.). 48p. (J). (gr. k-6). 1997. 12.95 (*1-57072-066-5*) Overmountain Pr.

Lonely Americans. Rollo W. Brown. LC 74-121452. (Essay Index Reprint Ser.). 1977. 23.95 (*0-8369-1699-9*) Ayer.

Lonely Christmas Tree. Donald Cripe. (Illus.). 24p. (Orig.). (J). (gr. k-3). 1995. pap. 6.95 (*0-9649625-0-0*) Buds Pubng.

Lonely Cries of Love. Shawn P. Henley. 1998. pap. write for info. (*1-57553-786-9*) Watermrk Pr.

Lonely Crowd: A Study of the Changing American Character. abr. ed. David Riesman et al. (Studies in National Policy: No. 3). (C). 1961. reprint ed. pap. 18.00 (*0-300-00193-2*, Y41) Yale U Pr.

Lonely Crusade. 2nd ed. Chester B. Himes. LC 98-162554. 398p. 1997. reprint ed. pap. 14.95 (*1-56025-142-5*, Thunders Mouth) Avalon NY.

Lonely Days Were Sundays: Reflections of a Jewish Southerner. Eli N. Evans. LC 92-42313. (Illus.). 288p. 1993. text 25.00 (*0-87805-627-0*) U Pr of Miss.

Lonely Days Were Sundays: Reflections of a Jewish Southerner. Eli N. Evans. LC 92-42313. (Illus.). 360p. 1994. pap. 15.95 (*0-87805-752-8*) U Pr of Miss.

Lonely Disciple: Monograph on T. Subba Row 1856-90. N. C. Ramanujachary. 1993. pap. 5.95 (*81-7059-215-1*, 7606, Quest) Theos Pub Hse.

Lonely Doll. Dare Wright. 64p. (J). (ps-3). 1998. 16.00 (*0-395-89926-5*); pap. 6.95 (*0-395-90112-X*) HM.

Lonely Dreamer. Hebe Elsna. 187p. 1996. reprint ed. spiral bd. 15.00 (*0-7873-0309-7*) Hlth Research.

Lonely Eagles. Robert C. Rose. (Illus.). 1976. 20.00 (*0-917612-00-0*) Aviation.

Lonely Eagles & Buffalo Soldiers: African-Americans in World War II see First Books

Lonely Fighter: One Man's Battle with the United States Government. John P. Hayes. 1979. 10.00 (*0-8184-0270-9*) Carol Pub Group.

Lonely Girl. Judy Baer. (Cedar River Daydreams Ser.: No. 17). 16p. (Orig.). (J). (gr. 7-10). 1992. mass mkt. 4.99 (*1-55661-280-X*) Bethany Hse.

Lonely Grass. large type ed. Nelson Nye. LC 93-25506. 290p. 1993. lib. bdg. 15.95 (*0-8161-5837-1*, G K Hall Lrg Type) Mac Lib Ref.

Lonely Grave: The Life & Death of William Redmond. Terence Denman. (Illus.). 208p. 1995. 29.50 (*0-7165-2561-5*, Pub. by Irish Acad Pr) Intl Spec Bk.

***Lonely Gun.** Luke Adams. 176p. 1999. mass mkt. 3.99 (*0-8439-4631-8*, Leisure Bks) Dorchester Pub Co.

Lonely Gun. Gordon D. Shirreffs. 176p. 1989. pap. 2.95 (*0-380-70640-7*, Avon Bks) Morrow Avon.

***Lonely Heart.** large type ed. Jacquelyn Webb. 224p. 2000. pap. 20.99 (*1-85389-992-5*, Dales) Ulverscroft.

***Lonely Heart: A Collection of Poetry.** Joseph E. Dicks. 48p. 2000. pap. 8.00 (*0-8059-4722-1*) Dorrance.

Lonely Hearts. Natty Bumppo. LC 91-78189. (Illus.). 325p. (Orig.). 1992. pap. 9.75 (*0-9604894-4-4*) Borf Bks.

Lonely Hearts. John Harvey. 288p. 1997. pap. 11.00 (*0-8050-5494-4*) H Holt & Co.

Lonely Hearts. John Harvey. 320p. 1990. mass mkt. 4.99 (*0-380-71006-4*, Avon Bks) Morrow Avon.

***Lonely Hearts.** Annie Kimberlin. 320p. 1998. mass mkt. 4.99 (*0-505-52256-X*, Love Spell) Dorchester Pub Co.

***Lonely Hearts, Changing Worlds.** Robert Winter. 2001. 22.00 (*1-57962-028-0*) Permanent Pr.

Lonely Hearts Club. Raul Nunez. Tr. by Ed Emery from SPA. (Masks Ser.). 160p. (Orig.). 1990. pap. 10.95 (*1-85242-137-1*) Serpents Tail.

***Lonely Hearts of the Cosmos: The Story of the Scientific Quest for the Secret of the Universe.** Dennis Overbye. LC 99-45792. 464p. 1999. pap. 16.95 (*0-316-64896-5*, Back Bay) Little.

Lonely House. Lowell Erdahl. (Orig.). 1989. pap. 7.95 (*1-55673-117-5*, 9828) CSS OH.

Lonely Hunter: A Biography of Carson McCullers. Lam Kam Chuen. 1975. 12.50 (*0-385-04028-8*) Doubleday.

Lonely Hunters: An Oral History of Lesbian & Gay Southern Life, 1948-1968. James T. Sears. (C). 1998. pap. text 25.00 (*0-8133-2475-0*, Pub. by Westview) HarpC.

Lonely Is the Valley. large type ed. Lynn Granger. (Linford Romance Library). 272p. 1992. pap. 16.99 (*0-7089-7195-4*, Linford) Ulverscroft.

Lonely Journey in a Foreign Land: Ambassadors Magazine Collection. Ed. by Edwin Su et al. (Ambassadors Magazine Collection: No. 5). (CHI.). 208p. (Orig.). 1994. pap. 7.50 (*1-882324-09-9*) Ambssdrs Christ.

Lonely Kind of War: Forward Air Controller, Vietnam. Marshall Harrison. (Illus.). 304p. 1997. reprint ed. pap. 15.95 (*0-89141-638-2*) Presidio Pr.

Lonely Knight. Christine Flynn. (Special Edition Ser.). 1993. per. 3.50 (*0-373-09826-X*, 5-09826-4) Silhouette.

Lonely Lady. Harold Robbins. 1993. per. 6.99 (*0-671-87490-X*) PB.

Lonely Lake der Einsame See. Arnold Zimmerman. Ed. by Chris Swansen. 40p. (Orig.). 1989. pap. 12.00 (*0-942018-04-4*) Schoolhouse WI.

Lonely Land. Sigurd F. Olson. LC 97-22181. (The Fesler-Lampert Minnesota Heritage Book Ser.). 1997. write for info. (*0-8166-2997-8*) U of Minn Pr.

Lonely Lands: A Guidebook to Inverarary, Kintyre, Glen Coe, Loch Awe, Loch Lomond, Cowal, The Kyles of Bute, & All of Central Argyll. Tom Atkinson. LC 99-185008. 171p. 1989. pap. text 9.95 (*0-946487-10-3*) Luath Pr Ltd.

Lonely Life. Jack Pierson. (Illus.). 144p. 1997. 39.95 (*3-908162-61-0*) Dist Art Pubs.

Lonely Lioness: A Masai Tale. Illus. by Yumi Heo. LC 94-48449. (J). 1996. 17.00 (*0-679-86934-4*, Pub. by Knopf Bks Yng Read) Random.

***Lonely Love.** Vivan Rosenburg. LC 00-190570. 475p. 2000. 25.00 (*0-7388-1717-1*); pap. 18.00 (*0-7388-1718-X*) Xlibris Corp.

Lonely Lula Cat. Joseph Slate. LC 84-48345. (Illus.). 32p. (J). (ps-1). 1985. 11.50 (*0-06-025806-3*) HarpC Child Bks.

Lonely Machines. Julia Vinograd. (Orig.). 1992. pap. 4.95 (*0-929730-42-9*) Zeitgeist Pr.

Lonely Man of Faith. Joseph Soloveitchik. LC 96-41174. 128p. 1997. 30.00 (*0-7657-5968-3*) Aronson.

Lonely Men. Louis L'Amour. 192p. 1984. mass mkt. 4.50 (*0-553-27677-8*) Bantam.

Lonely Men. Femi Olugbile. LC 88-139532. (Drumbeat Novel Ser.). 183 p. 1987. write for info. (*0-582-98500-5*) Longman.

Lonely Millionaire. Carol Grace. (Romance Ser.). 1995. per. 2.75 (*0-373-19057-3*, 1-19057-8) Silhouette.

Lonely on the Mountain. Louis L'Amour. 208p. 1984. mass mkt. 4.50 (*0-553-27678-6*) Bantam.

Lonely on the Mountain. Louis L'Amour. 1996. mass mkt. 4.99 (*0-553-85153-5*) Bantam.

Lonely Only Dog. Adele M. Brodkin. LC 98-7782. (Hello Reader! Ser.). (Illus.). 32p. (J). (gr. 1-3). 1998. 3.99 (*0-590-52280-9*) Scholastic Inc.

Lonely Other: A Woman Watching America. Diana H. George. LC 95-32488. (Creative Nonfiction Ser.). 224p. 1996. 14.95 (*0-252-06534-4*) U of Ill Pr.

Lonely Pain of Cancer: Home Care for the Terminally Ill. Kathleen L. Peabody & Margaret L. Mooney. Ed. by Bettye Ellison. LC 91-90114. (Illus.). 160p. (Orig.). (C). 1991. pap. 15.95 (*0-9629350-1-8*) Sharp Pub.

Lonely Passion of Judith Hearne. Brian Moore. 223p. 1988. pap. 11.95 (*0-316-57966-1*) Little.

***Lonely Passion of Judith Hearne.** Brian Moore. 1999. pap. write for info. (*0-316-57981-5*) Little.

Lonely Passion of Judith Hearne. Brian Moore. 248p. 1997. pap. text. write for info. (*0-7710-9992-4*) NCanadian Lib.

Lonely Pedestrian: Francis Marion Streamer. Ann Briley. 174p. 1986. 18.95 (*0-87770-534-8*) Ye Galleon.

Lonely Place. large type ed. Basil Copper. (Linford Mystery Library). 304p. 1997. pap. 16.99 (*0-7089-5060-4*) Ulverscroft.

Lonely Plains. Esther L. Vogt. LC 92-75484. (Heart for the Prairie Ser.: Bk. 2). 125p. (Orig.). 1993. pap. 8.99 (*0-88965-100-0*, Pub. by Horizon Books) Chr Pubns.

Lonely Planet. Steven Dietz. 1994. pap. 5.25 (*0-8222-1404-0*) Dramatists Play.

Lonely Planet Africa: On a Shoestring. 8th ed. Hugh Finlay et al. (Illus.). 1064p. 1998. pap. 29.95 (*0-86442-481-7*) Lonely Planet.

Lonely Planet Africa - the South. David Else et al. LC 98-100836. (Illus.). 928p. 1997. pap. 25.95 (*0-86442-473-6*) Lonely Planet.

Lonely Planet Afrique Du Sud. 2nd ed. Richard Everist. (FRE.). 700p. 1996. 27.95 (*2-84070-043-3*) Lonely Planet.

Lonely Planet Afrique Du Sud. 3rd ed. Lonely Planet Staff. 1998. pap. 29.95 (*2-84070-078-6*) Lonely Planet.

Lonely Planet Alaska. 5th ed. Jim DuFresne. (Illus.). 450p. 1997. pap. 16.95 (*0-86442-414-0*) Lonely Planet.

Lonely Planet Amsterdam. Rob Van Driesum. (Illus.). 224p. 1997. pap. 14.95 (*0-86442-444-2*) Lonely Planet.

Lonely Planet Amsterdam. Rob Van Driesum. (FRE.). 1997. 16.95 (*2-84070-067-0*) Lonely Planet.

***Lonely Planet Amsterdam Condensed: Amsterdam Condensed.** Jeremy Gray & Nikki Hall. (Condensed Guides Ser.). (Illus.). 128p. 2000. pap. 9.95 (*1-86450-133-2*) Lonely Planet.

Lonely Planet Andalousie. Lonely Planet Staff. (Lonely Planet Travel Guides Ser.). 1999. pap. text 19.95 (*2-84070-083-2*) Lonely Planet.

Lonely Planet Andalucia. Susan Forsyth & John Noble. (Illus.). 320p. 1999. pap. 16.95 (*0-86442-559-7*) Lonely Planet.

Lonely Planet Antarctica. Jeff Rubin. (Illus.). 352p. 1996. pap. 17.95 (*0-86442-415-9*) Lonely Planet.

***Lonely Planet Antarctica.** 2nd ed. Jeff Rubin. (Travel Guides Ser.). (Illus.). 384p. 2000. pap. 19.95 (*0-86442-772-7*) Lonely Planet.

Lonely Planet Arab Gulf States. 2nd ed. Gordon Robison. (Illus.). 528p. 1996. pap. 19.95 (*0-86442-390-X*) Lonely Planet.

Lonely Planet Argentina, Uruguay & Paraguay. 3rd ed. Wayne Bernhardson. 768p. 1999. pap. 21.95 (*0-86442-641-0*) Lonely Planet.

Lonely Planet Argentina, Uruguay & Paraguay: Travel Guide. 2nd ed. Wayne Bernhardson. (Illus.). 768p. 1996. pap. 19.95 (*0-86442-336-5*) Lonely Planet.

***Lonely Planet Australia.** 10th ed. Ed. by Lonely Planet Publications Staff. (Travel Guides Ser.). (Illus.). 1082p. 2000. pap. text 24.95 (*1-86450-068-9*) Lonely Planet.

***Lonely Planet Australia Travel Atlas.** Lonely Planet Publications Staff. (Travel Atlases Ser.). (Illus.). 128p. 2000. pap. 14.95 (*1-86450-065-4*) Lonely Planet.

Lonely Planet Australie. 2nd ed. (FRE.). 1997. 39.95 (*2-84070-048-4*) Lonely Planet.

Lonely Planet Australie. 3rd ed. Lonely Planet Staff. (Lonely Planet Travel Guides Ser.). 1999. pap. text 33.95 (*2-84070-085-9*) Lonely Planet.

Lonely Planet Austria. 2nd ed. Mark Honan. (Lonely Planet Travel Guides Ser.). (Illus.). 408p. 1999. pap. text 16.95 (*0-86442-577-5*) Lonely Planet.

Lonely Planet Backpacking in Alaska: A Walking Guide. Jim DuFresne. (Illus.). 256p. 1995. pap. 13.95 (*0-86442-266-0*) Lonely Planet.

Lonely Planet Bahamas, Turks & Caicos. Christopher P. Baker. (Illus.). 512p. 1998. pap. 17.95 (*0-86442-482-5*) Lonely Planet.

***Lonely Planet Bahrain, Kuwait & Qatar.** Gordon Robison & Paul Greenway. (Travel Guides Ser.). (Illus.). 24.95p. 2000. pap. 15.99 (*1-86450-132-4*) Lonely Planet.

Lonely Planet Baja California. Walt Peterson. LC 00-265951. (Diving & Snorkeling Guides Ser.). (Illus.). 128p. 1999. pap. text 16.95 (*0-86442-572-4*) Lonely Planet.

Lonely Planet Baja, California. 4th ed. Wayne Bernhardson. (Illus.). 328p. 1998. pap. 16.95 (*0-86442-445-0*) Lonely Planet.

An Asterisk (*) at the beginning of an entry indicates that the title is appearing for the first time.

Lonely Planet Bali & Lombok. 7th ed. Paul Greenway. (Lonely Planet Travel Guides Ser.). (Illus.). 456p. 1999. pap. text 15.95 (*0-86442-606-2*) Lonely Planet.

Lonely Planet Bali et Lombok. 2nd ed. Tom Brosnahan. (FRE.). 1997. 24.95 (*2-84070-057-3*) Lonely Planet.

Lonely Planet Bangkok. 4th ed. Joe Cummings. 240p. 1999. pap. 14.95 (*0-86442-666-6*) Lonely Planet.

Lonely Planet Bangladesh: Travel Guide. 3rd ed. Alex Newton et al. LC 96-181078. (Illus.). 288p. 1996. pap. 15.95 (*0-86442-296-2*) Lonely Planet.

Lonely Planet Barcelona. Damien Simonis. 244p. 1999. pap. 15.95 (*0-86442-607-0*) Lonely Planet.

Lonely Planet Beijing. 3rd ed. Robert Storey. (Illus.). 224p. 1998. pap. 14.95 (*0-86442-547-3*) Lonely Planet.

Lonely Planet Berlin. Andrea Shulte-Peevers & David Peevers. (Illus.). 256p. 1998. pap. 14.95 (*0-86442-560-0*) Lonely Planet.

Lonely Planet Bermuda. Ned Friary & Glenda Bendure. (Illus.). 176p. 1997. pap. 14.95 (*0-86442-417-5*) Lonely Planet.

Lonely Planet Bhutan. Stan Armington. (Illus.). 256p. 1998. pap. 19.95 (*0-86442-483-3*) Lonely Planet.

Lonely Planet Bolivia. 3rd ed. Deanna Swaney. (Illus.). 496p. 1996. pap. 19.95 (*0-86442-396-9*) Lonely Planet.

***Lonely Planet Boston.** Kim Grant. (Travel Guides Ser.). (Illus.). 256p. 2000. pap. 15.95 (*0-86442-642-9*) Lonely Planet.

Lonely Planet Boy. Barney Hoskyns. 208p. (Orig.). 1997. pap. text 13.99 (*1-85242-387-0*) Serpents Tail.

Lonely Planet Brazil. 4th ed. Nick Selby. (Lonely Planet Travel Guides Ser.). (Illus.). 720p. 1998. pap. text 19.95 (*0-86442-561-9*) Lonely Planet.

Lonely Planet Bresil. 2nd ed. R. Jones et al. (FRE.). 750p. 1989. 26.95 (*2-84070-038-7*) Lonely Planet.

Lonely Planet Britain. 2nd ed. Tom Smallman & Pat Yale. 1080p. 1999. pap. 25.95 (*0-86442-578-3*) Lonely Planet.

Lonely Planet Britain. 2nd ed. Bryn Thomas et al. (Illus.). 1040p. 1997. pap. 24.95 (*0-86442-518-X*) Lonely Planet.

***Lonely Planet British Phrasebook.** Elizabeth Bartsch-Parker et al. 320p. 1999. pap. 5.95 (*0-86442-484-1*) Lonely Planet.

***Lonely Planet Budapost.** Steve Fallon. (Travel Guides Ser.). (Illus.). 184p. 2000. pap. 14.95 (*1-86450-118-9*) Lonely Planet.

Lonely Planet Buenos Aires. 2nd ed. Wayne Bernhardson. 160p. 1999. pap. 12.95 (*0-86442-643-7*) Lonely Planet.

Lonely Planet Bushwalking in Australia: Walking Guide. 3rd ed. John Chapman & Monica Chapman. (Illus.). 360p. (Orig.). 1997. pap. 17.95 (*0-86442-391-8*) Lonely Planet.

Lonely Planet Cairo. Andrew Humphreys. (Illus.). 176p. 1998. pap. 14.95 (*0-86442-548-1*) Lonely Planet.

***Lonely Planet California: California Condensed.** Marisa Geirlich. Ed. by Lonely Planet Publications Staff. (Travel Guides Ser.). (Illus.). 128p. 2000. pap. text 9.95 (*1-86450-041-7*) Lonely Planet.

Lonely Planet California & Nevada: Travel Guide. Marisa Gierlich et al. (Illus.). 850p. 1996. pap. 19.95 (*0-86442-335-7*) Lonely Planet.

Lonely Planet Californie et Nevada. Tony Wheeler. (FRE.). 1997. 29.95 (*2-84070-045-X*) Lonely Planet.

Lonely Planet Cambodge. 2nd ed. Chris Taylor. (FRE.). 1992. 22.95 (*2-84070-055-7*) Lonely Planet.

***Lonely Planet Cambodia.** 3rd ed. Nick Ray. (Lonely Planet Travel Guides Ser.). 224p. 1999. pap. 15.95 (*0-86442-670-4*) Lonely Planet.

Lonely Planet Canada. 5th ed. Mark Lightbody & Dorinda Talbot. (Illus.). 976p. 1997. 21.95 (*0-86442-409-4*) Lonely Planet.

Lonely Planet Canary Islands. Damien Simonis. (Illus.). 280p. 1998. pap. 14.95 (*0-86442-522-8*) Lonely Planet.

Lonely Planet Cantonese. 3rd ed. Kam Y. Lan. 256p. 1999. pap. 6.95 (*0-86442-645-3*) Lonely Planet.

Lonely Planet Cape Town. 2nd ed. Jon Murray. (Illus.). 160p. 1998. pap. 12.95 (*0-86442-485-X*) Lonely Planet.

Lonely Planet Central America: On a Shoestring. 3rd ed. Nancy Keller et al. (Illus.). 832p. 1997. pap. 19.95 (*0-86442-418-3*) Lonely Planet.

Lonely Planet Central Asia: Travel Guide. Andrew Humphreys et al. LC 96-201803. (Illus.). 544p. 1996. pap. 17.95 (*0-86442-358-6*) Lonely Planet.

Lonely Planet Central Europe. 3rd ed. Steve Fallon. (On a Shoestring Ser.). (Illus.). 800p. 1999. pap. text 24.95 (*0-86442-608-9*) Lonely Planet.

Lonely Planet Chicago. Ryan V. Berkmoes. LC 99-230673. (Illus.). 256p. 1998. pap. 15.95 (*0-86442-549-X*) Lonely Planet.

Lonely Planet Chile & Easter Island. 4th ed. Wayne Bernhardson. (Illus.). 452p. 1997. pap. 19.95 (*0-86442-421-3*) Lonely Planet.

***Lonely Planet Chile & Easter Island.** 5th ed. Ed. by Lonely Planet Publications Staff. (Travel Guides Ser.). (Illus.). 2000. pap. text 19.95 (*1-86450-088-3*) Lonely Planet.

Lonely Planet Chile & Easter Island Travel Atlas: With Travel Information & Roadtesting. Wayne Bernhardson. (Lonely Planet Ser.). 1997. pap. text 14.95 (*0-86442-517-1*) Lonely Planet.

Lonely Planet Chine. 3rd ed. (FRE.). 1994. 39.95 (*2-84070-049-2*) Lonely Planet.

Lonely Planet City Map Bangkok. 1999. pap. 5.95 (*1-86450-004-2*) Lonely Planet.

Lonely Planet City Map Berlin. 1999. pap. 5.95 (*1-86450-005-0*) Lonely Planet.

Lonely Planet City Map Chicago. 1999. pap. 5.95 (*1-86450-006-9*) Lonely Planet.

***Lonely Planet CitySync.** Lonely Planet Publications Staff. 2000. pap. 49.95 (*1-86450-228-2*) Lonely Planet.

Lonely Planet Colombia: Travel Survival Kit. 2nd ed. Krzysztof Dydynski. (Illus.). 544p. 1995. pap. 15.95 (*0-86442-234-2*) Lonely Planet.

***Lonely Planet Corfu & the Lonians.** Sally Webb. Ed. by Lonely Planet Publications Staff. (Travel Guides Ser.). (Illus.). 208p. 2000. pap. text 14.95 (*1-86450-073-5*) Lonely Planet.

Lonely Planet Corse. Tony Wheeler et al. 304p. 1999. pap. 19.95 (*2-84070-092-1*) Lonely Planet.

Lonely Planet Corsica. Tony Wheeler et al. 256p. 1999. pap. 15.95 (*0-86442-792-1*) Lonely Planet.

***Lonely Planet Costa Rican Phrasebook.** Thomas Kohnstamm. (Lonely Planet Phrasebooks). (Illus.). 256p. 2000. pap. 7.95 (*1-86450-105-7*) Lonely Planet.

***Lonely Planet Crete.** Jeanne Oliver. Ed. by Lonely Planet Publications Staff. (Travel Guides Ser.). (Illus.). 256p. 2000. pap. text 15.95 (*1-86450-074-3*) Lonely Planet.

***Lonely Planet Crete: Crete Condensed.** Jeanne Oliver. Ed. by Lonely Planet Publications Staff. (Travel Guides Ser.). (Illus.). 128p. 2000. pap. text 9.95 (*1-86450-042-5*) Lonely Planet.

Lonely Planet Croatia. Jeanne Oliver. 288p. 1999. pap. 16.95 (*0-86442-646-1*) Lonely Planet.

Lonely Planet Cuba. D. Stanley. (FRE., Illus.). 530p. 1997. 24.95 (*2-84070-066-2*) Lonely Planet.

Lonely Planet Cuba. David Stanley. (Illus.). 400p. 1997. pap. 17.95 (*0-86442-403-5*) Lonely Planet.

***Lonely Planet Cyprus.** Paul Hellander. Ed. by Lonely Planet Publications Staff. (Travel Guides Ser.). (Illus.). 256p. 2000. pap. text 15.95 (*1-86450-075-1*) Lonely Planet.

Lonely Planet Czech & Slovak Republics. 2nd ed. Scott McNeely & Richard Nebeksy. (Illus.). 560p. 1998. pap. 19.95 (*0-86442-525-2*) Lonely Planet.

Lonely Planet Czech & Slovak Republics: Travel Survival Kit. John King, III & Richard Nebesky. (Illus.). 504p. 1995. pap. 15.95 (*0-86442-245-8*) Lonely Planet.

Lonely Planet Deep South. Kap Stann & Diane Marshall. (Illus.). 608p. (Orig.). 1998. pap. 19.95 (*0-86442-486-8*) Lonely Planet.

Lonely Planet Delhi: City Guide. Hugh Finlay. LC 96-133409. (Illus.). 320p. 1996. pap. 9.95 (*0-86442-349-7*) Lonely Planet.

Lonely Planet Denmark. 2nd ed. Glenda Bendure & Ned Friary. 384p. 1999. pap. 17.95 (*0-86442-609-7*) Lonely Planet.

Lonely Planet Denmark: Travel Guide. Glenda Bendure & Ned Friary. LC 96-223566. (Illus.). 384p. 1996. pap. 17.95 (*0-86442-330-6*) Lonely Planet.

Lonely Planet Diving & Snorkeling Australia's Great Barrier Reef. 2nd ed. Len Zell. 176p. 1999. pap. 17.95 (*0-86442-763-8*) Lonely Planet.

Lonely Planet Diving & Snorkeling Guide to Australia: Coral Sea & Great Barrier Reef. Carl Roessler. (Diving & Snorkeling Guides Ser.). 96p. 1991. pap. 14.95 (*1-55992-044-0*, Pisces Books) Lonely Planet.

Lonely Planet Diving & Snorkeling Guide to Australia: Southeast Coast & Tasmania. Peter Stone. (Diving & Snorkeling Guides Ser.). 96p. 1992. pap. 14.95 (*1-55992-059-9*, Pisces Books) Lonely Planet.

Lonely Planet Diving & Snorkeling Guide to Bahamas: Family Islands & Grand Bahama. 2nd ed. Bob Keller & Charlotte Keller. LC 94-18171. (Pisces Diving & Snorkeling Guides Ser.). 96p. 1994. 14.95 (*1-55992-078-5*, Pisces Books) Lonely Planet.

Lonely Planet Diving & Snorkeling Guide to Bahamas: Nassau & New Providence Island. 2nd ed. Steve Blount & Lisa Walker. (Pisces Diving & Snorkeling Guides Ser.). 1990. pap. 14.95 (*1-55992-040-8*, Pisces Books) Lonely Planet.

Lonely Planet Diving & Snorkeling Guide to Bali & the Komodo Region. Tim Rock. (Diving & Snorkeling Guides Ser.). (Illus.). 96p. 1996. pap. 14.95 (*1-55992-086-6*, 2086, Pisces Books) Lonely Planet.

Lonely Planet Diving & Snorkeling Guide to Belize. 2nd ed. Franz O. Meyer. (Illus.). 96p. 1998. pap. 15.95 (*0-86442-575-9*) Lonely Planet.

Lonely Planet Diving & Snorkeling Guide to Bermuda. Lawson Wood. (Pisces Diving & Snorkeling Guides Ser.). (Illus.). 128p. 1997. pap. 15.95 (*1-55992-096-3*, 2096, Pisces Books) Lonely Planet.

Lonely Planet Diving & Snorkeling Guide to Bermuda. Lawson Wood. (Illus.). 96p. 1998. pap. 15.95 (*0-86442-573-2*) Lonely Planet.

Lonely Planet Diving & Snorkeling Guide to Bonaire. Jerry Schnabel & Susan L. Swygert. (Pisces Diving & Snorkeling Guides Ser.). 96p. 1991. pap. 14.95 (*1-55992-043-2*, Pisces Books) Lonely Planet.

Lonely Planet Diving & Snorkeling Guide to Bonaire. 2nd ed. Susan Swygert & Jerry Schnabel. (Pisces Diving & Snorkeling Guides Ser.). (Illus.). 96p. 1997. pap. 14.95 (*1-55992-100-5*, 2100, Pisces Books) Lonely Planet.

Lonely Planet Diving & Snorkeling Guide to British Virgin Islands. Linda Sorensen. (Pisces Diving & Snorkeling Guides Ser.). (Illus.). 96p. 1991. pap. 14.95 (*1-55992-050-5*, 2050, Pisces Books) Lonely Planet.

Lonely Planet Diving & Snorkeling Guide to California's Central Coast: Including Southern Monterey County, San Luis Obispo County, Santa Barbara County, Ventura County. Darren Douglass. LC 94-20893. (Pisces Diving & Snorkeling Guides Ser.). 80p. 1994. pap. 14.95 (*1-55992-079-3*, Pisces Books) Lonely Planet.

Lonely Planet Diving & Snorkeling Guide to Cayman Islands: Grand Cayman, Little Cayman & Cayman Brac. 2nd ed. Carl Roessler. (Pisces Diving & Snorkeling Guides Ser.). 96p. 1993. pap. 14.95 (*1-55992-042-4*, Pisces Books) Lonely Planet.

Lonely Planet Diving & Snorkeling Guide to Cocos Island. Lucy Agace. LC 96-37859. (Pisces Diving & Snorkeling Guides Ser.). 96p. 1997. pap. 14.95 (*1-55992-092-0*, 2092, Pisces Books) Lonely Planet.

Lonely Planet Diving & Snorkeling Guide to Cozumel. 2nd ed. George S. Lewbel & Larry R. Martin. (Pisces Diving & Snorkeling Guides Ser.). 96p. 1991. pap. 14.95 (*1-55992-034-3*, Pisces Books) Lonely Planet.

Lonely Planet Diving & Snorkeling Guide to Cozumel. 3rd ed. George S. Lewbel & Larry R. Martin. (Illus.). 96p. 1998. pap. 14.95 (*0-86442-574-0*) Lonely Planet.

Lonely Planet Diving & Snorkeling Guide to Cuba. Diana Williams. LC 96-15505. (Diving & Snorkeling Guides Ser.). (Illus.). 96p. 1996. pap. 14.95 (*1-55992-090-4*, 2090, Pisces Books) Lonely Planet.

Lonely Planet Diving & Snorkeling Guide to Curacao. 2nd ed. George S. Lewbel. LC 96-39573. (Pisces Diving & Snorkeling Guides Ser.). 96p. 1997. 14.95 (*1-55992-095-5*, 2095, Pisces Books) Lonely Planet.

Lonely Planet Diving & Snorkeling Guide to Fiji Islands. W. Gregory Brown. LC 92-45216. (Pisces Diving & Snorkeling Guides Ser.). 96p. 1993. pap. 14.95 (*1-55992-063-7*, Pisces Books) Lonely Planet.

Lonely Planet Diving & Snorkeling Guide to Florida Keys. 2nd ed. John Halas et al. (Pisces Diving & Snorkeling Guides Ser.). 96p. 1992. pap. 14.95 (*1-55992-055-6*, Pisces Books) Lonely Planet.

Lonely Planet Diving & Snorkeling Guide to Great Lakes. Kathy Johnson & Greg Lashbrook. (Pisces Diving & Snorkeling Guides Ser.). 96p. 1991. pap. 14.95 (*1-55992-046-7*, Pisces Books) Lonely Planet.

Lonely Planet Diving & Snorkeling Guide to Guam & Yap. 2nd ed. Tim Rock. LC 99-462601. (Diving & Snorkeling Guides Ser.). 128p. 1999. pap. text 15.95 (*0-86442-744-1*) Lonely Planet.

Lonely Planet Diving & Snorkeling Guide to Hawaiian Islands. 2nd ed. Doug Wallin. (Pisces Diving & Snorkeling Guides Ser.). 112p. 1991. pap. 14.95 (*1-55992-038-6*, Pisces Books) Lonely Planet.

Lonely Planet Diving & Snorkeling Guide to Jamaica. Hannie Smit & Theo Smit. (Diving & Snorkeling Guides Ser.). (Illus.). 96p. 1996. pap. 14.95 (*1-55992-087-4*, 2087, Pisces Books) Lonely Planet.

Lonely Planet Diving & Snorkeling Guide to Northern California & the Monterey Peninsula. 2nd ed. Steve Rosenberg. (Diving & Snorkeling Guides Ser.). 96p. 1992. pap. 14.95 (*1-55992-052-1*, Pisces Books) Lonely Planet.

Lonely Planet Diving & Snorkeling Guide to Pacific Northwest: Includes Puget Sound, San Juan Islands, & Vancouver Island. Edward Weber. LC 92-23549. (Pisces Diving & Snorkeling Guides Ser.). 1993. pap. 14.95 (*1-55992-075-0*, Pisces Books) Lonely Planet.

Lonely Planet Diving & Snorkeling Guide to Palau. Tim Rock & Francis Toribiong. LC 93-27894. (Diving & Snorkeling Guides Ser.). (Illus.). 96p. 1994. pap. 14.95 (*1-55992-068-8*, Pisces Books) Lonely Planet.

Lonely Planet Diving & Snorkeling Guide to Puerto Rico: Includes Vieques, Culebra, & Desecheo. Steve Simonsen. (Diving & Snorkeling Guides Ser.). (Illus.). 96p. 1996. pap. 14.95 (*1-55992-084-X*, 2084, Pisces Books) Lonely Planet.

Lonely Planet Diving & Snorkeling Guide to Red Sea. John Ratterree. LC 94-25371. (Pisces Diving & Snorkeling Guides Ser.). 96p. 1994. 14.95 (*1-55992-081-5*, PISCES, Pisces Books) Lonely Planet.

Lonely Planet Diving & Snorkeling Guide to Roatan & Honduras' Bay Islands. Sharon Collins. LC 93-17943. (Diving & Snorkeling Guides Ser.). 96p. 1993. pap. 14.95 (*1-55992-074-2*, Pisces Books) Lonely Planet.

Lonely Planet Diving & Snorkeling Guide to Roatan & Honduras' Bay Islands. 2nd ed. Sharon Collins. LC 93-17943. (Pisces Diving & Snorkeling Guides Ser.). 96p. 1997. pap. 14.95 (*1-55992-093-9*, 2093, Pisces Books) Lonely Planet.

Lonely Planet Diving & Snorkeling Guide to Scotland: Includes Shetlands, Scapa Flow & Hebrides. Lawson Wood. (Diving & Snorkeling Guides Ser.). (Illus.). 96p. 1996. pap. 14.95 (*1-55992-094-7*, 2094, Pisces Books) Lonely Planet.

Lonely Planet Diving & Snorkeling Guide to Seychelles. Lawson Wood. LC 96-42214. (Diving & Snorkeling Guides Ser.). 96p. 1997. pap. 14.95 (*1-55992-097-1*, 2097, Pisces Books) Lonely Planet.

Lonely Planet Diving & Snorkeling Guide to Southern California: Includes Los Angeles, Orange & San Diego Counties. 2nd ed. Darren Douglas. LC 93-20673. (Pisces Diving & Snorkeling Guides Ser.). (Illus.). 112p. (Orig.). 1994. pap. 14.95 (*1-55992-057-2*, Pisces Books) Lonely Planet.

Lonely Planet Diving & Snorkeling Guide to St. Maarten, Saba & St. Eustatius. Jerry Schnabel & Susan L. Swygert. LC 94-8698. (Diving & Snorkeling Guides Ser.). 92p. 1994. pap. 14.95 (*1-55992-066-1*, Pisces Books) Lonely Planet.

Lonely Planet Diving & Snorkeling Guide to Texas. Barbara Dunn & Stephan Myers. (Diving & Snorkeling Guides Ser.). 96p. 1990. 14.95 (*1-55992-032-7*, Pisces Books) Lonely Planet.

Lonely Planet Diving & Snorkeling Guide to Texas: Includes Inland, Coastal, & Offshore Sites. 2nd ed. Barbara Dunn & Janet R. Edwards. LC 96-8596. (Pisces Diving & Snorkeling Guides Ser.). 96p. (Orig.). 1996. pap. 14.95 (*1-55992-091-2*, 2091, Pisces Books) Lonely Planet.

Lonely Planet Diving & Snorkeling Guide to the Best Caribbean Diving. Susanne Cummings & Stuart Cummings. LC 95-12828. (Diving & Snorkeling Guides Ser.). (Illus.). 96p. 1995. pap. 14.95 (*1-55992-082-3*, 2082, Pisces Books) Lonely Planet.

Lonely Planet Diving & Snorkeling Guide to Truk Lagoon. Tim Rock. LC 93-30789. (Diving & Snorkeling Guides Ser.). 96p. 1994. pap. 14.95 (*1-55992-069-6*, Pisces Books) Lonely Planet.

Lonely Planet Diving & Snorkeling Guide to Turks & Caicos Islands. Stuart Cummings & Susanne Cummings. LC 92-34115. (Pisces Diving & Snorkeling Guides Ser.). 1993. pap. 14.95 (*1-55992-067-X*, Pisces Books) Lonely Planet.

Lonely Planet Diving & Snorkeling Guide to U. S. Virgin Islands: St. Croix, St. Thomas & St. John. 2nd ed. Susanne Cummings & Stuart Cummings. (Pisces Diving & Snorkeling Guides Ser.). 96p. 1992. pap. 14.95 (*1-55992-053-X*, Pisces Books) Lonely Planet.

Lonely Planet Diving & Snorkeling Guide to Vanuatu. Brian Ansell et al. LC 94-23351. (Diving & Snorkeling Guides Ser.). 96p. 1995. pap. 14.95 (*1-55992-080-7*, Pisces Books) Lonely Planet.

Lonely Planet Dominica. Michael Lawrence. 128p. 1999. pap. 15.95 (*0-86442-764-6*) Lonely Planet.

Lonely Planet Dominican Republic & Haiti. Scott Doggett & Leah Gordon. 352p. 1999. pap. 15.95 (*0-86442-647-X*) Lonely Planet.

Lonely Planet Drive Thru America. Sean Condon. (Illus.). 300p. (Orig.). 1998. pap. 12.95 (*0-86442-506-6*) Lonely Planet.

***Lonely Planet Dubai.** Lou Callan. Ed. by Lonely Planet Publications Staff. (Travel Guides Ser.). (Illus.). 176p. 2000. pap. text 14.95 (*1-86450-131-6*) Lonely Planet.

Lonely Planet Dublin. 3rd ed. Tom Smallman. 192p. 1999. pap. 12.95 (*0-86442-610-0*) Lonely Planet.

Lonely Planet Dublin: City Guide. 2nd ed. Tony Wheeler et al. (Illus.). 288p. (Orig.). 1996. pap. 11.95 (*0-86442-351-9*) Lonely Planet.

Lonely Planet East Africa. 4th ed. Hugh Finlay & Geoff Crowther. (Illus.). 720p. 1997. pap. 21.95 (*0-86442-449-3*) Lonely Planet.

Lonely Planet Eastern Caribbean. 2nd ed. Glenda Bendure & Ned Friary. (Illus.). 560p. 1998. pap. 17.95 (*0-86442-422-1*) Lonely Planet.

Lonely Planet Eastern Europe. 5th ed. Steve Fallon. (On a Shoestring Ser.). (Illus.). 864p. 1999. pap. text 24.95 (*0-86442-611-9*) Lonely Planet.

Lonely Planet Ecuador & the Galapagos. 4th ed. Rob Rachowiecki. (Illus.). 512p. 1997. pap. 19.95 (*0-86442-348-9*) Lonely Planet.

Lonely Planet Edinburgh. Tom Smallman. 160p. 1999. pap. 11.95 (*0-86442-580-5*) Lonely Planet.

Lonely Planet Egypt. 4th ed. Damien Simonis et al. (Illus.). 512p. 1996. pap. 17.95 (*0-86442-395-0*) Lonely Planet.

Lonely Planet Egypt Travel Atlas. Contrib. by Leanne Logan & Geert Cole. (Illus.). 72p. 1996. pap. 14.95 (*0-86442-376-4*) Lonely Planet.

***Lonely Planet Estonia, Latvia & Lithuania.** 2nd ed. Nicola Williams et al. (Travel Guides Ser.). (Illus.). 398p. 2000. pap. 19.95 (*0-86442-678-X*) Lonely Planet.

Lonely Planet Estonia, Latvia & Lithvonia. John Noble et al. LC 98-118689. (Illus.). 464p. 1997. pap. 19.95 (*0-86442-416-7*) Lonely Planet.

Lonely Planet Etats Baltes et Kaliningrad. 11th ed. John Noble & Susan Forsyth. (FRE., Illus.). 300p. 1994. 23.95 (*2-84070-019-0*) Lonely Planet.

Lonely Planet Fiji: Travel Guide. 4th ed. Robyn Jones & Leonardo Pinheiro. (Illus.). 312p. 1997. pap. 14.95 (*0-86442-353-5*) Lonely Planet.

Lonely Planet Finland. 3rd ed. Jennifer Brewer. 400p. 1999. pap. 19.95 (*0-86442-649-6*) Lonely Planet.

Lonely Planet Florida. Nicholas Selby. (Illus.). 608p. 1997. pap. 19.95 (*0-86442-374-8*) Lonely Planet.

Lonely Planet France. 2nd ed. Steve Fallon & Daniel Robinson. (Illus.). 1118p. 1997. pap. 19.95 (*0-86442-331-4*) Lonely Planet.

Lonely Planet France. 3rd ed. Steve Fallon et al. 1100p. 1999. pap. 24.95 (*0-86442-612-7*) Lonely Planet.

Lonely Planet Gambia & Senegal. David Else. LC 99-461706. (Illus.). 256p. 1998. pap. 16.95 (*0-86442-593-7*) Lonely Planet.

Lonely Planet Germany. Steve Fallon et al. (Illus.). 864p. 1998. pap. 19.95 (*0-86442-487-6*) Lonely Planet.

Lonely Planet Goa. Bryn Thomas & Douglas Streatfeild-James. (Illus.). 256p. (Orig.). 1998. pap. 14.95 (*0-86442-488-4*) Lonely Planet.

Lonely Planet Great Reefs of the World. Carl Roessler. (Diving & Snorkeling Guides Ser.). (Illus.). 128p. 1992. pap. 19.95 (*1-55992-058-0*, 2058, Pisces Books) Lonely Planet.

Lonely Planet Greece. 3rd ed. Rosemary Hall et al. LC 98-149678. (Illus.). 752p. 1998. pap. 19.95 (*0-86442-527-9*) Lonely Planet.

***Lonely Planet Greek Islands.** David Willett. Ed. by Lonely Planet Publications Staff. (Travel Guides Ser.). (Illus.). 480p. 2000. pap. text 17.95 (*1-86450-109-X*) Lonely Planet.

***Lonely Planet Greek Phrasebook.** 2nd ed. Markella Mikkelsen. (Lonely Planet Phrasebooks). (ENG & GRE., Illus.). 320p. 2000. pap. 7.95 (*0-86442-683-6*) Lonely Planet.

Lonely Planet Guadeloupe et ses Iles. Isabelle Muller. (FRE.). 1997. 18.95 (*2-84070-068-9*) Lonely Planet.

Lonely Planet Guatemala & Belize. 2nd ed. (Lonely Planet Travel Guides Ser.). (FRE.). 1998. 24.95 (*2-84070-069-7*) Lonely Planet.

Lonely Planet Guatemala, Belize & Yucatan: La Ruta Maya. 3rd ed. Tom Brosnahan & Nancy Keller. (Illus.). 584p. 1997. pap. 19.95 (*0-86442-424-8*) Lonely Planet.

Lonely Planet Hawaii. 4th ed. Glenda Bendure & Ned Friary. (Illus.). 608p. 1997. pap. 19.95 (*0-86442-489-2*) Lonely Planet.

***Lonely Planet Hawaii.** 5th ed. Ed. by Lonely Planet Publications Staff. (Travel Guides Ser.). (Illus.). 2000. pap. text 19.95 (*1-86450-047-6*) Lonely Planet.

Lonely Planet Hindi & Urdu. 2nd ed. Richard Delacy. (Illus.). 256p. 1998. pap. 6.95 (*0-86442-425-6*) Lonely Planet.

An Asterisk (*) at the beginning of an entry indicates that the title is appearing for the first time.

Lonely Planet Ho Chi Minh (Saigon) City Guide. Robert Storey. (Illus.). 280p. 1995. pap. 9.95 (*0-86442-311-X*) Lonely Planet.

Lonely Planet Hong Kong. 1999. pap. 5.95 (*1-86450-007-7*) Lonely Planet.

Lonely Planet Hong Kong. Nicko Goncharoff. (Illus.). 352p. 1996. pap. 12.95 (*0-86442-426-4*) Lonely Planet.

Lonely Planet Hong Kong: City Guide. 2nd ed. Damian Harper. (Lonely Planet City Guides). (Illus.). 272p. 14.95 (*0-86442-583-X*) Lonely Planet.

Lonely Planet Hong Kong, Macau & Guangzhou. 8th ed. Robert Storey. (Illus.). 448p. 1997. pap. 15.95 (*0-86442-410-8*) Lonely Planet.

Lonely Planet Hong Kong, Macau & Guangzhou: Travel Survival Kit. 9th ed. Damian Harper. (Lonely Planet Travel Guides Ser.). (Illus.). 480p. 1998. pap. text 15.95 (*0-86442-584-8*) Lonely Planet.

Lonely Planet Hongrie. 11th ed. Steve Fallon. (FRE., Illus.). 440p. 1994. 19.95 (*2-84070-020-4*) Lonely Planet.

Lonely Planet Honolulu. 2nd ed. Glenda Bendure & Ned Friary. (Illus.). 184p. 1997. pap. 12.95 (*0-86442-490-6*) Lonely Planet.

Lonely Planet Hungary. 2nd ed. Steve Fallon. (Illus.). 448p. 1997. pap. 17.95 (*0-86442-452-3*) Lonely Planet.

***Lonely Planet Hungary.** 3rd ed. Steve Fallon. (Travel Guides Ser.). (Illus.). 400p. 2000. pap. 17.95 (*0-86442-685-2*) Lonely Planet.

Lonely Planet Iceland, Greenland & the Faroe Islands. 3rd ed. Deanna Swaney. (Illus.). 640p. 1997. pap. 19.95 (*0-86442-453-1*) Lonely Planet.

Lonely Planet Iles Grecques. 4th ed. Lonely Planet Staff. (Lonely Planet Travel Guides Ser.). 1999. pap. text 22.95 (*2-84070-084-0*) Lonely Planet.

Lonely Planet in Rajasthan. Royina Grewal. LC 97-147776. 264p. 1997. pap. text 10.95 (*0-86442-457-4*) Lonely Planet.

Lonely Planet Inde. 2nd ed. Bryn Thomas. (FRE.). 1200p. 1996. 32.95 (*2-84070-042-5*) Lonely Planet.

Lonely Planet Inde. 3rd ed. Bryn Thomas et al. (Illus.). 1176p. 1998. pap. 39.95 (*2-84070-070-0*) Lonely Planet.

Lonely Planet India. 7th ed. Bryn Thomas et al. (Illus.). 1056p. 1997. pap. 25.95 (*0-86442-491-4*) Lonely Planet.

Lonely Planet India & Bangladesh Travel Atlas. Hugh Finlay. (Illus.). 164p. 1995. pap. 14.95 (*0-86442-270-9*) Lonely Planet.

***Lonely Planet Indian Himalaya.** 2nd ed. Bradley Mahew et al. (Illus.). 496p. 2000. pap. 19.95 (*0-86442-688-7*) Lonely Planet.

***Lonely Planet Indian Subcontinent.** Hugh Finlay. (On a Shoestring Ser.). (Illus.). 736p. 2000. pap. 24.95 (*0-86442-689-5*) Lonely Planet.

***Lonely Planet Indonesia.** 6th ed. Peter Turner. (Illus.). 1136p. 2000. pap. 25.95 (*0-86442-690-9*) Lonely Planet.

Lonely Planet Indonesia's Eastern Islands. Peter Turner. (Illus.). 416p. 1998. pap. 17.95 (*0-86442-503-1*) Lonely Planet.

Lonely Planet Indonesie. 2nd ed. (FRE.). 1997. 39.95 (*2-84070-062-X*) Lonely Planet.

Lonely Planet Iran. 2nd ed. Paul Greenway. (Illus.). 416p. 1998. pap. 17.95 (*0-86442-455-8*) Lonely Planet.

Lonely Planet Iran: A Travel Survival Kit. David St. Vincent. (Illus.). 352p. (Orig.). 1992. pap. 14.95 (*0-86442-136-2*) Lonely Planet.

Lonely Planet Ireland. 3rd ed. Tom Smallman et al. (Illus.). 768p. 1998. pap. 19.95 (*0-86442-530-9*) Lonely Planet.

Lonely Planet Islands of Australia's Great Barrier Reef. 3rd ed. Hugh Finlay. (Lonely Planet Travel Guides Ser.). (Illus.). 280p. 1998. pap. text 14.95 (*0-86442-563-5*) Lonely Planet.

Lonely Planet Israel & Palestinian Territories Travel Atlas. Contrib. by Andrew Humphreys. (Illus.). 64p. 1996. pap. 12.95 (*0-86442-440-X*) Lonely Planet.

Lonely Planet Israel & the Palestinian Territories. 4th ed. Andrew Humphreys & Paul Hellander. 432p. 1999. pap. 17.95 (*0-86442-691-7*) Lonely Planet.

Lonely Planet Istanbul: City Guides. Tom Brosnahan. (Illus.). 260p. 1997. pap. 12.95 (*0-86442-388-8*) Lonely Planet.

Lonely Planet Istanbul: City Guides. 2nd ed. Tom Brosnahan. (Lonely Planet City Guides). (Illus.). 176p. 1999. pap. text 14.95 (*0-86442-585-6*) Lonely Planet.

***Lonely Planet Italy.** 4th ed. Helen Gillman et al. (Illus.). 816p. 2000. pap. 21.95 (*0-86442-692-5*) Lonely Planet.

Lonely Planet Jakarta: City Guide. Peter Turner. (Illus.). 280p. 1995. pap. 9.95 (*0-86442-290-3*) Lonely Planet.

Lonely Planet Jakarta: City Guide. 2nd ed. Peter Turner. (Lonely Planet City Guides). (Illus.). 192p. 1999. pap. text 14.95 (*0-86442-615-1*) Lonely Planet.

Lonely Planet Jamaica. Christopher P. Baker. LC 97-147759. (Illus.). 496p. 1996. pap. 17.95 (*0-86442-372-1*) Lonely Planet.

Lonely Planet Japan. 6th ed. Chris Taylor et al. (Illus.). 800p. 1997. pap. 25.95 (*0-86442-493-0*) Lonely Planet.

Lonely Planet Java: Travel Survival Kit. Peter Turner. (Illus.). 384p. 1995. pap. 14.95 (*0-86442-314-4*) Lonely Planet.

Lonely Planet Jerusalem. Andrew Humphreys. (Illus.). 240p. 1997. pap. 12.95 (*0-86442-298-9*) Lonely Planet.

Lonely Planet Jordan & Syria. 3rd ed. Damien Simonis & Hugh Finlay. (Illus.). 384p. 1997. pap. 17.95 (*0-86442-427-2*) Lonely Planet.

Lonely Planet Jordan, Syria & Lebanon Travel Atlas. Contrib. by Ann Jousiffe. (Illus.). 88p. 1997. pap. 14.95 (*0-86442-441-8*) Lonely Planet.

Lonely Planet Jordanie et Syrie. 2nd ed. (FRE.). 1996. 20.95 (*2-84070-047-6*) Lonely Planet.

Lonely Planet Karakoram Highway. 3rd ed. John King, III. (Illus.). 320p. 1998. pap. 17.95 (*0-86442-531-7*) Lonely Planet.

Lonely Planet Kenya. 3rd ed. Hugh Finlay & Geoff Crowther. (Illus.). 352p. 1997. pap. 17.95 (*0-86442-460-4*) Lonely Planet.

Lonely Planet Kenya Travel Atlas. Hugh Finlay. (Illus.). 80p. 1997. pap. 14.95 (*0-86442-442-6*) Lonely Planet.

Lonely Planet Korea. 4th ed. Robert Storey. (Illus.). 432p. 1997. pap. 17.95 (*0-86442-494-9*) Lonely Planet.

Lonely Planet Kyoto. Mason Florence. (Illus.). 224p. 1998. pap. 14.95 (*0-86442-564-3*) Lonely Planet.

Lonely Planet Laos. 2nd ed. (FRE.). 1996. 22.95 (*2-84070-050-6*) Lonely Planet.

Lonely Planet Laos. 2nd ed. Joe Cummings. (Illus.). 272p. 1996. pap. 15.95 (*0-86442-381-0*) Lonely Planet.

Lonely Planet Laos. 3rd ed. Lonely Planet Staff. (Lonely Planet Travel Guides Ser.). 1999. pap. text 22.95 (*2-84070-088-3*) Lonely Planet.

Lonely Planet Laos: Travel Survival Kit. 3rd ed. Joe Cummings. (Lonely Planet Travel Guides Ser.). (Illus.). 272p. 1998. pap. text 15.95 (*0-86442-617-8*) Lonely Planet.

Lonely Planet Laos Travel Atlas. Contrib. by Joe Cummings. (Illus.). 48p. 1997. pap. 12.95 (*0-86442-375-6*) Lonely Planet.

Lonely Planet Lebanon: Travel Survival Kit. Ann Jousiffe. LC 98-148460. (Illus.). 240p. 1998. pap. 15.95 (*0-86442-350-0*) Lonely Planet.

Lonely Planet Lisbon. Julia Wilkinson. (Illus.). 152p. 1998. pap. 14.95 (*0-86442-550-3*) Lonely Planet.

***Lonely Planet Loire.** Nicola Williams. Ed. by Lonely Planet Publications Staff. (Travel Guides Ser.). (Illus.). 320p. 2000. pap. text 17.99 (*1-86450-097-2*) Lonely Planet.

Lonely Planet London. 1999. pap. 5.95 (*1-86450-008-5*) Lonely Planet.

Lonely Planet London. Pat Yale. LC 98-172416. (Illus.). 304p. 1998. pap. 14.95 (*0-86442-495-7*) Lonely Planet.

***Lonely Planet London: London Condensed.** Steve Fallon. Ed. by Lonely Planet Publications Staff. (Travel Guides Ser.). (Illus.). 128p. 2000. pap. text 9.95 (*1-86450-043-3*) Lonely Planet.

Lonely Planet Londres. Pat Yale. (Illus.). 304p. 1998. pap. 16.95 (*2-84070-080-8*) Lonely Planet.

Lonely Planet Los Angeles. 2nd ed. John Gottberg et al. 256p. 1999. pap. 15.95 (*0-86442-551-1*) Lonely Planet.

Lonely Planet Madagascar & Comoros. 3rd ed. Paul Greenway & Deanna Swaney. (Illus.). 416p. 1997. pap. 17.95 (*0-86442-496-5*) Lonely Planet.

Lonely Planet Madagascar & the Comoros. (Lonely Planet Travel Guides Ser.). (FRE.). 1998. 24.95 (*2-84070-071-9*) Lonely Planet.

Lonely Planet Malaisie et Singapour. 3rd ed. Chris Rowthorn et al. 608p. 1999. pap. 29.95 (*2-84070-093-X*) Lonely Planet.

Lonely Planet Malawi, Mozambique & Zambia. David Else. (Illus.). 304p. 1997. pap. 15.95 (*0-86442-462-0*) Lonely Planet.

Lonely Planet Malaysia, Singapore & Brunei. 6th ed. Peter Turner & Chris Taylor. (Illus.). 608p. 1996. pap. 17.95 (*0-86442-393-4*) Lonely Planet.

Lonely Planet Malaysia, Singapore & Brunei: Travel Survival Kit. 7th ed. Chris Rowthorn. LC 97-649684. (Lonely Planet Travel Guides Ser.). (Illus.). 608p. 1999. pap. text 17.95 (*0-86442-618-6*) Lonely Planet.

Lonely Planet Malaysie et Singapour. 2nd ed. Peter Turner. (FRE.). 1997. 29.95 (*2-84070-051-4*) Lonely Planet.

Lonely Planet Maldives. 3rd ed. James Lyon et al. (Illus.). 160p. 1997. pap. 14.95 (*0-86442-497-3*) Lonely Planet.

***Lonely Planet Maldives.** 4th ed. James Lyon. (Travel Guides Ser.). (Illus.). 208p. 2000. pap. 15.95 (*0-86442-700-X*) Lonely Planet.

Lonely Planet Mali Blues. Lieve Joris. Tr. by Sam Garrett. 320p. 1998. pap. 12.95 (*0-86442-532-5*) Lonely Planet.

***Lonely Planet Mandarin Phrasebook.** 4th ed. Hua-Yuan L. Mowry. 2000. pap. 6.95 (*0-86442-652-6*) Lonely Planet.

Lonely Planet Maroc. 2nd ed. 1998. 26.95 (*2-84070-075-1*) Lonely Planet.

Lonely Planet Maroc. 3rd ed. Hugh Finlay et al. (FRE., Illus.). 420p. 1995. 23.95 (*2-84070-029-8*) Lonely Planet.

Lonely Planet Martinique. Michel McLeod. (FRE.). 1997. 18.95 (*2-84070-072-7*) Lonely Planet.

Lonely Planet Mauritius, Reunion & Seychelles: A Travel Survival Kit. 2nd rev. ed. Deanna Swaney et al. (Illus.). 392p. 1993. pap. 14.95 (*0-86442-188-5*) Lonely Planet.

Lonely Planet Mediterranean Europe. 4th ed. Steve Fallon. (On a Shoestring Ser.). (Illus.). 1048p. 1999. pap. text 25.95 (*0-86442-619-4*) Lonely Planet.

Lonely Planet Melbourne. 1999. pap. 5.95 (*1-86450-009-3*) Lonely Planet.

Lonely Planet Melbourne. 2nd ed. Mark Armstrong. (Illus.). 312p. 1997. pap. 12.95 (*0-86442-386-1*) Lonely Planet.

***Lonely Planet Melbourne.** 3rd ed. David McClymont & Mark Armstrong. (Travel Guides Ser.). (Illus.). 200p. 2000. pap. 14.95 (*1-86450-124-3*) Lonely Planet.

Lonely Planet Mexico. 6th ed. John Noble et al. (Illus.). 976p. 1998. pap. 19.95 (*0-86442-429-9*) Lonely Planet.

Lonely Planet Mexico City. John Noble. 256p. 1998. pap. 14.95 (*0-86442-499-X*) Lonely Planet.

***Lonely Planet Mexico City.** 2nd ed. John Noble. (Travel Guides Ser.). (Illus.). 224p. 2000. pap. 14.95 (*1-86450-087-5*) Lonely Planet.

Lonely Planet Mexique. 2nd ed. (FRE., Illus.). 924p. 1996. 31.95 (*2-84070-032-8*) Lonely Planet.

Lonely Planet Micronesia. 3rd ed. Glenda Bendure & Ned Friary. (Illus.). 336p. 1995. pap. 12.95 (*0-86442-310-1*) Lonely Planet.

***Lonely Planet Micronesia.** 4th ed. Kate Galbraith. (Travel Guides Ser.). (Illus.). 2000. pap. 16.95 (*1-86450-104-9*) Lonely Planet.

Lonely Planet Middle East. 2nd ed. Andrew Humphreys et al. (Illus.). 832p. 1997. pap. 21.95 (*0-86442-407-8*) Lonely Planet.

Lonely Planet Mongolia. 2nd ed. Paul Greenway. (Illus.). 224p. 1997. pap. 16.95 (*0-86442-500-7*) Lonely Planet.

Lonely Planet Morocco. 4th ed. Frances L. Gordon et al. (Illus.). 544p. 1998. pap. 17.95 (*0-86442-501-5*) Lonely Planet.

***Lonely Planet Moscow.** Ryan V. Berkmoes. (Travel Guides Ser.). (Illus.). 224p. 2000. pap. text 15.95 (*1-86450-054-9*) Lonely Planet.

Lonely Planet Myanmar (Birmanie) 2nd ed. Tony Wheeler. (FRE.). 350p. 1993. 22.95 (*2-84070-041-7*) Lonely Planet.

Lonely Planet Myanmar (Burma) Travel Survival Kit. 6th ed. Joe Cummings & Tony Wheeler. (Illus.). 400p. 1996. pap. 13.95 (*0-86442-324-1*) Lonely Planet.

Lonely Planet Namibie. Deanna Swaney. 272p. 1999. pap. 22.95 (*2-84070-094-8*) Lonely Planet.

Lonely Planet Nepal. 2nd ed. Tony Wheeler. (FRE.). 1997. 24.95 (*2-84070-052-2*) Lonely Planet.

Lonely Planet Nepal. 3rd ed. Hugh Finlay. (Illus.). 416p. 1996. pap. 17.95 (*0-86442-397-7*) Lonely Planet.

Lonely Planet Nepal. 4th ed. Hugh Finlay et al. 416p. 1999. pap. 19.95 (*0-86442-704-2*) Lonely Planet.

Lonely Planet New Caledonia. 3rd ed. Leanne Logan & Geert Cole. (Illus.). 256p. 1997. pap. 14.95 (*0-86442-533-3*) Lonely Planet.

Lonely Planet New England: Travel Survival Kit. Tom Brosnahan. (Illus.). 528p. 1996. pap. 19.95 (*0-86442-265-2*) Lonely Planet.

Lonely Planet New Orleans. Robert Raburn. (Illus.). 312p. 1997. pap. 11.95 (*0-86442-430-2*) Lonely Planet.

Lonely Planet New South Wales. 2nd ed. Tom Smallman & David Willett. (Illus.). 544p. 1997. pap. 17.95 (*0-86442-464-7*) Lonely Planet.

Lonely Planet New York City. 1999. pap. 5.95 (*1-86450-010-7*) Lonely Planet.

Lonely Planet New York City. David Ellis. (Illus.). 280p. 1997. pap. 15.95 (*0-86442-502-3*) Lonely Planet.

Lonely Planet New York City. David Ellis. (FRE.). 1997. 19.95 (*2-84070-076-X*) Lonely Planet.

***Lonely Planet New York City: New York City Condensed.** Dani Valent. Ed. by Lonely Planet Publications Staff. (Travel Guides Ser.). (Illus.). 128p. 2000. pap. text 9.95 (*1-86450-046-8*) Lonely Planet.

Lonely Planet New York, New Jersey & Pennsylvania. Tom Smallman et al. (Illus.). 688p. 1997. pap. 19.95 (*0-86442-408-6*) Lonely Planet.

Lonely Planet North-East Asia: On a Shoestring. 4th ed. Robert Storey et al. (Illus.). 640p. 1995. pap. 16.95 (*0-86442-250-4*) Lonely Planet.

Lonely Planet Norway. Deanna Swaney. 300p. 1999. pap. 17.95 (*0-86442-654-2*) Lonely Planet.

Lonely Planet Nouvelle-Zelande. 2nd ed. (FRE.). 1996. 29.95 (*2-84070-053-0*) Lonely Planet.

***Lonely Planet O'ahu.** Ed. by Lonely Planet Publications Staff. (Travel Guides Ser.). (Illus.). 288p. 2000. pap. text 14.95 (*1-86450-048-4*) Lonely Planet.

***Lonely Planet Oman & the Untied Arab Emirates.** Lou Callan & Gordon Robinson. (Travel Guides Ser.). (Illus.). 256p. 2000. pap. 15.99 (*1-86450-130-8*) Lonely Planet.

Lonely Planet Outback Australia. 2nd ed. Denis O'Byrne. (Illus.). 536p. 1998. pap. 21.95 (*0-86442-504-X*) Lonely Planet.

Lonely Planet Pacific Northwest: Travel Survival Kit. 2nd ed. Bill McRae et al. (Lonely Planet Travel Guides Ser.). (Illus.). 912p. 1999. pap. text 24.95 (*0-86442-534-1*) Lonely Planet.

Lonely Planet Pacific Northwest: U. S. A. Guide. Bill McRae & Judy Jewell. (Illus.). 896p. 1995. pap. 19.95 (*0-86442-240-7*) Lonely Planet.

Lonely Planet Pakistan. 5th ed. John King, III et al. (Illus.). 416p. 1998. pap. 17.95 (*0-86442-535-X*) Lonely Planet.

Lonely Planet Panama. Scott Doggett. (Illus.). 352p. 1999. pap. 16.95 (*0-86442-566-X*) Lonely Planet.

Lonely Planet Papua New Guinea: A Travel Survival Kit. 5th ed. Jon Murray & Tony Wheeler. (Illus.). 380p. 1993. pap. 15.95 (*0-86442-190-7*) Lonely Planet.

Lonely Planet Papua New Guinea - Diving & Snorkeling. Bob Halstead & Tim Rock. 176p. 1999. pap. 17.95 (*0-86442-776-X*) Lonely Planet.

Lonely Planet Papua/New Guinea. 6th ed. Adrian Lipscomb et al. (Illus.). 380p. 1998. pap. 17.95 (*0-86442-402-7*) Lonely Planet.

Lonely Planet Paris. 1999. pap. 5.95 (*1-86450-011-5*) Lonely Planet.

Lonely Planet Paris: City Guide. 2nd ed. Daniel Robinson & Tony Wheeler. (Lonely Planet City Guides). (Illus.). 264p. 1998. pap. text 14.95 (*0-86442-622-4*) Lonely Planet.

***Lonely Planet Paris: Paris Condensed.** Rob Flynn. Ed. by Lonely Planet Publications Staff. (Travel Guides Ser.). (Illus.). 128p. 2000. pap. text 9.95 (*1-86450-044-1*) Lonely Planet.

***Lonely Planet Peru.** 4th ed. Rob Rachowiecki. (Illus.). 512p. 2000. pap. 17.95 (*0-86442-710-7*) Lonely Planet.

Lonely Planet Philippines. 6th ed. Jens Peters. (Illus.). 528p. 1997. pap. 19.95 (*0-86442-466-3*) Lonely Planet.

Lonely Planet Poland. 3rd ed. Krysztof Dydinski. 552p. 1999. pap. 19.95 (*0-86442-655-0*) Lonely Planet.

Lonely Planet Pologne. 2nd ed. (FRE.). 1996. 27.95 (*2-84070-046-8*) Lonely Planet.

Lonely Planet Portugal. John King, III & Julia Wilkinson. (Illus.). 400p. 1997. pap. 17.95 (*0-86442-467-1*) Lonely Planet.

Lonely Planet Portugal. 2nd ed. Julia Wilkinson & John King, III. 544p. 1999. pap. 19.95 (*0-86442-623-2*) Lonely Planet.

Lonely Planet Portugal Travel Atlas. John King, III & Julia Wilkinson. (Illus.). 72p. 1997. pap. 14.95 (*0-86442-480-9*) Lonely Planet.

***Lonely Planet Portuguese Phrasebook.** Clara Vitorino. (Lonely Planet Phrasebooks). (POR & ENG.). 320p. 2000. pap. 7.95 (*0-86442-589-9*) Lonely Planet.

Lonely Planet Prague. 1999. pap. 5.95 (*1-86450-012-3*) Lonely Planet.

Lonely Planet Prague. John King, III & Richard Nebesky. 208p. 1999. pap. 16.95 (*2-84070-090-5*) Lonely Planet.

Lonely Planet Prague. 2nd ed. John King, III & Richard Nebesky. (Illus.). 332p. 1997. pap. 12.95 (*0-86442-468-X*) Lonely Planet.

Lonely Planet Prague. 3rd ed. John King, III & Richard Nebesky. 216p. 1999. pap. 14.95 (*0-86442-624-0*) Lonely Planet.

Lonely Planet Provence & the Cote D'Azur. Nicola Williams. 400p. 1999. pap. 17.95 (*0-86442-625-9*) Lonely Planet.

Lonely Planet Quebec et Ontario. Christine Coste. (FRE.). 1998. 24.95 (*2-84070-077-8*) Lonely Planet.

Lonely Planet Queensland: Australia Guide. Mark Armstrong. (Illus.). 672p. 1996. pap. 17.95 (*0-86442-318-7*) Lonely Planet.

Lonely Planet Queensland: Australia Guide. 2nd ed. Andrew Humphreys. (Lonely Planet Travel Guides Ser.). (Illus.). 600p. 1999. pap. text 17.95 (*0-86442-590-2*) Lonely Planet.

Lonely Planet Rajasthan. Michelle Coxall & Sarina Singh. (Illus.). 352p. 1997. pap. 15.95 (*0-86442-470-1*) Lonely Planet.

Lonely Planet Rarotonga & the Cook Islands. 4th ed. Nancy Keller. (Illus.). 192p. 1998. pap. 14.95 (*0-86442-553-8*) Lonely Planet.

Lonely Planet Rarotonga & the Cook Islands: A Travel Survival Kit. 3rd ed. Tony Wheeler & Nancy Keller. (Illus.). 192p. 1994. pap. 11.95 (*0-86442-232-6*) Lonely Planet.

Lonely Planet Republique Tcheque et Slovaquie. John King, III & Richard Nebesky. (FRE., Illus.). 484p. 1995. 25.95 (*2-84070-028-X*) Lonely Planet.

Lonely Planet Reunion et Maurice. Sarina Singh et al. (Illus.). 416p. 1998. pap. 24.95 (*2-84070-073-5*) Lonely Planet.

Lonely Planet Rio de Janeiro. 1999. pap. 5.95 (*1-86450-013-1*) Lonely Planet.

Lonely Planet Rio de Janeiro. 2nd ed. Andrew Draffen. (Lonely Planet Travel Guides Ser.). (Illus.). 200p. 1998. pap. text 14.95 (*0-86442-591-0*) Lonely Planet.

Lonely Planet Rocky Mountains. 2nd ed. Nicko Goncharoff. (Lonely Planet Travel Guides Ser.). (Illus.). 960p. 1999. pap. text 24.95 (*0-86442-536-8*) Lonely Planet.

Lonely Planet Romania & Moldova: Travel Guide. Nicola Williams. (Illus.). 496p. 1998. pap. 16.95 (*0-86442-329-2*) Lonely Planet.

Lonely Planet Rome. Helen Gillman. 304p. 1999. pap. 15.95 (*0-86442-626-7*) Lonely Planet.

Lonely Planet Russia, Ukraine & Belarus: Travel Survival Kit. Richard Nebesky et al. (Illus.). 1200p. 1996. pap. 27.95 (*0-86442-320-9*) Lonely Planet.

***Lonely Planet Russian Phrasebook: With Two-Way Dictionary.** 3rd ed. James Jenkin & Inna Zaitseva. (Lonely Planet Phrasebooks). 320p. 2000. pap. 7.95 (*1-86450-106-5*) Lonely Planet.

Lonely Planet Samoa. 3rd ed. Dorinda Talbot. (Illus.). 204p. 1998. pap. 14.95 (*0-86442-555-4*) Lonely Planet.

Lonely Planet San Francisco. 1999. pap. 5.95 (*1-86450-014-X*) Lonely Planet.

Lonely Planet San Francisco: City Guide. 2nd ed. Tom Downs & Tony Wheeler. (Lonely Planet City Guides). (Illus.). 256p. 1999. pap. text 15.95 (*0-86442-556-2*) Lonely Planet.

Lonely Planet Scandinavian & Baltic Europe. 3rd ed. Glenda Bendure et al. (Illus.). 576p. 1997. pap. 17.95 (*0-86442-434-5*) Lonely Planet.

Lonely Planet Scandinavian & Baltic Europe. 4th ed. Glenda Bendure. (On a Shoestring Ser.). (Illus.). 592p. 1999. pap. text 19.95 (*0-86442-628-3*) Lonely Planet.

Lonely Planet Scotland. Tom Smallman & Graeme Cornwallis. 384p. 1999. pap. 15.95 (*0-86442-592-9*) Lonely Planet.

Lonely Planet Seattle. Bill McRae. (Illus.). 222p. 1998. pap. 14.95 (*0-86442-537-6*) Lonely Planet.

Lonely Planet Senegal et Gambie. David Else.Tr. of Senegal & Gambia. 256p. 1999. pap. 19.95 (*2-84070-149-9*) Lonely Planet.

Lonely Planet Seoul. 3rd ed. Robert Storey. (Illus.). 192p. 1999. pap. 14.95 (*0-86442-779-4*) Lonely Planet.

***Lonely Planet Sicily.** Fionn Davenport. (Travel Guides Ser.). (Illus.). 2888p. 2000. pap. 15.95 (*1-86450-099-9*) Lonely Planet.

Lonely Planet Singapore. 3rd ed. Peter Turner. (Illus.). 288p. 1996. pap. 11.95 (*0-86442-400-0*) Lonely Planet.

Lonely Planet Singapore: City Guide. 4th ed. Paul Hellander. (Lonely Planet City Guides). (Illus.). 224p. 1999. pap. text 14.95 (*0-86442-630-5*) Lonely Planet.

Lonely Planet Slovenia: Travel Survival Kit. 2nd ed. Steve Fallon. (Lonely Planet Travel Guides Ser.). (Illus.). 344p. 1998. pap. text 15.95 (*0-86442-538-4*) Lonely Planet.

Lonely Planet Slovenie. Steve Fallon. (FRE.). 220p. 1996. 22.95 (*2-84070-034-4*) Lonely Planet.

Lonely Planet Solomon Islands. 3rd ed. Mark Honan. LC 98-118672. (Illus.). 288p. 1997. pap. 17.95 (*0-86442-405-1*) Lonely Planet.

Lonely Planet South Africa, Lesotho & Swaziland. 3rd ed. Jon Murray et al. (Illus.). 672p. 1997. pap. 21.95 (*0-86442-508-2*) Lonely Planet.

Lonely Planet South Africa Travel Atlas. Jon Murray. (Illus.). 80p. 1997. pap. 14.95 (*0-86442-443-4*) Lonely Planet.

An Asterisk (*) at the beginning of an entry indicates that the title is appearing for the first time.

L

*Lonely Planet South America on a Shoestring. 7th ed. James Lyon et al. (Illus.). 1176p. 2000. pap. 29.95 (0-86442-656-9) Lonely Planet.

Lonely Planet South Australia. Denis O'Byrne. (Illus.). 336p. 1996. pap. 14.95 (0-86442-383-7) Lonely Planet.

Lonely Planet South-East Asia on a Shoestring. 9th ed. Peter Turner et al. (Illus.). 1024p. 1997. pap. 21.95 (0-86442-412-4) Lonely Planet.

Lonely Planet South-East Asia on a Shoestring. 10th ed. Hugh Finlay et al. 1024p. 1999. pap. 21.95 (0-86442-632-1) Lonely Planet.

Lonely Planet South India. Christine Niven et al. (Illus.). 696p. 1998. pap. 24.95 (0-86442-594-5) Lonely Planet.

Lonely Planet South-West China. Bradley Mayhew & Thomas Huhti. (Illus.). 600p. 1998. pap. 19.95 (0-86442-596-1) Lonely Planet.

*Lonely Planet Southern Africa Travel Atlas. Lonely Planet Publications Staff. (Travel Atlases Ser.). (Illus.). 128p. 2000. pap. 14.95 (1-86450-101-4) Lonely Planet.

Lonely Planet Southwest. 2nd ed. Rob Rachowiecki. (Lonely Planet Travel Guides Ser.). (Illus.). 992p. 1999. pap. text 24.95 (0-86442-539-2) Lonely Planet.

Lonely Planet Spain. John Noble et al. (Illus.). 800p. 1997. pap. 19.95 (0-86442-474-4) Lonely Planet.

Lonely Planet Spain. 2nd ed. Damien Simonis et al. 1008p. 1999. pap. 21.95 (0-86442-633-X) Lonely Planet.

Lonely Planet Sri Lanka. 2nd ed. Christine Niven. (FRE.). 1997. 22.95 (2-84070-056-5) Lonely Planet.

Lonely Planet Sri Lanka. 6th ed. Christine Niven. (Illus.). 282p. 1996. pap. 14.95 (0-86442-476-0) Lonely Planet.

Lonely Planet St. Petersburg: City Guide. Nicholas Selby. (Illus.). 348p. 1996. pap. 11.95 (0-86442-326-8) Lonely Planet.

Lonely Planet St. Petersburg: City Guide. 2nd ed. Nick Selby. (Lonely Planet City Guides). 1999. pap. text 15.95 (0-86442-657-7) Lonely Planet.

*Lonely Planet Sweden. Graeme Cornwallis. (Travel Guides Ser.). (Illus.). 380p. 2000. pap. 17.95 (0-86442-721-2) Lonely Planet.

Lonely Planet Switzerland. 2nd ed. Mark Honan. (Illus.). 368p. 1997. pap. 16.95 (0-86442-404-3) Lonely Planet.

*Lonely Planet Switzerland. 3rd ed. Mark Honan. (Travel Guides Ser.). (Illus.). 384p. 2000. pap. 17.95 (0-86442-723-9) Lonely Planet.

Lonely Planet Sydney. 1999. pap. 5.95 (1-86450-015-8) Lonely Planet.

Lonely Planet Sydney. 3rd ed. Tom Smallman. (Illus.). 304p. 1997. pap. 12.95 (0-86442-510-4) Lonely Planet.

*Lonely Planet Sydney: Sydney Condensed. Nikki Hall & Dani Valent. Ed. by Lonely Planet Publications Staff. (Travel Guides Ser.). (Illus.). 128p. 2000. pap. text 9.95 (1-86450-045-X) Lonely Planet.

Lonely Planet Tahiti. 4th ed. Robert F. Kay. (FRE., Illus.). 220p. 1996. 24.95 (2-84070-036-0) Lonely Planet.

Lonely Planet Tahiti & French Polynesia: A Travel Survival Kit. 4th ed. Tony Wheeler & Rob Kay. (Illus.). 400p. 1997. pap. 16.95 (0-86442-287-3) Lonely Planet.

Lonely Planet Taiwan: Travel Survival Kit. 4th ed. Robert Storey. (Lonely Planet Travel Guides Ser.). (Illus.). 360p. 1998. pap. text 17.95 (0-86442-634-8) Lonely Planet.

Lonely Planet Tanzania, Zanzibar & Pemba. Mary Fitzpatrick. 320p. 1999. pap. 17.95 (0-86442-726-3) Lonely Planet.

Lonely Planet Tasmania. John Chapman & Monica Chapman. (Illus.). 304p. 1996. pap. 14.95 (0-86442-384-5) Lonely Planet.

Lonely Planet Texas. Nick Selby et al. 544p. 1999. pap. 19.95 (0-86442-571-6) Lonely Planet.

Lonely Planet Thailand. 8th ed. Joe Cummings. 976p. 1999. pap. 21.95 (0-86442-636-4) Lonely Planet.

Lonely Planet Thailand Travel Atlas. Joe Cummings. (Illus.). 44p. 1995. pap. 8.95 (0-86442-269-5) Lonely Planet.

*Lonely Planet Thailand, Vietnam, Laos & Cambodia Travel Atlas. Lonely Planet Publications Staff. (Travel Atlases Ser.). (Illus.). 112p. 2000. pap. 14.95 (1-86450-102-2) Lonely Planet.

*Lonely Planet Thailand's Islands & Beaches. 2nd ed. Joe Cummings. (Illus.). 496p. 2000. pap. 15.95 (0-86442-728-X) Lonely Planet.

Lonely Planet Tibet. 4th ed. Bradley Mayhew. 320p. 1999. pap. 17.95 (0-86442-637-2) Lonely Planet.

Lonely Planet Tibet: Travel Survival Kit. 3rd ed. Chris Taylor. (Illus.). 256p. 1995. pap. 14.95 (0-86442-289-X) Lonely Planet.

Lonely Planet Tokyo. Chris Rowthorn. LC 99-192646. (Illus.). 248p. 1998. pap. 14.95 (0-86442-567-8) Lonely Planet.

Lonely Planet Tonga: A Travel Survival Kit. 3rd ed. Nancy Keller. (Illus.). 208p. 1998. 14.95 (0-86442-568-6) Lonely Planet.

Lonely Planet Tramping in New Zealand: Walking Guide. 4th ed. Jim Du Fresne. (Lonely Planet Walking Guides). (Illus.). 352p. 1998. pap. text 17.95 (0-86442-598-8) Lonely Planet.

Lonely Planet Trekking en Himalaya-Nepal. 6th ed. Stan Armington. (FRE., Illus.). 372p. 1994. 22.95 (2-84070-023-9) Lonely Planet.

Lonely Planet Trekking in East Africa: A Walking Guide. 2nd ed. David Else. LC 98-130331. (Illus.). 304p. (Orig.). 1998. pap. 17.95 (0-86442-541-4) Lonely Planet.

Lonely Planet Trekking in Spain: A Walking Guide. Marc Dubin. (Illus.). 208p. (Orig.). 1990. pap. 11.95 (0-86442-088-9) Lonely Planet.

Lonely Planet Trekking in the Indian Himalaya: A Walking Guide. 3rd ed. Garry Weare. (Illus.). 272p. 1997. pap. 17.95 (0-86442-357-8) Lonely Planet.

Lonely Planet Trekking in the Karakoram & Hindukush. John Mock & Kimberly O'Neil. LC 97-126119. (Illus.). 304p. 1996. pap. 16.95 (0-86442-360-8) Lonely Planet.

Lonely Planet Trekking in the Nepal Himalaya: A Walking Guide. 7th ed. Stan Armington. (Illus.). 400p. 1997. pap. 17.95 (0-86442-511-2) Lonely Planet.

Lonely Planet Trekking in the Patagonian Andes: A Walking Guide. 2nd ed. Clem Lindenmayer. LC 98-130340. (Illus.). 224p. (Orig.). 1998. pap. 15.95 (0-86442-477-9) Lonely Planet.

Lonely Planet Tunisia. David Willett. (Illus.). 256p. (Orig.). 1998. pap. 15.95 (0-86442-512-0) Lonely Planet.

Lonely Planet Tunisie. David Willett. (Illus.). 256p. 1998. pap. 19.95 (2-84070-081-6) Lonely Planet.

Lonely Planet Turkey. 5th ed. Tom Brosnahan & Pat Yale. (Illus.). 752p. 1996. pap. 19.95 (0-86442-364-0) Lonely Planet.

Lonely Planet Turkey. 6th ed. Tom Brosnahan & Pat Yale. 848p. 1999. pap. 21.95 (0-86442-599-6) Lonely Planet.

Lonely Planet Turkey Travel Atlas. Contrib. by Tom Brosnahan. (Illus.). 112p. 1997. pap. 14.95 (0-86442-272-5) Lonely Planet.

Lonely Planet Turquie. Tom Brosnahan. (FRE.). 1997. 29.95 (2-84070-054-9) Lonely Planet.

Lonely Planet Turquie. 2nd ed. Tom Brosnahan. 800p. 1999. pap. 31.95 (2-84070-096-4) Lonely Planet.

*Lonely Planet Tuscany. Damien Simonis. (Travel Guides Ser.). (Illus.). 352p. 2000. pap. 16.99 (0-86442-733-6) Lonely Planet.

Lonely Planet U. S. A. James Lyon et al. (Illus.). 1200p. 1999. pap. 24.95 (0-86442-513-9) Lonely Planet.

*Lonely Planet Unpacked: Travel Disaster Stories. Tony Wheeler et al. 256p. 1999. pap. 12.95 (1-86450-062-X) Lonely Planet.

Lonely Planet Vancouver. Chris Wyness. 160p. 1999. pap. 14.95 (0-86442-659-3) Lonely Planet.

Lonely Planet Vanuatu. 3rd ed. Denis O'Byrne & David Harcombe. 304p. 1999. pap. 15.95 (0-86442-660-7) Lonely Planet.

Lonely Planet Vanuatu: A Travel Survival Kit. 2nd ed. David Harcombe & Denis O'Byrne. (Illus.). 304p. 1995. pap. 13.95 (0-86442-293-8) Lonely Planet.

Lonely Planet Venezuela. 2nd ed. Krzysztof Dydynski. (Illus.). 400p. 1998. pap. 19.95 (0-86442-514-7) Lonely Planet.

Lonely Planet Venezuela: Travel Survival Kit. Krzysztof Dydynski. (Illus.). 336p. 1994. pap. 14.95 (0-86442-229-6) Lonely Planet.

Lonely Planet Vienna. 2nd ed. Mark Honan. (Illus.). 182p. 1998. pap. 14.95 (0-86442-557-0) Lonely Planet.

Lonely Planet Vietnam. 3rd ed. Daniel Robinson. (FRE.). 1998. 27.95 (2-84070-079-4) Lonely Planet.

Lonely Planet Vietnam. 4th ed. 560p. 1999. pap. 27.95 (2-84070-097-2) Lonely Planet.

Lonely Planet Vietnam. 5th ed. Mason Florence. (Lonely Planet Travel Guides Ser.). (Illus.). 616p. 1999. pap. text 17.95 (0-86442-638-0) Lonely Planet.

Lonely Planet Vietnam Travel Atlas. Contrib. by Robert Storey. (Illus.). 56p. 1996. pap. 9.95 (0-86442-367-5) Lonely Planet.

*Lonely Planet Virginia & the Capital Region. Randy Peffer et al. (Travel Guides Ser.). (Illus.). 624p. 2000. pap. 21.95 (0-86442-769-7) Lonely Planet.

Lonely Planet Walking in Britain. David Else. LC 98-114693. (Illus.). 480p. 1997. pap. 17.95 (0-86442-478-7) Lonely Planet.

Lonely Planet Walking in Ireland. Sandra Bardwell et al. 352p. 1999. pap. 17.95 (0-86442-602-X) Lonely Planet.

Lonely Planet Walking in Italy. Helen Gillman et al. (Illus.). 352p. 1998. pap. 17.95 (0-86442-542-2) Lonely Planet.

Lonely Planet Walking in Spain. 2nd ed. Miles Robbis et al. 384p. 1999. pap. 17.95 (0-86442-543-0) Lonely Planet.

Lonely Planet Walking in Switzerland: Walking Guide. Clem Lindenmayer. (Illus.). 352p. 1996. pap. 14.95 (0-86442-327-6) Lonely Planet.

Lonely Planet Washington, D. C. & the Capital Region. Kap Stann et al. (Illus.). 624p. 1997. pap. 19.95 (0-86442-437-X) Lonely Planet.

Lonely Planet West Africa. 4th ed. David Else et al. 880p. 1999. pap. 29.95 (0-86442-569-4) Lonely Planet.

Lonely Planet West Africa: Travel Survival Kit. 3rd ed. Alex Newton & David Else. (Illus.). 928p. 1995. pap. 21.95 (0-86442-294-6) Lonely Planet.

Lonely Planet Western Australia. 2nd ed. Jeff Williams. (Illus.). 310p. 1998. pap. 14.95 (0-86442-544-9) Lonely Planet.

Lonely Planet Western Australia: Travel Survival Kit. Jeff Williams. (Illus.). 320p. 1995. pap. 13.95 (0-86442-268-7) Lonely Planet.

Lonely Planet Western Europe. 4th ed. Steve Fallon et al. (On a Shoestring Ser.). (Illus.). 1376p. 1999. pap. text 25.95 (0-86442-639-9) Lonely Planet.

Lonely Planet Yemen. 31st ed. P. Hamalainen. (FRE., Illus.). 820p. 1996. 22.95 (2-84070-040-9) Lonely Planet.

Lonely Planet Yemen: Travel Survival Kit. 3rd ed. Pertti Hamalainen. (Illus.). 256p. 1996. pap. 13.95 (0-86442-319-5) Lonely Planet.

*Lonely Planet Yucatan. Scott Doggett. (Travel Guides Ser.). (Illus.). 320p. 2000. pap. 17.95 (1-86450-103-0) Lonely Planet.

Lonely Planet Zimbabwe & Botswana. 2nd ed. Deanna Swaney. 560p. 1999. pap. 27.95 (2-84070-098-0) Lonely Planet.

Lonely Planet Zimbabwe, Botswana & Namibia. 3rd ed. Deanna Swaney. (Lonely Planet Travel Guides Ser.). (Illus.). 824p. 1999. pap. text 24.95 (0-86442-545-7) Lonely Planet.

Lonely Planet Zimbabwe, Botswana & Namibia: Travel Survival Kit. 2nd ed. Deanna Swaney & Myra L. Shackley. (Illus.). 800p. 1995. pap. 19.95 (0-86442-313-6) Lonely Planet.

Lonely Planet Zimbabwe, Botswana & Namibia Travel Atlas. Contrib. by Deanna Swaney. (Illus.). 60p. 1996. pap. 9.95 (0-86442-274-1) Lonely Planet.

Lonely Planet Zimbabwe, Botswana et Namibie. 2nd ed. Deanna Swaney & Myra Shackley. (FRE.). 600p. 1996. 30.95 (2-84070-035-2) Lonely Planet.

*Lonely Pony, Vol. 25. Jeanne Betancourt. (Pony Pals Ser.: No. 25). (Illus.). 144p. (J). (gr. 2-5). 2000. mass mkt. 3.99 (0-439-06491-0) Scholastic Inc.

Lonely Road. Rebera E. Foston. Ed. by Cynthia E. Garnett. (Orig.). Date not set. pap. write for info. (0-614-14897-9) Foston Adolescent.

Lonely Road. Nevil Shute. 1970. mass mkt. 0.95 (0-345-22089-7) Fawcett.

Lonely, Sad & Angry: A Parent's Guide to Depression in Children & Adolescents. Barbara D. Ingersoll & Sam Goldstein. 240p. 1996. pap. 12.95 (0-385-47642-6, Anchor NY) Doubleday.

Lonely Scarecrow. Tim Preston. LC 98-42030. (Illus.). 32p. (J). (ps-3). 1999. 14.99 (0-525-46080-2, Dutton Child) Peng Put Young Read.

Lonely Scoundrel: A Supplement to the Perishing Republic. Jerome Bahr. LC 73-80240. 89p. 1974. 12.95 (0-686-63592-2) Trempealeau.

Lonely Silver Rain. John D. MacDonald. LC 96-96201. 1996. mass mkt. 5.99 (0-449-22485-6) Fawcett.

Lonely Sky. William Bridgeman & Jacqueline Hazard. Ed. by James B. Gilbert. LC 79-7232. (Flight: Its First Seventy-Five Years Ser.). (Illus.). 1980. reprint ed. lib. bdg. 30.95 (0-405-12148-2) Ayer.

Lonely Stranger. Mike Sadler. (Junior African Writers Ser.). (Illus.). 80p. (J). (gr. 3 up). 1992. pap. 4.99 (0-7910-2922-0) Chelsea Hse.

*Lonely Street. Steve Brewer. (Bubba Mabry Mystery Ser.: No. 1). 256p. 1999. mass mkt. 5.95 (1-890768-19-7) Intrigue Press.

Lonely Street. Steve Brewer. Ed. by Doug Grad. 224p. 1994. mass mkt. 4.99 (0-671-74734-7) PB.

Lonely Wayfaring Man: Emerson & Some Englishmen. Townshend Scudder. LC 80-2545. reprint ed. 40.00 (0-404-19270-X) AMS Pr.

Lonely Wizard. Helmut Kollars. LC 97-38433.Tr. of Es War Einmal Zauberer Ganz Allein. (Illus.). 32p. (J). (gr. k-3). 1998. 16.95 (1-56711-804-6, Blackbirch Picturebk) Blackbirch.

Lonely Woman: Forugh Farrokhzad & Her Poetry. Michael C. Hillmann. LC 86-51008. (Illus.). 181p. 1987. reprint ed. 15.00 (0-89410-543-4, Three Contnts); reprint ed. pap. 15.00 (0-89410-544-2, Three Contnts) L Rienner.

Lonely Years: Don't Look Like I'll Be an Old Man. William Reynolds. (Illus.). 86p. (Orig.). 1996. pap. 7.50 (1-57502-270-2, P0956) Morris Pubng.

Lonely Years, 1925-1939: The Unpublished Stories & Correspondence. Isaac Babel. Tr. by Max Hayward & A. R. MacAndrew from RUS. (Verba Mundi Ser.). 432p. 1995. pap. 15.95 (0-87923-978-6) Godine.

Lonely's Game. R. W. Jones. 250p. 1994. pap. 16.95 (1-85411-096-9, Pub. by Seren Bks) Dufour.

Loner. Lass Small. (Desire Ser.: No. 594). 1990. per. 2.50 (0-373-05594-3) Silhouette.

Loner. Linda Turner. 1995. mass mkt. 3.75 (0-373-07673-8, 1-07673-6) Silhouette.

Loner. Ester Wier. 160p. (J). (gr. 4-7). 1992. pap. 2.99 (0-590-44352-6) Scholastic Inc.

Loner. large type ed. Elliot Conway. (Linford Western Library). 288p. 1992. pap. 16.99 (0-7089-7253-5, Linford) Ulverscroft.

Loner. large type ed. Linda Turner. (Silhouette Ser.). 1998. 20.95 (0-373-59865-3) Thorndike Pr.

Loner: Three Sketches of the Personal Life & Ideas of R. B. Bennett. P. B. Waite. (Joanne Goodman Lectures). 128p. 1992. text 30.00 (0-8020-2894-2); pap. text 15.95 (0-8020-7401-4) U of Toronto Pr.

Loner & the Lady see Caballero Solitario

Loner & the Lady. Eileen Wilks. (Desire Ser.). 1996. per. 3.50 (0-373-76008-6, 1-76008-1) Silhouette.

Loneran on Conversion: Applications for Religious Formation. Mary K. Kinberger. LC 91-31788. (American University Studies: Theology & Religion: Ser. VII, Vol. 124). X, 143p. (C). 1992. text 35.95 (0-8204-1743-2) P Lang Pubng.

Lonergan & Feminism. Ed. by Cynthia S. Crysdale. (Lonergan Studies). 228p. 1994. text 55.00 (0-8020-5024-7); pap. text 18.95 (0-8020-7432-4) U of Toronto Pr.

Lonergan & Kant: Five Essays on Human Knowledge. Giovanni B. Sala. Ed. by Robert M. Doran. Tr. by Joseph Spoerl from GER. (Lonergan Studies). 197p. 1994. text 65.00 (0-8020-0429-6) U of Toronto Pr.

Lonergan & Thomas on the Will: An Essay in Interpretation. Terry J. Tekippe. 164p. (Orig.). (C). 1993. pap. text 23.50 (0-8191-9073-X); lib. bdg. 49.00 (0-8191-9072-1) U Pr of Amer.

Lonergan on Conversion: The Development of a Notion. Michael L. Rende. 238p. (C). 1990. lib. bdg. 41.00 (0-8191-7525-0) U Pr of Amer.

Lonergan Reader. Ed. by Mark D. Morelli & Elizabeth A. Morelli. (Lonergan Studies). 400p. 1996. pap. text 24.95 (0-8020-7648-3) U of Toronto Pr.

Lonergan Reader. Ed. by Mark D. Morelli & Elizabeth A. Morelli. (Longergan Studies). 624p. 1997. text 75.00 (0-8020-4251-1) U of Toronto Pr.

Lonergan's Hermeneutics: Its Development & Application. Ed. by Sean E. McEvenue & Ben F. Meyer. LC 88-28383. 313p. 1989. 44.95 (0-8132-0670-7) Cath U Pr.

Lonergan's Retrieval of the Notion of Human Being: Clarifications of the Reflections on the Argument of Insight, Chapters I-XVIII. Frank P. Braio. LC 87-34585. 460p. (C). 1988. lib. bdg. 54.50 (0-8191-6851-3) U Pr of Amer.

Loners: The Life Path of Unusual Children. Sula Wolff. LC 94-39339. (Illus.). 208p. (C). (gr. 13). 1995. 80.00 (0-415-06504-6) Routledge.

Loners & Dreamers: The Cosmic Voyage of a Literary Outlaw. William Allen. 500p. 2000. 26.00 (0-9672117-1-9) Wolfhawk Bks.

Lonesome & Coping. unabridged ed. Winona H. Ondra. LC 96-95210. (Illus.). 320p. (Orig.). 1997. pap. 20.00 (0-9655858-0-8) Boyden Pub.

Lonesome Beauty of the Moment. Lee Bassett. 1996. pap. text 10.00 (0-911287-14-0) Blue Begonia.

Lonesome Cowboy. Lois F. Dyer. 1996. per. 3.99 (0-373-24038-4, 1-24038-1) Silhouette.

Lonesome Cowboy. Debbie Macomber. (Promo Ser.). 1998. per. 4.50 (0-373-83342-3, 1-83342-5) Harlequin Bks.

*Lonesome Cowboy. large type ed. Debbie Macomber. 1999. 25.99 (0-263-16058-0, Pub. by Mills & Boon) Ulverscroft.

Lonesome Dove. Larry McMurtry. 1993. pap. 6.99 (0-671-74471-2) PB.

Lonesome Dove. Larry McMurtry. Ed. by Bill Grose. 960p. 1993. per. 7.99 (0-671-79589-9) PB.

Lonesome Dove. Larry McMurtry. 848p. 1985. 26.50 (0-671-50420-7) S&S Trade.

Lonesome Dove. Larry McMurtry. 848p. 2000. pap. 15.00 (0-684-85752-9) S&S Trade.

Lonesome Dove. rev. ed. Larry McMurtry. 2000. mass mkt. 7.99 (0-671-68390-X) PB.

Lonesome Fox. Louise Kantenwein. (Illus.). (J). 1995. 7.95 (0-533-11338-5) Vantage.

Lonesome Gods. Louis L'Amour. 464p. 1984. mass mkt. 5.50 (0-553-27518-6) Bantam.

Lonesome Gun. large type ed. Theodore V. Olsen. (Linford Western Large Print Ser.). 1993. pap. 16.99 (0-7089-7367-1, Linford) Ulverscroft.

Lonesome Land. B. M. Bower. LC 96-49022. (Illus.). xiii, 326p. 1997. pap. 13.95 (0-8032-6134-9, Bison Books) U of Nebr Pr.

Lonesome Leo, the Little Lion. Drake Simpson & Debi Simpson. Ed. by Bill Csellak. (Illus.). 20p. (Orig.). (J). (gr. 2-5). 1997. pap. text 10.95 (0-9657850-0-9) Lion Eyes.

*Lonesome No More. Jean Brashear. (Special Edition Ser.: No. 1302). 2000. per. 4.50 (0-373-24302-2, 1-24302-1) Harlequin Bks.

Lonesome, Old Camp Fires. Howard L. Norskog. 40p. 1994. pap. 6.00 (0-9625171-6-X) H L Norskog.

***Lonesome Pine. Jane West. (Illus.). 64p. (J). 2000. 24.95 (0-9701025-7-7) Haylett Pubng.**

The Lonesome Pine is an inspirational story about a pine tree's dream of becoming what he was planted to be...a Christmas tree. In his eyes he is perfect, in other peoples he is not. "Please pick me," he shouted with glee, "I'd love to be a Christmas tree." But folks just seemed to pass him by. "No, I don't think so," he hears them cry. But what is wrong? He asked himself, I'm not different from anyone else. "Now I won't get dressed up in baubles & bows, or have bright shining lights from my head to my toes. I wanted to see the children with smiles, as they awoke to see their presents in piles" We are taken along on his unexpected journey, witnessing his hopes & dreams, fears & disappointments.Once reaching his final destination, it turns out to be more than he could have ever dreamed of. The Lonesome Pine is not just special in what he becomes, he is also unique in what he is....a sixty-four page fully illustrated triangular shaped book. This is a book that will be treasured by your child & the child within you, for years to come. *Publisher Paid Annotation.*

Lonesome Ranch. Charles A. Seltzer. 1976. reprint ed. lib. bdg. 24.95 (0-88411-118-0) Amereon Ltd.

Lonesome Rider. Heather G. Pozzessere. (Historical Short Stories Ser.). 1993. per. 4.99 (0-373-83259-1, 1-83259-1) Silhouette.

Lonesome River. 1990. mass mkt. 3.95 (0-445-77196-8, Pub. by Warner Bks) Little.

Lonesome River. Dorothy Garlock. 384p. 1987. mass mkt. 5.99 (0-445-20362-5, Pub. by Warner Bks) Little.

Lonesome River. large type ed. Dorothy Garlock. LC 98-41391. 1998. 27.95 (0-7838-0386-9, G K Hall Lrg Type) Mac Lib Ref.

Lonesome Road. Martha B. Stiles. LC 98-70542. 288p. 1998. 25.00 (0-917788-69-9) Gnomon Pr.

*Lonesome Roads. Peter Crowther. 145p. 1999. pap. 13.99 (0-9531468-1-2, Pub. by RazorBlade Pr) Firebird Dist.

Lonesome Run. Annie Bern. 192p. 1998. pap. 15.95 (1-58244-006-9) Rutledge Bks.

Lonesome Trail. John G. Neihardt. (Collected Works of John G. Neihardt). 303p. 1999. reprint ed. lib. bdg. 98.00 (1-58201-784-0) Classic Bks.

Lonesome Traveler. Jack Kerouac. LC 60-14613. 192p. 1989. pap. 11.00 (0-8021-3074-7, Grove) Grove-Atltic.

Lonesome Traveler: The Life of Lee Hays. Doris Willens. LC 93-13490. (Illus.). xxiii, 299p. 1993. pap. 12.95 (0-8032-9747-5, Bison Books) U of Nebr Pr.

Lonesome Traveller. Jack Kerouac. 174p. Date not set. 17.95 (0-8488-1746-X) Amereon Ltd.

Lonesome West. Martin McDonagh. 1998. pap. 5.25 (0-8222-1666-3) Dramatists Play.

Lonesome Whistle: A Story of Survival. Laurence Mark. 107p. (Orig.). 1996. pap. 10.95 (0-9655765-0-7) L Mark.

An Asterisk (*) at the beginning of an entry indicates that the title is appearing for the first time.

Lonestar & the Trapper Turf War, No. 146. 192p. (Orig.). 1994. mass mkt. 3.99 (*0-515-11477-4*, Jove) Berkley Pub.

Lonewolf's Cry: Episodes of an Haimeri Poetic Lifetime. Guichard Cadet. 1996. pap. 8.00 (*0-9647635-0-8*) La Caille-Nous.

Lonewolf's Woman. Deborah Camp. 384p. (Orig.). 1995. mass mkt. 4.99 (*0-380-77757-6*, Avon Bks) Morrow Avon.

Long: Biographical Sketch of Enoch Long, an Illinois Pioneer (with Genealogy) Harvey Reid. (Illus.). 134p. 1996. reprint ed. pap. 19.00 (*0-8328-5615-0*); reprint ed. lib. bdg. 29.00 (*0-8328-5614-2*) Higginson Bk Co.

Long: History of the Long Family of Pennsylvania. W. G. Long. 365p. 1993. reprint ed. pap. 56.00 (*0-8328-3706-7*); reprint ed. lib. bdg. 66.00 (*0-8328-3705-9*) Higginson Bk Co.

Long Acre. large type ed. Claire Rayner. 592p. 1992. 27.99 (*0-7089-2593-6*) Ulverscroft.

Long Acting Cephalosporins in Surgery. Ed. by K. Hell. (Journal: European Surgical Research: Vol. 21, Suppl. 1, 1989). 58p. 1989. pap. 20.00 (*3-8055-4971-7*) S Karger.

Long-Acting Nifedipine: End-Organ Protection & Prevention of Cardiovascular Disease: 3rd International Symposium, Berlin, September 1996: Proceedings. Ed. by Shimon Braun. (Cardiology Ser.: Vol. 88, Suppl. 3, 1997). (Illus.). iv, 74p. 1997. pap. 34.00 (*3-8055-6620-4*) S Karger.

Long Acting Steroid Contraception. Ed. by Daniel R. Mishell, Jr. LC 83-43027. (Advances in Human Fertility & Reproductive Endocrinology Ser.: No. 2). (Illus.). 216p. 1983. reprint ed. pap. 67.00 (*0-7837-9558-0*, 206030700005) Bks Demand.

Long Affair: Thomas Jefferson & the French Revolution, 1785-1800. Conor C. O'Brien. (Illus.). 360p. 1996. 29.95 (*0-226-61653-3*) U Ch Pr.

Long Affair: Thomas Jefferson & the French Revolution, 1785-1800. Conor C. O'Brien. (Illus.). 368p. 1998. pap. 15.00 (*0-226-61656-8*) U Ch Pr.

Long after Hannibal Had Passed with Elephants: Poems & Epigrams. Alan Jones. (Illus.). 614p. (Orig.). (C). 1995. pap. 10.00 (*0-9646466-0-9*) Edgewise Pr.

Long after Midnight. Ray Bradbury. 1994. lib. bdg. 24.95 (*1-56849-432-7*) Buccaneer Bks.

Long after Midnight. large type ed. Iris Johansen. LC 96-54266. (Romc-Hall Ser.). 560p. 1997. 27.95 (*0-7838-2040-2*, G K Hall Lrg Type) Mac Lib Ref.

Long after Midnight. Iris Johansen. 464p. 1997. reprint ed. mass mkt. 6.99 (*0-553-57181-8*) Bantam.

Long after Midnight, Set. abr. ed. Iris Johansen. 1997. audio 16.99 (*0-553-47779-X*, 394933) BDD Aud Pub.

Long Ago. Linda W. Beech et al. Ed. by Susan Evento. (Literature Based Reading Activities/Conversion Ser.). 64p. 1995. pap. 9.95 (*1-56784-517-7*) Newbridge Educ.

Long Ago. Margie Burton et al. Ed. by Susan Evento. (Early Connections Ser.). 16p. (J). (gr. k-2). 1998. pap. 4.25 (*1-892393-50-6*) Benchmark Educ.

Long Ago & Far Away, Vol. 1. Marylyle Rogers. 1997. mass mkt. 5.99 (*0-312-96314-9*) St Martin.

Long Ago & Far Away: And Other Short Plays. David Ives. 1994. pap. 5.25 (*0-8222-1397-4*) Dramatists Play.

Long Ago & Today, Vol. 3933. Rozanne L. Williams. (Social Studies Learn to Read Ser.). (Illus.). 16p. (J). (ps-2). 1996. pap. 2.75 (*1-57471-138-5*, 3933) Creat Teach Pr.

Long Ago & Today, Vol. 3976. Rozanne L. Williams. (Social Studies Big Bks.). (Illus.). 16p. (J). (ps-2). 1997. pap. 12.98 (*1-57471-184-9*, 3976) Creat Teach Pr.

***Long Ago & Today Series, 4 bks.** Peter Roop & Connie Roop. 24p. 1999. 79.68 (*1-57572-604-1*) Heinemann Lib.

Long Ago by Shannon Side. Edmund Lenihan. 1982. pap. 7.95 (*0-85342-671-6*) Dufour.

Long Ago God Spoke: How Christians May Hear the Old Testament Today. William L. Holladay. LC 95-11848. 352p. 1995. 42.00 (*0-8006-2932-9*, 1-2932, Fortress Pr); pap. 25.00 (*0-8006-2884-5*, 1-2884, Fortress Pr) Augsburg Fortress.

Long Ago in a Castle. Marie Farre. Tr. by Sarah Matthews from FRE. LC 87-33996. (Illus.). 38p. (J). (gr. k-5). 1988. 5.95 (*0-944589-06-5*, 065) Young Discovery Lib.

Long Ago in France: The Years in Dijon. M. F. K. Fisher. 176p. 1992. pap. 11.00 (*0-671-75514-5*, Touchstone) S&S Trade Pap.

Long Ago in France: The Years in Dijon. large type ed. M. F. K. Fisher. LC 92-16951. 281p. 1992. reprint ed. lib. bdg. 19.95 (*1-56054-471-6*) Thorndike Pr.

Long Ago in Lunenburg on Stony Creek of the Meherrin: With Callis, Elder, Fisher, Hudgins, Mize, Steagall & Related Families. June B. Evans. (Illus.). 144p. 1993. 31.50 (*0-9611114-5-3*) Bryn Ffyliaid.

Long Ago in Oregon. Claudia L. Lewis. LC 86-45781. (Charlotte Zolotow Bk.). (Illus.). 64p. (J). (gr. 3-7). 1987. 11.95 (*0-06-023839-9*) HarpC Child Bks.

Long Ago in Serafina. large type ed. Lee F. Gregson. (Western Library). 240p. 1995. pap. 16.99 (*0-7089-7689-1*, Linford) Ulverscroft.

Long Ago Is Far Away: Figuring Out How the Universe Began. Tony Rothman. LC 93-16340. (J). 1993. write for info. (*0-7167-9000-9*) W H Freeman.

Long Ago Love. Bonna L. DuBois. LC 85-10451. 192p. 1985. 14.95 (*0-8027-0861-7*) Walker & Co.

Long Ago, Not Far Away: An Illustrated History of Six Middlesex County Towns. Greater Middletown Preservation Trust Staff. LC 96-30300. (Illus.). 1996. write for info. (*0-89865-976-0*) Donning Co.

Long Ago Told. Harold Bell Wright. 1998. lib. bdg. 51.95 (*1-56723-108-X*) Yestermorrow.

Long Ago Yesterday. Anne Rockwell. LC 95-32657. (Illus.). 24p. (J). (ps up). 1999. 16.00 (*0-688-14411-X*, Greenwillow Bks) HarpC Child Bks.

Long Ago, Yesterday in Appalachia. Carmella M. Schnautz. Ed. by Paula N. Deal. (Illus.). 472p. 1988. 22.50 (*0-9619574-0-9*) C Schnautz.

Long & Happy Life. Reynolds Price. LC 61-12790. 208p. 1987. 20.00 (*0-689-11947-X*); pap. 4.95 (*0-689-10224-0*) Atheneum Yung Read.

***Long & Healthy Life: The Facts about High Level Wellness.** Neecie Moore. 144p. 1999. pap. 12.95 (*0-9660700-1-1*, Pub. by Validation Pr) ACCESS Pubs Network.

Long & Living Shadow. large type ed. Daoma Winston. LC 93-12737. 258p. 1993. lib. bdg. 19.95 (*1-56054-729-4*) Thorndike Pr.

***Long & Short of It.** Stephen Ellis. LC 99-31888. 104p. 1999. pap. 14.00 (*1-881471-40-3*, Pub. by S Duyvil) SPD-Small Pr Dist.

***Long & Short of It.** Stephen Ellis. LC 99-31888. 104p. 2000. 29.95 (*1-881471-41-1*) S Duyvil.

Long & Short of It. Cheryl Nathan & Lisa McCourt. (Illus.). 32p. (J). (ps-3). 1999. pap. 5.95 (*0-8167-5609-0*) BrdgeWater.

Long & Short of It. Pamela Painter. LC 98-71950. (Series in Short Fiction). 202p. 1999. pap. 15.95 (*0-88748-286-4*, Pub. by Carnegie-Mellon) Cornell U Pr.

Long & Short of It - Fun with Phonics: Fun with Phonics. Denise C. Schoemer. (Illus.). 64p. (Orig.). (J). (ps-1). 1996. pap. 1.95 (*1-885744-07-2*) Otter Creek.

Long & Short of Mother Goose: Reading Level 2-3, 2 bks. (Read to Me Bks.). (J). 1993. 3.00 (*0-88336-970-2*); 3.00 (*0-88336-969-9*); digital audio 7.00 (*0-88336-971-0*) New Readers.

Long & Short-Term Interest Rates: An Econometric Study. James L. Ford & T. Stark. LC 67-9408. (Illus.). x, 61p. 1967. 12.50 (*0-678-06255-2*) Kelley.

Long & Short Vowel Sounds. Walter B. Barbe. (Linking Learning to Sound - Symbol Relationships Ser.: Bk. B). 48p. (J). (gr. 2-3). 1997. pap., wbk. ed. 2.50 (*1-56762-079-5*) Modern Learn Pr.

***Long & Short Vowels: 20 Interactive Word Books That Help Every Child Become A Better Reader.** Mary Beth Spann. 1999. pap. text 9.95 (*0-439-08677-9*) Scholastic Inc.

Long & Terrible Shadow: White Values & Native Rights in the Americas Since 1492. 2nd ed. Thomas R. Berger. 183p. 1999. pap. text 17.95 (*0-295-97807-4*) U of Wash Pr.

Long & the Short. Tom Davis. LC 94-69062. (Illus.). 40p. (Orig.). 1994. pap. text 5.95 (*1-884778-05-4*) Old Mountain.

Long & the Short & the All. Osho. Ed. by K. Prabhu. LC 84-42806. (Early Writings & Discourses Ser.). 320p. 1984. pap. 4.95 (*0-88050-708-X*) Oshos.

Long & the Short & the Tall. Willis Hall. (Hereford Plays Ser.). 92p. (C). 1988. pap. 6.95 (*0-435-22390-9*, 22390) Heinemann.

Long, & the Short & the Tall: A Marine Combat Unit in the Pacific. Alvin M. Josephy, Jr. LC 79-20013. 1980. reprint ed. 25.95 (*0-89201-081-9*) Zenger Pub.

***Long & the Short & the Tall: Marines in Combat on Guam & Iwo Jima.** Chuck Lawliss. 2000. pap. 16.95 (*1-58080-080-7*) Burford Bks.

Long & Wearisome Journey: The Eakin Family Diaries, 1866. rev. ed. Ed. by Shirley Ecvart et al. (Illus.). 263p. 1993. reprint ed. pap. 12.95 (*0-918957-10-9*) Pika Oregon.

Long & Winding Road. Ted Greenwald. (Illus.). 128p. 1997. text 14.98 (*1-56799-623-X*, MetroBooks) M Friedman Pub Grp Inc.

Long & Winding Road. Ed. by Melisa Mitchell. LC 97-228380. 1997. 69.95 (*1-57553-407-X*) Watermrk Pr.

Long & Winding Road, 1. unabridged ed. Michael Lizza. (Illus.). 20p. (Orig.). 1994. pap. 5.00 (*1-929326-50-5*) Hal Bar Pubg.

Long & Winding Road: A History of the Beatles on Record Neville Stannard & John Tobler. LC 83-228674. 240p. 1983. write for info. (*0-907080-96-0*) Virgin Bks.

Long & Winding Road: A Spiritual Guide for Baby Boomers. Helen Neinast & Thomas C. Ettinger. LC 98-42482. 96p. 1998. pap. 8.00 (*0-687-01593-6*) Dimen for Liv.

***Long & Winding Road II, 9.** unabridged ed. Michael Lizza. (Illus.). 120p. (Orig.). 1999. pap. 25.00 (*1-929326-57-2*) Hal Bar Pubg.

Long Argument: English Puritanism & the Shaping of New England Culture, 1570-1700. Stephen Foster. LC 90-41564. (Institute of Early American History & Culture Ser.). xx, 415p. (C). 1991. 55.00 (*0-8078-1951-4*) U of NC Pr.

Long Argument: English Puritanism & the Shaping of New England Culture, 1570-1700. Stephen Foster. LC 90-41564. 415p. (C). 1996. pap. text 19.95 (*0-8078-4583-3*) U of NC Pr.

Long Arm & the Angel of Inferno, No. 208. Tabor Evans. 192p. (Orig.). 1996. mass mkt. 4.99 (*0-515-11843-5*, Jove) Berkley Pub.

Long Arm & the Arizona Ambush, No. 204. Tarbor Evans. 192p. (Orig.). 1995. mass mkt. 4.50 (*0-515-11766-8*, Jove) Berkley Pub.

Long Arm of Coincidence: The Frustrated Connection Between Beowulf & Grettis Saga. Magnus Fjalldal. LC 99-159648. 216p. 1998. text 50.00 (*0-8020-4301-1*); pap. text 16.95 (*0-8020-8128-2*) U of Toronto Pr.

Long Arm of Lee: The History of the Artillery of the Army of Northern Virginia, 2 vols., Vol. 1: Bull Run to Fredericksburg. Jennings C. Wise. LC 91-16846. (Illus.). vii, 463p. 1991. reprint ed. pap. 19.95 (*0-8032-9733-5*, Bison Books) U of Nebr Pr.

Long Arm of Lee: The History of the Artillery of the Army of Northern Virginia, 2 vols., Vol. 2: Chancellorsville to Appomattox. Jennings C. Wise. LC 91-16846. (Illus.). ix, 582p. 1991. reprint ed. pap. 15.95 (*0-8032-9734-3*, Bison Books) U of Nebr Pr.

Long Arm Quarterback. Matt Christopher. LC 99-26049. 144p. (J). (gr. 3-7). 1999. pap. 3.95 (*0-316-10562-7*) Little.

***Long Arm Quarterback.** Matt Christopher. LC 99-26049. 144p. (J). (gr. 3-7). 1999. 15.95 (*0-316-10571-6*) Little.

Long Arms of Dr. Octopus - Spiderman. LC 97-108158. (Stick to It Ser.). (Illus.). 12p. (J). (ps-3). 1995. 8.98 (*1-57082-226-3*, Pub. by Mouse Works) Time Warner.

Long Awaited Moment: The Working Class & the Italian Communist Party in Milan, 1943-1948. Tom Behan. LC 95-21799. (American University Studies: Vol. 174). (Illus.). XII, 310p. (C). 1997. 49.95 (*0-8204-2674-1*) P Lang Pubng.

Long Awaited Stork: A Guide to Parenting after Infertility. rev. ed. Ellen S. Glazer. LC 97-49626. 300p. 1998. pap. text 21.95 (*0-7879-4053-4*) Jossey-Bass.

Long-Awaited Wedding. Doris E. Fell. (Love Inspired Ser.: Bk. 62). 1999. per. 4.50 (*0-373-87062-0*, 1-87062-5, Steeple Hill) Harlequin Bks.

Long Balls, No Strikes: How Baseball Can Keep the Good Times Rolling. Joe Morgan & Richard Lally. LC 99-33098. 288p. 1999. 25.00 (*0-609-60524-0*, Crown) Crown.

Long Beach: A North Carolina Town: Its Origin & History. Wolfgang Furstenau. LC 95-227772. (Illus.). 372p. 1995. 17.95 (*0-9648233-0-6*) W Furstenau.

Long Beach: A Photography Survey. Ed. by Constance Glenn. (Illus.). 70p. pap. 40.00 (*0-936270-01-2*) CA St U LB Art.

***Long Beach: The City & its People.** William Hillburg. (Illus.). 300p. 2000. 39.95 (*1-886483-48-5*) Heritge Media.

Long Beach, Clayoquot & Beyond. Brian Payton. LC 96-910695. (Illus.). 96p. (Orig.). 1997. pap. 16.95 (*1-55192-063-8*) Raincoast Bk.

Long Beach in the Twenties. Historical Soc. of Long Beach Staff. (Illus.). 64p. 1969. pap. 11.00 (*0-9610250-0-X*) Hist Soc of Long Bch.

Long Beach Island Historical Postcards. 1995. pap. 8.95 (*0-945582-33-1*) Down the Shore Pub.

***Long Beach Peninsula Historic Picture Album.** (Illus.). 128p. 1998. 39.95 (*1-891395-15-7*) Pediment Grp.

Long Before Forty. C. S. Forester. 22.95 (*0-89190-605-3*) Amereon Ltd.

Long Binh Jail: An Oral History of Vietnam's Notorious U. S. Military Prison. Cecil B. Currey. LC 99-23634. (Illus.). 288p. 1999. 25.95 (*1-57488-186-8*) Brasseys.

Long Bitter Trail: Andrew Jackson & the Indians. Anthony F. Wallace. Ed. by Eric Foner. LC 92-32609. (Critical Issue Ser.). 144p. 1993. pap. 8.00 (*0-8090-1552-8*) Hill & Wang.

Long Black Coat. John Waters. (New Island Plays Ser.). 96p. 1996. pap. 12.95 (*1-85459-263-7*, Pub. by N Hern Bks) Theatre Comm.

Long Black Coat. John Waters & David Byrne. 64p. 1995. pap. 12.95 (*1-874597-22-7*) Dufour.

Long Black Song: Essays in Black American Literature & Culture. Houston A. Baker, Jr. 156p. 1990. pap. text 14.50 (*0-8139-1301-2*) U Pr of Va.

Long Black Song: Essays in Black American Literature & Culture. Houston A. Baker, Jr. LC 72-77261. 168p. reprint ed. pap. 52.10 (*0-608-17191-3*, 202699800053) Bks Demand.

Long Blue Blazer. Jeanne Willis & Susan Varley. (Illus.). 32p. (J). (ps-1). 1998. pap. 9.95 (*0-86264-790-8*, Pub. by Andersen Pr) Trafalgar.

Long Blue Edge of Summer: A Guide to the Shorelines of Michigan. Doris Scharfenberg. LC 92-13068. (Illus.). 240p. 1992. reprint ed. pap. 12.95 (*1-879094-09-6*) Momentum Bks.

Long Blue Line: A History of the Queensland Police Force. Ross Johnston. 400p. (C). 1990. 135.00 (*0-86439-128-5*, Pub. by Boolarong Pubns) St Mut.

Long Body of the Dream. Richard Grossinger. 256p. (Orig.). 1974. pap. 5.00 (*0-913028-28-2*) North Atlantic.

Long Boom: A Vision for the Coming Age of Prosperity. Peter Schwartz et al. LC 99-64774. 352p. 1999. text 26.00 (*0-7382-0074-3*, Pub. by Perseus Pubng) HarpC.

***Long Boom: A Vision for the Coming Age of Prosperity.** Peter Schwartz et al. 352p. 2000. reprint ed. pap. text 17.00 (*0-7382-0364-5*, Pub. by Perseus Pubng) HarpC.

Long Branch. Paul Sniffen. (Images of America Ser.). 128p. 1996. pap. 16.99 (*0-7524-0298-6*) Arcadia Publng.

Long Branch People & Places. Randall Gabrielan. LC 98-87873. (Images of America Ser.). 1998. write for info. (*0-7524-0809-7*) Arcadia Publng.

Long Campaign: History of the Fifteenth Fighter Group World War II. John William Lambert. 1982. 45.00 (*0-89745-032-9*) Beachcomber Bks.

Long Canoe. Malcolm A. Hoffmann. 294p. 1994. 20.00 (*1-57087-075-6*) Prof Pr NC.

Long Chance. Peter Kyne. 1976. lib. bdg. 14.85 (*0-89968-054-2*, Lghtyr Pr) Buccaneer Bks.

Long Circular Walks in the Peak District. John N. Merrill. 64p. 1986. 25.00 (*0-907496-42-3*, Pub. by JNM Pubns) St Mut.

Long Circulating Liposomes: Old Drugs, New Therapeutics. Martin C. Woodle. LC 97-30426. (Biotechnology Intelligence Unit (SV) Ser.). 205p. Date not set. 115.00 (*1-57059-508-9*) Landes Bioscience.

Long Circulating Liposomes: Old Drugs, New Therapeutics. Ed. by Martin C. Woodle. LC 97-30426. (Biotechnology Intelligence Unit (SV) Ser.). 205p. 1997. 149.00 (*3-540-63082-1*) Spr-Verlag.

Long Claws: An Arctic Adventure. James Houston. (Illus.). (J). (gr. 6). 1995. 9.28 (*0-395-73262-X*) HM.

Long Claws: An Arctic Adventure. James A. Houston. (Picture Puffin Ser.). (Illus.). (J). 1992. 10.19 (*0-606-01717-8*, Pub. by Turtleback) Demco.

Long Claws: An Arctic Adventure. large type ed. James Houston. (Illus.). 54p. (J). (gr. 6). 13.50 (*0-614-20603-0*, L-38201-00 APHB) Am Printing Hse.

Long Coffin. large type ed. Nigel Tranter. 1975. 27.99 (*0-85456-369-5*) Ulverscroft.

Long Cold Fall. Sam Reaves. 304p. 1992. mass mkt. 4.50 (*0-380-71641-0*, Avon Bks) Morrow Avon.

Long Compan Nazi Germany. Tim Kirk. LC 94-1131. (Companions to History Ser.). 288p. (C). 1995. pap. text 27.19 (*0-582-06375-2*, 76904, Pub. by Addison-Wesley) Longman.

***Long Corridor.** Catherine Cookson. 2000. pap. 8.95 (*0-552-14078-3*, Pub. by Transworld Publishers Ltd) Trafalgar.

Long Corridor: Selected Poetry of Mushakoji (Surname) Saneatsu. Mushakoji Saneatsu. Tr. & Intro. by Robert Epp. LC 95-60539. 398p. (C). 1996. text 30.00 (*1-880276-70-4*) Yakusha.

Long Crossing. Neva Powell. LC 98-85615. (Illus.). 124p. (YA). (gr. 5-8). 1998. pap. 12.95 (*0-9661072-2-5*) Avocet Pr.

Long Crossing & Other Labrador Stories. Elliott Merrick. LC 91-32226. (Illus.). 158p. (Orig.). (C). 1992. pap. 13.95 (*0-89101-074-2*) U Maine Pr.

Long Cycles in the History of Mathematics. Alexei Barabashev. Ed. by Irving H. Anellis. Tr. by Gregory Crowe from RUS. (Russian Philosophy & History of Logic, Mathematics & Science Ser.). (Illus.). xii, 176p. (Orig.). 1996. pap. 29.95 (*1-884905-02-1*) Modern Logic.

Long Cycles World Politics. G. Modelski. LC 86-15731. 256p. 1986. pap. 30.00 (*0-295-96430-8*) U of Wash Pr.

Long Dark Tea-Time of the Soul. Douglas Adams. 320p. 1991. per. 6.99 (*0-671-74251-5*) PB.

Long Dark Tea-Time of the Soul. Douglas Adams. 1988. 12.09 (*0-606-01764-X*, Pub. by Turtleback) Demco.

Long Darkness: Psychological & Moral Perspectives on Nuclear Winter. Ed. & Intro. by Lester Grinspoon. LC 85-40986. 217p. 1986. pap. 14.00 (*0-300-03664-7*, YF-31) Yale U Pr.

Long Darkness: Psychological & Moral Perspectives on Nuclear Winter. Ed. by Lester Grinspoon. LC 84-40986. 223p. reprint ed. pap. 69.20 (*0-7837-5199-0*, 208022800004) Bks Demand.

Long Day: The Story of a New York Working Girl. Dorothy Richardson. 320p. (C). 1990. reprint ed. pap. text 14.50 (*0-8139-1289-X*) U Pr of Va.

Long Day Monday. Peter Turnbull. 1995. per. 3.99 (*0-373-26160-8*, 1-26160-1) Harlequin Bks.

Long Day Monday. large type ed. Peter Turnbull. 1994. 27.99 (*0-7089-3175-8*) Ulverscroft.

Long Day Wanes: A Malayan Trilogy. Anthony Burgess. 512p. 1993. pap. 13.95 (*0-393-30943-6*) Norton.

Long Days Journey. Patricia Nieman. 1997. pap. write for info. (*1-57553-489-4*) Watermrk Pr.

***Long Day's Journey: The Steamboat & Stagecoach Era in the Northern West.** Carlos Arnoldo Schwantes. LC 99-29316. (Illus.). 408p. 1999. 60.00 (*0-295-97691-8*) U of Wash Pr.

Long Day's Journey into Night. 36p. 1998. 9.95 (*1-58130-564-8*, NU5648) Novel Units.

Long Day's Journey into Night. 40p. (YA). 1998. 11.95 (*1-58130-565-6*, NU5656SP) Novel Units.

Long Day's Journey into Night. Eugene O'Neill. 19.95 (*0-89190-370-4*) Amereon Ltd.

Long Day's Journey into Night. Eugene O'Neill. 176p. 1950. 20.00 (*0-300-04600-6*) Yale U Pr.

Long Day's Journey into Night. Eugene O'Neill. LC 89-50523. 176p. 1989. pap. 10.00 (*0-300-04601-4*) Yale U Pr.

Long Day's Journey Into Night: Curriculum Unit. Center for Learning Network Staff & Eugene O'Neill. (Drama Ser.). 67p. (YA). (gr. 9-12). 1993. spiral bd. 18.95 (*1-56077-245-X*) Ctr Learning.

Long Day's Journey into Night: Native Eloquence. Michael Hinden. (Twayne's Masterwork Studies: No. 49). 168p. (gr. 9 up). 1990. 29.00 (*0-8057-7995-7*, Twyne) Mac Lib Ref.

Long Death. Andrist. 1995. 14.00 (*0-684-82938-X*) S&S Trade.

Long Death of British Labourism. Willie Thompson. LC 92-47378. 195p. (C). 49.95 (*0-7453-0580-6*, Pub. by Pluto GBR); pap. 15.95 (*0-7453-0581-4*, Pub. by Pluto GBR) Stylus Pub VA.

Long, Deep Furrow: Three Centuries of Farming in New England. abr. ed. Howard S. Russell. Ed. & Abr. by Mark Lapping. LC 81-51605. (Illus.). 394p. 1982. pap. 24.95 (*0-87451-214-X*) U Pr of New Eng.

Long, Deep Furrow: 3 Centuries of Farming in New England. Howard S. Russell. LC 73-91314. 688p. reprint ed. 200.00 (*0-608-16641-3*, 202753400055) Bks Demand.

Long Dimanche de Finacailles see Very Long Engagement

Long Discourses of the Buddha: A Translation of the Digha Nikaya. Tr. by Maurice O. Walshe from PLI. LC 95-11288. (Teachings of the Buddha Ser.). (Illus.). 656p. 1995. 37.50 (*0-86171-103-3*, Pub. by Wisdom MA) Natl Bk Netwk.

Long Dispute: European Colonisation & Maori Land Rights in Southern New Zealand. rev. ed. Harry C. Evison. (Illus.). 380p. 1997. pap. 39.95 (*0-908812-57-4*, Pub. by Canterbury Univ) Accents Pubns.

Long Distance. Asher Reich. Ed. by Stanley H. Barkan & Karen Alkaley-Gut. (Review Israeli Writers Chapbook Ser.: No. 2). (ENG & HEB.). 48p. 1991. 15.00 (*0-89304-381-8*); 15.00 (*0-89304-383-4*); pap. 5.00 (*0-89304-382-6*); pap. 5.00 (*0-89304-384-2*) Cross-Cultrl NY.

Long Distance. Aleda Shirley. (Poetry Ser.). 1996. 19.95 (*1-881163-16-4*); pap. 11.95 (*1-881163-17-2*) Miami Univ Pr.

***Long Distance: A Year of Living Strenuously.** Bill McKibben. LC 00-55613. 2000. write for info. (*0-684-85597-6*) Simon & Schuster.

L

An Asterisk (*) at the beginning of an entry indicates that the title is appearing for the first time.

L

Long Distance Anaphora. Ed. by Jan Koster & Eric Reuland. (Illus.). 352p. (C). 1991. text 99.95 (0-521-39111-3) Cambridge U Pr.

Long Distance & Reseller Markets: Small Players Rise Again. Market Intelligence Staff. 295p. 1992. 1695.00 (1-56753-385-X) Frost & Sullivan.

Long Distance Bicycle Touring Primer. Harvey Botzman. (Illus.). 72p. 1995. pap. 10.95 (1-889602-01-9) Cyclotour Guide.

Long Distance Calls. Dave Margoshes. 192p. 1997. pap. 12.95 (1-55050-104-6, Pub. by Coteau) Genl Dist Srvs.

Long Distance Commuting in Minnesota: Final Report. John S. Adams et al. (Illus.). 93p. (Orig.). (C). 1995. pap. text 30.00 (0-7881-2017-4) DIANE Pub.

Long Distance Crystal Set, MRL 2. Elmer G. Osterhoudt. (MRL Handbook Ser.: Vol. HB-2). (Illus.). 24p. 1999. pap. write for info. (1-891501-01-1) Modern Radio.

Long Distance For Less: The Official Guide to Long Distance Telephone Services in the United States. 3rd rev. ed. Robert Self. LC 87-62959. 576p. 1998. reprint ed. pap. 75.00 (0-913761-05-2) Market Dyn.

***Long-Distance Genealogy.** Christine Crawford Oppenheimer. (Illus.). 208p. 2000. pap. 18.99 (1-55870-535-X, Betrwy Bks) F & W Pubns Inc.

Long-Distance Grandma: How to Stay Connected with Grandkids Far Away. Janet Teitsort. LC 98-5523. 160p. 1998. 14.99 (0-8010-1165-5) Baker Bks.

Long Distance Grandmother: How to Stay Close to Distant Grandchildren. 3rd ed. Selma Wassermann. (Illus.). 272p. 1996. pap. text 14.95 (0-88179-122-9) Hartley & Marks.

Long-Distance Grandparenting see Long-Distance Grandparenting Series

Long-Distance Grandparenting Series, 3. Jenelle Koftan & Kenneth Koftan. Incl. Long-Distance Grandparenting. (Illus.). 96p. (Orig.). (J). 1988. pap. 12.95 (0-945184-00-X); Bk. II. Long-Distance Grandparenting. Illus. by Carl Mar. 96p. (Orig.). (J). (gr. k-2). 1988. pap. 12.95 (0-945184-01-8); Bk. III. Long-Distance Grandparenting. Illus. by Carl Mar. 96p. (Orig.). (J). (gr. 3-5). 1988. pap. 12.95 (0-945184-02-6); 1990. 37.95 (0-945184-06-9) Spring Creek Pubns.

Long Distance-High Bit Rate Systems. rev. ed. IGIC, Inc. Staff. (Fiber Optics Reprint Ser.: Vol. 11). (Illus.). 333p. 1994. pap. 75.00 (1-56851-060-8) Info Gatekeepers.

Long-Distance Hiking: Lessons from the Appalachian Trail. Roland Mueser. LC 97-21278. (Illus.). 192p. 1997. pap. 16.95 (0-07-044458-7) McGraw.

Long Distance Life. Marita Golden. 1999. mass mkt. 6.99 (0-345-36711-1) Ballantine Pub Grp.

Long Distance, Love: Echoes in an Empty House. Date not set. write for info. (1-887822-04-6) Around Snd Pr.

Long Distance Markets, 2001. 176p. 1992. 1950.00 (0-89336-904-7, G-137) BCC.

Long-Distance Marriage. Sharon Kendrick. (Presents Ser.: Vol. 1969). 1998. per. 3.75 (0-373-11969-0, 1-11969-2) Harlequin Bks.

***Long-Distance Nationalism: Diasporas, Homelands & Indentities.** Zlatko Skrbis. (Research in Migration & Ethnic Relations Ser.). 222p. 1999. text 65.95 (1-85972-672-0, Pub. by Ashgate Pub) Ashgate Pub Co.

Long-Distance Neutrino Detection-Nineteen Seventy-Eight: C. L. Cowan Memorial Symposium, Catholic University. Ed. by A. W. Saenz & H. Uberall. LC 79-52078. (AIP Conference Proceedings Ser.: No. 52). (Illus.). 1979. lib. bdg. 16.50 (0-88318-151-7) Am Inst Physics.

Long Distance Oatmeal Eater. Marjorie Simon. 80p. (Orig.). 1985. pap. 5.95 (0-937310-30-1) Story Line.

Long Distance Propagation of HF Radio Waves. A. V. Gurevich & E. E. Tsedilina. (Physics & Chemistry in Space Ser.: Vol. 12). (Illus.). 350p. 1985. 175.95 (0-387-15139-7) Spr-Verlag.

***Long Distance Reflexives, Vol. 33.** Peter Cole. (Syntax & Semantics Ser.). 350p. 2000. 120.00 (0-12-613533-9) Acad Pr.

Long Distance Services: A Buyer's Guide. Daniel D. Briere. LC 90-42994. (Artech House Telecommunications Library). 310p. 1990. reprint ed. pap. 96.10 (0-608-00557-6, 206144000008) Bks Demand.

Long Distance Walkers' Handbook. 6th ed. Barbara Blatchford. (Illus.). 288p. 1998. pap. 19.95 (0-7136-4835-X, 93301, Pub. by A & C Blk) Midpt Trade.

Long Distance Walks in Pyrenees. Chris Townsend. (Illus.). 128p. 1992. pap. 29.95 (1-85223-391-5, Pub. by Cro1wood) Trafalgar.

Long Distance Walks in Scotland-NE. Arthur Stewart. (Illus.). 128p. 1994. pap. 24.95 (1-85223-824-0, Pub. by Cro1wood) Trafalgar.

***Long Distance Whisper - Artificial Words.** A. Molotkov et al. 200p. (C). 2000. write for info. (0-9678919-1-4) Discord.

Long Distances: Contemporary Theory, Technique & Training. 3rd ed. Ed. by Jess Jarver. (Contemporary Track & Field Ser.). (Illus.). 145p. 1995. pap. 16.50 (0-911521-41-0) Tafnews.

***Long Dream.** Richard Wright. LC 99-59961. (Library of Black Literature). 400p. 2000. pap. text 15.95 (1-55553-423-6) NE U Pr.

Long Drift. Sam Brown. 192p. 1995. 20.95 (0-8027-4146-0) Walker & Co.

Long Drift. large type ed. Sam Brown. LC 95-30258. 368p. 1995. 21.95 (0-7838-1448-8, G K Hall Lrg Type) Mac Lib Ref.

***Long Drive Home.** Stan Rogal. 177p. (Orig.). 1999. pap. write for info. (1-895837-56-1) Insomniac.

Long Drums & Canons: Teaching & Researching African Literatures. Bernth Lindfors. LC 94-37182. 200p. 1994. 49.95 (0-86543-436-0); pap. 16.95 (0-86543-437-9) Africa World.

Long Dry Season. Omar Eby. LC 88-15634. 216p. 1988. 14.95 (0-934672-60-1) Good Bks PA.

Long Dying of Baby Andrew. Peggy Stinson & Robert Stinson. 384p. 1983. 17.95 (0-316-81635-3, Little Brwn Med Div) Lppncott W & W.

Long-Eared Bats. Susan Swift. (Poyser Natural History Ser.). (Illus.). 192p. (C). 1998. boxed set 29.95 (0-85661-108-5) Poyser.

Long Eighteenth Century: British Political & Social History, 1688-1832. Frank O'Gorman. LC 97-14187. (The Arnold History of Britain Ser.). 432p. 1997. pap. text 24.95 (0-340-56751-1) OUP.

***Long Eighth Century: Production, Distribution & Demand.** Ed. by Chris Wickham & Inge Lyse Hansen. (Transformation of the Roman World Ser.). (Illus.). 369p. 2000. text 122.00 (90-04-11723-7) Brill Academic Pubs.

Long Engagements: Maturity in Modern Japan. David W. Plath. 248p. 1980. pap. 12.95 (0-8047-1176-3) Stanford U Pr.

Long Entanglement. Lawrence S. Kaplan. 280p. 1999. pap. 22.95 (0-275-96419-1, Praeger Pubs) Greenwood.

***Long Entanglement: The United States & NATO after Fifty Years.** Lawrence S. Kaplan. LC 98-37152. 280p. 1999. 65.00 (0-275-96418-3, Praeger Pubs) Greenwood.

Long est Presidency: France in the Mitterrand Years, 1981-1995. Julius W. Friend. 320p. 1998. pap. text 29.00 (0-8133-2851-9, Pub. by Westview) HarpC.

Long Exile. Georges Simenon. Tr. by Eileen Ellenbogen. LC 81-48019. (Helen & Kurt Wolff Bk.). 372p. 1983. 15.95 (0-15-152997-3) Harcourt.

Long Experience of Love. Jim Moore. LC 94-32531. 104p. (Orig.). 1995. pap. 12.95 (1-57131-401-6) Milkweed Ed.

Long Fall: Screenplay. Jim Ralston. Ed. & Intro. by Jorn K. Bramann. LC 95-70028. (Upper Potomacs Ser.). 120p. 1995. pap. 5.00 (0-945073-18-6) Nightsun MD.

Long Fall Short & Hairy Poems. S. McBraney. (Illus.). (J). 1996. mass mkt. 8.95 (0-340-66494-0, Pub. by Hodder & Stought Ltd) Trafalgar.

Long Falling. Keith Ridgway. LC 97-45669. 320p. 1998. 22.00 (0-395-90530-3) HM.

Long Falling. Keith Ridgway. 305p. 1999. pap. 13.00 (0-395-95782-6) HM.

Long Family History. Roy C. Long. (Illus.). 304p. 1989. write for info. (0-318-65517-9) R C Long.

Long Family History. Roy C. Long. Ed. by McClain Printing Co., Staff. (Illus.). 304p. 1989. 30.00 (0-9623739-0-7) R C Long.

Long Fatal Love Chase. Louisa May Alcott. 368p. 1996. mass mkt. 6.99 (0-440-22301-6) Dell.

Long Fatal Love Chase. large type ed. Louisa May Alcott. 1997. pap. 23.95 (0-7862-0623-3) Thorndike Pr.

Long Fifteenth Century: Essays for Douglas Gray. Ed. by Helen Cooper & Sally Mapstone. (Illus.). 374p. 1997. text 85.00 (0-19-818365-8) OUP.

Long Finish: An Aurelio Zen Mystery. Michael Dibdin. LC 98-15764. 272p. 1998. 24.00 (0-375-40429-5) Pantheon.

Long Finish: An Aurelio Zen Mystery. Michael Dibdin. 2000. pap. 12.00 (0-375-70401-9) Vin Bks.

***Long Finish: An Aurelio Zen Mystery.** large type ed. Michael Dibdin. LC 98-46980. 1999. 26.95 (0-7862-1762-6) Thorndike Pr.

Long Firm. Jake Arnott. LC 99-26932. 345p. 1999. 25.00 (1-56947-169-X) Soho Press.

Long Flight Home: Captain Ford's Epic Journey. Ed Dover. (Illus.). 192p. 1998. 30.00 (1-888962-07-0) Paladwr Pr.

Long Fuse. Laurence D. Lafore. LC 81-1514. (Critical Periods of History Ser.). 282p. 1981. reprint ed. lib. bdg. 67.50 (0-313-22969-4, LALF, Greenwood Pr) Greenwood.

Long Fuse: An Interpretation of the Origins of World War I. 2nd ed. Laurence Lafore. (Illus.). 284p. (C). 1997. reprint ed. pap. text 13.95 (0-88133-954-7) Waveland Pr.

Long Fuse: How England Lost the American Colonies: 1760-1785. Don Cook. LC 94-43632. 432p. 1996. pap. 14.00 (0-87113-661-9, Atlntc Mnthly) Grove-Atltic.

Long Game. Derek Lawrenceson. (Golf Basics Ser.). (Illus.). 112p. (Orig.). 1996. pap. 14.95 (1-57243-121-0) Triumph Bks.

Long-Germ Care Planning Guide: The Consumer Resource for Long-Term Care. Phyllis R. Shelton. 136p. 1997. pap. 19.95 (0-9633516-2-1, HG9396) Shelton Mktg.

Long Gestation: Irish Nationalist Life, 1891-1918. Patrick Maume. LC 99-22052. 2000. text 55.00 (0-312-22549-0) St Martin.

Long Gone. Dabney Stuart. LC 96-23191. 72p. 1996. pap. 10.95 (0-8071-2121-5); text 17.95 (0-8071-2120-7) La State U Pr.

Long Gone: The Mecklenberg Six & the Theme of Escape in Black Folklore. Daryl C. Dance. LC 86-7097. (Illus.). 208p. 1987. pap. 17.00 (0-87049-581-X) U of Tenn Pr.

***Long Gone Sun: Bilingual Edition.** Claire Malroux. Tr. by Marilyn Hacker from FRE. Orig. Title: Soleil de Jadis. 260p. 2000. pap. 15.95 (1-878818-87-2, Pub. by Sheep Meadow) U Pr of New Eng.

Long Good-Bye: The Withdrawal of Russian Military Forces from the Baltic States. John R. Beyrle. (Pew Case Studies in International Affairs). 50p. (C). 1996. text 3.50 (1-56927-371-5) Geo U Inst Dplmcy.

Long Good Friday. Barrie Keeffe. 45p. (C). 1988. pap. write for info. (0-413-55550-X, A0153, Methuen Drama) Methn.

Long Goodbye. Raymond Chandler. 1992. pap. 10.00 (0-679-74087-2) Random.

Long Goodbye. Raymond Chandler. LC 87-45920. (Crime Ser.). 384p. 1988. pap. 12.00 (0-394-75768-8) Vin Bks.

Long Goodbye. Raymond Chandler. 1992. pap. 10.00 (0-394-23910-5) Vin Bks.

Long Goodbye. Patty Davis. LC 97-2994. 1999. 20.00 (0-679-45092-0) McKay.

Long Goodbye: Reflections on Dealing with Alzheimers. Linda M. Combs. 200p. 1994. write for info. (0-9640312-0-5) Combs Pubng.

Long Goodbye & Beyond: Coping with Alzheimers. Linda Combs. LC 97-77070. 160p. 1998. pap. 12.95 (1-885221-83-5) BookPartners.

***Long Gray Line: The American Journey of West Point's Class of 1966.** Rick Atkinson. LC 99-15023. (Illus.). 608p. 1999. pap. text 15.00 (0-8050-6291-2) H Holt & Co.

***Long Green: The Rise & Fall of Tobacco in South Carolina.** Eldred E. Prince & Robert R. Simpson. LC 99-43773. (Illus.). 304p. 2000. 40.00 (0-8203-2176-1) U of Ga Pr.

Long Green Valley. Ray Crain. (Illus.). 372p. 1996. 35.00 (0-9641149-1-7) Main Graphics.

Long-Haired Cats. Ulrike Muller. (Pet Care Ser.). 1984. pap. 6.95 (0-8120-2803-1) Barron.

Long-Haired Cats. Jeanne Ramsdale. 80p. pap. 6.95 (0-86622-174-3) TFH Pubns.

Long-Haired Cats. Jeanne Ramsdale. (Illus.). 80p. 1984. pap. text 6.95 (0-86622-231-6, PB-116) TFH Pubns.

Long-Haired Kings & Other Studies in Frankish History. J. M. Wallace-Hadrill. (Medieval Academy Reprints for Teaching Ser.: No. 11). 272p. 1982. reprint ed. pap. text 14.95 (0-8020-6500-7) U of Toronto Pr.

Long Hammering: Essays on the Forging of an African American Presence in the Hudson River Valley to the Early Twentieth Century. A. J. Williams-Myers. 190p. 1994. 49.95 (0-86543-302-X); pap. 14.95 (0-86543-303-8) Africa World.

Long Hard Journey: The Story of the Pullman Porter. Patricia McKissack. (Illus.). 158p. (YA). 1995. pap. 9.95 (0-8027-7437-7) Walker & Co.

Long Hard Journey: The Story of the Pullman Porter. Patricia McKissack & Frederick McKissack. 144p. (J). (gr. 7-9). 1990. 17.95 (0-8027-6884-9); lib. bdg. 18.85 (0-8027-6885-7) Walker & Co.

Long Hard Road Out of Hell. Marilyn Manson. LC ML420.M233A3 1998. 288p. 1998. 24.00 (0-06-039258-4) HarpC.

Long Hard Road Out of Hell. Marilyn Manson & Neil Strauss. (Illus.). 288p. 1999. pap. 15.00 (0-06-098746-4, ReganBks) HarperTrade.

Long Haul: An Autobiography. Myles Horton et al. LC 97-40870. 1997. pap. 17.95 (0-8077-3700-3) Tchrs Coll.

Long Haul: Conversations with Southern Novelists. William Parrill. 194p. (Orig.). (C). pap. text 22.50 (0-8191-9078-0); lib. bdg. 47.50 (0-8191-9077-2) U Pr of Amer.

Long Haul: The Story of the New York State Barge Canal. Michele A. McFee. LC 98-26211. (Illus.). 221p. 1998. reprint ed. pap. 25.00 (0-935796-99-1) Purple Mnt Pr.

Long Haul, ATM & Multi-Media Networks, Vol. 2, NOC '98 - Networks & Optical Communication see Networks & Optical Communication '98

***Long Have I Loved You: A Theologian Reflects on His Church.** Walter J. Burghardt. LC 99-40097. 500p. 2000. pap. 20.00 (1-57075-296-6) Orbis Bks.

LONG HDBK MOD BRIT 1714. 3rd ed. Chris Cook & John Stevenson. LC 96-18356. (Longman Handbooks to History Ser.). 560p. (C). 1996. pap. text 26.25 (0-582-29304-9) Addison-Wesley.

Long Henry. Robert Kammen. 1987. pap. 2.50 (0-8217-2155-0) Kensgtn Pub Corp.

Long Highway Home. Amy Collier. LC 97-61415. 112p. 1998. pap. 8.95 (1-57921-044-9) WinePress Pub.

Long Hill Township. Mary Lou Weller. (Images of America Ser.). (Illus.). 128p. 1997. pap. 16.99 (0-7524-0519-5) Arcadia Publng.

Long Home. William Gay. LC 99-33496. 250p. 1999. 24.95 (1-878448-91-9) MacMurray & Beck.

Long Home. Christian Wiman. LC 98-36324. (Ruerich Poetry Prize Winner Ser.: Vol. 13). 88p. 1998. pap. 12.95 (1-885266-67-7) Story Line.

Long Hot Summer. K. S. Rodriguez. (Dawson's Creek Ser.: No. 1). (YA). (gr. 8 up). 1998. per. 4.99 (0-671-02474-4, Archway) PB.

***Long Hot Summer.** Wendy Rosnau. (Intimate Moments Ser.: Vol. 996). 2000. per. 4.50 (0-373-07996-6) Silhouette.

Long, Hot Summer. large type ed. Betty Burton. 608p. 1996. 27.99 (0-7089-8817-2, Charnwood) Ulverscroft.

Long Hot Summer. large type ed. Rosemary Friedman. 1991. 27.99 (0-7089-2531-6) Ulverscroft.

Long House of the Iroquois. Spencer L. Adams. LC 76-43640. (Illus.). reprint ed. 34.50 (0-404-15475-1) AMS Pr.

Long Hunt. Debra Doyle. 1996. mass mkt. 5.99 (0-8125-3496-4, Pub. by Tor Bks) St Martin.

Long Hunt: Death of the Buffalo East of the Mississippi. Ted F. Belue. (Illus.). 288p. 1996. 22.95 (0-8117-0968-X) Stackpole.

Long Hunters. Dodge Tyler. (Daniel Boone: No. 7). 176p. (Orig.). 1997. mass mkt. 3.99 (0-8439-4336-X, Leisure Bks) Dorchester Pub Co.

***Long Injustice: The Strange Story of Alex Alexandrowicz.** Alex Alexandrowicz & David Wilson. 175p. 1999. pap. 36.00 (1-872870-45-7, Pub. by Waterside Pr) Gaunt.

Long Interstate 80: Ohio. Steven C. Price. 76p. 1998. pap. 9.95 (0-9667091-0-1) Educ Tours.

Long Interview. Grant McCracken. (Qualitative Research Methods Ser.: Vol. 13). 96p. (C). 1988. text 24.00 (0-8039-3352-5); pap. text 10.50 (0-8039-3353-3) Sage.

Long Is a Dragon: Chinese Writing for Children. Peggy Goldstein. LC 90-81148. (Illus.). 32p. (J). (gr. 3-8). 1991. 17.95 (1-881896-01-3) Pacific View Pr.

Long Island: A Natural History. Robert Villani. LC 97-7632. (Illus.). 192p. 1997. 39.95 (0-8109-3591-0, Pub. by Abrams) Time Warner.

Long Island: Our Story. Newsday Staff. (Illus.). 418p. 1998. 44.95 (1-885134-14-2) Newsday.

Long Island: People & Places, Past & Present. rev. ed. Bernie Bookbinder. LC 98-21839. (Illus.). 280p. 1998. 39.95 (0-8109-4255-0, Pub. by Abrams) Time Warner.

Long Island: The Golden Isle. Paula Cohen et al. LC 96-42432. 1996. pap. write for info. (1-885352-51-4) Community Comm.

Long Island: The Suburban Experience. Ed. by Barbara M. Kelly. LC 90-30804. (Long Island Studies). (Illus.). 120p. (Orig.). 1990. 20.00 (1-55787-065-9, NY71055); pap. 10.00 (1-55787-058-6, NY71056) Hrt of the Lakes.

Long Island & Literature. Ed. by Joann P. Krieg. (Long Island Studies). (Illus.). 46p. (Orig.). 1989. pap. 6.00 (1-55787-055-1) Hrt of the Lakes.

Long Island Architecture. Ed. by Joann P. Krieg. (Long Island Studies). (Illus.). 168p. 1991. 30.00 (1-55787-069-1, NY71058); pap. 15.00 (1-55787-070-5, NY71057) Hrt of the Lakes.

Long Island Colonial Patents. Frederick Van Wyck. (Illus.). 191p. 1997. reprint ed. pap. 21.00 (0-8328-6085-9) Higginson Bk Co.

Long Island Country House, 1870-1930. Steven Bedford. LC 87-63536. (Illus.). 100p. (C). 1988. pap. 15.00 (0-943526-17-5) Parrish Art.

Long Island Country Houses, 2. Anthony Baker. Date not set. write for info. (0-393-03900-5) Norton.

Long Island Country Houses, 2 vols., Set. Anthony Baker. (Illus.). 1120p. Date not set. write for info. (0-393-03899-8) Norton.

Long Island Country Houses & Their Architects, 1860-1940. Ed. by Anthony K. Baker et al. (Illus.). 584p. 1997. 85.00 (0-393-03856-4) Norton.

Long Island Gazetteer. Karl H. Proehl & Barbara Shupe. 370p. 1984. 29.95 (0-935912-15-0) LDA Pubs.

Long Island Genealogical Source Material. Herbert F. Seversmith & Kenn Stryker-Rodda. 121p. 1962. lib. bdg. 18.00 (0-915156-24-5) Natl Genealogical.

Long Island Genealogies: Being Kindred Descendants of Thomas Powell of Bethpage, L.I., 1688. Mary P. Bunker. (Illus.). 350p. 1989. reprint ed. lib. bdg. 58.00 (0-8328-0574-2) Higginson Bk Co.

Long Island Green Directory. Ed. by Island-Metro Publications Staff. 1994. write for info. (0-9619832-6-4) Island-Metro Pubns.

Long Island Green Directory, 1995-96 Edition. Island-Metro Publications, Inc. Staff. 1995. write for info. (0-9619832-8-0) Island-Metro Pubns.

Long Island Guide to Dining & Wining. Robert Schoolsky. 1990. pap. 9.95 (0-317-93161-2) LI Restaurant Guide.

Long Island International Desk Manual. 4th rev. ed. Ed. by Island-Metro Publications, Inc. Staff. 1994. write for info. (0-9619832-5-6) Island-Metro Pubns.

Long Island International Trade Desk Manual. 3rd rev. ed. Ed. by Island-Metro Publications, Inc. Staff. 1993. write for info. (0-9619832-3-X) Island-Metro Pubns.

Long Island Job Source. Ed. by John McCrudden & Ellen Avenoso. 80p. (Orig.). 1989. pap. 4.95 (0-9623212-0-6) LIU SC.

Long Island Job Source. rev. ed. Ed. by John McCrudden & Ellen Avenoso. 125p. (Orig.). 1990. pap. text 4.95 (0-9623212-1-4) LIU SC.

Long Island Landscape, 1914-1946: The Transitional Years. Ronald G. Pisano. LC 82-81697. (Illus.). 40p. (Orig.). 1982. pap. 4.00 (0-943526-35-3) Parrish Art.

Long Island Modern: The First Generation of Modernist Architecture on Long Island, 1925-1960. Alastair Gordon & Helen A. Harrison. LC 87-80696. (Illus.). 36p. 1987. pap. 5.00 (0-933793-06-5) Guild Hall.

Long Island Native Plants for Landscaping: A Source Book: Sources on Long Island for Environmentally Sound & Beautiful Landscaping Alternatives. Karen Blumer. (Illus.). 70p. (Orig.). 1989. pap. 6.95 (0-685-28019-5) Growing Wild.

Long Island Nature Preserves Col. Book. Barlowe. 1998. pap. 2.95 (0-486-29406-4) Dover.

Long Island, New York: 1870 Census Index, 2 vols., Set. Ed. by Bradley W. Steuart. 1760p. 1989. lib. bdg. 195.00 (1-877677-05-1) Herit Quest.

Long Island (NY) Maps & Their Makers. David Y. Allen. LC 98-187438. 1997. 23.95 (0-8488-1804-0) Amereon Ltd.

Long Island Rail Road in Early Photographs. Ron Ziel. (Illus.). Date not set. pap. 16.95 (0-8488-0882-7); lib. bdg. 36.95 (0-8488-0881-9) Amereon Ltd.

Long Island Rail Road Photographs. Ron Ziel. (Illus.). 1990. pap. 13.95 (0-486-26301-0) Dover.

Long Island Rail Road Steam Locomotive Pictorial. David D. Morrison. Ed. by Linda A. Valenti. LC 87-36821. (Illus.). 60p. (Orig.). 1987. pap. 9.95 (0-945089-00-7) Cannon Ball.

***Long Island Resource Guide.** Jacqueline Henry. Ed. by Robert Lipper & Patricia Hall. 140p. 1999. pap. 25.00 (1-888465-06-9) Island-Metro Pubns.

***Long Island Resource Guide, Vol. 2.** Jacqueline Henry. Ed. by Robert Lipper. 140p. 2000. pap. 25.00 (1-888465-08-5) Island-Metro Pubns.

Long Island Seafood Cookbook. J. George Frederick. Ed. by Jean Joyce. 1971. pap. 6.95 (0-486-22677-8) Dover.

Long Island Shore Diver: A Diver's Guide to Long Island's Beach Dives. 2nd ed. Daniel Berg. (Illus.). 100p. 1992. pap. text. write for info. (0-9616167-7-6) Aqua Explorers.

Long Island Sound & the South Shore. A. P. Balder. (Illus.). 80p. 1994. pap. 39.95 (0-930151-11-9) Chartcrafters Pubs.

Long Island Sound Municipal Report Card: Environmental Assessments of 78 Coastal Communities. Dare Fuller & Laura Siegel. 180p. 1998. pap. write for info. (*1-893340-04-X*) Natl Resources Defense Coun.

Long Island Sports Resource Guide: An Events Planner's Directory to Nassau-Suffolk Athletic Facilities. Ed. by Island-Metro Publications Staff. 48p. 1993. write for info. (*0-9619832-4-8*) Island-Metro Pubns.

***Long Island the Way We Were.** Newsday Staff. 1999. pap. text 9.95 (*1-885134-23-1*) Newsday.

***Long Island 2001.** Ed. by Zagat Publishers Staff. (Illus.). 2000. pap. 10.95 (*1-57006-238-2*) Zagat.

***Long Island Ultimate Entertainment, 2000.** (Illus.). 854p. 1999. pap. 25.00 (*1-880248-38-7*, 0033) Enter Pubns.

Long Island Union List of Periodicals, 5 vols., Set. Ed. by Judith B. Neufeld. (Orig.). 1996. pap. write for info. (*0-938435-41-8*) LI Lib Resources.

Long Island Union List of Periodicals, Vol. 1. Ed. by Judith B. Neufeld. (Orig.). 1996. pap. write for info. (*0-938435-42-6*) LI Lib Resources.

Long Island Union List of Periodicals, Vol. 2. Ed. by Judith B. Neufeld. (Orig.). 1996. pap. write for info. (*0-938435-43-4*) LI Lib Resources.

Long Island Union List of Periodicals, Vol. 3. Ed. by Judith B. Neufeld. (Orig.). 1996. pap. write for info. (*0-938435-44-2*) LI Lib Resources.

Long Island Union List of Periodicals, Vol. 4. Ed. by Judith B. Neufeld. (Orig.). 1996. pap. write for info. (*0-938435-45-0*) LI Lib Resources.

Long Island Union List of Periodicals, Vol. 5. Ed. by Judith B. Neufeld. (Orig.). 1996. pap. write for info. (*0-938435-46-9*) LI Lib Resources.

Long Island Union List of Periodicals 1998. Ed. by Judith B. Neufeld. 1998. lib. bdg. 400.00 (*0-938435-47-7*) LI Lib Resources.

Long Island Women: Activists & Innovators. Ed. by Natalie A. Naylor & Maureen O. Murphy. (Illus.). 340p. 1998. 38.00 (*1-55787-151-5*, NY71067); pap. 20.00 (*1-55787-150-7*, NY71067) Hrt of the Lakes.

Long Island Writers. Ed. by Stanley H. Barkan & George Wallace. 1991. boxed set 75.00 (*0-685-49049-1*) Cross-Cultrl NY.

Long Island Writers. deluxe limited ed. Ed. by Martin Tucker. (Confrontation Special Anthology Issue Ser.). 288p. 1985. 30.00 (*0-685-58008-3*) Confront Mag Pr.

Long Island Writers & Writings. Ed. by Martin Tucker. (Confrontation Special Anthology Issue Ser.). 288p. 1985. pap. 10.00 (*0-913057-03-7*) Confront Mag Pr.

Long Island's History & Cultural Heritage: An Integrative Curriculum Resource for Educators. Natalie A. Naylor et al. LC 92-63132. (Illus.). 70p. 1992. pap. 7.00 (*0-943526-23-X*) Parrish Art.

Long John Dunn of Taos. Max Evans. LC 91-58932. (Illus.). 164p. 1992. reprint ed. 22.95 (*0-940666-20-0*); reprint ed. pap. 12.95 (*0-940666-16-2*) Clear Light.

Long John Silver. Bjorn Larsson. 1999. 26.00 (*1-86046-694-X*, Pub. by Harvill Press) FS&G.

***Long John Silver.** Bjorn Larsson. 2000. pap. text 12.00 (*1-86046-538-2*) Harvill Press.

Long Journey. Nanetta Andenoro. Ed. by Amy L. Andenoro. (Orig.). 1997. mass mkt. 5.95 (*0-9658602-0-5*) Three G.

***Long Journey.** unabridged ed. R. Gates Condre. (Illus.). 190p. 2000. pap. 12.00 (*0-9679040-3-X*) Exlent Pubng.

Long Journey: Literary Themes of French Canada. Jack Warwick. LC 68-117293. (University of Toronto Romance Ser.: No. 12). 182p. reprint ed. pap. 56.50 (*0-8357-6404-4*, 203576400096) Bks Demand.

Long Journey: South Africa's Quest for a Negotiated Settlement. Ed. by Steven Friedman. (Illus.). 216p. (Orig.). (C). 1993. pap. text 24.95 (*0-86975-444-0*, Pub. by Ravan Pr) Ohio U Pr.

Long Journey: The Autobiography of Pitirim A. Sorokin. Pitirim A. Sorokin. 1963. 22.95 (*0-8084-0203-X*) NCUP.

***Long Journey Home.** (Illus.). 180p. 2000. pap. 16.95 (*1-930897-01-4*) Wings Pubs.

Long Journey Home. large type ed. Mary Raymond. (Linford Romance Library). 320p. 1985. pap. 16.99 (*0-7089-6071-5*, Linford) Ulverscroft.

Long Journey Home: A Chronicle of Travel & Adventure. W. Fleming Reeder. Ed. by Don Williams. LC 98-60379. (Illus.). 280p. 1998. pap. 19.95 (*1-888338-10-5*) New Messenger Bks.

Long Journey Home: A Story of Separation & the Search for Love. Richard J. Delaney. (Illus.). 48p. (J). (gr. 3-7). 1997. pap. 10.95 (*1-885473-14-1*) Wood N Barnes.

Long Journey Home: Stories from Black History. Julius Lester. LC 98-115427. 160p. (YA). (gr. 6 up). 1998. pap. 4.99 (*0-14-038981-4*, PuffinBks) Peng Put Young Read.

Long Journey Home: Stories from Black History. Julius Lester. (J). 1998. 10.09 (*0-606-12987-1*, Pub. by Turtleback) Demco.

***Long Journey Home: Stories from Black History.** Julius Lester. (YA). (gr. 6 up). 2000. 19.25 (*0-8446-7148-7*) Peter Smith.

Long Journey Home: The Bluegrass Chronicles of Les Leverett. Les Leverett. 96p. 1998. pap. text 12.95 (*1-880756-15-3*) Riverwood Pr.

Long Journey Home: The Memoirs of Flora Leipman. large type ed. Flora Leipman. (Illus.). 464p. 1988. 15.95 (*0-7089-1801-8*) Ulverscroft.

Long Journey Home: The Story of a Jew's Modern-Day Pilgrimage to Christ. R. Levin. LC 94-76014. xvii, 171 p. 1995. pap. 10.00 (*0-9640720-0-9*) My Fathrs Busn SC.

***Long Journey Home: The 1932 Motorcycle Voyage by Robert Fulton Jr.** Caitlin Fitzgerald. (Illus.). 2000. 35.00 (*0-9672484-1-8*) AGW Lithographers.

Long Journey into North, Vol. 65. Mary Kay Rummell. (Juniper Books Ser.). 78p. 1998. pap. 8.50 (*1-55780-153-3*) Juniper Pr ME.

Long Journey to Deep Canon: A Western Quartet. T. T. Flynn. LC 97-27720. 246p. 1997. lib. bdg. 17.95 (*0-7862-0751-5*) Five Star.

Long Journey to Deep Canon: A Western Quintet. large type ed. Flynn. LC 98-30794. 1999. 30.00 (*0-7862-0774-4*) Thorndike Pr.

Long Journey to the Country of the Hurons, Vol. 25. Gabriel Sagard-Theodat. Ed. by George M. Wrong. Tr. by H. H. Langton. LC 68-28613. 411p. 1969. reprint ed. lib. bdg. 65.00 (*0-8371-3861-2*, SAJC, Greenwood Pr) Greenwood.

Long Journey to the Rose Garden: The Adventures of an Italian-American Who Pulls Himself up by the Bootstraps. John Tursi & Thelma Palmer. LC 89-81123. (Illus.). 192p. (Orig.). 1990. pap. 11.95 (*0-9624646-0-0*) Fidalgo Bay.

Long Jump: And Other Olympic Themes. Joe G. Emerson. 112p. 1992. pap. 9.50 (*0-9633083-0-0*) Quixote Pubns.

Long Kill. Patrick Ruell. 256p. 1989. reprint ed. pap. 3.50 (*0-380-70742-X*, Avon Bks) Morrow Avon.

Long Knife. James A. Thom. 1994. mass mkt. 5.99 (*0-345-38074-6*) Ballantine Pub Grp.

Long Lake. John Todd. LC 97-20466. 100p. 1997. reprint ed. pap. 12.50 (*0-935796-88-6*) Purple Mnt Pr.

Long Lance. Chief Buffalo Child & Sylvester Long. LC 95-18985. 320p. 1995. lib. bdg. 45.00 (*0-87805-829-X*) U Pr of Miss.

Long Lance. Sylvester Long. LC 95-18985. 320p. 1995. pap. 16.95 (*0-87805-830-3*) U Pr of Miss.

Long Land. Budington Swanson. 1977. 13.00 (*0-931068-07-X*) Purcells.

Long Landscape. Paul Wilson. 144p. 1999. pap. 11.95 (*1-55050-147-X*, Pub. by Coteau) Genl Dist Srvs.

Long-Lasting Hanging Plants. Rhonda M. Hart. 1995. 2.95 (*0-88266-057-8*, Storey Pub) Storey Bks.

Long Lavender Look. John D. MacDonald. 1996. mass mkt. 5.99 (*0-449-22474-0*) Fawcett.

Long Lavender Look. John D. MacDonald. (Travis McGee Mystery Ser.). 1998. mass mkt. 5.99 (*0-449-45717-6*) Fawcett.

***Long, Lean & Lethal.** Heather Graham. 400p. 2000. mass mkt. 6.99 (*0-451-40915-9*, Onyx) NAL.

Long Leather Cord. Larry Townsend. (Orig.). 1994. mass mkt. 4.95 (*1-56333-201-9*, Badboy) Masquerade.

Long-Legged Fly. James Sallis. 208p. 1992. 17.95 (*0-88184-810-7*) Carroll & Graf.

Long-Legged Fly. James Sallis. 192p. 1994. mass mkt. 4.99 (*0-380-72242-9*, Avon Bks) Morrow Avon.

***Long-legged Mary-ann.** Simon. 2003. write for info. (*0-15-100586-9*) Harcourt.

Long-Legged Wading Birds of the North American Wetlands. Photos by Lucian Niemeyer. LC 92-28154. (Illus.). 224p. 1993. 49.95 (*0-8117-1889-1*) Stackpole.

Long Legs & Short Nights: A Flight Attendant Story. Marilyn Tritt. Tr. & Illus. by Linda Lampman. LC 94-90016. 190p. 1996. pap. 8.95 (*0-9649577-0-1*) Air Time.

Long Life & How to Reach It. Joseph G. Richardson. Ed. by Barbara G. Rosenkrantz. LC 76-40640. (Public Health in America Ser.). 1977. reprint ed. lib. bdg. 19.95 (*0-405-09828-6*) Ayer.

Long Life Cookbook: Delectable Recipes for Two. Anne Casale. (Illus.). 400p. 1991. pap. 12.50 (*0-345-37376-6*) Ballantine Pub Grp.

Long Life, Good Health Through Tai-Chi Chuan. Simmone Kuo. (Illus.). 134p. 1991. pap. 14.95 (*1-55643-111-2*) North Atlantic.

Long Life, Honey in the Heart: A Story of Initation & Eloquence from the Shores of a Mayan Lake. Martin Prechtel. LC 99-27247. (Illus.). 384p. 1999. 25.95 (*0-87477-994-4*, Tarcher Putnam) Putnam Pub Group.

Long Life in Florida. Hilton Hotema. 240p. 1996. reprint ed. pap. 18.50 (*0-7873-0438-7*) Hlth Research.

Long Life Now: Strategies for Staying Alive. Lee R. Hitchcox. LC 95-19693. (Illus.). 388p. (Orig.). 1996. pap. 15.95 (*0-89087-763-7*) Celestial Arts.

***Long Life Short Stories.** Katrina Croswell. 1999. pap. write for info. (*1-58235-006-X*) Watermrk Pr.

Long Life to Your Children! A Portrait of High Albania. Marjorie Senechal. LC 96-37827. (Illus.). 240p. 1997. pap. 21.95 (*1-55849-097-3*); text 40.00 (*1-55849-096-5*) U of Mass Pr.

Long Like a River. Nancy Schoenberger. LC 97-45348. 104p. 1998. pap. 12.95 (*0-8147-8104-7*); text 25.00 (*0-8147-8105-5*) NYU Pr.

Long Line of Dead Men: A Matthew Scudder Novel. Lawrence Block. (Matthew Scudder Mystery Ser.). 1996. mass mkt. 5.99 (*0-380-72024-8*, Avon Bks) Morrow Avon.

Long Line of Dead Men: A Matthew Scudder Novel. Lawrence Block. (Matthew Scudder Mystery Ser.). 304p. 1999. pap. 12.50 (*0-380-80604-5*, Avon Bks) Morrow Avon.

Long Line of Dead Men: A Matthew Scudder Novel. large type ed. Lawrence Block. LC 94-47382. (Cloak & Dagger Ser.). 479p. 1995. lib. bdg. 23.95 (*0-7862-0407-9*) Thorndike Pr.

Long Line of Splendor, 1742-1992: The Genealogy of a Regiment, the 116th Infantry, the Stonewall Brigade. John W. Schildt. (U. S. Military History Ser.). (Illus.). 288p. 1994. 35.00 (*0-936772-09-3*) Antietam.

Long Lines. Sutton. 1989. mass mkt. 3.95 (*0-445-40079-X*, Pub. by Warner Bks) Little.

***Long Live Disco!** 120p. 1999. otabind 12.95 (*0-634-00237-6*) H Leonard.

Long Live Man. Gregory Corso. LC 62-16927. (Orig.). 1962. pap. 8.95 (*0-8112-0025-6*, NDP127, Pub. by New Directions) Norton.

Long Live Mary, Queen of Scots. Stewart Ross. (Illus.). 62p. (J). (gr. 3-5). 1998. 15.95 (*0-237-51787-6*) EVN1 UK.

Long Live Rock 'n' Roll: The Transmission of the Beat, 1961-1991. Heylin. 1999. 25.00 (*0-02-864660-6*) Macmillan.

Long Live Sandawara. Mudrooroo. 208p. pap. 12.95 (*0-947062-01-7*) Hyland Hse.

Long Live the Hodag! The Life & Legacy of Eugene Simeon Shepard, 1854-1923. (Illus.). x, 152p. (Orig.). 1996. pap. 12.00 (*0-9653745-0-5*) Hodag Pr.

Long Live the King. Lyn Tornabene. 1981. pap. 3.50 (*0-671-43569-8*) PB.

Long Live the Spy. large type ed. Terence Kelly. 352p. 1992. 11.50 (*0-7089-2611-8*) Ulverscroft.

Long Live the Strong: A History of Rural Society in the Apennine Mountains. Roland Sarti. LC 84-16347. (Illus.). 296p. 1985. lib. bdg. 32.50 (*0-87023-466-8*) U of Mass Pr.

Long Live the 2 of Spades. Daniel Crocker. 63p. 1999. pap. 7.00 (*1-891408-10-0*, GBP-11) Green Bean.

Long Lived & Short Lived Animal Book. David Conrad Taylor. LC 95-6729. (Animal Opposites Ser.). (Illus.). 32p. (J). 1995. lib. bdg. 5.00 (*0-8172-3952-9*) Raintree Steck-V.

Long-Lived Radionuclide Chemistry in Nuclear Waste Treatment. NEA Staff. LC 98-222844. (OECD Proceedings Ser.). 272p. 1998. pap. 65.00 (*92-64-16148-1*, 6698131P) OECD.

Long-Lived States in Collisions. S. Danko Bosanac. 208p. 1988. 108.00 (*0-8493-6871-5*, QC794, CRC Reprint) Franklin.

Long Lives: Chinese Elderly & the Communist Revolution. 2nd ed. Deborah Davis-Friedmann. LC 89-64240. (Illus.). 190p. 1991. pap. 12.95 (*0-8047-1808-3*) Stanford U Pr.

Long Loneliness - Reissue. Dorothy Day. LC 81-4727. (Illus.). 304p. 1997. pap. 15.00 (*0-06-061751-9*, RD363, Pub. by Harper SF) HarpC.

Long Lonely Highway: A 1950's Elvis Scrapbook. Ger J. Rijff. Ed. by Thomas Schultheiss. (Rock & Roll Remembrances Ser.: No. 8). (Illus.). 200p. 1988. reprint ed. 28.50 (*0-87650-237-0*) Popular Culture.

Long Lonely Time: A Woman's Search for Justice. Edythe Robinson. (Illus.). 160p. (Orig.). 1990. pap. 8.95 (*0-936101-11-3*) RBH.

Long, Long Ago. Gary A. Smith. 0.50 (*0-687-50171-7*) Abingdon.

Long Long Ago. Sharon Warren. LC 94-96536. (Illus.). 192p. (Orig.). 1995. pap. text 10.00 (*0-9636074-2-1*) Imagic Unltd.

Long, Long Ago. Alexander Woollcott. reprint ed. lib. bdg. 23.95 (*0-89190-146-9*, Rivercity Pr) Amereon Ltd.

***Long, Long Ago, in Bethlehem the Birth of Jesus.** Carine MacKenzie. 1999. 12.99 (*1-85792-386-3*) Christian Focus.

Long, Long Autumn Nights: Selected Poems of Oguma Hideo, 1901-1940. Oguma Hideo. Tr. & Intro. by David G. Goodman. LC 89-15726. (Michigan Monographs in Japanese Studies: No. 3). (Illus.). x, 125p. 1989. 11.95 (*0-939512-39-4*) U MI Japan.

Long, Long Autumn Nights: Selected Poems of Oguma Hideo, 1901-1940. Oguma Hideo. Tr. & Intro. by David G. Goodman. (Michigan Monograph Series in Japanese Studies: Vol. 3). 124p. 1999. pap. 8.95 (*0-939512-94-7*) U MI Japan.

Long Long Dances. large type ed. Eric Malpass. 354p. 1982. 27.99 (*0-7089-0825-X*) Ulverscroft.

Long, Long Letter. Elizabeth Spurr. LC 95-8073. (Illus.). 32p. (J). (ps-3). 1996. lib. bdg. 14.89 (*0-7868-2100-0*, Pub. by Hyprn Child) Little.

Long Long Letter. Elizabeth Spurr. 1997. 11.15 (*0-606-13579-0*, Pub. by Turtleback) Demco.

Long, Long Letter. Elizabeth Spurr. LC 95-8073. (Illus.). 32p. (J). (ps-3). 1997. reprint ed. pap. 5.95 (*0-7868-1202-8*, Pub. by Hyprn Ppbks) Little.

Long, Long Love. Walter Sullivan. LC 99-31905. (Voices of the South Ser.). 232p. 1999. pap. 15.95 (*0-8071-2448-6*) La State U Pr.

Long Long Time Ago: Korean Folk Tales. Illus. by Dong-Sung Kim. LC 97-74945. 128p. (J). (gr. k-7). 1998. 22.95 (*1-56591-083-4*, Pub. by Hollym Bks) Weatherhill.

Long Look at Life: Prose & Poetry. Sonny Long. 84p. 1999. pap. 7.95 (*0-9671441-0-8*) Pine Country.

***Long Look at Life Vol. 2: The Collected Columns.** Sonny Long. 140p. 1999. pap. 9.95 (*0-9671441-1-6*) Pine Country.

Long Look Home. Jeanne W. Torosian. LC 83-80374. (Illus.). 96p. 1983. pap. 5.95 (*0-88100-030-2*) Natl Writ Pr.

Long Lost. Ramsey Campbell. 448p. 1996. mass mkt. 6.99 (*0-8125-5086-2*, Pub. by Tor Bks) St Martin.

***Long-Lost Bride.** large type ed. Day Leclaire. 1999. per. 3.50 (*0-373-15825-4*, Harlequin) Harlequin Bks.

***Long-Lost Bride.** large type ed. Day Leclaire. (Harlequin Romance Ser.). 2000. 22.95 (*0-263-16408-X*) Mills & Boon.

***Long-Lost Bride: Fairytale Weddings.** Day Leclaire. (Harlequin Romance Ser.). 1999. per. 3.50 (*0-373-03579-9*, Harlequin) Harlequin Bks.

Long-Lost Heir. Amanda Stevens. (Intrigue Ser.). 1998. per. 3.99 (*0-373-22462-1*, 1-22462-5) Harlequin Bks.

Long Lost Husband. Joleen Daniels. 1994. per. 2.75 (*0-373-19043-3*, 1-19043-8) Harlequin Bks.

Long-Lost Mom. Jill Shalvis. 1998. per. 4.25 (*0-373-07905-2*, 1-07905-2, Mira Bks) Harlequin Bks.

Long Lost Recipes: Of Aunt Susan. Patty V. MacDonald. (Illus.). 198p. 1989. 15.95 (*0-9624490-0-8*) P V MacDonald.

Long-Lost Wife? Barbara Faith. 1996. per. 3.99 (*0-373-07730-0*, 1-07730-4) Silhouette.

Long Loud Silence. Wilson A. Tucker. 1993. reprint ed. lib. bdg. 18.95 (*0-89968-375-4*, Lghtyr Pr) Buccaneer Bks.

Long Love: New & Collected Poems, 1957-1998. Patricia C. Lamb. LC 98-93640. 220p. 1998. 14.95 (*0-9615145-3-1*) Harbottle Pr.

Long Made Short. Stephen Dixon. LC 93-11174. (Poetry & Fiction Ser.). 160p. (C). 1993. text 32.50 (*0-8018-4738-9*) Johns Hopkins.

Long March. Don Lawson. (J). 1983. 12.95 (*0-690-04271-X*) HarpC Child Bks.

Long March. Michael Mullen. 182p. 1997. pap. 7.95 (*1-85371-890-4*, Pub. by Poolbeg Pr) Dufour.

***Long March.** Keith Spalding. 203p. 1999. pap. 45.00 (*1-85072-227-7*, Pub. by W Sessions) St Mut.

Long March: A Reform Agenda for Latin America & the Caribbean in the Next Decade. Shahid J. Burki & Guillermo E. Perry. LC 97-13357. (Latin American & Caribbean Studies). 132p. 1997. pap. 22.00 (*0-8213-3985-0*, 13985) World Bank.

Long March: A Reform Agenda for Latin America & the Caribbean in the Next Decade (Spanish) Shahid J. Burki & Guillermo E. Perry. (Latin American & Caribbean Studies). 148p. 1998. pap. 22.00 (*0-8213-4281-9*, 14281) World Bank.

Long March: And, In the Clap Shack. William Styron. LC 92-56371. 1993. reprint ed. pap. 14.00 (*0-679-73675-1*) Vin Bks.

Long March: How the Cultural Revolution of the 1960's Changed America. Roger Kimball. LC 00-22211. 320p. 2000. 23.95 (*1-893554-09-0*) Encounter Bks.

Long March: The Choctaw's Gift to Irish Famine Relief. Marie-Louise Fitzpatrick. (Illus.). 32p. (YA). (gr. 2-7). 1999. 14.95 (*1-883672-91-0*) Tricycle Pr.

Long March: The Lives of Frank & Alice Baldwin. Robert H. Steinbach. (Illus.). 243p. 1990. 24.95 (*0-292-74659-8*) U of Tex Pr.

Long March Diary: China Epic. Charlotte Y. Salisbury. 208p. 1986. 16.95 (*0-8027-0904-4*) Walker & Co.

Long March to Freedom. Thomas R. Hargrove. 1995. 23.00 (*0-345-40508-0*) Ballantine Pub Grp.

Long Memory: The Black Experience in America. Mary F. Berry & John W. Blassingame. LC 80-24748. (Illus.). 508p. 1982. pap. text 26.95 (*0-19-502910-0*) OUP.

***Long Mournful Winter Has Turned into Spring.** Gerald J. Williams. LC 99-90642. 238p. 1999. pap. 9.95 (*1-57921-238-7*) WinePress Pub.

Long Narrow Strip of Land. Woodlief Brown. (Illus.). 97p. 1998. lib. bdg. 24.95 (*0-9670760-0-5*) H V Chapman.

Long Night. Poul Anderson. 1999. pap. 3.50 (*0-8125-1396-7*, Pub. by Tor Bks) St Martin.

Long Night. P. B. Gallagher. (Orig.). 1979. mass mkt. 2.25 (*0-685-96934-7*, Zebra Kensgtn) Kensgtn Pub Corp.

Long Night. David Perry. (Vampire: The Dark Ages). (Illus.). (Orig.). 1997. pap. 10.95 (*1-56504-509-2*, 5008) White Wolf.

Long Night. Dean Smith. (Star Trek: No. 14). 1996. mass mkt. 5.99 (*0-671-55165-5*) PB.

Long Night. large type ed. Hartley Howard. (Linford Mystery Library). 448p. 1997. pap. 16.99 (*0-7089-5098-1*, Linford) Ulverscroft.

Long Night. Andrew Lytle. LC 88-12101. (Library of Alabama Classics). 336p. 1988. reprint ed. pap. 14.95 (*0-8173-0415-0*) U of Ala Pr.

Long Night. rev. ed. Lowell D. Blanton. (Read-along Radio Dramas Ser.). (J). (gr. 6-9). 1984. ring bd. 38.00 (*1-878298-08-9*) Balance Pub.

Long Night Ahead: Poems & Art from the Line Club. Ed. by Lee Sharkey. 60p. 1992. pap. 8.95 (*0-9632651-0-5*) Borealis Pr.

Long Night of the Grave. Charles L. Grant. (Illus.). 1986. 20.00 (*0-937986-88-7*) D M Grant.

Long Night of White Chickens. Francisco Goldman. 472p. 1998. pap. text 13.00 (*0-8021-3547-1*, Grove) Grove-Atltic.

Long Night's Journey into Day: A Revised Retrospective on the Holocaust. rev. ed. Alice L. Eckardt & A. Roy Eckardt. LC 88-10668. 278p. (C). 1988. 39.95 (*0-8143-2085-6*); pap. 19.95 (*0-8143-2086-4*) Wayne St U Pr.

Long Night's Loving. Anne Mather. (Presents Ser.: No. 1887). 1997. per. 3.50 (*0-373-11887-2*, 1-11887-6) Harlequin Bks.

Long Night's Loving. large type ed. Anne Mather. (Harlequin Ser.). 1997. 20.95 (*0-263-15294-4*) Thorndike Pr.

Long Nineteenth Century: A History of Germany, 1780-1918. David Blackbourn. LC 97-29535. (Illus.). 624p. 1998. pap. 24.95 (*0-19-507672-9*); text 60.00 (*0-19-507671-0*) OUP.

Long-Nosed Pig: A Pop-Up Book. Keith Faulkner. LC 97-11311. (Illus.). 16p. (J). 1998. 12.99 (*0-8037-2296-6*, Dial Yng Read) Peng Put Young Read.

Long Obedience in the Same Direction. Eugene H. Peterson. LC 79-2715. 192p. (Orig.). 1980. pap. 11.99 (*0-87784-727-4*, 727) InterVarsity.

***Long Obedience in the Same Direction: Discipleship in an Instant Society.** Eugene H. Peterson. 128p. 2000. pap. 7.99 (*0-8308-2039-6*) InterVarsity.

***Long Obedience in the Same Direction: Discipleship in an Instant Society.** 20th anniversary ed. Eugene H. Peterson. 204p. 2000. 16.99 (*0-8308-2277-1*); pap. 11.99 (*0-8308-2257-7*) InterVarsity.

***Long Odds: Stories.** Gordon Weaver. 200p. 2000. pap. 17.95 (*0-8262-1291-3*) U of Mo Pr.

Long Ones. Joe R. Lansdale. 1999. write for info. (*1-889186-15-5*) Necro Publns.

Long Pale Corridor: Contemporary Poems of Bereavement. Ed. by Judi Benson & Agneta Falk. 320p. 1996. pap. 18.95 (*1-85224-317-1*, Pub. by Bloodaxe Bks) Dufour.

Long Path: The Search for a Tennessee Bicentennial Landmark. Kem G. Hinton. LC 97-23353. (Illus.). 224p. 1997. 49.95 (*1-57736-028-1*, Hillsboro Pr) Providence Hse.

L

L

Long Path to Nearness: A Contribution to a Corporeal Philosophy of Communication & the Groundwork for an Ethics of Relief. Ramsey E. Ramsey. LC 97-9253. 160p. 1997. 49.95 (*0-391-04048-0*) Humanities.

Long Path to Nearness: A Contribution to a Corporeal Philosophy of Communication & the Groundwork for an Ethics of Relief. Ramsey E. Ramsey. 160p. 1999. 49.95 (*1-57392-450-4*, Humanity Bks) Prometheus Bks.

Long Patrol. Brian Jacques. LC PZ7.J15317Lo 1997. (Redwall Ser.). (Illus.). 368p. (J). (gr. 4-8). 1998. 21.99 (*0-399-23165-X*, Philomel) Peng Put Young Read.

Long Patrol. Brian Jacques. (Redwall Ser.). (Illus.). 318p. (J). (gr. 4-7). 1999. reprint ed. pap. 5.99 (*0-441-00599-3*) Ace Bks.

Long Peace: Inquiries into the History of the Cold War. John L. Gaddis. 352p. 1989. reprint ed. pap. text 14.95 (*0-19-504335-9*) OUP.

Long Peace: Ottoman Lebanon, 1861-1920. Engin D. Akarli. LC 92-18987. 1993. 55.00 (*0-520-08014-9*, Pub. by U CA Pr) Cal Prin Full Svc.

Long-Period Global Variations of Incoming Solar Radiation. Anandu D. Vernekar. (Meteorological Monograph: Vol. 12, No. 34). (Illus.). 128p. 1972. 25.00 (*0-933876-37-8*) Am Meteorological.

Long Pig. Jon S. Fink. 324p. 1996. pap. 19.95 (*0-224-04081-2*, Pub. by Jonathan Cape) Trafalgar.

Long Point: Last Port of Call. Dave Stone. (Illus.). 144p. 1998. pap. 7.95 (*1-55046-079-X*, Pub. by Boston Mills) Genl Dist Srvs.

Long Polar Watch: Canada & the Defence of North America. Melvin Conant. LC 62-14889. 216p. reprint ed. pap. 67.00 (*0-608-30730-0*, 200215100012) Bks Demand.

Long Preparation Course Toefl Test with Answers. Phillips. 1997. 27.19 (*0-201-31521-1*) Addison-Wesley.

Long Pretense: Soviet Treaty Diplomacy from Lenin to Gorbachev. Arnold Beichman. 296p. (C). 1990. 39.95 (*0-88738-360-2*) Transaction Pubs.

***Long Program: Skating Toward Life's Victories.** Peggy Fleming & Peter Kaminsky. 272p. 1999. 24.95 (*0-671-03886-9*, PB Hardcover) PB.

***Long Program: Skating Toward Life's Victories.** Peggy Fleming & Peter Kaminsky. 224p. 2000. 13.95 (*0-671-03887-7*) PB.

Long Pull from Stavanger: The Reminiscences of a Norwegian Immigrant. Birger Osland. 263p. 1945. 15.00 (*0-87732-027-6*) Norwegian-Am Hist Assn.

Long QT Syndrome. Ed. by Peter J. Schwartz. LC 97-16499. (Clinical Approaches to Tachyarrhythmias Ser.: No. 7). (Illus.). 120p. 1997. 24.00 (*0-87993-680-0*) Futura Pub.

Long Quiet Highway: Waking up in America. Natalie Goldberg. 256p. 1994. pap. 13.95 (*0-553-37315-3*) Bantam.

Long Rain. Peter Gadol. LC 97-15662. 320p. 1997. text 23.00 (*0-312-15571-9*, Picador USA) St Martin.

***Long Rain.** Peter Gadol. 304p. 2000. pap. 13.00 (*0-312-26354-6*) St Martin.

Long Rain, Vol. 1. Peter Gadol. Vol. 1. 1998. pap. 6.99 (*0-312-96638-5*, Pub. by Tor Bks) St Martin.

Long Rainy Season: Haiku & Tanka. Ed. by Akemi Tomioka et al. LC 94-28749. (Contemporary Japanese Women's Poetry Ser.: Vol. 1). (Illus.). 200p. (Orig.). 1994. pap. 12.00 (*1-880656-15-9*) Stone Bridge Pr.

Long-Range Atmospheric Transport of Natural & Contaminant Substances: Proceedings of the NATO Advanced Research Workshop on "The Long-Range Atmospheric Transport of Natural & Contaminant Substances from Continent to Ocean & Continent to Continent" Held in St. Georges, Bermuda, January 10-17, 1988. Ed. by Anthony H. Knap & Mary-Scott Kaiser. (C). 1990. text 191.50 (*0-7923-0577-9*) Kluwer Academic.

Long-Range Casimir Forces: Theory & Recent Experiments on Atomic Systems. F. S. Levin & D. A. Micha. (Finite Systems & Multiparticle Dynamics Ser.: Vol. 1). (Illus.). 374p. (C). 1993. text 85.00 (*0-306-44385-6*, Kluwer Plenum) Kluwer Academic.

Long-Range Correlations in Astrophysical Systems Vol. 848: Annals of the New York Academy of Sciences. Ed. by J. Robert Buchler et al. LC 98-13137. 143p. 1998. 80.00 (*1-57331-112-X*); pap. 80.00 (*1-57331-113-8*) NY Acad Sci.

***Long-Range Dependence: Theory & Applications.** Paul Doukhan. (Illus.). 2000. 64.95 (*0-8176-4168-8*) Birkhauser.

***Long Range Desert Group.** W. B. Kennedy Shaw. (Military Paperbacks Ser.). 2000. pap. 18.95 (*1-85367-407-9*) Greenhill Bks.

Long Range Desert Group in the Mediterranean. R. L. kay. (World War II Monograph Ser.: No. 6). (Illus.). 38p. 1998. 19.50 (*1-57638-138-2*, M6-H); pap. 9.50 (*1-57638-137-4*, M6-S) Merriam Pr.

Long Range Desert Group 1940-1945, 32. Robin Jenner. 1999. pap. text 12.95 (*1-85532-958-1*) Ospry.

Long Range Deserter. large type ed. David Bingley. (Linford Mystery Library). 400p. 1997. pap. 16.99 (*0-7089-5100-7*, Linford) Ulverscroft.

Long-Range Effects of Early Childhood Sexual Experiences. Allie Kilpatrick. 224p. 1992. pap. 27.50 (*0-8058-0914-7*); text 49.95 (*0-8058-0913-9*) L Erlbaum Assocs.

Long Range Exploration Planning: A Guide to Preparing Goals, Strategies, & Action Plans. Robert E. Megill. 96p. 1985. 15.00 (*0-87814-286-X*, P4408) PennWell Bks.

***Long-Range Information Technology Plans: Strategies for the Future.** ICMA Staff. 184p. 1998. pap. 36.00i (*0-87326-163-1*) Intl City-Cnty Mgt.

Long Range Plan for the Federal Courts. Ed. by L. Ralph Mecham. 205p. (C). 1998. pap. text 35.00 (*0-7881-7159-3*) DIANE Pub.

Long Range Planning. Didactic Systems Staff. (Simulation Game Ser.). 1971. pap. 26.25 (*0-89401-049-2*) Didactic Syst.

Long Range Planning: A How-to-Do-It Manual for Public Libraries. Suzanne W. Bremer & Susan M. Palmatier. LC 94-5841. 109p. 1994. pap. 45.00 (*1-55570-162-0*) Neal-Schuman.

Long Range Planning Cumulative Index, Vols. 1-17. Ed. by B. Taylor. 1986. pap. 28.00 (*0-08-032664-1*, Pub. by PPL) Elsevier.

Long Range Planning Cumulative Index, Vols. 1-22. Ed. by B. Taylor. 80p. 1991. 145.25 (*0-08-040795-1*, Pergamon Pr) Elsevier.

Long-Range Planning for Your Business: An Operating Manual. Merritt L. Kastens. LC 75-41378. 172p. reprint ed. pap. 53.40 (*0-7837-4239-8*, 204392800012) Bks Demand.

Long Range Planning Manual for Board Members. Struck. 1996. 26.00 (*0-8342-0416-9*) Aspen Pub.

Long-Range Planning of Japanese Corporations. Toyohiro Kono. LC 92-18407. (Studies in Organization: No. 37). xiv, 390p. (C). 1992. pap. text 29.95 (*3-11-013793-3*); lib. bdg. 72.95 (*3-11-012914-0*) De Gruyter.

Long-Range Surveillance Unit Operations. 1990. lib. bdg. 79.95 (*0-8490-3986-X*) Gordon Pr.

Long-Range Surveillance Unit Operations. 1991. lib. bdg. 79.95 (*0-8490-4093-0*) Gordon Pr.

Long-Range Surveillance Unit Operations. 104p. 1990. pap. 14.00 (*0-87364-540-5*) Paladin Pr.

Long Range Transport of Pesticides. Ed. by David A. Kurtz. (Illus.). 480p. 1990. lib. bdg. 99.95 (*0-87371-168-8*, L168) Lewis Pubs.

Long-Range War: Sniping in Vietnam. Peter R. Senich. (Illus.). 268p. 1994. text 44.95 (*0-87364-789-0*) Paladin Pr.

Long-Range World Population Projections: Two Centuries of Population Growth. (Population Studies: No. 125). 35p. 1992. pap. 10.00 (*92-1-151241-7*, E.92.XIII.3) UN.

Long Reach. Susan Davis. LC 92-50343. 208p. (Orig.). 1993. pap. 12.95 (*0-936609-27-3*) QED Ft Bragg.

Long Reach. Michael Stone. LC 96-21141. 225p. 1998. pap. 5.99 (*0-14-024703-3*) Viking Penguin.

Long Reach. large type ed. Michael Stone. (Niagara Large Print Ser.). 320p. 1997. 29.50 (*0-7089-5875-3*) Ulverscroft.

Long Reach: New & Uncollected Poems, 1948-1984. Richard Eberhart. LC 83-23746. 240p. 1984. 17.95 (*0-8112-0885-0*, Pub. by New Directions); pap. 8.95 (*0-8112-0886-9*, NDP565, Pub. by New Directions) Norton.

Long Recess. Shirley T. Cicholas. LC 82-24389. 223p. 1985. 13.95 (*0-87949-235-X*) Ashley Bks.

Long Red Herring. Pat Cook. LC 94-226409. 1994. 5.50 (*0-87129-336-6*, L78) Dramatic Pub.

Long Red Sign. Dewitt L. Edenfield. 216p. mass mkt. 4.99 (*1-55197-170-4*) Picasso Publ.

Long Reinforced Concrete Columns. Reinforced Concrete Research Council Staff. (Bulletin Ser.: No. 21). 250p. 1986. 5.00 (*0-87262-537-0*) Am Soc Civil Eng.

***Long Remember.** Kantor. 416p. 2000. pap. 24.95 (*0-312-86552-X*) Forge NYC.

***Long Remember.** MacKinlay Kantor. 416p. 2000. pap. 14.95 (*0-312-87520-7*, Pub. by Forge NYC) St Martin.

Long Remember. Mackinlay Dantor. 1993. reprint ed. lib. bdg. 89.00 (*0-7812-5475-2*) Rprt Serv.

Long Remembered: Favorite Narrative Poems. large type ed. (General Ser.). 256p. 1992. 19.95 (*0-8161-5567-4*, G K Hall Lrg Type) Mac Lib Ref.

Long Rest. large type ed. Basil Copper. LC 94-12705. 221p. 1994. lib. bdg. 16.95 (*0-8161-7421-0*, G K Hall Lrg Type) Mac Lib Ref.

Long Retreat: The Calamitous Defense of New Jersey, 1776. Arthur S. Lefkowitz. LC 99-29035. 190p. 1999. text 25.00 (*0-8135-2759-7*) Rutgers U Pr.

Long Revolution. Raymond Williams. LC 75-16613. 369p. 1975. reprint ed. lib. bdg. 35.00 (*0-8371-8244-1*, WILR, Greenwood Pr) Greenwood.

Long Ride. Mary Bell. 250p. 2000. otabind 10.95 (*0-9653572-2-8*) Dry Store.

Long Ride. Bonnie Bryant. (Pine Hollow Ser.: No. 1). 192p. (YA). (gr. 5-9). 1998. mass mkt. 4.50 (*0-553-49242-X*) BDD Bks Young Read.

Long Ride Cookbook: Lighten Your Load & Take the Stress Out of Wilderness Cooking. Mary T. Bell & Judith Lynch. (Illus.). 150p. 2000. otabind 14.95 (*0-9653572-3-6*) Dry Store.

Long Ride Home. W. Michael Gear. 1991. mass mkt. 4.99 (*0-8125-1392-4*, Pub. by Tor Bks) St Martin.

Long Ride Home. Louis L'Amour. 192p. 1998. mass mkt. 4.50 (*0-553-28181-X*) Bantam.

Long Ride Home. Louis L'Amour. 1989. 9.09 (*0-606-01765-8*, Pub. by Turtleback) Demco.

Long Ride Home. large type ed. Louis L'Amour. LC 96-36267. 228p. 1998. 25.95 (*0-7838-1954-4*, G K Hall Lrg Type) Mac Lib Ref.

Long Ride in Texas: The Explorations of John Leonard Riddell. Ed. & Intro. by James O. Breeden. LC 93-27569. (Centennial Series of the Association of Former Students: No. 51). (Illus.). 136p. 1994. 25.95 (*0-89096-582-X*) Tex A&M Univ Pr.

Long Riders. large type ed. Dan Cushman. (Linford Western Library). 304p. 1995. pap. 16.99 (*0-7089-7697-2*, Linford) Ulverscroft.

Long Rides & Lucky Shots: Twenty-One Long Horseback Rides & Twenty One Lucky Shots. Fred N. Kimmel. LC 99-71094. 251p. 1999. pap. 19.95 (*0-9661115-2-4*) Zantanon Pr.

Long-Riding Man. large type ed. Clayton Nash. (Linford Western Large Print Ser.). 256p. 1998. pap. 17.99 (*0-7089-5272-0*, Linford) Ulverscroft.

Long Rifle. S. E. White. (Illus.). 544p. 1987. reprint ed. 25.00 (*0-935632-54-9*) Wolfe Pub Co.

Long Rifle. Stewart E. White. reprint ed. lib. bdg. 25.95 (*0-88411-885-1*) Amereon Ltd.

Long River: A Novel. Joseph Bruchac. 320p. 1995. 19.95 (*1-55591-213-3*) Fulcrum Pub.

***Long River Waltzes.** Michael J. Caduto. 20p. 2000. pap. 15.00 (*0-9670141-3-1*) LunaBlu.

Long Road. Fernando Galan. (Literacy Volunteers of America Readers Ser.). 32p. (Orig.). 1988. pap. text 3.00 (*0-8428-9604-X*) Cambridge Bk.

Long Road. Luis Garay. (Illus.). 32p. (J). (gr. 1-3). 1997. 15.95 (*0-88776-408-8*) Tundra Bks.

Long Road. Arthur E. Morgan. 1962. 3.50 (*0-910420-08-4*); pap. 2.50 (*0-910420-09-2*) Comm Serv OH.

Long Road. large type ed. Mary Minton. (Magna Large Print Ser.). 469p. 1997. 27.99 (*0-7505-0894-9*) Ulverscroft.

Long Road: From Oran to Pilsen. Ed. by Richard D. Wissolik et al. LC 99-10637. (Joe & Henny Heisel Ser.: No. VII). (Illus.). 416p. 1999. 40.00 (*1-885851-13-8*) St Vincent Coll.

Long Road Back: A Survivors Guide to Anorexia. Judy Tam Sargent. 208p. 1999. 23.95 (*1-880823-19-5*) N Star Pubns.

***Long Road Called Goodbye.** Charlotte A. Akin. (Illus.). 340p. 2000. 25.00 (*1-881871-33-9*, Pub. by Creighton U Pr); pap. write for info. (*1-881871-34-7*, Pub. by Creighton U Pr) BookMasters.

Long Road for Home: The Civil War Experiences of Four Farmboy Soldiers of the Twenty-Seventh Massachusetts Regiment of Volunteer Infantry as Told by Their Personal Correspondence, 1861-1864. Ed. by Henry C. Lind. LC 91-58579. (Illus.). 216p. (C). 1992. 36.50 (*0-8386-3464-8*) Fairleigh Dickinson.

Long Road Home. Danielle Steel. LC 97-37444. 408p. 1998. 25.95 (*0-385-31956-8*) Delacorte.

Long Road Home. Danielle Steel. LC 97-37444. 1998. 25.95 (*0-385-33285-8*) Delacorte.

Long Road Home. Danielle Steel. 448p. 1999. mass mkt. 7.99 (*0-440-22483-7*) Dell.

Long Road Home. aut. limited ed. Danielle Steel. 408p. 1998. 200.00 (*0-385-32410-3*) Delacorte.

Long Road Home. large type ed. Danielle Steel. LC 97-37444. 1998. 29.95 (*0-385-31992-4*) Delacorte.

Long Road Home. Lori Wick. (Place Called Home Ser.). 190p. 1997. reprint ed. pap. 8.99 (*1-56507-590-0*) Harvest Hse.

Long Road Home: A China Journal. Vera Schwarcz. LC 83-16657. (National Association of Baptist Professors of Religion Dissertion Ser.: No. 4). 284p. 1984. 42.50 (*0-300-03009-6*) Yale U Pr.

Long Road Home: An Autobiography. John Moody. LC 75-2650. (Wall Street & the Security Market Ser.). 1975. reprint ed. 25.95 (*0-405-06975-8*) Ayer.

Long Road Home: The Autobiography of a Canadian Soldier in Italy in World War II. Fred Cederberg. LC 99-203982. (Illus.). 257p. 1985. pap. 13.95 (*0-7737-5050-9*) Genl Dist Srvs.

***Long Road Home: The Autobiography of a Canadian Soldier in Italy in World War II.** Fred Cederberg. (Illus.). 262p. 2000. pap. 19.95 (*0-7737-6105-5*) Stoddart Publ.

Long Road of War: A Marine's Story of Pacific Combat. James W. Johnston. LC 97-23894. (Illus.). 178p. 2000. pap. 11.95 (*0-8032-7612-5*, Bison Books) U of Nebr Pr.

***Long Road South: The Pan American Highway.** Joseph R. Yogerst et al. LC 99-51315. 1999. write for info. (*0-7922-7844-5*) Natl Geog.

Long Road to a European Monetary Union. Sima Lieberman. 222p. (Orig.). (C). 1992. pap. text 26.50 (*0-8191-8591-4*); lib. bdg. 48.50 (*0-8191-8590-6*) U Pr of Amer.

Long Road to Boston. Bruce W. Tuckman. 176p. (Orig.). 1987. pap. 12.95 (*0-915297-04-3*) Cedarwinds.

Long Road to Dakota. Ardath Ewing. 97p. 1991. pap. 6.95 (*0-9630264-0-2*) A Ewing.

Long Road to Delano. Sam Kushner. LC 74-30123. 240p. reprint ed. pap. 74.40 (*0-608-12013-8*, 202286500030) Bks Demand.

Long Road to Freedom. large type ed. Ginette Spanier. 272p. 1990. 23.95 (*0-7451-1170-X*, G K Hall Lrg Type) Mac Lib Ref.

Long Road to Freedom: The Advocate History of the Gay & Lesbian Movement. Ed. by Mark Thompson. LC 95-5498. (Stonewall Inn Editions Ser.). 1995. pap. 24.95 (*0-312-13114-3*, Stonewall Inn) St Martin.

***Long Road to Gettysberg.** Jim Murphy. (Illus.). 128p. (J). (gr. 4-7). 2000. pap. 7.95 (*0-618-05157-0*, Clarion Bks) HM.

Long Road to Gettysburg. Jim Murphy. (Illus.). 128p. (J). (gr. 4-7). 1992. 17.00 (*0-395-55965-0*, Clarion Bks) HM.

Long Road to Recovery: Community Responses to Industrial Disaster. J. K. Mitchell. 313p. 30.00 (*92-808-0926-1*, UNUP-926) UN.

Long Road to Reform: Restructuring Public Education in Quebec. Henry Milner. 192p. (C). 1986. text 60.00 (*0-7735-0563-6*, Pub. by McG-Queens Univ Pr); pap. text 27.95 (*0-7735-0564-4*, Pub. by McG-Queens Univ Pr) CUP Services.

Long Road to Revolution: The Hungarian Gulag, 1945-1956. Istvan Fehervary et al. Ed. by Krisztina Fehervary. Tr. by Zsuzsa Gorka et al from HUN. LC 89-63286. (Illus.). 228p. (Orig.). 1990. 20.00 (*0-9622049-2-7*); pap. 12.95 (*0-9622049-3-5*) Pro Libertate Pub.

Long Road Turns to Joy: A Guide to Walking Meditation. Thich Nhat Hanh. Orig. Title: A Guide to Walking Meditation. (Illus.). 84p. (Orig.). 1996. pap. 8.00 (*0-938077-83-X*) Parallax Pr.

Long Roads, Short Distances: Teaching Writing & Writing Teachers. Brenda M. Power. LC 97-14455. 1997. pap. text 17.50 (*0-435-07240-4*) Heinemann.

Long Roll. Mary Johnston. 702p. Date not set. 37.95 (*0-8488-2343-5*) Amereon Ltd.

Long Roll. Mary Johnston. 204p. 1996. reprint ed. pap. 15.95 (*0-8018-5524-1*) Johns Hopkins.

Long Roll: Impressions of a Civil War Soldier. Charles Johnson. LC 86-4153. (Illus.). 298p. 1986. reprint ed. 19.95 (*0-938634-08-9*) Carabelle.

Long Roll on the Rhine: A Study of Hitler's Germany. E. Alexander Powell. 1976. 250.00 (*0-8490-2183-9*) Gordon Pr.

Long Routes: Mountaineering Rock Climbs in Snowdonia & the Lake District. Robin Ashcroft. 224p. 1998. pap. 29.95 (*1-85158-910-4*, Pub. by Mainstream Pubng) Trafalgar.

Long Row to Hoe. limited rev. ed. Billy C. Clark. Ed. by James M. Gifford. LC 91-40399. (Illus.). 285p. (YA). (gr. 6 up). 1992. reprint ed. 30.00 (*0-945084-28-5*) J Stuart Found.

Long Row to Hoe. rev. ed. Billy C. Clark. Ed. by James M. Gifford. LC 91-40399. (Illus.). 285p. 1992. reprint ed. 22.00 (*0-945084-27-7*) J Stuart Found.

Long Run. Joe Henderson. LC 75-20958. (Illus.). 1978. pap. 5.95 (*0-89037-101-6*); student ed. 7.95 (*0-89037-102-4*) Anderson World.

Long Run. large type ed. Ted Allbeury. LC 96-48664. 1997. lib. bdg. 22.95 (*0-7838-8041-3*, G K Hall Lrg Type) Mac Lib Ref.

Long Run: The Story of the Eagles. Marc Shapiro. (Illus.). 192p. (Orig.). 1995. pap. 21.95 (*0-7119-4817-8*, OP 47749, Pub. by Omnibus Press) Omnibus NY.

Long-Run Availability of Phosphorus: A Case Study in Mineral Resource Analysis. Frederick J. Wells. LC 74-6842. 144p. reprint ed. pap. 44.70 (*0-608-11247-X*, 202095200020) Bks Demand.

Long-Run Determination of the United Kingdom Monetary Aggregates. S. G. Hall et al. LC HG2937.. (Bank of England - Discussion Papers: No. 41). 46p. 1989. reprint ed. pap. 30.00 (*0-608-03149-6*, 206360200007) Bks Demand.

Long Run Economic Growth. 1996. text 79.95 (*3-7908-0959-4*) Spr-Verlag.

Long Run Economic Relations. R. F. Engle. (Illus.). 308p. 1992. pap. text 32.00 (*0-19-828339-3*) OUP.

Long-Run Economics: An Evolutionary Approach to Economic Growth. Norman Clark & Calestous Juma. 230p. 1992. pap. text 19.50 (*1-85567-062-3*) St Martin.

Long-Run Economics: An Evolutionary Approach to Economics. Norman Clark & Calestous Juma. 230p. 1992. 49.00 (*0-86187-903-1*) St Martin.

Long-Run Florida Processed Orange Outlook, 1993-94 Through 2002-03. (Illus.). 47p. (Orig.). (C). 1994. pap. text 30.00 (*0-7881-0351-2*) DIANE Pub.

Long Run of Myles Mayberry. Alfred Alcorn. LC 98-54296. (Illus.). 240p. 1999. pap. 13.00 (*1-58195-001-2*, Pub. by Zoland Bks) Consort Bk Sales.

Long-Run of New Reserves of Crude Oil in the U. S., 1966-1973. Abdallah R. Bouhabib. Ed. by Stuart Bruchey. LC 78-22665. (Energy in the American Economy Ser.). (Illus.). 1979. lib. bdg. 19.95 (*0-405-11968-2*) Ayer.

Long Sandy Hair of Neftoon Zamora. Michael Nesmith. LC 98-19510. 256p. 1998. 24.95 (*0-312-19296-7*, Thomas Dunne) St Martin.

Long Schoolroom: Lessons in the Bitter Logic of the Poetic Principle. Allen Grossman. LC 96-29634. 224p. (C). 1997. pap. 13.95 (*0-472-06637-4*, 06637); text 39.50 (*0-472-09637-0*, 09637) U of Mich Pr.

Long Sea Outfalls. Institution of Civil Engineers Staff. 230p. 1989. text 57.75 (*0-7277-1516-X*, Pub. by T Telford) RCH.

Long Search. Khurram Murad. 44p. (J). 1996. pap. 3.50 (*0-614-21023-2*, 733) Kazi Pubns.

Long Search. large type ed. Isabelle Holland. LC 90-29875. 406p. 1991. reprint ed. lib. bdg. 18.95 (*1-56054-127-X*) Thorndike Pr.

Long Season. Sam Brown. 1987. 16.95 (*0-8027-4073-1*) Walker & Co.

Long Season. James Brosnan. 1981. reprint ed. 19.95 (*0-941372-01-4*) Holtzman Pr.

Long Season. Sam Brown. Ed. by Doug Grad. 256p. 1994. reprint ed. mass mkt. 4.50 (*0-671-67186-3*) PB.

Long Season of Rain. Helen S. Kim. 1997. mass mkt. 4.50 (*0-449-70462-9*, Juniper) Fawcett.

Long Season of Rain. Helen S. Kim. LC 96-16597. 224p. (YA). (gr. 7 up). 1995. 15.95 (*0-8050-4758-1*, B Martin BYR) H Holt & Co.

Long Secret. Louise Fitzhugh. LC 65-23370. (Illus.). (YA). (gr. 5 up). 1965. 15.00 (*0-06-021410-4*) HarpC Child Bks.

Long Secret. Louise Fitzhugh. LC 65-23370. (Trophy Bk.). (Illus.). 288p. (J). (gr. 3-7). 1990. pap. 4.95 (*0-06-440332-7*, HarpTrophy) HarpC Child Bks.

Long Secret. Louise Fitzhugh. (J). 1965. 10.05 (*0-606-04469-8*, Pub. by Turtleback) Demco.

***Long Shadow.** large type ed. 1999. pap. 24.95 (*0-7862-2091-0*) Mac Lib Ref.

Long Shadow: Culture & Politics in the Middle East. Daniel Pipes. 320p. 1988. pap. 39.95 (*0-88738-220-7*) Transaction Pubs.

Long Shadow: Culture & Politics in the Middle East. Daniel Pipes. 320p. (C). 1990. pap. 24.95 (*0-88738-849-3*) Transaction Pubs.

Long Shadow: Emily Dickinson's Tragic Poetry. Clark Griffith. LC 63-16234. 318p. reprint ed. pap. 98.60 (*0-608-10696-8*, 200098800053) Bks Demand.

An Asterisk (*) at the beginning of an entry indicates that the title is appearing for the first time.

Long Shadow: Jefferson Davis & the Final Days of the Confederacy. Michael B. Ballard. LC 97-6957. 1997. pap. 15.95 (*0-8203-1941-4*) U of Ga Pr.

Long Shadow of Little Rock. Daisy Bates. LC 86-19129. 260p. 1987. reprint ed. pap. 16.00 (*0-938626-75-2*) U of Ark Pr.

Long-Shadowed Forest. Helen Hoover. 1998. pap. 14.95 (*0-8166-3172-7*) U of Minn Pr.

Long Shadows: Indian Leaders Standing in the Path of Manifest Destiny, 1600-1900. Jack Jackson. (Illus.). 128p. 1985. 17.95 (*0-942376-07-2*) Paramount TX.

Long Shadows: Stories. Marie L. Kaschnitz. Tr. & Intro. by Anni Whissen. LC 94-24281. (GERM Ser.). xvi, 150p. 1995. 45.00 (*1-57113-021-7*) Camden Hse.

Long Ships. Frans Bengtsson. 414p. 1992. reprint ed. lib. bdg. 35.95 (*0-89966-934-4*) Buccaneer Bks.

Long Shmooze: Everything the Gate Keepers to Hollywood Don't Have Time to Tell You... Again!! Judy Belshe. (Illus.). 461p. 1998. spiral bd., wbk. ed. 30.00 (*0-9655530-1-9*) J Belshe.

Long Shot. Michelle Martin. 336p. 1998. mass mkt. 5.50 (*0-553-57650-X*) Bantam.

Long Shot. Paul Monette. 328p. 1988. reprint ed. pap. 14.95 (*0-8216-2004-5*) Carol Pub Group.

Long Shot for Paul. Matt Christopher. 155p. (J). (gr. 3-7). 1990. pap. 3.95 (*0-316-14244-1*) Little.

Long Shot for Paul. Matt Christopher. (J). 1966. 9.05 (*0-606-04732-8*, Pub. by Turtleback) Demco.

Long Shots from the Flatlands. Richard Wiman. (Illus.). 240p. 1995. 19.95 (*0-9648701-0-X*) Greasy Bayou.

Long Siesta. large type ed. David Horsley. (Dales Large Print Ser.). 256p. 1996. pap. 18.99 (*1-85389-653-5*, Dales) Ulverscroft.

Long Sigh the Wind Makes: Poems by William Stafford. William Stafford. (Illus.). 62p. (Orig.). 1991. pap. 15.00 (*0-9629194-0-3*) Adrienne Lee.

Long Silence. Sylvie Desrosiers. (Novels in the Roman Plus Ser.). (FRE., Illus.). 160p. (YA). (gr. 8 up). 1996. pap. 8.95 (*2-89021-256-4*, Pub. by La Courte Ech) Firefly Bks Ltd.

***Long Silence: Civilian Life under the German Occupation of Northern.** Helen McPhail. 256p. 2000. text 59.50 (*1-86064-479-1*) St Martin.

Long Silk Line. Wendell Zehel. 192p. 1997. mass mkt. 5.95 (*1-56315-077-8*) SterlingHse.

Long Silk Strand: A Grandmother's Legacy to Her Granddaughter. Laura Williams. LC 94-78196. (Illus.). 32p. (J). (gr. k-4). 1995. 15.95 (*1-56397-236-0*) Boyds Mills Pr.

***Long Silk Strand: A Grandmother's Legacy to Her Granddaughter.** Laura E. Williams. LC 94-78196. (Illus.). 32p. (J). 2000. pap. 7.95 (*1-56397-856-3*) Boyds Mills Pr.

***Long Silk Strand: A Grandmother's Legacy to Her Granddaughter.** Laura E. Williams. (Illus.). (J). 2000. 13.40 (*0-606-18013-3*) Turtleback.

Long Skeleton. Frances Lockridge & Richard Lockridge. 1975. reprint ed. lib. bdg. 21.95 (*0-89190-909-5*, Rivercity Pr) Amereon Ltd.

Long Slim Slimy Ones, Short Fat Juicy Ones - Complete Guide to Worms in Your Garden see Worm Book: The Complete Guide to Worms in Your Garden

Long Slow Burn: Sexing up the Social Sciences. Kath Weston. LC 97-48675. 224p. (C). (gr. 13). 1998. 75.00 (*0-415-92043-4*) Routledge.

Long Slow Burn: Sexuality & Social Science. Kath Weston. LC 97-48675. 224p. 1998. pap. 18.99 (*0-415-92044-2*) Routledge.

Long Slow Death of Jack Kerouac. Jim Christy. LC 99-188146. (Illus.). 96p. 1998. pap. 12.95 (*1-55022-357-7*, Pub. by ECW) Genl Dist Srvs.

Long Snake Tattoo. Frank Downes. (Frontlines Ser.). 192p. 1998. pap. 12.95 (*1-899344-35-7*, Pub. by Do-Not Pr) Dufour.

Long Son. Peter Bowen. LC 98-48954. 272p. 1999. text 22.95 (*0-312-19917-1*) St Martin.

***Long Son: A Montana Mystery Featuring.** Peter Bowen. 272p. 2000. pap. 13.95 (*0-312-25398-2*) St Martin.

Long Song to the One I Love. Ravi Singh. Ed. by Kathy Cullen. LC 85-51790. (Illus.). 75p. (Orig.). 1985. pap. 8.95 (*0-9615707-0-9*) White Lion Pr.

Long Southern Nights. Heather Macallister. 1997. per. 3.50 (*0-373-25756-2*, 1-25756-7) Harlequin Bks.

***Long-Span Bridges & Aerodynamics.** Ed. by T. Miyata et al. (Illus.). viii, 304p. 1999. 112.00 (*4-431-70259-8*) Spr-Verlag.

Long Spikes. Jim Arnosky. (Illus.). 96p. (J). (gr. 3-7). 1992. 13.00 (*0-395-58830-8*, Clarion Bks) HM.

Long Star Politics. Paul Benson et al. LC 96-76366. 400p. (C). 1996. pap. text 41.50 (*0-15-503538-X*, Pub. by Harcourt Coll Pubs) Harcourt.

Long Steel Rail: The Railroad in American Folksong. Norm Cohen. LC 80-14874. (Music in American Life Ser.). (Illus.). 736p. 1981. pap. 18.95 (*0-252-01145-7*) U of Ill Pr.

***Long Steel Rail: The Railroad in American Folksong.** 2nd ed. Norm Cohen. (Illus.). 744p. 2000. pap. 32.95 (*0-252-06881-5*) U of Ill Pr.

Long Stem Rose. Briege Duffaud. 384p. 1995. pap. 13.95 (*1-85371-502-6*, Pub. by Poolbeg Pr) Dufour.

Long Storm. Ernest Haycox. 288p. 1993. mass mkt. 3.50 (*1-55817-724-8*, Pinncle Kensgtn) Kensgtn Pub Corp.

Long Storm. large type ed. Ernest Haycox. LC 93-7032. 369p. 1993. lib. bdg. 18.95 (*1-56054-699-9*) Thorndike Pr.

Long Story Short. Dennis O'Driscoll. 84p. 1993. pap. 17.95 (*0-85646-256-X*, Pub. by Anvil Press) Dufour.

Long Story Short. Dennis O'Driscoll. LC 94-132445. Date not set. pap. 11.95 (*1-873790-47-3*) Dufour.

Long Story Short. Mary G. Rodriguez. (Poesia Tejana Ser.: Vol. 4). (ENG & SPA.). x, 46p. 1999. pap. 12.00 (*0-930324-45-5*) Wings Pr.

Long Story Short. Nancy E. Shick. LC 90-63709. (Illus.). 145p. 1990. 19.95 (*1-878044-01-X*) Mayhaven Pub.

Long Stretch at First Base. Matt Christopher. (J). 1993. 9.05 (*0-606-05719-6*, Pub. by Turtleback) Demco.

Long Struggle of Eritrea for Independence & Constructive Peace. Ed. by Lionel Cliffe & Basil Risbridger Davidson. LC 88-62161. 230p. (C). 1988. 29.95 (*0-932415-36-9*); pap. 9.95 (*0-932415-37-7*) Red Sea Pr.

Long Summer. Dorothy E. Miller. (Illus.). 35p. (J). (gr. 3 up). 1998. pap. 9.00 (*0-9638844-1-7*) Miller & Seymour.

Long Sun. Janice Lucas. LC 93-48028. 266p. 1994. 22.00 (*1-56947-013-8*) Soho Press.

Long Sunset. Anthony M. Browne. 400p. 1997. pap. 24.95 (*0-575-40040-4*, Pub. by V Gollancz) Trafalgar.

Long Sunset: Memoirs of Winston Churchill's Last Private Secretary. Anthony M. Browne. LC 95-174752. 400p. 1997. 50.00 (*0-304-34478-8*, Pub. by V Gollancz) Trafalgar.

Long Swing in Historical Perspective: An Interpretive Study. John C. Soper. LC 77-14772. (Dissertations in American Economic History Ser.). 1978. 26.95 (*0-405-11057-X*) Ayer.

Long Swings in Urban Development. Manuel Gottlieb. (Urban & Regional Studies: No. 4). (Illus.). 384p. 1976. 99.90 (*0-87014-226-7*) Natl Bur Econ Res.

Long Sword & Scabbard Slide in Asia. William Trousdale. LC U 0853.. (Smithsonian Contributions to Anthropology Ser.: no. 17). 344p. reprint ed. pap. 106.70 (*0-608-13627-1*, 202030800016) Bks Demand.

Long-Tailed Parakeets: A Complete Pet Owner's Manual. Annette Wolter. 1992. pap. 6.95 (*0-8120-1351-4*) Barron.

***Long Tales, Short Tales & Tall Tales.** Colin West. (J). 2000. pap. 6.95 (*0-552-52798-X*, Pub. by Transworld Publishers Ltd) Trafalgar.

Long Tales, Short Tales & Tall Tales. large type ed. Colin West. (J). 1997. 16.95 (*0-7451-6903-1*, Galaxy Child Lrg Print) Chivers N Amer.

Long Talking Bad Conditions Blues. Ronald Sukenick. LC 79-52030. 1979. 15.95 (*0-914590-60-X*); pap. 6.95 (*0-914590-61-8*) Fiction Coll.

Long, Tall Temporary Husband. Anne Ha. (Silhouette Romance Ser.). 184p. 1998. per. 3.50 (*0-373-19297-5*, 1-19297-0) Silhouette.

Long Tall Texan Summer. Diana Palmer. 1997. per. 5.99 (*0-373-48342-2*, 1-48342-9) Harlequin Bks.

***Long Tall Texan Weddings.** 2000. per. 12.95 (*0-373-65211-9*) Harlequin Bks.

Long Tall Texans. Diana Palmer. 1994. per. 5.99 (*0-373-48320-1*, 1-48320-5) Silhouette.

Long, Tall Texans. Diana Palmer. (Silhouette Promo Ser.). 1999. pap. 12.95 (*0-373-48393-7*, 1-48393-2, Harlequin) Harlequin Bks.

Long, Tall Texans: Emmett; Regan's Pride; That Burke Man, 3 bks. in 1. rev. ed. Diana Palmer. (By Request Ser.). 1999. mass mkt. 5.99 (*0-373-20158-3*, 1-20158-1) Harlequin Bks.

Long, Tall Texans: Harden, Evan, Donavan. Diana Palmer. 1997. per. 5.99 (*0-373-20137-0*, 1-20137-5) Harlequin Bks.

Long Term. Frazier. 160p. 1995. pap. text 19.95 (*0-316-29419-5*, Little Brwn Med Div) Lppncott W & W.

Long Term Adaptations among Arctic Hunter-Gatherers: A Case Study from Southern Baffin Island. George Sabo, III. LC 90-27623. (Evolution of North American Indians: Series of Outstanding Dissertations). 424p. 1991. text 10.00 (*0-8240-6111-X*) Garland.

Long-Term Adequacy of World Timber Supply. Roger A. Sedjo & Kenneth S. Lyon. LC 89-8519. 230p. 1990. 30.00 (*0-915707-46-2*) Resources Future.

Long-Term Aging & Loss-of-Coolant Accident Testing of Electrical Cables: United States/French Cooperative Research Program. C. F. Nelson. 151p. 1996. per. 15.00 (*0-16-062784-2*) USGPO.

Long-Term Agricultural Projections to 2005. (Illus.). 48p. (Orig.). (C). 1997. pap. text 25.00 (*0-7881-3703-4*) DIANE Pub.

Long-Term Ambulatory Electrocardiography. Jos R. Roelandt & P. G. Hugenholtz. 1982. text 126.50 (*90-247-2664-6*) Kluwer Academic.

Long-Term & Short-Term Assays for Carcinogens: A Critical Appraisal. Ed. by R. Montesano et al. (IARC Scientific Publications: No. 83). (Illus.). 580p. 1987. pap. 70.00 (*92-832-1183-9*) OUP.

Long-Term & Short-Term Interest Rates in the United Kingdom. Frank W. Paish. LC 67-4633. vii, 56p. 1967. 15.00 (*0-678-06764-3*) Kelley.

Long-Term & Short-Term Screening Assays for Carcinogens - A Critical Appraisal: Evaluation of Carcinogenic Risks to Humans. (IARC Monographs). 426p. 1980. text, suppl. ed. 48.00 (*92-832-1404-8*) World Health.

Long-Term Animal Studies: Their Predictive Value for Man. Ed. by S. R. Walker & A. D. Dayan. 1986. text 124.00 (*0-85200-931-3*) Kluwer Academic.

Long-Term Behavior of Composites - STP 813. Ed. by T. Kevin O'Brien. LC 82-73765. 300p. 1983. 42.00 (*0-8031-0252-6*, STP813) ASTM.

Long-Term Brazilian Economic Growth, 1930-1994. Marcelo Abreu & Dorte Verner. LC 97-224735. (Long-Term Growth Ser.). 140p. 1997. pap. 25.00 (*92-64-15619-4*, 41-97-14-1, Pub. by Org for Econ) OECD.

Long-Term Budgetary Pressures & Policy Options. Douglas Hamilton & Joseph Antos. Ed. by Paul L. Houts. (Illus.). 53p. (Orig.). (C). 1997. pap. text 30.00 (*0-7881-4482-0*) DIANE Pub.

***Long-Term Budgetary Pressures & Policy Options.** Sherry Snyder. LC 98-156143. 89p. 1998. pap. 7.00 (*0-16-049591-1*, Congress) USGPO.

Long-Term Capital Flows & the Great Depression: The Role of the United States, 1927-1933. Heywood Fleisig. LC 75-2580. (Dissertations in American Economic History Ser.). 1979. 39.95 (*0-405-07200-7*) Ayer.

Long Term Care. Fred Reneau. 1996. 10.74 (*0-07-011925-2*) McGraw.

***Long Term Care.** 3rd ed. 198p. 1999. pap. 26.00 (*0-7931-3375-0*) Dearborn.

***Long Term Care.** 3rd ed. Sorrentino. 1999. teacher ed. write for info. (*0-323-00711-2*) Mosby Inc.

Long-Term Care: A Dollar & Sense Guide. LC 97-190253. 1999. pap. 18.00 (*0-944847-22-6*) United Sr Hlth Co-op.

***Long-Term Care: An Analysis of Access, Cost & Quality.** Laura Randa King. LC 99-49039. 96p. 2000. 42.00 (*0-7618-1557-0*); pap. 24.50 (*0-7618-1558-9*) U Pr of Amer.

Long Term Care: An Annotated Bibliography, 25. Theodore H. Koff. LC 94-39768. (Bibliographies & Indexes in Gerontology Ser.: Vol. 25). 152p. 1995. lib. bdg. 59.95 (*0-313-28583-7*, Greenwood Pr) Greenwood.

Long-Term Care: Current Issues & Future Directions. (Illus.). 33p. 1996. reprint ed. pap. text 20.00 (*0-7881-3203-2*) DIANE Pub.

Long-Term Care: Diverse, Growing Population Includes Millions of Americans of All Ages. (Illus.). 24p. 1996. reprint ed. pap. text 20.00 (*0-7881-3218-0*) DIANE Pub.

Long-Term Care: Economic Impacts & Financing Dilemmas. 104p. 1990. 20.00 (*0-929852-02-8*) Natl Health Coun.

Long-Term Care: Economic Issues & Policy Solutions. Ed. by Roland Eisen. LC 96-46172. (Developments in Health Economics & Public Policy Ser.). 352p. (C). 1996. lib. bdg. 157.50 (*0-7923-9824-6*) Kluwer Academic.

Long-Term Care: Federal, State & Private Options for the Future. Raymond C. O'Brien & Michael T. Flannery. LC 97-1573. 290p. (C). 1997. pap. 24.95 (*0-7890-0261-2*) Haworth Pr.

Long-Term Care: Federal, State & Private Options for the Future. Raymond C. O'Brien & Michael T. Flannery. LC 97-1573. 290p. (C). 1997. 49.95 (*0-7890-0173-X*) Haworth Pr.

Long Term Care: For Activity & Social Service Professionals. 2nd ed. Elizabeth B. Martini et al. (Illus.). 404p. (C). 1996. pap. text 35.00 (*1-882883-28-4*) Idyll Arbor.

Long-Term Care: Knowing the Risk, Paying the Price. Ed. by Bruce Boyd. LC 97-176580. 248p. 1997. pap. text 30.00 (*1-879143-34-8*) Health Ins Assn Am.

Long-Term Care: Knowing the Risk, Paying the Price Study Manual. HIAA Staff. 60p. 1997. pap. 10.00 (*1-879143-35-6*) Health Ins Assn Am.

Long Term Care: Legal Accountability for Nurses & Other Long Term Care Providers. J. Fiesta. LC 96-38258. (Professional Reference - Nursing Ser.). 208p. 1997. mass mkt. 31.95 (*0-8273-6726-0*) Delmar.

Long-Term Care: Management, Scope & Practical Issues. Ed. by John A. Toner et al. LC 92-49112. 240p. (Orig.). (C). 1993. pap. text 19.95 (*0-914783-66-1*) Charles.

Long-Term Care: Managing Across the Continuum. Pratt. LC 98-44807. 640p. 1999. pap. 55.00 (*0-8342-1032-0*, 10320) Aspen Pub.

Long-Term Care: Other Countries Tighten Budgets While Seeking Better Access. (Illus.). 44p. (Orig.). (C). 1995. pap. text 25.00 (*0-7881-1715-7*) DIANE Pub.

Long-Term Care: Principles, Programs & Policies. Rosalie A. Kane & Robert L. Kane. 462p. (C). 1987. 52.95 (*0-8261-6010-7*) Springer Pub.

Long-Term Care: Private Sector Elder Care Could Yield Multiple Benefits. (Illus.). 45p. (Orig.). (C). 1995. pap. text 25.00 (*0-7881-1755-6*) DIANE Pub.

Long-Term Care: Support for Elder Care Could Benefit the Government Workplace & the Elderly. (Illus.). 70p. (Orig.). (C). 1994. pap. text 25.00 (*0-7881-1439-5*) DIANE Pub.

Long Term Care: Test-Taking Review for Nurses Aide. Barbara A. Vitale & Patricia M. Nugent. (Illus.). 224p. (C). (gr. 13). 1990. pap. text 17.95 (*0-8016-5221-9*, 05221) Mosby Inc.

Long Term Care Administration: Teamwork & Effective Management. Ruby H. Neuhaus. 200p. (Orig.). (C). 1990. pap. text 23.50 (*0-8191-7861-6*); lib. bdg. 45.00 (*0-8191-7860-8*) U Pr of Amer.

Long-Term Care Administration: The Management of Institutional & Non-Institutional Components of the Continuum of Care. Ben Abramovice. LC 87-11949. (Series on Marketing & Health Services Administration: No. 1). 256p. (C). 1987. text 39.95 (*0-86656-399-7*) Haworth Pr.

Long-Term Care Administration Handbook. Ed. by Seth B. Goldsmith. LC 92-48287. 592p. 1993. 93.00 (*0-8342-0374-X*, 20374) Aspen Pub.

***Long Term Care Administration State Licensure Requirements & College Directory.** Susan J. Courtney & James E. Allen. 191p. 1999. pap. write for info. (*0-9635064-5-5*) Nat Assn Bds Exam.

***Long-Term Care Advocacy.** Eric M. Carlson. LC 99-43080. 1050p. 1999. 135.00 (*0-8205-4153-2*) Bender.

Long-Term Care & Ethnicity. Ada C. Mui et al. LC 98-11157. 232p. 1998. 59.95 (*0-86569-232-7*, Auburn Hse) Greenwood.

Long-Term Care & Its Alternatives. Charles B. Inlander et al. LC 95-52968. (Illus.). 256p. 1996. pap. 16.95 (*1-882606-56-6*) Peoples Med Soc.

Long-Term Care & the Law: A Legal Guide for Health Care Professionals. George D. Pozgar et al. 510p. 1992. 67.00 (*0-8342-0289-1*, 20289) Aspen Pub.

Long-Term Care Case Management: Design & Evaluation. Robert Applebaum & Carol Austin. LC 90-9483. 192p. 1990. 29.95 (*0-8261-6430-7*) Springer Pub.

Long-Term Care Case Management: State Experiences & Implications for Federal Policy. (Illus.). 45p. (Orig.). (C). 1995. pap. text 25.00 (*0-7881-2377-7*) DIANE Pub.

***Long-Term Care Clinical Assessment: A Guide for the Social Worker.** David Liebert. (Illus.). 100p. (C). 1999. pap. 29.50 (*0-929442-55-5*) Prof Prnting & Pub.

***Long-Term Care Compliance Manual.** D. Scott Jones. Ed. by Claudia Hoffacker. 210p. 2000. pap. text 249.00 (*1-57839-079-6*) Opus Communs.

***Long Term Care Compliance Resource Manual.** L. E. Zimmerman et al. Ed. by Aspen Health Law & Compliance Center Staff & Charles County Nursing & Rehabilitation Center Staff. LC 00-22787. (Illus.). 2000. write for info. (*0-8342-1730-9*) Aspen Pub.

Long-Term Care Crisis: Elders Trapped in the No-Care Zone. Carroll L. Estes & James H. Swan. LC 92-30579. (Illus.). 352p. (C). 1993. text 58.00 (*0-8039-3992-2*); pap. text 26.50 (*0-8039-3993-0*) Sage.

Long-Term Care Decisions: Ethical & Conceptual Dimensions. Ed. by Lawrence B. McCullough & Nancy L. Wilson. LC 94-37416. (Illus.). 304p. 1995. text 40.00 (*0-8018-4993-4*) Johns Hopkins.

Long-Term Care Documentation & Guidelines. Marilyn Stoner. 250p. (C). 1999. ring bd. 99.95 (*1-56930-079-8*) Skidmore Roth Pub.

Long-Term Care Experience Report for 1997. 6th rev. ed. Ed. by Jim Bugenhagen. 70p. (C). 1999. pap. 45.00i (*0-89382-594-8*, LTC-LR97) Nat Assn Insurance.

***Long-Term Care Experience Report for 1998.** 6th rev. ed. Ed. by Jim Bugenhagen. 70p. 2000. pap. 45.00 (*0-89382-663-4*) Nat Assn Insurance.

Long-Term Care Facilities & Facility Programs in Camden County & Their Utilization 1993-1994: Camden County Long Term Care Database. Text by Harmon T. Hicks. (Illus.). 67p. 1995. ring bd. 20.00 (*0-932965-33-4*) Old Cookbooks HT Hicks.

Long Term Care Facility Policy & Procedure Manual. Diane P. Atchinson. Ed. by Diana Johnson. 427p. 1996. ring bd. 225.00 (*1-929162-01-4*, ltcM006) DPA Assocs.

Long Term Care Facility Resident Assessment Instrument: User's Manual. James E. Allen. LC 97-3056. 496p. 1997. 42.95 (*0-8261-9900-3*) Springer Pub.

Long-Term Care Family Manual. Marylou Hughes. 97p. 1995. 30.00 (*1-877735-49-3*, 2300PP) Prof Prnting & Pub.

Long Term Care Financing: A Consumer's Agenda for Action. Betsy Abramson. 134p. 1989. 20.00 (*0-685-26153-0*) Ctr Public Rep.

Long-Term Care for Frail Older People: Reaching for the Ideal System. Ed. by John C. Campbell & Naoki Ikegami. LC 99-17631. (Keio University Symposia for Life Science & Medicine Ser.). 270p. 1999. 139.00 (*4-431-70250-4*) Spr-Verlag.

Long-Term Care for Older Persons: A Policy Perspective. Nancy Eustis et al. LC 83-7080. (Social Gerontology Ser.). 224p. (C). 1984. mass mkt. 20.00 (*0-534-02910-8*) Brooks-Cole.

Long-Term Care for the Elderly: A Factbook. David Rabin. (Illus.). 269p. 1986. pap. text 19.95 (*0-19-504106-2*) OUP.

Long-Term Care for the Functionally Dependent Elderly: PHS 90-1765. (Vital & Health Statistics Ser. 13: Data on Health Resources Utilization: No. 104). 58p. 3.00 (*0-685-61585-5*, 017-022-01116-6) Natl Ctr Health Stats.

Long Term Care for the Rural Elderly: New Directions in Services, Research, & Policy. Ed. by Graham D. Rowles et al. LC 96-28439. (Illus.). 216p. 1996. 39.95 (*0-8261-9380-3*) Springer Pub.

***Long-Term Care for the 21st Century: A Common Sense Proposal to Support Family Caregiver - Congressional Hearing.** Ed. by Charles E. Grassley. 74p. 2000. pap. text 20.00 (*0-7567-0152-X*) DIANE Pub.

Long Term Care Handbook: Legal, Operational & Financial Guideposts. Ed. by Thomas C. Fox et al. 377p. 1991. 35.00 (*0-918945-11-9*) Am Hlth Lawyers.

Long-Term Care Handbook: Resources for the Health Information Manager. Ed. by Teresa Ganser. 198p. 1999. pap. text 62.00 (*1-58426-027-0*, AB102499) Am Hlth Info.

Long-Term Care Human Resources Management: The Personnel Touch. John T. Cirn et al. (Learning the Continuum: AUPHA Modules for Management Education Ser.). (Illus.). (Orig.). (C). 1989. pap. text 20.00 (*0-910591-20-2*) AUPHA Pr.

Long-Term Care in an Aging Society: Choices & Challenges for the '90s. Ed. by Gerald A. Larue & Rich Bayly. LC 91-18979. (Golden Age Books - Perspectives on Aging Ser.). 170p. (Orig.). 1992. 26.95 (*0-87975-695-0*); pap. 18.95 (*0-87975-712-4*) Prometheus Bks.

Long-Term Care Industry. Ed. by Peter Allen. 200p. 1989. pap. 1795.00 (*0-317-01805-1*) FIND-SVP.

Long-Term Care Insurance: Guide to Comparing Insurance Rates. (Illus.). 61p. 1998. pap. text 20.00 (*0-7881-4785-4*) DIANE Pub.

Long-Term Care Insurance as an Employment Benefit: Hearing Before the Subcommittee on the Civil Service of the Committee on Government Reform & Oversight, House of Representatives, One Hundred Fifth Congress, Second Session, March 26, 1998. United States Government. LC 98-208334. iii, 160 p. 1998. write for info. (*0-16-057300-9*) USGPO.

Long-Term Care Insurance Experience Report for 1995. 2nd rev. ed. Ed. by Jim Bugenhagen. 84p. (C). 1997. pap. 25.00 (*0-89382-457-7*, LTC-LR) Nat Assn Insurance.

An Asterisk (*) at the beginning of an entry indicates that the title is appearing for the first time.

L

Long-Term Care Insurance Experience Reports for 1994. Ed. by Jim Bugenhagen. 76p. (Orig.). 1996. pap. 25.00 (*0-89382-385-6*, LTC-LR94) Nat Assn Insurance.

*__Long-Term Care Insurance Made Simple.__ Les Abramovitz. LC 99-12994. 220p. 1999. pap. 14.95 (*1-885987-14-5*, ME094, Health Info Pr) Practice Mgmt Info.

Long-Term Care Investment Strategies: A Guide to Start-Ups, Facility Conversions & Strategic Alliances. Ronald E. Mills. 200p. (C). 1995. text 55.00 (*1-55738-622-6*, Irwn Prfssnl) McGraw-Hill Prof.

Long-Term Care Marketing: A Management Primer. Frederick R. Eisele. (Learning the Continuum: AUPHA Modules for Management Education Ser.). (Illus.). 80p. (Orig.). (C). 1989. pap. text 20.00 (*0-910591-22-9*) AUPHA Pr.

Long Term Care Nursing. Peggy A. Grubbs & Barbara A. Blasband. 1995. pap., teacher ed. 20.80 (*0-8359-4955-9*) P-H.

Long-Term Care Nursing Assistant. Peggy A. Grubbs & Barbara A. Blasband. LC 94-18668. (C). 1994. 30.20 (*0-13-146747-6*) P-H.

Long-Term Care Nursing Assistant. Perspective Press Inc. Staff. (Illus.). 320p. (gr. 13). 1995. pap. text 24.95 (*0-8151-4550-0*, 25772) Mosby Inc.

Long Term Care Nursing Assistant. 2nd ed. (C). 1999. pap. 22.00 (*0-13-016399-6*) P-H.

Long Term Care Nursing Assistant. 2nd ed. (C). 2000. pap. 50.00 (*0-13-016390-2*); pap. 50.00 (*0-13-016401-1*); pap. 50.00 (*0-13-016402-X*) P-H.

*__Long-Term Care Nursing Assistant.__ 2nd ed. Peggy A. Grubbs & Barbara A. Blasband. LC 99-32629. (Illus.). 431p. 1999. pap. text 41.00 (*0-13-013253-5*) P-H.

Long-Term Care Nursing Assistant Training Manual. 2nd ed. Ed. by Mary Ann Anderson et al. LC 95-46849. (Illus.). 352p. (Orig.). 1996. pap. 29.95 (*1-878812-28-9*) Hlth Prof Pr.

Long Term Care Nursing Review for Practical Nurses: A Guide to Preparing for the Certification Exam. 100p. (Orig.). 1996. pap. 25.00 (*1-882515-21-8*) Hlth Educ Netwk.

Long Term Care Nursing Standards Manual, Policies, & Procedures, Suppl. 6. Ed. by O. Alice Leshem & Dorothy M. Varholak. 1998. ring bd. 69.00 (*0-8342-0331-6*, S5406) Aspen Pub.

Long-Term Care of Older People: A Practical Guide. Elaine Brody. LC 77-5944. 402p. 1977. 52.00 (*0-87705-274-3*, Kluwer Acad Hman Sci) Kluwer Academic.

Long Term Care of the Elderly: Public Policy Issues. Ed. by Charlene Harrington et al. LC 84-17754. (Sage Library of Social Research: Vol. 157). 280p. 1985. reprint ed. pap. 86.80 (*0-608-02987-4*, 205962700006) Bks Demand.

Long-Term Care Planning Guide. 8th ed. Phyllis R. Shelton. Orig. Title: Health Benefits Guide for Seniors. (Illus.). vii, 151p. 1998. pap. 19.95 (*0-9633516-4-8*) Shelton Mktg.

*__Long-Term Care Planning Guide: The Consumer Resource for Long-Term Care Financing.__ 10th rev. ed. Phyllis R. Shelton. Orig. Title: Health Benefits Guide for Seniors. (Illus.). 175p. 2000. pap. 15.99 (*0-9633516-8-0*) Shelton Mktg.

Long-Term Care Service Coordination: The Evolving Continuum. John A. Toner. (Learning the Continuum: AUPHA Modules for Management Education Ser.). (Illus.). 114p. (Orig.). (C). 1989. pap. text 20.00 (*0-910591-16-4*) AUPHA Pr.

*__Long-Term Care Suitability.__ Dearborn Financial Institute Staff. LC 00-28250. 2000. pap. 29.00 (*0-7931-3796-9*) Dearborn.

*__Long-Term Caring for Your Parents.__ Martha N. O'Tool & Mary B. Payne. iv, 44p. 1998. pap. 9.95 (*0-9664247-1-9*) Sndwch Pr.

Long-Term Changes in Coastal Benthic Communities. Ed. by C. H. Heip et al. (Developments in Hydrobiology Ser.). 1987. lib. bdg. 253.50 (*90-6193-637-3*) Kluwer Academic.

Long-Term Climate Monitoring by the Global Climate Observing System: International Meeting of Experts, Asheville, North Carolina, U. S. A., January 9-11, 1995. Ed. by Thomas R. Karl. 400p. (C). 1996. text 161.50 (*0-7923-3856-1*) Kluwer Academic.

Long-Term Climatic Variations: Data & Modelling. Ed. by Jean-Claude Duplessy & Marie-Therese Spyridakis. LC 94-12952. 1994. 229.00 (*0-387-58112-X*) Spr-Verlag.

Long Term Clinical Care of Parkinson's Disease: Journal: European Neurology, Vol. 30, Suppl. 1, 1990. Ed. by T. Nakanishi. vi, 42p. 1990. pap. text 21.00 (*3-8055-5161-4*) S Karger.

Long Term Clinical Care of Parkinson's Disease: 3rd Symposium, Tokyo, April 1988. Ed. by T. Nakanishi. (Journal: European Neurology: Vol. 29, Suppl. 1, 1988). 38p. 1989. pap. 19.25 (*3-8055-4969-5*) S Karger.

Long Term Clinical Care of Parkinson's Disease, Tokyo, April 1987: Second Symposium. Ed. by T. Nakanishi. (Journal: European Neurology: Vol. 28, Suppl. 1, 1988). vi, 42p. 1988. pap. 15.00 (*3-8055-4833-8*) S Karger.

Long Term Clinical Care of Parkinson's Disease, 5th Symposium, Tokyo, April 1990. Ed. by T. Nakanishi. (Journal: European Neurology: Vol. 31, Suppl. 1, 1991). (Illus.). iv, 60p. 1991. pap. 28.00 (*3-8055-5401-X*) S Karger.

Long-Term Complications of Therapy for Cancer in Childhood & Adolescence. Daniel M. Green. LC 88-8365. (Contemporary Medicine & Public Health Ser.). 184p. 1989. text 45.00 (*0-8018-3765-0*) Johns Hopkins.

Long-Term Consequences of Disasters: The Reconstruction of Friuli-Italy in Its International Context 1976-1988. R. Geipel. Ed. by R. S. DeSanto. (Environmental Management Ser.). (Illus.). xx, 171p. 1990. 123.00 (*0-387-97419-9*) Spr-Verlag.

Long-Term Consequences of Early Environment: Growth, Development & the Lifespan Developmental Perspective. Ed. by C. J. Henry & Stanley J. Ulijaszek. (Society for the Study of Human Biology Symposium Ser.: No. 37). (Illus.). 272p. (C). 1996. text 57.95 (*0-521-47108-7*) Cambridge U Pr.

Long Term Consequences of Early Feeding. Ed. by John Boulton et al. LC 95-23864. (Nestle Nutrition Workshop Ser.: Vol. 36). 256p. 1995. text 69.00 (*0-397-51728-9*) Lppncott W & W.

Long-Term Continuing Impacts & Legal Principles of Superfund, RCRA, & Related Law, 1996. 25p. Date not set. pap. text 20.00 (*1-56986-289-3*, ENV-96-25) Federal Bar.

Long Term Control of Exhaustable Resources, Vol. 13. Pierre Lasserre. (Fundamentals of Pure & Applied Economics Ser.). viii, 122p. 1991. pap. text 59.00 (*3-7186-5134-3*, Harwood Acad Pubs) Gordon & Breach.

*__Long-Term Day Trader: Short-Term Strategies to Boost Your Long-Term Profits.__ Michael Sincere & Deron Wagner. 256p. 2000. pap. 14.99 (*1-56414-453-4*) Career Pr Inc.

Long-Term Dynamical Behaviour of Natural & Artificial N-Body Systems. Ed. by Archie E. Roy. (C). 1988. text 266.50 (*90-277-2801-1*) Kluwer Academic.

Long-Term Economic & Military Trends, 1994-2015: The United States & Asia. Charles Wolf, Jr. et al. LC 95-30019. 64p. 1995. pap. 15.00 (*0-8330-2328-4*, MR-627) Rand Corp.

Long-Term Effects of Conservation Rates. Vista Consulting Group Staff et al. LC 97-203247. (Illus.). 95p. 1997. pap. 125.00 (*0-89867-904-4*, 90723) Am Water Wks Assn.

Long Term Effects of Sewage Sludge & Farm Slurries Applications: Proceedings of an EEC Seminar Held at Pisa, Italy, 25-27 September, 1984. Ed. by J. H. Williams et al. (Illus.). ix, 239p. 1985. 57.75 (*0-85334-399-3*) Elsevier.

Long-Term Effects of Vocational Education: Earnings, Employment, Education, & Aspirations. Jeanne Desy et al. 41p. 1984. 4.25 (*0-318-22146-2*, RD246) Ctr Educ Trng Employ.

Long-Term Energy Storage in Solar Systems. J. L. Rosenfeld & J. Morton. (C). 1984. 140.00 (*0-7855-4195-0*, Pub. by Interntl Solar Energy Soc) St Mut.

Long-Term Energy Storage in Solars Systems (C35) J. L. Rosenfeld & J. Morton. 77p. (C). 1984. 165.00 (*0-685-30221-0*, Pub. by Interntl Solar Energy Soc) St Mut.

Long-Term Environmental Effects of Offshore Oil & Gas Development. Ed. by D. F. Boesch & Nancy N. Rabalais. 720p. 1987. mass mkt. 271.50 (*1-85166-094-1*) Elsevier.

Long-Term Environmental Trends for ITV. Gregory Schmid. 25p. 1985. 6.00 (*0-318-19207-1*, R-63) Inst Future.

Long-Term Evolution of Planetary Systems. Ed. by R. Dvorak & J. Henrard. (C). 1989. text 278.00 (*0-7923-0120-X*) Kluwer Academic.

Long-Term Experiments in Agricultural & Ecological Sciences. Ed. by R. A. Leigh & A. E. Johnston. (Illus.). 448p. 1994. text 130.00 (*0-85198-933-0*) OUP.

Long-Term Experiments with Acid Rain in Norwegian Forest Ecosystems. Ed. by Gunnar Abrahamsen et al. LC 93-28646. (Ecological Studies: Vol. 104). 1993. 118.00 (*0-387-94119-3*) Spr-Verlag.

Long-Term Factors in American Economic Growth. Ed. by Stanley L. Engerman & Robert E. Gallman. LC 86-11408. (National Bureau of Economic Research Studies in Income & Wealth: Vol. 51). 898p. (C). 1987. lib. bdg. 96.00 (*0-226-20928-8*) U Ch Pr.

Long-Term Factors in American Economic Growth. Ed. by Stanley L. Engerman & Robert E. Gallman. LC 86-11408. xiv, 900p. 1992. pap. text 34.50 (*0-226-20929-6*) U Ch Pr.

Long-Term Family Recovery from Disaster. Robert C. Bolin. (Program on Environment & Behavior Monograph Ser.: No. 36). 280p. (Orig.). (C). 1982. pap. 20.00 (*0-685-28110-8*) Natural Hazards.

Long-Term Financial Planning: Creative Strategies for Local Government. Ed. by Jeffrey I. Chapman. LC 87-2613. (Practical Management Ser.). 188p. (Orig.). 1987. pap. 23.95 (*0-87326-076-7*) Intl City-Cnty Mgt.

Long-Term Forest Dynamics of the Temperate Zone. P. A. Delcourt & H. R. Delcourt. (Ecological Studies: Vol. 63). (Illus.). 450p. 1987. 152.00 (*0-387-96495-9*) Spr-Verlag.

Long-Term Fostering & the Children Act: A Study of Foster Parents Who Went on to Adopt. J. Rowe et al. (C). 1989. 60.00 (*0-903534-49-5*, Pub. by Brit Ag for Adopt & Fost) St Mut.

Long-Term Greedy: The Triumph of Goldman Sachs. Nils Lindskoog. LC 96-76405. (Illus.). 159p. 1998. 24.95 (*0-9652153-3-4*) McCrossen Pub.

*__Long-Term Greedy: The Triumph of Goldman Sachs.__ 2nd ed. Nils Lindskoog. LC 99-74730. 192p. 1999. 24.95 (*0-9652153-7-7*) McCrossen Pub.

Long-Term Growth in Tunisia. LC 97-109710. 135p. 1996. 23.00 (*92-64-14925-2*, 41-96-07-1, Pub. by Org for Econ) OECD.

Long-Term Hemodialysis. Nguyen-Khoa Man et al. LC 95-14248. 148p. (C). 1995. text 81.00 (*0-7923-3477-9*) Kluwer Academic.

Long-Term Historical Changes in the Forest Resource: Case Studies of Finland, France, Great Britain, Greece, Hungary, the Netherlands, Sweden & the United States of America. LC 97-133940. (Geneva Timber & Forest Studies: No. 10). 76p. pap. 16.00 (*92-1-116649-7*) UN.

Long Term Human-Computer Interaction: An Exploratory Perspective. Richard C. Thomas. LC 98-18111. 1998. pap. 79.95 (*3-540-76209-4*) Spr-Verlag.

Long-Term Imprisonment: Issues of Policy, Science & Correctional Practice. Timothy J. Flanagan. 184p. 1995. text 52.00 (*0-8039-7032-3*); pap. text 24.00 (*0-8039-7033-1*) Sage.

Long-Term Integration of Renewable Energy Sources into the European Energy System. Ed. by LTI-Research Group Staff. LC 98-3940. (Environmental & Resource Economics Ser.). (Illus.). x, 268p. 1998. pap. 67.00 (*3-7908-1104-1*) Spr-Verlag.

Long-Term Intragastric pH Measurement in Man: Basic & Methodological Aspects - Journal: Digestive Diseases, Vol. 8, Suppl. 1, 1990. Ed. by W. Londong et al. (Illus.). vi, 98p. 1990. pap. 29.75 (*3-8055-5274-2*) S Karger.

Long-Term Intravenous Immunoglobulin Treatment in Patients with AIDS-Related Complex: Journal: Vox Sanguinis, Vol. 59, Suppl. 1, 1990. Ed. by B. A. Perret et al. (Illus.). iv, 60p. 1990. pap. 19.25 (*3-8055-5256-4*) S Karger.

Long-Term Lease Planning & Drafting. Neil S. Hecht. LC 73-89537. 428p. reprint ed. pap. 132.70 (*0-608-13842-8*, 202043200017) Bks Demand.

Long-Term Leasing: Accounting, Evaluation, Consequences. Ahmed Riahi-Belkaoui. LC 97-22749. 160p. 1998. 59.95 (*1-56720-147-4*, Quorum Bks) Greenwood.

Long-Term Management of Patients after Myocardial Infarction. Ed. by C. Tissa Kappagoda & P. V. Greenwood. (Developments in Cardiovascular Medicine Ser.). (C). 1987. text 104.50 (*0-89838-352-8*) Kluwer Academic.

Long Term Monitoring for Epilepsy. American Journal of EEG Technology Staff & American END Society Committee. (Illus.). iv, 178p. 1995. per. 24.00 (*1-57797-004-7*) ASET.

Long Term Neurotoxic Effects of Paint Solvents. Royal Society of Chemistry Staff. 1990. 55.00 (*0-85186-339-6*) CRC Pr.

Long-Term Non-Operating Reliability of Electronic Products. Judy Pecht & Michael G. Pecht. LC 95-18275. (Electronics & Reliability Ser.). 144p. 1995. per. 44.95 (*0-8493-9621-2*, 9621) CRC Pr.

Long Term Oxygen Therapy: Scientific Basis & Clinical Application. Ed. by Walter J. O'Donohue, Jr. LC 94-48767. (Lung Biology in Health & Disease Ser.: Vol. 81). (Illus.). 416p. 1995. text 180.00 (*0-8247-9499-0*) Dekker.

Long-Term Patient Care Policies & Procedures Manual. Laura A. Luc & Michele Beattie. LC 92-48193. 174p. 1993. pap. 55.00 (*0-8342-0320-0*, 20320) Aspen Pub.

Long Term Performance & Aging Characteristics of Nuclear Plant Pressure Transmitters. H. M. Hashemian et al. (Illus.). 386p. (Orig.). 1993. per. write for info. (*1-882148-01-0*) Analysis & Measurement.

Long-Term Potentiation: A Debate of Current Issues. Ed. by Michel Baudry & Joel L. Davis. (Bradford Series in Complex Adaptive Systems). 464p. 1991. 70.00 (*0-262-02330-X*, Bradford Bks) MIT Pr.

Long Term Potentiation: A Debate of Current Issues, Vol. 2. Ed. by Michel Baudry & Joel L. Davis. (Illus.). 440p. 1994. 85.00 (*0-262-02370-9*, Bradford Bks) MIT Pr.

Long-Term Potentiation: A Debate of Current Issues, Vol. 3. Ed. by Michel Baudry & Joel L. Davis. LC 91-11092. Vol. 3. (Illus.). 448p. 1996. 75.00 (*0-262-02409-8*, Bradford Bks) MIT Pr.

Long-Term Practice: Skills for the Certified Nursing Assistant. Marjorie G. Frazier & Barbara A. Vitale. LC 95-7613. 1995. write for info. (*0-614-32285-5*, Little Brwn Med Div) Lppncott W & W.

Long-Term Profit Planning. Ernest H. Weinwurm & George F. Weinwurm. LC 71-150292. 272p. reprint ed. pap. 84.40 (*0-608-12140-1*, 202390400034) Bks Demand.

Long-Term Prognosis Following Valve Replacement: Proceedings. Conference on Cardiovascular Disease, 2nd, Snowmas. Ed. by J. H. Vogel. (Advances in Cardiology Ser.: Vol. 7). 1972. 86.25 (*3-8055-1299-6*) S Karger.

*__Long-term Projects Algebra 1 2001.__ HRW Staff. 2001. pap. text 40.40 (*0-03-054287-1*) Harcourt Schl Pubs.

Long-Term Psychiatric Patients: A Study in Community Care. Susan Lonsdale et al. 1980. 15.00 (*0-7855-0572-5*, Pub. by Natl Inst Soc Work) St Mut.

Long-Term Results & Indications in Otology & Otoneurosurgery. Ed. by R. Charachon & E. Garcia-Ibanez. LC 91-30815. (Illus.). 596p. 1991. lib. bdg. 171.50 (*90-6299-070-3*, Pub. by Kugler) Kugler Pubns.

Long-Term Results in Plastic & Reconstruction Surgery. Robert M. Goldwyn. 1980. 110.00 (*0-316-31972-4*, Little Brwn Med Div); 110.00 (*0-316-31973-2*, Little Brwn Med Div) Lppncott W & W.

Long-Term Results in Vascular Surgery. James S. Yao & William H. Pearce. (Illus.). 494p. (C). 1993. pap. text 160.00 (*0-8385-9385-2*, A9385-4, Apple Lange Med) McGraw.

Long-Term Results of Arterial Interventions. Ed. by Alain Branchereau & Michael Jacobs. LC 97-3245. (Illus.). 354p. 1997. 95.00 (*0-87993-679-7*) Futura Pub.

Long-Term Retention of Knowledge & Skills. M. J. Farr. (Recent Research in Psychology Ser.). 185p. 1989. 64.95 (*0-387-96531-9*) Spr-Verlag.

Long-Term Scenarios of Livestock-Crop-Land Use Interactions in Developing Country Land & Water. A. F. Bouwman. LC 98-126631. (Land & Water Bulletin Ser.: No. 6). 144p. 1997. pap. 19.00 (*92-5-103985-2*, F39852, Pub. by FAO) Bernan Associates.

*__Long-Term Secrets to Short-Term Trading.__ Larry Williams. LC 98-44949. (Trading Advantage Ser.). 272p. 1999. 69.95 (*0-471-29722-4*) Wiley.

Long-Term Serviceability of Concrete Structures. 293p. 1989. 41.75 (*0-685-45550-5*, SP-117BOW6) ACI.

*__Long Term Stability of High Temperature Materials: Proceedings Symposium, San Diego, California, 1999.__ Ed. by G. E. Fuchs et al. LC 99-75790. (Illus.). 230p. 1999. 74.00 (*0-87339-453-4*) Minerals Metals.

Long-Term Stewardship & the Nuclear Weapons Complex: The Challenge Ahead. Katherine N. Probst & Michael H. McGovern. LC 98-23013. (Illus.). 67p. 1998. pap. text 9.95 (*0-915707-97-7*) Resources Future.

Long-Term Studies in Ecology. Ed. by Gene E. Likens. (Illus.). 210p. 1990. 101.95 (*0-387-96743-5*) Spr-Verlag.

Long-Term Studies of Vertebrate Communities. Martin L. Cody & Jeffrey A. Smallwood. LC 96-12813. (Illus.). 597p. 1996. text 69.95 (*0-12-178075-9*) Acad Pr.

Long-Term Surveillance System for British Woodland Vegetation. H. C. Dawkins & D. R. Field. 1978. 45.00 (*0-85074-038-X*) St Mut.

Long-Term Tamoxifen Treatment for Breast Cancer. Ed. by Craig V. Jordan. LC 93-39744. 309p. 1994. reprint ed. pap. 95.80 (*0-608-01871-6*, 206252300003) Bks Demand.

Long Term Threats to Canada's James Bay from Human Development. Jan Beyea & Joyce Rosenthal. (Environmental Policy Analysis Department Reports). (Illus.). 34p. (Orig.). 1989. pap. text. write for info. (*0-930698-31-2*) Natl Audubon.

Long-term Treatment of Depression, Vol. 3. S. A. Montgomery & F. Rouillon. LC 91-40088. (Perspectives in Psychiatry Ser.: No. 1951). 286p. 1992. 235.95 (*0-471-92892-5*, Wiley-Liss) Wiley.

Long-Term Treatments of Anxiety Disorders. Ed. by Robert F. Prien & Matig R. Mavissakalian. 464p. 1996. 58.00 (*0-88048-656-2*, 8656) Am Psychiatric.

Long-Term Trends in Latin American Economic Development. Ed. & Intro. by Miguel Urrutia. 170p. (C). 1991. pap. text 14.50 (*0-940602-38-5*) IADB.

Long-Term Unemployed & the Elderly in Migrant Communities in Europe. Council of Europe Staff. 1992. 12.00 (*92-871-2019-6*, Pub. by Council of Europe) Manhattan Pub Co.

Long Term Unemployment. Odile Benoit-Guilbot. 1994. 18.00 (*1-85567-212-X*) St Martin.

Long-Term Unemployment. Ed. by Odile Benoit-Guilbot & Duncan Gallie. LC 94-13741. (Social Change in Western Europe Ser.). 182p. 1994. 45.00 (*1-85567-248-0*) St Martin.

*__Long-Term Unemployment & Reemployment Policies.__ Laurie J. Bassi & Stephen A. Woodbury. LC 00-30199. (Research in Employment Policy Ser.). 2000. write for info. (*0-7623-0577-0*) Jai Pr.

Long-Term Utilization of Space Station Freedom: Public Policy Workshop Report. 30p. 1992. pap. 14.95 (*0-685-75202-X*, PP-22) AIAA.

Long Term Variability of Pelagic Fish Populations & Their Environment: Proceedings of the International Symposium, Sendai, Japan, 14-18 November 1989. Tsuyoshi Kawasaki et al. LC 91-8859. 412p. 1991. 186.00 (*0-08-040266-6*, Pub. by Pergamon Repr) Franklin.

Long-term Viability of Amtrak & the Need for A Dedicated Funding Source: Hearing Before the Committee on Finance, United States Senate, One Hundred Fifth Congress, First Session on S. 436, April 23, 1997. United States. LC 98-212701. iv, 109p. 1997. write for info. (*0-16-057261-4*) USGPO.

Long-Throated Flumes & Broad-Crested Weirs. Ed. by M. G. Bos. 1984. text 136.00 (*90-247-3113-5*) Kluwer Academic.

Long Time Ago. write for info. (*0-9702281-9-8*) T Mooney.

Long Time Ago & Half a World Away. unabridged ed. Hugh Borrow. 169p. 1998. pap., per. 12.95 (*0-938911-14-7*) Indiv Ed - Poppy Ln.

Long Time Between Kisses. Sandra Scoppettone. LC 81-47853. 224p. (YA). (gr. 7 up). 1982. 12.95 (*0-06-025229-4*) HarpC Child Bks.

Long-Time Clinical Care of Parkinson's Disease, Symposium, Tokyo, April 1986: Journal: European Neurology, Vol. 26, Suppl. 1, 1987. Ed. by T. Nakanishi. (Illus.). iv, 56p. 1987. pap. 18.50 (*3-8055-4590-8*) S Karger.

Long Time Coming. Sandra Brown. 240p. 1997. mass mkt. 6.99 (*0-553-56278-9*, Fanfare) Bantam.

Long Time Coming: Racial Inequality in the Nonmetropolitan South, 1940-1990. Mark A. Fossett & M. Therese Siebert. Ed. by Forrest A. Desaran. LC 96-29842. (Rural Studies). 304p. (C). 1997. pap. 75.00 (*0-8133-8932-1*, Pub. by Westview) HarpC.

Long Time No See. Ed McBain, pseud. 272p. 1987. mass mkt. 4.99 (*0-380-70369-6*, Avon Bks) Morrow Avon.

Long Time No See. Ed McBain, pseud. 304p. 1997. mass mkt. 5.99 (*0-446-60449-6*, Pub. by Warner Bks) Little.

Long Time No See: Confessions of a Hollywood Ganster. Marc Lawrence. 240p. 1996. pap. text 18.95 (*1-880756-17-X*) Riverwood Pr.

Long Time No See: Confessions of a Movie Gangster. Marc Lawrence. (Illus.). 199p. (Orig.). (C). 1993. pap. text 19.95 (*0-9636700-0-X*) Ursus Pr CA.

Long Time Passing. Linda Crew. LC 96-54715. 208p. (YA). (gr. 5-9). 1997. 15.95 (*0-385-32496-0*) Delacorte.

Long Time Passing. Adrienne Jones. LC 90-4046. (Charlotte Zolotow Bk.). 256p. (YA). (gr. 7 up). 1990. 14.95 (*0-06-023055-X*) HarpC Child Bks.

Long Time Passing: Lives of Older Lesbians see Lesbian Passages: True Stories Told by Women over 40
Long-Time Performance of Concrete in a Seawater Exposure. 55p. 1995. pap. 25.00 (*0-89312-190-8*, RP337T) Portland Cement.
Long-Time Predictions in Dynamics: Proceedings of the NATO Advanced Study Institute held in Cortina d'Ampezzo, Italy, August 3-16, 1975. NATO Advanced Study Institute Staff. Ed. by Victor G. Szebehely & Byron D. Tapley. LC 76-7373. (NATO Advanced Study Institute Ser.: No. 26). 1975. lib. bdg. 112.00 (*90-277-0692-1*) Kluwer Academic.
Long to Reign over Us: Memories of Coronation Day & Life in the 1950s. large type ed. Kenneth McLeish & V. McLeash. (Charnwood Library). (Illus.). 336p. 1993. 11.50 (*0-7089-8740-0*, Charnwood) Ulverscroft.
Long Trail. Penny Hayes. 248p. 1986. pap. 8.95 (*0-930044-76-2*) Naiad Pr.
***Long Trail.** Bud Jones. LC 99-91157. 1999. 25.00 (*0-7388-0648-X*); pap. 18.00 (*0-7388-0649-8*) Xlibris Corp.
Long Trail. large type ed. Alan Irwin. (Linford Western Library). 240p. 1996. pap. 16.99 (*0-7089-7878-9*, Linford) Ulverscroft.
Long Trail see Collected Works of Hamlin Garland
Long Trail. Hamlin Garland. (Collected Works of Hamlin Garland). (YA). 1988. reprint ed. lib. bdg. 59.00 (*0-7812-1236-7*) Rprt Serv.
Long Trail. George Watts. (American Autobiography Ser.). 180p. 1995. reprint ed. lib. bdg. 69.00 (*0-7812-8659-X*) Rprt Serv.
Long Trail: Soldiers Songs & Slang, 1914-18. John Brophy & Eric Partridge. LC 72-8462. (Select Bibliographies Reprint Ser.). 1977. reprint ed. 20.95 (*0-8369-6966-9*) Ayer.
***Long Trail Back.** Todhunter Ballard. 1999. 19.00 (*0-7540-8070-6*, Gunsmoke) Chivers N Amer.
Long Trail Guide. 24th ed. Ed. by Sylvia L. Plumb. (Illus.). 238p. 1997. reprint ed. pap. 14.95 (*1-888021-01-2*) Green Mtn Club.
***Long Trail Home.** Stephen A. Bly. 2001. pap. 12.99 (*0-8054-2356-7*) Broadman.
Long Trail Home. Tracy Dunham. LC 96-96762. (Mythmaker Ser.: No. 3). 192p. 1996. 18.95 (*0-8034-9176-X*, Avalon Bks) Bouregy.
Long Trail North. John J. Conley. Ed. by Doug Grad. 192p. (Orig.). 1993. mass mkt. 4.50 (*0-671-74930-7*) PB.
Long Trail to Paradise: Linus Brooks - Founder of Brooks, Oregon Journal of 1850. Compiled by CCGS Staff. (Illus.). 162p. 1986. 15.00 (*1-892685-38-8*) Clark Cnty Gene.
Long Transition: Building Socialism in Tanzania. Idrian N. Resnick. LC 80-8089. 416p. 1982. 28.00 (*0-85345-554-6*, Pub. by Monthly Rev); pap. 12.00 (*0-85345-555-4*, Pub. by Monthly Rev) NYU Pr.
Long Trek to Solola. Inga Solonevich. LC 92-7262. (Illus.). 266p. (Orig.). 1992. 18.95 (*0-936015-35-7*); pap. 12.95 (*0-936015-34-9*) Pocahontas Pr.
Long Trick of Pennywise. John Pound. (C). 1990. pap. 35.00 (*0-7223-2457-X*, Pub. by A H S Ltd) St Mut.
Long Trip: The Prehistory of Psychedelia. Paul Devereux. LC 96-53444. (Illus.). 224p. 1997. pap. 15.95 (*0-14-019540-8*) Viking Penguin.
Long Trip: The Prehistory of Psychedelia. Paul Devereux. 1999. pap. 12.95 (*0-14-025378-5*) Viking Penguin.
Long Trip to Z. Fulvio Testa. LC 96-47336. (Illus.). 32p. (J). (ps-3). 1997. 15.00 (*0-15-201610-4*) Harcourt.
Long Turn Toward Light. Barbara Angell. (Illus.). 121p. (Orig.). 1991. pap. 10.00 (*0-914946-94-3*) Cleveland St Univ Poetry Ctr.
Long Tusk. Baxter. 2000. 23.00 (*0-06-105133-0*); mass mkt. 5.99 (*0-06-105135-7*) HarpC.
Long Twentieth Century. Giovanni Arrighi. 224p. (C). 1994. pap. 23.00 (*1-85984-015-9*, B4616, Pub. by Verso) Norton.
Long Vacation. large type ed. Mary Romney. 304p. 1987. 27.99 (*0-7089-1715-1*) Ulverscroft.
Long Valley. John Steinbeck. (Twentieth-Century Classics Ser.). 6304p. 1995. pap. 12.95 (*0-14-018745-6*, Penguin Classics) Viking Penguin.
Long Vegetable Fibres. R. R. Mukherjee & T. Radhakrishnan. 81p. 1972. 100.00 (*0-7855-7203-1*) St Mut.
Long View. Charles O. Hartman. LC 98-48771. (Wesleyan Poetry Ser.). 136p. 1999. pap. 12.95 (*0-8195-2253-8*, Wesleyan Univ Pr); text 27.00 (*0-8195-6380-3*, Wesleyan Univ Pr) U Pr of New Eng.
Long View. Elizabeth J. Howard. 384p. 1996. per. 12.00 (*0-671-00024-1*) PB.
Long View. Mary Richmond. (Russell Sage Foundation Reprint Ser.). (Illus.). 1971. reprint ed. lib. bdg. 37.00 (*0-697-00209-8*) Irvington.
Long View: Essays on the Discipline of Hope & Poetic Craft. Robert Pack. LC 91-13598. 296p. (C). 1991. lib. bdg. 32.50 (*0-87023-761-6*) U of Mass Pr.
Long View in Economic Policy: The Case of Agriculture & Food. Theodore W. Schultz. 16p. 1987. pap. 9.95 (*1-55815-006-4*) ICS Pr.
Long View of History. 3rd ed. George Novack. 46p. 1979. reprint ed. pap. 3.50 (*0-87348-428-2*) Pathfinder NY.
***Long View of Improved Putting: Using the Long Putter.** Richard E. Heyl & Glenn R. Apple. Ed. by Michelle S. Wright. (Illus.). xxvi, 146p. 1999. pap. text 25.95 (*0-9653532-4-9*) Leaning Pine Pub.
Long Vowel A. Dona H. Rice. (Vowel Workbks.). 32p. (J). (gr. k-2). 1997. pap. 2.95 (*1-57690-231-5*) Tchr Create Mat.
Long Vowel E. Dona H. Rice. (Vowel Workbks.). 32p. (J). (gr. k-2). 1997. pap. 2.95 (*1-57690-232-3*) Tchr Create Mat.
Long Vowel I. Dona H. Rice. (Vowel Workbks.). (J). (gr. k-2). 1997. pap. 2.95 (*1-57690-233-1*) Tchr Create Mat.
Long Vowel O. Dona H. Rice. (Vowel Workbks.). 32p. (J). (gr. k-2). 1997. pap. 2.95 (*1-57690-234-X*) Tchr Create Mat.
Long Vowel Readers, 5 vols., Set. E. Reid et al. (Start Reading Ser.: Set B). 40p. (J). (ps-3). 1986. pap. text 14.95 (*1-56422-037-0*) Start Reading.
Long Vowel Readers: Blue Book Kit. Yuriko Nichols. (Learning Language Arts Through Literature Ser.). (Illus.). 10p. (J). 1998. pap. 15.00 (*1-880892-58-8*) Com Sense FL.
Long Vowel Readers & Workbooks, 10 vols., Set. E. Reid et al. (Start Reading Ser.: Set B). 164p. (J). (ps-3). 1986. pap. text 28.95 (*1-56422-043-5*); pap. text 369.95 (*1-56422-047-8*) Start Reading.
Long Vowel Review. Dona H. Rice. (Vowel Workbks.). 32p. (J). (gr. k-2). 1997. pap. 2.95 (*1-57690-236-6*) Tchr Create Mat.
Long Vowel U. Dona H. Rice. (Vowel Workbks.). 32p. (J). (gr. k-2). 1997. pap. 2.95 (*1-57690-235-8*) Tchr Create Mat.
***Long Vowel Word Machines: Grade 1-3.** Jo Ellen Moore. Ed. by Marilyn Evans. (Word Machines Ser.). (Illus.). 28p. 2000. pap., teacher ed. 12.95 (*1-55799-758-6*, 781) Evan-Moor Edu Pubs.
Long Vowel Workbooks, 5 vols., Set. E. Reid et al. (Start Reading Ser.: Set B). 124p. (J). (ps-3). 1986. pap. text 14.95 (*1-56422-040-0*) Start Reading.
Long Vowels. Barbara Gregorich. Ed. by Joan Hoffman. (I Know It! Book Ser.). (Illus.). 32p. (ps-3). 1981. student ed. 2.49 (*0-938256-41-6*, 02041) Sch Zone Pub Co.
***Long Vowels.** Vicky Shiotsu. (Monster Phonics Ser.). (Illus.). 48p. (J). (gr. 1-2). 1999. pap. 5.95 (*0-7373-0218-6*, 02186w) NTC Contemp Pub Co.
***Long Vowels: CD-ROM Edition.** Steven Traugh & Susan Traugh. Ed. by Rozanne Lanczak Williams. (Fun Phonics Ser.: Vol. 8027). (Illus.). 24p. (J). (gr. k). 1999. pap. 12.98 incl. cd-rom (*1-57471-641-7*) Creat Teach Pr.
Long Vowels: Reading & Writing Skills. Jo Ellen Moore. (Illus.). 32p. (J). (gr. k-2). 1995. pap., wbk. ed. 2.50 (*1-58610-027-0*, Learn on the Go) Learn Horizon.
Long Vowels Vol. 8023: Fun Phonics. Steven Traugh & Rozanne L. Williams. (Fun Phonics Ser.: Vol. 3). (Illus.). 24p. (J). (gr. k-2). 1993. pap., wbk. ed. 10.98 (*1-57471-093-1*) Creat Teach Pr.
Long Vowels (Language) Jo E. Moore. (Reading & Writing Ser.). (Illus.). 32p. (J). (gr. 1-2). 1996. pap., teacher ed. 2.95 (*1-55799-406-4*, 4008) Evan-Moor Edu Pubs.
Long Voyage. Jorge Semprun. 1997. pap. 11.95 (*0-14-118029-3*) Viking Penguin.
Long Voyage. Jorge Semprun. 1999. pap. write for info. (*0-14-026262-8*) Viking Penguin.
Long Voyage Back. Luke Rhinehart. 1996. pap. text 14.95 (*0-07-052507-2*) McGraw.
Long Voyage Back: A Novel. Luke Rhinehart. LC 82-23586. (Bluejacket Paperback Ser.). 408p. 1995. pap. 15.95 (*1-55750-130-0*) Naval Inst Pr.
Long Voyage Home: 7 Plays of the Sea. Eugene O'Neill. 21.95 (*0-89190-369-0*) Amereon Ltd.
Long Voyage Home & Other Plays. unabridged ed. Eugene O'Neill. (Thrift Editions Ser.). (Illus.). 80p. 1995. reprint ed. pap. text 1.00 (*0-486-28755-6*) Dover.
***Long Wait.** Annie Cobb. LC 99-42682. (Math Matters Ser.). (Illus.). 32p. (J). (gr. 1-3). 2000. pap. 4.59 (*1-57565-094-0*) Kane Pr.
***Long Wait.** Annie Cobb. (Math Matters Ser.). (Illus.). (J). 2000. 10.40 (*0-606-18221-7*) Turtleback.
Long Wait. Mickey Spillane, pseud. 20.95 (*0-89190-835-8*) Amereon Ltd.
Long Wait. Budge Wilson. (Illus.). 32p. (J). (ps up). 13.95 (*0-7737-5851-8*) STDK.
Long Wait. large type ed. Patricia Robins. (Dales Large Print Ser.). 300p. 1996. pap. 18.99 (*1-85389-629-2*, Dales) Ulverscroft.
Long Wait. unabridged ed. Budge Wilson. (Illus.). 32p. (J). (ps up). 1997. 16.95 (*0-7737-3021-4*) STDK.
Long Wait: The Forging of the Anglo-American Nuclear Alliance 1945-58, 64. Timothy J. Botti. LC 87-7530. (Contributions in Military Studies Ser.: No. 64). 282p. 1987. 65.00 (*0-313-25902-X*, BLW/, Greenwood Pr) Greenwood.
Long Walk. Stephen King & Richard Bachman. 370p. 1999. mass mkt. 7.99 (*0-451-19671-6*, Sig) NAL.
Long Walk. Karl Lassiter. 416p. 1996. mass mkt. 5.99 (*0-7860-0305-7*, Pinncle Kensgtn) Kensgtn Pub Corp.
Long Walk. Slavomir Rawicz. 1995. reprint ed. lib. bdg. 27.95 (*1-56849-676-1*) Buccaneer Bks.
***Long Walk.** abr. deluxe ed. Slavomir Rawicz. LC 99-67831. (Adventure Library Ser.: Vol. 20). 268p. 1999. reprint ed. lib. bdg. 32.50 (*1-885283-20-2*) Advent Library.
Long Walk: A History of the Navajo Wars, 1846-1868. Lynn R. Bailey. (Illus.). 300p. 1979. 24.95 (*0-87026-047-2*) Westernlore.
Long Walk: The Placemaking Legacy of Howard University. Harry G. Robinson, III & Hazel R. Edwards. Ed. by Thomas C. Battle & Clifford L. Muse. LC 96-76220. (Illus.). xviii, 264p. 1996. 250.00 (*0-9652091-0-5*); pap. 50.00 (*0-9652091-2-1*); lthr. 1500.00 (*0-9652091-2-1*) Howard Univ.
Long Walk: The True Story of a Trek to Freedom. Slavomir Rawicz. LC 98-107014. 252p. 1997. reprint ed. 25.00 (*1-55821-634-0*); reprint ed. pap. 12.95 (*1-55821-684-7*) Lyons Pr.
Long Walk Home. Larsen. 1981. pap. 10.00 (*0-06-250980-2*, Perennial) HarperTrade.
Long Walk Home. Matt Mattingly. (Illus.). 168p. 1998. pap. 12.95 (*1-880710-38-2*) Monterey Pacific.
Long Walk Home. large type ed. Michael O'Donnell. (Adventure Suspense Ser.). 1989. 27.99 (*0-7089-2061-6*) Ulverscroft.
Long Walk in the Australian Bush. William J. Lires. LC 98-21240. 208p. 1998. pap. 16.95 (*0-8203-2055-2*) U of Ga Pr.
***Long Walk on the Isle of Skye: A New 75-Mile Island Trek.** David Paterson. (Illus.). 144p. 1999. pap. 27.50 (*0-9521908-4-2*, Pub. by Peak Pubg Ltd) Trans-Atl Phila.
Long Walk Through War: A Combat Doctor's Diary. Klaus H. Huebner. LC 86-30103. (Military History Ser.: No. 4). (Illus.). 224p. 1987. 19.95 (*0-89096-320-7*) Tex A&M Univ Pr.
Long Walk to Church: A Contemporary History of Russian Orthodoxy. Nathaniel Davis. (C). 1994. pap. 32.00 (*0-8133-2277-4*, Pub. by Westview) HarpC.
Long Walk to Forever: Based Upon an Episode from Kurt Vonnegut, Jr's "Welcome to the Monkey House"/by Brian Harnetiaux. Kurt Vonnegut, Jr. 20p. 1990. pap. 3.50 (*0-87129-625-X*, L61) Dramatic Pub.
Long Walk to Freedom: The Autobiography of Nelson Mandela. Nelson Mandela. (Illus.). 608p. 1995. pap. 14.95 (*0-316-54818-9*) Little.
***Long Walk to Freedom & Mandela.** HRW Staff. 2000. text 11.60 (*0-03-056581-2*) Harcourt Schl Pubs.
***Long Walk to Freedom & Mandela.** HRW Staff. 2000. pap. text, student ed. 13.20 (*0-03-056582-0*) Harcourt Schl Pubs.
Long Walk to Mulege. Howard Hale. 119p. (Orig.). 1980. pap. 12.95 (*0-9640189-1-8*) Pinkerton CA.
Long Walk up the Water Slide, Vol. 1. Don Winslow. 1998. 5.99 (*0-312-96617-2*, Pub. by Tor Bks) St Martin.
Long Walks & Intimate Talks. Grace Paley. LC 90-27844. (Illus.). 80p. 1991. 29.95 (*1-55861-043-X*); pap. 12.95 (*1-55861-044-8*) Feminist Pr.
Long Walks in the Afternoon, Poems. Margaret Gibson. LC 82-275. 63p. 1982. pap. 12.95 (*0-8071-1018-3*); text 15.95 (*0-8071-1017-5*) La State U Pr.
Long Wall Mining. (Illus.). 60p. (Orig.). (C). 1995. pap. text 20.00 (*0-7881-2515-X*) DIANE Pub.
Long War: The Intellectual People's Front & Anti-Stalinism, 1930-1940. Judy Kutulas. LC 94-26407. 352p. 1994. text 49.95 (*0-8223-1526-2*); pap. text 18.95 (*0-8223-1524-6*) Duke.
Long War: The IRA & Sinn Fein, 1985 to Today. Brendan O'Brien. 448p. 1995. 19.95 (*0-8156-0319-3*) Syracuse U Pr.
Long War: The IRA & Sinn Fein, 1985 to Today. 2nd ed. Brendan O'Brien. LC 99-21434. (Irish Studies). 345p. 1999. pap. 19.95 (*0-8156-0597-8*) Syracuse U Pr.
***Long War Against God: The History & Impact of the Creation/Evolution Conflict.** Henry Morris. LC 00-100214. 344p. 2000. pap. 13.99 (*0-89051-291-4*) Master Bks.
Long War Dead. Bryan A. Floyd. LC 83-63243. 96p. 1984. pap. 16.00 (*0-932966-45-4*) Permanent Pr.
Long Watch. Harvey Haislip. 1953. pap. 5.25 (*0-8222-0686-2*) Dramatists Play.
Long Wave in Economic Life. Jacob J. Duijn. 240p. (C). 1983. text 37.95 (*0-04-330330-7*); pap. text 18.95 (*0-04-330331-5*) Routledge.
Long Wave in the World Economy: The Current Crisis in Historical Perspective. Andrew Tylecote. 368p. (C). 1993. pap. 29.99 (*0-415-03691-7*, B2422) Routledge.
Long-Wave Optics, Vol. 1. George W. Chantry. 1984. text 162.00 (*0-12-168101-7*) Acad Pr.
Long Wave Polar Modes in Semiconductor Heterostructures. C. Trallero-Giner et al. LC 97-29180. 164p. 1998. 130.50 (*0-08-042694-8*, Pergamon Pr) Elsevier.
Long-Wave Rhythms in Economic Development & Political Behavior. Brian J. L. Berry. LC 90-4586. (Illus.). 280p. 1991. text 49.50 (*0-8018-4035-X*) Johns Hopkins.
Long-Wave Runup Models. LC 96-49412. 500p. 1997. lib. bdg. 82.00 (*981-02-2909-7*) World Scientific Pub.
Long Wave Theory. Ed. by Christopher Freeman. LC 96-5870. (International Library of Critical Writings in Economics: Vol. 69). 678p. 1996. 270.00 (*1-85278-954-9*) E Elgar.
Long Wavelength Infrared Detectors. Ed. by Manijeh Razeghi. (Optoelectronic Properties of Semiconducter Ser.). 488p. 1997. text 81.00 (*2-88449-208-9*); pap. text 48.00 (*2-88449-209-7*) Gordon & Breach.
Long Wavelength Infrared Detectors & Arrays: Physics & Applications. Ed. by S. S. Li et al. LC 95-61601. (Proceedings Ser.: Vol. 95-28). (Illus.). 264p. 1995. 44.00 (*1-56677-124-2*) Electrochem Soc.
Long Wavelength Infrared Detectors & Arrays: Physics & Applications: Second International Symposium. V. Swaminathan et al. (Proceedings Ser.: Vol. 94-30). 264p. 1995. pap. 44.00 (*1-56677-089-0*) Electrochem Soc.
***Long Wavelength Infrared Detectors & Arrays: Physics & Applications VI.** Ed. by S. S. Li et al. 242p. 1999. 46.00 (*1-56677-215-X*, PV 98-21) Electrochem Soc.
Long Wavelength Infrared Detectors & Arrays: Physics & Applications/State-of-the-Art Program on Compound Semiconductors XIX. Ed. by F. Radpour et al. LC 93-72863. (Proceedings Ser.: Vol. 94-5). (Illus.). 384p. 1995. 40.00 (*1-56677-034-3*) Electrochem Soc.
Long Wavelength Infrared Detectors & Arrays V: Physics & Applications. Ed. by S. S. Li et al. LC 98-158678. (Proceedings Ser.: Vol. 97-33). 280p. 1998. 46.00 (*1-56677-186-2*) Electrochem Soc.
***Long Wavelength Infrared Emitters Based on Quantum Wells & Superlattices.** Ed. by Manfred Helm. (Optoelectronic Properties of Semiconductor Ser.: Vol. 6). 412p. 2000. text 150.00 (*90-5699-683-5*, G & B Science) Gordon & Breach.
Long-Wavelength Semiconductor Devices, Materials & Processes Vol. 216: Materials Research Society Symposium Proceedings. Ed. by A. Katz et al. 543p. 1991. text 17.50 (*1-55899-108-5*) Materials Res.
Long Waves in Economic Development: Kondratieff, Schumpter & the Enigma of Long Waves. Jan Reijnders. (Illus.). 320p. 1990. text 95.00 (*1-85278-339-7*) E Elgar.
Long Waves of Capitalist Development: A Marxist Interpretation. 2nd rev. ed. Ernest Mandel. LC 95-3101. 174p. (C). 1995. pap. 23.00 (*1-85984-037-X*, C0480, Pub. by Verso) Norton.
Long Way. Jay Bern. LC 98-65641. 310p. 1998. pap. 18.95 (*1-57197-121-1*) Pentland Pr.
Long Way. Bernard Moitessier. 1996. pap. text 14.95 (*0-07-042958-8*) McGraw.
Long Way. Bernard Moitessier. (Illus.). 252p. 1995. pap. 14.95 (*0-924486-84-8*) Sheridan.
Long Way Down: A Novel. Douglas Hall. LC 72-191185. 184 p. (J). 1971. write for info. (*0-7737-0003-X*) Musson Publ.
***Long Way from Chicago.** Elizabeth Klar. Ed. by Dawn Michelle Robbins. (J). 2000. 9.95 (*1-58130-628-8*); 11.95 (*1-58130-629-6*) Novel Units.
***Long Way from Chicago.** Richard Peck. LC 98-10953. 148p. (J). (gr. 4-7). 1998. 15.99 (*0-8037-2290-7*, Dial Yng Read) Peng Put Young Read.
***Long Way from Chicago.** Richard Peck. (Illus.). 176p. (J). (gr. 5 up). 2000. pap. 4.99 (*0-14-130352-2*, PuffinBks) Peng Put Young Read.
***Long Way from Home.** Connie Briscoe. 416p. 2000. mass mkt. 6.99 (*0-06-103021-X*, Avon Bks) Morrow Avon.
Long Way from Home. Gordon Kahn. LC 88-34238. 464p. 1989. pap. 20.00 (*0-916950-90-5*) Biling Rev-Pr.
Long Way from Home. Claude McKay. LC 74-77507. (American Negro: His History & Literature. Series 2). 1980. reprint ed. 29.95 (*0-405-01880-0*) Ayer.
***Long Way from Home: A Memoir.** Robert L. Long. (Illus.). 80p. (Orig.). 1999. pap. 10.00 (*0-9674100-0-2*) New Sthrn Writers.
Long Way from Home: A Novel. Frederick Busch. 304p. 1994. reprint ed. pap. 12.00 (*0-449-90922-0*, Columbine) Fawcett.
Long Way from Home: A Sociological Exploration of Contemporary Idolatry. J. A. Walter. 217p. 1979. pap. 12.75 (*0-85364-260-5*, Pub. by Paternoster Pub) McClelland & Stewart.
Long Way from Home: An Autobiography. Claude McKay. (American Biography Ser.). 354p. 1991. reprint ed. lib. bdg. 79.00 (*0-7812-8282-9*) Rprt Serv.
Long Way from Home: Effects of Public High Schools on Village Children Away from Home. Judith Kleinfeld. LC 73-620228. (ISER Reports: No. 38). (Illus.). 215p. 1973. pap. 5.00 (*0-88353-011-2*) U Alaska Inst Res.
Long Way from Home: The Tuberculosis Epidemic among the Inuit. Pat S. Grygier. (McGill-Queen's Series in Health & Society). (Illus.). 272p. 1994. 60.00 (*0-7735-1216-0*, Pub. by McG-Queens Univ Pr) CUP Services.
Long Way from Home: The Tuberculosis Epidemic among the Inuit. Pat S. Grygier. (McGill-queen's Hannah Institute Studies in the History of Medicine, Health, & Society Ser.). (Illus.). 272p. 1997. pap. 22.95 (*0-7735-1637-9*, Pub. by McG-Queens Univ Pr) CUP Services.
Long Way from Hungary. John T. Gojack. 110p. 1996. 42.95 (*1-888672-10-2*) J Ciano Pubng.
Long Way from Hungary, Vol. 1. John T. Gojack. 110p. 1996. pap. 32.95 (*1-888672-11-0*) J Ciano Pubng.
Long Way from Solving That One: Psycho-Social & Ethical Implications of Ross Macdonald's Lew Archer Tales. Jeffrey H. Mahan. 166p. (C). 1990. lib. bdg. 37.50 (*0-8191-7710-5*) U Pr of Amer.
Long Way from St. Louie. Colleen J. McElroy. LC 96-53099. 200p. (Orig.). 1997. pap. 13.95 (*1-56689-059-4*) Coffee Hse.
Long Way from the Creek. Howard E. Blank. LC 97-76068. 389p. 1998. 24.00 (*0-9661751-1-5*) Pikesville Pr.
Long Way from the Road: The Wit & Wisdom of Prince Edward Island. David Weale. 116p. 1998. 13.95 (*0-9698606-3-3*) Acorn Pr.
Long Way from Tipperary: What a Former Monk Discovered in His Search for the Truth. John Dominic Crossan. LC 00-20477. 240p. 2000. 23.00 (*0-06-069974-4*, Pub. by Harper SF) HarpC.
Long Way from Zero. David Major. 246p. (Orig.). (J). (gr. 6-10). 1996. pap. 12.95 (*0-9655533-0-2*) Davdsn Pubng VA.
***Long Way Home.** Larry Dane Brimner. (Rookie Readers Ser.). (Illus.). (J). 2000. 18.00 (*0-516-22011-X*) Childrens.
Long Way Home. Connie Briscoe. LC 98-52053. 368p. 1999. 25.00 (*0-06-017278-9*) HarpC.
***Long Way Home.** Robert J. Conley. LC 00-37401. Vol. 5. 192p. 2000. pap. 11.95 (*0-8061-3276-0*) U of Okla Pr.
Long Way Home. Patricia Foster. 320p. 1999. pap. 23.95 (*0-525-94253-X*) NAL.
***Long Way Home.** Lydia Laube. 1998. pap. text 12.95 (*1-86254-325-9*) Wakefield Pr.
Long Way Home. Cheryl Reavis. (Special Edition Ser.: No. 1245). 1999. per. 4.25 (*0-373-24245-X*, 1-24245-2) Silhouette.
Long Way Home. Melissa Romero. (Illus.). 200p. (YA). 2000. pap. 11.00 (*1-883573-15-7*) Pride & Imprints.
Long Way Home, 1 vol. Wendy Corsi Staub. (Friends Ser.). 352p. 1999. mass mkt. 5.99 (*0-515-12440-0*, Jove) Berkley Pub.
Long Way Home: A Pacific Odyssey of World War II. James R. Schultz. (Illus.). 144p. (Orig.). 1996. pap. 12.50 (*0-88739-114-1*) Creat Arts Bk.
Long Way Home: Poems by Pat Schneider. Pat Schneider. 96p. 1993. pap. 14.00 (*0-941895-11-4*) Amherst Wri Art.
Long Way Home: Twelve Years of Words. Dwight Yoakam. LC 98-49549. 192p. 1999. 21.95 (*0-7868-6514-8*, Pub. by Hyperion) Time Warner.

L

An Asterisk (*) at the beginning of an entry indicates that the title is appearing for the first time.

Long Way Home . . . A Christmas Story. Stephen C. LaPanta. (Illus.). 56p. 1996. 15.95 (*0-9659048-0-6*) Homewrd Bound.

Long Way Home, the Short Way of Love. John F. Marshall. (Spirit & Life Ser.). viii, 114p. 1968. pap. 3.50 (*1-57659-090-9*) Franciscan Inst.

Long Way to a New Land. Joan Sandin. LC 80-8942. (I Can Read Bks.). (Illus.). 64p. (J). (ps-3). 1986. pap. 3.95 (*0-06-444100-8*, HarpTrophy) HarpC Child Bks.

Long Way to a New Land. Joan Sandin. (I Can Read Bks.). (Illus.). (J). (gr. 2-4). 1991. pap. 8.95 incl. audio (*1-55994-494-3*) HarperAudio.

Long Way to a New Land. Joan Sandin. (I Can Read Bks.). (J). (gr. 2-4). 1981. 8.95 (*0-606-00914-0*, Pub. by Turtleback) Demco.

Long Way to a New Land Literature Mini-Unit. Janet Lovelady. (Illus.). 32p. (J). (gr. 3-5). 1990. student ed. 4.95 (*1-56096-013-2*) Mari.

Long Way to a New Land Study Guide. Colleen Schreurs. 50p. (J). (gr. 1-3). 1993. reprint ed. student ed., ring bd. 9.99 (*1-58609-113-1*) Progeny Pr WI.

Long Way to Europe: Historical Observations from a Contemporary View. Ed. by Wolfgang Mommsen. LC 93-36819. 254p. 1994. 24.95 (*0-86715-270-2*) Edition Q.

Long Way to Go. large type ed. Una Rothwell. 320p. 1987. 27.99 (*0-7089-1617-1*) Ulverscroft.

Long Way to Go: A Story of Women's Right to Vote. Zibby O'Neal. (Once Upon America Ser.). (Illus.). 64p. (J). (gr. 2-6). 1992. pap. 4.99 (*0-14-032950-1*, PuffinBks) Peng Put Young Read.

Long Way to Go: A Story of Women's Right to Vote. Zibby O'Neal. (Once upon America Ser.). (J). 1992. 10.19 (*0-606-01718-6*, Pub. by Turtleback) Demco.

Long Way to Go: Black & White in America. Jonathan Coleman. 1997. 27.50 (*0-517-59087-5*, Crown) Crown Pub Group.

***Long Way to Go: Black & White in America.** Jonathan Coleman. 480p. 1998. reprint ed. pap. 15.00 (*0-87113-723-2*, Atlntc Mnthly) Grove-Atltic.

***Long Way to Los Gatos.** Verne R. Albright. (Illus.). 384p. 1999. 29.95 (*0-9658533-2-2*) Amigo Pubns.

Long Way to See: Images & Voices of North Dakota. Photos by Wayne Gudmundson. LC 87-71788. (Illus.). 112p. 1987. pap. 18.00 (*0-911042-36-9*) NDSU Inst Reg.

***Long Way up the Rock Dump: The Story of Life in a Little Western Pennsylvania Coal Town.** (Illus.). 220p. 2000. pap. 15.00 (*0-9676200-0-7*) C S K Stewart.

Long Way Westward. Joan Sandin. LC 89-2024. (I Can Read Bks.). (Illus.). 64p. (J). (ps-3). 1992. pap. 3.95 (*0-06-444198-9*, HarpTrophy) HarpC Child Bks.

Long Way Westward. Joan Sandin. (I Can Read Bks.). (J). (gr. 2-4). 1992. 8.95 (*0-606-02304-6*, Pub. by Turtleback) Demco.

Long Way Westward Study Guide. Colleen Schreurs. 44p. (J). (gr. 1-3). 1993. student ed., ring bd. 9.99 (*1-58609-114-X*) Progeny Pr WI.

Long Ways from Where I've Been: An African-American's Journey from the Jim Crow South to Chicago's Gold Coast. Roosevelt Richards. 176p. 1994. pap. 10.95 (*1-879360-35-7*) Noble Pr.

Long Week-End, 1897-1919: Part of a Life. Wilfred R. Bion. 299p. 1990. reprint ed. pap. text 41.95 (*0-9507895-0-X*, Pub. by H Karnac Bks Ltd) Brunner-Mazel.

Long Weekend 1897-1919: Part of a Life. Wilfred R. Bion. 287p. 1991. pap. 41.50 (*1-85575-000-7*, Pub. by H Karnac Bks Ltd) Other Pr LLC.

***Long Weekends.** Lee Bailey. LC 99-52841. 2000. 16.99 (*0-517-20899-7*) Random Hse Value.

Long Were the Nights: The Saga of a PT Squadron in the Solomons. Hugh B. Cave. 1981. reprint ed. 17.95 (*0-89201-091-6*) Zenger Pub.

Long White. Sharon Dilworth. LC 88-17307. (Iowa Short Fiction Award Ser.). 204p. 1988. 10.00 (*0-87745-216-4*) U of Iowa Pr.

Long White Con. Iceberg Slim & Robert Beck. 224p. 1988. mass mkt. 6.99 (*0-87067-974-0*) Holloway.

Long Wind. Beverly Lauderdale. LC 87-91110. 1988. 16.95 (*0-87212-211-5*) Libra.

Long-Winded Lady: Notes from the New Yorker. Maeve Brennan. LC 98-7925. 288p. 1998. pap. 13.00 (*0-395-89363-1*) HM.

Long Winter see Little House Books

Long Winter. Laura Ingalls Wilder. (Little House). (J). (gr. 3-6). 1995. pap. 2.50 (*0-590-30094-6*) Scholastic Inc.

Long Winter. Laura Ingalls Wilder. (Little House). (J). (gr. 3-6). 1981. 10.05 (*0-606-03846-9*, Pub. by Turtleback) Demco.

Long Winter. large type ed. Eva Burfield. 320p. 1987. 27.99 (*0-7089-1608-2*) Ulverscroft.

Long Winter. rev. ed. Laura Ingalls Wilder. LC 52-7530. (Little House). (Illus.). 352p. (J). (gr. 4-7). 1953. 16.95 (*0-06-026460-8*); lib. bdg. 16.89 (*0-06-026461-6*) HarpC Child Bks.

Long Winter Ends. Newton G. Thomas. LC 97-37105. (Great Lakes Books Publication). 368p. 1998. pap. 16.95 (*0-8143-2762-1*) Wayne St U Pr.

Long Winter Gone. Terry C. Johnston. (Sons of the Plains Ser.: No. 1). 480p. 1990. mass mkt. 6.99 (*0-553-28621-8*) Bantam.

Long Work, Short Life. Bernard Malamud. (Chapbooks in Literature Ser.). (Illus.). 1985. 5.00 (*0-9614940-1-8*) Bennington Coll.

Long Year. Ann Chidester. LC 74-26097. (Labor Movement in Fiction & Non-Fiction Ser.). reprint ed. 49.50 (*0-404-58411-X*) AMS Pr.

Long Years of Exile: Central Asian Refugees in Afghanistan & Pakistan. Audrey C. Shalinsky. LC 93-27034. (Illus.). 1993. lib. bdg. 43.00 (*0-8191-9286-4*) U Pr of Amer.

Long Years of Neglect: The Work & Reputation of William Gilmore Simms. John C. Guilds. LC 87-34297. 265p. 1989. text 26.00 (*1-55728-028-2*) U of Ark Pr.

Long Yesterday: The Story of Patrick & Rosie. Lynne Gladstone-Millar. 266p. 1996. 35.00 (*1-85821-306-1*, Pub. by Pentland Pr) St Mut.

Longaberger Story . . . And How We Did It. rev. ed. Steve Williford & Dave Longaberger. LC 90-63930. (Illus.). 216p. 1994. pap. 11.95 (*1-879111-25-X*) Lincoln-Bradley.

Longanimity: A Disposition to Bear Injuries Patiently. 2nd ed. Mary M. Paice. 103p. 1998. reprint ed. pap. 12.00 (*0-9666321-0-9*) Tucker Thompson.

Longarm, No. 230. Tabor Evans. 192p. (Orig.). 1998. mass mkt. 4.99 (*0-515-12230-0*, Jove) Berkley Pub.

Longarm & the Apache Plunder. Tabor Evans. (Longarm Ser.: No. 189). 192p. (Orig.). 1994. mass mkt. 3.99 (*0-515-11454-5*, Jove) Berkley Pub.

Longarm & the Backwoods Baroness. Tabor Evans. (Longarm Ser.: No. 222). 192p. 1997. mass mkt. 4.99 (*0-515-12080-4*, Jove) Berkley Pub.

Longarm & the Barbed Wire Bullies, No. 190. Tabor Evans. 192p. (Orig.). 1994. mass mkt. 3.99 (*0-515-11476-6*, Jove) Berkley Pub.

***Longarm & the Black Widow.** Tabor Evans. (Longarm Ser.: Vol. 259). 192p. 2000. mass mkt. 4.99 (*0-515-12839-2*, Jove) Berkley Pub.

Longarm & the Blossom Rock Banshee, Vol. 238. Tabor Evans. (Longarm Ser.). 192p. 1998. pap. 4.99 (*0-515-12372-2*, Jove) Berkley Pub.

***Longarm & the Blue-Eyed Squaw.** Tabor Evans. (Longarm Ser.: Vol. 19). 2000. mass mkt. 5.99 (*0-515-12705-1*, Jove) Berkley Pub.

Longarm & the Boardinghouse Widow. Tabor Evans. (Longarm Ser.: No. 218). 192p. 1997. mass mkt. 4.99 (*0-515-12016-2*, Jove) Berkley Pub.

Longarm & the Border Wildcat No. 229. Tabor Evans. 192p. 1998. mass mkt. 4.99 (*0-515-12209-2*, Jove) Berkley Pub.

Longarm & the Bounty Hunters. Tabor Evans. (Longarm Ser.: No. 187). 192p. (Orig.). 1994. mass mkt. 3.99 (*0-515-11407-3*, Jove) Berkley Pub.

Longarm & the Bounty of Blood, No. 181. Tabor Evans. LC 94-131134. 192p. (Orig.). 1994. mass mkt. 3.99 (*0-515-11283-6*, Jove) Berkley Pub.

Longarm & the Branded Beauty. Tabor Evans. (Longarm Ser.). 1998. mass mkt. 4.99 (*0-515-12278-5*, Jove) Berkley Pub.

Longarm & the Calgary Kid. Tabor Evans. (Longarm Ser.: Vol. 17). 1998. mass mkt. 5.50 (*0-515-12276-9*, Jove) Berkley Pub.

Longarm & the Chain Gang Women, Vol. 250. Tabor Evans. (Longarm Ser.). 1999. mass mkt. 4.99 (*0-515-12614-4*, Jove) Berkley Pub.

***Longarm & the Church Ladies.** Tabor Evans. (Longarm Ser.: Vol. 260). 2000. mass mkt. 4.99 (*0-515-12872-4*, Jove) Berkley Pub.

Longarm & the Colorado Counterfeiter, 241. Tabor Evans. (Longarm Ser.: Vol. 241). 192p. 1999. mass mkt. 4.99 (*0-515-12437-0*, Jove) Berkley Pub.

Longarm & the Counterfeit Corpse. Tabor Evans. (Longarm Ser.: No. 212). 192p. 1996. mass mkt. 4.99 (*0-515-11925-3*, Jove) Berkley Pub.

Longarm & the Cursed Corpse, 1 vol., Vol. 246. Tabor Evans. (Longarm Ser.). 1999. mass mkt. 4.99 (*0-515-12519-9*, Jove) Berkley Pub.

Longarm & the Danish Dames. Tabor Evans. (Longarm Ser.). 299p. 1999. mass mkt. 5.50 (*0-515-12435-4*, Jove) Berkley Pub.

Longarm & the Dead Man's Play, No. 225. Tabor Evans. 192p. 1997. mass mkt. 4.99 (*0-515-12144-4*, Jove) Berkley Pub.

Longarm & the Dead Man's Reward, Vol. 221. Tabor Evans. (Longarm Ser.: No. 22). 192p. 1997. mass mkt. 4.99 (*0-515-12069-3*, Jove) Berkley Pub.

Longarm & the Deadly Thaw. Tabor Evans. (Longarm Ser.: No. 198). 192p. (Orig.). 1995. mass mkt. 3.99 (*0-515-11634-3*, Jove) Berkley Pub.

Longarm & the Devil's Sister. Tabor Evans. 192p. 1999. 4.99 (*0-515-12485-0*, Jove) Berkley Pub.

***Longarm & the Diary of Madame Velvet, Vol. 251.** Tabor Evans. 1999. mass mkt. 4.99 (*0-515-12660-8*, Jove) Berkley Pub.

Longarm & the Double-Barrel Blowout, Vol. 223. Tabor Evans. (Longarm Ser.: No. 22). 192p. 1997. mass mkt. 4.99 (*0-515-12104-5*, Jove) Berkley Pub.

Longarm & the Double Eagles. Tabor Evans. (Longarm Ser.: No. 166). 192p. (Orig.). 1992. mass mkt. 3.99 (*0-515-10955-X*, Jove) Berkley Pub.

Longarm & the Durango Double-Cross. Tabor Evans. (Longarm Ser.). 1998. mass mkt. 4.99 (*0-515-12244-0*, Jove) Berkley Pub.

***Longarm & the Dynamite Damsel.** Tabor Evans. (Longarm Ser.: Vol. 256). 2000. mass mkt. 4.99 (*0-515-12770-1*, Jove) Berkley Pub.

***Longarm & the Four Corners Gang, 252.** Tabor Evans. Vol. 252. 192p. 1999. mass mkt. 4.99 (*0-515-12687-X*, Jove) Berkley Pub.

***Longarm & the Golden Goddess.** Tabor Evans. (Longarm Ser.: No. 261). 2000. mass mkt. 4.99 (*0-515-12890-2*) Berkley Pub.

Longarm & the Grand Slam Heist. Tabor Evans. (Longarm Ser.: No. 209). 1996. mass mkt. 4.99 (*0-515-11861-3*, Jove) Berkley Pub.

Longarm & the Grave Robbers, No. 239. Tabor Evans. 192p. 1998. pap. 4.99 (*0-515-12392-7*, Jove) Berkley Pub.

Longarm & the Hatchet Woman. Tabor Evans. (Longarm Ser.: Vol. 237). 183p. 1998. mass mkt. 4.99 (*0-515-12356-0*, Jove) Berkley Pub.

Longarm & the Helldorado. Tabor Evans. (Longarm Ser.: No. 196). 192p. (Orig.). 1995. mass mkt. 3.99 (*0-515-11591-6*, Jove) Berkley Pub.

Longarm & the High Rollers. Tabor Evans. (Longarm Ser.: No. 186). 192p. (Orig.). 1994. pap. 3.99 (*0-515-11391-3*, Jove) Berkley Pub.

Longarm & the Hostage Woman. Tabor Evans. (Longarm Ser.: No. 215). (Orig.). 1996. mass mkt. 4.99 (*0-515-11968-7*, Jove) Berkley Pub.

Longarm & the Indian War. Tabor Evans. (Longarm Ser.: No. 220). 192p. 1997. mass mkt. 4.99 (*0-515-12050-2*, Jove) Berkley Pub.

Longarm & the Jerkwater Bustout. Tabor Evans. (Longarm Ser.: No. 194). 192p. (Orig.). 1995. mass mkt. 3.99 (*0-515-11551-7*, Jove) Berkley Pub.

Longarm & the Kansas Jailbird. Tabor Evans. (Longarm Ser.: 243). 192p. 1999. mass mkt. 4.99 (*0-515-12468-0*, Jove) Berkley Pub.

Longarm & the Kansas Killer, No. 200. Tabor Evans. 192p. (Orig.). 1995. mass mkt. 4.50 (*0-515-11681-5*, Jove) Berkley Pub.

Longarm & the Lady Faire, No. 236. Tabor Evans. 192p. 1997. mass mkt. 4.99 (*0-515-12162-2*, Jove) Berkley Pub.

Longarm & the Lady from Tombstone, Vol. 247. Tabor Evans. (Longarm Ser.). 1999. mass mkt. 4.99 (*0-515-12533-4*, Jove) Berkley Pub.

Longarm & the Last Man. Tabor Evans. (Longarm Ser.: No. 184). 192p. (Orig.). 1994. mass mkt. 3.99 (*0-515-11356-5*, Jove) Berkley Pub.

Longarm & the Lusty Lady. Tabor Evans. (Longarm Ser.: No. 16). 256p. 1996. mass mkt. 5.50 (*0-515-11923-7*, Jove) Berkley Pub.

Longarm & the Maiden Medusa, Vol. 224. Tabor Evans. (Longarm Ser.). 192p. 1997. mass mkt. 4.99 (*0-515-12132-0*, Jove) Berkley Pub.

Longarm & the Man-Eaters. Tabor Evans. (Longarm Ser.: No. 192). 192p. (Orig.). 1994. mass mkt. 3.99 (*0-515-11505-3*, Jove) Berkley Pub.

Longarm & the Minute Men. Tabor Evans. (Longarm Ser.: No. 213). 1996. mass mkt. 4.99 (*0-515-11942-3*, Jove) Berkley Pub.

***Longarm & the Mustang Gang, 255.** Tabor Evans. 2000. mass mkt. 4.99 (*0-515-12755-8*, Jove) Berkley Pub.

Longarm & the Navaho Drums. Tabor Evans. (Longarm Ser.: No. 13). 288p. (Orig.). 1993. mass mkt. 4.50 (*0-515-11164-3*, Jove) Berkley Pub.

***Longarm & the Nevada Belly Dancer.** Tabor Evans. (Longarm Ser.: No. 257). 2000. mass mkt. 4.99 (*0-515-12790-6*, Jove) Berkley Pub.

Longarm & the Nevada Nymphs, Vol. 240. Tabor Evans. (Longarm Ser.). 1998. mass mkt. 4.99 (*0-515-12411-7*, Jove) Berkley Pub.

Longarm & the Nevada Swindle. Tabor Evans. (Longarm Ser.: No. 171). 192p. (Orig.). 1993. mass mkt. 3.99 (*0-515-11061-2*, Jove) Berkley Pub.

***Longarm & the Pistolero Princess.** Tabor Evans. (Longarm Ser.: Vol. 258). 192p. 2000. mass mkt. 4.99 (*0-515-12808-2*) Berkley Pub.

Longarm & the Racy Ladies. Tabor Evans. (Longarm Ser.: No. 214). 1996. mass mkt. 4.99 (*0-515-11956-3*, Jove) Berkley Pub.

Longarm & the Rebel Executioner, No. 227. Tabor Evans. 192p. 1997. mass mkt. 4.99 (*0-515-12178-9*, Jove) Berkley Pub.

Longarm & the Red-Light Ladies, 1 vol., Vol. 242. Tabor Evans. (Longarm Ser.). 1999. mass mkt. 4.99 (*0-515-12450-8*, Jove) Berkley Pub.

***Longarm & the Redhead's Ransom.** Tabor Evans. (Longarm Ser.: Vol. 54). 2000. mass mkt. 4.99 (*0-515-12734-5*, Jove) Berkley Pub.

Longarm & the Renegade Assassins. Tabor Evans. (Longarm Ser.: Vol. 234). 1998. mass mkt. 4.99 (*0-515-12292-0*, Jove) Berkley Pub.

Longarm & the River Pirates. Tabor Evans. (Longarm Ser.). 1998. mass mkt. 4.99 (*0-515-12340-4*, Jove) Berkley Pub.

Longarm & the San Angelo Showdown. Tabor Evans. (Longarm Ser.: No. 193). 192p. (Orig.). 1995. mass mkt. 3.99 (*0-515-11528-2*, Jove) Berkley Pub.

Longarm & the Secret Assassin. Tabor Evans. (Longarm Ser.: No. 216). 1996. mass mkt. 4.99 (*0-515-11982-2*, Jove) Berkley Pub.

***Longarm & the Sheep War.** Tabor Evans. (Longarm Ser.: Vol. 249). 185p. 1999. mass mkt. 4.99 (*0-515-12572-5*, Jove) Berkley Pub.

Longarm & the Shoshoni River. Tabor Evans. (Longarm Ser.: No. 168). 192p. (Orig.). 1992. mass mkt. 3.99 (*0-515-10997-5*, Jove) Berkley Pub.

Longarm & the Silver Mine Marauders. Tabor Evans. (Longarm Ser.: No. 197). (Orig.). 1995. mass mkt. 3.99 (*0-515-11612-2*, Jove) Berkley Pub.

***Longarm & the Sins of Sister Simone.** Tabor Evans. (Longarm Ser.: Vol. 262). 192p. 2000. mass mkt. 4.99 (*0-515-12910-0*, Jove) Berkley Pub.

Longarm & the Train Robbers. Tabor Evans. (Longarm Ser.: No. 182). 192p. (Orig.). 1994. mass mkt. 3.99 (*0-515-11313-1*, Jove) Berkley Pub.

Longarm & the Unwritten Law. Tabor Evans. (Longarm Ser.: No. 15). 288p. (Orig.). 1995. mass mkt. 4.99 (*0-515-11680-7*, Jove) Berkley Pub.

***Longarm & the Vanishing Virgin, 1 vol., Vol. 245.** Tabor Evans. (Longarm Ser.). 1999. mass mkt. 4.99 (*0-515-12511-3*, Jove) Berkley Pub.

Longarm & the Voodoo Queen, No. 228. Tabor Evans. 192p. 1997. mass mkt. 4.99 (*0-515-12191-6*, Jove) Berkley Pub.

Longarm & the Whiskey Creek Widow. Tabor Evans. (Longarm Ser.: Vol. 232). 1998. mass mkt. 4.99 (*0-515-12265-3*, Jove) Berkley Pub.

Longarm & the Whiskey Woman. Tabor Evans. (Longarm Ser.: No. 217). 1997. mass mkt. 4.99 (*0-515-11998-9*, Jove) Berkley Pub.

Longarm & the Wicked Schoolmarm. Tabor Evans. (Longarm Ser.: Vol. 235). 1998. mass mkt. 4.99 (*0-515-12302-1*, Jove) Berkley Pub.

Longarm & the Wronged Woman. Tabor Evans. (Longarm Ser.: No. 248). 1999. mass mkt. 4.99 (*0-515-12556-3*, Jove) Berkley Pub.

Longarm in the Cross Fire. Tabor Evans. (Longarm Ser.: No. 177). 192p. (Orig.). 1993. mass mkt. 3.99 (*0-515-11194-5*, Jove) Berkley Pub.

***Longarm in the Valley of Sin, Vol. 253.** Tabor Evans. (Longarm Ser.). 1999. mass mkt. 4.99 (*0-515-12707-8*, Jove) Berkley Pub.

***Longarm on a Bloody Vendetta.** Tabor Evans. (Longarm Bks.: Vol. 263). 2000. mass mkt. 4.99 (*0-515-12932-1*, Jove) Berkley Pub.

Longarm on the Fever Coast. Tabor Evans. (Longarm Ser.: No. 183). 192p. (Orig.). 1994. mass mkt. 3.99 (*0-515-11338-7*, Jove) Berkley Pub.

Longarm on the Santee Killing Grounds. Tabor Evans. (Longarm Ser.: No. 14). 288p. (Orig.). 1994. mass mkt. 4.99 (*0-515-11459-6*, Jove) Berkley Pub.

Longboarder's Start-Up: A Guide to Longboard Surfing. Doug Werner. LC 96-60497. (Start-Up Sports Ser.: No. 6). (Illus.). 160p. 1996. pap. 11.95 (*1-884654-06-1*) Tracks Pubng.

Longboat to Hawaii: An Account of the Voyage of the Clipper Ship Hornet of New York, Bound for San Francisco in 1886, As Recorded in the Journals in Captain Josiah A. Mitchell, Master, Henry Ferguson, Passenger, Samuel Ferguson, Passenger Together with Observations on the Burning of the Vessel by Mark Twain. Ed. by Alexander C. Brown. LC 74-22317. 256p. 1974. reprint ed. pap. 79.40 (*0-608-02468-6*, 206311200004) Bks Demand.

Longbow: A Social & Military History. Robert Hardy. LC 76-25029. 216p. 1977. 19.95 (*0-668-04080-7*, ARCO) Macmillan.

Longbow: A Social & Military History. Robert Hardy. LC 77-352712. 216 p. 1976. write for info. (*0-85059-218-6*) P Stephens.

Longbow: A Social & Military History. Robert Hardy. 1998. pap. text 24.95 (*0-9645741-3-6*) Bois dArc Pr.

Longbow: A Social & Military History 3rd ed. Robert Hardy. LC 92-85355. 244p. 1992. write for info. (*1-85260-412-3*) P Stephens.

Longbow No. 2: The Official Strategy Guide. Prima Publishing Staff. LC 97-69335. 304p. 1997. per. 19.99 (*0-7615-1206-3*) Prima Pub.

Longbow Country. E. Donnall Thomas, Jr. LC 96-134976. 146p. 1995. 19.95 (*0-9647096-0-0*) TBM.

Longbows of the Far North: An Archer's Adventures in Alaska & Siberia. E. Donnall Thomas, Jr. LC 93-3148. (Illus.). 144p. 1993. 18.95 (*0-8117-0956-6*) Stackpole.

Longcase Clock. rev. ed. Tom Robinson. (Illus.). 468p. 1995. 79.50 (*1-85149-232-1*) Antique Collect.

***Longcase Clocks.** Joanna Greenlaw. (Illus.). 1999. pap. 30.00 (*0-7478-0417-6*, Pub. by Shire Pubns) Parkwest Pubns.

Longcase Clocks & Standing Regulators Pt. 1: Machine Made Clocks. Tran D. Ly. (Illus.). 1994. 69.50 (*0-930163-60-5*) Arlington Bk.

Longcase Painted Dials: Their History & Restoration. M. F. Tennant. (Illus.). 256p. 1995. 50.00 (*0-7090-5529-3*, Pub. by R Hale Ltd) Antique Collect.

Longcase Painted Dials: Their History & Restoration. M. F. Tennant. (Illus.). 256p. 1997. 50.00 (*0-7198-0260-1*, Pub. by R Hale Ltd) Antique Collect.

Longeing & Long Lining the English & Western Horse: A Total Program. Cherry Hill. LC 98-28079. 256p. 1998. 29.95 (*0-87605-080-1*) Howell Bks.

Longer Combination Trucks. (Illus.). 56p. 1994. pap. text 35.00 (*1-57979-119-0*) DIANE Pub.

Longer Combination Trucks: Potential Infrastructure Impacts, Productivity Benefits, & Safety Concerns. (Illus.). 56p. (Orig.). (C). 1995. pap. text 25.00 (*0-7881-1967-2*) DIANE Pub.

Longer Essay Writing Text. Smilkstein. (C). Date not set. pap. text 28.00 (*0-15-501169-3*, Pub. by Harcourt Coll Pubs) Harcourt.

Longer Fly Casting. Lefty Kreh. (Illus.). 112p. 1991. pap. 12.95 (*1-55821-127-6*) Lyons Pr.

Longer Hours, Fewer Jobs: Employment & Unemployment in the United States. Michael Yates. LC 93-26615. (Illus.). 160p. (J). (ps-12). 1993. pap. 13.00 (*0-85345-888-X*, Pub. by Monthly Rev) NYU Pr.

Longer Hours or More Jobs? An Investigation of Amending Hours Legislation to Create Employment. Ronald G. Ehrenberg & Paul L. Schumann. LC 81-11284. (Cornell Studies in Industrial & Labor Relations: No. 22). 190p. 1982. pap. text 14.95 (*0-87546-091-7*, ILR Press) Cornell U Pr.

Longer Life for Your Pet: How to Increase the Lifespan of Your Dog or Cat. Robert Gilmore. LC 94-96037. (Orig.). 1994. pap. 4.95 (*0-9640710-0-2*) Dr Goodhlth.

Longer Life, More Joy: Techniques for Enhancing Health, Happiness & Inner Vision. Gay G. Luce. 1992. pap. 12.95 (*0-87877-171-9*) Newcastle Pub.

Longer-Term Issues in Transportation: Conference Papers. John Rickard. 400p. 1991. 112.95 (*1-85628-254-6*, Pub. by Avebry) Ashgate Pub Co.

Longer Thou Livest, & Enough Is As Good As a Feast. William Wager. Ed. by R. Mark Benbow. LC 67-15815. (Regents Renaissance Drama Ser.). 178p. 1967. reprint ed. pap. 55.20 (*0-608-02040-0*, 206269300003) Bks Demand.

Longer Thou Livest the More Fool Thou Art. William Wager. LC 73-133755. (Tudor Facsimile Texts. Old English Plays Ser.: No. 41). reprint ed. 59.50 (*0-404-53341-8*) AMS Pr.

An Asterisk (*) at the beginning of an entry indicates that the title is appearing for the first time.

Longer View. Harvey Jackins. 1987. 16.00 (*0-913937-17-7*); pap. 13.00 (*0-913937-18-5*) Rational Isl.

Longer View: Essays Toward a Critique of Political Economy. Paul A. Baran. LC 68-13656. 464p. 1972. pap. 10.00 (*0-85345-220-2*, Pub. by Monthly Rev) NYU Pr.

Longer Views: Extended Essays. Samuel R. Delany. LC 96-1237. 384p. 1996. pap. 19.95 (*0-8195-6293-9*, Wesleyan Univ Pr); text 50.00 (*0-8195-5281-X*, Wesleyan Univ Pr) U Pr of New Eng.

Longest. David Armentrout. LC 96-26509. (Fascinating Facts Ser.). 1996. lib. bdg. 14.60 (*1-57103-129-4*) Rourke Pr.

Longest Aisle: An Offbeat Guide to Wedding Planning. Richard Mintzer. LC 94-20506. (Illus.). 144p. 1994. pap. 9.95 (*0-8065-1575-9*) Carol Pub Group.

Longest Battle: RCN in the Atlantic 1939-45. John D. Harbron. (Illus.). 112p. 1997. pap. write for info. (*1-55125-019-5*, Vanwell Pub) Howell Pr VA.

Longest Breath: Poems. Greg Field. LC 98-211339. (Illus.). 96p. 1998. pap. 10.00 (*0-910479-01-1*) Mid-America Pr.

Longest Cave. Roger W. Brucker & Richard A. Watson. LC 86-15537. 360p. 1987. pap. 17.95 (*0-8093-1322-7*) S Ill U Pr.

Longest Cocktail Party: An Insider's Diary of the Beatles. Richard Di Lello. LC 72-85965. (Rock & Roll Remembrances Ser.: No. 2). (Illus.). 352p. 1983. 40.00 (*1-56075-044-8*) Popular Culture.

Longest Day. Michael Collier. (Doctor Who Ser.). 1998. pap. 5.95 (*0-563-40581-3*) BBC.

Longest Day: The Classic Epic of D-Day. Cornelius Ryan. 352p. 1994. pap. 12.00 (*0-671-89091-3*, Touchstone) S&S Trade Pap.

Longest Easter Egg Hunt Ever. (Illus.). 24p. (J). (gr. 1-3). 1996. 3.98 (*1-890095-01-X*) Nesak Intl.

***Longest Flight: Yuma's Quest for the Future.** Shirley Woodhouse Murdock & James A. Gillaspie. (Illus.). xv, 96p. 1999. pap. 10.00 (*0-9675508-0-7*) Longest Flight.

Longest Fraud: A Grace de Rossa Novel. Maggie Gibson. 256p. 1996. pap. 12.95 (*1-85371-549-2*, Pub. by Poolbeg Pr) Dufour.

Longest Game. Steven Krasner. LC 96-94053. (Illus.). 36p. (J). (gr. 4-6). 1996. 4.95 (*0-9642721-1-3*) Gorilla Prodns.

***Longest Hair in the World.** Lois Duncan. LC 98-53072. 32p. (J). (gr. k-2). 1999. 15.95 (*0-385-32113-9*) BDD Bks Young Read.

***Longest Hair In The World.** Lois Duncan. (J). 2001. pap. 5.99 (*0-440-41239-0*) BDD Bks Young Read.

Longest Home Run. Roch Carrier. Tr. by Sheila Fischman from FRE. LC 92-62364. Orig. Title: Le Plus Long Circuit. (Illus.). 24p. (J). (gr. 3 up). 1993. 15.95 (*0-88776-300-6*) Tundra Bks.

Longest Interurban Charter. Larry Plachno. Ed. by Eric Bronsky. LC 88-24784. (Illus.). 96p. 1988. pap. 16.00 (*0-933449-08-9*) Transport Trails.

Longest Journey. E. M. Forster. LC 97-206310. 304p. 1997. mass mkt. 4.95 (*0-553-21455-1*) Bantam.

Longest Journey. E. M. Forster. text. write for info. (*0-7131-6421-2*, Pub. by E A) Routldge.

Longest Journey. E. M. Forster. Ed. by Elizabeth Heine. (Abinger Edition of E. M. Forster Ser.: Vol. 2). 400p. 1985. 69.50 (*0-8419-5832-7*) Holmes & Meier.

Longest Journey. E. M. Forster. 1962. pap. 4.95 (*0-685-04270-7*, V40) Vin Bks.

Longest Journey. E. M. Forster. LC 93-11210. 320p. 1993. pap. 12.00 (*0-679-74815-6*) Vin Bks.

Longest Journey. E. M. Forster. 1989. reprint ed. lib. bdg. 27.95 (*0-89966-632-9*) Buccaneer Bks.

Longest Journey. E. M. Forster. 330p. 1999. reprint ed. lib. bdg. 29.95 (*0-7351-0068-3*) Replica Bks.

Longest Journey & Drawn Together by Fate, Vols. 1 & 2. Hsi-Wen Yin. (CHI.). 1997. pap. 10.00 (*1-890474-02-9*, 003) Nrth Amer Chinese Wrters.

Longest Line: Broadway's Most Singular Sensation, A Chorus Line. Gary Stevens & Alan George. (Illus.). 284p. 1995. 45.00 (*1-55783-221-8*) Applause Theatre Bk Pubs.

Longest Line: Broadway's Most Singular Sensation: A Chorus Line. Gary Stevens & Alan George. 284p. 1998. pap. 19.95 (*1-55783-363-X*) Applause Theatre Bk Pubs.

Longest Night: Chronicle of a Dead City. Petros Haris. Ed. by Theofanis G. Stavrou. Tr. by Theodore Sampson from GRE. (Modern Greek History & Culture Ser.). (Illus.). 128p. 1985. 20.00 (*0-932963-02-1*) Nostos Bks.

Longest Pleasure. Anne Mather. 384p. 1987. mass mkt. 3.50 (*0-373-97030-7*) Harlequin Bks.

***Longest Raid of the Civil War: Little-Known & Untold Stories of Morgan's Raid into Kentucky, Indiana & Ohio.** Lester V. Horwitz. LC 99-72224. (Illus.). 528p. 1999. 34.95 (*0-9670267-0-9*); pap. 29.95 pap. 29.95 (*0-9670267-1-7*) Farmcourt Pubg.

Longest Ride. Patrick Denise Lewis. LC 98-54828. 164p. (J). (gr. 5-7). 1995. 14.95 (*0-8050-4715-8*) H Holt & Co.

Longest Shadow: In the Aftermath of the Holocaust. Geoffrey H. Hartman. (Helen & Martin Schwartz Lectures in Jewish Civilization). 192p. 1996. 29.95 (*0-253-33033-5*) Ind U Pr.

Longest Shot: Lil E. Tee & the Kentucky Derby. John S. Eisenberg. LC 95-41243. (Illus.). 224p. 1996. 24.95 (*0-8131-1956-1*) U Pr of Ky.

Longest Silence: A Life in Fishing. Thomas McGuane. LC 99-27199. 320p. 1999. 25.00 (*0-679-45485-3*) Knopf.

***Longest Single Note.** Peter Crowther. 1999. write for info. (*1-881475-56-5*) Cemetery Dance.

Longest Step: Searching for God. James DiGiacomo et al. (Encounter Ser.). (Illus.). 1985. 5.95 (*0-86683-180-0*, 315) Harper SF.

Longest Street: A History of Lafourche Parish & GrandIsle. Tanya Ditto. Ed. by Doug Woolfolk. (Illus.). 136p. 1980. 13.00 (*0-86518-013-X*) Moran Pub Corp.

Longest Thread. Jennifer Ackerman. 2001. 24.95 (*0-670-86063-8*) Viking Penguin.

Longest Trek: My Tour of the Galaxy. Grace L. Whitney & Jim Denney. LC 98-12679. 208p. 1998. pap. 14.95 (*1-884956-03-3*) Quill Driver.

Longest Trek: My Tour of the Galaxy. Grace L. Whitney & Jim Denney. (Illus.). 256p. 1998. 45.00 (*1-884956-05-X*) Quill Driver.

Longest Voyage: Circumnavigators in the Age of Discovery. Robert Silverberg. LC 97-1812. 544p. 1997. pap. 19.95 (*0-8214-1192-6*) Ohio U Pr.

Longest Voyage & Slow Lightning. Poul Anderson & Steve Popkes. (Double Ser.: No. 30). 1991. pap. 3.95 (*0-8125-1170-0*, Pub. by Tor Bks) St Martin.

Longest Walk: The World of Bomb Disposal. Peter Birchall. LC 98-140295. (Illus.). 240p. 1998. 27.95 (*1-85409-398-3*, Pub. by Arms & Armour) Sterling.

Longest War: Sex Differences in Perspective. 2nd ed. Carol Tavris & Carole Wade. 416p. (Orig.). (C). 1984. write for info. (*0-318-57722-4*) Harcourt Coll Pubs.

Longest War: The Iran-Iraq Military Conflict. Dilip Hiro. (Illus.). 323p. (C). 1990. pap. 20.99 (*0-415-90407-2*, A5320) Routledge.

Longest War in History: The Platonic & Aristotelian Struggles over Idealism, Rationalism, Collectivism & Individuality. rev. ed. Ralph A. Hageman. 260p. 1998. pap. text 23.00 (*1-893760-02-2*) Eliopoulos.

***Longest Winter.** Ian Roy & Julie Doiron. (Illus.). 64p. 1999. pap. 14.00 (*0-921411-95-2*) Genl Dist Srvs.

Longest Winter. Daphney Wright. 288p. 1989. 24.95 (*0-385-25209-9*) Doubleday.

Longevity. (Fitness, Health & Nutrition Ser.). (Illus.). 144p. (gr. 7). 1999. 17.95 (*0-8094-6142-0*) Time-Life.

Longevity: To the Limits & Beyond. Ed. by J. M. Robine et al. LC 98-100706. (Research & Perspectives in Longevity Ser.). (Illus.). 148p. 1997. 89.95 (*3-540-62945-9*) Spr-Verlag.

Longevity & TAO: Mind-Body Transformation. (Alternative Medicine Ser.). 1992. lib. bdg. 86.95 (*0-8490-5390-0*) Gordon Pr.

Longevity Code: Your Personal Prescription for a Longer, Sweeter Life. Zorba Paster & Susan Meltsner. 336p. 2001. 25.00 (*0-609-60360-4*) C Potter.

Longevity Equation: How to Eat As Much As You Like & Still Live over 100 Years to Tell about It! Richard G. Deeb. 246p. 1992. pap. text 11.95 (*0-9634020-0-5*) Long Life Pr.

Longevity Factor: Chromium Picolinate. Richard A. Passwater. LC 93-5147. Orig. Title: Living Longer, Living Better, Slowing Aging with the Longevity Factor. 88p. (Orig.). 1993. pap. 4.95 (*0-87983-619-9*, 36199K, Keats Publng) NTC Contemp Pub Co.

Longevity Handbook: Flying Crane Kung for Health. Sheng Keng Yun. LC 98-55722. (Illus.). 176p. 1999. pap. 14.95 (*1-57863-108-4*) Weiser.

Longevity of Building Services Installations, Stage 1: Inventory of Operating Experiences for Estimating Longevity. A. Jonsson & S. Lindgren. (C). 1983. 175.00 (*0-7855-4407-0*, Pub. by Build Servs Info Assn) St Mut.

Longevity of Reptiles & Amphibians. Snider & Bowler. 1992. pap. write for info. (*0-916984-26-5*) SSAR.

Longevity, Senescence, & the Genome. Caleb E. Finch. (Illus.). xvi, 938p. 1994. pap. text 45.00 (*0-226-24889-5*) U Ch Pr.

Longevity, Senescence, & the Genome. Caleb E. Finch. (John D. & Catherine T. MacArthur Foundation Series on Mental Health & Development). (Illus.). 858p. 1995. 65.00 (*0-226-24888-7*) U Ch Pr.

Longevity Sourcebook. David Seidman. LC 97-30843. 336p. 1998. pap. 17.00 (*0-7373-0013-2*, 00132W) NTC Contemp Pub Co.

Longevity Strategy. Mahoney. 272p. 1999. pap. 14.95 (*0-471-32794-8*) Wiley.

Longevity Strategy: How to Live to 100 Using the Brain-Body Connection. David Mahoney & Richard Restak. LC 97-50639. 272p. 1998. 22.95 (*0-471-24867-3*) Wiley.

Longevity Therapy: An Innovative Approach to Nursing Home Care of the Elderly. Bobbie R. Graubarth-Szyller & Julianna D. Padgett. LC 89-821. 176p. (Orig.). 1989. pap. 20.95 (*0-914783-30-0*) Charles.

Longfellow: His Life & Work. Newton Arvin. LC 77-1342. 338p. 1977. reprint ed. lib. bdg. 65.00 (*0-8371-9505-5*, ARLO, Greenwood Pr) Greenwood.

Longfellow & His Poetry. Ed. by William H. Smeaton. LC 76-120966. (Poetry & Life Ser.). reprint ed. 27.50 (*0-404-52533-4*) AMS Pr.

Longfellow & His Poetry. William H. Smeaton. (BCL1-PS American Literature Ser.). 143p. 1992. reprint ed. lib. bdg. 69.00 (*0-7812-6782-X*) Rprt Serv.

Longfellow, & Other Essays. William P. Trent. LC 67-23276. (Essay Index Reprint Ser.). 1977. 20.95 (*0-8369-0950-X*) Ayer.

Longfellow Commemorative Conference: Papers Presented. Ed Tucker et al. LC 82-603663. (Illus.). 121p. (Orig.). 1983. pap. 5.00 (*0-9610844-0-5*) Longfellow.

Longfellow Evangeline Cas. abr. ed. Henry Wadsworth Longfellow. LC 66-1705. 1972. audio 14.00 (*0-694-50133-6*, SWC 1179, Caedmon) HarperAudio.

Longfellow Square. Kenneth Rosen. Ed. by Elizabeth Burke. (Illus.). 64p. (Orig.). 1992. pap. 11.95 (*1-878112-00-7*) Ascensius Pr.

Longfellows Letters, Vols. 1-2, 1814-1836 & 1837-1843 see Letters of Henry Wadsworth Longfellow

Longfellows Letters, Vols. 3-4, 1844-1856 & 1857-1865 see Letters of Henry Wadsworth Longfellow

Longhaired Cats: An Owner's Guide to a Happy Healthy Pet. Anna Sadler. LC 96-3951. (Illus.). 160p. 1996. 12.95 (*0-87605-476-9*) Howell Bks.

Longhi's: Recipes & Romance from Maui's Most Famous Restaurant. Bob Longhi. LC 97-45488. (Illus.). 172p. 1998. 29.95 (*0-89815-950-4*) Ten Speed Pr.

***Longhorn.** Evelyn Rogers. (Texas Empires Ser.). 400p. 2000. mass mkt. 5.99 (*0-8439-4679-2*, Leisure Bks) Dorchester Pub Co.

Longhorn Beetles of the British Isles. Norman Hickin. (Natural History Ser.: no. 22). (Illus.). 24p. 1989. pap. 5.25 (*0-85263-897-3*, Pub. by Shire Pubns) Parkwest Pubns.

Longhorn Hoops: The History of Texas Basketball. Richard Pennington. LC 98-60912. (Illus.). 480p. 1998. 35.00 (*0-292-76585-1*) U of Tex Pr.

***Longhorns.** J Frank Dobie. 1999. 9.99 (*0-7858-1130-3*) Book Sales.

Longhorns. J. Frank Dobie. LC 79-67706. (Illus.). 440p. 1980. reprint ed. pap. 16.95 (*0-292-74627-X*) U of Tex Pr.

***Longhouse.** Cynthia Breslin Beres. LC 00-27815. (Native American Homes Ser.). (Illus.). 2000. write for info. (*1-55916-247-3*) Rourke Bk Co.

Longhouse Legends see Storypole Legends: Legends of the Indians of Puget Sound

Longhunter Muzzleloading Big Game Record Book. 2nd ed. Robert H. Wallace. LC 95-92755. (Illus.). 200p. 1996. 35.00 (*0-9606428-8-9*) Natl Muzzle Load.

Longhunter Society Big Game Record Book. Ed. by Sharon Cunningham. (Illus.). 175p. 1992. 35.00 (*0-9606428-2-X*) Natl Muzzle Load.

Longi: Daphnis et Chloe. Ed. by Reeve. (GRE.). 1994. 29.95 (*3-8154-1932-8*, T1932, Pub. by B G Teubner) U of Mich Pr.

Longing. Maria Espinosa. LC 95-9763. 298p. 1995. pap. 9.95 (*1-55885-145-3*) Arte Publico.

***Longing.** James D. Landis. LC 00-35049. 592p. 2000. 26.00 (*0-15-100453-6*) Harcourt.

Longing. Bill Mayer. 90p. (Orig.). 1993. pap. 9.95 (*0-9636556-0-4*) Pangaea Bks.

Longing. Paul Reed. LC 88-14994. 192p. 1990. pap. 7.95 (*0-89087-597-9*) Celestial Arts.

Longing: Selected Poems. Jaime G. De Biedma. Tr. by James Nolan from SPA. 180p. (Orig.). 1993. pap. 9.95 (*0-87286-277-1*) City Lights.

Longing & Belonging: From the Faraway Nearby. Dick Hebdige. 1996. pap. text 65.00 (*0-9650583-1-X*) Site Santa Fe.

Longing & Belonging: From the Faraway Nearby. Text by Dick Hebdige et al. (Illus.). 192p. 1996. pap. 45.00 (*0-9650583-0-1*, 620822) Site Santa Fe.

Longing at Least Is Constant. Kathryn Payne. LC 98-215173. 64p. 1988. pap. 9.75 (*0-921411-68-5*) Genl Dist Srvs.

Longing for a Form: Essays on the Fiction of C. S. Lewis. Ed. by Peter J. Schakel. LC 77-2586. 254p. reprint ed. pap. 78.80 (*0-7837-0827-0*, 204114100020) Bks Demand.

***Longing for a Kiss: Treasury of Love Poems.** Michael A. Peszke. 128p. 1999. 19.95 (*0-7818-0671-2*) Hippocrene Bks.

Longing for Company. Judy Hamlin. 64p. (Orig.). 1993. pap. 1.00 (*1-56476-195-9*, 6-3195, Victor Bks) Chariot Victor.

Longing for Dad: Father Loss & Its Impact. Beth M. Erickson. LC 98-15536. 280p. 1998. pap. 11.95 (*1-55874-549-1*) Health Comm.

Longing for Darkness. China Galland. 1999. pap. 13.95 (*0-14-019566-1*) Viking Penguin.

Longing for Darkness. China Galland. 400p. 1991. reprint ed. pap. 14.95 (*0-14-012184-6*, Penguin Bks) Viking Penguin.

Longing for Darkness: Kamante's Tales from Out of Africa. Peter H. Beard. (Illus.). 264p. (ps up). 1998. pap. 24.95 (*0-8118-2105-6*) Chronicle Bks.

Longing for Darkness: Kamante's Tales from Out of Africa. Ed. by Peter Beard. (Illus.). 264p. 1991. reprint ed. 25.00 (*0-87701-724-7*); reprint ed. pap. 24.95 (*0-87701-680-1*) Chronicle Bks.

Longing for Dawn: The Jewish Guide to Consolation. Y. Y. Baifus. LC 95-18057. 1995. 20.95 (*0-87306-719-3*) Feldheim.

Longing for Death. Ed. by Alfred French. (GER., Illus.). 106p. (C). 1995. text 14.50 incl. audio (*0-930329-80-5*) Kabel Pubs.

Longing for God: Learning to Cultivate Your Spiritual Garden. J. K. Jones. LC 94-70790. 206p. 1994. 14.99 (*0-89900-683-3*) College Pr Pub.

Longing for God: Prayer & the Rhythms of Life. Glandion Carney & Bill Long. LC 93-41899. Orig. Title: The Rhythm of Live & the Psalms. 228p. 1993. pap. 10.99 (*0-8308-1665-8*, 1665) InterVarsity.

Longing for Heaven. large type ed. H. Bonar. 6.99 (*1-85792-011-2*, Pub. by Christian Focus) Spring Arbor Dist.

Longing for Holiness: Selected Writings of John Wesley see Upper Room Spiritual Classics: Series 1

Longing for Home. Ed. by Leroy S. Rouner. LC 96-30449. (Boston University Studies in Philosophy & Religion: Vol. 17). 248p. (C). 1997. text 34.00 (*0-268-01310-1*) U of Notre Dame Pr.

Longing for Home: Recollections & Reflections. Frederick Buechner. LC 96-1008. 192p. 1996. 21.00 (*0-06-061191-X*, Pub. by Harper SF) HarpC.

Longing for Land: Tradition & Change in a Swazi Agricultural Community. Paul N. Bowen. 256p. 1993. 72.95 (*1-85628-398-4*, Pub. by Avebry) Ashgate Pub Co.

Longing for Latitude. Alan C. Howard. LC 97-94737. 56p. 1998. pap. 8.95 (*0-9661463-0-1*) Greenroom Pr.

Longing for Love: A Woman's Conversations with a Compassionate Heavenly Father. Ruth Senter. 128p. 1997. pap. 7.99 (*1-55661-939-1*) Bethany Hse.

Longing for Paradise: Psychological Perspectives on an Archetype. Mario Jacoby. Tr. by Myron B. Gubitz from GER. LC 84-51937.Tr. of Die Sehnsucht-nach dem Paradies. 229p. 1985. 24.95 (*0-938434-21-7*); pap. 15.95 (*0-938434-20-9*) Sigo Pr.

Longing for Running Water: Ecofeminism & Liberation. Ivone Gebara. Tr. by David Molineaux from POR. LC 99-47658. 1999. pap. 22.00 (*0-8006-3183-8*, Fortress Pr) Augsburg Fortress.

Longing for the Harmonies: Themes & Variations from Modern Physics. Frank Wilczek & Betsy Devine. (Illus.). 1989. pap. 9.95 (*0-393-30596-1*) Norton.

L

Longing for the Light: Selected Poems of Vicente Aleixandre. Vicente Aleixandre. Ed. by Lewis Hyde. Tr. by Stephen Kessler et al from SPA. 284p. 1985. reprint ed. pap. 10.00 (*0-914742-89-2*) Copper Canyon.

Longing for Total Revolution: Philosophic Sources of Social Discontent from Rousseau to Marx & Nietzsche. Bernard Yack. (C). 1992. pap. 15.95 (*0-520-07852-7*, Pub. by U CA Pr) Cal Prin Full Svc.

Longing for Total Revolution: Philosophic Sources of Social Discontent from Rousseau to Marx & Nietzsche. Bernard Yack. LC 86-8184. (Studies in Moral, Political, & Legal Philosophy). 409p. 1986. reprint ed. pap. 126.80 (*0-608-07527-2*, 206774300009) Bks Demand.

Longing for Worldly Pleasures: Fifteen Strings of Cash, Vol. 2. Ed. by A. C. Scott. (Illus.). 172p. 1972. pap. 14.95 (*0-299-05374-1*) U of Wis Pr.

Longing Heart. Murad Khurram. 28p. (J). 1980. pap. 3.50 (*0-86037-138-7*) New Era Publns MI.

Longing to Be Loved. C. S. Lovett. 1982. pap. 7.95 (*0-938148-36-2*) Prsnl Christianity.

Longing to Be Loved: Can Their Marriage Survive Their Differences? Allan Kennedy et al. LC 96-37778. 1997. pap. 10.99 (*0-8163-1375-X*) Pacific Pr Pub Assn.

Longing to Die - Fighting to Live: An Incest Survivor's Story. Myrna R. Olson. LC 97-65412. 111p. 1997. pap. 10.00 (*0-9620254-1-0*) Nathan Star Pr.

Longings of Women. Marge Piercy. 448p. 1995. mass mkt. 6.99 (*0-449-22349-3*, Crest) Fawcett.

Longings of Women. large type ed. Marge Piercy. LC 94-18341. 752p. 1994. lib. bdg. 25.95 (*0-8161-7457-1*, G K Hall Lrg Type) Mac Lib Ref.

Longinus: On the Sublime. Tr. by James A. Arieti & John M. Crossett. LC 84-25435. (Texts & Studies in Religion: Vol.21). 275p. 1985. lib. bdg. 89.95 (*0-88946-554-1*) E Mellen.

Longinus - Longini de Sublimitate Lexicon. Longinus. Ed. by Ruth Neuberger. (Alpha-Reihe A Ser.). (GER.). viii, 118p. 1987. write for info. (*3-487-07896-1*) G Olms Pubs.

Longinus on the Sublime. Longinus. LC 78-41181. reprint ed. 32.50 (*0-404-14743-7*) AMS Pr.

Longinus on the Sublime: The Peri Hupsous in Translations by Nicolas Boileau-Despreaux (1674) & William Smith (1739) Longinus. LC 75-8892. 390p. 1975. lib. bdg. 60.00 (*0-8201-1153-8*) Schol Facsimiles.

Longitude: A Novel Carlos Cortes. LC 98-947580. xxiii, 410 p. 1998. write for info. (*971-542-154-7*) U of Philippines Pr.

Longitude: The True Story of a Lone Genius Who Solved the Greatest Scientific Problem of His Time. Dava Sobel. 1996. text 19.00 (*0-07-059593-3*) McGraw.

Longitude: The True Story of a Lone Genius Who Solved the Greatest Scientific Problem of His Time. Dava Sobel. LC 95-17402. 184p. 1996. pap. 11.95 (*0-14-025879-5*) Viking Penguin.

Longitude: The True Story of a Lone Genius Who Solved the Greatest Scientific Problem of His Time. Dava Sobel. 224p. 1995. 19.00 (*0-8027-1312-2*) Walker & Co.

Longitude: The True Story of a Lone Genius Who Solved the Greatest Scientific Problem of His Time. large type ed. Dava Sobel. (Isis Large Print Ser.). 1997. 24.95 (*0-7531-5036-0*) T T Beeler.

Longitude Prize: The Race Between the Moon & the Watch-Machine. Joan Dash. LC 97-44257. (Illus.). 208p. 2000. 16.00 (*0-374-34636-4*) FS&G.

Longitude Zero, 1884 to 1984: Proceedings of an International Symposium held at the National Maritime Museum, Greenwich, London, 9-13 July 1984 to Mark the Centenary of the Adoption of the Greenwich Meridian. Ed. by P. Beer et al. (Illus.). 408p. 1985. pap. 89.00 (*0-08-032726-5*, Pub. by PPL) Elsevier.

Longitudes. John Birkbeck. 64p. 1999. pap. 12.00 (*0-9671757-1-2*) Carmine Creek.

Longitudes & Latitudes in the U. S. Eugene Dernay. 128p. 1945. 13.00 (*0-86690-067-5*, D1062-014) Am Fed Astrologers.

Longitudes et Latitudes: Des Villes, Villages et Lieux du Quebec. Gilles Poulin. 117p. 1985. 14.95 (*2-920083-14-7*) Edns Roseau.

***Longitudinal Data Analysis: Designs, Models & Methods.** Ab Mooijaart et al. Ed. by Catrien C. J. H. Bijleveld & Leo Van Der Kamp. LC 98-61162. 432p. 1998. 94.00 (*0-7619-5537-2*) Sage.

***Longitudinal Endosonography: Atlas & Manual for Use in the Upper Gastrointestinal Tract** T. Rosch et al. LC 99-36126. 1999. write for info. (*3-540-65586-7*) Spr-Verlag.

Longitudinal Field Research Methods: Studying Processes of Organizational Change. Ed. by George P. Huber & Andrew Van De Ven. (Organizational Science Ser.). 400p. (C). 1995. 52.00 (*0-8039-7090-0*); pap. 24.95 (*0-8039-7091-9*) Sage.

Longitudinal Muscle in Esophageal Disease. O. Arthur Stiennon. LC 94-61983. (Illus.). 300p. (C). 1995. 150.00 (*0-9644594-0-X*) Radiology Pub.

Longitudinal Research, No. 76. Scott Menard. (Quantitative Applications in the Social Sciences Ser.: Vol. 76). (Illus.). 96p. 1991. pap. 10.95 (*0-8039-3753-9*) Sage.

An Asterisk (*) at the beginning of an entry indicates that the title is appearing for the first time.

L

Longitudinal Research: Methods & Uses in Behavioral Sciences. Ed. by Fini Schulsinger et al. (Longitudinal Research in the Behavioral, Social, & Medical Sciences Ser.). 368p. 1981. lib. bdg. 95.50 (*0-89838-056-1*) Kluwer Academic.

Longitudinal Research in Alcoholism. Ed. by Donald W. Goodwin & Sarnoff A. Mednick. 1984. lib. bdg. 97.00 (*0-89838-133-9*) Kluwer Academic.

Longitudinal Research on Individual Development: Present Status & Future Prospectives. Ed. by David Magnusson & Paul Casaer. LC 93-18120. (European Network on Longitudinal Studies on Individual Development: Vol. 7). (Illus.). 267p. (C). 1993. text 95.00 (*0-521-43478-5*) Cambridge U Pr.

Longitudinal Results of the Ypsilanti Perry Preschool Project. David P. Weikart et al. 152p. 1993. reprint ed. 15.95 (*0-929816-55-2*, R1037) High-Scope.

Longitudinal Retirement History Study: Instructor's Manual. James L. Peterson et al. (Gerontology Research Toolkit Ser.). 64p. (Orig.). 1994. pap. text, teacher ed. 30.00 (*0-8018-5046-0*) Johns Hopkins.

Longitudinal Retirement History Study: Student Workbook. Elinore E. Lurie et al. (Gerontology Research Toolkit Ser.). 168p. (Orig.). 1994. pap. text, student ed. 49.00 (*0-8018-5045-2*) Johns Hopkins.

Longitudinal Studies in Child Psychology & Psychiatry: Practical Lessons from Research Experience. Ed. by Arthur R. Nicol. LC 84-11802. (Wiley Series on Studies in Child Psychiatry). 423p. reprint ed. pap. 131.20 (*0-8357-4945-2*, 203787600009) Bks Demand.

Longitudinal Studies of Children of Psychological Risk: Cross-National Perspective. Ed. by Charles W. Greenbaum & Judith G. Auerbach. 288p. (C). 1992. text 73.25 (*0-89391-824-5*) Ablx Pub.

***Longitudinal Studies of Creativity: A Special Issue of Creativity Research Journal.** Ed. by Mark A. Runco. 72p. 1999. pap. 20.00 (*0-8058-9802-6*) L Erlbaum Assocs.

Longitudinal Studies of HIV Infection in Intravenous Drug Users. 1993. lib. bdg. 250.00 (*0-8490-8921-2*) Gordon Pr.

Longitudinal Study of Adolescent Growth. J. M. Buckler. (Illus.). 448p. 1990. 288.00 (*0-387-19569-6*) Spr-Verlag.

Longitudinal Study of Aging: Instructor's Manual. James L. Peterson et al. (Gerontology Research Toolkit Ser.). 62p. (Orig.). 1994. pap. text, teacher ed. 30.00 (*0-8018-5044-4*) Johns Hopkins.

Longitudinal Study of Aging: Student Workbook. Elinore E. Lurie et al. (Gerontology Research Toolkit Ser.). 182p. (Orig.). 1994. pap. text, student ed. 49.00 (*0-8018-5043-6*) Johns Hopkins.

Longitudinal Study of Dyslexia. H. J. Gjessing & B. Karlsen. (Illus.). 305p. 1989. 156.00 (*0-387-96948-9*) Spr-Verlag.

Longitudinal Study on Intelligence in the Second Year. J. Steven Reznick. 1997. pap. text 15.00 (*0-226-71041-6*) U Ch Pr.

Longitudinal Surveys of Children. National Research Council Staff. Ed. by Kirsten K. West et al. LC 98-87275. 128p. (C). 1998. pap. text 24.75 (*0-309-06192-X*) Natl Acad Pr.

Longknives: The U. S. Cavalry & Other Mounted Forces, 1845-1942. Kurt H. Cox & John P. Langellier. (GI: The Illustrated History of the American Soldier, His Uniform, & His Equipment Ser.). (Illus.). 80p. 1996. pap. 12.95 (*1-85367-233-5*, Pub. by Greenhill Bks) Stackpole.

Longknives: The U.S. Cavalry & Other Mounted Forces, 1845-1942. Kurt Hamilton Cox. LC 99-20252. (G.I. Ser.). (Illus.). 84p. 1999. 19.95 (*0-7910-5367-9*) Chelsea Hse.

Longleg. Glenda Adams. LC 92-52964. 339p. 1992. pap. 9.95 (*0-943433-09-6*) Cane Hill Pr.

Longlegs the Heron. Thornton W. Burgess. (J). 19.95 (*0-8488-0400-7*) Amereon Ltd.

Longlegs the Heron. Thornton W. Burgess. (J). 1992. reprint ed. lib. bdg. 17.95 (*0-89966-979-4*) Buccaneer Bks.

Longlining. Asmund Bjordal & Svein Lolkkeborg. 156p. (Orig.). 1996. text 75.00 (*0-85238-200-6*) Blackwell Sci.

Longliving of Soviet Georgia. G. Z. Pitskhelauri. Tr. by Gari Lesnoff-Caravaglia from RUS. LC 81-4176. (Illus.). 158p. 1982. 30.95 (*0-89885-073-8*, Kluwer Acad Hman Sci) Kluwer Academic.

Longman A-Level Reference Guide: Geography. Longman Publishing Staff. Date not set. pap. text. write for info. (*0-582-06388-4*) Addison-Wesley.

Longman Advanced Grammar: Reference & Practice. Alexander. 1992. pap. text. write for info. (*0-582-07978-0*, Pub. by Addison-Wesley) Longman.

Longman Annotated English Poems 1649-1681, Vol. I. John Dryden. Ed. by Paul Hammond. (Annotated English Poets Ser.). 480p. (C). 1995. 194.00 (*0-582-49213-0*, 76666) Longman.

Longman Annotated Englsh Poems V2 1682-1685, Vol. II. John Dryden. Ed. by Paul Hammond. 480p. (C). 1995. text 130.50 (*0-582-23944-3*, 76667) Addison-Wesley.

***Longman Anthology British Literature Volume 2.** 3024p. (C). 1998. write for info. (*0-321-04772-9*) Addison-Wesley.

Longman Anthology of American Drama. Ed. by Lee A. Jacobus. LC 80-21895. 512p. (C). 1982. text 34.95 (*0-582-28348-5*) Longman.

Longman Anthology of American Poetry see Anthology of American Poetry: Colonial to Contemporary

Longman Anthology of British Literature. Damrosch. 18.00 (*0-321-02737-X*) Addson-Wesley Educ.

***Longman Anthology of British Literature: Compact Version.** David Damrosch. LC 99-56300. 2648p. 1999. pap. 51.00 (*0-321-07670-2*) Longman.

***Longman Anthology Of British Literature Volume 1.** 3008p. (C). 1998. write for info. (*0-321-04771-0*) Addison-Wesley.

Longman Anthology of Contemporary American Poetry. 2nd ed. Ed. by Stuart Friebert & David G. Young. 629p. (C). 1989. pap. 65.00 (*0-8013-0046-0*, 75710) Longman.

***Longman Anthology of Drama & Theatre.** 2000. teacher ed. write for info. (*0-321-07790-3*) Addison-Wesley.

***Longman Anthology of Womens Literature.** 2000. teacher ed. write for info. (*0-321-07807-1*) Addison-Wesley.

Longman Atlas for Caribbean Examination. Morrissey. 1991. pap. text. write for info. (*0-582-07284-0*, Pub. by Addison-Wesley) Longman.

Longman Bibliography of Composition & Rhetoric, 1984 1985: Longman Series in College Composition & Communication, Vol. I, 1984-1985. Erika C. Lindemann. 318p. 1987. text 44.76 (*0-582-28376-0*, 71409) Longman.

***Longman Brain Trainer.** 58p. 2000. write for info. (*0-582-36875-8*) Longman.

Longman Business English Usage. Strutt. 1992. pap. text. write for info. (*0-582-07153-4*, Pub. by Addison-Wesley) Longman.

Longman Comp Euro Natlsm. Raymond Pearson. LC 92-46026. (Companions to History Ser.). 352p. (C). 1993. text 57.50 (*0-582-07229-8*, Pub. by Addison-Wesley) Longman.

***Longman Compact Anthology of British Literature.** David Damrosch. LC 99-56300. 1999. pap. text 35.00 (*0-321-07672-9*); pap. text 35.00 (*0-321-07673-7*) Longman.

***Longman Companion to America, Russia & the Cold War, 1941-98.** 2nd ed. John W. Young. LC 98-39550. (Longman Companions to History Ser.). 328p. 1998. pap. 33.06 (*0-582-36901-0*) Addison-Wesley.

Longman Companion Germany Since 1945. Adrian Webb. LC 98-20576. (Companions to History Ser.). (C). 1998. text 74.67 (*0-582-30736-8*) Addison-Wesley.

***Longman Companion Labour Party.** Harry Harmer. LC 98-51307. 1999. text 68.95 (*0-582-31214-0*) Longman.

Longman Companion to America: From Wilson to Roosevelt, 1910-45. Patrick Renshaw. Ed. by Chris Cook & John Stevenson. LC 95-23386. (Longman Companions to History Ser.). 256p. (C). 1995. text 55.00 (*0-582-09116-0*, Pub. by Addison-Wesley) Longman.

***Longman Companion to Britain in the Eighteenth Century, 1688-1820.** Jeremy Gregory & John Stevenson. LC 99-25136. 568p. (C). 1999. 75.95 (*0-582-27989-5*) Longman.

Longman Companion to Britain in the Eighteenth Century, 1688-1820. Jeremy Gregory & John Stevenson. LC 99-25136. (Companions to History Ser.). 568p. 1999. pap. text 25.95 (*0-582-27988-7*) Longman.

Longman Companion to Britain in the Era of the Two World Wars, 1914-45. Andrew Thorpe. (Longman Companions to History Ser.). 240p. (C). 1993. pap. text 33.25 (*0-582-07772-9*, Pub. by Addison-Wesley) Longman.

Longman Companion to Britain since 1945. Ed. by Chris Cook & John Stevenson. LC 94-49608. (Companions to History Ser.). 272p. (C). 1995. text 62.95 (*0-582-07030-9*, Pub. by Addison-Wesley) Longman.

Longman Companion to Britain since 1945. Ed. by Chris Cook & John Stevenson. LC 94-49608. (Companions to History Ser.). 272p. (C). 1995. pap. text 30.94 (*0-582-07031-7*) Longman.

Longman Companion to Cold War & Detente 1941-91: Longman Companions to History. John W. Young. LC 92-12765. (Longman Companions to History Ser.). (C). 1993. text 72.95 (*0-582-06173-3*, 79451) Longman.

Longman Companion to European Decolonization in the 20th Century. Muriel Chamberlain. LC 98-14251. (C). 1998. 73.13 (*0-582-07774-5*) Addison-Wesley.

Longman Companion to European Decolonization in the 20th Century. Muriel Chamberlain. LC 98-14251. 360p. (C). 1998. pap. text 25.50 (*0-582-07773-7*) Longman.

Longman Companion to European Nationalism 1789-1920. Raymond Pearson. LC 92-46026. (Companions to History Ser.). 352p. (C). 1995. pap. 45.00 (*0-582-07228-X*) Longman.

Longman Companion to Germany since 1945. Adrian Webb. LC 98-20576. (Companions to History Ser.). 360p. (C). 1998. pap. text 29.50 (*0-582-30737-6*) Longman.

***Longman Companion to Imperial Russia, 1689 - 1917.** David Longley. LC 99-57966. 496p. (C). 2000. write for info. (*0-582-31989-7*); pap. text 24.00 (*0-582-31990-0*) Longman.

Longman Companion to Napoleonic Europe. Clive Emsely. LC 92-12764. (Companions to History Ser.). 320p. (C). 1992. text 72.95 (*0-582-07224-7*, 79453) Longman.

Longman Companion to Nazi Germany. Tim Kirk. LC 94-1131. (Companions to History Ser.). 288p. (C). 1994. text 65.00 (*0-582-06376-0*, 76891, Pub. by Addison-Wesley) Longman.

***Longman Companion to Nineteenth Century Britain.** Chris Cook. LC 99-21551. (Companions to History Ser.). 368p. (C). 1999. 79.95 (*0-582-27991-7*) Longman.

***Longman Companion to Nineteenth Century Britain.** Chris Cook. LC 99-21551. (Companions to History Ser.). 368p. (C). 1999. pap. text 25.95 (*0-582-27990-9*) Longman.

***Longman Companion to Renaissance Europe, 1390-1530.** Stella Fletcher. LC 99-12941. 400p. 1999. pap. text 28.95 (*0-582-29882-2*) Addison-Wesley.

Longman Companion to the European Reformation, C. 1500-1618. Mark Greengrass. LC 97-14165. (Longman Companions to History Ser.). (C). 1998. 27.50 (*0-582-06174-1*); text 71.25 (*0-582-06175-X*) Longman.

Longman Companion to the European Union since 1945. Alasdair Blair. LC 98-51662. (Companions to History Ser.). 400p. 1999. pap. text 27.95 (*0-582-36884-7*) Longman.

***Longman Companion to the European Union, 1945-1999.** Alasdair Blair. LC 98-51662. 400p. 1999. 76.50 (*0-582-36885-5*) Addison-Wesley.

Longman Companion to the Labour Party, 1900-1998. Harry Harmer. LC 98-51307. (History Ser.). 328p. 1999. pap. text 28.50 (*0-582-31215-9*) Longman.

***Longman Companion to the Middle East since 1914.** 2nd ed. Ovendale. LC 98-14432. (Longman Companions to History Ser.). 408p. (C). 1998. pap. text, suppl. ed. 29.50 (*0-582-31555-7*) Longman.

Longman Companion to the Stuart Age, 1603-1714. John Wroughton. LC 96-43672. (Longman Companions to History Ser.). 320p. (C). 1997. 78.00 (*0-582-25776-X*); pap. text 20.75 (*0-582-25775-1*) Longman.

Longman Companion Tudor. Rosemary O'Day. LC 94-9970. (Longman Companions to History Ser.). 336p. (C). 1995. text 62.95 (*0-582-06725-1*, 77010, Pub. by Addison-Wesley) Longman.

Longman Coordinated Geography Text. Ross. Date not set. pap. text. write for info. (*0-582-06299-3*, Pub. by Addison-Wesley) Longman.

Longman Dictionary of American English. Marjorie Fuchs. 64p. 1992. pap. text, wbk. ed. 11.03 (*0-8013-0840-2*, 78906) Longman.

***Longman Dictionary of American English.** 2nd ed. (C). 2000. pap. 19.93 (*0-13-088450-2*) P-H.

Longman Dictionary of American English. 2nd ed. Addison-Wesley Longman, Inc. Staff. LC 96-51562. 1996. pap. text 19.04 (*0-8013-1823-8*) Longman.

Longman Dictionary of American English. 2nd ed. Longman Publishing Staff. 1997. text. write for info. (*0-201-49120-6*) Addison-Wesley.

Longman Dictionary of American English. 2nd ed. Longman U. K. Addison Wesley Staff. 80p. 1997. pap. text, wbk. ed. 11.75 (*0-8013-2027-5*) Addison-Wesley.

Longman Dictionary of American English: A Dictionary for Learners of English. Longman, Inc. Staff. 792p. (Orig.). (C). 1983. pap. text 28.67 (*0-582-90611-3*, 75187) Longman.

Longman Dictionary of American English: A Dictionary for Learners of English. 2nd ed. Addison-Wesley Longman, Inc. Staff. LC 96-51562. 1997. text 29.39 (*0-8013-1409-7*) Longman.

Longman Dictionary of American English Teacher's Companion. 2nd ed. Longman U. K. Addison Wesley Staff. 24p. 1997. pap. text, teacher ed. 10.28 (*0-8013-2028-3*) Addison-Wesley.

Longman Dictionary of Applied Linguistics. Jack Richards et al. 324p. 1985. pap. text 25.95 (*0-582-55708-9*, 74434) Longman.

Longman Dictionary of Business English. Adam. 1994. pap. text. write for info. (*0-582-25126-5*, Pub. by Addison-Wesley) Longman.

Longman Dictionary of Business English. J. H. Adam. Date not set. text. write for info. (*0-582-05029-4*, Pub. by Addison-Wesley) Longman.

Longman Dictionary of Business English: English-Hungarian. 2nd ed. J.H. Adam. (ENG & HUN.). 809p. 1993. 150.00 (*0-7859-8882-3*) Fr & Eur.

Longman Dictionary of Contemporary English. Ed. by Paul Proctor. (Illus.). 1229p. (C). 1987. pap. text 25.95 (*0-582-84223-9*, 75140) Longman.

Longman Dictionary Of Contemporary English. 3rd ed. Longman. 1995. 46.31 (*0-582-23751-3*, Pub. by Addison-Wesley) Longman.

Longman Dictionary of English Language & Culture. Longman Staff. (Illus.). 1995. pap. text 34.59 (*0-582-08676-0*, 70796) Longman.

Longman Dictionary of French Grammar & Idioms. Andre O. Hurtgen. (ENG & FRE.). 244p. 1991. 37.28 (*0-8013-0560-8*, 78466); pap. 22.60 (*0-8013-0547-0*, 78453) Longman.

Longman Dictionary of Geography. Audrey N. Clark. (C). 1986. pap. text 36.95 (*0-582-35261-4*) Longman.

Longman Dictionary of Geography. Audrey N. Clark. 750p. 1989. pap. 25.60 (*0-582-01779-3*, 78043) Longman.

Longman Dictionary of Poets: The Lives & Works of 1001 Poets in the English Language. Alan N. Bold. LC 86-129123. 320p. reprint ed. pap. 99.20 (*0-8357-6195-9*, 203448500090) Bks Demand.

Longman Dictionary of Spanish Grammar & Idioms. Andre O. Hurtgen. (ENG & SPA.). 232p. 1991. 37.28 (*0-8013-0627-2*, 78553); pap. 22.60 (*0-8013-0626-4*, 78552) Longman.

Longman Dictionary of the English Language. LC 84-185340. 1988. 29.95 (*0-582-55511-6*) Longman.

Longman Dictionary of Twentieth Century Biography. Frwd. by Asa Briggs. 480p. 1900. pap. text 16.95 (*0-582-89213-9*, TV3862) Longman.

Longman Dictionry Amer Engl Second Ed Wrkbk. 2nd ed. (C). 1997. pap. text 0.00 (*0-201-69520-0*) HEPC Inc.

Longman English & Chinese Dictionary. Longman Publishing Staff. Date not set. text. write for info. (*0-582-04944-X*, Pub. by Addison-Wesley) Longman.

Longman English-Chinese Illustrated Dictionary of Science. Erodman. (Illus.). 1992. text. write for info. (*962-359-590-5*) Addison-Wesley.

Longman English Collection: Arguing the Case. Griffin. 1993. pap. text. write for info. (*0-582-07877-6*, Pub. by Addison-Wesley) Longman.

Longman English Grammar. L. G. Alexander. 1989. pap. text 29.67 (*0-582-55892-1*, 78032) Longman.

Longman ESL Literacy. Yvonne Nishio. 256p. 1991. teacher ed. 29.95 (*0-8013-0579-9*, 78505) Longman.

Longman ESL Literacy. 2nd ed. Yvonne W. Nishio. LC 97-46997. 192p. 1998. pap. text, student ed. 17.64 (*0-201-35182-X*) Addison-Wesley.

Longman Essential Activator Put Your Ideas Into Words. 1997. write for info. (*0-582-24741-1*) Addison-Wesley.

Longman First Learning Dictionary. (ARA., Illus.). 156p. (J). 1987. pap. 3.50 (*0-86685-235-2*, LDL6899, Pub. by Librairie du Liban) Intl Bk Ctr.

Longman Grammar of Spoken & Written English. Douglas Biber. LC 99-29033. 1999. pap. text 119.00 (*0-582-23725-4*) Addison-Wesley.

***Longman Guide to Columbia Online Style.** Margaret Barber. 32p. (C). 1999. pap. 2.80 (*0-321-06745-2*) Addison-Wesley.

Longman Guide to English Usage. Sidney Greenbaum. pap. 17.95 (*0-14-051356-6*, Pub. by Pnguin Bks Ltd) Trafalgar.

Longman Guide to English Usage. Sidney Greenbaum & Janet Whitcut. 1989. 16.95 (*0-582-55619-8*) Longman.

Longman Guide to Living Religions. Harris et al. LC 95-162748. Date not set. pap. text. write for info. (*0-582-25297-0*, Pub. by Addison-Wesley) Longman.

Longman Guide to Sources in Contemporary British History, Vol. 1. Ed. by David Waller. LC 92-46024. 1993. text. write for info. (*0-582-20971-4*, Pub. by Addison-Wesley) Longman.

Longman Guide to the Advanced Placement Examination in United States History. 2nd ed. Ted Morse. LC 94-112381. 1994. text 18.16 (*0-8013-1143-8*) Addison-Wesley.

***Longman Guide to the Web.** Lester Faigley. LC 99-56549. 160p. 1999. spiral bd. 16.00 (*0-321-06730-4*) Longman.

Longman Handbook: Modern Language Association(Update) Anson. 862p. (C). 1999. 41.00 (*0-321-04966-7*) Addson-Wesley Educ.

***Longman Handbook Chapters 1-6.** 2nd ed. (C). 1999. write for info. (*0-321-07742-3*) Addison-Wesley.

***Longman Handbook Compact Edition.** (C). 1999. pap. text 6.00 (*0-321-06502-6*, Celebration) Addson-Wesley Educ.

Longman Handbook for UIC Writers & Readers. Anson & Schwegler. (C). 1998. text 34.67 (*0-201-45657-5*) Addison-Wesley.

Longman Handbook for Writers: Document Guide. Anson. (C). 1997. pap. text 10.00 (*0-673-97976-8*) Addison-Wesley.

***Longman Handbook For Writers & Readers.** (C). 2000. write for info. (*0-321-07733-4*) Addson-Wesley Educ.

Longman Handbook for Writers & Readers. Anson. 252p. (C). 1997. pap. text, wbk. ed. 26.73 (*0-673-98552-0*) Addison-Wesley.

Longman Handbook for Writers & Readers. Anson. (C). 1997. pap. text 13.00 (*0-673-98570-9*) Addison-Wesley.

Longman Handbook for Writers & Readers. Anson. (C). 1997. pap. text. write for info. (*0-321-40006-2*) Addson-Wesley Educ.

Longman Handbook for Writers & Readers. Anson. LC 97-154701. (C). 1997. pap. text. write for info. (*0-321-40007-0*) Addson-Wesley Educ.

Longman Handbook for Writers & Readers. Chris M. Anson & Robert A. Schwegler. LC 96-2037. (C). 1997. text 31.75 (*0-673-98550-4*) Longman.

***Longman Handbook for Writers & Readers.** 2nd ed. 320p. (C). 1999. pap. text 27.40 (*0-321-06492-5*, Celebration) Addson-Wesley Educ.

***Longman Handbook for Writers & Readers.** 2nd ed. 104p. (C). 1999. pap. text 26.00 (*0-321-06495-X*, Celebration); pap. text 0.00 (*0-321-06532-8*, Celebration) Addson-Wesley Educ.

***Longman Handbook for Writers & Readers.** 2nd ed. 152p. (C). 1999. pap. text 26.00 (*0-321-06496-8*, Celebration) Addson-Wesley Educ.

***Longman Handbook for Writers & Readers.** 2nd ed. (C). 1999. text. write for info. (*0-321-07793-8*) Addson-Wesley Educ.

Longman Handbook for Writers & Readers. 2nd ed. Anson. LC 99-30574. 979p. (C). 1999. 41.00 (*0-321-05804-6*) Addison-Wesley.

***Longman Handbook for Writers & Readers.** 2nd ed. Daedalus. 1999. 40.00 (*0-321-06490-9*) Longman.

Longman Handbook For Writers & Readers. 4th ed. (C). 1997. 11.00 (*0-673-97446-4*) Addison-Wesley.

Longman Handbook for Writers & Readers. 5th ed. Dornan. (C). 1996. pap. text 11.25 (*0-673-97363-8*) Addison-Wesley.

Longman Handbook for Writers & Readers: MAC. Anson. (C). 1997. pap. text 14.80 (*0-673-98571-7*) Addison-Wesley.

Longman Handbook for Writers & Readers-Answer Key. Anson. (C). 1997. pap. text 12.00 (*0-673-97974-1*) Addison-Wesley.

***Longman Handbook for Writers & Readers with MLA Updates.** Anson & Schwegler. 1999. pap. text 36.00 (*0-201-57608-2*) Addison-Wesley.

Longman Handbook of Modern American History, 1763-1996. Chris Cook & David Waller. LC 97-14206. (Companions to History Ser.). (C). 1997. text 76.88 (*0-582-08489-X*) Longman.

Longman Handbook of Modern European History, 1763-1991: Longman Handbooks to History. Chris Cook. (C). 1992. text 57.50 (*0-582-07291-3*) Addison-Wesley.

***Longman Handbook of the Modern World: International History & Politics since 1945.** Chris Cook & John Stevenson. LC 98-19337. (C). 1998. 74.95 (*0-582-30412-1*) Longman.

Longman Handy Learner's Dictionary. Longman Staff. (YA). (gr. 9-12). 1988. pap. text 11.95 (*0-582-96413-X*, 78324) Longman.

Longman Handy Learner's Dictionary of American English. Longman Staff. 1p. 1995. pap. 15.44 (*0-582-09483-6*) Addison-Wesley.

Longman Idioms Dictionary. Longman Publishing Group Staff. 1998. pap. text 32.89 (*0-582-30577-2*) Addison-Wesley.

Longman Idioms Dictionary: Over 6,000 Idioms. Stern. 1998. text 43.00 (*0-582-30578-0*, Prentice Hall) P-H.

An Asterisk (*) at the beginning of an entry indicates that the title is appearing for the first time.

Longman Illustrated Dictionary of Geography. John A. Kingston. (Illus.). 1989. lib. bdg. 8.95 (0-582-02163-4) Longman.

Longman Introductory Course for the TOEFL Test. Deborah Phillips. LC 96-1447. 1996. pap. text 21.00 (0-201-89899-3, Pub. by Addison-Wesley) Longman.

Longman Junior American Dictionary. Longman Staff. 1p. 1999. pap. text 12.67 (0-582-33251-6) Addison-Wesley.

Longman Modern History Germany, 1918 to 1945. Swinton. 1995. pap. text. write for info. (0-582-80469-8, Pub. by Addison-Wesley) Longman.

Longman New Junior English Dictionary. Longman Publishing Staff. 1993. pap. text. write for info. (0-582-09485-2, Pub. by Addison-Wesley) Longman.

Longman New Pocket English Dictionary. 2nd ed. Longman Publishing Staff. 1994. pap. text. write for info. (0-582-09484-4, Pub. by Addison-Wesley) Longman.

Longman Office Typing Step-by-Step, Bk. 3. Iris Kerry & Patricia Alderton. LC 73-8652. 144p. reprint ed. pap. 44.70 (0-608-13194-6, 202524700043) Bks Demand.

***Longman Penguin Reader.** 1998. write for info. (0-201-39702-1) Addison-Wesley.

Longman Photo Dictionary: Beginning & Intermediate. Marilyn S. Rosenthal & Daniel B. Freeman. 91p. (C). 1989. pap. text 14.70 (0-8013-0004-5, 75670) Longman.

Longman Photo Dictionary: Intermediate. Marilyn S. Rosenthal et al. (Illus.). 1989. pap. text, student ed. 12.13 (0-8013-0056-8, 75720) Longman.

Longman Photo Dictionary: Workbook-Beginning. Marjorie Fuchs. (Illus.). 1989. pap. text, student ed. 12.13 (0-8013-0249-8, 75904) Longman.

***Longman Picture Dictionary: American English.** Julie Ashworth. 1999. pap. text 14.67 (0-582-29981-0) Addison-Wesley.

***Longman Picture Dictionary: American-Japanese.** Julie Ashworth. 1999. pap. text 16.00 (0-582-33295-8) Addison-Wesley.

***Longman Picture Dictionary: American-Korean.** Julie Ashworth. 1999. pap. text 16.80 (0-582-33297-4) Addison-Wesley.

Longman-Pitman Office Dictionary. Longman Publishing Staff. 1990. pap. text. write for info. (0-582-06623-9, Pub. by Addison-Wesley) Longman.

Longman Polit Pamph Land. William Holton. 96p. (C). 1997. pap. text 7.86 (0-673-98467-2) Addison-Wesley.

Longman Political Pamphleteer. Ed. by Poli. 48p. (C). 1997. pap. text 7.86 (0-673-98329-3) Addison-Wesley.

Longman Political Pamphleteer: Sexual Harassment & the Courts. John C. Domino. (Political Pampheleteer Ser.). (C). 1997. pap. text 7.80 (0-673-99781-2) Addson-Wesley Educ.

Longman Political Pamplet. Canon. (Political Pampheleteer Ser.). (C). 1997. pap. text 8.00 (0-673-99775-8) Addson-Wesley Educ.

Longman Preparation Course for the TOEFL Test. Deborah Phillips. (C). 1999. pap. text 46.60 (0-201-37908-2) Addison-Wesley.

Longman Preparation Course for the TOEFL Test: CBE: Companion to Skills & Strategies, Vol. V. Deborah Phillips. (Longman Preparation Course for the TEOFL Ser.). 1999. 46.60 (0-201-52077-X) Addison-Wesley.

Longman Preparation Series for the TOEIC Test: Advanced Course. 2nd rev. ed. Linford Lougheed. LC 96-4683. (English for Business Success Ser.). Orig. Title: English the International Language. 1996. pap. text 23.10 (0-201-87791-0, Pub. by Addison-Wesley) Longman.

Longman Preparation Series for the TOEIC Test: Basic Course. 2nd rev. ed. Linford Lougheed. LC 96-2499. (English for Business Success Ser.). 1996. write for info. (0-614-98002-X) Longman.

***Longman Preparations Course for the TOEFL Test--CBT Volume.** Deborah Phillips. LC 98-43066. 1998. pap. text. write for info. (0-201-60437-X) Addison-Wesley.

Longman Pronunciation Dictionary. Wells. 1990. text. write for info. (0-582-96411-3, Pub. by Addison-Wesley) Longman.

Longman Pronunciation Dictionary. Wells. 1997. pap. text 32.89 (0-582-05383-8, Pub. by Addison-Wesley) Longman.

Longman Structural Readers, 8 bks., Stage 5. Incl. Valentine Generation & Other Stories. John Updike. 1981. pap. text 30.00 (0-582-53108-X); Winds of Change. 1981. pap. text 4.62 (0-582-53765-7); (English As a Second Language Bk.). Set pap. 4.25 (0-318-54111-4) Longman.

Longman Structural Readers, 8 bks., Stage 5. Incl. Valentine Generation & Other Stories. John Updike. 1981. pap. text 30.00 (0-582-53108-X); Winds of Change. 1981. pap. text 4.62 (0-582-53765-7); (English As a Second Language Bk.). 1981. 30.00 (0-582-74003-7) Longman.

Longman Structural Readers, Stage 6. Ed. by W. S. Allen. (English As a Second Language Bk.). 1981. pap. 4.25 (0-685-03098-9) Longman.

Longman Textbook Reader. 224p. (C). 1998. 0.16 (0-321-04617-X) Addison-Wesley.

Longman TOEFL Preparation Course User Guide. 2nd ed. Deborah Phillips. 1995. pap. text 11.58 (0-201-84678-0) Addison-Wesley.

Longman TOEFL Preparation Program: (Longman Preparation Course for the TOEFL) D. Phillips. 1989. pap. text 8.50 (0-8013-0212-9, 75870) Longman.

Longman Top Pocket Roget's Thesaurus. Longman Publishing Staff. Date not set. pap. text. write for info. (0-582-04793-5, Pub. by Addison-Wesley) Longman.

Longman Tropical Forest. Kenneth A. Longman & I. J. Jenik. LC 73-85681. (Illus.). 160p. 1974. pap. text 11.95 (0-582-44045-9) Longman.

Longman Twentieth Century History Series: A New Deal. 1987. pap. text 8.19 (0-582-22375-X, 70928) Longman.

Longman Twentieth Century History Series: China since 1900. 1988. pap. text 7.95 (0-582-22378-4, 78309) Longman.

Longman Twentieth Century History Series: Conflict in Palestine. 1989. pap. text 7.95 (0-582-34346-1, 78420) Longman.

Longman Twentieth Century History Series: Global War. (J). 1990. pap. text 7.95 (0-582-34348-8, 78448) Longman.

Longman Twentieth Century History Series: Italy & Mussolini. 1983. pap. text 8.19 (0-582-22371-7, 70924) Longman.

Longman Twentieth Century History Series: Roads to War. 1989. pap. text 7.95 (0-582-34344-5, 78426) Longman.

Longman Twentieth Century History Series: Russia in War & Revolution. 1986. pap. text 8.19 (0-582-22376-8, 70929) Longman.

Longman Twentieth Century History Series: Stalin & the Soviet Union. 1988. pap. text 7.95 (0-582-22377-6, 78261) Longman.

Longman Twentieth Century History Series: The Age Excess. 1986. pap. text 8.19 (0-582-22374-1, 70927) Longman.

Longman Workbook for Readers & Writers. Ed. by Weekes. (C). 1997. pap. text 47.00 (0-321-01238-0) Addson-Wesley Educ.

Longman World Guide: Birds. Whitefield. Date not set. pap. text. write for info. (0-582-89354-2, Pub. by Addison-Wesley) Longman.

***Longman Writers Companion.** Anson. 1999. pap. 30.67 (0-201-67713-X) Addison-Wesley.

***Longman Writer's Companion.** Anson. LC 99-36017. 471p. (C). 1999. spiral bd. 35.00 (0-8013-3157-9) Longman.

Longman Writing Environment. Daedalus. (C). 1999. text. write for info. (0-321-02405-2) Addison-Wesley.

Longman's Guide to the Advanced Placement Examination in European History. Mildred Alpern. 1993. pap. text 26.80 (0-8013-0943-3) Longman.

Longman's Medical Embryology. 7th ed. Thomas W. Sadler. LC 94-29937. (Illus.). 1996. 34.00 (0-683-07489-X) Lppncott W & W.

Longmen Grotto: The National Museums & Monuments of Ancient China. Liu J. Long. (National Museums & Monuments of Ancient China Ser.). (Illus.). 128p. 1997. 30.00 (0-85667-456-7) M T Train.

Longmont Album: History & Folklore of the St. Vrain Valley. Betty A. Newby. LC 95-25536. 1995. write for info. (0-89865-953-1) Donning Co.

Longneck Bird of Longboat Key: One of the Privileged Class. Jonathan Woe. (Land of Woefully Ser.: No. 2). (Illus.). 32p. (J). 1992. 14.95 (0-9627946-6-X) Hawk FL.

Longplaying. Richard W. Blevins. Ed. by Edward Mycue. (Took Modern Poetry in English Ser.: No. 43). 40p. 1994. pap. 5.00 (1-879457-45-8) Norton Coker Pr.

Longrider: A Tale of Just Passin' Through. unabridged ed. Mark Tiger Edmonds. LC 98-73130. 176p. 1998. pap. 10.95 (0-942979-51-6) Livingston U Pr.

Longrider: A Tale of Passin' Through. unabridged ed. Mark Tiger Edmonds. LC 98-73130. 104p. 1998. 20.95 (0-942979-52-4) Livingston U Pr.

Longrifles of North Carolina. 2nd ed. John Bivins, Jr. LC 87-63592. (Illus.). 240p. 1988. boxed set 50.00 (0-87387-097-2) Shumway.

Longrifles of Pennsylvania: Jefferson, Clarion & Elk Counties, Vol. 1. Russell Harriger. LC 83-51452. (Illus.). 256p. 1984. 50.00 (0-87387-087-5) Shumway.

Longrifles of Western Pennsylvania: Allegheny & Westmoreland Counties. Richard F. Rosenberger & Charles Kaufmann. LC 92-12625. (Illus.). 192p. (C). 1993. text 60.00 (0-8229-3727-1) U of Pittsburgh Pr.

Longrun Dynamics: A General Economic & Political Theory. Snooks. LC 97-52348. 304p. 1998. text 79.95 (0-312-21422-7) St Martin.

Longs-McHenrys Peak, CO. rev. ed. Ed. by Trails Illustrated Staff. (Illus.). 1997. 6.99 (0-925873-22-5) Trails Illustrated.

Longs Peak. Stephen A. Trimble. 1984. pap. 9.95 (0-930487-17-6) Rocky Mtn Nature Assn.

Longs Peak. Chester Wickwire. (Illus.). 80p. 1998. pap. 10.00 (0-932616-66-6) Brick Hse Bks.

Long's Preschool & Daycare Directory: Massachusetts Edition. Paula Long & Linda Robillard. 254p. (Orig.). 1996. pap. 14.95 (0-9651881-0-8) ABC Pubng Assn.

Longshore Textbook. 3rd ed. Compiled & Intro. by David E. Cisek. 400p. 1993. 49.00 (0-88450-086-1, 0861) Lawyers & Judges.

***Longshore Textbook.** 4th rev. ed. Ed. by Steven M. Birnbaum et al. LC 99-33489. 464p. 1999. 85.00 (0-913875-88-0, 0861-N) Lawyers & Judges.

Longshoremen. Charles B. Barnes. Ed. by Leon Stein. LC 77-70482. (Illus.). 1977. reprint ed. lib. bdg. 35.95 (0-405-10156-2) Ayer.

***Longshot.** Mark Ammerman. LC 99-80158. (Cross & the Tomahawk Ser.: Vol. 3). 318p. 2000. pap. 11.99 (0-88965-165-5, Pub. by Horizon Books) Chr Pubns.

Longshot. Dick Francis. 336p. 1999. mass mkt. 5.99 (0-449-21955-0, Crest); mass mkt. write for info. (0-449-45825-3, Crest) Fawcett.

***Longson.** 1999. mass mkt. write for info. (0-312-97059-5) St Martin.

***Longstreet Highroad Guide to the Arizona Mountains & Grand Canyon.** Stewart Aitchison. LC 00-104188. (Longstreet Highroad Coastal Ser.). (Illus.). 352p. 2000. pap. 18.95 (1-56352-593-3) Longstreet.

***Longstreet Highroad Guide to the California Coast.** Ken McKowen. LC 00-104187. (Illus.). 352p. 2000. pap. 18.95 (1-56352-594-1) Longstreet.

***Longstreet Highroad Guide to the California Sierra Nevada.** Mark Grossi. LC 00-104190. (Longstreet Highroad Coastal Ser.). (Illus.). 352p. 2000. pap. 18.95 (1-56352-592-5) Longstreet.

***Longstreet Highroad Guide to the Chesapeake Bay.** Deane Winegar & Garvey Winegar. LC 99-68569. (Longstreet Highroad Coastal Ser.). (Illus.). 320p. 2000. pap. 18.95 (1-56352-544-5) Longstreet.

***Longstreet Highroad Guide to the Colorado Mountains.** Hal Clifford. LC 99-61764. (Illus.). 352p. 1999. pap. 18.95 (1-56352-537-2) Longstreet.

Longstreet Highroad Guide to the Florida Keys & Everglades. Rick Farren. LC 98-89180. (Illus.). 320p. 1999. pap. 18.95 (1-56352-543-7) Longstreet.

Longstreet Highroad Guide to the Georgia Coast & Okefenokee, 5 vols. Georgia Conservancy Staff et al. LC 97-76537. (Illus.). 272p. 1998. pap. 18.95 (1-56352-461-9) Longstreet.

Longstreet Highroad Guide to the Georgia Coast & Okefenokee. Richard J. Lenz. LC 98-89179. (Illus.). 320p. 1999. pap. 18.95 (1-56352-542-9) Longstreet.

***Longstreet Highroad Guide to the Maine Coast.** Elizabeth Edwardsen. LC 99-61769. (Illus.). 320p. 1999. pap. 18.95 (1-56352-545-3) Longstreet.

Longstreet Highroad Guide to the New Hampshire Mountains. Carol C. Cushing. LC 98-89177. (Illus.). 320p. 1999. pap. 18.95 (1-56352-503-8) Longstreet.

Longstreet Highroad Guide to the New York Adirondacks. Philip Brown. LC 98-89176. (Illus.). 352p. 1999. pap. 18.95 (1-56352-505-4) Longstreet.

Longstreet Highroad Guide to the North Carolina Mountains, 5 vols. Lynda McDaniel. LC 97-76535. (Illus.). 308p. 1998. pap. 18.95 (1-56352-463-5) Longstreet.

***Longstreet Highroad Guide to the Northwest Coast.** Allan May. LC 00-104186. (Illus.). 352p. 2000. pap. 18.95 (1-56352-595-X) Longstreet.

***Longstreet Highroad Guide to the Oregon Cascades.** Terry W. Sheely. LC 99-68570. (Longstreet Highroad Coastal Ser.). (Illus.). 336p. 2000. pap. 18.95 (1-56352-538-0) Longstreet.

Longstreet Highroad Guide to the Vermont Mountains. Nancy Bazilchuk & G. Richard Strimbeck. LC 98-89178. (Illus.). 320p. 1999. pap. 18.95 (1-56352-504-6) Longstreet.

Longstreet Highroad Guide to the Washington Cascades. Allan May. LC 99-61768. (Illus.). 352p. 1999. pap. 18.95 (1-56352-536-4) Arthritis Found.

Longstreet's Aide: The Civil War Letters of Major Thomas J. Goree. Ed. by Thomas W. Cutrer. LC 94-37521. (Nation Divided Ser.). (Illus.). 304p. (C). 1995. 32.50 (0-8139-1574-0) U Pr of Va.

***Longstreet's Assault - Pickett's Charge: The Lost Record of Pickett's Wounded.** Jerry Frey. 240p. 2000. 29.95 (1-57249-195-7, Burd St Pr) White Mane Pub.

Longsword, Earl of Salisbury: An Historical Romance, 2 vols., Set. Thomas Leland. LC 73-22765. 420p. 1975. reprint ed. 87.95 (0-405-06016-5) Ayer.

Longsworth Family History: Descendants of Solomon Longsworth, Sr., of Maryland. Mary E. Breese. LC 52-23969. (Illus.). 281p. reprint ed. pap. 87.20 (0-608-10215-6, 205167600099) Bks Demand.

Longterm & Peakscan: Neutron Activation Analysis Computer Programs. Thomas Meyers & Mark Denies. (Technical Reports Ser.: No. 2). (Illus.). 1972. pap. 1.00 (0-932206-11-5) U Mich Mus Anthro.

Longterm Care of the Coronary Patient. Risteard Mulcahy. (Illus.). 124p. (Orig.). 1992. pap. text 35.00 (0-443-04673-5) Church.

Longtime Californ' A Documentary Study of an American Chinatown. Victor G. Nee & Brett De Bary Nee. 438p. 1986. reprint ed. pap. 16.95 (0-8047-1336-7) Stanford U Pr.

Longtime Companions: Autobiographies of Gay Male Fidelity. Ed. by Alfred Lees & Ronald Nelson. LC 98-46138. 225p. 1999. pap. 17.95 (1-56023-957-3, Harrington Park); lib. bdg. 39.95 (0-7890-0641-3, Harrington Park) Haworth Pr.

Longtime Friends: An Essence of Life. Ann M. Skelly. 1999. 6.95 (0-8362-7169-6) Andrews & McMeel.

Longue Reflexion Amoureuse. Paul Eluard. (Illus.). 9.95 (0-686-55976-2) Fr & Eur.

Longus. William E. McCulloh. LC 77-99541. (Twayne's World Authors Ser.). 1970. lib. bdg. 20.95 (0-8057-2540-7) Irvington.

Longus: Daphnis & Chloe. Longus. Ed. by Morgan. 1994. write for info. (0-85668-562-3, Pub. by Aris & Phillips); pap. write for info. (0-85668-563-1, Pub. by Aris & Phillips) David Brown.

Longview We Remember. Linda N. Jones. LC 89-52179. (Illus.). 290p. (Orig.). 1990. 29.95 (0-9625511-1-2); pap. text 19.95 (0-9625511-0-4) Storm Ridge Pr.

Longwalker's Journey: A Novel of the Choctaw Trail of Tears. Beatrice O. Harrell. Ed. by Cindy Kane. LC 98-9754. (Illus.). 144p. (J). (gr. 3-6). 1999. 15.99 (0-8037-2380-6, Dial Yng Read); lib. bdg. 15.89 (0-8037-2383-0, Dial Yng Read) Peng Put Young Read.

Longwall-Shortwall Mining, State of the Art. fac. ed. Ed. by R. V. Ramani. LC 81-67436. (Illus.). 306p. 1981. reprint ed. pap. 94.90 (0-7837-7849-X, 204760800007) Bks Demand.

Longwall Thick Seam Mining: Proceedings of the Indo-U. S. Seminar on Longwall Mining Systems for Thick Seam Mining - Assessment of Progress & Needs, Indian School of Mines, Dhanbad, 11-13 January 1986. Ed. by Raja V. Ramani & Ajoy K. Ghose. 270p. (C). 1988. text 136.00 (90-6191-901-0, Pub. by A A Balkema) Ashgate Pub Co.

***Longwood Guide to Writing.** 224p. 2000. teacher ed. write for info. (0-205-31092-3) Allyn.

***Longwood Guide to Writing: Website.** 1999. write for info. (0-205-31093-1) Allyn.

***Longwood Reader.** 4th ed. Ed. by Edward A. Dornan & Charles W. Dawe. LC 99-27491. 742p. (C). 1999. pap. text 36.00 (0-205-30801-5) Allyn.

Longwood to Writing. Andrea Lunsford & Bridges. LC 99-52642. 700p. 1999. 46.00 (0-205-27206-1) Allyn.

Longwood Writing Brief. Andrea Lunsford & Bridges. LC 99-52643. 612p. 1999. pap. text 42.00 (0-205-27207-X) Allyn.

Longyear: The Descendants of Jacob Longyear of Ulster County, New York. Edmund J. Longyear. 622p. 1992. reprint ed. pap. 89.00 (0-8328-2393-7); reprint ed. lib. bdg. 99.00 (0-8328-2392-9) Higginson Bk Co.

L

Lonidamine. Ed. by B. Silvestrini et al. (Journal: Oncology: Vol. 41, Suppl. 1). (Illus.). iv, 124p. 1984. pap. 76.75 (3-8055-3867-7) S Karger.

Lonidamine: A New Pharmacological Approach to the Study & Control of Spermatogenesis & Tumors. Ed. by B. Silvestrini & A. Caputo. (Journal: Chemotherapy: Vol. 27, Suppl.). (Illus.). 120p. 1981. pap. 31.50 (3-8055-3438-8) S Karger.

Lonigan. Louis L'Amour. 192p. 1988. mass mkt. 4.50 (0-553-27536-4) Bantam.

***Lonley Planet Cuba.** 2nd ed. David Stanley. (Travel Guides Ser.). (Illus.). 448p. 2000. pap. 19.99 (0-86442-750-6) Lonely Planet.

Lonnie Bailey's Zoo. Lonnie D. Bailey. 1998. pap. write for info. (1-57553-917-9) Watermrk Pr.

Lonnie Mack Vital Blues Guitar. Richard DeVinck. (Illus.). 216p. (Orig.). 1996. pap. 24.95 (1-56922-009-3, 07-4036) Creat Cncpts.

Lonny's Poems. Justin Franchi. 129p. 1998. pap. 11.95 (1-892896-32-X) Buy Books.

***Lonoke County, Arkansas, Will Books A & B, 1873-1913.** Tracey C. Converse. 65p. 1999. pap. 15.00 (1-56546-147-9) Arkansas Res.

Lonquen. Maximo P. Gomez. (SPA.). 303p. 1980. 8.00 (0-317-15033-2, 3013) Ediciones Norte.

***Lonsdale: Plays One.** Frederick Lonsdale. (Oberon Bks.). 2000. pap. 20.95 (1-84002-073-3) Theatre Comm.

Lonsdale's Belt: The Story of Boxing's Greatest Prize. John Harding. (Illus.). 352p. 1996. 31.95 (0-86051-846-9, Robson-Parkwest) Parkwest Pubns.

***Lonzie's Fried Chicken Vol. 2: A Journal of Accessible Southern Fiction & Poetry.** 2nd ed. Illus. by E. H. Goree. 112p. 1999. pap. 8.95 (0-9673427-0-8) Southern Escarpment.

***Lonzie's Fried Chicken Vol. 3: A Journal of Accessible Southern Fiction & Poetry.** Ed. by E. H. Goree. 100p. 2000. pap. 8.95 (0-9673427-1-6) Southern Escarpment.

Loo-Loo, Boo & Art You Can Do. Denis Roche. LC 95-21971. (Illus.). 32p. (J). (ps-4). 1996. 14.95 (0-395-75921-8) HM.

Loo Sanction. large type ed. Trevanian. 400p. 1983. 27.99 (0-7089-8095-3, Charnwood) Ulverscroft.

Look see Mira

Look. Nina Blanchard. 432p. 1996. mass mkt. 5.99 (0-451-18034-8, Sig) NAL.

***Look.** Michael Grejniec. LC 93-16066. (Illus.). 32p. (J). (ps-3). 1999. pap. 6.95 (0-7358-1197-0, Pub. by North-South Bks NYC) Chronicle Bks.

Look, Vol. 1. 80p. 1992. pap. 19.95 (88-7070-169-7) Belvedere USA.

Look, Vol. 2. 80p. 1992. pap. 19.95 (88-7070-170-0) Belvedere USA.

Look, Vol. 3. 80p. 1992. pap. 19.95 (88-7070-171-9) Belvedere USA.

Look . . . What Do You See? Jennifer Rye. LC 90-40231. (First Science Ser.). (Illus.). 32p. (J). (gr. k-3). 1991. pap. 3.95 (0-8167-2123-8); lib. bdg. 17.25 (0-8167-2122-X) Troll Communs.

Look - a Butterfly. David Cutts. LC 81-11369. (Now I Know Ser.). (Illus.). 32p. (J). (gr. k-2). 1997. pap. 3.50 (0-89375-663-6) Troll Communs.

Look - And Learn! Using Picture Books with Children Grades Five & Up. Sheryl L. Saunders. LC 98-31489. (Illus.). 96p. 1999. pap. 9.95 (0-325-00019-0) Heinemann.

Look about You. Date not set. write for info. (0-614-10752-0) U Delaware Pr.

Look about You. LC 79-133699. (Tudor Facsimile Texts. Old English Plays Ser.: No. 92). reprint ed. 49.50 (0-404-53392-2) AMS Pr.

Look after Yourself: The Health Handbook for Older People. Alan Stewart. (Illus.). 156p. (Orig.). 1991. pap. 14.95 (0-04-442259-8, Pub. by Allen & Unwin Pty) Paul & Co Pubs.

Look Again! Tana Hoban. LC 72-127469. 40p. (J). (ps-1). 1971. text 15.00 (0-02-744050-8, Mac Bks Young Read) S&S Childrens.

Look Again: Better Policies Are Possible. Lorna Hahn. LC 96-32402. 138p. 1996. pap. text 19.50 (0-7618-0434-X) U Pr of Amer.

Look Again! Clues to Modern Paintings. Sally Montanari. (Illus.). 68p. (Orig.). 1989. pap. 8.95 (0-913515-36-1, Starrhill Press) Black Belt Communs.

Look Again! The Second Ultimate Spot-the-Difference Book. A. J. Wood. (Illus.). 40p. (J). (gr. 1 up). 1995. pap. 5.99 (0-14-066459-9, PuffinBks) Peng Put Young Read.

Look Again Pictures: For Language Development & Lifeskills. rev. ed. Judy W. Olsen. (Illus.). xx, 112p. 1998. pap. text 19.95 (1-882483-70-7) Alta Bk Ctr.

Look Ahead. Andrew Carnegie. 1996. lib. bdg. 251.75 (0-8490-5940-2) Gordon Pr.

Look Ahead: Year 2020. (Special Reports: No. 220). 551p. 1988. 25.00 (0-309-04702-1, SR220) Transport Res Bd.

Look-Alike Bride. Laura Anthony. (Surprise Brides Ser.). 1997. per. 3.25 (0-373-19220-7, 1-19220-2) Silhouette.

Look-Alike Fiancee. Elizabeth Duke. (Romance Ser.: Vol. 395). 1998. mass mkt. 3.50 (0-373-17395-4, 1-17395-4) Harlequin Bks.

L

***Look-Alikes.** Little, Brown & Company Staff. (Illus.). 2000. 13.95 (*0-316-89077-4*) Little.
Look-ALikes: Discover a Land Where Things Are Not As They Appear. Joan Steiner. LC 97-32795. (Illus.). 32p. (J). (gr. k-3). 1998. 12.95 (*0-316-81255-2*) Little.
***Look-Alikes Jr.** Joan Steiner. (Illus.). 2000. 13.95 (*0-316-89073-1*) Little.
Look-Alikes Jr. Find More Than 700 Hidden Everyday Objects. Joan Steiner. LC 99-11683. (Illus.). 32p. (J). (gr. k-3). 1999. 13.95 (*0-316-81307-9*) Little.
Look-Alikes Winter Holidays. Joan Steiner. (J). 2001. write for info. (*0-316-81187-4*) Little.
Look & Cook Cookbook: Chicken. (Butterfly Bks.). (Illus.). 167p. 1997. 18.95 (*0-86685-714-1*) Intl Bk Ctr.
Look & Cook Cookbook: Chocolate Desserts. (Butterfly Bks.). (ARA., Illus.). 167p. 1997. 18.95 (*0-86685-715-X*) Intl Bk Ctr.
Look & Cook Cookbook: Fruit Desserts. (Butterfly Bks.). (Illus.). 167p. 1997. 18.95 (*0-86685-716-8*) Intl Bk Ctr.
Look & Cook Cookbook: Main Vegetables. (Butterfly Bks.). (Illus.). 167p. 1997. 18.95 (*0-86685-692-7*) Intl Bk Ctr.
Look & Cook Cookbook: Meat Classics. (Butterfly Bks.). (ARA., Illus.). 167p. 1997. 18.95 (*0-86685-691-9*) Intl Bk Ctr.
Look & Feel: Proceedings of the Oxford Symposium on Food & Cookery, 1993. Ed. by Harlan Walker. 246p. 1994. pap. 35.00 (*0-907325-56-4*) Food Words.
Look & Find. Illus. by John Wallner. 12p. (J). (ps-2). 1988. 7.95 (*0-448-19068-0*, G & D) Peng Put Young Read.
***Look & Find Activity Book.** Brighter Vision Publishing Staff. (Illus.). (J). 2000. pap. 1.39 (*1-55254-149-5*) Brighter Vision.
***Look & Find Casper the Friendly Ghost & the Ghostly Trio.** Howard Bender. 24p. (J). (gr. 2-7). 1999. pap. 3.95 (*0-8167-6292-9*) Troll Communs.
Look & Find Series, 19 vols., Set. (J). (gr. k-6). 1998. lib. bdg. 284.05 (*1-56674-907-7*) Forest Hse.
Look & Find Street Fighter II. 1994. write for info. (*0-7853-0699-4*) Pubns Intl Ltd.
Look & Learn, 6 bks. Nicola Tuxworth. Incl. First Book about Animal Homes. LC 98-31779. 24p. (J). (gr. 1 up). 1999. 19.93 (*0-8368-2285-4*); First Book about Bodies. LC 98-31772. 24p. (J). (gr. 1 up). 1999. 19.93 (*0-8368-2286-2*); First Book about Colors. LC 98-31780. 24p. (J). (gr. 1 up). 1999. lib. bdg. 19.93 (*0-8368-2287-0*); First Book about Growing. LC 98-31778. 24p. (J). (gr. 1 up). 1999. lib. bdg. 19.93 (*0-8368-2370-2*); First Book about Mixing & Matching. LC 98-31777. 24p. (J). (gr. 1 up). 1999. lib. bdg. 19.93 (*0-8368-2371-0*); First Book about Patterns. LC 98-31774. 24p. (J). (gr. 1 up). 1999. lib. bdg. 19.93 (*0-8368-2288-9*); (Illus.). (J). (gr. 1 up). 1999. Set lib. bdg. 119.60 (*0-8368-2284-6*) Gareth Stevens Inc.
Look & Learn: Basic Learning Concepts, 4 vols., Set. Istar Schwager. (Illus.). 144p. (J). (ps-2). 1993. lib. bdg. 55.80 (*1-56674-928-X*, HTS Bks) Forest Hse.
***Look & Learn: My Day.** . Southwater. (J). 2000. 7.95 (*1-84215-165-7*) Anness Pub.
***Look & Learn: My Home.** . Southwater. (J). 2000. 7.95 (*1-84215-169-X*) Anness Pub.
***Look & Learn: Outdoor Play.** . Southwater. (J). 2000. 7.95 (*1-84215-168-1*) Anness Pub.
***Look & Learn: Pets.** . Southwater. (J). 2000. 7.95 (*1-84215-167-3*) Anness Pub.
***Look & Learn: Wild Animals.** . Southwater. (J). 2000. 7.95 (*1-84215-166-5*) Anness Pub.
***Look & Learn - Farm Animals.** Southwater Staff. (J). 2000. 7.95 (*1-84215-091-X*) Anness Pub.
Look & Listen. Lorna Read. (My Big Little Fat Bks.). (Illus.). 20p. (J). (ps). 1996. bds. 3.49 (*1-85854-160-3*) Brimax Bks.
Look & Listen, Pt. C. Frances Clark. (Frances Clark Library for Piano Students). 48p. (Orig.). (J). (gr. k-12). 1962. pap. text 6.95 (*0-87487-178-6*) Summy-Birchard.
Look & Listen, Pt. D. Frances Clark. (Frances Clark Library for Piano Students). 48p. (Orig.). (J). (gr. k-12). 1962. pap. text 6.95 (*0-87487-179-4*) Summy-Birchard.
Look & Listen, Pt. A. Frances Clark. (Frances Clark Library for Piano Students). 48p. (Orig.). (J). (gr. k-6). 1962. pap. text 6.95 (*0-87487-176-X*) Summy-Birchard.
Look & Listen, Pt. B. Frances Clark. (Frances Clark Library for Piano Students). 48p. (Orig.). (J). (gr. k-12). 1962. pap. text 6.95 (*0-87487-177-8*) Summy-Birchard.
Look & Look Again: Lost in the Haunted Mansion. Maria Tropea. (Illus.). 24p. (Orig.). (J). 1991. 2.98 (*1-56156-044-8*); pap. 1.95 (*1-56156-050-2*) Kidsbks.
Look & Look Again: Lost in the Haunted Mansion. Maria Tropea. (Look & Look Again Ser.). (Illus.). 24p. (Orig.). (J). (gr. 4-7). 1990. pap. 1.95 (*1-878890-03-4*) Palisades Prodns.
Look & Look Again: Missing Snowman. Maria Tropea. (Illus.). 24p. (J). 1991. 2.98 (*1-56156-047-2*); pap. 1.95 (*1-56156-053-7*) Kidsbks.
Look & Look Again: Silly Schoolhouse. Maria Tropea. (Illus.). 24p. (J). 1991. pap. 1.95 (*1-56156-051-0*) Kidsbks.
Look & Look Again: Silly Schoolhouse. Maria Tropea. (Illus.). 24p. (J). 1991. 2.98 (*1-56156-045-6*) Kidsbks.
Look & Look Again: Where's Benjy Bunny? Maria Tropea. (Illus.). 24p. (J). 1991. 2.98 (*1-56156-046-4*); pap. 1.95 (*1-56156-052-9*) Kidsbks.
Look & Move On. Mohammed Mrabet. Tr. by Paul Bowles. 128p. 1989. 30.00 (*0-7206-0756-6*, Pub. by P Owen Ltd) Dufour.
Look & See, Vol. 4469. Sandi Hill. Ed. by Joel Kupperstein. (Learn to Read Math Ser.). (Illus.). 16p. (J). 1998. pap. 2.75 (*1-57471-376-0*, 4469) Creat Teach Pr.
Look & See H O T V or Letter E. LaVerne Stevens. LC 91-75641. (Illus.). 32p. (J). (ps-k). 1991. spiral bd. 8.00 (*0-9630441-0-9*) B&B Pr.
Look & See Marvelous Me: A Self Esteem Program. John Wolf & Judith A. Sahlin. LC 96-77637. (Illus.). 22p. (Orig.). (J). (gr. 4-6). 1996. pap. 13.95 (*1-884063-91-8*) Mar Co Prods.
Look & See the Town: Historic Sites of Nashville & Davidson County. Orphelia Paine. 68p. 1989. pap. write for info. (*0-9630176-0-8*) Metro Hist Comm.
Look & See What God Gave Me. Sally A. Conan. LC 97-7491. (Illus.). 32p. (J). (ps-2). 1998. pap. 7.95 (*0-8091-6645-3*, 6645-3) Paulist Pr.
***Look & Tremble: A Novel of West Florida.** Jesse Earle Bowden. 304p. 2000. 21.95 (*0-942407-53-9*) Father & Son.
Look Around You. William Read. LC 91-38758. 1992. 13.95 (*0-87949-364-X*) Ashley Bks.
Look at a Tree. Eileen Curran. LC 84-8843. (Illus.). 32p. (J). (gr. k-2). 1985. pap. 3.50 (*0-8167-0350-7*) Troll Communs.
Look at Annette. Marion Walter. LC 77-186592. (Illus.). 32p. (J). (ps-3). 1972. 5.95 (*0-87131-071-6*) M Evans.
Look at Architecture Columbus Indiana. 182p. 1998. pap. 19.95 (*0-9659299-1-4*) Visitors Ctr.
Look at Bump. Christopher James. (Illus.). 10p. (J). 1993. pap. 4.49 (*1-881445-16-X*) Sandvik Pub.
***Look at Commercial Buildings In 1995: Characteristics, Energy Consumption & Energy Expenditures.** 406p. 1998. per. 37.00 (*0-16-063545-4*) USGPO.
Look at Cross-Addiction. Saul Selby. 12p. (Orig.). 1985. pap. 1.55 (*0-89486-331-2*) Hazelden.
Look at Della Duck. Rozanne L. Williams. (Illus.). 12p. (J). (gr. k-2). write for info. (*1-58605-014-1*) Knowledge Kids.
Look at Derailment Today: North America & Europe. Jean B. Leslie & Ellen Van Velsor. LC 95-52011. 69p. 1996. pap. text 20.00 (*1-882197-15-1*) Ctr Creat Leader.
Look at Dogs. Monica Halpern. (Look at Science Ser.). 1998. pap. 4.95 (*0-8172-7986-5*) Raintree Steck-V.
Look at God's Book. Mary Schramm. (Illus.). 42p. (J). (gr. k-6). 1973. pap. text 14.99 (*1-55976-148-2*) CEF Press.
Look at Insects. Roma Bishop. 1994. pap. 3.95 (*0-671-88310-0*) Litle Simon.
Look at It This Way: Reframing Life's Experiences. Clifford E. Isaacson. LC 95-4941. 174p. (Orig.). 1996. pap. 9.95 (*0-945156-04-9*) Upper Des Moines Counsel.
Look at It This Way: Toys & Activities for Children with Visual Impairment. Roma Lear. LC 99-164788. (Illus.). 144p. 1998. pap. text 25.00 (*0-7506-3895-8*) Buttrwrth-Heinemann.
Look at Languages. 2nd ed. Arthur Frommer. (C). 1998. pap. 31.00 (*0-15-507826-7*, Pub. by Harcourt Coll Pubs) Harcourt.
Look at Latin American Lifestyles. 2nd ed. Marvin K. Mayers. (International Museum of Cultures Ser.: No. 2). 138p. 1982. pap. 12.50 (*0-88312-170-0*) S I L Intl.
Look at Life: A Collection of Poems. Raymond Mears. 72p. 1999. pap. 8.00 (*1-891774-13-1*, Path Pubng in Christ) Path Pubng.
***Look at Life: Exploring the Diversity of Organisms.** 3rd ed. Carol Crowder & Mary Durant. 284p. (C). 1999. pap. text, wbk. ed. 24.95 (*0-7872-6289-7*) Kendall-Hunt.
Look at Life: Exploring the Unity of Organisms. 3rd ed. Joe Anders et al. 256p. (C). 1996. pap. text 20.95 (*0-7872-2361-1*) Kendall-Hunt.
Look at Life from a Deer Stand. Chapman. 1996. pap. text 9.98 (*0-9653274-0-X*) S&A Family.
Look at Life from a Deer Stand: Hunting for the Meaning of Life. Steve Chapman. LC 97-42832. 130p. 1998. pap. 8.99 (*1-56507-864-0*) Harvest Hse.
Look at Loras One Hundred & Fiftieth Celebration. Loras College Sesquicentennial Committee Staff. Ed. by Anthony Farrington. (Illus.). 100p. 1989. 39.95 (*0-936875-04-6*) Loras Coll Pr.
***Look at Mars** Ray Spangenburg & Diane Moser. LC 99-37378. (Out of This World Ser.). 2000. 32.00 (*0-531-11717-0*) Watts.
Look at Me. Anita Brookner. 1997. pap. 12.00 (*0-679-73813-4*) Vin Bks.
Look at Me. Doris Dorrie. (Illus.). 128p. 1998. 35.00 (*3-908161-14-2*) Abbeville Pr.
Look at Me. Kathy Poelker. (Illus.). 64p. 1987. teacher ed. 7.95 (*0-945405-00-6*) LAM Co.
***Look at Me.** Christine H. Tangvald. Ed. by Jennifer Stewart. (Patty Cake Devotions Ser.). (Illus.). 14p. (J). (ps). 1999. bds. 3.99 (*0-7847-0980-7*, 04294) Standard Pub.
Look at Me! large type ed. Susan Lumpkin. (HRL Cuddle Bks.). (Illus.). 7p. (J). (ps-k). 1999. pap. text 10.95 (*1-57332-145-1*) HighReach Lrning.
***Look at Me: A Novel.** Lauren Porosoff Mitchell. LC 00-28747. 204p. 2000. pap. 14.95 (*0-9654578-1-8*, Pub. by Leapfrog Pr) Consort Bk Sales.
***Look at Me! Animals: My Own Photo Book.** Lynn Chang. (Illus.). 20p. (J). 2000. 6.95 (*0-8118-2255-9*) Chronicle Bks.
Look at Me in a Funny Hat! Richard Johnson. LC 93-32379. (Illus.). 14p. (J). (ps up). 1994. 4.99 (*1-56402-414-8*) Candlewick Pr.
Look at Me in Funny Clothes! Richard Johnson. LC 93-32380. (Illus.). 14p. (J). (ps up). 1994. 4.99 (*1-56402-415-6*) Candlewick Pr.
***Look at Me! Vehicles: My Own Photo Book.** Lynn Chang. (Illus.). 20p. (YA). 2000. 6.95 (*0-8118-2278-8*) Chronicle Bks.
Look at Me World. Gary Roen. LC 76-2745. (Illus.). 1976. pap. 2.50 (*0-88435-006-1*) Chateau Pub.
Look at Minerals: From Galena to Gold. Jo S. Kittinger. LC 98-22677. (First Books-Earth & Sky Science). 1998. lib. bdg. 22.00 (*0-531-20385-9*) Watts.
Look at Minerals: From Galena to Gold. Jo S. Kittinger. (First Bks.). (Illus.). 64p. (J). (gr. 4-6). 1999. pap. text 6.95 (*0-531-15925-6*) Watts.
Look at Moons Ray Spangenburg & Diane Moser. LC 99-15452. (Out of This World Ser.). (J). 2000. 32.00 (*0-531-11702-2*) Watts.
Look at Mormonism. Gary J. Coleman. pap. 4.95 (*0-89036-142-8*) Liahona Pub Trust.
Look at My Ugly Face: Myths & Musings on Beauty & Other Perilous Obsessions with Women's Appearance. Sara Halprin. 352p. 1996. pap. 12.95 (*0-14-023492-6*, Penguin Bks) Viking Penguin.
Look at My Ugly Face! Myths & Musings on Beauty & Other Perilous Obsessions with Women's Appearance. Sara Halprin. 344p. 1998. text 23.00 (*0-7881-5281-5*) DIANE Pub.
Look at My World. Kathy Poelker. (Illus.). 48p. 1983. teacher ed. 7.95 (*0-945405-04-9*) LAM Co.
Look at Opposites. Tori West. (Illus.). (J). (gr. k-2). 1998. write for info. (*1-892800-10-1*) Temp Tattoo.
Look at Pond Life. rev. ed. Rena K. Kirkpatrick. LC 84-26249. (Look at Science Ser.). (Illus.). 32p. (J). (gr. 2-4). 1985. pap. 4.95 (*0-8114-6901-8*) Raintree Steck-V.
Look at Relapse. Jacqueline Kennedy Onassis. 10p. 1974. pap. 1.65 (*0-89486-007-0*, 1380B) Hazelden.
Look at Revelation. Stanley Scism & Jimmy Stewart. (James Stewart Library). 256p. 1998. pap. 10.00 (*1-56722-226-9*) Word Aflame.
Look at Rocks: From Coal to Kimberlite. Jo S. Kittinger. LC 97-6727. (First Book Ser.). (J). 1997. lib. bdg. 22.00 (*0-531-20310-7*) Watts.
Look at Rocks: From Coal to Kimberlite. Jo S. Kittinger. (First Bks.). 1998. pap. 6.95 (*0-531-15887-X*) Watts.
Look at Snakes. Jerald Halpern. (Look at Science Ser.). 1998. pap. 4.95 (*0-8172-7984-9*) Raintree Steck-V.
Look at Spiders. Jerald Halpern. (Look at Science Ser.). 1998. pap. 4.95 (*0-8172-7985-7*) Raintree Steck-V.
Look at State & Local Tax Policies: Past Trends & Future Prospects. Ed. by Frederick D. Stocker. (Tax Policy Roundtable Papers: No. TPR17). 77p. (C). 1991. pap. text 7.00 (*1-55844-118-2*) Lincoln Inst Land.
***Look at Stewardship.** Ed. by R. M. Davis & P. D. Buford. 160p. 2000. mass mkt. 5.99 (*1-56722-253-6*) Word Aflame.
Look at Student Impact Sports: An Inside Approach to the Theory & Theology of Competitive Sports Programming for High School Youth Ministry. Student Impact Staff. (Student Impact Ser.). 1996. 24.99 incl. VHS (*0-310-20134-9*) Zondervan.
Look at Teeth. Allan Fowler. LC 98-46556. (Rookie Read-About Science Ser.). (Illus.). 32p. (J). (gr. 1-2). 1999. lib. bdg. 19.00 (*0-516-21217-6*) Childrens.
***Look at Teeth.** Allan Fowler. (Rookie Read-About Science Ser.). (Illus.). 32p. (J). (gr. 1-2). 2000. pap. text 4.95 (*0-516-26567-9*) Childrens.
Look at Television News. Henningham. Date not set. pap. text. write for info. (*0-582-71158-4*, Pub. by Addison-Wesley) Longman.
Look at the Americans with Disabilities Act: A Guide to Compliance for Tennessee Local Governments. 3rd ed. Leslie F. Schechter & Marie A. Murphy. 62p. (C). 1993. pap. text 30.00 (*0-7881-0096-3*) DIANE Pub.
Look at the Book: Traveling the Original Route 66. Charles R. Swindoll. 1998. pap., student ed. 5.95 (*1-57972-182-6*) Insight Living.
Look at the Child. Aline D. Wolf. LC 78-58153. (Illus.). 64p. 1978. pap. 5.95 (*0-9601016-2-4*) Parent-Child Pr.
Look at the Credit Approval Process. John A. Davis, Jr. LC 86-23855. (Illus.). 56p. 1986. pap. text 35.00 (*0-936742-36-4*) Robt Morris Assocs.
Look at the Evidence: Essays & Reviews. John Clute. 465p. 1996. 30.00 (*0-934933-05-7*); pap. 15.00 (*0-934933-06-5*) Serconia Pr.
Look at the Harlequins! Vladimir Nabokov. LC 89-40553. (Vintage International Ser.). 272p. 1990. pap. 14.00 (*0-679-72728-0*) Vin Bks.
Look at the Holidays. Kathy Poelker. (Illus.). 64p. (J). (ps-4). 1988. reprint ed. teacher ed. 7.95 (*0-317-91200-3*) LAM Co.
Look at the Moon. May Garelick. LC 95-49115. (Illus.). 32p. (J). (gr. 2-6). 1996. 14.95 (*1-57255-142-9*) Mondo Pubng.
Look at the Night. Michael O'Hearn. LC 95-61438. (Illus.). 48p. 1996. pap. 9.95 (*1-883650-24-0*) Windswept Hse.
Look at the Record: An Album of Toronto's Lyric Theatres, 1825-1984. Anno. & Compiled by Joan P. Baillie. (Illus.). 300p. 1995. 39.95 (*0-88962-326-0*) Mosaic.
Look at the Sky. George D. Durrant. 1994. 10.95 (*0-88494-925-7*) Bookcraft Inc.
Look at the Stars. Andrews & McMeel Staff. 1994. 4.95 (*0-8362-3092-2*) Andrews & McMeel.
Look at the Stars. Andrews & McMeel Staff. (Illus.). 80p. 1994. 4.95 (*0-8362-3109-0*) Andrews & McMeel.
Look at This. (Key Words Readers Ser.: B Series, No. 641-1b). (Illus.). pap. 3.50 (*0-7214-0013-2*, Ladybrd) Penguin Putnam.
Look at This. (Key Words Readers Ser.: Series S705, No. 1). (Illus.). student ed. 1.95 (*0-317-04001-4*, Ladybrd) Penguin Putnam.
Look at This Day. Louise D. Hall. vi, 152p. 1997. 20.00 (*0-9653578-0-5*) Haldean Pub.
Look at This Tree. Susan Canizares & Pamela Chanko. LC 97-34204. (Science Emergent Readers Ser.). (J). 1997. pap. 2.50 (*0-590-14998-9*) Scholastic Inc.
Look at Tomorrow Today. Leonard Cataldo & Robert Pelletier. LC 89-50770. (Illus.). 500p. 1989. pap. 18.95 (*0-914918-94-X*, Whitford) Schiffer.
Look at Tomorrow's Tactical Air Forces. Lane Pierrot et al. (Illus.). 89p. (C). 1997. pap. text 30.00 (*0-7881-4298-4*) DIANE Pub.
Look at Trees. Rena K. Kirkpatrick. (J). 1990. pap. text 6.95 (*0-8172-2384-3*) Raintree Steck-V.
Look at U. S., Bk. 1. Carole Cross. 1989. pap. 11.00 (*0-8092-4387-3*) NTC Contemp Pub Co.
Look at U. S., Bk. 2. Carole Cross. 1989. pap. 11.00 (*0-8092-4386-5*) NTC Contemp Pub Co.
Look at U. S., 2 bks., Bks. 1 & 2. Ed. by Contemporary Book Editors. 1989. pap., teacher ed. 8.75 (*0-8092-4380-6*) NTC Contemp Pub Co.
Look at U. S. Literacy Level. Contemporary Book Editors. 1989. pap., teacher ed. 8.75 (*0-8092-4328-8*) NTC Contemp Pub Co.
Look at U. S. Literacy Level. Ed. by Sally Wigginton. 1989. pap. 11.00 (*0-8092-4329-6*) NTC Contemp Pub Co.
Look at Weather. rev. ed. Rena K. Kirkpatrick. LC 84-26251. (Look at Science Ser.). (Illus.). 32p. (J). (gr. 2-4). 1985. pap. 5.25 (*0-8114-6906-9*) Raintree Steck-V.
Look at Your Eyes. Paul Showers. (J). 1962. pap. 4.95 (*0-690-01261-6*) HarpC Child Bks.
Look at Your Eyes. rev. ed. Paul Showers. LC 91-10167. (Let's-Read-&-Find-Out Science Bks.: Stage 1). (Illus.). 32p. (J). (ps-1). 1992. 14.00 (*0-06-020188-6*); pap. 4.50 (*0-06-445108-9*, HarpTrophy); lib. bdg. 15.89 (*0-06-020189-4*) HarpC Child Bks.
Look Away. Harold Coyle. 1996. mass mkt. 6.99 (*0-671-52819-X*) PB.
Look Away. Harold Coyle. 1997. per. 3.99 (*0-671-00991-5*) PB.
Look Away: Reality & Sentiment in Southern Art. Estill C. Pennington. LC 89-8731. (Illus.). 200p. 1989. 50.00 (*0-934601-92-5*) Saraland Pr.
Look Away, a Dixie Notebook. James H. Street. LC 75-142924. (Illus.). 241p. 1977. reprint ed. lib. bdg. 59.75 (*0-8371-5950-4*, SLA&) Greenwood.
Look Away from Dixie. fac. ed. Frank E. Smith. LC 65-23762. 100p. 1965. reprint ed. pap. 31.00 (*0-7837-7744-2*, 204750000007) Bks Demand.
Look, Baby! Sue Kueffner. (Illus.). 8p. (J). (ps). 1999. text 8.99 (*1-56799-882-8*) M Friedman Pub Grp Inc.
Look Baby Board Books What's on My Head? Margaret Miller. (Illus.). 14p. (J). (ps-4). 1998. 4.99 (*0-689-81912-9*) Litle Simon.
Look Back: The Birth of the Americans with Disabilities Act. Robert C. Anderson. LC 96-19551. (Journal of Religion in Disability & Rehabilitation Ser.: Vol. 2, No. 4). 90p. 1996. 39.95 (*0-7890-0007-5*, Haworth Pastrl) Haworth Pr.
Look Back - A Step Forward. Alfred D. Crimi. LC 86-33228. (Illus.). 242p. 1987. 19.95 (*0-934733-13-9*) CMS.
Look Back, a Look Ahead: Proceedings of the Attitude Research Conference, 10th, Hilton Head Island, SC, 1979. Attitude Research Conference Staff. Ed. by George B. Hafer. LC 80-10370. (American Marketing Association, Proceedings Ser.). 217p. reprint ed. pap. 67.30 (*0-608-14655-2*, 202335600032) Bks Demand.
***Look Back All the Green Valley.** Fred Chappell. LC 99-27227. 288p. 1999. text 24.00 (*0-312-24215-8*, Picador USA) St Martin.
***Look Back All the Green Valley.** Fred Chappell. LC 99-27227. 288p. 2000. pap. 13.00 (*0-312-24310-3*, Picador USA) St Martin.
***Look Back & Laugh.** Jean Desmond. 407p. 2000. 25.00 (*0-7388-1738-4*); pap. 18.00 (*0-7388-1739-2*) Xlibris Corp.
Look Back & See: Twenty Lively Tales for Gentle Tellers. Margaret R. MacDonald. (Illus.). 178p. (Orig.). 1991. 35.00 (*0-8242-0810-2*) Wilson.
Look Back in Anger. John Osborne. 1987. pap. 5.95 (*0-87129-222-X*, L29) Dramatic Pub.
Look Back in Anger. John Osborne. LC 57-9161. 96p. 1994. 23.95 (*0-87599-081-9*) S G Phillips.
Look Back in Anger. John Osborne. 96p. 1982. pap. 8.95 (*0-14-048175-3*, Penguin Bks) Viking Penguin.
Look Back in Anger: Mother-Daughter & Father-Daughter Relationships in Women's Autobiographical Writings of the 1970's & 1980's. Norgard Klages. LC 94-3636. (Studies in Modern German Literature: Vol. 71). 165p. (C). 1995. text 39.95 (*0-8204-2520-6*) P Lang Pubng.
Look Back in Gender: Sexuality & the Family in Post-War British Drama. Michelene Wandor. 171p. (C). 1988. pap. write for info. (*0-413-56730-3*, A0154, Methuen Drama) Methn.
Look Back, Moss. Betty Levin. LC 97-34510. (Illus.). 152p. (J). (gr. 3-7). 1998. 15.00 (*0-688-15696-7*, Grenwillow Bks) HarpC Child Bks.
Look Back, My Love. large type ed. Jean Carew. (Linford Romance Large Print Ser.). 288p. 1995. pap. 16.99 (*0-7089-7679-4*, Linford) Ulverscroft.
Look Back on Laurel Hills. Joseph P. Brennan. (Illus.). 54p. (Orig.). 1989. 30.00 (*0-9618918-1-5*); pap. 8.00 (*0-9618918-2-3*) Jwindz Pub.
Look Back on Murder. large type ed. Malcolm Gray. (Linford Mystery Library). 334p. 1989. pap. 16.99 (*0-7089-6630-6*, Linford) Ulverscroft.
***Look Backward & Forward at American Professional Women & Their Families.** Rita J. Simon. LC 99-52302. 176p. 2000. pap. 27.50 (*0-7618-1582-1*) U Pr of Amer.
***Look Backward & Forward at American Professional Women & Their Families.** Ed. by Rita J. Simon. LC 99-52302. 176p. 2000. 49.00 (*0-7618-1581-3*) U Pr of Amer.
Look Before You Bounce. Disney Enterprises, Inc. Staff. (Disney's "Out & about with Pooh" Library: Vol. 4). (Illus.). 44p. (J). (gr. 1-6). 1996. 3.49 (*1-885222-58-0*) Advance Pubs.
Look Before You Build: Geologic Studies for Safer Land Development in the San Francisco Bay Area. Martha B. Tyler. (Illus.). 54p. (C). 1997. pap. text 25.00 (*0-7881-4588-6*) DIANE Pub.
Look Before You Leap! see Walt Disney's Read & Grow Library

An Asterisk (*) at the beginning of an entry indicates that the title is appearing for the first time.

Look Before You Leap: Market Research Made Easy. Don Doman et al. (Business Ser.). 144p. 1993. pap. 14.95 (*0-88908-292-8*) Self-Counsel Pr.

Look Before You Lease: Secrets to Smart Vehicle Leasing. 2nd ed. Michael S. Kranitz. LC 97-76990. 200p. (Orig.). 1998. pap. 12.95 (*1-889093-04-1*) Buy-Rite.

Look Before You Love. Nancilee Wydra. LC 98-17925. (Illus.). 304p. 1998. 22.95 (*0-8092-2873-4*, 287340, Contemporary Bks) NTC Contemp Pub Co.

***Look Before You Love: Feng Shui Techniques for Revealing Anyone's True Nature.** Nancilee Wydra. 304p. 2000. pap. 14.95 (*0-8092-2512-3*, 251230, Contemporary Bks) NTC Contemp Pub Co.

Look Behind Every Hill & The Big Trouble. Steve Frazee. 1990. pap. 3.50 (*0-8125-0540-9*, Pub. by Tor Bks) St Martin.

Look Behind the Mirror. Allison Wegener. 32p. (Orig.). 1997. pap. 4.95 (*1-890424-06-4*) Dyn-Novel.

Look Beyond Jesus to Muhammad. Mohammed Abu-Bakr. 57p. 1993. pap. 4.50 (*1-882250-07-9*) Purple Dawn.

Look Beyond the Model Minority Image: Critical Issues in Asian America. Intro. by Grace Yun. 155p. (Orig.). (C). 1989. pap. text. write for info. (*0-318-65927-1*) Minority Rights.

Look Beyond Tomorrow: The Carola Spencer Story. Lillie Ammann. 80p. 1998. pap. 14.95 (*0-9665912-0-8*) Lillies Lovely.

Look Beyond Transcription: Mechanisms Determining MRNA Stability & Translation in Plants. Julia Bailey-Serres et al. LC 98-4694. 183p. 1998. pap. write for info. (*0-943088-36-4*) Am Soc of Plan.

Look Book. Tana Hoban. LC 96-46268. (Illus.). 40p. (J). (ps-3). 1997. 16.00 (*0-688-14971-5*, Grenwillow Bks) HarpC Child Bks.

Look Book. Photos by Tana Hoban. LC 96-46268. (Illus.). 40p. (J). (ps up). 1997. lib. bdg. 15.93 (*0-688-14972-3*, Grenwillow Bks) HarpC Child Bks.

Look Both Ways. James Hazard. 55p. (Orig.). (J). (gr. 4-6). 1987. pap. 4.25 (*0-935399-03-8*) Main St Pub.

Look Both Ways: City Math. Time-Life Books Editors. Ed. by Patricia Daniels et al. (I Love Math Ser.). (Illus.). 64p. (J). (gr. k-2). 1992. lib. bdg. write for info. (*0-8094-9959-2*) Time-Life.

***Look Both Ways: Helping Your Children Stay Innocent & Grow Wise.** Dan Hamilton & Elizabeth Hamilton. LC 99-15060. 132p. 1999. pap. text 9.99 (*0-8308-1921-5*) InterVarsity.

***Look! Bugs...** Karen Hooker. (Illus.). 8p. (J). (gr. k-2). 1999. pap. 3.75 (*1-58323-002-5*) Seedling Pubns.

Look, Christ. Philip Owens. (C). 1979. pap. 33.00 (*0-85088-601-5*, Pub. by Gomer Pr) St Mut.

Look Closely at the Child: Christmas Poems. Arthur O. Roberts. LC 97-76793. 70p. 1997. 17.00 (*0-913342-87-4*) Barclay Pr.

Look Closer: River Life. Barbara Taylor. LC 92-52822. (Look Closer Ser.). (Illus.). 32p. (J). (gr. 1-4). 1992. 9.95 (*1-56458-130-6*) DK Pub Inc.

Look Closer: Visual Thinking Skills & Activities. Nancy L. Johnson. (Illus.). 128p. (Orig.). 1995. pap. 12.95 (*1-880505-10-X*, CLC0182) Pieces of Lrning.

Look down from Clouds: New Poems. Marvin Levine. Ed. & Pref. by David B. Axelrod. 52p. 1997. pap. 12.00 (*0-925062-09-X*) Writers Ink Pr.

Look Fatter in Jeans: An Adventure in Growing Older & Wiser. Mary London. LC 97-155546. (Illus.). vi, 306p. (Orig.). 1997. pap. 12.95 (*0-9656648-0-5*) Boomer Pubns.

***Look Fear In The Face: From Adolescence to Adulthood Against All Odds.** Sandra M. Rubin. 206p. 1998. pap. 11.95 (*0-9657402-0-X*) Rubin & Kraus.

Look for a Bird. Edith T. Hurd. LC 76-58726. (I Can Read Science Bks.). (Illus.). (J). (ps-3). 1977. 9.95 (*0-06-022719-2*) HarpC Child Bks.

Look for a Field to Land: Poems. Elaine Preston. LC 94-7129. 74p. (Orig.). 1994. pap. 8.95 (*1-882593-06-5*) Bridge Wrks.

***Look for a Letter Tomorrow: A College Girl's Life 100 Years Ago.** Helen Fox. Ed. by Margaret Carmichael Emerson. (Illus.). 200p. 2000. pap. 15.00 (*0-945069-10-3*) Freedom Pr Assocs.

Look for Laura. Anthony Tallarico. (Where Are They? Ser.). (Illus.). 24p. (Orig.). (J). 1990. 9.95 (*0-942025-89-X*) Kidsbks.

Look for Laura. Anthony Tallarico. (Where Are They? Ser.). (Illus.). 24p. (Orig.). (J). 1991. pap. 2.95 (*0-942025-77-6*) Kidsbks.

Look for Lisa. Anthony Tallarico. (Where Are They? Ser.). (Illus.). 24p. (J). 1988. pap. 2.95 (*0-942025-66-0*) Kidsbks.

Look for Lisa. Anthony Tallarico. (Where Are They? Ser.). (Illus.). 24p. (J). 1990. 9.95 (*0-942025-61-X*) Kidsbks.

Look for Lisa. Anthony Tallarico. (Where Are They? Ser.). (Illus.). 24p. (J). (gr. 2-6). 1990. lib. bdg. 10.95 (*0-8167-1957-8*) Troll Communs.

Look for Lisa: Time Traveller. Tony Tallarico. (Where Are They? Ser.). (Illus.). 24p. (J). 1992. 9.95 (*1-56156-067-7*) Kidsbks.

Look for Me by Moonlight. Mary D. Hahn. LC 94-21892. 198p. (J). 1995. 15.00 (*0-395-69843-X*) HM.

Look for Me by Moonlight. Mary D. Hahn. 176p. (YA). (gr. 7 up). 1997. mass mkt. 4.50 (*0-380-72703-X*, Avon Bks) Morrow Avon.

Look for Me by Moonlight. Mary D. Hahn. LC 94-21892. (J). 1997. 9.60 (*0-606-11573-0*, Pub. by Turtleback) Demco.

Look for Me on the Mountain. Forrest Carter. 1976. 22.95 (*0-8488-1264-6*) Amereon Ltd.

Look for Me under the Rainbow. Bernard Jan. (Illus.). 61p. 1998. write for info. (*1-86106-831-X*, Pub. by Minerva Pr) Unity Dist.

Look for the Butterfly. Colleen Dahlgren. Ed. by Christina C. Wightman. 100p. 1999. pap. 9.95 (*1-888911-11-5*) Benson Smythe.

Look for the Lollipops. Emma D. Ricks. LC 98-91451. xii, 98p. 1998. pap. 9.95 (*0-9664071-0-5*) Lollipop Shoppe.

***Look for the Rainbow.** 3rd ed. (Illus.). 68p. 1999. pap. 10.00 (*0-9678211-0-X*) Stellar Creations.

Look for the Spirit. Slightly Off-Center Writers Group Staff. (To Be Your Own Ser.). (Illus.). 48p. (J). (gr. 4-6). 1994. pap. 6.95 (*1-56721-086-4*) Twnty-Fifth Cent Pr.

Look for the Union Label: A History of the International Ladies' Garment Workers' Union. Gus Tyler. LC 94-25223. (Labor & Human Resources Ser.). (Illus.). 360p. (gr. 13). 1995. 77.95 (*1-56324-409-8*); pap. 35.95 (*1-56324-410-1*) M E Sharpe.

Look for Yourself: The Science & Art of Self-Realization. Douglas E. Harding. LC 98-60142. (Illus.). 246p. 1998. pap. 16.95 (*1-878019-01-5*) Inner Drctns.

Look Good, Feel Good. Alexandra Parsons. LC 96-11727. (Life Education Ser.). (J). 1997. lib. bdg. 19.00 (*0-531-14428-3*) Watts.

Look Homeward . . . The Paintings of Deborah Morrissey McGoff. David T. Johnson. LC 97-68818. (Illus.). 44p. (Orig.). 1997. mass mkt. write for info. (*1-891122-01-0*) Spfld Mus Art.

Look Homeward Angel see Best American Plays: Fifth Series, 1958-1963

Look Homeward, Angel. Thomas Wolfe. (Hudson River Editions Ser.). 522p. 1977. 45.00 (*0-684-15158-8*, Scribners Ref) Mac Lib Ref.

Look Homeward, Angel. Thomas Wolfe. 544p. 1995. per. 14.00 (*0-684-80443-3*) S&S Trade.

Look Homeward, Angel. Thomas Wolfe. LC 97-13090. 1997. 29.50 (*0-684-84221-1*) S&S Trade.

Look Homeward, Angel. Thomas Wolfe. 359p. 1981. reprint ed. lib. bdg. 39.95 (*0-89966-293-5*) Buccaneer Bks.

Look How a Baby Grows. Alexandra E. Fischer. (Poke & Look Learning Ser.). (Illus.). 16p. (J). (ps-3). 1995. spiral bd., bds. 12.95 (*0-448-40925-9*, G & D) Peng Put Young Read.

***Look How a Baby Grows.** Alexandra E. Fischer. (Poke & Look Learning Bks.). (Illus.). 16p. (J). (ps-3). 2000. 9.99 (*0-448-42402-9*, Planet Dexter) Peng Put Young Read.

Look! I Can Cook! A Simplified Guide to Cooking & Household Skills. Kay Bryan. LC 79-89358. 269p. 1979. pap. 15.98 (*0-88290-130-3*) Horizon Utah.

***Look! I Can Read!** Susan Hood. LC 00-35354. (All Aboard Reading Ser.). (Illus.). 32p. (J). (ps-3). 2000. 13.89 (*0-448-42282-4*, G & D); pap. 3.99 (*0-448-41967-X*, G & D) Peng Put Young Read.

***Look! I Can Read! Level One.** Susan Hood. (All Aboard Reading Ser.). (Illus.). (J). 2000. 9.44 (*0-606-18470-8*) Turtleback.

Look, I Can Talk! Student Notebook in English. Blaine Ray. (Illus.). 100p. 1991. pap. text, teacher ed. 12.95 (*1-56018-456-6*) Sky Oaks Prodns.

Look, I Can Talk! Student Notebook in French. 2nd ed. Blaine Ray & Greg Buchan. Ed. by James J. Asher. (FRE., Illus.). 100p. (Orig.). 1995. pap. text, student ed. 12.95 (*1-56018-497-3*) Sky Oaks Prodns.

Look, I Can Talk! Student Notebook in Spanish. 2nd ed. Blaine Ray. Ed. by James J. Asher. (SPA., Illus.). 96p. (Orig.). 1997. pap. text, student ed. 12.95 (*1-56018-474-4*) Sky Oaks Prodns.

Look, I Can Talk! Teacher's Guidebook. 3rd ed. Blaine Ray. Ed. by James J. Asher. 52p. 1998. pap. text, teacher ed. 12.00 (*1-56018-008-0*) Sky Oaks Prodns.

Look, I Can Talk More! In English - Student Textbook. Blaine Ray et al. Ed. by James J. Asher. (Illus.). 120p. (Orig.). 1997. pap. text 13.95 (*1-56018-489-2*) Sky Oaks Prodns.

Look, I Can Talk More! - Mirame, Puedo Hablar Mas! In Spanish - Student Textbook. Blaine Ray et al. (Illus.). 120p. (Orig.). 1995. pap. text 13.95 (*1-56018-490-6*) Sky Oaks Prodns.

Look, I Can Talk More! - Regardez-Moi, Je Peux Parler Plus! In French - Student Textbook. Blaine Ray et al. (Illus.). 120p. 1999. pap. text 13.95 (*1-56018-491-4*, 123) Sky Oaks Prodns.

Look, I Can Talk! (Schau, Ich Kann Reden!: Deutsches Schuler Arbeitsbuch) Student Notebook in German. Blaine Ray. Ed. by James J. Asher. (GER., Illus.). 96p. 1998. pap. text 14.00 (*1-56018-461-2*) Sky Oaks Prodns.

Look, I'm Growing Up. Marilyn Knoepfel & Betty Farber. LC 90-72100. (Happy Day Bks.). (Illus.). 24p. (J). (ps). 1995. pap. 1.99 (*0-7847-0353-1*, 04233) Standard Pub.

Look, I'm Still Talking: A Step-by-Step Approach to Communication Through TPR Stories, Vol. 3. Blaine Ray & Joe Neilson. (Look, I Can Talk! Ser.). (Illus.). vi, 72p. (Orig.). (YA). (gr. 9-12). 1993. pap. text 12.95 (*0-929724-18-6*, 18-6) Command Performance.

Look in, Look up, Look Out! Be the Person You Were Meant to Be. Joyce L. Vedral. 288p. 1997. mass mkt. 12.99 (*0-446-67287-4*, Pub. by Warner Bks) Little.

Look in the Mirror: A Handbook for Widowers. Edward Ames. Ed. by Joy Johnson. (Illus.). 31p. (Orig.). 1995. pap. 4.95 (*1-56123-083-9*) Centering Corp.

Look Inside. Leonard Hilt & Joyce Hilt. (Illus.). 80p. (Orig.). 1995. pap. 10.00 (*1-886094-17-9*) Chicago Spectrum.

Look Inside. Carolyn A. O'Riley. (Illus.). 30p. (J). (ps-2). 1998. spiral bd. 10.00 (*1-891870-01-7*, 00200) Archangels Pen.

Look Inside: Affirmation for Kids. Charlotte Horning et al. (Illus.). 216p. (J). 1995. pap. 18.95 (*0-933025-42-4*) Blue Bird Pub.

Look Inside a Car. Alexandra E. Fischer. (Poke & Look Learning Ser.). (Illus.). 16p. (J). (ps-3). 1996. spiral bd., bds. 12.95 (*0-448-41315-9*, G & D) Peng Put Young Read.

Look Inside a Castle. Laura Driscoll. LC 98-71534. (Poke & Look Learning Ser.). (Illus.). 16p. (J). (ps-3). 1998. mass mkt. 9.99 (*0-448-41889-4*, G & D) Peng Put Young Read.

***Look Inside a Computer.** Emily Sollinger. (Poke & Look Learning Bks.). (Illus.). 16p. (J). (ps-3). 2000. 9.99 (*0-448-42178-X*, Planet Dexter) Peng Put Young Read.

Look Inside a Rainforest. Alexandra E. Fischer. LC 93-80549. (Poke & Look Learning Ser.). (Illus.). 16p. (J). (ps-3). 1999. bds. 9.99 (*0-448-42048-1*, G & D) Peng Put Young Read.

Look Inside a Ship. Denise Patrick. (Poke & Look Learning Ser.). (Illus.). 16p. (J). (ps-3). 1989. spiral bd., bds. 11.95 (*0-448-19352-3*, G & D) Peng Put Young Read.

Look Inside an Airplane. Tr. by Patrizia Malfatti. LC 93-77479. (Poke & Look Learning Ser.). (Illus.). 16p. (J). (ps-3). 1994. spiral bd., bds. 12.95 (*0-448-40543-1*, G & D) Peng Put Young Read.

***Look Inside an Airplane.** Patrizia Malfatti. (Poke & Look Learning Bks.). (Illus.). 16p. (J). (ps-3). 2000. 9.99 (*0-448-42401-0*, Planet Dexter) Peng Put Young Read.

Look Inside Cross-Sections: Jets. Moira Butterfield. (Look Inside Cross-Sections Ser.). (Illus.). 32p. (J). 1996. pap. 6.95 (*0-7894-0767-1*) DK Pub Inc.

Look Inside Cross-Sections: Planes. Stephen Biesty. (Illus.). 32p. (J). pap. 8.99 (*0-590-24341-1*) Scholastic Inc.

Look Inside Cross-Sections: Ships. Stephen Biesty. (Illus.). 32p. (J). pap. 8.99 (*0-590-24342-X*) Scholastic Inc.

Look Inside Cross-Sections: Tanks. Deni Bown. (Look Inside Cross-Sections Ser.). (Illus.). 32p. (J). 1996. pap. 6.95 (*0-7894-0768-X*) DK Pub Inc.

***Look Inside Cross-Sections: Tanks.** Kindersley Dorling. (J). 1999. pap. 14.50 (*0-613-03015-X*) Econo-Clad Bks.

Look Inside the Earth. Gina Ingoglia. (Poke & Look Learning Ser.). (Illus.). 16p. (J). (ps-3). 1991. spiral bd., bds. 12.95 (*0-448-40087-1*, G & D) Peng Put Young Read.

Look Inside the Earth. Gina Ingoglia. (Poke & Look Learning Ser.). (Illus.). 16p. (J). (ps-3). 1998. mass mkt. 9.99 (*0-448-41890-8*, G & D) Peng Put Young Read.

Look Inside the Ocean. Patrizia Malfatti. LC 99-202338. (Poke & Look Learning Ser.). (Illus.). 16p. (J). (ps-3). 1998. mass mkt. 9.99 (*0-448-41891-6*, G & D) Peng Put Young Read.

***Look Inside the Teenage Soul.** Mark Healy. (Illus.). 2000. pap. 5.99 (*0-14-131018-9*, PuffinBks) Peng Put Young Read.

Look Inside Your Body. Gina Ingoglia. (Poke & Look Learning Ser.). (Illus.). 16p. (J). (ps-3). 1989. spiral bd., bds. 12.99 (*0-448-21033-9*, G & D) Peng Put Young Read.

Look Inside Your Body. Gina Ingoglia. (Poke & Look Learning Ser.). (Illus.). 16p. (J). (ps-3). 1998. mass mkt. 9.99 (*0-448-41892-4*, G & D) Peng Put Young Read.

Look Inside Your Brain. Heather Alexander. (Poke & Look Learning Ser.). (Illus.). 16p. (J). (ps-3). 1998. mass mkt. 9.99 (*0-448-41893-2*, G & D) Peng Put Young Read.

Look into Japan. Ed. by Japan Travel Bureau Staff. (JTB's Illustrated Japan in Your Pocket Ser.: No. 1). (Illus.). 192p. 1986. pap. 17.95 (*4-533-00307-9*, Pub. by Japan Trvl Bur) Bks Nippan.

Look into My Eyes. Glenda Sanders. LC 96-3494. 217p. 1995. per. 3.25 (*0-373-25666-3*, 1-25666-8) Harlequin Bks.

Look into Space: A Supplement to Childcraft - The How & Why Library. World Book Editors. LC 65-25105. (Illus.). 224p. (J). (gr. 1-6). 1994. write for info. (*0-7166-0694-1*) World Bk.

***Look into Space Bumper.** J. Kirkwood. (Illus.). (J). 1999. pap. text. write for info. (*0-7613-0788-5*) Millbrook Pr.

Look into the Bible. Ed. by Eric Gower. (Illus.). 143p. 1993. 15.95 (*0-87508-714-0*) Chr Lit.

***Look into the Past Ancient Chinese.** Julia Waterlow. (Look into the Past Ser.). (Illus.). 1999. write for info. (*0-7398-1411-7*) Raintree Steck-V.

***Look into the Past Maya.** Peter Chrisp. 1999. 21.35 (*0-7398-1410-9*) Raintree Steck-V.

***Look Into the Soul of a Young Dreamer.** Derrick T. Holman. 60p. 2000. 6.00 (*1-58235-587-8*) Watermrk Pr.

Look into Tokyo. Ed. by Japan Travel Bureau Staff. (JTB's Illustrated Japan in Your Pocket Ser.: No. 7). (Illus.). 192p. 1986. pap. 17.95 (*4-533-00664-7*, Pub. by Japan Trvl Bur) Bks Nippan.

Look It Up! A Comprehensive Equine Glossary. Ed. by Toni M. Leland. LC 95-74741. (Illus.). 64p. (Orig.). 1996. pap. 6.95 (*1-887932-09-7*, GLS) Equine Graph Pubng.

***Look-It-Up Book of First Ladies.** Sydelle A. Kramer. LC 00-35306. (Illus.). 2000. pap. 11.99 (*0-679-99347-9*) Discovery.

Look-it-Up Book of Presidents. Wyatt Blassingame. (J). 1996. 14.09 (*0-606-11574-9*, Pub. by Turtleback) Demco.

Look-It-Up Book of Presidents. rev. ed. Wyatt Blassingame. LC 89-10519. (Illus.). 176p. (J). (gr. 4-7). 1990. pap. 8.99 (*0-679-80358-0*, Pub. by Random Bks Yng Read) Random.

Look-It-Up Book of Presidents. rev. ed. Wyatt Blassingame. LC 89-10519. (Illus.). (J). (gr. 5-9). 1990. lib. bdg. 14.99 (*0-679-90353-4*, Pub. by Random Bks Yng Read) Random.

Look It up Guide to Washington Libraries & Archives. Laura A. Bergheim. LC 95-41198. 377p. 1995. lib. bdg. 55.00 (*0-933833-35-0*) Beacham Pub Corp.

Look Like a Winner after 50. 2nd ed. Grinnig Idiot Press Staff. Date not set. 15.95 (*0-88100-089-2*) Natl Writ Pr.

Look Like a Winner after 50. 2nd ed. Grinnig Idiot Press Staff. LC 94-66013. 190p. 1995. pap. 15.95 (*0-88100-082-5*) Natl Writ Pr.

Look Like a Winner after 50! With Care, Color & Style. 3rd rev. ed. Jo Peddicord. LC 96-79098. (Illus.). 190p. 1997. pap. 15.95 (*0-9654434-0-X*) Golden Aspen.

Look Like Yourself & Love It! The 4-T Guide to Personal Style. 2nd ed. Jane Segerstrom. LC 80-50836. (Illus.). 168p. (Orig.). (C). 1980. pap. 14.95 (*0-936740-06-X*) Triad Pr TX.

Look, Listen & Learn. (Barbie Preschool Workbks.: Vol. 4). (Illus.). 72p. (J). 1998. pap. write for info. (*0-7666-0213-3*, Honey Bear Bks) Modern Pub NYC.

Look, Listen & Learn: Ways for Kids to Cope with Diabetes. Dan Brannan. 136p. 1996. pap. 22.95 incl. audio (*0-9650228-2-X*) D Brannan.

Look, Listen & Love. large type ed. Barbara Cartland. (Magna Large Print Ser.). 272p. 1996. 27.99 (*0-7505-0905-8*, Pub. by Mgna Lrg Print) Ulverscroft.

***Look, Listen & Love: The Powerpuff Girls.** Golden Books Staff. (Illus.). (J). 2000. 9.99 (*0-307-10107-X*, Goldn Books) Gldn Bks Pub Co.

Look, Listen & Read Alefbet: With Alfy & Betty. Sol Scharfstein. LC 98-164999. 1987. 4.95 (*0-88125-220-4*) Ktav.

Look, Listen & Trust: A Framework for Learning Through Drama. George Rawlins & Jillian Rich. LC 91-51056. 92p. (Orig.). 1992. pap. 17.00 (*0-88734-618-9*) Players Pr.

Look, Listen, Read. Claude Levi-Strauss. Tr. by Brian C. Singer from ENG. LC 96-51629. (Illus.). 224p. 1997. 24.00 (*0-465-06880-4*, Pub. by Basic) HarpC.

Look, Listen, Read. Claude Levi-Strauss. 224p. 2000. pap. 10.00 (*0-465-06881-2*, Pub. by Basic) HarpC.

Look! Listen! Vibrate! Smile! 5th rev. ed. Domenic Priore. (Dumb Angel Gazette Ser.: Vol. 2). (Illus.). 200p. 1995. pap. 19.95 (*0-86719-417-0*) Last Gasp.

Look! Look! Michael Foreman. (Illus.). 32p. (J). (ps-1). 1998. 17.95 (*0-86264-758-4*, Pub. by Andersen Pr) Trafalgar.

Look, Look! I Wrote A Book! Reproducible Little Books for Emergent Readers. Linda Ball. (Illus.). 176p. (J). 1997. pap. text 12.95 (*0-673-36357-0*, GoodYrBooks) Addson-Wesley Educ.

Look! Look! Look! Tana Hoban. LC 87-25655. (Illus.). 40p. (J). (ps-1). 1988. 17.00 (*0-688-07239-9*, Grenwillow Bks) HarpC Child Bks.

Look Ma, I'm Flying. Jean Walters-Lucy. Ed. & Illus. by Delight Tabesh. LC 92-13953. 48p. (Orig.). (J). (ps-5). 1992. per. 6.95 (*0-941992-28-4*) Los Arboles Pub.

Look Ma, No Hands! Boing! Tom Johnson. (Nickelodeon Hands: Free Guides Ser.: No. 1). (Illus.). 48p. (J). (gr. 1-5). 1996. pap. 12.95 (*0-689-80814-3*, Simon Spot) Litle Simon.

Look Ma, No Hands! Splash! Tom Johnson. (Nickelodeon Hands: Free Guides Ser.: No. 2). (Illus.). 48p. (J). (gr. 1-5). 1996. pap. 12.95 (*0-689-80815-1*) S&S Bks Yung.

Look, Ma, No Meat! 786 Hearty Vegetarian Main Dishes, No Meat, No Fish, No Eggs. Kathleen M. Corcoran. LC 88-70769. 550p. (Orig.). 1988. pap. 25.95 (*1-882055-01-2*) Butternut MN.

Look Me in the Eye: Old Women, Aging, & Ageism. 2nd ed. Barbara Macdonald & Cynthia Rich. LC 91-36595. 192p. (Orig.). 1991. pap. 8.95 (*0-933216-87-4*) Spinsters Ink.

Look Mom . . . No Cavities: How to Raise a Cavity Free Child. Gregory F. George & Jordana H. Geist. (Illus.). 68p. 1997. pap. 16.95 (*0-9662475-0-7*) PDC Pr.

Look Mom I Can Cook. Dot Gibson. 64p. 1986. pap. 7.95 (*0-941162-06-0*) D Gibson.

Look Mr. Kim I'm Being Haved! A Guide to Resolving Power Struggles with Small Children. Michael Jude & Kim Wallace. (Illus.). 138p. 1997. pap. 12.95 (*0-933025-57-2*) Blue Bird Pub.

***Look, No Hands!** deluxe ed. Clair Killen. Ed. by Kate Hitt. 106p. 1999. pap. 11.00 (*0-9652575-8-4*, Pub. by Many Names) Bookpeople.

Look, Now Hear This: Combined Auditory Training & Speechreading Instruction. Janet Jeffers & Margaret Barley. (Illus.). 230p. 1979. 42.95 (*0-398-03830-9*); pap. 30.95 (*0-398-06181-5*) C C Thomas.

Look of It: A Theory of Visual Form in English Peotry. Richard Bradford. LC 94-151247. 1993. 44.95 (*1-85918-000-0*) Intl Spec Bk.

Look of Long-Time Lovers. Glady Maring. 80p. 1998. pap. 8.00 (*1-57502-817-4*, PO2249) Morris Pubng.

***Look of Love, Vol. 1.** Monica Jackson. (Arabesque Ser.). 1999. mass mkt. 4.99 (*1-58314-069-7*) BET Bks.

Look of Love, Vol. 2, No. 1. unabridged ed. Ed. by Lana M. Wegeng et al. (Illus.). 66p. 1998. pap. 8.95 (*0-9659454-4-8*) Columbia Pubns.

Look of Love (Miradas de Amor) Lynda Sandoval. (SPA.). 1999. pap. 5.99 (*0-7860-1034-7*) Kensgtn Pub Corp.

Look of Maps: An Examination of Cartographic Design. Arthur H. Robinson. LC 85-22647. (Illus.). 119p. 1952. reprint ed. pap. 36.90 (*0-608-07546-9*, 206776100009) Bks Demand.

Look of Russian Literature: Avant-Garde Visual Experiments, 1900-1930. Gerald Janecek. LC 84-42578. (Illus.). 335p. reprint ed. pap. 103.90 (*0-608-06311-8*, 206667300008) Bks Demand.

Look of the Century. Michael Tambini. LC 96-11806. (Illus.). 288p. 1996. 39.95 (*0-7894-0950-X*) DK Pub Inc.

Look of the Century. 2nd ed. Michael Tambini. LC 98-11806. 512p. 1999. pap. 16.95 (*0-7894-4635-9*) DK Pub Inc.

Look of the West, 1860. Richard Burton. LC 63-17030. (Illus.). 363p. reprint ed. 112.60 (*0-8357-9710-4*, 201463000093) Bks Demand.

Look of Things. Philip Levine. 1996. pap. 13.00 (*0-614-20812-2*) Knopf.

Look of Things: Poems. Henri Cole. LC 94-23297. 71p. 1995. 20.00 (*0-679-43352-X*) Knopf.

Look of Things: Poems. Henri Cole. 1996. pap. 13.00 (*0-679-76593-X*) Knopf.

Look Once, Look Again, 24 bks., Set. David M. Schwartz. Incl. Among the Flowers. Photos by Dwight Kuhn. LC 98-6309. (Illus.). 24p. (J). (gr. 1 up). 1999. lib. bdg.

An Asterisk (*) at the beginning of an entry indicates that the title is appearing for the first time.

L

19.93 (0-8368-2241-2); Animal Ears. Photos by Dwight Kuhn. LC 99-48372. (Illus.). 24p. (J). (gr. 1 up). 1999. lib. bdg. 19.93 (0-8368-2576-4); Animal Eyes. Illus. by Dwight Kuhn. LC 99-18610. 24p. (YA). (gr. 1 up). 1999. lib. bdg. 19.93 (0-8368-2423-7); Animal Feathers & Fur. Illus. by Dwight Kuhn. LC 99-18611. 24p. (J). (gr. 1 up). 1999. lib. bdg. 19.93 (0-8368-2424-5); Animal Feet. Photos by Dwight Kuhn. LC 99-48371. (Illus.). 24p. (YA). (gr. 1 up). 1999. lib. bdg. 19.93 (0-8368-2577-2); Animal Mouths. Illus. by Dwight Kuhn. LC 99-18609. 24p. (J). (gr. 1 up). 1999. lib. bdg. 19.93 (0-8368-2425-3); Animal Noses. Photos by Dwight Kuhn. LC 99-48370. (Illus.). 24p. (J). (gr. 1 up). 1999. lib. bdg. 19.93 (0-8368-2578-0); Animal Skins & Scales. Photos by Dwight Kuhn. LC 99-47589. (Illus.). 24p. (YA). (gr. 1 up). 1999. lib. bdg. 19.93 (0-8368-2579-9); Animal Tails. Illus. by Dwight Kuhn. LC 99-18606. 24p. (J). (gr. 1 up). 1999. lib. bdg. 19.93 (0-8368-2426-1); At the Farm. Illus. by Dwight Kuhn. LC 98-15405. 24p. (J). (gr. 1 up). 1998. lib. bdg. 19.93 (0-8368-2221-8); At the Pond. Photos by Dwight Kuhn. LC 98-6310. (Illus.). 24p. (J). (gr. 1 up). 1999. lib. bdg. 19.93 (0-8368-2244-7); At the Seashore. Illus. by Dwight Kuhn. LC 98-15391. 24p. (J). (gr. 1 up). 1998. lib. bdg. 19.93 (0-8368-2224-2); At the Zoo. Illus. by Dwight Kuhn. LC 98-15402. 24p. (J). (gr. 1 up). 1998. lib. bdg. 19.93 (0-8368-2225-0); In a Tree. Photos by Dwight Kuhn. LC 98-6308. (Illus.). 24p. (J). (gr. 1 up). 1999. lib. bdg. 19.93 (0-8368-2245-5); In the Desert. Illus. by Dwight Kuhn. LC 98-15408. 24p. (J). (gr. 1 up). 1998. lib. bdg. 19.93 (0-8368-2220-X); In the Forest. Illus. by Dwight Kuhn. LC 98-15396. 24p. (J). (gr. 1 up). 1998. lib. bdg. 19.93 (0-8368-2222-6); In the Garden. Photos by Dwight Kuhn. LC 98-6312. (Illus.). 24p. (J). (gr. 1 up). 1999. lib. bdg. 19.93 (0-8368-2242-0); In the Meadow. Illus. by Dwight Kuhn. LC 98-15407. 24p. (J). (gr. 1 up). 1998. lib. bdg. 19.93 (0-8368-2223-4); In the Park. Photos by Dwight Kuhn. LC 98-6311. (Illus.). 24p. (J). (gr. 1 up). 1999. lib. bdg. 19.93 (0-8368-2243-9); Plant Blossoms. Illus. by Dwight Kuhn. LC 99-47588. 24p. (J). (gr. 1 up). 1999. lib. bdg. 19.93 (0-8368-2580-2); Plant Fruits & Seeds. Illus. by Dwight Kuhn. LC 99-18607. 24p. (J). (gr. 1 up). 1999. lib. bdg. 19.93 (0-8368-2427-X); Plant Leaves. Illus. by Dwight Kuhn. LC 99-18608. 24p. (J). (gr. 1 up). 1999. lib. bdg. 19.93 (0-8368-2428-8); Plant Stems & Roots. Photos by Dwight Kuhn. LC 99-47692. (Illus.). 24p. (YA). (gr. 1 up). 1999. lib. bdg. 19.93 (0-8368-2581-0); Underfoot. Photos by Dwight Kuhn. LC 98-6307. (Illus.). 24p. (J). (gr. 1 up). 1999. lib. bdg. 19.93 (0-8368-2246-3); (Illus.). 24p. (J). (gr. 1 up). Set lib. bdg. 478.32 (0-8368-2657-4) Gareth Stevens Inc.

Look Once, Look Again: Incl. Animal Ears, Animal Feet, Animal Noises, Animal Skin & Scales, Plant Blossoms & Plant Stems & Roots, 6 bks. David M. Schwartz. (Illus.). (J). (gr. 1 up). lib. bdg. 119.58 (0-8368-2575-6) Gareth Stevens Inc.

Look Once, Look Twice. Janet Marshall. LC 94-27259. (Illus.). 64p. (J). (gr. k-3). 1995. 13.95 (0-395-71644-6) Ticknor & Flds Bks Yng Read.

Look Out: A Nine-Session Program to Encourage African American Young Men to Help Prevent Alcohol-Related Birth Defects. Ed. by Kristen L. Glunz. 82p. (Orig.). 1996. pap. 24.95 (1-882145-01-1, 554) U WI Clearinghse.

Look Out Below! 2nd ed. Francis L. Sampson. (Illus.). 266p. 1989. reprint ed. 17.00 (0-318-42830-X) One Hund First Air.

Look Out, Bird! Marilyn Janovitz. LC 93-38765. (Illus.). 32p. (J). (ps-1). 1997. pap. 6.95 (1-55858-702-0, Pub. by North-South Bks NYC) Chronicle Bks.

***Look Out by the Water.** Steck-Vaughn Company Staff. (Read All about It Ser.). (Illus.). (J). 2000. pap. 4.95 (0-8114-3737-X) Raintree Steck-V.

***Look Out, Earth-Below!** Gail Herman. (Fairy School Ser.). 80p. (J). 2000. pap. 3.99 (0-553-48707-8, Skylark BDD) BDD Bks Young Read.

Look Out, Everybody! Watson Goodman. LC 85-82539. 352p. (Orig.). 1986. pap. 7.00 (0-9616332-0-4) Ent Emmanuel.

Look Out for Hydrophobia. Betsy Wing. 1990. 17.95 (1-55972-050-6, Birch Ln Pr) Carol Pub Group.

Look Out for Liza. Faith Baldwin. 1976. reprint ed. lib. bdg. 22.95 (0-88411-620-4) Amereon Ltd.

Look Out for Space. William F. Nolan. 192p. (Orig.). 1985. pap. 4.95 (0-930330-20-X) Intl Polygonics.

Look Out for Turtles! Melvin Berger. LC 90-36894. (Trophy Let's-Read-&-Find-Out Bk., Stage 2). (Illus.). 32p. (J). (gr. k-4). 1996. pap. 4.95 (0-06-445156-9, HarpTrophy) HarpC Child Bks.

Look Out for Turtles! Melvin Berger. LC 90-36894. (Let's-Read-&-Find-Out Science Bks.: Stage 2). (Illus.). 32p. (J). (ps-3). 2000. lib. bdg. 15.89 (0-06-022540-8) HarpC Child Bks.

Look Out for Turtles! Melvin Berger. (Let's Read-&-Find-Out Science Ser.). 1992. 10.15 (0-606-09572-1, Pub. by Turtleback) Demco.

Look Out Kindergarten, Here I Come! Nancy L. Carlson. LC 98-47039. (Illus.). 32p. (J). (ps-1). 1999. 15.99 (0-670-88378-6) Viking Penguin.

***Look Out! Letters Alive.** Keith Polette. (Illus.). 48p. 1999. pap. 8.95 (1-880505-44-4, CLC0228) Pieces of Lrning.

Look Out, Lion Cub! Michele Coxon. LC 99-70740. (Lift-the-Flap Bks.). (Illus.). 16p. (J). (ps). 1998. pap. 6.95 (1-887734-39-2) Star Brght Bks.

Look Out London. Louise Nicholson. (Illus.). 48p. (J). (gr. 1-4). 1998. pap. 9.95 (1-898304-84-X, Pub. by Bodley Head) Trafalgar.

Look Out, Look Out, It's Coming! Laura Geringer. LC 91-4707. (Illus.). 40p. (J). (ps-2). 1992. 15.00 (0-06-021711-1); lib. bdg. 14.89 (0-06-021712-X) HarpC Child Bks.

Look Out, Mr. Watson! Mack Yates. 24p. (J). 1992. pap. 5.00 (1-886210-05-5) Tyketoon Yng Author.

***Look Out on the Road.** Steck-Vaughn Company Staff. (Read All about It Ser.). (Illus.). (J). 2000. pap. 4.95 (0-8114-3736-1) Raintree Steck-V.

Look Out, Patrick! Paul Geraghty. LC 89-77850. (Illus.). 32p. (J). (ps-1). 1990. text 13.95 (0-02-735822-4, Mac Bks Young Read) S&S Childrens.

Look Out Tiger. Tony Potter. (J). (ps-3). 1998. 7.95 (1-902553-04-7) Grimond.

Look-Out Tower. Geoffrey Ursell. 1997. pap. 7.95 (0-88801-138-5, Pub. by Turnstone Pr) Genl Dist Srvs.

Look Out Washington. Patricia Reilly Giff. (J). 1996. pap. 4.99 (0-440-91121-4) BDD Bks Young Read.

Look Out Washington. Patricia Reilly Giff. (J). 1996. pap. 4.99 (0-440-91142-7) BDD Bks Young Read.

Look Out Washington. Patricia Reilly Giff. (J). 1996. pap. 4.99 (0-440-91166-4) BDD Bks Young Read.

Look Out, Washington, D. C.! Patricia Reilly Giff. (Polk Street Special Ser.). 1995. 9.19 (0-606-07803-7, Pub. by Turtleback) Demco.

Look Out, Washington, D. C.! The Polk Street Kids on Tour. Patricia Reilly Giff. (Polk Street Special Ser.: No. 6). (Illus.). 128p. (J). (gr. 1-4). 1995. pap. 3.99 (0-440-40934-9) Dell.

Look Out World . . . Here I Come! Ziggy's Down-to-Earth Humor: A Look at the Environment & Ourselves. Tom Wilson. (Illus.). 104p. (Orig.). 1991. pap. 5.95 (0-8362-1872-8) Andrews & McMeel.

Look Out World - I'm Me. Jamie Buckingham. 228p. 1993. pap. 9.99 (0-88419-318-7) Creation House.

Look over the Edge. Sharon Creedon. (Illus.). 16p. (J). (gr. k-4). 1987. pap. 5.95 (0-9620446-0-1) Sunset Mktg.

Look! Primary Technology. Gilbert. 1987. pap. text. write for info. (0-05-004180-0); pap. text, teacher ed. write for info. (0-05-004182-7) Addison-Wesley.

Look! Snow! Kathryn O. Galbraith. LC 91-28250. (Illus.). 32p. (J). (gr. k-3). 1992. 13.95 (0-689-50551-5) McElderry Bks.

Look 10 Years Younger, Live 10 Years Longer: A Man's Guide. David Ryback. 1999. 9.99 (1-57866-061-0) Galahad Bks.

Look 10 Years Younger, Live 10 Years Longer: A Man's Guide. David Ryback. LC 95-34064. 318p. (C). 1995. text 24.95 (0-13-079344-2) P-H.

Look 10 Years Younger, Live 10 Years Longer: A Man's Guide. David Ryback. LC 95-34064. 318p. (C). 1995. pap. text 13.95 (0-13-079336-1); pap. text 14.95 (0-13-079310-8) P-H.

Look 10 Years Younger, Live 10 Years Longer: A Woman's Guide. David Ryback. 1999. 9.99 (1-57866-062-9) Galahad Bks.

Look 10 Years Younger, Live 10 Years Longer: A Woman's Guide. David Ryback. LC 95-35882. 368p. (C). 1995. text 24.95 (0-13-079328-0) P-H.

***Look Ten Years Younger Live Ten Years Premium.** 1999. 4.95 (0-13-018412-8) P-H.

Look to Business, Not Government, for a Better Denver Airport: Why the Private Sector Can Best Decide Stapleton's Future. Frank Vorhies. 28p. 1989. pap. text 8.00 (1-57655-127-X) Independ Inst.

Look to Markets, Not Bureaucrats for More Recycling: Legislative Waste Control Efforts Could Prove Wasteful. James P. McMahon. (Issue Papers: No. 8-93). 5p. 1993. pap. text 8.00 (1-57655-075-3) Independ Inst.

Look to the Earth: Historical Archaeology & the American Civil War. Ed. by Clarence R. Geier, Jr. & Susan E. Winter. LC 94-4508. (Illus.). 344p. (C). 1996. pap. text 18.50 (0-87049-954-8) U of Tenn Pr.

Look to the East. 1994. pap. 10.00 (0-88053-064-2, M400) Macoy Pub.

Look to the East. Lester. 15.95 (0-685-22017-6) Wehman.

Look to the East. Ralph P. Lester. 15.00 (0-911164-18-9) Powner.

Look to the East! A Ritual of the First Three Degrees of Freemasonry. Ralph P. Lester. 220p. 1998. reprint ed. pap. 19.95 (0-7661-0465-6) Kessinger Pub.

Look to the Future in Industrial Gear Lubricants. D. S. Taber & D. J. Edwards. (Technical Papers: Vol. P254.30). (Illus.). 8p. 1970. pap. text 30.00 (1-55589-358-9) AGMA.

Look to the Hills. Hazel Krantz. 224p. (J). (gr. 3-8). 1995. pap. 9.95 (0-8276-0571-4) JPS Phila.

Look to the Horizon. Scott Keyes. 45p. 1985. pap. 6.00 (0-9633179-1-1); audio 10.00 (0-9633179-0-3) D Scott Pubs.

Look to the Lady see Margery Allingham Omnibus

***Look to the Lady.** large type unabridged ed. Margery Allingham. 2000. 26.95 (0-7531-6101-X, 16101X, Pub. by ISIS Lrg Prnt) ISIS Pub.

Look to the Light. Diane C. Esser. Ed. & Photos by Norma Hiller. (Illus.). 52p. (Orig.). 1995. pap. 15.95 (0-9648035-0-X) Fireside Gallerie.

Look to the Mountain. LeGrand Cannon, Jr. 416p. 1991. reprint ed. pap. 7.95 (0-88150-215-4, Pub. by Countryman) Norton.

Look to the Mountain: An Ecology of Indigenous Education. Gregory Cajete. LC 94-175203. (Illus.). 248p. (Orig.). (C). 1993. pap. 19.95 (1-882308-65-4) Kivaki Pr.

Look to the North: A Wolf Pup Diary. Jean Craighead George. LC 95-39162. (Illus.). 32p. (J). (gr. k-4). 1997. 14.95 (0-06-023641-8); lib. bdg. 15.89 (0-06-023640-X) HarpC Child Bks.

Look to the North: A Wolf Pup Diary. Jean Craighead George. LC 95-39162. (Illus.). 32p. (J). (gr. k-4). 1998. pap. 5.95 (0-06-443510-5, HarpTrophy) HarpC Child Bks.

Look to the Rainbow. Edmonde Haddad. 74p. 1997. write for info. (1-86106-643-0, Pub. by Minerva Pr) Unity Dist.

Look to the River. William A. Owens. LC 87-40267. (Texas Tradition Ser.: No. 8). 134p. 1988. reprint ed. pap. 11.95 (0-87565-026-0) Tex Christian.

Look to the Rose. Shirley Seifert. Date not set. reprint ed. lib. bdg. 17.95 (0-89190-135-3, Am Repr) Amereon Ltd.

Look to the Sky. Jerry DeBruin. 160p. (J). (gr. 4-12). 1988. student ed. 12.99 (0-86653-440-7, GA1051) Good Apple.

Look to the Stars. Emilie Loring. reprint ed. lib. bdg. 21.95 (0-88411-371-X) Amereon Ltd.

***Look to Your Front: Studies in the First World War.** British Commission for Military History Staff. Ed. by Brian Bond. 224p. 2000. pap. 60.00 (1-86227-065-1, Pub. by Spellmnt Pubs) St Mut.

Look, Touch, & Feel with Buster. Rod Campbell. (Illus.). 12p. (J). 1992. pap. 8.49 (1-881445-06-2) Sandvik Pub.

Look Twice: Mirror Reflections, Logical Thinking. Duncan Birmingham. (J). (gr. 3 up). 1991. pap. 7.50 (0-906212-86-3, Pub. by Tarquin Pubns) Parkwest Pubns.

Look unto Jesus. 1995. pap. 1.30 (0-8341-9420-1) Nazarene.

Look up & Hope: The Life & Prison Ministry of Maud Ballington Booth. 2nd ed. Susan F. Welty. 1998. reprint ed. pap. 9.95 (1-885287-00-3) Volunteers Amer.

Look up & Live: Dance in Prayer & Meditation. Margaret F. Taylor. Ed. by Doug Adams. 96p. 1980. pap. 6.95 (0-941500-12-8) Sharing Co.

Look up for Yes. Julia Tavalaro & Richard Tayson. LC 96-48597. 192p. 1997. 19.00 (1-56836-171-8) Kodansha.

Look up for Yes. Julia Tavalaro & Richard Tayson. LC 96-48597. 256p. 1998. pap. 12.95 (0-14-027282-8) Viking Penguin.

Look up, Look Down. Tana Hoban. LC 91-12613. 32p. (J). (ps up). 1992. 14.00 (0-688-10577-7, Grenwillow Bks) HarpC Child Bks.

Look up Look down Look All Around Bandelier National Monument. Bill Hallett & Jane Hallett. (Illus.). 32p. (Orig.). (J). (gr. 3-8). 1990. pap., student ed. 3.95 (1-877827-02-9) Look & See.

Look up Look Down Look All Around Chaco Culture National Historical Park. Bill Hallett & Jane Hallett. (Illus.). 32p. (Orig.). (J). (gr. 3-8). 1989. pap., student ed. 3.95 (1-877827-00-2) Look & See.

Look up Look down Look All Around El Morro National Monument. Bill Hallett & Jane Hallett. (Illus.). 32p. (Orig.). (J). (gr. 3-8). 1988. pap., student ed. 3.45 (0-943087-04-X) Look & See.

Look up, Look down, Look All Around Mesa Verde National Park. Bill Hallett & Jane Hallett. (Illus.). 32p. (Orig.). (J). (gr. 3-8). 1990. pap., student ed. 3.95 (1-877827-04-5) Look & See.

Look up, Look down, Look All Around Red River, New Mexico. Bill Hallett & Jane Hallett. (Illus.). 16p. (Orig.). (J). (gr. 3-8). 1990. pap., student ed. 2.50 (1-877827-03-7) Look & See.

Look up the Welsh: A Phrasebook Guide to the Welsh Language. Heini Gruffudd. 1979. pap. 6.50 (0-89979-024-0) British Am Bks.

Look We've Come Through: Manuscript Edition. Hugh Wheeler. 1963. pap. 13.00 (0-8222-0687-0) Dramatists Play.

***Look What Came from Australia.** Kevin Davis. 2000. pap. text 6.95 (0-531-16433-0) Watts.

Look What Came from Australia. Kevin A. Davis. LC 99-19254. (Look What Came From Ser.). 1999. 21.00 (0-531-11684-0) Watts.

Look What Came from China. Miles Harvey. LC 97-35689. (Look What Came From Ser.). (J). 1998. 20.00 (0-531-11495-3) Watts.

Look What Came from China. Miles Harvey. (Look What Came from Ser.). (Illus.). 32p. (J). (gr. 2-4). 1999. pap. text 6.95 (0-531-15936-1) Watts.

Look What Came from Egypt. Miles Harevy. LC 97-35688. (Look What Came from Ser.). (J). 1998. 20.00 (0-531-11498-8) Watts.

***Look What Came from Egypt.** Miles Harvey. (Look What Came from Ser.). (Illus.). 32p. (J). (gr. 2-4). 1999. pap. text 6.95 (0-531-15937-X) Watts.

***Look What Came from England.** Kevin Davis. (Look What Came from Ser.). (Illus.). (J). 2000. pap. 6.95 (0-531-16434-9) Watts.

Look What Came from England. Kevin A. Davis. LC 99-19258. (Look What Came from Ser.). 1999. 21.00 (0-531-11686-7) Watts.

***Look What Came from France.** Miles Harvey. (Illus.). (J). 1999. 12.40 (0-606-18153-9) Turtleback.

Look What Came from France. Miles Harvey. LC 98-36173. (Look What Came from Ser.). (J). 1999. 21.00 (0-531-11501-1) Watts.

Look What Came from France. Miles Harvey. (Look What Came from Ser.). 1999. pap. text 6.95 (0-531-15964-7) Watts.

***Look What Came from Germany.** Kevin Davis. (Look What Came from Ser.). (Illus.). (J). 2000. pap. 6.95 (0-531-16435-7) Watts.

Look What Came from Germany. Kevin A. Davis. LC 99-19256. (Look What Came from Ser.). 1999. 21.00 (0-531-11685-9) Watts.

Look What Came from Greece. Kevin A. Davis. LC 99-19257. (Look What Came from Ser.). 1999. write for info. (0-531-11744-8) Watts.

Look What Came from Greece. Miles Harvey. (Look What Came from Ser.). 1999. pap. text 6.95 (0-531-15974-4) Watts.

Look What Came from India. Miles Harvey. LC 98-35851. 1999. 20.00 (0-531-11587-9) Watts.

Look What Came from India. Miles Harvey. (Look What Came from Ser.). 1999. pap. text 6.95 (0-531-15965-5) Watts.

Look What Came from Italy. Miles Harvey. LC 97-33331. (Look What Came From Ser.). (J). 1998. 20.00 (0-531-11497-X) Watts.

Look What Came from Italy. Miles Harvey. (Look What Came from Ser.). (Illus.). 32p. (J). (gr. 2-4). 1999. pap. text 6.95 (0-531-15938-8) Watts.

Look What Came from Japan. Miles Harvey. LC 98-35845. (Look What Came from Ser.). (J). 1999. 21.00 (0-531-11500-3) Watts.

Look What Came from Japan. Miles Harvey. 1999. lib. bdg. 6.95 (0-531-15966-3) Watts.

Look What Came from Mexico. Miles Harvey. LC 97-30825. (Look What Came from Ser.). (J). 1998. 20.00 (0-531-11496-1) Watts.

***Look What Came from Russia.** Miles Harvey. (Illus.). (J). 1999. 12.40 (0-606-18154-7) Turtleback.

Look What Came from Russia. Miles Harvey. LC 98-35948. 1999. 20.00 (0-531-11499-6) Watts.

Look What Came from Russia. Miles Harvey. (Look What Came from Ser.). 1999. pap. text 6.95 (0-531-15967-1) Watts.

***Look What Came from the United States.** Kevin Davis. (Look What Came from Ser.). (Illus.). (J). 2000. pap. 6.95 (0-531-16436-5) Watts.

***Look What Came from the United States.** Kevin A. Davis. (Illus.). (J). 2000. 12.40 (0-606-18155-5) Turtleback.

Look What Came from the United States. Kevin A. Davis. LC 99-109255. (Look What Came from Ser.). 1999. 21.00 (0-531-11687-5) Watts.

Look What God Made! Stephen Mcintruff. 1999. pap. text 2.49 (0-7847-0887-8) Standard Pub.

Look What God Made! Linda J. Sattgast. Ed. by Julie Smith. LC 94-9201. (Illus.). 32p. (J). (ps-2). 1995. 6.99 (0-7814-0184-4, Chariot Bks) Chariot Victor.

Look What I Can Do. Jose Aruego. (J). 1988. 10.15 (0-606-03608-3, Pub. by Turtleback) Demco.

Look What I Can Do! Kees Moerbeek. (Little Spinners Ser.). (Illus.). 10p. (J). (ps-k). 1998. 7.95 (0-7613-0391-X, Copper Beech Bks) Millbrook Pr.

Look What I Can Do! Jose Aruego. LC 87-21743. (Illus.). 32p. (J). (ps-1). 1988. reprint ed. mass mkt. 4.95 (0-689-71205-7) Aladdin.

Look What I Did with a Leaf. Morteza E. Sohi. LC 92-35142. (NatureCraft Ser.). (Illus.). 32p. (Orig.). (J). (ps-3). 1993. 14.95 (0-8027-8215-9); lib. bdg. 15.85 (0-8027-8216-7) Walker & Co.

Look What I Did with a Leaf. Morteza E. Sohi. (Illus.). 32p. (Orig.). (J). (ps-3). 1995. pap. 5.95 (0-8027-7440-7) Walker & Co.

Look What I Did With a Leaf! Morteza E. Sohi. (Naturecraft Ser.). 1995. 11.15 (0-606-08808-3, Pub. by Turtleback) Demco.

***Look What I Did with a Shell.** Morteza E. Sohi. (Nature Craft Ser.). (Illus.). 32p. (J). (gr. 1-3). 2000. 15.95 (0-8027-8722-3) Walker & Co.

***Look What I Did with a Shell.** Morteza E. Sohi. LC 00-21532. (Nature Craft Ser.). (Illus.). 32p. (J). (gr. 1-4). 2000. lib. bdg. 16.85 (0-8027-8723-1) Walker & Co.

Look What I Found: The Young Conservationist's Guide to the Care & Feeding of Small Wildlife. Marshall T. Case. 95p. 1983. pap. 9.95 (0-8159-6119-7) Devin.

Look What I Made! Creative Crafts. Sarah H. Healton & Kay H. Whiteside. (J). (gr. 1-3). 1997. text 16.95 (0-07-027701-X) McGraw.

Look What I Made! Creative Crafts for Ages 6-8. Ed. by Sarah H. Healton & Kay H. Whiteside. (Illus.). 112p. (J). (gr. 1-3). 1992. 16.95 (0-8306-4037-1, 4181); pap. 9.95 (0-8306-4038-X, 4181) McGraw-Hill Prof.

Look What I Made! Easy Holiday Crafts for Young Children. Terri A. Pope. Ed. by Jennifer Weaver-Spencer. (Illus.). 96p. (J). (ps-1). 1998. pap. text 10.95 (0-88724-470-X, CD-0060) Carson-Dellos.

Look What I Made! 40 Craft Ideas & 120 Related Activities for Children Ages 2 to 5. Joan W. Buma. (Illus.). 96p. 1991. pap. 9.95 (1-55958-073-9) Prima Pub.

Look What I Made Now Vol. II: Interactive Nature Activities for Young Children. Joan W. Buma. (Look What I Made! Ser.). (Illus.). 96p. 1991. pap. 9.95 (1-55958-176-X) Prima Pub.

Look What the Stork Brought: Man of the Month. Dixie Browning. (Desire Ser.: No. 1111). 1997. per. 3.50 (0-373-76111-2, 1-76111-3) Harlequin Bks.

Look What They Have Done to the Blu. M. Blackaby. LC 97-179828. 1997. text 17.95 (0-575-06393-9, Pub. by V Gollancz) Trafalgar.

Look What We've Brought You from India: Crafts, Games, Recipes, Stories & Other Cultural Activities from Indian Americans. Phyllis Shalant. LC 97-414. (J). 1997. 18.95 (0-382-39465-8, Julian Messner); pap. write for info. (0-382-39465-8, Julian Messner) Silver Burdett Pr.

Look What We've Brought You from Korea: Crafts, Games, Recipes, Stories & Other Cultural Activities from Korean-Americans. Phyllis Shalant. (Illus.). (J). (gr. 2 up). pap. 7.95 (0-382-24994-1) Silver.

Look What We've Brought You from Korea: Crafts, Games, Recipes, Stories & Other Cultural Activities from Korean-Americans. Phyllis Shalant. LC 94-25829. (Illus.). (J). 1994. lib. bdg. 15.95 (0-671-88701-7, Julian Messner) Silver Burdett Pr.

Look What We've Brought You from Mexico. Phyllis Shalant. (J). (ps-3). 1992. pap. 6.95 (0-671-75257-X, Julian Messner) Silver Burdett Pr.

Look What We've Brought You from Mexico: Crafts, Games, Recipes, Stories & Other Cultural Activities from Mexican Americans. 2nd ed. Phyllis Shalant. LC 97-44493. (J). 1998. 18.95 (0-382-39979-X, Julian Messner); pap. 7.95 (0-382-39980-3, Julian Messner) Silver Burdett Pr.

An Asterisk (*) at the beginning of an entry indicates that the title is appearing for the first time.

L

Look What We've Brought You from the Caribbean: Crafts, Games, Recipes, Stories, & Other Cultural Activities. Phyllis Shalant. LC 97-6287. (J). 1998. 22.00 (*0-382-39925-0*, Julian Messner); pap. 11.00 (*0-382-39926-9*, Julian Messner) Silver Burdett Pr.

Look What We've Brought You from Vietnam: Crafts, Games, Recipes, Stories & Other Cultural Activities from New Americans. Phyllis Shalant. LC 87-20276. (Cultural Activities Ser.). (Illus.). 48p. (J). (gr. 2-6). 1988. pap. 6.95 (*0-671-65978-2*, Julian Messner) Silver Burdett Pr.

Look What We've Brought You from Vietnam: Crafts, Games, Recipes, Stories & Other Cultural Activities from Vietnamese Americans. 2nd ed. Phyllis Shalant. LC 97-42446. (J). 1998. 25.25 (*0-382-39981-1*, Julian Messner); pap. 10.60 (*0-382-39982-X*, Julian Messner) Silver Burdett Pr.

*__Look What You Can Do with Grids.__ Carolyn Kyle & Laura Tayne. (Illus.). 1999. pap. 17.95 (*0-935133-74-7*) CKE Pubns.

Look What You Can Make with Boxes: Over 90 Pictured Crafts & Dozens of More Ideas. Ed. by Lorianne Siomades. LC 97-76815. 48p. (J). (gr. 4-6). 1998. pap. text 5.95 (*1-56397-704-4*) Boyds Mills Pr.

*__Look What You Can Make with Egg Cartons.__ Ed. by Betsy Ochester. LC 00-100007. (Illus.). 48p. (J). (ps-7). 2000. pap. 5.95 (*1-56397-906-3*) Boyds Mills Pr.

Look What You Can Make with Paper Bags. Ed. by Judy Burke. LC 97-77904. (Illus.). 48p. (J). (ps-7). 1999. pap. 5.95 (*1-56397-717-6*) Boyds Mills Pr.

Look What You Can Make with Paper Plates. Highlights Staff. LC 96-85993. (Illus.). 48p. (J). (ps-5). 1997. pap., student ed. 5.95 (*1-56397-643-9*) Boyds Mills Pr.

Look What You Can Make with Tubes: Over 90 Pictured Crafts & Dozens of More Ideas. Ed. by Margie H. Richmond. LC 96-80396. (Illus.). 48p. (J). (gr. k-7). 1997. pap., student ed. 5.95 (*1-56397-677-3*) Boyds Mills Pr.

Look Whats Cooking at Spanish Point Lodge: Chef John Irish/American Cookbook. John S. Malone. (Illus.). 7p. (Orig.). 1997. pap. 10.00 (*0-9657105-0-5*) J S Malone.

Look What's Cooking in Richmond: Contains the Favorite Recipes from Virginia's Legislators. Ed. by Diana Worrell. (Illus.). 63p. (Orig.). 1984. pap. 5.95 (*0-9613647-0-X*) Va CARES.

Look What's Cooking Now: Minnesota Heritage Cookbook, Vol. II. American Cancer Society. Ed. by Sue Zelickson. (Illus.). 176p. (Orig.). 1985. pap. 10.00 (*0-9602796-1-X*) Am Cancer Minn.

Look Who Lives in the Arctic. Alan Baker. LC 99-46892. (Look Who Lives in--Ser.). 32p. (J). 1999. 14.95 (*0-87226-540-4*, 65404B, P Bedrick Books) NTC Contemp Pub Co.

Look Who Lives in the Desert. Alan Baker. (Look Who Lives in--Ser.). 32p. (J). 1999. 14.95 (*0-87226-541-2*, 65412B, P Bedrick Books) NTC Contemp Pub Co.

Look Who Lives in the Ocean. Alan Baker. LC 98-37549. (Look Who Lives in--Ser.). 32p. (J). 1999. 14.95 (*0-87226-539-0*, 65390B, P Bedrick Books) NTC Contemp Pub Co.

*__Look Who Lives in the Rain Forest.__ Alan Baker. LC 98-37562. (Look Who Lives in--Ser.). 32p. (J). 1999. 14.95 (*0-87226-538-2*, 65382B, P Bedrick Books) NTC Contemp Pub Co.

*__Look Whooo's Counting.__ Suse MacDonald. LC 99-87552. (Illus.). (J). (ps-1). 2000. 14.95 (*0-590-68320-9*) Scholastic Inc.

Look Who's a Grandmother. Dolli Tingle. 1996. 6.95 (*0-8378-9856-0*) Gibson.

Look Who's Adopted. Michael S. Taheri. 1997. pap. 11.19 (*1-879201-21-6*) WNY Wares.

*__Look Who's in the Thanksgiving Play!__ Andrew Clements. (Lift-the-Flap Bks.). (Illus.). (J). 1999. pap. 5.99 (*0-689-82807-1*) Litle Simon.

Look Who's Laughing Vol. 1: Studies in Gender & Comedy. Ed. by Gail Finney. LC 93-44165. (Studies in Gender & Humor: No. 1). 312p. 1994. text 48.00 (*2-88124-644-3*); pap. text 25.00 (*2-88124-645-1*) Gordon & Breach.

Look Who's Playing First Base. Matt Christopher. (Illus.). 131p. (J). (gr. 4-6). 1987. pap. 3.95 (*0-316-13989-0*) Little.

Look Who's Playing First Base. Matt Christopher. (J). 1971. 9.05 (*0-606-02401-8*, Pub. by Turtleback) Demco.

Look Who's Talking: A Guide for Lay Speakers in the Church. Ronald E. Sleeth. LC 77-1171. 1977. pap. 8.95 (*0-687-22630-9*) Abingdon.

Look Who's Talking: An Anthology of Voices in the Modern American Short Story. Ed. by Bruce Weber. 352p. 1989. pap. 6.50 (*0-671-68723-9*, WSP) PB.

Look Who's Talking: In the Bay Area, 1993. 36p. 1992. 5.95 (*1-883529-00-X*) Arts Made Lively.

Look Who's Talking: In the Bay Area, 1994. (Illus.). 28p. 1994. 5.95 (*1-883529-01-8*) Arts Made Lively.

Look Who's Talking! Strategies for Developing Group Interaction. Mary A. Christison & Sharron Bassano. (Illus.). 108p. 1995. pap. text 16.95 (*1-882483-33-2*) Alta Bk Ctr.

Look Who's Toast Now! Hot Truth about How the World Will End in the Year 2000--or Maybe Not! Kevin Johnson. LC 97-33843. 144p. (YA). 1997. pap. 7.99 (*0-7642-2004-7*) Bethany Hse.

Look with the Heart. Dan Miller. 365p. 1998. 24.95 (*0-9653086-2-6*) Phoenix Images.

*__Look with the Heart.__ large type ed. Barbara Cartland. LC 00-27787. 172p. (Orig.). 2000. 27.95 (*0-7838-9058-3*) Mac Lib Ref.

Look Within. Scott Free. 107p. 1996. pap. 9.95 (*0-9635673-0-6*) S Free.

Look Within: Inspirations of Love. Dadaji. Ed. by Ann Mills. LC 87-71489. (Illus.). 260p. (Orig.). 1995. pap. 11.95 (*0-942687-01-9*) Amida Pr.

*__Look Within or Do Without: The 13 Qualities Winners All Share.__ Tom Bay. 224p. 2000. pap. 14.99 (*1-56414-490-9*) Career Pr Inc.

Look You Like: Medical Answers to 400 Questions on Skin & Hair Care. Linda Allen Schoen & Paul Lazar. (Illus.). 336p. 1989. text 39.75 (*0-8247-8146-5*) Dekker.

Look Younger, Live Longer: Add 25 to 50 Years to Your Life, Naturally. Bruce Goldberg. LC 97-32142. (Illus.). 224p. (Orig.). 1999. pap. 12.95 (*1-56718-321-2*) Llewellyn Pubns.

*__Look Younger Longer... Without Plastic Surgery.__ Eleni-Dayle Iversen. Ed. by Richard Price. (Illus.). xii, 144p. 2000. otabind 21.95 (*0-9671932-0-6*) Young in Heart.

Looka Yonder: The Imaginary America of Populist Culture. Duncan Webster. 1988. 49.95 (*0-415-00715-1*); pap. 12.95 (*0-415-00716-X*) Routledge.

Looka Yonder: The Imaginary America of Populist Culture. Duncan Webster. LC 87-32914. 277p. reprint ed. pap. 85.90 (*0-608-20403-X*, 207165600002) Bks Demand.

Lookalike Love. large type ed. Nancy John. (Linford Romance Large Print Ser.). 320p. 1996. pap. 16.99 (*0-7089-7965-3*, Linford) Ulverscroft.

Looked for a City. Lydia Buksbazen. LC 58-17705. 1955. pap. 8.95 (*0-915540-15-0*) Frnds Israel.

Lookin' Back. Gary D. Trump. (Illus.). 64p. 1995. pap. 4.99 (*1-884366-01-5*, 13/14) AThreeTCO.

*__Lookin' for Luv.__ Carl Weber. 2000. pap. 14.00 (*1-57566-695-2*, Knsington) Kensgtn Pub Corp.

Lookin' Good: The Elements of Document Design for Beginners. Sharon Yoder & Irene Smith. (Illus.). 85p. 1995. spiral bd. 14.95 (*1-56484-081-6*) Intl Society Tech Educ.

Looking Across. Marcia L. Masters. 90p. (Orig.). 1990. pap. 7.95 (*0-939395-12-6*) Thorntree Pr.

Looking After: A Son's Memoir. John Daniel. 272p. 1997. pap. 14.00 (*1-887178-59-7*, Pub. by Counterpt DC) HarpC.

Looking after Cage Birds. David Alderton. (Illus.). 128p. 1996. pap. 14.95 (*0-7137-2578-8*, Pub. by Blandford Pr) Sterling.

Looking after Dad. Elizabeth Oldfield. (From Here to Paternity Ser.). 1997. per. 3.50 (*0-373-11879-1*, 1-11879-3) Harlequin Bks.

Looking after Dad. large type ed. Elizabeth Oldfield. (Mills & Boon Large Print Ser.). 288p. 1997. 23.99 (*0-263-15170-0*, Pub. by Mills & Boon) Ulverscroft.

Looking after Heritage Places: The Basics of Heritage Planning for Managers, Landowners & Administrators. Michael Pearson & Sharon Sullivan. 412p. 1995. pap. 39.95 (*0-522-84554-1*, Pub. by Melbourne Univ Pr) Paul & Co Pubs.

Looking after Lily. Cindy Bonner. LC 93-33730. 336p. 1999. 18.95 (*1-56512-045-0*) Algonquin Bks.

Looking after Myself. Sarah Levete. LC 97-41644. (How Do I Feel About... Ser.). (Illus.). 24p. (J). (gr. k-4). 1998. lib. bdg. 19.90 (*0-7613-0809-1*, Copper Beech Bks) Millbrook Pr.

Looking after Nietzsche. Ed. by Laurence A. Rickels. LC 89-4579. (SUNY Series, Intersections). 265p. (C). 1989. pap. text 21.95 (*0-7914-0157-X*) State U NY Pr.

Looking after Our Land. Will Critchley. (FRE., Illus.). 88p. (C). 1991. pap. 25.95 (*0-85598-171-7*, Pub. by Oxfam Pubns) St Mut.

Looking after Our Land: Environment. Will Critchley. (Illus.). 88p. (C). 1991. pap. 14.95 (*0-85598-170-9*, Pub. by Oxfam Pub) Stylus Pub VA.

Looking after the Babysitter. Rita Benson. LC 93-26221. (Voyages Ser.). (Illus.). (J). 1994. 4.25 (*0-383-03760-3*) SRA McGraw.

Looking Again at Indian Art. Vidya Dehejia. (Illus.). 156p. 1978. 16.95 (*0-318-36271-6*) Asia Bk Corp.

Looking Ahead, Level 2. Lellag. LC 98-128134. (Global Esl/Elt Ser.). 288p. (J). 1998. pap. 29.95 (*0-8384-7911-1*) Heinle & Heinle.

Looking Ahead, Level 3. Byleer. (Global Esl/Elt Ser.). 304p. (J). 1998. pap. 29.95 (*0-8384-7902-2*) Heinle & Heinle.

Looking Ahead: A Guide to Retirement. Fred Kemp & Bernard Battle. 140p. 1993. 30.00 (*1-85190-179-5*, Pub. by Tolley Pubng) St Mut.

Looking Ahead: Human Factors Challenges in a Changing World. Raymond S. Nickerson. 456p. 1992. text 89.95 (*0-8058-1150-8*) L Erlbaum Assocs.

Looking Ahead: Human Factors Challenges in a Changing World. Raymond S. Nickerson. 456p. 1992. pap. 45.00 (*0-8058-1151-6*) L Erlbaum Assocs.

Looking Ahead: Identifying Key Economic Issues for Business & Society in the 1980s. (CED Supplementary Paper). 54p. 1981. lib. bdg. 5.00 (*0-87186-333-2*) Comm Econ Dev.

Looking Ahead: Independent School Issues & Answers. Ed. by Patrick F. Bassett & Louis M. Crosier. LC 94-70106. 219p. (Orig.). 1994. pap. 19.95 (*0-9627671-6-6*) Avocus Pub.

Looking Ahead: Self-Conceptions, Race & Family as Determinants of Adolescent Orientation to Achievement. Chad Gordon. LC 77-183121. (Arnold & Caroline Rose Monograph Series in Sociology). v, 120 p. 1972. write for info. (*0-912764-02-3*) Am Sociological.

Looking Ahead: Twentieth Century Happenings. H. Pereira Mendes. LC 79-154451. (Utopian Literature Ser.). 1976. reprint ed. 29.95 (*0-405-03533-0*) Ayer.

Looking Ahead: Your Plan for a "Successful Career" As a Teenager. Marc Jacobs & Lenore Gilrane. (Illus.). 40p. 1991. wbk. ed. 5.00 (*1-878848-20-8*, 144C) Natl Res Ctr.

Looking Ahead Bk. 1: Introduction to Academic Writing. Sharon Cavusgil. LC 98-158909. 256p. (J). 1998. pap. 29.95 (*0-8384-7884-0*) Heinle & Heinle.

Looking Ahead Bk. 4: Mastering Academic Writing. Christine Holton & Judith Marasco. LC 98-134801. 336p. (J). 1998. pap. 29.95 (*0-8384-7893-X*) Heinle & Heinle.

Looking Ahead at Environmental Education. Ed. by Karen Flagstad. (Illus.). 34p. (Orig.). (C). 1995. pap. text 20.00 (*0-7881-2613-X*) DIANE Pub.

Looking Ahead Instructor's Manual, Bks. 1 & 2. Byleer. (J). 1998. pap. 19.25 (*0-8384-7832-8*) Heinle & Heinle.

Looking Ahead with Living Trusts. Galen F. Griepp. 200p. 1996. pap. text 15.95 (*1-888274-07-7*) Millennium Calif.

Looking & Feeling Your Best: A Guide for Guys see Need to Know Library: Lessons of Life

Looking & Seeing. Henry A. Pluckrose. LC 97-30964. (Senses Ser.). (J). 1998. 21.40 (*0-8172-5225-8*) Raintree Steck-V.

*__Looking Around.__ Steck-Vaughn Company Staff. (Read All about It Ser.). (Illus.). (J). 2000. pap. 4.95 (*0-8114-3721-3*) Raintree Steck-V.

Looking Around: A Journey Through Architecture. Witold Rybczynski. 320p. 1993. reprint ed. pap. 12.95 (*0-14-016889-3*, Penguin Bks) Viking Penguin.

Looking Around Corners: The Art of Problem Prevention. Andrew J. DuBrin. 303p. 1999. pap. 16.95 (*1-886284-33-4*, Pub. by Chandler Hse) Natl Bk Netwk.

*__Looking at a Far Mountain: A Study of Kendo Kata.__ Paul Budden. (Illus.). 2000. pap. 19.95 (*0-8048-3245-5*) Tuttle Pubng.

Looking at America. Bernard Drachman. LC 76-107696. (Essay Index Reprint Ser.). 1977. 23.95 (*0-8369-1499-6*) Ayer.

Looking at American Food: A Pictorial Introduction to American Language & Culture. Jann Huizenga. LC 98-38744. (Looking at America Ser.). 1998. 6.99 (*0-8325-0402-5*) NTC Contemp Pub Co.

Looking at American Holidays. Jann Huizenga. 48p. 1985. pap. 6.99 (*0-8325-0410-6*) NTC Contemp Pub Co.

*__Looking at Ants.__ Eleanor Christian & Lyzz Roth-Singer. LC 00-36474. (Illus.). (J). 2000. write for info. (*0-7368-0725-X*) Capstone Pr.

Looking at Art, 12 vols. (Illus.). (YA). (gr. 4-10). 1996. lib. bdg. 245.00 (*0-7172-7595-7*) Grolier Educ.

Looking at Art: A Guide to Responsive Viewing. Roy Sonnema. 152p. (C). 1998. per. 27.95 (*0-7872-5325-1*, 41532501) Kendall-Hunt.

Looking at Art from the Inside Out: The Psychoiconographic Approach to Modern Art. Mary M. Gedo. LC 93-46635. (Contemporary Artists & Their Critics Ser.). (Illus.). 333p. (C). 1994. pap. text 19.95 (*0-521-43567-6*) Cambridge U Pr.

Looking at Art from the Inside Out: The Psychoiconographic Approach to Modern Art. Mary M. Gedo. LC 93-46635. (Contemporary Artists & Their Critics Ser.). (Illus.). 333p. (C). 1994. text 85.00 (*0-521-43407-6*) Cambridge U Pr.

Looking at Australia. W. F. Henderson & R. A. Henderson. LC 76-29054. (Looking at Other Countries Ser.). (J). (gr. 4-6). 1977. 12.95 (*0-397-31703-4*, Lppncott) Lppncott W & W.

Looking at Ballet: Ashton & Balanchine, 1926-1936. Bruce Fleming et al. (Illus.). 48p. (Orig.). 1993. pap. 24.95 (*0-9632543-0-8*) R Sage Coll.

Looking at Bears. Dorothy H. Patent. LC 94-1834. (Illus.). 40p. (J). (gr. k-3). 1994. lib. bdg. 15.95 (*0-8234-1139-7*) Holiday.

Looking at Biology. 5th ed. Bleekman & Fiedler. 200p. 1993. pap. text, lab manual ed. 33.80 (*0-536-58399-4*) Pearson Custom.

Looking at Brazil. Sarita H. Kendall. LC 73-19605. (J). (gr. 4-6). 1974. 12.95 (*0-397-31527-9*) HarpC Child Bks.

Looking at Buildings East Riding. Moffat & Neave. 36p. text 11.95 (*0-14-071064-7*, Pub. by Pnguin Bks Ltd) Trafalgar.

Looking at Canada. Josephine Earn. LC 76-8481. (Looking at Other Countries Ser.). (Illus.). (J). 1977. 12.95 (*0-397-31704-2*) HarpC Child Bks.

Looking at Carriages. Sallie Walrond. 285p. 1990. 100.00 (*0-85131-552-6*, Pub. by J A Allen) Trafalgar.

Looking at Casino Chips & Tokens: A Guide to Technical Terms. Donald D. Spencer. LC 94-16021. (Illus.). 96p. (Orig.). 1994. pap. 13.95 (*0-89218-241-5*) Camelot Pub.

Looking at Children. Bjorklund. (Psychology Ser.). 1992. pap., student ed. 20.95 (*0-534-13705-9*) Brooks-Cole.

Looking at Children's Play: The Bridge from Theory to Practice. Patricia M. Monighan-Nourot et al. (Early Childhood Education Ser.). 176p. (C). 1987. pap. text 16.95 (*0-8077-2872-1*) Tchrs Coll.

Looking at Cities. Allan B. Jacobs. LC 84-19247. (Illus.). 176p. 1985. 34.50 (*0-674-53891-9*) HUP.

Looking at Class. H. Beynon. text 65.00 (*1-85489-120-0*) Rivers Oram.

*__Looking at Class.__ H. Beynon. (Illus.). 224p. 2000. pap. 24.95 (*1-85489-121-9*) Rivers Oram.

Looking at Death. Barbara Norfleet. (Imago Mundi Ser.). (Illus.). 144p. 1993. 40.00 (*0-87923-964-6*) Godine.

Looking at Each Other: Korean Western Cultures in Contrast. Marion E. Current. (Illus.). 96p. 1983. pap. 4.95 (*0-8048-1415-5*, Pub. by Seoul Intl Tourist) Tuttle Pubng.

*__Looking at Early Years Education & Care.__ Rose Drury. 2000. pap. 25.95 (*1-85346-659-X*) David Fulton.

Looking at English, Bk. 3. Fred Malkemes & Deborah S. Pires. (Illus.). 288p. (C). 1983. pap. text 14.00 (*0-13-540435-5*) P-H.

Looking at European Ceramics: A Guide to Technical Terms. David H. Cohen & Catherine Hess. LC 92-79943. (Looking at . . . Ser.). (Illus.). 92p. (Orig.). 1993. pap. 12.95 (*0-89236-216-2*) OUP.

Looking at European Sculpture: A Guide to Technical Terms. Jane Bassett & Peggy Fogelman. LC 96-39855. (Looking at . . . Ser.). (Illus.). 104p. (Orig.). 1997. pap. 12.95 (*0-89236-291-X*) OUP.

Looking at Faces in Art see How to Look at Art

Looking at Fashion: The Catalogue of the Florence Biennial. Ed. by Germano Celant. (Illus.). 684p. 1999. 75.00 (*88-8118-208-4*, Pub. by Skira IT) Abbeville Pr.

Looking at Figures. (Open Learning for Supervisory Management). 1986. pap. text 19.50 (*0-08-070028-4*, Pergamon Pr) Elsevier.

Looking at Figures. Nebsm Staff. (Open Learning for Supervisory Management). 1986. pap. text 19.50 (*0-08-033965-4*, Pergamon Pr) Elsevier.

Looking at Gay & Lesbian Life. rev. ed. Warren J. Blumenfeld & Diane Raymond. LC 92-30483. 448p. 1992. pap. 19.00 (*0-8070-7923-5*) Beacon Pr.

Looking at Geometry, Unit V. Albert B. Bennett et al. (Math & the Mind's Eye Ser.). (Illus.). 76p. (C). 1987. teacher ed., ring bd. 10.00 (*1-886131-17-1*, ME5) Math Lrning.

Looking at Giacometti. David Sylvester. LC 95-44742. 88p. 1995. 27.50 (*0-8050-4210-5*) H Holt & Co.

Looking at Giacometti. David Sylvester. (Illus.). 176p. 1997. pap. 14.95 (*0-8050-4163-X*, Owl) H Holt & Co.

Looking at Greek Vases. Ed. by Tom Rasmussen & Nigel J. Spivey. (Illus.). 300p. (C). 1991. pap. text 19.95 (*0-521-37679-3*) Cambridge U Pr.

Looking at Henry Moore's Elephant Skull Etchings During the Yom Kippur War, in Jerusalem. Shirley Kaufman & Henry Moore. LC 76-57422. (Illus.). 1977. pap. 9.95 (*0-87775-108-0*) Unicorn Pr.

Looking at History: Indiana's Hoosier National Forest Region, 1600 to 1950. Ellen Sieber & Cheryl A. Munson. LC 93-43983. (Illus.). 136p. 1994. pap. 12.95 (*0-253-28789-8*); text 26.95 (*0-253-35226-6*) Ind U Pr.

Looking at Indian Art of the Northwest Coast. Hilary Stewart. LC 78-73988. (Illus.). 112p. 1979. pap. 15.95 (*0-295-95645-3*) U of Wash Pr.

Looking at Insects. Colin Guthrie & Colin Dann. 88p. 1987. 45.00 (*0-7855-2143-7*, Pub. by K Mason Pubns Ltd) St Mut.

Looking at Insects. David Suzuki. LC 91-38974. (Illus.). 96p. (J). 1992. 29.95 (*0-471-54747-6*) Wiley.

Looking at Insects. David Suzuki & Brabara Hehner. (Illus.). 96p. (J). (gr. 3-6). 1992. pap. 9.95 (*0-471-54050-1*) Wiley.

Looking at Iran. Janine Wiedel. LC 78-6038. (Looking at Other Countries Ser.). (Illus.). (J). (gr. 4-7). 1979. 12.95 (*0-397-31797-2*) HarpC Child Bks.

Looking at Italian Renaissance Sculpture. Ed. & Contrib. by Sarah Blake McHam. LC 97-14906. (Illus.). 304p. (C). 1998. text 75.00 (*0-521-47366-7*) Cambridge U Pr.

Looking at Italian Renaissance Sculpture. Ed. & Contrib. by Sarah Blake McHam. LC 97-14906. (Illus.). 304p. (C). 2000. pap. text 27.95 (*0-521-47921-5*) Cambridge U Pr.

Looking at Language Classrooms: Trainer's Guide. Diana Lubelska & Margaret Matthews. LC 97-222165. (Illus.). 1997. write for info. (*0-521-58873-1*) Cambridge U Pr.

Looking at Languages. 2nd ed. Arthur Frommer. (C). 1994. wbk. ed. 31.00 (*0-15-500123-X*) Harcourt Coll Pubs.

Looking at Languages: Answer Key. 2nd ed. Arthur Frommer. (C). 1993. pap. text, teacher ed., suppl. ed. 40.00 (*0-15-500124-8*, Pub. by Harcourt Coll Pubs) Harcourt.

Looking at Law. 4th rev. ed. Stephen Gillers. LC 96-39769. 304p. 1997. pap. 14.95 (*0-452-01178-7*, Plume) Dutton Plume.

Looking at Law School: A Student Guide from the Society of American Law Teachers. rev. ed. Stephen Gillers. 1997. pap. 12.95 (*0-452-27795-7*, Plume) Dutton Plume.

Looking at Life from a Lily Pad: Verse Inspired from the Earth. Lin Simmons. viii, 118p. 1998. pap. 12.00 (*0-9659925-0-0*) Hopper Exped.

Looking at Life Piece by Piece. Kristen Kemper. 90p. 1996. pap. 14.95 (*1-57438-004-4*, 8255) Ed Ministries.

Looking at LISP. Tony Hasemer. 272p. 1984. pap. text 16.95 (*0-201-12080-1*) Addison-Wesley.

Looking at Literacy: Using Images of Literacy to Explore the World of Reading & Writing. Nigel Hall & Anne Robinson. 68p. 1995. pap. 16.95 (*1-85346-378-7*, Pub. by David Fulton) Taylor & Francis.

Looking at Literacy: Using Images of Literacy to Explore the World of Reading & Writing. Nigel Hall & Anne Robinson. LC 95-47135. 1996. pap. text 15.00 (*0-435-08898-X*) Heinemann.

Looking at Literature. Deakin University Press Staff. 86p. (C). 1986. 75.00 (*0-7300-0404-X*, Pub. by Deakin Univ) St Mut.

*__Looking at Looking: An Introduction to the Intelligence of Vision.__ Theodore E. Parks. LC 00-9062. 2000. pap. write for info. (*0-7619-2204-0*) Sage.

Looking at Love: With Guy de Maupassant. unabridged ed. Read by Adam Menken & Franette Liebow. 1996. 16.95 incl. audio (*1-882071-68-9*) B&B Audio.

Looking at Lovemaking: Constructions of Sexuality in Roman Art, 100 B.C., A.D. 250. John R. Clarke. LC 96-40380. 406p. 1998. 39.95 (*0-520-20024-1*, Pub. by U CA Pr) Cal Prin Full Svc.

*__Looking at Microbes: Viewers Guide.__ Erin Davis et al. (Illus.). (C). 1998. pap. text. write for info. (*0-7637-0760-0*) Jones & Bartlett.

*__Looking at Minibeasts, 4 vols.__ Incl. Butterflies & Moths. (Illus.). 32p. (J). (gr. 1-4). 2000. lib. bdg. (*1-929298-80-3*, Pub. by Thameside Pr); Ladybugs & Beetles. (Illus.). 32p. (J). (gr. 1-4). 2000. lib. bdg. (*1-929298-79-X*, Pub. by Thameside Pr); Slugs & Snails. (Illus.). 32p. (J). (gr. 1-4). 2000. lib. bdg. (*1-929298-81-1*, Pub. by Thameside Pr); Spiders & Centipedes. (Illus.). 32p. (J). (gr. 1-4). 2000. lib. bdg. (*1-929298-82-X*, Pub. by Thameside Pr); (Illus.). (J). (gr. 1-4). 2000. Set lib. bdg. 90.40 (*1-929298-83-8*, Pub. by Thameside Pr) Smart Apple.

L

Looking at Myself & Carrot: A 30-Day Performance. Coco Gordon. (Intimate Ser.: No. 5). (Illus.). 292p. 1987. 410.00 (0-943375-04-5) W Space.
Looking at Myself, Form I Booklet & Answer Folder. CFKR Career Materials Staff. Ed. by Robert Kauk. (Illus.). 20p. (J). (gr. 2-5). 1998. reprint ed. pap. 4.20 (0-934783-55-1) CFKR Career.
*****Looking at Myself, Form II.** Bob Kauk. (Illus.). 16p. (YA). (gr. 7). 1999. pap. 4.20 (0-934783-56-X) CFKR Career.
*****Looking at Nature.** Brigitte Baumbusch. Tr. by Erika Paoli from ITA. LC 99-29621. (Art for Children Ser.). (Illus.). 29p. (J). (ps-3). 1999. 9.95 (1-55670-971-4) STC Pubns.
Looking at Nature: A Fact Finder Book. Robin Robbins. (Illus.). 48p. (J). (gr. 7-9). 1992. pap. 8.95 (0-563-34499-7, BBC-Parkwest) Parkwest Pubns.
Looking at Old Prints. John Booth. 195p. (C). 1989. pap. text 65.00 (0-906853-06-0, Pub. by Cambdge Hse Bks) St Mut.
Looking at Our Lives: Picture Dictionary. Karen Carlisi & Robin Stevens. (Illus.). 72p. (J). (gr. k-9). 1996. pap. 12.95 incl. audio (0-9649379-0-5) EECI.
Looking at Our Lives Picture Dictionary. Karen Carlisi & Robin Stevens. (Illus.). (Orig.). (J). (gr. 4-6). 1997. pap. text, teacher ed. 19.95 (0-9649379-2-1); pap. text, wbk. ed. 9.95 (0-9649379-1-3); audio 16.95 (0-614-24873-6) EECI.
Looking at Paintings: A Guide to Technical Terms. Dawson Carr & Mark Leonard. LC 91-24329. (Looking at . . . Ser.). 84p. 1992. pap. 12.95 (0-89236-213-8) OUP.
Looking at Patronage: Recent Acquisitions of Asian Art. Asian Art Museum Curatorial Staff. LC 89-80817. (Illus.). 112p. (Orig.). 1989. pap. 19.95 (0-939117-03-7) Asian Art Mus.
Looking at Penguins. Dorothy H. Patent. LC 92-37673. (Illus.). 40p. (J). (gr. k-3). 1993. lib. bdg. 16.95 (0-8234-1037-4) Holiday.
Looking at Philosophy: The Unbearable Heaviness of Philosophy Made Lighter. 2nd ed. Donald Palmer. LC 93-4006. (Illus.). 412p. (C). 1994. pap. 21.95 (1-55934-230-7, 1230) Mayfield Pub.
Looking at Photographs: A Guide to Technical Terms. Gordon Baldwin. LC 90-28861. (Looking at...Ser.). (Illus.). 97p. 1991. pap. 12.95 (0-89236-192-1, Pub. by J P Getty Trust) OUP.
Looking at Photographs: 100 Pictures from the Collection of the Museum of Modern Art. John Szarkowski. LC 72-82885. (Illus.). 216p. 1976. pap. 32.50 (0-87070-514-8, 0-8109-6044-3, Pub. by Mus of Modern Art) Little.
Looking at Photographs: 100 Pictures from the Collection of the Museum of Modern Art. John Szarkowski & Museum of Modern Art Staff. (Illus.). 216p. 1999. pap. 37.50 (0-8212-2623-1, Pub. by Bulfinch Pr) Little.
Looking at Picture Books. John W. Stewig. (Illus.). 256p. 1995. text 39.00 (0-917846-29-X, 95575) Highsmith Pr.
Looking at Pictures see How to Look at Art
Looking at Pictures. Susan Woodford. LC 82-14613. (Cambridge Introduction to Art Ser.). (Illus.). 128p. 1983. pap. text 16.95 (0-521-28647-6) Cambridge U Pr.
Looking at Pictures: An Introduction to Art for Young People. Joy Richardson. LC 96-86476. (Illus.). 80p. 1997. 17.95 (0-8109-4252-6, Pub. by Abrams) Time Warner.
Looking at Plants. David Suzuki. LC 91-37451. (Illus.). 96p. (J). 1992. 29.95 (0-471-54748-4); pap. 9.95 (0-471-54049-8) Wiley.
Looking at Prints, Drawings & Watercolours: A Guide to Technical Terms. Paul Goldman. LC 88-13241. (Looking at...Ser.). (Illus.). 64p. 1989. pap. 12.95 (0-89236-148-4, Pub. by J P Getty Trust) OUP.
Looking at Schools: Instruments & Processes for School Analysis. Janet McGrail et al. 140p. 1991. reprint ed. pap. 23.95 (1-56602-038-7) Research Better.
Looking at Senses. David Suzuki & Barbara Hehner. LC 91-10772. (Illus.). 96p. (J). 1991. 24.95 (0-471-54751-4); pap. 9.95 (0-471-54048-X) Wiley.
Looking at Seventeenth-Century Dutch Art: Realism Reconsidered. Ed. by Wayne Franits. LC 96-36607. (Illus.). 296p. (C). 1998. pap. text 24.95 (0-521-49945-3) Cambridge U Pr.
Looking at Space. (Jump Ser.). 36p. (J). (gr. 2-7). pap. write for info. (1-882210-20-4) Action Pub.
Looking at Space. David Glover. (Launch Pad Library). (Illus.). 32p. (J). (gr. k-4). 1997. 11.95 (1-58087-000-7) C D Stampley Ent.
Looking At Space: First-Grade Friends. Grace Maccarone. LC 95-36016. (Hello Reader! Ser.). (Illus.). 32p. (J). (ps-3). 1996. pap. 3.50 (0-590-73878-X, Cartwheel) Scholastic Inc.
Looking at the Body. David Suzuki. LC 91-9720. (Illus.). 96p. (J). 1991. 24.95 (0-471-54752-2); pap. 9.95 (0-471-54052-8) Wiley.
Looking at the Comedia in the Year of the Quincentennial: Proceedings of the 1992 Symposium on Golden Age Drama at the University of Texas, El Paso, March 18-21. Ed. by Barbara Mujica et al. LC 93-2619. (ENG & SPA.). 1993. 62.50 (0-8191-9249-X); pap. 34.50 (0-8191-9357-7) U Pr of Amer.
Looking at the Environment. David Suzuki. (Illus.). 96p. (J). 1992. 29.95 (0-471-54749-2); pap. 9.95 (0-471-54051-X) Wiley.
Looking at the Episcopal Church. William Sydnor. LC 80-81103. 152p. 1990. reprint ed. pap. 10.95 (0-8192-1279-2) Morehouse Pub.
Looking at the Land of Promise: Pioneer Images of the Pacific Northwest. William H. Goetzmann. LC 87-37174. (Illus.). 122p. 1988. 26.25 (0-87422-025-4); pap. 15.00 (0-87422-024-6) Wash St U Pr.
Looking at the Liturgy: A Critical View of It's Contemporary Reform. Aidan Nichols. LC 96-83645. 128p. 1996. pap. text 9.95 (0-89870-592-4) Ignatius Pr.
Looking at the Moon. Kit Pearson. 224p. (J). (gr. 5 up). 1996. pap. 3.99 (0-14-034852-2, PuffinBks) Peng Put Young Read.
Looking at the Moon. Kit Pearson. (J). 1996. 9.09 (0-606-08562-9, Pub. by Turtleback) Demco.
Looking at the Overlooked: Four Essays on Still-Life Painting. Norman Bryson. (Illus.). 192p. 1990. 32.50 (0-674-53905-2) HUP.
Looking at the Overlooked: Four Essays on Still-Life Painting. Norman Bryson. 192p. (C). 1991. pap. text 22.50 (0-674-53906-0) HUP.
Looking at the Personal Diaries of William F. Dusenberry. Carrie Eldridge. (Illus.). 213p. 1992. reprint ed. spiral bd. 30.00i (1-928979-12-2) C Eldridge.
Looking at the Planets: A Book about the Solar System. Melvin Berger. (Illus.). 32p. (J). (gr. 1-3). 1995. pap. 5.95 (0-590-20300-2) Scholastic Inc.
Looking at the Planets: A Book about the Solar System. Melvin Berger. 1995. 11.15 (0-606-07804-5, Pub. by Turtleback) Demco.
Looking at the Sun. James M. Fallows. 1995. pap. 15.00 (0-679-76162-4) Random.
Looking at the Wolf: Biology, Behavior, Biases. Bruce Thompson. 12p. 1987. pap. 3.95 (0-911797-36-X) Roberts Rinehart.
Looking at the Words of Our People: An Anthology of First Nation Literary Criticism. Ed. by Jeannette C. Armstrong. 216p. 1993. pap. 10.95 (0-919441-52-1, Pub. by Theytus Bks) Orca Bk Pubs.
Looking at Things: Poems for Children. Doris Scheff. (Illus.). 47p. (J). (gr. 1-4). 1997. pap. write for info. (1-86106-596-5, Pub. by Minerva Pr) Unity Dist.
Looking at Totem Poles. Hilary Stewart. LC 93-14724. (Illus.). 192p. (C). 1993. reprint ed. pap. 15.95 (0-295-97259-9) U of Wash Pr.
Looking at Type. 3rd ed. Earle C. Page. LC 83-2028. (Illus.). 40p. 1997. pap. 5.75 (0-935652-09-4) Ctr Applications Psych.
Looking at Type: The Fundamentals. Charles R. Martin. 68p. 1997. pap. 7.00 (0-935652-31-0) Ctr Applications Psych.
Looking at Type & Learning Styles. Gordon D. Lawrence. 72p. 1997. pap. 7.00 (0-935652-33-7) Ctr Applications Psych.
Looking at Type & Spirituality. Sandra K. Hirsh & Jane A. Kise. 72p. 1997. pap. 7.00 (0-935652-30-2) Ctr Applications Psych.
Looking at Type in the Workplace. Larry Demarest. 68p. 1997. pap. 7.00 (0-935652-32-9) Ctr Applications Psych.
Looking at Weather. David Suzuki. LC 91-9258. (Illus.). 96p. (J). 1991. 24.95 (0-471-54753-0); pap. 9.95 (0-471-54047-1) Wiley.
Looking at Work, 4 vols. Stuart B. Schwartz. (J). 1998. 76.00 (0-516-29736-8) Childrens.
Looking at Work. Stuart Schwartz & Craig Conley. (Illus.). 32p. 21.26 (0-7368-0305-X) Capstone Pr.
Looking Awry: An Introduction to Jacques Lacan Through Popular Culture. Slavoj Zizek. (October Bks.). (Illus.). 200p. 1991. 35.00 (0-262-24031-9) MIT Pr.
Looking Awry: An Introduction to Jacques Lacan Through Popular Culture. Slavoj Zizek. (Illus.). 200p. 1992. reprint ed. pap. text 17.50 (0-262-74015-X) MIT Pr.
Looking Back. Fleur Adcock. 80p. 1998. pap. 13.95 (0-19-288068-3) OUP.
Looking Back. Jessie L. Alexander & Phil Hill. (Illus.). 160p. 1982. 24.95 (0-686-45748-X) At Speed Pr.
Looking Back. Pamela M. Green. (Illus.). 160p. 2000. pap. write for info. (1-929219-01-6) Image Ink.
Looking Back. Bess Burrows Rivett. (Illus.). 96p. pap. (0-9698752-8-2) Sh1oreline.
Looking Back. Norman Douglas. 1988. reprint ed. lib. bdg. 59.00 (0-7812-0058-X) Rprt Serv.
Looking Back. Norman Douglas. LC 70-144981. 1971. reprint ed. 69.00 (0-403-00795-X) Scholarly.
Looking Back: A Book of Memories. Lois Lowry. LC 98-11376. (Illus.). 192p. (YA). (gr. 5 up). 1998. 16.00 (0-395-89543-X) HM.
*****Looking Back: A Book of Memories.** Lois Lowry. (Illus.). (J). 2000. 18.30 (0-606-18106-7) Turtleback.
Looking Back: A Photographic History of New Zealand. Keith Sinclair & Wendy Harrex. (Illus.). 1979. text 39.95 (0-19-558036-2) OUP.
Looking Back: A Pictorial History of the Flathead Valley, Montana. Kathryn L. Mckay & Northwest Montana Historical Society Staff. LC 97-34848. 1997. write for info. (1-57864-019-9) Donning Co.
Looking Back: A Pictorial Look at the Lehigh Valley, 1850 to 1920. Ed. by Morning Call Staff. LC 98-66246. (Illus.). 152p. 1998. 24.95 (0-9664197-0-7) Morning Call.
Looking Back: A Reader on the Histories of Deaf Communities & Their Sign Languages. Ed. by Renate Fischer & Harlan Lane. 540p. (C). 1993. text 59.95 (3-927731-32-3, Pub. by Signum-Verlag) Gallaudet Univ Pr.
Looking Back: An Illustrated History of the American Ophthalmic Industry. Joseph L. Bruneni. LC 94-68862. (Illus.). 232p. (C). 1994. 68.00 (1-886308-00-4) Optical Lab.
Looking Back: An Immigrant in the New World. Marie Jastrow. 1986. 15.95 (0-393-02348-6) Norton.
Looking Back: Art in Savannah, 1900-1960. Harry H. DeLorme, Jr. & Pamela D. King. LC 96-61004. (Illus.). 120p. (Orig.). 1996. pap. 25.00 (0-933075-02-2) Telfair Mus.
Looking Back: Autobiography of Mehr Chand Mahajan. Ed. by Mehr C. Mahajan. (C). 1994. 28.00 (81-241-0194-9, Pub. by Har-Anand Pubns) S Asia.
Looking Back Childhood Extracts from Autobiographies. John Foster. LC 75-322130. 140 p. 1973. write for info. (0-7131-1812-1, Pub. by E A) Routldge.
Looking Back: Memoirs. Lou Andreas-Salome. (Illus.). 226p. 1995. pap. 12.95 (1-56924-848-6) Marlowe & Co.
Looking Back: Reminiscent Party Fun for Senior Citizens. Marge Knoth. (Illus.). 110p. (Orig.). 1996. per. 11.99 (0-927935-01-5) Valley Pr IN.
Looking Back: Tales of Olds Antioch & Other Places. Earl J. Hohlmayer. (Illus.). 240p. Date not set. pap. 19.95 (0-9651251-1-4) E & N Hohlmayer.
Looking Back: The Final Tale of Life on the Prairie. Linda K. Hubalek. LC 94-74378. (Butter in the Well Ser.: Bk. 4). (Illus.). 140p. (gr. 4-12). 1995. reprint ed. pap. 9.95 (1-886652-03-1) Butterfld Bks.
Looking Back: 32 People Facing Death Teach Us How to Live. Michael Shima. LC 95-90563. 208p. (Orig.). 1996. pap. 11.95 (0-9646749-2-0) Wyeth Hall Pr.
Looking Back No. II: Tales of Old East Contra Costa County. Earl S. Hohlmayer. (Illus.). 240p. (Orig.). 1996. pap. 19.95 (0-9651251-0-6) E & N Hohlmayer.
Looking Back . . . Moving Forward. Darrell Pugh. 140p. 1988. 27.95 (0-936678-10-0); pap. 17.95 (0-685-25268-X) Am Soc Pub Admin.
Looking Back - Moving Forward: History of the Billings YWCA, 1907-1988. Margaret Ping. Ed. by Rachel Schaffer. (Orig.). 1991. pap. write for info. (0-9629912-0-1) M Ping.
Looking Back a Moment . . . And Other Poems. Richard A. Booth. (Illus.). 84p. 1995. pap., per. 9.95 (1-885813-03-1) B & B Pubng.
Looking Back & Thinking Forward: Reexaminations of Teaching & Schooling. Lillian Weber & Beth Alberty. LC 97-20829. 1997. 40.00 (0-8077-3674-0); pap. 18.95 (0-8077-3673-2) Tchrs Coll.
Looking Back & Writing Forward: A Unique Approach to Lifewriting. Louise M. Cabral. Orig. Title: Islands of Recall: Write Your Life Story with Guided Imagery. 1998. pap. write for info. (1-891968-01-7) Knowop Inc.
*****Looking Back at Francis Bacon.** David Sylvester. LC 99-69757. (Illus.). 272p. 2000. 50.00 (0-500-01994-0, Pub. by Thames Hudson) Norton.
Looking Back... At Live Television & Other Matters. Delbert Mann. Ed. by Ira Skutch. LC 98-74095. (Illus.). 383p. 1999. 44.95 (1-882766-05-9); pap. 32.95 (1-882766-06-7) Dirs Guild Am.
Looking Back at My Own Career. Rishikesh Shaha. LC 98-904651. viii, 47 p. 1997. write for info. (81-7303-071-5, Pub. by Book Faith) S Asia.
Looking Back at Tennessee: A Photographic Retrospective. Wayne C. Moore & Mark Herbison. LC 96-78410. (Illus.). 224p. 1996. 29.95 (1-57736-014-1, Hillsboro Pr) Providence Hse.
*****Looking Back at the June 1967 War.** Ed. by Haim Gordon. LC 98-37154. 224p. 1999. 59.95 (0-275-96170-2, Praeger Pubs) Greenwood.
Looking Back at Washington, LA: The Memoirs of David Jasper McNicoll. Paul L. Lastrapes. LC 96-79501. (Illus.). xiv, 176p. 1997. reprint ed. 21.95 (0-9660421-0-7); reprint ed. pap. 11.95 (0-9660421-1-5) P L Lastrapes.
Looking Back from the Nineties: An Autobiography. Cicely McCall. LC 95-128656. viii, 127 p. 1994. write for info. (0-947893-32-6) Gliddon Bks.
Looking Back in Anger. Hernando J. Abaya. xv, 346p. (Orig.). (C). 1992. pap. 15.75 (971-10-0477-1, Pub. by New Day Pub) Cellar.
Looking Back in Post Cards. J. H. Johnston, III. (Illus.). 104p. 1991. 35.00 (0-9621374-1-3) J H Johnston.
Looking Back in Wonder: Diary of a Dance Critic. Walter Sorell. (Illus.). 298p. 1986. text 57.50 (0-231-06278-8) Col U Pr.
Looking Back into the Future. Robert S. Kreider. LC 99-163003. (Cornelius H. Wedel Historical Ser.: Vol. 11). (Illus.). 325p. 1998. pap. 25.00 (1-889239-00-3) Bethel Coll.
Looking Back, Looking Forward: An Adoptive Father's Sociological Testament. H. David Kirk. 32p. 1995. 5.00 (0-944934-14-5) Perspect Indiana.
*****Looking Back, Moving Forward.** Marita Littauer. LC 99-6613. 2000. pap. text 10.99 (0-7642-2275-9) Bethany Hse.
Looking Back, Moving Forward: A Guidebook for Communities Responding to Sexual Assault. 250p. (Orig.). (C). 1995. pap. text 55.00 (0-7881-1874-9) DIANE Pub.
Looking Back, Moving On. Sharon A. Jaeger. (Illus.). 48p. (Orig.). 1996. pap. 15.00 (0-912767-13-8) Intertxt AK.
*****Looking Back, Moving on: Memoir as Prologue.** Janice Rubin. 191p. 2000. pap. write for info. (1-889534-44-7) Jay St Pubs.
Looking Back on India. Hubert Evans. 286p. 1988. 32.00 (0-7146-3327-5, Pub. by F Cass Pubs) Intl Spec Bk.
Looking Back on Progress. Northbourne. 1996. pap. 17.95 (0-614-21232-4, 735) Kazi Pubns.
Looking Back on Progress. 2nd ed. Northbourne. Ed. & Frwd. by James R. Wetmore. (Perennial Wisdom Ser.). 122p. 1995. reprint ed. pap. text 16.95 (0-900588-03-9) S Perennis.
Looking Back on the End of the World. Ed. by Deitmar Kamper & Christoph Wulf. 119p. Date not set. 7.00 (0-936756-46-2) Autonomedia.
Looking Back on the Future: Building a Quality Foundation. Joseph T. Black. 192p. 1993. 16.95 (0-9628474-3-7) Life Vision Bks.
Looking Back on the Vietnam War: A 1990s Perspective on the Decisions, Combat, & Legacies. Ed. by William Head & Lawrence E. Grinter. LC 92-39177. (Contributions in Military Studies Ser.: No. 142). 288p. 1993. pap. 24.95 (0-275-94555-3, B4555) Greenwood.
Looking Back on the Vietnam War: A 1990s Perspective on the Decisions, Combat, & Legacies, 142. Ed. by William Head & Lawrence E. Grinter. LC 92-39154. (Contributions in Military Studies Ser.: No. 142). 288p. 1993. 69.50 (0-313-28869-0, GM8869) Greenwood.
Looking Back Reaching Forward. Charles Villa-Vicencio. pap. 25.00 (1-85649-820-4, Pub. by Zed Books); text 65.00 (1-85649-819-0, Pub. by Zed Books) St Martin.
Looking Back, Thinking Ahead: American School Reform, 1993-1995. Educational Excellence Network Staff & Education Policy Committee. 1994. 3.50 (0-614-17717-0) Hudson Instit IN.
Looking Back to See Ahead. Helen H. Perlman. LC 89-31900. 244p. 1989. pap. text 15.95 (0-226-66038-9); lib. bdg. 47.00 (0-226-66037-0) U Ch Pr.
Looking Back West. Elmer Kelton. LC 72-82123. 120p. 1992. reprint ed. 19.95 (0-9635599-0-7) Talley Pr.
Looking Back While Surging Forward. Lenore P. Job. (Orig.). 1984. pap. 12.95 (0-916645-01-0) Peters Wright.
*****Looking Back with Papaw's Little Gentleman.** Carroll B. McGarity. (Illus.). vi, 235p. 2000. 24.95 (0-615-11826-7) Look Back Pub.
Looking Backward. Edward Bellamy. Ed. by Frederic R. White. (University Classics Ser.). Orig. Title: Looking Backward, 2000-1887. 272p. 1979. pap. 12.95 (0-87532-107-0) Hendricks House.
Looking Backward. Edward Bellamy. Ed. & Intro. by Cecelia Tichi. (American Library). Orig. Title: Looking Backward, 2000-1887. 240p. 2000. pap. 11.95 (0-14-039018-9) Viking Penguin.
Looking Backward. Edward Bellamy. Orig. Title: Looking Backward, 2000-1887. 318p. reprint ed. lib. bdg. 24.95 (0-89190-238-4, Rivercity Pr) Amereon Ltd.
Looking Backward. unabridged ed. Edward Bellamy. LC 95-49596. (Thrift Editions Ser.). Orig. Title: Looking Backward, 2000-1887. 160p. 1996. reprint ed. pap. text 2.00 (0-486-29038-7) Dover.
Looking Backward: A Critical Appraisal of Communitarian Thought. Derek L. Phillips. 258p. (C). 1993. pap. text 17.95 (0-691-04484-8, Pub. by Princeton U Pr) Cal Prin Full Svc.
Looking Backward: A Critical Appraisal of Communitarian Thought. Derek L. Phillips. LC 92-36381. 280p. (C). 1993. text 42.50 (0-691-07425-9, Pub. by Princeton U Pr) Cal Prin Full Svc.
*****Looking Backward: From 2000 to 1887.** Edward Bellamy. 220p. 2000. pap. 14.95 (1-55709-506-X) Applewood.
Looking Backward & What I Saw. 2nd ed. W. W. Satterlee. LC 76-154461. (Utopian Literature Ser.). 1971. reprint ed. 25.95 (0-405-03543-8) Ayer.
Looking Backward at Us. William Raspberry. LC 91-21565. 1991. 20.00 (0-87805-535-5) U Pr of Miss.
Looking Backward, 1988-1888: Essays on Edward Bellamy. Ed. by Daphne Patai. LC 88-10621. 240p. (Orig.). (C). 1988. pap. 16.95 (0-87023-634-2); lib. bdg. 35.00 (0-87023-633-4) U of Mass Pr.
Looking Backward to Sweden: A Genealogical Research Book, & the Lind-Bure Family, 1000-1986. Marilyn Lind & Carl S. Lind. LC 86-81744. (Illus.). 154p. (Orig.). 1986. pap. text 14.50 (0-937463-11-6) Linden Tree.
*****Looking Backward, 2000-1887.** Edward Bellamy. 2000. pap. 10.95 (1-892295-59-8) Green Integer.
Looking Backward, 2000-1887. Edward Bellamy. 247p. (C). 1981. pap. 5.00 (0-07-554374-5) McGraw.
*****Looking Backward, 2000-1887.** Edward Bellamy. 2000. mass mkt. 5.95 (0-451-52763-1, Sig) NAL.
Looking Backward, 2000-1887. Edward Bellamy. (Modern Library College Editions). 275p. (C). 1982. pap. text 3.75 (0-685-04266-9) Random.
Looking Backward, 2000-1887. Edward Bellamy. Ed. by Daniel H. Borus. (Bedford Series in History & Culture). 214p. 1995. text 45.00 (0-312-12244-6) St Martin.
Looking Backward, 2000-1887. Intro. by Jackson Wilson. 1981. pap. 4.00 (0-685-03398-8, T42) Random.
Looking Backward, 2000-1887. Edward Bellamy. 1990. reprint ed. lib. bdg. 25.95 (0-89968-477-7) Buccaneer Bks.
Looking Backward, 2000-1887 see Looking Backward
Looking Before We Leap: Social Science & Welfare Reform. Ed. by R. Kent Weaver & William T. Dickens. 152p. 1995. pap. 16.95 (0-8157-9261-1) Brookings.
Looking Beneath the Surface: Through the Eyes of Faith. LaVerne Thomas. (Illus.). 42p. (Orig.). 1996. pap. 7.00 (1-57502-349-0, PO1146) Morris Pubng.
Looking Beyond. Ludwig A. Geissler. LC 77-154442. (Utopian Literature Ser.). 1976. reprint ed. 18.95 (0-405-03525-X) Ayer.
*****Looking Beyond Credit.** Jonathan Dawson & Andy Jeans. 56p. 1998. pap. 25.00 (1-85339-423-8, Pub. by Intermed Tech) Stylus Pub VA.
*****Looking Beyond Race: The Life of Otis Milton Smith.** Otis Milton Smith & Mary M. Stolberg. LC 00-38184. (Illus.). 248p. 2000. 24.95 (0-8143-2939-X, Great Lks Bks) Wayne St U Pr.
Looking Beyond the Ivy League: Finding the College That's Right for You. Loren Pope. LC 95-12252. 1995. pap. 12.95 (0-14-023952-9, Penguin Bks) Viking Penguin.
Looking Black. La Bo. 31p. (Orig.). 1993. pap. 5.95 (1-56411-123-7) Untd Bros & Sis.
Looking Black. LaBo. 31p. (Orig.). 1993. pap. text 3.95 (1-56411-055-9) Untd Bros & Sis.
Looking Both Ways: Poems. Jane O. Wayne. LC 84-2201. (Breakthrough Ser.: No. 45). 72p. 1984. pap. 12.95 (0-8262-0454-6) U of Mo Pr.
Looking Closely: Exploring the Role of Phonics in One Whole Language Classroom. Heidi Mills et al. (Illus.). 69p. (Orig.). 1992. pap. 11.95 (0-8141-3031-3) NCTE.
Looking Closer: Critical Writings on Graphic Design. Ed. by Michael Bierut et al. LC 93-71922. 256p. (Orig.). 1994. pap. 18.95 (1-880559-15-3) Allworth Pr.

An Asterisk (*) at the beginning of an entry indicates that the title is appearing for the first time.

Looking Closer No. 2: Critical Writings on Graphic Design. 2nd ed. Ed. by Michael Bierut et al. LC 93-83003. 256p. (Orig.). 1997. pap. 18.95 (*1-880559-56-0*) Allworth Pr.

Looking Closer Vol. 3: Classic Writings on Graphic Design. Ed. by Michael Bierut et al. LC 98-74536. 304p. 1999. pap. 18.95 (*1-58115-022-9*) Allworth Pr.

Looking Critically: 21 Years of Artforum Magazine. Ed. by Amy B. Sandback. LC 83-24345. (Illus.). 352p. reprint ed. pap. 109.20 (*0-8357-1536-1*, 207059000004) Bks Demand.

Looking Deep in the Southern Sky: Proceedings of the ESO/Australia Workshop Held at Sydney, Australia, 10-12 December, 1997. 2nd ed. Ed. by Rafaella O. Morganti & Warrick J. Couch. LC 98-32280. (ESO Astrophysics Symposia Ser.). (Illus.). xxi, 336p. 1999. 49.95 (*3-540-65286-8*) Spr-Verlag.

Looking Deeper: A Swan's Questions & Answers. Klong-chen Rab-byams Pa. Tr. by Herbert V. Guenther from TIB. LC 84-179. (Illus.). 64p. 1984. pap. 4.00 (*0-931454-09-3*) Timeless Bks.

Looking Deeply. Thich Nhat Hahn. 1987. 15.00 incl. audio (*0-938077-09-0*) Parallax Pr.

Looking Down. Margie Burton et al. Ed. by Susan Evento. (Early Connections Ser.). 16p. (J). (gr. k-2). 1998. pap. 4.25 (*1-892393-54-9*) Benchmark Educ.

Looking Down. Steve Jenkins. LC 94-38720. (Illus.). 32p. (J). (ps-2). 1995. 14.95 (*0-395-72665-4*) Ticknor & Flds Bks Yng Read.

Looking down Dark Holes & Climbing Mountains. Thomas Weinberg. (Illus.). 150p. (Orig.). (C). 1979. pap. 6.95 (*0-9603484-0-9*) T Weinberg.

Looking down from the Mountain Top: The Story of One Woman's Fight Against All Odds. Christine Michael. Ed. by Mary Plaut. LC 91-62562. (Illus.). 300p. 1992. pap. 24.95 (*0-9630571-0-3*) Spirit of Success.

*__Looking down on Human Intelligence.__ Ian J. Deary. (Oxford Psychology Ser.). (Illus.). 384p. 2000. text 85.00 (*0-19-852417-X*) OUP.

*__Looking Down the Road: A Systems Approach to Futures Studies.__ Douglas Raybeck. 131p. (C). 2000. pap. 10.95 (*1-57766-116-8*) Waveland Pr.

Looking East Leftwards, Vol. 2. David Mandel. (Former "State Socialist" World Ser.). 250p. 1997. 53.99 (*1-55164-099-6*, Pub. by Black Rose); pap. text 24.99 (*1-55164-098-8*, Pub. by Black Rose) Consort Bk Sales.

Looking for a Bluebird. Joseph Wechsberg. LC 73-16801. (Illus.). 210p. 1974. reprint ed. lib. bdg. 69.50 (*0-8371-7234-9*, WELO, Greenwood Pr) Greenwood.

Looking for a Bluebird: Music Book Index. Joseph Wechsberg. 210p. 1993. reprint ed. lib. bdg. 79.00 (*0-7812-9630-7*) Rprt Serv.

*__Looking for a Book.__ large type ed. Judy Mullican. (BB Ser.). (Illus.). 8p. (J). (ps-1). 2000. pap. text 10.95 (*1-57332-165-6*); pap. text 10.95 (*1-57332-166-4*) HighReach Lrning.

Looking for a City in America: Down These Mean Streets a Man Must Go . . . Andre Corboz. LC 91-14796. (Illus.). 96p. 1992. pap. 10.95 (*0-89236-211-1*, Getty Res Inst) J P Getty Trust.

Looking for a City in America: Down These Mean Streets a Man Must Go. Andre Corboz. (Illus.). 128p. 1992. pap. 17.95 (*0-87923-935-2*) Godine.

*__Looking For A Fight.__ Lynn Snowden Picket. 2000. 23.95 (*0-385-31584-8*, Dial Pr) Dell.

Looking for a Hero. Patti Berg. 384p. 1998. mass mkt. 5.99 (*0-380-79555-8*, Avon Bks) Morrow Avon.

Looking for a Miracle: Weeping Icons, Relics, Stigmata, Visions & Healing Cures. Joe Nickell. LC 93-25322. (Illus.). 253p. 1993. 26.95 (*0-87975-840-6*) Prometheus Bks.

Looking for a Miracle: Weeping Icons, Relics, Stigmata, Visions & Healing Cures. Joe Nickell. LC 98-43809. (Illus.). 253p. 1999. pap. 17.95 (*1-57392-680-9*) Prometheus Bks.

Looking for a Ship. John McPhee. 242p. 1990. 18.95 (*0-374-19077-1*) FS&G.

Looking for a Ship. John McPhee. 248p. 1991. pap. 12.00 (*0-374-52319-3*) FS&G.

Looking for a Soft Place to Land. Cin Salach. 64p. (Orig.). 1996. pap. 10.95 (*1-882688-11-2*) Tia Chucha Pr.

Looking for Alibrandi. Melina Marchetta. LC 98-35804. 256p. (YA). (gr. 9 up). 1999. 16.95 (*0-531-30142-7*); lib. bdg. 17.99 (*0-531-33142-3*) Orchard Bks Watts.

Looking for America: Prints of Rural Life from the 1930s & 1940s. Barbara J. MacAdam. LC 94-45118. (Illus.). 1994. 3.00 (*0-944722-18-0*) Hood Mus Art.

Looking for America: Seven Schools Experimenting with Intergroup Relations, Vol. 2. Delia Pompa & Michael Reilly. (Illus.). 116p. (Orig.). 1995. pap. 16.95 (*1-880002-11-6*) Natl Coal Advocates.

Looking for America: The People's History, Vol. 2. 2nd ed. Ed. by Stanley I. Kutler. Vol. 2. (Illus.). 2p. (C). 1980. pap. text 24.50 (*0-393-95013-1*) Norton.

Looking for America Vol. I: Promising School-Based Practices in Intergroup Relations. Lucia Gill et al. Ed. by Delia Pompa. (Illus.). 156p. (Orig.). 1994. pap. 16.95 (*1-880002-06-X*) Natl Coal Advocates.

Looking for America on the New Jersey Turnpike. Angus K. Gillespie. (C). 1993. pap. 12.95 (*0-8135-1955-1*) Rutgers U Pr.

Looking for America on the New Jersey Turnpike. Angus K. Gillespie & Michael A. Rockland. LC 89-6085. (Illus.). 288p. 1989. 24.95 (*0-8135-1466-5*) Rutgers U Pr.

Looking for an Opportunity see Buscando una Oportunidad

Looking for Angels. Valiska Gregory. LC 94-34341. (Illus.). 32p. (J). (ps-3). 1996. per. 17.00 (*0-689-80500-4*) S&S Bks Yung.

Looking for Angels: A Search for Truth about Heavenly Messengers. Steven P. Osborne. 126p. (Orig.). 1996. pap. 9.95 (*1-878423-23-1*) Morson Pub.

Looking for Angels & Answers. Howard S. Leavitt. LC 94-38175. 1995. pap. 12.95 (*1-883911-04-4*) Brandylane.

Looking for Angels in New York. Jacqueline Osherow. LC 88-4797. (Contemporary Poetry Ser.). 72p. 1988. 14.95 (*0-8203-1059-X*) U of Ga Pr.

Looking for Arthur: A Once & Future Travelogue. Richard Leviton. LC 96-48775. 600p. 1995. pap. text 16.95 (*1-886449-13-9*) Barrytown Ltd.

Looking for Atlanta. Marilyn D. Staats. LC 92-6016. 240p. 1992. 19.95 (*0-8203-1470-6*) U of Ga Pr.

Looking for Atlanta. Marilyn D. Staats. 240p. 1993. mass mkt. 5.99 (*0-446-36574-2*) Warner Bks.

Looking for Atlanta: A Novel. Marilyn Dorn Staats. 232p. 1999. pap. 12.95 (*0-8203-2120-6*) U of Ga Pr.

Looking for Atlantis. Colin Thompson. (J). 1997. pap. 6.99 (*0-679-88547-1*) Knopf.

Looking for Atlantis. Colin Thompson. (J). 1997. 12.19 (*0-606-11575-7*, Pub. by Turtleback) Demco.

Looking for Atlantis. Colin Thompson. (J). (gr. 1 up). 1997. reprint ed. pap. 6.99 (*0-614-28953-X*) Random Bks Yng Read.

*__Looking for Bears.__ Ann Mace. (Books for Young Learners). (Illus.). 12p. (J). (gr. k-2). 1999. pap. text 5.00 (*1-57274-268-2*, A2468) R Owen Pubs.

*__Looking for Bernie.__ Richard R. Karlen. LC 99-95282. 408p. 1999. 15.00 (*0-9660831-1-3*) IronBound Pr.

Looking for Binoculars. Robin Magowan. 50p. 1976. pap. 10.00 (*0-87711-062-X*) Story Line.

Looking for Birds & Other Wild Life. Nell Hutchinson. 1998. pap. 8.95 (*0-533-12600-2*) Vantage.

Looking For Brothers: Essays. Michael Rowe. 196p. 1999. pap. text 15.00 (*0-88962-671-5*) Mosaic.

Looking for Buddha in the Barbed-Wire Garden. Janet McCann. 62p. 1996. pap. 10.00 (*1-888105-08-9*) Avisson Pr.

*__Looking for Carroll Beckwith: The True Story of a Detective's Search for His Past Life.__ Robert L. Snow. LC 99-37795. 240p. 1999. 19.95 (*1-57954-101-1*, Daybrk) Rodale Pr Inc.

*__Looking for Chengdu: A Woman's Adventures in China.__ Hill Gates. LC 99-28430. 1999. 42.50 (*0-8014-3646-X*); pap. 16.95 (*0-8014-8632-7*) Cornell U Pr.

Looking for Cinderella. Charlotte Dematons. Tr. & Adapted by Leigh Sauerwein. LC 96-11515. (Illus.). 40p. (J). 1996. 15.95 (*1-886910-13-8*) Front Str.

Looking for Clark Gable & Other 20th-Century Pursuits: Collected Writings. Virginia V. Hamilton. LC 95-44926. (Illus.). 224p. (Orig.). 1996. pap. 21.95 (*0-8173-0834-2*) U of Ala Pr.

Looking for Crabs. Bruce Whatley. (Illus.). 81p. (J). (ps-1). 1999. pap. 7.00 (*0-207-17771-6*, Pub. by HarpC) Consort Bk Sales.

Looking for Data in All the Right Places: A Guidebook for Conducting Original Research with Young Investigators. Alane J. Starto & Gina D. Schack. 142p. (Orig.). 1991. pap. 19.95 (*0-936386-60-6*) Creative Learning.

Looking for De Soto: A Search Through the South for the Spaniard's Trail. Joyce R. Hudson. LC 92-17252. (Illus.). 248p. 1993. 29.95 (*0-8203-1497-8*) U of Ga Pr.

Looking for Dilmun. Geoffrey Bibby. (Illus.). 286p. 1997. 39.95 (*0-905743-90-3*, Pub. by Stacey Intl) Intl Bk Ctr.

Looking for Divine Transportation: Poetry by Karren Lalonde Alenier. Karren Lalonde Alenier. Ed. by Grace Cavalieri. 75p. (Orig.). 1999. pap. 10.00 (*0-938572-24-5*, Pub. by Bunny Crocodile) WrdWrks Pub.

Looking for Dr. Condom. William E. Kruck. (Publications of the American Dialect Society: No. 66). vii, 112p. (Orig.). 1981. pap. text 11.20 (*0-8173-0067-8*) U of Ala Pr.

Looking for Earths: The Race to Find New Solar Systems. Alan Boss. LC 97-49033. 256p. 1998. 27.95 (*0-471-18421-7*) Wiley.

*__Looking for Earths: The Race to Find New Solar Systems.__ Alan Boss. 256p. 2000. pap. 16.95 (*0-471-37911-5*) Wiley.

Looking for Employment in the United States. Luis A. Cardona. 1997. 11.95 (*0-914199-05-6*) Carreta Pr.

*__Looking for Estrellita.__ Brian Castro. 264p. 2000. pap. 19.95 (*0-7022-3115-0*, Pub. by Univ Queensland Pr) Intl Spec Bk.

*__Looking for Estrillita.__ Brian Castro. 1999. pap. 24.95 (*0-7022-3114-2*, Pub. by Univ Queensland Pr) Intl Spec Bk.

Looking for Eulabee Dix: The Illustrated Biography of an American Miniaturist. Jo A. Ridley. LC 97-29794. (Illus.). 304p. 1998. 45.00 (*0-940979-36-5*) Natl Museum Women.

Looking for Eulabee Dix: The Illustrated Biography of an American Miniaturist (1878-1961) Jo A. Ridley. LC 97-29794. (Illus.). 1997. pap. write for info. (*0-940979-37-3*) Natl Museum Women.

Looking for Farrakhan. Florence H. Levinsohn. LC 97-11335. 320p. 1997. 25.00 (*1-56663-157-2*, Pub. by I R Dee) Natl Bk Netwk.

Looking for Felix. Libby Hathorn. LC 92-34259. (Voyages Ser.). (Illus.). (J). 1993. 4.25 (*0-383-03638-0*) SRA McGraw.

*__Looking for Flavour.__ Barbara Santich. 249p. 2000. pap. 19.95 (*1-86254-395-X*, Pub. by Wakefield Pr) BHB Intl.

*__Looking for Flavour.__ Barbara Santich. (Illus.). 2000. pap. text 19.95 (*1-86254-385-2*) Wakefield Pr.

Looking for Friends in All the Right Places. Edward Ross. Ed. by Jennifer Zahgkuni. LC 98-96489. 264p. (Orig.). 1999. pap. 14.95 (*0-9666695-3-3*) Baxter Pubg.

Looking for Gatsby: My Life. Faye Dunaway & Betsy Sharkey. (Illus.). 416p. 1998. per. 14.00 (*0-671-67526-5*, PB Trade Paper) PB.

Looking for Gatsby: My Life. Faye Dunaway & Betsy Sharkey. LC 95-34651. 480p. 1995. 24.50 (*0-684-80841-2*) Simon & Schuster.

Looking for Genet: Literary Essays & Reviews. Alfred Chester. Ed. by Edward Field. LC 92-11477. 260p. (Orig.). 1992. 25.00 (*0-87685-873-6*); pap. 12.50 (*0-87685-872-8*) Black Sparrow.

Looking for God. Kirkwood. Date not set. pap. text. write for info. (*0-582-20255-8*, Pub. by Addison-Wesley) Longman.

Looking for God: A Complete Guide to the Religious & Spiritual Groups of the World. Steven Sadlier. 224p. 1999. pap. text 12.95 (*0-89529-930-5*, Avery) Penguin Putnam.

*__Looking for God: A Seeker's Guide to Religious & Spiritual Groups of the World.__ Steven Sadleir. 2000. pap. 15.95 (*0-399-52643-9*, Perigee Bks) Berkley Pub.

Looking for God in All the Wrong Places. Mark Finley & Steven R. Mosley. LC 95-46220. 1995. pap. 1.99 (*0-8163-1320-2*) Pacific Pr Pub Assn.

Looking for God in Brazil: The Progressive Catholic Church in Urban Brazil's Religious Arena. John Burdick. LC 92-32556. (C). 1993. 58.00 (*0-520-08000-9*, Pub. by U CA Pr) Cal Prin Full Svc.

Looking for God in Brazil: The Progressive Catholic Church in Urban Brazil's Religious Arena. John Burdick. LC 92-32556. (Illus.). 280p. (C). 1996. pap. 16.95 (*0-520-20503-0*, Pub. by U CA Pr) Cal Prin Full Svc.

Looking for God in the Suburbs: The Religion of the American Dream & Its Critics, 1945-1965. James Hudnut-Beumler. LC 93-41778. 240p. 1994. text 42.00 (*0-8135-2083-5*) Rutgers U Pr.

Looking for God in the Suburbs: The Religion of the American Dream & Its Critics, 1945-1965. James Hudnut-Beumler. LC 93-41778. 240p. (C). 1994. pap. text 18.00 (*0-8135-2084-3*) Rutgers U Pr.

Looking for God in Time & Memory: Psychology, Theology, & Spirituality in Augustine's "Confessions" J. G. Kristo. 154p. (C). 1991. pap. text 21.50 (*0-8191-8192-7*); lib. bdg. 44.00 (*0-8191-8191-9*) U Pr of Amer.

Looking for Gold. Bradford Angier. LC 74-23258. (Illus.). 224p. 1995. pap. 16.95 (*0-8117-2034-9*) Stackpole.

Looking for Gold: A Year in Jungian Analysis. Susan Tiberghien. 208p. 1995. pap. 15.95 (*3-85630-560-2*) Continuum.

*__Looking for Ground: Countertransference, Epistemology & the Problem of Value.__ Peter Carnochan. LC 00-26372. 2000. write for info. (*0-88163-324-0*) Analytic Pr.

Looking for Halloween see Set 1

Looking for Happiness. R. Kirkwood. Date not set. pap. text. write for info. (*0-582-20311-2*, Pub. by Addison-Wesley) Longman.

*__Looking for Harlem: Urban Aesthetics in African-American Literature.__ Maria Balshaw. 192p. 2000. 59.95 (*0-7453-1339-6*, Pub. by Pluto GBR); pap. 19.95 (*0-7453-1334-5*, Pub. by Pluto GBR) Stylus Pub VA.

Looking for History. Hugh Ogden. (Red Hill Ser.). 64p. 1991. pap. 8.95 (*1-879969-00-9*) CRS Outloudbooks.

Looking for Hogeye. Roy Reed. LC 85-28906. 142p. 1986. 16.00 (*0-938626-62-0*) U of Ark Pr.

Looking for Holes. Niko Scharer. (Illus.). 32p. (J). (gr. 1-5). 1995. 13.95 (*1-879085-92-5*, Whispering Coyote) Charlesbridge Pub.

Looking for Home. Jean Ferris. 176p. (YA). 1993. pap. 3.95 (*0-374-44566-4*) FS&G.

Looking for Home. Jean Ferris. (Aerial Fiction Ser.). (J). 1993. 9.05 (*0-606-05913-X*, Pub. by Turtleback) Demco.

Looking for Home: A Phenomenological Study of Home in the Classroom. Carollyne Sinclaire. LC 93-37842. 168p. (C). 1994. pap. text 17.95 (*0-7914-2040-X*) State U NY Pr.

Looking for Home: A Phenomenological Study of Home in the Classroom. Carollyne Sinclaire. LC 93-37842. 168p. (C). 1994. text 53.50 (*0-7914-2039-6*) State U NY Pr.

Looking for Honey. Henry C. Blount. (Illus.). (Orig.). 1984. 5.00 (*0-9614047-0-1*) McArthur Pub.

Looking for Jackie: American Fashion Icons. Ed. by Town & Country Editors. LC 99-29437. 208p. 1999. 50.00 (*0-688-16726-8*, Wm Morrow) Morrow Avon.

Looking for Jamie Bridger. Nancy Springer. LC 94-25484. (J). 1999. pap. 14.89 (*0-8037-1774-1*, Dial Yng Read) Peng Put Young Read.

Looking for Jesus. Virginia Stem Owens. 1997. 16.00 (*0-06-066399-5*) HarpC.

Looking for Jesus. Virginia Stem Owens. LC 98-39671. 240p. 1999. pap. 18.00 (*0-664-25819-0*) Westminster John Knox.

Looking for Jesus. N. T. Wright. 20p. (Orig.). (C). 1995. reprint ed. pap. 2.95 (*1-57383-039-9*) Regent College.

Looking for Josephine: And Other Stories. John Stewart. LC 98-159525. 184p. 1998. pap. 15.95 (*0-920661-71-8*, Pub. by TSAR Pubns) LPC InBook.

Looking for Juliette. Janet T. Lisle. LC 94-6922. 128p. (J). (gr. 3-5). 1994. lib. bdg. 16.99 (*0-531-08720-4*) Orchard Bks Watts.

Looking for Juliette. Janet T. Lisle. LC 94-6922. Vol. 2. 128p. (J). (gr. 4-7). 1994. 15.95 (*0-531-06870-6*) Orchard Bks Watts.

Looking for Juliette. Janet Taylor Lisle. LC 94-6922. (Investigators of the Unknown Ser.). 1996. 9.09 (*0-606-10255-8*, Pub. by Turtleback) Demco.

Looking for La Perouse: D/Entrecasteaux in Australia & the South Pacific 1792-1793. Frank Horner. (Illus.). 384p. (Orig.). 1997. 29.95 (*0-522-84758-7*, Pub. by Melbourne Univ Pr) Paul & Co Pubs.

Looking for Langston. Maria K. Mootry. (Illus.). 45p. 1998. pap. 10.00 (*0-9651768-2-7*) Hunan Pr.

Looking for Leaders: Episodes, Events & Travel. Dick Squires. LC 91-90452. (Illus.). 160p. (Orig.). 1991. per. 7.00 (*0-9624138-2-8*) D Squires.

Looking for Lemont: Place & People in an Illinois Canal Town. Ed. by Michale P. Conzen et al. LC 94-20130. (Studies on the Illinois & Michigan Canal Corridor: No. 7). 1994. 15.00 (*0-89065-142-6*) U Chicago Comm Geo.

Looking for Little Egypt. Donna Carlton. LC 94-79660. (Illus.). 120p. (Orig.). 1995. pap. 14.95 (*0-9623998-1-7*) Intl Dance Discovery.

Looking for Livingstone: An Odyssey of Silence. Marlene Nourbese Philip. 88p. 1995. per. 10.95 (*0-920544-88-6*, Pub. by Mercury Bk) LPC InBook.

Looking for Liz: A Sticker Book about Habitats. Scholastic, Inc. Staff. (J). (ps-3). 1995. pap. text 3.50 (*0-590-88128-0*) Scholastic Inc.

Looking for Lost. Taylor Graham. 94p. (Orig.). 1991. pap. 7.50 (*1-880575-04-3*) Hot Pepper.

*__Looking for Lost Bird: A Jewish Woman Discovers Her Navajo Roots.__ Yvette D. Melanson & Claire Safran. 240p. 2000. pap. 12.00 (*0-380-79553-1*, Avon Bks) Morrow Avon.

Looking for Lost Bird: A Jewish Woman's Discovery of Her Navajo Roots. Yvette D. Melanson & Claire Safran. LC 98-42110. 240p. 1999. 22.00 (*0-380-97601-3*, Avon Bks) Morrow Avon.

Looking for Love see Buscar del Amor: Seducing Nell

*__Looking for Love.__ (Illus.). 43p. 2000. pap. 7.00 (*0-615-11313-3*, M20001LL) Artworks mph.

Looking for Love. Tom Wood. 82p. 1990. pap. 37.95 (*0-89381-451-2*) Aperture.

Looking for Love in All the Wrong Places: Overcoming Romantic & Sexual Addictions. Jed Diamond. 256p. 1989. reprint ed. mass mkt. 4.99 (*0-380-70774-8*, Avon Bks) Morrow Avon.

Looking for Love On-Line. Richard M. Rogers. 1997. 12.95 (*0-614-19925-5*) Macmillan.

Looking for Love Through the Personals: The Write Way. Judy Knoll. Ed. by Janet Parkerson. (Orig.). 1989. pap. text 9.95 (*0-9623921-0-3*) Personal Connections.

Looking for Luck. Maxine Kumin. 96p. 1993. pap. 9.95 (*0-393-30947-9*) Norton.

*__Looking for Mary: Or, the Blessed Mother & Me.__ Beverly Donofrio. 304p. 2000. 23.95 (*0-670-88459-6*, Viking) Viking Penguin.

Looking for Mary Lou: Illegal Syntax. Ivan Arguelles. LC 88-92723. (Illus.). 169p. (Orig.). 1989. pap. 35.00 (*0-9621676-0-6*) Rock Steady Pr.

Looking for Meaning: Instructional Manual to Accompany Pixie. Matthew Lipman & A. M. Sharp. LC 81-71564. 390p. 1982. teacher ed., spiral bd. 45.00 (*0-916834-18-2*, TX932-050) Inst Advncmnt Philos Child.

Looking for Merlyn. Dilys Evans. LC 95-50725. (Illus.). (J). 1997. write for info. (*0-590-60191-1*) Scholastic Inc.

*__Looking for Mies.__ Ricardo Daza. (Illus.). 200p. 2000. pap. 24.95 (*3-7643-6238-3*, Pub. by Birkhauser) Princeton Arch.

*__Looking for Miracles, Vol. 97.__ Lynn Bulock. (Love Inspired Ser.). 2000. mass mkt. 4.50 (*0-373-87103-1*, Steeple Hill) Harlequin Bks.

Looking for Missy. large type ed. Heidi A. Spietz. Ed. by Frances Henderson. (Illus.). 27p. (J). (gr. 1-2). 1996. pap. 5.00 (*0-929487-28-1*) Am Montessori Consult.

Looking for Mr. Butterfingers: A Comedy of Love, Videodates & Nuclear Waste. Catherine Kitcho. LC 99-90158. 304p. 1999. pap. 14.00 (*0-9666604-1-2*, B3043099) Pele Pubns.

Looking for Mr. Goodbar. Judith Rossner. 1991. mass mkt. 5.95 (*0-671-73575-6*) PB.

Looking for Mr. Goodbar. Judith Rossner. 1997. per. 14.00 (*0-671-01901-5*) PB.

*__Looking for Mr. Nobody: The Secret Life of Goronwy Rees.__ Jenny Rees. 2000. pap. 24.95 (*0-7658-0688-6*) Transaction Pubs.

Looking for Mr. Nobody: The Secret Life of Goronwy Rees. Jenny Rees. (Illus.). 320p. 1995. 40.00 (*0-297-81430-3*, Pub. by Weidenfeld & Nicolson) Trafalgar.

Looking for Mo. Daniel Duane. LC 97-43486. 224p. 1998. 22.00 (*0-374-19083-6*) FS&G.

Looking for Mo. Daniel Duane. 229p. 1999. pap. 12.00 (*0-671-03483-9*, WSP) PB.

Looking for Mr. Claus. Dawn Stewardson. 1996. per. 3.99 (*0-373-70719-3*, 1-70719-9) Harlequin Bks.

Looking for Mr. Preston. Ed. by Laura Antoniou. 1995. 23.95 (*1-56333-288-4*, R Kasak Bks) Masquerade.

Looking for My Name. Ron Atkinson. 1973. pap. 10.00 (*0-912846-06-2*) Bookstore Pr.

Looking for Myself. Kurt B. Boone. 40p. 1995. pap. 6.00 (*0-8059-3570-3*) Dorrance.

Looking for Native Ground: Contemporary Appalachian Poetry. Rita Quillen. LC 89-83315. 1989. pap. 9.95 (*0-913239-58-5*) Appalach Consortium.

Looking for Normal. Shirley D. Rowland. 1997. pap. 56.95 (*1-57553-596-3*) Watermrk Pr.

Looking for Old Ontario. Thomas F. McIlwraith. LC 97-161352. (Illus.). 360p. 1997. pap. 19.95 (*0-8020-7658-0*); text 76.50 (*0-8020-0708-2*) U of Toronto Pr.

Looking for One's Shadow at Noon Vol. I: Looking for the Self in Family & Society. Mary M. Leue. 1993. pap. 7.95 (*1-878115-03-0*) Dwn-To-Erth Bks.

L

An Asterisk (*) at the beginning of an entry indicates that the title is appearing for the first time.

Looking for One's Shadow at Noon Vol. II: Finding the Self in School & Community. Mary M. Leue. 116p. (Orig.). 1993. pap. 7.95 (*1-878115-02-2*) Dwn-To-Erth Bks.

Looking for Patterns. Margie Burton et al. Ed. by Alison Adams. (Early Connections Ser.). 16p. (J). (gr. k-2). 1999. pap. 4.50 (*1-58344-070-4*) Benchmark Educ.

***Looking for Peace? Try Confession.** 2nd ed. Mary Ann Budnik. LC 00-190498. 184p. 1998. pap. 9.95 (*0-9700021-2-2*) R B Media.

Looking for Peoria: The Epicurean at Rest. Dennis McBride. (Orig.). 1995. pap. 9.95 (*1-882550-13-7*) Quiet Lion Pr.

***Looking for Perfection.** Valerie Kirkwood. (Bouquet Ser.: Vol. 39). 2000. mass mkt. 3.99 (*0-8217-6533-7*, Zebra Kensgtn) Kensgtn Pub Corp.

Looking for Perouse: D'Entrecasteaux in Australia & the South Pacific 1792-1793. Frank Horner. (The Miegunyah Press Ser.: No. 2). 384p. 1995. 49.95 (*0-522-84451-0*, Pub. by Melbourne Univ Pr) Paul & Co Pubs.

Looking for Phantoms: Flaws in the Khmer Rouge Screening Process. Stephen Golub. Ed. by Virginia Hamilton. 36p. 1986. write for info. (*0-318-60963-0*) US Comm Refugees.

Looking for Pythagoras: The Pythagorean Theorem. Glenda Lappan et al. Ed. by Catherine Anderson et al. (Connected Mathematics Ser.). (Illus.). 160p. (Orig.). 1997. teacher ed. 16.50 (*1-57232-181-4*, 21476); pap. text 5.95 (*1-57232-180-6*, 21475) Seymour Pubns.

Looking for Rachel Wallace. Robert B. Parker. 224p. 1987. mass mkt. 6.99 (*0-440-15316-6*) Dell.

***Looking for Reasons Why: The Antecedents of Adolescent Sexual Risk-Taking, Pregnancy & Childbearing.** Douglas Kirby. 35p. 1999. pap. write for info. (*1-58671-035-4*) Natl Cpgn Teen Preg.

***Looking for Samson.** large type ed. John Newton Chance. 216p. 2000. pap. 18.99 (*0-7089-5652-1*, Linford) Ulverscroft.

Looking for Scotland. Sally Evans. 1997. pap. 12.95 (*3-7052-0053-4*, Pub. by Poetry Salzburg) Intl Spec Bk.

Looking for Shapes. Margie Burton et al. Ed. by Alison Adams. (Early Connections Ser.). 16p. (J). (gr. k-2). 1999. pap. 4.50 (*1-58344-071-2*) Benchmark Educ.

Looking for Shiloh: Poems. Edsel Ford. LC 68-9420. 80p. 1968. pap. 12.95 (*0-8262-8012-9*) U of Mo Pr.

Looking for Signs. unabridged ed. Margaret Wright. (Select Poets Ser.: No. 1). 32p. 1998. pap. 5.00 (*1-891298-01-1*) Small Poetry.

Looking for Steinbeck's Ghost. Jackson J. Benson. LC 88-40205. (Illus.). 224p. 1988. 27.95 (*0-8061-2155-6*) U of Okla Pr.

Looking for Susie. Bernadine Cook. LC 90-41001. (Illus.). 32p. (J). (gr. 1-3). 1991. lib. bdg. 15.00 (*0-208-02241-4*, Linnet Bks) Shoe String.

Looking for Tara: The Gone with the Wind Guide to Margaret Mitchell's Atlanta. Don O'Briant. LC 94-77585. 112p. 1994. pap. 6.95 (*1-56352-172-5*) Longstreet.

***Looking for the Aliens.** Jenny Randles. (UFO Files Ser.). (Illus.). 241p. 2000. pap. 9.95 (*0-7137-2800-0*) Blandford Pr.

Looking for the Answer. John Benton. 1983. pap. 2.99 (*0-85234-202-0*, Pub. by Evangelical Pr) P & R Pubng.

Looking for the Armenians: Eli Smith's Missionary Adventure, 1830-1831. Margaret R. Leavy. (Transactions Ser.: Vol. 50, Pt. 4). (Illus.). 84p. 1992. pap. 16.00 (*1-878508-07-5*) CT Acad Arts & Sciences.

***Looking for the Cow: Modern Korean Poems.** Ed. by Kevin O'Rourke. 168p. 2000. pap. 14.95 (*1-901233-51-0*, Pub. by Dedalus) Dufour.

Looking for the Cow of Dao. Gail Gelburd. (Illus.). 16p. (Orig.). 1991. pap. 8.95 (*1-890789-00-3*) Coun for Creat Proj.

Looking for the Faces of God. Deena Metzger. LC 89-23139. 96p. (Orig.). 1989. pap. 8.00 (*0-938077-23-6*) Parallax Pr.

Looking for the Future. Leon Wofsy. 150p. 1995. pap. 10.00 (*0-9644667-0-8*); lib. bdg. 21.00 (*0-9644667-1-6*) IW Rose Pr.

Looking for the Last Percent: The Controversy over Census Undercounts. Harvey M. Choldin. LC 93-24224. 296p. (C). 1994. text 48.00 (*0-8135-2039-8*); pap. text 19.00 (*0-8135-2040-1*) Rutgers U Pr.

Looking for the Lilac Line & Other Stories from off the Road. Peter Anderson. 272p. 1991. 26.95 (*1-879601-03-6*); pap. 16.95 (*1-879601-02-8*) Semaphore Bks.

Looking for the Lost: Journeys Through a Vanishing Japan. Alan Booth. Ed. by John Urda. (Illus.). 416p. 1995. 25.00 (*1-56836-065-7*) Kodansha.

Looking for the Lost: Journeys Through a Vanishing Japan. Alan Booth. Ed. by Joshua Sitzer. (Illus.). 416p. 1996. pap. 15.00 (*1-56836-148-3*, Kodansha Globe) Kodansha.

Looking for the "Lost Colony" Tom Parramore & Barbara Parramore. (Illus.). 32p. 1984. pap. 3.00 (*0-318-03650-9*) Tanglewood Press.

Looking for the Lost Gods of England. Kathleen Herbert. LC 95-131777. 56p. 1994. pap. 12.95 (*1-898281-04-1*, Pub. by Anglo-Saxon Bks) Paul & Co Pubs.

Looking for the Mahdi. N. Lee Wood. 304p. 1996. pap. 12.00 (*0-441-00298-6*) Ace Bks.

Looking for the Mahdi. N. Lee Wood. 1997. mass mkt. 5.99 (*0-614-27693-4*); mass mkt. 5.99 (*0-441-00450-4*) Ace Bks.

Looking for the Other: Feminism & the Imperial Gaze. Ann E. Kaplan. LC 96-31257. (Illus.). 256p. (C). 1997. 80.00 (*0-415-91016-1*); pap. 21.99 (*0-415-91017-X*) Routledge.

Looking for the Other Side. Shemy S. Cohen. 1998. mass mkt. 6.99 (*0-425-16307-5*) Berkley Pub.

Looking for the Pale Eagle. Stephen Meats. 62p. (Orig.). 1993. pap. 8.00 (*0-939391-18-X*) B Woodley Pr.

Looking for the Parade. Murray. LC 98-50928. 124p. 1999. 21.00 (*0-393-04727-X*) Norton.

***Looking for the Parade.** Joan Murray. 144p. 2000. pap. 13.00 (*0-393-32064-2*) Norton.

Looking for the Past. Beverly A. Jurczak. 380p. 1994. 25.95 (*0-9647210-5-8*) Looking for Past.

Looking for the Perfect Beat: The Art & Culture of the DJ. Kurt B. Reighley. 244p. 2000. per. 12.95 (*0-671-03869-9*, MTV Bks) PB.

Looking for the Prehispanic Filipino & Other Essays in Philippine History. William H. Scott. 170p. (Orig.). 1993. pap. 15.00 (*971-10-0524-7*, Pub. by New Day Pub) Cellar.

Looking for the Worm. Diana Azar. 128p. 1989. 19.95 (*0-89754-057-3*); pap. 8.95 (*0-89754-056-5*) Dan River Pr.

***Looking for Trouble.** Leslie Cockburn. 288p. 1998. 24.95 (*0-385-48319-8*) Doubleday.

Looking for Trouble. Leslie Cockburn. 288p. 1999. pap. 12.95 (*0-385-48355-4*, Anchor NY) Doubleday.

Looking for Trouble. Marilyn Kaye. (Camp Sunnyside Friends Ser.: No. 5). 128p. (J). (gr. 4). 1990. pap. 2.95 (*0-380-75909-8*, Avon Bks) Morrow Avon.

Looking for Trouble: And Other Stories. R. J. March. LC 98-52511. 1999. pap. 12.95 (*1-55583-455-8*, Pub. by Alyson Pubns) Consort Bk Sales.

Looking for Trouble: Another Historical Novel of Ruben McNair's Adventures after Civil War. Jim L. McAlpin. Ed. by Rivers M. Wilson. (Historical Novels of Civil War & Aftermath: Vol. III). (Illus.). 1999. pap. write for info. (*0-9658220-2-8*) HHI.

Looking for Trouble: Cinderman, Cry for the Moon, Chasing Trouble. Anne Stuart. 2000. per. 6.99 (*0-373-20172-9*, 1-20172-2) Harlequin Bks.

Looking for Trouble: The Life & Times of a Foreign Correspondent. Richard Beeston. LC 97-12843. (Illus.). 178p. 1997. 42.50 (*1-85753-251-1*, Pub. by Brasseys) Brasseys.

Looking for Trouble: Writings on Film, Shopping & Gender. Suzanne Moore. 308p. (Orig.). (C). 1992. pap. 15.99 (*1-85242-242-4*) Serpents Tail.

Looking for Vincent. Thea Dubelaar. (Illus.). 56p. (J). (gr. 2-8). 1992. 9.95 (*1-56288-300-3*) Checkerboard.

***Looking for X.** Deborah Ellis. 144p. (J). (gr. 4-7). 2000. 15.95 (*0-88899-378-1*, Pub. by Grndwd Bks) Publishers Group.

***Looking for You All My Life.** Melody Carlson. (Whispering Pines Ser.). 300p. 2000. pap. 9.99 (*0-7369-0063-2*) Harvest Hse.

Looking for Your Name: A Collection of Contemporary Poems. Selected by Paul B. Janeczko. LC 92-25648. 160p. (YA). (gr. 7 up). 1993. lib. bdg. 17.99 (*0-531-08625-9*) Orchard Bks Watts.

Looking Forever Young. Michael Maris & Dennis Monton. (YA). 1995. write for info. (*1-879234-30-0*) Herit Pub TX.

Looking Forward. Franklin D. Roosevelt. LC 72-2382. (FDR & the Era of the New Deal Ser.). 284p. 1973. reprint ed. lib. bdg. 35.00 (*0-306-70477-3*) Da Capo.

Looking Forward: A Dream of the United States of the Americas in 1999. Arthur Bird. LC 76-154429. (Utopian Literature Ser.). 1974. reprint ed. 18.95 (*0-405-03512-8*) Ayer.

Looking Forward: A Guide to Futures Research. Olaf Helmer. LC 83-4520. (Illus.). 376p. reprint ed. pap. 116.60 (*0-8357-8430-4*, 203469300091) Bks Demand.

Looking Forward: A Guidebook for the Laryngectomee. 3rd ed. Robert L. Keith. LC 95-905. 1995. pap. 9.95 (*0-86577-567-2*) Thieme Med Pubs.

Looking Forward: Games, Rhymes & Exercises to Help Children Develop Their Learning Abilities. Molly Von Heider. 160p. 1995. per. 19.95 (*1-869890-67-1*, Pub. by Hawthorn Press) Anthroposophic.

Looking Forward: Participatory Economics for the Twenty-First Century. Michael Albert & Robin Hahnel. Orig. Title: Participatory Economics. (Illus.). 154p. 1991. 25.00 (*0-89608-406-X*); pap. 16.00 (*0-89608-405-1*) South End Pr.

Looking Forward: The Next 40 Years. Ed. by John M. Templeton. LC 92-55048. 256p. 1993. 25.00 (*0-88730-589-X*, HarpBusn) HarpInfo.

Looking Forward: The Next 40 Years. Ed. by John M. Templeton. 228p. 1997. pap. 14.95 (*1-890151-05-X*) Templeton Fnd.

***Looking Forward: Visions of the 21st Century by California High School Students** Larry Vogel. LC 98-89799. 49 p. 1998. write for info. (*0-9668074-0-5*) Xerox Corp.

Looking Forward, & Others. Booth Tarkington. LC 74-93381. (Essay Index Reprint Ser.). 1977. 23.95 (*0-8369-1384-1*) Ayer.

Looking Forward, Looking Backward, 100. Walter Laqueur. LC 83-11038. 154p. 1983. pap. 9.95 (*0-275-91578-6*, B1578, Praeger Pubs) Greenwood.

Looking Forward, Looking Black. Ed. by Jo Anna Isaac. 1999. pap. text 18.95 (*0-910969-03-5*) Hobart & Wm Smith.

Looking Forward to a New Day. LaNell Compton. 1984. 7.95 (*0-8158-0418-0*) Chris Mass.

***Looking Forward to Christmas: Family Devotions for the Season.** John Farrar. (Illus.). 64p. 2000. 11.99 (*0-8010-1200-7*) Baker Bks.

***Looking Forward to the First Day: American Philosophy--Primal & Pragmatic.** Bruce W. Wilshire. LC 99-47237. (American & European Philosophy Ser.). 2000. pap. write for info. (*0-271-02026-1*) Pa St U Pr.

Looking from the Inside/Out. AIT Staff. 104p. (Orig.). (J). (gr. 2-4). 1996. pap. text 8.95 (*0-7842-0812-3*) Agency Instr Tech.

Looking from Within: A Seeker's Guide to Attitudes for Mastery & Inner Growth. Sri Aurobindo. Ed. by A. S. Dalal. 185p. 1997. pap. 7.95 (*81-7058-406-X*, Pub. by SAA) E-W Cultural Ctr.

Looking from Within: A Seeker's Guide to Attitudes for Mastery & Inner Growth. Sri Aurobindo & Mother. LC 94-73075. 185p. 1995. pap. 6.95 (*0-941524-81-7*) Lotus Pr.

Looking Further Backward. Ed. by Arthur D. Vinton. LC 74-154466. (Utopian Literature Ser.). 1976. reprint ed. 21.95 (*0-405-03548-9*) Ayer.

Looking Further Forward: An Answer to Looking Backward. Richard Michaelis. LC 72-154452. (Utopian Literature Ser.). 1971. reprint ed. 16.95 (*0-405-03534-9*) Ayer.

***Looking Glass.** Richard Paul Evans. LC 99-43458. 336p. 1999. 17.95 (*0-684-86781-8*) S&S Trade.

Looking Glass. Ed. by Clifford E. Trafzer et al. (Illus.). 219p. 1991. pap. 15.00 (*0-934931-06-2*) SDSU Press.

Looking Glass. Doris Trinidad. 207p. (Orig.). (C). 1992. pap. 13.75 (*971-10-0446-1*, Pub. by New Day Pub) Cellar.

***Looking Glass.** abr. ed. Richard Paul Evans. 1999. audio 18.00 (*0-671-04574-1*) S&S Audio.

Looking Glass: Find Answers in Your Mind by Dreaming Them. Joan Hageman. Ed. & Illus. by T. E. Hall. Illus. by Michael Payne. LC 91-66268. 350p. (Orig.). 1992. pap. 16.95 (*1-880481-00-6*) Systs & More.

Looking Glass: New Poems. Isabella Gardner. LC 61-15932. 1961. pap. 1.50 (*0-226-28238-4*, PP4) U Ch Pr.

Looking Glass Dream Log. Joan Hageman. 130p. 1992. spiral bd. 15.95 (*1-880481-01-4*) Systs & More.

Looking-Glass for London & England. Thomas Lodge & Robert Greene. LC 71-133697. (Tudor Facsimile Texts. Old English Plays Ser.: No. 67). reprint ed. 59.50 (*0-404-53367-1*) AMS Pr.

Looking-Glass for Married Folkes. Robert Snawsel. LC 74-28886. (English Experience Ser.: No. 763). 1975. reprint ed. 25.00 (*90-221-0763-9*) Walter J Johnson.

***Looking-Glass Kate.** Ferent Mara. (J). 1999. pap. 21.00 (*963-13-4780-X*, Pub. by Corvina Bks) St Mut.

Looking Glass Lives: A Novel. Felice Picano. LC 98-21812. (Illus.). 240p. 1998. pap. 12.95 (*1-55583-481-7*) Alyson Pubns.

Looking-Glass Lover: A Novel. Ursula Perrin. 256p. 1989. 17.95 (*0-316-69961-6*) Little.

Looking-Glass Self: An Examination of Self-Awareness. John V. Canfield. LC 90-7143. 264p. 1990. 65.00 (*0-275-93586-8*, C3586, Praeger Pubs) Greenwood.

Looking Glass Sky. Deborah Whitaker-Duncklee. Ed. by Susan Remkus. LC 95-43720. (Illus.). 128p. (Orig.). 1995. pap. 12.95 (*1-880396-44-0*, JP9644-0) Jalmar Pr.

Looking Glass War. John Le Carre, pseud. 1997. pap. 12.00 (*0-345-41829-8*) Ballantine Pub Grp.

Looking-Glasse for London & England; George A. Greene, the Pinner of Wakefield; Selimus, Emperour of the Turkes; A Maidens Dreame, 1590-1599 see Life & Complete Works in Prose & Verse of Robert Greene

Looking Good, 8 bks., Set. Jacqueline Ball. (Illus.). 64p. (J). (gr. 5 up). 1990. lib. bdg. 127.52 (*0-86625-287-8*) Rourke Pubns.

Looking Good, 8 bks., Set 11. Jacqueline Ball. (Illus.). 64p. (J). (gr. 5 up). 1990. 95.60 (*0-685-58754-1*) Rourke Corp.

Looking Good: Learning to Improve Your Appearance. Mary J. Haugen. 50p. 1991. text, teacher ed. 49.95 (*1-884074-04-9*) PCI Educ Pubg.

***Looking Good: Male Body Image in Modern America.** Lynn Luciano. (Illus.). 272p. 2001. 25.00 (*0-8090-6637-8*) Hill & Wang.

Looking Good: Photographing Your Library. Raymond S. Bial. 1991. 15.00 (*0-8389-0575-7*) ALA.

Looking Good: Teenagers & Eating Disorders. Marion Crook. 128p. (Orig.). 1992. pap. 12.95 (*1-55021-077-7*, Pub. by NC Ltd) U of Toronto Pr.

Looking Good: Wardrobe Planning & Personal Style Development. Nancy Nix-Rice. (Illus.). 160p. 1996. pap. text 19.95 (*0-935278-42-7*) Palmer-Pletsch.

Looking Good & Doing Good: Corporate Philanthropy & Corporate Power. Jerome L. Himmelstein. LC 96-34217. (Philanthropic Studies). 1997. 29.95 (*0-253-33237-0*); pap. 12.95 (*0-253-21103-4*) Ind U Pr.

Looking Good at Any Age. Amy E. Newburger & Pam Proctor. LC 99-17984. 256p. 1999. 22.95 (*0-385-49218-9*) Doubleday.

Looking Good, Feeling Good: Fashion & Beauty for the over 50's. Ed. by Nancy Tuft. 156p. (C). 1991. 45.00 (*0-86242-102-0*, Pub. by Age Concern Eng) St Mut.

Looking Good, Feeling Good: Fashion & Beauty in Mid-Life & Beyond. 2nd large type ed. Nancy Tuft. (Illus.). 152p. 1993. 24.95 (*1-85695-045-X*, Pub. by ISIS Lrg Prnt) Transaction Pubs.

Looking Good Feeling Great. Joanna G. Zurek. (Illus.). 149p. (Orig.). (C). 1978. pap. text 12.95 (*0-9602076-1-9*) J G Zurek.

***Looking Good in Print.** 3rd ed. Roger C. Parker. 400p. 2000. pap. text 34.99 (*1-57610-616-0*) Coriolis Grp.

Looking Good Is Feeling Good. Trude See. (Simulation Game Ser.). 1975. pap. 26.25 (*0-89401-050-6*) Didactic Syst.

Looking Good Is Good Business: A Handbook of Publicity & Promotion Techniques Every Builder Should Use. John E. Bertram. LC 92-24918. (Illus.). 112p. (Orig.). 1992. pap. 12.00 (*0-86718-379-9*) Home Builder.

Looking Good, Living Long, Feeling Great: A Breakthrough 9-Step Program to Help You Look Your Best, Live a Long, Healthy Life & Feel Great in the Process. Edna W. Burt. LC 92-90004. 100p. (Orig.). 1992. pap. 14.95 (*0-9631972-0-7*) Edna FourCZNS.

Looking Good on Paper: How to Create Eye-Catching Reports, Proposals, Memos, & Other Business Documents. Garrett Soden. LC 94-27096. 144p. (Orig.). 1995. pap. 16.95 (*0-8144-7858-1*) AMACOM.

Looking Good on the Web. Daniel Gray. LC 99-43076. 200p. 1999. pap. text 29.99 (*1-57610-508-3*) Coriolis Grp.

Looking Good Outside, Feeling Bad Inside: Freedom from the Shame That Hides the Real You. Curtis Levang. 142p. (Orig.). 1995. pap. 9.99 (*1-883002-11-7*) Emerald WA.

Looking Good Puzzle Game. Mary J. Haugen. (Life Skills Educational Puzzle Game Ser.: No. 3). 4p. 1992. text 19.95 (*1-884074-13-8*) PCI Educ Pubg.

Looking Great... Linda Dano & Anne Kyle. (Illus.). 208p. 1998. pap. 15.00 (*0-399-52387-1*, Perigee Bks) Berkley Pub.

Looking Great, Staying Young. Dick Clark. LC 80-684. 256p. 1980. 11.95 (*0-672-52657-3*, Bobbs) Macmillan.

Looking High & Low: Art & Cultural Identity. Ed. by Brenda J. Bright & Liza Bakewell. LC 94-48508. (Illus.). 210p. 1995. 43.00 (*0-8165-1311-2*); pap. 18.95 (*0-8165-1516-6*) U of Ariz Pr.

Looking Homeward: A Thomas Wolfe Photo Album. Morton I. Teicher. LC 92-41925. (Illus.). 216p. (C). 1993. 29.95 (*0-8262-0893-2*) U of Mo Pr.

Looking In. Ewald W. Schnitzer. LC 77-91620. (Illus.). 1977. pap. 4.95 (*0-913612-03-0*) Strawberry Valley.

Looking In. Eugene Sisco, Jr. 120p. 1990. pap. 11.00 (*0-9616911-5-8*) M F Sohn Pubns.

Looking In: The Art of Viewing. Mieke Bal et al. (Illus.). 240p. 1999. text 60.00 (*90-5701-102-6*); pap. text 24.95 (*90-5701-112-3*) Gordon & Breach.

Looking In - Looking Out: La Mirada Extranjera. Jenaro Talens & Michael Nerlich. Ed. by Luis A. Ramos-Garcia. (GER & SPA., Illus.). 1989. 12.95 (*0-934840-09-1*) Studia Hispanica.

Looking in Classrooms. 7th ed. (C). 1997. 24.00 (*0-673-97924-5*, GoodYrBooks) Addson-Wesley Educ.

***Looking in Classrooms.** 8th ed. 144p. (C). 1999. pap. 26.00 (*0-321-06400-3*) Addison-Wesley.

Looking in Classrooms. 8th ed. Thomas L. Good. LC 99-22637. 540p. (C). 1999. pap. 71.00 (*0-321-04897-0*) Addison-Wesley.

Looking in Looking Out: Redefining Child Care & Early Education in a Diverse Society. Hedy N. Chang et al. Ed. by Carol Dowell. (Illus.). 240p. (C). 1996. pap. 27.00 (*1-887039-12-0*) Calif Tomorrow.

Looking in My Mirror Backwards: Reflections at Mid-Life. Jay Grooters. 1996. 13.95 (*0-9641395-0-2*) Urban Rancher.

Looking in on Music Teaching. Barrett. 1998. 22.00 (*0-697-38695-3*, WCB McGr Hill) McGrw-H Hghr Educ.

Looking in, Reaching Out: A Manual for Training Service Volunteers. Dorine Thomas & Ret Thomas. LC 96-21811. 192p. 1996. teacher ed., ring bd. 59.95 (*0-89390-376-0*) Resource Pubns.

Looking in, Seeing Out: Consciousness & Cosmos. Menas Kafatos & Thalia Kafatou. 1991. pap. 13.95 (*0-8356-0674-0*, Quest) Theos Pub Hse.

Looking in the Mirror: Self-Appraisal in the Local Church. Lyle E. Schaller. LC 83-15857. 208p. 1984. pap. 11.95 (*0-687-22635-X*) Abingdon.

Looking Inland. Christine Evans. 56p. 1983. pap. 8.95 (*0-907476-24-4*) Dufour.

Looking Inside: Machines & Constructions. Paul Fleisher & Patricia Keeler. LC 90-743. (Illus.). 40p. (J). (gr. 2-7). 1991. text 13.95 (*0-689-31483-3*) Atheneum Yung Read.

Looking Inside Cartoon Animation. Ron Schultz. (X-Ray Vision Ser.). (Illus.). 48p. (J). (gr. 3 up). 1992. pap. 6.95 (*1-56261-066-X*, J Muir) Avalon Travel.

Looking Inside Caves & Caverns. Ron Schultz. LC 93-13159. (X-Ray Vision Ser.). (Illus.). 48p. (J). (gr. 4-7). 1993. pap. 6.95 (*1-56261-126-7*, J Muir) Avalon Travel.

Looking Inside Sports Aerodynamics. Ron Schultz. (X-Ray Vision Ser.). (Illus.). 48p. (J). (gr. 3 up). 1992. pap. 6.95 (*1-56261-065-1*, J Muir) Avalon Travel.

Looking Inside Sunken Treasure. Ron Schultz. (X-Ray Vision Ser.). (Illus.). 48p. (J). (gr. 3 up). 1992. pap. 6.95 (*1-56261-074-0*, J Muir) Avalon Travel.

Looking Inside Telescopes & the Night Sky. Ron Schultz. LC 92-31621. (X-Ray Vision Ser.). (Illus.). 48p. (J). (gr. 4-7). 1992. pap. 6.95 (*1-56261-072-4*, J Muir) Avalon Travel.

Looking Inside the Brain. Ron Schultz. LC 91-44927. (X-Ray Vision Ser.). (Illus.). 48p. (J). (gr. 4-7). 1992. pap. 6.95 (*1-56261-064-3*, J Muir) Avalon Travel.

Looking into Degas: Uneasy Images of Women & Modern Life. Eunice Lipton. (Illus.). 1986. 60.00 (*0-520-05604-3*, Pub. by U CA Pr) Cal Prin Full Svc.

Looking into Literature & Seeing Myself. Laurie Chapin & Ellen Flagenheimer-Riggle. (Illus.). 128p. (J). (gr. k-3). 1992. student ed. 9.99 (*0-86653-706-6*, 1427) Good Apple.

Looking into Mind: How to Recognize Who You Are & How You Know. Anthony Damiani. Ed. by Widsom's Goldenrod Staff. 298p. (Orig.). 1990. pap. 14.95 (*0-943914-50-7*) Larson Pubns.

***Looking into Nature's Secrets.** Michael Bright. LC 98-68766. (Looking into Our World Ser.). (Illus.). 14p. (J). (ps-2). 1999. bds. 11.99 (*1-57584-316-1*, Pub. by Rdrs Digest) S&S Trade.

Looking into Primary Headship: A Research Based Interpretation. Geoff Southworth. LC 94-36872. 236p. 1995. 95.00 (*0-7507-0371-7*, Falmer Pr); pap. 29.95 (*0-7507-0372-5*, Falmer Pr) Taylor & Francis.

Looking into Space. Margie Burton et al. Ed. by Alison Adams. (Early Connections Ser.). 16p. (J). (gr. k-2). 1999. pap. 4.50 (*1-58344-072-0*) Benchmark Educ.

An Asterisk (*) at the beginning of an entry indicates that the title is appearing for the first time.

L

***Looking into the Earth: An Introduction to Geological Geophysics.** Allan E. Mussett & M. Aftab Khan. LC 00-20382. (Illus.). 608p. (C). 2000. 90.00 (*0-521-78085-3*); pap. 39.95 (*0-521-78574-X*) Cambridge U Pr.

Looking into the Eyes of a Killer: A Psychiatrist's Journey Through the Murderer's World. Drew Ross. LC 98-13245. (Illus.). 250p. (C). 1998. 26.95 (*0-306-45791-1*, Plenum Trade) Perseus Pubng.

Looking into the Heart of Light. William Hathaway. LC 88-19133. (University of Central Florida Contemporary Poetry Ser.). 104p. 1988. 14.95 (*0-8130-0901-4*) U Press Fla.

Looking into the Invisible: Intuition, Clairvoyance, Dreams. 3rd ed. Omraam M. Aivanhov. (Izvor Collection: Vol. 228). 217p. 1995. pap. 7.95 (*2-85566-469-1*, Pub. by Prosveta) Prosveta USA.

Looking into the Middle Ages. Huck Scarry. LC 84-47626. (Illus.). 12p. (J). (gr. 2 up). 1985. 12.50 (*0-06-025224-3*) HarpC Child Bks.

Looking Into the Past: People, Places & Customs. Intro. by Fred L. Israel. (Illus.). 64p. (J). (gr. 5). 1997. 203.40 (*0-7910-4674-5*) Chelsea Hse.

Looking into the Seeds of Time: The Price of Modern Development. 2nd rev. ed. Y. S. Brenner. LC 97-30355. 385p. 1997. pap. 24.95 (*1-56000-996-9*) Transaction Pubs.

Looking into Your Future Lives. Gloria Chadwick. 1996. pap. write for info. (*0-8092-3412-2*) NTC Contemp Pub Co.

Looking Inward: Observations on the Art of Meditation. Acharn K. Khao-suan-luang. 64p. 1991. 3.75 (*955-24-0084-8*, Pub. by Buddhist Pub Soc) Vipassana Res Pubns.

Looking It Up. M. Preston Foster. (J). (gr. 2-5). 1988. pap. 8.99 (*0-8224-4345-7*) Fearon Teacher Aids.

Looking Left: Socialism in Europe after the Cold War. Donald Sassoon. 1998. pap. 19.95 (*1-56584-428-9*, Pub. by New Press NY) Norton.

Looking, Listening & Learning: Observing & Assessing Young Readers. Carl Braun. 200p. (Orig.). 1993. pap., teacher ed. 18.00 (*1-895411-55-6*) Peguis Pubs Ltd.

Looking, Making & Learning: Thinking about Art & Design in the Primary School. Anthony Dyson. 112p. (Orig.). 1989. 20.95 (*0-8464-1417-1*) Beekman Pubs.

Looking Man's T. V. Cookbook - Recipes from the Cooking Man Show. Dawud Ujamaa. (Illus.). pap. 14.95 (*1-884938-05-1*) Dawud Ujamma.

Looking North: Art from the University of Alaska Museum. Aldona Jonaitis et al. LC 97-35363. (Illus.). 240p. 1998. 60.00 (*0-295-97693-4*) U of Wash Pr.

Looking North: Art from the University of Alaska Museum. University of Alaska Museum Staff et al. Ed. by Aldona Jonaitis. LC 97-35363. (Illus.). 206p. 1998. pap. text 35.00 (*0-295-97694-2*) U of Wash Pr.

Looking North to South-East Asia: The View from Australia. Australian Institute of International Affairs Staf. Ed. by Edward P. Wolfers. LC 76-50495. 288p. reprint ed. pap. 89.30 (*0-7837-0996-X*, 204130200020) Bks Demand.

Looking On. Rosemary Betterton. 1987. 22.95 (*0-86358-177-3*, Pub. by Pandora) Harper SF.

Looking Out. M. Hettich & C. Ahern. 30p. 1981. 3.00 (*0-943216-06-0*) MoonsQuilt Pr.

Looking Out: A Walk in the Park. Mary Lou Stahl. (My Nature Book). (Illus.). 8p. (Orig.). (J). (ps). 1993. pap. 6.00 (*1-886075-02-6*) Grass Rt Ent.

Looking Out: Perspectives on Dance & Criticism in a Multicultural World. Ed. by David Gere et al. LC 95-98941. (Illus.). 242p. 1995. 32.00 (*0-02-870683-8*, Schirmer Books) Mac Lib Ref.

Looking Out- Looking In. 7th ed. Ronald B. Adler & Neil Towne. (Illus.). 450p. (C). 1993. text. write for info. (*0-318-69103-5*) Harcourt Coll Pubs.

Looking Out for #1. Robert J. Ringer. 352p. 1985. mass mkt. 6.99 (*0-449-21010-3*, Crest) Fawcett.

Looking Out for Ollie. Sharon Montey. (Storybridge Ser.). 80p. (J). (gr. 3-7). 1995. pap. 9.95 (*0-7022-2734-X*, Pub. by Univ Queensland Pr) Intl Spec Bk.

***Looking Out for Sarah.** Glenna Lang. LC 00-37714. (Illus.). (J). 2001. write for info. (*0-88106-647-8*, Talewinds) Charlesbridge Pub.

Looking Out, Looking In. 8th ed. Adler. (C). 1995. pap. text, teacher ed. 42.00 (*0-15-502739-5*) Harcourt Coll Pubs.

Looking Out, Looking In. 8th ed. Ronald B. Adler. (C). 1995. text 47.50 (*0-15-501728-4*) Harcourt Coll Pubs.

Looking Out, Looking In. 9th ed. Adler. (C). 1998. text 47.50 (*0-15-505787-1*, Pub. by Harcourt Coll Pubs) Harcourt.

Looking Outward: Years of Crisis at the United Nations. Ed. by Robert L. Schiffer et al. LC 84-6708. 295p. 1984. reprint ed. lib. bdg. 65.00 (*0-313-24529-0*, STLO, Greenwood Pr) Greenwood.

Looking over My Shoulder. . . Dell W. Etheridge. Ed. by Shelah S. Bayuk. (Illus.). 30p. (Orig.). 1998. pap. write for info. (*1-892172-03-8*) Writing Matters.

***Looking over My Shoulder: Reflections on the 20th Century.** Ed. by Anne-Marie Oomen. LC 00-100916. (Illus.). 104p. 2000. pap. 15.00 (*0-9679632-0-6*) Nrthwst MI Col.

***Looking Past the Sky: Prayers by Young Teens.** Ed. by Marilyn Kielbasa. 152p. (YA). 1999. pap. 5.95 (*0-88489-582-3*) St Marys.

Looking Past Today. Gary Short. Ed. by Kirk Robertson. 36p. 1983. pap. 3.50 (*0-916918-24-6*); pap. text 12.00 (*0-916918-25-4*) Duck Down.

Looking Pretty, Feeling Fine: Total Beauty for Teens. Marjabelle Y. Stewart. (Illus.). 1979. 10.95 (*0-679-51178-4*) McKay.

Looking Queer: Body Image & Identity in Lesbian, Bisexual, Gay, & Transgender Communities. Ed. by Dawn Atkins. LC 98-14678. 467p. (C). 1998. 69.95 (*0-7890-0463-1*, Harrington Park); pap. 32.95 (*1-56023-931-X*, Harrington Park) Haworth Pr.

Looking South: Chapters in the Story of an American Region, 136. Ed. by Winfred B. Moore, Jr. & Joseph F. Tripp. LC 89-1888. (Contributions in American History Ser.: No. 136). 301p. 1989. 65.00 (*0-313-26694-8*, MLU, Greenwood Pr) Greenwood.

Looking the Tiger in the Eye: Confronting the Nuclear Threat. Carl B. Feldbaum & Ronald J. Bee. LC 85-48253. (Illus.). 320p. (YA). (gr. 7 up). 1988. 14.95 (*0-06-020414-1*) HarpC Child Bks.

Looking Through Glass. Mukul Kesavan. LC 94-24172. 375p. 1995. 25.00 (*0-374-19085-2*) FS&G.

Looking Through Glass. Mukul Kesavan. (C). 1995. 19.50 (*0-02-516006-0*, Pub. by Ravi Dayal) S Asia.

***Looking Through Grandmother's Glasses: A Journey into a Child's Heart.** Lynn Wendelbo. (Illus.). 114p. (J). (ps-4). 1999. pap. 16.95 (*1-885473-97-4*, PreProd Pr) Wood N Barnes.

Looking Through My Mother's Eyes: Life Stories of Nine Italian Immigrant Women in Canada. Giovanna Del Negro. LC 95-81766. 133p. 1996. pap. 12.00 (*1-55071-043-5*) Guernica Editions.

***Looking Through Rose-Tinted Bifocals: Lighthearted Views on Life by Angela F. Huston.** Angela F. Huston. 235p. 2000. pap. 12.95 (*0-9677085-1-6*) Porch Lite.

***Looking Through the Faraway End: Creating a Literature-Based Reading Curriculum with Second Graders.** Lee Galda et al. (Kids InSight Ser.). 2000. pap., teacher ed. 19.95 (*0-87207-263-0*, 263) Intl Reading.

Looking Through the Window: A Picture of God's Love for Each Day of the Year. Liam Hickey. 224p. 1996. pap. 39.95 (*0-85439-523-7*, Pub. by St Paul Pubns) St Mut.

Looking Through the Window: Real-Life Missionary Stories. Betty M. Hockett. LC 95-76811. (Illus.). 120p. (J). (gr. 3-8). 1995. pap. 9.00 (*0-943701-22-8*) George Fox Pr.

Looking Through the Window of Sociology. 2nd ed. Lynda Dodgen & Adrian M. Rapp. 476p. (C). 1996. pap. text 46.95 (*0-7872-1576-7*) Kendall-Hunt.

Looking to Europe: The EC Policies of the British Labour Party & the Danish SDP. Jens H. Haahr. 368p. (Orig.). (C). 1993. pap. 27.00 (*87-7288-449-5*, Pub. by Aarhus Univ Pr) David Brown.

***Looking to Learn: Visual Pedagogy at the University of Chicago.** Linda Seidel. LC 98-60521. 1998. pap. text 12.00 (*0-935573-21-6*) D & A Smart Museum.

Looking to Learn While Learning to Look. Phyllis Guthrie. 118p. (Orig.). (C). 1991. pap. text 13.95 (*0-89641-213-X*) American Pr.

Looking to the East with Western Eyes. Leah Maines. LC 99-187912. (New Women's Voices Ser.: Vol. 1). 25p. 1998. pap. 7.00 (*0-9664324-0-1*) Finishng Line.

***Looking to the Future.** (Overcoming Obstacles). 32p. (YA). (gr. 6-9). 1999. pap. text 11.50 (*1-929393-10-5*) Community for Ed.

Looking to the Future. Veritas Publications Staff. 1989. pap. 15.00 (*1-85390-062-1*, Pub. by Veritas Pubns) St Mut.

Looking to the Future: A Global Review of UNICEF's Facts for Life Initiative. 80p. 1997. write for info. (*92-806-3274-4*) U N I C E.

Looking to the Future: Papers Read at an International Symposium On Prospects For Worship, Religious Architecture & Socio-religious Studies, 1976. J. G. Davies & University of Birmingham Staff. LC 77-369107. 171p. 1976. write for info. (*0-7044-0234-3*) Univ of Birmingham.

Looking to the New Millenium: New Jersey's Plan for Higher Education. Ed. by Robert Albright et al. 42p. 1998. reprint ed. pap. text 20.00 (*0-7881-4152-X*) DIANE Pub.

Looking Together: Introducing Young Children to the Cleveland Museum of Art. Peneope Buchanan. LC 96-47689. 1996. write for info. (*0-940717-38-7*) Cleveland Mus Art.

Looking Together at Students' Work: A Companion Guide to Assessing Student Learning. Tina Blythe et al. LC 99-22561. 21. 64p. 1999. pap. 11.95 (*0-8077-3855-7*) Tchrs Coll.

Looking Toward Ararat: Armenia in Modern History. Ronald G. Suny. LC 92-19420. 304p. 1993. 41.95 (*0-253-35583-4*); pap. 19.95 (*0-253-20773-8*, MB-773) Ind U Pr.

***Looking Toward Pleiades: A Collection of Traditional Poetry.** Stephen R. Galati. (Illus.). 22p. 2000. pap. 10.00 (*0-9679403-0-3*, Pleiades-01) Pencraft Writ.

Looking Two Ways: Documentary Film's Relationship with Reality & Cinema. Toni De Bromhead. 148p. (C). 1996. pap. 30.00 (*87-89825-13-6*, Pub. by Intervention Pr) Smyrna.

Looking unto Jesus. 1988. pap. text 1.35 (*0-8474-0775-6*) Back to Bible.

Looking unto Jesus. Isaac Ambrose. 1994. 34.99 (*0-87377-998-3*) GAM Pubns.

Looking unto Jesus. Charles H. Spurgeon & Vic Lockman. 1976. mass mkt. 0.10 (*1-56186-505-2*) Pilgrim Pubns.

Looking Up. Jim N. Griffith. LC 93-14384. 197p. 1993. text 12.95 (*0-86554-427-1*, MUP/H341) Mercer Univ Pr.

Looking Up: Looking Back at Old Brisbane Watercolours. R. Wood & Grahame R. Readshaw. 80p. (C). 1990. 90.00 (*0-86439-032-7*, Pub. by Boolarong Pubns) St Mut.

Looking up . . . While Lying Down: Thoughts, Poems, & Prayers for Those in the Hospital. John E. Biegert. (Looking up Ser.). 24p. 1979. pap. 1.95 (*0-8298-0364-5*) Pilgrim OH.

Looking Up a Story. Ed. by Instructional Fair Staff. 1998. pap. 16.95 (*0-513-01794-1*) Instruct Fair.

Looking up at Down: The Emergence of Blues Culture. William Barlow. 464p. 1990. pap. 22.95 (*0-87722-722-5*) Temple U Pr.

Looking Up While Lying Down (Thoughts, Poems & Prayers for Those in the Hospital) see Mirando Hacia Arriba en Medio de la Enfermedad (Looking up . . . While Lying Down)

Looking West John D. Dorst. LC 98-37212. (Contemporary Ethnography Ser.). 1999. 19.95 (*0-8122-1440-4*) U of Pa Pr.

Looking West. John D. Dorst. LC 98-37212. 1999. 45.00 (*0-8122-3173-2*) U of Pa Pr.

***Looking West: Excursions in a Landscape of Vision & Display.** John D. Dorst. LC 98-37212. (Contemporary Ethnography Ser.). 1999. write for info. (*0-8122-1680-6*); write for info. (*0-8122-3500-2*) U of Pa Pr.

Looking West: Three Essays on Swedish American Life. Jules Mauritzson. Tr. by Conrad Bergendoff. xx, 73p. 1994. pap. 12.00 (*0-910184-42-9*) Augustana.

Looking White People in the Eye: Gender, Race & Culture in Courtrooms & Classrooms. Sherene H. Razack. LC 99-164793. 272p. 1998. text 55.00 (*0-8020-0928-X*); pap. text 21.95 (*0-8020-7898-2*) U of Toronto Pr.

Looking Within: How X-Ray, CT, MRI, Ultrasound, & Other Medical Images Are Created & How They Help Physicians Save Lives. Anthony B. Wolbarst. LC 98-3892. 224p. 1999. 50.00 (*0-520-21181-2*, Pub. by U CA Pr); pap. 19.95 (*0-520-21182-0*, Pub. by U CA Pr) Cal Prin Full Svc.

Looking Within: The Misleading Tendencies of Looking Backward Made Manifest. J. W. Roberts. LC 78-154459. (Utopian Literature Ser.). 1976. reprint ed. 24.95 (*0-405-03541-1*) Ayer.

Lookouts: Firewatchers of the Cascades & Olympics. 2nd rev. ed. Ira Spring & Byron Fish. LC 96-20760. (Illus.). 224p. 1996. pap. 16.95 (*0-89886-494-1*) Mountaineers.

Lookout's Letter. Cornel Lengyel. LC 75-148857. (Living Poets' Library). pap. 2.50 (*0-686-05006-1*) Dragons Teeth.

Lookout/Tagout & the Printing Industry: Videotape & Manual. 150.00 (*0-614-25591-0*, 00HR1940) Print Indus Am.

Looks & Frictions: Essays in Cultural Studies & Film Theory. Paul Willemen. 176p. (C). 1994. 35.00 (*0-253-36588-0*); pap. 14.95 (*0-253-36589-9*) Ind U Pr.

Looks Are Deceiving. Maggie Ferguson. (Intrigue Ser.). 1994. per. 2.99 (*0-373-22284-X*, 1-22284-3) Harlequin Bks.

Looks Are Deceiving. Maggie Ferguson. 1997. pap. 3.99 (*0-373-83334-2*, 1-83334-2) Harlequin Bks.

***Looks Good to Me.** John Chapman. Ed. by Connie Breithoff. 180p. 1999. pap. 23.95 (*0-9675838-0-2*) Chappys Inc.

Looks Like an Angel see Cara de Angel: Husband Not Included!

Looks Like (And More) Wordbook, No. 3. Jeannette A. Fidell. 1992. pap. write for info. (*1-881124-02-9*) Ctr Creat Endeavors.

Looks Perfect. Kim Moritsugu. 220p. 1996. pap. 14.95 (*0-86492-196-9*, Pub. by Goose Ln Edits) Genl Dist Srvs.

Loom & Other Stories. R. A. Sasaki. 124p. 1991. pap. 11.95 (*1-55597-157-1*) Graywolf.

Loom & Spindle. Harriet H. Robinson. LC 75-46389. 144p. (C). 1976. pap. 7.95 (*0-916630-02-1*) Pr Pacifica.

Loom & the Cloth: An Exhibition of the Fabrics of Jewish Life. Temple Museum of Religious Art Staff & Claudia Z. Fechter. (Illus.). 40p. (Orig.). (C). 1988. 7.00 (*0-9621087-0-7*) Temple-Tifereth.

Loom & the Lash. Sharon Fennessey. (J). (gr. 5-9). 1998. pap. 10.00 (*1-57960-042-5*) Disc Enter Ltd.

Loom of Destiny. Arthur J. Stringer. LC 74-103529. (Short Story Index Reprint Ser.). 1977. 19.95 (*0-8369-3272-2*) Ayer.

Loom of God: Mathematical Tapestries at the Edge of Time. Clifford A. Pickover. LC 96-45675. (Illus.). 292p. (C). 1997. 29.95 (*0-306-45411-4*, Plenum Trade) Perseus Pubng.

***Loom of Language.** Frederick Bodmer. 669p. 1999. reprint ed. pap. 19.95 (*0-85036-350-0*, Pub. by MRLN) Paul & Co Pubs.

Loom of Language. Frederick Bodmer. Ed. by Lancelot Hogben. (Illus.). 720p. 1985. reprint ed. pap. 19.95 (*0-393-30034-X*) Norton.

Loom of the Future: Weather Engineering. Trevor J. Constable. 18.95 (*0-945685-19-X*) Borderland Sciences.

Loom of the Tancred. large type ed. Diane Pearson. (Romance Ser.). 1974. 27.99 (*0-85456-303-2*) Ulverscroft.

Loomis Gang. George W. Walter. LC 53-7852. (Illus.). 272p. 1953. pap. 18.95 (*0-932052-47-9*) North Country.

Looms & Weaving. Anna Benson & Neil Warburton. (Album Ser.: Vol. 154). (Illus.). 32p. 4.75 (*0-85263-753-5*, Pub. by Shire Pubns) Lubrecht & Cramer.

Loon. Ivah J. Green. LC 65-22310. (Illus.). 32p. (J). (gr. 4 up). 1968. lib. bdg. 9.95 (*0-87783-025-8*) Oddo.

Loon. Kip Taylor. LC 87-90324. (Illus.). 184p. 1989. 45.00 (*0-9623422-0-3*) S Taylor.

Loon: Voice of the Wilderness. Joan Dunning. LC 85-50055. (Illus.). 144p. 1985. 17.95 (*0-89909-080-X*, 80-950-7) Yankee Bks.

Loon & Deer Were Traveling. (J). 1992. 22.60 (*0-516-07069-X*) Childrens.

Loon & Deer Were Traveling. (J). 1993. pap. text 5.67 (*0-516-05167-9*) Childrens.

Loon at Northwood Lake. Elizabeth Ring. (Smithsonian's Backyard Ser.). (Illus.). 32p. (J). (ps-2). 1997. 15.95 (*1-56899-393-5*); 19.95 incl. audio (*1-56899-397-8*, BC5013) Soundprints.

Loon at Northwood Lake, Including large book & large toy. Elizabeth Ring. (Smithsonian's Backyard Ser.). (Illus.). 32p. (J). (ps-2). 1997. 32.95 (*1-56899-395-1*); 36.95 incl. audio (*1-56899-399-4*) Soundprints.

Loon at Northwood Lake, Including Small & Lg. Plush Toy. Elizabeth Ring. LC 96-39101. (Smithsonian's Backyard Ser.). (Illus.). 32p. (J). (ps-2). 1997. 43.95 incl. audio (*1-56899-640-3*) Soundprints.

Loon at Northwood Lake, Micro bk. Elizabeth Ring. (Smithsonian's Backyard Ser.). (Illus.). 32p. (J). (ps-2). 1997. 4.95 (*1-56899-394-3*) Soundprints.

Loon at Northwood Lake: Micro Book & Toy. Elizabeth Ring. (Illus.). 32p. (J). (ps-2). 1997. 12.95 (*1-56899-459-1*) Soundprints.

***Loon Box.** Kristopher Scuccimarra. LC 00-103852. 78p. 2000. pap. 12.00 (*1-58776-050-9*, Straw Hse Pr) Vivisphere.

Loon Feather. Iola Fuller. LC 40-27210. 480p. 1967. pap. 14.00 (*0-15-653200-X*, Harvest Bks) Harcourt.

Loon in My Bathtub. Ronald Rood. LC 85-61031. (Illus.). 192p. (Orig.). 1985. reprint ed. pap. 12.95 (*0-933050-28-3*) New Eng Pr VT.

Loon Journal. Scott Miller. (Illus.). 40p. (Orig.). (J). (gr. 4 up). 1989. pap. 5.98 (*0-926147-01-3*) Loonfeather.

***Loon Lake.** Jonathan London & Susan Ford. LC 00-8935. (J). 2001. pap. write for info. (*0-8118-2003-3*) Chronicle Bks.

Loon Lake - Ash Valley Revisited. Ray O. Sims. LC 96-90648. (Illus.). 325p. 1998. 59.00 (*0-9666417-0-1*); pap. 44.95 (*0-9666417-1-X*) Ray O Sims.

***Loon Lake Fishing Derby.** Kathleen Cook Waldron. LC 98-89929. (Illus.). 32p. (J). (gr. k-3). 1999. 14.95 (*1-55143-142-4*) Orca Bk Pubs.

***Loon Laughter: Ecological Fables & Nature Tales.** Leet Paul Aird. 1999. pap. 11.95 (*1-55041-390-2*) Fitzhenry & W Ltd.

Loon Legends. Corinne A. Dwyer. LC 88-60995. (Illus.). 96p. 1988. pap. 9.95 (*0-87839-046-4*) North Star.

Loon Magic. 10th rev. ed. Tom Klein. LC 95-38568. (Illus.). 176p. 1996. pap. 19.95 (*1-55971-578-2*, NorthWord Pr) Creat Pub Intl.

Loon Magic for Kids. Tom Klein. LC 91-14114. 48p. (J). 1990. pap. 6.95 (*1-55971-121-3*, NorthWord Pr) Creat Pub Intl.

Loon Notes: A Citizen's Guide to Loon Preservation. Paul Strong. (Illus.). 48p. (Orig.). (C). 1990. pap. 3.95 (*0-9625573-0-7*) Northland Coll SOEI.

Loon Rock. Maxine Trotter. Tr. by Helen Sylliboy. (Illus.). 26p. (J). (gr. k-2). pap. 7.95 (*0-920336-84-1*, Pub. by U Coll Cape Breton) Genl Dist Srvs.

Loon Song. Marcia A. Wakeland. (Illus.). 32p. (J). (gr. k-4). 1995. pap. 7.95 (*0-9635083-7-7*) Misty Mtn.

Loon Song. Marcia M. Wakeland. (Illus.). 32p. (J). (gr. k-4). 1995. 14.95 (*0-9635083-6-9*) Misty Mtn.

Loon Spirit. Phil Harper. LC 94-24958. (Illus.). 32p. (J). (gr. 1-5). 1995. 11.95 (*1-55971-463-8*, NorthWord Pr) Creat Pub Intl.

Loonette's Puzzles & Mazes. (Big Comfy Couch Puzzles & Mazes Ser.). (Illus.). 24p. (J). (ps-1). 1997. pap. write for info. (*0-7666-0015-7*, Honey Bear Bks) Modern Pub NYC.

Looney Coon. S. Campbell. 1980. pap. 3.00 (*0-933062-16-8*) R H Sommer.

***Looney Limericks.** Ed. by Frank Jacobs. (Illus.). 64p. 1999. pap. 1.00 (*0-486-40615-6*) Dover.

Looney Toon Big Book of Cross Stitch: 99 Designs. Leisure Arts Staff. LC 98-65610. 1998. pap. 19.95 (*1-57486-097-6*) Leisure AR.

Looney Tune Bath Book Aquarium. (J). 1995. 2.25 (*1-56960-183-6*) Book Essentials.

Looney Tune Bath Book Bath Time. (J). 1995. 2.25 (*1-56960-182-8*) Book Essentials.

Looney Tune Bath Book Seashore Fun. (J). 1995. 2.25 (*1-56960-184-4*) Book Essentials.

Looney Tune Bath Book Water Fun. (J). 1995. 2.25 (*1-56960-185-2*) Book Essentials.

Looney Tunes. Western Publishing Co., Inc. Staff. (Illus.). (J). (gr. k-4). 1993. pap. 19.95 (*1-882954-06-8*) Aspen Press.

Looney Tunes: Piano 4H. 33p. 1989. pap. 7.95 (*0-7692-1150-X*, PF0607) Wrner Bros.

Looney Tunes & Merrie Melodies. Jerry Beck & Will Friedwald. (Illus.). 396p. 1995. pap. 15.95 (*0-8050-0894-2*, Owl) H Holt & Co.

Looney Tunes BN Color-Me. 30p. (J). 1990. pap. 6.95 (*0-7692-1149-6*, PF0672) Wrner Bros.

Looney Tunes Collectibles: Unauthorized Guide. Debra S. Braun. LC 98-83099. (Illus.). 160p. 1999. pap. 29.95 (*0-7643-0823-8*) Schiffer.

Looney Tunes in Plastic Canvas, Bk. 7. 96p. 1996. pap. text 16.95 (*1-57486-036-4*) Oxmoor Hse.

Looney Tunes' Magic Eye. N.E. Thing Enterprises Staff. (Illus.). 32p. (J). 1995. 14.95 (*0-8362-7053-3*) Andrews & McMeel.

Looney Tunes Musical Storybook: Bugs Bunny's Circus Job. Sideline. 1989. 12.99 (*0-88704-173-6*) Sight & Sound.

Looney Tunes 1998 Collector's Value Guide. Joe T. Nguyen et al. 1998. pap. 10.95 (*1-888914-26-2*) CheckerBee.

Looney Tunes Spooky Stories. Oliver Noone. LC 97-214310. (Looney Tunes Song & Sound Bks.). (Illus.). 24p. (J). (ps-2). 1997. 14.98 (*0-7853-2366-X*, PI24) Pubns Intl Ltd.

Looney Tunes Talk Back to the Movies. (Looney Tunes Song & Sound Bks.). (Illus.). 24p. (J). (ps-6). 14.98 (*0-7853-1253-6*, PI5) Pubns Intl Ltd.

An Asterisk (*) at the beginning of an entry indicates that the title is appearing for the first time.

L

Looney Xylo-Tunes: Make Your Own Merry Melody Music. Looney Tunes Books Staff. (Illus.). (J). 1999. 17.99 (0-8289-1019-7) Penguin Putnam.

***Looneyspoons: Low-Fat Food Made Fun.** Janet Podleski. (Illus.). 2000. pap. 19.95 (0-399-52563-7, Perigee Bks) Berkley Pub.

Looneyspoons: Low-Fat Food Made Fun! Janet Podleski & Greta Podleski. LC 97-13876. (Illus.). 192p. 1997. per. 19.95 (0-9680631-1-X) Granet Pub.

***Looneyville Zip Code 25259 Lore: Applachian Mountains Folklore - Popular Etmology - Colloquial Speech.** Jake Miller. LC 99-91441. 2000. 25.00 (0-7388-0782-6); pap. 18.00 (0-7388-0783-4) Xlibris Corp.

Loonie Louie Meets the Space Fungus. Oscar S. Senn. 112p. (J). 1991. pap. 2.95 (0-380-75894-6, Avon Bks) Morrow Avon.

Loonie Summer. Christiane Duchesne. (First Novels Ser.). (Illus.). 60p. (J). (gr. 1-4). 1995. mass mkt. 3.99 (0-88780-272-9, Pub. by Formac Publ Co); bds. 14.95 (0-88780-273-7, Pub. by Formac Publ Co) Formac Dist Ltd.

Loonies Arrive. Christiane Duchesne. (First Novels Ser.). (Illus.). 61p. (J). (gr. 1-4). 1995. mass mkt. 3.99 (0-88780-206-0, Pub. by Formac Publ Co); bds. 14.95 (0-88780-207-9, Pub. by Formac Publ Co) Formac Dist Ltd.

Loons see Birdbooks

Loons. Text by Robert Busch. (Illus.). 120p. 1999. 24.95 (1-55110-928-X) Whitecap Bks.

Loons. Roy Dennis. (WorldLife Library). (Illus.). 72p. (Orig.). (YA). 1993. pap. 16.95 (0-89658-224-8) Voyageur Pr.

Loons. Aubrey Lang. (Illus.). 144p. 1996. pap. text 19.95 (1-55209-017-5) Firefly Bks Ltd.

***Loons.** Aubrey Lang & Wayne Lynch. (Illus.). 144p. 2000. 15.98 (1-57145-241-9, Thunder Bay) Advantage Pubs.

Loons. Patrick Merrick. LC 98-38203. (Illus.). 32p. (J). 1999. lib. bdg. 22.79 (1-56766-595-0) Childs World.

Loons: Postcard Book. Ed. by BrownTrout Publishing Company Staff. (Illus.). 1997. pap. 7.95 (1-56313-881-6) BrownTrout Pubs Inc.

Loons: Song of the Wild. Ed. by Michael Dregnl. (Illus.). 108p. 1999. pap. 9.95 (0-89658-425-9) Voyageur Pr.

Loons: Song of the Wild: An Anthology of Writing, Photography, & Art from Throughout the World on the Five Species of Loons. Ed. by Michael Dregni. LC 95-40899. (Illus.). 108p. 1996. 9.95 (0-89658-279-5) Voyageur Pr.

Loon's Necklace. Illus. by Elizabeth Cleaver. 24 pp.p. (J). (ps up). 1990. pap. 7.95 (0-19-540675-3) OUP.

Loon's Necklace. Williama Toye. (J). 1977. 12.70 (0-606-04470-1, Pub. by Turtleback) Demco.

***Loony-Bin Trip.** Kate Millett. 320p. 2000. reprint ed. pap. 16.95 (0-252-06888-2) U of Ill Pr.

Loony Laws & Other Strange Happenings. Roberts. LC 98-56202. 1998. pap. 5.95 (0-8069-2056-4) Sterling.

Loony Laws & Silly Statutes. Sheryl Lindsell-Roberts. LC 93-42066. (Illus.). 128p. (J). 1994. pap. 5.95 (0-8069-0472-0) Sterling.

Loop. Joe Coomer. 216p. 1999. pap. 11.00 (0-684-85904-1) S&S Trade Pap.

Loop. Nicholas Evans. LC 98-12240. 448p. 1998. 25.95 (0-385-31700-X) Delacorte.

Loop. Nicholas Evans. 544p. 1999. mass mkt. 7.99 (0-440-22462-4) Dell.

Loop. Warren Leight. Date not set. pap. 5.95 (0-8222-1734-1) Dramatists Play.

Loop. John Taggart. (Sun & Moon Classics Ser.: No. 151). 240p. 1991. pap. 10.95 (1-55713-012-4) Sun & Moon CA.

Loop. large type ed. Nicholas Evans. LC 98-34897. 672p. 1998. 30.00 (0-7862-1633-6, G K Hall Lrg Type) Mac Lib Ref.

Loop. large type ed. Nicholas Evans. LC 98-34897. 672p. 1999. pap. 30.00 (0-7862-1634-4) Thorndike Pr.

Loop: Where the Skyscraper Began. (Skyline: Pt. II). 1992. write for info. (1-880005-02-6) Perspectvs Intl.

Loop Current. large type ed. Alan Sewart. (Linford Mystery Library). 1991. pap. 16.99 (0-7089-7028-1, Linford) Ulverscroft.

Loop Groups. Andrew Pressley & Graeme Segal. (Oxford Mathematical Monographs). (Illus.). 316p. 1988. pap. text 45.00 (0-19-853561-9) OUP.

Loop Groups, Discrete Versions of Some Classical Integrable Systems, & Rank 2 Extensions. Percy Deift et al. LC 92-28571. (Memoirs Ser.: No. 479). 101p. 1992. pap. 26.00 (0-8218-2540-2, MEMO/100/479) Am Math.

Loop in the Lone Kauri Road. Allen Curnow. 1987. pap. 8.95 (0-19-648053-1) OUP.

Loop Parallelization. Utpal Banerjee. LC 94-5029. (International Series in Engineering & Computer Science, VLSI, Computer Architecture, & Digital Screen Processing). 192p. (C). 1994. text 133.50 (0-7923-9455-0) Kluwer Academic.

Loop Spaces, Characteristic Classes, & Geometric Quantization. Jean-Luc Brylinski. LC 92-34421. (Progress in Mathematics Ser.: Vol. 107). xvi, 300p. 1994. 54.50 (0-8176-3644-7) Birkhauser.

Loop the Loop. Barbara Dugan. LC 90-21727. (Illus.). 32p. (J). (gr. k up). 1992. lib. bdg. 15.93 (0-688-09648-4, Grenwillow Bks) HarpC Child Bks.

Loop the Loop. Barbara Dugan. LC 90-21727. (Illus.). 32p. (J). (ps-3). 1992. 16.00 (0-688-09647-6, Grenwillow Bks) HarpC Child Bks.

Loop the Loop. Barbara Dugan. LC 92-40168. (Picture Puffin Ser.). (Illus.). (J). 1993. 10.19 (0-606-05444-8, Pub. by Turtleback) Demco.

Loop Transfer Recovery: Analysis & Design. Ali Saberi et al. LC 93-3306. (Communications & Control Engineering Ser.). 1993. 97.95 (0-387-19831-8) Spr-Verlag.

Loop Transformations for Restructuring Compilers: The Foundations. Uptal Banerjee. LC 92-41647. 328p. (C). 1993. text 141.50 (0-7923-9318-X) Kluwer Academic.

Loophole Logic: The Finest Audit-Proof Tax Breaks. Andrew Westhem & Donald J. Korn. 302p. 1998. 26.95 (0-9637899-7-X) Elliott & James Pubs.

***Looping Evaluation Book.** Char Forsten et al. Ed. by Cathy Kingery. LC 99-74299. 86p. 1999. pap. 19.95 (1-884548-29-6, 5743, Crystal Spgs) Soc Dev Educ.

Looping Handbook: Teachers & Students Progressing Together. Jim Grant et al. Ed. by Aldene Fredenburg. LC 96-83277. 160p. 1996. pap. 24.95 (1-884548-07-5, 4857, Crystal Spgs) Soc Dev Educ.

***Looping the Loop: Posters of Flight.** Henry Serrano Villard & Willis M. Allen, Jr. LC 99-80208. (Illus.). 160p. 2000. 40.00 (0-9670076-2-3, 130767AE, Pub. by Kales Pr) Motorbooks Intl.

***Loops.** Actar Staff. (Quaderns Ser.: Vol. 23). 2000. 29.95 (84-95273-16-0) Actar.

Loops & Interfaces of Man. Loran Forizs. LC 76-24283. 1977. 7.95 (0-87212-072-4) Libra.

Loops & Roots: The Conflict Between Official & Traditional Family Planning in India. Purnima Chattopadhayay-Dutt. LC 94-905654. (Illus.). xxxv, 655p. (C). 1995. 69.00 (81-7024-659-8, Pub. by Ashish Pub Hse) Nataraj Bks.

Loops for Learning: Memory Boosters Across the Curriculum, Grades 4-10. Dale Bulla. LC 95-13799. 1995. pap. 29.00 (1-56976-027-6) Zephyr Pr AZ.

Loops, Knots, Gauge Theories & Quantum Gravity. Rodolfo Gambini & Jorge Pullin. (Monographs on Mathematical Physics). (Illus.). 337p. (C). 1999. pap. text 44.95 (0-521-65475-0) Cambridge U Pr.

Loos Family Genealogy, 1535-1958. S. L. Bast. 245p. 1991. reprint ed. pap. 37.00 (0-8328-2040-7); reprint ed. lib. bdg. 47.00 (0-8328-2039-3) Higginson Bk Co.

Loose among the Lambs. large type ed. Jay Brandon. LC 94-922. 686p. 1994. lib. bdg. 23.95 (0-7862-0197-5) Thorndike Pr.

Loose among the Lambs. Jay Brandon. Ed. by Bill Grose. 1994. reprint ed. pap. 6.50 (0-671-88315-1) PB.

Loose among the Lambs. Jay Brandon. Ed. by Bill Grose. 400p. 1994. reprint ed. mass mkt. 5.99 (0-671-76033-5) PB.

Loose Balls: Easy Money, Hard Fouls, Cheap Laughs & True Love in the NBA. Jayson Williams & Steve Friedman. LC 99-41569. 288p. 2000. 23.95 (0-385-49226-X) Doubleday.

Loose Bolts? Peter Schlaifer. 1973. 225.00 (1-893139-08-5) Merrimack Films.

***Loose Boundary Hydraulics.** Arved J. Raudkivi. (Illus.). 512p. (C). 1998. text 100.00 (90-5410-447-3, Pub. by A A Balkema); pap. text, student ed. 53.00 (90-5410-448-1, Pub. by A A Balkema) Ashgate Pub Co.

Loose Boundary Hydraulics. 3rd ed. Arved J. Raudkivi. (Civil Engineering Ser.). (Illus.). 556p. 1990. pap. text 74.95 (0-08-034073-3, Prgamon Press) Buttrwrth-Heinemann.

***Loose Cannon.** Dean Ing. 2000. text 23.95 (0-312-87194-5) Forge NYC.

Loose Cannon. large type ed. Donald MacKenzie. LC 93-28769. 269p. 1994. lib. bdg. 16.95 (0-8161-5859-2, G K Hall Lrg Type) Mac Lib Ref.

Loose Cannons. Stan Seaberg. LC 97-75506. 208p. 1998. 19.95 (1-57197-093-2) Pentland Pr.

Loose Cannons: Devastating Dish from the World's Wildest Women. Autumn Stephens. LC 97-38649. 256p. 1998. pap. 11.95 (1-57324-107-5) Conari Press.

Loose Cannons: Devastating Dish from the World's Wildest Women. Autumn Stephens. 304p. 1999. 7.98 (1-56731-319-1, MJF Bks) Fine Comms.

Loose Canons. John Hoffman. Date not set. write for info. (0-06-099610-2); 13.00 (0-06-098748-0) HarpC.

Loose Canons. John Hoffman. 384p. 2000. 24.00 (0-06-039275-4, ReganBks) HarperTrade.

Loose Canons: Notes of the Culture Wars. Henry Louis Gates, Jr. 232p. 1992. text 30.00 (0-19-507519-6) OUP.

Loose Canons: Notes on the Cultural Wars. Henry Louis Gates, Jr. 224p. 1993. pap. 13.95 (0-19-508350-4) OUP.

Loose Change: 3 Women of the 60s. Sara Davidson. LC 96-37040. 381p. 1997. pap. 14.95 (0-520-20910-9, Pub. by U CA Pr) Cal Prin Full Svc.

Loose Change Blue Book for Slot Machines: A Price Guide to Relative Current Value 1997-1998 (Approved Through 2003) 4th rev. ed. Ed. by Daniel R. Mead. LC 96-94665. 368p. 1997. per. 39.95 (0-934422-52-4, BKS-100324) Mead Pub Corp.

Loose Change Red Book Price Guide for Trade Stimulators & Counter Games: A Price Guide to Relative Current Value - 1997-1998 (Approved Through 2003) 3rd ed. Daniel R. Mead. LC 96-94664. 110p. 1996. per. 17.95 (0-934422-48-6, BKS-100486) Mead Pub Corp.

Loose Chippings. Thomas G. Wheeler. LC 69-11990. (Illus.). (YA). (gr. 10 up). 1969. 26.95 (0-87599-152-1) S G Phillips.

***Loose Coins.** Joe L. Hensley & Guy M. Townsend. (WWL Mystery Ser.: Bk. 352). 2000. per. 5.99 (0-373-26352-X, 1-26352-4, Wrldwide Lib) Harlequin Bks.

Loose Coins. Joe L. Hensley & Guy M. Townsend. LC 98-21126. 208p. 1998. text 20.95 (0-312-19297-5) St Martin.

Loose Connection. M. R. Meek. 224p. 1991. per. 3.50 (0-373-26070-9) Harlequin Bks.

Loose Connections: Joining Together in America's Fragmented Communities. Robert Wuthnow. LC 98-14519. ix, 336p. 1998. 35.00 (0-674-53903-6) HUP.

Loose-Coupling Revisited: A Critical View of Weick's Contribution to Educational Administration. Ed. by William Foster. 125p. (C). 1983. 45.00 (0-7300-0004-4, Pub. by Deakin Univ) St Mut.

Loose Cow Party. Baxter Black. (Illus.). 1998. pap. 13.95 (0-939343-29-0) Coyote Cowboy.

***Loose Diamonds: A Novel.** Theodora Overton. 304p. 2001. pap. 14.95 (1-56474-355-1) Fithian Pr.

Loose Ends. John Hewitt. 62p. 1983. pap. 8.95 (0-85640-284-2, Pub. by Blackstaff Pr) Dufour.

Loose Ends: A Journaling Tool for Tying up the Incomplete Details of Your Life & Heart. Eldonna Bouton. (Illus.). 172p. 1999. pap. 13.95 (0-9670384-0-5) Whole Hrt.

***Loose Ends: A Novel.** Neal Bowers. LC 00-34166. 2001. write for info. (0-375-50499-0) Random.

Loose Ends: Closure & Crisis in the American Social Text. Russell J. Reising. LC 96-24672. (New Americanists Ser.). (Illus.). 392p. 1997. pap. text 18.95 (0-8223-1891-1); lib. bdg. 54.95 (0-8223-1887-3) Duke.

Loose Ends: Jottings from a Fractured Life Ned Sherrin. LC 93-53817. 205 p. 1991. write for info. (0-340-55908-X) St Martin.

Loose Ends: Poems. Vanessa Van Dyke. 64p. (Orig.). 1993. pap. 8.50 (1-56474-056-0) Fithian Pr.

Loose Ends: Poems from Hollywood. Mark Dunster. 11p. 1999. pap. 5.00 (0-89642-788-9) Linden Pubs.

Loose-fill Insulations. 8p. 1995. pap. 1.00 (0-16-063413-X) USGPO.

Loose Gems: Stories about Life, Love & Business. Sidney Taial. Ed. by Walt Crowley. (Illus.). 96p. 1998. 19.98 (0-9664745-0-3) Crowley Assocs.

Loose Herd of Texans. Billy Porterfield. LC 77-99277. 212p. 1978. 18.95 (0-89096-044-5) Tex A&M Univ Pr.

Loose Hints upon Education: 1782 Edition. Henry Home. 436p. 1996. reprint ed. 85.00 (1-85506-420-0) Bks Intl VA.

Loose-Leaf Lectionary: Green Binder. 1990. spiral bd. 24.95 (0-8146-1194-X) Liturgical Pr.

Loose-Leaf Lectionary: Red Binder. 1993. spiral bd. 24.95 (0-8146-2295-X) Liturgical Pr.

Loose-leaf 3-hole Punched Text-acct. 18th ed. Philip E. Fess & Carl S. Warren. (SWC-Accounting). 1995. ring bd. 79.95 (0-538-85910-5) S-W Pub.

Loose Leaves Fall: Selected Poems. Kerry S. Keys. LC 77-10170. 77p. 1977. pap. 10.00 (0-930502-00-0) Pine Pr.

Loose Leaves from a Busy Life. Morris Hillquit. LC 78-146160. (Civil Liberties in American History Ser.). 1971. reprint ed. lib. bdg. 42.50 (0-306-70102-2) Da Capo.

Loose Lips. Rita Mae Brown. LC 98-56079. 384p. 1999. 24.95 (0-553-09972-8) Bantam.

***Loose Lips.** Rita Mae Brown. 384p. 2000. pap. 13.95 (0-553-38067-2, Spectra) Bantam.

Loose Livers & Floatin Kidneys. Wayne Ates. 80p. 1997. pap. 8.00 (0-8059-4111-8) Dorrance.

Loose Nuts: Under the Hood & Behind the Wheel: A Glossary of Car Terms. Ed. by Brenda Star. (Illus.). 64p. 1997. pap. 14.95 (1-884886-06-X) Star Group.

Loose on Liquidators: The Role of a Liquidator in a Voluntary Winding-Up. Peter Loose. xxiii, 216p. 1972. 18.95 (0-85308-023-2) W S Hein.

Loose on Liquidators: The Role of a Liquidator in a Voluntary Winding-Up. Ed. by Peter Losse & Michael Griffiths. 400p. (C). 1989. 200.00 (0-7855-6040-8) St Mut.

Loose on the Wind. Will H. Hays, Jr. 342p. (Orig.). 1989. pap. write for info. (0-9624303-0-7) W H Hays.

Loose Papers & Sundry Chancery Causes. Jean M. Mihalyka. 1997. pap. 28.00 (1-886706-22-0) Hickory Hse.

Loose Screw. large type ed. Gerald Hammond. (Linford Mystery Library). 288p. 1988. pap. 16.99 (0-7089-6501-6, Linford) Ulverscroft.

***Loose Screws.** J. M. Powers & L. M. Stout. LC 99-90812. 1999. 25.00 (0-7388-0538-6); pap. 18.00 (0-7388-0539-4) Xlibris Corp.

Loose Shoes: The Story of Ralph Sutton. James D. Shacter. LC 93-80452. (Illus.). 470p. 1994. 30.00 (0-9639101-0-8) Jaynar Pr.

Loose Sugar. Brenda Hillman. LC 96-44572. (Wesleyan Poetry Ser.). 127p. 1997. pap. 12.95 (0-8195-2243-0, Wesleyan Univ Pr); text 25.00 (0-8195-2242-2, Wesleyan Univ Pr) U Pr of New Eng.

Loose That Man & Let Him Go see Hombre, Eres Libre-Desatad... Hombre!

Loose That Man & Let Him Go! T. D. Jakes. LC 97-149644. 224p. 1995. pap. 11.99 (1-880089-15-7, Pub. by Albury Pub) Appalach Bk Dist.

Loose That Man & Let Him Go! T. D. Jakes. 56p. 1996. pap., wbk. ed. 7.99 (1-880089-42-4, Pub. by Albury Pub) Appalach Bk Dist.

Loose That Man & Let Him Go! T. D. Jakes. 224p. 1996. 15.99 (1-880089-97-1, Pub. by Albury Pub) Appalach Bk Dist.

***Loose That Man & Let Him Go! So You Call Yourself a Man?** T. D. Jakes. 2000. 12.99 (0-88486-277-1, Inspirational Pr) Arrowood Pr.

Loose to the Wilds. 2nd ed. Martin McMurtrey. 162p. (YA). reprint ed. pap. 6.00 (0-9623961-0-9) M A McMurtrey.

Loose Tooth. Steven Kroll. (J). 1984. 10.19 (0-606-02729-7, Pub. by Turtleback) Demco.

Loose-Tooth Luke. Patsy Jensen. LC 97-31371. (Real Kids Readers Ser.). (Illus.). 48p. (J). (gr. 1-3). 1998. pap. 3.99 (0-7613-2034-2); lib. bdg. 17.90 (0-7613-2009-1) Millbrook Pr.

***Loose Watch: A Lost & Found Times Anthology.** Ed. by John M. Bennett. 205p. 1998. pap. 20.00 (0-9521256-8-4, Pub. by Invisible Bks) SPD-Small Pr Dist.

Loose Woman. Sandra Cisneros. LC 93-35937. 115p. 1994. 22.50 (0-679-41644-7) Knopf.

Loose Woman. Sandra Cisneros. LC 93-35937. 1995. pap. 10.00 (0-679-75527-6) Vin Bks.

Loose Women, Lecherous Men: A Feminist Philosophy of Sex. Linda J. LeMoncheck. LC 96-34477. 320p. 1997. pap. 22.00 (0-19-510556-7) OUP.

***Loosed to Live.** Rita L. Twiggs. Ed. by Norman O. Hall. (Illus.). 52p. 2000. pap. 10.00 (0-9667850-5-3) Black Pearl Pub.

LooseEnds. Owen Hill. 72p. (Orig.). 1996. pap. 6.95 (0-926664-15-8) Bay Area Ctr Art & Tech.

Loosen Up! Quick Activities to Build Confidence & Creativity. Greta Rasmussen & Ted Rasmussen. (Illus.). 64p. (Orig.). (J). (gr. 2-6). 1997. pap. 8.95 (0-936110-19-8) Tin Man Pr.

Loosening the Bonds. Joan M. Jensen. LC 85-22471. 273p. (C). 1988. pap. 19.00 (0-300-04265-5) Yale U Pr.

Loosening the Grip: A Handbook of Alcohol Information. 6th ed. Jean Kinney. LC 99-16744. (Illus.). 480p. 2000. write for info. (0-07-289106-8) McGraw-Hill HPD.

Loosening the Reins: Stories of a Father & His Son. John L. Moore. 224p. 1992. pap. 9.99 (0-310-57721-7) Zondervan.

***Loosening the Seams: Interpretations of Gerald Vizenor.** A. Robert Lee. LC 99-58862. (Illus.). 321p. 2000. pap. 29.95 (0-87972-802-7) Bowling Green Univ Popular Press.

***Loosening the Seams: Interpretations of Gerald Vizenor.** Ed. by A. Robert Lee. LC 99-58862. (Illus.). 321p. 2000. 59.95 (0-87972-801-9) Bowling Green Univ Popular Press.

Loosening Up: Getting Rid of Those Uptight Feelings. James Cisek & Anthea George. (Illus.). 40p. 1985. reprint ed. pap. 4.25 (0-9604510-7-2) Life Skills.

Loosestrife: Poems. Stephen Dunn. LC 96-1238. 80p. 1996. 19.00 (0-393-03982-X) Norton.

Loosestrife: Poems. Stephen Dunn. LC 96-1238. 96p. 1998. pap. 11.00 (0-393-31683-1) Norton.

Loot. Aaron Elkins. LC 98-35254. 320p. 1999. 24.00 (0-688-15927-3, Wm Morrow) Morrow Avon.

***Loot.** Aaron Elkins. LC 98-35254. 384p. 1999. mass mkt. 6.99 (0-380-73162-2, Avon Bks) Morrow Avon.

Loot. Aaron Elkins. LC 99-31996. 1999. write for info. (1-56895-750-5) Wheeler Pub.

***Loot!** large type ed. Albert Payson Terhune. LC 00-20840. 265p. 2000. 30.00 (0-7838-8746-9, G K Hall & Co) Mac Lib Ref.

Loot. Truman H. Alexander. LC 79-39077. (Black Heritage Library Collection). 1977. reprint ed. 21.95 (0-8369-9015-3) Ayer.

Loot of Cities. Arnold Bennett. LC 74-17025. (Collected Works of Arnold Bennett: Vol. 49). 1977. reprint ed. 25.95 (0-518-19130-3) Ayer.

Loot of the Cities. Arnold Bennett. 1972. 10.00 (1-880418-08-8) D M Grant.

Loot Players. Chalcey Mellowe & Elmer Spiezio. 170p. 1998. pap. 16.95 (1-57502-717-8) Morris Pubng.

Loot Players. Clancey Mellowe. 208p. 1998. pap. 19.95 (1-57502-608-2, PO1745) Morris Pubng.

Lootas, the Little Wave-Eater: An Orphaned Sea Otter's Story. Clare H. Meeker. LC 99-24722. (Illus.). 43p. (J). (gr. 3-5). 1999. pap. 12.95 (1-57061-164-5) Sasquatch Bks.

***Looted: The Philippines after the Bases.** Donald Kirk. 2000. pap. 21.95 (0-312-22769-8) St Martin.

Looted Democracy. Donald Kirk. LC 97-21844. 1998. text 45.00 (0-312-17423-3) St Martin.

Looters. Robert Minhinnick. LC 89-82059. 72p. 1990. pap. 14.95 (1-85411-019-5, Pub. by Seren Bks) Dufour.

***Looters of Eden.** Frank L. Hicks, Jr. (Illus.). 325p. 1999. 26.95 (1-929179-05-7) Solitude Solace.

Looters of the Public Domain. S. A. Puter. LC 70-38833. (Illus.). 495p. 1972. reprint ed. lib. bdg. 59.50 (0-306-70449-8) Da Capo.

Looters of the Public Domain: Embracing a Complete Exposure of the Fraudulent System of Acquiring Titles to the Public Lands of the United States. Stephen A. Futer & Horace Stevens. LC 72-2866. (Use & Abuse of America's Natural Resources Ser.). (Illus.). 500p. 1972. reprint ed. 36.95 (0-405-04530-1) Ayer.

Looting of Nicaragua. Rafael De Nogales. LC 70-111726. (American Imperialism: Viewpoints of United States Foreign Policy, 1898-1941 Ser.), 1970. reprint ed. 23.95 (0-405-02041-4) Ayer.

***Loouisiana Attorney's/Secretary's Handbook.** 13th ed. 520p. 2000. 55.00 (0-9631577-8-7) Cypress MN.

Lop Rabbits As Pets. Sandy Crook. (Illus.). 128p. 1986. 24.95 (0-86622-137-9, PS-809) TFH Pubns.

LOPADS: Fifth Annual Workshop on Input/Output in Parallel & Distributed Systems 1997. 114p. 1997. pap. write for info. (0-89791-966-1, 415973) Assn Compu Machinery.

Lopate Essays. Phillip Lopate. 1999. pap. 18.25 (0-670-81435-0) Viking Penguin.

Lope de Vega: El Arte Nuevo de Hacer "Novellas" Carmen R. Rabel. (Monografias A Ser.: No. A 150). 94p. (C). 1992. 54.00 (1-85566-016-4, Pub. by Tamesis Bks Ltd) Boydell & Brewer.

Lope de Vega & Spanish Drama. James Fitzmaurice-Kelly. LC 79-115860. (Studies in European Literature: No. 56). 63p. 1970. reprint ed. lib. bdg. 75.00 (0-8383-1073-7) M S G Haskell Hse.

***Lope De Vega & the Comedia De Santos.** Robert R. Morrison. LC 99-45899. (Iberica Ser.: Vol. 33). 432p. (C). 2000. 66.95 (0-8204-4856-7) P Lang Pubng.

Lope de Vega in Deutschland. Hermann Tiemann. xv, 310p. 1970. reprint ed. write for info. (0-318-71869-3) G Olms Pubs.

Lope de Vega in Deutschland. Hermann Tiemann. (Illus.). xv, 310p. 1970. reprint ed. write for info. (0-318-71640-2) G Olms Pubs.

An Asterisk (*) at the beginning of an entry indicates that the title is appearing for the first time.

Lope de Vega's El Brasil Restituido. Gino De Solenni & Lope de Vega. (ENG & SPA.). 306p. 1929. text 2.60 (*0-318-14282-1*) Hispanic Inst.

Lope de Vega's El Castigo del Discreto. William L. Fichter. (ENG & SPA.). 280p. 1925. text 2.00 (*0-318-14283-X*) Hispanic Inst.

Lope de Vega's "El Desden Vengado" Lope de Vega. Ed. & Intro. by Mabel M. Harlan. xliv, 196p. 1938. 3.60 (*0-318-22347-3*) Hispanic Inst.

Lope de Vega's El Palacio Confuso. Intro. by Charles H. Stevens. 138p. 1939. text 2.90 (*0-318-14284-8*) Hispanic Inst.

Lope de Vega's "La Desdichada Estefania" A Critical Edition of the Autograph Manuscript. Hugh W. Kennedy & Lope de Vega. LC 75-1049. (Romance Monographs: No. 13). 1975. 31.00 (*84-399-3628-1*) Romance.

Lope de Vega's "La Nueva Victoria de Don Gonzalo de Cordoua" Henryk Ziomek. 211p. 1939. 6.00 (*0-318-22348-1*) Hispanic Inst.

Lope de Vega's "Los Espanoles en Flandes" A Critical Edition. Lope de Vega. Ed. by Veronica M. Sauter. LC 95-13285. (Iberica Ser.: No. 17). (Illus.). X, 286p. (C). 1998. text 52.95 (*0-8204-2824-8*) P Lang Pubng.

Lope de Vega's Vida & Valores. Villanueva F. Marques. LC 87-25561. 369p. 1988. pap. 20.00 (*0-8477-3522-2*) U of PR Pr.

L'Opera Del Tradimento see Work of Betrayal

L'Opera del Tradimento see Work of Betrayal

L'Opera Del Tradimento see Work of Betrayal

L'Opera del Tradimento see Work of Betrayal

L'Opera, ou la Defaite des Femmes see Opera: The Undoing of Women

Lopharia & Porostereum (Corticiaceae) K. Hjortstam & Leif Ryvarden. (Synopsis Fungorum Ser.: No. 4). 68p. 1990. pap. text 27.50 (*82-90724-06-3*, Pub. by Fungi-Flora) Lubrecht & Cramer.

Lophophorates: Notes for a Short Course Organized by J. T. Dutro, Jr. & R. S. Boardman. Ed. by T. W. Broadhead. (Studies in Geology). (Illus.). iv, 251p. 1981. pap. 12.00 (*0-910249-03-2*) U of Tenn Geo.

Lopsided: A Comic Expose of Southern California. Richard Tyrone. LC 93-83954. 175p. (Orig.). 1993. pap. 8.95 (*0-9635908-3-9*) Pentrope Pub.

Lopsided Angel. Noan Carlson. LC 96-79034. (Illus.). 176p. (Orig.). 1996. pap. 9.95 (*1-882420-29-2*) Hearth KS.

Lopsided Growth: Political Economy of Indian Development. Pradhan H. Prasad. (Illus.). 136p. 1990. 14.95 (*0-19-562406-8*) OUP.

***Lopsided March for String Sextet.** Eugenia Schuler. 22p. 1999. write for info. (*0-934502-04-8*) Thursday Pubs.

L'Option Nucleaire see Nuclear Power Game

Loquacities. Charles M. Flandrau. LC 68-22912. (Essay Index Reprint Ser.). 1977. reprint ed. 19.95 (*0-8369-0445-1*) Ayer.

***Lora Brody Plugged In: The Definitive Guide to the Best Kitchen Appliances.** Lora Brody. Ed. by Pam Hoenig. LC 97-17682. 384p. 1998. 25.00 (*0-688-14961-8*, Wm Morrow) Morrow Avon.

***Lorain.** Black River Historical Society Staff. (Images of America Ser.). 128p. 1999. pap. 18.99 (*0-7385-0178-6*) Arcadia Publng.

Lorain & Medina Street Atlas. 24th ed. (Illus.). 1997. 4.95 (*1-879116-41-3*, 873-Y) Commercial Survey.

Loran-C Handbook. Bud Kaczor. 104p. (Orig.). 1986. pap. 12.95 (*0-9617593-0-5*) Sea Dog Marine Pub.

Loran-C User Handbook. (Illus.). 257p. (Orig.). (C). 1994. pap. text 40.00 (*0-7881-1102-7*) DIANE Pub.

Loran-C User Handbook. (Orig.). 1997. lib. bdg. 251.95 (*0-8490-8200-5*) Gordon Pr.

Loran-C User Handbook. (Commandant Instruction Ser.: No. M 16552.3). (Illus.). 257p. (Orig.). 1980. pap. 20.00 (*0-16-041594-2*, 050-012-00331-9) USGPO.

Loran C-User Handbook: Radionavigation System. 1995. lib. bdg. 252.75 (*0-8490-7516-5*) Gordon Pr.

Loran Cruise Plans: For Long Island Sound, Block Island Sound & Newport, Rhode Island, Vol. 2. Robert G. Adelson. 1986. 59.95 (*0-9615134-1-1*) Am Marine Corp.

Loran Cruise Plans: For Massachusetts, Rhode Island, Cape Cod & the Islands, Vol. 1. Robert G. Adelson. 1985. 59.95 (*0-9615134-0-3*) Am Marine Corp.

Loranthaceae of Southern India & Their Host Plants. Ed. by C. E. Fischer. 195p. 1978. reprint ed. 45.00 (*0-7855-3045-2*, Pub. by Intl Bk Distr) St Mut.

Loras College Story: 150 Years. Francis P. Friedl. (Illus.). 242p. 1990. 15.00 (*0-936875-05-4*) Loras Coll Pr.

Lorax see Lorax

Lorax. Dr. Seuss, pseud. (Illus.). (J). (gr. 2-3). 1971. lib. bdg. 15.99 (*0-394-92337-5*, Pub. by Random Bks Yng Read) Random.

Lorax. Dr. Seuss, pseud. (J). 1971. 14.00 (*0-606-03849-3*, Pub. by Turtleback) Demco.

Lorax. Dr. Seuss, pseud. (Illus.). 61p. (J). (ps-3). 1971. 14.00 (*0-394-82337-0*, Pub. by Random Bks Yng Read) Random.

Lorax. Dr. Seuss, pseud. (J). 1992. pap. 13.00 incl. audio (*0-679-82273-9*, Pub. by Random Bks Yng Read) Random.

Lorax. Dr. Seuss, pseud. Tr. by Aida E. Marcuse. Orig. Title: The Lorax. (Illus.). (J). (gr. 3-6). 1993. 14.95 (*1-880507-04-8*) Lectorum Pubns.

Lorax Mini. Dr. Seuss, pseud. (J). 1998. 4.99 (*0-679-88910-8*, Pub. by Random Bks Yng Read) Random.

Lorax Mini Book & Puppet. Dr. Seuss, pseud. (J). 1998. 14.99 (*0-679-88909-4*, Pub. by Random Bks Yng Read) Random.

Lorbeeren des Casar. Rene de Goscinny & M. Uderzo. (GER., Illus.). (J). 24.95 (*0-8288-4978-1*) Fr & Eur.

***Lorca: A Dream of Life.** Leslie Stainton. LC 98-51194. (Illus.). 496p. 1999. text 35.00 (*0-374-19097-6*) FS&G.

***Lorca: A Dream of Life.** Leslie Stainton. (Illus.). 496p. 2000. pap. 16.00 (*0-374-52702-4*) FS&G.

Lorca: An Appreciation of His Poetry. Roy Campbell. LC 76-137665. (Studies in Poetry: No. 38). (C). 1971. reprint ed. lib. bdg. 75.00 (*0-8383-1226-8*) M S G Haskell Hse.

Lorca: Plays 1. Federico Garcia Lorca. Tr. by Gwynne Edwards & Peter Luke. (Methuen World Dramatists Ser.). 208p. (C). 1988. pap. write for info. (*0-413-15780-6*, A0155, Methuen Drama) Methn.

Lorca: Plays 2. Federico Garcia Lorca. Tr. & Intro. by Gwynne Edwards. (Methuen World Dramatists Ser.). 181p. (C). 1990. pap. write for info. (*0-413-62260-6*, A0400, Methuen Drama) Methn.

Lorca: Plays 3. Federico Garcia Lorca. Tr. by Gwynne Edwards & Henry Livings. 224p. (C). 1993. pap. write for info. (*0-413-65240-8*, A0630, Methuen Drama) Methn.

Lorca: The Theater Beneath the Sand. Gwynne Edwards. 356p. 1982. 20.00 (*0-7145-2698-3*) M Boyars Pubs.

Lorca: The Theatre Beneath the Sand. Gwynne Edwards. 356p. 1995. pap. 16.95 (*0-7145-2771-8*) M Boyars Pubs.

Lorca, Alberti, & the Theater of Popular Poetry. Sandra Robertson. LC 91-17755. (American University Studies: Romance Languages & Literature: Ser. II, Vol. 170). 267p. 1992. 44.95 (*0-8204-1565-0*) P Lang Pubng.

Lorca & Jimenez: Selected Poems. Federico Garcia Lorca et al. Tr. & Compiled by Robert Bly. LC 96-52545. 208p. 1997. pap. 14.00 (*0-8070-6213-8*) Beacon Pr.

Lorca en la Lirica Puertorriquena. Juan A. Pagan. LC 80-17628. (Coleccion Mente y Palabra). (Illus.). 359p. 1981. 12.00 (*0-8477-0574-9*); pap. 9.60 (*0-8477-0575-7*) U of PR Pr.

Lorca Poesie d'Uove Vie. Joseph Velasco. (Iberian Studies: No. 8). (FRE.). 494p. (Orig.). 1997. pap. text 59.95 (*1-889431-09-5*) Univ Pr South.

Lorca, una Escritura en Trance: Libro de Poemas y Divan del Tamarit. Candelas Newton. LC 92-12286. (Purdue University Monographs in Romance Languages: Vol. 40). (SPA.). x, 250p. 1992. 80.00 (*1-55619-308-4*); pap. 27.95 (*1-55619-309-2*) J Benjamins Pubng Co.

Lorca, Valle-Inclan y Las Esteticas de la Disidencia: Ensayos Sobre Literatura Hispanica. Sumner Greenfield. LC 95-68280. (SPA.). 219p. (Orig.). 1996. pap. 35.00 (*0-89295-083-8*) Society Sp & Sp-Am.

Lorca Variations, Vols. I-VIII. Jerome Rothenberg. 1990. pap. 8.00 (*84-87467-02-4*, Pub. by Zasterle Pr) SPD-Small Pr Dist.

Lorca Variations: 1 to 33. Jerome Rothenberg. LC 93-794. 128p. (Orig.). 1993. pap. 10.95 (*0-8112-1253-X*, NDP771, Pub. by New Directions) Norton.

Lorca y las Vanguardias: Hacia el Teatro. Antonio Cao. (Monagrafias A Ser.: Vol. CXII). (SPA.). 106p. (C). 1984. 41.00 (*0-7293-0202-4*, Pub. by Tamesis Bks Ltd) Boydell & Brewer.

LorcaLines: Combinations Inspired by Federico Garcia Lorca. William Lemos. LC 94-72532. (Illus.). 60p. (Orig.). 1994. pap. 12.95 (*0-9642125-1-X*) Daylight Ducks.

Lorcan O'Herlihy. Ed. by Oscar R. Ojeda. (Contemporary World Architects Ser.). (Illus.). 132p. 1999. pap. 19.99 (*1-56496-504-X*) Rockport Pubs.

Lorca's Drawings & Poems: Forming the Eye of the Reader. Cecelia J. Cavanaugh. LC 95-4099. (Illus.). 208p. 1995. 39.50 (*0-8387-5302-7*) Bucknell U Pr.

Lorca's Poet in New York: The Fall into Consciousness. Betty J. Craige. LC 76-24339. (Studies in Romance Languages: No. 15). 106p. reprint ed. pap. 32.90 (*0-7837-5818-9*, 204548500006) Bks Demand.

Lorca's the Public: A Study of His Unfinished Play el Publico & of Love & Death in the Work of Federico Garcia Lorca. Rafael M. Nadal. 247p. (C). 1981. pap. 9.95 (*0-7145-2752-1*) M Boyars Pubs.

Lord. Romano Guardini. LC 96-22678. 535p. 1996. pap. 14.95 (*0-89526-714-4*, Gateway Editions) Regnery Pub.

Lord. C. E. Lord. (Illus.). 263p. 1991. reprint ed. pap. 42.00 (*0-8328-2026-1*); reprint ed. lib. bdg. 52.00 (*0-8328-2025-3*) Higginson Bk Co.

Lord: Certain Members of the Lord Family Who Settled in New York City in the Early 1800's, Descendants of Thomas Lord of Hartford, Connecticut. Kenneth Lord. 92p. 1995. reprint ed. pap. 18.00 (*0-8328-4924-3*); reprint ed. lib. bdg. 28.00 (*0-8328-4923-5*) Higginson Bk Co.

Lord: History of the Descendants of Nathan Lord of Ancient Kittery, Maine. C. C. Lord. Ed. by G. E. Lord. (Illus.). 218p. 1993. reprint ed. pap. 33.00 (*0-8328-3708-3*); reprint ed. lib. bdg. 43.00 (*0-8328-3707-5*) Higginson Bk Co.

***Lord Acton.** Roland Hill. LC 99-53065. (Illus.). 523p. 2000. 39.95 (*0-300-07956-7*) Yale U Pr.

Lord Acton: A Study in Conscience & Politics. Gertrude Himmelfarb. 1993. pap. 19.95 (*1-55815-270-9*) ICS Pr.

Lord Acton's History of Liberty. George Watson. 122p. 1994. 52.95 (*0-85967-995-0*, Pub. by Scolar Pr) Ashgate Pub Co.

Lord Advocate's Diary. Gordon Stott. 252p. 1991. 25.90 (*0-08-041399-4*, Pub. by Aberdeen U Pr) Macmillan.

Lord Alfred Tennyson see Victorian Poets: Critical Heritage

Lord & Christ: The Implications of Lordship for Faith & Life. Ernest C. Reisinger. LC 94-33274. 198p. (Orig.). 1994. pap. 8.99 (*0-87552-388-9*) P & R Pubng.

Lord & Giver of Life. John Paul, II, pseud. 120p. (Orig.). 1986. pap. 6.95 (*1-55586-103-2*) US Catholic.

Lord & Giver of Life see I Believe in the Holy Spirit

Lord & His Prayer. N. T. Wright. LC 97-8577. 96p. 1997. pap. 9.00 (*0-8028-4320-4*) Eerdmans.

Lord & His Prayer. N. T. Wright. 96p. 1997. pap. 8.00 (*0-88028-178-2*, 1407) Forward Movement.

***Lord & Lady of Heat: The Poem.** Lady Randy. 1999. pap. 14.00 (*0-9674838-0-8*, LLH-1) LadyRandy.

Lord & Peasant in Peru: A Paradigm of Political & Social Change. F. LaMond Tullis. LC 79-116738. 303p. reprint ed. pap. 94.00 (*0-7837-2340-7*, 205742800004) Bks Demand.

Lord & the General Din of the World. Jane Mead. LC 95-23868. 96p. 1996. pap. 12.95 (*0-9641151-1-5*) Sarabande Bks.

Lord Arthur Savile's Crime. Oscar Wilde. 20.95 (*0-8488-0328-0*) Amereon Ltd.

***Lord Arthur Savile's Crime.** Oscar Wilde. 2000. pap. 3.95 (*1-86092-016-0*, Pub. by Travelman Pub) IPG Chicago.

Lord Arthur Savile's Crime, The Portrait of Mr. W. H. see Works of Oscar Wilde

Lord Arundel & His Circle. David Howarth. LC 85-2515. 264p. 1986. 65.00 (*0-300-03469-5*) Yale U Pr.

Lord Atkin. Geoffrey Lewis. 288p. 1984. boxed set 50.00 (*0-406-27210-7*, UK, MICHIE) LEXIS Pub.

***Lord Atkin.** Geoffrey Lewis. 264p. 1999. reprint ed. 54.00 (*1-84113-057-5*, Pub. by Hart Pub) Intl Spec Bk.

Lord Baltimore. Loree Lough. (Colonial Leaders Ser.). (Illus.). 80p. (J). (gr. 3 up). 1999. pap. 8.95 (*0-7910-5692-9*) Chelsea Hse.

Lord Baltimore. Lori Lough. LC 99-33136. (Colonial Leaders Ser.). (Illus.). 80p. (YA). (gr. 3 up). 1999. 16.95 (*0-7910-5349-0*) Chelsea Hse.

Lord Barton's Honour. Elizabeth Michaels. (Regency Romance Ser.). 1993. mass mkt. 2.99 (*0-373-31201-6*, 1-31201-6) Harlequin Bks.

***Lord Be Glorified (Assembly Edition) Companion Hymnal for Blended Worship, 2 vols.** 223p. 1999. write for info. (*1-57992-050-0*) OR Catholic.

Lord Be Glorified (Keyboard/Vocal Edition) Companion Hymnal for Blended Worship. 224p. Date not set. write for info. (*1-57992-051-9*) OR Catholic.

Lord Be with You: A Visual Handbook. Don E. Saliers & Charles D. Hackett. (Illus.). 86p. (Orig.). 1990. pap. 24.95 (*1-878009-06-0*, OSL Pubns) Order St Luke Pubns.

Lord Beaconsfield. James A. Froude. LC 76-157333. (Select Bibliographies Reprint Ser.). 1977. reprint ed. 21.95 (*0-8369-5793-8*) Ayer.

***Lord Berners: The Last Eccentric.** Mark Amory. (Illus.). 272p. 2000. pap. 22.95 (*0-7126-6578-1*, Pub. by Pimlico) Trafalgar.

Lord Bishop: The Life of Samuel Wilberforce, 1805-1873. Standish Meacham. LC 70-102669. (Illus.). 338p. 1970. 29.00 (*0-674-53913-3*) HUP.

Lord, Bless My Child. William Carmichael & Nancie Carmichael. LC 95-12643. 256p. 1995. 19.99 (*0-8423-2047-4*) Tyndale Hse.

Lord, Bless This Marriage. William Carmichael & Nancie Carmichael. LC 98-31854. 226p. 1999. 19.99 (*0-8423-3855-1*) Tyndale Hse.

Lord Bolingbroke: Contributions to the Craftsman. Ed. by Simon Varey. 1983. 69.00 (*0-19-822386-2*) OUP.

Lord, Break Me. William MacDonald. 1972. pap. 3.00 (*0-937396-24-9*) Walterick Pubs.

***Lord Brocktree.** Brian Jacques. (Redwall Ser.). (Illus.). (J). (gr. 4-8). 2000. 22.95 (*0-399-23590-6*, G P Putnam) Peng Put Young Read.

Lord Burgie: Wish You Were Here & Others. I. Burgie. (Piano-Vocal-Guitar Ser.). 1989. 9.95 (*0-89524-420-9*, 02500560) Cherry Lane.

Lord Burlington: Architecture, Art & Life. Toby Barnard. 328p. 1995. 65.00 (*1-85285-094-9*) Hambledon Press.

Lord Burlington: The Man & His Politics : Questions of Loyalty. Edward T. Corp. LC 98-25036. (Studies in British History Ser.). xi, 212p. 1998. write for info. (*0-88946-450-2*) E Mellen.

Lord Burlington - The Man & His Politics. Edward Corp. LC 98-25036. (Studies in British History: Vol. 48). (Illus.). 252p. 1998. text 89.95 (*0-7734-8367-5*) E Mellen.

Lord Bute: Essays in Reinterpretation. Karl W. Schweizer. 280p. 1989. text 55.00 (*0-7185-1261-8*) St Martin.

Lord Butler: The 1984 Act in Retrospect. F. B. Sullivan. 44p. 1980. 8.00 (*0-8002-3648-3*) OpUniv Pr.

Lord Byron see Romantics: Critical Heritage

Lord Byron. George Gordon Byron. (Poets Ser.). 146p. 1993. 5.95 (*0-7117-0440-6*, Pub. by JARR UK) Seven Hills Bk.

Lord Byron. Graham. 1998. 32.00 (*0-8057-1654-8*, Twyne) Mac Lib Ref.

Lord Byron. Ed. by Jane Stabler. (Everyman's Poetry Ser.). 1997. pap. 3.50 (*0-460-87810-7*, Everyman's Classic Lib) Tuttle Pubng.

Lord Byron. 2nd ed. Paul G. Trueblood. (English Authors Ser.: No. 78). 200p. 1977. 28.95 (*0-8057-6694-4*, Twyne) Mac Lib Ref.

Lord Byron: A Sesquicentennial Exhibition Catalogue. Compiled by Sally Leach. (Illus.). 40p. 1975. pap. 7.00 (*0-87959-017-3*) U of Tex H Ransom Ctr.

Lord Byron: Selected Letters & Journals. George Gordon Byron. 408p. 1982. 32.00 (*0-674-53915-X*) Belknap Pr.

Lord Byron: Selected Letters & Journals. Ed. by Leslie A. Marchand. LC 82-9720. 408p. 1984. pap. 10.95 (*0-674-53912-5*) Belknap Pr.

Lord Byron: The Complete Miscellaneous Prose. George Gordon Byron. Ed. by Andrew Nicholson. (Oxford English Texts Ser.). (Illus.). 616p. (C). 1991. text 160.00 (*0-19-818543-X*) OUP.

***Lord Byron: The Major Works.** George Gordon Byron. Ed. by Jerome J. McGann. (Oxford World's Classics Ser.). 1080p. 2000. pap. 16.95 (*0-19-284040-1*) OUP.

Lord Byron Vol. X, Don Juan Cantos XIV & XV Manuscript: A Facsimile of the Original Draft Manuscripts in the Berg Collection at the New York Public Library. George Gordon Byron. Ed. by Andrew Nicholson. LC 94-42004. (Manuscripts of the Younger Romantics Ser.: Vol. 10). 192p. 1995. text 121.00 (*0-8153-1147-8*) Garland.

Lord Byron & His Circle. Willis S. Pratt. (Studies in Byron: No. 5). 1970. pap. 39.95 (*0-8383-0062-6*) M S G Haskell Hse.

Lord Byron & His Contemporaries: Essays from the 6th International Byron Seminar. Ed. by Charles E. Robinson. LC 80-66848. (Illus.). 256p. 1982. 35.00 (*0-87413-180-4*) U Delaware Pr.

Lord Byron & His Detractors. J. Murray. LC 77-119079. (Studies in Byron: No. 5). 1970. reprint ed. lib. bdg. 75.00 (*0-8383-1075-3*) M S G Haskell Hse.

Lord Byron & Some of His Contemporaries. Leigh Hunt. LC 24-23123. reprint ed. 59.50 (*0-404-03419-5*) AMS Pr.

Lord Byron & Some of His Contemporaries, 2 vols. in 1. Leigh Hunt. (Anglistica & Americana Ser.: No. 176). (Illus.). xxxix, 899p. 1976. reprint ed. 148.20 (*3-487-06059-0*) G Olms Pubs.

Lord Byron As a Satirist in Verse. Claude M. Fuess. LC 72-10825. (Studies in Byron: No. 5). 1974. lib. bdg. 75.00 (*0-8383-0554-7*) M S G Haskell Hse.

Lord Byron at the Opera. Herbert E. Read. (Dramascripts Ser.: Vol. 3). 1995. 5.95 (*0-900891-02-5*) Oleander Pr.

Lord Byron in His Letters. George Gordon Byron. Ed. by V. H. Collins. LC 72-3626. (Studies in Byron: No. 5). 1972. reprint ed. lib. bdg. 75.00 (*0-8383-1582-8*) M S G Haskell Hse.

Lord Byron the European: Essays from the International Byron Society. Ed. by Richard Cardwell. LC 97-24022. (Studies in British Literature: No. 31). 240p. 1997. text 89.95 (*0-7734-8593-7*) E Mellen.

Lord Byron's Cain: Twelve Essays & a Text with Variants & Annotations. Truman G. Steffan. LC 68-56131. 530p. reprint ed. pap. 164.30 (*0-8357-7715-4*, 203607200002) Bks Demand.

Lord Byron's Correspondence, 2 vols., Set. George Gordon Byron. (BCL1-PR English Literature Ser.). 1992. reprint ed. lib. bdg. 150.00 (*0-7812-7474-5*) Rprt Serv.

Lord Byron's Doctor: A Novel. Paul West. LC 90-47121. (Phoenix Fiction Ser.). vi, 288p. 1999. pap. 13.95 (*0-226-89401-0*) U Ch Pr.

Lord Byron's Iberian Pilgrimage. Gordon K. Thomas. LC 83-14274. (Illus.). xiii, 92p. 1983. pap. 9.95 (*0-8425-2139-9*, Friends of the Library) Brigham.

Lord Byron's Jackal: The Life of Edward John Trelawny. David Crane. LC 99-16413. (Illus.). 408p. 1999. 30.00 (*1-56858-143-2*) FWEW.

Lord Byron's Marriage. G. Wilson Knight. 298p. 1957. 69.50 (*0-614-00171-4*); 69.50 (*0-614-00276-1*) Elliots Bks.

Lord Byron's Strength: Romantic Writing & Commercial Society. Jerome Christensen. (Illus.). 416p. 1995. pap. text 17.95 (*0-8018-4356-1*) Johns Hopkins.

***Lord Caldwell & the Cat, Vol. 1.** Joy Reed. (Zebra Regency Romance Ser.). 1999. mass mkt. 4.99 (*0-8217-6356-3*, Zebra Kensgtn) Kensgtn Pub Corp.

***Lord Carlton's Courtship.** Debbie Raleigh. (Zebra Regency Romance Ser.). 256p. 2000. mass mkt. 4.99 (*0-8217-6463-2*, Zebra Kensgtn) Kensgtn Pub Corp.

Lord Chancellor. Nicholas Underhill. (Illus.). 1988. 120.00 (*0-900963-81-6*, Pub. by T Dalton) St Mut.

Lord Chandos Letter. Hugo Von Hofmannsthal. Tr. by Russell Stockman from GER. LC 85-63764. 64p. 1986. pap. 8.95 (*0-910395-18-7*) Marlboro Pr.

Lord, Change Me! see Cambiame, Senor!

Lord, Change Me! 2nd ed. Evelyn Christenson. 192p. 1993. pap. 9.99 (*1-56476-054-5*, 6-3054, Victor Bks) Chariot Victor.

Lord, Change Me! Leader's Guide. Evelyn Christenson. 64p. 1993. pap., teacher ed. 6.50 (*1-56476-055-3*, 6-3055, Victor Bks) Chariot Victor.

***Lord Charlemont's History of Italian Poetry from Dante to Metastasio Vol. I: A Critical Edition from the Autograph Manuscript.** Ed. by George Talbot. LC 99-58598. (Critical Editions & Translations Ser.: Vol. 4). 640p. 2000. text 129.95 (*0-7734-7780-2*) E Mellen.

***Lord Charlemont's History of Italian Poetry from Dante to Metastasio Vol. II: A Critical Edition from the Autograph Manuscript.** Ed. by George Talbot. LC 99-58598. (Critical Editions & Translations Ser.: Vol. 5). 420p. 2000. text 109.95 (*0-7734-7782-9*) E Mellen.

***Lord Charlemont's History of Italian Poetry from Dante to Metastasio Vol. III: A Critical Edition from the Autograph Manuscript.** Ed. by George Talbot. LC 99-58598. (Critical Editions & Translations Ser.: Vol. 6). 412p. 2000. text 109.95 (*0-7734-7784-5*) E Mellen.

Lord Chatham: A War Minister in the Making. Owen A. Sherrard. LC 75-2703. (Illus.). 323p. 1975. reprint ed. lib. bdg. 65.00 (*0-8371-8034-1*, SHCW, Greenwood Pr) Greenwood.

Lord Chatham: Pitt & the 7 Years' War. Owen A. Sherrard. LC 75-2701. (Illus.). 437p. 1975. reprint ed. lib. bdg. 75.00 (*0-8371-8033-3*, SHLC, Greenwood Pr) Greenwood.

Lord Chatham & America. Owen A. Sherrard. LC 75-2700. (Illus.). 395p. 1975. reprint ed. lib. bdg. 69.50 (*0-8371-8031-7*, SHLCA, Greenwood Pr) Greenwood.

Lord Chatham & the Whig Opposition. D. A. Winstanley. 460p. 1966. reprint ed. 35.00 (*0-7146-1527-7*, Pub. by F Cass Pubs) Intl Spec Bk.

Lord Chelmsford's Zululand Campaign, 1878-1879. John Laband. LC 94-26112. 1997. 53.95 (*0-7509-0665-0*, Pub. by Sutton Pub Ltd) Intl Pubs Mktg.

Lord Chesterfield: His Character & Characters. Colin Franklin. LC 93-1518. 166p. 1993. 51.95 (*0-85967-966-7*, Pub. by Scolar Pr) Ashgate Pub Co.

Lord Chesterfield & His World. Samuel Shellabarger. LC 72-156737. 1971. reprint ed. 32.00 (*0-8196-0271-X*) Biblo.

Lord Chesterfield's Letters. Lord Chesterfield. Ed. by David Roberts. LC 99-181683. 480p. 1998. pap. 13.95 (*0-19-283715-X*) OUP.

An Asterisk (*) at the beginning of an entry indicates that the title is appearing for the first time.

L

Lord Churchill's Coup: The Anglo-American Empire & Glorious Revolution Reconsidered. Stephen S. Webb. LC 95-22815. (Illus.). 416p. 1995. 30.00 (0-394-54980-5) Knopf.

Lord Churchill's Coup: The Anglo-American Empire & the Glorious Revolution Reconsidered. Stephen S. Webb. LC 98-40554. 1998. pap. text 22.95 (0-8156-0558-7) Syracuse U Pr.

Lord Clayborne's Fancy. Laura Matthews. 256p. 1989. mass mkt. 3.50 (0-446-35412-0, Pub. by Warner Bks) Little.

Lord Cochrane: Seaman, Radical, Liberator. Christopher Lloyd. LC 98-6484. 1998. 25.00 (0-8050-5986-5); pap. 14.00 (0-8050-5569-X, Owl) H Holt & Co.

Lord Conrad's Lady. Leo Frankowski. 1998. pap. 5.99 (0-345-91443-0, Del Rey) Ballantine Pub Grp.

Lord Cornbury Scandal: The Politics of Reputation in British America. Patricia U. Bonomi. LC 97-40318. (Published for the Omohundro Institute of Early American History & Culture Ser.). (Illus.). 304p. 1998. 29.95 (0-8078-2413-5) U of NC Pr.

***Lord Cornbury Scandal: The Politics of Reputation in British America.** Patricia U. Bonomi. LC 97-40318. (Published for the Omohundro Institute of Early American History & Culture, Williamsburg, Virginia Ser.). (Illus.). 304p. 2000. pap. 19.95 (0-8078-4869-7) U of NC Pr.

Lord Curzon: The Last of the British Moghuls. Nayana Goradia. (Illus.). 344p. (C). 1993. text 32.00 (0-19-562824-1, 14346) OUP.

Lord Curzon: The Last of the British Moghuls. Nayana Goradia. (Oxford India Paperbacks Ser.). (Illus.). 326p. 1998. reprint ed. pap. text 15.95 (0-19-564362-3) OUP.

Lord Curzon, 1859-1925: A Bibliography, 5. James G. Parker. LC 91-9473. (Bibliographies of British Statesmen Ser.: No. 5). 136p. 1991. lib. bdg. 59.95 (0-313-28122-X, PLZ, Greenwood Pr) Greenwood.

Lord Dearborn's Destiny. Brenda Hiatt. (Regency Romance Ser.). 1993. mass mkt. 2.99 (0-373-31191-5, 1-31191-9) Harlequin Bks.

***Lord Demon.** Roger Zelazny. 336p. 2000. mass mkt. 6.99 (0-380-77023-7, Avon Bks) Morrow Avon.

Lord Demon. Roger Zelazny & Jane Lindskold. LC 99-20950. 288p. 1999. 23.00 (0-380-97333-2, Avon Bks) Morrow Avon.

Lord Diablo's Demise. Meg-Lynn Roberts. 1996. mass mkt. 4.50 (0-8217-5338-X, Zebra Kensgtn) Kensgtn Pub Corp.

Lord Dismiss Us. Michael Campbell. LC 83-18173. (Phoenix Fiction Ser.). 384p. 1993. pap. 9.95 (0-226-09244-5) U Ch Pr.

Lord Do You Love Me? Frank Schaffer Publications Staff. 1997. pap. text 2.49 (0-7647-0243-2) Schaffer Pubns.

Lord, Do You Love Me? Frank Schaffer Publications Staff. 1997. pap. text 12.95 incl. audio (0-7647-0272-6) Schaffer Pubns.

Lord, Don't Let It Rain at Lunch: More Devotions for Teachers. Patricia A. Fisher. 176p. 1993. pap. 10.99 (0-310-60471-0) Zondervan.

Lord, Don't Let It Rain at Recess. Patricia A. Fisher. 224p. 1988. pap. 10.99 (0-310-44521-3, 12344P) Zondervan.

***Lord Dragoner's Wife.** Lynn Kerstan. (Signet Regency Romance Ser.). 224p. 1999. mass mkt. 4.99 (0-451-19861-1, Sig) NAL.

Lord Dunsany: A Bibliography. S. T. Joshi & Darrell Schweitzer. LC 93-8453. (Author Bibliographies Ser.: No. 90). (Illus.). 393p. 1993. 50.00 (0-8108-2714-X) Scarecrow.

Lord Dunsany: Master of the Anglo-Irish Imagination, 64. LC 94-24571. (Contributions to the Study of Science Fiction & Fantasy). 248p. 1995. 62.95 (0-313-29403-8) Greenwood.

Lord Edgeware Dies. Agatha Christie. 1984. 10.60 (0-606-00969-8, Pub. by Turtleback) Demco.

Lord Edgware Dies. Agatha Christie. 240p. 1986. mass mkt. 5.99 (0-425-09961-X) Berkley Pub.

Lord Elgin & the Marbles. 3rd rev. ed. William St. Clair. (Illus.). 456p. 1998. pap. text 16.95 (0-19-288053-5) OUP.

Lord, Empower Us! George P. Mocko. Ed. by Michael L. Sherer. (Orig.). 1987. pap. 3.50 (0-89536-851-X, 7810) CSS OH.

Lord Emsworth & Others. P. G. Wodehouse. 224p. 1975. pap. 9.95 (0-14-002568-5, Penguin Bks) Viking Penguin.

Lord Emsworth's Annotated Whiffle: The Care of the Pig. Ed. by James Hogg. (Illus.). 128p. 1995. 16.95 (0-87008-134-9) JAS Heineman.

Lord Fish. Walter De la Mare. LC 96-26253. (Candlewick Treasures Ser.). (Illus.). 128p. (J). (gr. 3-9). 1997. 11.99 (0-7636-0134-9) Candlewick Pr.

Lord for the Body. Albert B. Simpson. LC 95-70299. 156p. 1996. pap. 9.99 (0-87509-624-7) Chr Pubns.

Lord Fordington's Offer. large type ed. Sally James. (Dales Large Print Ser.). 272p. 1996. pap. 18.99 (1-85389-673-X, Dales) Ulverscroft.

Lord, Forgive Me, Cycle B. David L. Wade. 1987. 6.95 (0-89536-885-4, 7871) CSS OH.

Lord Fortune's Prize. Nancy Richards-Akers. 224p. (Orig.). 1993. mass mkt. 3.99 (0-380-77191-8, Avon Bks) Morrow Avon.

***Lord Foulgrin's Letters.** Randy Alcorn. LC 00-8460. 2000. 14.99 (1-57673-679-2) Multnomah Pubs.

Lord Foul's Bane: The Chronicles of Thomas Covenant, the Unbeliever, Vol. 1. Stephen R. Donaldson. (Del Rey Bk.). 496p. 1987. mass mkt. 3.99 (0-345-34865-6) Ballantine Pub Grp.

Lord Freddie's First Love, 1. Patricia Bray. 224p. 1999. mass mkt. 4.99 (0-8217-6322-9) Kensgtn Pub Corp.

Lord Galveston & the Ghost. Jeanne Savery. 256p. 1998. pap. 4.99 (0-8217-5869-1, Zebra Kensgtn) Kensgtn Pub Corp.

Lord Ganesha. Sant Keshavadas. (Illus.). 186p. (Orig.). 1988. pap. 21.00 (0-942508-19-X) Vishwa.

Lord George Bentinck: A Political Biography. Benjamin Disraeli & Robert W. Kamphuis. LC 89-34108. (Library of Conservative Thought). 396p. 1997. pap. text 24.95 (1-56000-947-0) Transaction Pubs.

Lord George Gordon. Yirmeyanu Bindman. 250p. 1991. 15.95 (1-56062-056-0); pap. 12.95 (1-56062-057-9) CIS Comm.

Lord Gifford & His Lectures: A Centenary Retrospect. Ed. by Stanley L. Jaki. viii, 138p. 1987. 19.95 (0-7073-0465-2, MUP/H213) Scot Acad Pr.

Lord Gilmore's Bride. Sheila Walsh. (Signet Regency Romance Ser.). 224p. (Orig.). 1990. pap. 3.95 (0-317-03017-5, Sig) NAL.

Lord, Give Me Eternal Life. (Image of God Ser.). (J). (gr. 8). 1996. pap. text 10.95 (0-89870-441-3) Ignatius Pr.

Lord, Give Me Wisdom: Practical Principles from Proverbs. Terry Powell. LC 98-83288. 160p. 1999. pap. 9.99 (1-57921-210-7, Pub. by WinePress Pub) BookWorld.

Lord Giveth & Taketh Away. Manly P. Hall. pap. 4.95 (0-89314-330-8) Philos Res.

Lord Glenraven's Return. large type ed. Anne Barbour. LC 94-48915. 336p. 1995. pap. 20.95 (0-7862-0417-6) Thorndike Pr.

Lord Gnome's Literary Companion. Ed. by Francis Wheen. 360p. 1996. pap. 20.00 (1-85984-045-0, Pub. by Verso) Norton.

Lord God Made a World. Carol Greene. LC 97-140002. (Read-n-Sing Bible Stories Ser.). (Illus.). 32p. (J). (ps-2). 1997. 6.99 (0-570-04879-6) Concordia.

Lord God Made Them All. James Herriot. 384p. 1984. mass mkt. 7.50 (0-553-26958-5) Bantam.

Lord God Made Them All. James Herriot. 320p. 1981. text 17.95 (0-312-49834-9) St Martin.

Lord God Made Them All. large type ed. James Herriot. LC 93-19646. 422p. 1993. reprint ed. lib. bdg. 22.95 (0-8161-5215-2, G K Hall Lrg Type) Mac Lib Ref.

Lord God Made Them All, Vol. 1. James Herriot. 384p. 1998. pap. 7.99 (0-312-96620-2, Pub. by Tor Bks) St Martin.

Lord God of Truth & Concerning the Teacher. Gordon H. Clark & Aurelius Augustine. Ed. & Intro. by John W. Robbins. 110p. 1994. pap. 7.95 (0-940931-40-0) Trinity Found.

Lord God of Truth Within. M. 1976. reprint ed. 18.00 (0-911662-56-1) Yoga.

Lord Grenville: A Bibliography, 2. A. D. Harvey. LC 89-2790. (Bibliographies of British Statesmen Ser.: No. 2). 104p. 1989. lib. bdg. 55.00 (0-313-28090-8, HWG/, Greenwood Pr) Greenwood.

Lord Grey of the Reform Bill, Being the Life of Charles, 2nd Earl Grey. George M. Trevelyan. LC 76-110874. 413p. 1971. reprint ed. lib. bdg. 38.50 (0-8371-4553-8, TRLG, Greenwood Pr) Greenwood.

Lord Grey, 1764-1845. E. A. Smith. (Illus.). 352p. 1996. pap. 26.95 (0-7509-1127-1, Pub. by Sutton Pub Ltd) Intl Pubs Mktg.

Lord Grizzly. Frederick Manfred, pseud. 1994. mass mkt. 4.50 (0-451-18413-0, Sig) NAL.

***Lord Hailey, the Colonial Office & the Politics of Race in the Second World War: The Loss of White Prestige.** Suke Wolton. LC 99-86154. 240p. 2000. text 65.00 (0-312-23214-4) St Martin.

Lord Hailsham: A Life. Geoffrey Lewis. (Illus.). 403p. 1998. 50.00 (0-224-04252-1, Pub. by Jonathan Cape) Trafalgar.

Lord Halewyn see Ghelderode: Seven Plays

Lord Harry. Catherine Coulter. 1995. mass mkt. 7.50 (0-451-40591-9, Topaz) NAL.

Lord Harry. large type ed. Catherine Coulter. LC 96-38767. (ROMC-Hall Ser.). 424p. 1997. lib. bdg. 27.95 (0-7838-2001-1, G K Hall Lrg Type) Mac Lib Ref.

Lord Hasting's Indentured Retainers, 1461-1483: The Lawfulness of Livery & Retaining under the Yorkists & the Tudors. William H. Dunham, Jr. (Connecticut Academy of Arts & Sciences Ser., Trans.: Vol. 39). 1955. pap. 69.50 (0-685-22896-7) Elliots Bks.

Lord, Heal My Hurts see Senor, Sana Mis Heridas

Lord, Heal My Hurts. Kay Arthur. 280p. 1996. pap. 12.99 (0-88070-879-4, Multnomah Bks) Multnomah Pubs.

Lord, Heal My Hurts. Kay Arthur. Tr. by Capstone Publishers Staff from CHI. 280p. 1996. pap. 9.95 (1-888655-55-0) Precept Ministries.

***Lord Hear Our Prayer.** rev. ed. William G. Storey & Thomas McNally. LC 99-41019. 416p. 2000. pap. 14.95 (0-87793-684-6) Ave Maria.

Lord, Hear Our Prayer: Prayer of the Faithful for Sundays, Holy Days, & Ritual Masses. Jay Cormier. 382p. 1995. text 49.95 (0-8146-2166-X) Liturgical Pr.

Lord, Hear Our Prayers: Invocations & Personal Prayers for Busy Times. Irene M. Howard. 106p. (Orig.). 1995. pap. 7.00 (0-9648223-0-X) Creat Synthesis.

Lord Heard My Cry. Charles E. Green. LC 95-71967. 96p. 1995. pap. 9.95 (1-881576-73-6) Providence Hse.

Lord Heartless. Barbara Metzger. 1998. mass mkt. 4.99 (0-449-00171-7, Crest) Fawcett.

Lord Heathbury's Revenge. large type ed. Rachelle Edwards. (Linford Romance Library). 256p. 1995. pap. 16.99 (0-7089-7780-4, Linford) Ulverscroft.

Lord, Help Me: I'm Grieving. R. Bareis Aviron-Violet. (Illus.). 24p. 1993. pap. 1.25 (0-915531-15-1) OR Catholic.

Lord, Help Me: I'm Sick. R. Bareis Aviron-Violet. (Illus.). 24p. 1993. pap. 1.25 (0-915531-14-3) OR Catholic.

Lord, Help Me! The Desperate Dieter. Beth Hammond. (Continued Applied Christianity Ser.). 80p. 1983. pap. 5.99 (0-570-03896-0, 12-2978) Concordia.

Lord Help Me Not to Have These Evil Thoughts! Harold D. Vaughan. 73p. (C). 1988. reprint ed. pap. 4.00 (0-942889-04-5) Christ Life Pubns.

Lord Help Us to Save Our Planet. Ernest Guthery. (Illus.). 53p. 1998. pap. 4.95 (0-9643619-4-9) Guthery Bks.

Lord Herbert of Chirbury (1582-1648) An Intellectual Biography. John Butler. (Studies in British History: Vol. 16). 592p. 1990. write for info. (0-88946-467-7) E Mellen.

Lord High Executioner: Unshamed Look at Handmen, Headsmen & Their Kind. Howard Engel. (Illus.). 256p. 1996. 29.95 (1-55013-790-5) Firefly Bks Ltd.

Lord Hornblower. C. S. Forester. 320p. Date not set. write for info. (0-8488-1324-3) Amereon Ltd.

Lord Hornblower. C. S. Forester. 1991. lib. bdg. 21.95 (1-56849-052-6) Buccaneer Bks.

Lord Hornblower. C. S. Forester. 322p. (YA). (gr. 7 up). 1989. reprint ed. pap. 13.00 (0-316-28943-4, Back Bay) Little.

Lord Hornblower, Vol. 1. C. S. Forester. (J). (gr. 7 up). 1946. 17.95 (0-316-28908-6) Little.

Lord Hugo's Bride. large type ed. Marina Oliver. (Linford Romance Library). 1991. pap. 16.99 (0-7089-7101-6, Linford) Ulverscroft.

Lord Hugo's Wedding. large type ed. Marina Oliver. (Linford Romance Library). 320p. 1993. pap. 16.99 (0-7089-7459-7, Linford) Ulverscroft.

Lord, I Can Resist Anything but Temptation. Harold L. Bussell. (Orig.). 1985. pap. 4.70 (0-310-37271-2, 12389P) Zondervan.

Lord, I Don't Know What to Do! Cynthia B. Hodge. 1991. 4.95 (0-9629305-0-4) Vertellim.

Lord, I Got Much More Than I Asked For. Jonita B. Carter. 144p. (Orig.). 1993. pap. 12.00 (0-9638881-0-2) S E T H Pubs.

Lord, I Haven't Talked to You since the Last Crisis, but... see Senor, No Te Hablo Desde la Ultima Crisis, Pero . . .

Lord, I Haven't Talked to You since the Last Crisis, But . . . The Purpose & Power of Prayer. Lorraine Peterson. LC 93-40579. 24p. (YA). (gr. 7-12). 1994. pap. 8.99 (1-55661-385-7) Bethany Hse.

Lord, I Miss My Time with You. T. D. Jakes. (Orig.). 1997. pap. 12.50 (1-890521-01-9) Jakes Ent.

Lord, I Need Grace to Make It. Kay Arthur. 252p. 1996. pap. 12.99 (0-88070-881-6, Multnomah Bks) Multnomah Pubs.

Lord, I Need Grace to Make It. Kay Arthur. Tr. by Capstone Publishers Staff from CHI. 247p. 1996. pap. 9.95 (1-888655-52-6) Precept Ministries.

Lord, I Said I Wouldn't Fail You, but I Did! T. D. Jakes. (Orig.). 1997. pap. 12.50 (1-890521-00-0) Jakes Ent.

Lord, I Want to Be A Christian Inna My Church. Donald F. Black. 1993. pap. 9.95 (1-55673-576-6, 7975, Fairway Pr) CSS OH.

***Lord, I Want to Be a Christian Inna My Church.** Donald F. Black. 125p. 1999. reprint ed. pap. 13.95 (1-885631-38-3, 38-3, Family Of Man Pr) G F Hutchison.

Lord, I Want to Know You. Kay Arthur. 219p. (Orig.). 1996. pap. 12.99 (0-88070-880-8, Multnomah Bks) Multnomah Pubs.

Lord, I Want to Know You. Kay Arthur. Tr. by Capstone Publishers Staff from CHI. 219p. (Orig.). 1995. pap. 9.99 (1-888655-53-4) Precept Ministries.

Lord, I Want to Love You More: A Daily Inspirational Calendar. Kay Arthur. 384p. (gr. 10). 1993. spiral bd. 11.99 (0-8007-7138-9) Revell.

***Lord, I Wish My Family Would Get Saved! Trusting God to Add Your Household to His Family.** Larry Keefauver. 228p. 2000. pap. 12.99 (0-88419-678-X) Creation House.

Lord, I Wish My Husband Would Pray with Me: Breaking down the Spiritual Walls Between You & Your Husband. Larry Keefauver. LC 97-48933. 216p. 1998. pap. 12.99 (0-88419-528-7) Creation House.

Lord, I Wish My Teenager Would Talk with Me. Larry Keefauver. LC 99-75007. 228p. 1999. pap. 12.99 (0-88419-639-9) Creation House.

Lord, I Would Follow Thee. Brent L. Top. LC 96-85274. 1996. 14.95 (1-57008-265-0) Bookcraft Inc.

Lord I'm Coming Home: Everyday Aesthetics in Tidewater, North Carolina. John Forrest. LC 88-47728. (Anthropology of Contemporary Issues Ser.). (Illus.). 296p. 1988. pap. text 18.95 (0-8014-9483-4) Cornell U Pr.

Lord, I'm Torn Between Two Masters. Kay Arthur. LC 96-15067. 264p. 1996. pap. 12.99 (0-88070-886-7, Multnomah Bks) Multnomah Pubs.

Lord in Waiting. Nigel Tranter. mass mkt. 11.95 (0-340-62587-2, Pub. by Hodder & Stought Ltd) Trafalgar.

Lord in Waiting. Nigel Tranter. 384p. 1995. 25.95 (0-340-58785-7, Pub. by Hodder & Stought Ltd) Trafalgar.

Lord, Increase Our Faith. Michael Landsman. LC 94-70706. 186p. (Orig.). 1994. mass mkt. 5.99 (0-88270-718-3) Bridge-Logos.

Lord, Increase Our Faith. Neal A. Maxwell. 1994. 11.95 (0-88494-919-2) Bookcraft Inc.

Lord Is Come. Barbour Publishing, Inc. Editors. 1999. pap. 0.99 (1-57748-437-1) Barbour Pub.

Lord, Is It Warfare? Kay Arthur. 350p. 1996. pap. 12.99 (0-88070-882-4, Multnomah Bks) Multnomah Pubs.

Lord, Is It Warfare? Teach Me to Stand. Kay Arthur. Tr. by Capstone Publishers Staff from CHI. 339p. (Orig.). 1996. pap. 10.95 (1-888655-54-2) Precept Ministries.

Lord Is My Light. Lloyd Pfautsch. 1.25 (0-687-07135-6) Abingdon.

Lord Is My Salvation. Lynn N. Austin. (Chronicles of the King Ser.: Bk. 3). 272p. (Orig.). 1996. pap. 12.99 (0-8341-1603-0) Beacon Hill.

Lord Is My Shepherd. Larry G. Herr. LC 96-18838. 32p. 1996. pap. 0.89 (0-8280-1064-1) Review & Herald.

Lord Is My Shepherd. Lois Veals. 2.99 (0-906731-62-3, Pub. by Christian Focus) Spring Arbor Dist.

Lord Is My Shepherd: A Devotional Study of the 23rd Psalm. Orlando Harms. 84p. (Orig.). 1990. pap. 5.00 (1-877941-01-8) Ctr Mennonite Brethren Studies.

Lord Is My Shepherd: A Psalm for the Grieving. Victor M. Parachin. LC 91-76660. 64p. (Orig.). 1992. pap. 3.95 (0-89243-415-5) Liguori Pubns.

***Lord is My Shepherd! From Psalm 23.** Joel Anderson. LC 98-89074. 24p. 1999. 9.95 (0-307-25176-4) Gldn Bks Pub Co.

***Lord Is My Shepherd: From Psalm 23.** Ingrid Beck. 1999. pap. 7.99 (1-85608-400-0) Hunt GBR.

Lord Is My Shepherd: From Psalm 23. Illus. by Ingrid Beck. 32p. 1999. 10.00 (0-664-22135-1) Westminster John Knox.

Lord Is My Shepherd: Reflections on God's Loving Care. Adrian Rogers. LC 98-51509. (Illus.). 111p. 1999. 14.99 (1-58134-048-6) Crossway Bks.

Lord Is My Shepherd: The Theology of a Caring God. Michael Samuel. LC 96-12052. 288p. 1996. pap. 30.00 (1-56821-912-1) Aronson.

Lord Is My Shepherd: The 23rd Psalm. Illus. by Tasha Tudor. LC 79-21734. 32p. (J). (gr. 2 up). 1980. 12.95 (0-399-20756-2, Philomel) Peng Put Young Read.

Lord Is My Shepherd: The 23rd Psalm. Tasha Tudor. 32p. (J). (ps-3). 1999. pap. 5.99 (0-698-11755-7) Putnam Pub Group.

Lord is My Shepherd: Words of Comfort. 1995. 7.50 (0-7459-3362-9, Pub. by Lion Pubng) Trafalgar.

Lord Is My Shepherd: 101 Thoughts of Encouragement. Compiled by Brownlow Publishing Company, Creative Department S. LC 99-236649. (Easelette Miniatures Ser.). 101p. 1998. spiral bd. 5.99 (1-57051-187-X, 187X) Brownlow Pub Co.

***Lord Is My Shepherd: 12 Promises for Every Woman.** Elizabeth George. LC 00-27812. 250p. 2000. pap. 9.99 (1-56507-989-2) Harvest Hse.

Lord Is My Shepherd Book. Pockets Learning Staff. (Illus.). 8p. (ps up). 1998. 35.00 (1-888074-99-X) Pckts Lrning.

Lord Is My Song. Lynn N. Austin. LC 96-227552. (Chronicles of the King Ser.: Bk. 2). 304p. (Orig.). 1996. pap. 12.99 (0-8341-1602-2) Beacon Hill.

Lord Is My Strength. Lynn N. Austin. (Chronicles of the King Ser.: Bk. 1). 304p. 1995. pap. 12.99 (0-8341-1538-7) Beacon Hill.

Lord Is Near: Experiencing the Presence of God. John M. Drescher. (Visitation Pamphlets Ser.). 16p. (Orig.). 1989. pap. 2.99 (0-8361-3508-3) Herald Pr.

Lord Is Near to All. Ruled. 1997. 7.98 (0-7824-7905-7) Antioch Pub Co.

Lord Is Present. Joseph M. Champlin. 1973. pap. 7.95 (0-87193-175-3) Dimension Bks.

Lord is Risen! He is Risen Indeed! He Really Is! Gospel Sermons for Lent/Easter. Richard L. Sheffield. 1998. pap. 10.95 (0-7880-1252-5) CSS OH.

Lord Is Risen! He Is Risen Indeed! He Really Is! Cycle A: Gospel Sermons for Lent - Easter. Richard L. Sheffield. LC 98-5114. 118p. 1998. pap. 10.50 (0-7880-1249-5) CSS OH.

Lord, It's Me Again. Judson Cornwall. 179p. (Orig.) 1994. pap. 7.99 (0-88270-666-7) Bridge-Logos.

Lord, I've Felt Like a Worm for So Long, It's Hard to Think Like a Butterfly! Joan Wilson. 128p. (Orig.). 1992. pap. 3.28i (0-9636259-0-X) J W Wilson Pubns.

Lord Jagannath: His Temple, Cult & Festivals. Himanshu S. Patnaik. (Illus.). 196p. (C). 1994. 67.00 (81-7305-051-1, Pub. by Aryan Bks Intl) Nataraj Bks.

***Lord Jakobovits in Conversation.** Immanuel Jakobovits & Michael Shashar. LC 00-32103. 2000. write for info. (0-85303-395-1, Pub. by M Vallentine & Co) Intl Spec Bk.

Lord Jesus, Teach Me to Pray: A 7 Week Course in Personal Prayer. 2nd ed. Lucy Rooney & Robert S. Faricy. LC 95-68113. 111p. 1994. pap. 5.95 (1-882972-55-4) Queenship Pub.

Lord Jesus, Think on Me. Lloyd Pfautsch. 1.00 (0-687-06188-1) Abingdon.

Lord Jim. Joseph Conrad. (Classics Illustrated Notes Ser.). (Illus.). (J). 1997. pap. text 4.99 (1-57840-066-X, Pub. by Acclaim Bks) Penguin Putnam.

Lord Jim. Joseph Conrad. (J). Date not set. lib. bdg. 24.95 (0-8488-1272-7) Amereon Ltd.

Lord Jim. Joseph Conrad. 288p. (J). 1981. mass mkt. 4.95 (0-553-21361-X, Bantam Classics) Bantam.

Lord Jim. Joseph Conrad. (J). 1988. lib. bdg. 25.95 (0-89966-057-6) Buccaneer Bks.

Lord Jim. Joseph Conrad. LC 98-41019. (Dover Thrift Editions Ser.). 256p. (J). 1999. pap. text 2.00 (0-486-40650-4) Dover.

Lord Jim. Joseph Conrad. (FRE.). 512p. (J). 1982. pap. 13.95 (0-7859-1962-7, 2070374033) Fr & Eur.

Lord Jim. Joseph Conrad. Ed. by Morton D. Zabel. LC 91-30904. (J). 1958. pap. 13.96 (0-395-05121-5, RivEd) HM.

Lord Jim. Joseph Conrad. (J). 1992. 17.00 (0-679-40544-5) Knopf.

Lord Jim. Joseph Conrad. (Illus.). 1999. 7.95 (3-8290-2842-3) Konemann.

Lord Jim. Joseph Conrad. 320p. (J). 1961. mass mkt. 4.95 (0-451-52234-6, CJ1195, Sig Classics) NAL.

Lord Jim. Joseph Conrad. Ed. & Intro. by John Batchelor. (World's Classics Paperback Ser.). 448p. (J). 1983. pap. 4.95 (0-19-281625-X) OUP.

***Lord Jim.** Joseph Conrad. (Oxford World's Classics Hardcovers Ser.). 368p. 2000. 15.00 (0-19-210044-0) OUP.

Lord Jim. Joseph Conrad. (Now Age Illustrated V Ser.). (Illus.). 64p. (gr. 4-12). 1979. student ed. 1.25 (0-88301-415-7) Pendulum Pr.

An Asterisk (*) at the beginning of an entry indicates that the title is appearing for the first time.

Lord Jim. Joseph Conrad. (Now Age Illustrated V Ser.). (Illus.). 64p. (J). (gr. 4-12). 1979. pap. text 2.95 (*0-88301-391-6*) Pendulum Pr.

Lord Jim. Joseph Conrad. (J). 1998. pap. text 4.95 (*84-320-3974-8*) Planeta.

Lord Jim. Joseph Conrad. (Signet Classics). (J). 1961. 9.05 (*0-606-02758-0*, Pub. by Turtleback) Demco.

***Lord Jim.** Joseph Conrad. 2000. pap. 7.95 (*0-460-87665-1*, Everyman's Classic Lib) Tuttle Pubng.

Lord Jim. Joseph Conrad. (Classics Library). 272p. (J). 1998. pap. 3.95 (*1-85326-037-1*, 0371WW, Pub. by Wrdsworth Edits) NTC Contemp Pub Co.

Lord Jim. Tessa Krailing. (Barron's Book Notes Ser.). (YA). (gr. 9-12). 1985. pap. 2.50 (*0-8120-3522-4*) Barron.

Lord Jim. large type ed. Joseph Conrad. 493p. (J). 1981. 27.99 (*0-7089-8014-7*, Charnwood) Ulverscroft.

Lord Jim. Joseph Conrad. LC 75-184734. 320p. (J). 1971. reprint ed. lib. bdg. 14.00 (*0-8376-0409-5*) Bentley Pubs.

Lord Jim. unabridged ed. Joseph Conrad. (Wordsworth Classics). (J). (gr. 6-12). 1998. 5.27 (*0-89061-037-1*, R0371WW, Jamestwn Pub) NTC Contemp Pub Co.

Lord Jim. 2nd ed. Ed. by D. H. Howe. (Illus.). 78p. 1993. pap. text 5.95 (*0-19-585263-X*) OUP.

Lord Jim: A Tale. Joseph Conrad. Ed. by John Batchelor. (Oxford World's Classics Ser.). 352p. (J). 2000. pap. 4.95 (*0-19-283512-2*) OUP.

Lord Jim: A Tale. Joseph Conrad. Ed. by Robert Hampson. 384p. 1989. pap. 5.95 (*0-14-018092-3*, Penguin Classics) Viking Penguin.

Lord Jim: After the Truth. Ross C. Murfin. (Masterwork Studies: No. 88). 160p. (C). 1992. 29.00 (*0-8057-8094-7*, Twyne); pap. 13.95 (*0-8057-8560-4*, Twyne) Mac Lib Ref.

Lord Jim: An Authoritative Text, Backgrounds, Essays in Criticism. 2nd ed. Joseph Conrad. Ed. by Thomas C. Moser & Norman Sherry. LC 95-1667. (Critical Editions Ser.). (C). 1996. pap. text 14.75 (*0-393-96335-7*) Norton.

***Lord Jim: 100th Anniversary.** Joseph Conrad. (Classics Ser.). 2000. mass mkt. 4.95 (*0-451-52767-4*, Sig) NAL.

Lord Jim & Nostromo. Joseph Conrad. LC 99-39913. 800p. 1999. pap. 11.95 (*0-375-75489-X*) Modern Lib NY.

Lord Jim Notes. J. M. Lybyer. (Cliffs Notes Ser.). 80p. 1962. pap. 4.95 (*0-8220-0762-5*, Cliff) IDG Bks.

Lord Jim's Many Marriages. Ruby B. Christian. 278p. (Orig.). 1995. pap. 12.00 (*0-9647882-0-9*) Bkshelf Pubns.

Lord John Russell: A Biography. Paul Scherer. LC 98-43989. 432p. 1999. 57.50 (*1-57591-021-7*) Susquehanna U Pr.

Lord John Ten. Ed. by Dennis Etchison. 200p. 1987. 25.00 (*0-935716-43-2*) Lord John.

Lord Jupiter. Morningland Publications, Inc. Staff & Gopi G. Donato. (Astrology Ser.). (Illus.). 283p. (Orig.). 1980. pap. 6.95 (*0-935146-50-4*) Morningland.

Lord Kelvin: His Influence on Electrical Measurements & Units. Paul Tunbridge. (History of Technology Ser.: No. 18). ix, 106p. 1992. 42.00 (*0-86341-237-8*, Pub. by Peregrinus) Dist Unknown.

Lord Kelvin: The Dynamic Victorian. Harold Sharlin & Tiby Sharlin. LC 78-50771. (Illus.). 1979. 35.00 (*0-271-00203-4*) Pa St U Pr.

Lord Kelvin & the Age of the Earth. Joe D. Burchfield. (Illus.). xx, 280p. 1990. pap. text 27.00 (*0-226-08043-9*) U Ch Pr.

Lord Kelvin's Machine. James P. Blaylock. LC 91-14048. (Illus.). 272p. 1992. 22.95 (*0-87054-163-3*) Arkham.

Lord Kirkle's Money, 2. Avi. (Beyond the Western Sea Ser.). (J). 1998. 10.34 (*0-606-13200-7*) Turtleback.

***Lord Kitchener & Mr. Churchill.** 200p. 2000. pap. 14.00 (*0-11-702423-6*, Pub. by Statnry Office) Balogh.

Lord Kito's Revenge. 2nd rev. ed. Soma Vira. (Planet Keepers Ser.: Vol. 4). 198p. 1996. pap. 12.95 (*0-9646057-4-0*) Space Link Bks.

Lord Krishna-Love Incarnate. M. Varma. 226p. 1978. 9.95 (*0-318-37163-4*) Asia Bk Corp.

Lord Krishna's Cuisine: The Art of Indian Vegetarian Cooking. Yamuna Devi. (Illus.). 824p. (Orig.). 1987. 34.95 (*0-525-24564-2*, Dutt) Dutton Plume.

Lord Langcliffe's Lady. Donna Davidson. (Zebra Regency Romance Ser.). 288p. 1998. mass mkt. 4.99 (*0-8217-5903-5*, Zebra Kensgtn) Kensgtn Pub Corp.

***Lord Langdon's Kiss.** Elena Greene. (Zebra Regency Romance Ser.). 2000. mass mkt. 4.99 (*0-8217-6583-3*, Zebra Kensgtn) Kensgtn Pub Corp.

***Lord Langdon's Tutor.** Laura Paquet. (Regency Romance Ser.). 224p. 2000. mass mkt. 4.99 (*0-8217-6675-9*, Zebra Kensgtn) Kensgtn Pub Corp.

Lord Leighton. Russell Ash. (Illus.). 96p. 1996. 45.00 (*1-85793-732-5*, Pub. by Pavilion Bks Ltd) Trafalgar.

Lord Leighton. Russell Ash. (Illus.). 96p. 1998. pap. 19.95 (*1-86205-150-X*, Pub. by Pavilion Bks Ltd) Trafalgar.

Lord Lenny Comes Home. large type ed. Judy Mullican. (HRL Big Bks.). (Illus.). 8p. (Orig.). (J). (ps-k). 1996. pap. text 10.95 (*1-57332-071-4*) HighReach Lrning.

Lord, Let Me Know You: Devotions to Saint Augustine. John E. Rotelle. 72p. 1987. pap. 1.00 (*0-941491-04-8*) Augustinian Pr.

Lord, Let Me Love. Marjorie Holmes. 288p. 1992. reprint ed. lib. bdg. 27.95 (*0-89966-895-X*) Buccaneer Bks.

Lord, Let Me Prove That Winning the Lottery Won't Spoil Me! Sandra Pittman. (Illus.). 144p. (Orig.). 1992. pap. 9.95 (*0-940873-92-3*) AKG.

Lord Liar. Laurie Grant. LC 95-7118. (Historical Ser.). 298p. 1995. per. 4.50 (*0-373-28857-3*, 1-28857-0) Harlequin Bks.

Lord, Life Becomes More Simple. Date not set. pap. 1.25 (*0-8341-9195-4*, AN-2643) Lillenas.

Lord Liverpool: The Life & Political Career of Robert Banks Jenkinson, Second Earl of Liverpool, 1770-1828. Norman Gash. (Illus.). 296p. 1985. 40.00 (*0-674-53910-9*) HUP.

Lord Liverpool & Liberal Toryism, 1820-1827. 2nd ed. William R. Brock. (Illus.). 300p. 1967. 35.00 (*0-7146-1457-2*, Pub. by F Cass Pubs) Intl Spec Bk.

Lord Liverpool's Administration: The Crucial Years, 1815-1822. J. E. Cookson. xiii, 422p. 1975. 89.50 (*0-208-01495-0*) Elliots Bks.

Lord Look Kindly on the Child. Regina Press Staff. 1994. pap. 6.25 (*0-88271-348-5*) Regina Pr.

Lord Looketh on the Heart. Max Molgard & Bette Molgard. 1998. 13.95 (*1-57008-438-6*) Bookcraft Inc.

Lord Lothian vs. Lord Lothian. Lothian Lord. 1991. lib. bdg. 76.00 (*0-8490-4420-0*) Gordon Pr.

Lord Lyndhurst: The Flexible Tory. Dennis Lee. (Illus.). 288p. 1994. 35.00 (*0-87081-358-7*) Univ Pr Colo.

Lord Lytton's Indian Administration, 1876-80: The Untold Story. Betty Balfour. (C). 1988. 58.50 (*81-212-0137-3*, Pub. by Gian Publng Hse) S Asia.

Lord Mahavira & His Times. Kailash C. Jain. (C). 1991. 20.00 (*81-208-0805-3*, Pub. by Motilal Bnarsidass) S Asia.

Lord Make Me New. Meta J. Townsand. 34p. 1998. pap. 5.00 (*1-55630-083-2*) Brentwood Comm.

Lord, Make My Life Count. Raymond C. Ortlund. LC 75-6188. 144p. (YA). (gr. 11). 1975. pap. 9.99 (*0-8307-0348-9*, S112175, Regal Bks) Gospel Lght.

Lord Marques Idlenes: Containing Mainfold Matters of Acceptable Devise. William Paulet. LC 79-84131. (English Experience Ser.: No. 949). 112p. 1979. reprint ed. lib. bdg. 15.00 (*90-221-0949-6*) Walter J Johnson.

Lord Mayor of Lisbon: The Portuguese Tribune of the People & His 24 Guilds. Harry Bernstein. (Atlantic Studies on Society in Change: No. 57). 208p. (C). 1989. lib. bdg. 41.50 (*0-8191-7235-9*) U Pr of Amer.

Lord Mayor's Court of London: Depositions Relating to Americans, 1641-1736. Peter W. Coldham. LC 80-80349. 119p. 1980. pap. 10.00 (*0-686-27217-X*); lib. bdg. 12.00 (*0-915156-23-7*, SP 44) Natl Genealogical.

Lord Melbourne, 1779-1848. L. G. Mitchell. LC 97-177477. (Illus.). 368p. 1997. text 55.00 (*0-19-820592-9*) OUP.

Lord Merlyn's Magic. Marcy Stewart. 1995. mass mkt. 4.50 (*0-8217-5112-3*, Zebra Kensgtn) Kensgtn Pub Corp.

Lord Methuen & the British Army: Failure & Redemption in South Africa. Stephen M. Miller. LC 98-24089. 288p. 1999. 39.50 (*0-7146-4904-X*, Pub. by F Cass Pubs); pap. 17.50 (*0-7146-4460-9*, Pub. by F Cass Pubs) Intl Spec Bk.

Lord Monboddo, 1990 Edition. William Knight. 336p. 1996. reprint ed. 75.00 (*1-85506-207-0*) Bks Intl VA.

Lord Montjoy's Country Inn. Cathleen Clare. (Zebra Regency Romance Ser.). 256p. 1998. mass mkt. 4.99 (*0-8217-5902-7*, Zebra Kensgtn) Kensgtn Pub Corp.

Lord Morley's Tryumphes of Fraunces Petrarcke: The First English Translation of the Trionfi. Francesco Petrarca. Ed. by D. D. Carnicelli. LC 72-164690. 302p. 1971. reprint ed. pap. 93.70 (*0-7837-2312-1*, 205740000004) Bks Demand.

Lord Mullion's Secret. large type ed. Michael Innes. 302p. 1993. 27.99 (*0-7505-0031-X*) Ulverscroft.

***Lord Mumford's Minx.** Debbie Raleigh. 2000. mass mkt. 4.99 (*0-8217-6673-2*) Kensgtn Pub Corp.

Lord My Portion. Watchman Nee. Ed. by Herbert L. Fader & James P. O'Dell. (Illus.). 246p. (Orig.). 1984. pap. 4.50 (*0-935008-61-6*) Christian Fellow Pubs.

Lord Needed a Prophet. 2nd ed. Susan A. Madsen. LC 96-31. (Illus.). 250p. (J). (gr. 3-6). 1996. 14.95 (*1-57345-088-X*) Deseret Bk.

Lord Nelson, 1, vol. 4. H. Nicholas. 1999. pap. text 32.95 (*1-86176-051-5*) CHPG.

Lord Nelson, 1, vol. 6. H. Nicholas. 1999. pap. text 32.95 (*1-86176-053-1*) CHPG.

Lord Nelson, 1, vol. 7. H. Nicholas. 1999. pap. text 32.95 (*1-86176-054-X*) CHPG.

Lord Nelson, 1, vol.5. H. Nicholas. 1999. pap. text 32.95 (*1-86176-052-3*) CHPG.

Lord Nelson, 1758-1805: A Bibliography, 7. Leonard W. Cowie. LC 89-12756. (Bibliographies of British Statesmen Ser.: No. 7). 200p. 1990. lib. bdg. 65.00 (*0-313-28082-7*, CBK/, Greenwood Pr) Greenwood.

***Lord Nightingale's Debut.** Judith A. Lansdowne. 2000. mass mkt. 4.99 (*0-8217-6671-6*) Kensgtn Pub Corp.

***Lord Nightingale's Love Song.** Judith A. Landsdowne. (Zebra Regency Romance Ser.). 2000. mass mkt. 4.99 (*0-8217-6688-0*, Zebra Kensgtn) Kensgtn Pub Corp.

***Lord Nightingale's Triumph.** Judith A. Lansdowne. (Regency Romance Ser.). 256p. 2000. mass mkt. 4.99 (*0-8217-6704-6*, Zebra Kensgtn) Kensgtn Pub Corp.

Lord Norman. Henry Clay. Ed. by Mira Wilkins. LC 78-3906. (International Finance Ser.). (Illus.). 1979. reprint ed. lib. bdg. 47.95 (*0-405-11211-4*) Ayer.

Lord North: The Prime Minister Who Lost America. Peter Whiteley. LC 96-49807. (Illus.). 256p. 1996. 45.00 (*1-85285-145-7*) Hambledon Press.

Lord Nottingham's Manual of Chancery Practice & Prolegomena of Chancery & Equity. D. E. Yale. LC 85-48159. (Cambridge Studies in English Legal History). 400p. 1986. reprint ed. 95.00 (*0-912004-28-2*) Gaunt.

Lord Nuffield. Peter Hull. (Lifelines Ser.: No. 39). (Illus.). 48p. 1989. pap. 7.50 (*0-7478-0203-3*, Pub. by Shire Pubns) Parkwest Pubns.

***Lord of a Visible World: An Autobiography in Letters.** H. P. Lovecraft. Ed. by S. T. Joshi & David E. Schultz. 424p. 2000. 49.95 (*0-8214-1332-5*, Ohio U Ctr Intl); pap. 24.95 (*0-8214-1333-3*, Ohio U Ctr Intl) Ohio U Pr.

Lord of Arabia: An Intimate Study of a King. H. C. Armstrong. LC 96-41813. (The Kegan Paul Arabia Library). 306 p. 1997. 110.00 (*0-7103-0568-0*, Pub. by Kegan Paul Intl) Col U Pr.

Lord of Arur the Tyagaraja Cult in Tamilnadu: Study in Conflict & Accommodation. Rajeshwari Ghose. LC 96-900873. (C). 1996. 38.00 (*81-208-1391-X*, Pub. by Motilal Bnarsidass) S Asia.

Lord of Attention: Gerald Stanley Lee & the Crowd Metaphor in Industrializing America. Gregory W. Bush. LC 90-37499. (Illus.). 240p. (C). 1991. lib. bdg. 30.00 (*0-87023-724-1*) U of Mass Pr.

***Lord of Bellavista: The Dramatic Story of a Prison Transformed.** David Miller. 1999. pap. text 10.95 (*0-281-05128-3*) Abingdon.

Lord of Chaos. Robert Jordan. LC 94-30173. (Wheel of Time Ser.: Bk. 6). 716p. 1994. text 25.95 (*0-312-85428-5*) St Martin.

Lord of Chaos. Robert Jordan. (Wheel of Time Ser.: Bk. 6). 1024p. 1995. mass mkt. 7.99 (*0-8125-1375-4*, Pub. by Tor Bks) St Martin.

Lord of Chaos. Robert Jordan. (Wheel of Time Ser.: BK. 6). 1995. 13.09 (*0-606-12079-3*, Pub. by Turtleback) Demco.

Lord of Chaos. deluxe limited ed. Robert Jordan. (Wheel of Time Ser.: Bk. 6). 704p. 1994. 200.00 (*0-312-85788-8*, Pub. by Tor Bks) St Martin.

Lord of Confusion. Ladislas M. Orsy. 1969. 10.00 (*0-87193-064-1*) Dimension Bks.

Lord of Dance. 1986. mass mkt. 4.50 (*0-446-73345-8*, Pub. by Warner Bks) Little.

Lord of Dance. Andrew M. Greeley. 1986. mass mkt. 4.95 (*0-446-34286-6*, Pub. by Warner Bks) Little.

Lord of Danger. Anne Stuart. 384p. 1997. mass mkt. 5.99 (*0-8217-5678-8*, Zebra Kensgtn) Kensgtn Pub Corp.

Lord of Dark Places. Hal Z. Bennett. LC 96-60145. 286p. (Orig.). 1997. pap. 13.95 (*1-885983-12-3*) Turtle Point Pr.

Lord of Desire. Nicole Jordan. 416p. (Orig.). 1992. mass mkt. 4.50 (*0-380-76621-3*, Avon Bks) Morrow Avon.

***Lord of Emperors: Book Two of the Sarantine Mosaic, , No. 2.** Guy Gavriel Kay. (Sarantine Mosaic Ser.: Vol. 2). 544p. 2000. 24.00 (*0-06-105121-7*, HarperPrism) HarpC.

Lord of Enchantment. Suzanne Robinson. 336p. 1994. mass mkt. 5.50 (*0-553-56344-0*) Bantam.

Lord of Falcon Ridge. Catherine Coulter. (Orig.). 1995. mass mkt. 6.99 (*0-515-11584-3*, Jove) Berkley Pub.

Lord of Falcon Ridge. large type ed. Catherine Coulter. (Large Print Bks.). (Orig.). 1995. pap. 20.95 (*1-56895-253-8*) Wheeler Pub.

Lord of Fire. Emma F. Merritt. 400p. (Orig.). 1994. mass mkt. 4.50 (*0-380-77288-4*, Avon Bks) Morrow Avon.

Lord of Glory. Emden C. Mace. 1986. pap. 5.99 (*0-88019-182-1*) Schmul Pub Co.

Lord Of Glory... Crucified: Meditations on the Passion of Christ. Tim Shenton. 1998. pap. 13.99 (*0-946462-52-6*) P & R Pubng.

Lord of Hawkfell Island. Catherine Coulter. 416p. 1993. mass mkt. 6.99 (*0-515-11230-5*, Jove) Berkley Pub.

Lord of Hawkfell Island. large type ed. Catherine Coulter. LC 95-17031. (Large Print Bks.). 1995. pap. 20.95 (*1-56895-235-X*) Wheeler Pub.

Lord of History. Edward C. Fredrich. 32p. (Orig.). 1976. pap. 4.00 (*0-8100-0087-3*, 22N0766) Northwest Pub.

Lord of Horses. Diana L. Paxson. 1996. 23.00 (*0-614-96768-6*, Avon Bks); 23.00 (*0-614-96938-7*, Avon Bks) Morrow Avon.

Lord of Horses. Diana L. Paxson. 1997. mass mkt. 5.99 (*0-380-76528-4*, Avon Bks) Morrow Avon.

***Lord of Horses (HC)** Diana L. Paxson. 2000. 23.00 (*0-380-97265-4*) HarpC.

Lord of Kestle Mount. large type ed. Jeanne F. Montague. (Dales Large Print Ser.). 389p. 1996. pap. 18.99 (*1-85389-666-7*, Dales) Ulverscroft.

Lord of Lackawaxen Creek. Zane Grey. (Miniature Bk.). (Illus.). 64p. 1981. 17.50 (*0-915998-18-1*) Lime Rock Pr.

Lord of Legend. Charlene Cross. 336p. 1993. mass mkt. 5.50 (*0-671-73825-9*) PB.

Lord of Life. 1994. pap. 6.95 (*1-55897-916-6*); pap. 7.00 (*1-55897-918-2*) Brentwood Music.

Lord of Light. Roger Zelazny. 288p. 2000. reprint ed. mass mkt. 6.50 (*0-380-01403-3*, Avon Bks) Morrow Avon.

Lord of Light & Shadow: The Many Faces of God. D. J. Conway. LC 96-39222. (Illus.). 224p. 1999. pap. 14.95 (*1-56718-177-5*) Llewellyn Pubns.

Lord of Light, Prince of Peace. Ed. by Dick Bolk. 1986. 6.99 (*0-685-68482-2*, MC-58) Lillenas.

Lord of Lords. Arranged by Tom Fettke & Camp Kirkland. 1997. pap. 6.99 (*0-8341-9689-1*) Lillenas.

Lord of Lyonsbridge. Ana Seymour. 1999. per. 4.99 (*0-373-29072-1*, 1-29072-5) Harlequin Bks.

Lord of Midnight. Jo Beverley. (Topaz Historical Romance Ser.). 378p. 1998. mass mkt. 6.50 (*0-451-40801-2*, Onyx) NAL.

Lord of Midnight. large type ed. Jo Beverley. LC 98-34893. 1998. 23.95 (*1-56895-662-2*) Wheeler Pub.

Lord of My Heart. Jo Beverley. 384p. (Orig.). 1992. mass mkt. 4.50 (*0-380-76784-8*, Avon Bks) Morrow Avon.

Lord of Raven's Peak. Catherine Coulter. 400p. (Orig.). 1994. mass mkt. 6.99 (*0-515-11351-4*, Jove) Berkley Pub.

Lord of Raven's Peak. large type ed. Catherine Coulter. LC 95-10893. (Large Print Bks.). (Orig.). 1995. 23.95 (*1-56895-223-6*) Wheeler Pub.

***Lord of Scoundrels.** Loretta Chase. LC 99-45472. 1999. 26.95 (*0-7862-2252-2*) Mac Lib Ref.

Lord of Scoundrels. Loretta Chase. 384p. 1995. mass mkt. 6.50 (*0-380-77616-2*, Avon Bks) Morrow Avon.

Lord of Springs. Bennie L. Sinclair. LC 90-30379. 40p. (Orig.). 1990. pap. 5.00 (*0-926487-06-X*) Rowan Mtn Pr.

Lord of Sunset. Parke Godwin. LC 97-50346. 480p. 1998. pap. 13.00 (*0-380-72675-0*, Avon Bks) Morrow Avon.

***Lord of Sunset.** Parke Godwin. 576p. 1999. mass mkt. 6.99 (*0-380-81064-6*, Avon Bks) Morrow Avon.

Lord of the Absurd. Raymond J. Nogar. LC 98-23394. 160p. 1998. reprint ed. pap. 12.00 (*0-268-01320-9*) U of Notre Dame Pr.

Lord of the Andes. Brian Lawless. LC 96-96321. 220p. (Orig.). 1996. pap., per. 12.95 (*0-9652387-0-9*, PO791) Brians Pub.

Lord of the Animals: A Miwok Indian Creation Myth. Fiona French. LC 96-21410. (Illus.). 32p. (J). (gr. k-3). 1997. 15.95 (*0-7613-0112-7*) Millbrook Pr.

***Lord of the Banquet: The Literary & Theological Significance of the Lukan Travel Narrative.** David P. Moessner. LC 98-3559. 384p. 1998. pap. 22.00 (*1-56338-242-3*) TPI PA.

***Lord of the Barn Yard: Killing the Fatted Calf & Arming the Aware in the Corn Belt.** Tristan Egolf. LC 98-35360. xxii, 410 p. 1999. 24.00 (*0-8021-1641-8*, Grove) Grove-Atltic.

***Lord of the Barnyard: Killing the Fatted Calf & Arming the Aware in the Cornbelt.** Tristan Egolf. 432p. 2000. pap. 12.00 (*0-8021-3672-9*, Pub. by Grove-Atltic) Publishers Group.

Lord of the Black Earth. Jeff L. Cline. Ed. by Catherine C. Cline. 200p. 1999. pap. 9.95 (*1-892009-04-8*) Maheshsvari Pub.

***Lord of the Cranes: A Chinese Tale.** Illus. by Jian Jiang Chen. LC 99-57811. 36p. (J). (gr. k-3). 2000. lib. bdg. 15.88 (*0-7358-1193-8*, Pub. by North-South Bks NYC) Chronicle Bks.

***Lord of the Cranes: A Chinese Tale.** Kerstin Chen. Tr. by J. Alison James. 36p. 2000. 15.95 (*0-7358-1192-X*) North-South Bks NYC.

Lord of the Dance. Sydney Carter. LC 99-204375. 1999. write for info. (*0-7459-3898-1*) Lion USA.

Lord of the Dance. Andrew M. Greeley. 544p. 1989. mass mkt. 5.95 (*0-446-35752-9*, Pub. by Warner Bks) Little.

Lord of the Dance: An African Retelling. Veronique Tadjo. LC 89-2785. (Illus.). 32p. (J). (gr. 1-4). 1989. 12.95 (*0-397-32351-4*); lib. bdg. 13.89 (*0-397-32352-2*) HarpC Child Bks.

Lord of the Dance: An Essay in Mysticism. 2nd ed. Anthony Duncan. 117p. (Orig.). 1996. reprint ed. pap. 10.95 (*0-9650839-5-0*) Sun Chalice.

Lord of the Dance: The Autobiography of a Tibetan Lama. Chagdud Tulku. LC 92-23341. 248p. 1992. pap. 16.95 (*1-881847-00-4*) Padma Pub CA.

***Lord of the Dance: The Mani Rimdu Festival in Tibet & Nepal.** Richard J. Kohn. (C). 2001. pap. text. write for info. (*0-7914-4892-4*) State U NY Pr.

***Lord of the Dance: The Mani Rimdu Festival in Tibet & Nepal.** Richard J. Kohn. (C). 2001. text. write for info. (*0-7914-4891-6*) State U NY Pr.

***Lord of the Dark Lake.** Ron Faust. 320p. 2000. pap. 13.95 (*0-312-87510-X*) Forge NYC.

Lord of the Dark Lake. Ron Faust. 1998. mass mkt. 6.99 (*0-8125-3023-3*, Pub. by Tor Bks) St Martin.

Lord of the Dawn: Quetzalcoatl & the Tree of Life. 2nd rev. ed. Tony Shearer. (Illus.). 176p. (C). 1995. pap. 12.95 (*0-87961-240-1*) Naturegraph.

Lord of the Dead. Tom Holland. (J). 1996. 15.00 (*0-671-53313-4*) PB.

Lord of the Dead. Tom Holland. 336p. 1998. mass mkt. 14.00 (*0-671-02411-6*, Pocket Books) PB.

Lord of the Dead: Slave of my Thirst. Tom Holland. 1997. per. 6.99 (*0-671-53426-2*) PB.

***Lord of the Desert.** Diana Palmer. 2000. mass mkt. 6.99 (*1-55166-617-0*, 1-66617-1, Mira Bks) Harlequin Bks.

Lord of the Dragon. Suzanne Robinson. 352p. 1995. mass mkt. 5.50 (*0-553-56345-9*, Fanfare) Bantam.

Lord of the Fantastic: Stories in Honor of Roger Zelazny. Ed. by Martin H. Greenberg. LC 98-18521. 373p. (YA). (gr. 8 up). 1998. pap. 14.00 (*0-380-78737-7*, Eos) Morrow Avon.

Lord of the Fantastic: Stories in Honor of Roger Zelazny, Vol. 1. Ed. by Martin H. Greenberg. 480p. 1999. mass mkt. 6.99 (*0-380-80886-2*, Avon Bks) Morrow Avon.

Lord of the Fire Lands: A Tale of the King's Blades. Dave Duncan. LC 99-33277. 368p. 1999. 23.00 (*0-380-97461-4*, Avon Bks) Morrow Avon.

***Lord of the Fire Lands: A Tale of the King's Blades.** Dave Duncan. 480p. 2000. mass mkt. 6.99 (*0-380-79127-7*) Morrow Avon.

Lord of the Flies. 40p. (YA). 1998. 11.95 (*1-56137-384-2*, NU3842SP) Novel Units.

***Lord of the Flies.** Ed. by Cliffs Notes Staff. (Cliffs Notes Ser.). 80p. 2000. pap. 4.99 (*0-7645-8597-5*) IDG Bks.

Lord of the Flies. Robert Golding. 208p. (YA). (gr. 7 up). pap. 6.95 (*0-8072-1364-0*) Listening Lib.

Lord of the Flies. William Golding. 20.95 (*0-88411-695-6*) Amereon Ltd.

Lord of the Flies. William Golding. 1959. pap. 6.95 (*0-399-50148-7*, Perigee Bks) Berkley Pub.

Lord of the Flies. William Golding. 1998. pap. text 4.95 (*0-7910-4135-2*) Chelsea Hse.

Lord of the Flies. William Golding. Ed. by Harold Bloom. LC 98-23884. (Modern Critical Interpretations Ser.). 176p. (YA). (gr. 8 up). 1999. 34.95 (*0-7910-4777-6*) Chelsea Hse.

Lord of the Flies. William Golding. 1990. 10.92 (*0-02-635121-8*) Glencoe.

***Lord of the Flies.** William Golding. 1999. 9.95 (*1-56137-383-4*) Novel Units.

Lord of the Flies. William Golding. (Assessment Packs Ser.). 15p. 1998. pap. text 15.95 (*1-58303-048-4*) Pthways Pubng.

Lord of the Flies. William Golding. 1954. 12.05 (*0-606-00196-4*, Pub. by Turtleback) Demco.

Lord of the Flies. William Golding. (Great Books of the 20th Century Ser.). 192p. 1999. pap. 12.95 (*0-14-028333-1*, Penguin Bks) Viking Penguin.

An Asterisk (*) at the beginning of an entry indicates that the title is appearing for the first time.

L

***Lord of the Flies.** William Golding & Mary M. Hartley. (Literature Made Easy Ser.). (Illus.). 96p. (YA). 1999. pap. 4.95 (*0-7641-0821-2*) Barron.

Lord of the Flies. Gillian C. Hanscombe. pap. 5.95 (*0-14-077046-1*, Pub. by Pnguin Bks Ltd) Trafalgar.

Lord of the Flies. Holt & Company Staff. 1989. pap., student ed. 11.00 (*0-03-023448-4*) Holt R&W.

Lord of the Flies. Tessa Krailing. (Barron's Book Notes Ser.). (C). 1984. pap. 3.95 (*0-8120-3426-0*) Barron.

Lord of the Flies. Ed. by Clarice Swisher. LC 97-5020. (Literary Companion Ser.). (YA). (gr. 9-12). 1997. pap. 16.20 (*1-56510-628-8*) Greenhaven.

Lord of the Flies, Set. abr. ed. William Golding. 1997. pap. 16.95 incl. audio (*0-14-086416-4*, 395312, Png AudioBks) Viking Penguin.

Lord of the Flies: A Study Guide. Joyce Friedland & Rikki Kessler. (Novel-Ties Ser.). (YA). (gr. 9-12). 1983. pap. text, teacher ed. 15.95 (*0-88122-026-4*) Lrn Links.

Lord of the Flies: A Unit Plan. Mary B. Collins. 154p. 1994. teacher ed., ring bd. 26.95 (*1-58337-109-5*) Teachers Pet Pubns.

Lord of the Flies: Curriculum Unit. Center for Learning Network Staff & William Golding. (Novel Ser.). 60p. (YA). (gr. 9-12). 1991. reprint ed. spiral bd. 18.95 (*1-56077-144-5*) Ctr Learning.

Lord of the Flies: Fathers & Sons. Patrick Reilly. (Masterwork Studies). 170p. 1992. 23.95 (*0-8057-7999-X*, Twayne); pap. 18.00 (*0-8057-8049-1*, Twayne) Mac Lib Ref.

Lord of the Flies: Reproducible Teaching Unit. rev. ed. James Scott. 38p. (YA). (gr. 7-12). 1985. teacher ed., ring bd. 29.50 (*1-58049-060-3*, TU25/U) Prestwick Hse.

Lord of the Flies: Text, Notes & Criticism. Ed. by James R. Baker & Arthur B. Siegler, Jr. 1964. mass mkt. 6.95 (*0-399-50643-8*, Perigee Bks) Berkley Pub.

Lord of the Flies: The Play. William Golding. 96p. 1996. pap. 8.95 (*0-571-16056-5*) Faber & Faber.

Lord of the Flies Notes. Denis M. Calandra. (Cliffs Notes Ser.). 72p. 1971. pap. 4.95 (*0-8220-0754-1*, Cliff) IDG Bks.

Lord of the Forest. Rachel Ford. (Presents Ser.: No. 1368). 1991. per. 2.75 (*0-373-11368-4*) Harlequin Bks.

Lord of the Forest. large type ed. Rachel Ford. 229p. 1992. 27.99 (*0-7505-0319-X*) Ulverscroft.

Lord of the Four Quarters: The Mythology of Kingship. John W. Perry. 1991. pap. 12.95 (*0-8091-3252-4*) Paulist Pr.

Lord of the Four Seasons. Malcolm Nygren. 144p. (Orig.). 1986. pap. 7.95 (*0-9617890-1-8*) Doxology Lane.

Lord of the Fries: And Other Stories. Tim Wynne-Jones. LC 98-41581. 224p. (YA). (gr. 5-9). 1999. 17.95 (*0-7894-2623-4*, D K Ink) DK Pub Inc.

Lord of the Geats. Thomas O. Jones. (Orig.). (YA). (gr. 9 up). 1995. pap. 9.99 (*0-88092-175-7*) Royal Fireworks.

Lord of the High Lonesome. Janet Dailey. (Janet Dailey Americana Ser.: No. 884). 1992. per. 3.59 (*0-373-89884-3*, 1-89884-0) Harlequin Bks.

Lord of the Hollow Dark. rev. ed. Russell Kirk. 384p. 1989. reprint ed. pap. 13.95 (*0-931888-35-2*) Christendom Pr.

Lord of the Horizon. Joan Grant. 300p. 1989. pap. 14.95 (*0-89804-147-3*, Pub. by Ariel GA) Alliance Bk Co.

Lord of the Horizon. Joan Grant. 1980. 29.95 (*0-405-11785-X*) Ayer.

Lord of the House of Dawn: Poems. John Oliver Simon. 64p. (Orig.). 1991. pap. 7.95 (*0-941017-17-6*) Bombshelter Pr.

Lord of the Impossible. Lloyd J. Ogilvie. LC 84-333. 224p. 1984. pap. 12.95 (*0-687-22710-0*) Abingdon.

Lord of the Isles. David Drake. LC 97-5761. (Lord of the Isles Ser.: Vol. 1). 448p. 1997. 25.95 (*0-312-85396-3*, Pub. by Tor Bks) St Martin.

Lord of the Isles. David Drake. (Lord of the Isles Ser.: Vol. 1). 625p. 1998. mass mkt. 6.99 (*0-8125-2240-0*, Pub. by Tor Bks) St Martin.

Lord of the Isles. Elizabeth Mayne. 1997. per. 4.99 (*0-373-28947-2*, 1-28947-9) Silhouette.

Lord of the Isles. Nigel Tranter. mass mkt. 11.95 (*0-340-36836-5*, Pub. by Hodder & Stought Ltd) Trafalgar.

Lord of the Isles. Sir Walter Scott. 1988. reprint ed. lib. bdg. 59.00 (*0-7812-0077-6*) Rprt Serv.

Lord of the Isles. Sir Walter Scott. 1971. reprint ed. 49.00 (*0-403-00716-X*) Scholarly.

***Lord of the Keep.** Ann Lawrence. 400p. (Orig.). 1999. mass mkt. 5.99 (*0-505-52351-5*, Love Spell) Dorchester Pub Co.

Lord of the Light: Exploring the Astrological Sun. Haydn Paul. (Illus.). 240p. 1993. pap. 17.95 (*1-85230-188-0*, Pub. by Element MA) Penguin Putnam.

Lord of the Lodge. large type ed. Miriam MacGregor. 285p. 1992. 11.50 (*0-7505-0315-7*) Ulverscroft.

Lord of the Manor. Shari Anton. (Historical Ser.: Vol. 434). 1998. per. 4.99 (*0-373-29034-9*, 1-29034-5) Harlequin Bks.

***Lord of the Mountain: The Sardiel Poems.** Rienzi Crusz. 160p. 1999. pap. 13.95 (*0-920661-82-3*) TSAR Pubns.

Lord of the Necropolis. Eugene Deweese. (Ravenloft Ser.). 1997. pap. 5.99 (*0-7869-0660-X*, Pub. by TSR Inc) Random.

Lord of the Night. Cara Miles. 384p. (Orig.). 1993. mass mkt. 4.50 (*0-380-76453-9*, Avon Bks) Morrow Avon.

***Lord of the Night.** Connie Mason. 384p. 1998. reprint ed. mass mkt. 5.50 (*0-505-52254-3*, Love Spell) Dorchester Pub Co.

Lord of the Panther Skin. Shota Rustaveli. Tr. by R. H. Stevenson. LC 76-13225. 240p. (C). 1977. text 29.50 (*0-87395-320-7*) State U NY Pr.

***Lord of the Rings.** Ed. by Harold Bloom. LC 99-52464. (Modern Critical Interpretations Ser.). 300p. 1999. 34.95 (*0-7910-5665-1*) Chelsea Hse.

Lord of the Rings. J. R. R. Tolkien. Ed. by Fotonovel Publications Staff. (Illus.). 1979. pap. 2.95 (*0-686-52700-3*) Fotonovel.

Lord of the Rings, 3 vols. J. R. R. Tolkien. 1988. boxed set 65.00 (*0-395-48932-6*) HM.

Lord of the Rings. J. R. R. Tolkien. LC 91-10298. (Illus.). 1200p. 1991. 70.00 (*0-395-59511-8*) HM.

Lord of the Rings, 3 vols. J. R. R. Tolkien. (Illus.). 1992. boxed set 90.00 (*0-395-64741-X*) HM.

Lord of the Rings. J. R. R. Tolkien. LC 99-26007. 1216p. 1999. pap. 20.00 (*0-395-97468-2*) HM.

Lord of the Rings. J. R. R. Tolkien. 1216p. pap. 20.00 (*0-8072-8344-4*) Listening Lib.

Lord of the Rings, 001. 2nd ed. J. R. R. Tolkien. LC 75-308399. 1232p. 1974. 75.00 (*0-395-19395-8*) HM.

Lord of the Rings: Curriculum Unit. Center for Learning Network Staff & J. R. R. Tolkien. (Novel Ser.). 96p. (YA). 1991. spiral bd. 18.95 (*1-56077-137-2*) Ctr Learning.

***Lord of the Rings: Millennium Edition, 7 vols., Vol. 7.** J. R. R. Tolkien. 2000. 70.00 (*0-618-03766-7*) HM.

Lord of the Rings: The Mythology of Power. Jane Chance. (Twayne's Masterwork Studies). 140p. 1992. 23.95 (*0-8057-9441-7*, Twyne) Mac Lib Ref.

Lord of the Rings: The Mythology of Power. Jane Chance. (Twayne's Masterwork Studies: Vol. 99). 140p. 1992. pap. 18.00 (*0-8057-8571-X*, Twyne) Mac Lib Ref.

***Lord of the Rings: The Two Towers & The Return of the King.** abr. ed. J. R. R. Tolkien. 1998. audio 12.00 (*0-89845-223-6*, CPN 1478) HarperAudio.

Lord of the Rings & the Hobbit. J. R. R. Tolkien. (Barron's Book Notes Ser.). 138p. 1986. pap. 3.95 (*0-8120-3523-2*) Barron.

Lord of the Rings & the Hobbit Notes. Gene B. Hardy. (Cliffs Notes Ser.). 80p. (Orig.). 1977. pap. text 4.95 (*0-8220-1286-3*, Cliff) IDG Bks.

Lord of the Rings Official Game Secrets. Steven Schwartz. 1994. pap. 12.95 (*1-55958-675-3*) Prima Pub.

Lord of the Rings Oracle. Terry Donaldson. (Illus.). 128p. 1998. 24.95 (*0-8069-2053-X*) Sterling.

Lord of the Rings Tarot. Terry Donaldson. LC 97-36503. 1997. pap. text 14.00 (*1-57281-054-8*, BK169) US Games Syst.

Lord of the Rings Tarot Deck & Book Set. Terry Donaldson. (Illus.). 224p. 1997. pap. 30.00 (*1-57281-055-6*, LRS99) US Games Syst.

Lord of the Rings Tarot Deck & Card Game. Terry Donaldson. 1997. 15.00 (*1-57281-017-3*) US Games Syst.

Lord of the Sacred City: The Episcopus Exclusus in Late Medieval & Early Modern Germany. J. Jeffrey Tyler. LC 98-41127. (Studies in Medieval & Reformation Thought). 1998. 100.00 (*90-04-11120-4*) Brill Academic Pubs.

Lord of the Saved: A Study of the Lordship Controversy. Kenneth L. Gentry, Jr. LC 92-24057. 1993. pap. 6.99 (*0-87552-265-3*) P & R Pubng.

Lord of the Sea. M. P. Sheil. 24.95 (*0-89190-788-2*) Amereon Ltd.

Lord of the Sea. Matthew P. Shiel. LC 74-16521. (Science Fiction Ser.). 504p. 1975. reprint ed. 41.95 (*0-405-06313-X*) Ayer.

Lord of the Shining Face: My House Is Empty: An Exploration into Creation. Margaret Kirk. Ed. by Lily Nova & Iven Lourie. LC 97-74400. (Illus.). 176p. 1997. pap. 14.95 (*0-9645181-0-4*) Artemis Bks.

***Lord of the Skies: Explore the Miracle of Weather & Rediscover God, His Son.** Alan S. Winfield. LC 99-63732. (Illus.). 144p. 2000. pap. 9.99 (*1-57921-233-6*, Pub. by WinePress Pub) BookWorld.

Lord of the Sky: Zeus. Doris Gates. (Greek Myths Ser.). (Illus.). (J). (gr. 3-7). 1982. pap. 4.99 (*0-14-031532-2*, PuffinBks) Peng Put Young Read.

Lord of the Sky: Zeus. Doris Gates. (Gods & Goddesses of Ancient Greece Ser.). (J). 1972. 10.09 (*0-606-02898-6*, Pub. by Turtleback) Demco.

Lord of the Three in One: The Spread of a Cult in Southeast China. Kenneth Dean. LC 97-46181. 393p. 1998. text 45.00 (*0-691-02881-8*, Pub. by Princeton U Pr) Cal Prin Full Svc.

Lord of the Trees. Philip Jose Farmer. 124p. 1991. reprint ed. lib. bdg. 35.95 (*0-89966-804-6*) Buccaneer Bks.

Lord of the Two Lands. Judith Tarr. 416p. 1994. mass mkt. 4.99 (*0-8125-2078-5*, Pub. by Tor Bks) St Martin.

Lord of the Valley: Hope for the Hurting. James Spruce. LC 93-219174. 80p. (Orig.). 1993. pap. 6.99 (*0-8341-1462-3*) Beacon Hill.

Lord of the Vampires: The Diaries of the Family Dracul. Jeanne Kalogridis. LC 96-13868. 1996. write for info. (*0-614-14341-1*) Delacorte.

Lord of the Vampires: The Diaries of the Family Dracul. Jeanne Kalogridis. 384p. 1997. mass mkt. 5.99 (*0-440-22442-X*) Dell.

Lord of the Wolves. Heather Graham. 416p. 1993. mass mkt. 6.99 (*0-440-21149-2*) Dell.

Lord of the Wolves. large type ed. Heather Graham. LC 93-37780. 565p. 1994. lib. bdg. 20.95 (*0-7862-0093-6*) Thorndike Pr.

Lord of the World. Robert H. Benson. LC 74-15951. (Science Fiction Ser.). 352p. 1975. reprint ed. 32.95 (*0-405-06277-X*) Ayer.

***Lord of the World.** unabridged ed. Robert H. Benson. LC 99-47255. (Catholic Writers Ser.). 384p. 2000. reprint ed. pap. 22.00 (*1-890318-38-8*, Pub. by St Augustines Pr) Chicago Distribution Ctr.

Lord of Thunder. Emma F. Merritt. 432p. (Orig.). 1994. mass mkt. 4.99 (*0-380-77290-6*, Avon Bks) Morrow Avon.

Lord of Vengeance. Tina St. John. 1999. mass mkt. 5.50 (*0-449-00425-2*) Fawcett.

Lord, Only You Can Change Me. Kay Arthur. 244p. 1996. pap. 12.99 (*0-88070-878-6*, Multnomah Bks) Multnomah Pubs.

Lord Ormont & His Aminta: A Novel see Works of George Meredith

Lord Palmerston. Muriel Chamberlain. LC 87-28827. (Political Portraits Ser.). 135p. 1988. 22.95 (*0-8132-0663-4*); pap. 9.95 (*0-8132-0664-2*) Cath U Pr.

Lord Palmerston. Anthony Trollope. Ed. by N. John Hall. LC 80-1901. (Selected Works of Anthony Trollope). 1981. reprint ed. lib. bdg. 27.95 (*0-405-14190-4*) Ayer.

Lord Palmerston, 1784-1865: A Bibliography, 16. Michael S. Partridge & Karen E. Partridge. LC 93-43710. (Bibliographies of British Statesmen Ser.: No. 16). 328p. 1994. lib. bdg. 95.00 (*0-313-28292-7*, Greenwood Pr) Greenwood.

Lord Peter: A Collection of All the Lord Peter Wimsey Stories. Dorothy L. Sayers. 31.95 (*0-8488-1153-4*) Amereon Ltd.

Lord Peter: A Collection of All the Lord Peter Wimsey Stories. Dorothy L. Sayers. 496p. 1995. mass mkt. 5.99 (*0-06-104361-3*) HarpC.

Lord Peter Views the Body: Lord Peter Views the Body. Dorothy L. Sayers. 320p. 1995. mass mkt. 5.99 (*0-06-104359-1*, Harp PBks) HarpC.

Lord Peter Wimsey Companion. Stephan Clarke. 1986. 49.95 (*0-89296-125-2*, Pub. by Mysterious Pr) Little.

"Lord, Please Don't Take Me in August" African Americans in Newport & Saratoga Springs. Myra Beth Young Armstead. LC 98-58092. 1999. 39.95 (*0-252-02485-0*) U of Ill Pr.

***"Lord, Please Don't Take Me in August" African Americans in Newport & Saratoga Springs.** Myra Beth Young Armstead. LC 98-58092. (Illus.). 208p. 1999. pap. 16.95 (*0-252-06801-7*) U of Ill Pr.

Lord, Please Zip Up My Armor. Mab G. Hoover. 112p. 1986. pap. 3.70 (*0-310-35642-3*, 11268P) Zondervan.

Lord, Please Zip Up My Armor. 2nd ed. Mab G. Hoover. 128p. 1988. pap. 6.95 (*0-310-35641-5*, 11267P) Zondervan.

Lord Pluto. Gopi Gyan. (Illus.). 171p. (Orig.). 1980. spiral bd. 6.95 (*0-935146-22-9*) Morningland.

Lord Prestimion. Robert Silverberg. LC 98-39208. 432p. 1999. 25.00 (*0-06-105028-8*) HarpC.

***Lord Prestimion: The Majipoor Cycle Continues.** Robert Silverberg. (Prestimion Trilogy Ser.: Vol. 2). 512p. (YA). 2000. mass mkt. 6.99 (*0-06-105810-6*, Avon Bks) Morrow Avon.

Lord Radcliffes Season, 1. Jo Ann Ferguson. 256p. 1999. mass mkt. 4.99 (*0-8217-6289-3*) Kensgtn Pub Corp.

Lord Radstock & the Russian Awakening. David Fountain. (Illus.). pap. 8.99 (*0-907821-04-9*) Revival Lit.

"Lord Randal" & Other British Ballads. Ed. by Francis J. Child. (Thrift Editions Ser.). (Illus.). 64p. (Orig.). 1996. pap. text 1.00 (*0-486-28987-7*) Dover.

Lord Randolph Churchill: A Political Life. R. F. Foster. (Illus.). 1983. pap. 24.95 (*0-19-822756-6*) OUP.

Lord Reigns: A Theological Handbook of the Psalms. James L. Mays. LC 94-10407. (Interpretation Ser.). 228p. (Orig.). 1994. pap. 22.95 (*0-664-25558-2*) Westminster John Knox.

Lord Returns. R. A. Torrey. 1997. pap. 8.99 (*1-898787-91-3*) Emerald House Group Inc.

Lord Rhys: Prince of Deheubarth. Roger Turvey. 1997. pap. 17.95 (*0-8464-4586-7*) Beekman Pubs.

Lord Rhys: Prince of Deheubarth. Roger Turvey. 1997. pap. 22.00 (*1-85902-430-0*, Pub. by Gomer Pr) St Mut.

Lord Rochester. Ed. by Paddy Lyons. (Everyman's Poetry Ser.). 116p. 1997. pap. 1.95 (*0-460-87819-0*, Everyman's Classic Lib) Tuttle Pubng.

Lord Rose up from Seir: Studies in the History & Tradition of the Negev & Southern Judah. Lars E. Axelsson. (Coniectanea Biblica. Old Testament Ser.: No. 25). 210p. (Orig.). 1987. pap. text 48.00 (*91-22-00876-4*) Coronet Bks.

Lord Said "Tell Them I Love Them" Not by Bread Alone: Amplified Edition, Pt. 1. Merle E. Koepke. 63p. 1985. reprint ed. pap. 4.95 (*1-891125-05-2*) Hands Jesus.

Lord Said "Tell Them I Love Them" Not by Bread Alone: Amplified Edition, Pt. 2. Merle E. Koepke. 67p. 1985. reprint ed. pap. 4.95 (*1-891125-06-0*) Hands Jesus.

Lord Said "Tell Them I Love Them" Not by Bread Alone: Amplified Edition, Pt. 3. Merle E. Koepke. 58p. 1985. reprint ed. pap. 4.95 (*1-891125-07-9*) Hands Jesus.

Lord Said "Tell Them I Love Them" Not by Bread Alone: Amplified Edition, Pt. 4. Merle E. Koepke. 78p. 1985. reprint ed. pap. 4.95 (*1-891125-08-7*) Hands Jesus.

Lord Said "Tell Them I Love Them" Not by Bread Alone: Amplified Edition, Pt. 5. Merle E. Koepke. 74p. 1985. reprint ed. pap. 4.95 (*1-891125-09-5*) Hands Jesus.

Lord Said "Tell Them I Love Them" Seek Him. Merle E. Koepke. 37p. 1984. reprint ed. pap. 2.95 (*1-891125-04-4*) Hands Jesus.

Lord Said "Tell Them I Love Them" Zoe Life. Merle E. Koepke. 35p. 1994. reprint ed. pap. 2.95 (*1-891125-03-6*) Hands Jesus.

Lord Salisbury: A Political Biography. David Steele. (Illus.). 472p. 1999. 66.00 (*1-85728-326-0*, Pub. by UCL Pr Ltd) Taylor & Francis.

Lord Saturn. (Illus.). 179p. (Orig.). 1980. spiral bd. 6.95 (*0-935146-23-7*) Morningland.

Lord Savage. Patricia Coughlin. 448p. 1996. mass mkt. 5.50 (*0-553-57520-1*, Fanfare) Bantam.

Lord Savage. Debra Dier. 320p. (Orig.). 1996. mass mkt. 4.99 (*0-8439-4119-7*) Dorchester Pub Co.

Lord Sayer's Ghost. Cindy Holbrok. 416p. 1996. mass mkt. 4.99 (*0-8217-5320-7*) Kensgtn Pub Corp.

Lord Scandal's Lady. Cathleen Clare. 256p. 1997. mass mkt. 4.99 (*0-8217-5591-9*, Zebra Kensgtn) Kensgtn Pub Corp.

Lord Selkirk's Diary, 1803-1804, Vol. 35. Thomas D. Selkirk. Ed. by Patrick White. LC 69-14504. 359p. 1969. reprint ed. lib. bdg. 65.00 (*0-8371-3864-7*, SESD, Greenwood Pr) Greenwood.

Lord Selkirk's Work in Canada. Chester B. Martin. (BCL1 - History - Canada Ser.). 240p. 1991. reprint ed. lib. bdg. 79.00 (*0-7812-6374-3*) Rprt Serv.

Lord Shaftesbury. John L. Hammond & Barbara Hammond. LC 70-169762. (Select Bibliographies Reprint Ser.). 1977. reprint ed. 25.95 (*0-8369-5982-5*) Ayer.

Lord Show Us Thy Glory. Ray H. Hughes. LC 97-66508. 215p. 1997. pap. 9.99 (*0-87148-534-6*) Pathway Pr.

Lord Sin. Catherine Archer. 1997. per. 4.99 (*0-373-28979-0*, 1-28979-2) Harlequin Bks.

Lord Soth. Edo Van Belkom. (DragonLance Warriors Ser.). 1997. pap. 5.99 (*0-7869-0519-0*, Pub. by TSR Inc) Random.

***Lord St. Claire's Angel.** Donna J. Simpson. 1999. mass mkt. 4.99 (*0-8217-6449-7*) Kensgtn Pub Corp.

***Lord Stanhope's Proposal.** Jessica Benson. (Regency Romance Ser.). 2000. mass mkt. 4.99 (*0-8217-6537-X*, Zebra Kensgtn) Kensgtn Pub Corp.

Lord Strafford. Henry D. Traill. LC 70-137386. (Select Bibliographies Reprint Ser.). 1977. 19.95 (*0-8369-5587-0*) Ayer.

Lord Swinton. J. A. Cross. 1982. 52.00 (*0-19-822602-0*) OUP.

***Lord Teach Me How to Love: Learning from the Ultimate Example.** Creflo A. Dollar, Jr. 2000. 19.99 (*1-57794-295-7*) Harrison Hse.

Lord, Teach Me How to Pray. Pattie Pendry. Ed. by Harold McDougal. 112p. 1998. pap. 7.99 (*1-884369-88-X*, Serenity Bks) McDougal Pubng.

Lord, Teach Me to Pray. Mary A. Isleib. 112p. (Orig.). Date not set. pap. 4.99 (*0-9629986-1-3*) M A Isleib.

Lord, Teach Me to Pray! Jean Paradis. (C). 1988. 39.00 (*0-85439-256-4*, Pub. by St Paul Pubns) St Mut.

Lord, Teach Me to Pray in 28 Days. Kay Arthur. LC 94-29310. 1995. pap. 8.99 (*1-56507-252-9*) Harvest Hse.

Lord, Teach Me to Pray in 28 Days. Kay Arthur. Tr. by Capstone Publishers Staff from CHI. 159p. 1996. pap. 3.95 (*1-888655-51-8*) Precept Ministries.

Lord Teach Me to Pray in 28 Days. large type ed. Kay Arthur. LC 96-22272. 172p. 1996. pap. 13.95 (*0-8027-2706-9*) Walker & Co.

Lord, Teach Me to Pray in 28 Days see Senor Esename a Orar en 28 Diaz

Lord, Teach Us: The Lord's Prayer & the Christian Life. Stanley Hauerwas & William H. Willimon. 128p. (Orig.). 1996. pap. 7.95 (*0-687-00614-7*) Abingdon.

Lord Teach Us How to Fight: Practical Expositions on Ephesians 6: 10-18. Dan Bond. 135p. 1989. write for info. (*1-877654-01-9*) Word Transfer.

Lord, Teach Us to Pray. Charles E. Cravey. 1989. pap. 9.95 (*0-938645-16-1*) In His Steps.

Lord Teach Us to Pray. Edward C. Fredrich. 40p. (Orig.). 1985. pap. 4.00 (*0-8100-0208-6*, 22N0797) Northwest Pub.

Lord, Teach Us to Pray. Nathaniel Holcomb. 190p. 1997. pap. write for info. (*1-930918-01-1*) Its All About Him.

Lord, Teach Us to Pray. Gerard Joubert. LC 88-91188. (Illus.). 344p. (C). 1988. pap. 10.00 (*0-9620592-0-X*) G Joubert.

Lord Teach Us to Pray. Leonard Mullens. 1963. pap. 1.00 (*0-686-75248-1*) Firm Foun Pub.

Lord, Teach Us to Pray. Lucille Walker. LC 86-2994. 1986. pap. 4.95 (*0-87148-525-7*) Pathway Pr.

Lord, Teach Us to Pray. Gerald Joubert. (Illus.). 330p. 1998. reprint ed. pap. 10.00 (*1-892873-06-0*) Ginger Pubns.

Lord, Teach Us to Pray, 2 bks., Set. Ed White. 52p. (Orig.). 1991. pap. text, teacher ed. 2.99 (*0-89900-349-4*) College Pr Pub.

Lord, Teach Us to Pray: A New Look at the Lord's Prayer. Arthur P. Boers. LC 92-71102. 192p. (Orig.). 1992. pap. 11.99 (*0-8361-3583-0*) Herald Pr.

Lord, Teach Us to Pray: A Powerful, Thought-Provoking Look at Jesus' Teaching on Prayer. Ancil Jenkins. 1988. pap. 6.99 (*0-89225-338-X*) Gospel Advocate.

***Lord, Teach Us to Pray! A Primer for Children & Adults.** rev. ed. Colleen T. Evans. Ed. by Wendelyn Martz. LC 99-96317. (Illus.). 72p. (J). (gr. k-5). 2000. 15.95 (*0-9674105-0-9*, 4000) H Davidson Pubg.

Lord, Teach Us to Pray: Sermons on Prayer. Alexander Whyte. 292p. (C). 1998. reprint ed. pap. 25.95 (*1-57383-106-9*) Regent College.

Lord, Teach Us to Pray Vol. I: The Father Fact. Nathaniel Holcomb. 53p. 1995. write for info. (*1-930918-02-X*) Its All About Him.

Lord, Teach Us to Pray Vol. II: Developing Friendship Through Fellowship. Nathaniel Holcomb. 50p. 1995. write for info. (*1-930918-03-8*) Its All About Him.

Lord, Teach Us to Pray Vol. III: A Focused Faith in the Father. Nathaniel Holcomb. 43p. 1995. pap. write for info. (*1-930918-04-6*) Its All About Him.

Lord, Teach Us to Pray Vol. IV: Fighting the Foe of the Flesh. Nathaniel Holcomb. 34p. 1995. pap. write for info. (*1-930918-05-4*) Its All About Him.

Lord Ted: The Dexter Enigma. Alan Lee. (Illus.). 256p. 1996. pap. 13.95 (*0-575-60040-3*, Pub. by V Gollancz) Trafalgar.

Lord, the Lion & Mutu. Del Delaney. (Literature Crusade Ser.). pap. 0.95 (*0-89985-379-X*) Christ for the Nations.

Lord, the Lion & Mutu. Del Delaney. 1974. pap. 1.95 (*0-89985-995-X*) Christ for the Nations.

Lord, the Lion & Mutu (Cristo, el Leon y Pablo) Gordon Lindsay. (Literature Crusade Ser.). (SPA.). pap. 0.95 (*0-89985-377-3*) Christ for the Nations.

Lord, Through Poetry. Pearlie Ponder. 208p. 1999. pap. write for info. (*0-9644034-1-2*) P Ponder.

Lord Tony's Wife. Emmuska Orczy. (J). 1986. reprint ed. lib. bdg. 37.95 (*0-89966-553-5*) Buccaneer Bks.

An Asterisk (*) at the beginning of an entry indicates that the title is appearing for the first time.

Lord Uranus. Gopi G. Donato. Ed. by Morningland Publications, Inc. Staff. (Astrology Ser.). (Illus.). 341p. (Orig.). 1981. spiral bd. 6.95 (*0-935146-52-0*) Morningland.

Lord Valentine's Castle. Robert Silverberg. Vol. 1. 528p. 1995. mass mkt. 6.50 (*0-06-105487-9*, HarperPrism) HarpC.

Lord Vanity. Samuel Shellabarger. 479p. Date not set. 30.95 (*0-8488-2389-3*) Amereon Ltd.

Lord Wakeford's Gold Watch. Paula T. Gerard. 256p. 1997. mass mkt. 4.99 (*0-8217-5840-3*, Zebra Kensgtn) Kensgtn Pub Corp.

Lord Wakeford's Gold Watch. Paula T. Girard. 256p. 1995. mass mkt. 3.99 (*0-8217-4979-X*, Pinncle Kensgtn) Kensgtn Pub Corp.

Lord, Where Are You When Bad Things Happen? Kay Arthur. 238p. 1996. pap. 12.99 (*0-88070-883-2*, Multnomah Bks) Multnomah Pubs.

Lord, Where Are You When Bad Things Happen? Kay Arthur. Tr. by Capstone Publishers Staff from CHI. 270p. 1996. pap. 8.99 (*1-888655-50-X*) Precept Ministries.

***Lord, Why Am I Crying? A Christian Perspective on Depression.** Lynda A. Doty. LC 99-38445. 142p. 1999. pap. 7.99 (*1-56722-234-X*) Word Aflame.

Lord, Why Not Me? A Mother's Story of an Autistic Child. Marean J. Price. (Illus.). 104p. (Orig.). pap. text 14.95 (*1-883372-00-3*) Rondelle Pub.

Lord Will Gather Me In: My Journey to Jewish Orthodoxy. David Klinghoffer. LC 98-26387. 272p. 1998. 24.00 (*0-684-82341-1*) Free Pr.

Lord Will Keep You Going. Ruth Boise. Ed. by Barry Lane. (Opening Doors Ser.: No. 1). (Illus.). 32p. (Orig.). 1989. pap. 4.00 (*1-877829-04-8*) Homegrown Bks.

Lord William Bentinck: The Making of a Liberal Imperialist, 1774-1839. John Rosselli. LC 72-95302. 386p. reprint ed. pap. 119.70 (*0-608-18297-4*, 203154700075) Bks Demand.

Lord William Russell & His Wife, 1815-1846. Georgiana Blakiston. LC 73-75710. 1974. 30.00 (*0-8420-1681-3*) Scholarly Res Inc.

Lord Willin' & the River Don't Rise. Joyce H. Smith. LC 97-41715. 231p. 1998. pap. 18.95 (*1-56072-490-0*, Nova Kroshka Bks) Nova Sci Pubs.

Lord Won't Mind. Gordon Merrick. 256p. 1996. reprint ed. pap. 11.95 (*1-55583-290-3*) Alyson Pubns.

Lord Wraxall's Fancy. Anna L. Saxby. (Black Lace Ser.). 300p. 1996. mass mkt. 5.95 (*0-352-33080-5*, Pub. by Virgin Bks) London Brdge.

Lord Wraybourne's Betrothed. large type ed. Jo Beverly. 351p. 1991. reprint ed. lib. bdg. 18.95 (*1-56054-087-7*) Thorndike Pr.

Lord Wyland Takes a Wife. Joy Reed. 256p. 1997. mass mkt. 4.99 (*0-8217-5767-9*, Zebra Kensgtn) Kensgtn Pub Corp.

Lord, You Must Be Joking! Bible Stories That Tell Your Story. Eugene J. Webb. LC 94-22722. 176p. (Orig.). 1994. pap. 10.95 (*0-89390-309-4*) Resource Pubns.

Lord, You Must Be Joking! Leader's Guide. John E. Barone & Eugene J. Webb. 80p. (Orig.). 1994. pap., teacher ed. 7.95 (*0-89390-310-8*) Resource Pubns.

***Lord Zip's Bubble Mystery.** Judy Mazzeo Zocchi. (Lord Zip Ser.). (Illus.). 8p. (J). (ps). 2000. mass mkt. 4.99 (*1-891997-11-4*) Dingles & Co.

Lordly Domains. rev. ed. Greg Stafford & Liam Routt. (Pendragon Role Playing Game Ser.). (Illus.). 128p. (Orig.). 1997. pap. 19.95 (*1-56882-050-X*, 2719) Chaosium.

Lords & Ladies. Terry Pratchett. 384p. 1994. mass mkt. 6.99 (*0-552-13891-6*) Bantam.

Lords & Ladies. Ed. by John Scognamiglio. 384p. 1996. mass mkt. 4.50 (*0-8217-5323-1*) Kensgtn Pub Corp.

Lords & Ladies MM. Terry Pratchett. 288p. 1996. mass mkt. 6.50 (*0-06-105692-8*, HarperPrism) HarpC.

Lords & the New Creatures. Jim Morrison. LC 74-107256. 142p. 1971. pap. 10.00 (*0-671-21044-0*, Touchstone) S&S Trade Pap.

Lord's Annointed. rev. ed. Ed. by Philip E. Satterthwaite et al. 320p. 1995. pap. 20.00 (*0-85364-685-6*, Pub. by Paternoster Pub) OM Literature.

Lord's Book of Life & Health. Jakob Lorber. Tr. by Gerhard Hanswille from GER. 265p. (Orig.). 1994. per. 17.95 (*1-885928-00-9*) Merkur Pubng.

Lord's Coming see Venida del Senor

Lord's Day. Kingdom Quotes Staff. pap. write for info. (*0-930179-13-7*) Johns Enter.

Lord's Day. Jo Pipa. 1996. pap. 9.99 (*1-85792-201-8*, Pub. by Christian Focus) Spring Arbor Dist.

Lord's Day. Paul K. Jewett. 1978. reprint ed. pap. text 8.95 (*0-9602638-0-2*) Fuller Seminary.

Lord's Day Seminar in Four Audio Cassettes: A Biblical Study of the Validity & Value of the Sabbath. unabridged ed. Samuele Bacchiocchi. (Biblical Perspectives Ser.: Vol. 1). 1995. audio 20.00 (*1-930987-25-0*, LDSA4) Biblical.

Lord's Dominion: The History of Canadian Methodism. Neil Semple. LC 97-158873. (Illus.). 544p. 1996. 65.00 (*0-7735-1367-1*, Pub. by McG-Queens Univ Pr) CUP Services.

Lord's Dominion: The History of Canadian Methodism. Neil Semple. LC 97-158873. (McGill-Queen's Studies in the History of Religion Ser.: No. 21). (Illus.). 544p. 1996. pap. 24.95 (*0-7735-1400-7*, Pub. by McG-Queens Univ Pr) CUP Services.

Lord's Fast see Ayuno del Senor

Lords First Night. Boureau. Tr. by Lydia G. Cochrane. LC 97-36598. 1998. pap. text 19.00 (*0-226-06743-2*); lib. bdg. 55.00 (*0-226-06742-4*) U Ch Pr.

Lord's Freedman. Keith W. Lamb. 266p. (Orig.). 1995. pap. 10.99 (*1-56043-829-0*, Treasure Hse) Destiny Image.

Lord's Harvest & the Rural Church: A New Look at Ministry in the Agri-Culture. Kent R. Hunter. 144p. (Orig.). 1993. pap. 8.99 (*0-8341-1503-4*) Beacon Hill.

Lord's Hidden Message in Money. Jo Vah. 50p. 1998. reprint ed. pap. text. write for info. (*1-57502-896-4*, PO2445) Morris Pubng.

Lord's House: A Guide to Creation Careful Management of Church Facilities. Frederick W. Krueger. LC 95-30414. 1995. 22.00 (*1-886158-06-1*) Macalester.

Lords House: A History of Sheffield's Roman Catholic Buildings 1570-1990. Denis Evinson. 190p. 1991. 16.95 (*1-85075-303-2*, Pub. by Sheffield Acad) CUP Services.

Lords' Jews: Magnate-Jewish Relations in the Polish-Lithuanian Commonwealth During the 18th Century. M. S. Rosman. (Harvard Ukrainian Research Institute Monograph). (Illus.). 260p. (C). 1990. reprint ed. text 32.95 (*0-916458-18-0*) Harvard Ukrainian.

Lords' Jews: Magnate-Jewish Relations in the Polish-Lithuanian Commonwealth During the 18th Century. M. S. Rosman. (Harvard Ukrainian Research Institute Monograph). (Illus.). 260p. (C). 1992. reprint ed. pap. text 18.00 (*0-916458-47-4*) Harvard Ukrainian.

Lords Last Call. Ross Norris. LC 98-73707. 287p. 1998. pap. 12.95 (*1-883697-19-0*) Hara Pub.

Lord's Motel: A Novel. Gail D. Storey. LC 92-10532. 224p. 1992. 19.95 (*0-89255-178-X*) Persea Bks.

Lord's Motel: A Novel. Gail D. Storey. 1993. reprint ed. pap. 9.95 (*0-89255-194-1*) Persea Bks.

Lords of All the World: Ideologies of Empire in Spain, Britain, & France, 1492-1830. Anthony Pagden. 256p. 1998. pap. 18.00 (*0-300-07449-2*) Yale U Pr.

Lords of Castle Weirwyck. Elaine F. Wells. 256p. (Orig.). 1980. mass mkt. 1.95 (*0-89083-668-X*, Zebra Kensgtn) Kensgtn Pub Corp.

Lords of Chaos: The Bloody Rise of the Satanic Metal Underground. Michael Moynihan & Didrik Soderlind. LC 98-168794. (Illus.). 358p. 1997. pap. 16.95 (*0-922915-48-2*) Feral Hse.

Lords of Creation. Timothy R. Sullivan. 256p. (Orig.). 1992. mass mkt. 3.99 (*0-380-76284-6*, Avon Bks) Morrow Avon.

***Lords of Death.** Alexander E. Presniakov. 260p. 2000. pap. 14.95 (*1-57532-294-3*, Pub. by Press-Tige Pub) Barnes & Noble Inc.

Lords of Destruction. Frank Frazetta. 1993. mass mkt. 4.99 (*0-8125-3422-0*, Pub. by Tor Bks) St Martin.

Lords of Discipline. Pat Conroy. 512p. 1982. mass mkt. 7.99 (*0-553-27136-9*) Bantam.

Lords of Discipline. Pat Conroy. 1980. 25.00 (*0-937036-01-3*) Old NY Bk Shop.

Lords of Discipline. Pat Conroy. 1995. 13.50 (*0-606-01637-6*, Pub. by Turtleback) Demco.

Lords of Discipline, Set. abr. ed. Pat Conroy. 1988. audio 18.00 (*0-553-45152-9*) BDD Aud Pub.

Lords of Dublin in the Age of Reformation. Colm Lennon. 320p. 1989. 45.00 (*0-7165-2419-8*, Pub. by Irish Acad Pr) Intl Spec Bk.

Lords of Fleet Street: The Harmsworth Dynasty Richard Bourne. LC 90-227554. 1990. write for info. (*0-04-440450-6*, Pub. by Allen & Unwin Pty) Paul & Co Pubs.

***Lords of Foggy Bottom.** Tom Lansford. LC 99-27661. 1999. write for info. (*0-914746-55-3*) G Kurian.

Lords of Human Kind: European Attitudes to Other Cultures in the Imperial Age. Victor Kiernan. LC 96-180106. 384p. 1998. pap. 24.95 (*1-897959-23-0*, Pub. by Serif) IPG Chicago.

Lords of Industry. Henry D. Lloyd. LC 73-2519. (Big Business; Economic Power in a Free Society Ser.). 1973. reprint ed. 24.95 (*0-405-05099-2*) Ayer.

Lords of Land. Matt Braun. 1996. mass mkt. 5.99 (*0-312-95831-5*, Pub. by Tor Bks) St Martin.

Lords of Light. Deepak Chopra & Martin Greenberg. 343p. 1999. mass mkt. 6.99 (*0-312-96892-2*, Thomas Dunne) St Martin.

Lords of Light: The Path of Initiation in the Western Mysteries. W. E. Butler. Ed. by Toni Geikie. 160p. (Orig.). 1990. pap. 10.95 (*0-89281-308-3*) Inner Tradit.

Lords of Magic: The Official Strategy Guide. Joe G. Bell. LC 97-69338. (Secrets of the Game Ser.). 320p. 1998. per. 19.99 (*0-7615-1147-4*) Prima Pub.

Lords of Midnight the Official Strategy Guide. Ron Wartow. 1995. pap. 19.95 (*0-7615-0071-5*) Prima Pub.

***Lords of Misrule.** 1999. pap. 17.95 (*1-56971-352-9*, Pub. by Dark Horse Comics) Penguin Putnam.

Lords of Misrule, Vol. 1. Nigel Tranter. mass mkt. 11.95 (*0-340-22303-0*, Pub. by Hodder & Stought Ltd) Trafalgar.

Lords of Misrule: Mardi Gras & the Politics of Race in New Orleans. James Gill. LC 96-32927. (Illus.). 272p. 1997. pap. 18.00 (*0-87805-916-4*) U Pr of Miss.

Lords of Parliament Studies, 1714-1914. Ed. by R. W. Davis. LC 94-17743. x, 230p. 1995. 45.00 (*0-8047-2476-8*) Stanford U Pr.

Lords of Poverty: The Power, Prestige & Corruption of the International Aid Business. Graham Hancock. LC 89-6893. 1992. pap. 12.00 (*0-87113-469-1*, Atlntc Mnthly) Grove-Atltic.

Lords of Speech. Edgar D. Jones. LC 68-58799. (Essay Index Reprint Ser.). 1977. 17.95 (*0-8369-1040-0*) Ayer.

Lords of the Ascendancy: The Irish House of Lords & Its Members, 1600-1800. Francis G. James. LC 95-11179. 192p. 1995. 39.95 (*0-8132-0840-8*) Cath U Pr.

Lords of the Ascendancy, 1600-1800. Francis James. 248p. 1995. 45.00 (*0-7165-2529-1*, Pub. by Irish Acad Pr) Intl Spec Bk.

Lords of the Cold: Mountaineering Tales in Verse. John Christopher. LC 93-84082. 64p. (Orig.). 1993. pap. 11.95 (*0-9630775-5-3*) PPC Bks.

Lords of the Expanse. (Star Wars). 1997. 30.00 (*0-87431-297-3*) West End Games.

Lords of the Fly: Drosophila Genetics & the Experimental Life. Robert E. Kohler. LC 93-29436. 344p. 1994. pap. text 18.95 (*0-226-45063-5*); lib. bdg. 45.00 (*0-226-45062-7*) U Ch Pr.

Lords of the Ghostland: A History of the Ideal. Edgar E. Saltus. LC 71-116003. reprint ed. 37.50 (*0-404-05539-7*) AMS Pr.

***Lords of the Harvest.** Charles. 2000. pap. 27.00 (*0-7382-0291-6*, Pub. by Perseus Pubng) HarpC.

Lords of the Horizons: A History of the Ottoman Empire. Jason Goodwin. LC 98-41601. (Illus.). 352p. 1999. 32.50 (*0-8050-4081-1*) H Holt & Co.

***Lords of the Horizons: A History of the Ottoman Empire.** Jason Goodwin. 2000. pap. 15.00 (*0-8050-6342-0*, Owl) H Holt & Co.

Lords of the Lake: The Naval War on Lake Ontario, 1812-1814. Robert Malcomson. LC 98-67770. (Illus.). 432p. 1999. 36.95 (*1-55750-532-2*) Naval Inst Pr.

Lords of the Lebanese Marches: Violence & Narrative in Arab Society. Michael Gilsenan. LC 95-50482. (Illus.). 495p. (C). 1996. pap. 24.95 (*0-520-20590-1*, Pub. by U CA Pr) Cal Prin Full Svc.

Lords of the Lebanese Marches: Violence & Narrative in Arab Society. Michael Gilsenan. LC 95-50482. (Illus.). 375p. (C). 1996. text 58.00 (*0-520-20589-8*, Pub. by U CA Pr) Cal Prin Full Svc.

Lords of the Left-Hand Path: A History of Spiritual Dissent. Stephen E. Flowers. (Illus.). xiv, 260p. 1997. pap. 36.00 (*1-885972-08-3*) Runa-Raven Pr.

Lords of the Middle Dark. Jack L. Chalker. (Rings of the Master Ser.: Bk. 1). 1986. mass mkt. 4.99 (*0-345-32560-5*, Del Rey) Ballantine Pub Grp.

Lords of the Mountain: Social Banditry & Peasant Protest in Cuba, 1878-1918. Louis A. Perez. LC 88-19815. (Pitt Latin American Ser.). 288p. reprint ed. pap. 89.30 (*0-608-20008-5*, 207128400010) Bks Demand.

Lords of the Night. Blayne et al. 320p. 1997. mass mkt. 4.99 (*0-8217-5593-5*, Zebra Kensgtn) Kensgtn Pub Corp.

Lords of the Ocean. James L. Nelson. LC 99-26943. 352p. 1999. 23.00 (*0-671-03490-1*, PB Hardcover) PB.

Lords of the Ocean. James L. Nelson. 368p. 2000. reprint ed. per. 13.95 (*0-671-01383-1*) PB.

Lords of the Plains: A Novel. Max Crawford. LC 96-41322. 320p. 1997. 14.95 (*0-8061-2908-5*) U of Okla Pr.

Lords of the Realm: The Real History of Baseball. John Helyar. 1995. mass mkt. 6.99 (*0-345-39261-2*) Ballantine Pub Grp.

Lords of the Realm No. II: The Official Strategy Guide. Bart Farkas. LC 96-70913. 168p. 1997. per. 16.99 (*0-7615-0947-X*) Prima Pub.

Lords of the Rivers. Nancy N. Baxter. LC 88-82312. (Heartland Chronicles Ser.: Bk. II). (Illus.). 500p. 1988. pap. 14.95 (*0-9617367-7-1*) Guild Pr IN.

Lords of the Savanna: The Bambara, Fulani, Lgbo, Mossi, Nupe. Philip Koslow. LC 97-7295. (Kingdoms of Africa Ser.). (Illus.). 72p. (J). (gr. 3 up). 1997. pap. 8.95 (*0-7910-3142-X*) Chelsea Hse.

Lords of the Secret Inner Circle. Dahk Knox. 600p. 1995. 21.95 (*1-881116-06-9*, Pub. by Black Forest Pr) Epic Bk Promo.

Lords of the Secret Inner Circle: The Series, 3 bks., Set, Vols. I-III. Dahk Knox. 600p. 1994. 21.95 (*1-881116-20-4*) Black Forest Pr.

Lords of the Seventh Swarm. Dave Wolverton. (Golden Queen Ser.). 1998. mass mkt. 6.99 (*0-8125-5032-3*, Pub. by Tor Bks) St Martin.

Lords of the Seventh Swarm, No. 2. Dave Wolverton. 352p. 1997. 24.95 (*0-312-85771-3*) Tor Bks.

Lords of the Sky. Angus Wells. 688p. 1995. mass mkt. 6.50 (*0-553-57266-0*, Spectra) Bantam.

Lords of the Sunset: A Tour in the Shan States. Maurice Collis. LC 77-87074. reprint ed. 42.50 (*0-404-16807-8*) AMS Pr.

Lords of the Valley: Including the Complete Text of "Our Unsheltered Lives" by Ed Lord. LaVerne Hanners & Ed Lord. LC 95-36291. (Illus.). 200p. 1996. 24.95 (*0-8061-2804-6*) U of Okla Pr.

Lords of the Wild. Joseph A. Altsheler. 24.95 (*0-8488-0905-X*) Amereon Ltd.

Lords of the Wild. Joseph A. Altsheler. 1993. reprint ed. lib. bdg. 21.95 (*0-89968-563-3*) Buccaneer Bks.

Lords of Tikal: Rulers of an Ancient Maya City. Peter D. Harrison. LC 98-61523. (New Aspects of Antiquity Ser.). (Illus.). 208p. 1999. 60.00 (*0-500-05094-5*, Pub. by Thames Hudson) Norton.

***Lords of Tikal: Rulers of an Ancient Maya City.** Peter D. Harrison. LC 98-61523. (Illus.). 208p. 2000. pap. 29.95 (*0-500-28129-7*, Pub. by Thames Hudson) Norton.

Lord's Own Church. Harvey A. Childress. 1980. pap. 2.25 (*0-88027-086-1*) Firm Foun Pub.

Lord's Oysters. Gilbert Byron. LC 57-6442. (Maryland Paperback Bookshelf Ser.). 344p. 1977. reprint ed. pap. 11.95 (*0-8018-1959-8*) Johns Hopkins.

Lord's Portion: A Scriptural View of Tithing. Roy L. Moss. LC 96-13479. 96p. 1996. pap. 5.99 (*1-56722-191-2*) Word Aflame.

Lord's Prayer see Padre Nuestro

***Lord's Prayer.** LC 99-179123. (Foundations in Faith Ser.). 80p. 1998. student ed. write for info. (*0-570-06867-3*) Concordia.

Lord's Prayer. William Barclay. (William Barclay Library). 128p. 1999. pap. 12.00 (*0-664-25815-8*) Westminster John Knox.

Lord's Prayer. Illus. by Helen Caswell. LC 95-5369. 1995. 5.95 (*0-687-01173-6*) Abingdon.

Lord's Prayer. Helen Caswell. 24p. (J). 1995. pap. 5.95 (*0-687-01589-8*) Abingdon.

***Lord's Prayer.** Martin Chemnitz. Ed. & Tr. by George Williams. LC 99-53101. 128p. 2000. 19.99 (*0-570-04283-6*) Concordia.

Lord's Prayer. Glenn Clark. pap. 1.95 (*0-910924-08-2*) Macalester.

Lord's Prayer. Robin Currie. LC 98-192069. 1998. 7.99 (*0-7814-3035-6*) Chariot Victor.

Lord's Prayer. Alice J. Davidson. (Alice in Bibleland Storybooks). (Illus.). (J). (gr. 3 up). 1989. 5.95 (*0-8378-1868-0*) Gibson.

Lord's Prayer. C. F. Evans. 1997. pap. 14.00 (*0-334-02715-2*) TPI PA.

Lord's Prayer. Antonio Gentili & Alberto Camici. 96p. 1996. pap. 39.95 (*0-85439-510-5*, Pub. by St Paul Pubns) St Mut.

Lord's Prayer. Romano Guardini. LC 96-33548. 124p. (Orig.). 1996. pap. 11.95 (*0-918477-46-8*) Sophia Inst Pr.

***Lord's Prayer.** Tim Ladwig. LC 98-52477. (Illus.). 32p. (J). (ps). 2000. 16.00 (*0-8028-5180-0*, Eerdmans Bks) Eerdmans.

Lord's Prayer. Roberta Letwenko & Edward Letwenko. (Jeremy the Bible Bookworm Ser.). (Illus.). 32p. (J). 3.95 (*0-614-22066-1*) Regina Pr.

Lord's Prayer. Philip N. Odhner. 77p. 1994. 12.50 (*1-883270-01-4*) Swedenborg Assn.

***Lord's Prayer.** Linda Parry. LC 99-74439. (Prayers with Bears Ser.). (Illus.). 16p. (J). (ps). 1999. 3.99 (*0-8499-5970-5*) Tommy Nelson.

Lord's Prayer. Mary S. Rosenberger. (Covenant Bible Studies). 48p. 1989. pap. 4.95 (*0-87178-541-2*, 8412) Brethren.

Lord's Prayer. St. Cyprian of Carthage. 1982. pap. 2.50 (*0-89981-054-3*) Eastern Orthodox.

Lord's Prayer. Maggie Swanson. (Maggie Swanson Board Books). 1999. 3.95 (*0-88271-711-1*) Regina Pr.

Lord's Prayer. Thomas Watson. 300p. 1994. pap. 14.99 (*0-85151-145-7*) Banner of Truth.

Lord's Prayer. Herman Witsius. 424p. 1994. 17.99 (*0-87552-873-2*) P & R Pubng.

***Lord's Prayer.** Illus. by Miriam Zook. (To Learn & Color Ser.). 32p. (J). (gr. 1-3). 1998. pap. 1.25 (*0-7399-0313-6*, 2918) Rod & Staff.

***Lord's Prayer.** Gerhard Ebeling. (Pocket Faith Ser.: Vol. 3). 136p. 2000. reprint ed. pap. 8.95 (*1-55725-254-8*, 930-054) Paraclete MA.

Lord's Prayer. Thomas Watson. 332p. 1993. reprint ed. text 21.99 (*0-85151-664-5*) Banner of Truth.

Lord's Prayer. rev. ed. Spiros Zodhiates. 407p. 1982. pap. 8.99 (*0-89957-049-6*) AMG Pubs.

Lord's Prayer: A Survey Theological & Literary. Nicholas Ayo. LC 90-50929. (C). 1993. pap. text 17.50 (*0-268-01292-X*) U of Notre Dame Pr.

Lord's Prayer: An Esoteric Study. Rudolf Steiner. Tr. by Floyd McKnight from GER. 26p. 1977. pap. 3.95 (*0-88010-029-X*) Anthroposophic.

Lord's Prayer: An Illustrated Bible Passage for Young Children. Ed. by David Meyer & Alice Meyer. LC 91-90826. (Illus.). 32p. (Orig.). (J). (ps-4). 1991. pap. 12.95 incl. audio (*1-879099-05-5*) Thy Word.

Lord's Prayer: Brass Quint. 9.95 (*0-7935-4085-2*, 5042375) H Leonard.

Lord's Prayer: Bridge to a Better World. C. G. Weeramantry. LC 97-52262. 304p. 1998. pap. 16.00 (*0-7648-0181-3*, Liguori Triumph) Liguori Pubns.

Lord's Prayer: For 2 or 3 Octave Handbells. A. Malotte. 4p. 1989. 3.50 (*0-7935-5540-X*, 50488973) H Leonard.

Lord's Prayer: Forgive Us Our Trespasses, Wall Chart. Roberta Collier-Morales. (Basic Bible Charts Ser.). (Illus.). (J). (gr. 2-8). 1997. pap. 12.95 (*0-9655082-5-0*, 509L) Rose Publshg.

Lord's Prayer: High E Flat Voice & Piano. A. Malotte. 8p. 1986. pap. 3.95 (*0-7935-5331-8*, 50279830) H Leonard.

***Lord's Prayer: How to Really Understand the Meaning of the Prayer, Study Guide.** Jack Hayford. (EZ Lesson Plan Ser.). 1999. pap. write for info. (*0-7852-9609-3*) Tommy Nelson.

***Lord's Prayer: In Above a Hundred Languages, Versions & Characters, 1713.** Greyden Press Staff. 1999. 25.00 (*1-57074-388-6*) Greyden Pr.

Lord's Prayer: Low in G with Voice & Organ. A. Malotte. 6p. 1986. pap. 3.95 (*0-7935-5355-5*, 50284400) H Leonard.

Lord's Prayer: Low Voice & Piano in G. A. Malotte. 6p. 1986. pap. 3.95 (*0-7935-5329-6*, 50284370) H Leonard.

Lord's Prayer: Medium High in D Flat. A. Malotte. 8p. 1986. pap. 3.95 (*0-7935-5327-X*, 50279710) H Leonard.

Lord's Prayer: Medium in C Voice & Piano. A. Malotte. 8p. 1986. pap. 3.95 (*0-7935-5317-2*, 50281100) H Leonard.

Lord's Prayer: Medium Low Voice & Piano. A. Malotte. 8p. 1986. pap. 3.95 (*0-7935-5322-9*, 50279720) H Leonard.

Lord's Prayer: String Quartet. 9.95 (*0-7935-4538-2*, 50482395) H Leonard.

***Lord's Prayer: The Prayer That Jesus Taught Two Thousand Years Ago.** Retold by Lois Rock. (Illus.). 32p. (J). (gr. k-3). 2000. 8.95 (*0-8091-6679-8*) Paulist Pr.

Lord's Prayer: Woodwind Quintet. 9.95 (*0-7935-4561-7*, 50482402) H Leonard.

Lord's Prayer, a Devotional Meditation: And Ye Shall Find Rest unto Your Souls. Scott Devon. LC 97-77064. 128p. 1998. 14.95 (*1-890394-16-5*) Rhodes & Easton.

Lord's Prayer & Other Prayer Texts from the Greco-Roman Era. Ed. by James H. Charlesworth et al. LC 94-31. 304p. (Orig.). (C). 1994. 25.00 (*1-56338-080-3*) TPI PA.

Lord's Prayer for Children, 1 vol. Lois Rock. (J). 1999. 9.99 (*0-7459-4092-7*) Lion USA.

Lords Prayer for Children. Lois Rock. 1999. 6.99 (*0-88486-232-1*, Inspirational Pr) Arrowood Pr.

***Lord's Prayer in My Life: The Basic Lessons of Prayer.** Marbury E. Anderson. 96p. 2000. pap. 9.95 (*1-886513-23-6*) Kirk Hse Pubs.

L

An Asterisk (*) at the beginning of an entry indicates that the title is appearing for the first time.

L

Lord's Prayer in the Light of Our Lord's Life & Preaching. Paul Hinnebusch. 192p. (Orig.). 1996. pap. 11.95 (*0-8198-4480-2*) Pauline Bks.

Lord's Sermons. Jakob Lorber. Tr. by Violet Ozols & Hildegard Von Koerber from GER. LC 80-50280. (Jakob Lorber Ser.). 256p. 1981. 12.95 (*0-934616-06-X*) Valkyrie Pub Hse.

Lord's Song: The Basis, Function & Significance of Choral Music in Chronicles. John W. Kleinig. (JSOT Supplement Ser.: No. 156). 236p. 1993. 70.00 (*1-85075-394-6*, Pub. by Sheffield Acad) CUP Services.

Lord's Song in a Foreign Land: The Psalms as Prayer. Thomas P. Wahl. LC 97-47370. 214p. (Orig.). 1998. pap. text 16.95 (*0-8146-2086-8*) Liturgical Pr.

***Lord's Song in a Strange Land: Music & Identity in Contemporary Jewish Worship.** Jeffrey A. Summit. LC 99-47436. 240p. 2000. 29.95 (*0-19-511677-1*) OUP.

Lord's Song in a Timely Music Primer. O. Talmadge Spence. (Illus.). 138p. 1997. pap. 10.95 (*1-882542-18-5*) Fndtns NC.

Lord's Supper. Martin Chemnitz. Tr. by J. A. Preus. 296p. 1979. 26.00 (*0-570-03275-X*, 15-2720) Concordia.

Lord's Supper. A. P. Gibbs. 1963. pap. 8.00 (*0-937396-25-7*) Walterick Pubs.

Lord's Supper. P. G. Jeffery. 1998. pap. text 6.99 (*0-85234-402-3*) P & R Pubng.

Lord's Supper. expanded ed. Martin E. Marty. LC 97-2472. 88p. (Orig.). 1997. pap. 7.99 (*0-8066-3339-5*, 9-3339, Augsburg) Augsburg Fortress.

Lord's Supper. John M. Talbot. Ed. by Phil Perkins. 80p. 1996. reprint ed. pap. text. write for info. (*1-883803-06-3*) Troubadour Lord.

Lord's Supper: Believers' Church Perspectives. Ed. by Dale R. Stoffer. LC 96-32559. 336p. (Orig.). 1997. pap. 24.99 (*0-8361-3119-3*) Herald Pr.

Lord's Supper: Historical Writings on Its Meaning to the Body of Christ. J. B. Rotherham et al. Ed. by Charles Gresham & Tom Lawson. 243p. (C). 1993. 13.99 (*0-89900-603-5*) College Pr Pub.

Lord's Supper: The Church's Love Feast. Donald L. Norbie. 1986. pap. 3.00 (*0-937396-67-2*) Walterick Pubs.

Lord's Supper: Toward an Ecumenical Understanding of the Eucharist. Philippe Larere. Tr. by Patrick Madigan. 100p. (Orig.). 1993. pap. 7.95 (*0-8146-2226-7*) Liturgical Pr.

Lord's Supper & the Bible. Cornelius R. Stam. 115p. 1982. 9.50 (*1-893874-07-9*) Berean Bibl Soc.

Lord's Supper from Wycliffe to Crammer. David B. Knox. 75p. 1986. pap. 7.95 (*0-85364-379-2*, Pub. by Paternoster Pub) McClelland & Stewart.

Lord's Supper in Anabaptism: A Study in the Christology of Balthasar Hubmaier, Pilgram Marpeck, & Dirk Philips. John D. Rempel. LC 93-78630. (Studies in Anabaptist & Mennonite History: Vol. 33). 272p. 1993. 29.99 (*0-8361-3112-6*) Herald Pr.

***Lord's Supper Is a Celebration of Grace: What the Bible Teaches about Communion.** Gordon J. Keddie. 1999. pap. 8.99 (*0-85234-425-2*) Evangelical Pr.

Lord's Supper Pocket Guide. F. Levon Hucks. (Pocket Guide Ser.). 64p. (Orig.). 1992. pap. 1.79 (*0-687-22648-1*) Abingdon.

Lord's Supper, Prayers, Thanksgiving. C. R. Nichol. 1957, pap. 8.95 (*0-915547-62-7*) Abilene Christ U.

Lord's Table. Andrew Murray. 1985. mass mkt. 5.99 (*0-87508-424-9*) Chr Lit.

Lord's Table: The Meaning of Food in Early Judaism & Christianity. Gillian Feeley-Harnik. LC 93-41414. 200p. (C). 1994. pap. text 15.95 (*1-56098-338-8*) Smithsonian.

Lords Temporal & Lords Spiritual: A Chronological Checklist of the Popes, Patriarchs, Katholikoi & Independent Archbishop & Metropolitans of the Monarch, Autocephalous Churches of the Christian East & West. 2nd ed. Michael Burgess. LC 87-6319. (Stokvis Studies in Historical Chronology & Thought: No. 1). 336p. 1995. pap. 31.00 (*0-89370-426-1*) Millefleurs.

Lord's Test, 1884-1989. Spellmount Ltd. Publishers Staff. (C). 1986. 100.00 (*0-946771-22-7*, Pub. by Spellmnt Pubs) St Mut.

Lord's University: Freedom & Authority at BYU. Bryan Waterman & Brian Kagel. LC 98-28933. (Illus.). 488p. 1998. pap. 19.95 (*1-56085-117-1*) Signature Bks.

Lord's Way. Dallin H. Oaks. LC 91-30610. x, 259p. 1991. 17.95 (*0-87579-578-1*) Deseret Bk.

Lord's Way. Dallin H. Oaks. LC 91-30610. x, 259p. 1995. pap. 9.95 (*0-87579-960-4*) Deseret Bk.

***Lord's Will.** O. Talmadge Spence. 101p. 1999. pap. 6.00 (*1-882542-22-3*) Fndtns NC.

Lord's Woods. Robert S. Arbib, Jr. LC 73-139373. 219p. 1971. 6.95 (*0-393-08639-9*) Norton.

***Lordsburg - LaVerne in Southern California.** Marlin Heckman. (Postcard History Ser.). (Illus.). 128p. 1999. pap. 18.99 (*0-7385-0249-9*) Arcadia Publng.

Lordship: Basic Discipleship. Floyd McClung. (Christian Basics Bible Studies: No. 15). 64p. (Orig.). 1996. pap., wbk. ed. 4.99 (*0-8308-2015-9*, 2015) InterVarsity.

***Lordship: The Lordship of Jesus Christ.** 2nd large type ed. Danah Trammel. (Spiritual Warfare Ser.: Vol. 3). 30p. 1998. pap. 6.95 (*0-9672108-0-1*, 9672108) Kingdom Pr GA.

Lordship & Community: Battle Abbey & Its Banlieu, 1066-1538. Eleanor Searle. 479p. 59.43 (*0-88844-026-X*) Brill Academic Pubs.

Lordship & Community: The Lestrange Family & the Village of Hunstanton, Norfolk, in the First Half of the Sixteenth Century. Cord Oestmann. (Illus.). 301p. (C). 1994. 75.00 (*0-85115-351-8*) Boydell & Brewer.

Lordship & Inheritance in Early Medieval Japan: A Study of the Kamakura Soryo System. Jeffrey P. Mass. 352p. 1989. 45.00 (*0-8047-1540-8*) Stanford U Pr.

Lordship & Landscape in Norfolk, 1250-1350: The Early Records of Holkham. Ed. by William Hassall & Jacques Beauroy. (Records of Social & Economic History, British Academy New Ser.: No. XX). (Illus.). 700p. 1994. text 125.00 (*0-19-726093-4*) OUP.

***Lordship & Tradition in Barbarian Europe.** Hermann Moisl. LC 99-13603. 1999. write for info. (*0-88946-684-X*) E Mellen.

***Lordship & Tradition in Barbarian Europe.** Hermann Moisl. LC 99-13603. (Studies in Classics: Vol. 10). 224p. 1999. text 89.95 (*0-7734-8151-6*) E Mellen.

Lordship, Kingship, & Empire: The Idea of Monarchy, 1400-1525. J. H. Burns. (Carlyle Lectures). 192p. 1992. text 55.00 (*0-19-820206-7*) OUP.

Lordship of Christ. James A. Stewart. pap. 1.49 (*1-56632-062-3*) Revival Lit.

Lordship of England: Royal Wardships & Marriages in English Society & Politics, 1217-1327. Scott L. Waugh. LC 88-1134. (Illus.). 343p. 1988. reprint ed. pap. 106.40 (*0-608-07514-0*, 206773700009) Bks Demand.

Lordship of Jesus Christ. William Pape. 145p. 1995. pap. 8.00 (*1-882840-06-2*) Comm Christian.

Lordship of the Holy Spirit. Derrick P. Gomez. Ed. by Phyllis Mackall. (Illus.). (Orig.). 1995. pap. text 11.95 (*0-9648336-0-3*) Sprt Life NY.

Lordship of the Isles. I. F. Grant. 520p. (C). 1986. 75.00 (*0-901824-68-2*, Pub. by Mercat Pr Bks) St Mut.

Lordship Salvation: Some Crucial Questions & Answers. Robert H. Lescelius. 1992. pap. 6.99 (*1-56632-001-1*) Revival Lit.

Lordship Salvation: The Only Kind There Is. Curtis I. Crenshaw. 250p. (Orig.). 1994. pap. 10.95 (*1-877818-12-7*) Footstool Pubns.

Lordship Salvation Grace Life Edition: A Biblical Evaluation & Response. Charles C. Bing. 205p. 1997. pap. 10.00 (*0-9701365-0-1*) Grace Life.

Lordship to Patronage. Rosalind Mitchison. 1991. pap. text 20.00 (*0-7486-0233-X*, Pub. by Edinburgh U Pr) Col U Pr.

Lore: Capturing Traditional Environmental Knowledge. Ed. by Martha Johnson. 1992. pap. 17.50 (*0-88936-644-6*, Pub. by IDRC Bks) Stylus Pub VA.

Lore: Capturing Traditional Environmental Knowledge. Ed. by Martha Johnson. (Illus.). 190p. (C). 1998. reprint ed. pap. text 40.00 (*0-7881-7046-5*) DIANE Pub.

Lore & Language of Schoolchildren. Iona Opie & Peter Opie. (Illus.). 448p. 1987. pap. 10.95 (*0-19-282059-1*) OUP.

Lore & Lure of the Coastal Banks. Billie J. Huling. (Illus.). 98p. (Orig.). 1994. pap. 15.00 (*1-880994-19-4*) Mt Olive Coll Pr.

Lore & Science in Ancient Pythagoreanism. Walter Burkert. Tr. by Edwin L. Minar, Jr. LC 70-162856. 543p. reprint ed. pap. 168.40 (*0-7837-2230-3*, 205732000004) Bks Demand.

Lore Kadden Lindenfeld: A Life in Textiles, 1945-1997. Sigrid Weltge. Ed. by James Thompson. (College Dossiers Ser.: Vol. 3). (Illus.). 51p. 1997. pap. 20.00 (*0-9649020-3-6*) Blck Mtn Coll.

Lore of Birthdays. Ed. by Ralph Linton & Adelin Linton. LC 97-20032. (Illus.). 116p. 1997. reprint ed. lib. bdg. 40.00 (*0-7808-0265-9*) Omnigraphics Inc.

Lore of Large Numbers. P. J. Davis. LC 61-13842. (New Mathematical Library: No. 6). 165p. 1961. pap. text 5.00 (*0-88385-606-9*, NML-06) Math Assn.

Lore of Running. 3rd ed. Timothy D. Noakes. LC 90-29001. (Illus.). 832p. 1991. pap. 22.95 (*0-88011-438-X*, PNOA0438) Human Kinetics.

Lore of the Fried Clam & a History of the Soft-Shell Clam Industry. Dean Merchant. (Illus.). 160p. 2000. pap. 19.95 (*0-914339-79-6*, Pub. by P E Randall Pub) U Pr of New Eng.

Lore of the Great Turtle: Indian Legends of Mackinac Retold. Dirk Gringhuis. LC 73-636148. (Illus.). 96p. 1999. pap. 6.00 (*0-911872-11-6*) Mackinac St Hist Pks.

Lore of the Lakes. Dana T. Bowen. 1940. pap. 13.75 (*0-912514-12-4*) Freshwater.

Lore of the Lumber Camps. enl. rev. ed. Earl C. Beck. LC 49-7123. (University of Michigan Studies & Publications). (Illus.). 378p. reprint ed. pap. 117.20 (*0-608-10836-7*, 205107800074) Bks Demand.

Lore of the Sacred Horse. Marion Davies. (Illus.). 219p. (Orig.). 1995. pap. 21.95 (*1-898307-17-2*) Holmes Pub.

Lore of the Unicorn. Odell Shepard. (Illus.). 336p. 1993. reprint ed. pap. 8.95 (*0-486-27803-4*) Dover.

Lore of the Whare-Wananga, 2 vols., Set. Ed. by Stephenson P. Smith. LC 75-35272. reprint ed. 79.50 (*0-404-14370-9*) AMS Pr.

Lore of Trout Fishing. Art Lee. LC 98-47330. 264p. 1999. pap. 26.95 (*0-88011-790-7*) Human Kinetics.

Lore of Wolverine Country. 2nd ed. Stanley C. Perkins. (Illus.). 244p. 1984. 15.00 (*0-940404-08-7*); pap. 12.00 (*0-9614640-3-8*) Broadblade Pr.

Lore Power Is "Man" Power. Thomas Adams. 64p. 1981. pap. write for info. (*0-9609242-0-5*) T Adams.

Loreena Mckennitt: Celtic Quest. Geoff Hancock. (Illus.). 224p. 1999. pap. 16.95 (*1-55082-254-3*) LPC InBook.

Lorelei. Mark A. Clements. 304p. 1995. pap. text, mass mkt. 4.99 (*0-8439-3867-6*) Dorchester Pub Co.

Loren Eiseley, a Modern Ishmael. Peter Heidtmann. LC 90-24756. (Illus.). xi, 133p. (C). 1991. lib. bdg. 29.50 (*0-208-02293-7*, Archon Bks) Shoe String.

Lorena. Fred Bean. 1998. mass mkt. 5.99 (*0-8125-4596-6*, Pub. by Forge NYC) St Martin.

***Lorentz Group, CPT & Neutrinos.** Ed. by Andrew E. Chubykalo et al. 350p. 2000. 86.00 (*981-02-4062-7*) World Scientific Pub.

Lorentzian Wormholes: From Einstein to Hawking. Matt Visser. (Computational & Applied Mathematical Physics Ser.). (Illus.). 400p. (C). 1995. text 59.95 (*1-56396-394-9*, AIP Pr) Spr-Verlag.

Lorentzian Wormholes - From Einstein to Hawking. Matt Visser. (Computational & Applied Mathematical Physics Ser.). (Illus.). 400p. 1997. pap. 29.95 (*1-56396-653-0*, AIP Pr) Spr-Verlag.

Lorenz Equations: Bifurcations, Chaos & Strange Attractors. C. Sparrow. (Applied Mathematical Sciences Ser.: Vol. 41). (Illus.). 288p. 1989. 52.95 (*0-387-90775-0*) Spr-Verlag.

Lorenz Hart: A Poet on Broadway. Fredrick Nolan. (Illus.). 416p. 1995. pap. 15.95 (*0-19-510289-4*) OUP.

Lorenz on Mount Fuji. Franz De Waal. Date not set. 26.00 (*0-465-04175-2*, Pub. by Basic); pap. write for info. (*0-465-04176-0*) Basic.

Lorenz Von Steins Arbeiten Fur Japan. Ed. by Kazuhiro Takii & Wilhelm Brauneder. (Rechts- und Sozialwissenschaftliche Ser.: Vol. 20). (Illus.). 286p. 1998. pap. 51.95 (*3-631-33039-1*) P Lang Pubng.

Lorenzaccio. Musset. (FRE.). (C). pap. 9.95 (*0-8442-1992-4*, VF1992-4) NTC Contemp Pub Co.

Lorenzaccio. Alfred Musset. (FRE., Illus.). 1964. pap. 10.95 (*0-8288-9647-X*, M2487) Fr & Eur.

Lorenzaccio. unabridged ed. Musset. (FRE.). pap. 6.95 (*2-87714-193-4*, Pub. by Bookking Intl) Distribks Inc.

Lorenzaccio: On Ne Badine Pas avec l'Amour et Autres Pieces. Alfred De Musset. (FRE.). 1988. pap. 16.95 (*0-7859-2991-6*) Fr & Eur.

Lorenzaccio. Andre del Sarto. Alfred De Musset. (Folio Ser.: No. 1026). (FRE.). 1978. pap. 9.95 (*2-07-037026-7*) Schoenhof.

Lorenzaccio Story. Paul Thompson. 72p. (Orig.). 1984. pap. 6.95 (*0-904383-85-7*, NO. 4137) Routledge.

Lorenza's Antipasti. Lorenza DeMedici. LC 98-4414. (Illus.). 176p. 1998. 40.00 (*0-609-60151-2*) C Potter.

Lorenza's Pasta: 200 Recipes for Family & Friends. Lorenza De' Medici. Date not set. 0.19 (*0-517-19915-7*) Random Hse Value.

***Lorenza's Pasta: 200 Recipes for Family & Friends.** Lorenza De'Medici. 2000. reprint ed. pap. 24.95 (*1-86205-039-2*, Pub. by Pavilion Bks Ltd) Trafalgar.

Lorenzetti's Golden Mean: The Riformatori of Siena, 1368-1885. Antonio Rutigliano. LC 91-19614. (American University Studies: History: Ser. IX, Vols. 101). 200p. (C). 1992. text 48.95 (*0-8204-1456-5*) P Lang Pubng.

Lorenzo Allegri: Il Primo Libro delle Musiche (Venice, 1618) Ed. by Andrew Dell'Antonio. LC 95-7387. (Italian Instrumental Music of the Sixteenth & Seventeenth Centuries Ser.: No. 27). 120p. 1995. text 77.00 (*0-8240-4526-2*) Garland.

Lorenzo Da Ponte in American Perspective: Two Lectures & a Review. Olga Ragusa. 77p. 1998. pap. 10.00 (*0-913298-88-3*) S F Vanni.

Lorenzo de Medici: A Verse Play. Francis Blessington. LC 92-11125. 66p. (Orig.). (C). 1992. pap. text 18.50 (*0-8191-8748-8*) U Pr of Amer.

Lorenzo de Medici: New Perspectives: Proceedings of the Internatinoal Conference Held at Brooklyn College & the Graduate Center of the City University of New York, April 30-May 2, 1992. Bernard Toscani. LC 93-17014. (Studies in Italian Culture: Literature in History: No. 13). XVI, 356p. (C). 1994. text 36.95 (*0-8204-2164-2*) P Lang Pubng.

Lorenzo de Medici: Selected Poems & Prose. Ed. & Tr. by Jon Thiem. 192p. 1992. 32.50 (*0-271-00772-9*) Pa St U Pr.

Lorenzo de Zavala: The Pragmatic Idealist, Vol. 1. Margaret S. Henson. LC 95-32720. (Texas Biography Ser.). (Illus.). 146p. 1996. 22.50 (*0-87565-150-X*) Tex Christian.

Lorenzo Ghiberti. Richard Krautheimer. LC 81-47999. (Princeton Monographs in Art & Archaeology: No. 31). (Illus.). 688p. reprint ed. pap. 200.00 (*0-608-20151-0*, 207142300011) Bks Demand.

Lorenzo Gomez - Dios Latino. Lorenzo Gomez. (Illus.). 100p. 2000. 49.95 (*1-890377-05-8*) Pohlmann Pr.

Lorenzo in Search of the Sun: D. H. Lawrence in Italy, Mexico & the American Southwest. Eliot G. Fay. LC 76-168012. reprint ed. 31.50 (*0-404-02373-8*) AMS Pr.

Lorenzo in Taos. Mabel D. Luhan. 1988. reprint ed. lib. bdg. 79.00 (*0-7812-0464-X*) Rprt Serv.

Lorenzo in Taos. Mabel G. Luhan. LC 78-145147. 352p. 1932. reprint ed. 59.00 (*0-403-01077-2*) Scholarly.

Lorenzo Lotto. Jacques Bonnet. (Illus.). 208p. 1997. 55.00 (*2-87660-190-7*, Pub. by Art Bks Intl) Partners Pubs Grp.

Lorenzo Lotto. Peter Humfrey & Lorenzo Lotto. LC 96-27624. 224p. 1997. 50.00 (*0-300-06905-7*) Yale U Pr.

Lorenzo Lotto: Rediscovered Master of the Renaissance. David A. Brown et al. LC 97-26418. 1997. write for info. (*0-89468-257-1*) Natl Gallery Art.

Lorenzo Lotto: Rediscovered Master of the Renaissance. David A. Brown et al. (Illus.). 272p. 1997. 55.00 (*0-300-07331-3*) Yale U Pr.

Lorenzo Lotto: The Frescoes in the Oratorio Suardi at Trescore. Francesca C. Bosco. (Illus.). 190p. 1999. boxed set 65.00 (*88-8118-319-6*, Pub. by Skira IT) Abbeville Pr.

Lorenzo Monaco. Marvin Eisenberg. (Illus.). 410p. (C). 1989. text 100.00 (*0-691-04042-7*, Pub. by Princeton U Pr) Cal Prin Full Svc.

Lorenzo the Naughty Parrot. large type ed. Tony Johnston. (Illus.). 1993. 9.50 (*0-614-09838-6*, L-34090-00) Am Printing Hse.

Lore's Life: At Eighty, a Time to Recall & Remember. Hanna Adler. LC 98-90458. 1998. pap. 10.95 (*0-533-12811-0*) Vantage.

***Loreto Fishing Chart & Guide.** (Illus.). 1999. 14.95 (*1-929394-05-5*, B005) Baja Directions.

Loretta & the Little Fairy. Gerda M. Scheidl. Tr. by J. Alison James. LC 92-33835. (Illus.). 64p. (J). (gr. 2-3). 1994. pap. 5.95 (*1-55858-353-X*, Pub. by North-South Bks NYC) Chronicle Bks.

Loretta Lynn: Coal Miner's Daughter see Coal Miner's Daughter

Loretta Mason Potts. Mary Chase. (J). (gr. 4-8). 1990. 23.25 (*0-8446-6428-6*) Peter Smith.

Loretta P. Sweeny, Where Are You? Patricia Reilly Giff. (Illus.). 144p. (J). (gr. 4-8). 1990. pap. 3.50 (*0-440-44926-X*, YB BDD) BDD Bks Young Read.

Loretta P. Sweeny, Where Are You? Patricia Reilly Giff. 1984. 8.60 (*0-606-03359-9*, Pub. by Turtleback) Demco.

Loretto & the Miraculous Staircase: How a Famous Staircase Was Built. Alice Bullock. LC 78-18526. (Illus.). 1978. pap. 2.95 (*0-931270-80-4*) Sunstone Pr.

Lorgnette. Donald G. Mitchell. (Notable American Authors Ser.). 1999. reprint ed. lib. bdg. 125.00 (*0-7812-4560-5*) Rprt Serv.

Lori. Gertrude Hoeksema. LC 87-62891. (Illus.). 153p. 1987. pap. 8.75 (*0-916206-33-5*) Refrd Free Pub Assn.

Lori. Ed. by John Wilson. 123p. (C). 1990. 33.00 (*0-9588101-3-3*, Pub. by Pascoe Pub) St Mut.

Lori, No. 3. John Benton. 176p. (Orig.). (YA). (gr. 7-12). 1990. reprint ed. mass mkt. 3.50 (*0-8007-8385-9*) J Benton Bks.

***Lori: My Daughter's Political Imprisonment in Peru.** Rhoda Berenson. (Illus.). 208p. 2000. (*1-893956-06-7*) Context Bks.

Lori . . . Where Are You? A Mother's Experience of Grief & Loss. Elaine Visitacion. LC 93-93835. 64p. 1993. 9.95 (*0-9635954-0-7*) E Visitacion.

Lori Lamb. Katherine Oana. Ed. by Tate Baird. (Fables for Today Ser.). (Illus.). 16p. (Orig.). (J). (ps). 1989. pap. 5.52 (*0-914127-09-8*) Univ Class.

***Loriana, Forever My Sweetheart.** Gina Prenz. LC 99-62. (Illus.). 288p. 1999. pap. 12.31 (*1-55212-312-X*) Trafford Pub.

***Loricariidae: The Tricks of the Trade.** Larry Lee Vires. (Illus.). ii, 93p. 1999. ring bd. 24.95 (*0-9670881-0-0*, 001) Vires Pubg.

***Loricariidae - The Most Beautiful L-Numbers.** Ulrich Glaser. (Aqualog Special Ser.: Vol. 2). (Illus.). 48p. 1998. 25.00 (*3-931702-34-0*, Pub. by Verlag ACS) Hollywood.

Loricariidae All L-Numbers. Ulrich Glaser & Wolfgang Glaser. (Aqualog Reference Bks.). (Illus.). 112p. 1995. pap. 39.10 (*3-931702-01-4*, Pub. by Verlag ACS) Hollywood.

Lorient City Plan. (Grafocarte Maps Ser.). 1992. 8.95 (*2-7416-0043-0*, 80043) Michelin.

Lorient to le Croisic. Imray, Laurie, Norie & Wilson Ltd. Staff. (Illus.). (C). 1990. text 60.00 (*0-7855-5785-7*, Pub. by Laurie Norie & Wilson Ltd) St Mut.

Lories & Lorikeets. Emmett Cestero. (Illus.). 1999. pap. 12.50 (*1-888417-77-3*) Dimefast.

Lories & Lorikeets: A Complete Pet Owner's Manual. Matthew M. Vriends. (Barron's Complete Pet Owner's Manuals). 80p. 1993. pap. 6.95 (*0-8120-1567-3*) Barron.

Lories & Lorikeets: The Brush-Tongued Parrots & Their Care. Alison Ruggles. (Illus.). 272p. 1996. 34.95 (*0-7137-2268-1*, Pub. by Blandford Pr) Sterling.

Lorinda Bewley & the Whitman Massacre. Myra S. Helm. 95p. (Orig.). 1984. pap. text 3.25 (*0-914019-06-6*) NW Interpretive.

Lorinda Leigh. large type ed. Una Horne. (Magna Large Print Ser.). (Illus.). 584p. 1996. 27.99 (*0-7505-0920-1*) Ulverscroft.

Lorinda's Diary. unabridged ed. Budge Wilson. 128p. (Orig.). (YA). (gr. 7 up). 1991. pap. 4.95 (*0-7736-7348-2*) STDK.

Lorine Niedecker: Solitary Player. Phyllis Walsh. (Juniper Bks.: Vol. 56). 48p. (Orig.). 1992. pap. 9.00 (*1-55780-116-9*) Juniper Pr ME.

Lorine Niedecker: Woman & Poet. Ed. & Intro. by Jenny Penberthy. (Man & Poet Ser.). (Illus.). 439p. 1996. 45.00 (*0-943373-38-7*); pap. 22.95 (*0-943373-39-5*) Natl Poet Foun.

Loring: A Trustee's Handbook. annuals Charles E. Rounds, Jr. & Eric P. Hayes. 384p. pap. 95.00 (*0-316-35243-8*, 52438) Aspen Law.

***Loring a Trustee's Handbook.** Charles E. Rounds. 1024p. 1999. boxed set 145.00 (*0-7355-0443-1*) Aspen Pub.

Loring's a Trustee's Handbook. 6th ed. James F. Farr. 1962. 30.00 (*0-316-27471-2*, Aspen Law & Bus) Aspen Pub.

Loris. Mark Dunster. (Rin Ser.: Pt. 1). (Orig.). 1980. pap. 4.00 (*0-89642-062-0*) Linden Pubs.

Lorita: A Novel. Prem N. Chopra. (C). 1997. pap. text. write for info. (*81-207-1848-8*) Sterling Pubs.

***Lorna Barrett.** Angus Balfour. 224p. 1999. mass mkt. 7.95 (*1-56201-159-6*, Pub. by Blue Moon Bks) Publishers Group.

Lorna Doone. Ed. by Jennifer Bassett. (Illus.). 80p. 1997. pap. text 5.95 (*0-19-422755-3*) OUP.

Lorna Doone. R. D. Blackmore. (Andre Deutsch Classics). 319p. (J). (gr. 5-8). 1996. 9.95 (*0-233-99076-3*, Pub. by Andre Deutsch) Trafalgar.

***Lorna Doone.** R. D. Blackmore. 1999. lib. bdg. 21.95 (*1-56723-172-1*) Yestermorrow.

Lorna Doone. Richard D. Blackmore. (Classics Library). Date not set. pap. 3.95 (*1-85326-076-2*, 0762WW, Pub. by Wrdsworth Edits) NTC Contemp Pub Co.

Lorna Doone. Jill Hyem & R. D. Blackmore. LC 99-165675. 93p. 1997. write for info. (*0-573-01827-8*) S French Trade.

Lorna Doone. Richard D. Blackmore. 345p. (J). 1976. reprint ed. lib. bdg. 27.95 (*0-89966-350-8*) Buccaneer Bks.

Lorna Doone. Richard D. Blackmore. 378p. (J). 1981. reprint ed. lib. bdg. 24.95 (*0-89967-024-5*, Harmony Rain) Buccaneer Bks.

Lorna Doone: A Romance of Exmoor. Richard D. Blackmore. Ed. by Sally Shuttleworth. (Oxford World's Classics Ser.). 710p. 1999. pap. 11.95 (*0-19-283627-7*) OUP.

An Asterisk (*) at the beginning of an entry indicates that the title is appearing for the first time.

Lorna Goodison. 2nd ed. Lorna Goodison. 31p. 1995. pap. text 9.00 (*0-9633741-4-1*) RI Study of Man.
Lorna Mouse Club. Alfonso Azpiri. (J). 1996. 14.95 (*1-882931-22-X*) Heavy Metal Magazine.
***Lorna Oppenheimer's Trade Secrets: Home Decorating Kit.** Lorna Oppenheimer. Ed. by Beth Weber. (Illus.). 67p. 1999. 49.95 (*1-893635-01-5*) Trade Sec.
Lorna Ruth My Life. Lorna R. Fosberg. Ed. by Harmeet K. Bhatia. LC 93-61049. (Illus.). 88p. (Orig.). 1993. 19.95 (*0-936029-32-3*); pap. 9.95 (*0-936029-33-1*) Western Bk Journ.
Lorna Sass' Complete Vegetarian Kitchen. Lorna J. Sass. LC 95-994. 1995. pap. 19.95 (*0-688-14185-4*, Hearst) Hearst Commns.
Lorna Sass' Short-Cut Vegetarian: Great Taste in No Time. Lorna Sass. (Orig.). 1997. pap. 15.00 (*0-614-28091-5*, Quil) HarperTrade.
Lorna Sass' Short-Cut Vegetarian: Great Taste in No Time. Lorna J. Sass. LC 96-48821. (Illus.). 176p. 1997. pap. 16.00 (*0-688-14599-X*, Grenwillow Bks) HarpC Child Bks.
Lorna Simpson: Untitled 54. Deborah Willis. Ed. by Michael Read. (Illus.). 72p. (Orig.). 1993. pap. 18.95 (*0-933286-60-0*) Frnds Photography.
Lorna's Wish. T. J. Bradstreet. (Darkest Wish Ser.: No. 2). (J). (gr. 3-7). 1996. pap. 3.99 (*0-380-77817-3*, Avon Bks) Morrow Avon.
Loros en Emergencias (Parrots in Danger) Emilio Carballido. (SPA., Illus.). 46p. (J). (gr. 5-6). 1993. pap. 5.99 (*968-16-4230-9*, Pub. by Fondo) Continental Bk.
Lorraine As in a Chagall Painting: Lorraine Comme Dans une Toile de Chagall. Gilbert Moore. Ed. by Harrison E. Livingstone. (ENG & FRE.). 96p. 1990. pap. text 8.95 (*0-941401-03-0*) Conservatory.
Lorraine Hansberry. Anne Cheney. (United States Authors Ser.: No. 430). 184p. 1984. 32.00 (*0-8057-7365-7*, Twyne) Mac Lib Ref.
Lorraine Hansberry Catherine Scheader. LC 77-7279. (They Found a Way Ser.). 78p. 1978. write for info. (*0-516-01851-5*) Childrens.
Lorraine Hansberry. Janet Tripp. LC 97-10846. (Importance of Ser.). (Illus.). (J). (gr. 4-12). 1997. lib. bdg. 22.45 (*1-56006-081-6*) Lucent Bks.
Lorraine Hansberry: A Research & Production Sourcebook, 13. Richard M. Leeson. LC 97-12283. (Modern Dramatists Research & Production Sourcebooks: Vol. 13). 192p. 1997. lib. bdg. 65.00 (*0-313-29312-0*, Greenwood Pr) Greenwood.
Lorraine Hansberry: Award-Winning Playwright & Civil Rights Activist. Susan Sinnott. LC 98-50507. 1998. pap. text 6.95 (*1-57324-093-1*) Conari Press.
Lorraine Hansberry: Playwright & Voice of Justice. Catherine Scheader. LC 97-35798. (African-American Biographies Ser.). (Illus.). 128p. (YA). (gr. 6 up). 1998. lib. bdg. 20.95 (*0-89490-945-2*) Enslow Pubs.
Lorraine Hansberry Playwriting Award: An Anthology of Prize-Winning Plays. 419p. 1996. pap. 16.67 (*0-931054-45-1*) Clark Pub.
Lorrie Morgan, Vol. 1. Collins1. LC 98-158128. 1998. 5.99 (*0-312-96608-3*, Pub. by Tor Bks) St Martin.
Lorscher Litanei. fac. limited ed. Ed. by J. Fried et al. (Codices Selecti A Ser.: Vol. IC). (GER.). 1994. 323.00 (*3-201-01622-5*, Pub. by Akademische Druck-und) Balogh.
Los Alamos. Joseph Kanon. 544p. 1998. mass mkt. 7.50 (*0-440-22407-1*, Island Bks) Dell.
Los Alamos. large type ed. Joseph Kanon. LC 97-32438. (Large Print Book Ser.). 1997. 26.95 (*1-56895-506-5*) Wheeler Pub.
Los Alamos: Beginning of an Era, 1943-1945. 5th ed. Los Alamos Scientific Laboratory Public Relations Staff. LC 92-8820. (Illus.). 64p. 1986. reprint ed. pap. 6.00 (*0-941232-07-7*) Los Alamos Hist Soc.
Los Alamos & the Development of the Atomic Bomb. Robert W. Seidel. LC 95-69167. (Illus.). 109p. 1995. pap. 6.95 (*0-9645703-0-0*) Otowi Crossing Pr.
***Los Alamos, New Mexico: A Survey to 1949.** Marjorie B. Chambers. Ed. by Linda K. Aldrich. LC 99-25047. (Los Alamos Story Ser.). (Illus.). 45p. 1999. pap. 10.00 (*0-941232-21-2*) Los Alamos Hist Soc.
Los Alamos, New Mexico: A Visitors & Newcomers Guide to the Area. Tom Ribe. (Illus.). 104p. 1997. pap. 8.95 (*0-9645703-4-3*) Otowi Crossing Pr.
Los Alamos Outdoors. 2nd ed. Dorothy Hoard. LC 93-41327. (Illus.). 132p. (Orig.). 1993. pap. 9.95 (*0-941232-12-3*) Los Alamos Hist Soc.
Los Alamos Place Names. Craig Martin & Los Alamos Historical Society Staff. LC 98-35807. (Illus.). 131p. 1998. pap. 10.95 (*0-941232-19-0*) Los Alamos Hist Soc.
Los Alamos Primer: The First Lectures on How to Build an Atomic Bomb. Robert Serber. Ed. & Intro. by Richard Rhodes. 1992. 32.50 (*0-520-07576-5*, Pub. by U CA Pr) Cal Prin Full Svc.
Los Alamos Trails. Craig Martin. (Illus.). 144p. 1998. pap. 13.95 (*0-9639040-2-7*) All Seasons.
Los Alamos WAACs-WACs: World War II, 1943-1946. Iris Y. Bell. (Illus.). 82p. (Orig.). 1993. 32.50 (*0-9637321-0-2*); pap. 18.50 (*0-9637321-1-0*) I Bell.
Los Alegres Ayudantes de Dios. Marilyn Lashbrook. (SPA.). 32p. 1997. pap. 3.50 (*0-8254-1418-0*, Edit Portavoz) Kregel.
Los Amantes del sol Poniente. Ramon Hernandez. LC 86-70336. (SPA.). 157p. reprint ed. pap. 48.70 (*0-608-08074-8*, 206903300002) Bks Demand.
***Los Angeles.** Olivier Boissiere. (Illus.). 160p. 1999. (*2-7450-0061-6*) Telleri Edit.
***Los Angeles.** Gheldere DeAlexis. (Illus.). 2000. pap. 14.95 (*2-89464-385-3*) Ulysses Travel.
***Los Angeles.** DK Publishing Staff. (Eyewitness City Maps Ser.). 2000. pap. 7.95 (*0-7894-5639-7*) DK Pub Inc.
Los Angeles. Insight Guides Staff. (Insight Guides). 1998. pap. text 7.95 (*0-88729-541-X*) Langenscheidt.
***Los Angeles.** Insight Guides Staff. (Insight Guides). 1998. pap. text 12.95 (*0-88729-895-8*) Langenscheidt.
Los Angeles. Paul Marshall & Nicola Williamson. (Rough Guide Ser.). (Illus.). 288p. (Orig.). 1998. pap. text 14.95 (*1-85828-344-2*, Pub. by Rough Guides) Penguin Putnam.
Los Angeles. Dian Phillips-Pulverman & Peter Lloyd. (Architecture Guides Ser.). (Illus.). 320p. 1997. pap. 5.95 (*3-89508-285-6*, 520195) Konemann.
Los Angeles. Chuck Place. LC 96-20832. (California Sights & Scenes Ser.). 64p. 1997. 14.95 (*0-88415-834-9*, 5834) Gulf Pub.
Los Angeles. St. Martin's Press Staff. (Marcellino's Restaurant Report Ser.). 1997. pap. 9.99 (*0-312-16920-5*) St Martin.
Los Angeles. James Steele. (World Cities Ser.: No. 2). (Illus.). 401p. 1994. 95.00 (*1-85490-293-8*, Pub. by Wiley) Wiley.
Los Angeles. Gail Stewart. (Great Cities of the U. S. A. Ser.). (Illus.). 48p. (YA). (gr. 5 up). 1989. lib. bdg. 23.93 (*0-86592-540-2*) Rourke Enter.
***Los Angeles.** Virgin Publishing Staff. (City Guides Ser.). (Illus.). 2001. pap. 17.95 (*0-7627-0784-4*) Globe Pequot.
Los Angeles. Santi Visalli. (Illus.). 192p. 1996. pap. 25.00 (*0-7893-0052-4*) St Martin.
Los Angeles. Morrow Mayo. 1992. reprint ed. lib. bdg. 75.00 (*0-7812-5064-1*) Rprt Serv.
Los Angeles. 2nd ed. Fodors Staff. (Citypacks Ser.). 1999. pap. 12.00 (*0-679-00249-9*) Fodors Travel.
Los Angeles. 2nd ed. Insight Guides Staff. (Insight Guides). 1998. pap. text 21.95 (*0-88729-704-8*) Langenscheidt.
Los Angeles. 2nd ed. Andrew F. Rolle. Ed. by Norris Hundley, Jr. & John A. Schutz. (Golden State Ser.). (Illus.). 240p. 1995. pap. 12.00 (*0-929651-01-4*) MTL.
Los Angeles. 1999th ed. Ed. by Macmillan Travel Staff. (Frommer's Travel Guides Ser.). 320p. 1999. pap. 14.95 (*0-02-862358-4*, Frommer) Macmillan Gen Ref.
***Los Angeles: A Century of Travel Experience in Every Guide.** Marael Johnson. (National Geographic Traveler Ser.). (Illus.). 2000. pap. 22.95 (*0-7922-7947-6*) Natl Geog.
Los Angeles: A Certain Style. Photos by John Vaughan. LC 94-41850. (Illus.). 204p. 1995. 35.00 (*0-8118-0882-3*) Chronicle Bks.
Los Angeles: A Guide to the City & Its Environs. Federal Writers' Project Staff. (American Guidebook Ser.). 1941. reprint ed. 59.00 (*0-403-02202-9*) Somerset Pub.
Los Angeles: A History of the Future. rev. ed. Paul Glover. (Illus.). 24p. 1995. pap. 3.50 (*0-9622911-0-2*) Greenplanners.
Los Angeles: Agentes Secretos de Dios. Billy Graham. Tr. by Juan Rojas from ENG. LC 76-20259.Tr. of Angels: God's Secret Agents. (SPA.). 176p. 1976. pap. 8.99 (*0-89922-069-X*) Caribe Betania.
Los Angeles: An Architectural Guide. David Gebhard & Robert W. Winter. LC 93-42654. (Illus.). 512p. 1994. pap. 21.95 (*0-87905-627-4*) Gibbs Smith Pub.
Los Angeles: Biography of a City. Ed. by John Caughey & LaRee Caughey. LC 75-17300. 1976. pap. 18.95 (*0-520-03410-4*, Pub. by U CA Pr) Cal Prin Full Svc.
Los Angeles: City of Dreams. Bill Boyarsky & Enrique Lavin. LC 98-56459. (Urban Tapestry Ser.). (Illus.). 1998. 44.95 (*1-881096-63-7*) Towery Pub.
Los Angeles: City of Dreams; Up the Mellow Yellow Brick Road. Mark St. George. LC 99-97833. (Illus.). 224p. 2000. pap. 18.95 (*0-9620541-5-1*, Prot 7.0) Proteus LA.
Los Angeles: Dream to Reality, 1885-1915. Judith Elias. (Santa Susana Press California Masters Ser.: No. 5). (Illus.). 112p. 1983. 70.00 (*0-937048-33-X*) Santa Susana.
Los Angeles: Escogidos y Malignos. Fred Dickason. (SPA.). 232p. 1995. pap. 8.99 (*0-8254-1164-5*, Edit Portavoz) Kregel.
Los Angeles: From Pueblo to City Future. Andrew F. Rolle. Ed. by Norris Hundley, Jr. & John A. Schutz. (Physical Education). (Illus.). 128p. 1981. pap. 8.75 (*0-87835-119-1*) Thomson Learn.
Los Angeles: Globalization, Urbanization, & Social Struggles. Roger Keil. LC 98-20621. (World Cities Ser.). 334p. 1998. pap. 34.95 (*0-471-98352-7*) Wiley.
Los Angeles: Know it Like a Native. 2nd ed. Griffin Trade Paperbacks Publishing Staff. (Let's Go Map Guides Ser.). 1999. pap. 8.95 (*0-312-19911-2*) St Martin.
Los Angeles: Not Paintings? David Pagel. 18p. (Orig.). 1993. 15.00 (*0-318-71699-2*) San Barb CAF.
Los Angeles: Place of Possibilities. Lynn C. Kronzek. LC 97-77580. (Illus.). 1998. 49.95 (*1-886483-13-2*) Heritge Media.
Los Angeles: Pocket Guide. Text by Donna Dailey. LC 99-222004. 1999. pap. text 8.95 (*2-8315-6327-5*) Berlitz.
Los Angeles: The End of the Rainbow. Merry Ovnick. LC 94-7219. (Illus.). 384p. (Orig.). 1995. pap. 34.95 (*0-9643119-0-9*) Balcony Pr.
Los Angeles A to Z: An Encyclopedia of the City & County. Leonard Pitt & Dale Pitt. LC 96-50261. (Illus.). 600p. 1997. 39.95 (*0-520-20274-0*, Pub. by U CA Pr) Cal Prin Full Svc.
Los Angeles A to Z: An Encyclopedia of the City & County. Leonard Pitt & Dale Pitt. LC 96-50261. (Illus.). 600p. 2000. pap. 24.95 (*0-520-20530-8*, Pub. by U CA Pr) Cal Prin Full Svc.
Los Angeles, a View from Crown Hill. Virginia L. Comer. LC 86-51391. (Illus.). 107p. (C). 1986. 24.95 (*0-9617800-0-2*); pap. 15.95 (*0-9617800-1-0*) Talbot Pr.
Los Angeles Access. rev. ed. Richard S. Wurman. (Access Travel Guides Ser.). (Illus.). 192p. 1987. pap. 12.95 (*0-318-39988-1*, Access Trvl) HarpInfo.
Los Angeles Agent Book: Get the Agent You Need for the Career You Want. 6th ed. K. Callan. 314p. 1998. pap. text 17.95 (*1-878355-09-0*) Sweden Pr.
***Los Angeles Agent Book: Get the Agent You Need for the Career You Want.** 7th ed. K. Callan. 315p. 2001. pap. 18.95 (*1-878355-12-0*, Pub. by Sweden Pr) SCB Distributors.
Los Angeles & Orange Country. 96p. text 11.95 (*88-8029-178-5*, Pub. by Bonechi) Eiron.
Los Angeles & the Automobile: The Making of the Modern City. Scott L. Bottles. (Illus.). 315p. 1991. pap. 17.95 (*0-520-07395-9*, Pub. by U CA Pr) Cal Prin Full Svc.
Los Angeles & the Great Depression. Leonard J. Leader. LC 91-25485. (Modern American History: New Studies & Outstanding Dissertations). 344p. 1991. text 25.00 (*0-8240-1903-2*) Garland.
Los Angeles & Vicinity. Georgia I. Hesse. Ed. by Robert C. Fisher. (Fisher Annotated Travel Guides Ser.). (Illus.). 1985. pap. 8.95 (*0-8116-0021-1*) NAL.
Los Angeles & Vicinity: The Best 200 Restaurants. Ed. by Tom Demaree. (New Epicure Ser.). (Illus.). 448p. (Orig.). 1993. pap. 12.95 (*0-9628274-5-2*) D Thomas Pub.
Los Angeles Architecture: The Contemporary Condition. James Steele. (Illus.). 232p. (C). 1993. text 59.95 (*0-7148-2869-6*, Pub. by Phaidon Press) Phaidon Pr.
Los Angeles Architecture: The Contemporary Condition. James Steele. (Illus.). 232p. 1998. pap. 34.95 (*0-7148-3756-3*, Pub. by Phaidon Press) Phaidon Pr.
Los Angeles at 25 MPH. Steve Diskin & Joseph Giovannini. LC 92-19303. 219p. 1993. pap. 39.95 (*0-442-01319-1*, VNR) Wiley.
Los Angeles at 25 MPH. Steve Diskin & Joseph Giovannini. 219p. 1993. pap. 39.95 (*0-471-28526-9*, VNR) Wiley.
Los Angeles Baby Resource Guide. Hazen Publishing Staff. 1998. pap. text 12.95 (*1-891506-00-5*) Im Expecting.
Los Angeles Barrio, 1850-1890: A Social History. Richard Griswold del Castillo. LC 78-65460. (Illus.). 232p. 1980. pap. 15.95 (*0-520-04773-7*, Pub. by U CA Pr) Cal Prin Full Svc.
Los Angeles Birds. James Kavanagh. (Pocket Naturalist Ser.). (Illus.). 1999. 5.95 (*1-889903-74-4*, Pub. by Waterford WA) Falcon Pub Inc.
***Los Angeles City Fire Apparatus: Photo Archive.** Chuck Madderom. LC 99-76048. (Illus.). 128p. 2000. pap. 29.95 (*1-58388-012-7*, 129956AE, Pub. by Iconografix) Motorbooks Intl.
Los Angeles, City of Dreams. Harry Carr. 1992. reprint ed. lib. bdg. 75.00 (*0-7812-5010-2*) Rprt Serv.
Los Angeles Citybook. (Torg Ser.). 128p. 18.00 (*0-87431-341-4*, 20524) West End Games.
Los Angeles Clippers see Pro Basketball Today
Los Angeles County: A Roadmap Thru the Government's Obstacle Course Specific to Los Angeles County. A. D. Skies. (Business Start-Up Quick Guide). 1997. pap. text 4.95 (*1-890998-00-1*) Mixed Bag.
Los Angeles County Mountain & Desert Explore Map AAA. Auto Club, Southern California Editors. (Illus.). 1997. 3.95 (*1-56413-354-0*) Auto Club.
***Los Angeles County Street Guide & Directory: 2000 Edition.** (Illus.). 336p. 1999. pap. 16.95 (*1-58174-122-7*) Thomas Bros Maps.
***Los Angeles County Street Guide & Directory, Zip Code Edition: 2000 Edition.** (Illus.). 336p. 1999. pap. 23.95 (*1-58174-123-5*) Thomas Bros Maps.
Los Angeles County Street Guide & Directory: 1999 Edition. Thomas Bros. Maps Staff. (Thomas Guides Ser.). (Illus.). 336p. 1998. spiral bd. 16.95 (*1-58174-015-8*) Thomas Bros Maps.
Los Angeles County Street Guide & Directory ZIP Code Edition: 1999 Edition. Thomas Bros. Maps Staff. (Illus.). 338p. 1998. pap. 23.95 (*1-58174-016-6*) Thomas Bros Maps.
***Los Angeles Diary 2000.** (Illus.). 214p. 1999. 17.00 (*1-57499-103-5*) Per Annum.
***Los Angeles Diary 2000, Leather.** (Illus.). 214p. 1999. 32.50 (*1-57499-102-7*) Per Annum.
***Los Angeles Diary 2001.** (Illus.). 214p. 2000. im. lthr. 18.00 (*1-57499-081-0*); lthr. 32.50 (*1-57499-080-2*) Per Annum.
Los Angeles Dodgers. Michael E. Goodman. (Baseball Ser.). (Illus.). 32p. (YA). (gr. 3 up). 1998. lib. bdg. 21.30 (*0-88682-912-7*, Creat Educ) Creative Co.
Los Angeles Dodgers. Chris W. Sehnert. LC 96-8143. (America's Game Ser.). (Illus.). 32p. (J). (gr. 3-8). 1997. lib. bdg. 16.48 (*1-56239-666-8*) ABDO Pub Co.
Los Angeles Dodgers Baseball Team. David Pietrusza. LC 98-25726. (Great Sports Teams Ser.). 48p. (J). (gr. 4-10). 1999. lib. bdg. 18.95 (*0-7660-1097-X*) Enslow Pubs.
Los Angeles Employer Directory. James R. Albin. 200p. 1994. 99.95 (*0-916210-81-2*) J R Albin.
Los Angeles Fire Department: A Century of Service. Paul Ditzel. (Fire Service History Ser.). (Illus.). 263p. (Orig.). 1988. pap. 39.95 (*0-925165-21-2*) Fire Buff Hse.
Los Angeles Fires of the Heart. Julie Bergman. (Illus.). 80p. (Orig.). 1995. pap. 14.00 (*0-9644458-5-9*) Undercover Bks.
Los Angeles for Less. Metropolis International Editors. 2000. pap. text 9.95 (*1-901811-51-4*) Metropolis International.
Los Angeles from the Days of the Pueblo. 2nd ed. W. W. Robinson. Ed. by Doyce B. Nunis, Jr. (Illus.). 128p. 1981. pap. 7.95 (*0-910312-45-1*) Calif Hist.
Los Angeles Graphic Design. Gerry Rosentswieg. 262p. 1993. 49.95 (*0-942604-33-4*) Madison Square.
Los Angeles Guide to Private Schools. Victoria Goldman. LC 98-5136. 560p. 1998. pap. 28.00 (*1-56947-113-4*) Soho Press.
Los Angeles House: Decoration & Design in America's 20th-Century City. Photos & Text by Tim Street-Porter. (Illus.). 1995. 60.00 (*0-517-70042-5*) C Potter.
Los Angeles in Fiction: A Collection of Essays. rev. ed. Ed. by David Fine. LC 95-9764. 305p. 1995. pap. 16.95 (*0-8263-1625-5*) U of NM Pr.
Los Angeles in the Thirties, 1931-1941. enl. rev. ed. David Gebhard & Harriette Von Breton. LC 89-1973. (California Architecture & Architects Ser.: No. 7). Orig. Title: L. A. in the Thirties. (Illus.). 192p. 1989. reprint ed. pap. 24.50 (*0-912158-97-2*) Hennessey.
Los Angeles in the Thirties, 1931-1941. enl. rev. ed. David Gebhard & Harriette Von Breton. LC 89-1973. (California Architecture & Architects Ser.: No. 7). Orig. Title: L. A. in the Thirties. (Illus.). 192p. 1989. 35.00 (*0-912158-98-0*) Hennessey.
Los Angeles International Airport: From Lindbergh's Landing Strip for World Air Center. Tom Moran. LC 93-36904. 1993. 29.95 (*1-884166-01-6*) Am Historical Pr.
Los Angeles International Airport Map AAA. Auto Club, Southern California Editors. (Illus.). 1998. 1.95 (*1-56413-347-8*) Auto Club.
***Los Angeles JobBank.** Contrib. by Adam Media Corporation Staff. (JobBank Ser.). 520p. 2000. pap. 16.95 (*1-58062-381-6*) Adams Media.
Los Angeles JobBank, 2000. Adams Media Corporation Staff. 512p. 1999. pap. 16.95 (*1-58062-229-1*) Adams Media.
Los Angeles Kings see NHL Today
Los Angeles Kings. Morgan Hughes. LC 98-13895. (Inside the NHL Ser.). (J). 1998. 16.48 (*1-57765-068-9*) ABDO Pub Co.
Los Angeles Koreatown: An Urban Geographical View of the Factors That Lead to Its Inception & Its Current Urbanization. Scott Shaw. (Illus.). 100p. (C). 1989. pap. 9.95 (*1-877792-09-8*) Buddha Rose.
Los Angeles Lakers see Pro Basketball Today
Los Angeles Lakers. Paul Joseph. LC 96-39616. (Inside the NBA Ser.). (Illus.). 32p. (J). (gr. 3-8). 1997. lib. bdg. 16.95 (*1-56239-762-1*) ABDO Pub Co.
Los Angeles Lakers Basketball Team. William W. Lace. LC 97-20074. (Great Sports Teams Ser.). (Illus.). 48p. (YA). (gr. 4-10). 1998. lib. bdg. 18.95 (*0-7660-1020-1*) Enslow Pubs.
***Los Angeles Lakers Basketball Team.** William W. Lace. LC 97-20074. (Great Sports Teams Ser.). (Illus.). 48p. (YA). (gr. 4-10). 1998. pap. 9.95 (*0-7660-1750-8*) Enslow Pubs.
Los Angeles Little Restaurant Guide. Camaro Editors. (Illus.). 1985. pap. 4.95 (*0-913290-85-8*) Camaro Pub.
***Los Angeles Marketplace 2001.** Ed. by Zagat Publishers Staff. (Illus.). 2000. pap. 10.95 (*1-57006-232-3*) Zagat.
Los Angeles Murals: A Book of Postcards. Robin J. Dunitz. (Illus.). 61p. (Orig.). 1995. pap. 9.95 (*0-9632862-3-4*) RJD Ent.
Los Angeles Murals by African-American Artists: A Book of Postcards. Robin J. Dunitz. (Illus.). 61p. (Orig.). 1995. pap. 9.95 (*0-9632862-2-6*) RJD Ent.
Los Angeles, 1939 . . . Street People & Friends. William Carroll. (Illus.). 144p. Date not set. pap. 25.00 (*0-910390-50-9*) Coda Publications.
Los Angeles Nude. Hisaka Kojima. (Illus.). 150p. 1994. pap. 29.95 (*4-416-89311-6*, Pub. by S Shinkosha) Bks Nippan.
Los Angeles One. Ed. by Derek Walker. (Academy Architecture Ser.). (Illus.). 176p. 1982. pap. 19.95 (*0-312-49877-2*) St Martin.
***Los Angeles/Orange Counties Street Guide & Thomas Guide Digital Edition: 2000 Edition.** (Illus.). 480p. 1999. pap. 44.95 incl. cd-rom (*1-58174-196-0*) Thomas Bros Maps.
Los Angeles-Orange Counties Street Guide & Directory, 1996 Census Tract Edition. Thomas Bros. Maps Staff. (Illus.). 484p. 1995. pap. 59.95 (*0-88130-765-3*) Thomas Bros Maps.
Los Angeles Painters of the 1920s. Nancy D. Moure. (Illus.). 40p. 1972. 2.00 (*0-915478-29-3*) Montgomery Gallery.
Los Angeles Peace Directory, 1989: A Guide to Peace & Social Change Groups in the Greater L. A. Area. 3rd rev. ed. Intro. by Eva Kataja. (Illus.). 160p. (Orig.). 1989. pap. 13.00 (*0-9621690-0-5*) UDWC.
Los Angeles Pocket Guide: Spanish ed. Berlitz Staff. 1999. pap. text 8.95 (*2-8315-7274-6*) Berlitz.
Los Angeles Poems: Poems from Hollywood. Mark Dunster. 11p. 1998. pap. 5.00 (*0-89642-558-4*) Linden Pubs.
Los Angeles Radio People, 1957-1997. Barrett. 1997. 4.95 (*0-9658907-0-8*) db Mkting.
Los Angeles R&B Groups & Duo's, 1945-1965. Steve Propes & Galen Gart. 200p. 1998. pap. write for info. (*0-936433-18-3*) Big Nickel.
Los Angeles Rebellion Against Racism. Movement for a Peoples Assembly Staff. 1992. pap. 2.50 (*0-89567-104-2*) World View Forum.
Los Angeles Restaurants. 3rd ed. Ed. by Alain Gayot. (Illus.). 416p. 1999. pap. 14.00 (*1-881066-47-9*) Gault Millau.
***Los Angeles Restaurants.** 4th ed. Ed. by Alain Gayot & Sharon Boorstin. (Illus.). 416p. 2000. pap. 14.00 (*1-881066-60-6*) Gault Millau.
Los Angeles Retirement & Relocation Guide. large type ed. Candyce Norvell. (Retirement & Relocation Guides Ser.). (Illus.). 350p. Date not set. pap. 24.95 (*1-56559-116-X*) HGI-Over Fifty.
Los Angeles Riots. Sue L. Hamilton. Ed. by John Hamilton. LC 92-28400. (Day of the Disaster Ser.). 32p. (J). 1992. lib. bdg. 12.98 (*1-56239-149-6*) ABDO Pub Co.
Los Angeles Riots. Ed. by Robert M. Fogelson. LC 70-90205. (Mass Violence in America Ser.). 1974. reprint ed. 24.95 (*0-405-01311-6*) Ayer.
***Los Angeles River: Its Life, Death, & Possible Rebirth.** Blake Gumprecht. LC 98-42432. (Illus.). 355p. 1999. 39.95 (*0-8018-6047-4*) Johns Hopkins.
Los Angeles Son Eternos. Illus. by Jenny Faw.Tr. of Angels Are Forever. (SPA.). 80p. 1998. text 4.95 (*0-88088-233-6*) Peter Pauper.

L

Los Angeles Sparks: Teamwork. Thomas S. Owens & Diana S. Helmer. LC 98-16492. (Women's Professional Basketball Ser.). 24p. (J). 1999. 18.60 (0-8239-5240-1, PowerKids) Rosen Group.

Los Angeles Sports Quiz. Brenda C. Alesii & Daniel Locche. LC 92-19306. (Illus.). 240p. 1992. pap. 10.95 (0-8065-1381-0, Citadel Pr) Carol Pub Group.

Los Angeles Spring. Photos by Robert Adams. (Illus.). 64p. 1986. 44.95 (0-89381-220-X) Aperture.

Los Angeles Stories. Ed. by John Miller. 176p. (Orig.). 1991. pap. 11.95 (0-87701-822-7) Chronicle Bks.

Los Angeles Streetcars: The Final Days. Ed. by John Heller. (Illus.). 48p. 1998. pap. 22.00 (0-9664304-1-7) Elctrc Rlwy Hist.

Los Angeles Struggles Toward Multiethnic Community: Asian American, African American & Latino Perspectives. Ed. by Edward T. Chang & Russell Leong. LC 94-32758. (Illus.). 192p. 1994. pap. 12.95 (0-295-97375-7) U of Wash Pr.

Los Angeles Survival Guide. Curt Northrup. LC 92-74429. (City Survival Guides Ser.). 156p. 1992. pap. 10.00 (0-9634720-0-3) Arkobaleno.

Los Angeles Times Crossword Companion, Vol. 1. 1995. pap. 25.00 (1-57495-041-X) Herbko Intl.

Los Angeles Times Crossword Companion, Vol. 2. 1995. pap. 12.00 (1-57495-042-8) Herbko Intl.

Los Angeles Times Crossword Companion, Vol. 3. 1995. pap. 12.00 (1-57495-043-6) Herbko Intl.

Los Angeles Times Crossword Companion, Vol. 4. 1995. pap. 12.00 (1-57495-044-4) Herbko Intl.

Los Angeles Times Crossword Companion, Vol. 5. 1995. pap. 12.00 (1-57495-045-2) Herbko Intl.

Los Angeles Times Duo-Crostic. Barry Tunick. 1996. pap. write for info. (0-8129-2226-3, Times Bks) Crown Pub Group.

Los Angeles Times Duo-Crostics, Vol. 1. Ed. by Barry Tunick. 1994. pap. 8.00 (0-8129-2225-5, Times Bks) Crown Pub Group.

Los Angeles Times Sunday Crossword, Vol. 5. Sylvia Bursztyn. Vol. 5. 1992. pap. 9.00 (0-8129-1917-3, Times Bks) Crown Pub Group.

Los Angeles Times Sunday Crossword, Vol. 6. Sylvia Bursztyn. 1992. pap. 8.50 (0-8129-1918-1, Times Bks) Crown Pub Group.

Los Angeles Times Sunday Crossword Omnibus, Vol. 2. 2nd ed. Sylvia Bursztyn. 1998. pap. 11.00 (0-8129-2973-X, Times Bks) Crown Pub Group.

Los Angeles Times Sunday Crossword Puzzles, Vol. 1. Sylvia Bursztyn. Vol. 1. 1991. pap. 8.50 (0-8129-1910-6, Times Bks) Crown Pub Group.

Los Angeles Times Sunday Crossword Puzzles, Vol. 2. Sylvia Bursztyn. 1991. pap. write for info. (0-685-47860-2, Times Bks) Crown Pub Group.

Los Angeles Times Sunday Crossword Puzzles, Vol. 5. Sylvia Bursztyn. 1992. pap. 7.00 (0-8129-2040-6, Times Bks) Crown Pub Group.

Los Angeles Times Sunday Crossword Puzzles, Vol. 6. Sylvia Bursztyn. 1992. pap. 7.00 (0-8129-2041-4, Times Bks) Crown Pub Group.

Los Angeles Times Sunday Crossword Puzzles, Vol. 7. Sylvia Bursztyn. Vol. 7. 1992. pap. 8.50 (0-8129-1919-X, Times Bks) Crown Pub Group.

Los Angeles Times Sunday Crossword Puzzles, Vol. 8. Sylvia Bursztyn. Vol. 8. 1992. pap. 8.50 (0-8129-1920-3, Times Bks) Crown Pub Group.

Los Angeles Times Sunday Crossword Puzzles, Vol. 10. 10th ed. Barry Tunick & Sylvia Bursztyn. 1993. pap. 8.50 (0-8129-2228-X, Times Bks) Crown Pub Group.

Los Angeles Times Sunday Crossword Puzzles, Vol. 11. 11th ed. Barry Tunick & Sylvia Bursztyn. Vol. 11. 1994. pap. 9.00 (0-8129-2229-8, Times Bks) Crown Pub Group.

Los Angeles Times Sunday Crossword Puzzles, Vol. 12. Barry Tunick & Sylvia Bursztyn. Vol. 12. 1994. pap. 9.00 (0-8129-2230-1, Times Bks) Crown Pub Group.

Los Angeles Times Sunday Crossword Puzzles, Vol. 13. Barry Tunick & Sylvia Bursztyn. Vol. 13. 1995. pap. 9.00 (0-8129-2231-X, Times Bks) Crown Pub Group.

Los Angeles Times Sunday Crossword Puzzles, Vol. 14. 14th ed. Sylvia Bursztyn & Barry Tunick. Vol. 14. 1995. pap. 9.00 (0-8129-2232-8, Times Bks) Crown Pub Group.

Los Angeles Times Sunday Crossword Puzzles, Vol. 15. Sylvia Bursztyn. Vol. 15. 1996. pap. 9.00 (0-8129-2788-5, Times Bks) Crown Pub Group.

Los Angeles Times Sunday Crossword Puzzles, Vol. 16. 16th ed. Sylvia Bursztyn. 1997. pap. 9.00 (0-8129-2938-1, Times Bks) Crown Pub Group.

Los Angeles Times Sunday Crossword Puzzles, Vol. 17. Barry Tunick & Sylvia Bursztyn. 1998. pap. 9.00 (0-8129-3020-7, Times Bks) Crown Pub Group.

***Los Angeles Times Sunday Crossword Puzzles, Vol. 19.** Sylvia Bursztyn. 64p. 2000. pap. 9.95 (0-8129-3352-4, Times Bks) Crown Pub Group.

Los Angeles Times Sunday Crosswork Omnibus, Vol. 1. Sylvia Bursztyn & Barry Tunick. 128p. 1996. pap. 11.00 (0-8129-2758-3, Times Bks) Crown Pub Group.

Los Angeles Town Compass: Vital Telephone Numbers Conveniently Organized to Save You Time, Money & Aggravation. Eric J. Makus. ix, 138p. (Orig.). 1996. pap. 14.95 (0-9654237-0-0) Town Compass.

Los Angeles 2000. Fodors Travel Publications, Inc. Staff. 1999. pap. 15.00 (0-679-00338-X) Fodors Travel.

***Los Angeles 2000.** Don McCormack. (Illus.). 1999. pap. 13.95 (1-929365-02-0, Pub. by McCormacks Guides) Bookpeople.

Los Angeles, 2000. Jane G. Pisano. (Urban Studies: No. 8). 48p. (Orig.). 1988. pap. 6.00 (0-913749-10-9) U MD Urban Stud.

***Los Angeles 2001.** Fodor's Staff. 2000. pap. 15.00 (0-679-00546-3) Fodors Travel.

Los Angeles Uncovered. Frank Thompson. LC 95-14522. 296p. 1995. pap. 16.95 (1-55622-391-9, Seaside Pr) Wordware Pub.

Los Angeles Watts Towers. Bud Goldstone & Arloa P. Goldstone. LC 97-27553. (Conservation & Cultural Heritage Ser.). 120p. 1997. pap. 24.95 (0-89236-491-2, Pub. by J P Getty Trust) OUP.

Los Angeles Wedding Planner. Tiger Oak Editors. (Publications - Regional Wedding Planners). (Illus.). 124p. 2000. pap. 16.95 (0-9663558-8-1, Pub. by Tiger Oak) Natl Bk Netwk.

Los Angeles with Love. Dorothy Rice. (Illus.). 100p. (Orig.). 1984. pap. text 17.95 (0-918269-00-8) Glen Hse.

Los Angeles Without a Map: A Love Story. Richard Rayner. LC 97-35013. 192p. 1997. pap. 12.00 (0-395-83809-6, Mariner Bks) HM.

Los Angeles/Long Beach Harbors Map AAA. Auto Club, Southern California Editors. (Illus.). 1999. 1.95 (1-56413-402-4) Auto Club.

***Los Angeles/Orange Counties Street Guide & Directory Zip Code Edition: 2000 Edition.** (Illus.). 480p. 1999. pap. 35.95 (1-58174-125-1) Thomas Bros Maps.

Los Angeles/Orange Counties Street Guide & Directory: 1999 Edition. Thomas Bros. Maps Staff. (Illus.). 480p. 1998. pap. 29.95 (1-58174-017-4) Thomas Bros Maps.

Los Angeles/Orange Counties Street Guide & Directory ZIP Code Edition: 1999 Edition. Thomas Bros. Maps Staff. (Illus.). 484p. 1998. pap. 35.95 (1-58174-018-2) Thomas Bros Maps.

***Los Angeles/Orange, 2000 Edition.** Thomas Brothers Maps Staff. 1999. pap. text 29.95 (1-58174-124-3) TBM.

***Los Angeles/Ventura Counties Street Guide & Directory: 2000 Edition.** (Illus.). 440p. 1999. pap. 27.95 (1-58174-126-X) Thomas Bros Maps.

***Los Angeles/Ventura Counties Street Guide & Thomas Guide Digital Edition: 2000 Edition.** (Illus.). 440p. 1999. pap. 42.95 incl. cd-rom (1-58174-199-5) Thomas Bros Maps.

***Los Angeles/Ventura Counties Street Guide & Directory, Zip Code Edition: 2000 Edition.** (Illus.). 440p. 1999. pap. 35.95 (1-58174-127-8) Thomas Bros Maps.

Los Angeles/Ventura Counties Street Guide & Directory: 1999 Edition. Thomas Bros. Maps Staff. (Illus.). 440p. 1998. pap. 27.95 (1-58174-021-2) Thomas Bros Maps.

Los Angeles/Ventura Counties Street Guide & Directory ZIP Code Edition: 1999 Edition. Thomas Bros. Maps Staff. (Illus.). 444p. 1998. pap. 35.95 (1-58174-023-9) Thomas Bros Maps.

***Los Angles.** 2nd ed. Ed. by Fodors Travel Publications, Inc. Staff. 2000. pap. 13.50 (0-679-00390-8) Fodors Travel.

Los Angles Clippers. Bob Italia. LC 96-39618. (Inside the NBA Ser.). (Illus.). 32p. (J). (gr. 3-8). 1997. lib. bdg. 16.95 (1-56239-761-3) ABDO Pub Co.

***Los Animales del Mundo - Great Animal Search.** (SPA., Illus.). 48p. (ps-3). 2000. pap. 9.95 (0-7460-3656-6, Pub. by Usbrne Pbng UK) EDC.

Los Animalitos/Big Bug Search. Ed. by Caroline Young. (Great Searches Ser.). (Illus.). 32p. (J). (ps up). 1999. pap. 8.95 (0-7460-3437-7, Usborne) EDC.

Los Anos Criticos: Desarrollo Del nino Del Nacimiento a Los Dos Anos. Judith Schneider. (SPA.). 53p. 1997. pap. 10.95 (0-944454-32-1) CAPE Center.

Los Anos de Juego: Desarrollo Del Nino De Dos a Seis Anos. Judith Schneider. (SPA.). 52p. 1997. pap. 10.95 (0-944454-35-6) CAPE Center.

Los Anos Indecisos. Gonzalo Forrente Ballester. 1999. pap. text 9.95 (84-08-02814-6) Planeta.

Los Aposentos Laterales del Corral de la Crux, 1582-1680: Estudio y Documentos. Ed. by Charles Davis & J. E. Varey. (Fuentes Para la Historia del Teatro en Espana Ser.: No. 0959-9487). (SPA.). 250p. 2001. 60.00 (1-85566-061-X) Boydell & Brewer.

Los Aztecas. Elizabeth Baquedano. 1997. pap. text 9.98 (968-38-0304-0) Panorama Edit.

Los Bandidos De Internet. Michael Coleman. 1990. pap. text 7.95 (84-406-7287-X) Lectorum Pubns.

LOS by DRG & Payment Source - North Central. 1994. write for info. (1-880678-93-4) HCIA.

LOS by DRG & Payment Source - Northeastern. 1994. write for info. (1-880678-92-6) HCIA.

LOS by DRG & Payment Source - Southern. 1994. write for info. (1-880678-94-2) HCIA.

LOS by DRG & Payment Source - United States. 1994. write for info. (1-880678-90-X) HCIA.

LOS by DRG & Payment Source - Western. 1994. write for info. (1-880678-91-8) HCIA.

LOS by Dx & Op - North Central. 1994. write for info. (1-880678-70-5) HCIA.

LOS by Dx & Op - Northeast. 1994. write for info. (1-880678-69-1) HCIA.

LOS by Dx & Op - Pediatric. 1994. write for info. (1-880678-73-X) HCIA.

LOS by Dx & Op - Southern. 1994. write for info. (1-880678-71-3) HCIA.

LOS by Dx & Op - United States. 1994. write for info. (1-880678-68-3) HCIA.

LOS by Dx & Op - Western. 1994. write for info. (1-880678-72-1) HCIA.

LOS by Dx & Op - Workers' Compensation. 1994. write for info. (1-880678-98-5) HCIA.

Los Cabos, La Paz. Stephane Marceau. (Due South Guide Ser.). (Illus.). 160p. 1999. pap. 10.95 (2-89464-186-9, Pub. by Ulysses Travel) Globe Pequot.

Los Capitalistas: Hispano Merchants on the Santa Fe Trail. Susan C. Boyle. LC 96-35705. 236p. 1997. 45.00 (0-8263-1789-8) U of NM Pr.

Los Carros Vacios: Level A. Pavon. text 7.95 (0-88436-281-7) EMC-Paradigm.

Los Cien Vestidos. Eleanor Estes. 1994. 11.15 (0-606-10861-0, Pub. by Turtleback) Demco.

***Los Cinco Lenguajes de Amor de los Ninos.** Gary Chapman & Ross Campbell. (SPA.). 2000. pap. 8.99 (0-7899-0508-6) Spanish Hse Distributors.

Los Cinco Sentidos En El Mundo Animal, 5 vols. Chelsea House Publishing Staff. (SPA.). 1997. 79.75 (0-7910-4000-3) Chelsea Hse.

Clasicos del Teatro Hispanoamericano, II (The Classics of Latin American Theater, II) Ed. by Gerardo Luzuriaga & Richard Reeve. (SPA.). 562p. 1975. pap. 17.99 (968-16-4486-7, Pub. by Fondo) Continental Bk.

Los Colores. Richard Scarry. (ps-3). 1998. 12.95 (84-08-01685-7) Planeta.

Los Colores de la Memoria see Colors of Memory: A Novel

Los Comanches: The Horse People, 1751-1845. Stanley Noyes. (Illus.). 393p. 1993. reprint ed. pap. 16.95 (0-8263-1548-8) U of NM Pr.

***Los Comentarios Al Ibis de Ovidio: El Largo Recorrido de Una Exegesis.** Rosario Guarino Ortega. 503p. 1999. 79.95 (3-631-34051-6) P Lang Pubng.

Los Cuadermos de Don Rigoberto: The Notebooks of Don Rigoberto. Mario Vargas Llosa. (SPA.). 1998. pap. 13.95 (0-14-027472-3) Viking Penguin.

Los Cuatro Cantantes de Guadalajara see Four Singers of Guadalajara

Los Cuentos del Cerdito. Jean Van Leeuwen. (Libro Puffin Facil-de-Leer Ser.). 1996. 8.70 (0-606-09573-X, Pub. by Turtleback) Demco.

Los de Abajo. Mariano Azuela. (SPA.). pap. 12.95 (968-16-0320-6, Pub. by Fondo) Continental Bk.

Los de Abel. Ana M. Matute. (SPA.). pap. 15.50 (84-233-1108-2, Pub. by Destino) Continental Bk.

Los Deportes. Chris Jaeggi. (I Know about Ser.). 1995. 7.70 (0-606-08809-1, Pub. by Turtleback) Demco.

***Los Descosidos Labios del Silencio.** Rafael Bordao. (SPA.). 51p. 2000. pap. 8.95 (1-881531-02-3, Palmar Pr) Ed Arcas.

***Los Desiertos.** Two Can Publishing Ltd. Staff. 2000. mass mkt. 4.95 (1-58728-970-9) Two Can Pub.

Lo's Diary. Pia Pera. Tr. by Ann Goldstein from ITA. 336p. 1999. 22.95 (1-56025-243-X, Thunders Mouth) Avalon NY.

Lo's Diary. Pia Pera. Tr. by Ann Goldstein. 293p. 1999. 22.95 (0-9643740-1-3) FoxRock.

***Los Diez Mandamientos.** (SPA.). 1999. 23.95 (84-08-01666-0) Planeta Edit.

Los Diez Pollitos. (SPA.). bds. 4.98 (1-85854-297-9) Brimax Bks.

Los Estilos Rio Bec, Chenes y Puuc en la Arquitectura Maya see Rio Bec, Chenes, & Puuc Styles in Maya Architecture

Los-Fat, Great-Tasting, Good-For-You Supermarket cookbook: More Than 150 Quick & Easy Recipes Using Today's Reduced-Fat Foods. Gary L. Rempe. 176p. 1998. pap. 14.95 (0-8092-2972-2) NTC Contemp Pub Co.

Los Hombres son de Marte, Las Mujeres son de Venus: Rivela,&Francisco. abr. ed. John Gray. (SPA.). 1996. audio 12.00 (0-694-51678-3, 394091, Pub. by HarperAudio) Lndmrk Audiobks.

***Los Horoscopos y To Futuro.** Joseph Baily. (SPA.). 1999. mass mkt. 4.99 (0-7899-0789-5) Spanish Hse Distributors.

Los Jovenes see Teenagers

Los Mapas. Chris Jaeggi. (I Know about Ser.). 1995. 7.70 (0-606-08810-5, Pub. by Turtleback) Demco.

Los Materiales. Karen Bryant-Mole. (Imagenes Ser.). 1997. 10.15 (0-606-10474-7, Pub. by Turtleback) Demco.

Los Mejores Remedios Caseros (The Best Home Remedies) 220 Consejos Practicos para Vencer Problemas Comunes de la Salud (220 Practical Tips to Conquer Common Health Conditions) Ed. by Abel Delgado & Prevention Health Books Editors. (SPA.). 192p. 1998. pap. 12.95 (1-57954-030-9) Rodale Pr Inc.

Los Miserables. Victor Hugo. 1998. pap. 23.95 (84-08-01939-2) Planeta.

***Los Montanas.** Two Can Publishing Ltd. Staff. (SPA.). 2000. mass mkt. 4.95 (1-58728-972-5) Two Can Pub.

Los Muertos no Hablan. S. R. Curtis. (Zorro Ser.). (SPA.). 1998. pap. text 9.95 (1-58105-165-4) Santillana.

Los Negocios en la Era Digital. Bill Gates. Tr. by Jose Antonio Bravo. (Illus.). 527p. 1999. pap. 17.95 (0-553-06101-1) Bantam.

Los Ninos Alfabeticos. Lourdes Ayala. (SPA.). 1995. 12.15 (0-606-09574-8, Pub. by Turtleback) Demco.

Los Nombres de Cristo. unabridged ed. Fray Luis De Leon. (SPA.). 187p. 1999. pap. 5.95 (84-410-0006-9, Pub. by Bookking Intl) Distribks Inc.

***Los Oceanos.** Two Can Publishing Ltd. Staff. (SPA.). 2000. mass mkt. 4.95 (1-58728-971-7) Two Can Pub.

Los Padres see Parents

***Los Paraisos Artificiales.** Benigno S. Nieto. 1999. 24.95 (84-239-7948-2) Planeta.

Los Pasos Hacia la Libertad en Cristo: Juvenil. N. Anderson & M. Park.Tr. of Steps to Freedom in Christ: Youth. 1.99 (0-7899-0376-8, 493782) Editorial Unilit.

Los Planetas. Chris Jaeggi. (I Know about Ser.). 1995. 7.70 (0-606-08811-3, Pub. by Turtleback) Demco.

Los Premios. Erich Segal. 1998. pap. text 11.95 (84-08-02186-9, Pub. by Planeta Edit) Planeta.

***Los Retos del Lider en el Siglo XXI.** J. R. Roman. 1998. 6.99 (0-8297-1581-9) Vida Pubs.

Los Reyes del Mambo Tocan Canciones de Amor: Novela. Oscar Hijuelos. LC 96-20227. (SPA.). 560p. 1996. pap. 14.00 (0-06-095214-8) HarpC.

Salmos I. Robert Alden. (Comentario Biblico Portavoz Ser.). Orig. Title: Psalms. (SPA.). 336p. 1994. pap. 9.99 (0-8254-1001-0, Edit Portavoz) Kregel.

Los Santos Inocentes. Miguel Delibes. 1997. pap. text 8.00 (84-08-02047-1) Planeta Editorial.

Los Secretos de las Obras de Arte II. Rose-Marie Hagen. 1997. 24.99 (3-8228-8011-6) Benedikt Taschen.

Los Secretos/Familia: Reader 2. Kay Jarvis Sladky. text 3.75 (0-88436-859-9) EMC-Paradigm.

Los Seis Ciegos y el Elefante. Karen Backstein. (Hello Reader! Ser.). 1999. pap. 3.99 (0-439-06338-8) Scholastic Inc.

Los Sivx. Robert Nicholson. Tr. by Jose R. Araluce from ENG. (Raices Ser.). (SPA., Illus.). 32p. (J). 1993. 16.95 (1-56492-092-5) Laredo.

Los Sonidos A Mi Alrededor. Paul Showers. (SPA.). 1996. 11.15 (0-606-09577-2, Pub. by Turtleback) Demco.

Los Sufis. Idries Shah. 1997. pap. text 24.00 (84-7245-339-1) Kairos Editorial.

Los topos see Moles

***Los Ultimos Gigantes.** Francois Place. (Illus.). 78p. (J). (gr. 3). 1999. 15.95 (980-257-235-7, Pub. by Ediciones Ekare) Kane-Miller Bk.

***Los Vencedores Que Dios Busca.** Ed. by Living Stream Ministry Staff. 1999. pap. 8.25 (0-7363-0651-X) Living Stream Ministry.

Los Viajes de Gulliver. Jonathan Swift. 1998. pap. 4.95 (84-08-01061-1) Planeta.

***Los Vita Nutrientes.** Robert C. Atkins. 1999. pap. 23.95 (970-05-1083-2) Distribks Inc.

***Los 7 Habitos De La Familias Altamente Efectivas.** Stephen R. Covey. 1999. pap. 23.95 (970-05-1004-2) Distribks Inc.

Losbuch In Deutschen Reimpaaren. fac. ed. Intro. by W. Abraham. (Codices Selecti A Ser.: Vol. XXXVIII). (GER., Illus.). 46p. 1972. lthr. 372.00 (3-201-00790-0, Pub. by Akademische Druck-und) Balogh.

Lose Fat. Leslie Kenton. 1997. mass mkt. 1.99 (0-8041-1624-5) Ivy Books.

Lose Fat While You Sleep: No Dieting, No Drugs, No Exercise. 7th ed. Pete Billac. Ed. by Cliff Evans. Tr. by Myra Patrick from ENG.Tr. of Pierda Grasa Mientras Usted Duerme. (SPA., Illus.). 96p. 1998. reprint ed. pap. 9.95 (0-943629-38-1) Swan Pub.

Lose Fat While You Sleep No Dieting No Drugs No Exercise. large type ed. Pete Billac. Ed. by Cliff Evans. LC 98-84047. 96p. 1998. pap. 9.95 (0-943629-33-0) Swan Pub.

Lose the Halo, Keep the Wings: Great Advise for Ministers' Wives. Virginia Wilson. (Illus.). 159p. 1996. pap. text 10.95 (1-56309-116-X, N964126, New Hope) Womans Mission Union.

Lose the Weight of the World: The Five Days Spiritual Fitness Plan for Your Soul. Charles Blair. LC 97-65168. 284p. 1997. pap. 11.95 (0-89221-346-9) New Leaf.

Lose This Book . . . And Find It Through Horary: A Practical Guide to Finding Lost Articles Through Horary Astrology. Alphee Lavoie. (Illus.). 140p. (Orig.). 1995. pap. 11.95 (0-9645621-0-3) AIR Soft.

***Lose Those Last 10 Pounds: The 28-Day Fool-Proof Plan to a Healthy Body.** Denise Austin. LC 99-49879. (Illus.). 288p. 2000. 21.95 (0-7679-0469-9) Broadway BDD.

***Lose Three, Win One.** Julian L. Nugent, Jr. 96p. 1999. pap. 10.00 (0-8059-4785-X) Dorrance.

Lose to Win: A Cardiologist's Guide to Weight Loss & Nutritional Healing. Stephen T. Sinatra. (Illus.). 228p. 1992. 19.95 (1-879111-26-8) Lincoln-Bradley.

Lose Ugly Fat Fast. Sylvan R. Lewis. (Illus.). 128p. 1980. pap. 2.00 (0-936320-04-4) Compact Books.

Lose Weight: Vettese,&Sirah. abr. ed. Harold H. Bloomfield & Sirah Vettese. 1991. audio 9.95 (1-55994-466-8, CPN 5013) HarperAudio.

***Lose Weight & Be Healthy: The Power of Knowledge.** Glen M. Todd. LC 99-97028. 2000. pap. 10.95 (0-533-13377-7) Vantage.

Lose Weight & Keep Fit: The Complete Handbook for Healthier Living. Aline McCarthy. 126p. 1990. pap. 19.95 (0-7463-0571-0, Pub. by How To Bks) Trans-Atl Phila.

Lose Weight Hypnosis Program. Petrie Method Inc., Staff. 1990. text 49.95 incl. audio (0-13-540360-X) P-H.

Lose Weight Naturally. Mark Bricklin. 374p. 1993. 9.98 (1-56731-027-3, MJF Bks) Fine Comms.

Lose Weight Naturally Cookbook. Sharon S. Claessens & Rodale Food Center Staff. (Illus.). 392p. 1994. 13.98 (1-56731-043-5, MJF Bks) Fine Comms.

Lose Weight Religiously. Trevor M. Phillips. 128p. 1990. pap. write for info. (0-9622708-3-0) Zubra Pub.

Lose Weight the Easy & Natural Way. 4.95 (0-686-40903-5, SR8) Transitions.

Lose Weight with Apple Vinegar: The Easy Way to the Ideal Body. Klaus Oberbeil. LC 99-168124.Tr. of Abnehmen mit Apfelessig. 136p. 1998. pap. 12.95 (1-882330-45-5) Magni Co.

Lose Weight with Dr. Art Ulene. 2nd ed. Art Ulene. LC 95-61971. (Illus.). 323p. 1995. pap. text 12.95 (1-56975-048-3) Ulysses Pr.

Lose Weight with Meridia. Larry S. Hobbs. LC 98-96365. (Illus.). 214p. 1999. pap. 14.95 (0-9639625-4-X, MER1) Pragmatic CA.

Lose Weight Without Going Hungry. Sylvan R. Lewis. (Illus.). 128p. 1981. pap. 2.00 (0-936320-10-9) Compact Books.

***Lose Your Gut Now! Drop Your Weight & Get in Shape Fast.** K. Winston Caine. LC 00-23906. 2000. write for info. (1-57954-277-8) Rodale Pr Inc.

Loser. Thomas Bernhard. Tr. by Jack Dawson. 200p. 1996. pap. 13.95 (0-226-04388-6) U Ch Pr.

Loser. Ed. by Frank Hardy. 230p. (C). 1990. 45.00 (0-9592104-5-8, Pub. by Pascoe Pub) St Mut.

Loser: The Real Seattle Music Story. 2nd rev. ed. Clark Humphrey. (Illus.). 239p. 1999. pap. 18.00 (1-929069-24-3) Misc Media.

***Loser Dies: A Satire.** Paul Morrissette. 215p. 2000. pap. 14.95 (0-7414-0376-5) Buy Books.

An Asterisk (*) at the beginning of an entry indicates that the title is appearing for the first time.

Loser Takes All. Graham Greene. 218p. 1993. pap. 9.95 (*0-14-018542-9*, Penguin Bks) Viking Penguin.
Loser Takes All: The Story of Bud Adams, Bad Football & Big Business. Ed Fowler. LC 97-71937. 208p. 1997. 21.00 (*1-56352-432-5*) Longstreet.
Losers. David Eddings. 1993. mass mkt. 5.99 (*0-345-38520-9*, Del Rey) Ballantine Pub Grp.
Losers: Gang Delinquency in an American Suburb. Gene Muhlbauer & Laura Dodder. LC 82-25497. 138p. 1983. 65.00 (*0-275-91048-2*, C1048, Praeger Pubs) Greenwood.
Losers Are Pirates: A Close Look at the PBS Series "Vietnam: A Television History" rev. ed. James Banerian. LC 85-61423. 416p. 1985. pap. 14.95 (*0-932729-01-0*) Sphinx Pub.
Loser's Blues. large type ed. Paula Gosling. 419p. 1982. 27.99 (*0-7089-0815-2*) Ulverscroft.
Loser's Club. mass mkt. write for info. (*0-312-97433-7*) St Martin.
Losers Club. Lisa S. Baker. 288p. 2000. text 23.95 (*0-312-24216-6*, Minotaur) St Martin.
Losers Fight Back. Barbara M. Joosse. LC 92-40783. (Illus.). 128p. (J). 1994. 15.00 (*0-395-62335-9*, Clarion Bks) HM.
Losers Fight Back: A Wild Willie Mystery. Barbara M. Joosse. LC 92-40783. 1996. 9.09 (*0-606-09578-0*, Pub. by Turtleback) Demco.
Losers Guide to, You Call This a Life. Doug Gordon. (Illus.). 81p. (Orig.). 1995. pap. text 9.95 (*0-9647318-1-9*) Gordon Ent Multimedia.
Losers, Inc. Claudia Mills. LC 96-30922. 150p. (J). (gr. 3-7). 1997. 16.00 (*0-374-34661-5*) FS&G.
Losers, Inc. Claudia Mills. LC 98-14221. 96p. (J). (gr. 3-7). 1998. pap. 4.95 (*0-7868-1274-5*, Pub. by Hyperion) Time Warner.
Losers, Inc. Claudia Mills. 160p. 1998. pap. 4.95 (*0-7868-1364-4*, Pub. by Hyprn Ppbks) Little.
Losers, Users & Parasites: A Host's Guide to Ridding Your Life of Unwanted People. Lance Q. Zedric. Ed. by Eugene D. Wheeler. LC 96-22252. (Illus.). 80p. (Orig.). 1996. pap. 9.95 (*0-934793-61-1*) Pathfinder CA.
Losing a Continent: France's North American Policy, 1753-1763, 62. Frank W. Brecher. LC 98-13974. (Contributions to the Study of World History Ser.: Vol. 62). 240p. 1998. 65.00 (*0-313-30786-5*, Greenwood Pr) Greenwood.
Losing a Parent. Fiona Marshall. LC 93-36599. 168p. (Orig.). 1993. pap. 12.95 (*1-55561-056-0*) Fisher Bks.
Losing a Parent: Passage to a New Way of Living. Alexandra Kennedy. LC 90-55786. 160p. 1991. pap. 15.00 (*0-06-250498-3*, Pub. by Harper SF) HarpC.
***Losing A Parent: Practical Help for You & Other Family Members.** 2nd ed. Fiona Marshall. LC 99-88893. 168p. 2000. pap. 14.00 (*1-55561-223-7*) Fisher Bks.
Losing Absalom. Alexs D. Pate. 320p. 1995. mass mkt. 7.50 (*0-425-15013-5*) Berkley Pub.
Losing Absalom. Alexs D. Pate. LC 93-23686. 220p. 1994. 5.00 (*1-56689-017-9*) Coffee Hse.
Losing America's Drug War: "Just Say No" to "Just Say Nothing": Hearing Before the Subcommittee on National Security, International Affairs & Criminal Justice of the Committee on Government Reform & Oversight, House of Representatives, 104th Congress, 2nd Session, October 10, 1996. USGPO Staff. LC 98-152295. iii, 159 p. 1998. pap. write for info. (*0-16-056026-8*) USGPO.
Losing & Fusing: Borderline Transitional Object & Self Relations. Roger A. Lewin & Clarence Schulz. LC 92-6219. 368p. 1992. 55.00 (*0-87668-490-8*) Aronson.
Losing Asia: Modernization & the Culture of Development. Bret Wallach. LC 95-12863. (Illus.). 256p. 1996. 28.00 (*0-8018-5170-X*) Johns Hopkins.
Losing Balance: The De-Democratization of America. William P. Kreml. LC 91-9148. 184p. (C). (gr. 13). 1991. text 59.95 (*0-87332-846-9*) M E Sharpe.
Losing Battles. Eudora Welty. LC 78-58857. (Vintage International Ser.). 416p. 1990. pap. 14.00 (*0-679-72882-1*) Vin Bks.
Losing Caitlin. Alexandra Flinn. 224p. (YA). (gr. 7 up). 14.95 (*0-06-029198-2*); lib. bdg. 14.89 (*0-06-029199-0*) HarpC Child Bks.
Losing Control: How & Why People Fail at Self-Regulation. Todd F. Heatherton et al. LC 94-17313. (Illus.). 307p. 1994. text 59.95 (*0-12-083140-6*) Acad Pr.
Losing Control: Sovereignty in an Age of Globalization. Saskia Sassen. 128p. 1996. 21.00 (*0-231-10608-4*) Col U Pr.
Losing Eddie: A Novel. Deborah J. Corey. LC 00-9. (Front Porch PB Ser.). (Illus.). 238p. 1994. pap. 8.95 (*1-56512-091-4*) Algonquin Bks.
Losing Eubie. Darlene T. Crist. (Illus.). 40p. (J). (gr. 3-5). 1998. pap. 9.95 (*0-9665072-0-7*) Red Bird Publ.
Losing Eugenio. Genevieve Brisac. Tr. by J. A. Underwood from FRE. LC 99-56674. 158p. 2000. 14.95 (*0-7145-3049-2*, Pub. by M Boyars Pubs) LPC InBook.
Losing Face: Status Politics in Japan. Susan J. Pharr. 1990. 40.00 (*0-520-06050-4*, Pub. by U CA Pr) Cal Prin Full Svc.
Losing Face: Status Politics in Japan. Susan J. Pharr. 1992. pap. 15.95 (*0-520-08092-0*, Pub. by U CA Pr) Cal Prin Full Svc.
Losing Face & Finding Grace: Twelve Bible Studies for Asian-American. Tom Lin. 80p. (Orig.). 1997. pap., student ed. 5.99 (*0-8308-1684-4*, 1684) InterVarsity.
Losing Faith in Faith: From Preacher to Atheist. Daniel E. Barker. 392p. (Orig.). 1992. pap. 20.00 (*1-877733-07-5*) Freedom Rel Found.
Losing from the Inside: The Cost of Conflict in the British Social Democratic Party. Patricia L. Sykes. 302p. 1989. 44.95 (*0-88738-223-1*); pap. 24.95 (*0-88738-815-9*) Transaction Pubs.
Losing Game. Freeman W. Crofts. 288p. Date not set. 23.95 (*0-8488-2240-4*) Amereon Ltd.
Losing Generations: Adolescents in High-Risk Settings. Ed. by National Research Council Staff. 288p. (Orig.). (C). 1993. pap. 19.95 (*0-309-05234-3*) Natl Acad Pr.
Losing Gravity. Kamala Ramy. LC 97-60120. 270p. (Orig.). 1997. pap. 12.95 (*0-9656598-0-1*) Word Wrap.
***Losing Ground.** Wylie. 2000. pap. 22.95 (*1-85702-918-6*, Pub. by Fourth Estate) Trafalgar.
Losing Ground: American Environmentalism at the Close of the Twentieth Century. Mark Dowie. (Illus.). 335p. 1996. pap. text 15.95 (*0-262-54084-3*) MIT Pr.
Losing Ground: American Social Policy, 1950-1980. 10th anniversary ed. Charles Murray. LC 94-241150. (Illus.). 352p. 1994. 16.00 (*0-465-04233-3*, Pub. by Basic) HarpC.
Losing Ground: Environmental Stress & World Food Prospects. Erik P. Eckholm. 223p. (C). 1976. pap. text 13.25 (*0-393-09167-8*) Norton.
Losing Ground: Human Rights Advocates under Attack in Colombia. Ed. by Washington Office on Latin America Staff. 61p. (C). 1997. pap. text 7.00 (*0-929513-41-X*) WOLA.
Losing Ground: Public Policy & the Displacement of Rural Black-Owned Homesteads. Housing Assistance Council Staff. 79p. 1984. 3.50 (*1-58064-067-2*) Housing Assist.
Losing Ground Against Drugs: The Erosion of America's Borders : Hearing Before the Committee on the Judiciary, United States Senate, One Hundred Fourth Congress, Second Session . . . July 31, 1996. United States Government. LC 98-115271. (S. Hrg. Ser.). iii, 91 p. 1997. write for info. (*0-16-055465-9*) USGPO.
***Losing Ground Against Drugs: The Erosion of America's Borders: Congressional Hearings.** Ed. by Orrin G. Hatch. 91p. (C). 1999. reprint ed. pap. text 20.00 (*0-7881-8292-7*) DIANE Pub.
Losing Hope: The Environment & Health in Russia. Olga Bridges & Jim Bridges. LC 95-83401. (Avebury Studies in Green Research). 288p. 1996. 78.95 (*1-85972-144-3*, Pub. by Avebry) Ashgate Pub Co.
Losing Isaiah. Seth J. Margolis. 400p. 1994. reprint ed. mass mkt. 5.99 (*0-515-11539-8*, Jove) Berkley Pub.
Losing It: America's Obsession with Weight & the Industry That Feeds on It. Laura Fraser. 1997. 24.95 (*0-614-25219-9*) NAL.
Losing It: America's Obsession with Weight & the Industry That Feeds on It. Laura Fraser. LC 98-184732. 336p. 1998. pap. 13.95 (*0-452-27291-2*) NAL.
Losing It: The Virginity Myth. Ed. by Louis M. Crosier. LC 93-71214. 195p. 1993. pap. 12.95 (*0-9627671-2-3*) Avocus Pub.
Losing It: The Virginity Myth. Ed. by Louis M. Crosier. LC 93-71214. 195p. 1994. 19.95 (*0-9627671-3-1*) Avocus Pub.
Losing It - Naturally: A Complete Holistic Weight Loss Program. Loretta Washburn. LC 98-73917. 296p. 1999. pap. 12.95 (*1-57174-122-4*) Hampton Roads Pub Co.
Losing It All & Find Yourself: How to Pick up the Pieces & Start Anew. Richard Dortch. LC 93-85812. 112p. (Orig.). 1993. pap. 6.95 (*0-89221-239-X*) New Leaf.
Losing Jessica. large type ed. Robby Deboer. LC 94-24146. 547p. 1995. 23.95 (*0-7862-0371-4*) Thorndike Pr.
Losing Joe's Place. Gordon Korman. LC 89-10627. 240p. (YA). (gr. 4-7). 1991. pap. 3.99 (*0-590-42769-5*, Point) Scholastic Inc.
Losing Joe's Place. Gordon Korman. (J). 1990. 9.09 (*0-606-00571-4*, Pub. by Turtleback) Demco.
***Losing Julia.** Jonathan Hull. LC 99-43316. 384p. 2000. 24.95 (*0-385-33375-7*) Delacorte.
Losing, Leaving, & Letting Go: Surviving the Change Points of Life. Marceal Clark. LC 94-6853. 144p. (Orig.). 1994. pap. 3.99 (*1-56722-022-3*) Word Aflame.
Losing Legitimacy: Street Crime & the Decline of Social Institutions in America. Gary Lafree. LC 98-13957. (Crime & Society Ser.). 1998. 27.00 (*0-8133-3450-0*, Pub. by Westview) HarpC.
Losing Legitimacy: Street Crime & the Decline of Social Institutions in America. Gary Lafree. (Crime & Society Ser.). (C). 1999. pap. text 20.00 (*0-8133-3451-9*) Westview.
Losing Less Money Raising Horses. rev. ed. Margaret Gardiner. (Illus.). 91p. 1986. reprint ed. pap. 7.95 (*0-9617808-0-0*) K Morgan Horse Farm.
Losing Liberty Judicially: Prohibitory & Kindred Laws Examined. Thomas J. North. xiv, 252p. 1981. reprint ed. 36.00 (*0-8377-0907-5*, Rothman) W S Hein.
Losing Little Sister. Ricardo A. Scott. (Ricardo Reggae Archives). (Illus.). 110p. (Orig.). 1996. pap. write for info. (*1-883427-85-1*) Crnerstone GA.
Losing Lou-Ann. Clinton A. Erb. 216p. (Orig.). 1996. pap. 14.95 (*0-9627232-6-6*) Psychology Pr.
Losing Louisa. Judith Caseley. LC 98-19501. 235p. (YA). (gr. 8 up). 1999. pap. text 17.00 (*0-374-34665-8*) FS&G.
***Losing Matt Shepard: Life & Politics in the Aftermath of Anti-Gay Murder.** Beth Loffreda. 2000. 22.95 (*0-231-11858-9*) Col U Pr.
Losing Mogadishu: Testing U. S. Policy in Somalia. Jonathan Stevenson. LC 94-23853. 224p. 1995. 28.95 (*1-55750-788-0*) Naval Inst Pr.
Losing My Virginity: How I've Survived, Had Fun & Made a Fortune Doing Business My Way. Richard Branson. LC 98-18979. (Illus.). 370p. 1998. 27.50 (*0-8129-3101-7*, Times Bks) Crown Pub Group.
***Losing My Virginity: How I've Survived, Had Fun & Made a Fortune Doing Business My Way.** Richard Branson. (Illus.). 384p. 1999. pap. 15.00 (*0-8129-3229-3*, Times Bks) Crown Pub Group.
Losing Nelson. Barry Unsworth. LC 99-28757. 352p. 1999. 23.95 (*0-385-48652-9*, N A Talese) Doubleday.
***Losing Nelson.** Barry Unsworth. 352p. 2000. pap. 14.00 (*0-393-32117-7*, Norton Paperbks) Norton.
Losing Our Democratic Spirit: Congressional Deliberation & the Dictatorship of Propaganda. Bill Granstaff. LC 99-18021. (Praeger Series in Political Communication). 248p. 1999. 59.95 (*0-275-96567-8*) Greenwood.
Losing Our Language: How Multicultural Classroom Instruction Is Undermining Our Children's Ability to Read, Write & Reason. Sandra Stotsky. LC 98-47124. 336p. 1999. 25.50 (*0-684-84961-5*) Free Pr.
Losing Our Souls: The American Experience in the Cold War. Edward Pessen. LC 93-11241. 256p. 1993. text 24.95 (*1-56663-037-1*) I R Dee.
Losing Our Souls: The American Experience in the Cold War. Edward Pessen. LC 95-32551. 256p. 1995. pap. text 12.95 (*1-56663-096-7*, Elephant Paperbacks) I R Dee.
Losing Our Virtue: Why the Church Must Recover Its Moral Vision. David F. Wells. 1999. pap. 20.00 (*0-8028-4672-6*, Eerdmans Bks) Eerdmans.
Losing Out: Sexuality & Adolescent Girls. Sue Lees. LC 86-3137. pap. 12.50 (*0-09-164101-2*) Hutchinson UK.
***Losing Paradise: The Growing Threat to Our Animals Our Environment & Ourselves.** Paul G. Irwin. 2000. pap. 14.95 (*0-7570-0003-7*) Square One.
Losing Parties: Out-Party National Committees, 1956-1993. Philip A. Klinkner. LC 94-16353. 288p. 1994. 40.00 (*0-300-06008-4*) Yale U Pr.
Losing Place: Refugee Populations & Rural Transformations in East Africa. Johnathan Bascom. LC 97-45095. (Refugee & Forced Migration Studies). 224p. 1998. 39.95 (*1-57181-083-8*) Berghahn Bks.
***Losing Proposition.** 1999. text. write for info. (*0-312-25324-9*) St Martin.
Losing Solitude. Martin Murie. LC 94-77619. 256p. (Orig.). 1996. pap. 14.95 (*0-943972-34-5*) Homestead WY.
Losing Strands in the Web of Life Vol. 141: Vertebrate Declines & the Conservation of Biological Diversity. John Tuxill. Ed. by Jane A. Peterson. 85p. 1998. pap. 5.00 (*1-878071-43-2*) Worldwatch Inst.
Losing the Edge: The Rise & Fall of Stanley Cup Champion New York Rangers. Barry Meisel. (Illus.). 256p. 1995. 23.00 (*0-684-81519-2*) S&S Trade.
Losing the Light: Terry Gilliam & the Munchausen Saga. Andrew Yule. (Illus.). 256p. 1991. 22.95 (*1-55783-060-6*) Applause Theatre Bk Pubs.
Losing the Light: Terry Gilliam & the Munchausen Saga. Andrew Yule. 256p. 1998. pap. 15.95 (*1-55783-346-X*) Applause Theatre Bk Pubs.
***Losing the Race: Self-Sabotage in Black America.** John McWhorter. 288p. 2000. 24.00 (*0-684-83669-6*) Free Pr.
Losing the Weight of the World: How to Lighten Your Burdens Through Meditation & Joyful Living. Jonathan Kramer & Diane D. Kramer. 336p. 1999. reprint ed. pap. 12.00 (*0-425-16543-4*) Berkley Pub.
Losing Time. Otis L. Graham. (Illus.). 384p. 1994. pap. 20.50 (*0-674-53935-4*) HUP.
Losing Time: The Industrial Policy Debate. Otis L. Graham, Jr. (Illus.). 384p. (C). 1992. text 39.00 (*0-674-53919-2*) HUP.
Losing to Win: The 1996 Elections & American Politics. James W. Ceaser & Andrew Busch. LC 97-1579. (Illus.). 198p. 1997. 51.00 (*0-8476-8405-9*); pap. 16.95 (*0-8476-8406-7*) Rowman.
Losing Touch. Margaret Hinxman. 256p. 1996. 24.00 (*0-7278-5100-4*) Severn Hse.
Losing Touch with the Living God (Malachi) John Benton. (Welwyn Commentary Ser.). 1985. pap. 8.99 (*0-85234-212-8*, Pub. by Evangelical Pr) P & R Pubng.
Losing Uncle Tim. MaryKate Jordan. Ed. by Abby Levine. LC 89-5280. (Illus.). 32p. (J). (gr. 2-6). 1989. pap. 5.95 (*0-8075-4758-1*); lib. bdg. 14.95 (*0-8075-4756-5*) A Whitman.
Losing Weight for Good: Developing Your Personal Plan of Action. Lawrence J. Cheskin. LC 96-31948. 264p. 1997. 24.95 (*0-8018-5499-7*) Johns Hopkins.
Losing Weight Permanently: Secrets of the 2Who Succeed. Gregory L. Jantz. LC 96-3837. 204p. 1996. pap. 11.99 (*0-87788-480-3*, H Shaw Pubs) Waterbrook Pr.
Losing Weight Thru Past Lives: or How I Lost 90 Pounds & Realized Ancient Monks Didn't Always Eat Well. Joe Vitale. 32p. (Orig.). 1986. pap. text 3.00 (*0-9617549-0-7*) Awareness Pubns.
Losing Weight with a High Protein Diet. 1994. lib. bdg. 250.95 (*0-8490-5662-4*) Gordon Pr.
Losing Weight Without Dieting. 1992. lib. bdg. 75.00 (*0-8490-8714-7*) Gordon Pr.
Losing You, Finding Me. Joanne Hargrove. 70p. 1995. pap. 9.95 (*1-884295-07-X*) Ananta Prnting.
Losing Your Best Friend. Corinne Bergstrom. LC 79-20622. (Illus.). 32p. (J). (ps-3). 1980. 16.95 (*0-87705-471-1*, Kluwer Acad Hman Sci) Kluwer Academic.
Losing Your Job, Reclaiming Your Soul: Stories of Resilience, Renewal & Hope. Mary L. Pulley. LC 97-4700. 1997. 24.50 (*0-7879-0937-8*) Jossey-Bass.
***Losing Your Parents, Finding Your Self: The Defining Turning Point of Adult Life.** Victoria Secunda. LC 99-35867. 368p. 2000. 24.95 (*0-7868-6312-9*, Pub. by Hyperion) Time Warner.
Losing Your Pounds of Pain: Breaking the Link Between Abuse, Stress, & Overeating. Doreen L. Virtue. LC 94-15864. 256p. (Orig.). 1994. pap. 12.95 (*1-56170-095-9*, 158) Hay House.
Losing Your Religion, Finding Your Faith: Spirituality & Young Adults. Brett C. Hoover. LC 97-35323. 144p. (YA). 1998. pap. 9.95 (*0-8091-3782-8*) Paulist Pr.
Losing Your Shirt: Recovery for Compulsive Gamblers & Their Families. Mary Heineman. 192p. 1996. pap. text 14.95 (*1-56838-126-3*) Hazelden.
Loss: A Novella & Two Short Stories. Vladimir Makanin. Tr. by Byron Lindsey from ENG. LC 98-15526. (Writings from an Unbound Europe Ser.). 136p. 1998. text 44.95 (*0-8101-1639-1*); pap. text 14.95 (*0-8101-1640-5*, Marlboro) Northwestern U Pr.
Loss: Sadness & Depression. John Bowlby. LC 79-2759. 492p. 2000. pap. text 24.00 (*0-465-04238-4*, Pub. by Basic) HarpC.
Loss - An Invitation to Grow. Jean C. Grigor. (C). 1990. pap. text 30.00 (*0-85305-269-7*, Pub. by Arthur James) St Mut.
Loss Abatement Through Project Management, Vol. 2. Steven S. Zumdahl. 20p. 19.50 (*0-614-05197-5*, LAPM06782M) ASFE.
Loss & Bereavement. Sheila Payne et al. LC 99-24181. (Health Psychology Ser.). 1999. 28.95 (*0-335-20105-9*) OpUniv Pr.
Loss & Bereavement: Managing Change. Ros Weston et al. LC 98-20838. 1998. 34.95 (*0-632-04787-9*) Blackwell Sci.
Loss & Bereavement in Childbearing. Rosemary Mander. LC 94-13658. (Illus.). 240p. 1994. pap. 24.95 (*0-632-03826-8*, Pub. by Blckwll Scitfc UK) Blackwell Sci.
Loss & Change in the Military Family. Carol B. Richardson. (Family Forum Library). 16p. 1993. 1.95 (*1-56688-074-2*) Bur For At-Risk.
Loss & Grief. Bob Wright. LC 92-30086. (Skills for Caring Ser.). (Illus.). 48p. 1992. pap. text 9.95 (*0-443-04619-0*) Church.
Loss & Grief Recovery: Help Caring for Children with Disabilities, Chronic, or Terminal Illness. Joyce M. Ashton & Dennis Ashton. LC 95-40492. 193p. 1996. 29.95 (*0-89503-138-8*) Baywood Pub.
Loss & Recovery of Transcendence: The Will to Power & the Light of Heaven. John C. Robertson, Jr. LC 95-5874. (Princeton Theological Monographs: Vol. 39). 1995. 14.00 (*1-55635-027-9*) Pickwick.
Loss & Restoration: Stories from Three Continents. Fred Flatow. LC 98-92655. (Illus.). 205p. 1998. pap. 12.95 (*0-9663933-0-9*) Brixton Pub.
Loss & Restoration of Regenerative Capacity in Tissues & Organs of Animals. L. V. Polezhaev. Tr. by Bruce M. Carlson. LC 71-160029. 395p. 1972. 34.00 (*0-674-53920-6*) HUP.
***Loss & Trauma: General & Close Relationship Perspectives.** Ed. by John H. Harvey & Eric D. Miller. 320p. 2000. text 59.95 (*1-58391-012-3*); pap. text 29.95 (*1-58391-013-1*) Brunner-Mazel.
Loss, Bereavement & Grief: A Guide to Effective Caring. Bob Spall & Stephen Callis. 160p. write for info. (*0-7487-3322-1*, Pub. by S Thornes Pubs) Trans-Atl Phila.
***Loss, Change & Grief: An Educational Perspective.** Erica Brown. 1998. pap. 25.95 (*1-85346-465-1*) Taylor & Francis.
Loss Control: If Disaster Strikes We're Ready. Margaret S. Cavallo. (Illus.). 1997. 3.5 ld. write for info. (*0-9658375-5-6*) O-Hill Pub.
Loss Control: If Disaster Strikes We're Ready. unabridged ed. Margaret S. Cavallo. (Illus.). 75p. 1997. ring bd. write for info. (*0-9658375-4-8*) O-Hill Pub.
Loss Control: If Disaster Strikes We're Ready. unabridged ed. Margaret S. Cavallo. (Illus.). 200p. 1997. ring bd. write for info. (*0-9658375-3-X*) O-Hill Pub.
Loss Control Program Module: Environmental Protection. Date not set. write for info. (*0-88061-077-8*) Intl Loss Cntrl.
Loss Control Program Module: Product Safety. Date not set. write for info. (*0-88061-076-X*) Intl Loss Cntrl.
Loss Control Program Module: Security. Date not set. write for info. (*0-88061-078-6*) Intl Loss Cntrl.
Loss Distributions. Robert V. Hogg & Stuart A. Klugman. LC 83-19663. (Probability & Mathematical Statistics: Applied Probability & Statistics Section Ser.: No. 1-346). 248p. 1984. 94.95 (*0-471-87929-0*, 1-346) Wiley.
Loss During Pregnancy or in the Newborn Period: Principles of Care with Clinical Cases & Analysis. Ed. by James R. Woods, Jr. & Jenifer L. Woods. LC 97-70847. (Illus.). 450p. 1997. text 34.95 (*0-9655310-0-7*) Jannetti Pubns.
Loss for Words: The Story of Deafness in a Family. Lou A. Walker. LC 85-42597. 224p. 1987. reprint ed. pap. 13.00 (*0-06-091425-4*, PL/1425, Perennial) HarperTrade.
Loss, Grief, & Bereavement: A Guide for Counseling, 4. Ed. by Otto S. Margolis et al. LC 85-12260. 176p. 1985. 49.95 (*0-275-90144-0*, C0144, Praeger Pubs) Greenwood.
Loss in China & the Revolutionary Legacy of Mao Tsetung. Bob Avakian. (Illus.). 1978. pap. 2.00 (*0-89851-017-1*) RCP Pubns.
Loss in Pregnancy: Guidelines for Pregnancy. Mcdonald. (C). 1996. pap. text 30.00 (*0-7020-1742-6*) Harcourt.
Loss Mitigation. rev. ed. Mortgage Bankers Association of America Staff. 175p. (C). 1997. pap. 270.00 (*1-57599-049-0*) Mortgage Bankers.
***Loss Models: From Data to Decisions.** Stuart A. Klugman et al. 192p. 1998. pap., student ed. 24.95 (*0-471-23885-6*) Wiley.
***Loss Models: From Data to Decisions, 1.** Stuart Klugman et al. LC 97-28718. (Wiley Series in Probability & Statistics). 672p. 1998. 94.95 (*0-471-23884-8*, Wiley-Interscience) Wiley.
Loss of a Parent: Understanding & Coping with Grief & Change after the Death of Our Parents. Alexander Levy. LC 99-64773. 208p. 1999. text 24.00 (*0-7382-0099-9*, Pub. by Perseus Pubng) HarpC.
Loss of a Pet. Wallace Sife. (Illus.). 160p. 1993. pap. 21.95 (*0-87605-625-7*) Howell Bks.
Loss of a Pet. expanded rev. ed. Wallace Sife. LC 97-41254. 208p. 1998. 12.95 (*0-87605-197-2*) Howell Bks.

L

An Asterisk (*) at the beginning of an entry indicates that the title is appearing for the first time.

Loss of Confidence: Politics & Policy in the 1970s. Ed. by David B. Robertson. LC 98-26747. (Issues in Policy History Ser.: No. 8). 184p. 1998. pap. 16.95 (*0-271-01845-3*) Pa St U Pr.

Loss of Habitat. Daniel J. Sundahl. LC 93-28614. 64p. 1993. pap. 14.95 (*0-7734-2777-5*, Mellen Poetry Pr) E Mellen.

Loss of Heaven. Jack Warner. 232p. 1991. pap. 16.95 (*1-879601-04-4*) Semaphore Bks.

Loss of Heaven. Jack Warner. 1992. reprint ed. 16.95 (*0-685-55209-8*) Semaphore Bks.

Loss of Innocence. Chassie West. 304p. 1997. mass mkt. 5.50 (*0-06-108111-6*, Harp PBks); mass mkt. 5.50 (*0-614-27745-0*, Harp PBks) HarpC.

Loss of Innocence: A True Story of Juvenile Murder. Eric J. Adams. 288p. (Orig.). 1991. mass mkt. 4.95 (*0-380-75987-X*, Avon Bks) Morrow Avon.

***Loss of Innocents: Child Killers & Their Victims.** Cara Elizabeth Richards. LC 99-39723. 280p. 2000. 55.00 (*0-8420-2602-9*, SR Bks); pap. 19.95 (*0-8420-2603-7*, SR Bks) Scholarly Res Inc.

Loss of Loved Ones. 2nd ed. David M. Moriarty. LC 79-50189. 312p. 1983. 27.50 (*0-87527-161-8*) Green.

Loss of Mastery: Puritan Historians in Colonial America. Peter Gay. LC 67-10969. (Jefferson Memorial Lectures). 176p. reprint ed. pap. 54.60 (*0-608-17991-4*, 202904500058) Bks Demand.

Loss of Roses. William Inge. 1963. pap. 5.25 (*0-8222-0688-9*) Dramatists Play.

Loss of Self. 2nd ed. Donna Cohen. 27.95 (*0-393-05016-5*) Norton.

Loss of Self: A Family Resource for the Care of Alzheimer's Disease & Related Disorders. Donna Cohen & Carl Eisdorfer. LC 85-15515. 1986. 19.95 (*0-393-02263-3*) Norton.

Loss of Self: A Resource for the Care of Alzheimer's Disease & Related Disorders. large type ed. Donna Cohen & Carl Eisdorfer. (Illus.). 574p. 1987. reprint ed. lib. bdg. 20.95 (*1-55736-005-7*) BDD LT Grp.

***Loss of Sexual Innocence.** Mike Figgis. (Screenplays Ser.). (Illus.). 128p. 1999. pap. 13.00 (*0-571-20153-9*) Faber & Faber.

***Loss of the Bismarck: An Avoidable Disaster.** Graham Rhys-Jones. (Illus.). 256p. 2000. 32.95 (*1-55750-533-0*) Naval Inst Pr.

Loss of the Culion. large type ed. Jeffrey Ashford. (Linford Mystery Library). 1991. pap. 16.99 (*0-7089-7154-7*) Ulverscroft.

Loss of the Miraculous. Ben Morreale. LC 95-82276. (Prose Ser.: No. 32). 150p. (C). 1997. pap. 13.00 (*1-55071-019-2*) Guernica Editions.

Loss of the S. S. Titanic. Lawrence Beesley. Date not set. 24.95 (*0-8488-2190-4*) Amereon Ltd.

***Loss of the S. S. Titanic: Its Story & Its Lessons.** Lawrence Beesley. LC 99-462121. (Illus.). 224p. 2000. pap. 13.00 (*0-618-05531-2*) HM.

Loss of the Self: In Modern Literature & Art. Wylie Sypher. LC 78-11790. 179p. 1979. reprint ed. lib. bdg. 38.50 (*0-313-20759-3*, SYLS, Greenwood Pr) Greenwood.

***Loss of the Ship Essex, Sunk by a Whale.** Thomas Nickerson. LC 00-20147. (Penguin Classics Ser.). 256p. 2000. pap. 12.95 (*0-14-043796-7*) Viking Penguin.

Loss of the Titanic, 1912. Tim Coates. 74p. 1998. 25.00 (*0-11-500499-8*, HM04998, Pub. by Statnry Office) Balogh.

***Loss of the Titanic, 1912.** Ed. by Tim Coates. (Uncovered Editions Ser.). 208p. 1999. pap. 14.00 (*0-11-702403-1*, Pub. by Statnry Office) Balogh.

Loss of Virtue: Moral Confusion & Social Disorder in Britain & America. 1995. 17.95 (*0-907631-50-9*) Login Pubs Consort.

Loss Prevention & Safety Promotion in the Process Industries: Proceedings of the 8th International Symposium, Antwerp, Belgium, June 6-9, 1995, 2 vols. Ed. by J. J. Mewis et al. LC 95-6875. 1500p. 1995. 376.75 (*0-444-82136-8*) Elsevier.

Loss Prevention & Safety Promotion in the Process Industries: Proceedings of the 8th International Symposium, Antwerp, Belgium, June 6-9, 1995, Vol. 1. Ed. by J. J. Mewis et al. LC 95-6875. 1995. 359.50 (*0-444-82131-7*) Elsevier.

Loss Prevention & Safety Promotion in the Process Industries: Proceedings of the 8th International Symposium, Antwerp, Belgium, June 6-9, 1995, Vol. 2. Ed. by J. J. Mewis et al. LC 95-6875. 1995. write for info. (*0-444-82134-1*) Elsevier.

Loss Prevention & Safety Research & Auditing. Bruce A. Hill. (Occupational Safety & Health Guide Ser.). 1999. 59.95 (*1-56670-330-1*) Lewis Pubs.

***Loss Prevention & the Small Business: The Security Professional's Guide to Asset Protection Strategies.** J. Robert Wyman. LC 99-18729. 208p. 1999. pap. 24.95 (*0-7506-7162-9*) Buttrwrth-Heinemann.

Loss Prevention Guide for Retail Businesses. Rudolph C. Kimiecik. 221p. 1995. 89.95 (*0-471-07636-8*) Wiley.

Loss Prevention in Process Industries, 2 vols. Frank P. Lees. (C). 1980. 1160.00 (*0-7855-4098-9*, Pub. by Witherby & Co) St Mut.

Loss Prevention, 1992 Conference Proceedings, Vol. 16. Ed. by Loss Prevention Committee of AICHE Safety & Health. (Technical Manual - Loss Prevention Ser.). 1992. ring bd. 35.00 (*0-8169-0571-1*, T-87) Am Inst Chem Eng.

Loss Prevention of Rotating Machinery: Papers Presented at ASME Petroleum Division Conference, Houston, Texas, September 1971. American Society of Mechanical Engineers Staff. LC 71-187881. 58p. reprint ed. pap. 30.00 (*0-608-11681-5*, 201132800078) Bks Demand.

Loss Prevention Professional. Bill Copeland. 404p. 1999. 40.00 (*0-9657659-5-4*) Absolutely Zero.

Loss Prevention Techniques & Training Manual. 2nd ed. Dana Turner. Ed. by Kris Bond. 320p. pap. text 125.00 (*0-8080-0492-1*) CCH INC.

Loss Prevention Test Kit. 45.00 (*0-318-17772-2*) ASFE.

Loss Prevention Test Kit. 2nd ed. Rev. by Lucie Martel. (FRE.). 45.00 (*0-614-05206-8*, LPTK06882M) ASFE.

Loss Prevention Through Crime Analysis. National Crime Prevention Institute Staff & Francis J. D'Addario. (Illus.). 96p. 1989. pap. 27.95 (*0-409-90191-1*) Buttrwrth-Heinemann.

***Loss Prevention Trilogy: How to Achieve Success!, 3 vols.** Bill Copeland. 1212p. 1999. 120.00 (*1-893763-46-3*) Absolutely Zero.

Loss Rate Concept in Safety Engineering. R. L. Browning. LC 80-22339. (Occupational Safety & Health Ser.: Vol. 6). (Illus.). 174p. reprint ed. pap. 54.00 (*0-608-08915-X*, 206955000005) Bks Demand.

Loss That Is Forever: The Lifelong Impact of the Early Death of a Mother or Father. Maxine Harris. 342p. 1998. text 24.00 (*0-7881-5694-2*) DIANE Pub.

Loss That Is Forever: The Lifelong Impact of the Early Death of a Mother or Father. Maxine Harris. 368p. 1996. pap. 13.95 (*0-452-27268-8*, Plume) Dutton Plume.

Losses & Lacunae in Early Insular Art. George Henderson. (C). 1988. 50.00 (*0-900657-66-9*, Pub. by W Sessions) St Mut.

Losses in Later Life: A New Way of Walking with God. 2nd ed. R. Scott Sullender. LC 99-17250. 188p. 1999. 39.95 (*0-7890-0627-8*); pap. 19.95 (*0-7890-0628-6*, Haworth Pastrl) Haworth Pr.

Losses in the Los Angeles Civil Unrest, April 29-May 1, 1992: Lists of the Damaged Properties & Korean Merchants & the L. A. Riot - Rebellion. Paul Ong & Suzanne Hee. 138p. 1993. pap. 6.95 (*1-883191-00-9*) U CA Ctr Pac Rim.

Losses of Moment. Lou Suarez. LC 95-5598. (Wick Poetry Chapbook Ser.: No. 8). 36p. (Orig.). 1995. pap. 4.75 (*0-87338-534-9*) Kent St U Pr.

Losses of Nations: Deadweight Politics vs. Public Rent Dividends. Fred Harrison et al. LC 99-171006. 278p. 1998. 40.00 (*1-901647-16-1*, Pub. by Othila Pr) Intl Spec Bk.

Losses of Nations: Deadweight Politics vs. Public Rent Dividends. Fred Harrison et al. LC 99-171006. 278p. 1998. pap. 20.00 (*1-901647-15-3*) Schalkenbach. DEADWEIGHT TAXES COST THE U.S. ECONOMY $1 TRILLION IN LOST OUTPUT & crush Britain's economy by more than $600 billion every year. Meanwhile, global trade war & depression loom, jobless people riot in France, Nazism rises again in Germany, & Asian prosperity evaporates. Economic analysis in THE LOSSES OF NATIONS traces this set of converging crises to a basic flaw in the governance of nations: the way in which nation-states finance themselves. TAXATION IN "DEVELOPED" COUNTRIES ABUSES WORKING PEOPLE, REWARDS LAND SPECULATION & FAVORS RECKLESS BANKING PRACTICES, which distorts the desire to save & invest, deprives millions of people of their right to work, & creates poverty & its attendant social problems. But politicians appear powerless to alter the flawed fiscal rules of the game, which are now also foisted upon former socialist countries. This is the crisis of governance that is alienating citizens from democratic politics. FORTUNATELY, THERE IS A VIABLE ALTERNATIVE WAY OF PUBLIC FINANCE that would increase & fairly distribute the wealth of nations. It is supported by the latest economic research, & presented by Ronald Banks, Mason Gaffney, Fred Harrison, Richard Noyes, Florenz Plassman, & Nicolaus Tideman, in THE LOSSES OF NATIONS. *Publisher Paid Annotation.*

Lossy Transmission Lines. Fred E. Gardiol. LC 87-3602. (Artech House Microwave Library). (Illus.). 396p. 1987. reprint ed. pap. 122.80 (*0-608-00564-9*, 206144700009) Bks Demand.

Lost. Mark Dunster. 12p. (Orig.). 1990. pap. 4.00 (*0-89642-187-2*) Linden Pubs.

Lost. Dennis B. Harris. Ed. by Kay Harris. (Illus.). 40p. (J). (gr. 1-4). 1996. 12.95 (*1-890022-00-4*) Lfestyle Min.

Lost. Paul B. Johnson & Celeste Lewis. LC 95-20846. (Illus.). 32p. (J). (ps-2). 1996. 15.95 (*0-531-09501-0*); lib. bdg. 16.99 (*0-531-08851-0*) Orchard Bks Watts.

Lost! David McPhail. (Illus.). 32p. (J). (gr. k-3). 1993. pap. 5.95 (*0-316-56336-6*, Joy St Bks) Little.

Lost. David M. McPhail. (J). 1990. 11.15 (*0-606-05916-4*, Pub. by Turtleback) Demco.

Lost. Helen R. Myers. 2000. per. 5.99 (*1-55166-572-7*, Mira Bks) Harlequin Bks.

Lost. John Peel. LC 98-113364. (Outer Limits Ser.: No. 4). 128p. (J). (gr. 3 up). 1997. mass mkt. 3.99 (*0-8125-9067-8*, Pub. by Tor Bks) St Martin.

Lost. John Peel. (Outer Limits Ser.). 1997. 9.09 (*0-606-13688-6*, Pub. by Turtleback) Demco.

Lost. Jessica Pierce. 1999. mass mkt. 3.50 (*0-8217-5056-9*) NAL.

Lost. Tott Publications Staff. 8p. (J). (gr. 1). 1988. pap. text 2.50 (*1-882225-10-4*) Tott Pubns.

***Lost!** Trimble. LC 99-50809. (Illus.). 20p. (ps-3). 2000. 10.95 (*0-15-202667-3*, Harcourt Child Bks) Harcourt.

***Lost!** Patti Trimble. LC 99-50809. (Illus.). 20p. (ps-3). 2000. pap. 3.95 (*0-15-202634-7*, Harcourt Child Bks) Harcourt.

***Lost.** Lucy Wadham. 320p. 2000. 24.95 (*0-7867-0785-2*, Pub. by Carroll & Graf) Publishers Group.

Lost, Vol. 1. David McPhail. (Illus.). (J). (ps-3). 1990. 14.95 (*0-316-56329-3*, Joy St Bks) Little.

Lost: A Novel. Hans-Ulrich Treichel. Tr. by Carol Brown Janeway from GER. LC 99-21533. 136p. 1999. 19.00 (*0-375-40627-1*) Pantheon.

Lost! A Ranger's Journal of Search & Rescue. Dwight McCarter & Ronald Schmidt. LC 97-73123. (Illus.). 180p. 1998. pap. 14.95 (*0-9641734-1-7*) Graphicom Pr.

***Lost! A Story in String.** Paul Fleischman. LC 99-27997. (Illus.). 32p. (ps-3). 1999. 15.95 (*0-8050-5583-5*) H Holt & Co.

***Lost a Job? Find a Life! Strategies for Charting a Successful Future after Losing a Job.** Regina McNamara. Ed. by Chris Amorosino. 70p. 1999. pap. 7.95 (*1-930311-01-X*) Kelsco.

Lost above the Timberline. Brock Cole. text. write for info. (*0-374-34660-7*) FS&G.

Lost Account of the Battle of Corinth & the Court Martial of General Van Dorn. Intro. by Monroe F. Cockrell. (Illus.). 88p. 1992. reprint ed. 25.00 (*0-916107-32-9*) Broadfoot.

Lost Acres Bride. Lynna Banning. 1998. per. 4.99 (*0-373-29037-3*, 1-29037-8) Harlequin Bks.

Lost Adulteries & Other Stories. William Davey. 174p. 1997. pap. 14.95 (*1-897722-39-7*, Pub. by Alyscamps Pr) Gotham.

Lost Adventures. Legend Staff. 1996. 22.50 (*1-880520-28-1*) Legend Enter.

Lost Agenda: Human Rights & U. N. Field Operations. Ed. by Human Rights Watch Staff. 184p. (Orig.). 1993. pap. 15.00 (*1-56432-103-7*) Hum Rts Watch.

Lost Airlines Liveries: Airline Color Schemes of the Past. John Morton. LC 97-118432. 112p. 1996. pap. text 21.95 (*0-7603-0258-8*) MBI Pubg.

Lost Allegory. Antony Oldknow. 35p. 1998. reprint ed. pap. text 5.00 (*1-881604-36-5*) Scopcraeft.

***Lost America.** Constance M. Greiff. 2001. 16.99 (*0-517-16268-7*) Crown Pub Group.

***Lost Americans.** Frank C. Hibben. (LC History-America-E). 196p. 1999. reprint ed. lib. bdg. 69.00 (*0-7812-4258-4*) Rprt Serv.

Lost & Buried Treasure of the Mississippi River. Netha Bell & Gary Scholl. Ed. by Bruce Carlson. (Illus.). 148p. (Orig.). 1991. pap. 9.95 (*1-878488-32-5*) Quixote Pr IA.

Lost & Buried Treasure of the Missouri River. Netha Bell. (Illus.). 172p. (Orig.). 1991. pap. 9.95 (*1-878488-57-0*) Quixote Pr IA.

Lost & Found see Word & Picture Books, Set 2: For Year C/A

Lost & Found see Perdida y Hallada

Lost & Found. (Illus.). 60p. (J). (gr. k-6). 1971. pap. text 8.99 (*1-55976-025-7*) CEF Press.

***Lost & Found.** (J). 2000. per. write for info. (*0-7434-0840-3*) PB.

Lost & Found. Judy Baer. (Cedar River Daydreams Ser.: No. 15). 144p. (Orig.). (J). (gr. 7-10). 1992. mass mkt. 4.99 (*1-55661-243-5*) Bethany Hse.

Lost & Found. Alyssa Satin Capucilli. 8p. (ps-1). pap. 6.95 (*0-694-01526-1*) HarpC.

***Lost & Found.** Jody Carr. 48p. 2000. mass mkt. write for info. (*0-06-101382-X*) HarpC.

***Lost & Found.** Janelle Cherrington. (Bear in the Big Blue House Shaped Board Bk.: Vol. 1). (Illus.). 16p. (ps-3). 2000. pap. 6.99 (*0-689-83222-2*, Simon Spot) Litle Simon.

***Lost & Found.** Cameron Dokey. (Enchanted Hearts Ser.). (Illus.). (J). 1999. 9.85 (*0-606-17965-8*) Turtleback.

Lost & Found. Jana Ellis. LC 89-36350. (Merivale Mall Ser.). 160p. (J). (gr. 7 up). 1989. pap. text 2.50 (*0-8167-1675-7*) Troll Communs.

Lost & Found. Beryl S. Glover. 163p. 1997. pap. 9.95 (*0-943487-49-8*) Sevgo Pr.

Lost & Found. Roberta Israeloff. 256p. 1997. per. 12.00 (*0-684-83344-1*) S&S Trade.

***Lost & Found.** Jayne Ann Krentz. 368p. 2000. 23.95 (*0-399-14669-5*) Putnam Pub Group.

Lost & Found. Jeff D. Marion. (Illus.). 64p. 1994. pap. 9.95 (*1-885912-02-1*) Sows Ear Pr.

Lost & Found. Caroline Moorehead. (Illus.). 336p. 1997. pap. 13.95 (*0-14-023950-2*) Penguin Putnam.

Lost & Found. Dallas Schulze. 1999. per. 4.50 (*0-373-83421-7*, 1-83421-7) Harlequin Bks.

Lost & Found. Mark Teague. LC 97-37357. (Illus.). 32p. (J). (ps-2). 1998. 15.95 (*0-590-84619-1*, Pub. by Scholastic) Scholastic Inc.

Lost & Found. Louise V. Tidd. LC 98-5575. (Real Kids Readers Ser.). (Illus.). 32p. (J). (gr. k-2). 1998. pap. 3.99 (*0-7613-2045-8*, Copper Beech Bks); lib. bdg. 16.90 (*0-7613-2020-2*, Copper Beech Bks) Millbrook Pr.

***Lost & Found.** Ed. by M. Jerry Weiss & Helen S. Weiss. LC 00-23538. 192p. (gr. 4-7). 2000. 19.95 (*0-312-87048-5*, Pub. by Forge NYC) St Martin.

Lost & Found. Joanna Wissinger. (Illus.). 144p. 1991. text 29.95 (*0-02-630590-9*) Macmillan.

Lost & Found. large type ed. Jim Lehrer. LC 91-13716. 249p. 1991. reprint ed. lib. bdg. 21.95 (*1-56054-180-6*) Thorndike Pr.

Lost & Found. 2nd ed. Wayne Holmes & Christine Pelletier. (Illus.). 90p. 1993. reprint ed. pap. text 25.00 (*1-58302-044-6*, BTU-06) One Way St.

Lost & Found: A Closer Look at Dying. Barbara Bernstein. 128p. (Orig.). 1994. pap. 9.95 (*0-87516-663-6*) DeVorss.

***Lost & Found: A Daughter's Tale of Violence & Redemption.** Babette Hughes. LC 99-57097. 168p. 2000. 22.00 (*1-57962-072-8*) Permanent Pr.

Lost & Found: A Kid's Book for Living through Loss. Marc Gellman & Thomas Hartman. LC 98-27779. (Illus.). 176p. (YA). (gr. 3-7). 1999. 15.00 (*0-688-15752-1*, Wm Morrow) Morrow Avon.

Lost & Found: A Musical Story Based on the Parables of the Lost Coin, the Lost Sheep, & the Prodigal Son: PreviewPak. Nylea L. Butler-Moore. 1996. pap. 6.00 incl. audio (*0-687-06514-3*) Abingdon.

Lost & Found: A Woman Revisits 8th Grade. Roberta Israeloff. 256p. 1996. 23.00 (*0-684-80081-0*) S&S Trade.

Lost & Found: Albany NY Area Church & Synagogue Vital Record Compendium. Diane S. Ptak. 30p. 1993. pap. 17.00 (*1-886905-03-7*) D S Ptak.

Lost & Found: Albany NY Area Church & Synagogue Vital Record Compendium, 1654-1925 - Supplement. Diane S. Ptak. LC 95-92177. (Illus.). 15p. (Orig.). 1995. pap. 11.00 (*1-886905-10-X*) D S Ptak.

Lost & Found: Christ's Teaching on Evangelism. Kenneth H. Good. 1990. pap. 4.99 (*0-85234-276-4*, Pub. by Evangelical Pr) P & R Pubng.

***Lost & Found: Critical Voices in New British Design.** Nick Barley & British Council Staff. LC 99-42385. 1999. write for info. (*0-8176-6095-X*) Birkhauser.

***Lost & Found: Critical Voices in New British Design.** British Council Staff. LC 99-42385. (Illus.). 128p. 1999. pap. 35.00 (*3-7643-6095-X*, Pub. by Birkhauser); pap. 35.00 (*3-7643-5998-6*, Pub. by Birkhauser); pap. 35.00 (*3-7643-6096-8*, Pub. by Birkhauser) Princeton Arch.

Lost & Found: Dogs, Cats & Everyday Heroes at a Country Animal Shelter. Elizabeth Hess. LC 97-51650. 240p. 1998. 24.00 (*0-15-100337-8*) Harcourt.

***Lost & Found: Dogs, Cats & Everyday Heroes at a Country Animal Shelter.** Elizabeth Hess. (Illus.). 240p. 2000. pap. 13.00 (*0-15-601288-X*) Harcourt.

Lost & Found: Finding the Extraordinary in the Ordinary. John A. Jenson. LC 98-23329. (Illus.). 144p. (J). 1998. 12.95 (*0-7868-6481-8*, Pub. by Hyperion) Time Warner.

Lost & Found: Impressions of an Ordinary Guy John A. Jenson. LC 98-151019. 139p. 1997. write for info. (*0-9661145-0-7*) Putt-Putt.

Lost & Found: Intro Pak. Nylea L. Butler-Moore. 1994. audio 29.95 (*0-687-22774-7*); audio 10.95 (*0-687-22775-5*) Abingdon.

Lost & Found: Intro Pak. Nylea L. Butler-Moore & Carol F. Krau. Ed. by Sandy Miller & Gary Smith. 1994. 19.95 (*0-687-22773-9*) Abingdon.

Lost & Found: Leader/Accompanist Edition. Nylea L. Butler-Moore. 1994. 14.95 (*0-687-22771-2*) Abingdon.

Lost & Found: Making & Remaking Working Partnerships with Parents of Children in the Care System. Ed. by Christine Harrison et al. LC 98-55930. 232p. 1999. pap. 34.95 (*1-85742-404-2*, Pub. by Ashgate Pub); text 69.95 (*1-85742-403-4*, Pub. by Ashgate Pub) Ashgate Pub Co.

***Lost & Found: Parables in Action.** Nancy I. Sanders. LC 99-58813. Vol. 1. (Illus.). 48p. (J). (ps-2). 2000. pap. text 4.99 (*0-570-07012-0*) Concordia.

Lost & Found: Singer's Edition. Nylea L. Butler-Moore. 1994. 2.95 (*0-687-22776-3*) Abingdon.

Lost & Found: The Adoption Experience. Betty J. Lifton. LC 87-45636. 320p. 1988. reprint ed. pap. 9.95 (*0-685-43848-1*, PL-7132, Perennial) HarperTrade.

Lost & Found, & Other Stories. Anne Marsella. LC 93-46128. 198p. (C). 1994. pap. 13.95 (*0-8147-5503-8*); text 25.00 (*0-8147-5502-X*) NYU Pr.

Lost & Found at Christmas. Caroline Grimshaw. 128p. 1999. pap. 5.95 (*1-902618-67-X*, Pub. by Onewrld Pubns) Penguin Putnam.

Lost & Found Bride. Modean Moon. (Desire Ser.: No. 1235). 1999. per. 3.75 (*0-373-76235-6*, 1-76235-5) Silhouette.

***Lost & Found Catholics: Voices of Vatican II.** Christopher M. Bellitto. (Illus.). 96p. 1999. pap. text 7.95 (*0-86716-312-7*, B3127) St Anthony Mess Pr.

Lost & Found Christmas. Judith Martin & Donald Ashwander. 14p. (J). (ps up). 1977. 5.00 (*0-87602-152-6*) Anchorage.

***Lost & Found Christmas: Rediscovering the True Spirit of Christmas.** John Jensen. 144p. 2000. 12.95 (*0-7868-6608-X*, Pub. by Hyperion) Time Warner.

Lost & Found Facilitator Manual. Vickie Kaczmarek. 14p. 1989. pap. text 14.95 (*1-882472-02-0*) Comm Grief Ctr.

***Lost & Found Groom.** Patricia McLinn. (Special Edition Ser.). 2000. mass mkt. 4.50 (*0-373-24344-8*, 1-24344-3) Silhouette.

Lost & Found in California: Four Decades of Assemblage Art. Contrib. by Sandra L. Starr. (Illus.). 119p. 1988. pap. 25.00 (*0-9620693-0-2*, Pub. by J Corcoran Gallery) RAM Publications.

***Lost & Found in the Land of Seduction.** Adam David. 2000. pap. 9.95 (*1-55279-026-6*) Picasso Publ.

Lost & Found Kit. (J). (gr. k-6). 1978. 19.99 (*1-55976-105-9*) CEF Press.

Lost & Found Lamb. Tracy Harrast. LC 98-206221. (Peek-a-Bible Ser.). (Illus.). 18p. (J). 1998. 6.99 (*0-310-97459-3*) Zondervan.

Lost & Found Lovers: Facts & Fantasies of Rekindled Romances. Nancy Kalish. 224p. 1997. 22.00 (*0-688-15181-7*, Wm Morrow) Morrow Avon.

***Lost & Found Mittens.** Robin Hansen. (Illus.). 128p. 2000. pap. 15.95 (*0-89272-457-9*) Down East.

Lost & Found: Poems, 1775-1982. Harry Guest. 126p. 1983. pap. 17.95 (*0-85646-089-3*, Pub. by Anvil Press) Dufour.

Lost & Found Puppy. Mary J. Flynn. (Illus.). 48p. (Orig.). (J). (gr. k-1). 1991. pap. 10.95 (*0-9623072-6-2*) S Ink WA.

Lost & Found Teen Manual. Vickie Kaczmarek. 7p. 1989. student ed. 8.95 (*1-882472-03-9*) Comm Grief Ctr.

Lost & Found Wallet. Mayer Bendet. 1997. 8.95 (*0-932351-37-9*) B P Marketing.

An Asterisk (*) at the beginning of an entry indicates that the title is appearing for the first time.

Lost & Old Rivers: Stories. Alan Cheuse. LC 98-25210. 224p. 1998. 19.95 (0-87074-432-1) SMU Press.

Lost & Saved. Caroline Sheridan Norton. LC 88-32738. 536p. 1989. 75.00 (0-8201-1434-0) Schol Facsimiles.

***Lost & Then Found: Turning Life's Disappointments into Hidden Treasures.** Trevor Griffiths. xii, 132p. 1999. reprint ed. pap. 12.99 (0-85364-966-9, Pub. by Paternoster Pub) OM Literature.

Lost & Won. Susan W. Petrie. 140p. 1990. 15.95 (0-945942-06-0); pap. 9.95 (0-945942-07-9) Portmanteau Editions.

Lost Angels. David J. Schow. Ed. by Arthur B. Cover & A. J. Krever. 1999. pap. 16.95 (1-893475-12-3) Alexander Pubg.

Lost Angels. Steve Toth. (Morning Coffee Chapbook Ser.). (Illus.). 19p. (Orig.). 1984. pap. 20.00 (0-915124-93-9) Coffee Hse.

***Lost Angels.** rev. ed. David J. Schow. 220p. 2000. pap. 17.95 (1-930235-06-2) Babbage.

Lost Angels: Psychoanalysis & Cinema. Vicky Lebeau. 168p. (C). 1994. pap. 22.99 (0-415-10721-0, B4795) Routledge.

Lost Angels: Tales of Los Angeles. Odie Hawkins. 208p. 1994. mass mkt. 3.95 (0-87067-735-7) Holloway.

Lost Anzacs: The Story of Two Brothers. Greg Kerr. (Illus.). 310p. 1998. reprint ed. pap. 27.95 (0-19-550663-4) OUP.

Lost Ark. Richard D. Gazowsky. (Orig.). (C). 1989. pap. 5.95 (0-317-93314-0) Voice Pentecost Pub.

Lost Arrow: And Other True Stories. Scott C. Davis. LC 94-92414. 64p. 1995. 19.95 (1-885942-75-3, 753); pap. 9.95 (1-885942-50-8, 508) Cune.

Lost Art of Church Fund Raising. Ashley Hale. 149p. 1993. 40.00 (0-944496-34-2) Precept Pr.

Lost Art of Declaring War. Brien Hallett. LC 98-8926. 232p. 1998. text 36.95 (0-252-02418-4); text 16.95 (0-252-06726-6) U of Ill Pr.

Lost Art of Disciple Making. Leroy Eims. 156p. (Orig.). 1978. mass mkt. 8.99 (0-310-37281-X, 9233P) Zondervan.

Lost Art of Forgiving: Stories of Healing from the Cancer of Bitterness. Johann Chistoph-Arnold. 149p. 1998. pap. text 13.00 (0-87486-950-1) Plough.

Lost Art of Healing. Agnes J. Galer. 74p. 1997. pap. 6.00 (0-89540-249-1, SB-249) Sun Pub.

Lost Art of Healing. Bernard Lown. LC R733.L684 1999. 344p. 1999. pap. 14.00 (0-345-42597-9) Ballantine Pub Grp.

Lost Art of Healing. Bernard Lown. LC 96-18184. 288p. 1996. 24.95 (0-395-82525-3) HM.

Lost Art of Intercession: Restoring the Power & Passion of the Watch of the Lord. Jim W. Goll. LC 98-132187. 182p. 1997. pap. 10.99 (1-56043-697-2, Revival Pr) Destiny Image.

Lost Art of Listening: How Learing to Listen Can Improve Relationships. Michael P. Nichols. LC 94-38111. (Family Therapy Ser.). 251p. 1995. lib. bdg. 32.95 (0-89862-267-0) Guilford Pubns.

Lost Art of Listening: How Learning to Listen Can Improve Relationships. Michael P. Nichols. LC 94-38111. (Guilford Family Therapy Ser.). 251p. 1996. pap. 15.95 (1-57230-131-7) Guilford Pubns.

Lost Art of Scratch Cooking: Recipes from the Kitchen of Natha Adkins Parker, 1. Robert Dederian. LC 97-94703. 1997. pap. 12.00 (0-9661872-0-2) C Parker.

***Lost Art of Tabby Redefined: Preserving Oglethorpe's Architectural Legacy.** Lauren B. Sickels-Taves & Michael S. Sheehan. (Illus.). v, 182p. 1999. pap. 21.95 (0-9675367-0-7) Architectural Cons Pr.

***Lost Art of the Great Speech: How to Write One - How to Deliver It.** Richard Dowis. LC 99-35742. 224p. 1999. pap. 14.95 (0-8144-7054-8) AMACOM.

Lost Art of War: The Recently Discovered Companion to the Bestselling "The Art of War" Sun Tzu, 2nd. Tr. by Thomas Cleary. LC 95-40157. 160p. 1997. pap. 12.00 (0-06-251405-9, Pub. by Harper SF) HarpC.

***Lost Arts: A Celebration of Culinary Traditions.** rev. ed. Lynn Alley. 176p. 2000. pap. 12.95 (1-58008-176-2) Ten Speed Pr.

Lost Artwork of Hollywood: Classic Images from Cinema's Golden Age. Fred E. Basten. (Illus.). 192p. 1996. 40.00 (0-8230-8345-4) Watsn-Guptill.

Lost Ashlar. Allen. 1952. pap. 1.00 (0-88053-017-0, M066) Macoy Pub.

Lost Aspect of Love. Tom Prinz & Reed Elliott. LC 98-60060. 144p. 1998. pap. 9.99 (1-57921-098-8, Pub. by WinePress Pub) BookWorld.

Lost at Birth: Saved by a Miracle. George E. Vandeman. Ed. by Glen Robinson. 46p. 1990. pap. 0.47 (0-8163-0929-9) Pacific Pr Pub Assn.

Lost at Sea. (Ready Readers Series II Stage II). (Illus.). 32p. (J). (gr. 1-3). 1996. pap. write for info. (1-56144-951-2, Honey Bear Bks) Modern Pub NYC.

***Lost at Sea.** Patrick Dillon. 288p. 2000. pap. 13.00 (0-684-86909-8, Touchstone) S&S Trade Pap.

Lost at Sea. A. A. Hoehling. LC 99-11922. 1999. pap. 12.95 (1-55853-744-9) Rutledge Hill Pr.

Lost at Sea, Vol. 1. Robert Parsons. 128p. 1991. reprint ed. pap. 9.95 (0-920021-96-4) Creative Bk Pub.

Lost at Sea, Vol. 2. Robert Parsons. 192p. 1995. reprint ed. pap. 9.95 (1-895387-09-4) Creative Bk Pub.

Lost at Sea: An American Tragedy. Patrick Dillon. LC 98-7013. 288p. 1998. 23.95 (0-385-31421-3, Dial Pr) Dell.

Lost at Sea: Ghost Ships & Other Mysteries. Michael Goss & George Behe. LC 94-20990. (Illus.). 359p. (C). 1994. 25.95 (0-87975-913-5) Prometheus Bks.

***Lost at Sea: Great Shipwrecks of History.** Ronald Pearsall. (Illus.). 1998. pap. 12.98 (1-880908-52-2) Todtri Prods.

Lost at Sea Leaders Manual. Pfeiffer. text 17.95 (0-88390-246-X) Jossey-Bass.

Lost at the White House: A 1909 Easter Story. Lisa Griest. LC 93-7945. (Carolrhoda On My Own Bks.). (Illus.). (J). (gr. k-3). 1993. lib. bdg. 18.60 (0-87614-726-0, Carolrhoda) Lerner Pub.

Lost at the White House: A 1909 Easter Story. Lisa Griest. (J). (gr. k-3). 1994. pap. 5.95 (0-87614-632-9, Carolrhoda) Lerner Pub.

***Lost Atlantis, & Other Ethnographic Studies.** Daniel Wilson. (LC History-America-E). 411p. 1999. reprint ed. lib. bdg. 99.00 (0-7812-4276-2) Rprt Serv.

***Lost Avenger.** Gene Machamer. LC 99-74432. (Illus.). 176p. 1999. pap. 9.00 (0-9627369-6-1) Carlisle Pr.

Lost Ballparks: A Celebration of Baseball's Legendary Fields. Lawrence S. Ritter. (Illus.). 224p. 1994. pap. 19.95 (0-14-023422-5) Studio Bks.

Lost Baltimore: A Portfolio of Vanished Buildings. Carleton Jones. (Maryland Paperback Bookshelf Ser.). (Illus.). 289p. 1997. reprint ed. pap. 15.95 (0-8018-5637-X) Johns Hopkins.

Lost Baltimore: A Portfolio of Vanished Buildings. Carlton Jones. LC 92-43452. (Illus.). 304p. (C). 1993. reprint ed. 40.00 (0-8018-4607-2) Johns Hopkins.

***Lost Band: A Novel.** Don Goldsmith. LC 99-56914. (Spanish Bit Ser.). 272p. 2000. 21.95 (0-8061-3226-4) U of Okla Pr.

Lost Bar Harbor. Ed. by G. W. Helfrich & Gladys O'Neil. LC 82-71103. (Illus.). 125p. 1982. pap. 9.95 (0-89272-142-1, PIC493) Down East.

***Lost Battalion.** Thomas M. Johnson & Fletcher Pratt. (Illus.). 352p. 2000. pap. 17.95 (0-8032-7613-3, Bison Books) U of Nebr Pr.

Lost Battalion. Orfalea. 1996. 24.95 (0-02-923455-7) Free Pr.

Lost Battalion. Gregory Orfalea. LC 96-43681. 448p. 1997. 27.00 (0-684-82804-9) Free Pr.

Lost Battalion: Controversy & Casualties in the Battle of Hue. Charles A. Krohn. LC 93-2867. 224p. 1993. 39.95 (0-275-94532-4, C4532, Praeger Pubs) Greenwood.

Lost Battalions: Going for Broke in the Vosges, Autumn, 1944. Franz Steidl. LC 96-54035. (Illus.). 256p. 1997. 21.95 (0-89141-622-6) Presidio Pr.

Lost Beatles Interviews. Geoffrey Giuliano. 400p. 1996. pap. 14.95 (0-452-27025-1, Plume) Dutton Plume.

Lost Beliefs of Northern Europe. Hilda E. Davidson. LC 92-40808. 240p. (C). (gr. 13). 1993. pap. 22.99 (0-415-04937-7) Routledge.

Lost Bellybutton. Margaret M. Gullette. LC 76-26377. (Illus.). 32p. (Orig.). (J). (ps-2). 1976. pap. 4.95 (0-914996-11-8) Lollipop Power.

Lost Beneath Manhattan. Sigmund Brouwer. (Accidental Detective Ser.: Vol. 1). 132p. (J). (gr. 3-7). 1994. pap. 5.99 (1-56476-370-6, 6-3370, Victor Bks) Chariot Victor.

***Lost Between Houses.** David Gilmour. 240p. 2000. pap. write for info. (0-679-31029-0) Random.

Lost Between the Cracks: Poems from the Neutral Zone. Compiled by Vicky Edmonds. 117p. 1996. pap. 12.00 (0-9639918-4-1) E All Above.

Lost Beyond Telling: Representations of Death & Absence in Modern French Poetry. Richard Stamelman. LC 90-55127. 264p. 1990. text 45.00 (0-8014-2408-9) Cornell U Pr.

***Lost Bird.** Margaret Coel. LC 99-22056. 304p. 1999. 21.95 (0-425-17059-4, Prime Crime) Berkley Pub.

***Lost Bird.** Margaret Coel. 304p. 2000. mass mkt. 6.50 (0-425-17030-6) Berkley Pub.

***Lost Bird.** large type ed. Margaret Coel. LC 99-59552. (Core Ser.). 332p. 2000. 28.95 (0-7838-8958-5, G K Hall Lrg Type) Mac Lib Ref.

Lost Bird of Wounded Knee: Spirit of the Lakota. Renee S. Flood. LC 97-34902. (Illus.). 392p. 1998. reprint ed. pap. 15.95 (0-306-80822-6) Da Capo.

Lost Birds of Paradise. Errol Fuller. (Illus.). 160p. 1996. 57.95 (1-85310-566-X, Pub. by Swan Hill Pr) Voyageur Pr.

Lost Body. Aime Cesaire. Tr. by Clayton Eshleman & Annette Smith from FRE. LC 86-1001. (Illus.). 132p. 1986. pap. 14.95 (0-8076-1148-4) Braziller.

Lost Body. Aime Cesaire. Tr. by Clayton Eshleman & Annette Smith from FRE. LC 86-1001. (Illus.). 132p. 1986. 25.00 (0-8076-1147-6, Pub. by Braziller) Norton.

Lost Body. Terry Ehret. LC 93-801. (National Poetry Ser.). 80p. 1993. pap. 11.00 (1-55659-057-1) Copper Canyon.

***Lost Bonanzas of Western Canada, Vol. 2.** (Illus.). 144p. 1999. reprint ed. pap. 14.95 (1-895811-86-4) Heritage Hse.

Lost Book of Paradise: Adam & Eve in the Garden of Eden. David Rosenberg. 192p. (J). 1995. pap. 12.45 (0-7868-8073-2, Pub. by Hyperion) Time Warner.

Lost Books of Africa Rediscovered - We Charge Genocide. Khalid A. Al-Mansour. (Illus.). 976p. (Orig.). (C). 1995. pap. 29.95 (1-883136-15-6) First Afr Arabian.

Lost Books of Merlyn: Druid Magic from the Age of Arthur. Douglas Monroe. LC 98-20787. (Illus.). 480p. 1998. pap. 14.95 (1-56718-471-5) Llewellyn Pubns.

Lost Books of the Bible. Frwd. by Solomen J. Schepps. (Illus.). 320p. 1988. 8.99 (0-517-27795-6) Random Hse Value.

Lost Books of the Bible: Being All the Gospels, Epistles, & Other Pieces Now Extant Attributed in the First Four Centuries to Jesus Christ, His Apostles & Their Companions. (Illus.). 350p. 1996. reprint ed. pap. 27.95 (1-56459-635-4) Kessinger Pub.

Lost Books of the Bible & the Forgotten Books of Eden. 658p. 12.99 (0-529-03385-2, 105OC); pap. 9.99 (0-529-02061-0, M312) World Publng.

Lost Books of the Bible & the Forgotten Books of Eden. Intro. by Frank Crane. LC 98-18468. 269p. 1994. pap. text 11.95 (1-881316-63-7) A&B Bks.

Lost Books of the Bible & the Forgotten Books of Eden. Rutherford Hayes Platt & J. Alden Brett. 1974. pap. 17.95 (0-452-00944-8) NAL.

Lost Borders. Mary H. Austin. (Collected Works of Mary Hunter Austin). 208p. 1998. reprint ed. lib. bdg. 88.00 (1-58201-523-6); reprint ed. lib. bdg. 88.00 (1-58201-522-8) Classic Bks.

***Lost Boston.** Jane Holtz Kay. LC 99-40639. 352p. 1999. pap. 25.00 (0-395-96610-8) HM.

***Lost Boy.** Noel Hynd. 1999. mass mkt. 5.99 (0-7860-1014-2, Pinncle Kensgtn) Kensgtn Pub Corp.

Lost Boy. New International Version of The Bible Staff. (Stories from the Great Book Ser.). (Illus.). (Orig.). (J). 1986. pap. 4.95 (0-918789-07-9) FreeMan Prods.

***Lost Boy.** Hans-Ulrich Treichel. (International Ser.). 2000. pap. 11.00 (0-375-70622-4) Vin Bks.

Lost Boy: A Foster Child's Search for the Love of a Family. Dave Pelzer. LC 97-17614. 250p. 1997. pap. 10.95 (1-55874-515-7) Health Comm.

Lost Boy: A Foster Child's Search for the Love of a Family, 3 Vols., Vol. 2. Dave Pelzer. LC 94-66665. 190p. 1994. pap. text 10.00 (0-929099-03-6) Omaha Pr Pub.

Lost Boy: A Novella. Thomas Wolfe. LC 92-53704. (Chapel Hill Bks.). (Illus.). xiv, 82p. (C). 1992. 24.95 (0-8078-2063-6) U of NC Pr.

Lost Boy: A Novella. Thomas Wolfe. Ed. by James W. Clark, Jr. LC 92-53704. (Chapel Hill Bks.). (Illus.). 95p. (C). 1994. pap. 11.95 (0-8078-4486-1) U of NC Pr.

Lost Boy & Other Stories. Emil Draitser. (RUS.). (Orig.). 1993. pap. 9.95 (5-239-01632-1) Maxims Bk NJ.

Lost Boy & the Monster. Craig K. Strete. LC 98-17333. (J). (ps-3). 1999. 15.95 (0-399-22922-1, G P Putnam) Peng Put Young Read.

***Lost Boys.** Willem Van der Walt. LC 99-194201. 1998. write for info. (0-19-571518-7) OUP.

Lost Boys: A Novel. Orson Scott Card. 544p. 1993. mass mkt. 6.99 (0-06-109131-6, Harp PBks) HarpC.

Lost Boys: Reflections on Psychoanalysis & Countertransference. Frederick Berenstein. 120p. (C). 1995. 20.00 (0-393-70188-3) Norton.

***Lost Boys: Why Our Sons Turn Violent & How We Can Save Them.** James Garbarino. LC 99-19897. 288p. 1999. 25.00 (0-684-85908-4) Free Pr.

***Lost Boys: Why Our Sons Turn Violet & How We Can Save Them.** James Garbarino. 288p. 2000. pap. 13.00 (0-385-49932-9, Anchor NY) Doubleday.

Lost Boys of Natinga: A School for Sudan's Young Refugees. Judy Walgren. LC 97-32210. 48p. (J). (gr. 3-7). 1998. 16.00 (0-395-70558-4) HM.

Lost Breeches: A Tale of Adventure, True Love- & Discipline! Louise Malatesta. (Illus.). 144p. 39.95 (1-899861-15-7, Pub. by AKS Bks) Xclusiv Distrib.

Lost Bride. Marianne Willman. 352p. 1998. mass mkt. 5.99 (0-312-96624-5) St Martin.

Lost Bride of Kildrummond. Lois Stewart. 1991. mass mkt. 3.95 (0-8217-3516-0, Zebra Kensgtn) Kensgtn Pub Corp.

Lost Broadway Theatres. 2nd rev. ed. Nicholas Van Hoogstraten. LC 97-23412. (Illus.). 288p. (Orig.). 1997. pap. 24.95 (1-56898-116-3) Princeton Arch.

Lost Brother. Rick Bennet. LC 96-32789. 240p. 1996. 21.45 (1-55970-367-9, Pub. by Arcade Pub Inc) Time Warner.

***Lost Burgundy.** Mary Gentle. (Book of Ash Ser.: 4). 464p. 2000. mass mkt. 6.50 (0-380-81114-6, Avon Bks) Morrow Avon.

Lost Campers. rev. ed. Paul Hutchens. (Sugar Creek Gang Ser.: No. 4). 128p. (J). mass mkt. 4.99 (0-8024-7008-4, 659) Moody.

Lost Car. Gilbert V. Beers. LC 94-239890. (Muffin Family Ser.). (Illus.). 32p. (Orig.). (J). 1994. pap. 3.50 (1-56476-314-5, 6-3314, Victor Bks) Chariot Victor.

Lost Cat. Tad Hardy. LC 94-23974. (Illus.). 32p. (J). (ps-2). 1996. 14.95 (0-395-73574-2) HM.

Lost Cause. Richard Greensted. 320p. 1997. pap. 11.95 (0-7472-5173-8, Pub. by Headline Bk Pub) Trafalgar.

Lost Cause. Edward A. Pollard. LC 74-117888. (Select Bibliographies Reprint Ser.). 1977. 60.95 (0-8369-5341-X) Ayer.

Lost Cause: Bill Clinton's Campaign for National Health Insurance. Nicholas Laham. LC 96-2197. 272p. 1996. 65.00 (0-275-95611-3, Praeger Pubs) Greenwood.

Lost Cause: John Wesley Hardin, the Taylor-Sutton Feud, & Reconstruction Texas. Jack Jackson. LC 98-7245. 150p. 1998. 29.95 (0-87816-619-X); pap. 16.95 (0-87816-618-1) Kitchen Sink.

Lost Cause: John Wesley Hardin, the Taylor-Sutton Feud & Reconstruction Texas. Jack Jackson. 150p. 1998. 24.95 (0-87816-623-8) Kitchen Sink.

Lost Cause: The Confederate Exodus to Mexico. Andrew Rolle. LC 65-11228. (Illus.). 272p. 1992. pap. 14.95 (0-8061-1961-6) U of Okla Pr.

Lost Cause of Rhetoric: The Relation of Rhetoric & Geometry in Aristotle & Lacan. David Metzger. LC 93-38231. 135p. (C). 1994. 31.95 (0-8093-1855-5) S Ill U Pr.

Lost Cause Regained. Edward A. Pollard. LC 78-117889. (Select Bibliographies Reprint Ser.). 1977. 20.95 (0-8369-5342-8) Ayer.

Lost Cause Regained. Edward A. Pollard. LC 70-174279. reprint ed. 27.50 (0-404-00097-5) AMS Pr.

Lost Causes: The Romantic Attraction of Defeated Yet Unvanquished Men & Movements. George Grant & Karen Grant. LC 99-27143. 224p. 1999. pap. 12.95 (1-58182-016-X) Cumberland Hse.

Lost Caves of St. Louis. Herbert Rother & Charlotte Rother. Ed. by Zellie Dunn. (Illus.). 144p. (Orig.). 1996. pap. 9.95 (0-9631448-7-1) VA Pub Corp.

***Lost Ceilings.** Janet Hamill. Ed. by Maureen Owen. LC 98-74413. 72p. 1999. pap. 7.95 (0-916382-35-4, Pub. by Telephone Bks) SPD-Small Pr Dist.

Lost Cement Mine. rev. ed. James W. Wright. Ed. by Richard E. Lingenfelter & Genny Smith. LC 84-7991. Orig. Title: The Cement Hunters. (Illus.). 120p. 1984. reprint ed. pap. 5.95 (0-931378-09-5) Live Oak.

Lost Center & Other Essays in Greek Poetry. Zissimos Lorenzatos. Tr. by Kay Cicellis. LC 79-3221. (Princeton Essays in Literature Ser.). 211p. reprint ed. pap. 65.50 (0-8357-4283-0, 203708200007) Bks Demand.

Lost Champion. Lawrence Wertan. LC 96-85021. 155p. (Orig.). (J). (gr. 5-12). 1996. pap. 15.00 (0-9653624-0-X) Boxer Books.

Lost Chapter of Acts of the Apostles. E. Raymond Capt. 32p. 1982. pap. 4.00 (0-934666-09-1) Artisan Pubs.

***Lost Chicago.** David Garrard Lowe. (Illus.). 272p. 2000. pap. 29.95 (0-8230-2871-2) Watsn-Guptill.

Lost Child: A Folk Tale. J. Janda. LC 97-26240. (Illus.). (J). (ps-5). 1999. pap. 6.95 (0-8091-6646-1) Paulist Pr.

Lost Child: Hope for Kids Without Hope. Tom Collins. 128p. 1992. pap. 9.95 (0-925190-52-7) Fairview Press.

Lost Child & Other Stories. Ed. by Lissa Gars. (Illus.). 80p. (J). (gr. 4-9). 1993. pap. 9.95 (1-882427-02-5) Aspasia Inc.

Lost Childhood. Yehuda Nir. 256p. 1989. 19.95 (0-15-158862-7) Harcourt.

***Lost Childhood: A World War II Memoir.** Yehuda Nir. LC 99-87444. (Illus.). 240p. (YA). (gr. 7 up). 2000. 15.95 (0-439-16389-7) Scholastic Inc.

***Lost Childhood: A World War II Memoir of a Jewish Boy.** Yehuda Nir. LC 99-87444. (Illus.). (J). 2000. pap. write for info. (0-439-16390-0) Scholastic Inc.

Lost Childhoods: The Plight of the Parentified Child. Gregory J. Jurkovic. LC 96-54241. xx, 252p. 1997. 34.95 (0-87630-825-6) Brunner-Mazel.

***Lost Children.** 1999. pap. 6.95 (1-881545-97-0) Angelas Bkshelf.

Lost Children. Barbara Crooker. 48p. (Orig.). 1989. pap. 17.00 (0-940592-23-1) Heyeck Pr.

Lost Children. Paul Goble. (Illus.). 40p. (J). 1998. per. 5.99 (0-689-81999-4) S&S Childrens.

***Lost Children.** Paul Goble. 1998. 11.19 (0-606-13582-0, Pub. by Turtleback) Demco.

Lost Children. Ed. by Brett Rutherford. 1988. 4.50 (0-318-64155-0) Poets Pr.

Lost Children: The Boys Who Were Neglected. Paul Goble. LC 91-44283. (Illus.). 40p. (J). (ps-12). 1993. text 14.95 (0-02-736555-7, Bradbury S&S) S&S Childrens.

***Lost Chord.** Jonathan Goldman. LC 99-93966. 208p. 1999. pap. 13.95 (0-9648776-1-9, Pub. by Spirit Music) New Leaf Dist.

Lost Chord: Essays on Victorian Music. Ed. by Nicholas Temperley. LC 88-45456. (Illus.). 192p. 1989. 15.95 (0-253-33518-3) Ind U Pr.

Lost Chord: Reaching the Person with Dementia Through the Power of Music. Melanie Chavin. 95p. (Orig.). 1991. pap. text 17.95 (1-879633-08-6) Eldersong.

Lost Chords: White Musicians & Their Contribution to Jazz. Richard M. Sudhalter. LC 97-42470. (Illus.). 912p. 1999. 35.00 (0-19-505585-3) OUP.

Lost Christianity: A Journey of Rediscovery to the Center of Christian Experience. 2nd ed. Jacob Needleman. (Classic Edition Ser.). 238p. 1993. pap. 15.95 (1-85230-132-5, Pub. by Element MA) Penguin Putnam.

Lost Chronicles of Love. Jonnie Dukes. 64p. (Orig.). 1997. pap. 6.95 (0-9641606-2-5) Easy Break.

Lost Chronicles of Terra Firma. Rosario Aguilar. Tr. by Edward W. Hood. LC 97-189499. 186p. (Orig.). 1998. pap. 13.00 (1-877727-62-8) White Pine.

***Lost Chronicles of the Maya Kings.** David Drew. 384p. 2000. 29.95 (0-520-22612-7, Pub. by U CA Pr) Cal Prin Full Svc.

Lost Cities. Joyce Goldenstern. LC 94-47099. (Weird & Wacky Science Ser.). 48p. (J). (gr. 4-10). 1996. lib. bdg. 18.95 (0-89490-615-1) Enslow Pubs.

Lost Cities: 50 Discoveries in World Archaeology. Ed. by Paul Bahn. (Illus.). 216p. 1999. pap. 24.95 (1-56649-002-2) Welcome Rain.

Lost Cities & Ancient Mysteries of Africa & Arabia. David Hatcher Childress. (Lost Cities Ser.: Bk. 4). (Illus.). 400p. (Orig.). 1987. pap. 14.95 (0-932813-06-2) Adventures Unltd.

Lost Cities & Ancient Mysteries of South America. David Hatcher Childress. (Lost Cities Ser.: Bk. 3). (Illus.). 400p. (Orig.). 1986. pap. 14.95 (0-932813-02-X) Adventures Unltd.

Lost Cities & Sunken Lands. Nigel Pennick. 1997. pap. 22.95 (1-898307-83-0, Pub. by Capall Bann Pubng) Holmes Pub.

Lost Cities of Africa. rev. ed. Basil Risbridger Davidson. 366p. 1988. pap. 16.95 (0-316-17431-9) Little.

Lost Cities of Ancient Lemuria & the Pacific. David Hatcher Childress. (Lost Cities Ser.). (Illus.). 400p. (Orig.). 1987. pap. 14.95 (0-932813-04-6) Adventures Unltd.

Lost Cities of Atlantis, Ancient Europe & the Mediterranean. David Hatcher Childress. (Lost Cities Ser.). 488p. 1995. pap. 16.95 (0-932813-25-9) Adventures Unltd.

Lost Cities of China, Central Asia & India. 2nd rev. ed. David Hatcher Childress. (Lost Cities Ser.). (Illus.). 400p. 1987. pap. 14.95 (0-932813-07-0) Adventures Unltd.

Lost Cities of Cibola. Richard G. Petersen. 292p. 1980. 5.95 (0-8199-0790-1, Frncscn Herld) Franciscan Pr.

Lost Cities of North & Central America. David Hatcher Childress. (Lost Cities Ser.). (Illus.). 400p. (Orig.). 1992. pap. 14.95 (0-932813-09-7) Adventures Unltd.

Lost Cities of the Ancient Southeast. Mallory M. O'Connor. LC 94-39265. (Illus.). 192p. 1995. 49.95 (0-8130-1350-X) U Press Fla.

Lost Cities of the Maya. Claude-Francois Baudez & Sydney Picasso. (Discoveries Ser.). (Illus.). 176p. 1992. pap. 12.95 (0-8109-2841-8, Pub. by Abrams) Time Warner.

***Lost Cities of the Mayas: The Life, Art & Discoveries of Frederick Catherwood.** Fabio Bourbon. LC 99-38982. (Illus.). 200p. (J). 2000. 35.00 (*0-7892-0623-4*, Abbeville Kids) Abbeville Pr.

Lost City. Scott Ciencin. LC 94-44454. (Dinotopia Ser.). (YA). (gr. 5-8). 1996. pap. 3.99 (*0-679-86983-2*, Pub. by Random Bks Yng Read) Random.

Lost City. Scott Ciencin. (Dinotopia Ser.). (YA). (gr. 5-8). 1996. 9.09 (*0-606-08564-5*, Pub. by Turtleback) Demco.

***Lost City.** Chuck Harman. 2000. pap. text 6.95 (*1-891736-10-8*) Studio Five.

LOST CITY PB. Alan Ehrenhalt. 320p. 1996. pap. 15.00 (*0-465-04193-0*) HarpC.

Lost City of Dunwich. N. Comfort. 1994. 50.00 (*0-86138-086-X*, Pub. by T Dalton) St Mut.

Lost City of Fruitvale. William P. Hansen. LC 89-52155. 120p. 1989. 34.95 (*0-938021-80-X*) Turner Pub KY.

***Lost City of Pompeii.** Dorothy Hinshaw Patent. LC 99-34980. (Frozen in Time Ser.). (J). (gr. 4-7). 2000. 27.07 (*0-7614-0785-5*, Benchmark NY) Marshall Cavendish.

Lost City of the Incas. Hiram Bingham. LC 81-7196. (Illus.). 263p. 1981. reprint ed. lib. bdg. 69.75 (*0-313-22950-3*, BILC, Greenwood Pr) Greenwood.

***Lost City of the Incas.** 2nd unabridged ed. Hiram Bingham. LC 99-26171. (Illus.). 288p. 2000. reprint ed. pap. 15.95 (*0-9613602-1-6*) Triune Bks.

Lost City of the Jedi. Paul Davids. (Star Wars: No. 2). (YA). (gr. 4 up). 1992. 9.09 (*0-606-00543-9*, Pub. by Turtleback) Demco.

Lost City of the Jedi. Paul Davids & Hollace Davids. LC 92-668025. (Star Wars: No. 2). 128p. (YA). (gr. 4-7). 1992. pap. 4.50 (*0-553-15888-0*, Starfire BDD) BDD Bks Young Read.

Lost City of the Jedi see Star Wars

***Lost City of the Jedi.** Paul Davids & Hollace Davids. (Star Wars: No. 2). (Illus.). 94p. (YA). (gr. 4 up). 1999. reprint ed. pap. text 10.00 (*0-7881-6480-5*) DIANE Pub.

***Lost Civilization of Petra.** Udi Levy. 2000. 45.00 (*0-86315-298-8*) Floris Bks.

Lost Civilizations. Leonard Cottrell. LC 73-15299. (International Library Ser.). 128 p. 1974. write for info. (*0-531-02119-X*) Watts.

Lost Civilizations. Anne Millard. LC 96-20486. (Mysteries of...Ser.). (Illus.). 40p. (J). (gr. 4-6). 1996. lib. bdg. 22.90 (*0-7613-0534-3*, Copper Beech Bks) Millbrook Pr.

Lost Civilizations of the Stone Age. Richard Rudgley. LC 98-37079. 320p. 1998. 26.00 (*0-684-85580-1*) S&S Trade.

***Lost Civilizations of the Stone Age.** Richard Rudgley. 320p. 2000. per. 15.00 (*0-684-86270-0*) S&S Trade.

Lost Civilizations Series, 24 bks. Incl. Africa's Glorious Legacy. Ed. by Dale Brown. LC 94-916. (Illus.). 168p. (gr. 11). 1999. 29.95 (*0-8094-9025-0*); Anatolica: Cauldron of Cultures. Dale Brown. LC 95-20268. (Illus.). 168p. (gr. 11). 1999. 29.95 (*0-8094-9108-7*); Ancient India: Land of Mystery. Ed. by Dale Brown. LC 94-29622. (Illus.). 168p. (gr. 11). 1999. 29.95 (*0-8094-9037-4*); Aztecs: Reign of Blood & Splendor. Ed. by Dale Brown. (Illus.). 168p. (gr. 11). 1999. 29.95 (*0-8094-9854-5*); Celts: Europe's People of Iron. Ed. by Dale Brown. (Illus.). 168p. (gr. 11). 1999. 29.95 (*0-8094-9029-3*); China's Buried Kingdoms. Time-Life Books Editors. LC 93-15068. (Illus.). 168p. (gr. 11). 1999. 29.95 (*0-8094-9891-X*); Early Europe: Mysteries in Stone. Time-Life Books Editors. LC 94-46002. (Illus.). 168p. (gr. 11). 1999. 29.95 (*0-8094-9100-1*); Egypt: Land of the Pharaohs. Ed. by Dale Brown. LC 91-36255. (Illus.). 168p. (gr. 11). 1999. 29.95 (*0-8094-9850-2*); Etruscans: Italy's Lovers of Life. Time-Life Books Editors. Ed. by Dale Brown. LC 94-43686. (Illus.). 168p. (gr. 11). 1999. 29.95 (*0-8094-9045-5*); Greece: Temples, Tombs, & Treasures. Ed. by Dale Brown. LC 93-43570. (Illus.). 168p. (gr. 11). 2000. 29.95 (*0-8094-9020-X*); Holy Land. Ed. by Dale Brown. (Illus.). 168p. (gr. 4-7). 1999. 29.95 (*0-8094-9866-9*); Incas: Lords of Gold & Glory. Ed. by Dale Brown. (Illus.). 168p. (gr. 4-7). 1999. 29.95 (*0-8094-9870-7*); Magnificent Maya. Ed. by Dale Brown. LC 92-39965. (Illus.). 168p. (gr. 4-7). 1999. 29.95 (*0-8094-9879-0*); Mesopotamia: The Mighty Kings. Ed. by Dale Brown. LC 94-24305. (Illus.). 168p. (gr. 11). 1999. 29.95 (*0-8094-9041-2*); Mound Builders & Cliff Dwellers. Time-Life Books Editors. Ed. by Dale Brown. LC 92-18534. (Illus.). 168p. (gr. 4-7). 1999. 29.95 (*0-8094-9858-8*); Persians: Masters of Empire. Time-Life Books Editors. LC 95-13943. (Illus.). 168p. (gr. 11). 1999. 29.95 (*0-8094-9104-4*); Pompeii: The Vanished City. Ed. by Dale Brown. (Illus.). 168p. (gr. 11). 1999. 29.95 (*0-8094-9862-6*); Ramses II: Magnificence on the Nile. Ed. by Dale Brown. LC 93-26270. (Illus.). 168p. (gr. 11). 1999. 29.95 (*0-8094-9012-9*); Rome: Echoes of Imperial Glory. Ed. by Dale Brown. LC 93-37766. (Illus.). 168p. (gr. 11). 1999. 29.95 (*0-8094-9016-1*); Search for El Dorado. Ed. by Dale Brown. LC 94-17846. (Illus.). 168p. (gr. 11). 1999. 29.95 (*0-8094-9033-1*); Southeast Asia: A Past Regained. Time-Life Books Editors. Ed. by Dale Brown. LC 95-34501. (Illus.). 168p. (gr. 11). 1999. 29.95 (*0-8094-9112-5*); Sumer: Cities of Eden. Ed. by Dale Brown. LC 92-38367. (Illus.). 168p. (gr. 11). 1999. 29.95 (*0-8094-9887-1*); Vikings: Raiders from the North. Ed. by Dale Brown. LC 93-14028. (Illus.). 168p. (gr. 11). 1999. 29.95 (*0-8094-9895-2*); Wondrous Realms of the Aegean. Time-Life Books Editors. Ed. by Dale Brown. LC 92-29449. (Illus.). 168p. (gr. 4-7). 1999. 29.95 (*0-8094-9875-8*); 359.10 (*0-8094-9149-4*) Time-Life.

***Lost Classics.** Michael Ondaatje. 2000. write for info. (*0-676-97299-3*, Pub. by Knopf) Random House.

Lost Classics. Robert Ruark. 1996. 35.00 (*1-57157-022-5*) Safari Pr.

Lost Coast. Benjamin Green. 24p. 1989. pap. 4.00 (*0-945251-03-3*) Great Elm.

Lost Coast. Nightingale Staff. LC 97-11288. 1997. pap. 11.95 (*0-312-15572-7*) St Martin.

***Lost Coast: A Moses Wine Mystery.** Roger L. Simon. 256p. 2000. reprint ed. per. 14.00 (*0-671-03904-0*, Pub. by ibooks) S&S Trade.

Lost Colonists: Their Fortune & Probable Fate. David B. Quinn. (America's 400th Anniversary Ser.). (Illus.). xviii, 53p. 1999. reprint ed. pap. 8.00 (*0-86526-204-7*) NC Archives.

Lost Colony. T. V. Olsen. LC 99-35658. (Westerns Ser.). 250p. 1999. 19.95 (*0-7862-1582-8*) Five Star.

Lost Colony. large type ed. T. V. Olsen. 275p. 2000. 30.00 (*0-7862-1588-7*) Thorndike Pr.

Lost Colony: A Martian Adventure. Michael McMurtrie. iii, 444p. 1998. pap. 20.00 (*0-9662885-0-5*) MERC Frontiers.

Lost Colony Activity Book. Carole Marsh Longmeyer. (Lost Colony Collection). (Illus.). (Orig.). (J). (gr. 3 up). 1994. pap. 19.95 (*0-935326-41-3*) Gallopade Intl.

Lost Colony Classroom Gamebook. Carole Marsh. (Carole Marsh Bks.). (Illus.). (Orig.). (J). (gr. 3-12). 1994. pap. 19.95 (*0-935326-86-3*) Gallopade Intl.

Lost Colony of Roanoke: Opposing Viewpoints. Thomas Schouweiler. LC 91-15188. (Great Mysteries Ser.). (Illus.). 80p. (J). (gr. 5-8). 1991. lib. bdg. 22.45 (*0-89908-093-6*) Greenhaven.

***Lost Colony of the Confederacy.** Eugene C. Harter. LC 00-37803. (Military History Ser.: Vol. 69). (Illus.). 160p. 2000. pap. 15.95 (*1-58544-102-3*) Tex A&M Univ Pr.

Lost Colony Storybook. Carole M. Longmeyer. (Lost Colony Collection). (Illus.). (J). (gr. 4 up). 1994. pap. 19.95 (*0-935326-38-3*) Gallopade Intl.

***Lost Columns of Ann Wells, 5 vols., Set.** unabridged ed. Incl. Vol. I. Lost Columns of Ann Wells. Ann Wells. Ed. by G. E. Reeves. 100p. 1999. pap. 24.95 (*0-9676285-1-2*); Vol. II. Lost Columns of Ann Wells. Ann Wells. Ed. by G. E. Reeves. (Illus.). 200p. 1999. pap. 24.95 (*0-9676285-0-4*); Vol. III. Lost Columns of Ann Wells. Ann Wells. Ed. by G. E. Reeves. 115p. 1999. pap. 24.95 (*0-9676285-2-0*); Vol. IV. Lost Columns of Ann Wells. Ann Wells. Ed. by G. E. Reeves. 105p. 1999. pap. 24.95 (*0-9676285-3-9*); Vol. V. 105p. 1999. pap. 24.95 (*0-9676285-4-7*); (Illus.). 1999. Set pap. 124.95 (*0-9676285-5-5*) GER Pubng.

Lost Columns of Ann Wells see Lost Columns of Ann Wells

Lost Comrades: Socialists of the Front Generation, 1918-1945. Dan S. White. (Illus.). 272p. 1992. 44.50 (*0-674-53924-9*) HUP.

Lost Conquistador Mine. David Cook. 1982. 5.50 (*0-394-52594-9*) Random.

***Lost Consonants.** Graham Rawle. 2000. pap. 13.95 (*1-872180-09-4*, Pub. by Fourth Estate) Trafalgar.

***Lost Consonants VI.** Graham Rawle. 2000. pap. 13.95 (*1-85702-563-6*, Pub. by Fourth Estate) Trafalgar.

***Lost Consonants VII.** Graham Rawle. 2000. pap. 13.95 (*1-85702-775-2*, Pub. by Fourth Estate) Trafalgar.

Lost Continent. Cutcliffe Hyne. 1974. 10.00 (*1-880418-09-6*) D M Grant.

Lost Continent. Cutcliffe Hyne. 368p. 1996. reprint ed. spiral bd. 21.50 (*0-7873-1272-X*) Hlth Research.

Lost Continent: Travels in Small Town America. Bill Bryson. LC 89-45027. 320p. 1990. reprint ed. pap. 13.50 (*0-06-092008-4*, Perennial) HarperTrade.

Lost Continent of Mu. James Churchward. 1991. lib. bdg. 300.00 (*0-8490-4801-X*) Gordon Pr.

Lost Continent of Mu. James Churchwood. write for info. (*0-85435-293-7*, Pub. by C W Daniel) Natl Bk Netwk.

Lost Continent of Mu. James Churchward. (Illus.). 335p. 1998. reprint ed. pap. 21.95 (*0-914732-19-6*) Bro Life Inc.

Lost Continent: or Slavery & the Slave Trade in Africa. Joseph Cooper. 130p. 1968. reprint ed. 49.50 (*0-7146-1890-X*, BHA-01890, Pub. by F Cass Pubs) Intl Spec Bk.

Lost Continents: The Atlantis Theme in History, Science & Literature. L. Sprague De Camp. (Illus.). 348p. 1970. reprint ed. pap. 9.95 (*0-486-22668-9*) Dover.

Lost Continents & the Hollow Earth: I Remember Lemuria & the Shaver Mystery. David Hatcher Childress & Richard Shaver. (Illus.). 280p. 1998. pap. 16.95 (*0-932813-63-1*) Adventures Unltd.

Lost Copper. Wendy Rose. LC 80-81849. 1992. pap. 10.00 (*0-939046-35-0*) Malki Mus Pr.

Lost Country. Dan Howell. LC 93-20045. 96p. 1993. pap. 10.95 (*0-87023-851-5*); lib. bdg. 20.00 (*0-87023-850-7*) U of Mass Pr.

Lost Country: Mongolia Revealed. Jasper Becker. (Illus.). 325p. 1992. lib. bdg. 35.00 (*0-340-55665-X*, Pub. by Hodder & Stought Ltd) Lubrecht & Cramer.

Lost Cove of Desiter. Timothy G. Saxe. LC 97-90880. 1998. pap. 8.95 (*0-533-12504-9*) Vantage.

Lost Covenant. Joan M. Sckrabulis. (Illus.). 90p. (Orig.). 1997. pap. 14.95 (*0-9657529-0-9*) Eclipse Prodns.

Lost Cowboy Ghost. James Buckley, Jr. (Nfl Adventures Ser.). 1996. 9.09 (*0-606-10893-9*, Pub. by Turtleback) Demco.

Lost Crops of Africa Vol. I: Grains. Ed. by F. R. Ruskin. (Illus.). 383p. (C). 1999. reprint ed. pap. text 50.00 (*0-7881-7512-2*) DIANE Pub.

Lost Crops of Africa Vol. I: Grains, Vol. I: Grains. National Research Council, Board on Science & Tech. LC 93-86876. 408p. (Orig.). (C). 1996. pap. 24.95 (*0-309-04990-3*) Natl Acad Pr.

***Lost Crown of Meleor.** George Teply. (Illus.). 32p. (J). (ps-2). 2000. pap. 6.95 (*1-55037-600-4*, Pub. by Annick Pr); lib. bdg. 16.95 (*1-55037-601-2*, Pub. by Annick Pr) Firefly Bks Ltd.

***Lost Crusade.** Howard C. Humphrey. LC 00-130511. 208p. 2000. write for info. (*1-57197-218-8*, Pub. by Pentland Pr) Assoc Pubs Grp.

Lost Crusade: America's Secret Cambodian Mercenaries. Peter Scott. LC 98-20797. (Special Warfare Ser.). (Illus.). 224p. 1998. 27.95 (*1-55750-846-1*) Naval Inst Pr.

Lost Daughters. Laurie Alberts. LC 98-48770. (Hardscrabble Bks. Ser.). 217p. 1999. 22.95 (*0-87451-898-9*) U Pr of New Eng.

Lost Daughters. large type ed. Jeanne Whitmee. (Charnwood Large Print Ser.). 656p. 1997. 27.99 (*0-7089-8930-6*, Charnwood) Ulverscroft.

Lost Daughters: A Micky Knight Mystery. J. M. Redmann. LC 99-10422. 320p. 1999. text 24.95 (*0-393-04028-3*) Norton.

Lost Daughters: Recovered Memory Therapy. Reinder Van Til. LC 97-21298. 301p. 1997. pap. 18.00 (*0-8028-4272-0*) Eerdmans.

***Lost Daughters of China: Abandoned Girls, Their Journey to America & the Search for a Missing Past.** Karin Evans. LC 99-87222. 288p. 2000. 23.95 (*1-58542-026-3*, Tarcher Putnam) Putnam Pub Group.

***Lost Day.** Judith Clarke. LC 98-55096. 154p. (YA). (gr. 9 up). 1999. 16.95 (*0-8050-6152-5*) H Holt & Co.

Lost Days of Agatha Christie. Carole Owens. 1996. pap. 12.95 (*0-918343-03-8*) Cottage Pr Inc.

Lost Death Valley Forty-Niner Journal of Louis Nusbaumer. George Koenig. LC 74-20026. (Illus.). 80p. 1974. pap. 5.95 (*0-912494-14-X*) Commun Print.

Lost Debate: German Socialist Intellectuals & Totalitarianism. William David Jones. LC 98-58029. 384p. 1999. 49.95 (*0-252-02480-X*) U of Ill Pr.

***Lost Debate: German Socialist Intellectuals & Totalitarianism.** William David Jones. LC 98-58029. 384p. 1999. pap. text 21.95 (*0-252-06796-7*) U of Ill Pr.

Lost Decade: America in the 70s. Ed. by Elsebeth Hurup. (Dolphin Ser.: No. 26). 217p. (C). 1996. pap. 19.95 (*87-7288-377-4*, Pub. by Aarhus Univ Pr) David Brown.

Lost Deep Thoughts: Don't Fight the Deepness. Jack Handey. (Illus.). 96p. (J). 1998. pap. 9.95 (*0-7868-8305-7*, Pub. by Hyperion) Time Warner.

Lost Destiny: Blood of Kerensky Trilogy. Michael A. Stackpole. (Battletech Ser.: No. 22). 288p. (Orig.). 1995. mass mkt. 6.99 (*0-451-45385-9*, ROC) NAL.

Lost Diaries of Cheng. Mark Slouka. write for info. (*0-375-40216-0*) Knopf.

Lost Diaries of Frans Hals. Michael Kernan. LC 95-843. 1995. pap. 13.95 (*0-312-13117-8*) St Martin.

Lost Diary. Marc Tolon Brown et al. LC 98-66850. (Arthur Chapter Book Ser.: Vol. 9). (Illus.). 64p. (J). (gr. 2-4). 1998. 12.95 (*0-316-11573-8*) Little.

Lost Diary. Dave Gustaveson. (Reel Kids Adventures Ser.: Bk. 7). 160p. (Orig.). (J). (gr. 3-8). 1996. pap. 5.99 (*0-927545-88-8*) YWAM Pub.

Lost Diary: A True War Story. Irwin B. Spandau. 80p. (Orig.). 1993. pap. 22.95 (*1-880365-74-X*) Prof Pr NC.

Lost Dimension. Paul Virilio. 130p. 1991. pap. 10.00 (*0-936756-73-X*) Autonomedia.

Lost Dimension. Paul Virilio. Tr. by Daniel Moshenberg. 146p. 1991. pap. 10.00 (*1-57027-044-9*) Autonomedia.

Lost Discipline & Hamartia. O. L. Wade. LC 72-305534. 20 p. 1972. write for info. (*0-85057-056-5*) Univ of Birmingham.

Lost Distilleries of Ireland. Brian Townsend. (Illus.). 192p. 1998. 24.95 (*1-897784-36-8*, Pub. by N Wilson Pubng) Interlink Pub.

***Lost Distilleries of Ireland.** Brian Townsend. 2000. pap. 16.95 (*1-897784-87-2*, Pub. by N Wilson Pubng) Interlink Pub.

Lost Dorsai. Gordon Rupert Dickson. 288p. 1993. mass mkt. 4.99 (*0-8125-0404-6*, Pub. by Tor Bks) St Martin.

Lost Dove: A Story for All Time. Eliane Wilson. LC 98-22913. (Illus.). 112p. 1998. 12.95 (*1-86204-311-6*, Pub. by Element MA) Penguin Putnam.

Lost Dreams. Nora Kay. 368p. 1997. mass mkt. 10.95 (*0-340-63999-7*, Pub. by Hodder & Stought Ltd) Trafalgar.

Lost Drum: The Myth of Sexuality in Papua New Guinea & Beyond. James F. Weiner. LC 95-7739. (New Directions in Anthropological Writing Ser.). 224p. 1995. 49.95 (*0-299-14860-2*); pap. 19.95 (*0-299-14864-5*) U of Wis Pr.

Lost Dutchman. Jacob Weiser. (Footprints in Time Ser.). (Illus.). 140p. (J). (gr. 3-6). 1989. pap. 9.95 (*0-944770-02-9*) Discovery GA.

Lost Dutchman & Superstition Mountain Who's Who. Mitchell Waite. LC 93-83367. (Illus.). 150p. (Orig.). (YA). 1993. pap. text 9.95 (*1-881260-07-0*) Southwest Pubns.

Lost Dutchman Mine. Sims Ely. 188p. 1992. reprint ed. lib. bdg. 22.95 (*0-89968-303-7*, Lghtyr Pr) Buccaneer Bks.

Lost Dutchman Mine Discoveries: And a History of Arizona Mining. Jay Fraser. (Illus.). 120p. 1988. pap. 9.95 (*0-918080-57-6*) Affil Writers America.

***Lost Dutchman Mine of Jacob Waltz Pt. 1: The Golden Dream.** T. E. Glover. (Illus.). 384p. 2000. pap. 19.95 (*0-9662091-8-4*) Cowboy Miner.

Lost Dutchman Newsletters, June 89-May 90, Vol. 1. Mitchell Waite. (Illus.). 139p. (Orig.). 1991. pap. text 9.95 (*1-881260-02-X*) Southwest Pubns.

Lost Dutchman Newsletters, June 1992-May 1993, Vol. 4. large type ed. Mitchell Waite. (Illus.). 130p. 1997. pap. text 9.95 (*1-881260-08-9*) Southwest Pubns.

Lost Dutchman Newsletters, June 91-May 92, Vol. 3. Mitchell Waite. (Illus.). 150p. (Orig.). 1993. pap. text 9.95 (*1-881260-05-4*) Southwest Pubns.

Lost Dutchman Newsletters, June 90-May 91, Vol. 2. Mitchell Waite. (Illus.). 153p. (Orig.). 1992. pap. text 9.95 (*1-881260-03-8*) Southwest Pubns.

Lost Dutchman Newsletters, June 93-May 95, Vol. 5. large type ed. Mitchell Waite. (Illus.). 130p. (Orig.). 1997. pap. text 9.95 (*1-881260-12-7*) Southwest Pubns.

Lost Earl & Other Poems. John T. Trowbridge. (Notable American Authors). 1999. reprint ed. lib. bdg. 125.00 (*0-7812-9817-2*) Rprt Serv.

Lost Earth: A Life of Cezanne. Philip Callow. LC 95-10065. (Illus.). 416p. 1995. 30.00 (*1-56663-084-3*) I R Dee.

Lost Ecstasy. Mary Roberts Rinehart. 400p. 1998. mass mkt. 5.99 (*1-57566-344-9*) Kensgtn Pub Corp.

Lost Edition of the Letters of Paul: A Reassessment of the Text of the Pauline Corpus Attested by Marcion. John J. Clabeaux. LC 88-28511. (Catholic Biblical Quarterly Monographs: No. 21). xiv, 181p. 1989. pap. 8.50 (*0-915170-20-5*) Catholic Bibl Assn.

Lost Egypt Vol. I: Epigraphic Survey. LC 92-61603. (Illus.). 8p. 1992. 2000.00 (*0-918986-88-5*) Orient Inst.

Lost Egypt Vol. II: Epigraphic Survey. LC 92-61603. (Illus.). 8p. 1992. 2000.00 (*0-918986-89-3*) Orient Inst.

Lost Egypt Vol. III: Epigraphic Survey. (Illus.). 8p. 1992. 2000.00 (*0-918986-90-7*) Orient Inst.

Lost Empire: The Life of Nikolai Rezanov. Hector Chevigny. LC 58-11484. 368p. 1965. pap. 9.95 (*0-8323-0345-3*) Binford Mort.

Lost Empire of the Gods. Earlyne C. Chaney. LC 93-72762. 224p. 1993. per. 15.95 (*0-918936-29-2*) Astara.

Lost Empires. J. B. Priestley. 1986. mass mkt. 4.95 (*0-394-74686-4*) Random.

Lost English County: Winchcombeshire in the 10th & 11th Centuries. Julian Whybra. (Studies in Anglo-Saxon History: Vol. 1). (Illus.). 146p. (C). 1990. 75.00 (*0-85115-500-6*) Boydell & Brewer.

Lost Epistles: Letters to the Faithful in the Early Church. Ed. by Robert Van de Weyer. (Little Gidding Bks.). 96p. 1997. 8.95 (*0-85305-356-1*, 744, Pub. by Arthur James) Morehouse Pub.

***Lost Europe: Images of a Vanished World.** Ed. by Jean Loussier & Robin Langley Sommer. (Illus.). 160p. 2000. reprint ed. text 30.00 (*0-7881-9008-3*) DIANE Pub.

***Lost Explorer: Finding Mallory on Mt. Everest.** Conrad Anker & David Roberts. LC 99-46131. 192p. 1999. 21.50 (*0-684-87151-3*) S&S Trade.

***Lost Face.** Jack London. (Collected Works of Jack London). 240p. 1998. reprint ed. lib. bdg. 88.00 (*1-58201-724-7*) Classic Bks.

Lost Faith of the Apostle & Prophets: History & Prophecy. Yisrayl Hawkins. (Illus.). 198p. (Orig.). 1985. pap. 19.00 (*1-890967-00-9*) Hse of Yahweh.

Lost Father. Mona Simpson. LC 92-56379. 1993. pap. 14.00 (*0-679-73303-5*) Vin Bks.

Lost Father. large type ed. Marina Warner. 497p. 1989. reprint ed. 19.95 (*1-85089-303-9*, Pub. by ISIS Lrg Prnt) Transaction Pubs.

Lost Fatherland: The Story of the Mennonite Emigration from Soviet Russia: 1921-1927. John B. Toews. (Studies in Anabaptist & Mennonite History). 262p. (C). 1995. reprint ed. pap. 20.50 (*1-57383-041-0*) Regent College.

Lost Fatherland: The Story of the Mennonite Emigration from Soviet Russia, 1921-1927. John B. Toews. LC 67-23294. (Studies in Anabaptist & Mennonite History: No. 12). 262p. reprint ed. pap. 74.70 (*0-608-12616-0*, 2025421) Bks Demand.

Lost Fathers: Politics of Fatherlessness in America. Daniels. 208p. 2000. pap. 16.95 (*0-312-22471-0*) St Martin.

Lost Fathers: The Politics of Fatherlessness. Cynthia R. Daniels. LC 97-48633. 224p. 1998. text 24.95 (*0-312-21107-4*) St Martin.

Lost Field Notes of Franklin R. Johnston's Life & Work among the American Indians. Franklin R. Johnston. Ed. by Bill Yenne. (Illus.). 200p. 1997. 22.95 (*1-885440-05-7*) First Glance.

Lost Films: Important Movies That Disappeared. Frank Thompson. LC 95-19250. (Illus.). 288p. 1996. pap. 16.95 (*0-8065-1604-6*, Citadel Pr) Carol Pub Group.

Lost Films, 1895-1917. Charles H. Tarbox. (Illus.). 280p. (C). 1983. 45.00 (*0-9610916-0-6*) Film Classic Exch.

Lost Films of the Fifties. Douglas Brode. (Illus.). 288p. (Orig.). (YA). 1988. pap. 15.95 (*0-8065-1092-7*, Citadel Pr) Carol Pub Group.

Lost Flower Children. Janet Taylor Lisle. LC 98-34912. (Illus.). 122p. (J). (gr. 3-6). 1999. 16.99 (*0-399-23393-8*, Philomel) Peng Put Young Read.

***Lost Foal.** Joanna Campbell. (Ashleighs Ser.: No. 8). 176p. 2000. mass mkt. 4.50 (*0-06-106632-X*) HarpC.

***Lost for the Cause: The Confederate Army in 1864.** Steven H. Newton. LC 99-67802. (Illus.). 384p. 2000. 29.95 (*1-882810-49-X*) Savas Pub.

***Lost for Words.** Deric Longden. 2000. pap. 8.95 (*0-552-13943-2*, Pub. by Transworld Publishers Ltd) Trafalgar.

***Lost for Words: The Psychoanalysis of Anorexia & Bulimia.** Em Farrell. LC 00-27707. 2000. pap. 17.95 (*1-892746-56-5*) Other Pr LLC.

Lost Forever, 4 bks. Jean-Christophe Balouet. Incl. Extinct Animals of the Islands. Barbara J. Behm. LC 96-50238. (Illus.). 32p. (J). (gr. 3 up). 1997. lib. bdg. 21.27 (*0-8368-1525-4*); Extinct Animals of the Northern Continents. Brenda Behm. LC 96-37610. (Illus.). 32p. (J). (gr. 3 up). 1997. lib. bdg. 21.27 (*0-8368-1526-2*); Extinct Animals of the Southern Continents. Barbara J. Behm. LC 96-37608. (Illus.). 32p. (J). (gr. 3 up). 1997. lib. bdg. 21.27 (*0-8368-1527-0*); Extinct Wildlife. Barbara J. Behm. LC 96-37603. (Illus.). 32p. (J). (gr. 3 up). 1997. lib. bdg. 21.27 (*0-8368-1524-6*); (Illus.). (J). 1997. Set lib. bdg. 85.07 (*0-8368-1523-8*) Gareth Stevens Inc.

Lost Fortune of Tsars. William Clarke. LC 96-24818. 336p. 1996. pap. 14.95 (*0-312-14672-8*) St Martin.

An Asterisk (*) at the beginning of an entry indicates that the title is appearing for the first time.

***Lost-Found Nation of Islam in America.** Clifton E. Marsh. 240p. 2000. pap. 17.95 (*1-57886-008-3*) Scarecrow Trade.

Lost-Found Nation of Islam in America. 2nd ed. Clifton E. Marsh. 240p. 2000. 37.50 (*0-8108-3089-2*) Scarecrow.

Lost Fragments. James Laughlin. LC 98-147172. 24p. 1998. pap. 10.95 (*1-901233-10-3*) Dufour.

Lost Frankenstein Pages. Berni Wrightson. (Illus.). 64p. 1991. pap. write for info. (*0-927203-08-1*) Apple Pr PA.

Lost Freedom. Herbert Kaufmann. Orig. Title: Kings Krokodile. (Illus.). (J). (gr. 7 up). 1969. 12.95 (*0-8392-3083-4*) Astor-Honor.

Lost Fremont Cannon Guidebook. Jamison Station Press Staff. (Desert Rat Guidebook Ser.: No. 4). (Illus.). 17p. 1985. 1.95 (*0-317-01480-3*) Jamison Stn.

Lost Frontier. Knut D. Peterson. LC 79-11657. 1981. 22.95 (*0-87949-172-8*) Ashley Bks.

Lost Frontier: Water Diversion in the Growth & Destruction of Owens Valley Agriculture. Robert A. Sauder. (Illus.). 208p. 1994. 43.00 (*0-8165-1381-3*) U of Ariz Pr.

Lost Futures: Our Forgotten Children. Stan Grossfeld. LC 96-78750. 1997. 68.00 (*0-89381-696-5*) Aperture.

Lost Galleon. Bret Harte. 1976. reprint ed. lib. bdg. 16.95 (*0-88411-591-7*) Amereon Ltd.

Lost Gallows. John Dickson Carr. 344p. 1986. pap. 3.50 (*0-88184-202-8*) Carroll & Graf.

***Lost Garden.** Annelies Strba. (Illus.). 96p. 2000. 50.00 (*3-907078-20-9*) Lars Muller.

Lost Garden. Laurence Yep. LC 95-53801. (Illus.). 144p. (J). (gr. 7 up). 1996. mass mkt. 4.95 (*0-688-13701-6*, Wm Morrow) Morrow Avon.

Lost Garden. Laurence Yep. (YA). 1998. 19.50 (*0-8446-6980-6*) Peter Smith.

Lost Garden. Laurence Yep. LC 95-53801. (J). 1996. 10.05 (*0-606-11579-X*, Pub. by Turtleback) Demco.

Lost Garden. large type ed. Jane A. Hodge. 1983. 15.95 (*0-7089-1027-0*) Ulverscroft.

Lost Gardens of Heligan. Tim Smit. (Illus.). 270p. 1998. 35.00 (*0-575-06422-6*, Pub. by V Gollancz) Trafalgar.

Lost Gems of Secret Knowledge. Ed. by Omar V. Garrison. 304p. 1973. 7.95 (*0-8216-0205-5*) Carol Pub Group.

Lost General. Elswyth Thane. 1974. reprint ed. lib. bdg. 22.95 (*0-88411-952-1*) Amereon Ltd.

Lost Generation. Kamlesh C. Kapur. (Illus.). 215p. (Orig.). 1994. 14.95 (*0-9624392-0-7*); pap. 15.95 (*0-9624392-1-5*) K S Kapur.

***Lost Geography.** Charlotte Bacon. LC 99-43958. 288p. 2000. 24.00 (*0-374-19160-3*) FS&G.

Lost Get-Back Boogie. James Lee Burke. Date not set. lib. bdg. 24.95 (*0-8488-1780-X*) Amereon Ltd.

Lost Get-Back Boogie. James Lee Burke. LC 94-33419. 256p. (J). 1995. pap. 10.45 (*0-7868-8101-1*, Pub. by Hyperion) Time Warner.

Lost Get-Back Boogie. James Lee Burke. LC 86-10662. 241p. 1986. 16.95 (*0-8071-1334-4*) La State U Pr.

***Lost Get-Back Boogie.** large type ed. James Lee Burke. 343p. 2000. lib. bdg. 28.95 (*1-58547-053-8*) Ctr Point Pubg.

Lost Get-Back Boogie. James Lee Burke. 256p. (J). 1997. reprint ed. mass mkt. 5.99 (*0-7868-8934-9*, Pub. by Hyperion) Time Warner.

Lost Giants. large type ed. Alan Scholefield. 1990. 11.50 (*0-7089-8554-8*, Charnwood) Ulverscroft.

Lost Girl. Nabiel Kanan. (Illus.). 96p. 1999. pap. 9.95 (*1-56163-229-5*, Comics Lit) NBM.

Lost Girl. D. H. Lawrence. 26.95 (*0-89190-611-8*) Amereon Ltd.

Lost Girl. D. H. Lawrence. Ed. by John Worthen. LC 80-40457. (Cambridge Edition of the Works of D. H. Lawrence). (Illus.). 483p. 1981. pap. text 39.95 (*0-521-29423-1*) Cambridge U Pr.

Lost Girls. Edward Hower. write for info. (*0-318-61695-5*) Viking Penguin.

***Lost Girls.** Andrew Pyper. LC 99-47397. 390p. 2000. 23.95 (*0-385-33446-X*) Delacorte.

***Lost Girls.** large type ed. Gwen Moffat. 360p. 2000. 31.99 (*0-7089-4172-9*) Ulverscroft.

Lost Glass Plates of Wilfred Eng: A Novel. Thomas Orton. LC 99-34803. 256p. 1999. text 24.00 (*1-58243-023-3*, Pub. by Counterpt DC) HarpC.

***Lost Glass Plates of Wilfred Eng: A Novel.** Thomas Orton. 2001. reprint ed. pap. 13.00 (*1-58243-125-6*) Counterpt DC.

***Lost Glory.** Dave Markee. 2000. pap. 10.99 (*1-85240-257-1*) SOV5.

Lost Goddesses of Early Greece: A Collection of Pre-Hellenic Myths. Charlene Spretnak. LC 91-41829. (Illus.). 152p. 1992. pap. 13.00 (*0-8070-1343-9*) Beacon Pr.

Lost Gods of Albion: The Chalk Hill-Figures of Britain. Paul Newman. LC 98-155071. (Illus.). 224p. 1998. 39.95 (*0-7509-1563-3*, Pub. by Sutton Pub Ltd) Intl Pubs Mktg.

***Lost Gods of Albion: The Chalk Hill-Figures of Britain.** Paul Newman. (Illus.). 224p. 1999. pap. 19.95 (*0-7509-1792-X*, Pub. by Sutton Pub Ltd) Bks Intl VA.

Lost Gods of England. Brian Branston. (Illus.). 194p. 1998. pap. 13.95 (*0-09-473340-6*, Pub. by Constable & Co) Trafalgar.

Lost Gods of England. Brian Branston. LC 83-72977. 1984. reprint ed. 10.95 (*0-500-27321-9*, Pub. by Thames Hudson) Norton.

Lost Gold & Buried Treasure: A Treasure Hunter's Guide to 250 Fortunes Waiting to Be Found. Kevin Randle. LC 95-34592. (Illus.). 288p. 1995. 19.95 (*0-87131-792-3*) M Evans.

Lost Gold & Silver Mines of the Southwest. unabridged ed. Eugene L. Conrotto. LC 96-20462. (Illus.). 288p. 1996. reprint ed. pap. text 7.95 (*0-486-29275-4*) Dover.

Lost Gold Mine of Juan Mondragon: A Legend from New Mexico Performed by Melaquias Romero. Charles L. Briggs. Ed. by Julian J. Vigil. LC 89-32119. 270p. 1990. 49.95 (*0-8165-0977-8*) U of Ariz Pr.

Lost Gold Mine of the Hudson. Tristram Coffin. 64p. pap. 5.95 (*0-941567-30-3*) J C & A L Fawcett.

Lost Gold Mines of Alaska: And Great Gold Robberies of the Alaska Gold Rush Era. Ron Wendt. (Illus.). 75p. 1998. pap. 10.95 (*1-886574-18-9*) Goldstream Pubns.

Lost Gospel: The Book of Q & Christian Origins. Burton L. Mack. LC 92-53921. 288p. 1994. reprint ed. pap. 15.00 (*0-06-065375-2*, Pub. by Harper SF) HarpC.

Lost Gospel Also Depth of Soul & Quest of Man. Moritz E. Pape. (Illus.). 24p. 1992. lib. bdg. 2.50 (*0-9630599-0-4*) Ltd Ex Pr.

Lost Gospel of Jesus: The Hidden Teachings of Christ. Gene Savoy. LC 78-71277. (Sacred Teachings of Light Ser.: Codex VIII). (Illus.). xv, 91p. 1984. text 39.50 (*0-936202-08-4*) Intl Comm Christ.

Lost Gospel of the Earth: A Call for Renewing Nature, Spirit & Politics. Tom Hayden. 280p. 1996. 22.00 (*0-87156-888-8*, Pub. by Sierra) Random.

Lost Gospel Q: The Original Sayings of Jesus. Ed. by Marcus Borg & Mark Powelson. Tr. by Ray Riegert. 128p. 1996. 15.00 (*1-56975-100-5*) Ulysses Pr.

Lost Gospel Q: The Original Sayings of Jesus. 2nd ed. Ed. by Marcus Borg et al. (Illus.). 128p. 1999. pap. 11.95 (*1-56975-189-7*) Ulysses Pr.

Lost Grizzlies: A Search for Survivors in the Wilderness of Colorado. Rick Bass. (Illus.). 220p. 1995. 22.95 (*0-395-71759-0*) HM.

Lost Grizzlies: A Search for Survivors in the Wilderness of Colorado. Rick Bass. 288p. 1997. pap. 13.00 (*0-395-85700-7*) HM.

Lost Grove: Autobiography of a Spanish Poet in Exile. Rafael Alberti. Ed. & Tr. by Gabriel Berns. LC 74-79760. 1977. pap. 13.95 (*0-520-04265-4*, Pub. by U CA Pr) Cal Prin Full Svc.

Lost Guardian. Ronald A. Cross. 1996. mass mkt. 5.99 (*0-8125-1595-1*) Tor Bks.

Lost Hardys a Concordance. 2nd rev. ed. Robert L. Crawford. (Illus.). 96p. 1996. spiral bd. 17.95 (*0-9639949-6-4*) SynSine Pr.

Lost Harvest: A Study of the Surface Mining Act's Failure to Reclaim Prime Farmland in the Midwest-Executive Summary. Russell Boulding. Ed. by Pamela Mavrolas & Chuck Sheketoff. (Illus.). (Orig.). 1984. pap. 5.00 (*0-943724-04-X*) Illinois South.

Lost Harvest: A Study of the Surface Mining Act's Failure to Reclaim Prime Farmland in the Midwest-Executive Summary. Russell Boulding. (Illus.). (Orig.). 1984. pap. 15.00 (*0-943724-05-8*) Illinois South.

Lost Harvests: Prairie Indian Reserve Farmers & Government Policy. Sarah Carter. (McGill-Queen's Native & Northern Ser.). 352p. (C). 1990. text 65.00 (*0-7735-0755-8*, Pub. by McG-Queens Univ Pr) CUP Services.

Lost Harvests: Prairie Indian Reserve Farmers & Government Policy. Sarah Carter. 352p. 1993. pap. 22.95 (*0-7735-0999-2*, Pub. by McG-Queens Univ Pr) CUP Services.

Lost Heart of Asia. Colin Thubron. 384p. 2000. pap. 14.00 (*0-06-092656-2*, Perennial) HarperTrade.

Lost Heritage. Mindy O. Block. 152p. 1997. pap. 15.00 (*0-9663197-0-2*) Sustaining Systs.

Lost Heritage. Natasha Borovsky. 686p. (Orig.). 1995. pap. 18.40 (*0-9647178-0-8*) Sila-Nova Pr.

Lost Heritage: The People of Old Butler, Tennessee & the Watauga Valley. Russ Calhoun. (Illus.). 387p. 1998. pap. 19.95 (*1-57072-081-9*) Overmountain Pr.

Lost Hero. Elizabeth S. Ward & Herbert D. Ward. LC 72-3106. (Black Heritage Library Collection). (Illus.). 1977. reprint ed. 16.95 (*0-8369-9090-0*) Ayer.

Lost Heroine of the Confederacy: The Diaries & Letters of Belle Edmondson. Ed. by William Galbraith & Loretta Galbraith. 239p. 1998. text 30.00 (*0-7881-5465-6*) DIANE Pub.

Lost Heroines: Little-Known Women Who Changed Their World. Rebecca Bartholomew. iv, 161p. 1997. pap. 10.95 (*0-9656117-0-1*) Uintah Springs.

Lost Highway. Richard Currey. 272p. 1998. pap. 12.00 (*0-395-92479-0*) HM.

Lost Highway. David Lynch & Barry Gifford. LC 97-161340. (Illus.). 128p. (Orig.). 1997. pap. 13.95 (*0-571-19150-9*) Faber & Faber.

***Lost Highway: Journeys & Arrivals of American Musicans.** Peter Guralnick. 1998. mass mkt. 15.95 (*0-316-19122-1*, Back Bay) Little.

Lost Highway: Journeys & Arrivals of American Musicians. Peter Guralnick. LC 98-73850. (Illus.). 368p. 1999. reprint ed. pap. 16.00 (*0-316-33274-7*, Back Bay) Little.

Lost Highways. Curtiss Ann Matlock. 1999. mass mkt. 5.99 (*1-55166-499-2*, 1-66499-4, Mira Bks) Harlequin Bks.

***Lost Highways: An Illustrated History of Road Movies.** Jack Sargeant. 1999. pap. text 19.95 (*1-871592-68-2*) Creation Books.

Lost History: Contras, Cocaine, the Press & 'Project Truth' unabridged ed. Robert Parry. 300p. 1999. pap. 19.95 (*1-893517-00-4*) Media Consort.

Lost History of the Canine Race: Our 15,000-Year Love Affair with Dogs. Mary E. Thurston. LC 96-11171. (Illus.). 320p. 1996. 24.95 (*0-8362-0548-0*) Andrews & McMeel.

Lost Hollywood. Jack Woody. (Illus.). 136p. 1987. 100.00 (*0-944092-00-4*) Twin Palms Pub.

Lost Honor of Katharina Blum. Heinrich Boll. Tr. by Leila Vennewitz. 160p. 1994. pap. 12.95 (*0-14-018728-6*, Penguin Classics) Viking Penguin.

***Lost Honour of Katharina Blum.** large type ed. Heinrich Boll. LC 99-46762. 259p. 1999. 24.95 (*1-56000-463-0*) Transaction Pubs.

Lost Horizon. James Hilton. 1976. 20.95 (*0-8488-0284-5*) Amereon Ltd.

Lost Horizon. James Hilton. 231p. 1988. mass mkt. 5.99 (*0-671-66427-1*) PB.

Lost Horizon. James Hilton. LC 90-61335. (World's Best Reading Ser.). 191 p. 1990. write for info. (*0-89577-361-9*) RD Assn.

Lost Horizon. James Hilton. 1933. 10.60 (*0-606-02843-9*, Pub. by Turtleback) Demco.

Lost Horizon. Anne Coulter Martene & Christopher Sergel. 133p. 1942. pap. 5.50 (*0-87129-868-6*, L30) Dramatic Pub.

Lost Horizon. Illus. by Charles Nicholas. (Contemporary Motivators Ser.). 32p. (Orig.). (J). (gr. 3-5). 1979. pap. text 2.25 (*0-88301-309-6*) Pendulum Pr.

Lost Horizon. James Hilton. 231p. 1983. reprint ed. lib. bdg. 28.95 (*0-89966-450-4*) Buccaneer Bks.

Lost Horizon: A Novel. James Hilton. LC 96-160022. 262p. 1996. 23.00 (*0-688-14656-2*, Wm Morrow) Morrow Avon.

Lost Horizon: Reproducible Teaching Unit. rev. ed. James Scott. 33p. (YA). (gr. 7-12). 1988. teacher ed., ring bd. 29.50 (*1-58049-061-1*, TU26/U) Prestwick Hse.

Lost Horizon Notes. Dale G. Hayes. (Cliffs Notes Ser.). 64p. 1966. pap. 4.95 (*0-8220-0771-1*, Cliff) IDG Bks.

Lost Horse. Ed Young. LC 96-52861. (Illus.). 32p. (J). (gr. k-3). 1998. 18.00 (*0-15-201016-5*) Harcourt.

***Lost Hound.** Robert L. Ashcom. (Illus.). 161p. 2000. lthr. 150.00 (*1-56416-176-5*) Derrydale Pr.

***Lost Hound: And Other Hunting Stories & Poems.** Robert L. Ashcom. LC 99-46004. (Illus.). 161p. 2000. 45.00 (*1-56416-173-0*) Derrydale Pr.

Lost Houses of East Yorkshire. David Neave & Edward Waterson. (C). 1989. text 35.00 (*0-9513966-0-9*) St Mut.

Lost Hunters. Joseph A. Altsheler. 1990. reprint ed. lib. bdg. 20.95 (*0-89968-463-7*) Buccaneer Bks.

Lost Hunters: A Story of Wild Man & Great Beasts. Joseph A. Altsheler. 311p. reprint ed. lib. bdg. 27.95 (*0-88411-949-1*) Amereon Ltd.

Lost Identity. Michiaki Horie & Hildegard Horie. Tr. by Dawn Huff from GER. 96p. (Orig.). (YA). (gr. 7 up). 1987. pap. 5.95 (*0-939925-09-5*) R C Law & Co.

Lost Illusion. Freda Utley. (American Autobiography Ser.). 288p. 1995. reprint ed. lib. bdg. 79.00 (*0-7812-8654-9*) Rprt Serv.

Lost Illusions. Honore de Balzac. Tr. by Kathleen Raine. LC 97-2727. 1997. 21.00 (*0-679-60264-X*) Modern Lib NY.

Lost Illusions. Honore de Balzac. Tr. by Herbert J. Hunt. LC 79-29738. (Classics Ser.). 384p. 1971. pap. 18.99 (*0-14-044251-0*, Penguin Classics) Viking Penguin.

Lost Illusions: Caribbean Minorities in Britain & the Netherlands. Ed. by Malcolm Cross & Hans Entzinger. 224p. (C). 1988. lib. bdg. 55.00 (*0-415-00628-7*) Routledge.

Lost Illusions: Caribbean Minorities in Britain & the Netherlands. Ed. by Malcolm Cross & Hans Entzinger. LC 89-101001. 326p. reprint ed. pap. 101.10 (*0-608-20328-9*, 207158100002) Bks Demand.

Lost Illusions: Latin American's Struggle for Democracy, as Recounted by Its Leaders. Paul Bocker. Ed. by Paul H. Boeker. 360p. 1990. pap. text 12.95 (*1-55876-024-5*) Wiener Pubs Inc.

Lost Illusions: Paul Leautaud & His World. James Harding. (Illus.). 230p. 1974. 29.50 (*0-8386-1744-1*) Fairleigh Dickinson.

Lost Illusions: Russian Policies Towards Bulgaria in 1877-1887. Karel Durman. (Uppsala Studies on the Soviet Union & Eastern Europe: No. 1). (Orig.). 1988. pap. 40.00 (*91-554-2153-9*, Pub. by Uppsala Univ Acta Univ Uppsaliensis) Coronet Bks.

Lost Impressionists: Masterpieces from Private Collections. Susanna De Vries-Evans. LC 92-80168. (Illus.). 192p. 1992. 40.00 (*1-879373-25-4*) Roberts Rinehart.

Lost in a Dream. Sandra Marton. (Presents Ser.: No. 457). 1992. per. 2.89 (*0-373-11457-5*, 1-11457-8) Harlequin Bks.

Lost in a Dream. large type ed. Sandra Marton. 1991. reprint ed. lib. bdg. 16.95 (*0-263-12685-4*) Mac Lib Ref.

Lost in a Labyrinth of Red Tape: The Story of an Immigration That Failed. Armin Schmid & Renate Schmid. (Jewish Lives Ser.). 150p. 1996. pap. 15.95 (*0-8101-1170-5*); text 39.95 (*0-8101-1185-3*) Northwestern U Pr.

Lost in America. David Connolly. (White Noise Poetry Ser.). 86p. (Orig.). (C). 1994. pap. 10.00 (*0-9628524-9-X*) Burning Cities Pr.

Lost in America. David Connolly. (White Noise Poetry Ser.). 70p. (Orig.). 1994. pap. 12.00 (*1-885215-00-2*) Burning Cities Pr.

Lost in America. Jonathan Dahl. 1992. write for info. (*0-679-74018-X*) McKay.

Lost in Blue Canyon. James Den Boer. (Orig.). 1979. pap. 5.00 (*0-87922-108-9*) Christophers Bks.

Lost in Boggley Woods. Will Ryan. Ed. by Mary Becker. (Teddy Ruxpin Adventure Ser.). (Illus.). 26p. (J). (ps). 1986. 9.95 (*0-934323-38-0*); audio. write for info. (*0-318-60973-8*) Alchemy Comms.

Lost in Care. Spencer Millham et al. 275p. 1986. text 66.95 (*0-566-00998-6*) Ashgate Pub Co.

Lost in Cyberspace. Richard Peck. (J). 1997. 10.09 (*0-606-10985-4*, Pub. by Turtleback) Demco.

Lost in Cyberspace. Richard Peck. LC 94-48330. (Illus.). 160p. (J). (gr. 5-9). 1997. pap. 4.99 (*0-14-037856-1*) Viking Penguin.

Lost in Cyberspace? Canada & the Information Revolution. Robert Chodos et al. LC 98-107658. 149p. 1997. 34.95 (*1-55028-519-X*, Pub. by J Lorimer); pap. 19.95 (*1-55028-518-1*, Pub. by J Lorimer) Formac Dist Ltd.

Lost in Cyberspace: Essays & Far-Fetched Tales. Val Schaffner. LC 93-22636. 192p. 1993. 17.95 (*1-882593-03-0*) Bridge Wrks.

Lost in Dino World. S. F. Black. (J). 1997. pap. 3.95 (*0-8167-4280-4*) Troll Communs.

Lost in Familiar Places: Creating New Connections Between the Individual & Society. Edward R. Shapiro & A. Wesley Carr. 224p. (C). 1991. 35.00 (*0-300-04947-1*) Yale U Pr.

Lost in Familiar Places: Creating New Connections Between the Individual & Society. Edward R. Shapiro & A. Wesley Carr. 224p. (C). 1993. pap. 16.00 (*0-300-05787-3*) Yale U Pr.

Lost in Gator Swamp. Franklin W. Dixon. (Hardy Boys Mystery Stories Ser.: No. 142). (J). (gr. 3-6). 1997. per. 3.99 (*0-671-00054-3*, Minstrel Bks) PB.

Lost in God: Rediscovering Modern Prayer Form in Traditional Saints. Terry Matz. LC 94-76023. 64p. (Orig.). 1994. pap. 2.95 (*0-89243-674-3*) Liguori Pubns.

***Lost in His Love.** Lyn Cote. LC 99-45167. (Blessed Assurance Ser.: No. 2). 256p. 2000. pap. 12.99 (*0-8054-1968-3*) Broadman.

Lost in Hypnagogia. Barbara Johns. (Illus.). 78p. 1997. pap. 4.95 (*1-890644-19-6*) Union Cnty.

***Lost in Jerusalem.** Jennifer Rees Larcombe. (Illus.). 24p. (J). (gr. k-3). 1999. pap. 2.99 (*1-58134-150-4*) Crossway Bks.

Lost in Language: Translations from the Japanese & Spanish. Dennis Maloney. 24p. (Orig.). 1989. pap. text 2.00 (*1-877800-00-7*) Springhse Editions.

Lost in Las Vegas. Monty Joynes. LC 98-72213. 304p. 1998. pap. text 12.95 (*1-57174-089-9*) Hampton Roads Pub Co.

Lost in Love. Michelle Reid. (Presents Ser.). 1994. per. 2.99 (*0-373-11665-9*, 1-11665-6) Harlequin Bks.

Lost in Merlin's Castle. P. J. Stray. LC 96-15647. (Passport Mystery Ser.: Vol. 3). (Illus.). 144p. (J). 1996. pap. 4.95 (*0-382-39680-4*); lib. bdg. 13.95 (*0-382-39679-0*) Silver Burdett Pr.

Lost in My Dreams. Faye Ashley. 1996. mass mkt. 5.99 (*0-312-95691-6*) Tor Bks.

Lost in New York, 2. John Escott. (Longman Originals Ser.). 1996. pap. text 5.51 (*0-582-07483-5*) Addison-Wesley.

Lost in North America: The Imaginary Canadian in the American Dream. John Gray. LC 94-242527. 208p. 1994. pap. 14.95 (*0-88922-350-5*, Pub. by Talonbks) Genl Dist Srvs.

Lost in Paradise. Edith R. Tjepkema. (Northwest Paradise Ser.: Vol. 4). 125p. (Orig.). (YA). (gr. 8-12). 1994. pap. 4.95 (*0-9620280-3-7*) Northland Pr.

Lost in Paradise: Stories. Constance H. Stewart. LC 96-27433. 144p. (Orig.). 1997. pap. 11.00 (*1-56474-203-2*) Fithian Pr.

Lost in Place: Growing up Absurd in Suburbia. Mark Salzman. 1996. pap. 12.00 (*0-679-76778-9*) Vin Bks.

Lost in Red Hawk Woods. Megan Stine & H. William Stine. (Brains & Parker McGoohan Ser.). 87p. (J). (gr. 4-6). 1993. pap. 3.95 (*1-56801-065-6*) Sundance Pub.

***Lost in Royalty: An Intimate Account of Monaco.** Cori Kirk. 1998. pap. write for info. (*0-9696960-4-3*) Mil2enia Pr.

Lost in Silence & Forgot. Grace J. Cooley. 208p. 1992. 17.50 (*0-87244-083-4*) Texian.

Lost in Space. Michael Dooley. LC 98-96508. 64p. 1998. pap. 5.95 (*0-9642168-2-5*) Totally Unique.

Lost in Space. Tim Grundmann. (Doug Chronicles: No. 1). 64p. (J). (gr. 2-4). 1998. pap. 3.50 (*0-7868-4232-6*, Pub. by Disney Pr) Time Warner.

Lost in Space. James Hatfield & George Burt. 368p. 1998. mass mkt. 6.99 (*0-7860-0550-5*, Pinncle Kensgtn) Kensgtn Pub Corp.

Lost in Space. Judy Katschke. LC 98-164527. 32p. (J). (gr. k-3). 1998. pap. 3.50 (*0-590-18936-0*, Cartwheel) Scholastic Inc.

Lost in Space. Brian McDonald & Gordon Purcell. (Illus.). 72p. (J). (gr. 3 up). 1998. pap. 7.95 (*1-56971-341-3*) Dark Horse Comics.

***Lost in Space: Digest.** Scholastic, Inc. Staff. (Illus.). (J). (gr. 3-7). 1998. pap. text 3.99 (*0-590-18934-4*) Scholastic Inc.

Lost in Space: Probing Feminist Science Fiction & Beyond. Marleen S. Barr. LC 93-12466. xvi, 232p. (C). 1993. pap. 19.95 (*0-8078-4421-7*); text 55.00 (*0-8078-2108-X*) U of NC Pr.

Lost in Space: Promised Land. large type ed. Pat Cadigan. LC 99-15812. 1999. pap. 30.00 (*0-7838-8675-6*) Mac Lib Ref.

Lost in Space: The True Story. Edward B. Shifres. Ed. by Will C. Gray. LC 98-60178. Orig. Title: Space Family Robinson: The True Story. (Illus.). 365p. 1998. reprint ed. pap. 14.95 (*1-881636-17-8*) Windsor Hse Pub Grp.

Lost in Space: The Ultimate Unauthorized Trivia Challenge for the Classic TV Series. James Hatfield & George Burt. (Classic TV Ser.). 368p. 1998. pap. 14.00 (*1-57566-299-X*, Knsington) Kensgtn Pub Corp.

Lost in Space: The Vault. Gene DeWeese. 320p. (Orig.). 1999. mass mkt. 5.99 (*0-06-105910-2*) HarpC.

Lost in Space & the Mortgage Due. Tim Kelly. 1979. pap. 3.00 (*0-686-38382-6*) Eldridge Pub.

Lost in Space Classic Postcard Book. Mark C. Vaz. 60p. 1998. pap. 9.99 (*0-06-105583-2*, HarperPrism) HarpC.

***Lost in Space Deluxe Storybook.** Scholastic, Inc. Staff. (Illus.). 48p. (J). (ps-3). 1998. pap. text 5.99 (*0-590-18935-2*, Cartwheel) Scholastic Inc.

Lost in Space Handbook. Paul Monroe. 174p. 1991. pap. 19.95 (*1-880417-02-2*) Star Tech.

***Lost in Space Hello Reader.** Scholastic, Inc. Staff. LC 98-175975. (Illus.). 48p. (J). (gr. 1-3). 1998. pap. text 3.99 (*0-590-18937-9*, Cartwheel) Scholastic Inc.

Lost in Space Scrapbook. Ed. by William E. Anchors, Jr. 150p. 1991. pap. 19.95 (*1-880417-04-9*) Star Tech.

L

Lost in Space Twenty-Fifth Anniversary Celebration. Flint Mitchell & William E. Anchors, Jr. 94p. 1991. pap. 11.95 (*1-880417-03-0*) Star Tech.

Lost in Space Yearbook. Robert Coyle, Jr. 100p. 1992. pap. 9.95 (*1-880417-06-5*) Star Tech.

***Lost in Spain.** John Wilson. (Illus.). 204p. (J). 1999. pap. 9.95 (*1-55041-523-9*) Fitzhenry & W Ltd.

***Lost in Spillville.** Sam Drexler, pseud & Fay Shelby. LC 00-190005. (Erika & Oz Adventures in American History Ser.: Vol. 1). 144p. (YA). (gr. 9-12). 2000. pap. 6.99 (*0-9669988-1-2*) Aunt Straw.

Lost in Stinkeye Swamp. R. L. Stine, pseud. (Give Yourself Goosebumps Ser.: No. 24). (J). 1997. pap. text 3.99 (*0-590-39775-3*, Little Apple) Scholastic Inc.

Lost in Stinkeye Swamp. R. L. Stine, pseud. (Give Yourself Goosebumps Ser.: No. 24). (J). 1997. 9.09 (*0-606-12988-X*, Pub. by Turtleback) Demco.

Lost in the Alps. R. Cosey. (Illus.). 120p. 1996. pap. 13.95 (*1-56163-160-4*, Comics Lit) NBM.

Lost in the Amazon: A Miss Mallard Mystery. Robert Quackenbush. (Illus.). 32p. (J). (gr. 1-4). 1990. lib. bdg. 15.95 (*0-945912-11-0*) Pippin Pr.

Lost in the Arctic with Pal Bear. Sherry C. Miller. (Molly Character - Color Me Ser.: No. 2). (Illus.). 32p. (Orig.). (J). (gr. k-5). 1984. pap. 1.95 (*0-913379-01-8*) Double M Pub.

Lost in the Barrens. Farley Mowat. 208p. (YA). 1985. mass mkt. 5.50 (*0-553-27525-9*, Starfire BDD) BDD Bks Young Read.

Lost in the Barrens. Farley Mowat. 1987. mass mkt. 6.99 (*0-7710-6681-3*) McCland & Stewart.

Lost in the Barrens. Farley Mowat. 1956. 9.09 (*0-606-00513-7*, Pub. by Turtleback) Demco.

Lost in the Big Thicket: A Mystery & Adventure in the Big Thicket of Texas. Wanda A. Landrey. LC 96-51663. (Illus.), 104p. (Orig.). (J). (gr. 5-6). 1997. pap. 10.95 (*1-57168-116-7*, Eakin Pr) Sunbelt Media.

Lost in the Blinded Blizzard. John R. Erickson. LC 99-19578. (Hank the Cowdog Ser.: No. 16). (Illus.). 144p. (J). (gr. 2-5). 1998. pap. 4.99 (*0-14-130392-1*, PuffinBks) Peng Put Young Read.

Lost in the Blinded Blizzard. John R. Erickson. (Hank the Cowdog Ser.: No. 16). (Illus.). 144p. (J). (gr. 2-5). 1998. 14.99 (*0-670-88423-5*) Viking Penguin.

Lost in the Blinding Blizzard. John R. Erickson. (Hank the Cowdog Ser.). (J). 1991. 12.05 (*0-606-01408-X*, Pub. by Turtleback) Demco.

***Lost in the Blizzard.** Constance Horne & Lori M. McCrae. 70p. (J). (gr. 3-6). 1999. pap. 5.95 (*1-895836-69-7*, Tesseract) Bk Collective.

Lost in the Blizzard. Paul Hutchens. LC 98-156156. (Sugar Creek Gang Ser.: Vol. 17). (J). 1998. mass mkt. 4.99 (*0-8024-7021-1*) Moody.

Lost in the Bone-Wheel Factory. Yusef Komunyakaa. LC 79-84583. 56p. 1979. pap. 7.00 (*0-89924-018-6*) Lynx Hse.

Lost in the Cave. Linda P. Silbert & Alvin J. Silbert. (Little Twirps Understanding People Bks.). (Illus.). (J). (gr. k-4). 1978. pap. 4.98 (*0-89544-057-1*) Silbert Bress.

Lost in the City: Tree of Desire & Serafin. Ignacio Solares et al. Tr. by Carolyn Brushwood & John S. Brushwood from SPA. LC 97-35001. (The Texas Pan American Ser.). 144p. 1998. 27.50 (*0-292-77731-0*, SOLLOS); pap. 14.95 (*0-292-77732-9*, SOLLOP) U of Tex Pr.

Lost in the Corn. Joyce Pond. (Illus.). 31p. (Orig.). (J). (gr. 6). 1992. pap. 6.95 (*0-9635877-0-6*) JBP Press.

Lost in the Cosmos: The Last Self-Help Book. Walker Percy. 262p. 1992. pap. 13.00 (*0-374-52346-0*) FS&G.

***Lost in the Cosmos: The Last Self-Help Book.** Walker Percy. LC 99-87846. 272p. 2000. pap. 14.00 (*0-312-25399-0*, Picador USA) St Martin.

Lost in the Cracks: Missing a Christian Lifestyle. Arthur Jaggard. 247p. (Orig.). 1992. pap. text 29.95 (*0-9632101-1-4*) Seth Pub.

Lost in the Customhouse: Authorship in the American Renaissance. Jerome Loving. LC 92-33051. 268p. 1993. text 36.95 (*0-87745-404-3*) U of Iowa Pr.

***Lost in the Dark Unchanted Forest.** John R. Erickson. (Hank the Cowdog Ser.: No. 11). (Illus.). (J). (gr. 2-5). 1999. pap. 12.25 (*0-8335-6824-8*) Econo-Clad Bks.

Lost in the Dark Unchanted Forest. John R. Erickson. LC 98-41815. (Hank the Cowdog Ser.: No. 11). (Illus.). 144p. (J). (gr. 2-5). 1998. pap. 4.99 (*0-14-130387-5*, PuffinBks) Peng Put Young Read.

Lost in the Dark Unchanted Forest. John R. Erickson. (Hank the Cowdog Ser.: No. 11). (Illus.). (J). (gr. 2-5). 1988. 12.05 (*0-606-01403-9*, Pub. by Turtleback) Demco.

Lost in the Devil's Desert. Gloria Skurzynski. LC 92-45656. (Illus.). 96p. (J). (gr. 5 up). 1993. pap. 3.95 (*0-688-04593-6*, Wm Morrow) Morrow Avon.

Lost in the Enchanted Forest. John Erickson. LC 98-41815. Vol. 11. (Illus.). 144p. (gr. 3-7). 1998. 14.99 (*0-670-88418-9*) Viking Penguin.

Lost in the Fire. David Clewell. 32p. (Orig.). 1993. pap. 6.95 (*0-9643009-0-7*) Garlic Pr MO.

Lost in the Fog. Irving Bacheller. LC 88-25923. (Illus.). (J). (gr. k-3). 1990. 14.95 (*0-316-07462-4*) Little.

Lost in the Forest. Nathan Aaseng. LC 96-18946. (Grubstake Adventure Ser.). 80p. (J). (gr. 5-9). 1996. pap. 5.99 (*0-8066-2790-5*, 9-2790, Augsburg) Augsburg Fortress.

Lost in the Funhouse. John Barth. 224p. 1988. reprint ed. pap. 12.00 (*0-385-24087-2*, Anchor NY) Doubleday.

Lost in the Funhouse: The Life & Mind of Andy Kaufman. Bill Zehme. LC 99-461996. (Illus.). 366p. 1999. 25.95 (*0-385-33371-4*) Delacorte.

Lost in the Funhouse: The Life & Mind of Andy Kaufman, Set. abr. ed. Bill Zehme. 1999. audio 17.95 (*1-55927-564-2*) Audio Renaissance.

Lost in the Great Atlantic Valley: or Frank Reade, Jr. & His Submarine Wonder the "Dart" Luis Senarens. (Frank Reade Library: Vol. 6). 1985. lib. bdg. 40.00 (*0-8240-3545-3*) Garland.

Lost in the Land of Enchantment: Travels in New Mexico. Art Latham. LC 95-30909. (Illus.). 232p. (Orig.). 1995. pap. 14.95 (*0-9623682-8-8*) Arroyo Pr.

Lost in the Land of Oz: Befriending Your Inner Orphan & Heading for Home. Madonna Kolbenschlag. LC 94-1247. 224p. 1994. reprint ed. pap. 13.95 (*0-8245-1402-5*) Crossroad NY.

Lost in the Material World: Man's Search for Happiness. Steve D. Petterson. Ed. by Athalie Bolinger. 215p. (Orig.). 1992. text 17.95 (*1-881353-07-9*); pap. text 12.95 (*1-881353-11-7*) Excaliber Pub.

Lost in the Mirror: An Inside Look at Borderline Personality Disorder. Richard A. Moskovitz. 208p. (Orig.). 1996. pap. 12.95 (*0-87833-936-1*) Taylor Pub.

Lost in the Museum. Miriam Cohen. 1995. 10.19 (*0-606-07808-8*, Pub. by Turtleback) Demco.

Lost in the Rentharpian Hills: Spanning the Decades with Carl Jacobi. R. Dixon Smith. LC 84-72634. 146p. 1985. 18.95 (*0-87972-287-8*) Bowling Green Univ Popular Press.

***Lost in the Sauce Cookbook.** Gerry Beaney. LC 99-91516. 285p. 1999. ring bd. 28.00 (*0-9677246-0-0*) Shorewood Cntrl.

Lost in the Secret Cave. Peter R. Doyle. LC 96-7656. (Daring Adventure Ser.: Bk. 10). (J). (gr. 4). 1996. pap. 5.99 (*1-56179-481-3*) Focus Family.

Lost in the Shuffle: The Co-Dependent Reality. Robert Subby. 160p. 1987. pap. text 8.95 (*0-932194-45-1*, 22H123) Health Comm.

***Lost in the Snow.** Ian Beck. LC 99-47802. 2000. pap. write for info. (*0-439-17521-6*) Scholastic Inc.

Lost in the Stars: Vocal Score. Ed. by Michael Lefferts. 184p. (Orig.). (C). 1981. per. 45.00 (*0-88188-031-0*, 00312251) H Leonard.

***Lost in the Store.** Clare Mishica. Ed. by Laura Ring. (Illus.). 24p. (J). (ps-2). 2000. pap. 1.99 (*0-7847-1102-X*, 04307) Standard Pub.

Lost in the Storm. Carol Carrick. (Illus.). 32p. (J). (ps-3). 1987. pap. 6.95 (*0-89919-493-1*, Clarion Bks) HM.

***Lost in the Suburbs: A Political Travelogue.** Stephen Dale. 304p. 1999. 20.95 (*0-7737-3204-7*, Pub. by Stoddart Publ) Genl Dist Srvs.

Lost in the System: Miss Tenn U. S. A.'s Triumphant Fight to Claim a Family of Her Own. Charlotte Lopez & Susan Dworkin. (Illus.). 192p. 1996. pap. 11.00 (*0-684-81199-5*, Fireside) S&S Trade Pap.

Lost in the Tunnel of Time. Sharon Draper. (Ziggy & the Black Dinosaurs Ser.). (Illus.). (YA). (gr. 5-9). 1996. 14.00 (*0-614-15661-0*) Just Us Bks.

Lost in the Tunnel of Time. Sharon M. Draper. LC 96-75037. (Ziggy & the Black Dinosaurs Ser.). (Illus.). 96p. (J). (gr. 3-7). 1996. pap. 6.00 (*0-940975-63-7*) Just Us Bks.

Lost in the Tunnel of Time. Sharon M. Draper. (Ziggy & the Black Dinosaurs Ser.). (Illus.). (YA). (gr. 5-9). 1996. pap. 6.00 (*0-614-15662-9*) Just Us Bks.

Lost in the Victory: Reflections of American War Orphans of World War II. Ed. by Calvin L. Chistman. LC 97-26872. (Illus.). 252p. 1998. 29.95 (*1-57441-033-4*) UNTX Pr.

***Lost in the War.** Nancy Antle. (Illus.). 144p. (YA). (gr. 6-12). 2000. pap. 4.99 (*0-14-130836-2*, PuffinBks) Peng Put Young Read.

Lost in the Wilds of Canada. J. Cadiz. (Illus.). 96p. pap. 9.95 (*0-7710-1828-2*, 867297Q) McCland & Stewart.

Lost in the Woods. Douglas Gast. LC 93-74994. 1994. pap. 9.95 (*1-55673-827-7*, 7998, Fairway Pr) CSS OH.

Lost in the Woods: Child Survival for Parents & Teachers. Colleen Politano. LC 93-25700. (Illus.). 64p. 1993. reprint ed. pap. 6.99 (*0-934802-83-1*) Globe Pequot.

Lost in the Yellowstone: Truman Evert's "Thirty-Seven Days of Peril" Ed. by Lee H. Whittlesey. LC 95-23911. (Illus.). 112p. (Orig.). 1995. pap. 10.95 (*0-87480-481-7*) U of Utah Pr.

***Lost in Time.** Hans Magnus Enzensberger. LC 00-21091. 256p. (gr. 6-9). 2000. write for info. (*0-8050-6571-7*) H Holt & Co.

***Lost in Time.** Michelle McKinney. 1999. pap. write for info. (*1-58235-074-4*) Watermrk Pr.

Lost in Time. unabridged ed. Linda Creech. (Illus.). 20p. (Orig.). 1997. pap. 5.00 (*1-929326-60-2*) Hal Bar Pubg.

Lost in Time & Space with Lefty Feep. Robert Bloch. Ed. by John Stanley. LC 86-71608. (Lefty Feep Ser.: Vol. 1). (Illus.). 276p. 1987. pap. 12.95 (*0-940064-01-4*) Creatures at Large.

Lost in Time & Space with Lefty Feep. Robert Bloch & John Stanley. LC 86-71608. 1987. write for info. (*0-940064-03-0*) Creatures at Large.

Lost in Translation. Margaret Ball. 1995. per. 5.99 (*0-671-87688-0*) Baen Bks.

Lost in Translation. Steven Harvey. LC 96-31224. 144p. 1997. 22.95 (*0-8203-1890-6*) U of Ga Pr.

Lost in Translation. Nicole Mones. LC PS3563.O519L67 1998. 384p. 1998. 23.95 (*0-385-31934-7*) Delacorte.

Lost in Translation. Nicole Mones. 366p. 1999. pap. 12.95 (*0-385-31944-4*, Delta Trade) Dell.

Lost in Translation: A Life in a New Language. Eva Hoffman. 288p. 1990. pap. 13.95 (*0-14-012773-9*, Penguin Bks) Viking Penguin.

Lost in Vegas! John Peel. (Secret World of Alex Mack Ser.: No. 23). (J). (gr. 3-6). 1984. pap. 3.99 (*0-671-00710-6*) PB.

***Lost in Washington: Finding the Way Back to Democracy in America.** Barry M. Casper. 416p. 2000. 60.00 (*1-55849-246-1*); pap. 19.95 (*1-55849-247-X*) U of Mass Pr.

Lost in Yonkers. Neil Simon. LC 92-29111. 128p. 1993. pap. 10.95 (*0-452-26883-4*, Plume) Dutton Plume.

Lost Indian Magic: A Mystery Story of the Red Man As He Lived Before the White Man Came. G. Moon & C. Moon. 1977. lib. bdg. 39.95 (*0-8490-2185-5*) Gordon Pr.

Lost Industries of Derbyshire. John N. Merrill. 120p. 1987. 35.00 (*0-907496-32-6*, Pub. by JNM Pubns) St Mut.

Lost Initiatives: Canada's Forest Industries, Forest Policy & Forest Conservation, 69. Peter Gillis & Thomas R. Roach. LC 86-3122. (Contributions in Economics & Economic History Ser.: No. 69). 339p. 1986. 65.00 (*0-313-25415-X*, GLT/) Greenwood.

Lost Innocence. Tina Vasilos. (Intrigue Ser.). 1994. per. 2.99 (*0-373-22274-2*) Harlequin Bks.

Lost Innocents. Patricia MacDonald. 368p. 1999. mass mkt. 7.50 (*0-446-60759-2*, Pub. by Warner Bks) Little.

***Lost Innocents.** Patricia J. MacDonald. LC 99-43651. 1999. 26.95 (*1-57490-216-4*) T T Beeler.

Lost Innocents. Patricia J. MacDonald. LC 97-23306. 304p. 1998. 24.00 (*0-446-51687-2*, Pub. by Warner Bks) Little.

***Lost Inside My Brain: A Discovery of a New Therapy for Brain Injury & the Hidden Problems of Recovery.** Maureen Del Giacco. Ed. by Booth Associates Staff. (Illus.). 100p. 2000. pap. 29.99 (*0-9701233-0-2*) Del Giaccos Art.

Lost Island. Eilis Dillon. 1986. 16.95 (*0-86278-119-1*) Dufour.

Lost Island. large type ed. Phyllis A. Whitney. 1983. 15.95 (*0-7089-0939-6*) Ulverscroft.

***Lost Islands: The Story of Islands That Have Vanished from Nautical Charts.** Henry Stommel. (Illus.). 146p. 1999. reprint ed. text 35.00 (*0-7881-6277-2*) DIANE Pub.

Lost Japan: Travel Literature. Alex Kerr. LC 96-189209. 280p. 1996. pap. 10.95 (*0-86442-370-5*) Lonely Planet.

Lost Jews. Emma Klein. LC 96-142238. 288p. 1996. text 39.95 (*0-312-12890-8*) St Martin.

Lost Keats: An Owen Keane Mystery. Terence Faherty. LC 96-7358. (Mystery Ser.). 250p. 1996. per. 5.50 (*0-373-26192-6*, 1-26192-4, Wrldwide Lib) Harlequin Bks.

Lost Keys of Freemasonry. Manly P. Hall. LC 76-12212. (Illus.). 110p. 1976. reprint ed. pap. 12.95 (*0-89314-838-5*) Philos Res.

Lost Keys of Freemasonry: or The Secret of Hiram Abiff. enl. rev. ed. Manly P. Hall. xxiv, 110p. 1994. reprint ed. text 12.00 (*0-88053-044-8*, M 300) Macoy Pub.

Lost King, No. 1. Margaret Weis. (Star of the Guardians Ser.: Vol. 1). 496p. 1990. mass mkt. 6.99 (*0-553-28600-5*, Spectra) Bantam.

***Lost King of England: The East European Adventures of Edward the Exile.** Gabriel Ronay. (Illus.). 222p. 2000. pap. 24.95 (*0-85115-785-8*) Boydell & Brewer.

Lost Kingdoms of Africa: Black Africa Before 1600. Stuart Kallen. 1990. lib. bdg. 15.98 (*1-56239-016-3*) ABDO Pub Co.

Lost Kingdoms of the Maya. Gene S. Stuart & George E. Stuart. LC 92-40803. (Illus.). 248p. 1993. 34.95 (*0-87044-928-1*) Natl Geog.

Lost Kingdoms of the Maya. deluxe ed. Gene S. Stuart & George E. Stuart. LC 92-40803. (Illus.). 248p. 1993. 41.95 (*0-87044-929-X*) Natl Geog.

Lost Kurds. Fuccaro. 256p. Date not set. text 55.00 (*1-86064-170-9*, Pub. by I B T) St Martin.

Lost Lady. Willa Cather. 1976. 19.95 (*0-8488-0450-3*) Amereon Ltd.

Lost Lady. Willa Cather. LC 98-34211. 160p. 1999. mass mkt. 4.95 (*0-451-52720-8*, Sig Classics) NAL.

Lost Lady. Willa Cather. Ed. by Charles W. Mignon et al. LC 96-20642. (Willa Cather Scholarly Edition Ser.). (Illus.). xii, 371p. 1997. text 60.00 (*0-8032-1427-8*) U of Nebr Pr.

Lost Lady. Willa Cather. 174p. 1990. pap. 9.00 (*0-679-72887-2*) Vin Bks.

Lost Lady. Willa Cather & Morris Dickstein. LC 98-11660. (Penguin Twentieth-Century Classics Ser.). 1999. 8.95 (*0-14-118131-1*) Viking Penguin.

Lost Lady. Jude Deveraux. Ed. by Linda Marrow. 1991. mass mkt. 6.99 (*0-671-73977-8*) PB.

Lost Lady. Willa Cather. 1990. reprint ed. lib. bdg. 19.95 (*0-89966-650-7*) Buccaneer Bks.

Lost Lady. Willa Cather. (Collected Works of Willa Cather). 173p. 1998. reprint ed. lib. bdg. 88.00 (*1-58201-569-4*) Classic Bks.

Lost Lady of Hathaway Manor. Anne Knoll. 1992. mass mkt. 3.99 (*0-8217-3634-5*, Zebra Kensgtn) Kensgtn Pub Corp.

Lost Lady of Old Years. John Buchan. 213p. 1995. pap. 13.95 (*1-873631-42-1*, Pub. by B&W Pub) Firebird Dist.

Lost Lagoon. Jonathan Schmidt. Date not set. 11.95 (*0-7373-0116-3*); pap. text 4.95 (*0-7373-0117-1*) Lowell Hse.

Lost Lake. Houghton Mifflin Company Staff. (Literature Experience 1993 Ser.). (J). (gr. 3). 1992. pap. 9.48 (*0-395-61783-9*) HM.

Lost Lake. Allen Say. (Illus.). 32p. (J). (gr. 1-4). 1989. 16.00 (*0-395-50933-5*) HM.

Lost Lake. Allen Say. 1989. 12.15 (*0-606-01434-9*, Pub. by Turtleback) Demco.

Lost Lake. Allen Say. (Illus.). 32p. (J). (gr. k-3). 1992. pap. 6.95 (*0-395-63036-3*, Sandpiper) HM.

Lost Lake. Mark Slouka. LC 97-49471. 2000. pap. 12.00 (*0-375-70208-3*) Knopf.

Lost Lake. Mark Slouka. LC 97-49471. 192p. 1998. 21.00 (*0-375-40215-2*) Random.

Lost Lake. Mary Swander. (Poetry Chapbook Ser.). (Orig.). 1986. pap. 7.00 (*0-937669-23-7*) Owl Creek Pr.

Lost Lamb. Melody Carlson. LC 99-13300. (Illus.). 40p. (J). (ps-3). 1999. 9.99 (*1-58134-072-9*) Crossway Bks.

Lost Lamb: The Story of the Good Shepherd. Patricia L. Nederveld. LC 98-15641. (God Loves Me Ser.). (Illus.). 24p. (J). (ps). 1998. pap. 2.45 (*1-56212-308-4*, 1105-0139) CRC Pubns.

Lost Land. Paul Startzman. 96p. 1998. pap. 9.00 (*0-8059-4302-1*) Dorrance.

Lost Land: Poems. Eavan Boland. LC 98-3214. 96p. 1998. 21.00 (*0-393-04663-X*) Norton.

***Lost Land: Poems.** Eavan Boland. 72p. 1999. pap. 11.00 (*0-393-31951-2*) Norton.

Lost Land: The Chicano Image of the Southwest. J. Chavez. LC 84-11950. 214p. 1984. pap. 13.95 (*0-8263-0750-7*) U of NM Pr.

Lost Lands & Cities Beneath the Sea: Legends, Folklore & Facts of the North Atlantic. Jon D. Singer. LC 97-91101. (Illus.). 150p. 1997. pap. 15.00 (*0-9660555-0-0*) J D Singer.

***Lost Lands of the Book of Mormon.** Phyllis Carol Olive. LC 94-98119. (Illus.). 348p. 2000. pap. write for info. (*0-9678223-0-0*) P C Olive.

Lost Landscapes: In Search of Isaac Bashevis Singer & the Jews of Poland. Agata Tuszynska. Tr. by Madeline G. Levine from POL. LC 97-21245. Orig. Title: Singer: Pejzaze Pamieci. 192p. 1998. 23.00 (*0-688-12214-0*, Wm Morrow) Morrow Avon.

Lost Landscapes & Failed Economics: The Search for a Value of Place. Thomas Michael Power. LC 95-32365. 316p. 1998. text 32.00 (*1-55963-368-9*) Island Pr.

Lost Landscapes & Failed Economies: The Search for a Value of Place. Thomas Michael Power. 350p. 1998. pap. 17.95 (*1-55963-369-7*) Island Pr.

Lost Language. Tracey West. LC 95-117230. 80p. (J). (gr. 5-9). 1995. pap. text 4.95 (*0-8114-9325-3*) Raintree Steck-V.

Lost Language of Cranes. David Leavitt. LC 97-18297. 352p. 1997. pap. 12.00 (*0-395-87733-4*) HM.

Lost Language of Symbolism, Vol. 1. Harold Bayley. (Illus.). 388p. 1988. reprint ed. pap. 10.95 (*0-8065-1100-1*, Citadel Pr) Carol Pub Group.

Lost Language of Symbolism, Vol. 2. Harold Bayley. 1990. pap. 10.95 (*0-8065-1163-X*, Citadel Pr) Carol Pub Group.

Lost Languages. Jonathan Minton. 30p. 1999. pap. 6.00 (*0-9670994-2-0*) Longleaf Meth Coll.

Lost Lawyer: Failing Ideals of the Legal Profession. Anthony T. Kronman. 434p. 1995. pap. 16.95 (*0-674-53927-3*, KROLOX) Belknap Pr.

Lost Lawyer: Failing Ideals of the Legal Profession. Anthony T. Kronman. 448p. 1993. 43.50 (*0-674-53926-5*) HUP.

Lost Laysen. Margaret Mitchell. write for info. (*0-614-96881-X*) Random.

Lost Laysen. Margaret Mitchell. (Illus.). 128p. 1996. 18.00 (*0-684-82428-0*) S&S Trade.

Lost Laysen, a One of a Kind Scrapbook for the Millions of Fans of Gone with the Wind. Margaret Mitchell. 1997. 14.05 (*0-606-12761-5*, Pub. by Turtleback) Demco.

Lost Leader: A Study of Wordsworth. Hugh I. Fausset. 447p. (C). 1966. reprint ed. lib. bdg. 75.00 (*0-8383-0547-4*) M S G Haskell Hse.

***Lost Leaves: Women Writers of Meiji Japan.** Rebecca L. Copeland. LC 99-58864. (Illus.). 320p. 2000. text 49.00 (*0-8248-2229-3*); pap. text 24.95 (*0-8248-2291-9*) UH Pr.

Lost Ledges of the West. H. Glenn Carson. 96p. 1991. pap. 7.95 (*0-941620-43-3*) Carson Ent.

Lost Left: Three Studies in Socialism & Nationalism. David Howell. LC 86-6968. (Illus.). 360p. 1993. lib. bdg. 40.00 (*0-226-35513-6*) U Ch Pr.

Lost Left: Three Studies in Socialism & Nationalism. David Howell. LC 86-6968. (Illus.). 360p. 1997. pap. text 15.95 (*0-226-35514-4*) U Ch Pr.

***Lost Legacy: Inspiring Women of Nineteenth-Century America.** Ed. by Susan F. Poole. LC 99-35264. (Illus.). 160p. (Orig.). 1999. pap. 14.95 (*0-87785-386-X*, Pub. by Swedenborg) Words Distrib.

Lost Legacy: The Mormon Office of Presiding Patriarch. Irene Bates & E. Gary Smith. LC 95-5370. (Illus.). 368p. 1995. text 32.50 (*0-252-02163-0*) U of Ill Pr.

***Lost Legend of the First Christmas.** J. L. Hardesty. (Lost Legend Trilogy Ser.). 1999. 19.95 (*0-9661305-1-0*) Ampelos Pr.

Lost Legends of Israel. Dagobert D. Runes. 1997. 6.99 (*0-517-18077-4*) Random Hse Value.

***Lost Legends of New Jersey: A Novel.** Frederick Reichen. LC 99-57774. 320p. 2000. 24.00 (*0-15-100507-9*) Harcourt.

Lost Legends of the West. Bard Williams. 192p. 1996. 8.98 (*0-88394-093-0*) Promntory Pr.

Lost Lemuria. W. Scott-Elliot. 44p. 1996. reprint ed. spiral bd. 8.00 (*0-7873-0754-8*) Hlth Research.

Lost Lemuria with 2 Maps Showing Distribution of Land Areas at Different Periods (1904) W. Scott Elliot. 50p. 1996. reprint ed. pap. 7.00 (*1-56459-832-2*) Kessinger Pub.

Lost Lennon Interviews. Geoffrey Giuliano. LC 96-28055. 288p. 1996. pap. text 12.95 (*1-55850-638-1*) Adams Media.

Lost Letters to Harriet. Percy Bysshe Shelley. LC 72-2571. (Select Bibliographies Reprint Ser.). 1977. reprint ed. 15.95 (*0-8369-6864-6*) Ayer.

Lost Lexicon: Secret Meanings in the Vocabulary of Spanish Literature During the Inquisition. Sanford Shepard. LC 82-70140. (Coleccion de Estudios Hispanicos - Hispanic Studies Collection). 143p. (Orig.). 1982. pap. 19.95 (*0-89729-309-6*) Ediciones.

Lost Lhasa: Heinrich Harrer's Tibet. Photos & Text by Heinrich Harrer. (Illus.). 224p. 1997. pap. 24.95 (*0-8109-2789-6*, Pub. by Abrams) Time Warner.

Lost Library of Cormanthyr. TSR Staff. 1998. pap. 5.99 (*0-7869-0735-5*, Pub. by TSR Inc) Random.

Lost Life of Horatio Alger, Jr. Gary Scharnhorst & Jack Bales. LC 84-48295. (Illus.). 224p. 1985. 35.00 (0-253-14915-0) Ind U Pr.
Lost Life of Horatio Alger, Jr. Gary Scharnhorst & Jack Bales. LC 84-48295. (Illus.). 224p. 1992. pap. 7.95 (0-253-20648-0, MB-648) Ind U Pr.
Lost Life of Horatio Alger, Jr. Gary Scharnhorst & Jack Bales. LC 84-48295. (Illus.). 221p. reprint ed. pap. 68.60 (0-608-09360-2, 205410600002) Bks Demand.
Lost Light: An Interpretation of Ancient Scriptures. Alvin B. Kuhn. 619p. 1992. reprint ed. pap. 39.00 (1-56459-177-8) Kessinger Pub.
Lost Lighthouses: Stories & Images of America's Vanished Lighthouses. Tim Harrison & Ray Jones. LC 99-37596. (Illus.). 128p. 1999. pap. text 15.95 (0-7627-0443-8) Globe Pequot.
Lost Liners: From the Titanic to the Andrea Doria: The Ocean Floor Reveals Its Greatest Lost Ships. Robert Duane Ballard. 224p. (J). 1998. pap. 29.45 (0-7868-8384-7, Pub. by Hyperion) Time Warner.
Lost Liners: From the Titanic to the Andrea Doria: The Ocean Floor Reveals It's Greatest Lost Ships. Robert Duane Ballard & Rick Archbold. LC 97-15270. (Illus.). 224p. (J). 1997. 60.00 (0-7868-6296-3, Pub. by Hyperion) Time Warner.
Lost Link Recovered. Edwin A. Sherman. (Illus.). 50p. 1994. reprint ed. pap. 8.95 (1-56459-443-2) Kessinger Pub.
Lost Little Angel. M. M. Ragz. LC 96-44989. (Illus.). 32p. (J). (ps-2). 1999. 16.00 (0-689-81067-9) S&S Bks Yung.
Lost Little Bunny. Joanne Barkan. (Sparkle & Glow Bks.). (Illus.). 24p. (J). (ps-3). 1995. pap. 3.95 (0-590-48932-1, Cartwheel) Scholastic Inc.
Lost Little Pig. Le Rap. (Nursery Rhymes Ser.). 15p. (J). (gr. k-2). 1991. pap. text 23.00 (1-56843-038-8); pap. text 4.50 (1-56843-085-X) EMG Networks.
Lost Little Robin. Howard Goldsmith. LC 98-25244. (Illus.). 30p. (J). (ps-3). 1998. 12.95 (0-07-024800-1) McGraw.
Lost Little Spirit. Connor Synder. (Illus.). 31p. (Orig.). (J). (gr. 4-6). 1995. pap. 7.95 (0-9651496-0-9) Valentine Publng.
***Lost Lives.** Nina Auerbach. 1998. 25.00 (0-226-03199-3) U Ch Pr.
Lost Locket. Carolyn Keene. (Nancy Drew Notebooks: No. 2). 80p. (J). (gr. 2-4). 1994. pap. 3.99 (0-671-87946-4) PB.
Lost Locket. Carolyn Keene. (Nancy Drew Notebooks: No. 2). (J). (gr. 2-4). 1994. 9.19 (0-606-06608-X, Pub. by Turtleback) Demco.
Lost Locket of Windbrace Hall. Beverly C. Warren. 1991. mass mkt. 3.95 (0-8217-3419-9, Zebra Kensgtn) Kensgtn Pub Corp.
Lost Locomotive of the Battle-Axe. Mike Savage. 16p. 1993. pap. 2.00 (1-886028-07-9) Savage Pr.
Lost Lore of a Man's Life: Lots of Cool Stuff Guys Used to Know But Forgot About the Great Outdoors. Denis Boyles. LC 97-9595. 224p. 1997. pap. 13.00 (0-06-095224-5, Perennial) HarperTrade.
Lost Love. Shirley Dummer. 188p. 1994. pap. 8.00 (0-9633479-2-6) Dummer Pub.
Lost Love: The Untold Story of Henrietta Szold. Baila R. Shargel. LC 97-2517. 345p. 1997. 21.95 (0-8276-0629-X) JPS Phila.
Lost Love Found. Bertrice Small. 512p. 1991. mass mkt. 4.99 (0-345-37419-3) Ballantine Pub Grp.
Lost Love, Last Love. Rosemary Rogers. (Steve & Ginny Ser.: Bk. 3). 384p. 1980. reprint ed. mass mkt. 5.99 (0-380-75515-7, Avon Bks) Morrow Avon.
Lost Love Letters. Sandra E. Sager. 1998. pap. write for info. (1-57553-711-7) Watermrk Pr.
Lost Love Letters of Heloise & Abelard: Perceptions of Dialogue in Twelfth-Century France. Constant J. Mews. Tr. by Neville Chiavaroli from LAT. LC 98-39073. 302p. 1999. text 49.95 (0-312-21604-1) St Martin.
Lost Love of a Child. Told to Dee Oglesby. 36p. (YA). (gr. 7-12). 1995. pap. 6.95 (1-57515-052-2) PPI Pubng.
Lost Lullaby. Deborah G. Alecson. LC 94-11712. 1995. 30.00 (0-520-08870-0, Pub. by U CA Pr) Cal Prin Full Svc.
Lost Lunar Baedeker: Poems of Mina Loy. Mina Loy. LC 95-7622. 184p. 1996. 20.00 (0-374-25872-4) FS&G.
Lost Lunar Baedeker: Poems of Mina Loy. Mina Loy. 256p. 1997. pap. 13.00 (0-374-52507-2, Noonday) FS&G.
Lost Magic. Berthe Amoss. LC 93-10082. 192p. (J). (gr. 5-9). 1993. 14.95 (1-56282-573-9, Pub. by Hyprn Child) Little.
Lost Magic of Christianity: Celtic Essene Connections. Michael Poynder. LC 98-105991. 180p. 1998. pap. 17.95 (1-898256-25-X) Dufour.
***Lost Magic of Christianity: Celtic Essene Connections.** Michael Poynder. (Illus.). 192p. 2000. pap. 16.99 (0-9536631-0-8, Pub. by Green Magic) SCB Distributors.
Lost Man's River. Peter Matthiessen. LC 97-10124. 1998. pap. 14.00 (0-679-73564-X) Random.
Lost Mansions of Mississippi. Mary C. Miller. LC 95-51855. (Illus.). 192p. (C). 1996. 35.00 (0-87805-888-5) U Pr of Miss.
Lost Manuscript of Martin Taylor Harrison. Stephen Bly. LC 95-2613. (Austin-Stoner Files Ser.: Bk. 1). 352p. 1995. pap. 11.99 (0-89107-852-5) Crossway Bks.
Lost Manuscript of Martin Taylor Harrison. large type ed. Stephen A. Bly. 465p. (Orig.). 1996. 21.95 (0-7838-1596-4, G K Hall Lrg Type) Mac Lib Ref.
***Lost Masterpieces.** Joseph F. Paxton. (Architecture 3s Ser.). 1999. 19.95 (0-7148-3872-1) Phaidon Pr.
***Lost Masters.** Peter Harclerode. 2000. 27.95 (1-56649-165-7) Welcome Rain.
Lost Meaning of Classical Architecture: Speculations on Ornament from Vitruvius to Venturi. George L. Hersey. (Illus.). 214p. (Orig.). 1988. pap. text 14.95 (0-262-58089-6) MIT Pr.
***Lost Memoirs of Edgar Cayce.** 2000. mass mkt. write for info. (0-312-97144-3) St Martin.
Lost Memories, Bk. 1. Suma C. Hai. (CHI., Illus.). 58p. 1997. pap. 12.00 (1-886544-13-1) Suma Ching Hai Intl.
Lost Memories, Bk. II. Suma C. Hai. (Illus.). 48p. 1997. pap. 12.00 (1-886544-14-X) Suma Ching Hai Intl.
Lost Message. Grace Livingston Hill. 20.95 (0-89190-403-4) Amereon Ltd.
Lost Milk Jar. Lucy Conley. (Illus.). 24p. (J). (ps-2). 1986. pap. 2.55 (0-7399-0029-3, 2327) Rod & Staff.
Lost Millennium. rev. ed. Walter Richmond & Leigh Richmond. xviii, 172p. 1986. pap. 10.95 (0-943975-00-X) Interdimens Sci.
Lost Millennium: Second Fire. Mike Moscoe. 320p. 1997. mass mkt. 5.99 (0-441-00458-X) Ace Bks.
Lost Millennium III: Lost Days. Mike Moscoe. 1998. mass mkt. 5.99 (0-441-00510-1) Ace Bks.
Lost Mind. Christopher Pike, pseud. 213p. (J). (gr. 6-10). 1995. 14.00 (0-671-87261-3, Archway) PB.
Lost Mind. Christopher Pike, pseud. 256p. (YA). (gr. 9 up). 1995. per. 3.99 (0-671-87269-9, Archway) PB.
Lost Mind. Christopher Pike, pseud. 1995. 9.09 (0-606-07809-6, Pub. by Turtleback) Demco.
Lost Mines & Buried Treasures along the Old Frontier. John D. Mitchell. LC 77-121730. (Beautiful Rio Grande Classics Ser.). (Illus.). 260p. 1982. reprint ed. pap. 12.00 (0-87380-114-X) Popular E Commerce.
Lost Mines & Historic Treasures. N. L. Barlee. Ed. by Herb Bryce. 96p. (Orig.). 1987. pap. 11.95 (0-88839-992-8) Hancock House.
Lost Mines of the Great Southwest. John D. Mitchell. LC 70-114964. (Beautiful Rio Grande Classics Ser.). (Illus.). 202p. 1984. reprint ed. pap. 10.00 (0-87380-013-3) Popular E Commerce.
***Lost Minnesota: Stories of Vanished Places.** Jack El-Hai. LC 00-8652. (Illus.). 2000. write for info. (0-8166-3515-3) U of Minn Pr.
Lost Moon: The Perilous Voyage of Apollo 13. Jim Lovell & Jeffrey Kluger. LC 99-89647. (Illus.). 384p. 1994. 25.00 (0-395-67029-2) HM.
Lost Moose. Jan Slepian. LC 94-6738. (Illus.). 40p. (J). (ps-3). 1995. 15.95 (0-399-22749-0, Philomel) Peng Put Young Read.
Lost Museum: The Nazi Conspiracy to Steal the World's Greatest Works of Art. rev. enl. ed. Hector Feliciano. (Illus.). 256p. 1998. pap. 15.00 (0-465-04191-4, Pub. by Basic) HarpC.
Lost Music. Katrina Porteous. LC 97-120487. 64p. 1997. pap. 15.95 (1-85224-380-5, Pub. by Bloodaxe Bks) Dufour.
Lost Music: Gustav Mole's War on Noise. Kathryn Meyrick. LC 91-33555. (Illus.). 32p. (J). (ps-5). 1992. 13.99 (0-85953-304-2); pap. 6.99 (0-85953-327-1) Childs Play.
Lost Music: Gustav Mole's War on Noise. unabridged ed. Kathryn Meyrick. (Theatre Ser.). (Illus.). (J). (ps-5). 1992. audio 6.99 (0-85953-378-6) Childs Play.
Lost Musicians. William Heinesen. Tr. by Erik J. Friis & Hedin Bronner from DAN. LC 70-163120. (Library of Scandinavian Literature). 1971. lib. bdg. 10.95 (0-8057-3337-X) Irvington.
Lost My Shoe. Marjorie Weinman Sharmat. (J). 2000. write for info. (0-15-202008-X) Harcourt.
***Lost Mysteries World.** Reader's Digest Association Staff. 2000. pap. 30.00 (1-876689-42-0, Pub. by RD Assn) Penguin Putnam.
Lost Name, 3 vols., 1. Joseph Sheridan Le Fanu. Ed. by Devendra P. Varma. LC 76-5272. (Collected Works). (Illus.). 1977. reprint ed. 29.95 (0-405-09221-0) Ayer.
Lost Name, 3 vols., Set. Joseph Sheridan Le Fanu. LC 76-5272. (Collected Works). (Illus.). 1977. reprint ed. 87.95 (0-405-09220-2) Ayer.
Lost Name, 3 vols., Vol. 2. Joseph Sheridan Le Fanu. Ed. by Devendra P. Varma. LC 76-5272. (Collected Works). (Illus.). 1977. reprint ed. 29.95 (0-405-09222-9) Ayer.
Lost Name, 3 vols., Vol. 3. Joseph Sheridan Le Fanu. Ed. by Devendra P. Varma. LC 76-5272. (Collected Works). (Illus.). 1977. reprint ed. 29.95 (0-405-09223-7) Ayer.
Lost Names: Scenes from Korean Boyhood. Richard E. Kim. LC 97-46168. 196p. 1998. pap. 12.95 (0-520-21424-2, Pub. by U CA Pr) Cal Prin Full Svc.
Lost Narratives: Popular Fictions, Politics & Recent History. Roger Bromley. 204p. 1989. pap. 14.95 (0-415-01873-0) Routledge.
Lost Narratives: Popular Fictions, Politics & Recent History. Roger Bromley. LC 88-14883. (Popular Fiction Ser.). 246p. reprint ed. pap. 76.30 (0-608-20321-1, 207157400002) Bks Demand.
Lost New Testament Book. Frederick Seaborne. 59p. 1996. reprint ed. spiral bd. 9.00 (0-7873-0756-4) Hlth Research.
***Lost New York.** Nathan Silver. 256p. 2000. pap. 25.00 (0-618-05475-8) HM.
***Lost No More.** 1999. 7.95 (1-57734-585-1, 01114409) Covenant Comms.
Lost Notebook. S. R. Ramanujan. xxvi, 419p. 1988. 69.00 (0-387-18726-X) Spr-Verlag.
Lost Notebooks of Loren Eiseley. Ed. by Kenneth Heuer. 1987. 22.95 (0-316-35921-1) Little.
Lost Oasis. Patrick Roscoe. 324p. (Orig.). 1995. pap. 14.95 (0-7710-7579-0) McCland & Stewart.
Lost on a Mountain in Maine. Donn Fendler. LC 77-99178. (Illus.). 112p. (J). (gr. 4 up). 1992. mass mkt. 5.95 (0-688-11573-X, Wm Morrow) Morrow Avon.
Lost on a Mountain in Maine. Donn Fendler. (J). 1994. 19.25 (0-8446-6772-2) Peter Smith.
Lost on a Mountain in Maine. Donn Fendler. LC 77-99178. (Illus.). 125p. 1999. 14.95 (0-89725-100-8, 1209) Picton Pr.
Lost on a Mountain in Maine: A Brave Boy's True Story of His Nine-Day Adventure Alone in the Mountains. Donn Fendler. (J). 1992. 9.05 (0-606-01378-4, Pub. by Turtleback) Demco.
Lost on Earth: Nomads of the New World. Mark Fritz. LC 98-26214. 304p. (gr. 8). 1999. 25.00 (0-316-29478-0) Little.
***Lost on Earth: Nomands of the New World.** Mark Fritz. LC 99-88060. (Illus.). 2000. pap. 16.00 (0-415-92609-2) Routledge.
***Lost on Earth: or Fateful Love.** Linda Kozlova. LC 99-91959. 2000. 25.00 (0-7388-1412-1); pap. 18.00 (0-7388-1413-X) Xlibris Corp.
***Lost on Everest: The Search for Mallory & Irvine.** P. L. Firstbrook. LC 00-31533. 2000. write for info. (0-8092-9736-1, Contemporary Bks) NTC Contemp Pub Co.
***Lost on Everest: The Search for Mallory & Irvine.** Peter Firstbrook. (Illus.). 224p. 1999. pap. 24.95 (0-8092-9892-9, 98929, Contemporary Bks) NTC Contemp Pub Co.
Lost on Sherman's Alley. Toby Gibbs & Jerry Voigt. (Illus.). 65p. 1993. pap. text 6.95 (1-883589-17-7) Clark Pub KY.
Lost on the Trail. Kenneth Taylor. Ed. by Tracy Moore. 96p. (J). (gr. 3-8). 1999. pap. 6.50 (1-891635-11-5) Moore Bks.
Lost on Victoria Lake. (Illus.). 76p. (Orig.). (J). (gr. 3-7). 1994. pap. 4.95 (0-9632074-3-1) Azimuth GA.
Lost One Found: Little Sames, 10 vols. Ed. by Chris Zarate. (Rays of Sunshine Ser.: Vol. 4). 55p. 1998. reprint ed. pap. 5.25 (1-893645-04-5) Born Again.
Lost Ones. Kevin J. Anderson. (Star Wars: No. 3). (Orig.). (J). (gr. 4-7). 1998. mass mkt. 5.99 (0-425-16999-5) Berkley Pub.
Lost Ones. Kevin J. Anderson & Rebecca Moesta. (Star Wars: No. 3). 232p. (Orig.). (J). (gr. 3-5). 1995. mass mkt. 4.99 (1-57297-052-9) Blvd Books.
Lost Ones. Margaret Greaves. (Duckling Ser.). (Illus.). 96p. (J). (gr. 4-6). 1993. 16.95 (0-460-88053-5, Pub. by J M Dent & Sons) Trafalgar.
Lost Ones. Samuel Beckett. LC 72-84341. Orig. Title: Le Depeupleur. 63p. 1988. reprint ed. pap. 9.95 (0-8021-3092-5, Grove) Grove-Atltic.
Lost Opportunities: The Civil Rights Record of the Bush Administration Mid-Term. Citizens' Commission on Civil Rights. Ed. by Susan M. Liss & William L. Taylor. LC 91-70979. 251p. (Orig.). 1991. pap. text 15.00 (0-9622865-1-6) CCCR.
Lost Opportunities: The Cyprus Question, 1950-1963. Evangelos Averoff-Tossizza. Tr. by Timothy Cullen & Susan Kyriakides from GRE. viii, 440p. 1986. 30.00 (0-89241-389-1) Caratzas.
Lost Opportunity: What Has Made Economic Reform in Russia So Difficult. Marshall I. Goldman. LC 94-16500. 300p. (C). 1994. text 24.00 (0-393-03700-2) Norton.
Lost Opportunity: What Has Made Economic Reform in Russia So Difficult. Marshall I. Goldman. LC 94-16500. 320p. 1996. pap. 13.95 (0-393-31485-5, Norton Paperbks) Norton.
Lost Orisha. Conrad E. Mauge. (Illus.). 224p. (Orig.). 1996. pap. 19.95 (0-9637516-4-6) Hse of Providence.
Lost Pages. Paul Di Filippo. LC 98-8394. 304p. 1998. pap. 15.95 (1-56858-099-1) FWEW.
Lost Paintings of Tunis Ponsen. William H. Gerdts & Susan S. Weininger. (Illus.). 115p. (Orig.). 1994. pap. 15.00 (0-614-29786-9) Muskegon Art.
Lost Paradise. Jean Clair. LC 96-135279. (Illus.). 600p. 1995. 125.00 (2-89192-194-1) Mont Mus Fine Arts.
***Lost Paradise.** Junichi Watanabe. 432p. 2000. 28.00 (4-7700-2324-3, Pub. by Kodansha Intl) Kodansha.
Lost Paradise. Robert P. Coffin. 1988. reprint ed. lib. bdg. 79.00 (0-7812-0366-X) Rprt Serv.
Lost Paradise: A Boyhood on a Maine Coast Farm. Robert P. Coffin. LC 78-144951. 1971. reprint ed. 49.00 (0-403-00904-9) Scholarly.
Lost Paradise: Early Reminiscences. Samuel Chotzinoff. LC 74-27970. (Modern Jewish Experience Ser.). 1975. reprint ed. 34.95 (0-405-06700-3) Ayer.
***Lost Passions of Jesus.** Don Milam, Jr. 2000. pap. 11.99 (0-9677402-0-7, Pub. by Mercy Place) Destiny Image.
Lost Patrol: The Mounties' Yukon Tragedy. Dick North. (Illus.). 160p. 1995. reprint ed. pap. 9.95 (1-895714-70-2) Raincoast Bk.
Lost Pensions: Settled Accounts of the Act of 6 April 1838. Craig R. Scott. 374p. 1996. pap. 28.00 (1-888265-03-5) Willow Bend.
Lost People Matter to God. Bill Hybels et al. (Defining Moments Ser.: Vol. 9). 1994. audio 12.99 (0-310-21059-3) Zondervan.
Lost Perspective? Trade Unions Between Ideology & Social Action in the New Europe Vol. 1: Ideological Persistence in National Traditions. Ed. by Patrick Pasture et al. (Perspectives on Europe Ser.: Vol. 1). 304p. 1996. 72.95 (1-85972-080-3, Pub. by Avebry) Ashgate Pub Co.
Lost Perspective? Trade Unions Between Ideology & Social Action in the New Europe Vol. 2: Significance of Ideology in European Trade Unionism. Ed. by Patrick Pasture et al. (Perspectives on Europe Ser.). 416p. 1996. 85.95 (1-85972-330-6, Pub. by Avebry) Ashgate Pub Co.
Lost Perspectives: The Art & Culture of Western Washington. Nile Thompson & Darrel Thiel. 1986. 3.95 (0-917048-60-1) Wash St Hist Soc.
Lost Perspectives? Trade Unions Between Ideology & Social Action in the New Europe, Vol. 1 & 2. Ed. by Patrick Pasture et al. (Perspectives on Europe Ser.). 720p. 1996. 149.95 (1-85972-331-4, Pub. by Avebry) Ashgate Pub Co.
Lost Pharaohs. Leornard Cottrel. 23.95 (0-88411-523-2) Amereon Ltd.
Lost Pharaohs: The Romance of Egyptian Archaeology. Leonard B. Cottrell. LC 72-90140. 256p. 1969. reprint ed. lib. bdg. 35.00 (0-8371-2260-0, COLP, Greenwood Pr) Greenwood.
Lost Pilot. James Tate. LC 75-21618. (Yale Series of Younger Poets: No. 62). reprint ed. 18.00 (0-404-53862-2) AMS Pr.
Lost Pilot. James Tate. LC 67-13449. (American Poetry Ser.: No. 22). 71p. 1982. reprint ed. pap. 5.95 (0-912946-97-0, Ecco Press) HarperTrade.
***Lost Plant!** Elizabeth S. Schussler & James H. Wandersee. LC 99-4. (Illus.). 40p. (J). (ps-6). 1999. spiral bd. 9.95 (1-55212-236-0, Thinking Log Pr) Trafford Pub.
Lost Plates of Laman. Bob Lewis. LC 97-33412. (Illus.). 76p. 1997. pap. 12.95 (1-56085-097-3) Signature Bks.
Lost Plays of Shakespeare's Age. Charles J. Sisson. LC 70-24859. x, 221p. 1971. write for info. (0-391-00151-5) Humanities.
Lost Plays of the Harlem Renaissance, 1920-1940. Ed. by James V. Hatch & Leo Hamalian. LC 96-29052. (African American Life Ser.). (Illus.). 416p. 1996. pap. 25.95 (0-8143-2580-7) Wayne St U Pr.
Lost Plays of the Irish Renaissance, Vol. 2. Ed. by William Feeney. 1979. 10.00 (0-912262-70-2) Proscenium.
Lost Pleiad & Other Poems. Thomas Holley Chivers. (Works of Thomas Holley Chivers Ser.). 1990. reprint ed. lib. bdg. 79.00 (0-7812-2284-2) Rprt Serv.
Lost Poet. Annabel Lee & Liz Levaar. LC 96-61964. 416p. 1997. 25.95 (1-890171-15-8); pap. 16.95 (1-890171-16-6) Unicorn Recs & Pub.
Lost Prime Minister: A Life of Sir Charles Dilke. David Nicholls. LC 95-6072. 1995. 55.00 (1-85285-125-2) Hambledon Press.
Lost Prince. Frances Hodgson Burnett. (J). 25.95 (0-8488-0691-3) Amereon Ltd.
Lost Prince. Peggy Downing. Orig. Title: Segra & Stargull. (Illus.). 216p. (J). (gr. 2-4). 1995. reprint ed. pap. 6.49 (0-89084-834-3, 088799) Bob Jones Univ.
Lost Princess. Paula Marshall. 1999. per. 4.99 (0-373-30337-8) Harlequin Bks.
Lost Princess. Rafe Martin. LC 98-4335. (J). 1999. 15.95 (0-399-22924-8, G P Putnam) Peng Put Young Read.
Lost Princess. Rabbi Nachman of Breslov. Ed. by Moshe Mykoff. (Illus.). 64p. (J). (gr. 1-4). 1996. 8.00 (0-930213-66-1) Breslov Res Inst.
Lost Princess. large type ed. Paula Marshall. (Mills & Boon Large Print Ser.). 350p. 1996. 23.99 (0-263-14759-2, Pub. by Mills & Boon) Ulverscroft.
***Lost Princess.** George MacDonald. Ed. by Glenn Edward Sadler. (Illus.). 134p. (J). 1999. reprint ed. text 25.00 (0-7881-6847-9) DIANE Pub.
Lost Princess of Oz. L. Frank Baum. (J). 22.95 (0-8488-0786-3) Amereon Ltd.
Lost Princess of Oz. L. Frank Baum & Peter Glassman. LC 97-78415. (Illus.). 352p. (J). (gr. 4-7). 1998. 24.00 (0-688-14975-8, Wm Morrow) Morrow Avon.
Lost Princess of Oz. unabridged ed. L. Frank Baum. LC 98-46178. (Illus.). 336p. (J). 1999. pap. 8.95 (0-486-40344-0) Dover.
Lost Profits in Patent Infringement Cases. Duane Burton. LC TX4-761-60. 800p. 1998. pap. 297.75 (1-928780-01-6) Big Foot Pr.
Lost Promise: An Intelligence Assessment. John A. Gentry. LC 92-36974. 324p. (C). 1993. lib. bdg. 49.00 (0-8191-8951-0) U Pr of Amer.
Lost Property. Bruce Ingman. LC 97-20638. (Illus.). 32p. (J). (ps-3). 1998. 15.00 (0-395-88900-6) HM.
Lost Property. Sylvia Kantaris. 1998. pap. 15.95 (1-85224-438-0, Pub. by Bloodaxe Bks) Dufour.
***Lost Property: Memoirs & Confessions of a Bad Boy.** Ben Sonnenberg. LC PN4874.S5753A3 1999. 264p. 1999. reprint ed. pap. text 15.00 (1-58243-045-4, Pub. by Counterpt DC) HarpC.
***Lost Property: The Woman Writer & English Literary History, 1380-1589.** Jennifer Summit. LC 99-87252. 1999. pap. text 18.00 (0-226-78013-9); lib. bdg. 45.00 (0-226-78012-0) U Ch Pr.
Lost Prophet: The Book of Enoch & Its Influence on Christianity. Margaret Barker. LC 88-35121. 128p. 1989. pap. 9.95 (0-687-22779-8) Abingdon.
Lost Prophets. Malabre. 1995. pap. 14.95 (0-07-103641-5) McGraw.
Lost Prophets: An Insider's History of the Modern Economists. Alfred L. Malabre, Jr. 272p. 1995. pap. 14.95 (0-87584-644-0) Harvard Busn.
Lost Province. Thomas McCarthy. LC 97-179141. 76p. 1996. pap. 15.95 (0-85646-276-4, Pub. by Anvil Press) Dufour.
Lost Puritan: A Life of Robert Lowell. Paul Mariani. (Illus.). 560p. 1996. pap. 15.00 (0-393-31374-3, Norton Paperbks) Norton.
Lost Pyramids of Rock Lake: Wisconsin's Sunken Civilization. Frank Joseph. LC 92-10283. (Illus.). 224p. 1992. pap. 14.95 (1-880090-04-X) Galde Pr.
Lost Quotes. John Marks. LC 94-60808. (Illus.). 81p. (Orig.). 1994. pap. 5.95 (0-9642648-0-3) Toranaga Pr.
Lost Race & Adult Fantasy Fiction Series, 69 bks., Set. Ed. by R. Reginald & Douglas Melville. (Illus.). 1978. lib. bdg. 2018.00 (0-405-10950-4) Ayer.
Lost Railroads of New England. 2nd rev. ed. Ronald D. Karr. LC 95-76497. (New England Rail Heritage Ser.). (Illus.). 167p. (Orig.). 1996. pap. 12.95 (0-942147-04-9) Branch Line Pr.

L

An Asterisk (*) at the beginning of an entry indicates that the title is appearing for the first time.

Lost Realms. Zecharia Sitchin. (Earth Chronicles Ser.: Bk. 4). 304p. 1990. mass mkt. 6.99 (0-380-75890-3, Avon Bks) Morrow Avon.

Lost Realms. Zecharia Sitchin. LC 89-91927. (Earth Chronicles Ser.: Bk. 4). (Illus.). 304p. 1990. reprint ed. 19.95 (0-939680-84-X) Bear & Co.

***Lost Rebellion.** Manoj Joshi. LC 99-936245. (Illus.). 1999. write for info. (0-14-027846-X) Penguin Books.

Lost Records: 1853 Pay Roster of the Washington (D. C.) Aqueduct. Carrie Eldridge. (Illus.). 60p. 1993. reprint ed. spiral bd. 15.00i (1-928979-16-5) C Eldridge.

Lost Reform: The Campaign for Compulsory Health Insurance in the United States from 1932 to 1943. Daniel S. Hirshfield. LC 71-115187. (Commonwealth Fund Publications). 235p. 1970. 26.50 (0-674-53917-6) HUP.

***Lost Religion of Jesus: Simple Living & Nonviolence in Early Christianity.** Keith Akers. 2000. pap. 20.00 (1-930051-26-3) Lantern Books.

***Lost Revolutions: The South in the 1950s.** Pete Daniel. LC 99-48066. (Illus.). 488p. 2000. 45.00 (0-8078-2537-9); pap. 19.95 (0-8078-4848-4) U of NC Pr.

Lost Rhythm Avenue. Jay Alamares. 48p. 1997. pap. 8.00 (1-888662-13-1) Vinegar Hill.

Lost Rib. Sharon Magnarelli. LC 83-46157. 232p. 1985. 38.50 (0-8387-5074-5) Bucknell U Pr.

***Lost Rider: A Bilingual Anthology - The Corvina Book of Hungarian Verse.** Corvina Books Staff. 432p. 1999. pap. 30.00 (963-13-4784-2, Pub. by Corvina Bks) St Mut.

Lost Rights: The Destruction of American Liberty. James Bovard. LC 95-20797. 416p. 1995. pap. 14.95 (0-312-12333-7, St Martin Griffin) St Martin.

***Lost River.** Richard Bangs. LC 99-13287. 266p. (YA). 1999. 25.00 (1-57805-026-X, Pub. by Sierra) Random.

Lost River. Paxton Riddle. 1999. mass mkt. 6.50 (0-425-16940-5) Berkley Pub.

Lost River. Roger Sheffer. LC 88-90528. 144p. (Orig.). 1988. pap. 14.95 (0-935939-02-4) Night Tree Pr.

Lost River Conspiracy. Dave Jackson. LC 95-31797. 220p. (YA). 1995. pap. 8.95 (1-56148-183-1) Good Bks PA.

***Lost River Mountain.** Charles Potts. 1999. pap. 13.00 (0-911287-32-9) Blue Begonia.

Lost Road & Other Writings: Language & Legend Before The Lord of the Rings. J. R. R. Tolkien. 1996. mass mkt. 6.99 (0-345-40685-0) Ballantine Pub Grp.

Lost Road & Other Writings: Language & Legend Before The Lord of the Rings. J. R. R. Tolkien. Ed. & Frwd. by Christopher Tolkien. (Illus.). 464p. 1987. 27.50 (0-395-45519-7) HM.

Lost Roads Project: A Walk-In Book of Arkansas. C. D. Wright. LC 94-30424. (Illus.). 112p. 1994. pap. text 16.00 (1-55728-362-1) U of Ark Pr.

***Lost Romance Ranch.** Annie Jones. LC 00-22410. (Route 66 Romantic Comedy Ser.: Vol. 3). (Illus.). 240p. 2000. pap. 6.95 (1-57856-135-3) Waterbrook Pr.

***Lost Runes.** Jane Welch. (Illus.). 608p. 1998. mass mkt. 11.95 (0-00-648200-7, Pub. by HarpC) Trafalgar.

Lost Russia: Photographing the Ruins of Russian Architecture. William C. Brumfield. LC 94-23065. (Illus.). 144p. 1995. 64.95 (0-8223-1557-2); pap. 27.95 (0-8223-1568-8) Duke.

Lost Sadists. Willard Gellis. 50p. (Orig.). 1988. pap. 7.00 (0-917455-07-X) Big Foot NY.

Lost Sahara Trail. Herbert Kaufmann. (J). (gr. 7 up). 1962. 10.95 (0-8392-3022-2) Astor-Honor.

***Lost Sailor.** Pam Conrad. LC 91-39640. 32p. (J). (gr. k-4). 1999. pap. 4.95 (0-06-443381-1, HarpTrophy) HarpC Child Bks.

Lost Saints: Gender & Victorian Literary Canonization. Tricia Lootens. (Victorian Literature & Culture Ser.). 288p. (C). 1996. text 35.00 (0-8139-1652-6) U Pr of Va.

Lost Sandstones & Lonely Skies & Other Essays. Jesse Stuart. LC 77-18066. 1979. 9.95 (0-89097-025-4) Archer Edns.

***Lost Science.** Gerry Vassilatos. 347p. 2000. pap. 16.95 (0-932813-75-5, Pub. by Adventures Unltd) SCB Distributors.

Lost Scout: A Garth Ryland Mystery. John R. Riggs. LC 97-32233. 352p. 1998. 17.95 (1-56980-121-5) Barricade Bks.

Lost Scrapbook. Evan Dara. 400p. 1995. 21.95 (1-57366-006-X) Fiction Coll.

Lost Scrapbook. Evan Dara. 475p. 1998. pap. 14.95 (1-57366-038-8) Fiction Coll.

***Lost Scrolls.** Chris Heimerdinger. LC 99-168698. (Tennis Shoes Adventure Ser.). 279 p. 1999. pap. 13.95 (1-57734-418-9, 01113747) Covenant Comms.

Lost Scrolls Medallion: Solid Brass Medallion, 1. Llewellyn. 1999. pap. text 10.00 (1-56718-058-2) Llewellyn Pubns.

Lost Scrolls of King Solomon. Richard Behrens. LC 98-5386. (Illus.). 432p. 1999. pap. 24.95 (1-56718-059-0) Llewellyn Pubns.

Lost Sea. Jan De Hartog. 1976. 22.95 (0-8488-0982-3) Amereon Ltd.

Lost Secrets of Ayurvedic Acupuncture: An Ayurvedic Guide to Acupuncture. Frank Ros. LC 93-80314. 206p. (Orig.). 1994. pap. 15.95 (0-914955-12-8) Lotus Pr.

Lost Secrets of Prayer: Practices for Self-Awakening. Guy Finley. LC 97-51713. 240p. 1999. reprint ed. pap. 9.95 (1-56718-276-3) Llewellyn Pubns.

Lost Secrets of the Mystery Schools: Coming of the Gods. Earlyne C. Chaney. 218p. 1991. per. 15.95 (0-918936-24-1) Astara.

Lost Sheep see **Oveja Perdida**

Lost Sheep see **Oveja Perdida**

Lost Sheep. Diane D. Fallon. (Illus.). 98p. (Orig.). 1987. pap. 9.95 (0-9618176-0-7) Full Dickens.

***Lost Sheep, 1.** Andy Robb. 1999. 6.00 (0-570-05586-5) Concordia.

Lost Ships. Bound. 192p. 1998. 30.00 (0-684-85077-X) S&S Trade.

Lost Ships: The Discovery & Exploration of the Ocean's Sunken Treasures. Mensun Bound. LC 98-36551. (Illus.). 192p. 1998. 35.00 (0-684-85251-9, S&S Edns) Simon & Schuster.

***Lost Shores, Forgotten Peoples: Spanish Explorations of the South East Maya Lowlands.** Ed. by Lawrence H. Feldman. (Illus.). 288p. 2000. pap. 18.95 (0-8223-2624-8); lib. bdg. 54.95 (0-8223-2630-2) Duke.

Lost Shrine of Bundushatur. Michael D. Wagner. 1998. 9.95 (0-7869-1194-8, Pub. by TSR Inc) Random.

Lost Sierra; Gold, Ghosts & Skis: Legendary Days of Skiing in the California Mining Camps. William B. Berry & Chapman Wentworth. 256p. 1992. 37.50 (0-9631721-0-7); pap. 25.00 (0-9631721-1-5) W&A Comms.

Lost Silk Hat. Edward J. Dunsany. LC 94-20189. 1994. pap. 5.00 (0-88734-335-X) Players Pr.

Lost Sir Massingberd: A Romance of Real Life. James Payn. LC 75-32794. (Literature of Mystery & Detection Ser.). 1976. reprint ed. 28.95 (0-405-07891-9) Ayer.

Lost Sisterhood: Prostitution in America, 1900-1918. Ruth C. Rosen. LC 81-23678. 272p. (C). 1983. pap. 15.95 (0-8018-2665-9) Johns Hopkins.

Lost Skiff. Donald Wetzel. LC 85-61541. 192p. 1986. reprint ed. 22.00 (0-933256-60-4) Second Chance.

Lost Slipper & the Curse of the Ramsbottoms. Tristan Davies. (Wallace & Gromit Comic Strip Bks.). 1998. pap. text 9.95 (0-8417-3035-0) Advent Med Kits.

Lost Snowman. Joyce. 32p. (ps-3). 15.95 (0-06-027430-1); lib. bdg. 15.89 (0-06-027431-X) HarpC.

***Lost Son, 1.** Andy Robb. (Illus.). 10p. (J). (ps). 1999. 6.00 (0-570-05587-3) Concordia.

Lost Son. Brent Spencer. 288p. 1995. 19.45 (1-55970-266-4, Pub. by Arcade Pub Inc) Time Warner.

Lost Songs: Political & Other Poems. Philip Ward. (Modern Poets Ser.: Vol. 11). (Illus.). 48p. 1981. pap. 5.95 (0-902675-51-6) Oleander Pr.

Lost Sonnets of Cyrano de Bergerac: A Poetic Fiction. James L. Carcioppolo. LC 97-92863. (Illus.). xiii, 115p. 1998. pap. 12.00 (0-9662204-0-4) Lost Sonnet Pubg.

Lost Soul. M. C. Summer. (Extreme Zone Ser.: No. 7). (YA). (gr. 6 up). 1997. per. 3.99 (0-671-01413-7, Archway) PB.

Lost Soul: The Confederate Soldier in New England. Les Rolston. LC 99-25079. 312p. 1998. pap. 12.95 (0-916489-88-4) Ancestry.

Lost Soul & Other Stories. Malavika Kapur. (New World Literature Ser.: No. 21). 1989. 12.75 (81-7018-563-7, Pub. by BR Pub) S Asia.

***Lost Soul Companion: Comfort & Constructive Advice for Struggling Actors, Musicians, Artists, Writers & Other Free Spirits.** Susan M. Brackney. LC 99-91690. (Illus.). 160p. 2000. 10.00 (0-9676323-0-7) Puckitt Pr.

Lost Soul of American Politics: Virtue, Self-Interest, & the Foundations of Liberalism. John P. Diggins. LC 86-10594. 424p. (C). 1986. pap. text 32.00 (0-226-14877-7) U Ch Pr.

***Lost Souls.** Ed. by Charles Boer. (Spring Journal Ser.: Vol. 65). 2000. pap. 17.50 (1-882670-17-5, Pub. by Spring Jrnl) Continuum.

Lost Souls. Poppy Z. Brite. 384p. 1993. mass mkt. 6.99 (0-440-21281-2) Dell.

***Lost Souls: A Bizarre Voyage into the Lives of the Desolate That Run Wild in Search of Deliverance.** Shawn P. Lytle. 112p. 1999. pap. 18.00 (0-9668764-1-5) One Way Out.

Lost Souls: A Cry to Recapture What's Disappearing in American Education. Tammi A. Lawrence. x, 231p. 1996. 22.00 (1-889934-01-1) Bs Hive Pub.

Lost Souls: Helping Young Adult Chronic Patients. Bert Pepper & Hilary Ryglewicz. 300p. 1996. 29.95 (0-02-924965-1) Free Pr.

***Lost Souls & Fallen Spirits, 1.** C. Carmelita. (Tien-Tu Ser.). 305p. 1999. pap. 15.00 (0-9668012-6-1) Enlighten Noah.

***Lost Source Exercise, 1997: Exercise of Radiological Response Through Cooperation & Coordination of Local, State & Federal Agency Resources under the National Contingency Plan.** B. Belanger. 48p. 1998. pap. 4.25 (0-16-062758-3) USGPO.

Lost Spanish Towns: Atascosito & Trinidad De Salcedo. Jean L. Epperson. (Illus.). 118p. (Orig.). 1996. pap. 10.00 (1-887745-07-6) Dogwood TX.

Lost Spirituals. Lily Y. Cohen. LC 74-39081. (Black Heritage Library Collection). (Illus.). 1977. reprint ed. 23.95 (0-8369-9019-6) Ayer.

Lost Stage Valley. Frank Bonham. 1998. 17.50 (0-7540-8022-6, Gunsmoke) Chivers N Amer.

Lost Stage Valley. large type ed. Frank Bonham. LC 97-44872. (Nightingale Ser.). 294p. 1998. pap. 18.95 (0-7838-8377-3, G K Hall & Co) Mac Lib Ref.

Lost Stamps of the United States. Ralph T. Foster. (Illus.). 160p. (Orig.). (J). (gr. 1-12). 1994. pap. text 29.99 (0-9643066-0-3) Foster Pubng.

Lost Star: The Search for Amelia Earhart. Randall Brink. (Illus.). 224p. 1995. pap. 12.95 (0-393-31311-5, Norton Paperbks) Norton.

Lost Star: The Story of Amelia Earhart. Patricia Lauber. LC 88-3043. 112p. (J). (gr. 4-7). 1990. pap. 3.50 (0-590-41159-4) Scholastic Inc.

Lost Stars: Lost, Missing & Troublesome Stars from the Catalogues of Johannes Bayer, Nicholas-Louis de Lacaille, John Flamsteed & Sundry Others. Morton Wagman. (Illus.). 250p. 2000. 49.95 (0-939923-78-5) M & W Pub Co.

Lost Steps. Andre Breton. Tr. & Intro. by Mark Polizzotti. LC 96-3479. (French Modernist Library). xxi, 135p. 1996. text 35.00 (0-8032-1242-9) U of Nebr Pr.

Lost Steps. Alejo Carpentier. Tr. by Harriet De Onis. 280p. 1989. pap. 12.00 (0-374-52199-9) FS&G.

Lost Steps of Reiki: The Channeled Messages of Wei Chi. Thomas A. Hensel & Kevin R. Emery. (Orig.). 1997. pap. 9.95 (1-890405-02-7) LightLines.

***Lost Stories for All Ages: Apocryphal Literature for the 21st Century.** W. Kent Smith. (Illus.). 198p. 1999. pap. 19.95 (0-9675869-0-9) Lodestar Cin Creat.

Lost Stories of Louisa May Alcott. Louisa May Alcott. Ed. by Daniel Shealy. LC 95-6897. 1995. 10.95 (0-8065-1654-2) Carol Pub Group.

Lost Stories of Louisa May Alcott, Set. unabridged ed. Louisa May Alcott. Ed. by Madeleine B. Stern et al. 1995. 16.95 incl. audio (1-882071-53-0, 393003, Pub. by B&B Audio) Lndmrk Audiobks.

Lost Stradivarius. John M. Falkner. Ed. by Edward Wilson. (World's Classics Ser.). 224p. 1991. pap. 7.95 (0-19-282848-7) OUP.

Lost Subjects, Contested Objects: Toward a Psychoanalytic Inquiry of Learning. Deborah P. Britzman. LC 97-35166. 256p. (C). 1998. text 59.50 (0-7914-3807-4); pap. text 19.95 (0-7914-3808-2) State U NY Pr.

Lost Subjects/Found Objects. Lawrence Fixel. Ed. by Jo-Anne Rosen. 30p. 1998. pap. 10.00 (1-879457-57-1, Finders Keepers Pr) Norton Coker Pr.

***Lost Suitcase: Reflections on the Literary Life.** Nicholas Delbanco. 227p. 2000. 24.95 (0-231-11542-3) Col U Pr.

Lost Summer. Elizabeth Feuer. LC 93-34212. 192p. (J). (gr. 7 up). 1995. 16.00 (0-374-31020-3) FS&G.

Lost Summer. Elizabeth Feuer. (J). 1997. 9.09 (0-606-11580-3, Pub. by Turtleback) Demco.

Lost Summer: The Heyday of the West End Theatre. Charles Duff. 272p. 1996. pap. 17.95 (0-435-07023-1) Heinemann.

Lost Summer: The '67 Red Sox & the Impossible Dream. Bill Reynolds. 328p. 1993. mass mkt. 5.50 (0-446-36427-4, Pub. by Warner Bks) Little.

Lost Sunshine. Clyde Bolton. LC 93-7775. 190p. 1994. 20.00 (1-881320-06-5, Black Belt) Black Belt Communs.

Lost Supper - The Last Generation. Phil Smith & Phil Demise. (Illus.). 72p. (Orig.). 1991. pap. 10.00 (0-685-47864-5) Gegenschein.

Lost Sword of the Confederate Ghost: A Mystery in Two Centuries. Emily C. Monte. LC 98-20332. (J). 1999. 5.99 (1-57249-132-9) White Mane Pub.

Lost T'ai-chi Classics from the Late Ch'ing Dynasty. Douglas Wile. LC 96-17699. (SUNY Series in Chinese Philosophy & Culture). 160p. (C). 1996. text 49.50 (0-7914-2653-X); pap. text 16.95 (0-7914-2654-8) State U NY Pr.

Lost Talent: Women in the Sciences. Sandra L. Hanson. LC 96-219. (Labor & Social Change Ser.). 224p. (C). 1996. lib. bdg. 39.95 (1-56639-446-5) Temple U Pr.

Lost Tales of Horatio Alger: Adventure, Romance & Moral Intrigue, the Best of Alger's Early Tales. Ed. by Gary Scharnhorst. LC 89-14919. 240p. (YA). (gr. 10 up). 1990. 6.95 (0-934745-11-0) Acadia Pub Co.

Lost Teachings of Atlantis. Jon Peniel. (Illus.). 371p. Date not set. pap. 17.95 (0-9660015-0-8, 2001) Windsor-Hill.

***Lost Temple.** DK Publishing Staff. (LEGO Game Bks.). 32p. (J). (gr. k-5). 1999. pap. 4.95 (0-7894-4706-1) DK Pub Inc.

Lost Temple of the Aztecs: What It Was When the Spaniards Invaded Mexico. Shelley Tanaka. LC 98-10986. (Illus.). 48p. (J). (gr. 4-9). 1998. 16.95 (0-7868-0441-6, Pub. by Hyperion) Time Warner.

***Lost Temple of Tula.** Gaby Goldsack. (Playmobil Pop-Ups Ser.). 10p. (J). (gr. k-3). 2000. 7.99 (1-57584-416-8) Rdrs Digest.

Lost Temple of Zorro. William McCay. (The Mask of Zorro Ser.). (J). (gr. 3-6). 1999. pap. 4.50 (0-671-51971-9) PB.

"Lost" Ten Tribes of Israel... Found! 2nd rev. ed. Steven M. Collins. 439p. 1992. pap. 16.00 (0-944379-11-7, 900-292) CPA Bk Pub.

Lost Theory of Asclepiades of Bithynia. J. T. Vallance. 174p. 1990. text 55.00 (0-19-824248-4) OUP.

Lost Threshold. Thomas G. Wheeler. LC 68-16349. (Illus.). (J). (gr. 7 up). 1968. 26.95 (0-87599-140-8) S G Phillips.

***Lost Time: On Remembering & Forgetting in Late Modern Culture.** David Gross. (Critical Perspectives on Modern Culture Ser.). 256p. 2000. 29.95 (1-55849-254-2) U of Mass Pr.

***Lost to the World.** A. Lynar. 1998. pap. text 35.00 (1-84018-066-8, Pub. by Mainstream Pubng) Trafalgar.

Lost to Them. Gaytri Saggar. 232p. 1997. 18.00 (0-8059-4001-4) Dorrance.

***Lost Tomb.** Kent R. Weeks. LC 98-21769. 384p. 1999. 27.50 (0-688-15087-X, Wm Morrow) Morrow Avon.

***Lost Tomb: In 1995, An American Egyptologist Discovered The Burial Site Of The Sons Of Ramesses Ii--this Is His.** Kent R. Weeks. LC 98-21769. (Illus.). 352p. 1999. reprint ed. pap. 16.00 (0-688-17224-5, Wm Morrow) Morrow Avon.

Lost Tooth Club. Arden Johnson. LC 97-29723. (Illus.). 32p. (J). (gr. k-2). 1998. 13.95 (1-883672-55-4) Tricycle Pr.

***Lost Tooth Club.** Arden Johnson. (Illus.). (J). (ps-3). 2000. pap. 5.95 (1-58246-041-8) Tricycle Pr.

Lost Toronto. William Dendy. (Illus.). 1979. 25.00 (0-19-540294-4) OUP.

Lost Town of Bledsoesborough, Tennessee: Its Beginning, Its End: Two Essays in the Record of Tennessee's Upper Cumberland of Old. Vernon Roddy. 1984. pap. 10.00 (0-318-03885-4) Upper Country.

***Lost Towns of Tidewater Maryland.** Donald G. Shomette. (Illus.). 376p. 2000. 34.95 (0-87033-527-8, Tidewtr Pubs) Cornell Maritime.

Lost Trade Routes. Shirley Toulson. 1989. pap. 25.00 (0-85263-649-0, Pub. by Shire Pubns) St Mut.

Lost Trails & Forgotten People: The Story of Jones Mountain. 2nd ed. Tom Floyd. LC 81-81883. 160p. 1985. pap. 7.50 (0-915746-21-2) Potomac Appalach.

Lost Trails of the Cimarron. 2nd ed. Harry E. Chrisman. LC 98-21220. (Illus.). 320p. 1998. pap. 16.95 (0-8061-3017-2) U of Okla Pr.

Lost Trappers. David H. Coyner. Ed. & Afterword by David J. Weber. LC 94-36584. (Illus.). 232p. 1995. pap. 12.95 (0-8061-2725-2) U of Okla Pr.

Lost Trappers. David H. Coyner. 1992. reprint ed. lib. bdg. 75.00 (0-7812-5020-X) Rprt Serv.

Lost Traveler. Sanora Babb. LC 95-7569. 314p. 1995. pap. 10.95 (0-8263-1568-2) U of NM Pr.

Lost Travellers: A Romantic Theme with Variations. Bernard Blackstone. LC 83-1546. 292p. 1983. reprint ed. lib. bdg. 65.00 (0-313-23882-0, BLLT, Greenwood Pr) Greenwood.

Lost Treasure Mazes. Roger Moreau. 1999. pap. text 5.95 (0-8069-7811-2) Sterling.

Lost Treasure of Captain Blood. Jonathan Stroud. (Candlewick Gamebook Ser.). (Illus.). 32p. (J). 1997. reprint ed. pap. 7.99 (0-614-16040-5) Candlewick Pr.

Lost Treasure of Captain Blood: A Pirate Puzzle Adventure. Jonathan Stroud. LC 95-41016. (Illus.). 32p. (J). (gr. 4-7). 1996. 14.99 (1-56402-875-5) Candlewick Pr.

***Lost Treasure of Captain Kidd.** Peter Lourie. (Illus.). 96p. (Orig.). (J). (gr. 4-7). 2000. pap. 8.95 (1-56397-851-2) Boyds Mills Pr.

Lost Treasure of Captain Kidd. Peter Lourie. LC 95-40852. (Illus.). 157p. (Orig.). (J). (gr. 3 up). 1996. pap. 10.95 (1-885482-03-5) Shawangunk Pr.

Lost Treasure of Casa Loma. Eric Wilson. 112p. (J). (gr. 3-6). 1992. pap. 3.95 (0-7736-7380-6) Stoddart Publ.

Lost Treasure of the Inca. Peter Lourie. (Illus.). 48p. (YA). (gr. 5-8). 1999. 18.95 (1-56397-743-5) Boyds Mills Pr.

Lost Treasure of the Knights Templar: Solving the Oak Island Mystery. Steven Sora. LC 98-48741. (Illus.). 293p. 1999. pap. 16.95 (0-89281-710-0, Destiny Bks) Inner Tradit.

Lost Treasure of the Rainforest. Judith M. Austin. (GlobalFriends Adventures Ser.). (Illus.). 64p. (J). (gr. 2-6). 1996. pap. 5.95 (1-58056-002-4, GlobalFr Pr) GlobalFriends.

Lost Treasure Ships of the Twentieth Century. Nigel Pickford. LC 99-14514. (Illus.). 192p. 1999. 40.00 (0-7922-7472-5) Natl Geog.

Lost Treasures. (Library of Curious & Unusual Facts). (Illus.). 128p. 1990. 17.27 (0-8094-7703-3); lib. bdg. 23.27 (0-8094-7704-1) Time-Life.

Lost Treasures: A guide to Buried Treasures, 1 vol. Bill Yenne. LC 99-174435. 1999. mass mkt. 6.99 (0-425-16742-9) Berkley Pub.

Lost Treasures & Wonders. Charles A. Mills. 55p. 1996. pap. 5.00 (0-945598-10-6) Apple Cheeks Pr.

Lost Treasures of Baja California. James Francez. Ed. by W. B. Knox & Martha Quinn. LC 96-228264. (ENG & SPA., Illus.). 100p. 1996. pap. 29.95 (1-881116-72-7) Black Forest Pr.

Lost Treasures of Scotland. Jack Forbes. (Illus.). 108p. 1986. pap. 9.95 (0-941402-03-7) Devon Pub.

Lost Treasures of the West: Legends of Bullion, Lost Shipwrecks, Hidden Mines & Stagecoach Stories. Brad Williams & Choral Pepper. 192p. 1997. pap. 7.99 (0-88394-097-3) Galahad Bks.

Lost Treasures on the Old Spanish Trail. George A. Thompson. 122p. 1987. pap. 13.95 (0-914740-31-8) Western Epics.

Lost Tribe. Mark Lee. LC 98-6905. 256p. 1998. text 22.00 (0-312-18695-9) St Martin.

Lost Tribe. Mark Lee. 288p. 1999. pap. 13.00 (0-312-20420-5, Picador USA) St Martin.

***Lost Tribe.** Edward Marriott. 2000. pap. 14.00 (0-8050-6449-4) H Holt & Co.

***Lost Tribe: A Harrowing Passage into New Guinea's Heart of Darkness.** Edward Marriott. 258p. 2000. 23.00 (0-7881-9341-4) DIANE Pub.

Lost Tribe: A Harrowing Passage into New Guinea's Heart of Darkness. Edward Marriott. LC 97-10420. 1997. 23.00 (0-8050-5318-2) H Holt & Co.

Lost Tribes: History, Doctrine, Prophecies & Theories about Israel's Lost Ten Tribes. R. Clayton Brough. 1992. 14.98 (0-88290-441-8) Horizon Utah.

Lost Tribes & Sunken Continents. Robert Wauchope. 1962. lib. bdg. 12.50 (0-226-87635-7) U Ch Pr.

Lost Tribes & Sunken Continents: Myth & Method in the Study of American Indians. Robert Wauchope. LC 62-18112. 177p. reprint ed. pap. 54.90 (0-608-16393-7, 202675000051) Bks Demand.

Lost Tribes of Israel: or The First of the Red Men. Charles Even. 1977. 29.95 (0-405-10243-7, 14436) Ayer.

Lost Tribes of North Carolina: Index & Digest to Hathaway's "North Carolina Historical & Genealogical Register", Pt. 1. Worth S. Ray. 192p. 1997. reprint ed. pap. 22.50 (0-8063-0479-0, 4795) Clearfield Co.

Lost Tribes of North Carolina: Old Albemarle & Its Absentee Landlords, Pt. IV. Worth S. Ray. LC 67-9767. 156p. 1998. reprint ed. pap. 17.50 (0-8063-0287-9) Clearfield Co.

Lost Tribes of the Irish in South. Irvin S. Cobb. (Collected Works of Irvin S. Cobb). 300p. 1998. reprint ed. lib. bdg. 88.00 (1-58201-598-8) Classic Bks.

Lost Trumpets: A Conservative Map to America's Destiny. Bruce Herschensohn. 282p. (C). 1994. 27.50 (0-930783-24-7) Claremont Inst.

***Lost Twin.** Peter Pereira. 37p. 2000. pap. 14.95 (1-58249-006-6) Grey Spider.

***Lost Twin.** limited deluxe ed. Peter Pereira. 37p. 2000. 45.00 (1-58249-005-8) Grey Spider.

Lost Twin, 3. Raymond Pizante. (Longman Originals Ser.). 1995. pap. text 5.51 (0-582-08142-4) Addison-Wesley.

An Asterisk (*) at the beginning of an entry indicates that the title is appearing for the first time.

Lost Twin Cities. Larry Millett. LC 92-10460. (Illus.). 336p. 1992. pap. 29.95 (0-87351-273-1) Minn Hist.

Lost Umbrella of Kim Chu. 2nd ed. Ed. by D. H. Howe. (Illus.). 62p. 1993. pap. text 5.95 (0-19-585493-4) OUP.

Lost Universe: Pawnee Life & Culture. Gene Weltfish. LC 77-7164. (Illus.). xx, 508p. 1977. reprint ed. pap. 16.95 (0-8032-5871-2, Bison Books) U of Nebr Pr.

Lost Valley: A Western Trio. Max Brand. LC 98-2606. 1998. 20.00 (0-7862-0997-6) Thorndike Pr.

Lost Valley: A Western Trio. large type ed. Max Brand. LC 99-11212. (Illus.). 1999. 23.95 (0-7862-1036-2) Mac Lib Ref.

Lost Valley, & Other Stories. Algernon Blackwood. LC 70-167442. (Short Story Index Reprint Ser.). (Illus.). 1977. reprint ed. 23.95 (0-8369-3968-9) Ayer.

Lost Victorian Architecture. James K. Kettlewell. (Illus.). 12p. 1977. 10.00 (0-685-70733-4) Gal Assn NY.

Lost Victories. Erich Von Manstein. Orig. Title: Verlorene Siege. 1994. lib. bdg. 37.95 (1-56849-383-5) Buccaneer Bks.

Lost Victories: The Military Genius of Stonewall Jackson. B. Alexander. 350p. 1996. 10.98 (0-7858-0722-5) Bk Sales Inc.

Lost Victories: War Memoirs of Hitlers Most Brilliant General. Erich Von Manstein. LC 82-3779. (Illus.). 592p. 1994. pap. 22.95 (0-89141-525-4) Presidio Pr.

Lost Village: Historic Driving Tours in the Catskills. Mary Robinson Sive. LC 98-172959. (Illus.). 176p. 1998. pap. 14.95 (1-892289-00-8) DCHA.

Lost Village: Portrait of an Irish Village in 1925. John McKenna. 71p. (Orig.). 1995. reprint ed. pap. 9.95 (1-874597-17-0, Pub. by New Island Books) Irish Bks Media.

***Lost Village of Central Park.** Hope L. Killcoyne. LC 99-22378. (Mysteries in Time Ser.: Vol. 9). (Illus.). 89p. (J). (gr. 3-7). 1999. lib. bdg. 14.95 (1-893110-02-8) Silver Moon.

Lost Villages of England. Maurice Beresford. LC 99-202683. (History Handbooks Ser.). (Illus.). 448p. 1998. pap. 29.95 (0-7509-1848-9, Pub. by Sutton Pub Ltd) Intl Pubs Mktg.

Lost Voices: Women, Chronic Pain, & Abuse. Nellie A. Radomsky. LC 94-29611. 1995. pap. 14.95 (1-56023-864-X) Haworth Pr.

Lost Voices: Women, Chronic Pain & Abuse. Nellie A. Radomsky. LC 94-29611. 172p. 1995. lib. bdg. 54.95 (1-56024-921-8, Harrington Park) Haworth Pr.

Lost Voices of World War One: An International Anthology of Writers, Poets & Playwrights. Ed. by Tim Cross. (Illus.). 414p. (Orig.). (C). 1990. pap. text 23.95 (0-87745-264-4) U of Iowa Pr.

Lost Voyages: Two Centuries of Shipwrecks in the Approaches to New York. Bradley Sheard. LC 97-32170. (Illus.). 216p. 1998. pap. 29.95 (1-881652-17-3) Aqua Quest.

***Lost Wagon Train.** large type ed. Zane Grey. LC 98-48133. 1999. 19.95 (1-57490-171-0, Sagebrush LP West) T T Beeler.

Lost Wake. Laban Hill. LC 98-84828. (X Games Extreme Mysteries). 96p. (J). (gr. 3-7). 1998. pap. 3.95 (0-7868-1263-X, Pub. by Hyperion) Time Warner.

Lost Wanderer: A Guide to Finding the Wandering Alzheimer's Disease Subject. Robert J. Koester & David Stooksbury. (Illus.). 150p. (Orig.). 1999. pap. text 9.95 (1-879471-16-7) DBS Prodns.

Lost Warriors. Rachel Lee. (And the Winner Is...Ser.). 1997. mass mkt. 3.99 (0-373-48347-3, 1-48347-8) Harlequin Bks.

Lost Warriors: American Hero, Conard County. Rachel Lee. (Intimate Moments Ser.). 1993. per. 3.50 (0-373-07535-9, 5-07535-3) Silhouette.

Lost Was the Key: A True Story of Alien Abduction. Leah A. Haley. LC 93-215739. 168p. 1995. reprint ed. pap. 16.95 (1-883729-03-3) Greenleaf Tenn.

Lost Wax: Poems. Heather Ramsdell. LC 97-33774. (National Poetry Ser.). 80p. 1998. pap. 11.95 (0-252-06706-1) Univ of Illinois at Chicago.

Lost-Wax Casting: A Practitioner's Manual. Wilburt Feinberg. (Illus.). 96p. 1983. pap. 17.50 (0-903031-88-4, Pub. by Intermed Tech) Stylus Pub VA.

Lost Weddings: A Novel. Maria Beig. Tr. by Peter Blickle & Jaimy Gordon from GER. 140p. 1990. 17.95 (0-89255-145-3) Persea Bks.

***Lost Weekend.** Billy Wilder et al. LC 00-23397. 150p. 2000. pap. 15.95 (0-520-21856-6, Pub. by U CA Pr) Cal Prin Full Svc.

Lost Weekend. Charles Jackson. LC 78-26163. 1979. reprint ed. lib. bdg. 14.00 (0-8376-0430-3) Bentley Pubs.

Lost Weekend. Charles Jackson. 1993. reprint ed. lib. bdg. 19.95 (1-56849-167-0) Buccaneer Bks.

Lost Weekend: A Novel. Charles Jackson. LC 96-9572. 244p. 1996. reprint ed. pap. 16.95 (0-8156-0419-X, JALWP) Syracuse U Pr.

Lost Wild America: The Story of Our Extinct & Vanishing Wildlife. enl. rev. ed. Robert M. McClung. LC 93-15657. (Illus.). xvi, 277p. (YA). (gr. 6-12). 1993. lib. bdg. 29.50 (0-208-02359-3, Linnet Bks) Shoe String.

***Lost Wilderness.** limited ed. Mohamed I. Ismail & Alice T. Pianfetti. (Illus.). 216p. 2000. 60.00 (1-57157-099-3) Safari Pr.

Lost with All Hands: A Family Forever Changed. Mary Melton. LC 98-88764. (Illus.). 254p. 1998. pap. 14.95 (0-89725-364-7, 1903, Penobscot Pr) Picton Pr.

***Lost Woman.** large type ed. Nara Lake. 272p. 2000. 31.99 (0-7089-4170-2) Ulverscroft.

Lost Women, Banished Souls. Garnett K. Cohen. 168p. (C). 1996. pap. 17.95 (0-8262-1073-2) U of Mo Pr.

Lost Woods. large type ed. Carson. LC 98-44509. 1999. 30.00 (0-7862-1697-2) Thorndike Pr.

Lost Woods: The Discovered Writing of Rachel Carson. Rachel Louise Carson. Ed. by Linda Lear. LC 98-20058. (Illus.). 288p. 1999. pap. 16.00 (0-8070-8547-2) Beacon Pr.

***Lost Word: A. U. M.; A Masonic Monograph.** Frank C. Higgins. (Illus.). 1999. pap. 8.95 (1-55818-465-1) Holmes Pub.

Lost Word Found. J. D. Buck. 50p. 1992. reprint ed. pap. 7.00 (0-922802-14-9) Kessinger Pub.

Lost Word of Freemasonry. Hilton Hotema. 58p. (Orig.). 1996. reprint ed. spiral bd. 12.00 (0-7873-0424-7) Hlth Research.

Lost Word of Freemasonry. Henry Pirtle. 240p. 1993. reprint ed. pap. 19.95 (1-56459-320-7) Kessinger Pub.

***Lost Words: Narratives of Language & the Brain, 1825-1926.** L. S. Jacyna. LC 99-89724. (Illus.). 256p. 2000. 45.00 (0-691-00413-7) Princeton U Pr.

Lost Words & Lost Worlds: Modernity & the Language of Everyday Life in Nineteenth-Century Stockholm. Allan R. Pred. (Cambridge Human Geography Ser.). (Illus.). 316p. (C). 1990. text 69.95 (0-521-37531-2) Cambridge U Pr.

Lost Work of Stephen King: A Guide to Unpublished Manuscripts, Story Fragments, Alternative Versions, & Oddities. Stephen J. Spignesi. LC 98-24116. 361p. 1998. 19.95 (1-55972-469-2, Birch Ln Pr) Carol Pub Group.

Lost Work of Stephen King: Complete & Uncut Signed Limited Edition. aut. limited ed. Stephen J. Spignesi. 400p. 1998. 60.00 (1-892950-03-0) Overlook Connect.

Lost Work of Stephen King: Complete & Uncut Signed Limited Edition - Lettered 1-52. aut. limited ed. Stephen J. Spignesi. 300p. 1998. 350.00 (1-892950-04-9) Overlook Connect.

Lost Works of William Carlos Williams: The Volumes of Collected Poetry as Lyrical Sequence. Robert J. Cirasa. LC 94-41572. 344p. 1995. 49.50 (0-8386-3576-8) Fairleigh Dickinson.

Lost World. Arthur Conan Doyle. 320p. 1989. pap. 5.95 (0-89733-331-4) Academy Chi Pubs.

Lost World. Arthur Conan Doyle. 1992. pap. text. write for info. (0-17-556535-X) Addison-Wesley.

Lost World. Arthur Conan Doyle. 1976. 21.95 (0-8488-0990-4) Amereon Ltd.

Lost World. Arthur Conan Doyle. 1988. lib. bdg. 18.95 (0-89966-233-1) Buccaneer Bks.

Lost World. Arthur Conan Doyle. 176p. 1998. pap. 1.50 (0-486-40060-3) Dover.

Lost World. Arthur Conan Doyle. (Twelve-Point Ser.). 1999. lib. bdg. 24.00 (1-58287-112-4) North Bks.

Lost World. Arthur Conan Doyle. Ed. by Ian Duncan. (Oxford World's Classics Ser.). 768p. 1998. pap. 8.95 (0-19-283352-9) OUP.

Lost World. Arthur Conan Doyle. (Puffin Classics Ser.). (Illus.). 288p. (YA). (gr. 5 up). 1995. pap. 4.99 (0-14-036748-9, PuffinBks) Peng Put Young Read.

Lost World. Arthur Conan Doyle. Ed. by Sarah Matthews. (Thornes Classic Novels Ser.). (Illus.). 243p. 1996. pap. 16.95 (0-7487-2481-8, Pub. by S Thornes Pubs) Trans-Atl Phila.

Lost World. Arthur Conan Doyle. 256p. 1993. mass mkt. 4.99 (0-8125-3468-9, Pub. by Tor Bks) St Martin.

Lost World. Arthur Conan Doyle. 256p. 1997. mass mkt. 4.99 (0-8125-6483-9, Pub. by Tor Bks) St Martin.

Lost World. Ed. by Microfax Staff. (J). 1997. pap. text 2.95 (0-7894-2117-8) DK Pub Inc.

Lost World. large type ed. Arthur Conan Doyle. (Large Print Heritage Ser.). 340p. 1998. lib. bdg. 31.95 (1-58118-034-9, 22017) LRS.

***Lost World, Set.** unabridged ed. Arthur Conan Doyle. (YA). (gr. 8 up). 1998. 35.95 incl. audio (1-55685-583-4) Audio Bk Con.

Lost World: A Novel. Michael Crichton. (YA). 1996. mass mkt. 7.99 (0-345-40288-X) Ballantine Pub Grp.

Lost World: A Novel. Michael Crichton. (YA). 1997. pap. 12.00 (0-345-41900-6); mass mkt. 7.99 (0-345-91166-0) Ballantine Pub Grp.

Lost World: A Novel, 4 vols. Michael Crichton. 1995. audio 27.50 (0-679-44763-6) Discovery.

Lost World: A Novel. Michael Crichton. (YA). 1997. 14.95 (0-679-45540-X) Knopf.

Lost World: A Novel. large type ed. Michael Crichton. 640p. (YA). 1995. 25.95 (0-7838-1589-1, G K Hall Lrg Type) Mac Lib Ref.

Lost World: And Other Stories. Arthur Conan Doyle. (Classics Library). 480p. 1998. pap. 3.95 (1-85326-245-5, 2455WW, Pub. by Wrdsworth Edits) NTC Contemp Pub Co.

Lost World: Jurassic Park. John Whitman & David Koepp. (Illus.). 320p. 1997. 9.95 (0-8118-1999-X) Chronicle Bks.

Lost World: Jurassic Park: The Movie Storybook. Jane Mason. LC 96-80479. (Illus.). 32p. (Orig.). (J). 1997. pap. 8.95 (0-448-41573-9, G & D) Peng Put Young Read.

Lost World: Jurassic Park 2 Official Guide. Brady Games Staff & Christine Cain. 112p. 1997. 11.99 (1-56686-711-8) Brady Pub.

Lost World: Tibet. Amaury De Riencourt. 320p. (C). 1990. 110.00 (0-907855-04-0, Pub. by Honeyglen Pub Ltd) St Mut.

Lost World No. 2: The End of the Third World. Marcio Souza. Tr. by Lana Santamaria. 368p. (Orig.). 1993. pap. 12.00 (0-380-89829-2, Avon Bks) Morrow Avon.

***Lost World Adventures.** Mark S. Smith. LC 99-67328. 2000. pap. 10.99 (0-89051-277-9) Master Bks.

Lost World, Does It Exist? Robert Johnstone. 1978. 13.95 (0-317-54306-7) Dufour.

Lost World, Does It Exist? Robert Johnstone. 1978. 21.00 (0-901072-75-3) Dufour.

Lost World Movie Scrapbook. Preller James. LC 97-177455. (J). 1997. pap. text 7.99 (0-590-37399-4) Scholastic Inc.

Lost World of Agharti: The Mystery of Vril Power. Alec MacLellan. (Illus.). 236p. 1997. pap. 12.95 (0-285-63314-7, Pub. by Souvenir Pr Ltd) IPG Chicago.

Lost World of Classical Legal Thought: Law & Ideology in America, 1886-1937. William M. Wiecek. LC 97-28858. 296p. 1998. text 65.00 (0-19-511854-5) OUP.

Lost World of the Craft Printer. Maggie Holtzberg-Call. (Folklore & Society Ser.). (Illus.). 256p. 1992. text 27.50 (0-252-01799-4) U of Ill Pr.

Lost World of the Kalahari. Laurens Van Der Post. LC 77-4292. (Illus.). 288p. 1977. reprint ed. pap. 13.00 (0-15-653706-0, Harvest Bks) Harcourt.

Lost World of Thomas Jefferson. Daniel J. Boorstin. LC 80-26835. 320p. 1981. pap. 12.95 (0-226-06496-4) U Ch Pr.

Lost World of Thomas Jefferson. Daniel J. Boorstin. LC 93-17196. xiv, 320p. 1993. pap. 14.95 (0-226-06497-2) U Ch Pr.

Lost World of Willis O'Brien: The Original Shooting Script of the 1925 Landmark Special Effects Dinosaur Film, with Photographs. Ed. by Roy Kinnard. LC 92-56657. (Illus.). 176p. 1993. lib. bdg. 34.50 (0-89950-861-8) McFarland & Co.

Lost World Piano Solos Jurassic Park. J. Williams. 40p. 1997. pap. 12.95 (0-7935-8540-6) H Leonard.

Lost Worlds. Damon Wilson. 1998. mass mkt. 9.95 (1-85487-698-8, Pub. by Scarlet Bks) London Brdge.

Lost Worlds: How Our European Ancestors Coped with Everyday Life & Why Life Is So Hard Today. Arthur E. Imhof. Tr. by Thomas Robisheaux from GER. LC 96-6721. (Studies in Early Modern German History). (Illus.). 224p. 1996. 29.95 (0-8139-1659-3) U Pr of Va.

Lost Worlds & Mad Elephants - Literature Science & Technology, 1700-1990: Proceedings International Conference on Science Technology. Illus. by Elmar Schenkel & Stefan Welz. (Leipzig Explorations in Literature & Culture Ser.: Vol. 2). 422p. 1999. 59.80 (3-931397-16-5) Galda & Wilch.

Lost Worlds Romance: From Dawn till Dusk, 51. Allienne R. Becker. LC 92-1130. (Contributions to the Study of Science Fiction & Fantasy Ser.: No. 51). 184p. 1992. 55.00 (0-313-26123-7, BKR/, Greenwood Pr) Greenwood.

Lost Wreck of the Isis. Robert Duane Ballard. (J). (gr. 4-7). 1994. pap. 4.95 (0-590-43853-0) Scholastic Inc.

Lost Wright: Frank Lloyd Wright's Vanished Masterpieces. Carla Lind. (Illus.). 176p. 1996. 34.50 (0-684-81306-8) S&S Trade.

Lost Writings. James Connolly & Aindrias O. Casthasaigh. LC 97-28160. 256p. 1997. 59.95 (0-7453-1297-7, Pub. by Pluto GBR) Stylus Pub VA.

Lost Writings. James Connolly & Aindrias O. Casthasaigh. 256p. 1997. pap. 21.95 (0-7453-1296-9, Pub. by Pluto GBR) Stylus Pub VA.

Lost Writings. Jack L. Saunders. 158p. 1998. reprint ed. pap. 10.00 (1-892590-28-X) Out Your Bk.

***Lost Years.** Ed. by Surrey Beatty Staff. 160p. 1999. pap. 68.00 (0-949324-64-7, Pub. by Surrey Beatty & Sons) St Mut.

Lost Years. large type ed. Diana Morgan. (General Ser.). 464p. 1993. 27.99 (0-7089-2882-X) Ulverscroft.

Lost Years. J. M. Dillard. Ed. by David Stern. (Star Trek Giant Novel Ser.). 448p. (Orig.). 1990. reprint ed. mass mkt. 5.99 (0-671-70795-7) PB.

Lost Years: A Memoir, 1945-1951. Isherwood. 256p. 2000. 25.00 (0-06-118001-7, HarpCollins) HarperTrade.

Lost Years: My 1632 Days in Vietnamese Reeducation Camps. Tran Tri Vu. LC 88-82258. (Indochina Research Monographs). 381p. (C). 1989. pap. 15.00 (1-55729-006-7) IEAS.

Lost Years & Other Stories. Deitz. 1994. pap. 6.95 (0-938985-12-4) Mntn Memories Bks.

Lost Years of Jesus Revealed. Charles F. Potter. 160p. 1985. mass mkt. 5.99 (0-449-13039-8, GM) Fawcett.

Lost Years of Merlin. T. A. Barron. LC 96-33920. (Lost Years of Merlin Ser.: No. 1). 336p. (J). (gr. 4-7). 1996. pap. 19.99 (0-399-23018-1, Philomel) Peng Put Young Read.

***Lost Years of Merlin.** T. A. Barron. (J). (gr. 4-7). 1998. mass mkt. 4.99 (0-8125-7777-9) Tor Bks.

Lost Years of Merlin. T. A. Barron. (Lost Years of Merlin Ser.: No. 1). 270p. (J). (gr. 4-7). 1999. reprint ed. mass mkt. 5.99 (0-441-00668-X) ACE.

Lost Yesterday. Jenny Lykins. (Time Passages Ser.). 352p. 1997. mass mkt. 5.99 (0-515-12013-8, Jove) Berkley Pub.

***Lostech: The Mechwarrior Equipment Guide, Vol. 172.** Bryan Nystul. (Mech Warrior Ser.). (Illus.). 2000. pap. 20.00 (1-55560-399-8) FASA Corp.

Lostman's River. Cynthia DeFelice. 160p. (J). (gr. 4-7). 1995. mass mkt. 4.50 (0-380-72396-4, Avon Bks) Morrow Avon.

Lostman's River. Cynthia DeFelice. (J). 1995. 9.60 (0-606-07810-X, Pub. by Turtleback) Demco.

Lostman's River. Cynthia C. DeFelice. LC 93-40857. 160p. (YA). (gr. 7 up). 1994. lib. bdg. 15.00 (0-02-726466-1) Atheneum Yung Read.

Lostness of Mankind: One Motivation for Evangelism. Louis L. King. (Heritage Ser.). (FRE.). 30p. (Orig.). 1991. pap. 1.59 (0-87509-449-X) Chr Pubns.

***Los/Tres Cerditos.** (SPA.). 1999. pap. 7.95 (88-8148-250-9) Europ Lang Inst.

Losungsansatze fur Grenzuberschreitende Umweltprobleme bei Internationaler Handelsverflechtung. Gerd Kodding. (Europaische Hochschulschriften: Reihe 5: Bd. 2028). (GER., Illus.). 209p. 1996. pap. 42.95 (3-631-31030-7) P Lang Pubng.

Lot: The Wordly Christian. John G. Butler. 224p. 1994. 15.50 (1-889773-10-7) LBC Publns.

Lot & Lot's Daughter. Ward Moore. 72p. 1996. pap. 10.00 (0-9648320-1-1) Tachyon Pubns.

Lot & Lot's Wife. Gordon Lindsay. (Old Testament Ser.: Vol. 5). 1964. pap. 1.95 (0-89985-958-5) Christ for the Nations.

Lot Lizards. Ray Garton. 1991. 22.00 (0-929480-59-7) Mark Ziesing.

Lot More Than Sex. Alexis Satchell. (Illus.). 65p. (Orig.). 1986. pap. 6.95 (0-931841-05-4) Satchells Pub.

Lot of Cowboys. William A. Grable. 40p. 1995. pap. text 9.50 (1-887508-02-3) MGM Sahara.

Lot of Otters. Barbara H. Berger. LC 95-50532. (Illus.). 32p. (J). (gr. k-1). 1997. 16.99 (0-399-22910-8, Philomel) Peng Put Young Read.

***Lot of Otters.** Barbara Helen Berger. (Picture Puffin Ser.). (Illus.). 32p. (J). (ps-1). 2000. pap. 6.99 (0-698-11863-4, PuffinBks) Peng Put Young Read.

Lot Sodom & God see Lot Sodoma y Dios

Lot, Sodom & God see Lot, Sodoma y Dios

Lot, Sodoma y Dios. Domingo Fernandez. (Actualidades Ser.).Tr. of Lot, Sodom & God. (SPA.). 1993. 2.29 (1-56063-455-3, 498159) Editorial Unilit.

Lot Sodoma y Dios. Domingo Fernandez. (Serie Actualidades - Actualities Ser.).Tr. of Lot Sodom & God. (SPA.). 42p. 1993. pap. write for info. (0-614-27077-4) Editorial Unilit.

Lot to Ask: A Life of Barbara Pym Hazel Holt. LC 90-228936. xi, 308p. 1990. write for info. (0-333-40614-1) Macmillan.

Lot to Be Thankful For: What Parents Want Children to Learn about America. Steve Farkas & Jean Johnson. 48p. 1998. pap. 10.00 (1-889483-58-3) Public Agenda.

Lot to Make up For. John Buell. 201p. 1990. 18.95 (0-374-19177-8) FS&G.

Lot to Remember. Joan Grant. 256p. 1994. pap. 10.95 (0-89804-160-0) Ariel GA.

Lot to Remember. Joan M. Grant. 1980. 21.95 (0-405-11781-7) Ayer.

Loteria: And Other Stories. Ruben Mendoza. LC 97-40636. 128p. 1998. pap. 12.95 (0-312-18129-9) St Martin.

***Loteria Cards & Fortune Poems: A Book of Lives.** Juan Felipe Herrera & Artemio Rodriguez. LC 99-16206. (Illus.). 208p. 1999. 15.95 (0-87286-359-X, Pub. by City Lights) SPD-Small Pr Dist.

Lotfi Mansouri: An Operatic Life. Lofti Mansouri & Aviva Layton. (Illus.). 140p. 1994. 19.95 (0-88962-179-9) Mosaic.

Lothair & Letters to His Sister see Works of Benjamin Disraeli

Lothar Baumgarten: Eklipse. limited ed. Text by Thomas Wagner. (Illus.). 72p. 1998. pap. 125.00 (3-928762-80-X, 810993, Pub. by Richter Verlag) Dist Art Pubs.

Lotharingian Apocalypse & The Dresden Manuscript, 2 vols., Set. deluxe ed. Ed. by Eckhard Hollmann et al. (ENG, FRE & GER., Illus.). 1987. 4500.00 (0-7855-1560-7) St Mut.

Lothian: Petronius - the Book. Andrew Lothian. 102p. 1988. pap. 24.00 (0-406-10396-8, MICHIE) LEXIS Pub.

Lothian Collection: 25 Tunes from the Great Houses of the Lothians. Alison Kinnaird. (Illus.). 33p. 1995. pap. 0.00 (0-9511204-8-4) Kinmor.

Lothian, Historical Guide. M. Collard. LC 99-488179. 1998. pap. 14.95 (1-874744-45-9, Pub. by Birlinn Ltd) Dufour.

Lotion Bullwhip Giraffe. Tan Lin. LC 95-51822. (New American Poetry Ser.: Vol. 26). 110p. 1996. pap. 10.95 (1-55713-258-5) Sun & Moon CA.

Lotions, Oils & Essences. (Gifts from Nature Ser.). (Illus.). 64p. 1998. 12.95 (1-85967-591-3, Lorenz Bks) Anness Pub.

Lotions, Potions, & Slime: Mudpies & More! Nancy Blakey. LC 95-41082. (Illus.). 120p. (J). (ps-7). 1996. pap. 8.95 (1-883672-21-X) Tricycle Pr.

Lotissement du Ciel. Blaise Cendrars. (FRE.). 1976. pap. 11.95 (0-7859-2209-1, 207036724X) Fr & Eur.

Loto Azul. Herge.Tr. of Blue Lotus. (SPA., Illus.). 62p. (J). 19.95 (0-8288-5049-6) Fr & Eur.

LOTOSphere: Software Development with LOTOS. Ed. by Tommaso Bolognesi et al. LC 94-39291. 524p. (C). 1995. text 139.00 (0-7923-9529-8) Kluwer Academic.

Lots-a-Dots. Helen Davis. LC 87-90414. 1987. 4.98 (0-916809-16-1) Scott Pubns MI.

Lots & Lots of Zebra Stripes: Patterns in Nature. Stephen R. Swinburne. LC 97-77909. (Illus.). 32p. (J). (ps-2). 1998. 15.95 (1-56397-707-9) Boyds Mills Pr.

Lot's Life. Tom Wakefield. 160p. 1991. pap. 9.95 (1-85242-152-5) Serpents Tail.

Lots More Tell & Draw Stories. Margaret J. Oldfield. (Illus.). (J). (ps-3). 1973. pap. 6.95 (0-934876-03-7) Creative Storytime.

Lots More Tell & Draw Stories. Margaret J. Oldfield. (Illus.). (J). (ps-3). 1973. lib. bdg. 11.95 (0-934876-07-X) Creative Storytime.

Lots of Bugs! Roberta K. Loman. 1999. pap. text 2.49 (0-7847-0888-6) Standard Pub.

Lots of 'Cots: Cooking with Apricots. 2nd ed. Illus. by Sari Gennis. LC 89-90853. 62p. (Orig.). 1989. pap. text 6.95 (0-9621547-1-7) Ben Ali Bks.

***Lots of Dads.** Shelley Rotner. (Picture Puffin Ser.). (Illus.). (J). 2000. pap. 5.99 (0-14-056516-7, PuffinBks) Peng Put Young Read.

***Lots of Dads.** Shelley Rotner. (Illus.). (J). 2000. 11.44 (0-606-18422-8) Turtleback.

Lots of Dads. Shelley Rotner & Sheila M. Kelly. LC 96-33714. (Illus.). 24p. (J). 1997. 12.99 (0-8037-2086-6, Dial Yng Read); 12.89 (0-8037-2089-0, Dial Yng Read) Peng Put Young Read.

Lots of Energy. Thomas-Cochran. (What a Wonderful World 1 Ser.). 1991. pap. text. write for info. (0-582-90955-4, Pub. by Addison-Wesley) Longman.

L

Lots of Hearts. Maryann Cocca-Leffler. LC 95-78720. (All Aboard Reading Picture Readers Ser.). (Illus.). 32p. (Orig.). (J). (ps-1). 1997. pap. 3.95 (*0-448-41304-3*, G & D) Peng Put Young Read.

Lots of Hugs in a Lunch Box: 75 More Tear-Out Notes to Brighten Your Child's Day. Joy Stevans. Ed. by Lise Caldwell. (Illus.). 160p. (J). (gr. 1-6). 2000. pap. 5.99 (*0-7847-1065-1*) Standard Pub.

Lots of Knots. Ian Boyd. (Illus.). 24p. (Orig.). (J). (gr. 3-7). 1996. pap. 5.95 (*0-8167-4066-6*) Troll Communs.

Lots of Lice. Bobbi Katz. LC 97-27254. (Hello Reader! Science Ser.). (Illus.). 40p. (J). (gr. 1-3). 1998. pap. 3.99 (*0-590-10834-4*, Pub. by Scholastic Inc) Penguin Putnam.

Lots of Lice. Bobbi Katz. (Hello Science Reader! Ser.). (J). (gr. 1-3). 1998. 9.19 (*0-606-13583-9*, Pub. by Turtleback) Demco.

Lots of Limericks. Illus. by Rebecca Perry. LC 91-329. 128p. (J). (gr. 4-7). 1991. 16.00 (*0-689-50531-0*) McElderry Bks.

Lots of Little Bears. Richard Hefter. LC 83-2184. (Stickybear Bks.). (Illus.). 32p. (J). (ps-1). 1983. 5.95 (*0-911787-04-6*) Optimum Res Inc.

Lots of Luckovich. Mike Luckovich. LC 96-221424. 96p. 1996. pap. 10.00 (*0-671-54519-1*) PB.

Lots of Meat. Dan Gilbert. 160p. 2000. reprint ed. pap. 5.95 (*1-930535-06-6*) Star Dists.

Lots of Pots see Take Along Stories

Lots To Do. Jane Brettle. 1999. 3.98 (*1-57717-101-2*) Todtri Prods.

Lot's Wife. Caryn Mirriam-Goldberg. Ed. & Intro. by Denise Low. 80p. 2000. pap. 8.00 (*0-939391-27-9*) B Woodley Pr.

Lot's Wife. Janice Thaddeus. LC 86-3984. (Eileen W. Barnes Award Ser.). (Illus.). 64p. (Orig.). 1986. pap. 6.50 (*0-938158-07-4*) Saturday Pr.

Lot's Wife. large type ed. Tom Wakefield. 288p. 1992. 27.99 (*0-7089-2688-6*) Ulverscroft.

Lot's Wife & the Venus of Milo: Conflicting Attitudes to the Cultural Heritage in Modern Russia. Boris Thomson. LC 77-77703. 177p. reprint ed. pap. 50.50 (*0-608-15614-0*, 2031734) Bks Demand.

Lotsa Luck. Diana G. Gallagher. (Sabrina, the Teenage Witch Ser.: NO. 10). 160p. (YA). (gr. 7-12). 1998. per. 4.50 (*0-671-01980-5*, Archway) PB.

Lotsizing & Scheduling for Production Planning. Knut Haase. LC 94-14149. (Lecture Notes in Economics & Mathematical Systems Ser.: Vol. 408). 1994. write for info. (*0-387-57833-1*) Spr-Verlag.

Lotta Malarkey. G. Z. Patten. (Illus.). 140p. 1998. pap. text 11.95 (*0-9612974-3-3*) Patten Pr Inc.

Lotta Schmidt & Other Stories. Anthony Trollope. Ed. by N. John Hall. LC 80-1886. (Selected Works of Anthony Trollope). 1981. reprint ed. lib. bdg. 49.95 (*0-405-14151-3*) Ayer.

Lotta's Christmas Surprise. Astrid Lindgren. LC 90-60542. (Illus.). 32p. (J). (ps-3). 1990. 13.95 (*91-29-59782-X*, Pub. by R & S Bks) FS&G.

Lotta's Easter Surprise. Astrid Lindgren. Tr. by Barbara Lucas. LC 90-9054. (Illus.). 32p. (J). (ps-3). 1991. 13.95 (*91-29-59862-1*) FS&G.

Lotta's Fountain. limited ed. Lois Rather. (Illus.). 1979. 35.00 (*0-686-15713-3*) Rather Pr.

Lotta's Progress. Norma Johnston. 160p. 1998. pap. 3.99 (*0-380-78916-7*, Avon Bks) Morrow Avon.

Lotta's Progress. Norma Johnston. 1998. 9.09 (*0-606-13584-7*, Pub. by Turtleback) Demco.

Lotte Hofmann: Textile Pictures (1950-1981) Heidrun Jecht. 1998. 40.00 (*3-925369-78-3*, Pub. by Arnoldsche Art Pubs) Antique Collect.

Lotte in Weimar: The Beloved Returns. Thomas Mann. Tr. by Helen T. Lowe-Porter. 475p. 1990. 30.00 (*0-520-07006-2*, Pub. by U CA Pr); pap. 17.95 (*0-520-07007-0*, Pub. by U CA Pr) Cal Prin Full Svc.

Lotte Soll Nicht Sterben: Level A. text 7.95 (*0-88436-039-3*) EMC-Paradigm.

Lotter Ticket. John T. Trowbridge. (Notable American Authors). 1999. reprint ed. lib. bdg. 125.00 (*0-7812-9811-3*) Rprt Serv.

Lotteries. Alan J. Karcher. 170p. (C). 1991. pap. text 24.95 (*1-56000-578-5*) Transaction Pubs.

Lotteries & Contests: A Broadcaster's Handbook. 3rd ed. 101p. (Orig.). 1990. pap. 40.00 (*0-89324-080-X*) Natl Assn Broadcasters.

Lotteries & Sweepstakes. C. L'Estrange Ewen. LC 72-80143. (Illus.). 1972. reprint ed. lib. bdg. 26.95 (*0-405-08493-5*) Ayer.

Lottery. Beverly Carradine. 72p. 1997. pap. 3.99 (*0-88019-363-8*) Schmul Pub Co.

Lottery. Shirley Jackson. 26p. (YA). (gr. 10 up). 1953. pap. 3.50 (*0-87129-264-5*, L31) Dramatic Pub.

Lottery. Edward M. Merrill. 336p. mass mkt. 4.99 (*1-55197-105-4*) Picasso Publ.

Lottery. large type ed. Anita Burgh. (Magna Large Print Ser.). 598p. 1997. 27.99 (*0-7505-0992-9*) Ulverscroft.

Lottery. Shirley Jackson. 1993. reprint ed. lib. bdg. 29.95 (*0-89968-429-7*, Lghtyr Pr) Buccaneer Bks.

Lottery: A History from Ancient to Modern Times. Samuel W. Valenza, Jr. (LOMAP Ser.: Vol. 6). 180p. 1988. pap. 9.95 (*0-936918-10-1*) Intergalactic NJ.

Lottery: America's Latest Financial Security. Nathaniel A. Dickens. (Orig.). 1985. pap. write for info. (*0-916191-02-8*) Dickens Pubns.

Lottery: And Other Stories. Shirley Jackson. 320p. (C). 1982. pap. 12.00 (*0-374-51681-2*) FS&G.

Lottery: And Other Stories. Shirley Jackson. 1982. 17.10 (*0-606-04385-3*, Pub. by Turtleback) Demco.

Lottery & Other Stories. Shirley Jackson. 1976. 23.95 (*0-8488-0369-8*) Amereon Ltd.

Lottery & Other Stories. Shirley Jackson. 320p. 2000. 19.95 (*0-679-64039-8*) Modern Lib NY.

Lottery Blues. Emily Costello. (Soccer Stars Ser.: No. 5). (J). (gr. 3-7). 1998. pap. 3.99 (*0-553-48648-9*) BDD Bks Young Read.

Lottery Book. Terri LaFleur. 167p. 1991. pap. 100.00 (*1-883567-52-1*) TLF Pubns.

Lottery Book: Play to Win! Ben E. Johnson. 224p. (Orig.). 1991. mass mkt. 3.99 (*0-380-76405-9*, Avon Bks) Morrow Avon.

Lottery Dictionary see Sus Suenos Convertidos en Numeros de Loteria: El Diccionario de la Loteria

Lottery Inspector. Jack Rudman. (Career Examination Ser.: C-451). 1994. pap. 27.95 (*0-8373-0451-2*) Nat Learn.

Lottery Lie: Gamblers, Money & Hungry Kids. Ivan Zabilka. 1998. pap. 11.95 (*1-885224-20-6*) Bristol Hse.

Lottery Marketing Aide. Jack Rudman. (Career Examination Ser.: C-3165). 1994. pap. 27.95 (*0-8373-3165-X*) Nat Learn.

Lottery Marketing Representative. Jack Rudman. (Career Examination Ser.: C-3166). 1994. pap. 27.95 (*0-8373-3166-8*) Nat Learn.

Lottery Number Dream Book: The Lottery Dictionary. Charles White. (Illus.). 100p. (Orig.). 1997. pap. 15.00 (*0-9657360-0-8*) Rainbow Enter CA.

Lottery Numbers Book, LOMAP-9. 2nd ed. Ron Shelly & Chas J. Vale. 1995. pap. write for info. (*0-936918-14-4*) Intergalactic NJ.

Lottery of Love. large type ed. Vicki Page. (Lythway Ser.). 208p. 1991. 19.95 (*0-7451-1276-5*, G K Hall Lrg Type) Mac Lib Ref.

Lottery of Love: The Romance Guide for the Next Century, an Astrological Handbook to Relationships - the Ultimate Formula for Marriage! Karon Christian. 160p. (Orig.). 1994. pap. 14.95 (*0-9648317-3-2*) Patterson CA.

Lottery: or The Adventures of James Harris. Shirley Jackson. LC 79-24173. 1980. reprint ed. lib. bdg. 20.00 (*0-8376-0455-9*) Bentley Pubs.

Lottery Player's Magazine Official Traveler's Guide to Lotteries. Samuel W. Valenza, Jr. (LOMAP Ser.: Vol. 1). (Illus.). 24p. 1983. 3.50 (*0-936918-04-7*) Intergalactic NJ.

Lottery Rose. 2000. 9.95 (*1-56137-501-2*) Novel Units.

Lottery Rose. Irene Hunt. (J). 1976. 10.05 (*0-606-01753-4*, Pub. by Turtleback) Demco.

Lottery Rose: A Study Guide. Marcia Tretler. (Novel-Ties Ser.). 22p. (J). (gr. 6-8). 1990. pap. text 15.95 (*0-88122-395-6*) Lrn Links.

Lottery Solution. William L. Atwood. LC 92-560. 110p. 1992. 9.95 (*0-944957-13-7*) Rivercross Pub.

Lottery Solution: With Accompanying Software. rev. ed. William L. Atwood. LC 96-24427. (Illus.). 176p. (Orig.). 1996. pap. 19.95 (*0-944957-96-X*) Rivercross Pub.

Lottery Systems: A Collection of the Best from Lottery Player's Magazine. Ed. by Chas J. Vale. (LOMAP Ser.: Vol. 5). (Illus.). 96p. pap. 9.95 (*0-936918-09-8*) Intergalactic NJ.

Lottery Winner. Mary Higgins Clark. 304p. 1995. mass mkt. 7.99 (*0-671-86717-2*, Pocket Books) PB.

Lottery Winner. Mary Higgins Clark. 1997. reprint ed. lib. bdg. 32.95 (*1-56849-588-9*) Buccaneer Bks.

Lottery Winner: Alvirah & Willy Stories. Mary Higgins Clark. 256p. 1994. 22.00 (*0-671-86716-4*) S&S Trade.

Lottie Deno: Gambling Queen of Hearts. Cynthia Rose. LC 93-5335. (Illus.). 116p. 1993. 22.95 (*0-940666-33-2*); pap. 12.95 (*0-940666-38-3*) Clear Light.

Lottie Moon Storybook. Carolyn E. Jones. (Illus.). 20p. (Orig.). (J). (gr. k-4). 1984. pap. 1.25 (*0-9616996-0-4*) Honor Pub.

Lottie Project. Wilson. 2000. 17.95 (*0-385-40703-3*, Pub. by Transworld Publishers Ltd) Trafalgar.

Lottie Project. Jacqueline Wilson. 2001. pap. 4.50 (*0-440-41617-5*) BDD Bks Young Read.

Lottie Project. Jacqueline Wilson. LC 99-11465. (Illus.). 214p. (J). (gr. 4-7). 1999. 15.95 (*0-385-32718-8*) Delacorte.

Lottie Trago. large type ed. E. V. Thompson. (Charnwood Library). 1991. 27.99 (*0-7089-8578-5*, Charnwood) Ulverscroft.

Lottie's New Beach Towel. Petra Mathers. LC 97-6689. 32p. (J). (ps-k). 1998. 15.00 (*0-689-81606-5*) Atheneum Yung Read.

Lottie's New Friend. Petra Mathers. LC 98-21625. 32p. (J). (ps-3). 1999. 15.00 (*0-689-82014-3*) S&S Childrens.

Lotto Cipher Book Game: A Journey into Alphanumeric Time! Frank Armanno, Sr. (Illus.). 48p. 1992. pap. 5.95 (*0-9671820-0-X*) Prog Time Corp.

Lotto Gameplans & Systems: Winning Strategies. Chas J. Vale. 50p. 1985. pap. 9.95 (*0-936918-06-3*) Intergalactic NJ.

Lotto Vendors Handbook. Denton S. Harewood. LC 95-79904. 100p. (Orig.). 1996. pap. 25.00 (*0-934789-04-5*) Hands-On Pub Co.

Lotto Winning Systems: How to Play the Lottery Smartly & Win. Aleksander Anakiev & Maya Anaklev. 128p. (Orig.). 1987. pap. 12.95 (*0-318-23367-3*) LWS Pub.

Lotton Art Glass. Thomas O'Connor. 1993. 49.95 (*0-915410-45-1*) McGraw.

Lotto's Losing Numbers: Fifteen Reasons Why Colorado Can't Afford a Bigger Lottery. David S. D'Evelyn. 6p. 1998. pap. text 8.00 (*1-57655-024-9*) Independ Inst.

Lotus. Graham Arnold. LC 99-185217. (Sutton's Photographic History of Railways Ser.). (Illus.). 160p. 1998. pap. 21.95 (*0-7509-1865-9*, Pub. by Sutton Pub Ltd) Intl Pubs Mktg.

Lotus. Myungkark Park. LC 91-67959. (Illus.). 130p. (Orig.). 1992. pap. write for info. (*1-877974-22-6*) Prompter Pubns.

Lotus. Graham Robson. (Album Ser.: no. 294). (Illus.). 32p. (C). 1989. pap. 4.75 (*0-7478-0217-3*, Pub. by Shire Pubns) Parkwest Pubns.

Lotus, Vol. 29. Ed. by Pievluigi Nicolin. 1981. pap. 29.95 (*0-8478-5339-X*) Rizzoli Intl.

Lotus: The Complete Story Chris Harvey. LC 87-126406. (Mini Marque History Ser.). 136 P. :p. 1982. write for info. (*0-85429-298-5*, Pub. by GT Foulis) Haynes Manuals.

Lotus: The Elite, Elan, Europa. Chris Harvey. LC 83-147188. 234 p. 1982. 14.95 (*0-902280-85-6*) Haynes Manuals.

Lotus: The Introductory Program, 1993. 1993. teacher ed. write for info. (*0-02-802509-1*) Glencoe.

Lotus among the Magnolias: The Mississippi Chinese. Robert S. Quan. LC 81-23991. (Illus.). 180p. reprint ed. pap. 55.80 (*0-7837-1071-2*, 204159400021) Bks Demand.

Lotus & Caterham Seven Racers for the Road. John Tipler. (Illus.). 192p. 1995. 34.95 (*1-85223-858-5*, Pub. by Cro1wood) Motorbooks Intl.

Lotus & Other Tales of Medieval Japan. Takeshi Umehara. Tr. by Paul McCarthy. LC 96-61006. 200p. 1997. 16.95 (*0-8048-2062-7*) Tuttle Pubng.

Lotus & the Flame. Dhooswan Sayami. 164p. (C). 1980. 40.00 (*0-89771-065-7*, Pub. by Ratna Pustak Bhandar) St Mut.

Lotus & the Maple Leaf: The Soka Gakkai Buddhist Movement in Canada. Daniel A. Metraux. 160p. 1996. lib. bdg. 32.00 (*0-7618-0271-1*) U Pr of Amer.

Lotus & the Rose. Scott Ciencin. 304p. (Orig.). 1993. mass mkt. 4.99 (*0-446-36249-2*, Pub. by Warner Bks) Little.

Lotus Approach. (Quick Study Computer Ser.). 4p. pap. 3.95 (*1-57222-325-1*) Barcharts.

An Asterisk (*) at the beginning of an entry indicates that the title is appearing for the first time.

***Lotus Approach Millennium Edition 9.0 Quick Source Guide.** (Illus.). 6p. 2000. pap. 4.95 (*1-930674-01-5*) Quick Source.

Lotus Be Brief. Robert W. Harris. 124p. 1990. pap. 9.95 (*0-931011-28-0*) Grapevine Pubns.

Lotus Bleu see Blue Lotus

Lotus Bleu. Herge.Tr. of Blue Lotus. (FRE.). (J). (gr. 2-9). 19.95 (*0-8288-5050-X*) Fr & Eur.

***Lotus Bleu.** Herge.Tr. of Blue Lotus. (FRE.). (gr. 4-7). 1999. 19.95 (*2-203-00104-6*) Midwest European Pubns.

Lotus Boat: The Origins of Chinese Tz'u Poetry in T'ang Popular Culture. Marsha L. Wagner. LC 83-20925. (Studies in Oriental Culture: No. 18). 192p. 1984. text 50.50 (*0-231-04276-0*) Col U Pr.

***Lotus Born.** Shambhala Publications Staff. 1999. pap. write for info. (*1-56957-119-8*, Pub. by Shambhala Pubns) Random.

Lotus-Born: The Life Story of Padmasambhava. Yeshe Tsogyal. LC 92-52516. 264p. 1993. 30.00 (*0-87773-909-9*, Pub. by Shambhala Pubns) Random.

Lotus-Born: The Life Story of Padmasambhava. Yeshe Tsogyal. LC 91-52516. (Dragon Editions Ser.). 264p. 1993. pap. 24.95 (*0-87773-869-6*, Pub. by Shambhala Pubns) Random.

Lotus Collection Book of Days. 112p. 1998. 14.95 (*0-945798-60-1*) Amber Lotus.

Lotus Crew. Stewart Meyer. (Midnight Classics Ser.). 150p. 1996. reprint ed. pap. 10.99 (*1-85242-417-6*) Serpents Tail.

***Lotus Domino Administration in a Nutshell.** Gregory G. Neilson. Ed. by Robert Denn. (In a Nutshell Ser.). (Illus.). 400p. 2000. pap. 24.95 (*1-56592-717-6*) OReilly & Assocs.

***Lotus Domino 5 Programming Bible.** Steve Oliver. (Illus.). 2000. pap. text 39.99 (*0-7645-4722-4*) IDG Bks.

Lotus Domino for the AS/400. Dick Bains et al. Ed. by Jelan Heidelberg. (AS/400 Ser.). (Illus.). 374p. 1999. 59.95 (*1-889671-29-0*) Advice Pr.

Lotus Domino Server. 2nd ed. Londergan. 1997. 39.95 (*0-8055-1574-7*, M&T Bks) IDG Bks.

Lotus Domino Server. 2nd ed. Steve Londergan. 640p. 1997. pap. 39.95 incl. cd-rom (*1-55851-511-9*, M&T Bks) IDG Bks.

Lotus Domino Web Site Development. Steve Oliver & Pete Wood. LC 98-24387. 615p. 1998. pap. 44.99 incl. cd-rom (*0-07-913755-5*) McGraw.

***Lotus Domino 5 Programming Bible.** Oliver. (Bible Ser.). 600p. 2000. 39.99 (*0-7645-4724-0*) IDG Bks.

Lotus Eater. Harriot Curtis. (Works of Harriot Curtis). 1990. reprint ed. lib. bdg. 79.00 (*0-685-44774-X*) Rprt Serv.

Lotus Eaters. Gerald Green. 1976. reprint ed. lib. bdg. 33.95 (*0-89190-122-1*, Rivercity Pr) Amereon Ltd.

Lotus Elise. John Tipler. (Illus.). 200p. 1999. 35.95 (*1-86126-213-2*, 128163AE, Pub. by Cro1wood) Motorbooks Intl.

Lotus Essential. 1997. 16.99 (*0-7686-0092-8*) Quest Custom.

Lotus Exhibition: Aristocratic Adornments of India: 3rd Century B. C. to 20th Century. Tsajon Von Lixfeld. (Illus.). 53p. 1998. 14.95 (*0-9633959-7-1*) Bowers Mus.

Lotus Fire. Arundale. 1976. 23.95 (*0-8356-7502-5*) Theos Pub Hse.

Lotus 5.0 for Windows: Tool Kit. Duffy. (Management Information Systems Ser.). 1996. pap. 17.95 (*0-7895-0402-2*) Course Tech.

Lotus Flowers. Ellen B. Voigt. 1988. pap. 8.95 (*0-393-30494-9*) Norton.

***Lotus Flowers.** Ellen Bryant Voigt. (Classic Contemporaries Ser.). (Illus.). 2000. pap. text 12.95 (*0-88748-310-0*) Carnegie-Mellon.

Lotus for Windows. Iris Blanc. 1993. pap. 12.00 (*1-56243-111-0*, LW-17) DDC Pub.

Lotus for Windows 4.0. DDC Publishing Staff. 1993. pap. 12.00 (*1-56243-138-2*, 03013) DDC Pub.

Lotus for Windows 95: Tutorial & Applications. Sandra Cable. 1997. pap. 32.75 (*0-538-71712-2*) Sth-Wstrn College.

Lotus for Windows Release 4.0. Sarah E. Hutchinson et al. LC 94-240411. 208p. (C). 1994. text 12.50 (*0-256-16464-9*, Irwn McGrw-H) McGrw-H Hghr Educ.

Lotus for Windows 2.4. Shelly Cashman. (C). 1994. text. write for info. (*0-318-70359-9*) S-W Pub.

Lotus 49. Michael Oliver. (Illus.). 256p. 1999. 49.95 (*1-901295-51-6*, 129154AE, Pub. by Vloce Pub) Motorbooks Intl.

Lotus Freelance Graphics 96 - Illustrated, Incl. instr. resource kit, test mgr., Web pg. Katherine Murray. (Illustrated Ser.). (Illus.). 192p. 1996. text. write for info. incl. 3.5 ld (*0-7600-3751-5*) Course Tech.

Lotus Freelance Graphics 2.1 for Windows. Rick Sullivan. (Computer Training Ser.). 140-180p. 1996. mass mkt., spiral bd. 21.95 incl. 3.5 hd (*0-538-66003-1*) S-W Pub.

Lotus Freelance Graphics 2.1 for Windows: Quick Course. Goldfarb. (DF - Computer Applications Ser.). 192p. 1995. mass mkt. 17.95 (*0-538-64904-6*) S-W Pub.

***Lotus Freelance Millennium Edition 9.0 Quick Source Guide.** Quick Source Staff. (Illus.). 6p. 2000. pap. 4.95 (*1-930674-00-7*) Quick Source.

Lotus Guide Agenda. Robert H. Flast & Lauren Flast. 304p. 1988. pap. 19.95 (*0-201-15786-1*) Addison-Wesley.

Lotus Guide to Add in Toolkit 1-2-3. Barton E. Listick. 1990. pap. text 22.95 (*0-201-52324-8*) Addison-Wesley.

Lotus Guide to Freelance Graphics for Windows, Release 2.0. Jeff Sutton. LC 93-16486. (Lotus Bks.). 1993. write for info. (*1-56860-741-5*) Brady Pub.

Lotus Guide to 1 2 3 Function. Mary Campbell. 256p. 1988. pap. 21.95 (*0-201-12948-5*) Addison-Wesley.

Lotus Guide to Learning 1-2-3 Macros. Lotus Development Corporation Staff. 1986. pap. text 19.18 (*0-201-16821-9*) Addison-Wesley.

Lotus Guide to Learning 123 REL2.2. Lotus Development Corporation Staff. 1989. pap. 22.95 (*0-201-52320-5*) Addison-Wesley.

Lotus Guide to Learning Symphony: Revised for Release 2.0. 3rd rev. ed. Lotus Development Corporation Staff. (Lotus Bks.). 1988. pap. 22.95 (*0-201-16699-2*) Addison-Wesley.

Lotus Guide to 1-2-3: Release 2.2. Peter G. Randall. 1990. pap. 24.95 (*0-13-539529-1*) P-H.

Lotus Guide to 1-2-3 Advanced MACRO Commands: Programming Techniques. Lotus Books Staff. LC 86-32213. 1987. pap. 23.95 (*0-201-16822-7*) Addison-Wesley.

Lotus Guide to 1-2-3-G. Mary Campbell. 1990. pap. write for info. (*0-201-55068-7*) Addison-Wesley.

Lotus Guide to 1 2 3 Release 3. David J. Bookbinder. 512p. 1988. pap. 22.95 (*0-201-15038-7*) Addison-Wesley.

Lotus Guide to 1-2-3 Release 3. write for info. (*0-318-62954-2*) Addison-Wesley.

Lotus Guide to Spreadsheet Publishing. Scott Tucker. LC 91-41236. 1991. pap. 24.95 (*0-13-539313-2*) P-H.

Lotus Heritage. Ian Adcock. (Color Library). (Illus.). 128p. 1995. pap. 15.95 (*1-85532-508-X*, Pub. by Ospry) Motorbooks Intl.

Lotus in the City: How to Combine Spiritual Practice with Everyday Life. David Fontana. 1995. pap. 14.95 (*1-85230-573-8*, Pub. by Element MA) Penguin Putnam.

Lotus in the Fire: The Healing Power of Zen. Jim Bedard. LC 98-31120. 160p. 1999. pap. 14.00 (*1-57062-430-5*, Pub. by Shambhala Pubns) Random.

Lotus in the Lab: Spreadsheet Applications for Scientists & Engineers. Glenn I. Ouchi. 196p. (C). 1988. pap. 24.95 (*0-201-14307-0*) Addison-Wesley.

***Lotus in the Stream: Essays in Basic Buddhism.** Hsing-yhun-ta-shih Staff & Tom Graham. LC 00-21589. 2000. write for info. (*0-8348-0441-7*) Weatherhill.

Lotus Land. Monica Highland. (McGraw-Hill Paperbacks Ser.). 480p. (C). 1995. pap. text 31.50 (*0-07-028793-7*) McGraw.

Lotus Language Dictionary Quick Reference. Edenfield & Hill. 400p. 1997. 29.95 (*0-7897-1395-0*) Que.

Lotus Moon. Janice Kaiser. 296p. 1995. per. 4.99 (*1-55166-029-6*, 1-66029-9, Mira Bks) Harlequin Bks.

Lotus Moon: The Poetry of the Buddhist Nun Rengetsu. Tr. by John Stevens from JPN. (Inklings Edition Ser.). (Illus.). 128p. (Orig.). 1994. pap. 7.95 (*0-8348-0303-8*, Inklings Edits) Weatherhill.

Lotus Notes: Administration Survival Guide. Leslie Lesnick & Andrew Dahl. 672p. 1996. 55.00 incl. cd-rom (*0-672-30844-4*, Bobbs) Macmillan.

Lotus Notes Administrator's Handbook. Nicolas Behrman. 1996. pap. write for info. (*1-55851-487-2*, M&T Bks) IDG Bks.

Lotus Notes & Domino Essential Reference. David Hatter & Tim Bankes. LC 98-88582. 676p. 1999. pap. 45.00 (*0-7357-0007-9*) New Riders Pub.

Lotus Notes & Domino 5. Lars Klander. (Certification Study Guide Ser.). 1008p. 1999. 49.99 (*0-7821-2489-5*) Sybex.

***Lotus Notes & Domino 5 Developer's Handbook.** Cate Richards. (Developer's Handbks.). 1104p. 1999. 54.99 (*0-7821-2424-0*) Sybex.

Lotus Notes & Domino 5 Development Unleashed. Deborah Lynd. (Unleashed Ser.). 1400p. 1999. pap. 49.99 (*0-672-31414-2*) Sams.

Lotus Notes & Domino 5 Scalable Network Design. John P. Lamb. LC 99-34198. 752p. 1999. pap. 49.95 incl. cd-rom (*0-07-913792-X*) McGraw.

Lotus Notes & Domino 4.5 Answers! Certified Tech Support. 2nd ed. Polly Kornblith. LC 97-203005. (Illus.). 448p. (Orig.). 1997. pap. text 24.99 (*0-07-882383-8*, Oracle Press) Osborne-McGraw.

Lotus Notes & Domino 4.5 Architecture, Administration, & Security. Scott Thomas. LC 97-23410. (Illus.). 478p. 1997. pap. 44.95 (*0-07-064562-0*) McGraw.

Lotus Notes & Domino R5 24Seven. 4th ed. Cate Richards & Laura Robinson. (24seven Ser.). 704p. 2000. 34.99 (*0-7821-2518-2*) Sybex.

***Lotus Notes & Domino 5 Bible.** Kenyon Brown. Ed. by Kevin Brown & Kyle Brown. LC 99-37073. (Bible Ser.). 936p. 2000. pap. 39.99 (*0-7645-4590-6*) IDG Bks.

Lotus Notes Application Development: Exams 190-171 & 190-272. Ed. by Schwartz. LC 98-43762. 1998. pap., student ed. 29.99 (*0-07-134569-8*) McGraw.

Lotus Notes Application Development Handbook. Erica Kerwien. 608p. 1995. pap. 39.99 (*1-56884-308-9*) IDG Bks.

Lotus Notes Certification Exam Guide: Application Development & System Administration. Scott L. Thomas & Amy E. Peasley. LC 97-27735. 624p. 1997. 54.95 incl. cd-rom (*0-07-913674-5*) McGraw.

Lotus Notes Developer's Guide. Rose Kelleher et al. LC 96-48472. (Illus.). 500p. 1997. pap. 39.95 incl. cd-rom (*1-55622-545-8*) Wordware Pub.

Lotus Notes Domino Server. 2nd ed. Steve Londergan. LC 97-30959. 672p. 1997. pap. 39.95 (*1-55851-574-7*, M&T Bks) IDG Bks.

Lotus Notes Domino Toolkit. Steve Gillmor. (Illus.). 608p. 1997. pap., pap. text 44.95 incl. cd-rom (*0-07-913262-6*) McGraw.

Lotus Notes Fat Faqs. Ken Yee. (McGraw Hill Fat Faqs Ser.). (Illus.). 560p. 1998. pap. text 39.95 incl. cd-rom (*0-07-913680-X*) McGraw.

Lotus Notes 5 Certification Exam Guide: Application Development I & II & System Administration I & II. Libby Schwarz. LC 99-59940. 832p. 2000. write for info. (*0-07-135090-X*) Osborne-McGraw.

Lotus Notes 5 for Dummies. Stephen Londergan & Pat Freeland. LC 99-61892. (For Dummies Ser.). (Illus.). 384p. 1999. pap. 19.99 (*0-7645-0320-0*) IDG Bks.

Lotus Notes 5 for Dummies Quick Reference. Stephen Londergan & Pat Freeland. LC 99-62475. (For Dummies). 224p. 1999. spiral bd. 12.99 (*0-7645-0319-7*) IDG Bks.

***Lotus Notes 5.0 Quick Source Guide.** Quick Source Staff. (Illus.). 6p. 1999. pap. 4.95 (*1-930674-04-X*) Quick Source.

Lotus Notes for Dummies. Paul Freeland. LC 94-239744. 384p. 1994. pap. 19.95 (*1-56884-212-0*) IDG Bks.

Lotus Notes for Web Workgroups. Robert Dale & Barbara Opyt. LC 96-14280. 280p. (C). 1996. pap. 36.95 (*1-56690-110-3*) Thomson Learn.

Lotus Notes 4.5 & Domino 4.5: Administrator's Professional Reference. New Riders Publishing Staff. LC 97-17298. 900p. 1997. 69.99 (*1-56205-757-X*) New Riders Pub.

Lotus Notes & Domino 4.5 Developer's Guide. Steven Kern. LC 97-65458. 788p. 1997. 49.99 incl. cd-rom (*0-672-31079-1*) Macmillan.

Lotus Notes 4.5 for Dummies. Stephen Londergan. LC 97-73622. 224p. 1997. spiral bd. 12.99 (*0-7645-0311-1*) IDG Bks.

Lotus Notes 4.5 for Dummies. Stephen Londergan & P. Freeland. LC 97-70731. (Illus.). 384p. 1997. pap. 19.99 (*0-7645-0185-2*) IDG Bks.

Lotus Notes 4.5, Quick Reference. Sean Keshxon. LC 98-100692. (Illus.). (Orig.). 1996. pap. 12.00 (*1-56243-351-2*, G-15) DDC Pub.

Lotus Notes 4.5 Essentials. 229p. 1997. teacher ed. 49.99 (*1-57576-500-4*) Sams.

Lotus Notes 4.5 Essentials. Steve Daly. LC 96-68974. (Illus.). 240p. 1997. 22.99 (*1-57576-436-9*) Sams.

***Lotus Notes 4.6.** ENI Publishing Ltd. Staff. (Straight to the Point Ser.). 1999. pap. 7.95 (*2-7460-0037-7*) ENI Publng.

***Lotus Notes 4.6.** Marie L. Texier. (On Your Side Ser.). 1999. pap. 15.95 (*2-7460-0056-3*) ENI Publng.

***Lotus Notes 4.6 Quick Source Guide.** Quick Source Staff. (Illus.). 6p. 1999. pap. 4.95 (*1-930674-05-8*) Quick Source.

Lotus Notes 4 Unleashed. Randall Tamura et al. LC 96-67719. 1000p. 1996. 55.00 (*0-672-30906-8*) Sams.

Lotus Notes Fundamentals. 1993. teacher ed. 49.95 (*1-56877-094-4*) Macmillan USA.

Lotus Notes Idea Book. Jeff Kovel & Kent Quirk. LC 95-44807. 416p. 1995. pap. 24.95 (*0-201-40787-6*) Addison-Wesley.

Lotus Notes Network Design. John P. Lamb. 1996. pap. 44.95 (*0-07-036160-6*) McGraw.

Lotus Notes Network Design Release 5. Peter Lew & John P. Lamb. LC 97-30082. (Illus.). 575p. 1997. pap., text 44.95 incl. cd-rom (*0-07-913241-3*) McGraw.

Lotus Notes Release 5. Rupert Clayton. LC 99-61233. (No Experience Required Ser.). (Illus.). 608p. 1999. pap. text 24.99 (*0-7821-2184-5*) Sybex.

Lotus Notes System Administration: Exams 190-174 & 190-275. Schwartz. LC 98-55299. 1999. pap. 29.99 (*0-07-134562-0*) McGraw.

Lotus Notes Three Revealed. David Gewirtz. LC 93-85333. 1994. pap. 24.95 (*1-55958-433-5*) Prima Pub.

Lotus Notes 2.1: Fundamentals. 1993. teacher ed. 49.95 (*1-56877-147-9*) Macmillan USA.

Lotus Notes 2.1 Fundamentals. 1993. student ed. 29.95 (*1-56877-146-0*) Macmillan USA.

Lotus Notes 1-2-3 5.0 for Windows Made Simple. Morris. 160p. Date not set. pap. text 19.95 (*0-7506-2307-1*) Buttrwrth-Heinemann.

Lotus Notes 4.6. (Quick Study Computer Ser.). 4p. pap. 3.95 (*1-57222-322-7*) Barcharts.

***Lotus Notes 5 Fast & Easy.** Katherine Murray. LC 98-65716. (Fast & Easy Ser.). (Illus.). 305p. 1999. pap. 16.99 (*0-7615-1393-0*) Prima Pub.

***Lotus Notes/Domino 5 System Administration.** Tony Aveyard. (CLP Fast Track Ser.). 600p. 2000. pap. 39.99 (*0-7357-0878-9*) New Riders Pub.

Lotus of the Wonderful Law: or The Lotus Gospel. William E. Soothill. LC 86-20970. 288p. (C). 1996. pap. text 19.00 (*0-7007-0198-2*, Pub. by Curzon Pr Ltd) UH Pr.

Lotus 1-2-3. Don Cassel. 114p. (C). 1993. pap. 9.33 (*0-13-013657-3*) P-H.

Lotus 1-2-3. 4th ed. Solomon. Date not set. pap. text, teacher ed. write for info. (*0-314-02209-0*) West Pub.

Lotus 1-2-3: A Classroom Approach with Practical Applications Release 2.3. Bonnie Holloway & Donna Sarber. 320p. (C). 1993. text 24.28 (*0-697-23237-9*) Bus & Educ Tech.

Lotus 1-2-3: A Classroom Approach with Practical Applications Release 2.3. Bonnie Holloway & Donna Sarber. 320p. (C). 1994. text 24.28 (*0-697-23239-5*) Bus & Educ Tech.

Lotus 1-2-3: A Practical Learning Guide. Alan D. Mazursky & Eileen B. Dlugoss. 500p. (C). 1988. teacher ed. 14.00 (*1-56118-087-4*); pap. text 25.95 (*1-56118-086-6*) Paradigm MN.

Lotus 1-2-3: Advanced Applications, Cases & Solutions. Fritz H. Grupe. 208p. (C). 1990. text 28.27 (*0-697-11725-1*) Bus & Educ Tech.

Lotus 1-2-3: Release 3.1. Sarah E. Hutchinson et al. 216p. (C). 1993. text 12.50 (*0-256-13490-1*, Irwn McGrw-H) McGrw-H Hghr Educ.

Lotus 1-2-3: Short Course. Alan D. Mazursky & Eileen B. Dlugoss. 208p. (C). pap. text 19.95 (*1-56118-089-0*) Paradigm MN.

Lotus 1-2-3: Step by Step. Judd Robbins. 1990. pap. 24.95 (*0-672-22712-6*, MICHIE) LEXIS Pub.

Lotus 1-2-3: The Useable Portable Guide. Jon Haber & Herbert R. Haber. 232p. (C). 1989. pap. text 12.95 (*0-945765-17-7*) Useable Portable Pubns.

Lotus 1-2-3 - A Hands-On Approach: Exercises in Business Productivity. Wallace Whistance-Smith. LC 95-24422. (Illus.). xii, 303p. (C). 1991. pap. 12.44 (*0-201-50633-5*) Addison-Wesley.

***Lotus 1-2-3 & Excel Manager.** Weygandt. 84p. 1999. pap. 22.95 incl. disk (*0-471-35321-3*) Wiley.

Lotus 1-2-3 at Work: The Joy of Lotus. McGrath. 1990. pap. 5.00 incl. 3.5 hd (*0-13-633835-6*) Macmillan USA.

Lotus 1-2-3 at Work: The Joy of Lotus. Jack McGrath. 1990. pap. 44.95 (*0-13-635327-4*) P-H.

Lotus 1-2-3 5.0 for Windows: Applications for Reinforcement. Rob Anderson. (Computer Applications Ser.). 1996. mass mkt. 31.95 (*0-538-71450-6*) S-W Pub.

Lotus 1-2-3 (for DOS) James E. Potter. Ed. by Alfred J. Garrotto. (FasTrak Jr. Ser.). 52p. 1993. spiral bd. 9.00 (*0-9632069-6-6*) Bridge Lrn Systs.

Lotus 1-2-3 for DOS: Intermediate. 1993. teacher ed. 49.95 (*1-56877-076-6*); teacher ed. 49.95 (*1-56877-139-8*) Macmillan USA.

Lotus 1-2-3 for DOS 3.0 3.1 3.1. 1993. teacher ed. 29.95 (*1-56877-075-8*) Macmillan USA.

Lotus 1-2-3 for DOS 2.2: Intermediate. 1992. 29.95 (*1-56877-024-3*) Macmillan USA.

Lotus 1-2-3 for Marketing & Sales. Michael V. Laric & M. Ronald Stiff. 256p. 1984. pap. 24.95 (*0-685-08556-2*) P-H.

Lotus 123 for the Business World. (C). 1996. write for info. (*0-8087-2481-9*) Pearson Custom.

Lotus 1-2-3 for Windows. Sarah E. Hutchinson et al. LC 94-103349. 216p. (C). 1993. text 12.50 (*0-256-14950-X*, Irwn McGrw-H) McGrw-H Hghr Educ.

Lotus 1-2-3 for Windows for Dummies. John Walkenbach. (For Dummies Ser.). 350p. 1993. pap. 16.95 (*1-56884-052-7*) IDG Bks.

Lotus 1-2-3 97 for Windows 95: Tutorial & Applications. Sandra Cable. 1997. pap., teacher ed. 34.95 (*0-538-71709-2*) Sth-Wstrn College.

Lotus 1-2-3 for Windows 95 Essentials AIE. Editorial Custom Staff. 1998. 49.99 (*1-57576-576-4*) Que Educ & Trng.

Lotus 1-2-3 for Windows 95 Essentials. Que Education & Training Staff. Date not set. 22.99 (*1-57576-598-5*) Que Educ & Trng.

Lotus 1-2-3 for Windows 95. Gary B. Shelly & T. Cashman. 448p. 1997. pap. 40.95 (*0-7895-1197-5*) Course Tech.

Lotus 1-2-3 for Windows 95 Essentials, Level 3. Que Education & Training Staff. Date not set. 22.99 (*1-57576-601-9*) Que Educ & Trng.

Lotus 1-2-3 for Windows 95: Quick Torial. Newberry. (DF - Computer Applications Ser.). 1998. mass mkt. 22.95 (*0-538-67981-6*) S-W Pub.

Lotus 1-2-3 for Windows 1.0: Beginners. 1993. teacher ed. 29.95 (*1-56877-077-4*); teacher ed. 49.95 (*1-56877-078-2*) Macmillan USA.

Lotus 1-2-3 for Windows 1.0: Intermediate. 1993. 29.95 (*1-56877-123-1*); teacher ed. 49.95 (*1-56877-122-3*) Macmillan USA.

Lotus 1-2-3 for Windows Release 4 & 5, Easy Reference Guide. Albin. (DF - Computer Applications Ser.). 1995. mass mkt. 9.95 (*0-538-63690-4*) S-W Pub.

Lotus 1-2-3 for Windows Release 5.0. Sarah E. Hutchinson et al. LC 95-137856. 224p. (C). 1994. text 12.50 (*0-256-18923-4*, Irwn McGrw-H) McGrw-H Hghr Educ.

Lotus 1-2-3 for Windows Release 4.0 Quick Start. Varnonstacy. (DF - Computer Applications Ser.). 1994. mass mkt. 19.95 (*0-538-63675-0*) S-W Pub.

Lotus 1-2-3 for Windows Release 4.0: Tutorial & Applications. Groneman. (DF - Computer Applications Ser.). 1994. mass mkt. 30.95 (*0-538-63692-0*) S-W Pub.

Lotus 1-2-3 for Windows, Release 4-5: Tutorial & Applications. large type ed. Nancy J. Groneman. 1995. 65.50 (*0-614-09597-2*, L-83781-00) Am Printing Hse.

Lotus 1-2-3 for Windows 2.O: Beginners. 1993. 29.95 (*1-56877-079-0*) Macmillan USA.

Lotus 1-2-3 for Windows 2.0: Beginners. 1993. teacher ed. 49.95 (*1-56877-080-4*) Macmillan USA.

Lotus 1-2-3 for Windows, Version 4. (Prisma Computer Courses Ser.). (Illus.). 200p. (Orig.). 1995. pap. 12.95 (*1-85365-390-X*, Pub. by Spectrum) Seven Hills Bk.

Lotus 1-2-3 4.0 for Windows. Rick Sullivan. 144p. 1996. text 18.95 (*0-538-63427-8*) S-W Pub.

Lotus 1-2-3 4.0 for Windows at a Glance: The Fastest & Easiest Way to Learn Lotus 1-2-3 4.0. Eugene W. Teglovic. LC 94-1447. 128p. (Orig.). 1994. pap. 15.95 (*1-55622-424-9*) Wordware Pub.

Lotus 1-2-3 4.0/5.0 for Windows: Quick Course. Thompson. (DF - Computer Applications Ser.). 1995. mass mkt. 15.95 (*0-538-64894-5*) S-W Pub.

Lotus 1-2-3 (Intro.) Quick Reference Guide. Iris Blanc & Elinore J. Hildebrandt. (DDC Quick Reference Guides Ser.). 40p. 1986. 12.00 (*0-936862-31-9*, L-17) DDC Pub.

Lotus 1-2-3 Made Easy: Book. M. Shamsul Haque. LC 84-63147. (Illus.). viii, 152p. 1985. per. 9.95 (*0-933057-01-6*) Namuk Intl Inc.

***Lotus 1-2-3 Millennium Edition 9.0 Quick Source Guide.** Quick Source Staff. (Illus.). 6p. 1999. pap. 4.95 (*1-930674-03-1*) Quick Source.

***Lotus 1-2-3 Millennium Intermediate.** (Illus.). 220p. (YA). 1999. pap. write for info. (*0-7423-0356-X*, LOT123M02LG) ComputerPREP.

***Lotus 1-2-3 Millennium Intermediate: Instructor Guide.** (Illus.). 220p. 1999. pap., teacher ed. write for info. (*0-7423-0419-1*) ComputerPREP.

***Lotus 1-2-3 Millennium Introduction.** (Illus.). (YA). 1999. pap. write for info. (*0-7423-0355-1*, LOT123M01LG) ComputerPREP.

***Lotus 1-2-3 Millennium Introduction: Instructor Guide.** (Illus.). 179p. 1999. pap., teacher ed. write for info. (*0-7423-0418-3*) ComputerPREP.

***Lotus 1-2-3 97: Module 2.** Niit. 2000. 8.00 (*0-619-02304-X*) Course Tech.

L

An Asterisk (*) at the beginning of an entry indicates that the title is appearing for the first time.

Lotus 1-2-3, 97 Fast & Easy. Diane Koers. LC 97-67397. 336p. 1997. per. 16.99 (*0-7615-1193-8*) Prima Pub.

Lotus 1-2-3 97 Guru. Bill Hartman. (Computer Guru Ser.). (Illus.). 20p. 1998. spiral bd. 5.99 (*1-58187-031-0*) Guru Books.

Lotus 1-2-3 Quick Course. Thompson. (DF - Computer Applications Ser.). 1994. mass mkt. 18.95 (*0-538-63535-5*) S-W Pub.

Lotus 1-2-3, Quick Start. Anthony W. Stacy & Sue V. Stacy. LC 93-8178. 109p. (C). 1994. mass mkt. 19.95 (*0-538-71046-2*) S-W Pub.

Lotus 1-2-3 R5 for Windows Visual Pack Guide: Visual Pocket Guide. Maran Graphics Staff & Ruth Maran. 256p. 1995. spiral bd. 14.99 (*1-56884-671-1*) IDG Bks.

Lotus 1-2-3 R5 Simplified. expanded ed. Maran Graphics Staff & Ruth Maran. LC 94-79403. 352p. 1994. pap. 19.99 (*1-56884-670-3*) IDG Bks.

Lotus 1-2-3 Release 5 for Windows Virtual Tutor. Que Education & Training Staff. (Essentials Ser.). 1997. pap. text 25.00 (*1-57576-112-2*) Que Educ & Trng.

Lotus 1-2-3 Release 5 for Windows Double Diamond Edition. Gary Shelly et al. (Shelly Cashman Ser.). 208p. 1995. pap., teacher ed. write for info. (*0-87709-993-6*) Course Tech.

Lotus 1-2-3 Release 5 for Windows. expanded ed. Marangraphics Staff. 1994. text 24.95 (*0-9695666-9-7*, Pub. by MaGr) IDG Bks.

Lotus 1-2-3 Release 5 for Windows - New Perspectives Introductory, Incl. instr. resource kit, test bank, transparency. Roger Hayen. (New Perspectives Ser.). (Illus.). 360p. (C). 1995. pap. 30.95 (*0-7600-3271-8*) Course Tech.

Lotus 1-2-3 Release 5 for Windows - New Perspectives Comprehensive, Incl. instr. resource kit, test bank, transparency. Roger Hayen. (New Perspectives Ser.). (Illus.). 600p. (C). 1995. pap. 42.95 (*0-7600-3370-6*) Course Tech.

Lotus 1-2-3 Release 5 for Windows - Illustrated, Incl. instr. resource kit, test bank, transparency. Jane Hosie-Bounar. (Illustrated Ser.). (Illus.). 200p. 1995. text, mass mkt. 20.95 incl. 3.5 ld (*1-56527-597-7*) Course Tech.

Lotus 1-2-3 Release 5 for Windows: A Professional Approach. Carole K. Tobias. LC 95-9802. 1995. write for info. (*0-02-802621-7*) Glencoe.

Lotus 1-2-3 Release 5 Virtual Tutor. Que Education & Training Staff. Date not set. pap. text 35.00 incl. cd-rom (*1-57576-099-1*) Que Educ & Trng.

Lotus 1-2-3 Release 4 for DOS: LTU Microcomputer Applications. Gary B. Shelly & T. Cashman. 384p. (C). 1995. mass mkt. 38.95 (*0-87709-901-4*) S-W Pub.

Lotus 1-2-3 Release 4 for Windows. Brenda Nielsen. (Illustrated Ser.). (Illus.). (C). 1994. pap. write for info. incl. disk (*1-56527-169-6*) Course Tech.

Lotus 1-2-3 Release 4 for Windows. Timothy J. O'Leary & Linda I. O'Leary. LC 93-80529. (C). 1994. pap. text 11.50 (*0-07-049008-2*) McGraw.

Lotus 123 Release 4 for Windows. Sullivan. (Computer Training Ser.). (C). 1995. spiral bd. 21.95 (*0-538-64097-9*) S-W Pub.

Lotus 1-2-3 Release 4 for Windows: Self Teaching Guide. 20th ed. Douglas J. Wolf. 272p. 1993. pap. 22.95 (*0-471-30324-0*) Wiley.

Lotus 1-2-3 Release 6 for Windows, Quick Reference. Glen Davis. LC 98-100711. (Quick Reference Guides Ser.). (Illus.). (Orig.). 1996. pap. 12.00 (*1-56243-348-2*, G-13) DDC Pub.

Lotus 1-2-3 Release 3.0-3.1 Quick Reference Guide with Template. 24.95 (*0-913365-01-7*, S138) Microref Educ Systs.

Lotus 1-2-3, Release 2.4. Timothy J. O'Leary & Linda I. O'Leary. (C). 1994. pap. text 11.50 (*0-07-048994-7*) McGraw.

Lotus 1-2-3, Release 2.4. Miguel Pendas. (Step-by-Step Ser.). 1995. teacher ed. write for info. (*0-02-800956-8*) Glencoe.

Lotus 1-2-3, Release 2.4: A Tutorial to Accompany Peter Norton's Introduction to Computers. Terrence P. O'Donnell. LC 93-38995. 1994. write for info. (*0-02-801326-3*) Glencoe.

Lotus 1-2-3 Release 2.4. Sarah E. Hutchinson & Stacey C. Sawyer. LC 94-140602. 228p. (C). 1993. text 12.50 (*0-256-13715-3*, Irwn McGrw-H) McGrw-H Hghr Educ.

Lotus 1-2-3, Release 2.2: A Ready Reference Manual. Catherine Garrison & Mercedes McGowen. (Illus.). 144p. (C). 1991. pap. text 12.95 (*0-201-18559-8*) Addison-Wesley.

Lotus 1-2-3, Release 2.3. Timothy J. O'Leary et al. 1992. pap. text 11.00 (*0-07-048818-5*) McGraw.

Lotus 1-2-3, Release 2.2. rev. ed. Timothy J. O'Leary & Linda I. O'Leary. (C). 1993. pap. text 11.50 (*0-07-048897-5*) McGraw.

Lotus 1-2-3 Release 2.3 Quick Reference Guide with Template. 24.95 (*1-56351-035-9*, S164) Microref Educ Systs.

Lotus 1-2-3 Release 2.3 Quick Reference Guide. 19.95 (*1-56351-031-6*, G164) Microref Educ Systs.

Lotus 1-2-3 Release 2.3 for Business. Roy Ageloff. (Illus.). 650p. (C). 1992. disk 49.95 (*1-878748-85-8*); disk 49.95 (*1-878748-86-6*); disk 30.95 (*1-878748-87-4*) Course Tech.

Lotus 1-2-3 Release 2.3 for Accounting: Principles. Jeffrey E. Michelman. (Illus.). 400p. (C). 1992. disk 53.35 (*1-878748-81-5*); disk 53.35 (*1-878748-82-3*); disk 24.95 (*1-878748-83-1*); disk 24.95 (*1-878748-84-X*) Course Tech.

Lotus 1-2-3 Release 2.2 for Business. Roy Ageloff. 512p. (C). 1991. disk 53.50 (*1-878748-28-9*); disk 31.00 (*1-878748-39-4*); disk 53.50 (*1-878748-27-0*); disk 31.00 (*1-878748-38-6*) Course Tech.

Lotus 1-2-3 Release 2.2 for Accounting. Jeffrey E. Michelman. (Illus.). 568p. (C). 1990. disk 56.75 (*1-878748-00-9*); disk 56.75 (*1-878748-01-7*); disk 31.00 (*1-878748-56-4*); disk 31.00 (*1-878748-57-2*) Course Tech.

Lotus 1-2-3 Self-Taught on the IBM PC. Ira H. Krakow. (Illus.). 320p. 19.95 (*0-317-13081-1*) P-H.

Lotus 1-2-3 Simplified: Including Version 2.0. 2nd ed. David Bolocan. (Illus.). 272p. 1986. pap. 16.95 (*0-8306-2748-0*) McGraw-Hill Prof.

Lotus 1-2-3 Simplified for the IBM PC. Don Cassel. 272p. 1985. pap. 53.95 (*0-671-93843-6*) S&S Trade.

Lotus 1-2-3 Simplified, Release 3.1. David Bolocan. (Illus.). 368p. 1991. pap. 19.95 (*0-8306-3772-9*, 3772) McGraw-Hill Prof.

Lotus 1-2-3 the Easy Way. Richard Montague & Joel Goldstein. (Illus.). 53p. (Orig.). (C). 1990. pap. text 5.95 (*0-936285-09-5*) U New Haven Pr.

Lotus 1-2-3 3.1: Beginners. 1993. 29.95 (*1-56877-073-1*); teacher ed. 49.95 (*1-56877-074-X*) Macmillan USA.

Lotus 1-2-3 3.0 Quick Reference Guide. 1990. pap. 19.95 (*0-913365-72-6*) Microref Educ Systs.

Lotus 1-2-3 Tutorial & Applications. Groneman. (DF - Computer Applications Ser.). 1992. mass mkt. 28.95 (*0-538-61593-1*) S-W Pub.

Lotus 1-2-3 2.3: Beginning. 1993. 29.95 (*1-56877-071-5*); teacher ed. 49.95 (*1-56877-072-3*) Macmillan USA.

Lotus 1-2-3 2.2: Advanced. 1993. 29.95 (*1-56877-121-5*); teacher ed. 49.95 (*1-56877-120-7*) Macmillan USA.

Lotus 1-2-3 2.2: Beginners. 1993. 29.95 (*1-56877-069-3*); teacher ed. 49.95 (*1-56877-070-7*) Macmillan USA.

Lotus 1-2-3 2.2: Intermediate. 1993. 29.95 (*1-56877-138-X*); teacher ed. 49.95 (*1-56877-119-3*) Macmillan USA.

Lotus 1-2-3 (2.2 & 2.3) Advanced. Douglas M. Finney. (Illus.). 188p. 1992. spiral bd. 29.95 incl. disk (*1-56435-033-9*) Finney Lrng Systs.

Lotus 1-2-3 (2.2 & 2.3) Beginning. 2nd ed. Douglas M. Finney. (Illus.). 152p. 1992. spiral bd. 29.95 incl. disk (*1-56435-032-0*) Finney Lrng Systs.

Lotus 1-2-3 2.2 Quick Reference with Template. 1990. pap. 24.95 (*0-913365-75-0*) Microref Educ Systs.

Lotus 1-2-3 User's Handbook. Weber Systems, Inc. Staff. (User's Handbook Ser.). 304p. (Orig.). 1984. pap. 9.95 (*0-345-31815-3*, Ballantine) Ballantine Pub Grp.

Lotus 1-2-3 (Ver. 3.1) Quick Reference Guide. Iris Blanc. (Illus.). 1992. spiral bd. 12.00 (*1-56243-031-9*, J-18) DDC Pub.

Lotus 1-2-3 (Ver. 2.2) Quick Reference Guide. Iris Blanc. (DDC Quick Reference Guides Ser.). (YA). (gr. 9-12). 1990. spiral bd. 12.00 (*1-56243-000-9*, L2-17) DDC Pub.

Lotus 1-2-3 Version 5.0 Windows Introduction. Computer Confidence Staff. (Illus.). 165p. 1994. spiral bd. 29.95 incl. disk (*1-57533-014-8*) Comput Confidence.

Lotus 1-2-3 Version 4.0 (DOS) Basics & Beyond. M. G. Detienne. 119p. 1995. pap. text 29.00 (*1-887580-00-X*) Tec Trek.

Lotus 1-2-3, Version 3.4. 2nd ed. Jim Edwards. (STAR Ser.). (C). 1994. pap. 12.95 (*0-87709-165-X*, BF165X) S-W Pub.

Lotus 1-2-3, Version 3.4, IBM PC: Quick Reference Guide. Iris Blanc. 1993. spiral bd. 12.00 (*1-56243-090-4*, L317) DDC Pub.

Lotus 1-2-3, Version 2.4. Anna L. Slepecky. LC 93-24433. (Glencoe Seminar Ser.). 1993. teacher ed. write for info. (*0-02-801077-9*); student ed. write for info. (*0-02-801076-0*) Glencoe.

Lotus 1-2-3 Version 2.4: Basics & Beyond. M. G. Detienne. 112p. 1993. pap. text 29.00 (*1-887580-01-8*) Tec Trek.

Lotus 1-2-3 Version 2.3. Sarah E. Hutchinson & Stacey C. Sawyer. 224p. (C). 1993. text 12.50 (*0-256-13712-9*, Irwn McGrw-H) McGrw-H Hghr Educ.

Lotus 1-2-3 Version 2.3. M-USA Video Staff. (LogicNotes Ser.). 1991. 24.95 (*0-929978-57-9*) M-USA Busn Systs.

Lotus 1-2-3 Version 2.2. Sarah E. Hutchinson et al. 224p. (C). 1993. text 12.50 (*0-256-13487-1*, Irwn McGrw-H) McGrw-H Hghr Educ.

Lotus 1-2-3 with Template. Micoref Educational Systems Staff. 1986. pap. 19.95 (*0-913365-05-X*) Microref Educ Systs.

Lotus 1-2-3 Workbook. Richard D. Spinetto. (Illus.). 304p. (C). 1989. spiral bd. write for info. (*0-318-69102-7*, Irwn McGrw-H) McGrw-H Hghr Educ.

Lotus 1-2-3/R5 for Windows: Illustrated Brief Edition. Christie Williams. (Illustrated Ser.). (Illus.). 96p. 1995. pap. 11.95 (*0-7600-3500-8*) Course Tech.

Lotus 1-2-3/R2.4 for Business. Ageloff. 680p. (C). 1993. pap. write for info. (*1-56527-078-9*) Course Tech.

***Lotus 123, 97.** ENI Publishing Ltd. Staff. (Triunfar Con Ser.). 2000. pap. text 7.95 (*2-84072-739-0*) ENI Publng.

Lotus 1-2-3 Quick Reference Guide with Template. 1989. pap. 24.95 (*0-913365-56-4*) Microref Educ Systs.

Lotus Organizer 97. (Quick Study Computer Ser.). 4p. pap. 3.95 (*1-57222-321-9*) Barcharts.

Lotus Path. Elizabeth D. King. 127p. 1997. pap. 10.00 (*0-89540-257-2*, SB-257) Sun Pub.

Lotus Prayer Book. Ed. by Swami Karunananda Ma. LC 86-10384. 224p. (Orig.). 1986. pap. 12.95 (*0-932040-33-0*) Integral Yoga Pubns.

Lotus Race Cars 1961-1994 Photo Album. Norman Hayes. LC 97-75279. (Photo Album Ser.). (Illus.). 112p. 1998. pap. 19.95 (*1-882256-84-0*) Iconografix.

***Lotus Racing Cars.** John Tipler. (Illus.). 160p. 2000. 24.95 (*0-7509-2389-X*) Sutton Publng.

Lotus Seed. Sherry Garland. LC 92-2913. (Illus.). 32p. (J). (gr. 1-5). 1993. 15.00 (*0-15-249465-0*) Harcourt.

Lotus Seed. Sherry Garland. LC 92-2913. (Illus.). 32p. (J). 1997. pap. 6.00 (*0-15-201483-7*) Harcourt.

Lotus Seed. Sherry Garland. LC 92-2913. (J). 1997. 11.20 (*0-606-11581-1*, Pub. by Turtleback) Demco.

Lotus Seeds & Lucky Stars: Asian Myths & Traditions on Pregnancy & Birthing. Shu Shu Costa. LC 97-53269. 144p. 1998. 17.45 (*0-684-84397-8*) S&S Trade.

Lotus 7: A Collector's Guide. Jeremy Coulter. (Collector's Guide Ser.). (Illus.). 128p. 1995. 19.98 (*0-947981-71-3*, Pub. by Motor Racing) Motorbooks Intl.

Lotus since the 70's Vol. 2: Esprit, Etna & V8 Engines Collector's Guide. Graham Robson. (Collector's Guide Ser.). (Illus.). 128p. 1993. 27.95 (*0-947981-69-1*, Pub. by Motor Racing) Motorbooks Intl.

Lotus Smartstart Essentials. Sue Plumley. 1995. teacher ed. 39.99 (*0-7897-0446-3*) Que.

Lotus Smartstart Essentials. John Preston. 1995. 49.99 (*0-7897-0421-8*) Que.

Lotus SmartSuite: A Practical Approach. Judi N. Fernandez. 600p. 1995. pap. 39.95 (*1-55828-423-0*, MIS Pr) IDG Bks.

Lotus Smartsuite Essential. 1997. 36.00 (*0-7686-0099-5*) Quest Custom.

Lotus SmartSuite Notes Bundle. Que Development Group Staff. 1994. pap. 100.00 (*1-56529-951-5*) Que.

Lotus SmartSuite Quickstart Bundle. Que Staff. 1994. pap. 75.00 (*1-56529-969-8*) Que.

Lotus SmartSuite 6-in-1 for Windows 95. Que Development Group Staff. (Illus.). (Orig.). 1996. 26.99 (*0-7897-0636-9*) Que.

Lotus SmartSuite 3 for Windows - Illustrated, Incl. instr. resource kit, test bank, transparency. Christie Williams. (Illustrated Ser.). (Illus.). 463p. (C). 1995. pap. 50.95 (*1-56527-562-4*) Course Tech.

Lotus Smartsuite 97 Essentials. 530p. (C). 1998. pap. text 55.00 (*1-58076-045-7*) Que Educ & Trng.

Lotus Sutra. Numata Center for Buddhist Translation & Research. Tr. by Kubo Tsugunari & Yuyama Akira from CHI. LC 91-60119. (BDK English Tripitaka Ser.: Vol. 13-I). 363p. (C). 1993. text 35.00 (*0-9625618-0-0*) Numata Ctr.

Lotus Sutra. Tr. by Burton Watson from CHI. LC 92-38410. (Translations from the Asian Classics Ser.). 352p. (C). 1993. 44.00 (*0-231-08160-X*) Col U Pr.

Lotus Sutra. Burton Watson. LC 92-38410. 358p. 1994. pap. 19.00 (*0-231-08161-8*) Col U Pr.

Lotus Sutra in Japanese Culture. Ed. by George J. Tanabe, Jr. & Willa J. Tanabe. LC 88-36735. (Illus.). 264p. 1989. text 29.00 (*0-8248-1198-4*) UH Pr.

Lotus Sutra Poems. Robley E. Whitson. 72p. 1995. pap. 12.00 (*1-55605-259-6*) Wyndham Hall.

Lotus Symphony - Made Easy: Understanding & Using Symphony Book. M. Shamsul Haque. LC 86-90505. (Illus.). xxx, 400p. 1990. pap., per. 23.95 (*0-933057-04-0*) Namuk Intl Inc.

Lotus Textbook. Kanjitsu Ijima. 62p. (Orig.). 1984. pap. 10.00 (*0-86627-010-8*) Crises Res Pr.

Lotus Tips: The Introductory Program. LC 92-39064. (Glencoe Ser.). 1993. write for info. (*0-02-802506-7*) Glencoe.

Lotus Tips: The Introductory Program. large type ed. 1993. 38.50 (*0-614-09839-4*, L-31417-00) Am Printing Hse.

Lotus Twin Cam Engine. Mike Wikens. (Illus.). 223p. 1996. 39.95 (*1-85532-645-0*, Pub. by Ospry) Motorbooks Intl.

Lotus 2.4. Don Cassel. (Source 1 Ser.). (C). 1993. pap. 9.33 (*0-13-834300-4*) P-H.

Lotus 2.3 2.4 Quick Reference Guide. 1993. pap. 14.95 (*1-56351-093-6*) Microref Educ Systs.

Lotus Web Development Exam 190-281: Accelerated Lotus Study Guide. Oliver. LC 98-55405. (Accelerated Ser.). 1999. pap., student ed. 29.99 (*0-07-134533-7*) McGraw.

Lotus Word Pro for Windows. Susan Jaderstrom. (Quicktorial Ser.). 1996. mass mkt. 20.95 (*0-538-71539-1*) S-W Pub.

Lotus Word Pro for Windows: Quick Course. Susan Jaderstrom. (DF - Computer Applications Ser.). 1996. mass mkt. 22.95 (*0-538-71527-8*) S-W Pub.

***Lotus Word Pro Millennium Edition 9.0 Quick Source Guide.** Quick Source Staff. (Illus.). 6p. 2000. pap. 4.95 (*1-930674-02-3*) Quick Source.

Lotus Word Pro 97. (Quick Study Computer Ser.). 4p. pap. 3.95 (*1-57222-296-4*) Barcharts.

Lotus WordPro 96 for Windows 95: Illustrated Brief Edition. 10th ed. Mary-Terese Cozzola. (Illustrated Ser.). (Illus.). 96p. (C). 1996. pap. 12.95 (*0-7600-4700-6*) Course Tech.

Lotus Worksheet File Formats: Essential Data File Facts about 1-2-3-, Symphony, & Jazz. Lotus Development Corporation Staff. write for info. (*0-318-60208-3*) Addison-Wesley.

Lotus 1 2 3. (C). 1989. text. write for info. (*0-201-51098-7*) Addison-Wesley.

Lotus 1-2-3. Kenneth S. Close. (SWC-General Business). (C). 1986. mass mkt. 34.25 (*0-538-10190-3*, J19) S-W Pub.

Lotus 1 2 3. Dolores M. Etter. (C). 1994. 28.95 (*0-8053-1783-X*) Benjamin-Cummings.

Lotus 1-2-3 For Windows 2.0: Intermediate. 1993. 29.95 (*1-56877-125-8*) Macmillan USA.

Lotus 1-2-3, Release 2.2: An Introduction to Problem Solving with Spreadsheets User's Manual. Diane Zak. 1993. write for info. incl. 3.5 hd (*0-8053-1346-X*) Benjamin-Cummings.

Lotus 1 2 3 Release 2.4. (Illus.). xvii, 168p. 1993. teacher ed., spiral bd., wbk. ed. 29.00 (*0-7402-0140-9*, LTOOD242IG) Accelerated Comput Train.

Lotus 1-2-3 Release 2.4 Macro Programming. (Illus.). iii, 78p. 1992. student ed., spiral bd., wbk. ed. 15.95 (*0-7402-0117-4*, LtOOD24M WB) Accelerated Comput Train.

Lotus 1 2 3 Release 3.4 Intermediate. (Illus.). xvii, 152p. 1993. teacher ed., spiral bd., wbk. ed. 29.00 (*0-7402-0175-1*, LTOOD342IG) Accelerated Comput Train.

Lotus. 1-2-3. Release 4 for Windows. Maroln Graphincs Staff. 1994. 6.00 (*1-56884-686-X*) IDG Bks.

Lotus 1-2-3 Tutorial Guide. O'Leary. (C). 1992. text, student ed. 32.00 incl. 3.5 hd (*0-201-60585-6*) Addison-Wesley.

Lotus 1-2-3, Version 2.2. (C). 1990. text. write for info. (*0-201-52290-X*) Addison-Wesley.

Lotus 1-2-3 (2.4 Dos) Made Simple. Robertson. 160p. Date not set. pap. text 19.95 (*0-7506-2066-8*) Buttrwrth-Heinemann.

Lotus 1 2 3 (3.1) Macros. (Illus.). iiii, 72p. 1992. student ed., spiral bd., wbk. ed. 15.95 (*0-7402-0122-0*, LTOOD31M WB) Accelerated Comput Train.

Lotus 1-2-3 97 - Illustrated Brief Edition. Christie Williams. (Illustrated Ser.). (Illus.). (C). 1997. pap. 12.95 (*0-7600-5348-0*) Course Tech.

Lotus 1-2-3 97 - Illustrated Standard Edition. Christy Williams & Jane Hosie-Bounar. (Illustrated Ser.). (Illus.). (C). 1997. pap. 21.95 (*0-7600-5347-2*) Course Tech.

Lotus 1-2-3 97 for Windows 95. Betsy Newberry. (Quicktorial Ser.). 1998. pap. text 21.95 (*0-538-68430-5*) S-W Pub.

Lotus 1 2 3/Release 3.1 Macro Programming. (Illus.). xvii, 144p. 1990. teacher ed., spiral bd., wbk. ed. 29.00 (*0-7402-0147-6*, LTOOD31MIG) Accelerated Comput Train.

Lotus 123 - Win 3.1. (Quick Study Computer Ser.). 4p. pap. 3.95 (*1-57222-166-6*) Barcharts.

Lotus 123 - 97. (Quick Study Computer Ser.). 4p. pap. 3.95 (*1-57222-273-5*) Barcharts.

Lotus 123 for Windows R 4/5: Tutorial & Applications. Groneman. 1995. wbk. ed. 46.50 (*0-538-64764-7*) Thomson Learn.

LOTUS 2.4 3.5 SE NAT PKG. Timothy J. O'Leary & Linda L. O'Leary. 524p. (C). 1994. pap. text, student ed. 44.99 incl. 3.5 hd (*0-8053-1353-2*) Benjamin-Cummings.

Lotusland: A Photographic Odyssey. Photos by W. B. Dewey et al. LC 95-14944. (Illus.). 144p. 1996. 65.00 (*0-9627297-5-2*) A A Knoll Pubs.

LotusScript Exam 190-273: Accelerated Lotus Study Guide. William Thompson. LC 98-55404. 1999. pap. text 29.99 (*0-07-134561-2*) McGraw.

LotusWorks 3.0: Everything You Need to Know: A Quick & Easy Guide to Getting the Most from LotusWorks. Sandra E. Schnyder. (Illus.). 496p. 1992. pap. 24.95 (*1-55958-184-0*) Prima Pub.

LOTUS123 R2.2 USER SE PK. Timothy J. O'Leary. 1991. student ed. 27.75 (*0-8053-1330-3*) Benjamin-Cummings.

Lotze's System of Philosophy. George Santayana et al. Ed. by Paul Grimley et al. LC 72-135008. 286p. reprint ed. pap. 88.70 (*0-608-10051-X*, 200575300059) Bks Demand.

Lou: Winning at Illinois. Lou Henson & Skip Myslenski. LC 89-62927. 266p. 1989. 18.95 (*0-915611-24-4*) Sports Pub.

Lou Andreas-Salome: Feministin Oder Antifeministin? Eine Standortbestimmung zur Wilhelminischen Frauenbewegung. Caroline Kreide. (Studies in Modern German Literature: Vol. 68). (GER.). VIII, 145p. (C). 1996. text 38.95 (*0-8204-2478-1*) P Lang Pubng.

Lou Austin Anthology. Lou Austin. 1983. 8.50 (*0-685-06307-0*) Partnership Foundation.

Lou Boudreau: Covering All of the Bases April, 1997. Lou Boudreau & Russell Schneider. LC 93-84610. (Illus.). 203p. 1997. 24.95 (*0-915611-72-4*) Sports Pub.

Lou Ferrigno's Guide to Personal Power. Lou Ferrigno. 224p. pap. 19.95 (*0-9643739-0-4*) L Ferrigno Ent.

Lou Ferrigno's Guide to Personal Power, Bodybuilding, & Fitness. Lou Ferrigno. LC 96-15171. (Illus.). 208p. 1996. pap. 14.95 (*0-8092-3125-5*, 312550, Contemporary Bks) NTC Contemp Pub Co.

Lou Gehrig. Norman L. Macht. (Baseball Legends Ser.). (Illus.). 64p. (J). (gr. 3 up). 1992. lib. bdg. 15.95 (*0-7910-1176-3*) Chelsea Hse.

Lou Gehrig. Richard Rambeck. LC 92-40673. (Sports Superstars Ser.). (Illus.). 32p. (J). (gr. 2-6). 1994. lib. bdg. 21.36 (*1-56766-073-8*) Childs World.

Lou Gehrig: An American Classic. Richard Bak. LC 94-46151. 208p. 1995. 29.95 (*0-87833-883-7*) Taylor Pub.

Lou Gehrig: Classic Sports Shots. Bruce Weber. 48p. (J). (gr. 4-6). 1993. pap. 1.25 (*0-590-47023-X*) Scholastic Inc.

Lou Gehrig: One of Baseball's Greatest. Guernsey Van Riper, Jr. LC 86-10951. (Childhood of Famous Americans Ser.). (Illus.). 192p. (J). (gr. 3-7). 1986. reprint ed. mass mkt. 4.95 (*0-02-041930-9*, Pub. by Macmillan) S&S Trade.

Lou Gehrig: The Luckiest Man Alive. David A. Adler. LC 95-7997. (Illus.). 32p. (J). (gr. k-4). 1997. 16.00 (*0-15-200523-4*, Gulliver Bks) Harcourt.

***Lou Gehrig: The Luckiest Man Alive.** David A. Adler. 2001. pap. write for info. (*0-15-202483-2*) Harcourt.

Lou Gehrig, One of Baseball's Greatest. Guernsey Van Riper. (Childhood of Famous Americans Ser.). (J). 1986. 10.05 (*0-606-03241-X*, Pub. by Turtleback) Demco.

Lou Gehrig, Pride of the Yankees. Keith Brandt. LC 85-1075. (Illus.). 48p. (J). (gr. 4-6). 1997. pap. 3.95 (*0-8167-0550-X*) Troll Communs.

Lou Gehrig, Pride of the Yankees. Keith Brandt. LC 85-1075. (Illus.). 48p. (J). (gr. 4-6). 1997. lib. bdg. 17.25 (*0-8167-0549-6*) Troll Communs.

Lou Gehrig, Pride of the Yankees. Keith Brandt. 1986. 8.70 (*0-606-01629-5*, Pub. by Turtleback) Demco.

***Lou Goes Too!** Jacqueline Sweeney. LC 98-43359. (We Can Read Ser.). (J). (gr. k-2). 1999. 21.36 (*0-7614-0921-1*, Benchmark NY) Marshall Cavendish.

Lou Grant: The Making of TV's Top Newspaper Drama. Douglass K. Daniel. (Illus.). 380p. 1995. 45.00 (*0-8156-2675-4*); pap. 19.95 (*0-8156-0363-0*) Syracuse U Pr.

An Asterisk (*) at the beginning of an entry indicates that the title is appearing for the first time.

Lou Harrison: Composing a World. Leta E. Miller & Frederic Lieberman. (Illus.). 416p. 1998. 35.00 (*0-19-511022-6*) OUP.

***Lou Harrison: Selected Keyboard & Chamber Music, 1937-1994.** Lou Harrison. Ed. by Leta E. Miller. (Music of the United States of America Ser.: Vol. MUSA8). (Illus.). lv, 162p. 1998. pap. 95.00 (*0-89579-414-4*) A-R Eds.

Lou Henry Hoover: Essays on a Busy Life. Ed. by Dale C. Mayer. LC 93-78297. (Illus.). 160p. 1994. 23.50 (*1-881019-04-7*) High Plns WY.

Lou Henry Hoover: The Duty to Serve. Nancy A. Colbert. LC 97-33329. (Notable Americans Ser.). (Illus.). 112p. (YA). (gr. 5 up). 1998. lib. bdg. 18.95 (*1-883846-22-6*) M Reynolds.

Lou-Lan & Other Stories. Yasushi Inoue. Tr. by J. Araki & Edward G. Seidensticker from JPN. LC 79-66239. 160p. 1994. reprint ed. pap. 10.00 (*0-87011-472-7*) Kodansha.

Lou Reed: Between the Lines. Michael Wrenn. 144p. 1994. per. 14.95 (*0-85965-164-9*, Pub. by Plexus) Publishers Group.

Lou Reed: Growing up in Public. Peter Doggett. (Illus.). 216p. 1997. pap. 17.95 (*0-7119-3002-3*, OP 46820) Omnibus NY.

Lou Sander's Tips & Tricks for Commodore. Louis F. Sander. 1991. 24.95 (*0-8306-7434-9*) McGraw-Hill Prof.

Lou Tabory's Guide to Saltwater Baits & Their Imitations: An All-Color Guide. Lou Tabory. (Illus.). 144p. 1995. pap. 16.95 (*1-55821-361-9*) Lyons Pr.

Lou Whittaker: Memoirs of a Mountain Guide. Lou Whittaker. (Illus.). 264p. 1995. pap. 16.95 (*0-89886-459-3*) Mountaineers.

Lou Who? The Odyssey of a French Poodle in England & America. Shirley Robertson. LC 93-84751. (Illus.). 216p. (Orig.). 1993. pap. text 13.95 (*1-880222-16-7*) Red Apple Pub.

Louanne Pig in Making the Team. unabridged ed. Nancy Carlson. (Illus.). (J). (gr. k-3). 1987. pap. 15.95 incl. audio (*0-87499-038-6*) Live Oak Media.

Louanne Pig in Making the Team, Set. unabridged ed. Nancy Carlson. (Illus.). (J). (gr. k-3). 1987. 24.95 incl. audio (*0-87499-040-8*); pap., teacher ed. 31.95 incl. audio (*0-87499-039-4*) Live Oak Media.

Louanne Pig in the Mysterious Valentine. Nancy Carlson. (Illus.). 32p. 1996. pap. text 4.95 (*1-57505-032-3*, Carolrhoda) Lerner Pub.

Louanne Pig in The Mysterious Valentine. unabridged ed. Nancy Carlson. (Illus.). (J). (gr. 1-3). 1988. pap. 15.95 incl. audio (*0-87499-086-6*) Live Oak Media.

Louanne Pig in The Mysterious Valentine, Set. Nancy Carlson. (Illus.). (J). (gr. 1-3). 1988. 24.95 incl. audio (*0-87499-087-4*) Live Oak Media.

Louanne Pig in The Mysterious Valentine, 4 bks., Set. unabridged ed. Nancy Carlson. (Illus.). (J). (gr. 1-3). 1988. pap., teacher ed. 31.95 incl. audio (*0-87499-088-2*) Live Oak Media.

Louanne Pig in the Perfect Family. unabridged ed. Nancy Carlson. (Illus.). (J). (gr. k-3). 1987. 24.95 incl. audio (*0-87499-037-8*); pap. 15.95 incl. audio (*0-87499-035-1*) Live Oak Media.

Louanne Pig in the Perfect Family, 4 bks., Set. Nancy Carlson. (Illus.). (J). (gr. k-3). 1987. pap., teacher ed. 31.95 incl. audio (*0-87499-036-X*) Live Oak Media.

Louanne Pig in Witch Lady. Nancy Carlson. (Nancy Carlson's Neighborhood Ser.). (Illus.). 32p. (J). (ps-2). 1997. pap. text 4.95 (*1-57505-234-2*, Carolrhoda) Lerner Pub.

Loucks: Genealogy of the Loucks Family, Beginning with Johann Dietrich Loucks & His Descendants in Direct Line to Joseph Louck, & All His Known & Traceable Descendants to Date. E. M. McBrier. (Illus.). 317p. 1991. reprint ed. pap. 48.50 (*0-8328-1727-9*); reprint ed. lib. bdg. 58.50 (*0-8328-1726-0*) Higginson Bk Co.

Loud. Dirck Toll. LC 92-73649. 72p. (Orig.). 1992. pap. 7.50 (*0-9634317-1-4*) Hill Pr NY.

Loud & Clear: How to Prepare & Deliver Effective Business & Technical Presentations. 4th ed. George L. Morrisey. LC 97-10309. 1997. pap. 15.00 (*0-201-12793-8*) Addison-Wesley.

Loud & Quiet. Jack Challoner. LC 95-48339. (Illus.). 32p. (J). (gr. 1-4). 1996. lib. bdg. 21.40 (*0-8172-4318-6*) Raintree Steck-V.

Loud Emily. Alexis O'Neill. LC 97-18217. (Illus.). 40p. (J). (ps-2). 1998. 16.00 (*0-689-81078-4*) S&S Childrens.

Loud Hawk: The United States vs. the American Indian Movement. Kenneth S. Stern. LC 93-6175. 384p. 1994. 25.95 (*0-8061-2587-X*) U of Okla Pr.

Loud Let It Ring: Adventist World Radio, Twenty-Five Years of Miracles. Allen R. Steele. LC 95-50945. 1996. pap. 1.97 (*0-8163-1335-0*) Pacific Pr Pub Assn.

Loud Mouthed Gun. James W. Schultz. (Indian Culture Ser.). 27p. (J). (gr. 4-8). 1984. pap. 4.95 (*0-89992-095-0*) Coun India Ed.

Loud, Proud & Passionate: Including Women with Disabilities in International Development Programming. Ed. by Sygall Lewis. (SPA.). 1997. 25.00 (*0-614-31254-X*) Mobility Intl.

Loud Silents: Origins of the Social Problem Film. Kay Sloan. (Illus.). 192p. 1988. text 24.95 (*0-252-01544-4*) U of Ill Pr.

Loud Singer & Little Bird: Nipalaaq & Ukillaq. Harley D. Shield & Martha Shield. (Illus.). 160p. 1998. pap. 12.95 (*0-9664583-0-3*) Arctic Pubns.

Louder!!! The Official James Scott LOUD Reading Poetry Book. James Scott. 60p. (J). (gr. 1-6). 1994. 9.95 (*1-886080-00-3*) Loud Lit.

Louder, I Can't Hear You. Bill Gleason. 30p. 1974. pap. 3.50 (*0-87129-553-9*, L32) Dramatic Pub.

Louder Than Words: A Third Collection. Ed. by William H. Shore. LC 94-20156. 336p. 1994. pap. 11.95 (*0-15-600117-9*) Harcourt.

***Loudest, Fastest, Best Drummer in Kansas.** Marguerite W. Davol. LC 99-29513. 32p. (J). (gr. k-4). 2000. 15.95 (*0-531-30191-5*); lib. bdg. 16.99 (*0-531-33191-1*) Orchard Bks Watts.

Loudest Scream. R. L. Stine, pseud. (Fear Street: No. 2). (YA). (gr. 7 up). 1996. per. 3.99 (*0-671-52956-0*) PB.

Loudest Scream. R. L. Stine, pseud. (Fear Street: No. 2). (YA). (gr. 7 up). 1996. 9.09 (*0-606-10808-4*, Pub. by Turtleback) Demco.

Loudmouth: Best of Bob Geldof & the Boomtown Rats. 1997. pap. 17.95 (*0-8256-1429-5*, AM 92224) Music Sales.

Loudmouth George & the Big Race. Nancy Carlson. LC 83-5191. (Illus.). 32p. (J). (ps-3). 1983. lib. bdg. 17.27 (*0-87614-215-3*, Carolrhoda) Lerner Pub.

Loudmouth George & the Bir Race. Nancy Carlson. (Illus.). 32p. 1996. pap. text 4.95 (*1-57505-033-1*, Carolrhoda) Lerner Pub.

Loudmouth George & the Cornet. Nancy Carlson. LC 82-22171. (Illus.). 32p. (J). (ps-3). 1983. lib. bdg. 17.27 (*0-87614-214-5*, Carolrhoda) Lerner Pub.

Loudmouth George & the Cornet. Nancy Carlson. (Nancy Carlson's Neighborhood Ser.). (Illus.). 32p. (J). (ps-2). 1997. pap. text 4.95 (*1-57505-235-0*, Carolrhoda) Lerner Pub.

Loudmouth George & the Fishing Trip. Nancy Carlson. LC 82-22159. (Illus.). 32p. (J). (ps-3). 1983. lib. bdg. 17.27 (*0-87614-213-7*, Carolrhoda) Lerner Pub.

Loudmouth George & the Fishing Trip. Nancy Carlson. (Illus.). 32p. (J). (ps-3). 1994. pap. 4.95 (*0-87614-623-X*, Carolrhoda) Lerner Pub.

Loudmouth George & the Fishing Trip. unabridged ed. Nancy Carlson. (Illus.). (J). (gr. k-3). 1986. 24.95 incl. audio (*0-87499-019-X*); pap. 15.95 incl. audio (*0-87499-017-3*) Live Oak Media.

Loudmouth George & the Fishing Trip, 4 vols., Set. Nancy Carlson. (Illus.). (J). (gr. k-3). 1986. pap., teacher ed. 31.95 incl. audio (*0-87499-018-1*) Live Oak Media.

Loudmouth George & the New Neighbors. Nancy Carlson. LC 83-7298. (Illus.). 32p. (J). (ps-3). 1983. lib. bdg. 17.27 (*0-87614-216-1*, Carolrhoda) Lerner Pub.

Loudmouth George & the New Neighbors. Nancy Carlson. (Nancy Carlson's Neighborhood Ser.). (Illus.). 32p. (J). (ps-2). 1997. pap. text 4.95 (*0-87614-622-1*) Lerner Pub.

Loudmouth George & the Sixth Grade Bully. Nancy Carlson. (Nancy Carlson's Neighborhood Ser.). (Illus.). 32p. (J). (ps-3). 1994. pap. 4.95 (*0-87614-624-8*, First Ave Edns); lib. bdg. 17.27 (*0-87614-217-X*, First Ave Edns) Lerner Pub.

Loudmouth George & the Sixth Grade Bully. unabridged ed. Nancy Carlson. (Illus.). (J). (gr. k-3). 1986. 24.95 incl. audio (*0-87499-016-5*); pap. 15.95 incl. audio (*0-87499-014-9*) Live Oak Media.

Loudmouth George & the Sixth Grade Bully, 4 bks., Set. Nancy Carlson. (Illus.). (J). (gr. k-3). 1986. pap., teacher ed. 31.95 incl. audio (*0-87499-015-7*) Live Oak Media.

Loudness of Sam. James Proimos. LC 98-29884. (Illus.). 32p. (J). (ps-3). 1999. 13.00 (*0-15-202087-X*) Harcourt.

Loudon's Encyclopaedia of Plants, 3 vols., Set. Prints India Staff. (C). 1988. 500.00 (*0-7855-0053-7*, Pub. by Print Hse) St Mut.

Loudon's Indian Narratives: A Selection of Some of the Most Interesting Narratives of Outrages Committed by the Indians in Their Wars with the White People. A. Loudon. LC 96-78507. (The Great Pennsylvania Frontier Ser.: Vol. 8). (Illus.). 658p. 1996. reprint ed. 49.95 (*1-889037-07-9*, 8) Wennawoods.

***Loudoun County: Blending Tradition with Innovation.** Julie Johnson. (American Enterprise Ser.). (Illus.). 136p. 2000. 44.95 (*1-58192-016-4*) Community Comm.

Loudoun County Street Guide & Directory: 1999 Edition. Thomas Bros. Maps Staff. (Illus.). 128p. 1998. pap. 9.95 (*1-58174-096-4*) Thomas Bros Maps.

Loudoun County, Virginia: Marriage Records to 1891. Aurelia M. Jewell. 100p. 1975. pap. 15.00 (*0-685-65071-5*) VA Bk.

***Loudoun County, Virginia: People & Places.** Mary Fishback. (Images of America Ser.). 128p. 2000. pap. 18.99 (*0-7385-0563-3*) Arcadia Publng.

***Loudoun County, Virginia: 250 Years of Towns & Villages.** Mary Fishback. (Images of America Ser.). (Illus.). 128p. 1999. pap. 18.99 (*0-7385-0060-7*) Arcadia Publng.

Loudoun County, Virginia Cemeteries: A Preliminary Index. Thomas Balch Library Staff. 354p. 1996. pap. 30.00 (*1-888265-08-6*) Willow Bend.

Loudoun County, Virginia Marriage Bonds, 1762-1850. Aurelia M. Jewell. 219p. 1997. reprint ed. pap. 21.00 (*0-8063-4699-X*, Pub. by Clearfield Co) ACCESS Pubs Network.

Loudoun County, Virginia Marriages, 1760-1850. John Vogt & T. William Kethley, Jr. 462p. 1985. pap. 20.00 (*0-935931-07-4*) Iberian Pub.

Loudoun County, Virginia Minute Book, 1780-1783. T.L.C. Genealogy Staff. 196p. (Orig.). 1990. pap., spiral bd. 12.00 (*1-886633-74-6*) TLC Genealogy.

Loudspeaker & Headphone Handbook. 2nd rev. ed. John Borwick. LC 94-22160. (Illus.). 608p. 1994. pap. text 95.00 (*0-240-51371-1*, Focal) Buttrwrth-Heinemann.

***Loudspeaker & Headphone Handbook.** 3rd ed. Ed. by John Borwick. (Illus.). 608p. 2000. pap. 120.00 (*0-240-51578-1*, Focal) Buttrwrth-Heinemann.

Loudspeaker Design Cookbook. 5th ed. Vance Dickason. (Illus.). 165p. 1995. pap. text 34.95 (*1-882580-10-9*) Audio Amateur.

Loudspeaker Handbook. John Eargle. (Electrical Engineering Ser.). 1996. 59.95 (*0-442-02033-3*, VNR) Wiley.

Loudspeaker Recipes: Four Two-Way Designs, Bk. 1. Vance Dickason. LC 94-71764. (Illus.). 144p. (Orig.). 1994. pap. 24.95 (*1-882580-04-4*) Audio Amateur.

Loudspeakers: The Why & How of Good Reproduction. G. A. Briggs. LC 90-81199. (Illus.). 88p. 1990. pap. text 6.95 (*0-9624191-3-3*) Audio Amateur.

Louella Mae, She's Run Away! Karen B. Alarcon. LC 96-12319. (Illus.). 32p. (J). (gr. 1-4). 1997. 14.95 (*0-8050-3532-X*) H Holt & Co.

Lough Corrib: Its Shores & Islands. William R. Wilde. (Illus.). 306p. 1971. 45.95 (*0-405-01719-7*) Arno Press.

Lough Corrib: Its Shores & Islands. William R. Wilde. 7.00 (*0-405-18975-3*, 16891) Ayer.

Lough Neagh: The Ecology of a Multipurpose Water Resource. Ed. by R. B. Wood & R. V. Smith. LC 92-44827. (Monographiae Biologicae: No. 69). 1993. text 343.00 (*0-7923-2112-X*) Kluwer Academic.

Lougheed. B. Byron Price. (Illus.). 148p. 1991. 65.00 (*0-9620327-2-7*) Nygard Pub.

Loughs of Ireland: An Angler's Guide. 3rd ed. Peter O'Reilly. (Fly Fishing International Ser.). (Illus.). 335p. 1999. 34.95 (*0-8117-1025-4*) Stackpole.

Louie. rev. ed. Ezra Jack Keats. LC 75-6766. (Illus.). 32p. (J). (ps-3). 1983. 14.89 (*0-688-02383-5*, Grenwillow Bks) HarpC Child Bks.

***Louie: A Country Lady.** large type unabridged ed. Doreen Louie West. 255p. 1999. 23.95 (*0-7531-5076-X*, 15076X, Pub. by ISIS Lrg Prnt) ISIS Pub.

Louie A. Gardella: Just Passing Through - My Work in Nevada Agriculture, Agricultural Extension, & Western Water Resources. Intro. by Mary E. Glass. 485p. 1975. lib. bdg. 66.50 (*1-56475-140-6*); fiche. write for info. (*1-56475-141-4*) U NV Oral Hist.

Louie & Dan Are Friends. Bonnie Pryor. LC 96-32444. (Illus.). 32p. (J). 1997. lib. bdg. 15.93 (*0-688-08561-X*, Wm Morrow) Morrow Avon.

Louie & Dan Are Friends. Bonnie Pryor. LC 96-32444. (Illus.). 32p. (J). (ps-3). 1997. 16.00 (*0-688-08560-1*, Wm Morrow) Morrow Avon.

Louie & Rosie. Harriet Ziefert. 1924. lib. bdg. write for info. (*0-688-17560-0*, Wm Morrow) Morrow Avon.

Louie Llama, the Beanstalk, & the Magic Ring: The Llama Family in America. 2nd rev. ed. Donald E. Black. Tr. by Georgetown University Professor & Professional Sta & Organization of American States Staff. (ENG & SPA., Illus.). 32p. (J). (gr. 3 up). 1997. pap. 9.95 (*0-9625753-4-8*) SuperAmerican Bks.

Louie, Louie: The History & Myth. Dave Marsh. (Illus.). 256p. (J). 1993. 19.45 (*1-56282-865-7*, Pub. by Hyperion) Time Warner.

Louie, Louie: The History & Myth. Dave Marsh. (Illus.). 256p. (J). 1994. pap. 12.45 (*0-7868-8028-7*, Pub. by Hyperion) Time Warner.

***Louie the Lifeguard.** large type ed. Lisa P. Gillen. (LB Ser.). (Illus.). 6p. (J). (ps-1). 2000. pap. text 10.95 (*1-57332-176-1*); pap. text 10.95 (*1-57332-175-3*) HighReach Lrning.

Louie the Lobster. John McGahee. LC 96-86374. 1996. mass mkt., spiral bd. 9.95 (*1-889131-04-0*) CasAnanda.

Louie's Big Break. Gregg Sanderson. (Fox Kids Funhouse Ser.). (J). 1998. pap. text 4.50 (*1-57840-220-4*) Acclaim Bks.

***Louie's Goose.** Illus. by Harriet Ziefert & Emily Bolam. LC 99-28566. 32p. (J). 2000. 15.00 (*0-618-03023-9*) HM.

***Louie's Search.** Ezra Jack Keats. LC 00-9594. 2001. pap. write for info. (*0-14-056761-5*, PuffinBks) Peng Put Young Read.

Louie's Search. Ezra Jack Keats. LC 89-15128. (Illus.). 40p. (J). (gr. k-3). 1989. reprint ed. mass mkt. 4.95 (*0-689-71354-1*) Aladdin.

Louis: The Louis Armstrong Story, 1900-1971. Max Jones & John Chilton. (Quality Paperbacks Ser.). (Illus.). 302p. 1988. reprint ed. pap. 12.95 (*0-306-80324-0*) Da Capo.

Louis "Aloysius" Bertrand's Gaspard de la Nuit: Fantasies in the Manner of Rembrandt & Callot. 2nd ed. Aloysius Bertrand. Tr. & Intro. by John T. Wright. 182p. (C). 1994. lib. bdg. 39.00 (*0-8191-9345-3*) U Pr of Amer.

Louis Althusser: A Bibliography. Ed. by Joan Nordquist. (Social Theory: A Bibliographic Ser.: No. 3). 50p. 1986. pap. 20.00 (*0-937855-04-9*) Ref Rsch Serv.

Louis & the Night Sky. unabridged ed. Nicola Morgan. LC 99-178828. (Illus.). 32p. (J). (ps-3). 1993. pap. 4.95 (*0-19-540970-1*) STDK.

Louis-Antoine De Bougainville, 1729-1811: A Study in French Naval History & Politics. Mary Kimbrough. LC 90-22129. (Studies in French Civilization: Vol. 7). 252p. 1990. lib. bdg. 89.95 (*0-88946-744-7*) E Mellen.

Louis Aragon. Lucille F. Becker. LC 70-110702. (Twayne's World Authors Ser.). 1971. lib. bdg. 20.95 (*0-8057-2056-1*) Irvington.

Louis Armstrong. Michel Boujut. LC 98-65883. (Illus.). 144p. 1998. 40.00 (*0-8478-2131-5*, Pub. by Rizzoli Intl) St Martin.

Louis Armstrong. Daruthula H. Millender. LC 96-24544. (Illus.). 192p. 1997. 4.99 (*0-689-80881-X*) S&S Bks Yung.

Louis Armstrong. Tutti Staff. (Legends Ser.: No. 1). 177p. 1995. pap. 16.95 incl. disk (*1-57301-050-2*) TuTTi USA.

Louis Armstrong. Adam Woog. LC 94-296. (Importance of Ser.). (J). (gr. 5-8). 1995. lib. bdg. 22.45 (*1-56006-059-X*) Lucent Bks.

Louis Armstrong. Hugues Panassie. LC 79-20828. (Roots of Jazz Ser.). (Illus.). 148p. 1979. reprint ed. pap. 7.95 (*0-306-80116-7*); reprint ed. lib. bdg. 25.00 (*0-306-79611-2*) Da Capo.

Louis Armstrong: A Jazz Master for B-Flat Instruments. 48p. 1985. pap. 8.95 (*0-7935-3530-1*, 00120549) H Leonard.

Louis Armstrong: A Self-Portrait, Special Edition. limited ed. Richard Meryman. LC 70-152507. (Illus.). 59p. 1996. boxed set 125.00 (*0-87130-026-5*, Pub. by Eakins) RAM Publications.

Louis Armstrong: An Extravagant Life. Laurence Bergreen. 592p. 1998. pap. 16.00 (*0-7679-0156-8*) Broadway BDD.

Louis Armstrong: Jazz Musician. Patricia McKissack & Fredrick McKissack. LC 91-12420. (Great African Americans Ser.). (Illus.). 32p. (J). (gr. 1-4). 1991. lib. bdg. 14.95 (*0-89490-307-1*) Enslow Pubs.

Louis Armstrong: King of Jazz. Wendie C. Old. LC 97-35860. (African-American Biographies Ser.). (Illus.). 128p. (YA). (gr. 6 up). 1998. lib. bdg. 20.95 (*0-89490-997-5*) Enslow Pubs.

Louis Armstrong: Musician. Sam Tanenhaus. Ed. by Nathan I. Huggins. (Black Americans of Achievement Ser.). (Illus.). 124p. (YA). (gr. 5 up). 1988. lib. bdg. 19.95 (*1-55546-571-4*) Chelsea Hse.

Louis Armstrong: Musician. Sam Tanenhaus. Ed. by Nathan I. Huggins. (Black Americans of Achievement Ser.). (Illus.). 112p. (YA). (gr. 5 up). 1989. pap. 8.95 (*0-7910-0221-7*) Chelsea Hse.

Louis Armstrong: Musician. Sam Tanenhaus. (Black American Ser.). (Illus.). 192p. (YA). 1989. reprint ed. mass mkt. 3.95 (*0-87067-558-3*, Melrose Sq) Holloway.

Louis Armstrong: Swinging, Singing Satchmo. Sandford Brown. (Impact Biographies Ser.). (Illus.). 144p. (YA). (gr. 7-12). 1993. pap. 6.95 (*0-531-15680-X*) Watts.

Louis Armstrong: The Definitive Biography. Tr. by Bertram Thompson. (GER.). 150p. (C). 1999. pap. text 24.95 (*0-8204-3103-6*) P Lang Pubng.

Louis Armstrong - A Self Portrait. Richard Meryman. LC 70-152507. 1971. pap. 25.00 (*0-87130-027-3*) Eakins.

Louis Armstrong Companion. Bernett. 1998. pap. 15.00 (*0-02-864718-1*) Mac Lib Ref.

***Louis Armstrong, in His Own Words.** Louis Armstrong. Ed. by Thomas Brothers. (Illus.). 304p. 2001. pap. 14.95 (*0-19-514046-X*) OUP.

***Louis Armstrong, in His Own Words: Selected Writings.** Louis Armstrong. Ed. by Thomas Brothers. LC 99-17040. (Illus.). 302p. 1999. 25.00 (*0-19-511958-4*) OUP.

Louis Armstrong Odyssey: From Jane Alley to America's Jazz Ambassador. Dempsey J. Travis. (Illus.). 240p. (J). (gr. 5-12). 1997. text 23.75 (*0-941484-26-2*) Urban Res Pr.

Louis Armstrong, Young Music Maker. Daruthula H. Millender. (Childhood of Famous Americans Ser.). (J). 1997. 10.09 (*0-606-11582-X*, Pub. by Turtleback) Demco.

Louis Auchincloss. David B. Parsell. (United States Authors Ser.: No. 534). 152p. 1988. 21.95 (*0-8057-7516-1*, Twyne) Mac Lib Ref.

Louis Auchincloss: Family Fortunes Three Collected Novels. Louis Auchincloss. 1993. 11.98 (*0-88365-825-9*) Galahad Bks.

Louis B. Wright: A Bibliography & an Appreciation. Frederick Hard. (Special Publications Ser.). 1978. 10.00 (*0-918016-66-5*) Folger Bks.

Louis Blanc: His Life & His Contribution to the Rise of French Jacobin-Socialism, Number 1. Leo A. Loubere. LC 80-23424. (Northwestern University Studies in History: No.1). 256p. 1980. reprint ed. lib. bdg. 65.00 (*0-313-22690-3*, LOBL) Greenwood.

Louis Braille. Margaret Davidson. (FRE.). (J). pap. 5.99 (*0-590-71110-5*) Scholastic Inc.

***Louis Braille.** Jayne Woodhouse. LC 97-13733. (Lives & Times Ser.). 1998. 19.92 (*1-57572-559-2*) Heinemann Lib.

Louis Braille: Inventor. Jennifer F. Bryant. (Great Achievers Ser.). (Illus.). 120p. (YA). (gr. 5 up). 1994. lib. bdg. 19.95 (*0-7910-2077-0*, Chelsea Juniors) Chelsea Hse.

Louis Braille: The Blind Boy Who Wanted to Read. Dennis Fradin. LC 96-6972. (Remarkable Children Ser.: No. 1). (Illus.). (J). 1996. pap. 5.95 (*0-382-39469-0*); lib. bdg. 15.95 (*0-382-39468-2*) Silver Burdett Pr.

Louis Braille: The Blind Boy Who Wanted to Read. Dennis Fradin. (Remarkable Children Ser.). (Illus.). (J). (gr. k-5). 1997. 15.95 (*0-614-29053-8*, Silver Pr NJ); pap. 6.95 (*0-614-29054-6*, Silver Pr NJ) Silver Burdett Pr.

Louis Braille: The Boy Who Invented Books for the Blind. Margaret Davidson. (Illus.). 80p. (J). (gr. 2-5). 1991. pap. 3.50 (*0-590-44350-X*) Scholastic Inc.

Louis Braille: The Boy Who Invented Books for the Blind. Margaret Davidson. LC 73-39630. (J). 1971. 8.70 (*0-606-03851-5*, Pub. by Turtleback) Demco.

Louis Braille, l'Enfant de la Nuit. Margaret Davidson. (Folio - Cadet Rouge Ser.: No. 225). (FRE., Illus.). 103p. (J). (gr. 3-7). 1990. pap. 10.95 (*2-07-031225-9*) Schoenhof.

Louis Brandeis. Marcus. 1997. 26.95 (*0-8057-7765-2*, Twyne) Mac Lib Ref.

Louis Brandeis: The People's Justice. Suzanne Freedman. LC 95-24503. (Justices of the Supreme Court Ser.). (Illus.). 104p. (YA). (gr. 6 up). 1996. lib. bdg. 20.95 (*0-89490-678-X*) Enslow Pubs.

Louis Brandeis Slept Here: A Slightly Cynical History of American Jews. David Gleicher. LC 96-36479. 1997. 14.95 (*965-229-167-6*, Pub. by Gefen Pub Hse) Gefen Bks.

Louis Bromfield. David D. Anderson. Ed. by Sylvia E. Bowman. LC 63-20614. (Twayne's United States Authors Ser.). 187p. (C). 1964. text 20.95 (*0-8290-1717-8*) Irvington.

Louis Bromfield: Ohio & Self-Discovery. James M. Hughes. (Illus.). 32p. (Orig.). 1997. pap. 2.95 (*1-888683-12-0*) Wooster Bk.

Louis Bromfield & the Malabar Farm Experience. John T. Carter. Date not set. pap. 11.95 (*0-8488-1716-8*); lib. bdg. 21.95 (*0-8488-1813-X*) Amereon Ltd.

Louis Bromfield at Malabar: Writings on Farming & Country Life. Ed. by Charles E. Little. LC 88-37841. 256p. 1988. 30.00 (*0-8018-3674-3*) Johns Hopkins.

L

An Asterisk (*) at the beginning of an entry indicates that the title is appearing for the first time.

L

Louis Bromfield, Novelist & Agrarian Reformer: The Forgotten Author. Ivan Scott. LC 98-5741. 688p. 1998. text 129.95 (*0-7734-8503-1*) E Mellen.

Louis Carlen: Aufsatze Zur Rechtsgeschichte der Schweiz. Hans C. Faussner & Louis C. Morsak. (GER.). xvi, 412p. 1994. 148.00 (*3-615-00100-1*, Pub. by Weidmann) Lubrecht & Cramer.

Louis Carlen: Sinnenfalliges Recht. (GER.). xviii, 508p. 1995. 138.00 (*3-615-00149-4*, Pub. by Weidmann) Lubrecht & Cramer.

Louis Comfort Tiffany. Alastair Duncan. (Library of American Art). (Illus.). 160p. 1992. 45.00 (*0-8109-3862-6*, Pub. by Abrams) Time Warner.

***Louis Comfort Tiffany.** William Warmus. (Essential Ser.). 2000. pap. 12.95 (*0-8109-5828-7*) Abrams.

***Louis Comfort Tiffany.** William Warmus. (Illus.). 112p. 2000. 12.95 (*0-7407-1304-3*) Andrews & McMeel.

Louis Comfort Tiffany. 2nd ed. Hugh F. McKean. Tr. by Heidewig Frankhanel. (ENG & GER., Illus.). 312p. (C). 1988. 118.00 (*3-8170-2012-0*, Pub. by Knstvrlag Weingrtn) Intl Bk Import.

Louis Comfort Tiffany: At the Metropolitan Museum of Art. Alice Cooney Frelinghuysen. (Illus.). 100p. 1999. pap. 19.95 (*0-8109-6535-6*, Pub. by Abrams) Time Warner.

Louis Comfort Tiffany: The Painting Career of a Colorist. Joan E. Price. (American University Studies, Series XX: Vol. 28). XXIV, 111p. (C). 1996. text 32.95 (*0-8204-2770-5*) P Lang Pubng.

Louis D. Brandeis: Justice for the People. Philippa Strum. (Illus.). 536p. 1984. 46.50 (*0-674-53921-4*) HUP.

Louis 'David' Riel. Thomas Flanagan. 214p. 1979. mass mkt. 5.95 (*0-88780-118-8*, Pub. by Formac Publ Co) Formac Dist Ltd.

Louis David Riel: Prophet of the New World. Thomas Flanagan. LC 78-18497. 226p. reprint ed. pap. 70.10 (*0-608-12900-3*, 202361700033) Bks Demand.

Louis 'David' Riel: Prophet of the New World. rev. ed. Thomas Flanagan. 248p. 1996. text 50.00 (*0-8020-0815-1*); pap. text 17.95 (*0-8020-7184-8*) U of Toronto Pr.

Louis Dembitz Brandeis, 1856-1941: A Bibliography. Roy M. Mersky. (Yale Law Library Publications: No. 15). ii, 44p. 1987. reprint ed. pap. 15.00 (*0-8377-2437-6*, Rothman) W S Hein.

Louis Dembitz Brandeis Papers. Louis D. Brandeis. LC 88-890709. (American Legal Manuscripts from the Harvard). 94 p. 1985. write for info. (*0-89093-801-6*) U Pubns Amer.

Louis Dollo's Papers on Paleontology & Evolution: Original Anthology. Ed. by Stephen Jay Gould. LC 79-8355. (History of Paleontology Ser.). (ENG & FRE., Illus.). 1980. lib. bdg. 69.95 (*0-405-12752-9*) Ayer.

Louis Dudek & His Works. Terry Goldie. (Canadian Author Studies). 65p. (C). 1985. pap. text 9.95 (*0-920802-83-4*, Pub. by ECW) Genl Dist Srvs.

Louis E. Eliasberg Sr., King of Coins. Q. David Bowers. (Illus.). 176p. 1996. text 62.50 (*0-943161-64-9*) Bowers & Merena.

Louis Evans' Creole Cookbook. Louis Evans. LC 90-20533. 240p. 1991. 18.95 (*0-88289-799-3*) Pelican.

Louis Farrakhan: Made in America. A. Marshall. 300p. (Orig.). 1996. pap. 22.95 (*0-9655729-0-0*) BSB Pub.

Louis Farrakhan - Political Activist: Political Activist. Therese DeAngelis. LC 98-6101. (Black Americans of Achievement Ser.). (Illus.). 144p. (YA). (gr. 5 up). 1999. 19.95 (*0-7910-4688-5*); pap. 8.95 (*0-7910-4689-3*) Chelsea Hse.

Louis Farrakhan & the Nation of Islam. Jim Haskins. LC 96-3607. (Illus.). (J). 1996. 15.95 (*0-8027-8422-4*); lib. bdg. 16.85 (*0-8027-8423-2*) Walker & Co.

Louis Farrakhan's New Nation of Islam: The Ambiguous Struggle for Self-Determination. Dennis Walker. 320p. 2000. pap. 18.95 (*0-932863-30-2*, Pub. by Clarity Pr) SCB Distributors.

Louis-Ferdinand Celine. Merlin Thomas. LC 79-20591. 1980. 16.50 (*0-8112-0754-4*, Pub. by New Directions) Norton.

Louis G. Redstone: From Israeli Pioneer to American Architect. Louis G. Redstone. LC 89-11119. (Illus.). 206p. 1989. reprint ed. pap. 63.90 (*0-608-00142-2*, 206092300006) Bks Demand.

Louis Ginzberg: Keeper of the Law. Eli Ginzberg. 360p. 1996. pap. 9.95 (*0-8276-0625-7*) JPS Phila.

Louis Guilloux. Jean-Claude Bourles. (FRE., Illus.). 1997. pap. write for info. (*2-86808-110-X*) Intl Scholars.

Louis Guttman on Theory & Methodology: Selected Writings. Ed. by Shlomit Levy. (Benchmark Ser.). 448p. 1994. 91.95 (*1-85521-389-3*, Pub. by Dartmth Pub) Ashgate Pub Co.

Louis Hammer: Essays in Criticism. Sharon A. Jaeger. (Illus.). 120p. (Orig.). 2000. pap. 22.95 (*0-912767-12-X*) Intertxt AK.

Louis Head Cemetery. M. Edward Burtt. (Illus.). i, 27p. (Orig.). 1994. pap. write for info. (*1-888913-12-6*) M E Burtt.

Louis Head Cemetery. rev. ed. M. Edward Burtt. (Illus.). i, 50p. (Orig.). 1996. pap. write for info. (*1-888913-21-5*) M E Burtt.

Louis Henry Sullivan. Mario M. Elia. (Illus.). 280p. 1996. 60.00 (*1-56898-092-2*) Princeton Arch.

Louis Henry Sullivan. Hans Frei. (Studio Paperback Ser.). (Illus.). 176p. 1992. pap. 29.95 (*3-7643-5574-3*, Pub. by Birkhauser) Princeton Arch.

Louis Horst: Musician in a Dancer's World. Janet M. Soares. LC 91-32933. (Illus.). 296p. 1992. 35.95 (*0-8223-1226-3*) Duke.

Louis I. Kahn. David B. Brownlee. (Illus.). 240p. 1997. pap. 25.00 (*0-7893-0099-0*, Pub. by Universe) St Martin.

***Louis I. Kahn.** Klaus-Peter Gast. LC 99-10835. (Studiopaperback Ser.). (Illus.). 192p. 1999. pap. 29.95 (*3-7643-5964-1*, Pub. by Birkhauser) Princeton Arch.

Louis I. Kahn Klaus-Peter Gast & Louis I. Kahn. LC 99-10835. 1999. write for info. (*0-8176-5964-1*) Birkhauser.

Louis I. Kahn: A Bibliography. Jack P. Brown. LC 86-25781. 112p. 1986. text 44.00 (*0-8240-9918-4*) Garland.

Louis I. Kahn: In the Realm of Architecture. David B. Brownlee & David G. DeLong. LC 91-9760. (Illus.). 448p. 1991. pap. 42.50 (*0-8478-1330-4*, Pub. by Rizzoli Intl) St Martin.

Louis I. Kahn: Light & Space. Urs Buttiker. Tr. by David Bean from GER. LC 93-17933.Tr. of Licht & Raum. (ENG & GER.). 1993. 69.00 (*0-8176-2297-7*) Birkhauser.

Louis I. Kahn: Light & Space. Urs Buttiker.Tr. of Licht & Raum. (ENG & GER., Illus.). 192p. 1998. 68.00 (*3-7643-2297-7*) Birkhauser.

Louis I. Kahn: The Construction of the Kimbell Art Museum. (Illus.). 168p. 1999. 35.00 (*88-8118-471-0*, Pub. by Skira IT) Abbeville Pr.

Louis I. Kahn: The Idea of Order. Klaus-Peter Gast. LC 98-10929. 1998. write for info. (*0-8176-5659-6*); write for info. (*3-7643-5860-2*) Birkhauser.

Louis I. Kahn: The Idea of Order. Klaus-Peter Gast. LC 98-10929. (Illus.). 200p. 1998. 75.00 (*3-7643-5659-6*, Pub. by Birkhauser) Princeton Arch.

Louis I. Kahn: The Library at Phillips Exeter Academy. Glenn E. Wiggins. 48p. 1997. 39.95 (*0-471-28831-4*, VNR) Wiley.

Louis I. Kahn: Unbuilt Masterworks. Kent Larson. LC 98-52140. (Illus.). 232p. 2000. 60.00 (*1-58093-014-X*, Pub. by Monacelli Pr) Penguin Putnam.

***Louis I. Kahn's Trenton Jewish Community Center.** Susan G. Solomon. (Building Studies). 2000. pap. 19.95 (*1-56898-226-7*) Princeton Arch.

Louis Icart Erotica. William R. Holland & Louis Icart. LC 98-5040. (Illus.). 1998. 49.95 (*0-7643-0515-8*) Schiffer.

Louis J. Isola: Immigrant: I Made Good in the United States. Ed. by Mary E. Glass. 112p. 1980. lib. bdg. 32.50 (*1-56475-195-3*); fiche. write for info. (*1-56475-196-1*) U NV Oral Hist.

Louis Kahn: Conversations with Students. Louis Kahn. (Architecture at Rice Ser.: Vol. 26). (Illus.). 112p. 1998. pap. 14.95 (*1-56898-149-X*) Princeton Arch.

Louis Kahn: The Library at Philips Exeter Academy. Glenn Wiggins. LC 97-6038. 1997. pap. 39.95 incl. cd-rom (*0-442-02531-9*, VNR) Wiley.

Louis L. Snyder's Historical Guide to World War II. Louis L. Snyder. LC 81-13433. 838p. 1982. lib. bdg. 110.00 (*0-313-23216-4*, SNH/, Greenwood Pr) Greenwood.

***Louis Laloy (1874-1944) on Dubussy, Ravel & Stravinsky.** Deborah Priest. LC 99-31934. (Illus.). 340p. 1999. text 83.95 (*1-84014-628-1*, Pub. by Ashgate Pub) Ashgate Pub Co.

Louis Lambert. Honore de Balzac. 272p. 1968. 10.95 (*0-8288-9357-8*) Fr & Eur.

Louis Lambert - Les Proscrits - Jesus-Christ en Flandres. Honore de Balzac. (FRE.). 320p. 1980. pap. 11.95 (*0-7859-1905-8*, 2070371611) Fr & Eur.

Louis L'Amour. rev. ed. Robert L. Gale. (Twayne's United States Authors Ser.: No. 491). 180p. (C). 1992. 21.95 (*0-8057-7649-4*, Twyne) Mac Lib Ref.

***Louis L'Amour: Sackett Boxed Set.** Louis L'Amour. 1999. mass mkt., boxed set 18.00 (*0-553-66738-6*) Bantam.

Louis L'Amour: The Long Trail. J. C. Elton. 1976. 21.95 (*0-8488-0885-1*) Amereon Ltd.

Louis L'Amour: The Sacketts, 4 vols., Set. Louis L'Amour. 1990. boxed set 17.50 (*0-553-60928-9*) Bantam.

***Louis L'Amour Boxed Gift Set.** Louis L'Amour. 1999. mass mkt. 14.97 (*0-553-66737-8*) Bantam.

Louis L'Amour Checklist. J. E. Clauss. pap. 17.95 (*0-88411-244-6*) Amereon Ltd.

Louis L'Amour Companion. Robert Weinberg. 448p. 1994. mass mkt. 5.99 (*0-553-56609-1*) Bantam.

***Louis le Vau: Mazarin's Collaege, Colbert's Revenge** Hilary Ballon. LC 99-25747. 1999. write for info. (*0-691-04895-9*) Princeton U Pr.

***Louis Le Vau: Mazarin's College, Colbert's Revenge.** Hillary Ballon. LC 99-25747. 1999. 45.00 (*0-691-00186-3*, Pub. by Princeton U Pr) Cal Prin Full Svc.

Louis Lecoin: A Chronology. V. Munoz. Tr. by W. Scott Johnson. (Libertarian & Anarchist Chronology Ser.). 1979. lib. bdg. 59.95 (*0-8490-3051-X*) Gordon Pr.

Louis Loucheur & the Shaping of Modern France, 1916-1931. Stephen D. Carls. LC 92-40840. (Illus.). 416p. 1993. text 60.00 (*0-8071-1787-0*) La State U Pr.

Louis MacNeice: The Poet in His Contexts. Peter McDonald. 252p. 1991. text 65.00 (*0-19-811766-3*) OUP.

Louis MacNeice & His Influence. Ed. by Kathleen Devine & Alan J. Peacock. (A Colin Smythe Publication). 180p. (C). 1998. text 60.00 (*0-86140-391-6*) OUP.

Louis Marshall: Defender of Jewish Rights. Morton Rosenstock. LC 65-19608. 335p. reprint ed. pap. 103.90 (*0-7837-3680-0*, 204355400009) Bks Demand.

Louis Massignon: Christian Ecumenist. Giulio Basetti-Sani. 262p. 1974. 6.95 (*0-8199-0496-1*, Frncscn Herld) Franciscan Pr.

Louis Massignon: The Crucible of Compassion. Mary L. Gude. LC 95-18778. (C). 1997. text 34.95 (*0-268-01308-X*) U of Notre Dame Pr.

Louis Moreau Gottschalk. William Korf. (Wissenschaftliche Abhandlungen-Musicological Studies: Vol. 37). 140p. 1983. lib. bdg. 54.00 (*0-931902-16-9*) Inst Mediaeval Mus.

Louis Motorists' Guide to the Soviet Union. 2nd ed. Victor E. Louis & Jennifer M. Louis. LC 85-21830. (Illus.). 625p. 1987. pap. 69.00 (*0-08-031816-9*, Pergamon Pr) Elsevier.

Louis Napoleon & the Recovery of France. Frederick A. Simpson. LC 75-8490. (Illus.). 400p. 1975. reprint ed. lib. bdg. 35.00 (*0-8371-8153-4*, SILN, Greenwood Pr) Greenwood.

Louis Navellier Modern Portrait Theory. Navellier. 1996. text 27.95 (*0-07-046482-0*) McGraw.

Louis-Nicolas Clerambault - Two Cantatas for Soprano & Chamber Ensemble. Louis-Nicolas Clerambault. Ed. by Donald H. Foster. (Recent Researches in Music of the Baroque Era Ser.: Vol. B27). (Illus.). xxiv, 89p. 1979. pap. 40.00 (*0-89579-104-8*) A-R Eds.

***Louis Osteen's Charleston Cuisine: Recipes from a Lowcountry Chef.** Louis Osteen. LC 99-32156. 320p. 1999. 24.95 (*1-56512-087-6*) Algonquin Bks.

Louis Pasteur. P. Debre. Tr. by Elborg Forster from FRE. LC 97-43686. (Illus.). 560p. 1998. 39.95 (*0-8018-5808-9*) Johns Hopkins.

***Louis Pasteur.** Patrice Debre. Tr. by Elborg Forster. 560p. 2000. pap. 19.95 (*0-8018-6529-8*) Johns Hopkins.

***Louis Pasteur.** Ann Fullick. LC 00-35015. (Groundbreakers Ser.). 2000. lib. bdg. write for info. (*1-57572-373-5*) Heinemann Lib.

Louis Pasteur: Disease Fighter. Linda W. Smith. LC 96-38082. (Great Minds of Science Ser.). (Illus.). 128p. (J). (gr. 4-10). 1997. lib. bdg. 20.95 (*0-89490-790-5*) Enslow Pubs.

Louis Pasteur: Founder of Modern Medicine. John H. Tiner. (Sower Ser.). 176p. (YA). (gr. 5-9). 1991. pap. 7.99 (*0-88062-159-1*) Mott Media.

Louis Pasteur: Free Lance of Science. Rene Jules Dubos. (Series in Science). (Illus.). 462p. 1986. reprint ed. pap. 14.95 (*0-306-80262-7*) Da Capo.

Louis Pasteur: Young Scientist. Francene Sabin. LC 82-15924. (Illus.). 48p. (J). (gr. 4-6). 1983. lib. bdg. 17.25 (*0-89375-853-1*) Troll Communs.

Louis Pasteur: Young Scientist. Francene Sabin. LC 82-15924. (Illus.). 48p. (J). (gr. 4-6). 1997. pap. 3.95 (*0-89375-854-X*) Troll Communs.

Louis Pasteur & Germs see Science Discoveries

Louis Pecour's 1700 Recueil de Dances. Anne L. Witherell. LC 82-13496. (Studies in Musicology: No. 60). (Illus.). 304p. reprint ed. pap. 94.30 (*0-8357-1367-9*, 207058700001) Bks Demand.

Louis-Philippe de Segur: An Intellectual in a Revolutionary Age. L. Apt. (International Archives of the History of Ideas Ser.: No. 25). 173p. 1969. lib. bdg. 71.50 (*90-247-0201-1*, Pub. by M Nijhoff) Kluwer Academic.

***Louis Prima Songbook: Jump, Jive An' Wail.** 64p. 1999. otabind 12.95 (*0-634-00287-2*) H Leonard.

Louis Ribak, the Late Paintings. Harry Rand. 36p. 1984. pap. 10.00 (*0-914983-00-8*) Roswell Mus.

Louis Rorimer: A Man of Style. Leslie A. Pina. LC 90-34121. (Illus.). 158p. 1990. 25.00 (*0-87338-418-0*) Kent St U Pr.

Louis Rukeyser's Book of Lists: The Best, the Worst, & the Funniest from the Worlds of Business, Finance, & Politics. Louis Rukeyser. LC 97-23136. 320p. 1997. 25.00 (*0-8050-5126-0*) H Holt & Co.

Louis Rukeyser's Book of Lists: The Best, the Worst & the Funniest from the Worlds of Business, Finance & Politics. Louis Rukeyser. 288p. 1999. pap. 14.95 (*0-8050-5127-9*, Owl) H Holt & Co.

Louis S. B. Leakey: Beyond the Evidence. Martin Pickford. LC 98-147155. (Illus.). 187p. 1998. pap. 25.00 (*1-85756-396-4*, Pub. by Janus Pubng) Paul & Co Pubs.

Louis Shores Biography: Defining Educational Librarianship. Orvin L. Shiflett. LC 95-50041. 316p. 1996. 36.00 (*0-8108-3114-7*) Scarecrow.

Louis Souris et Ses Amis, 1. Gonzalez. 1984. pap. text 13.80 (*0-685-32948-8*, 76147) Longman.

Louis Souris et Ses Amis, 11. Gonzalez. 1984. pap. text 14.00 (*0-8013-0111-4*, 75775) Longman.

Louis Stettner's New York. Louis Stettner. LC 96-34903. (Illus.). 128p. 1997. 24.95 (*0-8478-2004-1*, Pub. by Rizzoli Intl) St Martin.

Louis Sullivan: His Life & Work. Robert C. Twombly. LC 85-13583. (Illus.). xii, 544p. 1999. reprint ed. pap. 19.95 (*0-226-82006-8*) U Ch Pr.

Louis Sullivan: Prophet of Modern Architecture. rev. ed. Hugh Morrison. LC 97-46562. 352p. 1998. pap. 30.00 (*0-393-73023-9*) Norton.

Louis Sullivan: The Function of Ornament. David Van Zanten et al. (Illus.). 1996. pap. 35.00 (*0-393-30498-1*) Norton.

Louis Sullivan: The Poetry of Architecture. Robert Twombly. 75.00 (*0-393-04823-3*) Norton.

Louis Sullivan & the Chicago School. Nancy Frazier. (Illus.). 112p. 1999. pap. 19.95 (*1-57715-085-6*) Knckerbocker.

Louis Sullivan & the Polemics of Modern Architecture: The Present Against the Past. David S. Andrew. LC 83-18164. (Illus.). 216p. 1985. text 24.95 (*0-252-01044-2*) U of Ill Pr.

Louis the Eleventh. Pierre Champion. Tr. by Winifred S. Whale. LC 73-109617. (Select Bibliographies Reprint Ser.). 1977. 26.95 (*0-8369-5226-X*) Ayer.

Louis XV: The Monarchy in Decline. George P. Gooch. LC 75-36361. (Illus.). 285p. 1976. reprint ed. lib. bdg. 89.50 (*0-8371-8632-3*, GOLO, Greenwood Pr) Greenwood.

Louis XV & Madame de Pompadour: A Love Affair with Style. Penelope Hunter-Stiebel. (Illus.). 112p. 1990. 45.00 (*1-878799-00-2*) Rosenberg & Stiebel.

Louis the XV & the "Parlement" of Paris, 1737-1755. John Rogister. (Illus.). 314p. (C). 1995. text 69.95 (*0-521-40395-2*) Cambridge U Pr.

Louis XV's Army Vol. 2: French Infantry. Rene Chartrand. (Men-at-Arms Ser.: Vol. 302). (Illus.). 48p. pap. 12.95 (*1-85532-602-7*, Pub. by Osprey); pap. 12.95 (*1-85532-625-6*, Pub. by Osprey) Stackpole.

Louis XV's Army Vol. 3: Foreign Infantry. Rene Chartrand & Eugene Leliepvre. (Men-at-Arms Ser.: Vol. 304). (Illus.). 48p. 1997. pap. 12.95 (*1-85532-623-X*, Pub. by Osprey) Stackpole.

Louis XV's Army Vol. 4: Specialist & Light Troops. Rene Chartrand & Eugene Leliepvre. (Men-at-Arms Ser.: Vol. 308). (Illus.). 48p. 1997. pap. 12.95 (*1-85532-624-8*, Pub. by Osprey) Stackpole.

Louis XV's Army Vol. 5: Colonial & Naval Troops. Rene Chartrand & Eugene Leliepvre. (Men-at-Arms Ser.: No. 313). (Illus.). 48p. 1998. pap. 12.95 (*1-85532-709-0*, Pub. by Osprey) Stackpole.

Louis XV's Navy, 1748-1762: A Study of Organization & Administration. James S. Pritchard. 304p. 1987. 60.00 (*0-7735-0570-9*, Pub. by McG-Queens Univ Pr) CUP Services.

Louis the Fish. Arthur Yorinks. (Sunburst Ser.). (Illus.). 32p. (J). (ps up). 1986. pap. 5.95 (*0-374-44598-2*, Sunburst Bks) FS&G.

Louis XIV's Army. Rene Chartrand. (Men-at-Arms Ser.: No. 203). (Illus.). 48p. 1988. pap. 11.95 (*0-85045-850-1*, 9136, Pub. by Osprey) Stackpole.

Louis XIV. Peter Campbell. 184p. (C). 1995. pap. 15.00 (*0-582-01770-X*) Addison-Wesley.

Louis the Fourteenth. Michel Deon. (FRE.). 1991. pap. 15.95 (*0-7859-2174-5*, 2070384195) Fr & Eur.

Louis XIV. J. H. Shennan. (Lancaster Pamphlets Ser.). (Illus.). 52p. (C). 1995. pap. 11.99 (*0-415-09068-7*) Routledge.

Louis XIV. David L. Smith. (Topics in History Ser.). 136p. (C). 1992. pap. 18.95 (*0-521-40699-4*) Cambridge U Pr.

Louis XIV. Sturdy. LC 98-4786. 224p. 1998. pap. 19.95 (*0-312-21428-6*); text 55.00 (*0-312-21427-8*) St Martin.

***Louis the Fourteenth & Absolutism.** William Beik. 2000. pap. 15.95 (*0-312-13309-X*) St Martin.

Louis XIV & the Craft of Kingship. Ed. by John C. Rule. LC 72-79845. 500p. 1970. reprint ed. pap. 155.00 (*0-608-00918-0*, 206171200011) Bks Demand.

Louis XIV & the French Monarchy. Andrew Lossky. LC 93-39313. 312p. (C). 1994. text 59.00 (*0-8135-2081-9*) Rutgers U Pr.

Louis XIV & the Greatness of France. Maurice P. Ashley. 1965. pap. 14.95 (*0-02-901080-2*) Free Pr.

Louis XIV & the Twenty Million Frenchmen. Pierre Goubert. 352p. 1972. pap. 7.96 (*0-394-71751-1*, V751) Vin Bks.

Louis the Fourteenth & the Zenith of the French Monarchy. Arthur Hassall. LC 72-2558. (Select Bibliographies Reprint Ser.). 1977. reprint ed. 52.95 (*0-8369-6856-5*) Ayer.

Louis XIV, France & Europe, 1601-1715. Richard Wilkinson. (Access to History Ser.). 152p. 1993. write for info. (*0-614-97985-4*, Pub. by Hodder & Stought Ltd) Lubrecht & Cramer.

Louis XIV's Versailles. Guy Walton. LC 85-8680. (Illus.). 246p. 1994. pap. 14.95 (*0-226-87255-6*) U Ch Pr.

Louis XIV's Versailles. Guy Walton. LC 85-8680. (Illus.). 246p. 1994. lib. bdg. 35.00 (*0-226-87254-8*) U Ch Pr.

Louis the Great, King of Hungary & Poland: His Age & His People. Ed. by Steven B. Vardy. 1987. 79.50 (*0-88033-087-2*, Pub. by East Eur Monographs) Col U Pr.

Louis IX & the Challenge of the Crusade: A Study in Rulership. William C. Jordan. LC 79-83996. 309p. 1979. reprint ed. pap. 95.80 (*0-608-03309-X*, 206402100008) Bks Demand.

Louis II de Baviere du le Roi Foucroye. Guy Des Cars. 9.95 (*0-686-55666-6*) Fr & Eur.

Louis II de Baviere du le Roi Foucroye: Documents Hors Texte. Guy Des Cars. 318p. 1975. 19.95 (*0-686-55647-X*) Fr & Eur.

Louis XVII, 2 vols. Alcide Beauchesne. LC 78-161731. (Illus.). reprint ed. 164.50 (*0-404-07546-0*) AMS Pr.

Louis XVI. John Hardman. (Illus.). 288p. 1994. pap. 19.00 (*0-300-06077-7*) Yale U Pr.

Louis XVI & Marie Antoinette. Nesta H. Webster. 1976. 250.00 (*0-87968-364-3*) Gordon Pr.

Louis XIII, the Just. A. Lloyd Moote. 417p. (C). 1989. 55.00 (*0-520-06485-2*, Pub. by U CA Pr) Cal Prin Full Svc.

Louis XIII, the Just. A. Lloyd Moote. (Illus.). 417p. 1991. reprint ed. pap. 17.95 (*0-520-07546-3*, Pub. by U CA Pr) Cal Prin Full Svc.

Louis the Torch. Paul Metcalf. 56p. 1983. pap. 3.95 (*0-916696-20-0*) Cross Country.

Louis XII. Frederic J. Baumgartner. 319p. 1996. pap. 18.95 (*0-312-16173-5*) St Martin.

Louis the Twentieth. Thierry Ardisson. (FRE.). 249p. 1988. pap. 11.95 (*0-7859-2083-8*, 2070379124) Fr & Eur.

Louis Vierne: Organist of Notre Dame. Rollin Smith. LC 99-42128. (Complete Organ Ser.: Vol. 3). 805p. 2000. 76.00 (*1-57647-004-0*) Pendragon NY.

Louis Wain - King of the Cat Artists, 1860-1939: A Dramatized Biography. Heather Latimer. Ed. by Geoffrey Hutchison-Cleaves. LC 82-82032. (Illus.). 172p. 1982. lib. bdg. 25.00 (*0-943698-01-4*) Papyrus Letterbox.

Louis Wain - King of the Cat Artists, 1860-1939: A Dramatized Biography. limited ed. Heather Latimer. 1982. 25.00 (*0-943698-00-6*) Papyrus Letterbox.

Louis Wain - King of the Cat Artists, 1860-1939: A Dramatized Biography. Heather Latimer. Ed. by Geoffrey Hutchison-Cleaves. LC 82-82032. (Illus.). 172p. 1982. reprint ed. 25.00 (*0-943698-02-2*) Papyrus Letterbox.

Louis Wirth: A Bio-Bibliography, 1. Roger A. Salerno. LC 87-19631. (Bio-Bibliographies in Sociology Ser.: No. 1). 152p. 1987. lib. bdg. 55.00 (*0-313-25473-7*, SLU/, Greenwood Pr) Greenwood.

An Asterisk (*) at the beginning of an entry indicates that the title is appearing for the first time.

Louis Wirth on Cities & Social Life. Louis Wirth. Ed. by Albert J. Reiss, Jr. LC 64-24970. (Heritage of Sociology Ser.). 380p. 1996. pap. text 18.00 (0-226-90242-0) U Ch Pr.

Louis Wirth on Cities & Social Life: Selected Papers. Louis Wirth. Ed. by Albert J. Reiss, Jr. LC 64-24970. (Heritage of Sociology Ser.). 380p. reprint ed. pap. 117.80 (0-608-09555-9, 205435700005) Bks Demand.

***Louis XIV.** Ian Dunlop. (Illus.). 512p. 2000. text 27.95 (0-312-26196-9) St Martin.

***Louis XIV & Absolutism: A Brief Study with Documents.** William Beik. 2000. text 39.95 (0-312-22743-4) St Martin.

***Louis Xvi: The Silent King.** John Hardman. (An Arnold Publication). (Illus.). 224p. 2000. pap. 19.99 (0-340-70650-3, Pub. by E A); text 65.00 (0-340-70649-X, Pub. by E A) OUP.

Louis XVIII. Philip Mansel. 1999. pap. text 24.95 (0-7509-2217-6) Sutton Pub Ltd.

Louis Zukofsky: Man & Poet. Ed. by Carroll F. Terrell. LC 79-89637. (Man & Poet Ser.). 1979. 40.00 (0-915032-50-3); pap. 22.95 (0-915032-74-0) Natl Poet Foun.

Louis Zukofsky & the Poetry of Knowledge. Mark Scroggins. 312p. 1998. pap. text 24.95 (0-8173-0957-8) U of Ala Pr.

Louis Zukofsky & the Poetry of Knowledge. Mark Scroggins. LC 98-8879. 312p. 1998. text 49.95 (0-8173-0907-1) U of Ala Pr.

Louis Zukofsky & the Transformation of a Modern American Poetics. Sandra K. Stanley. LC 93-11118. 208p. 1994. 40.00 (0-520-07357-6, Pub. by U CA Pr) Cal Prin Full Svc.

***Louisa.** Simone Zelitch. 384p. 2000. 23.95 (0-399-14659-8) Putnam Pub Group.

Louisa: 50th Anniversary Edition. Brian Matthews. LC 99-208738. 1998. reprint ed. pap. 19.95 (0-7022-3071-5, Pub. by Univ Queensland Pr) Intl Spec Bk.

Louisa . . . A Southern Girls' Escape in 1864. Elizabeth Bowne. LC 96-166529. 1995. pap. 12.00 (0-9634826-5-3) New Hope AL.

Louisa & Louisa County, Virginia. Patty G. B. Cooke. (Images of America Ser.). (Illus.). 128p. 1996. pap. 16.99 (0-7524-0560-8) Arcadia Publng.

Louisa Catherine Johnson Adams. Ann Heinrichs. LC 97-47279. (Encyclopedia of First Ladies Ser.). 112p. (J). 1998. 33.00 (0-516-20845-4) Childrens.

Louisa Elliott. Ann V. Roberts. 800p. 1990. mass mkt. 5.95 (0-380-70991-0, Avon Bks) Morrow Avon.

***Louisa Matthiasdottir.** Jed Perl et al. (Illus.). 198p. 2000. 65.00 (1-55595-197-X) Hudson Hills.

Louisa May: A Modern Biography of Louisa May Alcott. Martha Saxton. LC 78-324902. xi, 428 p. 1978. 7.50 (0-233-96965-9) Andre Deutsch.

Louisa May: The World & Works of Louisa May Alcott. Norma Johnston. 1995. 10.05 (0-606-07812-6, Pub. by Turtleback) Demco.

Louisa May: The World & Works of Louisa May Alcott. Norma Johnston. LC 94-20624. (Illus.). 256p. (YA). (gr. 7 up). 1995. reprint ed. pap. 4.95 (0-688-12696-0, Wm Morrow) Morrow Avon.

***Louisa May Alcott.** Louisa May Alcott. LC 99-57115. (Portable Library). 704p. 2000. pap. 16.95 (0-14-027574-6, Penguin Bks) Viking Penguin.

Louisa May Alcott. Ednah D. Cheney. 1998. 39.95 (0-7910-4535-8) Chelsea Hse.

Louisa May Alcott. Patricia Reilly Giff. 1999. pap. write for info. (0-670-84566-3) Viking Penguin.

Louisa May Alcott. Jill C. Wheeler. Ed. by Julie Berg. (Illus.). 32p. (J). 1995. lib. bdg. 14.98 (1-56239-518-1) ABDO Pub Co.

Louisa May Alcott. Katharine S. Anthony. LC 77-2388. 304p. 1977. reprint ed. lib. bdg. 35.00 (0-8371-9552-7, ANLMA, Greenwood Pr) Greenwood.

Louisa May Alcott, No. 457. Ruth K. MacDonald. (United States Authors Ser.). 128p. 1983. 21.95 (0-8057-7397-5, Twayne) Mac Lib Ref.

***Louisa May Alcott: A Biography.** Madeleine B. Stern. LC 99-15688. 422p. 1999. pap. text 20.00 (1-55553-417-1) NE U Pr.

Louisa May Alcott: A Modern Biography. Martha Saxton. 1995. 27.50 (0-374-19210-3); pap. 15.00 (0-374-52460-2) FS&G.

Louisa May Alcott: American Storyteller. Amy Ruth. LC 97-47283. (A&E Biography Ser.). 128p. (J). (gr. 4-7). 1998. lib. bdg. 17.95 (0-8225-4938-7, Lerner Publctns) Lerner Pub.

Louisa May Alcott: An Intimate Anthology. Louisa May Alcott. LC 97-16454. 432p. 1997. 18.00 (0-385-48722-3) Doubleday.

***Louisa May Alcott: Aurthor of "Little Women"** Karen C. Warrick. LC 99-36476. (Historical American Biographies Ser.). (Illus.). 128p. (gr. 6 up). 2000. lib. bdg. 20.95 (0-7660-1254-9) Enslow Pubs.

Louisa May Alcott: From Blood & Thunder to Hearth & Home. Madeleine B. Stern. LC 97-45008. 246p. 1998. pap. text 17.95 (1-55553-348-5) NE U Pr.

Louisa May Alcott: Her Girlhood Diary. Louisa May Alcott. Ed. by Cary Ryan. LC 93-22343. (Illus.). 56p. (YA). (gr. 5 up). 1997. 14.95 (0-8167-3139-X) BrdgeWater.

Louisa May Alcott: Her Girlhood Diary. Louisa May Alcott. Ed. by Cary Ryan. LC 93-22343. (Illus.). 56p. (YA). (gr. 5 up). 1995. pap. 4.95 (0-8167-3150-0, Troll Medallion) Troll Communs.

Louisa May Alcott: Her Girlhood Diary. Louisa May Alcott. 1993. 10.15 (0-606-07811-8, Pub. by Turtleback) Demco.

Louisa May Alcott: Her Life, Letters & Journals. Louisa May Alcott. (American Biography Ser.). 404p. 1991. reprint ed. lib. bdg. 89.00 (0-7812-8009-5) Rprt Serv.

***Louisa May Alcott: The Girlhood Diary of a Young Author.** Kerry A. Graves. (Diaries, Letters & Memoirs Ser.). 32p. (J). (gr. 2-7). 2000. lib. bdg. 22.60 (0-7368-0599-0, Blue Earth Bks) Capstone Pr.

Louisa May Alcott: Young Novelist. Beatrice Gormley. LC 98-30236. (Childhood of Famous Americans Ser.). (Illus.). 192p. (J). (gr. 4-6). 1999. mass mkt. 4.99 (0-689-82025-9, 076714004993) Aladdin.

***Louisa May Alcott & Charlotte Bronte: Transatlantic Translations.** Christine Doyle. LC 99-50721. 232p. (C). 2000. text 28.00 (1-57233-083-X, Pub. by U of Tenn Pr) U Ch Pr.

***Louisa May Alcott Encyclopedia.** Ed. by Gregory K. Eiselein & Anne Phillips. 432p. 2001. lib. bdg. 95.00 (0-313-30896-9, Greenwood Pr) Greenwood.

Louisa May Alcott on Race, Sex, & Slavery. Louisa May Alcott. Ed. & Intro. by Sarah Elbert. LC 96-48085. (Illus.). 1997. text 42.50 (1-55553-308-6); pap. text 15.95 (1-55553-307-8) NE U Pr.

Louisa May Alcott Unmasked: Collected Thrillers. Louisa May Alcott. Ed. & Intro. by Madeleine B. Stern. (Illus.). 780p. 1995. text 55.00 (1-55553-225-X); pap. text 24.95 (1-55553-226-8) NE U Pr.

Louisa May Alcott Unmasked: Collected Thrillers, Set. unabridged ed. Louisa May Alcott. Ed. & Intro. by Madeleine B. Stern. 1996. 16.95 incl. audio (1-882071-63-8, 393916, Pub. by B&B Audio) Lndmrk Audiobks.

Louisa May Alcott, Young Writer. Laurence Santrey. LC 85-1086. (Illus.). 48p. (J). (gr. 4-6). 1986. pap. 3.95 (0-8167-0564-X) Troll Communs.

Louisa May Alcott, Young Writer. Laurence Santrey. 1986. 8.70 (0-606-01630-9, Pub. by Turtleback) Demco.

Louisa May Alcott's Fairy Tales & Fantasy Stories. Louisa May Alcott. Ed. by Daniel Shealy. LC 91-43144. (Illus.). 432p. (J). 1992. pap. 24.95 (0-87049-758-8) U of Tenn Pr.

Louisa May Alcott's Little Women at Christmas. Louisa May Alcott. LC 99-13474. (J). 1999. 14.95 (0-8249-4161-6) Ideals.

Louisa Pallant see Works of Henry James Jr.: Collected Works

Louisa S. McCord: Poems, Drama, Biography, Letters. Ed. by Richard C. Lounsbury. (Southern Texts Society Ser.). 480p. (C). 1996. text 37.50 (0-8139-1653-4) U Pr of Va.

Louisa S. McCord: Political & Social Essays. Ed. by Richard C. Lounsbury. (Southern Texts Society Ser.). (Illus.). 608p. (C). 1995. text 45.00 (0-8139-1570-8) U. Pr of Va.

Louisa S. McCord: Selected Writings. Ed. by Richard C. Lounsbury. LC 97-8829. (Southern Texts Society Ser.). 288p. 1997. pap. text 14.50 (0-8139-1760-3) U Pr of Va.

Louisana Automotive Directory. Ed. by T. L. Spelman. 1985. 24.95 (1-55527-015-8) Auto Contact Inc.

Louisa's Wonder Book: An Unknown Alcott Juvenile. Louisa May Alcott. Ed. by Madeline B. Stern. LC 76-358119. (Clarke Historical Press Juvenile Ser.: No. 1). Orig. Title: Will's Wonder Book. (Illus.). (J). 1975. reprint ed. 7.50 (0-916699-08-0) CMU Clarke Hist Lib.

Louisbourg: Un Guide en Couleurs a Histoire Vivante. Susan Biagi. Tr. by Marie-Claude Rioux. LC 97-950059.Tr. of Louisbourg - A Living History Colourguide. (ENG & FRE., Illus.). 72p. 1997. pap. 16.95 (0-88780-363-6, Pub. by Formac Publ Co) Formac Dist Ltd.

Louisbourg - A Living History Colour Guide. Susan Biagi. LC 96-950145. (Illus.). 72p. (Orig.). 1997. pap. 10.95 (0-88780-362-8, Pub. by Formac Publ Co) Seven Hills Bk.

Louisbourg - A Living History Colourguide see Louisbourg: Un Guide en Couleurs a Histoire Vivante

Louise. large type ed. Sarah A. Shears. 1978. 12.00 (0-7089-0228-6) Ulverscroft.

Louise & Walter Arensberg Collection: Pre-Columbian Sculpture. Ed. by George Kubler. (Illus.). 222p. 1954. 5.00 (0-87633-001-4) Phila Mus Art.

***Louise Arner Boyd: Arctic Explorer.** Durlynn Anema. LC 99-59448. (Notable Americans Ser.). (Illus.). 112p. (YA). (gr. 5 up). 2000. lib. bdg. 19.95 (1-883846-42-0) M Reynolds.

Louise Bogan. Elizabeth Frank. LC 86-2639. (Illus.). 460p. 1986. pap. text 27.00 (0-231-06315-6) Col U Pr.

Louise Bogan: A Reference Source. Claire E. Knox. (Author Bibliographies Ser.: No. 86). 337p. 1991. 45.00 (0-8108-2379-9) Scarecrow.

Louise Bogan's Aesthetic of Limitation. Gloria Bowles. LC 86-45954. 166p. 1987. reprint ed. pap. 51.50 (0-608-01048-0, 205935600001) Bks Demand.

Louise Bourgeois. Marie-Laure Bernadac. (Illus.). 192p. 1996. 35.00 (2-08-013600-3, Pub. by Flammarion) Abbeville Pr.

Louise Bourgeois. Paul Gardner. LC 93-2081. (Series on Women Artists). (Illus.). 128p. 1994. pap. 14.95 (0-87663-639-3, Pub. by Universe) St Martin.

Louise Bourgeois. Charlotta Kotik et al. 1994. write for info. (0-87273-130-8) Bklyn Mus.

Louise Bourgeois. Peter Weiermair et al. (Illus.). 196p. 1995. 45.00 (3-905514-84-2) Dist Art Pubs.

Louise Bourgeois: Blue Days & Pink Days. Jerry Gorovoy & Louise Bourgeois. (Illus.). 320p. 1998. pap. 45.00 (88-87029-03-2, 810502, Pub. by Fondazione Prada) Dist Art Pubs.

Louise Bourgeois: Drawings & Observations. Louise Bourgeois & Lawrence Rinder. LC 95-80663. 192p. 1996. 27.50 (0-8212-2299-6, Pub. by Bulfinch Pr) Little.

Louise Bourgeois: The Locus of Memory, Works, 1982-1993. Charlotta Kotik et al. LC 93-28375. (Illus.). 144p. 1994. 49.50 (0-8109-3127-3, Pub. by Abrams) Time Warner.

Louise Bourgeois: The Personages. Jeremy Strick. Ed. by Mary A. Steiner. LC 94-66473. (Illus.). 72p. (Orig.). 1994. pap. text 19.95 (0-89178-040-8) St Louis Art Mus.

Louise Bourgeois: The Secret of Cells. Rainer Crone & Petrus Graf Schaesberg. LC 98-231844. (Illus.). 160p. 1998. 65.00 (3-7913-1610-9) te Neues.

***Louise Bourgeois Meret Oppenheim Ilse Weber: Drawings & Works on Paper.** Stephan Kunz et al. (Illus.). 88p. 2000. pap. 25.00 (3-908617-00-6, Pub. by Unikate) Dist Art Pubs.

***Louise Brooks: A Biography.** Barry Paris. 2000. reprint ed. pap. 19.95 (0-8166-3781-4) U of Minn Pr.

Louise Brooks: Portrait of an Anti-Star. Ed. by Roland Jaccard. Tr. by Gideon Y. Schein from FRE. (Illus.). 160p. 1986. pap. 19.95 (0-918432-77-4) Baseline Bks.

Louise Built House. Louise Pfanner. 1999. text 10.95 (0-312-02015-5) St Martin.

***Louise Dahl-Wolfe: A Retrospective.** Intro. by Dorothy Twining Globus. (Illus.). 196p. 2000. 45.00 (0-8109-4051-5, Pub. by Abrams) Time Warner.

Louise de la Valliere. Alexandre Dumas. Ed. & Intro. by David Coward. (Oxford World's Classics Ser.). 764p. 1998. pap. 14.95 (0-19-283465-7) OUP.

Louise de la Valliere. Alexandre Dumas. 1994. reprint ed. lib. bdg. 37.95 (1-56849-274-X) Buccaneer Bks.

Louise de Marillac: A Light in the Darkness. Kathryn LaFleur. LC 96-6432. 254p. 1996. pap. 12.95 (1-56548-075-9) New City.

Louise Durman's Recipes upon Request. Louise Durham. (Illus.). pap. text 12.00 (1-881092-00-3) Knoxville News-Sentinel.

Louise Erdrich: A Critical Companion. Lorena L. Stookey. LC 99-21709. (Critical Companions to Popular Contemporary Writers Ser.). 184p. 1999. 29.95 (0-313-30612-5, GR0612, Greenwood Pr) Greenwood.

Louise Erdrich & Michael Dorris. Rosenberg. 1998. 22.95 (0-8057-4573-4, Twyne) Mac Lib Ref.

Louise Erdrich's Love Medicine: A Casebook. Hertha D. Sweet Wong. LC 98-37962. (Casebooks in Contemporary Fiction Ser.). 256p. 1999. pap. 14.95 (0-19-512722-6); text 35.00 (0-19-512721-8) OUP.

Louise Farrenc, 1804-1875: Composer, Performer, Scholar. Bea Friedland. Ed. by George J. Buelow. LC 80-22465. (Studies in Musicology: No. 32). 283p. 1980. reprint ed. pap. 87.80 (0-8357-1111-0, 207028400065) Bks Demand.

Louise Fitzhugh. Virginia L. Wolf. (Twayne's United States Authors Ser.: No. 589). 158p. 1991. 21.95 (0-8057-7614-1, Twyne) Mac Lib Ref.

Louise Goes Wild. Stephen Krensky. LC 98-24824. (Illus.). (J). 1999. lib. bdg. 16.01 (0-8037-2308-3, Dial Yng Read) Peng Put Young Read.

Louise Goes Wild. Stephen Krensky. Ed. by Cindy Kane. LC 98-24824. (Illus.). 80p. (J). (gr. 2-4). 1999. 13.99 (0-8037-2307-5, Dial Yng Read) Peng Put Young Read.

Louise Imogen Guiney. Henry C. Fairbanks. Ed. by Sylvia E. Bowman. LC 73-2361. (Twayne's United States Authors Ser.). 163p. (C). 1973. lib. bdg. 20.95 (0-8290-1719-4) Irvington.

Louise Lateau: Her Stigmas & Ecstasy. Augustus Rohling. 55p. 1994. reprint ed. spiral bd. 14.00 (0-7873-1288-6) Hlth Research.

Louise Lawler: For Sale. Jenny Holzer. (Reihe Cantz Ser.). 1994. pap. 14.95 (3-89322-269-3, Pub. by Edition Cantz) Dist Art Pubs.

Louise Lucas Story: This Time Tomorrow. James F. Wright. LC 65-28219. (Emulation Bk.). 141p. reprint ed. pap. 43.80 (0-8357-6439-7, 203581000097) Bks Demand.

Louise Moillon Seventeenth Century Still-Life Artist. Helen Chastain Sowa. LC 98-73394. (Illus.). vii, 96p. (C). 1998. 29.95 (0-9666424-0-6) Chateau Pubg.

Louise Murdock's Living Legacy: A History of the Wichita Art Museum. Intro. by J. Richard Gruber. LC 91-67475. (Illus.). 55p. (Orig.). 1991. pap. 15.00 (0-939324-44-X) Wichita Art Mus.

***Louise Nevelson - Essay by Michael Klein.** LC 99-67528. (Illus.). 58p. 1999. pap. 20.00 (1-879173-43-3) Locks Gallery.

Louise Nicholson's India Companion. Louise Nicholson. (Illus.). 352p. 1998. pap. 19.95 (0-7472-7757-5, Pub. by Headline Bk Pub) Trafalgar.

***Louise Soccer Star.** Stephen Krensky. (Illus.). 80p. (J). (gr. 2-4). 2000. 13.99 (0-8037-2495-0, Dial Yng Read) Peng Put Young Read.

Louise Swesey Schmidt: Memories of Childhood in Gerlach Area--1910-1916. Ed. by Mary E. Glass. 76p. 1977. lib. bdg. 27.50 (1-56475-171-6); fiche. write for info. (1-56475-172-4) U NV Oral Hist.

Louise Takes Charge. Stephen Krensky. LC 97-37441. (Illus.). (J). (gr. 2-4). 1998. 13.99 (0-8037-2305-9, Dial Yng Read) Peng Put Young Read.

***Louise Takes Charge.** Stephen Krensky. (Puffin Chapters Ser.). (Illus.). 80p. (J). (gr. 2-5). 2000. pap. 3.99 (0-14-130822-2, PuffinBks) Peng Put Young Read.

***Louise Takes Charge.** Stephen Krensky. (Illus.). (J). 2000. 9.34 (0-606-18423-6) Turtleback.

Louise the One & Only. Elizabeth Koehler-Pentacoff. LC 95-19112. (Illus.). 64p. (J). (gr. 1-4). 1995. pap. 2.95 (0-8167-3757-6, Little Rainbow) Troll Communs.

Louise von Francois & Die Letze Reckenburgerin: A Feminist Reading. Thomas C. Fox. (New York University Ottendorfer Ser.: Vol. 28). X, 269p. 1988. text 37.00 (0-8204-0767-4) P Lang Pubng.

Louise von Gall: Her World & Work. Hugh Powell. (GERM Ser.). x, 230p. 1993. 65.00 (1-879751-55-0) Camden Hse.

Louise's Leaves: Around the Calendar with Local Garden Produce. Louise Frazier. (Illus.). 84p. 1994. spiral bd. 15.95 (0-938250-50-7) Bio-Dynamic Farm.

Louise's Legacy: Hamm Family Stories. Ed. by Moira F. Harris. LC 98-67648. (Illus.). 160p. 1998. pap. 15.95 (1-880654-14-8) Pogo Pr.

Louisiana see Official Precancel Catalog, State Sections

Louisiana see From Sea to Shining Sea

Louisiana see Atlas of Historical County Boundaries

Louisiana see One Nation Series

Louisiana see Celebrate the States - Group 2

***Louisiana.** (Switched on Schoolhouse Ser.). (Illus.). (J). 2000. pap. 24.95 (0-7403-0270-1) Alpha AZ.

Louisiana. Richard Bizier. (Illus.). 416p. 1999. pap. text 23.95 (1-56554-350-5) Pelican.

Louisiana. Capstone Press Geography Department Staff. (One Nation Ser.). (Illus.). 48p. (J). (gr. 3-7). 1996. 19.00 (0-516-20269-3) Childrens.

Louisiana. Childrens Press Staff. (From Sea to Shining Sea Ser.). (Illus.). 64p. (J). 1995. pap. 7.95 (0-516-43818-2) Childrens.

***Louisiana.** Robb Johnstone. (American States Ser.). (Illus.). 32p. (J). (gr. 3-7). 2000. write for info. (1-930954-55-7) Weigl Pubs.

Louisiana. Rita C. LaDoux. LC 92-13365. (Hello U. S. A. Ser.). (Illus.). 72p. (J). (gr. 3-6). 1993. lib. bdg. 19.93 (0-8225-2740-5, Lerner Publctns) Lerner Pub.

Louisiana. Emily McAuliffe. (States & Their Symbols Ser.). 1998. 14.00 (0-531-11605-0) Childrens.

***Louisiana.** Rand McNally Staff. 1998. pap. 5.95 (0-528-96666-9) Rand McNally.

Louisiana. Kathleen Thompson. LC 85-9976. (Portrait of America Library). 48p. (J). (gr. 4-8). 1996. pap. 5.95 (0-8114-7443-7) Raintree Steck-V.

Louisiana. Kathleen Thompson. LC 85-9976. (Portrait of America Library). (Illus.). 48p. (YA). (gr. 3-6). 1996. lib. bdg. 22.83 (0-8114-7338-4) Raintree Steck-V.

Louisiana. Anne Welsbacher. LC 97-24614. (United States Ser.). (Illus.). 32p. (J). 1998. lib. bdg. 19.93 (1-56239-880-6, Checkerboard Library) ABDO Pub Co.

Louisiana. 2nd ed. Martin Hintz. LC 98-11032. (America the Beautiful Ser.). (J). 1998. 32.00 (0-516-20634-6) Childrens.

Louisiana: A Geography. Henry W. Bullamore. (Westview Geographies of the United States Ser.). (C). 1996. text 35.00 (0-86531-310-5); pap. text 20.00 (0-86531-472-1) Westview.

Louisiana: A Guide to the State. Federal Writers' Project Staff. (American Guidebook Ser.). 711p. 1941. reprint ed. 95.00 (0-403-02169-3) Somerset Pub.

Louisiana: A Guide to the State. Federal Writers' Project Staff & Writers Program-WPA Staff. (American Guide Ser.). 1989. reprint ed. lib. bdg. 79.00 (0-7812-1017-8, 1017) Rprt Serv.

***Louisiana: A Guide to Unique Places.** 5th ed. Gay Martin. (Off the Beaten Path Ser.). (Illus.). 2000. pap. 12.95 (0-7627-0805-0) Globe Pequot.

Louisiana: A History. Joe G. Taylor. (States & the Nation Ser.). (Illus.). 1984. pap. 12.95 (0-393-30174-5) Norton.

Louisiana: A History. 3rd ed. Bennett H. Wall et al. (Illus.). 440p. (C). 1997. pap. text 26.95 (0-88295-932-8) Harlan Davidson.

Louisiana: A Land Apart. Ed. by Barry J. Ancelet et al. LC 84-72896. (Illus.). 144p. 1985. 35.00 (0-917541-01-4) Galerie Pr.

Louisiana: A Novel. Erna Brodber. LC 97-21363. 168p. (Orig.). 1997. pap. 17.00 (1-57806-031-1) U Pr of Miss.

Louisiana: A Record of Expansion. Albert Phelps. LC 72-3748. (American Commonwealths Ser.: No. 18). reprint ed. 42.50 (0-404-57218-9) AMS Pr.

Louisiana! A(lligator) to Z(ydeco) Carole Marsh. (Carole Marsh Louisiana Bks.). (J). 1994. pap. text 19.95 (0-7933-7320-4); lib. bdg. 29.95 (0-7933-7321-2); disk 29.95 (0-7933-7322-0) Gallopade Intl.

Louisiana: Its Land & People. fac. ed. Fred B. Kniffen. LC 68-13448. (Illus.). 202p. 1968. reprint ed. pap. 62.70 (0-7837-7766-3, 204752200007) Bks Demand.

***Louisiana: Microcosm of a Mixed Jurisdiction.** Vernon Valentine Palmer. LC 99-67316. 336p. 1999. 39.95 (0-89089-892-8) Carolina Acad Pr.

Louisiana: Off the Beaten Path: A Guide to Unique Places. 4th ed. Gay Martin. Ed. by Carolyn Kolb. LC 98-45558. (Off the Beaten Path Ser.). (Illus.). 256p. 1998. pap. 12.95 (0-7627-0268-0) Globe Pequot.

Louisiana: Sketches of Historical Homes & Sights. M. S. Hays. 1965. lib. bdg. 6.95 (0-87511-058-4) Claitors.

Louisiana: The Land & Its People. 4th ed. Manie Culbertson. (Illus.). 128p. (C). 1986. teacher ed. 9.95 (0-88289-894-9) Pelican.

Louisiana: The Land & Its People. 4th ed. Sue Eakin & Manie Culbertson. (Illus.). 560p. 1998. text 27.50 (1-56554-289-4) Pelican.

Louisiana: The Land & Its People Student Skill Builder. 4th ed. Sue Eakin & Manie Culbertson. (Illus.). 128p. (C). 1986. student ed. 9.95 (0-88289-634-2) Pelican.

Louisiana: The Land & Its People Student Skillbuilder. 2nd ed. Manie Culbertson. (Illus.). 128p. (J). (gr. 4-7). 1999. pap. 9.95 (1-56554-625-3) Pelican.

Louisiana: Why Stop?: A Guide to Louisiana Roadside Historical Markers. Marael Johnson. LC 96-36283. 192p. 1996. pap. 14.95 (0-88415-924-8, 5924) Gulf Pub.

Louisiana - Collected Works of Federal Writers Project. Federal Writers' Project Staff. 1991. reprint ed. lib. bdg. 98.00 (0-7812-5600-3) Rprt Serv.

Louisiana Almanac, 2000-2001. Milburn Calhoun. (Illus.). 672p. 1997. pap. 16.95 (1-56554-771-3) Pelican.

Louisiana Almanac, 2000-2001. Ed. by Milburn Calhoun. (Illus.). 704p. 1997. 26.00 (1-56554-770-5) Pelican.

Louisiana Ancients of Man: Archaeology. J. A. Sibley. 1967. 15.00 (0-87511-107-6) Claitors.

Louisiana & Arkansas Railway: The Story of a Regional Line. James R. Fair. LC 96-53960. (Railroads in America Ser.). (Illus.). 215p. 1997. 47.95 (0-87580-219-2) N Ill U Pr.

L

An Asterisk (*) at the beginning of an entry indicates that the title is appearing for the first time.

L

Louisiana & Other State Greats (Biographies) Carole Marsh. (Carole Marsh Louisiana Bks.). (Illus.). (J). (gr. 3-8). 1994. pap. 19.95 (*1-55609-403-5*); lib. bdg. 29.95 (*1-55609-404-3*) Gallopade Intl.

Louisiana & Other State Greats (Biographies) Carole Marsh. (Carole Marsh Louisiana Bks.). (Illus.). (J). (gr. 3-8). 1997. disk 29.95 (*0-7933-1677-4*) Gallopade Intl.

Louisiana & Quebec: Bilateral Relations & Comparative Sociopolitical Evolution, 1673-1993. Alfred O. Hero, Jr. (Tulane Studies in Political Science: No. 20). 350p. (C). 1995. text 51.00 (*0-8191-9630-4*) U Pr of Amer.

Louisiana & Quebec: Bilateral Relations & Comparative Sociopolitical Evolution, 1673-1993. Alfred O. Hero, Jr. LC 96-7147. (Tulane Studies in Political Science: No. 20). (Illus.). 350p. (C). 1995. pap. text 26.50 (*0-8191-9631-2*) U Pr of Amer.

Louisiana Appellate Practice Handbook. Louisiana Appellate Court Handbook Committee. LC 86-81536. 1986. 115.00 (*0-318-21801-1*) West Group.

Louisiana Appellate Practice Handbook: Supplement, 1992. Louisiana Appellate Court Handbook Committee. LC 86-81536. 1992. suppl. ed. 52.50 (*0-317-04348-X*) West Group.

***Louisiana Architecture: A Handbook on Styles.** Jonathan Fricker. LC 98-71639. 112p. (C). 1998. pap. 10.00 (*1-887366-23-7*) Univ LA Lafayette.

Louisiana Architecture of William King Stubbs. F. Lestar Martin. LC 94-78826. (Illus.). 76p. 1995. 32.00 (*0-9644513-0-1*) LA Tech Univ.

Louisiana Atlas & Gazetteer. DeLorme. LC 99-462943. 1998. pap. 16.95 (*0-89933-217-X*) DeLorme Map.

Louisiana Attorney's - Secretarys Handbook. 10th ed. James D. Slaten. 496p. 1997. 54.00 (*0-9631577-5-2*) Cypress MN.

Louisiana Attorneys/Secretarys Handbook. 12th ed. James D. Slaten. 439p. 1999. 55.00 (*0-9631577-7-9*) Cypress MN.

Louisiana Backroads & Bayous. Pat Louviere. (Illus.). 128p. 1992. vinyl bd. 60.00 (*0-9620814-2-6*) Louviere Fine Arts.

Louisiana Backroads & Bayous. deluxe ed. Pat Louviere. (Illus.). 128p. 1992. lthr. 200.00 (*0-9620814-1-8*) Louviere Fine Arts.

Louisiana Backyard Wildlife Management. Bill Vermillion. (Illus.). 99p. 1997. pap. 5.00 (*0-9638600-5-4*) LA Dept Wldlife.

Louisiana Bandits, Bushwackers, Outlaws, Crooks, Devils, Ghosts, Desperadoes & Other Assorted & Sundry Characters! Carole Marsh. (Carole Marsh Louisiana Bks.). (Illus.). (J). (gr. 3-8). 1994. pap. 19.95 (*0-7933-0501-2*); lib. bdg. 29.95 (*0-7933-0502-0*); disk 29.95 (*0-7933-0503-9*) Gallopade Intl.

Louisiana "BIO" Bingo! 24 Must Know State People for Kids to Learn about While Having Fun! Carole Marsh. (Bingo! Ser.). (Illus.). (J). (gr. 2-8). 1998. pap. 14.95 (*0-7933-8576-8*) Gallopade Intl.

Louisiana Birds. James Kavanagh. (Pocket Naturalist Ser.). (Illus.). 1999. 5.95 (*1-58355-007-0*, Pub. by Waterford WA) Falcon Pub Inc.

Louisiana Blue see Treasured Horses Collection

Louisiana Blue: A Tiller Galloway Thriller, Vol. 1. David Poyer. 1995. mass mkt. 5.99 (*0-312-95422-0*) St Martin.

***Louisiana Blueprint.** Nola Mae Ross. (Illus.). 126p. 2000. 40.00 (*1-887144-13-7*) N M Ross.

Louisiana Bookstore Book: A Surprising Guide to Our State's Bookstores & Their Specialties for Students, Teachers, Writers & Publishers. Carole Marsh. (Carole Marsh Louisiana Bks.). (Illus.). 1994. pap. 19.95 (*0-7933-2910-8*); lib. bdg. 29.95 (*0-7933-2909-4*); disk 29.95 (*0-7933-2911-6*) Gallopade Intl.

Louisiana Buildings, 1720-1940: The Historic American Buildings Survey. Ed. by Jessie Poesch & Barbara S. Bacot. LC 96-16959. (Illus.). 472p. (C). 1996. 59.95 (*0-8071-2054-5*) La State U Pr.

***Louisiana Business Directory, 2000 Edition.** rev. ed. American Business Directories Staff. 1680p. 1999. boxed set 520.00 incl. cd-rom (*0-7687-0173-2*) Am Busn Direct.

Louisiana Cajun Seafood Cookbook. Mercedes Vidrine. 1989. pap. 9.95 (*0-87511-894-1*) Claitors.

Louisiana Cajuns - Cajuns de la Louisiane. Turner Browne. Tr. by James Spohrer & Elisabeth Spohrer. LC 77-24171. (ENG & FRE.). 118p. 1977. pap. 36.60 (*0-7837-8454-6*, 204925900010) Bks Demand.

Louisiana Capitol: Its Art & Architecture. Vincent Kubly. LC 76-49889. (Illus.). 152p. 1977. text 34.95 (*0-88289-082-4*) Pelican.

Louisiana Catahoula Leopard Dog. Don Abney. Ed. by Luana Luther. LC 95-83697. (Illus.). 113p. (Orig.). 1996. pap. text 19.95 (*0-944875-44-0*) Doral Pub.

Louisiana Census Index, 1850 Slave Schedule. (Illus.). 1988. lib. bdg. 85.00 (*0-89593-353-5*, Accel Indexing) Genealogical Srvcs.

Louisiana Census Index, 1850 Mortality Schedules. (Illus.). lib. bdg. 48.00 (*0-89593-352-7*, Accel Indexing) Genealogical Srvcs.

Louisiana Census Index, 1890 Union Vets. Ronald V. Jackson. (Illus.). lib. bdg. 54.00 (*0-89593-671-2*, Accel Indexing) Genealogical Srvcs.

Louisiana Census Index, 1860 Slave Schedule. (Illus.). 1988. lib. bdg. 100.00 (*0-89593-356-X*, Accel Indexing) Genealogical Srvcs.

Louisiana Census Index, 1860 Mortality Schedules. (Illus.). 1987. lib. bdg. 82.00 (*0-89593-355-1*, Accel Indexing) Genealogical Srvcs.

Louisiana Census Index, 1880 (Excludes Orleans Parish) (Illus.). lib. bdg. write for info. (*0-89593-358-6*, Accel Indexing) Genealogical Srvcs.

Louisiana Census Records: Avoyelles & St. Landr. Robert B. Ardoin. 114p. 1995. reprint ed. pap. 14.00 (*0-8063-0446-4*, 151) Clearfield Co.

Louisiana Census Records Vol. II: Iberville, Natchitoches. Robert B. Ardoin. 216p. 1995. reprint ed. pap. 21.50 (*0-8063-0507-X*, 152) Clearfield Co.

Louisiana Children's Code Handbook Lucy S. McGough. LC 98-159679. (West's Louisiana Deskbks.). 1005 p. 1998. write for info. (*0-314-23268-0*) West Pub.

Louisiana Civil Practice Forms 2d. Roger M. Denton. LC 84-52338. 1985. 135.00 (*0-318-04535-4*) West Group.

Louisiana Classic Christmas Trivia: Stories, Recipes, Activities, Legends, Lore & More! Carole Marsh. (Carole Marsh Louisiana Bks.). (Illus.). (J). (gr. 3-8). 1994. pap. 19.95 (*0-7933-0504-7*); lib. bdg. 29.95 (*0-7933-0505-5*); disk 29.95 (*0-7933-0506-3*) Gallopade Intl.

Louisiana Coastales. Carole Marsh. (Carole Marsh Louisiana Bks.). (J). 1994. lib. bdg. 29.95 (*0-7933-7283-6*) Gallopade Intl.

Louisiana Coastales. Carole Marsh. (Carole Marsh Louisiana Bks.). (Illus.). (J). (gr. 3-8). 1994. pap. 19.95 (*1-55609-119-2*); lib. bdg. 29.95 (*1-55609-400-0*); disk 29.95 (*0-7933-1673-1*) Gallopade Intl.

Louisiana Code of Civil Procedure: As Amended Through the 1983 Regular Session of the Legislature. Ed. by William E. Crawford. LC 84-131708. 1983. pap. 24.00 (*0-317-13475-2*) West Pub.

Louisiana Code of Evidence Pocket Manual. unabridged ed. Bobby M. Harges & Gaynell Williams. 94p. 1997. pap. 5.95 (*0-9659797-5-X*) B M Harges.

Louisiana Code of Evidence Practice Guide. 2nd ed. Richard K. Leefe. LC 98-87232. 640p. 1998. 130.00 (*0-327-00303-0*, 6878011) LEXIS Pub.

Louisiana Code of Evidence Practice Guide. 2nd ed. Richard K. Leefe. 30p. 1999. 35.00 (*0-327-01155-6*, 6878512) LEXIS Pub.

Louisiana Code Research Guide. Lawyers Cooperative Publishing Staff. 1988. 95.00 (*0-318-43161-0*) West Group.

***Louisiana Coloring Book.** Carole Marsh. (Louisiana Experience! Ser.). (Illus.). (J). (gr. k-5). 2000. pap. 3.95 (*0-7933-9551-8*) Gallopade Intl.

Louisiana Commercial Financing Forms, 2 vols. Philip D. Claverie & James A. Stuckey. 1994. ring bd., suppl. ed. 85.00 (*0-685-74615-1*, MICHIE) LEXIS Pub.

Louisiana Commercial Financing Forms, 2 vols., Set. Philip D. Claverie & James A. Stuckey. 600p. 1994. spiral bd. 170.00 (*0-8342-0195-X*, 81317-10, MICHIE) LEXIS Pub.

Louisiana Commercial Law: The Antebellum Period. Richard H. Kilbourne, Jr. xix, 233p. 1980. 17.00 (*0-940448-06-8*) LSU Law Pubns.

Louisiana Contemporaries: Selections from the ARCO Collection. Terrington Calas et al. (Illus.). 32p. (Orig.). 1992. 7.00 (*0-936819-06-5*) USL Art Museum.

Louisiana Cookery. Mary Land. 1972. pap. 8.95 (*0-87511-070-3*) Claitors.

Louisiana Corporations, 2 vols. James S. Holliday, Jr. & Rick J. Norman. LC 83-81051. (Louisiana Practice Systems Library). 1983. 220.00 (*0-318-00429-1*) West Group.

Louisiana Corporations, 2 vols. James S. Holliday, Jr. & Rick J. Norman. LC 83-81051. (Louisiana Practice Systems Library). 1993. suppl. ed. 85.00 (*0-317-03238-0*) West Group.

Louisiana Courtroom Evidence. Roy C. Cheatwood et al. 400p. 1993. ring bd. 115.00 (*1-55943-150-4*, MICHIE) LEXIS Pub.

Louisiana Creole & Cajun, Vol. 7. Margaret Maring. 64p. 1984. pap., per. 3.95 (*0-942320-14-X*) Am Cooking.

Louisiana Creole & Cajun Cooking: At Its Best. Tyrone A. Willis. LC 91-91168. (Illus.). 105p. (Orig.). 1992. 9.95 (*0-9630753-0-6*) Chef Willis.

Louisiana Creole Poems. Calvin A. Claudel. LC 82-80025. (Illus.). 50p. (Orig.). 1982. pap. 3.50 (*0-942544-00-5*) Negative Capability Pr.

***Louisiana Crime in Perspective 2000.** Ed. by Kathleen O'Leary Morgan & Scott E. Morgan. 22p. 2000. spiral bd. 19.00 (*0-7401-0317-2*) Morgan Quitno Corp.

Louisiana Crime Perspective, 1998. Ed. by Kathleen O'Leary Morgan & Scott E. Morgan. 20p. 1998. pap. 19.00 (*1-56692-917-2*) Morgan Quitno Corp.

Louisiana Crime Perspectives, 1999. Kathleen O'Leary Morgan. 22p. 1999. spiral bd. 19.00 (*0-7401-0117-X*) Morgan Quitno Corp.

Louisiana Criminal Law & Motor Vehicle Handbook: Annual Edition. annuals rev. ed. Ed. by Gould Editorial Staff. 1180p. (C). pap. 24.95 (*0-87526-367-4*) Gould.

Louisiana "Crinkum-Crankum" A Funny Word Book about Our State. Carole Marsh. (Carole Marsh Louisiana Bks.). (Illus.). (J). 1994. pap. 19.95 (*0-7933-4863-3*); lib. bdg. 29.95 (*0-7933-4862-5*); disk 29.95 (*0-7933-4864-1*) Gallopade Intl.

Louisiana Dawn. Jennifer Blake. (Orig.). 1993. mass mkt. 5.99 (*0-449-14820-3*, GM) Fawcett.

Louisiana Dayride: 52 Short Trips from New Orleans. Shelley N. Holl. LC 95-31370. (Illus.). 134p. 1995. pap. 14.95 (*0-87805-822-2*) U Pr of Miss.

Louisiana Dingbats! A Fun Book of Games, Stories, Activities & More about Our State That's All in Code! for You to Decipher, Bk. 1. Carole Marsh. (Carole Marsh Louisiana Bks.). (Illus.). (J). (gr. 3-12). 1994. pap. 19.95 (*0-7933-3828-X*); lib. bdg. 29.95 (*0-7933-3827-1*); disk 29.95 (*0-7933-3829-8*) Gallopade Intl.

Louisiana Divorce. Robert C. Lowe. LC 83-82099. (Louisiana Practice Systems Library). 1984. ring bd. 120.00 (*0-317-00651-7*) West Group.

Louisiana Divorce. Robert C. Lowe. LC 83-82099. (Louisiana Practice Systems Library). 1993. suppl. ed. 70.00 (*0-317-03231-3*) West Group.

Louisiana During World War II: Politics & Society, 1939-1945. Jerry P. Sanson. LC 98-51457. 336p. 1999. text 60.00 (*0-8071-2308-0*) La State U Pr.

Louisiana Early Census Records, Vol. 2. Ronald V. Jackson. 1988. 33.00 (*0-89593-278-4*, Accel Indexing) Genealogical Srvcs.

Louisiana Early Census Records 1700s, Vol. 1. (Illus.). lib. bdg. 33.00 (*0-89593-277-6*, Accel Indexing) Genealogical Srvcs.

Louisiana Economy. Ed. by Thomas R. Beard. LC 69-17622. (Louisiana State University Studies: No. 15). 240p. 1969. pap. 74.40 (*0-7837-8462-7*, 204926700010) Bks Demand.

Louisiana Entertains. Hope J. Norman. 1981. 12.95 (*0-9603758-0-5*) Rapides Symphony.

Louisiana Entertains: Featured As "A Best Cookbook" by Town & Country Magazine. Ed. by Hope J. Norman & Louise A. Simon. LC 83-60953. (Illus.). 312p. (Orig.). 1983. pap. 11.95 (*0-9603758-1-3*) Rapides Symphony.

Louisiana Environmental Handbook, 2 vols., Set. Roger A. Stetter. LC 92-81220. 1992. ring bd. 220.00 (*0-317-05357-4*) West Group.

Louisiana Environmental Law. Stephen Schott. 382p. 1993. pap. text 94.00 (*0-86587-364-X*) Gov Insts.

Louisiana Estate Planning, Will Drafting, & Estate Administration. Jack Nadel. 1994. disk 75.00 (*0-614-03737-9*, MICHIE) LEXIS Pub.

Louisiana Estate Planning, Will Drafting, & Estate Administration, 3 vols. Max Nathan, Jr. & Carole C. Neff. 1994. suppl. ed. 85.00 (*0-685-74479-5*, MICHIE) LEXIS Pub.

Louisiana Estate Planning, Will Drafting, & Estate Administration, 3 vols. Nathan & Neff. LC 98-87232. 2000p. 1998. ring bd. 340.00 (*0-327-00260-3*, 81329-11) LEXIS Pub.

***Louisiana Estate Planning, Will Drafting & Estate Administration, Issue 1.** 2nd ed. Max Nathan, Jr. & Carole C. Neff. 100p. 1999. spiral bd. write for info. (*0-327-01525-X*, 8133621) LEXIS Pub.

Louisiana Estate Planning, Will Drafting, & Estate Administration, 3 vols., Set. Max Nathan, Jr. & Carole C. Neff. 1800p. 1992. spiral bd. 255.00 (*1-56257-952-5*, 813310-10, MICHIE) LEXIS Pub.

Louisiana Evidence: Problems & Materials. Bobby M. Hargas & Russell Jones. 237p. (C). 1998. ring bd. 40.00 (*1-879581-56-6*) Lupus Pubns.

Louisiana Experience. M. A. Fontenot & J. Landry. 1983. 20.00 (*0-87511-646-9*) Claitors.

***Louisiana Experience Pocket Guide.** Carole Marsh. (Louisiana Experience! Ser.). (Illus.). (J). 2000. pap. 6.95 (*0-7933-9546-1*) Gallopade Intl.

***Louisiana Faces: Images from a Renaissance.** Photos by Philip Gould. (Illus.). 160p. 2000. 39.95 (*0-8071-2621-7*) La State U Pr.

***Louisiana Faces: Images from a Renaissance.** Philip Gould & Jason Berry. LC 00-9246. 2000. write for info. (*0-8071-2646-2*) La State U Pr.

Louisiana Facts & Factivities. Carole Marsh. (Carole Marsh State Bks.). (Illus.). (J). (gr. 4-7). 1996. pap., teacher ed. 19.95 (*0-7933-7883-4*, C Marsh) Gallopade Intl.

Louisiana Facts & Symbols. Emily McAuliffe. LC 98-16600. (States & Their Symbols Ser.). 24p. (J). 1999. write for info. (*0-7368-0081-6*, Hilltop Bks) Capstone Pr.

Louisiana Family Law. Christopher L. Blakesley. 450p. 1993. spiral bd. 110.00 (*0-250-42752-4*, MICHIE) LEXIS Pub.

Louisiana Family Law. Christopher L. Blakesley. 1995. ring bd. 110.00 (*0-327-03964-7*, 81341-10, MICHIE) LEXIS Pub.

Louisiana Federal Census Index 1860. LC 99-197282. (Illus.). 1985. lib. bdg. 125.00 (*0-89593-354-3*, Accel Indexing) Genealogical Srvcs.

Louisiana Federal Census Index 1870. (Illus.). lib. bdg. 235.00 (*0-89593-357-8*, Accel Indexing) Genealogical Srvcs.

Louisiana Federal Census Index 1810. Ronald V. Jackson. LC 77-85938. (Illus.). lib. bdg. 48.00 (*0-89593-049-8*, Accel Indexing) Genealogical Srvcs.

Louisiana Federal Census Index 1820. Ronald V. Jackson. LC 77-85939. (Illus.). lib. bdg. 54.00 (*0-89593-050-1*, Accel Indexing) Genealogical Srvcs.

Louisiana Federal Census Index 1830. Ronald V. Jackson. LC 77-85941. (Illus.). lib. bdg. 58.00 (*0-89593-051-X*, Accel Indexing) Genealogical Srvcs.

Louisiana Federal Census Index 1840. Ronald V. Jackson. LC 77-85942. (Illus.). lib. bdg. 64.00 (*0-89593-052-8*, Accel Indexing) Genealogical Srvcs.

Louisiana Federal Census Index, 1850. Ronald V. Jackson. LC 77-85960. (Illus.). lib. bdg. 67.00 (*0-89593-053-6*, Accel Indexing) Genealogical Srvcs.

Louisiana Festival & Events Guide. Julie Posner. (Illus.). 225p. (Orig.). 1997. pap. write for info. (*0-9654906-2-9*) Huli Pub.

Louisiana Festival Fun for Kids! Carole Marsh. (Carole Marsh Louisiana Bks.). (Illus.). (YA). (gr. 3-12). 1994. pap. 19.95 (*0-7933-3981-2*); lib. bdg. 29.95 (*0-7933-3980-4*); disk 29.95 (*0-7933-3982-0*) Gallopade Intl.

Louisiana Festivals Cookbook. Lou A. Gardens. 218p. 1994. spiral bd. 21.95 (*0-925417-10-6*, 17106) Gulf Pub.

Louisiana Fever. D. J. Donaldson. 288p. 1996. 21.95 (*0-312-14362-1*) St Martin.

Louisiana Fever. D. J. Donaldson. 1997. mass mkt. 5.99 (*0-312-96257-6*) St Martin.

Louisiana French Grammar, Vol. 1, Phonology, Morphology, & Syntax. Marilyn Conwell & Alphonse Juilland. (Janua Linguarum, Ser. Practica: No. 1). 1963. text 55.40 (*90-279-0621-1*) Mouton.

Louisiana Gardener's Guide: The What, Where, When, How & Why of Gardening in Louisiana. Joe White & Dan Gill. LC 97-46051. (Illus.). 424p. (Orig.). 1997. pap. 19.95 (*1-888608-33-1*) Cool Springs Pr.

Louisiana Gardens. Mary Fonseca. LC 98-56086. (Illus.). 128p. 1999. pap. 19.95 (*1-56554-306-8*) Pelican.

***Louisiana Gardens.** Mary Fonseca. LC 98-56086. (Illus.). 128p. 1999. 29.95 (*1-56554-305-X*) Pelican.

Louisiana "GEO" Bingo! 38 Must Know State Geography Facts for Kids to Learn While Having Fun! Carole Marsh. (Bingo! Ser.). (Illus.). (J). (gr. 2-8). 1998. pap. 14.95 (*0-7933-8577-6*) Gallopade Intl.

Louisiana Government! The Cornerstone of Everyday Life in Our State! Carole Marsh. (Carole Marsh Louisiana Bks.). (Illus.). (J). (gr. 3-12). 1996. pap. 19.95 (*0-7933-6236-9*); lib. bdg. 29.95 (*0-7933-6235-0*); disk 29.95 (*0-7933-6237-7*) Gallopade Intl.

Louisiana Governments Performance Standards, 1990. Ed. by Greg Michels. (Governments Performance Standards Ser.). (Illus.). 150p. 1990. text 125.00 (*1-55507-486-3*) Municipal Analysis.

Louisiana Governors: From Iberville to Edwards. Ed. by Joseph G. Dawson, III. LC 89-27333. (Illus.). 360p. 1990. text 50.00 (*0-8071-1527-4*) La State U Pr.

Louisiana Gumbo: A Cajun Cookbook. Shelby Camp & Mildred Camp. 250p. (Orig.). 1986. pap. 10.00 (*0-935687-00-9*, 186) Best Cookbks.

***Louisiana Gumbo Cookbook.** Bea Weber. (Illus.). 2000. 15.95 (*0-925417-13-0*) Acadian Hse Pub.

Louisiana Hayride Years. Logan et al. 1999. pap. 14.95 (*0-312-20661-5*, St Martins Paperbacks) St Martin.

***Louisiana Health Care in Perspective 2000.** Ed. by Kathleen O'Leary Morgan & Scott E. Morgan. 21p. 2000. spiral bd. 19.00 (*0-7401-0217-6*) Morgan Quitno Corp.

Louisiana Health Care Perspective, 1998. Ed. by Kathleen O'Leary Morgan & Scott E. Morgan. 20p. 1998. pap. 19.00 (*1-56692-817-6*) Morgan Quitno Corp.

Louisiana Health Care Perspective, 1999. Ed. by Kathleen O'Leary Morgan. 21p. 1999. spiral bd. 19.00 (*0-7401-0067-X*) Morgan Quitno Corp.

Louisiana Heron-Snowy Egert Nesting Area. Ronald Everhart. (Illus.). 112p. 1984. 25.00 (*0-915261-00-6*) World Nature.

Louisiana "HISTO" Bingo! 42 Must Know State History Facts for Kids to Learn While Having Fun! Carole Marsh. (Bingo! Ser.). (Illus.). (J). (gr. 2-8). 1998. pap. 14.95 (*0-7933-8578-4*) Gallopade Intl.

Louisiana Historical & Biographical Index, Vol. 1. Ronald V. Jackson. LC 78-53698. (Illus.). 1984. lib. bdg. 30.00 (*0-89593-183-4*, Accel Indexing) Genealogical Srvcs.

Louisiana Historical Quarterly, 37 vols., Set. Louisiana Historical Quarterly Staff. 1995. reprint ed. 3439.50 (*0-614-07691-9*) AMS Pr.

Louisiana Historical Society Publications, 10 vols., Set. Louisiana Historical Society Staff & Parish of St. Mary Labeth Staff. 1995. reprint ed. 700.00 (*0-404-19531-8*) AMS Pr.

Louisiana Historical Society Publications, Vol. 1-10. reprint ed. lib. bdg. 60.00 (*0-404-19574-1*) AMS Pr.

Louisiana History: Bossier Parish. Samuel J. Touchstone. LC 89-83726. (Illus.). 125p. (Orig.). 1989. pap. text 6.95 (*0-914917-02-1*) Folk-Life.

Louisiana History: Sabine Parish. Samuel J. Touchstone. LC 97-202075. (Illus.). 135p. 1997. pap. text 6.95 (*0-914917-07-2*) Folk-Life.

Louisiana History! Surprising Secrets about Our State's Founding Mothers, Fathers & Kids! Carole Marsh. (Carole Marsh Louisiana Bks.). (Illus.). (J). (gr. 3-12). 1996. pap. 19.95 (*0-7933-6083-8*); lib. bdg. 29.95 (*0-7933-6082-X*); disk 29.95 (*0-7933-6084-6*) Gallopade Intl.

Louisiana Hot Air Balloon Mystery. Carole Marsh. (Carole Marsh Louisiana Bks.). (Illus.). (J). (gr. 2-9). 1994. pap. 19.95 (*0-7933-2481-5*); disk 29.95 (*0-7933-2482-3*) Gallopade Intl.

Louisiana Hot Air Balloon Mystery. Carole Marsh. (Carole Marsh Louisiana Bks.). (Illus.). (J). (gr. 2-9). 1997. 29.95 (*0-7933-2480-7*) Gallopade Intl.

Louisiana Hot Zones! Viruses, Diseases, & Epidemics in Our State's History. Carole Marsh. (Hot Zones! Ser.). (Illus.). (J). (gr. 3-12). 1998. pap. 19.95 (*0-7933-8883-X*); lib. bdg. 29.95 (*0-7933-8882-1*) Gallopade Intl.

Louisiana Houses of A. Hays Town. Cyril E. Vetter. LC 98-48589. (Illus.). 176p. 1999. 39.95 (*0-8071-2371-4*) La State U Pr.

***Louisiana Hurricane, 1860.** Kathleen Duey. 256p. (YA). 2000. per. 4.99 (*0-671-03926-1*, Archway) PB.

***Louisiana Hurricane, 1860.** Kathleen Duey. (Illus.). (J). 2000. 10.34 (*0-606-18802-9*) Turtleback.

Louisiana IceGators Phenomenon. Trent Angers et al. (Illus.). 56p. (Orig.). 1996. 11.95 (*0-925417-27-0*); pap. 8.95 (*0-925417-24-6*) Acadian Hse Pub.

Louisiana in Perspective, 1998. Ed. by Kathleen O'Leary Morgan & Scott E. Morgan. 24p. 1998. pap. 19.00 (*1-56692-867-2*) Morgan Quitno Corp.

***Louisiana in Perspective, 1999.** Ed. by Kathleen O'Leary Morgan. 26p. 1999. spiral bd. 19.00 (*1-56692-967-9*) Morgan Quitno Corp.

***Louisiana in Perspective 2000.** Ed. by Kathleen O'Leary Morgan & Scott E. Morgan. 26p. 2000. spiral bd. 19.00 (*0-7401-0267-2*) Morgan Quitno Corp.

Louisiana in the Age of Jackson: A Clash of Cultures & Personalities. Joseph G. Tregle, Jr. LC 98-24708. 344p. 1999. text 37.50 (*0-8071-2292-0*) La State U Pr.

Louisiana in the Confederacy. Jefferson D. Bragg. LC 96-49698. 339p. 1997. pap. 16.95 (*0-8071-2179-7*) La State U Pr.

Louisiana in the Short Story. L. C. McVoy. LC 73-130264. (American History & Americana Ser.: No. 47). 1970. reprint ed. lib. bdg. 75.00 (*0-8383-1171-7*) M S G Haskell Hse.

Louisiana Indian Dictionary for Kids! Carole Marsh. (Carole Marsh State Bks.). (J). (gr. 2-9). 1996. 29.95 (*0-7933-7698-X*, C Marsh); pap. 19.95 (*0-7933-7699-8*, C Marsh) Gallopade Intl.

An Asterisk (*) at the beginning of an entry indicates that the title is appearing for the first time.

Louisiana Indian Studies: A Selected Bibliography. Michael J. Foret. LC 95-74714. 284p. 1995. 25.00 (*0-940984-98-9*) Univ LA Lafayette.

Louisiana Indians. Carrel Muller & Brenda Muller. (Illus.). 64p. (J). (gr. 3 up). 1985. 7.50 (*0-915785-01-3*) Bonjour Books.

Louisiana Insurance Laws. Louisiana Law Staff. LC 98-66269. 1998. write for info. (*0-89246-498-4*) NILS Pub.

Louisiana International Trade Directory. 3rd ed. Ed. by International Marketing Institute Staff. 135p. 1980. 25.00 (*0-942286-01-4*) Intl Mktg.

*__Louisiana Investment & Business Guide: Business, Investment, Export-Import Opportunities, 50 vols., Vol. 18.__ Global Investment Center, USA Staff. (U. S. Regional Investment & Business Library-99: Vol. 18). (Illus.). 350p. (Orig.). 1999. pap. 59.95 (*0-7397-1117-2*) Intl Business Pubns.

Louisiana Iris: The History & Culture of Five Native American Species & Their Hybrids. Ed. by Marie Caillet & Joseph K. Mertzweiller. (Illus.). 1988. 23.95 (*0-317-65674-0*) TX Gardener Pr.

*__Louisiana Iris: The Taming of a Native American Wildflower.__ 2nd ed. Marie Caillet & Society for Louisiana Irises Staff. LC 99-57037. (Illus.). 272p. 2000. 34.95 (*0-88192-477-6*) Timber.

Louisiana Iris History & Culture. Marie Caillet. 1988. 23.95 (*0-914641-09-3*) TX Gardener Pr.

*__Louisiana Jeopardy.__ Carole Marsh. (Louisiana Experience! Ser.). (Illus.). (J). (gr. 2-6). 2000. pap. 7.95 (*0-7933-9548-8*) Gallopade Intl.

Louisiana Jeopardy! Answers & Questions about Our State! Carole Marsh. (Carole Marsh Louisiana Bks.). (Illus.). (J). (gr. 3-12). 1994. pap. 19.95 (*0-7933-4134-5*); lib. bdg. 29.95 (*0-7933-4133-7*); disk 29.95 (*0-7933-4135-3*) Gallopade Intl.

*__Louisiana Jography.__ Carole Marsh. (Louisiana Experience! Ser.). (Illus.). (J). (gr. 2-6). 2000. pap. 7.95 (*0-7933-9549-6*) Gallopade Intl.

Louisiana "Jography" A Fun Run Thru Our State! Carole Marsh. (Carole Marsh Louisiana Bks.). (Illus.). (J). (gr. 3-8). 1994. pap. 19.95 (*1-55609-108-7*); lib. bdg. 29.95 (*1-55609-396-9*); disk 29.95 (*0-7933-1663-4*) Gallopade Intl.

Louisiana Journey. Neil Johnson. LC 97-26862. (Illus.). 160p. 1997. 39.95 (*0-8071-2229-7*) La State U Pr.

Louisiana Keepsake, 1985. Lillie P. Gallagher. (Illus.). 128p. (J). 1984. 10.00 (*0-9610174-7-3*) Petit Press.

Louisiana-Keepsake, 1987, Louisiane-Recueil 1987. Lillie P. Gallagher. (ENG & FRE.). 128p. 1986. 10.00 (*0-9610174-5-7*) Petit Press.

Louisiana Keepsake, 1986. Lillie P. Gallagher. (ENG & FRE.). 1985. 10.00 (*0-9610174-6-5*) Petit Press.

Louisiana Keepsake, 1990. write for info. (*0-9610174-2-2*) Petit Press.

Louisiana Keepsake, 1991. write for info. (*0-9610174-1-4*) Petit Press.

Louisiana Kid's Cookbook: Recipes, How-To, History, Lore & More! Carole Marsh. (Carole Marsh Louisiana Bks.). (Illus.). (J). (gr. 3-8). 1994. pap. 19.95 (*0-7933-0513-6*); lib. bdg. 29.95 (*0-7933-0514-4*); disk 29.95 (*0-7933-0515-2*) Gallopade Intl.

Louisiana Land & Exploration (LL&E) A Report on the Company's Environmental Policies & Practices. (Illus.). 13p. (C). 1994. reprint ed. pap. text 40.00 (*0-7881-0979-0*, Coun on Econ) DIANE Pub.

Louisiana Land Surveying Law: Questions & Answers. John E. Keen. 56p. (C). 1995. pap. text 25.00 (*1-56569-027-3*) Land Survey.

Louisiana Landlord & Tenant Law. 16th ed. George M. Armstrong, Jr. 400p. 1994. ring bd. 120.00 (*0-614-05887-2*, MICHIE) LEXIS Pub.

Louisiana Landlord & Tenant Law, 1987-1993. George M. Armstrong, Jr. 400p. 1989. suppl. ed. 55.00 (*0-250-42071-6*, MICHIE) LEXIS Pub.

Louisiana Landscape & Genre Painting of the 19th Century. LC 81-50951. (Illus.). 44p. 1981. pap. 6.00 (*0-913060-19-4*) Norton Art.

Louisiana Law of Obligations in General: A Precis. Alain A. Levasseur. 350p. (C). 1988. pap. 39.50 (*0-409-25390-1*, MICHIE) LEXIS Pub.

Louisiana Law of Quasi-Contracts or Unjust Enrichment: A Precis. Alain A. Levasseur. LC 92-28451. 1992. pap. 35.00 (*0-409-25521-1*, MICHIE) LEXIS Pub.

Louisiana Law of Unjust Enrichment in Quasi-Contracts. Alain A. Levasseur. 490p. 1991. ring bd. 110.00 (*0-409-25600-5*, MICHIE) LEXIS Pub.

Louisiana Leaders. Louisiana Pen Women Staff. 1970. 20.00 (*0-87511-067-3*) Claitors.

Louisiana Legacy: A Rich Tradition of Artistry with Food & Joy in Life. Thibodaux Service League Members Staff. Ed. by Gloria E. Lynch & Katherine D. Silverberg. LC 82-50498. (Illus.). 288p. 1982. 11.95 (*0-9608800-0-3*) Thibodaux.

Louisiana Legacy: A Rich Tradition of Artistry with Food & Joy in Life. Thibodaux Service League Members Staff. Ed. by Louise C. Coleman. (Illus.). 283p. 1992. reprint ed. 14.95 (*0-944681-04-2*) Celestial Pub.

Louisiana Legal Advisor. 3rd ed. Stephen E. Covell & Lauren K. Covell. LC 93-70673. 302p. 1993. pap. 11.95 (*0-935773-23-1*) Charleston Pr.

Louisiana Legal Research. 2nd ed. Win-Shin S. Chiang. 260p. 1990. boxed set 60.00 (*0-409-25172-0*, MICHIE) LEXIS Pub.

Louisiana Legal Services Desk Manual. 468p. 1984. 28.50 (*0-317-03730-7*, 37,357B) NCLS Inc.

Louisiana Library Book: A Surprising Guide to the Unusual Special Collections in Libraries Across Our State for Students, Teachers, Writers & Publishers - Includes Reproducible Mailing Labels Plus Activities for Young People! Carole Marsh. (Carole Marsh Louisiana Bks.). (Illus.). 1994. pap. 19.95 (*0-7933-3060-2*); lib. bdg. 29.95 (*0-7933-3059-9*); disk 29.95 (*0-7933-3061-0*) Gallopade Intl.

Louisiana Light: Low-Fat, Low-Calorie, Low-Cholesterol, Low-Salt Cajun & Creole Cookery. Roy F. Guste, Jr. 1989. 29.95 (*0-393-02714-7*) Norton.

Louisiana Limited Liability Company Forms & Practice Manual. James M. Fantaci et al. LC 96-40896. 592p. 1997. ring bd. 219.90 (*1-57400-018-7*) Data Trace Pubng.

Louisiana Lovely: John Slocum. Jake Logan. (Slocum Ser.: Vol. 224). 192p. 1997. mass mkt. 4.99 (*0-515-12176-2*, Jove) Berkley Pub.

Louisiana Manufacturers Register. 9th rev. ed. Ed. by Frank Lambing. 1999. 71.00 (*1-58202-052-3*) Manufacturers.

Louisiana Marriages Index, Early to 1850. Liahona Research Staff. 185p. lib. bdg. 35.00 (*0-945433-45-X*) Herit Quest.

Louisiana Math! How It All Adds up in Our State. Carole Marsh. (Carole Marsh Louisiana Bks.). (Illus.). (YA). (gr. 3-12). 1996. pap. 19.95 (*0-7933-6542-2*); lib. bdg. 29.95 (*0-7933-6541-4*) Gallopade Intl.

Louisiana Media Book: A Surprising Guide to the Amazing Print, Broadcast & Online Media of Our State for Students, Teachers, Writers & Publishers - Includes Reproducible Mailing Labels Plus Activities for Young People! Carole Marsh. (Carole Marsh Louisiana Bks.). (Illus.). 1994. pap. 19.95 (*0-7933-3216-8*); lib. bdg. 29.95 (*0-7933-3215-X*); disk 29.95 (*0-7933-3217-6*) Gallopade Intl.

Louisiana Museum: Jorgen Bo, Vilhelm Wohlert. Photos by Jens Frederiksen. (Opus Ser.: Vol. 3). (Illus.). 64p. 1993. 39.95 (*3-8030-2703-9*, Pub. by E J Wasmuth) Dist Art Pubs.

*__Louisiana Music.__ Koster. 2000. 24.00 (*0-306-81003-4*) Da Capo.

Louisiana Mystery Van Takes Off! Handicapped Louisiana Kids Sneak off on a Big Adventure, Bk. 1. Carole Marsh. (Carole Marsh Louisiana Bks.). (Illus.). (J). (gr. 3-12). 1994. 29.95 (*0-7933-5015-8*); pap. 19.95 (*0-7933-5016-6*); disk 29.95 (*0-7933-5017-4*) Gallopade Intl.

Louisiana, Napoleon & the United States: An Autobiography of Pierre-Clement de Laussat (1756-1835) Pierre-Clement De Laussat. LC 89-32164. (Illus.). 226p. (Orig.). (C). 1989. pap. text 22.00 (*0-8191-7448-3*); lib. bdg. 39.00 (*0-8191-7447-5*) U Pr of Amer.

Louisiana Native Guards: The Black Military Experience During the Civil War. James G. Hollandsworth, Jr. LC 95-34787. (Illus.). 176p. (C). 1995. 24.95 (*0-8071-1939-3*) La State U Pr.

Louisiana Native Guards: The Black Military Experience During the Civil War. James G. Hollandsworth, Jr. LC 95-34787. (Illus.). 168p. 1998. pap. 12.95 (*0-8071-2336-6*) La State U Pr.

Louisiana New Notary Kit. LA Notary Association Staff. 1996. ring bd. 30.00 (*0-87511-805-4*, LLANOT) Claitors.

Louisiana Notarial Manual. 2nd ed. M. Truman Woodward. 1962. text, suppl. ed. 35.00 (*0-87473-016-3*, 68505-10, MICHIE) LEXIS Pub.

Louisiana Notorial Manual: 1973 Supplement. M. Truman Woodward. 1985. pap. 7.50 (*0-87473-188-7*, 68506-10, MICHIE) LEXIS Pub.

Louisiana One Hundred Years Ago. Edward King. (Historical Ser.). (Illus.). 1976. pap. 3.50 (*0-89540-026-X*, SB-026); pap. 3.50 (*0-89540-027-8*, SB-027) Sun Pub.

Louisiana-Pacific Corp. A Report on the Company's Environmental Policies & Practices. (Illus.). 55p. (C). 1994. reprint ed. pap. text 40.00 (*0-7881-0961-8*, Coun on Econ) DIANE Pub.

Louisiana Parks Guide. Chris Boyer. Ed. by Barbara McCarg. 100p. (Orig.). 1988. pap. text 4.95 (*0-935201-33-5*) Affordable Adven.

Louisiana Plantation Homes: A Return to Splendor. Paul Malone. LC 84-25369. (Illus.). 160p. 1986. 39.95 (*0-88289-403-X*) Pelican.

*__Louisiana Plantation Homes Postcard Book.__ Paul Malone. 1999. pap. 9.95 (*1-56554-641-5*) Pelican.

Louisiana Political Hijinks. C. Vidrine. 1985. pap. 7.95 (*0-87511-723-6*) Claitors.

Louisiana Power & Light. John Dufresne. LC 95-31672. 320p. 1995. pap. 12.95 (*0-452-27502-4*, Plume) Dutton Plume.

Louisiana Proud. Andy Smith & Andrew M. Smith, Sr. LC 87-80958. (Illus.). 176p. 1987. 19.95 (*0-9618564-0-8*) LA Proud Pr.

Louisiana Proud, Vol. II. Andy Smith & Andrew M. Smith, Sr. LC 87-80958. (Illus.). 176p. 1989. 19.95 (*0-9618564-1-6*) LA Proud Pr.

Louisiana Proud, Vol. III. Andy Smith & Andrew M. Smith, Sr. (Illus.). 176p. 1990. 19.95 (*0-9618564-2-4*) LA Proud Pr.

Louisiana Proud Vol. 4: Historical Pictorial of Louisiana Towns. Andy Smith. Ed. by J. Kirby Ward. (Illus.). 176p. (C). 1994. 19.95 (*0-9618564-6-7*) LA Proud Pr.

Louisiana Proud Collection of Home Cooking. Andy Smith & Andrew M. Smith, Sr. (Illus.). 303p. 1991. pap. 12.95 (*0-9618564-3-2*) LA Proud Pr.

Louisiana Proud Collection of Sweet Things. Andy Smith & Kirby Ward. Ed. by Evelyn Duke. (Illus.). 320p. 1993. pap. write for info. (*0-9618564-5-9*) LA Proud Pr.

Louisiana Public Records Doctrine & the Civil Law Tradition. Alejandro M. Garro. 398p. 1989. lib. bdg. 35.00 (*0-940448-19-X*) LSU Law Pubns.

*__Louisiana Purchase.__ James A. Corrick. LC 00-9156. (World History Ser.). 2000. write for info. (*1-56006-637-7*) Lucent Bks.

Louisiana Purchase. A. E. Hotchner. 400p. 1996. 24.00 (*0-7867-0309-1*) Carroll & Graf.

Louisiana Purchase. Carl J. Richard. LC 94-74141. (Louisiana Life Ser.: No. 7). (Illus.). 59p. (Orig.). 1995. pap. 5.00 (*0-940984-91-1*) Univ LA Lafayette.

Louisiana Purchase. Gail Sakurai. LC 97-12015. (Cornerstones to Freedom Ser.). 32p. (J). 1998. lib. bdg. 19.50 (*0-516-20791-1*) Childrens.

Louisiana Purchase. Gail Sakurai. Ed. by Brendon January. (Cornerstones to Freedom Ser.). (Illus.). 32p. (J). 1998. pap. 5.95 (*0-516-26336-6*) Childrens.

Louisiana Purchase. A. E. Hotchner. 384p. 1997. reprint ed. pap. 14.95 (*1-891442-00-7*) VA Pub Corp.

*__Louisiana Purchase: An Encyclopedia.__ Junius P. Rodriguez. 2002. lib. bdg. 99.00 (*1-57607-188-X*) ABC-CLIO.

Louisiana Purchase: Vocal Selections. Irving Berlin. 40p. 1997. pap. 8.95 (*0-7935-7351-3*) H Leonard.

*__Louisiana Purchase & its Aftermath, 1800-1830.__ Dolores E. Labbbe & University of Southwestern Louisiana Staff. LC 98-209973. (Bicentennial Series in Louisiana History). x, 637p. 1998. 40.00 (*1-887366-21-0*) Univ LA Lafayette.

*__Louisiana Purchase in American History.__ Ann Gaines. LC 99-24659. (In American History Ser.). (Illus.). 128p. (gr. 5 up). 2000. lib. bdg. 20.95 (*0-7660-1301-4*) Enslow Pubs.

Louisiana Quiz Bowl Crash Course! Carole Marsh. (Carole Marsh Louisiana Bks.). (Illus.). (J). (gr. 3-8). 1994. pap. 19.95 (*1-55609-401-9*); lib. bdg. 29.95 (*1-55609-402-7*); disk 29.95 (*0-7933-1672-3*) Gallopade Intl.

Louisiana Reading Adventures. Zenobia M. Johnson & Lucretia-del J. Broussard. (Illus.). 32p. (Orig.). (J). (gr. 4-7). 1984. 3.50 (*0-9617411-0-4*) Z M Johnson.

Louisiana Real & Rustic. Emeril Lagasse & Marcelle Bienvenu. LC 95-46653. (Illus.). 288p. 1996. 25.00 (*0-688-12721-5*, Wm Morrow) Morrow Avon.

Louisiana Reconstructed, 1863-1877. Joe G Taylor. LC 74-77327. 574p. 1974. pap. 178.00 (*0-7837-8504-6*, 204931200011) Bks Demand.

Louisiana Related Laws to the Insurance Laws. Louisiana. LC 97-65766. 1997. write for info. (*0-89246-470-4*) NILS Pub.

Louisiana Republican Party, 1948-1984, Vol. 18. Stella Z. Theodoulou. 1985. 18.95 (*0-930598-19-9*) Tulane Stud Pol.

Louisiana Republication Party, 1948-1984: The Building of a State Political Party. Stella Z. Theodoulou. Ed. by N. V. Baker. LC 88-107190. (Tulane Studies in Political Science). (Illus.). 185p. Date not set. reprint ed. pap. 57.40 (*0-608-20650-4*, 207208700003) Bks Demand.

Louisiana Retirement & Relocation Guide. large type ed. (Retirement & Relocation Guides Ser.). (Illus.). 350p. Date not set. pap. 24.95 (*1-56559-142-9*) HGI-Over Fifty.

Louisiana Rollercoasters! Carole Marsh. (Carole Marsh Louisiana Bks.). (Illus.). (YA). (gr. 3-12). 1994. pap. 19.95 (*0-7933-5279-7*); lib. bdg. 29.95 (*0-7933-5278-9*); disk 29.95 (*0-7933-5280-0*) Gallopade Intl.

Louisiana Rose. Elizabeth Sherwood. 416p. 1994. pap. 4.50 (*1-55817-893-7*) Kensgtn Pub Corp.

Louisiana Sampler: Recipes from Our Fairs & Festivals. John D. Folse. LC 96-90707. (Illus.). 208p. (C). 1996. 19.95 (*0-9625152-3-X*) Chef John Folse.

Louisiana Sampler Cookbook. ACS Staff. 1980. pap. text 10.95 (*0-87511-514-4*) Claitors.

Louisiana Scenes: The Lower Mississippi Valley. Morgan & Kerr. 1962. 24.95 (*0-87511-088-6*) Claitors.

Louisiana School Trivia: An Amazing & Fascinating Look at Our State's Teachers, Schools & Students! Carole Marsh. (Carole Marsh Louisiana Bks.). (Illus.). (J). (gr. 3-8). 1994. pap. 19.95 (*0-7933-0510-1*); lib. bdg. 29.95 (*0-7933-0511-X*); disk 29.95 (*0-7933-0512-8*) Gallopade Intl.

Louisiana Secured Transactions Practice Guide. David S. Willenzik. Ed. by Karen Morgan & John Wierzbieki. LC 96-75836. 1000p. 1996. text. write for info. (*0-7620-0051-1*) West Group.

Louisiana Security Rights in Personal Property. Henry D. Gabriel. 380p. 1991. ring bd. 85.00 (*0-409-25599-8*, MICHIE); suppl. ed. 100.00 (*0-250-42734-6*, MICHIE) LEXIS Pub.

Louisiana Security Rights in Personal Property. Henry D. Gabriel. (FRE.). 24p. 1994. ring bd., suppl. ed. 45.00 (*0-614-03739-5*, MICHIE) LEXIS Pub.

Louisiana Sentencing Guidelines Manual. 1992nd ed. Cheney C. Joseph, Jr. et al. 270p. 1992. pap. text. write for info. (*0-314-00749-0*) West Pub.

Louisiana Silly Basketball Sportsmysteries, Vol. I. Carole Marsh. (Carole Marsh Louisiana Bks.). (Illus.). (J). (gr. 3-8). 1994. pap. 19.95 (*0-7933-0507-1*); lib. bdg. 29.95 (*0-7933-0508-X*); disk 29.95 (*0-7933-0509-8*) Gallopade Intl.

Louisiana Silly Basketball Sportsmysteries, Vol. II. Carole Marsh. (Carole Marsh Louisiana Bks.). (Illus.). (J). (gr. 3-8). 1994. pap. 19.95 (*0-7933-1679-0*); lib. bdg. 29.95 (*0-7933-1678-2*); disk 29.95 (*0-7933-1680-4*) Gallopade Intl.

Louisiana Silly Football Sportsmysteries, Vol. I. Carole Marsh. (Carole Marsh Louisiana Bks.). (Illus.). (J). (gr. 3-8). 1994. pap. 19.95 (*1-55609-398-5*); lib. bdg. 29.95 (*1-55609-399-3*); disk 29.95 (*0-7933-1665-0*) Gallopade Intl.

Louisiana Silly Football Sportsmysteries, Vol. II. Carole Marsh. (Carole Marsh Louisiana Bks.). (Illus.). (J). (gr. 3-8). 1994. pap. 19.95 (*0-7933-1667-7*); lib. bdg. 29.95 (*0-7933-1666-9*); disk 29.95 (*0-7933-1668-5*) Gallopade Intl.

Louisiana Silly Trivia! Carole Marsh. (Carole Marsh Louisiana Bks.). (Illus.). (J). (gr. 3-8). 1994. pap. 19.95 (*1-55609-041-2*); lib. bdg. 29.95 (*1-55609-395-0*); disk 29.95 (*0-7933-0522-5*) Gallopade Intl.

*__Louisiana since the Longs: 1960 to Century's End.__ Ed. by Michael L. Kurtz & Glenn R. Conrad. LC 96-84494. (Louisiana Purchase Bicentennial Series in Louisiana History: Vol. 9). (Illus.). 731p. 1998. 45.00 (*1-887366-26-1*) Ctr for Louisiana Studies.

*__Louisiana Sky.__ Kimberly W. Holt. 208p. (YA). (gr. 5 up). 2000. pap. 4.99 (*0-440-41570-5*, YB BDD) BDD Bks Young Read.

Louisiana Sojourns: Travelers' Tales & Literary Journeys. Ed. by Frank De Caro. LC 97-50292. (Illus.). 432p. 1998. 39.95 (*0-8071-2239-4*); pap. 22.95 (*0-8071-2240-8*) La State U Pr.

*__Louisiana Soldiers in the War of 1812.__ Marion John Bennett Pierson. 126p. 1999. pap. 22.50 (*0-8063-4912-3*) Clearfield Co.

Louisiana Spelling Bee! Score Big by Correctly Spelling Our State's Unique Names. Carole Marsh. (Carole Marsh Louisiana Bks.). (Illus.). (YA). (gr. 3-12). 1996. pap. 19.95 (*0-7933-6695-X*); lib. bdg. 29.95 (*0-7933-6694-1*) Gallopade Intl.

Louisiana Sports Legends: The Men & Women of the Louisiana Sports Hall of Fame. Jerry Byrd. Ed. by Neill Cameron. (Illus.). 336p. 1992. pap. 19.95 (*0-917898-18-4*) NSU Pr LA.

*__Louisiana State Bird Beauty Pageant.__ Todd-Michael St. Pierre. LC 00-191007. (Illus.). 2000. 15.95 (*0-9675170-0-1*) Word Blossoms Pubg.

Louisiana State Constitution: A Reference Guide, 4. Lee Hargrave. LC 90-40732. (Reference Guides to the State Constitutions of the United States Ser.: No. 4). 264p. 1990. lib. bdg. 69.50 (*0-313-26654-9*, HLS, Greenwood Pr) Greenwood.

*__Louisiana State Credit Directory, 2000 Edition.__ rev. ed. American Business Directories Staff. 400p. 1999. boxed set 165.00 incl. cd-rom (*0-7687-0304-2*) Am Busn Direct.

Louisiana Stories. Ed. by Ben Forkner. LC 89-25575. 400p. 1990. pap. 15.95 (*0-88289-737-3*) Pelican.

*__Louisiana Stories: Growing Up in the Bayou State.__ Ron LeLeux. 80p. 2000. 29.95 (*0-9700746-0-3*) Sat Morn Pubng.

Louisiana Successions. 2nd ed. Laura J. Carman. LC 98-89051. 800p. 1998. 150.00 (*0-327-00707-9*, 6879011) LEXIS Pub.

Louisiana Successions. 2nd ed. Laura Junge Carman. 914p. 115.00 (*0-327-10171-7*) LEXIS Pub.

*__Louisiana Successions, 1999 Supplement: Pocketpart.__ Laura J. Carman. 100p. 1999. suppl. ed. write for info. (*0-327-01690-6*, 6879413) LEXIS Pub.

Louisiana Sugar Plantations. R. B. Howell. 1969. 14.95 (*0-87511-060-6*) Claitors.

Louisiana Sugar Plantations During the Civil War. Charles P. Roland. LC 97-24368. (Illus.). 160p. 1997. pap. text 11.95 (*0-8071-2221-1*) La State U Pr.

Louisiana Survival. Betty L. Hall & Marjorie M. King. 160p. (Orig.). (gr. 10-12). 1979. pap. text 5.84 (*0-03-046871-X*) Westwood Pr.

Louisiana Tapestry: Ethnicity in St. Landry Parish. Vaughan B. Baker & Jean T. Kreamer. (Illus.). (Orig.). (gr. 7-12). 1983. pap. text 10.00 (*0-940984-07-5*) Univ LA Lafayette.

Louisiana Tech University - Then & Now. Photos by Philip Gould. (First Edition Ser.). (Illus.). 112p. 1992. 39.95 (*0-916509-84-2*) Harmony Hse Pub.

Louisiana Temptations. Louisiana Farm Bureau Federation Staff. LC 96-84999. 1996. 16.95 (*0-9652035-0-6*) LA Farm Bureau.

Louisiana-Texas Frontier. Isaac J. Cox. 1993. reprint ed. lib. bdg. 75.00 (*0-7812-5871-5*) Rprt Serv.

Louisiana Timeline: A Chronology of Louisiana History, Mystery, Trivia, Legend, Lore & More. Carole Marsh. (Carole Marsh Louisiana Bks.). (Illus.). (J). (gr. 3-12). 1994. pap. 19.95 (*0-7933-5930-9*); lib. bdg. 29.95 (*0-7933-5929-5*); disk 29.95 (*0-7933-5931-7*) Gallopade Intl.

Louisiana Tort Law. Frank L. Maraist & Thomas C. Galligan, Jr. 612p. 105.00 (*1-55834-406-3*) LEXIS Pub.

Louisiana Tort Law. Frank L. Maraist & Thomas C. Galligan, Jr. 1996. 105.00 (*1-55834-385-7*, 83175, MICHIE) LEXIS Pub.

Louisiana Tort Law, 1998 Cumulative Supplement. Frank L. Maraist & Thomas C. Galligan, Jr. 125p. 1998. suppl. ed. write for info. (*0-327-00343-X*, 8317611) LEXIS Pub.

Louisiana Trade Tokens. 2nd ed. Louis Crawford & Glyn Farber. Ed. & Photos by David E. Schenkman. LC 96-61243. (Illus.). 559p. 1997. 44.95 (*0-918492-11-4*) TAMS.

Louisiana Trees & Shrubs. Clair Brown. 1965. pap. 20.00 (*0-87511-012-6*) Claitors.

*__Louisiana Troops, 1720-1770.__ Winston De Ville. 136p. 1999. pap. 16.50 (*0-8063-4921-2*, Pub. by Clearfield Co) ACCESS Pubs Network.

Louisiana 2000! Coming Soon to a Calendar Near You - The 21st Century! - Complete Set of AL 2000 Items. Carole Marsh. (Two Thousand! Ser.). (Illus.). (J). (gr. 3-12). 1998. pap. 75.00 (*0-7933-9345-0*); lib. bdg. 85.00 (*0-7933-9346-9*) Gallopade Intl.

Louisiana 2000! Coming Soon to a Calendar Near You-The 21st Century! Carole Marsh. (Two Thousand! Ser.). (Illus.). (J). (gr. 3-12). 1998. pap. 19.95 (*0-7933-8730-2*); lib. bdg. 29.95 (*0-7933-8729-9*) Gallopade Intl.

Louisiana UFO's & Extraterrestrials! A Look at the Sightings & Science in Our State. Carole Marsh. (Carole Marsh Louisiana Bks.). (Illus.). (J). (gr. 3-12). 1997. pap. 19.95 (*0-7933-6389-6*); lib. bdg. 29.95 (*0-7933-6388-8*) Gallopade Intl.

Louisiana under the Rule of Spain, France & the United States, 1785-1807, 2 vols, Set. Ed. by James A. Robertson. LC 72-102254. (Select Bibliographies Reprint Ser.). 1977. 68.95 (*0-8369-5139-5*) Ayer.

L

L

Louisiana Voices: Remembering World War II. Ed. by Janet Barnwell. LC 99-169781. (Williams Center for Oral History Ser.: Vol. 2). (Illus.). 176p. (Orig.). 1998. pap. text 19.95 (0-8071-2236-X) La State U Pr.
Louisiana Women Writers: New Essays & a Comprehensive Bibliography. Ed. by Dorothy H. Brown & Barbara C. Ewell. LC 92-48. (Southern Literary Studies). 328p. (C). 1992. text 45.00 (0-8071-1743-9) La State U Pr.
Louisiana Women's Yellow Page Network. Ed. by C. L. Greco. 102p. 1987. pap. 6.95 (0-943615-00-3) LA WYPN.
Louisiana Women's Yellow Pages. C. L. Greco. 100p. 1988. pap. 6.95 (0-943615-01-1) LA WYPN.
Louisiana Workers' Compensation, 2 vols. 2nd ed. Denis P. Juge. LC 99-60917. 600p. 1999. ring bd. 140.00 (0-327-01070-3, 6880511) LEXIS Pub.
Louisiana Wrongful Death & Survival Actions. 2nd ed. Thomas J. Andre, Jr. 500p. 1992. ring bd. 120.00 (1-56257-954-1, MICHIE) LEXIS Pub.
Louisiana Wrongful Death & Survival Actions. 2nd ed. Thomas J. Andre, Jr. 1993. ring bd., suppl. ed. 60.00 (0-685-74597-X, MICHIE) LEXIS Pub.
Louisiana, Yesterday & Today: A Historical Guide to the State. John Wilds et al. LC 95-47383. (Illus.). 298p. (C). 1996. 24.95 (0-8071-1892-3); pap. 12.95 (0-8071-1893-1) La State U Pr.
Louisiana's Acadian Homes & Their History. Nola M. Ross. (Illus.). 72p. 1999. lib. bdg. 25.00 (1-887144-11-0) N M Ross.
Louisiana's Antebellum Architecture. John Desmond. 1970. 25.00 (0-87511-023-1) Claitors.
***Louisiana's BIG Activity Book.** Carole Marsh. (Louisiana Experience! Ser.). (Illus.). (J). (gr. k-5). 2000. pap. 9.95 (0-7933-9550-X) Gallopade Intl.
Louisiana's Capitols: The Power & the Beauty. Lawrence N. Powell. (Illus.). 144p. 1995. 35.00 (0-917541-03-0) Galerie Pr.
Louisiana's Cooking Secrets: Starring Louisiana's Finest Cajun & Creole Cookery. Kathleen D. Fish. Ed. by Judy Marks. LC 97-71560. (Illus.). 272p. 1997. pap. text 15.95 (1-883214-16-5) Bon Vivant Pr.
Louisiana's French Heritage. abr. rev. ed. Truman Stacey. (Illus.). 192p. 1990. 14.95 (0-925417-02-5) Acadian Hse Pub.
Louisiana's German Heritage: Louis Voss' Introductory History. Ed. by Don H. Tolzmann. (Illus.). 121p. 1994. reprint ed. pap. text 14.50 (1-55613-979-9) Heritage Bk.
Louisiana's Gothic Revival Architecture. Philippe Oszuscik. 1973. 15.00 (0-87511-093-2) Claitors.
***Louisiana's Historic Towns: Techland Edition.** Jess R. DeHart. Ed. by Melanie Hamlet DeHart. (Illus.). 71p. 2000. pap. 9.95 (0-913861-04-9) Hamlet Hse.
Louisiana's Loss, Mississippi's Gain: A History of Hancock County, Mississippi: From the Stone Age to the Space Age. Robert G. Scharff. LC 98-28171. 741p. 1999. 39.95 (1-55618-176-0) Brunswick Pub.
Louisiana's (Most Devastating!) Disasters & (Most Calamitous!) Catastrophies! Carole Marsh. (Carole Marsh Louisiana Bks.). (Illus.). (J). (gr. 3-8). 1994. pap. 19.95 (0-7933-0498-9); lib. bdg. 29.95 (0-7933-0499-7) Gallopade Intl.
Louisiana's (Most Devastating!) Disasters & (Most Calamitous!) Catastrophies! Carole Marsh. (Carole Marsh Louisiana Bks.). (Illus.). (J). (gr. 3-8). 1997. disk 29.95 (0-7933-0500-4) Gallopade Intl.
Louisiana's Native Americans: A Mournful Memory - Written in Blood. Margot Soule. Ed. by Margaret Thornton. (Illus.). 200p. Date not set. pap. write for info. (1-887875-14-X) Neshoba tek Pr.
Louisiana's Native Americans: A Mournful Memory - Written in Blood. Margot Soule. Ed. by Margaret Thornton. (Illus.). 200p. 1998. lib. bdg. write for info. (1-887875-15-8) Neshoba tek Pr.
Louisiana's New Garde. Nancy R. Ryan. Ed. by Carolyn Miller. LC 94-76410. (Illus.). 162p. 1994. 29.95 (0-929714-63-6); pap. 24.95 (0-929714-64-4) Great Chefs TV.
Louisiana's Plantation Homes: The Grace & Grandeur. Joe Arrigo. LC 90-44419. (Illus.). 112p. (Orig.). 1991. pap. 19.95 (0-89658-122-5) Voyageur Pr.
Louisiana's Unsolved Mysteries (And Their "Solutions") Includes Scientific Information & Other Activities for Students. Carole Marsh. (Carole Marsh Louisiana Bks.). (Illus.). (J). (gr. 3-12). 1994. pap. 19.95 (0-7933-5777-2); lib. bdg. 29.95 (0-7933-5776-4); disk 29.95 (0-7933-5778-0) Gallopade Intl.
Louisiane. Marcel Ayme. (FRE.). 248p. 1961. pap. 22.95 (0-7859-0415-8, M83980) Fr & Eur.
Louisiane. 2nd ed. Richard Bilzer. LC 99-23998. (FRE., Illus.). 416p. 1999. pap. text 23.95 (1-56554-678-4) Pelican.
Louisiane Aujourd'hui. 2nd ed. Michel Tauriac. (Illus.). 240p. 26.95 (1-56554-053-0) Pelican.
Louisiane Aujourd'hui. 6th ed. Michel Tauriac. (FRE., Illus.). 240p. 1998. 26.95 (1-56554-406-4) Pelican.
Louisiane Aujourhui. 3rd ed. Michel Tauric. 1998. 26.95 (1-56554-366-1) Pelican.
Louisianians All. Jeanne Frois. LC 92-19208. (Illus.). 144p. (J). 1991. 11.95 (0-88289-824-8) Pelican.
Louisville: A River Serenade. Bob Hill et al. LC 95-51557. (Urban Tapestry Ser.). (Illus.). 240p. 1995. 39.50 (1-881096-26-2) Towery Pub.
Louisville: Architecture & the Urban Environment. William Morgan. LC 79-631. 1979. 15.00 (0-87233-050-8) Bauhan.
Louisville: In Celebration Of. Martin E. Biemer. 368p. (YA). (gr. 7 up). 1988. 39.95 (0-89781-239-5) Am Historical Pr.
Louisville & Nashville: The Old Reliable. Charles Castner. (Illus.). 240p. 1996. 29.95 (1-883089-19-0) TLC VA.
***Louisville & Nashville Passenger Trains: The Pan American Era, 1921-1971.** Charles B. Castner et al. (Illus.). 240p. 2000. 33.95 (1-883089-49-2, Pub. by TLC VA) Motorbooks Intl.
***Louisville & Nashville Railroad, 1850-1963.** Kincaid A. Herr. (Illus.). 408p. 2000. reprint ed. 35.00 (0-8131-2184-1) U Pr of Ky.
***Louisville Cardinal Football.** Jim Bolus & Billy Reed. (Illus.). 160p. 1999. 24.95 (1-58382-048-5, Pub. by Sports Masters) Partners-West.
Louisville Diamonds. Turner Publishing Company Staff. 192p. Date not set. 34.95 (1-56311-323-6) Turner Pub KY.
Louisville Easy Finder Plus. Rand McNally Staff. LC 98-681876. (Easy Finder Plus Ser.). 1998. 9.95 (0-528-97214-6) Rand McNally.
Louisville Fire Department, Vol. II. Louisville Division of Fire Staff. LC 88-51134. (Illus.). 144p. 1988. 39.95 (1-56311-337-6) Turner Pub KY.
Louisville Guide Book for Kids. Buchart & Associates, Inc. Staff. 36p. (J). (ps-5). 1993. pap. 2.75 (1-883900-02-6) Buchart & Assocs.
Louisville-Nashville Diesel Locomotives. Ron Flanery. 168p. 1998. 26.95 (1-883089-31-X) TLC VA.
***Louisville Slugger Book of Great Hitters.** D. W. Crisfield. LC 97-45744. (Louisville Slugger Ser.). 192p. (J). (gr. 4-8). 1998. pap. 12.95 (0-471-19772-6) Wiley.
***Louisville Slugger Complete Book of Pitching.** Doug Myers & Mark Gola. LC 99-46713. 224p. 2000. pap. 17.95 (0-8092-2668-5, 266850, Contemporary Bks) NTC Contemp Pub Co.
Louisville Slugger Complete Book of Women's Fast-Pitch Softball. John Monteleone & Deborah Crisfield. LC 98-55221. (Illus.). 240p. 1999. pap. 19.95 (0-8050-5809-5, Pub. by H Holt & Co) VHPS.
***Louisville Slugger Presents Batting Around: A Comprehensive Collection of Hitting Achievements, Anecdotes & Analyses.** Doug Myers. LC 99-86838. (Illus.). 400p. 2000. pap. 19.95 (0-8092-2519-0, Contemporary Bks) NTC Contemp Pub Co.
Louisville Slugger Ultimate Book of Hitting. John J. Monteleone & Mark Gola. LC 96-46283. 1995. pap. 16.95 (0-8050-4413-2) H Holt & Co.
Louisville's Early Medicine Bottles. Gene Blasi. (Illus.). 95p. 1992. pap. write for info. (0-9645406-0-6) G Blasi.
Louisville's First Families: A Series of Genealogical Sketches. Kathleen Jennings. (Illus.). 176p. 1997. reprint ed. lib. bdg. 25.00 (0-8328-6736-5) Higginson Bk Co.
***Louisville/Southern Indiana Entertainment, 2000.** (Illus.). 518p. 1999. pap. 25.00 (1-58553-036-0, 0056) Enter Pubns.
Loukoum: The Little Prince of Belleville. Calixthe Beyala. LC 96-145955. (African Writers Ser.). 160p. 1995. pap. 10.95 (0-435-90968-1) Heinemann.
***Loula Grace Erdman.** Steck-Vaughn Company Staff. (Southwest Writers Ser.). (Illus.). (J). 2000. pap. 15.75 (0-8114-3896-1) Raintree Steck-V.
***LouLou's Dot-to-Dot.** Illus. by J. J. Rudisill et al. 32p. (J). 1999. pap. 2.99 (0-88724-485-8) Carson-Dellos.
***LouLou's Lemonade Stand.** Illus. by J. J. Rudisill et al. (Wimzie's House Bks.). 24p. (J). 1999. pap. 3.99 (0-88724-541-2, CD-4847) Carson-Dellos.
Lounge Lizard Journal. (Illus.). 128p. 18.95 (0-8118-2027-0) Chronicle Bks.
***Lounge Music.** 160p. 1998. otabind 14.95 (0-7935-9650-5) H Leonard.
Lounge Music Collection. 192p. 1997. per. 14.95 (0-7935-7593-1) H Leonard.
Loup-Garou. Boris Vian. (FRE.). 192p. 1984. pap. 13.95 (0-686-55701-8, 2264009314) Fr & Eur.
Loup-Garou of Cote Gelee. Morris Raphael. (Illus.). 48p. (J). (gr. 3-9). 1990. 19.95 (0-9608866-7-2) M Raphael.
Lourdes see Trois Villes
***Lourdes.** Rene Lauterin. (SPA.). 1999. 24.95 (84-08-02180-X) Planeta Edit.
***Lourdes.** Emile Zola. LC 99-89218. (Literary Classics). 504p. 2000. pap. 9.95 (1-57392-828-3) Prometheus Bks.
Lourdes. Emile Zola. Tr. by Ernest Alfred Vizetelly from FRE. LC 93-20801. (Pocket Classics Ser.). xii, 492p. 1993. pap. 10.95 (0-7509-0452-6, Pub. by Sutton Pub Ltd) Intl Pubs Mktg.
***Lourdes: Body & Spirit in the Secular Age.** Ruth Harris. 2000. pap. 17.00 (0-14-019618-8) Penguin Putnam.
Lourdes: City of the Sick. Catherine T. Watling. 124p. 1996. pap. 39.95 (0-85439-445-1, Pub. by St Paul Pubns) St Mut.
Lourdes: English Edition. Giulia Menotti. Tr. by Merry Orling. 64p. pap. text 9.95 (88-7009-025-6, Pub. by Bonechi) Eiron.
Lourdes: The Original File by a Skeptic Turned Believer. unabridged ed. J. B. Estrade. Tr. by J. H. LeBreton Girdlestone from FRE. LC 99-71180. 222p. 1999. pap. 14.95 (0-87243-244-0) Templegate.
Lourdes City Plan. (Grafocarte Maps Ser.). 1994. 8.95 (2-7416-0076-7, 80076) Michelin.
Lourdes of Arizona. Carlos Amantea. 150p. 1989. 17.95 (0-917320-30-1); pap. 10.95 (0-917320-11-5) Mho & Mho.
Louring Skies. William Radice. 72p. 1985. pap. 14.95 (0-85646-153-9, Pub. by Anvil Press) Dufour.
Lourmarin in the Eighteenth Century: A Study of a French Village. Thomas F. Sheppard. LC 79-126803. (Johns Hopkins University Studies in Historical & Political Science: Vol. 88 No. 2). 264p. reprint ed. pap. 81.90 (0-608-14484-3, 202530200043) Bks Demand.
L'Ourse Blanche see White Bear
Lou's Easy Cooking for One. Lou D. Taylor. LC 96-79732. (Illus.). 152p. 1997. 16.95 (0-9655612-1-6) Laurel Pub SC.
***Lou's on First: A Biography of Lou Costello.** Chris Costello. 2000. pap. 17.95 (0-8154-1083-2) Cooper Sq.
Lou's on First: The Biography of Lou Costello. Chris Costello. (Illus.). 384p. 1982. pap. 9.95 (0-312-49914-0) St Martin.
Louse: A Novel. David Grand. LC 98-20281. 272p. 1998. 23.95 (1-55970-449-7, Pub. by Arcade Pub Inc) Time Warner.
Louse: A Novel. David Grand. LC 99-45563. 2000. pap. 13.00 (0-15-600900-5) Harcourt.
Louisiana Mounds Society Newsletter Vol. 2: Years Six & Seven. Ed. by Jean Hunt. (Illus.). 305p. 1993. pap. 25.00 (0-9626812-5-3) Hunt Asso LA.
Lousy Foreigner: A Memoir. 2nd ed. H. M. Payan. LC 98-75084. 420p. 1998. reprint ed. pap. 12.95 (1-891231-10-3) Word Assn.
Lousy Reb. large type ed. John Dyson. (Dales Large Print Ser.). 242p. 1997. pap. 18.99 (1-85389-764-7, Dales) Ulverscroft.
Lout Rampage! Dan Clowes. 96p. 1992. per. 14.95 (1-56097-070-7) Fantagraph Bks.
Louth, Mablethorpe & Willoughby Loop. A. J. Ludlam. 64p. (C). 1985. 39.00 (0-85361-354-0) St Mut.
Louth to Bardney Branch. A. J. Ludlam & W. B. Herbert. 52p. (C). 1985. 39.00 (0-85361-348-6) St Mut.
Louvain Faculty of Theology in the Nineteenth Century: A Bibliography of the Professors in Theology & Canon Law: With Biographical Notes. Leo Kenis. LC 95-109425. (Annua Nuntia Lovaniensia Ser.). 229p. 1994. write for info. (90-6831-583-8) Peeters Pub.
Louves. Boileau-Narcejac. (FRE.). 1973. pap. 10.95 (0-7859-1744-6, 2070363856) Fr & Eur.
***Louvre.** Alexandra Bonfante-Warren. (Illus.). 320p. 2000. 75.00 (0-88363-501-1, Pub. by H L Levin) Publishers Group.
***Louvre.** Konemann Inc. Staff. 2000. 14.95 (3-8290-2647-1) Konemann.
Louvre. Michel Laclotte. (Illus.). 1996. pap. 4.95 (0-89659-097-6) Abbeville Pr.
***Louvre.** Anette Robinson. 1998. pap. text 12.95 (2-86656-121-X) Scala Edit.
Louvre: An Architectural History. Genevieve Bresc. LC 95-15362. (Illus.). 224p. 1995. text 75.00 (0-86565-963-X) Vendome.
***Louvre: Egyptian Antiquities.** (Illus.). 360p. 2000. 24.95 (2-86656-153-8, Pub. by Scala Edit) Antique Collect.
Louvre: Egyptian Antiquities. Christiane Ziegler. 1993. 19.95 (2-86656-077-9, Pub. by Scala Edit) Rizzoli Intl.
Louvre: European Paintings. Michel Laclotte & Jean-Pierre Cuzin. LC 82-61016. (Illus.). 256p. 1983. 40.00 (0-935748-49-0) Scala Books.
***Louvre: European Paintings.** (Illus.). 288p. 2000. 24.95 (2-86656-154-6, Pub. by Scala Edit) Antique Collect.
Louvre: European Paintings. Michel Laclotte & Jean-Pierre Cuzin. (Illus.). 288p. 1997. 40.00 (1-85759-026-0) Scala Books.
Louvre: Greek, Etruscan & Roman Antiquities. Alain Pasquier. (Illus.). 96p. 1991. 30.00 (1-870248-79-1) Scala Books.
Louvre: Near Eastern Antiquities. Annie Caubet & Marthe Bernus-Taylor. (Illus.). 96p. 1991. 30.00 (1-870248-80-5) Scala Books.
Louvre: Portrait of a Museum. Nicholas D. Archimbaud. LC 98-17163. 336p. 1998. 60.00 (1-55670-625-1) Stewart Tabori & Chang.
***Louvre & the Musee d'Orsay, 2 vols.** Alexandra Bonfante-Warren. 2000. boxed set 100.00 (0-88363-503-8, Pub. by H L Levin) Publishers Group.
Louvre Egyptian Antiquities. Ziegler & Michel Laclotte. (Illus.). 296p. 1994. 30.00 (1-85754-857-4) Scala Books.
Louvre European Sculpture. Jean-Rene Gaborit. (Illus.). 128p. 1994. 30.00 (1-85759-044-9) Scala Books.
***Louvre 500 Masterpieces.** Scala Editors. (Illus.). 1999. pap. 19.95 (2-86656-207-0) Scala Edit.
***Louvre 500 Pieces.** Scala Editors. 1999. pap. 19.95 (2-86656-152-X) Scala Edit.
Louvre, Green, Etruscan & Roman Antiquities. Scala Editors. (Illus.). 1993. 19.95 (2-86656-082-5, Pub. by Scala Edit) Rizzoli Intl.
Louvre, Objets d'Art. Daniel Alcouffe & Jannic Durand. (Illus.). 128p. 1995. 30.00 (0-302-00675-3) Scala Books.
Lovable Character Cakes. Debbie Brown. (Illus.). 1999. 14.95 (1-85391-727-3) Tuttle Pubng.
Lovable Furry Old Grover's Resting Places. Jon Stone. LC 83-21087. (Pictureback Ser.). (Illus.). 32p. (J). (ps-3). 1984. pap. 3.25 (0-394-86056-X, Pub. by Random Bks Yng Read) Random.
***Lovable Ladybug.** Becky Freeman. LC 99-53239. (Gabe & Critters Ser.). (Illus.). 32p. (J). (ps-3). 2000. 9.99 (0-7814-3341-X) Chariot Victor.
Lovable Lulaby. Haynes. 1995. 6.98 (1-57042-328-8) Warner Bks.
Lovable Lyle. Bernard Waber. LC 69-14728. (Lyle Ser.). (Illus.). 48p. (J). (ps-3). 1977. 16.00 (0-395-19858-5); pap. 5.95 (0-395-25378-0) HM.
Lovable Lyle. Bernard Waber. (Lyle Ser.). (J). (ps-3). 1979. 11.15 (0-606-00908-6, Pub. by Turtleback) Demco.
Lovable Mini Dolls. Terumi Otaka. (Illus.). 96p. 1982. pap. 17.00 (0-87040-518-7) Japan Pubns USA.
Lovables. Diane Loomans. (Illus.). 10p. (J). (ps). 1996. bds. 4.95 (0-915811-71-5, Starseed) H J Kramer Inc.
Lovables in the Kingdom of Self-Esteem. Diane Loomans. Ed. by Nancy Carleton. LC 90-52633. (Illus.). 32p. (J). (ps-5). 1991. 15.95 (0-915811-25-1, Starseed) H J Kramer Inc.
LovaBULL Stories & Adventures, Vol. 1. Tony Bosserman. LC 96-97175. (Illus.). 92p. (Orig.). (J). (gr. 4-6). 1997. 18.95 (0-9654673-0-9) Cncord Pr.
Love see Human Outcry: Chapbook Collection
Love. Ariel Books Staff. 128p. 1996. 3.95 (0-8362-0969-9, Arie Bks) Andrews & McMeel.
Love. Ariel Books Staff. LC 99-163154. (Tiny Tomes Ser.). 12p. 1997. 3.95 (0-8362-2957-6) Andrews & McMeel.
Love. Jacqueline Syrup Bergan & S. Marie Schwan. (Take & Receive Ser.). 144p. 1985. pap. 6.95 (0-88489-168-2) St Marys.
Love. Alexandra Bonfante-Warren. (Celebrations in Art Ser.). 72p. 1995. 12.98 (1-56799-167-X, MetroBooks) M Friedman Pub Grp Inc.
***Love.** Susan Branch. 2000. pap. 4.95 (0-7683-2184-0) CEDCO Pub.
Love. Leo F. Buscaglia. 1996. pap. 10.00 (0-449-91162-4) Fawcett.
Love. Leo F. Buscaglia. LC 72-92810. 147p. 1972. 9.95 (0-913590-07-X); 15.00 (0-685-72905-2) SLACK Inc.
Love. Ernesto Cardenal. 142p. 1994. pap. 21.00 (0-85532-344-2, Pub. by Srch Pr) St Mut.
Love. Angela Carter. 128p. 1988. pap. 10.95 (0-14-010851-3, Penguin Bks) Viking Penguin.
Love. Concordia Publishing Staff. (Connections Ser.). 1994. pap. 4.50 (0-570-09369-4, 20-2466) Concordia.
***Love.** Disney Staff. (Illus.). 48p. (J). (ps-3). 2000. pap. 4.95 (0-7407-1039-7) Andrews & McMeel.
***Love.** Linda Eyre & Richard Eyre. (Teaching Your Children Values Ser.). 32p. (J). (ps-7). 2000. pap. 16.95 incl. audio (1-56015-786-0) Penton Overseas.
Love. Elaine Goley. (Learn the Value Ser.). (Illus.). 32p. (J). (gr. 1-4). 1987. 11.95 (0-685-67578-5); lib. bdg. 132.66 (0-317-60399-X) Rourke Corp.
Love. Carolyn J. Griffin. (Lyrics on Matters Relating to Ser.). 10p. 1985. 8.00 (1-929388-06-3) Griffin Pubg Co Inc.
Love. Keith Haring. LC 98-49697. 80p. 1999. 12.95 (0-8212-2556-1, Pub. by Bulfinch Pr) Little.
***Love.** Honor Books Publishing Staff. (Fruit of the Spirit Ser.). 96p. 2000. 9.99 (1-56292-658-6) Honor Bks OK.
***Love.** Yves Saint Laurent & Marie-Paule Pelle. (Illus.). 80p. 2000. 12.95 (0-8109-3584-8, Pub. by Abrams) Time Warner.
Love. Love. 100p. 1982. pap. 4.75 (0-9608692-0-4) Love.
Love. Valerie Martin. (Illus.). 1976. pap. 4.50 (0-89924-004-6) Lynx Hse.
Love. Mary. 1959. pap. 4.50 (0-87516-056-5) DeVorss.
***Love.** Peter Nadas. Tr. by Imre Goldstein from HUN. LC 00-27908. 128p. 2000. 20.00 (0-374-19228-6) FS&G.
***Love.** SOLLY OZROVECH. 1999. pap. 3.95 (0-86997-708-3) Lux Verbi.
Love. Peter L. Scazzero. (Fruit of the Spirit Bible Studies). 48p. 1991. pap. 5.99 (0-310-53721-5) Zondervan.
Love. St. Paul Publications Staff. (C). 1990. text 29.00 (0-85439-355-2, Pub. by St Paul Pubns) St Mut.
Love. Stendhal, pseud. Tr. by Gilbert Sale & Suzanne Sale. (Classics Ser.). 336p. 1975. pap. 11.95 (0-14-044307-X, Penguin Classics) Viking Penguin.
Love, 9 vols. Robert Strand. LC 99-64007. (Nine Fruits of the Spirit Ser.). 48p. 1999. 3.99 (0-89221-461-9) New Leaf Pr.
Love. Christine Tarantino. 14p. 1997. ring bd. 2.95 (1-887480-45-5) Wrds Lght Intl.
Love. Luegenia Van Buskirk. 1997. pap. write for info. (1-57553-600-5) Watermrk Pr.
Love. Illus. & Des. by Gian B. Vanni. LC 64-24622. 78p. (J). 1997. 20.00 (0-8076-1426-2) Braziller.
***Love.** Lux Vergi. 1999. pap. 4.95 (0-86997-772-5) Lux Verbi.
Love. VITTORIA STUDIOS Staff. 1999. 8.95 (0-7683-2108-5) CEDCO Pub.
***Love.** Warner Press Publishers Staff. (Lion Cub Upside-Down Books Ser.). (Illus.). (J). 2000. pap. 5.95 (0-87162-826-0) Warner Pr.
Love. Sherryl Woods. 1992. per. 3.39 (0-373-09769-7, 5-09769-6) Silhouette.
Love. Lao Russell. (Illus.). 207p. 1980. reprint ed. text 4.00 (1-879605-21-X) U Sci & Philos.
Love. Elizabeth Von Arnim. Ed. by Donna Ng. 288p. 1995. reprint ed. per. 12.00 (0-671-88392-5, WSP) PB.
Love. rev. ed. Jane Belk Moncure. (Child's World of Values Ser.). (Illus.). 24p. (J). (ps-3). 1996. lib. bdg. 18.50 (1-56766-298-6) Childs World.
***Love.** unabridged ed. Charles Ferry. LC 00-90402. (Illus.). 91p. 2000. pap. 12.00 (0-9632799-4-7) DaisyHill Pr.
Love: A Book of Poetry. (Illus.). 80p. 1992. 4.95 (0-8362-3009-4) Andrews & McMeel.
Love: A Book of Quotations. Ed. by Herb Galewitz. LC 99-207579. 64p. 1998. pap. 1.00 (0-486-40004-2) Dover.
Love: A Book of Remembrances. Nichol. 134p. pap. 14.95 (0-88922-038-7, Pub. by Talonbks) Genl Dist Srvs.
Love: A Celebration. Ed. by Helen Exley. (Suedel Giftbooks Ser.). (Illus.). 64p. 1993. 12.00 (1-85015-453-8) Exley Giftbooks.
Love: A Celebration in Art & Literature. Ed. by Jane Lahr & Lena Tabori. LC 82-5680. (Illus.). 240p. 1982. 45.00 (0-941434-20-6) Stewart Tabori & Chang.
Love: A Century of Love & Passion. Florence Montreynaud. (Illus.). 400p. 1998. 39.99 (3-8228-7645-3) Taschen Amer.
Love: A Fairy Tale for Grown-Up Children. Leo F. Buscaglia. 1995. 9.95 (0-03-063201-3) Harcourt Coll Pubs.
***Love: A Giftbook with Envelope.** Nancy Cogan Akmon. Tr. & Des. by Roni Akmon. (Giftbook Ser.). (Illus.). 48p. 1999. 6.95 (1-884807-40-2, EC 708) Blushing Rose.
Love: A Philosophical Perspective. 2nd ed. Marty Richards & Richard C. Richardson. 192p. (C). 1994. 41.00 (0-536-58501-6) Pearson Custom.
Love: A Pop-Up Book. (Tiny Tomes Ser.). 12p. 1997. 3.95 (0-614-24602-4, Arie Bks) Andrews & McMeel.
Love: A Somatic View. Stanley Keleman. (Clinical Education in Somatic Process Ser.). 90p. (Orig.). 1994. pap. 12.00 (0-934320-15-2) Center Pr.
Love: A User's Guide. Clare Naylor. LC 98-49247. 1999. pap. 12.95 (0-449-00556-9) Fawcett.

An Asterisk (*) at the beginning of an entry indicates that the title is appearing for the first time.

Love: A User's Guide - Intimacy from Birth to Death. Jane Knowles. 224p. 1991. pap. 17.50 (*0-04-440855-2*, Pub. by Rivers Oram) NYU Pr.

Love: Animals & the Law. Mark Love. 1997. pap. write for info. (*0-406-04967-X*, LAL, MICHIE) LEXIS Pub.

Love: Christian Romance, Marriage, Friendship. 2nd ed. Diogenes Allen. 168p. (Orig.). 1997. reprint ed. pap. write for info. (*0-9653625-1-5*) Caroline Pr.

Love: Classics from Modern Library. Modern Library Staff. LC 98-34560. 224p. 1999. pap. 12.95 (*0-375-75309-5*) Modern Lib NY.

Love: Emotion, Myth, & Metaphor. Robert C. Solomon. LC 89-39922. 383p. 1990. pap. 21.95 (*0-87975-569-5*) Prometheus Bks.

Love: Jewels from the Words of Abdu'l-Baha. Abdu'l-Baha. 48p. 1994. pap. 5.95 (*1-870989-34-1*) Bahai.

Love: Leap of the Heart & a Sweet Tear. 112p. 1996. 16.95 (*0-9617268-5-7*) Satori Pr.

Love: Making It Last. Barry St. Clair & Bill Jones. (Love/Sex/Dating Series). 140p. (YA). 1993. pap. 7.99 (*1-56476-188-6*, 6-3188, Victor Bks) Chariot Victor.

***Love: Meditations on Love.** Wendy Beckett. 48p. 2000. 9.95 (*0-7894-5338-X*, D K Ink) DK Pub Inc.

Love: Poems. Danielle Steel. 256p. 1989. mass mkt. 6.99 (*0-440-15377-8*) Dell.

Love: Poems. abr. ed. Danielle Steel. 168p. 1984. 19.95 (*0-385-29363-1*) Delacorte.

***Love: Poems for the Romantic Heart.** D. N. Sutton. vi, 26p. 1999. pap. 10.00 (*0-940361-20-5*) Sherwood-Spencer Pub.

Love: Proverbs of the Heart. Wolfgang Mieder. LC 89-63662. (Illus.). 80p. (Orig.). 1989. pap. 6.95 (*0-933050-63-1*) New Eng Pr VT.

***Love Quotations from the Heart, Mini Edition.** Running Press Staff. 1999. 4.95 (*0-7624-0665-8*) Running Pr.

***Love: Short Stories.** Valerie Martin. LC 99-28391. 79p. 1999. pap. 14.95 (*0-9668612-3-X*, Pub. by Lost Horse) SPD-Small Pr Dist.

Love: Ten Poems by Pablo Neruda. Pablo Neruda. LC 97-193693. 48p. (J). 1995. pap. 6.70 (*0-7868-8148-8*, Pub. by Hyperion) Time Warner.

Love: The Breath of Life. Asher. 160p. (Orig.). 1995. pap. 8.50 (*0-9636109-1-0*) Nuf-Love Pub.

Love: The Course They Forgot to Teach You in School. Gregory J. Godek. LC 97-22797. 480p. 1997. pap. 14.95 (*1-57071-199-2*, Casablanca) Sourcebks.

Love: The Greatest Gift of All. Phyllis J. Le Peau. (LifeGuide Bible Studies). 64p. 1997. pap. 4.99 (*0-8308-1083-8*, 1083) InterVarsity.

Love: The Greatest Thing in the World : A Classic Devotional Study On 1 Corinthians 13. rev. ed. Lewis A. Drummond & Henry Drummond. LC 97-30340. 208p. 1998. pap. 6.99 (*0-8254-2470-4*) Kregel.

Love: The "L" Word. 2nd rev. ed. Jay Carter. Ed. by Margaret Verhulst. (Illus.). 80p. Date not set. pap. 9.95 (*0-937004-13-8*) Unicorn PA.

Love: The Secret to Your Success. Gloria Copeland. 13p. 1992. pap. 1.00 (*0-88114-798-2*) K Copeland Pubns.

Love: The Story of Elizabeth Barrett Browning. Mary Logue. LC 95-44422. (Value Biographies Ser.). (Illus.). 32p. (J). 1997. lib. bdg. 21.36 (*1-56766-225-0*, 62250) Childs World.

Love: The Way to Victory. Kenneth E. Hagin. LC 96-117827. 290p. 1994. pap. 9.95 (*0-89276-523-2*) Faith Lib Pubns.

Love: 31 Reflections on Christian Virtue, 3 vols., Vol. 1. Carl Koch. (31 Reflections on Christian Virtue Ser.). 96p. 1996. pap. 6.95 (*0-88489-383-9*) St Marys.

***Love Vol. 3034: 16 Acid-Free Papers for Scrapbooks & More!** Ed. by Suzanne McNeill. (Illus.). 16p. 1999. 6.30 (*1-893749-17-7*) Fiskars.

Love - A Fruit Always in Season: Daily Meditations from the Words of Mother Teresa of Calcutta. Ed. by Dorothy S. Hunt. LC 86-81472. (Illus.). 260p. (Orig.). 1987. pap. 10.95 (*0-89870-167-8*) Ignatius Pr.

Love - & Other Things. Beth D. Nordby. 1992. 14.95 (*0-533-10026-7*) Vantage.

Love, - & the Philosopher: A Study in Sentiment (1923) Marie Corelli. 287p. 1996. reprint ed. pap. 17.95 (*1-56459-727-X*) Kessinger Pub.

LOVE - From Black Men to Black Women. Ed. by Frances J. Barnes. 78p. 1996. reprint ed. pap. 9.95 (*0-9650742-0-X*) LOVE LINE.

LOVE - From Black Women to Black Men. Ed. by Frances J. Barnes. 79p. 1996. pap. 9.95 (*0-9650742-1-8*) LOVE LINE.

Love - Impact on Physical & Mental Health: The Lack of Love, While Interacting with a Multitude of Other Co-Factors, Is the Most Significant & Influential Contributing Factor in the Majority (Not All) of Both Mental & Physical Illnesses. Peter R. Schemm. 207p. (Orig.). 1996. pap. 10.00 (*0-9656746-0-6*, 9625448) P Schemm.

Love - The Driving Force: Mary Ward's Spirituality: Its Significance for Moral Thought. Jeanne Cover. LC 96-51198. (Studies in Theology: No. 13). 217p. (Orig.). 1997. pap. 25.00 (*0-87462-637-4*) Marquette.

Love - Where to Find It, How to Keep It. Elle Becker. 106p. (Orig.). 1991. pap. 6.95 (*0-915708-32-9*) Cheever Pub.

Love--or Mush? Six Action-Packed Lessons on 1 Corinthians 13: 1-6 to Use with Junior Highers. Scott E. Osenbaugh. LC 87-80603. (Illus.). 96p. (gr. 4-7). 1988. pap., teacher ed. 7.95 (*0-88243-745-3*, 02-0745) Gospel Pub.

Love, a Celebration. Ed. by Helen Exley. (Sharon Bassin Covers Ser.). (Illus.). 64p. 1997. 9.00 (*1-85015-897-5*) Exley Giftbooks.

Love a Hostage. large type ed. Grace Lang. (Linford Romance Library). 272p. 1993. pap. 16.99 (*0-7089-7324-8*, Linford) Ulverscroft.

Love a Journey of Discovery: Selected Poems. Erika H. Niemann. LC 99-94714. xvi, 125p. 1999. pap. 10.95 (*0-9670746-0-6*, 1) Close Connects Pubg.

Love a Rebel . . . Love a Rogue. Shirl Henke. 448p. 1998. mass mkt. 5.99 (*0-8439-4406-4*, Leisure Bks) Dorchester Pub Co.

Love a Rebel, Love a Rogue. Shirl Henke. 448p. (Orig.). 1994. pap. text, mass mkt. 4.99 (*0-8439-3673-8*) Dorchester Pub Co.

Love Abounding. G. D. Watson. 1988. pap. 13.99 (*0-88019-230-5*) Schmul Pub Co.

Love above All & Other Drawings. George Grosz. Tr. by Stanley Appelbaum. (GER., Illus.). 120p. (Orig.). 1971. pap. text 7.95 (*0-486-22675-1*) Dover.

***Love According to Teresa.** Florence Boutwell. LC 99-89760. (Illus.). (YA). 2000. write for info. (*0-87062-298-6*, Millwood Pub) A H Clark.

Love Across Color Lines: Ottilie Assing & Frederick Douglass. Maria Diedrich. LC 98-25224. (Illus.). 352p. 1999. 25.00 (*0-8090-1613-3*) Hill & Wang.

***Love Across Color Lines: Ottilie Assing & Frederick Douglass.** Maria Diedrich. (Illus.). 512p. 2000. pap. 15.00 (*0-8090-6686-6*) Hill & Wang.

Love Across the Color Line: The Letters of Alice Hanley to Channing Lewis. Helen L. Horowitz & Kathy Peiss. LC 95-49936. (Illus.). 144p. (C). 1996. 35.00 (*1-55849-023-X*); pap. 15.95 (*1-55849-024-8*) U of Mass Pr.

***Love Across the Water.** Julia Clarke. 224p. 2000. 18.99 (*0-7089-5700-5*) Ulverscroft.

Love Addiction: A Guide to Emotional Independence. Martha R. Bireda & Mike Link. (Illus.). 224p. 1990. pap. 14.95 (*0-934986-91-6*) New Harbinger.

Love Addiction: Help Yourself Out. Brenda Schaeffer. 36p. (Orig.). 1986. pap. 3.25 (*0-89486-383-5*, 5208B) Hazelden.

Love Adds a Little Chocolate: 100 Stories to Brighten Your Day & Sweeten Your Life. Medard Laz. 224p. 1998. 14.00 (*0-446-52424-7*, Pub. by Warner Bks) Little.

***Love Adds the Chocolate.** Linda Andersen. (Illus.). 32p. 2000. 10.95 (*1-57856-325-9*) Waterbrook Pr.

***Love Adds the Chocolate.** Linda Andersen. (Illus.). 32p. 2000. 10.95 (*1-57856-377-1*) Waterbrook Pr.

Love Aesthetics of Maurice Sceve: Poetry & Struggle. Jerry C. Nash. (Cambridge Studies in French: No. 34). 217p. (C). 1991. text 64.95 (*0-521-39412-0*) Cambridge U Pr.

***Love Affair: A Memoir of Jackson Pollock.** Ruth Kligman. LC 99-44604. (Illus.). 224p. 1999. pap. 16.95 (*0-8154-1009-3*) Cooper Sq.

Love Affair: A Prayer Journal. Andrew M. Greeley. 192p. 1993. reprint ed. pap. 10.95 (*0-8245-1369-X*) Crossroad NY.

Love Affair: The Story of the Sirak Art Collection. Babette Sirak & Kirsten Chapman. (Illus.). 73p. 1991. pap. 22.95 (*0-918881-29-3*) Columbus Mus Art.

Love Affair As a Work of Art. Dan Hofstadter. 304p. 1996. 24.00 (*0-374-19231-6*) FS&G.

Love Affair As a Work of Art. Dan Hofstadter. 336p. 1997. pap. text 13.00 (*0-374-52485-8*, Noonday) FS&G.

Love Affair of Fran & Maurie. Fran Sumner. Ed. by Judy Horst. (Illus.). 154p. 1997. 15.00 (*0-88197-100-6*) Group Fore Prods.

Love Affair of Mr. Ding & Mrs. Dong. Lionel Koechlin. (Child's World Library). (Illus.). 32p. (J). (gr. k-5). 1992. lib. bdg. 18.50 (*0-89565-817-8*) Childs World.

Love Affair with God. Anthony J. Asalone. Date not set. pap. write for info. (*0-9673212-1-2*) Gods Love Pub.

Love Affair with Life. Mira Mataric. LC 98-85388. 325p. 1998. 25.00 (*0-9663501-9-7*); pap. 15.00 (*0-7388-0025-2*) Xlibris Corp.

Love Affair with Life & Smithsonian. Edward K. Thompson. LC 95-31054. (Illus.). 320p. (C). 1995. 26.95 (*0-8262-1026-0*) U of Mo Pr.

Love Affair with 100 Cars: And Ultimately with the Ultimate Woman. W. Lawson Jones. Ed. by Terry Dawson. LC 96-92610. (Illus.). viii, 180p. 1997. 17.95 (*0-9654055-0-8*, LV100-1) Schobert Pubng.

Love Affairs: Marriage & Infidelity. Richard Taylor. LC 96-50919. 210p. 1997. pap. 18.95 (*1-57392-128-9*) Prometheus Bks.

Love Affairs: What Everyone Should Know. Francis H. Wise. Ed. & Intro. by Joyce M. Wise. LC 86-51159. 278p. (Orig.). 1986. pap. 8.00 (*0-915766-65-5*) Wise Pub.

Love Affairs of a Bibliomaniac. Eugene Field. (Notable American Authors Ser.). 1992. reprint ed. lib. bdg. 75.00 (*0-7812-2652-X*) Rprt Serv.

Love Affairs of Some Famous Men. Edward J. Hardy. LC 72-4514. (Essay Index Reprint Ser.). 1977. reprint ed. 25.95 (*0-8369-2948-9*) Ayer.

Love Affairs with Barely Any People in Them. Bruce Isaacson. 76p. (Orig.). 1990. pap. 5.95 (*0-929730-18-6*) Zeitgeist Pr.

Love after Death. Mary Jones. 76p. 1994. pap. 12.95 (*1-85302-287-X*) Taylor & Francis.

Love after Life see Power of Love: A Promise Kept

***Love after Life.** D. Patrick Miller. 240p. 2000. pap. 14.95 (*0-9656809-3-2*) Fearless Bks.

Love after the Riots. Juan F. Herrera. 64p. (Orig.). 1996. pap. 10.95 (*1-880684-28-4*) Curbstone.

Love, Again. large type ed. Doris Lessing. LC 96-8526. (Large Print Bks). 1996. 25.95 (*1-56895-341-0*, Compass) Wheeler Pub.

Love Again: Novel, A. Doris Lessing. LC 95-53317. 368p. 1997. pap. 13.00 (*0-06-092796-8*, Perennial) HarperTrade.

Love Against Hate. Karl Augustus Menninger. LC 42-50183. 320p. 1959. pap. 10.95 (*0-15-653892-X*, Harvest Bks) Harcourt.

Love Against the Grey Winter Mean. Sam Silva. (Dog River Review Poetry Ser.). 36p. (Orig.). (YA). 1993. pap. 4.00 (*0-916155-23-4*) Trout Creek.

***Love Air: Occasional Lyrics & Poems of the Heart.** Charlotte Ann Frick. (Love Poem Trilogy Ser.: Bk. 1). viii, 106p. 1999. pap. write for info. (*0-9676746-1-1*) J Grey Pr.

Love All. large type ed. Mary Barham. (Linford Romance Library). 256p. 1998. pap. 17.99 (*0-7089-5226-7*, Linford) Ulverscroft.

Love All Creatures. M. S. Kayani. 36p. (J). 1996. pap. 3.50 (*0-614-21024-0*, 737) Kazi Pubns.

Love All Start. large type ed. Margaret A. Carr. (Linford Romance Library). 1991. pap. 16.99 (*0-7089-7043-5*) Ulverscroft.

Love Alone: Eighteen Elegies for Rog. Paul Monette. (Stonewall Inn Editions Ser.). 80p. 1988. pap. 8.95 (*0-312-02602-1*) St Martin.

Love Alone: The Way of Revelation. Hans U. Von Balthasar. 128p. 1989. pap. 22.00 (*0-7220-7728-9*, Pub. by Veritas Pubns) St Mut.

***Love along the Way: A Love Story of a Young Army Soldier & a Cherokee Indian Girl, That Started with the "Trail of Tear" Time 1839-1950.** Ed. by Norman R. Martin & Judy C. Martin Mallins. (Illus.). 96p. 1999. lib. bdg. 8.85 (*0-9646489-8-9*) Martain Pub.

***Love Always.** 80p. 1999. otabind 16.95 (*0-634-00248-1*) H Leonard.

Love Always. Mildred R. Gaston. 1999. mass mkt. 5.99 (*0-345-43258-4*) Ballantine Pub Grp.

Love Always. Mildred E. Riley. 306p. 1997. pap. 10.95 (*1-885478-15-1*, Pub. by Genesis Press) BookWorld.

Love Always: A Novel. Ann Beattie. LC 85-40866. (Vintage Contemporaries Ser.). 256p. 1986. pap. 12.00 (*0-394-74418-7*) Vin Bks.

Love Always Answers: Walking the Path of a Course in Miracles. Diane Berke. 176p. (Orig.). 1994. pap. 11.95 (*0-8245-1432-7*) Crossroad NY.

Love Always, Ginner. Virginia Murrell. 200p. 1996. 19.95 (*1-888321-03-2*) Semco Bks.

Love Always, Mom: How a Family Fights Cancer. Judith Rolfs. 130p. (Orig.). 1997. pap. 11.95 (*1-57502-365-2*, PO1170) Morris Pubng.

***Love Always, Patsy: Patsy Cline's Letters to a Friend.** Cindy Hazen & Mike Freeman. LC 99-39442. 1999. pap. 13.95 (*0-425-17168-X*) Berkley Pub.

Love among Orientals. Maxine Glassman. LC 97-46046. 208p. 1998. pap. 23.95 (*1-55611-529-6*, Pub. by D I Fine) Penguin Putnam.

Love Among the Artists. David Bunn. (Illus.). 160p. 1996. 275.00 (*1-888979-00-3*) D Bunn.

Love among the Centralians. Gertrude Fass. Ed. by William-Alan Landes. LC 96-48549. 72p. 1997. pap. 6.00 (*0-88734-244-2*) Players Pr.

Love among the Guilty. Helen Kitson. 64p. 1996. pap. 16.95 (*1-85224-309-0*, Pub. by Bloodaxe Bks) Dufour.

Love among the Haystacks. D. H. Lawrence. reprint ed. lib. bdg. 20.95 (*0-88411-676-X*) Amereon Ltd.

Love among the Haystacks & Other Pieces. D. H. Lawrence. (Select Bibliographies Reprint Ser.). 1977. reprint ed. 18.95 (*0-518-19074-9*) Ayer.

Love among the Ruins. Angela M. Thirkell. LC 97-6463. 464p. 1997. pap. 13.95 (*1-55921-204-7*) Moyer Bell.

Love among the Ruins: Manuscript Edition. Elmer Rise. 1963. pap. 13.00 (*0-8222-0917-9*) Dramatists Play.

Love Among the Walnuts. Ferris. LC 97-50291. 228p. (YA). (gr. 7 up). 1998. 16.00 (*0-15-201590-6*) Harcourt.

Love among the Wild Gods: Reclaiming True Power & Peace. Joyce Bleiman & Kathleen Boisen. LC 98-21177. 144p. 1998. 17.95 (*1-56474-277-6*) Fithian Pr.

Love among the Xoids. John Sladek. (Booklet Ser.: No. 15). 15p. (Orig.). 1984. pap. 1.00 (*0-936055-12-X*) C Drumm Bks.

Love, an Inner Connection: Based on Principles Drawn from the I Ching. Carol K. Anthony. 168p. (Orig.). 1993. pap. 12.95 (*0-9603832-6-3*) Anthony Pub Co.

Love Analyzed. Ed. by Roger Lamb. LC 96-38902. 288p. (C). 1996. pap. 27.00 (*0-8133-3223-0*, Pub. by Westview); text 75.00 (*0-8133-8891-0*, Pub. by Westview) HarpC.

Love-Ananda Gita (1990), the Santosha Avatara Gita (1995) see Da Love-Ananda Gita: The "Late Time" Avataric Revelation of the Great Means to Worship & Realize the True & Spiritual Divine Person

Love, Anarchy, & Emma Goldman: A Biography. abr. rev. ed. Candace S. Falk. LC 89-10967. (Illus.). 350p. 1990. pap. 16.95 (*0-8135-1513-0*) Rutgers U Pr.

Love & a Wooden Spoon. Charmaine Solomon. (Illus.). 126p. 1994. 20.95 (*0-85572-214-2*, Pub. by Hill Content Pubng) Seven Hills Bk.

Love & Addiction. Stanton Peele & Archie Brodsky. LC 74-5818. 284p. 1975. 16.95 (*0-8008-5041-6*) Taplinger.

Love & Admiration & Respect: The O'Neill-Commins Correspondence. Eugene O'Neill. Ed. by Dorothy Commins. LC 86-6195. xxi, 248p. 1986. text 41.00 (*0-8223-0668-9*) Duke.

Love & Anger. John L. Bell & Graham Maule. 80p. 1998. pap. 8.95 (*1-57999-031-2*, G-4947) GIA Pubns.

Love & Anger. George F. Walker. 96p. 1990. pap. 10.95 (*0-88910-369-0*, Pub. by Talonbks) Genl Dist Srvs.

Love & Anger: Essays on AIDS, Activism, & Politics. Peter F. Cohen. LC 97-51814. 194p. 1998. 39.95 (*0-7890-0455-0*, Harrington Park); pap. 16.95 (*1-56023-930-1*, Harrington Park) Haworth Pr.

Love & Anger: Managing Family Conflict. Mary Tjosvold et al. 180p. (Orig.). 1991. pap. text 12.95 (*0-9621542-1-0*) Team Media.

Love & Anger: The Parental Dilemma. Nancy Samalin & Catherine Whitney. 256p. 1992. pap. 12.95 (*0-14-012992-8*, Penguin Bks) Viking Penguin.

Love & Anger in Marriage. 1984. pap. 7.99 (*0-310-45291-0*, 11258P) Zondervan.

Love & Attachment: Contemporary Issues & Treatment Considerations. Carol Tosone & Theresa G. Aiello. LC 98-36489. 1999. 40.00 (*0-7657-0185-5*) Aronson.

Love & Attachment: or Falling in Love Is B. S. An Unauthorized Psychological Approach. Don Rothbardt & Paul N. Harris. LC 92-34014. 208p. (Orig.). 1992. pap. 11.95 (*0-915180-35-9*) Harrowood Bks.

Love & Awakening: Discovering the Sacred Path of Intimate Relationship. John Welwood. 272p. 1997. pap. 13.00 (*0-06-092797-6*, Perennial) HarperTrade.

Love (And Baby Powder) Covers All. Marilyn G. Barnes. 148p. (Orig.). 1992. pap. 7.95 (*0-939513-88-9*) Joy Pub SJC.

Love & Baseball: Poems. Mark O'Brien & Susan Fernbach. 36p. 1997. pap. 6.00 (*1-891420-04-6*) Lemonade Factory.

Love & Be Loved: Making Love the Most Wonderful Experience in Life. rev. ed. John A. Tamiazzo. 144p. 1989. reprint ed. pap. 9.95 (*0-9621459-0-4*) TPREP.

Love & Being: An Investigation into the Metaphysics of St. Thomas Aquinas. Bernard J. Diggs. 180p. 1947. 15.00 (*0-913298-45-X*) S F Vanni.

Love & Betrayal. Carolyn Keene. (Nancy Drew on Campus Ser.: No. 21). (YA). (gr. 8 up). 1997. per. 3.99 (*0-671-00213-9*, Archway) PB.

Love & Betrayal: A Novel. Muriel Maddox. LC 96-16304. 288p. 1997. 22.95 (*0-86534-249-0*) Sunstone Pr.

Love & Betrayal: Broken Trust in Intimate Relationships. John Amodeo. 304p. (Orig.). 1994. pap. 11.00 (*0-345-37856-3*) Ballantine Pub Grp.

***Love & Bile: Sayings of a Gadfly.** Max Maxwell. (Illus.). xiv, 142p. 2000. pap. 12.95 (*0-9679344-0-0*) Gadfly Pr PA.

Love & Charity. large type ed. Veronica Denham. (Linford Romance Large Print Ser.). 256p. 1998. pap. 17.99 (*0-7089-5239-9*, Linford) Ulverscroft.

Love & Cherish. Dorothy Garlock. 1982. mass mkt. 2.50 (*0-89083-897-6*, Zebra Kensgtn) Kensgtn Pub Corp.

Love & Cherish. large type ed. Dorothy Garlock. LC 98-15573. 1998. 25.95 (*0-7862-1493-7*) Mac Lib Ref.

Love & Cherish. Dorothy Garlock. 352p. 1995. reprint ed. mass mkt. 5.99 (*0-446-36524-6*, Pub. by Warner Bks) Little.

Love & Cherish: Special Edition. Dorothy Garlock. 352p. 1998. reprint ed. mass mkt. 3.99 (*0-446-60648-0*, Pub. by Warner Bks) Little.

Love & Conflict: A Covenantal Model of Christian Ethics. Joseph L. Allen. 336p. (C). 1995. reprint ed. pap. text 28.50 (*0-8191-9763-7*) U Pr of Amer.

Love & Cooking. Venita Cibak. 1991. 21.95 (*0-9629320-0-0*) Cibak & Assocs.

Love & Crush: Poems. Barry Wallenstein. (Orig.). 1991. pap. 10.95 (*0-89255-158-5*) Persea Bks.

Love & Dating. rev. ed. George B. Eager. LC 93-80760. (Illus.). 96p. (YA). (gr. 6-12). 1994. 12.95 (*1-879224-18-6*); pap. 7.95 (*1-879224-11-9*) Mailbox.

Love & Dating & Other Natural Disasters! Ron Wheeler. (Illus.). 96p. (Orig.). (YA). (gr. 7-12). 1993. pap. 6.99 (*0-8341-1505-0*) Beacon Hill.

Love & Death. Vardis Fisher. 21.95 (*0-88411-558-5*) Amereon Ltd.

***Love & Death.** Carolyn G. Hart. LC 00-33692. 2001. write for info. (*0-425-17805-6*, Prime Crime) Berkley Pub.

Love & Death. 5th ed. Sri Aurobindo. 27p. 1990. pap. 1.50 (*81-7058-162-1*, Pub. by SAA) E-W Cultural Ctr.

Love & Death: A Study in Censorship. Gershon Legman. 1963. pap. 1.75 (*0-87817-012-X*) Hacker.

Love & Death, & Other Disasters: Stories, 1977-1995. Jenifer Levin. LC 96-41687. 144p. (Orig.). 1996. pap. 10.95 (*1-56341-078-8*) Firebrand Bks.

Love & Death, & Other Disasters: Stories, 1977-1995. Jenifer Levin. LC 96-41687. 144p. (Orig.). 1996. lib. bdg. 22.95 (*1-56341-079-6*) Firebrand Bks.

Love & Death in Charleston. Patricia Robinson. LC 98-96228. 192p. 1998. 18.95 (*0-8034-9306-1*, Avalon Bks) Bouregy.

Love & Death in London. Created by Francine Pascal. (Sweet Valley High Ser.: No. 104). 224p. (YA). (gr. 7 up). 1994. mass mkt. 3.50 (*0-553-56227-4*) Bantam.

Love & Death in London. Kate William. (Sweet Valley High Ser.: No. 104). (YA). (gr. 7 up). 1994. 8.60 (*0-606-06027-8*, Pub. by Turtleback) Demco.

Love & Death in the American Novel. Leslie A. Fiedler. LC 97-25221. 520p. 1998. reprint ed. pap. 16.95 (*1-56478-163-1*) Dalkey Arch.

Love & Death in the Ancient Near East: Essays in Honor of Marvin H. Pope. Ed. by John H. Marks & Robert M. Good. LC 86-29441. ix, 258p. 1987. text 39.50 (*0-931500-06-0*) Eisenbrauns.

Love & Death on Long Island. Gilbert Adair. LC 98-22274. 144p. 1998. pap. 12.00 (*0-8021-3592-7*, Grove) Grove-Atltic.

Love & Deborah. large type ed. Netta Muskett. 382p. 1982. 27.99 (*0-7089-0776-8*) Ulverscroft.

***Love & Desire: Photoworks.** William A. Ewing. LC 99-34572. (Illus.). 400p. 1999. pap. 35.00 (*0-8118-2621-X*) Chronicle Bks.

Love & Desire & Hate. Joan Collins. Ed. by Julie Rubenstein. 480p. 1991. reprint ed. mass mkt. 5.99 (*0-671-66581-2*) PB.

Love & Devotion. Nitya C. Yati. (C). 1995. reprint ed. 16.00 (*81-246-0058-9*, Pub. by DK Pubs Ind) S Asia.

***Love & Diamonds in 90 Days: A Guide for Everything You Must Know to Play the Dating & Marriage Game for Keeps!** Holly Stabin. LC 00-190101. 95p. 2000. pap. 19.95 (*0-9677067-0-X*, LD101) SOW Pubns.

Love & Dishes: Scene-Stealing Recipes from Your Favorite Soap Stars. Ed. by Irene Krause Keene. (Illus.). 128p. 1998. text 17.00 (*0-7881-5940-2*) DIANE Pub.

Love & Dreams. Patricia Hagan. 352p. 1988. pap. 3.95 (*0-380-75159-3*, Avon Bks) Morrow Avon.

L

An Asterisk (*) at the beginning of an entry indicates that the title is appearing for the first time.

Love & Duty. Wall. 1988. per. 3.95 (*0-671-63448-8*) PB.

Love & Duty. G. D. Watson. 1996. pap. 7.99 (*0-88019-165-1*) Schmul Pub Co.

Love & Emotion - Stevie B. (Piano-Vocal-Guitar Ser.). (Illus.). 48p. (Orig.). 1991. pap. 10.95 (*0-7935-0749-9*, 00308102) H Leonard.

Love & Estrangement in the Baha'i Community. Arnie Nerenberg. 137p. (Orig.). 1986. 14.95 (*0-933770-47-2*) Kalimat.

Love & Exile: A Memoir. Isaac Bashevis Singer. 1986. pap. 16.00 (*0-374-51992-7*) FS&G.

Love & Exile: A Memoir. large type ed. Isaac Bashevis Singer. (Illus.). 480p. 1987. reprint ed. lib. bdg. 19.95 (*1-55736-006-5*) BDD LT Grp.

Love & Family: Raising a Traditional Family in a Secular World. Mercedes A. Wilson. LC 96-75715. 400p. 1996. pap. text 19.95 (*0-89870-607-6*) Ignatius Pr.

Love & Family Life. Swami Rama. LC 92-37512. 130p. (Orig.). 1992. pap. 12.95 (*0-89389-133-9*) Himalayan Inst.

Love & Fear. Ed. by Natasha Perova & Arch Tait. (Glas Ser.: No. 4). (Illus.). 224p. 1993. pap. 14.95 (*0-939010-35-6*) I R Dee.

Love & Fertility: How to Avoid or Achieve Pregnancy . . . Naturally. 3rd rev. ed. Mercedes A. Wilson. (Illus.). 88p. 1998. pap. text 17.90 (*0-9633125-4-5*) Family Amer Fnd.

Love & Fertility: How to Avoid or Achieve Pregnancy . . . Naturally! (Includes 6-month Record Keeping Chart) 2nd ed. Mercedes A. Wilson. (Illus.). 65p. 1992. pap. text 17.90 (*0-9633125-0-2*) Family Amer Fnd.

Love & Forgiveness: A Workbook for Self Healing & Healing Relationships. Leonard M. Shaw. 109p. 1989. pap. 10.00 (*0-9630184-9-3*) L M Shaw.

Love & Forgiveness in Yeats's Poetry. Catherine Cavanaugh. LC 85-20692. (Studies in Modern Literature: No. 57). (Illus.). 186p. reprint ed. pap. 57.70 (*0-8357-1728-3*, 207053700001) Bks Demand.

Love & Fortune. Charlotte McPherren. LC 94-147303. 368p. (Orig.). 1994. pap. text, mass mkt. 4.50 (*0-8439-3560-X*) Dorchester Pub Co.

Love & Freedom: An Englishwoman's Life in Czechoslovakia. Rosemary Kavan. 288p. 1988. 19.95 (*0-8090-4680-6*) Hill & Wang.

Love & Freedom: Professional Women & the Reshaping of Personal Life. Alison MacKinnon. LC 96-28526. (Illus.). 314p. 1997. text 59.95 (*0-521-49736-1*); pap. text 22.95 (*0-521-49761-2*) Cambridge U Pr.

Love & Friendship. Allan Bloom. 592p. 1994. pap. 15.00 (*0-671-89120-0*, Touchstone) S&S Trade Pap.

Love & Friendship. Alison Lurie. LC 97-2226. 1997. pap. text 12.00 (*0-8050-5178-3*, Owl) H Holt & Co.

Love & Friendship. Alison Lurie. 304p. 1993. pap. 9.00 (*0-380-71945-2*, Avon Bks) Morrow Avon.

Love & Friendship: An Integrated Unit. Kathy Rogers. (Primary Thematic Units Ser.). (Illus.). 96p. (Orig.). 1994. pap. 12.95 (*0-944459-88-9*) ECS Lrn Systs.

Love & Friendship: The Heart of the Catholic. Ann Gallagher et al. (Grade School Chastity - Project Genesis Ser.). (Illus.). 148p. (Orig.). (J). (gr. 6). 1996. pap. text, teacher ed. write for info. (*1-885845-16-2*); pap. text, student ed. write for info. (*1-885845-17-0*) Leaflet Missal.

Love & Friendship in Plato & Aristotle. A. W. Price. 278p. 1990. reprint ed. pap. text 27.00 (*0-19-824899-7*) OUP.

Love & Friendship Treasures. Maurine McGowan. 22p. (Orig.). 1997. mass mkt. 8.00 (*0-9657234-1-0*, 97-001) W & M Pub.

Love & Fury. Patricia Hagan. 384p. 1986. pap. 3.95 (*0-380-89614-1*, Avon Bks) Morrow Avon.

Love & Garbage. Ivan Klima. Tr. by Ewald Osers from CZE. LC 92-50713.Tr. of Laska a Smeti. (Illus.). 223p. 1993. pap. 13.00 (*0-679-73755-3*) Vin Bks.

Love & Glory. Robert Funderburk. LC 94-27177. (Innocent Years Ser.: No. 1). 34p. 1994. pap. 8.99 (*1-55661-460-8*) Bethany Hse.

Love & Glory. Patricia Hagan. (Trilogy Bks.: No. 3). 384p. 1982. pap. 3.95 (*0-380-79665-1*, Avon Bks) Morrow Avon.

Love & Glory. Robert B. Parker. 224p. 1984. mass mkt. 6.99 (*0-440-14629-1*) Dell.

***Love & Glory.** large type ed. Robert Funderburk. LC 99-58241. (Christian Fiction Ser.). 2000. 24.95 (*0-7862-2375-8*) Thorndike Pr.

***Love & Glory: A Question of Honor, No Surrender, Return of a Hero.** Lindsay McKenna. 2000. per. 6.99 (*0-373-20173-7*, 1-20173-0) Harlequin Bks.

Love & Glory: Women of the Old West. Larry D. Underwood. LC 90-63202. (Illus.). 200p. (Orig.). 1997. reprint ed. pap. 10.95 (*1-886225-21-4*) Dageforde Pub.

Love & God. Maharishi Mahesh Yogi. 56p. 1973. 9.00 (*0-89186-003-7*) Age Enlight Pr.

Love & Hate: The Natural History of Behavior Patterns. Irenaus Eibl-Eibesfeldt. Tr. by Geoffrey Strachan from GER. LC 95-37462. (Evolutionary Foundations of Human Behavior Ser.). (Illus.). 289p. 1996. pap. text 24.95 (*0-202-02038-X*) Aldine de Gruyter.

Love & Hate in the Analytic Setting. pap. 40.00 (*0-7657-0291-6*) Aronson.

Love & Hate in the Nursery & Beyond. Jule Eisenbud. 220p. 1991. 35.00 (*0-9622885-3-5*) Psyche Pr NY.

Love & Hate in the Nursery & Beyond: Voices from the Unconscious. Jule Eisenbud. LC 96-24594. (Illus.). 228p. (Orig.). 1996. pap. 16.95 (*1-883319-52-8*) Frog Ltd CA.

***Love & Hatred: The Stormy Marriage of Leo & Sonya Tolstoy.** William Shirer. (Illus.). 400p. 2000. reprint ed. 25.00 (*0-7881-9397-X*) DIANE Pub.

Love & Hisses: The National Society of Film Critics Sound off on the Hottest Movie Controversies. Ed. by Peter Rainer. LC 92-11175. 560p. 1992. pap. 16.95 (*1-56279-031-5*) Mercury Hse Inc.

Love & Honor. Patricia Hagan. 336p. (Orig.). 1989. pap. 3.95 (*0-380-75557-2*, Avon Bks) Morrow Avon.

Love & Honor. Melody Morgan. 320p. (Orig.). 1998. mass mkt. 4.99 (*0-8439-4341-6*, Leisure Bks) Dorchester Pub Co.

Love & Hope: Fromm & Education. Adir Cohen. Ed. by Roy Evans. (Special Aspects of Education Ser.: Vol. 10). xiv, 114p. 1990. pap. text 69.00 (*2-88124-294-4*) Gordon & Breach.

Love & Human Remains - Unidentified Human Remains & the True Nature of Love. Brad Fraser. (Illus.). 250p. 1996. pap. 18.95 (*1-896300-04-9*) NeWest Pubs.

Love & Ideology in the Afternoon: Soap Opera, Women, & Television Genre. Laura S. Mumford. LC 94-44239. (Arts & Politics of the Everyday Ser.). 176p. 1995. 27.95 (*0-253-32879-9*); pap. 12.95 (*0-253-20965-X*) Ind U Pr.

Love & Infamy. Frank Deford. 576p. 1995. mass mkt. 5.99 (*0-8217-0122-3*, Zebra Kensgtn); mass mkt. 5.99 (*0-7860-0122-4*, Pinncle Kensgtn) Kensgtn Pub Corp.

***Love & Inspirational Thoughts.** Eunice Webb-Matthews. 1999. pap. write for info. (*1-58235-090-6*) Watermrk Pr.

***Love & Intimate Relationships: Journeys of the Heart.** Norman M. Brown & Ellen S. Amatea. LC 99-53202. 2000. 34.95 (*0-87630-979-1*) Brunner-Mazel.

Love & Its Meaning in the World. Rudolf Steiner. LC 98-30549. 208p. 1998. pap. 16.95 (*0-88010-441-4*, 1977) Anthroposophic.

Love & Its Place in Nature: A Philosophical Interpretation of Freudian Psychoanalysis. Jonathan Lear. 243p. 1991. pap. 10.00 (*0-374-52320-7*) FS&G.

Love & Its Place in Nature: A Philosophical Interpretation of Freudian Psychoanalysis. Pref. by Jonathan Lear. LC 98-28023. 256p. 1998. pap. 12.50 (*0-300-07467-0*) Yale U Pr.

Love & Its Place in Nature: A Philosophical Interpretation of Freudian Psychoanalysis. Jonathan Lear. 243p. 1999. reprint ed. text 19.00 (*0-7881-6269-1*) DIANE Pub.

Love & Its Sounding: Explorations of T. S. Eliot. Christopher Southgate. LC 98-199482. 1997. pap. 10.95 (*3-7052-0098-4*, Pub. by Poetry Salzburg) Intl Spec Bk.

Love & Joy: Law, Language, & Religion in Ancient Israel. Yochanan Muffs. (Jewish Theological Seminary of America Ser.). 240p. (Orig.). (C). 1995. pap. text 15.95 (*0-674-53932-X*) HUP.

Love & Joy, Law, Language, & Religion in Ancient Israel. Yochanan Muffs. LC 92-11977. 1992. 29.95 (*0-674-53931-1*) Jewish Sem.

Love & Justice. Eva O'Diam. (Covenant Bible Studies). 48p. 1990. pap. 4.95 (*0-87178-543-9*, 8439) Brethren.

Love & Justice: Selections from the Shorter Writings of Reinhold Niebuhr. Reinhold Niebuhr. Ed. by D. B. Robertson. 1990. 16.50 (*0-8446-2659-7*) Peter Smith.

Love & Justice: Selections from the Shorter Writings of Reinhold Niebuhr. Reinhold Niebuhr. Ed. by D. B. Robertson. (Library of Theological Ethics). 320p. 1992. pap. 16.00 (*0-664-25322-9*) Westminster John Knox.

Love & Kisses. Anita R. Block. 1964. pap. 5.25 (*0-8222-0689-7*) Dramatists Play.

Love & Kisses. Sarah Wilson. LC 98-23820. (Illus.). 32p. (J). (ps-3). 1999. 9.99 (*1-56402-792-9*) Candlewick Pr.

Love & Kisses & a Halo of Truffles: Letters to Helen Evans Brown. James Beard. Ed. by John Ferrone. (Illus.). 448p. 1995. pap. 13.45 (*1-55970-318-0*, Pub. by Arcade Pub Inc) Time Warner.

Love & Kisses & a Halo of Truffles: Letters to Helen Evans Brown. James Beard. Ed. by John Ferrone. LC 94-9548. (Illus.). 416p. 1994. 25.45 (*1-55970-264-8*, Pub. by Arcade Pub Inc) Time Warner.

***Love & Kisses, Kitty.** Max Haynes. LC 99-188748. (Illus.). 16p. (J). (ps-k). 1999. 6.99 (*0-525-46150-7*, Dutton Child) Peng Put Young Read.

Love & Knishes: An Irrepressible Guide to Jewish Cooking. 3rd ed. Sara Kasdan. Ed. by Kathryn Hall. LC 97-74952. (Illus.). 192p. 1994. pap. 14.95 (*1-57090-076-0*) Alexander Dist.

***Love & Knowledge: The Quest for Personal Meaning.** James Donnelly. 84p. 1999. pap. 12.95 (*0-9672775-0-7*) South Garden.

***Love & Laments.** Joanna Mallet. vi, 26p. (C). 2000. pap. 5.95 (*0-9700740-0-X*) Athena Press NY.

Love & Language: A Study of the Classical French Moralist Writers. Louise K. Horowitz. LC 76-57232. 179p. reprint ed. pap. 55.50 (*0-608-09688-1*, 206980300006) Bks Demand.

***Love & Laughter.** large type ed. Lilian Harry. 432p. 2000. write for info. (*0-7505-1455-8*, Pub. by Mgna Lrg Print) Ulverscroft.

Love & Laughter: Lady on Top. Judy G. Gill. 1997. per. 3.50 (*0-373-44025-1*) Harlequin Bks.

Love & Laughter: One Way Ticket; The Marrying Man; Gus Is Back. Elise Title et al. (Promo Ser.). 1994. per. 4.99 (*0-373-83298-2*, 1-83298-9) Harlequin Bks.

***Love & Laughter: The True Story of an Online Cancer Survivors Support Group.** Marilyn R. Moody. LC 99-91489. 1999. 25.00 (*0-7388-0830-X*); pap. 18.00 (*0-7388-0831-8*) Xlibris Corp.

Love & Law in Europe. Ed. by Hanne Petersen. 158p. 1998. 76.95 (*1-85521-994-8*, K487.P75L68, Pub. by Ashgate Pub) Ashgate Pub Co.

Love & Learning. Sidney E. Mead. Ed. by Mary L. Doyle. 1978. pap. 5.00 (*0-914914-12-X*); lib. bdg. 12.95 (*0-914914-13-8*) New Horizons.

Love & Libido: Index of Modern Authors & Subjects with Guide for Rapid Research. Ann D. Crist. LC 90-56243. 190p. 1991. 47.50 (*1-55914-236-7*); pap. 44.50 (*1-55914-237-5*) ABBE Pubs Assn.

Love & Lies (Bride's Bay). Dawn Stewardson. (Intrigue Ser.). 1996. per. 3.75 (*0-373-22362-5*, 1-22362-7) Harlequin Bks.

Love & Life: A Christian Sexual Morality Guide for Teens. Coleen K. Mast. (Illus.). 155p. 1986. pap., teacher ed. 11.95 (*0-89870-108-2*) Ignatius Pr.

Love & Life: A Christian Sexual Morality Guide for Teens. Coleen K. Mast et al. LC 86-80693. (Illus.). 119p. 1986. pap. 8.95 (*0-89870-106-6*); pap., teacher ed. 6.95 (*0-89870-107-4*) Ignatius Pr.

Love & Limerence: The Experience of Being in Love. 2nd ed. Dorothy Tennov. LC 98-47912. 357p. 1999. pap. 17.95 (*0-8128-6286-4*, Pub. by Madison Bks UPA) Natl Bk Netwk.

Love & Limits. Anthony Coletta. 40p. (Orig.). 1992. pap. text 6.00 (*0-935493-93-X*) Modern Learn Pr.

Love & Limits: Achieving a Balance in Parenting. Ronald Huxley. LC 98-5413. (Illus.). 172p. 1998. pap. 29.95 (*1-56593-936-0*, 1834) Thomson Learn.

Love & Limits: Guidance Tools for Creative Parenting. Elizabeth Crary. LC 93-49556. (Star Parenting Bk.). 48p. (Orig.). 1994. pap. 6.95 (*1-884734-04-9*); lib. bdg. 16.95 (*1-884734-05-7*) Parenting Pr.

Love & Limits: Guidance Tools for Creative Parenting see Amor y Limites: Una Guia para Ser Padres Creativos

Love & Living. Thomas Merton. Ed. by Naomi B. Stone & Patrick Hart. LC 79-14717. 240p. (C). 1985. pap. 11.00 (*0-15-653895-4*, Harvest Bks) Harcourt.

Love & Living Together. Dale Robb. LC 77-15242. 110p. (Orig.). reprint ed. pap. 34.10 (*0-608-16313-9*, 202718000054) Bks Demand.

***Love & Logic: Poetry of Romance & Reason.** Michael C. Hinson. 80p. 2000. pap. 12.00 (*1-56474-347-0*) Fithian Pr.

***Love & Logic Magic for Early Childhood: Practical Parenting from Birth to Six Years.** Jim Fay & Charles Fay. Ed. by Adryan Russ. 192p. 2000. pap. 24.95 (*1-930429-00-2*, Pub. by Cline-Fay Inst) Midpt Trade.

Love & Longing in Bombay. Vikram Chandra. 288p. 1998. pap. 13.00 (*0-316-13677-8*) Little.

Love & Longing in Bombay. Vikram Chandra. 1998. pap. 13.00 (*0-316-18970-7*, Back Bay) Little.

Love & Longing in the Age of Chivalry. Martha Yeilding Scribner. LC 98-29772. 1998. 8.95 (*1-55853-672-8*) Rutledge Hill Pr.

Love & Lore. Edgar E. Saltus. LC 76-126647. reprint ed. 37.50 (*0-404-05516-8*) AMS Pr.

***Love & Loss: American Portrait & Mourning Miniatures.** Robin J. Frank. (Illus.). 360p. 2000. 35.00 (*0-300-08724-1*) Yale U Pr.

Love & Loveless. Intro. by Anne Williamson. LC 97-175651. (Pocket Classics Ser.). 384p. 1997. pap. 12.95 (*0-7509-1471-8*, Pub. by Sutton Pub Ltd) Intl Pubs Mktg.

***Love & Lucia.** large type ed. Barbara Cartland. 320p. 1999. 31.99 (*0-7505-1419-1*, Pub. by Mgna Lrg Print) Ulverscroft.

Love & Marriage see Amor y Matrimonio

Love & Marriage see Amor & Matrimonio

***Love & Marriage.** (In Classical Mood Ser.: Vol. 52). (Illus.). 30p. 1999. write for info. (*1-892207-05-2*) Intl Masters Pub.

Love & Marriage. Bill Cosby. 304p. 1990. mass mkt. 6.50 (*0-553-28467-3*) Bantam.

Love & Marriage. Kahlil Gibran. 1999. 4.95 (*0-375-40458-9*) Knopf.

Love & Marriage. Mayhew. 1996. 5.95 (*0-88271-498-8*) Regina Pr.

Love & Marriage. John Osteen. 32p. 1980. mass mkt. 0.75 (*0-912631-23-6*) J O Pubns.

Love & Marriage: An International Collection of Literature, Philosophy, & Poetry Specially Selected for Book Discussion Groups by the Great Books Foundation. Ed. & Intro. by Great Bks. Foundation Staff. LC 98-123588. (Fiftieth Anniversary Ser.). 332p. (Orig.). 1997. pap. 14.95 (*1-880323-75-3*) Great Bks Found.

Love & Marriage: Making Sure of Sarah; Something Blue - 50th Anniversary. anniversary ed. Betty A. Neels & Emma Goldrick. (Romance Ser.: No. 3554). 1999. per. 3.50 (*0-373-03554-3*, 1-03554-2) Harlequin Bks.

Love & Marriage: Making Sure of Sarah; Something Blue - 50th Anniversary. anniversary large type ed. Betty A. Neels & Emma Goldrick. (Romance Ser.: No. 3554). 1999. per. 3.50 (*0-373-15800-9*, 1-15800-5) Harlequin Bks.

***Love & Marriage & Divorce.** Bob Zahn. Ed. by Cliff Carle. 144p. 2000. pap. 6.95 (*1-57644-098-2*) CCC Pubns.

Love & Marriage Around the World. Carol Gelber. LC 97-1695. (Illus.). 72p. (J). (gr. 5-7). 1998. lib. bdg. 21.40 (*0-7613-0102-X*) Millbrook Pr.

Love & Marriage in Africa. Mbiti. 1974. pap. text. write for info. (*0-582-64122-5*, Pub. by Addison-Wesley) Longman.

Love & Marriage in Late Medieval London. Tr. & Intro. by Shannon McSheffrey. LC 94-47339. (Documents of Practice Ser.). 1995. pap. 6.00 (*1-879288-53-2*) Medieval Inst.

Love & Marriage in the Age of Chaucer. Henry A. Kelly. LC 74-10414. 360p. 1975. pap. 111.60 (*0-7837-7445-1*, AU0045200011) Bks Demand.

Love & Marriage in the Middle Ages. Georges Duby. 232p. (C). 1996. reprint ed. pap. 14.95 (*0-226-16774-7*) U Ch Pr.

Love & Marriage in the Twelfth Century. Ed. by W. Van Hoecke & A. Welkenhuysen. No. 8. 316p. (Orig.). 1981. pap. 52.50 (*90-6186-120-9*, Pub. by Leuven Univ) Coronet Bks.

Love & Marriage Thru the Years. 256p. (Orig.). Date not set. pap. 12.95 (*0-7692-1038-4*, SF0145) Wrner Bros.

Love & Mary Ann. large type ed. Catherine Cookson. 1970. 15.95 (*0-85456-657-0*) Ulverscroft.

Love & Memories. Louis R. Samuels. 1998. pap. write for info. (*1-57553-789-3*) Watermrk Pr.

Love & Memory. Jamal Gabobe. (Illus.). 36p. 1996. pap. 9.95 (*1-885942-01-X*) Cune.

Love & Mr. Lewisham. H. G. Wells. Ed. by Jeremy Lewis. 256p. 1994. pap. text 6.95 (*0-460-87420-9*, Everyman's Classic Lib) Tuttle Pubng.

Love & Mr. Lewisham. H. G. Wells. (Everyman's Library). 1994. pap. 6.95 (*0-460-87305-9*, Everyman's Classic Lib) Tuttle Pubng.

Love & Murder. Created by Francine Pascal. (Sweet Valley University Thriller Edition Ser.: No. 11). 288p. (YA). (gr. 7 up). 1998. mass mkt. 4.50 (*0-553-49225-X*, Sweet Valley) BDD Bks Young Read.

Love & Narcissism in Psychoanalytic Practice. Ed. by Herbert S. Strean. LC 85-7644. (Current Issues in Psychoanalytic Practice Ser.: Vol. 2, No. 1). 107p. 1985. text 3.95 (*0-86656-386-5*) Haworth Pr.

Love & Nature, Unity & Doubling in the Novels of Maupassant. Ed. by Helen Roulston. (American Univ. Studies: Romance Languages & Literature: Ser. 2, Vol. 79). XIV, 152p. 1989. 28.50 (*0-8204-0635-X*) P Lang Pubng.

Love & Oranges. Marvin Payne. (Keepsake Paperbacks Ser.). 62p. 1988. reprint ed. pap. 3.95 (*0-88494-402-6*) Jackman Pubng.

Love & Oranges. 2nd ed. Marvin Payne. 64p. (YA). (gr. 9 up). 1988. reprint ed. pap. 3.95 (*0-929985-08-7*) Jackman Pubng.

Love & Orgasm: A Revolutionary Guide to Sexual Fulfillment. Alexander Lowen. (Illus.). 319p. 1975. pap. 7.00 (*0-02-077320-X*) Macmillan.

***Love & Other Four-Letter Words.** Carolyn Mackler. 2000. 14.95 (*0-385-32743-9*) Delacorte.

Love & Other Infectious Diseases: A Memoir. Molly Haskell. 304p. 1992. pap. 12.95 (*0-8065-1326-8*, Citadel Pr) Carol Pub Group.

Love, & Other Poems. deluxe limited ed. Dan Woodward. (Illus.). 50p. (YA). (gr. 11 up). 1994. 15.95 (*1-882935-12-8*) Westphalia.

Love & Other Stories. Anton Chekhov. Tr. by Constance Garnett from RUS. (Tales of Anton Chekhov Ser.: Vol. 13). 351p. 1987. reprint ed. pap. 9.50 (*0-88001-060-6*) HarpC.

Love & Passion see Amor y Pasion

Love & Pedagogy. Miguel de Unamuno. Tr. by Michael Vande Berg from SPA. LC 92-36951.Tr. of Amor y Pedagogia. XXV, 187p. (C). 1996. text 39.95 (*0-8204-1725-4*) P Lang Pubng.

Love & Politics: A New Commentary on the Song of Songs. Luis Stadelmann. LC 92-17162. 256p. 1992. pap. 9.95 (*0-8091-3290-7*) Paulist Pr.

Love & Politics: Radical Feminist & Lesbian Theories. Carol A. Douglas. LC 90-4218. (Illus.). 363p. (Orig.). (C). 1990. 18.00 (*0-910383-18-9*); pap. 12.00 (*0-910383-17-0*) Ism Pr.

Love & Politics in Wartime: Letters to My Wife, 1943-45. Benedict S. Alper. Ed. by Joan W. Scott. 248p. 1992. 26.50 (*0-252-01877-X*) U of Ill Pr.

Love & Power. Lynn V. Andrews. LC 97-8458. 256p. 1997. 23.00 (*0-06-018646-1*) HarpC.

Love & Power. Lynn V. Andrews. 176p. 1998. pap. 13.00 (*0-06-092955-3*, Perennial) HarperTrade.

***Love & Power.** Y. S. Wang. 402p. 2000. pap. 18.00 (*0-7388-2020-2*) Xlibris Corp.

Love & Power: How to Raise Competent, Confident Children. Glenn Austin. 244p. 1994. reprint ed. pap. 12.95 (*0-471-02498-8*) Wiley.

Love & Power: The Psychology of Interpersonal Creativity. Paul Rosenfels. LC 66-25081. 1966. 12.95 (*0-87212-009-0*) Libra.

Love & Power: The Role of Religion & Morality in American Politics. Michael J. Perry. 240p. 1993. reprint ed. pap. text 19.95 (*0-19-508355-5*) OUP.

Love & Power in the Nineteenth Century: The Marriage of Violet Blair. Virginia J. Laas. (Illus.). 192p. 1998. 32.00 (*1-55728-505-5*); pap. 16.00 (*1-55728-506-3*) U of Ark Pr.

Love & Power in the Peasant Family. Martine Segalen. Tr. by Sarah Matthews. LC 82-50495. (Illus.). 224p. 1992. 25.00 (*0-226-74451-5*) U Ch Pr.

Love & Power in the Peasant Family: Rural France in the Nineteenth Century. Martine Segalen. Tr. by Sarah Matthews. LC 82-50495. (Illus.). 216p. reprint ed. pap. 67.00 (*0-608-09528-1*, 205433000005) Bks Demand.

Love & Power Journal: A Workbook for the Fine Art of Living. Lynn V. Andrews. (Illus.). 208p. 1999. text, wbk. ed. 15.95 (*1-56170-605-1*, 574) Hay House.

Love & Profit: The Art of Caring Leadership. James A. Autry. 224p. 1992. pap. 12.50 (*0-380-71749-2*, Avon Bks) Morrow Avon.

Love & Reading: An Essay in Applied Psychoanalysis. Gerald J. Butler. (American University Studies: Comparative Literature: Ser. III, Vol. 25). X, 192p. (C). 1988. text 32.95 (*0-8204-0763-1*) P Lang Pubng.

Love & Reality. Eli Siegel. 1977. pap. write for info. (*0-911492-22-4*) Aesthetic Realism.

***Love & Remembrance: A Memory Book for Parents Whose Child Has Died.** Margot Burkle. 1998. 6.95 (*1-56123-104-5*) Centering Corp.

Love & Remembrance: The Poetry of Jorge Manrique. Frank A. Dominguez. LC 88-21627. 232p. 1988. 28.00 (*0-8131-1651-1*) U Pr of Ky.

Love & Responsibility. Karol Wojtyla. Tr. by H. T. Willetts from POL. LC 92-75063. 319p. 1993. reprint ed. pap. 14.95 (*0-89870-445-6*) Ignatius Pr.

Love & Responsibility. rev. ed. Karol Wojtyla. Tr. by H. T. Willetts. LC 81-2261. 320p. 1994. 15.00 (*0-374-19247-2*) FS&G.

An Asterisk (*) at the beginning of an entry indicates that the title is appearing for the first time.

***Love & Riot in Los Angeles: The Biography of Oscar Zeta Acosta.** Burton M. Moore. Ed. by Andrea Cabello. (Nuestra Historia Ser.: Vol. 4). 160p. 2000. pap. 24.95 (*0-915745-29-1*) Floricanto Pr.

Love & Rockets: Hernandez Satryeon, Vol. 15. Jaime Hernandez & Gilbert Hernandez. pap. 14.95 (*1-56097-271-8*, Pub. by Fantagraph Bks) Seven Hills Bk.

Love & Rockets: Lost Women. Jaime Hernandez. (Illus.). 144p. 1988. pap. 10.95 (*0-930193-66-0*) Fantagraph Bks.

Love & Rockets: Poison River, Vol. 12. Jaime Hernandez & Gilbert Hernandez. 39.95 (*1-56097-152-5*, Pub. by Fantagraph Bks) Seven Hills Bk.

Love & Rockets: X. Gilbert Hernandez. Ed. by Gary Groth. (Complete Love & Rockets Ser.: Vol. 10). (Illus.). 96p. 1993. 35.00 (*1-56097-102-9*); pap. 12.95 (*1-56097-101-0*) Fantagraph Bks.

Love & Rockets Bk. 14: Luba Conquers the World. Gilbert Hernandez. 136p. 1996. 34.95 (*1-56097-260-2*); pap. 18.95 (*1-56097-259-9*) Fantagraph Bks.

Love & Rockets Vol. 1: Music for Mechanics. Gilbert Hernandez et al. (Complete Love & Rockets Ser.). (Illus.). 144p. 1985. 35.00 (*0-930193-16-4*); pap. 18.95 (*0-930193-13-X*) Fantagraph Bks.

Love & Rockets Vol. 2: Chelo's Burden. Gilbert Hernandez et al. (Complete Love & Rockets Ser.). (Illus.). 144p. (Orig.). 1986. 35.00 (*0-930193-26-1*) Fantagraph Bks.

Love & Rockets Vol. 3: Las Mujeres Perdidas. Gilbert Hernandez & Jaime Hernandez. (Complete Love & Rockets Ser.). (Illus.). 144p. 1990. reprint ed. 35.00 (*0-930193-32-6*, Pub. by Fantagraph Bks) Seven Hills Bk.

Love & Rockets Vol. 4: Tears from Heaven. Gilbert Hernandez & Jaime Hernandez. (Complete Love & Rockets Ser.). (Illus.). 128p. (Orig.). 1988. 30.00 (*0-930193-45-8*); pap. 16.95 (*0-930193-44-X*) Fantagraph Bks.

Love & Rockets Vol. 5: House of Raging Women. Gilbert Hernandez & Jaime Hernandez. (Complete Love & Rockets Ser.). (Illus.). 128p. (Orig.). 1988. 35.00 (*0-930193-70-9*) Fantagraph Bks.

Love & Rockets Vol. 6: Duck Feet. Gilbert Hernandez & Jaime Hernandez. (Complete Love & Rockets Ser.). (Illus.). 128p. 1989. 35.00 (*0-930193-82-2*); pap. 15.95 (*0-930193-81-4*) Fantagraph Bks.

Love & Rockets Vol. 7: The Death of Speedy. Jaime Hernandez. (Illus.). 136p. 1989. 39.95 (*1-56097-004-9*); pap. 16.95 (*1-56097-003-0*) Fantagraph Bks.

Love & Rockets Vol. 8: Blood of Palomar. Gilbert Hernandez. (Illus.). 136p. 1989. 39.95 (*1-56097-006-5*); pap. 16.95 (*1-56097-005-7*) Fantagraph Bks.

Love & Rockets Vol. 9: "Flies on the Ceiling" Jaime Hernandez & Gilbert Hernandez. (Illus.). 120p. 1991. 35.00 (*1-56097-072-3*, Pub. by Fantagraph Bks); pap. 16.95 (*1-56097-071-5*) Fantagraph Bks.

Love & Rockets Vol. 11: Wig Wam Bam. Jaime Hernandez. 128p. 1993. per. 14.95 (*1-56097-120-7*) Fantagraph Bks.

Love & Rockets Vol. 11: Wig Wam Bam, Vol. 11. Jaime Hernandez. (Love & Rockets Ser.). 128p. 1993. 35.00 (*1-56097-121-5*) Fantagraph Bks.

Love & Rockets Vol. 12: Poison River. Gilbert Hernandez. 1994. pap. text 19.95 (*1-56097-151-7*) Fantagraph Bks.

Love & Rockets Vol. 13: Chester Square. Jaime Hernandez. 160p. 1996. pap. 18.95 (*1-56097-255-6*) Fantagraph Bks.

Love & Rockets Vol. 13: Chester Square. Jaime Hernandez. 160p. 1996. 34.95 (*1-56097-256-4*) Fantagraph Bks.

Love & Rockets Sketchbook, Vol. 1. Gilbert Hernandez & Jaime Hernandez. Ed. by Doug Erb. (Illus.). 192p. 1989. 39.95 (*0-930193-85-7*) Fantagraph Bks.

Love & Rockets Sketchbook, Vol. II. Gilbert Hernandez & Jaime Hernandez. 144p. 1992. 39.95 (*1-56097-100-2*); pap. 19.95 (*1-56097-099-5*) Fantagraph Bks.

***Love & Romance.** Ed. by Helen Exley. (Words for Life Ser.). (Illus.). 80p. 1999. 7.00 (*1-86187-154-6*) Exley Pubns Ltd.

Love & Romance: A Pictorial Archive from 19th-Century. Carol B. Grafton. (Illus.). 128p. 1989. pap. 8.95 (*0-486-25938-2*) Dover.

Love & Romance: True Stories of Passion on the Road. Ed. by Judith Babcock Wylie. (Travelers' Tales Guides Ser.). 319p. 1998. pap. 17.95 (*1-885211-18-X*, 18-X) Trvlers Tale.

Love & Saint Augustine. Hannah Arendt. Ed. by Joanna V. Scot & Judith C. Stark. LC 95-12866.Tr. of Libesbegrieff bei Augustine. 254p. 1995. 22.50 (*0-226-02596-9*) U Ch Pr.

Love & Saint Augustine. Hannah Arendt. Ed. by Joanna V. Scot & Judith C. Stark. LC 95-12866.Tr. of Libesbegrieff bei Augustine. 234p. 1998. pap. 16.00 (*0-226-02597-7*) U Ch Pr.

Love & Salt Water. Ethel Wilson. 178p. 1996. pap. text 6.95 (*0-7710-8957-0*) McCland & Stewart.

Love & Savagery. Des Walsh. 56p. 1989. reprint ed. pap. 9.95 (*0-88922-270-3*, Pub. by Talonbks) Genl Dist Srvs.

Love & Science: Selected Music-Theatre Texts. Richard Foreman. LC 90-29042. 204p. 1991. pap. 13.95 (*1-55936-021-6*) Theatre Comm.

***Love & Scorn: New & Selected Poems.** Carol Frost. 136p. 2000. 49.95 (*0-8101-5098-0*, TriQuart); pap. 16.95 (*0-8101-5099-9*, TriQuart) Northwestern U Pr.

Love & Selected Poems. Aharon Shabtai. Tr. by Peter Cole from HEB. LC 97-5231. 248p. 1997. text 24.95 (*1-878818-53-8*, Pub. by Sheep Meadow) U Pr of New Eng.

Love & Selected Poems. Aharon Shabtai. Tr. by Peter Cole from HEB. LC 97-5231. 248p. 1997. pap. 12.95 (*1-878818-78-3*) U Pr of New Eng.

Love & Service of God, Infinite Love. Margaret Louise Margaret Claret de la Touche. Tr. by Patrick O'Connell from FRE. LC 86-51580. 230p. 1994. reprint ed. pap. 12.50 (*0-89555-310-4*) TAN Bks Pubs.

Love & Sex: Cross Cultural Perspectives. Elaine Hatfield & Richard L. Rapson. LC 95-13436. 320p. (C). 1995. pap. text 23.00 (*0-205-16103-0*) Allyn.

Love & Sex after Forty: A Guide for Men & Women for Their Mid & Later Years. large type ed. Robert N. Butler & Myrna I. Lewis. (Illus.). 322p. 1987. reprint ed. lib. bdg. 19.95 (*1-55736-008-1*) BDD LT Grp.

Love & Sex after Sixty. Robert N. Butler & Myrna I. Lewis. (Illus.). 320p. 1993. pap. 11.50 (*0-345-38034-7*) Ballantine Pub Grp.

Love & Sex after Sixty. 2nd large type ed. Robert N. Butler & Myrna I. Lewis. LC 96-45183. (Spec-Hall Ser.). 375p. 1996. lib. bdg. 21.95 (*0-7838-2027-5*, G K Hall Lrg Type) Mac Lib Ref.

***Love & Sex By the Numbers: A Numerology Guide to Romance.** Pam Bell. 256p. 2000. pap. 13.00 (*0-380-80840-4*, Quil) HarperTrade.

Love & Sex in Plain Language. 3rd ed. Eric W. Johnson. LC 77-5705. (Illus.). (YA). (gr. 7 up). 1977. 13.95 (*0-397-01231-4*) HarpC Child Bks.

Love & Sex in Twelve Cultures. Robert Endleman. 150p. (Orig.). (C). 1989. text 30.00 (*0-9622885-1-9*); pap. text 14.95 (*0-9622885-0-0*) Psyche Pr NY.

Love & Sex Signs: Venus, Mars & Astrology. Joanne Madeline Moore. 1998. pap. text 14.95 (*0-7318-0667-0*) Simon & Schuster.

Love & Sex Tests: Twenty-Four Psychological Tests to Help You Evaluate Your Readiness for Relationships, Love, & Sex. Louis H. Janda. LC 98-20209. 256p. 1998. pap. 9.95 (*1-58062-002-7*) Adams Media.

Love & Sex Without Conflict. Buryl Payne. (Illus.). 64p. 1993. 7.95 (*0-9635600-0-X*) Psycho Physics.

Love & Sexuality. 4th ed. Omraam M. Aivanhov. 283p. 1997. pap. 14.95 (*2-85566-740-2*, Pub. by Prosveta) Prosveta USA.

Love & Sexuality, Pt. I. 3rd ed. Omraam M. Aivanhov. (Complete Works: Pt. I, Vol. 14). (Illus.). 250p. 1989. pap. 14.95 (*2-85566-423-3*, Pub. by Prosveta) Prosveta USA.

Love & Sexuality, Pt. II. 4th ed. Omraam M. Aivanhov. (Complete Works: Vol. 15). 301p. 1992. pap. 14.95 (*2-85566-440-3*, Pub. by Prosveta) Prosveta USA.

Love & Sexuality: An Exploration of Venus & Mars. Baba Kirby & Janey Stubbs. LC 92-17966. 255p. 1992. pap. 15.95 (*1-85230-358-1*, Pub. by Element MA) Penguin Putnam.

Love & Sexuality in Literature. Fonseca. 128p. 1998. pap. text 25.00 (*1-56226-420-6*) CAT Pub.

Love & Sexuality Through Palmistry: Playing the "Love Game" Rhoda Hamilton. (Illus.). 157p. 1996. mass mkt. 16.95 (*0-9655382-1-4*) Rhoda.

Love & Shadows see De Amor y de Sombra

Love & Society in Shakespearean Comedy: A Study of Dramatic Form & Content. Richard Levin. LC 84-40060. 208p. 1985. 32.50 (*0-87413-266-5*) U Delaware Pr.

Love & Solitude: Selected Poems, 1916-1923. 3rd ed. Edith Sodergran. Tr. by Stina Katchadourian from FIN. LC 92-13509. (International Poetry Ser.: No. 1). (SWE.). 185p. (Orig.). 1996. pap. 14.00 (*0-940242-14-1*) Fjord Pr.

Love & Splendor. Patricia Hagan. 352p. 1987. pap. 3.95 (*0-380-75158-5*, Avon Bks) Morrow Avon.

Love & Strategy in the Eighteenth Century French Novel. Vera Lee. 150p. (Orig.). 1986. pap. 14.95 (*0-87047-019-1*); text 19.95 (*0-87047-018-3*) Schenkman Bks Inc.

Love & Superstition. Said Salah. (Arabian Story Masterpiece Ser.). 62p. 1990. 8.00 (*1-887584-25-0*) Intl Prom Art.

Love & Survival: The Scientific Basis for the Healing Power of Intimacy. Dean Ornish. 320p. 1999. pap. 14.00 (*0-06-093020-9*) HarpC.

***Love & Survival: The Scientific Basis for the Healing Power of Intimacy.** abr. ed. Dean Ornish. 1998. audio 18.00 (*0-694-51875-1*, CPN2685) HarperAudio.

Love & Survival: The Scientific Basis for the Healing Power of Intimacy. large type ed. Dean Ornish. LC 98-26645. 450p. 1998. 26.95 (*0-7862-1550-X*) Thorndike Pr.

Love & Sympathy in Theravada Buddhism. Harvey B. Aronson. viii, 127p. 1986. 12.00 (*81-208-0049-4*, Pub. by Motilal Bnarsidass) S Asia.

Love & Terror. William Herrick. LC 80-25140. 256p. 1981. 13.95 (*0-8112-0791-9*, Pub. by New Directions) Norton.

Love & Terror. William Herrick. LC 80-25140. 256p. 1982. pap. 5.95 (*0-8112-0841-9*, NDP538, Pub. by New Directions) Norton.

Love & Terror. Alan Jolis & Atlantic Monthly Staff. LC 98-14734. 352p. 1998. 24.00 (*0-87113-715-1*, Atlntc Mnthly) Grove-Atltic.

Love & the American Delinquent: The Theory & Practice of "Progressive" Juvenile Justice, 1825-1920. Steven L. Schlossman. LC 76-17699. (Illus.). 1994. lib. bdg. 20.00 (*0-226-73857-4*) U Ch Pr.

Love & the American Delinquent: The Theory & Practice of "Progressive" Juvenile Justice, 1825-1920. Steven L. Schlossman. LC 76-17699. (Illus.). 1994. pap. text 10.00 (*0-226-73858-2*) U Ch Pr.

***Love & the American Dream: The Art of Robert Indiana.** Aprile Gallant. (Illus.). 136p. 1999. 40.00 (*0-916857-18-2*, Pub. by Port Mus Art) U of Wash Pr.

Love & the American Dream: The Art of Robert Indiana. Aprile Gallant et al. Ed. by Fronia W. Simpson. LC 98-68099. (Illus.). 136p. 1998. pap. 25.00 (*0-916857-17-4*, Pub. by Port Mus Art) U of Wash Pr.

***Love & the Bottle.** Don Kerr. 192p. 2000. pap. 14.95 (*1-55050-161-5*, Pub. by Coteau) Genl Dist Srvs.

Love & the Caribbean: Tales, Characters & Scenes of the West Indies. Alec Waugh. 310p. 1994. pap. 12.95 (*1-56924-997-0*) Marlowe & Co.

Love & the Expansion of Self. Arthur Aron & Elaine N. Aron. (Clinical & Community Psychology Ser.). 420p. 1986. pap. 29.95 (*0-89116-459-6*) Hemisp Pub.

Love & the Golden Rule. (Universal Truths Ser.). 72p. 1990. reprint ed. pap. 3.95 (*0-685-29332-7*) Golden Rule.

Love & the Intellectual: A Pair of Blue Eyes. Brian Crick. (C). 1989. 35.00 (*0-907839-20-7*, Pub. by Brynmill Pr Ltd) St Mut.

Love & the Novel: The Poetics & Politics of Romantic Fiction. George Paizis. LC 98-13758. 256p. 1998. text 65.00 (*0-312-21547-9*) St Martin.

Love & the Philosopher, a Study in Sentiment. Marie Corelli. 287p. 1972. reprint ed. spiral bd. 18.50 (*0-7873-0204-X*) Hlth Research.

Love & the Quest for Identity in the Fiction of Henry James. Philip Sicker. LC 79-17311. 213p. reprint ed. pap. 66.10 (*0-8357-2776-9*, 203990200014) Bks Demand.

***Love & the Single Corpse.** Annie Griffin. 288p. 2000. mass mkt. 5.99 (*0-425-17612-6*, Prime Crime) Berkley Pub.

Love & the Soul. Alan Williamson. LC 95-8679. (Phoenix Poets Ser.). 74p. 1995. pap. 10.95 (*0-226-89933-0*); lib. bdg. 25.00 (*0-226-89932-2*) U Ch Pr.

Love & the Soul: Psychological Interpretations of the Eros & Psyche Myth. James Gollnick. 200p. (C). 1992. pap. 19.95 (*0-88920-212-5*) W Laurier U Pr.

Love & the Soul Maker. Mary H. Austin. (Collected Works of Mary Hunter Austin). 286p. 1998. reprint ed. lib. bdg. 88.00 (*1-58201-524-4*) Classic Bks.

Love & the Symbolic Journey in the Poetry of Cavafy, Eliot & Seferis. C. Capri-Karka. LC 82-81629. 374p. 1982. pap. text 12.00 (*0-918618-21-5*) Pella Pub.

Love & Theft: Blackface Minstrelsy & the American Working Class. Eric Lott. (Race & American Culture Ser.). (Illus.). 328p. 1995. pap. text 18.95 (*0-19-509641-X*) OUP.

Love & Time. Ou-Yang Hsiu. Tr. by J. P. Seaton from CHI. LC 89-61457. 96p. (Orig.). 1989. pap. 9.00 (*1-55659-024-5*) Copper Canyon.

Love & Toil: Motherhood in Outcast London, 1870-1918. Ellen M. Ross. LC 92-40849. (Illus.). 336p. 1993. pap. text 22.00 (*0-19-508321-0*) OUP.

Love & Tradition: Marriage Between Jews & Christians. Egon Mayer. LC 85-6588. 311p. reprint ed. pap. 96.50 (*0-608-08571-5*, 206909400002) Bks Demand.

***Love & Transformation: An Ovid Reader.** 2nd ed. Richard A. Lafleur & Ovid. LC 98-218230. x, 192 p. 1999. write for info. (*0-673-58920-X*) Addison-Wesley.

Love & Tribulation. Leslie Kelemen. 1992. 16.95 (*0-533-10197-2*) Vantage.

Love & Triumph. Patricia Hagan. 320p. (Orig.). 1991. mass mkt. 4.95 (*0-380-75558-0*, Avon Bks) Morrow Avon.

Love & Truth in the Ramayana of Tulsidas. Anantanand Rambachan. 72p. 1989. pap. 5.00 (*0-9634164-0-5*) Vijnana Pubns.

Love & Understanding. Joe Penhall. 1998. pap. 5.25 (*0-8222-1688-4*) Dramatists Play.

***Love & Valor: Intimate Civil War Letters Between Captain Jacob & Emeline Ritner.** Prod. by Floating Gallery Staff. 350p. 2000. pap. 18.95 (*0-9673863-0-6*, Pub. by Sigourney Pr Inc) ACCESS Pubs Network.

***Love & Valor: Intimate Civil War Letters Between Captain Jacob & Emeline Ritner.** Charles F. Larimer. LC 99-72882. (Illus.). 453p. 2000. 27.95 (*0-9673863-1-4*) Sigourney Pr Inc.

Love & Vengeance: or Little Viola's Victory. Theodore E. Nash. LC 78-173016. reprint ed. 27.50 (*0-404-00095-9*) AMS Pr.

Love & War. (Cross-Cultural Review Chapbook Ser.: No. 37). 48p. 1991. 15.00 (*0-89304-320-6*); 15.00 (*0-89304-322-2*); pap. 5.00 (*0-89304-321-4*); pap. 5.00 (*0-89304-323-0*) Cross-Cultrl NY.

Love & War. Patricia Hagan. (Trilogy Bks.: No. 1). 544p. 1978. pap. 3.95 (*0-380-01947-7*, Avon Bks) Morrow Avon.

***Love & War.** James Hewitt. (Illus.). 296p. 1999. 28.00 (*1-85782-318-4*, Pub. by Blake Publng) Seven Hills Bk.

***Love & War.** John Jakes. (North & South Trilogy Ser.: Vol. 2). 1088p. 2000. mass mkt. 7.99 (*0-451-20082-9*, Sig) NAL.

Love & War. Peg Sutherland. (Hometown Reunion Ser.). 1996. per. 4.50 (*0-373-82551-X*, 1-82551-2) Harlequin Bks.

Love & War. Ed. by Margaret Weis & Tracy Hickman. LC 86-51589. (DragonLance Tales Ser.: Vol. 3). (Illus.). 352p. (Orig.). 1987. pap. 5.99 (*0-88038-519-7*, Pub. by TSR Inc) Random.

***Love & War.** large type ed. Barbara Cartland. LC 98-26225. 168 p. 1998. pap. write for info. (*0-7540-3506-9*, G K Hall Lrg Type) Mac Lib Ref.

***Love & War: A New Camfield Novel of Love.** large type ed. Barbara Cartland. LC 98-26225. 165p. 1998. 30.00 (*0-7838-0311-7*, G K Hall Lrg Type) Mac Lib Ref.

Love & War: Adventures from the Firuz Shah Namah of Sheikh Bighami. Muhammad Ibn A. Bighami. LC 74-6039. (Unesco Collection of Representative Works). 224p. 1974. 50.00 (*0-8201-1126-0*) Schol Facsimiles.

Love & War: Pearl Harbor Through V-J Day. Robert Easton & Jane Easton. LC 90-50686. (Illus.). 400p. 1991. 27.95 (*0-8061-2336-2*) U of Okla Pr.

Love & War: Poetry. Marvin Jackmon. LC 95-83140. 140p. (Orig.). pap. 15.00 (*0-9649672-0-0*) Black Bird Pr.

Love & War: Wartime Love Letters. Susan B. Wallace. LC 97-4848. (Illus.). 96p. 1996. 19.99 (*1-56530-219-2*, Pub. by Summit TX) BookWorld.

Love & War Between the Signs: Astrological Secrets to Finding & Creating a Happy Relationship. Amy Keehn. 272p. 1996. per. 15.00 (*0-7615-0834-1*) Prima Pub.

Love & War in the Apennines. Eric Newby. (Lonely Planet Journeys (Travel Literature) Ser.). 276p. 1999. pap. 12.95 (*0-86442-765-4*) Lonely Planet.

Love & War in the Middle English Romances. Margaret A. Gist. LC 78-63499. reprint ed. 42.50 (*0-404-17147-8*) AMS Pr.

Love & Wedding Piano Solos. 104p. 1991. pap. 12.95 (*0-7935-0611-5*, 00311507) H Leonard.

Love & Work Enough: The Life of Anna Jameson. Clara Thomas. LC 67-3186. (Canadian University Paperbooks Ser.: No. 211). 272p. reprint ed. pap. 84.40 (*0-8357-4150-8*, 203692300007) Bks Demand.

Love & Zen in the Outer Hebrides. Kevin MacNeil. 1998. pap. 12.95 (*0-86241-812-7*, Pub. by Canongate Books) Interlink Pub.

Love-Anger. Karen O. Savalan. 206p. 1981. 16.00 (*0-86690-316-X*, S1448-014) Am Fed Astrologers.

Love Anyhow: Famous Fathers Write to Their Children. Ed. by Reid Sherline. LC 94-1996. (Illus.). 108p. 1994. 14.95 (*0-943221-19-6*) Timken Pubs.

Love Around the House: Helpful Household Tips You Won't Find in Any Martha Stewart Book. Ava Cadell. Ed. by Andrew S. Ross. (Illus.). 160p. 1998. pap. 12.95 (*0-9662623-0-1*, 40001) Peters Publishing.

Love Arrives, Chapter 1-9, Vol. 1. 138p. 1999. lib. bdg. 31.00 (*0-9628982-6-0*, LA#1) Gemini Group.

Love Arts: The Foundation for Love, Romance & Intimacy. Marcia Singer. 275p. (Orig.). 1996. pap. 16.00 (*1-887110-08-9*) Allian Pubng.

Love As Energy. R. Wayne Kraft. (Teilhard Studies: No. 19). 1988. pap. 3.50 (*0-89012-056-0*) Am Teilhard.

Love As Passion: The Codification of Intimacy. Niklas Luhmann. Tr. by Jeremy Gaines & Doris L. Jones from GER. LC 86-14929. 256p. 1987. 43.00 (*0-674-53923-0*) HUP.

Love As Passion: The Codification of Intimacy. Nuklas Luhmann. Tr. by Jeremy Gaines & Doris L. Jones from ENG. LC 98-17103. (Cultural Memory in the Present Ser.). 248p. 1998. pap. 18.95 (*0-8047-3253-1*) Stanford U Pr.

Love As Strong As Ginger. Lenore Look. LC 96-43459. (Illus.). 40p. (J). (gr. k-4). 1999. 15.00 (*0-689-81248-5*) S&S Childrens.

Love Ascending. Ruth De Menezes. 90p. 1987. 7.95 (*0-937495-18-2*) Claremont CA.

Love at Every Step: My Concept of Poetry. Darshan Singh. LC 89-92182. (Illus.). 108p. 1989. pap. 10.00 (*0-918224-23-3*) S K Pubns.

Love at First Bite. Ed. by Fotonovel Publications Staff. (Illus.). (Orig.). 1979. pap. 2.75 (*0-686-52701-1*) Fotonovel.

Love at First Byte. Lin Hsin Hsin. 300p. 1992. pap. text 21.00 (*981-02-1026-4*) World Scientific Pub.

Love at First Byte: Surviving Cyberspace. Steven J. Baumrucker. (Illus.). 224p. (Orig.). 1995. pap. 14.95 (*0-9646312-1-0*) LMAO Pub Co.

***Love at First Sight.** B. J. Daniels. (Intrigue Ser.: Vol. 555). 2000. per. 4.25 (*0-373-22555-5*) Harlequin Bks.

Love at First Sight. Sandra Lee. 336p. 1999. mass mkt. 5.50 (*0-553-58008-6*) Bantam.

***Love At First Sight.** Earl Naumann. 2001. pap. 18.95 (*1-57071-623-4*, Casablanca) Sourcebks.

Love at First Sight. large type unabridged ed. (Harlequin Ser.). (C). 1990. lib. bdg. 18.95 (*0-263-12372-3*) Mac Lib Ref.

Love at Home. Khurram Murad. 48p. (J). 1996. pap. 3.50 (*0-614-21025-9*, 738) Kazi Pubns.

Love at Home - Starring Grandpa. George D. Durrant. LC 95-81232. 1995. pap. 7.95 (*1-57008-197-2*) Bookcraft Inc.

Love at Leisure. large type ed. Daisy Thomson. (Linford Romance Library). 320p. 1995. pap. 16.99 (*0-7089-7683-2*, Linford) Ulverscroft.

Love at Midlife: Building & Re-Building Relationships at Midlife. Richard A. Osing. LC 98-20707. 1998. pap. 13.95 (*0-945213-31-X*) Rudi Pub.

Love at Risk see Amor en Peligro: Looking after Dad

Love at Second Sight. large type ed. Peggy Gaddis. (Romance Ser.). 1994. pap. 16.99 (*0-7089-7604-2*, Linford) Ulverscroft.

Love at Second Sight. large type ed. Paul McLaughlin. (Large Print Ser.). (Illus.). 384p. 1996. 27.99 (*0-7089-3593-1*) Ulverscroft.

Love at Second Sight. large type ed. Elizabeth Ward. (Dales Large Print Ser.). 201p. 1995. pap. 18.99 (*1-85389-552-0*, Dales) Ulverscroft.

Love at the Egyptian Theatre. Barbara Drake. LC 78-50183. 1978. pap. 2.50 (*0-686-09378-X*) Red Cedar.

Love at the Heart of Things. Douglas V. Steele. LC 98-5450. 1998. 27.00 (*0-87574-959-3*) Pendle Hill.

Love at the Heart of Things: A Biography of Douglas V. Steere. Glenn E. Hinson. LC 98-13580. 1998. 16.50 (*0-8358-0860-2*) Upper Room Bks.

Love at the Heart of Things: A Biography of Douglas V. Steere. Douglas V. Steele & E. Glenn Hinson. LC 98-5450. 1998. pap. 17.00 (*0-87574-929-1*, 6016) Pendle Hill.

Love at Work: Using Your Job to Find a Mate. Margaret Kent & Robert Feinschreiber. LC 88-40078. 208p. 1989. mass mkt. 3.95 (*0-446-35635-2*, Pub. by Warner Bks) Little.

Love Awakens the Heart: Whatever Tomorrow Brings & As Time Goes By. Lori Wick. (Californians Ser.). 464p. 1998. 12.99 (*0-88486-194-5*, Inspirational Pr) Arrowood Pr.

Love Bade Me Welcome: Daily Readings with George Herbert. Gerrit S. Dawson. LC 97-92692. 249p. 1997. 16.00 (*0-9660973-1-9*) Glen Lorien Bks.

An Asterisk (*) at the beginning of an entry indicates that the title is appearing for the first time.

***Love Ballads.** 72p. 1999. pap. 7.95 (*1-57560-298-9*, Pub. by Cherry Lane) H Leonard.

***Love Ballads.** 216p. 1999. otabind 14.95 (*1-57560-294-6*, Pub. by Cherry Lane) H Leonard.

Love Ballads, Vol. 45. 48p. 1970. pap. 6.95 (*0-7935-4977-9*, 00100460) H Leonard.

Love Ballads of Lionel Richie (Piano - Vocal) Ed. by Milton Okun. (Illus.). 95p. (Orig.). 1990. pap. text 14.95 (*0-89524-343-1*) Cherry Lane.

Love Be Mine. Shirlee Busbee. 416p. 1998. mass mkt. 6.99 (*0-446-60530-1*, Pub. by Warner Bks) Little.

Love Bears All Things. gif. ed. LC 97-196974. (Illus.). 48p. 1997. 8.99 (*0-310-97067-9*) Zondervan.

Love, Beauty, & Harmony in Sufism. Nasrollah S. Fatemi et al. 12.95 (*0-8453-2248-6*, Cornwall Bks) Assoc Univ Prs.

Love Before the Law. Jacques Doyon. (C). 1988. 39.00 (*0-85439-250-5*, Pub. by St Paul Pubns) St Mut.

***Love Bein' Black: Poems in Celebration of Blackness.** (Illus.). 1999. pap. 10.95 (*0-9671226-0-0*) Honor Pr.

***Love Betrayed.** large type ed. Morag Lewis. 304p. 1999. pap. 18.99 (*0-7089-5579-7*, Linford) Ulverscroft.

Love Between Equals: A Philosophical Study of Love & Sexual Relationships. John Wilson. LC 95-10677. 240p. 1995. text 59.95 (*0-312-12729-4*) St Martin.

Love Between Equals: How Peer Marriage Really Works. Pepper Schwartz. 208p. 1995. per. 12.00 (*0-02-874061-0*) Free Pr.

Love Between Equals: How Peer Marriage Really Works. Pepper Schwartz. LC 94-4771. 1994. 19.95 (*0-02-931715-0*) Free Pr.

Love Between Fathers & Daughters. Ed. by Helen Exley. (Love Between Ser.). (Illus.). 60p. 1995. 9.00 (*1-85015-643-3*) Exley Giftbooks.

Love Between Fathers & Daughters. Ed. by Helen Exley. (Love Between (Suedels) Ser.). (Illus.). 60p. 1997. 12.00 (*1-85015-892-4*) Exley Giftbooks.

Love Between Fathers & Sons. Ed. by Helen Exley. (Love Between Ser.). (Illus.). 60p. 1995. 9.00 (*1-85015-642-5*) Exley Giftbooks.

Love Between Grandmothers & Grandchildren. Ed. by Helen Exley. (Love Between Ser.). (Illus.). 64p. 1997. 9.00 (*1-85015-852-5*) Exley Giftbooks.

Love Between Grandmothers & Grandchildren. Helen Exley. 1998. 12.00 (*1-86187-091-4*) Exley Giftbooks.

Love Between Men: Enhancing Intimacy & Keeping Your Relationship Alive. Rik Isensee. 224p. 1996. reprint ed. pap. text 12.95 (*1-55583-362-4*) Alyson Pubns.

Love Between Men in English Literature. Paul Hammond. LC 96-8834. 272p. 1996. pap. 18.95 (*0-312-16327-4*) St Martin.

Love Between Mothers & Daughters. Ed. by Helen Exley. (Love Between Ser.). (Illus.). 60p. 1995. 9.00 (*1-85015-640-9*) Exley Giftbooks.

Love Between Mothers & Daughters. Ed. by Helen Exley. (Love Between (Suedels) Ser.). (Illus.). 60p. 1997. 12.00 (*1-85015-890-8*) Exley Giftbooks.

Love Between Mothers & Sons. Ed. by Helen Exley. (Love Between Ser.). (Illus.). 60p. 1995. 9.00 (*1-85015-641-7*) Exley Giftbooks.

Love Between Mothers & Sons. Ed. by Helen Exley. (Love Between (Suedels) Ser.). (Illus.). 60p. 1997. 12.00 (*1-85015-891-6*) Exley Giftbooks.

Love Between Sisters. Ed. by Helen Exley. (Love Between Ser.). (Illus.). 64p. 1997. 9.00 (*1-85015-957-2*) Exley Giftbooks.

Love Between Women: Early Christian Responses to Female Homoeroticism. Bernadette J. Brooten. (Illus.). 416p. 1996. 34.95 (*0-226-07591-5*) U Ch Pr.

Love Between Women: Early Christian Responses to Female Homoeroticism. Bernadette J. Brooten. 1998. pap. 19.00 (*0-226-07592-3*) U Ch Pr.

Love Beyond Death: The Anatomy of a Myth in the Arts. Rudolph Binion. LC 92-35152. (C). 1993. text 45.00 (*0-8147-1189-8*) NYU Pr.

Love Beyond Desire. Jessica Marchant. 400p. (Orig.). 1997. mass mkt. 3.99 (*1-85487-925-1*, Pub. by Scarlet Bks) London Brdge.

Love Beyond Forever. Diana Haviland. 320p. 1999. mass mkt. 4.99 (*0-505-52293-4*, Love Spell) Dorchester Pub Co.

Love Beyond Life: The Healing Power of After-Death Communications. Joel Martin & Patricia Romanowski. 336p. 1998. mass mkt. 5.99 (*0-440-22649-X*) Dell.

***Love Beyond Reach.** Gillian Kaye. 200p. 2000. 18.99 (*0-7089-5704-8*) Ulverscroft.

Love Beyond Reason. Sandra Brown. 256p. 1994. reprint ed. mass mkt. 7.50 (*0-446-36070-8*, Pub. by Warner Bks) Little.

Love Beyond Reason. Sandra Brown. 256p. 1997. reprint ed. mass mkt. 3.99 (*0-446-60568-9*, Pub. by Warner Bks) Little.

Love Beyond Reason: Moving God's Love from Your Head to Your Heart. John Ortberg. LC 98-26062. 208p. 1998. 16.99 (*0-310-21215-4*) Zondervan.

Love Beyond Surrender. Susan C. Feldhake. (Serenade Saga Ser.: No. 10). 192p. (Orig.). 1984. pap. 2.50 (*0-310-46602-4*, 15519P) Zondervan.

Love Beyond the Stars: Spiritual Warriors. Maggie Chambers. Ed. by David Miller & Linda Miller. (Illus.). 106p. (Orig.). 1990. pap. 8.95 (*0-9624206-1-1*) Inner Mind Dynamics.

***Love Beyond Time.** Judie Aitken. (Time Passages Romance Ser.). 2000. mass mkt. 5.99 (*0-515-12744-2*, Jove) Berkley Pub.

Love Beyond Time. Marsha Newman. 329p. 1987. 14.95 (*0-9608658-3-7*) Wellspring Utah.

Love Beyond Time, 1 vol. Flora Speer. (Love Spell Ser.). 448p. 1999. mass mkt. 5.50 (*0-505-52326-4*) Dorchester Pub Co.

***Love Beyond Time: A Novel.** Nancy Campbell Allen. LC 99-36448. 1999. pap. 12.95 (*1-57734-540-1*, 01114344) Covenant Comms.

***Love Beyond Words.** Sandra Kuck. LC 99-40856. 64p. 2000. 16.99 (*0-7369-0284-8*) Harvest Hse.

***Love Binds Us Together.** Stormie Omartian. (Moment Meditation Ser.). 64p. 2000. pap. 7.99 (*0-7369-0193-0*) Harvest Hse.

Love Bite. Sherry Gottlieb. 288p. (Orig.). 1994. mass mkt. 5.99 (*0-446-36537-8*, Pub. by Warner Bks) Little.

***Love Bite: Alien Interference in Human Love Relationships.** Eve F. Lorgen. (Illus.). 224p. 1999. 24.95 (*0-918501-97-0*, Archives Pr); pap. 19.95 (*0-918501-98-9*, Archives Pr) Media Assocs.

***Love Bite: Alien Interference in Human Love Relationships.** large type ed. Ed. by G. H. Harrison. LC 99-64144. (Illus.). xi, 224p. 1999. pap. 19.95 (*0-9677737-0-9*, EL-011) ELogos & HHC.

Love Bites. Ed. by Amarantha Knight. LC 95-206267. (Orig.). 1995. pap. 12.95 (*1-56333-234-5*, R Kasak Bks) Masquerade.

Love Bites. Margaret St. George. LC 95-8351. (American Romance Ser.). 249p. 1995. mass mkt. 3.50 (*0-373-16582-X*, 1-16582-8) Harlequin Bks.

Love Bitter & Sweet. David L. Porter. LC 97-17489. (Illus.). 96p. 1997. pap. 10.00 (*0-7867-0470-5*) Carroll & Graf.

Love Blossom. Leroy Nabauns. Ed. by Yvette B. McCann. 136p. (Orig.). 1997. pap. 14.00 (*0-9660263-2-2*) Vol Pr.

Love Boat (Collector's Edition), 2 bks. Jeraldine Saunders. (Illus.). 336p. 1998. pap. 24.95 (*1-56718-614-9*) Llewellyn Pubns.

Love Boats: Above & Below Decks with Jeraldine Saunders. Jeraldine Saunders. LC 98-35514. (Illus.). 336p. 1999. 12.95 (*1-56718-607-6*, K607) Llewellyn Pubns.

Love Book. John R. Price. 112p. 1998. pap. 7.00 (*1-56170-503-9*, 869) Hay House.

Love Book. Norma J. Stodden & Linda McCormick. Ed. by Gail Levy. (Baby Sign Bks.). (Illus.). 18p. (J). (ps). 1988. bds. 3.95 (*0-943693-04-7*) TRI Pubns.

Love Book for Couples: Building a Healthy Relationship. E. Michael Lillibridge. LC 83-81431. 144p. (Orig.). 1984. lib. bdg. 26.95 (*0-89334-209-2*, 209-2) Humanics Ltd.

Love Books of Ovid. Ovid. 20.00 (*0-8196-2769-0*) Biblo.

Love Breaks. Oscar Hahn. Tr. by James Hoggard from SPA. LC 90-26915. (Discoveries Ser.). (ENG & SPA.). 64p. 1991. pap. 10.50 (*0-935480-49-8*) Lat Am Lit Rev Pr.

Love Breaks Through. K. Mackinnon. 6.99 (*1-85792-027-9*, Pub. by Christian Focus) Spring Arbor Dist.

Love Broke Through: The True Story of Tom Stribling. Thomas B. Stribling & Verne Becker. 224p. 1990. pap. 8.99 (*0-310-52861-5*) Zondervan.

Love Bug. Scott Sorrentino. LC 97-80150. (Wonderful World of Disney Ser.). 80p. (J). (gr. 3-7). 1997. pap. 3.25 (*0-7868-4211-3*, Pub. by Disney Pr) Time Warner.

***Love Bug & Other Tales of Psychotherapy.** Dan Briddell. LC 00-27327. 272p. 2000. text 24.95 (*0-312-24249-2*) St Martin.

Love Bugs. David A. Carter. LC 95-141692. (Bug Bks.: No. 1). (Illus.). 10p. (J). (ps-2). 1995. per. 12.95 (*0-671-86629-X*) Little Simon.

***Love Bugs.** Havoc Publishing Staff. 1999. 8.00 (*1-57977-661-2*) Havoc Pub.

Love Burning Deep: Poems & Lyrics. Kathy Galloway. (Illus.). pap. 15.95 (*0-687-85711-2*) Abingdon.

Love Busters: Overcoming the Habits that Destroy Romantic Love. 2nd rev. ed. Willard F. Harley, Jr. LC 97-1794. 192p. 1997. 16.99 (*0-8007-1739-2*) Revell.

Love by Chocolate. Rosanne Bittner et al. 320p. 1997. mass mkt. 5.99 (*0-515-12014-6*, Jove) Berkley Pub.

Love by Degree & The Boardroom Bridegroom, 2 bks. in 1, Bk. 1. 50th anniversary ed. Debbie Macomber & Renee Roszel. (Harlequin 50th Anniversary Collection Ser.). 377p. 1999. mass mkt. 6.99 (*0-373-83409-8*, 1-83409-2, Harlequin) Harlequin Bks.

Love by Design. Marcella Sanders. 1999. mass mkt. 4.99 (*1-58314-022-0*) BET Bks.

Love by Mail: The International Guide to Personal Advertising. Richard N. Cote. LC 92-28035. 1992. pap. 9.95 (*0-910155-22-4*, Enigma Bks) Bartleby Pr.

Love by Proxy. Diana Palmer. 1994. per. 3.59 (*0-373-45163-6*) Silhouette.

Love by the Bolt. Georges Feydeau. Tr. by J. Paul Marcoux. 78p. 1984. pap. 5.50 (*0-87129-176-2*, L55) Dramatic Pub.

Love by the Numbers: Form & Meaning in the Poetry of Catullus. Helena Dettmer. LC 96-41571. (Lang Classical Studies: No. 10). XVIII, 366p. (C). 1997. text 58.95 (*0-8204-3663-1*) P Lang Pubng.

Love Bytes. Sally Chapman. (WWL Mystery Ser.). 1996. per. 4.99 (*0-373-26197-7*, 1-26197-3, Wrldwide Lib) Harlequin Bks.

Love Bytes: Cafe 1. Elizabeth Craft. 224p. (J). (gr. 7). 1997. per. 3.99 (*0-671-00445-X*, Archway) PB.

Love Calendar: The Secrets of Love. Peggy R. Thorne. LC 93-83848. (Illus.). 160p. (Orig.). 1993. pap. 9.95 (*0-9626762-2-5*) PM Pubs.

Love Calls the Doctor. Elizabeth Seifert. 1974. reprint ed. lib. bdg. 23.95 (*0-88411-039-7*) Amereon Ltd.

Love Calls Us to the Things of This World: The Return to Belmont in the Merchant of Venice. Jeanne Heifetz. (LeBaron Russell Briggs Prize Honors Essays in English Ser.). 80p. 1982. pap. 4.25 (*0-674-53922-2*) HUP.

Love Came Laughing By. Emilie Loring. 20.95 (*0-89190-128-0*) Amereon Ltd.

Love Can Be Repaired. Dale E. Galloway. 178p. 1990. pap. 8.95 (*1-885605-08-0*) Scott-Twnty-Twnty.

Love Can Be Sweet Even with Diabetes. Janet Meirelles. 1999. pap. 18.95 (*1-58040-012-4*) Am Diabetes.

Love Can Build a Bridge. Naomi Judd. LC 96-2393. (Illus.). 32p. (J). 1999. 15.95 incl. audio (*0-06-027206-6*) HarpC Child Bks.

Love Can Build a Bridge. Naomi Judd & Bud Schaetzle. LC 92-50239. 1994. mass mkt. 6.99 (*0-449-22274-8*, Crest) Fawcett.

Love Canal: The Story Continues... Lois M. Gibbs. 240p. 1998. pap. 16.95 (*0-86571-382-0*) New Soc Pubs.

***Love Canal: Toxic Waste Tragedy.** Victoria Sherrow. LC 00-9474. (American Disasters Ser.). (Illus.). (J). 2001. write for info. (*0-7660-1553-X*) Enslow Pubs.

Love Cards: What Your Birthday Reveals about You & Your Personal Relationships. 3rd ed. Robert Camp. LC 97-1800. 384p. 1997. otabind 24.95 (*1-57071-145-3*) Sourcebks.

***Love Carried Me Home: Women Surviving Auschwitz.** Joy Erlichman Miller. 250p. 2000. pap. 11.95 (*1-55874-824-5*, Simcha Press) Health Comm.

Love, Celibacy & the Inner Marriage. John P. Dourley. 128p. 1987. pap. 16.00 (*0-919123-28-7*, Pub. by Inner City Bks) BookWorld.

***Love-Centered Life: Eileen M. Dooling-Plecki & Christine A. Ruddy.** Eileen M. Dooling-Plecki & Christine A. Ruddy. (Illus.). 240p. 2000. 22.95 (*1-58151-071-3*, Pub. by BookPartners) Midpt Trade.

Love-Centered Marriage in a Self-Centered World. Irving Sarnoff & Suzanne Sarnoff. 1989. 79.95 (*0-89116-927-X*) Hemisp Pub.

Love Chains: Stories. Margaret B. Young. LC 96-14253. 216p. (Orig.). 1997. pap. 17.95 (*1-56085-084-1*) Signature Bks.

Love Changes Everything. Kalu Okpi. (Heartbeats Ser.). 112p. (YA). (gr. 7 up). 1994. pap. 4.99 (*0-7910-2934-4*) Chelsea Hse.

Love Changes Everything. ArLynn Presser. (Love Stories Ser.). 176p. (Orig.). (YA). (gr. 7-12). 1995. mass mkt. 3.99 (*0-553-56665-2*) BDD Bks Young Read.

Love Charade. large type ed. Janet Beaton. (Linford Romance Library). 1991. pap. 16.99 (*0-7089-7053-2*) Ulverscroft.

Love Charm. Pamela Morsi. 384p. 1996. mass mkt. 5.99 (*0-380-78641-9*, Avon Bks) Morrow Avon.

***Love Charm.** large type ed. Pamela Morsi. LC 98-24628. 424 p. 1998. 25.95 (*0-7838-0307-9*, G K Hall & Co) Mac Lib Ref.

Love Charms & Spells. Jade. 1997. pap. 5.95 (*0-942272-47-1*) Original Pubns.

Love Charms & Spells. 2nd ed. Jade. Ed. by Judith DeFrain. (Illus.). 86p. 1984. reprint ed. pap. 10.00 (*0-9619008-0-6*) Eye Cat.

***Love Checks.** Ed. by Michael Omara Books U. K. Staff. 80p. 2000. pap. 5.95 (*1-57071-519-X*) Sourcebks.

Love Chef Cooks Pasta. Francis Anthony. LC 97-48319. (Illus.). 224p. 1998. 20.00 (*0-688-14969-3*, Hearst) Hearst Commns.

Love, Cherish Me. Rebecca Brandewyne. 576p. 1999. mass mkt. 5.99 (*0-505-52302-7*) Dorchester Pub Co.

Love Child. Meg Alexander. 1999. per. 4.99 (*0-373-30336-X*) Harlequin Bks.

***Love Child.** I. Carr. 1999. text 35.00 (*0-340-68951-X*, Pub. by Hodder & Stought Ltd) Trafalgar.

Love Child. Patricia Coughlin. (Silhouette Ser.: No. 245). 1992. mass mkt. 4.99 (*0-373-48245-0*) Silhouette.

Love Child. Angela Drake. (Scarlet Ser.). 1997. mass mkt. 3.99 (*1-85487-987-1*, Pub. by Scarlet Bks) London Brdge.

***Love Child.** Angela Drake. 496p. 2000. 31.99 (*0-7505-1509-0*) Ulverscroft.

Love-Child. Kathryn Ross. (Presents Ser.: No. 1938). 1998. per. 3.75 (*0-373-11938-0*, 1-11938-7) Harlequin Bks.

Love Child. Eve Shelnutt. LC 78-27484. 160p. (Orig.). 1979. pap. 9.00 (*0-87685-384-X*) Black Sparrow.

Love Child. large type ed. Catherine Cookson. 512p. 1992. lib. bdg. 14.95 (*1-56054-935-1*) Thorndike Pr.

Love Child: Where There Is Love: Upon the Storm, 2 vols. in 1. Annette Broadrick & Justine Davis. (By Request 2's Ser.). 2000. per. 4.99 (*0-373-21704-8*, 1-21704-1) Harlequin Bks.

Love, Chrissie. Delores Stacy. 1986. pap. 3.95 (*0-317-89499-4*) Delcy Bks.

Love Clan: The Family of Daniel Love & Sarah McColl. Mabel R. Love. (Illus.). 192p. (Orig.). 1992. pap. 20.00 (*0-9632429-0-3*) Love Pubs.

Love Classic: Secret Sexual. James L. Gong. Ed. by Weihua Ma. (CHI., Illus.). 1998. pap. 18.00 (*0-9663964-2-1*) Pacific Internat.

Love Clinic: There Is a Doctor in the House. Sheron C. Patterson. (Illus.). 1999. pap. 10.00 (*0-9667850-0-2*) Black Pearl Pub.

***Love Coach: You Have Never Been Taught How to Make Love Work, until Now.** Susan Quilliam. 2000. pap. 12.95 (*0-7225-3986-X*) Thorsons PA.

Love Come of Age: Reflections on Christian Spirituality. John H. Miller. 135p. 1998. pap. 10.00 (*1-887567-11-9*) CBCCU Amer.

Love Comes Softly. Janette Oke. LC 79-16421. (Love Comes Softly Ser.: Vol. 1). 192p. 1979. pap. 8.99 (*0-87123-342-8*) Bethany Hse.

Love Comes Softly. Janette Oke. 1979. 14.09 (*0-606-03052-2*, Pub. by Turtleback) Demco.

Love Comes Softly, 4 vols., Vol. 5-8. Janette Oke. 1993. boxed set 35.99 (*1-55661-778-X*) Bethany Hse.

Love Comes Softly: Gift Set, 4 vols., Vol. 1-4. Janette Oke. (Orig.). 1993. pap. text 35.99 (*1-55661-777-1*) Bethany Hse.

Love Commandments: Essays in Christian Ethics & Moral Philosophy. Ed. by Edmund N. Santurri & William Werpehowski. LC 90-49503. 327p. (Orig.). 1992. pap. text 25.00 (*0-685-64839-7*) Georgetown U Pr.

Love, Commandments & Values: An Interfaith Perspective. Sajjad Haider. 1997. pap. 14.95 (*0-614-27518-0*) Kazi Pubns.

Love Communings: Soul Embracings with the Spirit of the Unborn Child. Thaemas A. Maharriyum. (Illus.). 68p. (Orig.). 1985. write for info. (*0-912323-02-7*); pap. write for info. (*0-912323-01-9*) Apollo Phonic.

Love, Conflict, & Marriage. Paul H. Eichar. 1994. pap. 5.95 (*1-55673-589-8*, 7988) CSS OH.

Love Conquers All: Essays on Holy Living. W. E. McCumber. 100p. (Orig.). 1993. pap. 7.99 (*0-8341-1455-0*) Beacon Hill.

Love Conquers Nothing: A Glandular History of Civilization. Emily Hahn. LC 70-148215. (Biography Index Reprint Ser.). 1977. reprint ed. 23.95 (*0-8369-8062-X*) Ayer.

Love Constrained. Michael Howard. Ed. by Rozella Heyns. (Illus.). 244p. (Orig.). 1996. pap. 8.00 (*1-888529-02-4*) Out of Africa Pub.

Love Contracts. Helen Duncan. 144p. 1998. pap. 6.95 (*0-9652813-3-7*) Dello & Assoc.

Love Coupons. Gregory J. P. Godek. LC 96-50432. (Illus.). 128p. 1996. pap. 5.95 (*1-57071-155-0*, Casablanca) Sourcebks.

Love, Covenant & Meaning. Jonathan Mills. 140p. 1997. pap. 14.95 (*1-57383-091-7*) Regent College.

Love Covers see O Amor Cobre Todo

Love Covers. Paul E. Billheimer. 1980. pap. 8.99 (*0-87508-006-5*) Chr Lit.

Love Crazy: Outrageous but True Stories of How Couples Met & Married. Allan Zullo & Kathryn Zullo. (Illus.). 112p. (Orig.). 1996. pap. 7.95 (*0-8362-1049-2*) Andrews & McMeel.

Love Creates Balance. Melford Okilo. 1991. 3.00 (*1-879605-04-X*) U Sci & Philos.

Love Cry-Poems. Franklin W. Hamilton. 1970. pap. 2.95 (*0-911938-03-6*) Walden Pr.

Love Cure: Therapy Erotic & Sexual. John R. Haule. 176p. 1996. pap. 18.50 (*0-88214-513-4*) Spring Pubns.

Love Customs in Eighteenth-Century Spain. Carmen M. Gaite. Tr. by Maria G. Tomsich from SPA. LC 90-24575. 273p. 1991. 45.00 (*0-520-07043-7*, Pub. by U CA Pr) Cal Prin Full Svc.

***Love Cuts.** John Hegley. LC 97-148536. 128p. 1998. mass mkt. write for info. (*0-7493-2194-6*) Random House.

Love Cycles: The Science of Intimacy. Winnifred B. Cutler. (Illus.). 330p. 1996. reprint ed. write for info. (*0-9651753-0-8*) Athena Inst.

Love, Dad see Con Todo Mi Amor Papa

Love, Dad see Con Todo Mi Amor, Papa

Love, Dad: Letters of Faith to My Children. Herbert Brokering. LC 98-9577. 1998. pap. text 10.99 (*0-8066-3619-X*, 9-3619, Augsburg) Augsburg Fortress.

Love Dance. Maureen Stephenson. (Rainbow Romances Ser.: No. 902). 160p. 1994. 14.95 (*0-7090-4981-1*) Parkwest Pubns.

Love Dance. large type ed. Maureen Stephenson. (Linford Romance Library). 256p. 1996. pap. 16.99 (*0-7089-7891-6*, Linford) Ulverscroft.

Love Dances. Molefi K. Asante. LC 95-71324. (Illus.). 80p. 1996. pap. text 9.95 (*0-9635245-9-3*) Sungai Bks.

Love Dances. Van V. Heffner. (Illus.). 200p. (Orig.). 1995. pap. 12.95 (*0-9649610-0-8*) H&A Pubng.

Love Dances: Poems. Harvey Grady. 80p. 1993. pap. write for info. (*1-883876-02-8*) Ctr Human Potent.

Love Dangerously. large type ed. Peggy L. Jones. (Linford Romance Library). 320p. 1989. pap. 16.99 (*0-7089-6699-3*, Linford) Ulverscroft.

Love Dat Cat: 165 Wonderful Things You Can Do for Your Cat. Jill Kramer. Ed. by Cliff Carle. 176p. 1996. mass mkt. 6.95 (*1-57644-006-0*) CCC Pubns.

Love, Dating & Marriage. George B. Eager. LC 86-90552. (Illus.). 136p. (Orig.). (YA). (gr. 6-12). 1987. pap. 5.95 (*0-9603752-5-2*) Mailbox.

Love, Dating & Sex: What Teens Want to Know. George B. Eager. (Illus.). 208p. (YA). (gr. 7-12). 1988. lib. bdg. 16.95 (*0-9603752-9-5*) Mailbox.

Love, Dating & Sex: What Teens Want to Know. George B. Eager. (Illus.). 208p. (YA). (gr. 7-12). 1989. pap. text 10.95 (*0-9603752-8-7*) Mailbox.

Love, Death & Exile: Poems Translated from Arabic. Abdul W. Al-Bayati. Tr. by Bassam K. Frangieh from ARA. LC 90-20394. 314p. (Orig.). (C). 1991. pap. 14.95 (*0-87840-218-7*) Georgetown U Pr.

Love, Death, & the Changing of the Seasons. Marilyn Hacker. 216p. 1995. pap. 11.00 (*0-393-31225-9*) Norton.

Love, Death & the Prom. Jon Jory. 54p. 1991. pap. 5.50 (*0-87129-120-7*, L69) Dramatic Pub.

Love Debate Poems of Christine de Pizan. Barbara K. Altmann. LC 97-43642. 336p. 1998. 49.95 (*0-8130-1578-2*) U Press Fla.

Love, Debra. Fritz Hamilton. LC 90-7412. 132p. (Orig.). 1990. 19.95 (*0-940880-30-X*); pap. 9.95 (*0-940880-29-6*) Open Hand.

***Love Denied.** Willa Johnson. 64p. 2000. pap. 6.95 (*1-58597-016-6*) Leathers Pub.

Love Derived. Gary Taylor, Sr. (Illus.). 37p. (Orig.). 1994. pap. 4.00 (*1-56411-081-8*) Untd Bros & Sis.

Love Diatribe. Harry Kondoleon. 1991. pap. 5.25 (*0-8222-0690-0*) Dramatists Play.

Love Dipped in Blackness. Mansa K. Ra'Ifa. 48p. 1999. pap. 8.00 (*0-8059-4718-3*) Dorrance.

***Love Disconsoled: Meditations on Christian Charity.** Timothy P. Jackson. LC 99-12129. (Cambridge Studies in Religion & Critical Thought: No. 7). (Illus.). 280p. (C). 1999. 59.95 (*0-521-55493-4*) Cambridge U Pr.

Love Diseases. Paul Redfern. (Illus.). 150p. 1981. reprint ed. pap. 4.95 (*0-8065-0772-1*, Citadel Pr) Carol Pub Group.

***Love Disorder.** Conrad Boeding. Ed. by Judith Champion. (Illus.). 170p. 1998. per. 17.00 (*0-9668302-0-2*, Pub. by Human Pass Inst) Herveys Bklink.

An Asterisk (*) at the beginning of an entry indicates that the title is appearing for the first time.

Love Divine. Alexandra Ripley. 832p. 1997. mass mkt. 7.99 (*0-446-60472-0*, Pub. by Warner Bks); mass mkt. 215.73 (*0-446-16428-3*) Warner Bks.

Love Divine: Studies in Bhakti & Devotional Mysticism. Ed. by Karel Werner. (Durham Indological Ser.: No. 3). (Illus.). 244p. (C). 1996. text 45.00 (*0-7007-0235-0*, Pub. by Curzon Pr Ltd) UH Pr.

Love Does No Harm: Sexual Ethics for the Rest of Us. Marie M. Fortune. 156p. 1998. reprint ed. pap. 12.95 (*0-8264-1128-2*) Continuum.

Love Does Not Condemn: The World, the Flesh, & the Devil According to Platonism, Christianity, Gnosticism, & "A Course in Miracles" Kenneth Wapnick. LC 89-16887. 614p. 1989. 25.00 (*0-933291-07-8*) Foun Miracles.

Love down Under. large type ed. James Leasor. (Adventure Suspense Ser.). 512p. 1993. 27.99 (*0-7089-2969-9*) Ulverscroft.

Love Drug: Marching to the Beat of Ecstasy. Richard S. Cohen. LC 97-39231. 166p. 1998. 39.95 (*0-7890-0453-4*, Hawrth Medical); pap. 19.95 (*0-7890-0454-2*, Hawrth Medical) Haworth Pr.

Love Duets One Piano Four Hands Piano Duet: Seven Romatic Ballads. 56p. 1997. pap. 8.95 (*0-7935-6951-6*) H Leonard.

***Love Each Other.** Ed. by Porchlight Entertainment Staff. (Jay Jay the Jet Plane Board Bks.: Vol. 3). (Illus.). 12p. (J). (ps). 2000. 5.99 (*0-8499-7552-2*) Tommy Nelson.

Love Earth: The Beauty Makeover. Shelly Nielsen & Julie Berg. LC 93-18954. (Target Earth Ser.). (J). 1993. pap. 7.49 (*1-56239-409-6*) ABDO Pub Co.

Love Earth: The Beauty Makeover. Shelly Nielsen & Julie Berg. LC 93-18954. (Target Earth Ser.). (Illus.). (J). (ps-7). 1993. lib. bdg. 15.98 (*1-56239-198-4*) ABDO Pub Co.

Love Eaters & The Kiss of Kin. Mary Lee Settle. LC 95-32164. (Mary Lee Settle Collection). 388p. (C). 1995. reprint ed. pap. 14.95 (*1-57003-098-7*) U of SC Pr.

Love Eclipsed: Joyce Carol Oates' Faustian Moral Vision. Nancy A. Watanabe. 1997. write for info. (*0-614-29715-X*) U Pr of Amer.

Love Eclipsed: Joyce Carol Oates's Faustian Moral Vision. Nancy A. Watanabe. LC 97-38946. 216p. (C). 1997. text 39.50 (*0-7618-0934-1*) U Pr of Amer.

Love Elegies of the Renaissance: Marot, Louise Labe & Ronsard. Gertrude S. Hanisch. (Stanford French & Italian Studies: No. 15). viii, 145p. 1979. pap. 56.50 (*0-915838-24-9*) Anma Libri.

***Love, Ellen: A Mother/Daughter Journey.** Betty DeGeneres. 384p. 2000. pap. 14.00 (*0-688-17688-7*, Quil) HarperTrade.

Love, Ellen: A Mother/Daughter Journey. Betty DeGeneres. LC 98-50367. (Illus.). 366p. 1999. 24.00 (*0-688-16274-6*, Wm Morrow) Morrow Avon.

Love Em . . . And Leave Em. Leamon T. Reynolds. 184p. (Orig.). (C). 1989. pap. 6.95 (*1-877917-06-0*) Alpha Bible Pubns.

Love 'Em & Lead 'Em. Paul B. Malone, III. LC 86-60237. (Illus.). 192p. (Orig.). 1986. 18.95 (*0-9616548-1-3*); pap. 10.95 (*0-9616548-0-5*) Synergy Pr.

Love 'Em or Lose 'Em: Getting Good People to Stay. Beverly L. Kaye & Sharon Jordan-Evans. LC 99-38557. (Illus.). 233p. 1999. 17.95 (*1-57675-073-6*) Berrett-Koehler.

Love Embraces Destiny: The Cambridge Chronicles. Donna F. Crow. (Cambridge Chronicles Ser.). 1999. 11.99 (*0-88486-225-9*, Inspirational Pr) Arrowood Pr.

Love Enter. Paul Kafka. 336p. 1997. pap. 12.00 (*0-395-86001-6*) HM.

Love Enthroned. Daniel Steele. 1984. 8.99 (*0-88019-077-9*) Schmul Pub Co.

***Love, Etc.** Julian Barnes. 2001. 24.00 (*0-375-41161-5*) Knopf.

Love Eternal: A Heart Cries, Yet Love E'er Abides. Jerry D. Babb. LC 95-62094. (Illus.). 128p. (Orig.). 1996. 19.95 (*0-9649513-1-2*); pap. 9.95 (*0-9649513-0-4*) White Buck.

Love Everlastin' Mickee Madden. 352p. 1998. pap. 5.99 (*0-7860-0527-6*, Pinncle Kensgtn) Kensgtn Pub Corp.

Love Everlasting. Charlotte Austen. 352p. (Orig.). 1988. mass mkt. 3.95 (*0-446-34966-6*, Pub. by Warner Bks) Little.

Love Everlasting. Anna Larence. (Arabesque Ser.). 256p. 1998. pap. 4.99 (*0-7860-0512-2*, Pinncle Kensgtn) Kensgtn Pub Corp.

Love Every Woman Needs: Intimacy with Jesus. Jan McCray. LC 97-13496. 256p. 1997. pap. 12.99 (*0-8007-9253-X*) Chosen Bks.

Love Exchange: An Adventure in Prayer. Margaret Therkelsen. LC 97-43970. 160p. 1998. pap. 9.99 (*0-8007-5660-6*) Revell.

Love Experience. Roger Christopherson. Ed. by Sheri Hirst. 124p. (Orig.). 1984. pap. 5.95 (*0-914597-01-9*) Pubs West AZ.

Love Express. Sierra Leone. 256p. (Orig.). 1995. pap. 3.95 (*1-877606-01-4*) R Romance.

Love, Face to Face. Yvonne Hendrix. LC 97-90446. 64p. 1998. pap. 8.95 (*0-533-12404-2*) Vantage.

Love, Faith, & Hope: A Collection of Inspirational Poems, Short Stories, Essays, & Treasures. Kenya R. Martin et al. 210p. 1998. 15.00 (*0-9664022-0-0*) Martin Triplts.

***Love, Fear & Other Things That Cry Out in the Night: Moments Alone with Agoraphobia.** Marilyn R. Moody. LC 99-91490. 2000. 25.00 (*0-7388-0832-6*); pap. 18.00 (*0-7388-0833-4*) Xlibris Corp.

Love-Fear Tapestry. large type ed. Muriel Janes. (Linford Romance Library). 240p. 1994. pap. 16.99 (*0-7089-7509-7*, Linford) Ulverscroft.

Love Feast. Robert Stowe. 12p. (Orig.). 1987. pap. 5.95 (*0-940754-41-X*) Ed Ministries.

Love Feud. Martha Corson. 1983. pap. 1.95 (*0-373-46067-8*) Harlequin Bks.

Love-Fifteen. Antonio Skarmeta. Tr. by Jonathan Tittler from SPA. LC 96-4268. (Discoveries Ser.). 128p. (Orig.). (C). 1996. pap. 13.95 (*0-935480-82-X*) Lat Am Lit Rev Pr.

Love Finds a Home. large type ed. Janette Oke. (Love Comes Softly Ser.: Vol. 8). 224p. 1989. pap. 8.99 (*1-55661-086-6*) Bethany Hse.

***Love First: A New Approach to Intervention.** Jeff Jay & Debra Erickson Jay. 208p. 2000. pap. 14.00 (*1-56838-521-8*) Hazelden.

Love Flight: A Poetic Journey. LaVonne Sullivan. (Flight Ser.: Vol. III). (Illus.). 16p. 1996. pap. 3.00 (*1-885800-06-1*) PineTree Pr.

Love Flower. Joan Elizabeth Lloyd. 224p. 1998. pap. 10.95 (*0-7867-0531-0*) Carroll & Graf.

Love Flute. Goble. (J). 1998. pap. 5.99 (*0-87628-517-5*) Ctr Appl Res.

Love Flute. Paul Goble. LC 91-19716. (Illus.). 32p. (J). (ps up). 1992. text 16.00 (*0-02-736261-2*, Bradbury S&S) S&S Childrens.

Love Flute. Paul Goble. LC 91-19716. (Illus.). 32p. (J). (gr. k-3). 1997. per. 5.99 (*0-689-81683-9*) S&S Childrens.

Love Flute. Paul Goble. 1997. 11.19 (*0-606-12404-7*, Pub. by Turtleback) Demco.

Love Follows the Heart. large type ed. June M. Bacher. 352p. (Orig.). 1991. pap. 8.95 (*0-8027-2662-3*) Walker & Co.

***Love Food, Lose Weight: 3 Essential Steps to Enjoying Food for Perfect Helath.** Stephen Twigg. 2000. pap. 13.95 (*0-452-28152-0*, Plume) Dutton Plume.

Love for a Lifetime see Amor Para Toda la Vida

Love for a Lifetime. audio compact disk 15.99 (*1-57673-629-6*) Multnomah Pubs.

Love for a Lifetime: Building a Marriage That Will Go the Distance. James Dobson. 143p. 1994. pap. 5.99 (*0-88070-683-X*, Multnomah Bks) Multnomah Pubs.

Love for a Lifetime: Building a Marriage That Will Go the Distance. James Dobson. 1999. 19.99 (*1-57673-588-5*) Multnomah Pubs.

Love for a Night see Amor de una Noche

Love for All Life see Amor para Toda la Vida

Love for All Seasons. Denise Domning. 1996. mass mkt. 5.99 (*0-451-40704-0*, Onyx) NAL.

Love for All Seasons: A Do It Yourself Resourcebook to Enhance Marital Relationships. Patrick J. Aspell & Dee Dee Aspell. 114p. 1995. spiral bd. 17.95 (*1-881773-02-7*) Lifewings.

Love for Hire. Jasmine Cresswell. (Romance Ser.: No. 176). 1992. per. 2.79 (*0-373-03176-9*, 1-03176-4) Harlequin Bks.

***Love for Ivy.** Virginia Hart. LC 98-96846. 192p. 1999. lib. bdg. 18.95 (*0-8034-9335-5*, Avalon Bks) Bouregy.

Love for Life. Robert L. Brotzman. 63p. 1999. pap. 9.95 (*0-7414-0109-6*) Buy Books.

Love for Love. William Congreve. Ed. by Emmett L. Avery. LC 66-20827. (Regents Restoration Drama Ser.). 165p. 1966. reprint ed. pap. 51.20 (*0-608-02042-7*, 206269500003) Bks Demand.

Love for Love. 2nd ed. Malcolm Kelsall. (C). 1999. pap. text 8.00 (*0-393-90084-3*) Norton.

Love for Lydia, 1. Jeanne Savery. 256p. 1999. mass mkt. 4.99 (*0-8217-6321-0*) Kensgtn Pub Corp.

Love for Other Things: New & Selected Poems. Tom Hennen. 1993. 4.00 (*0-941127-13-3*) Dacotah Terr Pr.

Love for Priscilla. Glenda Moriwaki. (Illus.). 28p. (Orig.). (J). (ps-3). 1991. pap. 4.95 (*0-9627956-7-4*) Meadora Pub.

Love for Sale. John Leslie. (Gideon Lowry Mystery Ser.). 272p. 1997. per. 6.50 (*0-671-51126-2*) PB.

Love for Sale. Sharon Stewart. (Love & Laughter Ser.: No. 36). 1998. per. 3.50 (*0-373-44036-7*) Harlequin Bks.

Love for Sale: A Gideon Lowry Mystery. John Leslie. LC 96-8554. 1997. 22.00 (*0-671-51127-0*) PB.

Love for Sale: Materialist Readings of the Troubadour Razo Corpus. William E. Burgwinkle. LC 97-30606. (New Middle Ages Ser.: Vol. 5). (Illus.). 360p. 1997. text 70.00 (*0-8153-2842-7*, H2067) Garland.

Love for Sale: The Words & Pictures of Barbara Kruger. Kate Linker. (Illus.). 96p. 1996. pap. 16.95 (*0-8109-2651-2*, Pub. by Abrams) Time Warner.

Love for the Living: Meditations on the Meaning of Marriage & Life. Dan Saferstein. LC 99-47908. 224p. 2000. 22.95 (*0-7868-6530-X*, Pub. by Hyperion) Time Warner.

Love Forever: Yayoi Kusama in New York 1958-1968. Yayoi Kusama. LC 97-75136. (Illus.). 192p. 1998. pap. 29.95 (*0-87587-181-X*, 810021) LA Co Art Mus.

Love Forever - Poetry for Lovers. Johnny Walker. 69p. 1998. pap. 16.00 (*0-9662701-0-X*) Aspire Bks.

***Love Forever True.** Nelson Word Publishing Group Staff. (Precious Moments Seasons of Faith Ser.). (Illus.). 32p. 2000. 7.99 (*0-7852-5534-6*) Nelson.

Love Forevermore. Madeline Baker. 432p. 1997. mass mkt. 5.99 (*0-8439-4267-3*, Leisure Bks) Dorchester Pub Co.

Love Formula: A Unique Way to Evaluate Your Love Partner. 2nd ed. Blair MacArthur. 287p. 1990. 15.95 (*0-944052-00-2*) Cayman Isle Ent.

Love Formulas: The Works! Nance McCullough. (Illus.). 85p. 1980. pap. 4.40 (*0-936916-01-X*) NAMAC.

Love Formulas: The Works. rev. ed. Nance McCullough. (Illus.). 85p. 1981. pap. 8.45 (*0-936916-02-8*, Pub. by NAMAC) New Leaf Dist.

Love Forty: A Play. Frank Vickery. LC 98-145398. 70 p. 1997. write for info. (*0-573-01826-X*) S French Trade.

***Love Found a Way: Stories of Christmas.** Ron Mehl. LC 99-33692. 160p. 1999. 12.95 (*1-57856-276-7*) Waterbrook Pr.

Love Foundation. Cristie M. Buckley. 32p. (Orig.). 1989. pap. 0.75 (*0-88144-140-6*) Christian Pub.

Love Foundation. Cristie M. Buckley. (Orig.). 1987. pap. 0.75 (*0-9618333-0-0*) Renais Pub.

Love from Below. Wild Goose Publications Staff. (C). 1990. 25.00 (*0-947988-34-3*, Pub. by Wild Goose Pubns) St Mut.

Love, from Grandma: Words of Wisdom & Hope from America's Grandmothers. Rebecca Amble. (Illus.). 144p. (Orig.). 1994. pap. 10.95 (*0-9643203-0-4*) Future Focus.

Love from Grandma Gift Book. Illus. by Jennifer Parker. 96p. 1998. 12.99 (*1-58375-422-9*) Garborgs.

Love, from Grandma Gift Book: Words of Wisdom & Hope from Grandmothers Around the World. Compiled by Becky L. Amble. 144p. 1995. pap. 9.99 (*1-881830-23-3*, DS18386) Garborgs.

Love from Shakespeare to Coward: An Enlightening Entertainment. Elizabeth Sharland. 96p. 1999. pap. text 7.95 (*1-55783-369-9*) Applause Theatre Bk Pubs.

Love, from the Ends of the Earth: Poems. Enoch Dillon. LC 90-3627. 64p. (Orig.). 1990. pap. 7.50 (*0-931832-64-0*) Fithian Pr.

Love, from the Fifth-Grade Celebrity. Patricia Reilly Giff. 128p. (J). (gr. k-6). 1987. pap. 3.99 (*0-440-44948-0*, YB BDD) BDD Bks Young Read.

Love, from the Fifth Grade Celebrity. Patricia Reilly Giff. (J). 1986. 9.09 (*0-606-03610-5*, Pub. by Turtleback) Demco.

***Love from the Heart of the Home.** Susan Branch. 1998. 11.95 (*0-316-18950-2*) Little.

Love from the Heart of the Home: A Keepsake Book. Susan Branch. 64p. (gr. 8). 1994. 11.95 (*0-316-10658-5*) Little.

Love from the Inside Out. 2nd ed. Dina B. Evan. 128p. (Orig.). 1994. mass mkt. write for info. (*0-9650536-0-1*) D Evan.

Love from the Living Bible. Perry Tanksley. 1976. 4.95 (*0-686-17793-2*) Allgood Bks.

Love from the Sea. Ronald W. Cutburth. Ed. by Cynthia E. Naumann. Tr. by Hannelore Witt. (GER., Illus.). 27p. (J). (gr. 5-8). 1989. pap. write for info. (*1-878291-03-3*) Love From Sea.

Love from the Sea. Ronald W. Cutburth. Ed. by Cynthia E. Naumann. Tr. by Hannelore Witt. (FRE., Illus.). 27p. (J). (gr. 5-8). 1989. pap. write for info. (*1-878291-07-6*) Love From Sea.

Love from the Sea. Ronald W. Cutburth. Ed. by Cynthia E. Naumann. Tr. by Kerstin Lander. (SWE., Illus.). 27p. (J). (gr. 5-8). 1989. pap. write for info. (*1-878291-06-8*) Love From Sea.

Love from the Sea. Ronald W. Cutburth. Ed. by Cynthia E. Naumann. (Illus.). 27p. (J). (gr. 4-7). 1990. pap. 3.50 (*1-878291-01-7*) Love From Sea.

Love from the Sea. Ronald W. Cutburth. Ed. by Cynthia E. Naumann. Tr. by Rocio G. Tostado. (SPA., Illus.). 27p. (J). (gr. 5-8). 1990. pap. write for info. (*1-878291-09-2*) Love From Sea.

Love from the Sea. Ronald W. Cutburth. Ed. by Cynthia E. Naumann. Tr. by Bobbie West. (CHI., Illus.). 27p. (J). (gr. 5-8). 1990. pap. write for info. (*1-878291-11-4*) Love From Sea.

***Love from the Spirit: A Compilation of Poetry.** G. A. Beck. LC 99-96655. 2000. pap. 7.95 (*0-533-13282-7*) Vantage.

Love from Wales: An Anthology. Ed. by Sian James & Tony Curtis. 175p. (Orig.). 1991. 35.00 (*1-85411-064-0*, Pub. by Seren Bks); pap. 17.95 (*1-85411-067-5*, Pub. by Seren Bks) Dufour.

Love from Your Friend, Hannah. Mindy W. Skolsky. LC 97-29819. 246p. (J). (gr. 1-5). 1998. 16.95 (*0-7894-2492-4*) DK Pub Inc.

Love from Your Friend, Hannah. Mindy W. Skolsky. LC 99-27015. (Illus.). 256p. (J). (gr. 3-7). 1999. mass mkt. 5.95 (*0-06-440746-2*) HarpC.

Love from Your Friend, Hannah. Mindy Warshaw Skolsky. 256p. (J). (gr. 4-6). pap. 5.95 (*0-8072-1546-5*) Listening Lib.

Love Fugue. Shulamith W. Caine. Ed. by Rodger Moody. 80p. (Orig.). 1997. pap. 10.00 (*1-878851-10-1*) Silverfish Rev Pr.

Love Full Circle: The Golden Rule. Douglas M. McIntosh. (Foundations of the Faith Ser.). 1999. pap. 9.99 (*0-8024-6647-8*) Moody.

Love Game. Mallory Rush. LC 96-323. 250p. 1995. per. 4.99 (*0-373-83313-X*, 1-83313-6) Harlequin Bks.

Love-Game Comedy. David L. Stevenson. reprint ed. 20.00 (*0-404-06263-6*) AMS Pr.

Love Games. Deborah Aydt. (J). 1984. pap. 2.25 (*0-590-32431-4*) Scholastic Inc.

Love Games. Jacqui Deevoy. 144p. (J). 1997. pap. 6.95 (*0-09-925142-6*, Pub. by Random) Trafalgar.

***Love Games: How to Deepen Communication, Resolve Conflict, & Discover Who Your Partner Really Is.** Mark R. Waldman. LC 99-32737. (Illus.). 272p. 2000. 23.95 (*1-58542-005-0*, Tarcher Putnam) Putnam Pub Group.

***Love Games: Over 100 Creative Relationship Exercises to Deepen Communications, Resolve Conflict, & Discover Who Your Partner Really Is.** Mark R. Waldman. 2000. 23.95 (*1-58542-005-5*, Tarcher Putnam) Putnam Pub Group.

Love Games: Secret Fantasies. Mallory Rush. 1995. pap. 2.99 (*0-614-00493-4*, 1-25622-1) Harlequin Bks.

Love Garden. rev. ed. James Sunwall. LC 96-18321. 55p. (Orig.). 1996. pap. 5.00 (*0-88734-305-8*) Players Pr.

Love Garden Colors Poetry. Steven NurAhmed. 1992. pap. text. write for info. (*0-9629532-2-9*) Black Angels.

Love Germ: A Novel. Jill Neville. LC 98-24038. 160p. 1998. pap. 12.00 (*1-85984-285-2*, Pub. by Verso) Norton.

Love Ghosts & Nose Hair. Steven Herrick. (Illus.). (YA). 1996. pap. 14.95 (*0-7022-2878-8*, Pub. by Univ Queensland Pr) Intl Spec Bk.

Love Gift. Judith Saxton. 192p. 1999. 24.00 (*0-7278-5418-6*, Pub. by Severn Hse) Chivers N Amer.

Love God . . . Clean House . . . Help Others. Duane F. Reinert. 72p. 1996. pap. 4.95 (*0-8091-3643-0*, 3643-0) Paulist Pr.

Love God & Do As You Please. Morris L. Venden. (Anchor Ser.). 93p. 1992. pap. 8.99 (*0-8163-1089-0*) Pacific Pr Pub Assn.

Love, God & You. Ann L. Ramsey. (Illus.). 28p. 1999. pap. write for info. (*0-9645663-3-8*) Crown Peak Pubns.

Love Goes to Press: A Comedy in Three Acts. Martha E. Gellhorn & Virginia Cowles. Ed. & Afterword by Sandra W. Spanier. LC 94-22925. (Illus.). xiv, 94p. 1995. text 45.00 (*0-8032-2154-1*) U of Nebr Pr.

Love Gone Wrong. Toni J. Turner. Ed. by Nancy Gustafson. 96p. 1995. 13.95 (*0-9643316-4-0*) Frnd Pubng.

Love Grants No Choice. large type ed. Sarah Westbury. (Linford Romance Library). 1995. pap. 16.99 (*0-7089-7789-8*, Linford) Ulverscroft.

Love, Greatly Enlarged. Leo Vroman. Ed. by Stanley H. Barkan. (International Writers Ser.: No. 1). (DUT & ENG.). 112p. 1991. 25.00 (*0-89304-125-4*); pap. 15.00 (*0-89304-126-2*) Cross-Cultrl NY.

Love, Groucho: Letters from Groucho Marx to His Daughter Miriam. unabridged ed. Ed. by Miriam M. Allen. (Illus.). 241p. 1993. pap. 14.95 (*0-571-19809-0*) Faber & Faber.

Love Grows in Brooklyn. Jack Fulton. 378p. 1992. pap. 17.95 (*0-9635312-0-4*) Hillcraft Pub.

Love Guaranteed: Better Marriage in 8 weeks. 2nd ed. Edward E. Ford. 124p. 1987. reprint ed. pap. 9.00 (*0-9616716-3-7*) Brandt Pub.

Love, Guilt & Reparation & Other Works, 1921-1945. Melanie Klein. (Writings of Melanie Klein Ser.: Vol. 1). 480p. (C). 1984. 45.00 (*0-02-918420-7*) Free Pr.

Love Had a Compass: Journals & Poetry. Robert Lax. Ed. by Jim Uebbing. 272p. 1996. 22.00 (*0-8021-1587-X*, Grove) Grove-Atltic.

Love Handbook for Singles: What Every Single Needs to Know about Love, Dating & Finding a Lifelong Partner. Nancy J. Carroll. Orig. Title: Finding & Keeping a Loving Relationship. 179p. 1993. pap. 12.95 (*0-9663204-0-9*) Life Skills Dev.

Love Handles. Laura J. Walker. 176p. 1998. pap. 8.99 (*0-7642-2092-6*, 212092) Bethany Hse.

Love Hangs upon An Empty Door. Bruce Wright. LC 98-24616. 122p. 1998. pap. 12.00 (*1-56980-129-0*) Barricade Bks.

Love Happens. (J). 1997. write for info. (*0-614-29175-5*) BDD Bks Young Read.

Love Happens. Elizabeth Chandler. (Love Stories Super Edition Ser.: No. 5). 208p. (Orig.). (YA). (gr. 7 up). 1997. mass mkt. 4.50 (*0-553-49217-9*) BDD Bks Young Read.

Love Has a Price Tag. Elisabeth Elliot. 180p. 1979. reprint ed. pap. 9.99 (*0-89283-153-7*) Servant.

Love Has a Thousand Ways to Tell. Paul T. Dahlstrom. 69p. (Orig.). 1993. pap. 8.00 (*0-9635690-3-1*) TA Pubns.

Love Has Come My Way. Langston O. Harris. (Illus.). 400p. (Orig.). 1997. pap. 10.00 (*0-9631730-5-7*) DRL Bks.

Love Has Everything to Do with It. Beverly J. Hudson. (Illus.). 20p. (Orig.). 1996. pap. 10.00 (*0-9658040-1-1*) Talents From God.

***Love Has Many Faces: When You Find a Friend You Find a Circle of Love.** Denise Turney. 374p. 2000. 20.00 (*0-9663539-1-9*) Chistell Pub.

Love Has No Bonds. Devereaux Macy Staff. 1990. pap. write for info. (*1-886716-04-8*) Devereaux.

Love Has No Fear: One Couple's Search for Healing. rev. ed. Joan Peterson. LC 97-93355. (Orig.). 1997. pap. 12.95 (*0-9656017-5-7*) Merkaba Pr.

Love, Hate, & Everything in Between: Put Your Feelings into Words. Mamiko Murakami. Tr. by Ralph F. McCarthy. (Power Japanese Ser.). 144p. 1997. pap. 13.00 (*4-7700-2089-9*) Kodansha.

***Love, Hate & Other Feelings.** Pete Sanders & Steve Myers. LC 99-45964. (What Do You Know about... Ser.). 32p. (J). (gr. 4-6). 2000. lib. bdg. 21.90 (*0-7613-1150-5*, Copper Beech Bks) Millbrook Pr.

Love, Hate & Reparation. Ed. by Melanie Klein & Joan Riviere. (Orig.). 1964. pap. 9.95 (*0-393-00260-8*) Norton.

Love-Hate Anthology: Releasing the Bitch Within . . . Alex Prayson. (Illus.). 52p. (Orig.). 1993. pap. 10.00 (*0-9639301-0-9*) A Prayson.

Love, Hate or Communicate. Mack Timberlake. LC 98-116927. 1997. pap. 8.99 (*0-89274-953-9*) Harrison Hse.

Love, Hawaii-Style: Stories, Spells & Fables from the World's Most Romantic Island. Toni Polancy & Holly Lang. (Illus.). (Orig.). 1999. pap. 19.95 (*0-9666253-2-3*, Pub. by Barefoot Pub) Booklines Hawaii.

Love Head see Love Killers

Love Heals: A Spiritual Program for the Sick. 5th rev. ed. Ed. by Mary J. Gilliland. (Illus.). 128p. (C). 1984. reprint ed. pap. text 6.50 (*1-878268-02-3*) Lit Comm Pubs.

Love Heals All. Leslie Brannen. 288p. 1997. mass mkt. 5.99 (*0-515-12188-6*, Jove) Berkley Pub.

Love Hear My Heart. Sonya T. Pelton. 1990. mass mkt. 4.50 (*0-8217-2913-6*, Zebra Kensgtn) Kensgtn Pub Corp.

***Love Hexagon.** William Sutcliffe. 224p. 2000. pap. 12.00 (*0-14-029609-3*) Penguin Putnam.

***Love Him Forever.** Cherie Bennett. (Illus.). (J). 1999. 9.85 (*0-606-17968-2*) Turtleback.

Love Holds No Grievances: The Ending of Attack. 3rd ed. Tara Singh. LC 88-9341. 112p. (Orig.). 1988. pap. 5.95 (*1-55531-226-8*) Life Action Pr.

L

An Asterisk (*) at the beginning of an entry indicates that the title is appearing for the first time.

L

Love, Honor & a Pregnant Bride: Do You Take This Stranger? Karen R. Smith. (Silhouette Romance Ser.: No. 1326). 1998. per. 3.50 (*0-373-19326-2*, 1-19326-7) Harlequin Bks.

***Love, Honor & Cherish.** Sherryl Woods. 2000. per. 6.99 (*0-373-20174-5*, 1-20174-8) Harlequin Bks.

Love, Honor & Cherish: The Greatest Wedding Moments from All My Children, General Hospital, & One Life to Live. Warner. LC 98-4406. (Illus.). 384p. (J). 1998. 29.95 (*0-7868-6368-4*, Pub. by Hyperion) Time Warner.

Love, Honor & Forgive: A Guide for Married Couples. Bill Farrel & Pam Farrel. LC 99-55903. 192p. 2000. pap. 10.99 (*0-8308-2227-5*) InterVarsity.

Love, Honor & Negotiate: Making Your Marriage Work. Betty Carter & Joan K. Peters. 320p. 1996. 23.00 (*0-671-89624-5*) PB.

***Love, Honor & Obey Yourself.** Iyanla Vanzant. (Inner Visions Practicing the Principles Ser.). 2000. pap. 14.95 (*0-684-87262-5*, Fireside) S&S Trade Pap.

Love, Honor, Cherish. Julie Otlewis. (Orig.). 1994. pap. 7.95 (*1-56245-081-6*) Great Quotations.

***Love, Honour & Kill.** Molly Katz. 504p. 2000. 31.99 (*0-7089-4290-3*) Ulverscroft.

Love, Hope & Recovery: Healing the Pain of Addiction. Joann Breeden. LC 93-36924. 272p. (Orig.). 1993. pap. 12.95 (*0-931892-77-5*) B Dolphin Pub.

Love, Hope & Tragedy: A Brooklyn Memoir. Joan Calciano. Ed. by Don Gabor & Eileen Cowell. 204p. 1998. pap. 12.00 (*1-879834-06-5*) Convstn Arts.

Love Hostage see Rehenes de un Amor: Held Hostage

Love, Human & Divine: The Heart of Christian Ethics. Edward C. Vacek. LC 93-37944. (Moral Traditions & Moral Arguments Ser.). 336p. (C). 1996. pap. 21.95 (*0-87840-627-1*) Georgetown U Pr.

Love Hunger see Hambre de Amor

Love Hunger: Recovery from Food Addiction. Frank Minirth et al. 1991. pap. 12.00 (*0-449-90613-2*) Fawcett.

Love Hunger Action Plan. Sharon Sneed. LC 92-23652. 288p. 1993. 12.99 (*0-8407-3461-1*) Nelson.

Love Hunter. Jon Hassler. 1996. pap. 12.00 (*0-345-41019-X*) Ballantine Pub Grp.

Love Hunter. Jon Hassler. 336p. 1988. reprint ed. mass mkt. 5.99 (*0-345-35017-0*) Ballantine Pub Grp.

***Love Hurts.** (Rock & Pop Classics: Vol. 3). (Illus.). 30p. 1999. write for info. incl. audio compact disk (*1-892207-32-X*) Intl Masters Pub.

***Love Hurts.** Laura Peyton Roberts. (Clearwater Crossing Ser.). (YA). (gr. 5-8). 2000. mass mkt. 3.99 (*0-553-49299-3*) BDD Bks Young Read.

Love Hurts. large type ed. Mary-Beth Williams. (Linford Romance Library). 256p. 1996. pap. 16.99 (*0-7089-7963-7*, Linford) Ulverscroft.

Love Idylls. Samuel R. Crockett. LC 73-130055. (Short Story Index Reprint Ser.). 1977. 20.95 (*0-8369-3572-1*) Ayer.

Love in a Bare Room. Mario Pelaccio. Ed. by Stanley H. Barkan. Tr. by Nat Scammacca & Nina Scammacca. (Review Italian-American Writers Ser.: No. 1). 48p. 1992. 15.00 (*0-685-49050-5*); 15.00 (*0-685-49051-3*); pap. 5.00 (*0-89304-668-X*); pap. 5.00 (*0-685-49052-1*) Cross-Cultrl NY.

Love in a Blue Time: Short Stories. Hanif Kureishi. LC 97-19118. 212p. 1997. 21.50 (*0-684-83794-3*) S&S Trade.

Love in a Blue Time: Short Stories. Hanif Kureishi. 256p. 1999. pap. 11.00 (*0-684-84818-X*) S&S Trade.

Love in a Chinese Garden. Rachel May. 1997. per. 5.99 (*0-373-83348-2*, 1-83348-2) Harlequin Bks.

Love in a Dead Language. Lee Siegel. LC 98-31296. (Illus.). 312p. 1999. 25.00 (*0-226-75697-1*) U Ch Pr.

Love in a Different Climate: Men Who Have Sex with Men in India. Jeremy Seabrook. LC 99-17438. 224p. 1999. 25.00 (*1-85984-837-0*, Pub. by Verso) Norton.

***Love in a Different Climate: Men Who Have Sex with Men in India.** Jeremy Seabrook. 192p. 2000. pap. 19.00 (*1-85984-168-6*, Pub. by Verso) Norton.

Love in a Dry Season. Shelby Foote. 1992. pap. 12.00 (*0-679-73618-2*) Vin Bks.

Love in a Green Shade: Idyllic Romances Ancient to Modern. Richard F. Hardin. LC 99-36931. (Illus.). 288p. 2000. text 50.00 (*0-8032-2394-3*) U of Nebr Pr.

Love in a Hate Situation. Christian P. Lodewyk. 156p. 1987. pap. 5.95 (*0-88144-107-4*) Christian Pub.

Love in a Lunch Box: Poems & Parables for Children's Worship. Elaine Ward. 160p. (Orig.). 1996. pap. 12.95 (*0-687-00660-0*) Abingdon.

Love in a Manger. June Tink. 1992. pap. 4.95 (*1-55673-461-1*, 7914) CSS OH.

Love in a Small Town. Curtiss A. Matlock. 1997. mass mkt. 5.99 (*0-380-78107-7*, Avon Bks) Morrow Avon.

Love in a Time of Hate: Liberation Psychology in Latin America. Nancy C. Hollander. LC 97-9639. 240p. (C). 1997. text 50.00 (*0-8135-2425-3*); pap. text 21.95 (*0-8135-2426-1*) Rutgers U Pr.

***Love in a Time of Loneliness: Three Essays on Drives & Desires.** Paul Verhaeghe. LC 99-13536. 222p. 1999. 22.00 (*1-892746-31-X*) Other Pr LLC.

Love in Action: UMCOR: Fifty Years of Service. Norma Kehrberg. LC 89-17841. 144p. 1989. pap. 2.39 (*0-687-22808-5*) Abingdon.

Love in Action: Writings on Nonviolent Social Change. Thich Nhat Hanh. LC 93-31443. 154p. 1993. pap. 13.50 (*0-938077-63-5*) Parallax Pr.

Love in Alaska. John O'Neill. 96p. 1994. pap. text 11.95 (*0-88982-135-6*, Pub. by Oolichan Bks) Genl Dist Srvs.

Love in Ambush. large type ed. K. Summerfield. (Linford Romance Library). 1990. pap. 16.99 (*0-7089-6829-5*, Linford) Ulverscroft.

Love in America: Gender & Self-Development. Francesca M. Cancian. (Illus.). 224p. 1987. text 59.95 (*0-521-34202-3*) Cambridge U Pr.

Love in Ancient Rome. Pierre Grimal. Tr. by Arthur Train, Jr. from FRE. LC 86-40087. 328p. (Orig.). 1986. reprint ed. pap. 14.95 (*0-8061-2014-2*) U of Okla Pr.

Love in Another Room. Claire O'Connor. 254p. 1997. pap. 13.95 (*1-86023-019-9*, Pub. by Martello Bks) Irish Amer Bk.

Love in Another Town. Barbara Taylor Bradford. LC 95-36834. 240p. 1996. mass mkt. 5.99 (*0-06-109209-6*) HarpC.

Love in Another Town. large type ed. Barbara Taylor Bradford. LC 95-42560. 208p. 1996. pap. 22.95 (*0-7838-1560-3*, G K Hall Lrg Type) Mac Lib Ref.

Love in Another Town. large type ed. Barbara Taylor Bradford. 224p. 1999. 24.95 (*0-7838-1559-X*, G K Hall Lrg Type) Mac Lib Ref.

Love in Another Town: Banes,&Lisa, Set. abr. ed. Barbara Taylor Bradford. 1995. audio 17.00 (*0-694-51598-1*, 393244) HarperAudio.

Love in Asian Art & Culture. Vidya Dehejia et al. LC 98-29249. (Asian Art & Culture Ser.). (Illus.). 120 p. 1998. pap. 24.95 (*0-295-97759-0*) U of Wash Pr.

Love in Atlantis. Bonnie Barrett. LC 90-53327. 182p. 1991. 22.00 (*0-933256-77-9*) Second Chance.

Love in Baroque Art. Frederick N. Hartt. LC 62-19124. (Illus.). 18.00 (*0-685-71752-6*) J J Augustin.

Love in Black & White: If Only Man Could See the Truth to Life. Ricardo A. Scott. (Ras Cardo Lectures to Humanity). (Illus.). 150p. 1995. pap. text 25.95 (*1-883427-97-5*, GRTS67-3/97) Crnerstone GA.

Love in Bloom. Bartholomew. 1998. mass mkt. 12.95 (*0-373-80515-2*, 1-80515-9) Harlequin Bks.

***Love in Bloom.** Michaila Callan. (Zebra Bouquet Ser.: Vol. 51). 256p. 2000. pap. 3.99 (*0-8217-6625-2*, Zebra Kensgtn) Kensgtn Pub Corp.

Love in Camera. Louise Anthony. (Rainbow Romances Ser.). 160p. 1993. 14.95 (*0-7090-4890-4*) Parkwest Pubns.

Love in Chaos: Spiritual Growth & the Search for Peace in Northern Ireland. Mary McAleese. LC 82-40254. 124p. 1998. reprint ed. pap. 11.95 (*0-8264-1137-1*) Continuum.

Love in Deed: Preparing for Christian Marriage. rev. ed. Judith Tate-O'Brien. (Illus.). 72p. 1981. pap. 3.95 (*0-936098-27-9*) Intl Marriage.

Love in E-Flat. Norman Krasna. 1967. pap. 5.25 (*0-8222-0691-9*) Dramatists Play.

Love in Every Room: The Heartbeat of the Home. Karla Dornacher. 80p. 1998. 12.99 (*0-8499-5400-2*) Word Pub.

Love in Excess or the Fatal Enquiry: Eliza Haywood. Ed. by David Oakleaf. (Literary Texts Ser.). 240p. 1994. pap. 12.95 (*1-55111-016-4*) Broadview Pr.

Love in Exile: An American Writer's Memoir of Life in Divided Berlin. Edith Anderson. LC 99-13795. (Illus.). 408p. 1999. 29.50 (*1-883642-67-1*) Steerforth Pr.

Love in Father's Plan. Thomas Washington. pap. 7.50 (*1-55517-419-1*) CFI Dist.

Love in Greenwich Village. Floyd Dell. LC 73-128730. (Short Story Index Reprint Ser.). 1977. 20.95 (*0-8369-3621-3*) Ayer.

Love in Hazard. large type ed. Jean Marsh. (Linford Romance Library). 272p. 1993. pap. 16.99 (*0-7089-7325-6*, Linford) Ulverscroft.

Love in Her Life. large type ed. Angela Gordon. LC 94-3327. 228p. 1994. lib. bdg. 16.95 (*0-8161-7450-4*, G K Hall Lrg Type) Mac Lib Ref.

Love-In-Idleness: The Poetry of Roberto Zingarello. John Bradley. LC 89-51372. 72p. 1989. 10.00 (*0-915380-24-2*) Word Works.

Love in Las Vegas. Ivy Preston. (Rainbow Romances Ser.). 160p. 1993. 14.95 (*0-7090-4830-0*) Parkwest Pubns.

Love in Las Vegas. large type ed. Ivy Preston. (Linford Romance Library). 1994. pap. 16.99 (*0-7089-7622-0*, Linford) Ulverscroft.

Love in Late Season: New Poems. Anne Marx. LC 92-38177. 1992. 17.50 (*0-87233-108-3*) Bauhan.

Love in Later Life. H. B. Gibson. LC 98-231242. 160p. 1998. pap. 27.95 (*0-7206-1026-5*, Pub. by P Owen Ltd) Dufour.

Love in Literature: Studies in Symbolic Expression. Wallace Fowlie. LC 70-37836. (Essay Index Reprint Ser.). 1977. reprint ed. 20.95 (*0-8369-2589-0*) Ayer.

Love in London. Theodor Kramer. Tr. by Max Brainin & Jorg Thunecke. LC 94-29276. (Studies in Austrian Literature, Culture, & Thought). (ENG & GER.). 161p. 1995. pap. 15.95 (*1-57241-009-4*) Ariadne CA.

Love in Marriage: A Translation of E. Swedenborg's Sensible Joy in Married Love & Foolish Pleasures of Illicit Love. Emanuel Swedenborg. Tr. by David F. Gladish. LC 92-60085. 530p. 1992. pap. 24.95 (*0-87785-141-7*) Swedenborg.

Love in Mid-Winter Night: Korean Sijo Poetry. Tr. by Chung Chong-wha from KOR. (KOR., Illus.). 112p. 1986. 35.00 (*0-7103-0104-9*) Routledge.

Love in Modern American Drama. Naresh K. Jain. (C). 1991. 14.00 (*81-85425-23-X*, Pub. by Manohar) S Asia.

Love in Motion. Jean R. Desarmes. 1998. pap. 8.95 (*0-533-12773-4*) Vantage.

Love in Motion. Theresa Goldstrand. LC 97-97115. 192p. 1998. 18.95 (*0-8034-9276-6*, Avalon Bks) Bouregy.

Love in Old Cloathes & Other Stories. Henry C. Bunner. LC 78-94706. (Short Story Index Reprint Ser.). (Illus.). 1977. 20.95 (*0-8369-3084-3*) Ayer.

Love in Opposing Colors: An Unsanctioned Romance. Calvin Davis. LC 93-93664. 170p. write for info. (*0-9639770-0-8*) T Z Leether Pubs.

Love in Pasadena. Richard Hoe. 288p. mass mkt. 4.99 (*1-55197-048-1*) Picasso Publ.

Love in Sanskrit & Tamil Literature: A Study of Characters & Nature. Devapoopathy Nadarajah. (C). 1995. 26.00 (*81-208-1215-8*, Pub. by Motilal Bnarsidass) S Asia.

***Love in Store.** Linda Sheel. 1998. pap. 6.95 (*0-09-926373-4*, Pub. by Random) Trafalgar.

***Love in the Ancient World.** Christopher Miles. 2000. pap. 21.95 (*1-84188-010-8*) Seven Dials.

Love in the Ancient World. Christopher Miles & John Julius Norwich. LC 98-125216. 1997. text 27.50 (*0-312-17988-X*) St Martin.

Love in the Armpit, Tzeltal Tales of Love, Murder & Cannibalism: Modern Folk Tales from the Tzeltal Maya Town of Tenejapa, Chiapas, Pt. 1. Ed. by Lawrence H. Feldman. LC 77-151846. (Museum Briefs Ser.: No. 23). (Illus.). iii, 27p. 1977. pap. text 1.80 (*0-913134-23-6*) Mus Anthro MO.

Love in the Balance. Marianne Martin. LC 97-52958. 240p. (Orig.). 1998. pap. 11.95 (*1-56280-199-6*) Naiad Pr.

Love in the Bible. Michael Penny. 48p. (Orig.). 1997. pap. 3.00 (*1-880573-34-2*) Bible Search Pubns.

Love in the Catskills: The Novel. Beverly Friend. (Illus.). 108p. 1998. pap. 10.00 (*0-9669525-0-2*) B Friend.

***Love in the Church.** 2nd ed. (Illus.). 176p. 2000. write for info. (*0-9677966-2-8*) Same Found.

***Love in the "Corral" Conjugal Spirituality & Antitheatrical Polemic in Early Modern Spain, 31.** Thomas Austin O'Connor. (Iberica Ser.: Vol. 31). 395p. (C). 2000. text 64.95 (*0-8204-4493-6*) P Lang Pubng.

Love in the Economy: Social Doctrine of the Church for the Individual in the Economy. Christopher McQustra. 220p. (C). 1996. pap. 39.95 (*0-85439-324-2*, Pub. by St Paul Pubns) St Mut.

Love in the Film. William K. Everson. (Illus.). 256p. (C). 1981. pap. 7.95 (*0-8065-0778-0*, Citadel Pr) Carol Pub Group.

Love in the First Degree: Romantic Traditions. Patricia Coughlin. (Intimate Moments Ser.). 1995. per. 3.75 (*0-373-07632-0*, 1-07632-2) Silhouette.

***Love in the Garden.** Jean-Pierre Otte. Tr. by Moishe Black & Maria Green. 2000. 20.00 (*0-8076-1467-X*) Braziller.

Love in the Keys. 3rd ed. David B. Axelrod. 28p. 1991. pap. 6.00 (*0-925062-17-0*) Writers Ink Pr.

Love in the Lead: The Miracle of the Seeing Eye Dog. 2nd ed. Peter B. Putnam. LC 97-15322. (Illus.). 304p. 1997. reprint ed. pap. 16.95 (*0-7618-0777-2*) U Pr of Amer.

Love in the Mortar Joints: The Story of Habitat for Humanity. Millard Fuller & Diane Scott. LC 81-86084. 150p. 1980. pap. 6.95 (*0-8329-1444-4*) New Win Pub.

Love in the 90s, B. B. & Jo: The Story of a Lifelong Love, a Granddaughter's Portrait. Keri Pickett. (Illus.). 112p. 1995. 14.95 (*0-446-52032-2*, Pub. by Warner Bks) Little.

Love in the Palm of Your Hand: How to Use Palmistry for Successful Relationships. Ghanshyam S. Birla. LC 98-38310. (Illus.). 208p. 1998. pap. 19.95 (*0-89281-718-6*) Inner Tradit.

Love in the Persian Way. Harry Barba. (C). 1970. pap. 5.95 (*0-911906-07-X*) Harian Creative Bks.

Love in the Phalanstery. Victor A. Hennequin. Tr. by Henry James, Sr. LC 78-72345. (Free Love in America Ser.). reprint ed. 32.50 (*0-404-60960-0*) AMS Pr.

Love in the Promised Land: The Story of Anzia Yezierska & John Dewey. Mary V. Dearborn. (Illus.). 350p. 1988. text 29.95 (*0-02-908090-8*) Free Pr.

Love in the Rain: Hebeh Tahtal Matar. Naguib Mahfouz. (ARA.). pap. 9.95 (*0-86685-154-2*) Intl Bk Ctr.

Love in the Ruins. Barbara Cartland. 176p. (Orig.). 1995. mass mkt. 4.50 (*0-515-11733-1*, Jove) Berkley Pub.

Love in the Ruins. Walker Percy. LC 71-143301. 416p. 1971. 27.95 (*0-374-19302-9*) FS&G.

Love in the Ruins. Walker Percy. 352p. 1989. mass mkt. 5.99 (*0-8041-0378-X*) Ivy Books.

***Love in the Ruins: Novel.** Walker Percy. LC 99-32173. 384p. 1999. pap. 15.00 (*0-312-24311-1*) St Martin.

Love in the Sixth: An Extraordinary & Sensual Love Story. Kim Hamlet. LC 97-72595. 178p. (Orig.). 1997. pap. 17.00 (*1-890622-00-1*) Leathers Pub.

Love in the Spotlight. large type ed. Katrina Wright. (Romance Ser.). 1994. pap. 16.99 (*0-7089-7605-0*, Linford) Ulverscroft.

Love in the Suds, a Town Eclogue: Being the Lamentation of Roscius for the Loss of His Nyky. Third Edition with Preface "A Letter to David Garick, Esq. from William Kenrick, L. K. D." & Appendix. William Kenrick. LC 92-22033. (Augustan Reprints Ser.: No. 246). 1987. reprint ed. 14.50 (*0-404-70246-5*) AMS Pr.

Love in the Time of Cholera see Amor en los Tiempos del Colera - Love in the Time of Cholera

Love in the Time of Cholera. Gabriel Garcia Marquez. Tr. by Edith Grossman from SPA. LC 98-119521. xxxiii, 422p. 1997. 20.00 (*0-375-40069-9*) Everymns Lib.

Love in the Time of Cholera. Gabriel Garcia Marquez. Tr. by Edith Grossman from SPA. LC 87-40484. 348p. 1988. 30.00 (*0-394-56161-9*) Knopf.

Love in the Time of Cholera. Gabriel Garcia Marquez. Tr. by Edith Grossman. 352p. 1989. pap. 13.95 (*0-14-011990-6*, Penguin Bks) Viking Penguin.

Love in the Time of Cholera. Gabriel Garcia Marquez. Tr. by Edith Grossman from SPA. LC 99-205033. (Penguin Great Books of the 20th Century Ser.). 348p. (C). 1999. pap. 14.95 (*0-14-028164-9*) Viking Penguin.

Love in the Time of Victoria: Sexuality, Class & Gender in Nineteenth-Century London. Francoise Barret-Ducrocq. Tr. by John Howe. 304p. 1991. 29.95 (*0-685-50118-3*, A5362) Verso.

Love in the Trenches: A Couples Guide to Transforming the Power Struggle. Al Crowell. 155p. (Orig.). 1996. pap. 49.95 (*0-9652992-0-1*) A Crowell Publ.

Love in the Upstairs Flat. Mary Minock. LC 95-8692. 92p. 1995. pap. 14.95 (*0-7734-2729-5*, Mellen Poetry Pr) E Mellen.

Love in the Western World. Denis De Rougemont. Tr. by Montgomery Belgion from FRE. LC 82-48560. (ENG.). 400p. 1983. reprint ed. pap. text 16.95 (*0-691-01393-4*, Pub. by Princeton U Pr) Cal Prin Full Svc.

Love in the Wind. Madeline Baker. 448p. (Orig.). 1997. mass mkt. 5.99 (*0-8439-4227-4*) Dorchester Pub Co.

Love in the Wind, 1. Madeline Baker. 432p. (Orig.). 1999. reprint ed. mass mkt. 5.99 (*0-8439-4589-3*, Leisure Bks) Dorchester Pub Co.

Love in the Wings. Doreen Griffen. (Rainbow Romances Ser.). 160p. 1994. 14.95 (*0-7090-5048-8*, 913) Parkwest Pubns.

Love in the Wings. large type ed. Doreen Griffin. (Linford Romance Library). 272p. 1995. pap. 16.99 (*0-7089-7745-6*, Linford) Ulverscroft.

Love in the Winter: Stories. fac. ed. Daniel Curley. LC 76-7541. (Illinois Short Fiction Ser.). 124p. 1994. pap. 38.50 (*0-7837-7618-7*, 204737000007) Bks Demand.

Love in Times of Reformation. William P. Balkenende. Tr. by Judy Den Hertog from DUT. (Illus.). 105p. (Orig.). (YA). 1991. pap. 7.90 (*0-921100-32-9*) Inhtce Pubns.

Love in Vain. Charles Miller. (Illus.). 50p. (Orig.). (C). 1997. pap. 20.00 (*0-935645-16-0*) AJFP.

Love in Vain: A Vision of Robert Johnson. rev. ed. Alan Greenberg. (Illus.). 274p. 1994. reprint ed. pap. 13.95 (*0-306-80557-X*) Da Capo.

Love in Vein (MM) Poppy Z. Brite. 416p. 1995. mass mkt. 6.50 (*0-06-105490-9*) HarpC.

Love in Vein II. 448th ed. Ed. by Poppy Brite & Martin H. Greenberg. 544p. 1998. mass mkt. 5.99 (*0-06-105657-X*, HarperPrism) HarpC.

***Love in Vein II: 18 More Original Tales of Vampire Erotica.** Poppy Z. Brite. 2000. 9.99 (*0-7858-1211-3*) Bk Sales Inc.

Love in Verse. Kathleen Blease. LC 97-29400. 128p. 1999. pap. 10.00 (*0-449-00128-8*) Fawcett.

***Love in Verse.** Kathleen Blease. 1999. pap. 10.00 (*0-449-45904-7*) Fawcett.

Love in Wartime. Liesel Kulig. (Orig.). 1992. mass mkt. 6.95 (*1-56333-044-X*, Rhinoceros) Masquerade.

Love in Your Life: A Jewish View of Teenage Sexuality. Roland B. Gittelsohn. (YA). (gr. 7-9). 1991. pap. 9.95 (*0-8074-0460-8*, 142685) UAHC.

Love, Intimacy, & Sex. Jack D. Douglas & Freda C. Atwell. LC 87-20658. (Sociological Observations Ser.: No. 20). (Illus.). 304p. 1988. reprint ed. pap. 94.30 (*0-608-01166-5*, 205946600001) Bks Demand.

Love Invents Us. Amy Bloom. LC 97-21966. 224p. 1998. pap. 12.00 (*0-375-75022-3*) Vin Bks.

***Love Irony: Spacial Fashion.** Ronald J. McMillan. (Illus.). 459p. 2000. write for info. (*0-7541-0915-1*, Pub. by Minerva Pr) Unity Dist.

Love Is . . . 32p. (J). 1993. pap. 12.95 (*0-7935-2375-3*, 00330608); pap. 9.95 (*0-7935-2376-1*, 00330609) H Leonard.

***Love Is.** Carolyn Brown. LC 99-94443. 192p. 1999. 18.95 (*0-8034-9366-5*, Avalon Bks) Bouregy.

Love Is. Patricia T. Cousin et al. (Visions: African-American Experiences: No. 15). (Illus.). 8p. (Orig.). (J). (gr. k-1). 1995. pap. text 3.00 (*1-57518-014-6*) Arborlake.

Love Is... Dee Frances. Date not set. pap. 3.00 (*1-885519-62-1*) DDDD Pubns.

***Love Is...** Criswell Freeman. 128p. 2000. pap. 4.95 (*1-58334-062-9*, Pub. by Walnut Gr Pr) Midpt Trade.

Love Is . . . Laurie Lechlitner. 80p. 1988. pap. 3.95 (*0-88144-125-2*) Christian Pub.

Love Is . . . Shonda LeJeune. LC 96-204003. (Illus.). 28p. (J). 1996. 12.95 (*0-87516-691-1*); pap. 9.95 (*0-87516-690-3*) DeVorss.

Love Is: Meditations for Couples on I Corinthians 13. Les Parrott & Leslie Parrot. LC 98-44037. 1999. 12.99 (*0-310-21666-4*) Zondervan.

Love Is . . . 25 Songs of Love. Ed. by Milton Okun. 128p. (YA). 1995. pap. 14.95 (*0-89524-978-2*) Cherry Lane.

Love Is a Baby. Joan W. Anglund. LC 91-1224. (Illus.). 32p. (J). 1992. 8.95 (*0-15-200517-X*, Harcourt Child Bks) Harcourt.

***Love Is a Beautiful Thing.** Esther L. Beilenson. (Pocket Gold Ser.). (Illus.). 64p. 1999. 5.95 (*0-88088-110-0*) Peter Pauper.

Love Is a Challenge. Hope Dube. (Junior African Writers Ser.). (Illus.). 80p. (J). (gr. 3 up). 1992. pap. 5.00 (*0-7910-2923-9*) Chelsea Hse.

Love Is a Child. Kenyette Adrine-Robinson. Ed. by Charlotte T. Durant & Ethel Pye. (Illus.). 40p. (Orig.). 1992. pap. 4.00 (*0-913678-23-6*) New Day Pr.

Love Is a Choice: Recovery for Codependent Relationships. Robert Hemfelt et al. 288p. 1991. pap. 12.99 (*0-8407-3189-2*) Nelson.

Love Is a Choice: Recovery for Codependent Relationships. Robert Hemfelt et al. 288p. 1991. pap., wbk. ed. 16.99 (*0-8407-3337-2*) Nelson.

Love Is a Choice: Recovery for Codependent Relationships. Robert Hemfelt et al. 284p. 1996. pap. 5.99 (*0-7852-7530-4*) Nelson.

Love Is a Circle Songbook. unabridged ed. Phyllis U. Hiller. 18p. (Orig.). (J). (ps-3). 1994. mass mkt. 6.95 (*1-884877-15-X*, 1992221SB) Creat Mats Lib.

Love Is a Dangerous Game. large type ed. Marjorie Lewty. (Linford Romance Library). 304p. 1985. pap. 16.99 (*0-7089-6064-2*, Linford) Ulverscroft.

Love Is a Decision see Amor es una Decision

Love Is a Decision. Gary Smalley & John Trent. 1992. pap. 12.99 (*0-8499-3362-5*) Word Pub.

Love Is a Decision. Gary Smalley & John Trent. Ed. by Denise Silvestro. 256p. 1993. reprint ed. per. 6.50 (*0-671-75048-8*) Word Pub.

Love Is a Derivative of Attracted Differences Between a Man & a Woman. Ike D. Coleman. LC 98-90074. 1998. pap. 12.95 (*0-533-12702-5*) Vantage.

Love Is a Dog from Hell: Poems, 1974-1977. Charles Bukowski. LC 77-10501. 312p. 1998. reprint ed. 25.00 (*0-87685-363-7*); reprint ed. pap. 15.00 (*0-87685-362-9*) Black Sparrow.

An Asterisk (*) at the beginning of an entry indicates that the title is appearing for the first time.

*Love Is a Fire. Llewellyn Vaughan-Lee. LC 00-27915. 256p. 2000. pap. write for info. (1-890350-03-6, Pub. by Golden Sufi Ctr) Words Distrib.

Love is a Flame of the Lord: More Homilies on the Just Word. Walter J. Burghardt. LC 95-22767. 192p. (Orig.). 1996. pap. 14.95 (0-8091-3603-1) Paulist Pr.

Love Is a Four Letter Word. Anita R. Block. LC 73-116940. (Short Story Index Reprint Ser.). 1977. 21.95 (0-8369-3442-3) Ayer.

*Love Is a Gambler. large type ed. Maysie Greig. 352p. 1999. 31.99 (0-7089-4122-2, Linford) Ulverscroft.

Love Is a Gentle Stranger. large type ed. June M. Bacher. 1987. pap. 8.95 (0-8027-2611-9) Walker & Co.

*Love Is a Handful of Honey. Giles Andreae. LC 99-12767. (Illus.). 32p. (J). (ps-2). 1999. 14.95 (1-888444-58-4) Little Tiger.

Love Is a Happy Cat. Michael W. Fox. LC 82-14216. (Illus.). 96p. 1996. pap. 6.95 (1-55704-279-9, Pub. by Newmarket) Norton.

Love Is a Hot Fudge Sundae. Steve Hotchner. 1987. 3.50 (0-87129-413-3, L51) Dramatic Pub.

*Love Is a Journey: Couples Facing Cancer. Jan Latona & Gary J. Stricklin. LC 99-66209. (Illus.). xv, 110p. 1999. pap. 14.95 (0-9673715-0-3) Greyrock.

Love Is a Many Splendored Thing: And 56 Classic Love Songs. Ed. by Tony Esposito. 192p. (YA). 1995. pap. text 14.95 (0-89724-636-5, MF9528) Wrner Bros.

Love is a Racket. John Ridley. 1999. mass mkt. 6.99 (0-345-43409-9) Ballantine Pub Grp.

Love Is a Racket: A Novel. John Ridley. LC 98-15879. 288p. 1998. 24.00 (0-375-40142-3) Random.

*Love Is a Rainbow. large type ed. Juliet Gray. 256p. 2000. pap. 18.99 (0-7089-5644-0, Linford) Ulverscroft.

*Love Is a Secret. large type ed. 2000. 30.00 (0-7838-8794-9, G K Hall Lrg Type) Mac Lib Ref.

Love Is a Solitary Game. Esther Tusquets. Tr. by Bruce Penman from SPA. LC 85-10878. 160p. (Orig.). 1986. pap. 10.95 (0-7145-4042-0) Riverrun NY.

Love Is a Space. Mary A. Welch. 49p. (Orig.). 1988. pap. 7.95 (0-9618342-0-X) M A Welch Prod.

*Love Is a Special Way of Feeling. Joan Walsh Anglund. LC 99-32782. (J). 1999. 9.95 (0-15-202358-5) Harcourt.

Love Is a Special Way of Feeling: Silver Anniversary Edition. Joan W. Anglund. LC 84-19296. (Illus.). 32p. (J). 1985. reprint ed. 10.00 (0-15-249724-2, Harcourt Child Bks) Harcourt.

Love Is a Start: The Real Challenges of Raising Children with Emotional Disorders. Donna Shilts. LC 98-96487. (Illus.). 328p. 1999. pap. 14.95 (0-9666313-0-7) LookAgain Pubg.

Love Is a Story: A New Theory of Relationships. Robert J. Sternberg. 256p. 1998. 23.00 (0-19-510642-3) OUP.

Love Is a Story: A New Theory of Relationships. Robert J. Sternberg. (Illus.). 256p. 1999. pap. 14.95 (0-19-513102-9) OUP.

Love Is a Stranger. Tr. by Kabir Helminski. 96p. 1996. pap. 9.00 (0-614-21306-1, 739) Kazi Pubns.

Love Is a Stranger. Frances Paige. 192p. 25.00 (0-7278-5525-5) Severn Hse.

*Love Is a Stranger: Selected Lyric Poetry of Jalaluddin Rumi. Jalal Al-Din Rumi. Tr. by Kabir Helminski. LC 99-49893. 96p. 2000. pap. 10.95 (1-57062-527-1, Pub. by Shambhala Pubns) Random.

Love Is a Stranger: Selected Lyric Poetry of Jalaluddin Rumi. Jalal Al-Din Rumi. Tr. & Intro. by Kabir E. Helminski. 96p. 1993. pap. 10.00 (0-939660-32-6) Threshold CA.

Love Is a Tempest. large type ed. Angela Gordon. LC 97-36288. (Paperback Ser.). 220p. 1997. lib. bdg. 21.95 (0-7838-8317-X, G K Hall Lrg Type) Mac Lib Ref.

Love Is a Time of Day. John Patrick. 1970. pap. 5.25 (0-8222-0692-7) Dramatists Play.

Love Is a Verb. Mary E. Edmunds. LC 94-24070. x, 133p. 1995. 13.95 (0-87579-890-X) Deseret Bk.

Love Is a Verb. Louis Gittner. 200p. 1987. 12.95 (0-9605492-3-4) Touch Heart.

Love Is A Verb: How to Stop Analyzing Your Relationship, Start Making It Great! Bill O'Hanlon & Pat Hudson. 160p. 1995. 19.95 (0-393-03734-7) Norton.

Love is a Wild Assault. Elithe H. Kirkland. 504p. 1991. reprint ed. pap. 15.95 (0-940672-58-8) Shearer Pub.

Love Is All You Need. Regina A. Burch. 242p. 1998. pap. 12.95 (1-880849-10-0) Chapel Hill NC.

Love Is Always Right see Amor Siempre Tiene Razon

Love Is Always Right. Josh McDowell & Norm Giesler. 196p. 1996. pap. 12.99 (0-8499-3965-8) Word Pub.

Love Is Always There. Lisa Kent. LC 93-20412. (Illus.). 32p. (J). (ps-5). 1993. pap. 4.95 (0-8091-6611-9) Paulist Pr.

Love Is an Awesome Thing. Richard Oxley. Ed. by Tim Ohr. (Illus.). 1996. 12.95 (1-884942-01-6) Wrld Tampa.

Love Is an Inside Job. Cliff Custer. 196p. 1993. pap. text. write for info. (0-9637419-1-8) Cyber Pub.

Love Is Better Than Wine. Herbert Lockyer. LC 80-84903. 128p. 1981. pap. 3.95 (0-89221-083-4) New Leaf.

Love Is Blind. Marvin Heiferman. 1990. pap. 10.95 (0-679-72097-9) McKay.

Love Is Blind. Ed. by Marvin Heiferman & Carole Kismaric. (Illus.). 96p. 1997. 19.95 (1-57687-007-3, 620061, pwerHse Bks) pwerHse Cultrl.

*Love Is by God: A World Tour of Wisdom for Finding Inner Peace. David James. 265p. 1999. pap. 9.95 (0-9671928-3-8) Chicago Pr.

Love Is Contagious. Patricia McLaine. 1961. pap. 5.25 (0-8222-0693-5) Dramatists Play.

Love Is Dynamite. Lester Sumrall. 57p. 1987. pap. text 10.00 (0-937580-02-3) Sumrall Pubng.

Love Is Enough. Miriam. 1962. 6.50 (0-8159-6112-X) Devin.

*Love Is Enough: Poems & Paintings Celebrating Love. Raymond Simon. LC 99-48903. (Illus.). 96p. 2000. 14.95 (0-8092-2476-5, 242670, Contemporary Bks) NTC Contemp Pub Co.

Love Is Enough, Poems by the Way see Collected Works of William Morris

Love Is Eternal. Perry Tanksley. 4.50 (0-686-15452-5) Allgood Bks.

Love Is Eternal. large type ed. Irving Stone. 1976. 27.99 (0-85456-551-5) Ulverscroft.

Love Is Eternal. Irving Stone. 1994. reprint ed. lib. bdg. 27.95 (1-56849-556-0) Buccaneer Bks.

Love Is Everywhere! Special Edition Coloring Book. Golden Books Staff. 84p. (J). (ps-4). 1997. pap. text 2.99 (0-307-05843-3, 05843, Goldn Books) Gldn Bks Pub Co.

Love Is for Life. Irish Bishop's Pastoral Staff. 115p. (Orig.). 1986. pap. 3.95 (0-86217-154-7, Pub. by Veritas Pubns) St Mut.

Love Is for the Dogs. Patricia R. Mauser. (J). 1989. pap. 2.50 (0-380-75723-0, Avon Bks) Morrow Avon.

Love Is for the Lucky. large type ed. Susanne McCarthy. 1990. lib. bdg. 18.95 (0-263-12347-2) Mac Lib Ref.

Love Is Forever. Joan W. Anglund. LC 97-14793. (Illus.). 32p. (J). 1998. 10.00 (0-15-201680-5) Harcourt.

Love Is Forever. Karol Cooper. 1999. pap. text 6.95 (1-58334-000-9) Walnut Gr Pr.

Love Is Forever. Wallace Piroyan. 143p. (Orig.). 1983. pap. 2.50 (0-9613129-1-2) Chiwaukee Pub Co.

Love Is Forever: Poems in Family Life. Mildred Fielder. 198p. (Orig.). 1992. pap. 11.95 (0-9620162-2-5) M Fielder.

Love Is Hard Work. Miguel Algarin. 1997. 24.50 (0-684-83999-7) S&S Trade.

Love Is Hell: Tenth Anniversary Edition. 10th anniversary ed. Matt Groening. LC 96-150061. (Illus.). 56p. 1994. pap. 12.00 (0-679-75665-5) Pantheon.

Love Is Here to Stay. large type ed. Peggy Gaddis. 1994. 27.99 (0-7089-3185-5) Ulverscroft.

Love Is His Word. Richard Proulx. pap. write for info. (1-58459-068-8, 4037) Wrld Lib Pubns.

Love Is in the Cards. Emma Goldrick. (Presents Ser.: No. 1360). 1991. per. 2.75 (0-373-11360-9) Harlequin Bks.

Love Is in the Earth - A Kaleidoscope of Crystals Update: The Reference Book Describing the Metaphysical Properties of the Mineral Kingdom. A Melody. Ed. by R. R. Jackson. LC 94-61710. (Illus.). 728p. (Orig.). 1995. pap. 18.95 (0-9628190-3-4) Earth-Love Pub Hse.

Love Is in the Earth - Kaleidoscopic Pictorial: Supplement A. A. Melody. LC 96-86276. (Illus.). 384p. (Orig.). 1996. pap. 18.95 (0-9628190-7-7) Earth-Love Pub Hse.

Love Is in the Earth - Kaleidoscopic Pictorial Supplement Z. Melody. Ed. by Laodeciae Augustine. (Illus.). 384p. 1998. pap. 18.95 (0-9628190-5-0) Earth-Love Pub Hse.

Love Is in the Earth - Laying-on-of-Stones: The Journey Continues. A Melody. Ed. by R. R. Jackson & L. Augustine. LC 91-771320. (Illus.). 273p. (Orig.). 1992. pap. 12.95 (0-9628190-1-8) Earth-Love Pub Hse.

Love Is in the Earth - Mineralogical Pictorial: Treasures of the Earth. A Melody. Ed. by Bob Jackson. LC 93-73772. (Illus.). 416p. (Orig.). 1994. pap. 27.95 (0-9628190-2-6) Earth-Love Pub Hse.

Love Is Lasting. John Boynton. 96p. (Orig.). 1971. pap. 3.50 (0-917814-01-0) AstroArt Ent.

Love Is Layers of Sharing see Curriculum Written for Partners in Parenting Education

Love Is Letting Go of Fear. Gerald G. Jampolsky. LC 79-52027. 144p. 1995. pap. 8.95 (0-89087-246-5) Celestial Arts.

Love Is Letting Go of Fear. Gerald G. Jampolsky. (SPA., Illus.). 160p. 1989. pap. 7.95 (0-925776-00-9) Cogent Publishing.

Love Is Letting Go of Fear. Gerald G. Jampolsky. 1995. audio 16.00 (0-671-51993-X) S&S New Media.

Love Is Like the Lion's Tooth. Ed. by Frances McCullough. LC 77-25659. 96p. (YA). (gr. 7 up). 1984. 12.95 (0-06-024138-1) HarpC Child Bks.

Love Is Little: A Sampling of Shaker Spirituals. Ed. & Compiled by Roger L. Hall. (Illus.). 48p. 1992. spiral bd. 12.00 (0-944178-01-4) World Shaker.

Love Is My Only Master: Affirmations & Reflections for the Heart & Soul. Kathryn M. Peters. 316p. 1993. pap. 14.95 (0-9638490-0-X) Heartlght Prodns.

Love Is My Reason. large type ed. Grace Goodwin. (Linford Romance Library). 336p. 1992. pap. 16.99 (0-7089-7279-9, Linford) Ulverscroft.

Love Is Needed see Se Necesita Amor: Accidental Nanny

Love Is Never Enough: How Couples Can Overcome Misunderstandings, Resolve Conflicts, & Solve Relationship Problems Through Cognitive Therapy. Aaron T. Beck. LC 88-45010. 432p. 1989. reprint ed. pap. 14.00 (0-06-091604-4, Perennial) HarperTrade.

Love Is No Laughing Matter. Pedro Calderon de la Barca. (Hispanic Classics Ser.). 1986. 59.95 (0-85668-365-5, Pub. by Aris & Phillips); pap. 25.00 (0-85668-366-3, Pub. by Aris & Phillips) David Brown.

Love Is Not . . . Because. Ruth F. Boorstin. LC 98-84271. 192p. 1998. lib. bdg. 14.95 (1-883477-24-7) Lone Oak MN.

Love Is Not a Consolation: It Is a Light. Primus St. John. LC 82-71661. 1982. pap. 9.95 (0-915604-75-2) Carnegie-Mellon.

Love Is Not Enough. Bruno Bettelheim. 1950. 27.95 (0-02-903280-6) Free Pr.

Love Is Now. rev. ed. Peter E. Gillquist. 1970. 5.95 (0-310-36941-X, 18054P) Zondervan.

*Love Is Patient & Kind: St. Paul's Letter: 1 Corinthians 13. Ariel Books Staff. 2000. pap. 4.95 (0-7407-1036-2) Andrews & McMeel.

Love Is Patient, Love Is Kind. Charles L. Allen. LC 88-37589. 1989. 4.95 (0-687-22812-3) Abingdon.

Love Is Recognition. limited ed. Evelyn Eaton. LC 78-183569. (Living Poets' Library). pap. 2.50 (0-686-01282-8) Dragons Teeth.

*Love Is, Ribbon Book. Brownlow Publishing Co. Staff. LC 99-235832. 1999. pap. 8.99 (1-57051-250-7) Brownlow Pub Co.

Love Is Shown in Little Ways. Ken Michel. LC 96-148300. (Illus.). 80p. 1995. 4.95 (0-8362-3126-0) Andrews & McMeel.

Love Is Starving for Itself. Patric Roscoe. 240p. Date not set. pap. 16.50 (1-55128-015-9, Pub. by Mercury Bk) LPC InBook.

Love Is Straight from the Heart: A Collection of Poetry. Diana L. Byrd. 72p. (Orig.). 1997. pap. 7.00 (0-8059-3993-8) Dorrance.

Love Is Strange: Stories of Postmodern Romance. Ed. by Joel Rose & Catherine Texier. LC 92-15411. 288p. 1993. pap. 12.95 (0-393-30965-7) Norton.

Love Is Strength: Love Has No Weakness, 2 vols. in 1. Michael B. Stone. (Illus.). 1979. 9.50 (0-9603448-0-2) M B Stone.

*Love Is Strong As Death. James D. Freeman. LC 99-16621. (Illus.). 154p. 1999. 14.95 (0-87159-246-0) Unity Bks.

Love Is Stronger Than Death. Peter J. Kreeft. LC 91-76753. 141p. 1992. reprint ed. pap. 9.95 (0-89870-392-1) Ignatius Pr.

*Love Is Stronger Than Death: The Mystical Union of Two Souls. Cynthia Bourgeault. LC 98-56526. 224p. 1999. 21.00 (0-609-60473-2, CPG Pr) IDG Bks.

Love Is the Answer! Cora Hussey. LC 98-93752. x, 76p. 1998. pap. 5.95 (0-9661830-1-0) C Hussey.

Love Is the Answer. Albert Krassner. (Orig.). 1987. pap. 4.95 (0-912061-13-8) Veridon Edns.

*Love Is the Answer. S. Lee. 1998. pap. text 14.95 (0-575-60246-5, Pub. by V Gollancz) Trafalgar.

*Love Is the Answer! 2nd ed. Cora Hussey. 1999. reprint ed. per. 5.95 (0-9661830-2-9) C Hussey.

Love Is the Answer: Creating Positive Relationships. Gerald G. Jampolsky. 256p. 1990. pap. 14.95 (0-553-35268-7) Bantam.

Love Is the Contingency. 176p. 1997. pap. 9.95 (0-9624427-3-9) Procrustes Pr.

Love Is the Crooked Thing. Lee K. Abbott. LC 96-15039. 182p. 1996. pap. 16.00 (0-8142-0713-8) Ohio St U Pr.

Love Is the Crooked Thing. Barbara Wersba. LC 87-171. (Charlotte Zolotow Bk.). 160p. (YA). (gr. 7 up). 1987. 11.95 (0-06-026366-0) HarpC Child Bks.

Love Is the Cure. large type ed. Helen Upshall. (Magna General Fiction Ser.). 306p. 1992. 27.99 (0-7505-0431-5, Pub. by Mgna Lrg Print) Ulverscroft.

Love Is the Enemy. large type ed. Marjorie Harding. 432p. 1985. 27.99 (0-7089-1311-3) Ulverscroft.

*Love Is the Hardest Lesson: A Memoir. Margaret Hope Bacon. LC 99-45314. 1999. 10.00 (0-87574-936-4) Pendle Hill.

Love Is the Key. Irene Brand. 224p. 1988. pap. 5.95 (0-310-47801-4, 15657P) Zondervan.

Love Is the Key. Mary Lyons. (Presents Ser.). 1994. per. 2.99 (0-373-11633-0, 1-11633-4) Harlequin Bks.

Love Is the Link: A Hospice Doctor Shares Her Experience of Near Death & Dying. Pamela M. Kircher. Ed. by Paul Cash. LC 95-78976. 144p. (Orig.). 1995. pap. 11.95 (0-943914-76-0) Larson Pubns.

Love Is the Measure: A Biography of Dorothy Day. rev. ed. Jim Forest. LC 93-41162. 234p. 1994. reprint ed. pap. 17.00 (0-88344-942-0) Orbis Bks.

Love Is the Only Reality. Merle Waldbaum. Ed. by Burton Waldbaum. 1988. 6.00 (0-9614248-5-0) Gentle World.

Love Is the Silence: Poems, 1948-1974. Stuart Z. Perkoff. 1975. pap. 4.00 (0-88031-018-9) Invisible-Red Hill.

Love Is the Target: An Answer for Troubled Americans, Today. Art Fettig. (Illus.). 96p. (Orig.). 1992. pap. 5.95 (0-916927-16-4) Growth Unltd.

Love Is the Wine: Talks of a Sufi Master in America. 2nd ed. Sheikh Muzaffer Ozak. LC 98-83050. 1999. pap. 9.95 (0-89314-425-8) Philos Res.

Love Is Touching. John Boynton. (Illus.). 48p. 1972. pap. 2.95 (0-917814-03-7) AstroArt Ent.

*Love Is Triumph. large type ed. Amber Dana. 320p. 1999. pap. 18.99 (0-7089-5545-2, Linford) Ulverscroft.

Love Is Walking Hand-in-Hand. Charles M. Schulz. (Illus.). 1983. pap. 4.95 (0-915696-80-0) Determined Prods.

Love Is Walking Hand-in-Hand. Charles M. Schulz. LC 79-63490. (Illus.). 1982. reprint ed. 6.95 (0-915696-14-2) Determined Prods.

Love Is Where It Falls. Simon Callow. LC 99-26551. 208p. 1999. 23.00 (0-88064-239-4) Fromm Intl Pub.

*Love Is Where It Falls. Simon Callow. 2001. reprint ed. pap. 13.00 (0-88064-257-2) Fromm Intl Pub.

Love Is Your Calling. Josef Heinzmann. (C). 1988. 39.00 (0-85439-222-X, Pub. by St Paul Pubns) St Mut.

Love Is Your Disguise: Sermons for Lent/Easter. Frank Luchsinger. LC 98-13655. (Second Lessons Ser.). 110p. 1998. pap. 9.95 (0-7880-1269-X) CSS OH.

Love Isn't Always Easy. Ed. by Susan Polis Schutz. LC 82-74104. (Illus.). 96p. 1983. 16.95 (0-88396-182-2) Blue Mtn Art.

*Love Isn't Love... Until. K. L. Morgan. LC 99-67790. 84p. 1999. pap. write for info. (1-58308-128-3, 81283) TriQuest.

Love It, Don't Label It: A Practical Guide for Using Spiritual Principles in Everyday Life. Carlin J. Diamond. Ed. by Kim Peterson. (Illus.). 200p. (Orig.). 1986. pap. 10.00 (0-911761-03-9) Fifth Wave Pr.

Love, Janis: A Revealing Biography of Janis Joplin. 2nd rev. ed. Laura Joplin. (Illus.). 352p. 1999. pap. 16.00 (1-888358-08-4) Acid Test Prodns.

Love, Judy: Letters of Hope & Healing for Women with Breast Cancer. Judy Hart. 250p. (Orig.). 1993. pap. 10.95 (0-943233-52-6) Conari Press.

Love Just in Time. Flora Speer. 448p. 1998. mass mkt. 5.50 (0-505-52289-6, Love Spell) Dorchester Pub Co.

Love Just in Time. Flora M. Speer. 448p. (Orig.). 1995. mass mkt. 4.99 (0-505-52004-4, Love Spell) Dorchester Pub Co.

Love Just Screws Everything Up. Lynn Johnston. LC 96-84531. (For Better or for Worse Collection). (Illus.). 128p. (Orig.). 1996. pap. 9.95 (0-8362-2128-1) Andrews & McMeel.

Love, Justice, Then Spirituality: Indigenous Women of North America on Ways of Seeing Beyond Apology, Dominance & Resistance. Indigenous Women of North America. (Common Ground Ser.: Vol. 6). (Illus.). 70p. (Orig.). 1992. pap. 10.00 (1-884478-05-0) Common Grnd.

Love Keys: The Art of Magnetic Sex: A Unique Guide to Love & Sexual Fulfilment Diana Richardson. LC 98-55290. 1999. write for info. (1-86204-387-6) Element MA.

*Love-Kill. James Saporito. LC 99-91418. 1999. 25.00 (0-7388-0762-1); pap. 18.00 (0-7388-0763-X) Xlibris Corp.

Love Killer. John McDowell & Bob Hostetler. LC 93-25122. (Powerlink Chronicle Ser.: Vol. 2). (YA). (gr. 6 up). 1993. pap. 9.99 (0-8499-3509-1) Word Pub.

Love Killers. Jackie Collins. Orig. Title: Love Head. 1991. per. 5.99 (0-671-73786-4) PB.

Love Kills. Ed. by Ed Gorman & Martin H. Greenberg. LC 96-53912. 432p. 1997. pap. 12.95 (0-7867-0426-8) Carroll & Graf.

Love Kills: The Stalking of Diane Newton King. Andy Hoffman. 264p. (Orig.). 1994. mass mkt. 5.50 (0-380-77274-4, Avon Bks) Morrow Avon.

Love Knot. Elizabeth Chadwick. 474p. 1999. text 27.95 (0-312-24407-X) St Martin.

Love Knot: A Comedy in One Act. Michael McFaden. (Illus.). 32p. 1975. pap. 3.25 (0-88680-118-4) I E Clark.

*Love Knot: Ties That Blind Cancer Partners. Robert Ross. 2000. pap. 15.00 (0-7637-1412-7) Jones & Bartlett.

Love, Knowledge, & Discourse in Plato: Dialogue & Dialectic in "Phaedrus", "Republic", "Parmenides" Herman L. Sinaiko. LC 65-24431. (Midway Reprint Ser.). 1979. pap. text 13.50 (0-226-76018-9) U Ch Pr.

Love Known: Theology & Experience in George Herbert's Poetry. Richard Strier. LC 83-6798. xxii, 278p. 1994. 25.00 (0-226-77716-2) U Ch Pr.

Love Known: Theology & Experience in George Herbert's Poetry. Richard Strier. LC 83-6798. xxii, 300p. 1997. pap. 15.95 (0-226-77717-0) U Ch Pr.

*Love Knows No Distance. Nora B. Hawthorne. 1999. pap. 19.95 (1-892861-03-8) Vision Pubg Grp.

Love Knows No Limit. Elliot. 1992. pap. text 1.50 (0-8474-1191-5) Back to Bible.

Love, Labour & Loss: Stillbirth & Neonatal Death. Jo Benson. 192p. 1996. pap. text 17.95 (1-85727-063-0, Pub. by Scarlet Pr) LPC InBook.

Love Labours Lost. Miriam Gilbert. (Illus.). 137p. 1997. text 24.95 (0-7190-4624-6, Pub. by Manchester Univ Pr) St Martin.

Love Laws see Leyes del Amor: (The Laws of Love)

Love, Lawyers & Lies. Courtney Ross et al. 200p. 1991. per. write for info. (0-8187-0147-1) Harlo Press.

Love Leads Home. large type ed. June M. Bacher. 1988. pap. 8.95 (0-8027-2624-0) Walker & Co.

Love Leap of the Heart. B. Shih. LC 96-167155. 1997. pap. 9.95 (0-9617268-0-6) Satori Pr.

Love Leaves at Midnight. large type ed. Barbara Cartland. (Magna Large Print Ser.). 288p. 1997. 27.50 (0-7505-1111-7) Thorndike Pr.

*Love Lesson. Sheridon Smythe. 1999. mass mkt. 5.99 (0-515-12682-9) Berkley Pub.

Love Lessons. Marian Oaks. 480p. 1992. mass mkt. 4.50 (0-8217-3959-X, Zebra Kensgtn) Kensgtn Pub Corp.

Love Lessons. Dale R. Starks. 116p. 1991. pap. 6.95 (0-9630790-0-X) D R Starks.

*LOVE LESSONS. Brenda Wade. 256p. 1999. pap. 21.95 (1-56743-005-8, Amistad) HarperTrade.

*Love Lessons. large type ed. Lois S. Brady. LC 99-38388. 1999. 25.95 (1-56895-772-6, Wheeler) Wheeler Pub.

Love Lessons: A Guide to Transforming Relationships. Brenda Wade & Brenda L. Richardson. 272p. 1994. pap. 12.95 (1-56743-062-7, Amistad) HarperTrade.

Love Lessons: African Americans & Sex, Romance & Marriage the Nineties. George Davis. LC 97-28865. 256p. 1998. pap. 12.00 (0-688-14864-6, Wm Morrow) Morrow Avon.

Love Lessons: Twelve Real-Life Love Stories. Lois Smith-Brady. LC 99-13485. (Illus.). 240p. 1999. 17.50 (0-684-85234-9) S&S Trade.

Love, Let Me Not Hunger. large type ed. Paul Gallico. 1974. 27.99 (0-85456-286-9) Ulverscroft.

*Love Letter. Cathleen Schine. LC 97-37247. 272p. 1998. pap. 12.95 (0-452-27948-8) NAL.

*Love Letter. Cathleen Schine. 362p. 1999. mass mkt. 6.99 (0-451-19867-0, Sig) NAL.

*Love Letter: The Heartbreaking Tale of the Incredible Bond. Sandro Mayer. 2000. pap. 12.95 (88-7301-404-6) Gremese Intl.

Love Letter from an Impossible Land. William Meredith. LC 70-144748. (Yale Series of Younger Poets: No. 42). reprint ed. 18.00 (0-404-53842-8) AMS Pr.

Love Letter from God. Bride of Christ. (Illus.). 77p. 1997. mass mkt. 8.95 (1-885351-77-1) Cheval Intl.

Love Letter to America. T. Schuman. 46p. 1984. pap. 5.00 (0-935090-13-4) Almanac Pr.

L

An Asterisk (*) at the beginning of an entry indicates that the title is appearing for the first time.

Love Letter to the Blue Planet. Elaine Emans. LC 91-31755. 92p. 1992. pap. 5.95 (*0-936015-29-2*) Pocahontas Pr.

Love Letters. Arnold Adoff. LC 96-19982. (Illus.). 40p. (J). (ps-3). 1997. 15.95 (*0-590-48478-8*) Scholastic Inc.

Love Letters. Ed. by Helen Exley. (Illus.). 60p. 1997. 8.00 (*1-85015-934-3*) Exley Giftbooks.

Love Letters. A. R. Gurney. 1989. spiral bd. 5.95 (*0-8222-0694-3*) Dramatists Play.

Love Letters. Madeleine L'Engle. 303p. 1996. 19.99 (*0-87788-528-1*, H Shaw Pubs) Waterbrook Pr.

Love Letters. Candice Poarch & Janice Sims. 288p. 1997. mass mkt. 4.99 (*0-7860-0366-9*, Pinncle Kensgtn) Kensgtn Pub Corp.

Love Letters. JoAnna Poehlmann. LC 95-33393. (Post Impressions Ser.). (Illus.). 72p. 1996. bds. 5.95 (*0-7892-0091-0*) Abbeville Pr.

Love Letters. Ed. by Peter Washington. 256p. 1996. 12.50 (*0-679-44689-3*) Knopf.

Love Letters, Vol. 2. Orley R. Herron. 80p. 1996. write for info. (*1-889555-01-0*) Stephen Aubry.

***Love Letters: A Is for Always, B Is for Baby, C Is for Cowboy.** Lisa Jackson. (By Request 3's Ser.). 2000. mass mkt. 6.99 (*0-373-20177-X*, 1-20177-1) Harlequin Bks.

***Love Letters: A Novel.** Kirby Roy, III. LC 98-55254. 383p. (Orig.). 1999. pap. 18.95 (*0-9644932-7-6*, NanKira Bks) Kujichagulia Pr.

Love Letters: A Women's Story. Celia M. Halas. 1982. pap. 6.95 (*0-9608560-0-5*) Schalaco Pub.

Love Letters: An Illustrated Anthology. Antonia Fraser. (Illus.). 192p. 1989. 19.95 (*0-8092-4314-8*) NTC Contemp Pub Co.

Love Letters: And Two Other Plays: The Golden Age & What I Did Last Summer. A. R. Gurney. 264p. 1990. pap. 11.95 (*0-452-26501-0*, Plume) Dutton Plume.

Love Letters: Gibran. Tr. by Suheil Bushrui & Salma H. Al-Kuzbari. (Illus.). 136p. 1995. pap. 11.95 (*1-85168-106-X*, Pub. by Onewrld Pubns) Penguin Putnam.

***Love Letters: How to Unlock the Secrets in Your Lover's Handwriting.** Paula Roberts. 2000. pap. 9.95 (*1-86204-693-X*, Pub. by Element MA) Penguin Putnam.

Love Letters: Reading Level 3. (Sundown Fiction Collection). 1993. 3.95 (*0-88336-214-7*); audio 9.95 (*0-88336-776-9*) New Readers.

Love Letters Before Birth & Beyond. Mary Knight. 184p. (Orig.). 1997. pap. 14.95 (*0-9654970-0-3*) Single Eye Pub.

Love Letters Between a Certain Late Nobleman & the Famous Mr. Wilson. Michael S. Kimmel. LC 90-4409. (Journal of Homosexuality Ser.: No. 19, No. 2). (Illus.). 124p. 1990. pap. text 19.95 (*0-918393-69-8*, Harrington Park) Haworth Pr.

Love Letters Between a Certain Late Nobleman & the Famous Mr. Wilson. Michael S. Kimmel. LC 90-4229. (Journal of Homosexuality: Vol. 19, No. 2). (Illus.). 124p. 1990. text 3.95 (*0-86656-985-5*) Haworth Pr.

Love Letters, Death Threats & Suicide Notes: New & Selected Poems & Essays (1991-1998) Eric C. Webb. LC 98-90817. 115p. (Orig.). 1999. pap. 12.95 (*0-9667368-0-X*) Souls Commun.

Love Letters for Sale. Kate William. (Sweet Valley High Ser.: No. 88). (YA). (gr. 7 up). 1992. 8.35 (*0-606-00685-0*, Pub. by Turtleback) Demco.

***Love Letters from God.** Anthony J. Asalone. xii, 142p. 1999. pap. 12.99 (*0-9673212-0-4*) Gods Love Pub.

Love Letters from God. Connie Witter. LC 96-123524. 160p. 1995. mass mkt. 5.99 (*0-89274-829-X*, HH-829) Harrison Hse.

***Love Letters from God: Affirmations for Your Soul.** Bonnie Schluter. 2000. pap. 14.99 (*1-56292-630-6*) Honor Bks OK.

Love Letters from Spirit to You. 2nd ed. Jacob Beilhart. 112p. 1986. reprint ed. pap. 4.95 (*0-918588-07-3*, 505-100) Barksdale Foun.

Love Letters, Lust Letters. Karrie Psuik. 45p. (Orig.). 1994. pap. 7.95 (*0-9645010-1-5*, Karrie Angel) Prem Raja Baba.

***Love Letters of a Lifetime: Romance in America.** Lifetime Television for Women Staff. 192p. 2001. 15.95 (*0-7868-6705-1*, Pub. by Hyperion) Time Warner.

Love Letters of a Portugese Nun. Gabriel De Lavergne. 48p. 1998. mass mkt. 7.95 (*1-86046-034-8*) Harvill Press.

Love Letters of Abelard & Heloise. Peter Abelard & Heloise. 1991. lib. bdg. 250.00 (*0-8490-4152-X*) Gordon Pr.

Love Letters of J. Timothy Owen. Constance C. Greene. LC 85-45846. 192p. (YA). (gr. 7 up). 1986. 11.95 (*0-06-022156-9*) HarpC Child Bks.

Love-Letters of Margaret Fuller, 1845-1846. Margaret Fuller. (American Biography Ser.). 228p. 1991. reprint ed. lib. bdg. 69.00 (*0-7812-8139-3*) Rprt Serv.

Love Letters of Margaret Fuller, 1845-1846. Margaret S. Ossoli. LC 72-122592. reprint ed. 41.50 (*0-404-04835-8*) AMS Pr.

Love-Letters of Margaret Fuller, 1845-1846. Sarah M. Ossoli. (BCL1-PS American Literature Ser.). 228p. 1992. reprint ed. lib. bdg. 79.00 (*0-7812-6817-6*) Rprt Serv.

Love Letters of Nathaniel Hawthorne, 1839-1863. Nathaniel Hawthorne. (American Biography Ser.). 1991. reprint ed. lib. bdg. 99.00 (*0-7812-8173-3*) Rprt Serv.

Love Letters of Thomas Carlyle & Jane Welsh, 2 vols. Thomas Carlyle. Ed. by Alexander Carlyle. LC 75-30016. (Illus.). reprint ed. 135.00 (*0-404-14050-5*) AMS Pr.

Love Letters That Work: Create Some Excitement in Your Life. Scott A. McIntosh. (Illus.). 80p. (Orig.). 1992. pap. 7.95 (*0-9632879-0-7*) McIntosh Pubns.

Love Letters to God. Joyce O'Kelley. 1989. 7.95 (*0-86544-053-0*) Salv Army Suppl South.

Love Letters to His Bride. Moses Mendelssohn. Tr. by Frauke Regan from GER. (Illus.). 120p. 1991. 21.95 (*0-941062-55-4*) Begos & Rosenberg.

Love Letters to Louise. Jack Tilley. LC 97-90557. 217p. 1998. 18.95 (*0-533-12423-9*) Vantage.

***Love Letters to My Baby: A Guided Journal for Expectant & New Mothers.** Vickey L. Banks. LC 99-57662. (Illus.). 96p. 2000. 14.99 (*1-57673-580-X*, Pub. by Multnomah Pubs) GL Services.

Love Letters to Remember: A Collection of Romance & Passion. Ed. by Elizabeth Belew. LC 96-204759. (Illus.). 96p. 1996. boxed set 15.95 (*1-889116-02-5*) Penbrooke Pub.

Love Lettes to Elizabeth. Elizabeth R. Masterson. v, 114p. 1999. 10.00 (*0-9670541-0-9*) E D Rupp.

Love, Liberation, & the Law. J. Vernon McGee. LC 95-154353. 1995. 15.99 (*0-7852-7828-1*) Nelson.

Love Lies. Fern Kupfer. 1995. pap. 4.99 (*0-8217-5155-7*) NAL.

Love, Lies & Alibis: Love the Man. Linda Markowiak. (Love That Man Ser.: No. 819). 1998. per. 4.25 (*0-373-70819-X*, 1-70819-7) Harlequin Bks.

Love, Lies & Jessica Wakefield see Libertad Incondicional

Love, Lies, & Jessica Wakefield. Laurie John. (Sweet Valley University Ser.: No. 2). (YA). (gr. 7 up). 1993. 9.09 (*0-606-05656-4*, Pub. by Turtleback) Demco.

Love, Lies, & Jessica Wakefield. Created by Francine Pascal. (Sweet Valley University Ser.: No. 2). 240p. (YA). (gr. 7 up). 1993. mass mkt. 4.50 (*0-553-56306-8*) Bantam.

Love, Lies, & Video. Cherie Bennett & Jeff Gottesfeld. (Trash Ser.). (YA). (gr. 7-12). 1997. pap. 3.99 (*0-614-28636-0*) Berkley Pub.

Love, Lies, & Video. Cherie Bennett & Jeff Gottesfeld. (Trash Ser.: No. 2). 224p. 1997. mass mkt. 3.99 (*0-425-15907-8*) Berkley Pub.

Love Lies Bleeding. Edmund Crispin. 20.95 (*0-89190-693-2*) Amereon Ltd.

***Love-Lies-Bleeding.** Barbara Haworth-Attard. (On Time's Wing Ser.). 144p. (J). (gr. 5 up). 1999. pap. 5.95 (*1-896184-60-X*) Roussan Pubs.

Love Lies Bleeding: A China Bayles Mystery. Susan Wittig Albert. LC 96-53666. 320p. 1997. pap. 21.95 (*0-425-15969-8*, Prime Crime) Berkley Pub.

Love Lies Bleeding: A China Bayles Mystery. Susan Wittig Albert. (China Bayles Mystery Ser.). 320p. 1998. reprint ed. pap. 5.99 (*0-425-16611-2*, Prime Crime) Berkley Pub.

Love Lies Bleeding: A Novel. Robert K. Swisher, Jr. LC 88-2095. (Contemporary Life Fiction Ser.). 96p. (Orig.). 1989. pap. 8.95 (*0-86534-121-4*) Sunstone Pr.

Love Lies Slain. large type ed. L. L. Blackmur. LC 90-10849. 397p. 1990. 17.95 (*0-89621-995-X*) Thorndike Pr.

Love Lies Waiting. large type ed. Mary Romney. (General Ser.). 432p. 1993. 27.99 (*0-7089-2867-6*) Ulverscroft.

***Love Life.** Zeruya Shalev. Tr. by Dalya Bilu from HEB. LC 99-36112. 272p. 2000. 24.00 (*0-8021-1655-8*, Pub. by Grove-Atltic) Publishers Group.

Love Life. Charlotte Vale Allen. 272p. 1998. reprint ed. pap. 20.00 (*0-9657437-4-8*) Isld Nation.

Love Life: I Cor. 13. W. Graham Scroggie. LC 79-2551. (W. Graham Scroggie Library). 96p. 1980. reprint ed. pap. 5.99 (*0-8254-3733-4*) Kregel.

Love, Life & Chocolate Chip Cookies. Donna L. Montgomery. 120p. (Orig.). 1995. pap. 6.95 (*0-938577-10-7*) St Johns Pub.

Love, Life, & Laughter. Charles Lee. Ed. by Paul N. Harris. 180p. 1990. 12.50 (*0-915180-32-4*) Harrowood Bks.

Love, Life, & Laughter. Charles Lee. Ed. by Paul N. Harris. 180p. 1991. pap. 9.95 (*0-915180-34-0*) Harrowood Bks.

Love, Life & Laughter. Leisure Arts Staff. 1998. pap. text 19.95 (*1-57486-113-1*) Oxmoor Hse.

***Love, Life & Learning: A Poetic Diary Featuring Poetry by Darlene.** Darlene M. Washington. 1999. spiral bd. 9.95 (*0-9674396-0-4*) D M Washington.

Love, Life & Living: Book of Poems. Johnetta Glaspie. Ed. by Beverly Hayes. LC 97-94339. 70p. (C). 1997. spiral bd. 10.00 (*0-9660356-0-7*) Jsha Pubns.

Love, Life & War. Frank N. Kautzmann. 34p. (Orig.). 1996. pap. 6.95 (*0-614-13540-0*) Austin Press.

Love, Life & Work (1906) Elbert Hubbard. 160p. 1998. reprint ed. pap. 19.95 (*0-7661-0299-8*) Kessinger Pub.

Love Life for Every Married. Ed Wheat. 1996. mass mkt. 5.99 (*0-310-21486-6*) Zondervan.

Love Life for Every Married Couple see Amor que No Se Apaga

Love Life for Every Married Couple. Ed Wheat. 251p. 1980. pap. 9.99 (*0-310-42511-5*, 10266P) Zondervan.

Love Life for Every Married Couple. Ed Wheat. 288p. 1987. 12.95 (*0-310-42510-7*, 10264) Zondervan.

Love Life for Every Married Couple. Ed Wheat & Gloria O. Perkins. 272p. 1987. pap. 12.95 (*0-310-42518-2*, 10264G) Zondervan.

Love Life for Parents: How to Have Kids & a Sex Life Too. David Arp & Claudia Arp. LC 97-39951. 1997. pap. 10.99 (*0-310-20715-0*) Zondervan.

Love-Life Poems, Vol. 2. Anthony Repici. (Orig.). 1997. pap. write for info. (*1-57553-490-8*) Watermrk Pr.

Love Life Rhythm. Sahar Muakasa. LC 87-71849. (ARA & ENG.). 181p. 1987. 30.00 (*0-944025-00-5*) Advance Research.

Love Life Wisdom. Paul F. Ernst. LC 99-90514. 365p. 1999. 25.00 (*0-7388-0418-5*); pap. 15.00 (*0-7388-0419-3*) Xlibris Corp.

***Love Lifted Me: The Unfinished Journey of Harlow Fullwood Jr.** Harlow Fullwood, Jr. & Frederick Douglass, IV. (Illus.). 275p. (YA). (gr. 8-12). 2000. pap. 20.00 (*0-935132-28-7*) C H Fairfax.

Love, Light & a Dream: Television's Past, Present & Future. James Roman. LC 95-47213. 320p. 1998. pap. 24.95 (*0-275-96437-X*, Praeger Pubs) Greenwood.

Love, Light & Life. Mosie Lister. 60p. 1987. 5.99 (*0-8341-9156-3*, MC-64) Lillenas.

Love Like Gold. large type ed. Valerie Parv. 1993. 19.95 (*0-263-13319-2*) Thorndike Pr.

Love Like Gumbo. Nancy Rawles. LC 97-31392. (Discoveries Ser.: No. 2). 272p. 1997. pap. 14.00 (*0-940242-75-3*) Fjord Pr.

Love Like Rage. Wendy-o Matik. 64p. (Orig.). 1994. pap. 7.00 (*0-916397-31-9*) Manic D Pr.

Love Like Romeo & Juliet. Natalie Bishop. 1993. per. 3.50 (*0-373-09840-5*, 5-09840-5) Silhouette.

Love Like That. large type unabridged ed. (Harlequin Ser.). 1994. lib. bdg. 19.95 (*0-263-13584-5*) Mac Lib Ref.

Love Like This! 1998. pap. write for info. (*0-9660541-1-3*) GMW Ents.

Love Lines. 4th ed. Jayne May & Dick Murdock. 130p. 1978. pap. 5.00 (*0-932916-01-5*) May-Murdock.

***Love Lines: Every Girls Guide to First Love.** Caroline Plaisted. (J). 2000. pap. text 5.95 (*1-902618-77-7*, Pub. by Element Childrns) Penguin Putnam.

Love Listen Discipline: 52 Weekly Parenting Tips for Fathers. Tafuta Fundisha-Bey. (Illus.). v, 88p. (Orig.). 1997. pap. 10.00 (*0-9657772-0-0*) Father in Action.

Love Lists: What Every Woman Wants Her Man Can Know. L. Casselberry & F. Candy. Ed. by Barbara Lehman & G. Morgan. (Illus.). 144p. 1998. pap. 14.95 (*0-9660772-0-2*) Access Ability.

Love, Live & Share. Susan Polis Schutz. LC 80-66672. (Illus.). 96p. 1980. 16.95 (*0-88396-118-0*) Blue Mtn Art.

Love Lived Too Long. Scott Shaw. 73p. (Orig.). 1990. pap. 9.95 (*1-877792-21-7*) Buddha Rose.

Love Lives: Have the Perfect Relationship with the Star-Sign of Your Choice. Carole Golder. 272p. (Orig.). 1995. pap. 8.95 (*0-8050-1311-3*, Owl) H Holt & Co.

Love Lives for Believers Journal. Katherine E. Anderson. 150p. 1998. pap., spiral bd. 15.95 (*1-57876-400-9*, Love Lives) Triple U Enterprises.

Love Lives for Believers Journal & Calendar Set. Katherine E. Anderson. 1998. pap., spiral bd. 21.95 (*1-57876-494-7*, Love Lives) Triple U Enterprises.

Love Lives for Families. Katherine E. Anderson. 150p. 1998. pap., spiral bd. 15.95 (*1-57876-402-5*, Love Lives) Triple U Enterprises.

Love Lives for Families Journal & Calendar Set. Katherine E. Anderson. 1998. pap., spiral bd. 21.95 (*1-57876-496-3*, Love Lives) Triple U Enterprises.

Love Lives for Friends Journal. Katherine E. Anderson. 150p. 1998. pap., spiral bd. 15.95 (*1-57876-403-3*, Love Lives) Triple U Enterprises.

Love Lives for Friends Journal & Calendar Set. Katherine E. Anderson. 1998. pap., spiral bd. 21.95 (*1-57876-497-1*, Love Lives) Triple U Enterprises.

Love Lives for the Faithful Journal. Katherine E. Anderson. 150p. 1998. pap., spiral bd. 15.95 (*1-57876-401-7*, Love Lives) Triple U Enterprises.

Love Lives for the Faithful Journal & Calendar Set. Katherine E. Anderson. 1998. pap., spiral bd. 21.95 (*1-57876-495-5*, Love Lives) Triple U Enterprises.

Love Lives for Those Who Wait Journal. Katherine E. Anderson. 150p. 1998. pap., spiral bd. 15.95 (*1-57876-404-1*, Love Lives) Triple U Enterprises.

Love Lives for Those Who Wait Journal & Calendar Set. Katherine E. Anderson. 1998. pap., spiral bd. 21.95 (*1-57876-498-X*, Love Lives) Triple U Enterprises.

Love Lives for True Lovers Journal & Calendar Set. Katherine E. Anderson. 1998. pap., spiral bd. 21.95 (*1-57876-499-8*, Love Lives) Triple U Enterprises.

Love Lives Here, Vol. 2. Mary L. Lewis. (Illus.). 98p. 1988. pap. 6.50 (*1-56770-185-X*) S Scheewe Pubns.

Love Lives Here, Vol. 3. Mary L. Lewis. 100p. 1988. pap. text 6.50 (*1-56770-195-7*) S Scheewe Pubns.

Love Lives of the Great Composers. Basil Howitt. 288p. (Orig.). 1995. pap. 17.95 (*0-920151-18-3*, Pub. by Sound & Vision) Firefly Bks Ltd.

Love Loops: A Divorced Father's Personal Journey. William Sturner. LC 81-90983. 1983. 10.95 (*0-87212-166-6*) Libra.

Love, Loss & Healing: A Woman's Guide to Transforming Grief. Susan T. De Lone. Ed. by Marge Columbus. (Illus.). 232p. 1998. pap. 14.95 (*1-889531-01-4*) Sibyl Pubns.

Love, Loss, & What I Wore. Ilene Beckerman. LC 95-20460. (Illus.). 164p. 1995. 14.95 (*1-56512-111-2*, 72111) Algonquin Bks.

***Love Lost & Found.** Carolyn Campbell. 2000. mass mkt. 7.50 (*0-425-17627-4*) Berkley Pub.

***Love Lost & Other Poems.** Gabrielle Della-Bescat. LC 99-90828. 1999. pap. 8.95 (*1-56167-556-3*, Five Star Spec Ed) Am Literary Pr.

***Love, Lost, Love Gained.** Claire M. Ford. LC 99-65238. 192p. 2000. pap. 12.95 (*1-58501-020-0*, Pub. by CeShore Pubg) Natl Bk Netwk.

***Love Lounge.** Havoc Publishing Staff. 1999. pap. 5.00 (*0-7416-1122-8*) Havoc Pub.

Love, Love see I Love You

Love Love Love. Ariel Books Staff. LC 97-193805. 12p. 1997. 4.95 (*0-8362-2945-2*, Arie Bks) Andrews & McMeel.

Love, Love, Love. Andy Warhol. LC 95-2261. (Illus.). 96p. 1996. 10.95 (*0-8212-2132-9*, Pub. by Bulfinch Pr) Little.

Love, Love, Love: The "Little Mandate" of Catherine De Hueck Doherty, 1896-1985. Robert Wild. LC 88-34243. 111p. (Orig.). 1989. pap. 7.95 (*0-8189-0549-2*) Alba.

Love, Loving, & Being Loved: What Men & Women Have to Say about It. SeMia Bray. Ed. by Wanda Santos-Bray et al. (Illus.). 80p. (Orig.). 1996. pap. 14.95 (*0-9653264-0-3*, 1001) Noisemaker Pub.

Love, Lucy. large type ed. Lucille Ball. LC 96-48275. 1999. pap. 24.95 (*0-7862-0966-6*) Thorndike Pr.

Love, Lucy. large type ed. Lucille Ball & Betty H. Hoffman. LC 96-48275. (Americana Series). 368p. 1997. lib. bdg. 26.95 (*0-7862-0965-8*) Thorndike Pr.

Love, Lust, & Handcuffs: Understanding the Sex Abuser. Sharie McCrary. LC 92-45167. 166p. (Orig.). 1993. pap. 8.95 (*1-880489-03-1*) Hoopuka Pr.

***Love, Lust & Longing in the White House: The Romantic Relationships of America's President's.** Webb Garrison. (Illus.). 320p. 2000. pap. 14.95 (*1-58182-081-X*, Cumberland Hearthside) Cumberland Hse.

Love, Lust & Rebellion: New Approaches to Georg Buchner. Reinhold Grimm. LC 84-40497. 280p. 1985. text 30.00 (*0-299-09860-5*) U of Wis Pr.

Love, Lust & Rebellion: New Approaches to Georg Buchner. Reinhold Grimm. LC 84-40497. 279p. reprint ed. pap. 86.50 (*0-608-20437-4*, 207169000002) Bks Demand.

Love Lust Pages Vol. 1: An Anthology of Erotic Poetry from the Writer's Corner. 45p. 1996. pap. 10.00 (*1-890799-01-7*, LLP214) Writers Corner.

Love Lyrics. Stan Proper. 40p. 1996. pap. 2.00 (*0-9619992-7-6*) Walden Sudbury.

Love Lyrics: Poetry by Jeanette Adams. Jeanette Adams. (Illus.). 32p. (Orig.). 1982. pap. 5.00 (*0-9627018-2-3*) J Adams Pubns.

Love Lyrics from the Carmina Burana. Ed. & Tr. by P. G. Walsh. LC 92-30358. xxxviii, 218p. (C). 1993. 55.00 (*0-8078-2068-7*); pap. text 19.95 (*0-8078-4400-4*) U of NC Pr.

***Love Lyrics in Light & Shadow.** Helen H. Gordon. (Life Enhancement Ser.: No. 4). 48p. 1999. pap. 7.95 (*0-9666192-3-4*) Anacade Intl.

Love Lyrics of Ancient Egypt. Tr. by Barbara H. Fowler from EGY. LC 94-5721. (Illus.). xvi, 85p. 1994. 29.95 (*0-8078-2159-4*); pap. 14.95 (*0-8078-4468-3*) U of NC Pr.

Love Machine. Jacqueline Susann. LC 97-27295. 512p. 1998. pap. 12.00 (*0-8021-3544-7*, Grove) Grove-Atltic.

Love Made Manifest. Edward M. Cook. LC 94-79089. 230p. 1994. 14.95 (*0-914927-21-3*) Higher Ed Pubns.

Love Made Perfect: Foundations for the Holy Life. LC 97-34246. 152p. 1997. pap. 9.99 (*0-8341-1654-5*); pap., teacher ed. 4.99 (*0-8341-1682-0*) Beacon Hill.

Love Madness: Medicine, the Novel, & the Female Insanity, 1800-1865. Helen Small. (Illus.). 274p. 1998. reprint ed. pap. text 24.95 (*0-19-818491-3*) OUP.

Love Magic. Marina Medici. LC 93-3847. 256p. 1994. pap. 16.00 (*0-671-79684-4*, Fireside) S&S Trade Pap.

***Love Magic.** Sally Morningstar. LC 00-28504. (Illus.). 128p. 2000. pap. 14.95 (*0-8069-2781-X*) Sterling.

Love Magic: The Way to Love Through Rituals, Spells, & Magical Life. Laurie Cabot & Tom Cowan. 288p. 1992. pap. 12.95 (*0-385-30570-2*, Delta Trade) Dell.

Love-Magic & Butterfly People: The Slim Curly Version of the Ajilee & Mothway Myths. Berard Haile & Irvy W. Goossen. Ed. by Karl W. Luckert. LC 78-59705. (American Tribal Religions Ser.: No. 2). (ENG & NAV.). 184p. reprint ed. pap. 57.10 (*0-7837-4615-6*, 204433600002) Bks Demand.

Love Magnetics. abr. ed. Roger W. Breternitz. 1985. pap. 9.95 incl. audio (*1-893417-13-1*) Vector Studios.

Love-Makers. Judith Gould. 512p. 1986. mass mkt. 7.50 (*0-451-15957-8*, Sig) NAL.

Love Makes a Family: Portraits of Lesbian, Gay, Bisexual & Transgendered Parents & Their Families. Photos by Gigi Kaeser. LC 98-30266. (Illus.). 208p. 1999. text 40.00 (*1-55849-160-0*); pap. text 19.95 (*1-55849-161-9*) U of Mass Pr.

Love Makes the Air Light. Raymond Roseliep. (Orig.). 1965. pap. 1.95 (*0-393-04243-X*) Norton.

Love Makes the World Go Round. Helen Exley. 1998. 7.00 (*1-86187-049-3*) Exley Giftbooks.

Love Makes Thinking Dark. Barbara Henning. 1995. pap. 7.00 (*0-935992-03-0*) United Art Bks.

Love Map Playbook: Charting Your Course to a Loving Relationship. Lowell J. Arthur. 32p. 1995. student ed. 12.95 (*1-884180-07-8*) LifeStar.

Love Maps: A Guide & Discussion Workbook. Tony Picchioni. 1998. text, wbk. ed. 7.94 (*1-56870-318-X*) RonJon Pub.

Love, Marriage & Divorce. Contrib. by Stephen P. Andrews et al. 121p. 1985. reprint ed. 39.00 (*0-932051-63-4*) Rprt Serv.

Love, Marriage, & Divorce, & the Sovereignty of the Individual. Ed. by Charles Shively. 1975. 20.00 (*0-87730-010-0*) M & S Pr.

Love, Marriage, & Family in Jewish Law & Tradition. Michael Kaufman. LC 91-38088. 416p. 1992. 40.00 (*0-87668-515-7*) Aronson.

Love, Marriage, & Family in Jewish Law & Tradition. Michael Kaufman. LC 91-38088. 416p. 1996. pap. 30.00 (*1-56821-884-2*) Aronson.

Love, Marriage & Family 101. Anne Peters. 1997. per. 3.25 (*0-373-19254-1*, 1-19254-1) Silhouette.

Love, Marriage & Friendship in the Soviet Union: Ideals & Practice. Vladimir Shlapentokh. LC 84-15943. 276p. 1984. 65.00 (*0-275-91266-3*, C1266, Praeger Pubs) Greenwood.

Love, Marriage, & Money. Gail Liberman & Alan Lavine. LC 98-12784. 208p. 1998. pap. 15.95 (*0-7931-2661-4*) Dearborn.

Love, Marriage & Other Calamities. Debbi Rawlins. 1997. per. 3.75 (*0-373-16675-3*, 1-16675-0) Harlequin Bks.

Love, Marriage & Righteousness by Faith. Morris L. Venden. (Anchor Ser.). 92p. 1989. pap. 7.99 (*0-8163-0784-9*) Pacific Pr Pub Assn.

Love, Marriage, & Sex in the Christian Tradition from Antiquity to Today. Jeffrey E. Ford. LC 98-9745. 350p. 1998. 74.95 (*1-57309-265-7*) Intl Scholars.

An Asterisk (*) at the beginning of an entry indicates that the title is appearing for the first time.

L

Love, Marriage & Sex in the Christian Tradition from Antiquity to Today. Jeffrey E. Ford. LC 98-9745. 350p. 1998. pap. 54.95 (1-57309-264-9) Intl Scholars.

Love, Marriage & the Family: Yesterday & Today. James A. Mohler. LC 82-8699. 224p. (Orig.). 1982. pap. 7.95 (0-8189-0434-8) Alba.

Love Massage. (Illus.). 120p. (Orig.). 1995. pap. text 10.00 (0-9625732-0-5) C Glanville.

Love Massage. Cecil E. Glanville. (Illus.). 120p. (Orig.). (C). 1995. write for info. (0-318-69810-2) C Glanville.

Love Match. Valerie King. 1991. mass mkt. 3.99 (0-8217-3579-9, Zebra Kensgtn) Kensgtn Pub Corp.

Love Match. Judy A. Nelson & Sandra Faulker. (Illus.). 256p. 1993. 19.95 (1-55972-157-X, Birch Ln Pr) Carol Pub Group.

Love Match Robert Westall. LC 98-165845. 184p. 1997. write for info. (0-416-19220-3) Routledge.

Love Match. Arnold Bennett. LC 74-16481. (Collected Works of Arnold Bennett: Vol. 50). 1977. reprint ed. 19.95 (0-518-19131-1) Ayer.

Love Matters: A Book of Lesbian Romance. Linda Sutton. LC 98-41558. 6p. 1999. 29.95 (0-7890-0288-4, Harrington Park) Haworth Pr.

***Love Matters: A Book of Lesbian Romance.** Linda Sutton. LC 98-41558. 198p. 1999. pap. 14.95 (1-56023-918-2, Harrington Park) Haworth Pr.

Love, Me. Denise K. Simon. 252p. 1993. pap. 9.95 (0-9637019-0-8) Gabriel Pr FL.

Love, Me. Tiffany White. 1994. per. 2.99 (0-373-25590-X) Harlequin Bks.

Love Me No. 1: Study Companion Workbook, No. 1. Denise K. Simon & Ronald D. Simon. 128p. (Orig.). 1995. pap., wbk. ed. 12.95 (0-9637019-1-6) Gabriel Pr FL.

Love, Me No. 2: Study Companion Workbook, No. 2. Denise K. Simon & Ronald D. Simon. 128p. (Orig.). 1996. pap., wbk. ed. 12.95 (0-9637019-2-4) Gabriel Pr FL.

Love, Me Vol. 3: Study Companion Workbook. Denise J. Simon & Ronald D. Simon. 128p. (Orig.). 1996. pap., wbk. ed. 12.95 (0-9637019-3-2) Gabriel Pr FL.

Love Me Again. Ann Major. (Family Continuity Program Ser.: No. 22). 1999. per. 4.50 (0-373-82170-0, 1-82170-1) Harlequin Bks.

Love Me Always. Created by Francine Pascal. (Sweet Valley University Ser.: No. 44). 240p. (YA). (gr. 7 up). 1998. mass mkt. 3.99 (0-553-57032-3) BDD Bks Young Read.

Love Me Forever. Desiree Dupont. LC 97-178736. 142p. 1996. pap. 12.95 (81-7328-065-7) Intl Spec Bk.

Love Me Forever. Johanna Lindsey. 348p. 1996. mass mkt. 6.99 (0-380-72570-3, Avon Bks) Morrow Avon.

***LOVE ME FOREVER (HC)** Lindsey. 2000. 22.00 (0-380-97263-8) Morrow Avon.

Love Me, Hate Me: But Don't Turn Me Off. Wallace R. Wirths. 72p. (Orig.). 1987. pap. 5.95 (0-940797-00-3) Media Spec.

Love Me, I'm a Criminal: or How to Get Away with Murder. Nathaniel N. Noble. Ed. by Gwen Costa. 1990. pap. 14.95 (0-87949-356-9) Ashley Bks.

Love Me, I'm a Criminal: or How to Get Away with Murder. Nathaniel N. Noble. 1996. pap. 19.95 (0-614-20719-3) Rainbow Bks.

Love Me Like You Mean It. Leslea Newman. 100p. (Orig.). 1987. reprint ed. pap. 8.95 (1-878533-14-2) Pride & Imprints.

Love Me, Live Me, I Am the Eternal Force: Being with Sai Baba. 208p. 1995. 12.00 (0-929839-04-8) Wisdom Works Pr.

Love Me Long. Doris Frankel. 1950. pap. 5.25 (0-8222-0695-1) Dramatists Play.

Love Me, Love Me Not. Cameron Dokey. 1995. mass mkt. 3.99 (0-7860-4983-9, Pinncle Kensgtn) Kensgtn Pub Corp.

Love Me, Love My Bed. Rita C. Estrada. (Harlequin Temptation Ser.: No. 595). 1996. per. 3.50 (0-373-25695-7, 1-25695-7) Harlequin Bks.

Love Me, Love My Bookie: Petting & Betting. Joe E. Palmer. 200p. (Orig.). 1989. pap. 9.95 (0-9622549-1-6, TXU 161-521) Remlap Pub.

Love Me, Love My Broccoli. Julie Anne Peters. 160p. (J). (gr. 3-7). 1999. mass mkt. 3.99 (0-380-79899-9, Avon Bks) Morrow Avon.

Love Me, Love My Doggerel. Louise F. Kerr. LC 70-107863. (Illus.). 1969. 3.00 (0-937684-02-3) Tradd St Pr.

Love Me, Love My Planet P. L. A. Y. Book: An Environmental Guide. Marcia Singer. LC 91-91308. (Illus.). 64p. (Orig.). (J). (gr. 1-7). 1991. pap. 7.95 (0-9622543-2-0) PLAY House.

Love Me Never. Edith Courtney. 256p. 25.00 (0-7278-5213-2) Severn Hse.

Love Me Not. Barbara Stewart. (Great Escapes Ser.). 1994. pap. 1.99 (0-373-83276-1, 1-83276-5) Harlequin Bks.

Love Me Now. large type ed. John McPartland. (Linford Mystery Library). 400p. 1994. pap. 16.99 (0-7089-7475-9, Linford) Ulverscroft.

Love Me Only. Hebby Roman. 384p. 1999. mass mkt. 4.99 (0-8217-6206-0) Kensgtn Pub Corp.

***Love Me or Leave Me.** large type ed. Josephine Cox. 400p. 1999. 31.99 (0-7089-9077-0) Ulverscroft.

Love Me Tender. Sandra Hill. 400p. 1998. mass mkt. 5.99 (0-8439-4457-9, Leisure Bks) Dorchester Pub Co.

Love Me Tender. Barbara Kaye. (Superromance Ser.: No. 495). 1992. per. 3.39 (0-373-70495-X, 1-70495-6) Harlequin Bks.

Love Me Tender. Elvis Presley. (Illus.). 32p. (J). 15.95 (0-06-027797-1) HarpC.

***Love Me Tender, Vol. 15.** Michaila Callan. (Zebra Bouquet Ser.). 1999. mass mkt. 3.99 (0-8217-6350-4, Zebra Kensgtn) Kensgtn Pub Corp.

Love Me Tender: The True Story of Marilyn & the King As Told by Karma Karen. Karma Karen. LC 97-91687. (Illus.). 304p. (Orig.). 1997. pap. 16.95 (0-9657228-0-5) Read Head.

Love Me, Thorn. Kim A. Brown. 320p. (Orig.). 1996. pap. 5.50 (0-9637762-5-8) Binders Keepers.

Love Me to Death. Linda Wolfe. 272p. 1999. per. 14.00 (0-671-51732-5) S&S Trade.

Love Me to Death: A Journalist's Memoir of the Hunt for Her Friend's Killer. Linda Wolfe. (Illus.). 254p. 1998. 24.00 (0-671-51720-1) PB.

Love Me Tomorrow. Rosanne Bittner. 320p. 1998. mass mkt. 5.99 (0-8217-5818-7, Zebra Kensgtn) Kensgtn Pub Corp.

Love Me Tomorrow. large type ed. Patricia Robins. (Dales Large Print Ser.). 254p. 1996. pap. 18.99 (1-85389-679-9, Dales) Ulverscroft.

Love Me True: Man of the Month/ Anniversary. anniversary ed. Ann Major. (Desire Ser.: No. 1213). 1999. per. 3.75 (0-373-76213-5, 1-76213-7) Silhouette.

Love Me When I'm Most Unlovable, Vol. II. Robert Ricken. 32p. (J). (gr. 6-9). 1987. pap. 4.00 (0-88210-198-6) Natl Assn Principals.

Love Me with Fury. Connie Mason. 384p. 1997. mass mkt. 5.50 (0-505-52215-2, Love Spell) Dorchester Pub Co.

Love Me with Fury. Cara Miles. 384p. (Orig.). 1991. mass mkt. 4.50 (0-380-76450-4, Avon Bks) Morrow Avon.

Love Me with Fury. Janelle Taylor. 496p. 1992. mass mkt. 4.99 (0-8217-3827-5, Zebra Kensgtn) Kensgtn Pub Corp.

Love Me with Fury. Janelle Taylor. 493p. 1996. pap. 5.99 (0-8217-5452-1) Kensgtn Pub Corp.

Love Medicine. Louise Erdrich. 88p. 1995. 19.95 (0-8050-1716-X) H Holt & Co.

Love Medicine. expanded ed. Louise Erdrich. LC 93-15166. 352p. 1995. 24.00 (0-8050-2798-X) H Holt & Co.

Love, Medicine & Miracles: Lessons Learned about Self-Healing from a Surgeon's Experience with Exceptional Patients. 60th ed. Bernie S. Siegel. LC 89-46437. (Illus.). 256p. 1998. reprint ed. pap. 14.00 (0-06-091983-3, Perennial) HarperTrade.

Love, Medicine & Miracles: Siegel,&Bernie. abr. ed. Bernie Siegel. 1992. audio 18.00 (0-89845-767-X, CPN 2107) HarperAudio.

Love Medicine RI. exp. ed. Louise Erdrich. LC 92-56263. 384p. 1998. pap. 13.00 (0-06-097554-7, Perennial) HarperTrade.

***Love Meets Alzheimers.** Gene Guerreno. LC 00-100852. 80p. 2000. 14.95 (1-58244-062-X) Rutledge Bks.

Love Meets the Dragon: A Field Manual for Ministers. Tom Owen-Towle. LC 97-69514. 174p. 1997. pap. 12.95 (0-931104-46-7) SunInk Pubn.

***Love Mends a Broken Heart.** Brenda Duke-Barber. 200p. 1999. pap. 8.99 (0-7392-0292-8, PO3630) Morris Pubng.

Love Merry-Go-Round. William F. Brown. 116p. 1999. pap. 25.00 (1-881936-13-9) WFB Ent.

Love Message see Mensaje de Amor

Love Minus. Mary Gallagher. 1989. pap. 5.25 (0-8222-0696-X) Dramatists Play.

Love Minus Zero. A. Macdonald. 8.50 (0-906731-92-5, Pub. by Christian Focus) Spring Arbor Dist.

Love Minus Zero - No Limits No. 15: Io Journal. Frank Zero. (Illus.). 96p. 1972. pap. 15.00 (0-913028-02-9) North Atlantic.

Love, Miracles & Animal Healing: A Veterinarian's Journey from Physical Medicine to Spiritual Understanding. Allen M. Schoen & Pam Procter. LC 95-1389. 240p. 1995. 21.50 (0-684-80207-4) S&S Trade.

Love, Miracles & Animal Healing: A Veterinarian's Journey from Physical Medicine to Spiritual Understanding. Allen M. Schoen & Pam Proctor. 240p. 1996. per. 12.00 (0-684-82273-3, Fireside) S&S Trade Pap.

Love, Mom: Stories from the Life of a Global Activist, Teacher & Mother of Six. unabridged ed. Miriam L. Levering et al. (Illus.). 196p. 1996. pap. 14.95 (0-9656330-1-2) Orchard Gap Pr.

***Love Money.** Sara Manning. 1998. pap. 6.95 (0-09-926376-9, Pub. by Random) Trafalgar.

Love More Precious. Marilyn Austin. (Serenade Serenata Ser.: No. 40). 1986. pap. 1.49 (0-310-47482-5, 15594P) Zondervan.

Love Must Be Tough see Amor Debe Ser Firme

Love Must Be Tough: Proven Hope for Families in Crisis. James Dobson. 256p. 1996. 19.99 (0-8499-1341-1) Word Pub.

Love Must Be Tough - Straight Talk. James C. Dobson. 14.99 (0-8499-1654-2) Word Pub.

Love Must Not Be Forgotten. Zhang Jie. LC 86-70557. (New Chinese Fiction Ser.). 244p. 1986. 16.95 (0-8351-1699-9); pap. 8.95 (0-8351-1698-0) China Bks.

Love Must Wait. large type ed. Patricia Robins. (Dales Large Print Ser.). 326p. 1997. pap. 18.99 (1-85389-678-0, Dales) Ulverscroft.

Love My Elna, Vol. 1. Janet Stocker & Gay. (Illus.). 68p. (Orig.). 1988. student ed. 14.95 (0-9620826-0-0) G & J Pub.

***Love My Vitamins.** Cindy Devine Dalton. LC 00-28017. (Why Should I... Ser.). 2000. write for info. (1-55916-306-2) Rourke Bk Co.

Love, Mystery & Misery: Feeling in Gothic Fiction. Coral A. Howells. (C). 1995. pap. 25.00 (0-485-12111-5, Pub. by Athlone Pr) Humanities.

***Love N Kisses.** Lavinia Hart. (Illus.). 24p. (J). 2000. pap. text 8.95 (1-902618-91-2, Pub. by Element Childrns) Penguin Putnam.

Love Never Dies. Cherie Bennett. (Teen Anges Ser.: No. 2). (J). 1996. mass mkt. 3.99 (0-380-78248-0, Avon Bks) Morrow Avon.

Love Never Dies: Working Through Grief to Contact Your Mate Who... Joan T. Williams. LC 98-86690. 325p. 1998. pap. 25.00 (0-7388-0067-8); pap. 15.00 (0-7388-0068-6) Xlibris Corp.

Love Never Faileth: Eknath Easwaran on St. Francis, St. Augustine, St. Paul & Mother Teresa. 2nd ed. Eknath Easwaran. LC 84-20756. (Classics of Christian Inspiration Ser.). 288p. 1996. 22.00 (0-915132-90-7); pap. 12.95 (0-915132-89-3) Nilgiri Pr.

Love Never Fails see Amor Nunca Deja de Ser

Love Never Fails. Kenneth Copeland. 24p. 1987. pap. 0.75 (1-57562-094-4) K Copeland Pubns.

Love Never Fails. Kenneth Copeland. 12p. 1987. pap. 1.00 (0-88114-792-3) K Copeland Pubns.

Love Never Fails. Kenneth E. Hagin. 1984. pap. 1.00 (0-89276-264-0) Faith Lib Pubns.

Love Never Forgets: A Small Books of Verse. Alta M. Rymer. (Illus.). 32p. 1998. pap. 9.95 (0-934723-09-5) Rymer Bks.

Love Never Found. Mike Scheiner. 70p. 1997. write for info. (1-57074-355-X) Greyden Pr.

Love Not a Rebel. Heather Graham. 448p. 1989. mass mkt. 6.50 (0-440-20237-X) Dell.

Love Not Human. Gordon Rupert Dickson. 256p. 1988. pap. 2.95 (0-8125-3554-5, Pub. by Tor Bks) St Martin.

Love Not the World see No Ameis al Mundo

Love Not the World. Watchman Nee. 124p. 1993. pap. text 5.70 (1-883137-05-5) Christ Stewards.

Love Not the World. rev. ed. Watchman Nee. 13p. 1998. mass mkt. 5.99 (0-87508-489-3, 489) Chr Lit.

***Love Notes, 64 vols.** Susan Branch. 2000. pap. text 13.95 (0-7683-2182-4) CEDCO Pub.

Love Notes. Carolyn Keene. (Nancy Drew Files: No. 109). (J). (gr. 6 up). 1995. mass mkt. 3.99 (0-671-88200-7) PB.

Love Notes. Carolyn Keene. (Nancy Drew Files: No. 109). (YA). (gr. 6 up). 1995. 9.09 (0-606-07929-7, Pub. by Turtleback) Demco.

Love Notes. Neil Wilson. 112p. 1996. pap. 4.99 (0-8423-2151-9) Tyndale Hse.

Love Notes, Vol. 1. Orley R. Herron. 80p. 1996. write for info. (1-889555-00-2) Stephen Aubry.

Love Notes: Boys on the Brain & Other Junior-High Stories. Karle Dickinson. LC 93-44343. (Illus.). 128p. (YA). (gr. 6-9). 1994. pap. 3.50 (0-8167-3468-2) Troll Communs.

***Love Notes: First Books.** Janet H. von Stein & Margaret von Stein. (Illus.). 35p. 2000. pap. 8.00 (0-9674448-0-2) J&M Pubn.

Love Notes: From My Heart to Yours. Dianna Booher. LC 98-131733. (Illus.). 7p. 1997. 9.99 (0-8499-5263-8) Word Pub.

Love Notes: Nurture Activities for Families. Angela D. Bottom & Mary M. Stowers. 54p. (Orig.). 1996. pap. text, spiral bd. 10.00 (1-888406-01-1) Phoenix Access.

***Love Note's: Poetic Justice for the Soul.** Kristina R. Nelson. 72p. 1999. pap. text 10.00 (0-9678537-0-2, 1337) New Hope Local.

***Love Notes: Quotations from the Heart.** unabridged ed. Gil Friedman. Orig. Title: A Dictionary of Love. 224p. 2000. pap. 12.95 (0-913038-00-8) Yara Pr.

Love Now! The Secret to Happiness. Christine L. Assad. LC 95-94720. 128p. (Orig.). 1995. pap. 10.00 (0-9647984-0-9) Inner Lght Pubs.

Love Nuances: Twelve Great Love Stories. unabridged ed. Mary Nicholaou. LC 97-90865. (Illus.). 54p. 1998. pap. 12.95 (1-890812-01-3) EROS.

***Love Numbers.** Margaret Arnold. 2000. 7.99 (0-517-16184-2) Crown Pub Group.

Love Numbers: How to Use Numerology to Make Love Count. Margaret Arnold. LC 97-40972. (Illus.). 272p. (Orig.). 1999. pap. 9.95 (1-56718-040-X) Llewellyn Pubns.

Love Object. Jere Cunningham. 198p. 1985. lib. bdg. 12.50 (0-910489-03-3) Scream Pr.

Love Observed: Joy Davidman's Life & Marriage to C. S. Lewis. Lyle W. Dorsett. LC 98-10029. 168p. 1998. pap. 11.99 (0-87788-479-X, H Shaw Pubs) Waterbrook Pr.

***Love of a Good Woman: Stories.** Alice Munro. LC 98-36721. 352p. 1999. pap. 13.00 (0-375-70363-2) Knopf.

***Love of Annie.** Gladys Zellgert. LC 99-63386. 240p. 1999. pap. 12.95 (1-57921-225-5) WinePress Pub.

Love of Art: European Art Museums & Their Public. Pierre Bourdieu & Alain Darbel. Tr. by Caroline Beattie & Nick Merriman from FRE. LC 90-70310. 190p. 1991. 35.00 (0-8047-1558-0) Stanford U Pr.

Love of Art & Art of Love. Tullah Hanley. LC 75-24839. (Illus.). 504p. 1975. 15.00 (0-87832-017-2) Piper.

***Love of Choon Hyang.** Chi S. Rhee. 2000. pap. 7.95 (1-57087-518-9) Prof Pr NC.

Love of Christ see Mother Teresa Treasury: Mother Teresa of Calcutta

Love of Dogs: The Ultimate Tribute to Our Best Friend. Ed. by Todd R. Berger. LC 98-37543. (PetLife Library). (Illus.). 160p. 1999. 29.95 (0-89658-412-7) Voyageur Pr.

Love of Eating: Another Simple Delicious Cookbook. Renny Darling. LC 77-85732. (Illus.). 1977. pap. 14.95 (0-930440-01-3) Royal Hse.

Love of Eternal Wisdom. Saint Louis Grignon de Montfort. 1960. pap. 4.95 (0-910984-05-0) Montfort Pubns.

***Love of Fat Men.** large type unabridged ed. Helen Dunmore. 189p. 1999. 26.95 (0-7531-5898-1, 158981, Pub. by ISIS Lrg Prnt) ISIS Pub.

Love of Food, Love of God. Pitt-Rivers. 300p. (C). 2000. lib. bdg. 34.95 (0-226-67005-8) U Ch Pr.

Love of Four Colonels. Peter Ustinov. 1953. pap. 5.25 (0-8222-0697-8) Dramatists Play.

***Love of Freedom Has No Fatherland: The Politicization of Armenians & the Iranian Constitutiona.** Houri Berberian. 216p. 2000. pap. 30.00 (0-8133-3817-4) Westview.

Love of Friends. Nancy Bond. LC 96-38087. 304p. (YA). (gr. 7 up). 1997. per. 17.00 (0-689-81365-1) Atheneum Yung Read.

Love of Friends. Constance Jones. LC 97-2116. 1997. 26.00 (0-684-81409-9) S&S Trade.

Love of Friends: A Celebration of Women's Friendship. Barbara Albert. 288p. 1997. pap. 11.00 (0-425-16058-0) Berkley Pub.

Love of Frog: Ranaphilia, 3 vols., 3. Malachi McCormick. 96p. 1993. 35.00 (0-318-70248-7) Stone St Pr.

Love of Frog: Ranaphilia, 3 vols., Vol. 1. Malachi McCormick. (Special Paste Paper Miniature Collections Ser.). 84p. 1993. write for info. (0-943984-57-2) Stone St Pr.

Love of Frog: Ranaphilia, 3 vols., Vol. 2. Malachi McCormick. (Special Paste Paper Miniature Collections Ser.). 84p. 1993. write for info. (0-943984-58-0) Stone St Pr.

Love of Frog: Ranaphilia, 3 vols., Vol. 3. Malachi McCormick. (Special Paste Paper Miniature Collections Ser.). 84p. 1993. write for info. (0-943984-59-9) Stone St Pr.

Love of German Shepherds: The Ultimate Tribute. Ed. by Todd R. Berger. LC 99-13245. (PetLife Library). (Illus.). 160p. 1999. 29.95 (0-89658-446-1) Voyageur Pr.

Love of Glory & the Common Good: Aspects of the Political Thought of Thucydides. Michael Palmer. 188p. (C). 1992. text 54.50 (0-8476-7731-1); pap. text 22.95 (0-8476-7732-X) Rowman.

Love of God. Oswald Chambers. 1986. pap. 8.95 (0-87508-293-9) Chr Lit.

Love of God. Oswald Chambers. 128p. 1988. pap. 8.99 (0-929239-04-0) Discovery Hse Pubs.

Love of God, 4 vols. Marie-Agnes Gaudrat & Ulises Wensell. (What Is God Like? Ser.). (Illus.). 10p. (J). 1992. bds. 4.95 (0-8146-2137-6) Liturgical Pr.

Love of God. D. Martyn Lloyd-Jones. LC 94-15386. (Studies in First John: Bk. 4). 208p. 1994. pap. 10.99 (0-89107-814-2) Crossway Bks.

Love of God. Bernard N. Schneider. 1985. pap. 5.99 (0-88469-167-5) BMH Bks.

Love of God. Charles Stanley. 24p. 1995. pap. 2.50 (1-56476-532-6, 6-3532, Victor Bks) Chariot Victor.

Love of God: Hymns of Faith & Assurance. Arranged by Lavawan Riley. 1998. pap. 8.99 (0-8341-9768-5) Nazarene.

Love of God & Social Duty in the Ramcaritmanas. Edmour J. Babineau. 1979. 13.95 (0-89684-050-6, Pub. by Motilal Bnarsidass) S Asia.

Love of Gods. large type ed. Alan Hunter. (General Ser.). 1998. pap. 21.95 (0-7862-1288-8) Thorndike Pr.

Love of Goldens. Ed. by Todd R. Berger. LC 98-17603. (Petlife Library). (Illus.). 160p. 1998. 29.95 (0-89658-385-6) Voyageur Pr.

***Love of Goldens: The Ultimate Tribute to Golden Retrievers.** Todd R. Berger. LC 99-88399. (PetLife Library). (Illus.). 160p. 2000. pap. 19.95 (0-89658-469-0) Voyageur Pr.

Love of Good Women. Isabel Miller. 224p. 1986. pap. 8.95 (0-930044-81-9) Naiad Pr.

Love of Her Life. Laurie John. (Sweet Valley University Ser.: No. 6). (YA). (gr. 7 up). 1994. 8.60 (0-606-06791-4, Pub. by Turtleback) Demco.

***Love of Her Own, Vol. 1.** Bettye Griffin. 1999. mass mkt. 4.99 (1-58314-053-0) BET Bks.

Love of Highland Mary. Jess Bolton. 288p. 1994. pap. write for info. (1-874640-01-7, Pub. by Argyll Pubng) St Mut.

Love of Irish Women. Ed. by Malachi McCormick. 32p. 1984. 9.00 (0-943984-15-7) Stone St Pr.

Love of Jesus & the Love of Neighbor. Karl Rahner. (C). 1988. 39.00 (0-85439-224-6, Pub. by St Paul Pubns) St Mut.

Love of Knowledge. Tarthang Tulku. LC 87-24452. 447p. (Orig.). 1987. 30.00 (0-89800-169-2); pap. 16.95 (0-89800-138-2) Dharma Pub.

***Love of Labs: The Ultimate Tribute to Labrador Retrievers.** Todd R. Berger. LC 99-86897. (PetLife Library). (Illus.). 160p. 2000. pap. 19.95 (0-89658-468-2) Voyageur Pr.

Love of Labs: The Ultimate Triibute to Labrador Retrievers. Ed. by Michael Dregni & Todd R. Berger. LC 97-7939. (World's Greatest Dogs Ser.). (Illus.). 160p. 1997. 29.95 (0-89658-356-2) Voyageur Pr.

Love of Lace. Cynthia Hart & Catherine Calvert. LC 92-50288. (Illus.). 112p. 1992. 17.95 (1-56305-300-4, 3300) Workman Pub.

Love of Landry. Paul Laurence Dunbar. LC 70-81113. (Black Heritage Library Collection). 1977. reprint ed. 35.95 (0-8369-8559-1) Ayer.

Love of Landry. Paul Laurence Dunbar. LC 70-81113. (Black Heritage Library Collection). 1991. reprint ed. pap. text 24.95 (0-88143-126-5) Ayer.

Love of Landry. Paul Laurence Dunbar. LC 72-88408. 200p. 1969. reprint ed. lib. bdg. 59.50 (0-8371-1810-7, DUL&) Greenwood.

Love of Landry. Paul Laurence Dunbar. (Notable American Authors Ser.). 1992. reprint ed. lib. bdg. 75.00 (0-7812-2712-7) Rprt Serv.

Love of Learning: Desire for Justice: Undergraduate Education & the Option for the Poor. Ed. by William E. Reiser. LC 94-60876. 138p. 1995. 22.00 (0-940866-41-2) U Scranton Pr.

Love of Learning & Desire for God: A Study of Monastic Culture. 3rd ed. Jean Leclercq. LC 60-53004. viii, 282p. 1982. pap. 18.00 (0-8232-0407-3) Fordham.

Love of Liberty. Leonard E. Read. 173p. 1975. pap. 3.95 (0-910614-54-7) Foun Econ Ed.

An Asterisk (*) at the beginning of an entry indicates that the title is appearing for the first time.

Love of Life. Jack London. lib. bdg. 20.95 (*0-8488-2000-2*) Amereon Ltd.

Love of Life. rev. ed. Jack London. (Read-along Radio Dramas Ser.). (YA). (gr. 6-12). 1986. ring bd. 38.00 (*1-878298-21-6*) Balance Pub.

***Love of Life & Other Stories.** Jack London. (Collected Works of Jack London). 240p. 1998. reprint ed. lib. bdg. 88.00 (*1-58201-725-5*) Classic Bks.

Love of Long Age & Other Stories. Marie Corelli. 271p. 1978. reprint ed. 17.50 (*0-7873-0222-8*) Hlth Research.

Love of Loons. M. Link & Kate Crowley. (Voyageur Wilderness Ser.). (Illus.). 96p. (Orig.). 1990. pap. 16.95 (*0-89658-072-5*) Voyageur Pr.

Love of Mary. D. Roberto. LC 83-51545. 240p. 1985. reprint ed. pap. 8.00 (*0-89555-235-3*) TAN Bks Pubs.

Love of Mountains: Two Stories by Uno Koji. Koji Uno. Tr. by Elaine T. Gerbert. LC 96-9711. 1997. pap. text 23.00 (*0-8248-1756-7*) UH Pr.

Love of My Heart. Emma Richmond. LC 95-4593. (Romance Ser.). 185p. 1995. per. 2.99 (*0-373-03349-4*, 1-03349-7) Harlequin Bks.

***Love of Old Egypt.** PHILIP MARKHAM. 224p. 1999. pap. 14.99 (*0-352-33354-5*) Virgin Bks.

Love of Order: South Carolina's First Secession Crisis. John Barnwell. LC 81-11441. xv, 256p. 1982. 49.95 (*0-8078-1498-9*) U of NC Pr.

Love of Parson Lord, & Other Stories by Mary E. Wilkins Freeman. Mary E. Wilkins Freeman. LC 76-75776. (Short Story Index Reprint Ser.). 1977. 19.95 (*0-8369-3001-0*) Ayer.

Love of Seven Dolls. 126p. 1989. reprint ed. pap. 7.95 (*1-55882-013-2*, Lib Crime Classics) Intl Polygonics.

***Love of Spaniels: The Ultimate Tribute to Cockers, Springers & Other Great Spaniels.** Todd R. Berger. (PetLife Library). (Illus.). 160p. 2000. 29.95 (*0-89658-453-4*) Voyageur Pr.

Love of the Father. Jeffrey B. Rice. LC 98-60603. (Illus.). 32p. (J). (gr. 3-6). 1998. 14.95 (*1-890394-24-6*); pap. 9.95 (*1-890394-23-8*) Rhodes & Easton.

Love of the Infidel. Chrystom G. Horattas. Ed. by Sam Chekwas. 240p. 1998. pap. 14.95 (*1-885778-49-X*) Seaburn.

Love of the Land. Darrell Sifford. LC 80-18379. (Illus.). 288p. 1980. 11.95 (*0-89795-010-0*) Farm Journal.

Love of the Last Tycoon. F. Scott Fitzgerald. Ed. by Matthew J. Bruccoli. 228p. 1995. per. 10.00 (*0-02-019985-6*, Pub. by Macmillan) S&S Trade.

Love of "The Last Tycoon" A Western. F. Scott Fitzgerald. Ed. by Matthew J. Bruccoli. (Works of F. Scott Fitzgerald). (Illus.). 448p. (C). 1994. 42.95 (*0-521-40231-X*) Cambridge U Pr.

Love of the Nightingale. rev. ed. Timberlake Wertenbaker. 67p. 1989. pap. 5.95 (*0-87129-045-6*, L68) Dramatic Pub.

Love of the Nightingale & The Grace of Mary Traverse. Timberlake Wertenbaker. 96p. 1990. pap. 10.95 (*0-571-15383-6*) Faber & Faber.

Love of the Samurai Thousand Years of Japanese Homosexuality. Tsuneo Watanabe & Junlchi Iwata. 1995. 19.95 (*0-85449-115-5*, Pub. by Gay Mens Pr) LPC InBook.

Love of the Soule. Gregory Martin et al. LC 78-320571. (English Recusant Literature, 1558-1640 Ser.). 400p. 1978. write for info. (*0-85967-447-8*) Scolar Pr.

***Love of Women.** Falconer. 2000. pap. 11.95 (*0-552-99623-8*, Pub. by Transworld Publishers Ltd) Trafalgar.

Love of Worker Bees. Alexandra M. Kollontai. Tr. by Cathy Porter from RUS. 232p. 1978. reprint ed. pap. 10.00 (*0-89733-001-3*) Academy Chi Pubs.

Love of Your Life. Gregory E. Penn. 1996. 20.00 (*0-614-96867-4*) Harper SF.

Love on a Branch Line. large type ed. John Hadfield. 21.95 (*1-85695-394-7*, Pub. by ISIS Lrg Prnt) Transaction Pubs.

Love on a Dark Island. large type ed. Katrina Wright. (Linford Romance Library). 1991. pap. 16.99 (*0-7089-7064-8*) Ulverscroft.

Love on a Far Island. large type ed. Nina Shaldon. (Dales Romance Ser.). 1993. pap. 13.95 (*1-85389-324-2*, Dales) Ulverscroft.

Love on a Leash: Giving Joy to Others Through Pet Therapy. Liz Palika. Ed. by Catherine Ohala. LC 94-3877. (Illus.). 176p. 1996. pap. 14.95 (*0-931866-76-6*) Alpine Pubns.

***Love on a Plate.** large type ed. Betty Grass. 248p. 2000. pap. 18.99 (*0-7089-5643-2*, Linford) Ulverscroft.

***Love on a Shoestring.** Felicia Kalapos. 112p. 1999. pap. 11.95 (*1-58244-055-7*) Rutledge Bks.

Love on a String. large type ed. Celia A. Scott. LC 96-34322. 322p. 1993. 27.99 (*0-7505-0568-0*) Ulverscroft.

Love on an Animal Farm: A Story for Children. Altina Miranda. (Illus.). 32p. (Orig.). (J). 1993. pap. 8.95 (*0-86534-202-4*) Sunstone Pr.

Love on Fire - More Joy & Sexual Science: Love-Sex & the Reverse-Effect Phenomenon. Walter A. Heiby. LC 94-40011. 812p. 1996. 39.50 (*0-938869-04-3*, HQ31.H4715) MediSci Pubs.

Love on Ice. large type ed. Petra Sawley. (Linford Romance Library). 256p. 1994. pap. 16.99 (*0-7089-7536-4*) Ulverscroft.

Love on Its Own. Hadaya. 1998. 23.00 (*0-8050-5998-9*) H Holt & Co.

Love On-Line. Carolyn Keene. (Nancy Drew on Campus Ser.: No. 19). (YA). (gr. 8 up). 1997. mass mkt. 3.99 (*0-671-00211-2*) PB.

Love on Line. Deanna Warren. Ed. by Stanley C. Coy. (Illus.). 104p. (Orig.). 1994. pap. 10.00 (*1-881459-18-7*) Eagle Pr SC.

***Love on-Line: 50 Ways to Net Your Lover: How to Find True Romance by E-Mail.** Bonnie Estridge & Mandy Gold. 160p. 1998. 10.00 (*0-7225-3565-1*, Pub. by Thorsons MD) Natl Bk Netwk.

Love on the Air - Gundell. A. J. Gundell. 1994. pap. 19.95 incl. cd-rom (*0-89524-798-4*) Cherry Lane.

Love on the Alexander Hamilton. Ron Overton. 88p. 1985. pap. 6.00 (*0-914610-39-2*) Hanging Loose.

Love on the Dole. Ronald Gow & Walter Greenwood. (Hereford Plays Ser.). 125p. (Orig.). (C). 1988. pap. 6.95 (*0-435-22360-7*, 22360) Heinemann.

Love on the Left Bank. Ed Van Der Elsken. 112p. 1999. 39.95 (*1-899235-22-1*, Pub. by Dewi Lewis) Dist Art Pubs.

Love on the Mountain: Chronicle of a Camaldolse Monk. Robert Hale. LC 99-38722. (Illus.). 206p. 1999. pap. 14.95 (*0-940147-45-9*) Source Bks CA.

Love on the Nile. large type ed. Katrina Wright. (Linford Romance Library). 1991. pap. 16.99 (*0-7089-7114-8*) Ulverscroft.

***Love on the Rocks.** Anne Harris. 1998. pap. 6.95 (*0-09-926375-0*, Pub. by Random) Trafalgar.

***Love on the Run.** Shari MacDonald. LC 00-34720. 2000. write for info. (*0-7862-2708-7*) Five Star.

***Love on the Run.** Shari MacDonald. LC 98-231258. (Salinger Sisters Romantic Comedy Ser.: Bk. 1). 256p. 1998. pap. 6.95 (*1-57856-084-5*) Waterbrook Pr.

Love on the Run. Jeanne Rose. (Silhouette Romance Ser.). 1994. per. 2.75 (*0-373-19027-1*, 1-19027-1) Harlequin Bks.

***Love on the Run, 37.** Lee Greenwood. (Bouquet Ser.: Vol. 37). 2000. mass mkt. 3.99 (*0-8217-6531-0*, Zebra Kensgtn) Kensgtn Pub Corp.

***Love on the Run: A Novel.** Rachel Ann Nunes. LC 99-88762. 2000. write for info. (*1-57734-604-1*) Covenant Comms.

Love on the Wild Side. Penny Porter. (Illus.). 234p. 1997. pap. 12.95 (*0-9656923-1-0*) Singing Valley.

***Love on Trial: An American Scandal in Black & White.** Earl Lewis. (Illus.). 320p. 2000. 26.95 (*0-393-05013-0*) Norton.

Love on Turtle Island. large type ed. Theresa Murphy. (Linford Romance Library). 240p. 1998. pap. 17.99 (*0-7089-5236-4*, Linford) Ulverscroft.

Love Once & Forever. Flora Speer. 400p. 1999. mass mkt. 5.99 (*0-505-52291-8*, Love Spell) Dorchester Pub Co.

Love One Another. Joan W. Anglund. LC 81-67305. (Illus.). 5.95 (*0-915696-45-2*) Determined Prods.

Love One Another. Elaine Cannon. 1995. pap. 3.95 (*1-57008-194-8*) Bookcraft Inc.

Love One Another. J. Marshall. 1990. pap. 36.00 (*0-7220-5175-1*) St Mut.

Love One Another. Watchman Nee. Tr. by Stephen Kaung. (Basic Lesson Ser.: Vol. 6). 235p. 1975. 7.00 (*0-935008-09-8*); pap. 5.50 (*0-935008-10-1*) Christian Fellow Pubs.

Love One Another. John C. Schwarz. 23p. 1996. pap. text 2.95 (*1-55612-604-2*, LL1604) Sheed & Ward WI.

***Love One Another: How to Let God's Heart Shine Through Your Life.** Gloria Chisholm. LC 00-22846. 128p. 2000. pap. 8.95 (*1-57856-310-0*) Waterbrook Pr.

Love One Another: In Defense of Our Catholic Brothers & Sisters. Wayne F. Monbleau. 47p. (Orig.). 1983. pap. 4.00 (*0-944648-03-7*) Loving Grace Pubns.

***Love One Another: The Last Days of Jesus.** Lauren Thompson. LC 99-25157. (Illus.). 32p. (J). (gr. 1-5). 2000. 15.95 (*0-590-31830-6*, Scholastic Ref) Scholastic Inc.

Love One Another: With Skedaddle Skunk & Friends. Diane M. Stortz. (Coloring Bks.). (Illus.). 16p. (J). 1995. pap. 1.49 (*0-7847-0275-6*, 02565) Standard Pub.

***Love One Another from Your Heart.** Zondervan Publishing House Staff. 40p. 1999. 7.99 (*0-310-97885-8*) Zondervan.

***Love One Day at a Time.** Mark Allen. 384p. 1998. pap. 9.95 (*2-921556-58-8*) Modus Viv.

Love 101: To Love Oneself Is the Beginning of a Lifelong Romance. Peter McWilliams. (Life 101 Ser.). 432p. (Orig.). 1995. pap. 11.95 (*0-931580-70-6*) Prelude Press.

Love 101: To Love Oneself Is the Beginning of a Lifelong Romance. Peter McWilliams. (Orig.). 1997. pap. text 5.95 (*0-931580-72-2*) Prelude Press.

Love 101: A Lifelong Course on How to Truly Live & Love. Robert Strand. LC 93-84143. 192p. 1993. pap. 8.95 (*0-89221-237-3*) New Leaf.

Love Online: A Practical Guide to Digital Dating. Phyllis Phlegar. 192p. (C). 1995. pap. text 9.95 (*0-201-40965-8*) Addison-Wesley.

Love Online: A Practical Guide to Digital Dating. Phyllis Phlegar. 192p. (C). 1995. pap. 119.40 (*0-201-41038-9*) Addison-Wesley.

Love Only Once. Johanna Lindsey. 352p. 1985. mass mkt. 6.99 (*0-380-89953-1*, Avon Bks) Morrow Avon.

Love: or A Reasonable Facsimile. 2nd ed. Gloree Rogers. 160p. (Orig.). 1989. pap. 10.00 (*0-932112-27-7*) Carolina Wren.

Love or Honor. Joan Barthel. 1990. mass mkt. 4.95 (*0-380-71105-2*, Avon Bks) Morrow Avon.

Love or Loneliness, You Decide. Robert H. Schuller. 108p. 1991. 12.95 (*1-879989-03-4*) New Hope Pub.

Love or Money. Jackie Calhoun. 256p. (Orig.). 1996. pap. 10.95 (*1-56280-147-3*) Naiad Pr.

Love or Money. Ed. by Tricia Hedge. (Illus.). 48p. 1989. pap. text 5.95 (*0-19-421651-9*) OUP.

Love Organs: A Novel. Bruce Walters. LC 96-97155. 430p. 1997. 24.95 (*0-9654832-7-4*) Dunewood Pr.

Love, Otto: The Legacy of Anne Frank see Letters from Otto Frank

Love Pain Hope: Poetic Thoughts. Barbara-Marie Green. 50p. 1993. reprint ed. pap. 7.95 (*1-883414-00-8*) Bar JaMae.

Love Pains Expose: When Love Dies. Zulma Gonzalez-Parker. (Orig.). pap. 4.00 (*0-685-28957-5*) Heartfelt Pr.

Love Paints Beauty in the Soul: A Book Sequel to Mysterious Stranger Aboard. John Johnson & Alice Johnson. 172p. (Orig.). 1996. pap. 9.95 (*0-964827l-1-5*) Mal-Jonal Prodns.

Love Passion & Solitude. Moneim A. Fadali. 144p. (Orig.). 1994. pap. 9.95 (*1-885113-54-4*) Hidden Springs.

Love, Passion & Soul. abr. ed. Barbara De Angelis et al. (Quest love Ser.: Vol. 1). 1998. 12.00 incl. audio (*0-671-57895-2*, Sound Ideas) S&S Trade.

Love, Passion & Tears. Gayle Ponthier. 1159p. write for info. (*0-9658038-0-5*) G Ponthier.

Love, Passion & Tears. Gayle Ponthier. Ed. by Geneva Mars et al. LC 98-88599. (Illus.). 352p. 1999. pap. 14.95 (*1-888224-04-5*) Prestige LA.

***Love Pat's from God: How Much My Father Loves Me.** fac. ed. Michele Langford. (Illus.). 2000. pap. 9.95 (*0-9675234-1-9*) JEMS Pubns.

Love, Peace & Joy: Devotion to the Sacred Heart of Jesus According to St. Gertrude. Andre Prevot. LC 84-51822. 224p. 1985. reprint ed. pap. 7.00 (*0-89555-255-8*) TAN Bks Pubs.

Love, Peace, & Other Major Issues: Selected Poems. Robert F. Allen. 113p. (Orig.). 1991. pap. 9.95 (*0-941703-09-6*) Healthyculture.

***Love Pearls: From a Mother to Her Daughter.** Nancy Swan Drew. (Illus.). 112p. 2000. 12.95 (*0-89087-983-4*) Celestial Arts.

Love Period. Islah Beyand & Jaleelah Karriem. (Illus.). 48p. (Orig.). 1988. pap. text 5.00 (*0-317-92553-9*) We Did It.

***Love Photo Memory Album: A Gift of Memory.** Linda Spivey. 1998. write for info. (*1-57977-227-7*) Havoc Pub.

Love Play. Rosemary Rogers. 384p. 1982. mass mkt. 6.50 (*0-380-81190-1*, Avon Bks) Morrow Avon.

Love Play. Mallory Rush. 1999. per. 5.99 (*0-373-83359-8*, 1-83359-9) Harlequin Bks.

Love Play of Anthony & Cleopatra: A Critical Study of Shakespeare's Play. Philip J. Traci. LC 77-106458. (Studies in English Literature). 1970. text 53.85 (*90-279-0535-5*) Mouton.

Love + Marriage = Death: And Other Essays on Representing Difference. Sander L. Gilman. LC 98-23979. (Studies in Jewish History & Culture). 254p. 1998. 49.50 (*0-8047-3261-2*); pap. 17.95 (*0-8047-3262-0*) Stanford U Pr.

Love Poem for a Bank Robber. Jane Teller. (Chapbooks Ser.). (Illus.). (Orig.). 1981. pap. 3.00 (*0-914140-09-4*) Carpenter Pr.

Love Poem to a Black Junkie. Paulette C. White. 37p. (YA). (gr. 7-12). 1975. pap. 5.00 (*0-916418-04-9*) Lotus.

Love Poems. Betty B. Choate. (Illus.). 78p. 1986. 6.95 (*0-9616352-0-7*) B B Choate.

Love Poems. Erich Fried. 280p. (Orig.). pap. 19.95 (*0-7145-4185-0*) Riverrun NY.

***Love Poems.** Charles Ghigna. LC 99-41350. 48p. 1999. pap. 7.95 (*1-57587-115-7*) Crane Hill AL.

Love Poems. Nikki Giovanni. 1997. 12.00 (*0-614-20397-X*, Wm Morrow); 13.00 (*0-688-14989-8*, Wm Morrow) Morrow Avon.

Love Poems. Sheila Kohler. Ed. & Selected by Peter Washington. (Everyman's Library Pocket Poets Ser.). 256p. 1993. 12.50 (*0-679-42906-9*) Random.

Love Poems. James Laughlin. LC 97-10980. 96p. 1998. pap. 7.95 (*0-8112-1387-0*, NDP865, Pub. by New Directions) Norton.

Love Poems. Ed. by Masson. (Poetry Library). 240p. 1998. pap. 7.95 (*1-85326-445-8*, 4458WW, Pub. by Wrdsworth Edits) NTC Contemp Pub Co.

Love Poems. Ovid. Tr. by A. D. Melville. 304p. 1999. pap. 10.95 (*0-19-283633-1*) OUP.

Love Poems. Rene Ricard. (Illus.). 37p. 1999. pap. 5.95 (*0-9666328-6-9*) CUZ Ed.

Love Poems. Compiled by Elizabeth Riley. LC 68-58827. (Granger Index Reprint Ser.). 1977. 15.95 (*0-8369-6040-8*) Ayer.

Love Poems. Sonia Sanchez. LC 73-83168. 208p. (Orig.). pap. 15.00 (*0-89388-104-X*) Okpaku Communications.

Love Poems. Anne Sexton. 1977. write for info. (*0-318-53411-8*) HM.

Love Poems. Anne Sexton. 80p. 1999. pap. 14.00 (*0-395-95777-X*, Mariner Bks) HM.

Love Poems. Anne Sexton. 1969. 18.20 (*0-606-01799-2*, Pub. by Turtleback) Demco.

Love Poems. Bruce B. Wilmer. 114p. (Orig.). 1990. pap. 9.95 (*0-9615967-2-4*) Wilmer Graphics.

Love Poems. Selected by Michael Wylie. (Jarrold Poets Ser.). 146p. (Orig.). 1994. 5.95 (*0-7117-0678-6*) Seven Hills Bk.

Love Poems. Lois Wyse. 80p. 1996. 8.98 (*0-88365-929-8*) Galahad Bks.

Love Poems: From Spain & Spanish America. Tr. by Perry Higman from SPA. 160p. (Orig.). 1986. pap. 12.95 (*0-87286-183-X*) City Lights.

Love Poems: Selected Poems, Bilingual Edition. Salvatore Di Giacomo. Tr. by Frank Palescandolo from ITA. (Essential Poets Ser.: Vol. 79). 151p. 1999. pap. 15.00 (*1-55071-060-5*) Guernica Editions.

Love Poems & Humourous Ones: Written at the End of a Volume of Small Printed Books, A.D. 1614-1619, in the British Museum, Labelled "Various Poems" Frederick J. Furnivall. LC 76-51941. (Ballad Society, London. Publications: No. 11). reprint ed. 20.00 (*0-404-50825-1*) AMS Pr.

Love Poems & New Beginnings: A Collection of Zen Sketches, Poems & Haiku. John Terninko. (Illus.). 139p. (Orig.). 1994. pap. 7.00 (*1-882382-05-6*) Respons Mgmt.

Love Poems & Other Revolutionary Actions. Bobbi Sykes. (Poetry Ser.). 57p. (Orig.). 1989. reprint ed. pap. text 14.95 (*0-7022-2173-2*, Pub. by Univ Queensland Pr) Intl Spec Bk.

Love Poems & Sonnets of William Shakespeare. William Shakespeare. LC 57-11411. 160p. 1957. 14.95 (*0-385-01733-2*) Doubleday.

Love Poems by Women. Wendy Mulford. LC 90-82345. 320p. 1991. pap. 10.00 (*0-449-90538-1*, Columbine) Fawcett.

Love Poems for Cards & Letters. Ara J. Movsesian. LC 88-81507. (Illus.). 90p. 1988. pap. 9.95 (*0-916919-60-9*) Electric Pr.

Love Poems for the Millennium. Peter Johnson. LC 99-188918. 36p. 1998. pap. 5.00 (*0-9656161-2-6*) Quale Pr.

***Love Poems for You.** Felicia Dkeke-Ibezim. LC 99-94658. 62p. 1999. per. 6.95 (*0-9661598-1-0*) Ekwike Bks & Pub.

Love Poems from a Poor Man. Lee Netzler. LC 84-91012. 54p. (Orig.). 1984. pap. 6.95 (*0-9647696-1-1*) Netzler Pubng.

Love Poems from Around the World. Hippocrene Books Staff. 500p. 1999. pap. 14.95 (*0-7818-0752-2*) Hippocrene Bks.

Love Poems from the Japanese. Ed. by Sam Hamill. Tr. by Kenneth Rexroth from JPN. (Pocket Classics Ser.). 144p. (Orig.). 1994. pap. 6.00 (*0-87773-982-X*, Pub. by Shambhala Pubns) Random.

Love Poems of Anne Sexton. Anne Sexton. 80p. 1989. pap. 13.00 (*0-395-51760-5*) HM.

Love Poems of Friendship: And the Joys & Sorrows of Life. Helene L. Kohen. LC 90-83593. 61p. (Orig.). 1990. pap. 9.95 (*0-910147-85-X*) World Poetry Pr.

Love Poems of Ghanand. K. P. Bahadur. (C). 1991. reprint ed. 12.50 (*81-208-0836-3*, Pub. by Motilal Bnarsidass) S Asia.

Love Poems of John Keats: In Praise of Beauty. 6th ed. John Keats. LC 90-36880. xiii, 64p. 1990. text 9.95 (*0-312-05105-0*) St Martin.

Love Poems of Lord Byron: A Romantic's Passion. 8th ed. George Gordon Byron. 75p. 1990. text 9.95 (*0-312-05124-7*) St Martin.

Love Poems of May Swenson. May Swenson. 96p. 1991. pap. 14.00 (*0-395-59222-4*) HM.

Love Poems of Rumi. Ed. & Tr. by Deepak Chopra. Tr. by Fereydoun Kia. LC 97-35690. 1998. 12.00 (*0-609-60243-8*) Harmony Bks.

***Love Poems of Shakespeare.** William Shakespeare. 2001. 12.99 (*0-517-16364-0*) Crown Pub Group.

Love Poems of Six Centuries. Ed. by Helen Husted. LC 70-86798. (Granger Index Reprint Ser.). 1977. 23.95 (*0-8369-6105-6*) Ayer.

***Love Poems of the Sacred Heart.** unabridged ed. Scott G. Betton. Ed. by Diana J. Thornton. 202p. (Orig.). 2000. pap. 15.00 (*1-930507-00-3*) Eternal Pubng.

Love Poems with an After-Bite! For Bitter & Battered Lovers. Julia M. Busch. LC 94-94645. (Illus.). 128p. (Orig.). 1996. pap. 9.95 (*0-9632907-0-3*) Anti Aging Pr.

Love Poetry Across the Centuries. Lion. 1995. 7.50 (*0-7459-3363-7*, Pub. by Lion Pubng) Trafalgar.

Love Poetry in Sixteenth-century France: A Study in Themes & Traditions Stephen Minta. LC 78-313941. vi, 173 p. 1977. write for info. (*0-7190-0676-7*) Manchester Univ Pr.

Love Poetry of Shakespeare. Ed. by Roy Booth. 162p. 1995. 14.95 (*1-85626-138-7*, Pub. by Cathie Kyle) Trafalgar.

Love Poetry Written to Moo Lei Before She Threw Herself from a Twenty-Five Story Taipei Hotel Room Window. Scott Shaw. 69p. (Orig.). 1990. pap. 6.95 (*1-877792-12-8*) Buddha Rose.

***Love Police/Rough & Rugged.** Annette Sanford. (Duets Ser.). 2000. mass mkt. 5.99 (*0-373-44088-X*, Harlequin) Harlequin Bks.

Love, Politics, & "Rescue" in Lesbian Relationships. Diana Rabenold. (Lesbian-Feminist Essay Ser.). 24p. (Orig.). 1987. pap. 3.50 (*0-939821-29-X*) HerBooks.

***Love Potion.** Sandra Hill. 400p. (Orig.). 1999. mass mkt. 5.99 (*0-505-52349-3*, Love Spell) Dorchester Pub Co.

Love Potion. Rebecca Paisley et al. 272p. (Orig.). 1995. mass mkt. 4.99 (*0-515-11549-5*, Jove) Berkley Pub.

Love Potion. Created by Francine Pascal. (Sweet Valley Twins Ser.: No. 72). 144p. (J). (gr. 3-7). 1993. pap. 3.50 (*0-553-48058-8*) Bantam.

***Love Potion.** Janet Quin-Harkin. (Enchanted Hearts Ser.). (Illus.). (J). 1999. 9.85 (*0-606-17966-6*) Turtleback.

Love Potion. Jamie Suzanne. (Sweet Valley Twins Ser.: No. 72). (J). (gr. 3-7). 1993. 8.60 (*0-606-05652-1*, Pub. by Turtleback) Demco.

Love Potion, No. 5. Cathy G. Thacker. 1994. per. 3.50 (*0-373-16556-0*, 1-16556-2) Harlequin Bks.

Love Potion #9, 1 vol. Claire Cross. (Magical Love Ser.). 309p. 1999. mass mkt. 5.99 (*0-515-12529-6*, Jove) Berkley Pub.

Love Potion Number Nine. Kate Hoffmann. (Temptation Ser.). 1994. per. 2.99 (*0-373-25587-X*, 1-25587-6) Harlequin Bks.

Love Potions: A Guide to Aphrodisia & Sexual Pleasure. Cynthia M. Watson & Angela Hynes. LC 92-35363. 288p. (Orig.). 1993. pap. 13.95 (*0-87477-724-0*, Tarcher Putnam) Putnam Pub Group.

Love Power. Tom Battle. Ed. by Schar Battle. 124p. 1994. pap. 4.00 (*0-9627066-4-7*) Battle Minist.

Love Power: Centerfolds. Susan Carroll. (Desire Ser.). 1994. per. 2.99 (*0-373-05876-4*, 1-05876-7) Silhouette.

Love Power: New Dimensions for Building Strong Families. Alan Stine. LC 78-70360. 1978. 11.98 (*0-88290-105-2*) Horizon Utah.

Love, Power & Justice. Paul Johannes Tillich. 140p. 1960. pap. 10.95 (*0-19-500222-9*) OUP.

An Asterisk (*) at the beginning of an entry indicates that the title is appearing for the first time.

L

Love, Power & Justice. Paul Johannes Tillich. 1980. 22.00 (*0-8446-5694-1*) Peter Smith.

Love, Power, & Knowledge: Towards a Feminist Transformation of the Sciences. Hilary Rose. LC 94-1883. 352p. 1994. 45.00 (*0-253-35046-8*); pap. 19.95 (*0-253-20907-2*) Ind U Pr.

Love, Power, & Political Interests see Why Women Are Oppressed

Love Present: And Other Stories. John Montague. 1999. pap. 11.95 (*0-86327-672-5*) Wolfhound Press.

Love Project. Ed. & Illus. by Thomas Taylor. 88p. 1993. pap. 12.00 (*1-930259-07-7*) Anabasis.

Love Project. rev. ed. Arleen Lorrance. LC 78-15162. (Illus.). 103p. 1978. pap. 6.95 (*0-916192-14-8*) L P Pubns.

Love Project Way. Arleen Lorrance & Diane K. Pike. 216p. (Orig.). 1980. pap. 10.95 (*0-916192-15-6*) L P Pubns.

Love Psalms: God's Gift of Lover Everlasting. (Psalms Ser.). (Illus.). 128p. 1999. 15.99 (*1-56292-804-X*) Honor Bks OK.

Love Quest. Carol Batdorf. 224p. 1994. pap. 14.95 (*0-88839-337-7*) Hancock House.

Love Quest: A Sexual Odyssey. Anne Cumming. 200p. 1992. 33.00 (*0-7206-0835-X*, Pub. by P Owen Ltd) Dufour.

Love Quest: Powerful Insights That Will Guide You to Creating the Loving Relationship You Desire. Willie C. Hooks. 150p. 1990. pap. 19.95 (*0-9623440-2-8*) JTE Assocs.

Love Quotations. Ed. by Helen Exley. (Quotations Bks.). (Illus.). 60p. 1992. reprint ed. 8.00 (*1-85015-059-1*) Exley Giftbooks.

Love Race. large type ed. Grace Richmond. (Linford Romance Library). 304p. 1992. pap. 16.99 (*0-7089-7276-4*, Linford) Ulverscroft.

***Love Re-Membered: Resources for a House Eucharist.** Jim Cotter. 64p. 1999. pap. 24.00 (*0-85305-347-2*, Pub. by Arthur James) St Mut.

***Love Rekindled: Practising Hospitality.** Jim Cotter. 64p. 1999. pap. 24.00 (*0-85305-348-0*, Pub. by Arthur James) St Mut.

Love Relations: Normality & Pathology. Otto F. Kernberg. LC 94-38369. 224p. 1995. 40.00 (*0-300-06031-9*) Yale U Pr.

Love Relations: Normality & Pathology. Otto F. Kernberg. 224p. 1998. pap. 16.00 (*0-300-07435-2*) Yale U Pr.

Love Relationships: A Moving Sea. Charles T. Cayce & Leslie G. Cayce. LC 95-30994. (Edgar Cayce's Wisdom for the New Age Ser.). 215p. 1995. pap. 12.95 (*0-87604-347-3*, 457) ARE Pr.

Love, Religion, & Politics in Fifteenth Century Spain. Angus MacKay & Ian R. MacPherson. LC 98-36907. (Medieval Iberian Peninsula Ser.). 1998. 97.25 (*90-04-10810-6*) Brill Academic Pubs.

Love, Remember Me. Corinne Everett. 368p. (Orig.). 1997. mass mkt. 5.50 (*0-505-52183-0*) Dorchester Pub Co.

Love, Remember Me. Bertrice Small. 1996. mass mkt. 5.99 (*0-345-40926-4*) Ballantine Pub Grp.

Love Remembers. Thelma B. Hill. LC 82-81128. (Illus.). 192p. 1982. 12.95 (*0-88100-004-3*) Natl Writ Pr.

***Love Renewed in Oakbrook City.** Kathryn Jameson. LC 98-61306. 144p. 1998. pap. 7.95 (*1-57921-149-6*, Pub. by WinePress Pub) BookWorld.

Love Responds: Reflections on Christian Morality. John H. Miller. 149p. (Orig.). 1990. pap. 7.00 (*0-9626257-0-1*) CBCCU Amer.

Love Rides the Rails: or Will the Mail Train Run Tonight? Morland Cary. 1940. pap. 5.25 (*0-8222-0698-6*) Dramatists Play.

Love Rights of Women. Havelock Ellis. 1991. lib. bdg. 79.95 (*0-8490-4313-1*) Gordon Pr.

Love Rimes of Petrarch. Francesco Petrarca. Tr. by Morris Bishop from ITA. LC 79-12820. (Illus.). 61p. 1980. reprint ed. lib. bdg. 39.75 (*0-313-22002-6*, PELR, Greenwood Pr) Greenwood.

Love Ripples of the Sunstar's Tree. Chad Crispo & Cassand Crispo. LC 91-70114. (Illus.). 75p. (Orig.). 1991. pap. 15.95 (*0-945306-01-6*) W F Garnett.

Love Ruins Everything. Karen X. Tulchinsky. LC PR9199.3.T76L68 1998. 280p. 1998. pap. 14.95 (*0-88974-082-8*, Pub. by Press Gang Pubs) LPC InBook.

Love Run. Jay Parini. (Orig.). 1989. mass mkt. 4.95 (*0-929654-22-6*, 66) Blue Moon Bks.

Love Runs True. Rachel Evans. LC 98-96226. 192p. 1998. 18.95 (*0-8034-9304-5*, Avalon Bks) Bouregy.

Love Russian Style. Ed. by Natasha Perova & Arch Tait. (Glas Ser.: No. 8). (Illus.). 224p. pap. 14.95 (*0-939010-44-5*) I R Dee.

***Love, Ruth: A Son's Memoir.** Charles C. Lovett. (Illus.). 240p. 1999. pap. 17.00 (*0-9672040-4-6*) Callanwolde.

Love Scene. Elaine M. Starkman. (Illus.). 1980. pap. 5.00 (*0-9601254-2-6*) Sheer Pr.

Love Scrolls: Love Passages. Edward Hayes. 56p. 1999. pap. 8.00 (*0-8059-4553-9*) Dorrance.

Love Season. large type ed. Peggy L. Jones. (Romance Ser.). 1994. pap. 16.99 (*0-7089-7615-8*, Linford) Ulverscroft.

Love Secured: How to Prevent a Drifting Marriage. Donald R. Harvey. LC 87-28460. 240p. (YA). (gr. 10). 1994. pap. 11.99 (*0-8010-4392-1*, Ravens Ridge) Baker Bks.

Love Serenade: Screenplay. Shirley Barrett. 1997. pap. 17.95 (*0-86819-529-4*, Pub. by Currency Pr) Accents Pubns.

Love Set Free: Meditations on the Passion According to John. Martin L. Smith. LC 98-25268. 1998. 7.95 (*1-56101-153-3*) Cowley Pubns.

Love, Sex & Astrology. Teri King. 336p. 1994. mass mkt. 5.99 (*0-06-109245-2*, HarpPBks) HarpC.

Love, Sex & Astrology. Teri King. 276p. 1993. pap. 14.95 (*0-572-01960-2*, Pub. by W Foulsham) Trans-Atl Phila.

Love, Sex & Feminism: A Philosophical Essay. John Wilson. (Modern Revivals in Philosophy Ser.). 136p. (C). 1994. text 53.95 (*0-7512-0160-X*, Pub. by Gregg Revivals) Ashgate Pub Co.

***Love, Sex & Gender in the World Religions.** Joseph Runzo. 2000. pap. 19.95 (*1-85168-223-6*, Pub. by Onewrld Pubns) Penguin Putnam.

Love, Sex & God see Learning about Sex Series

Love, Sex & God. Bill Ameiss & Jane Graver. (Learning about Sex Ser.: Bk. 5). 128p. (YA). (gr. 9 up). 1988. pap. 8.99 (*0-570-03556-2*, 14-2105) Concordia.

Love, Sex & Intimacy. Lorenz Staff. 1998. 30.00 (*1-85967-088-1*) Anness Pub.

Love, Sex & Intimacy: Their Psychology, Biology & History. Elain Hatfield & Richard Rapson. 520p. (C). 1997. pap. text 62.00 (*0-06-500702-6*) Addson-Wesley Educ.

***Love, Sex & Kids: God's Plan for the Family.** Casey Treat. LC 97-62470. 96p. 1999. pap. 12.00 (*1-57921-082-1*) WinePress Pub.

Love, Sex, & Magic: Exploring the Spiritual Union Between Male & Female. Sirona Knight. LC 98-52835. 192p. 1998. pap. 12.00 (*0-8065-2043-4*, Citadel Pr) Carol Pub Group.

Love, Sex & Marriage. Harold E. Buttram & Paul P. Ricchio. 64p. (Orig.). 1983. pap. 2.95 (*0-916285-42-1*) Humanitarian.

Love, Sex & Marriage in the Civil War. Charles A. Mills. 48p. 1994. pap. 6.00 (*0-945598-09-2*) Apple Cheeks Pr.

Love, Sex & Marriage Not Necessarily in That Order: Poetic Commentary by Sol the Sage. Sol Finkelman. 104p. 1994. pap. 14.95 (*0-9641973-1-6*) Genie Pubng.

Love, Sex, & Murder. Sue Cameron. 416p. 1997. mass mkt. 6.99 (*0-446-60438-0*, Pub. by Warner Bks) Little.

Love, Sex & Nutrition: A Nutritional Guide to Improving & Energizing Your Intimate Relationship. Bernard Jensen. LC 88-8124. 256p. (Orig.). pap. 10.95 (*0-89529-395-1*, Avery) Penguin Putnam.

Love, Sex & Power in Later Life: A Libertarian Perspective. Tony Gibson. 104p. (Orig.). 1992. pap. 7.50 (*0-900384-65-4*) Left Bank.

Love, Sex & PSA: Living & Loving with Prostate Cancer. Robert Hitchcox. (Illus.). 109p. 1997. pap. 12.95 (*0-9659734-0-9*) TMC Pr.

***Love, Sex & Relationships.** Sherman. 1999. pap. 11.99 (*1-57658-141-1*) YWAM Pub.

Love, Sex & Relationships. Dean Sherman. 196p. Date not set. pap. 11.99 (*0-927545-56-X*) YWAM Pub.

***Love, Sex & Tractors.** Roger Welsch. LC 00-28178. (Illus.). 224p. 2000. pap. 14.95 (*0-7603-0868-3*) MBI Pubg.

Love, Sex, Death, & the Meaning of Life: The Films of Woody Allen. rev. ed. Foster Hirsch. LC 90-40288. (Illus.). 305p. 1990. reprint ed. pap. 12.95 (*0-87910-143-1*) Limelight Edns.

Love, Sex, Feminism. John Wilson. LC 79-24902. 125p. 1980. 45.00 (*0-275-91695-2*, C1695, Praeger Pubs) Greenwood.

Love, Sexuality & Matriarchy: About Gender. Erich Fromm. Ed. by Rainer Funk. LC 97-38333. 256p. 1997. 24.95 (*0-88064-186-X*) Fromm Intl Pub.

Love, Sexuality & Matriarchy: About Gender. Erich Fromm. Ed. by Rainer Funk. 240p. 1999. pap. 14.00 (*0-88064-240-8*) Fromm Intl Pub.

Love, Sexuality, & the Sacrament of Marriage. John Chryssavgis. LC 96-9464. 100p. (Orig.). (C). 1996. pap. 7.95 (*1-885652-03-8*, Pub. by Holy Cross Orthodox) BookWorld.

Love Shack. Richard Van Lieven. LC 96-204622. 163p. (Orig.). 1997. pap. 12.95 (*1-86448-073-4*, Pub. by Allen & Unwin Pty) IPG Chicago.

Love Shadows: An Unbelievable Tryst with the Holy Ghost. Mary Moline. 380p. 1999. pap. 10.00 (*0-913444-13-8*) M Moline.

Love Shook My Heart: Lesbian Love Stories. Ed. by Irene Zahava. LC 97-32629. 250p. 1998. pap. 11.95 (*1-55583-404-3*) Alyson Pubns.

***Love Sick: Lessons on Relationships from Biological Psychiatry.** Andrew Abarbanel. 2000. pap. 18.95 (*0-923521-54-2*) Bull Pub.

***Love Signs.** Celeste B. Longacve. 360p. 2000. 24.00 (*0-930043-13-8*) Sweet Fern.

Love Signs: Find Your True Love Using Astrology, Numbers, Handwriting, Palm Reading & Face Reading. 3rd rev. expanded ed. Jeraldine Saunders. LC 98-20404. 336p. 1999. pap. 12.95 (*1-56718-618-1*) Llewellyn Pubns.

Love Signs for Beginners. Kristyna Arcarti. (Headway Guide for Beginners Ser.). (Illus.). 96p. 1996. mass mkt. 11.95 (*0-340-64805-8*, Pub. by Headway) Trafalgar.

Love, Sin & Survival: Three Women in 1930s Utah. Lavon B. Carroll. LC 99-60983. 454p. 1999. pap. 12.95 (*1-888106-94-8*) Agreka Bks.

Love Sketches from Aleppo: Bilingual: English-Arabic. Adnan Jarkess. (ARA.). 1993. 15.95 (*0-86685-612-9*, JAR1629, Pub. by Librairie du Liban) Intl Bk Ctr.

Love Slave. Mallory Rush. (Temptation Ser.). 1993. mass mkt. 2.99 (*0-373-25548-9*, 1-25548-8) Harlequin Bks.

Love Slave. Bertrice Small. 448p. (Orig.). 1995. pap. 10.00 (*0-345-38598-5*) Ballantine Pub Grp.

Love Slave. Bertrice Small. (Orig.). 1997. mass mkt. 6.50 (*0-345-41658-9*) Ballantine Pub Grp.

Love Slave. Bertrice Small. (Orig.). 1997. mass mkt. 6.50 (*0-449-00213-6*, Crest) Fawcett.

***Love Slave.** Terry Wakelin. 256p. 2000. pap. 9.95 (*1-901388-54-9*, Pub. by Chimera Pubns) Firebird Dist.

Love Slaves. Samuel L. Brengle. 104p. 1996. pap. 7.99 (*0-88019-352-2*) Schmul Pub Co.

Love Slaves. Samuel L. Brengle. 1960. reprint ed. 4.95 (*0-86544-004-2*) Salv Army Suppl South.

Love Smarts: A Singles Guide to Finding That Special Someone. Kathy Tait. (Personal Self-Help Ser.). 264p. (Orig.). 1994. pap. 11.95 (*0-88908-797-0*) Self-Counsel Pr.

Love Snare. James Irungu. (Heartbeats Ser.). 112p. (YA). (gr. 7 up). 1994. pap. 5.95 (*0-7910-2935-2*) Chelsea Hse.

Love So Amazing. Robert Moyer. 1997. pap. 5.99 (*0-907927-54-8*) Emerald House Group Inc.

Love So Amazing . . . Memories of Meher Baba. Bili Eaton. LC 84-23597. 144p. 1984. pap. 8.95 (*0-913078-55-7*) Sheriar Pr.

Love So Fine. Linda Ladd. 352p. 1999. mass mkt. 6.99 (*0-451-19509-4*, Topaz) NAL.

Love So True. Loure Bussey. 256p. 1999. mass mkt. 4.99 (*0-7860-0608-0*) Kensgtn Pub Corp.

Love So Wild. large type ed. Deborah Chester. 473p. 1982. 27.99 (*0-7089-0764-4*) Ulverscroft.

Love Someone Today: Stories of Encouragement & Inspiration for the Times of Our Lives. Delilah. Date not set. write for info. (*0-7432-1078-6*) S&S Trade.

***Love Song.** Wilma Fasano. LC 99-90982. 192p. 1999. 18.95 (*0-8034-9387-8*, Avalon Bks) Bouregy.

Love Song. Sharon Gillenwater. 246p. (Orig.). 1995. pap. 9.99 (*0-88070-747-X*, Palisades OR) Multnomah Pubs.

Love Song. Andrew M. Greeley. LC 88-40088. 1989. mass mkt. 5.95 (*0-446-35619-0*, Pub. by Warner Bks) Little.

Love Song. Keiko Nishi. (Illus.). 208p. 1998. pap. text 15.95 (*1-56931-255-9*, Viz Comics) Viz Comms Inc.

***Love Song.** large type ed. Charlotte Bingham. 472p. 1999. 31.99 (*0-7089-9107-6*) Ulverscroft.

Love Song for a Raven. Elizabeth Lowell. 1996. per. 5.50 (*1-55166-311-2*, 1-66311-1, Mira Bks) Harlequin Bks.

Love Song for a Raven. Elizabeth Lowell. (Mira Bks.). 1998. per. 5.50 (*1-55166-422-4*, 1-66422-6, Mira Bks) Harlequin Bks.

Love Song for a Raven. Elizabeth Lowell. 1993. mass mkt. 4.50 (*0-373-48276-0*, 5-48276-5) Silhouette.

Love Song for Brenda: A Father's Love for His Disabled Daughter. Ray Snook. 96p. (Orig.). 1991. pap. 7.95 (*0-89827-090-1*, BK045) Wesleyan Pub Hse.

Love Song for Sicily. Rolando Certa. Ed. by Stanley H. Barkan. Tr. by Nina Scammacca & Nat Scammacca. (Review Chapbook Ser.: No. 30: Italian (Sicilian Poetry) 1).Tr. of Ital. & Sicilian & Eng.. (Illus.). 16p. 1982. 15.00 (*0-89304-879-8*, CCC153); pap. 5.00 (*0-89304-854-2*) Cross-Cultrl NY.

Love Song for Ulster. Bill Morrisson. 192p. 1994. pap. 19.95 (*1-85459-260-2*, Pub. by N Hern Bks) Theatre Comm.

Love Song of Alfred J. Prufrock. T. S. Eliot. 1976. 16.95 (*0-8488-0997-1*) Amereon Ltd.

Love Song of J. Edgar Hoover. Kinky Friedman. LC 97-93936. 240p. 1997. pap. 11.95 (*0-345-41509-4*) Ballantine Pub Grp.

Love Song of J. Edgar Hoover. Kinky Friedman. 1996. 23.00 (*0-684-80377-1*) S&S Trade.

Love Song of J. Edgar Hoover. large type ed. Kinky Friedman. LC 96-45016. 1996. pap. 22.95 (*1-56895-394-1*) Wheeler Pub.

Love Song of the Dark Lord: Jayadeva's Gitagovinda. Barbara S. Miller. 131p. 1997. pap. 17.50 (*0-231-11097-9*) Col U Pr.

Love Song of the Little Bear. Margaret Wise Brown. (Illus.). 32p. 2000. 15.49 (*0-7868-2445-X*, Pub. by Hyprn Child) Little.

Love Song of the Little Bear. Margaret Wise Brown. (Illus.). 32p. Date not set. 4.99 (*0-7868-1361-X*, Pub. by Hyprn Ppbks) Little.

Love Song of the Little Bear. Margaret Wise Brown. (Illus.). 32p. 2000. pap. 14.99 (*0-7868-0509-9*, Pub. by Hyprn Ppbks) Little.

Love Song to a Long Gone Time: Memoirs of a Moviegoer from Way Back. Chris O'Grady. LC 86-90178. 258p. 1991. 19.95 (*0-9631753-0-0*) C-C OGrady.

Love Song to the Messiah. Jamie S. Lash. 16p. 1987. reprint ed. pap. 2.95 (*0-915775-05-0*) Love Song Mess Assn.

Love Song to the Plains. Mari Sandoz. LC 61-6441. (Illus.). x, 305p. 1966. pap. 12.95 (*0-8032-5172-6*, Bison Books) U of Nebr Pr.

***Love Songs.** 80p. 1999. pap. 8.95 (*0-7935-9835-4*) H Leonard.

***Love Songs.** 256p. 2000. per. 6.95 (*0-634-01227-4*) H Leonard.

Love Songs. Perf. by Elton John. 72p. 1996. otabind 17.95 (*0-7935-6446-8*) H Leonard.

Love Songs. Lawrence Sanders. 400p. 1989. mass mkt. 6.99 (*0-425-11273-X*) Berkley Pub.

Love Songs. Katherine Stone. 480p. 1996. mass mkt. 6.99 (*0-8217-5205-7*, Zebra Kensgtn) Kensgtn Pub Corp.

Love Songs. large type ed. Katherine Stone. LC 96-16363. 1996. 24.95 (*1-56895-327-5*) Wheeler Pub.

Love Songs, No. 7. 64p. 1984. pap. 5.95 (*0-7935-3296-5*, 00243453) H Leonard.

Love Songs, Vol. 29. 48p. Date not set. pap. 5.95 (*0-7935-1965-9*, 00100135) H Leonard.

Love Songs: Simplified for Piano. Ed. by Tony Esposito. 96p. 1995. pap. text 11.95 (*0-89724-759-0*, BP3339A) Wrner Bros.

***Love Songs: The Book.** 184p. 1998. otabind 16.95 (*0-7935-8508-2*) H Leonard.

Love Songs & Graffiti. Jack Little. 82p. (Orig.). pap. 7.00 (*0-913057-08-8*) Confront Mag Pr.

Love Songs & Graffiti. deluxe limited ed. Jack Little. 82p. (Orig.). 20.00 (*0-913057-07-X*) Confront Mag Pr.

Love Songs & Lullabyes for Daddy's Little Dreamer. J. Aaron Brown. (Illus.). 8p. (J). (gr. 3). 1995. 15.95 incl. audio compact disk (*0-927945-14-2*) Someday Baby.

Love Songs & Lullabyes for Daddy's Little Dreamer. J. Aaron Brown. (Illus.). 8p. (J). (ps). 1995. 12.95 incl. audio (*0-927945-13-4*) Someday Baby.

Love Songs & Sonnets. Ed. by Pater Washington. (Everyman's Library Pocket Poetry Ser.). 1997. pap. 12.50 (*0-614-29415-0*) Knopf.

***Love Songs at the Piano.** 104p. 1999. otabind 12.95 (*0-634-00417-4*) H Leonard.

Love Songs For All God's Children: 100 or Today's Sacred Favorites. Compiled by R. W. Stringfield. 224p. pap. 19.99 (*0-8341-9957-2*) Lillenas.

Love Songs for Singers. 192p. 1995. per. 16.95 (*0-7935-5052-1*, 00310087) H Leonard.

***Love Songs for the Dead.** Gisela Huberman. LC 99-48638. 2000. 25.95 (*1-56492-285-5*) Laredo.

Love Songs from Al-Andalus: History, Structure & Meaning of the Kharja. Otto Zwartjes. LC 97-2841. (Medieval Iberian Peninsula Ser.: Vol. 11). xiii, 443p. 1997. 92.00 (*90-04-10694-4*) Brill Academic Pubs.

Love Songs from Broadway. 80p. 1996. pap. 12.95 (*0-7935-6023-3*) H Leonard.

Love Songs from Stage & Screen. Friedman-Fairfax & Sony Music Staff. (CD Ser.). (Illus.). 72p. 1994. pap. 15.98 incl. audio compact disk (*1-56799-124-6*, Friedman-Fairfax) M Friedman Pub Grp Inc.

***Love Songs from the Man'yoshu: Selections from a Japanese Classic.** Ian Hideo Levy. 2000. pap. 25.00 (*4-7700-2642-0*) Kodansha.

Love Songs from the Movies. 160p. 1994. per. 14.95 (*0-7935-3312-0*, 00311671) H Leonard.

Love Songs from the Movies. (E-Z Play Today Ser.: Vol. #096). 112p. 1997. otabind 9.95 (*0-7935-8089-7*) H Leonard.

Love Songs from the Movies in Easy Piano. (Easy Play Ser.). 152p. 1995. per. 14.95 (*0-7935-3832-7*, 00222589) H Leonard.

Love Songs in Sumerian Literature: Critical Edition of the Dumuzi[001b]b-[001b]sinanna Songs. Yitzhak Sefati. LC 98-210112. (Studies in Near Eastern Languages & Culture). 445p. 1998. write for info. (*965-226-203-X*) Bar Ilan U Pr.

Love Songs Make You Cry. Lasana M. Sekou. LC 88-80157. (Illus.). 95p. 1989. pap. 10.00 (*0-913441-07-4*) Hse of Nehesi.

Love Songs of Arnhem Land. Ronald M. Berndt. LC 77-83828. (Illus.). 274p. reprint ed. pap. 85.00 (*0-608-09387-4*, 205413200004); reprint ed. pap. 84.40 (*0-608-21012-9*, 2054540) Bks Demand.

Love Songs of Childhood. Eugene Field. LC 74-98081. (Granger Index Reprint Ser.). 1977. 15.95 (*0-8369-6077-7*) Ayer.

Love Songs of Children. Eugene Field. (Notable American Authors Ser.). (J). 1992. reprint ed. lib. bdg. 75.00 (*0-7812-2645-7*) Rprt Serv.

Love Songs of John Denver (Piano - Vocal) Ed. by Mark Phillips. (Illus.). 79p. (Orig.). 1990. pap. text 9.95 (*0-89524-378-4*) Cherry Lane.

Love Songs of Kabir. G. N. Das. (C). 1992. 17.50 (*81-7017-288-8*, Pub. by Abhinav) S Asia.

Love Songs of Sappho. Sappho. Tr. by Paul Roche from GRE. LC 98-38950. (Literary Classics Ser.). (Illus.). 251p. 1998. reprint ed. pap. 8.95 (*1-57392-251-X*) Prometheus Bks.

Love Songs of the Beatles. 80p. 1987. pap. 12.95 (*0-7935-2504-7*, 00356224) H Leonard.

Love Songs of the Beatles, No. 179. 48p. 1994. pap. 8.95 (*0-7935-3365-1*, 00102325) H Leonard.

Love Songs of the 80's. Leonard, Hal, Corporation Staff. (Decades of Love Songs Ser.). 160p. 1995. per. 14.95 (*0-7935-4592-7*) H Leonard.

Love Songs of the 80s & 90s. 224p. 1997. otabind 16.95 (*0-7935-8344-6*) H Leonard.

***Love Songs of the 50s & 60s for Easy Guitar.** 64p. 1998. pap. 8.95 (*0-7935-8502-3*) H Leonard.

Love Songs of the 50's. Leonard, Hal, Corporation Staff. (Decades of Love Songs Ser.). 160p. 1995. per. 14.95 (*0-7935-4457-2*) H Leonard.

***Love Songs of the 40s & 50s.** 200p. 1998. otabind 14.95 (*0-7935-8341-1*) H Leonard.

Love Songs of the 40's. Leonard, Hal, Corporation Staff. (Decades of Love Songs Ser.). 160p. 1995. per. 14.95 (*0-7935-4445-9*) H Leonard.

Love Songs of the Irish. James N. Healy. 64p. 8.95 (*1-900428-20-2*, OS 00114, Pub. by Ossian) Music Sales.

Love Songs of the Irish. James N. Healy. 64p. 1996. reprint ed. 9.95 (*0-85342-697-X*, OS 00114) Music Sales.

Love Songs of the New Kingdom. Tr. & Illus. by John L. Foster. LC 92-11889. 141p. 1992. reprint ed. 20.00 (*0-292-72476-4*); reprint ed. pap. 10.95 (*0-292-72477-2*) U of Tex Pr.

Love Songs of the 90's. Leonard, Hal, Corporation Staff. 160p. 1995. otabind 14.95 (*0-7935-4593-5*) H Leonard.

***Love Songs of the 90s for Easy Guitar.** 80p. 1998. pap. 9.95 (*0-7935-8506-6*) H Leonard.

Love Songs of the 70's. Leonard, Hal, Corporation Staff. (Decades of Love Songs Ser.). 160p. 1995. otabind 14.95 (*0-7935-4591-9*) H Leonard.

***Love Songs of the 70s & 80s for Easy Guitar.** 64p. 1998. pap. 8.95 (*0-7935-8504-X*) H Leonard.

Love Songs of the 60's. Leonard, Hal, Corporation Staff. 160p. 1995. per. 14.95 (*0-7935-4456-4*) H Leonard.

Love Songs of the 60s & 70s. 232p. 1997. otabind 16.95 (*0-7935-8343-8*) H Leonard.

Love Songs of the 30's. Leonard, Hal, Corporation Staff. (Decades of Love Songs Ser.). 160p. 1995. per. 14.95 (*0-7935-4441-6*) H Leonard.

Love Songs of the Tone-Deaf. Asher Brauner. LC 99-94657. 300p. 1999. pap. 11.95 (*0-9670861-0-8*) Brown Bear Bks.

Love Songs of the 20's. Leonard, Hal, Corporation Staff. (Decades of Love Songs Ser.). 160p. 1995. per. 14.95 (*0-7935-4442-4*) H Leonard.

Love Songs of Vidyapati. W. G. Archer. 1987. 14.00 (81-208-0291-8, Pub. by Motilal Bnarsidass) S Asia.

Love Sonnets & Madrigals to Tommaso de'Cavalieri. Michelangelo di Lodovico Buonarroti Simoni. Tr. by Michael Sullivan from ITA. LC 98-111568. (Illus.). 128p. 1998. 32.00 (0-7206-1040-0, Pub. by P Owen Ltd) Dufour.

Love Sonnets of the Renaissance. Lawrence Kitchin. LC 89-82409. 96p. 1990. pap. 16.95 (0-948259-60-4) Dufour.

Love, Sorrow & Rage: Destitute Women in a Manhattan Residence. Alisse Waterston. LC 98-32269. (Illus.). 224p. 1999. 59.50 (1-56639-706-5); pap. 19.95 (1-56639-707-3) Temple U Pr.

Love, Soul & Freedom: Dancing with Rumi on the Mystic Path. Denise Breton & Christopher Largent. Tr. by Coleman Barks. LC 97-48972. 320p. 1998. 21.95 (1-56838-207-3) Hazelden.

Love Speed. Lemieux. 2001. per. 4.50 (0-689-81799-1) S&S Childrens.

Love Spell. Karen Williams. Ed. by Lee Boojamra & Alice Frier. 192p. (Orig.). 1993. pap. 9.95 (0-9628938-2-X) Rising AZ.

***Love Spell Box: 30 Potent Spells to Enhance Your Love Life.** Gillian Kemp. 96p. 2000. 16.95 (0-8212-2690-8) Bulfinch Pr.

Love Spells & Rituals Gift Set. Sue Bowes. (Illus.). 64p. 1998. 19.95 (0-8069-2439-X) Sterling.

Love Spells for More Fulfilling & Intimate Relationships. James L. Page. 144p. (Orig.). 1992. pap. 14.95 (0-572-01621-2, Pub. by W Foulsham) Trans-Atl Phila.

Love, Stars & All That. Kirin Narayan. Ed. by Jane Rosenman. 320p. 1995. pap. 10.00 (0-671-79396-9) PB.

Love Stories. Ursula K. Le Guin. write for info. (0-06-105201-9, HarperPrism) HarpC.

Love Stories. Charles Mills & Ruth Brand. LC 95-168509. (Professor Appleby & the Maggie B. Tapes Ser.: Vol. 3). 128p. (J). (gr. 4-7). 1995. pap. 8.99 (0-8280-0934-1) Review & Herald.

Love Stories. Rosamunde Pilcher. 1996. mass mkt. 5.99 (0-312-95756-4, Pub. by Tor Bks) St Martin.

Love Stories. large type ed. 576p. 1992. 27.99 (0-7089-2582-0, Linford) Ulverscroft.

***Love Stories: Granta 68, Winter 1999.** Ed. by Ian Jack. (Magazine Ser.: Vol. 68). 256p. 2000. pap. 12.95 (0-9645611-8-2) Granta.

Love Stories: Reading Level 2-3. Illus. by Cheri Bladholm. LC 93-12038. (Timeless Tales Ser.). 1993. 4.95 (0-88336-462-X); audio 9.95 (0-88336-539-1) New Readers.

Love Stories Are Too Violent for Me. William Viharo. LC 95-61613. (Orig.). 1995. pap. 10.00 (0-9645931-0-6) Wild Card Pr.

Love Stories for All Centuries. Barbara Rodman. 96p. 1984. 8.95 (0-89697-143-0) Intl Univ Pr.

Love Stories for the Rest of Us. Ed. by Genie D. Chipps & Bill Henderson. 500p. 1994. 29.50 (0-916366-90-1, Pub. by Pushcart Pr) Norton.

Love Stories for the Rest of Us. Ed. by Genie D. Chipps & Bill Henderson. 500p. 1995. pap. 15.00 (0-916366-93-6, Pub. by Pushcart Pr) Norton.

Love Stories for the Time Being. Ed. by Genie D. Chipps & Bill Henderson. 450p. 1987. 25.00 (0-916366-42-1, Pub. by Pushcart Pr) Norton.

Love Stories for the Time Being. Ed. by Genie D. Chipps & Bill Henderson. 450p. 1989. pap. 12.95 (0-916366-53-7, Pub. by Pushcart Pr) Norton.

Love Stories for the Time Being. Ed. by Genie D. Chipps & Bill Henderson. 459p. 1999. pap. 19.00 (0-916366-22-7, Pub. by Pushcart Pr) Norton.

Love Stories God Told: Great Romances from the Bible. David Kopp & Heather Kopp. LC 97-34260. 242p. 1998. 19.99 (1-56507-823-3) Harvest Hse.

Love Stories-Love Poems. Ed. by Joe D. Bellamy & Roger Weingarten. LC 82-84443. 258p. (Orig.). 1982. pap. 12.95 (0-931362-07-5) Fiction Intl.

Love Stories of Old California. Cora M. Older. LC 94-43777. 320p. 1995. pap. 15.95 (1-55709-400-4) Applewood.

Love Stories of Old California. Cora M. Older. LC 75-167465. (Short Story Index Reprint Ser.). 1977. reprint ed. 26.95 (0-8369-3991-3) Ayer.

Love Storm. Susan Johnson. 416p. 1995. mass mkt. 5.99 (0-553-56328-9) Bantam.

Love Story. CRM Staff. (CHI.). 111p. 1984. pap. 4.50 (1-56582-086-X) Christ Renew Min.

Love Story. Gabriel Delgado. 64p. (Orig.). 1975. pap. 1.25 (0-89228-046-8) Impact Christian.

Love Story. Erich Segal. 144p. 1988. mass mkt. 7.50 (0-553-27528-3) Bantam.

Love Story. large type ed. Erich Segal. reprint ed. 10.00 (0-318-65669-8) NAVH.

Love Story. Erich Segal. 1994. reprint ed. lib. bdg. 25.95 (1-56849-334-7) Buccaneer Bks.

***Love Story: The Unauthorized Biography of Jennifer Love Hewitt.** Marc Shapiro. LC 99-167163. 134 p. 1998. pap. 5.99 (0-425-16755-0) Blvd Books.

Love Story from Nineteenth Century Quebec: The Diary of George Stephen Jones. Ed. by Peter Ward. 120p. 1990. 19.95 (0-921149-47-6) Broadview.

Love Story from the Bridal Chamber of Ishi & the Lily. Bobbi Troyer. LC 97-77735. (Illus.). 132p. (Orig.). 1997. per. 15.00 (0-9661507-6-7, 1) Ishi.

Love Story in Shakespearean Comedy. Anthony J. Lewis. LC 91-45643. 248p. 1992. 29.95 (0-8131-1786-0) U Pr of Ky.

***Love Strong as Death.** Ronald Walls. LC 99-26704. 250p. 1999. pap. write for info. (1-879007-41-X) St Bedes Pubns.

***Love Styles: Re-Engineering Marriage for the New Millennium.** Bryan Brook. 92p. 2000. pap. 9.95 (0-9637285-3-9) Prose Assocs.

***Love Success.** Richard Starr. 1999. pap. 24.95 (1-888221-25-9) Results Now.

Love Sucks: New York Stories of Love, Hate, & Anonymous Sex. Ken Shakin. 240p. 1997. pap. 14.95 (0-85449-254-2, Pub. by Gay Mens Pr) LPC InBook.

Love Suicide at Amijima: A Study of a Japanese Domestic Tragedy by Chikamatsu Monzaemon. Donald H. Shively. LC 91-318. (Michigan Classics in Japanese Studies: No. 5). viii, 173p. 1991. reprint ed. pap. 8.95 (0-939512-51-3) U MI Japan.

Love Suicide at Schofield Barracks: Full Length. Romulus Linney. 1972. pap. 5.25 (0-8222-0702-8) Dramatists Play.

Love Suicide at Schofield Barracks: One-Act. Romulus Linney. Date not set. pap. 5.95 (0-8222-1773-2) Dramatists Play.

Love Suicide at Schofield Barracks: One-Act. Romulus Linney. 1985. pap. 3.25 (0-8222-0701-X) Dramatists Play.

Love Suicides. John Romeril. 1997. pap. 14.95 (0-86819-515-4, Pub. by Currency Pr) Accents Pubns.

Love Supreme. Pauline Hopkins. (X Press Black Classics Ser.). 175p. 1996. pap. 9.95 (1-874509-27-1, Pub. by X Pr) LPC InBook.

Love Supreme: Real-Life Stories of Black Love. TaRessa Stovall & Calvin Stovall. LC 99-33750. (Illus.). 208p. 2000. 23.95 (0-446-52171-X, Pub. by Warner Bks) Little.

***Love Supreme: Real-Life Stories of Black Love.** TaRessa Stovall & Calvin Stovall. 2001. pap. write for info. (0-446-67662-4) Warner Bks.

Love Surrounds Us. Carol A. Vercz. 1993. 5.00 (0-910119-22-8) SOCO Pubns.

***Love Survives.** large type ed. Christina Good. 240p. 2000. pap. 18.99 (0-7089-5642-4, Linford) Ulverscroft.

Love Sweeter Love: Creating Relationships of Simplicity & Spirit. Jann Mitchell. LC 97-49137. (Sweet Simplicity Ser.). (Illus.). 192p. 1998. pap. 12.95 (1-885223-73-0) Beyond Words Pub.

Love Tactics: How to Win the One You Want. Thomas W. McKnight & Robert H. Phillips. LC 87-31935. 144p. pap. 7.95 (0-89529-367-6, Avery) Penguin Putnam.

Love Tactics: How to Win the One You Want. unabridged ed. Thomas W. McKnight & Robert Phillips. 1996. 16.95 incl. audio (1-882071-62-X) B&B Audio.

Love-Tactics: Strategic Psychology to Win the One You Want. Thomas W. McKnight. (Illus.). 76p. 1985. pap. 4.95 (0-9615050-0-1) Wisdom Pr.

Love Takes a Country Road, Vol. 1. Janet Hayward Burnham. LC 99-21839. 1999. pap. 21.95 (0-7838-8614-4) Thorndike Pr.

Love Takes Time. Kathleen R. Acker. LC 96-90032. 1996. 11.95 (0-533-11784-4) Vantage.

Love Takes Time. Herring. 1992. pap. text. write for info. (0-17-556002-1) Addison-Wesley.

Love Takes Wing. Janette Oke. LC 88-19276. (Love Comes Softly Ser.: Vol. 7). 224p. (Orig.). 1988. pap. 8.99 (1-55661-035-1) Bethany Hse.

Love Takes Wing. large type ed. Janette Oke. LC 94-43842. 322p. (Orig.). 1995. 22.95 (0-7838-1206-X, G K Hall Lrg Type) Mac Lib Ref.

Love Tales of the Soul: Selected Writings by G. Shanier. G. Shanier. (Illus.). 86p. 1998. pap. 5.95 (0-7392-0002-X) Morris Pubng.

Love Talk: A Communication Guide for Married Couples. Eugene Stehura. LC 90-62652. 96p. (Orig.). 1991. pap. 7.95 (1-55612-403-1, LL1403) Sheed & Ward WI.

Love Talker. Elizabeth Peters, pseud. 1990. pap. 4.99 (0-8125-0727-4, Pub. by Tor Bks) St Martin.

Love Talker. Deborah Pryor. 1992. pap. 5.25 (0-8222-1384-2) Dramatists Play.

Love Tangles. Eddy. Ed. by Windsor Company Staff. 85p. 1993. 19.95 (0-9637631-0-5) Windsor VA.

Love Tarot: Uses the Powers of the Mystic Deck to Guide You in Love, Romance & Sex. Sarah Bartlett. 96p. 1995. 17.95 (0-8212-2223-6, Pub. by Bulfinch Pr) Little.

Love Teachings of Kama Sutra: With Extracts from Koka Shastra, Anaga Ranga & Other Famous Individuals. Indra Sinha. LC 98-163031. 192p. 1997. pap. text 22.95 (1-56924-779-X) Marlowe & Co.

Love Test. 1999. mass mkt. 3.95 (0-446-73736-4, Pub. by Warner Bks) Little.

Love Test: Romance & Relationship Self-Quizzes Developed by Psychologists & Therapists. Virginia B. Rutter & Pepper Schwartz. LC 97-33452. 240p. 1998. pap. 12.00 (0-399-52403-7, Perigee Bks) Berkley Pub.

***Love That Baby: Nurture Your Child with Spiritual Assurance.** LC 99-98111. (Illus.). 312p. 2000. pap. write for info. (0-9677944-0-4) Peaceful Parent.

Love That Bunch. Aline Kominsky-Crumb. 144p. 1990. 35.00 (1-56097-034-0); pap. 16.95 (1-56097-017-0) Fantagraph Bks.

Love That Comes from God: Reflections on the Family. Chiara Lubich. Tr. by Julian Stead from ITA. (Spirituality of Unity Ser.). 96p. 1995. pap. 6.95 (1-56548-030-9) New City.

Love That Ended Yesterday in Texas. Cathy S. Bowers. x, 86p. 1992. 16.50 (0-89672-301-1) Tex Tech Univ Pr.

Love That Endures. Claudia Jameson. (Romance Ser.: No. 189). 1992. per. 2.89 (0-373-03189-0, 1-03189-7) Harlequin Bks.

Love That God Forgot. large type ed. Alexander Cordell. (Ulverscroft Large Print Ser.). 496p. 1997. 27.99 (0-7089-3770-5) Ulverscroft.

Love That Heals. Norman W. Cooper. 1977. pap. 7.00 (0-87516-228-2) DeVorss.

***Love That Keeps Us Sane: Living the Little Way of St. Therese of Lisieux.** Marc Foley. (IlluminationBook Ser.). 2000. pap. 5.95 (0-8091-4002-0) Paulist Pr.

Love That Lasts: Making a Magnificent Marriage. Gary Ricucci & Betsy Ricucci. Ed. by Greg Somerville. 176p. 1992. pap. 8.99 (1-881039-02-1) PDI Ministries.

***Love that Latin Beat.** (E-Z Play Today Ser.: Vol. #269). 56p. 1998. pap. 7.95 (0-7935-8940-1) H Leonard.

Love That Never Ends: A Key to the Catechism of the Catholic Church. J. Augustine DiNoia et al. LC 96-68289. 160p. 1996. 14.95 (0-87973-852-9, 852) Our Sunday Visitor.

Love That Never Fails: 1 Corinthians 13. H. Dale Burke. (Guidelines for Living Ser.). 208p. 1999. pap. 9.99 (0-8024-8198-1) Moody.

Love That Will Not Let Me Go: My Time with Theodore Dreiser. Marguerite Tjader. Ed. by Lawrence E. Hussman. (Modern American Literature Ser.: Vol. 19). XX, 131p. (C). 1998. pap. text 19.95 (0-8204-4034-5) P Lang Pubng.

Love the Body You Were Born With: A Ten-Step Workbook for Women. Monica A. Dixon. 192p. 1996. pap. 13.00 (0-399-51975-0, Perigee Bks) Berkley Pub.

Love the Earth! Barbara B. Linse & Marilyn Knight. Ed. by Ginny Dresser. (Illus.). 32p. (J). 1991. pap. write for info. (0-318-68833-6) Arts Pubns.

Love the Earth! Annalisa Suid. (Illus.). 48p. (J). (gr. 1-3). 1993. pap. 9.95 (1-878279-48-3) Monday Morning Bks.

Love the Earth! An Ecology Resource Book. Barbara B. Linse & Marty Links. (Illus.). (J). 1991. 5.95 (1-878079-01-8); 4.95 (0-685-59046-1) Arts Pubns.

Love the Earth, Exploring Environmental Activities for Young Children. Patty Claycomb. 1991. pap. 12.95 (0-933212-47-X) Partner Pr.

Love the Essence of Life. Pradeep Rampersad. 1997. pap. write for info. (1-57553-454-1) Watermrk Pr.

Love the Eternal Link. Carolyn De la Hey. 1999. pap. 21.00 (1-85072-038-X, Pub. by W Sessions) St Mut.

Love the Evil. Suzanne C. Leiphart. 224p. 1999. pap. 14.95 (0-7414-0013-8) Buy Books.

***Love the Evil: A Psychological Thriller about Overcoming Destructive Relationships.** Suzanne Leiphart. LC 99-91487. 218p. 2000. 25.00 (0-7388-0826-1) Xlibris Corp.

Love, the Family Circus. Bil Keane. (Illus.). 104p. 1983. pap. 5.95 (0-8362-2007-2) Andrews & McMeel.

Love, the Fiddler. Lloyd Osbourne. LC 73-103526. (Short Story Index Reprint Ser.). 1977. 20.95 (0-8369-3268-4) Ayer.

Love the Least of My Children. Elvira Bellegoni. (Illus.). 64p. 1999. pap. 12.95 (0-9662542-4-4) Etta Pub Co.

***Love, the Magician.** Brian Bouldrey. LC 00-28183. 179p. (C). 2000. 49.95 (1-56023-993-X, Harrington Park) Haworth Pr.

***Love, the Magician.** Brian Bouldrey. LC 00-28183. 179p. 2000. pap. text 19.95 (1-56023-994-8) Haworth Pr.

***Love the One You Love.** Beth Kitzinger & Linda D. Rockey. 192p. 1999. 7.98 (1-56731-325-6, MJF Bks) Fine Comms.

Love, the Town Couldn't Stop. Ed Smith. 210p. 1996. pap. text 7.99 (1-887827-02-1) New Authors Pubns.

Love Them In: The Life & Theology of D. L. Moody. Stanley N. Gundry. 279p. 1999. pap. 12.99 (0-8024-9057-3) Moody.

Love Theme Greetings to Duplicate & Use. Lamp Light Press Staff. (Illus.). 70p. 1993. ring bd. 29.95 (0-917593-22-7, Lamp Light Pr) Prosperity & Profits.

Love Theory in Later Hanbalite Islam. Joseph N. Bell. LC 78-5904. 280p. (C). 1979. text 24.50 (0-87395-244-8) State U NY Pr.

***Love They Lost: Living with the Legacy of Our Parents' Divorce.** Stephanie Staal. LC 00-38366. 256p. 2000. 23.95 (0-385-33409-5) Delacorte.

Love Thine Enemas & Heal Thyself. Jerry G. Knox. (Illus.). 425p. 1997. pap. text 29.95 (0-9625908-1-9) Lifeknox Pub.

Love Thine Enemy. Fred Caesar. 190p. 1984. 8.95 (0-89697-147-3) Intl Univ Pr.

Love Thing. Dixie Browning. 1994. per. 3.59 (0-373-45170-9) Silhouette.

***Love Through All Time.** Jean Nash. 392p. 1999. pap. 9.95 (1-893896-03-X) Ima Jinn.

***Love Through the Generations: The Inspirational Journey of an African-American Family for Children of All Ages.** Johnson et al. (Illus.). 104p. 1999. pap. 3.98 (0-9655064-8-7) Amber Books.

Love Through Time. Terri Brisbin. (Time Passages Romance Ser.). 532p. 1998. mass mkt. 5.99 (0-515-12403-6, Jove) Berkley Pub.

Love Thy Neighbor: A Story of War. Peter Maass. LC 95-39250. 305p. 1996. 25.00 (0-679-44433-5) Knopf.

Love Thy Neighbor: A Story of War. Peter Maass. LC 95-39250. 305p. 1997. pap. 13.00 (0-679-76389-9) Vin Bks.

***Love Tickles Your Fancy.** Tome Tiny. 2000. 3.95 (0-7407-0113-4) Andrews & McMeel.

Love till Death. Cesar Moro. Tr. by Frances Lefevre.Tr. of Amour a Mort. 140p. 1971. 25.00 (0-931106-05-2) TVRT.

Love Time see Tiempo de Amor: A Wife in Time

Love Times Three. Carolyn Keene. (River Heights Ser.: No. 1). (Orig.). (YA). (gr. 6 up). 1991. pap. 3.50 (0-671-96703-7, Archway) PB.

Love Times Two: International Edition. Stephanie Foster. (YA). 1994. pap. 3.50 (0-553-24153-2) Bantam.

Love to All, Jim: A Young Man's Letters from Vietnam. James G. Rowe, Jr. Ed. by Gary R. Prescott. LC 88-35579. (Illus.). 128p. (Orig.). 1989. pap. 9.95 (0-89407-096-7) Strawberry Hill.

Love to Be Happy: The Secrets of Sustainable Joy. Mehdi N. Bahadori. LC 93-6410. 176p. (Orig.). 1993. pap. 10.95 (0-931892-71-6) B Dolphin Pub.

Love to Be Loved: A Collection of Poetry in Emotion. John F. Ramsey. 64p. 1998. pap. 14.95 (0-9647940-7-1) Adventura Pubng.

Love to Cherish. Beverly Clark. LC 98-206080. (Indigo Love Stories Ser.). 287p. 1998. 15.95 (1-885478-35-6, Pub. by Genesis Press) BookWorld.

Love to Cherish. Connie Mason. 1997. mass mkt. 5.99 (0-380-77999-4, Avon Bks) Morrow Avon.

Love to Cherish. unabridged ed. Beverly L. Clark. 287p. 1999. pap. 8.95 (1-885478-84-4, Pub. by Genesis Press) BookWorld.

Love to Christ (Necessary to Escape the Curse at His Coming) Thomas Doolittle. 215p. 1994. reprint ed. 18.95 (1-877611-84-0) Soli Deo Gloria.

Love to Cook, Vol. 1. Louise Thompson-Childs. (Illus.). 1994. 17.95 (0-9644445-0-X) Louise Childs.

Love to Cook: A Collection of Recipes. Martha S. Schrier. Ed. by Kathryn McKee & Dorothy Weigand. (Illus.). 482p. (Orig.). 1992. write for info. (0-9628403-0-0) M S Schrier.

Love to Die For. Christine T. Jorgensen. (Mystery Ser.). 256p. 1997. per. 4.99 (0-373-26231-0, 1-262310, Wrldwide Lib) Harlequin Bks.

Love to Die For. Christine T. Jorgensen. 214p. 1994. 19.95 (0-8027-3188-0) Walker & Co.

***Love to Die For.** Patricia Springer. 2000. mass mkt. 6.50 (0-7860-1086-X, Pinncle Kensgtn) Kensgtn Pub Corp.

Love to Eat, Hate to Eat: Breaking the Bondage of Destructive Eating Habits. Elyse Fitzpatrick. LC 98-44305. 250p. 1999. pap. 9.99 (0-7369-0013-6) Harvest Hse.

***Love to Jump!, 1 vol.** Scholastic, Inc. Staff. (Illus.). 20p. (ps-k). 1999. bds. 4.99 (0-439-07795-8) Scholastic Inc.

Love to Learn. (Barbie Preschool Learning Pads Ser.: Vol. 3). (Illus.). 48p. (J). 1998. pap. write for info. (0-7666-0196-X, Honey Bear Bks) Modern Pub NYC.

Love to Learn, Nature, Learn to Love. Gary N. Yaker. 44p. (Orig.). 1986. student ed. 4.00 (0-937055-00-X) Yaker Enviro.

Love to Live - Live to Love. Dorothy C. Hulbert. 1984. write for info. (0-318-58393-3) Rector Pub.

Love to Quilt Bears Bears Bears. Karen K. Buckley. LC 96-37102. (Love to Quilt Ser.). 48p. 1997. pap. 14.95 (0-89145-881-6, 4815, Am Quilters Soc) Collector Bks.

Love to Quilt Men's Neckties: Sampler Blocks. Janet B. Elwin. LC 96-49789. (Love to Quilt Ser.). (Illus.). 48p. 1997. pap. 14.95 (0-89145-882-4, 4816, Am Quilters Soc) Collector Bks.

Love to Quilt Penny Squares. Willa Baranowski. (Illus.). 56p. (Orig.). 1996. pap. 12.95 (0-89145-879-4, 4753, Am Quilters Soc) Collector Bks.

Love to Read! Activities to Foster a Love of Reading. Cindy Barden. Ed. by Judy Mitchell. (Illus.). 160p. (Orig.). (J). (gr. 3-6). 1995. pap., teacher ed. 14.95 (1-57310-032-3) Teachng & Lrning Co.

***Love to Roll!** (Teletubbies Ser.). (Illus.). 20p. (ps-k). 1999. bds. 4.99 (0-439-07794-X) Scholastic Inc.

Love to the Highest Bidder. Rachel Ann Nunes. LC 98-24031. 1998. pap. 12.95 (1-57734-278-X, 01113429) Covenant Comms.

Love to Water My Soul. Jane Kirkpatrick. (Dreamcatcher Ser.: Vol. 2). 366p. 1996. pap. 12.99 (0-88070-938-3, Multnomah Bks) Multnomah Pubs.

Love to William & Vincent. Christine Tarantino. 22p. 1997. ring bd. 4.95 (1-887480-50-1) Wrds Lght Intl.

Love to Write! Activities to Sharpen Creative Writing Skills. Cindy Barden. Ed. by Judy Mitchell. (Illus.). 144p. (Orig.). (gr. 3-6). 1995. pap. 13.95 (1-57310-017-X) Teachng & Lrning Co.

Love Tokens. Tricia L. Vicedomine. (Illus.). 100p. 1998. 39.95 (0-9661413-2-6); pap. 24.95 (0-9661413-3-4) Series Script.

Love Tokens As Engraved Coins. Lloyd L. Entenmann. LC 91-92019. (Illus.). 250p. 1991. pap. 45.00 (0-9629326-0-4) L L Entenmann.

Love Too Beautiful. Manuel M. Mediero. Ed. by Martha T. Halsey. Tr. by Hazel Cazorla from SPA. LC 94-61737. (Contemporary Spanish Plays Ser.: Vol. 8).Tr. of Juana del Amor Hermoso. (Illus.). 80p. (Orig.). 1995. pap. 6.00 (0-9631212-7-8) Estreno.

***Love Took My Hand: The Spirituality of George Herbert.** Philip Sheldrake. LC 99-58742. 128p. 2000. pap. 10.95 (1-56101-179-7) Cowley Pubns.

Love Touch, Vol. 1. Jill Matthews. Ed. by John M. Spafford. (Illus.). 50p. (Orig.). 1996. pap. 3.95 (1-890538-00-0, Pulp Friction) Rhiannon Pubns.

Love Touch, Vol. 2. Jill Matthews. Ed. by John M. Spafford. (Illus.). 50p. (Orig.). 1996. pap. 3.95 (1-890538-01-9, Pulp Friction) Rhiannon Pubns.

Love Touch, Vol. 3. Jill Matthews. Ed. by John M. Spafford. (Illus.). 50p. (Orig.). 1996. pap. 3.95 (1-890538-02-7, Pulp Friction) Rhiannon Pubns.

Love Touch, Vol. 4. Jill Matthews. Ed. by John M. Spafford. (Illus.). 50p. (Orig.). 1996. pap. 3.95 (1-890538-03-5, Pulp Friction) Rhiannon Pubns.

Love Touch, Vol. 5. Jill Matthews. Ed. by John M. Spafford. (Illus.). 50p. (Orig.). 1996. pap. 3.95 (1-890538-04-3, Pulp Friction) Rhiannon Pubns.

Love Touch, Vol. 6. Jill Matthews. Ed. by John M. Spafford. (Illus.). 50p. (Orig.). 1996. pap. 3.95 (1-890538-05-1, Pulp Friction) Rhiannon Pubns.

Love Touch, Vol. 7. Jill Matthews. Ed. by John M. Spafford. (Illus.). 50p. (Orig.). 1996. pap. 3.95 (1-890538-06-X, Pulp Friction) Rhiannon Pubns.

Love Touch, Vol. 8. Jill Matthews. Ed. by John M. Spafford. (Illus.). 50p. (Orig.). 1996. pap. 3.95 (1-890538-07-8, Pulp Friction) Rhiannon Pubns.

Love Touch, Vol. 9. Jill Matthews. Ed. by John M. Spafford. (Illus.). 50p. (Orig.). 1996. pap. 3.95 (1-890538-08-6, Pulp Friction) Rhiannon Pubns.

Love Touch, Vol. 10. Jill Matthews. Ed. by John M. Spafford. (Illus.). 50p. (Orig.). 2000. pap. 3.95 (1-890538-09-4, Pulp Friction) Rhiannon Pubns.

Love Touch, Vol. 11. Jill Matthews. Ed. by John M. Spafford. (Illus.). 50p. (Orig.). 2000. pap. 3.95 (*1-890538-10-8*, Pulp Friction) Rhiannon Pubns.

Love Touch, Vol. 12. Jill Matthews. Ed. by John M. Spafford. (Illus.). 50p. (Orig.). 2000. pap. 3.95 (*1-890538-11-6*, Pulp Friction) Rhiannon Pubns.

Love Touch, Vol. 13. Jill Matthews. Ed. by John M. Spafford. (Illus.). 50p. (Orig.). 2000. pap. 3.95 (*1-890538-12-4*, Pulp Friction) Rhiannon Pubns.

Love Transcending in Reaction see Lay Counseling Series

Love Trauma Syndrome: Free Yourself from the Pain of a Broken Heart. R. B. Rosse. LC RC543.R67 1999. (Illus.). 305p. (C). 1999. 26.95 (*0-306-46006-8*, Pub. by Perseus Pubng) HarpC.

Love Treasures: "The Mother", Book One. Sri Aurobindo. (Illus.). 98p. 1985. 36.00 (*0-89071-333-2*, Pub. by SAA) Acrpls Bks CO.

Love Triangle. Pavlik. 48p. 1997. spiral bd. 7.81 (*0-07-292788-7*) McGraw.

***Love Triangle.** Joseph Testa. 2000. pap. 8.00 (*0-8059-4919-4*) Dorrance.

Love Triangle: Role Play Peacegames. David W. Felder. 48p. 1996. pap. text 8.95 (*0-910959-81-1*, B&G 16B) Wellington Pr.

Love Triangles. Rasul. 1998. pap. 12.95 (*1-890301-05-1*) M Bey.

Love Triumphs. Pearl Wood. 96p. 1997. pap. 7.99 (*0-8059-4097-9*) Dorrance.

Love Trouble. Jeffery M. Jones. (Sun & Moon Classics/American Theater in Literature Ser.: No. 78). 102p. (Orig.). 1994. pap. 10.95 (*1-55713-198-8*) Sun & Moon CA.

Love Trouble: New & Collected Work. Veronica Geng. Tr. by Ian Frazier. LC 98-47177. 312p. 1999. pap. 14.00 (*0-395-94557-7*) HM.

Love, Truth & Perception. Kathy Oddenino. 288p. (Orig.). (C). 1993. pap. 14.95 (*0-923081-03-8*) Joy Pubns MD.

Love Twin. Patty Salier. (Desire Ser.: No. 1121). 1998. per. 3.50 (*0-373-76121-X*, 1-76121-2) Silhouette.

***Love U Mama.** Mouseworks Staff. 10p. (J). 1999. bds. 6.99 (*1-57082-985-3*, Pub. by Mouse Works) Time Warner.

Love Uncut: Poems, 1986. Bill Kushner. 85p. 1990. pap. 6.00 (*0-935992-05-7*) United Art Bks.

Love under Cover. Justin Davis. (Silhouette Romance Ser.). 1998. 21.95 (*0-373-59923-4*) Silhouette.

***Love Undercover.** Tamara Sneed. 2000. mass mkt. 5.99 (*1-58314-142-1*) BET Bks.

Love Undetectable: Notes on Friendship, Sex, & Survival. Andrew Sullivan. LC 98-13502. 256p. 1998. 23.00 (*0-679-45119-6*) Knopf.

Love Undetectable: Notes on Friendship, Sex & Survival. Andrew Sullivan. 272p. 1999. pap. 13.00 (*0-679-77315-0*) Knopf.

Love Undone. 2nd ed. Pamela Irich. LC 97-97128. 295p. 1997. per. 15.00 (*0-9663794-0-3*) Aphrodite Bks.

Love Unlimited: Insights on Life & Love. Barry White & Marc Eliot. LC 99-32563. 256p. 1999. 23.00 (*0-7679-0364-1*) Broadway BDD.

Love Unmerited. Donna F. Crow. (Serenade Serenata Ser.: No. 38). 1986. pap. 1.49 (*0-310-47442-6*, 15590P) Zondervan.

Love Untangled. large type ed. Frances Peploe. (Linford Romance Library). 1989. pap. 16.99 (*0-7089-6789-2*, Linford) Ulverscroft.

Love Unwilling. Shirl Henke. 464p. (Orig.). 1987. mass mkt. 3.95 (*0-446-32306-3*, Pub. by Warner Bks) Little.

***Love upon the Throne.** Patrick Barlow. 1999. pap. 15.95 (*1-85459-421-4*, Pub. by Theatre Comm) Consort Bk Sales.

Love Valley: An American Utopia. Conrad E. Ostwalt. LC 98-23595. 202p. 1998. 45.95 (*0-87972-759-4*); pap. 21.95 (*0-87972-760-8*) Bowling Green Univ Popular Press.

Love! Valour! Compassion! Terrence McNally. 1995. pap. 5.25 (*0-8222-1467-9*) Dramatists Play.

Love! Valour! Compassion! & a Perfect Ganesh: Two Plays. Terrence McNally. (Orig.). 1997. pap. 12.95 (*0-452-27930-5*, Plume) Dutton Plume.

Love Verse. A. Alexander Volenski. LC 95-96144. 93p. (Orig.). 1995. pap. 16.95 (*0-9644554-6-3*) Alexander Pub.

Love Verse 96. A. Alexander Volenski. LC 96-96046. 96p. (Orig.). 1996. pap. 16.95 (*0-9644554-8-X*) Alexander Pub.

Love Vignettes. 2nd ed. Donald W. Murphy. LC 97-70957. 84p. 1997. pap. 11.95 (*0-9655599-2-0*) LaRena Pr.

Love Vignettes. 2nd rev. ed. Donald w. Murphy. v, 84p. 1997. 15.95 (*0-9655599-1-2*) LaRena Pr.

Love Vignettes: Poetry of Love & Light. Donald W. Murphy. LC 83-82452. 78p. 1982. 7.95 (*0-9655599-0-4*) LaRena Pr.

Love Virtue. Carl Japikse. 1999. pap. text 9.95 (*0-89804-087-6*) Ariel Prods.

Love, Virtues & Commandments: An Interfaith Perspective. Sajjad Haider. 156p. (C). 1997. pap. 12.95 (*0-934905-79-7*) Kazi Pubns.

***Love Virus: Why We Jump from Youthful Purpose to Mature Confusion.** Ted Borgeas. 100p. 2000. spiral bd. 9.95 (*0-9666110-3-9*) Age-Trott.

Love Visions. Geoffrey Chaucer. Tr. by Brian Stone. (Classics Ser.). 272p. 1983. pap. 11.95 (*0-14-044408-4*, Penguin Classics) Viking Penguin.

Love-Voices from the Heart. William J. Crockett. 15p. 1985. pap. text 3.00 (*0-934383-03-0*) Pride Prods.

Love vs. Illusion. M. J. Rodgers. (Intrigue Ser.). 1996. per. 3.75 (*0-373-22375-7*, 1-22375-9) Harlequin Bks.

Love Waits. Maureen E. Broderick. 256p. 1999. 25.00 (*0-9664483-6-7*); pap. write for info. (*0-9664483-5-9*) Baxter Bks.

Love Waits at Penrhyn. large type ed. Pat Phillips. LC 97-36278. (Candlelights Ser.). 217p. 1997. lib. bdg. 18.95 (*0-7862-1240-3*) Thorndike Pr.

Love Waits on Welcome: And Other Miracles. rev. ed. Corinne Edwards. 160p. 1997. 10.95 (*1-57789-001-9*) Crest Hse.

Love, War & Remembrance. Rosemarie Werkman. 1992. pap. 12.50 (*0-89824-524-9*) Lib Res.

Love, War, & the 96th Engineers (Colored) The World War II New Guinea Diaries of Captain Hyman Samuelson. Ed. by Gwendolyn Midlo Hall. LC 95-5729. (Illus.). 342p. 1995. 26.95 (*0-252-02179-7*) U of Ill Pr.

Love Warps the Mind a Little. John Dufresne. LC 97-39784. 336p. 1998. pap. 13.95 (*0-452-27898-8*) NAL.

Love Warps the Mind a Little. John Dufresne. LC 96-3112. 352p. 1997. 23.00 (*0-393-04013-5*) Norton.

Love Warps the Mind a Little. John Dufresne. 1998. pap. text. write for info. (*0-393-10166-5*) Norton.

Love Warps the Mind a Little. large type ed. John Dufresne. LC 97-9217. (Core Ser.). 553p. 1997. 26.95 (*0-7838-8127-4*, G K Hall Lrg Type) Mac Lib Ref.

Love Was Born at Christmas. Susan E. Luttrell. (Orig.). (J). (gr. k-4). 1981. pap. 3.50 (*0-89536-483-2*, 1234) CSS OH.

Love Was Waiting. Joyce H. Frost. (Wellspring Romance Ser.). 176p. (Orig.). 1987. pap. 4.95 (*0-9614712-2-0*) Wellspring Bks.

***Love Wears No Mask.** Johnnie Jammer. 352p. 2000. 14.95 (*1-56167-590-3*) Am Literary Pr.

***Love Whispers.** Swami Rama. 120p. 2000. pap. 13.95 (*0-89389-178-9*) Himalayan Inst.

Love Wild & Fair. Bertrice Small. 672p. 1978. mass mkt. 6.99 (*0-380-40030-8*, Avon Bks) Morrow Avon.

Love Will Find a Way: Poems for Soul Seekers. David Macy. 40p. 1999. pap. 3.95 (*0-9668443-3-5*) Macy Intl.

Love Will Have to Wait. large type ed. Michelle Grahame. (Linford Romance Large Print Ser.). 256p. 1998. pap. 17.99 (*0-7089-5251-8*, Linford) Ulverscroft.

Love Will Live & Other Selected Poems. Robert T. Rogers. Ed. & Frwd. by Claude Ware. (Illus.). 80p. 1995. pap. 8.00 (*0-9640995-1-9*) Mitram Bks.

***Love Wisdom: Hold a Question in Your Mind & Wherever You open This Book, There Will Be Your Answer.** Carolyn Temsi & Caro Handley. LC 99-40380. 128p. 1999. per. 10.00 (*0-671-03647-5*, PB Trade Paper) PB.

***Love with a Difference.** large type ed. Ruth Bridge. 272p. 1999. pap. 18.99 (*0-7089-5520-7*, Linford) Ulverscroft.

Love with a Few Hairs. Mohammed Mrabet. Tr. by Paul Bowles from ARA. 176p. 1986. reprint ed. pap. 8.95 (*0-87286-192-9*) City Lights.

Love with a Long, Tall Texan. Diana Palmer. 1999. per. 6.99 (*0-373-48379-1*) Harlequin Bks.

Love with a Stranger. Janelle Taylor. 480p. 1996. mass mkt. 6.99 (*0-8217-5416-5*, Zebra Kensgtn) Kensgtn Pub Corp.

***Love with a Stranger.** large type ed. Janelle Taylor. (G. K. Hall Romance Ser.). 2000. 28.95 (*0-7838-8973-9*, G K Hall Lrg Type) Mac Lib Ref.

Love with Honor. Loring. LC 98-29031. 1998. 24.95 (*0-7862-1628-X*) Thorndike Pr.

Love with the Proper Stranger. Suzanne Brockmann. (Intimate Moments Ser.: No. 831). 1998. per. 3.99 (*0-373-07831-5*, 1-07831-0) Silhouette.

Love with Your Eyes Open. Clement Renirkens. Tr. by Marc Lucas & Claudia Lucas from FRE. LC 85-28669. 145p. (Orig.). 1986. pap. 7.95 (*0-8189-0491-7*) Alba.

Love Within. Penelope Neri. 320p. 1997. mass mkt. 5.99 (*0-8217-5398-3*, Zebra Kensgtn) Kensgtn Pub Corp.

Love Without Conditions: Reflections of the Christ Mind. Paul Ferrini. (Reflections of the Christ Mind Ser.: Pt. 1). (Illus.). 177p. 1994. 12.00 (*1-879159-15-5*) Heartways Pr.

Love Without End. Beatrice A. Patton. (Illus.). 175p. (Orig.). 1987. pap. 10.00 (*0-914916-79-3*) Ku Paa.

"Love Without End" Jesus Speaks. Glenda Green. Ed. by Wanda Evans. LC 98-73963. 344p. 1999. pap. 18.95 (*0-9666623-1-8*) Heartwings Pubng.

Love Without Limits: Responsible Nonmonogamy & the Quest for Sustainable Intimate Relationships. Deborah Anapol. LC 91-77439. 192p. (Orig.). 1992. pap. 16.00 (*1-880789-06-X*) IntiNet Res Ctr.

Love Without Marrying. James L. Park. LC HQ728.P37 1996. (Love among Authentic Persons Ser.: No. 6). 1995. pap. 3.75 (*0-89231-506-7*) Existential Bks.

Love Without Measure: Extracts from the Writings of St. Bernard of Clairvaux. Paul Dimier. (Cistercian Studies: No. 127). 154p. 1990. pap. 10.95 (*0-87907-727-1*) Cistercian Pubns.

Love Without Pretense: Romans 12.9-21 & Hellenistic-Jewish Wisdom Literature. Walter T. Wilson. (Wissenschaftliche Untersuchungen Zum Neuen Testament Ser.: No. 2, Pt. 46). 264p. (Orig.). 1991. pap. 62.50 (*3-16-145756-0*, Pub. by JCB Mohr) Coronet Bks.

Love Without Reason. Alison Fraser. (Presents Ser.). 1994. per. 2.99 (*0-373-11675-6*, 1-11675-5) Harlequin Bks.

Love Without Reason. large type ed. Antonia Fraser. (Harlequin Ser.). 1994. lib. bdg. 19.95 (*0-263-13657-4*) Thorndike Pr.

Love Without Shame: Sexuality in Biblical Perspective. David B. Wyrtzen. LC 90-24576. 176p. (Orig.). 1991. pap. 10.99 (*0-929239-34-2*) Discovery Hse Pubs.

Love Without Wings: Some Friendships in Literature & Politics. Louis Auchincloss. 187p. 1999. reprint ed. pap. text 19.00 (*0-7881-6266-7*) DIANE Pub.

Love Won Out. John Paulk. LC 99-27731. 1999. 17.99 (*1-56179-783-9*) Focus Family.

***Love Won Out.** John Paulk & Anne Paulk. LC 99-27731. 1999. pap. 10.99 (*1-56179-816-9*) Focus Family.

Love Words: The Self & the Text in Medieval & Renaissance Poetry. Mariann S. Regan. LC 81-15126. 288p. 1982. text 39.95 (*0-8014-1415-6*) Cornell U Pr.

Love, Work, & Death: Jewish Life in Medieval Umbria. Ariel Toaff. Tr. by Judith Landry from ITA. LC 95-42748. (Illus.). 300p. 1996. text 55.00 (*1-874774-19-6*, Pub. by Littman Lib) Intl Spec Bk.

Love, Work & Death: Jewish Life in Medieval Umbria. Ariel Toaff. Tr. by Judith Landry from ITA. (Illus.). 308p. 1998. pap. 24.95 (*1-874774-33-1*, Pub. by Littman Lib) Intl Spec Bk.

***Love Workbook: A Guide to Happiness in Your Personal Relationships.** David R. Lima. 192p. 2000. pap., wbk. ed. 14.95 (*1-893733-00-9*, DL01, Pub. by Super Six) ACCESS Pubs Network.

***Love Worth Finding: King James Version, 100.** Adrian Rogers. 1999. pap. 8.75 (*5-553-91952-5*, Goodnews); pap. text 8.75 (*5-553-91960-6*, Goodnews) Black Bayou.

Love Ya: Meditations by Eleanor Rost. Eleanor Rost. iv, 98p. 1998. 14.95 (*0-9662189-0-6*) New Paradigms.

Love Ya Like a Sister: A Story of Friendship from the Journals of Katie Ouriou. Katie Ouriou. Ed. by Julie Johnston. 208p. (YA). (gr. 5 up). 1999. pap. 7.95 (*0-88776-454-1*) Tundra Bks.

Love Ye One Another. Lao Russell. 45p. 1996. pap. 2.00 (*1-879605-46-5*) U Sci & Philos.

Love Ye One Another: In Light, Love & Peace. Walter Spivey & Colleen Spivey. 342p. (Orig.). 1985. pap. 13.00 (*0-318-59206-1*) Coleman Pub.

Love You Can Touch: Gift Ideas That Show You Care. Jane Jarrell. LC 99-18850. (Illus.). 80p. 1999. pap. 12.99 (*0-7369-0159-0*) Harvest Hse.

Love you Deserve: Ten Keys to Perfect Love. M. Scott Peck. LC 97-94328. (Illus.). 270p. 1998. pap. 13.95 (*0-9659976-3-4*) Lifepath Pub.

Love You Forever see Siempre Te Querre

Love You Forever. Robert Munsch. (Illus.). 32p. (J). (gr. 4-10). 1986. 12.95 (*0-920668-36-4*); pap. 4.95 (*0-920668-37-2*) Firefly Bks Ltd.

***Love You Forever.** Robert Munsch. (Illus.). 32p. 2000. 17.95 (*1-55209-109-0*) Firefly Bks Ltd.

Love You Forever. Robert Munsch. 1986. 10.15 (*0-606-02470-0*, Pub. by Turtleback) Demco.

Love You Forever. deluxe ed. Robert Munsch. (Illus.). 32p. (J). 1995. boxed set 19.95 (*1-895565-66-9*) Firefly Bks Ltd.

Love You Forever: A Big Book. Robert Munsch. (Illus.). 32p. (J). (ps-3). 1994. pap. 19.95 (*1-895565-37-5*) Firefly Bks Ltd.

Love You Forever: (The Cowboy Club) Janice Kaiser. (Temptation Ser.: Vol. 702). 1998. per. 3.75 (*0-373-25802-X*, 1-25802-9) Harlequin Bks.

***Love You Leave Behind: Book One.** Stan Hill. LC 00-190546. 525p. 2000. 25.00 (*0-7388-1810-0*); pap. 18.00 (*0-7388-1811-9*) Xlibris Corp.

***Love You Leave Behind: Book Two.** Stan Hill. LC 00-190547. 477p. 2000. 25.00 (*0-7388-1812-7*); pap. 18.00 (*0-7388-1813-5*) Xlibris Corp.

Love You Like a Sister: Thirty Cool Rules for Making & Being a Better Best Friend. Camy Baker. 176p. (J). (gr. 3-8). 1998. pap. 3.99 (*0-553-48656-X*) Bantam.

***Love You Promised Me.** Silvia Molina. Tr. by David Unger from SPA. LC 99-27587. 152p. 1999. pap. 14.95 (*1-880684-62-4*, Pub. by Curbstone) SPD-Small Pr Dist.

Love You, Soldier. Amy Hest. 1993. 9.19 (*0-606-02730-0*, Pub. by Turtleback) Demco.

***Love You, Soldier.** Amy Hest & Sonja Lamut. LC 99-46874. (Illus.). 80p. (J). (gr. 3-7). 2000. 14.99 (*0-7636-0943-9*) Candlewick Pr.

Love You, Soldier. large type ed. Amy Hest. 1995. 13.50 (*0-614-09598-0*, L-34812-00) Am Printing Hse.

Love You to Bits & Pieces: Life with David Helfgott. Gillian Helfgott & Alissa Tanskaya. 1997. pap. 11.95 (*0-14-026644-5*, Penguin Bks) Viking Penguin.

Love You to Death. Eileen Goudge. 1999. pap. 3.50 (*0-14-036079-4*, Viking) Viking Penguin.

Love You to Death. Grant Michaels. LC 92-37742. (Stonewall Inn Mysteries Ser.). 1993. text 8.95 (*0-312-08841-8*) St Martin.

Love You to Death, Darling. Wensley Clarkson. 1996. mass mkt. 4.99 (*1-85782-012-6*, Pub. by Blake Publng) Seven Hills Bk.

Love You to Pieces. J. R. Sansevere & Erica Farber. (Illus.). (J). 1997. pap. 6.99 (*0-679-88709-1*, Pub. by Random Bks Yng Read) Random.

Love You Until... Lisa McCourt. LC 98-32045. (Illus.). 32p. (J). (gr. k-2). 1999. 16.95 (*0-8091-6658-5*) Paulist Pr.

Love, Your Bear Pete. Dyan Sheldon. LC 93-2883. (Illus.). 32p. (J). (ps-3). 1996. reprint ed. pap. 5.99 (*1-56402-968-9*) Candlewick Pr.

Love Your Body. Louise L. Hay. 128p. 1998. pap. 7.00 (*1-56170-602-7*, 880) Hay House.

Love Your Body. Viktoras Kulvinskas. (Illus.). 94p. (Orig.). 1972. pap. text 9.95 (*0-933278-01-2*) Twen Fir Cent.

Love Your Body: A Guide to Transforming Body Language. Lisa Licavoli & Tami Brannon. LC 96-86301. 200p. (Orig.). 1996. pap. 12.50 (*1-57502-304-0*, P01043) Morris Pubng.

Love Your Body: A Positive Affirmation Guide for Loving & Appreciating Your Body! rev. ed. Louise L. Hay. LC 89-84644. 112p. 1995. pap. 5.00 (*0-937611-66-2*, 103A) Hay House.

Love Your Body, Stay Healthy: Mini Page Resource Book. Betty Debnam. (Illus.). 32p. (J). 1994. pap. 4.95 (*0-8362-4321-8*) Andrews & McMeel.

Love Your Brother, Love Your Neighbor. Khurram Murad. 32p. (J). 1996. pap. 3.50 (*0-614-21026-7*, 740) Kazi Pubns.

Love Your Cat. Elizabeth Loonan. 93p. 1994. write for info. (*1-57215-006-8*) World Pubns.

Love Your Disease: It's Keeping You Healthy! John Harrison. LC 88-82395. 416p. (Orig.). 1988. reprint ed. pap. 12.95 (*0-937611-36-0*, 109) Hay House.

Love Your Dog. Sheila Buff. 93p. 1994. write for info. (*1-57215-005-X*) World Pubns.

Love Your Enemies. F.C.D.T. Trustees Staff. 1989. pap. write for info. (*1-887621-24-5*) Found Ch Divine Truth.

Love Your Enemies: Discipleship, Pacifism, & Just War Theory. Lisa S. Cahill. LC 93-35461. 288p. 1994. pap. 20.00 (*0-8006-2700-8*, 1-2700, Fortress Pr) Augsburg Fortress.

Love Your Enemy. Ellen James. (Romance Ser.: No. 202). 1992. per. 2.89 (*0-373-03202-1*, 1-03202-8) Harlequin Bks.

Love Your Fat Away. Ali Guggenheim. 1991. write for info. (*0-9628958-0-6*) Guggenheim CA.

Love Your God. Khurram Murad. 36p. (J). 1996. pap. 3.50 (*0-614-21027-5*, 741) Kazi Pubns.

Love Your God with All Your Mind: The Role of Reason in the Life of the Soul. James P. Moreland. LC 97-2300. 249p. (Orig.). 1997. pap. 14.00 (*1-57683-016-0*) NavPress.

Love Your Job! Loving the Job You Have . . . Finding a Job You Love. Paul Powers & Deborah Russell. (Illus.). 210p. (Orig.). 1993. pap. 12.95 (*1-56592-036-8*) Thomson Learn.

Love Your Neighbor: Stories of Values & Virtues. Arthur Dobrin. LC 97-44212. (Illus.). 64p. (J). (ps-3). 1999. 16.95 (*0-590-04410-9*) Scholastic Inc.

Love Your Neighbor As Yourself: Blessing Your Neighborhood Through Love & Prayer. 2nd rev. ed. Mary L. Sisk. Ed. by Teresa T. Gillis. (Illus.). 60p. 1998. pap. 5.00 (*0-9664295-1-6*) M L V Sisk.

Love Your Neighbor to Life. 1994. pap. 3.95 (*0-87162-455-9*) Warner Pr.

Love Your Neighbour: A Woman's Workshop on Fellowship. Lawrence O. Richards. (Woman's Workshop Ser.). 160p. (Orig.). 1981. pap. 2.95 (*0-310-43451-3*, 18139P) Zondervan.

Love Your Work. David McKenna. 168p. 1990. pap. text 7.99 (*0-89693-036-X*, Victor Bks) Chariot Victor.

Love Your Work, Love Your Life: What Would You Like to Be When You Grow Up. 2nd ed. Pam Gross. 200p. 1999. pap. 12.95 (*1-893075-05-2*) Spirit Pr OR.

Love Yourself. J. B. Livingston. 1972. 4.95 (*0-89137-421-3*) Quality Pubns.

Love Yourself, Heal Your Life Workbook. Louise L. Hay. (SPA.). 189p. pap. 12.95 (*84-86344-91-3*, 141) Hay House.

Love Yourself, Heal Your Life Workbook. Louise L. Hay. Ed. by Glenn Kolb. LC 90-35636. 169p. 1990. pap., wbk. ed. 12.95 (*0-937611-69-7*, 117) Hay House.

Love Yourself, So . . . Hate the Weight! 100 Practical Tips That Really Work - You Can Feel Better, Look Better, Even Be Better. Brother Craig. LC 96-34357. (Illus.). 128p. (Orig.). 1996. pap. 9.95 (*0-88007-215-6*) Woodbridge Pr.

Love Yourself Thin: The Revolutionary Spiritual Approach to Weight Loss. Victoria Moran. 352p. 1999. mass mkt. 6.99 (*0-451-19721-6*, Sig) NAL.

Love Yourself Thin: The Revolutionary Spiritual Approach to Weight Loss. Victoria Moran. LC 97-15793. (Illus.). 256p. 1997. text 19.95 (*0-87596-461-3*) Rodale Pr Inc.

Love, Zena Beth. Diane Salvatore. LC 92-12741. 224p. 1992. 18.95 (*1-56280-015-9*) Naiad Pr.

Love, Zena Beth. Diane Salvatore. 224p. 1993. reprint ed. pap. 10.95 (*1-56280-030-2*) Naiad Pr.

Loveable Katie Lovewell. Emma Goldrick. 1993. per. 2.89 (*0-373-11520-2*, 1-11520-3) Harlequin Bks.

Loveable Katie Lovewell. large type ed. Emma Goldrick. (Harlequin Ser.). 1992. reprint ed. 18.95 (*0-263-12988-8*) Mac Lib Ref.

Lovebird. Pamela L. Higdon. LC 97-14731. (Owner's Guide to a Happy, Healthy Pet Ser.). 1997. write for info. (*0-08-760543-0*) Howell Bks.

Lovebird: An Owner's Guide to a Happy Healthy Pet. Pam Higdon. LC 97-14731. 126p. 1997. 12.95 (*0-87605-430-0*) Macmillan.

Lovebirds: Everything about Housing, Care, Nutrition, Breeding, & Diseases: with a Special Chapter, Understanding Lovebirds. 2nd ed. Matthew M. Vriends. LC 95-18372. (Complete Pet Owner's Manual Ser.). (Illus.). 1995. pap. 6.95 (*0-8120-9014-4*) Barron.

Lovebirds: International Edition. Janet Quin-Harkin. (YA). 1994. pap. 3.50 (*0-553-24181-8*) Bantam.

Lovebirds As a Hobby. Kenny Le Breton. (TT Ser.). (Illus.). 96p. 1992. pap. 8.95 (*0-86622-411-4*, TT011) TFH Pubns.

Lovebirds As a New Pet. Oliver Denton. (Illus.). 64p. (Orig.). 1990. pap. 6.95 (*0-86622-617-6*, TU-009) TFH Pubns.

Lovebirds Today. Karl-Herbert Delpy. (Illus.). 64p. 1996. 12.95 (*0-7938-0118-4*, WW021) TFH Pubns.

Lovebirds Today: A Complete & Up-to-Date Guide. Karl-Herbert Deply & American Society for the Prevention of Cruelty to. LC 97-3626. (Basic Domestic Pet Library). 76p. (J). (gr. 3 up). 1997. 19.95 (*0-7910-4614-1*) Chelsea Hse.

Lovechild. Metsy Hingle. (Desire Ser.). 1997. per. 3.50 (*0-373-76055-8*, 1-76055-2) Silhouette.

Lovecraft: A Study in the Fantastic. Maurice Levy. Tr. by S. T. Joshi from FRE. LC 87-36470. 148p. 1988. 31.95 (*0-8143-1955-6*); pap. 16.95 (*0-8143-1956-4*) Wayne St U Pr.

Lovecraft: Disturbing the Universe. Donald R. Burleson. LC 90-37366. 184p. 1990. text 24.95 (*0-8131-1728-3*) U Pr of Ky.

Lovecraft Lexicon: A Dictionary of People & Places in Lovecraft's Novels. Anthony B. Pearsall. LC 97-65816. 288p. 2000. pap. 16.95 (*1-56184-129-3*) New Falcon Pubns.

Lovecraft Remembered. Ed. by Peter Cannon. LC 98-43006. (Illus.). 489p. 1998. 29.95 (*0-87054-173-0*) Arkham.

Lovecraft's Legacy: A Centennial Celebration of H. P. Lovecraft. Ed. by Robert E. Weinberg & Martin H. Greenberg. 352p. 1996. pap. 13.95 (*0-312-86140-0*, Pub. by Tor Bks) St Martin.

Loved & Lost: The Journey Through Dying, Death, & Bereavement. John Quinlan. LC 96-8727. 108p. (Orig.). 1997. pap. text 9.95 (*0-8146-2439-1*, Liturg Pr Bks) Liturgical Pr.

Loved & the Envied. Enid Bagnold. LC 75-110820. 276p. 1970. reprint ed. lib. bdg. 38.50 (*0-8371-2700-9*, BALE, Greenwood Pr) Greenwood.

Loved & the Unloved. Thomas H. Phillips. LC 97-42205. 260p. 1998. pap. 17.00 (*1-57806-056-7*, Banner Bk) U Pr of Miss.

Loved by Angels: Angels Are Right Beside Us . . . Sabrina Fox. LC 98-16736.Tr. of Wie Engel Uns Lieben. 272p. 1999. pap. 14.95 (*1-885394-32-2*) Bluestar Communs.

Loved Dead. H. P. Lovecraft. 224p. 1997. mass mkt. 4.95 (*0-7867-0445-4*) Carroll & Graf.

Loved One. Evelyn Waugh. lib. bdg. 20.95 (*1-56723-177-2*) Yestermorrow.

***Loved One.** large type ed. Evelyn Waugh. LC 99-46177. (Perennial Bestsellers Ser.). 1999. 27.95 (*0-7838-8787-6*, G K Hall & Co) Mac Lib Ref.

Loved One. Evelyn Waugh. 1994. reprint ed. lib. bdg. 27.95 (*1-56849-358-4*) Buccaneer Bks.

Loved One. rev. ed. Evelyn Waugh. LC 77-88216. (Illus.). 164p. 1977. pap. 13.95 (*0-316-92608-6*, Back Bay) Little.

Loveday. large type ed. Barbara Whitnell. 576p. 1992. 11.50 (*0-7089-8610-2*, Charnwood) Ulverscroft.

Lovedeath. Dan Simmons. 384p. 1994. reprint ed. mass mkt. 5.99 (*0-446-60077-6*, Pub. by Warner Bks) Little.

Lovegram. 1994. pap. 59.88 (*0-7860-8873-7*) Kensgtn Pub Corp.

Lovegram. 1995. pap. 79.84 (*0-7860-8874-5*) Kensgtn Pub Corp.

Lovehuman: How to Be Who You Love. Betsy O. Thompson. LC 91-71181. (Orig.). 1992. pap. 9.95 (*1-879023-06-7*) Ascension Pub.

Lovejoy's College Guide. 23rd ed. C. T. Straughton & B. S. Lovejoy. 1600p. 1998. 50.00 incl. cd-rom (*0-02-862489-0*) Macmillan.

Lovejoy's College Guide. 25th ed. C. T. Straughton & B. S. Lovejoy. 1600p. 1998. 25.95 incl. cd-rom (*0-02-862488-2*) Macmillan.

Lovejoy's College Guide 1998. 24th ed. Charles T. Straughn, II & Barbarasue L. Straughn. 1557p. 1997. pap. 25.95 incl. 3.5 ld (*0-02-861689-8*, Arc) IDG Bks.

Lovejoy's College Guide 1998. 24th ed. Charles T. Straughn, II & Barbarasue L. Straughn. 1557p. 1997. pap. 50.00 (*0-02-861687-1*, Arco) Macmillan Gen Ref.

Lovejoy's Guide to Graduate Programs in Engineering & Computer Science. Wintergreen Orchard House Staff. LC 97-116438. 496p. pap. 24.95 (*0-02-861317-1*, Arco) Macmillan Gen Ref.

Lovejoy's Guide to Graduate Programs in Engineering & Computer Science. 2nd ed. Wintergreen. 432p. 1998. pap. 22.95 (*0-02-862039-9*, Arco) Macmillan Gen Ref.

Lovejoy's Guide to Graduate Programs in the Biological Sciences. Wintergreen. 432p. 1998. pap. 22.95 (*0-02-862041-0*, Arco) Macmillan Gen Ref.

Lovejoy's Guide to Graduate Programs in the Humanities & Social Sciences. 2nd ed. Wintergreen. 608p. 1998. pap. text 22.95 (*0-02-862040-2*, Arco) Macmillan Gen Ref.

Lovejoy's Guide to Graduate Programs in the Humanities Arts & Social Science. Wintergreen Orchard House Staff. LC 97-112120. 496p. 1996. 21.95 (*0-02-861316-3*, Arco) Macmillan Gen Ref.

Lovejoy's Shortcuts & Strategies for the LSAT. Charles E. Kohlhase. 1985. pap. 7.95 (*0-685-09990-3*) S&S Trade.

Loveknot. Marisa Carroll. (Tyler Ser.: No. 12). 1999. mass mkt. 3.99 (*0-373-82512-9*, 0-82512-5) Harlequin Bks.

Loveland. Jane Alexander. 288p. 1998. pap. 4.99 (*0-7860-0556-4*, Pinncle Kensgtn) Kensgtn Pub Corp.

Loveland: Constitutional Law - a Critical Introduction. Ian Loveland. 1996. pap. write for info. (*0-406-04968-8*, LCLC, MICHIE) LEXIS Pub.

Loveland Pass - Idaho Springs - Georgetown, CO. rev. ed. Ed. by Trails Illustrated Staff. (Illus.). 1996. 8.99 (*0-925873-25-X*) Trails Illustrated.

Lovelaw: Love, Sex, & Marriage Around the World. Anthony Clare. (Illus.). 200p. 1988. pap. 14.95 (*0-563-20412-5*, Pub. by BBC) Parkwest Pubns.

Loveless Fables. Camilo Jose Cela. 1994. 19.95 (*0-02-523330-0*) Macmillan.

Loveless Marriage. Barbara Cartland. (Camfield Ser.: No. 139). 176p. 1995. mass mkt. 3.99 (*0-515-11572-X*, Jove) Berkley Pub.

Loveless Marriage. large type ed. Barbara Cartland. LC 97-32590. 220p. 1998. 19.95 (*0-7838-1893-9*, G K Hall Lrg Type) Mac Lib Ref.

Lovelet Kingdom. Glenda Walker & Leah Adriana. (Illus.). 45p. (J). (gr. 5-7). 1999. pap. 7.95 (*0-7392-0039-9*, PO2808) Morris Pubng.

Lovelich's Romance of Merlin, Pt. II. Ed. by Ernst A. Kock. (EETS ES Ser.: No. 112). 1969. reprint ed. pap. 30.00 (*0-8115-4844-9*) Periodicals Srv.

Loveliest to Me. Alice H. Yoder. (Illus.). 68p. (Orig.). 1989. reprint ed. pap. 5.95 (*0-9620651-2-0*) Grace Oregon.

Lovelife: Entries. 3rd rev. ed. Virge MacLeod. 435p. 1996. pap. write for info. (*0-9610402-1-1*) Solus Impress.

Lovelines for a Goat-Born Lady. John Agard. LC 90-60288. (Illus.). 80p. (Orig.). 1991. pap. 12.95 (*1-85242-201-7*) Serpents Tail.

Loveliness of Christ. Samuel Rutherford. 54p. 1990. 3.00 (*1-882840-04-6*) Comm Christian.

Lovelink. Tess N. Kimber. (Rainbow Romances Ser.: No. 890). 160p. 1994. 14.95 (*0-7090-4953-6*) Parkwest Pubns.

Lovelink. large type ed. Tess N. Kimber. (Linford Romance Library). 256p. 1995. pap. 16.99 (*0-7089-7676-X*, Linford) Ulverscroft.

Lovell & Winter's Pediatric Orthopaedics. 5th ed. Raymond T. Morrissy & Stuart L. Weinstein. 1552p. text. write for info. (*0-7817-2580-1*); text. write for info. (*0-7817-2581-X*); text 275.00 (*0-7817-2582-8*) Lppncott W & W.

Lovell & Winter's Pediatric Orthopaedics, 2 vols., Set. 4th ed. Ed. by Raymond T. Morrissy & Stuart L. Weinstein. LC 95-31125. 1334p. 1995. text 293.00 (*0-397-51397-6*) Lppncott W & W.

Lovell & Winter's Pediatric Orthopaedics, Vol. 1. Ed. by Raymond T. Morrissy & Stuart L. Weinstein. LC 95-31125. 1995. write for info. (*0-397-51598-7*) Lppncott W & W.

Lovell & Winter's Pediatric Orthopaedics, Vol. 2. Ed. by Raymond T. Morrissy & Stuart L. Weinstein. LC 95-31125. 1995. write for info. (*0-397-51599-5*) Lppncott W & W.

Lovell. Biographical Genealogy of the Lovell Family in England & America. L. Rhodes & T. G. Rhodes. 219p. 1998. reprint ed. pap. 33.50 (*0-8328-9677-2*); reprint ed. lib. bdg. 43.50 (*0-8328-9676-4*) Higginson Bk Co.

***Lovell Legend.** Alonda Cyrkozuch. LC 99-93969. (Illus.). 28p. (J). (ps-12). 1999. pap. 5.95 (*1-929098-00-6*, 01) Stry Teller.

Lovell White Durrant: Guide to Corporation Tax. Elaine M. Davies. 307p. 1995. pap. 50.00 (*1-85941-037-5*, Pub. by Cavendish Pubng) Gaunt.

Lovelock. Orson Scott Card & Kathryn H. Kidd. 320p. 1995. 5.99 (*0-8125-1805-5*, Pub. by Tor Bks) St Martin.

Lovelock Cave. fac. ed. Llewellyn L. Loud & M. R. Harrington. (University of California Publications in American Archaeology & Ethnology: Vol. 25: 1). (Illus.). 259p. (C). 1929. reprint ed. pap. text 27.50 (*1-55567-026-1*) Coyote Press.

Lovelorn Lady. large type ed. Jeanne Bowman. 272p. 1992. pap. 16.99 (*0-7089-7133-4*, Linford) Ulverscroft.

Lovely Ambition. Mary E. Chase. 1960. 5.95 (*0-393-08477-9*) Norton.

Lovely Are the Messengers. Daniel Plasman. LC 98-61617. 203p. 1998. pap. 12.95 (*1-881636-36-4*) Windsor Hse Pub Grp.

Lovely Country. Lawton. 1996. pap. 12.00 (*0-15-600466-6*) Harcourt.

Lovely Country: A Novel. David Lawton. 288p. 1995. 22.00 (*0-15-100171-5*) Harcourt.

Lovely Cross Stitch Designs. Nihon Vogue Staff. (Illus.). 84p. (Orig.). 1983. pap. 11.95 (*0-87040-529-2*) Japan Pubns USA.

Lovely Day. large type ed. Barbara Redmayne. (Romance Ser.). 320p. 1988. 27.99 (*0-7089-1747-X*) Ulverscroft.

Lovely Embroidery Patterns. Ondori Publishing Company Staff. LC 79-66301. (Illus.). 1980. pap. 13.95 (*0-87040-465-2*) Japan Pubns USA.

***Lovely in Her Bones.** Sharyn McCrumb. 1999. 5.99 (*0-345-91574-7*) Ballantine Pub Grp.

Lovely in Her Bones. J. Jill Robinson. 188p. 1993. per. 12.95 (*0-88978-260-1*, Pub. by Arsenal Pulp) LPC InBook.

***Lovely in Her Bones.** large type ed. Sharyn McCrumb. LC 00-22871. 2000. pap. 22.95 (*1-56895-859-5*) Wheeler Pub.

Lovely in Her Bones. Sharyn McCrumb. 224p. 1999. reprint ed. mass mkt. 5.99 (*0-345-36035-4*) Ballantine Pub Grp.

Lovely Laces: Crochet, Knit & Tat. Workbasket Magazine Staff. (Illus.). 80p. 1994. pap. 9.95 (*0-86675-306-0*) KC Pub.

Lovely Lady. Mary H. Austin. (Collected Works of Mary Hunter Austin). 272p. 1998. reprint ed. lib. bdg. 88.00 (*1-58201-525-2*) Classic Bks.

Lovely Lady. D. H. Lawrence. LC 77-38721. (Short Story Index Reprint Ser.). 1977. reprint ed. 15.95 (*0-8369-4134-9*) Ayer.

Lovely Lady Dressed in Blue (Bella Dama Vestida en Azul) And the Knights of Our Lady (Los Caballeros de Nuestra Senora) Joan A. Bell et al. Tr. by Carmen A. Emmanuelli Klosterman. (Stories of the Faith Ser.). (ENG & SPA., Illus.). 60p. (gr. k-10). 1994. pap. 9.95 (*1-889733-01-6*, 01003) Precious Life Bks.

Lovely Me: The Life of Jacqueline Susann. 2nd ed. Barbara Seaman. LC 96-30736. 480p. 1996. pap. 14.95 (*1-888363-37-1*) Seven Stories.

Lovely Mover: A Harpur & Iles Mystery. Bill James. LC 99-11489. (Harpur & Iles Mysteries Ser.). 264p. 1999. 23.00 (*0-393-04763-6*, Foul Play) Norton.

***Lovely Mover: A Harpur & Iles Mystery.** Bill James. (Harpur & Iles Mysteries Ser.). 272p. 2000. pap. 7.95 (*0-393-32034-0*) Norton.

Lovely Mover: A Harpur & Iles Mystery. large type ed. Bill James. LC 98-44505. Date not set. 30.00 (*0-7862-1680-8*) Thorndike Pr.

Lovely Peggy: A Play in Three Acts Based on the Love Romance of Margaret Woffington & David Garrick. J. R. Crawford. 1911. 49.50 (*0-686-51412-2*) Elliots Bks.

Lovely Reed: An Enthusiast's Guide to Building Bamboo Fly Rods. Jack Howell. LC 97-51371. (Illus.). 191p. 1998. 50.00 (*0-87108-868-1*) Pruett.

Lovely Shadow. large type ed. Ursula Bloom. (Lythway Ser.). 265p. 1992. 15.95 (*0-7451-1613-2*, G K Hall Lrg Type) Mac Lib Ref.

Lovely Sunday for Creve Coeur. Tennessee Williams. LC 79-20589. 1980. pap. 8.95 (*0-8112-0757-9*, NDP497, Pub. by New Directions) Norton.

Lovely Tale of Photography. Peter Nadas. 120p. 1999. pap. 14.50 (*80-902171-6-8*, Pub. by Twisted Spoon) SPD-Small Pr Dist.

Lovely Treachery of Words: Essays Selected & New. Robert Kroetsch. 216p. 1989. pap. text 24.95 (*0-19-540694-X*) OUP.

Lovemaking: A No-Nonsense Practical Solution. Diana Piacere & Nicholas Piacere. 64p. 1992. pap. 9.95 (*0-9640117-0-0*) InFour Grp.

***Lovemap Guidebook.** John Money. LC 99-28248. 300p. 1999. 39.50 (*0-8264-1203-3*) Continuum.

Lovemaps: Clinical Concepts of Sexual-Erotic Health & Pathology, Paraphilia & Gender Transposition in Childhood, Adolescence & Maturity. John Money. LC 85-24153. (Illus.). 350p. (C). 1986. 34.50 (*0-8290-1589-2*) Irvington.

Lovemaps: Clinical Concepts of Sexual-Erotic Health & Pathology, Paraphilia & Gender Transposition in Childhood, Adolescence & Maturity. John Money. LC 85-24153. 351p. 1986. pap. 19.95 (*0-87975-456-7*) Prometheus Bks.

Lovemaps: Clinical Concepts of Sexual-Erotic Health & Pathology, Paraphilia & Gender Transposition in Childhood, Adolescence & Maturity. John Money. LC 85-24153. (Illus.). 350p. (C). 1989. reprint ed. pap. 18.95 (*0-8290-1892-1*) Irvington.

Lovenotes: Music for the Unborn Child. Lorna Zemke. 1989. teacher ed. 89.95 incl. audio, VHS (*0-9625034-1-X*) Silver Lake Col Pr.

LoveNotes for Lovers: Words That Make Music for Two Hearts Dancing! Larry James. LC 95-92143. 216p. (Orig.). 1995. pap. 9.95 (*1-881558-03-7*) Career Assurance.

***Loveonline.com: The Story of an Email Romance.** Niamh McAnally. 191p. 1999. pap. 8.00 (*0-9673237-1-1*) Keenore Pubg.

Loveparent: How to Be the Parent You Hope to Be. Betsy O. Thompson. LC 90-82467. (Orig.). 1991. pap. 8.95 (*1-879023-08-3*) Ascension Pub.

Loveplay. Conrad Bishop & Elizabeth Fuller. 90p. (Orig.). 1993. pap. 5.00 (*0-9624511-1-8*) WordWorkers.

Lovepoems. Penny Harter. (Illus.). 72p. (Orig.). 1981. pap. 4.95 (*0-89120-016-9*, Old Plate) From Here.

Lover. Carter Brown. 1980. mass mkt. 1.75 (*0-451-09121-3*, E9121, Sig) NAL.

Lover. Marguerite Duras. LC 99-166709. 1998. pap. 10.00 (*0-375-70052-8*) Random.

Lover. Nicole Jordan. 384p. (Orig.). 1997. mass mkt. 5.99 (*0-380-78560-9*, Avon Bks) Morrow Avon.

Lover. Harold Pinter. 1965. pap. 3.25 (*0-8222-0704-4*) Dramatists Play.

***Lover.** Robin Schone. 384p. 2000. pap. text 12.00 (*1-57566-570-0*) Kensgtn Pub Corp.

Lover. Abraham B. Yehoshua. Tr. by Philip Simpson. 368p. 1993. pap. 14.00 (*0-15-653912-8*, Harvest Bks) Harcourt.

Lover. Harriet Zinnes. LC 89-862. 160p. (Orig.). 1988. pap. 9.95 (*0-918273-46-3*) Coffee Hse.

Lover. Bertha Harris. (Cutting Edge: Lesbian Life & Literature Ser.). 320p. (C). 1993. reprint ed. text 45.00 (*0-8147-3504-5*); reprint ed. pap. text 16.50 (*0-8147-3505-3*) NYU Pr.

Lover & a Friend. Beatrice Joyner. 1999. pap. write for info. (*0-9659035-3-2*) Busy As A Bea.

Lover & Deceiver. Beverly Barton. (Intimate Moments Ser.). 1994. per. 3.50 (*0-373-07557-X*, 5-07557-7) Silhouette.

Lover & the Beloved: A Way of Franciscan Prayer. John M. Talbot. 123p. 1994. reprint ed. pap. 8.00 (*1-883803-04-7*) Troubadour Lord.

Lover Awaits: Seven Sins. Patricia Rosemoor. 1998. per. 3.99 (*0-373-22499-0*, 1-22499-7, Mira Bks) Harlequin Bks.

Lover Betrayed. large type ed. Vivian Stuart. (Linford Romance Library). 1988. pap. 10.95 (*0-7089-6476-1*, Linford) Ulverscroft.

Lover Boy. Leila Davis. 176p. 1989. pap. 2.95 (*0-380-75722-2*, Avon Bks) Morrow Avon.

***Lover by Deception.** large type ed. Penny Jordan. 1999. 21.95 (*0-263-16206-0*, Pub. by Mills & Boon) Ulverscroft.

***Lover by Deception: Sweet Revenge/Seduction.** Penny Jordan. (Harlequin Presents Ser.). 1999. mass mkt. 3.75 (*0-373-12068-0*, Harlequin) Harlequin Bks.

Lover for a Night see Amante de una Noche

Lover in Pursuit. Stephanie James. (Promo Ser.). 1999. per. 4.50 (*0-373-80668-X*, 1-80668-6) Harlequin Bks.

Lover in the Rough. Elizabeth Lowell. 320p. 1994. mass mkt. 6.99 (*0-380-76760-0*, Avon Bks) Morrow Avon.

Lover in the Shadows. Lindsay Longford. (Shadows Ser.). 1994. per. 3.50 (*0-373-27029-1*, 5-27029-3) Silhouette.

Lover, Is This Exile? Robert Gibbons. 1989. pap. 10.00 (*0-911623-07-8*) I Klang.

Lover Man. Dallas Murphy. 1988. pap. 4.99 (*0-671-66188-4*) PB.

Lover of Horses. Tess Gallagher. 192p. 1992. pap. 12.95 (*1-55597-160-1*) Graywolf.

Lover of My Soul. Hanan Hamada. LC 98-60752. 176p. 1998. pap. 10.99 (*1-57921-122-4*, Pub. by WinePress Pub) BookWorld.

Lover of My Soul: A Search for Ecstasy & Wisdom. Perry Brass. Ed. by Tom Laine. LC 97-73677. (Illus.). 96p. (Orig.). 1997. pap. 8.95 (*0-9627123-8-8*) Belhue Pr.

Lover of My Soul: Delighting in God's Passionate Love. Alan S. Wright. LC 98-18707. 192p. 1998. pap. 12.99 (*1-57673-269-X*) Multnomah Pubs.

Lover of Truth: A Health Novel (1923) Marie Winchell Walker. 198p. 1998. reprint ed. pap. 17.95 (*0-7661-0481-8*) Kessinger Pub.

***Lover, Stranger: A Memory Away . . .** Amanda Stevens. 1999. per. 3.99 (*0-373-22511-3*, 1-22511-9) Harlequin Bks.

Lover under Cover (Trinity Street West) Justine Davis. LC 96-7309. (Intimate Moments Ser.). 250p. 1996. per. 3.99 (*0-373-07698-3*, 1-07698-3) Silhouette.

Lover Unknown. Shawna Delacorte. (Lawman Ser.). 1997. per. 3.75 (*0-373-22413-3*, 1-22413-8) Harlequin Bks.

Lover Within: Accessing the Lover in the Male Psyche. Robert Moore & Douglas Gillette. 288p. 1995. pap. 12.50 (*0-380-72071-X*, Avon Bks) Morrow Avon.

Lover Within: Opening to Energy in Sexual Practice. Julie Henderson. Ed. by George Quasha. LC 86-30066. (Illus.). 118p. 1987. 18.95 (*0-88268-023-4*) Station Hill Pr.

***Lover Within: Opening to Energy in Sexual Practice.** 2nd rev. ed. Julie Henderson. LC 98-28526. 144p. 1998. pap. 13.95 (*1-58177-017-0*, Pub. by Barrytown Ltd) Consort Bk Sales.

***Loverboy.** (Rock & Pop Classics: Vol. 18). (Illus.). 30p. 2000. write for info. (*1-892207-47-8*) Intl Masters Pub.

Loverboy. R. G. Belsky. LC 96-27120. 1997. mass mkt. 23.00 (*0-380-97439-8*, Avon Bks) Morrow Avon.

Loverboy. R. G. Belsky. 352p. 1998. mass mkt. 6.50 (*0-380-79068-8*, Avon Bks) Morrow Avon.

Loverboy. Vicki L. Thompson. (Temptation Ser.). 1994. per. 2.99 (*0-373-25584-5*, 1-25584-3) Harlequin Bks.

Loverboys. Ana Castillo. LC 96-29904. 224p. 1997. pap. 11.95 (*0-452-27773-6*, Plume) Dutton Plume.

Loverboys. Ana Castillo. 220p. 1996. 21.00 (*0-393-03959-5*) Norton.

Loveroot. Erica Jong. LC 74-15483. 89p. 1995. 4.95 (*0-03-014046-3*) H Holt & Co.

Lovers. Brian Friel. 1968. pap. 5.95 (*0-87129-245-9*, L34) Dramatic Pub.

Lovers. Judith Krantz. 544p. 1995. mass mkt. 7.99 (*0-553-56135-9*) Bantam.

Lovers. Heather Macauley. 96p. (Orig.). (C). 1996. pap. 9.95 (*0-9648093-7-0*) HOME Pubng.

Lovers. Rod McKuen. (Orig.). 1982. pap. 2.95 (*0-671-43615-5*) PB.

Lovers. Valerie Sherwood. 1991. 20.00 (*0-7278-4211-0*) Severn Hse.

Lovers. Padraig Standun. 162p. (Orig.). 1991. pap. 10.95 (*1-85371-166-7*, Pub. by Poolbeg Pr) Dufour.

Lovers. Linda Sunshine. (Illus.). 204p. 1998. text 27.00 (*0-7881-5950-X*) DIANE Pub.

Lovers. large type ed. Judith Krantz. Date not set. pap. 4.99 (*0-517-19680-8*) Random Hse Lrg Prnt.

Lovers. large type ed. Philippa Wat. 1994. 27.99 (*0-7089-3177-4*) Ulverscroft.

Lovers. large type ed. Morris West. LC 93-38621. 478p. 1994. lib. bdg. 23.95 (*0-7862-0101-0*) Thorndike Pr.

Lovers. large type ed. Morris West. LC 93-38621. 478p. 1994. pap. 14.95 (*0-7862-0102-9*) Thorndike Pr.

Lovers. Philip Jose Farmer. 1993. reprint ed. lib. bdg. 18.95 (*0-89968-339-8*, Lghtyr Pr) Buccaneer Bks.

Lovers, Vol. 1. Morris West. 1994. mass mkt. 5.99 (*0-312-95346-1*) St Martin.

***Lovers: Great Romances of Our Time Through the Eyes of Legendary Writers.** John Miller & Aacon Kenedi. (Illus.). 128p. 1999. 29.95 (*0-8212-2612-6*, Pub. by Bulfinch Pr) Little.

***Lovers: The Legend of Trystan & Yseult.** Kate Hawks. LC 99-20840. 336p. 1999. pap. 13.50 (*0-380-72676-9*, Avon Bks) Morrow Avon.

Lovers - Killers. Robert Trammell. LC 80-21523. (Lucky Heart Bk.). 58p. 1980. reprint ed. pap. 30.00 (*0-7837-9155-0*, 204985500003) Bks Demand.

Lover's Almanac. Maureen Howard. 288p. 1999. pap. 12.95 (*0-14-027512-6*, Penguin Classics) Viking Penguin.

Lovers & Agnostics. Kelly Cherry. LC 94-68940. (Classic Contemporaries Ser.). 88p. 1995. reprint ed. pap. 12.95 (*0-88748-208-2*) Carnegie-Mellon.

Lovers & Celebrations. Joel Rudinger. (Orig.). 1984. pap. 7.95 (*0-918342-20-1*) Cambric.

***Lovers & Executioners.** John Strand. 154p. (C). 1999. pap. 5.60 (*0-87129-910-0*, L98) Dramatic Pub.

Lovers & Friends. Elizabeth James. 1991. 22.00 (*0-7278-4217-X*) Severn Hse.

Lovers & Friends. Camille Marchetta. 480p. 1991. mass mkt. 4.95 (*0-380-70812-4*, Avon Bks) Morrow Avon.

Lovers & Friends. Camille Marchetta. Ed. by William Grose. 480p. 1995. mass mkt. 5.99 (*0-671-86926-4*) PB.

Lovers & Gamblers. Jackie Collins. 592p. 1991. reprint ed. mass mkt. 7.99 (*0-446-35660-3*, Pub. by Warner Bks) Little.

Lovers & Liars. Sally Beauman. 1995. mass mkt. 6.99 (*0-449-22368-X*, Crest) Fawcett.

Lovers & Liars. Sally Beauman. 1997. pap. text 6.99 (*0-449-45793-1*) Fawcett.

Lovers & Liars. Sally Steward. 400p. 1997. mass mkt. 3.99 (*1-85487-927-8*, Pub. by Scarlet Bks) London Brdge.

***Lovers & Other Lunatics.** Eugenia Riley. (Time of Your Life Ser.). 400p. 2000. mass mkt. 5.99 (*0-505-52371-X*, Love Spell) Dorchester Pub Co.

Lovers & Other Strangers. Carol Malyon. 176p. 1996. pap. text. write for info. (*0-88984-169-1*) Porcup Quill.

Lovers & Others. Laurel Speer. LC 80-17078. (Illus.). 40p. (Orig.). 1980. pap. 1.95 (*0-937212-00-8*) Truedog.

Lovers & Others: A Musical. Neil K. Newell. 1997. pap. 5.00 (*1-57514-307-0*, 0102) Encore Perform Pub.

Lovers & Strangers. Candace Schuler. LC 96-649. (Temptation Ser.). 218p. 1995. per. 3.25 (*0-373-25649-3*, 1-25649-4) Harlequin Bks.

Lovers & Survivors: A Partner's Guide to Living with & Loving a Sexual Abuse Survivor. S. Yvette De Beixedon. 225p. 1995. pap. 14.95 (*1-885003-09-9*) R D Reed Pubs.

Lovers & Tyrants. Francine Du Plessix Gray. 1988. pap. 7.95 (*0-393-30547-3*) Norton.

***Lovers Are Special.** Lucy Mead. 2000. 5.99 (*0-517-16183-4*) Crown Pub Group.

An Asterisk (*) at the beginning of an entry indicates that the title is appearing for the first time.

Lover's Bedside Companion see Lover's Companion: Romantic Inspiration & Creative Ideas

Lovers' Book of Days. Wendy Hobson. 1994. 12.98 (0-7858-0086-7) Bk Sales Inc.

Lover's Charm. Sandy Hingston. 1999. mass mkt. 5.99 (0-440-22371-7) Dell.

Lovers' Choice. Becky Birtha. LC 87-17281. 152p. (Orig.). 1994. pap. 10.95 (1-878067-41-9) Seal Pr WA.

Lovers, Clowns, & Fairies: An Essay on Comedies. Stuart M. Tave. LC 92-42650. 290p. (C). 1993. pap. 16.50 (0-226-79020-7); lib. bdg. 52.50 (0-226-79019-3) U Ch Pr.

***Lover's Companion: Romantic Inspiration & Creative Ideas.** Gregory Godek. Orig. Title: The Lover's Bedside Companion. 160p. 2000. pap. 7.95 (1-57071-516-5, Casablanca) Sourcebks.

Lover's Credo: Poetry. Corliss Lamont. LC 82-13909. 1994. pap. 8.95 (0-87233-114-8) Bauhan.

Lovers Dark & Dangerous. Ed. by Harlequin Books Staff. (Romance Digest Ser.: Vol. 82744). 1998. mass mkt. 3.50 (0-373-82744-X, 1-82744-3) Harlequin Bks.

Lovers Dark & Dangerous. Lindsay McKenna et al. 1994. mass mkt. 4.99 (0-373-48310-4, 1-48310-6) Harlequin Bks.

Lover's Dictionary: How to Be Amorous in Five Delectable Languages. 2nd ed. NTC Publishing Group Staff. (ENG, FRE, GER, ITA & SPA., Illus.). 128p. 1994. pap. 5.95 (0-8442-9097-1, Natl Textbk Co) NTC Contemp Pub Co.

Lover's Dictionary: How to Be Amorous in Five Languages. (ENG, FRE, GER, ITA & SPA.). 125p. 1981. pap. 12.95 (0-8288-1447-3, M9778) Fr & Eur.

Lover's Discourse. Roland Barthes. LC 78-7794. 224p. 1979. pap. text 11.00 (0-374-52161-7) FS&G.

Lovers Don't Lie. Chrissie Loveday. (Scarlet Ser.). 1998. mass mkt. 3.99 (1-85487-565-5, Pub. by Scarlet Bks) London Brdge.

Lover's Eye. Michael S. Glaser. LC 88-92836. 65p. 1990. pap. 7.00 (0-938572-01-6) Bunny Crocodile.

Lovers for a Day: New & Collected Stories on Love. Ivan Klima. Tr. by Gerald Turner from CZE. LC 99-27586. 240p. 1999. 24.00 (0-8021-1651-5, Grove) Grove-Atltic.

***Lovers for a Day: New & Collected Stories on Love.** Ivan Klima. 2000. pap. text 12.00 (0-8021-3747-4, Grove) Grove-Atltic.

Lovers for Life: Creating Lasting Passion, Trust & True Partnership. Daniel Ellenberg & Judith Bell. (Illus.). 320p. (Orig.). 1995. pap. 16.95 (0-944031-61-7) Aslan Pub.

Lovers Forever. Shirlee Busbee. 1996. mass mkt. 5.99 (0-446-60219-1, Pub. by Warner Bks) Little.

Lover's Gift & Crossing. Rabindranath Tagore. 94p. 1985. 5.50 (0-333-90010-3) Asia Bk Corp.

Lovers' Guide: The Art of Better Lovemaking. 4th ed. Andrew Stanway. (Illus.). 128p. 1993. text 23.95 (0-312-10413-8) St Martin.

Lovers' Guide Encyclopedia: The Definitive Guide to Sex & You. Ed. by Doreen Massey. LC 96-61220. (Illus.). 248p. 1997. pap. 24.95 (1-56025-111-5, Thunders Mouth) Avalon NY.

Lover's Guide to Japan: Where the Action Is . . . And How to Get Some! Boye L. De Mente. LC 89-50659. 184p. (Orig.). 1989. pap. 5.95 (0-8048-1589-5) Tuttle Pubng.

Lovers Guide to Massage. Roger Hicks & Victoria Day. (Illus.). 80p. 1996. 9.95 (0-7063-7512-2, Pub. by WrLock) Sterling.

Lover's Handbook. K. B. Randolph. 154p. (Orig.). 1995. pap. 12.00 (0-9643139-0-1) Hawkins Kelly Pub.

Lover's Handbook: Handwriting & Personal Relationships. Gloria Hargreaves. (Illus.). 128p. (Orig.). 1990. pap. 15.95 (0-7206-0791-4, Pub. by P Owen Ltd) Dufour.

Lovers I Ching. Burr. (Illus.). 144p. 2000. text 19.95 (0-312-24082-1) St Martin.

***Lover's I Ching.** Stephen Karcher. (Illus.). 2000. 16.95 (1-86204-484-8, Pub. by Element MA) Penguin Putnam.

Lovers in Evolution. Carolyn M. Kleefeld. LC 83-82753. 81p. (Orig.). 1983. pap. 7.95 (0-9602214-0-9) Atoms Mirror.

***Lovers in Lisbon.** large type ed. Barbara Cartland. LC 99-54983. 2000. pap. 23.95 (0-7838-8929-1, G K Hall & Co) Mac Lib Ref.

Lovers in Midsummer. Luella E. McMahon. 46p. 1970. pap. 3.50 (0-87129-148-7, L35) Dramatic Pub.

Lover's Knot Placemats. Cynthia Martin. (Illus.). 24p. 1993. 6.95 (0-922705-45-3) Quilt Day.

Lover's Knot Quilt. Eleanor Burns. (Illus.). 59p. (Orig.). 1985. pap. 8.95 (0-922705-04-6) Quilt Day.

Lover's Leap. Pamela Browning. (American Romance Ser.). 1996. per. 3.75 (0-373-16632-X, 1-16632-1) Harlequin Bks.

Lover's Leap. Linda Wing. 24p. (Orig.). 1995. pap. 3.95 (0-9641986-6-5) Poetry Harbor.

Lovers' Lies. Daphne Clair. (Presents Ser.: Vol. 1970). 1998. per. 3.75 (0-373-11970-4, 1-11970-0) Harlequin Bks.

Lover's Lies. large type ed. Daphne Clair. (Mills & Boon Large Print Ser.). 288p. 1997. 23.99 (0-263-15166-2, Pub. by Mills & Boon) Ulverscroft.

Lovers Living, Lovers Dead. Richard Lortz. 224p. 1980. 22.00 (0-933256-28-0) Second Chance.

Lover's Meeting. I. Carr. mass mkt. 13.95 (0-340-68950-1, Pub. by Hodder & Stought Ltd) Trafalgar.

***Lovers Meeting.** large type ed. Irene Carr. 384p. 1999. 31.99 (0-7089-4154-0) Ulverscroft.

Lovers Meeting: Discussions of Five Plays by Shakespeare. Ed. by Carnegie Institute of Technology, Department of En. LC 72-1335. (Essay Index Reprint Ser.). 1977. reprint ed. 15.95 (0-8369-2836-9) Ayer.

Lovers Melancholy. John Ford. LC 70-25576. (English Experience Ser.: No. 271). 88p. 1970. reprint ed. 35.00 (90-221-0271-8) Walter J Johnson.

Lover's Moon. Jane Toombs. 256p. 1997. mass mkt. 4.99 (0-8217-5600-1, Zebra Kensgtn) Kensgtn Pub Corp.

Lovers Not Friends. large type ed. Helen Brooks. (Harlequin Romance Ser.). 284p. 1995. lib. bdg. 18.95 (0-263-14125-X) Mac Lib Ref.

Lovers of Cinema: The First American Film Avant-Garde, 1919-1945. Ed. by Jan-Christopher Horak. LC 95-7399. (Studies in Film). (Illus.). 416p. 1995. 49.95 (0-299-14680-4) U of Wis Pr.

Lovers of Cinema: The First American Film Avant-Garde, 1919-1945. Ed. by Jan-Christopher Horak. LC 95-7399. (Wisconsin Studies in Film). (Illus.). 416p. 1998. pap. text 24.95 (0-299-14684-7) U of Wis Pr.

Lovers of Lapula. Mike Sadler. (Heartbeats Ser.). 112p. (YA). (gr. 7 up). 1994. pap. 5.95 (0-7910-2939-5) Chelsea Hse.

Lovers of Louisiana see Collected Works of George W. Cable

Lovers of Louisiana. George W. Cable. (Works of George Cable). 1988. reprint ed. 59.00 (0-685-48944-2) Rprt Serv.

Lovers of the Place: Monasticism Loose in the Church. Francis Kline. LC 96-34650. 144p. (Orig.). 1997. pap. text 11.95 (0-8146-2428-6, Liturg Pr Bks) Liturgical Pr.

Lovers of Truth. Roy D. Mixon. 43p. (Orig.). 1986. pap. 2.25 (0-934942-64-1, 3874) White Wing Pub.

Lovers of Wisdom. Kolak. (Philosophy Ser.). (C). 1997. student ed. 15.75 (0-534-23935-8) Wadsworth Pub.

Lovers of Wisdom. Daniel Kolak. LC 96-37020. (Philosophy Ser.). 900p. (C). 1997. 47.95 (0-534-23934-X) Wadsworth Pub.

***Lovers of Wisdom: A Historical Introduction to Philosophy.** 2nd ed. Kolak. (Philosophy Ser.). (C). 2000. text 34.25 (0-534-54146-1) Wadsworth Pub.

Lovers Only. Christine Pacheco. (Desire Ser.). 1997. per. 3.50 (0-373-76054-X, 1-76054-5) Silhouette.

Lovers Paradise: 222 Love Quotations. Sam Majdi. LC 96-95509. 72p. 1997. pap. 9.95 (0-9658378-0-7) Saman Publ.

Lovers, Parricides & Highwaymen: Aspects of Sturm und Drang Drama. Bruce Duncan. LC 99-18276. 260p. 1999. 60.00 (1-57113-086-1) Camden Hse.

Lover's Picnic: How to Prepare the Most Romantic Picnic Ever. Patrick F. Pease. 24p. (Orig.). 1989. pap. 3.95 (0-9624137-0-4) Spirit Originals.

Lovers' Quarrels: The Other Side of Romance. William A. Ross & Judy Ford. Ed. by Robert Carlson. 96p. (Orig.). 1988. pap. 4.95 (0-9619246-1-6) Playful Wisdom.

***Lovers, Queens & Strangers: Strong Women in Celtic Myth.** Anne Bernard Kearney. 148p. 2000. pap. 15.95 (1-899047-50-6, Pub. by A A Farmar) Irish Bks Media.

***Lover's Question: Selected Stories.** Thomas Farber. LC 00-34611. 2000. write for info. (0-88739-298-9) Creat Arts.

Lovers' Reunion see Reunion de Enamorados

Lover's Reunion. Anne M. Winston. (Desire Ser.: Bk. 1226). 1999. per. 3.75 (0-373-76226-7, 1-76226-9) Silhouette.

Lover's Revolt see Collected Works of John W. De Forest

Lover's Revolt. John W. De Forest. (Collected Works of John W. De Forest). 1988. reprint ed. lib. bdg. 59.00 (0-7812-1165-4) Rprt Serv.

Lovers' Secrets. Glenda Sanders. (Temptation Ser.). 1993. mass mkt. 2.99 (0-373-25554-3, 1-25554-6) Harlequin Bks.

***Lover's Tale.** Maurice Hewlett. 184p. 2000. pap. 9.95 (0-594-00840-9) Eightn Hundrd.

Lover's Tarot: For Affairs of the Heart. Jane Lyle. (Illus.). 144p. 1992. text 28.95 (0-312-08258-4) St Martin.

Lovers Touch. Penny Jordan. (Promo Ser.). 1999. per. 4.50 (0-373-83374-1, 1-83374-8) Harlequin Bks.

Lovers' Treasury of Verse. Ed. by John W. Chadwick & Annie H. Chadwick. LC 70-139758. (Granger Index Reprint Ser.). 1977. 18.95 (0-8369-6212-5) Ayer.

Lovers Voice. Donna Deneze. 50p. 1997. pap. text 10.00 (1-886706-21-2) Hickory Hse.

***Lovers' Waltz - Solo Piano Edition.** Jay Unger & Molly Mason. 6p. 1998. pap. 3.95 (0-7866-4349-8, 97516) Mel Bay.

***Lover's Waltz - Violin Duet & Piano Edition.** Jay Ungar & Molly Mason. 12p. 1998. pap. 9.95 (0-7866-4350-1, 98048) Mel Bay.

Lovers Workbook: Who Am I? Who Are You? Richard A. Sardi. 176p. 1997. pap. 29.95 (0-9654424-0-3) Search Publng.

Loves Of Judith. Meir Shalev. Tr. by Barbara Harshav from HEB. LC 98-22747. 315p. 1998. 25.00 (0-88001-635-3) HarpC.

Love's Abiding Joy. Janette Oke. LC 83-15503. (Love Comes Softly Ser.: Vol. 4). 224p. (Orig.). 1983. pap. 8.99 (0-87123-401-7) Bethany Hse.

Love's Alien Shore. large type ed. Lillie Holland. 336p. 1992. pap. 16.99 (0-7089-7142-3, Linford) Ulverscroft.

Love's Ambush. Theresa Scott. 400p. (Orig.). 1997. mass mkt. 5.99 (0-8439-4199-5) Dorchester Pub Co.

Love's Answer. Michael Heffernan. LC 93-38321. (Iowa Poetry Prize Ser.). 96p. (Orig.). 1994. pap. 11.95 (0-87745-451-5) U of Iowa Pr.

Love's Apprentice: Confessions from the School of Romance. Shirley Abbott. LC 97-44865. 288p. 1998. 23.00 (0-395-67369-0) HM.

Love's Apprentice: The Romantic Education of a Modern Woman. Shirley Abbott. 288p. 1999. pap. 13.00 (0-395-95785-0) HM.

Love's Argument: Gender Relations in Shakespeare. Marianne Novy. LC 84-3553. 249p. 1984. reprint ed. pap. 77.20 (0-7837-9031-7, 204978200003) Bks Demand.

Love's Awakening. large type ed. Rachel Ford. 220p. 1992. 27.99 (0-7505-0249-5) Ulverscroft.

Love's Bitter Memories. large type ed. Peggy Gaddis. (Linford Romance Library). 288p. 1994. pap. 16.99 (0-7089-7507-0, Linford) Ulverscroft.

Love's Blood. Clark Howard. 1994. mass mkt. 6.50 (0-312-95301-1) St Martin.

Love's Body. Norman O. Brown. 285p. 1990. 48.00 (0-520-07105-0, Pub. by U CA Pr); pap. 15.95 (0-520-07106-9, Pub. by U CA Pr) Cal Prin Full Svc.

Love's Brazen Fire. Betina M. Krahn. 384p. 1997. mass mkt. 5.99 (0-8217-5691-5, Zebra Kensgtn) Kensgtn Pub Corp.

Love's Calendar, Lays of the Hudson, & Other Poems. Charles F. Hoffman. (Notable American Authors Ser.). 1992. reprint ed. lib. bdg. 75.00 (0-7812-3136-1) Rprt Serv.

Love's Changelinges Change. Philip Sidney. Ed. & Intro. by John P. Cutts. LC 74-84570. (North American Mentor Texts & Studies: No. 2). 1974. pap. 16.50 (0-87423-009-8) Westburg.

Love's Charade. Jane Feather. 478p. 1996. mass mkt. 5.50 (0-8217-5285-5, Zebra Kensgtn) Kensgtn Pub Corp.

Love's Cherished Refrain. Kay D. Rizzo. LC 94-27523. (Chloe Celeste Chronicles Ser.: 4). 1994. pap. 9.99 (0-8163-1222-2) Pacific Pr Pub Assn.

Love's Children. Judith Chernaik. 1992. 20.00 (0-685-55206-3) Knopf.

Love's Choices. Penny Jordan. LC 95-21491. 383p. 1995. mass mkt. 5.99 (0-373-15309-0, 1-15309-7) Harlequin Bks.

Love's Choices. Penny Jordan. 1996. mass mkt. 5.99 (0-373-83327-X, 1-83327-6) Harlequin Bks.

Love's Chosen Love: A Record of Events . . . Gail M. Weatherbe. LC 96-119381. 22p. 1995. pap. 4.00 (1-879135-01-9) Emma Pub Soc.

Love's Coming-of-Age: A Series of Papers on the Relations of the Sexes (1912) Edward Carpenter. 164p. 1999. reprint ed. pap. 16.95 (0-7661-0737-X) Kessinger Pub.

Love's Compass: A Natural History of the Heart. Daniel M. Epstein. 1990. 17.26 (0-201-15667-9) Addison-Wesley.

Love's Compass: A Natural History of the Heart. Daniel M. Epstein. 1991. pap. 9.57 (0-201-57094-7) Addison-Wesley.

Love's Courtly Ethic in "The Faerie Queene" From Garden to Wilderness. John Rooks. LC 91-37408. (University of Kansas Humanistic Studies: Vol. 58). XIII, 244p. (C). 1992. text 38.95 (0-8204-1708-4) P Lang Pubng.

Love's Cradle: Selected Poems by Wilson Reid Ogg. Wilson R. Ogg. (Illus.). 75p. (Orig.). 1988. pap. 5.00 (0-929707-01-X) Pinebrook CA.

Love's Dark Shadow. Grace Green. (Romance Ser.). 1995. pap. 2.99 (0-373-17215-X, 1-17215-4) Harlequin Bks.

Love's Deadly Silhouette, Vol. II. Leslie Richards. (Illus.). 1979. mass mkt. 1.95 (0-89083-438-5, Zebra Kensgtn) Kensgtn Pub Corp.

***Love's Deception.** Adrianne Byrd. (Arabesque Ser.). 288p. 2000. mass mkt. 5.99 (1-58314-136-7) BET Bks.

Love's Deceptions. Charlene Berry. 1996. pap. 10.95 (1-885478-11-9) Genesis Press.

Love's Desire. large type ed. Jane Toombs. (Black Satin Romance Ser.). 440p. 1996. 27.99 (1-86110-005-1) Ulverscroft.

***Love's Destiny.** Louise M. Quezada. 1999. pap. text 8.95 (1-885478-68-2, Pub. by Genesis Press) BookWorld.

***Love's Dialectic: Mimesis & allegory in the romances of Lope de Vega.** (Illus.). 202p. 2000. 40.00 (1-889441-05-8) Romance.

Love's Diamond. Adeline Foster. (Illus.). 100p. (Orig.). 1982. pap. 4.95 (0-9609794-0-9) A Foster.

Love's Dilemmas. Robert Herrick. LC 73-113677. (Short Story Index Reprint Ser.). 1977. 19.95 (0-8369-3406-7) Ayer.

Love's Dilemmas see Collected Works of Robert Herrick

Love's Dilemmas. Robert Herrick. (Collected Works of Robert Herrick). 1988. reprint ed. lib. bdg. 59.00 (0-7812-1263-4) Rprt Serv.

Love's Double Fool. large type ed. Alison A. York. (Magna Large Print Ser.). 245p. 1996. 27.99 (0-7505-1011-0, Pub. by Mgna Lrg Print) Ulverscroft.

Love's Elusive Flame. Phoebe Conn. 1983. mass mkt. 3.75 (0-8217-1267-5, Zebra Kensgtn) Kensgtn Pub Corp.

Love's Enchantment: Story Poems & Ballads. Compiled by Helen Ferris. LC 73-86796. (Granger Index Reprint Ser.). 1977. 18.95 (0-8369-6076-9) Ayer.

Love's Encore. Sandra Brown. LC 98-24003. 228 p. 1998. 26.95 (1-56895-566-9) Wheeler Pub.

Love's Encore. Sandra Brown. 256p. 1997. reprint ed. mass mkt. 6.50 (0-446-36428-2, Pub. by Warner Bks) Little.

Love's Enduring Hope: A Pioneer Romance. large type ed. June M. Bacher. 296p. 1992. reprint ed. pap. 9.95 (0-8027-2670-4) Walker & Co.

Love's Enduring Promise. Janette Oke. LC 80-22993. (Love Comes Softly Ser.: Vol. 2). 208p. 1980. pap. 8.99 (0-87123-345-2) Bethany Hse.

Love's Enduring Promise. large type ed. Janette Oke. LC 80-22993. (Love Comes Softly Ser.: Vol. 2). 28p. 1985. pap. 10.99 (0-87123-829-2) Bethany Hse.

Love's Energies. 2nd ed. June Singer. 1990. pap. 16.95 (0-938434-51-9) Sigo Pr.

Love's Eternal Legacy. Arvin S. Gibson. 208p. 1994. 14.98 (0-88290-504-X, 1955) Horizon Utah.

Love's Eternal Light: Poems. Cora Slaghta. 1990. 9.00 (0-917560-49-3) Woman Activist.

***Love's Executioner: And Other Tales of Psychotherapy.** Irvin D. Yalom. (Perennial Classics Ser.). 288p. 2000. pap. 14.00 (0-06-095834-0) HarpC.

Love's Executioner: And Other Tales of Psychotherapy. Irvin D. Yalom. LC 89-46494. 288p. 1990. reprint ed. pap. 13.50 (0-06-097334-X, Perennial) HarperTrade.

Love's Face. Margaret Montreuil. 163p. 1997. mass mkt. 11.00 (0-9659320-2-8) Lvg Waters.

Love's Fatal Glance: A Study of Eye Imagery in the Poets of the Ecole lyonnaise. Lancelot K. Donaldson-Evans. LC 80-10415. (Romance Monographs: No. 39). 155p. 1980. 24.00 (84-499-3694-2) Romance.

***Love's Fatal Illusions: 25 Romantic Illusions That Destroy Loving Relationships.** viii, 200p. 2000. pap. 11.95 (0-9675537-0-9) Upstart Pubng Co.

***Love's Fiery Jewel.** Elaine Barbieri. 512p. 2000. pap. 5.99 (0-505-52391-4, Love Spell) Dorchester Pub Co.

Love's Fire: Re-creations of Rumi. Andrew Harvey. 120p. (Orig.). 1989. pap. 9.95 (0-9622973-0-5) Meeramma Pubns.

Love's Fire: Seven New Plays Inspired by Seven Shakespearean Sonnets. Contrib. by Eric Bogosian et al. LC 98-14725. 128p. 1998. pap. 16.00 (0-688-16172-3, Quil) HarperTrade.

Love's Fools: Aucassin, Troilus, Calisto & the Parody of the Courtly Lover. June H. Martin. (Monagrafias A Ser.: Vol. XXI). 156p. (Orig.). (C). 1972. pap. 41.00 (0-900411-33-3, Pub. by Tamesis Bks Ltd) Boydell & Brewer.

Love's Fortune. Jeanne Innes. 384p. 1995. pap. 4.99 (0-8217-4967-6) NAL.

Love's Full Circle. Lurlene McDaniel. (Serenade Serenata Ser.: No. 33). 1986. pap. 1.49 (0-310-47302-0) Zondervan.

***Love's Funny That Way.** Pamela Burford. (Temptation Ser.). 2000. mass mkt. 3.99 (0-373-25912-3, 1259126) Harlequin Bks.

Love's Gentle Journey, No. 21. Kay Cornelius. (Serenade Saga Ser.). 1985. pap. 2.50 (0-310-47002-1, 15555P) Zondervan.

Love's Glittering Web. large type ed. Kate Bowe. 512p. 1984. 27.99 (0-7089-1096-3) Ulverscroft.

Love's Glory: Recreations of Rumi. Andrew Harvey. LC 96-12370. 111p. (Orig.). 1996. pap. 10.95 (1-55643-225-9) North Atlantic.

Love's Golden Touch. large type ed. Jane Lester. (Linford Romance Library). 272p. 1985. pap. 16.99 (0-7089-6055-3, Linford) Ulverscroft.

Love's Golden Wings. LaJoyce Martin. LC 87-17346. (Pioneer Trilogy Ser.). (Illus.). 256p. (Orig.). (YA). (gr. 7 up). 1987. pap. 8.99 (0-932581-19-6) Word Aflame.

***Love's Got Everything to Do with It.** Rosemarie Karlebach. 168p. 2000. 14.99 (1-56322-070-9) Hensley Pub.

Love's Harvest: Family, Faith, Friends. Christopher De Vinck. LC 98-9847. 216p. 1998. pap. 14.95 (0-8245-1749-0, Crsrd) Crossroad NY.

***Love's Healing Power.** Terry Zahniser McDermid. LC 99-90978. 192p. 1999. 18.95 (0-8034-9383-5, Avalon Bks) Bouregy.

Love's Heavenly Dream. unabridged ed. William C. Stuber. LC 95-68352. (Illus.). 54p. (Orig.). 1995. pap. text 14.95 incl. audio (1-887198-00-8); pap. text 14.95 incl. cd-rom (1-887198-02-4) Shabda Pub.

Love's Hidden Symmetry: What Makes Love Work in Relationships. Bert Hellinger et al. LC 98-13152. 1998. 38.00 (1-891944-00-2) Zeig Tucker.

***Love's Hidden Symmetry: What Makes Love Work in Relationships.** expanded ed. Bert Hellinger et al. LC 00-32067. 2000. write for info. (1-891944-66-5) Zeig Tucker.

Love's Illusion. Katherine Sutcliffe. 1998. mass mkt. 6.99 (0-451-40836-5, Onyx) NAL.

Love's Image. Rosalyn Alsobrook. 288p. 1996. mass mkt. 4.99 (0-8217-5332-0, Zebra Kensgtn) Kensgtn Pub Corp.

Love's Inner Beauty. large type ed. Peggy O'More. (Linford Romance Library). 1991. pap. 16.99 (0-7089-6984-4, Linford) Ulverscroft.

Love's Instruments. Melvin Dixon. LC 95-68621. 80p. (Orig.). 1995. pap. 10.95 (1-882688-07-4) Tia Chucha Pr.

***Love's Intrigue.** June Francis. 336p. 1999. 20.99 (1-85389-878-3) Ulverscroft.

Love's Journey. Tim Holcomb & Brian Marsh. 24p. (Orig.). 1995. pap. 3.00 (1-57514-175-2, 3079) Encore Perform Pub.

Love's Journey. Curt Philips. LC 84-70262. (Illus.). 139p. (Orig.). (C). 1984. pap. text 6.95 (0-918899-00-1) Dragonscales & Mane Pub.

Love's Journey, Vol. 1. Marilyn Thielen. LC 96-67621. 101p. (Orig.). 1996. pap. 11.95 (1-882792-22-X) Proctor Pubns.

Love's Kitchen: Give a Little Heart Today. Danielle K. Szczepanik. 120p. 1994. 8.95 (0-9645814-0-X) D K Szczepanik.

Love's Knowledge: Essays on Philosophy & Literature. Martha C. Nussbaum. 432p. 1992. pap. text 22.00 (0-19-507485-8) OUP.

Love's Labor: Essays on Equality, Dependency, & Care. Eva F. Kittay. LC 98-18629. 256p. (C). 1998. 70.00 (0-415-90412-9) Routledge.

Love's Labor: Essays on Equality, Dependency & Care. Eva F. Kittay. LC 98-18629. xvii, 238p. (C). 1999. pap. 19.99 (0-415-90413-7) Routledge.

***Love's Labors: A Memoir of a Young Marriage & Divorce.** Daniel Roche. 288p. 1999. pap. 13.00 (1-57322-775-7, Riverhd Trade) Berkley Pub.

Love's Labors: A Story of Marriage & Divorce. Daniel Roche. LC 98-45432. (Illus.). 304p. 1999. 23.95 (1-57322-067-1, Riverhead Books) Putnam Pub Group.

***Love's Labor's Lost.** William Shakespeare. (Pelican Shakespeare Ser.). 144p. 2000. pap. 5.95 (0-14-071477-4, Pelican Bks) Viking Penguin.

L

An Asterisk (*) at the beginning of an entry indicates that the title is appearing for the first time.

Love's Labor's Lost: A Midsummer Night's Dream: The Merchant of Venice. William Shakespeare. Ed. by Clifford C. Huffman. LC 95-8285. (Shakespeare Bibliographies Ser.: Vol. 2). 80p. 1995. pap. 9.95 (*0-86698-177-2*, P28) Pegasus Pr.

Love's Labor's Lost: Granville Barker's Prefaces to Shakespeare. William Shakespeare. Ed. by Granville Barker. LC 95-165799. 75p. (gr. 8-12). 1995. pap. 6.95 (*0-435-08651-0*) Heinemann.

***Love's Labors Tossed: Trust & the Final Fling.** Robert F. Smith. LC 00-24711. (Trust Williams Trilogy Ser.). 2000. write for info. (*1-57345-648-9*) Deseret Bk.

Love's Labour Lost. 3rd ed. William Shakespeare. (English). (C). 1998. mass mkt. 45.00 (*0-17-443557-6*) Wadsworth Pub.

***Love's Labour Lost.** 3rd ed. William Shakespeare. (English). 400p. (C). 1998. pap. 11.95 (*0-17-443500-2*) Wadsworth Pub.

Love's Labour's Lost. Miriam Gilbert. LC 92-14074. (Shakespeare in Performance Ser.). 1993. pap. write for info. (*0-7190-2750-0*, Pub. by Manchester Univ Pr) St Martin.

Love's Labour's Lost. William Shakespeare. (BBC Television Plays Ser.). 1986. pap. 7.95 (*0-563-20278-5*, Pub. by BBC) Parkwest Pubns.

Love's Labour's Lost. William Shakespeare. 1996. pap. 3.99 (*0-671-66921-4*) Folger.

Love's Labour's Lost. William Shakespeare. Ed. by John Arthos. 1965. mass mkt. 4.95 (*0-451-52267-2*) NAL.

Love's Labour's Lost. William Shakespeare. Ed. by George Hibbard. (Oxford Shakespeare Ser.). (Illus.). 272p. 1990. 59.00 (*0-19-812947-5*) OUP.

Love's Labour's Lost. William Shakespeare. Ed. by G. R. Hibbard. LC 94-13246. (Oxford Shakespeare Ser.). (Illus.). 272p. 1990. pap. 7.95 (*0-19-281940-2*) OUP.

***Love's Labour's Lost.** William Shakespeare. (Big Works Collection). (Illus.). 1p. 1999. 29.95 (*1-929142-08-0*) One Page Bk.

Love's Labour's Lost. William Shakespeare. Ed. by John Kerrigan. (New Penguin Shakespeare Ser.). 256p. 1982. pap. 5.95 (*0-14-070738-7*, Penguin Classics) Viking Penguin.

Love's Labour's Lost. William Shakespeare. (Classics Library). 1998. pap. 3.95 (*1-85326-259-5*, 2595WW, Pub. by Wrdsworth Edits) NTC Contemp Pub Co.

Love's Labour's Lost see New Variorum Edition of Shakespeare

Love's Labour's Lost. 5th ed. William Shakespeare. Ed. by Richard W. David. (Arden Shakespeare Ser.). 1956. reprint ed. pap. 8.95 (*0-416-10440-1*, NO. 2475) Routledge.

Love's Labour's Lost: Critical Essays. Ed. by Felicia H. Londre. LC 97-526. (Shakespeare Criticism Ser.: Vol. 13). (Illus.). 496p. 1997. text 110.00 (*0-8153-0984-8*, H1643) Garland.

Love's Labour's Lost: Modern Text with Introduction. William Shakespeare. Ed. & Intro. by A. L. Rowse. (Contemporary Shakespeare Ser.: Vol. IV). 126p. (Orig.). (C). 1986. pap. text 3.45 (*0-8191-3923-8*) U Pr of Amer.

Loves Labour's Lost & Henry VIII see Shakespeare Yesterday - Today, 1989-1998

Love's Lance. Diane Conrad. 46p. (Orig.). 1996. pap. 8.00 (*0-614-32387-8*) Phantsml Pr.

Love's Last Barrier. large type ed. Irene Lawrence. (Linford Romance Library). 1990. pap. 16.99 (*0-7089-6881-3*, Linford) Ulverscroft.

***Love's Last Chance: A Nigel & Nicky Mystery.** Krandall Kraus. (Illus.). 288p. 2000. pap. 11.95 (*1-55583-505-8*, Pub. by Alyson Pubns) Consort Bk Sales.

Love's Late Spring. Lydia Heerman. (Serenade Serenata Ser.: No. 4). 192p. (Orig.). 1983. pap. 2.50 (*0-310-50002-8*, 17100P) Zondervan.

Love's Legacy. Madeline Baker et al. Ed. by Heather Graham et al. 448p. 1996. pap. text 6.99 (*0-8439-4000-X*) Dorchester Pub Co.

Love's Legacy. Denise Daniels. 384p. 1998. mass mkt. 4.99 (*0-8217-6060-2*, Zebra Kensgtn) Kensgtn Pub Corp.

Love's Litany: The Writing of Modern Homoerotics. Kevin Kopelson. LC 93-39677. xii, 194p. 1994. 39.50 (*0-8047-2299-4*); pap. 12.95 (*0-8047-2345-1*) Stanford U Pr.

Love's Little Instruction Book. Annie Pigeon. 96p. 1994. mass mkt. 4.99 (*1-55817-774-4*, Pinncle Kensgtn) Kensgtn Pub Corp.

***Love's Little Instruction Book: Romantic Hints for Lovers of All Ages.** Annie Pigeon. 2000. mass mkt. 5.99 (*0-7860-1261-7*, Pinncle Kensgtn) Kensgtn Pub Corp.

Love's Little Suggestion Book. Sylvia Kreng. (Books for the Soul). (Illus.). 52p. 1995. pap. 5.95 (*1-891210-95-5*, LLSB13) Bartlett Pub.

Loves Lives for True Lovers Journal. Katherine E. Anderson. 150p. 1998. pap., spiral bd. 15.95 (*1-57876-405-X*, Love Lives) Triple U Enterprises.

Love's Long Journey. large type ed. Janette Oke. LC 82-9469. (Love Comes Softly Ser.: Vol. 3). 28p. 1982. pap. 8.99 (*0-87123-315-0*) Bethany Hse.

Love's Lost Melody. Therese Martini. 448p. 1984. mass mkt. 3.50 (*0-446-32236-9*, Pub. by Warner Bks) Little.

Love's Madness Vol. 17: Complete Plays 17. Manuel P. Garcia. 56p. 1998. 4.95 (*1-885901-67-4*, Liberts) Presbyters Peartree.

Love's Mansion. Paul West. 339p. 1993. pap. 13.95 (*0-87951-503-1*, Pub. by Overlook Pr) Penguin Putnam.

Love's Masks: Identity, Intertextuality & Meaning in the Old French Tristan Poems. Merritt R. Blakeslee. LC 88-22225. (Arthurian Studies: No. XV). 175p. 1989. 70.00 (*0-85991-264-7*) Boydell & Brewer.

Love's Masquerade. Violet Hamilton. 304p. 1996. mass mkt. 4.99 (*0-8217-5409-2*, Zebra Kensgtn) Kensgtn Pub Corp.

Love's Masquerade. Cynthia Richey. 1990. 19.95 (*0-8027-1117-0*) Walker & Co.

Loves Me . . . Loves Me Not: The Art of Choosing Who's Right for You (Includes Interactive Cards), Incl. cards. Tom DuFresne. 90p. 1997. 24.95 (*0-9641461-3-4*) AP Pr.

Loves Me, Loves Me Not. Anilu Bernardo. 169p. (J). (gr. 6-12). 1998. pap. 9.95 (*1-55885-259-X*, Pinata Bks) Arte Publico.

***Loves Me, Loves Me Not.** Barbara Jean Hicks. (Once Upon a Dream Ser.: Vol. 3). 256p. 2000. pap. 9.95 (*1-57856-124-8*) Waterbrook Pr.

Love's Medallion. Martha LaFave. Ed. by Liz Severn. (Illus.). 180p. 1997. pap. 8.95 (*1-888701-04-8*) Jarrett Pr.

Love's Meinie & Proserpina see Complete Works of John Ruskin

***Loves Me/Loves Me Not.** Havoc Publishing Staff. 1999. pap. 9.00 (*0-7416-1004-3*) Havoc Pub.

Love's Memories. Brenda Duke-Barber. 206p. 1998. pap. 8.99 (*1-57502-929-4*, PO2556) Morris Pubng.

Love's Memories. Heidi Strasser. 1988. 2.50 (*0-517-00669-3*) Random Hse Value.

Love's Mended Wings. LaJoyce Martin. LC 86-33955. (Pioneer Trilogy Ser.: Bk. 2). (Illus.). 272p. (Orig.). 1987. pap. 8.99 (*0-932581-09-9*) Word Aflame.

Love's Mind: An Essay on Contemplative Life. John S. Dunne. LC 93-13910. (C). 1993. text 23.00 (*0-268-01303-9*) U of Notre Dame Pr.

***Love's Mind: An Essay on Contemplative Life.** John S. Dunne. LC 93-13910. 170p. 2000. reprint ed. pap. 14.00 (*0-268-01331-4*, Pub. by U of Notre Dame Pr) Chicago Distribution Ctr.

***Love's Miracle.** Jacquelin Thomas. (Arabesque Ser.). 2000. mass mkt. 5.99 (*1-58314-126-X*) BET Bks.

Love's Moment. Albert Krassner. (Illus.). 20p. 1984. pap. 10.95 (*0-912061-05-7*) Veridon Edns.

Loves Music, Loves to Dance. Mary Higgins Clark. 1996. reprint ed. lib. bdg. 35.95 (*1-56849-265-0*) Buccaneer Bks.

Loves Music, Loves to Dance. Mary Higgins Clark. Ed. by Julie Rubenstein. 336p. 1992. reprint ed. per. 7.99 (*0-671-75889-6*) PB.

Love's Not a Three Dollar Fare. Terry LaBan. 128p. 1995. pap. 14.95 (*1-56097-165-7*) Fantagraph Bks.

***Loves of Catrin.** Gower. 2000. pap. 8.95 (*0-552-13631-X*, Pub. by Transworld Publishers Ltd) Trafalgar.

Loves of Harry Dancer. Lawrence Sanders. 288p. 1986. mass mkt. 6.50 (*0-425-08473-6*) Berkley Pub.

Loves of Joao Vencio. Vencio. 1991. 14.95 (*0-15-146390-5*) Harcourt.

Loves of Lord Granton. Marion Chesney. 1997. mass mkt. 4.50 (*0-449-22260-8*, Crest) Fawcett.

Loves of Lord Granton. large type ed. Marion Chesney. LC 97-30533. (ROMC-Hall Ser.). 206p. 1997. lib. bdg. 25.95 (*0-7838-8301-3*, G K Hall Lrg Type) Mac Lib Ref.

Loves of Ricardo Sanchez. Ricardo Sanchez. 220p. (C). 1997. 22.95 (*1-882688-13-9*); pap. 12.95 (*1-882688-14-7*) Tia Chucha Pr.

Loves of Ruby Dee. Curtiss A. Matlock. 1996. mass mkt. 5.99 (*0-380-78106-9*, Avon Bks) Morrow Avon.

Loves of Sean O'Malley: Risk the Hazard Trail. Florence B. Smith. 288p. 1998. pap. 7.00 (*1-893463-03-6*) F B Smith.

***Loves of Sundry Philosophers & other Great Men: A Translation of Madame de Villedieu's les Amours des Grands Hommes.** Yanick Villedieu & Nancy Deighton Klein. LC 99-89312. (Studies in French Literature: Vol. 37). 112p. 2000. text 59.95 (*0-7734-7867-1*) E Mellen.

Loves of the Cat: An Illustrated Anthology of Old & Modern Cat Poems. Kim Wheeler. LC 85-63189. (Illus.). 101p. (Orig.). (J). (gr. 5 up). 1985. pap. 5.00 (*0-9615937-0-9*) Star City Pubns.

Loves of the Gods: Mythological Painting from Watteau to David. Colin B. Bailey. LC 91-40371. (Illus.). 588p. 1992. pap. 29.95 (*0-912804-26-2*) Kimbell Art.

Loves of the Plants. Erasmus Darwin. 214p. 1991. reprint ed. 85.00 (*1-85477-065-9*) Continuum.

Loves of the Poets: Poems. David H. Rosenthal. 86p. 1989. 17.95 (*0-89255-139-9*); pap. 9.95 (*0-89255-132-1*) Persea Bks.

Loves of Their Lives: Enduring Romantic Relationships from Antony & Cleopatra to Today. Louis Baldwin. (Illus.). 320p. 1993. 21.95 (*1-55972-190-1*, Birch Ln Pr) Carol Pub Group.

Love's Own Crown. Laurie Grant. 352p. (Orig.). 1989. mass mkt. 3.95 (*0-445-20875-9*, Pub. by Warner Bks) Little.

Love's Own Dream. large type ed. Jacqueline Hacsi. (Linford Romance Library). 322p. 1993. pap. 16.99 (*0-7089-7454-6*, Linford) Ulverscroft.

Love's Perfect Image, No. 9. Judy Baer. (Serenade Serenata Ser.). 1984. pap. 1.49 (*0-310-46522-2*, 15512P) Zondervan.

***Love's Pilgrimage.** Upton Sinclair. (Collected Works of Upton Sinclair). 663p. 1999. reprint ed. lib. bdg. 148.00 (*1-58201-824-3*) Classic Bks.

Love's Prism: Reflections from the Heart of a Woman. Alla R. Bozarth. LC 86-63272. 76p. (Orig.). 1987. pap. 4.95 (*1-55612-044-3*) Wisdom House.

Love's Prisoner (Presents Plus) Elizabeth Oldfield. LC 96-551. 189p. 1995. mass mkt. 3.25 (*0-373-11773-6*) Harlequin Bks.

Love's Promise. Karen A. Bale. 416p. 1996. mass mkt. 4.99 (*0-8217-5234-0*, Zebra Kensgtn) Kensgtn Pub Corp.

Love's Promise. Adrienne E. Reeves. 1998. 4.99 (*0-7860-0568-8*) Kensgtn Pub Corp.

Love's Promised Land. Diana Haviland. 1999. 26.95 (*0-7862-1957-2*) Mac Lib Ref.

***Love's Quiet Corner.** large type ed. Laura Parrish, pseud. (Paperback Ser.). 2000. pap. 23.95 (*0-7838-8981-X*, G K Hall Lrg Type) Mac Lib Ref.

Love's Raging Fires. large type ed. Joanna Makepeace. LC 94-19598. 597p. 1995. pap. 19.95 (*0-7862-0300-5*) Thorndike Pr.

Love's Remedies: Recantation & Renaissance Lyric Poetry. Patricia B. Phillippy. LC 94-21457. 1995. 39.50 (*0-8387-5263-2*) Bucknell U Pr.

***Love's Revolution: Racial Intermarriage.** Maria P. P. Root. (Illus.). 264p. 2001. 69.50 (*1-56639-825-8*); pap. 22.95 (*1-56639-826-6*) Temple U Pr.

Love's Reward. Jean R. Ewing. 224p. 1997. mass mkt. 4.99 (*0-8217-5812-8*, Zebra Kensgtn) Kensgtn Pub Corp.

***Love's Sacred Order: The Four Loves Revisited.** Erasmo Leiva-Merikakis. 165p. 2000. pap. 12.95 (*0-89870-791-9*, Pub. by Ignatius Pr) Midpt Trade.

Loves Sacrifice. John Ford. LC 76-25887. (English Experience Ser.: No. 314). 88p. 1971. reprint ed. 20.00 (*90-221-0314-5*) Walter J Johnson.

Love's Second Blooming. Grace Gooodwin. (Rainbow Romances Ser.). 160p. 1995. 14.95 (*0-7090-5494-7*, 924) Parkwest Pubns.

Love's Second Blooming. large type ed. Grace Goodwin. (Linford Romance Library). 320p. 1996. pap. 16.99 (*0-7089-7888-6*, Linford) Ulverscroft.

Love's Second Chances. Terry Blackstock. 1999. 24.99 (*0-310-23045-4*) HarpC.

Love's Silent Song. large type ed. June M. Bacher. (Orig.). 1987. pap. 8.95 (*0-8027-2610-0*) Walker & Co.

***Love's Song.** Ivette Gonzalez. (Encanto Ser.). 384p. 2000. mass mkt. 5.99 (*0-7860-1116-5*, Pinncle Kensgtn) Kensgtn Pub Corp.

Love's Story Told: A Life of Henry A. Murray. Forrest G. Robinson. LC 92-8705. 490p. 1992. 29.95 (*0-674-53928-1*) HUP.

Love's Story Told: A Life of Henry A. Murray. Forrest G. Robinson. (Illus.). 496p. (C). 1995. pap. 18.95 (*0-674-53929-X*) HUP.

***Love's Strategy: The Political Theology of Johann Baptist Metz.** Ed. by John K. Downey. LC 99-40925. 192p. 1999. pap. 25.00 (*1-56338-285-7*) TPI PA.

Love's Subtle Signature. Maria Bakkum. Ed. by janet Leih. (Illus.). 66p. 1993. pap. 5.00 (*1-877649-17-1*) Tesseract SD.

Love's Sweet. Clyde Watsom. 1999. 4.99 (*0-14-054291-4*) NAL.

Love's Sweet. Clyde Watson. LC 98-14273. (Illus.). 32p. (J). (gr. 3-4). 1998. 15.99 (*0-670-83453-X*) Viking Penguin.

Love's Sweet Freedom. large type ed. Jacqueline Wallace. 240p. 1994. 27.99 (*0-7089-3141-3*) Ulverscroft.

Love's Sweet Music. large type ed. Jean Saunders. (Dales Romance Ser.). 301p. 1993. pap. 18.99 (*1-85389-398-6*, Dales) Ulverscroft.

Love's Sweet Promise. Susan Feldhake. (Serenade Serenata Ser.: No. 2). 192p. (Orig.). 1983. pap. 1.49 (*0-310-46462-5*, 15506P) Zondervan.

Love's Sweet Return: The Harlequin Story. Margaret A. Jensen. 250p. pap. 8.95 (*0-88961-086-X*, Pub. by Womens Pr) LPC InBook.

Love's Sweet Return: The Harlequin Story. Margaret A. Jensen. LC 84-72407. 188p. 1984. 20.95 (*0-87972-318-1*) Bowling Green Univ Popular Press.

Love's Sweet Surrender. Arlene Hale. LC 83-17850. (Orig.). 1983. reprint ed. pap. 11.95 (*0-89621-478-8*) Thorndike Pr.

Love's Tangled Web. large type ed. Joy St. Clair. (Dales Large Print Ser.). 204p. 1996. pap. 18.99 (*1-85389-602-0*, Dales) Ulverscroft.

Love's Tender Portrait. large type ed. Alice Sharpe. LC 93-10506. 1993. pap. 14.95 (*1-56054-748-0*) Thorndike Pr.

Love's Tender Prelude. Kay D. Rizzo. LC 94-5442. (Chloe Celeste Chronicles Ser.: No. 1). 1994. pap. 9.99 (*0-8163-1219-2*) Pacific Pr Pub Assn.

***Loves That Bind: A Novel.** Julian Rios. (Vintage International Ser.). 256p. 1999. pap. 12.00 (*0-375-70060-9*) Vin Bks.

Love's the Best Doctor see Miser & Other Plays

Love's Theatre. Ed. by Esther Selsden. 365p. 1995. pap. 10.95 (*0-7867-0157-9*) Carroll & Graf.

Love's Tortured Headland: A Continuation of Lapped Furrows. Peter Kavanagh. 45p. 1978. 50.00 (*0-914612-10-7*) Kavanagh.

Love's Tour. Qi-Jia Chen. 110p. 1996. pap. text 5.00 (*0-614-13434-X*) New Wrld Poetry.

Love's Treasure. large type ed. Helen McCabe. (Linford Romance Library). 192p. 1997. pap. 16.99 (*0-7089-5084-1*, Linford) Ulverscroft.

Love's Turbulent Tides. Ali O'Coy. 238p. (Orig.). Date not set. pap. 14.95 (*0-9659023-9-0*) A C Seale.

Love's Unending Legacy. Janette Oke. LC 84-18412. (Love Comes Softly Ser: Vol. 5). 224p. 1984. pap. 8.99 (*0-87123-616-8*) Bethany Hse.

Love's Unfolding Dream. large type ed. Janette Oke. LC 87-15780. (Love Comes Softly Ser.: Vol. 6). 224p. (J). (gr. 4 up). 1987. pap. 8.99 (*0-87123-979-5*) Bethany Hse.

Love's Unfolding Dream. large type ed. Janette Oke. LC 84-18412. 224p. 1987. pap. 10.99 (*0-87123-980-9*) Bethany Hse.

Love's Velvet Chains. LaJoyce Martin. LC 89-24983. (Illus.). 240p. (Orig.). 1989. pap. 8.99 (*0-932581-56-0*) Word Aflame.

Love's Vendetta. Stephanie Howard. 1994. per. 2.99 (*0-373-17171-4*) Harlequin Bks.

Love's Virtues. Mike W. Martin. 224p. 1996. 35.00 (*0-7006-0766-8*); pap. 14.95 (*0-7006-0767-6*) U Pr of KS.

Love's Voyage. Sherry Landgraf. Ed. by Dianne Bradbury & Wanda Bare. LC 95-67506. 436p. 1995. 23.95 (*0-9644981-0-3*) Donnabelle Pub.

Love's Wild Desire. Jennifer Blake. LC 96-96440. 1996. mass mkt. 4.99 (*0-449-14878-5*) Fawcett.

Love's Wild Desire. large type ed. Jennifer Blake. LC 97-3568. (Large Print Book Ser.). 1997. 25.95 (*1-56895-419-0*) Wheeler Pub.

Love's Wild Wager: March Madness. Taylor Ryan. LC 95-7081. (Historical Ser.). 296p. 1995. per. 4.50 (*0-373-28862-X*, 1-28862-0) Harlequin Bks.

Love's Witness: Five Centuries of Love Poetry by Women. Ed. by Jill Hollis. 352p. 1993. pap. 10.95 (*0-7867-0030-0*) Carroll & Graf.

Love's Work. Gillian Rose. 1997. pap. 2.99 (*0-8052-1078-4*) Schocken.

Love's Work: A Reckoning with Life. Gillian Rose. 160p. 1996. 20.00 (*0-8052-4135-3*) Schocken.

***Lovescene Limousine & Company.** unabridged ed. Damon Ferguson. 160p. 2000. pap. 11.95 (*0-9701925-0-9*) New Model.

Lovescenes. large type ed. Sandra Marton. 298p. 1993. 27.99 (*0-7505-0439-0*) Ulverscroft.

Lovesick. large type ed. Angeles Mastretta. Tr. by Margaret Sayers Peden from SPA. LC 97-5817. 538p. 1997. 24.95 (*0-7862-1083-4*) Thorndike Pr.

Lovesick: A Novel. Angeles Mastretta. Tr. by Margaret Sayers Peden. 400p. 1998. pap. 13.00 (*1-57322-655-6*, Riverhd Trade) Berkley Pub.

Lovesick: Modernist Plays of Same-Sex Love, 1894-1925. Laurence Senelick. LC 98-27240. (Illus.). 210p. 1999. pap. 23.99 (*0-415-18557-2*) Routledge.

Lovesick: Modernist Plays of Same-Sex Love, 1894-1925. Ed. by Laurence Senelick. LC 98-27240. (Illus.). 201p. 1999. 75.00 (*0-415-18556-4*) Routledge.

Lovesick: The Best Quotes about Love & Sex. Bruce Lansky. LC 96-43476. (Orig.). 1997. write for info. (*0-88166-270-4*) Meadowbrook.

Lovesick: The Best Quotes about Love & Sex. Ed. by Bruce Lansky. LC 96-43476. 110p. (Orig.). 1997. 7.00 (*0-671-57499-X*) S&S Trade.

Lovesick Computer. William T. Crow. 25p. (YA). (gr. 10 up). 1982. pap. 3.50 (*0-87129-840-6*, L47) Dramatic Pub.

Lovesickness in the Middle Ages: The Viaticum & Its Commentaries. Mary F. Wack. LC 89-22450. (Middle Ages Ser.). (Illus.). 372p. (C). 1990. text 44.95 (*0-8122-8142-X*) U of Pa Pr.

LoveSmart: Transforming the Emotional Patterns That Sabotage Relationships. Sandra Michaelson. (Illus.). 280p. (Orig.). 1996. pap. 15.95 (*1-882631-28-5*) Prospect NM.

Lovesome Hill. Jean S. MacLeod. 224p. 1996. 22.00 (*0-7278-4981-6*) Severn Hse.

***Lovesong.** Elizabeth Jolley. 252p. 1998. pap. 16.95 (*0-14-027275-5*) Penguin Bks.

Lovesong. Geraldine McCaughrean. 424p. 1997. pap. 17.95 (*1-86066-040-1*, Pub. by R Cohen Bks) Trafalgar.

Lovesong. Paula Williams. 1988. 2.50 (*0-517-00639-1*) Random Hse Value.

Lovesong: Becoming a Jew. Julius Lester. (Illus.). 256p. 1995. reprint ed. pap. 12.45 (*1-55970-316-4*, Pub. by Arcade Pub Inc) Time Warner.

Lovesong for Miss Lydia. Don Evans. 1986. pap. 5.25 (*0-8222-0700-1*) Dramatists Play.

Lovesong for the Giant Contessa. Steven T. Culbert. LC 96-51156. xiii, 278 p. 1997. 20.00 (*1-56858-082-7*) FWEW.

Lovesongs. Katherine Stone. 480p. 1991. mass mkt. 4.95 (*0-8217-3362-1*, Zebra Kensgtn) Kensgtn Pub Corp.

Lovespell. large type ed. Jennifer Taylor. 1991. reprint ed. lib. bdg. 18.95 (*0-263-12599-8*) Mac Lib Ref.

Loves's Labour's Lost. William Shakespeare. Ed. by Barbara A. Mowat & Paul Werstine. (New Folger Library). (Illus.). 352p. 1996. mass mkt. 3.99 (*0-671-72274-3*) S&S Trade.

Lovest Thou Me? Frances J. Roberts. 1967. pap. 3.25 (*0-932814-19-0*) Kings Farspan.

LoveStart: Pre-Birth Bonding. Eve Marnie. (SPA.). 142p. (Orig.). pap. 10.00 (*84-86344-88-3*, 139) Hay House.

Lovestorm. Judith E. French. 384p. 1990. pap. 3.95 (*0-380-75553-X*, Avon Bks) Morrow Avon.

Lovestorm. Joann Ross. (Temptation Ser.). 1993. per. 2.99 (*0-373-25571-3*, 1-25571-0) Harlequin Bks.

***Lovestruck.** (Rock & Pop Classics: Vol. 10). (Illus.). 30p. 2000. write for info. (*1-892207-39-7*) Intl Masters Pub.

Lovestruck. Charlotte Lamb. (Presents Ser.: No. 1935). 1998. per. 3.75 (*0-373-11935-6*, 1-11935-3) Harlequin Bks.

Lovestruck. Kate William. (Sweet Valley High Ser.: No. 27). (YA). (gr. 7 up). 1986. 9.09 (*0-606-01636-8*, Pub. by Turtleback) Demco.

Lovestruck. large type ed. Charlotte Lamb. (Harlequin Romance Ser.). 288p. 1998. 20.95 (*0-263-15491-2*) Thorndike Pr.

Lovestyles: How to Celebrate Your Differences. Tina B. Tessina. 368p. (Orig.). 1987. pap. 9.95 (*0-87877-097-6*) Newcastle Pub.

Lovett's Lights on Acts. C. S. Lovett. 1972. pap. 8.95 (*0-938148-28-1*) Prsnl Christianity.

Lovett's Lights on I Corinthians with Gems from II Corinthian. C. S. Lovett. (Illus.). 392p. (Orig.). (C). 1996. pap. 14.95 (*0-938148-48-6*) Prsnl Christianity.

Lovett's Lights on Galatians, Ephesians, Philippians, Colossians, 1 & 2 Thessalonians. C. S. Lovett. 1970. pap. 7.95 (*0-938148-25-7*) Prsnl Christianity.

Lovett's Lights on Hebrews. C. S. Lovett. 1976. pap. 8.45 (*0-938148-32-X*) Prsnl Christianity.

Lovett's Lights on John. C. S. Lovett. 1970. pap. 8.45 (*0-938148-24-9*) Prsnl Christianity.

Lovett's Lights on Revelation. C. S. Lovett. (Illus.). 352p. 1992. pap. 12.95 (*0-938148-44-3*) Prsnl Christianity.

Lovett's Lights on Romans. C. S. Lovett. 1975. pap. 8.95 (*0-938148-30-3*) Prsnl Christianity.

An Asterisk (*) at the beginning of an entry indicates that the title is appearing for the first time.

Lovett's Lights on the Sermon on the Mount. C. S. Lovett. 176p. (Orig.). 1985. pap. 7.45 (*0-938148-40-0*) Prsnl Christianity.

Lovetypes: Discover Your Romantic Style & Find Your Soul Mate. Alexander Avila. LC 98-46457. 304p. 1999. pap. 13.50 (*0-380-80014-4*, Avon Bks) Morrow Avon.

Lovewell: The Expeditions of Captain John Lovewell & His Encounters with the Indians, with a Biographical Sketch of Captain Lovewell. Frederic Kidder. (Illus.). 123p. 1993. reprint ed. pap. 19.00 (*0-8328-3368-1*); reprint ed. lib. bdg. 29.00 (*0-8328-3367-3*) Higginson Bk Co.

***Lovewords: Poetry from a Place Called Love.** Fisiwe. Ed. by Chuora Whahid Rasul. (Illus.). 96p. 1999. pap. 10.00 (*0-9666802-2-7*) Pauline Publishing.

Loveworks: Coming to Terms with Intimacy & Equality. Ronald W. Heilmann & Mary A. Massey. 172p. (Orig.). 1995. pap. 14.95 (*1-883520-09-6*) Jeremiah Pr.

Lovey - A Book of Poems. Geraldine E. Lamkin. 72p. 1983. pap. 5.00 (*0-9612632-0-2*) Lamkin.

Lovey Mary. Alice H. Rice. 211p. 20.95 (*0-8488-1133-X*) Amereon Ltd.

Lovhers. Nicole Brossard. 96p. 1987. pap. 5.00 (*0-919349-93-5*) Guernica Editions.

***Lovies: Cherished Objects of Affection.** Ed. & Photos by Susan Swick Morrow. (Illus.). 50p. 2000. pap. 19.95 (*0-9700122-0-9*) S S Morrow.

***Lovin' Ain't Over: The Couple's Guide to Better Sex after Prostate Disease.** Ralph J. Alterowitz. 2000. pap. write for info. (*1-883257-03-4*) Hlth Edu Lit.

Lovin' Dutch Ovens: A Cook Book for the Dutch Oven Enthusiast. Joan S. Larsen. Ed. by Carolyn Bessey & Julie Ware. LC 91-90722. (Illus.). 241p. 1991. 19.95 (*1-880415-03-8*) L F S Pubns.

Lovin' for a Lifetime: 365 Ways to Keep Romance in Your Marriage. Lisa J. Peck. 128p. 1998. pap. 6.98 (*0-88290-640-2*, 1092) Horizon Utah.

Lovin' Leo: Your Leonardo DiCaprio Scrapbook. Ed. by Scholastic, Inc. Staff. (Illus.). 48p. (J). (gr. 4-7). 1998. pap. 5.99 (*0-590-04855-4*) Scholastic Inc.

Lovin' Spoonful: A Collection of Favorite Recipes. St. Luke's Regional Medical Center Auxiliary Staff. LC 92-1727. 1992. spiral bd. 10.00 (*0-87197-342-1*) Favorite Recipes.

***Lovina's Song: A Pioneer Girl's Journey with the Donner Party.** Marian Rudolph. LC 99-61583. (Illus.). 187p. (YA). (gr. 5-8). 1999. pap. 11.95 (*1-928595-01-4*) Citron Bay.

Lovina's Song: A Pioneer Girl's Journey with the Donner Party. Marian Rudolph. (Illus.). 192p. (J). 1998. pap. 11.95 (*1-883965-43-8*) Rattle OK Pubns.

Loving. (Self-Concept Ser.). 64p. (J). (gr. 3-8). 1984. 8.99 (*0-86653-180-7*, GA 540) Good Apple.

Loving. Ann Morris. (Illus.). 32p. (J). 1990. 16.00 (*0-688-06340-3*); lib. bdg. 15.93 (*0-688-06341-1*) Lothrop.

Loving. Ann Morris. LC 90-33844. 1994. 10.15 (*0-606-06547-4*, Pub. by Turtleback) Demco.

Loving. Danielle Steel. 384p. (Orig.). 1981. mass mkt. 6.99 (*0-440-14657-7*) Dell.

Loving. Ann Morris. Ed. by Amy Cohn. LC 90-33844. (Illus.). 32p. (J). (ps-3). 1994. reprint ed. mass mkt. 4.95 (*0-688-13613-3*, Wm Morrow) Morrow Avon.

Loving: Poetry & Art. Ed. by Charles Sullivan. (Illus.). 160p. 1992. 29.95 (*0-8109-3562-7*, Pub. by Abrams) Time Warner.

Loving a Happy Dog. Mary Shields. (Illus.). 32p. (J). 1992. pap. 12.00 (*0-9618348-3-8*) Pyrola Pub.

Loving a Lowly Stranger. large type ed. Christina Cordaire. LC 97-51959. (Romance Ser.). 1998. 24.95 (*0-7862-1372-8*) Thorndike Pr.

Loving a Prodigal: A Survival Guide For Parents of Rebellious Children. Norman Wright. LC 99-21017. 1999. 18.99 (*1-56476-743-4*, Victor Bks) Chariot Victor.

***Loving Across the Color Line: A White Adoptive Mother Learns about Race.** Sharon Rush. LC 99-89362. 192p. 2000. 23.95 (*0-8476-9912-9*) Rowman.

Loving Again. Joseph A. Ryan. 160p. 1991. pap. 7.99 (*0-310-53631-6*) Zondervan.

***Loving A.J., Vol. 1.** Marisa Jackson. 1999. per. 6.99 (*0-689-83471-3*) S&S Childrens.

Loving an Imperfect Man. Ellen S. Stern. LC 96-41487. 1997. 22.00 (*0-671-52516-6*) PB.

Loving an Imperfect Man. Ellen S. Stern. 1998. per. 12.00 (*0-671-52901-3*, PB Trade Paper) PB.

Loving & Giving. Gina Ferris. (Special Edition Ser.). 1994. per. 3.50 (*0-373-09879-0*, 5-09879-3) Silhouette.

Loving & Giving. Beatrice Hewitt. 63p. (C). 1989. text 35.00 (*0-936270-77-2*, Pub. by Pentland Pr) St Mut.

Loving & Healing Your Inner Adolescent. 2nd rev. ed. Martha B. Beveridge. Ed. by Terrisa Bruce-Phipps. 25p. 1994. pap. 3.50 (*1-889237-05-1*) Options Now.

Loving & Leaving the Good Life. Helen Nearing. (Illus.). 198p. 1993. reprint ed. pap. 16.95 (*0-930031-63-6*) Chelsea Green Pub.

Loving & Letting Go: Parents Who Decide Against Medical Intervention. Deborah Davis. (Illus.). 64p. (Orig.). 1992. pap. 5.95 (*1-56123-060-X*, LLGC) Centering Corp.

Loving & Listening: A Parent's Book of Daily Inspirations for Rebuilding the Family after Divorce. Melinda Blau. LC 95-45918. 384p. (Orig.). 1996. pap. 13.00 (*0-399-52202-6*, Perigee Bks) Berkley Pub.

Loving & Losing. Carolyn Keene. (Nancy Drew on Campus Ser.: No. 15). (YA). (gr. 8 up). 1996. per. 3.99 (*0-671-56804-3*) PB.

Loving & Losing a Pet: A Psychologist & a Veterinarian Share Their Wisdom. Michael Stern & Susn Cropper. LC 97-23339. (Illus.). 232p. 1998. 35.00 (*0-7657-0116-2*) Aronson.

Loving Argument. Margery Snyder. 56p. (Orig.). 1991. pap. 5.00 (*1-880298-06-6*) Viridiana.

Loving Arms: British Women Writing the Second World War. Karen Schneider. LC 96-5744. 232p. (C). 1996. text 34.95 (*0-8131-1980-4*) U Pr of Ky.

***Loving Arms of God: Biblical Truths for God's Family.** Elizabeth S. Stickney. LC 00-23829. (Illus.). 2000. write for info. (*0-8028-5171-1*) Eerdmans.

Loving Arms of the Law. Mary Curtis. (Special Edition Ser.: No. 730). 1992. per. 3.39 (*0-373-09730-1*, 5-09730-8) Harlequin Bks.

Loving As Jesus Loved, Vol. 10. Sharon Steele. (Aglow Bible Study Ser.). 1999. 6.99 (*0-8307-2504-0*) Gospel Lght.

Loving As Jesus Loves. Albert B. Simpson. LC 95-70301. 104p. 1996. pap. 8.99 (*0-87509-604-2*) Chr Pubns.

Loving Boldly: Issues Facing Lesbians. Esther D. Rothblum & Ellen Cole. LC 88-21415. (Women & Therapy Ser.: Vol. 8, Nos. 1-2). (Illus.). 224p. 1989. pap. text 14.95 (*0-918393-58-2*, Harrington Park) Haworth Pr.

Loving Care. large type ed. Margaret Barker. 1995. 27.99 (*0-7505-0746-2*, Pub. by Mgna Lrg Print) Ulverscroft.

Loving Care of Pet Parrots. Rosemary Low. (Illus.). 160p. 1999. pap. 12.95 (*0-88839-439-X*) Hancock House.

Loving Change: The Secrets of Lifelong, Joy, Fulfillment & Opportunity. Jeremy Birch. (Illus.). 267p. (Orig.). 1994. pap. 19.95 (*0-9613102-5-1*) StressPress.

Loving Changes: A Journal for Mothers in Times of Transition. (Illus.). 304p. 1998. 16.95 (*0-8298-1239-3*) Pilgrim OH.

***Loving Charity.** Catherine Archibald. 320p. 2000. mass mkt. 4.99 (*0-8439-4704-7*, Leisure Bks) Dorchester Pub Co.

Loving Children: Words of Love about Kids from Those Who Cherish Them. Bob West. LC 92-35196. 128p. 1993. pap. 9.95 (*1-879904-10-1*) Halo Bks.

Loving Chloe: A Novel. Jo-Ann Mapson. LC 97-20578. 368p. 1999. pap. 13.00 (*0-06-093028-4*) HarpC.

Loving Chloe: A Novel. Jo-Ann Mapson. LC 98-24006. 1998. write for info. (*1-56895-567-7*) Wheeler Pub.

Loving Choices: A Growing Experience. Bruce Fisher & Nina Hart. (Illus.). 240p. (Orig.). 1995. pap. text 12.00 (*0-9607250-3-2*) Fisher Pubng.

***Loving Choices: An Experience in Growing Relationships.** Bruce Fisher & Nina Hart-Fisher. 224p. 2000. pap. 14.95 (*1-886230-30-7*, Rebuilding Bks) Impact Pubs CA.

Loving Choices Facilitators Manual: A Growing Experience. Bruce Fisher & Nina Hart. (Illus.). (Orig.). 1996. pap. text, teacher ed. write for info. (*0-9607250-5-9*) Fisher Pubng.

Loving Choices Workbook: A Growing Experience. Bruce Fisher & Nina Hart. (Illus.). 118p. (Orig.). 1995. pap. text 12.00 (*0-9607250-4-0*) Fisher Pubng.

Loving Community. Forrest M. Plants. (Eagle Bible Ser.). 1989. pap. 0.99 (*0-87162-551-2*, D9153) Warner Pr.

Loving Companions: Our Jewish Wedding Album. Ronald H. Isaacs & Leora W. Isaacs. LC 90-40487. 144p. 1991. 30.00 (*0-87668-736-2*) Aronson.

Loving Contract: How to Be Lovers for Life & Create a Happy, Successful Marriage. Mark Jones. Ed. by Heddy Oliver. 96p. (Orig.). 1983. pap. text 9.95 (*0-686-36407-4*) Evolvement.

Loving Correction: First Corinthians 16. rev. ed. Spiros Zodhiates. (Exegetical Commentary Ser.). 1998. pap. 8.99 (*0-89957-477-7*) AMG Pubs.

Loving Daughters. large type ed. Olga Masters. LC 93-11696. (General Ser.). 458p. 1993. lib. bdg. 18.95 (*0-7862-0032-4*) Thorndike Pr.

Loving Discipline A to Z. 2nd rev. ed. Esther Wright. LC 94-90641. 80p. 1996. pap. text 9.95 (*0-9642947-1-0*) Teaching From Heart.

Loving Dominant. 2nd ed. John Warren. (Orig.). 1998. mass mkt. 7.95 (*1-56333-600-6*, Rhinoceros) Masquerade.

***Loving Dominant.** 2nd rev. ed. John Warren. 220p. 2000. pap. 11.95 (*1-890159-20-4*) Greenery Pr.

Loving Each Day. John Roger. 1989. 10.00 (*0-914829-26-2*) Mandeville LA.

Loving Each One Best: A Caring & Practical Approach to Raising Siblings. Nancy Samalin & Catherine Whitney. 224p. 1997. pap. 13.95 (*0-553-37834-1*) Bantam.

Loving Each Other. Leo F. Buscaglia. 208p. 1986. pap. 10.00 (*0-449-90157-2*, Columbine) Fawcett.

Loving Each Other. Leo F. Buscaglia. LC 84-50590. 208p. 1984. 13.95 (*0-943432-27-8*) SLACK Inc.

Loving Each Other: The Challenge of Human Relationships. Leo Buscaglia. 1995. audio 16.00 (*0-671-52070-9*) S&S Trade.

Loving Each Other for Better & for Best, 2 vols. in 1. Gary Smalley. 480p. 1997. 11.99 (*0-88486-079-5*) Arrowood Pr.

Loving Edith. large type ed. Mary Tannen. 272p. 1995. lib. bdg. 24.95 (*1-57490-026-9*, Beeler LP Bks) T T Beeler.

Loving Elizabeth. 304p. 1999. mass mkt. 4.99 (*0-8217-6320-2*) Kensgtn Pub Corp.

Loving Endlessly Bk. I: Awakening. Thelma Williams. (Illus.). 16p. 1999. pap. 4.00 (*0-945768-03-6*) A-Town Pub Co.

Loving Endlessly Bk. II: Searching for Answers. Thelma Williams. (Illus.). 16p. 1999. pap. 4.00 (*0-945768-06-0*) A-Town Pub Co.

Loving Endlessly Bk. III: Lost Love. Thelma Williams. (Illus.). 16p. 1999. pap. 4.00 (*0-945768-08-7*) A-Town Pub Co.

Loving Endlessly Bk. IV: One Way Love. Thelma Williams. (Illus.). 16p. 1999. pap. 4.00 (*0-945768-12-5*) A-Town Pub Co.

Loving Endlessly Bk. V: Just Lonely. Thelma Williams. (Illus.). 16p. 1999. pap. 4.00 (*0-945768-07-9*) A-Town Pub Co.

Loving Endlessly Bk. VI: Still Loving. Thelma Williams. (Illus.). 16p. 1999. pap. 4.00 (*0-945768-14-1*) A-Town Pub Co.

Loving Endlessly Bk. VII: Forbidden Love. Thelma Williams. (Illus.). 16p. 1999. pap. 4.00 (*0-945768-10-9*) A-Town Pub Co.

Loving Endlessly Bk. VIII: Inside Stuff. Thelma Williams. (Illus.). 16p. 1999. pap. 4.00 (*0-945768-13-3*) A-Town Pub Co.

Loving Endlessly Bk. IX: Complete Love. Thelma Williams. (Illus.). 16p. 1999. pap. 4.00 (*0-945768-11-7*) A-Town Pub Co.

Loving Endlessly Bk. X: Sharing. Daniel F. Williams. (Illus.). 16p. 1999. pap. 4.00 (*0-945768-15-X*) A-Town Pub Co.

Loving Endlessly Bk. XI: Living Learning Loving. Cynthia Ross. (Illus.). 16p. 1999. pap. 4.00 (*0-945768-16-8*) A-Town Pub Co.

Loving Enemies. Rachel Davis & Deana James. 416p. 1996. mass mkt. 5.99 (*0-8217-5418-1*, Zebra Kensgtn) Kensgtn Pub Corp.

Loving Enemy. large type ed. Catherine Cross. (Dales Large Print Ser.). 124p. 1996. pap. 18.99 (*1-85389-606-3*, Dales) Ulverscroft.

Loving Evangeline. Linda Howard. (Mira Bks.). 249p. 1998. mass mkt. 5.50 (*1-55166-457-7*, 1-66457-2, Mira Bks) Harlequin Bks.

Loving Evangeline. large type ed. Linda Howard. (Silhouette Ser.). 1997. 20.95 (*0-373-59828-9*) Thorndike Pr.

Loving Food: A Collection of Recipes for All Occasions. Ed. by Sara J. Kasperzak. (Illus.). 236p. 1991. 25.00 (*0-9630254-0-6*) Comm Alum Ckware.

***Loving for Life: Building a Covenant Marriage.** 2nd ed. LeeAnn Rawlins. 1999. pap. 9.95 (*1-929125-02-X*, Pub. by Loyal Pubng) BookWorld.

Loving Freely Without Needing. rev. ed. James L. Park. LC BD436.P37 1996. (Love among Authentic Persons Ser.: No. 2). Orig. Title: Authentic Love: An Existential Vision. 1995. pap. 3.75 (*0-89231-502-4*) Existential Bks.

Loving from Your Soul: Creating Powerful Relationships. Shepherd Hoodwin. LC 94-92317. (Summerjoy Michael Ser.). 160p. 1995. pap. 11.95 (*1-885469-02-0*) Summerjoy.

Loving Fury. Phoebe Conn. 1986. mass mkt. 3.95 (*0-317-39260-3*, Zebra Kensgtn) Kensgtn Pub Corp.

Loving Game. Sylvia Baker. 288p. 1997. pap. 11.95 (*0-7472-5124-X*, Pub. by Headline Bk Pub) Trafalgar.

Loving Game. large type ed. Sylvia Baker. (Black Satin Romance Ser.). 442p. 1997. 27.99 (*1-86110-027-2*, Pub. by Mgna Lrg Print) Ulverscroft.

***Loving Ganesa: Hinduism's Endearing Elephanat - Faced God.** 2nd rev. ed. Satguru Sivaya Subramuniyaswami. LC 99-73601. (Rishi Collection Ser.). (Illus.). 800p. 2000. pap. 29.85 (*0-945497-77-6*) Himalayan Acad.

***Loving Glory.** Geri Borcz. (Splendor Historical Romances Ser.). 320p. 2000. mass mkt. 4.99 (*0-8217-6469-1*, Zebra Kensgtn) Kensgtn Pub Corp.

Loving God. Charles Colson. 1997. mass mkt. 5.99 (*0-310-21439-4*) Zondervan.

Loving God. Charles Colson. 320p. 1997. pap. 12.99 (*0-310-21914-0*) Zondervan.

Loving God. Carolyn Nystrom. (Christian Character Bible Studies). 64p. (Orig.). 1992. pap., wbk. ed. 4.99 (*0-8308-1141-9*, 1141) InterVarsity.

Loving God. Eleanor Snyder & Susan Pries. LC 95-61974. (Living Stones Ser.). 206p. (J). (ps-8). 1996. pap. 32.95 (*0-87303-173-3*) Faith & Life.

Loving God. large type ed. Charles M. Colson. 1987. pap. 16.95 (*0-8027-2594-5*) Walker & Co.

Loving God: Journey to a More Mature Faith. David S. Rose. (Illus.). 70p. (Orig.). 1990. pap. text 9.50 (*0-9627687-0-7*) Proctors Hall Pr.

Loving God, Loving Family. Ann Gallagher et al. (Grade School Chastity - Project Genesis Ser.). (Illus.). 148p. (Orig.). (J). (gr. 5). 1996. pap. text, teacher ed. write for info. (*1-885845-14-6*); pap. text, student ed. write for info. (*1-885845-15-4*) Leaflet Missal.

***Loving God Through the Darkness: Selected Writings of John of the Cross.** John of the Cross. Ed. by Stephen S. Wilburn. LC 99-37741. (Spiritual Classics). 95p. 2000. pap. 5.00 (*0-8358-0904-8*) Upper Room Bks.

Loving God with All Your Mind see **Ama a Dios con Toda Tu Mente**

Loving God with All Your Mind. Elizabeth George. 252p. 1998. pap. 9.99 (*1-56507-861-6*) Harvest Hse.

Loving God's Way: A Fresh Look at the One Another Passages. Gary DeLashmutt. LC 95-37015. 144p. 1996. pap. 9.99 (*0-8254-2454-2*) Kregel.

***Loving Graham Greene: A Novel.** Gloria Emerson. LC 99-86033. 192p. 2000. 22.95 (*0-679-46324-0*) Random.

Loving Guide to the World As a Two Year-Old Says It. Mary Field & Elliot Field. (Illus.). 14p. (Orig.). (J). (ps up). 1983. pap. 5.95 (*0-914445-00-6*) Palm Springs Pub.

Loving Hands: The Traditional Art of Baby Massage. Frederick Leboyer. LC 97-25335. (Illus.). 1997. pap. 16.95 (*1-55704-314-0*, Pub. by Newmarket) Norton.

Loving, Hating & Survival: A Handbook for All Who Work with Troubled Children & Young People. Ed. by Andrew Hardwick & Judith Woodhead. LC 98-40536. 250p. 1999. text 43.95 (*1-85742-424-7*, RJ499.3.L68, Pub. by Arena) Ashgate Pub Co.

Loving Hearts, Gentle Voices, Treasured Love, Embraces . . . Sharon R. Edler. 134p. 1997. pap. 12.00 (*0-8059-4047-2*) Dorrance.

Loving Help? or Control? Which? Dee Frances. Date not set. pap. 3.00 (*1-885519-63-X*) DDDD Pubns.

Loving Her. Ann A. Shockley. LC 97-18233. (Northeastern Library of Black Literature). 208p. 1997. reprint ed. pap. text 14.95 (*1-55553-329-9*) NE U Pr.

Loving Highwayman. large type ed. Pamela Bennetts. (Ulverscroft). 336p. 1994. 27.99 (*0-7089-3035-2*) Ulverscroft.

Loving Him Without Losing You: How to Stop Disappearing & Start Being Yourself. Beverly Engel. LC 99-52075. 304p. 2000. text 24.95 (*0-471-35558-5*) Wiley.

Loving in the War Years: Lo Que Nunca Paso por Sus Labios. Cherrie Moraga. LC 86-61474. 153p. 1983. 30.00 (*0-89608-196-6*); pap. 14.00 (*0-89608-195-8*) South End Pr.

***Loving in the War Years: Lo Que Nunca Paso por Sus Labios.** Cherrie Moraga. (Classics Ser.: Vol. 6). 208p. 2000. 40.00 (*0-89608-627-5*); pap. 17.00 (*0-89608-626-7*) South End Pr.

***Loving in Time of War.** Jody Aliesan. 1999. pap. 13.00 (*0-911287-31-0*) Blue Begonia.

Loving Is Many Things: Reflections on Love. G. Leo Robertson. 32p. 1987. pap. 5.00 (*0-9618775-0-2*) G L Robertson.

Loving Is Natural, Parenting Is Not: Creating a Value-Centered Family. Gilbert C. Gockley & Tanya T. Gockley. LC 96-85939. (Illus.). 216p. (Orig.). 1997. pap. 14.95 (*0-9651889-0-6*) Coleman Press.

Loving Jack. Nora Roberts. (Language of Love Ser.: No. 42). 1994. mass mkt. 3.59 (*0-373-51042-X*, 1-51042-9) Silhouette.

***Loving Jessie.** Dallas Schulze. 2001. mass mkt. 5.99 (*1-55166-791-6*, Mira Bks) Harlequin Bks.

Loving Jesus. Mother Teresa of Calcutta. 166p. 1991. pap. 6.99 (*0-89283-676-8*, Charis) Servant.

Loving Joseph Smith Out of Hell. Marci Moles. LC 94-96578. 188p. 1994. pap. write for info. (*1-886389-02-0*) Inside Job.

Loving Journeys Guide to Adoption. Elaine L. Walker. LC 92-93516. (Illus.). 394p. (Orig.). 1992. pap. 24.95 (*0-9633642-0-0*) Loving Journeys.

Loving Julia. Karen Robards. 384p. 1986. reprint ed. mass mkt. 6.99 (*0-446-30057-8*, Pub. by Warner Bks) Little.

Loving Justice: God's Acceptable Worship. Bob Hunter & Carol Hunter. (LifeGuide Bible Studies). 59p. (Orig.). 1990. pap., wbk. ed. 4.99 (*0-8308-1066-8*, 1066) InterVarsity.

Loving Katherine. Carolyn Davidson. (Harlequin Historical Ser.: No. 325). 1996. per. 4.99 (*0-373-28925-1*, 1-28925-5) Harlequin Bks.

Loving Kindness: The Mitzuah of Gemilut Chassadim. Jacob I. Schocnet. Orig. Title: Gemilut Chassadim. 24p. 1999. pap. 2.75 (*0-8266-0187-1*, Merkos LInyonei Chinuch) Kehot Pubn Soc.

Loving Leader: The Man's Role at Home see **Liderazgo con Amor: Funcion Hombre Hogar**

Loving Leadership. Willow Creek Resources Staff. (Defining Moments Ser.: Vol. 13). 1995. audio 9.99 (*0-310-20433-X*) Zondervan.

Loving Legacy. large type ed. Marion Lennox. 301p. 1995. 11.50 (*0-7505-0817-5*, Pub. by Mgna Lrg Print) Ulverscroft.

Loving Lesbian. Claire McNab & Sharon Gedan. LC 96-45485. 208p. (Orig.). 1997. pap. 14.95 (*1-56280-169-4*) Naiad Pr.

Loving Letters. Liz N. Connery. (Illus.). 60p. (Orig.). 1985. pap. text 7.00 (*0-9614333-0-2*) L Newkirk Connery.

Loving Letters: An Islamic Alphabet. LC 95-80319. (Illus.). 26p. (J). (ps up). 1995. 12.50 (*0-915957-53-1*) amana pubns.

Loving Life: Living Vision. Robert J. Wright. write for info. (*0-9661401-5-X*) Except Liv Pr.

Loving Life: The Seven Journeys. Robert J. Wright. Date not set. write for info. (*0-9661401-2-5*) Except Liv Pr.

Loving Life after 60: Celebrating the Autumn of Your Life. Tom Paugh. LC 99-31679. 176p. 2000. pap. 9.50 (*1-57223-283-8*) Willow Creek Pr.

Loving Linsey. Rachelle Morgan. 1999. mass mkt. 5.99 (*0-380-80040-3*, Avon Bks) Morrow Avon.

Loving Literature. Ed. by Scholastic, Inc. Staff. 240p. (gr. 3-7). 1993. pap. 19.95 (*0-590-49038-9*) Scholastic Inc.

Loving, Living, & Party Going. Henry Green, pseud. 528p. 1993. pap. 14.95 (*0-14-018691-3*, Penguin Classics) Viking Penguin.

Loving Lucy. Bart Andrews & Thomas Watson. (Illus.). 383p. 1982. pap. 14.95 (*0-312-49975-2*) St Martin.

Loving Madly/Loving Sanely. Andrew Abarbanel. 240p. 1998. pap. 13.00 (*1-57566-251-5*, Knsington) Kensgtn Pub Corp.

Loving Madly/Loving Sanely. Andrew Ararbanel. LC 96-79080. 224p. 1997. 22.00 (*1-57566-161-6*, Knsington) Kensgtn Pub Corp.

Loving Mariah. Beverly Bird. (Intimate Moments Ser.: No. 790). 1997. per. 3.99 (*0-373-07790-4*, 1-07790-8) Silhouette.

***Loving Max, Vol. 13.** Wendy Morgan. (Zebra Bouquet Ser.). 1999. mass mkt. 3.99 (*0-8217-6348-2*, Zebra Kensgtn) Kensgtn Pub Corp.

Loving Me: The Sisterfriend's Guide to Being Single & Happy. Claudette Sims. LC 98-24341. 128p. 1998. 12.95 (*0-8050-5160-0*, Owl) H Holt & Co.

Loving Me, Loving You: Balancing Love & Power in a Co-Dependent World. Brenda Schaeffer. 168p. (Orig.). pap. 11.95 (*0-89486-747-4*, 5154A) Hazelden.

Loving Me-Loving You: Loving Me Frees Me for Loving You. Donna Reed. 151p. 1993. pap. 10.00 (*0-9641434-0-2*) Westbury Pubng.

***Loving Memories.** Penny Boylan. 2000. 16.95 (*0-7548-0479-8*, Lorenz Bks) Anness Pub.

***Loving Memories.** Great Quotations Staff. 2000. 5.99 (*1-56245-423-4*) Great Quotations.

***Loving Memories: Trans-Mississippi, 1898 - Greater America, 1899 Expositions.** (Illus.). xii, 204p. 1999. ring bd. 19.95 (*0-9679494-9-1*) C Drehsen.

Loving Memories from Dog to Dog. Howard W. Gabriel, III. (Illus.). 32p. (Orig.). (J). (gr. k-6). 1987. pap. 2.95 (*0-936997-01-X*) M & H Enter.

L

Loving Men: Gay Partners, Spirituality, & AIDS. Richard P. Hardy. LC 98-20737. 190p. 1998. pap. 17.95 (0-8264-1138-X) Continuum.

Loving Men More, Needing Men Less. Judith Sills. 1997. pap. 11.95 (0-14-024223-6) Viking Penguin.

Loving Midlife Marriage. Betty Polston & Susan K. Golant. LC 99-17025. 272p. (C). 1999. pap. 14.95 (0-471-31453-6) Wiley.

***Loving Monday: Succeeding in Business Without Selling Your Soul, 2 vols.** 1999. text 14.99 incl. audio (0-8308-2260-7) InterVarsity.

Loving Monday: Succeeding in Business Without Selling Your Soul. John D. Beckett. LC 98-17886. 177p. 1998. 15.99 (0-8308-1926-6, 1926) InterVarsity.

Loving More: The Primer. 4th rev. ed. Orig. Title: Loving More: The Polyfidelity Primer. 196p. 1999. pap. 16.00 (0-9622144-2-6) PEP.

Loving More: The Polyfidelity Primer see Loving More: The Primer

Loving Mozart: A Past Life Memory of the Composer's Final Years. Mary Montano. 239p. 1995. pap. 21.00 (0-9642577-0-X) Cantus Verus.

Loving My Jewishness: Jewish Self Pride & Self-Esteem. Ed. by Dov Peretz Elkins. LC 78-58511. 1978. pap. 10.00 (0-918834-04-X) Growth Assoc.

Loving Nature: Ecological Integrity & Christian Responsibility. James A. Nash. 1991. pap. 16.95 (0-687-22824-7) Abingdon.

Loving Nature . . . The Right Way Vol. 1: A Family Guide to Viewing & Photographing Scenic Areas & Wildlife. William W. Hartley. Ed. by Bruce R. Hopkins. 160p. (Orig.). 1996. pap. 19.95 (1-888859-00-8) Prtnrship Pr.

Loving Neighbors Across Time: A Christian's Guide to Protecting the Earth. Robert Parham. Ed. by Becky Nelson. (Illus.). 114p. 1991. pap. text 6.95 (1-56309-042-2, N924106, New Hope) Womans Mission Union.

***Loving Obedience.** William J. Richardson. LC 00-26977. 2000. pap. 12.99 (1-881273-26-1) Northfield Pub.

Loving One Another. Gene Getz. LC 79-63450. 143p. 1979. pap. 1.80 (0-88207-786-4, 6-2786, Victor Bks) Chariot Victor.

Loving One Another. Carolyn Nystrom. (Christian Character Bible Studies). 64p. (Orig.). 1992. pap., wbk. ed. 4.99 (0-8308-1142-7, 1142) InterVarsity.

Loving One Another: Choretz Chayir's Ahavas Yisroel. Aaron Werner. 60p. 1994. text 7.95 (1-885006-34-9); pap. text 4.95 (1-885006-35-7) Three Beacons.

Loving Parent's Guide to Discipline. Marilyn E. Gootman. 208p. (Orig.). 1995. mass mkt. 4.99 (0-425-14571-9) Berkley Pub.

***Loving Parents' Guide to Discipline: How to Teach Your Child to Behave Responsibly--With Kindness, Understanding & Respect.** Marilyn E. Gootman. 208p. 2000. pap. 12.00 (0-425-17450-6) Berkley Pub.

Loving Parents/Happy Kids. Ivan W. Fitzwater. LC 86-63128. (Illus.). 117p. (Orig.). 1986. pap. 10.00 (0-931722-53-5) Corona Pub.

***Loving Pedro Infante.** Denise Chavez. 272p. 2001. 24.00 (0-374-19411-4) FS&G.

Loving Power: Stories. Robert Flanagan. (Contemporary Midwest Fiction Ser.: No. 1). 160p. (Orig.). (C). 1990. pap. 8.95 (0-933087-17-9) Bottom Dog Pr.

Loving Promises. Helen Steiner Rice. (Illus.). 128p. (gr. 10). 1988. 16.99 (0-8007-1600-0) Revell.

Loving Rachel. Jane Bernstein. 1994. pap. text 15.00 (0-941038-01-7) Coyne & Chenoweth.

Loving Reading: Erotics of the Text. Steven G. Kellman. LC 85-1320. 114p. (C). 1985. lib. bdg. 27.50 (0-208-02077-2, Archon Bks) Shoe String.

Loving Relationships. Sondra Ray. LC 79-55633. 192p. 1995. pap. 9.95 (0-89087-244-9) Celestial Arts.

Loving Relationships II. Sondra Ray. 192p. 1995. pap. 9.95 (0-89087-661-4) Celestial Arts.

Loving Remedy. large type ed. Joanna Neil. 288p. 1995. 23.99 (0-263-14338-4, Pub. by Mills & Boon) Ulverscroft.

Loving Reminders for Couples: 60 Affectionate Notes for Those Close to Your Heart. John Cast & Flanklin Covey Company Staff. 1998. pap. 9.95 (1-883219-92-2) Franklin Covey.

***Loving Reminders for Families.** Franklin Covey Company Staff. (Loving Reminders Ser.). 1999. pap. text 9.95 (1-883219-84-1) Franklin Covey.

Loving Reminders for Kids: 60 Nurturing Notes Sealed with Hugs & Kisses! Franklin Covey Company Staff. 1998. pap. 9.95 (1-883219-74-4) Franklin Covey.

Loving Reminders for Teen to Teen. Franklin Covey Company. 1999. pap. text 9.95 (1-883219-83-3) Franklin Covey.

***Loving Sabotage.** Amalie Nothomb. Tr. by Andrew Wilson from FRE. 2000. 21.95 (0-8112-1459-1, Pub. by New Directions) Norton.

Loving Samantha. Robin Gideon. 1996. mass mkt. 4.99 (0-8217-5293-6, Zebra Kensgtn) Kensgtn Pub Corp.

Loving Sander. Joseph Geraci. 160p. 1996. pap. 12.95 (0-85449-231-3, Pub. by Gay Mens Pr) LPC InBook.

Loving Search for God: Contemplative Prayer & "The Cloud of Unknowing" William A. Meninger. LC 82-40274. 142p. (C). 1995. pap. 11.95 (0-8264-0851-6) Continuum.

Loving Search for the Lost Servant. Swami B. Sridhar. (Illus.). 104p. 1987. pap. 10.95 (0-945475-22-5, 1016, Pub. by Mandala Pub Grp) Words Distrib.

Loving Sex: A Pocket Guide. Jane Hertford. (Illus.). 96p. 1999. 10.95 (0-7867-0659-7) Carroll & Graf.

Loving Shepherd see Word & Picture Books, Set 1: For Year B/C

Loving Smart: Putting Your Cards on the Table. Jeffrey Title et al. LC 92-32441. 246p. 1993. mass mkt. 12.99 (0-446-39433-5) Warner Bks.

Loving Solutions: Overcoming Barriers in Your Marriage. Gary Chapman. LC 98-196852. 214p. 1998. 19.99 (1-881273-25-3) Moody.

Loving Solutions: Overcoming Barriers in Your Marriage. Gary Chapman. 214p. 1999. pap. 11.99 (1-881273-91-1) Northfield Pub.

Loving Someone Gay. rev. ed. Don Clark. LC 87-13846. 290p. 1995. pap. 9.95 (0-89087-505-7) Celestial Arts.

Loving Someone Gay. 3rd ed. Don Clark. LC 97-13372. 256p. 1997. pap. 14.95 (0-89087-837-4) Celestial Arts.

Loving Spirit. Daphne Du Maurier. LC 71-184733. 384p. 1971. reprint ed. lib. bdg. 20.00 (0-8376-0415-X) Bentley Pubs.

Loving Spirits. Melinda Pryce. 208p. 1994. mass mkt. 4.50 (0-515-11474-X, Jove) Berkley Pub.

Loving Spoonfuls. Covenant House Texas Guild Staff. (Illus.). 224p. 1995. 15.50 (0-9648928-2-0) Covenant House TX.

Loving Stitch: A History of Knitting & Spinning in New Zealand. Heather Nicholson. (Illus.). 320p. 1998. pap. 45.00 (1-86940-188-3, Pub. by Auckland Univ) Paul & Co Pubs.

Loving Stitches: A Guide to Fine Hand Quilting. Jeana Kimball. Ed. by Barbara Weiland. LC 92-23450. (Joy of Quilting Ser.). (Illus.). 52p. 1993. pap. 12.95 (1-56477-014-1, B147) Martingale & Co.

Loving Subject: Desire, Eloquence, & Power in Romanesque France. Gerald A. Bond. LC 95-17882. (Middle Ages Ser.). 296p. 1995. text 39.95 (0-8122-3322-0) U of Pa Pr.

Loving Surrender. large type ed. Catherine Grant. (Linford Romance Library). 288p. 1992. pap. 16.99 (0-7089-7196-2, Linford) Ulverscroft.

Loving Tea. 1996. pap. 5.99 (0-425-16249-4) Berkley Pub.

Loving Tea. Jane Resnick. LC 98-127241. 1997. mass mkt. 6.50 (0-425-16119-6) Berkley Pub.

***Loving Teens to Fruitful Maturity: Biblical Studies for Parents of Teens.** Cynthia J. Henry. Ed. by Sarah E. Henry. (Illus.). 24p. 1999. pap. 5.99 (1-891287-18-4) C J Studios.

***Loving Teens to Fruitful Maturity: Biblical Studies for Parents of Teens.** 2nd rev. ed. Cynthia J. Henry. Ed. by Sarah E. Henry. (Illus.). 24p. 1999. 24.95 (1-891287-19-2) C J Studios.

Loving the Church. Christoph Schonborn. LC 97-76859. 1998. pap. text 14.95 (0-89870-676-9) Ignatius Pr.

Loving the City God Loves. J. Kip Givens. 1994. pap. write for info. (0-9641158-3-2) Redemp Fellowship.

Loving the Earth. Fredric Lehrman. (Illus.). 48p. (YA). (gr. 6-12). 1990. 14.95 (0-89087-603-7) Celestial Arts.

Loving the Enemy. Rebecca Daniels. (Romance Ser.). 1994. per. 2.75 (0-373-08987-2, 5-08987-5) Silhouette.

Loving the Enemy. Created by Francine Pascal. (Sweet Valley University Thriller Edition Ser.: No. 15). 272p. (YA). (gr. 7 up). 1999. mass mkt. 4.50 (0-553-49263-2) BDD Bks Young Read.

Loving the Everyday: Meditations for Moms. Elizabeth B. Barkley. LC 94-207366. 206p. 1994. pap. 8.95 (0-86716-191-4) St Anthony Mess Pr.

Loving the Good Driver: Poems. Rustin Larson. LC 95-39507. 64p. 1996. pap. 14.95 (0-7734-2672-8, Mellen Poetry Pr) E Mellen.

Loving the Questions: An Exploration of the Nicene Creed. Marianne H. Micks. LC 93-22816. 134p. 1993. pap. 9.95 (1-56101-081-2) Cowley Pubns.

Loving the Questions: An Exploration of the Nicene Creed. Marianne H. Micks. LC 93-22816. 144p. (C). 1993. pap. 11.00 (1-56338-072-2) TPI PA.

Loving the Teens in Your World. Mark Schaufler. 24p. 1996. spiral bd. 2.00 (1-886904-27-8) MST Minist.

Loving the World. Carolyn Nystrom. (Christian Character Bible Studies). 64p. (Orig.). 1992. pap., wbk. ed. 4.99 (0-8308-1143-5, 1143) InterVarsity.

Loving Those We'd Rather Hate. Joseph M. Stowell. 64p. pap. 4.99 (0-8024-4690-6, 209) Moody.

Loving Thoughts for a Perfect Day. Louise L. Hay. Ed. by Dan Olmos. LC 93-13178. (Loving Thoughts Ser.). (Illus.). 64p. 1993. 5.95 (1-56170-069-X, 182) Hay House.

Loving Thoughts for Health & Healing. Louise L. Hay. Ed. by Dan Olmos. LC 93-13177. (Loving Thoughts Ser.). (Illus.). 64p. 1993. 5.95 (1-56170-070-3, 183) Hay House.

Loving Thoughts for Increasing Prosperity. Louise L. Hay. Ed. by Dan Olmos. LC 93-13180. (Loving Thoughts Ser.). (Illus.). 64p. 1993. 5.95 (1-56170-068-1, 181) Hay House.

Loving Thoughts for Loving Yourself. Louise L. Hay. Ed. by Dan Olmos. LC 93-13179. (Loving Thoughts Ser.). (Illus.). 64p. 1993. 5.95 (1-56170-067-3, 180) Hay House.

Loving Time. Leslie Glass. 432p. 1997. reprint ed. mass mkt. 5.99 (0-553-57209-1) Bantam.

Loving to Audition: The Audition Workbook. Larry Silverberg. LC 96-40242. (Young Actors Ser.). 160p. 1996. pap. 14.95 (1-57525-007-1) Smith & Kraus.

Loving to Survive: Sexual Terror, Men's Violence & Women's Lives. Dee L. Graham et al. LC 94-3057. (Feminist Crosscurrents Ser.). 321p. (C). 1994. text 45.00 (0-8147-3058-2) NYU Pr.

Loving to Survive: Sexual Terror, Men's Violence & Women's Lives. Edna I. Rawlings et al. LC 94-3057. (Feminist Crosscurrents Ser.). 321p. (C). 1995. pap. text 19.50 (0-8147-3059-0) NYU Pr.

Loving Touch: A Guide to Being a Better Lover. Andrew Stanway. (Illus.). 192p. 1994. pap. 17.95 (0-7867-0097-1) Carroll & Graf.

Loving Touch: The Sacred Covenant of Divine Communion. Sri Akhenaton. LC 96-72257. (Illus.). 331p. 1998. pap. 24.95 (0-9621839-8-9) Portal MD.

Loving Touches. Lory Freeman. LC 85-62434. (Illus.). 32p. (Orig.). (J). (ps-3). 1985. lib. bdg. 15.95 (0-943990-21-1) Parenting Pr.

Loving Touches. Lory Freeman. LC 85-62434. (Illus.). 32p. (Orig.). (J). (ps-3). 1985. pap. 5.95 (0-943990-20-3) Parenting Pr.

Loving Touches. David Hellerstein. 256p. 1988. reprint ed. mass mkt. 3.95 (0-446-34412-5, Pub. by Warner Bks) Little.

Loving Tough, Loving Smart, Loving You: You & the Alcoholic. Arnie Wallace & Adryan Russ. LC 89-82160. 98p. (Orig.). 1990. per. 9.95 (0-9625341-0-2) Challenger CA.

Loving Truth & Peace: The Grand Religious Worldview of Rabbi Benzion Uziel. Marc Angel. LC 98-42912. 1999. 30.00 (0-7657-6034-7) Aronson.

***Loving v. Virginia: Interracial Marriage.** Karen Alonso. LC 99-50541. (Landmark Supreme Court Cases Ser.). (Illus.). 112p. (YA). (gr. 6 up). 2000. lib. bdg. 20.95 (0-7660-1338-3) Enslow Pubs.

Loving Voice: A Caregiver's Book of Read-Aloud Stories for the Elderly. Ed. by Carolyn Banks & Janis Rizzo. LC 91-34876. 320p. 1992. pap. 14.95 (0-914783-59-9) Charles.

Loving Voice: A Caregiver's Book of Read-Aloud Stories for the Elderly. large type ed. Ed. by Carolyn Banks & Janis Rizzo. LC 92-42562. (General Ser.). 417p. 1993. lib. bdg. 21.95 (0-8161-5620-4, G K Hall Lrg Type) Mac Lib Ref.

Loving Voice: A Caregiver's Book of Read-Aloud Stories for the Elderly. large type ed. Ed. by Carolyn Banks & Janis Rizzo. LC 92-42562. (General Ser.). 417p. 1994. 18.95 (0-8161-5621-2, G K Hall Lrg Type) Mac Lib Ref.

Loving Voice Vol. II: A Caregiver's Book of More Read-Aloud Stories for the Elderly. Ed. by Carolyn Banks & Janis Rizzo. LC 94-1593. 296p. (Orig.). 1994. pap. 14.95 (0-914783-70-X) Charles.

Loving Wanda Beaver: Novella & Stories. Alison Baker. LC 95-12600. 208p. 1995. 16.95 (0-8118-1064-X) Chronicle Bks.

Loving Wanda Beaver: Novella & Stories. Alison Baker. 1997. pap. text 11.95 (0-8118-1788-1) Chronicle Bks.

Loving Who You Are Where You Are. Theta Burke. LC 82-71079. 80p. 1982. pap. 5.95 (0-916872-07-6) Delafield Pr.

Loving Wild. Lisa Ann Verge. (Temptation Ser.: No. 671). 1998. per. 3.75 (0-373-25771-6, 1-25771-6) Harlequin Bks.

Loving with a Vengeance: Mass-Produced Fantasies for Women. Tania Modleski. 140p. (C). 1984. pap. 18.99 (0-415-90136-7, NO. 9176) Routledge.

Loving with a Vengeance: Mass-Produced Fantasies for Women. Tania Modleski. LC 82-8687. 141p. (C). 1982. lib. bdg. 29.50 (0-208-01945-6, Archon Bks) Shoe String.

Loving with Back Pain: Good Sex with a Bad Back. Kathy Ulrich & Vicki Chandler. (Illus.). ii, 71p. (Orig.). 1996. pap. 12.00 (0-9655410-0-2) Wondersight.

Loving with Passion: Your Guide to the Joy of Sexual Intimacy. Donald Etkes. LC 94-69182. (Illus.). 224p. 1995. pap. 12.95 (0-9641850-5-9) Claremont Pubng.

Loving Without Being Vulnerable. Bill Bissett. LC 98-135811. 144p. 1997. pap. 12.95 (0-88922-372-6, Pub. by Talonbks) Genl Dist Srvs.

Loving Without Tears. large type ed. Molly Keane. LC 98-6679. xii, 320p. 1998. write for info. (0-7540-3368-6) Chivers N Amer.

Loving Without Tears. large type ed. Molly Keane. LC 98-6679. xii, 320p. pap. 21.95 (0-7862-1487-2) Thorndike Pr.

Loving Words: And Gentle Barbs from Cupid's Arrow. Tom C. Armstrong. LC 95-80286. 60p. (Orig.). 1995. pap. 5.99 (0-9638661-1-7) AD HOC Bks.

Loving Words Every Child Needs to Hear, 1. Edwin Anderson. 96p. 1999. 9.99 (0-8499-5404-5) Word Pub.

Loving Words Every Woman Wants to Hear. Edwin Anderson & John Peterson. (Illus.). 96p. 1999. 9.99 (0-8499-5402-9) Word Pub.

Loving Work. Frank Price. 255p. 1995. 56.95 (0-566-07634-9, Pub. by Gower) Ashgate Pub Co.

Loving You. Jim Wortham. LC 75-25329. 64p. (Orig.). 1975. pap. 2.95 (0-915216-03-5) Marathon Intl Bk.

Loving You Forever: Keeping Your Man/Woman Happy & at Home. Jan. 36p. 1995. pap. 10.99 (1-891884-84-0) J H Harris.

Loving You Was My Undoing: A Novel. Javier Gonzalez-Rubio. Tr. by Yareli Arizmendi & Stephen Lytle from SPA. LC 98-5712. 160p. 1999. 21.00 (0-8050-4878-2) H Holt & Co.

Loving Your Child Is Not Enough: Positive Discipline That Works. Nancy Samalin. LC 98-167678. 288p. 1998. pap. 12.95 (0-14-027053-1) Viking Penguin.

Loving Your City into the Kingdom: City-Reaching Strategies for a 21st Century Revival. Ted Haggard & Jack W. Hayford. LC 96-52722. 204p. 1997. pap. 11.99 (0-8307-1895-8, Regal Bks) Gospel Lght.

Loving Your Husband: Building an Intimate Marriage in a Fallen World. Cynthia Heald. 120p. 1989. pap. 7.00 (0-89109-544-6) NavPress.

***Loving Your Job, Finding Your Passion: Work & the Spiritual Life.** Joseph G. Allegretti. LC 99-87529. 208p. 2000. pap. 10.95 (0-8091-3939-1) Paulist Pr.

Loving Your Long-Distance Relationship. Stephen Blake. 96p. 1996. pap. 6.99 (0-9680971-0-3) Anton.

Loving Your Long-Distance Relationship, Vol. 1. Stephen Blake. 1998. text 13.95 incl. audio (0-9680971-1-1) Anton.

***Loving Your Long Distance Relationship for Women.** Stephen Blake. 1998. text 6.99 (0-9680971-6-2) Anton.

Loving Your Marriage Enough to Protect It. Jerry B. Jenkins. pap. 10.99 (0-8024-3492-4, 210) Moody.

***Loving Your Marriage Enough to Protect It.** Jerry B. Jenkins. 2000. pap. 12.99 (0-8024-4086-X) Moody.

Loving Your Wife: Building an Intimate Marriage in a Fallen World. Jack Heald & Cynthia Heald. 120p. (Orig.). 1989. pap. 7.00 (0-89109-575-6) NavPress.

Loving Yourself First: A Woman's Guide to Personal Power. abr. ed. Linda Coleman-Willis. (Illus.). 250p. 1997. pap. 12.95 (1-890368-00-8, WLW Pub) L Coleman-Willis.

Loving Yourself for God's Sake. Adolfo Quezada. LC 96-72288. 96p. 1997. pap. 5.95 (1-878718-35-5, Resurrection Pr) Catholic Bk Pub.

Loving Yourself More: One Hundred One Meditations for Women. Virginia A. Froehle. LC 93-71890. (Illus.). 128p. (Orig.). 1993. pap. 6.95 (0-87793-513-0) Ave Maria.

Loving Yourself Well: Affirming the Challenge of Illness. Topf. 1992. per. 10.95 (0-13-540261-1) P-H.

Lovingkindness. Anne Roiphe. 256p. 1989. mass mkt. 5.99 (0-446-35274-8, Pub. by Warner Bks) Little.

Lovingkindness. Anne Roiphe. LC 97-25388. 272p. 1997. mass mkt. 11.99 (0-446-67388-9, Pub. by Warner Bks) Little.

Lovingkindness. Sharon Salzberg. 208p. 1997. pap. 12.00 (1-57062-176-4, Pub. by Shambhala Pubns) Random.

Lovingly: Poems for All Seasons. Helen Steiner Rice. LC 77-123061. 96p. (gr. 11). 1987. 13.99 (0-8007-1521-7) Revell.

Lovingood Papers, 1965. Ed. by Ben H. McClary. LC 63-22059. 77p. reprint ed. pap. 30.00 (0-8357-6544-X, 203590700097) Bks Demand.

Lovingood Papers, 1964. Ed. by Ben H. McClary. LC 63-22059. 51p. reprint ed. pap. 30.00 (0-8357-6543-1, 203590600097) Bks Demand.

Loving's Love: A Black American's Experience in Aviation. Neal V. Loving. LC 93-24418. (History of Aviation Ser.). (Illus.). 304p. 1994. 29.95 (1-56098-342-6) Smithsonian.

Lovis Corinth. Ed. by Peter-Klaus Schuster et al. LC 96-31056. (Illus.). 392p. 1996. 75.00 (3-7913-1682-6, Pub. by Prestel) te Neues.

Lovis Corinth. Horst Uhr. LC 89-20317. (California Studies in the History of Art: No. 27). (Illus.). 400p. 1990. 65.00 (0-520-06776-2, Pub. by U CA Pr) Cal Prin Full Svc.

Lovis Corinth: Postcard Book. Prestel Staff. 1997. pap. text 8.95 (3-7913-1744-X, Pub. by Prestel) te Neues.

Lovis Corinth: The Graphic Work. Karl Schwarz. (GER., Illus.). 1985. 150.00 (0-915346-73-7) A Wofsy Fine Arts.

Lovis Corinth: The Late Graphic Work, Die Spate Graphik. rev. ed. Heinrich Muller. (ENG & GER., Illus.). 224p. 1994. 150.00 (1-55660-171-9) A Wofsy Fine Arts.

Lovis Corinth: The Paintings - Catalogue Raisonne. 2nd rev. ed. Charlotte Berend-Corinth & Beatrice Hernad. (GER., Illus.). 960p. 1992. boxed set 275.00 (1-55660-197-2) A Wofsy Fine Arts.

Lovisa: Angel from Norway. Louise R. Afeltra. LC 96-27675. (Illus.). 96p. (Orig.). 1997. pap. 9.95 (1-56474-206-7) Fithian Pr.

Lovtsov Atlas of the North Pacific Ocean, Compiled at Bol'sheretsk, Kamchatka, in 1782. Ed. by Richard A. Pierce. Tr. by Lydia T. Black from RUS. LC 96-30697. (Alaska History Ser.: No. 38). (Illus.). 62p. 1991. pap. 12.50 (0-919642-38-1) Limestone Pr.

Low: Good & Evil in the Work of Nayland Blake. Kathy Acker. (Illus.). 39p. 1990. 20.00 (0-902825-33-X) Petersburg Pr.

Low Achieving Children: The First Seven Years. Ed. by Sarah H. Broman et al. 184p. (C). 1985. text 36.00 (0-89859-637-8) L Erlbaum Assocs.

Low Advanced Technical English. Vannaerssen. (College ESL Ser.). (J). 1995. student ed., suppl. ed. 29.95 incl. audio (0-8384-4291-9) Heinle & Heinle.

Low-Altitude Wind Shear & Its Hazard to Aviation. Low-Altitude Wind Shear & Its Hazard to Aviation C & National Research Council Staff. 112p. 1983. pap. text 14.95 (0-309-03432-9) Natl Acad Pr.

Low & Equatorial Latitudes in the International Reference Ionosphere: Proceedings of the COSPAR International Scientific Symposium Held in New Delhi, India, 9-13 January 1995. Ed. by K. Rawer et al. (Advances in Space Research Ser.: No. 18). 338p. 1995. pap. text 92.75 (0-08-042673-5, Pergamon Pr) Elsevier.

Low & High Dielectric Constant Materials: Materials Science, Processing & Reliability Issues. Ed. by H. S. Rathore et al. LC 98-100811. (Proceedings Ser.: Vol. 97-8). 262p. 1997. 48.00 (1-56677-135-8) Electrochem Soc.

***Low & High Dielectric Constant Materials: Materials Science, Processing & Reliability Issues & Thin Film Materials for Advanced Packaging Technologies.** Ed. by R. Singh et al. 226p. 2000. 64.00 (1-56677-229-X, PV 99-7) Electrochem Soc.

Low & High Dielectric Constant Materials & Their Applications. Nalwa. LC 98-43222. 750p. (C). 1999. write for info. (0-12-513906-3); write for info. (0-12-513907-1) Acad Pr.

Low & High Style in Italian Renaissance Art. Patricia Emison & Raymond Waddington. LC 97-13222. (Studies in the Renaissance: Vol. 8). (Illus.). 288p. 1997. text 66.00 (0-8153-2530-4, H02033) Garland.

***Low & Inside: A Book of Baseball Anecdotes, Oddities & Curiosities.** H. Allen Smith & Ira L. Smith. (Illus.). 240p. 2000. reprint ed. pap. 13.00 (1-891369-14-8, Pub. by Breakaway Bks) Consort Bk Sales.

Low & Intermediate Energy Kaon-Nuclear Physics. Ed. by Ezio Ferrari & Galileo Violini. 424p. 1981. text 141.50 (90-277-1183-6) Kluwer Academic.

***Low & Slow: A Personal History of a Liaison Pilot in World War II.** Don Moore. LC 99-70896. 234 p. 1999. write for info. (0-9670334-0-3) SA Hts Pub Co.

Low-Aptitude Men in the Military: Who Profits, Who Pays? Janice H. Laurence & Peter F. Ramsberger. LC 91-20081. 200p. 1991. 52.95 (0-275-94060-8, C4060, Praeger Pubs) Greenwood.

Low Back & Leg Pain. 5th ed. James M. Cox. (Illus.). 20p. 1988. write for info. (0-9616488-3-X) Alef Bet Comns.

Low Back & Leg Pain from Herniated Cervical Disk. Herman Kabat. 154p. 1980. pap. 17.50 (0-87527-246-0) Green.

Low Back & Neck Pain: Causes & Conservative Treatment. P. C. Williams. (Illus.). 96p. 1982. pap., spiral bd. 18.95 (0-398-03193-2) C C Thomas.

Low Back & Pelvis: Clinical Applications. Chris J. Hutcheson. 200p. 1996. 48.00 (0-8342-0689-7, 20689) Aspen Pub.

***Low-Back, Ladder-Back, Cane-Bottom Chair: Biblical Meditations.** James S. Lowry. 128p. 1999. pap. 12.95 (0-88489-566-1) St Marys.

Low Back Pain. A. Delitto. (Monograph Ser.). 1998. pap. write for info. (1-887759-62-X) Am Phys Therapy Assn.

Low Back Pain. William Hunter. 56p. 1985. 5.00 (0-8187-0058-0) Harlo Press.

Low Back Pain. 2nd ed. Sam W. Wiesel et al. (Illus.). 931p. 1989. 65.00 (0-87473-449-5, 62021-10, MICHIE) LEXIS Pub.

***Low Back Pain.** 3rd ed. Sam W. Wiesel et al. 931p. 1999. 65.00 (0-327-10013-3, 6202111) LEXIS Pub.

Low Back Pain. 5th ed. James Cox et al. (Illus.). 645p. 1990. 100.00 (0-683-02152-4) Lppncott W & W.

Low Back Pain: A Scientific & Clinical Overview. Ed. by James Weinstein & Steve Gordon. LC 96-44528. 480p. 1996. 105.00 (0-89203-160-3) Amer Acad Ortho Surg.

Low Back Pain: A Symptom-Based Approach to Diagnosis & Treatment. Karen S. Rucker et al. (Illus.). 368p. 2000. 40.00 (0-7506-9485-8) Buttrwrth-Heinemann.

Low Back Pain: Care & Prevention with Traditional Chinese Medicine. Douglas Frank. Ed. & Intro. by Bob Flaws. LC 95-80458. (Illus.). 125p. (Orig.). 1995. pap. 9.95 (0-936185-66-X) Blue Poppy Pr.

Low Back Pain: Clinical Diagnosis & Management. 2nd ed. Leonard P. Seimon. (Illus.). 352p. 1995. 99.00 (0-939957-40-X) Demos Medical.

Low Back Pain: Health Care Needs Asessment: The Epidemiologically Based Needs Assessment Reviews, Second Series. Wessex Institute for Health Research & Development. LC 97-13355. 1997. write for info. (1-85775-201-5, Radcliffe Med Pr) Scovill Paterson.

Low Back Pain: Mechanisms, Diagnosis & Treatment. 6th ed. James M. Cox. LC 98-17984. 736p. 1998. 89.00 (0-683-30358-9) Lppncott W & W.

Low Back Pain: Medical Diagnosis & Comprehensive Management. 2nd ed. David G. Borenstein et al. LC 93-41601. 1994. text. write for info. (0-7216-5411-8, W B Saunders Co) Harcrt Hlth Sci Grp.

Low Back Pain Handbook: A Practical Guide for the Primary Care Clinician. Ed. by Andrew J. Cole & Stanley Herring. LC 96-20355. 500p. (Orig.). 1996. pap. text 46.00 (1-56053-152-5) Hanley & Belfus.

Low Back Pain Handbook: Evaluation & Management. D'Orazio. 336p. 1998. text 40.00 (0-7506-9618-4) Buttrwrth-Heinemann.

Low Back Pain Syndrome. 5th ed. Renee Cailliet. LC 94-22969. (Pain Ser.). (Illus.). 381p. 1994. pap. text 25.95 (0-8036-1607-4) Davis Co.

Low-Back Patient: Treatment by Physical Therapy. Joan G. Lafreniere. (C). (gr. 13). 1979. 31.50 (0-89352-033-0) Mosby Inc.

Low-Background High-Efficiency Geiger-Muller Counter. (Technical Reports: No. 33). (Illus.). 32p. 1964. pap. 13.00 (92-0-135064-3, IDC33, Pub. by IAEA) Bernan Associates.

***Low Birthweight in Minority & High-Risk Women: Patient Outcome Research Team (Port)-Final Report.** Ed. by Robert L. Goldenberg. (Illus.). 100p. (C). 1999. reprint ed. pap. text 20.00 (0-7881-8415-6) DIANE Pub.

Low Black Schooner: Yacht America, 1851-1945. John Rousmaniere. (Illus.). 71p. 1998. pap. text 20.00 (0-7881-5274-2) DIANE Pub.

Low Black Schooner: Yacht America, 1851-1945. John Rousmaniere. 80p. (C). 1990. text 59.00 (0-7855-7002-0, Pub. by Fernhurst Bks) St Mut.

Low Blood Sugar. M. A. Budd. 224p. 1998. pap. 11.00 (0-7225-3119-2, 902624Q) Thorsons PA.

Low Blood Sugar. Clement G. Martin. 192p. 1985. per. 5.00 (0-671-76410-1, Fireside) S&S Trade Pap.

Low Blood Sugar Cookbook: Sugarless Cooking for Everyone. Patricia Krimmel & Edward A. Krimmel. LC 85-80481. (Illus.). 192p. (Orig.). 1992. pap. 12.95 (0-916503-01-1) Franklin Pubs.

Low Blood Sugar Handbook. rev. ed. Patricia T. Krimmel & Edward A. Krimmel. LC 91-73247. (Illus.). 192p. 1992. pap. 12.95 (0-916503-04-6) Franklin Pubs.

Low Blood Sugar (Hypoglysemia) The Twentieth Century Epidemic? Martin L. Budd. LC 83-5053. 128 sp. (Orig.). 1983. pap. 9.95 (0-8069-7792-2) Sterling.

Low Bridge & Punk Pungs. Sam Hellman. LC 78-134965. (Short Story Index Reprint Ser.). (Illus.). 1977. 15.95 (0-8369-3695-7) Ayer.

Low Bridges & High Water: On the New York State Barge Canal. Charles T. O'Malley. (Illus.). 284p. 1991. pap. 19.95 (0-925168-38-6) North Country.

Low Brow Art of Robert Williams. Robert Williams. (Illus.). 96p. 1995. 24.95 (0-86719-418-9) Last Gasp.

Low-Budget, High-Quality Design. Steven Heller & Anne Fink. (Illus.). 160p. 1990. 35.00 (0-8230-2880-1) Watsn-Guptill.

***Low Budget Marketing Techniques.** Secrets of Small Business Ownership Editors. 48p. 1999. pap. 7.95 (1-929369-00-X) Free State Pr.

Low-Budget Program for Multi-Ethnic Gifted Students. Riggs. 1989. pap. 14.99 (0-89824-133-2) Trillium Pr.

***Low Budget Video Bible: Film School Edition: The Essential Guide to Making Top Notch Student Video.** 3rd ed. Cliff Roth. (Illus.). 524p. (C). 1999. pap. text 27.95 (0-9635216-5-9) Desktop Vid.

Low Budget Video Bible: The Essential Do-It-Yourself Guide to Making Top Notch Video on a Shoestring Budget. 2nd rev. ed. Cliff Roth. (Illus.). 458p. (Orig.). (C). 1997. pap. 27.95 (0-9635216-1-6) Desktop Vid.

Low Budget/High Quality Design: The Art of Inexpensive Visual Communication. Steven Heller. (Illus.). 160p. 1997. pap. text 24.95 (0-8230-2879-8) Watsn-Guptill.

Low Cal Country: Taking the Calories & Cholesterol Out of Hearty Country Cooking. Louise B. Dillow. LC 91-75620. (Illus.). 264p. 1992. pap. 13.95 (0-931722-91-8) Corona Pub.

Low Calorie: For Dieters. Ed. by G & R Publishing Staff. (Uni-Bks.). 160p. (Orig.). 1994. pap. text 3.00 (1-56383-014-0, 1700) G & R Pub.

Low Calorie & Special Dietary Foods. Ed. by Basant K. Dwivedi. (Uniscience Ser.). 144p. 1978. 89.00 (0-8493-5249-5, RM258, CRC Reprint) Franklin.

Low Calorie Cookbook. Darlene Kronschnabel. (Illus.). 64p. (Orig.). 1985. pap. 3.95 (0-8249-3003-7) Ideals.

Low-Calorie Desserts. Christine France. 1998. pap. text 12.95 (1-85967-697-9, Lorenz Bks) Anness Pub.

Low-Calorie Foods Handbook. Aaron M. Altschul. (Food Science & Technology Ser.: Vol. 56). (Illus.). 608p. 1993. text 225.00 (0-8247-8812-5) Dekker.

***Low-Calorie Sweeteners: Present & Future: ISA-IUFoST World Conference on Low-Calorie Sweeteners, Barcelona, April 1999.** Ed. by A. Corti. LC 99-48944. (World Review of Nutrition & Dietetics Ser.: Vol. 85). (Illus.). xiv, 244p. 1999. 198.25 (3-8055-6938-6) S Karger.

Low Calorie Way. Barbara Kyte & Kathy Greenberg. LC 80-84335. (Illus.). 1981. pap. 2.95 (0-915942-17-8) SF Design.

Low-Capacity Cryogenic Refrigeration. G. Walker & E. R. Bingham. LC 93-46643. (Monographs on Cryogenics: No. 9). (Illus.). 318p. 1994. text 75.00 (0-19-851760-2, Clarendon Pr) OUP.

Low-Carb Cookbook: The Complete Guide to the Healthy Low Carbohydrate Lifestyle - With over 250 Delicious Recipes, Everything You Need to Know about Stocking the Pantry, & Sources for the Best Prepared Foods & Ingredients. Frances M. McCullough. LC 96-49343. (Illus.). 400p. 1997. 22.95 (0-7868-6273-4, Pub. by Hyperion) Time Warner.

***Low-Carb Cookbook: The Complete Guide to the Healthy Low-Carbohydrate Lifestyle - With over 250 Recipes.** Fran McCullough. (Illus.). 2001. mass mkt. 7.99 (0-7868-8991-8) Hyperion.

***Low-Carb Cooking with Stevia: The Naturally Sweet & Calorie-Free Herb.** James Kirkland. LC 99-98116. (Illus.). 256p. 2000. pap. 14.95 (1-928906-14-1) Crystal Health.

***Low-Carb Ideas - Good Food.** 2nd ed. 1999. 14.95 (0-9671579-1-9) IdeasByMe.

***Low-Carb Meals in Minutes.** Linda Gassenheimer. 192p. 2000. pap. 18.95 (1-57959-512-X, Pub. by BB&T Inc) Publishers Group.

***Low Carb Recipes, Fast & Easy.** Belinda Schweinhart. Ed. by Chaddie Letson. 100p. 1999. spiral bd. 15.95 (0-9671821-0-7) Brass Pig.

Low Carbon Comfort Pt. 5: Space Heating Efficiency & Low Carbon Comfort. Florentin Krause et al. (Energy Policy in the Greenhouse Ser.: Vol. 2). 140p. (Orig.). 1998. pap. 35.00 (1-883774-08-X) IPSEP.

Low-Carbon High Strength Ferrous Alloys: Proceedings of the Indo-U. S. Workshop LCFA 1992. Indo-U. S. Workshop LCFA Staff. Ed. by O. N. Mohanty. (Key Engineering Materials Ser.: Vols. 84-85). 700p. 1993. text 216.00 (0-87849-656-4, Pub. by Trans T Pub) Enfield Pubs NH.

Low-Central & Low-Back Vowels in the English of the Eastern United States. Thomas H. Wetmore. (Publications of the American Dialect Society: No. 32). (Illus.). 131p. 1959. pap. text 4.40 (0-8173-0632-3) U of Ala Pr.

Low Cholesterol - Low Sodium: For Good Health. Ed. by G & R Publishing Staff. (Uni-Bks.). 160p. (Orig.). 1994. pap. text 3.00 (1-56383-026-4, 3400) G & R Pub.

Low-Cholesterol Chinese Cuisine. Cheo Chao Teng & Chen Hsueh-Hsia. (CHI & ENG.). 124p. 1990. pap. 19.95 (0-941676-22-6) Wei-Chuan Pub.

Low Cholesterol, Healthy Eating. Lorenz Staff. 1998. 12.95 (1-85967-671-5) Anness Pub.

Low Cholesterol Low Calorie Desserts. Leinwoll. 1986. pap. 6.95 (0-684-13380-6, Scribners Ref) Mac Lib Ref.

Low Cholesterol Oat Plan. Barbara Earnest & Sarah Schlesinger. 352p. 1990. pap. 7.95 (0-380-70839-6, Avon Bks) Morrow Avon.

Low Cholesterol Three Ingredient Cookbook, Vol. IV. Ruthie Wornall. (Illus.). 67p. 1991. spiral bd. 6.95 (0-9624467-3-4) Wornall Pub.

Low City, High City: Tokyo from Edo to the Earthquake. Edward G. Seidensticker. 302p. (C). 1991. pap. text 14.95 (0-674-53939-7) HUP.

Low City, High City, Tokyo from Edo to the Earthquake: How the Shogun's Ancient Capital Became a Great Modern City, 1867-1923. Edward G. Seidensticker. LC 84-70646. (Illus.). 320p. (C). 1985. reprint ed. pap. 13.95 (0-916870-88-X) Creat Arts Bk.

Low-Cost & Energy Saving Construction Materials, Vol. 1. Ed. by K. Ghavami & Hsai-Yang Fang. LC 84-80024. 640p. (Orig.). 1984. pap. 50.00 (0-932871-08-9) Envo Pub Co.

Low-Cost & Energy-Saving Wastewater Treatment Technologies: Proceedings of ISLEWTT Harbin '90 held at Harbin Institute of Architecture & Civil Engineering, Harbin, China. Ed. by B. Z. Wang et al. (Water Science & Technology Ser.: No. 24). (Illus.). 264p. 1991. pap. 118.75 (0-08-041158-4, Pergamon Pr) Elsevier.

Low-Cost Approach to PCR: Appropriate Transfer of Biomolecular Techniques. Eva Harris. LC 98-16653. (Illus.). 328p. 1998. pap. text 39.95 (0-19-511926-6) OUP.

Low Cost Automation. Paiuk & Weisz. LC 96-223480. (IFAC Postprint Ser.). 432p. 1995. pap. 82.25 (0-08-042239-X, Pergamon Pr) Elsevier.

Low Cost Automation: Components, Instruments, Techniques & Applications: Selected Papers from the IFAC Symposium, Milan, Italy, 8-10 November 1989. Ed. by A. De Carli. (IFAC Symposia Ser.: 9015). (Illus.). 528p. 1990. 246.00 (0-08-037866-8, Pergamon Pr) Elsevier.

Low Cost Automation 1998. Z. Y. Chen & T. Y. Chai. LC 99-39975. (IFAC Proceedings Ser.). 1999. pap. 75.50 (0-08-043027-9, Pub. by Elsevier) Elsevier.

Low Cost Automation, 1992: Techniques, Components & Instruments, Applications. Ed. by Peter Kopacek & P. Albertos. LC 93-36687. (IFAC Symposia Ser.: No. 13). 348p. 1993. 129.25 (0-08-041716-7, Pergamon Pr) Elsevier.

Low Cost CAD in Building Services. C. McLeeland & I. Baird. (C). 1987. 120.00 (0-86022-114-8, Pub. by Build Servs Info Assn) St Mut.

Low Cost CAD Systems. 89.00 (0-686-40544-7) C I M Systems.

Low Cost Compensation Secrets. (C). 1990. pap. text 6.85 (0-13-539537-2, Macmillan Coll) P-H.

Low-Cost Condition Monitoring for Engineering Services. J. Armstrong & P. Taylor. 160p. 1988. text 50.00 (0-419-14450-1, E & FN Spon) Routledge.

Low Cost Conversions. George D. Myers. iii, 27p. 1997. spiral bd. 5.00 (1-892365-01-4) Epic Conver.

Low-Cost Development of Small Water Power Sites. Hans W. Hamm. 43p. 1982. pap. 9.50 (0-86619-014-7); pap. 9.50 (0-86619-015-5); pap. 9.50 (0-86619-016-3) Vols Tech Asst.

Low Cost Earth Shelters. Jim Eggert. LC 81-18244. (Illus.). 159p. (Orig.). reprint ed. pap. 49.30 (0-8357-8581-5, 203495000091) Bks Demand.

***Low-Cost Electrification.** Nigel Smith. 38p. 1999. pap. 25.00 (1-85339-454-8, Pub. by Intermed Tech) Stylus Pub VA.

Low-Cost Energy-Efficient House or Shelter. 1991. lib. bdg. 88.95 (0-8490-4670-X) Gordon Pr.

Low-Cost FDDI. 111p. 1992. pap. 1495.00 (1-56851-010-1, IGIC-60) Info Gatekeepers.

Low-Cost FDDI Conference Proceedings. 1997. 125.00 (0-614-26569-X, LCEP92) Info Gatekeepers.

Low Cost FDOI '92, Boston, MA. 1992. 250.00 (0-614-26536-3, LCFP92) Info Gatekeepers.

***Low Cost Flip Chip Technologies: Direct Chip Attack.** John H. Lau. LC 99-88307. (Professional Engineering Ser.). (Illus.). 600p. 2000. 89.95 (0-07-135141-8) McGraw-Hill Prof.

Low-Cost Housing in Developing Countries. G. C. Mathur. (C). 1993. 24.00 (81-204-0774-1, Pub. by Oxford IBH) S Asia.

Low Cost Jigs, Fixtures & Gages for Limited Production. Ed. by W. Boyes. LC 85-62533. 320p. 1985. 58.00 (0-87263-207-5) SME.

Low-Cost Load-Carrying Devices: The Design & Manufacture of Some Basic Means of Transport. Ron Dennis & Alan Smith. 192p. 1995. pap. 29.50 (1-85339-265-0, Pub. by Intermed Tech) Stylus Pub VA.

Low-Cost Main Dishes. Ed. by Nancy A. Hecht. LC 73-90911. (Family Circle Bks.). (Illus.). 128p. 1977. 12.95 (0-405-11405-2) Ayer.

Low-Cost Maintenance Control. W. Colebrook Cooling. LC 73-75670. (Illus.). 71p. reprint ed. pap. 30.00 (0-608-11638-6, 205152900085) Bks Demand.

Low-Cost Marketing Research: A Guide for Small Businesses. 2nd ed. Keith Gorton & Isobel Doole. LC 88-27012. (Illus.). 165p. reprint ed. pap. 51.20 (0-608-05298-1, 206583600001) Bks Demand.

Low-Cost Marketing Strategies: Field-Tested Techniques for Tight Budgets. Elisabeth Deran. LC 86-30640. 160p. 1987. 47.95 (0-275-92341-X, C2341, Praeger Pubs) Greenwood.

Low Cost, No Cost Ideas for Youth Ministry. Ed. by Steve Saavedra. (SPA.). 112p. 1998. per. 9.99 (0-7644-2123-9, Vital Ministry) Group Pub.

Low-Cost, Personal-Computer-Based Investment Decision Systems. Jerry Felsen. LC 77-83508. 1977. pap. 34.00 (0-916376-03-6) CDS Pub.

Low Cost Planet: Energy & Environmental Problems, Solutions & Costs. David Toke. LC 94-49666. 224p. (C). 1995. 63.00 (0-7453-0843-0, Pub. by Pluto GBR); pap. 16.95 (0-7453-0844-9, Pub. by Pluto GBR) Stylus Pub VA.

Low Cost Pole Building Construction. rev. ed. Ralph Wolfe et al. LC 80-10232. (Illus.). 192p. 1983. pap. 14.95 (0-88266-170-1) Storey Bks.

Low Cost Prefabricated Wooden Houses: A Manual for Developing Countries. 99p. pap. 6.00 (92-1-106260-8) UN.

Low Cost Printing for Development. Jonathan Zeitlyn. 120p. 1988. pap. 19.50 (1-85339-065-8, Pub. by Intermed Tech) Stylus Pub VA.

Low Cost Road Construction in Indonesia: Labour-Based Road Projects in Manggarai District, Vol. I, Documentation. A. Beusch et al. 48p. 1998. pap. 19.50 (3-906494-01-2, Pub. by Intermed Tech) Stylus Pub VA.

Low Cost Road Construction in Indonesia: Labour-Based Road Projects in Manggarai District, Vol. II, Workbook. A. Beusch et al. 110p. 1998. pap., wbk. ed. 17.50 (3-906494-02-0, Pub. by Intermed Tech) Stylus Pub VA.

Low Cost Rural Health Care & Health Manpower Training: An Annotated Bibliography with Special Emphasis on Developing Countries. 165p. 1975. write for info. (0-88936-051-0) IDRC Bks.

Low Cost Rural Health Care & Health Manpower Training: An Annotated Bibliography with Special Emphasis on Developing Countries. 182p. 1976. write for info. (0-88936-093-6) IDRC Bks.

Low Cost Rural Health Care & Health Manpower Training: An Annotated Bibliography with Special Emphasis on Developing Countries, Vol. 3. F. M. Delaney. 187p. 1977. write for info. (0-88936-138-X) IDRC Bks.

Low Cost Rural Health Care & Health Manpower Training: An Annotated Bibliography with Special Emphasis on Developing Countries, Vol. 4. F. M. Delaney. 186p. 1979. write for info. (0-88936-201-7) IDRC Bks.

Low-Cost Sanitation: A Survey of Practical Experience. John Pickford. 176p. 1995. pap. 19.50 (1-85339-233-2, Pub. by Intermed Tech) Stylus Pub VA.

Low-Cost Sewerage. Ed. by D. Duncan Mara. LC 96-15925. 238p. 1996. pap. 70.00 (0-471-96691-6) Wiley.

Low-Cost Smart Sensor Interfacing. Fransiscus M. Van der Goes. (Illus.). 180p. (Orig.). 1996. pap. 57.50 (90-407-1324-3, Pub. by Delft U Pr) Coronet Bks.

Low-Cost Test Equipment Projects You Can Build. Delton T. Horn. LC 92-9565. 208p. 1992. 22.95 (0-8306-4154-8, 3886); pap. 13.95 (0-8306-4155-6, 3886) McGraw-Hill Prof.

Low-Cost Urban Food Distribution Systems in Latin America. 65p. 1994. 12.00 (92-5-103450-8, F34508, Pub. by FAO) Bernan Associates.

Low Cost Urban Sanitation. D. Duncan Mara. LC 95-42464. 240p. 1996. pap. 75.00 (0-471-96163-9) Wiley.

Low Cost Vehicles: Options for Moving People & Goods. Gordon Hathway. (Illus.). 112p. 1985. pap. 19.50 (0-946688-02-8, Pub. by Intermed Tech) Stylus Pub VA.

Low-Cost Water Supply & Sanitation Technology. (SEARO Regional Health Papers: No. 4). 40p. 1984. pap. text 5.00 (92-9022-173-9) World Health.

Low Cost Ways to Brighten Displays. Linda Milliken. Ed. by Deneen Celecia. (Illus.). 48p. 1994. pap., student ed. 6.95 (1-56472-051-9) Edupress Inc.

Low-Cost Windmill for Developing Nations. Hartmut Bossel. 45p. 1970. pap. 9.50 (0-86619-035-X) Vols Tech Asst.

Low Countries: History of the Northern & Southern Netherlands. 1994. lib. bdg. 250.95 (0-8490-5676-4) Gordon Pr.

Low Countries: Multidisciplinary Studies. Ed. by Margriet B. Lacy. LC 89-24778. (Publications of the American Association for Netherlandic Studies: Vol. 3). (Illus.). 266p. (C). 1990. lib. bdg. 45.00 (0-8191-7587-0) U Pr of Amer.

Low Countries & Beyond. Ed. by Robert S. Kirsner. 340p. (C). 1993. lib. bdg. 59.50 (0-8191-8943-X) U Pr of Amer.

Low Countries in the Early Modern World. Herman Van der Wee. 320p. 1994. 86.95 (0-86078-384-7, Pub. by Variorum) Ashgate Pub Co.

Low Countries, 1780-1940. E. H. Kossman. (History of Modern Europe Ser.). (Illus.). 790p. 1978. text 95.00 (0-19-822108-8) OUP.

Low Country. large type ed. Anne Rivers Siddons. LC 98-25215. 1999. pap. 26.95 (0-7862-1425-2) Thorndike Pr.

Low Country: A Novel. Anne Rivers Siddons. LC 98-7771. 304p. 1998. 25.00 (0-06-017616-4) HarpC.

***Low Country: A Novel.** Anne Rivers Siddons. 480p. 1999. mass mkt. 7.99 (0-06-109332-7, Harp PBks) HarpC.

Low Country: A Novel. large type ed. Anne Rivers Siddons. LC 98-25215. 509p. 1998. write for info. (0-7540-2156-4) Chivers N Amer.

Low Country: A Novel. large type ed. Anne Rivers Siddons. LC 98-25215. 1998. 28.95 (0-7862-1424-4) Thorndike Pr.

***Low Country: Monk,&Debra, Set.** abr. ed. Anne Rivers Siddons. 1998. audio 25.00 (0-694-51996-0, 696012) HarperAudio.

Low Country Carolina Genealogies: Including the Following Families, DeSaussure, Huger, Horry, Laurens, Bishop Smith, Ford, Mitchel King, Boone. Charlton deSaussure. LC 97-67552. (Illus.). write for info. (0-89308-395-X) Southern Hist Pr.

Low Country Commonwealth. Jean Francois Le Petit. Tr. by E. Grimeston. LC 72-25634. (English Experience Ser.: No. 208). 1969. reprint ed. 45.00 (90-221-0208-4) Walter J Johnson.

Low Country Liar. Janet Dailey. 1992. per. 3.59 (0-373-89890-8, 1-89890-7) Harlequin Bks.

Low Country Quake Tales. Joyce B. Bagwell. 88p. (YA). 1986. pap. 7.50 (0-89308-593-6, SC 84) Southern Hist Pr.

Low Country Scenes: Charleston, S. C. rev. ed. Photos by Wm. Bryan Riggs et al. (Illus.). 24p. 1996. pap. 4.95 (0-9649686-3-0) Chrlstn Post Card.

Low Country Stories. Lisa Harris. Ed. by Bertha Rogers. (Fiction Award Ser.). 33p. (Orig.). 1997. pap. 6.00 (0-9646844-5-4) Bright Hill.

Low Cycle & Static Bending Strength of Carburized & High Hardness Through Hardened Gear Teeth. W. Pizzichil. (Nineteen Ninety-One Fall Technical Meeting Ser.: Vol. 91FTM7). (Illus.). 13p. 1991. pap. text 30.00 (1-55589-604-9) AGMA.

Low Cycle Fatigue. Ed. by H. D. Solomon et al. LC 87-23714. (Special Technical Publication Ser.: No. 942). (Illus.). 1300p. 1987. 165.00 (0-8031-0944-X, STP942) ASTM.

Low Cycle Fatigue: A Symposium. American Society for Testing & Materials Staff. LC 87-23714. 1306p. reprint ed. pap. 200.00 (0-7837-5975-4, 204577900007) Bks Demand.

Low Cycle Fatigue & Elasto-Plastic Behaviour of Materials. K. T. Rie & P. D. Portella. LC 98-34273. 1998. 253.00 (0-08-043326-X) Elsevier.

Low-Cycle Fatigue & Life Prediction- STP 770. Ed. by Claude Amzallag et al. 646p. 1982. 60.00 (0-8031-0713-7, STP770) ASTM.

Low Density, High Temperature Powder Metallurgy Alloys. Ed. by William E. Frazier et al. LC 91-60684. (Illus.). 281p. 1991. reprint ed. pap. 87.20 (0-608-02487-2, 206313100004) Bks Demand.

Low-Dielectric Constant Materials V Vol. 565: Materials Research Society Symposium Proceedings. Ed. by J. P. Hummel et al. 306p. 1999. text 77.00 (1-55899-472-6) Materials Res.

Low-Dielectric Constant Materials III: Materials Research Society Symposium Proceedings, Vol. 476. Ed. by C. Case et al. LC 97-48258. 300p. 1997. text 66.00 (1-55899-380-0) Materials Res.

Low-Dielectric Constant Materials II. Ed. by K. Uram et al. LC 97-18162. (Materials Research Society Symposium Proceedings Ser.: No. 443). 203p. 1997. text 72.00 (1-55899-347-9) Materials Res.

Low-Dimensional Applications of Quantum Field Theory: Proceedings of a NATO ASI Held in Cargese, France, July 11-29, 1995. Ed. by Laurent Baulieu et al. LC 97-17158. (NATO ASI Ser.: Vol. 362). 384p. (C). 1997. text 129.50 (0-306-45686-9) Plenum.

Low-Dimensional Conductors & Superconductors. Ed. by D. Jerome & L. G. Caron. (NATO ASI Series B, Physical Sciences: Vol 155). (Illus.). 540p. 1987. 125.00 (0-306-42587-4, Plenum Trade) Perseus Pubng.

Low-Dimensional Conductors & Superconductors: Electron-Electron Correlation Effects In. Ed. by A. A. Ovchinnikov & I. I. Ukrainskii. (Research Reports in Physics). (Illus.). ix, 161p. 1991. pap. 69.00 (0-387-54248-5) Spr-Verlag.

Low Dimensional Electronic Properties of Molybdenum Bronzes & Oxides. Ed. by Claire Schlenker. (C). 1989. text 303.50 (0-7923-0085-8) Kluwer Academic.

Low-Dimensional Electronic Systems: New Concepts, Proceedings of the Seventh International Winter School, Mauterndorf, Austria, February 24-28, 1992. Ed. by G. Bauer et al. LC 92-36489. (Solid-State Sciences Ser.: Vol. 111). 1993. 119.95 (0-387-55998-1) Spr-Verlag.

Low-Dimensional Models in Statistical Physics & Quantum Field Theory: Proceedings of the 34th Internationale Universit Atswochen fur Kern- & Teilchenphysik, Schladming, Austria, March 4-11, 1995. Ed. by Harald Grosse & Ludwig Pittner. LC 96-5683. (Lecture Notes in Physics Ser.: Vol. 469). 339p. 1996. 84.00 (3-540-60990-3) Spr-Verlag.

Low-Dimensional Organic Conductors. A. Graja. 320p. (C). 1992. text 74.00 (981-02-0477-9); pap. text 40.00 (981-02-0478-7) World Scientific Pub.

Low-Dimensional Properties of Solids: Proceedings of Nobel Jubilee Symposium. M. Jonson. 220p. 1993. text 109.00 (981-02-1217-8); pap. text 61.00 (981-02-1218-6) World Scientific Pub.

Low-Dimensional Quantum Field Theories for Condensed Matter Physicists - Lecture Notes of ICTP. Yu Lu et al. (Series on Modern Condensed Matter Physics: Vol. 6). 624p. 1995. text 109.00 (981-02-2140-1) World Scientific Pub.

***Low Dimensional Semiconductor Structures: Fundamentals & Device Applications.** Ed. by Keith Barnham & Dimitri Vvedensky. LC QC611.6.S9L67 2000. (Illus.). 410p. (C). 2000. 59.95 (0-521-59103-1) Cambridge U Pr.

Low-Dimensional Semiconductors: Materials, Physics, Technology, Devices. Michael J. Kelly. (Series on Semiconductor Science & Technology: No. 3). (Illus.). 564p. 1996. text 120.00 (0-19-851781-5); pap. text 60.00 (0-19-851780-7) OUP.

Low Dimensional Sigma Models. W. J. Zakrzewski. (Illus.). 304p. 1989. 39.00 (0-85274-231-2) IOP Pub.

Low Dimensional Structures in Semiconductors: From Basic Physics to Applications. A. R. Peaker & H. G. Grimmeiss. (NATO ASI Ser.: Vol. 281). (Illus.). 440p. (C). 1992. text 110.00 (0-306-44086-5, Kluwer Plenum) Kluwer Academic.

Low Dimensional Structures Prepared by Epitaxial Growth or Regrowth on Patterned Subtrates: Proceedings of the NATO Advanced Research Workshop, Ringberg in Rottach Egern, Germany, February 20-24, 1995. Piet Demeester. Ed. by Karl Eberl & Pierre M. Petroff. LC 95-34347. (NATO Advanced Science Institutes Ser.: Series E, Vol. 289). 400p. (C). 1995. text 206.00 (0-7923-3679-8) Kluwer Academic.

***Low-Dimensional Systems: Interactions & Transport Properties.** Ed. by T. Brandes. (Lecture Notes in Physics Ser.: Vol. 554). (Illus.). vii, 219p. 2000. 72.80 (3-540-67237-0) Spr-Verlag.

Low-Dimensional Topology. Ed. by K. Johannson. (Monographs in Geometry & Topology). xiv, 239p. 1994. 25.00 (1-57146-018-7) Intl Pr Boston.

Low Dimensional Topology. Ed. by Samuel J. Lomonaco, Jr. LC 83-10022. (Contemporary Mathematics Ser.: Vol. 20). 346p. 1983. pap. 38.00 (0-8218-5016-4, CONM/20) Am Math.

Low Dimensional Topology. Hanna Nencka. LC 99-14986. (Contemporary Mathematics Ser.). 1999. write for info. (0-8218-0884-2) Am Math.

Low-Dimensional Topology & Quantum Field Theory. H. Osborn. (NATO ASI Ser.: Vol. 315). (Illus.). 332p. (C). 1993. text 110.00 (0-306-44578-6, Kluwer Plenum) Kluwer Academic.

Low-Dose Extrapolation of Cancer Risks: Issues & Persepectives. Ed. by W. Farland et al. LC 95-77850. (Illus.). 355p. 1995. pap. 50.00 (0-944398-33-2) ILSI.

Low-Dose Methotrexate-Therapy in Rheumatic Diseases. Ed. by R. Rau. (Rheumatology Ser.: Vol. 9). (Illus.). xii, 268p. 1986. 155.75 (3-8055-4236-4) S Karger.

Low Down - A Century Remembered. W. Edward Sedl. 320p. 1995. write for info. (0-9646415-0-X) U Pittsburgh LAA.

Low-Down Laundry Line Blues. C. M. Millen. LC 97-41117. (Illus.). 32p. (J). (ps-3). 1999. 15.00 (0-395-87497-1) HM.

Low-Down on Entropy & Interpretive Thermodynamics. Stephen J. Kline. LC 99-61990. (Illus.). 120p. 1999. pap. 25.00 (1-928729-01-0) DCW Industries.

Low-E Glazing Design Guide. Timothy E. Johnson. (Illus.). 208p. 1991. pap. text 52.95 (0-7506-9147-6) Buttrwrth-Heinemann.

Low Earth Orbital Satellites in Personal Communication Networks. Abbas Jamilipour. LC 97-32244. 1997. 93.00 (0-89006-955-7) Artech Hse.

Low East. David Henderson. 80p. 1980. pap. 4.95 (0-913028-72-X) North Atlantic.

Low East. David Henderson. 80p. 1980. 15.00 (0-913028-73-8) North Atlantic.

Low Emission Vehicle Technologies. 1997. 61.00 (1-56091-972-8, SP-1260) Soc Auto Engineers.

Low End of Nowhere: A Streeter Mystery. Michael Stone. 224p. 1997. pap. 5.95 (0-14-024694-0) Viking Penguin.

Low End of Nowhere: A Streeter Mystery. large type ed. Michael Stone. (Niagara Large Print Ser.). 290p. 1997. pap. 29.50 (0-7089-5863-X, Linford) Ulverscroft.

Low Energy Antimatter: Proceedings of the Workshop on the Design of a Low Energy Antimatter Facility, Madison, Wisconsin, October 1985. Ed. by D. B. Cline. 220p. 1986. text 60.00 (9971-5-0163-5) World Scientific Pub.

Low-Energy Antiproton Physics: Proceedings of the Third Biennial Conference on Low Energy Physics. G. Kernel et al. 800p. 1995. text 170.00 (981-02-2236-X) World Scientific Pub.

Low Energy Electron Diffraction. Ed. by David H. Templeton & Gabor A. Somorjai. (Transactions of the American Crystallographic Association Ser.: Vol. 4). 144p. 1968. pap. 25.00 (0-686-60375-3) Polycrystal Bk Serv.

Low Energy Electron Diffraction. M. A. Van Hove et al. (Surface Sciences Ser.: Vol. 6). (Illus.). 610p. 1986. 91.95 (0-387-16262-3) Spr-Verlag.

Low Energy Hadron Interactions: Compilation of Coupling Constants & Low Energy Parameters. Ed. by G. Hoehler. LC 25-9130. (Tracts in Modern Physics Ser.: Vol. 55). (Illus.). 1971. 73.95 (0-387-05250-X) Spr-Verlag.

Low-Energy Ion Beam & Plasma Modification of Materials Vol. 223: Materials Research Society Symposium Proceedings. Ed. by J. M. Harper et al. 397p. 1991. text 71.00 (1-55899-117-4) Materials Res.

Low Energy Ion Beams: Proceedings of the LEIB Conference, 3rd, Loughborough, U. K., March 28-31, 1983. Ed. by W. A. Grant. 120p. 1984. pap. 30.00 (0-08-030553-9, Pergamon Pr) Elsevier.

Low-Energy Ion Beams, 1980: Invited & Contributed Papers Presented at the Second International Conference on Low-Energy Ion Beams Held at the University of Bath, 14-17 April 1980, Organised by the Atomic Collisions in Solids Group of the Institute of Physics. International Conference on Low-Energy Ion Beams S. Ed. by I. H. Wilson & K. G. Stephens. LC 84-2005. (Conference Ser.: No. 54). 366p. reprint ed. pap. 113.50 (0-7837-3252-X, 204327100007) Bks Demand.

Low-energy Ion Irradiation of Solid Surfaces. Herbert Gnaser. LC 98-44834. 1998. 169.00 (3-540-65007-5) Spr-Verlag.

Low Energy Ion-Surface Interactions. Ed. by J. Wayne Rabalais. LC 93-21244. (Current Topics in Ion Chemistry & Physics Ser.). 610p. 1994. 375.00 (0-471-93891-2) Wiley.

Low Energy Tests of Conservation Laws in Particle Physics: Conference Proceedings, Blacksburg, Virginia, 1983. Ed. by M. Blecher & K. Gotow. LC 84-71157. (AIP Conference Proceedings Ser.: No. 114, Subseries on Particles & Fields No. 33). 322p. 1984. lib. bdg. 40.50 (0-88318-313-7) Am Inst Physics.

Low Energy X-Ray Diagnostics: Monterey, 1981. Ed. by D. T. Attwood & B. L. Henke. (AIP Conference Proceedings Ser.: No. 75). 394p. 1981. lib. bdg. 44.00 (0-88318-174-6) Am Inst Physics.

Low-Expansion Materials: Proceedings: Low-Expansion Ceramics Symposium (96th: 1994: Indianapolis, Indiana) Ed. by David P. Stinton & Santosh Y. Limaye. LC 95-12136. (Ceramic Transactions Ser.: Vol. 52). (Illus.). 256p. 1995. 88.00 (0-944904-92-0, CT052) Am Ceramic.

Low Fancy. Catriona Strang. 64p. 1993. pap. 12.00 (1-55022-197-3, Pub. by ECW) Genl Dist Srvs.

***Low Fat.** Penny Stephens & Smithmark Publishing Staff. (Portable Chef Ser.). (Illus.). 256p. 1999. 7.98 (0-7651-0877-1) Smithmark.

Low Fat & Happy: Flavorful Family-Style Recipes That Will Leave You Feeling Satisfied Not Deprived. Teresa R. Collins. LC 97-94333. 223p. 1997. pap. 11.95 (0-9660238-7-0) Aspire Pub.

Low-Fat & Healthy One-Pot Meals. Surrey Books Staff. LC 98-213565. (Collector's Ser.: Vol. 41). (Illus.). 64p. 1997. per. 3.95 (0-942320-59-X) Am Cooking.

Low Fat & Light Four Ingredient Cookbook. Emily Cale & Linda Coffee. 144p. 1996. pap. 9.95 (0-9628550-2-2) Coffee & Cale.

Low Fat & Luscious. Better Homes & Gardens. LC 95-81715. 160p. 1996. 16.95 (0-696-20373-1) Meredith Bks.

Low-Fat & Luscious Italian. Better Homes & Gardens. LC 96-78798. (Illus.). 160p. 1997. 16.95 (0-696-00063-6) Meredith Bks.

Low-Fat & Luscious Vegetarian. Ed. by Kristi Fuller. LC 97-71331. (Illus.). 160p. 1997. 16.95 (0-696-20727-3, Better Homes) Meredith Bks.

Low-Fat Back Packing. 2nd ed. Alex Roman. Ed. by Yvonne McCall. LC 97-66525. (Illus.). 40p. (Orig.). (YA). 1997. reprint ed. pap. text 15.95 (1-887003-41-X) Dancng Jester.

***Low-Fat Bed & Breakfast Cookbook: 225 Tried-&-True Recipes from North American B&Bs.** M. J. Smith. LC 98-231224. 272p. 1998. pap. 13.95 (1-56561-149-7) Wiley.

***Low Fat Bed & Breakfast Cookbook: 300 Tried & True Recipes from North American B & Bs.** M. J. Smith. 240p. 1998. pap. 13.95 (0-471-34746-9) Wiley.

Low Fat Chicken. Anne Hildyard. 1997. pap. text 12.95 (1-85967-472-0, Lorenz Bks) Anness Pub.

Low-Fat Chicken Breasts: 120 Healthy & Delicious Recipes for Skinless, Boneless Chicken Breasts. Diane Rozas. (Particular Palate Ser.). (Illus.). 144p. 1996. 10.00 (0-517-88634-0, Crown) Crown Pub Group.

***Low Fat Cookbook.** Sue Kreitzman. (Living Ser.). (Illus.). 160p. 2000. pap. 13.95 (0-7894-6145-5) DK Pub Inc.

Low Fat Cooking. 200p. 1995. spiral bd. 19.95 (1-870049-97-7) Oliver Bks.

Low-Fat Cooking. (Popular Brands Cookbooks Ser.). (Illus.). 24p. 1997. pap. write for info. (0-7666-0090-4, Honey Bear Bks) Modern Pub NYC.

Low-Fat Cooking. Brigit Binns. (Complete Idiot's Guides Ser.). 320p. 1999. pap. text 16.95 (0-02-862888-8) Macmillan Gen Ref.

***Low Fat Cooking: Dishes For Deliciously Nutritious Healthy Eating.** Anne Sheasby. 96p. 1999. pap. 12.95 (0-7548-0552-2) Anness Pub.

Low-Fat Cooking: Recipes for Today's Lifestyle. 160p. 1998. pap. 12.99 (1-896891-32-2) Companys Coming.

Low-Fat Cooking for Good Health: 200+ Delicious Quick & Easy Recipes. Gloria Rose. LC 93-617. 384p. 1993. pap. 13.95 (0-89529-577-6, Avery) Penguin Putnam.

Low-Fat Cooking for Good Health: 200+ Delicious Quick & Easy Recipes Without Added Fat, Sugar or Salt. Gloria Rose. (Illus.). 384p. 1996. pap. 14.95 (0-89529-686-1, Avery) Penguin Putnam.

***Low Fat Cooking to Beat the Clock: Delicious, Inspired Meals in 15 Minutes.** Sam Gugino. 2001. pap. 19.95 (0-8118-2712-7) Chronicle Bks.

***Low Fat Cook's Companion: Over 300 Delicious Recipes for Healthy Eating.** (Illus.). 416p. 2000. 40.00 (1-85967-794-0, Lorenz Bks) Anness Pub.

Low-Fat Country Cooking. Taste of Home Staff. LC 97-65129. 292p. 1997. 24.95 (0-89821-210-3, 24495) Reiman Pubns.

Low-Fat Cuisine. 320p. 1999. 16.95 (0-02-862853-5, Pub. by Macmillan) S&S Trade.

Low-Fat Down Home Cook Book. Mary Stangl. 458p. spiral bd. 19.95 (0-9631854-2-X) Stangl Pub.

Low-Fat Epicure. Sallie Twentyman. (Orig.). 1995. pap. 5.50 (0-425-14766-5) Berkley Pub.

Low-Fat Fast Food Guide. Jamie Pope-Cordle & Martin Katahn. 64p. 1993. pap. 3.99 (0-393-31007-8) Norton.

Low-Fat Favorites: Flavorful Recipes for Healthful Meals. Members of Moosewood College Staff. LC 96-49430. (Moosewood Collective Ser.). 1996. 35.00 (0-517-70210-X) Crown.

Low-Fat Favorites: Flavorful Recipes for Healthful Meals. Moosewood Collective Staff. Ed. by Pam Krauss. LC 96-49430. (Moosewood Collective Ser.). (Illus.). 466p. 1996. pap. 22.00 (0-517-88494-1) Crown Pub Group.

Low Fat Finales: Reduced Fat Dessert Recipes Collected by Chris Brito-Millard, Certified Personal Trainer. rev. ed. Chris Brito-Millard. (Illus.). 92p. 1995. 12.95 (0-9649659-1-7) B A Brito.

Low-Fat for Life: An Integrated Program for Making the Change to a Healthier, Low-fat Lifestyle. rev. ed. Mike Heus et al. LC 93-91552. (Illus.). 494p. 1998. pap. 16.95 (0-937373-05-2) Micamar Pub.

Low Fat for Life Cookbook. Sue Kreitzman. LC 97-32261. 1998. 24.95 (0-7894-2753-2) DK Pub Inc.

Low-Fat Good Food Cookbook: Combo Prepack. Martin Katahn & Terri Katahn. LC 94-6548. 1994. pap. 209.10 (0-393-31186-4) Norton.

Low-Fat Good Food Cookbook: For a Lifetime of Fabulous Food. Martin Katahn. (Illus.). 1994. pap. 9.95 (0-393-31149-X) Norton.

Low-Fat Gourmet Chicken: 225 Delicious, Low-Cholesterol Chicken Recipes, Each with Complete Nutritional Analysis. Jackie Eddy & Eleanor Clark. 288p. 1991. spiral bd. 14.95 (1-55958-139-5) Prima Pub.

Low Fat Great Tasting Kids' Snacks: Healthy & Delicious Recipes. Mary A. Melone & Carol Parik. (Cooking Books for Children: Vol. 5). (Illus.). 96p. (J). (gr. 3-8). 1996. lib. bdg. 18.95 (1-56674-177-7, HTS Bks) Forest Hse.

Low-Fat Grilling. Melanie Barnard. LC 94-33253. 192p. 1995. pap. 10.00 (0-06-095073-0, Perennial) HarperTrade.

Low Fat Handbook. Consumer Guide Editors. 1996. mass mkt. 7.99 (0-451-82314-1) NAL.

Low-Fat, High-Flavor Cookbook. Oxmoor House Staff. 240p. 1996. 29.95 (0-8487-1454-7) Oxmoor Hse.

Low Fat Home Cooking with Kay: Recipes Passed down for Three Generations from Mother to Daughter. Kay S. Schaal. x, 99p. 1998. pap. 14.96 (0-9668982-0-6) By The Bk Pub.

Low Fat Indian Cookbook. Roshi Razzaq. 128p. 1993. 12.98 (1-55521-898-9) Bk Sales Inc.

Low-Fat Italian. Cole Group Editors Staff. (Cole's Cooking Companion Ser.). (Illus.). 96p. 1996. pap. 7.95 (1-56426-814-4) Cole Group.

Low Fat Kitchen. Donna Deane. (Illus.). 208p. 1998. pap. 18.95 (1-883792-22-3, Pub. by LA Times) Sunbelt Pubns.

Low-Fat Korean Cooking: Fish, Shellfish & Vegetables, 3 vols., Vol. 2. Chin-hwa Noh. LC 85-80451. (Illus.). 64p. 1997. 16.98 (0-930878-47-7) Hollym Intl.

Low Fat Kosher Cookbook. Faye Levy. LC 96-29192. 1997. 24.95 (0-517-70364-5) Random Hse Value.

Low-Fat Kroger Cookbook. Michelle Lombardo & Karen McNamara. LC 95-91064. (Illus.). 176p. (Orig.). 1996. pap. 4.95 (0-9648438-1-1) Wellness GA.

Low-Fat Latin Cooking. Rafael Palomino. 2001. write for info. (0-688-16725-X, Hearst) Hearst Commns.

Low-Fat Lies: High-Fat Frauds & the Healthiest Diet in the World. Kevin Vigilante & Mary Flynn. LC 99-21204. (Illus.). 334p. 1999. 19.95 (0-89526-321-1, Pub. by Regnery Pub) Natl Bk Netwk.

***Low-Fat Lies: High Fat Frauds & the Healthiest Diet in the World.** Mary Flynn & Kevin Vigilante. 334p. 2000. reprint ed. pap. 14.95 (0-89526-220-7, LifeLine Press) Regnery Pub.

Low-Fat Living: Turn off the Fat Makers, Turn on the Fat Burners for Longevity, Energy, Weight Loss, Freedom from Disease. Robert K. Cooper & Leslie L. Cooper. (Illus.). 496p. 1996. text 27.95 (0-87596-295-5) Rodale Pr Inc.

Low-Fat Living: Turn off the Fat-Makers; Turn on the Fat-Burners for Longevity, Energy, Weight Loss, Freedom from Disease. Robert K. Cooper & Leslie L. Cooper. (Illus.). 478p. 1998. pap. 14.95 (1-57954-021-X) Rodale Pr Inc.

Low-Fat Living Cookbook: 250 Easy, Great-Tasting Recipes. Leslie L. Cooper. LC 97-41540. 400p. 1998. 27.95 (0-87596-435-4) Rodale Pr Inc.

***Low-Fat Living Cookbook: 250 Easy, Great-Tasting Recipes.** Leslie L. Cooper. LC 97-41540. (Illus.). 448p. 2000. pap. 17.95 (0-87596-436-2) Rodale Pr Inc.

Low-Fat Living for Real People: The Fat-Free Chocolate-Covered Creme-Filled Mini-Cakes Diet & Other Confusions of Low-Fat Eating Explained. 2nd rev. ed. Linda Levy & Francine Grabowski. LC 97-75607. 1998. pap. text 14.95 (0-9627403-9-X) Lake Isle Pr.

Low Fat Living Menu Planner: Time Saving Tips to Cook & Look Lean. Cheryl Larson. (Illus.). 1995. 24.95 (0-9648696-0-8) Nutrilife.

***Low Fat Low Cholesterol Recipes For A Healthy Heart.** Christine France. 160p. 2000. pap. 14.95 (1-84215-093-6) Anness Pub.

***Low Fat, Low Sugar: Essential Vegetarian Collection.** Rose Elliot. (Illus.). 2000. pap. 16.95 (0-7225-3949-5, Pub. by Thorsons PA) HarpC.

Low-Fat Meals. Better Homes & Gardens. (Better Homes & Gardens Ser.). 128p. 1990. 12.95 (0-696-01889-6) Meredith Bks.

***Low-Fat Meals in Minutes: Home Library Cookbooks.** Home Library Editors. 120p. 1999. pap. 11.95 (1-56426-155-7, Pub. by Cole Group) ACCESS Pubs Network.

Low-Fat Meats: Design Strategies & Human Implications. Ed. by Harold D. Hafs & Robert G. Zimbelman. (Illus.). 330p. 1994. text 73.00 (0-12-313260-6) Acad Pr.

Low-Fat Mexican Cooking. Patrick J. Earvolino. LC 95-40342. (Illus.). 224p. 1996. pap. 4.95 (0-89658-277-9) Voyageur Pr.

Low-Fat Mexican Cooking. Patrick J. Earvolino. (Illus.). 224p. 1999. reprint ed. pap. text 17.00 (0-7881-6305-1) DIANE Pub.

Low Fat Mexican Recipes. Lee Fischer et al. LC 97-46337. (Illus.). 96p. 1997. ring bd. 6.95 (1-885590-12-1) Golden West Pub.

Low Fat No Fat If I Can You Can. 1996. 11.80 (0-9655197-0-8) D S Sharp.

Low Fat Sauces. Linda Fraser. 1997. pap. text 12.95 (1-85967-484-4, Lorenz Bks) Anness Pub.

Low-Fat Snack Diet: How to Lose Weight Through Snacking. 1992. lib. bdg. 79.95 (0-8490-5467-2) Gordon Pr.

Low-Fat Soul. Jonell Nash. LC 97-97059. 224p. 1997. pap. 14.00 (0-345-41363-6) Ballantine Pub Grp.

Low-Fat Supermarket: A Guide to Weight Loss, Cholesterol Control & Good Nutrition for the Entire Family. Judith S. Smith & Scott D. Smith. LC 92-80422. 304p. 1993. pap. 10.95 (0-914984-43-8) Starburst.

Low-Fat Supermarket Shopper's Guide: Making Healthy Choices from Thousands of Brand-Name Items. Jaime Pope & Martin Katahn. 88p. 1996. pap. 5.95 (0-393-31488-X, Norton Paperbks) Norton.

Low-Fat Supermarket Shopper's Guide: Making Healthy Choices from Thousands of Brand-Name Items. Jamie Pope. 72p. 1993. pap. 3.99 (0-393-30923-1) Norton.

Low Fat Supermarket Shopping Guide. Jane Pope-Cordle. 1993. pap. 69.80 (0-393-30982-7) Norton.

Low-Fat Three Ingredient Cookbook. Ruthie Wornall. 1995. pap. 6.95 (0-9624467-7-7) Wornall Pub.

Low Fat Times: Delicious Recipes 20 Fat & Less. Karen Cole. 277p. (Orig.). 1995. pap. 13.95 (0-9644225-0-6) Karon Assocs.

***Low-Fat Top Secret Recipes.** Todd Wilbur. LC 00-23732. (Illus.). 240p. 2000. pap. 12.95 (0-452-28149-0, Plume) Dutton Plume.

Low Fat Vegetarian Cooking: Classic Slim Cuisine. Sue Kreitzman. (Vegetarian Cooking Ser.). (Illus.). 208p. (Orig.). 1996. pap. 14.95 (0-89594-834-6) Crossing Pr.

***Low-Fat Way.** (Mini Cook Bks.). 148p. 1998. pap. 1.95 (3-8290-0376-5, 770252) Konemann.

An Asterisk (*) at the beginning of an entry indicates that the title is appearing for the first time.

Low-Fat Way to Cook. Oxmoor House Staff. LC 93-84154. 256p. 1993. 29.99 (*0-8487-1125-4*) Oxmoor Hse.

Low-Fat Way to Cook Chicken. Oxmoor House Staff. LC 94-74793. (Illus.). 144p. 1995. spiral bd. 18.95 (*0-8487-2200-0*) Oxmoor Hse.

Low-Fat Way to Cook Pasta. Oxmoor House Staff. LC 94-62126. (Illus.). 144p. 1995. spiral bd. 18.95 (*0-8487-2201-9*) Oxmoor Hse.

Low-Fat Ways to Bake. Leisure Arts Staff. (Illus.). 144p. 1998. 18.95 (*0-8487-2216-7*) Oxmoor Hse.

Low-Fat Ways to Cook Desserts. Oxmoor House Staff. LC 95-74600. 144p. 1995. spiral bd. 18.95 (*0-8487-2204-3*) Oxmoor Hse.

Low-Fat Ways to Cook Family Favorites. Leisure Arts Staff. LC 96-71086. (Illus.). 144p. 1997. 18.95 (*0-8487-2215-9*) Oxmoor Hse.

Low Fat Ways to Cook Fish & Shellfish. Oxmoor House Staff. LC 96-71083. 144p. 1997. spiral bd. 18.95 (*0-8487-2207-8*) Oxmoor Hse.

Low-Fat Ways to Cook for the Holidays. Ed. & Compiled by Susan M. McIntosh. LC 98-67025. (Illus.). 144p. 1998. spiral bd. 29.95 (*0-8487-2217-5*) Oxmoor Hse.

Low-Fat Ways to Cook for Two. 1999. 18.95 (*0-8487-2218-3*) Oxmoor Hse.

Low-Fat Ways to Cook Meats. Oxmoor House Staff. LC 95-74601. 144p. 1996. spiral bd. 18.95 (*0-8487-2205-1*) Oxmoor Hse.

Low-Fat Ways to Cook One-Dish Meals. Oxmoor House Staff. LC 95-97712. 144p. 1995. spiral bd. 18.95 (*0-8487-2202-7*) Oxmoor Hse.

Low-Fat Ways to Cook Quick & Easy. Oxmoor House Staff. LC 95-67713. 144p. 1995. spiral bd. 18.95 (*0-8487-2203-5*) Oxmoor Hse.

Low Fat Ways to Cook Regional Fare. Oxmoor House Staff. LC 96-71084. 144p. 1997. spiral bd. 18.95 (*0-8487-2213-2*) Oxmoor Hse.

Low-Fat Ways to Cook Salads & Side Dishes. 144p. 1999. 18.95 (*0-8487-2210-8*) Oxmoor Hse.

Low-Fat Ways to Cook Soups & Stews. Leisure Arts Staff. LC 96-71085. (Illus.). 144p. 1997. 18.95 (*0-8487-2214-0*) Oxmoor Hse.

Low-Fat Ways to Cook Vegetarian. Leisure Arts Staff. LC 96-67710. 144p. 1996. spiral bd. 18.95 (*0-8487-2206-X*, 104006) Oxmoor Hse.

Low-Fat Ways to Lose Weight. Leisure Arts Staff. LC 96-68032. 144p. 1996. spiral bd. 18.95 (*0-8487-2208-6*, 104007) Oxmoor Hse.

Low-Fat Ways to Stir-Fry. Oxmoor House Staff. LC 96-67711. 144p. 1996. spiral bd. 18.95 (*0-8487-2209-4*, 104008) Oxmoor Hse.

Low Fire: Other Ways to Work in Clay. Leon I. Nigrosh. LC 79-56377. (Illus.). 112p. (YA). (gr. 7-12). 1980. 20.75 (*0-87192-120-0*) Davis Mass.

***Low Flammability Polymeric Materials.** Ed. by G. E. Zaikov & N. A. Khalturinskii. 1999. 85.00 (*1-56072-703-9*) Nova Sci Pubs.

***Low Flow Anaesthesia.** 2nd ed. Jan A. Baum. (Illus.). 256p. 2000. text 80.00 (*0-7506-4672-1*) Buttrwrth-Heinemann.

Low-Flow Anaesthesia: The Theory & Practice of Low Flow, Minimum Flow & Closed System Anaesthesia. Jan A. Baum & Geoffrey Nunn. LC 96-167207. 192p. 1996. text 80.00 (*0-7506-2127-3*) Buttrwrth-Heinemann.

Low Flying Aircraft: Stories by T. M. McNally. T. M. McNally. LC 91-14100. (Flannery O'Connor Award for Short Fiction Ser.). 176p. 1991. 19.95 (*0-8203-1378-5*) U of Ga Pr.

Low Frequency Astrophysics from Space: Proceedings of an International Workshop Held in Crystal City, Virginia, U. S. A., on 8 & 9 January 1990. Ed. by N. E. Kassim et al. (Lecture Notes in Physics Ser.: Vol. 362). xii, 280p. 1990. 40.95 (*0-387-52891-1*) Spr-Verlag.

Low Frequency Electromagnetic Design. Michael P. Perry. (Electrical Engineering & Electronics Ser.: Vol. 28). (Illus.). 256p. 1985. text 150.00 (*0-8247-7453-1*) Dekker.

Low Frequency Properties of Dielectric Crystals: Piezoelectric, Pyroelectric & Related Constants see Crystal & Solid State Physics: Group III

Low Frequency Properties of Dielectric Crystals: Second & Higher Order Elastic Constants see Crystal & Solid State Physics: Group III

***Low Frequency Scattering.** George Dassios & Ralph E. Kleinman. LC 99-32310. (Oxford Mathematical Monographs). 320p. 2000. text 115.00 (*0-19-853678-X*) OUP.

Low-Frequency Sound & Marine Mammals: Current Knowledge & Research Needs. National Research Council Staff. LC 93-61700. (Illus.). 93p. 1994. pap. 30.00 (*0-608-04831-3*, 206548800004) Bks Demand.

Low-Frequency Waves & Irregularities in the Ionosphere: Proceedings of the ESRIN-ESLAB Symposium, 2nd, Frascati, Italy, Sept 23-27, 1968. ESRIN-ESLAB Symposium Staff. Ed. by N. D'Angelo. (Astrophysics & Space Science Library: No.14). 218p. 1969. text 146.50 (*90-277-0114-8*) Kluwer Academic.

Low Friction Arthroplasty of the Hip: Theory & Practice. J. Charnley. (Illus.). 1978. 176.00 (*0-387-08893-8*) Spr-Verlag.

Low German (Platt Duutsch) A Brief History of the Low German Language & People. Robert L. Stockman. LC 98-91589. (Illus.). 445p. 1998. pap. 20.00 (*0-9665502-0-X*) Low German Pr.

Low-Grade & Nonconventional Sources of Manganese. David B. Brooks. LC 66-24411. 135p. reprint ed. pap. 41.90 (*0-608-12256-4*, 202378700034) Bks Demand.

Low-Grade Metamorphism. Doug Robinson & Martin Frey. LC 98-18900. (Illus.). 8p. 1998. pap. 75.00 (*0-632-04756-9*) Blackwell Sci.

Low-Grade Metamorphism of Mafic Rocks. Ed. by Peter Schiffman & Howard W. Day. LC 94-43589. (Special Papers: Vol. 296). 1995. 50.00 (*0-8137-2296-9*) Geol Soc.

Low-Gravity Fluid Dynamics & Transport Phenomena. Ed. by Jan N. Koster & R. L. Sani. (PAAS Ser.: Vol. 130). 1990. 99.95 (*0-930403-74-6*, V-130) AIAA.

Low-Gravity Fluid Mechanics: Mathematical Theory of Capillary Phenomena. Ed. by A. D. Myshkis et al. Tr. by R. S. Wadhwa from RUS. (Illus.). 610p. 1987. 175.95 (*0-387-16189-9*) Spr-Verlag.

Low-Gravity Sciences, Seminar Series 1986, University of Colorado at Boulder. Ed. by Jean N. Koster. (Science & Technology Ser.: Vol. 67). (Illus.). 290p. 1987. 55.00 (*0-87703-270-X*, Am Astronaut Soc); pap. 45.00 (*0-87703-271-8*, Am Astronaut Soc) Univelt Inc.

Low-Hanging Fruit. G. B. Mann. LC 96-94783. 128p. 1997. 18.95 (*0-9655117-0-7*, LHF001) GrapeVinePress.

Low Head Hydro-Electricity. Ed. by L. J. Duckers & J. Morton. (C). 1988. 125.00 (*0-7855-4210-8*, Pub. by Interntl Solar Energy Soc) St Mut.

Low Head Hydro-Electricity (C52) L. J. Duckers & J. Morton. 57p. (C). 1988. 120.00 (*0-7855-3810-0*, Pub. by Interntl Solar Energy Soc) St Mut.

Low Impact Service - A Guide to Automotive Service & Warranty Complaints, How to Avoid Them, How to Resolve Them: The Complete Handbook & Directory for the Mechanically Disinclined. Peter A. Ciullo. LC 92-80997. 176p. (Orig.). 1992. pap. 12.95 (*0-9626043-6-4*) Maradia Pr.

Low Incidence Conditions. Ed. by Margaret C. Wang et al. (Handbook of Special Education: Research & Practice Ser.: Vol. 3). 380p. 1988. 133.50 (*0-08-033385-0*, Pergamon Pr) Elsevier.

Low Incident Ion Energies see Ion Implantation Range & Energy Deposition Distributions

Low-Income Families & Economic Stability. 1991. lib. bdg. 69.95 (*0-8490-4509-6*) Gordon Pr.

Low-Income Housing: Overview of State-Federal Issues. Jon Dunlap & William Waren. (State-Federal Issue Brief Ser.: Vol. 5, No. 3). 22p. 1992. pap. text 6.50 (*1-55516-897-3*, 8500-0503) Natl Conf State Legis.

Low Income Housing: Technology & Policy: Proceedings of the International Conference, Bangkok, June 1977, 3 vols. Ed. by R. P. Pama et al. 1978. 674.00 (*0-08-023241-8*, Pub. by Pergamon Repr) Franklin.

***Low-income Housing Credit.** 235p. 1999. ring bd. 24.00 (*0-16-059033-7*) USGPO.

Low Income Housing Tax-Exempt Bond Handbook. Michael J. Novogradac. 1998. spiral bd. 89.95 (*0-9663962-0-0*) Novogradac & Co.

Low Income Rural Housing. D. R. Veena. 141p. 1986. 19.00 (*81-7024-027-1*, Pub. by Ashish Pub Hse) S Asia.

Low Income Self-Employment: Work, Benefits & Living Standards. Tony Eardley & Anne Corden. LC 95-83044. 336p. 1996. 87.95 (*1-85972-241-5*, Pub. by Avebry) Ashgate Pub Co.

Low-Intensity Conflict: A Guide for Tactics, Techniques, & Procedures. James Gallagher. LC 92-11174. (Illus.). 208p. 1992. pap. 14.95 (*0-8117-2552-9*) Stackpole.

Low Intensity Conflict: The New Battlefield in Central America. Tom Barry. 70p. (Orig.). 1986. pap. 5.95 (*0-911213-05-8*) Interhemisp Res Ctr.

Low-Intensity Conflict & Modern Technology: Terrorism & "Small Wars", 2 vols., Set. 1995. lib. bdg. 602.99 (*0-8490-7554-8*) Gordon Pr.

Low-Intensity Conflict in American History. Claude C. Sturgill. LC 93-17648. 160p. 1993. 55.00 (*0-275-93987-1*, Praeger Pubs) Greenwood.

Low-Intensity Conflict in the Third World. Lewis B. Ware. 1988. pap. 7.50 (*1-58566-022-1*) Air Univ.

Low Intensity Democracy: Political Power in the New World Order. Barry Gills et al. LC 93-25787. 250p. (C). 1993. 49.95 (*0-7453-0535-0*, Pub. by Pluto GBR); pap. 19.95 (*0-7453-0536-9*, Pub. by Pluto GBR) Stylus Pub VA.

***Low K Dielectric Materials Technology.** 1999. 185.00 (*1-892568-35-7*) Smicndctr Equip.

Low-Key Politics: Local-Level Leadership & Change in the Middle East. Richard T. Antoun. LC 77-19018. (Illus.). 285p. (C). 1979. text 19.50 (*0-87395-373-8*) State U NY Pr.

Low Latitude Aeronomical Processes: Proceedings of the COSPAR 22nd Plenary Meeting, Bangalore, India, 1979. COSPAR, Twenty-Second Plenary Meeting Staff. Ed. by A. P. Mitra. LC 79-41341. 1980. 84.00 (*0-08-024439-4*, Pergamon Pr) Elsevier.

Low-Latitude Ionospheric Physics. Kuo Fu-Shong. (CP Ser.: No. 7). 328p. 1994. 215.00 (*0-08-042134-2*, Pergamon Pr) Elsevier.

Low-Level Aggression: First Steps on the Ladder to Violence. Arnold P. Goldstein. 240p. 1999. pap. text 19.95 (*0-87822-423-8*) Res Press.

Low Level Attack: The Pacific. Jack Lambert. (Air Combat Photo History Ser.). 1997. pap. 18.95 (*0-933424-83-3*) Specialty Pr.

***Low Level Attack Vol. 3: The Mediterranean & Europe.** Jock Lambert. (Illus.). 112p. 1998. pap. 18.95 (*1-58007-005-1*) Specialty Pr.

Low-Level Environmental Radioactivity: Sources & Evaluation. Josef Sabol & Richard Tykva. LC 94-60049. 341p. 1995. pap. text 64.95 (*1-56676-189-1*) Technomic.

***Low Level Hell: A Scout Pilot in the Big Red One.** Hugh L. Mills, Jr. & Robert Anderson. 336p. 2000. pap. 19.95 (*0-89141-719-2*) Presidio Pr.

Low-Level Ionizing Radiation: A Source Guide. 1991. lib. bdg. 76.00 (*0-8490-4851-6*) Gordon Pr.

Low Level Liberators: The Story of Patrol Bombing Squadron 104 in the South Pacific During World War II. Paul F. Stevens. LC 98-194223. 318 p. 1997. write for info. (*1-889553-06-9*) WhitMar Elect.

Low-Level Measurements & Their Applications to Environmental Radioactivity: Proceedings of la Rabida International Summer School. Ed. by M. Garcia-Leon & G. Madurga. 596p. (C). 1988. text 125.00 (*9971-5-0461-8*) World Scientific Pub.

Low-Level Measurements of Man-Made Radionuclides in the Environment. M. Garcia-Leon & G. Madurga. 484p. 1991. text 137.00 (*981-02-0397-7*) World Scientific Pub.

Low-Level Measurements of Man-Made Radionuclides in the Environment: Proceedings. M. Garcia-Leon & R. G. Tenorio. 584p. 1994. text 121.00 (*981-02-1632-7*) World Scientific Pub.

Low Level Mission. Leon Wolff. LC 75-169443. (Literature & History of Aviation Ser.). 1972. reprint ed. 23.95 (*0-405-03786-4*) Ayer.

Low Level Path Marking & Lighting Systems, UL 1994. 2nd ed. (C). 1997. pap. text 330.00 (*0-7629-0145-4*) Underwrtrs Labs.

***Low Level Radiation & Immune System Damage: An Atomic Era Legacy.** Joseph J. Mangano. LC 98-18138. 1998. lib. bdg. 49.95 (*1-56670-334-4*, L1334) Lewis Pubs.

Low Level Radiation & Living State. Ed. by N. G. Huilgol et al. (Illus.). viii,189p. 1994. text 69.00 (*0-387-57313-5*) Spr-Verlag.

Low Level Radiation Effects: A Fact Book. 2nd ed. A. Bertrand Brill. Ed. by James Adelstein et al. LC 82-16939. 153p. 1982. ring bd. 20.00 (*0-932004-14-8*) Soc Nuclear Med.

Low-Level Radioactive Waste: A Legislator's Guide. Barbara Foster et al. LC 97-206122. 98p. 1994. 15.00 (*1-55516-498-6*, 4640) Natl Conf State Legis.

***Low-Level Radioactive Waste Disposal Market: Supply & Demand in the U. S.** Susan A. Kaplan. 36p. 1999. pap. 250.00 (*0-9652661-1-7*, E-175-1) Kapline Ent.

Low-Level Radioactive Waste Regulation: Science, Politics, & Fear. Ed. by Michael Burns. (Illus.). 311p. 1987. lib. bdg. 89.95 (*0-87371-026-6*, L026) Lewis Pubs.

Low-Level Radioactive Waste Repositories: An Analysis of Costs. NEA Staff. 180p. 1999. pap. 50.00 (*92-64-16154-6*, 66 99 03 1 P) Org for Econ.

***Low-Level Waste Data Base Development Program.** J. W. McConnell. 448p. 1998. per. 35.00 (*0-16-062954-3*) USGPO.

Low Life: Lures & Snares of Old New York. Luc Sante. (Illus.). 326p. 1991. 27.50 (*0-374-19414-9*) FS&G.

Low Life: Lures & Snares of Old New York. Luc Sante. LC 91-58051. 1992. pap. 16.00 (*0-679-73876-2*) Vin Bks.

Low Life & Moral Improvement in Mid-Victorian England. Ed. by John K. Walton & Alastair Wilcox. 268p. 1993. pap. 17.95 (*0-7185-1491-2*, Pub. by Leicester U Pr) Cassell & Continuum.

Low Life & Moral Improvement in Mid-Victorian England. Ed. by John Walton & Alastair Wilcox. 1991. text 59.00 (*0-7185-1351-7*) St Martin.

Low Light & Thermal Imaging Systems: March 3-5, 1975, London. International Conference on Low Light & Thermal Im. LC TK8315.I5. (Institution of Electrical Engineers Conference Report Ser.: No. 124). 244p. reprint ed. pap. 75.70 (*0-608-11060-4*, 201213000080) Bks Demand.

Low Light Level Imaging Systems: Proceedings, Two-Day Seminar. Society of Photographic Scientists & Engineers Sta. Ed. by A. C. Langord. LC 70-151457. 193p. reprint ed. pap. 59.90 (*0-608-15002-9*, 202570200046) Bks Demand.

Low Light Photography: Pro-Photo Series. Jonathan Hilton. (Pro-Photo Ser.). 120p. 1999. pap. 35.00 (*2-88046-444-7*) Watsn-Guptill.

Low Limit Seven-Card Stud. Gary Oliver. 28p. (Orig.). 1991. pap. 6.95 (*0-9635909-1-X*) Poker Tips Pr.

Low, Low Tide & Collected Stories. Stephen E. McCallum. LC 98-89475. 375p. 1998. text 25.00 (*0-7388-0277-8*); pap. text 15.00 (*0-7388-0278-6*) Xlibris Corp.

Low Magnetic Fields in Anisotropic Superconductors. Allan J. Greer & William J. Kossler. Ed. by W. Beiglbock et al. LC 95-13008. (Lecture Notes in Physics Ser.: Vol. 30). xiii, 149p. 1995. 49.95 (*3-540-59167-2*) Spr-Verlag.

***Low-Maintenance Garden: A Complete Guide to Designs, Plants & Techniques for Easy-Care Gardens.** Susan Berry & Steve Bradley. LC SB473.B47 2000. (Illus.). 144p. 2000. 29.95 (*1-55209-514-2*); 19.95 (*1-55209-531-2*) Firefly Bks Ltd.

Low-Maintenance Gardening. Ed. by Sunset Books Staff. LC 98-86297. (Illus.). 240p. 1998. pap. 19.95 (*0-376-03512-9*) Sunset Books.

Low Maintenance Gardening. Time-Life Books Editors. Ed. by Janet Cave. LC 94-40455. (Time-Life Complete Gardener Ser.). (Illus.). 160p. (gr. 11). 1999. pap. 16.95 (*0-7835-4101-5*) Time-Life.

Low Maintenance Gardening. Anne M. Zeman. LC 92-19074. (Illus.). 1993. write for info. (*1-880281-09-0*) NK Lawn & Garden.

Low Maintenance Gardening. Anne M. Zeman. (NK Lawn & Garden Step-by-Step Visual Guides Ser.). (Illus.). 80p. (Orig.). 1993. pap. 6.95 (*0-380-76804-6*, Avon Bks) Morrow Avon.

Low-Maintenance Gardening: Beautiful Gardens in Half-An-Hour a Week. Peter McHoy. 1998. pap. text 12.95 (*1-85967-698-7*, Lorenz Bks) Anness Pub.

Low-Maintenance Landscaping. Susan A. McClure & Erin Hynes. (Successful Organic Gardening Ser.). (Illus.). 160p. 1994. pap. 14.95 (*0-87596-614-4*); text 24.95 (*0-87596-613-6*) Rodale Pr Inc.

Low-Maintenance Water Gardens. Helen Nash. (Illus.). 128p. 1998. pap. 17.95 (*0-8069-4283-5*) Sterling.

Low Maintenance Water Gardens. Helen Nash. Date not set. pap. 17.95 (*0-676-57331-2*) Random.

Low Maintenance Water Gardens. Storey Publishing Staff. 1997. 24.95 (*0-676-57206-5*) Random.

Low Maintenence Bonsai. Herb Gustafson. LC 99-14533. 96p. 1999. write for info. (*0-8069-6211-9*) Sterling.

Low Mid-Volume Competitive Analysis. Laurel A. Ranger. Ed. by Juneann Kasper. (Copier Productivity Ser.). 50p. (Orig.). 1994. pap. 45.00 (*0-9629936-2-X*) Minnella Ent.

Low Molecular Weight Heparin & Its Clinical Use: Journal: Haemostasis, Vol. 16, No. 1, 1985. 124p. 1986. pap. 68.00 (*3-8055-4230-5*) S Karger.

***Low Molecular Weight Heparin Therapy: An Evaluation of Clinical Trials Evidence.** Monique Sarret et al. LC 99-39512. 474p. 1999. 165.00 (*0-8247-8213-5*) Dekker.

Low-Molecular-Weight Heparins: A New Therapeutic Approach to Thrombosis Proceedings. Ed. by J. Monasterio & M. M. Samama. (Journal Ser.: Vol. 26, No. 2, 1996). (Illus.). iv, 66p. 1996. pap., suppl. ed. 21.75 (*3-8055-6277-2*) S Karger.

Low Molecular Weight Heparins: Pharmacology, In-Vivo & Ex-Vivo Effects & Clinical Results - Journal: Haemostasis, Vol. 18, Suppl. 2, 1988. Ed. by H. K. Breddin et al. (Illus.). iv, 88p. 1988. pap. 28.00 (*3-8055-4787-0*) S Karger.

Low Molecular Weight Heparins in Clinical Practice. Ed. by Doutremepuich. (Illus.). 264p. 1992. text 160.00 (*0-8247-8640-8*) Dekker.

Low 'n Slow: Lowriding in New Mexico. Carmella Padilla & Jack Parsons. LC 98-31198. (Illus.). 120p. 1999. 39.95 (*0-89013-372-7*) Museum NM Pr.

Low Noise Electronic System Design. C. D. Motchenbacher & J. A. Connelly. LC 92-39598. 448p. 1993. 104.95 (*0-471-57742-1*) Wiley.

Low Noise Marine Gears. W. Haller. (Nineteen Ninety-One Fall Technical Meeting Ser.: Vol. 91FTM4). (Illus.). 11p. 1991. pap. text 30.00 (*1-55589-601-4*) AGMA.

Low-Noise Wide-Band Amplifiers in Bipolar & CMOS Technologies. Zhong Y. Chang & Willy M. Sansen. (International Series in Engineering & Computer Science, VLSI, Computer Architecture, & Digital Screen Processing). 224p. (C). 1990. text 110.00 (*0-7923-9096-2*) Kluwer Academic.

Low on the Go: Quick Lowfat Recipes for Busy People. 2nd rev. ed. Terri Petersen. (Illus.), 234p. 1991. pap. 15.95 (*0-9639826-0-5*) Lean for Life.

Low or No Tuition: The Feasibility of a National Policy for the First Two Years of College: An Analytical Report. Carnegie Council on Policy Studies in Higher Educa. LC 75-4276. 96p. reprint ed. pap. 30.00 (*0-608-12985-2*, 202387300034) Bks Demand.

Low Oxalate Cookbook. LC 97-60098. (Illus.). 224p. 1997. spiral bd. 27.00 (*0-9656223-0-4*) Vulvar Pain.

Low Pay: Its Causes & the Post-War Trade Union Response. Colin Duncan. LC 81-30555. (Social Policy Research Monographs: No. 3). (Illus.). 175p. reprint ed. pap. 54.30 (*0-8357-8940-3*, 203333300085) Bks Demand.

Low Pay & Earnings Mobility in Europe. Ed. by Rita Asplund et al. LC 98-17708. 296p. 1998. 90.00 (*1-85898-854-3*) E Elgar.

Low-Power CMOS Design. Anantha P. Chandrakasan & Robert Brodersen. LC 97-38651. 644p. 1998. 99.95 (*0-7803-3429-9*, PC 5703) Inst Electrical.

Low Power CMOS VLSI Circuit Design. Kaushik Roy & Sharat Prasad. LC 98-19426. 359p. 2000. 79.95 (*0-471-11488-X*) Wiley.

Low-Power CMOS Wireless Communications: A Wideband CDMA System Design. Samuel Sheng & Robert w. Brodersen. LC 97-42147. 284p. 1998. text 108.00 (*0-7923-8085-1*) Kluwer Academic.

Low Power Design in Deep Submicron Electronics. Ed. by Wolfgang Nebel & Jean P. Mermet. LC 97-16495. 1997. text 318.00 (*0-7923-4569-X*) Kluwer Academic.

Low Power Design in Deep Submicron Electronics. Ed. by Wolfgang Nebel & Jean P. Mermet. LC 97-42789. 596p. 1998. pap. text 120.00 (*0-7923-8103-3*) Kluwer Academic.

Low Power Design Methodologies. Jan M. Rabaey & Massoud Pedram. LC 95-37557. (Kluwer International Series in Engineering & Computer Science). 367p. (C). 1995. text 127.00 (*0-7923-9630-8*) Kluwer Academic.

Low Power Digital CMOS Design. Anantha P. Chandrakasan & Robert W. Broderson. LC 95-16761. 424p. (C). 1995. text 115.00 (*0-7923-9576-X*) Kluwer Academic.

Low-Power Digital VLSI Design: Circuits & Systems. Abdellatif Bellaouar & Mohamed I. Elmasry. LC 95-16756. (Illus.). 552p. (C). 1995. text 133.00 (*0-7923-9587-5*) Kluwer Academic.

Low-Power HF Microelectronics: A Unified Approach. Ed. by Gerson A. Machado. (IEE Circuits & Systems Ser.: No. 8). 960p. 1996. boxed set 99.00 (*0-85296-874-4*) INSPEC Inc.

Low Power PCs: Personal Access Communications Systems (PACS) (C). 1999. text 65.00 (*0-13-906009-X*, Prentice Hall) P-H.

Low Power VLSI Design & Technology. LC 97-107084. 128p. 1996. 34.00 (*981-02-2518-0*) World Scientific Pub.

***Low-Power Wireless Infrared Communications.** Rob Otte et al. LC 99-45811. 1999. text 105.00 (*0-7923-8643-4*) Kluwer Academic.

Low-Power Wireless Optical Transmission: Systems for Communications, Telemetry & Control. Rob Otte. (Illus.). 167p. 1998. pap. 44.50 (*90-407-1609-9*, Pub. by Delft U Pr) Coronet Bks.

Low Pressure Boilers. 3rd ed. Frederick M. Steingress. (Illus.). 236p. 1994. 26.96 (*0-8269-4412-4*) Am Technical.

Low Pressure Membrane Filtration for Particle Removal. (Illus.). 200p. 1992. pap. 76.00 (*0-89867-624-X*, 90603) Am Water Wks Assn.

Low-Pressure Synthetic Diamond: Manufacturing & Applications. Bernard Dischler & C. Wild. LC 98-2582. 193p. 1997. 109.00 (3-540-63619-6) Spr-Verlag.

Low-Profile Amateur Radio. 1993. pap. 8.00 (0-87259-411-4) Am Radio.

Low Profile Selling: Act Like a Lamb, Sell Like a Lion. Tom Hopkins. Ed. by Tom Murphy & Judy Slack. 249p. 1994. 24.95 (0-938636-29-4) T Hopkins Intl.

Low Protein Cookery for Phenylketonuria. 3rd ed. Virginia E. Schuett. LC 97-5931. (Illus.). 572p. 1997. pap. 24.95 (0-299-15384-3) U of Wis Pr.

Low Protein Diet & Progression of Chronic Renal Failure. Ed. by M. Strauch & Sergio Giovannetti. (Contributions to Nephrology Ser.: Vol. 53). (Illus.). viii, 146p. 1986. 29.75 (3-8055-4364-6) S Karger.

Low-Protein Diets in Renal Patients: Composition & Absorption. Ed. by N. Gretz. (Contributions to Nephrology Ser.: Vol. 72). (Illus.). x, 106p. 1989. 29.75 (3-8055-4963-6) S Karger.

Low Rank Representations & Graphs for Sporadic Groups. Cheryl E. Praeger & Leonard H. Soicher. (Australian Mathematical Society Lecture Ser.: No. 8). 153p. 1997. pap. text 39.95 (0-521-56737-8) Cambridge U Pr.

Low-Relaxation Strand: Practical Applications in Precast Prestressed Concrete. (PCI Journal Reprints Ser.). 20p. 1983. pap. 14.00 (0-318-19794-4, JR281) P-PCI.

Low Rent: A Decade of Prose & Photographs from the Portable Lower East Side. Ed. & Intro. by Kurt Hollander. LC 94-13395. 320p. 1994. pap. 13.00 (0-8021-3408-4, Grove) Grove-Atltic.

Low Reynolds Number Hydrodynamics. John R. Happel & Howard Brenner. (Mechanics of Fluids & Transport Processes Ser.). 1983. pap. text 110.00 (90-247-2877-0) Kluwer Academic.

Low Rider. Phillip Reed. LC 98-15898. 336p. 1998. 23.00 (0-671-00166-3, Pocket Books) PB.

Low Rider. Phillip Reed. 1999. mass mkt. 6.50 (0-671-00167-1) S&S Trade.

Low Rider. large type ed. Philip Reed. LC 98-50508. 1999. 26.95 (0-7862-1758-8) Mac Lib Ref.

Low Rider Hydraulics Basic Installation Manual. large type ed. Ray G. DeLeon. (Illus.). 108p. (Orig.). 1995. pap. 49.95 (0-9650586-0-3) D C D T.

***Low Riders.** Ann Parr. (Illus.). 2000. 16.95 (0-7910-5849-2) Chelsea Hse.

***Low Riders.** Ann Parr. (Illus.). 2001. pap. 5.95 (0-7910-5850-6) Chelsea Hse.

Low-Risk High-Performance Investing with Convertible Bonds. Jeffrey J. Pritchard. 256p. 1990. 39.95 (0-88730-396-X, HarpBusn) HarpInfo.

***Low Risk, High Reward: Starting & Growing a Business with Minimal Risk.** Bob Reiss & Jeffrey L. Cruikshank. 352p. 2000. 27.50 (0-684-84962-3) Free Pr.

Low Risk Investing: How to Get a Good Return on Your Money Without Losing Any Sleep. Gordon K. Williamson. LC 94-15477. 1994. pap. 10.95 (1-55850-384-6) Adams Media.

Low Risk Neonatal Nursing. Rudman. (Certified Nurse Examination Ser.: CN-22). pap. 23.95 (0-8373-6122-2) Nat Learn.

Low Road. Ed. by Richard Hill. 192p. 1998. 24.00 (0-7278-5335-X) Severn Hse.

***Low Road.** large type ed. Reginald Hill. 224p. 1999. 31.99 (0-7089-9108-4) Ulverscroft.

Low Road Home: Collected Poems. Donald Gordon. 66p. 1987. pap. text 7.75 (0-08-035073-9, Pub. by Aberdeen U Pr) Macmillan.

Low-Salt Cookbook. Michelle Berriedale-Johnson. (Healthy Eating Library). 1999. pap. 12.95 (0-7548-0184-5, Lorenz Bks) Anness Pub.

Low Self-Esteem: Your Questions Answered. Elaine Sheehan. (Element Guide Ser.). 128p. 1999. pap. 9.95 (1-86204-373-6, Pub. by Element MA) Penguin Putnam.

Low-Sew Bathroom Projects. Handcraft Illustrated Magazine Editorial Staff. LC 98-5472. (Fast & Fabulous Ser.). (Illus.). 128p. 1998. 24.95 (0-7621-0091-5, Pub. by RD Assn) Penguin Putnam.

Low-Sew Bedroom. Carol E. Sterbenz. LC 97-31658. (Fast & Fabulous Ser.). (Illus.). 128p. 1998. 24.95 (0-7621-0028-1, Pub. by RD Assn) Penguin Putnam.

Low Sew Window Treatments. Cowles Creative Publishing Staff & Home Decorating Institute Staff. LC 97-37376. (Creative Textiles Ser.). (Illus.). 112p. 1997. pap. 16.95 (0-86573-413-5) Creat Pub Intl.

Low Smoke, Halogen-Free Polymeric Jackets. Date not set. 30.00 (0-614-18693-5, T-33-655-1994) Insulated Cable.

Low-Solvent Coatings for Structural Steel. John D. Keane & J. A. Bruno, Jr. 133p. 1982. pap. text 45.00 (0-938477-48-X, SSPC 82-07) SSPC.

Low Speed Aerodynamics. Katz. 1992. text, student ed. 31.25 (0-07-050447-4) McGraw.

Low-Speed Aerodynamics. Joseph Katz & Allen Plotkin. (C). 1991. text. write for info. (0-07-050446-6) McGraw.

Low Speed Automobile Accidents: Accident Reconstruction & Occupant Kinematics, Dynamics & Biomechanics. 2nd ed. Dale R. Atkinson et al. LC 96-23978. 688p. 1999. 115.00 (0-913875-23-6, 5236-N) Lawyers & Judges.

***Low Speed Automobile Accidents: Accident Reconstruction & Occupant Kinematics, Dynamics & Biomechanics.** 2nd ed. Alan J. Watts et al. LC 99-40415. (Illus.). 660p. 1999. kivar 115.00 (0-913875-74-0) Lawyers & Judges.

***Low Speed Automobile Accidents: Investigation, Documentation & Case Preparation.** Peter Rast & Robert E. Stearns. 144p. 2000. spiral bd. 45.00 (0-913875-87-2, 5872-N) Lawyers & Judges.

Low Speed Marine Diesel Engines. John B. Woodward. LC 87-36570. 284p. (C). 1988. reprint ed. lib. bdg. 37.50 (0-89464-284-7) Krieger.

Low-Speed Wind Tunnel Testing. 2nd ed. William H. Rae & Alan Pope, Jr. LC 84-3700. 552p. 1984. 150.00 (0-471-87402-7) Wiley.

***Low Speed Wind Tunnel Testing.** 3rd ed. Jewel B. Barlow et al. LC 98-28891. 728p. 1999. 89.95 (0-471-55774-9) Wiley.

Low Stakes Blackjack: How to Play & Win with One Dollar-Five Dollar Bets. John Sharpe. 88p. 1995. pap. 9.95 (0-9644808-0-8) Poco Libro Pr.

Low Stress Grinding. Guy Bellows. (Machining Process Ser.: MDC 83-103). (Illus.). 136p. 1983. pap. 17.50 (0-936974-09-5) Inst Adv Manuf.

Low Sugar Three Ingredient Cookbook. Ruthie Wornall. (Three Ingredient Cookbook Ser.). 1996. spiral bd. 6.95 (0-9624467-8-5) Wornall Pub.

***Low Surface Brightness Universe: IAU Colloquium 171, Vol. 170.** Ed. by J. I. Davies et al. (ASP Conference Series Proceedings). (C). 1999. text 52.00 (1-886733-92-9) Astron Soc Pacific.

Low Tech Education in a High Tech World: Corporations & Classrooms in the New Information Society. Elizabeth L. Useem. LC 85-16044. (AAAS Issues in Science & Technology Ser.). 288p. reprint ed. pap. 82.10 (0-7837-6746-3, 2046374) Bks Demand.

Low-Tech, Light-Tech, High-Tech: Building in the Information Age. Klaus Daniels. (Illus.). 240p. 1998. 60.00 (3-7643-5861-0) Birkhauser.

***Low-Tech, Light-Tech, High-Tech: Special Edition.** Klaus Daniels. (Illus.). 240p. 2000. pap. 49.95 (3-7643-6329-0) Birkhauser.

Low Temperature Air Cooling Design Considerations. P. M. Rose & F. Alamdari. 1992. 60.00 (0-86022-326-4, Pub. by Build Servs Info Assn) St Mut.

Low Temperature & General Plasmas. Ed. by M. Milosavljevic & Z. Petrovic. 317p. (C). 1996. lib. bdg. 145.00 (1-56072-399-8) Nova Sci Pubs.

Low Temperature & Solar Grain Drying Handbook. Midwest Plan Service Engineers Staff. LC 80-12869. (Illus.). 86p. 1980. pap. 6.00 (0-89373-048-3, MWPS-22) MidWest Plan Serv.

Low Temperature Behavior & Acceptance Criteria for Elastomeric Bridge Bearings. (National Cooperative Highway Research Program Report Ser.: No. 325). 69p. 1989. 9.00 (0-309-04622-X, NR325) Transport Res Bd.

Low Temperature Chemistry of the Atmosphere. Moortgat Geert et al. (NATO ASI Ser.: Vol. 21). 1994. write for info. (3-540-58111-1) Spr-Verlag.

Low-Temperature Chemistry of the Atmosphere. Ed. by G. K. Moortgat et al. (Global Environmental Change Ser.). 544p. 1994. 287.95 (0-387-58111-1) Spr-Verlag.

Low-Temperature Combustion & Autoignition. M. J. Pilling. LC 97-44671. (Comprehensive Chemical Kinetics Ser.). 818p. 1997. 462.50 (0-444-82485-5) Elsevier.

Low Temperature Cracking: Binder Validation. D. H. Jung & Ted S. Vinson. (SHRP-A Ser.: No. 399). 106p. (Orig.). (C). 1994. pap. text 15.00 (0-309-05805-8) Natl Res Coun.

Low-Temperature Cracking: Field Validation of the Thermal Stress Restrained Speciment Test. Hannele K. Kanerva et al. (SHRP Ser.: A-401). (Illus.). 116p. (C). 1994. pap. text 15.00 (0-309-05808-2, PA401) Natl Res Coun.

Low-Temperature Cracking: Test Selection. D. H. Jung & Ted S. Vinson. (SHRP Ser.: No. A-400). (Illus.). 106p. (Orig.). (C). 1994. pap. text 15.00 (0-309-05807-4, PA400) Natl Res Coun.

Low-Temperature Electronics. Ed. by Randall K. Kirschman. LC 86-10265. 504p. 1986. 89.95 (0-87942-206-8, PC01974) Inst Electrical.

***Low Temperature Electronics: Physics, Devices, Circuits, & Applications.** Ed. by Edmundo A. Gutierrez-D et al. 704p. 2000. 165.00 (0-12-310675-3) Acad Pr.

Low Temperature Electronics & High Temperature Superconductivity. C. L. Claeys et al. (Proceedings Ser.: Vol. 95-9). 446p. 1995. 62.00 (1-56677-103-X) Electrochem Soc.

Low Temperature Electronics & High Temperature Superconductivity: 4th International Symposium. Ed. by C. Claeys et al. LC 97-197087. (Proceedings Ser.: Vol. 97-2). (Illus.). 412p. 1997. 64.00 (1-56677-129-3) Electrochem Soc.

Low Temperature Epitaxial Growth of Semiconductors. Ed. by T. Hariu. 352p. (C). 1990. text 137.00 (9971-5-0839-7) World Scientific Pub.

Low-Temperature Geochemistry. Ed. by Tu Guangzhi. (Illus.). 220p. 1996. 97.50 (90-6764-230-4, Pub. by VSP) Coronet Bks.

Low Temperature (LT) GaAs & Related Materials. Ed. by E. Weber et al. (Symposium Proceedings Ser.: Vol. 241). 297p. 1992. text 60.00 (1-55899-135-2) Materials Res.

Low Temperature Lubricant Rheology Measurement & Relevance to Engine Operation. Ed. by Robert B. Rhodes. LC 92-39198. (Special Technical Publication Ser.: No. 1143). (Illus.). 90p. 1993. 47.00 (0-8031-1438-9, STP1143) ASTM.

Low-Temperature Mechanical Properties of Asphalt Concrete. 60p. 1982. 15.00 (0-318-17747-1, RR-82-3) Asphalt Inst.

Low Temperature Mechanical Properties of Copper & Selected Copper Alloys. National Bureau of Standards Staff. 165p. 1967. 24.75 (0-317-34537-0, 50) Intl Copper.

Low Temperature Methods in Biological Electron Microscopy. Ed. by Anthony W. Robards et al. (Practical Methods in Electron Microscopy Ser.: Vol. 10). 552p. 1986. pap. 108.75 (0-444-80684-9) Elsevier.

Low-Temperature Microscopy & Analysis. P. Echlin. (Illus.). 568p. (C). 1991. text 120.00 (0-306-43984-0, Kluwer Plenum) Kluwer Academic.

Low Temperature Molecular Spectroscopy: Proceedings of the NATO Advanced Study Institute, Sintra, Portugal, September 3-15, 1995. Ed. by R. Fausto. LC 96-2942. (NATO Advanced Science Institutes Series C). 640p. (C). 1996. text 316.00 (0-7923-4083-3) Kluwer Academic.

Low Temperature Oxidation. AGARD-NATO Staff. (Agardographs Ser.: No. 86). xiv, 412p. 1967. text 506.00 (0-677-10540-1) Gordon & Breach.

Low-Temperature Oxidation: The Role of Vitreous Oxides. Francis P. Fehlner. LC 85-22491. (Corrosion Monograph Ser.). 257p. 1986. 185.00 (0-471-87448-5) Wiley.

Low Temperature Physics: Proceedings of the International Conference on Low Temperature Physics, 9th, Columbus, Ohio, 1964, 2 Pts., Pt. A. International Conference on Low Temperature Physic. Ed. by J. G. Daunt & D. O. Edwards. LC 65-14085. 640p. 1965. reprint ed. pap. 198.40 (0-608-08261-9, 201940300001) Bks Demand.

Low Temperature Physics: Proceedings of the International Conference on Low Temperature Physics, 9th, Columbus, Ohio, 1964, 2 Pts., Pt. B. International Conference on Low Temperature Physic. Ed. by J. G. Daunt & D. O. Edwards. LC 65-14085. 654p. 1965. reprint ed. pap. 200.00 (0-608-08262-7, 201940300002) Bks Demand.

Low Temperature Physics: Proceedings of the Summer School Held at Blydepoort, Eastern Transvaal, South Africa 15-25 January 1991. Ed. by M. J. Hoch et al. (Lecture Notes in Physics Ser.: Vol. 394). x, 374p. 1991. 70.95 (0-387-54923-4) Spr-Verlag.

Low Temperature Physics One see Encyclopedia of Physics

Low Temperature Physics Research in the Soviet Union. Vladimir Kresin. Ed. by Ben Armfield. 101p. (Orig.). 1985. pap. text 75.00 (1-55831-024-X) Delphic Associates.

Low Temperature Physics Two see Encyclopedia of Physics

Low Temperature Preservation of Foods & Living Matter. Ed. by Owen R. Fennema et al. (Food Science & Technology Ser.: Vol. 3). (Illus.). 616p. 1973. text 199.00 (0-8247-1185-8) Dekker.

Low-Temperature Properties of Bithuminous Materials & Compacted Bithuminous Paving Mixtures - STP 628. Ed. by Charles R. Marek. 1977. 11.00 (0-8031-0194-5, STP628) ASTM.

Low-Temperature Properties of Silver. David R. Smith & F. R. Fickett. (Illus.). 53p. (Orig.). (C). 1995. pap. text 25.00 (0-7881-2417-X) DIANE Pub.

Low-Temperature Pumpability Characteristics of Engine Oils in Full-Scale Engines - DS 57. American Society for Materials & Testing Staff. 104p. 1975. pap. 16.00 (0-8031-0392-1, DS57) ASTM.

Low Temperature Stress Physiology in Crops. Ed. by Paul H. Li. 208p. 1988. 124.00 (0-8493-6567-8, SB781, CRC Reprint) Franklin.

Low Temperature Techniques in Experimental Condensed Matter Physics. Richardson & Smith. (Orig.). 1988. pap. 41.95 (0-318-33228-0, 15002) Addison-Wesley.

Low Temperature X-Ray Diffraction Tutorial (LTXRD-Tutorial) (American Crystallographic Association Lecture Notes Ser.: No. 3). 48p. 1977. pap. 15.00 (0-686-47226-8) Polycrystal Bk Serv.

Low Tension Elecric Energy Distribution Equipment in Argentina: A Strategic Entry Report, 1996. Compiled by Icon Group International Staff. (Illus.). 161p. 1999. ring bd. 1610.00 incl. audio compact disk (0-7418-1426-9) Icon Grp.

Low Thermal Expansion Alloys & Composites: Proceedings of a Symposium Co-Sponsored by the Refractory Metals Committee of the Structural Materials Division (SMD) & the Electronic Packaging & Photonics Materials Division (EMPMD), Held at the Fall Meeting of the Minerals, Metals & Materials Society in Chicago, Illinois, November 2-5, 1992. Minerals, Metals & Materials Society, Meeting (1992: Chicago, IL) Staff. Ed. by John J. Stephens & Darrel R. Frear. LC 94-76982. (Illus.). 233p. reprint ed. pap. 72.30 (0-608-04983-2, 206560100004) Bks Demand.

Low Thermal Expansion Glass Ceramics. Ed. by Hans Bach. (Schott Series on Glass & Glass Ceramics). (Illus.). 304p. 1996. 149.00 (3-540-58598-2) Spr-Verlag.

Low Tide. David Frum. 224p. Date not set. pap. 14.00 (0-465-04196-5, Pub. by Basic) HarpC.

Low Tide in the Desert: Nevada Stories. David Kranes. LC 96-22466. (Western Literature Ser.). 192p. (Orig.). 1996. pap. 15.00 (0-87417-287-X) U of Nev Pr.

Low Twelve: "By Their Deeds Ye Shall Know Them" Edward S. Ellis. 252p. 1997. reprint ed. 19.95 (0-7661-0100-2) Kessinger Pub.

***Low Vibration Design of a Helical Gear Pair.** K. Umezawa. (Technical Papers: Vol. 98FTM5). 13p. 1998. pap. 30.00 (1-55589-723-1) AGMA.

Low Virtues: The Value of Human Scale Architecture to Birmingham Urbanism. Photos by John O'Hagan. (Illus.). 28p. 1998. 4.00 (0-943994-23-3) Birmingham Hist Soc.

Low Vision. Ed. by G. C. Woo. (Illus.). 600p. 1987. 89.00 (0-387-96538-6) Spr-Verlag.

Low Vision: A Resource Guide with Adaptations for Students with Visual Impairments. 2nd ed. Nancy Levack. LC 94-6108. 1994. pap. 25.00 (1-880366-12-6) TSBVI.

Low Vision: Proceedings of Vision 1993, the International Conference on Low Vision, 5-9 July 1993, Groningen, Netherlands. A. C. Kooijman et al. LC 93-80286. (Studies in Health Technology & Informatics: Vol. 11). 608p. (gr. 12). 1994. 130.00 (90-5199-144-4) IOS Press.

Low Vision: Reflections of the Past, Issues for the Future. Ed. by Virginia E. Bishop et al. 181p. 1993. pap. 29.95 (0-89128-218-1) Am Foun Blind.

Low Vision Care. C. Allyn Uniacke. (Illus.). 500p. (C). 1995. text 49.95 (0-397-51330-5, Lippnctt) Lppncott W & W.

Low Vision Handbook. Barbara Brown. LC 97-10169. (Basic Bookshelf for Eyecare Professionals Ser.). (Illus.). 160p. 1997. pap. text 30.00 (1-55642-329-2, 63292) SLACK Inc.

Low Vision in Optometric Practice. Christine Dickinson. LC 98-28062. (Illus.). 320p. 1998. pap. text 65.00 (0-7506-2262-8) Buttrwrth-Heinemann.

Low Vision Rehabilitation. Donald C. Fletcher. LC 98-41362. (Ophthalmology Monographs Ser.). xiv, 162 p. 1999. write for info. (1-56055-170-4) American Academic Assn for Research.

Low-Voltage AC & DC Power Circuit Breakers Used in Enclosures UL 1066. 3rd ed. (C). 1997. pap. text 95.00 (0-7629-0179-9) Underwrtrs Labs.

Low-Voltage CMOS Operational Amplifiers: Theory, Design & Implementation. Satoshi Sakurai. (International Series in Engineering & Computer Science). 254p. (C). 1994. text 120.00 (0-7923-9507-7) Kluwer Academic.

Low-Voltage CMOS VLSI Circuits. James B. Kuo & Jea-Hong Lou. LC 98-37315. 456p. 1998. 98.95 (0-471-32105-2) Wiley.

Low-Voltage Fuses Pt. 1: General Requirements, UL 248-1. (C). 1994. pap. text 95.00 (1-55989-662-0) Underwrtrs Labs.

Low-Voltage Fuses Pt. 2: Class C Fuses. 1996. write for info. (0-7629-0005-9, UL 248-2) Underwrtrs Labs.

Low-Voltage Fuses Pt. 3: Class CA & CB Fuses. 1996. write for info. (0-7629-0006-7, UL 248-3) Underwrtrs Labs.

Low-Voltage Fuses Pt. 5: Class G Fuses. 1996. write for info. (0-7629-0007-5, UL 248-5) Underwrtrs Labs.

Low-Voltage Fuses Pt. 6: Class H Non-Renewable Fuses. 1996. write for info. (0-7629-0008-3, UL 248-6) Underwrtrs Labs.

Low-Voltage Fuses Pt. 7: Class H Renewable Fuses. 1996. write for info. (0-7629-0009-1, UL 248-7) Underwrtrs Labs.

Low-Voltage Fuses Pt. 9: Class K Fuses. 1996. write for info. (0-7629-0010-5, UL 248-9) Underwrtrs Labs.

Low-Voltage Fuses Pt. 11: Plug Fuses. 1996. write for info. (0-7629-0011-3, UL 248-11) Underwrtrs Labs.

Low-Voltage Fuses Pt. 13: Semiconductor Fuses. 1996. write for info. (0-7629-0012-1, UL 248-13) Underwrtrs Labs.

Low-Voltage Fuses Pt. 16: Test Limiters. 1996. write for info. (0-7629-0013-X, UL 248-16) Underwrtrs Labs.

Low Voltage Landscape Lighting Systems, UL 1838. 2nd ed. (C). 1996. pap. text 95.00 (1-55989-575-6) Underwrtrs Labs.

***Low Voltage Level One.** NCCER Staff. 1999. pap. text 50.00 (0-13-014874-1, Prentice Hall); pap. text 50.00 (0-13-014875-X, Prentice Hall) P-H.

Low Voltage Lighting Fixtures for Use in Recreational Vehicles, UL 234. 4th ed. (C). 1994. pap. text 95.00 (1-55989-519-5) Underwrtrs Labs.

Low-Voltage Low-Power Analog Integrated Circuits. Ed. by Wouter A. Serdijn. LC 95-21368. (Kluwer International Series in Engineering & Computer Science). 124p. (C). 1995. text 103.00 (0-7923-9608-1) Kluwer Academic.

Low-Voltage Low-Power Digital BiCMOS Circuits: Circuit Design, Comparative Study & Sensitivity. Samir S. Rofail & Kiat Seng Yeo. LC 99-11804. 384p. (C). 1999. 75.00 (0-13-011380-8) P-H.

Low Voltage Marine Lighting Fixtures, UL 1149. (C). 1994. pap. text 95.00 (1-55989-611-6) Underwrtrs Labs.

Low-Voltage/Low-Power Integrated Circuits & Systems. Edgar Sanchez-Sinencio & Andreas Andreou. 450p. 1998. 69.95 (0-7803-1081-0, PC4341) Inst Electrical.

Low-Voltage/Low-Power Integrated Circuits & Systems: Low Voltage Mixed-Signal Circuits. Ed. by Edgar Sanchez-Sinencio & Andreas Andreou. LC 98-36702. 592p. 1998. 69.95 (0-7803-3446-9, PC4341-QOE) Inst Electrical.

Low-Volume Roads: Environmental Planning & Assessment, Modern Timber Bridges, & Other Issues (TRR 1426) Ed. by Norman Solomon. (Transportation Research Record Ser.). (Illus.). 88p. 1994. pap. text 25.00 (0-309-05573-3) Natl Res Coun.

Low-Wage Challenge to Global Growth: The Labor Cost-Productivity Imbalance in Newly Industrialized Countries. Walter R. Mead. 48p. 1990. 12.00 (0-944826-21-0) Economic Policy Inst.

Low-Wage Employment in Europe. Ed. by Stephen Bazen et al. LC 98-27888. 240p. 1999. 80.00 (1-85898-932-9) E Elgar.

Low Wage Jobs & Workers: Trends & Options for Change, Final Report. Displaced Homemakers Network Staff & Institute for Women's Policy Research Staff. 348p. 1989. pap. 30.00 (0-685-29929-5) Inst Womens Policy Rsch.

Low Wage Jobs & Workers: Trends & Options for Change: Summary of Findings. Displaced Homemakers Network Staff & Institute for Women's Policy Research Staff. 23p. 1989. pap. 5.00 (0-685-29942-2) Inst Womens Policy Rsch.

Low-Wage Labor Market Indicators by City & State: The Constraints Facing Welfare Reform. Jared Bernstein. (Illus.). 100p. (C). 1998. pap. text 20.00 (0-7881-7516-5) DIANE Pub.

Low Wages & the Working Poor. Barry Bluestone et al. LC 73-620152. (Policy Papers in Human Resources & Industrial Relations Ser.: No. 22). 215p. 1973. pap. 5.00 (0-87736-127-4) U of Mich Inst Labor.

An Asterisk (*) at the beginning of an entry indicates that the title is appearing for the first time.

Low Wages & the Working Poor. Mary H. Stevenson et al. LC 73-620152. (Policy Papers in Human Resources & Industrial Relations Ser.: No. 22). 215p. 1973. 10.00 (0-87736-126-6) U of Mich Inst Labor.

Low-Waste Technologies in Engineering Industries. Economic Commission for Europe Staff. LC 94-203644. 176p. 32.00 (92-1-116582-2) UN.

Low-Water Flower Gardener: 270 Unthirsty Plants for Color, Including Perennials, Ground Covers, Grasses & Shrubs. Eric A. Johnson & Scott Millard. LC 92-73645. (Illus.). 144p. (Orig.). 1993. pap. 16.95 (0-9628236-1-9) Ironwood AZ.

Low-Water Gardening: Creating & Running the Ideal Garden with Less Water. John Lucas. (Illus.). 176p. 1993. pap. 16.95 (0-460-86151-4) Trafalgar.

***Low-Water-Use Plants.** Carol Shuler. (Illus.). 144p. 2000. pap. 19.95 (1-55561-271-7) Fisher Bks.

Low-Water-Use Plants for California & the Southwest. Carol Shuler. LC 92-34627. (Illus.). 144p. (Orig.). 1993. pap. 17.95 (1-55561-037-4) Fisher Bks.

Low Wit. Werner Low. LC 81-69178. 79p. (Orig.). 1982. pap. 3.95 (0-917976-15-0, White Ewe Pr) Thunder Baas Pr.

Low x Physics: Proceedings of the 5th Workshop Madrid, Spain 1997. F. Barreiro. 1998. 58.00 (981-02-3514-3) World Scientific Pub.

Lowcountry: The Natural Landscape. Tom Bladgen et al. (Illus.). 106p. 1988. 49.95 (0-933101-12-0) Legacy Pubns.

Lowcountry Child. Monica Simmons. (Multicultural Ser.). (Illus.). 48p. (J). (gr. 2-8). 1996. 14.99 (0-9646889-0-5) Todays Kids.

Lowcountry Daytrips. William P. Baldwin, Jr. (Illus.). 287p. (Orig.). 1995. pap. 9.95 (0-933101-07-4) Legacy Pubns.

Lowden of Illinois: The Life of Governor Frank O. Lowden. William T. Hutchinson. Incl. Vol. 1. LC 57-6274. xiv, 382p. 1993. pap. text 12.50 (0-226-36245-0); LC 57-6274. (Midway Reprint Ser). 1975. reprint ed. Set pap. text 12.50 (0-685-04989-2) U Ch Pr.

Lowden of Illinois - The Life of Frank O. Lowden Vol. 1: City & State. William T. Hutchinson. LC 57-6274. (Midway Reprint Ser.). (Illus.). 396p. reprint ed. pap. 122.80 (0-608-09406-4, 205420700001) Bks Demand.

Lowden of Illinois - The Life of Frank O. Lowden Vol. 2: Nation & Countryside. William T. Hutchinson. LC 57-6274. (Midway Reprint Ser.). (Illus.). 393p. reprint ed. pap. 121.90 (0-608-09407-2, 205420700002) Bks Demand.

Lowder Family in America. William N. Hurley, Jr. (Illus.). 393p. (Orig.). 1996. pap. 31.50 (0-7884-0487-3, H870) Heritage Bk.

Lowdown on Higher Education: Straight Talk to Returning Students. Sandra L. Quinn & Sanford Kantner. 125p. (C). 1988. pap. 9.95 (0-8290-1437-3); text 19.50 (0-8290-1436-5) Irvington.

***Lowdown on Modern Economics: Adam Smith's Micro to Current U. S. Macro.** Stephen K. Happle. 210p. 2000. pap. text 35.95 (0-913878-62-6) T Horton & Dghts.

Lowe Art Museum Selected Works: Handbook of the Permanent Collection. LC 95-36220. (Illus.). 1996. write for info. (0-614-08632-9) Lowe Art Mus.

Lowe Art Museum Selected Works: Handbook of the Permanent Collection. Lowe Art Museum Staff. 176p. 1996. pap. 19.95 (0-9648614-0-2) Lowe Art Mus.

Lowe/Lerner Camelot see Classical Connections: Complete Program

Lowell. John Pendergast. (Images of America Ser.). 128p. 1996. pap. 16.99 (0-7524-0410-5) Arcadia Publng.

Lowell, Vol. II. John Pendergast. (Images of America Ser.). 1997. pap. 16.99 (0-7524-0539-X) Arcadia Publng.

Lowell: An Industrial City, Lowell National Historical Park & Lowell Heritage State Park, Lowell, Massachusetts. 113p. 1993. per. 8.00 (0-16-061652-2) USGPO.

Lowell: The Corporations & the City. Heidi Vernon-Wortzel. LC 92-27524. (Studies in Entrepreneurship). 232p. 1992. text 20.00 (0-8153-0996-1) Garland.

Lowell: The Story of an Industrial City. Thomas Dublin. LC 91-28814. (Official National Park Handbook Ser.: No. 140). (Illus.). 112p. 1993. pap. 8.00 (0-912627-46-8, 024-005-01097-1) Natl Park Serv.

Lowell: The Story of an Industrial City: A Guide to Lowell National Historical Park & Lowell Heritage State Park, Lowell, Massachusetts. Thomas Dublin & Paul Marion. (Illus.). 111p. 1998. pap. text 20.00 (0-7881-4825-7) DIANE Pub.

***Lowell: The True Story of an Existential Pig.** Gay L. Balliet. LC 99-75938. (Illus.). 260p. 2000. 23.95 (0-88282-193-8) New Horizon NJ.

Lowell & His Poetry. William Henry Hudson. LC 78-120988. (Poetry & Life Ser.). reprint ed. 16.00 (0-404-52517-2) AMS Pr.

Lowell & Mars. William G. Hoyt. (Illus.). 392p. 1976. pap. 12.50 (0-8165-0514-4) U of Ariz Pr.

Lowell, As It Was, & As It Is. Henry A. Miles. LC 72-5063. (Technology & Society Ser.). (Illus.). 234p. 1976. reprint ed. 18.95 (0-405-04714-2) Ayer.

Lowell Connector: Lines & Shots from Kerovac's Town. John Yau et al. 111p. 1993. pap. 12.95 (0-9638433-0-3) Hard Pr MA.

Lowell L. Bennion: Teacher, Counselor, Humanitarian. Mary L. Bradford. LC 95-40866. (Illus.). 410p. 1996. 24.95 (1-56085-081-7) Signature Bks.

Lowell, MA: Where Jack Kerouac's Road Begins. Jack Kerouac et al. (Illus.). (Orig.). 1996. pap. 39.95 (0-934953-47-3) Water Row Pr.

Lowell Mason: A Bio-Bibliography, 11. Carol A. Pemberton. LC 87-37569. (Bio-Bibliographies in Music Ser.: No. 11). 219p. 1988. lib. bdg. 55.00 (0-313-25881-3, PLL/, Greenwood Pr) Greenwood.

Lowell Mill Girls: Life in the Factory. JoAnne W. Deitch. (Perspectives on History Ser.: Pt. I). 52p. 1998. pap. 6.95 (1-57960-041-7) Disc Enter Ltd.

Lowell Mill Girls: Life in the Factory. JoAnne B. Weisman. (Perspectives on History Ser.). 48p. (YA). (gr. 5-12). 1991. pap. 6.95 (1-878668-06-4) Disc Enter Ltd.

Lowell Offering: A Repository of Original Articles Written by "Factory Girls" Ed. by Nancy Zaroulis. 23p. 1981. pap. 0.50 (0-942472-03-9) Lowell Museum.

Lowell Offering: Writings by New England Mill Women (1840-1845) Benita Eisler. 224p. 1997. pap. 12.95 (0-393-31685-8) Norton.

Lowen Kinder-Busch see Lion Family Book

Lowenfeld Lectures: Viktor Lowenfeld on Art Education & Therapy. Ed. by John A. Michael. LC 80-29265. (Illus.). 420p. (C). 1982. text 40.00 (0-271-00283-2) Pa St U Pr.

Lowenfeld Mosaic Test. 2nd ed. Margaret Lowenfeld. 1994. reprint ed. pap. 55.00 (0-9521788-1-8, Pub. by M Lowenfeld) Intl Spec Bk.

Lowengrab von Milet. Elke Forbeck & Huberta Heres. 65p. 1997. pap. 40.00 (3-11-016101-X) De Gruyter.

Lowenskold Ring. Selma Lagerlof. Tr. by Linda Schenck from SWE. (Norvik Press Series B: No. 8). 117p. 1991. pap. 19.95 (1-870041-14-3, Pub. by Norvik Pr) Dufour.

Lower: Some Account of the Lower Family in America, Principally of the Descendants of Adam Lower, Who Settled in Williamsport, PA in 1779. J. L. Lower. (Illus.). 144p. 1993. reprint ed. pap. 25.00 (0-8328-3710-5); reprint ed. lib. bdg. 35.00 (0-8328-3709-1) Higginson Bk Co.

Lower & Middle Egypt. Jaromir Malek. (Topographical Bibliography of Ancient Egyptian Hieroglyphic Texts Ser.: Reliefs & Paintings, Vol. 4). 35.00 incl. fiche (0-900416-20-3, Pub. by Aris & Phillips) David Brown.

Lower Atlantic: North Carolina, South Carolina. Thomas G. Aylesworth & Virginia L. Aylesworth. LC 94-40429. (State Studies). 88p. (J). (gr. 4 up). 1995. pap. 8.95 (0-7910-3419-4); lib. bdg. 18.95 (0-7910-3401-1) Chelsea Hse.

Lower Bajocian (Jurassic) Cephalopod Faunas from Western Canada, & Proposed Assemblage Zones for the Lower Bajocian of North America see Palaeontographica Americana: Vol. 9

Lower Blackstone River Valley. Charles E. Savoie. (Images of America Ser.). 1998. pap. 16.99 (0-7524-0922-0) Arcadia Publng.

Lower Body Solutions: Middle Age Fat - Stubborn "Pear" Shapes - 50 Pounds Plus - Lose It All. Laura Dayton. (Illus.). 160p. 1998. pap. 24.95 (0-9662752-2-5) Dayton Pubns.

Lower Brainstem & Bodily Homeostasis. William W. Blessing. (Illus.). 592p. 1997. text 89.50 (0-19-507511-0) OUP.

Lower Cape Cod. Cheryl J. Huban. (Twelve Short Hikes Ser.). (Illus.). 32p. 1997. pap. 4.95 (1-57540-096-0) Falcon Pub Inc.

Lower Carboniferous Echinoderms from Northern Utah & Western Wyoming. Gary D. Webster. LC 97-184394. (Bulletin of the Utah Geological Survey Ser.: Vol. 128). (Illus.). 65p. 1997. pap. 6.50 (1-55791-600-4, B-128) Utah Geological Survey.

Lower Class Culture As a Generating Milieu of Gang Delinquency. Walter B. Miller. (Reprint Series in Sociology). (C). 1993. reprint ed. pap. text 1.00 (0-8290-2623-1, S-197) Irvington.

Lower-Class Heresy: Poems. T. R. Hummer. LC 86-19278. 96p. (Orig.). 1987. 9.95 (0-252-01389-1) U of Ill Pr.

Lower Columbia River, Hugh Keenleyside Dam to Birchbank: Water Quality Assessment & Objectives : Technical Appendix G. A. Butcher. LC 93-206922. 1992. write for info. (0-7726-1650-7) GovofBC.

Lower Cretaceous Bivales: From the Eastern Heilongjiang Province of China. Guan Jian. (Chinese Science Studies). (Illus.). 301p. 1998. 79.95 (7-03-005851-8) Intl Scholars.

Lower Cretaceous Stratigraphy, Northern Coahuila, Mexico. C. I. Smith. (Reports of Investigations: RI 65). (Illus.). 101p. 1970. pap. 4.00 (0-318-03166-3) Bur Econ Geology.

Lower Danube River: In the Southeastern European Political & Economic Complex from Antiquity to 1948. Spiridon G. Focas. Tr. by Rozeta J. Metes. (East European Monographs). 697p. 1987. text 108.50 (0-88033-123-2, Pub. by East Eur Monographs) Col U Pr.

Lower Denture Problems? The Worlds Only Self-Help Book on Dentures. Michael Mackenzie. LC 98-74385. (Illus.). 136p. 1999. 19.95 (0-9668234-9-4) First Bite Pubg.

***Lower Depths.** Maksim Gorky & Jenny Covan. LC 99-54723. (Thrift Ser.). 2000. pap. 1.50 (0-486-41115-X) Dover.

***Lower Depths.** unabridged ed. Maxim Gorky. Ed. by William-Alan Landes. Tr. by Jennie Covan from RUS. LC 99-51846. 64p. (YA). (gr. 4-12). 1999. pap. 7.00 (0-88734-815-7) Players Pr.

Lower Depths: Scenes from Russian Life. Maxim Gorki. Tr. by Edwin Hopkins. 1995. pap. 5.95 (0-8283-1445-4) Branden Bks.

Lower Depths & Other Plays. Maxim Gorky. Tr. by Alexander Bakshy & Paul S. Nathan. xx, 220p. 1959. pap. 13.00 (0-300-00100-2, Y-4) Yale U Pr.

Lower Depths & Other Plays. Maksim Gor'kii. Tr. by Alexander Bakshy & Paul S. Nathan. LC 75-41116. reprint ed. 36.00 (0-404-14773-9) AMS Pr.

Lower Devonian Conodonts (Hesperius-Kindlei Zones), Central Nevada. Michael A. Murphy & Jonathan C. Matti. LC 82-8638. (University of California Publications in Social Welfare: No. 123). (Illus.). 97p. reprint ed. pap. 30.10 (0-8357-6863-5, 203556100095) Bks Demand.

Lower Devonian Fenestrata (Bryozoa) of the Prague Basin, Barrandian Area, Bohemia, Czechoslovakia. Frank K. McKinney & Jiri Kriz. LC 86-80770. (Field Museum of Natural History, Publication 1368, Geology Ser.: Vol. 15). 96p. 1986. reprint ed. pap. 30.00 (0-608-03778-8, 206462200009) Bks Demand.

Lower Dimensional Gravity. J. D. Brown. 164p. 1988. text 33.00 (9971-5-0622-X) World Scientific Pub.

Lower-Dimensional Systems & Molecular Electronics. Ed. by R. M. Metzger et al. (NATO ASI Ser.: Vol. 248). (Illus.). 756p. (C). 1990. text 198.00 (0-306-43826-7, Kluwer Plenum) Kluwer Academic.

Lower Downtown Historic District. Barbara Gibson. (Historic Denver Guides Ser.). (Illus.). 96p. (Orig.). 1995. pap. 8.95 (0-914248-07-3) Hist Denver.

Lower East Side Jews: An Immigrant Generation. Ronald Sanders. LC 99-35299. 512p. 1999. pap. text 13.95 (0-486-40901-5) Dover.

***Lower East Side Memories: A Jewish Place in America.** Hasia R. Diner. LC 00-21148. (Illus.). 264p. 2000. 27.95 (0-691-00747-0) Princeton U Pr.

Lower East Side Shopping Guide. Ellen Telzer & Sharon Greene. 88p. 1982. pap. 5.95 (0-934758-01-8) Shopping Experience.

Lower East Side Tourbook. 6th ed. Oscar Israelowitz. 150p. 1998. pap. 9.95 (1-878741-38-1) Israelowitz Pub.

***Lower Engine Assembly: Reher-Morrison Racing Engines.** Robert Colesworthy & David Reher. Ed. & Photos by James Barfield. (Illus.). 150p. 1999. pap. 79.95 (0-9669002-2-7) Educ Tech Consul.

Lower Extremity Amputation. Wesley S. Moore & Malone. 352p. 1989. text 105.00 (0-7216-6485-7, W B Saunders Co) Harcrt Hlth Sci Grp.

Lower Extremity Amputation: A Guide to Functional Outcomes in Physical Therapy Management. 2nd ed. Linda A. Karacoloff et al. LC 92-7054. 288p. 1992. 67.00 (0-8342-0291-3) Aspen Pub.

Lower Extremity & Spine in Sports Medicine. 2nd ed. Ed. by James A. Nicholas. LC 94-26126. (Illus.). 1808p. (C). (gr. 13). 1994. text 280.00 (0-8151-6391-6, 23615) Mosby Inc.

Lower Extremity Reconstruction. John B. McCaw & Phillip G. Arnold. LC 87-82108. (Illus.). 246p. 1987. text 163.50 (0-939789-04-3) Lppncott W & W.

Lower Extremity Vascular Disease. Ed. by Kenneth Ouriel. LC 95-6842. 1995. text 152.00 (0-7216-4749-9, W B Saunders Co) Harcrt Hlth Sci Grp.

Lower Fairfores Baptist Church, Union County, South Carolina: Minutes, 1809-1872, Membership Lists Through 1906. Ed. by Brent H. Holcomb. LC 97-67952. 124p. 1997. 20.00 (0-913363-27-8) SCMAR.

Lower Female Genital Tract: A Clinicopathologic Approach. Debra S. Heller. LC 97-40571. 339p. 1998. write for info. (0-683-30340-6) Lppncott W & W.

Lower 48. Joel Dailey. (Illus.). 96p. 1999. pap. 9.00 (0-9663846-2-8) Lavender Ink.

***Lower Genital Tract Precancer.** 2nd ed. Albert Singer & John M. Monaghan. LC 99-16649. (Illus.). 344p. 2000. 195.00 (0-632-04769-0) Blackwell Sci.

Lower Gulf Islands, the Abu Musa & Tunbs Dispute, 6 vols. Ed. by P. L. Toye. (Arabian Geopolitics Ser.: Vol. 2). 4000p. 1993. reprint ed. lib. bdg. 1495.00 (1-85207-490-6, Pub. by Archive Editions) N Ross.

Lower! Higher! You're a Liar! Miriam Chaikin. LC 83-48445. (Charlotte Zolotow Bk.). (Illus.). 160p. (J). (gr. 3-7). 1984. 12.95 (0-06-021186-5) HarpC Child Bks.

Lower Income Americans, Higher Cost Financial Services. John P. Caskey. 75p. 1997. pap. 100.00 (1-880572-26-5) Filene Res.

Lower K & L-Theory. A. A. Ranicki. (London Mathematical Society Lecture Note Ser.: No. 178). 182p. (C). 1992. pap. text 39.95 (0-521-43801-2) Cambridge U Pr.

Lower Kern River Country, 1850-1950: Wilderness to Empire. William H. Boyd. (Illus.). 233p. 1997. 18.95 (0-943500-15-X) Kern Historical.

***Lower Level Reading Skills.** Ed. by Allyn & Bacon Incorporated Staff. 2000. 34.00 (0-205-30755-8) Allyn.

Lower Limb see Physiology of the Joints

Lower Limb see Jamieson's Illustrations of Regional Anatomy

Lower Limb Amputations: A Guide to Rehabilitation. Gloria T. Sanders. LC 85-10439. (Illus.). 607p. 1986. text 62.00 (0-8036-7723-5) Davis Co.

Lower Merion: A History. Ed. by Phyllis C. Maier & Mary M. Wood. 120p. 1988. text 20.00 (0-9649368-1-X) Lower Merion.

Lower Merion: A History. rev. ed. Ed. by Phyllis C. Maier & Mary M. Wood. (Illus.). 128p. 1992. text 20.00 (0-9649368-2-8) Lower Merion.

Lower Merion Academy: Legend in Learning. Jo A. Debes. 24p. (Orig.). 1997. pap. write for info. (0-9649368-3-6) Lower Merion.

Lower Merrimack, an Illustrated History: The Valley & Its Peoples. Paul Hudon. LC 82-50186. (Illus.). 176p. 1982. 22.95 (0-89781-047-3) Am Historical Pr.

Lower-Middle-Class Education. Robert M. Davis. LC 96-4378. (Illus.). 192p. (C). 1996. 24.95 (0-8061-2848-8) U of Okla Pr.

Lower Miocene Foraminifera of Florida. J. A. Cushman. 1972. reprint ed. 10.00 (0-934454-58-2) Lubrecht & Cramer.

Lower Mississippi Valley Expeditions of Clarence Bloomfield Moore. Clarence Bloomfield Moore. LC 98-19292. (Classics in Southeastern Archaeology Ser.). 472p. 1998. pap. text 39.95 (0-8173-0949-7) U of Ala Pr.

Lower Moments in Higher Education. Otto F. Bauer. (Illus.). x, 155p. (Orig.). 1997. pap. 11.95 (0-9659052-0-9) Rockbrook Pr.

Lower Mount Washington Valley. Jean Ulitz & Mabel Hidden. LC 96-228072. (Images of America Ser.). 128p. 1996. pap. 16.99 (0-7524-0275-7) Arcadia Publng.

Lower Niger & Its Tribes. Arthur G. Leonard. 564p. 1968. reprint ed. 57.50 (0-7146-1687-7, Pub. by F Cass Pubs) Intl Spec Bk.

Lower Oil Prices: Mapping the Impact. Richard N. Cooper et al. LC 87-83646. (International Energy Studies: No. 4). x, 109p. (Orig.). 1988. pap. 21.50 (0-942781-03-1) Harvard EEPC.

Lower Palaeozoic of North-Western & West-Central Africa. Ed. by Charles H. Holland. LC 83-6543. (Lower Palaeozoic Rocks of the World Ser.: Vol. 4). (Illus.). 536p. reprint ed. pap. 166.20 (0-608-17584-6, 203042300069) Bks Demand.

Lower Palaeozoic of the Middle East, Eastern & Southern Africa, & Antarctica: With Essays on Lower Palaeozoic Trace Fossils of Africa & Lower Palaeozoic Palaeoclimatology. Ed. by Charles H. Holland. LC 80-41688. (Lower Palaeozoic Rocks of the World Ser.: Vol. 3). (Illus.). 371p. reprint ed. pap. 115.10 (0-608-18410-1, 203042400069) Bks Demand.

Lower Paleolithic Site at Hoxne, England. Ronald Singer et al. LC 91-35934. (Illus.). 256p. 1993. 75.00 (0-226-76111-8) U Ch Pr.

Lower Penobscot River Region. Richard R. Shaw. (Images of America Ser.). 128p. 1999. pap. 18.99 (0-7524-0264-1) Arcadia Publng.

Lower Piedmont Country. Herman C. Nixon. LC 78-142685. (Essay Index Reprint Ser.). 1977. 20.95 (0-8369-2064-3) Ayer.

Lower Piedmont Country: The Uplands of the Deep South. Herman C. Nixon. LC 83-24164. (Library of Alabama Classics). (Illus.). 296p. 1980. reprint ed. pap. 19.95 (0-8173-0214-X) U of Ala Pr.

Lower Plants of the Indian Subcontinent: A Collection of Papers. Indian Scientists Staff. (Nova Hedwigia Beiheft Ser.: No. 47). (Illus.). 648p. 1974. pap. text 120.00 (3-7682-5447-X) Lubrecht & Cramer.

Lower Plants of the Indian Subcontinent II: Another Collection of Papers by Indian Scientists. (Illus.). 1979. lib. bdg. 120.00 (3-7682-5463-1) Lubrecht & Cramer.

Lower Power Design: A Collection of CSEM Papers. Ed. by Eric Vittoz et al. (Illus.). 300p. (C). 1995. pap. 120.00 (0-932905-09-9) Penton Pub.

Lower St. Lawrence. Ivan S. Brookes. (Illus.). 1974. 10.75 (0-912514-13-2) Freshwater.

Lower Shenandoah Valley in the Civil War: The Impact of War upon the Civilian Population & upon Civil Institutions. Edward H. Phillips. (Virginia Civil War Battles & Leaders Ser.). (Illus.). 224p. 1993. 19.95 (1-56190-042-7) H E Howard.

Lower Sort: Philadelphia's Laboring People, 1750-1800. Billy G. Smith. LC 89-46174. (Illus.). 272p. 1994. text 39.95 (0-8014-2242-6); pap. text 14.95 (0-8014-8163-5) Cornell U Pr.

Lower South in American History. W. G. Brown. LC 68-24973. (American History & Americana Ser.: No. 47). 1969. reprint ed. lib. bdg. 75.00 (0-8383-0919-4) M S G Haskell Hse.

Lower South in American History. William G. Brown. LC 69-13843. 271p. 1969. reprint ed. lib. bdg. 35.00 (0-8371-0925-6, BRO&, Greenwood Pr) Greenwood.

Lower South in American History. William G. Brown. (BCL1 - United States Local History Ser.). 271p. 1991. reprint ed. text 79.00 (0-7812-6283-6) Rprt Serv.

Lower South in American History. William G. Brown. LC 71-108464. 1970. reprint ed. 15.00 (0-403-00446-2) Scholarly.

Lower Tanana Athabaskan Listening & Writing Exercises. James Kari et al. 27p. 1991. pap. 4.00 (1-55500-041-X) Alaska Native.

Lower Tertiary Biostratigraphy of the California Coast Ranges. Virgil S. Mallory. LC 59-1390. 460p. reprint ed. pap. 142.60 (0-608-13923-8, 202374500033) Bks Demand.

Lower Than Angels: A Memoir of War & Peace. W. W. Windstaff. LC 92-28335. (Illus.). 1993. 19.95 (0-910155-24-0, Enigma Bks) Bartleby Pr.

Lower Than the Angels. Anthony Phillips. 68p. 1996. pap. 8.95 (1-85311-136-8, 846, Pub. by Canterbury Press Norwich) Morehouse Pub.

***Lower Than the Angels: All New, All American Tales.** 300p. 2000. mass mkt. 11.95 (1-893362-10-8) Jean Hse.

***Lower Than the Angels: Science Fact, Science Fiction & Fantasy.** Ed. by Vonnie Winslow Crist & David W. Kriebel. 192p. 1999. pap. 14.95 (0-9641622-2-9) Lite Circle.

Lower Tiers of the Space Transportation Industrial Base. 25p. (Orig.). (C). 1995. pap. text 20.00 (0-7881-2505-2) DIANE Pub.

Lower Tiers of the Space Transportation Industrial Base. (Orig.). 1996. lib. bdg. 250.99 (0-8490-6353-1) Gordon Pr.

Lower-Track Classrooms: A Curricular & Cultural Perspective. Reba Page. 288p. (C). 1991. text 48.00 (0-8077-3092-0); pap. text 22.95 (0-8077-3093-9) Tchrs Coll.

Lower-Track Classrooms: A Curricular & Cultural Perspective. Reba N. Page. LC 91-3141. 287p. reprint ed. pap. 89.00 (0-608-20002-6, 207127900010) Bks Demand.

L

An Asterisk (*) at the beginning of an entry indicates that the title is appearing for the first time.

L

Lower Triassic Temnospondyli of Tasmania. John Cosgriff. LC 73-87235. (Geological Society of America, Special Paper: No. 149). (Illus.). 140p. reprint ed. pap. 43.40 (0-608-15186-6, 202737300055) Bks Demand.

Lower Umpqua Texts & Notes on the Kusan Dialects. Leo J. Frachtenberg. LC 72-82341. (Columbia Univ. Contributions to Anthropology Ser.: Vol. 4). 1969. reprint ed. 34.50 (0-404-50554-6) AMS Pr.

Lower Urinary Tract Diseases of Dogs & Cats. Gerald V. Ling. LC 94-41538. (Illus.). 256p. (C). (gr. 13). 1995. text 90.00 (0-8151-5446-1, 23970) Mosby Inc.

Lower Urinary Tract Obstruction in Childhood. Bradford W. Young. LC 72-175467. 215p. reprint ed. pap. 66.70 (0-608-14010-4, 205544900022) Bks Demand.

Lower Your Blood Pressure with Food & Herbs. Date not set. pap. 6.95 (1-930329-01-6) R M Khalilullah.

Lower Yukon River. Alaska Geographic Society Staff. Ed. by Penny Rennick. LC 72-92087. (Alaska Geographic Ser.: Vol. 17, No. 4). (Illus.). 96p. pap. 19.95 (0-88240-195-5) Alaska Geog Soc.

Lower Zambezi Basin in Mozambique. Shubi L. Ishemo. LC 95-77011. 304p. 1995. 87.95 (1-85628-450-6, Pub. by Avebry) Ashgate Pub Co.

Lowerberg Genealogy Vol. 1: Descendants of Abraham Lowerberg. Howard E. Krehbiel. (Illus.). 269p. 1997. text 30.00 (1-890050-18-0) Carlisle Press.

***Lowercase Abcs: Preschool Activity Book.** Ed. by Ralph Cosentino. (Illus.). 32p. (J). (ps-k). 1999. pap., student ed. 2.95 (1-58610-000-9) Learn Horizon.

***Lowercase Alphabet.** Dalmatian Press Staff. (Tools Ser.). (Illus.). (J). (ps). 1999. pap. text 2.29 (1-57759-143-7) Dalmatian Pr.

***Lowercase Curvise Practice.** Donald N. Thurber. (D'nealian Handwriting from A to Z Ser.). (Illus.). (J). 1999. pap. 7.95 (0-673-59236-7, GoodYrBooks) Addson-Wesley Educ.

***Lowercase Letters.** Liane Onish. (Jumpstart Workbooks Ser.). (Illus.). (J). (ps-k). 2000. pap. text 3.99 (0-439-16418-4) Scholastic Inc.

Lowering Cholesterol in High-Risk Individuals & Populations. Ed. by Basil M. Rifkind. LC 94-45081. (Fundamental & Clinical Cardiology Ser.: No. 24). (Illus.). 384p. 1995. text 145.00 (0-8247-9412-5) Dekker.

Lowering Skies. Pamela Oldfield. 400p. 1998. 25.00 (0-7278-2205-5) Severn Hse.

Lowering the Cost of Emission Reduction: Joint Implementation in the Framework Convention on Climate Change. Michael A. Ridley. LC 97-49849. (Environment & Policy Ser.). 188p. 1998. 84.00 (0-7923-4914-8) Kluwer Academic.

Lowering the Risk: A Self-Care Plan for Relapse Prevention. Merlene Miller & Terence Gorski. 31p. 1991. pap. 4.00 (0-8309-0609-6) Herald Pub Hse.

Lowering the Wings of Humility. Janet Good. (Illus.). 24p. (J). 1998. pap. 5.95 (0-9661602-5-8) Hadassah Invest.

Lowering Your Handicap. Steve Newell. 1999. 12.99 (1-84100-170-8) Quadrillion Media.

***Lowery Collection - A Descriptive List of Maps of the Spanish Possessions... of the United States.** Ed. by Phillip Lee Phillips. 567p. 1999. reprint ed. 75.00 (1-57898-163-8) Martino Pubng.

Lowest Blue Flame Before Nothing. Lara Stapleton. LC 98-30108. 196p. 1998. pap. 10.95 (1-879960-54-0) Aunt Lute Bks.

Lowest of the Low. Gunter Wallraff. 1987. 16.95 (0-317-62634-5) Freundlich.

Lowestoft: East Coast Port. Robert Malster. 128p. 1994. pap. 21.00 (0-86138-013-4, Pub. by T Dalton) St Mut.

Lowfat American Favorites. Goldie Silverman & Jacqueline Williams. (Illus.). 160p. 1990. pap. 8.95 (0-911954-95-3, Nitty Gritty Ckbks) Bristol Pub Ent CA.

Lowfat Beef. Jackie Eddy & Eleanor Clark. LC 96-18472. 288p. 1997. per. 15.00 (0-7615-0191-6) Prima Pub.

Lowfat Cooking for Dummies. Lynn Fischer. LC 97-70748. (For Dummies Ser.). 432p. 1997. pap. 19.99 (0-7645-5035-7) IDG Bks.

Lowfat Grill. Conna Rodnitzky. 336p. 1998. per. 18.00 (0-7615-1789-8) Prima Pub.

Lowfat Jewish Vegetarian Cookbook: Healthy Traditions from Around the World, Vol. 1. Debra Wasserman. LC 93-61354. 224p. (Orig.). 1994. pap. 15.00 (0-931411-12-2) Vegetarian Resc.

Lowfat Korean Cooking. Susan Kim. Ed. & Photos by Thomas Wilson. Photos by Lee Whiting. (Illus.). iv, 131p. 1995. 24.99 (0-9656125-9-7) S Kims Cookbks.

Lowfat Recipes Tried & True by Nancy, 2 vols., Vol. 1. Nancy Vanover. (Illus.). 142p. 1996. spiral bd. 12.00 (0-9651397-0-0) N Vanover.

Lowfat Wholegrain Cookbook. Zoe M. Caywood. (Illus.). 175p. (Orig.). 1993. pap. write for info. (0-9616521-3-6) War Eagle Cks.

Lowland Dry Forests of Santa Cruz, Bolivia: A Global Conservation Priority. Theodore A. Parker, 3rd et al. LC 93-72263. 104p. 1995. pap. 7.00 (1-881173-02-X, Pub. by Conser Intl) U Ch Pr.

Lowland Floodplain Rivers: Geomorphological Perspectives. Paul A. Carling & G. E. Petts. LC 91-21774. (British Geomorphological Research Group Symposia Ser.). 318p. 1992. 315.00 (0-471-93119-5) Wiley.

Lowland Huasteca: Archaeological Survey & Excavation, 1957 Field Season. William T. Sanders. (Illus.). vii, 214p. 1978. pap. 11.00 (0-913134-85-6) Mus Anthro MO.

Lowland Maya Civilization in the Eighth Century A. D. A Symposium at Dumbarton Oaks, 7th & 8th October 1989. Ed. by Jeremy A. Sabloff & John S. Henderson. LC 92-8249. (Illus.). 496p. 1993. 35.00 (0-88402-206-4, Dumbarton Rsch Lib) Dumbarton Oaks.

Lowlands: Development & Management. Ed. by N. Miura et al. LC 99-225806. (Illus.). 498p. (C). 1994. text 126.00 (90-5410-603-4, Pub. by A A Balkema) Ashgate Pub Co.

Lowly Manger Empty Tomb. Alan Roberts. LC 98-68273. 80p. 1999. pap. 9.95 (1-57197-152-1) Pentland Pr.

Lowly Worm's Shapes & Sizes. Richard Scarry. (Busy World of Richard Scarry Ser.). (Illus.). 14p. (J). (ps-k). 1998. 4.99 (0-689-81654-5) S&S Childrens.

Lowndes County, Georgia, Probate Records: Recorded July Term 1847-January Term 1852. Charles R. Corbett. (Illus.). xxvi, 259p. 1998. 35.00 (0-9661041-0-2) C R Corbett.

Lowndes of South Carolina, an Historical & Genealogical Memoir. G. B. Chase. (Illus.). 81p. 1990. reprint ed. pap. 16.00 (0-8328-1497-0); reprint ed. lib. bdg. 24.00 (0-8328-1496-2) Higginson Bk Co.

Lowrey's International Trumpet Discography. Alvin L. Lowrey. LC 89-23960. 1200p. 1990. 180.00 (0-938100-79-3) Camden Hse.

Lowriders & Other Customized Cars see Wheels

Lowriders & Other Customized Cars. E. D. Lake. (Wheels Ser.). (Illus.). 48p. (J). (gr. 3-6). 1995. 19.00 (0-516-35217-2) Childrens.

***Lowry: A Visionary Artist.** Michael Howard. 1999. 75.00 (1-902970-00-4) Lowry Hse.

Lowry Ruin in Southwestern Colorado. Paul S. Martin. (Chicago Field Museum of Natural History Fieldiana Anthropology Ser.: Vol. 23). 1969. reprint ed. 70.00 (0-527-01883-X) Periodicals Srv.

Lowry's, Bryan's, & Chapman's Batteries of Virginia Artillery. J. L. Scott. (Virginia Regimental Histories Ser.). (Illus.). 108p. 1988. 19.95 (0-930919-56-4) H E Howard.

Lowrys' Handbook of Right-to-Know & Emergency Planning. George G. Lowry & Robert C. Lowry. (Illus.). 421p. 1988. lib. bdg. 119.00 (0-87371-112-2, L112) Lewis Pubs.

Lowry's Revenge. large type ed. Ron Watkins. (Linford Western Library). 208p. 1997. pap. 16.99 (0-7089-5057-4, Linford) Ulverscroft.

***Loyal Ansar.** Noura Durkee. Ed. by Huda Quraishi-Ahmed et al. (Stories of the Sahabah Ser.: Vol. 3). (Illus.). 170p. (YA). (gr. 7-10). 1999. pap. text 10.00 (1-56316-452-3) Iqra Intl Ed Fdtn.

Loyal Butterfly: A Story about Loyalty. (Excellence in Character Series Storybks.). (Illus.). 30p. (J). (gr. k-8). 1998. pap. 6.00 (1-58259-022-2) Global Classrm.

Loyal Cat. Illus. by Aki Sogabe. LC 94-10937. 40p. (J). (gr. k-4). 1995. 15.00 (0-15-200092-5, Harcourt Child Bks) Harcourt.

Loyal Customer: A Lesson from a Cab Driver. Shep Hyken. 64p. (Orig.). pap. 8.95 (0-9637820-1-0) Alan Pr.

Loyal Disloyalty. Jeffrey Ashford. LC 99-31889. 1999. 25.95 (0-7862-2048-1) Mac Lib Ref.

Loyal Disloyalty. Jeffrey Ashford. LC 98-47511. 192p. 1998. text 20.95 (0-312-19918-X) St Martin.

Loyal for Life! Building Lasting Bonds with Customers. Jerry Wilson. LC 97-76825. 240p. Date not set. pap. 14.95 (1-885221-82-7) BookPartners.

***Loyal Hearts.** Sarah Westleigh. 1999. per. 4.99 (0-373-30335-1) Harlequin Bks.

Loyal Letters: Studies on Mediaeval Alliterative Poetry & Prose. Ed. by L. A. Houwen & A. A. MacDonald. xii, 300p. 1994. pap. 49.00 (90-6980-075-6, Pub. by Egbert Forsten) Hod1der & Stoughton.

Loyal Mountaineers of Tennessee. Thomas William Humes. (Illus.). 411p. 1998. reprint ed. 27.95 (1-57072-078-9) Overmountain Pr.

Loyal Opposition: Americans in North Vietnam, 1965-1972. James W. Clinton. (Illus.). 432p. 1996. 29.95 (0-87081-412-5) Univ Pr Colo.

***Loyal Opposition: Struggling with the Church on Homosexuality.** Tex Sample & Amy S. DeLong. LC 99-50271. 192p. 2000. pap. 16.00 (0-687-08425-3) Abingdon.

Loyal Opposition: Tudor Traditionalist Polemics, 1535-1558. Ellen A. Macek. (Studies in Church History: Vol. 7). XV, 299p. (C). 1996. text 53.95 (0-8204-3059-5) P Lang Pubng.

Loyal Opposition in Time of War: The Republican Party & the Politics of Foreign Policy from Pearl Harbor to Yalta, 49. Richard E. Darilek. LC 75-44655. (Contributions in American History Ser.: No.49). 239p. (Orig.). 1976. 55.00 (0-8371-8773-7, DLO/) Greenwood.

Loyal Physician: Roycean Ethics & the Practice of Medicine. Griffin Trotter. LC 97-4638. (Library of American Philosophy). 312p. 1997. 29.95 (0-8265-1291-7) Vanderbilt U Pr.

Loyal Rebels: Andreas Hofer & the Tyrolean Uprising of 1809. F. Gunther Eyck. LC 86-1571. 298p. 1986. pap. 27.00 (0-8191-5280-3) U Pr of Amer.

***Loyal Refugees.** Robert Livesey. (Discovering Canada Ser.). 1999. pap. text 9.95 (0-7737-6043-1) STDK.

Loyal Subject. Heinrich Mann. Ed. by Helmut Peitsch. LC 97-22094. (The German Library). 348p. 1997. pap. 24.00 (0-8264-0955-5) Continuum.

Loyal Subjects Looking-Glasse. William Willymat. LC 73-38231. (English Experience Ser.: No. 495). 76p. 1972. reprint ed. 15.00 (90-221-0495-8) Walter J Johnson.

Loyal to the Land: The History of a Greenwich Connecticut Family. Deborah W. Ray & Gloria P. Stewart. LC 90-46740. (Illus.). 192p. 1990. 45.00 (0-914659-50-2) Phoenix Pub.

Loyal Volunteers of London & Environs Infantry & Cavalry in Their Respective Uniforms. Thomas Rowlandson. 1981. 325.00 (0-238-78977-2) St Mut.

Loyal West Virginia, 1861-1865. Theodore F. Lang. (Illus.). 476p. 1998. 35.00 (1-885033-19-2) Blue Acorn Pr.

Loyalism in New York During the American Revolution. Alexander C. Flick. LC 75-120214. (Columbia University. Studies in the Social Sciences: No. 37). reprint ed. 37.50 (0-404-51037-X) AMS Pr.

Loyalism in New York During the American Revolution. Alexander C. Flick. LC 72-90175. (Mass Violence in America Ser.). 1977. reprint ed. 27.95 (0-405-01310-8) Ayer.

Loyalism in Revolutionary Virginia: The Norfolk Area & the Eastern Shore. Adele Hast. Ed. by Robert Berkhofer. LC 81-16357. (Studies in American History & Culture: No. 34). 239p. 1982. reprint ed. pap. 74.10 (0-8357-1277-X, 207009200064) Bks Demand.

Loyalism in Virginia: Chapters in the Economic History of the Revolution. Isaac S. Harrell. LC 26-18312. reprint ed. 32.50 (0-404-03135-8) AMS Pr.

Loyalist Millenarians see Millennium in America: From the Puritan Migration to the Civil War

Loyalist Mind: Joseph Galloway & the American Revolution. John E. Ferling. LC 77-22369. 1977. 28.50 (0-271-00514-9) Pa St U Pr.

Loyalist Narratives from Upper Canada, Vol. 27. Ed. by James J. Talman. LC 69-14505. 411p. 1969. reprint ed. lib. bdg. 65.00 (0-8371-5064-7, TALN, Greenwood Pr) Greenwood.

Loyalist Resolve: Patient Fortitude in the English Civil War. Raymond A. Anselment. LC 87-40514. 240p. 1989. 36.50 (0-87413-338-6) U Delaware Pr.

Loyalist Runaway. Donna Smyth. 136p. (YA). (gr. 5 up). 1995. pap. 8.95 (0-88780-086-6); bds. 16.95 (0-88780-087-4) Formac Dist Ltd.

Loyalists: Revolution, Exile, Settlement. Christopher Moore. 280p. 1994. pap. 16.95 (0-7710-6093-9) McCland & Stewart.

Loyalists: War & Peace in Northern Ireland. Peter Taylor. (Illus.). 304p. 1999. 27.50 (1-57500-047-4, Pub. by TV Bks) HarpC.

Loyalists & Community in North America, 158. Robert M. Calhoon et al. LC 93-49539. (Contributions in American History Ser.: No. 158). 240p. 1994. 59.95 (0-313-28947-6, Greenwood Pr) Greenwood.

Loyalists & Revolutionaries: Political Leaders Compared. Kay Phillips & Mostafa Rejai. LC 87-27888. (Illus.). 203192p. 1988. 49.95 (0-275-92915-9, C2915, Praeger Pubs) Greenwood.

Loyalists in East Florida, 1774-1785: The Most Important Documents Pertaining Thereto..., 2 vols., 1. Wilbur H. Siebert. LC 72-8750. (American Revolutionary Ser.). (Illus.). 734p. reprint ed. lib. bdg. 63.00 (0-8290-1684-8) Irvington.

Loyalists in East Florida, 1774-1785: The Most Important Documents Pertaining Thereto..., 2 vols., 2. Wilbur H. Siebert. LC 72-8750. (American Revolutionary Ser.). (Illus.). 734p. reprint ed. 70.00 (0-685-02671-X) Irvington.

Loyalists in North Carolina During the Revolution. Robert O. DeMond. LC 78-65828. 286p. 1979. reprint ed. pap. 28.50 (0-8063-0839-7) Clearfield Co.

Loyalists in Ontario: The Sons & Daughters of the American Loyalists of Upper Canada. William D. Reid. (Illus.). 418p. 1994. reprint ed. 27.00 (0-8063-1440-0, 4865) Clearfield Co.

Loyalists in the American Revolution. Claude H. Van Tyne. (BCL1 - U. S. History Ser.). 360p. 1991. reprint ed. lib. bdg. 89.00 (0-7812-6120-1) Rprt Serv.

***Loyalists in the American Revolution.** 2nd unabridged ed. Claude H. Van Tyne. 372p. 1999. reprint ed. pap. 18.95 (0-87928-128-6) Corner Hse.

Loyalists in the Southern Campaign of the Revolutionary War Vol. 1: Official Rolls of Loyalists Recruited from North & South Carolina, Georgia, Florida, Mississippi, & Louisiana. Murtie J. Clark. LC 80-84321. 635p. 1999. pap. 47.50 (0-8063-0924-5) Clearfield Co.

Loyalists in the Southern Campaign of the Revolutionary War Vol. II: Official Rolls of Loyalists Recruited from Maryland, Pennsylvania, Virginia, & Those Recruited from Other Colonies. Murtie J. Clark. LC 80-84321. 687p. 1999. pap. 49.95 (0-8063-0941-5) Clearfield Co.

Loyalists in the Southern Campaign of the Revolutionary War Vol. III: Official Rolls of Loyalists Recruited from the Middle Atlantic Colonies, with Lists of Refugees from Other Colonies. Murtie J. Clark. LC 80-84321. 484p. 1999. pap. 37.50 (0-8063-0952-0) Clearfield Co.

Loyalists of America & Their Times, 1620-1816, 2 Vols. A. E. Ryerson. LC 68-31273. (American History & Americana Ser.: No. 47). 1969. reprint ed. lib. bdg. 150.00 (0-8383-0195-9) M S G Haskell Hse.

***Loyalists of Massachusetts: And the Other Side of the American Revolution.** James H. Stark. 509p. 1999. pap. 45.00 (0-8063-4939-5) Clearfield Co.

Loyalists of Massachusetts: And the Other Side of the American Revolution. James H. Stark. (Illus.). viii, 510p. 1988. reprint ed. pap. 35.00 (1-55613-131-3) Heritage Bk.

Loyalists of Massachusetts: And the Other Side of the American Revolution. James H. Stark. LC 68-58022. (Illus.). vii, 569p. 1972. reprint ed. lib. bdg. 57.50 (0-678-00791-8) Kelley.

Loyalists of Massachusetts: Their Memorials, Petitions & Claims. Alfred E. Jones. (Illus.). 365p. 1995. reprint ed. pap. 29.95 (0-8063-0196-1, 3075) Clearfield Co.

Loyalists of Pennsylvania. Wilbur H. Siebert. LC 72-8736. (American Revolutionary Ser.). reprint ed. lib. bdg. 39.50 (0-8398-1882-3) Irvington.

Loyalists of Revolutionary Delaware: A University of Delaware Bicentennial Book. Harold B. Hancock. LC 76-14768. 159p. 1977. 27.50 (0-87413-116-2) U Delaware Pr.

Loyalists, Pacifists & Prisoners see Lancaster County During the American Revolution Series

Loyalists to Canada: The 1783 Settlement of Quakers & Others at Passamaquoddy. Theodore C. Holmes. LC 92-60928. (Illus.). 352p. 1992. 36.50 (0-89725-087-7, 1339) Picton Pr.

Loyalty & Locality: Popular Allegiance in Devon During the English Civil War. Mark Stoyle. LC 95-114283. (Illus.). 304p. 1995. text 50.00 (0-85989-428-2, Pub. by Univ Exeter Pr) Northwestern U Pr.

Loyalties. Patricia L. Barnes-Svarney. (Starfleet Academy Ser.: No. 10). (J). (gr. 3-6). 1996. pap. 3.99 (0-671-55280-5, Minstrel Bks) PB.

Loyalties. Patricia L. Barnes-Svarney. (Starfleet Academy Ser.). 1996. 9.09 (0-606-09893-3, Pub. by Turtleback) Demco.

Loyalties. Daniel P. Moynihan. LC 83-22666. 112p. 1984. 9.95 (0-15-154748-3) Harcourt.

***Loyalties, Set.** unabridged ed. John Galsworthy. (YA). (gr. 9 up). 1998. 20.95 incl. audio (1-55685-544-3) Audio Bk Con.

***Loyalties of Lieutenant Hawk.** Gordon B. Clark. LC 98-94263. viii, 349p. 1999. per. write for info. (0-9661371-2-4) Long Pt Pr.

Loyalties of Lieutenant Hawk. Gordon B. Clark. 224p. 1997. pap. 9.95 (1-882265-52-1) Tandem Alley.

Loyalties of Voters: A Lifetime Learning Model. Richard Rose & Ian McAllister. 256p. (C). 1990. text 45.00 (0-8039-8274-7); pap. text 19.95 (0-8039-8275-5) Sage.

Loyalty. Shelagh Canning. (Illus.). 1997. pap. 3.25 (0-614-27577-6) S&S Childrens.

Loyalty, Bk. 8. Shelagh Canning. LC 96-29809. (Adventures from the Book of Virtues). (Illus.). 24p. (J). 1997. 3.25 (0-689-81280-9) S&S Childrens.

Loyalty, Reading Level 2. Rita Petrucelli. (Learn the Value Ser.: Set II). (Illus.). 32p. (J). (gr. 1-4). 1989. 11.95 (0-685-58786-X) Rourke Corp.

Loyalty: An Essay on the Morality of Relationships. George P. Fletcher. LC 92-460. 224p. (C). 1993. 25.00 (0-19-507026-7) OUP.

Loyalty: An Essay on the Morality of Relationships. George P. Fletcher. 224p. 1995. pap. 11.95 (0-19-509832-3) OUP.

***Loyalty: Move Beyond Faithfulness - Dare to Reach the Heights.** James L. Zirkle. 54p. 2000. pap. 4.00 (0-9679934-0-7) Living Water Teach.

Loyalty: Teacher & Parent Handbook. (Excellence in Character Ser.). (Illus.). 90p. 1998. pap. text 14.95 (1-58259-007-9); pap. text 14.95 (1-58259-037-0) Global Classrm.

***Loyalty & Dependability.** Linda Eyre & Richard Eyre. (Teaching Your Children Values Ser.). 32p. (J). (ps-7). 2000. pap. 16.95 incl. audio (1-56015-792-5) Penton Overseas.

Loyalty & Integrity. W. L. Martin. 1996. pap. text 19.99 (0-9682646-0-3) CPRE.

Loyalty & Leadership in an Early Islamic Society. rev. ed. Roy Mottahedeh. 239p. 1998. pap. text 24.50 (1-86064-181-4) I B T.

Loyalty & Locality: Popular Allegiance in Devon During the English Civil War. Mark Stoyle. (Illus.). 346p. 1996. pap. 24.95 (0-85989-500-9, Pub. by Univ Exeter Pr) Northwestern U Pr.

Loyalty & Security: Employment Tests in the United States. Ralph Brown, Jr. 1958. 89.50 (0-685-26658-3) Elliots Bks.

Loyalty & Security: Employment Tests in the United States. Ralph S. Brown, Jr. LC 79-151417. (Civil Liberties in American History Ser.). 522p. 1972. reprint ed. lib. bdg. 59.50 (0-306-70218-5) Da Capo.

Loyalty & Security in a Democratic State. Ed. by Richard Rivere. LC 75-54570. (Great Contemporary Issues Ser.). 1977. lib. bdg. 27.95 (0-405-09864-2) Ayer.

***Loyalty, Betrayal & Other Contact Sports.** Brown Bear. LC 99-95057. v, 347p. 1999. pap. 12.00 (0-9673933-0-2) Erzse.

***Loyalty, Betrayal, & Other Contact Sports: (Bravo)** Brown Bear, pseud. LC 99-91753. xxii, 317p. 2000. pap. write for info. (0-9673933-2-9) Erzse.

Loyalty by Oath. Hallock Hoffman. (C). 1957. pap. 4.00 (0-87574-094-4) Pendle Hill.

Loyalty Defiled. Alison Stuart. 448p. 1997. pap. 11.95 (0-7472-5220-3, Pub. by Headline Bk Pub) Trafalgar.

Loyalty Demands Dissent: The Autobiography of an Engaged Buddhist. Sulak Sivaraksa. LC 98-9467. (Illus.). 272p. 1998. 22.50 (1-888375-10-8) Parallax Pr.

Loyalty Effect: The Hidden Force Behind Growth, Profits, & Lasting Value. Harvard Business Review Staff. 336p. 1996. 24.95 (0-07-103666-0) McGraw.

Loyalty Effect: The Hidden Force Behind Growth, Profits, & Lasting Value. Frederick F. Reichheld & Thomas Teal. (Illus.). 323p. (C). 1996. 24.95 (0-87584-448-0) Harvard Busn.

Loyalty Factor: A Management Guide to the Changing Dynamics of Loyalty in the Workplace. Carol K. Goman. (Illus.). 105p. (Orig.). (C). 1990. pap. 13.95 (0-9625435-0-0) KCS Pub.

Loyalty Factor: Building Trust in Today's Workplace. Carol K. Goman. LC 90-63423. 1991. pap. 9.95 (0-942361-29-6) MasterMedia Pub.

Loyalty in America. John H. Schaar. LC 82-972. 217p. 1982. lib. bdg. 38.50 (0-313-23416-7, SCLO, Greenwood Pr) Greenwood.

Loyalty in Death. J. D. Robb, pseud. 358p. 1999. mass mkt. 6.99 (0-425-17140-X) Berkley Pub.

***Loyalty in Death.** large type ed. J. D. Robb, pseud. (Americana Series). 2000. 30.95 (0-7862-2443-6) Thorndike Pr.

***Loyalty in Death.** large type ed. J. D. Robb, pseud. LC 99-87731. 2000. pap. write for info. (0-7862-2444-4) Thorndike Pr.

An Asterisk (*) at the beginning of an entry indicates that the title is appearing for the first time.

Loyalty in the Spirituality of St. Thomas More. Brian Byron. 171p. 1972. text 57.50 (*90-6004-293-X*, Pub. by B De Graaf) Coronet Bks.

Loyalty Is My Honor: Waffen-SS Soldiers Talking. Gordon Williamson. LC 96-191688. (Illus.). 192p. 1995. 24.95 (*0-7603-0012-7*) MBI Pubg.

Loyalty Link: How Loyal Employees Create Loyal Customers. Dennis McCarthy. LC 96-46702. 198p. 1997. 19.95 (*0-471-16389-9*) Wiley.

***Loyalty Marketing for the Internet Age: How to Identify, Attract, Serve, & Retain Customers in an E-Commerce Environment.** Kathleen Sindell. 2000. pap. 24.95 (*0-7931-4033-1*) Dearborn.

Loyalty Marketing Resource Book. Neil Raphel & Janis Raye. 171p. 1998. pap. 79.95 (*0-9624808-9-4*) Raphel Mktg.

Loyalty on the Frontier. A. W. Bishop. Ed. by Phillip A. Sperry. (Illus.). 244p. 1993. reprint ed. 34.95 (*1-56869-046-0*); reprint ed. pap. 22.95 (*1-56869-047-9*) Oldbuck Pr.

Loyalty to Church & State: The Mind of His Excellency Francis Archbishop Satolli, Apostolic Delegate. Ed. by J. R. Slattery. LC 71-38461. (Religion in America, Ser.: No. 2). 256p. 1972. reprint ed. 21.95 (*0-405-04082-2*) Ayer.

Loyalty to God: The Apostles Creed in Life & Liturgy. Theodore W. Jennings, Jr. 256p. (Orig.). 1992. pap. 18.95 (*0-687-22821-2*) Abingdon.

Loyalty to the Hunt. Dorina Michelutti. 56p. pap. 5.00 (*0-919349-70-6*) Guernica Editions.

***Loyalty.com: Customer Relationship Management in the New Era of Marketing.** Fred Newell. LC 99-58215. 325p. 2000. 29.95 (*0-07-135775-0*) McGraw.

Loydene in Love. Lael J. Littke. LC 86-12000. 160p. (YA). (gr. 7 up). 1986. 13.95 (*0-15-249888-5*, Harcourt Child Bks) Harcourt.

Loyola. Thomas Hughes. 1988. reprint ed. lib. bdg. 75.00 (*0-7812-0468-2*) Rprt Serv.

Loyola & the Educational System of the Jesuits. Thomas A. Hughes. 1892. 49.00 (*0-403-00121-8*) Scholarly.

Loyola & the Educational System of the Jesuits. Thomas A. Hughes. LC 83-45594. reprint ed. 35.00 (*0-404-19887-2*) AMS Pr.

Loyola Freshman Experience. 2nd ed. Steven DiSalvo. 104p. (C). 1997. per. 32.95 (*0-7872-4163-6*, 41416301) Kendall-Hunt.

***Loyola Law School: A Sense of Purpose & a Sense of Mission.** deluxe ed. Ed. by Gerald T. McLaughlin. (Illus.). 134p. (C). 2000. 49.00 (*0-9679921-0-9*) Loyola Law.

Loyola University of Chicago Law Journal, 1970-1995/96, 28 vols., Set. 1970. 1255.00 (*0-8377-9107-3*, Rothman) W S Hein.

Loyola's Acts: The Rhetoric of the Self. Marjorie O'Rourke Boyle. LC 97-2132. (New Historicism Ser.: Vol. 36). (Illus.). 277p. 1997. 48.00 (*0-520-20937-0*, Pub. by U CA Pr) Cal Prin Full Svc.

Lozana Andaluza. Francisco Delicado. (Nueva Austral Ser.: Vol. 38). (SPA.). 1991. pap. text 24.95 (*84-239-1838-6*) Elliots Bks.

Lozana Andaluza: A Traves de los Siglos. Bruno M. Damiani & Louis Imperiale. (SPA.). 244p. 1997. 74.95 (*1-57309-250-9*) Intl Scholars.

***Lozen.** ROBSON. 1999. mass mkt. write for info. (*0-8125-7609-8*) Tor Bks.

Lozi. Ernest D. Brown, Jr. LC 96-45306. (Heritage Library of African Peoples: Set 4). (Illus.). 64p. (YA). (gr. 7-12). 1996. lib. bdg. 16.95 (*0-8239-2015-1*, D2015-1) Rosen Group.

Lozowick (Prints of Louis) A Catalogue Raisonne. Janet Flint. (Illus.). 224p. 1982. 150.00 (*0-933920-30-X*) A Wofsy Fine Arts.

LP Boundedness of Fourier Integral Operators. R. Michael Beals. LC 82-8754. (Memoirs of the American Mathematical Society Ser.: Vol. 38/264). 57p. 1982. pap. 16.00 (*0-8218-2264-0*, MEMO/38/264) Am Math.

LP-CD Master: Record Album Reference & Price Guide 1940-1987. Joseph P. Rausch. LC 87-92216. 378p. (Orig.). 1988. pap. 39.95 (*0-9620095-0-4*) Standard Music.

***LP for HR: The Loss Prevention Guide for Human Resources Professionals.** Bill Copeland. xii, 182p. 2000. 40.00 (*1-893763-00-5*) Absolutely Zero.

LP-Gas Engine Fuels: A Symposium Presented at the Seventy-Fifth Annual Meeting, ASTM, Los Angeles, CA, 25-30 June 1972. Symposium on LP-Gas Engine Fuels Staff. LC 72-93838. (ASTM Special Technical Publication: No. 525). 140p. reprint ed. pap. 43.40 (*0-7837-4700-4*, 204484600003) Bks Demand.

LP-Gas Safety Handbook. (Illus.). 150p. 1996. 185.00 (*0-317-35195-8*) NPGA.

LP-Gas Training Guidebooks, 5 vols., Set. Larry Carley. Ed. by John B. Fox. 1984. pap. 100.00 (*0-88466-004-4*) NPGA.

LPC Case Study: Civil Litigation. Michelle Robson & Tim Clarke. 239p. 1994. pap. 24.00 (*1-85431-388-6*, Pub. by Blackstone Pr) Gaunt.

LPC Case Study: Civil Litigation, 1995/96. Michelle Robson & Tim Clarke. 266p. 1995. 9.95 (*1-85431-476-9*, Pub. by Blackstone Pr) Gaunt.

LPC Case Study: Civil Litigation, 1996/97. 3rd ed. Michelle Robson & Tim Clarke. 264p. 1996. pap. 26.00 (*1-85431-579-X*, Pub. by Blackstone Pr) Gaunt.

LPC Case Study: Civil Litigation, 1997/98. 4th rev. ed. Michelle Robson & Tim Clarke. 285p. 1997. pap. 28.00 (*1-85431-697-4*, Pub. by Blackstone Pr) Gaunt.

LPC Case Study: Civil Litigation, 1998-99. 5th ed. Michelle Robson & Tim Clarke. (Legal Practice Course Guides Ser.). 304p. 1998. pap. 36.00 (*1-85431-789-X*) Gaunt.

LPC Case Study: Criminal Litigation. Hugh Brayne. 167p. 1994. pap. 24.00 (*1-85431-387-8*, Pub. by Blackstone Pr) Gaunt.

LPC Case Study: Criminal Litigation, 1995/96. Hugh Brayne. 202p. 1995. 9.95 (*1-85431-477-7*, Pub. by Blackstone Pr) Gaunt.

LPC Case Study: Criminal Litigation, 1996/97. 3rd ed. Hugh Brayne. 191p. 1996. pap. 26.00 (*1-85431-578-1*, Pub. by Blackstone Pr) Gaunt.

LPC Case Study: Criminal Litigation, 1997/98. 4th rev. ed. Hugh Brayne & Philip Plowden. 193p. 1997. pap. 28.00 (*1-85431-696-6*, Pub. by Blackstone Pr) Gaunt.

LPC Case Study: Criminal Litigation, 1998-99. 5th ed. Hugh Brayne & Philip Plowden. (Legal Practice Course Guides Ser.). 218p. 1998. pap. 36.00 (*1-85431-790-3*) Gaunt.

LPCVD Silicon Nitride & Oxynitride Films: Material & Applications in Integrated Circuit Technology. Ed. by F. H. Habraken. ix, 159p. 1991. 29.00 (*0-387-53954-9*) Spr-Verlag.

***Lpg & Natural Gas Equipment in Peru: A Strategic Entry Report, 1998.** Compiled by Icon Group International Staff. (Country Industry Report). (Illus.). 135p. 1999. ring bd. 1350.00 incl. audio compact disk (*0-7418-0273-2*) Icon Grp.

***LPG Bottling Plants in India: A Strategic Entry Report, 1995.** Compiled by Icon Group International Staff. (Illus.). 182p. 1999. ring bd. 1820.00 incl. audio compact disk (*0-7418-1620-2*) Icon Grp.

***LPGA's Guide to Every Shot.** Ladies Professional Golf Association Staff. LC 99-89363. (Illus.). 200p. 2000. pap. 19.95 (*0-88011-980-2*) Human Kinetics.

LPI-Facilitator's Guide & Scoring Software. 2nd ed. James M. Kouzes & Barry Z. Posner. 112p. 1997. ring bd. 139.95 (*0-7879-0973-4*) Jossey-Bass.

LPI-IC Facilitator's Guide & Scoring Software. James M. Kouzes & Barry Z. Posner. 112p. 1997. ring bd. 139.95 (*0-7879-0983-1*) Jossey-Bass.

***LPI Linux Certification Fast Track: Level 1 Basic Administration.** New Riders Development Group Staff. (Fast Tracks Ser.). 500p. 2000. pap. 59.95 (*0-7357-0942-4*) New Riders Pub.

LPI Psychometric Properties. Pfeiffer. 1992. text. write for info. (*0-88390-331-8*, Pfffr & Co) Jossey-Bass.

***LPIC Linux Level I Exam Guide.** Theresa Hadden. 368p. 2000. pap. 39.99 (*0-7897-2292-5*) Que.

***LPIC Linux Level I Cheat Sheet: Covers Test 1.** Jim Richardson. (Cheat Sheet Ser.). 350p. 2000. pap. 24.99 (*0-7897-2289-5*) Que.

***LPN Nursing Pearls of Wisdom.** Hunter S. Thompson. (Pearls of Wisdom Ser.). 1999. pap. 26.00 (*1-58409-002-2*) Boston Medical.

LPN Photo Manual: A Step-by-Step Guide to Patient Care. Springhouse Publishing Company Staff. Ed. by June Norris. (Illus.). 512p. 1996. pap. text 26.95 (*0-87434-851-X*) Springhouse Corp.

LPN to RN Transitions. Nicki Harrington et al. LC 95-40073. 416p. 1995. pap. text 24.00 (*0-397-55065-0*) Lppncott W & W.

LPN/LVN Review: Medical/Surgical Tutor. Gary W. Stogsdill. (LPN/LVN Nursing Ser.). (C). 1995. 20.95 (*0-8273-6545-4*) Delmar.

LPRA Cumulative Supplement, 1999, 39 vols. Incl. Tables I 99CS. (SPA.). 30p. 1999. (*0-327-08494-4*, 84258-16); Tables II 99CS. annot. ed. (SPA.). 35p. 1999. (*0-327-08495-2*, 84260-16); Title 8-9 99CS. annot. ed. (SPA.). 187p. 1999. (*0-327-08470-5*, 84229-16); Title 18 Section 861-End & Title 19 99CS. annot. ed. (SPA.). 15p. 1999. (*0-327-08479-0*, 84239-16); Title 18 Section 1-860 99CS. annot. ed. (SPA.). 124p. 1999. (*0-327-08478-2*, 84238-16); Title 11-12 99CS. annot. ed. (SPA.). 103p. 1999. (*0-327-08472-3*, 84231-16); Title 5 99CS. annot. ed. (SPA.). 35p. 1999. (*0-327-08468-5*, 84227-16); Title 4 99CS. annot. ed. (SPA.). 101p. 1999. (*0-327-08467-7*, 84225-16); Title 14-16 Section 1-700 99CS. annot. ed. (SPA.). 264p. 1999. (*0-327-08476-6*, 84236-16); Title 1 Hist Docs 99CS. annot. ed. (SPA.). 185p. 1999. (*0-327-08463-4*, 84221-16); Title 6-7 99CS. annot. ed. (SPA.). 268p. 1999. (*0-327-08469-3*, 84228-16); Title 16 Section 701-End & Title 17 99CS. annot. ed. (SPA.). 212p. 1999. (*0-327-08477-4*, 84237-16); Title 10 99CS. annot. ed. (SPA.). 67p. 1999. (*0-327-08471-5*, 84230-16); Title 13 Section 8561-End 99CS. annot. ed. (SPA.). 220p. 1999. (*0-327-08475-8*, 84234-16); Title 13 Section 1-6000 99CS. annot. ed. (SPA.). 15p. 1999. (*0-327-08473-1*, 84232-16); Title 13 Section 6001-8560 99CS. annot. ed. (SPA.). 133p. 1999. (*0-327-08474-X*, 84233-16); Title 34 & Rules 99CS. annot. ed. (SPA.). 108p. 1999. (*0-327-08493-6*, 84257-16); Title 30 99CS. annot. ed. (SPA.). 19p. 1999. (*0-327-08485-5*, 84249-16); Title 31 Section 4171-End 99CS. annot. ed. (SPA.). 41p. 1999. (*0-327-08489-8*, 84253-16); Title 31 Section 1-1270 99CS. annot. ed. (SPA.). 186p. 1999. (*0-327-08486-3*, 84250-16); Title 31 Section 1271-2990 99CS. annot. ed. (SPA.). 38p. 1999. (*0-327-08487-1*, 84251-16); Title 31 Section 2991-4143 99CS. annot. ed. (SPA.). 32p. 1999. (*0-327-08488-X*, 84252-16); Title 33 99CS. annot. ed. (SPA.). 130p. 1999. (*0-327-08492-8*, 84256-16); Title 32 99CS. annot. ed. (SPA.). 57p. 1999. (*0-327-08490-1*, 84254-16); Title 32 Rules 99CS. annot. ed. (SPA.). 145p. 1999. (*0-327-08491-X*, 84255-16); Title 3 Sections 881-End 99CS. 244p. 1999. (*0-327-08466-9*, 84224-16); Title 3 Sections 451-880 99CS. annot. ed. (SPA.). 94p. 1999. (*0-327-08465-0*, 84223-16); Title 29 99CS. annot. ed. (SPA.). 146p. 1999. (*0-327-08484-7*, 84248-16); Title 20 99CS. annot. ed. (SPA.). 20p. 1999. (*0-327-08480-4*, 84240-16); Title 21 99CS. annot. ed. (SPA.). 302p. 1999. (*0-327-08481-2*, 84241-16); Title 27-28 99CS. annot. ed. (SPA.). 212p. 1999. (*0-327-08483-9*, 84247-16); Title 26 99CS. annot. ed. (SPA.). 29p. 1999. (*0-327-08482-0*, 84246-16); Title 2-3 Sections 1-450 99CS. annot. ed. (SPA.). 8p. 1999. (*0-327-08464-2*, 84222-16); (SPA.). 1999. write for info. (*0-327-08393-X*, 47505-15) LEXIS Pub.

LPRA Engl: 95-96 Sup, Vol. 27-28. Date not set. suppl. ed. write for info. (*0-327-06620-2*, 84179-13) LEXIS Pub.

LPRA Engl: 95-96 Sup, Vol. T3(881-END) Date not set. suppl. ed. write for info. (*0-327-06602-4*, 84158-13) LEXIS Pub.

LPRA Engl: 95-96 Sup, Vol. T4(1-2000) Date not set. suppl. ed. write for info. (*0-327-06603-2*, 84159-13) LEXIS Pub.

LPRA Engl: 95-96 Sup, Vol. T5. Date not set. suppl. ed. write for info. (*0-327-06604-0*, 84161-13) LEXIS Pub.

LPRA Engl: 95-96 Sup, Vol. T6-7. Date not set. suppl. ed. write for info. (*0-327-06605-9*, 84162-13) LEXIS Pub.

LPRA Engl: 95-96 Sup, Vol. T8-9. Date not set. suppl. ed. write for info. (*0-327-06606-7*, 84163-13) LEXIS Pub.

LPRA Engl: 95-96 Sup, Vol. T10. Date not set. suppl. ed. write for info. (*0-327-06607-5*, 84164-13) LEXIS Pub.

LPRA Engl: 95-96 Sup, Vol. T11-12. Date not set. suppl. ed. write for info. (*0-327-06608-3*, 84165-13) LEXIS Pub.

LPRA Engl: 95-96 Sup, Vol. T13(1-6K) Date not set. suppl. ed. write for info. (*0-327-06609-1*, 84166-13) LEXIS Pub.

LPRA Engl: 95-96 Sup, Vol. T13(6001-8560) Date not set. suppl. ed. write for info. (*0-327-06610-5*, 84167-13) LEXIS Pub.

LPRA Engl: 95-96 Sup, Vol. T13(END) Date not set. suppl. ed. write for info. (*0-327-06611-3*, 84168-13) LEXIS Pub.

LPRA Engl: 95-96 Sup, Vol. T14-16. Date not set. suppl. ed. write for info. (*0-327-06612-1*, 84169-13) LEXIS Pub.

LPRA Engl: 95-96 Sup, Vol. T16-17. Date not set. suppl. ed. write for info. (*0-327-06613-X*, 84170-13) LEXIS Pub.

LPRA Engl: 95-96 Sup, Vol. T21. Date not set. suppl. ed. write for info. (*0-327-06614-8*, 84174-13) LEXIS Pub.

LPRA Engl: 95-96 Sup, Vol. T22-23(1-230) Date not set. suppl. ed. write for info. (*0-327-06615-6*, 84175-13) LEXIS Pub.

LPRA Engl: 95-96 Sup, Vol. T23(231-END) Date not set. suppl. ed. write for info. (*0-327-06616-4*, 84176-13) LEXIS Pub.

LPRA Engl: 95-96 Sup, Vol. T24. Date not set. suppl. ed. write for info. (*0-327-06617-2*, 84177-13) LEXIS Pub.

LPRA Engl: 95-96 Sup, Vol. T25. Date not set. suppl. ed. write for info. (*0-327-06618-0*, 84178-13) LEXIS Pub.

LPRA Engl: 95-96 Sup, Vol. T26. Date not set. suppl. ed. write for info. (*0-327-06619-9*, 84179-13) LEXIS Pub.

LPRA Engl: 95-96 Sup, Vol. T29. Date not set. suppl. ed. write for info. (*0-327-06621-0*, 84181-13) LEXIS Pub.

LPRA Engl: 95-96 Sup, Vol. T30. Date not set. suppl. ed. write for info. (*0-327-06622-9*, 84183-13) LEXIS Pub.

LPRA Engl: 95-96 Sup, Vol. T31(1-1270) Date not set. suppl. ed. write for info. (*0-327-06623-7*, 84148-13) LEXIS Pub.

LPRA Engl: 95-96 Sup, Vol. T31(1271-2990) Date not set. suppl. ed. write for info. (*0-327-06624-5*, 84185-13) LEXIS Pub.

LPRA Engl: 95-96 Sup, Vol. T31(2991-4143) Date not set. suppl. ed. write for info. (*0-327-06625-3*, 84186-13) LEXIS Pub.

LPRA Engl: 95-96 Sup, Vol. T31(4171-END) Date not set. suppl. ed. write for info. (*0-327-06626-1*, 84187-13) LEXIS Pub.

LPRA Engl: 95-96 Sup, Vol. T32. Date not set. suppl. ed. write for info. (*0-327-06627-X*, 84188-13) LEXIS Pub.

LPRA Engl: 95-96 Sup, Vol. T32(RULES) Date not set. suppl. ed. write for info. (*0-327-06628-8*, 84189-13) LEXIS Pub.

LPRA Engl: 95-96 Sup, Vol. T33. Date not set. suppl. ed. write for info. (*0-327-06629-6*, 84190-13) LEXIS Pub.

LPRA Engl: 95-96 Sup, Vol. T34(RULES) Date not set. suppl. ed. write for info. (*0-327-06630-X*, 84191-13) LEXIS Pub.

LPRA Engl Hist: 95-96 Sup, Vol. T1. Date not set. suppl. ed. write for info. (*0-327-06600-8*, 84155-13) LEXIS Pub.

LPRA Engl Index A-I: 95-96 Sup. Date not set. write for info. (*0-327-06633-4*, 84195-13) LEXIS Pub.

LPRA Engl Index J-Z: 95-96 Sup. Date not set. write for info. (*0-327-06634-2*, 84196-13) LEXIS Pub.

LPRA Engl Tables I: 95-96 Sup. Date not set. write for info. (*0-327-06631-8*, 84192-13) LEXIS Pub.

LPRA Engl Tables II: 95-96 Sup. Date not set. write for info. (*0-327-06632-6*, 84193-13) LEXIS Pub.

***LPRA T. 14-15 Replacement Volume.** 540p. 2000. write for info. (*0-327-13650-2*, 4747412) LEXIS Pub.

***LPRA T. 24 Replacement Volume (English)** 750p. 1999. write for info. (*0-327-09407-9*, 4755311) LEXIS Pub.

***LPRA T. 25 Replacement Volume English.** 500p. 1999. write for info. (*0-327-09437-0*, 4755411) LEXIS Pub.

LPRA T.23 Pt. 2: 521-End. (SPA.). 440p. 1999. write for info. (*0-327-08772-2*, 47503-10) LEXIS Pub.

LPS 1998 - Proceedings of the 32nd Annual Loss Prevention Symposium. Contrib. by Loss Prevention Committee of AIChE'S Safety & Heal & M. L. Griffin. 618p. 1998. pap. 125.00 (*0-8169-0765-X*, T-105) Am Inst Chem Eng.

LPS, 1997: Proceedings of the 31st Annual Loss Prevention Symposium. Ed. by Loss Prevention Committee of AIChE Safety & Health et al. (Technical Manual - Loss Prevention Ser.). 744p. 1997. 120.00 (*0-8169-0726-9*, T-102) Am Inst Chem Eng.

LRFD Bridge Design Specifications, E. M. 2nd ed. (Bridges & Structures Ser.: Vol. LRDF-EM-2). (Illus.). 2432p. (C). 1998. pap. 230.00 (*1-56051-095-1*) AASHTO.

LRFD Bridge Design Specifications, S. I. 2nd ed. (Bridges & Structures Ser.: Vol. LRFD-SI-2). (Illus.). 1216p. (C). 1998. pap. 120.00 (*1-56051-094-3*) AASHTO.

LRFD Bridge Design Specifications, U. S. 2nd ed. (Bridges & Structures Ser.: Vol. LRFD-US-2). (Illus.). 1216p. (C). 1998. pap. 120.00 (*1-56051-093-5*) AASHTO.

LRFD Steel Design. William T. Segui. LC 93-23170. 1993. mass mkt. 75.95 (*0-534-93353-X*) PWS Pubs.

***LRFD Steel Design.** 2nd ed. William T. Segui. (C). 1998. pap. 90.95 (*0-534-95155-4*) Thomson Learn.

LRFD Steel Design Using Advanced Analysis. Wai-Fah Chen & Seung-Eock Kim. LC 96-36957. (New Directions in Civil Engineering Ser.). 464p. 1997. boxed set 84.95 (*0-8493-7432-4*) CRC Pr.

Lrng Bus Math With Elec Calc. Richard R. McCready. (Math). 1975. mass mkt. 12.75 (*0-534-00396-6*) PWS Pubs.

LRRP Team Leader. John Burford. 1994. mass mkt. 4.99 (*0-8041-1051-4*) Ivy Books.

LRRP's in Action. John Burford. (Combat Troops in Action Ser.). (Illus.). 50p. 1994. pap. 9.95 (*0-89747-313-2*) Squad Sig Pubns.

LRTA (Leisure, Recreation, & Tourism Abstracts) A User Handbook. M. Leighfield. 125p. (Orig.). 1990. pap. text 35.00 (*0-85198-676-5*) OUP.

LS Fortran: Language Reference. 1994. pap. write for info. (*1-885644-02-7*) Fortner Sftware.

LS Fortran: Macintosh User's Guide. 1995. pap. write for info. (*1-885644-03-5*) Fortner Sftware.

LS Fortran: Power Macintosh User's Guide. 1994. pap. write for info. (*1-885644-04-3*) Fortner Sftware.

LSA Chairman's Manual. 24p. 1989. pap. 4.95 (*0-909991-13-8*) Bahai.

LSA Secretary's Manual. 12p. 1989. pap. 4.95 (*0-909991-04-9*) Bahai.

LSA Treasurer's Manual. 20p. 1989. pap. 4.95 (*0-909991-02-2*) Bahai.

LSAT. 6th ed. Thomas H. Martinson. 1995. pap. 29.00 incl. disk (*0-671-89970-8*) Macmillan USA.

LSAT: Law School Admission Test. 6th ed. 1995. pap. 12.95 (*0-671-89968-6*, Arco) Macmillan Gen Ref.

LSAT: Law School Admission Test. 7th ed. Thomas H. Martinson. 400p. 1996. pap. 13.95 (*0-02-861072-5*, Arco) Macmillan Gen Ref.

LSAT: Law School Admission Test, 2000 Edition. 2000th ed. Thomas H. Martinson. (Illus.). 480p. 1999. pap. 16.95 (*0-02-863216-8*, Arc) IDG Bks.

***LSAT: The Official Tripleprep, 1.** Test Prep Guides Staff. 144p. 1999. pap. 15.95 (*0-8129-3244-7*, Times Bks); pap. 15.95 (*0-8129-3246-3*, Times Bks) Crown Pub Group.

LSAT: Triple Prep, Vol. 1. Kaplan Law School Admission Staff. 128p. 1994. pap. 14.95 (*0-553-85164-0*) Bantam.

LSAT: Triple Prep, Vol. 2. Kaplan Law School Admission Staff. 128p. 1996. pap. 14.95 (*0-553-85167-5*) Bantam.

LSAT: Triple Prep, Vol. 2. Law School Admissions Services Staff. (Kaplan Source Ser.). 128p. 1994. pap. 14.95 (*0-553-06226-3*) Bantam.

LSAT - Law School Admission Test. rev. ed. Research & Education Association Staff. LC 97-68607. (Illus.). 688p. 1998. pap. text 20.95 (*0-87891-854-X*) Res & Educ.

LSAT, Law School Admission Test. 6th ed. Thomas H. Martinson. LC 95-7730. 384p. 1995. pap. 12.95 (*0-02-860326-5*) Macmillan.

LSAT Law School Admission Test with Tests on CD - Rom: 1999 Edition. Thomas H. Martinson. LC 97-81121. 392p. 1998. pap. 29.95 incl. cd-rom (*0-02-862480-7*, Arco) Macmillan Gen Ref.

LSAT, 1998. Kaplan Staff. 1997. 20.00 (*0-684-83679-3*); 34.95 incl. cd-rom (*0-684-83683-1*) S&S Trade.

LSAT, 1998-99. Kaplan Staff. 304p. 1998. 20.00 (*0-684-84760-4*) S&S Trade.

Kaplan LSAT, 1998-99: Law Scool Admission Test. Kaplan. 304p. 1998. pap. 34.95 incl. cd-rom (*0-684-84761-2*) S&S Trade.

LSAT Power. Cambridge Review Staff. 384p. 1996. 16.95 (*0-02-861077-6*) Macmillan.

LSAT Power. Cambridge Review Staff & Joyce L. Vedral. 1997. pap. text 29.95 incl. disk (*0-02-861516-6*, Arco) Macmillan Gen Ref.

LSAT Power, 1998. 336p. 17.95 (*0-02-861686-3*) Macmillan.

LSAT Preparation Guide: Law School Admission Test. Peter Z. Orton. (Cliffs Test Preparation Ser.). 336p. (Orig.). (C). 1993. pap. text 9.95 (*0-8220-2066-1*, Cliff) IDG Bks.

LSAT Success. 2nd ed. Thomas O. White. (Peterson's Test Success Ser.). 237p. 1998. pap. text 16.95 (*0-7689-0024-7*) Petersons.

LSAT Success: Complete Advice on Preparing for the Law School Admission Test. 2nd rev. ed. Thomas O. White. (Test Success Ser.). 240p. (C). 1996. pap. 12.95 (*1-56079-585-9*) Petersons.

***LSAT Success 2000.** 6th ed. Peterson's Guides Staff. 245p. 1999. pap. 16.95 incl. cd-rom (*0-7689-0224-X*) Petersons.

***LSAT Success 2001.** 7th ed. Peterson's Guides Staff. 245p. 2000. pap. 16.95 (*0-7689-0411-0*) Petersons.

LSAT Supercourse. 5th ed. Thomas H. Martinson. LC 96-232940. 752p. 1996. 19.95 (*0-02-861184-5*, Arc) IDG Bks.

LSAT Supercourse. 5th ed. Thomas H. Martinson. 1996. 34.95 incl. disk (*0-02-860613-2*, Arc) IDG Bks.

LSAT Supercourse. 6th ed. Thomas H. Martinson. 720p. 1998. pap. text 18.95 (*0-02-862486-6*, Arco) Macmillan Gen Ref.

LSAT TestBuster. Anita P. Davis. 250p. 2000. pap. 19.95 (*0-87891-144-8*) Res & Educ.

LSAT the Official Triple Prep, Vol. 1. Law School Admissions Services Staff. LC 97-221989. (Kaplan Source Ser.). 128p. (C). 1994. pap. 15.95 (*0-553-06222-0*) Bantam.

L

LSAT Triple Prep Volume 2, Vol. 2. Kaplan Law School Admission Staff. LC 97-221989. 128p. (C). 1996. pap. 15.95 (*0-553-06642-0*) Bantam.

***LSAT 2000-2001: Law School Admission Test.** Kaplan Staff et al. (Illus.). 486p. 2000. pap. 20.00 (*0-684-87011-8*) Kaplan.

LSAT with Testware. Research & Education Association Staff. 510p. 1999. pap. text 34.95 incl. disk (*0-87891-471-4*) Res & Educ.

***LSD.** Sean Connolly. LC 00-25655. 2000. lib. bdg. write for info. (*1-57572-258-5*) Heinemann Lib.

LSD. Mary A. Littell. LC 96-6864. (Drug Library Ser.). (Illus.). 112p. (YA). (gr. 6 up). 1996. lib. bdg. 20.95 (*0-89490-739-5*) Enslow Pubs.

LSD: A Total Study. D. Siva Sankar et al. LC 72-95447. 1975. 69.95 (*0-9600290-3-6*) PJD Pubns.

LSD: Still with Us after All These Years. Leigh A. Henderson & William J. Glass. LC 94-20172. 163p. 1994. 22.95 (*0-02-914395-0*) Jossey-Bass.

LSD: Still with Us after All These Years. Leigh A. Henderson & William J. Glass. LC 98-19895. (Psychology Ser.). 176p. 1998. reprint ed. pap. 18.95 (*0-7879-4379-7*) Jossey-Bass.

LSD: Visions or Nightmares? Michael E. Trulson. (Encyclopedia of Psychoactive Drugs Ser.: No. 1). (Illus.). 124p. (YA). (gr. 7 up). 1985. lib. bdg. 19.95 (*0-87754-752-1*) Chelsea Hse.

LSD, PCP & Hallucinogen Drug Dangers. Judy Monroe. LC 99-14105. (Drug Dangers Ser.). (Illus.). 64p. (gr. 4-10). 2000. lib. bdg. 19.95 (*0-7660-1318-9*) Enslow Pubs.

LSD, PCP & Other Hallucinogens. Ed. by Steven L. Jaffe. LC 99-22299. (Illus.). 80p. (J). (gr. 4-8). 1999. lib. bdg. 19.95 (*0-7910-5183-8*) Chelsea Hse.

LSD Psychotherapy: Exploring the Frontiers of the Hidden Mind. 2nd ed. Stanislav Grof. LC 92-1429. (Illus.). 352p. 1994. 34.95 (*0-89793-166-1*); pap. 22.95 (*0-89793-158-0*) Hunter Hse.

LSD-25 & Tryptamine Syntheses: Overview & Reference Guide for Professionals. Otto Snow. LC 98-90045. (Psychoactive Synthesis Ser.: No. 2). (Illus.). xix, 131p. 1998. pap. 19.95 (*0-9663128-1-3*, Pub. by Thoth Pr) Homestead Bk.

LSE - Inquiry Currency Principle. Thomas Tooke. 120p. (C). 1997. 60.00 (*0-415-14395-0*) Routledge.

LSI Interfacing. Mike James. 1988. 32.00 (*0-434-90889-4*) CRC Pr.

LSM-LSMR: WWII Amphibious Forces. Turner Publishing Company Staff. LC 94-60250. (Illus.). 168p. 1994. 49.95 (*1-56311-140-3*) Turner Pub KY.

LSU College of Engineering Vol. I: Origins & Establishment, 1860-1908. Dan R. Frost & Kou K. Nelson. LC 94-38639. 200p. 1995. text 30.00 (*0-8071-1997-0*) La State U Pr.

LSU College of Engineering Vol. II: Growth & Maturity, 1909-1970. Dan R. Frost. (Illus.). 248p. 1999. text 30.00 (*0-8071-2484-2*) La State U Pr.

LT: Recreation Development in the American Countryside. 1987. pap. 1.75 (*0-88314-373-9*) AAHPERD.

Lt. Charles Wilkes & the Great U. S. Exploring Expedition. Cheri Wolfe. Ed. by William H. Goetzmann. (World Explorers Ser.). (Illus.). 120p. (YA). (gr. 5 up). 1991. lib. bdg. 19.95 (*0-7910-1320-0*) Chelsea Hse.

Lt. John T. McLaughlin, USN: Mystery Man of the Second Seminole War. Nell C. Weidenbach. (Illus.). 128p. (Orig.). 1995. pap., spiral bd. write for info. (*0-9638968-2-2*) Foxcord Hse.

Lt. Joshua Hewes, a New England Pioneer, & Some of His Descendants. Eben Putnam. (Illus.). 673p. 1989. reprint ed. pap. 101.00 (*0-8328-0654-4*); reprint ed. lib. bdg. 109.00 (*0-8328-0653-6*) Higginson Bk Co.

***LTC Ancillary Services Acquisition Report, 1999.** Irving Levin Associates, Inc. Staff. (Illus.). v, 111p. 1999. pap. 295.00 (*1-930625-06-5*) I Levin.

LTU Micro Applications: Wordperfect 5.1 Step-by-Step. Gary B. Shelly & T. Cashman. LC 95-201586. 1995. mass mkt. 38.95 (*0-7895-0006-X*) S-W Pub.

LTU Quattro Pro 6.0 for Windows. Gary B. Shelly & T. Cashman. 208p. 1995. mass mkt. 22.95 (*0-7895-0344-1*) S-W Pub.

LTU Windows Applications: Power Point 4.0 for Windows. Green et al. 352p. 1995. pap. 38.95 (*0-7895-0130-9*) S-W Pub.

LTU Wordperfect 6.1 for Windows. Gary B. Shelly & T. Cashman. (Double Diamond Ser.). 208p. 1995. mass mkt. 22.95 (*0-7895-0337-9*) S-W Pub.

***L2TP: Implementation & Operation.** Richard Shea. LC 99-37615. 288p. 1999. pap. text 19.95 (*0-201-60448-5*) Addison-Wesley.

Lu Ann Hampton Laverty Oberlander. Preston Jones. 1977. pap. 5.25 (*0-8222-0705-2*) Dramatists Play.

Lu Gwei-Djen: A Commemoration. Pentland Press Ltd. Staff. (C). 1989. text 59.00 (*1-85821-034-8*, Pub. by Pentland Pr) St Mut.

Lu Hong, Art & Life. Wenkuang Chang & Jeffrey Goldberg. (Illus.). 83p. (Orig.). 1989. pap. write for info. (*0-318-65508-X*) Segal Fine Art.

Lu Hshun & His Predecessors. Vladimir I. Semanov. Ed. by Charles J. Alber. LC 80-50885. 204p. 1980. reprint ed. pap. 63.30 (*0-8357-2622-3*, 204011000014) Bks Demand.

Lu Hsun: Complete Poems - A Translation with Introduction & Annotation. David Y. Ch'en. LC 88-70039. (Monograph Ser.: No. 22). 275p. (Orig.). 1988. pap. 10.00 (*0-939252-19-8*) ASU Ctr Asian.

Lu Hsun Reader. Compiled by William J. Lyell, Jr. 1976. 14.95 (*0-88710-046-5*) Yale Far Eastern Pubns.

Lu Pavone: Poesia in Dialetto - The Peacock: Poems in the Molisan Dialect. Giuseppe Jovine. Tr. by Luigi Bonaffini from ITA. LC 93-14212. (Studies in Southern Italian & Italian-American Culture: Vol. 5). (ENG & MIS.). LII, 371p. (C). 1994. text 59.95 (*0-8204-2238-X*) P Lang Pubng.

Lu Xun & Evolution. James R. Pusey. LC 97-13018. (SUNY Series in Philosophy & Biology). 288p. (C). 1998. text 65.50 (*0-7914-3647-0*); pap. text 21.95 (*0-7914-3648-9*) State U NY Pr.

Lu Xun Xiao Shuo Ji: Vocabulary (Selected Short Stories) rev. ed. Tr. & Compiled by D. C. Lau. 220p. 1987. pap. 14.95 (*962-201-391-0*, Pub. by Chinese Univ) U of Mich Pr.

Lu Xun Xiao Shuo Ji: Vocabulary (Selected Short Stories of Lu Xun) Lu Hsun, pseud. (Illus.). 207p. 1979. reprint ed. pap. 14.95 (*0-917056-22-1*) Cheng & Tsui.

Lua Getsiner: Herald of the Covenant. Velda P. Metelmann. LC 97-182240. (Illus.). 250p. (Orig.). 1997. pap. 29.95 (*0-85398-416-6*) G Ronald Pub.

Luann: Dear Diary. Greg Evans. 1991. pap. 3.50 (*0-8125-1416-5*, Pub. by Tor Bks) St Martin.

Luann: Homework Is Ruining My Life. Greg Evans. 128p. 1989. pap. 2.95 (*0-8125-0635-9*, Pub. by Tor Bks) St Martin.

Luann: If Confusion Were a Class I'd Get an "A" Greg Evans. 128p. (Orig.). 1995. pap. 3.99 (*0-8125-1732-6*, Pub. by Tor Bks) St Martin.

Luann: I'm Not Always Confused, I Just Look That Way. Greg Evans. (Illus.). 128p. (Orig.). 1993. pap. 3.50 (*0-8125-1734-2*, Pub. by Tor Bks) St Martin.

Luann: My Bedroom & Other Environmental Hazards. Greg Evans. (Illus.). 128p. (Orig.). 1993. pap. 3.50 (*0-8125-1735-0*, Pub. by Tor Bks) St Martin.

Luann: Pizza Isn't Everything. Greg Evans. (Illus.). 128p. 1991. pap. 3.50 (*0-8125-1174-3*, Pub. by Tor Bks) St Martin.

Luann: School's OK If You Can Stand the Food. Greg Evans. (Illus.). 128p. 1992. pap. 3.50 (*0-8125-1733-4*, Pub. by Tor Bks) St Martin.

Luann: The Plunge. Greg Evans. LC 98-29141. (Illus.). 127p. 1998. pap. 9.95 (*1-55853-667-1*) Rutledge Hill Pr.

Luann: There's Nothing Worse Than First Period P.E. Greg Evans. (Illus.). 128p. 1992. pap. 3.50 (*0-8125-1731-8*, Pub. by Tor Bks) St Martin.

Luann: Who Invented Brothers Anyway? Greg Evans. 1989. pap. 2.95 (*0-8125-7225-4*, Pub. by Tor Bks) St Martin.

Luann: Will We Be Tested on This? Greg Evans. (Illus.). 128p. 1992. pap. 3.50 (*0-8125-1729-6*, Pub. by Tor Bks) St Martin.

Luapula, Dependence or Development: Zambia Geographical Association Handbook, No. 6. Jeremy Gould. (Finnish Society for Development Studies: No. 3). 252p. (Orig.). 1990. 47.50 (*951-96156-1-X*) Coronet Bks.

Luba. M. Nooter & Allen F. Roberts. LC 96-31073. (Heritage Library of African Peoples). (Illus.). 64p. (YA). (gr. 7-12). 1996. lib. bdg. 16.95 (*0-8239-2002-X*) Rosen Group.

Luba & the Wren. Patricia Polacco. LC 98-16353. 32p. (J). (ps-3). 1999. 16.99 (*0-399-23168-4*, Philomel) Peng Put Young Read.

Luba Gurdjieff: A Memoir with Recipes. 2nd ed. Luba G. Everitt & Marina C. Bear. LC 97-24599. (Illus.). 120p. 1997. reprint ed. pap. 15.95 (*0-943389-22-4*, SLG Bks) Snow Lion-SLG Bks.

Lubaroff & Altman on Delaware Limited Partnerships. Martin I. Lubaroff & Paul M. Altman. LC 95-43524. 1270p. 1998. ring bd. 185.00 (*1-56706-288-1*) Aspen Law.

Lubavitcher Rabbi's Memoirs, Vol. 1. abr. ed. Yosef Y. Schneersohn. Tr. by Nissan Mindel from YID. 336p. (YA). 1960. 12.00 (*0-8266-0428-5*) Kehot Pubn Soc.

Lubavitcher Rabbi's Memoirs, Vol. 2. Yosef Yitchak Scneersohn. Tr. by Nissan Mindel from YID. 296p. (YA). 1960. reprint ed. 15.00 (*0-8266-0429-3*) Kehot Pubn Soc.

Lubavitcher Women in America: Identity & Activism in the Postwar Era. Bonnie J. Morris. LC 97-28021. 192p. (C). 1998. text 44.50 (*0-7914-3799-X*); pap. text 14.95 (*0-7914-3800-7*) State U NY Pr.

***Lubb Dup.** Anne Tyler. (Illus.). 36p. 1998. pap. 35.00 (*1-888636-11-4*) Sara Ranchouse.

Lubbock: City of Land & Sky. Freda McVay et al. LC 94-21463. (Urban Tapestry Ser.). (Illus.). 256p. 1994. 39.50 (*1-881096-09-2*) Towery Pub.

Lubbock: From Town to City. Lawrence L. Graves et al. Ed. by Gale Richardson. (Museum Journals). (Illus.). 438p. (Orig.). 1986. 30.00 (*0-911618-11-2*) Mus Texas.

Lubbock & the South Plains. 2nd rev. ed. Donald Abbe et al. (Illus.). 128p. 1995. 29.95 (*0-89781-481-9*) Am Historical Pr.

Lubbock Lake: Late Quaternary Studies on the Southern High Plains. Ed. by Eileen Johnson. LC 87-1888. (Illus.). 192p. 1988. lib. bdg. 49.50 (*0-89096-321-5*) Tex A&M Univ Pr.

Lube Recommendations & Capacities Booklet, 1986. 48p. student ed. 5.55 (*0-88098-084-2*, H M Gousha) Prntice Hall Bks.

Lubeck, 1900 Proceedings see International Congress on the History of Art

Lubertha Johnson: Civil Rights Efforts in Las Vegas, 1940s-1960s. Ed. by Jamie Coughtry & R. T. King. (Illus.). 88p. 1988. write for info. (*1-56475-334-4*); lib. bdg. 32.50 (*1-56475-333-6*); fiche. write for info. (*1-56475-335-2*) U NV Oral Hist.

Lubok: Russian Folk Pictures of the 17th & 19th Centuries. Ed. by Alla Sytova. (Illus.). 1984. 150.00 (*0-7855-1653-0*) St Mut.

Luboml: The Memorial Book of a Vanished Shtetl. Berl Kagan. LC 97-6197. 1997. 39.50 (*0-88125-580-7*) Ktav.

Lubricant Base Oil & Wax Processing. Arilino Sequeira, Jr. (Chemical Industries Ser.: Vol. 60). (Illus.). 304p. 1994. text 145.00 (*0-8247-9256-4*) Dekker.

Lubricants & Lubrication: Proceedings of the 21st Leeds-Lyon Symposium on Tribology, University of Leeds, Institute of Tribology, Leeds, U. K., 6-9 September, 1994. Leeds-Lyons Symposium on Tribology Staff. Ed. by D. Dowson et al. LC 95-20695. (Tribology Ser.: Vol. 30). 708p. 1995. 263.00 (*0-444-82263-1*) Elsevier.

Lubricants & Lubrication in Metalworking Operations. Elliot Nachtman & Serope Kalpakjian. (Manufacturing Engineering & Materials Processing Ser.: Vol. 14). (Illus.). 288p. 1985. text 150.00 (*0-8247-7401-9*) Dekker.

***Lubricants & Lubrications.** Theo Mang. 528p. 2000. text 184.95 (*3-527-29536-4*) Wiley.

Lubricants & Related Products: Synthesis, Properties & Application International Standards. Dieter Klamann. Tr. by Alfred Killer from GER. (Illus.). 489p. 1984. 140.00 (*3-527-26022-6*, Wiley-VCH) Wiley.

Lubricants & Special Fluids. rev. ed. Vaclav Stepina & Vaclav Vesely. LC 92-30804. (Tribology Ser.: Vol. 22).Tr. of Maziva a Specialni Oleje. xiv, 704p. 1992. 294.00 (*0-444-98674-X*) Elsevier.

Lubricants & Their Applications see Eurotrib, '81: Proceedings of the Third International Tribology Congress, Warsaw

Lubricants for Passenger Car & Diesel Engines. 110p. 1998. pap. 35.00 (*0-7680-0205-2*, SP-1368) Soc Auto Engineers.

Lubricants for Passenger Car & Heavy Duty Diesel Engines. 1997. pap. 75.00 (*0-7680-0073-4*) Soc Auto Engineers.

Lubricating Oils & Greases. C. Broyles. 385p. 1998. 1195.00 (*0-318-04168-5*) Busn Trend.

Lubricating Polymer Surfaces. Yoshito Idaka & Yoshikimi Uyama. LC 93-60803. 175p. 1993. pap. 59.95 (*1-56676-013-5*) Technomic.

Lubrication. (Principles of Steam Generation Ser.: Module 4). (Illus.). 90p. 1982. spiral bd. 25.00 (*0-87683-254-0*); write for info. (*0-87683-275-3*) GP Courseware.

Lubrication. Multimedia Development Services Staff. (Plant Fundamentals Ser.: Vol. XI, Module III). (Illus.). 1995. teacher ed. 49.95 (*1-57431-076-3*); student ed. 30.00 (*1-57431-036-4*) Tech Trng Systs.

Lubrication: A Tribology Handbook. Michael J. Neale. 148p. 1993. 39.00 (*1-56091-392-4*, R-130) Soc Auto Engineers.

***Lubrication & Reliability Handbook.** M. J. Neale. (Illus.). 224p. 2000. 59.95 (*0-7506-7364-8*, Newnes) Buttrwrth-Heinemann.

***Lubrication at the Frontier: The Role of the Interface & Surface Layers in the Thin Film & Boundary Regime: Proceedings of the 25th Leeds-Lyon Symposium on Tribology: Held in the Institut National des Science Appliqubees des Lyon, France, 8th-11th September, 1998.** Leeds-Lyon Symposium on Tribology Staff et al. LC 99-34741. (Tribology Ser.). 908p. 1999. 276.50 (*0-444-50267-X*) Elsevier.

Lubrication Engineers Manual. 2nd ed. AISE Staff. LC 96-85885. (Illus.). 650p. 1996. text 245.00 (*0-930767-01-2*) Assn Iron & Steel.

Lubrication for Industry. Kenneth E. Bannister. 200p. 1996. text 32.95 (*0-8311-3061-X*) Indus Pr.

Lubrication Fundamentals. J. George Wills. (Mechanical Engineering Ser.: Vol. 3). (Illus.). 480p. 1980. text 110.00 (*0-8247-6976-7*) Dekker.

Lubrication in Practice. 2nd ed. W. L. Robertson. (Mechanical Engineering Ser.: Vol. 27). (Illus.). 240p. 1984. text 125.00 (*0-8247-7204-0*) Dekker.

Lubrication of Enclosed Gear Drives. J. L. Draper. (Technical Papers: Vol. P125). (Illus.). 9p. 1935. pap. text 30.00 (*1-55589-354-6*) AGMA.

Lubrication of Involute Gearing. B. W. Kelley & A. J. Lemanski. (Technical Papers: Vol. P254.28). (Illus.). 17p. (Orig.). 1967. pap. text 30.00 incl. audio compact disk (*1-55589-356-2*) AGMA.

Lubrication Recommendations Guide, 1990. 48p. 1990. 7.00 (*0-13-130618-9*, H M Gousha) Prntice Hall Bks.

Lubrication Recommendations Wall Chart, 1990. 12p. 1990. 5.50 (*0-13-130600-6*, H M Gousha) Prntice Hall Bks.

Lubrication Techniques. Tel-A-Train, Inc. Staff. 1987. student ed. 6.50 (*1-56355-037-7*) Tel-A-Train.

Lubrication Technology for Advanced Engines: An Assessment of Future Needs. (CRTD Ser.: Vol. 26). 104p. 1993. write for info. (*0-7918-0689-8*, 100352) ASME.

Luby's Story: Good Food from Good People. Steve Barnhill. Ed. by Alice Evett. LC 88-51273. (Illus.). xvi, 108p. (Orig.). 1989. pap. 6.95 (*0-934955-12-3*) Watercress Pr.

Luc Besson. Hayward. (Illus.). 160p. 1998. pap. 19.95 (*0-7190-5076-6*, Pub. by Manchester Univ Pr); text 69.95 (*0-7190-5075-8*, Pub. by Manchester Univ Pr) St Martin.

Luc le theologien: Vingt-cinq ans de recherches (1950-1975) see Luke the Theologian: Thirty-Three Years of Research (1950-1983)

Luc Tuymans. Ulrich Loock. (Contemporary Artists Ser.). (Illus.). 160p. 1996. pap. 29.95 (*0-7148-3551-X*, Pub. by Phaidon Press) Phaidon Pr.

Luca & Andrea Della Robbia. Maud Crutwell. LC 79-155625. (Illus.). reprint ed. 39.50 (*0-404-01869-6*) AMS Pr.

Luca di Tomme: A Sienese Fourteenth-Century Painter. Sherwood A. Fehm, Jr. LC 83-20400. (Illus.). 234p. 1986. text 62.00 (*0-8093-0941-6*) S Ill U Pr.

Luca Marenzio: Complete Five Voice Madrigals, 6 vols. John Steele. Incl. Vol. I. 246p. 1996. pap. 25.00 (*1-888471-08-5*); Vol. II. 268p. 1996. pap. 25.00 (*1-888471-09-3*); Vol. III. 268p. 1996. pap. 25.00 (*1-888471-10-7*); Vol. IV. 268p. 1996. pap. 25.00 (*1-888471-11-5*); Vol. V. 268p. 1996. pap. 25.00 (*1-888471-12-3*); Vol. VI. 268p. 1996. pap. 25.00 (*1-888471-13-1*); (Renaissance Voices). 149.70 (*1-888471-07-7*) Gaudia Mus & Arts.

Luca Marenzio: The Complete Four Voice Madrigals. John Steele. (Renaissance Voices Ser.). 256p. 1995. pap. 25.00 (*1-888471-06-9*) Gaudia Mus & Arts.

Luca Marenzio & the Italian Madrigal, 1577-1593, 2 vols., 1. James M. Chater. LC 81-13095. (Studies in British Musicology). 273p. reprint ed. pap. 84.70 (*0-8357-1255-9*, 207025900001) Bks Demand.

Luca Marenzio & the Italian Madrigal, 1577-1593, 2 vols., 2. James M. Chater. LC 81-13095. (Studies in British Musicology). 243p. reprint ed. pap. 75.40 (*0-8357-1256-7*, 207025900002) Bks Demand.

Luca Signorelli. Antonio Paolucci. Tr. by Lisa C. Pelletti from ITA. (Library of Great Masters). (Illus.). 80p. (Orig.). 1990. pap. 12.99 (*1-878351-12-5*) Riverside NY.

Luca Signorelli. Antonio Paolucci. (Grandes Maestros del Arte Ser.). (SPA., Illus.). 80p. (Orig.). 1993. pap. 12.99 (*1-878351-31-1*) Riverside NY.

Luca Signorelli. Maud Cruttwell. LC 75-131677. (Illus.). xi, 144p. 1972. reprint ed. 59.00 (*0-403-00912-X*) Scholarly.

Luca Signorelli: The San Brizio Chapel, Orvieto. Jonathan B. Riess. LC 93-21668. (Great Fresco Cycles of the Renaissance Ser.). (Illus.). 104p. 1995. 25.00 (*0-8076-1312-6*) Braziller.

Lucadia Pease & the Governor. Ed. by Katherine Hart & Elizabeth Kemp. (Illus.). 350p. 1974. 20.00 (*0-88426-037-2*) Encino Pr.

Lucado 3 in 1: In the Eye of the Storm, He Still Moves Stones, a Gentle Thunder. Max Lucado. 1998. 16.99 (*0-8499-1552-X*) Word Pub.

***Lucado 3 in 1: In the Grip of Grace/When God Whispers Your Name/Applause of Heaven.** Max Lucado. 2000. 16.99 (*0-8499-1664-X*) Tommy Nelson.

Lucan: De Bello Civili I. Ed. by R. Getty. (Bristol Latin Texts Ser.). (LAT.). 224p. 1992. pap. 25.95 (*1-85399-357-3*, Pub. by Brist Class Pr) Focus Pub-R Pullins.

Lucan: De Bello Civili VII. Ed. by O. A. Dilke. (Bristol Latin Texts Ser.). (LAT.). 192p. 1978. reprint ed. 25.95 (*0-906515-04-1*, Pub. by Brist Class Pr) Focus Pub-R Pullins.

Lucan: Spectacle & Engagement. Matthew Leigh. (Oxford Classical Monographs). 376p. 1997. text 85.00 (*0-19-815067-9*) OUP.

Lucan No. VIII: Civil War. Lucan. Ed. by R. Mayer. (Classical Texts Ser.). 1981. 59.99 (*0-85668-155-5*, Pub. by Aris & Phillips) David Brown.

Lucan VIII: Civil War. Lucan. Ed. by R. Mayer. (Classical Texts Ser.). 1981. pap. 28.00 (*0-85668-176-8*, Pub. by Aris & Phillips) David Brown.

Lucan Bellum Civile Nine. David P. Kubiak. (Latin Commentaries Ser.). 128p. (Orig.). (C). 1985. pap. text 7.00 (*0-929524-43-8*) Bryn Mawr Commentaries.

Lucani Bk. X: De Bello Civili. Shackleton Bailey. (LAT.). 1997. 95.00 (*3-519-11502-6*, T1502, Pub. by B G Teubner) U of Mich Pr.

Lucan's Civil War. Tr. by P. F. Widdows. LC 87-45586. (Illus.). 320p. 1988. 52.95 (*0-253-31399-6*) Ind U Pr.

Lucanus - Concordantia in Lucanum. Ed. by Manfred Wacht. (Alpha-Omega, Reihe A Ser.: Bd. CXXV). 891p. 1992. write for info. (*3-487-09494-0*) G Olms Pubs.

Lucas. (Comentario Biblico Mundo Hispano Ser.: Vol. 16).Tr. of Luke. (SPA.). pap. 10.99 (*0-311-03116-1*, Edit Mundo) Casa Bautista.

Lucas. Paul N. Benware. (Comentario Biblico Portavoz Ser.). Orig. Title: Luke (Everyman's Bible Commentary). (SPA.). 152p. 1994. pap. 6.99 (*0-8254-1059-2*, Edit Portavoz) Kregel.

Lucas. Alistair Highet. LC 98-50907. 2001. write for info. (*1-56846-127-5*) Creative Co.

Lucas: El Evangelio para Todos, Vol. 3. Frank Stagg.Tr. of Studies in the Gospel of Luke. (SPA.). 144p. 1967. pap. 8.99 (*0-311-04328-3*) Baptist Spanish.

Lucas: The Loner. Cindy Gerard. (Desire Ser.). 1996. per. 3.25 (*0-373-05975-2*, 1-05975-7) Silhouette.

Lucas Afuera, Lucas Adentro (Lucas Outside, Lucas Inside) Carmen Lenero. (SPA., Illus.). (J). (gr. 5-6). 1997. pap. 5.99 (*968-16-5434-X*, Pub. by Fondo) Continental Bk.

Lucas & Company. 1990. 3.95 (*0-9627894-0-2*) LNR Pubns.

Lucas Case & Modern Takings Theory. Carolynne C. White & Gerard G. Alberts. (State Legislative Reports: Vol. 18, No. 9). 3p. 1993. pap. text 15.00 (*1-55516-098-0*, 7302-1809) Natl Conf State Legis.

Lucas Cranach. Alexander Stepanov. (Great Painters Ser.). (Illus.). 176p. 1997. 40.00 (*1-85995-266-6*) Parkstone Pr.

Lucas Fishbone. Gregory Maguire. LC 89-39772. (Illus.). 48p. (J). (gr. k-3). 1990. 14.95 (*0-06-024089-X*) HarpC Child Bks.

***Lucas Gets Hurt.** Katherine Applegate. (Making Out Ser.: No. 7). 192p. (YA). (gr. 7-12). 1998. mass mkt. 3.99 (*0-380-80217-1*, Avon Bks) Morrow Avon.

Lucas (Luke) Anonimo. (Biblia de Bosquejos y Sermones (The Preacher's Outline & Sermon Bible) Ser.). (SPA.). 448p. 1998. pap. 24.99 (*0-8254-1009-6*, Edit Portavoz) Kregel.

Lucas (Luke) Holman & Broadman Staff. 100p. 1999. pap. 5.95 (*0-8054-9358-1*) Broadman.

Lucas Samaras: Cubes, Pragmata & Trapezoids. Text by Jan Avgikos. (Illus.). 48p. (Orig.). 1994. pap. write for info. (*1-878283-48-0*) PaceWildenstein.

Lucas Samaras: Gold. Barbara Rose. LC 98-88819. (Illus.). 64p. 1998. pap. write for info. (*1-878283-81-2*) PaceWildenstein.

An Asterisk (*) at the beginning of an entry indicates that the title is appearing for the first time.

Lucas Samaras: Objects & Subjects, 1969-1986. Thomas McEvilley et al. (Illus.). 224p. 1988. 65.00 (*0-89659-803-9*) Abbeville Pr.

Lucas Samaras: Pastels. Mildred Glimcher. LC 93-83248. (Illus.). 48p. (Orig.). 1993. pap. write for info. (*1-878283-29-4*) PaceWildenstein.

Lucas Samaras: Photo-Transformations. limited ed. University Art Museum Staff. (Illus.). 64p. (Orig.). (C). 1976. pap. text 30.00 (*0-685-46240-4*) CA St U LB Art.

Lucas Samaras: Sketches, Drawings, Doodles, & Plans. limited ed. Ed. by Jack Glenn & Constance W. Glenn. (Reproduction Sketchbook Ser.). (Illus.). 80p. 1987. 300.00 (*0-8109-4995-4*) Abrams.

Lucas vs. the Green Machine: Landmark Supreme Court Property Rights Decision by the Man Who Won It Against the Odds. David Lucas. Ed. by Lorna Bolkey et al. LC 95-12090. (Illus.). 319p. (Orig.). 1995. pap. 16.95 (*1-57090-011-6*) Alexander Dist.

Lucas y Virginia (Benjamin & Tulip) Rosemary Wells. (SPA.). (J). (gr. k-1). pap. 5.95 (*0-88272-321-9*) Santillana.

Lucasfilm Alien Chronicles: Exodus. Julia Ecklar. (Orig.). 1997. mass mkt. 5.99 (*0-614-27728-0*) Blvd Books.

Lucasfilm's Alien Chronicles: The Golden One. Deborah Chester. (Lucasfilm Alien Chronicles Bk.: No. I). 1997. mass mkt. 5.99 (*1-57297-278-5*) Blvd Books.

Lucasfilm's Alien Chronicles Book Bk. III: The Crystal Eye. Deborah Chester. 1999. mass mkt. 6.99 (*0-441-00635-3*) Ace Bks.

Lucasta Smirk Goes Beserk! large type ed. David Tinkler. (Illus.). (J). 1997. 16.95 (*0-7451-5493-X*, Galaxy Child Lrg Print) Chivers N Amer.

Lucca, 1430-1494: The Reconstruction of an Italian City-Republic. M. E. Bratchel. (Illus.). 358p. 1995. text 85.00 (*0-19-820484-1*) OUP.

Luce d'Inverno: English & Italian Poetry. Maria Mazziotti. Tr. by Nina Scammacca & Nat Scammacca.Tr. of Winter Light. (Illus.). 67p. 1988. 15.00 (*0-89304-525-X*); pap. 7.50 (*0-89304-524-1*) Cross-Cultrl NY.

Luce Irigaray: Philosophy in the Feminine. Margaret Whitford. 304p. (C). 1991. pap. 22.99 (*0-415-05969-0*, A5481) Routledge.

Lucero Isaac: Night People's Theater. Intro. by Gabriel Garcia Marquez. LC 91-65620. (Illus.). 24p. 1991. pap. 10.00 (*0-935037-41-1*) G Peters Gallery.

Luceros de Amor. Ana T. Merced de Mendez. (Illus.). 100p. 1990. write for info. (*0-9627442-0-4*) A T Merced de Mendez.

Luces & la Civilization: The Social Reforms of Mariano Galvez see Applied Enlightenment: Nineteenth Century Liberalism, 1800-1839

Luces de Bohemia. Ramon Del Valle-Inclan. Ed. by Alonso Zamora Vicente. (Nueva Austral Ser.: Vol. 1). (SPA.). 1991. pap. text 24.95 (*84-239-1801-7*) Elliots Bks.

Luces de Candilejas, los Espectaculos en Espana, 1898-1936. Andres Ameros. (Nueva Austral Ser.: No. 196). (SPA.). 1991. pap. text 24.95 (*84-239-1996-X*) Elliots Bks.

Luces Encendidas para Cada Dia: Lights for Each Day. Miguel Limardo. 376p. 1985. reprint ed. 11.99 (*0-311-40038-8*) Casa Bautista.

Luces y Tiempos (Lights & Time) Lazaro Blanco. (SPA., Illus.). 64p. 1987. pap. 8.99 (*968-16-2639-7*, Pub. by Fondo) Continental Bk.

Lucet Braiding: Variations on a Renaissance Cord. Elaine Fuller. (Illus.). 32p. 1998. pap. 12.00 (*1-891656-06-6*, LE60) Lacis Pubns.

Luch Sveta see Ray of Light: Instructions in Piety & the State of the World at the End of Time

Lucha. Constance Urdang. LC 86-20765. 112p. (Orig.). 1986. pap. 9.95 (*0-918273-23-4*) Coffee Hse.

Lucha: The Struggles of Latin American Women. Ed. by Connie Weil. (Minnesota Latin American Ser.). (Illus.). 200p. (Orig.). 1988. pap. text 12.95 (*0-910235-32-5*) Prisma Bks.

*__Lucha con el Angel.__ Manuel De la Puebla. (SPA.). 54p. 1998. lib. bdg. 6.00 (*1-881708-19-5*) Edcnes Mairena.

Lucha Contra Principados Demoniacos. Rita Cabeza.Tr. of Fight Demonic Principalities. (SPA.). 99p. 1995. 3.50 (*1-56063-997-0*, 550170) Editorial Unilit.

Lucha de los Chicanos por la Liberacion: La Posicion del Portido Comunista, 20th National Convention. Communist Party Convention Staff.Tr. of Toward Chicano Liberation: the Communist Party Position. (SPA.). 24p. 1972. pap. 0.40 (*0-87898-092-X*) New Outlook.

Lucha Justa para Toda la Familia. Fran Schmidt & Alice Friedman. Ed. by Yvonne W. Sepulveda. Tr. by Jorge Larrazabal & Mariana Larrazabal. (ENG & SPA., Illus.). 32p. (Orig.). 1994. pap. text 12.95 (*1-878227-25-4*) Peace Educ.

Lucha Maya see Mayan Struggle: Portrait of a Guatemalan People in Danger

Lucha Obrera de Cuba. Efren Naranjo. LC 91-75690. (Coleccion Cuba y sus Jueces). (SPA.). 80p. (Orig.). 1992. pap. 9.95 (*0-89729-621-4*) Ediciones.

Lucha Por El Sufragio Femenino En Puerto Rico, 1896-1935. Barcelo Miller, Maria de F. LC 97-60512. write for info. (*0-929157-45-1*) Ediciones Huracan.

Luchando por el Amor: Daddy's Choice. Doreen O. Malek. (Deseo Ser.). (SPA.). 1996. per. 3.50 (*0-373-35157-7*, 1-35157-6) Harlequin Bks.

Luchar por Vivir. Irving Sanchez. (SPA.). 1987. pap. 7.95 (*0-317-02856-1*) Phoenix Soc.

Luchevaia Diagnostika Endofitnogo Raka Zheludka see Radiodiagnosis of Endophytic Gastric Cancer

Luchino Visconti. Tonetti. 1998. pap. 20.00 (*0-8057-1641-6*) Mac Lib Ref.

Luchino Visconti: Three Screenplays. Luchino Visconti. LC 82-49273. (Cinema Classics Ser.). 313p. 1985. lib. bdg. 11.00 (*0-8240-5784-8*) Garland.

Luchino Visconti: Two Screenplays. Luchino Visconti. LC 82-49279. (Cinema Classics Ser.). 184p. 1985. lib. bdg. 11.00 (*0-8240-5785-6*) Garland.

Luchon/Andorre/Perpignan Map. 1997. 6.95 (*2-06-700086-1*, 86) Michelin.

Luchow's German Cookbook. Jan Mitchell. Date not set. lib. bdg. 21.95 (*0-8488-1752-4*) Amereon Ltd.

Luchow's German Cookbook. Leonard J. Mitchell. 1994. lib. bdg. 21.95 (*1-56849-510-2*) Buccaneer Bks.

Lucia Ames Mead (1856-1936) & the American Peace Movement. John M. Craig. LC 89-12887. (Studies in World Peace: Vol. 4). 232p. 1990. lib. bdg. 89.95 (*0-88946-094-9*) E Mellen.

Lucia di Lammermoor: Vocal Score. G. Donizetti. (ENG & ITA.). 256p. 1986. pap. 24.95 (*0-7935-2862-3*, 50337150) H Leonard.

Lucia di Lammermoor in Full Score. Gaetano Donizetti. 384p. 1992. reprint ed. pap. text 23.95 (*0-486-27113-7*) Dover.

Lucia di Lammermoor Libretto. G. Donizetti. (ENG & ITA.). 36p. 1986. pap. 4.95 (*0-7935-2829-1*, 50340290) H Leonard.

Lucia in London. E. F. Benson. LC 98-37616. 232p. 1999. pap. 11.95 (*1-55921-277-2*) Moyer Bell.

Lucian: A Selection. Lucian. Ed. by M. C. McLeod. (Classical Texts Ser.). 320p. (C). 1991. pap. 32.00 (*0-85668-416-3*, Pub. by Aris & Phillips) David Brown.

Lucian: A Selection. M. D. Lucian. Ed. by M. C. McLeod. (Classical Texts Ser.). 320p. (C). 1991. 59.99 (*0-85668-415-5*, Pub. by Aris & Phillips) David Brown.

Lucian: Satirical Sketches. Paul Turner. LC 89-26834. 320p. 1990. 31.95 (*0-253-36097-8*); pap. 6.95 (*0-253-20581-6*, MB-581) Ind U Pr.

Lucian: Selections. Ed. by K. C. Sidwell. (GRE.). 150p. 1986. pap. 18.95 (*0-906515-36-X*, Pub. by Brist Class Pr) Focus Pub-R Pullins.

Lucian & His Influence in Europe. Christopher Robinson. LC 79-16580. (Illus.). 258p. reprint ed. pap. 80.00 (*0-7837-3758-0*, 204357500010) Bks Demand.

Lucian & the Latins: Humor & Humanism in the Early Renaissance. David Marsh. LC 98-25390. (Recentiores Ser.). 248p. 1998. text 49.50 (*0-472-10846-8*, 10846) U of Mich Pr.

Lucian Blaga - Ein Rumanischer Dichter und die Deutsche Literatur. Mircea Vaida-Voevod. (GER.). 1992. write for info. (*3-487-09260-3*) G Olms Pubs.

*__Lucian Freud, Etchings from the PaineWebber Art Collection.__ Scott Willcox & David Cohen. LC 98-75233. (Illus.). 1999. write for info. (*0-930606-88-4*) Yale Ctr Brit Art.

Lucian Freud Nudes. Lucian Freud. 1998. write for info. (*0-679-45290-7*) Random.

Lucian Freud Paintings. Robert Hughes. LC 89-51234. (Illus.). 136p. 1997. reprint ed. pap. 34.95 (*0-500-27535-1*, Pub. by Thames Hudson) Norton.

Lucian of Samosata in the Two Hesperias: An Essay in Literary & Cultural Translation. Michael Zappala. 1990. 49.50 (*0-916379-71-X*) Scripta.

Lucian und Menipp. Rudolf Helm. 392p. 1967. reprint ed. write for info. (*0-318-70933-3*) G Olms Pubs.

Lucian Vera Historia. C. S. Jerram. (Illus.). 104p. 1991. reprint ed. 15.00 (*0-86516-240-9*) Bolchazy-Carducci.

Luciana Miotto. Henri E. Ciriani. 1998. pap. 7.99 (*88-86502-88-5*, Pub. by Canal & Stamperia) Antique Collect.

Luciani. Ed. by Steindl. (GRE.). 1970. 16.95 (*3-322-00227-6*, T1988, Pub. by B G Teubner) U of Mich Pr.

Luciani: Piscator. Itzkowitz. (GRE.). 1992. pap. 43.50 (*3-519-01515-3*, T1515, Pub. by B G Teubner) U of Mich Pr.

Luciano Berio: Two Interviews. Luciano Berio et al. Ed. & Tr. by David Osmond-Smith from ITA. LC 84-12346. (Illus.). 192p. 1989. reprint ed. pap. 12.95 (*0-7145-2898-6*) M Boyars Pubs.

Luciano Pavarotti: The Myth of the Tenor. Jurgen Kesting. Tr. by Susan H. Ray. LC 96-14972. 208p. 1996. text 26.95 (*1-55553-282-9*) NE U Pr.

Luciano Story. Sid Feder & Joachim Joesten. 1999. lib. bdg. 26.95 (*1-56723-202-7*) Yestermorrow.

Luciano Story. Sid Feder & Joachim Joesten. 336p. 1994. reprint ed. pap. 14.95 (*0-306-80592-8*) Da Capo.

Luciano's Luck see Jack Higgins Omnibus

Luciano's Luck. Jack Higgins. Ed. by Julie Rubenstein. 256p. 1992. reprint ed. mass mkt. 5.50 (*0-671-67618-0*) PB.

Lucian's Atticism: The Morphology of the Verb. R. J. Deferrari. 81p. 1916. reprint ed. lib. bdg. 25.00 (*0-685-13370-2*, Pub. by AM Hakkert) Coronet Bks.

Lucian's Satire. rev. ed. Jennifer Hall. Ed. by W. R. Connor. LC 80-2652. (Monographs in Classical Studies). 1981. lib. bdg. 100.95 (*0-405-14039-8*) Ayer.

Lucian's Science Fiction Novel, True Histories: Interpretation & Commentary. Aristoula Georgiadou & David H. Larmour. LC 98-11432. (Mnemosyne, Bibliotheca Classica Batava Ser.). 220p. 1998. 98.50 (*90-04-10667-7*) Brill Academic Pubs.

Lucianus: Index et Rerum et Verborum. C. Jacobitz. xii, 744p. 1966. reprint ed. write for info. (*0-318-72046-9*) G Olms Pubs.

Lucia's Little Houses: A Portfolio of Small-House Designs by Maine Architect Robert W. Knight. 3rd rev. ed. Robert W. Knight. Ed. by Lucia Knight. (Illus.). 60p. (Orig.). 1997. pap. 15.00 (*0-9656464-1-6*) Lucias Little Hses.

Lucia's Progress. E. F. Benson. LC 98-53775. 234p. 2000. pap. 11.95 (*1-55921-233-0*) Moyer Bell.

Lucid Dreaming. Stephen LaBerge. 304p. 1986. mass mkt. 5.95 (*0-345-33355-1*) Ballantine Pub Grp.

Lucid Dreaming: The Paradox of Consciousness During Sleep. Celia Green & Charles McCreery. LC 93-50637. 224p. (C). (gr. 13). 1994. pap. 18.99 (*0-415-11239-7*, B4223) Routledge.

Lucid Dreaming Kit: How to Awaken Within, Control & Use Your Dreams. Paul Devereux & Charla Devereux. LC 98-86146. (Illus.). 128p. 1998. pap. 22.95 (*1-885203-66-7*) Jrny Editions.

Lucid Dreams. Richard Doerflor. 240p. 1998. mass mkt. 5.99 (*1-880090-68-6*) Galde Pr.

Lucid Dreams in 30 Days: The Creative Sleep Program. Keith Harary & Pamela Weintraub. 1989. pap. 5.95 (*0-318-42740-0*); pap. 8.95 (*0-312-03389-3*) St Martin.

Lucid Dreams in 30 Days: The Creative Sleep Program. Keith Harary & Pamela Weintraub. LC 98-53743. 1999. pap. 9.95 (*0-312-19988-0*) St Martin.

Lucid Interval: Subjective Writing & Madness in History. George MacLennan. 232p. 1992. 38.50 (*0-8386-3505-9*) Fairleigh Dickinson.

Lucid Stars. Andrea Barrett. 336p. 1997. pap. 12.95 (*0-385-31943-6*, Delta Trade) Dell.

*__Lucid Suitcase.__ Diane Wald. 64p. 1999. pap. 10.95 (*1-888996-16-1*, Red Hen Press) Valentine CA.

Lucid Waking: Mindfulness & the Spiritual Potential of Humanity. Georg Feuerstein. LC 97-7875. 192p. 1997. 22.95 (*0-89281-613-9*) Inner Tradit.

Lucid Wind. LC 96-95078. (Illus.). 87p. (Orig.). 1996. pap. 12.00 (*0-9655481-4-7*) J Kashubeck.

Lucida Intervalla: Containing Divers Miscellaneous Poems, Written at Finsbury & Bethlem by the Doctors Patient Extraordinary. James Carkesse. LC 92-25461. (Augustan Reprints Ser.: Nos. 195-196). 1979. reprint ed. 21.50 (*0-404-70195-7*, PR339) AMS Pr.

Lucida Locura del Dr. Laban. Monica Goldemberg.Tr. of Apparent Insanity of Dr. Laban. (SPA.). 1991. pap. 3.50 (*1-56063-061-2*, 497707) Editorial Unilit.

Lucidario in Musica di Alcune oppenioni Antiche et Moderne. fac. ed. Pietro Aaron. (Monuments of Music & Music Literature in Facsimile Ser., Series II: Vol. 68). (Illus.). 1978. lib. bdg. 35.00 (*0-8450-2268-7*) Broude.

"Lucidarium" of Marchetto of Padua: A Critical Edition, Translation & Commentary. Jan Herlinger. LC 83-6895. 584p. (C). 1985. lib. bdg. 60.00 (*0-226-32762-0*) U Ch Pr.

Lucidarius. Deutschen Akademie der Wissenschaften Staff & Felix Heidlauf. (Deutsche Texte des Mittelalters Ser.: Band XXVIII). (GER.). xviii, 98p. write for info. (*3-296-17228-9*, Pub. by Weidmann) Lubrecht & Cramer.

Lucie Babbidge's House. Sylvia Cassedy. 256p. (J). 1993. pap. 4.50 (*0-380-71812-X*, Avon Bks) Morrow Avon.

Lucie Hupp's Gardening Without Tears: The Diary of a Fancy Dirt Gardener. Lucie Hupp. Ed. by James G. Hupp et al. LC 98-94094. (Illus.). 357p. 1998. pap. 27.50 (*0-9668032-0-5*) J G Hupp.

Lucie Rie - Hans Cooper: Potters in Parallel. Ed. by Margot Coatts. (Illus.). 161p. 1997. 55.00 (*1-889250-07-4*) Gentle Br.

Lucie Rie - Hans Coper. J. Stewart Johnson. (Illus.). 1994. pap. 9.95 (*0-614-07043-0*) Metro Mus Art.

Lucien et la Pensee Religieuse de Son Temps. Ed. by Leonardo Taran. (Ancient Greek Literature Ser.). 562p. 1988. lib. bdg. 25.00 (*0-8240-7753-9*) Garland.

Lucien Leuwen, 2 vols. Stendhal, pseud. 1973. write for info. (*0-318-63481-3*) Fr & Eur.

Lucien Leuwen. Stendhal, pseud. (FRE.). 414p. 1982. pap. 13.95 (*0-7859-1645-8*, 2080703501) Fr & Eur.

Lucien Leuwen. unabridged ed. Stendhal, pseud. (FRE.). pap. 7.95 (*2-87714-215-9*, Pub. by Bookking Intl) Distribks Inc.

Lucien Leuwen, 2 vols., 1. Stendhal, pseud. (Folio Ser.: Nos. 515 & 516). 1973. 10.95 (*2-07-036515-8*) Schoenhof.

Lucien Leuwen, 2 vols., 2. Stendhal, pseud. (Folio Ser.: Nos. 515 & 516). 1973. 10.95 (*2-07-036516-6*) Schoenhof.

*__Lucien Maxwell: Villain or Visionary.__ Harriet Freiberger. LC 99-10210. (Illus.). 160p. 1999. pap. 14.95 (*0-86534-286-5*) Sunstone Pr.

Lucienne. Jules Romains, pseud. (Folio Ser.: No. 1671). (FRE.). 280p. 1922. 14.95 (*2-07-037671-0*) Schoenhof.

Lucienne - Le Dieu des Corps Quand le Navire: Psyche I, II, III. Jules Romains, pseud. (FRE.). 1985. pap. 18.95 (*0-7859-4228-9*) Fr & Eur.

Lucienne et le Boucher. Marcel Ayme. (FRE.). 348p. 1959. pap. 16.95 (*0-7859-4881-3*) Fr & Eur.

Lucien's Story. Aleksandra Kroh & Lucien Duckstein. LC 96-22214. 80p. 1996. 39.95 (*0-8101-6020-X*, Marlboro); pap. 11.95 (*0-8101-6021-8*, Marlboro) Northwestern U Pr.

Lucifer. 3rd rev. ed. B. R. Hicks. (Illus.). 557p. 1990. pap. 14.95 (*1-58363-056-2*, SW-6603) Christ Gospel.

Lucifer: A Theological Tragedy. George Santayana. LC 75-104561. reprint ed. lib. bdg. 36.00 (*0-8398-1850-5*) Irvington.

Lucifer: The Devil in the Middle Ages. Jeffrey B. Russell. LC 84-45153. (Illus.). 356p. 1986. pap. text 16.95 (*0-8014-9429-X*) Cornell U Pr.

Lucifer at Large. C. John McCole. LC 68-16949. (Essay Index Reprint Ser.). 1977. reprint ed. 19.95 (*0-8369-0643-8*) Ayer.

Lucifer at Large. C. John McCole. LC 68-57457. (Studies in Fiction: No. 34). 1969. reprint ed. lib. bdg. 75.00 (*0-8383-0595-4*) M S G Haskell Hse.

Lucifer Before Sunrise, Vol. 14. Henry Williamson. 1999. pap. text 15.95 (*0-7509-2156-0*) A Sutton.

Lucifer, Bischof von Calaris und das Schisma der Luciferianer. Gustav Kruger. vi, 130p. 1969. reprint ed. write for info. (*0-318-70776-4*) G Olms Pubs.

Lucifer Crusade. Mack Maloney. (Wingman Ser.: No. 3). 432p. 1987. mass mkt. 3.95 (*0-8217-2232-8*, Zebra Kensgtn) Kensgtn Pub Corp.

Lucifer Crusade. Mack Maloney. (Wingman Ser.: No. 3). 416p. 1997. mass mkt. 4.99 (*0-7860-0388-X*, Pinncle Kensgtn) Kensgtn Pub Corp.

Lucifer Destronado. William Schnoebelen & Sharon Schnoebelen. (SPA., Illus.). 352p. 1993. pap. 11.99 (*0-937958-42-5*) Chick Pubns.

Lucifer Dethroned: A True Story. William Schnoebelen & Sharon Schnoebelen. (Illus.). 352p. 1993. pap. 11.99 (*0-937958-41-7*) Chick Pubns.

Lucifer Diary: Story of an Angel. Lewis R. Walton. 441p. (Orig.). 1997. pap. 13.95 (*0-9656834-0-0*) Aralon Pr.

Lucifer Directive. John Land. 1984. mass mkt. 4.95 (*0-8217-3354-0*, Zebra Kensgtn) Kensgtn Pub Corp.

Lucifer in Harness: American Meter, Metaphor & Diction. Edwin S. Fussell. LC 72-4040. 197p. 1973. reprint ed. pap. 61.10 (*0-608-02511-9*, 206315500004) Bks Demand.

Lucifer, Lucifer, How You Have Fallen. John K. Seagrove. LC 95-94599. 204p. (Orig.). 1996. per. 15.00 (*0-9647633-0-3*) Kendall Pubng.

Lucifer Principle: A Scientific Expedition into the Forces of History. Howard Bloom. LC 94-11464. 480p. 1997. reprint ed. pap. 15.00 (*0-87113-664-3*, Atlntc Mnthly) Grove-Atltic.

*__Lucifer Rising.__ Sharon Bowers. 352p. 2000. pap. 16.99 (*0-9677687-2-1*, Pub. by Justice Hse) BkMstrs TX.

*__Lucifer Rising: A Book of Sin, Devil-Worship & Rock-'N'-Roll.__ Gavin Baddeley. 1999. pap. 16.95 (*0-85965-280-7*, Pub. by Plexus) Publishers Group.

Lucifer State: A Novel Approach to Rhetoric. 2nd ed. Trevor Melia & Nova Ryder. (Illus.). 208p. (C). 1994. per. 16.95 (*0-8403-6847-X*, 40305701) Kendall-Hunt.

Lucifer Stationen eines Motivs. Ernst Osterkamp. (Komparatistische Studien: Vol. 9). (C). 1979. 104.60 (*3-11-007804-X*) De Gruyter.

Lucifer Unemployed. Aleksander Wat. Tr. by Lillian Vallee from POL. 123p. 1990. pap. 9.95 (*0-8101-0840-2*) Northwestern U Pr.

Lucifer, with Angels. Evangeline Paterson. 58p. 1994. pap. 11.95 (*1-873790-64-3*) Dufour.

Lucifer's Army: The Power Behind Fortune Telling, Charms & Demons. B. R. Hicks. 241p. 1990. reprint ed. 12.95 (*1-58363-057-0*, SW-6604) Christ Gospel.

Lucifer's Eye. Hugh B. Cave. 1991. pap. 3.95 (*0-8125-1079-8*, Pub. by Tor Bks) St Martin.

Lucifer's Hammer. Larry Niven & Jerry Pournelle. 640p. 1985. mass mkt. 5.95 (*0-449-20813-3*, Crest) Fawcett.

Lucifer's Handbook: A Simplified Critique of Popular Religion. Lee Carter. LC 76-55893. 1977. pap. text 7.95 (*0-918260-01-9*) Acad Assoc.

Lucifer's Lady. large type ed. Claire Tremaine. (Ulverscroft Large Print Ser.). 336p. 1997. 27.99 (*0-7089-3801-9*) Ulverscroft.

*__Lucifer's Legacy: The Meaning of Asymmetry.__ Frank Close. (Illus.). 272p. 2000. 27.50 (*0-19-850380-6*) OUP.

Lucifer's Lexicon. L. A. Rollins. 144p. (Orig.). 1987. pap. text 8.95 (*0-915179-43-1*) Loompanics.

Lucilio. Nicola Terzaghi. 449p. 1979. reprint ed. write for info. (*3-487-06841-9*) G Olms Pubs.

Lucilius: Index Lucilianus. Ed. by Luci Berkowitz & Theodore F. Brunner. xiv, 171p. 1968. 40.00 (*0-318-71974-6*) G Olms Pubs.

Lucilius & Horace: A Study in the Classical Theory of Imitation. George C. Fiske. (University of Wisconsin Studies in Language & Literature: No. 7). 524p. 1966. reprint ed. 83.20 (*0-685-66464-3*, 05101336) G Olms Pubs.

Lucilius & Horace, a Study in Classical Theory of Imitation. George C. Fiske. LC 78-109732. 524p. 1971. reprint ed. lib. bdg. 79.50 (*0-8371-4222-9*, FILH, Greenwood Pr) Greenwood.

Lucilius. Laws of the XII Tables see Remains of Old Latin

Lucille. Arnold Lobel. LC 64-11616. (I Can Read Bks.). (Illus.). 64p. (J). (gr. k-3). 1964. lib. bdg. 12.89 (*0-06-023966-2*) HarpC Child Bks.

Lucille Ball: Pioneer of Comedy. Katherine E. Krohn. (Achievers Ser.). (Illus.). 64p. (J). (gr. 4-8). 1992. lib. bdg. 18.60 (*0-8225-0543-6*, Lerner Publctns) Lerner Pub.

Lucille Clifton Library. (J). 1995. lib. bdg. 101.14 (*0-8050-3074-3*) H Holt & Co.

Lucille Lortel: A Bio-Bibliography, 42. Sam McCready. LC 93-23892. (Bio-Bibliographies in the Performing Arts Ser.: No. 42). 304p. 1993. lib. bdg. 69.50 (*0-313-27605-6*, MUC/, Greenwood Pr) Greenwood.

Lucille Sweats. Kathryn Lasky. LC 99-462101. (Illus.). 32p. (ps up). 2000. 14.95 (*0-517-80037-3*) Crown Pub Group.

Lucille Sweats. Kathryn Lasky. LC 99-462102. (Illus.). 32p. (ps up). 2000. lib. bdg. 16.99 (*0-517-80038-1*) Random Hse Value.

Lucille's Car Care: Everything You Need to Know from under the Hood - By America's Most Trusted Mechanic. Lucille Treganowan & Gina Catanzarite. (Illus.). 272p. (J). 1996. 19.45 (*0-7868-6201-7*, Pub. by Hyperion) Time Warner.

Lucille's Car Care: Everything You Need to Know from under the Hood-by America's Most Trusted Mechanic. Lucille Treganowan & Gina Catanzarite. (Illus.). 272p. (J). 1997. pap. 12.45 (*0-7868-8243-3*, Pub. by Hyperion) Time Warner.

Lucinda Legacy. Robert Mitchell. 281p. (C). 1990. pap. 65.00 (*0-646-03980-6*, Pub. by Boolarong Pubns) St Mut.

Lucinda Marries the Doctor. Elizabeth Seifert. 1974. reprint ed. lib. bdg. 22.95 (*0-88411-029-X*) Amereon Ltd.

Lucinda Parker: Paintings, 1976-1981. Paul Sutinen. (Illus.). 1981. pap. 2.00 (*0-914435-06-X*) Marylhurst Art.

Lucinda Williams - Sweet Old World. Ed. by Milton Okun. pap. 14.95 (*0-89524-744-5*) Cherry Lane.

Lucinderella. Berry Fleming. LC 87-62812. 192p. 1988. 22.00 (*0-933256-70-1*) Second Chance.

L

L

*Lucio Fontana. Sarah Whitfield. (Illus.). 208p. 2000. pap. 35.00 (0-520-22622-4) U CA Pr.
Lucio Fontana: Catalogue Rome, 1998. Ed. by Enrico Crispolti & Rosella Siligato. (Illus.). 375p. 1998. pap. 65.00 (88-435-6521-4) Gingko Press.
Lucio Fontana, 1899-1968: A Retrospective. Erika Billeter. LC 77-88448. (Illus.). 1977. pap. 6.98 (0-89207-010-2) S R Guggenheim.
Lucio Fulci: Beyond the Gates of Hell - A Tribute to the Maestro. 2nd ed. Charles Balun. LC 97-60427. (Illus.). 80p. 1997. reprint ed. pap. 12.95 (1-888214-07-4) Fantasma Bks.
*Lucio Fulci's "Zombie" We Are Going to Eat You! deluxe ed. Photos by Michael Broom & Derek Rook. (Illus.). 120p. 2000. pap. 24.99 (0-9667514-1-8) Blackest Heart.
Lucio Silla. Ed. by Ernest Warburton. (Johann Christian Bach, 1735-1782 The Collected Works). 575p. 1986. text 165.00 (0-8240-6057-1) Garland.
Lucio's Confession. 2nd ed. Maria De Sa-Carnejio. Tr. by Margaret J. Costa from POR. (Decadence Ser.). 121p. 1999. reprint ed. pap. 10.99 (1-873982-80-1, Pub. by Dedalus) Hippocrene Bks.
Lucita Regresa a Oaxaca (Lucita Comes Home to Oaxaca) Robin B. Cano. Tr. by Rafael E. Ricardez. LC 98-24323. (ENG & SPA., Illus.). 32p. (J). (gr. 3-6). 1998. 16.95 (1-56492-111-5) Laredo.
Lucius, Adventures of a Roman Boy. Alfred J. Church. LC 60-16706. (YA). (gr. 7-11). 1969. 22.00 (0-8196-0108-X) Biblo.
Lucius Annaeus Seneca: A Concordance to the Epigrams Attributed to Seneca the Younger. Lucius Annaeus Seneca. Ed. by Christopher J. Reagan. (Alpha-Omega, Reihe A Ser.: No. XXVII). vi, 118p. 1972. 28.87 (3-487-04493-5) G Olms Pubs.
Lucius Annaeus Seneca - Opera Philosophica: Index Verborum, Listes de Frequence, Releves Grammaticaux, 2 vols., Set. Lucius Annaeus Seneca. Ed. by Louis Delatte et al. (Alpha-Omega, Reihe A Ser.: Bd. XLI). 1042p. 1981. write for info. (3-487-07074-X) G Olms Pubs.
Lucius B. Swift: A Biography. William D. Foulke. LC 77-164600. (Select Bibliographies Reprint Ser.). 1977. reprint ed. 19.95 (0-8369-5884-5) Ayer.
Lucius Cary. Kurt Weber. LC 41-2183. reprint ed. 22.50 (0-404-06887-1) AMS Pr.
Lucius Chittenden's Journey to "The Inside of the Earth" Lucius E. Chittenden. (Occasional Papers: No. 17). (Illus.). 87p. 1995. pap. text 7.50 (0-944277-31-4) U VT Ctr Rsch VT.
Lucius Junius Brutus. Nathaniel Lee. Ed. by John Loftis. LC 67-12644. (Regents Restoration Drama Ser.). xxiv, 107p. 1967. pap. text 8.95 (0-8032-5362-1) U of Nebr Pr.
Lucius Lyon: An Eminently Useful Citizen. Kit Lane. LC 91-60196. (Illus.). 352p. 1991. 19.50 (1-877703-21-4) Pavilion Pr.
Lucius Q. C. Lamar: His Life, Times & Speeches, 1825-1893. Edward Mayes. LC 70-173065. reprint ed. 115.00 (0-404-04613-4) AMS Pr.
Lucius Q. C. Lamar, Secession & Reunion. Wirt A. Cate. (History - United States Ser.). 594p. 1993. reprint ed. lib. bdg. 99.00 (0-7812-4907-4) Rprt Serv.
Lucius, the First Christian King of Britain: A Tragedy. Delariviere Manley. LC 92-24018. (Augustan Reprints Ser.: Nos. 253-254). 1989. reprint ed. 21.50 (0-404-70253-8) AMS Pr.
Luck. Max Brand. LC 96-37391. ix, 204p. 1997. text 30.00 (0-8032-1277-1) U of Nebr Pr.
Luck. Mark Dunster. 15p. (Orig.). 1987. pap. 4.00 (0-89642-147-3) Linden Pubs.
*Luck. Eric Martin. 288p. 2000. 23.95 (0-393-04912-4) Norton.
Luck. John Perreault. 7.00 (0-686-09743-2); pap. 3.50 (0-686-09744-0) Kulchur Foun.
Luck. deluxe limited ed. Lex Runciman. 72p. 1981. pap. 12.00 (0-937669-02-4) Owl Creek Pr.
*Luck. large type ed. Max Brand. LC 99-30781. 1999. 20.95 (1-57490-196-6, Sagebrush LP West) T T Beeler.
Luck. Mary Arden. LC 72-4425. (Short Story Index Reprint Ser.). 1977. reprint ed. 21.95 (0-8369-4167-5) Ayer.
Luck: A Secular Faith. Wayne E. Oates. LC 94-19996. 128p. (Orig.). 1995. pap. 13.95 (0-664-25536-1) Westminster John Knox.
Luck! How to Get It & Keep It! James Sasse. LC 98-29528. (Illus.). 124p. (J). (gr. 4-7). 1998. pap. 4.95 (1-901881-12-1, Pub. by Element MA) Penguin Putnam.
Luck: The Brilliant Randomness of Everyday Life. Nicholas Rescher. LC 95-17421. 237p. 1995. 19.00 (0-374-19428-9) FS&G.
Luck Alone Is Not Enough see Gluck Allein Genugt Nicht: Eines Mannes Odyssee in Die Freiheit
Luck Alone Is Not Enough: From P. O. W. to P. O. G. I. rev. ed. Hans B. Thielemann. Ed. by Jan C. Thielemann & Hanna Bayer. (From Metropolis to Hick-Town, U. S. A. Ser.: Vol. 1). (Illus.). 341p. 1999. pap. 18.95 (1-890634-05-0) Hugelwilhelm Pub.
Luck & Chutzpah, Against All Odds. Hans G. Kahn. 264p. 1997. 19.95 (965-229-159-5) Gefen Bks.
Luck & Lucifer. Carolyn J. Griffin. (Lyrics on Matters Relating to Ser.). 10p. 1985. 8.00 (1-929388-07-1) Griffin Pubg Co Inc.
Luck Business: The Devastating Consequences of America's Gambling Explosion. Robert Goodman. LC 95-17929. 220p. 1995. 22.50 (0-02-912483-2) Free Pr.
*Luck Doesn't Happen by Chance. Claire Doyle Beland. 1999. pap. 12.95 (1-886940-05-3) Ozark Mountn.
Luck Family: Genealogical Findings. Mary Inglis-Sims. 64p. 1979. pap. 8.00 (0-930595-06-8) Sims Pub.
Luck Follows Me. Laurie Lawlor. (Heartland Ser.: No. 3). 176p. (J). (gr. 3-6). 1996. per. 3.99 (0-671-53718-0) PB.
Luck Follows Me. Laurie Lawlor. (Heartland Ser.). 1996. 9.09 (0-606-10862-9, Pub. by Turtleback) Demco.
Luck in the Head. M. John Harrison & Ian Miller. (Illus.). 80p. (Orig.). 1993. pap. 11.95 (1-878574-46-9) Dark Horse Comics.
Luck in the Shadows. Lynn Flewelling. (Nightrunner Ser.: Bk. 1). 496p. 1996. mass mkt. 6.50 (0-553-57542-2) Bantam.
Luck Is Where You Find It. large type ed. Amy Sadler. (Linford Western Library). 256p. 1996. pap. 16.99 (0-7089-7887-8) Ulverscroft.
*Luck of Barry Lyndon: A Romance of the Last Century. William Makepeace Thackeray. Ed. by Edgar F. Harden. LC 99-21755. (Thackeray Edition Ser.). 256p. 1999. text 75.00 (0-472-11042-X, 11042) U of Mich Pr.
Luck of Charlie Spinoza. B. E. Levine. 265p. (Orig.). 1995. pap. 12.00 (0-9646002-1-8) Off the Grid.
Luck of Roaring Camp. Bret Harte. Date not set. pap., teacher ed. 7.32 (0-89070-055-9, Jamestwn Pub) NTC Contemp Pub Co.
Luck of Roaring Camp. Bret Harte. (Jamestown Classics Ser.). (J). 1995. pap., student ed. 7.32 (0-89061-054-1, Jamestwn Pub) NTC Contemp Pub Co.
*Luck of Roaring Camp. Bret Harte. (Works of Bret Harte: Vol. 7). 1999. reprint ed. lib. bdg. 90.00 (0-7812-7839-2) Rprt Serv.
Luck of Roaring Camp & Other Short Stories. Bret Harte. 96p. 1992. reprint ed. pap. text 1.00 (0-486-27271-0) Dover.
Luck of the Bodkins. P. G. Wodehouse. 228p. 1954. pap. 12.99 (0-14-000986-8, Penguin Bks) Viking Penguin.
Luck of the Draw. Catherine Dain. (Orig.). 1996. mass mkt. 5.99 (0-425-15230-8) Berkley Pub.
Luck of the Draw. Candace Schuler. (Temptation Ser.). 1996. per. 3.50 (0-373-25708-2, 1-25708-8) Harlequin Bks.
Luck of the Irish. Sharon Brondos. (Superromance Ser.). 1994. per. 3.50 (0-373-70588-3, 1-70588-8) Harlequin Bks.
Luck of the Irish. Illus. by Susan Hood. (Charming Petites Ser.). 80p. 1996. 4.95 (0-88088-794-X) Peter Pauper.
Luck of the Irish. Niall Williams & Christine Breen. LC 94-26199. 260p. 1995. 20.00 (1-56947-022-7) Soho Press.
Luck of the Irish: Our Life in County Clare. Niall Williams & Christine Breen. LC 94-26199. 234p. 1996. pap. 11.00 (1-56947-078-2) Soho Press.
Luck of the Miss L. Lee Kingman. (J). (gr. 4-6). 1986. 12.95 (0-685-11813-4) HM.
Luck of the Year. Edward V. Lucas. LC 76-90657. (Essay Index Reprint Ser.). 1977. 19.95 (0-8369-1224-1) Ayer.
Luck or Cunning? see Shrewsbury Edition of the Works of Samuel Butler
Luck Runs Out. Charlotte MacLeod. 192p. 1981. pap. 3.50 (0-380-54171-8, Avon Bks) Morrow Avon.
Luck Was with Me: A Collection of Stories. Lew Strogat, pseud. Tr. by Jack E. Evans from RUS. LC 91-58180. (Illus.). 112p. 1991. pap. 12.00 (0-911971-69-6) Effect Pub.
Luck with Potatoes. Helen Ketteman. LC 94-48806. (Illus.). 32p. (J). (gr. k-3). 1995. 14.95 (0-531-09473-1); lib. bdg. 15.99 (0-531-08773-5) Orchard Bks Watts.
Luckee's Elbow Room. Mac S. Rutherford, II. (Illus.). 249p. (Orig.). 1988. pap. 4.95 (0-922510-00-8) Lucky Bks.
Lucker & Tiffany Peel Out. Eroica Mildmay. 192p. 1994. pap. 12.99 (1-85242-285-8) Serpents Tail.
Luckey's Hummel Figurines & Plates: ID & Value Guide. 11th ed. Carl F. Luckey. LC 97-73775. (Illus.). 456p. 1997. pap. 24.95 (0-89689-119-4, HUM11) Krause Pubns.
Luckham: Plays. Clare Luckham. 220p. 1999. pap. 19.95 (1-870259-68-8, Pub. by Theatre Comm) Consort Bk Sales.
Luckiest Day of Your Life. Edward Packard. (Choose Your Own Adventure Ser.: No. 132). (Illus.). (J). (gr. 4-8). 1993. 16.25 (0-553-63484-4) Bantam.
Luckiest Day of Your Life. Edward Packard. (Choose Your Own Adventure Ser.: No. 132). (J). (gr. 4-8). 1993. 8.60 (0-606-02732-7, Pub. by Turtleback) Demco.
Luckiest Girl. Beverly Cleary. LC 58-6667. 228p. (J). (gr. 7 up). 1970. 16.89 (0-688-31741-3, Wm Morrow) Morrow Avon.
Luckiest Girl. Beverly Cleary. 240p. (J). (gr. 4-7). 1996. pap. 4.99 (0-380-72806-0, Avon Bks) Morrow Avon.
Luckiest Girl. Beverly Cleary. 1996. 9.60 (0-606-10256-6, Pub. by Turtleback) Demco.
Luckiest Girl. Beverly Cleary. 224p. (J). (gr. 5-6). 1991. reprint ed. mass mkt. 4.50 (0-380-70922-8, Avon Bks) Morrow Avon.
Luckiest Girl in the World. Steven Levenkron. LC 96-44353. 192p. 1998. pap. 9.95 (0-14-026625-9) Viking Penguin.
*Luckiest Girl in the World. Verity Purdy. LC 98-232365. (Illus.). 192p. 1998. pap. 18.95 (1-895811-57-0) Heritage Hse.
*Luckiest Guy in the World. T. Boone Pickens. LC 00-31192. 2000. write for info. (1-58798-019-3) Beard Bks.
Luckiest Kid on the Planet. Lisa C. Ernst. LC 93-36329. (Illus.). 40p. (J). (ps-2). 1994. mass mkt. 14.95 (0-02-733566-6, Mac Bks Young Read) S&S Childrens.
Luckiest Kid on the Planet. Lisa Campbell Ernst. LC 93-36329. (Illus.). 40p. (J). (ps-2). 1999. per. 5.99 (0-689-82426-2) Aladdin.
*Luckiest Leprechaun. Illus. by Justine Korman & Denise Brunkus. LC 99-37016. (J). 1999. lib. bdg. 15.95 (0-8167-6604-5) Troll Communs.
Luckiest Man in the World. Randall Silvis. LC 84-4217. (Drue Heinz Literature Prize Ser.). 212p. 1984. text 22.50 (0-8229-3476-0) U of Pittsburgh Pr.
Luckiest One of All, 001. Bill Peet. (Illus.). 32p. (J). (gr. k-3). 1982. 16.00 (0-395-31863-7) HM.
Luckiest One of All, 001. Bill Peet. (Illus.). 32p. (J). (gr. k-3). 1985. pap. 7.95 (0-395-39593-3) HM.
Luckiest One of All. Bill Peet. (J). 1982. 12.15 (0-606-02818-8, Pub. by Turtleback) Demco.
Luckiest Orphans: A History of the Hebrew Orphan Asylum of New York. Hyman Bogen. LC 91-28913. (Illus.). 304p. (C). 1992. 34.95 (0-252-01887-7) U of Ill Pr.
Luckiest Unlucky Man Alive: A Wild Ride Overcoming Life's Greatest Challenges - And How You Can Too! Bill Goss. LC 97-72027. (Illus.). 211p. 1997. 19.95 (1-884962-17-3); pap. 14.95 (1-884962-12-2) Allnce Hse.
*Luckiest Unlucky Man Alive: A Wild Ride Overcoming Life's Greatest Challenges - And How You Can Too! Bill Goss. LC 97-72027. (Illus.). xxii, 214p. 2000. pap. 14.95 (0-9665234-2-3) Allnce Hse.
*Luckless Lady. large type ed. George Douglas. 296p. 1999. pap. 18.99 (0-7089-5560-6, Linford) Ulverscroft.
Luckman at Quarterback. Sidney Luckman. (American Autobiography Ser.). 233p. 1995. reprint ed. lib. bdg. 79.00 (0-7812-8582-8) Rprt Serv.
Luckmann & Sorensen's Medical-Surgical Nursing: A Psychophysiologic Approach. 4th ed. Ed. by Joyce M. Black & Esther Matassarin-Jacobs. (Illus.). 1993. teacher ed. write for info. (0-7216-3786-8, W B Saunders Co) Harcrt Hlth Sci Grp.
Luckmann & Sorensen's Medical-Surgical Nursing: A Psychophysiologic Approach, Manual of Test Questions. 4th ed. Ed. by Joyce M. Black & Esther Matassarin-Jacobs. (Illus.). 1993. write for info. (0-7216-3891-0, W B Saunders Co) Harcrt Hlth Sci Grp.
Luckmann Core Private Practice. Arlene L. Polaski. LC 97-115800. 1996. pap. text, student ed. 17.95 (0-7216-6771-6, W B Saunders Co) Harcrt Hlth Sci Grp.
Luckmann's Core Princ Prac. Polaski. 1996. 275.00 (0-7216-5998-5) Harcourt.
Luckmann's Core Principles & Practice of Medical-Surgical Nursing. Arlene L. Polaski & Suzanne E. Tatro. 1996. teacher ed. write for info. (0-7216-5995-0, W B Saunders Co) Harcrt Hlth Sci Grp.
Luckmann's Core Principles & Practice of Medical-Surgical Nursing. Arlene L. Polaski & Suzanne E. Tatro. Ed. by Thomas Eoyang. (Illus.). 1840p. 1996. text 68.00 (0-7216-5994-2, W B Saunders Co) Harcrt Hlth Sci Grp.
Luckmann's Core Principles & Practice of Medical-Surgical Nursing. Arlene L. Polaski & Suzanne E. Tatro. LC 96-166595. 1996. pap. text 19.95 (0-7216-6817-8, W B Saunders Co) Harcrt Hlth Sci Grp.
Luckmann's Core Principles & Practice of Medical-Surgical Nursing, Test Manual. Arlene L. Polaski & Suzanne E. Tatro. 1996. write for info. (0-7216-5996-9, W B Saunders Co) Harcrt Hlth Sci Grp.
Lucknow: Memories of a City. Ed. by Violette Graff. (Illus.). 336p. 1999. pap. 14.95 (0-19-564887-0) OUP.
Lucknow, Fire of Grace: The Story of Its Revolution, Renaissance & the Aftermath. Amaresh Misra. LC 98-908915. xix, 369p. 1998. write for info. (81-7223-338-8) CE25.
Lucknow Law Times 1990. E. B. C. Staff. (C). 1990. ring bd. 180.00 (0-89771-465-2) St Mut.
Lucks & Talismans: A Chapter of Popular Superstition. Charles R. Beard. LC 72-80494. 278p. 1972. reprint ed. 24.95 (0-405-08246-0, Pub. by Blom Pubns) Ayer.
Lucky. Pam Adams. (Illus.). 10p. (ps-1). 1999. pap. text 9.99 (0-85953-613-0) Childs Play.
Lucky. Terry Berger. LC 73-18617. (Lead-off Bks.). 48p. (J). (ps-3). 1976. 6.95 (0-87955-110-0); write for info. (0-87955-710-9) O'Hara.
Lucky. Jackie Collins. 1987. pap. 4.95 (0-317-59662-4, Sig) NAL.
Lucky. Jackie Collins. 1987. pap. 6.99 (0-671-70419-2) PB.
*Lucky. Jackie Collins. 624p. 1998. per. 7.99 (0-671-02348-9, Pocket Books) PB.
Lucky. Roger Hargreaves. (Little Miss ... Ser.). 32p. 1999. pap. 2.99 (0-8431-7504-4, Price Stern) Peng Put Young Read.
Lucky. Suzanne Taylor-Moore. 1977. 8.95 (0-938758-04-7) MTM Pub Co.
*Lucky: A Rape. Alice Sebold. LC 99-19697. 256p. 1999. 21.50 (0-684-85782-0) Scribner.
*Lucky - A Skunk's Adventure in the Endless Mountains of Pennsylvania. Barbara R. Sheely. (Illus.). 20p. (J). (gr. k-5). 1999. pap. 8.00 (0-9672077-0-3) B Sheeley.
Lucky American Childhood. Paul Engle. LC 95-25871. (Singular Lives Ser.). (Illus.). 228p. 1996. 24.95 (0-87745-540-6) U of Iowa Pr.
*Lucky at Love: Stories & Essays from Asia. Eric Browning-Larsen. 336p. 1999. pap. 12.00 (0-9673413-0-2) Pacific Path Inc.
Lucky Baldwin: The Story of an Unconventional Success. Carl B. Glasscock. (Illus.). 330p. 1993. pap. 14.95 (0-913814-27-X) Nevada Pubns.
Lucky Baseball Bat. Matt Christopher. 58p. (J). (gr. k-3). 1993. pap. 4.50 (0-316-14260-3) Little.
Lucky Baseball Bat. Matt Christopher. (Springboard Bks.). (J). 1991. 9.70 (0-606-05720-X, Pub. by Turtleback) Demco.
Lucky Bastard Club: A B-17 Pilot in Training & in Combat, 1943-45. Eugene Fletcher. (Illus.). 510p. (C). 1993. 29.95 (0-295-97232-7) U of Wash Pr.
Lucky Bear. Joan Phillips. LC 85-14467. (Step into Reading Ser.: A Step 1 Book). (Illus.). 32p. (J). (ps-1). 1986. pap. 3.99 (0-394-87987-2, Pub. by Random Bks Yng Read) Random.
Lucky Bear. Joan Phillips. (Step into Reading Ser.: A Step 1 Book). (J). (ps-1). 1986. 9.19 (0-606-12406-3, Pub. by Turtleback) Demco.
*Lucky Break: How I Became a Writer. Ed. by Howard Junker. 176p. 1999. pap. 17.95 (0-325-00156-1) Heinemann.
Lucky Bride. Ana Seymour. 1997. mass mkt. 4.99 (0-373-28950-2, 1-28950-3) Silhouette.
Lucky Bucky in Oz. John R. Neill. (Illus.). 289p. (J). (gr. 3 up). 1992. 24.95 (0-929605-17-9) Books of Wonder.
Lucky Bus. Richard G. Boyer. LC 73-87801. (Safety Ser.). (Illus.). 32p. (J). (gr. k-2). 1974. ring bd. 12.35 (0-87783-131-9) Oddo.
Lucky Charms. Houghton Mifflin Company Staff. (Literature Experience 1991 Ser.). (J). (gr. 3). 1990. pap. 9.48 (0-395-55153-6) HM.
Lucky Classis Friendly Tale. Mouse Works Staff. 10p. 1999. 6.99 (0-7364-1010-4, Pub. by Mouse Works) Time Warner.
Lucky Come Hawaii. 2nd ed. Jon Shirota. LC 65-28053. 256p. (Orig.). 1988. pap. 8.95 (0-935848-54-1) Bess Pr.
Lucky Comes Home. Dean Hughes. LC 94-30762. (Lucky Ladd Ser.: Bk. 10). 138p. (Orig.). (J). (gr. 4-6). 1994. pap. 4.95 (0-87579-941-8, Cinnamon Tree) Deseret Bk.
*Lucky Corner: The Biography of Congressman Alfred E. Santangelo & the Rise of Italian-Americans in Politics. Betty L. Santangelo. LC 99-30501. 348p. 1999. 24.95 (1-57703-010-9) CMS.
Lucky Day. abr. ed. Mary Higgins Clark. 1992. pap. 11.00 incl. audio (0-671-76017-3) PB.
Lucky Devil (Dangerous Men) Patricia Rosemoor. (Intrigue Ser.). 1996. per. 3.75 (0-373-22361-7, 1-22361-9) Harlequin Bks.
Lucky Dip. (Sunstart Ser.: No. 747-1). (Illus.). 50p. (J). (ps-5). 3.50 (0-7214-8000-4, Ladybrd) Penguin Putnam.
Lucky Dip, Vol. A. (Sunstart Ser.: Series S50). (Illus.). (J). (ps-5). student ed. 1.95 (0-7214-8007-1, Ladybrd) Penguin Putnam.
*Lucky Dog & Other Tales of Murder. Dick Lochte. LC 00-34753. (First Edition Mystery Ser.). 2000. write for info. (0-7862-2688-9) Five Star.
Lucky Dog Days. Judy Delton. (Pee Wee Scouts Ser.: No. 3). 80p. (J). (gr. k-3). 1988. pap. 3.99 (0-440-40063-5, YB BDD) BDD Bks Young Read.
Lucky Dog Days. Judy Delton. (Pee Wee Scouts Ser.). (J). 1988. 9.44 (0-606-08003-1) Turtleback.
Lucky Duck. Barbara DeRubertis. LC 96-75015. (Let's Read Together Ser.). (Illus.). 32p. (J). (ps-2). 1996. pap. 4.95 (1-57565-004-5) Kane Pr.
*Lucky Duck. Sarah Durkee. LC 99-87425. (Between the Lions Ser.). (Illus.). (J). 2000. 7.99 (0-307-16502-7, Goldn Books) Gldn Bks Pub Co.
*Lucky Duck. Illus. by Sarah Durkee & David Prebenna. LC 99-87425. (J). 2000. 10.99 (0-307-36502-6) Gldn Bks Pub Co.
Lucky Duck. Sue Kueffner. LC 99-19689. (Illus.). 32p. (J). (gr. k-3). 1999. pap. 3.99 (1-57584-309-9, Pub. by Rdrs Digest) S&S Trade.
Lucky Dust. Christopher Logue. Date not set. pap. 11.95 (0-85646-157-1, Pub. by Anvil Press) Dufour.
Lucky Dust. Christopher Logue. 8p. 1985. pap. 7.95 (0-85646-158-X, Pub. by Anvil Press) Dufour.
Lucky Eyes & a High Heart see Maud Gonne
Lucky Fights Back. Dean Hughes. LC 91-31416. (Lucky Ladd Ser.: Bk. 4). 150p. (Orig.). (J). (gr. 3-6). 1991. pap. text 4.95 (0-87579-559-5, Cinnamon Tree) Deseret Bk.
Lucky Generation: A Positive View of the 21st Century. William Davis. 320p. 1996. mass mkt. 13.95 (0-7472-4744-7, Pub. by Headline Bk Pub) Trafalgar.
Lucky Ghosts. Eddy Shah. 784p. 1991. pap. 7.99 (0-385-40239-2) Doubleday.
Lucky Glasses. (Happy Endings Padded Storybooks Ser.). (Illus.). 32p. (J). (ps-1). 1998. pap. write for info. (0-7666-0157-9, Honey Bear Bks) Modern Pub NYC.
*Lucky Gourd Shop. Joanna C. Scott. 2000. 25.00 (1-878448-01-3) MacMurray & Beck.
Lucky Hans: Story Pak. Jacob W. Grimm & Wilhelm K. Grimm. (Graphic Learning Literature Program Series: Folk Tales). (ENG & SPA., Illus.). (J). (gr. k). 1992. 45.00 (0-87746-229-1) Graphic Learning.
Lucky Hares & Itchy Bears. Susan Ewing. LC 96-7640. (Illus.). 32p. (J). (gr. 1 up). 1996. 15.95 (0-88240-475-X, Alaska NW Bks) Gr Arts Ctr Pub.
Lucky Horse. Bonnie Bryant. (Saddle Club Ser.: No. 89). 160p. (J). (gr. 4-6). 1999. pap. 3.99 (0-553-48675-6) BDD Bks Young Read.
Lucky Horseshoes. Carolyn Keene. (Nancy Drew Notebooks: No. 26). (Illus.). (J). (gr. 2-4). 1998. pap. 3.99 (0-671-00827-0-3, Minstrel Bks) PB.
Lucky in Love. Dean Hughes. LC 93-33301. (Lucky Ladd Ser.: No. 9). 161p. (Orig.). (J). (gr. 3-7). 1993. pap. 4.95 (0-87579-805-5, Cinnamon Tree) Deseret Bk.
Lucky in Love. Rebecca Robbins. 224p. (Orig.). 1994. mass mkt. 3.99 (0-380-77485-2, Avon Bks) Morrow Avon.
Lucky in Love. Tracy Sinclair. 1998. per. 4.25 (0-373-24167-4, 1-24167-8) Silhouette.
Lucky Jim. Kingsley Amis. 254p. 1993. pap. 11.95 (0-14-018630-1, Penguin Classics) Viking Penguin.
Lucky Jim. Kingsley Amis. 256p. 1976. reprint ed. lib. bdg. 22.95 (0-89244-069-4, Queens House) Amereon Ltd.
Lucky Jim. Kingsley Amis. 1990. reprint ed. lib. bdg. 29.95 (0-89968-473-4) Buccaneer Bks.
Lucky Kristoffer. Martin A. Hansen. Tr. by John J. Egglishaw from DAN. LC 73-9298. (Library of Scandinavian Literature). 377p. 1974. lib. bdg. 7.50 (0-8057-3339-6) Irvington.
Lucky LAD-LP. Robert Leeson. 1999. pap. text 16.95 (0-7540-6042-X) Chivers N Amer.
Lucky Lady. Susan Saunders. Date not set. pap. 4.95 (0-380-80756-4, Wm Morrow) Morrow Avon.
*Lucky Lady. Susan Saunders. LC 99-42648. 128p. (J). (gr. 4-7). 2000. 14.95 (0-380-97784-2, Avon Bks) Morrow Avon.
Lucky Lady & Navy Mystique: The Chenango in WWII. Brooke Hindle. 1991. 17.95 (0-533-08893-3) Vantage.

An Asterisk (*) at the beginning of an entry indicates that the title is appearing for the first time.

L

Lucky Life. Gerald Stern. LC 94-68939. (Classic Contemporaries Ser.). 88p. 1995. reprint ed. pap. 12.95 (*0-88748-207-4*) Carnegie-Mellon.

***Lucky Lizard.** Ellen Kelley. (Illus.). 96p. (J). (gr. 2-5). 2000. 14.99 (*0-525-46142-6*, Dutton Child) Peng Put Young Read.

***Lucky Logan Finds Love.** Barbara Cartland. LC 00-42583. .p. 2000. write for info. (*0-7862-2787-7*) Thorndike Pr.

Lucky Lookdown: A Tale of a Funny Fish. Suzanne Tate. LC 89-92221. (Suzanne Tate's Nature Ser.: No. 6). (Illus.). 28p. (J). (gr. k-4). 1989. pap. 4.95 (*0-9616344-8-0*) Nags Head Art.

Lucky Lookdown: A Tale of Funny Fish. Suzanne Tate. LC 89-92221. 1989. 9.15 (*0-606-10324-4*) Turtleback.

***Lucky Lottery.** Ron Roy. (A to Z Mysteries Ser.: Vol. 12). (Illus.). (J). 2000. pap. 3.99 (*0-679-89460-8*) Random.

***Lucky Lottery.** Ron Roy. (A to Z Mysteries Ser.: Vol. 12). (Illus.). (J). 2000. 11.99 (*0-679-99460-2*) Random Bks Yng Read.

Lucky, Lucky Day. Suzanne Weyn & Laura O'Neil. (Full House Michelle Ser.: Vol. 4). (J). (gr. 4-7). 1995. pap. 3.99 (*0-671-52272-8*) PB.

***Lucky Man.** Tony Dunbar. 240p. 1999. mass mkt. 5.99 (*0-440-22662-7*) Dell.

Lucky Man, Lucky Woman. Jack Driscoll. 272p. 2000. pap. 13.00 (*0-393-31945-8*) Norton.

Lucky Man, Lucky Woman: A Love Story. Jack Driscoll. 264p. 1999. 24.50 (*1-888889-08-X*, Pub. by Pushcart Pr) Norton.

Lucky Me. Lisa Fiedler. LC 98-5531. 172p. (YA). (gr. 6-12). 1998. 15.00 (*0-395-89131-0*, Clarion Bks) HM.

Lucky Me! Lisa Papademetriou. (Illus.). 48p. (J). 1999. 17.90 (*0-7613-2071-7*, Copper Beech Bks) Millbrook Pr.

***Lucky Me!** Lisa Papademetriou. (Real Kids Readers Ser.). (Illus.). 48p. (J). (gr. 1-3). 1999. pap. write for info. (*0-7613-2096-2*, Copper Beech Bks) Millbrook Pr.

Lucky Me! An Adoption Story. Anna Fairbank. LC 88-60649. (Illus.). 32p. (Orig.). (J). (ps-1). 1988. pap. 8.95 (*0-945436-01-7*) Mariah Pr.

Lucky Mouse. Elizabeth Ring. LC 94-46948. (Illus.). 32p. (J). (gr. k-3). 1995. lib. bdg. 21.40 (*1-56294-344-8*) Millbrook Pr.

***Lucky Mrs. Ticklefeather.** Dorothy Kunhardt. (Family Storytime Ser.). (Illus.). (J). 2000. 9.95 (*0-307-16853-0*) Gldn Bks Pub Co.

***Lucky Numbers Oracle: Discover the Power of Numerology.** Sonia Ducie. 2000. pap. 8.00 (*0-7225-3880-4*) Thorsons PA.

Lucky Nurse & Other Musical Plays. Michael J. LaChuisa. 1993. spiral bd. 16.00 (*0-8222-1354-0*) Dramatists Play.

Lucky O'Leprechaun. Jana Dillon. LC 98-18304. (Illus.). 32p. (J). (gr. k-3). 1998. text 14.95 (*1-56554-333-5*) Pelican.

Lucky O'Leprechaun Comes to America. Jana Dillon. 14.95 (*1-56554-816-7*) Pelican.

Lucky 130. M. K. Silver. (Illus.). 50p. 1999. pap. 11.95 (*0-9669913-0-3*) M Silver.

Lucky Ones. Doris Mortman. LC 96-80069. 407p. 1997. 22.95 (*1-57566-204-3*) Kensgtn Pub Corp.

Lucky Ones. Doris Mortman. 480p. 1998. pap. 6.99 (*0-8217-5920-5*, Zebra Kensgtn) Kensgtn Pub Corp.

Lucky Ones. large type ed. Doris Mortman. LC 97-47191. (Large Print Bks.). 1998. pap. 23.95 (*1-56895-532-4*) Wheeler Pub.

Lucky Pants & Other Golf Myths. Joe Kohl. LC 96-20826. (Illus.). 96p. (Orig.). 1996. pap. 7.95 (*0-914457-80-2*) Mustang Pub.

***Lucky Pennies & Hot Chocolate.** Carol Diggory Shields. LC 00-20967. (Illus.). 32p. (J). (ps-2). 2000. 13.99 (*0-525-46450-6*, Dutton Child) Peng Put Young Read.

Lucky Penny. Elizabeth August. (Romance Ser.). 1993. per. 2.75 (*0-373-08945-7*, 5-08945-3) Silhouette.

Lucky Penny. Harry Schorsch. Ed. by Eldonna Lay & Richard Lay. (Illus.). 245p. (Orig.). 1991. pap. 13.95 (*0-9619184-2-X*) E P Lay Assocs.

Lucky Poet: A Self-Study in Literature & Political Ideas: Being the Autobiography of Hugh MacDiarmid (Christopher Murray Grieve) Hugh MacDiarmid. LC 73-152431. xxiv, 43p. 1972. write for info. (*0-224-00715-7*) Jonathan Cape.

Lucky Prince. (Ladybird Bks.). (ARA., Illus.). 52p. 4.50 (*0-614-09118-7*, LDL184, Pub. by Librairie du Liban) Intl Bk Ctr.

Lucky Pup. Teacher Created Materials Staff. (Go Bks.). 8p. (J). (gr. k-1). 1997. pap. 2.49 (*1-57690-821-6*) Tchr Create Mat.

Lucky Science: Accidental Discoveries from Gravity to Velcro, with Experiments. Royston M. Roberts & Jeanie Roberts. LC 94-10373. 128p. (gr. 4-7). 1994. pap. 12.95 (*0-471-00954-7*) Wiley.

Lucky 7. Michael Lee. 64p. (J). (gr. 3 up). 1995. text 15.95 (*1-884187-19-6*) AMICA Pub Hse.

Lucky Seven. Jordan Smith. LC 86-32431. (Wesleyan Poetry Ser.). 78p. 1988. pap. 12.95 (*0-8195-1142-0*, Wesleyan Univ Pr) U Pr of New Eng.

Lucky Seventh: Tales of the Big League. Charles E. Van Loan. LC 78-130075. (Short Story Index Reprint Ser.). (Illus.). 1977. 20.95 (*0-8369-3656-6*) Ayer.

Lucky 6, 6 bks., Set. Robert W. Lucky. 1993. 164.75 (*0-7803-1018-7*) Inst Electrical.

Lucky Slots: How to Beat the Casino Bandits. Jack Kiely. 32p. 1997. pap. 7.95 (*0-934650-14-4*) Sunnyside.

Lucky Sods: A Play John Godber. LC 99-165607. 80p. 1995. write for info. (*0-573-01825-1*) S French Trade.

Lucky Sods & Passion Killers. John Godber. 1996. pap. 11.95 (*0-413-70170-0*, Methuen Drama) Methn.

Lucky Song. Vera B. Williams. LC 96-7151. (Illus.). 24p. (J). (ps-3). 1997. 15.00 (*0-688-14459-4*, Grenwillow Bks) HarpC Child Bks.

Lucky Song. Vera B. Williams. LC 96-7151. (Illus.). 24p. (J). (ps-3). 1997. 14.93 (*0-688-14460-8*, Grenwillow Bks) HarpC Child Bks.

Lucky Spot. Beth Henley. 1987. pap. 5.25 (*0-8222-0706-0*) Dramatists Play.

***Lucky Star.** Illus. by Megan McDonald & Andrea Wallace. LC 99-24652. (Road to Reading Ser.). 2000. 3.99 (*0-307-26329-0*, Whitman Coin) St Martin.

Lucky Starr & the Rings of Saturn. Isaac Asimov. (Lucky Starr Ser.). 176p. 1984. mass mkt. 1.95 (*0-345-31830-7*, Ballantine) Ballantine Pub Grp.

Lucky Stars. David A. Adler. LC 94-33629. (Houdini Club Magic Mystery Ser.). (J). 1996. 9.19 (*0-606-09579-9*, Pub. by Turtleback) Demco.

Lucky Stars. Patricia Roy. 384p. 1998. mass mkt. 5.99 (*0-446-60504-2*, Pub. by Warner Bks) Little.

Lucky Stone. Clifton. 1979. 12.50 (*0-440-05121-5*) Delacorte.

Lucky Stone. Lucille Clifton. (Illus.). 64p. (J). (gr. 2-5). 1986. pap. 3.99 (*0-440-45110-8*, YB BDD) BDD Bks Young Read.

Lucky Stone. Lucille Clifton. 1979. 8.70 (*0-606-02407-7*, Pub. by Turtleback) Demco.

Lucky Strike for God: And Other Stories. Karen Pietkiewicz. 144p. 1995. pap. 14.95 (*0-88962-588-3*) Mosaic.

Lucky Strikes... Again: Feats & Foibles of Engineers. Robert Lucky. LC 92-30769. (Illus.). 296p. (C). 1993. 34.95 (*0-7803-0433-0*, PC03301) Inst Electrical.

Lucky System Slot Book: Las Vegas Pro Reveals "Insider Slot Tricks" That Score Big Jackpot Wins. Donald Currier. 32p. (Orig.). 1996. pap. 10.00 (*1-890030-02-3*) Las Vegas Insider.

Lucky That Way: Stories of Seizing the Moment While Creating the Games Millions Play. Brad Fregger & Rodney Charles. LC 98-89350. 211p. 1998. 14.95 (*1-887472-56-8*) Sunstar Pubng.

Lucky, the Detective. Dean Hughes. LC 92-24537. (Lucky Ladd Ser.: Bk. 7). 149p. (Orig.). (J). (gr. 3-7). 1992. pap. 4.95 (*0-87579-654-0*, Cinnamon Tree) Deseret Bk.

Lucky Thing. Alice Schertle. LC 97-43166. (Illus.). 32p. (J). 1999. 17.00 (*0-15-200541-2*) Harcourt.

Lucky Thirteen. Hank Bedard. 1980. pap. 1.75 (*0-686-38385-0*) Eldridge Pub.

Lucky Thirteen. Hugh Godefroy. (Illus.). 284p. 1987. pap. 15.95 (*0-7737-5102-5*) Genl Dist Srvs.

***Lucky Thirteen.** Marilyn Kaye. 160p. (YA). 2000. pap. 4.50 (*0-553-48712-4*, Skylark BDD) BDD Bks Young Read.

Lucky 13: Short Plays about Arizona, Nevada & Utah. Ed. by Red Shuttleworth. (Illus.). 208p. 1995. pap. 17.95 (*0-87417-263-2*) U of Nev Pr.

Lucky 13th: Jump Pay. Rick Shelley. (Jump Play Ser.: No. 3). 288p. (Orig.). 1997. mass mkt. 5.99 (*0-441-00230-7*) Ace Bks.

Lucky Thirteenth: Side Show. Rick Shelley. 240p. (Orig.). 1994. pap. text 4.99 (*0-441-00123-8*) Ace Bks.

Lucky 13th: Until Relieved. Rick Shelley. 240p. (Orig.). 1994. mass mkt. 5.50 (*0-441-00019-3*) Ace Bks.

Lucky Tiger Combat Operations. Warren A. Trest. 55p. 1993. reprint ed. pap. 9.50 (*0-923135-53-7*) Dalley Bk Service.

***Lucky War: Third Army in Desert Storm.** Richard M. Swain. (Illus.). 390p. (C). 1999. pap. text 35.00 (*0-7881-7865-2*) DIANE Pub.

Lucky We Found Each Other. Perry Tanksley. 4.50 (*0-686-17143-8*) Allgood Bks.

Lucky You. Carl Hiaasen. 496p. 1998. mass mkt. 7.50 (*0-446-60465-8*, Pub. by Warner Bks) Little.

Lucky You. deluxe limited ed. Carl Hiaasen. 368p. 1997. boxed set 150.00 (*1-890885-01-0*) B E Trice.

Lucky You: A Novel. Carl Hiaasen. LC 97-36885. 320p. 1997. 24.00 (*0-679-45444-6*) Knopf.

Luckynuts & Real People. Tom Smario. LC 78-59481. 40p. pap. 3.00 (*0-932264-22-0*) Trask Hse Bks.

Lucky's Collectors Guide to 20th Century Yo-Yos: History & Values. Lucky J. Meisenheimer. LC 99-612740. (Illus.). 240p. 1998. write for info. (*0-9667612-1-9*); pap. 29.95 (*0-9667612-0-0*) Lucky Js Swim & Surf.

Lucky's Cool Club. Dean Hughes. LC 93-28534. (Lucky Ladd Ser.: No. 8). 141p. (Orig.). (J). (gr. 3-7). 1993. pap. 4.95 (*0-87579-786-5*, Cinnamon Tree) Deseret Bk.

Lucky's Gold Mine. Dean Hughes. LC 90-31072. (Lucky Ladd Ser.: Bk. 3). 132p. (Orig.). (J). (gr. 3-6). 1990. pap. 4.95 (*0-87579-350-9*, Cinnamon Tree) Deseret Bk.

Lucky's Lady. Tami Hoag. 368p. 1992. mass mkt. 6.99 (*0-553-29534-9*) Bantam.

Lucky's Mud Festival. Dean Hughes. LC 91-34494. (Lucky Ladd Ser.: Bk. 5). 141p. (Orig.). (J). (gr. 3-6). 1991. pap. text 4.95 (*0-87579-566-8*, Cinnamon Tree) Deseret Bk.

Lucky's Tricks. Dean Hughes. LC 92-25025. (Lucky Ladd Ser.: Bk. 6). 167p. (Orig.). (J). (gr. 3-7). 1992. pap. 4.95 (*0-87579-655-9*, Cinnamon Tree) Deseret Bk.

Lucky's 24 Hour Garage. Daniel Kirk. LC 95-43561. (Illus.). 32p. (J). 1996. lib. bdg. 14.89 (*0-7868-2168-X*, Pub. by Hyprn Child) Little.

Lucrar Com Opcoes de Futuros (Portuguese Profiting with Futures Options) David Caplan. (POR.). 52p. 1997. pap. 7.95 (*0-915513-86-2*) Ctr Futures Ed.

Lucrative Differences: Gender, Class & the Work of the Women's Movement in Hanover, 1880-1933. Nancy R. Reagin. LC 94-39348. 1995. pap. text 19.95 (*0-8078-4525-6*); lib. bdg. 59.95 (*0-8078-2210-8*) U of NC Pr.

Lucrece Borgia. Victor Hugo. 4.95 (*0-686-54079-4*) Fr & Eur.

Lucrecia's Dreams: Politics & Prophecy in Sixteenth-Century Spain. Richard L. Kagan. 229p. 1995. pap. 15.95 (*0-520-20158-2*, Pub. by U CA Pr) Cal Prin Full Svc.

Lucreti, T. Cari. 6th ed. Ed. by Martin. (LAT.). 1992. reprint ed. pap. 27.95 (*3-8154-1518-7*, T1518, Pub. by B G Teubner) U of Mich Pr.

Lucretia Ann on the Oregon Trail. 8th ed. Ruth G. Plowhead. LC 31-25267. (Illus.). 250p. (J). (gr. 4-8). 1997. reprint ed. pap. 10.95 (*0-87004-360-9*, 036090) Caxton.

Lucretia Borgia. Ferdinand Gregorovius. LC 68-20226. (Illus.). 401p. 1972. reprint ed. 26.95 (*0-405-08580-X*, Pub. by Blom Pubns) Ayer.

Lucretia Lombard. Kathleen Norris. (Collected Works of Kathleen Norris). 316p. 1999. reprint ed. lib. bdg. 98.00 (*1-58201-795-6*) Classic Bks.

Lucretia Mott. Lucile Davis. (Read-&-Discover Biographies Ser.). (J). 1998. 14.00 (*0-516-21272-9*, Bridgestone Bks) Capstone Pr.

Lucretia Mott. Dorothy Sterling. LC 98-48967. 240p. (J). (gr. 4-7). 1999. pap. 12.95 (*1-55861-217-3*, Pub. by Feminist Pr) Consort Bk Sales.

Lucretia Mott: Friend of Justice. Kem K. Sawyer. LC 91-70822. (Picture-Book Biography). (Illus.). 48p. (J). (gr. 5-8). 1991. pap. 7.95 (*1-878668-08-0*) Disc Enter Ltd.

Lucretia Mott: Friend of Justice. Kem K. Sawyer. (Illus.). 64p. (YA). 1998. pap. 7.95 (*1-57960-040-9*) Disc Enter Ltd.

Lucretia Mott: Her Complete Speeches & Sermons. Ed. by Dana Greene. LC 80-81885. (Studies in Women & Religion: Vol. 4). x, 412p. 1980. lib. bdg. 109.95 (*0-88946-968-7*) E Mellen.

***Lucretia Mott: Woman Suffragist.** Gina DeAngelis. (Women of Achievement Ser.). (Illus.). 112p. (YA). (gr. 5 up). 2000. write for info. (*0-7910-5295-8*); pap. text 9.95 (*0-7910-5296-6*) Chelsea Hse.

Lucretia Mott Speaking: Excerpts from the Sermons & Speeches of a Famous 19th Century Quaker Minister & Reformer. Margaret H. Bacon. LC 80-84980. 31p. (Orig.). 1980. pap. 4.00 (*0-87574-234-3*) Pendle Hill.

***Lucretia or the Children of Night (1853)** Edward Bulwer Lytton. 238p. 1999. reprint ed. pap. 18.00 (*0-7661-0796-5*) Kessinger Pub.

Lucretia Rudolph Garfield, 1832-1918. Ann Heinrichs. LC 97-48241. 112p. (J). 1998. 32.50 (*0-516-20846-2*) Childrens.

Lucretius: De Rerum Natura I. P. M. Brown. (Bristol Latin Texts Ser.). (LAT.). 292p. 1984. 29.95 (*0-86292-076-0*, Pub. by Brist Class Pr) Focus Pub-R Pullins.

Lucretius: De Rerum Natura V. Lucretius. Ed. by C. D. Costa. (C). 1985. pap. 17.95 (*0-19-814457-1*) OUP.

Lucretius: The Way Things Are: The De Rerum Natura of Titus Lucretius Carus. Lucretius. Tr. by Rolfe Humphries. LC 68-27349. (Greek & Latin Classics Ser.). 256p. 1968. reprint ed. pap. 10.95 (*0-253-20125-X*, MB-125) Ind U Pr.

Lucretius Bk. III: De Rerum Natura. P. Michael Brown. (Classical Texts Ser.). 232p. 1997. 59.99 (*0-85668-694-8*); pap. 28.00 (*0-85668-695-6*) David Brown.

Lucretius No. VI: De Rerum Natura. Lucretius. Ed. by Godwin. 1991. pap. 28.00 (*0-85668-500-3*, Pub. by Aris & Phillips) David Brown.

Lucretius - Concordantia in Lucretium. Ed. by Manfred Wacht. (Alpha-Omega, Reihe A Ser.: Bd. CXXII). vii, 845p. 1991. write for info. (*3-487-09404-5*) G Olms Pubs.

Lucretius & His Intellectual Background. Ed. by K. A. Algra et al. (Verhandelingen der Koninklijke Nederlandse Akademie van Wetenschappen, Afd. Letterkunde, Nieuwe Reeks Ser.: Vol. 172). 276p. 1997. pap. 51.50 (*0-444-85818-0*) Elsevier.

Lucretius & Scientific Thought. fac. ed. Alban D. Winspear. LC 63-17242. (Emulation Bk.). 164p. pap. 50.90 (*0-7837-7544-X*, 204692500005) Bks Demand.

Lucretius & the Transformation of Greek Wisdom. David N. Sedley. LC 97-35277. 304p. (C). 1998. 59.95 (*0-521-57032-8*) Cambridge U Pr.

Lucretius on Love & Sex. R. D. Brown. 1987. 54.00 (*90-04-08512-2*, CSCT, 15) Brill Academic Pubs.

Lucretius Selections from de Rerum Natura. Bonnie Catto & Lucretius. LC 97-43158. 304p. 1997. pap. 26.00 (*0-86516-399-5*) Bolchazy-Carducci.

Lucrezia Floriani. George Sand. Tr. by Julius Eker from FRE. 230p. 1985. reprint ed. pap. 11.00 (*0-89733-397-7*) Academy Chi Pubs.

***Luc's Revenge.** Catherine Geroge. (Presents Ser.: Bk. 2113). 2000. per. 3.99 (*0-373-12113-X*, 1-12113-6) Harlequin Bks.

***Luc's Revenge.** large type ed. Catherine George. 288p. 1999. 25.99 (*0-263-16136-6*, Pub. by Mills & Boon) Ulverscroft.

Lucus Furrinae & the Syrian Sanctuary on the Janiculum. Nicholas Goodhue. 175p. 1975. pap. 58.00 (*90-256-0730-6*, Pub. by AM Hakkert) BookLink Distributors.

Lucy. Jamaica Kincaid. LC 91-24905. (Contemporary Fiction Ser.). 163p. 1991. pap. 10.95 (*0-452-26677-7*, Plume) Dutton Plume.

Lucy. Jamaica Kincaid. LC 90-83987. 163p. 1990. 17.95 (*0-374-19434-3*) FS&G.

Lucy. Nazneen Sadiq. (Degrassi Book Ser.). 171p. (J). (gr. 6-9). 1995. mass mkt. 4.95 (*1-55028-238-7*); bds. 16.95 (*1-55028-239-5*) Formac Dist Ltd.

Lucy. large type ed. Jamaica Kincaid. LC 91-14173. (General Ser.). 169p. 1991. lib. bdg. 19.95 (*0-8161-5201-2*, G K Hall Lrg Type) Mac Lib Ref.

Lucy. large type ed. Jennie Tremaine, pseud. (Nightingale Ser.). 251p. 1991. lib. bdg. 14.95 (*0-8161-4997-6*, G K Hall Lrg Type) Mac Lib Ref.

Lucy: A Life in Pictures. Tim Frew. LC 96-32637. 96p. 1996. 12.98 (*1-56799-386-9*, MetroBooks) M Friedman Pub Grp Inc.

Lucy - Beginnings of Humankind. Donald E. Johanson & Maitland Edey. (Illus.). 416p. 1990. pap. 14.00 (*0-671-72499-1*) S&S Trade.

Lucy & Desi. large type ed. Warren G. Harris. LC 91-46294. 663p. 1992. lib. bdg. 15.95 (*1-56054-936-X*) Thorndike Pr.

Lucy & Her Times. Picq. 1996. write for info. (*0-8050-5284-4*) H Holt & Co.

Lucy & Mickey. Red J. Arobateau. (Orig.). 1995. mass mkt. 6.95 (*1-56333-311-2*, Hard Candy) Masquerade.

Lucy & the Loner. Elizabeth Bevarly. (Man of the Month Ser.). 1997. per. 3.50 (*0-373-76063-9*, 1-76063-6) Silhouette.

Lucy & the Pirates. Glen Petrie. (Illus.). 32p. (J). (gr. k-4). 1996. bds. 14.95 (*1-896580-02-5*, Pub. by Tlrad Bks) Tricycle Pr.

Lucy & the Sea Monster. K. Dolby & C. Church. (Puzzle Stories Ser.). (Illus.). 32p. (J). (ps-2). 1994. pap. 5.95 (*0-7460-1462-7*, Usborne); lib. bdg. 13.95 (*0-88110-679-8*, Usborne) EDC.

Lucy & the Sea Monster to the Rescue. Karen Dolby. Ed. by Michelle Bates. (Young Puzzle Adventures Ser.). (Illus.). 32p. (Orig.). (J). (ps-2). 1997. pap. 5.95 (*0-7460-2292-1*, Usborne); lib. bdg. 13.95 (*0-88110-934-7*, Usborne) EDC.

Lucy & the Stone. Dixie Browning. 1994. per. 2.99 (*0-373-05853-5*) Silhouette.

Lucy & Tom's Christmas. Shirley Hughes. (J). Date not set. pap. text. write for info. (*0-05-004509-1*) Addison-Wesley.

Lucy & Tom's 1-2-3. Shirley Hughes. 1999. pap. write for info. (*0-14-050782-5*) NAL.

***Lucy Anna & the Finders.** Sarah Hayes. LC 99-89378. 32p. (J). (gr. k-2). 2000. 15.99 (*0-7636-1200-6*) Candlewick Pr.

Lucy Audubon: A Biography. Carolyn E. DeLatte. LC 82-15205. (Southern Biography Ser.). 264p. 1982. pap. 81.90 (*0-7837-8449-X*, 204925400010) Bks Demand.

Lucy Bears Baby Album. Gibson. 1986. 25.00 (*0-8378-8133-1*) Gibson.

Lucy Blue & the Daughters of Light. Dana Redfield. LC 98-71588. 320p. 1998. pap. 13.95 (*1-57174-107-0*) Hampton Roads Pub Co.

***Lucy Book: Her Life in Television.** Geoffrey M. Fidelman. LC 99-18747. (Illus.). 432p. 1999. pap. 19.95 (*1-58063-051-0*, Pub. by Renaissance) St Martin.

Lucy Breckinridge of Grove Hill: The Journal of a Virginia Girl, 1862-1864. Lucy Breckinridge. Ed. by Mary D. Robertson. LC 79-88609. 251p. reprint ed. pap. 77.90 (*0-7837-1979-5*, 204225300002) Bks Demand.

Lucy Breckinridge of Grove Hill: The Journal of a Virginia Girl, 1862-1864. rev. ed. Ed. by Mary D. Robertson. LC 93-46329. (Women's Diaries & Letters of the Nineteenth-Century South Ser.). (Illus.). 267p. (C). 1994. reprint ed. pap. text 15.95 (*0-87249-999-5*) U of SC Pr.

Lucy Breckinridge of Grove Hill: The Journal of a Virginia Girl, 1862-1864 ; Edited by Mary D. Robertson. Lucy Gilmer Breckinridge & Mary D. Robertson. LC 79-88609. xvi, 235 p. 1979. 14.00 (*0-87338-234-X*) Kent St U Pr.

Lucy Church Amiably. Gertrude Stein. 240p. 1969. text 125.00 (*0-89366-280-1*) Ultramarine Pub.

***Lucy Church Amiably.** Gertrude Stein. LC 00-20975. 240p. 2000. reprint ed. pap. 12.95 (*1-56478-240-9*, Pub. by Dalkey Arch) Chicago Distribution Ctr.

Lucy Cousins Book of Nursery Rhymes. Lucy Cousins. 64p. (ps-k). 1999. 16.99 (*0-525-46133-7*, Dutton Child) Peng Put Young Read.

Lucy Cousins Book of Nursery Rhymes. Lucy Cousins. 32p. (J). (ps-1). 1999. pap. 5.99 (*0-14-056495-0*, PuffinBks) Peng Put Young Read.

Lucy Cousins Book of Nursery Rhymes & Beanbag. Lucy Cousins. (Illus.). (J). (ps up). 2000. 14.99 (*0-525-46081-0*, Dutton Child) Peng Put Young Read.

***Lucy Crocker 2.0.** Caroline Preston. LC 99-88095. 352p. 2000. 23.00 (*0-684-85449-X*) Scribner.

Lucy Davis Crowell: One Hundred Years at Nevada's Capital. Intro. by Mary E. Glass. 104p. 1965. lib. bdg. 30.50 (*1-56475-007-8*); fiche. write for info. (*1-56475-008-6*) U NV Oral Hist.

Lucy Dove. Janice Del Negro. LC 97-43607. (Illus.). (J). (gr. 3-6). 1998. 16.95 (*0-7894-2514-9*) DK Pub Inc.

Lucy Forever & Miss Rosetree, Shrinks. Susan Shreve. LC 96-17578. 128p. (J). (gr. 4-7). 1996. mass mkt. 4.95 (*0-688-14958-8*, Wm Morrow) Morrow Avon.

Lucy Forever & Miss Rosetree, Shrinks. Susan Shreve. (J). 1996. 10.05 (*0-606-11583-8*, Pub. by Turtleback) Demco.

Lucy Gayheart. Willa Cather. 1976. 21.95 (*0-8488-0451-1*) Amereon Ltd.

Lucy Gayheart. Willa Cather. 240p. 1995. pap. 12.00 (*0-679-72888-0*) Random.

Lucy Gayheart. large type ed. Willa Cather. 225p. 1992. reprint ed. lib. bdg. 19.95 (*1-56054-483-X*) Thorndike Pr.

Lucy Goes to the Country. Joe Kennedy. LC 97-43636. (Illus.). 32p. (J). (gr. k-2). 1998. 15.95 (*1-55583-428-0*, Alyson Wonderland) Alyson Pubns.

Lucy Grey. large type ed. Janis Coles. 288p. 1994. 27.99 (*0-7089-3090-5*) Ulverscroft.

Lucy Hutchinson's Lucretius. Hugh De Quehen. LC 97-132283. (LAT & ENG.). 270p. (C). 1996. text 42.50 (*0-472-10778-X*, 10778) U of Mich Pr.

Lucy in the Afternoon: An Intimate Memoir of Lucille Ball. large type ed. Jim Brochu. (General Ser.). 367p. 1991. lib. bdg. 21.95 (*0-8161-5077-X*, G K Hall Lrg Type) Mac Lib Ref.

Lucy in the Sky . . . Poems by Lucy McCurn. Lucy McCurn. 108p. (J). (gr. 4-8). 1997. spiral bd. 5.95 (*1-887480-23-4*) Wrds Lght Intl.

An Asterisk (*) at the beginning of an entry indicates that the title is appearing for the first time.

Lucy in the Wings. Joan Thompson. (Lucy Russell, Centerstage Ser.). 1995. 8.60 (*0-606-07814-2*, Pub. by Turtleback) Demco.

Lucy is Lost. Illus. by Ed King. LC 90-27675. (Gus Is Gone Ser.). 24p. (J). (1). 1991. pap. 3.95 (*1-56288-009-8*) Checkerboard.

Lucy Kemp-Welch, 1869-1958: The Spirit of the Horse. Laura Wortley. LC 97-145848. (Illus.). 260p. 1996. 49.50 (*1-85149-252-6*) Antique Collect.

Lucy Larcom: Life, Letters & Diary. Daniel D. Addison. LC 74-154143. (Select Bibliographies Reprint Ser.). 1977. reprint ed. 23.95 (*0-8369-5759-8*) Ayer.

Lucy Lawless & Renee O'Connor: Warrior Stars of Xena. Nikki Stafford. (Illus.). 300p. 1998. pap. text 16.95 (*1-55022-347-X*, Pub. by ECW) LPC InBook.

Lucy Lawless, Warrior Princess! Marc Shapiro. LC 99-199709. 1998. mass mkt. 5.99 (*0-425-16545-0*) Blvd Books.

Lucy Leighton's Journey. large type ed. Genevieve Lyons. LC 96-53886. 258p. 1997. lib. bdg. 21.95 (*0-7838-8075-8*, G K Hall Lrg Type) Mac Lib Ref.

Lucy Lettuce: A Story about Grief. Patrick Lorning & Joy Johnson. (Illus.). 16p. 1994. pap. 4.95 (*1-56123-072-3*) Centering Corp.

Lucy Lobster & Her Clacky Claws. Paul Flemming. (Snappy Fun Bks.: Vol. 7). (Illus.). 12p. (J). (gr. k-3). 1999. bds. 3.99 (*1-57584-249-1*, Pub. by Rdrs Digest) Random.

Lucy M. Lewis: American Indian Potter. Susan Peterson. (Illus.). 220p. 1984. 65.00 (*0-87011-685-1*) Kodansha.

Lucy M. Lewis: American Indian Potter. Susan Peterson. (Illus.). 220p. 1992. reprint ed. pap. 39.95 (*4-7700-1698-0*) Kodansha.

Lucy Maud & the Cavendish Cat. Lynn Manuel. (Illus.). 32p. (J). (gr. 1-3). 1997. 15.95 (*0-88776-397-9*) Tundra Bks.

***Lucy Maud Montgomery.** Mollie Gillen. (Canadians Ser.). (Illus.). 64p. (J). 1999. pap. text 6.95 (*1-55041-461-5*) Fitzhenry & W Ltd.

Lucy Maud Montgomery Album. Ed. by Kevin McCabe & Alexandra Heilbron. (Illus.). 544p. 1999. text 40.00 (*1-55041-386-4*) Fitzhenry & W Ltd.

Lucy Maxym Collection of Russian Lacquer. Lucy Maxym. (Illus.). 50p. (Orig.). 1989. 15.00 (*0-940202-10-7*) Crnrs of the Wrld.

***Lucy Meets Alfonse.** Margaret Sarkissian. 1999. lib. bdg. 28.00 (*0-226-73498-6*) U Ch Pr.

***Lucy of the Trail of Tears: Survivor of the Trail - Oklahoma Seminary Girl & Andrews Wichita Bride.** James D. Yoder. LC 99-91894. 2000. 25.00 (*0-7388-9960-7*); pap. 18.00 (*0-7388-9961-5*) Xlibris Corp.

***Lucy on the Loose.** Ilene Cooper. LC 00-21432. (Road to Reading Ser.). (Illus.). (J). 2000. pap. 3.99 (*0-307-26508-0*, Goldn Books) Gldn Bks Pub Co.

***Lucy on the Loose.** Ilene Cooper. (Road to Reading Mile 5 Ser.). (Illus.). (J). 2000. 10.99 (*0-307-46508-X*) Gldn Bks Pub Co.

***Lucy Parson Speaks.** Lucy Parsons. 208p. 2000. 28.00 (*0-88286-247-2*) C H Kerr.

Lucy Parsons, American Revolutionary. Carolyn Ashbaugh. LC 75-23909. (Illus.). 288p. 1976. pap. 30.00 (*0-88286-014-3*) C H Kerr.

Lucy Peale. Colby Rodowsky. 208p. (YA). 1992. 15.00 (*0-374-36381-1*) FS&G.

Lucy Peale. Colby Rodowsky. (Aerial Fiction Ser.). 176p. (YA). (gr. 7 up). 1994. pap. text 3.95 (*0-374-44659-8*, Sunburst Bks) FS&G.

Lucy Peale. large type ed. Colby Rodowksy. 216p. 1993. reprint ed. lib. bdg. 15.95 (*1-56054-611-5*) Thorndike Pr.

Lucy Poems: A Case Study in Literary Knowledge. Mark Jones. 336p. 1995. text 55.00 (*0-8020-0434-2*) U of Toronto Pr.

Lucy Russell, Centerstage: Lucy in the Wings. Joan Thompson. (Lucy Russell, Centerstage Ser.: No. 1). 144p. (Orig.). (J). (gr. 5-9). 1995. pap. 3.50 (*0-380-77450-X*, Avon Bks) Morrow Avon.

Lucy Russell, Centerstage: Stardom & Stinkwater. Joan Thompson. (Lucy Russell, Centerstage Ser.: No. 2). 160p. (Orig.). (J). (gr. 5-9). 1995. pap. 3.50 (*0-380-77451-8*, Avon Bks) Morrow Avon.

Lucy Russell, Centerstage: The Stagestruck Summer. Joan Thompson. (Lucy Russell, Centerstage Ser.: No. 3). 144p. (Orig.). (J). (gr. 5-9). 1995. pap. 3.50 (*0-380-77452-6*, Avon Bks) Morrow Avon.

Lucy Steps Through the Wardrobe. C. S. Lewis. LC 96-23200. (World of Narnia Ser.: Bk. 1). (Illus.). 40p. (J). (gr. k-4). 1997. 12.95 (*0-06-027450-6*) HarpC.

Lucy Steps Through the Wardrobe. C. S. Lewis. LC 96-23200. (World of Narnia Ser.). (Illus.). 40p. (J). (gr. k-4). 1998. pap. 5.95 (*0-06-443505-9*) HarpC.

***Lucy Stone: Pioneer of Woman's Rights.** Alice Stone Blackwell. 324p. 2000. pap. 17.50 (*0-8139-1990-8*) U Pr of Va.

Lucy Stone: Speaking Out for Equality. Andrea M. Kerr. LC 92-6159. (Illus.). 416p. 1992. 45.00 (*0-8135-1859-8*); pap. 19.00 (*0-8135-1860-1*) Rutgers U Pr.

***Lucy Sullivan Is Getting Married.** Marian Keyes. LC 99-20998. 448p. 1999. 24.00 (*0-380-97618-8*, Avon Bks) Morrow Avon.

***Lucy Sullivan Is Getting Married.** Marian Keyes. 624p. 2000. mass mkt. 6.99 (*0-380-79610-4*, Avon Bks) Morrow Avon.

Lucy Sullivan Is Getting Married. Marian Keyes. LC 96-201620. 740p. 1996. pap. 12.95 (*1-85371-615-4*, Pub. by Poolbeg Pr) Dufour.

Lucy Takes a Holiday. Salvatore Murdocca. LC 97-10789. (Illus.). (J). 1998. 15.95 (*1-57255-560-2*) Mondo Pubng.

Lucy Temple. Susanna Haswell Rowson. Ed. by Christine Levendusk. (Masterworks of Literature Ser.). 1991. 12.95 (*0-8084-0433-4*) NCUP.

Lucy Terry Prince. Robert L Merriam. (Illus.). 32p. 1983. 35.00 (*0-686-40220-0*) R L Merriam.

Lucy Terry Prince: Singer of History. David R. Proper. LC 97-65748. (Illus.). 56p. (Orig.). 1997. pap. 5.95 (*1-882374-02-9*) Pocumtuck Valley Mem.

Lucy, the Curiously Comical Cow. Corrine Vanderwerff. LC 97-32651. (Julius & Friends Ser.). (J). 1998. 6.99 (*0-8163-1582-5*) Pacific Pr Pub Assn.

Lucy Truman Aldrich Collection of European Porcelain Figures of the Eighteenth Century. Elizabeth T. Casey. LC 65-28229. (Illus.). 157p. 1965. 9.00 (*0-911517-26-X*) Mus of Art RI.

Lucy Willis: Light in Watercolor. Lucy Willis & Sally Bulgin. LC 96-29892. (Illus.). 128p. 1997. 19.95 (*0-8230-2776-7*) Watsn-Guptill.

Lucy Winchester. Christmas Carol Kauffman. 1992. pap. 5.95 (*0-87813-549-9*) Christian Light.

***Lucy's Bones, Sacred Stones & Einstein's Brain.** Harvey Rachlin. 2000. pap. 15.00 (*0-8050-6406-0*) St Martin.

Lucy's Bones, Sacred Stones & Einstein's Brain: The Remarkable Stories Behind the Great Objects. Harvey Rachlin. (Illus.). 416p. 1995. pap. 16.95 (*0-8050-3965-1*, Owl) H Holt & Co.

Lucy's Bones, Sacred Stones & Einstein's Brain: The Remarkable Stories Behind the Great Objects & Artifacts of History, From Antiquity to the Modern Era. Harvey Rachlin. LC 95-19935. (Reference Bks.). (Illus.). 416p. 1995. 27.50 (*0-8050-3964-3*) H Holt & Co.

Lucy's Challenge. large type ed. Hazel Fisher. 270p. 1994. 27.99 (*0-7505-0671-7*) Ulverscroft.

Lucy's Christmas. Hall. LC 92-46292. (Illus.). 40p. (J). (gr. k-3). 1998. pap. 7.00 (*0-15-201943-X*) Harcourt.

Lucy's Christmas. Donald Hall. LC 92-46292. (Illus.). 40p. (J). (ps-3). 1994. 14.95 (*0-15-276870-X*, Harcourt Child Bks) Harcourt.

Lucy's Cottage. large type ed. Pamela Bennetts. (Linford Romance Library). 336p. 1998. pap. 17.99 (*0-7089-5227-5*, Linford) Ulverscroft.

Lucy's Early Day. Don Estep. (Baby Shaped Board Bks.). (Illus.). 28p. (J). (ps). 1990. 2.95 (*0-02-689485-8*) Checkerboard.

Lucy's Eyes & Margaret's Dragon: The Lives of the Virgin Saints. Giselle Potter. LC 97-854. (J). (gr. 4 up). 1997. 17.95 (*0-8118-1515-3*) Chronicle Bks.

Lucy's Feet. Stephanie Stein. LC 92-4602. (Illus.). 32p. (J). (ps-5). 1992. 14.00 (*0-944934-05-6*) Perspect Indiana.

***Lucy's Legacy: Sex & Intelligence in Human Evolution.** Alison Jolly. 499p. 1999. 29.95 (*0-674-00069-2*) HUP.

Lucy's List: A Comprehensive Sourcebook for Making Larger Living Easier. Lucy D. Curtis. LC 96-15769. 272p. 1996. mass mkt. 14.99 (*0-446-67283-1*, Pub. by Warner Bks) Little.

Lucy's Summer. Donald Hall. LC 93-17130. (Illus.). 40p. (J). 1998. pap. 6.00 (*0-15-201723-2*, Harcourt Child Bks) Harcourt.

***Lucy's Summer.** Donald Hall. 1998. 11.20 (*0-606-13585-5*, Pub. by Turtleback) Demco.

Lucy's Village. Harrison. 1979. 12.95 (*0-85967-524-6*) Ashgate Pub Co.

Lucy's Winter Tale. Amy Ehrlich. 1999. pap. 4.99 (*0-14-055581-1*) NAL.

Lucy's Wish. Joan Lowery Nixon. LC 97-21529. (Orphan Train Ser.: No. 1). (Illus.). 128p. (J). (gr. 4-6). 1998. 9.95 (*0-385-32293-3*, Delacorte Pr Bks) BDD Bks Young Read.

Lucy's Wish. Joan Lowery Nixon. (Orphan Train Ser.: No. 1). (J). 1999. pap. 4.50 (*0-440-41306-0*) BDD Bks Young Read.

Lud-in-the-Mist. Hope Mirrlees. 315p. 1998. reprint ed. lib. bdg. 24.00 (*1-58287-006-3*) North Bks.

Lud of Lunden, Vol. 1. Talbot Mundy. (Tros of Samothrace Ser.). 1978. mass mkt. 2.25 (*0-89083-372-9*, Zebra Kensgtn) Kensgtn Pub Corp.

Ludden's Adult Guide to Colleges & Universities. LaVerne L. Ludden & Marsha J. Ludden. LC 96-34855. (Illus.). 576p. (Orig.). (C). 1996. pap. 19.95 (*1-57112-076-9*, P0769) Park Ave.

Luddite Rebellion. Brian Bailey. 1998. pap. text 33.95 (*0-7509-1353-3*, Pub. by Sutton Pub Ltd) Intl Pubs Mktg.

Luddite Rebellion. Brian J. Bailey. LC 98-6214. 240p. 1998. text 38.00 (*0-8147-1335-1*) NYU Pr.

Luddites: Machine-Breaking in Regency England. Malcolm I. Thomis. (Modern Revivals in Economic & Social History Ser.). 196p. 1993. 61.95 (*0-7512-0157-X*, Pub. by Gregg Pub) Ashgate Pub Co.

Luddites, 1812-1839. LC 72-2533. (British Labour Struggles Before 1850 Ser.). 1974. 33.95 (*0-405-04426-7*) Ayer.

Ludell's New York Time. Brenda Wilkinson. LC 79-3173. 192p. (YA). (gr. 7 up). 1980. 11.95 (*0-06-026497-7*) HarpC Child Bks.

Ludendorff: The Tragedy of a Military Mind. Karl Tschuppik. Tr. by W. H. Johnston from GER. LC 74-14118. (Illus.). 282p. 1975. reprint ed. lib. bdg. 35.00 (*0-8371-7788-X*, TSLU, Greenwood Pr) Greenwood.

Ludendorff Brucke in Remagen am 7, Merz 1945 - Im Lichte Bekannter und Neuer Ameinkanischer Quellen. Luther A. Dittmer. (De Medicinae Rebus Ser.: No. 3). (GER & ENG.). 1996. pap. 8.00 (*0-931902-35-5*) Inst Mediaeval Mus.

Ludendorff's Own Story, 2 Vols., Set. Erich Von Ludendorff. LC 72-165647. (Select Bibliographies Reprint Ser.). 1977. reprint ed. 60.95 (*0-8369-5956-6*) Ayer.

Ludi Medi Aevi: Studies in the History of Medieval Sport. John M. Carter. 1981. pap. text 30.95 (*0-89126-102-8*) MA-AH Pub.

Ludic Feminism & After. Teresa L. Ebert. LC 95-4333. (Critical Perspectives on Women & Gender Ser.). 352p. 1995. pap. 17.95 (*0-472-06576-9*, 06576); text 47.50 (*0-472-09576-5*, 09576) U of Mich Pr.

Ludic Imagination: A Reading of Joseph Conrad. Kenneth Simons. LC 84-23753. (Studies in Modern Literature: No. 41). 170p. reprint ed. pap. 52.70 (*0-8357-1593-0*, 207057600001) Bks Demand.

Ludic Self in Seventeenth-Century English Literature. Anna K. Nardo. LC 90-44797. (SUNY Series, the Margins of Literature). 263p. (C). 1991. pap. text 21.95 (*0-7914-0722-5*) State U NY Pr.

Ludicrous Demon: Aspects of the Grotesque in German Post-Romantic Prose. Lee B. Jennings. LC 63-64542. (University of California Publications in Social Welfare: Vol. 71). 224p. reprint ed. pap. 63.90 (*0-608-10023-4*, 2013771) Bks Demand.

Ludicrous Laws & Mindless Misdemeanors. Lance S. Davidson. LC 98-2672. 256p. 1998. pap. 14.95 (*0-471-13897-5*) Wiley.

***Ludlow.** Karen Pilon. (Images of America Ser.). 128p. 1999. pap. 18.99 (*0-7385-0224-3*) Arcadia Publng.

Ludlow Fair & Home Free: Two One-Act Plays in Volume. Lanford Wilson. 1998. pap. 5.25 (*0-8222-1628-0*) Dramatists Play.

Ludlow Grows Up. Kelli C. Foster. LC 95-21027. (Get Ready - Get Set - Read! Ser.). 1996. 8.70 (*0-606-10257-4*, Pub. by Turtleback) Demco.

Ludlow Grows Up. Kelli C. Foster & Gina Clegg Erickson. LC 95-21027. (Get Ready...Get Set...Read! Ser.). (Illus.). 26p. (J). (gr. k-3). 1996. pap. 3.50 (*0-8120-9247-3*) Barron.

Ludlow Grows Up, Set 5. Kelli C. Foster & Gina C. Erickson. (Get Ready...Get Set...Read! Ser.). (Illus.). (J). 1996. lib. bdg. 11.95 (*1-56674-197-1*) Forest Hse.

Ludlow Laughs. Jon Agee. LC 85-45466. (Illus.). 32p. (J). (ps up). 1987. pap. 4.95 (*0-374-44663-6*) FS&G.

Ludlow Massacre: Mini-Play. (Labor Studies). (J). (gr. 5 up). 1978. 6.50 (*0-89550-321-2*) Stevens & Shea.

Ludlow, 1085-1660: A Social, Economic, & Political History M. A. Faraday. LC 92-185290. 257 p. 1991. write for info. (*0-85033-804-2*) Phillimore & Co.

Ludmila Zhivkova: Her Many Worlds-New Culture & Beauty-Concepts & Action. Ed. by L. Zhivkova. 300p. 1982. 16.50 (*0-08-028171-0*, Pergamon Pr) Elsevier.

Ludovic Morateur Ou le Plus Que Parfait. Pierre Daninos. (FRE.). 248p. 1970. 10.95 (*0-8288-9178-8*, M3357); pap. 8.95 (*0-686-55565-1*) Fr & Eur.

Ludovico Ariosto: An Annotated Bibliography of Criticism, 1956-1980. Robert J. Rodini & Salvatore Di Maria. LC 84-2196. 288p. 1985. text 34.95 (*0-8262-0445-7*) U of Mo Pr.

Ludus Coventriae. Ed. by K. S. Block. (EETS, ES Ser.: Vol. 120). 1969. reprint ed. 30.00 (*0-8115-3412-X*) Periodicals Srv.

Ludus Coventriae: or The Place Called Corpus Christi. Ed. by K. S. Block. (ES 120 Ser.). 466p. 1970. reprint ed. 35.00 (*0-19-722560-8*) OUP.

Ludus Heliconius: And Other Latin Poems. Emanuel Swedenborg. Ed. & Tr. by Hans Helander. LC 95-204761. (Acta Universitatis Upsaliensis Ser.). 255p. 1995. write for info. (*91-554-3572-6*) Uppsala Univ Acta Univ Uppsaliensis.

Ludvig Holberg. F. J. Jansen. LC 74-2171. (Twayne's World Authors Ser.). 135p. (C). 1974. lib. bdg. 20.95 (*0-8057-2431-1*) Irvington.

Ludvig Holberg's Comedies. Gerald S. Argetsinger. LC 82-5796. (Illus.). 208p. 1983. 20.95 (*0-8093-1058-9*) S Ill U Pr.

Ludwig Achim von Arnime Kritische Schriften: Erstdrucke und Unbekanntes. Helene M. Kastinger Riley. (GER.). 626p. 1989. 65.00 (*1-929751-00-1*) Sagas Pubg.

Ludwig Achim von Arnim's Novellas of 1812. Ludwig Achim von Arnim. Tr. by Bruce Duncan. LC 97-41110. (Studies in German Language & Literature: Vol. 18). 228p. 1997. 89.95 (*0-7734-8439-6*) E Mellen.

Ludwig Alsdorf & Indian Studies. Ed. by Klaus Bruhn et al. (C). 1990. 23.50 (*81-208-0681-6*, Pub. by Motilal Bnarsidass) S Asia.

Ludwig Bamberger: German Liberal Politician & Social Critic, 1823-1899. Stanley Zucker. LC 74-17839. 355p. reprint ed. 110.10 (*0-8357-9756-2*, 201786200009) Bks Demand.

Ludwig Bemelmans, Vol. 665. Jackie F. Eastman. LC 96-20001. 150p. 1996. 32.00 (*0-8057-4535-1*, Twyne) Mac Lib Ref.

Ludwig Bemelmans: A Comprehensive Bibliography. Ed. by Murray Pomerance. (Illus.). 416p. 1995. 75.00 (*0-87008-140-3*) JAS Heineman.

Ludwig Boltzmann: Man, Physicist, Philosopher. Engelbert Broda. LC 82-80707. (Illus.). 179p. (C). 1983. 27.50 (*0-918024-24-2*) Ox Bow.

Ludwig Boltzmann: The Man Who Trusted Atoms. Carlo Cercignani. (Illus.). 348p. 1998. text 49.95 (*0-19-850154-4*) OUP.

Ludwig Boltzmann Bk. 1: His Later Life & Philosophy, 1900-1906: A Documentary History. Ed. by John T. Blackmore. LC 94-39753. (Boston Studies of Philosophy & History: Vol. 168). 280p. (C). 1995. lib. bdg. 102.50 (*0-7923-3231-8*, Pub. by Kluwer Academic) Kluwer Academic.

Ludwig Boltzmann Bk. 2: His Later Life & Philosophy, 1900-1906. John T. Blackmore. (Boston Studies in the Philosophy of Science: Vol. 174). 332p. 1995. lib. bdg. 132.50 (*0-7923-3464-7*, Pub. by Kluwer Academic) Kluwer Academic.

Ludwig Bottner & His Sons: The Beginning of the Boatner Family in America. Paula S. Felder. LC 84-81370. (Illus.). 280p. 1985. 25.00 (*0-9608408-1-8*) Hist Pubns.

Ludwig Feuerbach & the Outcome of Classical German Philosophy. Friedrich Engels. LC 76-42701. 104p. reprint ed. 20.00 (*0-404-15369-0*) AMS Pr.

Ludwig Feuerbach & the Outcome of Classical German Philosophy. Friedrich Engels. 95p. 1995. reprint ed. pap. 4.50 (*0-7178-0120-9*) Intl Pubs Co.

Ludwig II. Taschen America Staff. 1998. pap. 5.99 (*3-8228-7174-5*) Taschen Amer.

Ludwig II, Vol. II. Hans F. Nohbauer. 1998. pap. 9.99 (*3-8228-7430-2*) Taschen Amer.

Ludwig Meidner: An Expressionist Master. Victor Miesel. (Illus.). 71p. 1978. pap. 6.00 (*0-912303-16-6*) Michigan Mus.

Ludwig Mies Van der Rohe: The Tugendthat House. Daniela Hammer-Tugendthat. Ed. by Wolf Tegethoff. LC 99-58308. (ENG & GER., Illus.). 220p. 1998. 48.00 (*3-211-83065-0*, Pub. by Spr-Verlag) Princeton Arch.

Ludwig-Missionsverein & the Church in the United States, 1838-1918. Theodore Roemer. LC 73-3571. (Catholic University of America. Studies in Romance Languages & Literatures: No. 16). reprint ed. 32.50 (*0-404-57766-0*) AMS Pr.

Ludwig of Bavaria: A Verse Biography & a Play for Single Performer. Robert Peters. 128p. (Orig.). 1986. pap. 7.00 (*0-916156-82-5*) Cherry Valley.

Ludwig Richard Conradi: Missionar, Evangelist Und Organisator der Siebenten-tags-adventisten in Europa 3., Erweiterte Und Aktualisierte Auflage. 3rd ed. Daniel Heinz. (Illus.). 138p. 1998. 28.95 (*3-631-33744-2*) P Lang Pubng.

Ludwig Schuncke (1810-1834) & His Piano Music: Robert Schumann's Closest "Jugendfreund" Ruskin Cooper. Ed. by Joachim Draheim & Michael Schuncke. (GER., Illus.). 278p. 1997. write for info. (*3-926435-16-X*, Pub. by Fischer & Partner) Lichtental Pubns.

Ludwig II of Bavaria. Christopher McIntosh. LC 98-202794. (Illus.). 240p. 1998. pap. 19.95 (*1-86064-314-0*, Pub. by I B T) St Martin.

Ludwig the Tomato. Sid Rowland. (Illus.). 76p. 1990. pap. 8.00 (*0-9217158-05-4*) Del Valley.

Ludwig Tieck: A Guide to Research. Dwight A. Klett. LC 93-624. 224p. 1993. text 15.00 (*0-8240-5622-1*, H902) Garland.

Ludwig Tieck: A Literary Biography. Roger Paulin. (Illus.). 448p. 1987. reprint ed. pap. text 28.00 (*0-19-815852-1*) OUP.

Ludwig Tieck & America. Percy Matenko. LC 54-62860. (North Carolina. University. Studies in the Germanic Languages & Literatures: No. 12). reprint ed. 27.00 (*0-404-50912-6*) AMS Pr.

Ludwig Tieck & the Medieval Church. Mary M. Scheiber. LC 74-140028. (Catholic University Studies in German: No. 12). reprint ed. 37.50 (*0-404-50232-6*) AMS Pr.

Ludwig Tieck, the German Romanticist. Edwin H. Zeydel. 422p. 1935. reprint ed. lib. bdg. 63.70 (*3-487-04144-8*) G Olms Pubs.

Ludwig Tieck's Early Concept of Catholic Clergy & Church. Edgar A. Lang. LC 74-140044. (Catholic University Studies in German: No. 8). reprint ed. 37.50 (*0-404-50228-8*) AMS Pr.

Ludwig Tiecks Historische Romane: Untersuchungen zur Entwicklung Seiner Erzahlkunst. Christine Harte. Ed. by Rolf Tarot. (Arbeiten zur Geschichte und Theorie der Erzahlkunst Ser.: Bd. 12). 315p. 1997. 46.95 (*3-906759-13-X*, Pub. by P Lang) P Lang Pubng.

Ludwig Uhland & His Critics. Victor G. Doerksen. LC 94-26818. (Studies in German Literature, Linguistics & Culture). xii, 136p. 1994. 55.00 (*1-57113-002-0*) Camden Hse.

Ludwig Van Beethoven. David Brownell. (Illus.). 64p. 1980. pap. 3.95 (*0-88388-057-1*) Bellerophon Bks.

Ludwig Van Beethoven. Friedman-Fairfax & Sony Music Staff. (CD Ser.). 1995. pap. 16.98 incl. audio compact disk (*1-56799-180-7*, Friedman-Fairfax) M Friedman Pub Grp Inc.

Ludwig Van Beethoven. Stephen Johnson. (Classic FM Lifelines Ser.). 112p. 1997. pap. 9.95 (*1-86205-001-5*, Pub. by Pavilion Bks Ltd) Trafalgar.

Ludwig Van Beethoven. Mike Venezia. LC 95-40234. (Getting to Know the World's Greatest Composers Ser.). (Illus.). 32p. (J). (ps-4). 1996. lib. bdg. 21.00 (*0-516-04542-3*) Childrens.

Ludwig Van Beethoven: A Guide to Research. Theodore Albrecht. (Composer Resource Manuals Ser.). 900p. lib. bdg. 121.00 (*0-8240-8807-7*) Garland.

Ludwig Van Beethoven: Approaches to His Music. Carl Dahlhaus. Tr. by Mary Whittall. (Illus.). 304p. 1991. text 55.00 (*0-19-816148-4*) OUP.

Ludwig Van Beethoven: Approaches to His Music. Carl Dahlhaus. Tr. by Mary Whittall. (Illus.). 282p. 1994. pap. text 24.95 (*0-19-816399-1*) OUP.

Ludwig Van Beethoven: Fidelio. Paul Robinson. (Cambridge Opera Handbooks Ser.). 202p. (C). 1996. text 59.95 (*0-521-45221-X*) Cambridge U Pr.

Ludwig Van Beethoven: Fidelio. Paul Robinson. (Cambridge Opera Handbooks Ser.). (Illus.). 202p. (C). 1996. pap. text 18.95 (*0-521-45852-8*) Cambridge U Pr.

Ludwig Van Beethoven: Getting to Know the World's Greatest Composers. Mike Venezia. LC 95-40234. (Getting to Know the World's Greatest Artists Ser.). (Illus.). 32p. (J). (ps-4). 1996. pap. 6.95 (*0-516-20069-0*) Childrens.

Ludwig Van Beethoven: Leben und Schaffen, 2 vols. in 1. Adolf B. Marx. 709p. 1979. reprint ed. write for info. (*3-487-06720-X*) G Olms Pubs.

Ludwig Van Beethoven: Prometheus of the Modern World. Edmond B. Szekely. (Illus.). 24p. 1973. pap. 2.95 (*0-89564-060-0*) IBS Intl.

Ludwig van Beethoven: Selected Lieder for High Voice. Ed. & Tr. by Dietrich Erbelding from GER. (German Lieder Ser.: No. 6). (ENG & GER.). 42p. 1997. spiral bd. 10.95 (*1-58126-957-9*, GL#6BLv-Bhi) Pocket Coach.

An Asterisk (*) at the beginning of an entry indicates that the title is appearing for the first time.

Ludwig Van Beethoven: The Composer Who Continued to Write Music after He Became Deaf see Great Achievers: Lives of the Physically Challenged

Ludwig Van Beethoven: Young Composer. Louis Sabin. LC 91-18616. (Illus.). 48p. (J). (gr. 4-6). 1997. lib. bdg. 17.25 (*0-8167-2511-X*) Troll Communs.

Ludwig Van Beethoven: Young Composer. Louis Sabin. LC 91-18616. (Illus.). 48p. (J). (gr. 4-6). 1997. pap. 3.95 (*0-8167-2512-8*) Troll Communs.

Ludwig van Beethovens Leben, 5 vols., Set. Alexander W. Thayer. 1972. reprint ed. write for info. (*3-487-03185-X*) G Olms Pubs.

Ludwig Van Beethoven's Pianoforte Sonatas. William Behrend. Tr. by Ingeborg Lund. LC 74-24038. (Illus.). reprint ed. 54.50 (*0-404-12861-0*) AMS Pr.

Ludwig von Mises: An Annotated Bibliography. David Gordon. 64p. (Orig.). (C). 1988. pap. text 5.00 (*0-945466-03-X*) Ludwig von Mises.

Ludwig von Mises: Notes & Recollections. Ludwig Von Mises. LC 76-29877. 181p. 1978. 11.95 (*0-910884-04-8*) Libertarian Press.

Ludwig von Saint-Martin, Vol. V. Johannes Claasen. 456p. reprint ed. write for info. (*0-318-71433-7*) G Olms Pubs.

Ludwig Wittgenstein. Jaakko Hintikka. 1996. pap. text 53.50 (*0-7923-4280-1*) Kluwer Academic.

Ludwig Wittgenstein: A Comprehensive Bibliography. Compiled by Francois H. Lapointe. LC 79-6565. 312p. 1980. lib. bdg. 55.00 (*0-313-22127-8*, LAW/, Greenwood Pr) Greenwood.

Ludwig Wittgenstein: Cambridge Letters: Correspondence with Russell, Keynes, Moore, Ramsey & Graffi. Ed. by Brian McGuiness & George H. Von Wright. LC 94-40727. 352p. (C). 1996. text 55.95 (*0-631-19015-5*) Blackwell Pubs.

Ludwig Wittgenstein: Cambridge Letters: Correspondence with Russell, Keynes, Moore, Ramsey & Graffi. Ed. by Brian McGuiness & George H. Von Wright. LC 94-40727. 352p. 1997. pap. text 31.95 (*0-631-20758-9*) Blackwell Pubs.

Ludwig Wittgenstein: Critical Assessments, 4 vols., Set. Ed. by Stuart G. Shanker. 1986. 525.00 (*0-7099-2384-8*, Pub. by C Helm) Routldge.

Ludwig Wittgenstein: Critical Assessments, a Wittgenstein Biography, Vol 5. V. A. Shanker & Stuart G. Shanker. 1986. 95.00 (*0-685-11837-1*, Pub. by C Helm) Routldge.

Ludwig Wittgenstein: Eine Existenzielle Deutung. L. Adler. 1976. 35.00 (*3-8055-2390-4*) S Karger.

Ludwig Wittgenstein: Half-Truths & One-&-a-Half-Truths. Jaakko Hintikka. LC 96-21692. (Jaakko Hintikka Selected Papers HISP: Vol. 1). 368p. (C). 1996. lib. bdg. 124.00 (*0-7923-4091-4*) Kluwer Academic.

Ludwig Wittgenstein: His Place in the Development of Semantics. Tullio De Mauro. (Foundations of Language Supplementary Ser.: No. 3). 62p. 1967. text 100.50 (*90-277-0029-X*) Kluwer Academic.

Ludwig Wittgenstein: Personal Recollections. Ed. by Rush Rhees. LC 79-28474. 246p. 1981. 53.50 (*0-8476-6253-5*) Rowman.

Ludwig Wittgenstein: Philosophy & Language. Ed. by Alice Ambrose & Morris Lazerowitz. (Wittgenstein Studies). 325p. 1996. pap. 27.00 (*1-85506-488-X*) Bks Intl VA.

Ludwig Wittgenstein: The Duty of Genius. Ray Monk. (Illus.). 654p. 1990. 40.00 (*0-02-921670-2*) Free Pr.

Ludwig Wittgenstein: The Duty of Genius. Ray Monk. (Illus.). 672p. 1991. reprint ed. pap. 19.95 (*0-14-015995-9*, Penguin Bks) Viking Penguin.

Ludwig Wittgenstein - Vienna Edition Vol. 3: Bemerkungen Philosophische Bemerkungen. Ed. by M. Nedo. xv, 334p. 1995. 159.95 (*3-211-82534-7*) Spr-Verlag.

***Ludwig Wittgenstein, Weiner Ausgabe Studien Texte, Bande 1-5.** Ed. by M. Nedo. (ENG & GER.). 1999. pap. 143.00 (*3-211-83271-8*) Spr-Verlag.

***Ludwig Wittgenstein, Weiner Ausgabe Studien Texte Band 1: Philosophische Bemerkungen.** Ed. by M. Nedo. (ENG & GER.). xix, 196p. 1999. pap. 36.00 (*3-211-83266-1*) Spr-Verlag.

***Ludwig Wittgenstein, Weiner Ausgabe Studien Texte Band 2: Philosophische Betrachtungen. Philosophische Bemerkungen.** Ed. by M. Nedo. (ENG & GER.). xiii, 333p. 1999. pap. 36.00 (*3-211-83267-X*) Spr-Verlag.

***Ludwig Wittgenstein, Weiner Ausgabe Studien Texte Band 3: Bemerkungen. Philosophische Bemerkungen.** Ed. by M. Nedo. (ENG & GER.). xv, 334p. 1999. pap. 36.00 (*3-211-83268-8*) Spr-Verlag.

***Ludwig Wittgenstein, Weiner Ausgabe Studien Texte Band 4: Bemerkungen zur Philosophie. Bemerkungen zur Philosophischen Grammatik.** Ed. by M. Nedo. (ENG & GER.). xiii, 240p. 1999. pap. 36.00 (*3-211-83269-6*) Spr-Verlag.

***Ludwig Wittgenstein, Weiner Ausgabe Studien Texte Band 5: Philosophische Grammatik.** Ed. by M. Nedo. (ENG & GER.). xxvii, 195p. 1999. pap. 36.00 (*3-211-83270-X*) Spr-Verlag.

Ludwig Wittgenstein-Wiener Ausgable: Einfuhrung-Introduction. M. Nedo. (Illus.). 148p. 1994. 26.95 (*0-387-82498-7*) Spr-Verlag.

Ludwigsburger Porcelain: Faience, Earthenware, Stove, & Wall Tiles. Hans D. Flach. (GER., Illus.). 960p. 1997. 110.00 (*3-925369-30-9*, Pub. by Arnoldsche Art Pubs) Antique Collect.

Ludwigson: Selected Poems. Susan Ludwigson. 160p. (Orig.). pap. 13.95 (*0-7145-4187-7*) Riverrun NY.

***Lue Language: Glossaries, Texts & Translations.** William J. Gedney. Ed. by Thomas J. Hudak. (Illus.). (C). 1999. text 100.00 (*0-89148-076-5*) Ctr S&SE Asian.

Lueneburg, Ratsbuecherei, Mus. Ant. Pract. KN 1198. Ed. by Alexander Silbiger. (Seventeenth-Century Keyboard Music Ser.: Vol. 22). 225p. 1987. text 25.00 (*0-8240-8021-1*) Garland.

Luftartsteknisk Ordbog Engelsk-Dansk. H. Bach & J. Florant. (DAN & ENG.). 255p. 1968. 49.95 (*0-7859-0801-3*, M1280) Fr & Eur.

Luften des Schleiers. Ulrich Erker-Sonnabend. (Anglis-Tische und Amerikanistische Texte und Studien Ser.: Vol. 5). x, 310p. 1987. write for info. (*3-487-07946-1*) G Olms Pubs.

***Lufthansa.** Mike Hooks. (Images of Aviation Ser.). (Illus.). 128p. 1999. pap. 18.99 (*0-7524-1702-9*, Tempus Publng) Arcadia Publng.

Lufthansa: An Airline & Its Aircraft. R. E. Davies. (Great Airlines of the World Ser.). (Illus.). 96p. 1991. 30.00 (*0-9626483-3-7*) Paladwr Pr.

Luftverunreinigung und Herz-Kreislauf-System. L. Laszt & R. Schaad. (Illus.). viii, 140p. 1980. pap. 24.50 (*3-8055-3067-6*) S Karger.

Luftwaffe: Creating the Operational Air War, 1918-1940. James S. Corum. LC 97-6943. (Modern War Studies). (Illus.). 378p. 1999. 39.95 (*0-7006-0836-2*); pap. 19.95 (*0-7006-0962-8*) U Pr of KS.

Luftwaffe: From Training School to the Front - An Illustrated Study, 1933-1945. Michael Meyer & Paul Stipdonk. (Illus.). 288p. (C). (gr. 13). 1996. 39.95 (*0-88740-924-5*) Schiffer.

Luftwaffe: The Illustrated History of the German Air Force in WW II. John Pimlott. LC 98-2581. (Illus.). 176p. 1998. 24.95 (*0-7603-0516-1*) MBI Pubg.

Luftwaffe Airfield Equipment. Joachim Dressel & Manfred Griehl. Tr. by Don Cox. LC 92-62385. (Illus.). 52p. (Orig.). 1993. pap. 9.95 (*0-88740-482-0*) Schiffer.

Luftwaffe Album: Bomber & Fighter Aircraft of the German Air Force 1933-1945. Joachim Dressel. LC 97-185341. (Illus.). 352p. 1997. 34.95 (*1-85409-409-2*, Pub. by Arms & Armour) Sterling.

Luftwaffe Album: Bomber & Fighter Aircraft of the German Air Force 1933-1945. Joachim Dressel. 352p. 1999. pap. text 24.95 (*1-85409-519-6*) Strlng Pub CA.

Luftwaffe Camouflage & Markings 1935-1940, Pt. 1. G. Wrobel & Malowanie Oznakowanie. (Camouflage & Markings). (Illus.). 50p. 1995. pap. 15.95 (*83-86208-08-2*) MBI Pubg.

Luftwaffe Codes, Markings & Units, 1939-1945. Barry C. Rosch. LC 95-67631. (Illus.). 368p. 1995. 59.95 (*0-88740-796-X*) Schiffer.

Luftwaffe Colors. Kenneth A. Merrick. LC 74-14272. 1975. write for info. (*0-668-03652-4*, Arco) Macmillan Gen Ref.

Luftwaffe Colour Schemes & Markings 1935-45, 2 vols. Martin Windrow & Richard Ward. LC 71-155422. (Arco-Aircam Aviation Series, No. 25 & 26). 1971. write for info. (*0-668-02307-4*, ARCO) Macmillan.

Luftwaffe Data Book. Alfred Price. LC 97-18382. (Illus.). 240p. 1997. 34.95 (*1-85367-293-9*, Pub. by Greenhill Bks) Stackpole.

Luftwaffe Diary, Vol. 1. Uwe Feist & Thomas McGuirl. 150p. 35.00 (*0-9633824-1-1*) Ryton Pubns.

Luftwaffe Diary, Vol. 2. Uwe Feist & Thomas McGuirl. 160p. 40.00 (*0-9633824-3-8*) Ryton Pubns.

Luftwaffe Emblems, 1939-1945. Ed. by Barry Ketley. (Illus.). 96p. 1999. pap. 24.95 (*0-9519899-7-9*, Pub. by Hikoki Pubns) Howell Pr VA.

Luftwaffe Field Divisions, 1941-45. Kevin Conley. (Men-at-Arms Ser.: No. 229). (Illus.). 48p. pap. 11.95 (*1-85532-100-9*, 9187, Pub. by Ospry) Stackpole.

Luftwaffe Fighter Aces: The Jagdflieger & Their Combat Tactics & Techniques. Mike Spick. 1997. mass mkt. 5.99 (*0-8041-1696-2*) Ivy Books.

Luftwaffe Fighter Aces: The Jagdflieger & Their Combat Tactics & Techniques. Mike Spick. LC 96-32210. 248p. 1996. 34.95 (*1-85367-255-6*) Stackpole.

Luftwaffe Fighter Aircraft in Profile. Claes Sundin & Christer Berstrom. LC 97-66511. 160p. 1997. 35.00 (*0-7643-0291-4*) Schiffer.

Luftwaffe Fighter Force: The View from the Cockpit. Adolf Galland & Dave C. Isby. LC 98-7164. (Illus.). 256p. 1998. 39.95 (*1-85367-327-7*) Stackpole.

Luftwaffe Fledglings, 1935-1945: Luftwaffe Training Units & Their Aircraft. Ed. by Barry Ketley. (Illus.). 88p. 1999. pap. 24.95 (*0-9519899-2-8*, Pub. by Hikoki Pubns) Howell Pr VA.

Luftwaffe from the North Cape to Tobruk, 1939-1945: An Illustrated History. Holger Nauroth. LC 91-61441. (Illus.). 236p. 1991. 29.95 (*0-88740-361-1*) Schiffer.

Luftwaffe in Camera: The Years of Victory, 1939-1942. Alfred Price. (Illus.). 192p. 1998. 35.95 (*0-7509-1635-4*, Pub. by Sutton Pub Ltd) Intl Pubs Mktg.

Luftwaffe in Camera, 1942-1945: The Years of Desperation. Alfred Price. (Illus.). 192p. 1998. 39.95 (*0-7509-1636-2*, Pub. by Sutton Pub Ltd) Intl Pubs Mktg.

Luftwaffe in Chaos. Nicholas Rinaldi. 83p. 1985. 10.00 (*0-685-14614-6*) Negative Capability Pr.

Luftwaffe in the North African Campaign: A Photo Chronicle, 1941-1943. Werner Held & Ernst Obermaier. Tr. by Don Cox from GER. LC 91-66336. (Illus.). 238p. 1992. 29.95 (*0-88740-343-3*) Schiffer.

Luftwaffe Methods in the Selection of Offensive Weapons: Karlsruhe Study, Vol. 1. Paul Deichmann. (USAF Historical Studies: No. 187). 102p. 1955. reprint ed. pap. text 28.95 (*0-89126-149-4*) MA-AH Pub.

Luftwaffe Methods in the Selection of Offensive Weapons: Karlsruhe Study, Vol. 2. E. A. Marquard. (USAF Historical Studies: No. 187). 182p. 1955. reprint ed. pap. text 32.95 (*0-89126-150-8*) MA-AH Pub.

Luftwaffe, 1933-45: Strategy for Defeat. Williamson Murray. 391p. 1983. per. 12.00 (*0-16-002160-X*) USGPO.

Luftwaffe, 1933-45: Strategy for Defeat. Williamson Murray. (Illus.). 392p. 1996. reprint ed. pap. 22.95 (*1-57488-125-6*) Brasseys.

Luftwaffe Profile Series: Junkers Ju 52. Manfred Griehl. 14. (Illus.). 48p. 1999. pap. 14.95 (*0-7643-0952-8*) Schiffer.

Luftwaffe Profile Series: Messerschmitt Bf 109F. Manfred Griehl. 13. (Illus.). 48p. 1999. pap. 14.95 (*0-7643-0912-9*) Schiffer.

Luftwaffe Profile Series No. 3: Heinkel HE 219 UHU. Joachim Dressel & Manfred Griehl. Tr. by David Johnston from GER. LC 95-67545. (Illus.). 52p. (Orig.). 1995. pap. 14.95 (*0-88740-819-2*) Schiffer.

Luftwaffe Profile Series No. 4: Focke-Wulf FW 190. Tr. by David Johnston from GER. LC 95-67543. (Illus.). 52p. (Orig.). 1995. pap. 14.95 (*0-88740-817-6*) Schiffer.

Luftwaffe Profile Series No. 6: Flettner FL 282. (Illus.). 32p. (YA). (gr. 10-13). 1996. pap. 12.95 (*0-88740-921-0*) Schiffer.

Luftwaffe Profile Series No. 9: Heinkel He 111H. Manfred Griehl. (Illus.). 64p. 1996. pap. 14.95 (*0-7643-0165-9*) Schiffer.

***Luftwaffe Secret Projects.** Dieter Herwig & Heinz Rode. (Illus.). 144p. 2000. 39.95 (*1-85780-092-3*, Pub. by Midland Pubng) Specialty Pr.

Luftwaffe Secret Projects: Fighters, 1939-1945. Walter Schick & Ingolf Meyer. (Illus.). 176p. 1997. pap. 44.95 (*1-85780-052-4*) Specialty Pr.

Luftwaffe vs. RAF: Flying Equipment Of The Air War, 1939-45. Mick J. Prodger. LC 97-80324. 144p. 1998. 49.95 (*0-7643-0249-3*) Schiffer.

Luftwaffe vs. RAF-Flying Clothing of the Air War, 1939-1945, Vol. I. Mick J. Prodger. LC 96-70829. (Illus.). 160p. 1997. 49.95 (*0-7643-0234-5*) Schiffer.

Luftwaffe War Diaries: The German Air Force in World War II. Cajus Bekker. Tr. by Frank H. Ziegler from GER. LC 94-11183.Tr. of Angriffsh Ohe 4000. (Illus.). 447p. 1994. reprint ed. pap. 17.50 (*0-306-80604-5*) Da Capo.

***Luftwaffe's Way of War: German Air Force Doctrine, 1911-1945.** Tr. by Richard Muller & James S. Corum. LC 97-11252. (Illus.). 320p. 1998. 34.95 (*1-877853-47-X*) Nautical & Aviation.

Luftwarfe Profile Series No. 5: Junkers JU 87A. Dressel et al. LC 96-160359. (Illus.). 48p. (YA). (gr. 10-13). 1996. pap. 14.95 (*0-88740-920-2*) Schiffer.

Lug Dukhovnij. Tr. of Spiritual Meadow. 400p. reprint ed. 20.00 (*0-317-28903-9*); reprint ed. pap. 15.00 (*0-317-28904-7*) Holy Trinity.

Lug of Days to Come: New & Selected Poems & Translations. Daniel Haberman. LC 95-13869. 136p. 1996. 20.00 (*1-880284-13-8*) J Daniel.

Luganda-English Dictionary. John D. Murphy. 652p. 1972. 95.00 (*0-7859-3733-1*, M591) Fr & Eur.

Lugano & San Sebastian Conventions. 200p. 1990. pap. 175.00 (*0-406-04010-9*, U.K., MICHIE) LEXIS Pub.

Lugano Report: On Preserving Capitalism in the Twenty-First Century. Susan George. 208p. 1999. pap. 14.95 (*0-7453-1532-1*, Pub. by Pluto GBR) Stylus Pub VA.

***Lugano Report: On Preserving Capitalism in the Twenty-first Century.** Susan George. LC 99-12828. 208p. 1999. 49.95 (*0-7453-1537-2*, Pub. by Pluto GBR) Stylus Pub VA.

Lugar Celestial. Jaci Velasquez & Tom Granger. (SPA.). 128p. 1998. per. 10.00 (*0-684-84985-2*) S&S Trade.

***Lugar Donde Estuvo el Paraiso.** Carlos Franz. 1998. 25.95 (*84-08-02391-8*) Planeta Edit.

Lugar Donde Recuerda el Mar: A Place Where the Sea Remembers. Sandra Benitez. 176p. 1996. per. 10.00 (*0-684-82388-8*) Simon & Schuster.

Lugar en las Sombras. Walter Dean Myers.Tr. of Somewhere in the Darkness. (SPA.). 176p. (J). (gr. 7-9). 1994. pap. 3.50 (*0-590-47701-3*) Scholastic Inc.

Lugar Entre Las Sombras. Walter Dean Myers. (Mariposa Scholastica en Espanol Ser.). 1994. 8.60 (*0-606-06834-1*, Pub. by Turtleback) Demco.

Lugar Llamado Alli. John Osteen.Tr. of Place Called There. (SPA.). 32p. 1996. mass mkt. 0.75 (*0-912631-76-7*) J O Pubns.

Lugar para Sonar: The Honeymoon House. Patty Salier. (Silhouette Deseo Ser.: Vol. 240).Tr. of Place for Dreaming. (SPA.). 1998. per. 3.50 (*0-373-35240-9*, 1-35240-0) Harlequin Bks.

***Lugar Preparado para Ti...** R. A. Russell.Tr. of A Place Prepared for You. (SPA.). 10p. 1998. 1.00 (*1-56722-251-X*) Word Aflame.

Lugar Sin Limites (Hell Has No Limits) Jose Donoso. 208p. 1995. pap. 12.50 (*0-679-76527-1*) Vin Bks.

Lugar Tranquilo en Medio de un Mundo Loco. Joni Eareckson Tada.Tr. of Quiet Place in a Crazy World. (SPA.). 182p. 1995. 7.99 (*1-56063-637-8*, 498598) Editorial Unilit.

***Lugar Vacio.** Planeta Publishers Staff. 2000. pap. 13.95 (*84-239-8840-6*) Espasa Calpe.

Lugard & the Abeokuta Uprising: The Demise of Egba Independence. Harry A. Gailey. 148p. 1982. 45.00 (*0-7146-3114-0*, Pub. by F Cass Pubs) Intl Spec Bk.

Lugard & the Amalgamation of Nigeria: A Documentary Record. Ed. by Anthony H. Kirk-Greene. 281p. 1968. 45.00 (*0-7146-1685-0*, Pub. by F Cass Pubs) Intl Spec Bk.

Lugard in Hong Kong: Empires, Education & a Governor at Work, 1907-1912. Bernard Mellor. (Illus.). 232p. 1992. 68.50 (*962-209-316-7*, Pub. by HK Univ Pr) Coronet Bks.

Lugard's Bridge. Stewart Brown. LC 89-82060. 72p. (Orig.). 1990. pap. 14.95 (*1-85411-013-6*, Pub. by Seren Bks) Dufour.

Lugares Mas Famosos del Mundo. Editorial America, S. A. Staff. Ed. by Maria E. Del Real. (SPA., Illus.). 352p. 1990. pap. write for info. (*0-944499-87-2*) Editorial Amer.

Lugbara of Uganda. 2nd ed. John Middleton. (Orig.). (C). 1992. pap. text 23.50 (*0-15-500622-3*) Harcourt Coll Pubs.

***Lugbara Religion.** John Middleton & Thomas O. Beidelman. 344p. 1999. 56.95 (*3-8258-4034-4*); pap. 29.95 (*3-8258-4033-6*, Pub. by CE24) Transaction Pubs.

Lugbara Religion: Ritual & Authority among an East African People. John Middleton. LC 60-51074. 294p. reprint ed. pap. 91.20 (*0-608-13679-4*, 205538700017) Bks Demand.

Lugengeschichten. Walser. (GER.). (C). 1964. 11.95 (*0-8442-2864-8*, X2864-8) NTC Contemp Pub Co.

Lugenia Burns Hope: Black Southern Reformer. Jacqueline A. Rouse. LC 88-17521. (Brown Thrasher Bks.). (Illus.). 198p. 1992. reprint ed. pap. 15.95 (*0-8203-1464-1*) U of Ga Pr.

Luger. Jorgen Schlegel. 205p. 1984. 9.95 (*0-89697-177-5*) Intl Univ Pr.

Luger Handbook. Aarron Davis. LC 97-215928. 112p. 1997. pap. 9.95 (*0-87341-501-9*, LH01) Krause Pubns.

Luger Story: The Standard History of the World's Most Famous Handgun. John Walter. LC 95-15136. (Illus.). 256p. 1995. 39.95 (*1-85367-209-2*, Pub. by Greenhill Bks) Stackpole.

Luger Tips. rev. ed. Michael Reese, II. 1992. reprint ed. 14.95 (*0-913150-36-3*) Pioneer Pr.

Luggage Labels: Mementos from the Golden Age of Travel. David Craig. (Illus.). 120p. 1988. pap. 14.95 (*0-87701-531-7*) Chronicle Bks.

Luggage Labels & the Golden Age of Travel. Harold Darling. (Illus.). 56p. (Orig.). 1992. pap. 20.00 (*0-9621131-1-5*) Laughing Elephant.

Luggage of Life. Frank W. Boreham. 256p. 1985. pap. 12.99 (*0-8254-2164-0*, 95-007) Kregel.

Lughat Al-Arab (The Arabic Language) Arabic Dictionary, Vol. I. George M. Abdul-Massih. (ARA.). 487p. 1993. 25.00 (*0-86685-580-7*, LDL5807, Pub. by Librairie du Liban) Intl Bk Ctr.

Lugosi: His Life in Film, on Stage, & in the Hearts of Horror Lovers. Gary D. Rhodes. LC 96-46131. (Illus.). 430p. 1997. boxed set 55.00 (*0-7864-0257-1*) McFarland & Co.

Luigi Balugani's Drawings of African Plants. Paul Hulton et al. (Illus.). 275p. 1990. 176.00 (*90-6191-779-4*, Pub. by A A Balkema) Ashgate Pub Co.

Luigi Balugani's Drawings of African Plants. Paul Hulton et al. LC 87-51371. (Illus.). 140p. 1991. 95.00 (*0-930606-56-6*) Yale Ctr Brit Art.

Luigi Boccherini's Guitar Quintets - New Evidence. Matanya Ophee. LC 82-181560. (Studies in Guitar History Ser.). (Illus.). 88p. (Orig.). 1981. pap. 7.00 (*0-936186-06-2*) Edit Orphee.

Luigi Dallapiccola. Roman Vlad. 1988. reprint ed. lib. bdg. 59.00 (*0-7812-0297-3*) Rprt Serv.

Luigi Fabbri: A Chronology. V. Munoz. Tr. by W. Scott Johnson. (Libertarian & Anarchist Chronology Ser.). 1979. lib. bdg. 59.95 (*0-8490-3040-4*) Gordon Pr.

Luigi Jazz Dance Technique see Luigi's Jazz Warm Up: An Introduction to Jazz Style & Technique

***Luigi Lucioni in the Collection of the Elizabeth Dec. Wilson Museum on the Occasion of the Museum's Grand Opening, Southern Vermont Art Center, 22 July, 2000.** Luigi Lucioni. LC 00-26276. (Illus.). 2000. pap. write for info. (*0-9669382-3-2*) Gallery Press.

Luigi Ontani: A Monograph. Peter Weiermair. LC 97-226591. (Illus.). 192p. 1996. 55.00 (*3-908162-31-9*, Pub. by Edit Stemmle) Dist Art Pubs.

***Luigi Pirandelio, 1867-1936 Vol. I: His Plays in Sicilian.** Luigi Pirandello. Tr. by Joseph F. Privitera. LC 98-24056. (Studies in Italian Literature: Vol. 5a & 5b). 272p. 1998. text 89.95 (*0-7734-8337-3*) E Mellen.

***Luigi Pirandelio, 1867-1936 Vol. II: His Plays in Sicilian.** Luigi Pirandello. Tr. by Joseph F. Privitera. LC 98-24056. (Studies in Italian Literature: Vol. 5a & 5b). 284p. 1998. text 89.95 (*0-7734-8339-X*) E Mellen.

Luigi Pirandello: Lettere a Marta Abba. Benito Ortolani. 1700p. 1996. text 75.00 (*88-04-39379-3*, Pub. by Mondadori & Il) Princeton U Pr.

Luigi Pirandello: The Theatre of Paradox. Ed. by Julie R. Dashwood. LC 97-29102. 300p. 1997. text 89.95 (*0-7734-8746-8*) E Mellen.

Luigi Pirandello in the Theatre: A Documentary Record. Ed. by Susan Bassnett & Jennifer Lorch. LC 92-41548. (Contemporary Theatre Studies: Vol. 3). 224p. 1993. text 30.00 (*3-7186-5375-3*); pap. text 14.00 (*3-7186-5376-1*) Gordon & Breach.

Luigi Snozzi. Claude Lichtenstein. LC 97-13750. (Studio Paperback Ser.). (Illus.). 224p. 1997. pap. 29.95 (*3-7643-5439-9*, Pub. by Birkhauser) Princeton Arch.

Luigi Snozzi - Monte Carasso. Flavio Buidottis. (Illus.). 128p. 1995. 45.00 (*3-7643-5596-4*, Pub. by Birkhauser) Princeton Arch.

Luigi's Jazz Warm Up: An Introduction to Jazz Style & Technique. Lorraine Kriegel et al. Orig. Title: The Luigi Jazz Dance Technique. (Illus.). 181p. 1997. pap. 19.95 (*0-87127-202-4*) Princeton Bk Co.

***Luigo Pirardello from Novelle.** Luigo Pirardello. Ed. by Maurizio Falyhera & Cristina Giocometti. 1999. 29.95 incl. audio compact disk (*1-58214-121-5*) Mltilingl Bks.

Luirgean Eachainn Nill: Folktales from Cape Breton. Ed. by Margaret MacDonnell & John Shaw. 1985. 35.00 (*0-86152-086-6*, Pub. by Acair Ltd); pap. 25.00 (*0-7855-1321-3*, Pub. by Acair Ltd) St Mut.

***Luis Barragan.** Rene Burri. (Illus.). 2000. 15.95 (*0-7148-3960-4*) Phaidon Pr.

Luis Barragan. Canal & Stamperia Staff. 1998. pap. write for info. (*88-86502-86-9*, Pub. by Canal & Stamperia) Antique Collect.

Luis Barragan. Antonio R. Martinez. LC 96-77648. (Illus.). 252p. 1996. 60.00 (*1-885254-44-X*, Pub. by Monacelli Pr) Penguin Putnam.

L

Luis Barragan: The Architecture of Light, Color, & Form. Photos by Armando S. Portugal. LC 92-15545. (Illus.). 168p. 1992. 50.00 (0-8478-1482-3, Pub. by Rizzoli Intl) St Martin.
Luis Barragan: The Phoenix Papers. unabridged ed. Ed. by Ignacio San Martin. LC 97-418. (ENG & SPA., Illus.). 1997. 65.00 (0-87918-088-9) ASU Lat Am St.
Luis Barragan: The Phoenix Papers. unabridged ed. Ed. by Ignacio San Martin. LC 97-418. (ENG & SPA., Illus.). 144p. 1997. pap. 50.00 (0-87918-085-4) ASU Lat Am St.
Luis Barragan, 1902-1988. Martinez Riggen. (ITA., Illus.). 256p. 1997. 139.95 (88-435-4866-2, Pub. by Art Bks Intl) Partners Pubs Grp.
Luis Bunuel: A Critical Biography. Francisco Aranda. Ed. by David Robinson. LC 76-7621. 1976. reprint ed. lib. bdg. 35.00 (0-306-70754-3) Da Capo.
Luis Bunuel: A Critical Biography. Francisco Aranda. Ed. by David Robinson. LC 76-7621. (Illus.). 327p. 1976. reprint ed. pap. 11.95 (0-306-80028-4) Da Capo.
Luis Bunuel's "The Discreet Charm of the Bourgeoisie" Ed. by Marsha Kinder. LC 98-25859. (Cambridge Film Handbks.). (Illus.). 244p. (C). 1999. 49.95 (0-521-56064-0); pap. 14.95 (0-521-56831-5) Cambridge U Pr.
Luis Cernuda: A Study of the Poetry. Derek Harris. (Monagrafias A Ser.: Vol. XXXIII). 188p. (Orig.). (C). 1973. pap. 41.00 (0-900411-70-8, Pub. by Tamesis Bks Ltd) Boydell & Brewer.
*__Luis Cruz Azaceta: Bound.__ Text by Edward J. Sullivan & Susana Torruella Leval. (Illus.). 24p. 1998. pap. 15.00 (1-930191-04-9) M Martin Fine Art.
Luis de Leon. Manuel Duran. LC 79-19352. (Twayne's World Authors Ser.). 1971. lib. bdg. 20.95 (0-8057-2524-5) Irvington.
Luis de Leon: Names of Christ. Tr. by Manuel Duran & William Kluback. (Classics of Western Spirituality Ser.). (C). 1984. 14.95 (0-8091-0346-X); pap. 11.95 (0-8091-2561-7) Paulist Pr.
Luis de Morales & Leonardesque Influences in Spain. Elizabeth D. Trapier. (Illus.). 1953. reprint ed. 5.00 (0-87535-079-8) Hispanic Soc.
Luis Durand. Donald M. Decker. LC 79-120022. (Twayne's World Authors Ser.). 1971. lib. bdg. 20.95 (0-8057-2276-9) Irvington.
Luis Gonzalez Palma: Poems of Sorrow. Photos by Luis Gonzalez Palma. (Illus.). 152p. 1999. 65.00 (1-892041-05-7, Pub. by Arena Editions) Dist Art Pubs.
Luis Goytisolo's Narrative & the Quest for Literary Autonomy. Andrew M. Sobiesuo. LC 96-71722. 107p. 1997. 25.00 (0-938972-28-6) Spanish Lit Pubns.
Luis Jimenez: Working-Class Heroes: Images from the Popular Culture. Michael Brenson et al. (Illus.). 84p. (Orig.). 1997. pap. 24.00 (1-882603-05-2) Mid Am Arts.
*__Luis Leal: An Auto/Biography.__ Mario T. Garcia. LC 99-52635. (Illus.). 240p. 2000. 40.00 (0-292-72828-X); pap. 19.95 (0-292-72829-8) U of Tex Pr.
Luis Llorens Torres: Antologia Verso y Prosa. Arcadio D. Quinones. LC 86-83002. (Clasicos Ser.). (SPA.). 168p. 1996. pap. 8.75 (0-940238-87-X) Ediciones Huracan.
Luis Llorens Torres en Su Centenario. Seminario de Estudios Hispanicos Staff & Federico De Onis. LC 80-21479. (UPREX, Estudios Literarios Ser.: No. 57). 67p. 1983. pap. 2.00 (0-8477-0057-7) U of PR Pr.
Luis Luna Dejo de Banarse. Frank B. Edwards.Tr. of Mortimer Mooner Stopped Taking A Bath. (SPA., Illus.). 24p. (Orig.). (J). (ps-3). 1997. pap. 5.95 (0-921285-62-0, Pub. by Bungalo Books) Firefly Bks Ltd.
Luis Marsans Drawings & Paintings. 1986. pap. write for info. (0-936827-03-3) C Bernard Gallery Ltd.
Luis Martin Santos a la Luz de la Psicologia. Esperanza G. Saludes. LC 81-65512. (Coleccion de Estudios Hispanicos - Hispanic Studies Collection). 172p. (Orig.). 1981. pap. 15.95 (0-89729-291-X) Ediciones.
Luis Mi Rey. Ed. by Javier L. Herrera. (SPA.). 338p. 1998. pap. 15.00 (84-605-6348-0, Pub. by Fundacion EFE) IBD Ltd.
Luis Milan on Sixteenth-Century Performance Practice. Luis Gasser. LC 95-47996. (Publications of the Early Music Institute). (Illus.). 232p. 1996. pap. 24.95 (0-253-21018-6) Ind U Pr.
*__Luis Munoz Marin: Father of Modern Puerto Rico.__ Linda George. (Community Builders Ser.). (J). 2000. pap. text 6.95 (0-516-26513-X) Childrens.
Luis Munoz Marin: Father of Modern Puerto Rico. Linda George & Charles George. LC 98-37338. (Community Builders Ser.). 48p. (J). (gr. 3-5). 1999. lib. bdg. 23.00 (0-516-21586-8) Childrens.
Luis Munoz Marin y Sus Campanas Politicas: Memorias de Su Secretario-Taquigrafo Personal. Lieban Cordova. LC 83-26083. (SPA., Illus.). 175p. (Orig.). 1985. pap. 7.00 (0-8477-2472-7) U of PR Pr.
Luis Palau. W. T. Whalin. (Young Reader's Christian Library). (Illus.). 192p. (J). (gr. 3-7). 1998. pap. 1.39 (1-57748-367-7) Barbour Pub.
Luis Palau. W. T. Whalin. (Men of Faith Ser.). 16p. 1996. mass mkt. 4.99 (1-55661-842-5) Bethany Hse.
Luis Palau: Calling America & the Nations to Christ. Luis Palau & David Sanford. LC 94-21741. 1994. pap. text 8.99 (0-7852-7984-9) Nelson.
*__Luis Palau: Evangelist to the World.__ Ellen Bascuti. (Heroes of the Faith Ser.). 208p. 2000. pap. 3.97 (1-57748-803-2) Barbour Pub.
Luis Pales Matos. Rafael Tufino. (Puerto Rico Ser.). 1979. lib. bdg. 39.95 (0-8490-2996-X) Gordon Pr.
Luis Rafael Sanchez: Critica y Bibliografia. Nelida H. Vargas & Daisy C. Abreu. 292p. 1985. 7.00 (0-8477-3550-8) U of PR Pr.
Luis Rodriguez. Michael Schwartz. LC 96-28450. (Contemporary Hispanic Americans Ser.). (Illus.). 48p. (J). (gr. 3-7). 1997. lib. bdg. 24.26 (0-8172-3990-1) Raintree Steck-V.
Luis Rodriguez. Michael Schwartz. (Contemporary African Americans Ser.). (Illus.). 48p. (J). (gr. 3-7). 1998. pap. 7.95 (0-8172-6879-0) Raintree Steck-V.
Luis Tlon, Uqbar, Orbis Tertius. Jorge Luis Borges. 78p. 1983. pap. write for info. (0-88984-072-5) Porcup Quill.
Luis Valdez - Early Works: Actos, Bernabe & Pensamiento Serpentino. Teatro Campesino Staff & Luis Valdez. LC 89-35438. 189p. 1990. pap. text 11.95 (1-55885-003-1) Arte Publico.
Luis Vives, el Gran Valenciano. Foster Watson. 1987. reprint ed. pap. 10.00 (0-87535-013-5) Hispanic Soc.
Luisa Capetillo, 1879-1922. Ed. by Amilcar Tirado et al. (Puerto Rican Bibliographies Ser.). 15p. (C). 1986. reprint ed. pap. 1.00 (1-878483-40-4) Hunter Coll CEP.
Luisa Domic & Shawno. George Dennison. LC 94-6469. 213p. 1994. reprint ed. pap. 12.00 (1-883642-49-3) Steerforth Pr.
Luisa in Realityland. Claribel Alegria. Tr. by Darwin J. Flakoll. LC 87-71705. 152p. 1987. 17.95 (0-915306-70-0) Curbstone.
Luisa in Realityland. Claribel Alegria. Tr. by Darwin J. Flakoll. LC 87-71705. 152p. 1988. pap. 9.95 (0-915306-69-7) Curbstone.
Luisa Michel: A Chronology. V. Munoz. Tr. by W. Scott Johnson. (Libertarian & Anarchist Chronology Ser.). 1979. lib. bdg. 59.95 (0-8490-3028-5) Gordon Pr.
Luisa Miller, 2 vols., Set. Giuseppe Verdi. Ed. by Jeffrey Kallberg. (Works of Giuseppe Verdi: No. 1: Operas, Vol. 15). lvi, 696p. 1992. lib. bdg. 275.00 (0-226-85312-8) U Ch Pr.
Luisa Tetrazzini: The Florentine Nightingale. Charles N. Gattey. (Opera Biography Ser.: No. 5). (Illus.). 288p. 1995. 39.95 (0-931340-87-X, Amadeus Pr) Timber.
Luise. ein Beitrag Zur Geschichte der Konvenienz. Therese Huber. (Fruhe Frauenliteratur in Deutschland Ser.: Vol. 2). (GER.). xxiv, 224p. 1991. reprint ed. write for info. (3-487-09492-4) G Olms Pubs.
Luise Hensel Als Dichterin. F. Spiecker. LC 79-133463. (Northwestern University. Humanities Ser.: No. 3). 1970. reprint ed. 42.50 (0-404-50703-4) AMS Pr.
Luise Reichardt Als Musikpadagogin und Komponistin: Untersuchungen zu den Bedingungen Beruflicher Musikausubung Durch Frauen im Fruhen 19, Jahrhundert. Iris Boffo-Stetter. (Beitrage zur Geschichte der Musikpadagogik Ser.: Bd. 4). (GER., Illus.). 179p. 1996. 42.95 (3-631-30123-5) P Lang Pubng.
Luiseno Social Organization. Raymond C. White. (University of California Publications in American Archaeology & Ethnology Ser.: Vol. 48(2)). (Illus.). 110p. (C). 1963. pap. text 12.19 (1-55567-699-5) Coyote Press.
*__Luka Ke'elikolani.__ Ku'ulei Higashi. (HAW., Illus.). 21p. (J). (gr. 2). 1999. pap. 6.95 incl. audio (1-58191-065-7) Aha Punana Leo.
Lukacs after Communism: Interviews with Contemporary Intellectuals. Eva L. Corredor. LC 96-34207. (Post-Contemporary Interventions Ser.). 248p. 1997. pap. text 15.95 (0-8223-1763-X); lib. bdg. 49.95 (0-8223-1754-0) Duke.
Lukacs & Brecht. David Pike. LC 84-17406. xviii, 337p. 1985. text 55.00 (0-8078-1640-X) U of NC Pr.
Lukacs & Heidegger: Towards a New Philosophy. Lucien Goldmann. Tr. by William Q. Boelhower. 136p. pap. 12.95 (0-7100-8794-2, Routledge Thoemms) Routledge.
Lukacs Reader. Georg Lukacs. Ed. by Arpad Kadarky. 352p. (C). 1995. pap. 28.95 (1-55786-571-X) Blackwell Pubs.
Lukacs Reads Goethe: From Aestheticism to Stalinism. Nicholas Vazsonyi. LC 97-15666. (Studies in German Literature, Linguistics, & Culture). 210p. 1997. 50.00 (1-57113-114-0) Camden Hse.
Lukacs Reappraised. Ed. by Agnes Heller. LC 83-7182. 192p. 1983. pap. text 19.00 (0-231-05803-9) Col U Pr.
Lukacs' Road to God: The Early Criticism Against Its Pre-Marxist Background. Michael Holzman. (Current Continental Research Ser.: No. 208). 196p. (Orig.). 1985. pap. text 22.50 (0-8191-4720-6) U Pr of Amer.
Lukacs Today. Ed. by Tom Rockmore. 284p. (C). 1988. text 153.00 (90-277-2661-2, D Reidel) Kluwer Academic.
*__Lukan.__ Anna M. Hanberg. 2000. pap. 10.95 (0-533-13469-2) Vantage.
*__Lukan Passion Narrative: The Markan Material in Luke 22,54 - 23,25.__ Jay M. Harrington. (New Testament Tools & Studies Ser.). 1000p. 2000. 206.00 (90-04-11590-0) Brill Academic Pubs.
Lukan Voice: Confusion & Irony in the Gospel of Luke. James M. Dawsey. LC 86-19173. 208p. 1986. 24.95 (0-86554-193-0, MUP-H178) Mercer Univ Pr.
Lukang: Commerce & Community in a Chinese City. Donald R. DeGlopper. LC 95-2525. (SUNY Series in Chinese Local Studies). 296p. (C). 1995. text 59.50 (0-7914-2689-0); pap. text 19.95 (0-7914-2690-4) State U NY Pr.
Lukas at Auction. Joe Bagan. 300p. (Orig.). 1989. pap. 25.00 (0-9622850-0-5) Sachs Lawlor.
Lukas Foss: A Bio-Bibliography, 37. Karen L. Perone. LC 90-29280. (Bio Bibliographies in Music Ser.: No. 37). 296p. 1991. lib. bdg. 65.00 (0-313-26811-8, PLB, Greenwood Pr) Greenwood.
Luka's Quilt. Georgia Guback. LC 93-12241. (Illus.). 32p. (J). (ps-3). 1994. 14.95 (0-688-12154-3, Grenwillow Bks) HarpC Child Bks.
*__Luka's Story.__ Bel Ami Books Staff. 2000. pap. 15.95 (1-902644-25-5) Prowler Pr.
Luke see Commentaries on the New Testament
Luke see IVP New Testament Commentary
Luke see Lucas
Luke. (Life Application Bible Study Guide Ser.). 160p. 1992. pap. 5.99 (0-8423-2877-7, 02-2877-7) Tyndale Hse.
Luke. William Barclay. 312p. 1993. pap. 24.00 (0-7152-0273-1, Pub. by St Andrew) St Mut.
Luke. Bruce B. Barton et al. LC 97-27767. (Life Application Bible Commentary Ser.). 1998. 16.99 (0-8423-2852-1) Tyndale Hse.
Luke. Bentley. 1991. pap. text. write for info. (0-582-03579-1, Pub. by Addison-Wesley) Longman.
Luke. Jennifer Blake. 1999. mass mkt. 5.99 (1-55166-490-9, 1-66490-3, Mira Bks) Harlequin Bks.
Luke, 2. Darrell L. Bock. (Baker Exegetical Commentary on the New Testament Ser.). 2,150p. 1993. 80.00 (0-8010-1051-9) Baker Bks.
Luke. Darrell L. Bock. (NIV Application Commentary Ser.). 608p. 1996. 27.99 (0-310-49330-7) Zondervan.
*__Luke.__ Trent C. Butler. (Holman New Testament Commentary Ser.: Vol. 3). 2000. 16.99 (0-8054-0203-9) Broadman.
Luke. Cline. 1988. write for info. (0-88027-117-5) Firm Foun Pub.
Luke. Fred B. Craddock. (Interpretation: a Bible Commentary for Preaching & Teaching Ser.). 300p. 1990. text 27.00 (0-8042-3123-0) Westminster John Knox.
Luke. William E. Fischer. LC 88-61644. (People's Bible Ser.). 32p. 1994. student ed. 4.00 (0-8100-0512-3, 22N0851) Northwest Pub.
Luke. Victor P. Furnish. (Abingdon New Testament Commentaries Ser.). 416p. 1996. pap. 24.95 (0-614-18862-8) Abingdon.
Luke. Dana Gould. LC 97-37018. (Shepherd's Notes Ser.). 1997. 5.95 (0-8054-9004-3) Broadman.
Luke. Ed. by William M. Greathouse & Willard H. Taylor. (Bible Exposition Ser.: Vol. 3). 222p. 1974. 14.99 (0-8341-0314-1) Beacon Hill.
Luke. William Hendriksen. LC 78-58717. (New Testament Commentary Ser.). 1136p. 1978. 39.99 (0-8010-4191-0) Baker Bks.
Luke. Arthur A. Just. LC 96-17930. (Concordia Commentary Ser.). 1996. 30.00 (0-570-04254-2, 15-6019) Concordia.
Luke. Jonathan Knight. LC 97-30043. (New Testament Readings Ser.). 240p. (C). 1998. pap. 24.99 (0-415-17322-1) Routledge.
Luke. Jonathan Knight. LC 97-30043. (New Testament Readings Ser.). 240p. (C). 1998. 75.00 (0-415-17321-3) Routledge.
Luke. L. La Verdiere. 1989. pap. 21.00 (0-86217-008-7, Pub. by Veritas Pubns) St Mut.
Luke. B. Larson. (Mastering the Old & New Testament Ser.: Vol. 3). pap. 14.99 (0-8499-3319-6) Word Pub.
Luke. Bruce Larson. (Communicator's Commentary Ser.: Vol. 3). 347p. 22.99 (0-8499-0156-1) Word Pub.
Luke. Eugene LaVerdiere. LC 80-65618. (New Testament Message Ser.: Vol. 5). 296p. 1980. pap. 16.95 (0-8146-5128-3) Liturgical Pr.
Luke. Ana Leigh. (Mackenzies Ser.: No. 1). 384p. (Orig.). 1996. mass mkt. 5.50 (0-380-78098-4, Avon Bks) Morrow Avon.
Luke. J Vernon Mcgee. (Thru the Bible Commentary Ser.: Vol. 37). 1997. pap. 6.97 (0-7852-0668-X) Nelson.
Luke. Navpress Staff. (LifeChange Ser.). 1996. pap. 7.00 (0-89109-930-1) NavPress.
Luke. Jane Osborne & Chris Sugden. (Bible Study Commentaries Ser.). 1987. pap. 4.95 (0-87508-168-1) Chr Lit.
Luke. C. Marvin Pate. (Gospel Commentaries Ser.). 475p. pap. 22.99 (0-8024-5622-7, 517) Moody.
Luke. Victor H. Prange. (People's Bible Commentary Ser.). 266p. (Orig.). 1992. pap. 10.99 (0-570-04586-X, 12-8004) Concordia.
Luke. Victor H. Prange. LC 88-61644. (People's Bible Ser.). 266p. (Orig.). 1989. pap. 11.99 (0-8100-0297-3, 15N0453) Northwest Pub.
Luke. Sharon H. Ringe. Ed. by David L. Bartlett & Patrick D. Miller. (Westminster Bible Companion Ser.). 291p. 1995. pap. 20.00 (0-664-25259-1) Westminster John Knox.
Luke. Robert H. Stein. LC 92-30024. (New American Commentary Ser.: Vol. 24). 1993. 27.99 (0-8054-0124-5) Broadman.
Luke. Robert C. Tannehill. LC 96-30769. (Abington New Testament Commentaries Ser.). 1996. pap. 24.95 (0-687-06132-6) Abingdon.
Luke. Christopher M. Tuckett. (New Testament Guides Ser.: Vol. 3). 121p. 1996. pap. 12.50 (1-85075-751-8, Pub. by Sheffield Acad) CUP Services.
Luke. Tyndale House Publishers Staff. (Life Application Bible Studies). 139p. 1999. pap. 5.99 (0-8423-3416-5) Tyndale Hse.
*__Luke.__ Tom Walker. (Illus.). 112p. 2000. pap. 7.95 (0-664-50075-7) Westminster John Knox.
Luke. abr. ed. J. C. Ryle. LC 97-17281. (Classic Commentaries Ser.). 304p. 1997. pap. 17.99 (0-89107-955-6) Crossway Bks.
Luke. J. C. Ryle. (Expository Thoughts on the Gospel Ser.: Vol. 1). 390p. 1986. reprint ed. pap. 9.99 (0-85151-497-9) Banner of Truth.
Luke. J. C. Ryle. (Expository Thoughts on the Gospel Ser.: Vol. 2). 530p. 1986. reprint ed. pap. 9.99 (0-85151-498-7) Banner of Truth.
Luke see Preacher's Outline & Sermon Bible - New Testament Set
Luke, Vol. 3. Craig A. Evans. LC 96-4128. (New International Biblical Commentary Ser.). 398p. 1990. pap. 11.95 (0-943575-31-1) Hendrickson MA.
Luke see Layman's Bible Commentary
Luke: A Critical Study. Friedrich Daniel Ernst Schleiermacher. Ed. by Terrence N. Tice. Tr. by Connop Thirlwall from GER. LC 93-17976. (Schleiermacher Studies & Translations: Vol. 13). 556p. 1993. text 119.95 (0-7734-9326-3) E Mellen.
Luke: A Gospel for Today. Smith. 1989. pap. 16.95 (0-7459-1503-5, Pub. by Lion Pubng) Trafalgar.
Luke: A New Paradigm. M. D. Goulder. (JSNT Supplement Ser.: No. 20). 824p. 1989. pap. 39.50 (1-85075-101-3, Pub. by Sheffield Acad) CUP Services.
Luke: ESL Study Edition. Martha A. Lane. (Passport to the World of English Ser.: Bk. 4). (Illus.). 194p. 1997. teacher ed., ring bd. 23.00 incl. audio (1-877596-33-7); student ed., ring bd. 20.00 incl. audio (1-877596-34-5) Literacy & Evangelism.
Luke: Following Jesus. Sharrel Keyes. (Fisherman Bible Studyguide Ser.). 96p. 1983. pap. 4.99 (0-87788-511-7, H Shaw Pubs) Waterbrook Pr.
Luke: Following Jesus - Chinese Edition. Sharrel Keyes. Tr. by John Zheng. (CHI.). 109p. 1998. pap. 6.00 (1-56582-005-3) Christ Renew Min.
Luke: Good News & Great Joy. rev. ed. Marilyn Kunz & Catherine Schell. 96p. 1997. pap. 5.99 (1-880266-27-X) Neighborhood Bible.
Luke: Good News of Hope & Joy. Ada Lum. (LifeGuide Bible Studies). 112p. (Orig.). 1992. pap., wbk. ed. 4.99 (0-8308-1005-6, 1005) InterVarsity.
Luke: Gospel of God's Man. Keith L. Brooks. (Teach Yourself the Bible Ser.). pap. 5.99 (0-8024-5047-4, 521) Moody.
Luke: Gospel of the Son of Man. Paul N. Benware. (Everyman's Bible Commentaries Ser.). pap. 9.99 (0-8024-2074-5, 484) Moody.
Luke: Historian & Theologian see New Testament Profiles
Luke: Historian & Theologian. J. Howard Marshall, II. 252p. 1997. reprint ed. pap. 12.99 (0-85364-486-1, Pub. by Paternoster Pub) OM Literature.
Luke: Interpreter of Paul, Critic of Matthew. Eric Franklin. (JSNT Supplement Ser.: No. 92). 414p. 1994. 85.00 (1-85075-452-7, Pub. by Sheffield Acad) CUP Services.
Luke: Our Compassionate Savior. Robert Knopp. LC 99-214675. (Gospel Images for Prayer Ser.). 224p. 1998. pap. 7.95 (0-8198-3087-9) Pauline Bks.
Luke: That You May Know the Truth, Vol. 1. R. Kent Hughes. LC 98-29830. (Preaching the Word Ser.). 1998. 24.99 (1-58134-028-1) Crossway Bks.
Luke: That You May Know the Truth, Vol. 2. R. Kent Hughes. LC 98-29830. (Preaching the Word Ser.: Vol. 2). 480p. 1998. 24.99 (1-58134-029-X) Crossway Bks.
*__Luke: The Good News of God's Mercy.__ Kevin Perrotta. (Catholic Perspectives Six Weeks with the Bible). 83p. 2000. pap. 6.95 (0-8294-1370-7) Loyola Pr.
Luke: The Perennial Spirituality. Leonard Doohan. LC 85-71858. (Scripture for Worship Ser.). 228p. (Orig.). (C). 1993. pap. text 10.95 (0-89390-262-4) Resource Pubns.
Luke: 1849 - On the Golden Trail. Bonnie Pryor. LC 98-47498. (American Adventures Ser.). (Illus.). 176p. (YA). (gr. 3-7). 1999. 15.00 (0-688-15670-3, Wm Morrow) Morrow Avon.
*__Luke: 1849 - On the Golden Trail.__ Bonnie Pryor. LC 98-47498. (American Adventures Ser.). (Illus.). 176p. (J). (gr. 3-7). 2000. mass mkt. 4.50 (0-380-73102-9, Avon Bks) Morrow Avon.
*__Luke: 1849-On the Golden Trail.__ Bonnie Pryor. (Illus.). (J). 2000. 9.85 (0-606-17977-1) Turtleback.
Luke Vol. 1: 1: 1-9:50, 1. Darrell L. Bock. LC 94-33507. (Baker Exegetical Commentary on the New Testament Ser.: Vol. 1). 988p. (J). 1994. 44.99 (0-8010-1053-5) Baker Bks.
Luke Vol. 2: 9:51-24:53, 2. Darrell L. Bock. LC 94-33507. (Baker Exegetical Commentary on the New Testament Ser.). 1,162p. 1996. 44.99 (0-8010-1052-7) Baker Bks.
Luke, a Devotional Commentary: Meditations on the Gospel According to St. Luke. Ed. by Leo Zanchettin. 1999. pap. 22.95 (0-932085-27-X) Word Among Us.
Luke Acts: A Story of Prophet & People. Luke T. Johnson. LC 81-4520. 65p. 1980. pap. 1.00 (0-8199-0524-0, Frncscn Herld) Franciscan Pr.
Luke Acts: Angels, Christology & Soteriology. Crispin H. Fletcher-Louis. LC 97-182178. (WissUnt Zum Neuen Testament 2/94 Ser.). 372p. 1997. pap. 89.50 (3-16-146764-7, Pub. by JCB Mohr) Coronet Bks.
Luke-Acts & New Testament Historiography. Joel Green & Michael McKeever. LC 94-40065. (IBR Bibliographies Ser.). 160p. 1995. pap. 10.99 (0-8010-3872-3) Baker Bks.
Luke & Acts. Ed. by Gerald O'Collins & Gilberto Marconi. Tr. by Matthew J. O'Connell. LC 92-35226. 320p. 1993. pap. 10.95 (0-8091-3360-1) Paulist Pr.
Luke & Acts Study Guide, Bk. 1. Constance. 97p. 1988. pap., student ed. 12.99 (1-889015-47-4) Explrs Bible.
Luke & Acts Study Guide, Bk. 2. Constance. 89p. 1988. pap., student ed. 12.99 (1-889015-48-2) Explrs Bible.
Luke & Acts Study Guide, Bk. 3. Constance. 92p. 1988. pap., student ed. 12.99 (1-889015-49-0) Explrs Bible.
Luke & John. Ben C. Johnson. 160p. (Orig.). (C). 1995. pap. text 7.95 (0-929263-09-X) Great Love Church Intl.
Luke & John. Contrib. by Leander E. Keck. (New Interpreter's Bible: Vol. 9). 1996. 55.00 (0-687-27822-8) Abingdon.
Luke & the Gentile Mission: Gospel Anticipates Acts. Thomas J. Lane. (European University Studies: Series 23, Vol. 571). (GER.). 240p. 1996. pap. 44.95 (3-631-49999-X) P Lang Pubng.
Luke & the Restoration of Israel. David A. Ravens. (JSNT Supplement Ser.: No. 119). 287p. 1996. 80.00 (1-85075-565-5, Pub. by Sheffield Acad) CUP Services.
Luke & the Van Zandt County War. Judith M. Alter. LC 84-101. (Chaparral Bks.). (Illus.). 132p. (J). (gr. 4 up). 1984. 10.95 (0-912646-88-8) Tex Christian.
Luke & the Wolf. Roger Bell. 40p. 1997. 3.75 (0-9694127-3-8) Genl Dist Srvs.
Luke Comes Alive. John Blanchard. 1986. pap. 4.99 (0-85234-223-3, Pub. by Evangelical Pr) P & R Pubng.
Luke (Everyman's Bible Commentary) see Lucas
Luke Howard, 1772-1864. D. F. Scott. (C). 1988. 40.00 (0-900657-36-7, Pub. by W Sessions) St Mut.

An Asterisk (*) at the beginning of an entry indicates that the title is appearing for the first time.

L

Luke-John. William G. Scroggie. 1981. pap. 4.95 (*0-87508-485-0*) Chr Lit.

Luke, John see Interpreter's Bible

***Luke, Judaism & the Scholars: Critical Approaches to Luke-Acts.** Joseph B. Tyson. LC 99-6596. 224p. 1999. 29.95 (*1-57003-334-X*) U of SC Pr.

Luke Karamazov. Conrad Hilberry. LC 86-28218. (Great Lakes Bks.). 190p. 1987. 19.95 (*0-8143-1856-8*) Wayne St U Pr.

Luke Lea of Tennessee. Mary L. Tidwell. LC 93-70239. 330p. 1993. 39.95 (*0-87972-624-5*); pap. 15.95 (*0-87972-575-3*) Bowling Green Univ Popular Press.

Luke Leader's Guide: Taking up the Master's Mission. Joel Kok. (Revelation Ser.). 64p. 1997. pap., teacher ed. 6.75 (*1-56212-246-0*, 1312-8740); pap., student ed. 4.95 (*1-56212-245-2*, 1312-8700) CRC Pubns.

Luke Loader Helps Build a Road. Jen Koury. Ed. by Pat Linden & Steve Hilko. (Johnny Tractor Toybks.). (Illus.). 10p. (J). (ps-1). 1997. mass mkt. write for info. (*1-887327-13-4*) Ertl Co.

Luke Miver's Harvest. N. Walter Swan. Ed. by Harry Heseltine. 314p. pap. 32.95 (*0-86840-284-2*, Pub. by New South Wales Univ Pr) Intl Spec Bk.

Luke 19-24. Nolland. (Word Biblical Commentary Ser.: Vol. 35C). 1993. 29.99 (*0-8499-1072-2*) Word Pub.

Luke 9:21-18, Vol.35c. John Nolland. (Biblical Commentary Ser.: Vol. 35B). 1993. 29.99 (*0-8499-0254-1*) Word Pub.

Luke on the High Seas. Bonnie Pryor. (American Adventures Ser.). (J). Date not set. pap. 4.95 (*0-380-73286-6*, Wm Morrow) Morrow Avon.

Luke 1:1-9:20. John Nolland. (Biblical Commentary Ser.: Vol. 35A). 1993. 29.99 (*0-8499-0234-7*) Word Pub.

Luke Perry. Rosemary Wallner. LC 92-16036. (Reaching for the Stars Ser.). (Illus.). 32p. (J). 1992. lib. bdg. 13.98 (*1-56239-146-1*) ABDO Pub Co.

Luke Pryor Blackburn: Physician, Governor, Reformer. Nancy D. Baird. LC 79-888. (Kentucky Bicentennial Bookshelf Ser.). 136p. reprint ed. pap. 42.20 (*0-7837-5817-0*, 204548400006) Bks Demand.

Luke Short. Wayne Short. (Illus.). 260p. (Orig.). 1996. pap. 14.95 (*0-9644980-7-3*) Devils Thumb.

Luke Short's Best of the West. Luke Short. 1990. mass mkt. 3.95 (*0-8217-3003-7*, Zebra Kensgtn) Kensgtn Pub Corp.

Luke Skywalker. Mouse Works Staff. LC 98-127247. (Star Wars Ser.). (J). 1998. 6.98 (*1-57082-824-5*, Pub. by Mouse Works) Time Warner.

Luke Swetland's Captivity & Rescue from the Indians: An Early Settler of the Wyoming Valley & a Soldier of the American Revolution. Edward Merrifield. LC 98-88847. (Pennsylvania History & Legends Ser.). (Illus.). 66p. 1998. reprint ed. pap. 8.95 (*1-889037-15-X*) Wennawoods.

Luke the Lionhearted. Antonie Schneider. LC 98-11242. (Illus.). 32p. (J). (gr. k-3). 1998. lib. bdg. 15.88 (*1-55858-977-5*, Pub. by North-South Bks NYC) Chronicle Bks.

Luke the Lionhearted. Antonie Schneider. LC 98-11242. (Illus.). 32p. (J). (gr. k-3). 1998. 15.95 (*1-55858-976-7*, Pub. by North-South Bks NYC) Chronicle Bks.

Luke the Theologian: Thirty-Three Years of Research (1950-1983) Francois Bovon. Tr. by Ken McKinney from FRE. LC 87-7969. (Princeton Theological Monographs: No. 12).Tr. of Luc le theologien: Vingt-cinq ans de recherches (1950-1975). (Orig.). 1987. pap. 25.00 (*0-915138-93-X*) Pickwick.

Luke Walton. Horatio Alger, Jr. (Works of Horatio Alger Jr.). 1989. reprint ed. lib. bdg. 79.00 (*0-685-44745-6*) Rprt Serv.

Luke Walton: or The Chicago Newsboy. Horatio Alger. 1976. reprint ed. lib. bdg. 25.95 (*0-88411-813-4*) Amereon Ltd.

Luke Was There: A Study Guide. Marcia Tretler. Ed. by Joyce Friedland & Rikki Kessler. (Novel-Ties Ser.). 19p. (J). (gr. 4-6). 1990. pap. text 15.95 (*0-88122-400-6*) Lrn Links.

***Luke/Journeys Pack.** (J). 2000. pap. 9.49 (*0-06-449200-1*, HarpTrophy) HarpC Child Bks.

Luker Families: A History & Genealogy. write for info. (*0-318-59850-7*) V Luker.

Luke's Academic List. Joyce M. Herzog. Ed. by Tom Herzog. (Luke's List Ser.: Vol. 2). (Illus.). 146p. (Orig.). (J). (gr. k-8). 1997. pap. text. write for info. (*1-887225-13-7*) Simplified Lrn.

***Luke's Daughters.** Lynnette Kent. (Superromance Ser.: Vol. 901). 2000. per. 4.50 (*0-373-70901-3*) Harlequin Bks.

Luke's Life of Jesus. R. C. Sproul. 1997. pap. 16.99 (*1-85792-260-3*, Pub. by Christian Focus) Spring Arbor Dist.

Luke's Lifelong List. Joyce M. Herzog. Ed. by Tom J. Herzog. (Luke's List Ser.: Vol. 1). (Illus.). 126p. (Orig.). (J). (ps up). 1997. pap. text. write for info. (*1-887225-12-9*) Simplified Lrn.

Luke's Literary Achievement: Collected Essays. Ed. by C. M. Tuckett. (JSNT Supplement Ser.: No. 116). 232p. 1995. 70.00 (*1-85075-556-6*, Pub. by Sheffield Acad) CUP Services.

***Luke's Message.** Val Webb. 1999. pap. 5.00 (*0-687-02193-6*) Abingdon.

Luke's Message: Good News for the New Millennium. J. Ellsworth Kalas. LC 98-225086. 72p. 1997. pap. 5.00 (*0-687-05654-3*) Abingdon.

***Luke's Portrait of Gentiles Prior to Their Coming to Faith.** Christoph W. Stenschke. (Wissenschaftliche Untersuchungen Zum Neuen Testament Ser.: Vol. 108). 450p. 1999. 97.50 (*3-16-147139-3*, Pub. by JCB Mohr) Coronet Bks.

Luke's Portrait of Jesus. Bennie Goodwin. 96p. (Orig.). 1993. pap. text 4.95 (*0-940955-25-3*) Urban Ministries.

***Luke's Stories of Jesus: Theological Reading of Gospel Narrative & the Legacy of Hans Frei.** David Lee. (Journal for the Study of the New Testament, Supplement Ser.: No. 185). 408p. 1999. 85.00 (*1-84127-013-X*, Pub. by Sheffield Acad) CUP Services.

Luke's Summer Secret. Randall Wisehart. LC 91-786. 165p. 1991. pap. 9.00 (*0-944350-17-8*) Friends United.

Luke's Thrilling Gospel. Ivor C. Powell. LC 84-9637. (Ivor Powell Commentaries Ser.). 508p. 1984. lib. bdg. 19.99 (*0-8254-3513-7*) Kregel.

Luke's Would-Be Bride. Sandra Steffen. (Romance Ser.: No. 1230). 1997. per. 3.25 (*0-373-19230-4*, 1-19230-1) Silhouette.

Lukewarmness. rev. ed. Francis F. Carvajal. 142p. 1992. pap. 9.95 (*0-933932-59-6*) Scepter Pubs.

Lukian von Samosata, Alexander the False Prophet see Lukian von Samosata, Alexandros Oder der Lugenprophet: Eingeleitet, Herausgegeben, Ubersetzt und Erklart von Ulrich Victor

Lukian von Samosata, Alexandros Oder der Lugenprophet: Eingeleitet, Herausgegeben, Ubersetzt und Erklart von Ulrich Victor. (Religions in the Graeco-Roman World Ser.: No. 132).Tr. of Lukian von Samosata, Alexander the False Prophet. (GER.). viii, 184p. 1997. 72.50 (*90-04-10792-4*) Brill Academic Pubs.

Lukians Parasitendialog: Untersuchungen und Kommentar. Heinz-Gunther Nesselrath. (Untersuchungen zur Antiken Literatur und Geschichte Ser.: Vol. 22). (GER.). xi, 559p. 1985. 234.65 (*3-11-010277-3*) De Gruyter.

Lukrez - Versuch Einer Deutung. Marc Rozelaar. (GER.). xvi, 267p. 1988. reprint ed. write for info. (*3-487-09026-0*) G Olms Pubs.

Lukurmata: Household Archaeology in Prehispanic Bolivia. Marc Bermann. LC 93-23366. 328p. 1994. text 65.00 (*0-691-03359-5*, Pub. by Princeton U Pr) Cal Prin Full Svc.

Luky Jack & the Giant. Janet P. Johnson. LC 97-221865. (Legends of the World Ser.). (Illus.). (J). (gr. 2-6). 1997. pap. 35.95 incl. audio (*0-8167-4348-7*) Troll Communs.

Lulac: The Evolution of a Mexican American Political Organization. Benjamin Marquez. LC 92-28983. 159p. 1993. reprint ed. pap. 49.30 (*0-608-03571-8*, 206439400009) Bks Demand.

Lulie: The Iceburg. Takamado Hih Princess. (J). (gr. 3 up). 1998. 17.00 (*1-56836-272-2*) Kodansha.

Lull after the Storm: Poverty & Integrated Rural Development. Nadeem Mohsin. 1989. 28.50 (*81-7169-035-1*, Pub. by Commonwealth) S Asia.

***Lull & Bruno, Vol. 8.** Frances A. Yates. LC 99-15955. (Selected Works). 1999. write for info. (*0-415-22043-2*) Routledge.

Lull & Bruno: Collected Essays, Vol. 1. Francis A. Yates. (Illus.). 1982. 32.50 (*0-7100-0952-6*, Routledge Thoemms) Routledge.

***Lullabible: A Musical Treasury for Mother & Baby.** Stephen Elkins. (Illus.). 2000. 21.99 (*0-8054-2390-7*) Broadman.

***LullaBible: A Musical Treasury for Mother & Baby.** Stephen Elkins & Ellie Colton. (Illus.). 224p. (J). (ps). 2000. 14.99 (*0-8054-2388-5*) Broadman.

Lullabies. 1999. 15.00 (*1-56170-633-7*) Hay House.

Lullabies, 1 Vol. Kristen Matieu & Publications International, Ltd. Editorial Staff. LC 98-193914. (Baby Looney Tunes Song Bks.). (Illus.). (J). 1998. write for info. (*0-7853-2672-3*) Pubns Intl Ltd.

Lullabies: An Illustrated Songbook. Metropolitan Museum of Art Staff. (Illus.). 96p. (J). (gr. k up). 1997. 23.00 (*0-15-201728-3*) Harcourt.

Lullabies & Bedtime Stories. Friedman-Fairfax & Sony Music Staff. (CD Ser.). (Illus.). 72p. 1994. pap. 15.98 incl. audio (*1-56799-080-0*, Friedman-Fairfax) M Friedman Pub Grp Inc.

Lullabies & Daydreams: With Lullabies & Daydreams CD. 2nd ed. Suzanne Siegel Zenkel. (BookNotes Ser.). (Illus.). 64p. 1998. 13.99 incl. audio compact disk (*0-88088-411-8*) Peter Pauper.

Lullabies & Good Night. Illus. by Mary Cassatt. 32p. (J). 1989. 13.95 (*0-8249-8441-2*, Ideals Child); 17.95 incl. audio (*0-8249-7351-8*, Ideals Child) Hambleton-Hill.

***Lullabies & Lamentations.** Emma Zerik. 16p. 1999. pap. 12.00 (*1-929624-04-2*) Circle Creative.

Lullabies & Night Songs. Ed. by William Engvick. LC 65-22880. (Illus.). (J). (ps-3). 1965. 26.00 (*0-06-021820-7*) HarpC Child Bks.

Lullabies for Everyone: Musical Security Blanket. Sherry L. Keitz. Ed. by Herbert W. Ernst. (Illus.). 150p. (Orig.). Date not set. 17.99 incl. disk (*0-9647564-2-0*) Mystic Romance.

Lullabies for Little Hearts. Carol Smith. (Bibles for Little Hearts Ser.). 1999. pap. text 9.99 (*0-8423-3876-4*); pap. text 12.99 (*0-8423-3877-2*) Tyndale Hse.

Lullabies, Lyrics & Gallows Songs. Christian Morgenstern. LC 94-40351. (Illus.). 48p. (J). (gr. 2-4). 1995. 16.95 (*1-55858-364-5*, Pub. by North-South Bks NYC) Chronicle Bks.

Lullaby. Don Appell. 1954. pap. 5.25 (*0-8222-0707-9*) Dramatists Play.

Lullaby. J. M. Le Clezio. (Folio - Junior Ser.: No. 448). (FRE., Illus.). (J). (gr. 5-10). 1995. pap. 6.95 (*2-07-033448-1*) Schoenhof.

Lullaby: An 87th Precinct Novel. Ed McBain, pseud. 352p. 1990. mass mkt. 5.99 (*0-380-70384-X*, Avon Bks) Morrow Avon.

Lullaby Aggie of Sweet Potato Cave. Charles E. Price. 80p. 1996. pap. 6.95 (*1-57072-055-X*) Overmountain Pr.

Lullaby & Good Night. Berthe Amoss. (Illus.). 10p. (J). (ps-7). 1989. pap. 2.95 (*0-922589-13-5*) More Than a Card.

Lullaby & Good Night. Illus. by Julie Downing. LC 97-47306. 31p. (J). (ps). 1999. 15.00 (*0-689-81085-7*) S&S Bks Yung.

Lullaby & Goodnight. 8p. (J). 1991. 34.99 (*1-888074-15-9*) Pckts Lrning.

Lullaby & Goodnight. D. T. Hughes. Ed. by Linda Marrow. 288p. (Orig.). 1992. mass mkt. 4.99 (*0-671-72405-3*) PB.

***Lullaby & Goodnight.** Susan Kearney. (Intrigue Ser.). 2000. mass mkt. 4.25 (*0-373-22594-6*, 1225945) Harlequin Bks.

Lullaby & Goodnight: Bundles of Joy. Sandra Steffen. (Romance Ser.). 1995. per. 2.99 (*0-373-19074-3*, 1-19074-3) Silhouette.

Lullaby & Goodnight Sleepkit: The Gift of Sweet Dreams & Family Memories. Karen Carson et al. LC 91-67933. 32p. (J). (ps-3). 1992. pap. 2.95 (*1-880444-03-8*) Times to Treas.

Lullaby & Goodnight Sleepkit: The Gift of Sweet Dreams & Family Memories. Michael J. Rosen et al. LC 91-67933. (Illus.). 32p. (J). (ps-3). 1992. pap. 14.95 (*1-880444-01-1*) Times to Treas.

Lullaby & Goodnight Sleepkit: The Gift of Sweet Dreams & Family Memories, Mini Edition. Michael J. Rosen. (Illus.). 32p. (J). (ps-3). 1992. 14.95 incl. audio (*1-880444-02-X*) Times to Treas.

Lullaby & Goodnight Sleepkit: The Gift of Sweet Dreams & Family Memories, Set. Michael J. Rosen et al. LC 91-67933. (Illus.). 32p. (J). (ps-3). 1992. teacher ed., boxed set 28.95 incl. audio (*1-880444-00-3*) Times to Treas.

Lullaby Baby. C. R. Gibson Company, Staff. 1997. 22.00 (*0-7667-0705-9*) Gibson.

***Lullaby Bible.** Melody Carlson. LC 97-43520. (Illus.). 48p. (J). (ps). 1998. 10.99 (*1-57673-252-5*, Gold n Honey) Zondervan.

Lullaby Book. Richard Carlin. (Illus.). 64p. 1997. pap. 9.95 (*0-8256-2337-5*, AM37029) Music Sales.

Lullaby Cherub. Lynda Bell. (Illus.). 30p. (J). (ps-6). 1994. write for info. (*0-9641771-1-0*) Cherub Prods.

Lullaby Deception. Susan Kearney. (Intrigue Ser.). 1997. per. 3.75 (*0-373-22410-9*, 1-22410-4) Harlequin Bks.

Lullaby for a King. Jeffery Bell-Hanson. 1.25 (*0-687-50153-9*) Abingdon.

Lullaby for Daddy. Eddie Smith. LC 94-9773. (Illus.). 32p. (J). (ps). 1994. 16.95 (*0-86543-403-4*); pap. 8.95 (*0-86543-404-2*) Africa World.

Lullaby for Emily. David Kherdian. (J). 1995. 15.95 (*0-8050-2957-5*) H Holt & Co.

Lullaby Land. Eugene Field. (Notable American Authors Ser.). (J). 1992. reprint ed. lib. bdg. 75.00 (*0-7812-2646-5*) Rprt Serv.

Lullaby of Broadway: A Biography of Al Dubin. Patricia D. McGuire. (Illus.). 256p. 1983. 14.95 (*0-8065-0871-X*, Citadel Pr) Carol Pub Group.

Lullaby of Broadway Showstoppers: Piano/Vocal/Chords. 160p. (Orig.). 1996. pap. 16.95 (*0-7692-1039-2*, MF9617) Wrner Bros.

Lullaby of Murder. Dorothy S. Davis. 224p. 1989. reprint ed. spiral bd. 3.50 (*0-373-26021-0*) Harlequin Bks.

Lullaby of the Wind. Karen Whiteside. LC 83-47702. (Illus.). 32p. (J). (ps). 1984. 10.95 (*0-06-026411-X*) HarpC Child Bks.

Lullaby Raft. Naomi Shihab Nye. LC 96-22425. (Illus.). 32p. (J). (ps-1). 1997. 16.00 (*0-689-80521-7*) S&S Trade.

Lullaby Songbook. Jane Yolen. LC 85-752885. (Illus.). 32p. (J). (ps up). 1986. 13.95 (*0-15-249903-2*, Harcourt Child Bks) Harcourt.

Lullaby Town. Robert Crais. 352p. 1993. mass mkt. 6.50 (*0-553-29951-4*) Bantam.

Lullabyhullaballoo. M. Inkpen. (Illus.). (J). 1995. mass mkt. 13.95 (*0-340-62686-0*, Pub. by Hodder & Stought Ltd) Trafalgar.

Lullabys for Starry Nights. Contrib. by Dorian. (J). pap. 10.98 (*0-9647786-1-0*, 3001-4) Baby Music.

Lullahits. Ed. by Carol Cuellar. 36p. (Orig.). (YA). 1996. pap. text 9.95 (*1-57623-538-6*, MF9631) Wrner Bros.

Lullaway of Rockabye. Karla Kuskin. 32p. (J). (ps up). Date not set. lib. bdg. 13.89 (*0-06-027716-5*) HarpC Child Bks.

***Lullaway of Rockabye.** Karla Kuskin. 32p. (J). (ps up). 1999. 13.95 (*0-06-027715-7*) HarpC Child Bks.

Lully. Lionel D. La Laurencie. LC 77-3976. (Music Reprint Ser.). (FRE., Illus.). 1977. reprint ed. lib. bdg. 32.50 (*0-306-70894-9*) Da Capo.

Lully. 2nd ed. Lionel D. La Laurencie. LC 76-43923. (Music & Theatre in France in the 17th & 18th Centuries Ser.). (FRE.). reprint ed. 39.50 (*0-404-60167-7*) AMS Pr.

***Lully Studies.** Ed. by John Hajdu Heyer. LC 00-20313. (Illus.). 275p. (C). 2000. text Price not set. (*0-521-62183-6*) Cambridge U Pr.

Lulu: A Romance. Annamarie Jagose. LC 98-196873. 208p. 1998. write for info. (*0-86473-332-1*) Victoria Univ Pr.

Lulu: A Sex Tragedy. Peter Barnes. Tr. by Charlotte Beck from GER. 82p. (Orig.). (C). 1989. pap. write for info. (*0-413-61390-9*, A0366, Methuen Drama) Methn.

Lulu & the Ant: A Message of Love. Louise L. Hay & Dan Olmos. (J). (ps-3). 1991. 8.00 incl. audio (*1-56170-029-0*, 256) Hay House.

Lulu & the Artist. Lionel Koechlin. (Child's World Library). (Illus.). 32p. (J). (gr. k-5). 1992. lib. bdg. 18.50 (*0-89565-741-4*) Childs World.

Lulu & the Dark: Conquering Fears. Louise L. Hay & Dan Olmos. (J). (ps-3). 1991. 8.00 incl. audio (*1-56170-030-4*, 257) Hay House.

Lulu & the Ten Most Popular Excuses. Julie A. Waterman. 9p. (Orig.). 1982. pap. 1.25 (*0-943334-06-3*) Carmonelle Pubns.

Lulu & Willy the Duck: Learning Mirror Work. Louise L. Hay & Dan Olmos. (J). (ps-3). 1991. 8.00 incl. audio (*1-56170-031-2*, 258) Hay House.

Lulu Crow's Garden: A Silly Old Story with Brand-New Pictures. Lizi Boyd. LC 96-49012. (Illus.). 32p. (J). (gr. k-3). 1998. 14.95 (*0-316-10419-1*) Little.

Lulu Goes to Witch School. Jane O'Connor. (I Can Read Bks.). (Illus.). 64p. (J). (gr. 1-3). 1987. 13.00 (*0-06-024628-6*) HarpC Child Bks.

Lulu Goes to Witch School. Jane O'Connor. LC 87-37. (I Can Read Bks.). (Illus.). 64p. (J). (ps-3). 1990. pap. 3.95 (*0-06-444138-5*, HarpTrophy) HarpC Child Bks.

Lulu Goes to Witch School. Jane O'Connor. (I Can Read Bks.). (J). (gr. 1-3). 1991. 8.95 (*0-606-04734-4*, Pub. by Turtleback) Demco.

***Lulu in Hollywood.** expanded ed. Louise Brooks. 2000. pap. 19.95 (*0-8166-3731-8*) U of Minn Pr.

Lulu on the Bridge. Paul Auster. LC 98-17750. (Illus.). 304p. 1998. pap. 15.00 (*0-8050-5978-4*, Owl) H Holt & Co.

Lulu Plays: Earth Spirit; Pandora's Box; Death & Devil; Castle Wetterstein. Frank Wedekind. Tr. by Stephen Spender from GER. (German Expressionist Ser.). (Orig.). 1997. pap. 14.95 (*0-7145-0868-3*) Riverrun NY.

Lulu Turns Four. Lynn R. Horowitz. (Illus.). 32p. (J). (ps). 1993. 13.95 (*0-9625620-5-X*) DOT Garnet.

Lulu's Birthday. Howard. (J). 1999. 17.00 (*0-689-81073-3*) S&S Childrens.

Lulu's Birthday. Elizabeth F. Howard. LC 98-32206. (J). 2001. write for info. (*0-688-15944-3*, Grenwillow Bks); lib. bdg. write for info. (*0-688-15945-1*, Grenwillow Bks) HarpC Child Bks.

***Lulu's Busy Day.** Caroline Uff. LC 99-36100. (Illus.). (J). 2000. write for info. (*0-8027-8717-7*) Walker & Co.

***Lulu's Busy Day.** Caroline Uff. LC 99-36100. (Illus.). 24p. (J). (ps-k). 2000. 14.95 (*0-8027-8716-9*) Walker & Co.

***Lulu's Lemonade.** Barbara De Rubertis. (Illus.). (J). 2000. 10.40 (*0-606-18222-5*) Turtleback.

***Lulu's Lemonade.** Barbara DeRubertis. LC 99-42677. (Math Matters Ser.). (Illus.). 32p. (J). (gr. k-2). 2000. pap. 4.95 (*1-57565-093-2*) Kane Pr.

Lulu's Library. Louisa May Alcott. (Works of Louisa May Alcott). 1989. reprint ed. lib. bdg. 79.00 (*0-7812-1641-9*) Rprt Serv.

Lum: Genealogy of the Lum Family. Edward H. Lum. 270p. 1993. reprint ed. pap. 42.50 (*0-8328-3712-1*); reprint ed. lib. bdg. 52.50 (*0-8328-3711-3*) Higginson Bk Co.

Lum: Uruseiyatsura, Graphic Novel, Vol. 1. Rumiko Takahashi. Ed. by Seiji Horibuchi. Tr. by Satoru Fujii & Gerard Jones from JPN. (Illus.). 194p. 1990. pap. 14.95 (*0-929279-64-6*) Viz Commns Inc.

Lum: Uruseiyatsura, Graphic Novel, Vol. 2. Rumiko Takahashi. Ed. by Seiji Horibuchi. Tr. by Satoru Fujii & Gerard Jones from JPN. (Illus.). 214p. 1990. pap. 14.95 (*0-929279-63-8*) Viz Commns Inc.

Lum Hat & Other Stories: Last Tales of Violet Jacob. Ed. by R. J. Garden. (Illus.). 172p. 1982. text 17.90 (*0-08-028449-3*, Pergamon Pr); pap. text 11.00 (*0-08-028450-7*, Pergamon Pr) Elsevier.

Lum Urusei Yatsura: Perfect Collection. Viz Takahashi. 19.95 (*0-614-25035-8*, Viz Comics) Viz Commns Inc.

Lum Urusei Yatsura Perfect Collection. Rumiko Takahashi. (Illus.). 400p. 1997. pap. 19.95 (*1-56931-019-X*, Viz Comics) Viz Commns Inc.

Lumb & Jones' Veterinary Anesthesia. 3rd ed. Ed. by John C. Thurmon et al. LC 95-46509. (Illus.). 928p. 1996. 85.00 (*0-683-08238-8*) Lppncott W & W.

Lumbale Discectomie. Oliver D. Grin & Dorothy L. Bouwman. Tr. by John Vriend et al. (Patient Education Ser.). (DUT., Illus.). 18p. (Orig.). 1992. pap. text 4.00 (*0-929689-55-0*) Ludann Co.

Lumbar Disc Disease. Ed. by Russell W. Hardy, Jr. LC 82-7667. (Seminars in Neurological Surgery Ser.). (Illus.). 344p. 1982. reprint ed. pap. 106.70 (*0-608-00590-8*, 206117700007) Bks Demand.

Lumbar Disc Disease. 2nd ed. Ed. by Russell W. Hardy, Jr. LC 92-529. 384p. 1992. text 131.50 (*0-88167-951-8*) Lppncott W & W.

Lumbar Disc Herniation. F. Postacchini. LC 98-54151. (Illus.). 700p. 1998. 299.00 (*3-211-83118-5*) Spr-Verlag.

Lumbar Fusion & Stabilization. Ed. by K. Ono et al. LC 92-46674. 1993. 174.00 (*0-387-70116-8*) Spr-Verlag.

Lumbar Microdiskectomy. Oliver D. Grin & Dorothy L. Bouwman. (Patient Education Ser.). (Illus.). 24p. (Orig.). 1993. pap. text 4.00 (*0-929689-57-7*) Ludann Co.

Lumbar Segmental Instability. Marek Szpalski. LC 98-44132. 1998. 99.00 (*0-7817-1906-2*) Lppncott W & W.

Lumbar Spinal Stenosis. F. Postacchini. (Illus.). 230p. 1989. 120.00 (*0-387-82111-2*) Spr-Verlag.

***Lumbar Spinal Stenosis.** Marek Szpalski & Robert Gunzburg. LC 99-44476. 1999. write for info. (*0-7817-2380-9*) Lppncott W & W.

Lumbar Spine. Ed. by Martin B. Camins & Patrick F. O'Leary. LC 86-24862. (Illus.). 511p. 1987. reprint ed. pap. 158.50 (*0-608-05799-1*, 205976400007) Bks Demand.

Lumbar Spine: CT & MRI. J. George Teplick. LC 91-40944. (Illus.). 542p. 1992. reprint ed. pap. 168.10 (*0-608-05884-X*, 205985000007) Bks Demand.

Lumbar Spine: Mechanical Diagnosis & Therapy. Robin A. McKenzie. (Illus.). 164p. 1989. reprint ed. text 39.00 (*0-473-00064-4*, Pub. by Spinal Pubns Ltd) Orthopedic Phys.

Lumbar Spine & Back Pain. 4th ed. Ed. by Malcolm I. Jayson. (Illus.). 637p. 1992. text 189.00 (*0-443-04189-X*) Church.

Lumbar Spine Disorders: Current Concepts. Ed. by R. M. Aspden & R. W. Porter. LC 95-2988. 260p. 1995. text 74.00 (*981-02-2175-4*) World Scientific Pub.

Lumbar Spine Disorders Current Concepts, 2. 250p. 1996. lib. bdg. 41.00 (*981-02-2792-2*) World Scientific Pub.

L

Lumbar Spine Syndromes. Gunnar B. Andersson & T. W. McNeill. (Illus.). 250p. 1989. 118.00 (*0-387-82070-1*) Spr-Verlag.

Lumbar Vertebrae & Injuries: Medical Subject Analysis with Reference Bibliography. Trudy E. Allyson. LC 85-48091. 150p. 1987. 47.50 (*0-88164-454-4*); pap. 44.50 (*0-88164-455-2*) ABBE Pubs Assn.

Lumbee Indian Histories: Race, Ethnicity & Indian Identity in the Southern United States. Gerald M. Sider. 336p. (C). 1994. pap. text 18.95 (*0-521-46669-5*) Cambridge U Pr.

Lumbee Indians: An Annotated Bibliography, with Chronology & Index. Glenn E. Starr. LC 89-43629. 296p. 1994. lib. bdg. 75.00 (*0-89950-511-2*) McFarland & Co.

Lumbee Problem: The Making of an American Indian People. Karen I. Blu. LC 79-12908. (Cambridge Studies in Cultural Systems: No. 5). 292p. pap. 83.30 (*0-608-15695-7*, 2031622) Bks Demand.

Lumber. Louis Colman. LC 74-22773. (Labor Movement in Fiction & Non-Fiction Ser.). reprint ed. 36.50 (*0-404-58413-6*) AMS Pr.

Lumber & Labor. Vernon H. Jensen. LC 74-156444. (American Labor, Ser. 2). 1977. reprint ed. 25.95 (*0-405-02928-4*) Ayer.

*__Lumber Camp Library.__ Kinsey-Warnock. 2000. 14.95 (*0-06-029321-7*); lib. bdg. 15.89 (*0-06-029322-5*); mass mkt. 4.95 (*0-06-444292-6*) HarpC.

Lumber Drying Sourcebook: 40 Years of Practical Experience. Ed. by Gene Wengert & Richard Toennisson. (Illus.). 372p. 1998. pap. 30.00 (*0-935018-98-0*, 7274) Forest Prod.

Lumber from Local Woodlots. Robert L. Edmonds et al. (Illus.). 42p. 1988. pap. text 8.00 (*0-935817-09-3*, 27) NRAES.

Lumber Ghosts: A Travel Guide to the Historic Lumber Towns of the Pacific Northwest. Kenneth A. Erickson. LC 93-49503. (Illus.). 132p. 1994. pap. 16.95 (*0-87108-854-1*) Pruett.

Lumber Industry, 2 vols. U. S. Dept. of Commerce & Labor-Bureau of Corporat. LC 72-2873. (Use & Abuse of America's Natural Resources Ser.). 616p. 1972. reprint ed. 51.95 (*0-405-04540-9*) Ayer.

Lumber Industry in Early Modern Japan. Conrad Totman. LC 94-38136. (Illus.). 1995. text 35.00 (*0-8248-1665-X*) UH Pr.

Lumber Manufacturing: The Design & Operation of Sawmills & Planer Mills. rev. ed. Ed M. Williston. (Illus.). 512p. 1988. 55.00 (*0-87930-174-0*) Miller Freeman.

Lumber Recovery from Ponderosa Pine in the Black Hills, South Dakota. Marlin E. Plank. (Illus.). 24p. 1998. reprint ed. pap. 3.40 (*0-89904-519-7*, Ecosytems Resrch) Crumb Elbow Pub.

Lumber Room. Charles C. Todd. LC 98-91129. (Illus.). ii, 112p. 1999. pap. 12.95 (*0-9670482-0-6*) C C Todd.

Lumber Spine. 2nd ed. International Society for the Study of the Lumber. Ed. by Wiesel, Weinstein, Herkowitz, Dvorak, & Bell Staff et al. LC 95-10052. (Illus.). 1056p. 1996. text 260.00 (*0-7216-4953-X*, W B Saunders Co) Harcrt Hlth Sci Grp.

Lumbering in Early Twentieth Century Michigan: The Kneeland-Bigelow Company Experience. Herman L. Miller. (Illus.). 86p. (Orig.). 1995. pap. 19.95 (*0-9645716-0-9*) Walnut Hll Pr.

Lumbering Songs of the Northern Woods. rev. ed. Edith Fowke. 232p. 1986. text 19.95 (*0-920053-51-3*, Pub. by NC Ltd) U of Toronto Pr.

Lumberjack. William Kurelek. (Illus.). 48p. (YA). (gr. 5 up). 1996. pap. 9.95 (*0-88776-378-2*) Tundra Bks.

Lumberjack Frontier. Walker D. Wyman & Lee Prentice. (Illus.). 88p. 1969. pap. 7.95 (*0-686-27296-X*) U Wisc-River Falls Pr.

Lumberjacks & Logging: Coloring Books. Chet Kozlak. (Illus.). (J). 1981. pap. text 3.50 (*0-87351-158-1*) Minn Hist.

Lumberjacks & Rivermen in the Central Adirondacks, 1850-1950. Harold K. Hochschild. (Illus.). 1993. reprint ed. pap. 7.95 (*0-910020-09-4*) Adirondack Mus.

Lumbermen. Gail Stewart. (Wild West in American History Ser.). (Illus.). 32p. (J). (gr. 3-8). 1990. lib. bdg. 23.93 (*0-86625-407-2*) Rourke Pubns.

Lumbermen & Log Sawyers: Life, Labor, & Culture in the North Florida Timber Industry, 1830-1930. Jeffrey Drobney. LC 97-18523. (Illus.). 384p. 1997. 39.95 (*0-86554-546-4*, H417) Mercer Univ Pr.

Lumberton Report: UFO Activity in Southern North Carolina, April 3-9, 1975. Jennie Zeidman et al. (Illus.). 65p. (C). 1976. pap. 6.00 (*0-929343-51-4*) J A Hynek Ctr UFO.

Lumboischialgie. Ed. by W. Miller et al. (Fortbildungskurse fuer Rheumatologie Ser.: Vol. 6). (Illus.). xii, 264p. 1982. pap. 62.75 (*3-8055-2207-X*) S Karger.

Lumbosacral & Spinopelvic Fixation. Joseph Margulies. LC 93-34226. (Illus.). 976p. 1996. text 209.00 (*0-397-51388-7*) Lppncott W & W.

Lumbrera a Nuestro Camino. Ed. by Pablo A. Jimenez.Tr. of Light upon Our Path. (SPA.). 179p. 1994. 9.99 (*0-89922-531-4*, C066-5314) Caribe Betania.

Lumen: A Novel. Ben Pastor. LC 98-40703. 279p. 1999. 24.00 (*0-9657639-4-3*) Van Neste.

Lumen: Food for a New Age. G. J. Caton. LC 86-62413. (Illus.). 245p. 1986. pap. 4.95 (*0-939955-00-8*) Grand Union.

Lumen Lights the Way. Virginia Fullarton. (Illus.). 214p. (Orig.). (J). (gr. 3-6). 1997. pap. write for info. (*1-57502-424-1*, PO1304) Morris Pubng.

Lumenagerie. Michael Manning. (Illus.). 72p. 1996. pap. 11.95 (*1-56163-151-5*, Amerotica) NBM.

Lumi-Imager F1: Lab Protocols. Onno Bakker. LC 98-39227. 1998. pap. write for info. (*3-540-64794-5*) Spr-Verlag.

Lumiere D'Aout. William Faulkner. (FRE.). 1974. pap. 13.95 (*0-7859-2349-7*, 2070366219) Fr & Eur.

Lumiere de Fifty Chef d'Oeuvres. Jean De Hillerin. (FRE., Illus.). 206p. 1963. lib. bdg. 50.00 (*0-8288-3988-3*) Fr & Eur.

Lumiere de la Nuit les 18 Derniers Mois de Therese of Lisieux see Light of the Night: The Last Eighteen Months in the Life of Therese of Lisieux

Lumiere des Justes Vol. 1: Les Compagnons de Cocquelicot. Henri Troyat. (FRE.). 1970. pap. 11.95 (*0-7859-3267-4*, 2277122726) Fr & Eur.

Lumiere des Justes Vol. 2: La Barynia. Henri Troyat. (FRE.). 1970. pap. 11.95 (*0-7859-3268-2*, 2277122742) Fr & Eur.

Lumiere des Justes Vol. 3: La Gloire des Vaincus. Henri Troyat. (FRE.). 1970. pap. 11.95 (*0-7859-3269-0*, 2277122769) Fr & Eur.

Lumiere des Justes Vol. 4: Les Dames de Siberie. Henri Troyat. (FRE.). 1970. pap. 11.95 (*0-7859-3270-4*, 2277122785) Fr & Eur.

Lumiere des Justes Vol. 5: Sophie ou La Fin de Combats. Henri Troyat. (FRE.). 1970. pap. 11.95 (*0-7859-3271-2*, 2277122807) Fr & Eur.

Lumiere D'Oeil. Paula Jacques. (FRE.). 288p. 1983. pap. 11.95 (*0-7859-2479-5*, 2070374904) Fr & Eur.

Lumieres d'Homme. Charles Peguy. pap. 6.25 (*0-685-37052-6*) Fr & Eur.

*__Lumieres et commerce: L'exemple bordelais, 28.__ Jean Mondot & Catherine Larrere. 201p. 2000. 33.95 (*3-906764-35-4*, Pub. by P Lang) P Lang Pubng.

Lumieres sur Ma Vie Vol. 1: Inventaire de l'Aimbe (1884-1901) Georges Duhamel. (FRE.). 244p. 1949. pap. 16.95 (*0-7859-5419-8*) Fr & Eur.

Lumieres sur Ma Vie Vol. 2: Biographies de Mes Fantomer (1901-1906) Georges Duhamel. (FRE.). 256p. 1949. pap. 9.95 (*0-7859-5420-1*) Fr & Eur.

Lumieres sur Ma Vie Vol. 3: Le Temps de la Recherche (1906-1914) Georges Duhamel. 9.95 (*0-686-55183-4*) Fr & Eur.

Lumieres sur Ma Vie Vol. 4: La Pesee des Ames (1914-1919) Georges Duhamel. (FRE.). 336p. 1949. pap. 16.95 (*0-685-73299-1*) Fr & Eur.

Lumieres sur Ma Vie Vol. 5: Les Espoirs et les Epreuves (1919-1928) Georges Duhamel. (FRE.). 1928. pap. 16.95 (*0-7859-5422-8*) Fr & Eur.

Luminance: Lux Three. Linda Connor. 58p. 1994. pap. 19.95 (*0-9630393-2-6*) Ctr for Photo.

Luminare. Nancy Watt. 84p. (Orig.). 1988. pap. 9.99 (*0-925037-06-0*) Great Lks Poetry.

Luminaries: Princeton Faculty Remembered. Ed. by Patricia H. Marks. (Illus.). 250p. 1996. text 39.95 (*0-691-01167-2*, Pub. by Princeton U Pr) Cal Prin Full Svc.

Luminaries: The Psychology of the Sun & Moon in the Horoscope. Liz Greene & Howard Sasportas. LC 91-43968. (Seminars in Psychological Astrology Ser.: Vol. 3). 256p. (Orig.). 1992. reprint ed. pap. 14.95 (*0-87728-750-3*) Weiser.

Luminaries of the Humble. Elizabeth Woody. LC 94-10191. (Sun Tracks Ser.: Vol. 30). 127p. (Orig.). 1994. pap. 16.95 (*0-8165-1465-8*); lib. bdg. 38.00 (*0-8165-1488-7*) U of Ariz Pr.

Luminescence. Ed. by H. J. Cantow et al. (Advances in Polymer Science Ser.: Vol. 40). (Illus.). 200p. 1981. 57.00 (*0-387-10550-6*) Spr-Verlag.

Luminescence: Phenomena, Materials & Devices. Ed. by R. P. Rao. (Solid State Physics, Luminescence Ser.). 448p. (C). 1991. text 195.00 (*1-56072-013-1*) Nova Sci Pubs.

Luminescence Vol. 9: Scanning Microscopy Supplement. G. Remond et al. (Illus.). 288p. 1998. pap. 66.00 (*0-931288-48-7*) Scanning Microscopy.

Luminescence & Anisotropy of Zinc Sulfide Crystals. Ed. by M. D. Galanin. (Proceedings of the Lebedev Physics Institute Ser.: Vol. 175 Supplemental Volume). 169p. 1988. text 165.00 (*0-941743-20-9*) Nova Sci Pubs.

Luminescence & Energy Transfer. Ed. by J. D. Dunitz et al. (Structure & Bonding Ser.: Vol. 42). (Illus.). 133p. 1980. 58.95 (*0-387-10395-3*) Spr-Verlag.

Luminescence & Nonlinear Optics. Ed. by D. V. Skobel'tsyn. Tr. by Albin Tybulewicz from ENG. LC 73-83897. (Proceedings of the P. N. Lebedev Physics Institute Ser.: No. 59). (Illus.). 295p. 1973. reprint ed. pap. 91.50 (*0-608-05519-0*, 206598700006) Bks Demand.

*__Luminescence & Scintillation of Ce3+ Doped Inorganic Materials for Gamma-Ray Detection.__ J. C. van't Spijker. (ENG & DUT., Illus.). 160p. 1999. pap. 43.50 (*90-407-1844-X*, Pub. by Delft U Pr) Coronet Bks.

Luminescence & the Light Emitting Diode. E. W. Williams & R. Hall. LC 77-4427. 1978. 118.00 (*0-08-020442-2*, Pub. by Pergamon Repr) Franklin.

Luminescence & the Solid State. R. C. Ropp. (Studies in Inorganic Chemistry: Vol. 12). xvi, 454p. 1991. 250.75 (*0-444-88940-X*) Elsevier.

Luminescence Applications in Biological, Chemical, Environmental, & Hydrological Sciences. Ed. by Marvin C. Goldberg. LC 88-39131. (Symposium Ser.: No. 383). (Illus.). xi, 255p. 1989. 59.95 (*0-8412-1560-X*) Am Chemical.

Luminescence Applications in Biological, Chemical, Environmental, & Hydrological Sciences. Ed. by Marvin C. Goldberg. LC 88-39131. (ACS Symposium Ser.: Vol. 383). 264p. 1989. reprint ed. pap. 81.90 (*0-608-03285-9*, 206380300007) Bks Demand.

Luminescence Centers in Crystals. Ed. by N. G. Basov. Tr. by Albin Tybulewicz from RUS. LC 76-41167. (Proceedings of the P. N. Lebedev Physics Institute Ser.: No. 79). (Illus.). 182p. 1976. reprint ed. pap. 56.50 (*0-608-05538-7*, 206600600006) Bks Demand.

Luminescence Centers of Rare Earth Ions in Crystal Phosphors. Ed. by M. D. Galanin. (Proceedings of the Lebedev Physics Institute Ser.: Vol. 175). 161p. (C). 1988. text 165.00 (*0-941743-10-1*) Nova Sci Pubs.

Luminescence Dosimetry: Proceedings. Ed. by Frank H. Attix. LC 67-60038. (AEC Symposium Ser.). 527p. 1967. pap. 21.25 (*0-87079-263-6*, CONF-650637); fiche 9.00 (*0-87079-264-4*, CONF-650637) DOE.

Luminescence Immunoassay & Molecules Applications. Ed. by Knox VanDyke. 352p. 1990. 259.00 (*0-8493-5865-5*, QP519) CRC Pr.

Luminescence of Molecules & Crystals. M. D. Galanin. 150p. 1995. pap. 65.00 (*1-898326-33-9*, Pub. by CISP) Balogh.

Luminescence of Organic Substances see Atomic & Molecular Physics: Group II

Luminescence of Semiconductor Microstructures. Benoit Deveaud. 300p. 1998. text 53.00 (*981-02-2214-9*) World Scientific Pub.

Luminescence of Solids. D. R. Vij. LC 98-18247. (Illus.). 424p. (C). 1998. text 115.00 (*0-306-45643-5*, Kluwer Plenum) Kluwer Academic.

Luminescence of Wideband Semiconductors. Ed. by M. D. Galanin. Tr. by Michael L. Allen from RUS. LC 88-38658. (Proceedings of the Lebedev Physics Institute Ser.: Vol. 182). 257p. (C). 1989. text 175.00 (*0-941743-48-9*) Nova Sci Pubs.

Luminescence Techniques in Chemical & Biochemical Analysis. Ed. by Willy R. Baeyens et al. (Practical Spectroscopy Ser.: Vol. 12). (Illus.). 664p. 1990. text 235.00 (*0-8247-8369-7*) Dekker.

Luminescence Techniques in Solid State Polymer Research. L. Zlatkevich. 328p. 1989. text 145.00 (*0-8247-8045-0*) Dekker.

Luminescent Assays: Perspectives in Endocrinology & Clinical Chemistry. Mario Serio & Mario Pazzagli. LC 81-40363. (Serono Symposia Publications from Raven Press: No. 1). (Illus.). 302p. 1982. reprint ed. pap. 93.70 (*0-608-00619-X*, 206120600007) Bks Demand.

Luminescent Banner Designs. Koehlinger Mari Pierce-Ruhland. 96p. 1998. pap. 9.99 (*0-570-05341-2*) Concordia.

Luminescent Materials. G. Blasse & B. C. Grabmaier. LC 94-20336. 1994. 62.95 (*0-387-58019-0*) Spr-Verlag.

Luminescent Materials Vol. 560: Materials Research Society Symposium Proceedings. Ed. by J. McKittrick et al. LC 99-42465. 368p. 1999. text 73.00 (*1-55899-467-X*) Materials Res.

Luminescent Materials VI. Ed. by C. Ronda et al. LC 98-218280. (Proceedings Ser.: Vol. 97-29). 1998. 73.00 (*1-56677-182-X*) Electrochem Soc.

Luminescent Spectroscopy of Proteins. Eugene A. Permiakov. 176p. 1992. lib. bdg. 110.00 (*0-8493-4553-7*, QP551) CRC Pr.

Luminieres de la Democratie: Historie de l'Ecole Primaire Publique a Geneve au XIXe Siecle. Rita Hofstetter. (Exploration Ser.). vii, 378p. 1998. 27.95 (*3-906760-21-9*, Pub. by P Lang) P Lang Pubng.

*__Luminol Synthesis & Chemiluminescence.__ Carl T. Wigal. Ed. by Joe Jeffers. (Modular Laboratory in Chemistry Ser.). 12p. (C). 1999. pap. text 1.75 (*0-87540-731-5*, SYNT 731-5) Chem Educ Res.

Luminosa - She Kept on Playing: A Biography of Margarita Bavosi. Alfred Zirondoli. Tr. by Jerry Hearne from ITA. LC 94-15721. 144p. (Orig.). 1994. pap. 8.95 (*1-56548-069-4*) New City.

Luminosity. Alternative Museum Staff. LC 86-71975. (Illus.). (Orig.). 1986. pap. 5.00 (*0-932075-11-8*) Alternative Mus.

*__Luminosity.__ Frank McEnaney & Gillian Hemstock. 1999. pap. write for info. (*0-679-31004-5*) Random.

*__Luminosity: The Paintings of Stephen Hannock.__ Illus. by Stephen Hannock. LC 99-87349. 2000. pap. 50.00 (*0-8118-2832-8*) Chronicle Bks.

*__Luminous.__ Peter Quest. 142p. 1999. pap. 13.95 (*0-7414-0201-7*) Buy Books.

Luminous Animal. Tony Moffeit. 56p. (Orig.). 1989. pap. 6.00 (*0-916156-86-9*) Cherry Valley.

Luminous Blue Variables: Massive Stars in Transition: Proceedings of a Workshop Held in Kona, Hawaii, October 6-12, 1996. Ed. by Antonella Nota & Henny J. Lamers. (ASP Conference Series Proceedings: Vol. 120). 404p. 1997. 34.00 (*1-886733-40-6*) Astron Soc Pacific.

Luminous Brush: Painting with Egg Tempera. Altoon Sultan. LC 99-37390. (Illus.). 128p. 1999. pap. text 19.95 (*0-8230-2888-7*) Watsn-Guptill.

Luminous Darkness. Howard Thurman. LC 89-30926. 115p. 1989. reprint ed. 11.00 (*0-944350-07-0*) Friends United.

*__Luminous Darkness: A Commentary on the "Mystical Theology" of Dionysius the...__ Jim Wilson. 2000. 16.00 (*0-9677158-3-0*) Hse of Ho Tei.

Luminous Debris: Reflecting on Vestige in Provence & Languedoc. Gustaf Sobin. LC 99-20904. 304p. 1999. 45.00 (*0-520-21775-6*, Pub. by U CA Pr) Cal Prin Full Svc.

*__Luminous Debris: Reflecting on Vestige in Provence & Languedoc.__ Gustaf Sobin. LC 99-20904. 304p. 1999. pap. text 18.95 (*0-520-22245-8*, Pub. by U CA Pr) Cal Prin Full Svc.

Luminous Debris: Reflecting on Vestige in Southern France. Gustaf Sobin. 250p. 1997. 24.00 (*1-56886-043-9*) Marsilio Pubs.

Luminous Details. Brian Daldorph. 38p. (Orig.). 1992. pap. 3.00 (*1-880575-12-4*) Hot Pepper.

*__Luminous Disarray.__ Mary E. Martin. LC 98-71748. 1998. write for info. (*0-89002-339-5*) Northwoods Pr.

Luminous Essence: Body Talks to Body. Daniel Santos. (Illus.). 271p. (Orig.). 1994. pap. 13.95 (*0-9642416-0-9*) Luminous Pr.

Luminous Essence: New Light on the Healing Body an Alternative Healer's Story. Daniel Santos. LC 97-4460. 288p. 1997. pap. 14.00 (*0-8356-0755-0*, Quest) Theos Pub Hse.

Luminous Eye: The Spiritual World Vision of St. Ephrem the Syrian. 2nd ed. Sebastian Brock. (Cistercian Studies: No. 124). 250p. 1992. 36.95 (*0-87907-524-4*); pap. 15.95 (*0-87907-624-0*) Cistercian Pubns.

Luminous High-Latitude Stars. Ed. by D. D. Sasselov. (ASP Conference Series Proceedings: Vol. 45). 518p. 1993. 34.00 (*0-937707-64-3*) Astron Soc Pacific.

Luminous Image: Painted Glass Roundels in the Lowlands, 1480-1560. Timothy Husband. LC 95-11656. 234p. 1995. pap. 29.95 (*0-87099-748-3*) Metro Mus Art.

Luminous Island, Wondrous Self. Douglas C. Vest. LC 96-14447. (Illus.). 128p. 1996. pap. 9.95 (*0-940147-41-6*) Source Bks CA.

Luminous Land: Artists Discover Greece. Richard Stoneman. LC 97-31228. 188p. 1998. 39.95 (*0-89236-467-X*) OUP.

Luminous Life: How to Shine Like the Sun. Peter Rosen. Ed. by Carol Iozzi. 420p. (Orig.). 1994. pap. 20.00 (*1-878682-01-6*) Roaring Lion Pub.

Luminous Mind: The Way of the Buddha. Kalu Rinpoche. LC 96-24689. (Illus.). 352p. 1996. pap. 18.95 (*0-86171-118-1*) Wisdom MA.

Luminous Mysteries. John Holman. LC 98-20997. 240p. 2000. pap. 12.00 (*0-15-600757-6*, Harvest Bks) Harcourt.

Luminous Mysteries: A Novel. John Holman. LC 98-20997. 240p. (C). 1998. 22.00 (*0-15-100349-1*) Harcourt.

Luminous Night's Journey: An Autobiographical Fragment. A. H. Almaas. LC 96-84412. 131p. 1995. pap. 14.00 (*0-936713-08-9*, 11300) Diamond Bks CA.

Luminous Ones: A History of the Great Actresses. Elizabeth Nash. LC 91-19225. (American University Studies: Theatre Arts: Ser. XXVI, Vol. 10). 224p. 1992. 43.95 (*0-8204-1577-4*) P Lang Pubng.

Luminous Passage: The Practice & Study of Buddhism in America. Charles S. Prebish. LC 98-20767. 329p. 1999. 45.00 (*0-520-21696-2*, Pub. by U CA Pr) Cal Prin Full Svc.

*__Luminous Passage: The Practice & Study of Buddhism in America.__ Charles S. Prebish. LC 98-20767. 329p. 1999. pap. 18.95 (*0-520-21697-0*, Pub. by U CA Pr) Cal Prin Full Svc.

Luminous Sanity: Literary Criticism Written by John G. Neihardt. John T. Richards. 1973. pap. 5.00 (*0-9605980-6-X*) J T Richards.

Luminous Star Finder: Glow-In-The-Dark with Zodiac Dial. Rand McNally Staff. (Illus.). 1989. pap. 5.95 (*0-528-83374-X*) Rand McNally.

Luminous Starfinder. rev. ed. Hubbard Scientific Company Staff. 1995. pap. 6.45 (*0-8331-0431-4*, 431) Hubbard Sci.

Luminous Stars & Associations in Galaxies. Ed. by Camiel W. De Loore et al. 1986. pap. text 82.50 (*90-277-2273-0*); lib. bdg. 194.00 (*90-277-2272-2*) Kluwer Academic.

*__Luminous Web: Essays on Science & Religion.__ Barbara Brown Taylor. LC 99-57233. 120p. 2000. pap. 10.95 (*1-56101-169-X*) Cowley Pubns.

Lummi Indians of Northwest Washington. Bernhard J. Stern. LC 71-82357. (Columbia University. Contributions to Anthropology Ser.: Vol. 17). reprint ed. 29.50 (*0-404-50567-8*) AMS Pr.

Lummox. Mike Magnuson. 2000. 24.00 (*0-06-019372-7*); pap. 13.00 (*0-06-093188-4*) HarpC.

Lump. Tish Rabe. LC 99-162318. 1998. 4.99 (*0-679-89243-5*, Pub. by Random Bks Yng Read) Random.

Lump Gulch Tales. Jane Wodening. (Illus.). 150p. (Orig.). 1997. reprint ed. pap. 12.00 (*1-887997-08-3*) Baksun Bks.

Lump in the Middle. C. S. Adler. 160p. (YA). 1991. pap. 3.50 (*0-380-71176-1*, Avon Bks) Morrow Avon.

Lump It or Leave It. Florence King. 192p. 1991. pap. 10.95 (*0-312-06568-X*) St Martin.

*__Lump Sum Advisor.__ 1999. 25.00 (*0-13-018290-7*) P-H.

Lump Sum Advisor. 2nd ed. Gallea. LC 99-12188. (Illus.). 288p. 1999. 25.00 (*0-7352-0073-4*) P-H.

Lump Sum Handbook: Investment & Tax Strategies for a Secure Retirement. Anthony Gallea. 1993. pap. 14.95 (*0-13-199306-2*) P-H.

Lumpa Lou Elephant see Yea Us Series (Tails with a Moral)

Lumped Pulses & Discrete Displacements: A Physical Way to Understand Numerical Dynamics. A. W. Kok. 141p. (Orig.). 1995. pap. 59.50 (*90-407-1118-6*, Pub. by Delft U Pr) Coronet Bks.

Lumpenbourgeoisie: Lumpendevelopment: Dependence, Class, & Politics in Latin America. Andre G. Frank. Tr. by Marion D. Berdicio from SPA. LC 72-81764. 160p. 1973. pap. 10.00 (*0-85345-285-7*, Pub. by Monthly Rev) NYU Pr.

Lumps & Bumps: A Children's Book for Parents & a Parent's Book for Children. Denton L. Roberts. (Illus.). 22p. 1997. pap. 7.50 (*0-9613559-2-1*) Human Esteem Pub.

Lumpy Bumpy Alli Gator. Argentina Grader. (Illus.). 24p. (J). 1996. pap. 7.95 (*0-9670529-0-4*) Argentina Pubns.

Lumpy Bumpy Pumpkin: A Halloween Tale. Sandra Robbins. (See-More's Stories Ser.). (Illus.). 32p. (Orig.). (J). (ps-4). 1993. pap. 9.98 incl. audio (*1-882601-18-1*); pap. 4.95 (*1-882601-19-X*) See-Mores Wrkshop.

Lumumba's Congo. Washington Okumu. 1962. 12.95 (*0-8392-1062-0*) Astor-Honor.

Lun Yu of Kung Fu. Martin J. O'Malley. LC 75-19749. 20p. 1975. pap. 1.00 (*0-9606610-0-X*) M J O'Malley.

*__Luna.__ Sharon Butala. 246p. 2000. pap. 18.95 (*0-00-648540-5*) HarpC.

An Asterisk (*) at the beginning of an entry indicates that the title is appearing for the first time.

Luna & the Big Blur: A Story for Children Who Wear Glasses. Shirley Day. (Illus.). 32p. (J). (ps-3). 1995. 11.95 (*0-945354-66-5*) Am Psychol.

Luna Bella Luna: A Portrait of Vesale, Italy. Mike Noble. Tr. by Alba Rosso. (Illus.). 100p. 1997. 100.00 (*0-9657333-0-0*); pap. 40.00 (*0-9657333-1-9*) P Elledge Photo.

Luna Blanca de Chesed. Juan M. Borrero. (Nueva Austral Ser.: No. 91). (SPA.). 1991. pap. text 24.95 (*84-239-1891-2*) Elliots Bks.

***Luna de Cal.** Olivia Maciel.Tr. of Limestone Moon. (SPA & ENG.). 2000. pap. 16.00 (*0-9678808-0-7*, El Cisne) Black Swan Pr IL.

Luna de Pasion: Texas Moon. Joan E. Pickart. (Deseo Ser.: Vol. 115).Tr. of Passion Moon. (SPA.). 1998. per. 3.50 (*0-373-35245-X*, 1-35245-9) Harlequin Bks.

Luna e i Falo. Cesare Pavese. Ed. by Mark Musa. LC 68-13431. (ITA., Illus.). (C). 1968. pap. text 6.95 (*0-89197-281-1*) Irvington.

Luna e i Falo. Cesare Pavese. Ed. by Doug Thompson. 240p. 1995. text 19.95 (*0-7190-4383-2*, Pub. by Manchester Univ Pr) St Martin.

Luna, Luna: Creative Writing Ideas from Spanish, Latin American, & Latino Literature. Ed. by Julio Marzan. LC 96-44822. 248p. (Orig.). 1997. pap. 15.95 (*0-915924-52-8*) Tchrs & Writers Coll.

Luna Marine: Book Two of the Heritage Trilogy. Ian Douglas. LC 98-94799. (Heritage Trilogy Ser.: Bk. 2). 416p. 1999. mass mkt. 5.99 (*0-380-78829-2*, Eos) Morrow Avon.

Luna Moth's Life. John Himmelman. LC 97-20016. (Nature Upclose Ser.). 32p. (J). (ps-4). 1998. 23.00 (*0-516-20821-7*) Childrens.

Luna Moth's Life. John Himmelman. Ed. by Melissa Stewart. (Nature Upclose Ser.). (Illus.). 32p. (J). 1998. pap. 6.95 (*0-516-26354-4*) Childrens.

Luna Papers, 2 vols, Set. Ed. by Herbert I. Priestley. LC 75-165803. (Select Bibliographies Reprint Ser.). 1977. reprint ed. 49.95 (*0-8369-5959-0*) Ayer.

Luna Park: Cleveland's Fairyland of Pleasure. David W. Francis & Diane D. Francis. LC 95-83957. (Illus.). 156p. 1996. 27.95 (*0-935408-05-3*) Amusement Pk Bks.

Luna Rising: PSI Order: ISRA. Robert S. Martin. (Trinity Ser.). (Illus.). 1998. pap. 17.95 (*1-56504-760-5*, 9002) White Wolf.

Luna se Fue de Fiesta. Matthew Gollub. Tr. by Martin L. Guzman. LC 97-90855.Tr. of Moon Was at a Fiesta. (SPA., Illus.). 32p. (J). (gr. k-6). 1997. pap. 6.95 (*1-889910-14-7*) Tortuga Pr.

Luna se Fue de Fiesta. large type ed. Matthew Gollub. Tr. by Martin L. Guzman. LC 97-90855.Tr. of Moon Was at a Fiesta. (Illus.). 32p. (J). (gr. k-6). 1997. 15.95 (*1-889910-12-0*) Tortuga Pr.

Luna y las Olas. Frances Sainz. (Foundations Ser.). 24p. (J). (ps-1). 1992. pap. text 4.50 (*1-56843-096-5*) EMG Networks.

Luna y las Olas: Big Book. Frances Sainz. (Foundations Ser.). 24p. (J). (ps-1). 1992. pap. text 23.00 (*1-56843-049-3*) EMG Networks.

Luna Yoga: Vital Fertility & Sexuality. Adelheid Ohlig. Tr. by Meret Liebenstein from GER. LC 94-71324. (Best of Europe Ser.). (Illus.). 192p. (Orig.). 1995. pap. 11.95 (*0-9614620-6-X*) Ash Tree.

Lunacy & Letters. G. K. Chesterton. Ed. by Dorothy Collins. LC 72-4607. (Essay Index Reprint Ser.). 1977. reprint ed. 18.95 (*0-8369-2937-3*) Ayer.

Lunacy & the Arrangement of Books. Terry Belanger. ii, 28p. 1985. pap. 10.00 (*0-938768-08-5*) Oak Knoll.

Lunacy of Light: Emily Dickinson & the Experience of Metaphor. Wendy Barker. LC 86-6455. (Ad Feminam Ser.). 235p. 1991. pap. 16.95 (*0-8093-1707-9*) S Ill U Pr.

Lunalilo. rev. ed. Peter Galuteria. (Kamehameha Schools Intermediate Reading Program Ser.). (Illus.). 94p. (J). (gr. 3-7). 1993. pap. 7.95 (*0-87336-019-2*) Kamehameha Schools.

Lunar see Moonlit: Short Stories by Antonio Lupez Ortega

Lunar: Official Guide. J. Douglas Arnold & Zach Meston. (Gaming Mastery Ser.). (Illus.). 136p. (Orig.). 1994. pap. 11.95 (*1-884364-00-4*) Sandwich Islands.

Lunar: Silver Star Story Complete: Unauthorized Strategy. Christine Cain. LC 98-65941. (Illus.). 126p. 1999. pap. 12.99 (*0-7615-1642-5*) Prima Pub.

Lunar Attractions. Clark Blaise. 300p. 1990. pap. write for info. (*0-88984-105-5*) Porcup Quill.

Lunar-Based Analytical Laboratory. Ed. by Charles W. Gehrke et al. LC 97-16530. (Illus.). 332p. 1997. 60.00 (*0-937194-41-7*) A Deepak Pub.

Lunar-Based Chemical Analysis Laboratory: Proceedings of the Ninth College Colloquium on Chemical Evolution. Ed. by Cyril Ponnamperuma & Charles W. Gehrke. LC 91-40702. (Illus.). 281p. 1992. 50.00 (*0-937194-25-5*) A Deepak Pub.

Lunar Bases & Space Activities of the Twenty-First Century. Ed. by W. W. Mendell. LC 86-50. (Illus.). 865p. (C). 1986. 20.00 (*0-942862-02-3*) Lunar & Planet Inst.

Lunar Calendar: Dedicated to the Goddess in Her Many Guises. Ed. by Nancy Passmore. 32p. Date not set. 20.00 (*1-877920-10-X*) Luna Pr MA.

Lunar Concrete. 300p. 1991. 42.95 (*0-685-60172-2*, SP-125BOW6) ACI.

Lunar Consciousness. 2nd ed. Ingrid Naiman. 120p. Date not set. pap. 25.00 (*1-882834-00-3*) Seventh Ray.

***Lunar Eclipse.** Alona Kimchi. 2000. write for info. (*1-902881-28-1*, Pub. by Toby Pr Ltd); pap. 12.95 (*1-902881-29-X*, Pub. by Toby Pr Ltd) Toby Pr.

***Lunar Encounter: Science Fiction with a Sojourn into Cosmology & Philosophy.** Harold W. G. Allen. LC 00-190493. 232p. 2000. pap. 12.95 (*0-9624555-2-0*) Perspective Bks.

Lunar, Eternal Blue: Official Strategy Guide. J. Douglas Arnold & Zach Meston. (Gaming Mastery Ser.). (Illus.). 220p. (Orig.). 1995. pap. 16.95 (*1-884364-07-1*) Sandwich Islands.

Lunar Excursion to the Fifth Dimension. Joseph A. Uphoff, Jr. 68p. 1998. pap. text 4.00 (*0-943123-35-6*) Arjuna Lib Pr.

Lunar Flight Programs, 10th Annual AAS Meeting, May 4-7, 1964, New York, NY: 10th Annual AAS Meeting, New York, NY, May 4-7, 1964. Ed. by Ross Fleisig. LC 57-43769. (Advances in the Astronautical Sciences Ser.: Vol. 18). 630p. 1964. 45.00 (*0-87703-020-0*, Am Astronaut Soc) Univelt Inc.

Lunar Justice. Charles L. Harness. 192p. (Orig.). 1991. pap. 3.95 (*0-380-76010-X*, Avon Bks) Morrow Avon.

Lunar Light of Whitman's Poetry. M. Wynn Thomas. LC 86-12141. (Illus.). 336p. 1987. 36.50 (*0-674-53952-4*) HUP.

Lunar Nodes. Bernice P. Grebner. LC 76-23538. 72p. 1980. 14.00 (*0-86690-186-8*, G1154-014) Am Fed Astrologers.

Lunar Nodes. Mohan Koparkar. 96p. 1977. pap. 6.95 (*0-918922-04-6*) Mohan Ents.

Lunar Notes: Zoot Horn Rollo's Captain Beefheart Experience. Bill Harkleroad. 1998. pap. 17.95 (*0-946719-21-7*, Pub. by Helter Skelter) Interlink Pub.

Lunar Perspectives: Field Notes from the Culture Wars. Michael Keefer. 256p. (Orig.). 1996. pap. 15.95 (*0-88784-570-3*, Pub. by Hse of Anansi Pr) Genl Dist Srvs.

Lunar Rocks. Brian H. Mason & William G. Melson. LC 73-129659. 185p. reprint ed. pap. 57.40 (*0-608-30347-X*, 205512800008) Bks Demand.

Lunar Tables & Programs 4000 B.C. to A.D. 8000. Chapront-Touze & Chapront. 1991. pap. 19.95 (*0-943396-33-6*) Willmann-Bell.

Lunar Voices: Of Tragedy, Poetry, Fiction & Thought. David F. Krell. LC 94-46119. 204p. 1995. pap. text 14.95 (*0-226-45277-8*); lib. bdg. 39.95 (*0-226-45275-1*) U Ch Pr.

Lunar Wake. Catherine Hunter. 119p. 1997. pap. 7.95 (*0-88801-184-9*, Pub. by Turnstone Pr) Genl Dist Srvs.

Lunarcal: A Program for Determining the First Visibility of the Moon, Prayer Times, & Direction to Mecca. Bradley E. Schaefer. (Astronomy & Astrophysics Ser.). (Illus.). 32p. 1989. pap. 10.00 (*0-934525-17-X*); disk 48.00 (*0-934525-18-8*) West Research.

***Luna's California Poppies.** Alma Luz Villanueva. 2000. pap. write for info. (*0-927534-96-7*) Biling Rev-Pr.

Lunatic. Anthony Winkler. 224p. 1987. pap. 9.95 (*0-8184-0428-0*) Carol Pub Group.

Lunatic Cafe. Laurell K. Hamilton. (Anita Blake Vampire Hunter Ser.). 369p. 1996. mass mkt. 6.99 (*0-441-00293-5*) Ace Bks.

Lunatic Fringe. Gerald W. Johnson. LC 72-12626. 248p. 1973. reprint ed. lib. bdg. 38.50 (*0-8371-6680-2*, JOLF, Greenwood Pr) Greenwood.

Lunatic Guide to the David Letterman Show. Bradford Keeney. LC 94-23675. 1994. pap. 9.95 (*0-88268-188-5*) Station Hill Pr.

Lunatic Lover: Plays by French Women of the 17th & 18th Centuries. Ed. by Perry Gethner. LC 94-47317. 344p. (C). 1994. pap. 17.95 (*0-435-08637-5*, 08637) Heinemann.

Lunatic Lovers of Language: Imaginary Languages & Their Inventors. Marina Yaguello. LC 89-46430. 1991. 39.50 (*0-8386-3410-9*) Fairleigh Dickinson.

Lunatic on a Limb with Jesus. Jackie Kendall. LC 98-183267. 1998. pap. 10.99 (*1-56043-306-X*, Treasure Hse) Destiny Image.

Lunatics, Lovers, Poets, Jet & Bargirls: Poems by Gerald Nicosia. Gerald Nicosia. (Illus.). 80p. (Orig.). 1991. pap. text 9.50 (*0-924047-05-4*) Host Pubns.

Lunation Cycle: A Key to the Understanding of Personality. Dane Rudhyar. 208p. 1986. pap. 16.95 (*0-943358-26-4*) Aurora Press.

Lunations & Predictions. rev. ed. Sophia Mason. 66p. 1993. 12.00 (*0-86690-364-X*) Am Fed Astrologers.

Lunations & Transits - Step-by-Step: New Moon Through Signs & Houses. 2nd unabridged ed. Sophia Mason. (Illus.). 80p. 1996. spiral bd. 13.00 (*1-889805-06-8*) A-C Tapes.

Lunch see Set 3

Lunch. Steven Berkoff. 15p. 1985. pap. 10.00 (*0-929741-09-9*) Playsmith.

Lunch. Denise Fleming. LC 92-178. (Illus.). 32p. (J). (ps-2). 1995. 14.95 (*0-8050-1636-8*, Bks Young Read) H Holt & Co.

Lunch. Denise Fleming. (J). 1995. pap. 5.95 (*0-8050-4646-1*) H Holt & Co.

Lunch. Denise Fleming. 30p. (J). 1998. bds. 6.95 (*0-8050-5696-3*) H Holt & Co.

Lunch. Denise Fleming. LC 92-178. 1995. 11.15 (*0-606-09580-2*, Pub. by Turtleback) Demco.

Lunch. Karen Moline. 336p. 1996. mass mkt. 6.50 (*0-380-72306-9*, Avon Bks) Morrow Avon.

***Lunch.** D. A. Powell. 2000. 12.95 (*0-8195-6426-5*); pap. 12.95 (*0-8195-6427-3*) U Pr of New Eng.

Lunch: Vocal Selections. Ed. by Sy Feldman. 152p. (Orig.). (C). 1996. pap. text 10.95 (*1-57623-546-7*, PF9633) Wrner Bros.

Lunch at the Calories - Don't - County Cafe. Susan Sturgill. (Illus.). 50p. 1995. pap. 10.00 (*0-9626108-5-2*) Laughing Acad Pr.

Lunch at the 5 & 10. rev. ed. Miles Wolff. (Illus.). 208p. 1990. reprint ed. pap. text 10.95 (*0-929587-31-6*, Elephant Paperbacks) I R Dee.

Lunch at the Table of Opposites. Roger Hecht. 32p. (Orig.). 1996. pap. 5.00 (*1-881168-44-1*) Red Danceflr.

***Lunch at the Zoo.** Altman. LC 00-22430. (Illus.). 80p. (gr. 2-5). 1999. text 15.95 (*0-8050-6070-7*) St Martin.

***Lunch Book & Bag: A Guide to Making Delicious (And Nutritious) Lunches.** Kinny Kreiswirth & Jolene Bodily. (Illus.). 56p. (J). 1998. pap. 12.95 (*0-921051-66-2*) Somerville Hse.

Lunch Box. R. L. Chapman. (Illus.). 104p. 1997. pap. 10.00 (*0-8059-4168-1*) Dorrance.

Lunch Box. Charles Reasoner. (Little Box Bks.). (Illus.). 8p. (J). (ps up). 1995. bds. 8.95 (*0-614-03672-0*, Price Stern) Peng Put Young Read.

Lunch-Box Chronicles: Notes from the Parenting Underground. Marion Winik. LC 97-26753. 240p. 1998. 22.95 (*0-375-40156-3*) Pantheon.

Lunch-Box Chronicles: Notes from the Parenting Underground. Marion Winik. 240p. 1999. pap. 12.00 (*0-375-70170-2*) Vin Bks.

***Lunch Box Laughs: Over 75 Tear-Out Jokes to Make Your Child Giggle.** Tony Nappa & Mike Nappa. Ed. by Lise Caldwell. (Illus.). 160p. (J). (gr. 1-6). 2000. pap. 5.99 (*0-7847-1064-3*) Standard Pub.

***Lunch Box Letters: Writing Notes of Love & Encouragement to Your Children.** Carol Sperandeo & Bill Zimmerman. (Illus.). 216p. 2000. pap. 8.95 (*1-55209-526-6*) Firefly Bks Ltd.

***Lunch Box Notes.** (Illus.). 96p. 2000. pap. 5.95 (*1-57071-546-7*) Sourcebks.

Lunch Box Notes (From Those Who Care) Norm Caldwell. LC 97-33611. 160p. (Orig.). 1997. pap. 7.95 (*1-56273-177-7*) My Mothers Pub.

***Lunch Box Promises.** Tony Nappa & Mike Nappa. 160p. (J). (gr. 1-6). 2000. pap. 6.99 (*0-7847-1181-X*, 04326) Standard Pub.

Lunch Box Surprise. Grace Maccarone. LC 95-10284. (Hello Reader! Ser.: Bk. 1). (Illus.). 32p. (J). (ps-3). 1995. pap. 2.95 (*0-590-26267-X*, Cartwheel) Scholastic Inc.

Lunch Box Surprise. Grace Maccarone. (First-Grade Friends Ser.). (J). 1995. 8.70 (*0-606-07517-8*, Pub. by Turtleback) Demco.

***Lunch Box Trivia: Over Seventy-five Tear-Out Fun Facts about the Bible & Other Cool Stuff.** Tony Nappa & Mike Nappa. 160p. (J). (gr. 1-6). 2000. pap. 6.99 (*0-7847-1180-1*, 04325) Standard Pub.

Lunch Boxes. Fred Ehrlich. LC 93-2724. (Easy-to-Read Bks.: Level 2, Red). (Illus.). (J). (ps-3). 1993. pap. 3.99 (*0-14-036555-9*, PuffinBks) Peng Put Young Read.

Lunch Bugs: Simba's Book about Color. LC 96-123261. (Touch & Play Ser.). (Illus.). 20p. (J). (ps-k). 1995. 8.98 (*1-57082-125-9*, Pub. by Mouse Works) Time Warner.

Lunch Bunch. Margo Finch. LC 97-31377. (Real Kids Readers Ser.). (Illus.). 32p. (J). (gr. k-2). 1998. pap. 3.99 (*0-7613-2030-X*) Millbrook Pr.

***Lunch Bunch.** Margo Finch. LC 97-31377. (Real Kids Readers Ser.). (Illus.). 32p. (J). (gr. k-2). 1998. lib. bdg. 16.90 (*0-7613-2005-9*) Millbrook Pr.

Lunch Bunnies. Kathryn Lasky. LC 92-31554. (Illus.). 32p. (J). (gr. k-3). 1996. 14.95 (*0-316-51525-6*, Joy St Bks) Little.

Lunch Bunnies. Kathryn Lasky. (Illus.). 32p. (J). (ps-3). 1999. pap. 5.95 (*0-316-51586-8*) Little.

Lunch for a Bunch. Howard Goldthwaite. (Illus.). 6p. (J). 1994. 5.99 (*1-56476-172-X*, 6-3172, Victor Bks) Chariot Victor.

Lunch for Three. JoAnn Vandine. LC 92-31954. (Voyages Ser.). (Illus.). (J). 1993. 4.25 (*0-383-03582-1*) SRA McGraw.

Lunch Is on the Table! 40 Complete Menus with Step-by-Step Recipes for Midday Enjoyment. Robert Ackart. (Illus.). 132p. 1960. pap. 12.95 (*1-887678-03-4*) Finley-Greene Pubns.

Lunch Line. Caleen Jennings. 92p. 1989. pap. write for info. (*0-932720-50-1*) New Plays Inc.

Lunch Line. Karen B. Nagel. LC 96-14354. (Hello Math Reader Ser.: Level 3). (Illus.). 32p. (J). (gr. 1-4). 1996. 3.50 (*0-590-60246-2*, Cartwheel) Scholastic Inc.

Lunch Line. Karen Berman Nagel. (Hello Math Reader Ser.). (J). 1996. 8.70 (*0-606-11584-6*, Pub. by Turtleback) Demco.

Lunch Money: And Other Poems about School. Carol Diggory Shields. LC 95-7332. (Picture Puffin Ser.). (Illus.). 40p. (J). (ps-3). 1998. pap. 5.99 (*0-14-055890-X*, PuffinBks) Peng Put Young Read.

Lunch Money & Other Poems about School. Carol Diggory Shields. LC 95-7332. (Illus.). 40p. (J). (gr. 2-4). 1995. 15.99 (*0-525-45345-8*, Dutton Child) Peng Put Young Read.

***Lunch Money & Other Poems about School.** Carol Diggory Shields. 1998. 11.19 (*0-606-13586-3*, Pub. by Turtleback) Demco.

Lunch Poems. Frank O'Hara. LC 64-8689. (Pocket Poets Ser.: No. 19). 1964. pap. 7.95 (*0-87286-035-3*) City Lights.

Lunch That Mom Made. Margaret Beames. LC 92-21454. (Voyages Ser.). (Illus.). (J). 1993. 4.25 (*0-383-03639-9*) SRA McGraw.

Lunch with Cat & Dog, Vol. 3730. Contrib. by Rozanne L. Williams. (Emergent Reader Bks.). 16p. (J). (gr. k-2). 1995. pap. 2.49 (*0-916119-92-0*) Creat Teach Pr.

Lunch with Cat & Dog, Vol. 3973. Rozanne L. Williams. (Emergent Reader Big Bks.). (Illus.). 16p. (J). (gr. k-2). 1996. pap. 12.98 (*1-57471-111-3*) Creat Teach Pr.

***Lunch with Elizabeth David: A Novel.** Roger Williams. 352p. 2000. 24.95 (*0-7867-0707-0*) Carroll & Graf.

Lunch with Milly. Jeanne Modesitt. LC 93-33808. (Illus.). 32p. (J). (ps-2). 1997. 13.95 (*0-8167-3388-0*) BrdgeWater.

Lunch with Milly. Jeanne Modesitt. LC 93-33808. (Illus.). 32p. (J). (gr. k-2). 1996. pap. 4.95 (*0-8167-3389-9*, Troll Medallion) Troll Communs.

Lunch with Milly. Jeanne Modesitt. LC 93-33808. 1995. 10.15 (*0-606-09581-0*, Pub. by Turtleback) Demco.

Lunchbox Food: For School, Office & Picnics. Deona Tait. 1999. pap. text 14.95 (*0-7981-3841-6*) Human & Rousseau.

Lunchbox Love Notes: Notes for a Child. Ideals Children's Books Editors. (Love Notes Ser.). (Illus.). 112p. (Orig.). (J). (ps-5). 1995. pap., per. 5.95 (*1-57102-050-0*, Ideals Child) Hambleton-Hill.

Luncheon of the Boating Party. Stewart Conn. 64p. 1993. pap. 14.95 (*1-85224-142-X*, Pub. by Bloodaxe Bks) Dufour.

***Lunches.** MacDonald. (J). 2000. 29.95 (*0-385-40765-3*, Pub. by Transworld Publishers Ltd) Trafalgar.

Lunches & Snacks: With Lessons for Children. 2nd rev. ed. Sue Gregg & Emilie Barnes. (Eating Better Cookbooks: Basic Set: Vol. 4). (Illus.). 193p. (J). (gr. 2-12). 2000. spiral bd. 14.00 (*1-878272-03-9*) S Gregg Cookbks.

Lunching with the AntiChrist: A Family History. Michael Moorcock. 1994. 25.00 (*0-929480-46-5*) Mark Ziesing.

Lunching with the AntiChrist: A Family History. limited ed. Michael Moorcock. 1994. 60.00 (*0-929480-47-3*) Mark Ziesing.

Lunchroom Waste: A Study of "How Much & How Come" Clista Dow. Ed. by Linda H. Smith. (Triad Prototype Ser.). 44p. 1978. pap. 5.00 (*0-936386-04-5*) Creative Learning.

Lunchtime in Pittsburgh. Margaret Marquis. 40p. (Orig.). 1988. pap. 4.95 (*0-9621737-0-3*) Pittsburgh Promo.

Lunchtime Walks in Downtown San Francisco. Gail Todd. LC 98-24699. (Illus.). 220p. 1998. 11.95 (*0-89997-217-9*) Wilderness Pr.

Lund Model. Bo Andersson. LC 97-32156. (Cambridge Monographs on Particle Physics, Nuclear Physics & Cosmology: No. 4). (Illus.). 484p. (C). 1998. text 130.00 (*0-521-42094-6*) Cambridge U Pr.

Lunda under Belgian Rule: The Politics of Ethnicity. Edouard Bustin. (Illus.). 302p. 1975. 37.95 (*0-674-53953-2*) HUP.

Lunderston Tales. Robin Jenkins. 216p. 1996. 17.95 (*0-7486-6221-9*, Pub. by Polygon) Subterranean Co.

Lundstrom Collection of Terra Sigillata in the Museum of the Department of Classical Archaeology & Ancient History Goteborg University. Carin Wetter. (Acta Instituti Romani Regni Sueciae, Series in 4 Degrees: Vol. XIX). (Illus.). 97p. 1993. pap. 39.50 (*91-7042-147-1*, Pub. by P Astroms) Coronet Bks.

Lundwall. Lundwalls, Gustavsons, & Allied Swedish Families: Family History, Biography & More. Paul W. Lundwall. Ed. by Wm. E. Wright. (Illus.). 71p. 1998. pap. 15.50 (*0-8328-9679-9*) Higginson Bk Co.

Lundwall. Lundwalls, Gustavsons, & Allied Swedish Families: Family History, Biography & More. Paul W. Lundwall. Ed. by William E. Wright. (Illus.). 71p. 1998. lib. bdg. 25.50 (*0-8328-9678-0*) Higginson Bk Co.

Lundy & Irish Sea Pilot: Land's End to Portpatrick. David Conrad Taylor. (Illus.). 200p. 1994. pap. 125.00 (*0-85288-249-1*, Pub. by Laurie Norie & Wilson Ltd) St Mut.

Lundy, Fastnet & Irish Sea Pilot: The Bristol Channel. David Conrad Taylor. (Illus.). 95p. (C). 1988. pap. 69.00 (*0-85288-133-9*, Pub. by Laurie Norie & Wilson Ltd) St Mut.

Lundy Summer. large type ed. Peggy L. Jones. (Linford Romance Library). 1991. pap. 16.99 (*0-7089-7051-6*) Ulverscroft.

Lundy's: A Cookbook with Reminiscences from Brooklyn's Legendary Restaurant. Robert Cornfield & Kathy Gunst. LC 97-35343. 224p. 1998. 25.00 (*0-06-018741-7*) HarpC.

Lundy's Letter. Gerald Dawe. 50p. 1985. pap. 10.95 (*0-904011-84-4*) Dufour.

Lune see Encyclopedic Poetique: Anthologie Thematique de la Poesie Francaise Contemporaine

***Luneberg Variation.** Paolo Maurensig. LC 98-34459. 144p. 1998. pap. 11.00 (*0-8050-6028-6*, Owl) H Holt & Co.

Lunenburg: An Illustrated History. Brian Cuthbertson. (Illus.). 66p. 1997. pap. 16.95 (*0-88780-358-X*, Pub. by Formac Publ Co) Formac Dist Ltd.

***Lunenburg County, Virginia, Court Order Book 10, 1764-1765.** T.L.C. Genealogy Staff. 239p. 1999. pap. 20.00 (*1-57445-061-1*) TLC Genealogy.

***Lunenburg County, Virginia, Court Order Book 9, 1763-1764.** T.L.C. Genealogy Staff. 213p. 1999. pap. 15.00 (*1-57445-052-2*) TLC Genealogy.

Lunenburg County, Virginia Court Orders, 1746-1748. T.L.C. Genealogy Staff. LC 90-71808. 219p. (Orig.). 1991. pap., spiral bd. 15.00 (*1-886633-89-4*) TLC Genealogy.

Lunenburg County, Virginia, Court Orders, 1752-1762: An Every-Name Index to Order Books 2 1/2A, 2 1/2B, 3, 4, 5, 6, 7, & 8. LC 96-105821. 165p. 1995. pap., spiral bd. 20.00 (*1-57445-018-2*) TLC Genealogy.

Lunenburg County, Virginia Deed 1-16, 1746-1795: An Every-Name Index. T.L.C. Genealogy Staff. 204p. 1992. spiral bd. 15.00 (*1-886633-76-2*) TLC Genealogy.

Lunenburg County, Virginia Deeds, 1746-1752. T.L.C. Genealogy Staff. 98p. (Orig.). 1990. pap., spiral bd. 12.00 (*1-886633-77-0*) TLC Genealogy.

Lunenburg County, Virginia Deeds, 1752-1757. T.L.C. Genealogy Staff. 137p. (Orig.). 1990. pap., spiral bd. 12.00 (*1-886633-78-9*) TLC Genealogy.

Lunenburg County, Virginia Deeds, 1757-1761. T.L.C. Genealogy Staff. LC 90-70915. 143p. (Orig.). 1990. pap., spiral bd. 12.00 (*1-886633-79-7*) TLC Genealogy.

Lunenburg County, Virginia Deeds, 1764-1771. T.L.C. Genealogy Staff. LC 90-70915. 126p. (Orig.). 1990. pap., spiral bd. 12.00 (*1-886633-82-7*) TLC Genealogy.

Lunenburg County, Virginia Deeds, 1771-1777. T.L.C. Genealogy Staff. LC 90-190139. 114p. (Orig.). 1990. pap., spiral bd. 12.00 (*1-886633-83-5*) TLC Genealogy.

Lunenburg County, Virginia Deeds, 1777-1784. T.L.C. Genealogy Staff. LC 91-61467. 142p. (Orig.). 1991. pap., spiral bd. 12.00 (1-886633-84-3) TLC Genealogy.

Lunenburg County, Virginia Deeds, 1784-1787. T.L.C. Genealogy Staff. 79p. (Orig.). 1990. pap., spiral bd. 10.00 (1-886633-85-1) TLC Genealogy.

Lunenburg County, Virginia Deeds, 1787-1790. T.L.C. Genealogy Staff. LC 91-61466. 78p. (Orig.). 1991. pap., spiral bd. 9.00 (1-886633-86-X) TLC Genealogy.

Lunenburg County, Virginia Deeds, 1790-1795. T.L.C. Genealogy Staff. LC 92-70871. 147p. (Orig.). 1992. pap., spiral bd. 12.00 (1-886633-87-8) TLC Genealogy.

Lunenburg County, Virginia Deeds, 1763-1764, Bk. 9. T.L.C. Genealogy Staff. LC 90-71189. 66p. (Orig.). 1990. pap., spiral bd. 9.00 (1-886633-81-9) TLC Genealogy.

Lunenburg County, Virginia Deeds, 1761-1764, Bks. 7-8. T.L.C. Genealogy Staff. LC 90-70915. 134p. (Orig.). 1990. pap., spiral bd. 12.00 (1-886633-80-0) TLC Genealogy.

Lunenburg County, Virginia Land Patents, 1746-1916. T.L.C. Genealogy Staff. LC 90-71297. 169p. (Orig.). 1990. pap., spiral bd. 12.00 (1-886633-88-6) TLC Genealogy.

Lunenburg County, Virginia, Marriages, 1750-1853. John Vogt & T. William Kethley, Jr. LC 88-34673. 210p. 1988. pap. 12.00 (0-935931-39-2) Iberian Pub.

Lunenburg County, Virginia, Personal Property Tax Lists, 1782 & 1785. T.L.C. Genealogy Staff. 82p. (Orig.). 1992. pap., spiral bd. 10.00 (1-886633-90-8) TLC Genealogy.

Lunenburg County, Virginia, Will Book No. 1, with Inventories, Accounts, Etc., 1746-1762. 125p. 1999. spiral bd. 10.00 (1-57445-057-3) TLC Genealogy.

Lunenburg County, Virginia Will Book 2, 1760-1778. T.L.C. Genealogy Staff. LC 91-66027. 145p. 1991. spiral bd. 16.00 (1-886633-75-4) TLC Genealogy.

Lunenburg the Old Free State: A Contribution to the History of Lunenburg County & Southside Virginia, 2 vols., Set. Landon C. Bell. (Illus.). 1267p. 1995. reprint ed. lib. bdg. 132.00 (0-8328-5132-9) Higginson Bk Co.

Lunenburgh: or The Old Eastern District: Its Settlement & Early Progressm with Personal Recollections of the Town of Cornwall from 1824. J. F. Pringle. (Illus.). 423p. 1996. reprint ed. lib. bdg. 46.00 (0-8328-5156-6) Higginson Bk Co.

Lung: Molecular Basis of Disease. Jerome S. Brody. Ed. by Judy Fletcher. LC 97-27841. (Illus.). 240p. (C). 1998. text 50.00 (0-7216-6814-3, W B Saunders Co) Harcrt Hlth Sci Grp.

Lung: Research Accomplishments & Frontiers. 70p. 10.00 (0-685-14559-X) Am Lung Assn.

Lung: Scientific Foundations, 2 vols. 2nd ed. Ed. by Ronald G. Crystal et al. LC 96-14140. 2,710p. 1996. text 352.00 (0-397-51632-0) Lppncott W & W.

Lung & Heart-Lung Transplantation. V. Gallucci. (Illus.). 166p. 1991. text. write for info. (88-299-0983-1, Pub. by Piccin Nuova) Gordon & Breach.

Lung & Heart-Lung Transplantation. V. Gallucci et al. 166p. 1991. text 50.00 (1-57235-040-7) Piccin Nuova.

Lung at Depth. Ed. by Claes Lundgren & John M. Miller. LC 99-22838. (Lung Biology in Health & Disease Ser.). (Illus.). 712p. 1999. text 225.00 (0-8247-0158-5) Dekker.

Lung Cancer. Ed. by Desmond N. Carney. (An Arnold Publication). 280p. 1995. text 95.00 (0-340-56759-7, Pub. by E A) OUP.

***Lung Cancer.** Robert J. Ginsberg. (ACS Atlas of Clinical Oncology Ser.). 352p. 2000. boxed set 89.95 incl. cd-rom (1-55009-099-2) DEKR.

Lung Cancer. Ed. by Heine H. Hansen. (Cancer Treatment & Research Ser.). 1986. text 152.50 (0-89838-763-9) Kluwer Academic.

Lung Cancer. Ed. by Bruce E. Johnson & David H. Johnson. (Current Clinical Oncology Ser.). 368p. 1994. 145.00 (0-471-01285-8) Wiley.

Lung Cancer. Ed. by Robert B. Livingston. (Cancer Treatment & Research Ser.: No. 1). (Illus.). 320p. 1981. text 175.50 (90-247-2394-9) Kluwer Academic.

Lung Cancer. Ed. by Joseph Aisner. LC 84-12095. (Contemporary Issues in Clinical Oncology Ser.: No. 3). (Illus.). 352p. reprint ed. pap. 109.20 (0-7837-6257-7, 204596900010) Bks Demand.

Lung Cancer. 2nd ed. Jack A. Roth et al. LC 97-37264. (Illus.). 1998. 110.00 (0-86542-573-6) Blackwell Sci.

Lung Cancer. 2nd ed. Chris Williams. (Facts Ser.). (Illus.). 152p. (C). 1995. reprint ed. pap. 19.95 (0-19-262250-1) OUP.

Lung Cancer, Vol. 2. John G. Gruhn. 1989. 65.00 (0-938607-10-3) Field & Wood Inc Medical.

Lung Cancer, Vol. 2. John G. Gruhn. 1989. 75.00 (0-938607-17-0) Field & Wood Inc Medical.

Lung Cancer: A Comprehensive Treatise. Bitran & Golomb. 1987. 94.00 (0-685-18913-9, Grune & Strat) Harcrt Hlth Sci Grp.

***Lung Cancer: A Guide to Diagnosis & Treatment.** Walter Scott. (Illus.). 160p. 2000. pap. 14.95 (1-886039-43-7) Addicus Bks.

Lung Cancer: A Practical Guide to Management. Fergus R. Macbeth. 148p. 1996. pap. text 15.00 (3-7186-5860-7, Harwood Acad Pubs) Gordon & Breach.

Lung Cancer: A Practical Guide to Management. Fergus R. Macbeth et al. 148p. 1996. text 39.00 (3-7186-5859-3, Harwood Acad Pubs) Gordon & Breach.

Lung Cancer: Advances in Basic & Clinical Research. Ed. by Heine H. Hansen. LC 94-10350. (Cancer Treatment & Research Ser.: Vol. 72). 416p. (C). 1994. text 318.00 (0-7923-2835-3) Kluwer Academic.

***Lung Cancer: Ancient Truths, Natural Remedies & the Latest Findings for Your Health Today.** Don Colbert. (Bible Cure Ser.). 2000. pap. 5.99 (0-88419-680-1) Creation House.

***Lung Cancer: Principles & Practice.** Harvey I. Pass. LC 99-51908. (Illus.). 2000. 159.00 (0-7817-1791-4) Lppncott W & W.

Lung Cancer: Principles & Practice. Harvey I. Pass et al. 982p. 1995. text 151.00 (0-397-51361-5) Lppncott W & W.

Lung Cancer: Progress in Therapeutic Research. fac. ed. Ed. by Franco M. Muggia & Marcel Rozencweig. LC 77-84552. (Progress in Cancer Research & Therapy Ser.: No. 11). (Illus.). 640p. pap. 198.40 (0-7837-7179-7, 204712000005) Bks Demand.

Lung Cancer: Textbook for General Practitioners. Ed. by Europe Against Cancer Staff & H. H. Hansen. (EC Series for General Practitioners). (Illus.). xi, 58p. 1990. pap. 38.00 (0-387-53075-4) Spr-Verlag.

Lung Cancer: The Art of Detection by Conventional Radiography. Alfred Szamosi. Ed. by Swedish Heart & Lung Foundation Staff. (Illus.). 117p. 1995. 67.50 (91-630-2980-4) Coronet Bks.

Lung Cancer Chronicles. John A. Meyer. LC 89-11000. (Illus.). 250p. (Orig.). 1990. 35.00 (0-8135-1492-4); pap. 12.95 (0-8135-1493-2) Rutgers U Pr.

Lung Cancer Differentiation: Implications for Diagnosis & Treatment. Ed. by Samuel D. Bernal & Paul J. Hesketh. (Lung Biology in Health & Disease Ser.: Vol. 58). (Illus.). 496p. 1992. text 230.00 (0-8247-8638-6) Dekker.

Lung Cancer Handbook: Evaluation & Management. Christine M. Dela Cruz & Harubumi Kato. LC 92-1694. 189p. 1993. pap. text 35.00 (3-7186-5294-3) Gordon & Breach.

Lung Cancer, 1980: Post-Graduate Course II. Ed. by Heine H. Hansen & M. Roth. (International Congress Ser.: Vol. 525). 1981. pap. 47.25 (0-444-90160-4) Elsevier.

Lung Carcinomas. Ed. by Elizabeth M. McDowell. LC 86-33361. (Current Problems in Tumor Pathology Ser.). (Illus.). 410p. 1987. text 72.00 (0-443-03165-7) Church.

Lung Cell Biology. Donald Massaro. LC 88-33549. (Lung Biology in Health & Disease Ser.: Vol. 41). (Illus.). 1461p. 1989. reprint ed. pap. 200.00 (0-608-08006-3, 206797100012) Bks Demand.

Lung Circulation, 2 vols., Set, Vols. 1 & 2. D. M. Aviado. LC 64-24302. 1965. 633.00 (0-08-010988-8, Pub. by Pergamon Repr) Franklin.

Lung Connective Tissue: Location, Metabolism, & Response to Injury. Ed. by John A. Pickrell. 224p. 1981. 98.95 (0-8493-5749-7, RC756) CRC Pr.

***Lung Development.** Ed. by Claude Gaultier et al. LC 98-44090. (Clinical Physiology Ser.). (Illus.). 472p. 1999. text 89.50 (0-19-511278-4) OUP.

Lung Disease: State-of-the-Art, 1984-1986. Ed. by Reuben M. Cherniack. (Lung Disease: State-of-the-Art Ser.). (Illus.). 224p. 1987. 20.50 (0-915116-05-7, 9807) Am Lung Assn.

Lung Disease: State of the Art, 1986-1987. Ed. by Reuben M. Cherniack. (State of the Art Ser.). (Illus.). 202p. 1988. write for info. (0-915116-06-5, 9801) Am Lung Assn.

Lung Disease: State of the Art, 1987-1988. Ed. by Reuben M. Cherniack. (Illus.). 224p. 1989. 35.00 (0-915116-07-3, 9622) Am Lung Assn.

Lung Disease: State of the Art, 1988-1989. Ed. by Reuben M. Cherniack. (State of the Art Ser.). (Illus.). 230p. 1990. 50.00 (0-915116-08-1, 9620) Am Lung Assn.

Lung Disease: State of the Art, 1989-90. Ed. by Robert A. Klocke. (State of the Art Ser.). (Illus.). 226p. 1991. 60.00 (0-915116-09-X, 9611) Am Lung Assn.

Lung Disease: State of the Art, 1990-92. Ed. by Robert A. Klocke. (State of the Art Ser.). (Illus.). 348p. 65.00 (0-915116-10-3, 9775) Am Lung Assn.

Lung Disease: State of the Art, 1993-94. Ed. by Robert A. Klocke. (State of the Art Ser.). 256p. 50.00 (0-915116-11-1, 9776) Am Lung Assn.

Lung Disease: State of the Art, 1995-1996. ATS (Hansen) Staff. 356p. 1997. per. 65.00 (0-7872-3709-4) Kendall-Hunt.

Lung Disease in the Tropics. Ed. by Om P. Sharma. (Lung Biology in Health & Disease Ser.: Vol. 51). (Illus.). 624p. 1990. text 255.00 (0-8247-8398-0) Dekker.

Lung Diseases: Directory of Authors of New Medical & Scientific Reviews with Subject Index. Science & Life Consultants Association Staff. 160p. 1995. 47.50 (0-7883-0604-9); pap. 44.50 (0-7883-0605-7) ABBE Pubs Assn.

Lung Diseases of Adults. 110p. 1985. 12.00 (0-685-12131-3, 0032) Am Lung Assn.

Lung Diseases of Children: An Introduction. 110p. 17.00 (0-685-43333-1, 3511) Am Lung Assn.

Lung Dosimetry Models for Inhaled Radon Progeny. Martonen Hofmann. 1994. write for info. (0-8493-5830-2) CRC Pr.

Lung Function in Children & Adolescents. Ed. by A. Zapletal et al. (Progress in Respiratory Research Ser.: Vol. 22). (Illus.). viii, 220p. 1987. 152.25 (3-8055-4495-2) S Karger.

Lung Function Tests: A Guide to Their Interpretation. William J. M. Kinnear. 162p. 1999. pap. 80.00 (1-897676-80-8, Pub. by Nottingham Univ Pr) St Mut.

Lung Growth & Development. Ed. by John A. McDonald. LC 96-52512. (Lung Biology in Health & Disease Ser.: Vol. 100). (Illus.). 768p. 1997. text 215.00 (0-8247-9772-8) Dekker.

Lung in Rheumatic Diseases. Grant W. Cannon & Zimmerman. (Lung Biology in Health & Disease Ser.: Vol. 45). (Illus.). 576p. 1990. text 205.00 (0-8247-8211-9) Dekker.

Lung in Transition Between Health & Disease. Ed. by Peter T. Macklem & S. Permutt. (Lung Biology in Health & Disease Ser.: Vol. 12). (Illus.). 464p. 1979. text 190.00 (0-8247-7750-6) Dekker.

Lung Injury. Ed. by Ronald G. Crystal & John B. West. LC 91-32568. (Illus.). 416p. 1992. reprint ed. pap. 129.00 (0-608-07188-9, 206741300009) Bks Demand.

Lung Liquids. CIBA Foundation Staff. LC 76-870. (CIBA Foundation Symposium: New Ser.: No. 38). 340p. reprint ed. pap. 105.40 (0-608-14317-0, 202216600024) Bks Demand.

Lung Sounds: A Practical Guide. 2nd ed. Robert H. Wilkins et al. (Illus.). 114p. (C). (gr. 13). 1996. pap. text 43.00 (0-8151-9287-8, 25632) Mosby Inc.

Lung Sounds: A Practical Guide. 2nd ed. Wilkins et al. (Illus.). 128p. 1996. pap. text 49.00 (0-8151-9417-X, 28150) Mosby Inc.

Lung Surfactant: Basic Research in the Pathogenesis of Lung Disorders. Ed. by B. Mueller & P. Von Wichert. (Progress in Respiratory Research Ser.: Vol. 27). (Illus.). x, 266p. 1994. 208.75 (3-8055-5837-6) S Karger.

Lung Surfactant: Cellular & Molecular Processing. Seamus A. Rooney. LC 98-9173. (Molecular Biology Intelligence Unit Ser.). 227p. 1998. pap. 99.00 (1-57059-479-1) Landes Bioscience.

***Lung Surfactants: Basic Science & Clinical Applications.** Robert H. Notter. LC 00-31583. (Lung Biology in Health & Disease Ser.). 2000. write for info. (0-8247-0401-0) Dekker.

Lung Transplantation. R. Hetzer. 80p. 1999. 40.00 (3-7985-1062-8, Pub. by D Steinkopff) Spr-Verlag.

Lung Transplantation, No. 3. Ed. by Alec Patterson & Louis Couraud. LC 94-43203. (Current Topics in General Thoracic Surgery Ser.: Vol. 3). 612p. 1994. 281.50 (0-444-81567-8) Elsevier.

Lung Tumors. Ed. by B. Hoogstraten. (Illus.). 300p. 1988. 85.95 (0-387-16920-2) Spr-Verlag.

Lung Vascular Injury: Molecular & Cellular Response. Ed. by Arnold Johnson & Thomas J. Ferro. LC 92-18425. (Lung Biology in Health & Disease Ser.: Vol. 60). (Illus.). 368p. 1992. text 180.00 (0-8247-8718-8) Dekker.

Lung Viability after Circulatory Arrest: An Experimental Study in Rabbits. Dirk Van Raemdonck. (Acta Biomedica Lovaniensia Ser.). (Illus.). 166p. 1998. pap. 46.50 (90-6186-879-3, Pub. by Leuven Univ) Coronet Bks.

Lung Water & Solute Exchange. Ed. by Norman C. Staub. LC 77-15047. (Lung Biology in Health & Disease Ser.: No. 7). (Illus.). 584p. 1978. reprint ed. pap. 181.10 (0-608-00204-6, 206098700006) Bks Demand.

Lungbarrow. Marc Platt. (New Adventures Ser.). 256p. 1997. mass mkt. 5.95 (0-426-20502-2, Pub. by Virgin Bks) London Brdge.

Lungeing. G. N. E. F. Staff. (Official Instruction Handbook of the German National Equestrian Foundation Ser.: No. 6). (Illus.). 79p. 1990. pap. 20.95 (1-872082-16-5) Half Halt Pr.

Lungeing. Harvey. (Threshold Picture Guide Ser.: No. 36). (Illus.). 24p. 1996. pap. 12.00 (1-872082-82-3) Half Halt Pr.

Lungeing & Long Reining. Jennie Loriston-Clarke. (Illus.). 95p. 1994. 34.95 (1-872082-14-9, Pub. by Kenilworth Pr) Half Halt Pr.

Lunging at Life's Problems. Roch L. Mirabeau. LC 97-90796. 61p. 1998. pap. 8.95 (0-533-12476-X) Vantage.

***LungMouth.** Frank D'Andrea. 28p. 1999. pap. 2.79 (1-892061-01-5) Future Tense.

Lungo le Acque Tranquille see Beside Still Waters

Lungs. Steve Parker. LC 96-7961. (Look at Your Body Ser.). (Illus.). 32p. (J). (gr. 4-6). 1996. lib. bdg. 20.90 (0-7613-0530-0, Copper Beech Bks) Millbrook Pr.

Lungs. 3rd ed. Ed. by B. Corrin. (Systemic Pathology Ser.: Vol. 5). (Illus.). 467p. 1990. text 185.00 (0-443-03094-4) Church.

Lungs & Breathing. Mark Lambert. (How Our Bodies Work Ser.). (Illus.). 48p. (J). (gr. 5-8). 1988. lib. bdg. 12.95 (0-382-09701-7) Silver Burdett Pr.

Lungs & Respiratory System. Steve Parker. LC 96-43516. (Human Body Ser.). (Illus.). 48p. (J). (gr. 5-10). 1997. lib. bdg. 25.68 (0-8172-4803-X) Raintree Steck-V.

Lungscapes. Ed. by Pier C. Braga & Luigi Allegra. LC 92-9560. (Illus.). 112p. 1992. 108.00 (0-387-55249-9) Spr-Verlag.

Luni Sul Mignone Vol. II, Fasc. 2: The Zone of the Iron Age Building. Pontus Hellstrom. (Acta Instituti Romani Regni Sueciae, Series in 4 Degrees: Vol. XXVII:II,2). (Illus.). 186p. 1975. pap. 69.50 (91-7042-048-3, Pub. by P Astroms) Coronet Bks.

L'Unita e Gesu Abbandonato see Jesus - The Heart of His Message: Unity & Jesus Forsaken

***L'Univers Mythique de Tchicaya U Tam'si a Travers Son Oeuvre en Prose.** Kahiudi Claver Mabana. (Publications Universitaires Europeennes: Vol. 237). xii, 400p. 1998. 52.95 (3-906760-76-6, Pub. by P Lang) P Lang Pubng.

L'Universite Aujourdhui: Elements de Reflexion. A. Borrero Cabal. (FRE., Illus.). xxiv, 300p. 1995. pap. 19.00 (0-88936-729-9, Pub. by IDRC Bks) Stylus Pub VA.

L'Universo see Universe

***Lunkers! 130 Hilarious Cartoons about Fishing.** John Troy. LC 00-34928. 128p. 2000. 14.95 (1-58574-153-1) Lyons Pr.

Lunn Family Album. Hugh Lunn. (Illus.). 200p. 1995. pap. 19.95 (0-7022-2563-0, Pub. by Univ Queensland Pr) Intl Spec Bk.

Lunnettes d'Or et Autres Histoires de Ferrare. Giorgio Bassani. (FRE.). 448p. 1982. pap. 11.95 (0-7859-1959-7, 2070373940) Fr & Eur.

Lunsford Lane: or Another Helper from North Carolina. William G. Hawkins. LC 78-88542. (Black Heritage Library Collection). 1977. 18.95 (0-8369-8591-5) Ayer.

Lunt: The Ancestry of Abel Lunt. W. G. Davis. (Illus.). 269p. 1991. reprint ed. pap. 42.00 (0-8328-2085-7); reprint ed. lib. bdg. 52.00 (0-8328-2084-9) Higginson Bk Co.

Luo, 14 vols. Awor Ayodo & Atieno Odhiambo. Ed. by George Boud. (Heritage Library of African Peoples). (Illus.). 64p. (YA). (gr. 7-12). 1995. lib. bdg. 16.95 (0-8239-1758-4) Rosen Group.

L'Uomo Immagine Somigliante Di Dio see In God's Image & Likeness

Luoyang Museum. Wang Xiu. (National Museums & Monuments of Ancient China Ser.). (Illus.). 64p. 1997. 25.00 (0-85667-459-1, Pub. by P Wilson) Scala Books.

Lupa Maravillosa. Nomi Joval. (SPA., Illus.). 24p. (J). (ps-4). 1993. lib. bdg. 13.95 (1-879567-22-9, Valeria Bks) Wonder Well.

Lupang Tinubuan & Selected Works in English. Narciso G. Reyes. 118p. (Orig.). (C). 1991. pap. 10.75 (971-10-0407-0, Pub. by New Day Pub) Cellar.

Lupe & Me. Elizabeth Spurr. LC 91-35824. (Illus.). 40p. (J). (gr. 1-5). 1995. 13.00 (0-15-200522-6, Red Wagon Bks) Harcourt.

Lupe Luna Se Quedo Despierta Toda la Noche. Frank B. Edwards.Tr. of Melody Mooner Stayed up All Night. (SPA., Illus.). 24p. (Orig.). (J). (ps-3). 1997. pap. 5.95 (0-921285-60-4, Pub. by Bungalo Books) Firefly Bks Ltd.

Lupi, Servati. Ed. by Marshall. (LAT.). 1984. 39.50 (3-322-00191-1, T1370, Pub. by B G Teubner) U of Mich Pr.

Lupin Development Guide. Miles Dracup & Michael Kirby. LC 97-106174. 112p. 1996. pap. 19.95 (1-875560-66-1, Pub. by Univ of West Aust Pr) Intl Spec Bk.

Lupins as Crop Plants: Biology, Production & Utilization. Ed. by J. S. Gladstones et al. (A CAB International Publication). 480p. 1998. 135.00 (0-85199-224-2) OUP.

Lupita Manana. Patricia Beatty. LC 81-505. 192p. (J). (gr. 7 up). 1992. pap. 4.95 (0-688-11497-0, Wm Morrow) Morrow Avon.

***Lupita Manana.** Patricia Beatty. LC 81-505. (SPA.). 192p. (J). 2000. mass mkt. 4.95 (0-380-73247-5) Morrow Avon.

Lupita Manana. Patricia Beatty. (J). 1992. 10.05 (0-606-01376-8, Pub. by Turtleback) Demco.

***Lupus: A Patient Care Guide for Nurses & Other Health Professionals.** Terri Nass. Ed. by Julia Freeman & Anne Brown Rodgers. 130p. (C). 2000. reprint ed. pap. text 30.00 (0-7567-0062-0) DIANE Pub.

***Lupus: Alternative Therapies That Work.** Sharon Moore. 256p. 2000. pap. 14.95 (0-89281-889-1) Inner Tradit.

Lupus: Everything You Need to Know. Robert G. Lahita & Robert H. Phillips. LC 97-34718. 224p. 1999. pap. 12.95 (0-89529-833-3, Avery) Penguin Putnam.

Lupus: Living with It. Suzy Szasz. LC 95-31006. 243p. 1995. pap. 17.95 (1-57392-023-1) Prometheus Bks.

Lupus: Molecular & Cellular Pathogenesis. Gary M. Kammer & George C. Tsokos. LC 99-13238. (Contemporary Immunology Ser.: Vol. 7). 728p. 1999. 195.00 (0-89603-556-5) Humana.

Lupus: My Search for a Diagnosis. Eileen Radziunas. LC 89-24683. 144p. 1989. pap. 9.95 (0-89793-065-7) Hunter Hse.

***Lupus: The Facts.** Graham Hughes. LC 99-39046. (The Facts Ser.). (Illus.). 144p. 2000. pap. text 19.95 (0-19-263145-4) OUP.

Lupus - What's It All About? Claudia Pagano & Mary M. Goulding. xi, 210p. 1997. pap. 14.95 (0-9661036-3-7) Abiding Health.

***Lupus Book: A Guide for Patients & Their Families.** rev. ed. Daniel J. Wallace. LC 99-13841. (Illus.). 288p. 2000. 25.00 (0-19-513281-5) OUP.

Lupus Erythematoles. Schneider. 1996. text 19.95 (3-540-00962-0) Spr-Verlag.

Lupus Handbook for Women: Up-to-Date Information on Understanding & Managing the Disease Which Affects One in Five Hundred Women. Robin Dibner & Carol Colman. LC 94-17984. 176p. 1994. per. 11.00 (0-671-79031-5) S&S Trade.

Lupus Nephritis. Ed. by Edmund J. Lewis et al. LC 98-39265. (Oxford Clinical Nephrology Ser.). (Illus.). 336p. 1999. text 125.00 (0-19-262755-4) OUP.

Lupus Novice: Toward Self-Healing. 2nd rev. expanded ed. Laura Chester. LC 99-11490. 224p. 1999. pap. 13.95 (1-58177-020-0, P2083, Pub. by Barrytown Ltd) Consort Bk Sales.

Lupus Novice: Towards Self Healing. Laura Chester. Ed. by George Quasha. LC 87-9758. 192p. (C). 1987. 16.95 (0-88268-037-4) Station Hill Pr.

Lupus Viator Atlanta. Illus. by Darya Von Berner. 220p. boxed set 50.00 (0-932526-58-6) Nexus Pr.

Lurching from One Near Disaster to the Next. Warren Miller. (Illus.). 288p. 1998. pap. 14.95 (0-9636144-2-8) W Miller Prods.

***Lurching from One near Disaster to the Next.** Warren Miller. 288p. 1998. 24.95 (0-9636144-3-6) W Miller Prods.

Lure. Felice Picano. 1996. reprint ed. mass mkt. 6.95 (1-56333-398-8, Hard Candy) Masquerade.

Lure & Loathing: Essays on Race, Identity, & the Ambivalence of Assimilation. Intro. by Gerald Early. LC 92-50353. 1992. 22.00 (0-670-84185-4, Viking) Viking Penguin.

Lure & Loathing: Essays on Race, Identity, & the Ambivalence of Assimilation. Ed. by Gerald Early. 384p. 1994. pap. 14.95 (0-14-015937-1, Penguin Bks) Viking Penguin.

Lure & Lore of Language. Hilda Attride. 302p. (C). 1994. text 69.00 (0-536-58651-9) Pearson Custom.

An Asterisk (*) at the beginning of an entry indicates that the title is appearing for the first time.

Lure & Lore of the Golden Isles. Don Farrant. LC 93-37413. (Illus.). 192p. (Orig.). 1993. pap. 8.95 (*1-55853-262-5*) Rutledge Hill Pr.
Lure & Lore of Trout Fishing. Alvin R. Grove, Jr. (Illus.). 336p. 1971. boxed set 9.95 (*0-88395-010-3*) Freshet Pr.
Lure & Romance of Alchemy: A History of the Secret Link Between Magic & Science. C. J. Thompson. (Illus.). 249p. 1998. reprint ed. text 20.00 (*0-7881-5328-5*) DIANE Pub.
Lure & the Lore of Language. Attride Hilda & Valerie Davis. 198p. (C). 1990. pap. 69.00 (*0-536-57852-4*) Pearson Custom.
Lure & the Truth of Painting: Selected Essays on Art. Yves Bonnefoy. Ed. & Afterword by Richard Stamelman. LC 94-49686. (Illus.). 256p. 1995. 40.00 (*0-226-06444-1*) U Ch Pr.
Lure, Lore & Legends: A History of Northern New Mexico's Moreno Valley. Moreno Valley Writers Guild Staff. Ed. by Jack C. Urban. LC 97-66712. (Illus.). 208p. (Orig.). 1997. pap. 12.95 (*0-9643161-7-X*) Columb Pub.
Lure of Adventure. Robert K. Jones. LC 89-34753. (Starmont Pulp & Dime Novel Studies: No. 4). (Illus.). iv, 80p. 1989. pap. 15.00 (*1-55742-142-0*) Millefleurs.
Lure of Bells. (Illus.). 50p. 1989. 9.95 (*0-9607944-5-X*) World of Bells.
Lure of Dreams: Sigmund Freud & the Construction of Modernity. Harvie Ferguson. LC 95-38490. 264p. (C). 1996. 80.00 (*0-415-04835-4*); pap. 24.99 (*0-415-04836-2*) Routledge.
Lure of Esther Mountain: Matriarch of the Adirondack High Peaks. Sandra Weber. LC 95-4724. (Illus.). 80p. 1995. pap. 12.00 (*0-935796-65-7*) Purple Mnt Pr.
Lure of Fishing. Herb Berry. (Illus.). 154p. (Orig.). 1988. write for info. (*0-9620934-3-2*); pap. 14.95 (*0-9620934-0-8*); lib. bdg. 19.95 (*0-9620934-1-6*) XLN Pubs.
***Lure of Fishing: Mini Edition.** Andrews & McMeel Staff. 272p. 2000. mass mkt. 5.95 (*0-7407-0539-3*) Andrews & McMeel.
Lure of God: A Biblical Background for Process Theism. Lewis S. Ford. 158p. 1985. reprint ed. lib. bdg. 18.50 (*0-8191-4902-0*) U Pr of Amer.
Lure of Knowledge: Lesbian Sexuality & Theory. Judith Roof. Ed. by Lillian Faderman & Larry Gross. (Gay & Lesbian Ser.). 285p. (C). 1991. text 57.50 (*0-231-07486-7*) Col U Pr.
Lure of Knowledge: Lesbian Sexuality & Theory. Judith Roof. Ed. by Lillian Faderman & Larry Gross. (Gay & Lesbian Ser.). 285p. (C). 1993. pap. 19.00 (*0-231-07487-5*) Col U Pr.
Lure of Medford: Railroads, Airplanes, Buildings, Pipe Organs. Bert Webber & Margie Webber. LC F884 W 1996. (Illus.). 1996. pap. 12.95 (*0-936738-47-2*) Webb Research.
Lure of Modern Science: Fractal Thinking. B. J. West & B. Deering. (Studies of Nonlinear Phenomena in Life Sciences: Vol. 3). 432p. 1995. text 74.00 (*981-02-2197-5*) World Scientific Pub.
Lure of Neptune: German-Soviet Naval Collaboration & Ambitions, 1919-1941. Tobias R. Philbin, III. LC 94-3207. (Studies in Maritime History). 214p. 1994. text 34.95 (*0-87249-992-8*) U of SC Pr.
Lure of Paris: Nineteenth-Century American Painters & Their French Teachers. H. Barbara Weinberg. (Illus.). 296p. 1991. 95.00 (*1-55859-018-8*) Abbeville Pr.
Lure of Satyria. Cheryl Mildenhall. (Black Lace Ser.). 1995. mass mkt. 5.95 (*0-352-32994-7*, Pub. by Virgin Bks) London Brdge.
Lure of Tahiti. Ed. by A. Grove Day. LC 86-62756. 324p. 1987. mass mkt. 5.95 (*0-935180-31-1*) Mutual Pub HI.
Lure of the Antique & the Cult of Machine: The Kunstkammer & the Evolution of Nature, Art & Technology. Horst Bredekamp. Tr. by Allison Brown from GER. LC 95-16753. (Cultural & Museum Studies). (Illus.). 168p. (C). 1995. pap. text 18.95 (*1-55876-094-6*) Wiener Pubs Inc.
Lure of the Antique & the Cult of Machine: The Kunstkammer & the Evolution of Nature, Art & Technology. Horst Bredekamp. Tr. by Allison Brown from GER. LC 95-16753. (Cultural & Museum Studies). (Illus.). 168p. (C). 1995. text 42.95 (*1-55876-093-8*) Wiener Pubs Inc.
Lure of the Arctic. Bernice M. Chappel. Tr. by Marjorie N. Klein. LC 86-50153. (Illus.). 267p. (Orig.). 1986. pap. 8.95 (*0-9611596-2-6*) Wilderness Adventure Bks.
Lure of the Bush. Arthur W. Upfield. (Napoleon Bonaparte Mysteries Ser.). 21.95 (*0-89190-569-3*) Amereon Ltd.
Lure of the Decoy: An Exhibition of Selected Decoys from the Collection of the Cleveland Museum of Natural History. Ellen Walters. (Illus.). 32p. (Orig.). 1979. pap. 4.50 (*1-878600-03-6*) Cleve Mus Nat Hist.
Lure of the Falcon. large type ed. Dilys A. Gater. (Linford Romance Library). 256p. 1994. pap. 16.99 (*0-7089-7511-9*, Linford) Ulverscroft.
Lure of the Integers. Joseph Roberts. LC 91-62053. (MAA Spectrum Ser.). 300p. 1992. pap. text 12.00 (*0-88385-502-X*, LURE) Math Assn.
Lure of the Italian Treasure. Franklin W. Dixon. (Hardy Boys Mystery Stories Ser.: No. 157). (J). (gr. 3-6). 1999. pap. 3.99 (*0-671-03445-6*) PB.
Lure of the Land: A Social History of the Public Lands from the Articles of Confederation to the New Deal. Everett N. Dick. LC 66-13015. (Illus.). 460p. 1970. pap. 142.60 (*0-608-05113-6*, 206567200005) Bks Demand.
***Lure of the Lighthouse.** Alan Ross. 1999. pap. 6.95 incl. 5.25 hd (*1-58334-045-9*) Walnut Gr Pr.
Lure of the Links: Great Golf Stories. Ed. by David Owen & Joan Bingham. LC 97-2979. 400p. 1997. 23.00 (*0-87113-685-6*, Atlntc Mnthly) Grove-Atltic.
Lure of the Links: Great Golf Stories. Ed. by David Owen & Joan Bingham. 400p. 1999. reprint ed. pap. 14.00 (*0-87113-749-6*, Atlntc Mnthly) Grove-Atltic.
Lure of the Local: Senses of Place in a Multicentered Society. Lucy R. Lippard. 1998. pap. 19.95 (*1-56584-248-0*, Pub. by New Press NY) Norton.
Lure of the Local: The Sense of Place in a Multicentered Society. Lucy Lippard. LC 96-23879. (Illus.). 150p. 1997. 40.00 (*1-56584-247-2*, Pub. by New Press NY) Norton.
Lure of the Lone Trail: Writings from the North Woods. Glen Sheppard. LC 92-30391. (Illus.). 261p. (Orig.). 1993. pap. 15.95 (*1-879094-20-7*) Momentum Bks.
Lure of the Millennium: The Year 2000 & Beyond. rev. ed. Raymond F. Bulman. LC 99-18537. (Illus.). 250p. 1999. pap. 18.00 (*1-57075-253-2*) Orbis Bks.
Lure of the Occult. Kurt E. Koch. LC 79-160690. 192p. 1972. pap. 8.99 (*0-8254-3003-8*) Kregel.
Lure of the Phoenix: Sculpture by Doris Sams. John L. Cobbs & Lisa T. Barnes. (Illus.). 1992. 10.00 (*0-9624021-4-1*) Ursinus College.
Lure of the Riviera. F. H. Gostling. 1976. lib. bdg. 59.95 (*0-8490-2187-1*) Gordon Pr.
Lure of the Sea. deluxe ed. Ed. by Joseph E. Brown. (Wilderness Experience Ser.). (Illus.). 100p. 1996. 30.00 (*1-887656-28-6*) Tehabi Bks.
Lure of the Sea: The Discovery of the Seaside in the Western World. Alain Corbin. Tr. by Jocelyn Phelps from FRE. (Illus.). 380p. (C). 1994. 45.00 (*0-520-06638-3*, Pub. by U CA Pr) Cal Prin Full Svc.
***Lure of the Sinister: The Unnatural History of Satanism.** Gareth J. Medway. LC 99-49577. 2000. 29.95 (*0-8147-5645-X*) NYU Pr.
***Lure of the Sky.** Fred Donaldson. LC 99-91583. 326p. 2000. 25.00 (*0-7388-0906-3*); pap. 18.00 (*0-7388-0907-1*) Xlibris Corp.
Lure of the Transcendent: Collected Essays by Dwayne E. Huebner. Ed. by William Pinar & Vikki Hillis. LC 98-35222. (Studies in Curriculum Theory Ser.). 496p. 1999. 89.95 (*0-8058-2533-9*); pap. 36.00 (*0-8058-2534-7*) L Erlbaum Assocs.
***Lure of the West.** Amy Pastan. (Treasures from the Smithsonian American Art Museum). (Illus.). 112p. 2000. pap. 19.95 (*0-8230-0191-1*) Watsn-Guptill.
Lure of Wisdom. James D. Collins. LC 62-13514. (Aquinas Lectures). 1962. 15.00 (*0-87462-127-5*) Marquette.
Lure of Zion: The Case of Iraqi Jews. Abbas Shiblak. pap. 9.95 (*0-86356-033-4*, Pub. by Saqi) Intl Spec Bk.
Luremaking: The Art & Science of Spinnerbaits, Buzzbaits, Jigs, & Other Leadheads. A. D. Livingston. 161p. 1993. pap. 16.95 (*0-07-038152-6*) McGraw.
Luremaking: The Art & Science of Spinnerbaits, Buzzbaits, Jigs, & Other Leadheads. A. D. Livingston. (Illus.). 192p. 1993. pap. 16.95 (*0-87742-372-5*, Ragged Mntain) McGraw-Hill Prof.
Lures for Lunker Bass. Bud Andrews & W. Horace Carter. LC 89-84506. (Illus.). 246p. (Orig.). 1989. 12.95 (*0-937866-20-2*) Atlantic Pub Co.
Lurid Dreams. Charles L. Harness. 192p. (Orig.). 1990. pap. 3.50 (*0-380-75761-3*, Avon Bks) Morrow Avon.
Lurid Lady Lockport. Kasey Michaels. 208p. (Orig.). 1984. pap. 2.95 (*0-380-86231-X*, Avon Bks) Morrow Avon.
***Luring Largemouth Bass: Sure-Fire Strategies for Catching More & Bigger Bass.** Creative Publishing International, Inc. Staff. LC 99-59784. (Freshwater Angler Ser.). (Illus.). 192p. 2000. pap. 12.95 (*0-86573-117-9*) Creat Pub Intl.
***Luristan Excavation Documents: Djub-i Gauhar & Gul Khanan Murdah Iron Age III--Graveyards in the Aivan Plain.** B. Overlaet & E. Haerinck. Vol. 3. 1999. 81.50 (*90-429-0718-5*, Pub. by Peeters Pub) Bks Intl VA.
Lurker at the Threshold. H. P. Lovecraft & August Derleth. 192p. 1988. mass mkt. 4.50 (*0-88184-408-X*) Carroll & Graf.
Lurkers in the Water. Evan Skolnick. (Lion King Ser.). (J). 1997. pap. text 4.50 (*1-57840-162-3*, Pub. by Acclaim Bks) Penguin Putnam.
Lurking Fear & Other Stories. H. P. Lovecraft. 192p. 1985. mass mkt. 5.99 (*0-345-32604-0*) Ballantine Pub Grp.
Lurking Feminism: The Ghost Stories of Edith Wharton. Jenni Dyman. LC 94-36238. (American University Studies Series XXIV: American Literature: Vol. 62). XX, 199p. (C). 1996. text 44.95 (*0-8204-2697-0*) P Lang Pubng.
***Lurking Gun.** D. B. Newton. LC 98-47715. 191 p. 1999. write for info. (*0-7540-3647-2*) Chivers N Amer.
Lurking Gun. large type ed. D. B. Newton. LC 98-47715. Date not set. 30.00 (*0-7838-0447-4*, G K Hall Lrg Type) Mac Lib Ref.
Lurking on the Railroad. Dutton Foster et al. 1987. pap. 5.95 (*1-58342-001-0*, L03) Dramatic Pub.
Lurleen B. Wallace Foundation: A Legacy of Love. Bruce L. Patterson. (Illus.). 128p. (Orig.). 1996. pap. 9.95 (*0-9652910-0-6*) Comprehen Cancer.
Lurning: 147 Inspiring Thoughts for Learning on the Job. Sharon G. O'Neill. LC 93-1277. 93p. 1993. pap. 7.95 (*0-89815-536-3*) Ten Speed Pr.
Lus - The Light: Ermanna Montanari Performs Nevio Spadoni. Nevio Spadoni. Ed. & Tr. by Teresa Picarazzi from ITA. LC 99-24519. (Crossings Ser.: Vol. 3). 70p. 1999. pap. 7.00 (*1-884419-22-4*) Bordighera.
Lus de la Casa (The Light of the Home) A. H. Mottesi. (SPA.). 1.79 (*0-685-74950-9*, 498501) Editorial Unilit.
Luscher Color Test. Max Luscher. 224p. 1990. per. 6.99 (*0-671-73145-9*, PB Trade Paper) PB.
Luscious & Creamy Dessert Classics. (Recipes of the World Ser.). (Illus.). 1998. write for info. (*1-886614-83-0*) Intl Masters Pub.
Luscious Low Calorie Recipes by Maxine. Maxine T. Vaneven. LC 75-34770. (Illus.). 1975. pap. 4.95 (*0-916774-01-5*) Tolvan Co.
Lush Life. Bill Berkson. Ed. by Kenward Elmslie. LC 84-51752. 52p. (Orig.). 1985. pap. 6.00 (*0-915990-26-1*) Z Pr.
Lush Life. Dallas Murphy. 288p. (Orig.). 1993. mass mkt. 4.99 (*0-671-68556-2*) PB.
Lush Life: A Biography of Billy Strayhorn. David Hajdu. (Illus.). 306p. 1996. 27.50 (*0-374-19438-6*) FS&G.
Lush Life: A Biography of Billy Strayhorn. David Hajdu. 1997. pap. 15.00 (*0-86547-512-1*) N Point Pr.
Lush Life: The Billy Strayhorn Songbook. 56p. Date not set. 15.95 (*0-8256-1600-X*) Music Sales.
Lush on the Law of Husband & Wife. 4th ed. S. N. Grant-Bailey. clxvii, 753p. 1999. reprint ed. 230.00 (*1-56169-514-9*) Gaunt.
Lushai Girl. large type ed. Roberta Forrest. 592p. 1988. 27.99 (*0-7089-8452-5*, Charnwood) Ulverscroft.
Lushai Grammar & Dictionary. Lorrain. (ENG.). 346p. 1984. 24.95 (*0-7859-7514-4*) Fr & Eur.
Lushan Memories. Ed. by Paul Sherertz. (Illus.). 236p. 1989. pap. 18.00 (*0-9622179-0-5*) P C Sherertz.
Lushei Kuki Clans. John Shakespear. LC 77-87057. reprint ed. 41.50 (*0-404-16866-3*) AMS Pr.
Lushootseed Culture & the Shamanic Odyssey: An Anchored Radiance. Jay Miller. LC 98-38249. (Illus.). 334p. 1999. text 45.00 (*0-8032-3200-4*) U of Nebr Pr.
Lushootseed Dictionary. rev. ed. Bates et al. LC 94-5716. Orig. Title: Dictionary of Puget Salish. 381p. 1994. reprint ed. pap. 35.00 (*0-295-97323-4*) U of Wash Pr.
Lushootseed Reader with Intermediate Grammar Vol. II: Four Stories from Martha Lamont. Thom Hess. ix, 174p. (Orig.). 1998. pap. 20.00 (*1-879763-14-1*) U MT UMOPL.
Lushootseed Reader with Introductory Grammar Vol. 1: Four Stories from Edward Sam. Thom Hess. LC 95-60060. (University of Montana Occasional Papers in Linguistics: No. 11, 1995). ix, 202p. 1995. pap. 20.00 (*1-879763-11-7*) U MT UMOPL.
Lushootseed Texts: An Introduction to Puget Salish Narrative Aesthetics. Ed. & Tr. by Crisca Bierwert. Tr. by Vi Hilbert & Thomas M. Hess. LC 95-37060. (Studies in the Anthropology of North American Indians). (Illus.). xii, 325p. 1996. text 55.00 (*0-8032-1262-3*) U of Nebr Pr.
Lusiads. Tommaso Campanella. Tr. by Landeg White. LC 97-19376. (The World's Classics Ser.). (Illus.). 286p. 1998. pap. 7.95 (*0-19-283191-7*) OUP.
Lusiads. Luis V. De Camoens. 1975. 300.00 (*0-87968-318-X*) Gordon Pr.
Lusiads of Luis de Camoes. Tr. by Leonard Bacon from POR. (Illus.). 435p. 1980. reprint ed. pap. text 10.00 (*0-87535-128-X*) Hispanic Soc.
Lusions. James Ragan. LC 96-35090. 96p. 1997. 20.00 (*0-8021-1603-5*, Grove) Grove-Atltic.
Lusitania: Kultura Control. Ed. by Martin Avillez. (Illus.). 128p. (Orig.). (C). 1990. pap. text 8.00 (*0-936756-65-9*) Autonomedia.
Lusitania: Sites & Stations: Provisional Utopias. David Hickey et al. (Illus.). 256p. 1995. pap. text 15.00 (*1-882791-03-7*) Lusitania Pr.
***Lusitania: The Life & Legacy of an Ocean Legend.** Daniel Allen Butler. 2000. 29.95 (*0-8117-0989-2*) Stackpole.
Lusitania: Unraveling the Mysteries. Paddy O'Sullivan. LC 98-235776. (Illus.). 144p. 1998. 49.95 (*1-898256-51-9*, Pub. by Collins Press) Dufour.
***Lusitania: Unraveling the Mysteries.** Patrick O'Sullivan. (Illus.). 144p. 2000. 34.95 (*1-86227-086-4*, Pub. by Spellmnt Pubs) St Mut.
***Lusitania: Unravelling the Mysteries.** Patrick O'Sullivan. LC 99-48198. 240p. 2000. pap. 16.50 (*1-57409-094-1*) Sheridan.
Lusitania Controversies: Book One: Atrocity of War & a Wreck-Diving History. Gary Gentile. LC 99-193060. (Illus.). 312p. 1998. 25.00 (*1-883056-06-3*) GGP.
Lusitania Controversies Bk. 2: Dangerous Descents into Shipwrecks & Law. Gary Gentile. LC 99-193060. (Illus.). 392p. 1999. 25.00 (*1-883056-07-1*) GGP.
Luso-Brazilian Catalogues see Catalogues of the Canning House Library: Author & Subject Catalogues
Lusophone Africa, Portugal, & the United States: Possibilities for More Effective Cooperation. Kimberley A. Hamilton. LC 92-33552. (Significant Issues Ser.: Vol. 14, No. 11). 64p. 1993. pap. text 8.00 (*0-89206-205-3*) CSIS.
Lusophone African Liberators: The University Years. David Amaral. (Graduate Student Papers Competition). 20p. (Orig.). 1979. pap. text 2.00 (*0-941934-27-6*) Indiana Africa.
Lust. Elfriede Jelinek. (Masks Ser.). 256p. 1993. pap. 14.99 (*1-85242-183-5*) Serpents Tail.
Lust. Richard A. Melheim. 336p. 1994. 19.95 (*0-9635106-3-0*) Creat Outlet.
Lust: Lascivious Love Stories & Passionate Poems. Ed. by John Miller & Kirsten Miller. LC 93-28053. (Illus.). 144p. 1994. 14.95 (*0-8118-0691-X*) Chronicle Bks.
Lust: Licentious Underground Sexy True Gay Encounters, Vol. 1. Winston Leyland. (Illus.). 176p. (Orig.). 1994. reprint ed. pap. 14.95 (*0-943595-48-7*) Leyland Pubns.
Lust: Love & Longing. Eileen Morgan. (Sin Series). (Illus.). 128p. 1999. 24.95 (*0-9669573-1-8*) Red Rock.
Lust: Stories from Australian & New Zealand Writers Michael Gifkins. LC 95-176755. 182 p. 1995. write for info. (*1-86941-243-5*) Random.
***Lust: What We Know about Human Sexual Desire.** Pamela C. Regan & Ellen Berscheid. LC 99-6175. 173p. 1999. 49.95 (*0-7619-1792-6*) Sage.
Lust: What We Know about Human Sexual Desire. Pamela C. Regan & Ellen Berscheid. LC 99-6175. (Series on Close Relationships). 1999. write for info. (*0-7619-1793-4*) Sage.
Lust & Liberty. Joseph Tusiani. 1963. 12.95 (*0-8392-1063-9*) Astor-Honor.
Lust & Other Stories. Susan Minot. 160p. 1990. per. 10.00 (*0-671-70455-9*, WSP) PB.
***Lust & Other Stories.** Susan Minot. (Contemporaries Ser.). 160p. 2000. pap. text 11.00 (*0-375-70925-8*) Vin Bks.
Lust & Romance: Rated X Fine Art Photographs Michael A. Rosen. LC 98-91662. 63 p. 1998. write for info. (*0-86719-460-X*) Last Gasp.
***Lust & Spirituality: Episobic Ruminations Concerning Ontotheology & the Esoteric in Plato.** unabridged ed. John W. McGinley. 46p. 2000. pap. 5.00 (*0-9679316-1-4*) Golem Enter.
Lust at Large. N. Amos. mass mkt. 6.95 (*0-7472-4329-8*, Pub. by Headline Bk Pub) Trafalgar.
Lust for Blood. Olga Hoyt. 1990. pap. 10.95 (*0-8128-8511-2*, Scrbrough Hse) Madison Bks UPA.
***Lust for Blueprints.** Jody Azzouni. (Illus.). 88p. 1999. pap. 14.95 (*0-922558-07-8*) Poets Pr.
Lust for Fame: The Stage Career of John Wilkes Booth. Gordon Samples. LC 81-20882. (Illus.). 256p. 1998. pap. 25.00 (*0-7864-0586-4*) McFarland & Co.
Lust for Innocence Vol. 1: A Guide to Recognizing Pedophilia. unabridged ed. Thomas K. Meredith. (Illus.). xi, 91p. 1997. pap. 19.95 (*0-9661056-0-5*) World Patriot.
Lust for Life. Irving Stone. 29.95 (*0-89190-127-2*) Amereon Ltd.
Lust for Life. Irving Stone. 1994. lib. bdg. 29.95 (*1-56849-480-7*) Buccaneer Bks.
Lust for Life. Irving Stone. LC 83-24666. 1984. pap. 15.95 (*0-452-26249-6*, Plume) Dutton Plume.
Lust for Living. John B. Lust. 1982. 12.95 (*0-87904-036-X*) Lust.
Lust for Power: Nationalism, Slovakia & the Communists, 1918-1948. Yeshayahu Jelinek. (East European Monographs: No. 130). 105p. 1983. text 60.00 (*0-88033-019-8*, Pub. by East Eur Monographs) Col U Pr.
Lust in America: And Other Odd Views of Reality. Randall Garrison. Ed. by Daniel Waldron. LC 97-16023. 152p. (Orig.). 1997. pap. 12.95 (*0-941543-15-3*) Sun Dog Pr.
Lust in America: And Other Odd Views of Reality. limited ed. Randall Garrison. Ed. by Daniel Waldron. LC 97-16023. 152p. (Orig.). 1997. pap. 19.95 (*0-941543-16-1*) Sun Dog Pr.
Lust, Inc. Erica Bronte. (Orig.). 1996. mass mkt. 6.50 (*1-56333-467-4*) Masquerade.
Lust Killer. Andy Stack, pseud. (True Crime Annals Ser.: No. 1). 176p. 1983. mass mkt. 6.99 (*0-451-16687-6*, Sig) NAL.
Lust Lizard of Melancholy Cove. Christopher Moore. LC 98-46850. 320p. 1999. 23.00 (*0-380-97506-8*, Avon Bks) Morrow Avon.
***Lust Lizard of Melancholy Cove.** Christopher Moore. 320p. 2000. pap. 13.00 (*0-380-79274-5*, Avon Bks) Morrow Avon.
Lust Never Sleeps. Randy Turoff. (Orig.). 1997. mass mkt. 6.50 (*1-56333-475-5*, Rosebud) Masquerade.
Lust of Seeing: Themes of the Gaze & Sexual Rituals in the Fiction of Felisberto Hernandez. Frank Graziano. LC 96-12340. 280p. 1997. 42.50 (*0-8387-5338-8*) Bucknell U Pr.
Lust of the Cossacks. 2nd ed. Paul Little. 1998. reprint ed. mass mkt. 6.95 (*1-56333-664-2*) Masquerade.
Lust to Annihilate: A Psychoanalytic Study of Violence in Ancient Greek Culture. Eli Sagan. 231p. 1993. pap. text 10.00 (*1-882231-01-5*) FishDrum Pr.
Lust, Violence, Sin, Magic: Sixty Years of Esquire Fiction. Ed. by Rust Hills et al. 608p. 1994. pap. 15.00 (*0-87113-581-7*, Atlntc Mnthly) Grove-Atltic.
Lustathon. T. Andrews. 1996. mass mkt. 11.95 (*0-340-65811-8*, Pub. by Hodder & Stought Ltd) Trafalgar.
Luster of Jade: Poetry, Painting, & Music. Catherine Yi-yu Chu Woo. (University Research Lectures: No. 7). (Illus.). 86p. 1992. 30.00 (*1-879691-10-8*) SDSU Press.
Lustful Desires. Jodie Raye. 112p. (Orig.). 1997. pap. 10.95 (*0-9659250-2-1*) Whte Wlf Pr.
Lustful Maidens & Ascetic Kings: Buddhist & Hindu Stories of Life. Roy C. Amore & Larry D. Shinn. (Illus.). 210p. 1981. pap. text 10.95 (*0-19-502839-2*) OUP.
***Lustful Memoirs.** Ed. by Blue Moon Book Staffs. 2000. mass mkt. 7.95 (*1-56201-199-5*) Blue Moon Bks.
Lustgarten: Eine Sammlung Deutsche Lieder Zu Vierefuenf, Sechs, und Acht Stimmen, 1601. Hans L. Hassler. Ed. by Robert Eitner & Friedrich Zelle. (Publikation alterer praktischer und theoretischer Musikwerke Ser.: Vol. 15). (GER., Illus.). 1966. reprint ed. lib. bdg. 75.00 (*0-8450-1715-2*) Broude.
Lustgarten Um Bayreuth Vol. V: Eremitage, Sanspareil und Fantaisie in Beschreibungen Aus Dem 18. und 19. Jahrhundert. Ed. by Ingo Toussaint & Gerhard Hojer. (GER.). 332p. 1998. write for info. (*3-487-08401-5*) G Olms Pubs.
Lustige Dialogue. Harry A. Walbruck. (Graded Reader Ser.). (Illus.). 1990. pap., teacher ed. 6.99 (*0-8442-2138-4*, X2138-4) NTC Contemp Pub Co.
Lustige Dialogue. Harry A. Walbruck. (Graded Reader Ser.). (GER., Illus.). 176p. (C). 1990. pap. 12.65 (*0-8442-2136-8*, X2136-8) NTC Contemp Pub Co.
Lustige Geschichten. Harry A. Walbruck & Henschel. (Graded Reader Ser.). (GER.). 1988. pap., teacher ed. 6.99 (*0-8442-2145-7*, X2145-7) NTC Contemp Pub Co.
Lustige Geschichten. Harry A. Walbruck & Henschel. (Graded Reader Ser.). (GER.). 192p. (C). 1988. pap. 12.65 (*0-8442-2139-2*, X2139-2) NTC Contemp Pub Co.
Lustmord: Sexual Murder in Weimar Germany. Maria M. Tatar. LC 94-48601. 232p. 1995. text 35.00 (*0-691-04338-8*, Pub. by Princeton U Pr) Cal Prin Full Svc.
Lustmord: The Writings & Artifacts of Murderers. Ed. by Brian King. (Illus.). 328p. (Orig.). 1996. pap. 14.95 (*0-9650324-0-X*) Bloat.

L

Lustra. Ezra Pound. LC 72-11762. (Studies in Poetry: No. 38). 1973. reprint ed. lib. bdg. 75.00 (*0-8383-1688-3*) M S G Haskell Hse.

Lustre of Gold. (Freeman Classics Ser.). 157p. (Orig.). 1995. pap. 9.95 (*1-57246-005-9*) Foun Econ Ed.

Lustre of Our Country: The American Experience of Religious Freedom. John T. Noonan, Jr. LC 97-49327. 430p. 1998. 35.00 (*0-520-20997-4*, Pub. by U CA Pr) Cal Prin Full Svc.

***Lustre of Our Country: The American Experience of Religious Freedom.** John T. Noonan. LC 97-49327. 436p. 2000. pap. text 17.95 (*0-520-22491-4*) U CA Pr.

Lustre Pottery. Alan Caiger-Smith. (Illus.). 246p. (Orig.). 1985. pap. 38.00 (*0-9650786-5-5*) Gentle Br.

***Lustreware.** Michael Gibson. (Illus.). 40p. 1999. pap. 30.00 (*0-7478-0397-8*, Pub. by Shire Pubns) Parkwest Pubns.

Lustro Crucial, 1893-1898: El Concierto Conduce al Pacto, 1891-1896. Pilar Darbosa e Rosario. LC 83-10612. 182p. 1986. 12.00 (*0-8477-0879-9*); pap. 8.00 (*0-8477-0880-2*) U of PR Pr.

***Lustrous Tradeq: Material Culture & the History of Sculpture in England & Italy, C.1700-C.1860.** Cinzia Maria Sicca & Alison Yarrington. LC 00-22171. (Illus.). 2000. write for info. (*0-7185-0209-4*, Pub. by Leicester U Pr) Cassell & Continuum.

***Lust's Labour Won.** Patrick Henden. 224p. 1999. pap. 7.95 (*1-56201-140-5*, Pub. by Blue Moon Bks) Publishers Group.

Lust's Last. Richard A. Spiegel. (Illus.). 21p. (Orig.). 1976. pap. 1.00 (*0-934776-00-8*) Bard Pr.

Lusts of the Libertines. Marquis De Sade, pseud. Tr. by Julian Jones from FRE. 96p. 1998. reprint ed. pap. 12.95 (*1-871592-59-3*, Velvet Pub) Creation Books.

Lusts of the Prairie Preachers. Jerry Klein & Jack L. Bradley. (Illus.). 103p. (Orig.). 1996. pap. 14.95 (*1-889849-01-4*) Riverbeach Pub.

Lusty Juventus. Richard Wever. LC 76-133761. (Tudor Facsimile Texts. Old English Plays Ser.: No. 35). reprint ed. 59.50 (*0-404-53335-3*) AMS Pr.

Lusty Lady. Erika Langley. (Illus.). 208p. 1997. pap. 34.95 (*3-931141-59-4*) Dist Art Pubs.

***Lusty Life of Loon Lake Lloyd: True Life Western Tales.** Lloyd Keeland & Ellen Keeland. (Illus.). 2000. pap. 14.95 (*0-8323-0535-9*) Binford Mort.

Lusty Man. Terry Griggs. 192p. 1996. pap. text. write for info. (*0-88984-159-4*) Porcup Quill.

Lusty Wind for Carolina. Inglis Fletcher. 1976. reprint ed. lib. bdg. 33.95 (*0-89244-003-1*, Queens House) Amereon Ltd.

Lusty Wind for Carolina. Inglis Fletcher. 1990. reprint ed. lib. bdg. 39.95 (*0-89968-504-8*) Buccaneer Bks.

Lusty Wind for Carolina. Inglis Fletcher. LC 90-28349. 512p. 1995. reprint ed. 34.95 (*0-87797-225-7*) Cherokee.

***Lute in Britain: A History of the Instrument & Its Music.** Matthew Spring. (Early Music Ser.). (Illus.). 512p. 2001. text 99.00 (*0-19-816620-6*) OUP.

Lute Music of Francesco Canova da Milano. Ed. by Arthur J. Ness. LC 79-103671. (Harvard Publications in Music: Vols. 3 & 4). 507p. 1970. reprint ed. pap. 157.20 (*0-608-02224-1*, 205794600011) Bks Demand.

Lute of Jade: Selections from the Classical Poets of China. Launcelot A. Cranmer-Byng. LC 77-26072. 112p. 1978. reprint ed. lib. bdg. 45.00 (*0-313-20080-7*, CBLJ, Greenwood Pr) Greenwood.

Lute Songs of John Dowland. John Dowland. 1997. 10.95 (*0-486-29935-X*) Dover.

Lute Works of John Johnson, 3 Vols. John Johnson. Ed. by John M. Ward & Matanya Ophee. (Monuments of the Lutenist Art Ser.: Vol. III). 456p. (C). 1994. pap. 140.00 (*0-936186-72-0*, LUTE 3) Edit Orphee.

Lute Works of John Johnson: Guitar. John Johnson. Ed. by John M. Ward & Matanya Ophee. (Monuments of the Lutenist Art Ser.: Vol. III). 144p. (C). 1994. pap. 40.00 (*0-936186-95-X*, LUTE 3C) Edit Orphee.

Lute Works of John Johnson: Keyboard. John Johnson. Ed. & Intro. by John M. Ward. (Monuments of the Lutenist Art Ser.: Vol. III). 168p. (C). 1994. pap. 50.00 (*0-936186-93-3*, LUTE 3A) Edit Orphee.

Lute Works of John Johnson: Tablature. John Johnson. Ed. & Intro. by John M. Ward. (Monuments of the Lutenist Art Ser.: Vol. III). 144p. (C). 1994. pap. 60.00 (*0-936186-94-1*, LUTE 3B) Edit Orphee.

Luteal Phase. Ed. by S. L. Jeffcoate. LC 84-17424. (Current Topics in Reproductive Endocrinology Ser.: No. 4). (Illus.). 136p. reprint ed. pap. 42.20 (*0-8357-8638-2*, 203506200092) Bks Demand.

Lutece Cookbook. Andre Soltner. LC 94-45978. (Illus.). 512p. 1995. 37.50 (*0-679-42273-0*) Knopf.

Lutefisk Ghetto. Ed. by Art Lee. 224p. 1978. pap. 7.95 (*0-934860-02-5*) Adventure Pubns.

Lutefisk on the Lens. Anne Loesch. 19.95 (*0-9642763-0-5*) Pilot Pubng.

Luteinizing Hormone Receptors & Actions. Ed. by Mario Ascoli. 248p. 1985. 142.00 (*0-8493-5674-1*, QP572, CRC Reprint) Franklin.

Luteoviridae. Ed. by H. G. Smith & H. Barker. LC 99-489887. (CABI Publishing Ser.). 320p. 1999. 110.00 (*0-85199-324-9*) OUP.

Luther. Heiko A. Oberman. 400p. 1992. pap. 16.95 (*0-385-42278-4*) Doubleday.

Luther. John Osborne. 1961. pap. 5.95 (*0-87129-208-4*, L37) Dramatic Pub.

Luther: Fount Christian Thinker. Hans P. Grosshans. 1997. pap. 8.95 (*0-00-628027-7*, Pub. by HarpC) Trafalgar.

Luther: Letters of Spiritual Counsel. Martin Luther. Ed. & Tr. by T. G. Tappert. 465p. (C). 1997. pap. 26.95 (*1-57383-092-5*) Regent College.

Luther: Theologian for the Catholics & Protestants. Ed. by George Yule. 208p. 1985. pap. 27.95 (*0-567-29119-7*, Pub. by T & T Clark) Bks Intl VA.

Luther: To Justify Is to Heal. Loren W. Hellwig. 96p. (Orig.). 1994. pap. 7.99 (*0-88019-317-4*) Schmul Pub Co.

Luther & Calvin on Secular Authority. Ed. by Harro Hopfl. (Cambridge Texts in the History of Political Thought Ser.). 142p. (C). 1991. text 44.95 (*0-521-34208-2*); pap. text 12.95 (*0-521-34986-9*) Cambridge U Pr.

Luther & Erasmus: Free Will & Salvation. Desiderius Erasmus. Ed. by E. Gordon Rupp & Philip S. Watson. LC 76-79870. (Library of Christian Classics). 356p. 1978. pap. 28.95 (*0-664-24158-1*) Westminster John Knox.

Luther & German Humanism. Lewis W. Spitz. LC 95-23340. (Collected Studies: CS507). 350p. 1996. 101.95 (*0-86078-499-1*, Pub. by Variorum) Ashgate Pub Co.

Luther & His Katie. D. MacCuish. Date not set. pap. 4.99 (*0-906731-34-8*, Pub. by Christian Focus) Spring Arbor Dist.

Luther & His Mother. Ian D. Siggins. LC 80-2386. 96p. (Orig.). reprint ed. pap. 30.00 (*0-608-15326-5*, 202961300061) Bks Demand.

Luther & His Times: The Reformation from a New Perspective. Ernest G. Schwiebert. (Illus.). 892p. (J). 1950. 32.00 (*0-570-03246-6*, 15-1164) Concordia.

Luther & Learning: The Wittenberg University Luther Symposium. Marilyn J. Harran. LC 84-40810. (Illus.). 144p. 1985. 27.50 (*0-941664-13-9*) Susquehanna U Pr.

***Luther & Melanchthon in the Educational Thought in Middle & Eastern Europe.** Ed. by Reinhard Golz & Wolfgang Mayrhofer. (Textson Theory & History of Education Ser.: Vol. 10). 232p. 1999. pap. 32.95 (*3-8258-3490-5*, Pub. by CE24) Transaction Pubs.

Luther & the English Bible. Albert H. Gerberich. LC 83-45643. reprint ed. 29.50 (*0-404-19852-X*) AMS Pr.

Luther & the False Brethren. Mark U. Edwards, Jr. LC 75-181. xii, 242p. 1975. 37.50 (*0-8047-0883-5*) Stanford U Pr.

Luther & the Germany Reformation. Thomas M. Lindsay. LC 71-133524. (Select Bibliographies Reprint Ser.). 1977. reprint ed. 20.95 (*0-8369-5556-0*) Ayer.

Luther & the Modern State in Germany. Ed. by James D. Tracy. (Sixteenth Century Essays & Studies: Vol. VII). 110p. 1986. 40.00 (*0-940474-07-7*, SCJP) Truman St Univ.

Luther & the Old Testament. Heinrich Bornkamm. Ed. by Victor I. Gruhn. Tr. by Eric W. Gritsch & Ruth C. Gritsch from GEH. 320p. 1997. reprint ed. pap. 22.00 (*0-9623642-8-2*) Sigler Pr.

Luther & the Papacy: Stages in a Reformation Conflict. Scott H. Hendrix. LC 80-2393. 225p. reprint ed. pap. 69.80 (*0-608-17176-X*, 202787400056) Bks Demand.

Luther & the Peasants' War. Hubert Kirchner. LC 73-171507. (Facet Books-Historical Ser.: No. 22). 48p. (Orig.). reprint ed. pap. 30.00 (*0-608-16316-3*, 202718100054) Bks Demand.

Luther & the Reformation, 4 vols., Set. James Mackinnon. LC 83-45648. reprint ed. 157.50 (*0-404-19857-0*) AMS Pr.

Luther & the Reformation in the Light of Modern Research. Heinrich Boehmer. LC 83-45639. reprint ed. 67.50 (*0-404-19823-6*) AMS Pr.

Luther As an Educator. Gustav M. Bruce. LC 77-114482. (Illus.). 318p. 1979. reprint ed. lib. bdg. 65.00 (*0-8371-4771-9*, BRLD, Greenwood Pr) Greenwood.

Luther Bible Research in the Context of Volkish Nationalism in the Twentieth Century. Julie M. Winter. LC 97-26601. (Literature & the Sciences of Man Ser.: Vol. 19). 144p. (C). 1998. 38.95 (*0-8204-3879-0*) P Lang Pubng.

Luther Burbank: Mini-Play. (California History Ser.). (J). (gr. 5 up). 1978. 6.50 (*0-89550-330-1*) Stevens & Shea.

Luther Burbank, Our Beloved Infidel, His Religion of Humanity. Frederick W. Clampett. LC 73-109720. (Illus.). 144p. 1970. reprint ed. lib. bdg. 35.00 (*0-8371-4210-5*, CLLB, Greenwood Pr) Greenwood.

***Luther Corherns' Salmon Camp Chronicles.** Herb Curtis. 196p. 2000. pap. text 14.95 (*0-86492-268-X*) Goose Ln Eds.

Luther, Erasmus & the Reformation: A Catholic-Protestant Reappraisal. Ed. by John C. Olin et al. LC 68-8749. 160p. reprint ed. pap. 45.60 (*0-7837-0460-7*, 2040783) Bks Demand.

Luther, Erasmus & the Reformation: A Catholic-Protestant Reappraisal. Ed. by John C. Olin et al. LC 82-15500. 150p. 1982. reprint ed. lib. bdg. 55.00 (*0-313-23652-6*, OLLE, Greenwood Pr) Greenwood.

Luther Halsey Gulick. Ethel J. Dorgan. LC 78-143055. 1982. 20.95 (*0-8434-0450-7*, Pub. by McGrath NH) Ayer.

Luther in Context. David C. Steinmetz. LC 95-40111. 146p. 1996. pap. 15.99 (*0-8010-2082-4*, Labyrinth) Baker Bks.

Luther Lives. Edward C. Fredrich. LC 85-62568. 168p. 1983. 19.99 (*0-8100-0177-2*, 15N0408) Northwest Pub.

Luther Martin of Maryland. Paul S. Clarkson & R. Samuel Jett. LC 76-94392. 348p. reprint ed. pap. 107.90 (*0-608-15144-0*, 202580900046) Bks Demand.

***Luther, Ministry & the Ordination Rites in the Early Reformation Church.** Ralph F. Smith. (Renaissance & Baroque: Vol. 15). 304p. 1999. reprint ed. pap. text 35.95 (*0-8204-4945-8*) P Lang Pubng.

Luther North, Frontier Scout. Jeff O'Donnell. 1995. pap. 13.95 (*0-934904-10-3*) J & L Lee.

Luther on Conversion: The Early Years. Marilyn J. Harran. LC 83-7194. 219p. reprint ed. pap. 67.90 (*0-608-08095-0*, 206905400002) Bks Demand.

Luther Rector Hare. Ray Meketa. 1976. 25.95 (*0-8488-1097-X*) Amereon Ltd.

Luther Rice - Pioneer in Missions & Education. Edward B. Pollard & Daniel G. Stevens. (Ministry Helps Ser.). 125p. 1995. pap. 5.00 (*1-883265-07-X*) Richbarry Pr.

Luther, Servant of God. large type ed. write for info. (*0-318-68654-6*, 7005) LBW.

Luther the Expositor. Ed. by Jaroslav J. Pelikan. 286p. 1959. 29.00 (*0-570-06431-7*, 15-1741) Concordia.

Luther the Leader. 96p. 1997. pap. 5.95 (*1-881545-78-4*) Angelas Bkshelf.

Luther the Reformer: The Story of the Man & His Career. James M. Kittelson. LC 86-17266. (Illus.). 336p. (C). 1986. pap. 17.99 (*0-8066-2315-2*, 10-4151, Augsburg) Augsburg Fortress.

Luther und die Kirchengeschichte. Walther Kohler. (GER.). 371p. 1984. reprint ed. write for info. (*3-487-07401-X*) G Olms Pubs.

Luther Vandross Songs. 80p. 1995. per. 14.95 (*0-7935-3921-8*, 00306005) H Leonard.

Luther Whiting Mason, International Music Educator. Sondra W. Howe. LC 97-45591. (Detroit Monographs in Musicology/Studies in Music: Vol. 21). 1997. 37.50 (*0-89990-080-1*) Harmonie Park Pr.

Lutheran Basics for Teachers. 2.29 (*0-8066-3718-8*) Augsburg Fortress.

Lutheran Book of Prayer. rev. ed. Ed. by J. W. Acker. LC 76-119916. 203p. 1970. 6.99 (*0-570-03005-6*, 06-1141) Concordia.

Lutheran Book of Worship. large type ed. Contrib. by InterLutheran Worship Commission. LC 77-92160. (Lutheran Book of Worship Ser.). 1978. 80.00 (*0-8006-3395-4*, 3-395, Fortress Pr) Augsburg Fortress.

Lutheran Book of Worship: Braille Edition, 3 vols. Contrib. by InterLutheran Worship Commission. LC 77-92160. (Lutheran Book of Worship Ser.). 1978. 110.00 (*0-8006-3370-9*, 3-370, Fortress Pr) Augsburg Fortress.

Lutheran Book of Worship: Holy Communion. large type ed. Contrib. by InterLutheran Worship Commission. LC 77-92160. (Lutheran Book of Worship Ser.). 1978. 7.00 (*0-8006-3385-7*, 3-385, Fortress Pr) Augsburg Fortress.

Lutheran Book of Worship: Hymnal Companion. Ed. by Marilyn K. Stulken. LC 81-707. 670p. 1981. 55.00 (*0-8006-0300-1*, 1-300, Fortress Pr) Augsburg Fortress.

Lutheran Book of Worship: Hymns Large. Contrib. by InterLutheran Worship Commission. LC 77-92160. (Lutheran Book of Worship Ser.). 1978. 15.00 (*0-8006-3380-6*, 3-380, Fortress Pr) Augsburg Fortress.

Lutheran Book of Worship: Minister's Desk Edition. Contrib. by InterLutheran Worship Commission. LC 77-92169. (Lutheran Book of Worship Ser.). 1978. 30.00 (*0-8006-3341-5*, 3-341, Fortress Pr) Augsburg Fortress.

Lutheran Book of Worship: Minister's Edition. Contrib. by InterLutheran Worship Commission. LC 77-92169. (Lutheran Book of Worship Ser.). 1978. 110.00 (*0-8006-3334-2*, 3-340, Fortress Pr) Augsburg Fortress.

Lutheran Book of Worship: Occasional Service. Contrib. by InterLutheran Worship Commission. LC 77-92160. (Lutheran Book of Worship Ser.). 1978. 35.00 (*0-8006-3390-3*, 3-390, Fortress Pr) Augsburg Fortress.

Lutheran Christians & Their Beliefs. Jerry L. Schmalenberger. 1984. 3.95 (*0-89536-979-6*) CSS OH.

Lutheran Church & the East German State: Political Conflict & Change under Ulbricht & Honecker. Robert F. Goeckel. LC 90-31313. 344p. reprint ed. pap. 106.70 (*0-608-20894-9*, 207199300003) Bks Demand.

Lutheran Church Basement Women. Janet L. Marten & Allen Todman. LC 91-67641. 1992. 10.95 (*0-9613437-6-1*) Redbird Prods.

Lutheran Churches in the World: A Handbook. E. Theodore Bachmann & Mercia B. Bachmann. LC 89-31064. 640p. 1989. text 54.99 (*0-8066-2371-3*, 10-4157, Augsburg) Augsburg Fortress.

Lutheran Cyclopedia: A Concise In-Home Reference for the Christian Family. Ed. by Erwin L. Lueker. 845p. 1975. 29.99 (*0-570-03255-5*, 15-2163) Concordia.

Lutheran Ethic: The Impact of Religion on Laymen & Clergy. Lawrence K. Kersten. LC 71-102200. 310p. reprint ed. pap. 96.10 (*0-608-10585-6*, 207120600009) Bks Demand.

Lutheran Higher Education: An Introduction for Faculty. Ernest L. Simmons. LC 98-8147. 1998. 9.99 (*0-8066-3849-4*) Augsburg Fortress.

Lutheran Martyr. Neelak S. Tjernagel. 1982. 9.99 (*0-8100-0147-0*, 15N0375) Northwest Pub.

Lutheran Milieu of the Films of Ingmar Bergman. R. A. Blake. LC 77-22905. (Dissertation on Film Ser.). 1978. lib. bdg. 29.95 (*0-405-10751-X*) Ayer.

Lutheran People. Martin E. Marty. 32p. 1989. pap. write for info. (*1-889711-03-9*) Cathedral Direct.

Lutheran Worship. 1986. 14.50 (*0-570-01019-5*) Concordia.

Lutheran Worship: History & Practice. Ed. by Fred L. Precht. LC 93-23460. 608p. 1994. 26.00 (*0-570-04255-0*, 53-1015) Concordia.

Lutheran Worship Concordance. Prod. by Commission on Worship of the Lutheran Church, Miss. LC 94-41445. 1994. 19.95 (*0-570-01348-8*, 99-1527) Concordia.

Lutheran Worship-Little Agenda. 224p. 1987. pap. 14.00 (*0-570-03983-5*, 12-3010) Concordia.

Lutheran Worship-Little Agenda. deluxe ed. 224p. 1987. 25.00 (*0-570-04221-6*, 15-2183) Concordia.

Lutheran Zion-Pine Church Record, 1786-1827: Stony Creek, Virginia, Set, Vols. I & II. Ed. by Klaus Wust. Tr. by Ilse Martin & George M. Smith from GER. (Genealogical Source Bk.: Nos. 8 & 9). (Illus.). 1985. pap. 20.00 (*0-917968-13-1*) Shenandoah Hist.

Lutheranism: A Restaurant in Question & Answer Form. Martin E. Marty. 44p. 1989. pap. write for info. (*1-889711-04-7*) Cathedral Direct.

Lutheranism: The Theological Movement & Its Confessional Writings. Eric W. Gritsch & Robert W. Jenson. LC 76-7869. 224p. 1976. pap. 20.00 (*0-8006-1246-9*, 1-1246, Fortress Pr) Augsburg Fortress.

Lutheranism & Anglicanism in Colonial New Jersey: An Early Ecumenical Experiment in Swedesboro. Suzanne Geissler. LC 88-1648. (Studies in American Religion: Vol. 29). 136p. 1988. lib. bdg. 69.95 (*0-88946-673-4*) E Mellen.

Lutheranism in Colonial New York. Harry J. Kreider. LC 78-38452. (Religion in America, Ser. 2). 184p. 1972. reprint ed. 16.95 (*0-405-04072-5*) Ayer.

Lutherans. L. DeAne Lagerquist. (Denominations in America Ser.: No. 9). 192p. 1999. pap. 19.95 (*0-275-96393-4*, Greenwood Pr) Greenwood.

Lutherans, 9. L. DeAne Lagerquist. LC 99-22099. 272p. 1999. lib. bdg. 69.50 (*0-313-27549-1*, Greenwood Pr) Greenwood.

Lutherans & Catholics in Dialogue: Personal Notes for a Study. Paul C. Empie. Ed. by Raymond Tiemeyer. LC 80-69754. 160p. (Orig.). reprint ed. pap. 49.60 (*0-608-15325-7*, 202961200061) Bks Demand.

Lutherans in Berks County, Pennsylvania: Two Centuries of Continuous Organized Church Life, 1723-1923. H. S. Kidd. (Illus.). 503p. 1997. reprint ed. lib. bdg. 52.00 (*0-8328-7159-1*) Higginson Bk Co.

Lutherans in North America. rev. ed. Ed. by E. Clifford Nelson. LC 74-26337. (Illus.). 576p. 1980. 45.00 (*0-8006-1409-7*, 1-1409) Augsburg Fortress.

Lutherianism, Anti-Judaism, & Bach's St. John's Passion: Witha an Annotated Literal Translation of the Libretto. Michael Marissen. LC 97-40060. 128p. 1998. 16.95 (*0-19-511471-X*) OUP.

Lutherie et les luthiers. Louis Antoine Vidal. (FRE., Illus.). 348p. 1969. reprint ed. lib. bdg. 55.00 (*0-8450-2584-8*) Broude.

Lutherie, the Manufacture of Musical Instruments. Tr. by Helen Tullberg. (Illus.). 49p. (C). 1987. reprint ed. 42.00 (*0-902633-41-4*, Pub. by Picton) St Mut.

Lutherie Tools: Making Hand & Power Tools for String Instrument Building. Tim Olsen & Cyndy Burton. (Guild of American Luthiers Resource Bk.: No. 1). 122p. 1990. 25.00 (*0-9626447-0-6*) Guild Amer Luthiers.

Lutherie Woods & Steel String Guitars: A Guide to Tonewoods with a Compilaition of Repair & Construction Techniques. Tim Olsen & Cyndy Burton. (Guild of American Luthiers Resource Bk.: No. 2). 154p. 1998. 25.00 (*0-9626447-1-4*) Guild Amer Luthiers.

Luther's Approach to Scripture As Seen in His Commentaries on Galatians, 1519-1538. Kenneth Hagen. 194p. 1993. 115.00 (*3-16-145977-6*, Pub. by JCB Mohr) Coronet Bks.

Luthers Briefe see Luthers Werke in Auswahl

Luther's Catechism. David P. Kuske. (Illus.). 350p. (J). (gr. 7-8). 1982. pap. 6.00 (*0-938272-13-6*, 072151); text 13.50 (*0-938272-11-X*, 07N2153) WELS Board.

Luther's Catechism Comes to America: Theological Effects on the Issues of the Small Catechism Prepared in or for America Prior to 1850. Arthur C. Repp, Sr. LC 82-5453. (American Theological Library Association Monograph: No. 18). 329p. 1982. text 34.50 (*0-8108-1546-X*) Scarecrow.

Luther's Catechism EXERCISES. 1991. ring bd. 69.99 (*0-8100-0421-6*, 07N0759) WELS Board.

Luther's Catholic Christology. Franz Posset. LC 87-63002. 267p. (Orig.). 1988. pap. 10.99 (*0-8100-0275-2*, 15N0443) Northwest Pub.

Luthers Deutsch: Sprachliche Leistung und Wirkung. Herbert Wolf. (GER.). 1996. 61.95 (*3-631-49458-0*) P Lang Pubng.

Luther's Faith: The Cause of the Gospel in the Church. D. Olivier. LC 12-2961. 240p. 1982. pap. 17.00 (*0-570-03868-5*, 12-2961) Concordia.

Luther's Family Devotions for Every Day of the Church Year. Martin Luther. Ed. by George Link. Tr. by Joel Baseley from GER. Orig. Title: Luther's Taeglich Hausandacht auf Alle Tage des Kirchenjahres. 688p. 1996. 22.00 (*0-9652403-0-4*) M V Publns.

Luther's German Bible. Johann M. Reu. LC 83-45651. reprint ed. 75.00 (*0-404-19860-0*) AMS Pr.

Luther's Heirs Define His Legacy: Studies on Lutheran Confessionalization. Robert Kolb. LC 96-10221. (Collected Studies: No. CS539). (Illus.). 320p. 1996. 99.95 (*0-86078-592-0*, Pub. by Variorum) Ashgate Pub Co.

Luther's House of Learning: Indoctrination of the Young in the German Reformation. Gerald Strauss. LC 77-18705. 405p. reprint ed. pap. 125.60 (*0-608-11991-1*, 202300300030) Bks Demand.

Luther's Hymns. James F. Lambert. LC 83-45646. reprint ed. 34.50 (*0-404-19855-4*) AMS Pr.

Luther's Large Catechism: A Contemporary Translation with Study Questions. Martin Luther. 1988. 5.65 (*0-570-03539-2*, 14-2021) Concordia.

Luther's Legacy: Salvation & English Reformers, 1525-1556. Carl R. Trueman. LC 93-35766. 320p. 1994. text 65.00 (*0-19-826352-X*, Clarendon Pr) OUP.

Luther's Ninety-Five Theses. Martin Luther. Tr. by C. M. Jacobs. 18p. 1957. pap. 4.99 (*0-8006-1265-5*, 1-1265, Fortress Pr) Augsburg Fortress.

Luther's Ninety-Five Theses. Ernest G. Schwiebert. 35p. 1968. pap. 1.50 (*0-570-03519-8*, 14-1253) Concordia.

Luther's Prayers. Ed. by Herbert F. Brokering. LC 94-24889. 1994. pap. 10.99 (*0-8066-2755-7*, 9-2755, Augsburg) Augsburg Fortress.

Luther's Scottish Connection. James E. McGoldrick. LC 88-46054. 128p. 1989. 28.50 (*0-8386-3357-9*) Fairleigh Dickinson.

Luther's Small Catechism. Martin Luther. 32p. 1992. pap. text 0.95 (*1-58572-010-0*) Ambasdor Pubns.

Luther's Small Catechism Explained. abr. rev. ed. Martin Luther & H. U. Sverdrup. Ed. by John A. Loukom. Tr. by H. A. Urseth. 128p. 1995. reprint ed. text 4.95 (*1-58572-015-1*) Ambasdor Pubns.

An Asterisk (*) at the beginning of an entry indicates that the title is appearing for the first time.

***Luther's Small Dictionary: From Aal to Zululand: This Is Most Certainly True.** Janet Letnes Martin & Suzann Johnson Nelson. 252p. 1999. pap. 9.95 (*1-886627-06-1*, Pub. by Redbird Prods) Bookmen Inc.

Luthers Stellung zum Heidentum im Spannungsfeld von Tradition, Humanismus und Reformation. Herbert Blochle. (Europaische Hochschulschriften Ser.: Reihe 23, Bd. 531). (GER.). 534p. 1995. 74.95 (*3-631-48662-6*) P Lang Pubng.

Luther's Table Talk. Preserved Smith. LC 78-127457. (Columbia University. Studies in the Social Sciences: No. 69). 1970. reprint ed. 31.50 (*0-404-51069-8*) AMS Pr.

Luther's Taeglich Hausandacht auf Alle Tage des Kirchenjahres see Luther's Family Devotions for Every Day of the Church Year

Luther's Theological Development from Erfurt to Augsburg. Albert Hyma. LC 76-137247. reprint ed. 20.00 (*0-404-03479-9*) AMS Pr.

Luther's Theological Testament: The Schmalkald Articles. William R. Russell. 224p. 1995. 33.00 (*0-8006-2660-5*, 1-2660, Fortress Pr) Augsburg Fortress.

Luther's Theology of the Cross. Alister E. McGrath. 208p. 1990. pap. 28.95 (*0-631-17549-0*) Blackwell Pubs.

Luther's Thought: Essay on the Development of Luther's Thought on Justice, Law, & Society. F. Edward Cranz. 210p. 1998. reprint ed. pap. 19.00 (*1-888961-01-5*, 1015) Sigler Pr.

Luther's Variations in Sentence Arrangement from the Modern Literary Usage with Primary Reference to the Position of the Verb. Paul Curts. 1910. pap. 49.50 (*0-686-83611-1*) Elliots Bks.

Luthers Werke, 4 vols., Set. Martin Luther. (GER.). 1920p. 1982. pap. 113.85 (*3-11-008942-4*) De Gruyter.

Luthers Werke in Auswahl, 8 vols. Martin Luther. Ed. by Otto Clemen & Albert Leitzmann. Incl. Vol. 1. Schriften von 1517 bis 1520. 6th rev. ed. (Illus.). xxxii, 512p. 1966. 28.00 (*3-11-003152-3*); Vol. 2. Schriften von 1520 bis 1524. 6th rev. ed. vi, 464p. 1967. 28.00 (*3-11-003153-1*); Vol. 3. Schriften von 1524 bis 1528. 6th rev. ed. vi, 516p. 1966. 28.00 (*3-11-003154-X*); Vol. 4. Schriften von 1529 bis 1545. 6th rev. ed. vi, 428p. 1967. 28.00 (*3-11-003151-5*); Vol. 5. Junge Luther. 3rd rev. ed. Ed. by Erich Vogelsang. xi, 434p. 1963. 32.00 (*3-11-005609-7*); Vol. 6. Luthers Briefe. 3rd rev. ed. Ed. by Hanns Rueckert. xv, 451p. 1966. 32.00 (*3-11-005610-0*); Vol. 7. Predigten. 3rd ed. Ed. by Emanuel Hirsch. xii, 420p. 1962. 32.00 (*3-11-005611-9*); Vol. 8. Tischreden. 3rd ed. x, 387p. 1962. 32.00 (*3-11-005612-7*); write for info. (*0-318-51629-2*) De Gruyter.

Luther's Works, Vol. 6. Martin Luther. Tr. by Paul D. Pahl. LC 55-9893. 1969. 29.00 (*0-570-06406-6*, 15-1748) Concordia.

Luther's Works, Vol. 7. Martin Luther. Tr. by Paul D. Pahl. LC 55-9893. 1964. 29.00 (*0-570-06407-4*, 15-1749) Concordia.

Luther's Works, Vol. 9. Martin Luther. Ed. by Jaroslav J. Pelikan. LC 55-9893. 1960. 29.00 (*0-570-06409-0*, 15-1751) Concordia.

Luther's Works, Vol. 12. Martin Luther. LC 55-9893. 1955. 29.00 (*0-570-06412-0*, 15-1754) Concordia.

Luther's Works, Vol. 14. Martin Luther. LC 55-9893. 1958. 29.00 (*0-570-06414-7*, 15-1756) Concordia.

Luther's Works, Vol. 15. Martin Luther. Tr. by Jaroslav J. Pelikan et al from LAT. LC 55-9893. 1971. 29.00 (*0-570-06415-5*, 15-1757) Concordia.

Luther's Works, Vol. 17. Martin Luther. Tr. by Herbert J. Bouman. LC 55-9893. 1972. 29.00 (*0-570-06417-1*, 15-1759) Concordia.

Luther's Works, Vol. 21. Martin Luther. Tr. by Jaroslav J. Pelikan & A. T. Steinhaeu. LC 55-9893. 1968. 29.00 (*0-570-06421-X*, 15-1763) Concordia.

Luther's Works, Vol. 22. Martin H. Luther. Ed. by Jaroslav J. Pelikan. Tr. by Martin Bertram. LC 55-9893. 1957. 29.00 (*0-570-06422-8*, 15-1764) Concordia.

Luther's Works, Vol. 24. Martin Luther. Ed. by Jaroslav J. Pelikan. Tr. by Martin H. Bertram. LC 55-9893. 1961. 29.00 (*0-570-06424-4*, 15-1766) Concordia.

Luther's Works, Vol. 28. Martin H. Luther. Tr. by E. Sittler et al. LC 55-9893. 1973. 29.00 (*0-570-06428-7*, 15-1770) Concordia.

Luther's Works: Career of the Reformer, Vol. 31. Ed. by Harold J. Grimm & Helmut T. Lehmann. LC 55-9893. 1957. 30.00 (*0-8006-0331-1*, 1-331, Fortress Pr) Augsburg Fortress.

Luther's Works: Career of the Reformer II, Vol. 32. Ed. by George W. Forell & Helmut T. Lehmann. LC 55-9893. 1958. 30.00 (*0-8006-0332-X*, 1-332, Fortress Pr) Augsburg Fortress.

Luther's Works: Career of the Reformer III, Vol. 33. Ed. by Philip S. Watson & Helmut T. Lehmann. LC 55-9893. 1972. 30.00 (*0-8006-0333-8*, 1-333, Fortress Pr) Augsburg Fortress.

Luther's Works: Career of the Reformer IV, Vol. 34. Ed. by Lewis W. Spitz & Helmut T. Lehmann. LC 55-9893. 1960. 30.00 (*0-8006-0334-6*, 1-334, Fortress Pr) Augsburg Fortress.

Luther's Works: Catholic Epistles, Vol. 30. Martin H. Luther. Ed. by Jaroslav J. Pelikan. Tr. by M. Bertram & W. A. Hansen. LC 55-9893. 1967. 29.00 (*0-570-06430-9*, 15-1772) Concordia.

Luther's Works: Church & Ministry I, Vol. 39. Ed. by Eric W. Gritsch & Helmut T. Lehmann. LC 55-9893. 356p. 1970. 30.00 (*0-8006-0339-7*, 1-339, Fortress Pr) Augsburg Fortress.

Luther's Works: Church & Ministry II, Vol. 40. Ed. by Conrad Bergendoff & Helmut T. Lehman. LC 55-9893. 432p. 1958. 30.00 (*0-8006-0340-0*, 1-340, Fortress Pr) Augsburg Fortress.

Luther's Works: Church & Ministry III, Vol. 41. Ed. by Helmut T. Lehmann & Eric W. Gritsch. LC 55-9893. 1966. 30.00 (*0-8006-0341-9*, 1-341, Fortress Pr) Augsburg Fortress.

Luther's Works: Devotional Writings I, Vol. 42. Ed. by Martin O. Dietrich & Helmut T. Lehmann. LC 55-9893. 1969. 30.00 (*0-8006-0342-7*, 1-342, Fortress Pr) Augsburg Fortress.

Luther's Works: Devotional Writings II, Vol. 43. Ed. by Gustav K. Wiencke & Helmut T. Lehmann. LC 55-9893. 1968. 30.00 (*0-8006-0343-5*, 1-343, Fortress Pr) Augsburg Fortress.

Luther's Works: Genesis Chapters 1-5, Vol. 1. Jaroslav J. Pelikan & George V. Schick. LC 55-9893. 1958. 29.00 (*0-570-06401-5*, 15-1743) Concordia.

Luther's Works: Genesis Chapters 15-20, Vol. 3. Martin Luther. Ed. by Jaroslav J. Pelikan. Tr. by George V. Schick. LC 55-9893. 1961. 29.00 (*0-570-06403-1*, 15-1745) Concordia.

Luther's Works: Genesis Chapters 21-25, Vol. 4. Tr. by George V. Schick. LC 55-9893. 1964. 29.00 (*0-570-06404-X*, 15-1746) Concordia.

Luther's Works: Genesis Chapters 26-30, Vol. 5. Martin Luther. Tr. by George V. Schick. LC 55-9893. 1967. 29.00 (*0-570-06405-8*, 15-1747) Concordia.

Luther's Works: Genesis Chapters 45-50, Vol. 8. Martin Luther. Tr. by Paul D. Pahl. LC 55-9893. 1965. 29.00 (*0-570-06408-2*, 15-1750) Concordia.

Luther's Works: Genesis Chapters 6-11, Vol. 2. Martin Luther. Ed. by Jaroslav J. Pelikan. Tr. by George V. Schick. LC 55-9893. 1960. 29.00 (*0-570-06402-3*, 15-1744) Concordia.

Luther's Works: Lectures on Galatians, Vol. 27. Martin Luther. Ed. by Jaroslav J. Pelikan. Tr. by Richard Jungkuntz. LC 55-9893. 1963. 29.00 (*0-570-06427-9*, 15-1769) Concordia.

Luther's Works: Lectures on Galatians (Chapters 1 - 4), Vol. 26. Martin Luther. Ed. by Jaroslav J. Pelikan. LC 55-9893. 1968. 29.00 (*0-570-06426-0*, 15-1768) Concordia.

Luther's Works: Lectures on Isaiah (Chs. 1-29), Vol. 16. Martin Luther. Tr. by Herbert J. Bouman. 1968. 29.00 (*0-570-06416-3*, 15-1758) Concordia.

Luther's Works: Lectures on Minor Prophets III, Vol. 20. Martin Luther. Tr. by R. J. Dinda & W. B. Miller. LC 55-9893. 300p. 1973. 29.00 (*0-570-06420-1*, 15-1762) Concordia.

Luther's Works: Lectures on Romans Glosses & Scholia, Vol. 25. Martin Luther. Tr. by J. A. Preus & W. G. Tillmanns. LC 55-9893. (Luther's Works). 1972. 29.00 (*0-570-06425-2*, 15-1767) Concordia.

Luther's Works: Lectures on the Minor Prophets, 2: Jonah & Habakkuk, Vol. 19. Martin H. Luther. Ed. by Hilton C. Oswald. Tr. by M. Bertram & C. Froelich from GER. LC 55-9893. 1974. 29.00 (*0-570-06419-8*, 15-1761) Concordia.

Luther's Works: Lectures on the Psalms I, Vol. 10. Martin Luther. Tr. by H. J. Bouman. 1981. 29.00 (*0-570-06410-4*, 15-1752) Concordia.

Luther's Works: Lectures on the Psalms III, Vol. 11. Martin Luther. Ed. by Hilton C. Oswald. Tr. by Herbert J. Bowman from LAT. LC 55-9893. 560p. 1976. 29.00 (*0-570-06411-2*, 15-1753) Concordia.

Luther's Works: Lectures on Titus, Philemon, Hebrews, Vol. 29. Martin Luther. Tr. by Jaroslav J. Pelikan & W. A. Hansen. 1968. 29.00 (*0-570-06429-5*, 15-1771) Concordia.

Luther's Works: Letters I, Vol. 48. Ed. by Gottfried G. Krodel & Helmut T. Lehmann. LC 55-9893. 1963. 30.00 (*0-8006-0348-6*, Fortress Pr) Augsburg Fortress.

Luther's Works: Letters II, Vol. 49. Ed. & Tr. by Gerhard A. Krodel from GER. LC 55-9893. 480p. 1972. 30.00 (*0-8006-0349-4*, 1-349, Fortress Pr) Augsburg Fortress.

Luther's Works: Letters III, Vol. 50. Ed. by Gottfried G. Krodel & Helmut T. Lehmann. LC 74-76934. 416p. 1975. 30.00 (*0-8006-0350-8*, 1-350, Fortress Pr) Augsburg Fortress.

Luther's Works: Liturgy & Hymns, Vol. 53. Ed. by Ulrich S. Leupold & Helmut T. Lehmann. LC 55-9893. 1965. 30.00 (*0-8006-0353-2*, 1-353, Fortress Pr) Augsburg Fortress.

Luther's Works: Selected Psalms 2, Vol. 13. Martin Luther. Ed. by Jaroslav J. Pelikan. LC 55-9893. 1956. 29.00 (*0-570-06413-9*, 15-1755) Concordia.

Luther's Works: Sermons I, Vol. 51. Ed. by Helmut T. Lehmann & John W. Doberstein. LC 55-9893. 1959. 30.00 (*0-8006-0351-6*, 1-351, Fortress Pr) Augsburg Fortress.

Luther's Works: Sermons II, Vol. 52. Ed. by Hans J. Hillerbrand & Helmut T. Lehmann. LC 55-9893. 416p. 1974. 30.00 (*0-8006-0352-4*, 1-352, Fortress Pr) Augsburg Fortress.

Luther's Works: Sermons on the Gospel of St. John, Vol. 23. Martin Luther. Tr. by Martin H. Bertram. LC 55-9893. 1958. 29.00 (*0-570-06423-6*, 15-1765) Concordia.

Luther's Works: Table Talk, Vol. 54. Ed. by Theodore G. Tappert & Helmut T. Lehmann. LC 55-9893. 1967. 30.00 (*0-8006-0354-0*, 1-354, Fortress Pr) Augsburg Fortress.

Luther's Works: The Christian in Society I, Vol. 44. Ed. by Helmut T. Lehmann & James Atkinson. LC 55-9893. 1966. 30.00 (*0-8006-0344-3*, 1-344, Fortress Pr) Augsburg Fortress.

Luther's Works: The Christian in Society II, Vol. 45. Ed. by Walter I. Brandt & Helmut T. Lehmann. LC 55-9893. 1962. 30.00 (*0-8006-0345-1*, Fortress Pr) Augsburg Fortress.

Luther's Works: The Christian in Society III, Vol. 46. Ed. by Robert C. Schultz & Helmut T. Lehmann. LC 55-9893. 1967. 30.00 (*0-8006-0346-X*, 1-346, Fortress Pr) Augsburg Fortress.

Luther's Works: The Christian in Society IV, Vol. 47. Ed. by Franklin Sherman & Helmut T. Lehmann. LC 55-9893. 1971. 30.00 (*0-8006-0347-8*, 1-347, Fortress Pr) Augsburg Fortress.

Luther's Works: Word & Sacrament I, Vol. 35. Ed. by Theodore Bachmann & Helmut T. Lehmann. LC 55-9893. 426p. 1960. 30.00 (*0-8006-0335-4*, 1-335, Fortress Pr) Augsburg Fortress.

Luther's Works: Word & Sacrament II, Vol. 36. Ed. by Abdel R. Wentz & Helmut T. Lehmann. LC 55-9893. 400p. 1959. 30.00 (*0-8006-0336-2*, 1-336, Fortress Pr) Augsburg Fortress.

Luther's Works: Word & Sacrament III, Vol. 37. Ed. by Robert H. Fischer & Helmut T. Lehmann. LC 55-9893. 1961. 30.00 (*0-8006-0337-0*, 1-337, Fortress Pr) Augsburg Fortress.

Luther's Works: Word & Sacrament IV, Vol. 38. Ed. by Martin E. Lehman & Helmut T. Lehmann. LC 55-9893. 1971. 30.00 (*0-8006-0338-9*, 1-338, Fortress Pr) Augsburg Fortress.

Luther's Works-Index, Vol. 55. Ed. by Joel W. Lundeen. LC 86-45197. 512p. 1986. 30.00 (*0-8006-0355-9*, 1-355, Fortress Pr) Augsburg Fortress.

Luthien's Gamble. R. A. Salvatore. 336p. 1996. mass mkt. 5.99 (*0-446-60361-9*, Pub. by Warner Bks) Little.

Luthiers Scrap Book. rev. ed. Harry S. Wake. LC 81-186554. (Illus.). 110p. (Orig.). 1980. pap., student ed. 18.50 (*0-9607048-2-5*) H S Wake.

Luthistes Espagnols du XVIe Siecle, 2 vols in 1. Guillermo Morphy. (FRE & GER., Illus.). 306p. 1967. reprint ed. lib. bdg. 95.00 (*0-8450-1008-5*) Broude.

Lutrin: An Heroick Poem. Nicolas Boileau-Despreaux. LC 92-22030. (Augustan Reprints Ser.: No. 126). 1967. reprint ed. 14.50 (*0-404-70126-4*, PQ1721) AMS Pr.

Lutte Contre la Carence en Fer: Etude de Cas Realisee au Chili. Vivian Beyda et al. Ed. by Catherine E. Adams et al. Tr. by Catherine DeMaeyer. (FRE., Illus.). 64p. (Orig.). 1986. pap. text 3.50 (*0-318-35292-3*) ILSI.

Lutte Contre le Pauvrete & les Fonds d'Investissement Social: Le Cas de l'Amerique Latine. Philip J. Glaessner et al. (Discussion Paper Ser.: No. 261). (FRE.). 76p. 1995. pap. 22.00 (*0-8213-3369-0*, 13369) World Bank.

Lutte Contre L'Hypertension, Lucha Contra la Hypertension see Hypertension Control: Report of a WHO Expert Committee

Lutte pour un Parti Proletarien. James P. Cannon. 58p. 1997. pap. 8.00 (*0-87348-865-2*) Pathfinder NY.

Luttrell Village: Country Life in the Middle Ages. Sheila Sancha. LC 82-45588. (Illus.). 64p. (J). (gr. 6-9). 1983. 13.95 (*0-690-04323-6*); lib. bdg. 13.89 (*0-690-04324-4*) HarpC Child Bks.

Lutuing Pilipino. A. Charing. (Illus.). 170p. 1976. 8.95 (*0-318-36297-X*) Asia Bk Corp.

Lutyens in Italy. H. Petter. (Illus.). 55p. 1992. pap. 13.50 (*0-904152-21-9*, Pub. by British Schl Rome) David Brown.

***Lutzen 1632.** Richard Brzezinski. (Campaign Ser.: Vol. 68). 2000. pap. 17.95 (*1-85532-552-7*) Ospry.

Luuanda. J. L. Vieira. Tr. by Tamara L. Bender. (African Writers Ser.). 118p. (Orig.). (C). 1980. pap. 8.95 (*0-435-90222-9*, 90222) Heinemann.

Luv. Murray Schisgal. 1966. pap. 5.25 (*0-8222-0709-5*) Dramatists Play.

***Luv, Amelia - Luv, Nadia.** Marissa Moss. (J). 1999. pap. text 7.95 (*1-56247-823-0*) Pleasant Co.

***Luv, Amelia - Luv, Nadia.** Marissa Moss. (American Girl Backpack Bks.). (Illus.). 32p. (J). (ps-3). 1999. 14.95 (*1-56247-839-7*) Pleasant Co.

***Luv@first Site.** Tess Kindig. Vol. 5. 144p. (J). (gr. 5-9). 2000. pap. 5.99 (*0-8499-7582-4*) Tommy Nelson.

***Luvy, the Bull.** Orig. Title: Der Stier Liebevoll. (Illus.). 48p. (gr. 1-3). 1999. 8.95 (*1-890841-05-6*, S605en) Universal Life.

Lux Orientalis: or An Enquiry into the Opinion of the Eastern Sages Concerning the Praeexistence of Souls. Joseph Glanvill. Ed. by Bernhard Fabian. (Collected Works: Vol. II). 192p. 1978. reprint ed. 48.62 (*3-487-02688-0*) G Olms Pubs.

Lux Presents Hollywood: A Show-by-Show History of the Lux Radio Theater & the Lux Video Theater, 1934-1957. Connie J. Billips & Arthur Pierce. LC 94-11517. (Illus.). 739p. 1995. lib. bdg. 95.00 (*0-89950-938-X*) McFarland & Co.

Luxemborg see Cultures of the World - Group 14

Luxembourg. Ed. by Robert L. Collison. (World Bibliographical Ser.: No. 23). 184p. 1981. lib. bdg. 45.00 (*0-903450-37-2*) ABC-CLIO.

Luxembourg, Vol. 23. 2nd rev. ed. Jul Christophory & Emile Thoma. LC 97-188274. (World Bibliographical Ser.). 361p. 1997. lib. bdg. 90.00 (*1-85109-249-8*) ABC-CLIO.

***Luxembourg: A Country Study Guide.** Global Investment & Business Center, Inc. Staff. (World Country Study Guides Library: Vol. 101). (Illus.). 350p. 2000. pap. 59.00 (*0-7397-2399-5*) Intl Business Pubns.

Luxembourg - A Country Study Guide: Basic Information for Research & Pleasure. Global Investment Center, USA Staff. (World Country Study Guide Library: Vol. 101). (Illus.). 350p. 1999. pap. 59.00 (*0-7397-1498-8*) Intl Business Pubns.

***Luxembourg Business Intelligence Report, 190 vols.** Global Investment & Business Center, Inc. Staff. (World Business Intelligence Library: Vol. 101). (Illus.). 350p. 2000. pap. 99.95 (*0-7397-2599-8*) Intl Business Pubns.

***Luxembourg Business Law Handbook, 190 vols.** Global Investment & Business Center, Inc. Staff. (Global Business Law Handbooks Library: Vol. 101). (Illus.). 350p. 2000. pap. 99.95 (*0-7397-1998-X*) Intl Business Pubns.

***Luxembourg Business Opportunity Yearbook.** Global Investment & Business Center, Inc. Staff. (Global Business Opportunity Yearbooks Library: Vol. 101). (Illus.). 2000. pap. 99.95 (*0-7397-2199-2*) Intl Business Pubns.

***Luxembourg Business Opportunity Yearbook: Export-Import, Investment & Business Opportunities.** International Business Publications, U. S. A. Staff & Global Investment Center, U. S. A. Staff. (Global Business Opportunity Yearbooks Library: Vol. 101). (Illus.). 350p. 1999. pap. 99.95 (*0-7397-1299-3*) Intl Business Pubns.

***Luxembourg Country Review 2000.** Robert C. Kelly et al. (Illus.). 60p. 1999. pap. 39.95 (*1-58310-525-5*) CountryWatch.

***Luxembourg Foreign Policy & Government Guide.** Global Investment & Business Center, Inc. Staff. (World Foreign Policy & Government Library: Vol. 97). (Illus.). 350p. 1999. pap. 99.00 (*0-7397-3595-0*) Intl Business Pubns.

***Luxembourg Foreign Policy & Government Guide.** Global Investment & Business Center, Inc. Staff. (World Foreign Policy & Government Library: Vol. 97). (Illus.). 350p. 2000. pap. 99.95 (*0-7397-3799-6*) Intl Business Pubns.

***Luxembourg Investment & Business Guide.** Global Investment & Business Center, Inc. Staff. (Global Investment & Business Guide Library: Vol. 101). (Illus.). 2000. pap. 99.95 (*0-7397-1799-5*) Intl Business Pubns.

***Luxembourg Investment & Business Guide: Export-Import, Investment & Business Opportunities.** International Business Publications, USA Staff & Global Investment Center, USA Staff. (World Investment & Business Guide Library-99: Vol. 101). (Illus.). 350p. 1999. pap. 99.95 (*0-7397-0296-3*) Intl Business Pubns.

***Luxemburg Export-Import & Business Directory: Ultimate Directory for Conducting Export-Import Operations in the Country. Largest Exporters & Importers, Strategic Government & Business Contacts, Selected Export-Import Regulations & More.** International Business Publications, USA Staff & Global Investment Center, USA Staff. (World Export-Import & Business Library: 21). (Illus.). 250p. 2000. pap. 99.95 (*0-7397-3379-6*) Intl Business Pubns.

Luxford's Police Law in New Zealand. 4th ed. David Bates & T. G. Maxwell. 675p. 1991. boxed set 144.00 (*0-409-78728-0*, NZ, MICHIE) LEXIS Pub.

Luxor Museum of Ancient Egyptian Art Catalog. J. F. Romano et al. (American Research Center in Egypt, Catalogs Ser.: Vol. 1). (Illus.). xv, 219p. 1979. 32.50 (*0-913696-30-7*, Pub. by Amer Res Ctr Egypt) Eisenbrauns.

Luxorius: Simply to See. Tr. by Art Beck. 64p. 1990. pap. 80.00 (*0-918395-12-7*) Poltroon Pr.

Luxury: The Concept in Western Thought, Eden to Smollett. John Sekora. LC 77-4545. 360p. reprint ed. pap. 111.60 (*0-608-06107-7*, 206643900008) Bks Demand.

***Luxury & Austerity.** Ed. by Jacqueline Hill & Colm Lennon. LC 99-197891. (Illus.). 256p. 1999. 59.95 (*1-900621-22-3*, Pub. by Univ Coll Dublin Pr) Dufour.

Luxury Apartment Houses of Manhattan: An Illustrated History. Andrew Alpern. LC 92-26286. (Illus.). 192p. (Orig.). 1993. pap. 12.95 (*0-486-27370-9*) Dover.

***Luxury Car Book, 2000.** Ed. by Jack Gillis. (Illus.). 336p. 2000. pap. 11.00 (*0-06-273690-6*, HarpRes) HarpInfo.

Luxury Custom Home Collection B, 3,000 to 3,900 Square Feet - 104 Plans: Collection B. Mike Tecton. LC 94-90433. (Illus.). 64p. (Orig.). 1998. reprint ed. pap. 20.00 (*0-922070-21-0*, B) M Tecton Pub.

Luxury Dream Homes: 154 Luxury Home Plans from Eleven Leading Designers. rev. ed. Home Planners Staff. LC 94-75201. (Illus.). 192p. 1994. pap. 14.95 (*1-881955-16-8*) Home Planners.

***Luxury Fever: Why Money Fails to Satisfy in an Era of Excess.** Robert H. Frank. LC 98-45030. 336p. 1999. 25.00 (*0-684-84234-3*) Free Pr.

***Luxury Fever: Why Money Fails to Satisfy in an Era of Excess.** Robert H. Frank. LC 00-38499. 326p. 2000. pap. 18.95 (*0-691-07011-3*, Pub. by Princeton U Pr) Cal Prin Full Svc.

"Luxury Fleet" The Imperial German Navy, 1888-1918. Holger H. Herwig. LC 98-54432. 1998. write for info. (*1-57392-286-2*, Humanity Bks) Prometheus Bks.

Luxury Fleet: The Imperial German Navy, 1888-1918. 2nd rev. ed. Holger H. Herwig. LC 87-1448. (Illus.). 332p. (C). 1987. pap. 19.95 (*0-948660-03-1*, Pub. by Ashfield Pr) Humanities.

Luxury Home Plans. Sunset Books Staff. (Best Home Plans Ser.). (Illus.). 224p. 1997. pap. 6.95 (*0-376-01190-4*) Sunset Books.

Luxury Home Plans. 5th ed. Garlinghouse Company Staff. LC 98-75667. 1999. pap. text 7.95 (*0-938708-85-6*) L F Garlinghouse Co.

***Luxury Homes & Lifestyles: Elements for the New Millennium.** Orren T. Pickell. 1999. per. 39.95 (*0-9642057-4-2*) Ashley Group.

Luxury in the Rough. Ed Landgraf. LC 97-75984. 144p. 1998. pap. 12.95 (*1-57197-102-5*) Pentland Pr.

Luxury Leisure for Less: A Complete Guidebook. Lisa M. Turner. (Illus.). 132p. (Orig.). 1992. pap. 19.95 (*1-880115-01-8*) HUB Pub.

Luxury Nurse. large type ed. Peggy Gaddis. (Linford Romance Library). 1991. pap. 16.99 (*0-7089-7117-2*, Linford) Ulverscroft.

***Luxury of Adversity: Lessons from a Roman Prison.** Andrew Sloan. Ed. by Jim Eichenberger. (Solid Foundation Bible Studies Ser.). 64p. 2000. pap. 9.99 (*0-7847-1201-8*, 41110) Standard Pub.

L

An Asterisk (*) at the beginning of an entry indicates that the title is appearing for the first time.

Luxury Paradise: Brazil Our Love, Vol. 2. Sochitl S. Cotman. Ed. by Jacqueline N. Cotman & Peggy M. Peterman. LC 97-92167. (Illus.). 40p. (Orig.). 1997. pap. 10.00 (*0-9652390-3-9*) J N Cotman.

Luxury Paradise Vol. 1: Cayman Islands. Sochitl S. Cotman. Ed. & Photos by Jacqueline N. Cotman. (Illus.). 32p. (Orig.). 1995. pap. text 13.09 (*0-9652390-0-4*) J N Cotman.

Luxury Trades & Consumerism in Ancien Regime Paris: Studies in the History of the Skilled Workforce. Ed. by Robert Fox. LC 97-35615. 360p. 1998. text 86.95 (*0-86078-664-1*, Pub. by Ashgate Pub) Ashgate Pub Co.

Luxury Trains. Book Sales, Inc. Staff. 1995. 17.98 (*0-7858-0225-8*) Bk Sales Inc.

Luxury Travel for the Unrich & Unfamous: How to See the U. S. A. in an Affordable Way - a Family Guidebook. Beth Hubbell. Ed. by Gayle Harris. (Illus.). 136p. (Orig.). 1992. pap. 7.95 (*0-9631131-6-X*) Jeremiah Pubns.

Luxus Fuhrwerk: Ein Handbuch fur Equipagenbesitzer. Carl G. Wrangel. viii, 192p. 1992. write for info. (*3-487-08236-5*) G Olms Pubs.

Luy Tre Xua. (VIE.). 328p. (Orig.). 1995. pap. 10.00 (*1-889880-01-9*) Nguoi Dan.

Luyties Homeopathic Practice. Edward L. Perry. 165p. 1974. pap. 1.95 (*0-89378-052-9*) Formur Intl.

Luyties Reference Handbook. 1975. pap. 1.50 (*0-685-01665-X*) Formur Intl.

Luz. Ana M. Cetto. (Ciencia para Todos Ser.). (SPA.). pap. 6.99 (*968-16-2565-X*, Pub. by Fondo) Continental Bk.

Luz. Jason Cooper. (Secretos de la Ciencia Ser.).Tr. of Light. 24p. (J). (gr. k-4). Date not set. lib. bdg. 10.95 (*0-86593-326-X*) Rourke Corp.

***Luz: Contemporary Latino Art in the United States.** Andrew Connors. 2000. pap. 20.00 (*0-89013-375-1*) Museum NM Pr.

Luz Adicional con Respecto a la Edificacion del Cuerpo de Cristo. Witness Lee.Tr. of FURTHER LIGHT CONCERNING THE BUILDING UP OF THE BODY OF CHRIST. (SPA.). 81p. 1988. pap. 4.50 (*0-87083-426-6*, 08-009-002) Living Stream Ministry.

Luz de Estrellas a Traves de las Sombras. large type ed. Frances R. Havergal.Tr. of Starlight Through the Shadows. (SPA.). 72p. 1989. pap. 3.50 (*1-56063-336-0*, 494024) Editorial Unilit.

Luz de Invierno. Maria M. Gillan. (ENG & SPA.). 1992. 5.00 (*0-9617589-7-X*) Lincoln Springs Pr.

Luz de Mexico (The Light of Mexico) Cristina Pacheco. (SPA.). 355p. 1995. pap. 10.99 (*968-16-4308-9*, Pub. by Fondo) Continental Bk.

Luz Del Oriente: Orientale Lumen. John Paul, II, pseud. Tr. by Vatican Staff. (SPA.). 56p. (Orig.). 1995. pap. 5.95 (*1-57455-022-5*) US Catholic.

Luz Diaria Para el Camino Diario: Daily Light for the Daily Plan. 284p. 1984. pap. 10.50 (*0-311-40045-0*) Casa Bautista.

Luz En la Marisma. Javier Alfaya. (J). (gr. 4-7). 1998. pap. text 11.95 (*84-204-4806-0*) Santillana.

Luz en las Sombras: Return to Sender. Rebecca Winters. (Bianca Ser.).Tr. of A Light in the Shadows. (SPA.). 1997. per. 3.50 (*0-373-33430-3*, 1-33430-9) Harlequin Bks.

Luz en Sion: Cronicas IV. Bodie Thoene.Tr. of Light in Zion. (SPA.). 340p. 1995. 9.99 (*1-56063-683-1*, 494583) Editorial Unilit.

Luz Es Progreso? Manuel Glave Testino. (SPA.). 98p. 1988. pap. 17.00 (*1-85339-360-6*, Pub. by Intermed Tech) Stylus Pub VA.

Luz Navidena de Dios. Gladys Doonan. Ed. by Bernice Hilliker. (SPA., Illus.). 24p. 1998. pap. 1.25 (*1-879892-49-9*, EP-101) Editorial Bautista.

Luz Que Regresa. Salvador Elizondo. (SPA.). pap. 8.99 (*968-16-1796-7*, Pub. by Fondo) Continental Bk.

Luz y Sombra. Ana Roque. 200p. 1991. pap. 8.50 (*0-8477-3648-2*) U of PR Pr.

Luzac's Semitic Text & Translation Series, 20 vols. in 18. reprint ed. write for info. (*0-404-11290-0*) AMS Pr.

Luzerne County, PA Tombstone Inscriptions, Vol. 3. Norm Drasher & Peggy Drasher. 236p. 1995. per. 19.95 (*1-55856-207-9*, 043) Closson Pr.

Luzerne County, PA Tombstone Inscriptions, Vol. IV. Norm Drasher & Peggy Drasher. LC 94-177840. 1993. per. 18.95 (*1-55856-262-1*, 044) Closson Pr.

Luzerne Legal Register, Vols. 57-88. 1220.00 (*1-57588-326-0*, 302700) W S Hein.

Luzon. Malcolm Champlin & Steven Goldsberry. 448p. 1997. boxed set 22.95 (*1-56647-185-0*) Mutual Pub HI.

Luzon: A Novel. Malcolm Champlin & Steven Goldsberry. 448p. 1997. pap. 15.95 (*1-56647-190-7*) Mutual Pub HI.

Luzon: The United States Army Campaigns of World War 2. Dale Andrade. 31p. 1996. pap. 1.75 (*0-16-045115-9*) USGPO.

Lvov Ghetto Diary. David Kahane. Tr. by Jerzy Michalowicz from HEB. LC 90-11042. 176p. (C). 1990. lib. bdg. 25.00 (*0-87023-726-8*) U of Mass Pr.

Lvov-Warsaw School & Contemporary Philosophy. Katarzyna Kijania-Placek & Jan Wolenski. LC 98-24185. (Synthese Library). 1998. 157.00 (*0-7923-5105-3*) Kluwer Academic.

Lwaano Lwanyika: Tonga Book of the Earth. Tonga Reynolds & Colleen C. Cousins. (Illus.). 250p. 1994. pap. 19.95 (*1-870670-30-2*) Paul & Co Pubs.

LWR Diagnostic Inventory: A Placement & Assessment Guide. 1993. 2.60 (*0-88336-978-8*); teacher ed. 4.95 (*0-88336-979-6*); teacher ed., student ed. 7.95 (*0-88336-980-X*); 2.60 (*0-88336-975-3*); 2.60 (*0-88336-976-1*); 2.60 (*0-88336-977-X*) New Readers.

LWR Fuel Performance, West Palm Beach, FL, April 17-21, 1994. 735p. 1994. 88.00 (*0-89448-190-8*, 700200) Am Nuclear Soc.

LWR Fuel Performance, Williamsburg, VA, April 17-20, 1988: Proceedings. 1988. 45.00 (*0-89448-032-4*, 700131) Am Nuclear Soc.

LWR Pressure Components. Ed. by Folker H. Wittmann. (Structural Mechanics in Reactor Technology Ser.: Vol. F). 418p. (C). 1987. text 168.00 (*90-6191-767-0*, Pub. by A A Balkema) Ashgate Pub Co.

LWR Series. Nicky Ann. (ENG & SPA., Illus.). 1993. 10.95 (*0-9638312-0-8*) LWR Pubs.

LWR Trial Evaluation Kit. 1993. teacher ed. 40.00 (*0-88336-918-4*) New Readers.

LX: Memoirs of a Jugoslav. Vane Ivanovic. LC 76-27414. (Illus.). 1977. 14.95 (*0-15-154797-1*) Harcourt.

LXX Version: A Guide to the Translation Technique of the Septuagint. Staffan Olofsson. (Coniectanea Biblica. Old Testament Ser.: No. 30). 105p. (Orig.). 1990. pap. 36.50 (*91-22-01392-X*) Coronet Bks.

***LY or Zero Suffix? A Study in Variation of Dual-Form Adverbs in Present-Day English Volume 1: Overview & Volume 2: Adverbial Profiles.** Lise Opdahl. LC 99-86060. 862p. 2000. pap. 89.95 (*0-8204-4399-9*) P Lang Pubng.

Lyapunov Exponents. Ed. by L. Arnold & V. Wihstutz. (Lecture Notes in Mathematics Ser.: Vol. 1186). vi, 374p. 1986. 63.95 (*0-387-16458-8*) Spr-Verlag.

Lyapunov Exponents: Proceedings of a Conference Held in Oberwolfach, FRG, May 28-June 2, 1990. Ed. by L. Arnold et al. (Lecture Notes in Mathematics Ser.: Vol. 1486). viii, 365p. 1991. 65.95 (*0-387-54662-6*) Spr-Verlag.

Lyapunov Matrix Equation in System Stability & Control. Zoran Gajic & Muhammad T. Qureshi. (Mathematics in Science & Engineering Ser.: Vol. 195). (Illus.). 255p. 1995. text 53.00 (*0-12-273370-3*) Acad Pr.

Lyapunov Theorems for Operator Algebras. C. Akemann & J. Anderson. LC 91-28168. (Memoirs Ser.). 88p. 1991. pap. 19.00 (*0-8218-2516-X*, MEMO/94/458) Am Math.

Lyautey. Andre Maurois. 17.95 (*0-685-36945-5*) Fr & Eur.

Lycanthrope Leo. Kengo Kaji. (Illus.). 272p. 1998. pap. text 19.95 (*1-56931-237-0*, Viz Comics) Viz Commns Inc.

Lycanthropes. Mayfair Games Staff. 1991. 12.00 (*0-923763-30-9*) Mayfair Games.

***Lycanthropia.** Frederick Bloxham. LC 99-67824. 288p. 2000. 25.00 (*1-885003-40-4*, Pub. by R D Reed Pubs) Midpt Trade.

Lycanthropy Reader: Werewolves in Western Culture. Ed. by Charlotte F. Otten. (Illus.). 352p. 1986. pap. text 24.95 (*0-8156-2384-4*) Syracuse U Pr.

Lycanthropy Reader: Werewolves in Western Culture. Charlotte F. Otten. LC 86-14443. (Illus.). 357p. 1986. reprint ed. pap. 110.70 (*0-608-06965-5*, 206717300009) Bks Demand.

Lyceum Arcanum Mystery. Beverly M. Saling & Rick S. Marshall. (Talislanta Ser.). 64p. 1994. pap. 9.95 (*1-880992-13-2*) Wizards Coast.

***Lychnis & Silene in the Garden.** James L. Jones. 1999. pap. 9.95 (*0-9675093-2-7*) North Amer Rock.

Lycian Turkey. George E. Bean. (Illus.). 256p. 1990. pap. 24.95 (*0-7195-4764-4*, Pub. by John Murray) Trafalgar.

Lycian Turkey: An Archaeological Guide. George E. Bean. LC 78-326329. 197 p. 1978. write for info. (*0-510-03205-2*) Tolley UK.

Lycidas & the Italian Critics. Clay Hunt. LC 78-15344. 206p. reprint ed. pap. 63.90 (*0-7837-3300-3*, 205770200006) Bks Demand.

Lycoming County, PA Cemeteries, Vol. I. Des Warzel. 161p. 1996. per. 15.95 (*1-55856-212-5*, 108) Closson Pr.

Lycoperdaceae der DDR. Hans Kreisel. 1973. reprint ed. 32.00 (*3-7682-0852-4*) Lubrecht & Cramer.

Lycophron - Lexicon Zu Lycophron. Ed. by Maria G. Ciani. (Alpha-Omega, Reihe A Ser.: Bd. XXII). iv, 359p. 1975. 80.00 (*3-487-05593-7*) G Olms Pubs.

Lycopsid Stems & Roots & Sphenopsid Fructifications & Stems from the Upper Freeport Coal of Southeastern Ohio see Palaeontographica Americana: Vol. 6

Lycos Personal Gaming Guide. Marc A. Saltzman. 1998. pap. text 12.99 (*0-7897-1832-4*) Que.

Lycos Personal Internet Guide. Mike Miller. LC 98-86987. 1998. pap. text 12.99 (*0-7897-1831-6*) Que.

Lycos Personal Online Investment Guide. Duff Young. 1998. pap. text 12.99 (*0-7897-1833-2*) Que.

***Lycos Personal Web Page Guide.** Ben Sawyer. 1998. pap. text 12.99 (*0-7897-1834-0*) Que.

Lycurgi. Ed. by Conomis. (GRE.). 1970. 27.50 (*3-322-00152-0*, T1520, Pub. by B G Teubner) U of Mich Pr.

Lycurgus see Minor Attic Orators

***Lycurgus Lais.** M. Lyle Johnson. LC 99-64389. 260p. 1998. 25.00 (*0-7388-0490-8*); pap. 18.00 (*0-7388-0491-6*) Xlibris Corp.

Lyddie. Katherine Paterson. 240p. (YA). (gr. 5-9). 1991. 15.99 (*0-525-67338-5*, Dutton Child) Peng Put Young Read.

Lyddie. Katherine Paterson. LC 92-20304. 182p. (YA). (gr. 5-12). 1992. pap. 4.99 (*0-14-034981-2*, PuffinBks) Peng Put Young Read.

Lyddie. Katherine Paterson. 182p. (YA). (gr. 7-12). 1995. pap. 5.99 (*0-14-037389-6*, PuffinBks) Peng Put Young Read.

Lyddie. Katherine Paterson. (J). 1992. 10.09 (*0-606-00880-2*, Pub. by Turtleback) Demco.

***Lyddie.** Anne Troy. 40p. 1999. 9.95 (*1-56137-502-0*) Novel Units.

Lyddie. large type ed. Katherine Paterson. (J). 1995. 49.50 (*0-614-09599-9*, L-81891-00) Am Printing Hse.

Lyddie. large type ed. Katherine Paterson. 277p. (YA). 1993. reprint ed. lib. bdg. 15.95 (*1-56054-616-6*) Thorndike Pr.

***Lyddie, No. 18.** Katherine Paterson. Vol. 18. (SPA., Illus.). (J). (gr. 9-12). 1999. pap. 9.95 (*84-239-9015-X*) Espasa Calpe.

Lyddie: A Study Guide. Lorraine Sintetos. Ed. by J. Friedland & R. Kessler. (Novel-Ties Ser.). (J). (gr. 5-7). 1995. pap. text, student ed. 15.95 (*1-56982-313-8*) Lrn Links.

Lyddy. Eugenia J. Bacon. LC 77-37582. (Black Heritage Library Collection). 1977. reprint ed. 22.95 (*0-8369-8958-9*) Ayer.

Lyddy: A Tale of the Old South. Eugenia J. Bacon & Lucinda H. MacKethan. LC 97-31436. iix, 287p. 1998. pap. 17.00 (*0-8203-1967-8*) U of Ga Pr.

Lydeard Beauty. large type ed. Audrey Blanshard. 336p. 1994. 27.99 (*0-7089-3037-9*) Ulverscroft.

Lydgate's Fall of Princes, Pt. I. Ed. by Henry Bergen. (EETS, ES Ser.: Vol. 121). 1969. reprint ed. 30.00 (*0-8115-3413-8*) Periodicals Srv.

Lydgate's Fall of Princes, Pt. II. Ed. by Henry Bergen. (EETS, ES Ser.: Vol. 122). 1969. reprint ed. 30.00 (*0-8115-3414-6*) Periodicals Srv.

Lydgate's Fall of Princes, Pt. III. Ed. by Henry Bergen. (EETS, ES Ser.: Vol. 123). 1969. reprint ed. 30.00 (*0-8115-3415-4*) Periodicals Srv.

Lydgate's Fall of Princes, Pt. IV. Ed. by Henry Bergen. (EETS, ES Ser.: Vol. 124). 1969. reprint ed. 30.00 (*0-8115-3416-2*) Periodicals Srv.

Lydgate's Fall of Princes, Vol. I. Ed. by Henry Bergen. (EETS Extra Ser.: Vol. 121). 1967. reprint ed. 30.00 (*0-19-722572-1*, Pub. by EETS) Boydell & Brewer.

Lydgate's Fall of Princes, Vol. II. Ed. by Henry Bergen. (EETS Extra Ser.: Vol. 122). 1967. reprint ed. 30.00 (*0-19-722573-X*, Pub. by EETS) Boydell & Brewer.

Lydgate's Fall of Princes, Vol. III. Ed. by Henry Bergen. (EETS Extra Ser.: Vol. 123). 1967. reprint ed. 30.00 (*0-19-722574-8*, Pub. by EETS) Boydell & Brewer.

Lydgate's Fall of Princes, Vol. IV. Ed. by Henry Bergen. (EETS Extra Ser.: Vol. 124). 1967. reprint ed. 30.00 (*0-19-722575-6*, Pub. by EETS) Boydell & Brewer.

Lydgate's Fall of Princes Pt. 4: Bibliographical Introduction, Notes, & Glossary. John Lydgate. Ed. by Henry Bergen. LC 23-17910. (Carnegie Institution of Washington Publication Ser.: Vol. 262). 538p. reprint ed. pap. 166.80 (*0-608-06206-5*, 206644300004) Bks Demand.

Lydgate's Minor Poems: The Two Nightingale Poems. John Lydgate. Ed. by Otto Glauning. (EETS, ES Ser.: No. 80). 1969. reprint ed. 36.00 (*0-527-00282-8*) Periodicals Srv.

Lydgate's Minor Poems Pt. 1: Religious Poems. Ed. by H. N. Maccracken. (EETS, ES Ser.: Vol. 107). 1969. reprint ed. 30.00 (*0-8115-3409-X*) Periodicals Srv.

Lydgate's Minor Poems Pt. 2: Secular Poems. Ed. by H. N. Maccracken. (EETS, OS Ser.: Vol. 192). 1969. reprint ed. 30.00 (*0-8115-3380-8*) Periodicals Srv.

Lydgate's Reson & Sensuallyte, Vol. I. Ed. by Ernst Sieper. (EETS, ES Ser.: Vol. 84). 1969. reprint ed. 30.00 (*0-8115-3404-9*) Periodicals Srv.

Lydgate's Reson & Sensuallyte, Vol. II. Ed. by Ernst Sieper. (EETS, ES Ser.: Vol. 89). 1969. reprint ed. 20.00 (*0-8115-3406-5*) Periodicals Srv.

Lydgate's Reson & Sensuallyte: Studies & Notes, Vol. II. John Lydgate. Ed. by Ernst Sieper. (ES 89 Ser.). 1967. reprint ed. 9.95 (*0-19-722534-9*) OUP.

Lydgate's Reson & Sensuallyte I: Manuscripts, Text & Glossary. Ed. by Ernst Sieper. (EETS Extra Ser.: Vol. 84). 1965. reprint ed. 30.00 (*0-19-722567-5*, Pub. by EETS) Boydell & Brewer.

Lydgate's Siege of Thebes, Pt. 2. John Lydgate. Ed. by Axel Erdmann. (EETS, ES Ser.: No. 125). 1969. reprint ed. 40.00 (*0-527-00311-5*) Periodicals Srv.

Lydgate's "Siege of Thebes" Pt. 1: The Text. Ed. by Axel Erdmann. (EETS, ES Ser.: Vol. 108). 1969. reprint ed. 50.00 (*0-8115-4474-5*) Periodicals Srv.

Lydgate's Temple of Glass. John Lydgate. Ed. by J. Schick. (EETS, ES Ser.: No. 60). 1969. reprint ed. 54.00 (*0-527-00263-1*) Periodicals Srv.

Lydgate's Troy Book, Pt. 1. John Lydgate. Ed. by Henry Bergen. (EETS, ES Ser.: Nos. 97, 103, 106, 126). 1969. reprint ed. 90.00 (*0-527-00298-4*) Periodicals Srv.

Lydgate's Troy Book, Pt. 4. John Lydgate. Ed. by Henry Bergen. (EETS, ES Ser.: Nos. 97, 103, 106, 126). 1969. reprint ed. 70.00 (*0-527-00300-X*) Periodicals Srv.

Lydgate's Troy Book, Pts. 2-3. John Lydgate. Ed. by Henry Bergen. (EETS, ES Ser.: Nos. 97, 103, 106, 126). 1969. reprint ed. 65.00 (*0-527-00299-2*) Periodicals Srv.

Lydia. Marty R. Figley. LC 96-21210. (Illus.). 32p. (J). (ps-3). 1999. pap. 7.50 (*0-8028-5141-X*) Eerdmans.

Lydia. Elizabeth Lane. LC 96-3683. (Historical Ser.). 299p. 1996. per. 4.50 (*0-373-28902-2*, 1-28902-4) Harlequin Bks.

Lydia. Marilynn M. Moe. 69p. (Orig.). 1995. pap. 5.95 (*1-884816-04-5*) M M Moe.

Lydia. unabridged ed. Katherine Greegor. (Young Reader's Christian Library). (Illus.). 224p. (J). (gr. 3-7). 1996. pap. 1.39 (*1-55748-776-6*) Barbour Pub.

Lydia, Vol. 4. Marilyn Kaye. LC 87-12763. (Sisters Ser.). 144p. (J). (gr. 3-7). 1987. 13.95 (*0-15-200510-2*, Gulliver Bks); pap. 4.95 (*0-15-200511-0*, Gulliver Bks) Harcourt.

Lydia: A Novel. large type ed. Lois T. Henderson. 1987. pap. 7.95 (*0-8027-2608-9*) Walker & Co.

Lydia: Filling the Fibers with Faith. Phyllis Vos Wezeman & Colleen A. Wiessner. (Celebrate: A Creative Approach to Bible Studies). 24p. (Orig.). (J). (gr. 1-6). 1989. pap. 5.95 (*0-940754-71-1*) Ed Ministries.

Lydia: Seller of Purple. Robert W. Faid. LC 91-60795. 346p. 1991. reprint ed. pap. 9.95 (*0-89221-197-0*) New Leaf.

Lydia & the Purple Paint. Pam DeVito. Ed. by Jane Weinberger. LC 89-50681. (Illus.). 52p. (J). (ps-4). 1989. pap. 4.00 (*0-932433-59-6*) Windswept Hse.

Lydia Becomes a Follower of Jesus. Daphna Flegal. (Great Big Bks.). 16p. (J). 1997. pap. text 14.95 (*0-687-00152-8*) Abingdon.

Lydia Cheng '85. Robert Mapplethorpe. 1992. 25.00 (*0-8212-1946-4*, Pub. by Bulfinch Pr) Little.

Lydia Maria Child Reader. Carolyn L. Karcher. LC 96-35357. (New Americanists Ser.). 416p. 1997. pap. text 17.95 (*0-8223-1949-7*) Duke.

Lydia Maria Child Reader. Carolyn L. Karcher & Lydia Maria Child. LC 96-35357. (New Americanists Ser.). 416p. 1997. lib. bdg. 49.95 (*0-8223-1954-3*) Duke.

Lydia Mendoza: A Family Autobiography. Lydia Mendoza. LC 92-45111. 400p. 1993. pap. 17.95 (*1-55885-066-X*); text 32.95 (*1-55885-065-1*) Arte Publico.

Lydia, Queen of Palestine. Uri Orlev. 1995. 9.09 (*0-606-07817-7*, Pub. by Turtleback) Demco.

Lydia Sigourney: An Anthology in Memoriam, 1791-1865. Ed. by M. A. Myers. LC 95-79334. 160p. (Orig.). 1995. pap. 24.95 (*1-879183-27-7*) Bristol Banner.

Lydia Thrippe: A Critic's Diary Followed by the Lydiad, Vol. 1. Daniel Sloate. LC 98-73308. (Prose Ser.: Vol. 53). 96p. 1999. pap. 10.00 (*1-55071-073-7*) Guernica Editions.

Lydia Trendennis. large type ed. Frederick E. Smith. 432p. 1987. 27.99 (*0-7089-1632-5*) Ulverscroft.

Lydian Houses & Architectural Terracottas. Andrew Ramage. LC 78-15507. (Archaeological Exploration of Sardis, Monograph Ser.: No. 5). 104p. 1978. reprint ed. pap. 32.30 (*0-7837-2317-2*, 205740500004) Bks Demand.

Lydia's Daughter. large type ed. Grace Goodwin. 1991. 27.99 (*0-7089-2444-1*) Ulverscroft.

Lydia's Impatient Sisters: A Feminist Social History of Early Christianity. Luise Schottroff. Tr. by Barbara Rumscheidt & Martin Rumscheidt. 320p. 1995. 32.95 (*0-664-22072-X*) Westminster John Knox.

Lydia's Scream Date. Ruth Ashby. (Beetlejuice Ser.: No. 2). 96p. (J). 1992. pap. 2.99 (*0-671-75553-6*) PB.

Lydie Breeze. John Guare. 1982. pap. 5.25 (*0-8222-0710-9*) Dramatists Play.

Lydisches Woerterbuch. Roberto Gusmani. (GER.). 1964. 125.00 (*0-8288-6779-8*, M-7546) Fr & Eur.

Lydon "US" & "Our Neighbors" Historical Genealogical Directory of More Than 3200 Men, Women & Children Who Live about Lyndon, Osage County. C. R. Green. (Illus.). 39p. 1997. reprint ed. pap. 8.00 (*0-8328-6720-9*) Higginson Bk Co.

Lyell in America: The Transatlantic Years, 1841-1853. Leonard G. Wilson. LC 98-10319. (Illus.). 472p. 1998. 45.00 (*0-8018-5797-X*) Johns Hopkins.

Lyfe of Syr Thomas More. Ro Ba. Ed. by E. V. Hitchcock & P. E. Hallett. (EETS Original Ser.: Vol. 222). 1996. reprint ed. 30.00 (*0-19-722222-6*, Pub. by EETS) Boydell & Brewer.

Lygdamus: Corpus Tibullianum III, 1-6: Lygdami Elegiarum Liber. Fernando N. Antolin. LC 95-20759. (Mnemosyne, Bibliotheca Classica Batava Ser.: Vol. 154). 1996. 202.50 (*90-04-10210-8*) Brill Academic Pubs.

Lying for Truth: Understanding Yaakov's Deception of Esau. Nosson Slifkin. 1996. pap. 7.95 (*1-56871-106-9*) Targum Pr.

Lying. Sylvia Penny. 24p. (Orig.). 1995. pap. text 2.00 (*1-880573-23-7*) Bible Search Pubns.

***Lying.** Wendy Perriam. 2000. 32.95 (*0-7206-1108-3*, Pub. by P Owen Ltd) Dufour.

Lying: A Critical Analysis. Warren Shibles. LC 85-80835. 242p. 1985. 10.00 (*0-912386-20-7*) Language Pr.

Lying: A Metaphorical Memoir. Lauren Slater. LC 99-56284. 224p. 2000. 21.95 (*0-375-50112-6*) Random.

Lying: Moral Choice in Public & Private Life. Sissela Bok. 1989. pap. 14.00 (*0-679-72470-2*) Vin Bks.

***Lying Updated Edition.** Sissela Bok. 1999. pap. 14.00 (*0-375-70528-7*) Knopf.

Lying about the Landscape. Ed. by Geoff Levitus. 1997. text 30.00 (*90-5704-031-X*, Pub. by Craftsman House) Gordon & Breach.

Lying about the Wolf: Essays in Culture & Education. David Solway. LC 96-900920. 336p. 1997. pap. 19.95 (*0-7735-1536-4*, Pub. by McG-Queens Univ Pr) CUP Services.

Lying about the Wolf: Essays in Culture & Education. David Solway. LC 96-900920. 336p. 1997. 60.00 (*0-7735-1535-6*, Pub. by McG-Queens Univ Pr) CUP Services.

Lying Abroad. Brind. 2000. text 39.50 (*1-86064-377-9*) I B T.

Lying & Deception in Everyday Life. Ed. by Michael Lewis & Carolyn Saarni. LC 92-36145. 221p. 1993. lib. bdg. 32.00 (*0-89862-894-6*) Guilford Pubns.

Lying & Its Detection: A Study of Deception & Deception Tests. John A. Larson et al. LC 69-16241. (Criminology, Law Enforcement, & Social Problems Ser.: No. 78). 1969. reprint ed. 30.00 (*0-87585-078-2*) Patterson Smith.

Lying & Poetry from Homer to Pindar: Falsehood & Deception in Archaic Poetics. Louise Pratt. LC 92-45214. (Monographs in Classical Antiquity). 270p. 1993. text 44.50 (*0-472-10417-9*, 10417) U of Mich Pr.

Lying Awake. Catherine Carswell. 272p. 1997. pap. 12.95 (*0-86241-683-3*, Pub. by Canongate Books) Interlink Pub.

Lying Awake. Mark Salzman. 1999. pap. 0.00 (*0-375-70606-2*) Knopf.

***Lying Awake.** Mark Salzman. LC 99-89890. (Illus.). 192p. 2000. 21.00 (*0-375-40632-8*) Knopf.

Lying, Cheating & Stealing: Great Writers on Getting What You Want When You Want It. Ed. by Sara Nickles. LC 97-26165. 224p. 1997. pap. text 12.95 (*0-8118-1820-9*) Chronicle Bks.

Lying Days. Nadine Gordimer. 1994. lib. bdg. 24.95 (*1-56849-395-9*) Buccaneer Bks.

Lying Days. Nadine Gordimer. 352p. 1994. pap. 12.95 (*0-14-023367-9*, Penguin Bks) Viking Penguin.

An Asterisk (*) at the beginning of an entry indicates that the title is appearing for the first time.

Lying Doggo: He Sometimes Tells a Fib. Graham Rawle. (Illus.). 23p. 1997. pap. 13.95 (0-330-33999-0, Pub. by Macmillan) Trafalgar.

Lying Down Together: Law, Metaphor & Theology. Milner S. Ball. LC 85-40361. (Rhetoric of the Human Sciences Ser.). 224p. 1985. text 24.00 (0-299-10450-8) U of Wis Pr.

***Lying Down with the Lions: A Public Life from the Streets of Oakland to the Halls of Power.** Ronald V. Dellums & H. Lee Halterman. LC 99-32097. (Illus.). 240p. 2000. 25.00 (0-8070-4318-4) Beacon Pr.

***Lying down with the Lions: A Public Life from the Streets of Oakland to the Halls of Power.** Ronald V. Dellums & H. Lee Halterman. 2001. pap. 14.00 (0-8070-4319-2) Beacon Pr.

Lying Eyes. Erika Rand. (Intrigue Ser.). 1994. per. 2.99 (0-373-22259-9, 1-22259-5) Harlequin Bks.

***Lying for Fun & Profit: The Truth about the Media.** Kurt Butler. 304p. 1999. pap. 22.95 (0-9673281-0-1) Hlth Wise Prods.

Lying for Truth: Understanding Yaakov's Deception of Yitzchak. Nosson Slifkin. 91p. 1996. pap. 7.95 (0-614-23679-7) Targum Pr.

Lying Game. Jennifer Baker. (Class Secrets Ser.: No. 4). (YA). (gr. 7 up). 1996. mass mkt. 3.99 (0-671-51036-3, Pocket Books) PB.

Lying-In: A History of Childbirth in America. expanded ed. Richard W. Wertz & Dorothy C. Wertz. LC 89-50512. 344p. (C). 1989. pap. 19.00 (0-300-04087-3) Yale U Pr.

Lying in Bed: A Novel. J. D. Landis. LC 94-43078. 294p. 1995. 19.95 (1-56512-068-X) Algonquin Bks.

Lying in State. Eric Alterman. 2000. write for info. (0-316-03888-1) Little.

Lying in Wait. J. A. Jance. (J.P. Beaumont Ser.). 400p. 1996. mass mkt. 6.99 (0-380-71841-3, Avon Bks) Morrow Avon.

Lying Low. Diane Johnson. LC 97-43290. 288p. 1998. pap. 12.95 (0-452-27945-3, Plume) Dutton Plume.

Lying on the Couch: A Novel. Irvin D. Yalom. 384p. 1997. pap. 14.00 (0-06-092851-4, Perennial) HarperTrade.

Lying on the Eastern Slope: James Townsend's Comic Journalism on the Mining Frontier. Richard A. Dwyer & Richard E. Lingenfelter. LC 84-2251. (Illus.). 175p. 1984. reprint ed. pap. 54.30 (0-608-04495-4, 206524000001) Bks Demand.

***Lying Stones of Marrakech: Penultimate Reflections in Natural History.** Stephen Jay Gould. LC 99-36148. 384p. 2000. 25.95 (0-609-60142-3) Harmony Bks.

***Lying up a Nation.** Ronald M. Radano. 1998. pap. text 13.95 (0-226-70198-0); lib. bdg. 39.95 (0-226-70197-2) U Ch Pr.

Lying Voices. large type ed. E. X. Ferrars. LC 98-49015. Date not set. 30.00 (0-7838-8472-9, G K Hall Lrg Type) Mac Lib Ref.

Lying with the Enemy. Tim Binding. 368p. 1999. 24.00 (0-7867-0657-0) Carroll & Graf.

***Lying with the Enemy.** Tim Binding. 368p. 2000. reprint ed. pap. 12.95 (0-7867-0809-3, Pub. by Carroll & Graf) Publishers Group.

Lying with the Heavenly Woman: Understanding & Integrating the Feminine Archetypes in Men's Lives. Robert A. Johnson. LC 93-39206. 128p. 1995. pap. 10.00 (0-06-251066-5, Pub. by Harper SF) HarpC.

Lying Wonders: Evil Encounters of a Close Kind. Bob Kaminski. LC 96-228432. 224p. (Orig.). 1996. pap. 8.95 (1-883893-47-X) WinePress Pub.

Lykanthropus. W. P. Blake. LC 98-90442. 1998. pap. 11.95 (0-533-12809-9) Vantage.

Lyle: The Lyles of Pennsylvania, Being an Account of the Origin, Migrations & Generations of the Family. Alvin D. White. (Illus.). 343p. 1992. reprint ed. pap. 53.00 (0-8328-2415-1); reprint ed. lib. bdg. 63.00 (0-8328-2414-3) Higginson Bk Co.

Lyle: There's a Fortune in Your Attic. Compiled by Anthony Curtis. (Illus.). 512p. (Orig.). 1991. pap. 14.95 (0-399-51677-8, Perigee Bks) Berkley Pub.

Lyle: What's It Worth? Anthony Curtis. (Illus.). 1995. pap. 15.95 (0-399-51937-8, Perigee Bks) Berkley Pub.

***Lyle: 1001 More Antiques Worth a Fortune.** Anthony Curtis. LC 99-12453. 512p. 1999. pap. 15.95 (0-399-52507-6, Perigee Bks) Berkley Pub.

Lyle & the Birthday Party. Bernard Waber. (Lyle Ser.). (Illus.). 48p. (J). (ps-3). 1966. 16.00 (0-395-15080-9) HM.

Lyle & the Birthday Party. Bernard Waber. (Lyle Ser.). (J). (ps-3). 1966. 12.15 (0-606-00910-8, Pub. by Turtleback) Demco.

Lyle & the Birthday Party. Bernard Waber. (Lyle Ser.). (Illus.). 48p. (J). (ps-3). 1973. reprint ed. pap. 6.95 (0-395-17451-1, 4-97508, Sandpiper) HM.

Lyle Antique Dealers Pocket Guide. Compiled by Anthony Curtis. (Illus.). 256p. (Orig.). 1994. pap. 10.95 (0-399-51852-5, Perigee Bks) Berkley Pub.

Lyle at Christmas. Bernard Waber. LC 98-5381. (Lyle Ser.). 48p. (J). (ps-3). 1998. 16.00 (0-395-91304-7) HM.

Lyle at the Office. Bernard Waber. LC 93-49644. (Lyle Ser.). (Illus.). 48p. (J). (ps-3). 1994. 14.95 (0-395-70563-0) HM.

Lyle at the Office. Bernard Waber. LC 93-49644. (Lyle Ser.). (Illus.). 48p. (J). (ps-3). 1996. pap. 5.95 (0-395-82743-4) HM.

Lyle at the Office. Bernard Waber. (Lyle Ser.). (J). (ps-3). 1994. 11.15 (0-606-10863-7, Pub. by Turtleback) Demco.

Lyle Cashing in on Collecting Americana. Anthony Curtis. (Illus.). 512p. (Orig.). 1993. pap. 15.95 (0-399-51809-6, Perigee Bks) Berkley Pub.

Lyle Cavaneau & the Dark Specter. T. B. Foley. 96p. (Orig.). 1996. pap. 12.00 (1-887159-07-X) Preston-Speed.

***Lyle Family, the Ancestry & Posterity of Matthew, John, Daniel & Samual Lyle, Pioneer Settlers in Virginia.** Oscar K. Lyle. 361p. 2000. reprint ed. pap. 38.50 (0-8063-4986-7, Pub. by Clearfield Co) ACCESS Pubs Network.

Lyle Film & Rock n' Roll Collectibles. Anthony Curtis. (Illus.). 512p. (Orig.). 1996. pap. 14.95 (0-399-52205-0, Perigee Bks) Berkley Pub.

Lyle Finds His Mother. Bernard Waber. LC 74-5336. (Lyle Ser.). (Illus.). 48p. (J). (ps-3). 1974. 16.00 (0-395-19489-X) HM.

Lyle Finds His Mother. Bernard Waber. (Lyle Ser.). (Illus.). 48p. (J). (ps-3). 1978. pap. 5.95 (0-395-27398-6) HM.

Lyle Finds His Mother. Bernard Waber. (Lyle Ser.). (J). (ps-3). 1974. 11.15 (0-606-01533-7, Pub. by Turtleback) Demco.

***Lyle, Lyle Crocodile.** (J). 1999. 9.95 (1-56137-327-3) Novel Units.

Lyle, Lyle, Crocodile. Garrett Christopher. Ed. by J. Friedland & R. Kessler. (Little Novel-Ties Ser.). (J). (gr. k-2). 1994. pap. text, student ed. 14.95 (1-56982-083-X) Lrn Links.

Lyle, Lyle Crocodile. Houghton Mifflin Company Staff. (Literature Experience 1991 Ser.). (J). 1990. pap. 9.48 (0-395-55150-1) HM.

Lyle, Lyle Crocodile. Houghton Mifflin Company Staff. (Literature Experience 1993 Ser.). (J). 1992. pap. 9.48 (0-395-61790-1) HM.

Lyle, Lyle Crocodile. Bernard Waber. LC 65-19305. (Lyle Ser.). 48p. (J). (ps-3). 1987. pap. 5.95 (0-395-13720-9) HM.

Lyle, Lyle, Crocodile. Bernard Waber. (Lyle Ser.). (Illus.). 48p. (J). (ps-3). 1965. 15.00 (0-395-16995-X) HM.

Lyle, Lyle, Crocodile. Bernard Waber. (Lyle Ser.). (J). (ps-3). 1965. 11.15 (0-606-01005-X, Pub. by Turtleback) Demco.

Lyle, Lyle, Crocodile. unabridged ed. Bernard Waber. (Lyle Ser.). 1p. (J). (ps-3). 1993. pap. 9.95 incl. audio (0-395-66502-7, 497530) HM.

Lyle Mays Keyboard Styles & Techniques. 19.95 (0-7935-2793-7, 00292034) H Leonard.

Lyle Official Antiques Review, 1995. Anthony Curtis. 672p. (Orig.). 1994. pap. 13.95 (0-399-52146-1, Perigee Bks) Berkley Pub.

Lyle Official Antiques Review, 1996. Anthony Curtis. (Illus.). 672p. (Orig.). 1995. pap. 13.95 (0-399-52164-X, Perigee Bks) Berkley Pub.

Lyle Official Antiques Review, 1997. Anthony Curtis. (Illus.). 672p. (Orig.). 1996. pap. 13.95 (0-399-52246-8, Perigee Bks) Berkley Pub.

***Lyle Official Antiques Review 2000.** Anthony Curtis. 1999. pap. 16.95 (0-399-52545-9, Perigee Bks) Berkley Pub.

Lyle Official Antiques Review 1999. Anthony Curtis. (Illus.). 672p. 1998. pap. 15.95 (0-399-52450-9, Perigee Bks) Berkley Pub.

Lyle Price Guide to American Furniture. Anthony Curtis. LC 98-9793. 512p. 1998. pap. 15.95 (0-399-52410-X, Perigee Bks) Berkley Pub.

Lyle Price Guide to China. Anthony Curtis. LC 97-12649. 512p. 1997. pap. 15.95 (0-399-52310-3, Perigee Bks) Berkley Pub.

Lyle Price Guide to Collectibles & Memorabilia. Compiled by Anthony Curtis. (Illus.). 512p. 1988. pap. 13.00 (0-399-51445-7, Perigee Bks) Berkley Pub.

Lyle Price Guide to Collectibles & Memorabilia, No. 2. Compiled by Anthony Curtis. (Illus.). 512p. 1990. pap. 13.00 (0-399-51515-1, Perigee Bks) Berkley Pub.

Lyle Price Guide to Collectibles & Memorabilia, No. 3. Compiled by Anthony Curtis. (Illus.). 512p. 1994. pap. 15.95 (0-399-51855-X, Perigee Bks) Berkley Pub.

***Lyle Price Guide to Uncommon Antiques & Oddities.** Anthony Curtis. LC 00-27104. 512p. 2000. pap. 16.95 (0-399-52606-4, Perigee Bks) Berkley Pub.

Lyle Saxon: A Critical Biography. James W. Thomas. LC 91-65040, (Southern Literary Ser.: Vol. 3). 258p. (Orig.). 1991. pap. 23.95 (0-917786-83-1) Summa Pubns.

Lyle Stuart on Baccarat. rev. ed. Lyle Stuart. LC 96-44078. (Illus.). 272p. 1997. pap. 20.00 (1-56980-105-3) Barricade Bks.

Lylene. Vivian Vande Velde. 240p. 1997. mass mkt. 4.99 (0-06-105704-5, HarperPrism) HarpC.

Lyle's Administration of the College Library. Caroline M. Coughlin & Alice Gertzog. LC 97-8758. 208p. 1997. 38.00 (0-8108-3333-6); pap. 29.50 (0-8108-3330-1) Scarecrow.

Lyle's Administration of the College Library. 5th ed. Caroline M. Coughlin & Alice Gertzog. LC 92-6328. (Illus.). 621p. 1992. 61.00 (0-8108-2552-X); 73.00 (0-8108-2578-3) Scarecrow.

Lyle's Official Antiques Review, 1998. rev. ed. Anthony Curtis. (Illus.). 672p. 1997. pap. 14.95 (0-399-52352-9, Perigee Bks) Berkley Pub.

Lyle's One Thousand One Antiques Worth a Fortune: Which Not a Lot of People Know About. Compiled by Anthony Curtis. (Illus.). 512p. (Orig.). 1992. pap. 14.95 (0-399-51757-X, Perigee Bks) Berkley Pub.

Lyman Beecher: Selected Works see Millennium in America: From the Puritan Migration to the Civil War

Lyman Beecher & the Reform of Society: Four Sermons, 1804-1828. Lyman Beecher. LC 71-38437. (Religion in America, Ser. 2). 214p. 1977. reprint ed. 21.95 (0-405-04058-X) Ayer.

Lyman Briggs School Physics Laboratory Manual. Walter Benenson. 188p. 1994. spiral bd. 20.95 (0-8403-8853-5) Kendall-Hunt.

Lyman's Diary. Lyman Whitney. Ed. by Megen Phillips. (Illus.). 1998. pap., teacher ed. 25.00 (1-878406-17-5, Paintbrsh) Parker Dstb.

Lyman's History of Old Walla Walla County: Embracing Walla Walla, Columbia, Garfield & Asotin Counties, 2 vols. W. D. Lyman. (Illus.). 1577p. 1997. reprint ed. lib. bdg. 144.50 (0-8328-6938-4) Higginson Bk Co.

Lyme Borreliosis. J. S. Axford & D. H. Rees. (NATO ASI Ser.: Vol. 260). (Illus.). 344p. (C). 1994. text 115.00 (0-306-44664-2, Kluwer Plenum) Kluwer Academic.

Lyme Borreliosis II: Zentralblatt fuer Bakteriologie, Suppl. #18. Ed. by G. Stanek. (Illus.). 365p. 1994. 145.00 (3-437-11283-X, Pub. by Gustav Fischer) Lubrecht & Cramer.

Lyme Disease. Ronald L. Hoffman. (Good Health Guides Ser.). 1994. pap. 3.95 (0-87983-617-2, 36172K, Keats Publng) NTC Contemp Pub Co.

***Lyme Disease.** Alvin Silverstein et al. LC 99-42674. (Library Ser.). (J). 2000. 24.00 (0-531-11751-0) Watts.

Lyme Disease. Scott Veggeberg. LC 97-34042. (Diseases & People Ser.). (Illus.). 104p. (YA). (gr. 6 up). 1998. lib. bdg. 20.95 (0-7660-1052-X) Enslow Pubs.

***Lyme Disease.** Elaine Landau. (Illus.). 63p. (J). (gr. 5-7). 2000. reprint ed. text 17.00 (0-7881-9055-5) DIANE Pub.

Lyme Disease. 5th ed. Ed. by Daniel Rahn & Janine Evans. LC 97-3304. (Key Diseases Ser.). 254p. (Orig.). (C). 1998. pap. text 35.00 (0-943126-58-4) Amer Coll Phys.

Lyme Disease: A Mother's Perspective. Karen Angotti. 112p. (Orig.). 1993. pap. 6.95 (0-9633902-3-6) Anarek Pubns.

Lyme Disease: Molecular & Immunologic Approaches. Ed. by Steven E. Schutzer. LC 92-20115. (Current Communications in Cell & Molecular Biology Ser.: Vol. 6). 327p. 1992. 25.00 (0-87969-377-0) Cold Spring Harbor.

Lyme Disease: My Search for a Diagnosis. Linda Hanner. Ed. by Carol J. Frick. 215p. 1991. pap. 8.95 (0-9622669-1-4) Kashan Pub.

Lyme Disease: The Cause, the Cure, the Controversy. Alan G. Barbour. (Health Bks.). (Illus.). 272p. (C). 1996. 35.95 (0-8018-5224-2); pap. 15.95 (0-8018-5245-5) Johns Hopkins.

Lyme Disease - The Untold Story. Dennis Lakin. 174p. 1998. pap. 20.00 (1-890622-15-X) Leathers Pub.

Lyme Disease & the Nervous System. L. Reik. (Illus.). 192p. 1991. text 59.00 (0-86577-394-7) Thieme Med Pubs.

Lyme Regis. Ted Gosling & Lyn Marshall. LC 94-26100. (Towns & Villages of England Ser.). 1994. pap. 12.95 (0-7509-0570-0, Pub. by Sutton Pub Ltd) Intl Pubs Mktg.

Lymes' Heritage Cookbook. Ed. by Elizabeth M. Schuler. (Lymes' Heritage Ser.). (Illus.). 305p. (Orig.). 1991. pap. 14.95 (1-880897-01-6) Lyme Hist.

Lymington: A Pictorial Past. Brian Down. (C). 1989. 39.00 (1-85455-074-8, Pub. by Ensign Pubns & Print) St Mut.

Lymph Node Biopsy see Lymph Node Pathology

Lymph Node Biopsy Interpretation. 2nd ed. Ed. by Alfred G. Stansfeld & A. J. D'Ardenne. (Illus.). 512p. 1992. text 231.00 (0-443-04072-9) Church.

Lymph Node Pathology. 2nd ed. Harry L. Ioachim. LC 93-10712. Orig. Title: Lymph Node Biopsy. 736p. (C). 1993. reprint ed. text 195.00 (0-397-50807-7) Lppncott W & W.

Lymph Stasis: Pathophysiology, Diagnosis, & Treatment. Waldemar L. Olszewski. (Illus.). 592p. 1991. lib. bdg. 259.00 (0-8493-6499-X, RC646) CRC Pr.

Lymphatic & Non-Lymphatic Fluid Loss from the Peritoneal Cavity. Ed. by N. J. Ofsthun et al. (Journal: Blood Purification: Vol. 10, Nos. 3-4, 1992). (Illus.). 132p. 1993. pap. 88.75 (3-8055-5769-8) S Karger.

***Lymphatic Drainage of the Skin & Breast.** Roger Uren & John Thompson. 196p. 1999. text 80.00 (90-5702-410-1, Harwood Acad Pubs) Gordon & Breach.

Lymphatic Filariasis. (Technical Report Ser.: No. 702). 112p. 1984. pap. text 9.00 (92-4-120702-7) World Health.

Lymphatic Filariasis. Ed. by Thomas B. Nutman. 250p. 1998. pap. text 16.00 (1-86094-059-5) World Scientific Pub.

Lymphatic Filariasis: The Disease & Its Control: Fifth Report of the WHO Expert Committee on Filariasis. (Technical Reports: No. 821). (ENG, FRE & SPA.). vi, 71p. 1992. pap. text 10.00 (92-4-120821-X, 1100821) World Health.

***Lymphatic Metastasis & Sentinel Lymphonodectomy: Future Perspectives.** Ed. by P. M. Schlag. (Recent Results in Cancer Research Ser.). (Illus.). 300p. 2000. 175.00 (3-540-66642-7) Spr-Verlag.

Lymphatic System. Thomas Braem. 1994. pap. 19.95 (1-878576-26-7) Flash Anatomy Inc.

Lymphatic System & Cancer: Mechanisms & Clinical Management. Ed. by J. L. Meyer & J. M. Vaeth. (Frontiers of Radiation Therapy & Oncology Ser.: Vol. 28). (Illus.). x, 240p. 1994. 205.25 (3-8055-5889-9) S Karger.

Lymphatic Tissues & in Vivo Immune Responses. B. A. Imhof. 1032p. 1991. text 250.00 (0-8247-8528-2) Dekker.

Lymphatic Transport of Drugs. William N. Charman. 352p. 1992. lib. bdg. 159.00 (0-8493-6394-2, RM301) CRC Pr.

Lymphatics. 2nd ed. text. write for info. (0-7131-4410-6, Pub. by E A) Routldge.

***Lymphedema: A Breast Cancer Patient's Guide to Prevention & Healing.** Gwen White & Jeannie Burt. LC 99-32471. (Illus.). 204p. 1999. 22.95 (0-89793-265-X, Pub. by Hunter Hse); pap. 12.95 (0-89793-264-1, Pub. by Hunter Hse) Publishers Group.

Lymphocyte: Structure & Function. 2nd ed. John J. Marchalonis. (Immunology Ser.: Vol. 37). (Illus.). 440p. 1987. text 199.00 (0-8247-7797-2) Dekker.

Lymphocyte Activation. Ed. by L. E. Samelson. (Chemical Immunology Ser.: Vol. 59). (Illus.). xii, 220p. 1994. 182.75 (3-8055-5976-3) S Karger.

Lymphocyte Activation & Differentiation: Fundamental & Clinical Aspects. Ed. by J. C. Mani & J. Dornand. 960p. (C). 1988. lib. bdg. 276.95 (3-11-010760-0) De Gruyter.

Lymphocyte Circulation: Experimental & Clinical Aspects. Maria S. De Sousa. LC 80-40848. (Illus.). 287p. reprint ed. pap. 89.00 (0-608-17663-X, 203037700069) Bks Demand.

Lymphocyte Development: Cell Election Events & Signals During Immune Ontogeny. S. Pillai. (Illus.). 350p. 1997. 74.50 (0-8176-3853-9) Birkhauser.

Lymphocyte Hybridomas: Second Workshop. Ed. by F. Melchers et al. (Illus.). 1979. 34.95 (0-387-09670-1) Spr-Verlag.

Lymphocyte Signalling: Mechanisms, Subversion, & Manipulation. Maggie Harnett & Kevin Rigley. LC 96-19084. 470p. 1997. 235.00 (0-471-95903-0) Wiley.

Lymphocyte Stimulation: Differential Sensitivity to Radiation, Biochemical, & Immunological Processes. Ed. by Amleto Castellani. LC 80-19883. (Illus.). 196p. 1980. reprint ed. pap. 60.80 (0-608-05440-2, 206590900006) Bks Demand.

***Lymphocytes: A Practical Approach.** 2nd ed. Rowland-Jones, Sarah & Andrew J. McMichael. LC 99-54711. 384p. 2000. write for info. (0-19-963817-9); 55.00 (0-19-963816-0) OUP.

Lymphocytes & Their Interactions. fac. ed. Ed. by Ralph C. Williams, Jr. LC 75-14592. (Kroc Foundation Ser.: No. 4). (Illus.). 240p. pap. 74.40 (0-7837-7218-1, 204708000005) Bks Demand.

Lymphocytes in Comparative Immunology. Pilet. (Comparative Immunology, Microbiology Ser.). 1981. pap. 24.00 (0-08-026841-2, Pergamon Pr) Elsevier.

Lymphocytes in Immunotherapy of Cancer. Ed. by P. Koldovsky et al. (Illus.). 120p. 1989. 70.95 (0-387-50457-5) Spr-Verlag.

Lymphocytes in the Liver: Immunobiology, Pathology, & Host Defense. Ed. by I. Nicholas Crispe. LC 98-7962. 256p. 1999. 104.95 (0-471-19218-X, Wiley-Liss) Wiley.

Lymphocytes, Macrophages, & Cancer. Ed. by G. Mathe et al. LC 76-26538. (Recent Results in Cancer Research Ser.: Vol. 56). 1976. 35.00 (3-540-07902-5) Spr-Verlag.

Lymphocytic Choriomeningitis. Ed. by F. Lehmann-Grube. LC 70-167276. (Virology Monographs: Vol. 10). 1972. 47.00 (0-387-81017-X) Spr-Verlag.

Lymphoedema: Methods of Treatment & Control. unabridged ed. Michael Foldi & Ethel Foldi. 136p. 1993. pap. text 19.00 (0-646-22342-9, Pub. by Lymphoedema) Medicina Bio.

Lymphohaematopoietic Growth Factors in Cancer Therapy. Ed. by R. Mertelsmann & U. Veronesi. (EOS Monographs). (Illus.). vii, 90p. 1990. 62.95 (0-387-53086-X) Spr-Verlag.

Lymphohaematopoietic Growth Factors in Cancer Therapy II. Ed. by R. Mertelsmann. LC 92-49430. 1993. 123.00 (0-387-55953-1) Spr-Verlag.

Lymphoid Cells. Ed. by John I. Gallin & Anthony S. Fauci. LC 83-2848. (Advances in Host Defense Mechanisms Ser.: No. 2). (Illus.). 383p. 1983. reprint ed. pap. 118.80 (0-7837-9556-4, 206030500005) Bks Demand.

Lymphoid Malignancy. Masao Hanaoka. 1989. 95.00 (0-938607-24-3) Field & Wood Inc Medical.

Lymphokines. Ann S. Hamblin. (In Focus Ser.). (Illus.). 82p. 1988. pap. text 19.95 (1-85221-055-9) OUP.

Lymphokines & Interferons: A Practical Approach. Ed. by M. J. Clemens et al. (Practical Approach Ser.: 34). 396p. 1987. 72.00 (1-85221-036-2); pap. 49.95 (1-85221-035-4) OUP.

Lymphokines & Interleukins. Dawson. 1991. 109.00 (0-8493-7103-1, QR185) CRC Pr.

Lymphokines & the Immune Response. Ed. by Stanley Cohen. 304p. 1989. lib. bdg. 230.00 (0-8493-6427-2, QR185) CRC Pr.

Lymphoma. Ed. by A. C. Wotherspoon. LC 98-224243. (Cancer Surveys: No. 30). (Illus.). 360p. 1997. text 90.00 (0-87969-519-6) Cold Spring Harbor.

Lymphoma Project Report: Current Issues in Research & Treatment of AIDS-Associated Lymphoma. Michael Marco. (Illus.). 64p. (Orig.). (C). 1995. pap. text 20.00 (0-7881-1841-2) DIANE Pub.

Lymphomas. George P. Canellos et al. Ed. by Richard Lampert. LC 97-22034. 544p. 1997. text 175.00 (0-7216-5030-9, W B Saunders Co) Harcrt Hlth Sci Grp.

Lymphomas, Vol. I. Ed. by J. M. Bennett. 1981. text 226.00 (90-247-2479-1) Kluwer Academic.

Lymphomes Epidermotropes: Proceedings of the International Symposium, Bruxelles, March, 1977. Ed. by R. Schuppli. (Dermatologica Ser.: Vol. 157, No. 6). (Illus.). 1978. pap. 22.75 (3-8055-2982-1) S Karger.

Lymphoproliferative Diseases. Ed. by D. B. Jones & D. H. Wright. (Immunology & Medicine Ser.). (C). 1990. text 146.00 (0-85200-965-8) Kluwer Academic.

Lymphoproliferative Diseases: Pathogenesis, Diagnosis, Therapy. Ed. by P. K. Pattengale et al. (Developments in Oncology Ser.). 1985. text 147.00 (0-89838-725-6) Kluwer Academic.

Lymphoproliferative Disorders: Handbook of Investigation, Diagnosis & Management. J. A. Child. (Illus.). 420p. 1999. text 59.95 (0-412-58030-6, Pub. by E A) OUP.

Lyn Blumenthal: Force of Vision. Kate Horsfield et al. (Illus.). 20p. (Orig.). (C). 1989. pap. 4.00 (0-937335-08-8) LA Contemp Exhib.

Lyn Hancock's North. Lyn Hancock. 1995. 45.00 (1-55046-097-8, Pub. by Boston Mills) Genl Dist Srvs.

Lyn Lifshin: A Critical Study. Hugh Fox. LC 84-52092. vi, 184p. (C). 1985. 30.00 (0-87875-299-4) Whitston Pub.

L

***Lyn Peterson's Real Life Decorating.** Lyn Peterson. (Illus.). 304p. 2000. pap. 27.95 (*1-58011-028-2*) Creative Homeowner.

Lyn St. James: Driven to Be First. Ross Robert Olney. LC 96-16239. (Achievers Ser.). (J). 1997. lib. bdg. 19.93 (*0-8225-2890-8*, Lerner Publctns) Lerner Pub.

Lyn St. James: Driven to Be First. Ross Robert Olney. LC 96-16239. (Achievers Ser.). (Illus.). 64p. (J). 1997. pap. 5.95 (*0-8225-9749-7*, Lerner Publctns) Lerner Pub.

Lynch Families of the Southern States: Lineages & Court Records. L. D. Hines. Ed. by Dorothy F. Wulfeck. 373p. 1992. reprint ed. pap. 57.00 (*0-8328-2489-5*); reprint ed. lib. bdg. 67.00 (*0-8328-2488-7*) Higginson Bk Co.

Lynch Law. Jim Conover & James Brecher. (Illus.). vi, 297p. 1998. pap. 18.00 (*0-9669472-0-7*) Lynch Law.

Lynch Law. large type ed. William S. Brady. 1984. 12.00 (*0-685-29739-X*) Ulverscroft.

Lynch-Law: An Investigation into the History of Lynching in the United States. James E. Cutler. LC 69-14920. (Criminology, Law Enforcement, & Social Problems Ser.: No. 70). (Illus.). 1969. reprint ed. 18.00 (*0-87585-070-7*) Patterson Smith.

Lynch Law Legacy. large type ed. Lee Kimber. (Dales Western Ser.). 220p. 1993. pap. 18.99 (*1-85389-311-0*, Dales) Ulverscroft.

Lynch Law Through Due Process. Prince A. Cuba. (Illus.). 12p. (Orig.). reprint ed. pap. 3.00 (*1-56411-145-8*) Untd Bros & Sis.

Lynch Mob: Wicked Sensation. 1991. 16.95 (*0-7935-0386-8*, 00694758) H Leonard.

Lynch Mob - Wicked Sensation. (Guitar Recorded Versions Ser.). (Illus.). 160p. 1991. pap. 19.95 (*0-7935-0312-4*, 00660199) H Leonard.

Lynch on Lynch. Chris Rodley. 304p. 1999. pap. 15.95 (*0-571-19548-2*) Faber & Faber.

Lynch Record, Containing Biographical Sketches of Men of the Name Lynch, 16th-20th Century, Together with Information Regarding the Origin of the Name. Elizabeth C. Lynch. 154p. 1993. reprint ed. pap. 25.00 (*0-8328-3150-6*); reprint ed. lib. bdg. 35.00 (*0-8328-3149-2*) Higginson Bk Co.

Lynch Street: The May 1970 Slayings at Jackson State College. Tim Spofford. LC 87-21502. (Illus.). 228p. 1988. pap. 14.00 (*0-87338-371-0*) Kent St U Pr.

Lynch Years. T. P. O'Mahony. 125p. 1986. pap. 10.95 (*0-85105-449-8*, Pub. by Smyth) Dufour.

Lynchburg, an Architectural History. S. Allen Chambers, Jr. LC 81-3000. (Illus.). xiv, 576p. 1981. text 39.50 (*0-8139-0882-5*) U Pr of Va.

Lynchburg & Its Neighbors. 2nd ed. Rosa F. Yancey. 472p. 1997. reprint ed. 35.00 (*1-890306-04-5*) Warwick Hse.

Lynchburg & Its People. William A. Christian. (Illus.). 463p. 1995. reprint ed. lib. bdg. 49.00 (*0-8328-5133-7*) Higginson Bk Co.

Lynchburg College Symposium Readings Vol. I: Tyranny & Freedom. Lynchburg College Faculty Staff. LC 93-26942. 408p. (Orig.). 1993. pap. 24.95 (*0-8191-9284-8*); lib. bdg. 45.00 (*0-8191-9323-2*) U Pr of Amer.

Lynchburg in the Civil War. George G. Morris & Susan L. Foutz. (Virginia Civil War Battles & Leaders Ser.). (Illus.). 146p. 1984. 19.95 (*0-930919-11-4*) H E Howard.

Lynchburg, Virginia, & Nelson County, Virginia: Wills, Deeds & Marriages, 1807-1831. Bailey F. Davis. 252p. 1985. reprint ed. 30.00 (*0-89308-289-9*) Southern Hist Pr.

Lynchburg's Pioneer Quakers & Their Meeting House. 3rd rev. ed. Douglas S. Brown. (Illus.). 125p. 1997. reprint ed. 14.95 (*1-890306-06-1*) Warwick Hse.

***Lynched Man.** J. R. Roberts. (Gunsmith Ser.: Vol. 222). 192p. 2000. mass mkt. 4.99 (*0-515-12840-6*, Jove) Berkley Pub.

Lynchers. large type ed. Steven C. Lawrence. LC 98-21238. (Western Ser.). 162 p. 1998. pap. write for info. (*0-7540-3437-2*) Chivers N Amer.

Lynchers. large type ed. Steven C. Lawrence. LC 98-21238. (Nightingale Western Ser.). 172p. 1998. pap. 19.95 (*0-7838-0246-3*, G K Hall Lrg Type) Mac Lib Ref.

***Lynching.** Jordan. 2000. pap. 16.00 (*0-465-04297-X*, Pub. by Basic) HarpC.

Lynching. Bennie L. Sinclair. LC 91-23605. 208p. 1992. 19.95 (*0-8027-3201-1*) Walker & Co.

Lynching: The Dark Metaphor. Emma C. Jordan. 288p. 1997. 25.00 (*0-465-04294-5*, Pub. by Basic) HarpC.

Lynching - History & Analysis: A Legal Studies Monograph. Dwight D. Murphey. (Journal of Social, Political & Economic Studies: No. 24). 1995. pap. text 10.00 (*0-930690-53-2*) Coun Soc Econ.

Lynching & Vigilantism in the United States: An Annotated Bibliography, 34. Norton H. Moses. LC 96-44068. (Bibliographies & Indexes in American History Ser.: Vol. 34). 464p. 1997. lib. bdg. 85.00 (*0-313-30177-8*, Greenwood Pr) Greenwood.

Lynching in the New South: Georgia & Virginia, 1880-1930. W. Fitzhugh Brundage. LC 92-26034. (Blacks in the New World Ser.). (Illus.). 432p. 1993. 14.95 (*0-252-06345-7*); text 39.95 (*0-252-01987-3*) U of Ill Pr.

Lynching of Cleo Wright. Dominic J. Capeci, Jr. LC 98-5635. (Illus.). 352p. 1998. 29.95 (*0-8131-2048-9*) U Pr of Ky.

Lynching of Language: Gender, Politics, & Power in the Hill-Thomas Hearings. Ed. by Sandra L. Ragan et al. LC 95-32458. 304p. (C). 1996. text 39.95 (*0-252-02126-6*); pap. text 18.95 (*0-252-06517-4*) U of Ill Pr.

Lynching, Racial Violence, & Law. Ed. by Paul Finkelman. LC 91-42594. (Race, Law & American History, 1700-1990 Ser.: Vol. 9). 368p. 1992. text 10.00 (*0-8153-0542-7*) Garland.

***Lynching Tree.** Michael Stein. 254p. 2000. 25.00 (*1-57962-070-1*) Permanent Pr.

Lynchings: Extralegal Violence in Florida During the 1930s. Walter T. Howard. LC 94-36198. (Illus.). 208p. 1995. 35.00 (*0-945636-75-X*) Susquehanna U Pr.

***Lynchings in Duluth.** Michael W. Fedo. LC 00-21027. (Illus.). 208p. 2000. pap. 14.95 (*0-87351-386-X*, 386-x, Borealis Book) Minn Hist.

Lynch's Medical Laboratory Technology. 4th ed. Stanley S. Raphael. (Illus.). 864p. 1983. text 93.00 (*0-7216-7465-8*, W B Saunders Co) Harcrt Hlth Sci Grp.

Lynch's Revenge. Jack Cummings. 256p. 1993. mass mkt. 3.50 (*1-55817-752-3*, Pinncle Kensgtn) Kensgtn Pub Corp.

Lynch's Revenge. large type ed. Jack Cummings. LC 94-9244. 290p. 1994. lib. bdg. 18.95 (*0-7862-0219-X*) Thorndike Pr.

Lynda Benglis & Keith Sonnier: A Ten Year Retrospective, 1977-1987. Carter Ratcliff. Ed. by Audrey Hammill. LC 87-19544. (Illus.). 56p. (Orig.). 1987. pap. text 14.00 (*0-944564-00-3*) Alex Mus.

Lynda Field's 60 Tips for Self-Esteem: Quick Ways to Boost Your Confidence. Lynda Field. LC 97-19272. 128p. 1997. pap. 9.95 (*1-86204-103-2*, Pub. by Element MA) Penguin Putnam.

Lynda Ladybug. Dolores Bersen. 24p. (J). (ps-2). 1995. 13.95 (*0-9640986-2-8*); pap. 4.95 (*0-9640986-5-2*); lib. bdg. 14.95 (*0-9640986-3-6*) DUB Pubng.

Lynda Madaras' Growing-Up Guide for Girls see My Feelings, My Self: A Growing-Up Guide for Girls

***Lynda Morley's Outings & Adventures with Children Ages 1-5.** 3rd rev. ed. Lynda T. Morley. 370p. (Orig.). 1999. pap. 17.95 (*0-9662888-1-5*) Morley Pr.

Lynda Weinman's Web Graphics Resource Library. Lynda Weinman. 1997. pap. text 90.00 (*1-56205-774-X*) New Riders Pub.

***Lyndhurst: A Guide to the House & Landscape.** Amelia Peck et al. Ed. by Pamela T. Barr. (Illus.). 51p. 1998. pap. 10.00 (*0-9671404-0-4*) Lyndhurst.

Lyndon. Harriet Fletcher Fisher. (Images of America Ser.). 1998. pap. 16.99 (*0-7524-0915-8*) Arcadia Publng.

***Lyndon B. Johnson.** Scott Barbour. LC 00-28333. 2000. pap. write for info. (*0-7377-0500-0*) Greenhaven.

Lyndon B. Johnson. Jim Hargrove. LC 87-15890. (Encyclopedia of Presidents Ser.). (Illus.). 100p. (J). (gr. 3 up). 1987. lib. bdg. 24.00 (*0-516-01396-3*) Childrens.

Lyndon B. Johnson. Paul Joseph. LC 97-50200. (United States Presidents Ser.). (Illus.). 32p. (J). 1999. lib. bdg. 18.60 (*1-56239-814-8*, Checkerboard Library) ABDO Pub Co.

Lyndon B. Johnson. Tony Kaye. (World Leaders Past & Present Ser.). (Illus.). 120p. (YA). (gr. 5 up). 1988. lib. bdg. 19.95 (*0-87754-536-7*) Chelsea Hse.

Lyndon B. Johnson. Michael Schuman. LC 97-43693. (United States Presidents Ser.). 128p. (YA). (gr. 5 up). 1998. lib. bdg. 20.95 (*0-89490-938-X*) Enslow Pubs.

Lyndon B. Johnson. Ed. by Unger. (C). 1992. text. write for info. (*0-673-52109-5*) Addison-Wesley.

Lyndon B. Johnson: Mini-Play. (President's Choice Ser.). (YA). (gr. 8 up). 1978. 6.50 (*0-685-42322-0*) Stevens & Shea.

Lyndon B. Johnson: Thirty-Sixth President of the United States. Lucille Falkof. Ed. by Richard G. Young. LC 88-31003. (Presidents of the United States Ser.). (Illus.). (J). (gr. 5-9). 1989. lib. bdg. 21.27 (*0-944483-20-8*) Garrett Ed Corp.

Lyndon B. Johnson: Young Texan. 2nd ed. Barton. (J). 1995. pap. 3.95 (*0-689-71654-0*) Aladdin.

Lyndon B. Johnson & American Liberalism: A Brief Biography with Documents. Bruce J. Schulman. 269p. 1994. pap. text 11.95 (*0-312-08351-3*) St Martin.

Lyndon B. Johnson & American Liberalism: A Brief Biography with Documents. Bruce J. Schulman. (Bedford Series in History & Culture). 269p. 1995. text 45.00 (*0-312-10282-8*) St Martin.

Lyndon B. Johnson National Security Files: National Security Files, November 1963-June 1965. Lyndon Baines Johnson Library. LC 89-955812. (The Presidential Documents Ser.). 17 p. 1985. write for info. (*0-89093-461-4*) U Pubns Amer.

Lyndon B. Johnson National Security Files: National Security Files, 1963-1969 Robert Lester et al. LC 93-629993. 15p. 1987. write for info. (*0-89093-996-9*); write for info. (*1-55655-018-9*) U Pubns Amer.

Lyndon B. Johnson National Security Files: National Security Files, 1963-1969 Robert Lester et al. LC 98-159133. (National Security Files Ser.). 12 p. 1996. write for info. (*1-55655-642-X*) U Pubns Amer.

Lyndon B. Johnson National Security Files: National Security Files, 1963-1969. Robert Lester et al. LC 87-27901. 1 p. 1987. write for info. (*0-89093-966-7*); write for info. (*1-55655-004-9*) U Pubns Amer.

Lyndon B. Johnson National Security Files: National Security Files, 1963-1969. Robert Lester et al. LC 93-47284. (National Security Files Ser.). 34p. 1993. write for info. (*1-55655-470-2*) U Pubns Amer.

Lyndon B. Johnson National Security Files, 1963-1969: Project Coordinator, Robert E. Lester. Lyndon Baines Johnson Library. LC 98-159189. (National Security Files Ser.). 18 p. 1996. write for info. (*1-55655-643-8*) U Pubns Amer.

Lyndon B. Johnson's Vietnam Papers: A Documentary Collection. Ed. by David M. Barrett. LC 96-37250. 896p. (C). 1997. text 99.95 (*0-89096-741-5*) Tex A&M Univ Pr.

Lyndon Baines Johnson. Dennis Eskow. LC 92-43687. (Impact Biographies Ser.). (Illus.). 176p. (YA). (gr. 7-12). 1993. lib. bdg. 24.00 (*0-531-13019-3*) Watts.

Lyndon Baines Johnson & the Uses of Power, 221. Ed. by Bernard J. Firestone & Robert C. Vogt. LC 88-10250. (Contributions in Political Science Ser.: No. 221). 435p. 1988. 79.50 (*0-313-26395-7*, FJS/, Greenwood Pr) Greenwood.

Lyndon Baines Johnson, President. John Devaney. LC 85-31751. (Presidential Biography Ser.). 128p. (J). (gr. 5 up). 1986. 12.95 (*0-8027-6638-2*); lib. bdg. 13.85 (*0-8027-6639-0*) Walker & Co.

***Lyndon Institute: Vermont.** Harriet Fletcher Fisher. LC 99-69487. (Images of America Ser.). (Illus.). 128p. 2000. pap. 18.99 (*0-7385-0093-3*) Arcadia Publng.

Lyndon Johnson: The Tragic Self - A Psychohistorical Portrait. H. L. Muslin. LC 91-210. (Illus.). 250p. 1990. 23.95 (*0-306-43563-2*, Plen Insight) Perseus Pubng.

Lyndon Johnson & the American Dream. Doris Kearns Goodwin. 448p. 1991. pap. 16.95 (*0-312-06027-0*) St Martin.

Lyndon Johnson & the Great Society. John A. Andrew, III. LC 97-38966. (American Ways Ser.). 224p. 1998. 24.95 (*1-56663-184-X*, Pub. by I R Dee) Natl Bk Netwk.

Lyndon Johnson & the Great Society. John A. Andrew, III. LC 97-38966. (American Ways Ser.). 224p. 1999. pap. text 12.95 (*1-56663-185-8*) I R Dee.

Lyndon Johnson Confronts the World: American Foreign Policy, 1963-1968. Ed. by Warren I. Cohen & Nancy B. Tucker. 352p. (C). 1995. text 54.95 (*0-521-41428-8*); pap. text 19.95 (*0-521-42479-8*) Cambridge U Pr.

Lyndon Johnson's Dual War: Vietnam & the Press. Kathleen J. Turner. LC 84-16389. 368p. 1995. pap. text 18.00 (*0-226-81732-6*) U Ch Pr.

Lyndon Johnson's Dual War: Vietnam & the Press. Kathleen J. Turner. LC 84-16389. 368p. 1995. 30.00 (*0-226-81731-8*) U Ch Pr.

Lyndon Johnson's War: America's Cold War Crusade in Vietnam, 1945-1965: A Critical Issue. Michael H. Hunt. Ed. by Eric Foner. LC 95-26361. 144p. 1996. 18.00 (*0-8090-5023-4*) Hill & Wang.

Lyndon Johnson's War: America's Cold War Crusade in Vietnam, 1945-1968. Michael H. Hunt. 1997. pap. text 11.00 (*0-8090-1604-4*) Hill & Wang.

Lyndon Johnson's War: The Road to Stalemate in Vietnam. Larry Berman. 1991. pap. 9.95 (*0-393-30778-6*) Norton.

Lyndon's Complete Pace Chart for Runners. Rick Selig. 20p. 1987. pap. text 1.95 (*0-9618355-0-8*) Lyndon Prods.

Lyndon's Legacy: A Candid Look at Some Presidential Policymakers. Frank L. Kluckhohn. 1964. 9.95 (*0-8159-6113-8*) Devin.

Lyndon's Legacy: A Candid Look at the President's Policymakers. Frank L. Kluckhohn. LC 64-23751. 351p. reprint ed. pap. 108.90 (*0-608-13473-2*, 202270900029) Bks Demand.

Lyndora Chronicles, the Legendary Decades, 1902-1921. Peter Baycura & John F. Baycura. LC 99-185532. (Illus.). 286p. 1998. pap. 25.00 (*0-9665813-0-X*) J Baycura.

***Lynelle by the Sea.** Laurie Albanese. LC 99-42638. 240p. 2000. 22.95 (*0-525-94536-9*, Dutt) Dutton Plume.

***Lynelle by the Sea.** Laurie Lico Albanese. 2001. reprint ed. pap. 13.00 (*0-452-28218-7*, Plume) Dutton Plume.

***Lynette.** Sue W. Kramer. LC 00-190971. 2000. pap. 18.00 (*0-7388-2161-6*) Xlibris Corp.

Lynn. Joanne S. Foley. (Images of America Ser.). (Orig.). 1995. pap. 16.99 (*0-7524-0208-0*) Arcadia Publng.

Lynn: A Novel. Ruth Tolmie. LC 98-51126. 1999. pap. 15.95 (*0-936389-63-X*) Tudor Pubs.

Lynn: Postcards. Lynn Historical Society Staff. LC 98-87445. (Postcard History Ser.). (Illus.). 128p. 1998. pap. 16.99 (*0-7524-1278-7*) Arcadia Publng.

Lynn Album: A Pictoral History. Elizabeth Hope Cushing. (Illus.). 192p. 1990. 38.10 (*0-89865-807-1*) Lynn Hist Soc.

Lynn Album II: A Pictorial History. Kathryn Grover. LC 96-76791. (Illus.). 120p. 1996. 32.95 (*1-882162-12-9*) Lynn Hist Soc.

Lynn & Alice Going to School. Lynn Switzky & Alice Switzky. Ed. by Rodger A. Switzky. (Illus.). 36p. (J). (ps-4). 1999. pap. 7.50 (*0-9671080-0-4*) My Kids Bk.

Lynn & Hunst Anton Railway & the West Norfolk Branch. Stanley C. Jenkins. 140p. (C). 1985. 45.00 (*0-85361-330-3*) St Mut.

Lynn & Surroundings. Clarence W. Hobbs. LC 98-120261. (Illus.). 165p. 1998. reprint ed. pap. 16.00 (*0-7884-0789-9*, H500) Heritage Bk.

Lynn Andrews in Conversation with Michael Toms. Michael Toms. Ed. by Hal Z. Bennett. LC 94-11148. (New Dimensions Bks.). 128p. (Orig.). 1993. pap. 8.95 (*0-944031-42-0*) Aslan Pub.

Lynn Beach Painters: Art along the North Shore, 1880-1920. D. Roger Howlett. LC 98-66125. (Illus.). 96p. 1998. 35.00 (*1-882162-13-7*); pap. 23.00 (*1-882162-14-5*) Lynn Hist Soc.

Lynn Chadwick: Sculptor: A Complete Illustrated Catalog. Dennis Farr & Eva Chadwick. (Illus.). 374p. 1991. text 115.00 (*0-19-817213-3*) OUP.

Lynn Cohen: Lost & Found. Lynn Cohen. (Illus.). 108p. 1993. pap. 30.00 (*2-908257-08-4*, Pub. by F R A C) Dist Art Pubs.

Lynn Davis: Monument. Ed. by David Whitney. (Illus.). 136p. 1999. 65.00 (*1-892041-07-3*, Pub. by Arena Editions) Dist Art Pubs.

Lynn Fischer's Quick Low Cholesterol Gourmet. Lynn Fischer. 300p. 1993. pap. 12.95 (*1-879326-21-3*) Living Planet Pr.

Lynn Hershman: Paranoid Mirror. Abigail S. Godeau et al. Ed. by Helen Abbott & Mary Ribesky. Tr. by Don Reneau. (Illus.). 48p. (Orig.). 1995. pap. 9.95 (*0-932216-46-3*) Seattle Art.

(Lynn) Lin: Or Notable People & Notable Things in the Early History of Lynn, the Third Plantation of Massachusetts Colony (History & Reminiscences) Obadiah Oldpath. (Illus.). 500p. 1998. reprint ed. lib. bdg. 52.00 (*0-8328-7120-6*) Higginson Bk Co.

Lynne Alvarez Vol. 1: Collected Plays, Vol. I. Lynne Alvarez. LC 98-24129. (Contemporary Playwrights Ser.). 320p. 1998. pap. 19.95 (*1-57525-146-9*) Smith & Kraus.

Lynne Palmer's Astrological Almanac for 1998. Lynne Palmer. 286p. 1997. pap. 19.95 (*0-9652296-3-7*) Star Bright.

Lynne Reid Banks, 3 vols. Lynne Reid Banks. (J). (gr. 4-7). 1991. pap., boxed set 11.97 (*0-380-71680-1*, Avon Bks) Morrow Avon.

***Lynnette's Lyrics: Straight from the Heart.** Lynnette Tellis. 2000. pap. write for info. (*1-58235-381-6*) Watermrk Pr.

Lynnfield. Warren Falls. LC 98-85859. (Images of America Ser.). (Illus.). 128p. 1998. pap. 16.99 (*0-7524-1290-6*) Arcadia Publng.

Lynnfield, a Heritage Preserved, 1895-1977: History of Lynnfield, NH see History of the Town of Lynnfield, Massachusetts: 1635-1895

Lynton & Barnstaple Railway. L. T. Catchpole. 84p. (C). 1985. 45.00 (*0-85361-363-X*) St Mut.

Lynx. Jalma Barrett. LC 98-9881. (Wildcats of North America Ser.). (Illus.). 24p. (J). (gr. 3-5). 1998. lib. bdg. 16.95 (*1-56711-259-5*) Blackbirch.

Lynx. Julian J. Savarin. 240p. (J). 1986. 15.95 (*0-8027-0890-0*) Walker & Co.

Lynx. Jost W. Schneider. LC 94-2119. (J). (gr. 2-5). 1994. lib. bdg. 19.95 (*0-87614-844-5*, Carolrhoda) Lerner Pub.

Lynx: A Carolrhoda Nature Watch Book. Jost Schneider. (Illus.). 48p. (J). 1997. pap. text 7.95 (*1-57505-063-3*, Carolrhoda) Lerner Pub.

***Lynyrd Skynyrd: An Oral History.** Lee Ballinger. 256p. 1999. pap. 13.50 (*0-380-80154-X*, Avon Bks) Morrow Avon.

Lynyrd Skynyrd: With Notes & Tablature. 80p. 1991. per. 14.95 (*0-7935-0279-9*, 00660122) H Leonard.

Lynyrd Skynyrd Bass Book: With Notes & Tablature. 88p. 1991. per. 14.95 (*0-7935-0338-8*, 00660121) H Leonard.

Lynyrd Skynyrd Best of the Early Years: Guitar Personality. 36p. (Orig.). 1994. pap. 12.95 (*0-89724-271-8*, GF0648) Wrner Bros.

Lynyrd Skynyrd I'll Never Forget You. Gene Odom. 130p. 1983. pap. text 9.95 (*0-9656619-0-3*) A S C Pubng.

Lynyrd Skynyrd Songbook. 96p. 1985. otabind 17.95 (*0-7935-1085-6*, 00120558) H Leonard.

Lyon & de Cruz: Parents, Children & the Law. C. M. Lyon & Stephen De Cruz. 400p. 1994. pap. 36.00 (*0-406-50800-3*, MICHIE) LEXIS Pub.

Lyon Banlieue City Plan. (Grafocarte Maps Ser.). 1993. 8.95 (*2-7416-0019-8*, 80019) Michelin.

Lyon Campaign in Missouri: Being a History of the First Iowa Infantry. Eugene F. Ware. LC 91-70971. (Illus.). 424p. 1991. reprint ed. 24.95 (*0-9628936-0-9*) Pr Camp Pope.

Lyon Hunts & Humor: True Life Hunting & Adventure Stories. Tolbert J. Lyon. LC 90-37549. 1990. pap. 12.95 (*0-86534-148-6*) Sunstone Pr.

Lyon Legacy: 50th Anniversary, 3 bks. in 1. 50th ed. Peg Sutherland et al. (Superromance Ser.: Vol. 847). 1999. per. 4.25 (*0-373-70847-5*, 1-70847-8) Harlequin Bks.

Lyon Memorial: Massachusetts Families, Including Descendants of the Immigrant William Lyon of Roxbury, Peter & George of Dorchester, with an Introduction Treating the English Ancestry of the American Families. A. B. Lyon et al. (Illus.). 491p. 1989. reprint ed. pap. 73.50 (*0-8328-0796-6*); reprint ed. lib. bdg. 81.50 (*0-8328-0795-8*) Higginson Bk Co.

Lyon Memorial: New York Families, Descendants from the Immigrant Thomas Lyon of Rye. Ed. by R. B. Miller & A. B. Lyons. (Illus.). 539p. 1989. reprint ed. pap. 81.00 (*0-8328-0798-2*); reprint ed. lib. bdg. 89.00 (*0-8328-0797-4*) Higginson Bk Co.

Lyon Street Map. 1992. 9.95 (*2-06-700030-6*, 30) Michelin.

Lyon Street Map with Index. 1997. 12.95 (*2-06-700031-4*, 31) Michelin.

Lyon Uprising of 1834: Social & Political Conflict in the Early July Monarchy. Robert J. Bezucha. LC 74-75780. (Studies in Urban History). 288p. 1974. 36.50 (*0-674-53965-6*) HUP.

Lyon Villeurbanne City Plan. (Grafocarte Maps Ser.). 1993. 8.95 (*2-7416-0020-1*, 80020) Michelin.

Lyon/Chambery/Geneve Map. 1997. 6.95 (*2-06-700074-8*) Michelin.

Lyonel Feininger. Ulrich Luckhardt. (Illus.). 188p. 1989. 65.00 (*3-7913-1022-4*, Pub. by Prestel) te Neues.

Lyonel Feininger: Awareness, Recollection, & Nostalgia. Reinhold Heller. Ed. by Stephanie D'Alessandro. (Illus.). 20p. (Orig.). 1992. pap. 7.95 (*0-935573-13-5*) D & A Smart Museum.

Lyonel Feininger: Die Halle-Bilder. Ed. by Peter Romanus. (GER., Illus.). 120p. 1991. 64.00 (*3-7913-1155-7*, Pub. by Prestel) te Neues.

Lyonesse. Gladys Taber. 22.95 (*0-8488-1193-3*) Amereon Ltd.

Lyonhurst. large type ed. Rona Randall. (Ulverscroft Large Print Ser.). 448p. 1997. 27.99 (*0-7089-3831-0*) Ulverscroft.

Lyons American Government. Date not set. pap. text. write for info. (*0-314-05279-8*) West Pub.

Lyons Contrapunctus (1528), Pt. I. Ed. by David A. Sutherland. (Recent Researches in Music of the Renaissance Ser.: Vol. RRR21). (Illus.). xxvi, 95p. 1976. pap. 45.00 (*0-89579-066-1*) A-R Eds.

Lyons Contrapunctus (1528), Pt. II. Ed. by David A. Sutherland. (Recent Researches in Music of the Renaissance Ser.: Vol. RRR22). (Illus.). 100p. 1976. pap. 35.00 (*0-89579-067-X*) A-R Eds.

***Lyon's Crown.** M. L. Stainer. (Lyon Saga Ser.: No. 5). (Illus.). 165p. (YA). (gr. 5-9). 2000. lib. bdg. 9.95 (*1-893337-03-0*, Pub. by Chicken Soup) Herveys Bklink.

An Asterisk (*) at the beginning of an entry indicates that the title is appearing for the first time.

***Lyon's Crown.** unabridged ed. M. L. Stainer. (Lyon Saga Ser.: No. 5). (Illus.). 165p. (YA). (gr. 5). 2000. pap. 6.95 (*1-893337-04-9*, Pub. by Chicken Soup) Herveys Bklink.

Lyon's Cub. unabridged ed. M. L. Stainer. LC 97-47239. (Lyon Saga Ser.: Bk. 2). (Illus.). 162p. (YA). (gr. 5-9). 1998. lib. bdg. 9.95 (*0-9646904-5-4*) Chicken Soup.

Lyon's Cub. unabridged ed. M. L. Stainer. LC 97-47239. (Lyon Saga Ser.: Bk. 2). (Illus.). 162p. (YA). (gr. 5-10). 1998. pap. 6.95 (*0-9646904-6-2*) Chicken Soup.

Lyons, 1473 to 1503: The Beginnings of Cosmopolitanism. James B. Wadsworth. LC 62-14827. (Medieval Academy Bks.: No. 73). 1962. 25.00 (*0-910956-47-2*) Medieval Acad.

Lyon's Gift. Tanya A. Crosby. 384p. 1997. mass mkt. 5.99 (*0-380-78571-4*, Avon Bks) Morrow Avon.

Lyons' Guide to the Career Jungle: Workplace Ethics. Laura Lyons. LC 89-91730. 85p. 1989. pap. text 12.95 (*0-9623216-0-5*, Pub. by Odenwald Pr) Career Dynamics Inter.

Lyons on Horses. John Lyons. 240p. 1991. 29.95 (*0-385-41398-X*) Doubleday.

Lyon's Pride. Anne McCaffrey. (Rowan Ser.: Vol. 4). 336p. 1995. mass mkt. 6.99 (*0-441-00141-6*) Ace Bks.

Lyon's Pride. Maris Soule. (Romance Ser.). 1993. pap. 2.69 (*0-373-08930-9*, 5-08930-5) Silhouette.

Lyon's Pride. large type ed. Maris Soule. LC 93-7533. 266p. 1993. lib. bdg. 15.95 (*1-56054-738-3*) Thorndike Pr.

Lyon's Pride. unabridged ed. M. L. Stainer. LC 98-23980. (Lyon Saga Ser.: Bk. 3). (Illus.). 163p. (YA). (gr. 5 up). 1998. pap. 6.95 (*0-9646904-9-7*); lib. bdg. 9.95 (*0-9646904-8-9*) Chicken Soup.

Lyon's Roar. M. L. Stainer. LC 97-2128. (Lyon Saga Ser.: Bk. 1). (Illus.). 160p. (YA). (gr. 5 up). 1997. pap. 6.95 (*0-9646904-3-8*) Chicken Soup.

Lyon's Roar. unabridged ed. M. L. Stainer. LC 97-2128. (Lyon Saga Ser.: Bk. 1). (Illus.). 175p. (YA). (gr. 5 up). 1997. lib. bdg. 9.95 (*0-9646904-2-X*) Chicken Soup.

Lyon's Share. Janet Dailey. (Americana Ser.: No. 863). 1991. per. 3.50 (*0-373-89863-0*) Harlequin Bks.

Lyon's Share. Janet Dailey. LC 99-34773. 2000. pap. 30.00 (*0-7862-2073-2*) Thorndike Pr.

***Lyon's Throne.** M. L. Stainer. LC 99-18190. (Lyon Saga Ser.: Bk. 4). (Illus.). 153p. (YA). (gr. 6-9). 1999. pap. 6.95 (*1-893337-02-2*); lib. bdg. 9.95 (*1-893337-01-4*) Chicken Soup.

Lyophilization: Introduction & Basic Principles. Ed. by Thomas A. Jennings. LC 99-22039. 1999. 195.00 (*1-57491-081-7*) Interpharm.

***Lyotard: Just Education.** Pradeep Ajit Dillon & Paul Standish. LC 00-32830. 2000. write for info. (*0-415-21547-1*) Routledge.

Lyotard: Towards a Modern Philosophy. James Williams. LC 98-23964. (Key Contemporary Thinkers Ser.). 208p. 1998. 54.95 (*0-7456-1099-4*); pap. 21.95 (*0-7456-1100-1*) Blackwell Pubs.

***Lyotard & Political.** James Williams. LC 99-32750. 1999. pap. write for info. (*0-415-18349-9*) Routledge.

***Lyotard & the End of Grand Narratives.** Gary Browning. 192p. 2000. 49.95 (*0-7083-1507-0*, Pub. by U Wales Pr); pap. 27.50 (*0-7083-1479-1*, Pub. by U Wales Pr) Paul & Co Pubs.

***Lyotard & the Political.** James Williams. LC 99-32750. (Thinking the Political Ser.). 168p. (C). 2000. text. write for info. (*0-415-18348-0*) Routledge.

Lyotropic Liquid Crystals & the Structure of Biomembranes: A Symposium Based on the Fifth International Liquid Crystal Conference: Proceedings Held in Stockholm, Sweden, June 17-21, 1974. Ed. by Stig Friberg. LC 76-18704. (Advances in Chemistry Ser.: No. 152). (Illus.). 167p. 1976. reprint ed. pap. 51.80 (*0-608-06748-2*, 206694500009) Bks Demand.

Lyotropic State of Matter: Molecular Physics & Living Matter Physics. Alexander G. Petrov. 572p. 1999. text 140.00 (*90-5699-638-X*, ECU124, Harwood Acad Pubs) Gordon & Breach.

Lyra Celtica. Sharp & Matlay Staff & J. Matlay. LC 70-129343. (English Literature Ser.: No. 33). 496p. 1970. reprint ed. lib. bdg. 75.00 (*0-8383-1157-1*) M S G Haskell Hse.

Lyra Germanica. Catherine Winkworth. 1976. 250.00 (*0-87968-366-X*) Gordon Pr.

Lyra Heroica. Ed. by William E. Henley. LC 73-128154. (Granger Index Reprint Ser.). 1977. 20.95 (*0-8369-6181-1*) Ayer.

Lyra Historica: Poems of British History, A. D. 61-1910. Ed. by M. E. Windsor & J. Turral. LC 76-160913. (Granger Index Reprint Ser.). 1977. reprint ed. 20.95 (*0-8369-6278-8*) Ayer.

Lyra Historica: Poems of British History, A. D. 61-1910, 3 vols. in 1. Ed. by M. E. Windsor & J. Turral. LC 79-50854. (Granger Poetry Library). 1979. reprint ed. 25.00 (*0-89609-174-0*) Roth Pub Inc.

Lyra System of Relaxation No. 1: Star Songs, Star Path, Star Dance, Star Thoughts. Leigh Melander. Ed. by Rita Ferrandino. 1998. 39.95 (*1-58425-004-6*) Lyra Enterprises.

***Lyran Alliance.** Ed. by FASA Corp, Staff. (Battletech Field Manual Ser.). (Illus.). 2000. pap. 22.00 (*1-55560-396-3*) FASA Corp.

Lyre & the Flute: Garcilaso & the Pastoral. Dario Morera. (Monografias A Ser.: Vol. LXXXI). 128p. (C). 1982. 51.00 (*0-7293-0114-1*, Pub. by Tamesis Bks Ltd) Boydell & Brewer.

Lyre in the Pawn Shop: Essays on Literature & Survival, 1974-1984. Fay Zwicky. 297p. pap. 2.95 (*0-85564-267-X*, Pub. by Univ of West Aust Pr) Intl Spec Bk.

Lyre of Orpheus. Robertson Davies. 480p. 1990. pap. 13.95 (*0-14-011433-5*, Penguin Bks) Viking Penguin.

Lyrebird. (Picture Roo Bks.). (Illus.). 32p. (J). pap. 6.95 (*0-86417-615-5*, Pub. by Kangaroo Pr) Seven Hills Bk.

Lyrebird: A Natural History. Pauline Reilly. (Illus.). 102p. 1988. pap. 24.95 (*0-86840-083-1*, Pub. by New South Wales Univ Pr) Intl Spec Bk.

Lyrebird Rising: Louise Hanson-Dyer of l'Oiseau-Lyre, 1884-1962. Jim Davidson. (Illus.). 578p. 1994. 35.00 (*0-931340-72-1*, Amadeus Pr) Timber.

Lyrebird That Is Too Busy to Dance. Pauline Reilly. (Picture Roo Bks.). (Illus.). 32p. (Orig.). (J). 1993. pap. 6.95 (*0-86417-086-6*, Pub. by Kangaroo Pr) Seven Hills Bk.

Lyres. Francis Ponge. (FRE.). 1980. pap. 11.95 (*0-7859-2781-6*) Fr & Eur.

Lyres. Francis Ponge. (Poesie Ser.). (FRE.). 176p. 1980. pap. 9.95 (*2-07-032188-6*) Schoenhof.

Lyric: Poems along a Broken Road. G. Winston James. LC 98-89075. 96p. 1999. pap. 12.00 (*0-9655117-1-5*, LYR001) GrapeVinePress.

Lyric & Dramatic Tenor see Singer's Repertoire

***Lyric & Fate of Senses.** Susan Stewart. 1999. pap. text 16.00 (*0-226-77414-7*); lib. bdg. 45.00 (*0-226-77413-9*) U Ch Pr.

Lyric & Labour in the Romantic Tradition. Anne Janowitz. LC 97-40831. (Cambridge Studies in Romanticism: No. 30). (Illus.). 282p. (C). 1998. 59.95 (*0-521-57259-2*) Cambridge U Pr.

Lyric & Modern Poetry: Olson, Creeley, Bunting. Brian Conniff. (American University Studies: English Language & Literature: Ser. IV, Vol. 60). 218p. (C). 1988. text 39.90 (*0-8204-0533-7*) P Lang Pubng.

Lyric & Polemic: The Literary Personality of Roy Campbell. Rowland Smith. LC 72-82245. 261p. reprint ed. pap. 81.00 (*0-608-12276-9*, 202384300034) Bks Demand.

Lyric Art of Pierre Perrin Vol. 60/3B, Pt. 1: Birth of French Opera. L. Auld. (Wissenschaftliche Abhandlungen - Musicological Studies). 1996. 75.00 (*0-931902-28-2*) Inst Mediaeval Mus.

Lyric Art of Pierre Perrin Vol. 62, Pt.4: Recueil de Paroles. L. Auld. (Wissenschaftliche Abhandlungen - Musicological Studies). 1996. 75.00 (*0-931902-34-7*) Inst Mediaeval Mus.

Lyric Concerto: For Flute & Orchestra Piano Reduction. 56p. 1995. pap. 20.00 (*0-7935-4577-3*, 00841006) H Leonard.

Lyric Contingencies: Emily Dickinson & Wallace Stevens. Margaret Dickie. LC 90-48495. 192p. (C). 1991. text 28.50 (*0-8122-3077-9*) U of Pa Pr.

Lyric Descent in the German Romantic Tradition. Brigitte Peucker. LC 86-23393. 242p. reprint ed. pap. 75.10 (*0-7837-4542-7*, 208031700005) Bks Demand.

Lyric Impulse. Cecil Day Lewis. LC 65-16682. (Charles Eliot Norton Lectures, 1964-1965). 174p. reprint ed. pap. 54.00 (*0-7837-4103-0*, 205792600011) Bks Demand.

***Lyric Incarnate: The Dramas of Aleksandr Blok.** Timothy C. Westphalen. (Illus.). 212p. 1998. text 46.00 (*90-5755-020-2*, Harwood Acad Pubs); pap. text 24.00 (*90-5755-021-0*, Harwood Acad Pubs) Gordon & Breach.

Lyric Journey: Poetic Painting in China & Japan. James Cahill. LC 95-23906. (Edwin O. Reischauer Lectures). (Illus.). 296p. 1996. 45.00 (*0-674-53970-2*) HUP.

Lyric Language: French, Series 1. unabridged ed. Illus. by Bil Keane. LC 94-745817. (FRE & ENG.). (J). (ps-8). 1991. pap. 9.95 incl. audio (*1-56015-225-7*) Penton Overseas.

Lyric Language: French, Series 2. unabridged ed. Illus. by Bil Keane. (FRE & ENG.). (J). (ps-8). 1992. pap. 9.95 incl. audio (*1-56015-238-9*) Penton Overseas.

Lyric Language: French, Spanish, German, Italian, Series 1. 1994. teacher ed., per. 9.95 (*1-56015-318-0*) Penton Overseas.

Lyric Language: French, Spanish, German, Italian, Series 2. 1994. teacher ed., per. 9.95 (*1-56015-319-9*) Penton Overseas.

Lyric Language: German, Series 1. unabridged ed. Illus. by Bil Keane. (GER & ENG.). (J). (ps-8). 1991. pap. 9.95 incl. audio (*1-56015-227-3*) Penton Overseas.

Lyric Language: German, Series 2. unabridged ed. Illus. by Bil Keane. (ENG & GER.). (J). (ps-8). 1997. pap. 9.95 incl. audio (*1-56015-240-0*) Penton Overseas.

Lyric Language: Italian, Series 1. unabridged ed. Illus. by Bil Keane. (ITA & ENG.). (J). (ps-8). 1991. pap. 9.95 incl. audio (*1-56015-228-1*) Penton Overseas.

Lyric Language: Italian, Series 2. unabridged ed. Illus. by Bil Keane. (ITA & ENG.). (J). (ps-8). 1992. pap. 9.95 incl. audio (*1-56015-241-9*) Penton Overseas.

Lyric Language: Japanese, Series 1. unabridged ed. Illus. by Bil Keane. (ENG & JPN.). (J). (ps up). 1995. pap. 9.95 incl. audio (*1-56015-230-3*) Penton Overseas.

Lyric Language: Spanish, Series 1. unabridged ed. Illus. by Bil Keane. (SPA & ENG.). (J). (ps-8). 1991. pap. 9.95 incl. audio (*1-56015-226-5*) Penton Overseas.

Lyric Language: Spanish, Series 2. unabridged ed. Illus. by Bil Keane. (SPA & ENG.). (J). (ps-8). 1992. pap. 9.95 incl. audio (*1-56015-239-7*) Penton Overseas.

Lyric Language: Swedish, Series 1. unabridged ed. Illus. by Bil Keane. (SWE & ENG.). (J). (ps up). 1992. pap. 9.95 incl. audio (*1-56015-229-X*) Penton Overseas.

Lyric Language Spanish/English. (ENG & SPA.). 1992. pap. 14.95 (*1-56015-276-1*) Penton Overseas.

Lyric Lyric. Kelvin Corcoran. 1993. pap. 9.00 (*1-874400-00-8*, Pub. by Reality St Edits) SPD-Small Pr Dist.

Lyric Modes. Shirley Warren. 8p. (Orig.). 1990. pap. 3.00 (*1-877801-11-9*) Still Waters.

Lyric Moments, Bk. 1. Catherine Rollin. 24p. 1995. pap. 5.95 (*0-7390-0367-4*, 14663) Alfred Pub.

Lyric of the Circle Heart: The Bowman Family Trilogy. rev. ed. William Eastlake. LC 96-7666. 518p. 1996. pap. 14.95 (*1-56478-136-4*) Dalkey Arch.

Lyric Philosophy. Jan Zwicky. (Studies in Philosophy). 608p. 1992. text 65.00 (*0-8020-5014-X*); pap. text 25.00 (*0-8020-6943-6*) U of Toronto Pr.

Lyric Pieces for the Young: For Piano. N. Dello Joio. 16p. 1984. pap. 3.95 (*0-7935-2053-3*, 00009283) H Leonard.

Lyric Pieces Opus 68/71: Piano. Edvard Grieg. 44p. 1986. pap. 4.95 (*0-7935-4520-X*, 50263180) H Leonard.

Lyric Pieces Opus 62/65: Piano. E. Grieg. 60p. 1986. pap. 4.95 (*0-7935-4478-5*, 50263170) H Leonard.

Lyric Pioneers of Modern Germany. Solomon Liptzin. LC 28-5277. reprint ed. 27.50 (*0-404-03995-2*) AMS Pr.

Lyric Poems. John Keats. LC 91-9655. (Thrift Editions Ser.). viii, 80p. 1991. reprint ed. pap. 1.00 (*0-486-26871-3*) Dover.

Lyric Poems & Ballads. Heinrich Heine. Tr. by Ernst Feise. LC 61-9402. 221p. 1961. reprint ed. pap. 68.60 (*0-608-00907-5*, 206170100010) Bks Demand.

Lyric Poetry. Ernest Rhys. LC 70-174315. (Channels of English Literature Ser.: No. 6). reprint ed. 43.50 (*0-404-07816-8*) AMS Pr.

Lyric Poetry & the Drama of Position: Catullan Provocations. William Fitzgerald. LC 94-40303. (Classics & Contemporary Thought Ser.: Vol. 1). 340p. 1996. 52.50 (*0-520-20062-4*, Pub. by U CA Pr) Cal Prin Full Svc.

Lyric Poetry of the Italian Renaissance: An Anthology with Verse Translations. A. R. Lind. 1954. 59.50 (*0-685-26673-7*) Elliots Bks.

Lyric Preludes. William L. Gillock. 32p. (gr. 4-12). 1958. pap. text 5.95 (*0-87487-649-4*) Summy-Birchard.

Lyric Provinces in the English Renaissance. Harold E. Toliver. LC 85-10569. 259p. reprint ed. pap. 80.30 (*0-608-09890-6*, 206985600006) Bks Demand.

Lyric Quotation in Plato. Marian Demos. LC 98-36861. (Greek Studies: Vol. 38). 112p. 1999. 53.00 (*0-8476-8908-5*); pap. 21.95 (*0-8476-8909-3*) Rowman.

Lyric Singer: A Biography of Ella Higginson. Koert. (Special Papers: Vol. 3). 1986. pap. 9.95 (*0-318-23342-8*) WWU CPNS.

Lyric Soprano Arias: Master Class, Vol. 1. 1991. pap. 15.95 incl. audio (*0-7935-0434-1*) H Leonard.

Lyric Soprano Arias: Master Class, Vol. 2. 1991. pap. 15.95 (*0-7935-0433-3*) H Leonard.

Lyric Speakers of Old English Poetry. Lois Bragg. LC 89-46414. 1991. 32.50 (*0-8386-3403-6*) Fairleigh Dickinson.

Lyric Time: Dickinson & the Limits of Genre. Sharon Cameron. LC 78-9983. 292p. reprint ed. pap. 90.60 (*0-608-06275-8*, 206660400008) Bks Demand.

Lyric Voices: Approaches to the Poetry of Contemporary Song. Barbara F. Graves & Donald J. McBain. LC 77-165947. 222p. reprint ed. pap. 68.90 (*0-608-13616-6*, 205512900008) Bks Demand.

Lyric Wonder: Rhetoric & Wit in Renaissance English Poetry. James Biester. LC 96-35473. (Rhetoric & Society Ser.). 232p. 1996. text 39.95 (*0-8014-3313-4*) Cornell U Pr.

Lyric Year: One Hundred Poems. Ed. by Ferdinand Earle. LC 70-168781. (Granger Index Reprint Ser.). 1977. reprint ed. 23.95 (*0-8369-6301-6*) Ayer.

Lyrica Graece Selecta. Ed. by Denys L. Page. (Oxford Classical Texts Ser.). 276p. 1968. text 24.95 (*0-19-814567-5*) OUP.

Lyrical-Analysis: The Unconscious Through Jane Eyre. Angelyn Spignesi. 368p. (Orig.). 1990. pap. 3.95 (*0-933029-54-3*) Chiron Pubns.

Lyrical & Critical Essays. Albert Camus. LC 67-18621. 384p. 1970. pap. 12.00 (*0-394-70852-0*, V626) Vin Bks.

***Lyrical Aviators: Traveling America's Airways in a Small Place.** Sandra McClinton. LC 97-62092. (Illus.). 232p. 2000. 29.95 (*0-9659300-0-9*, Pub. by Whistling Swan) ACCESS Pubs Network.

Lyrical Ballads. R. L. Brett. 1987. pap. 12.00 (*0-416-29720-X*) Routledge.

Lyrical Ballads. Michael Mason. (Annotated Texts Ser.). 336p. (C). 1992. text 58.50 (*0-582-03302-0*) Longman.

Lyrical Ballads. William Wordsworth. Ed. by Michael Mason. (Annotated Texts Ser.). 336p. (C). 1992. pap. text 28.50 (*0-582-03303-9*) Longman.

Lyrical Ballads. William Wordsworth. LC 97-9672. (Revolution & Romanticism, 1789-1834 Ser.). 504p. 1997. 85.00 (*1-85477-200-7*) Continuum.

Lyrical Ballads. William Wordsworth & Samuel Taylor Coleridge. 236p. 1993. reprint ed. pap. 17.95 (*1-85477-124-8*) Continuum.

Lyrical Ballads: William Wordsworth & S. T. Coleridge. 2nd ed. William Wordsworth & Samuel Taylor Coleridge. Ed. by R. L. Brett & A. R. Jones. 340p. (C). 1991. pap. 18.99 (*0-415-06388-4*, A6612) Routledge.

Lyrical Ballads: Wordsworth & Coleridge, 1798-1805. 2nd ed. Ed. by R. L. Brett & A. R. Jones. 1968. pap. 14.95 (*0-415-02790-X*, NO. 2112) Routledge.

Lyrical Ballads & Other Poems, 1797-1800. William Wordsworth. Ed. by James Butler & Karen Green. LC 92-20343. (Cornell Wordsworth Ser.). (Illus.). 872p. 1993. text 105.00 (*0-8014-2572-7*) Cornell U Pr.

Lyrical Ballads, 1798. 2nd ed. William Wordsworth & Samuel Taylor Coleridge. Ed. by W. J. Owen. 220p. 1970. text 15.95 (*0-19-911006-9*) OUP.

Lyrical Bridge: Essays from Holderlin to Benn. Philip Grundlehner. LC 76-46765. (Illus.). 177p. 1978. 28.50 (*0-8386-1792-1*) Fairleigh Dickinson.

Lyrical Drama, 2 vols. Henry S. Edwards. LC 80-2274. reprint ed. 67.50 (*0-404-18840-0*) AMS Pr.

Lyrical Existentialists. Thomas Hanna. 299p. 1985. reprint ed. pap. 9.95 (*0-918236-02-9*) Freeperson.

Lyrical Heritage. Ed. by Melissa Mitchell. 1996. 69.95 (*1-57553-157-7*) Watermrk Pr.

Lyrical Ireland. Tom Kelly & Peter Somerville-Large. (Illus.). 156p. 1999. 35.00 (*1-57098-295-3*, Pub. by Roberts Rinehart) Publishers Group.

Lyrical Life Science. Douglas C. Eldon. (Orig.). (J). (gr. 3-10). 1995. audio 9.95 (*0-9646367-1-9*) Lyrical Lrng.

Lyrical Life Science. Douglas C. Eldon. LC 96-209814. (Illus.). 94p. (Orig.). (J). (gr. 3-10). 1995. pap. 19.95 incl. audio (*0-9646367-0-0*) Lyrical Lrng.

Lyrical Life Science: The Human Body, Vol. 3. Dorry Eldon. (Illus.). 94p. (YA). (gr. 4-9). 1998. pap. 19.95 incl. audio (*0-9646367-4-3*) Lyrical Lrng.

Lyrical Life Science, Vol. 2: Mammals, Ecology & Biomes, Vol. 2. Dorry Eldon et al. (Illus.). 114p. (J). (gr. 3-10). 1996. pap. 19.95 incl. audio (*0-9646367-2-7*) Lyrical Lrng.

Lyrical Life Science, Vol. 2: Mammals, Ecology & Biomes, Vol. 2. Douglas C. Eldon et al. (J). (gr. 3-10). 1996. pap. 9.95 incl. audio (*0-9646367-3-5*) Lyrical Lrng.

Lyrical Lu Xun: A Study of His Classical-Style Verse. Jon Kowallis. LC 95-17223. 392p. (C). 1996. text 37.50 (*0-8248-1511-4*) UH Pr.

Lyrical Pieces. Composed by Edvard Grieg. 224p. pap. 7.95 (*963-8303-05-0*) Konemann.

Lyrical Poetry from Blake to Hardy. Herbert J. Grierson. (BCL1-PR English Literature Ser.). 158p. 1992. reprint ed. lib. bdg. 69.00 (*0-7812-7070-7*) Rprt Serv.

Lyrical Poetry from Blake to Hardy. Herbert J. Grierson. LC 74-158903. 1971. reprint ed. 49.00 (*0-403-01309-7*) Scholarly.

Lyrical Poetry of the Nineteenth Century. Solomon F. Gingerich. (BCL1-PR English Literature Ser.). 159p. 1992. reprint ed. lib. bdg. 59.00 (*0-7812-7071-5*) Rprt Serv.

Lyrical Poetry of the Nineteenth Century. Herbert J. Grierson. LC 70-124768. reprint ed. 20.00 (*0-404-02915-9*) AMS Pr.

Lyrical Poetry of Thomas Hardy. Cecil M. Bowra. LC 75-22227. (Studies in Thomas Hardy: No. 14). 1975. lib. bdg. 75.00 (*0-8383-2098-8*) M S G Haskell Hse.

Lyrical Protest: Black Music's Struggle Against Discrimination. Mary Ellison. LC 89-3881. (Media & Society Ser.). 168p. 1989. 57.95 (*0-275-92757-1*, C2757, Praeger Pubs) Greenwood.

***Lyrical Romantic.** Samuel Taylor Coleridge. (Illus.). 1999. 19.95 (*1-86019-313-7*) Chelsea Hse.

Lyrical Symbols & Narrative Transformations: Essays in Honor of Ralph Freedman. Ed. by Kathleen L. Komar & Ross Shideler. LC 97-25500. (COMPLIT Ser.). 258p. 1998. 65.00 (*1-57113-120-5*) Camden Hse.

Lyrical Translation of Lao Tzu's Tao-Te Ching in English & Korean. Lao-tzu. LC 90-91956. (Illus.). 300p. (Orig.). 1986. pap. 20.00 (*0-942049-03-9*) One Mind Pr.

Lyricality in English Literature. Daniel Albright. LC 84-10455. 286p. 1985. reprint ed. pap. 88.70 (*0-608-02665-4*, 206331800004) Bks Demand.

***Lyrically Speaking.** (Illus.). 81p. 1998. pap. write for info. (*0-9673648-0-9*) Daniel Connell.

Lyricism & the Electric: Poems. Michael J. Laurence. (Illus.). 70p. (Orig.). 1996. pap. write for info. (*0-9649233-0-0*) Space Los Angeles.

Lyrico: The Only Horse of His Kind. 2nd ed. Elizabeth V. Foster. (Illus.). 247p. (J). (gr. 6-8). 1991. reprint ed. pap. 10.95 (*0-930407-21-0*) Parabola Bks.

Lyrics & Laments: Selected Translations from Hebrew & Yiddish. Tr. by Howard Schwartz. LC 79-54403. 1980. pap. 3.95 (*0-933532-03-2*) BkMk.

Lyrics by Oscar Hammerstein II. rev. ed. Lyrics by Oscar Hammerstein, II. 292p. 1985. per. 19.95 (*0-88188-379-4*, 00183452) H Leonard.

Lyrics for Re-Creation: Language for the Music of the Universe. James A. Conlon. 124p. 1996. pap. 14.95 (*0-8264-0921-0*) Continuum.

Lyrics for the Bride of God. Nathaniel Tarn. LC 74-23354. 160p. 1975. 7.95 (*0-8112-0565-7*, Pub. by New Directions); pap. 3.75 (*0-8112-0566-5*, NDP391, Pub. by New Directions) Norton.

Lyrics for the Centuries Cycle B: Sermons for the Sundays after Pentecost (First Third): First Lesson Texts. Arthur H. Kolsti. LC 96-10702. (Orig.). 1996. pap. 7.50 (*0-7880-0777-7*) CSS OH.

Lyrics from Arabia. 2nd ed. Ed. & Tr. by Ghazi A. Algosaibi from ARA. Tr. by Qazi Saleem from ARA. LC 84-51201. (ARA, ENG & URD., Illus.). 108p. 1983. reprint ed. pap. 8.95 (*0-89410-447-0*, Three Contnts) L Rienner.

Lyrics from English Airs, 1596-1622. Edward Doughtie. LC 78-115474. 679p. reprint ed. pap. 200.00 (*0-7837-6082-5*, 205912800007) Bks Demand.

Lyrics from Old Song Books. Ed. by Edmondstoune Duncan. LC 77-168780. (Granger Index Reprint Ser.). 1977. reprint ed. 30.95 (*0-8369-6300-8*) Ayer.

Lyrics from the Chinese. Helen Wadell. LC 74-75811. pap. 6.00 (*0-87957-003-2*) Brookville Bks.

Lyrics from the Dramatists of the Elizabethan Age see Collections of Lyrics & Poems: Sixteenth & Seventeenth Centuries

Lyrics from the Dramatists of the Elizabethan Age. Ed. by Arthur H. Bullen. LC 72-38342. (Select Bibliographies Reprint Ser.). 1977. reprint ed. 23.95 (*0-8369-6759-3*) Ayer.

Lyrics from the Song-Books of the Elizabethan Age see Collections of Lyrics & Poems: Sixteenth & Seventeenth Centuries

Lyrics, 1962-1985. 2nd ed. Bob Dylan. 500p. 1985. 35.00 (*0-394-54278-9*) Knopf.

Lyrics, 1962-1998. rev. ed. Bob Dylan. LC 97-17101. 1999. 35.00 (*0-679-43913-7*) Villard Books.

Lyrics of a Lowly Life. Paul Laurence Dunbar. LC 70-78996. (American Negro: His History & Literature. Series 2). (C). 1975. reprint ed. 36.95 (*0-405-01858-4*) Ayer.

Lyrics of a Lowly Life. Paul Laurence Dunbar. LC 70-78996. (American Negro: His History & Literature. Series 2). (C). 1991. reprint ed. pap. 27.95 (*0-88143-129-X*) Ayer.
***Lyrics of an Angel: Poetry in Reality.** Amani Abdul. 110p. 1999. pap. 12.95 (*1-929985-00-2*) Angel Hrt Pub.
Lyrics of Basotho Migrants. Ed. & Tr. by David B. Coplan. Tr. by Seakhi Santho. 1995. write for info. (*0-942615-27-1*) U Wis African Stud.
Lyrics of Blessings: Love Praises, Vol. I. Margaret A. Barnes. 50p. Date not set. pap. write for info. (*1-891597-57-4*, SDC Pr) Mleecole.
Lyrics of Blessings: Love Praises, Vol. II. Margaret A. Barnes. 50p. Date not set. pap. write for info. (*1-891597-58-2*, SDC Pr) Mleecole.
***Lyrics of Civility: Biblical Images & Popular Music Lyrics in American Culture.** Kenneth G. Bielen. LC 99-33782. 1999. write for info. (*0-8153-3193-2*) Garland.
Lyrics of Life. Barbara Scarantino. 92p. 1996. pap. 11.95 (*0-943172-96-9*) New Wave.
Lyrics of Life & Love. William S. Braithwaite. LC 70-88540. (Black Heritage Library Collection). 1988. 12.95 (*0-88143-081-1*) Ayer.
Lyrics of Love. Francine Craft. 320p. 1998. pap. 4.99 (*0-7860-0531-9*) Kensgtn Pub Corp.
Lyrics of Love. John D. Schuetze. 48p. 1996. pap. 37.99 (*0-8100-0588-3*, 22N0865) Northwest Pub.
Lyrics of Love Vol. 1: Songs & Poems. Jacques Melek. 120p. 1981. write for info. (*0-318-56567-6*, Sunrise Pubns); pap. 6.00 (*0-686-96966-9*, Sunrise Pubns) J Melek.
Lyrics of Love & Laughter. Paul Laurence Dunbar. 1993. reprint ed. lib. bdg. 89.00 (*0-7812-5359-4*) Rprt Serv.
Lyrics of Lowly Life. Paul Laurence Dunbar. 224p. 1984. pap. 9.95 (*0-8065-0922-8*, Citadel Pr) Carol Pub Group.
Lyrics of Lowly Life. Paul Laurence Dunbar. (Notable American Authors Ser.). 1992. reprint ed. lib. bdg. 75.00 (*0-7812-2709-7*) Rprt Serv.
Lyrics of Loyalty. Frank Moore. (Notable American Authors Ser.). 1999. reprint ed. lib. bdg. 125.00 (*0-7812-4579-6*) Rprt Serv.
Lyrics of Noel Coward. Noel Coward. 1978. pap. 6.95 (*0-670-44470-7*, Viking) Viking Penguin.
Lyrics of Noel Coward. Noel Coward. LC 73-77884. 432p. 1973. reprint ed. 25.00 (*0-87951-197-4*, Pub. by Overlook Pr) Penguin Putnam.
Lyrics of Noel Coward. Noel Coward. LC 73-77884. 432p. 1983. reprint ed. pap. 12.95 (*0-87951-187-7*, Pub. by Overlook Pr) Penguin Putnam.
Lyrics of Prince: A Literary Look at a Musical Poet, Philosopher & Storyteller. C. Liegh McInnis. LC 96-92619. (Illus.). ix, 112p. (Orig.). 1997. per. 15.00 (*0-9655775-0-3*) Psychedelic Lit.
Lyrics of Richard de Semilli: A Critical Edition & Musical Transcription. Ed. by Susan M. Johnson. (Medieval & Renaissance Texts & Studies: Vol. 81). 112p. 1992. 20.00 (*0-86698-092-X*, MR81) MRTS.
Lyrics of Sunshine & Shadow. Paul Laurence Dunbar. LC 70-83919. (Black Heritage Library Collection). 1977. 35.95 (*0-8369-8561-3*) Ayer.
Lyrics of Sunshine & Shadow. Paul Laurence Dunbar. LC 77-164801. reprint ed. 19.50 (*0-404-00038-X*) AMS Pr.
Lyrics of Sunshine & Shadow. Paul Laurence Dunbar. (Illus.). 1991. reprint ed. pap. 22.95 (*0-88143-125-7*) Ayer.
Lyrics of the Afro-American Spiritual: A Documentary Collection. Erskine Peters. LC 92-27574. (Encyclopedia of Black Music Ser.). 480p. 1993. lib. bdg. 75.00 (*0-313-26238-1*, PLY/, Greenwood Pr) Greenwood.
Lyrics of the Hearthside. Paul Laurence Dunbar. LC 70-164802. reprint ed. 19.50 (*0-404-00037-1*) AMS Pr.
Lyrics of the Hearthside. Paul Laurence Dunbar. LC 74-83920. (Black Heritage Library Collection). (C). 1977. reprint ed. 38.95 (*0-8369-8562-1*) Ayer.
Lyrics of the Hearthside. Paul Laurence Dunbar. LC 74-83920. (Black Heritage Library Collection). (C). 1991. reprint ed. pap. 27.95 (*0-88143-135-4*) Ayer.
Lyrics of the Letter H. Charles G. Halpine. (Notable American Authors Ser.). 1992. reprint ed. lib. bdg. 75.00 (*0-7812-2995-2*) Rprt Serv.
Lyrics of the Middle Ages: An Anthology. Ed. by James J. Wilhelm. LC 89-25639. (Illus.). 341p. 1990. pap. text 23.95 (*0-8240-7049-6*, 1268) Garland.
Lyrics of the Troubadours & Trouveres: An Anthology & a History. Ed. & Tr. by Frederick Goldin. 1990. 19.75 (*0-8446-5036-6*) Peter Smith.
Lyrics of the Trouveres: A Research Guide, 1970-1990. Ed. by Eglal Doss-Quinby. LC 93-38222. (Medieval Bibliographies Ser.: Vol. 17). 280p. 1994. text 20.00 (*0-8153-0085-9*, H1423) Garland.
Lyrics of Thomas Hardy: Pearls of Pity. Brian Green. LC 96-34812. 256p. 1996. text 49.95 (*0-312-15965-X*) St Martin.
Lyrics on Several Occasions. Ira Gershwin. 424p. 1997. reprint ed. 35.00 (*0-87910-050-8*); reprint ed. pap. 20.00 (*0-87910-094-X*) Limelight Edns.
Lyric's World. Nancy A. Richardson. (Star Wars: No. 2). (J). (gr. 4-7). 1998. pap. text 4.50 (*0-425-16762-3*) Berkley Pub.
Lyric's World. Nancy A. Richardson. (Star Wars: No. 2). 128p. (J). (gr. 3-5). 1996. mass mkt. 4.50 (*1-57297-068-5*) Blvd Books.
Lyrik - Twenty-Five Jahre, 2 pts., Pt. 1: Einzeltitel. Hans-Jurgen Schlutter. (Bibliographien Zur Deutschen Literature Ser.: Vol. 1). 1983. write for info. (*3-487-05453-1*) G Olms Pubs.
Lyrik - Twenty-Five Jahre, Pt. 2. Hans-Jurgen Schlutter. (Bibliographien Zur Deutschen Literature Ser.: Vol. 1). 514p. 1983. write for info. (*3-487-05454-X*) G Olms Pubs.
***Lyrik Chinesischer Dichterinnen: Von Den Anfangen (11. JH. V. CHR.) Bis Zum 10. JH. N. CHR.** Susanne Becker. (Frankfurter China-Studien. BD. 5 Ser.). 307p. 1999. 52.95 (*3-631-34861-4*) P Lang Pubng.
Lyrik Philipp von Zesens: Praxis und Theorie. Josef Keller. (European University Studies: German Language & Literature: Ser. 1, Vol. 606). (GER.). 246p. 1983. 40.00 (*3-261-03237-5*) P Lang Pubng.
***Lyrik Von Octavio Paz: Hauptthemen und Deren Synasthetische Vermittlung (Con un Resumen en Espanol)** Gabriele Wawerla. 192p. 1999. 37.95 (*3-631-34431-7*) P Lang Pubng.
Lyris: Poems & Selections by Lyris Hyatt. Lyris Hyatt. Ed. & Intro. by Vera P. Glenn. (Illus.). 50p. (Orig.). 1988. pap. 12.00 (*0-910557-21-7*) Acad New Church.
***Lyrische Kunst des Publius Papinius Statius in Silve II.** Andreas Kruger. (Europaische Hochschulschriften Ser.). 263p. 1999. 45.95 (*3-631-33077-4*) P Lang Pubng.
Lyron's Lament Bk. 1: Sanctum Trilogy. James Reasoner & Livia Reasoner. (Margaret Weis Presents Crusade Ser.). 224p. 1995. pap. 9.95 (*0-9647973-0-5*) Westvenge.
Lys dans la Vallee. Honore de Balzac. (Coll. Prestige). 49.95 (*0-685-34088-0*) Fr & Eur.
Lys dans la Vallee. Honore de Balzac. (FRE.). 1972. pap. 12.95 (*0-7859-1698-9*, 2070361128) Fr & Eur.
Lys dans la Vallee. Honore de Balzac. (Folio Ser.: No. 112). (FRE.). 1965. pap. 9.95 (*2-07-036112-8*) Schoenhof.
Lys dans la Vallee. unabridged ed. Honore de Balzac. (FRE.). pap. 7.95 (*2-87714-170-5*, Pub. by Bookking Intl) Distribks Inc.
Lys Rouge. Anatole France, pseud. (FRE.). 378p. 1964. 10.95 (*0-8288-9759-X*, F101271) Fr & Eur.
Lysander Spooner Reader. Intro. by George H. Smith. xxii, 343p. 1992. 24.95 (*0-930073-06-1*) Fox & Wilkes.
Lysander Spooner Reader. Ed. by George H. Smith. 343p. 1998. pap. 14.95 (*0-930073-26-6*) Fox & Wilkes.
Lysander's Lady. large type ed. Elizabeth Hawksley. 1995. 27.99 (*0-7089-3415-3*) Ulverscroft.
***Lysbeth: A Tale of the Dutch.** H. Rider Haggard. 252p. 2000. pap. 9.95 (*0-594-00765-8*) Eightn Hundrd.
Lysenko Affair. David Joravsky. LC 86-11303. xii, 472p. (C). 1986. pap. text 19.50 (*0-226-41031-5*) U Ch Pr.
Lysenko & the Tragedy of Soviet Science. Valery N. Soyfer. Tr. by Leo Gruliow & Rebecca Gruliow. (Illus.). 400p. (C). 1994. text 39.95 (*0-8135-2087-8*) Rutgers U Pr.
Lysenkoism in China: Proceeding of the 1956 Qingdao Gentics Conference. Ed. by Laurence Schneider. 120p. (gr. 13). 1986. pap. text 34.95 (*0-87332-410-2*) M E Sharpe.
Lysia Epitaphios, Pts. I & II. Lysias. Ed. by W. R. Connor. LC 78-18608. (Greek Texts & Commentaries Ser.). 1979. reprint ed. lib. bdg. 21.95 (*0-405-11448-6*) Ayer.
Lysianassoid Amphipoda (Crustacea) from Deepsea Thermal Vents. Jerry L. Barnard & Camilla Ingram. LC 90-9991. (Smithsonian Contributions to Zoology Ser.: No. 499). 84p. reprint ed. pap. 30.00 (*0-8357-2750-5*, 203986400013) Bks Demand.
***Lysias.** Lysias. LC 99-6344. 462p. 2000. 24.95 (*0-292-78166-0*); 55.00 (*0-292-78165-2*) U of Tex Pr.
Lysias. Tr. by W. R. Lamb. LC 76-29460. reprint ed. 45.00 (*0-404-15315-1*) AMS Pr.
Lysias: Five Speeches, Nos. 10, 12, 14, 19 & 22. E. S. Shuckburgh. (Bristol Greek Texts Ser.). (GRE.). 204p. 1979. reprint ed. 25.95 (*0-906515-44-0*, Pub. by Brist Class Pr) Focus Pub-R Pullins.
***Lysias: Five Speeches: 10, 12, 14, 19, 22.** M. Edwards. (GRE.). 198p. (C). 1999. pap. text 22.95 (*1-85399-447-2*, Pub. by Brist Class Pr) Focus Pub-R Pullins.
Lysias: Selected Speeches. Ed. by Charles D. Adams. LC 79-123339. (Oklahoma Series in Classical Culture: Vol. 3). 408p. 1989. reprint ed. pap. 19.95 (*0-8061-1396-0*) U of Okla Pr.
Lysias & the Corpus Lysiacum. Kenneth J. Dover. LC 68-63337. (Sather Classical Lectures: No. 39). 1968. 60.00 (*0-520-00351-9*, Pub. by U CA Pr) Cal Prin Full Svc.
Lysias Orations, One, Three. Ruth Scodel. (Greek Commentaries Ser.). 55p. (Orig.). (C). 1986. pap. text 6.00 (*0-929524-19-5*) Bryn Mawr Commentaries.
Lysimeter Concept: Environmental Behavior of Pesticides. Ed. by F. Fuhr et al. LC 98-16897. (Illus.). 304p. 1998. text 110.00 (*0-8412-3568-6*) OUP.
Lysimeters for Evapotranspiration & Environmental Measurements. Ed. by Richard G. Allen et al. LC 91-21900. 456p. 1991. pap. text 41.00 (*0-87262-813-2*) Am Soc Civil Eng.
Lysine & Its Uses. 1996. lib. bdg. 250.75 (*0-8490-5879-1*) Gordon Pr.
Lysine, Tryptophan & Other Amino Acids. Robert Garrison, Jr. Ed. by Richard A. Passwater & Earl R. Mindell. (Good Health Guide Ser.). 32p. (Orig.). 1982. pap. 2.95 (*0-87983-268-1*, 32681K, Keats Pubing) NTC Contemp Pub Co.
Lysis: A Proteolysis Database for the PC. B. Keil & N. T. Tong. 146p. 1992. 559.95 incl. 3.5 hd, 5.25 hd (*0-387-14123-5*) Spr-Verlag.
Lysis, Symposium, Gorgias, Vol. III. Tr. by W. R. Lamb. (Loeb Classical Library: No. 166). 558p. 1925. text 18.95 (*0-674-99184-2*) HUP.
Lysistrata see Aristophanes: Four Comedies
Lysistrata see Ten Greek Plays in Contemporary Translations
Lysistrata. Aristophanes. Tr. by Donald Sutherland. (C). 1997. pap. text 13.40 (*0-8102-0031-7*) Addson-Wesley Educ.
Lysistrata. Aristophanes. Date not set. lib. bdg. 17.95 (*0-8488-1953-5*) Amereon Ltd.
Lysistrata. Aristophanes. Ed. & Tr. by Matt Neuburg. (Crofts Classics). 128p. 1992. pap. text 4.95 (*0-88295-127-0*) Harlan Davidson.
Lysistrata. Aristophanes. Tr. by Nicholas Rudall from GRE. (Plays for Performance Ser.). 65p. 1991. pap. 7.95 (*0-929587-57-X*, Pub. by I R Dee); lib. bdg. 15.95 (*0-929587-61-8*, Pub. by I R Dee) Natl Bk Netwk.
Lysistrata. Aristophanes. Ed. & Tr. by Douglass Parker. 128p. 1970. mass mkt. 5.99 (*0-451-62495-5*, Ment) NAL.
Lysistrata. Aristophanes. Ed. by William-Alan Landes. Tr. by S. H. Landes. 44p. 1995. pap. 7.00 (*0-88734-345-7*) Players Pr.
Lysistrata. Jeffrey Henderson. 308p. 1990. reprint ed. pap. text 28.00 (*0-19-814496-2*) OUP.
Lysistrata. unabridged ed. Aristophanes. 64p. 1994. pap. text 1.00 (*0-486-28225-2*) Dover.
***Lysistrata: The Sex Strike.** Aristophanes. et al. (Absolute Classics Ser.). 96p. 2000. pap. 16.95 (*0-9536757-0-X*) Theatre Comm.
Lysistrata & Other Plays. Aristophanes. Tr. by Alan H. Sommerstein. (Classics Ser.). 256p. 1973. pap. 12.99 (*0-14-044287-1*, Penguin Classics) Viking Penguin.
Lysistrata, the Birds, the Clouds, & the Frogs Notes. W. John Campbell. (Cliffs Notes Ser.). 80p. (C). 1983. pap. text 4.95 (*0-8220-0776-2*, Cliff) IDG Bks.
Lysistrate. Aristophanes. Ed. by Ulrich Von Wilamowitz-Moellendorff. ii, 223p. 1964. 50.00 (*3-296-10600-6*) G Olms Pubs.
***Lysomal Pathways of Protein Degradation.** J. Fred Dice. LC 99-27040. (Molecular Biology Intelligence Ser.). 2000. write for info. (*1-57059-568-2*) Landes Bioscience.
Lysophosphatidate Signaling: Cellular Effects & Molecular Mechanisms. Marcel E. Durieux. LC 95-4044. (Molecular Biology Intelligence Unit Ser.). 244p. 1995. 89.00 (*1-57059-248-9*) Landes Bioscience.
Lysosomal Cysteine Proteases. 2nd ed. Heidrun Kirschke et al. (Protein Profile Ser.). (Illus.). 144p. 1998. pap. text 45.00 (*0-19-850249-4*) OUP.
***Lysosomal Pathways of Protein Degradation.** J. Fred Dice. (Molecular Biology Intelligence Unit Ser.). 144p. 2000. 99.00 (*1-58706-003-5*, Pub. by Eurekah) Landes Bioscience.
Lysosomes. E. Holtzman. LC 88-32085. (Cellular Organelles Ser.). (Illus.). 456p. (C). 1988. text 44.50 (*0-306-43126-2*, Kluwer Plenum) Kluwer Academic.
Lysosomes. E. Holtzman. LC 88-32085. (Cellular Organelles Ser.). (Illus.). 456p. (C). 1988. 89.00 (*0-306-42966-7*, Plenum Trade) Perseus Pubng.
Lysosomes: A Survey. E. Holtzman. (Cell Biology Monographs: Vol. 3). (Illus.). 300p. 1976. 98.00 (*0-387-81316-0*) Spr-Verlag.
Lysosomes: Their Role in Protein Breakdown. Hans Glaumann & John Ballard. 752p. 1987. text 104.00 (*0-12-286182-5*) Acad Pr.
Lysosomes & Lysosomal Storage Diseases. fac. ed. Ed. by John W. Callahan & J. Alexander Lowden. LC 79-5315. (Advances in Pediatric Research Ser.). (Illus.). 456p. pap. 141.40 (*0-7837-7298-X*, 204700800005) Bks Demand.
Lysozymes: Model Enzymes in Biochemistry & Biology. Ed. by Pierre Jolles. (EXS Ser.: Vol. 75). 1996. 189.95 (*0-8176-5121-7*); 189.95 (*3-7643-5121-7*) Birkhauser.
Lyssa & the Pirates: Blue Moon: A One & a Two. Charlie Wise. (Illus.). 64p. (Orig.). 1995. pap. 4.95 (*1-883847-10-9*) MU Press.
***Lyte Funkie Ones: An Unauthorized Biography.** Leah Furman & Elina Furman. 160p. 2000. mass mkt. 4.99 (*0-312-97536-8*, St Martins Paperbacks) St Martin.
Lytell Treatise for to Lerne Englisshe & Frensshe. LC 73-6167. (English Experience Ser.: No. 630). 27p. 1973. reprint ed. 15.00 (*90-221-0630-6*) Walter J Johnson.
Lytic Compartment of Plant Cells. P. Matile. LC 75-5931. (Cell Biology Monographs: Vol. 1). (Illus.). xiii, 183p. 1975. 87.95 (*0-387-81296-2*) Spr-Verlag.
Lytle-Tate Letters: The Correspondence of Andrew Lytle & Allen Tate. Ed. by Thomas D. Young & Elizabeth Sarcone. LC 87-16014. 1987. text 42.50 (*0-87805-326-3*) U Pr of Miss.
Lytle Treatise Composed by Johan Stadysshe . . . Against the Protestaci. John Standish. LC 79-85138. (English Experience Ser.: No. 955). 100p. 1979. reprint ed. lib. bdg. 15.00 (*90-221-0955-0*) Walter J Johnson.
Lytle Treatise of the Maner & Forme of Confession made by the most excellent & famous clerke M. Eras. of Roterdame. Desiderius Erasmus. LC 79-39487. (English Experience Ser.: No. 553). (Illus.). 232p. 1973. reprint ed. 27.50 (*90-221-0553-9*) Walter J Johnson.
Lyttel Cronycle: Richard Pynson's Translation (c. 1520) of La Fleur des Histoires de la Terre d'Orient (1307) Hetoum. Ed. by Glenn Burger. (Illus.). 286p. (C). 1988. text 50.00 (*0-8020-2626-5*) U of Toronto Pr.
Lyttelton-Hart-Davis Letters, Vol. II, 1956-57. Ed. by Rupert Hart-Davis. 226p. 1985. 20.00 (*0-89733-135-4*) Academy Chi Pubs.
Lyttelton-Hart-Davis Letters, Vol. III, 1958. Ed. by Rupert Hart-Davis. 152p. 1986. 20.00 (*0-89733-151-6*) Academy Chi Pubs.
Lyttelton-Hart-Davis Letters, Vol. IV: 1959. Ed. by Rupert Hart-Davis. 186p. 1987. 20.00 (*0-89733-250-4*) Academy Chi Pubs.
Lyttelton-Hart-Davis Letters, Vols. V & VI, 1960 & 1961-62. Ed. by Rupert Hart-Davis. 152p. 1990. 32.00 (*0-89733-305-5*) Academy Chi Pubs.
Lytton Manuscripts. Noel H. Osborne. 79p. 1967. 65.00 (*0-900801-10-7*) St Mut.
Lytton Strachey. Max Beerbohm. LC 74-7186. (English Literature Ser.: No. 33). 1974. lib. bdg. 75.00 (*0-8383-1936-X*) M S G Haskell Hse.
Lytton Strachey. John Ferns. (Twayne's English Authors Ser.: No. 462). 152p. (C). 1988. 22.95 (*0-8057-6966-8*, Twyne) Mac Lib Ref.
Lytton Strachey: A Biography. Michael Holroyd. LC 74-159435. 1144p. 1973. write for info. (*0-434-34579-2*) Buttrwrth-Heinemann.
Lytton Strachey: A Biography. Michael Holroyd. LC 72-175874. 1144p. 1971. write for info. (*0-14-003198-7*, PuffinBks) Peng Put Young Read.
Lytton Strachey: The New Biography. Michael Holroyd. LC 94-24632. 800p. 1995. 35.00 (*0-374-19439-4*) FS&G.
Lytton Strachey: The New Biography. Michael Holroyd. 374p. 1995. pap. 17.00 (*0-374-52465-3*, Noonday) FS&G.
LZ Cowboy: A Cowboy's Journal, 1979-1981. John Erickson. LC 96-40038. (Western Life Ser.: Vol. 3). (Illus.). 181p. 1997. 24.95 (*1-57441-024-5*) UNTX Pr.

M

M. Dennis J. Browne. 238p. 1992. 19.95 (*0-9614382-0-7*) Filmbook Pr.
***M.** Anton Kaes. 80p. 2000. pap. 10.95 (*0-85170-370-4*, Pub. by British Film Inst) Ind U Pr.
M. John Sack. (Vietnam Ser.). 224p. 1985. reprint ed. mass mkt. 5.99 (*0-380-69866-8*, Avon Bks) Morrow Avon.
***M.** 2nd ed. George Rosenberg. (New Voices in American Fiction Ser.). 95p. 2000. reprint ed. pap. 12.95 (*1-883938-72-4*) Dry Bones Pr.
M: Writings '67-'72. John Cage. LC 72-11051. (Illus.). 233p. 1974. pap. 18.95 (*0-8195-6035-9*, Wesleyan Univ Pr) U Pr of New Eng.
M - E: The God Within. Joseph R. Abrahamson. 130p. 1992. 22.00 (*0-9633462-0-2*); pap., per. 10.00 (*0-9633462-1-0*) Waverly Pubns.
M - PCpS-Cpk Software: Software for Machine - Process Capability Studies. Mario Perez-Wilson. (Variation Reduction Program Ser.). 120p. 1993. 800.00 incl. disk (*1-883237-02-5*) Adv Systs Cnslts.
M. A. & Sarah Lipschultz Art Collection. Jan Van der Marck. Ed. by Ruth A. Matinko-Wald & Betty L. Curry. LC 87-62754. (Illus.). 48p. (Orig.). (C). 1988. pap. 5.00 (*0-942461-03-7*) Mus Art Fl.
M. A. C. Mission Action Committee Guidelines. 28p. 1981. pap. 1.00 (*0-8341-1020-2*) Nazarene.
M. A. C. C. en Fiesta. M.A.C.C. Team Staff. (SPA.). 96p. 1982. write for info. (*0-614-04891-5*) Mex Am Cult.
M. A. Czaplicka Collected Works, 4 vols. David N. Collins. 1998. 600.00 (*0-7007-1001-9*, Pub. by Curzon Pr Ltd) Paul & Co Pubs.
M. A. P. for Algebra I. Charles T. Gatje & John F. Gatje. (Orig.). 1996. pap. text 2.95 (*0-937534-05-6*) G & G Pubs.
M. A. P. for Decimals. Charles T. Gatje & John F. Gatje. (SPA.). (Orig.). 1981. pap. text 2.25 (*0-937534-09-9*) G & G Pubs.
M. A. P. for Decimals. Charles T. Gatje & John F. Gatje. (Orig.). 1996. pap. text 2.95 (*0-937534-02-1*) G & G Pubs.
M. A. P. for Fractions. Charles T. Gatje & John F. Gatje. Tr. by Rafael Marcos. (SPA.). (Orig.). (YA). (gr. 5 up). 1981. pap. text 2.25 (*0-937534-07-2*) G & G Pubs.
M. A. P. for Fractions. Charles T. Gatje & John F. Gatje. (Orig.). 1996. pap. text 2.95 (*0-937534-01-3*) G & G Pubs.
M. A. P. for Geometry & Measurement. Charles T. Gatje & John F. Gatje. (Orig.). 1996. pap. text 2.95 (*0-937534-04-8*) G & G Pubs.
M. A. P. for Ratio, Proportion, Percent. Charles T. Gatje & John F. Gatje. (Orig.). 1996. pap. text 2.95 (*0-937534-03-X*) G & G Pubs.
M. A. P. for Whole Numbers. Charles T. Gatje & John F. Gatje. (Orig.). 1996. pap. text 2.95 (*0-937534-00-5*) G & G Pubs.
M & A in the Netherlands: Acquisitions, Takeovers, & Joint Ventures : Legal & Taxation. Steven R. Schuit & Jan-Erik Janssen. LC 96-52299. 1997. write for info. (*90-411-0319-8*) Kluwer Law Intl.
M & E Contracting Industry in Great Britain. G. Samuelsson-Brown & S. Whittome. 1993. 1580.00 (*0-86022-352-3*, Pub. by Build Servs Info Assn) St Mut.
***M & M & the Bad News Babies.** Pat Ross. (Illus.). (J). 1999. pap. 12.40 (*0-8085-3696-6*) Econo-Clad Bks.
M & M & the Bad News Babies. Pat Ross. (M & M Ser.). (Illus.). 48p. (J). (ps-3). 1985. pap. 4.99 (*0-14-031851-8*, PuffinBks) Peng Put Young Read.
M & M & the Bad News Babies. Pat Ross. (Picture Puffin Ser.). (Illus.). (J). 1985. 9.70 (*0-606-01684-8*, Pub. by Turtleback) Demco.
M & M & the Haunted House Game. Pat Ross. (Puffin Chapters Ser.). (Illus.). 64p. (J). (gr. 2-5). 1997. pap. 3.99 (*0-14-038730-7*, PuffinBks) Peng Put Young Read.
M & M & the Haunted House Game. Pat Ross. (Young Puffin Ser.). (J). 1990. 10.19 (*0-606-04735-2*, Pub. by Turtleback) Demco.
***M & M & the Mummy Mess.** Pat Ross. (Illus.). (J). 1999. 8.40 (*0-606-18424-4*) Turtleback.
M & M & the Santa Secrets. Pat Ross. (Puffin Chapters for Readers on the Move Ser.). 48p. (J). (gr. 2-5). 1998. pap. 3.99 (*0-14-130094-9*, PuffinBks) Peng Put Young Read.
M & M & the Santa Secrets. Pat Ross. (Illus.). (J). (gr. 1-4). reprint ed. pap. 2.95 (*0-317-62234-X*, PuffinBks) Peng Put Young Read.
M & M in Butte, Montana, & Other Faces. Photos by Harley E. Straus. LC 97-61520. (Illus.). 92p. 1997. pap. 19.95 (*1-891057-05-7*) Wordz & Ink.

An Asterisk (*) at the beginning of an entry indicates that the title is appearing for the first time.

***M & M's Around the World: Collector's Guide.** Ken Clee & Joyce Losonsky. (Illus.). 160p. 2000. pap. 29.95 (*0-7643-1078-X*) Schiffer.

"M & M's" Brand Chocolate Candies Counting Book. Barbara B. McGrath. (Illus.). 32p. (J). (ps-3). 1994. 15.95 (*0-88106-854-3*); pap. 6.95 (*0-88106-853-5*) Charlesbridge Pub.

"M & M's" Brand Chocolate Candies Counting Book. Barbara Barbieri McGrath. LC 95-72220. (Illus.). 10p. (J). (ps-k). 1997. bds. 4.95 (*0-88106-948-5*) Charlesbridge Pub.

M & M's Brand Counting Book. Barbara Barbieri McGrath. 1994. 12.15 (*0-606-07028-1*, Pub. by Turtleback) Demco.

M & Other Poems. John Peck. LC 96-24855. 136p. 1996. 29.95 (*0-8101-5055-7*, TriQuart); pap. 12.95 (*0-8101-5056-5*, TriQuart) Northwestern U Pr.

M. Annael Lucani de Bello Civili, Liber I. D. Lucan. Ed. by W. R. Connor & R. J. Getty. LC 78-67133. (Latin Texts & Commentaries Ser.). (ENG & LAT.). 1979. reprint ed. lib. bdg. 22.95 (*0-405-11603-9*) Ayer.

M. Annaeus Lucanus Bellum Civile: A Commentary, Bk. III. Vincent Hunink. 329p. 1992. pap. 50.00 (*90-5063-078-2*, Pub. by Gieben) J Benjamins Pubng Co.

M. Annei Lucani Belli Civilis Liber V: A Commentary. Pamela Barrat. xvi, 284p. 1979. pap. 82.00 (*90-256-0806-X*, Pub. by AM Hakkert) BookLink Distributors.

M As All a del Consenso de Washington: La Hora de la Reforma Institucional. Shahid J. Burki & Guillermo Perry. LC 98-37364. (World Bank Latin American & Caribbean Studies Ser.). 184p. 1998. pap. 22.00 (*0-8213-4347-5*) World Bank.

M. Blundeville, His Exercises Containing Sixe Treatises. Thomas Blundeville. LC 78-171736. (English Experience Ser.: No. 361). (Illus.). 718p. 1971. reprint ed. 75.00 (*90-221-0361-7*) Walter J Johnson.

M-Boats of World War I. Kelly K. Lydon. (Illus.). xii, 124p. 1998. pap. 20.00 (*0-9663091-0-3*) New Eng Seafarer.

M. Butterfly. David Henry Hwang. 1988. pap. 5.25 (*0-8222-0712-5*) Dramatists Play.

M. C. Escher: Art & Science. Ed. by H. S. Coxeter et al. xiv,402p. 1986. 133.50 (*0-444-70011-0*, North Holland) Elsevier.

M. C. Escher: His Life & Complete Graphic Work. Ed. by J. L. Locher. (Illus.). 352p. 1982. 65.00 (*0-8109-0858-1*) Abrams.

M. C. Escher: His Life & Complete Graphic Work. Ed. by J. L. Locher. (Illus.). 352p. 1992. pap. 29.98 (*0-8109-8113-0*, Pub. by Abrams) Time Warner.

M. C. Escher: Twenty-Nine Master Prints. Intro. by William Wegman & M. C. Escher. (Illus.). 64p. 1983. pap. 16.95 (*0-8109-2268-1*, Pub. by Abrams) Time Warner.

M. C. Escher: 6 Posters. Taschen Publishing Staff. (Taschen Posterbook Ser.). 1996. pap. 11.99 (*3-8228-0766-4*) Benedikt Taschen.

M. C. Escher, Calidocielos. Taschen, Benedikt Staff. (SPA.). 1996. pap. 12.99 (*3-8228-0675-7*) Taschen Amer.

M. C. Escher Coloring Book: Twenty-Four Images to Color. M. C. Escher. (Illus.). 24p. 1995. pap. 9.95 (*0-8109-2635-0*, Pub. by Abrams) Time Warner.

M. C. Escher, Estampas y Dibujos. Taschen, Benedikt Staff. 1996. pap. 12.99 (*3-8228-0678-1*) Taschen Amer.

M. C. Escher Kaleidocycles. Doris S. Schattschneider & Wallace Walker. (Illus.). 76p. 1985. pap. 18.95 (*0-906212-28-6*, Pub. by Tarquin Pubns) Parkwest Pubns.

M. C. Escher Postcard Book. M. C. Escher. 1998. pap. 5.99 (*3-8228-8693-9*) Taschen Amer.

M. C. Escher Sticker Book: Seventy-Nine Imaginative Stickers. M. C. Escher. 24p. 1995. pap. 9.95 (*0-8109-2638-5*) Abrams.

M. C. Higgins, the Great. Virginia Hamilton. LC 99-14288. (Illus.). 256p. (J). 1999. per. 18.00 (*0-689-83074-2*) S&S Bks Yung.

M. C. Higgins, the Great. Virginia Hamilton. LC 72-92439. 288p. (YA). (gr. 7 up). 1974. lib. bdg. 17.00 (*0-02-742480-4*, Mac Bks Young Read) S&S Childrens.

M. C. Higgins, the Great. Virginia Hamilton. (J). 1987. 9.60 (*0-606-02497-2*, Pub. by Turtleback) Demco.

M. C. Higgins the Great. Virginia Hamilton. (J). 1998. pap. 4.50 (*0-87628-568-X*) Ctr Appl Res.

***M. C. Higgins, the Great.** Elizabeth Klar. (J). 1999. 11.95 (*1-58130-603-2*); 9.95 (*1-58130-602-4*) Novel Units.

M. C. Higgins, the Great. Virginia Hamilton. LC 87-6330. 288p. (YA). (gr. 7 up). 1987. reprint ed. mass mkt. 3.95 (*0-02-043490-1*) Macmillan.

M. C. Higgins, the Great. 2nd ed. Virginia Hamilton. LC 92-27919. 288p. (J). (gr. 3-7). 1993. reprint ed. mass mkt. 3.95 (*0-689-71694-X*) Aladdin.

M. C. Higgins, the Great: A Study Guide. Kathleen Fischer. Ed. by J. Friedland & R. Kessler. (Novel-Ties Ser.). (J). (gr. 5-7). 1993. pap. text 15.95 (*0-88122-904-0*) Lrn Links.

M. C. Lilley & Co. Catalogue of Military Clothing & Equipments, 1882. 1989. reprint ed. 10.00 (*0-913150-92-4*) Pioneer Pr.

M. C. Lilley & Co. Catalogue of Regulation United States Army Uniforms & Equipments for National Guard Officers, No. 24. 1989. reprint ed. 10.00 (*0-913150-93-2*) Pioneer Pr.

M. C. Q. & Self Assessment Manual in Medicine. A. C. Tripathy. 224p. (C). 1990. 40.00 (*81-85017-47-6*, Pub. by Interprint) St Mut.

M. C. Q. in Clinical Subjects. L. C. Gupta. 324p. (C). 1991. 60.00 (*0-7855-6742-9*, Pub. by Interprint) St Mut.

M. C. Q. in Obstetrics & Gynecology. Ed. by A. C. Tripathy. 154p. (C). 1990. 60.00 (*0-7855-6743-7*, Pub. by Interprint) St Mut.

M. C. Q. in Ophthalmology. M. L. Agarwal. 185p. (C). 1991. 50.00 (*81-85017-54-9*, Pub. by Interprint) St Mut.

M. C. Q. in Pathology. V. H. Talib. 170p. (C). 1991. 50.00 (*81-85017-55-7*, Pub. by Interprint) St Mut.

M. C. Q. in Radiology. Ed. by L. C. Gupta. 172p. (C). 1990. 35.00 (*81-85017-45-X*, Pub. by Interprint) St Mut.

M. C. Turtle & the Hip Hop Hare: A Happenin' Rap. David Vozar. (Illus.). 32p. (J). (ps-2). 1997. pap. 5.99 (*0-440-41394-X*) Dell.

M. C. Turtle & the Hip Hop Hare, a Happenin' Rap. David Vozar. (Dell Picture Yearling Ser.). (J). 1997. 11.19 (*0-606-11585-4*, Pub. by Turtleback) Demco.

M-Chloronitrobenzene P-Chloronitrobenzene. Ed. by GDCh-Advisory Committee on Existing Chemicals of E. (BUA Report Ser.: No. 11). 97p. 1992. pap. 48.00 (*3-527-28451-6*, Wiley-VCH) Wiley.

M. Cornelii Frontonis Epistulae, Adnotatione Critica Instructae. Marcus C. Fronto. LC 75-7349. (Roman History Ser.). (LAT., Illus.). 1975. reprint ed. 29.95 (*0-405-07070-5*) Ayer.

M. D. Anderson Solid. Steven A. Curley. Ed. by Raphael E. Pollock. LC 97-41042. (Tumor Oncology Ser.). (Illus.). 264p. 1998. 89.95 (*0-387-98370-8*) Spr-Verlag.

M. D. Anderson Surgical Oncology Handbook. Ed. by David Berger et al. LC 94-3421. 464p. 1994. pap. text 36.95 (*0-316-56431-1*, Little Brwn Med Div) Lppncott W & W.

M. D. Anderson Surgical Oncology Handbook. 2nd ed. M. D. Anderson Cancer Center Department of Surgica & Barry W. Feig. LC 98-37038. 448p. 1998. pap. text 42.95 (*0-7817-1581-4*) Lppncott W & W.

M. D. Anderson Volunteers Cooking for Fun. Volunteers & Volunteer Staff. 288p. 1991. 15.00 (*0-9630631-0-3*) Anderson Cancer Ctr.

M. D. Geist Data Album 1. John Ott. (Illus.). 96p. 1996. pap. 9.95 (*1-56219-903-X*, CMX 0601) Central Pk Media.

M. D. Mad's Show Stoppers, Vol. 1. Drucker. 1985. mass mkt. 4.95 (*0-446-38179-9*, Pub. by Warner Bks) Little.

***M. D. P. O. W. A Firsthand Account of 42 Months of Imprisonment in Japanese Hands.** Julien M. Goodman. LC 99-93650. 218p. 2000. 18.95 (*0-533-13106-5*) Vantage.

***M. D. She Had to Marry.** Christine Rimmer. (Special Edition Ser.: Vol. 1345). 2000. mass mkt. 4.50 (*0-373-24345-6*, 1-24345-0) Harlequin Bks.

M Dayspring of Youth. (Illus.). 357p. 1985. reprint ed. 18.00 (*0-911662-67-7*) Yoga.

M. Derings Workes: More at Large Than Ever Hath Heer-to-Fore Been Printed, 3 pts. Edward Dering. LC 74-38171. (English Experience Ser.: No. 448). 692p. 1972. reprint ed. 105.00 (*90-221-0448-6*) Walter J Johnson.

M. Domesticus: The Short-Tailed Possum. Pat Storer & Betty Thomas. (Illus.). 116p. 1994. pap. 21.00 (*1-888144-08-4*) Country Storer Ent.

M. E. Beverly Hunter Great Masterpiece. 3rd ed. Marjorie E. Hunter. (Illus.). 100p. reprint ed. pap. 30.00 incl. audio (*0-685-35652-3*); reprint ed. pap. 20.00 (*0-685-35653-1*); reprint ed. audio 50.00 (*0-685-35654-X*) MH & Pr.

M. E. Beverly Hunter Great Masterpiece, 2 vols., Set. 3rd ed. Marjorie E. Hunter. (Illus.). 100p. reprint ed. pap. 60.00 incl. audio (*0-685-35651-5*) MH & Pr.

M. E. Beverly Hunter Great Masterpiece: Beverly Entertaining & Interesting Thoughts & Beverly Entertaining Melody. Marjorie B. Hunter. (Illus.). (Orig.). (J). (gr. 5 up). 1986. pap. text 30.00 (*0-317-93273-X*); audio 10.00 (*0-317-93274-8*) MH & Pr.

***M. E. Sharpe Library of Franklin D. Roosevelt Studies, 2 vols., Set.** Ed. by William D. Pederson et al. Incl. Franklin D. Roosevelt & Congress: The New Deal & Its Aftermath. Ed. & Intro. by Thomas Phillip Wolf. LC 99-87719. (Illus.). 288p. 2000. text 69.95 (*0-7656-0622-4*); Franklin D. Roosevelt & the Shaping of American Political Culture. Ed. & intro. by Nancy Beck Young. LC 99-88090. 224p. 2000. text 56.95 (*0-7656-0620-8*); 2000. Set text 119.95 (*0-7656-0648-8*) M E Sharpe.

***M. E. T. Publication No. 515: Rules & Regulations for Foreign Vessels Operating in the United States, Bks. 1 & 2.** 6th rev. ed. Ed. by Richard A. Block. 794p. 1999. pap. 146.00 (*1-879778-84-X*) Marine Educ.

M. Eberhart Mystery. Eberhart. 1988. mass mkt. 3.95 (*0-446-34921-6*, Pub. by Warner Bks) Little.

M-80. Jim Daniels. LC 92-62335. 100p. (C). 1993. pap. 10.95 (*0-8229-5497-4*); text 19.95 (*0-8229-3747-6*) U of Pittsburgh Pr.

M F Horn: Maynard Ferguson's Life in Music. William F. Lee. LC 98-130080. (Illus.). 1997. write for info. (*0-89745-982-2*) Sunflower U Pr.

M. F. K. Fisher: A Life in Letters: Correspondence, 1929-1991. Compiled by Norah K. Barr et al. (Illus.). 520p. 1998. reprint ed. pap. 21.00 (*1-887178-93-7*, Pub. by Counterpt DC) HarpC.

M. F. K. Fisher & Me: A Memoir of Food & Friendship. Jeannette Ferrary. LC 98-34544. 240p. 1998. pap. 14.95 (*0-312-19442-0*, Pub. by Tor Bks) St Martin.

M-Factor. Guy Beining. 36p. (Orig.). 1993. pap. 5.00 (*0-926935-82-8*) Runaway Spoon.

M Factor. Andrew Pattison. 1999. pap. text 12.00 (*0-7318-0697-2*) Simon & Schuster.

M-Files: True Reports of Minnesota's Unexplained Phenomena. Jay Rath. Ed. by Elizabeth McBride & Chris Roerden. LC 98-61219. (Illus.). 120p. 1998. pap. 14.95 (*0-915024-66-7*) Trails Media.

M-Fit Grocery Shopping Guide: Your Guide to Healthier Choices. 4th rev. ed. Nelda Mercer et al. LC 96-177886. 397p. 1995. pap. 18.95 (*0-9649656-0-7*) U MI Med Ctr.

M5 Anti-Boredom Guide. Richard Shurey. (C). 1988. pap. 29.00 (*0-946328-11-0*, Pub. by Thornhill Pr) St Mut.

***M for Mother.** Marjorie Riddell. 2000. pap. 12.95 (*0-552-99747-1*, Pub. by Transworld Publishers Ltd) Trafalgar.

M for Mother. large type ed. Marjorie Riddell. 1998. 23.95 (*0-7531-5802-7*, Pub. by ISIS Lrg Prnt) Transaction Pubs.

***M for Mother.** large type unabridged ed. Marjorie Riddell. 109p. 1999. pap. 19.95 (*0-7531-5814-0*, 158140, Pub. by ISIS Lrg Prnt) ISIS Pub.

M-Form Society. William G. Ouchi. 352p. 1986. mass mkt. 4.95 (*0-380-69914-1*, Avon Bks) Morrow Avon.

M48 Financial Planning for Physician. Timothy Carse & Jeffrey Slater. 1995. text 35.00 (*0-07-413101-X*, Irwn McGrw-H) McGrw-H Hghr Educ.

M-41 Walker Bulldog in Action. Jim Mesko. (Armor in Action Ser.). (Illus.). 50p. 1991. pap. 9.95 (*0-89747-262-4*, 2029) Squad Sig Pubns.

M-47 & M-48 Patton Tanks. Steven J. Zaloga. (Vanguard Ser.: No. 29). (Illus.). 48p. pap. 10.95 (*0-85045-466-2*, 9318, Pub. by Ospry) Stackpole.

M. G. Krein's Lectures on Entire Operators. M. L. Gorbachuk et al. LC 97-25604. (Operator Theory, Advances & Applications Ser.). 1997. write for info. (*0-8176-5704-5*) Birkhauser.

M. G. Krein's Lectures on Entire Operators. M. L. Gorbachuk et al. LC 97-25604. (Operator Theory, Advances & Applications Ser.). 232p. 1997. text. write for info. (*3-7643-5704-5*) Birkhauser.

M Grandma Franks' Cookbook. Ed. by James A. Franks & Elizabeth McKenzie. (Cookbook Ser.). 332p. 1998. 24.95 (*0-9657173-1-3*) Wld Goose Pr.

M. H. Baillie Scott & the Arts & Crafts Movement: Pioneers of Modern Design. James D. Kornwolf. LC 70-135661. (Illus.). 620p. reprint ed. pap. 192.20 (*0-608-11324-7*, 202222700025) Bks Demand.

M. I. A. Accounting for the Missing in Southeast Asia. 1997. lib. bdg. 251.95 (*0-8490-6163-6*) Gordon Pr.

M. I. A. Accounting for the Missing in Southeast Asia. Paul D. Mather. (Illus.). 207p. (Orig.). (C). 1995. pap. text 40.00 (*0-7881-2533-8*) DIANE Pub.

M. I. A. Accounting for the Missing in Southeast Asia. Paul D. Mather. 231p. (Orig.). 1995. per. 10.00 (*0-16-036391-8*) USGPO.

M. I. A. (Missing in Action) 2nd ed. H. Phillip Causer. LC 77-88747. (Illus.). 1995. pap. 12.95 (*0-918442-00-1*) Phipps Pub.

M. I. A.: or Mythmaking in America. H. Bruce Franklin. LC 93-24778. 246p. 1993. pap. 9.95 (*0-8135-2001-0*) Rutgers U Pr.

M. I. A. Saigon. W. J. Amos. 224p. 1986. mass mkt. 2.50 (*0-87067-274-6*, BH274) Holloway.

M I Carbine. Larry Ruth. pap. 19.95 (*0-88227-020-6*) Gun Room.

M. I. Hummel: The Golden Anniversary Album. Robert L. Miller. 1989. 19.98 (*0-88365-745-7*) Galahad Bks.

M. I. Hummel Album. Robert Miller. 320p. 1994. 19.98 (*0-88365-878-X*) Galahad Bks.

***M. I. Hummel Figurines, Plates, Miniatures & More Price Guide.** 8th ed. Robert L. Miller. (Illus.). 2000. pap. 24.95 (*0-942620-35-6*) Portfolio Pr.

M. I. Master. 72p. 1992. pap. 22.95 (*0-89898-989-2*, CPM001CD) Wrner Bros.

M. I. Master Trax Rock/Tape. 72p. 1994. pap. 19.95 (*0-89898-988-4*, CPM0001AT) Wrner Bros.

M. I. N. D. over Weight: How to Stay Slim the Rest of Your Life. William M. Macleod & Gael S. Macleod. 126p. (Orig.). 1985. reprint ed. 19.95 incl. audio (*0-934439-05-2*); reprint ed. pap. 9.95 (*0-934439-03-6*); reprint ed. 9.95 (*0-934439-04-4*) W G M Pub.

***M. I. T. Can Be Murder!** Frank M. Weyer. 196p. 2000. pap. 18.00 (*0-7388-2074-1*) Xlibris Corp.

M-Ideas in Banach Spaces & Banach Algebras. Peter Harmand et al. LC 93-16064. (Lecture Notes in Mathematics Ser.: Vol. 1547). viii, 384p. 1993. 69.95 (*0-387-56814-X*) Spr-Verlag.

M Is for Malice. Sue Grafton. LC 97-90543. 337p. 1998. mass mkt. 7.99 (*0-449-22360-4*, Crest) Fawcett.

M Is for Malice. Sue Grafton. LC 96-30897. (Illus.). 304p. 1995. 25.00 (*0-8050-3637-7*) H Holt & Co.

M Is for Malice. large type ed. Sue Grafton. LC 96-43539. (Core Ser.). 429p. 1997. lib. bdg. 27.95 (*0-7838-1833-5*, G K Hall Lrg Type) Mac Lib Ref.

M Is for Malice. large type ed. Sue Grafton. LC 96-43539. 458p. 1997. pap. 25.95 (*0-7838-1834-3*, G K Hall Lrg Type) Mac Lib Ref.

***M Is for Massachusetts.** Mary D. Wade. (Alpha Flight Bks.). (Illus.). 60p. (ps-3). 2000. 17.95 (*1-892920-42-5*) G H B Pubs.

***M Is for Michigan.** Julie Douglas. (Alpha Flight Bks.). (Illus.). 60p. (ps-3). 2000. 17.95 (*1-892920-43-3*) G H B Pubs.

M Is for Minnesota. Dori H. Butler. LC 98-13074. (Illus.). 32p. (J). (gr. 1-6). 1998. 16.95 (*0-8166-3041-0*) U of Minn Pr.

M Is for Minnesota. Debra M. Chial. LC 93-34643. (Illus.). 32p. (J). 1994. 12.95 (*0-89658-234-5*) Voyageur Pr.

M Is for Mirror. Duncan Birminham. (Illus.). 33p. (J). (ps-3). 1989. pap. 7.50 (*0-906212-66-9*, Pub. by Tarquin Pubns) Parkwest Pubns.

M Is for Mississippi: An Irreverent Guide to the Magnolia State. Jim Fraiser. 80p. (Orig.). 1992. pap. text 10.00 (*0-9627737-0-0*) Persimmon Pr MS.

***"M" Is for Missouri.** Carol Greene. (Alpha Flight Bks.). (Illus.). 60p. (J). 2000. 17.95 (*1-892920-26-3*) G H B Pubs.

***"M" Is for Missouri's Rocks & Minerals.** Judy Oetting. (Alpha Flight Bks.). (Illus.). 64p. (J). 2000. 17.95 (*1-892920-29-8*) G H B Pubs.

M Is for Mitten: The Michigan Alphabet Book. Annie Appleford. LC 99-33497. (Illus.). 32p. 1999. 15.95 (*1-886947-73-2*) Sleepng Bear.

M Is for Monster. Mel Gilden. 96p. (J). 1987. pap. 2.75 (*0-380-75423-1*, Avon Bks) Morrow Avon.

M Is for Montana. Gayle C. Shirley. LC 87-73310. (Illus.). 30p. (J). 1988. pap. 9.95 (*0-937959-32-4*) Falcon Pub Inc.

***M. J. The Life & Times of M. J. Coldwell.** Walter Stewart. (Illus.). 288p. 2000. 35.00 (*0-7737-3232-2*) Stoddart Publ.

M. J. Bienvenu. James Hatfield. text 25.95 (*0-312-30000-X*) St Martin.

M. J. Saffon's Bodylift. M. J. Saffon. 128p. 1984. mass mkt. 5.95 (*0-446-37363-X*, Pub. by Warner Bks) Little.

M. John Berry Nomination: Hearing Before the Committee on Energy & Natural Resources, United States Senate, One Hundred Fifth Congress, First Session, to Consider the Nomination of M. John Berry to Be Assistant Secretary for Policy, Management, & Budget, Department of the Interior, October 9, 1997. United States. LC 98-160471. 49p. 1998. write for info. (*0-16-056126-4*) USGPO.

M. K. Gandhi's Wit & Wisdom. Mohandas Karamchand Gandhi. Ed. by Arun Gandhi. (Illus.). 47p. 1996. pap. 10.00 (*0-9674549-0-5*) M K Gandhi.

M. K. Ghandi. Verinder Grover. (C). 1991. 56.00 (*81-7100-249-8*, Pub. by Deep & Deep Pubns) S Asia.

M-KdV Solitons on the Background of Quasi-Periodic Finite-Gap Solutions. Fritz Gesztesy & Roman Svirsky. LC 95-34456. (Memoirs of the American Mathematical Society Ser.: No. 563). 88p. 1995. pap. 33.00 (*0-8218-0406-5*, MEMO/118/563) Am Math.

M. L. Wilson & the Campaign for the Domestic Allotment. William D. Rowley. LC 69-19106. 233p. reprint ed. pap. 72.30 (*0-8357-2952-4*, 203920800011) Bks Demand.

M. M. S. County Buying Power Index. Magazine Marketing Service Staff. LC 75-22826. (America in Two Centuries Ser.). 1976. reprint ed. 20.95 (*0-405-07698-3*) Ayer.

M-M Service System with Ranked Servers in Heavy Traffic. G. F. Newell. (Lecture Notes in Economics & Mathematical Systems Ser.: Vol. 231). xi, 126p. 1984. 28.00 (*0-387-13377-1*) Spr-Verlag.

M. M. Warburg & Company, 1798-1938: Merchant Bankers of Hamburg. Eduard Rosenbaum & A. J. Sherman. LC 79-511. (Illus.). 190p. 1979. 39.95 (*0-8419-0477-4*) Holmes & Meier.

M. N. Roy's Memoirs. M. N. Roy. 1985. 17.50 (*0-8364-1296-6*, Pub. by Ajanta) S Asia.

M-1911A1 Automatic Pistol: Proud American Legend. Ed. by American Historical Foundation Staff. (Illus.). (Orig.). 1985. pap. 8.95 (*0-933489-03-X*) Amer Hist Found.

M. O. M. S. Handbook: Understanding Your Personality Type in Mothering. 2nd ed. Janet P. Penley & Diane W. Stephens. 64p. (Orig.). 1999. pap. text 14.00 (*0-9646974-0-8*, Mothers of Many Styles) Penley & Assocs.

M. O. R. E. Perfect Union. Nicholas Souchik, Jr. LC 97-90159. 194p. (Orig.). 1997. pap. 14.95 (*0-533-12314-3*) Vantage.

M. O. R. L. Middle of the Road Lizard. write for info. (*0-318-58235-X*) P-H.

M. O. S. T. Integrated Circuit Engineering. Ed. by J. Mavor. LC 73-87027. (Illus.). 172p. reprint ed. pap. 53.40 (*0-608-17790-3*, 203225500079) Bks Demand.

M1 - Selective Muscarinic Antagonists in Peptic Ulcer Therapy: Journal: Pharmacology, Vol. 37, Suppl. 1, 1988. Ed. by W. Kromer et al. (Illus.). vi, 66p. 1988. pap. 21.75 (*3-8055-4925-3*) S Karger.

M-1 Abrams Battle Tank. Steven J. Zaloga. (Vanguard Ser.: No. 41). (Illus.). 48p. pap. 10.95 (*0-85045-584-7*, 9322, Pub. by Ospry) Stackpole.

M-1 Abrams Main Battle Tank, 1982-92. Steven J. Zaloga. (New Vanguard Ser.: No. 2). (Illus.). 48p. pap. 12.95 (*1-85532-283-8*, 9337, Pub. by Ospry) Stackpole.

M-2 Bradley Infantry Fighting Vehicle. Steven J. Zaloga. (Vanguard Ser.: No. 43). (Illus.). 48p. pap. 10.95 (*0-85045-655-X*, 9332, Pub. by Ospry) Stackpole.

M-1 Does My Talking! The U. S. M-1 Garand Rifle in Pictures, World War II & Korea, Vol. 1. 2nd rev. ed. Ed. by Robert Bruce. (Weapons in Action Ser.). (Illus.). 80p. (Orig.). 1993. pap. 12.95 (*0-9631495-1-2*) R Bruce Photo.

M1 Garand: Owner's Guide. Scott A. Duff. 126p. 1995. pap. 16.95 (*1-888722-03-7*) S A Duff.

M1 Garand: Post World War II. Scott A. Duff. 139p. 1989. pap. 19.95 (*1-888722-00-2*) S A Duff.

M1 Garand: Serial Numbers & Data Sheets. Scott A. Duff. 101p. 1995. pap. 9.95 (*1-888722-05-3*) S A Duff.

M1 Garand: World War II. Scott A. Duff. 320p. 1993. 69.95 (*1-888722-02-9*); pap. 34.95 (*1-888722-01-0*) S A Duff.

M1 Garand, 1936-1957. 2nd ed. Joe Poyer & Craig Riesch. (For Collectors Only Ser.). (Illus.). 223p. 1997. pap. 19.95 (*1-882391-19-5*) N Cape Pubns.

M-1 Helmet: A History of the U. S. M-1 Helmet in World War II. Mark A. Reynosa. (Illus.). 112p. 1996. 39.95 (*0-7643-0074-1*) Schiffer.

***M1 Tank Platoon 3.** Prima Temp Authors. (Illus.). 240p. 2000. pap. 19.99 (*0-7615-2670-6*) Prima Pub.

M. or N., 2 vols. George J. Whyte-Melville. LC 75-32792. (Literature of Mystery & Detection Ser.). 1976. reprint ed. 51.95 (*0-405-07908-7*) Ayer.

M. P. B. Cerillera. Andersen. (SPA., Illus.). (J). (ps-k). 1997. pap. 2.49 (*968-13-2434-X*) Edit Diana.

M. P. Cardiff - Half & Half a Capital. Rhodri Morgan. Ed. by Meic Stephens. (Changing Wales Ser.). 80p. 1998. pap. 12.95 (*0-8464-4744-4*) Beekman Pubs.

M Programming: A Comprehensive Guide. Richard F. Walters. LC 97-6513. 407p. 1997. pap. text 44.95 (*1-55558-167-6*, Digital DEC) Buttrwrth-Heinemann.

M

An Asterisk (*) at the beginning of an entry indicates that the title is appearing for the first time.

M. R. C. S. M. C. Q.s for the Surgical Membership. P. A. Sylvester et al. 240p. 1997. pap. text 37.50 (0-7506-2606-2) Buttrwrth-Heinemann.

M. Seguin's Goat see Chevre de M. Seguin

M-16 Controversies: Military Organizations & Weapons Acquisition. Thomas L. McNaugher. LC 83-24574. 211p. 1984. 57.95 (0-275-91741-X, C1741, Praeger Pubs) Greenwood.

M68000 8-, 16-, 32-Bit Microprocessor's: Programmer's Reference Manual. 5th ed. Motorola, Inc. Staff. 240p. 1986. 26.95 (0-13-541475-X) P-H.

M Sixty-Three - Motorway Through a Town. Old Vicarage Publications Staff. 80p. (C). 1982. pap. text 39.00 (0-9508635-0-5, Pub. by Old Vicarage) St Mut.

M. Stambuloff. Ardern H. Beaman. LC 70-135791. (Eastern Europe Collection). 1971. reprint ed. 23.95 (0-405-02733-8) Ayer.

M. Stambuloff: With Six Portraits. Ardern H. Beaman. LC 72-5471. (Select Bibliographies Reprint Ser.). 1977. reprint ed. 20.95 (0-8369-6896-4) Ayer.

M Street Radio Directory. 8th ed. Ed. by Robert Unmacht. (Orig.). 1997. pap. text 68.06 (0-9647930-7-5) M St Corp.

M Street Radio Directory: 1997 Edition, Vol. 8. rev. ed. Ed. by Robert Unmacht & Pat McCrummen. 920p. (Orig.). 1997. pap. 49.00 (0-9647930-4-0) M St Corp.

M. T. V. Beavis & Butthead's Ensucklopedia. Mike Judge et al. LC 96-105785. (Illus.). 96p. 1994. per. 10.00 (0-671-52149-7) PB.

M10 Strategic Thinking. 144p. 1995. pap. text, per. 28.70 (0-7872-1407-8) Kendall-Hunt.

M. Terenti Varronis Antiquitatum Rerum: Divinasum: Libri 1, 14, 15, 16. Marcus T. Varro. Ed. by Reinholdo Agahd. LC 75-10661. (Ancient Religion & Mythology Ser.). (LAT.). 1976. reprint ed. 18.95 (0-405-07268-6) Ayer.

M. Terenti Varronis de Lingua Latina Libra. Marcus T. Varro. Ed. by W. R. Connor. LC 78-67154. (Latin Texts & Commentaries Ser.). 1979. reprint ed. lib. bdg. 28.95 (0-405-11621-7) Ayer.

M-Theory. Edward Witten. 1998. VHS 54.95 (0-8218-1350-1) Am Math.

M3D: Mechanics & Mechanisms of Material Damping. Ed. by Vikram K. Kinra & Alan Wolfenden. LC 92-28001. (Special Technical Publication Ser.: No. 1169). (Illus.). 590p. 1992. text 123.00 (0-8031-1495-8, STP1169) ASTM.

M3D Show, Vol. 1. (J). 1993. pap. write for info. (1-884069-50-9) MthreeD.

M3D Show, Vol. 2. (J). 1993. pap. write for info. (1-884069-51-7) MthreeD.

M3D Show, Vol. 3. (J). 1993. pap. write for info. (1-884069-52-5) MthreeD.

M3 Half-Track in Action. Jim Mesko. (Armor in Action Ser.: No. 34). (Illus.). 50p. 1996. pap. 9.95 (0-89747-363-9, 2034) Squad Sig Pubns.

M3 Halftrack, 1940-73. Steven Zaloga. (New Vanguard Ser.: Vol. 11). (Illus.). 48p. pap. 12.95 (1-85532-467-9, Pub. by Osprey) Stackpole.

M-3 Lee - Grant in Action. Jim Mesko. (Armor in Action Ser.). (Illus.). 50p. 1995. pap. 9.95 (0-89747-346-9) Squad Sig Pubns.

M. Tomchuk Graphic Work. Franz G. Geierhaas. LC 88-50984. (Illus.). 144p. 1989. 30.00 (0-9621400-0-7) M Tomchuk.

M. Tulli Ciceronis Ad M Brutum Orator. Marcus Tullius Cicero. Ed. by W. R. Connor & John E. Sandys. LC 78-67148. (Latin Texts & Commentaries Ser.). (ENG & LAT.). 1979. reprint ed. lib. bdg. 28.95 (0-405-11616-0) Ayer.

M. Tulli Ciceronis de Divinatione, 2 vols. Marcus Tullius Cicero. Ed. by W. R. Connor. LC 78-67146. (Latin Texts & Commentaries Ser.). (ENG & LAT.). 1979. reprint ed. lib. bdg. 48.95 (0-405-11614-4) Ayer.

M. Tulli Ciceronis de Domo Sua Ad Pontifices Oratio. Marcus Tullius Cicero. Ed. by W. R. Connor & Robert G. Nisbert. LC 78-67143. (Latin Texts & Commentaries Ser.). (ENG & LAT.). 1979. reprint ed. lib. bdg. 29.95 (0-405-11612-8) Ayer.

M. Tulli Ciceronis de Natura Deorum, 2 vols., Set. Marcus Tullius Cicero. Ed. by W. R. Connor. LC 78-67145. (Latin Texts & Commentaries Ser.). 1979. reprint ed. lib. bdg. 82.95 (0-405-11613-6) Ayer.

M. Tulli Ciceronis de Oratore, 3 vols. Marcus Tullius Cicero. Ed. by W. R. Connor. LC 78-67162. (Latin Texts & Commentaries Ser.). (ENG & LAT.). 1979. reprint ed. lib. bdg. 56.95 (0-405-11624-1) Ayer.

M. Tulli Ciceronis de Provinciis Consularibus Oratio Ad Senatum. Marcus Tullius Cicero. Ed. by W. R. Connor. LC 78-67125. (Latin Texts & Commentaries Ser.). (ENG & LAT.). 1979. reprint ed. lib. bdg. 23.95 (0-405-11596-2) Ayer.

M. Tulli Ciceronis Tusculanarum Disputationum Libra Quinque, 2 vols. Marcus Tullius Cicero. Ed. by W. R. Connor. LC 78-67129. (Latin Texts & Commentaries Ser.). (ENG & LAT.). 1979. reprint ed. lib. bdg. 66.95 (0-405-11599-7) Ayer.

M. Tullius Cicero, the Fragmentary Speeches. 2nd ed. Marcus Tullius Cicero. LC 94-41803. (American Philological Association American Classical Studies : No. 37). 350p. 1994. pap. 34.95 (0-7885-0075-9) OUP.

M2/M3 Bradley: Infantry Fighting Vehicle, 1983-95. Steven J. Zaloga. (Illus.). 48p. 1996. pap. 12.95 (1-85532-538-1, Pub. by Osprey) Stackpole.

M. V. Brewington: A Bibliography & Catalogue of the Brewington Press. Stuart M. Frank & Robert L. Webb. 36p. 1982. 6.50 (0-685-06347-X); pap. 5.00 (0-937854-20-4) Kendall Whaling.

"M" Word: A Bel Barrett Mystery. Jane Isenberg. 224p. 1999. mass mkt. 5.99 (0-380-80280-5, Avon Bks) Morrow Avon.

M. Y. T. H. Inc. in Action. Robert L. Asprin. 1991. mass mkt. 5.99 (0-441-55282-X) Ace Bks.

M. Y. T. H. Inc. Link. Robert L. Asprin. (Myth Ser.: No. 7). 176p. (Orig.). 1988. mass mkt. 5.50 (0-441-55277-3) Ace Bks.

M-47 & M-48 Patton Tanks, 31. rev. ed. Steven J. Zaloga. 1999. pap. text 12.95 (1-85532-825-9) Ospry.

Ma: The Cosmic Order. Dibinga W. Said. LC 95-92497. (Unity of Thought in Kaffric, Kushanic, Ani & Kemetic Civilizations Ser.: No. 005, Pt. I). 50p. (Orig.). (J). 1995. pap. text 5.00 (0-943324-74-2) Omenana.

Ma alim fi at-Tariq see Milestones

MA & PA: A History of the Maryland & Pennsylvania Railroad. 2nd ed. George W. Hilton. LC 99-32830. (Illus.). 179p. 1999. pap. 17.95 (0-8018-6294-9) Johns Hopkins.

Ma & Pa Dracula. Ann M. Martin. 128p. (J). (gr. 4-6). 1991. pap. 2.95 (0-590-43828-X) Scholastic Inc.

Ma & Pa Murders & Other Perfect Crimes. Louis Solomon. LC 76-56080. (J). (gr. 5 up). 1977. 12.95 (0-397-31577-5) HarpC Child Bks.

Ma Babouche pour Toujours. Gilles Gauthier. (Novels in the Premier Roman Ser.). (FRE.). 64p. (J). (gr. 2-5). 1996. pap. 7.95 (2-89021-128-2, Pub. by Les Editions) Firefly Bks Ltd.

Ma Barker. Sue Hamilton. Ed. by John Hamilton. LC 89-84925. (America's Most Wanted Ser.). (Illus.). 32p. (J). (gr. 4). 1989. lib. bdg. 11.96 (0-939179-65-2) ABDO Pub Co.

Ma Cinderella. Harold Bell Wright. 1998. lib. bdg. 36.95 (1-56723-109-8) Yestermorrow.

MA Criminal Law Sourcebook, 1998. R. Marc Kamrowitz & Timothy E. Maquire. LC 97-76385. 1998. pap. text 50.00 (1-57589-083-6, 199806.13) Mass CLE.

Ma de Proverbis. limited ed. Shuzo Takiguchi. (Ediciones Especiales y de Bibliofilo Ser.). (CAT, ENG, FRE, GER & JPN., Illus.). 1993. 7500.00 (84-343-0114-8) Elliots Bks.

Ma Dear's Aprons. Patricia C. McKissack. LC 94-48450. (Illus.). 1997. lib. bdg. 16.99 (0-679-95099-0, Apple Soup Bks) Knopf Bks Yng Read.

Ma Dear's Aprons. Patricia C. McKissack. LC 94-48450. (Illus.). 32p. (J). (ps-2). 1997. 16.00 (0-689-81051-2) S&S Childrens.

***Ma Dear's Aprons.** Patricia C. McKissack. (Illus.). (J). 2000. 11.44 (0-606-17928-3) Turtleback.

Ma Dear's Aprons. Patricia C. McKissack. (Illus.). 32p. (J). (gr. k-3). 2000. reprint ed. per. 5.99 (0-689-83262-1) Aladdin.

Ma Dent Va Tomber see My Tooth Is about to Fall Out

Ma Hea 'O Ia E Noho Ai? Illus. by 'Umi Kahalio'umi & Kahanano'eau Morita. (HAW.). (J). (gr. k). 1992. 6.95 (1-58191-046-0) Aha Punana Leo.

Ma Hezhi & the Illustration of the Book of Odes. Julia K. Murray. (Illus.). 272p. (C). 1993. text 115.00 (0-521-41787-2) Cambridge U Pr.

Ma, I Want a Name. 3rd ed. Claire F. Fafard. 141p. (Orig.). (YA). (gr. 6 up). 1995. pap. text 8.95 (0-9646084-0-5) C F G Fafard.

Ma Jeeter's Girls. Dorothy Thomas. LC 85-28851. (Illus.). vi, 197p. 1986. reprint ed. pap. 6.95 (0-8032-9405-0, Bison Books) U of Nebr Pr.

***Ma Jiang & the Orange Ants.** Barbara A. Porte. LC 99-30234. (Illus.). 32p. (J). (gr. k-4). 2000. lib. bdg. 17.99 (0-531-33241-1) Orchard Bks Watts.

***Ma Jiang & the Orange Ants.** Barbara Ann Porte. LC 99-30234. 32p. (J). (gr. k-4). 2000. 16.95 (0-531-30241-5) Orchard Bks Watts.

Ma-Ka: Diasporic Juks: Contemporary Writing by Queers of African Descent. Ed. by Debbie Douglas et al. LC 98-140945. 264p. 1997. pap. write for info. (1-896705-14-6) Sister Vis Pr.

Ma Ke 'Ano Kuloko: Healthy Cooking - Island Style. rev. ed. Lisa Bravo et al. (Illus.). 188p. 1995. spiral bd. 12.00 (0-9647939-1-1) Project LEAN HI.

Ma Kiley: The Life of Railroad Telegrapher. Thomas C. Jepsen. (Southwestern Studies Ser.). 1997. pap. text 12.50 (0-87404-275-5) Tex Western.

Ma Liang & His Magic Brush. 1981. pap. 3.95 (0-8351-0912-7) China Bks.

Ma-Ma. R.J. Jensen. 1989. pap. 3.95 (0-8217-2950-0) NAL.

Ma Ma Hu Hu: An Introduction to Chinese Writing. Peggy R. Goldstein. (Illus.). 40p. (J). 1995. pap. 10.95 (1-885340-16-8) Coming of Age.

Ma MacDonald. Joanne Arnott. (Illus.). 24p. (J). pap. 5.95 (0-88961-180-7, Pub. by Womens Pr) LPC InBook.

***Ma Maison en Dentelle de Bois.** Evelyne Trouillot. (FRE.). 77p. 1999. pap. write for info. (1-58437-001-7) Edit Memo.

Ma Maman. Debbie Bailey & Susan Huszar.Tr. of My Mom. (FRE., Illus.). 14p. (J). (ps). 1992. bds. 4.95 (1-55037-267-X, Pub. by Annick) Firefly Bks Ltd.

Ma mere et les Betes. Sidonie-Gabrielle Colette. (POR.). 24.95 incl. audio (0-685-21216-5) Fr & Eur.

Ma Mission au Japan, 1907-1914. Auguste Gerard. LC 72-168109. reprint ed. 55.00 (0-404-02713-X) AMS Pr.

Ma Murray: And the Newspapering Murrays. Georgina Keddells. 302p. 1967. mass mkt. 5.95 (0-88780-130-7, Pub. by Formac Publ Co) Formac Dist Ltd.

Ma Rainey's Black Bottom. August Wilson. LC 84-27156. 128p. 1985. pap. 9.95 (0-452-26113-9, Plume) Dutton Plume.

Ma Tzu: The Empty Mirror: The Present Day Awakened One Speaks on the Ancient Masters of Zen. Osho. Ed. by Deva Ashik. LC 98-103005. (Zen Ser.). 202p. 1989. 14.95 (3-89338-065-5, Pub. by Rebel Hse) Oshos.

Ma Vie. C. G. Jung. (FRE.). 528p. 1991. pap. 13.95 (0-7859-2618-6, 2070384071) Fr & Eur.

Ma Vie au Paradis. Anthony Borgia. 286p. 1989. 19.95 (2-920083-39-2) Edns Roseau.

Ma Vie et la Psychoanlyse. Sigmund Freud. (FRE.). 1971. pap. 10.95 (0-7859-2834-0) Fr & Eur.

Ma Vie et Mon Art Souvenirs. Felia Litvinne. Ed. by Andrew Farkas. LC 76-29950. (Opera Biographies Ser.).Tr. of My Life & My Art. (FRE., Illus.). 1977. reprint ed. lib. bdg. 28.95 (0-405-09691-7) Ayer.

Ma Xiangbo & the Mind of Modern China: 1840-1939. Ed. by Ruth Hayoe & Youngling Lu. LC 95-52845. 340p. (C). (gr. 13). 1996. text 69.95 (1-56324-831-X, East Gate Bk) M E Sharpe.

Ma, You're Driving Me Crazy! Toni Goffe. LC 92-40565. 32p. (J). 1993. 4.99 (0-85953-401-4) Childs Play.

Maacama Trio for ATB Recorders. Ridgway Banks. (Contemporary Consort Ser.: No. 1). 21p. 1989. pap. text 8.00 (1-56571-006-1) PRB Prods.

Maafa & Beyond: Remembrance, Ancestral Connections & Nation Building for the African Global Community. Erriel D. Roberson. LC 94-74578. 200p. (Orig.). 1995. pap. 15.00 (0-9644932-0-9) Kujichagulia Pr.

Maaglei Zedek: Rabbi's Manual. Ed. by David Polish. 263p. 1988. 12.50 (0-88123-004-9) Central Conf.

Maajabu Ya Utepe Wenye Madoadoa: The Adventure of the Speckled Band in Kiswahili. Arthur Conan Doyle. Tr. by George Gateno. (SWA., Illus.). 31p. (Orig.). 1993. pap. 8.00 (0-9695673-3-2) Battered Silicon.

Ma'ajim Marhalat Al-Hadanah: Dalil al-Murabbi. Abd-al-Wahid Ulwani. (Majalis Bi'r 'Ajam Ser.: Al-Hadanah). 288p. (J). 1994. 47.95 (1-57547-002-0) Dar Al-Fikr.

***Maakies.** Tony Millionaire. 2000. pap. 14.95 (1-56097-391-9) Fantagraph Bks.

Maalesh: A Theatrical Tour in the Middle-East. Jean Cocteau. Tr. by Mary C. Hoeck. LC 77-26022. (Illus.). 136p. 1978. reprint ed. lib. bdg. 49.50 (0-313-20054-8, COMT, Greenwood Pr) Greenwood.

Ma'alim Al Manhaj Al Islami: Outlines of the Islamic Method. 2nd ed. Muhammad Imarah. LC 90-5169. (Silsilat al Manhajiyah al Islamiyah Ser.: No. 3). (ARA.). 290p. 1990. 15.00 (0-912463-66-X); pap. 10.00 (0-912463-65-1) IIIT VA.

Ma'alos Ha-Torah. Avraham B. Zalman. Tr. by Elimelech Lepon. 155p. 1996. 16.95 (1-56871-098-4, Pub. by Targum Pr) Feldheim.

***Maalstrom.** Glenn L. Roberts. 244p. 1999. pap. 12.00 (0-9675809-0-0) Dark Lotus.

Ma'am Jones of the Pecos. Eve Ball. LC 68-9336. 265p. reprint ed. pap. 82.20 (0-608-13353-1, 202555000044) Bks Demand.

Maamarei Admur Hatzemach Tzedek, 5614-5615. Ed. by Eliyahu Matusof. (HEB.). 326p. 1998. 18.00 (0-8266-6014-2) Kehot Pubn Soc.

Maamorei Admor Hoemtzoee: Bamidbor, Vol. 1. Dov B. Schneuri. (HEB.). 320p. 1986. reprint ed. 17.00 (0-8266-5579-3) Kehot Pubn Soc.

Maamorei Admor Hoemtzoee: Bamidbor, Vol. 2. Dov B. Schneuri. 574p. reprint ed. 17.00 (0-8266-5580-7) Kehot Pubn Soc.

Maamorei Admor Hoemtzoee: Bamidbor, Vol. 3. Dov B. Schneuri. (HEB.). 415p. reprint ed. 17.00 (0-8266-5581-5) Kehot Pubn Soc.

Maamorei Admor Hoemtzoee: Bamidbor, Vol. 5. Dov B. Schneuri. (HEB.). 382p. reprint ed. 17.00 (0-8266-5483-5) Kehot Pubn Soc.

Maamorei Admor Hoemtzoee: Beraishes. Dov B. Schneuri. (HEB.). 592p. reprint ed. 17.00 (0-8266-5488-6) Kehot Pubn Soc.

Maamorei Admor Hoemtzoee: Devorim, Vol. 1. Dov B. Schneuri. (HEB.). 368p. reprint ed. 17.00 (0-8266-5583-1) Kehot Pubn Soc.

Maamorei Admor Hoemtzoee: Devorim, Vol. 2. Dov B. Schneuri. (HEB.). 282p. reprint ed. 17.00 (0-8266-5484-3) Kehot Pubn Soc.

Maamorei Admor Hoemtzoee: Devorim, Vol. 3. Dov B. Schneuri. (HEB.). 532p. reprint ed. 17.00 (0-8266-5485-1) Kehot Pubn Soc.

Maamorei Admor Hoemtzoee: Devorim, Vol. 4. Dov B. Schneuri. (HEB.). 367p. reprint ed. 17.00 (0-8266-5486-X) Kehot Pubn Soc.

Maamorei Admor Hoemtzoee: Drushai Chassunah, Vol. 1. Dov B. Schneuri. (HEB.). 395p. reprint ed. 17.00 (0-8266-5487-8) Kehot Pubn Soc.

Maamorei Admor Hoemtzoee: Drushay Chassunah, Vol. 2. Dov B. Schneuri. (HEB.). 386p. reprint ed. 17.00 (0-8266-5491-6) Kehot Pubn Soc.

Maamorei Admor Hoemtzoee: Nach. Dov B. Schneuri. (HEB.). 624p. 1990. 17.00 (0-8266-5493-2) Kehot Pubn Soc.

Maamorei Admor Hoemtzoee: Shemois, Vol. 1. Dov B. Schneuri. (HEB.). 320p. reprint ed. 17.00 (0-8266-5489-4) Kehot Pubn Soc.

Maamorei Admor Hoemtzoee: Shemois, Vol. 2. Dov B. Schneuri. (HEB.). 383p. reprint ed. 17.00 (0-8266-5490-8) Kehot Pubn Soc.

Maamorei Admor Hoemtzoee: Vayikro, Vol. 1. Dov B. Schneuri. (HEB.). 448p. reprint ed. 17.00 (0-8266-5577-7) Kehot Pubn Soc.

Maamorei Admor Hoemtzoee: Vayikro, Vol. 2. Dov B. Schneuri. (HEB.). 496p. 1986. reprint ed. 17.00 (0-8266-5578-5) Kehot Pubn Soc.

Maamorei Admur Hazoken. Schneur Z. Baruchovitch. 460p. reprint ed. 17.00 (0-8266-5566-1, 5566); reprint ed. 17.00 (0-8266-5569-6, 5569); reprint ed. 17.00 (0-8266-5570-X, 5570) Kehot Pubn Soc.

Maamorei Admur Hazoken, Vol. 2. 2nd ed. Schneur Zalman. (HEB.). 328p. 1975. reprint ed. 17.00 (0-8266-5461-4) Kehot Pubn Soc.

Maamorei Admur Hazoken: Bereishes Ushemos. Schneur Z. Baruchovitch. 574p. reprint ed. 17.00 (0-8266-5472-X) Kehot Pubn Soc.

Maamorei Admur Hazoken: Hanochos. Schneur Z. Baruchovitch. 238p. reprint ed. 17.00 (0-8266-5559-9) Kehot Pubn Soc.

Maamorei Admur Hazoken: Inyonim. Shneur Z. Baruchovitch. 608p. reprint ed. 17.00 (0-8266-5476-2) Kehot Pubn Soc.

Maamorei Admur Hazoken: Nevi'im. Shneur Z. Baruchovitch. 376p. reprint ed. 17.00 (0-8266-5474-6) Kehot Pubn Soc.

Maamorei Admur Hazoken: Vayikro Devorim. Shneur Z. Baruchovitch. 606p. reprint ed. 17.00 (0-8266-5473-8) Kehot Pubn Soc.

Maamorei Admur Hazoken: 5563, Vol. 1. Schneur Zalman. (HEB.). 480p. 1981. 17.00 (0-8266-5463-0) Kehot Pubn Soc.

Maamorei Admur Hazoken: 5563, Vol. 2. Schneur Zalman. (HEB.). 412p. 1981. 17.00 (0-8266-5464-9) Kehot Pubn Soc.

Maamorei Admur Hazoken: 5564. Schneur Zalman. (HEB.). 368p. 1980. 17.00 (0-8266-5564-5) Kehot Pubn Soc.

Maamorei Admur Hazoken: 5565, Vol. 1. Schneur Z. Baruchovitch. 592p. reprint ed. 17.00 (0-8266-5465-7, 5565) Kehot Pubn Soc.

Maamorei Admur Hazoken: 5565, Vol. 2. Schneur Z. Baruchovitch. 556p. reprint ed. 17.00 (0-8266-5466-5, 5565) Kehot Pubn Soc.

Maamorei Admur Hazoken: 5571. Schneur Zalman. LC 86-1856. (HEB.). 332p. 1995. 20.00 (0-8266-5571-8) Kehot Pubn Soc.

Maamorei Admur Hazoken Vol. 2: Ketubim. Shneur Z. Baruchovitch. 602p. reprint ed. 17.00 (0-8266-5475-4) Kehot Pubn Soc.

Maamorei Admur Hazoken Vol. 2: 5562. Schneur Z. Baruchovitch. (HEB.). 426p. reprint ed. 17.00 (0-8266-5462-2, 5562); reprint ed. 17.00 (0-8266-5469-X, 5568) Kehot Pubn Soc.

Maamorei Admur Hazoken Ha'ktzorim: Hakzorim. Schneur Z. Baruchovitch. (HEB.). 653p. reprint ed. 17.00 (0-8266-5561-0) Kehot Pubn Soc.

Maamorei Admur Hoemtzoee: Kuntresim. Dov B. Schneersohn. (HEB.). 612p. 1991. 17.00 (0-8266-5291-3) Kehot Pubn Soc.

Maamorei Admur Hoemtzoee Vol. 4: Bamidbar. Dov B. Schneuri. LC 86-18516. (HEB.). 334p. 1987. reprint ed. 17.00 (0-8266-5582-3) Kehot Pubn Soc.

Maamorei Admur Hoemtzoee Hanacnos. Dovber Schneersohn. Ed. by Alexander Z. Piekarski. LC 86-18516.Tr. of Discourses by Rabbi Dovber Schneersohn. (HEB.). 464p. 1994. 17.00 (0-8266-5492-4) Kehot Pubn Soc.

Ma'Aneh Lashon. (HEB.). 46p. 1995. pap. 5.00 (0-8266-0242-8) Kehot Pubn Soc.

Maaneh Lashon with English Translation. Tr. by Eliyahu Touger. 94p. 1996. pap. 6.50 (0-8266-0243-6) Kehot Pubn Soc.

Maarei Mekomos Lisefer Mishne Torah. (HEB.). 864p. 1984. 20.00 (0-8266-5307-3) Kehot Pubn Soc.

Maaroof the Cobler. (Butterfly Bks.). (ARA., Illus.). 31p. 8.95 (0-86685-742-7, LDL274, Pub. by Librairie du Liban) Intl Bk Ctr.

Maarouf & the Dream Caravan. Tr. by Denys Johnson-Davies. (Tales from Egypt & the Arab World Ser.). (ARA., Illus.). 48p. (Orig.). (J). (gr. 3-8). 1996. pap. 6.95 (977-5325-42-0, Pub. by Hoopoe Bks) AMIDEAST.

Maasai. Carol Beckwith. (Illus.). 276p. 1990. pap. 34.98 (0-8109-8099-1, Pub. by Abrams) Time Warner.

Maasai. Tepilit O. Saitoti & Ole Saitoti. (Illus.). 1980. 49.50 (0-8109-1303-8) Abrams.

Maasai. Paul White. (Jungle Doctor Novels Ser.). (J). 1993. 5.99 (0-85892-280-0) O M Lit.

Maasai. Tiyambe Zeleza. LC 94-5058. (Heritage Library of African Peoples). (Illus.). 64p. (YA). (gr. 7-12). 1994. lib. bdg. 16.95 (0-8239-1757-6) Rosen Group.

Maasai Identitat und sozialer Wandel bei den Maasai, 20. Raphael Laube. 1986. 20.95 (3-906764-10-9, Pub. by P Lang) P Lang Pubng.

Maasai of East Africa, 6 vols., Set. Jamie Hetfield. LC 95-51762. (Celebrating the Peoples & Civilizations of Africa Ser.). (Illus.). 24p. (J). (gr. k-4). 1996. lib. bdg. 15.93 (0-8239-2330-4, PowerKids) Rosen Group.

Maasai of Matapato: A Study of Rituals of Rebellion. Paul Spencer. LC 87-26035. (International African Library). (Illus.). 312p. 1988. 39.95 (0-253-33625-2) Ind U Pr.

Maasailand Ecology: Pastoralist Development & Wildlife Conservation in Ngorongoro, Tanzania. K. M. Holmwood & W. A. Rodgers. (Cambridge Studies in Ecology). (Illus.). 318p. (C). 1991. text 100.00 (0-521-40002-3) Cambridge U Pr.

Ma'asar U'geulat Admor Ha'emtzai. Ed. by Shalom D. Levin. (HEB.). 214p. 1997. pap. 5.00 (0-8266-5339-1) Kehot Pubn Soc.

Maasaw: Profile of a Hopi God. Ekkehart Malotki & Michael Lomatuway'ma. LC 87-163. (American Tribal Religions Ser.: No. 11). 283p. 1987. reprint ed. pap. 87.80 (0-608-01407-9, 206217000002) Bks Demand.

Maaser Kesafim. 1982. 18.95 (0-87306-304-X) Feldheim.

Ma'asse-Buch. Entstehung und Quellengeschichte. Jakob Meitlis. (GER.). xiv, 152p. 1987. reprint ed. write for info. (3-487-07833-3) G Olms Pubs.

Maastricht & Beyond: Building the European Union. Andrew Duff et al. Ed. by Roy Pryce & John Pinder. LC 94-8621. 328p. (C). 1994. pap. 24.99 (0-415-10818-7, B3523) Routledge.

Maastricht Treaty & the Economic & Monetary Union. Alfredo Panarella. (Law Ser.: Vol. 2). 83p. (Orig.). 1995. pap. 34.00 (90-6186-689-8, Pub. by Leuven Univ) Coronet Bks.

An Asterisk (*) at the beginning of an entry indicates that the title is appearing for the first time.

Maastricht Way to EMU. Michele Fratianni et al. LC 92-21840. (Essays in International Finance Ser.: No. 187). 50p. 1992. pap. 10.00 (*0-88165-094-3*) Princeton U Int Finan Econ.

MAAT: The American African Path of Sankofa. Gbonde I. Wase. 160p. 1998. pap. 12.95 (*0-9663880-0-3*) MBADU Publ.

Maat in Egyptian Autobiographies & Related Studies. Miriam Lichtheim. (Orbis Biblicus et Orientalis Ser.: Vol. 120). 211p. 1992. text 45.00 (*3-7278-0846-2*, Pub. by Presses Univ Fribourg) Eisenbrauns.

Maat Magick: A Guide to Self-Initiation. Nema. LC 95-18084. 256p. 1995. reprint ed. pap. 14.95 (*0-87728-827-5*) Weiser.

***Maathir - Ul - Umara.** Tr. by Beveridge. 1999. reprint ed. 64.00 (*81-7536-159-X*, Pub. by Low Price) S Asia.

Maatics: African Ethical Foundations. Omenana Collective Research Group Staff. (Laying the Foundations into the Heart Ser.). 60p. (Orig.). 1985. pap. 5.95 (*0-943324-21-1*) Omenana.

Maatskappywet 61 Van 1973 en Wet Op Beslote Korporasies 69 Van, 1984. 2nd ed. J. T. Pretorius. 634p. 1993. pap. write for info. (*0-7021-2918-6*, Pub. by Juta & Co) Gaunt.

Ma'avak Medini Be-Malkodet see No Way Out: The Politics of Polish Jewry, 1935-1939

Maayan Bais Hasho'Eivah. Shimon Schwab. (HEB.). 26.99 (*0-89906-031-5*, MAAY) Mesorah Pubns.

MAB Beg Memorial Volume. Ed. by A. Ali & P. Hoodbhoy. 304p. (C). 1991. text 89.00 (*981-02-0714-X*) World Scientific Pub.

Mab und Zahl in der Gotischen Baukunst. Konrad Hecht. (Abhandlungen der Braunschweigischen Wissenschaftlichen Gesellschaft Ser.: Bds. XXI, XXII, XXIII). (GER.). xii, 484p. 1997. reprint ed. 80.00 (*3-487-06753-6*) G Olms Pubs.

Mabbott As Poe Scholar: The Early Years. Maureen C. Mabbott. Ed. by Averil J. Kadis. (Orig.). 1980. pap. 2.95 (*0-910556-14-8*) Enoch Pratt.

Mabbul. Jill Storm. 220p. (YA). 1999. pap. 10.95 (*1-929078-18-8*, MABOO) Gods Kids.

Mab'Ei Hakittah: A Curriculum of Classroom Hebrew Expressions. Debby Leibenstein. 1997. pap. 3.75 (*1-878895-04-4*, C015) Torah Umesorah.

Mabel. Suzanne M. Coil. LC 94-9791. (Illus.). 32p. (J). (ps-3). 1994. 15.95 (*0-87905-602-9*) Gibbs Smith Pub.

***Mabel Dancing.** Amy Hest. LC 99-34807. (Illus.). 40p. (J). 2000. 15.99 (*0-7636-0746-0*) Candlewick Pr.

Mabel Dodge Luhan. Jane V. Nelson. (Western Writers Ser.: No. 55). (Illus.). 50p. (Orig.). 1982. pap. 4.95 (*0-88430-029-3*) Boise St U W Writ Ser.

Mabel Dodge Luhan: New Woman, New Worlds. Lois Palken Rudnick. LC 84-7415. (Illus.). 384p. 1987. reprint ed. pap. 19.95 (*0-8263-0995-X*) U of NM Pr.

Mabel Dwight: A Catalogue Raisonne of the Lithographs. Susan B. Robinson & John Pirog. LC 95-48281. (Illus.). 344p. 1996. 65.00 (*1-56098-646-8*) Smithsonian.

Mabel in Her Twenties. Rosaire Appel. (Illus.). 1992. 18.95 (*0-932511-43-0*); pap. 8.95 (*0-932511-44-9*) Fiction Coll.

***Mabel Lucie Attwell.** Chris Beetles. (Illus.). 110p. 1999. pap. 19.50 (*1-871136-56-3*, Pub. by Beetles Ltd) Antique Collect.

Mabel Lucie Attwell's Going to Bed Tales. Mabel L. Attwell. (Illus.). 128p. (J). 1996. 14.95 (*1-85479-938-X*, Pub. by M OMara) Assoc Pubs Grp.

Mabel McKay: Weaving the Dream. Greg Sarris. LC 93-38188. (Portraits of American Genius Ser.: No. 1). 1994. 40.00 (*0-520-08612-0*, Pub. by U CA Pr) Cal Prin Full Svc.

Mabel McKay: Weaving the Dream. Greg Sarris. LC 93-38188. (Portraits of American Genius Ser.: Vol. 1). (Illus.). 1997. pap. 12.95 (*0-520-20968-0*, Pub. by U CA Pr) Cal Prin Full Svc.

***Mabel Mercer.** James Haskins. 220p. 2000. pap. 12.95 (*1-56649-132-0*) Welcome Rain.

Mabel Murple. Sheree Fitch. (Illus.). 24p. 1997. pap. 4.95 (*0-385-25634-5*) Doubleday.

Mabel Normand: A Source Book to Her Life & Films. William T. Sherman. LC 94-93892. (Illus.). 475p. (Orig.). 1994. 95.00 (*0-9643760-0-8*); pap. 65.00 (*0-9643760-4-0*) W T Sherman.

***Mabel Ran Away with the Toys.** Jan Wahl. (Illus.). 32p. (J). (ps-3). 2000. 16.95 (*1-58089-059-8*); pap. 6.95 (*1-58089-067-9*, Whispering Coyote) Charlesbridge Pub.

Mabel Takes a Sail. Emily Chetkowski. (Illus.). 64p. (J). (gr. k-4). 1999. pap. text 10.50 (*1-880158-26-4*) J N Townsend.

Mabel Takes the Ferry. Emily Chetkowski. Ed. by Donald McIntire. LC 95-199886. (Illus.). 32p. (Orig.). (J). (ps-4). 1995. pap. text 7.95 (*0-929537-01-7*) Herit Pub Inc.

Mabel the Whale. Margaret Hillert. (Illus.). (J). (ps-2). 1958. pap. 5.10 (*0-8136-5546-3*); lib. bdg. 7.95 (*0-8136-5046-1*) Modern Curr.

Mabel Walker Willebrandt: A Study of Power, Loyalty, & Law. Dorothy M. Brown. LC 83-6651. (Illus.). 348p. 1984. 42.50 (*0-87049-402-3*) U of Tenn Pr.

***Mabela the Clever.** Margaret Read MacDonald. LC 00-8307. (Illus.). (J). 2000. write for info. (*0-8075-4902-9*) A Whitman.

Mabel's Santa Fe & Taos: Bohemian Legends (1900-1950) Elmo Baca. LC 99-16868. (Illus.). 184p. 1999. 29.95 (*0-87905-913-3*) Gibbs Smith Pub.

Mabinogi: A Book of Essays. Ed. by C. W. Sullivan, III. LC 95-52929. (Medieval Casebooks Ser.: Vol. 16). (Illus.). 416p. 1996. reprint ed. text 80.00 (*0-8153-1482-5*, H1791) Garland.

Mabinogi & Other Medieval Welsh Tales. Ed. by Patrick K. Ford. LC 76-3885. 1977. pap. 17.95 (*0-520-03414-7*, Pub. by U CA Pr) Cal Prin Full Svc.

Mabinogion. Jeffrey Gantz. (Classics Ser.). 372p. 1976. pap. 9.95 (*0-14-044322-3*, Penguin Classics) Viking Penguin.

Mabinogion. Ed. by Gwyn Jones & Thomas Jones. 356p. 1993. pap. 5.95 (*0-460-87297-4*, Everyman's Classic Lib) Tuttle Pubng.

Mabinogion. Tr. by Charlotte E. Guest. LC 96-49016. (Thrift Editions Ser.). 192p. 1997. reprint ed. pap. text 2.00 (*0-486-29541-9*) Dover.

Mabinogion. Ivor B. John. LC 70-139174. (Popular Studies in Mythology, Romance & Folklore: No. 11). reprint ed. 12.50 (*0-404-53511-9*) AMS Pr.

***Mable Hoffman's Complete Crockery Cookery.** Mable Hoffman. LC 00-25623. (Illus.). 2000. write for info. (*1-55788-349-1*, HP Books) Berkley Pub.

Mable Murple. Sheree Fitch. (Illus.). 32p. 1995. 8.95 (*0-385-25480-6*) Doubleday.

Mable Murple. Sheree Fitch. (Illus.). 24p. 1996. pap. 9.95 (*0-385-25614-0*) Doubleday.

Mabo: A Judicial Revolution: Aboriginal Land Rights Decision & Its Impact on Australian Law. Ed. by M. A. Stephenson & Suri Ratnapala. 225p. 1993. pap. text 19.95 (*0-7022-2546-0*, Pub. by Univ Queensland Pr) Intl Spec Bk.

Mabo: The Native Title Legislation. Ed. by M. A. Stephenson. LC 95-162125. 209p. 1995. pap. 24.95 (*0-7022-2746-3*, Pub. by Univ Queensland Pr) Intl Spec Bk.

Mabo: What the High Court Said. Peter Butt & Robert Eagleson. 128p. 1993. pap. 21.00 (*1-86287-118-3*, Pub. by Federation Pr) Gaunt.

Mabo Vol. 1: What the High Court Said & What the Government Did. 2nd ed. Peter Butt & Robert Eagleson. 99p. 1996. pap. 24.00 (*1-86287-207-4*, Pub. by Federation Pr) Gaunt.

Mabou Pioneers: A Genealogical, 2 vols., Vol. 1. A. D. MacDonald. 880p. text 29.95 (*0-88780-005-X*, Pub. by Formac Publ Co) Formac Dist Ltd.

Mabregelrecht: Kriminalpolitik, Normgenese und Systematische Struktur einer Schuldunabhangigen Gefahrenabwehr. Heinz Kammeier. xvi, 316p. 1996. write for info. (*3-11-014850-1*) De Gruyter.

Mabry Bass's Tarboro: From 1950 to 1990. Mabry Bass. Ed. by Roland Taylor. 480p. 1997. pap. 19.95 (*1-884570-77-1*) Research Triangle.

Mabuhay: Sentimental Journey World War II Experience. Ralph G. Myers. (Illus.). 62p. (Orig.). (C). 1989. pap. 7.95 (*0-9625571-0-2*) R E Myers.

Mabuto. Agnes Adachi. 112p. 2000. pap. 11.00 (*0-8059-4676-4*) Dorrance.

Mac. John MacLean. 192p. 1989. reprint ed. pap. 2.95 (*0-380-70700-4*, Avon Bks) Morrow Avon.

Mac - Microbiology Electron. Turney. 1994. 84.74 (*0-697-22259-4*, WCB McGr Hill) McGrw-H Hghr Educ.

MAC-AE: Business Ethics 96/97. 8th ed. Richardson. 1996. (*0-697-31618-1*, WCB McGr Hill) McGrw-H Hghr Educ.

MAC-AE: Human Development 96/97. 24th ed. Freiberg. 1996. (*0-697-31668-8*, WCB McGr Hill) McGrw-H Hghr Educ.

Mac Almanac. Sharon Aker. (Illus.). 960p. (Orig.). 1994. pap. 29.95 (*1-56276-143-9*, Ziff-Davis Pr) Que.

Mac Anatomy: A Graphical Guide. Jeff Baudin & John Bradley. 1995. pap. 32.95 incl. cd-rom (*1-55828-438-9*, MIS Pr) IDG Bks.

Mac & His Dog, Sir John. Margaret J. Roach.Tr. of Mac y Su Perro, Don Juan. (SPA., Illus.). (Orig.). (J). (gr. k-8). 1993. pap. 13.50 (*1-882666-01-1*); pap. 13.50 (*1-882666-00-3*) M Roach & Assocs.

Mac & His Dog, Sir John. Margaret J. Roach.Tr. of Mac y Su Perro, Don Juan. (ITA., Illus.). (Orig.). (J). (ps-8). 1996. pap. 15.00 (*1-882666-03-8*) M Roach & Assocs.

Mac & Ray's Olympiad Cookbook. Ron Hokanson. (Illus.). 86p. (Orig.). 1996. 14.95 (*0-9651297-0-5*) Harbor Rest.

Mac & Zach from Hackensack. George L. Rogers. (Illus.). 32p. (J). (gr. k-6). 1992. pap. 4.95 (*0-938399-06-3*); lib. bdg. 12.95 (*0-938399-07-1*) Acorn Pub MN.

***Mac Answers!** 2nd ed. Shelly Brisbin. 1999. pap. 24.99 (*0-07-212399-0*) McGraw-H Intl.

Mac Answers! Certified Tech Support. Bob LeVitus & Shelly Brisbin. LC 99-176038. 458p. 1998. pap. 24.99 (*0-07-211919-5*) McGraw.

Mac Assembly System Version 2.0. William Ford & William Topp. (Computer Science Ser.). 1992. spiral bd. 35.00 (*0-669-32716-6*) Jones & Bartlett.

Mac Assembly System Version 2.0 with Disk. William Ford & William Topp. (Computer Science). 1992. spiral bd. 35.00 incl. disk (*0-7637-0595-0*) Jones & Bartlett.

Mac Attack! The Road to 62!, Collectors Ed. Honor Books Staff. LC 99-226693. 1998. pap. 6.99 (*1-57757-062-6*) Trade Life.

Mac Basic Statistics. Moore. 1995. 48.00 (*0-7167-2679-3*) W H Freeman.

Mac Bathroom Reader. Owen W. Linzmayer. LC 94-67199. 320p. 1994. pap. 12.99 (*0-7821-1531-4*) Sybex.

Mac Bible Goodies Pack. Ed. by Victor Gavenda. 1996. pap. 24.95 incl. cd-rom (*0-201-88677-4*) Peachpit Pr.

Mac Biology Explor Essentials Of Biology. Graham. 1997. text 18.00 (*0-13-351926-0*) P-H.

Mac Chapter Disk. Douglas W. Nance. (Computer Science Ser.). (C). 1993. pap. write for info. (*0-314-00445-9*) West Pub.

Mac Classic & SE Repair & Upgrade Secrets. Larry Pina. (Illus.). 296p. (C). 1995. pap. text 28.00 (*1-56609-022-9*) Peachpit Pr.

Mac Club! Debra Schepp et al. LC 93-8520. (Illus.). 82p. (J). (gr. 1-3). 1993. 19.60 (*0-8306-4253-6*) McGraw-Hill Prof.

Mac Cognitive Psychology. 4th ed. Anderson. (C). 48.00 (*0-7167-2686-6*) W H Freeman.

Mac Computerized Testbank Abnormal Psychology Version B. Ronald Comer. (C). 1993. 48.00 (*0-7167-2455-3*) W H Freeman.

Mac de Design. (Illus.). 216p. 1995. 39.95 (*4-900781-01-0*, Pub. by AG Pubs) Bks Nippan.

Mac de Design, Vol. 2. AG Publishers Editors. (Illus.). 213p. 1997. 79.95 (*4-900781-13-4*, Pub. by AG Pubs Inc) Bks Nippan.

Mac Demystified: The Uncompromised Desktop Reference. Sandy Clark et al. LC 98-216405. xv, 736p. 1998. write for info. (*1-56784-425-1*) Newbridge Educ.

Mac Excel 4.0. 1993. 29.95 (*1-56877-033-2*); teacher ed. 49.95 (*1-56877-034-0*) Catapult WA.

Mac Excel 3.0: Beginners. 1993. 29.95 (*1-56877-027-8*); teacher ed. 49.95 (*1-56877-028-6*) Catapult WA.

Mac for the Teacher: ClarisWorks Version. Gregg Brownell et al. Ed. by Baxter. LC 93-41588. 450p. (C). 1994. mass mkt. 27.25 (*0-314-02505-7*) West Pub.

Mac for the Teacher: ClarisWorks Version. 2nd ed. Gregg Brownell. LC 96-19129. 350p. 1996. pap. 44.95 (*0-314-20057-6*) West Pub.

Mac Frog Nerve Experiments. Gunther. 1993. 91.00 (*0-697-21235-1*, WCB McGr Hill) McGrw-H Hghr Educ.

Mac Fundamentals with System 6. 1993. 29.95 (*1-56877-035-9*); teacher ed. 49.95 (*1-56877-036-7*) Catapult WA.

Mac Graphics: A Basic Design Workshop. Bo Numata. (Illus.). 144p. 1995. pap. 39.95 (*4-7661-0830-2*, Pub. by Graphic-Sha) Bks Nippan.

Mac-Graphics: A Designer's Visual Guide to Graphics for the Apple Macintosh. Ching S. Lim & Gim Lee. (Illus.). 288p. 1991. pap. 49.95 (*0-8306-1072-3*, 3864, Windcrest) TAB Bks.

Mac-Graphics Interactive Workshop: A Step-by-Step Visual Guide to Graphics for the Apple Macintosh. 3rd ed. Octogram Publishing Staff. (Illus.). 290p. 1995. pap. 79.95 incl. cd-rom (*0-201-88365-1*) Peachpit Pr.

Mac Is Not a Typewriter. Robin Williams. 72p. (C). 1995. pap. text 9.95 (*0-938151-31-2*, Pub. by Peachpit Pr) Addison-Wesley.

***Mac Laren's Bride.** Debra Dier. 368p. 2000. pap. 5.50 (*0-8439-4768-3*, Leisure Bks) Dorchester Pub Co.

Mac Maple Notebook - Calculus. 6th ed. Swokowski & Michael Olinick. (Mathematics Ser.). 1994. mass mkt. 8.00 (*0-534-93635-0*) PWS Pubs.

Mac Mathematica Notebook - Calculus. 6th ed. Swokowski & Michael Olinick. (Mathematics Ser.). 1994. mass mkt. 8.00 (*0-534-93633-4*) PWS Pubs.

Mac Mathematics Human Endeavor. Jacobs. 1994. 48.00 (*0-7167-2612-2*) W H Freeman.

Mac Multimedia & CD-ROMS for Dummies. Deke McClelland. 400p. 1995. pap. 19.99 (*1-56884-910-9*) IDG Bks.

Mac Multimedia & CD-ROMs for Dummies, Interactive Multimedia Value Pack. Deke McClelland. LC 95-77669. 416p. 1995. pap. 29.99 (*1-56884-911-7*); pap. 29.99 (*1-56884-912-5*) IDG Bks.

Mac OS 8: Visual QuickStart Guide. Maria Langer. LC 97-221091. 320p. (C). 1997. pap. text 17.95 (*0-201-69645-2*) Peachpit Pr.

Mac OS 8 for Dummies. Bob LeVitus. LC 97-80123. 432p. 1997. pap. 19.99 (*0-7645-0271-9*) IDG Bks.

***MAC OS 8.x: Module 2.** Niit. (CT Course Instructor Training Ser.). 2000. 8.00 (*0-619-02318-X*) Course Tech.

Mac OS 8.5: Visual QuickStart Guide. Maria Langer. LC 99-167854. (Visual QuickStart Guide Ser.). 336p. (C). 1998. pap. text 17.95 (*0-201-35357-1*, Pub. by Peachpit Pr) Addison-Wesley.

Mac OS 8.2 Black Book. Mark R. Bell. LC 98-33996. (Black Book Ser.). (Illus.). 754p. 1998. pap. 49.99 (*1-57610-304-8*) Coriolis Grp.

Mac OS 8 Unleashed. Lisa Lee. 1997. pap. text 39.99 incl. cd-rom (*1-56830-419-6*) Hayden.

***Mac OS 8 Web Server Cookbook.** David L. Hart & Philip E. Bourne. LC 98-24444. 400p. 1998. pap. text 39.99 (*0-13-520016-4*, Prentice Hall) P-H.

Mac OS 8.5 for Dummies. Bob LeVitus. LC QA76.76.O63L48684. (For Dummies Ser.). 432p. 1998. pap. 19.99 (*0-7645-0397-9*) IDG Bks.

Mac OS in a Nutshell. Rita F. Lewis. Ed. by Mark Stone. (In a Nutshell Ser.). (Illus.). 376p. 2000. pap. 24.95 (*1-56592-533-5*) OReilly & Assocs.

***Mac OS 9: The Complete Reference.** Gene Steinberg. 916p. 2000. pap. 39.99 (*0-07-212506-3*) McGraw.

***Mac OS 9: The Missing Manual.** David Pogue. (Illus.). 460p. 2000. pap. 19.95 (*1-56592-857-1*) OReilly & Assocs.

***Mac OS 9: Visual QuickStart Guide.** Maria Langer. 376p. 1999. pap. text 17.99 (*0-201-70004-2*) Peachpit Pr.

***Mac OS 9 for Dummies.** Bob LeVitus. LC 99-66422. (For Dummies Ser.). (Illus.). 432p. 1999. pap. 19.99 (*0-7645-0652-8*) IDG Bks.

***MAC OS 9 Guide.** Brad Miser. 450p. 2000. pap. 29.99 (*0-7897-2312-3*) Que.

***Mac OS 9.1 Book: The Most Up-to-Date Guide to the Newest Features of the Mac OS.** Mark R. Bell. (Illus.). 600p. 2000. pap. write for info. (*1-57610-776-0*) Coriolis Grp.

***Mac OS X.** David Pogue. (Missing Manuals Ser.). 2000. pap. 19.95 (*1-56592-867-9*) OReilly & Assocs.

***Mac OS X Administrator's Guide.** Andrew G. Russell. 500p. 2000. pap. 39.99 (*0-7615-2415-0*) Prima Pub.

***Mac OS X Black Book: The Reference Guide for Power Users.** Mark Bell. (Illus.). 700p. 2000. pap. 49.99 (*1-57610-606-3*) Coriolis Grp.

***Mac OS X Book: A Beginner's Guide to the Newest Mac OS.** Mark Bell. (Illus.). 580p. 2000. pap. 39.99 (*1-57610-605-5*) Coriolis Grp.

***Mac OS X Clearly Explained.** John Rizzo. (Illus.). 2000. pap. 44.95 (*0-12-589327-2*) Morgan Kaufmann.

***Mac OS X for Dummies.** Robert Le Vitus. (For Dummies Ser.). (Illus.). 424p. 2000. pap. 19.95 (*0-7645-0706-0*) IDG Bks.

Mac OS 8. (Quick Study Computer Ser.). 4p. pap. 3.95 (*1-57222-241-7*) Barcharts.

Mac OS 8.5 Book. Mark R. Bell. LC 99-18767. 599p. 1999. pap. text 39.99 (*1-57610-443-5*) Coriolis Grp.

***Mac OS 8.6 Fast & Easy.** Valda Hilley. (Fast & Easy Ser.). 1999. pap. 16.99 (*0-7615-1984-X*) Prima Pub.

***Mac OS/X Server Black Book: The System Administrator's Guide to Mac OS/X Server.** Mark Bell et al. (Black Book Ser.). (Illus.). 700p. 2000. pap. 49.99 (*1-57610-539-3*) Coriolis Grp.

Mac Perry's Florida Lawn & Garden Care. Mac Perry. LC 84-80148. (Illus.). 128p. 1984. pap. 6.95 (*0-9613236-0-4*) Florida Flair Bks.

***Mac Perry's Florida Lawn & Garden Care.** Mac Perry et al. LC 99-64731. (Illus.). 128p. 1999. pap. 8.95 (*0-8200-0417-0*) Great Outdoors.

Mac pour les Nuls. David Pogue. (FRE.). 338p. 1995. 49.95 (*0-7859-9852-7*) Fr & Eur.

Mac Powerpoint 3.0: Beginners. 1993. 29.95 (*1-56877-037-5*); teacher ed. 49.95 (*1-56877-038-3*) Catapult WA.

Mac Printer Secrets. Larry Pina. 1990. 34.95 (*0-672-48463-3*, Bobbs) Macmillan.

Mac Programming for Dummies. Dan Parks Sydow. LC 94-76644. 350p. 1994. pap. 19.95 (*1-56884-173-6*) IDG Bks.

Mac Programming for Dummies. 3rd ed. Dan Parks Sydow. LC 99-61115. (For Dummies Ser.). 432p. 1999. pap. 29.99 incl. cd-rom (*0-7645-0544-0*) IDG Bks.

Mac ROM Reference: A Programmer's Guide to Manintosh Macros. Keith Mattews & Jay Friedland. (Illus.). 650p. 1988. 29.95 (*0-685-18871-X*) P-H.

***Mac School Primer: A User's Guide to the Mac School Student Information System.** Lawrence Bickford. 206p. 1998. spiral bd. 32.00 (*0-9637294-9-7*) Sugar Hill Pr.

Mac Shareware 500: The Last Word on the Virus-Free Mac Shareware, 1994. 2nd ed. Ruffin Prevost & Rob Terrell. (Illus.). 458p. 1998. pap. 20.00 incl. disk (*0-7881-5767-1*) DIANE Pub.

***Mac Side Up.** Bob Elsdale. (Illus.). 32p. (J). (gr. k-3). 2000. 15.99 (*0-525-46467-0*, Dutton Child) Peng Put Young Read.

Mac TB Social Animal. 7th ed. Gary A. Thibodeau et al. 1994. 48.00 (*0-7167-2689-0*) W H Freeman.

Mac Test Bank Abnormal Psychology. 2nd ed. Comer. 1995. 48.00 (*0-7167-2693-9*) W H Freeman.

Mac Testbank Development of Children. Cole. (C). 1993. 48.00 (*0-7167-2473-1*) W H Freeman.

Mac3D: Three Dimensional Modeling & Rendering on the Macintosh. Stuart Mealing. (Illus.). 246p. (Orig.). 1994. pap. text 34.95 (*1-871516-46-3*, Pub. by Intellect) Cromland.

Mac Tips & Tricks: Essential Book for the Mac User. Caroline Bassett. LC 94-221889. 1994. pap. 14.95 (*1-55958-537-4*) Prima Pub.

Mac Tutorial Software-Mechanics. Raines et al. 1992. text 410.25 (*0-534-93076-X*) PWS Pubs.

Mac User Guide to Shareware. Gregory Wasson. (Guide to...Ser.). 421p. (Orig.). 1993. pap. 34.95 incl. disk (*1-56276-076-9*, Ziff-Davis Pr) Que.

Mac-V-SOG Command History Annex B, 1971-1972: The Last Secret of the Vietnam War, 2 vols., Set. Charles F. Reske. (Illus.). 350p. (Orig.). 1990. pap. 49.95 (*0-939427-63-X*, 09053) Alpha Pubns OH.

Mac-V-SOG Command History Annex B, 1971-1972: The Last Secret of the Vietnam War, 2 vols., Vol. 1. Charles F. Reske. (Illus.). 350p. (Orig.). 1990. pap. 26.95 (*0-939427-60-5*) Alpha Pubns OH.

Mac-V-SOG Command History Annex B, 1971-1972: The Last Secret of the Vietnam War, 2 vols., Vol. 2. Charles F. Reske. (Illus.). 350p. (Orig.). 1990. pap. 26.95 (*0-939427-61-3*) Alpha Pubns OH.

***Mac Wingate Series Assignments V & VI: Mission Code Echo: Springboard & Mission Code Foxtrot: Snow Queen.** Bryan Swift. 294p. 1999. pap. 17.95 (*1-58444-064-3*) DiscUs Bks.

***Mac Wingate Series Assignments IX, X & XI: Mission Code India: Track & Destroy, Mission Code Juiette: Survival & Mission Code Kilo: Scorpion.** Bryan Swift. 411p. 1999. pap. 19.95 (*1-58444-066-X*) DiscUs Bks.

***Mac Wingate Series Assignments I & II: Mission Code Alpha: Symbol & Mission Code Bravo: King's Pawn.** Bryan Swift. 286p. 1999. pap. 17.95 (*1-58444-062-7*) DiscUs Bks.

***Mac Wingate Series Assignments VII & VIII: Mission Code Golf: Acropolis & Mission Code Hotel: Volcano.** Bryan Swift. 285p. 1999. pap. 17.95 (*1-58444-065-1*) DiscUs Bks.

***Mac Wingate Series Assignments III & IV: Mission Code Charlie: Minotaur & Mission Code Delta: Granite Island.** Bryan Swift. 301p. 1999. pap. 17.95 (*1-58444-063-5*) DiscUs Bks.

Mac with Basic: Testbank. Steven L. Mandell. Date not set. pap. text, teacher ed. write for info. (*0-314-00706-7*) West Pub.

Mac Without Drugs. Maxx. 1994. 395.00 (*0-316-99689-0*) Little.

Mac Word 5.0: Beginners. 1993. 29.95 (*1-56877-039-1*); teacher ed. 49.95 (*1-56877-040-5*) Catapult WA.

Mac Word 5.1. 1993. 29.95 (*1-56877-103-7*); teacher ed. 49.95 (*1-56877-102-9*) Catapult WA.

Mac Word 5.1: Beginners. 1993. 29.95 (*1-56877-041-3*); teacher ed. 49.95 (*1-56877-042-1*) Catapult WA.

Mac World Mac & Power Mac Secrets. 2nd ed. David Pogue & Joseph Schorr. (Illus.). 1072p. 1998. pap. 30.00 incl. disk (*0-7881-5663-2*) DIANE Pub.

M

***Mac World OS 9 Bible.** Lon Poole. LC 99-58029. 936p. 2000. pap. 39.99 (*0-7645-3414-9*) IDG Bks.

Mac y Su Perro, Don Juan see Mac & His Dog, Sir John

***Macadonia Government & Business Contacts Handbook: Strategic Government & Business Contacts for Conducting Succesful Business, Export-Import & Investment Activity, 110.** International Business Publications, USA Staff & Global Investment Center, USA Staff. (World Export-Import & Business Library: 52). (Illus.). 250p. 2000. pap. 99.95 (*0-7397-6091-2*) Intl Business Pubns.

Macadonian & Eng. see Winter Song

Macady: A Novel. Jennie Hansen. LC 95-19135. 1995. pap. 10.95 (*1-55503-820-4*, 01111949) Covenant Comms.

Macalister: or Dying in the Dark. Douglas LePan. LC 95-157703. 144p. 1995. pap. 14.95 (*1-55082-139-3*, Pub. by Quarry Pr) LPC InBook.

Macallister's Task. Julian Jay Savarin. 1999. 25.00 (*0-7278-2278-0*) Severn Hse.

Macanche Island, el Peten, Guatemala: Excavations, Pottery, & Artifacts. Prudence M. Rice. LC 87-2040. (Illus.). 280p. (C). 1987. 49.95 (*0-8130-0838-7*) U Press Fla.

Macao: Mysterious Decay & Romance. Ed. by Donald Pittis & Susan J. Henders. (Illus.). 284p. 1998. pap. text 32.00 (*0-19-590569-5*) OUP.

***Macao Business & Investment Opportunities Yearbook: Investment, Export-Import & Other Business Opportunities & Contacts, 110 vols.** International Business Publications, USA Staff & Global Investment Center, USA Staff. (World Business Opportunities Library Ser.: Vol. 199). (Illus.). 350p. 2000. pap. 99.95 (*0-7397-1092-3*) Intl Business Pubns.

***Macao Business Law Handbook: Basic Business Legislation & Regulations Affecting Business & Investment Activities, 110 vols.** International Business Publications, USA Staff & Global Investment Center, USA Staff. (World Law Handbooks Library: Vol. 199). (Illus.). 2000. pap. 99.95 (*0-7397-1081-8*) Intl Business Pubns.

***Macao Investment & Business Guide: Investment, Export-Import, Foreign Economic Assistance Projects, Contacts & More.** International Business Publications, USA Staff & Global Investment Center, USA Staff. (World Investment Guides Library Ser.: Vol. 203). (Illus.). 350p. 2000. pap. 99.95 (*0-7397-1080-X*) Intl Business Pubns.

***Macao Remembers.** Jill McGivering. LC 99-36869. (Illus.). 248p. 1999. text 27.00 (*0-19-591735-9*) OUP.

***Macao Streets.** Cesar Guillen Nunez. LC 99-31642. (Illus.). 148p. 1999. text 45.00 (*0-19-587766-7*) OUP.

***Macao 2000.** Jean Berlie. LC 99-44985. 256p. 2000. text 35.00 (*0-19-592074-0*) OUP.

Macarena & Party Time Favorites. Ed. by Carol Cuellar. (Illus.). 144p. (Orig.). (YA). 1996. pap. text 14.95 (*1-57623-640-4*, MF9646) Wrner Bros.

Macaria: or Altars of Sacrifice. Augusta J. Evans. LC 91-30680. (Library of Southern Civilization). 448p. (C). 1992. text 55.00 (*0-8071-1661-0*); pap. text 24.95 (*0-8071-1662-9*) La State U Pr.

Macario. B. Traven. (SPA.). 1997. pap. 9.98 (*968-403-015-0*) Selector.

Macario. 3rd ed. Bruno Traven. Ed. by Sheilah R. Wilson. (Illus.). 153p. (C). 1995. pap. 9.95 (*0-942566-26-2*) LinguaText.

Macario, el Mono Sabio. Natalio Dominguez. (Fabulas Creaticas Ser.). (SPA.). 28p. (J). 1994. pap. write for info. (*0-929441-61-3*) Pubns Puertorriquenas.

***Macaroni & Cheese, Hot Dogs & Peas.** Christine Hickson. (Illus.). 34p. (J). (ps-k). 2000. 7.99 (*0-570-07044-9*) Concordia.

***Macaroni Math.** Ohanesian. 27p. (J). 2000. pap. 7.95 (*0-07-134826-3*) McGraw.

Macaroni Mess. Created by Francine Pascal. (Sweet Valley Kids Ser.: No. 72). 96p. (J). (gr. 1-3). 1997. pap. 3.50 (*0-553-48339-0*, Sweet Valley) BDD Bks Young Read.

Macaroni Mess. Created by Francine Pascal. (Sweet Valley Kids Ser.: No. 72). (J). (gr. 1-3). 1997. 8.60 (*0-606-11952-3*, Pub. by Turtleback) Demco.

***Macaroni on Tuesdays.** Daniel Roturra. 198p. 2000. pap. 10.95 (*1-929416-24-5*) Magner Pubg.

Macaroni Penguins. large type ed. Erik D. Stoops. Ed. by Graphic Arts & Production Staff. (Young Explorer Series II: Vol. 4). (Illus.). 32p. (J). (gr. 3-7). 1997. lib. bdg. 12.95 (*1-890475-09-2*) Faulkners Pub.

Macaronic Sermons: Bilingualism & Preaching in Late Medieval England. Siegfried Wenzel. (Recentiores: Later Latin Texts & Contexts Ser.). 376p. (C). 1994. text 57.50 (*0-472-10521-3*, 10521) U of Mich Pr.

MacArthur. Gavin Long. (Military Commanders Ser.). 1998. pap. 18.95 (*0-938289-14-4*, 289144) Combined Pub.

MacArthur: His Rendezvous with History. Courtney Whitney. LC 77-2965. 547p. 1977. reprint ed. lib. bdg. 75.00 (*0-8371-9564-0*, WHMA, Greenwood Pr) Greenwood.

MacArthur: Melbourne to Tokyo. Edward T. Imparato. LC 97-1453. 156p. 1997. 19.95 (*1-57249-050-0*, Burd St Pr) White Mane Pub.

MacArthur & Sutherland: The Good Years. Paul P. Rogers. LC 89-27560. 408p. 1990. 75.00 (*0-275-92918-3*, C2918, Praeger Pubs) Greenwood.

***MacArthur & the American Century: A Reader.** Ed. by William M. Leary. (Illus.). 480p. 2000. 40.00 (*0-8032-2930-5*) U of Nebr Pr.

MacArthur CDI Words & Gestures: Re-order Set of 20 Forms. Larry Fenson. 1993. 24.50 (*1-56593-155-6*, 0490) Singular Publishing.

MacArthur CDI Words & Sentences: Re-Order Set of 20 Forms. Larry Fenson. 1993. 24.95 (*1-56593-156-4*, 0491) Thomson Learn.

MacArthur Communicative Development Inventories: User's Guide & Technical Manual & Forms. Larry Fenson et al. (Illus.). 100p. (Orig.). (C). 1993. pap. text 154.95 (*1-56593-154-8*, 0489) Thomson Learn.

MacArthur Communicative Development Inventories (CDI) Users Guide & Technical Manual. Larry Fenson. (Illus.). 100p. (Orig.). (C). 1993. pap. 37.50 (*1-56593-259-5*, 0572) Thomson Learn.

MacArthur Competence Assessment Tool for Treatment. Thomas Grisso & Paul S. Appelbaum. LC 98-19161. 54p. 1998. 23.95 (*1-56887-041-8*) Pro Resource.

MacArthur New Testament Commentary Series, 9 bks., Set. John J. MacArthur, Jr. 174.91 (*0-8024-7587-6*) Moody.

***MacArthur Strikes Back: Decision at Buna: New Guinea, 1942-1943.** Harry A. Gailey. LC 00-38521. (Illus.). 272p. 2000. 27.95 (*0-89141-702-8*) Presidio Pr.

MacArthur Study Bible, 1. Macarther Study Staff. 1998. 49.99 (*0-8499-5421-5*) Word Pub.

MacArthur Study Bible. John MacArthur. 1998. 69.99 (*0-8499-1562-7*) Word Pub.

MacArthur Study Bible. Ed. by John MacArthur. 1998. 89.99 (*0-8499-1563-5*); 69.99 (*0-8499-5422-3*); lthr. 129.99 (*0-8499-5423-1*) Word Pub.

MacArthur Study Bible. Ed. by John F. MacArthur, Jr. (Illus.). 2200p. 1997. bond lthr. 59.99 (*0-8499-1223-7*) Word Pub.

MacArthur Study Bible. Ed. by John R. MacArthur. (Illus.). 1997. cd-rom 39.99 (*0-8499-5335-9*) Word Pub.

MacArthur Study Bible, 1. MacArthur Study Group Staff. 1997. 39.97 (*0-8499-1635-6*) Word Pub.

***MacArthur Topical Bible.** John MacArthur. 1632p. 1999. 34.99 (*0-8499-1572-4*) Word Pub.

MacArthur's Airman: General George C. Kenney & the War in the Southwest Pacific. Thomas E. Griffith, Jr. LC 98-15696. (Modern War Studies). 352p. 1998. 39.95 (*0-7006-0909-1*) U Pr of KS.

MacArthur's Japanese Constitution: A Linguistic & Cultural Study of Its Making. Kyoko Inoue. 392p. 1991. 47.95 (*0-226-38391-1*) U Ch Pr.

MacArthur's Jungle War: The 1944 New Guinea Campaign. Stephen R. Taaffe. LC 97-25228. 256p. 1998. 35.00 (*0-7006-0870-2*) U Pr of KS.

MacArthur's New Guinea Campaign: March-August, 1944. Nathan Prefer. (Illus.). 288p. 1995. 24.95 (*0-938289-51-9*, 289519) Combined Pub.

MacArthur's ULTRA: Codebreaking & the War Against Japan, 1942-1945. Edward J. Drea. LC 91-16842. (Modern War Studies). (Illus.). xvi, 296p. 1991. pap. 15.95 (*0-7006-0576-2*) U Pr of KS.

MacArthur's Undercover War: Spies, Saboteurs, Guerrillas & Secret Missions. William B. Breuer. LC 94-48706. 257p. 1995. 24.95 (*0-471-11458-8*) Wiley.

***MacArthur's War: Korea & the Undoing of an American Hero.** Stanley Weintraub. LC DS919.W46 1999. 375p. 2000. 27.50 (*0-684-83419-7*) Free Pr.

Macau. Richard L. Edmonds. LC 90-154365. (World Bibliographical Ser.: Vol. 105). 168p. 1989. lib. bdg. 45.00 (*1-85109-090-8*) ABC-CLIO.

Macau. Insight Guides Staff. (Insight Guides). 1998. pap. text 12.95 (*0-88729-442-1*) Langenscheidt.

Macau. Shann Daules. LC 90-63332. (China Guides Ser.). (Illus.). 158p. 1992. reprint ed. pap. 12.95 (*0-8442-9797-6*, Passprt Bks) NTC Contemp Pub Co.

***Macau: A Country Study Guide, 110 vols.** International Business Publications, USA Staff & Global Investment Center, USA Staff. (World Country Study Guides Library Ser.: Vol. 210). (Illus.). 350p. 2000. pap. 69.95 (*0-7397-1033-8*) Intl Business Pubns.

***Macau: The Imaginary City.** Jonathan Porter. LC 99-47016. 256p. 2000. pap. 16.00 (*0-8133-3749-6*, Pub. by Westview) HarpC.

Macau: Tourism in Transition. 72p. 1994. 35.00 (*1-882866-76-2*) Pac Asia Trvl.

***Macau - A Cultural Janus.** Christina M. Cheng. 232p. 1999. pap. (*962-209-486-4*) HK Univ Pr.

Macau Business & Investment Opportunities Yearbook-98: Business, Investment, Export-Import. Contrib. by Russian Information & Business Center, Inc. Staff. (Business & Investment Opportunity Library-98). (Illus.). 350p. 1998. pap. 99.00 (*1-57751-975-2*) Intl Business Pubns.

Macau Business Law Handbook-98. Russian Information & Business Center, Inc. Staff. (World Business Law Library-98 Ser.). (Illus.). 350p. 1998. pap. 99.00 (*1-57751-649-4*) Intl Business Pubns.

Macau, China: A Political History of the Portuguese Colony's Transition to Chinese Rule. Steve Shipp. LC 96-47117. (Illus.). 237p. 1997. lib. bdg. 35.00 (*0-7864-0233-4*) McFarland & Co.

Macau Investment & Business Guide: Economy, Export-Import, Business & Investment Climate, Business Contacts. Contrib. by Russian Information & Business Center, Inc. Staff. (Russia, NIS & Emerging Markets Investment & Business Library-98). (Illus.). 350p. 1998. pap. 99.00 (*1-57751-871-3*) Intl Business Pubns.

Macau on a Plate. Annabel Doling. (Illus.). 126p. 1996. pap. 19.95 (*962-7992-01-1*, Pub. by Saqi) Intl Spec Bk.

Macau Tourism Marketing: A New Focus for the Millennium. 47p. 1996. pap. 35.00 (*1-882866-40-1*) Pac Asia Trvl.

Macaulay: The Shaping of the Historian. John Clive. LC 86-26515. 576p. 1987. pap. 21.00 (*0-674-54005-0*) Belknap Pr.

Macaulay & the Whig Tradition. Joseph Hamburger. LC 75-27892. 288p. 1996. lib. bdg. 21.00 (*0-226-31472-3*) U Ch Pr.

Macaulay Culkin. Rosemary Wallner. LC 93-19061. (Reaching for the Stars Ser.). (Illus.). 32p. (J). 1993. lib. bdg. 13.98 (*1-56239-227-1*) ABDO Pub Co.

Macauley's Thumb. Lex Williford. LC 93-26433. (Iowa Short Fiction Award Ser.). 156p. 1994. 11.50 (*0-87745-443-4*) U of Iowa Pr.

Macaws. Roger G. Sweeney. (Complete Pet Owner's Manual Ser.). (Illus.). 64p. 1992. pap. 6.95 (*0-8120-4768-0*) Barron.

***Macaws & More.** Loren Spiotta. (Illus.). 1999. 12.95 (*0-7938-3021-4*) TFH Pubns.

Macaws As a Hobby. H. Schmidt. (Illus.). 96p. 1995. pap. text 8.95 (*0-7938-0096-X*, TT039) TFH Pubns.

***Macayo: A Prehistoric Settlement in the Upper Santa Cruz River Valley.** William L. Deaver. 240p. 2000. pap. text 25.00 (*1-879442-74-4*) Stats Res.

MACB. 1995. pap. text 17.00 (*0-8053-6297-5*) Addison-Wesley.

Macbeth see Major Literary Characters

Macbeth. 1987. write for info. (*0-201-43895-X*) Addison-Wesley.

Macbeth. 36p. (YA). 1998. 9.95 (*1-56137-436-9*, NU4369); 11.95 (*1-56137-437-7*, NU4377SP) Novel Units.

Macbeth. Steven M. Berner. (Quick Study Shakespeare Ser.). 4p. pap. 3.95 (*1-57222-261-1*) Barcharts.

***Macbeth.** Ed. by Cliffs Notes Staff. (Cliffs Complete Ser.). 240p. 2000. pap. 9.99 (*0-7645-8572-X*) IDG Bks.

***Macbeth.** Ed. by Cliffs Notes Staff. LC 00-35106. (Cliffs Notes Ser.). 128p. 2000. pap. 4.99 (*0-7645-8602-5*) IDG Bks.

***MacBeth.** Cass Foster. Ed. by Paul M. Howey. (Sixty-Minute Shakespeare Ser.). 75p. 2000. pap. 8.99 (*1-877749-41-9*) Five Star AZ.

***Macbeth.** Wendy Greenhill & Paul Wignall. LC 99-55121. (Shakespeare Library). 2000. lib. bdg. write for info. (*1-57572-283-6*) Heinemann Lib.

Macbeth. William Shakespeare. Ed. by Sylvan Barnet. 280p. 1999. mass mkt. 3.95 (*0-451-52444-6*) Addson-Wesley Educ.

Macbeth. William Shakespeare. (Illustrated Classics Shakespeare Collection). 64p. 1994. pap. 4.95 (*0-7854-0807-X*, 40603) Am Guidance.

Macbeth. William Shakespeare. LC 95-77830. (Classroom Reading Plays Ser.). 32p. (YA). (gr. 6-12). 1995. pap. 3.95 (*0-7854-1127-5*, 40202) Am Guidance.

Macbeth. William Shakespeare. Ed. by R. A. Foakes. (Shakespeare Library). 192p. 1996. pap. 7.95 (*1-55783-180-7*) Applause Theatre Bk Pubs.

Macbeth. William Shakespeare. (Cyber Classics Ser.). 1997. pap. text 14.95 (*1-55701-202-4*) BNI Pubns.

Macbeth. William Shakespeare. Ed. by David Bevington et al. (Classics Ser.). 176p. 1988. mass mkt. 3.95 (*0-553-21298-2*, Bantam Classics) Bantam.

Macbeth. William Shakespeare. Ed. by Robert Owen Scott. (Barron's Book Notes Ser.). (C). 1984. pap. 3.95 (*0-8120-3427-9*) Barron.

Macbeth. William Shakespeare. Ed. by Maynard Mack & Robert W. Boynton. LC 90-31129. (Shakespeare Ser.). 141p. (YA). (gr. 9-12). 1990. pap. text 7.50 (*0-86709-021-9*, 0021, Pub. by Boynton Cook Pubs) Heinemann.

Macbeth. William Shakespeare. (Illus.). 32p. (J). (gr. 3-5). 1997. 8.00 (*1-85854-272-3*) Brimax Bks.

Macbeth. William Shakespeare. Ed. by Rex Gibson. (Cambridge School Shakespeare Ser.). (Illus.). 176p. (C). 1993. pap. 9.95 (*0-521-42621-9*) Cambridge U Pr.

Macbeth. William Shakespeare. Ed. by A. R. Braunmuller. (New Cambridge Shakespeare Ser.). (Illus.). 302p. (C). 1997. text 44.95 (*0-521-22340-7*); pap. text 11.95 (*0-521-29455-X*) Cambridge U Pr.

Macbeth. William Shakespeare. Ed. by Roma Gill. (Oxford School Shakespeare Ser.). (C). 1994. text 10.72 (*0-669-40352-0*) HM Trade Div.

Macbeth. William Shakespeare. Ed. by Kortes. 1989. pap., student ed. 12.00 (*0-7747-1270-8*) Harcourt Schl Pubs.

Macbeth. William Shakespeare. Ed. by Mark Dunster. 40p. 1995. pap. 5.00 (*0-89642-260-7*) Linden Pubs.

Macbeth. William Shakespeare. 1986. pap. text 2.95 (*0-582-52711-2*) Longman.

Macbeth. William Shakespeare. Ed. by Linda Cookson. 1988. pap. 5.72 (*0-582-33191-9*, 72069) Longman.

Macbeth. William Shakespeare. Ed. by Roy Blatchford. (Literature Ser.). 1993. pap. 5.95 (*0-582-08827-5*, TG7662) Longman.

Macbeth. William Shakespeare. (C). 1997. pap. text. write for info. (*0-8013-3140-4*) Longman.

Macbeth. William Shakespeare. Ed. & Illus. by Diane Davidson. LC 83-12312. (Shakespeare on Stage Ser.: Vol. 1). 111p. (YA). (gr. 8-12). 1983. pap. 6.95 (*0-934048-02-9*) Lrn Links.

Macbeth. William Shakespeare. Ed. by R. A. Foakes. LC 67-29974. (Shakespeare Ser.). 1968. 7.50 (*0-672-51125-8*, SS2, Bobbs) Macmillan.

Macbeth. William Shakespeare. (Shorter Shakespeare Ser.). 1996. 9.95 (*0-02-861230-2*) Macmillan.

Macbeth. William Shakespeare. (Signet Classics Ser.). 288p. 2000. mass mkt. write for info. (*0-451-52677-5*) NAL.

Macbeth. William Shakespeare. Ed. by Bachman. (Shakespeare Ser.). 1994. pap., teacher ed. 6.99 (*0-8442-5738-9*) NTC Contemp Pub Co.

Macbeth. William Shakespeare. (Shakespeare Ser.). (Illus.). 216p. 1995. pap. 8.95 (*0-8442-5737-0*, 57370, Natl Textbk Co) NTC Contemp Pub Co.

***Macbeth.** William Shakespeare. (Big Works Collection). (Illus.). 1p. 1999. 29.95 (*1-929142-01-3*) One Page Bk.

Macbeth. William Shakespeare. Ed. by Paul Werstine & Barbara A. Mowat. (New Folger Library Ser.). 272p. 1992. per. 3.99 (*0-671-72275-1*, Folger Shake Ser) PB.

Macbeth. William Shakespeare. Ed. by S. H. Coote. pap. 5.95 (*0-14-077008-9*, Pub. by Pnguin Bks Ltd) Trafalgar.

Macbeth. William Shakespeare. 1996. 18.00 incl. audio (*0-679-44928-0*) Random Hse Value.

Macbeth. William Shakespeare. Ed. by Neil King. (Illustrated Shakespeare Ser.). 96p. 1995. pap. 17.95 (*0-85950-765-3*, Pub. by S Thornes Pubs) Trans-Atl Phila.

Macbeth. William Shakespeare. 350p. 1999. text 39.95 (*0-312-21068-X*); pap. text 9.95 (*0-312-14454-7*) St Martin.

Macbeth. William Shakespeare. (Shakespeare Made Easy Ser.). 1985. 12.05 (*0-606-01100-5*, Pub. by Turtleback) Demco.

Macbeth. William Shakespeare. Ed. by John F. Andrews. (Everyman Shakespeare Ser.). 211p. 1993. pap. 3.95 (*0-460-87182-X*, Everyman's Classic Lib) Tuttle Pubng.

Macbeth. William Shakespeare. Ed. by Alfred Harbage. (Pelican Shakespeare Ser.). 112p. (YA). (gr. 9 up). 1956. pap. 4.95 (*0-14-071401-4*, Pelican Bks) Viking Penguin.

Macbeth. William Shakespeare. Ed. by George K. Hunter. (New Penguin Shakespeare Ser.). 208p. 1981. pap. 5.95 (*0-14-070705-0*, Penguin Classics) Viking Penguin.

***Macbeth.** William Shakespeare. (Pelican Shakespeare Ser.). 128p. 2000. pap. 3.95 (*0-14-071478-2*, Penguin Bks) Viking Penguin.

Macbeth. William Shakespeare. Ed. by Voyager Company Staff. 1995. 49.95 (*1-55940-684-4*) Voyager NY.

Macbeth. William Shakespeare. (English Ser.). (C). 2001. mass mkt. 9.95 (*0-17-443525-8*) Wadsworth Pub.

Macbeth. William Shakespeare. LC 81-43787. (Illus.). 96p. 1982. pap. 6.95 (*0-89480-205-4*, 405) Workman Pub.

Macbeth. William Shakespeare. (Classics Library). 112p. 1997. pap. 3.95 (*1-85326-035-5*, 0355WW, Pub. by Wrdsworth Edits) NTC Contemp Pub Co.

***Macbeth.** William Shakespeare & Steve Eddy. (Literature Made Easy Ser.). (Illus.). 96p. 1999. pap. 4.95 (*0-7641-0830-1*) Barron.

Macbeth. Ed. by Southwick. 1993. text. write for info. (*0-582-24592-3*, Pub. by Addison-Wesley) Longman.

***Macbeth.** Steck-Vaughn Company Staff. (Illus.). (J). 2000. pap. 26.95 (*0-8114-6968-9*) Raintree Steck-V.

Macbeth. John Turner. (Open Guides to Literature Ser.). 128p. 1992. 99.95 (*0-335-09448-1*) OpUniv Pr.

Macbeth. Giuseppe Verdi. Ed. by Nicholas John. Tr. by Jeremy Sams from ITA. (English National Opera Guide Series: Bilingual Libretto, Articles: No. 41). (Illus.). 128p. (Orig.). 1991. pap. 9.95 (*0-7145-4148-6*) Riverrun NY.

Macbeth. large type ed. William Shakespeare. 1997. pap. 19.95 (*1-55701-223-7*) BNI Pubns.

Macbeth. large type ed. William Shakespeare. 1994. pap. 24.95 (*0-7089-4509-0*, Charnwood) Ulverscroft.

Macbeth see New Variorum Edition of Shakespeare

Macbeth. William Shakespeare. LC 93-21799. (Thrift Editions Ser.). 96p. 1994. reprint ed. pap. 1.00 (*0-486-27802-6*) Dover.

Macbeth. William Shakespeare. 96p. 1999. reprint ed. pap. 6.95 (*1-57002-107-4*) Univ Publng Hse.

***MacBeth.** William Shakespeare. 272p. 2000. reprint ed. per. 8.95 (*0-671-04287-4*) PB.

Macbeth. unabridged ed. William Shakespeare. (Wordsworth Classics). (YA). (gr. 6-12). 1998. 5.27 (*0-89061-035-5*, R0355WW, Jamestwn Pub) NTC Contemp Pub Co.

***Macbeth.** 2nd ed. William Shakespeare. Ed. by Daniel Leary. LC 99-195658. (Shakespeare Parallel Text Ser.). (Illus.). xx, 199p. 1998. write for info. (*0-7807-7034-X*, Covercraft) Perfection Learn.

Macbeth. 2nd ed. William Shakespeare. (English). 1997. 11.95 (*0-17-443466-9*) Thomson Learn.

Macbeth. 2nd rev. ed. William Shakespeare. Ed. by Roma Gill. (Oxford School Shakespeare Ser.). (Illus.). 138p. (YA). (gr. 6 up). 1994. pap. text 7.95 (*0-19-831970-3*) OUP.

Macbeth. 9th ed. William Shakespeare. Ed. by Kenneth Muir. (Arden Shakespeare Ser.). 276p. 1982. mass mkt. 45.00 (*0-416-47320-2*, NO. 2476) Routledge.

Macbeth. 9th ed. William Shakespeare. (English Ser.). (C). 2001. mass mkt. 45.00 (*0-17-443558-4*) Wadsworth Pub.

Macbeth: A Guide to the Play. Herbert R. Coursen. LC 96-49733. (Greenwood Guides to Shakespeare Ser.). 224p. 1997. lib. bdg. 49.95 (*0-313-30047-X*, Greenwood Pr) Greenwood.

***MacBeth: A Kid's Cautionary Tale Concerning Greed, Power, Mayhem & Other Current Events.** Nancy U. Charles. 52p. 1999. pap. 5.50 (*0-87129-948-8*, MB8) Dramatic Pub.

Macbeth: A Play Packet to Accompany Elementary, My Dear Shakespeare. Barbara Engen & Joy Campbell. (Illus.). 39p. 1989. reprint ed. teacher ed. 8.95 (*0-922947-01-5*) Mkt Masters.

Macbeth: A Study Guide. K. Fischer. Ed. by J. Friedland & R. Kessler. (Novel-Ties Ser.). (YA). (gr. 9-12). 1997. pap. text, student ed. 15.95 (*0-7675-0167-5*) Lrn Links.

Macbeth: A Unit Plan. Mary B. Collins. 172p. 1994. teacher ed., ring bd. 26.95 (*1-58337-072-2*) Teachers Pet Pubns.

***Macbeth: Arden Playgoers' Edition.** 3rd ed. William Shakespeare. Ed. by Kenneth Muir. 320p. 1998. 24.95 (*0-17-443621-1*) Thomson Learn.

Macbeth: Dual Edition. James Scott. 84p. (YA). (gr. 7-12). 1999. pap., wbk. ed. 6.75 (*1-58049-505-2*, DE05) Prestwick Hse.

Macbeth: Granville Barker's Prefaces to Shakespeare. William Shakespeare & Harley G. Barker. 68p. 1995. pap. 6.95 (*0-435-08652-9*, 08652) Heinemann.

MacBeth: High King of Scotland, 1040-57. Peter B. Ellis. (Illus.). 152p. (Orig.). 1990. pap. 11.95 (*0-85640-448-9*, Pub. by Blackstaff Pr) Dufour.

Macbeth: Libretto. Composed by Giuseppe Verdi. (ENG & ITA.). 1986. pap. 4.95 (*0-7935-5390-3*, 50340190) H Leonard.

***Macbeth: Man & Myth.** Nick Aitchison. 1999. 34.95 (*0-7509-1891-8*, Pub. by Sutton Publng) Intl Pubs Mktg.

M

An Asterisk (*) at the beginning of an entry indicates that the title is appearing for the first time.

Macbeth: Modern English Version Side-by-Side with Full Original Text. William Shakespeare. Ed. by Alan Durband. (Shakespeare Made Easy Ser.). (Illus.). 223p. (YA). (gr. 9-12). 1985. pap. 6.95 (*0-8120-3571-2*) Barron.

Macbeth: One-Act Adaptation - Director's Script. William Shakespeare. (Illus.). 27p. 1965. pap. 10.00 (*0-88680-120-6*) I E Clark.

Macbeth: One-Act Adaptation of Shakespeare's Masterpiece. William Shakespeare. (Illus.). 27p. 1965. pap. 3.25 (*0-88680-119-2*) I E Clark.

Macbeth: Original Text & Modern Verse. William Shakespeare. Ed. by Alan Durband. (Shakespeare Made Easy Ser.). (Orig.). 1995. pap. 17.95 (*0-7487-0256-3*, Pub. by S Thornes Pubs) Trans-Atl Phila.

Macbeth: Quayle,&Anthony, Set. unabridged ed. William Shakespeare. 1996. audio 18.00 (*0-89845-979-6*, CPN 231) HarperAudio.

Macbeth: Reproducible Teaching Unit. rev. ed. James Scott. 40p. (YA). (gr. 7-12). 1995. teacher ed., ring bd. 29.50 (*1-58049-063-8*, TU27/U) Prestwick Hse.

Macbeth: The Global Shakespeare. Ed. by International Thomson Publishing Staff. LC 96-990042. (Global Shakespeare Ser.). 1996. mass mkt. 12.95 (*0-17-605789-7*) S-W Pub.

Macbeth: The Inessential Shakespeare. William Shakespeare. Ed. by John Hort & Leela Hort. (Shakespeare in Modern English Ser.). 48p. 1992. pap. 7.00 (*0-948662-04-2*, Pub. by Kabet Pr) Empire Pub Srvs.

***Macbeth & King John & Timon of Athens: The Shakespeare Novels, Vol. IV, Vol. 4.** Coleman Thomas Randall. LC 00-190576. 2000. 25.00 (*0-7388-1414-8*); pap. 18.00 (*0-7388-1415-6*) Xlibris Corp.

Macbeth & Midsummer Night's Dream see Shakespeare Yesterday - Today, 1989-1998

Macbeth Classic Script. abr. ed. William Shakespeare. Ed. & Intro. by William-Alan Landes. LC 98-13052. (Classicscript Ser.). 64p. (YA). 1998. pap. 6.00 (*0-88734-531-X*) Players Pr.

Macbeth Complete Study Edition. William Shakespeare. Ed. by Sidney Lamb. 101p. 1964. pap. text, student ed. 6.95 (*0-8220-1428-9*, Cliff) IDG Bks.

Macbeth Did It. John Patrick. 1972. pap. 5.25 (*0-8222-0711-7*) Dramatists Play.

Macbeth for Kids. Lois Burdett. (Illus.). 64p. (YA). (gr. 3 up). 1996. text. write for info. (*0-88753-287-X*, Pub. by Black Moss) Firefly Bks Ltd.

Macbeth for Kids. Lois Burdett. (Shakespeare Can Be Fun! Ser.). 1996. 14.15 (*0-606-12762-3*, Pub. by Turtleback) Demco.

MacBeth for Kids. Lois Burdett. LC 96-900262. (Illus.). 64p. (YA). (gr. 2-7). 1996. pap. 8.95 (*0-88753-279-9*) Black Moss.

Macbeth for Young People. William Shakespeare. Ed. & Illus. by Diane Davidson. LC 86-5955. (Shakespeare for Young People Ser.: Vol. 4). 64p. (J). (gr. 5-8). 1986. pap. 5.95 (*0-934048-21-5*) Lrn Links.

Macbeth Notes. William Shakespeare. Ed. by Denis M. Calandra & Cliffs Notes Staff. (Cliffs Notes Ser.). 80p. 1960. pap. 4.95 (*0-8220-0046-6*, Cliff) IDG Bks.

MacBeth, Oliver Twist, Connecticut Yankee in King Arthur's Court & Les Miserables. Acclaim Books Staff. (Classics Illustrated Ser.). (Illus.). 1997. pap. text 179.64 (*1-57840-019-8*, Pub. by Acclaim Bks) Penguin Putnam.

Macbeth Prophecy. large type ed. Anthea Fraser. LC 97-6916. 335p. 1997. pap. 21.95 (*0-7838-8101-0*, G K Hall Lrg Type) Mac Lib Ref.

Macbeth Readalong. William Shakespeare. (Illustrated Classics Shakespeare Collection). (Illus.). 64p. 1994. pap. 14.95 incl. audio (*0-7854-0823-1*, 40605) Am Guidance.

Macbeth Reconsidered. John P. Kemble. LC 70-144645. reprint ed. 32.50 (*0-404-03646-5*) AMS Pr.

***Macbeth Study Guide.** Michael S. Gilleland. 68p. (YA). (gr. 9-12). 2000. student ed., ring bd. 14.99 (*1-58609-170-0*) Progeny Pr WI.

Macbeth the King. Nigel Tranter. mass mkt. 11.95 (*0-340-26544-2*, Pub. by Hodder & Stought Ltd) Trafalgar.

Macbett. Eugene Ionesco. (Coll. Le Manteau d'Arlequin). pap. 3.95 (*0-685-34255-7*) Fr & Eur.

Macbett. Eugene Ionesco. (FRE.). 1975. pap. 10.95 (*0-8288-3692-2*, M3583); pap. 10.95 (*0-7859-2362-4*, 2070366944) Fr & Eur.

Macbett. Eugene Ionesco. (Folio Ser.: No. 694). (FRE.). 1975. pap. 6.95 (*2-07-036694-4*) Schoenhof.

MacBride of Tordarroch. large type ed. Essie Summers. 384p. 1995. 27.99 (*0-7089-3439-0*) Ulverscroft.

MacBride Principles & U. S. Companies in Northern Ireland. Kenneth A. Bertsch. 150p. (Orig.). 1991. pap. 25.00 (*0-931035-87-2*) IRRC Inc DC.

***Macbride's Brigade: Irish Commandos in the Anglo-Boer War.** Donal P. McCraken. (Illus.). 224p. 1999. 29.95 (*1-85182-499-5*, Pub. by Four Cts Pr) Intl Spec Bk.

MacBride's Daughter. large type ed. Patricia Wilson. (Mills & Boon Large Print Ser.). 288p. 1997. 23.99 (*0-263-15126-3*, Pub. by Mills & Boon) Ulverscroft.

MacBugs Reference & DeBugging Guide: For MacBugs Version 6.2. Apple Computer, Inc. Staff. 464p. (C). 1991. pap. text 26.95 (*0-201-56767-9*) Addison-Wesley.

Macbush: A Comedy in Five Acts. Peter Gould. 107p. (Orig.). (C). 1988. pap. 6.95 (*0-915731-02-9*) Whetstone Bks.

Maccabean Martyrs As Saviours of the Jewish People: A Study of 2 & 4 Maccabees. Jan W. Van Henten. LC 97-35506. 368p. 1997. 115.00 (*90-04-10976-5*) Brill Academic Pubs.

Maccabean Revolt: Anatomy of a Biblical Revolution. Daniel J. Harrington. LC 88-81307. (Old Testament Message Ser.: Vol. 1). 143p. (Orig.). 1988. pap. 12.95 (*0-8146-5655-2*) Liturgical Pr.

Maccabee Jamboree: A Hanukkah Countdown. Cheri Holland. LC 98-4199. (Illus.). 24p. (J). (ps-2). 1998. pap. 4.95 (*1-58013-019-4*) Kar-Ben.

Maccabees One. Tr. & Intro. by Jonathan A. Goldstein. LC 75-32719. (Anchor Bible Ser.: Vol. 41). (Illus.). 624p. 1976. 42.50 (*0-385-08533-8*, Anchor NY) Doubleday.

MacCarthys of Munster, the History of a Great Irish Sept: A Facsimile Edition with an Extended Commentary Thereon by the MacCarthy Mor. Samuel T. McCarthy. (Illus.). 570p. 1997. 60.00 (*0-9654220-1-1*) Gryfons Pubs & Dist.

Macchi C.202 in Action. Roberto Gentilli. (Aircraft in Action Ser.: Vol. 41). (Illus.). 50p. 2000. pap. 9.95 (*0-89747-100-8*, 1041) Squad Sig Pubns.

Macchi MC.205 "Veltro" 2nd rev. ed. Maurizio Di Terlizzi. Ed. by Angelo Napoleone. Tr. by Kay Charlesworth. (Aviolibri Ser.: Vol. 1). (Illus.). 64p. 1997. pap. 14.95 (*88-86815-55-7*, Pub. by Istituto Bibliograf) Pacific Coast Mod.

***Macchi MC.202 Folgore, Pt. 1.** Maurizio Di Terlizzi. Ed. by Angelo Napoleone. Tr. by Stephen Richards. (Aviolibri Special Ser.: Vol. 1). (ITA & ENG., Illus.). 64p. 1999. pap. 21.95 (*88-86815-42-5*, Pub. by Istituto Bibliograf) Pacific Coast Mod.

Macchiaioli: Italian Painters of the Nineteenth Century. Norma Broude. LC 86-28270. 306p. 1988. 75.00 (*0-300-03547-0*) Yale U Pr.

Macclesfield Collection of Egyptian Antiquities. David. (Modern Egyptology Ser.). 1980. 49.95 (*0-85668-129-6*, Pub. by Aris & Phillips) David Brown.

***Maccordion Format: An Integrating Mosaic of American Society.** William J. Regan. (Illus.). 272p. 2000. write for info. (*0-9701015-0-3*) Pandemic.

MacDermots of Ballycloran, 3 vols. Anthony Trollope. Ed. by N. John Hall. LC 80-1874. (Selected Works of Anthony Trollope). 1981. reprint ed. lib. bdg. 115.95 (*0-405-14118-1*) Ayer.

Macdermots of Ballycloran: (trollope 1991) Skilton. 1991. 40.00 (*1-870587-16-2*) Ashgate Pub Co.

MacDiarmid: A Critical Biography. Alan Bold. LC 89-20452. (Illus.). 504p. (C). 1990. lib. bdg. 40.00 (*0-87023-714-4*) U of Mass Pr.

MacDonald Countries, 8 bks. Incl. Belgium & Luxembourg. Joan Marey & George Morey. 1985. lib. bdg. 14.96 (*0-382-06118-7*); Canada. Jeanette Harris. 1985. lib. bdg. 14.96 (*0-382-06110-1*); Egypt. Michael Von Haag. 1985. lib. bdg. 14.96 (*0-382-06112-8*); India. Natasha Talyarkhan. 1985. lib. bdg. 14.96 (*0-382-06113-6*); Mexico. John Howard. 1985. lib. bdg. 14.96 (*0-382-06114-4*); Netherlands. Frank E. Huggett. 1985. lib. bdg. 14.96 (*0-382-06117-9*); Nigeria. Richard Synge. 1985. lib. bdg. 14.96 (*0-382-06115-2*); Turkey. David Hotham. 1985. lib. bdg. 14.96 (*0-382-06116-0*); (J). (gr. 5 up). 1985. lib. bdg. write for info. (*0-686-57952-6*) Silver Burdett Pr.

MacDonald for the Prince. Alasdair MacLean. 104p. 1999. pap. 26.00 (*0-86152-002-5*, Pub. by Acair Ltd) St Mut.

MacDonald Presentation Volume: A Tribute to Duncan Black MacDonald, Consisting of Articles by Former Students, Presented to Him on His Seventieth Birthday, April 9, 1933. LC 68-22109. (Essay Index Reprint Ser.). 1977. 26.95 (*0-8369-0645-4*) Ayer.

MacDonald's Immigration Law & Practice. Ian A. MacDonald & Nicholas J. Blake. 1996. suppl. ed. write for info. (*0-406-99903-1*, MBIL4S, MICHIE) LEXIS Pub.

MacDonough-Hackstaff Ancestry. R. MacDonough. (Illus.). 526p. 1989. reprint ed. pap. 79.00 (*0-8328-0847-4*); reprint ed. lib. bdg. 87.00 (*0-8328-0846-6*) Higginson Bk Co.

***Macdougal Alley: A Novel.** Tatheena Roberts. 288p. 2001. pap. 11.95 (*1-55583-540-6*, Pub. by Alyson Pubns) Consort Bk Sales.

MacDougall's Darling. Emilie Richards. (Intimate Moments Ser.). 1995. per. 3.75 (*0-373-07655-X*, 1-07655-3) Silhouette.

MacDougall's Darling. large type ed. Emilie Richards. (Silhouette Romance Ser.). 1998. 20.95 (*0-373-59856-4*) Thorndike Pr.

MacDowell Poems. limited ed. R. D. Lakin. 1977. bds. 20.00 (*0-930126-00-9*) Typographeum.

Mace & the Gavel. Silvio A. Bedini. LC 97-30718. (Transactions Ser.: Vol. 87, Pt. 4). (Illus.). 84p. 1997. pap. 15.00 (*0-87169-874-9*, T874-bes) Am Philos.

Mace Bowman: Texas Feudist, Western Lawman. James S. Peters et al. (Illus.). 230p. 1996. 39.95 (*0-614-13835-3*) Hartmann Heritage.

Mace Bowman: Texas Feudist, Western Lawman - Collector's Edition. James S. Peters et al. (Illus.). 230p. 1996. 79.95 (*0-614-28587-9*) Hartmann Heritage.

Mace of Souls. Bruce Fergusson. 320p. 1991. reprint ed. pap. 3.95 (*0-380-71180-X*, Avon Bks) Morrow Avon.

Macedonia. Tikhomir R. Dordevic. LC 77-87529. reprint ed. 37.50 (*0-404-16586-9*) AMS Pr.

Macedonia: From Philip II to the Roman Conquest. Rene Ginouves & Iannis Akamatis. Tr. by David Hardy. LC 93-38156. (FRE.). 256p. 1994. text 79.50 (*0-691-03635-7*, Pub. by Princeton U Pr) Cal Prin Full Svc.

Macedonia: Human Rights Violations in Macedonia: A Threat to "Stability" Human Rights Watch/Helsinki Staff. LC 96-77111. 114p. (Orig.). 1996. pap. 10.00 (*1-56432-170-3*) Hum Rts Watch.

Macedonia: Its People & History. Stoyan Pribichevich. LC 82-80455. (Illus.). 304p. 1982. 32.50 (*0-271-00315-4*) Pa St U Pr.

Macedonia: Its Place in Balkan Power Politics. Elisabeth Barker. LC 80-16769. (Illus.). 129p. 1980. reprint ed. lib. bdg. 35.00 (*0-313-22587-7*, BAMI, Greenwood Pr) Greenwood.

Macedonia: Its Races & Their Future. H. N. Brailsford. LC 78-135796. (Eastern Europe Collection). 1980. reprint ed. 43.95 (*0-405-02738-9*) Ayer.

Macedonia - A Country Study Guide: Basic Information for Research & Pleasure. Global Investment Center, USA Staff. (World Country Study Guide Library: Vol. 102). (Illus.). 350p. 1999. pap. 59.00 (*0-7397-1499-6*) Intl Business Pubns.

Macedonia & Greece: The Struggle to Define a New Balkan Nation. John Shea. LC 96-32035. 429p. 1997. lib. bdg. 45.00 (*0-7864-0228-8*) McFarland & Co.

Macedonia & Greece in Late Classical & Early Hellenistic Times. National Gallery of Art Staff. Ed. by Beryl Barr-Sharrar & Eugene N. Borza. LC 82-150109. (Studies in the History of Art: Vol. 10, No. 1). (Illus.). 266p. reprint ed. pap. 82.50 (*0-608-10428-0*, 207106200010) Bks Demand.

Macedonia Business & Investment Opportunities Yearbook-98: Business, Investment, Export-Import. Contrib. by Russian Information & Business Center, Inc. Staff. (Business & Investment Opportunity Library-98). (Illus.). 350p. 1998. pap. 99.00 (*1-57751-937-X*) Intl Business Pubns.

***Macedonia Business Law Handbook, 190 vols.** Global Investment & Business Center, Inc. Staff. (Global Business Law Handbooks Library: Vol. 102). (Illus.). 350p. 2000. pap. 99.95 (*0-7397-2000-7*) Intl Business Pubns.

Macedonia Business Law Handbook-98. Russian Information & Business Center, Inc. Staff. (World Business Law Library-98). (Illus.). 350p. 1998. pap. 99.00 (*1-57751-807-1*) Intl Business Pubns.

***Macedonia Country Review 2000.** Robert C. Kelly et al. (Illus.). 60p. 1999. pap. 39.95 (*1-58310-526-3*) CountryWatch.

Macedonia Investment & Business Guide: Economy, Export-Import, Business & Investment Climate, Business Contacts. Contrib. by Russian Information & Business Center, Inc. Staff. (Russia, NIS & Emerging Markets Investment & Business Library-98). (Illus.). 350p. 1998. pap. 99.00 (*1-57751-857-8*) Intl Business Pubns.

***Macedonia, Republic Business Intelligence Report, 190 vols.** Global Investment & Business Center, Inc. Staff. (World Business Intelligence Library: Vol. 102). (Illus.). 350p. 2000. pap. 99.95 (*0-7397-2600-5*) Intl Business Pubns.

***Macedonia, Republic Foreign Policy & Government Guide.** Global Investment & Business Center, Inc. Staff. (World Foreign Policy & Government Library: Vol. 98). (Illus.). 350p. 1999. pap. 99.00 (*0-7397-3596-9*) Intl Business Pubns.

***Macedonia, Republic Foreign Policy & Government Guide.** Global Investment & Business Center, Inc. Staff. (World Foreign Policy & Government Library: Vol. 98). (Illus.). 350p. 2000. pap. 99.95 (*0-7397-3800-3*) Intl Business Pubns.

***Macedonia, Republic Investment & Business Guide.** Global Investment & Business Center, Inc. Staff. (Global Investment & Business Guide Library: Vol. 102). (Illus.). 2000. pap. 99.95 (*0-7397-1800-2*) Intl Business Pubns.

***Macedonia, Republic of, Business Opportunity Yearbook.** Global Investment & Business Center, Inc. Staff. (Global Business Opportunity Yearbooks Library: Vol. 102). (Illus.). 2000. pap. 99.95 (*0-7397-2200-X*) Intl Business Pubns.

***Macedonia, Republic of, Business Opportunity Yearbook: Export-Import, Investment & Business Opportunities.** International Business Publications, U. S. A. Staff & Global Investment Center, U. S. A. Staff. (Global Business Opportunity Yearbooks Library: Vol. 102). (Illus.). 350p. 1999. pap. 99.95 (*0-7397-1300-0*) Intl Business Pubns.

***Macedonia, the Former Yugoslav Republic: A Country Study Guide.** Global Investment & Business Center, Inc. Staff. (World Country Study Guides Library: Vol. 102). (Illus.). 350p. 2000. pap. 59.00 (*0-7397-2400-2*) Intl Business Pubns.

Macedonia, the Former Yugoslav Republic Investment & Business Guide: Export-Import, Investment & Business Opportunities. International Business Publications, USA Staff & Global Investment Center, USA Staff. (World Investment & Business Guide Library-99: Vol. 102). (Illus.). 350p. 1999. pap. 99.95 (*0-7397-0297-1*) Intl Business Pubns.

Macedonia to America & Back: A Biographical History of Dmitri Nasos. Thomay Nestor. LC 96-69028. 335p. (Orig.). 1996. pap. 18.95 (*1-880222-25-6*) Red Apple Pub.

***Macedonia'a Secret Army: The IMRO Militia & Volunteer Battalions, 1943-44.** Victoria Nichols. (Illus.). 700p. 2000. per. write for info. (*1-891227-21-1*, Axis Europa Bks) Axis Europa.

Macedonian: A Course for Beginning & Intermediate Students. Christina Elizabeth Kramer. LC 99-18931. 1999. pap. write for info. incl. audio compact disk (*0-299-16170-6*) U of Wis Pr.

***Macedonian: A Couse for Beginning & Intermediate Students - (Makedonski Jazik)** Christina Elizabeth Kramer. LC 99-18931. 1999. 34.95 (*0-299-16174-9*) U of Wis Pr.

Macedonian Conflict: Ethnic Nationalism in a Transnational World. Loring M. Danforth. (Illus.). 290p. 1995. pap. text 15.95 (*0-691-04356-6*, Pub. by Princeton U Pr) Cal Prin Full Svc.

Macedonian Empire: The Era of Warfare under Phillip II & Alexander the Great, 359-323 B. C. James R. Ashley. LC 97-40332. 496p. 1998. lib. bdg. 62.50 (*0-7864-0407-8*) McFarland & Co.

Macedonian-English - English-Macedonian Concise Dictionary. Davidovic Mladen. LC 97-21876. (ENG & MAC.). 180p. (Orig.). 1997. pap. 14.95 (*0-7818-0516-3*) Hippocrene Bks.

Macedonian-English Dictionary. Peter M. Hill & Suncica Mircevska. LC 97-23301. 712p. (C). 1998. 200.00 (*0-415-16046-4*) Routledge.

Macedonian Folk Songs for Voice & Tambura, Vol. 1. David G. Bilides et al. (Illus.). 113p. (Orig.). 1997. pap. 42.00 (*0-9658579-0-5*) Izvor Music.

Macedonian Folk Songs for Voice & Tambura, Vol. 2. David G. Bilides et al. 110p. (Orig.). 1999. pap. 42.00 (*0-9658579-1-3*) Izvor Music.

***Macedonian Question: Cultural, Historiography, Politics.** Victor Roudometof. 320p. 2000. 42.00 (*0-88033-451-7*, 553, Pub. by East Eur Monographs) Col U Pr.

Macedonian Question: 1893-1908. Madine Lange-Akhund. LC 97-74978. 320p. 1997. lib. bdg. 45.00 (*0-88033-383-9*, 486, Pub. by East Eur Monographs) Col U Pr.

Macedonian State. Nicholas G. Hammond. (Illus.). 440p. 1993. pap. text 35.00 (*0-19-814927-1*) OUP.

Macedonian Verbal Morphology: A Structural Analysis. Mark J. Elson. 147p. (Orig.). 1989. pap. 18.95 (*0-89357-201-2*) Slavica.

M

Macedonio Fernandez. Naomi Lindstrom. LC 80-53826. 138p. (Orig.). 1981. pap. 18.00 (*0-89295-018-8*) Society Sp & Sp-Am.

Macedonio, Selected Writings in Translation. Macedonio Fernandez. Ed. by Jo A. Englebert. LC 84-81373. 124p. 1989. pap. 10.00 (*0-941179-45-1*) Latitudes Pr.

MacEnvelop Professional: Reference Manual. Allen Lubow. 192p. 1992. pap. text 250.00 incl. disk (*1-880773-06-6*) SNX.

MacEnvelope. Allen Lubow. 131p. 1990. pap. text. write for info. (*1-880773-05-8*) SNX.

Macer Floridus De Viribus Herbarum see Macer's Virtue of Herbs

Macer's Virtue of Herbs. Tr. by Daniel P. O'Hanlon from LAT. Orig. Title: Macer Floridus De Viribus Herbarum. 125p. (C). 10.00 (*0-89744-243-1*) Auromere.

MacFroggy Teaches BASIC. Amy Barger & Andrew Barger. LC 93-9551. 127p. (J). (gr. 5-10). 1993. pap. text 8.95 (*0-944838-39-1*) Med Physics Pub.

Macgillivray on Insurance Law: Relating to All Risks Other Than Marine. 9th ed. Evan James MacGillivray & Nicholas Leigh-Jones. LC 98-198138. (Insurance Practitioners Library). 1024 p. 1997. write for info. (*0-421-50480-3*) Sweet & Maxwell.

MacGillivrays of Skye. Harold A. Steiner & Doris M. Steiner. LC 85-90308. (Illus.). 616p. 1985. lib. bdg. 35.00 (*0-9614517-0-X*) Haldor Co.

MacGregor Across Scotland: A Long-Distance Walk from Montrose to Ardnamurchan. Jimmie MacGregor. LC 92-80836. (Illus.). 96p. (Orig.). 1992. pap. 7.95 (*0-563-36187-5*, BBC-Parkwest) Parkwest Pubns.

MacGregor Brides. Nora Roberts. 384p. 1997. per. 6.99 (*0-373-48350-3*) Harlequin Bks.

MacGregor Grooms. Nora Roberts. 384p. 1998. per. 6.99 (*0-373-48369-4*, 1-48369-2) Silhouette.

MacGregor Trilogy. Nigel Tranter. 612p. 1996. mass mkt. 19.95 (*0-340-40572-4*, Pub. by Hodder & Stought Ltd) Trafalgar.

***MacGregors: Alan & Grant.** Nora Roberts. 512p. 1999. pap. 6.99 (*0-373-48389-9*, 1-48389-0) Silhouette.

***MacGregors: Ian & Daniel.** Nora Roberts. 1999. per. 6.99 (*0-373-48390-2*, 1-48390-8, Harlequin) Harlequin Bks.

MacGregors: Serena-Caine Playing the Odds; Tempting Fate. Nora Roberts. (Silhouette Promo Ser.). 1998. per. 6.99 (*0-373-48388-0*, 1-48388-2, Harlequin) Harlequin Bks.

MacGregor's Gathering. N. Tranter. 1993. mass mkt. 11.95 (*0-340-34914-X*, Pub. by Hodder & Stought Ltd) Trafalgar.

MacGregor's Mixture. Forbes MacGregor. 144p. (C). 1989. 35.00 (*0-903065-15-0*, Pub. by G Wright Pub) St Mut.

MacGuffin. Stanley Elkin. LC 99-35095. 288p. 1999. reprint ed. pap. 12.95 (*1-56478-223-9*, Pub. by Dalkey Arch) Chicago Distribution Ctr.

Mach Bands: Quantitative Studies on Neural Networks in the Retina. Floyd Ratliff. LC 65-10436. 1965. 38.00 (*0-8162-7045-7*) Holden-Day.

Mach One & Beyond: The Illustrated Guide to High-Speed Flight. Larry W. Reithmaier. LC 94-1421. (Illus.). 273p. 1994. pap. text 24.95 (*0-07-052021-6*) McGraw-Hill Prof.

Mach 1, the First Decade: The Art of Aviation Photography. Brian Shul. (Illus.). 180p. 1996. write for info. (*0-929823-23-0*) Mach One.

Macha of Chira, Costa Rica: Confessions of an Anthropologist. Ethelyn G. Orso. (Illus.). 170p. (Orig.). (C). 1991. pap. 13.95 (*0-9630475-0-7*) Lakeview LA.

Machado: A Dialogue with Time: Nature as an Expression of Temporality in the Poetry of Antonio Machado. Norma L. Hutman. LC 70-78554. 207p. 1969. text 32.50 (*0-8290-0186-7*) Irvington.

Machado: Campos de Castilla. Ed. by R. Havard. (BCP Spanish Texts Ser.). (SPA.). 128p. (C). 1997. pap. text 18.95 (*1-85399-484-7*, Pub. by Brist Class Pr) Focus Pub-R Pullins.

Machado de Assis. Earl E. Fitz. (World Authors Ser.). 160p. (C). 1989. 28.95 (*0-8057-8244-3*, TWAS 809, Twyne) Mac Lib Ref.

Machado de Assis. Richard Graham. LC 99-12681. 144p. 1999. 25.00 (*0-292-72821-2*); pap. 11.95 (*0-292-72822-0*) U of Tex Pr.

An Asterisk (*) at the beginning of an entry indicates that the title is appearing for the first time.

Machado de Assis & Feminism: Re-Reading the Heart of the Companion. Maria M. Lisboa. LC 96-4911. (Women's Studies: Vol. 11). 284p. 1996. 89.95 (*0-7734-8828-6*) E Mellen.

Machado de Assis, the Brazilian Pyrrhonian. Jose R. Maia Neto. LC 94-3008. (Studies in Romance Literatures: Vol. 5). 248p. 1994. 42.95 (*1-55753-051-3*) Purdue U Pr.

Machaut's Mass: An Introduction. Daniel Leech-Wilkinson. (Illus.). 224p. 1992. reprint ed. pap. text 19.95 (*0-19-816306-1*) OUP.

Mache Chache: Text Comprehension Exercises in Haitian Creole. Cauvin Paul. Ed. by Fequiere Vilsaint. 101p. (YA). (gr. 6-12). Date not set. wbk. ed. 10.00 (*1-881839-44-3*) Educa Vision.

Machete & the Cross: Campesino Rebellion in Yucatan. Don E. Dumond. LC 96-32949. (Illus.). xvii, 573p. 1997. text 60.00 (*0-8032-1706-4*) U of Nebr Pr.

Machias. Index of Surnames to George W. Drisko's "Narrative of the Town of Machias," Above. Compiled by Wade F. Harmon. 93p. 1995. reprint ed. pap. 18.00 (*0-8328-4618-X*); reprint ed. lib. bdg. 28.00 (*0-8328-4617-1*) Higginson Bk Co.

Machias, Maine, Families, 1767-1827. Ed. by Michael J. Denis. 24p. (Orig.). 1985. pap. 3.50 (*0-935207-99-6*) Danbury Hse Bks.

Machias, Maine, Marriages, 1767-1827. Michael J. Denis. 20p. 1984. pap. 3.00 (*0-935207-14-7*) Danbury Hse Bks.

Machias (ME) Genealogies. 29p. 1986. reprint ed. pap. 4.00 (*0-935207-41-4*) Danbury Hse Bks.

Machiavel the Prince. Connell. 2000. pap. text. write for info. (*0-312-14978-6*) St Martin.

*__Machiavelli.__ Quentin Skinner. (Very Short Introductions Ser.). 112p. 2000. pap. 8.95 (*0-19-285407-0*) OUP.

Machiavelli. Ed. by Maurizio Viroli. (Founders of Modern Political & Social Thought Ser.). 260p. 1998. pap. text 16.95 (*0-19-878089-3*) OUP.

Machiavelli. Ed. by Maurizio Viroli. (Founders of Modern Political & Social Thought Ser.). 260p. 1999. text 55.00 (*0-19-878088-5*) OUP.

Machiavelli see Aquinas

Machiavelli: In the Classroom & Board Room. John C. Williams. 123p. (C). 1994. pap. text 29.95 (*1-885827-01-6*) NatureGraphics.

Machiavelli: The Chief Works & Others, 1. Tr. by Allan H. Gilbert. LC 64-16192. 542p. 1996. reprint ed. pap. text 21.95 (*0-8223-0945-9*) Duke.

Machiavelli: The Chief Works & Others, 2. Tr. by Allan H. Gilbert. LC 64-16192. 499p. 1996. reprint ed. pap. text 21.95 (*0-8223-0946-7*) Duke.

Machiavelli: The Chief Works & Others, Set. Tr. by Allan Gilbert. LC 64-16192. 1996. reprint ed. pap. text 59.95 (*0-8223-0931-9*) Duke.

Machiavelli: The Chief Works & Others, Set. Tr. by Allan H. Gilbert. LC 64-16192. 1996. reprint ed. text 119.95 (*0-8223-0913-0*) Duke.

Machiavelli: The Chief Works & Others, Vol. 1. Tr. by Allan H. Gilbert. LC 64-16192. 546p. 1996. reprint ed. text 49.95 (*0-8223-0920-3*) Duke.

Machiavelli: The Chief Works & Others, Vol. 2. Tr. by Allan H. Gilbert. LC 64-16192. 512p. 1996. reprint ed. text 49.95 (*0-8223-0921-1*) Duke.

Machiavelli: The Chief Works & Others, Vol. 3. Tr. by Allan H. Gilbert. LC 64-16192. 504p. 1996. reprint ed. pap. text 21.95 (*0-8223-0947-5*) Duke.

Machiavelli: The Chief Works & Others, Vol Iii. Allan H. Gilbert. LC 64-16192. 501p. 1996. text 49.95 (*0-8223-0922-X*) Duke.

Machiavelli: The History of Florence & Other Selections. Niccolo Machiavelli. Ed. by Myron P. Gilmore. Tr. by Judith A. Rawson. 1970. 32.50 (*0-671-48364-1*) Irvington.

Machiavelli & His Friends: Their Personal Correspondence. James B. Atkinson et al. Tr. by David Sices. LC 96-31069. 600p. 1996. lib. bdg. 48.00 (*0-87580-210-9*) N Ill U Pr.

Machiavelli & Mystery of State. Peter S. Donaldson. 241p. (C). 1992. pap. text 19.95 (*0-521-43790-3*) Cambridge U Pr.

Machiavelli & the Discourse of Literature. Ed. by Albert R. Ascoli & Victoria Kahn. (Illus.). 312p. 1993. 49.95 (*0-8014-2870-X*); pap. text 19.95 (*0-8014-8109-0*) Cornell U Pr.

Machiavelli & the History of Prudence. Eugene Garver. LC 86-40454. (Rhetoric of the Human Sciences Ser.). 256p. 1987. text 32.95 (*0-299-11080-X*) U of Wis Pr.

Machiavelli & the History of Prudence. Eugene Garver. LC 86-40454. (Rhetoric of the Human Sciences Ser.). 253p. 1987. reprint ed. pap. 78.50 (*0-608-06999-X*, 206720700009) Bks Demand.

Machiavelli & the United States: 500th Anniversary Edition, 6 vols. in 1. Anthony J. Pansini. LC 70-108252. 1371p. 1969. 20.00 (*0-911876-02-2*) Greenvale.

Machiavelli & Us. Louis Althusser. LC 99-13811. 1999. 30.00 (*1-85984-711-0*, Pub. by Verso) Norton.

*__Machiavelli & Us.__ Louis Althusser. Ed. by Francois Matherson. Tr. by Gregory Elliott. 160p. 2001. pap. 19.00 (*1-85984-282-8*, Pub. by Verso) Norton.

Machiavelli '500. Ed. by Anne Paolucci. LC 77-126039. (Review of National Literatures Ser.: Vol. 1, No. 1). 1970. 6.95 (*0-918680-56-5*) Griffon House.

Machiavelli in Hell. Sebastian De Grazia. LC 92-50594. 1994. pap. 18.00 (*0-679-74342-1*) Vin Bks.

Machiavelli in 90 Minutes. Paul Strathern. LC 98-36091. (Philosophers in 90 Minutes Ser.). 96p. 1998. pap. 5.95 (*1-56663-213-7*, Pub. by I R Dee); lib. bdg. 14.95 (*1-56663-212-9*, Pub. by I R Dee) Natl Bk Netwk.

Machiavelli in Sixteenth-Century French Fiction. Heather Ingman. (American University Studies: Comparative Literature: Ser. III, Vol. 10). XII, 267p. (C). 1988. text 39.00 (*0-8204-0612-0*) P Lang Pubng.

Machiavelli Interface. Steve Perry. (Matador Trilogy Ser.: No. 3). 208p. 1986. mass mkt. 4.99 (*0-441-51356-5*) Ace Bks.

Machiavelli, Leonardo & the Science of Power. Roger D. Masters. LC 94-40484. (Frank M. Covey, Jr., Loyola Lectures in Political Analysis). (C). 1996. text 32.95 (*0-268-01416-7*) U of Notre Dame Pr.

Machiavelli, Leonardo, & the Science of Power. Roger D. Masters. LC 94-40484. (Frank M. Covey, Jr., Loyola Lectures in Political Analysis). 384p. (C). 1998. reprint ed. pap. text 24.95 (*0-268-01433-7*) U of Notre Dame Pr.

Machiavelli on Modern Leadership: Why Machiavelli's Iron Rules Are As Timely & Important Today As Five Centuries Ago. Michael A. Ledeen. LC 99-19366. 240p. 2000. text 22.95 (*0-312-20471-X*) St Martin.

*__Machiavelli on Modern Leadership: Why Machiavelli's Iron Rules Are as Timely & Important Today as Five Centuries Ago.__ Michael A. Ledeen. 224p. 2000. pap. 13.95 (*0-312-26356-2*, St Martin Griffin) St Martin.

Machiavelli Redeemed: Retrieving His Humanist Perspectives on Equality, Power, & Glory. Robert A. Kocis. LC 09-342234. 264p. (C). 1998. 41.50 (*0-934223-42-4*) Lehigh Univ Pr.

Machiavelli, the Prince: The Official Strategy Guide. William Possidente. LC 95-68589. 1995. pap. text 12.95 (*0-7615-0138-X*) Prima Pub.

Machiavelli to Bentham, 3 vols. W. T. Jones. Ed. by Edward M. Sait. (Essay Index Reprint Ser.: Vol. 2). 1977. reprint ed. 22.95 (*0-518-10155-X*) Ayer.

Machiavelli to Marx: Modern Western Political Thought. Dante Germino. LC 77-181415. 416p. 1979. pap. text 23.00 (*0-226-28850-1*, P810) U Ch Pr.

Machiavellian Cosmos. Anthony J. Parel. 216p. (C). 1992. 37.50 (*0-300-05169-7*) Yale U Pr.

Machiavellian Enterprise: A Commentary on the Prince. Leo Paul S De Alvarez. LC 98-54214. 205p. 1999. 32.00 (*0-87580-247-8*) N Ill U Pr.

Machiavellian Intelligence II: Evaluations & Extensions. Ed. by Andrew Whiten & Richard W. Byrne. LC 96-48233. (Illus.). 415p. (C). 1997. text 80.00 (*0-521-55087-4*); pap. text 34.95 (*0-521-55949-9*) Cambridge U Pr.

Machiavellian Legacy. Femia. LC 98-20171. 1998. text 59.95 (*0-312-21511-8*) St Martin.

Machiavellian Management: Playing & Winning the Corporate Power Game. Gerald R. Griffen. LC 90-7804. 256p. 1991. 57.95 (*0-275-93699-6*, C3699, Praeger Pubs) Greenwood.

Machiavellian Marquess. Freda Michel. 1979. mass mkt. 1.75 (*0-449-50014-4*, Coventry) Fawcett.

Machiavellian Moment: Florentine Political Thought & the Atlantic Republican Tradition. J. G. Pocock. LC 73-2490. 576p. 1975. pap. text 29.95 (*0-691-10029-2*, Pub. by Princeton U Pr) Cal Prin Full Svc.

Machiavellian Rhetoric: From the Counter-Reformation to Milton. Victoria Kahn. LC 93-45883. 336p. 1994. text 39.50 (*0-691-03491-5*, Pub. by Princeton U Pr) Cal Prin Full Svc.

*__Machiavellianism & Its Alternatives: Essays in Honor of Harvey Mansfield.__ Harvey Claflin Mansfield et al. LC 00-37283. 2000. write for info. (*0-7425-0827-7*) Rowman.

Machiavellians. James Burnham. LC 70-117762. (Essay Index Reprint Ser.). 1977. 19.95 (*0-8369-1785-5*) Ayer.

Machiavellians: A Social Psychological Study of Moral Character & Organizational Milieu. Stanley S. Guterman. LC 69-19104. 196p. reprint ed. pap. 60.80 (*0-608-17992-2*, 202911800058) Bks Demand.

Machiavellians: Defenders of Freedom. James Burnham. LC 87-23253. 246p. 1987. pap. 7.95 (*0-89526-785-3*) Regnery Pub.

Machiavellian's Guide to Womanizing. Nick Casanova. 128p. 1995. pap. 8.95 (*0-7867-0203-6*) Carroll & Graf.

Machiavellian's Guide to Womanizing. Nick Casanova. 1999. pap. text 5.99 (*0-7858-1074-9*) Bk Sales Inc.

Machiavelli's Mandragola. Stark Young. 175p. 1996. pap. 35.00 (*0-87556-799-1*) Saifer.

Machiavelli's Romans: Liberty & Greatness in the Discourses on Livy. J. Patrick Coby. LC 99-19460. (Applications of Political Theory Ser.). 384p. 1999. 65.00 (*0-7391-0069-6*); pap. 23.95 (*0-7391-0070-X*) Lxngtn Bks.

*__Machiavelli's "The Republican" The Best Possible America & How to Achieve It.__ Nelson A. Blue. 176p. 2000. pap. 14.95 (*1-880849-19-4*) Chapel Hill NC.

Machiavelli's Three Romes: Religion, Human Liberty, & Politics Reformed. Vickie B. Sullivan. LC 96-10830. 245p. 1996. lib. bdg. 32.00 (*0-87580-213-3*) N Ill U Pr.

Machiavelli's Virtue. Harvey C. Mansfield. LC 95-24115. 388p. 1996. 29.95 (*0-226-50368-2*) U Ch Pr.

Machiavelli's Virtue. Harvey C. Mansfield. 372p. 1998. pap. 15.00 (*0-226-50369-0*) U Ch Pr.

Machiavellism. Friedrich Meinecke. Tr. by Douglas Scott. LC 97-16855. 480p. 1997. pap. text 27.95 (*1-56000-970-5*) Transaction Pubs.

Machido-Once More: An American Family in Japan--the Second Year. Kenneth Fenter. Ed. by Lora Fenter. (Illus.). 1985. pap. 10.45 (*0-930693-01-9*) Cross Cult Pr.

Machig Labdron & the Foundations of Chod. Jerome Edou. LC 94-40283. 244p. 1994. pap. 16.95 (*1-55939-039-5*) Snow Lion Pubns.

Machina Ex Dea: Feminist Perspectives on Technology. Ed. by Joan Rothschild. (Athene Ser.). 264p. 1983. text 48.50 (*0-08-029404-9*, Pergamon Pr); pap. text 19.95 (*0-08-029403-0*, Pergamon Pr) Elsevier.

Machinability of Engineering Materials. B. Mills & A. H. Redford. (Illus.). 200p. 1983. 54.00 (*0-85334-183-4*) Elsevier.

Machinability Testing & Utilization of Machining Data: Proceedings of an International Conference on Machinability Testing & Utilization of Machining Data, 1978, Oak Brook, IL. LC 79-21143. (Materials-Metalworking Technology Ser.). (Illus.). 472p. reprint ed. pap. 146.40 (*0-8357-6196-7*, 203271400080) Bks Demand.

Machinal. Sophie Treadwell. 96p. 1993. pap. 12.95 (*1-85459-211-4*, Pub. by N Hern Bks) Theatre Comm.

Machination: Top Secret Lethal Defect. Wilson Sherman. Ed. by Darrell Fields. LC 94-70053. 179p. (Orig.). 1994. pap. 9.00 (*0-9639964-7-9*) ASF Pubns.

Machinations: The Writings of Three Generations of Hollingsworth Women Telling of Wealth & Power - The Textile Machinery Empire & the Family Tragedy That Created A Billionaire. Mary J. Crolley et al. (Illus.). 431p. (Orig.). (C). 1988. pap. 19.95 (*0-9621955-0-2*) MJH Crolley.

Machinations Photographs. Tress. (Illus.). 1995. per. 25.00 (*0-85449-086-8*, Pub. by Gay Mens Pr) LPC InBook.

*__Machine: Labor Confronts the Future.__ Ed. by John Earhurst & Andrew Parkin. (Illus.). 400p. 2000. pap. 35.00 (*1-86448-721-6*, Pub. by Allen & Unwin Pty) Paul & Co Pubs.

Machine - Process Capability Study: A Five Stage Methodology for Optimizing Manufacturing Processes. rev. ed. Mario Perez-Wilson. (Variation Reduction Program Ser.). 238p. 1993. reprint ed. 74.95 (*1-883237-00-9*) Adv Systs Cnslts.

Machine Age, Vol. 1. Plowden. 1995. text 60.00 (*0-8050-2902-8*) St Martin.

Machine-Age Ideology: Social Engineering & American Liberalism, 1911-1939. John M. Jordan. LC 93-2108. (Illus.). xviii, 332p. (C). 1994. 55.00 (*0-8078-2123-3*) U of NC Pr.

Machine Age Maya: The Industrialization of a Guatemalan Community. Manning Nash. LC 67-20810. 1992. pap. text 3.95 (*0-226-56863-6*, P262) U Ch Pr.

Machine Age to Jet Age: Radiomania's Guide to Tabletop Radios 1930-1959, Vol. 2. Mark V. Stein. (Illus.). 360p. (Orig.). 1997. pap. 28.95 (*0-9647953-1-0*) Radiomania Bks.

Machine Age to Jet Age: Radiomania's Guide to Tabletop Radios, 1933-1959, Vol. I. 2nd ed. Mark V. Stein. 272p. 1998. pap. 24.95 (*0-9647953-0-2*) Radiomania Bks.

*__Machine Age to Jet Age Vol. 3: Guide to Tabletop Radios 1930-1962 with Market Prices.__ Mark V. Stein. (Illus.). (Orig.). 1999. pap. 29.95 (*0-9647953-2-9*, Pub. by Radiomania Bks) Wash Bk Distrib.

Machine & Assembler Language Simulation. Art Rowland. 112p. (C). 1994. pap. text 20.55 (*1-56226-195-9*) CAT Pub.

Machine Applique. Jan Brooke. 96p. (C). 1989. 100.00 (*1-85368-059-1*, Pub. by New5 Holland) St Mut.

Machine Art. Philip Johnson. LC 77-86423. (Museum of Modern Art Publications in Reprint). (Illus.). 116p. 1969. reprint ed. 20.95 (*0-405-01542-9*) Ayer.

Machine Art: Sixtieth Anniversary Edition. 2nd ed. Pref. by Philip Johnson. LC 94-74587. (Illus.). 120p. 1995. pap. 12.95 (*0-87070-135-5*) Mus of Modern Art.

Machine Art--Museum of Modern Art: Sixtieth - Anniversary Edition, 1934-1994. Pref. by Philip Johnson. (Illus.). 116p. 1999. reprint ed. pap. text 18.00 (*0-7881-6107-5*) DIANE Pub.

Machine Art & Other Writings. Ezra Pound. Ed. & Intro. by Maria L. Ardizzone. LC 95-50858. (Illus.). 232p. 1996. pap. 16.95 (*0-8223-1765-6*); text 39.95 (*0-8223-1756-7*) Duke.

Machine As Metaphor & Tool. Ed. by H. Haken et al. (Illus.). 174p. 1993. 29.95 (*0-387-55816-0*) Spr-Verlag.

Machine at the Bedside: Strategies for Using Technology in Patient Care. Ed. by Stanley J. Reiser & Michael Anbar. (Illus.). 384p. 1984. pap. text 28.95 (*0-521-31832-7*) Cambridge U Pr.

Machine at Work: Technology, Work & Organization. Keith Grint & Steve Woolgar. LC 96-37740. 1997. 58.95 (*0-7456-0924-4*); pap. 25.95 (*0-7456-0925-2*) Blackwell Pubs.

Machine Beauty. Gelernter. 2000. pap. 11.00 (*0-465-04316-X*, Pub. by Basic) HarpC.

Machine Blacksmithing. 1996. lib. bdg. 250.75 (*0-8490-8347-8*) Gordon Pr.

Machine Calculation for Business & Personal Use. Gilbert J. Ribera. 200p. (C). 1994. pap. text, spiral bd. 27.01 (*0-8403-9483-7*) Kendall-Hunt.

Machine Calculation for Business & Personal Use. 2nd ed. Gilbert J. Ribera. LC 79-83523. 1979. pap. text 18.95 (*0-8162-7180-1*); teacher ed. 5.00 (*0-8162-7181-X*) Holden-Day.

Machine Controls: A Selection from the Tool & Manufacturing Engineers Handbook. Ed. by Thomas J. Drozda. LC 82-60312. (Illus.). 102p. 1988. reprint ed. pap. 31.70 (*0-7837-8190-3*, 204789500008) Bks Demand.

*__Machine Conversations.__ Yorick Wilks. LC 99-30264. (International Series In Engineering & Computer Science). 221p. 1999. write for info. (*0-7923-8544-6*) Kluwer Academic.

Machine Cryptography & Modern Cryptanalysis. Cipher Deavours & Louis Kruh. 259p. (C). 1985. text. write for info. (*0-89006-161-0*) Artech Hse.

Machine Cryptography & Modern Cryptanalysis. Cipher A. Deavours & Louis Kruh. LC 84-73275. (Artech House Telecommunications Library). 274p. 1985. reprint ed. pap. 85.00 (*0-608-00556-8*, 206143900008) Bks Demand.

Machine Cycle - Student's Manual: The Molding Process, Module One, Lesson 6. (Illus.). 1997. pap., student ed. write for info. (*1-58677-012-8*) Polymer Train.

Machine Design. A. S. Hall et al. 352p. (Orig.). (C). 1968. pap. 16.95 (*0-07-025595-4*) McGraw.

Machine Design. 2nd ed. Anthony Esposito & James R. Thrower. 540p. 1990. pap., teacher ed. 16.00 (*0-8273-4082-6*) Delmar.

Machine Design. 2nd ed. Anthony Esposito & James R. Thrower. 540p. 1991. mass mkt. 53.50 (*0-8273-4081-8*) Delmar.

Machine Design: A Solution Manual. 3rd ed. Robert H. Creamer. LC 83-2567. 540p. 1984. pap. text, teacher ed. 1.50 (*0-201-11281-7*) Addison-Wesley.

*__Machine Design: An Integrated Approach.__ 2nd ed. Robert L. Norton. 875p. 2000. 110.00 (*0-13-017706-7*) P-H.

*__Machine Design: Integrated Approach.__ 2nd ed. 2000. teacher ed. write for info. (*0-13-019196-5*) P-H.

Machine Design: Theory & Practice. Aaron D. Deutschman et al. (Illus.). 768p. (C). 1975. text 72.00 (*0-02-329000-5*, Macmillan Coll) P-H.

Machine Design for Mobile & Industrial Applications. Gary W. Krutz et al. 548p. 1994. 69.00 (*1-56091-389-4*, R-128) Soc Auto Engineers.

Machine Design for Mobile & Industrial Applications. 2nd ed. Gary W. Krutz et al. LC 98-46074. 700p. 1999. 79.00 (*0-7680-0013-0*, R-201) Soc Auto Engineers.

Machine Design Fundamentals: A Practical Approach. Hindhede. 672p. 1987. 90.00 (*0-13-541764-3*) P-H.

Machine Design Problem Solver. rev. ed. Research & Education Association Staff. (Illus.). 928p. 1994. pap. text 29.95 (*0-87891-605-9*) Res & Educ.

Machine Designed Mathcad Solutions. Cook. 1998. pap. text 38.00 (*0-13-287434-2*) P-H.

Machine Developments in Upholstery Sewing. 1985. 110.00 (*0-7855-1061-3*) St Mut.

Machine Discovery. Ed. by Jan M. Zytkow. LC 96-52468. (Spinoff FODA Ser.). 150p. (C). 1997. lib. bdg. 57.00 (*0-7923-4406-5*) Kluwer Academic.

Machine Drafting. Jack Rudman. (Occupational Competency Examination Ser.: OCE-24). 1994. pap. 27.95 (*0-8373-5724-1*) Nat Learn.

*__Machine Dreams.__ Joshua Mertz. LC 00-104542. 304p. 2000. pap. 16.00 (*0-9661664-4-2*, Pub. by Bald Mtn Bks) Partners Pubs Grp.

*__Machine Dreams.__ Jayne Anne Phillips. LC 99-18315. 352p. 1999. pap. 14.00 (*0-375-70525-2*) Vin Bks.

Machine Dreams. Jayne Anne Phillips. Ed. by Jane Rosenman. LC 91-2014. 400p. 1999. reprint ed. pap. 14.00 (*0-671-74235-3*, WSP) PB.

Machine Elements & Machine Dynamics: Proceedings of the 23rd Biennial Mechanisms Conference, 1994, Minneapolis, MN. 548p. 1994. pap. 90.00 (*0-7918-1285-5*) ASME.

Machine Elements & Mechanics. 3rd ed. Robert L. Mott. LC 98-34439. 852p. 1998. 105.00 (*0-13-841446-7*) P-H.

Machine Embroidery: Stitches & Techniques Instruction Workbook. Mary R. Osmus. 130p. 1990. student ed., spiral bd. 22.95 (*1-883118-01-8*) MRayOs Fiberwrks.

Machine Embroidery Vol. I: Beginning & Intermediate Patterns. Mary R. Osmus. 64p. 1992. student ed. 15.95 (*1-883118-02-6*) MRayOs Fiberwrks.

Machine Embroidery Vol. II: Intermediate & Advanced Patterns. Mary R. Osmus. 106p. 1992. student ed. 19.95 (*1-883118-03-4*) MRayOs Fiberwrks.

Machine Embroidery Handbook: Designing Fabrics with Stitching, Manipulation & Color. D. J. Bennett. Ed. by Carol Parks. LC 97-13888. (Illus.). 128p. 1997. 24.95 (*1-887374-45-0*, Pub. by Lark Books) Random.

Machine-God Laughs. Pragnell. 3.50 (*0-686-05843-7*); pap. 1.50 (*0-686-05844-5*) Fantasy Pub Co.

Machine Guarding. Keller, J. J., & Associates, Inc. Staff. LC 96-79538. (Workplace Safety in Action Ser.). 190p. 1996. spiral bd. 49.00 (*1-877798-70-3*, 1-SLG-6) J J Keller.

Machine Guarding: A Historical Perspective. Verne L. Roberts. LC 80-84798. (Illus.). 282p. 1980. text 39.95 (*0-938830-00-7*) Inst Product.

*__Machine Guarding Handbook: A Practical Guide to OSHA Compliance & Injury Prevention.__ Frank R. Spellman & Nancy E. Whiting. (Illus.). 106p. 1999. pap. 59.00 (*0-86587-662-2*, 662) Gov Insts.

Machine-Gun Diplomacy. John A. Hopkins & Melinda Alexander. 1980. lib. bdg. 59.95 (*0-8490-3174-5*) Gordon Pr.

Machine Gun Kelly. Sue Hamilton. Ed. by John Hamilton. LC 89-84924. (America's Most Wanted Ser.). (Illus.). 32p. (J). (gr. 4). 1989. lib. bdg. 11.96 (*0-939179-64-4*) ABDO Pub Co.

Machine Gun Kelly: To Right a Wrong. Bruce Barnes. 292p. (Orig.). 1992. pap. 12.95 (*0-9632609-0-1*) Tipper Pubns.

Machine-Gun Man: The True Story of George "Machine-Gun Kelly" As Told to Jim Dobkins & Ben Jorden. 252p. 1988. pap. 6.95 (*0-943247-04-7*) UCS Press.

Machine Gun Manual, 1886: 1886. Ed. by Jacques N. Jacobsen. 1989. 10.00 (*0-913150-99-1*) Pioneer Pr.

Machine-Gunners. Robert Westall. LC 76-13630. 192p. (J). (gr. 7 up). 1997. mass mkt. 4.95 (*0-688-15498-0*, Wm Morrow) Morrow Avon.

Machine-Gunners. Robert Westall. (J). 1997. 10.05 (*0-606-11586-2*, Pub. by Turtleback) Demco.

Machine Guns of World War I: Live Firing Classic Military Weapons in Color Photographs. Robert Bruce. (Illus.). 128p. 1997. 29.95 (*1-85915-078-0*, Pub. by W & G) Motorbooks Intl.

Machine Guns over the White House. Grant Stockbridge & Don Hutchison. (Spider Ser.: No. 48). (Illus.). 96p. 1998. per. 10.00 (*1-891729-05-5*) Pulp Advents.

Machine in America: A Social History of Technology. Carroll Pursell. (Illus.). 256p. 1995. text 45.00 (*0-8018-4817-2*); pap. text 17.95 (*0-8018-4818-0*) Johns Hopkins.

Machine in Me: An Anthropologist Sits among Computer Engineers. Gary L. Downey. LC 97-45228. 270p. (C). 1998. pap. 22.99 (*0-415-92022-1*) Routledge.

Machine in Me: An Anthropologist Sits among Computer Engineers. Gary L. Downey. LC 97-45228. (Illus.). 270p. (C). 1998. 80.00 (*0-415-92021-3*) Routledge.

Machine in the Garden: Technology & the Pastoral Ideal in America. Leo Marx. (Illus.). 400p. 1967. pap. 14.95 (*0-19-500738-7*) OUP.

Machine in the Garden: Technology & the Pastoral Ideal in America. 2nd ed. Leo Marx. LC 99-34697. (Illus.). 430p. 2000. pap. text 16.95 (*0-19-513351-X*) OUP.

***Machine in the Garden: Technology & the Pastoral Ideal in America.** 2nd ed. Leo Marx. LC 99-34697. (Illus.). 430p. 2000. text 35.00 (*0-19-513350-1*) OUP.

Machine in the Nursery: Incubator Technology & the Origins of Newborn Intensive Care. Jeffrey P. Baker. LC 95-40320. (Illus.). 256p. (C). 1996. text 45.00 (*0-8018-5173-4*) Johns Hopkins.

Machine in the Studio. Jones Staff. 1998. pap. text 27.50 (*0-226-40649-0*) U Ch Pr.

Machine in the Studio: Constructing the Postwar American Artist. Caroline A. Jones. (Illus.). 536p. 1996. 49.95 (*0-226-40648-2*) U Ch Pr.

Machine Infernale: Theatre. Jean Cocteau. (FRE.). 1962. 17.50 (*0-685-11299-3*, 854); pap. 10.95 (*0-8288-9128-1*, F96621) Fr & Eur.

Machine Intelligence: An International Bibliography with Abstracts of Sensors in Automated Manufacturing. Alan Gomersall. 240p. 1985. 103.95 (*0-387-13191-4*) Spr-Verlag.

Machine Intelligence: Intelligent Systems Practice & Perspective. Jean Hayes et al. (Business Data Processing; A Wiley Ser.: Vol. 10). 576p. 1982. text 145.00 (*0-470-27323-2*) P-H.

Machine Intelligence: Machine Expertise & the Human Interface. J. E. Hayes et al. LC 79-40785. (Machine Intelligence Ser.: Vol. 9). 492p. 1979. text 145.00 (*0-470-26714-3*) P-H.

Machine Intelligence: Perspectives on the Computational Model see Artificial Intelligence & Cognitive Science: Conceptual Issues

Machine Intelligence Vol. 11: Logic & the Acquisition of Knowledge. J. E. Hayes et al. (Illus.). 472p. 1988. 89.00 (*0-19-853718-2*) OUP.

Machine Intelligence Vol. 13: Machine Intelligence & Inductive Learning. Ed. by K. Furukawa et al. (Illus.). 488p. 1994. text 95.00 (*0-19-853850-2*) OUP.

Machine Intelligence & Autonomy for Aerospace Systems. Ed. by Ewald Heer & Henry Lum. (PAAS Ser.: Vol. 115). 355p. 1989. 69.95 (*0-930403-48-7*) AIAA.

Machine Intelligence & Knowledge Engineering for Robotic Applications. A. K. Wong & A. Pugh. (NATO Asi Series F: Vol. 33). xiv, 483p. 1987. 116.95 (*0-387-17844-9*) Spr-Verlag.

Machine Intelligence & Related Topics. Donald Michie. xii, 316p. 1982. text 161.00 (*0-677-05560-9*) Gordon & Breach.

***Machine Intelligence 15: Intelligent Agents.** Ed. by Koichi Furukawa et al. (Illus.). 528p. 2000. text 225.00 (*0-19-853867-7*) OUP.

Machine Intelligence 14: Applied Machine Intelligence. Ed. by Donald Michie et al. (Illus.). 470p. (C). 1996. text 115.00 (*0-19-853860-X*) OUP.

Machine Intelligence 12: Towards an Automated Logic of Human Thought. Ed. by J. E. Hayes. LC 97-228615. (Illus.). 352p. 1991. text 125.00 (*0-19-853823-5*) OUP.

Machine Interpretation of Line Drawing Images: Technical Drawings, Maps & Diagrams. Sergey V. Ablameyko & Tony Pridmore. LC 99-17199. 1999. write for info. (*3-540-76207-8*) Spr-Verlag.

Machine Interpretation of Line Drawings. Kokichi Sugihara. (Illus.). 245p. 1986. 32.50 (*0-262-19254-3*) MIT Pr.

Machine Interpretations of Patterson Functions & Alternative Direct Approaches & the Austin Symposium on Gas Phase Molecular Structure. Ed. by W. F. Bradley & Harold P. Hanson. (Transactions of the American Crystallographic Association Ser.: Vol. 2). 1966. pap. 25.00 (*0-686-60373-7*) Polycrystal Bk Serv.

Machine Knits. Valerie Carter. LC 86-81960. (Illus.). 128p. (Orig.). 1987. pap. 17.95 (*0-937274-29-1*) Lark Books.

Machine Knitting Textbook: Using the Passap E-6000. Marika Simon. (Illus.). 145p. 1997. pap. 39.95 (*0-9665734-0-4*) Simon Publns.

Machine Knitting Textbook: Using the Passap E-6000. 2nd rev. ed. Marika Simon. (Illus.). 160p. 1998. pap. 39.95 (*0-9665734-1-2*) Simon Publns.

Machine Language. Melissa Monroe. (Series of Poetry & Translation). 48p. (Orig.). 1997. pap. 12.00 (*1-882509-05-6*) Alef Bks.

Machine Language Disk I-O & Other Mysteries. Michael J. Wagner. (TRS-80 Information Ser.: Vol. 5). (Illus.). 288p. (Orig.). 1982. pap. 29.95 (*0-936200-06-5*) Blue Cat.

Machine Learning. Thomas M. Mitchell. LC 97-7692. (Illus.). 432p. (C). 1997. 83.44 (*0-07-042807-7*) McGraw.

Machine Learning: A Guide to Current Research. Ed. by Tom M. Mitchell et al. 1986. reprint ed. text 140.50 (*0-89838-214-9*) Kluwer Academic.

Machine Learning: A Multi-Strategy Approach, Vol. 4. Ed. by Ryszard S. Michalski & George Tecuci. 782p. (Orig.). (C). 1993. text 63.95 (*1-55860-251-8*) Morgan Kaufmann.

Machine Learning: A Theoretical Approach. Balas K. Natarajan. 250p. 1991. text 46.95 (*1-55860-148-1*) Morgan Kaufmann.

Machine Learning: An Artificial Intelligence Approach, Vol. 1. Ed. by Tom M. Mitchell et al. LC 86-2953. (Illus.). 572p. 1983. reprint ed. text 53.95 (*0-934613-09-5*) Morgan Kaufmann.

Machine Learning: An Artificial Intelligence Approach, Vol. II. Ed. by Ryszard S. Michalski et al. LC 82-10654. (Illus.). 738p. 1986. text 53.95 (*0-934613-00-1*) Morgan Kaufmann.

Machine Learning: An Artificial Intelligence Approach, Vol. 3. Ed. by Yves Kodratoff & Ryszard S. Michalski. 825p. 1990. text 58.95 (*1-55860-119-8*) Morgan Kaufmann.

Machine Learning: Applications in Expert Systems & Information Retrieval. Richard Forsyth & Roy Rada. LC 86-3054. (Artificial Intelligence Ser.). 277p. 1986. text 68.95 (*0-470-20309-9*); pap. text 29.95 (*0-470-20318-8*) P-H.

Machine Learning: ECML - 95: Proceeding of the 8th European Conference on Machine Learning, Held at Heraclion, Greece, April 25-27, 1995. Eighth European Conference on Machine Learning Sta. Ed. by S. Wrobel & Nada Lavrac. (Lecture Notes in Computer Science: Lecture Notes in Artificial Intelligence Ser.: Vol. 912). 370p. 1995. 62.00 (*3-540-59286-5*) Spr-Verlag.

***Machine Learning: ECML 2000: 11th European Conference on Machine Learning, Barcelona, Catalonia, Spain, May 31-June 2, 2000.** Ramon Lopez de Mantaras & Enric Plaza. LC 00-40012. (Lecture Notes in Computer Science Ser.). 2000. pap. write for info. (*3-540-67602-3*) Spr-Verlag.

Machine Learning: ECML '97: 9th European Conference on Machine Learning, Prague, Czech Republic, April 23-25, 1997, Proceedings. Ed. by M. Van Someren et al. LC 97-13121. (Lecture Notes in Artificial Intelligence Ser.: No. 1224). xi, 361p. 1997. pap. 61.00 (*3-540-62858-4*) Spr-Verlag.

Machine Learning: EMCL-94. Ed. by Francesco Bergadano & Luc DeRaedt. LC 94-8266. (Lecture Notes in Computer Science, Lecture Notes in Artificial Intelligence Ser.: Vol. 784). 1994. write for info. (*3-540-57868-4*) Spr-Verlag.

Machine Learning: EMCL-94. Ed. by Francesco Bergadano & Luc Raedt. LC 94-8266. (Lecture Notes in Computer Science, Lecture Notes in Artificial Intelligence Ser.: Vol. 784). 1994. 61.95 (*0-387-57868-4*) Spr-Verlag.

Machine Learning: From Theory to Applications - Cooperative Research at Siemens & MIT. Ed. by S. J. Hanson et al. LC 93-2796. (Lecture Notes in Computer Science Ser.: Vol. 661). 1993. 44.95 (*0-387-56483-7*) Spr-Verlag.

Machine Learning: Meta-Reasoning & Logics. Ed. by Pavel B. Brazdil & Kurt Konolige. (C). 1989. text 118.50 (*0-7923-9047-4*) Kluwer Academic.

Machine Learning: Neural Networks, Genetic Algorithms, & Fuzzy Systems. Hojjat Adeli & Shih-Lin Hung. 211p. 1994. pap. 64.99 (*0-471-01633-0*) Wiley.

Machine Learning: Proceedings of the Eighth International Workshop. Ed. by Lawrence A. Birnbaum & Gregg C. Collins. 1998. pap. text 39.95 (*1-55860-200-3*) Morgan Kaufmann.

Machine Learning: Proceedings of the Eleventh International Conference. Ed. by William W. Cohen & Haym Hirsh. LC 94-21011. 381p. (C). 1998. pap. text 49.95 (*1-55860-335-2*) Rutgers U Pr.

Machine Learning: Proceedings of the Fourteenth International Conference. 558p. 1998. pap. text 69.95 (*1-55860-486-3*) Morgan Kaufmann.

Machine Learning: Proceedings of the Ninth International Workshop (ML92) Ed. by Derek Sleeman & Peter Edwards. LC 92-17244. 1998. pap. text 44.95 (*1-55860-247-X*) Morgan Kaufmann.

Machine Learning: Proceedings of the Sixth International Conference. Ed. by Alberto M. Segre. 450p. (Orig.). (C). 1998. pap. text 29.95 (*1-55860-036-1*) Morgan Kaufmann.

Machine Learning: Proceedings of the Thirteenth International Conference. Ed. by Lorenza Saitta. (Orig.). (C). 1998. pap. text 69.95 (*1-55860-419-7*) Morgan Kaufmann.

Machine Learning - ECML-98: Proceedings 10th European Conference on Machine Learning, Chemnitz, Germany, April 21-23, 1998. Ed. by Claire Nedellec & Celine Rouveirol. LC 98-18109. (Lecture Notes in Artificial Intelligence: Vol. 1398). xii, 420p. 1998. pap. 67.00 (*3-540-64417-2*) Spr-Verlag.

Machine Learning - ECML '94: Proceedings of the European Conference on Machine Learning, Heraclion, Crete, Greece, April 1995. European Conference on Machine Learning Staff. Ed. by Nada Lavrac. LC 95-14637. (Lecture Notes in Computer Science, Vol. 912: Lecture Notes in Artificial Intelligence). 1995. write for info. (*0-387-59286-5*) Spr-Verlag.

Machine Learning - EWSL '91: European Working Session on Learning Porto, Portugal, March 6-8, 1991 Proceedings. Ed. by Yves Kodratoff & Joerg H. Siekmann. (Lecture Notes in Artificial Intelligence: Vol. 482). xi, 537p. 1991. 53.95 (*0-387-53816-X*) Spr-Verlag.

Machine Learning & Data Mining: Methods & Applications. Ed. by Ryszard Michalski et al. 456p. 1998. 84.99 (*0-471-97199-5*) Wiley.

***Machine Learning & Data Mining in Pattern Recognition: Proceedings of the First International Workshop, MLDM'99, Leipzig, Germany, September 16-18, 1999.** rev. ed. Ed. by P. Perner & M. Petrou. (Lecture Notes in Artificial Intelligence Ser.: Vol. 1715). viii, 215p. 1999. pap. 45.00 (*3-540-66599-4*) Spr-Verlag.

Machine Learning & Image Interpretation. T. Caelli & W. F. Bischof. LC 97-36803. (Advances in Computer Vision & Machine Intelligence Ser.). 448p. (C). 1997. 115.00 (*0-306-45761-X*, Kluwer Plenum) Kluwer Academic.

Machine Learning & Perception. LC 96-200740. 216p. 1996. pap. text 19.00 (*981-02-2642-X*) World Scientific Pub.

Machine Learning & Statistics: The Interface. Ed. by G. Nakhaeizadeh & C. C. Taylor. LC 96-4668. (Sixth-Generation Computer Technologies Ser.). 343p. 1996. 105.00 (*0-471-14890-3*) Wiley.

Machine Learning & Uncertain Reasoning. Ed. by Brian R. Gaines & John H. Boose. (Knowledge Based Systems Ser.: Vol. 3). 498p. 1990. text 83.00 (*0-12-273252-9*) Acad Pr.

Machine Learning, ECML '93: European Conference on Machine Learning, Vienna, Australia, April 5-7, 1993, Proceedings. Ed. by Pavel B. Brazdil. LC 93-12645. (Lecture Notes in Computer Science Ser.: Vol. 667). 1993. 65.95 (*0-387-56602-3*) Spr-Verlag.

***Machine Learning for Information Extraction: Papers from the AAAI Workshop.** Ed. by Mary E. Califf. (Technical Reports: Vol. WS-99-11). (Illus.). 52p. 1999. spiral bd. 25.00 (*1-57735-095-2*) AAAI Pr.

Machine Learning in Computer Vision - What, Why, & How? Papers from the 1993 Fall Symposium. Ed. by Kevin Bowyer & Lawrence Hall. (Technical Reports). (Illus.). 166p. (Orig.). 1994. spiral bd. 25.00 (*0-929280-53-9*) AAAI Pr.

Machine Learning in Information Access: Papers from the 1996 Spring Symposium. Ed. by Marti Hearst & Haym Hirsh. (Technical Reports). (Illus.). 128p. 1996. spiral bd. 25.00 (*1-57735-007-3*) AAAI Pr.

Machine Learning International Workshop on Machine Learning: Proceedings of the 5th International Conference. Ed. by John Laird. 467p. (C). 1998. pap. text 19.95 (*0-934613-64-8*) Morgan Kaufmann.

Machine Learning International Workshop, 4th, Irvine, CA: Proceedings. Ed. by Pat Langley. LC 87-3803. 416p. (Orig.). (C). 1998. pap. text 34.95 (*0-934613-41-9*) Morgan Kaufmann.

***Machine Learning Methods for Ecological Applications.** Alan Fielding. LC 99-33708. 280p. 1999. 125.00 (*0-412-84190-8*) Kluwer Academic.

Machine Learning Methods for Planning. Ed. by Steven Minton. LC 92-19279. (Series in Machine Learning). 550p. 1993. text 48.95 (*1-55860-248-8*) Morgan Kaufmann.

Machine Learning, 1990: Proceedings of the Seventh International Conference. Ed. by Bruce Porter & Raymond Mooney. 404p. (C). 1998. pap. text 39.95 (*1-55860-141-4*) Morgan Kaufmann.

Machine Learning of Design Concepts. Heng Li. LC 94-68172. (Topics in Engineering Ser.: Vol. 23). 180p. 1994. 91.00 (*1-56252-281-7*, 3587) Computational Mech MA.

Machine Learning of Design Concepts. Hengde Li. 180p. 1995. 91.00 (*1-85312-358-7*) Computational Mech MA.

Machine Learning of Inductive Bias. Paul E. Utgoff. 1986. text 86.50 (*0-89838-223-8*) Kluwer Academic.

Machine Learning of Natural Language. D. M. Powers. (Illus.). x, 358p. 1989. 49.00 (*0-387-19557-2*) Spr-Verlag.

Machine Learning of Robot Assembly Plans. Alberto M. Segre. (C). 1988. text 95.50 (*0-89838-269-6*) Kluwer Academic.

Machine Lockout (Reference Card) Tel-A-Train, Inc. Staff. 1989. student ed. 0.15 (*1-56355-173-X*) Tel-A-Train.

Machine Man & Other Writings. Ann Thomson. (Cambridge Texts in the History of Philosophy Ser.). 209p. 1996. text 59.95 (*0-521-47258-X*) Cambridge U Pr.

Machine, Metaphor, & the Writer: A Jungian View. Bettina L. Knapp. LC 88-7696. 272p. 1989. lib. bdg. 35.00 (*0-271-00664-1*) Pa St U Pr.

Machine Models of Music. Stephan Schwanauer & David Levitt. (Illus.). 556p. 1993. 55.00 (*0-262-19319-1*) MIT Pr.

***Machine Musicianship.** Robert Rowe. LC 00-38699. 2001. pap. write for info. (*0-262-18206-8*) MIT Pr.

Machine Needlelace & Other Embellishment Techniques. Judy Simmons. Ed. by Barbara Weiland. LC 96-50427. (Illus.). 96p. (Orig.). 1997. pap. 24.95 (*1-56477-162-8*, B273) Martingale & Co.

Machine Plays Chess. A. G. Bell. 1978. text 21.00 (*0-08-021221-2*, Pergamon Pr); pap. text 8.95 (*0-08-021222-0*, Pergamon Pr) Elsevier.

Machine Politics: A Study of Albany's O'Connells. Frank S. Robinson. LC 76-3785. Orig. Title: Albany's O'Connell Machine. (Illus.). 262p. 1977. reprint ed. 39.95 (*0-87855-147-6*) Transaction Pubs.

Machine Politics: Chicago Model. Harold F. Gosnell. LC 70-100507. reprint ed. 20.00 (*0-404-00591-8*) AMS Pr.

Machine Politics: Chicago Model. Harold F. Gosnell. LC 69-13914. (Illus.). 229p. 1970. reprint ed. lib. bdg. 45.00 (*0-8371-0451-3*, GOMP, Greenwood Pr) Greenwood.

Machine Politics: Chicago Model. 2nd ed. Harold F. Gosnell. LC 68-16692. (Midway Reprint Ser.). 279p. reprint ed. pap. 86.50 (*0-608-16571-9*, 202677600052) Bks Demand.

Machine Politics & Money in Elections in New York City. William Ivins. LC 71-112552. (Rise of Urban America Ser.). 1974. reprint ed. 16.95 (*0-405-02459-2*) Ayer.

Machine Politics in Transition: Party & Community in Chicago. Thomas M. Guterbock. LC 79-16131. (Studies of Urban Society). (Illus.). 352p. 1980. 33.00 (*0-226-31114-7*) U Ch Pr.

Machine Politics, Sound Bites, & Nostalgia: On Studying Political Parties. Ed. by John C. Green & Michael Margolis. LC 92-32648. 78p. (Orig.). (C). 1992. pap. text 16.00 (*0-8191-8856-5*); lib. bdg. 37.00 (*0-8191-8855-7*) U Pr of Amer.

Machine Proofs in Geometry: Automated Production of Readable Proofs for Geometry Theorems. Shang C. Chou et al. LC 94-5809. (Series on Applied Mathematics: Vol. 6). 480p. 1994. text 86.00 (*981-02-1584-3*) World Scientific Pub.

Machine Quilting Made Easy. Maurine Noble. Ed. by Ursula G. Reikes. (Joy of Quilting Ser.). (Illus.). 56p. 1994. pap. 12.95 (*1-56477-074-5*, B200) Martingale & Co.

Machine Quilting Primer. Cynthia Martin. Ed. by Eleanor Burns. (Illus.). 96p. (Orig.). 1996. 24.95 (*0-922705-90-9*) Quilt Day.

Machine Quilting with Decorative Threads. Maurine Noble & Elizabeth Hendricks. Ed. by Ursula Reikes. LC 97-44178. (Illus.). 88p. 1998. pap. 21.95 (*1-56477-216-0*, B333, That Patchwrk Pl) Martingale & Co.

Machine-Readable Coding Guidelines for the Book Industry. rev. ed. Joint Committee of the Book Industry Study Group &. (Illus.). 22p. 1997. pap. 7.50 (*0-940016-64-8*) Bk Indus Study.

Machine-Readable Version of Hegel's "Lectures on the Philosophy of Religion" (Produced under License with the University of California Press) Georg Wilhelm Friedrich Hegel. Ed. & Tr. by Peter C. Hodgson. (GER.). 123p. (C). 1992. ring bd. 75.00 incl. 3.5 hd (*1-878933-03-5*) Geotown Ctr Text Tech.

Machine-Readable Version of Ludwig Feuerbach's "Gesammelte Werke" (Produced under License with Akademie-Verlag, Berlin) Ludwig Feuerbach. Ed. by Werner Schuffenhauer. (GER.). 101p. (C). 1994, pap. 350.00 incl. 3.5 hd (*1-878933-05-1*) Geotown Ctr Text Tech.

Machine-Readable Version of the Phenomenology of Mind. Georg Wilhelm Friedrich Hegel. Tr. by J. B. Baillie from GER. 750p. (C). 1990. student ed. 35.00 (*1-878933-00-0*) Geotown Ctr Text Tech.

Machine Safety Set. 160p. 1993. ring bd. 445.00 (*1-57053-001-7*) Global Eng Doc.

Machine Scheduling Problems. A. H. Kan & A. H. Rinnooy-Kan. 1976. pap. text 78.50 (*90-247-1848-1*) Kluwer Academic.

Machine Sewn Rag Baskets. 2nd rev. ed. Wanda R. Melchert. LC 95-136447. (Illus.). 64p. (Orig.). 1994. pap. 11.95 (*0-9641199-0-0*) Desert Cntry.

Machine Shop. Sheldon Erickson et al. Ed. by Betty Cordel et al. (Illus.). 169p. (J). (gr. 5-9). 1993. 16.95 (*1-881431-39-8*, 1311) AIMS Educ Fnd.

Machine Shop Pt. 1: Testbook. California Department of Education Staff. (Apprenticeship Instructional Materials Ser.). 134p. 1973. pap. 6.25 (*0-8011-0567-6*) Calif Education.

Machine Shop Pt. 1: Workbook. California Department of Education Staff. (Apprenticeship Instructional Materials Ser.). (Illus.). 192p. 1973. pap. 8.25 (*0-8011-0566-8*) Calif Education.

Machine Shop Pt. 2: Testbook. California Department of Education Staff. (Apprenticeship Instructional Materials Ser.). 80p. 1977. pap. 6.25 (*0-8011-0570-6*) Calif Education.

Machine Shop Pt. 2: Workbook. California Department of Education Staff. (Apprenticeship Instructional Materials Ser.). (Illus.). 112p. 1977. pap. 8.25 (*0-8011-0569-2*) Calif Education.

Machine Shop Pt. 3: Testbook. California Department of Education Staff. (Apprenticeship Instructional Materials Ser.). 110p. 1976. pap. 6.25 (*0-8011-0572-2*) Calif Education.

Machine Shop Pt. 3: Workbook. California Department of Education Staff. (Apprenticeship Instructional Materials Ser.). (Illus.). 136p. 1976. pap. 8.25 (*0-8011-0571-4*) Calif Education.

Machine Shop Pt. 4: Testbook. California Department of Education Staff. (Apprenticeship Instructional Materials Ser.). 88p. 1969. pap. 3.75 (*0-8011-0575-7*) Calif Education.

Machine Shop Pt. 4: Workbook. California Department of Education Staff. (Apprenticeship Instructional Materials Ser.). (Illus.). 176p. 1969. pap. 7.25 (*0-8011-0574-9*) Calif Education.

Machine Shop Fundamentals. Stephen F. Krar. (Machine Tools Ser.). 1996. teacher ed. 17.50 (*0-8273-6946-8*) Delmar.

Machine Shop Fundamentals. Stephen F. Krar. (Machine Tools Ser.). 1997. text 37.95 (*0-8273-6945-X*) Delmar.

Machine Shop Operations & Setups. 4th ed. Orville D. Lascoe et al. (Illus.). 582p. 1973. 25.96 (*0-8269-1842-5*) Am Technical.

Machine Shop Practice, Vol. 1. 2nd ed. K. H. Moltrecht. LC 79-91236. (Illus.). 496p. (C). 1981. 20.95 (*0-8311-1126-7*) Indus Pr.

Machine Shop Practice, Vol. 2. 2nd ed. K. H. Moltrecht. LC 79-91236. (Illus.). 517p. (C). 1981. 20.95 (*0-8311-1132-1*) Indus Pr.

Machine Shop Skill Manual: Parallel Clamps. Thomas Wasiloff. LC TH5663.W3. (Illus.). 240p. reprint ed. pap. 74.40 (*0-608-11533-9*, 201157300079) Bks Demand.

Machine Shop Tools & Techniques. Robert H. Smith. (Illus.). 800p. 1991. reprint ed. pap. 19.00 (*1-877767-47-6*) Univ Publng Hse.

Machine Shop Training Course, 2 Vols., Vol. 1. 5th ed. Franklin D. Jones. (Illus.). 570p. 1964. 19.95 (*0-8311-1039-2*) Indus Pr.

Machine Shop Training Course, 2 Vols., Vol. 2. 5th ed. Franklin D. Jones. (Illus.). 566p. 1964. 19.95 (*0-8311-1040-6*) Indus Pr.

Machine Shop Workbook. Jack Rudman. (Workbook (W) Ser.: Vol. 2920). 43.95 (*0-8373-7928-8*) Nat Learn.

Machine Shop Workbook. Jack Rudman. (Workbook Ser.: W-2920). 1994. pap. 23.95 (*0-8373-7903-2*) Nat Learn.

Machine Shuts Down. Rod Tulloss. 40p. (Orig.). 1982. pap. 9.95 (*0-917658-15-9*) BPW & P.

***Machine-Stitched Cathedral Windows: Updating an Old Favorite.** Shelley Swanland. LC 99-44334. (Illus.). 96p. 1999. pap. 26.95 (*1-56477-285-3*, B402, That Patchwrk Pl) Martingale & Co.

Machine Stops & Other Stories. E. M. Forster. Ed. by Rod Mengham. LC 98-130653. 206p. 1998. 35.00 (*0-233-99167-0*, Pub. by Andre Deutsch) Trafalgar.

Machine Support Design Based on Vibration Calculus. Mihaly Makhult. 136p. 1977. 60.00 (*963-05-1150-9*, Pub. by Akade Kiado) St Mut.

Machine Takeover: The Growing Threat to Human Freedom in a Computer-Controlled Society. F. H. George. LC 76-27722. 208p. 1977. 96.00 (*0-08-021229-8*, Pub. by Pergamon Repr) Franklin.

Machine That Changed the World. Daniel Jones et al. LC 89-63284. 320p. (C). 1990. 150.00 (*0-89771-128-9*, Pub. by Inst Pur & Supply) St Mut.

Machine That Changed the World. James P. Womack et al. LC 89-63284. 336p. 1990. 24.95 (*0-89256-350-8*, Rawson Assocs) Macmillan.

Machine That Changed the World: The Story of Lean Production. James P. Womack et al. LC 91-55106. 336p. 1991. reprint ed. pap. 14.00 (*0-06-097417-6*, Perennial) HarperTrade.

Machine That Could: PNGV, a Government-Industry Partnership. Robert M. Chapman. LC 98-217140. (Illus.). 94p. 1998. pap. 15.00 (*0-8330-2657-7*, MR-1011-DOC) Rand Corp.

Machine That Would Go of Itself: The Constitution in American Culture. Michael G. Kammen. 550p. 1993. pap. text 26.95 (*0-312-09127-3*) St Martin.

Machine Tool. 6th ed. Neely. (C). 1998. pap. text, student ed., wbk. ed. write for info. (*0-13-099671-8*) P-H.

Machine Tool & Manufacturing Technology. Stephen F. Krar. (Machine Tools Ser.). 128p. 1997. pap., teacher ed. 17.95 (*0-8273-7863-7*) Delmar.

Machine Tool & Manufacturing Technology Workbook. Rappisarda et al. (Machine Tools Ser.). 224p. (C). 1997. text, wbk. ed. 19.50 (*0-8273-7587-5*) Delmar.

Machine Tool Condition Monitoring. L. E. Stockline. (Nineteen Ninety-One Fall Technical Meeting Ser.: Vol. 91FTM5). (Illus.). 6p. 1991. pap. text 30.00 (*1-55589-573-5*) AGMA.

***Machine Tool Design, Vol. 1.** N. Acherkan. 604p. 2000. pap. 56.25 (*0-89875-046-6*) U Pr Pacific.

***Machine Tool Design, Vol. 4.** N. Acherkan. 496p. 2000. pap. 56.25 (*0-89875-049-0*) U Pr Pacific.

Machine-Tool Dynamics: An Introduction. D. B. Welbourn & J. D. Smith. LC 71-101447. 152p. reprint ed. pap. 43.40 (*0-608-12915-1*, 2024558) Bks Demand.

Machine Tool Operations. Stephen F. Krar. LC 81-185871. (Illus.). 416p. (gr. 9-12). 1983. text 82.95 (*0-07-035430-8*) McGraw.

Machine Tool Practices. 3rd ed. Richard R. Kibbe et al. 1987. pap. text 15.50 (*0-471-85406-9*) P-H.

Machine Tool Practices. 6th ed. Richard R. Kibbe. LC 97-42905. 822p. 1998. 90.67 (*0-13-270232-0*) P-H.

Machine Tool Structures, Vol. 1. F. Koenigsberger & J. Tlusty. LC 79-84073. 1970. 236.00 (*0-08-013405-X*, Pub. by Pergamon Repr) Franklin.

Machine Tool Technology. Repp & McCarthy. 1999. teacher ed. 19.03 (*0-02-671600-3*) Glencoe.

Machine Tool Technology, No. 5. 5th ed. Willard McCarthy. 1984. 35.72 (*0-02-671570-8*) Macmillan.

Machine Tool Technology: Study Guide 1. 5th ed. Repp & McCarthy. (Illus.). 70p. (gr. 6-12). 1999. student ed. 11.61 (*0-02-671580-5*) Glencoe.

Machine Tool Technology: Study Guide 2. 5th ed. Repp & McCarthy. (Illus.). 137p. (gr. 6-12). 1999. student ed. 11.61 (*0-02-671590-2*) Glencoe.

Machine Tool Technology & Manufacturing Processes. C. Thomas Olivo. Ed. by H. G. Putnam. LC 86-18216. (Illus.). 640p. 1987. teacher ed. 15.95 (*0-938561-10-3*); student ed. 8.95 (*0-938561-09-X*) C T Olivo.

Machine Tool Technology & Manufacturing Processes. C. Thomas Olivo. Ed. by H. G. Putnam. LC 86-18216. (Illus.). 640p. 1986. pap. 42.75 (*0-938561-08-1*) Thomson Learn.

Machine Tools: U. S. & World Dynamics. R. Ebbin. 255p. 1998. 1995.00 (*0-945235-61-5*) Lead Edge Reports.

***Machine Tools & Metalworking Equipment in Colombia: A Strategic Entry Report, 1996.** Compiled by Icon Group International Staff. (Illus.). 165p. 1999. ring bd. 1650.00 incl. audio compact disk (*0-7418-1333-5*) Icon Grp.

***Machine Tools & Metalworking Equipment in Israel: A Strategic Entry Report, 1998.** Compiled by Icon Group International Staff. (Country Industry Report). (Illus.). 118p. 1999. ring bd. 1180.00 incl. audio compact disk (*0-7418-0515-4*) Icon Grp.

***Machine Tools & Metalworking Equipment in Vietnam: A Strategic Entry Report, 1999.** Compiled by Icon Group International. (Illus.). 158p. 1999. ring bd. 1580.00 incl. audio compact disk (*0-7418-1729-2*) Icon Grp.

Machine Tools Dictionary: English-French-German-Arabic. A. M. Abd-El-Wahed. (ARA, ENG, FRE & GER.). 334p. 1977. 75.00 (*0-8288-5498-X*, M9757) Fr & Eur.

***Machine Tools in Guangdong Province in China: A Strategic Entry Report, 1996.** Compiled by Icon Group International Staff. (Illus.). 158p. 1999. ring bd. 1580.00 incl. audio compact disk (*0-7418-1334-3*) Icon Grp.

Machine Tools, What They Are & How They Work: An Introduction to the Fundamentals of Mass Production. Horace E. Linsley. Ed. by Herbert D. Hall. LC 57-7456. 448p. reprint ed. pap. 138.90 (*0-608-11573-8*, 200190700008) Bks Demand.

Machine Trades. Jack Rudman. (Occupational Competency Examination Ser.: OCE-22). 1994. pap. 27.95 (*0-8373-5722-5*) Nat Learn.

Machine Trades Blueprint Reading. Taylord. (Blueprint Reading & Drafting Ser.). 1985. teacher ed. 13.50 (*0-8273-1912-6*) Delmar.

Machine Trades Blueprint Reading. David L. Taylord. (Blueprint Reading & Drafting Ser.). 1985. pap. 29.50 (*0-8273-1911-8*) Delmar.

***Machine Trades Print Reading.** Michael A. Barsamian & Richard Gizelbach. LC 00-34076. (Illus.). 2000. write for info. (*1-56637-594-0*) Goodheart.

Machine Trades Print Reading. Michael Barsamian & Richard Gizelbach. LC 92-32497. (Illus.). 240p. 1996. 27.60 (*1-56637-269-0*) Goodheart.

Machine Trades Printreading. Thomas E. Proctor et al. LC 95-171166. (Illus.). 298p. 1995. 28.96 (*0-8269-1864-6*) Am Technical.

Machine Trades Projects & Procedures: Standard & Metric. Frank Accurso. LC 77-8691. 1978. pap. text 11.50 (*0-672-97101-1*, Bobbs) Macmillan.

Machine Trans Spec: Cassettes. 2nd ed. Edith E. Ennis et al. 306p. (C). 1987. audio 432.50 (*0-15-551198-X*) Dryden Pr.

Machine Transcription. Blanche Ettinger & Edda Perfetto. 1992. text 150.00 incl. audio (*1-56118-067-X*) Paradigm MN.

Machine Transcription. 3rd ed. Ennis. (C). 1995. pap. text, spiral bd. 45.00 incl. 3.5 ld (*0-03-015879-6*, Pub. by Harcourt Coll Pubs) Harcourt.

Machine Transcription. 3rd ed. Blanche Ettinger & Edda Perfetto. LC 97-49881. 1998. 27.95 (*0-7638-0142-9*) Paradigm MN.

Machine Transcription: A Comprehensive Approach for Today's Office Professional - Short Course. 3rd ed. Carol A. Mitchell. 1995. teacher ed. 12.90 (*0-02-802226-2*) Glencoe.

Machine Transcription: A Comprehensive Approach for Today's Office Specialist. Carol A. Mitchell. 176p. (C). 1983. teacher ed. write for info. (*0-672-97987-X*); pap. text. write for info. (*0-672-97986-1*); write for info. (*0-672-97988-8*); audio. write for info. (*0-672-97989-6*) Macmillan.

Machine Transcription: A Comprehensive Approach for Today's Office Specialist. 3rd ed. Carol A. Mitchell. LC 94-36538. 1995. write for info. (*0-02-802221-1*) Glencoe.

Machine Transcription: A Comprehensive Approach for Today's Office Specialist, Short Course, Student Text. 3rd ed. Carol A. Mitchell. LC 94-24755. 1995. write for info. (*0-02-802220-3*) Glencoe.

Machine Transcription: Language Skills for Information Processing. 2nd ed. Blanche Ettinger & Edda Perfetto. 316p. (C). 1992. pap. text 25.95 (*1-56118-064-5*) Paradigm MN.

Machine Transcription: Language Skills for Information Processing. 2nd ed. Blanche Ettinger & Edda Perfetto. 316p. (C). 1992. teacher ed. 14.00 (*1-56118-065-3*); 12.50 (*1-56118-066-1*) Paradigm MN.

Machine Transcription & Word Processing. 2nd ed. William R. Pasewark. (KH - Office Machines Ser.). 1986. mass mkt. 15.50 (*0-538-23250-1*) S-W Pub.

Machine Transcription, Dictation & Proofreading. William R. Pasewark. (KH - Office Machines Ser.). 1987. mass mkt. 11.00 (*0-538-23350-8*) S-W Pub.

Machine Transcription for Document Processing. 3rd ed. Pasewark. (C). 1994. 400.00 (*0-538-71075-6*) Thomson Learn.

Machine Transcription for Document Processing. 3rd ed. William R. Pasewark. LC 94-15008. (C). 1994. mass mkt. 18.00 (*0-538-71074-8*) S-W Pub.

Machine Transcription: Language Skills for Information Processing: Instructor's guide with Disk. 3rd ed. Blanche Ettinger & Edda Perfetto. text, teacher ed. 18.00 incl. 3.5 hd (*0-7638-0139-9*) EMC-Paradigm.

Machine Transcription: Language Skills for Information Processing: Text with data disk, 3.5. 3rd ed. Blanche Ettinger & Edda Perfetto. 365p. text 27.95 (*0-7638-0138-0*) EMC-Paradigm.

Machine Transcription Specialist: A Text-Workbook. 2nd ed. Edith E. Ennis et al. 306p. (C). 1987. pap. text, teacher ed. 3.50 (*0-15-551196-3*) Dryden Pr.

Machine Transcription Word Processing. 2nd ed. Pasewark. (Office Machines Ser.). 1986. teacher ed. 16.50 (*0-538-23257-9*) S-W Pub.

Machine Transcriptionist. 3rd ed. Marilyn E. Price et al. LC 94-72573. 398p. (C). 1994. pap. text 38.00 (*0-03-094917-3*) Dryden Pr.

Machine Translation. Bozena Henisz-Dostert et al. (Trends in Linguistics, Studies & Monographs: No. 16). 1979. text 80.00 (*90-279-7836-0*) Mouton.

Machine Translation. Richard K. Miller & Terri C. Walker. LC 88-80494. (Survey on Technology & Markets Ser.: No. 2). 50p. 1989. pap. text 200.00 (*1-55865-001-6*) Future Tech Surveys.

Machine Translation: A View from the Lexicon. Bonnie J. Dorr. LC 92-35158. (Artificial Intelligence Ser.). (Illus.). 456p. 1993. 52.50 (*0-262-04138-3*) MIT Pr.

Machine Translation: Past, Present & Future. W. John Hutchins. LC 86-7465. (Computers & Their Applications Ser.). 382p. 1986. text 61.95 (*0-470-20313-7*) P-H.

Machine Translation & the Information Soup: Proceedings of the Third Conference of the Association for Machine Translation in the Americas, AMTA'98, Langhorne, PA, USA, October 28-31, 1998. Ed. by David Farwell et al. LC 98-48079. xix, 532p. 1998. pap. 79.00 (*3-540-65259-0*) Spr-Verlag.

Machine Translation & the Lexicon: Proceedings of the Third International EAMT Workshop, Held in Heidelberg, Germany, April 26-28, 1993. International EAMT Workshop Staff. Ed. by Petra Steffens. LC 95-2773. (Lecture Notes in Artificial Intelligence; Lecture Notes in Computer Science Ser.: Vol. 898). 251p. 1995. 49.00 (*0-387-59040-4*) Spr-Verlag.

Machine Translation & Translation Theory. Ed. by Susanne Heizmann & Christa Hauenschild. LC 97-25859. (Text, Translation, Computational Processing Ser.: Vol. 1). 260p. (C). 1997. lib. bdg. 87.45 (*3-11-015486-2*) Mouton.

Machine Translation in Japan. Ed. by Elaine Rich. (JTEC Panel Reports). vi, 142p. 1992. pap. write for info. (*1-883712-17-3*, JTEC) Intl Tech Res.

Machine Translation of Languages: Fourteen Essays. Ed. by William N. Locke & E. Donald Booth. LC 75-29339. 243p. 1976. reprint ed. lib. bdg. 38.50 (*0-8371-8434-7*, LOMT, Greenwood Pr) Greenwood.

Machine Translation Today. Ed. by Margaret King. 447p. 1987. 85.00 (*0-85224-519-X*, Pub. by Edinburgh U Pr) Col U Pr.

Machine Vision. Jack Hollingum. (Illus.). 100p. 1984. pap. 39.00 (*0-387-13837-4*) Spr-Verlag.

Machine Vision. Richard K. Miller & Terri C. Walker. LC 88-80902. (Survey on Technology & Markets Ser.: No. 18). 50p. 1989. pap. text 200.00 (*1-55865-017-2*) Future Tech Surveys.

Machine Vision. Nello Zeuch & Richard K. Miller. (Illus.). 209p. (gr. 13). 1989. text 72.95 (*0-442-23737-5*) Chapman & Hall.

Machine Vision: A Practical Technology for Advanced Image Processing, Vol. 1. M. Ejiri. xvi, 128p. 1989. pap. text 137.00 (*2-88124-353-3*) Gordon & Breach.

Machine Vision: Advent. Michael Brady. 1986. pap. text 95.95 (*0-201-11616-2*) Addison-Wesley.

Machine Vision: General Systems, Robotic Systems, Special Systems, Components, Accessories, Optical Inspection. Society of Manufacturing Engineers Staff. LC 84-51428. (Productivity Equipment Ser.). 396p. reprint ed. pap. 122.80 (*0-8357-7684-0*, 203585800002) Bks Demand.

Machine Vision: The Advent of Intelligent Robots. Michael Brady. 1986. pap. text 95.95 (*0-201-11629-4*) Addison-Wesley.

Machine Vision: Theory, Algorithms, Practicalities. 2nd ed. E. R. Davies. (Signal Processing & Its Applications Ser.). (Illus.). 784p. 1996. text 49.95 (*0-12-206092-X*) Acad Pr.

***Machine Vision Algorithms in Java: Techniques & Implementation.** Paul F. Whelan & Derek Molloy. LC 00-30072. 2000. write for info. (*1-85233-218-2*) Spr-Verlag.

Machine Vision & Advanced Image Processing in Remote Sensing. Ed. by I. Kanellopoulos et al. LC 99-30759. (Illus.). x, 335p. 1999. 109.00 (*3-540-65571-9*) Spr-Verlag.

Machine Vision & Digital Image Processing. Louis Galbiati. 240p. (C). 1990. text 58.60 (*0-13-542044-X*) P-H.

Machine Vision Applications, Architectures & Systems Integration III: 31 October-2 November, 1994, Boston, Massachusetts Bruce G. Batchelor et al. LC 94-67544. (Proceedings Ser.). x, 446p. 1994. pap. write for info. (*0-8194-1682-7*) SPIE.

Machine Vision Applications, Architectures & Systems Integration IV: 23-24 October, 1995, Philadelphia, Pennsylvania. Bruce G. Batchelor et al. LC 95-69915. x, 326 p. 1995. write for info. (*0-8194-1961-3*) SPIE.

Machine Vision Applications, Architectures & Systems Integration V, Vol. 2908. Ed. by Susan S. Solomon et al. LC 96-69760. (Proceedings Ser.). 284p. 1996. 66.00 (*0-8194-2310-6*) SPIE.

Machine Vision Applications, Architectures & Systems Integration VI, Vol. 3205. Ed. by Susan S. Solomon et al. LC 98-122588. 308p. 1997. 69.00 (*0-8194-2637-7*) SPIE.

Machine Vision Applications in Character Recognition & Industrial Inspection. Ed. by W. Blanz et al. 1992. 20.00 (*0-8194-0815-8*, 1661) SPIE.

Machine Vision Applications in Industrial Inspection V, Vol. 3029. Ed. by A. R. Rao & Ning Chang. LC 97-175319. 206p. 1997. 69.00 (*0-8194-2440-4*) SPIE.

Machine Vision Applications in Industrial Inspection VI, Vol. 3306. Ed. by A. R. Rao & Ning Chang. 164p. 1998. 48.00 (*0-8194-2746-2*) SPIE.

***Machine Vision Applications in Industrial Inspection VII.** Ed. by Kenneth W. Tobin & Ning S. Chang. 272p. 1999. pap. text 72.00 (*0-8194-3123-0*) SPIE.

Machine Vision for Advanced Production. LC 96-210434. 188p. 1996. 48.00 (*981-02-2526-1*) World Scientific Pub.

Machine Vision for Neural Networks. C. Davidson. 1993. text. write for info. (*0-442-01476-7*, VNR) Wiley.

Machine Vision for Robotics & Automated Inspection: Technical Report for Engineers & Managers, 3 Vols. Incl. Vol. 1. Fundamentals. Vol. 2. Applications. Vol. 3. Manufacturers-Systems. 1984. 1984. 185.00 (*0-685-08420-5*) SEAI Tech Pubns.

Machine Vision Sourcebook. D. Braggins & J. Hollingham. (Illus.). 250p. 1986. 205.95 (*0-387-16355-7*) Spr-Verlag.

Machine Vision Systems for Inspection & Metrology VII, Vol. 3521. Ed. by Bruce G. Batchelor et al. LC 99-159849. 1998. 89.00 (*0-8194-2982-1*) SPIE.

***Machine Vision Systems for Inspection & Metrology VIII.** Ed. by John W. Miller et al. 260p. 1999. pap. text 72.00 (*0-8194-3429-9*) SPIE.

Machine Vision Systems Integration: Critical Reviews. Ed. by B. G. Batchlor & F. M. Waltz. 1991. pap. 20.00 (*0-8194-0471-3*, VOL. CR36) SPIE.

Machine Work: Advanced, 2 vols. 1994. lib. bdg. 625.95 (*0-8490-5688-8*) Gordon Pr.

Machine Wreckers. Ernst Toller. 96p. (Orig.). 1996. pap. 14.95 (*1-85459-288-2*, Pub. by N Hern Bks) Theatre Comm.

Machine Writing & Typesetting. Frank J. Romano. (Illus.). 146p. 1986. lib. bdg. 24.95 (*0-938853-00-7*) GAMA Comns.

Machinehead Burn My Eyes. 95p. (YA). pap. 19.95 (*0-89524-946-4*, 02501259, Pub. by Cherry Lane) H Leonard.

Machinery Act of North Carolina: 1999 Edition. 299p. 15.00 (*0-327-10453-8*) LEXIS Pub.

Machinery Act of North Carolina, 1998 Supplement. 43p. 1999. write for info. (*0-327-07973-8*, 30562-10) LEXIS Pub.

Machinery Adhesives for Locking, Retaining & Sealing. Girard S. Haviland. (Mechanical Engineering Ser.: Vol. 44). (Illus.). 360p. 1986. text 155.00 (*0-8247-7467-1*) Dekker.

Machinery & Mechanical Devices: A Treasury of Nineteenth-Century Cuts. William Rowe. (Pictorial Archive Ser.). (Illus.). 64p. (Orig.). 1987. pap. 5.95 (*0-486-25445-3*) Dover.

Machinery Component Maintenance & Repair, Vol. 3. 2nd rev. ed. Heinz P. Bloch & Fred K. Geitner. LC 84-15738. (Practical Machinery Management for Process Plants Ser.). (Illus.). 370p. 1990. 95.00 (*0-87201-781-8*, 1781) Gulf Pub.

Machinery Dynamics, Applications & Vibration Control Problems: Presented at the 1989 ASME Design Technical Conferences, 12th Biennial Conference on Mechanical Vibration & Noise, Montreal, Quebec, Canada, September 17-21, 1989. Ed. by T. S. Sankar et al. LC 89-45939. (DE Ser.: Vol. 18-2). 386p. reprint ed. pap. 119.70 (*0-7837-1447-5*, 205242200017) Bks Demand.

Machinery Failure Analysis & Troubleshooting. fac. ed. Heinz P. Bloch & Fred K. Geitner. LC 83-10731. (Practical Machinery Management for Process Plants Ser.: No. 2). (Illus.). 668p. pap. 200.00 (*0-7837-7429-X*, 204722400006) Bks Demand.

Machinery Failure Analysis & Troubleshooting. 2nd ed. Heinz P. Bloch & Fred K. Geitner. LC 93-4776. (Practical Machinery Management for Process Plants Ser.: Vol. 2). (Illus.). 726p. 1994. reprint ed. pap. 200.00 (*0-608-07293-1*, 206752100009) Bks Demand.

Machinery Failure Analysis & Troubleshooting. 3rd ed. Heinz Bloch & Fred K. Geitner. LC 97-12229. (Practical Machinery Management for Process Plants Ser.: Vol. 2). 600p. 1997. 95.00 (*0-88415-662-1*, 5662) Gulf Pub.

Machinery for Horticulture. Brian Bell & Stewart Cousins. (Illus.). 304p. 1991. 34.95 (*0-85236-231-5*, Pub. by Farming Pr) Diamond Farm Bk.

Machinery for the Construction Industry in Australia: A Strategic Entry Report, 1996. Compiled by Icon Group International Staff. (Illus.). 134p. 1999. ring bd. 1340.00 incl. audio compact disk (*0-7418-0741-6*) Icon Grp.

Machinery for the Construction Industry in Australia: A Strategic Entry Report, 1997. Compiled by Icon Group International Staff. (Country Industry Report). (Illus.). 132p. 1999. ring bd. 1320.00 incl. audio compact disk (*0-7418-0145-0*) Icon Grp.

Machinery Maintenance. 2nd rev. ed. Ed. by Deere & Company Staff. (Fundamentals of Machine Operation Ser.). (Illus.). 101p. 1991. pap. text, teacher ed. 22.55 (*0-86691-158-8*, FMW10502T) Deere & Co.

Machinery Maintenance. 3rd rev. ed. Ed. by Deere & Company Staff. (Fundamentals of Machine Operation Ser.). (Illus.). 150p. 1991. pap. text 19.95 (*0-86691-130-8*, FMW10103NC) Deere & Co.

Machinery Malfunction Analysis & Correction. Robert C. Eisenmann. LC 97-31974. (d). 820p. (C). 1997. 84.00 (*0-13-240946-1*) P-H.

Machinery Management. 4th rev. ed. Ed. by Deere & Company Staff. (Farm Business Management Ser.). (Illus.). 182p. 1992. pap. text 35.95 (*0-86691-262-2*, FBM17105NC); pap. text, teacher ed. 40.95 (*0-86691-183-9*, FBM17504T); pap. text, student ed. 19.95 (*0-86691-184-7*, FBM17604W) Deere & Co.

Machinery, Money & the Millennium: From Moral Economy to Socialism, 1815-1860. Gregory Claeys. LC 87-2372. 275p. 1987. reprint ed. pap. 85.30 (*0-7837-9497-5*, 206024100004) Bks Demand.

Machinery of Death: A Shocking Indictment of Capital Punishment in the United States. Amnesty International Staff. 216p. (Orig.). (C). 1995. pap. 17.95 (*0-939994-94-1*) Amnesty Intl USA.

Machinery of Dominance: Women, Men, & Technical Know-How. Cynthia Cockburn. (Northeastern Series in Feminist Theory). 282p. 1988. text 45.00 (*1-55553-041-9*); pap. text 16.95 (*1-55553-046-X*) NE U Pr.

Machinery of Life. David S. Goodsell. LC 92-2303. (Illus.). 160p. 1994. 31.95 (*0-387-97846-1*); write for info. (*3-540-97846-1*) Spr-Verlag.

Machinery of Life. David S. Goodsell. (Illus.). 156p. 1997. 19.00 (*0-387-98273-6*) Spr-Verlag.

***Machinery of Life & Life of Machine.** Langton. 2000. 29.95 (*0-7382-0193-6*, Pub. by Perseus Pubng) HarpC.

Machinery of Succession. 2nd ed. J. Gareth Miller. (Illus.). 400p. 1996. text 96.95 (*1-85521-442-3*, Pub. by Dartmth Pub) Ashgate Pub Co.

Machinery of the Body. enl. rev. ed. Anton J. Carlson et al. LC 61-14536. 1993. lib. bdg. 30.00 (*0-226-09279-8*) U Ch Pr.

Machinery of the Body. 5th enl. rev. ed. Anton J. Carlson et al. LC 61-14536. (Illus.). 752p. reprint ed. pap. 200.00 (*0-608-09280-0*, 205415400004) Bks Demand.

Machinery of the Government. Sallis. (C). 1982. pap. write for info. (*0-03-910368-4*) Harcourt Coll Pubs.

Machinery of the Mind. E. Roy John. 1990. 127.50 (*0-8176-3461-4*) Birkhauser.

Machinery Replacement Strategies. Wendell Bowers. Ed. by Ralph Reynolds & Robert G. Holmes. (Farm Business Management Ser.). (Illus.). 104p. (C). 1994. pap. text 39.95 incl. disk (*0-86691-233-9*, FBM13101NC) Deere & Co.

Machinery Replacement Strategies. Wendell Bowers. Ed. by Ralph Reynolds & Robert G. Holmes. (Farm Business Management Ser.). 90p. (C). 1994. teacher ed. 33.95 incl. trans. (*0-86691-213-4*, FBM13501T) Deere & Co.

An Asterisk (*) at the beginning of an entry indicates that the title is appearing for the first time.

Machinery Replacement Strategies. Wendell Bowers. Ed. by Ralph Reynolds & Robert G. Holmes. (Farm Business Management Ser.). (Illus.). 42p. 1994. student ed. 21.95 (*0-86691-214-2*, FBM13601W) Deere & Co.

Machinery Safety: The Risk Based Approach. H. Raafat. 1996. pap. 129.00 (*1-85953-006-0*, Pub. by Tech Comm) St Mut.

Machinery, Vessels & Piping Etc. Recommendations for the Protection of Diesel Engines Operating in Hazardous Areas. EEMUA Staff. 1988. 125.00 (*0-85931-043-4*, Pub. by EEMUA) St Mut.

Machinery Vibration. Wowk. 322p. 1998. pap. 55.00 (*0-07-134861-1*) McGraw.

Machinery Vibration: Measurement & Analysis. Victor Wowk. 368p. 1991. 59.95 (*0-07-071936-5*) McGraw.

Machinery Vibration Alignment. Victor Wowk. LC 00-21019. (Illus.). 320p. 1998. 54.95 (*0-07-071939-X*) McGraw-Hill Prof.

Machinery's Handbook. Erik Oberg. 1998. pap. 89.95 (*0-8311-2600-0*) Industrial Products Corp.

Machinery's Handbook. 25th ed. Erik Oberg et al. 2545p. 1996. 94.00 (*0-8311-2575-6*) ASM.

Machinery's Handbook. 25th large type ed. Erik Oberg et al. 2543p. 1997. 95.00 (*0-8311-2595-0*) Indus Pr.

*__Machinery's Handbook.__ 26th ed. Ed. by Industrial Press Staff. (Illus.). 2640p. 2000. 99.95 (*0-8311-2635-3*) Indus Pr.

*__Machinery's Handbook: Toolbox Edition.__ 25th ed. Erik Oberg. (Illus.). 1998. 159.95 (*0-8311-2602-7*) Indus Pr.

*__Machinery's Handbook Toolbox Edition.__ 26th ed. Ed. by Industrial Press Staff. (Illus.). 2640p. 2000. 85.00 (*0-8311-2625-6*) Indus Pr.

Machinery's Handbook Guide. 25th ed. 224p. 1996. text 12.95 (*0-8311-2599-3*) Indus Pr.

*__Machinery's Handbook Guide.__ 26th ed. Ed. by Industrial Press Staff. (Illus.). 224p. 2000. pap. 12.95 (*0-8311-2699-X*) Indus Pr.

*__Machinery's Handbook Pocket Reference.__ Dick Pohanish. 1999. text 19.95 (*0-8311-3089-X*) Indus Pr.

Machinery's Handbook, Toolbox Edition. Erik Oberg. 1998. 149.95 (*0-8311-2601-9*) Indus Pr.

Machines see Young Scientist Concepts & Projects

Machines. (Make it Work Ser.). 42p. (J). (gr. 4-8). pap. write for info. (*1-882210-48-4*) Action Pub.

Machines. (Learn about Ser.). (Illus.). 64p. (J). (gr. 3-7). 1997. 8.95 (*1-85967-583-2*, Lorenz Bks) Anness Pub.

Machines. (Illustrated Science Dictionary Ser.). (Illus.). 160p. (J). (gr. 4-9). 1993. 19.00 (*0-671-84696-5*) Prntice Hall Bks.

*__Machines.__ (Make it Work Ser.). 2000. 12.95 (*1-58728-368-9*); 6.95 (*1-58728-357-3*) Two Can Pub.

Machines. Karen Bryant-Mole. LC 95-48064. (Illus.). 24p. (J). 1996. pap. 4.95 (*0-382-39624-3*); lib. bdg. 10.95 (*0-382-39588-3*) Silver Burdett Pr.

Machines. Center for Occupational Research & Development Staff. (Mechanical Technology Ser.). (Illus.). 142p. (C). 1983. pap. text 22.00 (*1-55502-154-9*) CORD Commns.

Machines. John Farndon. LC 93-20841. (Picturepedia Ser.). (Illus.). 48p. (J). (gr. k-3). 1993. write for info. (*1-56458-384-8*) DK Pub Inc.

Machines. Clive Gifford. (Understanding Science Ser.). (Illus.). 32p. (YA). (gr. 7-13). 1994. pap. 7.95 (*0-7460-1962-9*, Usborne) EDC.

Machines. Clive Gifford. (Understanding Science Ser.). (Illus.). 32p. (J). (gr. 7-12). 1999. lib. bdg. 15.95 (*0-88110-699-2*, Usborne) EDC.

Machines. David Glover & Jon Barnes. (Make It Work! Ser.). (Illus.). 48p. (J). pap. 7.95 (*0-590-24401-9*) Scholastic Inc.

Machines. Vic Lockman. (Big Book of Cartooning: No. 5). (Illus.). 48p. (Orig.). (YA). (gr. 8 up). 1992. pap. 6.00 (*0-936175-20-6*) V Lockman.

Machines. Ron Marson. (Task Cards Ser.: No. 22). (Illus.). 48p. 1989. teacher ed. 8.00 (*0-941008-99-1*) Tops Learning.

Machines. 2nd ed. Ann Morris. (Let Me Read Ser.). (Illus.). 16p. (J). (ps). 1995. bds. 2.95 (*0-673-36268-X*, GoodYrBooks) Addson-Wesley Educ.

*__Machines, 68.__ Eduardo Paolozzi. 254p. 1999. pap. 12.95 (*1-885490-19-4*, Pub. by Grnd St Pr) Dist Art Pubs.

Machines a Papier. Jean Bonin. (FRE., Illus.). 298p. 1988. pap. text (*2-9800538-3-X*) CA66.

Machines Always Existed: Skullcarrier, Coathanger Boy, Octopus' Lover. John Stoss. 1984. 20.00 (*0-916620-57-3*) Portals Pr.

Machines & Economic Growth: The Implications for Growth Theory, 156. Natalie McPherson. LC 93-44509. (Contributions in Economics & Economic History Ser.). 280p. 1994. 59.95 (*0-313-29255-8*, Greenwood Pr) Greenwood.

Machines & How They Work. David Burnie. LC 91-60147. (See & Explore Library). (Illus.). 64p. (J). (gr. 3 up). 1991. 12.95 (*1-879431-15-7*) DK Pub Inc.

Machines & How They Work. Weiss. (J). (gr. 4-7). 1983. 11.95 (*0-690-04299-X*) HarpC Child Bks.

Machines & Intelligence: A Critique of Arguments Against the Possibility of Artificial Intelligence, 2. Stuart Goldkind. LC 86-25712. (Contributions to the Study of Computer Science Ser.: No. 2). 149p. 1987. 45.00 (*0-313-25450-8*, GMA/) Greenwood.

Machines & Inventions see Understanding Science & Nature Series

Machines & Inventions see Record Breakers

Machines & Inventions. LC 92-35710. (Understanding Science & Nature Ser.). (J). 1993. lib. bdg. write for info. (*0-8094-9705-0*) Time-Life.

Machines & Liberty, a Portrait of Europe, 1789-1914. Martin Roberts. (Portrait of Europe Ser.). (Illus.). 360p. 1972. pap. 19.95 (*0-19-913040-X*) OUP.

Machines & Mechanisms. Myszka. 1999. pap. text, student ed. write for info. (*0-13-973322-1*) P-H.

Machines & Mechanisms: Applied Kinematic Analysis. David Myszka. LC 98-20255. 482p. 1998. 93.00 (*0-13-597915-3*) P-H.

*__Machines & Motion: Hands on Elementary School Science.__ (Illus.). 44p. 2000. teacher ed. 35.00 (*1-883410-49-5*) L Poore.

Machines & Structures: Fun Facts & Magnetic Picture Puzzles. Shirley Granahan. (Junior Builder Ser.). (Illus.). 32p. (J). (gr. 1-4). 1999. 12.99 (*1-58476-007-9*) Innovative Kids.

Machines & Thought: The Legacy of Alan Turing. Ed. by Peter Millican & Andy Clark. (Illus.). 308p. 1999. pap. text 24.95 (*0-19-823876-2*) OUP.

Machines & Thought: The Legacy of Alan Turing, Vol. I. Ed. by Peter Millican & Andy Clark. (Mind Association Occasional Ser.). (Illus.). 308p. 1997. text 55.00 (*0-19-823593-3*) OUP.

Machines & Work. Frank Schaffer Publications, Inc. Staff. (Science Notes Ser.). (Illus.). 8p. 1996. 2.49 (*0-86734-896-8*, 62033) Schaffer Pubns.

Machines As the Measure of Men: Science, Technology, & Ideologies of Western Dominance. Michael Adas. LC 89-845. (Cornell Studies in Comparative History). (Illus.). 484p. 1990. reprint ed. pap. text 18.95 (*0-8014-9760-4*) Cornell U Pr.

Machines at Work. Byron Barton. LC 86-24221. (Illus.). 32p. (J). (ps-1). 1987. lib. bdg. 15.89 (*0-690-04573-5*) HarpC Child Bks.

Machines at Work. Byron Barton. LC 86-24221. (Illus.). 32p. (J). (ps-3). 1987. 15.95 (*0-694-00190-2*) HarpC Child Bks.

Machines at Work, 4, Set. Henry Arthur Pluckrose. 1998. 72.00 (*0-531-19436-1*) Watts.

Machines at Work: A Very First Picture Book see Pictures & Words

Machines at Work Board Book. Byron Barton. (Illus.). 32p. (J). (ps up). 1997. 6.95 (*0-694-01107-X*, HarpFestival) HarpC Child Bks.

Machines, Buildings, Weaponry of Biblical Times. Max Schwartz. LC 97-3072. (Illus.). 208p. 1997. reprint ed. pap. 16.99 (*0-8007-5320-8*) Revell.

Machines for Earthmoving Work: Theory & Calculations. T. V. Alekseeva et al. Tr. by M. M. Sivaramakrishnan from RUS. 529p. (C). 1985. text 220.00 (*90-6191-447-7*, Pub. by A A Balkema) Ashgate Pub Co.

Machines for Loving. Robert Novak. 1973. 4.00 (*0-686-16137-8*) Windless Orchard.

Machines for Moving the Earth: Fundamentals of the Theory of Soil Loosening, Modeling of Working Processes & Forecasting Machine Parameters. Ed. by A. N. Zelenin et al. Tr. by C. B. Malvavkar from RUS. 566p. (C). 1986. text 190.00 (*90-6191-451-5*, Pub. by A A Balkema) Ashgate Pub Co.

Machines for Power Farming. 3rd ed. Archie Stone & Harold E. Gulvin. LC 76-42244. 542p. reprint ed. pap. 168.10 (*0-608-13677-8*, 205539400017) Bks Demand.

*__Machines in Our Hearts: The Cardiac Pacemaker, the Implantable Defibrillator & American Health Care.__ Kirk Jeffrey. LC 00-9627. (Illus.). 2001. write for info. (*0-8018-6579-4*) Johns Hopkins.

Machines in the Office. Rodney Dale & Rebecca Weaver. (Discoveries & Inventions Ser.). (Illus.). 64p. (YA). (gr. 7 up). 1994. lib. bdg. 20.00 (*0-19-521000-X*) OUP.

Machines, Languages & Complexity. Ed. by J. Dassow & J. Keleman. (Lecture Notes in Computer Science Ser.: Vol. 381). vi, 244p. 1989. 34.00 (*0-387-51516-X*) Spr-Verlag.

Machines That Kill. Fred Saberhagen. 1992. pap. 3.50 (*0-8125-2059-9*, Pub. by Tor Bks) St Martin.

Machines That Walk: The Adaptive Suspension Vehicle. Shin-Min Song & Kenneth J. Waldron. 327p. 1988. 47.50 (*0-262-19274-8*) MIT Pr.

Machines That Work. Caroline Young & Harriet Castor. (Young Machines Ser.). (Illus.). 96p. (J). (ps-3). 1993. pap. 14.95 (*0-7460-0990-9*, Usborne) EDC.

Machines We Use. Sally Hewitt. LC 97-2154. (It's Science Ser.). 32p. (J). 1998. lib. bdg. 20.00 (*0-516-20793-8*) Childrens.

Machines We Use. Sally Hewitt. Ed. by Helaine Cohen. (It's Science Ser.). (Illus.). 32p. (J). (gr. k-3). 1998. pap. 6.95 (*0-516-26392-7*) Childrens.

Machines Who Think. Pamela McCorduck. LC 79-13809. (Illus.). 375p. 1981. pap. text 12.00 (*0-7167-1135-4*) W H Freeman.

Machines with a Purpose. Howard Rosenbrock. (Illus.). 234p. 1990. text 55.00 (*0-19-856346-9*) OUP.

Machineworks: Vito Acconci, Alice Aycock, Kay Larson, Dennis Oppenheim. Janet Kardon. (Illus.). 1981. pap. 14.00 (*0-904540-26-X*) U of Pa Contemp Art.

*__Machining Center Programming & Operation Answers.__ Mike Lynch. (Illus.). 90p. 1998. pap. text. write for info. (*1-930861-02-8*, CC-MCPO-A) C N C Con.

*__Machining Center Programming & Operation Manual.__ Mike Lynch. (Illus.). 205p. 1998. pap. text. write for info. (*1-930861-00-1*, CC-MCPO-M) C N C Con.

*__Machining Center Programming & Operation Workbook.__ rev. ed. Mike Lynch. (Illus.). 90p. 1998. pap. text. write for info. (*1-930861-01-X*, CC-MCPO-W) C N C Con.

*__Machining Centers in Germany: A Strategic Entry Report, 1996.__ Compiled by Icon Group International Staff. (Illus.). 102p. 1999. ring bd. 1020.00 incl. audio compact disk (*0-7418-1335-1*) Icon Grp.

Machining Data Handbook, 2 vols., Set. 3rd ed. Ed. by Machinability Data Center Technical Staff. LC 80-81480. (Illus.). 1980. 150.00 (*0-936974-00-1*) Inst Adv Manuf.

Machining for Toolmaking & Experimental Work, 3 vols. 1989. 125.00 (*0-7855-2864-4*) St Mut.

Machining Fundamentals. Fitzpatrick. (Machine Tools Ser.). 1999. pap. 55.50 (*0-8273-5820-2*) Delmar.

Machining Fundamentals. Smith. (Machine Tools Ser.). 1996. pap., teacher ed. 15.95 (*0-8273-6410-5*, VNR) Wiley.

*__Machining Fundamentals: From Basic to Advanced Techniques.__ John R. Walker. LC 99-17776. 640p. 2000. text 49.28 (*1-56637-662-9*) Goodheart.

Machining Hard Materials. Ed. by Roy L. Williams. LC 82-50538. (Illus.). 257p. reprint ed. pap. 79.70 (*0-7837-6271-2*, 204598600010) Bks Demand.

Machining Impossible Shapes: IFIP TC5 WG5.3 International Conference on Sculptured Surfaces (SSM98), November 5-11, 1998 Chrysler Technology Center, Michigan / G. J. Olling et al. LC 99-30260. (International Federation for Information Processing Ser.). 1999. write for info. (*0-412-84680-2*) Chapman & Hall.

Machining Manufacturing Technology: Manufacturing Technology. Mario Rapisarda et al. LC 95-25386. (Machine Tools Ser.). (Illus.). 800p. 1997. mass mkt. 87.95 (*0-8273-6351-6*) Delmar.

Machining of Advanced Composites. Ed. by R. Ramulu & R. Komanduri. LC 93-73268. 227p. pap. 60.00 (*0-7918-1033-X*) ASME.

Machining of Advanced Materials: Proceedings of the International Conference on Machining of Advanced Materials. (Illus.). 165p. (Orig.). (C). 1994. pap. text 65.00 (*0-7881-1123-X*) DIANE Pub.

Machining of Advanced Materials Vol. 208-59: Machining of Advanced Materials. Ed. by Sanjeev Jain & Daniel C. Yang. LC 95-77287. (1995 Joint ASME Applied Mechanics & Materials Summer Meeting Ser.: Vol. 208). 148p. 1995. 88.00 (*0-7918-1323-1*, H00955) ASME.

*__Machining of Ceramics & Composites.__ Ed. by Said Jahanmir & M. Ramulu. LC 98-31684. (Mechanical Engineering Ser.). (Illus.). 720p. 1999. text 225.00 (*0-8247-0178-X*) Dekker.

Machining of Composite Materials: Proceedings of the Machining of Composite Materials Symposium, ASM/TMS Materials Week Held November 1-5, 1992, Chicago, IL. Ed. by T. S. Srivatsan & D. M. Bowden. LC 92-82924. (Illus.). 219p. 1992. reprint ed. pap. 67.90 (*0-608-02654-9*, 206331400004) Bks Demand.

Machining of Composite Materials No. 2: Proceedings of ASM 1993 Materials Congress, Materials Week '93, October 17-21, 1993, Held in Pittsburgh, PA. Ed. by T. S. Srivatsan et al. LC 93-74804. (Illus.). 187p. 1994. reprint ed. pap. 58.00 (*0-608-02616-6*, 206327400004) Bks Demand.

*__Machinist.__ Tracey Boraas. LC 99-54148. (Career Exploration Ser.). 48p. (YA). (gr. 5 up). 2000. lib. bdg. 21.26 (*0-7368-0491-9*, Capstone Bks) Capstone Pr.

Machinist. Jack Rudman. (Career Examination Ser.: C-460). 1994. pap. 23.95 (*0-8373-0460-1*) Nat Learn.

Machinist: Basic Skill Development. George Lehrling. LC 77-73238. 256p. reprint ed. pap. 79.40 (*0-608-11689-0*, 201157500079) Bks Demand.

Machinists: A New Study in American Trade Unionism. Mark Perlman. LC 61-16695. (Wertheim Publications in Industrial Relations). (Illus.). 350p. 1961. 22.50 (*0-674-54050-6*) HUP.

*__Machinists' & Metalworkers' Pocket Reference.__ Ronald A. Walsh. LC 00-26292. 448p. 2000. pap. 29.95 (*0-07-136092-1*) McGraw.

Machinists Formulas, Compositions & Receipts: A Handbook. 1996. lib. bdg. 261.99 (*0-8490-7594-7*) Gordon Pr.

Machinist's Helper. Jack Rudman. (Career Examination Ser.: C-461). 1994. pap. 23.95 (*0-8373-0461-X*) Nat Learn.

Machinists Library: Basic Machine Shop, 3 vols., Set. 4th ed. Rex Miller. 1983. 57.95 (*0-672-23380-0*, Bobbs) Macmillan.

Machinists' Ready Reference. 8th rev. ed. Compiled by C. Weingartner. (Illus.). 296p. 1994. spiral bd. 17.95 (*0-911168-90-7*) Prakken.

Machinist's Semi-Automated Life. Roger Tulin. 48p. (Orig.). 1984. pap. 5.95 (*0-917300-15-7*) Singlejack Bks.

Machismo y Educacion en Puerto Rico. Isabel Pico et al. (SPA.). 135p. 1989. pap. 6.25 (*0-8477-2466-2*) U of PR Pr.

Macho! Victor Villasenor. 240p. 1997. pap. 12.95 (*0-385-31118-4*, Delta Trade) Dell.

Macho: Is This What I Really Want? Bateman Mahoney & Bill Mahoney. (J). 1986. pap. 6.00 (*0-87738-024-4*) Youth Ed.

Macho au Coeur Tendre. Charlotte Lamb. (Azur Ser.: No. 782). (FRE.). 1999. mass mkt. 3.99 (*0-373-34782-0*, 1-34782-2) Harlequin Bks.

*__Macho Camacho's Beat.__ Luis Rafael Sanchez & Gregory Rabassa. 211p. (Orig.). 2000. pap. 11.95 (*1-56478-258-1*) Dalkey Arch.

*__Macho Love: Sex Behind Bars in Central America.__ Jacobo Schifter. LC 99-28342. 115p. 1999. pap. 14.95 (*1-56023-966-2*, Harrington Park); lib. bdg. 39.95 (*1-56023-965-4*, Harrington Park) Haworth Pr.

Macho Marines: True Homosexual Military Stories, Vol. 6. Ed. by Winston Leyland. 160p. 1997. pap. 14.95 (*0-943595-67-3*) Leyland Pubns.

Macho Medicine: A History of the Anabolic Steroid Epidemic. William N. Taylor. LC 91-52506. 208p. 1991. lib. bdg. 32.50 (*0-89950-613-5*) McFarland & Co.

Macho Sluts. Pat Califia. 296p. (Orig.). 1988. pap. 11.95 (*1-55583-115-X*) Alyson Pubns.

Macho Women with Guns. 3rd ed. Greg Porter. (Illus.). 72p. 1994. pap. text 9.95 (*0-943891-27-2*, 3005) Blacksburg Tactical.

Machos, Maricones, & Gays: Cuba & Homosexuality. Ian Lumsden. 288p. (Orig.). (C). 1996. pap. text 22.95 (*1-56639-371-X*); lib. bdg. 69.95 (*1-56639-370-1*) Temple U Pr.

Machos, Mistresses & Madonnas: Contesting the Power of Latin American Gender Imagery. Marit Melhuus & Kristi Anne. LC 96-48949. (C). 1996. pap. 20.00 (*1-85984-160-0*, Pub. by Verso) Norton.

Mach's Principle: From Newton's Bucket to Quantum Gravity. Ed. by J. Barbour & H. Pfister. (Einstein Studies: Vol. 6). 536p. 1996. 64.50 (*0-8176-3823-7*) Birkhauser.

Mach's Principle: From Newton's Bucket to Quantum Gravity. Ed. by Julian B. Barbour & Herbert Pfister. (Einstein Studies: Vol. 6). 1995. pap. write for info. (*3-7643-3823-7*) Birkhauser.

Machshevet Hataharah - Family Purity Charts: A Guide to Understanding & Practice. Yekusiel Farkash. 324p. 1989. 20.00 (*0-940118-61-0*) Moznaim.

Macht Als Gefahr Beim Helfer. 5th ed. Adolf Guggenbuehl-Craig. (Psychologische Praxis Ser.: No. 45). vi, 106p. 1987. pap. 16.75 (*3-8055-4562-2*) S Karger.

*__Macht der Vier: Von der Pythagoreischen Zahl Zum Modernen Mathematischen Strukturbegriff in Jacques Roubauds Oulipotischer Erzahlung.__ Elvira Laskowski-Caujolle. (Artefakt. Schriften Zur Soziosemiotik und Komparatistik Ser.). 376p. 1999. 56.95 (*3-631-34872-X*) P Lang Pubng.

Macht des Wortes: Eine Sprachsoziologie: The Power of the Word: A Sociology of Language. Torgny T. Segerstedt. LC 74-25783. (European Sociology Ser.). 182p. 1975. reprint ed. 21.95 (*0-405-06536-1*) Ayer.

Macht und Medien: Eine Medienwissenschaftliche Adaptationsanalyse von Shakespeares "Richard III" Joachim Kind. (Europaische Hochschulschriften, Reihe 40 Ser.: No. 64). (Illus.). 326p. 1997. 57.95 (*3-631-31932-0*) P Lang Pubng.

Machtergreifung von Links - Thuringen, 1945/46. Manfred Overesch. (GER.). 198p. 1993. write for info. (*3-487-09786-9*) G Olms Pubs.

Machtige Im Schmelzofen des Mitleids: Eine Interpretation Von 2 Sam 24. Adrian Schenker. (Orbis Biblicus et Orientalis Ser.: Vol. 42). 1982. pap. 18.75 (*3-7278-0255-3*, Pub. by Ed Univ Fri) Eisenbrauns.

*__Machu Picchu: A Civil Engineering Marvel.__ Kenneth R. Wright & Alfredo Valencia Zegarra. LC 00-24452. 2000. write for info. (*0-7844-0444-5*) Am Soc Civil Eng.

*__Machu Picchu: The Story of the Amazing Incas & Their City in the Clouds.__ Elizabeth Mann. LC 99-55172. (Wonders of the World Bks.: Vol. 6). (Illus.). 48p. (J). (gr. 3-6). 2000. 19.95 (*0-9650493-9-6*, Pub. by Mikaya Pr) Firefly Bks Ltd.

Machzor, 2 vols. Incl. Rosh Hashana - Ashkenaz: Zichron Reuven. 712p. 1985. 25.99 (*0-89906-676-3*); Rosh Hashana - Ashkenaz: Zichron Reuven. deluxe ed. 712p. 1985. ring bd. 44.95 (*0-89906-686-0*); Rosh Hashanah Sefard: Zichron Moshe. Nosson Scherman. 712p. 1986. 22.95 (*0-89906-679-8*); Rosh Hashanah Sefard: Zichron Moshe. deluxe ed. Nosson Scherman. 712p. 1986. ring bd. 44.95 (*0-89906-689-5*); (ArtScroll Siddur Ser.). 47.95 (*0-89906-678-X*) Mesorah Pubns.

Machzor, 2 vols. Nosson Scherman. (ArtScroll Siddur Ser.). boxed set 56.99 (*0-89906-681-X*) Mesorah Pubns.

Machzor, 2 vols. deluxe ed. Incl. Rosh Hashana - Ashkenaz: Zichron Reuven. 712p. 1985. 25.99 (*0-89906-676-3*); Rosh Hashana - Ashkenaz: Zichron Reuven. deluxe ed. 712p. 1985. ring bd. 44.95 (*0-89906-686-0*); Rosh Hashanah Sefard: Zichron Moshe. Nosson Scherman. 712p. 1986. 22.95 (*0-89906-679-8*); Rosh Hashanah Sefard: Zichron Moshe. deluxe ed. Nosson Scherman. 712p. 1986. ring bd. 44.95 (*0-89906-689-5*); (ArtScroll Siddur Ser.). Set ring bd. 89.95 (*0-89906-688-7*) Mesorah Pubns.

Machzor. Schneur Zalman of Liadi. (HEB.). 676p. 1991. reprint ed. 12.00 (*0-8266-0270-3*, Merkos LInyonei Chinuch) Kehot Pubn Soc.

Machzor, 2 vols., Set. Nosson Scherman. (ArtScroll Siddur Ser.). 1985. boxed set 47.95 (*0-89906-682-8*) Mesorah Pubns.

Machzor, 2 vols., Set. deluxe ed. Nosson Scherman. (ArtScroll Siddur Ser.). 1985. 89.95 (*0-89906-691-7*) Mesorah Pubns.

Machzor: Ashkenaz, 5 vols., Set. deluxe ed. boxed set 100.00 (*0-89906-021-8*, MPH5) Mesorah Pubns.

Machzor: Large Type Rosh Hashanah - Ashkenaz. 34.99 (*0-89906-723-9*, MRLA) Mesorah Pubns.

Machzor: Large Type Yom Kippur - Ashkenaz. 34.99 (*0-89906-724-7*, MYLA) Mesorah Pubns.

Machzor: Pesach - Ashkenaz. 25.99 (*0-89906-696-8*, MAPH) Mesorah Pubns.

Machzor: Pesach - Sefard. 25.99 (*0-89906-875-8*, MSPH) Mesorah Pubns.

Machzor: Pesach Pocket - Ashkenaz. 18.99 (*0-89906-921-5*, MPPH); pap. 15.99 (*0-89906-922-3*, MPPP) Mesorah Pubns.

Machzor: Rosh Hashanah Pocket - Ashkenaz. 18.99 (*0-89906-698-4*, MPRH); pap. 15.99 (*0-89906-699-2*, MPRP) Mesorah Pubns.

Machzor: Shavuos. Ashkenaz. 26.99 (*0-89906-876-6*, MAVH) Mesorah Pubns.

Machzor: Shavuos - Ashkenaz. 25.99 (*0-89906-697-6*, MAVH) Mesorah Pubns.

Machzor: Shavuos - Sefard. 25.99 (*0-89906-877-4*, MSVH) Mesorah Pubns.

Machzor: Succos - Sefard. 25.99 (*0-89906-695-X*, MSSH) Mesorah Pubns.

Machzor: Succos Pocket - Ashkenaz. 18.99 (*0-89906-888-X*, MPSH); pap. 15.99 (*0-89906-889-8*, MPSP) Mesorah Pubns.

Machzor: Yom Kippur - Sefard. 25.99 (*0-89906-680-1*, MSYH) Mesorah Pubns.

Machzor: Yom Kippur Pocket - Ashkenaz. 18.99 (*0-89906-896-0*, MPYH); pap. 15.99 (*0-89906-897-9*, MPYP) Mesorah Pubns.

Machzor Companion. M. Eisenmann. (Liturgy Ser.). 1993. 14.99 (*0-89906-425-6*); 11.99 (*0-89906-426-4*) Mesorah Pubns.

Machzor for Rosh Hashanah. 9th ed. Schneur Zalman of Liadi. LC 83-81224. 438p. 1982. reprint ed. 14.00 (*0-8266-0275-4*, Merkos LInyonei Chinuch) Kehot Pubn Soc.

Machzor for Rosh Hashanah with Tehillim. Schneur Zalman of Liadi. (HEB.). 468p. 1991. 18.00 (*0-8266-0273-8*, Merkos LInyonei Chinuch) Kehot Pubn Soc.

Machzor for Yom Kippur. 9th ed. Schneur Zalman of Liadi. LC 83-81224. 630p. 1982. reprint ed. 14.00 (*0-8266-0277-0*, Merkos LInyonei Chinuch) Kehot Pubn Soc.

Machzor for Yom Kippur with Tehillim. Schneur Zalman of Liadi. (HEB.). 564p. 1991. 18.00 (*0-8266-0274-6*, Merkos LInyonei Chinuch) Kehot Pubn Soc.

Machzor Succos Ashkenaz: Machzor Bais Yosef. Nosson Scherman & Meir Zlotowitz. Ed. by Avie Gold. (ArtScroll Siddur Ser.). 1350p. 1987. 25.99 (*0-89906-683-6*) Mesorah Pubns.

Machzor Succos Ashkenaz: Machzor Bais Yosef. deluxe ed. Nosson Scherman & Meir Zlotowitz. Ed. by Avie Gold. (ArtScroll Siddur Ser.). 1350p. 1987. ring bd. 49.95 (*0-89906-692-5*) Mesorah Pubns.

Macias. Mariano J. De Larra. Ed. by Luis Lorenzo-Rivero. (Nueva Austral Ser.: Vol. 155). (SPA.). 1991. pap. text 15.95 (*84-239-1955-2*) Elliots Bks.

M

Macias. Mariano J. De Larra. 224p. 1990. pap. 10.95 (*0-7859-5170-9*) Fr & Eur.

Macintosh. 1997. write for info. (*1-884486-30-4*) Wave Tech.

***Macintosh.** MacMillan. 216p. 1998. pap. text 33.33 incl. cd-rom (*0-13-013161-X*) P-H.

Macintosh: Basic Operations. Against the Clock. 1998. pap. text 33.33 (*0-13-921461-5*) P-H.

Macintosh: Quick Start. David W. Cochran. (C). 1991. mass mkt. 19.95 (*0-538-70475-6*) S-W Pub.

Macintosh Bible. 6th ed. Ed. by Jeremy Judson. LC 96-220176. 1009p. (C). 1996. pap. text 29.95 (*0-201-88636-7*) Peachpit Pr.

***Macintosh Bible.** 7th ed. Sharon Zardetto Aker. LC 99-167870. (Illus.). 1024p. (C). 1998. pap. 34.99 (*0-201-87483-0*, Pub. by Peachpit Pr) Addison-Wesley.

Macintosh Bible Guide to ClarisWorks 4. Charles Rubin. (Illus.). 520p. (C). 1995. pap. 24.95 (*0-201-88406-2*) Peachpit Pr.

Macintosh Bible Guide to Word 6. Maria Langer. (Illus.). 750p. (C). 1995. pap. text 24.95 (*1-56609-073-3*) Peachpit Pr.

Macintosh Bible/CD-ROM Combo. 6th ed. Ed. by Jeremy Judson & Victor Gavenda. 1000p. (C). 1996. pap. 44.95 incl. cd-rom (*0-201-68812-3*) Peachpit Pr.

Macintosh Book of Fonts: A Desktop Publishing Handbook for Font Lovers. Tim Ryan & Douglas G. Miles. LC 87-9607. 400p. 1988. pap. 24.95 (*0-915051-02-8*) SourceNet.

Macintosh Book of the Dead. Andy Inhatko. 1996. pap. text. write for info. (*0-201-40654-3*) Addison-Wesley.

MacIntosh C Programming Primer, Vol. II. Mark Toppan. (C). 1991. pap. text. write for info. (*0-201-55602-2*) Addison-Wesley.

Macintosh C Programming Primer Vol. 1: Inside the Toolbox Using THINK C, Vol. I. 2nd ed. Dave Mark & Cartwright Reed. 672p. (C). 1992. pap. text 32.95 (*0-201-60838-3*) Addison-Wesley.

Macintosh Companion: The Basics & Beyond. Sharon Z. Aker. 608p. 1991. pap. text 22.95 (*0-201-57754-2*) Addison-Wesley.

Macintosh Computerized Testbank T/A Medical-Surgical Nursing. 4th ed. Sharon Lewis. 1996. write for info. (*0-8151-5320-1*) Mosby Inc.

Macintosh Data Files. David Miller. (Illus.). 232p. 14.95 (*0-685-09444-8*) P-H.

Macintosh Design to Production: The Definitive Guide. Betsy Kopshina. 1995. pap. 34.95 (*1-55958-751-2*) Prima Pub.

Macintosh Designer's Guide to Digital Imaging: Controlling Black & White. Carl Sesto. LC 95-49195. 289p. 1996. pap. 29.95 (*0-471-13750-2*) Wiley.

Macintosh F-X: Tools & Techniques for Outrageous Effects. David Busch. LC 94-22446. 445p. 1994. pap. 34.95 incl. cd-rom (*1-55828-363-3*, MIS Pr) IDG Bks.

Macintosh Font Book. 3rd ed. Erfert Fenton. (Illus.). 400p. (C). 1995. pap. text 24.95 (*0-201-88364-3*) Peachpit Pr.

Macintosh for Kids. Martin Ouverson. write for info. (*0-318-58226-0*) P-H.

MacIntosh Fundamental Concepts 1995 Using the Mac SE. Danny Goodman. (Danny Goodman's Educational Series for the MacIntosh). Date not set. teacher ed. write for info. (*0-02-801056-6*) Glencoe.

Macintosh Game Programming Techniques. Cary Torkelson. LC 96-19483. 89p. 1996. pap. 39.95 incl. cd-rom (*1-55851-461-9*) IDG Bks.

Macintosh Graphics in Modula II. Russell L. Schnapp. (Illus.). 176p. 1986. 19.95 (*0-13-542309-0*) P-H.

MacIntosh Guide: Journeys Through Microsoft Excel 4.0. Jan O'Sullivan. (C). 1993. pap. text. write for info. (*0-201-59487-0*) Addison-Wesley.

Macintosh Human Interface Guidelines. Apple Computer, Inc. Staff. 416p. (C). 1992. pap. text 29.95 (*0-201-62216-5*) Addison-Wesley.

Macintosh Hypermedia Vol. 1: Reference Guide. Michael Fraase. (Illus.). 352p. (C). 1990. pap. 27.66 (*0-673-38791-7*, Scott Frsmn) Addson-Wesley Educ.

Macintosh Microsoft BASIC. Rick Dayton. write for info. (*0-318-58183-3*) P-H.

MacIntosh Mountain. Victor J. Kelly. 256p. 1983. pap. 4.95 (*0-310-35181-2*, 10497P) Zondervan.

Macintosh Notebook: Chart. Nancy Reel. write for info. (*0-318-59656-3*) S&S Trade.

Macintosh Notebook: Lotus JAZZ. John Heilborn. write for info. (*0-318-59658-X*) S&S Trade.

Macintosh Notebook: MACPASCAL. John Heilborn. write for info. (*0-318-59659-8*) S&S Trade.

Macintosh OLE 2.0 Developer's Reference: Programmer's Reference. Barry Potter. LC 94-233825. 871p. 1994. pap. 44.95 incl. cd-rom (*1-55851-420-1*, M&T Bks) IDG Bks.

Macintosh Online Handbook. Barbara Cooley. pap. 13.50 (*0-393-96279-2*) Norton.

***Macintosh OS 8.6: Visual QuickStart Guide.** 3rd ed. Maria Langer. LC 99-462548. 352p. (C). 1999. pap. 17.99 (*0-201-35472-1*, Pub. by Peachpit Pr) Addison-Wesley.

Macintosh Pascal Programming Primer Vol. 1: Inside the Toolbox Using THINK Pascal, Vol. I. Dave Mark. 544p. 1990. pap. text 26.95 (*0-201-57084-X*) Addison-Wesley.

Macintosh Programming Faqs. Stephen H. Baker. 656p. 1996. pap. 39.99 (*0-7645-4001-7*) IDG Bks.

Macintosh Programming MS-BASIC. Richard C. Vile. 1991. 19.95 (*0-8306-6241-3*) McGraw-Hill Prof.

MacIntosh Programming Primer: Inside the Toolbox Using Think C. Dave Mark. (C). 1991. pap. text. write for info. (*0-201-55644-8*) Addison-Wesley.

Macintosh Programming Techniques. 2nd ed. Dan P. Sydow. 89p. 1996. pap. 39.95 incl. cd-rom (*1-55851-458-9*) IDG Bks.

Macintosh Programming Techniques: A Foundation for All Macintosh Programmers. Dan Sydow. LC 93-46619. 1994. pap. 34.95 (*1-55828-326-9*, MIS Pr) IDG Bks.

Macintosh Revelations. 2nd ed. Ken Maki. LC 97-37449. 640p. 1998. pap., pap. text 44.99 incl. cd-rom (*0-471-19563-4*) Wiley.

***Macintosh Software Guide for the Law Office.** Randy B. Singer. (Illus.). 183p. 2000. pap. 34.95 (*1-57073-768-1*, Pub. by Amer Bar Assn) IPG Chicago.

Macintosh System Fitness Plan: Easy Exercises to Improve Performance & Reclaim Disk Space. Dan Shafer. LC 95-2556. 176p. (C). 1995. pap. text 14.95 (*0-201-48329-7*) Addison-Wesley.

Macintosh System 7.5 for Dummies. Bob LeVitus. LC 94-77742. 432p. 1994. pap. 19.95 (*1-56884-197-3*) IDG Bks.

Macintosh Teaching Materials. Flynn. Date not set. pap. text 21.95 (*0-314-86229-3*) West Pub.

Macintosh Technical. Smith. 1985. 24.95 (*0-13-542358-9*) P-H.

MacIntosh Technology in the Common Hardware Reference Platform. Apple Computer, Inc. Staff. 224p. (C). 1995. pap. text 43.95 (*1-55860-393-X*) Morgan Kaufmann.

Macintosh 3D Handbook. Craig Lyn. Orig. Title: Macintosh 3D. (Illus.). 450p. 1997. pap. 39.95 (*1-886801-63-0*) Thomson Learn.

Macintosh 3D Handbook. 3rd ed. Craig Lyn & Ben Long. Orig. Title: Macintosh 3D. (Illus.). 530p. 1999. pap. 49.95 (*1-886801-83-5*) Chrles River Media.

Macintosh User Reference. Apple Computer, Inc. Staff. 1994. pap. text. write for info. (*0-201-62279-3*) Addison-Wesley.

Macintosh Version to a Survey of Mathematics with Applications. 4th ed. Allen Angel. (C). 1995. 0.00 (*0-201-59059-X*) Addison-Wesley.

Macintosh VisiRef. Que Development Group Staff. LC 94-67593. (Illus.). 146p. (Orig.). 1994. 12.99 (*1-56529-831-4*) Que.

Macintosh Way. Guy Kawasaki. 224p. (C). 1989. 22.00 (*0-673-46175-0*) Addson-Wesley Educ.

Macintosh Windows Integration: Integrating Your Macintosh with Windows 95 & Windows NT Environment. John Rizzo. 400p. 1999. pap. text 44.95 incl. cd-rom (*0-12-589325-6*) Morgan Kaufmann.

Macintosh 3D see Macintosh 3D Handbook

MacIntyre Mine: From Failure to Fortune. Harold K. Hochschild. (Illus.). 27p. 1962. pap. 6.95 (*0-8156-8024-4*) Syracuse U Pr.

MacIntyre Mine - From Failure to Fortune. rev. ed. Harold K. Hochschild. (Township Thirty-Four Ser.). (Illus.). 1993. reprint ed. 6.95 (*0-910020-10-8*) Adirondack Mus.

MacIntyre Reader. Ed. by Kelvin Knight. LC 98-24229. 1999. 40.00 (*0-268-01436-1*); pap. 19.95 (*0-268-01437-X*) U of Notre Dame Pr.

Maciora & Mik Families Genealogy: Historia Rodzin Mikow i Maciorow. Joseph G. Maciora. LC 83-62000. (Illus.). 30p. (Orig.). 1983. pap. 7.00 (*0-9613407-0-3*) J G V Maciora.

***Mack & Leeann's Guide to Short-Term Missions.** J. Mack Stiles. 192p. 2000. pap. 11.99 (*0-8308-2269-0*) InterVarsity.

Mack & Mabel: Vocal Selections. (Illus.). 72p. 1982. pap. 8.95 (*0-88188-094-9*, 00384205) H Leonard.

Mack AP Super Duty Trucks 1926-1938 Photo Archive. Ed. by Thomas E. Warth. LC 96-76226. (Photo Archive Ser.). (Illus.). 128p. 1996. pap. 14.95 (*1-882256-54-9*) Iconografix.

Mack Bolan: Terminal Velocity. Don Pendleton. (Gold Eagle Ser.: No. 2). 384p. 1984. pap. 2.95 (*0-373-61402-0*) Harlequin Bks.

Mack Bolan: The Executioner. Don Pendleton. 1998. 63.88 (*0-373-96225-8*) Harlequin Bks.

***Mack Buses, 1900-1960: Photo Archive.** Ed. by Harvey Eckart. LC 99-76049. (Illus.). 128p. 2000. pap. 29.95 (*1-58388-020-8*, 129959AE, Pub. by Iconografix) Motorbooks Intl.

Mack EB, EC, ED, EE, EF, EG, DE 1936-1951 Photo Archive. Ed. by Thomas E. Warth. LC 94-74210. (Photo Archive Ser.). (Illus.). 144p. 1995. pap. 14.95 (*1-882256-29-8*) Iconografix.

Mack EH, EJ, EM, EQ, ER, ES 1936-1950 Photo Archive. Ed. by Thomas E. Warth. LC 95-77487. (Photo Archive Ser.). (Illus.). 128p. 1995. pap. 14.95 (*1-882256-39-5*) Iconografix.

Mack FC, FCSW & NW 1936-1947 Photo Archive. Ed. by Thomas E. Warth. LC 94-74209. (Photo Archive Ser.). (Illus.). 144p. 1995. pap. 14.95 (*1-882256-28-X*) Iconografix.

Mack FG, FH, FJ, FK, FN, FP, FT, FW 1937-1950 Photo Archive. Ed. by Thomas E. Warth. LC 95-77484. (Photo Archive Ser.). (Illus.). 128p. 1995. pap. 14.95 (*1-882256-35-2*) Iconografix.

Mack LF, LH, LJ, LM, LT, 1940-1956 Photo Archive. Ed. by Thomas E. Warth. LC 95-77488. (Photo Archive Ser.). (Illus.). 128p. 1995. pap. 14.95 (*1-882256-38-7*) Iconografix.

Mack Model AB Photo Archive. Ed. by Thomas E. Warth. LC 94-76265. (Photo Archive Ser.). (Illus.). 144p. 1994. pap. 14.95 (*1-882256-18-2*) Iconografix.

Mack Model B Fire Trucks, 1954-1966 Photo Archive. Ed. by Harvey Eckart. LC 96-78347. (Photo Archive Ser.). (Illus.). 128p. 1997. pap. 29.95 (*1-882256-62-X*) Iconografix.

Mack Model B 1953-1966 Photo Archive, Vol. 1. Ed. by Thomas E. Warth. LC 94-76264. (Photo Archive Ser.). (Illus.). 144p. 1994. pap. 29.95 (*1-882256-19-0*) Iconografix.

Mack Model B 1953-1966 Photo Archive, Vol. 2. Ed. by Thomas E. Warth. LC 94-76264. (Photo Archive Ser.: Vol. 2). (Illus.). 128p. 1995. pap. 29.95 (*1-882256-34-4*) Iconografix.

***Mack Model C Fire Trucks, 1957-1967: Photo Archive.** Ed. by Harvey Eckart. LC 99-76043. (Illus.). 128p. 2000. pap. 29.95 (*1-58388-014-3*, 129957AE, Pub. by Iconografix) Motorbooks Intl.

Mack Model CF Fire Trucks, 1967-1981 Photo Archive. Ed. by Harvey Eckart. LC 96-78340. (Photo Archive Ser.). (Illus.). 128p. 1997. pap. 29.95 (*1-882256-63-8*) Iconografix.

Mack Model L Fire Trucks 1940-1954 Photo Archive. Harvey Eckart. LC 98-71286. (Illus.). 128p. 1998. pap. 29.95 (*1-882256-86-7*) Iconografix.

Mack Trucks Photo Gallery. Tom E. Warth. LC 98-71285. (Illus.). 224p. 1998. pap. 24.95 (*1-882256-88-3*) Iconografix.

Macke. Anna Meseure. 1997. 12.99 (*3-8228-0671-4*) Benedikt Taschen.

Macke. Anna Meseure. 1994. pap. 9.99 (*3-8228-0551-3*) Taschen Amer.

Macken Charm. Jack Hodgins. 320p. 1996. pap. 14.95 (*0-7710-4185-3*) McCland & Stewart.

Macken, McCarry & Sappideen: The Law of Employment. 4th ed. James Macken et al. 650p. 1997. pap. 80.00 (*0-455-21454-9*, 14604, Pub. by LawBk Co) Gaunt.

MacKenna's Gold. Will Henry, pseud. 128p. 1988. pap. 2.75 (*0-380-70592-3*, Avon Bks) Morrow Avon.

MacKenna's Gold. Will Henry, pseud. 224p. 1997. reprint ed. mass mkt. 4.50 (*0-8439-4154-5*) Dorchester Pub Co.

MacKennas of Truagh. rev. ed. C. Eugene Swezey, III. (Illus.). 240p. (Orig.). 1993. pap. text 28.50 (*1-55613-849-0*) Heritage Bk.

MacKenna's Promise. Elizabeth Lane. (Historical Ser.). 1994. per. 3.99 (*0-373-28816-6*, 1-28816-6) Harlequin Bks.

Mackenzie. Leslie Roberts. LC 73-20906. 276p. 1974. reprint ed. lib. bdg. 65.00 (*0-8371-5864-8*, ROMR, Greenwood Pr) Greenwood.

MacKenzie: Yesterday & Beyond. Alfred P. Aquilina. (Illus.). 204p. 1981. pap. 7.95 (*0-88839-083-1*) Hancock House.

Mackenzie Basin Impact Study (MBIS) Final Report. Stewart J. Cohen et al. LC 98-141416. vii, 372 p. 1997. write for info. (*0-660-16973-8*, Pub. by Can7 Govern Pub) Intl Spec Bk.

Mackenzie Collection: A Study of West African Carved Gambling Chips. Morris Siegel. LC 41-25906. (American Anthropological Association Memoirs Ser.: No. 55). 1940. pap. 25.00 (*0-527-00554-1*) Periodicals Srv.

Mackenzie Eskimos. Knud J. Rasmussen. LC 76-21643. (Thule Expedition, 5th, 1921-1924 Ser.: Vol. 10, No. 2). reprint ed. 42.50 (*0-404-58326-1*) AMS Pr.

Mackenzie Family. Linda Howard. (Promo Ser.). 1998. per. 9.99 (*0-373-48376-7*, 1-48376-7) Silhouette.

Mackenzie King of Canada: A Biography. Henry R. Hardy. LC 77-135245. (Illus.). 390p. 1970. reprint ed. lib. bdg. 69.50 (*0-8371-5164-3*, HAMK, Greenwood Pr) Greenwood.

Mackenzie King Record, 1945-1946, Vol. 3. Ed. by J. W. Pickersgill & Donald F. Forster. 424p. 1970. text 75.00 (*0-8020-1713-4*) U of Toronto Pr.

Mackenzie King Record, 1947-48, Vol. 4. Ed. by J. W. Pickersgill & Donald F. Forster. 338p. 1990. text 75.00 (*0-8020-1714-2*) U of Toronto Pr.

Mackenzie-McNaughton Wartime Letters. Chalmers J. Mackenzie. Ed. by Mel Thistle. LC 72-185741. 192p. reprint ed. pap. 59.60 (*0-608-30165-5*, 201443300094) Bks Demand.

***Mackenzie Thorpe: From the Heart.** Mackenzie Thorpe. (Illus.). 2000. 35.00 (*0-7893-0509-7*) Universe.

Mackenzies. Linda Howard. 1996. mass mkt. 9.99 (*1-55166-246-9*, 1-66246-9, Mira Bks) Harlequin Bks.

Mackenzies: David. Ana Leigh. 384p. 1998. mass mkt. 5.99 (*0-380-79337-7*, Avon Bks) Morrow Avon.

MacKenzies: Flint. Ana Leigh. 384p. (Orig.). 1996. mass mkt. 5.50 (*0-380-78096-8*, Avon Bks) Morrow Avon.

***Mackenzies: Jake.** Ana Leigh. 384p. 1999. mass mkt. 5.99 (*0-380-79339-3*, Avon Bks) Morrow Avon.

***MacKenzies: Josh.** Ana Leigh. 384p. 2000. mass mkt. 5.99 (*0-380-81102-2*, Avon Bks) Morrow Avon.

Mackenzies: Peter. Ana Leigh. LC 98-93176. (Mackenzies Trilogy Ser.: Vol. 2). 384p. 1998. mass mkt. 5.99 (*0-380-79338-5*, Avon Bks) Morrow Avon.

Mackenzie's Baby. Anne McAllister. (American Romance Ser.). 1992. per. 3.39 (*0-373-16459-9*, 1-16459-9) Harlequin Bks.

Mackenzie's Baby. Anne McAllister. (Born in the U. S. A. Ser.). 1997. mass mkt. 4.50 (*0-373-47195-5*, 1-47195-2) Harlequin Bks.

Mackenzie's Mission. Linda Howard. (Intimate Moments Ser.). 1992. per. 3.39 (*0-373-07445-X*, 5-07445-5) Silhouette.

***Mackenzie's Mission.** Linda Howard. 2000. mass mkt. 6.99 (*0-373-48408-9*) Silhouette.

Mackenzie's Mountain. Linda Howard. 2000. per. 5.99 (*1-55166-574-3*) Harlequin Bks.

Mackenzie's Pleasure. Linda Howard. (Intimate Moments Ser.). 1996. per. 3.99 (*0-373-07691-6*, 1-07691-8) Silhouette.

Mackenzie's Pleasure. large type ed. Linda Howard. 1999. 21.95 (*0-373-59540-9*) Harlequin Bks.

Mackenzie's Rock. Alexander Mackenzie. (Shorey Historical Ser.). 39p. reprint ed. pap. 10.00 (*0-8466-0048-X*, S48) Shoreys Bkstore.

MacKenzie's Woman. large type ed. Jan Constant. LC 93-14408. 269p. 1993. lib. bdg. 15.95 (*0-8161-5842-8*, G K Hall Lrg Type) Mac Lib Ref.

Mackenzie's Woman: Bachelor Auction. Joann Ross. 1999. mass mkt. 3.75 (*0-373-25817-8*, Harlequin) Harlequin Bks.

Mackeral Sky. unabridged ed. Margeaux Herman. 243p. 1998. pap. 11.95 (*1-893667-01-4*) Sugar Mtn.

***Mackerel & the Making of Baltimore, Co. Cork, 1879-1913.** Seamus Fitzgerald. LC 99-27212. (Maynooth Studies in Local History). 64p. 1999. pap. 10.95 (*0-7165-2681-6*, Pub. by Irish Acad Pr) Intl Spec Bk.

Mackerel by Moonlight. William F. Weld. 256p. 1999. per. 6.99 (*0-671-03874-5*) PB.

Mackerel by Moonlight. William F. Weld. LC 98-3731. 240p. 1998. 23.00 (*0-684-85346-9*) S&S Trade.

Mackerel Sharks. Robert L. Buyer. (Carving Sea Life Ser.). (Illus.). 40p. 1996. pap. 7.95 (*0-8117-2468-9*) Stackpole.

MacKeurtan's Sale of Goods in South Africa. 5th ed. G. R. Hackwill. 346p. 1984. 39.00 (*0-7021-1413-8*, Pub. by Juta & Co) Gaunt.

Mackey's Jurisprudence of Freemasonry. Albert G. Mackey. 406p. 1994. reprint ed. 16.50 (*0-88053-026-X*, M 073) Macoy Pub.

Mackie & McCartney's Medical Microbiology, Vol. 2. 13th ed. Collee et al. (Illus.). 928p. 1989. text 59.00 (*0-443-02332-8*) Church.

Mackie Compact Mixers. Rudy Trubitt. 264p. 2000. per. 27.95 (*0-634-00670-3*) H Leonard.

Mackinac. Donna Winters. Ed. by Pamela Q. Chambers. LC 88-92702. (Great Lakes Romances Ser.). (Illus.). 208p. 1993. pap. 10.95 (*0-923048-75-8*) Bigwater Pub.

Mackinac: An Island Famous in These Regions. Phil Porter. (Illus.). 96p. 1998. 16.95 (*0-911872-69-8*); pap. 9.95 (*0-911872-68-X*) Mackinac St Hist Pks.

Mackinac & Lake Stories. Mary H. Catherwood. 1972. reprint ed. lib. bdg. 19.50 (*0-8422-8023-5*) Irvington.

Mackinac & the Porcelain City. Eugene T. Petersen. (Illus.). 40p. (Orig.). 1985. pap. 5.00 (*0-911872-53-1*) Mackinac St Hist Pks.

Mackinac Connection: The Insider's Guide to Mackinac Island. 3rd rev. ed. Amy McVeigh. LC 92-23695. (Illus.). 152p. 1998. pap. 12.95 (*0-9623213-3-8*) Mackinac Pub.

Mackinac Island: Historic Frontier, Vacation Resort, Timeless Wonderland. Pamela A. Piljac & Thomas M. Piljac. LC 88-4962. (Illus.). 320p. (Orig.). 1988. pap. 9.95 (*0-913339-07-5*) Bryce-Waterton Pubns.

Mackinac Island: Historic Frontier, Vacation Resort, Timeless Wonderland. Pamela A. Piljac & Thomas M. Piljac. (Illus.). 320p. (Orig.). 1996. pap. 14.95 (*1-55652-305-X*) Chicago Review.

Mackinac Island: Its History in Pictures. Eugene T. Petersen. LC 74-17184. (Illus.). 103p. (Orig.). 1973. 18.00 (*0-911872-13-2*) Mackinac St Hist Pks.

MacKinac Island & Sault Saint Marie. Stanley Newton. LC 76-4405. 1990. reprint ed. pap. 12.00 (*0-912382-19-8*) Black Letter.

Mackinac Island Annals of Fort Mackinac. rev. ed. Dwight H. Kelton. (Illus.). 129p. 1997. reprint ed. pap. 17.50 (*0-8328-6772-1*); reprint ed. lib. bdg. 27.50 (*0-8328-6771-3*) Higginson Bk Co.

Mackinac Island for Kids-on-the-Go. Susan D. Jolliffe & Amy McVeigh. (Illus.). 32p. (Orig.). 1993. pap. 5.00 (*0-9623213-2-X*) Mackinac Pub.

Mackinac Island Memories. deluxe ed. Ed. by Len Trankina & Sean O'Dell. (Travel Memories Ser.). (Illus.). viii, 72p. 1999. 12.00 (*0-89730-233-8*) R J Berg.

Mackinac Maze. Jerry Prescott. LC 97-75369. (Illus.). 350p. 1997. 22.50 (*1-882792-55-6*) Proctor Pubns.

Mackinac Passage: A Summer Adventure. Robert A. Lytle. (Illus.). 184p. 1995. pap. 11.95 (*1-882376-11-0*) Thunder Bay Pr.

Mackinac Passage: The Boathouse Mystery. Robert A. Lytle. (Illus.). 172p. (J). (gr. 3-10). 1996. pap. 11.95 (*1-882376-29-3*) Thunder Bay Pr.

Mackinac Passage: The General's Treasure. Robert A. Lytle. (Illus.). 172p. (YA). (gr. 9-12). 1997. pap. 12.95 (*1-882376-45-5*) Thunder Bay Pr.

Mackinac, the Gathering Place. Ed. by Russell McKee. LC 81-620009. 176p. 1981. 27.95 (*0-941912-02-7*) Mich Nat Res.

Mackinac to Miami: Exploring the Mississippi River. Burton D. Morgan. (Illus.). 96p. 1983. 45.00 (*0-9609310-1-5*) Summit Pub OH.

An Asterisk (*) at the beginning of an entry indicates that the title is appearing for the first time.

Mackinaw - Honolulu Connection. Ronald J. Lewis. LC 98-72209. 224p. 1998. pap. 12.95 (*0-9642436-2-8*) Agawa Pr.

Mackinaws down the Missouri: John C. Anderson's Journal of a Trip from Saint Louis, Mo., to Virginia City, Montana & Return, 1866. John C. Anderson. Ed. by Glen Barrett. LC 73-79903. (Illus.). 111p. reprint ed. pap. 34.50 (*0-8357-6197-5*, 203460500090) Bks Demand.

Mackinnon's Bride. Tanya A. Crosby. 384p. 1996. mass mkt. 5.99 (*0-380-77682-0*, Avon Bks) Morrow Avon.

Mackintosh Architecture. J. Cooper et al. 1984. 35.00 (*0-312-50244-3*) St Martin.

Mackintosh Architecture. Jackie Cooper et al. (Illus.). 128p. 1984. pap. 25.00 (*0-312-50243-5*) St Martin.

MackIntosh, MacIntosh, McIntosh: Descendants of Alexander MacIntosh. Frances S. Drisko. (Illus.). 319p. (Orig.). 1993. pap. text 43.00 (*1-55613-876-8*) Heritage Bk.

Mackintosh Postcard Book. Mackintosh Staff. 1996. pap. 5.99 (*3-8228-8630-0*) Taschen Amer.

Mackintosh Style: Design & Decor. Elizabeth Wilhide. LC 94-44478. (Illus.). 160p. 1995. 29.95 (*0-8118-1032-1*) Chronicle Bks.

Mackintosh Style: Design & Decor. Elizabeth Wilhide. 1998. pap. 19.95 (*0-8118-1946-9*) Chronicle Bks.

Mackintosh Watercolours. R. Billcliffe. pap. text 34.95 (*0-7195-3678-2*, Pub. by John Murray) Trafalgar.

Mackintosh's Masterwork: Charles Rennie Mackintosh & the Glasgow School of Art. William Buchanan et al. (Illus.). 224p. 1989. 40.00 (*0-87701-663-1*) Chronicle Bks.

Mackintosh's Masterwork: Charles Rennie Mackintosh & the Glasgow School of Art. William Buchanan et al. (Illus.). 224p. 1995. reprint ed. pap. 22.95 (*0-8118-0932-3*) Chronicle Bks.

Macklis-Wash Package. Roger M. Macklis. 1984. 26.90 (*0-316-54248-2*) Little.

Maclab for Psych 3.0 - Documentation. 3rd ed. Chute. (Psychology Ser.). 1994. pap. 14.00 (*0-534-23869-6*) Wadsworth Pub.

Maclab for Psychology V3.0: Student Lab Manual, Version 3. 3rd ed. Chute. (Psychology Ser.). 1994. mass mkt., lab manual ed. 25.50 (*0-534-23198-5*) Brooks-Cole.

Maclab-Powerlab for Mac-Documentation. Chute. LC 98-102058. (Psychology Ser.). 1996. pap. 60.75 (*0-534-34132-2*) Wadsworth Pub.

MacLarens. large type ed. C. L. Skelton. 465p. 1982. 27.99 (*0-7089-8040-6*, Charnwood) Ulverscroft.

MacLarens: A History of Clan Labhran. Margaret MacLaren. 153p. (C). 1989. text 60.00 (*0-946270-10-4*, Pub. by Pentland Pr) St Mut.

MacLaurin's Lady. Julie Tetel. LC 96-529. 354p. 1995. per. 4.50 (*0-373-28887-5*, 1-28887-7) Harlequin Bks.

*__MacLean Groom.__ Kathleen Harrington. LC 99-94452. (Highland Lairds Trilogy). 384p. 1999. mass mkt. 5.99 (*0-380-80727-0*, Avon Bks) Morrow Avon.

MacLean. Historical & Genealogical Account of the Clan MacLean, from Its First Settlement at Castle Duart, in the Isle of Mull, to the Present Period (1838) Seneachie. 358p. 1997. reprint ed. pap. 54.00 (*0-8328-9465-6*); reprint ed. lib. bdg. 64.00 (*0-8328-9464-8*) Higginson Bk Co.

Maclennan's Gaelic-English - English-Gaelic Dictionary. Malcolm Maclennan. 1985. 125.00 (*0-317-54667-8*, Pub. by Acair Ltd); pap. 80.00 (*0-7855-2996-9*, Pub. by Acair Ltd) St Mut.

MacLeod: A Short Sketch of Their Clan, History, Folk-Lore, Tales & Biographical Notices of Some Eminent Clansmen. R. C. MacLeod. 118p. 1992. reprint ed. pap. 19.00 (*0-8328-2681-2*); reprint ed. lib. bdg. 29.00 (*0-8328-2680-4*) Higginson Bk Co.

MacLeod & Levitt: Taxation of Insurance Business. 4th ed. J. S. MacLeod. 1997. write for info. (*0-406-04606-9*, MLTI4, MICHIE) LEXIS Pub.

MacLeod Evaporite Basin, Western Australia: Holocene Environments, Seidments & Geological Evolution. Brian W. Logan. LC 87-33455. (AAPG Memoir Ser.: Vol. 44). 152p. 1987. reprint ed. pap. 47.20 (*0-608-02775-8*, 206384100007) Bks Demand.

MacLeod's Clinical Examination. 8th ed. Christopher R. Edwards. (Illus.). 432p. 1990. pap. text 32.95 (*0-443-04079-6*) Church.

MacLeod's Clinical Examination. 9th ed. Munro. 1995. pap. text 31.50 (*0-443-04856-8*, W B Saunders Co) Harcrt Hlth Sci Grp.

Maclopedia: The Macintosh Hardware & Software Compendium. James C. McCroskey. 1990. pap. 24.95 (*0-13-541947-6*) P-H.

Maclopedia: The Ultimate Reference to Everything Macintosh. Hayden Development Group Staff. 1392p. 1996. 60.00 (*1-56830-281-9*) Hayden.

MacMath: A Dynamical Systems Software Package for the Macintosh. J. R. Hubbard & B. J. West. (Illus.). 168p. 1991. pap. 49.95 (*0-387-97416-4*) Spr-Verlag.

MacMath: A Dynamical Systems Software Package for the Macintosh. 2nd ed. J. Hubbard & B. J. West. (Illus.). viii, 162p. 1993. 54.95 (*0-387-94135-5*) Spr-Verlag.

Macmillan. John Turner. LC 93-11786. (Profiles in Power Ser.). 288p. (C). 1993. text 52.95 (*0-582-21880-2*, Pub. by Addison-Wesley) Longman.

MacMillan: The American Grain Family. W. Duncan MacMillan et al. LC 98-10694. xi, 336 p. 1998. 30.00 (*1-890434-04-3*) Afton Hist Soc.

*__Macmillan Animal Encyclopedia, 3.__ 1999. 50.00 (*0-02-865419-6*) Mac Bks.

Macmillan Animal Encyclopedia for Children. Roger Few. LC 91-3982. (Macmillan Children's Reference Ser.). (Illus.). 120p. (J). (gr. 2 up). 1991. text 17.00 (*0-02-762425-0*, Mac Bks Young Read) S&S Childrens.

Macmillan Atlas of Irish History. Thomas Crean. LC 97-28623. 144p. 1997. 27.50 (*0-02-862011-9*) Macmillan.

Macmillan Atlas of War & Peace: Bosnia Herzegovina. Macmillan Publishing Company Staff. 48p. 1996. 12.95 (*0-02-861265-5*) Macmillan.

MacMillan Baseball Encyclopedia. Simon & Schuster Staff. 1996. pap. 29.55 (*1-57595-014-6*) Macmillan Digit.

Macmillan Baseball Encyclopedia Update, 1997, Update 1. Macmillan Publishing Company Staff. 208p. 1997. pap. text 14.95 (*0-02-861512-3*) Macmillan.

Macmillan Bible Atlas. 3rd rev. ed. Yohanan Aharoni et al. LC 77-4313. (Illus.). 192p. 1993. 35.00 (*0-02-500605-3*) Macmillan.

Macmillan Book of Baseball Stories. Terry Egan et al. LC 92-6447. (Illus.). 128p. (J). (gr. 3 up). 1992. lib. bdg. 16.00 (*0-02-733280-2*, Mac Bks Young Read) S&S Childrens.

Macmillan Book of Bonsai. Horst Daute. (Gardening Guides Ser.). (Illus.). 128p. 1986. pap. 9.95 (*0-02-062660-6*) Macmillan.

MacMillan Book of Earliest Christian Prayers. F. Forrester Church & Terrence J. Mulry. 256p. 1990. pap. 9.95 (*0-02-031080-3*) Macmillan.

Macmillan Book of Greek Gods & Heroes. Alice Low. LC 85-7170. (Illus.). 192p. (J). (gr. 2-6). 1985. lib. bdg. 17.00 (*0-02-761390-9*, Mac Bks Young Read) S&S Childrens.

Macmillan Book of Proverbs, Maxims & Famous Phrases. Burton E. Stevenson. 2976p. 1987. text 75.00 (*0-02-614500-6*) Macmillan.

*__Macmillan Centennial Atlas of the World.__ rev. ed. 1999. 185.00 (*0-02-865370-X*) Mac Lib Ref.

Macmillan Centennial Atlas of World & Planet Earth World Atlas. Bertelsmann. 1997. 175.00 (*0-02-864901-X*) Mac Lib Ref.

Macmillan Children's Guide to Dinosaurs & Other Prehistoric Animals. Philip Whitfield. LC 91-45562. (Illus.). 96p. (J). (gr. 2 up). 1992. lib. bdg. 18.95 (*0-02-762362-9*, Mac Bks Young Read) S&S Childrens.

Macmillan Children's Guide to Endangered Animals. Roger Few. LC 92-41433. (Illus.). 96p. (J). (gr. 2 up). 1993. lib. bdg. 17.95 (*0-02-734545-9*, Mac Bks Young Read) S&S Childrens.

Macmillan Children's Thesaurus. Paul Hellweg. LC 93-21773. (J). (gr. 1-8). 1995. text 14.95 (*0-02-743525-3*, Mac Bks Young Read) S&S Childrens.

Macmillan College Handbook. 2nd ed. Gerald Levin. (C). 1990. teacher ed. write for info. (*0-02-370232-X*, U4240-0) Allyn.

Macmillan College Handbook. 2nd ed. Gerald Levin. LC 90-36315. 834p. (C). 1990. 46.00 (*0-02-370231-1*, Macmillan Coll) P-H.

Macmillan Compendium: African-American History. Macmillan Library Reference Staff. LC 98-36730. 1153p. 1998. per. 115.00 (*0-02-864979-6*) Macmillan Gen Ref.

Macmillan Compendium: American History. Macmillan Library Reference Staff. LC 98-36732. 1198p. 1998. per. 115.00 (*0-02-864978-8*) Macmillan Gen Ref.

Macmillan Compendium: Everyday Life: A Social History. Macmillan Library Reference Staff. LC 98-35920. 1078p. 1998. 115.00 (*0-02-864976-1*) Macmillan Gen Ref.

Macmillan Compendium: Select World Cultures. 1999. 125.00 (*0-02-865382-3*) Macmillan.

Macmillan Compendium: Sex, Genetics & Human Reproduction. Macmillan Staff. LC 97-25526. 1152p. 1997. 125.00 (*0-02-864919-2*) Mac Lib Ref.

Macmillan Compendium: Supreme Court. Ed. by Philip Weinberg. LC 99-22507. 1999. 125.00 (*0-02-865369-6*) Macmillan.

Macmillan Compendium: The Confederacy. Macmillan Staff. LC 97-23462. 1200p. 1997. 125.00 (*0-02-864920-6*) Mac Lib Ref.

Macmillan Compendium America at War: Selected Biographies from the Three-Volume Encyclopedia of the American Military. Macmillan Staff. LC 98-41961. 846p. 1998. 115.00 (*0-02-865061-1*) Mac Lib Ref.

*__Macmillan Compendium of How Government Works.__ Macmillan Staff. LC 98-49352. 1200p. 1998. per. 125.00 (*0-02-864975-3*) Macmillan Gen Ref.

*__Macmillan Compendium of Social Issues.__ Benford. 942p. 1998. 115.00 (*0-02-865055-7*) Macmillan Gen Ref.

*__Macmillan Compendium of Twenty First Century.__ Al. LC 98-50677. 999p. 1998. 125.00 (*0-02-864977-X*) Macmillan Gen Ref.

*__Macmillan Continental History Atlas Bundle, 5 Vols.__ (Illus.). 160p. 1998. 125.00 (*0-02-865051-4*) Mac Lib Ref.

Macmillan Dictionary. Macmillan Publishing Company Staff. 1973. write for info. (*0-02-195340-6*) Macmillan.

Macmillan Dictionary for Children. Ed. by Robert Costello. LC 97-12732. (Illus.). 896p. (J). (gr. 3-7). 1997. per. 16.95 (*0-689-81384-8*) S&S Childrens.

Macmillan Dictionary for Children. Ed. by W. D. Halsey & C. G. Morris. 784p. (J). 1982. 19.95 (*0-8288-1512-7*, M14143) Fr & Eur.

Macmillan Dictionary for Children: Multimedia Edition. (Illus.). (J). 1992. 59.95 (*1-56574-000-9*) Macmlln New Media.

Macmillan Dictionary for Students. Macmillan Publishing Company Staff. LC 84-3880. (Illus.). 1216p. (YA). (gr. 6-12). 1984. lib. bdg. 19.95 (*0-02-761560-X*, Mac Bks Young Read) S&S Childrens.

Macmillan Dictionary of English Spelling. Martin Manser. 512p. 1997. pap. 19.95 (*0-333-65777-2*, Pub. by Macmillan) Trans-Atl Phila.

Macmillan Dictionary of Measurement. John Clark. 512p. 1994. 27.50 (*0-02-525750-1*) Macmillan.

Macmillan Dictionary of Military Biography. Alan Axelrod. LC 97-31779. 463p. 1997. 39.95 (*0-02-861994-3*) Macmillan.

Macmillan Dictionary of Political Quotations: More than 11,000 Entries, from John Adams to Ron Ziegler. Lewis D. Eigen & Jonathan P. Siegel. LC 91-40116. 785p. 1993. 40.00 (*0-02-610650-7*) Macmillan.

Macmillan Dictionary of Psychology 2nd ed. N. S. Sutherland. LC 96-214801. ix, 515 p. 1995. write for info. (*0-333-62324-X*) Macmillan.

*__MacMillan Dictionary of Quotations.__ Book Sales, Inc. Staff. 2000. 17.99 (*0-7858-1191-5*) Bk Sales Inc.

Macmillan Dictionary of the First World War. Elizabeth-Anne Wheal & Stephen Pope. (Illus.). 480p. 1995. 67.50 (*0-333-61822-X*, Pub. by Pan) Trans-Atl Phila.

Macmillan Early Science Big Books, 4 vols., Set. Melvin Berger. (Illus.). (J). (ps-2). 1995. pap. write for info. (*1-56784-645-9*) Newbridge Educ.

Macmillan Encyclopedia, Vol. 4. John S. Rigden. 1997. 100.00 (*0-02-864589-8*) Macmillan.

Macmillan Encyclopedia of Architects, Vol. 1. Ed. by Adolf K. Placzek. 1982. 110.00 (*0-02-925010-2*) Mac Lib Ref.

Macmillan Encyclopedia of Computers, Vol. 1. Ed. by Bitter. 1992. 110.00 (*0-02-897046-2*) Mac Lib Ref.

Macmillan Encyclopedia of Computers, Vol. 2. Ed. by Gary G. Bitter. 1992. 110.00 (*0-02-897047-0*) Mac Lib Ref.

*__Macmillan Encyclopedia of Energy , 3 vol. set.__ John Zumerchik. 2000. 325.00 (*0-02-865021-2*) Macmillan.

Macmillan Encyclopedia of Energy. 2nd ed. Zumerchik. 2000. 110.00 (*0-02-865019-0*) Macmillan.

Macmillan Encyclopedia of Energy. 3rd ed. Zumerchik. 2000. 110.00 (*0-02-865020-4*) Macmillan.

Macmillan Encyclopedia of Health, 8 vols., 1. Visual Education Corporation Staff. (YA). (gr. 7-12). 1993. 45.00 (*0-02-897431-X*) Macmillan.

Macmillan Encyclopedia of Health, 8 vols., 2. Visual Education Corporation Staff. (YA). (gr. 7-12). 1993. 45.00 (*0-02-897432-8*) Macmillan.

Macmillan Encyclopedia of Health, 8 vols., 3. Visual Education Corporation Staff. (YA). (gr. 7-12). 1993. 45.00 (*0-02-897433-6*) Macmillan.

Macmillan Encyclopedia of Health, 8 vols., 4. Visual Education Corporation Staff. (YA). (gr. 7-12). 1993. 45.00 (*0-02-897434-4*) Macmillan.

Macmillan Encyclopedia of Health, 8 vols., 5. Visual Education Corporation Staff. (YA). (gr. 7-12). 1993. 45.00 (*0-02-897435-2*) Macmillan.

Macmillan Encyclopedia of Health, 8 vols., 6. Visual Education Corporation Staff. (YA). (gr. 7-12). 1993. 45.00 (*0-02-897436-0*) Macmillan.

Macmillan Encyclopedia of Health, 8 vols., 7. Visual Education Corporation Staff. (YA). (gr. 7-12). 1993. 45.00 (*0-02-897437-9*) Macmillan.

Macmillan Encyclopedia of Health, 8 vols., 8. Visual Education Corporation Staff. (YA). (gr. 7-12). 1993. 45.00 (*0-02-897438-7*) Macmillan.

Macmillan Encyclopedia of Military History, Vol. 1. Ed. by Chandler. 1996. 50.00 (*0-02-897106-X*) Mac Lib Ref.

Macmillan Encyclopedia of Military History, Vol. 2. Ed. by Chandler. 1996. 50.00 (*0-02-897107-8*) Mac Lib Ref.

Macmillan Encyclopedia of Military History, Vol. 2. Chandler. 1996. 100.00 (*0-02-897105-1*) Macmillan.

*__Macmillan Encyclopedia of Native American Tribes.__ Michael Johnson. LC 99-30114. 288p. 1999. write for info. (*0-00-286349-9*) Mac Lib Ref.

Macmillan Encyclopedia of Native American Tribes. 2nd ed. Michael Johnson. 288p. 1999. 80.00 (*0-02-865409-9*) Macmillan.

Macmillan Encyclopedia of Science, 12 vols. Incl. Vol. 1. Matter & Energy. Peter Lafferty. (J). 1991. 35.00 (*0-02-941141-6*); Vol. 2. Heavens, Stars, Galaxies, & the Solar System. Kerrod. (J). 1991. 35.00 (*0-02-941142-4*); Vol. 3. Earth Our Planet: Its Land Sea & Air. Dixon. (J). 1991. 35.00 (*0-02-941143-2*); Vol. 4. Life on Earth: Fossils & Human Ancestors. Twist. (J). 1991. 35.00 (*0-02-941144-0*); Vol. 5. Plants & Animals. John Stidworthy. (J). 1991. 35.00 (*0-02-941145-9*); Vol. 6. Body & Health. Walpole. (J). 1991. 35.00 (*0-02-941146-7*); Vol. 7. Environment, Ecology, Pollution, & Agriculture. Twist. (YA). 1991. 35.00 (*0-02-941147-5*); Vol. 8. Industry, Mining, & Manufacturing. Kerrod. (J). 1991. 35.00 (*0-02-941341-9*); Vol. 9. Fuel & Power. Twist. (J). 1991. 35.00 (*0-02-941342-7*); Vol. 10. Transportation from Bicycle to Spacecraft. Kerrod. (J). 1991. 35.00 (*0-02-941343-5*); Vol. 11. Communications: Print, Images, & Sound. Lewis. (J). 1991. 35.00 (*0-02-941344-3*); Vol. 12. Tools & Tomorrow. Kerrod. (J). 1991. 35.00 (*0-02-941345-1*); 1991. 375.00 (*0-02-941346-X*) Free Pr.

Macmillan Encyclopedia of Science, 12 vols., Set. 2nd ed. Andromeda. LC 96-36597. 1997. 375.00 (*0-02-864556-1*, Hall Reference) Macmillan.

Macmillan Encyclopedia of Science, Vol. 1. 2nd rev. ed. Andromeda. 1997. 35.00 (*0-02-864557-X*, Hall Reference) Macmillan.

Macmillan Encyclopedia of Science, Vol. 2. 2nd rev. ed. Andromeda. 1998. 35.00 (*0-02-864558-8*, Hall Reference) Macmillan.

Macmillan Encyclopedia of Science, Vol. 3. 2nd rev. ed. Andromeda. 1997. 35.00 (*0-02-864559-6*, Hall Reference) Macmillan.

Macmillan Encyclopedia of Science, Vol. 4. 2nd rev. ed. Andromeda. 1997. 35.00 (*0-02-864560-X*, Hall Reference) Macmillan.

Macmillan Encyclopedia of Science, Vol. 5. 2nd rev. ed. Andromeda. 1997. 35.00 (*0-02-864561-8*, Hall Reference) Macmillan.

Macmillan Encyclopedia of Science, Vol. 6. 2nd rev. ed. Andromeda. 1997. 35.00 (*0-02-864562-6*, Hall Reference) Macmillan.

Macmillan Encyclopedia of Science, Vol. 7. 2nd rev. ed. Andromeda. 1997. 35.00 (*0-02-864563-4*, Hall Reference) Macmillan.

Macmillan Encyclopedia of Science, Vol. 8. 2nd rev. ed. Andromeda. 1997. 35.00 (*0-02-864564-2*, Hall Reference) Macmillan.

Macmillan Encyclopedia of Science, Vol. 9. 2nd rev. ed. Andromeda. 1997. 35.00 (*0-02-864565-0*, Hall Reference) Macmillan.

Macmillan Encyclopedia of Science, Vol. 10. 2nd rev. ed. Andromeda. 1997. 35.00 (*0-02-864566-9*, Hall Reference) Macmillan.

Macmillan Encyclopedia of Science, Vol. 12. 2nd rev. ed. Andromeda. 1997. 35.00 (*0-02-864568-5*, Hall Reference) Macmillan.

Macmillan Encyclopedia of the Environment. Book Builders, Incorporated Staff. LC 96-29045. 1997. 50.00 (*0-02-897385-2*) S&S Trade.

Macmillan Encyclopedia of the Environment, 6 vols. Stephen R. Kellert. LC 96-29045. (Illus.). 864p. (J). 1997. 300.00 (*0-02-897381-X*) Macmillan.

Macmillan Encyclopedia of the Environment, Vol. 1. Book Builders, Inc. Staff. LC 96-29045. 1997. 50.00 (*0-02-897382-8*) Mac Lib Ref.

Macmillan Encyclopedia of the Environment, Vol. 2. Book Builders, Inc. Staff. LC 96-29045. 1997. 50.00 (*0-02-897383-6*) Mac Lib Ref.

Macmillan Encyclopedia of the Environment, Vol. 3. Book Builders, Inc. Staff. LC 96-29045. 1997. 50.00 (*0-02-897384-4*) Mac Lib Ref.

Macmillan Encyclopedia of the Environment, Vol. 5. Book Builders, Inc. Staff. LC 96-29045. 1997. 50.00 (*0-02-897386-0*) Mac Lib Ref.

Macmillan Encyclopedia of the Environment, Vol. 6. Book Builders, Inc. Staff. LC 96-29045. 1997. 50.00 (*0-02-897387-9*) Mac Lib Ref.

Macmillan Encyclopedia of World Slavery, 2 vols. Ed. by Paul Finkelman & Joseph C. Miller. LC 98-30610. (Illus.). 1020p. 1998. 210.00 (*0-02-864607-X*) Mac Lib Ref.

Macmillan Encyclopedia of World Slavery, Vol. 1. Finkelman & Miller. LC 98-30610. 1998. 110.00 (*0-02-864780-7*) S&S Trade.

Macmillan Encyclopedia of World Slavery, Vol. 2. Finkelman & Miller. LC 98-30610. 1998. 100.00 (*0-02-864781-5*) S&S Trade.

Macmillan Encyclopediaclopedia of Energy. Zumerchik. 2000. 110.00 (*0-02-865018-2*) Macmillan.

MacMillan Encyclopedic Numismatic Dictionary. W. Doty. (Illus.). lib. bdg. 45.00 (*0-02-532270-2*) S J Durst.

Macmillan Family Reference Atlas of the U. S. A. Mark T. Mattson. (Illus.). 377p. 1997. 27.95 (*0-02-864889-7*) Mac Lib Ref.

Macmillan Field Guide to Bird Identification. Alan Harris et al. (Illus.). 224p. (Orig.). 1993. pap. 29.50 (*0-333-59280-8*, Pub. by Pan) Trans-Atl Phila.

Macmillan Field Guide to Geological Structures. John L. Roberts. (Illus.). 256p. 1996. reprint ed. pap. 29.50 (*0-333-66295-4*, Pub. by Macmillan) Trans-Atl Phila.

Macmillan Field Guide to Trees & Shrubs. Robert H. Mohlenbrock. 1987. pap. 12.95 (*0-02-063430-7*) Macmillan.

Macmillan Field Guides: Rocks & Minerals. Macmillan Publishing Company Staff et al. (Illus.). 192p. 1985. pap. 12.95 (*0-02-079640-4*) Macmillan.

Macmillan First Atlas. Tony Potter & Nicola Wright. LC 91-31257. (Macmillan Children's Reference Ser.). (Illus.). 40p. (J). (ps-2). 1992. lib. bdg. 12.95 (*0-02-774920-7*, Mac Bks Young Read) S&S Childrens.

Macmillan First Dictionary. rev. ed. Ed. by Judith Levey. LC 90-6062. (Dictionaries Ser.). (Illus.). 416p. (J). (gr. k-4). 1990. lib. bdg. 14.00 (*0-02-761731-9*, Mac Bks Young Read) S&S Childrens.

Macmillan Good English Handbook. Godfrey Howard. 320p. 1997. 28.50 (*0-333-64806-4*, Pub. by Macmillan) Trans-Atl Phila.

Macmillan Government & Europe: A Study in the Process of Policy Development. Jacqueline Tratt. LC 96-23688. 192p. 1996. text 65.00 (*0-312-16369-X*) St Martin.

MacMillan Health Encyclopedia, 9 Vols. Macmillan Publishing Company Staff. LC 99-23432. 1999. write for info. (*0-02-865036-0*) Macmillan.

MacMillan Health Encyclopedia, vol 7. 7. 1999. 375.00 (*0-02-865046-8*) S&S Trade.

MacMillan Health Encyclopedia, vol 8. 8. 1999. 375.00 (*0-02-865047-6*) S&S Trade.

Macmillan Health Encyclopedia, Vol. 9. 1993. 45.00 (*0-02-897453-0*) Mac Lib Ref.

MacMillan Health Encyclopedia, vol 9. 9. 1999. 375.00 (*0-02-865048-4*) S&S Trade.

Macmillan Health Encyclopediaclopedia. LC 99-23432. 1999. 375.00 (*0-02-865040-9*) Macmillan.

Macmillan Health Encyclopediaclopedia. 2nd ed. LC 99-23432. 1999. 375.00 (*0-02-865041-7*) Macmillan.

Macmillan Health Encyclopediaclopedia. 3rd ed. 1999. 375.00 (*0-02-865042-5*) Macmillan.

Macmillan Health Encyclopediaclopedia. 4th ed. 1999. 375.00 (*0-02-865043-3*) Macmillan.

Macmillan Health Encyclopediaclopedia. 5th ed. 1999. 375.00 (*0-02-865044-1*) Macmillan.

Macmillan Health Encyclopediaclopedia. 6th ed. 1999. 375.00 (*0-02-865045-X*) Macmillan.

Macmillan Illustrated Encyclopedia of Dinosaurs & Prehistoric Animals. Ed. by Dougal Dixon. (Illus.). 312p. 1988. 39.95 (*0-02-580191-0*) Macmillan.

Macmillan Illustrated Encyclopedia of Myths & Legends. Arthur Cotterell. (Illus.). 256p. 1995. 24.95 (*0-02-860851-8*) Macmillan.

M

M

Macmillan Information Now Encyclopedia of Sexual Ethics. LC 98-180593. 750p. 1998. 39.95 (*0-02-864917-6*) Mac Lib Ref.

Macmillan Information Now Encyclopedia of the Confederacy. 750p. 1998. 39.95 (*0-02-864916-8*) Mac Lib Ref.

Macmillan Information Now Encyclopedia of World Religions. 640p. 1998. 39.95 (*0-02-864921-4*) Mac Lib Ref.

Macmillan Millennium Atlas of the World. David Prebenna. LC 96-20353. (Illus.). 1996. 175.00 (*0-02-861264-7*, H M Gousha) Prntice Hall Bks.

Macmillan Multicultural Big Books, 5 bks., Set. (Illus.). 1994. pap. 74.00 (*1-56784-525-8*) Newbridge Educ.

MacMillan on Options. Lawrence G. McMillan. LC 96-27174. 592p. 1996. 69.95 (*0-471-11960-1*) Wiley.

Macmillan Picture Wordbook. rev. ed. Ed. by Judith Levey. LC 90-8274. (Dictionaries Ser.). (Illus.). 64p. (J). (ps-1). 1990. lib. bdg. 8.95 (*0-02-754641-1*, Mac Bks Young Read) S&S Childrens.

Macmillan Portable World Atlas. Bertelsmann Cartographic Staff. 96p. 1997. pap. 17.95 (*0-02-862105-0*, Pub. by Macmillan) S&S Trade.

Macmillan Profiles: Festivals & Holidays. LC 99-26394. (Profiles Ser.). 1999. 75.00 (*0-02-865378-5*) Macmillan.

Macmillan Profiles: Heroes of the Holocaust. Macmillan Reference Library. LC 98-56458. (Profiles Ser.). 1999. 75.00 (*0-02-865362-9*) Macmillan.

Macmillan Profiles: Hispanic Americans. LC 99-23058. (Profiles Ser.). 1999. 75.00 (*0-02-865373-4*) Macmillan.

Macmillan Profiles: Humanitarians & Reformers. LC 99-38793. (Profiles Ser.). 400p. 1999. 75.00 (*0-02-865377-7*) Macmillan.

Macmillan Profiles: Kings & Queens. LC 99-37943. (Profiles Ser.). 400p. 1999. 75.00 (*0-02-865375-0*) Macmillan.

Macmillan Profiles: Monuments & Historic Places. LC 99-51559. 400p. 1999. 75.00 (*0-02-865374-2*) Macmillan.

Macmillan Profiles: Myths & Legends. Judy Culligan. LC 99-51558. (Profiles Ser.). 400p. 1999. 75.00 (*0-02-865376-9*) Macmillan.

Macmillan Profiles Scientists Entrepreneurs. Al. LC 98-28744. 389p. (J). 1998. 75.00 (*0-02-864983-4*) Macmillan Gen Ref.

Macmillan Profiles Tycoons Entrepreneurs. Al. LC 98-39089. 349p. 1998. per. 75.00 (*0-02-864982-6*) Macmillan Gen Ref.

***Macmillan Quick Reference Encyclopedia: Alcohol.** Macmillan Publishing Company Staff. 1998. 24.95 (*0-02-864959-1*) Macmillan.

***Macmillan Quick Reference Encyclopedia: Drugs.** Macmillan Publishing Company Staff. 1998. 24.95 (*0-02-864958-3*) Macmillan.

Macmillan Quick Reference Encyclopedia: Tobacco & Caffeine. Macmillan Staff. 1998. 24.95 (*0-02-864957-5*) Macmillan.

Macmillan Reader. 3rd ed. Judith Nadell et al. (Illus.). 768p. (C). 1992. teacher ed. write for info. (*0-318-69337-2*) Macmillan.

Macmillan Reader. 5th ed. Nadell et al. LC 98-21422. 762p. 1998. pap. 37.00 (*0-205-28216-4*) Allyn.

***Macmillan Reeds Nautical Almanac 2000: European Edition.** Ed. by Basil D'Oliveira & Brian Goulder. (Illus.). 1136p. 2000. pap. 69.50 (*0-333-80277-2*, Pub. by S1 & J) Trans-Atl Phila.

Macmillan School Dictionary. Macmillan Publishing Company Staff. 1974. 21.04 (*0-02-195310-4*) Macmillan.

MacMillan Transportation Encyclopedia, 6 Vols. Macmillan Publishing Company Staff. LC 99-33371. 649p. 1999. write for info. (*0-02-865361-0*) Macmillan.

Macmillan Visual Almanac: More Than 2,000 Charts, Graphs, Maps, & Visuals That Provide Essential Information in the Blink of an Eye. Ed. by Bruce S. Glassman. (Illus.). 608p. 1996. 19.95 (*0-02-861247-7*) Macmillan.

Macmillan Visual Desk Reference. Diagram Group Staff. (Illus.). 608p. 1993. 29.95 (*0-02-531310-X*) Macmillan.

Macmillan Visual Dictionary. Compiled by Jean-Claude Corbeil & Ariane Archambault. LC 95-20838. (Illus.). 864p. 1996. 65.00 (*0-02-860814-3*) Macmillan.

Macmillan Visual Dictionary. Diagram Group Staff. (Illus.). 864p. 1992. 45.00 (*0-02-528160-7*) Macmillan.

Macmillan Visual Dictionary. abr. ed. Compiled by Jean-Claude Corbeil & Ariane Archambault. LC 95-20838. (Illus.). 864p. 1995. 24.95 (*0-02-860810-0*) Macmillan.

MacMillan Visual Dictionary: Spanish/English. Jean-Claude Corbeil & Ariane Archambault. 896p. 1997. 39.95 (*0-02-861434-8*) Macmillan.

Macmillan Visual Dictionary for Children. 224p. 1998. 19.95 (*0-02-862693-1*) Macmillan.

Macmillan Visual Dictionary, Multilingual Edition: English, French, Spanish, German. Macmillan Publishing Company Staff. (Illus.). 928p. 1994. 65.00 (*0-02-578115-4*) Macmillan.

Macmillan World Atlas. 288p. 1997. 59.95 (*0-02-862244-8*) Macmillan.

Macmillan World Atlas. Macmillan Books Staff. 1996. 75.00 incl. cd-rom (*0-02-861445-3*) Macmillan.

Macmillan World Atlas. Macmillan Staff. LC 95-34908. (Illus.). 440p. 1996. 59.95 (*0-02-860812-7*) Macmillan.

Macmillan Writer. 4th ed. (C). 1999. write for info. (*0-205-31103-2*) S&S Trade.

Macmillan Writer: Rhetoric, Reader & Handbook. 4th ed. Nadell et al. LC 99-22375. 718p. 1999. pap. 47.00 (*0-205-29854-0*, Longwood Div) Allyn.

Macmillan Writer Brief. 4th ed. Nadell et al. 653p. 1999. pap. text 44.00 (*0-205-29855-9*, Longwood Div) Allyn.

Macmillian Profiles: African American Women. Macmillian & Library Reference Staff. LC 98-56447. (Profiles Ser.). 1999. 75.00 (*0-02-865363-7*, Macmillan Coll) P-H.

MacMillian Profiles Villains Outlaws. LC 98-37088. (Macmillan Profiles Ser.). 361p. 1998. 75.00 (*0-02-865058-1*) Macmillan.

Macnab's Backache. 3rd ed. John A. Mcculloch et al. LC 96-21766. (Illus.). 795p. 1997. 75.00 (*0-683-05797-9*) Lppncott W & W.

Macnamara's Irish Colony & the United States Taking of California in 1846. John Fox. LC 99-16977. (Illus.). 240p. 1999. lib. bdg. 35.00 (*0-7864-0687-9*) McFarland & Co.

MacNamara's Woman. Alicia Scott. 1997. per. 3.99 (*0-373-07813-7*, 1-07813-8) Silhouette.

MacNeal's Master Atlas of Decision Making: A New Kind of Guide to the Maps People Use in Making up Their Minds. Edward MacNeal. Ed. & Comment by Russell Joyner. LC 97-2441. (Illus.). 144p. (Orig.). 1997. pap. 19.95 (*0-918970-44-X*) Intl Gen Semantics.

MacNeil: The Clan MacNeil (Clann Niall) of Scotland. MacNeil of Barra. (Illus.). 227p. 1993. reprint ed. pap. 34.00 (*0-8328-3370-3*); reprint ed. lib. bdg. 44.00 (*0-8328-3369-X*) Higginson Bk Co.

***MacNeils of Tokyo.** Jack Seward. 192p. 2000. pap. 14.95 (*0-8048-3236-6*) Tuttle Pubng.

MacNeil/Vid Guide Intl Bus. Ricky Griffin. Ed. by Mary C. McEwing. 26p. 1996. pap. text 173.00 (*0-201-88473-9*) Addison-Wesley.

Macomb: A Pictorial History. John E. Hallwas. (Illinois Pictorial History Ser.). (Illus.). 1989. write for info. (*0-943963-14-1*) G Bradley.

Macon: An Architectural & Historical Guide. Middle Georgia Historical Society, Inc. Members. Orig. Title: A Guide to Macon's Architectural & Historical Heritage. (Illus.). 132p. (Orig.). 1996. 25.00 (*0-9651017-1-1*); pap. 10.00 (*0-9651017-0-3*) Middle Georgia.

Macon: The Center of Georgia. Tracy M. Maurer & Joni W. Woolf. Ed. by Robyn Putz. (Illus.). 208p. 1995. 39.00 (*1-885352-20-4*) Community Comm.

Macon County NC in the 1850 Census: A Snapshot in Time. Barbara McRae & Rebekah Leverette. 183p. 1997. pap. 22.00 (*0-9638930-3-3*) Teresita Pr.

Macon County, Missouri Pictorial History. Donna Lester. (Illus.). 110p. 1993. 35.00 (*0-88107-214-1*) Curtis Media.

Macon County, North Carolina, Marriages, 1829-1939. James E. Wooley. 156p. 1984. pap. 22.50 (*0-89308-342-9*) Southern Hist Pr.

***Macon, GA.** Vickie Prater. (Images of America Ser.). (Illus.). 128p. 1999. pap. 18.99 (*0-7385-0200-6*) Arcadia Publng.

Macon, the Center of Georgia: City Business Profiles. Tracy M. Maurer et al. 1995. pap. write for info. (*1-885352-23-9*) Community Comm.

Maconaquah's Story: The Saga of Frances Slocum. Kitty Dye. LC 96-765780. (Illus.). 110p. (YA). (gr. 7-12). 1996. pap. 8.95 (*0-9642058-2-3*) InChem Pubng.

Macon's Black Heritage: The Untold Story. Catherine Meeks. 1997. 34.95 (*0-9657119-9-4*) Tubmn African Amer.

Macoy's Short Addresses & Ceremonies for Matron's Use. Vee Hansen et al. 24p. 1995. reprint ed. pap. 3.00 (*0-88053-330-7*, S-084) Macoy Pub.

Macoy's Short Addresses for Matron: Forty-Five Sentiments. Vee Hansen & Opal Shaw. 28p. 1993. reprint ed. pap. 3.00 (*0-88053-329-3*, S-83) Macoy Pub.

Macoy's Star Songs. Nissenson. 48p. 1966. reprint ed. pap. 1.00 (*0-88053-311-0*, S301) Macoy Pub.

MacPac for Teachers: Hands-On Macintosh Applications. Annette Lamb. (Illus.). 148p. (C). 1997. pap. text 19.95 (*0-9641581-4-0*) Vision to Action.

MacPaint. write for info. (*0-318-58185-X*) P-H.

MacPelican's American Adventure. Scoular Anderson. LC 97-37127. (Gamebook Ser.). (Illus.). 32p. (J). (gr. 1-3). 1998. 12.99 (*0-7636-0443-7*) Candlewick Pr.

MacPerl: Power & Ease. Vicki Brown. 1998. pap. text 40.00 (*1-881957-32-2*) PT Freeware.

***MacPhails: Baseball's First Family of the Front-Office.** G. Richard McKelvey. LC 99-54849. (Illus.). 352p. 2000. 29.95 (*0-7864-0639-9*) McFarland & Co.

MacPherson's Lament. Sharyn McCrumb. (Elizabeth MacPherson Ser.). 1993. mass mkt. 6.99 (*0-345-38474-1*) Ballantine Pub Grp.

MacPlots Two Users Manual. 2nd ed. Laura Steinberg. (Powercadd Ser.). (Illus.). 79p. 1984. 250.00 (*1-878250-02-7*) Eng Soft NC.

MacPower. John Heilborn. write for info. (*0-318-58186-8*) P-H.

MacQueen: Studying Scots Law. Hector L. MacQueen. 170p. 1993. pap. 20.00 (*0-406-00013-1*, U.K., MICHIE) LEXIS Pub.

MacQueen & Thomson: Contract Law in Scotland. Hector L. MacQueen & J. M. Thomson. 1997. write for info. (*0-406-05397-9*, MSLC, MICHIE) LEXIS Pub.

Macrae: History of the Clan Macrae, with Genealogies. Alexander Macrae. (Illus.). xxii, 442p. 1992. reprint ed. pap. 71.00 (*0-8328-2683-9*); reprint ed. lib. bdg. 81.00 (*0-8328-2682-0*) Higginson Bk Co.

MacRae's Blue Book, 1997. 104th ed. Ed. by Mary O. Smith. 1568p. (Orig.). 1997. pap. 170.00 (*0-89910-243-3*) MacRaes Blue Bk.

MacRae's Blue Book, 1996. Ed. by Mary O. Smith. 1568p. (Orig.). 1996. pap. 170.00 (*0-89910-242-5*) MacRaes Blue Bk.

Macrame. braille large type ed. pap. 7.50 (*0-614-32400-9*) Cath Guild Blind.

Macrame: Sources of Fine Knotting. Ed. by Jules Kliot & Kaethe Kliot. (Illus.). 112p. 1998. per. 20.00 (*0-916896-97-8*, LE49) Lacis Pubns.

Macrame Book. Helene Bress. 1999. pap. text 27.95 (*1-886388-15-6*) Flower Valley Pr.

Macreconomics with Macrosolve Software/Windows. 5th ed. 1997. pap. 58.00 (*0-393-97060-4*) Norton.

Macrizi's Geschichte der Copten. Ahmad ibn Ali Magrizi. (GER.). 142p. 1979. reprint ed. write for info. (*3-487-06763-3*) G Olms Pubs.

Macro. 2nd ed. Robert Hall. (C). pap. text (*0-393-95768-3*) Norton.

Macro: Priciples & Policies. 7th ed. William J. Baumol. 1997. pap. text 73.00 (*0-03-025049-8*, Pub. by Harcourt Coll Pubs) Harcourt.

Macro: Test Item File. 5th ed. Robert Hall. (C). 1997. pap. text, teacher ed. write for info. (*0-393-96837-5*) Norton.

Macro Accounting & Modern Money Supplies. G. A. Swanson. LC 92-38001. 208p. 1993. 62.95 (*0-89930-794-9*, ZMA/, Quorum Bks) Greenwood.

***Macro & Close-Up Photography Handbook.** Stan Sholik & Ron Eggers. (Illus.). 120p. 2000. pap. 29.95 (*1-58428-026-3*) Amherst Media.

Macro & Micro: A Brief Introduction. 3rd ed. L. Tepperman. 432p. 1997. pap. 61.27 (*0-13-857897-4*) P-H.

***Macro & Micro Data Analyses & Their Integration.** Nancy D. Ruggles & Richard Ruggles. LC 99-17050. 576p. 1999. 115.00 (*1-85898-991-4*) E Elgar.

Macro & Micro-Mechanics of High Velocity Deformation & Fracture. Ed. by Kozo Kawata & Jumpei Shioiri. (International Union of Theoretical & Applied Mechanics Symposia Ser.). (Illus.). xviii, 427p. 1988. 103.95 (*0-387-16363-8*) Spr-Verlag.

Macro & Microemulsions: Theory & Applications. Ed. by Dinesh O. Shah. LC 84-28358. (ACS Symposium Ser.: No. 272). 488p. 1985. lib. bdg. 93.95 (*0-8412-0896-4*) Am Chemical.

Macro & Microemulsions: Theory & Applications. Ed. by Dinesh O. Shah. LC 84-28358. (ACS Symposium Ser.: No. 272). (Illus.). 512p. 1985. reprint ed. pap. 158.80 (*0-608-03262-X*, 206378100007) Bks Demand.

Macro Assembler & Toolkit 80386. Penn Brumm & Don Brumm. (Illus.). 608p. (Orig.). 1989. 35.95 (*0-8306-0247-X*) McGraw-Hill Prof.

Macro Cafe Cookbook: Macrobiotic Cooking Made Easy. Margaret Lawson. 1997. pap. 12.95 (*0-9660712-0-4*) Lawson Pubns.

Macro Case Studies in Social Work. Ed. by Robert W. McCelland et al. 160p. 1998. pap. 24.95 (*0-87304-296-4*) Manticore Pubs.

***Macro Ecomony Today.** 8th ed. Bradley R. Schiller. LC 99-16175. 512p. 1999. pap. 60.00 (*0-07-366277-1*) McGraw.

***Macro-Economia.** 4th ed. McEachern. 1999. pap. 62.95 (*968-7529-51-2*) Thomson Learn.

Macro-Economic Issues of Recovery in Transition Economies. Ed. by Pal Gaspar. LC 97-190744. 204p. 1997. pap. 44.00 (*963-05-7435-7*, Pub. by New South Wales Univ Pr) Intl Spec Bk.

Macro-Economic Management & Bureaucracy: The Case of Botswana. Jan Isaksen. (Research Report Ser.: No. 59). 53p. 1981. write for info. (*91-7106-192-4*, Pub. by Nordic Africa) Transaction Pubs.

Macro-Economic Planning with Conflicting Goals: Proceedings of a Workshop Held at the Vrije Universiteit of Brussels, Beligum, December 10, 1982. M. Despontin et al. (Lecture Notes in Economics & Mathematical Systems Ser.: Vol. 230). vi, 297p. 1984. 41.00 (*0-387-13367-4*) Spr-Verlag.

Macro-Economic Primer. Russell E. Moffett. 240p. (C). 1993. pap. text, per. 24.95 (*0-8403-8526-9*) Kendall-Hunt.

Macro Economic Theory. Roy G. Allen. LC 67-12508. (C). 1969. reprint ed. pap. text 10.50 (*0-312-50330-X*) St Martin.

Macro Economics. William A. McEachern. (SWC-Economics). 832p. (C). 1988. mass mkt. 37.75 (*0-538-08845-1*, H85) S-W Pub.

Macro-Economics in Question: The Keynesian-Monetarist Orthodoxies & the Kaleckian Alternative. Malcolm C. Sawyer. LC 82-3221. 244p. (gr. 13). 1982. pap. text 40.95 (*0-87332-220-7*) M E Sharpe.

Macro-Economics in Question: The Keynesian-Monetarist Orthodoxies & the Kaleckian Alternative. Malcolm C. Sawyer. LC 82-3221. (Illus.). 204p. 1982. reprint ed. pap. 63.30 (*0-7837-9958-6*, 206068500006) Bks Demand.

Macro-86: Programming Algorithms. J. David Hamilton & Robert G. Trenary. Ed. by John D. Hubbard. LC 84-12805. (Macro-86 Software Design Ser.). (Illus.). 498p. 1984. ring bd. 59.95 (*0-87119-089-3*, EC-1202) Heathkit-Zenith Ed.

Macro 86 Assembly Language Programming. Lawrence P. Larsen. LC 84-19295. (Macro-86 Software Design Ser.). (Illus.). 900p. 1984. ring bd. 59.95 (*0-87119-100-8*, EC-1201) Heathkit-Zenith Ed.

Macro Engineer: A 1-2-3 Macro Developer's Toolkit-2 Disks Included. Richard W. Ridington. 1990. pap. 79.95 (*0-13-543331-2*) P-H.

Macro-Engineering: Mit Brunel Lectures on Global Infrastructure Frank P. Davidson et al. LC 98-202039. (Horwood Series in Engineering Science). 206p. 1997. write for info. (*1-898563-33-0*, Pub. by Horwood Pub) Paul & Co Pubs.

***Macro-Engineering & the Earth: World Projects for the Year 2000 & Beyond: A Festchrift in Honour of Frank Davidson.** Uwe Kitzinger & Ernst G. Frankel. 350p. 1999. 65.00 (*1-898563-59-4*, Pub. by Horwood Pub) Paul & Co Pubs.

Macro-Environmental Policy: Principles & Design: With Cases on Milk Packaging, Cadmium, Phosphorus & Nitrogen, & Energy & Global Warming. G. Huppes. (Developments in Environmental Economics Ser.). 438p. 1993. 204.50 (*0-444-81657-7*) Elsevier.

Macro-Harmonic Music Manuscript Workbook. Faruq Z. Bey. (Illus.). 70p. (C). 1992. 15.00 (*1-56439-015-2*) Ridgeway.

Macro-History: A Theoretical Approach to Comparative World History. Lee D. Snyder. LC 98-31828. 736p. 1999. text 139.95 (*0-7734-8271-7*) E Mellen.

Macro-Ion Characterization: From Dilute Solutions to Complex Fluids. Ed. by Kenneth S. Schmitz. LC 93-39732. (Symposium Ser.: Vol. 548). 640p. 1994. text 140.00 (*0-8412-2770-5*, Pub. by Am Chemical) OUP.

Macro-Level Practice in the Human Services: An Introduction to Planning, Administration & Evaluation. Thomas M. Meenaghan et al. (Illus.). 288p. (C). 1982. 29.95 (*0-02-920850-5*) Free Pr.

Macro Magic with Turbo Assembler. Jim Mischel. Ed. by Jeff Duntemann. 368p. 1992. pap. 39.95 incl. disk (*0-471-57815-0*) Wiley.

Macro Marketing. 2nd ed. Reed Moyer et al. LC 77-26816. (Wiley Hamilton Series in Marketing). (Illus.). 213p. reprint ed. pap. 66.10 (*0-608-10690-9*, 202018600016) Bks Demand.

Macro Mellow. Sherry A. Rogers & Shirley Gallinger. (Orig.). 1992. pap. 12.95 (*0-9618821-4-X*) Prestige NY.

Macro-Micro Framework for Analysis of the Impact of Structural Adjustment on the Poor in Sub-Saharan Africa. Alexander H. Sarris. (Monographs). (Illus.). 140p. (C). 1990. pap. text 12.00 (*1-56401-005-8*) Cornell Food.

Macro-Micro Linkages in Sociology. Joan Huber. (American Sociological Association Presidential Ser.). (Illus.). 336p. 1991. 55.00 (*0-8039-4103-X*); pap. 25.95 (*0-8039-4104-8*) Sage.

Macro-Micro Linkages in Sociology. Joan Huber. LC 90-24238. (American Sociological Association Presidential Ser.). 304p. 1991. reprint ed. pap. 94.30 (*0-608-02767-7*, 206383300007) Bks Demand.

Macro-Models of the National Economy of the U. S. S. R. Vyacheslav V. Kolbin. 1985. lib. bdg. 191.00 (*90-277-1670-6*) Kluwer Academic.

Macro-Nationalisms: A History of the Pan-Movements, 112. Louis L. Snyder. LC 83-18600. (Contributions in Political Science Ser.: No. 112). 308p. 1984. 65.00 (*0-313-23191-5*, SMN/, Greenwood Pr) Greenwood.

Macro Perspective on Technology Transfer. Allan C. Reddy. LC 95-51413. 160p. 1996. 57.95 (*0-89930-977-1*, Quorum Bks) Greenwood.

Macro Plays. Ed. by David M. Bevington. Incl. Castle of Perserverance. Wisdom & Mankind. (Facsimiles Ser.). 42.00 (*0-686-16149-1*) Folger Bks.

Macro Plays: The Castle of Perseverance, Wisdom, Mankind. Ed. by Mark Eccles. (OS 262 Ser.). 1969. 24.95 (*0-19-722265-X*) OUP.

Macro Practice: A Generalist Approach. Ralph Brody & Murali D. Nair. 214p. 1999. pap. 30.00 (*0-911541-61-6*) Gregory Pub.

Macro-Preview Book. Stockman. (C). 1996. pap. 4.00 (*0-03-016503-2*) Harcourt.

Macro Processors & Techniques for Portable Software. Peter J. Brown. LC 73-17597. (Wiley Series in Computing). 258p. reprint ed. pap. 80.00 (*0-608-18442-X*, 203265400080) Bks Demand.

Macro Programming Lotus 1 2 3 Release 3.4. (Illus.). iii, 64p. 1993. student ed., spiral bd., wbk. ed. 15.95 (*0-7402-0152-2*, LTOOD34M WB) Accelerated Comput Train.

Macro Programming with Lotus 1 2 3 Release 3.4. (Illus.). xvii, 128p. 1993. teacher ed., spiral bd., wbk. ed. 29.00 (*0-7402-0177-8*, LTOOD34MIG) Accelerated Comput Train.

Macro-Sexology, Sex, Sweet Sour. Gustave F. Ado. LC 98-65642. 64p. 1998. pap. 9.95 (*1-57197-122-X*) Pentland Pr.

Macro SG Macro Sftwr PK. 6th ed. Gordon Staff. (C). 1993. 169.66 (*0-673-78821-0*) Addison-Wesley.

Macro Skills Workbook: A Generalist Approach. Karen K. Kirst-Ashman & Grafton H. Hull, Jr. LC 98-181092. 512p. (C). 1998. pap. text 43.95 (*0-8304-1491-6*) Thomson Learn.

***Macro Skills Workbook: A Generalist Approach.** 2nd ed. Hull Kirst-Ashman. 2000. 31.25 (*0-534-51302-6*) Brooks-Cole.

***Macro Social Work Practice.** 2nd ed. Brueggemann. (Social Work Ser.). 2000. 44.50 (*0-534-57322-3*) Wadsworth Pub.

Macro Socio-Economics: From Theory to Activism. Ed. by David Sciulli. LC 95-17028. 314p. (C). 1995. text 77.95 (*1-56324-650-3*) M E Sharpe.

Macro Socio-Economics: From Theory to Activism. Ed. by David Sciulli. LC 95-17028. 314p. (C). (gr. 13). 1995. pap. text 36.95 (*1-56324-651-1*) M E Sharpe.

Macro Split-Economics. 3rd ed. Robert B. Ekelund & Robert D. Tollison. (C). 1991. pap. text 42.66 (*0-673-52097-8*) Addson-Wesley Educ.

Macro Split-Principles of Economic Omics. 2nd ed. Gottheil. LC 98-7443. (Miscellaneous/Catalogs Ser.). 1998. pap. 66.95 (*0-538-86819-8*) S-W Pub.

Macro Study Guide & Workbook. Thea Alexander. 48p. (Orig.). 1984. pap., student ed., wbk. ed. 10.00 (*0-913080-11-X*) Macro Bks.

Macro Study Series, 7 vols., Set. Thea Alexander. 336p. (Orig.). 1984. pap. 44.95 (*0-913080-12-8*) Macro Bks.

Macro Systems in the Social Environment. Dennis D. Long & Martha C. Holle. LC 96-71591. 200p. (C). 1997. pap. text 25.00 (*0-87581-409-3*, MSSE) F E Peacock Pubs.

Macro: Theory/pol. William J. Boyes. (Thomson Executive Press). 552p. (C). 1984. mass mkt. 34.25 (*0-538-08700-5*, H70) S-W Pub.

Macro to Microscale Heat Transfer: The Lagging Behavior. D. Y. Tzou. LC 96-30320. (Chemical & Mechanical Engineering Ser.). 304p. 1996. 60.00 (*1-56032-435-X*) Taylor & Francis.

An Asterisk (*) at the beginning of an entry indicates that the title is appearing for the first time.

***Macro Trading & Investment Strategies: Macroeconomic Arbitrage in Global Markets.** Gabriel Burstein. LC 98-39938. (Trading Advantage Ser.). 228p. 1999. 59.95 (*0-471-31586-9*) Wiley.

Macro und Quickassembler. Ed. by P. Monadjemi. (GER.). (C). 1990. text. write for info. (*0-201-55938-2*) Addison-Wesley.

Macro View of Economics Today. 10th ed. Roger Leroy Miller. 288p. (C). 1998. pap. text, student ed. 24.00 (*0-321-03351-5*) Addison-Wesley.

Macro Writing Guide. Kevin Duggan. 60p. (C). 1987. pap., spiral bd. 12.95 (*0-9613848-2-4*) MARIS.

Macroassembler. 2nd ed. Monadjemi. (C). 1990. text. write for info. (*0-201-55908-0*) Addison-Wesley.

***Macroberts on Scottish Building Contracts** LC 99-34837. 1999. write for info. (*0-632-03411-4*) Blackwell Sci.

Macrobii Vol. I: Saturnalia. Ed. by Willis. (LAT.). 1994. reprint ed. 89.50 (*3-8154-1527-6*, T1527, Pub. by B G Teubner) U of Mich Pr.

Macrobii Vol. II: Indices. Ed. by Willis. (LAT.). 1994. reprint ed. 46.50 (*3-8154-1526-8*, T1526, Pub. by B G Teubner) U of Mich Pr.

Macrobiotic Approach to Cancer: Towards Preventing & Controlling Cancer with Diet & Lifestyle. 2nd rev. expanded ed. Michio Kushi & Edward Esko. LC 91-18034. (Illus.). 184p. (Orig.). 1991. pap. 9.95 (*0-89529-486-9*, Avery) Penguin Putnam.

Macrobiotic Brown Rice Cookbook. rev. ed. Craig Sams. (Illus.). 128p. 1983. pap. 9.95 (*0-89281-447-0*, Heal Arts VT) Inner Tradit.

Macrobiotic Cancer Prevention Cookbook: Recipes for the Prevention & Control of Cancer. Aveline Kushi & Wendy Esko. LC 88-24250. (Illus.). 176p. (Orig.). pap. 9.95 (*0-89529-391-9*, Avery) Penguin Putnam.

Macrobiotic Community Cookbook: Favorite Recipes from America's Macrobiotic Leaders. Andrea B. Lerman. LC 88-32260. (Illus.). 224p. (Orig.). pap. 12.95 (*0-89529-396-X*, Avery) Penguin Putnam.

Macrobiotic Cooking for Everyone. Edward Esko & Wendy Esko. LC 79-89344. (Illus.). 272p. (Orig.). 1981. pap. 21.00 (*0-87040-469-5*) Japan Pubns USA.

Macrobiotic Diet. rev. ed. Michio Kushi & Aveline Kushi. LC 92-70444. (Illus.). 352p. 1993. pap. 21.00 (*0-87040-878-X*) Japan Pubns USA.

Macrobiotic Guidebook for Living: And Other Essays. rev. ed. George Ohsawa. 130p. 1985. pap. 7.95 (*0-918860-41-5*) G Ohsawa.

Macrobiotic Health & Travel Directory. Alex Jack. 64p. 1997. pap. 6.95 (*1-882984-27-X*) One Peaceful World.

Macrobiotic Home Remedies. Michio Kushi & Marc Van Cauwenberghe. (Illus.). 224p. (Orig.). 1985. pap. 19.95 (*0-87040-554-3*) Japan Pubns USA.

Macrobiotic Miracle: A Woman Cures Herself of Cancer. Virginia Brown & Susan Stayman. (Illus.). 240p. 1985. pap. 15.00 (*0-87040-573-X*) Japan Pubns USA.

Macrobiotic Palm Healing. Michio Kushi & Olivia Oredson. LC 86-81326. (Illus.). 176p. 1987. pap. 25.00 (*0-87040-672-8*) Japan Pubns USA.

Macrobiotic Pregnancy & Care of the Newborn. Michio Kushi & Aveline Kushi. (Illus.). 240p. (Orig.). 1983. pap. 25.00 (*0-87040-531-4*) Japan Pubns USA.

Macrobiotic Resource Guide: A Directory to the Most Healthful, Affordable & Enviromentally Safe Foods, Products & Service. Ed. by Alex Jack. 160p. 1997. pap. 10.95 (*1-882984-26-9*) One Peaceful World.

Macrobiotic Seminars of Michio Kushi: Classic Lectures on Health & Diet, Oriental Medicine, & Self-Healing. Michio Kushi. Ed. by Edward Esko. 96p. 1998. pap. 10.95 (*1-882984-29-3*) One Peaceful World.

Macrobiotic Way: The Complete Macrobiotic Diet & Exercise Book. 2nd ed. Michio Kushi. LC 85-1324. 272p. pap. 9.95 (*0-89529-524-5*, Avery) Penguin Putnam.

Macrobiotics: An Invitation to Health & Happiness. George Ohsawa. 77p. 1984. reprint ed. pap. 5.95 (*0-918860-02-4*) G Ohsawa.

Macrobiotics & Beyond: A Guide to Total Living. Marcea Weber & Daniel Weber. 208p. pap. 9.95 (*0-89529-445-1*, Avery) Penguin Putnam.

Macrobiotics & Oriental Medicine: An Introduction to Holistic Health. Michio Kushi & Phillip Janetta. LC 85-81366. 288p. 1991. pap. 22.00 (*0-87040-659-0*) Japan Pubns USA.

***Macrobiotics & Oriental Medicine: An Introduction to Holistic Health.** Michio Kushi & Phillip Jannetta. (Illus.). 272p. 2000. reprint ed. pap. 22.00 (*0-7881-9415-1*) DIANE Pub.

Macrobiotics Beyond Food: A Guide to Health & Well-Being. Roanld E. Kotzsch. LC 86-81324. 242p. 1987. 27.00 (*0-87040-674-4*) Japan Pubns USA.

Macrobytes Software for IBM Computer to Accompany Mankiw Macroeconomics. David Weil. 1991. 14.95 incl. 3.5 hd (*0-87901-505-5*) Worth.

Macrocephalen Oolith von Hildesheim. Ed. by Eckhard Monnig. (GER.). xx, 77p. 1995. 25.00 (*3-487-10060-6*) G Olms Pubs.

Macroclimate & Plant Forms: An Introduction to Predictive Modeling in Phytogeography. E. O. Box. (Tasks for Vegetation Science Ser.: No. 1). 272p. 1981. text 234.00 (*90-6193-941-0*) Kluwer Academic.

Macrocosm: The Meaning of Numbers - The Key to the Cosmos. Oronzo Abbotecola. (Illus.). 29p. 1996. pap. 17.00 (*0-8059-3843-5*) Dorrance.

Macrocosm: Unified Energy Matter Gravity Life. Vernon J. David. LC 92-90127. (Illus.). 1992. write for info. (*0-9632581-0-9*) David Pub KS.

Macrocosm & Microcosm. Rudolf Steiner.Tr. of Makrokosmos und Mikosmos. Seelenfragen, Lebensfragen, Geistesfragen. 205p. 1986. 20.00 (*0-88010-201-2*); pap. 10.95 (*0-88010-200-4*) Anthroposophic.

Macrocosm U. S. A. Possibilities for a New Progressive Era... Ed. by Sandi Brockway. LC 92-80678. (Illus.). 464p. 1993. pap. 24.95 (*0-9632315-5-3*) Macrocosm.

Macrocycles. Ed. by Eicke R. Weber. (Topics in Current Chemistry Ser.: Vol. 161). (Illus.). ix, 278p. 1991. 144.95 (*0-387-54348-1*) Spr-Verlag.

Macrocyclic Compounds in Analytical Chemistry. Aleksei K. Zolotov. LC 96-44724. (Chemical Analysis Ser.). 448p. 1997. 129.00 (*0-471-17262-6*) Wiley.

Macrocyclic Lactone (Lactam) Antibiotics see Handbook of Antibiotic Compounds

Macrocyle Synthesis: A Practical Approach. Ed. by David Parker. (Practical Approach in chemistry Ser.). (Illus.). 266p. 1996. text 90.00 (*0-19-855841-4*); spiral bd. 45.00 (*0-19-855840-6*) OUP.

Macrodynamics: Toward a Theory on the Organization of Human Populations. Jonathan H. Turner. LC 94-40290. (Arnold & Caroline Rose Series of the ASA). 219p. (C). 1995. text 50.00 (*0-8135-2162-9*) Rutgers U Pr.

Macrodynamics of Advanced Market Economies. Alfred S. Eichner. LC 87-9693. (Illus.). 955p. 1987. reprint ed. pap. 200.00 (*0-7837-9970-5*, 206069700006) Bks Demand.

Macrodynamics of Advanced Market Economies. rev. ed. Alfred S. Eichner. LC 91-10741. (Illus.). 1088p. (gr. 13). 1991. text 99.95 (*0-87332-541-9*) M E Sharpe.

Macroecology. James H. Brown. 284p. 1995. pap. text 15.95 (*0-226-07615-6*); lib. bdg. 42.50 (*0-226-07614-8*) U Ch Pr.

Macroeconometric Modelling, 2 vols. Ed. by Kenneth F. Wallis. (International Library of Critical Writings in Econometrics: Vol. 2). 976p. 1994. 375.00 (*1-85278-664-7*) E Elgar.

Macroeconometrics: Developments, Tensions & Prospects. Ed. by Kevin D. Hoover. LC 95-16697. (Recent Economic Thought Ser.). 592p. (C). 1995. lib. bdg. 230.00 (*0-7923-9589-1*) Kluwer Academic.

Macroeconomia. 2nd ed. 656p. (C). 1995. pap. text 26.66 (*0-201-65383-4*) HEPC Inc.

Macroeconomic Activity & Income Inequality in the United States. William R. Russell et al. LC 89-42429. (Contemporary Studies in Economic & Financial Analysis: Vol. 55). 191p. 1989. 78.50 (*1-55938-003-9*) Jai Pr.

Macroeconomic Adjustment: Policy Instruments & Issues. Ed. by Jeffrey M. Davis. LC 92-22870. 90p. 1992. pap. 12.50 (*1-55775-303-2*) Intl Monetary.

Macroeconomic Adjustment & the Poor: The Case of Madagascar. Paul A. Dorosh et al. (Monographs). (Illus.). 160p. (C). 1990. pap. text 12.00 (*1-56401-009-0*) Cornell Food.

Macroeconomic Adjustment & the Poor: Toward a Research Policy. Grant M. Scobie. (Monographs). (Illus.). 121p. (C). 1989. pap. text 12.00 (*1-56401-001-5*) Cornell Food.

Macroeconomic Adjustment & the Poor in Madagascar: A CGE Analysis. Paul A. Dorosh. (Working Papers: No. 61). 33p. (C). 1994. pap. 7.00 (*1-56401-161-5*) Cornell Food.

Macroeconomic Analysis: An Intermediate Text. 2nd ed. David P. Cobham. LC 97-51476. 1998. pap. write for info. (*0-582-27452-4*) Longman.

Macroeconomic Analysis: An Introduction to Comparative Statics & Dynamics. Thomas F. Dernburg & Judith D. Dernburg. LC 75-76072. 302p. reprint ed. pap. 93.70 (*0-608-15177-7*, 205607900046) Bks Demand.

Macroeconomic Analysis & the Developing Countries, 1970-1990. Ian M. Little. LC 93-19069. 1993. pap. 9.95 (*1-55815-257-1*) ICS Pr.

Macroeconomic Analysis of Environmental Policy. E. C. van Ierland. (Developments in Environmental Economics Ser.: Vol. 2). 298p. 1992. 163.75 (*0-444-89998-7*) Elsevier.

Macroeconomic Conditions & Trade Liberalization. Ed. by Adolfo Canitrot & Silvia Junco. 224p. 1993. 14.50 (*0-940602-66-0*) IADB.

Macroeconomic Consequences of Energy Supply Shocks in Ukraine. H. Quan Chu & Wafik Grais. LC 94-16199. (Studies of Economies in Transformation: No. 12). 54p. 1994. pap. 22.00 (*0-8213-2837-9*) World Bank.

Macroeconomic Consequences of Farm Support Policies. Ed. by Andrew B. Stoeckel et al. LC 89-1559. (Duke Press Policy Studies). 432p. 1989. text 64.95 (*0-8223-0911-4*); pap. text 23.95 (*0-8223-0928-9*) Duke.

Macroeconomic Consequences of the 1986-87 Boom in the Mexican Stock Exchange & Treasury Bill Markets. Gonzalo Castaneda. LC 91-28444. (Developing Economies of the Third World Ser.). 136p. 1991. text 10.00 (*0-8153-0734-9*) Garland.

Macroeconomic Considerations in the Choice of an Agriculture Policy: A Study into Sectoral Independence with Reference to India. Ser Vaas Storm. 400p. 1993. 77.95 (*1-85628-616-9*, Pub. by Avebry) Ashgate Pub Co.

Macroeconomic Crises, Politics, & Growth in Brazil, 1964-90. Donald V. Coes. LC 94-31420. (World Bank Comparative Macroeconomic Studies). 256p. 1995. pap. 22.00 (*0-8213-2299-0*, 12299) World Bank.

Macroeconomic Debate: Models of the Closed & Open Economy. 2nd ed. Brian Hillier. 256p. (C). 1991. pap. text 34.95 (*0-631-17758-2*) Blackwell Pubs.

Macroeconomic Decision Making. 4th ed. Michael G. Rukstad. (C). Date not set. pap. text, teacher ed. 29.75 (*0-03-012099-3*) Harcourt Coll Pubs.

Macroeconomic Decision Making. 4th ed. Michael G. Rukstad. (C). 1999. pap. text 44.00 (*0-03-007334-0*, Pub. by Harcourt Coll Pubs) Harcourt.

Macroeconomic Decision Making in the World Economy. 3rd ed. Michael G. Rukstad. 720p. (C). 1992. pap. text 81.00 (*0-03-074733-3*) Dryden Pr.

Macroeconomic Decision Making in the World Economy. 3rd ed. Michael G. Rukstad. 481p. (C). 1993. pap. text, teacher ed. 27.50 (*0-03-076346-0*) Dryden Pr.

Macroeconomic Dimensions of Public Finance: Essays in Honour of Vito Tanzi. Ed. by Mario I. Blejer & Teresa M. Ter-Minassian. LC 95-497779. (Studies in the Modern World Economy: Vol. 5). 528p. (C). 1997. 115.00 (*0-415-14111-7*) Routledge.

Macroeconomic Diplomacy in the 1980's: Domestic Politics & International Conflict among the United States, Japan & Europe. C. Randall Henning. (Atlantic Papers: No. 65). 80p. 1987. lib. bdg. 16.95 (*0-7099-3794-6*, Pub. by C Helm) Routldge.

Macroeconomic Dynamics. Keizo Nagatani. LC 80-28883. (Illus.). 272p. 1981. text 85.00 (*0-521-23515-4*) Cambridge U Pr.

Macroeconomic Dynamics: An Essay in Circulation Analysis. Bernard Lonergan. Ed. by Frederick G. Lawerence et al. 368p. 1999. text 60.00 (*0-8020-4384-4*) U of Toronto Pr.

Macroeconomic Dynamics: An Essay in Circulation Analysis. Bernard Lonergan. Ed. by Frederick G. Lawrence et al. 368p. 1999. pap. text 21.95 (*0-8020-8195-9*) U of Toronto Pr.

Macroeconomic Effects & Diffusion of Alternative Technologies Within a Social Accounting Matrix: The Case of Indonesia. Haider A. Khan & Erik Thorbecke. 215p. 1988. text 46.95 (*0-566-05681-X*, Pub. by Avebry) Ashgate Pub Co.

Macroeconomic Effects of the Loma Prieta Earthquake. 48p. 1991. 7.00 (*0-317-05676-X*, P91001EQK) Assn Bay Area.

Macroeconomic Effects of War Finance in the United States: Taxes, Inflation & Deficit Finance. rev. ed. Lee E. Ohanian. LC 98-39521. (Financial Sector of the American Economy Ser.). (Illus.). 144p. 1998. 42.00 (*0-8153-3040-5*) Garland.

Macroeconomic Environment. 4th ed. (C). 1995. 24.16 (*0-8087-2515-7*) Pearson Custom.

Macroeconomic Environment & Health: With Case Studies for Countries in Greatest Need. (ENG & FRE.). x, 351p. 1993. pap. text 22.50 (*0-614-08024-X*, 1930042) World Health.

Macroeconomic Fluctuations & Individual Behaviour: The Implications of Real & Nominal Inertia. Hans Van Ees. 206p. 1991. text 82.95 (*1-85628-229-5*, Pub. by Avebry) Ashgate Pub Co.

Macroeconomic Forecasting A Sociological Appraisal. Robert Evans. LC 98-53742. 1999. write for info. (*0-415-20694-4*) Routledge.

Macroeconomic Information & Financial Trading. Robert I. Webb. (Advances in Theoretical & Applied Economics Ser.). (Illus.). 216p. 1994. 52.95 (*1-55786-325-3*) Blackwell Pubs.

***Macroeconomic Instability & Coordination: Selected Essays of Axel Leijonhufvud.** Axel Leijonhufvud. LC 00-34121. (Economists of the Twentieth Century Ser.). 2000. write for info. (*1-85278-967-0*) E Elgar.

Macroeconomic Instability in Post-Communist Countries. Jacek Rostowski. (Illus.). 396p. 1998. text 90.00 (*0-19-829048-9*) OUP.

Macroeconomic Interactions Between North & South. Ed. by David Currie & David Vines. 304p. 1988. text 69.95 (*0-521-36121-4*) Cambridge U Pr.

Macroeconomic Issues & Policies: The Case for Bangladesh. Akhtar Hossain. LC 95-51258. 344p. (C). 1996. 38.00 (*0-8039-9279-3*) Sage.

Macroeconomic Issues Facing ASEAN Countries. John Hicklin et al. LC 97-25968. 1997. write for info. (*1-55775-637-6*) Intl Monetary.

Macroeconomic Issues from a Keynesian Perspective Vol. 2: Selected Essays of A. P. Thirlwall, Vol. 2. A. P. Thirlwall. LC 96-54834. (Economists of the Twentieth Century Ser.). 416p. (C). 1997. text 110.00 (*1-85898-605-2*) E Elgar.

Macroeconomic Issues Today: Alternative Approaches. 5th ed. Robert B. Carson. 211p. (C). 1990. teacher ed. write for info. (*0-318-68118-8*) St Martin.

Macroeconomic Issues Today: Alternative Approaches. 6th ed. Robert B. Carson et al. LC 98-29532. 208p. 1999. pap. text 24.95 (*0-7656-0363-2*) M E Sharpe.

Macroeconomic Linkage: Savings, Exchange Rates, & Capital Flows. Ed. by Takatoshi Ito & Anne O. Krueger. LC 93-30295. (National Bureau of Economic Research East Asia Seminar on Economics Ser.: Vol. 3). 416p. 1994. 75.00 (*0-226-38669-4*) U Ch Pr.

Macroeconomic Management. Ed. by Soumitra Sharma. LC 94-44699. 1995. text 85.00 (*0-312-12608-5*) St Martin.

Macroeconomic Management & Fiscal Decentralization. Ed. by Jayanta Roy. (EDI Seminar Ser.). 264p. 1996. pap. 22.00 (*0-8213-3409-3*, 13409) World Bank.

Macroeconomic Management in China: Proceedings of a Conference in Dalian, June 1993. Ed. by Peter Harrold et al. LC 93-39544. (Discussion Paper Ser.: No. 222). 190p. 1994. pap. 22.00 (*0-8213-2722-4*, 12722) World Bank.

Macroeconomic Management under the Economic Reform. Ruifang Wang. 59.95 (*1-85972-563-5*) Ashgate Pub Co.

Macroeconomic Modelling. S. G. Hall & S. G. Henry. (Contributions to Economic Analysis Ser.: No. 172). 416p. 1988. 153.25 (*0-444-70429-9*, North Holland) Elsevier.

Macroeconomic Modelling & Policy Implications: In Honour of Perti Kukkonen. Ed. by Seppo Honkapohja & Mikael Ingberg. LC 93-18103. (Contributions to Economic Analysis Ser.: Vol. 216). 218p. 1993. 93.00 (*0-444-89626-0*, North Holland) Elsevier.

Macroeconomic Modelling in a Changing World: Expectations & the Supply Side. Ed. by Stephen Hall. LC 96-22708. 324p. 1997. 115.00 (*0-471-95791-7*) Wiley.

Macroeconomic Models & Controversies. Giuseppe Chirichiello. LC 93-44299. 1994. text 75.00 (*0-312-12097-4*) St Martin.

Macroeconomic Models for Adjustment in Developing Countries. Ed. by Mohsin S. Khan et al. vii, 323p. (Orig.). 1991. pap. 20.00 (*1-55775-219-2*) Intl Monetary.

Macroeconomic Performance, Stabilization & Adjustment: The Experience of Bangladesh in the 1980s. Sultan H. Rahman. (C). 1992. 12.00 (*81-85182-74-4*, Pub. by Indus Pub) S Asia.

Macroeconomic Policies & Structural Reform. OECD Staff. 344p. 1996. pap. 42.00 (*92-64-15326-8*, Pub. by Org for Econ) OECD.

Macroeconomic Policies & the Development of Markets in Transition Economies. Fabrizio Coricelli. 176p. (C). 1998. pap. text 16.95 (*963-9116-08-4*) Ctrl Europ Univ.

Macroeconomic Policies & the Development of Markets in Transition Economies. Fabrizio Coricelli. (Illus.). 176p. (C). 1998. 39.95 (*963-9116-05-X*) Ctrl Europ Univ.

Macroeconomic Policies, Crises, & Long-Run Growth: The Case of Indonesia, 1965-90. Wing T. Woo et al. LC 93-10909. (Comparative Macroeconomic Studies). 228p. 1994. pap. 22.00 (*0-8213-2212-5*, 12212) World Bank.

Macroeconomic Policies in an Interdependent World. Ed. by Ralph C. Bryant et al. vi, 420p. 1989. pap. 17.50 (*1-55775-111-0*) Intl Monetary.

M

Macroeconomic Policy. Robert J. Barro. (Illus.). 384p. 1990. 55.50 (*0-674-54080-8*) HUP.

Macroeconomic Policy. Barry Bosworth et al. (Seminar Ser.). 59p. 1990. 12.00 (*0-944826-20-2*) Economic Policy Inst.

Macroeconomic Policy. Alan Marin. 224p. (C). (gr. 13). 1992. text 74.95 (*0-415-08379-6*, A9691) Routledge.

Macroeconomic Policy after the Conservative Era: Studies in Investment, Saving & Finance. Ed. by Gerald A. Epstein & Herbert M. Gintis. 483p. (C). 1996. text 69.95 (*0-521-46290-8*) Cambridge U Pr.

Macroeconomic Policy & Adjustment in Korea, 1970-1990. Stephan Haggard et al. LC 94-10736. (Harvard Studies in International Development). 331p. 1994. text 30.00 (*0-674-54085-9*, HAGMAC) HUP.

Macroeconomic Policy & Agricultural Development Concepts & Case Studies of Egypt, Morocco & Jordan. Maury E. Bredahl. (Illus.). 70p. (C). 1998. reprint ed. pap. text 20.00 (*0-7881-4888-5*) DIANE Pub.

Macroeconomic Policy & Public Choice. David Kiefer. LC 96-50899. (Illus.). 251p. 1996. 99.95 (*3-540-61757-4*) Spr-Verlag.

Macroeconomic Policy & Public Choice. David Kiefer. LC 98-48120. 1998. pap. text, student ed. 39.95 (*3-540-64872-0*) Spr-Verlag.

***Macroeconomic Policy & the Exchange Rate.** Ed. by Julio De Brun & Rolf Luders. LC 99-32276. (Illus.). xii, 292p. 1999. pap. 19.95 (*0-9656930-5-8*) Intl Ctr Economic.

Macroeconomic Policy & the Future of Capitalism: The Revenge of the Rentiers & the Threat to Prosperity. John N. Smithin. LC 95-51454. 160p. 1996. 85.00 (*1-85278-731-7*) E Elgar.

Macroeconomic Policy & the Future of Capitalism: The Revenge of the Rentiers & the Threat to Prosperity. John N. Smithin. LC 95-51454. 160p. 1997. pap. 25.00 (*1-85278-745-7*) E Elgar.

Macroeconomic Policy as Implicit Industrial Policy: Its Industry & Enterprise Effects. John R. Norsworthy & Diana H. Tsai. LC 97-38536. 280p. 1997. 126.50 (*0-7923-8075-4*) Kluwer Academic.

Macroeconomic Policy Coordination in Europe: The ERM & Monetary Union. Ray Barrell & John Whitley. 288p. 1993. pap. 24.95 (*0-8039-8765-X*) Sage.

Macroeconomic Policy Coordination in Europe: The ERM & Monetary Union. Ed. by Ray Barrell & John Whitley. 304p. (C). 1993. text 69.95 (*0-8039-8764-1*) Sage.

Macroeconomic Policy, Credibility & Politics, Vol. 38. Torsten Persson. (Fundamentals of Pure & Applied Economics Ser.). 187p. 1990. pap. text 71.00 (*3-7186-5029-0*) Gordon & Breach.

Macroeconomic Policy Games. A. Riedl & G. Winckler. (Studies in Empirical Economics). (Illus.). xii, 123p. 1996. 70.00 (*3-7908-0857-1*) Spr-Verlag.

Macroeconomic Policy in Britain, 1974-1987. Andrew Britton. (NIESR Economic & Social Studies: No. 34). (Illus.). 400p. (C). 1991. 65.00 (*0-521-41004-5*) Cambridge U Pr.

Macroeconomic Policy in Britain, 1974-1987. Andrew Britton. (National Institute of Economic & Social Research Occasional Papers: No. 34). (Illus.). 384p. (C). 1994. pap. text 24.95 (*0-521-47833-2*) Cambridge U Pr.

Macroeconomic Policy in Open Economies, 5. Michele Fratianni et al. LC 96-18228. (Handbook of Comparative Economic Policies Ser.). 600p. 1997. lib. bdg. 135.00 (*0-313-28989-1*) Greenwood.

Macroeconomic Policy Modelling for Developing Countries. Victor Murinde. 462p. 1993. 96.95 (*1-85628-448-4*, Pub. by Avebry) Ashgate Pub Co.

Macroeconomic Policy Reforms, Poverty, & Nutrition: Analytical Methodologies. Per Pinstrup-Andersen. (Monographs). (C). 1990. pap. text 12.00 (*1-56401-003-1*) Cornell Food.

Macroeconomic Position of Botswana. Bertil Oden. (Research Report Ser.: No. 60). 84p. 1981. write for info. (*91-7106-193-2*, Pub. by Nordic Africa) Transaction Pubs.

Macroeconomic Principles. Fred Abraham. 136p. (C). 1995. pap. text, per. 17.95 (*0-7872-1395-0*) Kendall-Hunt.

***Macroeconomic Principles Coursebook '99.** David O. Whitten. (Illus.). 195p. (C). 1999. ring bd. 25.00 (*1-928841-00-7*) Goosedown Pr.

M

Macroeconomic Problems of Transformation: Stabilization Policies & Economic Restructuring. Ed. by Hansjorg Herr et al. LC 94-5497. 328p. 1994. 100.00 (*1-85898-060-7*) E Elgar.

Macroeconomic Prospects for a Small Oil Exporting Country. Ed. by Olav Bjerkholt & E. Offederal. 1985. lib. bdg. 160.00 (*90-247-3183-6*) Kluwer Academic.

Macroeconomic Reform in China: Laying the Foundation for a Socialist Economy. Lou Jiwei. LC 97-30276. (Discussion Paper Ser.: No. 374). 165p. 1997. pap. 22.00 (*0-8213-4018-2*, 14018) World Bank.

Macroeconomic Reform Policies in the Disadvantaged Economies Transition. 120p. pap. 17.50 (*92-1-119261-7*) UN.

Macroeconomic Reforms in Indo-China: Lessons from the Development Experiences of Indonesia, Malaysia & Singapore. Economic & Social Commission for Asia & the Pacific Staff. 119p. 1995. pap. text 20.00 (*0-614-26944-X*) UN.

Macroeconomic Reforms in the Economies in Transition. LC 95-947886. (Development Papers: No. 18). 103p. 25.00 (*92-1-119696-5*) UN.

Macroeconomic Stabilization in Transition Economies. Mario I. Blejer & Marko Skreb. LC 96-46103. 347p. 1997. text 47.95 (*0-521-58177-X*) Cambridge U Pr.

Macroeconomic Strategy for the 1990's: Getting the Long Run Right. Robert A. Levine & Peter J. Estan. LC 93-6415. 1993. pap. 15.00 (*0-8330-1449-8*, MR-325-RC) Rand Corp.

Macroeconomic Theory. 2nd ed. Charles H. Sargent. 1987. pap. text, student ed. 25.00 (*0-12-619752-0*) Acad Pr.

Macroeconomic Theory. 2nd ed. Thomas J. Sargent. (Economic Theory, Econometrics & Mathematical Economics Ser.). 510p. 1987. text 69.95 (*0-12-619751-2*) Acad Pr.

Macroeconomic Theory. 5th rev. ed. M. L. Jhingan. 726p. 1990. text 40.00 (*81-220-0108-4*, Pub. by Konark Pubs Pvt Ltd) Advent Bks Div.

Macroeconomic Theory. 6th enl. rev. ed. M. L. Jhingan. 1992. pap. 20.00 (*81-220-0242-0*, Pub. by Konark Pubs Pvt Ltd) Advent Bks Div.

Macroeconomic Theory: A Mathematical Introduction. Paul Burrows & Theodore Hitiris. LC 73-2779. 224p. reprint ed. pap. 69.50 (*0-608-15785-6*, 203102300073) Bks Demand.

Macroeconomic Theory: A Textbook on Macroeconomic Knowledge & Analysis. Edmond Malinvaud. LC 98-15139. (Advanced Textbooks in Economics). 1998. write for info. (*0-444-82862-1*); pap. 95.00 (*0-444-82863-X*) Elsevier.

Macroeconomic Theory: Diversity & Convergence. Ed. by Gary Mongiovi & Christof Ruhl. 272p. 1993. 95.00 (*1-85278-368-0*) E Elgar.

Macroeconomic Theory & Policy Vol. 2: The Selected Essays of Richard G. Lipsey, Vol. 2. Richard G. Lipsey. LC 96-35916. (Economists of the Twentieth Century Ser.). 480p. 1997. 110.00 (*1-85278-127-0*) E Elgar.

Macroeconomic Theory & Stabilization Policy. Willem H. Buiter. LC 89-5010. 384p. 1989. text 65.00 (*0-472-10138-2*, 10138) U of Mich Pr.

Macroeconomic Theory & Stabilization Policy. Andrew Stevenson et al. 1988. pap. 79.50 (*0-389-20782-9*, N8341) B&N Imports.

Macroeconomic Theory of Workable Competition. Charles E. Ferguson. LC 64-11624. 237p. reprint ed. 73.50 (*0-8357-9111-4*, 201790200010) Bks Demand.

Macroeconomic Thought see Methodology of Macroeconomic Thought: A Conceptual Analysis of Schools of Thought in Economics

Macroeconomic Uncertainty: International Risks & Opportunities for the Corporation. Clas G. Wihlborg & Lars Oxelheim. LC 87-8333. 268p. 1988. pap. 120.00 (*0-471-92013-4*) Wiley.

Macroeconomic Wall Street Journal. 3rd ed. Colander. 560p. 1997. pap. 74.06 (*0-256-26612-3*) McGraw.

***Macroeconomics.** 1999. teacher ed. write for info. (*0-321-40428-9*) Addison-Wesley.

Macroeconomics. (Quick Study Academic Ser.). 4p. pap. 2.95 (*1-57222-052-X*) Barcharts.

Macroeconomics. (C). 2001. pap. text 0.00 (*0-321-03135-0*, Celebration) Addson-Wesley Educ.

Macroeconomics. John M. Barron et al. (Illus.). 715p. (C). 1989. 77.00 (*0-201-13623-6*) Addison-Wesley.

Macroeconomics. Oliver J. Blanchard. 596p. (C). 1996. text 82.00 (*0-13-148099-5*) P-H.

Macroeconomics, 2 vols. Boyes. (C). Date not set. text, teacher ed., suppl. ed. 54.76 (*0-395-69064-1*) HM.

Macroeconomics. Ralph T. Byrns & Gerald W. Stone, Jr. (C). 1997. text 49.33 (*0-673-46567-5*) Addson-Wesley Educ.

Macroeconomics. Robert D. Cherry. LC 79-3130. (Economics Ser.). 1980. text. write for info. (*0-201-00911-0*) Addison-Wesley.

Macroeconomics. Delong. 2001. 60.25 (*0-07-232848-7*) McGraw.

Macroeconomics. Evans. 2000. 62.50 (*0-07-234578-0*) McGraw.

Macroeconomics. Lauren Feinstone & Steven E. Landsburg. LC 96-45453. 640p. (C). 1996. 83.44 (*0-07-020496-9*) McGraw.

Macroeconomics. John Kenneth Galbraith. LC 93-78636. (C). 1993. text 75.16 (*0-395-52241-2*) HM.

Macroeconomics. Paul R. Gregory & Roy J. Ruffin. (C). 1997. 47.00 (*0-673-99043-5*) Addson-Wesley Educ.

Macroeconomics. Steven E. Landsburg & Lauren Feinstone. (C). 1996. pap. text, student ed. 23.44 (*0-07-020498-5*) McGraw.

Macroeconomics. Richard G. Lipsey. 592p. (C). 1993. pap. 51.33 (*0-06-501023-X*) Addson-Wesley Educ.

Macroeconomics. N. Gregory Mankiw. (C). 1997. pap. text, teacher ed. 23.75 (*0-03-020189-6*) Harcourt Coll Pubs.

Macroeconomics. Authur O'Sullivan & Steven M. Sheffrin. LC 97-24092. 384p. 1997. pap. text 63.00 (*0-13-742842-1*) P-H.

Macroeconomics. Osullivan & Sheffrin. 1997. pap. text, student ed. 21.33 (*0-13-855172-3*) P-H.

Macroeconomics. Ed. by Prabhat Patnaik. (Oxford in India Readings Ser.; Themes in Economics). (Illus.). 256p. (C). 1995. 24.00 (*0-19-563534-5*) OUP.

Macroeconomics. Jack Rudman. (Advanced Placement Test (AP) Ser.: Vol. AP-6). 1997. pap. 23.95 (*0-8373-6206-7*) Nat Learn.

Macroeconomics. Roy J. Ruffin & Paul R. Gregory. (C). 1997. pap. text, student ed. 25.33 (*0-673-46588-8*) Addson-Wesley Educ.

Macroeconomics. Jae K. Shim & Joel G. Siegel. LC 91-3525. (Barron's EZ-101 Study Keys Ser.). 144p. (C). 1993. pap. 6.95 (*0-8120-4619-6*) Barron.

Macroeconomics. Gary Smith. (Illus.). 579p. (C). 1985. teacher ed. 3.20 (*0-7167-1709-3*) W H Freeman.

Macroeconomics. Stanlake. 1985. pap. text. write for info. (*0-582-35446-3*, Pub. by Addison-Wesley) Longman.

Macroeconomics. Taylor. (C). 1995. pap. text, student ed. 17.56 (*0-395-72199-7*) HM.

Macroeconomics. Tim Tregarthen. 527p. 1995. pap. text 40.60 (*1-57259-095-5*) Worth.

Macroeconomics. Tim Tregarthen. 208p. 1996. pap. text, student ed. 13.20 (*1-57259-045-9*) Worth.

Macroeconomics. Irvin B. Tucker. LC 96-20560. 1997. 43.00 (*0-314-09242-0*) West Pub.

Macroeconomics. Ed. by Tuerck. (C). 1999. pap. text, student ed. write for info. (*0-321-01445-6*) Addson-Wesley Educ.

Macroeconomics. Kenneth E. Weiher. Date not set. pap. text, teacher ed. write for info. (*0-314-96665-X*) West Pub.

Macroeconomics. Weiler. (C). 1990. pap. 19.00 (*0-06-047002-X*, Perennial) HarperTrade.

Macroeconomics. David Demery et al. LC 83-710. (Surveys in Economics Ser.). 288p. reprint ed. pap. 89.30 (*0-7837-1589-7*, 204188100024) Bks Demand.

Macroeconomics. Ed. by Prabhat Patnaik. (Oxford in India Readings Ser.). (Illus.). 254p. 1997. reprint ed. pap. text 10.95 (*0-19-564164-7*) OUP.

***Macroeconomics.** 2nd ed. (C). 2000. text. write for info. (*0-13-017327-4*); text. write for info. (*0-13-030469-7*) P-H.

***Macroeconomics.** 2nd ed. 2000. teacher ed. write for info. (*0-13-017268-5*) P-H.

***Macroeconomics.** 2nd ed. Olivier Blanchard. LC 99-49531. (Illus.). 548p. 1999. 90.00 (*0-13-013306-X*) P-H.

Macroeconomics, 2 vols. 2nd ed. Boyes. LC 93-78702. (C). 1993. pap. text 54.76 (*0-395-67542-1*) HM.

Macroeconomics, 2 vols. 2nd ed. Boyes. (C). 1993. pap. text, student ed. 16.76 (*0-395-67544-8*) HM.

Macroeconomics. 2nd ed. David C. Colander. LC 94-32398. (Series in Economics). 1994. write for info. (*0-256-16820-2*, Irwn McGrw-H) McGrw-H Hghr Educ.

Macroeconomics. 2nd ed. Mankiw & Scarth. 1994. text 68.95 (*1-57259-001-7*) Worth.

Macroeconomics. 2nd ed. Mcconnell. 1998. 47.00 (*0-07-229579-1*) McGraw.

Macroeconomics. 2nd ed. Michael Parkin. LC 92-15486. 624p. (C). 1993. pap. text 40.95 (*0-201-54699-X*) Addison-Wesley.

Macroeconomics. 2nd ed. Michael Parkin. LC 93-46052. 640p. (C). 1994. text 47.00 (*0-201-50033-7*) Addison-Wesley.

Macroeconomics. 2nd ed. Michael Parkin. (C). 1995. pap. text 25.33 (*0-201-62876-7*); pap. text 54.33 (*0-201-76574-8*) Addison-Wesley.

Macroeconomics. 2nd ed. Michael Parkin & Robin Bade. 718p. (C). 1992. text 56.20 (*0-13-544255-9*) P-H.

Macroeconomics. 2nd ed. Richard Startz. 1981. pap. text. write for info. (*0-07-017756-2*) McGraw.

Macroeconomics, 2 vols. 2nd ed. Taylor. (C). 1998. pap. text, student ed. 17.56 (*0-395-87455-6*) HM.

Macroeconomics. 2nd ed. Allen R. Thompson. LC 87-916. (C). 1988. pap. text 38.75 (*0-201-09684-6*) Addison-Wesley.

Macroeconomics. 2nd ed. Tregarthen. write for info. (*1-57259-885-9*) St Martin.

Macroeconomics. 2nd ed. Tregarthen. 2000. pap. text, student ed. 22.95 (*1-57259-887-5*) St Martin.

Macroeconomics. 2nd ed. Tregarthen. LC 99-42154. 2000. pap. write for info. (*1-57259-419-5*) Worth.

Macroeconomics. 2nd rev. ed. Andrew Abel & Ben S. Bernanke. Ed. by Beth Toland. (C). 1996. text 45.00 (*0-201-84788-4*) Addison-Wesley.

Macroeconomics. 3rd ed. Abel. 672p. (C). 1997. text. write for info. (*0-201-33906-4*) Addison-Wesley.

Macroeconomics. 3rd ed. Andrew Abel. (C). 1997. text. write for info. (*0-201-49897-9*) Addison-Wesley.

Macroeconomics. 3rd ed. Arnold. 1996. pap., student ed. 17.75 (*0-314-08937-3*) West Pub.

***Macroeconomics.** 3rd ed. Ben S. Bernanke. 1998. 92.00 (*0-201-44132-2*) Addison-Wesley.

Macroeconomics, 3 vols. 3rd ed. Boyes. LC 95-76929. (C). 1995. pap. text 29.16 (*0-395-74433-4*) HM.

Macroeconomics, 3 vols. 3rd ed. Boyes. (C). 1995. pap. text, student ed. 16.76 (*0-395-74435-0*) HM.

Macroeconomics, 3 vols. 3rd ed. Boyes. (C). 1996. pap. 13.96 (*0-395-78007-1*) HM.

Macroeconomics, 3 vols. 3rd ed. Martin Bronfenbrenner et al. (C). 1990. pap. text 3.96 (*0-395-52910-7*); pap. text, teacher ed. 5.16 (*0-395-52909-3*) HM.

Macroeconomics, 3 vols. 3rd ed. Martin Bronfenbrenner et al. (C). 1990. trans. 149.56 (*0-395-52911-5*) HM.

Macroeconomics. 3rd ed. Colander. 1997. pap. 20.31 (*0-07-109300-1*) McGraw.

Macroeconomics. 3rd ed. David C. Colander. LC 97-25686. 1997. write for info. (*0-07-115226-1*) McGraw.

Macroeconomics. 3rd ed. David C. Colander. LC 97-25681. 560p. 1997. pap. 60.94 (*0-256-17266-8*) McGraw.

Macroeconomics. 3rd ed. Rudiger Dornbusch & Stanley Fischer. 1984. pap. text. write for info. (*0-07-017771-6*) McGraw.

Macroeconomics. 3rd ed. David N. Hyman. LC 93-39680. 1993. write for info. (*0-256-15694-8*, Irwn McGrw-H) McGrw-H Hghr Educ.

Macroeconomics. 3rd ed. N. Gregory Mankiw. LC 96-60597. 532p. 1996. text 51.80 (*1-57259-141-2*) Worth.

Macroeconomics. 3rd ed. N. Gregory Mankiw. 339p. 1996. pap. text, student ed. 13.20 (*1-57259-233-8*) Worth.

Macroeconomics. 3rd ed. Michael Parkin. LC 95-690. 560p. (C). 1995. pap. text 70.00 (*0-201-60982-7*) Addison-Wesley.

Macroeconomics. 3rd ed. Michael Parkin. 1996. pap. text, student ed. 66.56 (*0-201-87873-9*) Addison-Wesley.

Macroeconomics. 3rd ed. Michael Parkin. (C). 1996. pap. text. write for info. (*0-201-88058-X*); pap. text, student ed. 26.25 (*0-201-60984-3*) Addison-Wesley.

Macroeconomics. 3rd ed. Michael Parkin. 608p. (C). 1996. pap. text. write for info. (*0-201-87428-8*); pap. text 45.00 (*0-201-30346-9*) Addison-Wesley.

Macroeconomics. 3rd ed. Michael Parkin. (C). 1997. pap. text, student ed. 25.00 (*0-201-30932-7*) Addison-Wesley.

Macroeconomics. 3rd ed. Michael Parkin. (C). 1997. pap. text, student ed. write for info. (*0-201-30584-4*) Addison-Wesley.

Macroeconomics. 3rd ed. Richard Startz. 1984. pap. text. write for info. (*0-07-017772-4*) McGraw.

Macroeconomics. 3rd ed. Trieff. 1997. pap. 17.19 (*0-256-17267-6*) McGraw.

Macroeconomics. 3rd rev. ed. Michael Parkin. LC 96-36836. 608p. (C). 1996. pap. text 75.00 (*0-201-97696-X*) Addison-Wesley.

***Macroeconomics.** 4th ed. Andrew B. Abel. (C). 2001. text 86.00 (*0-201-44133-0*) Addison-Wesley.

Macroeconomics. 4th ed. Roger A. Arnold. LC 97-37734. (HD - Intermediate Macroeconomics Ser.). (C). 1997. mass mkt. 67.95 (*0-538-88045-7*); mass mkt. 19.95 (*0-538-88052-X*) S-W Pub.

Macroeconomics. 4th ed. Jon L. Boyes. LC 98-71995. 1998. pap. text 44.97 (*0-395-90806-X*) HM.

Macroeconomics. 4th ed. Colander. 2000. 47.74 (*0-07-231795-7*) McGraw.

Macroeconomics. 4th ed. David N. Hyman. LC 96-210616. 544p. (C). 1996. text 46.75 (*0-256-16157-7*, Irwn McGrw-H) McGrw-H Hghr Educ.

Macroeconomics. 4th ed. Mankiw. LC 99-22254. 1999. text. write for info. (*1-57259-644-9*) Worth.

***Macroeconomics.** 4th ed. Mankiw. 1999. pap. text, student ed. 22.95 (*1-57259-645-7*) Worth.

***Macroeconomics.** 4th ed. Cohen K. Parkin. 256p. 2000. pap., student ed. 19.95 (*0-201-61389-1*) Addison-Wesley.

Macroeconomics. 4th ed. Michael Parkin. (C). 1997. pap. text 69.00 (*0-201-33626-X*) Addison-Wesley.

Macroeconomics. 4th ed. Michael Parkin. LC 97-11786. (Illus.). 512p. (C). 1997. pap. text 75.00 (*0-201-31691-9*) Addison-Wesley.

Macroeconomics. 4th ed. Michael Parkin. 528p. (C). 1998. pap. text. write for info. (*0-201-32264-1*) Addison-Wesley.

Macroeconomics. 4th ed. Stephen L. Slavin. 512p. (C). 1995. text 39.50 (*0-256-17174-2*, Irwn McGrw-H) McGrw-H Hghr Educ.

Macroeconomics. 4th ed. G. F. Stanlake. 1989. pap. text. write for info. (*0-582-04013-2*, Pub. by Addison-Wesley) Longman.

***Macroeconomics.** 5th ed. 320p. (C). 1999. pap. text 24.00 (*0-201-65712-0*) Addison-Wesley.

***Macroeconomics.** 5th ed. 336p. (C). 1999. text 25.20 (*0-201-63789-8*) S&S Trade.

***Macroeconomics.** 5th ed. 1p. (C). 1999. text 27.40 (*0-201-65726-0*) S&S Trade.

***Macroeconomics.** 5th ed. Roger A. Arnold. LC 00-36552. 2000. write for info. (*0-324-01747-2*) Sth-Wstrn College.

Macroeconomics. 5th ed. Robert J. Barro. LC 97-26136. 150p. 1997. 65.00 (*0-262-02436-5*) MIT Pr.

***Macroeconomics.** 5th ed. Michael Parkin. 352p. (C). 1999. pap. text, student ed. 26.40 (*0-201-63787-1*) Addison-Wesley.

Macroeconomics 5th ed. Michael Parkin. LC 98-55284. 568p. 2000. pap. 67.00 (*0-201-47386-0*) Addison-Wesley.

Macroeconomics. 5th ed. Stephen L. Slavin. LC 98-16408. 1998. 33.75 (*0-256-26327-2*, Irwn Prfssnl) McGraw-Hill Prof.

Macroeconomics. 6th ed. Adams. (C). 1998. pap. text, student ed. write for info. (*0-13-011236-4*) P-H.

Macroeconomics. 6th ed. Ralph T. Byrns & Gerald Stone. 496p. (C). 1997. pap. text 70.00 (*0-673-99329-9*) Addson-Wesley Educ.

Macroeconomics. 6th ed. Ralph T. Byrns & Gerald W. Stone. (C). 1995. pap. text, student ed. 24.38 (*0-673-99345-0*) Addson-Wesley Educ.

Macroeconomics. 6th ed. Rudiger Dornbusch & Stanley Fischer. LC 93-20536. (C). 1993. text 63.25 (*0-07-017844-5*) McGraw.

Macroeconomics. 6th ed. Robert Ekelund. LC 99-51527. (C). 1999. text 72.00 (*0-201-68028-9*) Addison-Wesley.

Macroeconomics. 6th ed. Robert J. Gordon. (C). 1993. pap. text, student ed. 29.06 (*0-673-52192-3*) Addson-Wesley Educ.

Macroeconomics. 6th ed. Slavin. 2001. 26.00 (*0-07-237412-8*) McGraw.

Macroeconomics. 6th ed. Richard Startz. (C). 1994. pap. text, student ed. 21.25 (*0-07-017846-1*) McGraw.

Macroeconomics. 6th ed. Swan. (C). 1994. pap. text, student ed. 32.00 (*0-03-098607-9*) Harcourt Coll Pubs.

Macroeconomics. 7th ed. Baumol. (C). 1997. pap. 66.50 (*0-03-023163-9*) Harcourt.

Macroeconomics. 7th ed. Baumol. 1997. 256.00 (*0-03-011728-3*, Pub. by Harcourt Coll Pubs) Harcourt.

Macroeconomics. 7th ed. Baumol. (C). 1997. pap. text, student ed. 29.50 (*0-03-011724-0*, Pub. by Harcourt Coll Pubs) Harcourt.

Macroeconomics. 7th ed. Byrns & Stone. 540p. (C). 2001. pap. text. write for info. (*0-321-03067-2*) Addison-Wesley.

Macroeconomics. 7th ed. Edwin G. Dolan & David E. Lindsey. LC 93-71249. 464p. (C). 1993. pap. text 51.00 (*0-03-097570-0*) Dryden Pr.

Macroeconomics. 7th ed. Rudiger Dornbusch et al. LC 97-30777. 576p. (C). 1997. 80.94 (*0-07-017985-9*) McGraw.

Macroeconomics. 7th ed. Robert J. Gordon. (C). 1998. text. write for info. (*0-201-31656-0*) Addison-Wesley.

Macroeconomics. 7th ed. Ed. by Robert J. Gordon. (C). 1998. pap. text, student ed. write for info. (*0-321-01439-1*) Addson-Wesley Educ.

Macroeconomics. 7th ed. Robert J. Gordon. 384p. (C). 1998. pap. text, student ed. 21.56 (*0-321-01762-5*) Addson-Wesley Educ.

Macroeconomics. 7th ed. RobertJ. Gordon. 656p. (C). 1998. text 92.00 (*0-321-02097-9*) Addison-Wesley.

***Macroeconomics.** 8th ed. (C). 2000. write for info. (*0-321-07739-3*) Addson-Wesley Educ.

***Macroeconomics.** 8th ed. 2000. write for info. (*0-321-08606-6*) P-H.

***Macroeconomics.** 8th ed. 464p. (C). 1999. pap. text 71.00 (*0-321-06277-9*, Celebration) Addson-Wesley Educ.

***Macroeconomics.** 8th ed. 416p. (C). 2000. pap. text 34.67 (*0-321-06276-0*, Celebration) Addson-Wesley Educ.

***Macroeconomics.** 8th ed. (C). 2000. pap. text 0.00 (*0-321-06278-7*, Celebration) Addson-Wesley Educ.

***Macroeconomics.** 8th ed. Dornbusch. 2000. 63.25 (*0-07-231485-0*) McGraw.

***Macroeconomics.** 8th ed. Robert J. Gordon. LC 99-27266. 656p. (C). 1999. 94.00 (*0-321-05229-3*) Addison-Wesley.

Macroeconomics. 8th ed. Gwartne. 1996. 246.00 (*0-03-019299-4*, Pub. by Harcourt Coll Pubs) Harcourt.

Macroeconomics. 8th ed. Gwartne. 1997. pap. text 33.50 (*0-03-019303-6*) Harcourt Coll Pubs.

***Macroeconomics.** 10th ed. Lipsey. 260p. (C). 2000. pap., student ed. 22.95 (*0-201-66472-0*) Addison-Wesley.

Macroeconomics. 11th ed. Richard G. Lipsey & Paul N. Courant. LC 95-35432. (Illus.). 560p. (C). 1996. text 56.25 (*0-673-99478-3*) Addson-Wesley Educ.

Macroeconomics. 11th ed. Mutti & Fredric C. Menz. LC 95-35432. (C). 1997. pap. text, student ed. 33.00 (*0-673-99928-9*) Addson-Wesley Educ.

Macroeconomics. 12th ed. Lipsey. 560p. (C). 1998. pap. text 70.00 (*0-201-36012-8*) Addison-Wesley.

***Macroeconomics.** 12th ed. Lipsey. 320p. (C). 1999. pap. text, student ed. 23.20 (*0-201-45841-1*) Addison-Wesley.

Macroeconomics. 13th ed. Campbell R. McConnell & Stanley L. Brue. (C). 1995. pap. text 67.50 (*0-07-046819-2*) McGraw.

Macroeconomics. 13th ed. William B. Walstad. (C). 1995. pap. text, student ed. 13.25 (*0-07-046822-2*) McGraw.

Macroeconomics. 14th ed. McConnell. 1998. pap., student ed. 17.19 (*0-07-289839-9*) McGraw.

Macroeconomics. 15th ed. Campbell R. McConnell. 2001. 45.74 (*0-07-234089-4*) McGraw.

Macroeconomics. 15th ed. Laurence Miners & Kathryn Nantz. (C). 1995. pap. text, student ed. 17.50 (*0-07-054998-2*) McGraw.

Macroeconomics. 15th ed. Paul Anthony Samuelson & William D. Nordhaus. (C). 1994. pap. text 46.74 (*0-07-054992-3*) McGraw.

Macroeconomics. 16th ed. Samuelson. 1998. 19.69 (*0-07-057952-0*) McGraw.

Macroeconomics. 16th ed. Paul Anthony Samuelson & William D. Nordhaus. LC 97-38897. 496p. (C). 1997. pap. 60.00 (*0-07-057951-2*) McGraw.

Macroeconomics. 17th ed. Samuelson. 2000. 46.74 (*0-07-231489-3*) McGraw.

***Macroeconomics.** 17th ed. Paul Anthony Samuelson. 2000. text, student ed. 17.50 (*0-07-237238-9*) McGraw.

Macroeconomics, Macrobytes Software 3.0 Windows. 3rd ed. N. Gregory Mankiw & David Weil. 1996. disk 14.80 (*1-57259-309-1*) Worth.

***Macroeconomics: A Contemporary Intro.** 5th ed. William A. McEachern. LC 99-11638. 530p. 1999. pap. text 64.95 (*0-538-88847-4*) Thomson Learn.

Macroeconomics: A Contemporary Introduction. 3rd ed. McEachern. (HB - Economics Ser.). (C). 1994. mass mkt., student ed. 16.00 (*0-538-82854-4*) S-W Pub.

Macroeconomics: A Contemporary Introduction. 4th ed. McEachern. (HB - Economics Ser.). 1996. mass mkt., student ed. 20.95 (*0-538-85522-3*) S-W Pub.

Macroeconomics: A Contemporary Introduction. 4th ed. William A. McEachern. LC 96-18535. 1996. mass mkt. 48.95 (*0-538-85515-0*) S-W Pub.

Macroeconomics: A European Text. 2nd ed. Michael Burda. (Illus.). 638p. 1997. text 85.00 (*0-19-877469-9*) OUP.

Macroeconomics: A European Text. 2nd ed. Michael Burda & Charles Wypolsz. LC 96-24643. (Illus.). 638p. 1997. pap. text 49.95 (*0-19-877468-0*) OUP.

Macroeconomics: A Microcomputer Modeling Approach with Emphasis on the Agribusiness Sector. 2nd ed. James Ralph Edwards. (C). 1994. pap. text. write for info. (*0-07-020511-6*) McGraw.

Macroeconomics: A Neoclassical Introduction. Merton H. Miller & Charles W. Upton. LC 73-90598. xvi, 384p. (C). 1986. pap. text 17.00 (*0-226-52623-2*) U Ch Pr.

An Asterisk (*) at the beginning of an entry indicates that the title is appearing for the first time.

Macroeconomics: A Strategic Survey: A Survey of Research Strategies. Ed. by Alessandro Vercelli & Nicola Dimitri. (Illus.). 504p. 1993. 95.00 (*0-19-877314-5*); pap. 39.95 (*0-19-877315-3*) OUP.
Macroeconomics: An Alternative Approach. Henry Vallet. (Illus.). 204p. (C). 1990. pap. text 34.95 (*0-9627882-1-X*) Bradley Mann.
Macroeconomics: An Integrated Approach. 2nd ed. Alan J. Auerbach & Laurence J. Kotlikoff. LC 98-6765. (Illus.). 500p. 1998. 65.00 (*0-262-01170-0*) MIT Pr.
Macroeconomics: An Integrated Approach. 2nd ed. Alan J. Auerbach & Laurence J. Kotlikoff. 1998. pap. text 35.00 (*0-262-51103-7*) MIT Pr.
Macroeconomics: An Integrated Approach, Study Guide to Accompany. 2nd ed. Debra Patterson. (Illus.). 171p. 1998. pap. text, student ed. 16.95 (*0-262-66146-2*) MIT Pr.
***Macroeconomics: An Open Economy Approach.** Eric J. Pentecoste. 2000. text 72.00 (*0-312-23368-X*) St Martin.
Macroeconomics: Analysis & Policy. 3rd ed. Lloyd G. Reynolds. (C). 1979. 14.95 (*0-256-02173-2*, Irwn McGrw-H) McGrw-H Hghr Educ.
Macroeconomics: Casebook. N. Gregory Mankiw. 514p. (C). 1991. text 54.95 (*0-87901-502-0*) Worth.
Macroeconomics: Casebook. N. Gregory Mankiw. 514p. (C). 1991. pap., student ed. 10.95 (*0-87901-503-9*) Worth.
Macroeconomics: Casebook. N. Gregory Mankiw. 121p. (C). 1992. pap. text 8.95 (*0-87901-597-7*) Worth.
Macroeconomics: Custom Edition. Colander. 1994. 34.00 (*0-256-18680-4*) McGraw.
Macroeconomics: Individual Choice & Its Consequences. Neil T. Skaggs & J. Lon Carlson. LC 95-35300. 1995. pap. 41.95 (*1-55786-736-4*) Blackwell Pubs.
Macroeconomics: Instructor's Resource Manual. 3rd ed. Andrew John & Patricia Pollard. 1997. teacher ed., ring bd. write for info. (*1-57259-234-6*); teacher ed., ring bd. write for info. (*1-57259-351-2*) Worth.
Macroeconomics: Principles & Applications. Lieberman. LC 97-17926. (AB - Accounting Principles Ser.). (C). 1997. 67.95 (*0-538-84759-X*) S-W Pub.
***Macroeconomics: Principles & Applications.** 2nd ed. Hall & Lieberman. 2000. pap. 47.00 (*0-324-01954-8*) Thomson Learn.
***Macroeconomics: Principles & Tools.** 2nd ed. 2000. write for info. (*0-13-018976-6*) P-H.
***Macroeconomics: Principles & Tools.** 2nd ed. Arthur O'Sullivan & Steven M. Sheffrin. 448p. 2000. pap. 61.33 (*0-13-018975-8*) P-H.
***MacRoeconomics: Principles & Tools Cdn: Cbc Video Library.** 2000. VHS. write for info. (*0-13-030904-4*) S&S Trade.
Macroeconomics: Principles, Problems, & Policies. 14th ed. Campbell R. McConnell & Stanley L. Brue. LC 98-19045. 1998. 60.50 (*0-07-289841-0*) McGraw.
Macroeconomics: Private & Public Choice. 8th ed. James D. Gwartney et al. 728p. (C). 1996. write for info. (*0-614-25316-0*) Harcourt Coll Pubs.
Macroeconomics: Private & Public Choice. 9th ed. James D. Gwartney. (C). 1999. pap. text 44.50 (*0-03-025781-6*) Harcourt Coll Pubs.
Macroeconomics: Private Markets & Public Choice. 5th ed. Robert B. Ekelund & Robert D. Tollison. LC 96-38799. 816p. (C). 1996. 70.00 (*0-201-91897-8*) Addison-Wesley.
MacRoeconomics: Private Markets & Public Choice. 5th ed. Robert B. Ekelund & Robert D. Tollison. LC 96-38799. (C). 1997. pap. text 31.60 (*0-201-85318-3*) Addison-Wesley.
Macroeconomics: Private Markets & Public Choice. 8th ed. Robert Gordon. (C). 1999. pap., student ed. 29.40 (*0-321-06275-2*) Addson-Wesley Educ.
Macroeconomics: Solutions Manual. 3rd ed. John Fernald & Jason Furman. 1997. write for info. (*1-57259-449-7*) Worth.
Macroeconomics: Study Guide. Jeremy R. Rudin & David Papell. pap. 12.00 (*0-393-96590-2*) Norton.
Macroeconomics: Study Guide. 5th ed. Robert Hall. (C). 1997. pap., student ed. 16.50 (*0-393-96836-7*) Norton.
Macroeconomics: Test Bank. 3rd ed. Nancy Jianakoplos. 1997. write for info. (*1-57259-235-4*) Worth.
Macroeconomics: The Brief Edition. Bernanke Abel. (C). 1999. text. write for info. (*0-201-36010-1*) Addison-Wesley.
Macroeconomics: The Canadian Economy. 2nd ed. Robert E. Hall et al. LC 93-34405. (C). 1994. pap. text 42.00 (*0-393-96544-9*) Norton.
Macroeconomics: The Dynamics of Commodity Production. Amit Bhaduri. LC 85-18249. (Illus.). 290p. (Orig.). 1986. reprint ed. pap. 89.90 (*0-7837-9930-6*, 206065700006) Bks Demand.
Macroeconomics: Theories & Applications. Elizabeth C. Bogan & Joseph J. Kiernan. LC 86-24643. (Illus.). 569p. (C). 1987. pap. text, student ed. 20.00 (*0-314-34713-5*) West Pub.
Macroeconomics: Theories & Policies. 6th ed. Froyen. LC 98-34929. 481p. (C). 1998. 92.00 (*0-13-099817-6*) P-H.
Macroeconomics: Theory & Policy. David C. Colander. LC 85-27863. (Illus.). 580p. reprint ed. pap. 179.80 (*0-7837-4742-X*, 204455100004) Bks Demand.
Macroeconomics: Theory & Policy. 3rd ed. William H. Branson. 656p. (C). 1997. 121.00 (*0-06-040932-0*) Addson-Wesley Educ.
Macroeconomics: Theory & Policy in the U. K. 3rd ed. David Greenaway et al. LC 96-23268. 490p. (C). 1997. pap. text 36.95 (*0-631-20019-3*) Blackwell Pubs.
Macroeconomics: Theory & Policy. Anthony J. Westaway & T. G. Weyman-Jones. LC 76-54984. (Modern Economics Ser.). 347p. reprint ed. pap. 107.60 (*0-7837-1607-9*, 204189900024) Bks Demand.
***Macroeconomics: Theory Performance & Policy.** 6th ed. 2000. write for info. (*0-393-97515-0*) Norton.
Macroeconomics: Wall Street Journal Edition. 4th ed. David N. Hyman. 544p. (C). 1996. text 53.00 (*0-256-22214-2*, Irwn McGrw-H) McGrw-H Hghr Educ.
Macroeconomics: Wall Street Journal Edition. 4th ed. Stephen L. Slavin. 528p. (C). 1995. text 48.00 (*0-256-21699-1*, Irwn McGrw-H) McGrw-H Hghr Educ.
Macroeconomics after Keynes: A Reconsideration of the General Theory. Victoria Chick. 356p. 1983. 32.50 (*0-262-03095-0*); pap. text 22.50 (*0-262-53045-7*) MIT Pr.
Macroeconomics & Business: An Interactive Approach. MacDonald. (ITBP Acquisitions Ser.). 400p. 1999. pap. 22.99 (*1-86152-450-1*) Thomson Learn.
Macroeconomics & Economic Policy Vol.1: The Selected Essays of Assar Lindbeck, Vol. 1. Assar Lindbeck. (Economists of the Twentieth Century Ser.). 352p. 1993. 100.00 (*1-85278-720-1*) E Elgar.
Macroeconomics & Imperfect Competition. Ed. by Jean-Pascal Benassy. LC 94-44342. (International Library of Critical Writings in Economics: Vol. 46). 544p. 1995. 230.00 (*1-85278-849-6*) E Elgar.
Macroeconomics & Macroeconomic Policy Issues. Thomas Mayer & Franco Spinelli. 271p. 1991. text 82.95 (*1-85628-219-8*, Pub. by Avebry) Ashgate Pub Co.
Macroeconomics & Macroeconomics. 4th ed. Michael Parkin. (C). 1998. pap. text, student ed. write for info. (*0-201-33635-9*) Addison-Wesley.
Macroeconomics & Micropolitics: The Electoral Effects of Economic Issues. D. Roderick Kiewiet. LC 82-21985. (Illus.). 184p. (C). 1999. pap. text 7.00 (*0-226-43533-4*) U Ch Pr.
Macroeconomics & Monetary Theory Vol. 1: The Selected Essays of Meghnad Desai. Meghnad Desai. (Economists of the Twentieth Century Ser.). 336p. 1995. 95.00 (*1-85278-689-2*) E Elgar.
Macroeconomics & New Macroeconomics. Bernhard Felderer & Stefan Homburg. (Illus.). 320p. (C). 1986. 54.00 (*0-387-16961-X*) Spr-Verlag.
Macroeconomics & New Macroeconomics. Bernhard Felderer & Stefan Homburg. (Illus.). xiii, 329p. 1992. pap. 35.00 (*0-387-18004-4*) Spr-Verlag.
Macroeconomics & New Macroeconomics. 2nd ed. Bernhard Felderer & Stefan Homburg. LC 92-15191. (Illus.). 352p. 1995. 49.00 (*0-387-55318-5*) Spr-Verlag.
Macroeconomics & the Environment, Seminar. Ed. by Ved P. Gandhi. 1996. pap. 22.50 (*1-55775-536-1*) Intl Monetary.
Macroeconomics & the Financial System. 3rd ed. Eileen Appelbaum & Lowell S. Young. LC 97-70708. 295p. (C). 1997. text 41.00 (*0-89463-075-X*) Am Inst FCPCU.
Macroeconomics & the Japanese Economy. Hiroshi Yoshikawa. (Illus.). 492p. 1996. text 80.00 (*0-19-823326-4*) OUP.
***Macroeconomics & the Real World: Econometric Techniques & Macroeconomic, Vol. 1.** Ed. by Roger E. Backhouse & Andrea Salanti. 384p. 2000. text 90.00 (*0-19-829795-5*) OUP.
***Macroeconomics & the Real World: Keynesian Economics, Unemployment, Vol. 2.** Ed. by Roger E. Backhouse & Andrea Salanti. 432p. 2000. text 90.00 (*0-19-829796-3*) OUP.
Macroeconomics & the U. S. Financial Systems. 264p. (C). 1995. text 29.40 (*0-536-58850-3*) Pearson Custom.
Macroeconomics & the Wage Bargain: A Modern Approach to Employment, Inflation, & the Exchange Rate. Wendy Carlin & David W. Soskice. (Illus.). 496p. 1990. 78.00 (*0-19-877245-9*); pap. text 38.00 (*0-19-877244-0*) OUP.
Macroeconomics & Wall Street Journal. 3rd ed. Stephen L. Slavin & David Hyman. (C). 1995. text 41.95 (*0-256-18108-X*, Irwn McGrw-H) McGrw-H Hghr Educ.
Macroeconomics (Canadian) David Colander & Peter Sephton. LC 95-78245. 528p. (C). 1996. per. 39.95 (*0-256-17572-1*, Irwn McGrw-H) McGrw-H Hghr Educ.
Macroeconomics Drill & Review. 2nd ed. David Colander. (C). 1995. text, student ed. 21.25 (*0-256-22261-4*, Irwn McGrw-H) McGrw-H Hghr Educ.
Macroeconomics, Economics in Action & Economic Times, Vol. 31. 2nd ed. Michael Parkin. (C). 1993. 57.66 incl. 5.25 hd (*0-201-63310-8*) Addison-Wesley.
Macroeconomics, Economics in the News & Economic Times. 2nd ed. Michael Parkin. 1993. 58.00 (*0-201-54089-4*) Addison-Wesley.
***Macroeconomics Essentials for Media Interpretation.** 2nd ed. Peter Kennedy. LC 99-52796. (Illus.). 400p. 2000. 60.00 (*0-262-11251-5*); pap. 29.50 (*0-262-61150-3*) MIT Pr.
Macroeconomics Exam, 3 vols. Boyes. (C). 1996. pap. 54.76 (*0-395-74658-2*) HM.
***Macroeconomics Fifth Edition Michael.** 5th ed. 336p. (C). 1999. text 25.20 (*0-201-63791-X*) S&S Trade.
Macroeconomics Finance Market Readings Pr. 2nd ed. Baily-Friedman. 1994. 22.00 (*0-256-13746-3*, Irwn McGrw-H) McGrw-H Hghr Educ.
Macroeconomics, Financial Markets & the International Sector. 2nd ed. Martin N. Baily & Philip Friedman. LC 94-27884. (Economics Ser.). 608p. (C). 1995. text 69.75 (*0-256-12552-X*, Irwn McGrw-H) McGrw-H Hghr Educ.
Macroeconomics Financial Markets & the International Sector: International Version. Martin N. Baily & Philip Friedman. (C). 1992. text, student ed. 32.50 (*0-256-11401-3*, Irwn McGrw-H) McGrw-H Hghr Educ.
Macroeconomics for Developing Countries. Raghbendra Jha. LC 94-4394. (Illus.). 352p. (C). 1995. pap. 29.99 (*0-415-10026-7*, B4218) Routledge.
Macroeconomics for Developing Countries. Raghbendra Jha. LC 94-4394. (Illus.). 456p. (C). (gr. 13). 1995. 100.00 (*0-415-10025-9*, B4214) Routledge.
Macroeconomics for Managers. J. R. Clark et al. 600p. 1990. teacher ed. write for info. (*0-318-66333-3*, H22114); student ed. 18.00 (*0-685-29826-4*, H22122); disk 13.33 (*0-685-29827-2*, H24342) P-H.
Macroeconomics for Open Economies. Murshed. 1998. pap. 21.99 (*1-86152-457-9*) Thomson Learn.
Macroeconomics for Today. Tucker. (Miscellaneous/Catalogs Ser.). (C). 1997. mass mkt., student ed. 19.95 (*0-314-20849-6*) S-W Pub.
Macroeconomics for Today. 2nd ed. Tucker. LC 99-29727. (SWC-Economics Ser.). 540p. 1999. pap. 64.95 (*0-324-00622-5*) Thomson Learn.
Macroeconomics for Today. 2nd ed. Tucker. (SWC-Economics Ser.). 1999. pap., student ed. 15.75 (*0-324-00785-X*) Thomson Learn.
Macroeconomics Global Economy. (C). Date not set. text. write for info. (*0-201-34745-8*) Addison-Wesley.
Macroeconomics in Brief. Peter M. Gutmann. LC 96-233351. 142p. (Orig.). (C). 1996. pap. text 13.95 (*0-943025-89-3*) Cummngs & Hath.
Macroeconomics in the Global Economy. Jeffrey Sachs & B. Larrain. 1993. 98.33 (*0-13-102252-0*) P-H.
Macroeconomics Model & Stabilization Policies for OPEC Countries: With Special Reference to the Iraqi Economy. A. Khalik Salman. LC 97-74448. (Illus.). 271p. 1997. text 70.95 (*1-85972-343-8*, Pub. by Ashgate Pub) Ashgate Pub Co.
Macroeconomics of European Agriculture. Thorvaldur Gylfason. LC 95-15803. (Studies in International Finance: No. 78). 56p. 1995. pap. 13.50 (*0-88165-250-4*) Princeton U Int Finan Econ.
Macroeconomics of Financing Government Expenditure: A Survey of the Static Consequences. Ramkishen S. Rajan & Mukul G. Asher. LC 97-945648. (Illus.). 123p. (Orig.). 1997. pap. 37.50 (*9971-69-200-7*, Pub. by Sngapore Univ Pr) Coronet Bks.
Macroeconomics of International Currencies: Theory, Policy & Evidence. Ed. by Paul Mizen & Eric J. Pentecost. LC 96-5321. (Illus.). 272p. (C). 1996. text 95.00 (*1-85898-077-1*) E Elgar.
Macroeconomics of Open Economies under Labour Mobility. George M. Agiomirgianakis. LC 99-72843. 186p. 1999. text 65.95 (*1-84014-949-3*, Pub. by Ashgate Pub) Ashgate Pub Co.
Macroeconomics of Populism in Latin America. Ed. by Rudiger Dornbusch & Sebastian Edwards. (National Bureau of Economic Research Project Report Ser.). (Illus.). 411p. 1991. pap. text 24.95 (*0-226-15844-6*) U Ch Pr.
Macroeconomics of Populism in Latin America. Ed. by Rudiger Dornbusch & Sebastian Edwards. (National Bureau of Economic Research Project Report Ser.). (Illus.). 416p. 1994. lib. bdg. 65.00 (*0-226-15843-8*) U Ch Pr.
Macroeconomics of Saving, Finance, & Investment. Ed. by Robert Pollin. LC 97-4499. 416p. (C). 1997. text 75.00 (*0-472-10787-9*, 10787) U of Mich Pr.
Macroeconomics of Self-Fulfilling Prophecies. 2nd ed. Roger E. Farmer. LC 98-48432. (Illus.). 300p. 1999. 40.00 (*0-262-06203-8*) MIT Pr.
Macroeconomics Plus Macroeconomics Study Guide. 2nd ed. Michael Parkin. 1994. text, student ed. write for info. (*0-201-87629-9*) Addison-Wesley.
Macroeconomics Policies, Crises & Growth in Sri Lanka, 1969-90. Premachandra Athukorala & Sisira Jayasuriya. LC 94-31612. (Comparative Macroeconomic Studies). 192p. 1994. pap. 22.00 (*0-8213-2297-4*, 12297) World Bank.
Macroeconomics Policy Analysis: Open Economies with Quantity Constraints. Michael P. Amos. 88p. 1989. text 47.95 (*0-521-34387-9*) Cambridge U Pr.
Macroeconomics, Prices, & Quantities: Essays in Memory of Arthur M. Okun. Ed. by James Tobin. LC 82-45981. 305p. 1983. 36.95 (*0-8157-8486-4*); pap. 16.95 (*0-8157-8485-6*) Brookings.
Macroeconomics Rational Expectations Approach. 2nd ed. Paul Labinski. (C). 1990. 49.00 (*0-536-57766-8*) Pearson Custom.
Macroeconomics Reader. Ed. by Brian Snowdon & Howard Vane. 688p. (C). 1997. 125.00 (*0-415-15715-3*); pap. 32.99 (*0-415-15716-1*) Routledge.
Macroeconomics Ready Notes. 2nd ed. Paul Estenson. 106p. (C). 1995. text 8.12 (*0-256-13816-8*, Irwn McGrw-H) McGrw-H Hghr Educ.
Macroeconomics Split - Economics: A Contemporary Introduction. 3rd ed. McEachern. (HB - Economics Ser.). (C). 1994. mass mkt. 40.00 (*0-538-82851-X*) S-W Pub.
Macroeconomics Student Workbook. 2nd ed. David Colander & Douglas Copeland. 304p. (C). 1995. text, student ed., wbk. ed. 18.12 (*0-256-18628-6*, Irwn McGrw-H) McGrw-H Hghr Educ.
Macroeconomics Study Guide. 4th ed. David N. Hyman. 432p. (C). 1996. text, student ed. 21.25 (*0-256-16158-5*, Irwn McGrw-H) McGrw-H Hghr Educ.
Macroeconomics Study Guide. 7th ed. Dornbusch. 1997. pap., student ed. 23.44 (*0-07-109309-5*) McGraw.
***Macroeconomics Theory Policy.** 2nd ed. Miller & Van Hoose. 2000. pap., student ed. 20.00 (*0-324-05498-X*) Sth-Wstrn College.
Macroeconomics 2.0. Muraoka. Date not set. pap. text, student ed. write for info. (*0-314-00840-3*) West Pub.
Macroeconomics under Debate. Alan S. Blinder. 216p. 1990. text 54.50 (*0-472-10140-4*, 10140) U of Mich Pr.
Macroeconomics Update Version with Economics in Action. 2nd ed. Michael Parkin. 1994. text, student ed. 53.25 (*0-201-76584-5*) Addison-Wesley.
Macroeconomics with EIA 3.0. 4th ed. Michael Parkin. (C). 1997. pap. text. write for info. (*0-201-34738-5*) Addison-Wesley.
Macroeconomics with TAG SW Windows. 8th ed. Gwartne. (C). 1997. 66.50 (*0-03-019882-8*) Harcourt.
Macroeconomics, 2e. 2nd ed. Roger A. Arnold. Ed. by Clyde Perlee. (SWC-Economics). 508p. (C). 1992. pap. 47.25 (*0-314-88425-4*) West Pub.
***MacroEconomy.** Saul H. Hymans. 182p. 1999. pap. write for info. (*0-9671766-2-X*) Huron Valley.
Macroeconomy. Michael B. McElroy. 1995. text 87.00 (*0-02-378801-1*, Macmillan Coll) P-H.
Macroeconomy: A Business Perspective. 3rd ed. Keith Cuthbertson & Peter Gripaios. LC 97-3292. 1997. pap. 17.99 (*1-86152-088-3*) Thomson Learn.
Macroeconomy: A Guide for Business. 2nd ed. Keith Cuthbertson & Peter Gripaios. LC 92-11036. 160p. 1992. pap. 24.95 (*0-415-08673-6*) Thomson Learn.
Macroeconomy: A Guide for Business. 2nd ed. Keith Cuthbertson & Peter Gripaios. LC 92-11036. 160p. (C). (gr. 13). 1992. pap. 60.95 (*0-415-08672-8*, A9715) Thomson Learn.
Macroeconomy: A Textbook View. Dipankar Dasgupta. (Illus.). 234p. 1998. text 8.95 (*0-19-564306-2*) OUP.
Macroeconomy of the Middle East & North Africa: Exploiting Potential for Growth. LC 96-190437. 1996. pap. write for info. (*1-55775-565-5*) Intl Monetary.
Macroeconomy Today. 7th ed. Bradley R. Schiller. (C). 1996. pap., student ed. 20.31 (*0-07-057805-2*); pap. text 45.74 (*0-07-057715-3*) McGraw.
***Macroeconomy Today.** 8th ed. (C). 2000. pap., student ed. 20.31 (*0-07-242957-7*) McGrw-H Hghr Educ.
Macroeconomy Today. 8th ed. Schiller. 1999. pap., student ed. 20.31 (*0-07-366280-1*) McGraw.
***Macroeconomy Today.** 8th ed. Schiller. 1999. 58.25 (*0-07-366279-8*) McGraw.
Macroevolution: Pattern & Process. Steven M. Stanley. LC 97-40163. (Illus.). 332p. 1998. reprint ed. pap. text 29.95 (*0-8018-5735-X*) Johns Hopkins.
Macrofungus Flora of China's Guangdong Province. Bi Zhishu et al. (Illus.). 756p. (C). 1997. 135.00 (*962-201-556-5*, Pub. by Chinese Univ) U of Mich Pr.
***Macrohistory: Essays in Sociology of the Long Run.** Randall Collins. LC 99-31771. 312p. 1999. 65.00 (*0-8047-3523-9*) Stanford U Pr.
***Macrohistory: Essays in The Sociology of Then Long Run.** Randall Collins. LC 99-31771. 1999. pap. text 18.95 (*0-8047-3600-6*) Stanford U Pr.
Macrohistory & Macrohistorians: Perspectives on Individual Social & Civilizational Change. Ed. by Johan Galtung & Sohail Inayatullah. LC 97-8811. 288p. 1997. 65.00 (*0-275-95755-1*, Praeger Pubs) Greenwood.
Macroions in Solution & Colloidal Suspension. K. Schmitz. 401p. 1992. 185.00 (*0-471-18763-1*, Wiley-VCH) Wiley.
Macroions in Solution & Colloidal Suspension. Kenneth S. Schmitz. 402p. 1992. 125.00 (*0-89573-778-7*, Wiley-VCH) Wiley.
Macrolichens of South Georgia. D. C. Lindsay. (British Antarctic Survey Report Ser.: No. 89). 98p. 1974. 25.00 (*0-85665-028-5*, Pub. by Brit Antarctic Surv) Balogh.
Macrolichens of the Northern Rocky Mountains. Bruce McCune & Trevor Goward. (Illus.). 200p. (Orig.). 1995. pap. 24.95 (*0-916422-82-8*) Mad River.
Macrolichens of the Pacific Northwest. Bruce McCune & Linda Geiser. LC 97-3549. (Illus.). 400p. (Orig.). 1997. pap. 25.95 (*0-87071-394-9*) Oreg St U Pr.
Macrolides, Chemistry, Pharmacology & Clinical Uses. A. Bryskier. (Illus.). 714p. 1993. 225.00 (*2-7184-0589-9*) Blackwell Sci.
Macrolinkages Between the Farm & Nonfarm Sectors & the Impact of Monetary Policy Decisions, Vol. 87-M1. S. Devadoss et al. (Illus.). 110p. (Orig.). 1988. pap. text 15.00 (*0-936911-00-X*) Ctr Agri & Rural Dev.
Macrologistics Management. Martin Stein & Frank Voehl. (Total Quality Ser.). (Illus.). 304p. 1997. boxed set 49.95 (*1-884015-39-5*) St Lucie Pr.
Macromarketing: A Canadian Perspective. Donald N. Thompson et al. LC 79-16031. (American Marketing Association, Proceedings Ser.). 326p. reprint ed. pap. 101.10 (*0-608-11937-7*, 202335000032) Bks Demand.
Macromedia Authoware 3.0 Internal Systems Functions Professional Reference. Joe Ganci. 608p. 1996. 65.00 (*1-56205-599-2*) New Riders Pub.
Macromedia Director Advanced Lingo Workshop. Terry Schussler. 1996. pap. text 45.00 (*1-56830-285-1*) Hayden.
Macromedia Director Design Guide. Matthew Manuel. 400p. (Orig.). 2000. pap. 34.99 (*0-7897-2146-5*) S&S Trade.
Macromedia Director Design Guide for Windows. Cathy Clarke & Lee Swearingen. (Illus.). 198p. (Orig.). 1995. pap. 30.00 (*1-56830-202-9*, Alpha Ref) Macmillan Gen Ref.
Macromedia Director 5.0 Revealed. Bernt Qahl. 1996. pap. text 50.00 (*1-56830-284-3*) Hayden.
Macromedia Director 4 for Macs for Dummies. Lauren Steinhauer & David Drucker. 384p. 1995. pap. 19.99 (*1-56884-916-8*) IDG Bks.
Macromedia Director Lingo Workshop. John J. Thompson & Sam Gottlieb. (Illus.). 352p. 1995. 45.00 (*1-56830-201-0*) Hayden.
Macromedia Director Lingo Workshop for Macintosh. 2nd ed. John Thompson. LC 96-77061. 368p. 1996. 45.00 (*1-56830-287-8*) Hayden.
***MacroMedia Director 7: Creating Powerful Multimedia.** 2000. teacher ed. write for info. (*0-13-019959-1*) P-H.
Macromedia Director X for Dummies. 2nd ed. Lauren Steinhauer. 384p. 1996. pap. 24.99 (*0-7645-0024-4*) IDG Bks.
Macromedia Dreamweaver Bible. Joseph W. Lowrey. LC TK5105.8885.D74L69. 816p. 1998. pap. 39.99 (*0-7645-3225-1*) IDG Bks.
***Macromedia Dreamweaver X.** (Sams Teach Yourself... in 24 Hours Ser.). 456p. 2000. 24.99 (*0-672-31883-0*) Sams.
Macromedia Flash 5 from Scratch. 512p. 39.99 (*0-7897-2461-8*) Que.
***Macromedia Flash 4.** (Sams Teach Yourself... in 24 Hours Ser.). 400p. 2000. 19.99 (*0-672-31892-X*) Sams.

M

An Asterisk (*) at the beginning of an entry indicates that the title is appearing for the first time.

M

***Macromedia Flash-illustrated.** TBD. (Illustrated Ser.). (C). 2001. text. write for info. (0-619-01766-X) Course Tech.
***Macromedia (R) Director (R) 7: Creating Powerful Multimedia.** Against the Clock, Inc. Staff. LC 99-55647. 2000. write for info. (0-13-016658-8) P-H.
Macromedia Web Publishing Unleashed. Dennis Hamilton et al. LC 96-71507. 1170p. 1997. 49.99 (1-57521-251-X) Sams.
Macro/Micro Divide. Paul Colomy. (Key Ideas Ser.). 200p. (C). 2000. pap. write for info. (0-415-08187-4) Routledge.
Macromolecular Architectures. Ed. by J. G. Hilborn et al. (Advances in Polymer Science Ser.: Vol. 147). (Illus.). 180p. 1999. 179.00 (3-540-65576-X) Spr-Verlag.
Macromolecular Aspects of Medical Biochemistry. J. P. Luzio & R. J. Thompson. (Illus.). 278p. (C). 1990. text 85.00 (0-521-26083-3); pap. text 30.95 (0-521-27828-7) Cambridge U Pr.
Macromolecular Assemblies in Polymeric Systems. Ed. by Pieter Stroeve & Anna C. Balazs. LC 92-15020. (ACS Symposium Ser.: Vol. 493). (Illus.). 326p. 1992. text 89.00 (0-8412-2427-7, Pub. by Am Chemical) OUP.
Macromolecular Biomaterials. Ed. by Garth W. Hastings & Paul Ducheyne. LC 83-7094. (Structure Property Relationship Biomaterials Ser.). 320p. 1984. 157.00 (0-8493-6263-6, R857, CRC Reprint) Franklin.
Macromolecular Biorecognition: Principles & Methods. Ed. by Irwin M. Chaiken et al. LC 87-29304. (Experimental Biology & Medicine Ser.: Vol. 19). (Illus.). 850p. (C). 1988. 125.00 (0-89603-141-1) Humana.
Macromolecular Chemistry, Vol. 1. Royal Society of Chemistry Staff. 1991. 128.00 (0-85186-840-1) CRC Pr.
Macromolecular Chemistry, Vol. 2. Royal Society of Chemistry Staff. 1989. 192.00 (0-85186-866-5) CRC Pr.
Macromolecular Chemistry, Vol. 3. Royal Society of Chemistry Staff. 1989. 236.00 (0-85186-876-2) CRC Pr.
Macromolecular Chemistry: Special Lectures Presented at the International Symposium on Macromolecular Chemistry Held in Prague, Czechoslovakia, 30 August-4 September 1965, Vol. 2. International Symposium on Macromolecular Chemistr. LC 67-83242. (Illus.). 648p. reprint ed. pap. 200.00 (0-608-10726-3, 2020711000018) Bks Demand.
Macromolecular Chemistry Vol. 4: Plenary & Main Lectures Presented at the International Symposium on Macromolecular Chemistry Held in Brussels-Louvain, Belgium 12-16 June 1967. International Symposim on Macromolecular Chemistry. LC 68-54464. (Illus.). 321p. reprint ed. pap. 99.60 (0-608-10713-1, 2020712000018) Bks Demand.
Macromolecular Complexes: Dynamic Interactions & Electronic Processes. Ed. by E. Tsuchida. 400p. 1991. 199.00 (0-471-18770-4, Wiley-VCH) Wiley.
Macromolecular Complexes: Dynamic Interactions & Electronic Processes of Macromolecular Complexes. Ed. by Eishun Tsuchida. 400p. 1991. lib. bdg. 140.00 (0-89573-784-1, Wiley-VCH) Wiley.
Macromolecular Complexes in Chemistry & Biology. P. Dubin et al. LC 93-38677. 1994. 131.95 (0-387-57166-3) Spr-Verlag.
Macromolecular Concept & Strategy for Humanity in Science, Technology & Industry. Ed. by B. Ranby et al. 160p. 1996. 117.00 (3-540-60315-8) Spr-Verlag.
Macromolecular Crystallography, Pt. A. Ed. by John N. Abelson et al. (Methods in Enzymology Ser.: Vol. 276). (Illus.). 700p. 1997. text 99.00 (0-12-182177-3) Morgan Kaufmann.
Macromolecular Crystallography, Pt. B. Ed. by Charles W. Carter, Jr. et al. (Methods in Enzymology Ser.: Vol. 277). (Illus.). 664p. 1997. text 99.95 (0-12-182178-1) Morgan Kaufmann.
Macromolecular Crystallography with Synchrotron Radiation. John R. Helliwell. (Illus.). 615p. (C). 1992. text 190.00 (0-521-33467-5) Cambridge U Pr.
Macromolecular Design: Concept & Practice: Macromonomers, Macroinitiator, Macroiniferter, Macroinifer - Macroiniter. Ed. by Munmaya K. Mishra. LC 92-85448. (Advanced Polymers Via Macromolecular Engineering Ser.). 500p. 1994. 125.00 (0-9639138-0-8) Polymer Frontiers.
Macromolecular Design of Polymeric Materials. Ed. by Koichi Hatada et al. LC 96-47256. (Plastics Engineering Ser.: Vol. 40). (Illus.). 896p. 1997. text 225.00 (0-8247-9465-6) Dekker.
Macromolecular Engineering: Recent Advances: International Conference on Advanced Polymers Via Macromolecular Engineering (1995: Poughkeepsie, New York) Ed. by Munmaya K. Mishra et al. LC 95-32590. (Illus.). 342p. (C). 1995. text 115.00 (0-306-45112-3, Kluwer Plenum) Kluwer Academic.
Macromolecular Interactions in Food Technology. Ed. by Nicholas Parris et al. LC 96-36455. (ACS Symposium Ser.: No. 650). (Illus.). 322p. 1996. text 105.00 (0-8412-3466-3, Pub. by Am Chemical) OUP.
Macromolecular Interplay in Brain Associative Mechanisms. Ed. by A. Neugebauer. LC 98-214620. 350p. 1997. text 78.00 (981-02-3212-8) World Scientific Pub.
Macromolecular Liquids Vol. 177: Materials Research Society Symposium Proceedings. Ed. by C. R. Safinya et al. 430p. 1990. text 17.50 (1-55899-065-8) Materials Res.
Macromolecular Mechanochemistry, 2 vols. C. Oprea & F. Dan. Incl. Polymer Mechanochemistry. 380p. 1999. 149.00 (1-898326-72-X); Polymers with Chemomechanical Function. 360p. 2000. 146.00 (1-898326-73-8); 1999. 146.00 (1-898326-76-2) CISP.
Macromolecular Physics Vol. 3: Crystal Melting. Bernhard Wunderlich. LC 72-82632. 1980. text 133.00 (0-12-765603-0) Acad Pr.
Macromolecular Reactions: Peculiarities, Theory & Experimental Approaches. Nicolai A. Plate et al. LC 94-30634. 450p. 1995. 345.00 (0-471-94392-4) Wiley.
Macromolecular Science & Engineering. Y. Tanabe. LC 99-11671. 432p. 1999. 104.00 (3-540-64378-8) Spr-Verlag.
Macromolecular Sequences in Systematic & Evolutionary Biology. Ed. by Morris Goodman. LC 82-15138. (Monographs in Evolutionary Biology). 432p. 1982. 85.00 (0-306-41061-3, Plenum Trade) Perseus Pubng.
***Macromolecular Symposia, No. 124.** Hartwig Hocker. Ed. by W. Guth et al. 158p. 1999. pap. 40.00 (3-527-29888-6) Wiley.
***Macromolecular Symposia 128.** A. Yu. Bilibin et al. Ed. by B. Jung et al. 264p. 1998. pap. 75.00 (3-527-29886-X) Wiley.
***Macromolecular Symposia 132.** Ed. by Hartwig Hocker et al. 474p. 1998. 250.00 (3-527-29800-2) Wiley.
***Macromolecular Symposia 133: Molecular Modeling of Polymers.** Rutledge. 120p. 1999. 69.95 (3-527-29801-0) Wiley.
***Macromolecular Symposia 135.** J. Kahovec & Hartwig Hocker. Ed. by Waltraut Guth et al. 386p. 1999. 150.00 (3-527-29803-7) Wiley.
***Macromolecular Symposia 136.** Ed. by V. B. Alescovskii. 150p. 1999. 65.00 (3-527-29804-5) Wiley.
***Macromolecular Symposia 139.** Hartwig Hocker & J. Kahovec. Ed. by W. Guth et al. 144p. 1999. 60.00 (3-527-29807-X) Wiley.
***Macromolecular Symposia 142.** P. Adler et al. Ed. by W. Guth et al. 225p. 1999. 105.00 (3-527-29902-5) Wiley.
Macromolecular Syntheses, Vol. II. Ed. by David A. Tirrell. (C). 1992. pap. 20.00 (1-881035-02-6); lib. bdg. 35.00 (1-881035-01-8) MRG Polymer.
Macromolecule-Metal Complexes. Ed. by F. Ciardelli et al. (Illus.). 276p. 1995. 163.95 (3-540-59383-7) Spr-Verlag.
Macromolecules. John G. Kirkwood. Ed. by P. L. Auer. (Documents on Modern Physics Ser.). xii, 192p. (Orig.). 1967. text 216.00 (0-677-00340-4) Gordon & Breach.
Macromolecules, Vol. 1. 2nd ed. Ed. by Hans-George Elias. Tr. by John W. Stafford from GER. LC 83-19294. (Illus.). 564p. (C). 1984. text 140.00 (0-306-41077-X, Kluwer Plenum) Kluwer Academic.
Macromolecules: Synthesis, Order & Advanced Properties. Contrib. by K. A. Armitstead et al. (Advances in Polymer Science Ser.: Vol. 100). (Illus.). xi, 422p. 1992. 200.00 (0-387-54490-9) Spr-Verlag.
Macromolecules Vol. 2: Synthesis, Materials & Technology, Vol. 2. 2nd ed. H. G. Elias. LC 83-19294. (Illus.). 862p. (C). 1984. text 165.00 (0-306-41085-0, Kluwer Plenum) Kluwer Academic.
Macromolecules in Solution. 2nd ed. Herbert Morawetz. LC 83-11991. (High Polymer Ser.: Vol. 21). 572p. (C). 1983. reprint ed. text 61.50 (0-89874-659-0) Krieger.
Macromolecules, 1992: Special Lectures of the 34th International Symposium. Ed. by J. Kahovec. x, 542p. 1993. 205.00 (90-6764-155-3) Coronet Bks.
Macromorphology, Brain Structures, Tables & Atlases Vol. 1: Comparative Neurobiology in Chiroptera. 532p. 1996. 118.00 (3-7643-5370-8) Spr-Verlag.
Macromycetes & Air Pollution: Mycocoenological Studies in Three Oligotrophic Spruce Forests in Europe. By Gulden et al. (Bibliotheca Mycologica: Vol. 144). (GER., Illus.). 11, 81p. 1992. 30.00 (3-443-59045-4, Pub. by Gebruder Borntraeger) Balogh.
Macronutrients: Investigating Their Role in Cancer. Marc S. Micozzi & Thomas E. Moon. (Illus.). 496p. 1992. text 210.00 (0-8247-8593-2) Dekker.
Macronutrients, Electrolytes & Macroelements in Sports Nutrition. Judy A. Driskell & Ira Wolinsky. LC 99-234359. (Nutrition in Exercise & Sport Ser.). 1999. 89.95 (0-8493-8196-7) CRC Pr.
Macropedius. Thomas W. Best. LC 70-185265. (Twayne's World Authors Ser.). 185p. (C). 1972. 20.95 (0-8290-1755-0) Irvington.
Macrophage. Nancy N. Pearsall & Russell S. Weiser. LC 77-85844. (Illus.). 214p. reprint ed. 66.40 (0-8357-9410-5, 201457600090) Bks Demand.
Macrophage. B. Vernon-Roberts. LC 72-184141. (Biological Structure & Function Ser.: 2). 250p. reprint ed. pap. 71.30 (0-608-12919-4, 2024552) Bks Demand.
Macrophage-Derived Cell Regulatory Factors. (Cytokines Ser.: Vol. 1). viii, 234p. 1989. 172.25 (3-8055-4793-5) S Karger.
Macrophage-Mediated Antibody-Dependent Cellular Cytotoxicity. fac. ed. Hillel S. Koren. LC 83-18924. (Immunology Ser.: No. 21). 383p. 1983. reprint ed. pap. 118.80 (0-7837-8323-X, 204911000010) Bks Demand.
Macrophage, 1990, Pt. 1. Ed. by R. Andreesen. (Journal: Vol. 59, No. 3, 1991). (Illus.). 92p. 1991. pap. 51.50 (3-8055-5407-9) S Karger.
Macrophage, 1990, Pt. 2. Ed. by R. Andreesen. (Journal: Pathobiology: Vol. 59, No. 4, 1991). (Illus.). 100p. 1991. pap. 51.50 (3-8055-5408-7) S Karger.
Macrophage, 1992: Abstracts, European Conference on Basic & Clinical Aspects of Macrophage Biology, Regensburg, FRG, September 1992. Ed. by R. Andreesen. (Journal: Pathobiology: Vol. 60, Suppl. 1, 1992). (Illus.). x, 42p. 1992. pap. 24.50 (3-8055-5689-6) S Karger.
Macrophage-Pathogen Interactions. Ed. by Bruce S. Zwilling & Eisenstein. (Immunology Ser.: Vol. 60). (Illus.). 664p. 1993. text 245.00 (0-8247-9124-X) Dekker.
Macrophages & Cancer. Ed. by Gloria H. Heppner & Amy M. Fulton. 240p. 1988. 132.00 (0-8493-4998-2, QR188, CRC Reprint) Franklin.
Macrophages & the Nervous System. V. Hugh Perry. (Molecular Biology Intelligence Unit Ser.). 118p. 1994. 99.00 (1-57059-044-3, LN9044); 99.00 (1-57059-173-3) Landes Bioscience.
***Macrophages in Anti-Inflammation: Molecular Mechanisms, Apoptosis & Tolerance Induction 2nd Teupitzer Colloquium, Teupitz, September 1999.** Ed. by S. Goerdt et al. (Illus.). 128p. 2000. pap. 39.25 (3-8055-7061-9) S Karger.
Macropolitics: Essays on the Philosophy & Science of Politics. Morton A. Kaplan. LC 68-8153. (C). 1968. 32.50 (0-89197-833-X) Irvington.
Macropolitics of Nineteenth-Century Literature: Nationalism, Exoticism, Imperialism. Ed. by Jonathan Arac & Harriet Ritvo. LC 94-41318. (New Americanists Ser.). 328p. 1995. pap. text 17.95 (0-8223-1612-9) Duke.
Macropolitics of Nineteenth-Century Literature: Nationalism, Exoticism, Imperialism. Ed. by Jonathan Arac & Harriet Ritvo. LC 90-44874. (New Cultural Studies). 320p. (C). 1991. text 39.95 (0-8122-8208-6) U of Pa Pr.
***Macroprudential Indicators of Financial System Soundness.** Owen Evans & International Monetary Fund Staff. LC 00-37013. 2000. write for info. (1-55775-891-3) Intl Monetary.
Macroscale & Microscale Organic Experiments. Kenneth L. Williamson. 765p. (C). 1994. teacher ed. 2.66 (0-669-24347-7) HM Trade Div.
Macroscale & Microscale Organic Experiments. 2nd ed. Kenneth L. Williamson. 765p. (C). 1994. text 67.96 (0-669-24346-9) HM Trade Div.
Macroscale & Microscale Organic Experiments. 3rd ed. Kenneth L. Williamson. LC 98-72094. xv, 799 p. 1999. text 58.47 (0-395-90220-7) HM.
***Macroscale Models of Flow Through Highly Heterogeneous Porous Media.** Mikhail Panfilov. LC 99-86779. (Theory & Applications of Transport in Porous Media Ser.). 2000. write for info. (0-7923-6176-8) Kluwer Academic.
Macroscope. Piers Anthony. 480p. 1976. mass mkt. 4.95 (0-380-00209-4, Avon Bks) Morrow Avon.
Macroscopic & Technical Properties of Matter: Group IV. Incl. Densities of Nonaqueous Solutions. Ed. by K. H. Hellwege. 1974. 1040.00 (0-387-06269-6); Heats of Mixing & Solution. G. Beggerow. 1976. 1015.00 (0-387-07443-0); High-Pressure Properties of Matter. G. Beggerow. (Illus.). 1979. 682.95 (0-387-09370-2); Liquid Crystals Subvol. D: Transition Temperatures & Related Properties of Three-Ring Systems with One Bridging Group. Ed. by J. Thiem & V. Vill. viii, 527p. 1994. 1903.95 (0-387-56757-7); Liquid Crystals Subvol. E: Three-Ring Systems with Two Bridging Systems. 1995. 2358.00 (0-387-56758-5); Phase Equilibria, Crystallographic Data & Values of Thermodynamic Properties of Binary Alloys Subvol. E: Phase Equilibria, Crystallographic & Thermodynamic Data of Binary Alloys. B. Predel. Ed. by W. Martienssen. (Illus.). 400p. 1995. 1804.95 (3-540-58428-5); Thermodynamic Equilibria of Boiling Mixtures. J. Weishaupt. Ed. by H. Hausen. (Illus.). 385p. 1975. 605.95 (0-387-07203-9); Pt. B. Densities of Binary Aqueous Systems & Heat Capacities of Liquid Systems. J. D'Ans. LC 62-53136. (Illus.). 1977. 490.00 (0-387-08272-7); (Landolt-Bornstein: Numerical Data & Functional Relationships in Science & Technology Ser.). write for info. (0-614-32367-3) Spr-Verlag.
Macroscopic Behavior of Heterogeneous Materials from the Microstructure. Ed. by S. Torquato & Dusan Krajcinovic. (AMD Ser.: Vol. 147). 192p. 1992. 52.50 (0-7918-1101-8, G00745) ASME.
Macroscopic Modelling of Turbulent Flows. Ed. by U. Frisch et al. LC 85-12655. (Lecture Notes in Physics Ser.: Vol. 230). x, 360p. 1985. 42.95 (0-387-15644-5) Spr-Verlag.
Macroscopic Ocular Pathology. F. H. Stefani & G. Hasenfratz. (Illus.). 170p. 1987. 192.00 (0-387-17404-4) Spr-Verlag.
Macroscopic Processes & Discharges see Electrical Breakdown & Discharges in Gases
Macroscopic Properties of Disordered Media: Proceedings 1981, New York. R. Burridge et al. (Lecture Notes in Physics Ser.: Vol. 154). 307p. 1982. 33.95 (0-387-11202-2) Spr-Verlag.
Macroscopic Quantum Coherence: Proceedings of the International Conference Northeastern University, Boston, U. S. A. 11-13 July, 1997. Ed. by E. Sassaroli et al. 480p. 1998. 106.00 (981-02-3368-X) World Scientific Pub.
Macroscopic Quantum Phenomena: Proceedings of the Workshop, Sussex, UK, August 23-24, 1990. Ed. by T. D. Clark et al. 250p. 1990. pap. 32.00 (981-02-0383-7); text 101.00 (981-02-0382-9) World Scientific Pub.
Macroscopic Quantum Phenomena & Coherence in Superconducting Networks. C. Giovanella & M. Tinkham. LC 96-122945. 500p. 1995. text 138.00 (981-02-2354-4) World Scientific Pub.
Macroscopic Quantum Tunneling of the Magnetic Moment. Eugene M. Chudnovsky & Javier Tejada. LC 97-26060. (Studies in Magnetism: No. 4). (Illus.). 188p. (C). 1998. text 54.95 (0-521-47404-3) Cambridge U Pr.
Macrosociology. 4th ed. Sanderson. (C). 1999. pap. text, student ed. write for info. (0-321-03973-4) Addson-Wesley Educ.
***Macrosociology: An Introduction to Human Societies.** 4th ed. Stephen K. Sanderson. LC 98-22973. 512p. (C). 1998. pap. text 75.00 (0-321-01846-X) Allyn.
Macrosociology: Introduction Human Societies. 3rd ed. (C). 1997. 13.00 (0-06-502158-4) Addson-Wesley Educ.
***Macrosociology: Introductn Human Societies.** 4th ed. (C). 1998. text 24.00 (0-321-03972-6) Addson-Wesley Educ.
Macrosomy, Obesity & Cancer. Lev M. Berstein. (Illus.). 207p. (C). 1996. lib. bdg. 135.00 (1-56072-202-9) Nova Sci Pubs.
Macross II Spaceships & Deck Plans, Vol. 3. Marc-Alexandre Vezina et al. Ed. by Alex Marciniszyn et al. (Illus.). 64p. (YA). 1994. pap. 9.95 (0-916211-75-4, 594) Palladium Bks.
Macrossan Street. Greg Chupita. 1998. pap. write for info. (1-57553-916-0) Watermrk Pr.
Macrosystems Theory & Its Applications: Equilibrium Models. Yury S. Popkov. Ed. by M. Thoma. LC 95-15124. (Lecture Notes in Control & Information Sciences: Vol. 203). 323p. 1995. 69.00 (3-540-19955-1) Spr-Verlag.
Macrothesaurus. 4th ed. 1991. 40.00 (0-685-48025-9, 91.I.3) UN.
Macrothesaurus for Information Processing in the Field of Economic & Social Development. 3rd ed. 347p. 35.00 (92-1-100272-9, E.85.I.15) UN.
Macrothesaurus for Information Processing in the Field of Economic & Social Development. 3rd ed. Jean Viet et al. LC 86-108126. xiv, 347p. 1985. write for info. (92-1-100282-6) UN.
Macrothesaurus for Information Processing in the Field of Economic & Social Development. 5th ed. OECD Staff. LC 98-197885. 436p. 1998. pap. 67.00 (92-64-16025-6, 40 98 01 1 P, Pub. by European Conference Ministers Transp) OECD.
Macrothesaurus para el Procesamiento de la Informacibon Relativa Al Desarrollo Econbomico y Social 3rd ed. Jean Viet. LC 86-197404. (ENG & SPA.). xvi, 346p. 1985. write for info. (92-1-300101-0) UN.
Macrotransport Processes. Howard Brenner & David A. Edwards. (Series in Chemical Physics). 744p. 1993. text 105.00 (0-7506-9332-0) Buttrwrth-Heinemann.
MACRS Depreciation Handbook. Mel Orenstein. 160p. 1995. pap. text 39.50 (0-7811-0106-9) Res Inst Am.
Mac's Choice. Debra L. Wert. LC 89-60200. (Illus.). 39p. (J). (gr. 1-6). 1995. wbk. ed. 5.00 (0-944576-15-X) Rocky River Pubs.
Mac's Choice. rev. ed. Debra L. Wert. LC 89-60200. (Illus.). 40p. (J). (gr. 1-6). 1995. pap. 11.95 (0-944576-14-1) Rocky River Pubs.
***Mac's Field Guide to Denali National Park.** Craig MacGowan. 2000. per. 4.95 (0-89886-745-2) Mountaineers.
***Mac's Field Guide to Midwest Garden Bugs.** Craig MacGowan. 2000. per. 4.95 (0-89886-746-0) Mountaineers.
Mac's Field Guide to Mount Rainier National Park: Flowers & Trees. Craig MacGowan. (Mac's Field Guide Ser.). (Illus.). 1998. pap. 4.95 (0-89886-596-4) Mountaineers.
Mac's Field Guide to Mount Rainier National Park: Mammals & Birds. Craig MacGowan. (Mac's Field Guide Ser.). (Illus.). 1998. pap. 4.95 (0-89886-595-6) Mountaineers.
***Mac's Field Guide to Southeast Garden Bugs.** Craig MacGowan. 2000. per. 4.95 (0-89886-747-9) Mountaineers.
***Mac's Field Guide to Yellowstone & Grand Teton National Parks: Trees & Wildflowers.** 2nd ed. Craig MacGowan. LC 99-6541. (Field Guide Ser.). (Illus.). 1999. pap. 4.95 (0-89886-673-1) Mountaineers.
Mac's Field Guide to Yosemite National Park: Birds & Mammals. Craig MacGowan. (Mac's Field Guide Ser.). 1999. 4.95 (0-89886-674-X) Mountaineers.
Mac's Field Guide to Yosemite National Park: Trees & Wildflowers. Craig MacGowan. (Orig.). 1999. pap. 4.95 (0-89886-675-8) Mountaineers.
MAC's Field Guides: Alaskan Wildlife. Craig MacGowan. (Illus.). 1997. pap. 4.95 (0-89886-393-7) Mountaineers.
MAC's Field Guides: California Coastal Birds. Craig MacGowan. (Illus.). 1990. pap. 4.95 (0-89886-261-2) Mountaineers.
Mac's Field Guides: California Coastal Fish. Craig MacGowan. (Illus.). 1997. pap. 4.95 (0-89886-570-0) Mountaineers.
MAC's Field Guides: California Coastal Invertebrates. Craig MacGowan. (Illus.). 1997. pap. 4.95 (0-89886-532-8) Mountaineers.
MAC's Field Guides: North America/Birds of Prey. Craig MacGowan. (Illus.). 1990. pap. 4.95 (0-89886-260-4) Mountaineers.
MAC's Field Guides: North America/Dinosaurs. Craig MacGowan. (Illus.). 1997. pap. 4.95 (0-89886-530-1) Mountaineers.
MAC's Field Guides: North America/Freshwater Fish. Craig MacGowan. (Illus.). 1998. pap. 4.95 (0-89886-217-5) Mountaineers.
MAC's Field Guides: North America/Land Mammals. Craig MacGowan. (Illus.). 1990. pap. 4.95 (0-89886-243-4) Mountaineers.
MAC's Field Guides: North America/Marine Mammals. Craig MacGowan. (Illus.). 1988. pap. 4.95 (0-89886-218-3) Mountaineers.
MAC's Field Guides: North America/Reptiles. Craig MacGowan. (Illus.). 1992. pap. 4.95 (0-89886-339-2) Mountaineers.
MAC's Field Guides: North America/Salmon & Trout. Craig MacGowan. (Illus.). 1994. pap. 4.95 (0-89886-392-9) Mountaineers.
MAC's Field Guides: Northeast Coast Water Birds. Craig MacGowan. (Illus.). 1988. pap. 4.95 (0-89886-214-0) Mountaineers.
MAC's Field Guides: Northeast Coastal Fish. Craig MacGowan. (Illus.). 1990. pap. 4.95 (0-89886-244-2) Mountaineers.
MAC's Field Guides: Northeast Coastal Invertebrates. Craig MacGowan. (Illus.). 1988. pap. 4.95 (0-89886-215-9) Mountaineers.
MAC's Field Guides: Northeast Park/Backyard Birds. Craig MacGowan. (Illus.). 1990. pap. 4.95 (0-89886-245-0) Mountaineers.

An Asterisk (*) at the beginning of an entry indicates that the title is appearing for the first time.

MAC's Field Guides: Northeast Wildflowers. Craig MacGowan. (Illus.). 1992. pap. 4.95 (*0-89886-337-6*) Mountaineers.

MAC's Field Guides: Northern California Park/Garden Birds. Craig MacGowan. (Illus.). 1991. pap. 4.95 (*0-89886-314-7*) Mountaineers.

MAC's Field Guides: Northern California Wildflowers. Craig MacGowan. (Illus.). 1991. pap. 4.95 (*0-89886-288-4*) Mountaineers.

MAC's Field Guides: Northwest Coast Water Birds. Craig MacGowan. (Illus.). 1988. pap. 4.95 (*0-89886-213-2*) Mountaineers.

MAC's Field Guides: Northwest Coastal Fish. Craig MacGowan. (Illus.). 1988. pap. 4.95 (*0-89886-211-6*) Mountaineers.

MAC's Field Guides: Northwest Coastal Invertebrates. Craig MacGowan. (Illus.). 1997. pap. 4.95 (*0-89886-212-4*) Mountaineers.

MAC's Field Guides: Northwest Garden Bugs. Craig MacGowan. (Illus.). 1997. pap. 4.95 (*0-89886-531-X*) Mountaineers.

MAC's Field Guides: Northwest Park/Backyard Birds. Craig MacGowan. (Illus.). 1990. pap. 4.95 (*0-89886-246-9*) Mountaineers.

MAC's Field Guides: Northwest Trees. Craig MacGowan. (Illus.). 1994. pap. 4.95 (*0-89886-391-0*) Mountaineers.

MAC's Field Guides: Pacific Northwest Wildflowers. Craig MacGowan. (Illus.). 1991. pap. 4.95 (*0-89886-287-6*) Mountaineers.

MAC's Field Guides: Rocky Mountain Wildflowers. Craig MacGowan & Sauskojus. (Illus.). 1992. pap. 4.95 (*0-89886-336-8*) Mountaineers.

MAC's Field Guides: San Juan Islands. Craig MacGowan. (Illus.). 1992. pap. 4.95 (*0-89886-338-4*) Mountaineers.

MAC's Field Guides: Southern California - Wildflowers. Craig MacGowan. (Illus.). 1991. pap. 4.95 (*0-89886-289-2*) Mountaineers.

MAC's Field Guides: Southern California Park/Garden Birds. Craig MacGowan. (Illus.). 1991. pap. 4.95 (*0-89886-315-5*) Mountaineers.

MAC's Field Guides: Southwest Cacti, Shrubs, Trees. Craig MacGowan. (Illus.). 1991. pap. 4.95 (*0-89886-295-7*) Mountaineers.

MAC's Field Guides: Southwest Park/Garden Birds. Craig MacGowan. (Illus.). 1991. pap. 4.95 (*0-89886-294-9*) Mountaineers.

Macs for Dummies. David Pogue. (Illus.). 336p. 1993. pap. 16.95 (*1-878058-53-3*) IDG Bks.

Macs for Dummies. 2nd ed. David Pogue. 350p. 1993. pap. 19.95 (*1-56884-051-9*) IDG Bks.

Macs for Dummies. 3rd ed. David Pogue. 432p. 1995. pap. 19.99 (*1-56884-239-2*) IDG Bks.

Macs for Dummies. 6th ed. David Pogue. LC QA76.8.M3P617 1998. (For Dummies Ser.). 432p. 1998. pap. 19.99 (*0-7645-0398-7*) IDG Bks.

***Macs for Dummies.** 7th ed. David Pogue. (For Dummies Ser.). (Illus.). 432p. 2000. pap. 19.99 (*0-7645-0703-6*) IDG Bks.

Macs for Teachers. Michelle Robinette. 384p. 1995. pap. 19.99 (*1-56884-601-0*) IDG Bks.

Macs for Teachers. 3rd ed. Michelle Robinette. LC 97-80224. 384p. 1997. pap. 24.99 (*0-7645-0226-3*) IDG Bks.

Macsbug Reference & Debugging Guide: For Macsbug 6.2. Apple Computer, Inc. Staff. 1991. pap. 34.95 incl. disk (*0-201-56768-7*) Addison-Wesley.

MacSheme: Users Guide & Language Reference Manual. Lightship Software Staff. 216p. 1990. pap. text 37.50 (*0-262-62077-4*) MIT Pr.

MacSpartan Plus User's Guide & Tutorial, Version 1.0. 223p. 1996. lab manual ed. 35.00 (*0-9643495-7-4*) Wavefunction.

***MacSpartan Pro/MacSpartan Plus.** Warren J. Hehre. (Illus.). 126p. 2000. pap. 35.00 (*1-890661-14-7*) Wavefunction.

***MacSpartan Pro/MacSpartan Plus: (version 2.0) Tutorial.** Warren J. Hehre. (Illus.). 136p. 2000. pap. 20.00 (*1-890661-16-3*) Wavefunction.

MACSpeed. Don Crabb. (Illus.). (Orig.). 1995. pap. 40.00 (*1-56830-227-4*) Hayden.

MACSYMA for Statisticians. Barbara Heller. LC 91-2471. (Probability & Mathematical Statistics Ser.). 264p. 1991. 115.00 (*0-471-62590-6*) Wiley.

Macsyma O. D. E. Lab Book. Dareen Redfern et al. LC 97-34233. (Math Ser.). 192p. 1997. pap. 28.75 (*0-7637-0532-2*) Jones & Bartlett.

Macsyma Tutorial for Calculus. Richard N. Fell. LC 97-29110. (Math Ser.). 109p. 1997. pap. 18.75 (*0-7637-0622-1*) Jones & Bartlett.

MACtivities: Learning to Use the Macintosh Computer. Kenneth W. Auvil. 1990. mass mkt. 22.95 (*0-538-60704-1*) S-W Pub.

Maculaitis Assessment Batteries. Jean D. Maculaitis. 1982. 19.10 (*0-88084-079-X*); 21.85 (*0-88084-088-9*); 33.70 (*0-88084-089-7*); 26.00 (*0-88084-094-3*); 26.00 (*0-88084-099-4*); 43.90 (*0-88084-104-4*); 34.50 (*0-88084-109-5*); 19.75 (*0-88084-108-7*) Alemany Pr.

Macular & Retinal Diseases: New Approaches in the Diagnosis & Therapy of Macular & Retinal Diseases, Leipzig, November 1996. Ed. by Peter Wiedemann & Leon Kohen. LC 97-34801. (Developments in Ophthalmology Ser.: No. 29). (Illus.). viii, 100p. 1997. 119.25 (*3-8055-6553-4*) S Karger.

***Macular Degeneration: A Comprehensive Guide to Treatment, Breakthroughs & Coping Strategies.** Robert D'Amato & Joan Snyder. (Illus.). 192p. 2000. pap. 14.95 (*0-8027-1359-9*) Walker & Co.

Macular Degeneration: Living Positively with Vision Loss. Betty Wason & James J. McMillan. LC 98-42145. (Illus.). 256p. 1998. pap. 14.95 (*0-89793-239-0*) Hunter Hse.

Macular Degeneration: Living Positively with Vision Loss. large type ed. Betty Wason & James J. McMillan. (Illus.). 256p. 1998. 24.95 (*0-89793-240-4*) Hunter Hse.

Macular Degeneration: The Complete Guide to Saving & Maximizing Your Sight. Lylas Mogk & Marja Mogk. LC 98-46041. (Illus.). 416p. 1999. pap. 13.95 (*0-345-42598-7*) Ballantine Pub Grp.

Macular Degeneration Handbook: Natural Ways to Prevent & Reverse It. Chet Cunningham. LC 98-61570. (Illus.). 278p. 1998. pap. 14.95 (*1-887053-11-5*) United Res CA.

Macular Disease. Lim Sternberg. 1995. 39.00 (*0-316-06079-8*, Little Brwn Med Div) Lppncott W & W.

Macular Disorders: An Illustrated Diagnostic Guide. Anthony A. Cavallerano & Rodney K. Gutner. LC 96-39906. (Illus.). 304p. 1997. text 97.50 (*0-7506-9224-3*) Buttrwrth-Heinemann.

***Macular Edema: Current Concepts.** Thomas J. Wolfensberger. LC 00-42661. (Illus.). 2000. write for info. (*0-7923-6441-4*) Kluwer Academic.

Macular Hole: Pathogenesis, Diagnosis, & Treatment. Steven A. Madreperla & Brooks McCuen. LC 98-20598. (Illus.). 192p. 1998. pap. text 59.95 (*0-7506-9960-4*) Buttrwrth-Heinemann.

Macular Surgery. Jerald A. Bovino. (Illus.). 184p. (C). 1994. pap. text 135.00 (*0-8385-6082-2*, A6082-0, Apple Lange Med) McGraw.

Macular Surgery. Hugo Quiroz-Mercado et al. 400p. text 135.00 (*0-7817-1531-8*) Lppncott W & W.

Maculate Muse: Obscene Language in Attic Comedy. Jeffrey Henderson. LC 74-82746. 265p. reprint ed. pap. 82.20 (*0-8357-8212-3*, 203375200087) Bks Demand.

Maculate Muse: Obscene Language in Attic Comedy. 2nd ed. Jeffrey Henderson. 288p. 1991. pap. text 19.95 (*0-19-506685-5*) OUP.

Macumba: The Teachings of Marie-Jose, Mother of the Gods. Serge Bramly. LC 94-290. (Illus.). 240p. (Orig.). 1994. pap. 14.95 (*0-87286-286-0*) City Lights.

Macumba Killer. Ramsay Thorne. (Renegade Ser.: No. 5). 224p. (Orig.). 1982. mass mkt. 2.25 (*0-446-30775-0*, Pub. by Warner Bks) Little.

MacUser Guide to Connectivity. John Rizzo. (Guide to...Ser.). (Illus.). 380p. (Orig.). 1992. pap. 27.95 (*1-56276-056-4*, Ziff-Davis Pr) Que.

MACV-SOG Command Histories (Annexes A, N & M), 1964-1966: First Secrets of the Vietnam War. Charles F. Reske. LC 92-82789. (Illus.). 178p. (Orig.). 1992. pap. 19.95 (*0-939427-62-1*) Alpha Pubns OH.

MacWeek Guide to Desktop Video. Erik Holsinger. (Guide to...Ser.). (Illus.). 368p. 1993. pap. 34.95 incl. cd-rom (*1-56276-127-7*, Ziff-Davis Pr) Que.

MacWeek Guide to System 7. Don Crabb. (Guide to...Ser.). (Illus.). 296p. (Orig.). 1991. pap. 24.95 (*1-56276-029-7*, Ziff-Davis Pr) Que.

Macworld: Complete Mac Handbook. Jim Heid. LC 91-70289. 548p. 1991. pap. 26.95 (*1-878058-17-7*) IDG Bks.

***MacWorld AppleWorks 6 Bible.** Steven A. Schwartz. (Illus.). 700p. 2000. pap. text 39.99 (*0-7645-3434-3*) IDG Bks.

Macworld Clarisworks 2.0-2.1 Companion. 2nd ed. Steven A. Schwartz. LC 94-76642. 550p. 1994. pap. 24.95 (*1-56884-180-9*) IDG Bks.

MacWorld Complete MAC Handbook. 3rd ed. Jim Heid. LC 94-77629. 1000p. 1994. pap. 39.95 incl. cd-rom (*1-56884-192-2*) IDG Bks.

MacWorld Creating Cool Web Pages with Adobe Pagemill. Bud E. Smith. LC 96-76247. 352p. 1996. pap. 29.99 (*0-7645-3006-2*) IDG Bks.

Macworld Creating Cool Web Pages with HTM. Dave Taylor. 384p. 1995. pap. 19.99 incl. disk (*1-56884-705-X*) IDG Bks.

MacWorld Excel 5 Companion. 2nd ed. Christopher Van Buren & David Maguiness. LC 94-77527. 448p. 1994. pap. 24.95 (*1-56884-081-0*) IDG Bks.

MacWorld Filemaker Pro 2.0-2.1 Bible. Steven Schwartz. LC 94-77749. 648p. 1994. pap. 34.95 (*1-56884-201-5*) IDG Bks.

MacWorld Freehand 4.0 Bible. Deke McClelland. LC 94-75904. 700p. 1994. pap. 29.95 (*1-56884-170-1*) IDG Bks.

MacWorld Guide to ClarisWorks 2. Steven A. Schwartz. (Illus.). 500p. 1993. pap. 22.95 (*1-56884-018-7*) IDG Bks.

MacWorld Guide to Microsoft Excel 4. David Maguiness. (Illus.). 432p. 1992. 22.95 (*1-878058-40-1*) IDG Bks.

MacWorld Guide to Microsoft Word 5.1. Jim Heid. LC 91-77219. (Illus.). 448p. 1992. 22.95 (*1-878058-39-8*) IDG Bks.

MacWorld Guide to Microsoft Works 3, Vol. 3. Barrie Sosinsky. (Illus.). 464p. 1992. pap. 22.95 (*1-878058-42-8*) IDG Bks.

Macworld Guide to System 7.0. Lon Poole. LC 91-72754. 356p. 1991. pap. 24.95 (*1-878058-16-9*) IDG Bks.

Macworld Guide to System 7.1. 2nd ed. Lon Poole. (Illus.). 432p. 1992. pap. 24.95 (*1-878058-65-7*) IDG Bks.

MacWorld Home Office Companion. Kathi Vian. LC 95-81939. 500p. 1996. pap. 24.99 (*1-56884-792-0*) IDG Bks.

MacWorld Illustrator 5.0/5.5 Bible. Ted Alspach. LC 94-75905. 650p. 1994. pap. 39.95 (*1-56884-097-7*) IDG Bks.

MacWorld Illustrator 6 Bible. 2nd ed. Ted Alspach. (Illus.). 850p. 1996. pap. 39.99 (*1-56884-494-8*) IDG Bks.

MacWorld Mac & Power Mac Secrets. 2nd ed. David Pogue. LC 94-77529. 1020p. 1994. pap. 39.95 (*1-56884-175-2*) IDG Bks.

MacWorld Mac & Power Mac Secrets. 3rd ed. David Pogue. LC 95-81815. 1088p. 1996. pap. 39.99 incl. disk (*1-56884-791-2*) IDG Bks.

MacWorld Mac Faqs. David Pogue. 456p. 1995. pap. 19.99 (*1-56884-480-8*) IDG Bks.

Macworld Mac OS 8.5 Bible. Lon Poole. LC QA76.76.O63P6583. (Bible Ser.). (Illus.). 1008p. 1998. pap. 39.99 (*0-7645-4042-4*) IDG Bks.

Macworld Mac Secrets. 5th ed. David Pogue & Joseph Schorr. LC QA76.8.M3P619 1999. (Secrets Ser.). 1344p. 1998. pap. 49.99 incl. cd-rom (*0-7645-4040-8*) IDG Bks.

MacWorld Mac Upgrade & Repair Bible. Todd Stauffer. LC 98-72476. (Bible Ser.). (Illus.). 984p. 1998. pap. 39.99 (*0-7645-3217-0*) IDG Bks.

Macworld Macintosh Secrets. David Pogue & Joseph Schorr. (Illus.). 1000p. 1993. pap. 39.95 incl. disk (*1-56884-025-X*) IDG Bks.

***MacWorld Microsoft Office "X" Bible.** Bob LeVitus. (Bible Ser.). (Illus.). 900p. 2000. pap. text 39.99 (*0-7645-3462-9*) IDG Bks.

Macworld Music & Sound Bible. Christopher Yavelow. 1398p. 1992. pap. 37.95 (*1-878058-18-5*) IDG Bks.

MacWorld Networking Bible. 2nd ed. David R. Kosiur. LC 94-77528. 750p. 1994. pap. 29.95 (*1-56884-194-9*) IDG Bks.

MacWorld Networking Handbook. David R. Kosiur. 584p. 1992. 29.95 (*1-878058-31-2*) IDG Bks.

MacWorld New Complete Mac Handbook. 2nd ed. Jim Heid. (Illus.). 1000p. 1993. pap. 39.95 incl. cd-rom (*1-56884-033-0*) IDG Bks.

MacWorld Pagemaker 5 Bible. Craig Danuloff. LC 93-61312. (Bible Ser.). 650p. 1994. pap. 39.95 (*1-878058-84-3*) IDG Bks.

MacWorld Pagemaker 6 Bible. 2nd ed. William Harrel & Craig Danuloff. LC 95-81547. 712p. 1995. pap. 39.99 incl. cd-rom (*1-56884-589-8*) IDG Bks.

MacWorld Photoshop 5 Bible. Deke McClelland. (Bible Ser.). (Illus.). 960p. 1998. pap. text 49.99 incl. cd-rom (*0-7645-3231-6*) IDG Bks.

MacWorld Photoshop 3.0 Bible. 2nd ed. Deke McClelland. LC 94-79605. 894p. 1994. pap. 39.95 (*1-56884-158-2*) IDG Bks.

MacWorld Photoshop 2.5 Bible. Deke McClelland. (Illus.). 650p. 1993. pap. 29.95 (*1-56884-022-5*) IDG Bks.

MacWorld Quarkxpress 3.2/3.3 Bible. Barbara Assadi & Galen Gruman. 650p. 1994. pap. 39.95 (*1-878058-85-1*) IDG Bks.

Macworld Read Me First Book. Jerry Borrell. LC 91-75702. 298p. 1991. pap. 22.95 (*1-878058-19-3*) IDG Bks.

MacWorld System 7.5 Bible. 3rd ed. Lon Poole. LC 94-77526. 560p. 1994. pap. 29.95 (*1-56884-098-5*) IDG Bks.

MacWorld Ultimate CD-ROM. Jim Heid. LC 94-79602. 96p. 1994. pap. 19.99 (*1-56884-477-8*) IDG Bks.

MacWorld Ultimate Mac CD-ROM. Gruman. 96p. 1994. 19.99 (*1-56884-479-4*) IDG Bks.

MacWorld Ultimate Mac Programming: Methods Of. Dave Mark. LC 94-72744. 592p. 1995. pap. 39.95 (*1-56884-195-7*) IDG Bks.

MacWorld Web Essentials. Charles Seiter & Cameron Crotty. LC 95-81814. 336p. 1996. pap. 24.99 (*1-56884-785-8*) IDG Bks.

MacWorld Word 6 Companion. 2nd ed. Jim Heid. LC 94-77625. 576p. 1994. pap. 24.95 (*1-56884-082-9*) IDG Bks.

MacWrite. write for info. (*0-318-58187-6*) P-H.

MacWrite: The Useable Portable Guide. Jon Haber & Herbert R. Haber. (Illus.). 32p. (Orig.). 1989. pap. 5.95 (*0-945765-10-X*) Useable Portable Pubns.

Macwrite Guidebook. Claris & Coleman. 1992. pap. 38.40 incl. cd-rom (*0-673-46723-6*) Addson-Wesley Educ.

Macy Family Cookbook. 2nd large type ed. Ed. by Randy D. Macy. (Illus.). 100p. 1996. pap. 19.95 (*0-9674622-0-7*) Macy Family.

***Macy Gray: Still Waiting.** Lindsey Kai. 128p. 2000. pap. write for info. (*1-58754-003-7*, Pub. by Olmstead Pr) LPC Group.

Mad. Roger Edwing. 1989. mass mkt. 3.50 (*0-446-35570-4*) Little.

***Mad: Cover to Cover, 48 Years, 6 Months & 3 Days of Mad Magazine Covers.** Comment by Frank Jacobs. (Illus.). 224p. 2000. pap. 24.95 (*0-8230-1684-6*) Watsn-Guptill.

MAD: The Half-Wit & Wisdom of Alfred E. Neuman. DC Comics Staff. LC 97-151527. (Illus.). 96p. 1997. 8.95 (*0-446-91200-X*, Pub. by Warner Bks) Little.

Mad about Cheddar. Angela Clubb. (Illus.). 88p. 1998. pap. text 10.00 (*0-7881-5305-6*) DIANE Pub.

Mad about Cheddar. Angela Clubb. (Illus.). 88p. 1983. pap. 5.95 (*0-7720-1436-1*) Genl Dist Srvs.

***Mad about Eggplant.** Shirly Smalheiser. LC 99-40467. 2000. 19.95 (*965-229-204-4*) Gefen Pub Hse.

Mad about Garlic. Pat Reppert. (Illus.). 157p. 1997. spiral bd. 9.95 (*1-57166-106-9*) Hearts N Tummies.

Mad about Islands: Novelists of a Vanished Pacific. A. Grove Day. 320p. 1987. 13.95 (*0-935180-46-X*); pap. 9.95 (*0-935180-47-8*) Mutual Pub HI.

***Mad about Macaroni: Rodale's New Classics Cookbooks.** Anne Egan. 2001. pap. 14.95 (*1-57954-343-X*) Rodale Pr Inc.

Mad about Madeline: The Complete Tales. Ludwig Bemelmans. (Madeline Ser.). (Illus.). 352p. (J). (ps-3). 1993. 35.00 (*0-670-85187-6*, Viking Child) Peng Put Young Read.

***Mad about Madeline: The Complete Tales.** Ludwig Bemelmans. (Madeline Ser.). (J). (ps-3). 1999. 35.00 (*0-670-88816-8*) Viking Penguin.

Mad about Madeline: The Complete Tales. Ludwig Bemelmans. (Madeline Ser.). (J). (ps-3). 1999. pap. 35.00 (*0-670-85297-X*) Viking Penguin.

Mad about Maggie: Fabulous Father. Pepper Adams. (Romance Ser.). 1993. per. 2.75 (*0-373-08964-3*, 5-08964-4) Silhouette.

Mad about Martha: The Fabulous Paper Doll Book. Illus. by Robert Rodriguez. 32p. (Orig.). 1997. pap. 9.95 (*0-8362-2432-9*, Cader Bks) Andrews & McMeel.

Mad about Mead: Nectar of the Gods. Pamela Spence. LC 97-39519. (Illus.). 208p. (Orig.). 1999. pap. 12.95 (*1-56718-683-1*) Llewellyn Pubns.

Mad about Mission: The Story of Thomas Coke. Cyril Davey. 127p. 1987. pap. 3.95 (*0-310-55242-7*, 19024P) Zondervan.

Mad about Muffins. Dot Vartan. LC 98-22871. (Illus.). 160p. 1998. write for info. (*0-8362-6994-2*) Andrews & McMeel.

Mad about Muffins: A Cookbook for Muffin Lovers. Dot Vartan. LC 96-85410. (Illus.). 128p. 1996. write for info. (*0-9653117-1-6*) Among Friends.

***Mad about NewYorkTown.** Terry Quinn. 140p. 2000. pap. 16.00 (*1-892323-22-2*) Vivisphere.

Mad about Physics: Braintwisters, Paradoxes & Curiosities. Christopher P. Jargodzki & Potter Franklin. 320p. 2000. pap. 16.95 (*0-471-56961-5*) Wiley.

***Mad About Plaid.** Jill McElmurry. LC 99-28800. (Illus.). 40p. (J). (gr. k-5). 2000. 14.95 (*0-688-16951-1*); lib. bdg. 14.89 (*0-688-16952-X*, Wm Morrow) Morrow Avon.

Mad about the Boys. J. Patrick. 1997. pap. 14.95 (*1-877978-78-7*, STARbks Pr) FL Lit Foundation.

Mad about the Buoy. Mad Magazine Editors. Ed. by Albert B. Feldstein. (Mad Ser.: No. 53). 1986. mass mkt. 3.95 (*0-446-30506-5*) Warner Bks.

Mad about the '80s: By the Usual Gang of Idiots. LC 99-33898. 1999. pap. 19.95 (*1-55853-774-0*) Rutledge Hill Pr.

Mad about the Fifties: The Best of the Decade. Usual Gang of Idiots & Joyce L. Vedral. LC 97-4376. (Illus.). 288p. 1997. pap. 19.95 (*0-316-55808-7*) Little.

Mad about the Major: In Uniform. Roz Denny Fox. (In Uniform Ser.: No. 821). 1998. per. 4.25 (*0-373-70821-1*, 1-70821-3) Harlequin Bks.

Mad about the Movies: Special WB Edition. Ed. by Nick Meglin & John Ficarra. LC 99-165891. (Illus.). 256p. 1998. pap. text 14.95 (*1-56389-459-9*, Pub. by DC Comics) Time Warner.

Mad about the Seventies: The Best of the Decade. Usual Gang of Idiots Staff. (Illus.). 288p. 1996. pap. 19.95 (*0-316-32802-2*) Little.

Mad about the Sixties: The Best of the Decade, Vol. 1. Mad Magazine Editors. LC 95-22337. (Illus.). 240p. 1995. pap. 20.00 (*0-316-33418-9*) Little.

Mad about Theatre. Richard Hornby. 272p. 1996. pap. 19.95 (*1-55783-260-9*) Applause Theatre Bk Pubs.

***Mad about TV.** Usual Gang of Idiots Staff. 272p. 1999. mass mkt. 14.95 (*1-56389-569-2*, Pub. by DC Comics) Time Warner.

Mad about You. Alyssa Dean. LC 95-4600. (Temptation Ser.: No. 524). 218p. 1995. per. 2.99 (*0-373-25624-8*, 1-25624-7) Harlequin Bks.

***Mad about You.** Roberta Gayle. (Arabesque Ser.). 2000. mass mkt. 5.99 (*1-58314-108-1*) BET Bks.

Mad about You: Dealing with Anger in Relationships. rev. ed. Tim Downs. 4p. (C). 1995. teacher ed., ring bd. 1.25 (*1-57334-011-1*, 742-002t); student ed., ring bd. 3.25 (*1-57334-010-3*, 742-002s) WSN Pr.

Mad about You Because . . . Linda Christel. LC 97-221668. 80p. 1997. 4.95 (*0-88088-817-2*) Peter Pauper.

Mad Ads: Advertising in Today's Marketplace. Paula K. Kuchmey. 173p. (Orig.). (YA). (gr. 7-12). 1995. pap. 6.95 (*1-57515-083-2*) PPI Pubng.

Mad Amadeus Sued a Madam. Allan Miller. LC 97-3303. (Illus.). 64p. (Orig.). 1997. pap. 10.01 (*1-56792-077-2*) Godine.

Mad Among Us: A History of the Care of America's Mentally Ill. Gerald N. Grob. 300p. 1994. 24.95 (*0-02-912695-9*) Free Pr.

Mad Among Us: A History of the Care of America's Mentally Ill. Gerald N. Grob. (Illus.). 416p. (C). 1995. pap. 16.95 (*0-674-54112-X*) HUP.

Mad Amos. Alan Dean Foster. 1996. mass mkt. 5.99 (*0-345-39362-7*, Del Rey) Ballantine Pub Grp.

Mad & Bad Fairies. Attic Pr. Staff. 1991. 34.95 (*0-946211-40-X*) St Mut.

Mad Angels: The Plays of Larry Kirwan. Larry Kirwan. 264p. 1994. pap. 10.00 (*0-9639601-0-5*) Forty Seven Bks.

Mad Angels & Amphetamines: An Anthology. Nik Beat et al. LC 96-136690. 96p. pap. 12.95 (*1-895837-14-6*) Insomniac.

Mad Around the World. 1980. mass mkt. 1.75 (*0-446-94445-9*, Pub. by Warner Bks) Little.

Mad As a Hatter. Sergio Aragones. 192p. (Orig.). 1987. mass mkt. 3.95 (*0-446-34741-8*, Pub. by Warner Bks) Little.

Mad As a Wet Hen! And Other Funny Idioms. Marvin Terban. 1987. 12.15 (*0-606-01805-0*, Pub. by Turtleback) Demco.

Mad As a Wet Hen & Other Funny Idioms. Marvin Terban. LC 86-17575. (Illus.). 64p. (J). (ps-3). 1987. pap. 7.95 (*0-89919-479-6*, Clarion Bks) HM.

Mad As Hell. 96p. 1997. pap. 19.95 (*0-932905-12-9*) Penton Pub.

Mad As Hell. Mike Lupica. LC 97-40087. 256p. 1997. pap. 14.95 (*0-8092-3008-9*, 300890, Contemporary Bks) NTC Contemp Pub Co.

Mad As Usual. Sergio Aragones. 192p. 1990. mass mkt. 3.50 (*0-446-35860-6*, Pub. by Warner Bks) Little.

Mad at Your Lawyer. Tanya Starnes. Ed. by Robin Leonard. LC 96-27640. (Illus.). 352p. 1996. pap. 21.95 (*0-87337-326-X*) Nolo com.

***Mad Ave: Award-Winning Advertising in the 20th Century.** The Art Directors Club Staff. LC 99-42238. (Illus.). 256p. 2000. 39.95 (*0-7893-0369-8*) Universe.

Mad Bear. Doug Boyd. 368p. 1994. pap. 12.00 (*0-671-75945-0*, Touchstone) S&S Trade Pap.

M

M

Mad Blake. Elyse Curtis. LC 97-94169. 76p. 1997. pap. 7.95 (*1-891058-07-X*, 117) Astral Projections.

Mad Blood Stirring: Vendetta & Factions in Friuli During the Renaissance. Edward Muir. LC 92-15211. 424p. 1993. text 49.95 (*0-8018-4446-0*) Johns Hopkins.

Mad Blood Stirring: Vendetta in Renaissance Italy. abr. ed. Edward Muir. LC 97-41775. (Illus.). 208p. 1998. pap. text 15.95 (*0-8018-5849-6*) Johns Hopkins.

Mad Book of Revenge. Stan Hart, Jr. (Illus.). 192p. (Orig.). 1988. mass mkt. 2.95 (*0-446-35072-9*, Pub. by Warner Bks) Little.

Mad Boy Chronicles. Michael O'Brien. LC 97-124270. 154p. 1997. pap. text 11.95 (*0-88754-509-2*) Theatre Comm.

Mad Boys: A Novel. Ernest Hebert. LC 93-969. 228p. 1993. 22.00 (*0-87451-643-9*) U Pr of New Eng.

***Mad Broom Of Life.** Kyoji Takahashi. 1999. 60.00 (*4-7713-0361-4*) Korinsha.

Mad Capades. E. C. Publications Staff. 192p. (Orig.). 1992. mass mkt. 3.99 (*0-446-36310-3*, Pub. by Warner Bks) Little.

Mad Chopper. Kent Allard. 320p. 1998. pap. 5.99 (*0-7860-0557-2*, Pinncle Kensgtn) Kensgtn Pub Corp.

Mad Clowns Around. 2000. mass mkt. 1.95 (*0-446-90372-8*, Pub. by Warner Bks) Little.

Mad Cooler. 192p. 1988. mass mkt. 2.95 (*0-446-35000-1*, Pub. by Warner Bks) Little.

Mad Cow Crisis: Health & the Public Good. Scott C. Ratzan. LC 97-38913. 1998. text 55.00 (*0-8147-7510-1*); pap. text 18.50 (*0-8147-7511-X*) NYU Pr.

Mad Cow Crisis: Health & the Public Good. Scott C. Ratzan. 256p. 1997. pap. text 24.95 (*1-85728-812-2*, Pub. by UCL Pr Ltd) Taylor & Francis.

Mad Cow Crisis: Health & the Public Good. Ed. by Scott C. Ratzan. 256p. 1997. 69.95 (*1-85728-828-9*, Pub. by UCL Pr Ltd) Taylor & Francis.

Mad Cow U. S. A. Could the Nightmare Happen Here? Sheldon Rampton & John Stauber. LC 97-22500. 224p. 1997. 24.95 (*1-56751-111-2*) Common Courage.

Mad Cowboy. Howard Lyman. LC 97-51961. 224p. 1998. 22.50 (*0-684-84516-4*) S&S Trade.

Mad Cows & Milk Gate. Virgil M. Hulse. LC 96-78006. 288p. (Orig.). 1996. pap. 20.00 (*0-9654377-0-1*) Marble Mtn.

Mad Cows & Mother's Milk: The Perils of Poor Risk Communication. Douglas Powell & William Leiss. LC 99-203404. 308p. 1997. text 65.00 (*0-7735-1618-2*, Pub. by McG-Queens Univ Pr) CUP Services.

Mad Cows & Mother's Milk: The Perils of Poor Risk Communication. Douglas Powell & William Leiss. LC 99-203404. 320p. 1998. pap. 19.95 (*0-7735-1619-0*, Pub. by McG-Queens Univ Pr) CUP Services.

Mad Cub. Michael McClure. 230p. 1996. pap. 10.95 (*1-56201-087-5*) FoxRock.

Mad Dad's Quips & Quotes: A Syndicated Daily Cartoon Strip. (Illus.). 1997. write for info. (*1-885170-05-X*) Walden Press.

Mad Disasters. Duck Edwing. 192p. (Orig.). 1992. mass mkt. 3.99 (*0-446-36202-6*, Pub. by Warner Bks) Little.

Mad Dog: Stories. Heinrich Boll. Tr. by Breon Mitchell. LC 97-16104. 144p. 1997. text 19.95 (*0-312-16757-1*) St Martin.

Mad Dog: Stories. Heinrich Boll. 176p. 1998. pap. 12.00 (*0-312-19549-4*) St Martin.

***Mad Dog & Annie.** Virginia Kantra. 2001. 4.50 (*0-373-27118-2*, 1-27118-8) Silhouette.

***Mad Dog & Englishman, Vol. 27.** J. M. Hayes. 2000. 23.95 (*1-890208-49-3*) Poisoned Pen.

Mad Dog McGraw. Mike Uhlberg. LC 98-41169. (Illus.). 32p. (J). (ps-3). 2000. 15.99 (*0-399-23308-3*, G P Putnam) Peng Put Young Read.

Mad Dog Mom: Or If all Else Fails, Lower Your Expectations. Susan Murphy. LC 97-17538. 96p. 1997. pap. 5.95 (*1-57587-064-9*) Crane Hill AL.

Mad Dog of Lobo Mountain. rev. ed. Lee Roddy. (D.J. Dillon Adventure Ser.). 132p. (J). 1996. pap. 5.99 (*1-56476-506-7*, 6-3506, Victor Bks) Chariot Victor.

Mad-Dog Prosecutors & Other Hazards of American Business. Michael Zinn. LC 99-45817. 278p. 1999. 22.95 (*1-58177-056-1*, Pub. by Barrytown Ltd) Consort Bk Sales.

Mad Dogs: The New Rabies Plague. Don Finley. LC 97-34672. (Illus.). 232p. 1998. pap. 14.95 (*0-89096-822-5*) Tex A&M Univ Pr.

Mad Dogs & Scotsmen. large type ed. Gerald Hammond. LC 96-25010. 1996. 20.95 (*0-7838-1890-4*, G K Hall Lrg Type) Mac Lib Ref.

Mad Dogs, Englishmen, & the Errant Anthropologist: Fieldwork in Malaysia. 20th ed. Douglas Raybeck. LC 97-205614. (Illus.). 248p. (C). 1996. pap. text 12.50 (*0-88133-906-7*) Waveland Pr.

***Mad Dogs of Trieste: New & Selected Poems.** Janine Pommy Vega. LC 00-23658. 275p. 2000. 30.00 (*1-57423-127-8*) Black Sparrow.

***Mad Dogs of Trieste: New & Selected Poems.** Janine Pommy Vega. 275p. 2000. pap. 16.00 (*1-57423-126-X*) Black Sparrow.

***Mad Dogs of Trieste: New & Selected Poems.** aut. ed. Janine Pommy Vega. LC 00-23658. 275p. 2000. 40.00 (*1-57423-128-6*) Black Sparrow.

Mad Ducks & Bears: Football Revisited. George Plimpton. 256p. 1993. pap. 14.95 (*1-55821-240-X*) Lyons Pr.

Mad Family Gets Their Mads Out: Fifty Things Your Family Can Say & Do to Express Anger Constructively. Lynne Namka. LC 94-60804. (Illus.). 48p. (Orig.). 1994. pap. 10.95 (*0-9642167-0-1*) Talk Trust & Feel.

MAD Fantasy, Fables, & Other Foolishness. Don Edwing. 192p. (Orig.). 1989. mass mkt. 3.50 (*0-446-35366-3*, Pub. by Warner Bks) Little.

Mad Folk of the Theatre. Cornelia Otis Skinner. LC 70-93380. (Essay Index Reprint Ser.). 1977. 26.95 (*0-8369-1851-7*) Ayer.

***Mad for Max.** Holly Fuhrmann. 2000. pap. 8.50 (*1-893896-05-6*) Ima Jinn.

Mad for Modernism: Earl Horter & His Collection. Innis H. Shoemaker et al. LC 98-56052. (Illus.). 192p. 1999. 45.00 (*0-87633-127-4*); pap. write for info. (*0-87633-134-7*) Phila Mus Art.

***Mad for Newyorktown.** Terry Quinn. LC 00-101732. 98p. 2000. pap. 12.00 (*1-58776-031-2*, Straw Hse Pr) Vivisphere.

Mad for the Dad. Terry Essig. 1997. per. 3.25 (*0-373-19198-7*, 1-19198-0) Silhouette.

Mad Forest: A Play from Romania. Caryl Churchill. 96p. 1996. pap. text 9.95 (*1-55936-114-X*) Theatre Comm.

***Mad Game.** Roland Lazenby. LC 99-45112. 256p. 1999. 21.95 (*1-57028-225-0*, 82250H, Mstrs Pr) NTC Contemp Pub Co.

***Mad Game: The NBA Education of Kobe Bryant.** Roland Lazenby. (Illus.). 2000. pap. 14.95 (*0-8092-9605-5*, Contemporary Bks) NTC Contemp Pub Co.

Mad Gasser of Bessledorf Street. Phyllis Reynolds Naylor. 112p. (J). 1992. pap. 3.50 (*0-380-71350-0*, Avon Bks) Morrow Avon.

Mad Genius: The Odyssey, Pursuit & Capture of the Unabomber Suspect. Nancy Gibbs et al. Ed. by Time Magazine Editors. 288p. 1996. mass mkt. 5.99 (*0-446-60459-3*, Pub. by Warner Bks) Little.

Mad Genius Controversy: A Study in the Sociology of Deviance. George Becker. LC 78-875. (Sociological Observations Ser.: No. 5). 152p. reprint ed. pap. 47.20 (*0-608-09954-6*, 202186900026) Bks Demand.

Mad Girl Drives in a Daze. Lyn Lifshin. (Illus.). 20p. (Orig.). 1995. 4.95 (*1-878116-37-1*) JVC Bks.

***Mad Girls in Love.** Michael Lee West. 2001. write for info. (*0-06-018406-X*) HarpC.

***Mad Girls in Love.** Michael Lee West. 2002. pap. write for info. (*0-06-098506-2*, Perennial) HarperTrade.

Mad Goes Wild. Frank Jacobs & Bob Clarke. (Illus.). 192p. (Orig.). 1981. mass mkt. 1.75 (*0-446-94283-9*, Pub. by Warner Bks) Little.

***Mad Hatter.** Illus. by Barry Moser. (Barry Moser Ser.). 160p. 1998. 9.95 (*1-55156-080-1*, Pub. by Paperblank) Andrews & McMeel.

Mad Heroes. Joseph Tenenbaum. LC 75-134983. (Short Story Index Reprint Ser.). 1977. 17.95 (*0-8369-3713-9*) Ayer.

***Mad Herringtons.** Jane Myers Perrine. 200p. 2000. 19.95 (*1-929085-22-2*); 17.95 (*1-929085-23-0*); mass mkt. 4.95 (*1-929085-21-4*) Rgncy Pr.

***Mad Herringtons.** large type ed. Jane Myers Perrine. 336p. 2000. 23.95 (*1-929085-24-9*); per. 19.95 (*1-929085-25-7*) Rgncy Pr.

Mad House. Kelly O'Rourke. (Halloween Ser.). 1998. mass mkt. 4.50 (*1-57297-342-0*) Blvd Books.

Mad House: Growing Up in the Shadows of Mentally Ill Siblings. Clea Simon. LC 96-26893. 224p. 1998. mass mkt. 12.95 (*0-14-027434-0*) Viking Penguin.

Mad in Orbit. Mad Magazine Editors. (Mad Ser.). (Illus.). 192p. 1981. mass mkt. 1.75 (*0-446-94591-9*, Pub. by Warner Bks) Little.

***Mad in Pursuit.** Violette Leduc. LC 99-29869. 1999. pap. text 14.00 (*1-57322-740-4*, Riverhead Books) Putnam Pub Group.

Mad in U. S. A. Gary Huck & Mike Konopacki. 112p. (Orig.). 1993. pap. 12.00 (*0-88286-223-5*) C H Kerr.

***Mad Isn't Bad: A Child's Book about Anger.** Michaelene Mundy. LC 99-72094. (Elf-Held Books for Kids). (Illus.). 32p. (J). (ps-3). 1999. pap. 5.95 (*0-87029-331-1*, 20106) Abbey.

***Mad Jack.** Catherine Coulter. 352p. 1999. mass mkt. 7.50 (*0-515-12420-6*, Jove) Berkley Pub.

***Mad Jack.** Catherine Coulter. LC 99-46172. 1999. 26.95 (*1-56895-784-X*, Wheeler) Wheeler Pub.

Mad Jack. Dave Sargent & Pat L. Sargent. (Animal Pride Ser.: No. 16). (Illus.). 42p. (J). (gr. 2-8). 1996. lib. bdg. 12.95 (*1-56763-034-0*) Ozark Pub.

Mad Jack: The Biography of Captain John Percival, USN, 1779-1862, 136. David F. Long. LC 92-31763. (Contributions in Military Studies Ser.: No. 136). 288p. 1993. 62.95 (*0-313-28567-5*, LMJ, Greenwood Pr) Greenwood.

Mad Jackpot. 192p. (Orig.). 1989. mass mkt. 3.50 (*0-446-35322-1*, Pub. by Warner Bks) Little.

Mad King: The Life & Times of Ludwig II of Bavaria. Greg King. LC 96-24034. (Illus.). 320p. 1996. 24.95 (*1-55972-362-9*, Birch Ln Pr) Carol Pub Group.

***Mad Libs.** Roger Price & Leonard Stern. (J). 1999. pap. 10.99 (*0-8431-7464-1*, Price Stern) Peng Put Young Read.

***Mad Libs for President.** Roger Price. (Illus.). 48p. (J). (gr. 4-7). 2000. pap. 3.99 (*0-8431-7623-7*, Price Stern) Peng Put Young Read.

Mad Libs 40th Anniversary. deluxe ed. Leonard Stern. (Mad Libs Ser.). 96p. (J). (gr. 4-7). 1998. pap. 3.99 (*0-8431-7823-X*) Peng Put Young Read.

Mad Libs from Outer Space. Leonard Stern & Roger Price. (Mad Libs Ser.). (Illus.). 48p. (Orig.). (J). (gr. 4-7). 1989. pap. 3.99 (*0-8431-2443-1*, Price Stern) Peng Put Young Read.

Mad Libs Halloween: Night of the Living Mad Libs-Monster Mad Libs, Vol. 1. Roger Price. 1999. pap. 3.99 (*0-8431-7466-8*, Price Stern) Peng Put Young Read.

Mad Libs in Love. Leonard Stern & Roger Price. pap. 3.99 (*0-8431-7628-8*, Price Stern) Peng Put Young Read.

Mad Libs on the Road: World's Greatest Word Game. Roger Price. (Mad Libs Ser.). 48p. (J). (gr. 4-7). 1999. pap. 3.99 (*0-8431-7498-6*, Price Stern) Peng Put Young Read.

***Mad Libs 2001 Desk Calendar.** Roger Price & Leonard Stern. 640p. 2000. pap. 10.99 (*0-8431-7573-7*) Peng Put Young Read.

Mad Look at the Future. Lou Silverstone & Jack Rickard. (Illus.). 192p. (Orig.). 1978. mass mkt. 1.50 (*0-446-88174-0*, Pub. by Warner Bks) Little.

Mad Look at the Sixties. Mad Magazine Editors. Ed. by Nick Meglin. (Illus.). 192p. (Orig.). 1989. mass mkt. 3.95 (*0-446-35499-6*, Pub. by Warner Bks) Little.

Mad Love. Andre Breton. Tr. by Mary A. Caws from FRE. LC 86-24889. (French Modernist Library). (Illus.). xviii, 129p. 1997. pap. 12.00 (*0-8032-6072-5*, Bison Books) U of Nebr Pr.

***Mad Loves: Women & Music in Offenbach's Les Contes d'Hoffmann.** Heather Hadlock. LC 00-23688. (Illus.). 192p. 2000. 29.95 (*0-691-05802-4*) Princeton U Pr.

Mad-ly Yours. Sergio Aragones. 1989. mass mkt. 3.95 (*0-446-35815-0*, Pub. by Warner Bks) Little.

Mad Mad Mad Mad Mad Libs: World's Greatest Word Game. Roger Price & Leonard Stern. (Mad Libs Ser.). 48p. (J). 1998. pap. 3.99 (*0-8431-7441-2*, Price Stern) Peng Put Young Read.

Mad, Mad, Mad World: A Life in Hollywood. Stanley Kramer & Thomas M. Coffey. 1997. 25.00 (*0-614-28254-3*) Harcourt.

Mad, Mad Monday. Herma Silverstein. (YA). (gr. 7-9). 1989. pap. 2.99 (*0-671-67403-X*, Archway) PB.

Mad Maddie Maxwell. STACIE MASLYN. 2000. 7.99 (*0-310-23207-4*) HarpC.

Mad Madonna. Susan A. Holton. 205p. (Orig.). 1987. pap. 14.95 (*0-943456-21-5*) Bearly Ltd.

Mad Mag's Woof. John Byrne. (Illus.). 80p. (J). pap. 7.95 (*0-14-130043-4*, Pub. by Pnguin Bks Ltd) Trafalgar.

Mad Man. Samuel R. Delany. (Orig.). 1994. 23.95 (*1-56333-193-4*, R Kasak Bks) Masquerade.

Mad Man. Samuel R. Delany. (Orig.). 1996. mass mkt. 8.95 (*1-56333-408-9*, Rhinoceros) Masquerade.

Mad Maria. Marcio Souza. 1985. mass mkt. 4.95 (*0-380-89871-3*, Avon Bks) Morrow Avon.

Mad Martin. Patricia Windsor. LC 76-3837. (Trophy Bk.). (J). (gr. 4-6). 1978. reprint ed. pap. 1.95 (*0-06-440093-X*, HarpTrophy) HarpC Child Bks.

Mad Me: Anger Control Activity Book. Jim Boulden & Joan Boulden. Ed. by JoAnn Farness. (Illus.). 16p. (J). (gr. k-2). 1995. pap. 5.95 (*1-878076-46-9*) Boulden Pub.

Mad Mechs: Paranoia. (Paranoia Ser.). 6.00 (*0-87431-160-8*, 12031) West End Games.

***Mad Men & Medusas: Reclaiming Hysteria.** Mitchell. 2000. pap. 18.00 (*0-465-04614-2*, Pub. by Basic) HarpC.

***Mad Men & Medusas: Reclaiming Hysteria.** Juliet Mitchell. 352p. 2000. 30.00 (*0-465-04613-4*, Pub. by Basic) HarpC.

Mad Menagerie. Sergio Aragones. 1989. mass mkt. 3.50 (*0-446-35419-8*, Pub. by Warner Bks) Little.

***Mad Merlin.** J. Robert King. LC 00-25946. 304p. 2000. 23.95 (*0-312-86963-0*, Pub. by Tor Bks) St Martin.

Mad Mike. large type ed. George Goodchild. (Ulverscroft Large Print Ser.). 368p. 1998. 29.99 (*0-7089-3939-2*) Ulverscroft.

Mad Mike: A Biography of Brigadier Michael Calvert. 35.00 (*0-85052-543-8*) Leo Cooper.

***Mad Millennium Joke Book.** Ladybird Books Staff. 1999. text 6.99 (*0-7214-9743-8*) Ladybird Bks.

Mad Minute. Lamont B. Steptoe. (Illus.). 70p. (Orig.). (C). 1989. write for info. (*0-318-64262-X*) Whirlwind Pr.

Mad Minute. Lamont B. Steptoe. 84p. (Orig.). 1990. pap. 15.00 (*0-922827-08-7*) Whirlwind Pr.

Mad Minutes & Vietnam Months. Michael Clodfelter. 384p. 1996. mass mkt. 5.99 (*0-7860-0337-5*, Pinncle Kensgtn) Kensgtn Pub Corp.

Mad Minutes & Vietnam Months: A Soldier's Memoir. Micheal Clodfelter. LC 87-43170. 1989. mass mkt. 4.50 (*0-8217-2604-8*, Zebra Kensgtn) Kensgtn Pub Corp.

Mad Minutes & Vietnam Months: A Soldier's Memoir. Micheal Clodfelter. LC 87-43170. (Illus.). 254p. 1988. pap. 22.95 (*0-89950-326-8*) McFarland & Co.

Mad Money: How to Preserve, Protect & Multiply Your Personal Injury Lawsuit Settlement. Linda Oldt. Ed. by Thomas R. Oldt. LC 94-96293. 160p. (Orig.). 1994. pap. 24.95 (*0-9642868-0-7*) Invest Informat.

Mad Money: When Markets Outgrow Governments. Susan Strange. LC 98-34303. 220p. 1998. pap. 20.95 (*0-472-06693-5*, 06693) U of Mich Pr.

Mad Monkton & Other Stories. Wilkie Collins. Ed. & Intro. by Norman Page. (Oxford World's Classics). 432p. 1999. pap. 10.95 (*0-19-283772-9*) OUP.

Mad Monkton & Other Stories. Wilkie Collins. reprint ed. lib. bdg. 19.95 (*0-89190-247-3*, Rivercity Pr) Amereon Ltd.

Mad Moon of Dreams. Brian Lumley. LC 87-82043. (Illus.). 192p. 1987. 21.00 (*0-932445-28-4*); pap. 7.50 (*0-932445-27-6*) Ganley Pub.

Mad Moon of Dreams. Brian Lumley. 256p. 1994. mass mkt. 4.99 (*0-8125-2421-7*, Pub. by Tor Bks) St Martin.

***Mad Morgan.** Kerry Newcomb. LC 00-25936. 288p. 2000. text 24.95 (*0-312-26197-7*) St Martin.

***Mad Myths Mind the Door.** Steve L. Barlow. (Illus.). 128p. (J). 1998. pap. 7.95 (*0-14-037725-5*, Pub. by Pnguin Bks Ltd) Trafalgar.

Mad Myths Stone Me. Steve Barlow. (Illus.). 124p. (J). 1997. pap. 7.95 (*0-14-037108-7*, Pub. by Pnguin Bks Ltd) Trafalgar.

Mad Nap-Pulon Matt: Anonymous Sixteenth Century Romagnol Poem in English Verse Translation. Ed. by D. B. Gregor. (Language & Literature Ser.: Vol. 7). 1976. 35.00 (*0-902675-37-0*) Oleander Pr.

Mad National Geogery. David Canalos et al. Ed. by Brian Richards & Larry Smith. (Wild Dog Ser.: No. 3). (Illus.). 40p. (Orig.). 1990. pap. 12.00 (*0-933087-16-0*) Bottom Dog Pr.

Mad Overboard. Mad Magazine Editors. (Mad Ser.: No. 47). (Illus.). 192p. (Orig.). 1983. mass mkt. 1.95 (*0-446-30407-7*, Pub. by Warner Bks) Little.

Mad Painter Poems. Judith Minty. Ed. by Robert Bixby. 36p. (Orig.). 1996. pap. 6.00 (*1-882983-25-4*) March Street Pr.

Mad Pantomimes. Sergio Aragones. 192p. 1987. mass mkt. 3.99 (*0-446-34397-8*, Pub. by Warner Bks) Little.

Mad Parts of Sane People in Analysis. Ed. by Murray Stein. LC 92-39057. (Chiron Clinical Ser.). (Illus.). 240p. (Orig.). 1993. pap. 24.95 (*0-933029-67-5*) Chiron Pubns.

Mad People's History of Madness. Ed. by Dale Peterson. LC 81-50430. (Contemporary Community Health Ser.). 382p. 1982. pap. 118.50 (*0-7837-8541-0*, 204935600011) Bks Demand.

Mad Polyunsa. Title. 2000. mass mkt. 1.95 (*0-446-90595-X*, Pub. by Warner Bks) Little.

Mad Pomegranate & the Praying Mantis: An Andalusian Adventure. Peter Luke. 238p. 1984. 27.00 (*0-86140-200-6*, Pub. by Smyth) Dufour.

Mad Potter of Biloxi: The Art & Life of George E. Ohr. Garth Clark et al. (Illus.). 192p. 1989. 85.00 (*0-89659-927-2*) Abbeville Pr.

Mad Princes of Renaissance Germany. H. C. Midelfort. LC 93-39116. (Studies in Early Modern German History). (Illus.). 224p. (C). 1994. text 30.00 (*0-8139-1500-7*) U Pr of Va.

Mad Princes of Renaissance Germany. H. C. Midelfort. 1996. pap. 14.50 (*0-8139-1501-5*) U Pr of Va.

Mad Punter Strikes Again. Charles M. Schulz. (Peanuts Classics Ser.). 128p. 1995. pap. 6.95 (*0-8050-1894-8*, Owl) H Holt & Co.

Mad Raccoons Collection. Cathy Hill. Ed. by Chuck Melville. (Illus.). 144p. (Orig.). 1995. pap. 14.95 (*1-883847-12-5*) MU Press.

Mad Reader. E. C. Publications. LC 54-13035. 1979. mass mkt. 1.50 (*0-345-28190-X*) Ballantine Pub Grp.

Mad River. Jan Beatty. LC 95-31468. (Poetry Ser.). 63p. 1996. pap. 10.95 (*0-8229-5570-9*) U of Pittsburgh Pr.

Mad River. Jan Beatty. LC 95-31468. (Poetry Ser.). 63p. (C). 1996. text 24.95 (*0-8229-3897-9*) U of Pittsburgh Pr.

***Mad Scientist Handbook: The Do-It-Yourself Guide to Making Your Own Rock Candy, Anti-Gravity Machine, Edible Glass, Rubber & Fake Blood.** Joey Green. (Illus.). (J). 2000. 17.30 (*0-606-18425-2*) Turtleback.

***Mad Scientist Handbook: The Do-It-Yourself Guide to Making Your Own Rock Candy, Antigravity Machine, Edible Grass, Rubber Eggs, Fake Blood, Green Slime & Much, Much More.** Joey Green. LC 99-57902. (Illus.). 192p. 2000. pap. 11.95 (*0-399-52593-9*, Perigee Bks) Berkley Pub.

Mad Scientists see Monsters

Mad Scientists of Sound Gravikords, Whirlies & Pyrophones: Experimental Musical Instruments. Bart Hopkin. (Illus.). 96p. 1996. 28.95 incl. audio compact disk (*1-55961-382-3*, Ellipsis Arts) Relaxtn Co.

Mad Scientist's Secret: Amazing Adventure Puzzle Thrillers. Marvin Miller. 112p. (J). (gr. 4-6). 1994. pap. 2.50 (*0-590-49438-4*) Scholastic Inc.

Mad Season. Nancy M. Wright. (WWL Mystery Ser.). 1998. per. 4.99 (*0-373-26270-1*, 1-26270-8, Wrldwide Lib) Harlequin Bks.

Mad Season, Vol. 1. Nancy M. Wright. 208p. 1996. 20.95 (*0-312-14819-4*, Thomas Dunne) St Martin.

Mad Shadows. Marie-Claire Blais. 134p. 1996. pap. text 7.95 (*0-7710-9867-7*) McCland & Stewart.

Mad Shelley. James R. Ullman. LC 74-18406. 134p. 1975. reprint ed. 45.00 (*0-87752-178-6*) Gordian.

Mad Shelley. James R. Ullman. 1970. reprint ed. pap. 39.95 (*0-8383-0078-2*) M S G Haskell Hse.

Mad Shepherds & Other Human Studies. Lawrence P. Jacks. LC 73-125223. (Short Story Index Reprint Ser.). 1977. 19.95 (*0-8369-3590-X*) Ayer.

***Mad Ship.** Robin Hobb. (Liveship Traders Ser.). 864p. 2000. mass mkt. 6.99 (*0-553-57564-3*) Bantam.

Mad Ship. Robin Hobb. LC 98-51188. (Liveship Traders Ser.). 704p. 1999. reprint ed. 24.95 (*0-553-10333-4*, Spectra) Bantam.

Mad Spy vs. Spy: The Updated Files. Mad Magazine Editors. 192p. (Orig.). 1989. mass mkt. 3.95 (*0-446-35400-7*, Pub. by Warner Bks) Little.

***Mad Summer Night's Dream.** Ruth Brown. LC 98-43734. (Illus.). 32p. (J). (ps-2). 1999. 15.99 (*0-525-46010-1*, Dutton Child) Peng Put Young Read.

Mad Survival Handbook. Stan Hart, Jr. & Paul Coker. (Illus.). 192p. (Orig.). 1980. mass mkt. 1.75 (*0-446-94015-1*, Pub. by Warner Bks) Little.

MAD Takes the Cake, No. 90. E. C. Publications Staff. 192p. (Orig.). 1992. mass mkt. 3.99 (*0-446-36311-1*, Pub. by Warner Bks) Little.

Mad Tales from the School of Hard Yocks. Dick DeBartolo. (Illus.). 192p. (Orig.). 1991. mass mkt. 3.99 (*0-446-36203-4*, Pub. by Warner Bks) Little.

Mad Tell-It-Like-It-Is Book. Lou Silverstone & Bob Jones, Jr. 192p. 1989. mass mkt. 3.50 (*0-446-35764-2*, Pub. by Warner Bks) Little.

Mad, the Bad & the Dangerous. Sara Orwig. (Superromance Ser.). 1993. mass mkt. 3.50 (*0-373-70563-8*, 1-70563-1) Harlequin Bks.

Mad, the Bad, & the Innocent: The Criminal Mind on Trial. Barbara Kirwin. 352p. 1998. mass mkt. 5.99 (*0-06-101344-7*, Harp PBks) HarpC.

Mad, the Bad & the Innocent: The Criminal Mind on Trial. Barbara R. Kirwin. LC 97-7833. 320p. 1997. 23.95 (*0-316-49499-2*) Little.

Mad to Be Normal: Conversations with R. D. Laing. Bob Mullan. 406p. (C). 1995. pap. 23.00 (*1-85343-395-0*, Pub. by Free Assoc Bks) NYU Pr.

An Asterisk (*) at the beginning of an entry indicates that the title is appearing for the first time.

Mad to Be Saved: The Beats, the '50s, & Film. David Sterritt. LC 97-43376. 320p. 1998. 29.95 (*0-8093-2180-7*) S Ill U Pr.

Mad Trapper of Rat River. Dick North. (Illus.). 144p. 1991. pap. 5.95 (*0-7736-7307-5*) Genl Dist Srvs.

Mad Travelers: Reflections on the Reality of Transient Mental Illness. Ian Hacking. LC 98-20894. (Page-Barbour Lectures Ser.). 174p. 1998. 27.95 (*0-8139-1823-5*) U Pr of Va.

Mad Tuesdays. Katy Perry. Ed. by Lisa Lyons. (Illus.). 160p. (Orig.). 1992. pap. 12.95 (*0-9626823-3-0*) Perry ME.

Mad User Guide. Michael Cook & Margaret Procter. 1989. text 19.95 (*0-566-03621-5*) Ashgate Pub Co.

Mad Wives & Island Dreams: Shimao Toshio & the Margins of Japanese Literature. Philip Gabriel. LC 98-16634. 328p. (C). 1999. text 49.00 (*0-8248-2012-6*); pap. text 28.95 (*0-8248-2089-4*) UH Pr.

Mad World, My Masters. Barrie Keeffe. (Methuen Modern Plays Ser.). 100p. (C). 1988. pap. write for info. (*0-413-47410-0*, A0158, Methuen Drama) Methn.

***Mad World, My Masters.** Thomas Middletown. 1999. pap. 15.00 (*0-87830-099-6*) Routledge.

Mad World, My Masters. Thomas Middleton. Ed. by Standish Henning. LC 65-10544. (Regents Renaissance Drama Ser.). 131p. reprint ed. pap. 40.70 (*0-8357-7877-0*, 203629500002) Bks Demand.

Mad World; My Masters & Other Plays. Thomas Middleton. (Oxford World's Classics Ser.). 416p. 1999. pap. 9.95 (*0-19-283455-X*) OUP.

Mad World, My Masters, & Other Prose Works, 2 vols., Set. Nicholas Breton. (BCL1-PR English Literature Ser.). 1992. reprint ed. lib. bdg. 150.00 (*0-7812-7194-0*) Rprt Serv.

Mad World, My Masters, & Other Prose Works, 2 vols., Set. Nicholas Breton. Ed. by Ursula Kentish-Wright. LC 30-11771. 1968. reprint ed. 49.00 (*0-403-00108-0*) Scholarly.

Mada: An Erotic Novel. Kleya Forte Escamilla. 162p. 1994. per. 10.95 (*0-920813-69-0*) Sister Vis Pr.

Madaba Plains Project Vol. I: The 1984 Season at Tell el-Umeiri & Vicinity & Subsequent Studies. Ed. by Lawrence T. Geraty et al. (Madaba Plains Project Ser.: Vol. 1). (Illus.). 526p. (C). 1989. text 79.99 (*0-943872-96-0*) Andrews Univ Pr.

Madaba Plains Project Vol. II: The 1987 Season at Tell el-Umeiri & Vicinity & Subsequent Studies. Ed. by Larry G. Herr et al. LC 91-73700. (Madaba Plains Project 2 Ser.: Vol. 2). (Illus.). 633p. (C). 1991. text 79.99 (*0-943872-98-7*) Andrews Univ Pr.

Madaba Plains Project Vol. III: The 1989 Season at Tell el-'Umeiri & Vicinity. Ed. by Larry G. Herr et al. LC 97-71219. (Illus.). 385p. 1997. write for info. (*0-943872-71-5*) Andrews Univ Pr.

***Madaba Plains Project Database Entry & Information Retrieval System Manual.** Karen A. Borstad. (Illus.). 93p. 1999. pap. 10.00 (*0-9642060-3-X*) Inst of Archaeol.

Madachy's Mathematical Recreations. Joseph S. Madachy. LC 78-74116. (Illus.). 1979. pap. 4.95 (*0-486-23762-1*) Dover.

Madagascar see Cultures of the World - Group 15

Madagascar see Festivals of the World

Madagascar. Gian P. Barbieri. (Photo & Sexy Bks.). 1997. 29.99 (*3-8228-8262-3*) Taschen Amer.

Madagascar. Hilary Bradt. LC 94-178370. (World Bibliographical Ser.). 138p. 1994. lib. bdg. 46.50 (*1-85109-179-3*) ABC-CLIO.

Madagascar. Daniel W. Gade. (American Geographical Society Around the World Program Ser.). (Illus.). 64p. (Orig.). 1995. 18.95 (*0-939923-61-0*); pap. 13.95 (*0-939923-60-2*) M & W Pub Co.

Madagascar. Martin J. Gutnik & Natalie Browne-Gutnik. LC 94-41785. (Wonders of the World Ser.). (Illus.). 64p. (J). 1995. lib. bdg. 25.64 (*0-8114-6372-9*) Raintree Steck-V.

Madagascar. Ed. by Alison Jolly et al. LC 83-17394. (Key Environment Ser.). (Illus.). 250p. 1984. text 73.00 (*0-08-028002-1*, Pergamon Pr) Elsevier.

***Madagascar.** Mary N. Oluonye. LC 99-38138. (Ticket to Ser.). (Illus.). 48p. (J). (gr. k-2). 2000. lib. bdg. 22.60 (*1-57505-145-1*, Carolrhoda) Lerner Pub.

Madagascar. Mary N. Oluonye. LC 98-54225. (Globe-Trotters Club Ser.). (Illus.). 48p. (J). (gr. 3-5). 2000. lib. bdg. 22.60 (*1-57505-120-6*, Carolrhoda) Lerner Pub.

***Madagascar: A Country Study Guide.** Global Investment & Business Center, Inc. Staff. (World Country Study Guides Library: Vol. 103). (Illus.). 350p. 2000. pap. 59.00 (*0-7397-2401-0*) Intl Business Pubns.

Madagascar: A Natural History. Ken Preston-Mafham. (Illus.). 224p. 1991. 45.00 (*0-8160-2403-0*) Facts on File.

Madagascar: A World Out of Time. Photos by Frans Lanting. (Illus.). 144p. 1990. 60.00 (*0-89381-422-9*) Aperture.

***Madagascar: An Agenda for Growth & Poverty Reduction.** LC 99-32772. (Country Studies Ser.). 94p. 1999. pap. 22.00 (*0-8213-4551-6*, 14551); pap. 22.00 (*0-8213-4558-3*, 14558) World Bank.

Madagascar: An Environmental Profile. IUCN Conservation Monitoring Center Staff. (International Union for the Conservation of Nature & Natural Resources: A Belhaven Press Book Ser.). 388p. 1987. pap. 30.00 (*2-88032-607-9*) St Martin.

Madagascar: Major World nations. Rita Stevens. (Major World Nations Ser.). (Illus.). 144p. (YA). (gr. 5 up). 1999. lib. bdg. 19.95 (*0-7910-4762-8*) Chelsea Hse.

Madagascar: Politics, Economics & Society. Maureen Covell. (Marxist Regimes Ser.). 225p. 1987. text 49.00 (*0-86187-428-5*); text 17.50 (*0-86187-429-3*) St Martin.

Madagascar: Society & History. Ed. by Conrad P. Kottak et al. LC 83-70313. (Illus.). 451p. 1986. lib. bdg. 39.95 (*0-89089-252-0*) Carolina Acad Pr.

Madagascar: Spanish. Taschen Staff. (SPA.). 1997. 29.99 (*3-8228-8041-8*, Pub. by Benedikt Taschen) Bks Nippan.

***Madagascar: The Bradt Travel Guide.** 6th ed. Hilary Bradt. LC 99-44249. 368p. 2000. pap. 18.95 (*1-898323-97-6*) Bradt Pubns.

Madagascar - A Country Study Guide: Basic Information for Research & Pleasure. Global Investment Center, USA Staff. (World Country Study Guide Library: Vol. 103). (Illus.). 350p. 1999. pap. 59.00 (*0-7397-1500-3*) Intl Business Pubns.

Madagascar & the Protestant Impact: The Work of the British Missions, 1818-95. Bonar A. Gow. LC BR1470.M2G68. (Dalhousie African Studies). 284p. reprint ed. pap. 88.10 (*0-608-13138-5*, 202522900043) Bks Demand.

Madagascar Before the Conquest: The Island, the Country & the People. James Sibree. LC 74-15090. reprint ed. 39.50 (*0-404-12140-3*) AMS Pr.

Madagascar Business & Investment Opportunities Yearbook-98: Business, Investment, Export-Import. Contrib. by Russian Information & Business Center, Inc. Staff. (Business & Investment Opportunity Library-98). (Illus.). 350p. 1998. pap. 99.00 (*1-57751-976-0*) Intl Business Pubns.

***Madagascar Business Intelligence Report, 190 vols.** Global Investment & Business Center, Inc. Staff. (World Business Intelligence Library: Vol. 103). 350p. 2000. pap. 99.95 (*0-7397-2601-3*) Intl Business Pubns.

***Madagascar Business Law Handbook, 190 vols.** Global Investment & Business Center, Inc. Staff. (Global Business Law Handbooks Library: Vol. 103). (Illus.). 350p. 2000. pap. 99.95 (*0-7397-2001-5*) Intl Business Pubns.

***Madagascar Business Opportunity Yearbook.** Global Investment & Business Center, Inc. Staff. (Global Business Opportunity Yearbooks Library: Vol. 103). (Illus.). 2000. pap. 99.95 (*0-7397-2201-8*) Intl Business Pubns.

***Madagascar Business Opportunity Yearbook: Export-Import, Investment & Business Opportunities.** International Business Publications, U. S. A. Staff & Global Investment Center, U. S. A. Staff. (Global Business Opportunity Yearbooks Library: Vol. 103). (Illus.). 350p. 1999. pap. 99.95 (*0-7397-1301-9*) Intl Business Pubns.

Madagascar Corundum. Eugene R. Black. Ed. by Lawrence Baber. 256p. 1979. pap. 6.95 (*0-9666256-0-9*, B10011) Hardwick Pubns.

***Madagascar Country Review 2000.** Robert C. Kelly et al. (Illus.). 60p. 1999. pap. 39.95 (*1-58310-527-1*) CountryWatch.

***Madagascar Foreign Policy & Government Guide.** Global Investment & Business Center, Inc. Staff. (World Foreign Policy & Government Library: Vol. 99). (Illus.). 350p. 1999. pap. 99.00 (*0-7397-3597-7*) Intl Business Pubns.

***Madagascar Foreign Policy & Government Guide.** Global Investment & Business Center, Inc. Staff. (World Foreign Policy & Government Library: Vol. 99). (Illus.). 350p. 2000. pap. 99.95 (*0-7397-3801-1*) Intl Business Pubns.

Madagascar in Pictures. rev. ed. Department of Geography, Lerner Publications. (Visual Geography Ser.). (Illus.). 64p. (YA). (gr. 5 up). 1988. lib. bdg. 19.93 (*0-8225-1841-4*, Lerner Publctns) Lerner Pub.

***Madagascar Investment & Business Guide.** Global Investment & Business Center, Inc. Staff. (Global Investment & Business Guide Library: Vol. 103). (Illus.). 2000. pap. 99.95 (*0-7397-1801-0*) Intl Business Pubns.

Madagascar Investment & Business Guide: Economy, Export-Import, Business & Investment Climate, Business Contacts. Contrib. by Russian Information & Business Center, Inc. Staff. (Russia, NIS & Emerging Markets Investment & Business Library-98). (Illus.). 350p. 1998. pap. 99.00 (*1-57751-872-1*) Intl Business Pubns.

***Madagascar Investment & Business Guide: Export-Import, Investment & Business Opportunities.** International Business Publications, USA Staff & Global Investment Center, USA Staff. (World Investment & Business Guide Library-99: Vol. 103). (Illus.). 350p. 1999. pap. 99.95 (*0-7397-0298-X*) Intl Business Pubns.

***Madagascar, Mayoette & Comoros.** James Penrith. (Travellers Survival Kit Ser.). 2000. pap. 18.95 (*1-85458-241-0*) Vac Wrk Pubns.

Madagascar: or Robert Drury's Journal During Fifteen Years' Captivity on That Island, & a Further Description of Madagascar by Alexis Rochon. Robert Drury & Daniel Defoe. LC 69-19359. (Illus.). 398p. 1970. reprint ed. lib. bdg. 35.00 (*0-8371-1403-9*, DRM&) Greenwood.

Madagascar Revisited. William C. Ellis. LC 72-5541. (Black Heritage Library Collection). 1977. reprint ed. 39.95 (*0-8369-9139-7*) Ayer.

Madagascar Wildlife. Hilary Bradt et al. LC 96-13766. (Bradt Country Guides Ser.). (Illus.). 138p. 1996. pap. 19.95 (*1-56440-947-3*, Pub. by Bradt Pubns) Globe Pequot.

Madagassisch-Deutsch Woerterbuch. Henning Bergenholtz. (GER.). 656p. 1991. 135.00 (*0-7859-8555-7*, 3924690626) Fr & Eur.

Madaket Millie. Frances Ward Weller. (Illus.). 32p. (ps-3). 1999. pap. 5.99 (*0-698-11774-3*) Putnam Pub Group.

Madaline: Love & Survival in Antebellum New Orleans. Ed. by Dell Upton. LC 95-14156. 1996. 29.95 (*0-8203-1758-6*) U of Ga Pr.

Madalyn Murray O'Hair: Most Hated Woman in America. Jon Rappoport. 170p. 1998. mass mkt. 6.95 (*0-939040-04-2*, 184) Truth Seeker.

***Madam: Chronicles of a Nevada Cathouse.** Lora Shaner. 1999. pap. write for info. (*0-929712-58-7*) Huntington Pr.

Madam: Chronicles of a Nevada Cathouse. Lora Shanor. 320p. 1999. 24.95 (*0-929712-57-9*) Huntington Pr.

Madam & Eve's Greatest Hits. S. Francis et al. LC 97-198879. (Illus.). 1997. write for info. (*0-14-027068-X*) Penguin Books.

Madam Anna's Palm Faxts. (Illus.). 50p. 1999. write for info. (*1-893125-08-4*) Womens Studio Wrkshop.

Madam As Entrepreneur: Career Management in House Prostitution. Barbara S. Heyl. LC 76-50329. 276p. 1978. 34.95 (*0-87855-211-1*) Transaction Pubs.

Madam Butterfly. Giacomo Puccini. Ed. by Nicholas John. Tr. by R. H. Ellcin from ITA. (English National Opera Guide Series: Bilingual Libretto, Articles: No. 26). (Illus.). (Orig.). 1984. pap. 9.95 (*0-7145-4038-2*) Riverrun NY.

Madam C. J. Walker: Building a Business Empire. Penny Colman. LC 93-13824. (Gateway Biographies Ser.). (Illus.). 48p. (J). (gr. 2-4). 1994. lib. bdg. 21.90 (*1-56294-338-3*) Millbrook Pr.

Madam C. J. Walker: Entrepreneur. Alelia Bundles. Ed. by Nathan I. Huggins. (Black Americans of Achievement Ser.). (Illus.). 124p. (YA). (gr. 5 up). 1991. lib. bdg. 19.95 (*1-55546-615-X*) Chelsea Hse.

Madam C. J. Walker: Entrepreneur. Alelia Bundles. Ed. by Nathan I. Huggins. (Black Americans of Achievement Ser.). (Illus.). 124p. (YA). (gr. 5 up). 1992. pap. 8.95 (*0-7910-0251-9*) Chelsea Hse.

Madam C. J. Walker: Self-Made Millionaire. Patricia McKissack & Fredrick McKissack. LC 92-6189. (Great African Americans Ser.). (Illus.). 32p. (J). (gr. 1-4). 1992. lib. bdg. 14.95 (*0-89490-311-X*) Enslow Pubs.

Madam Cama: A True Nationalist. B. D. Yadav. (Indian Freedom Fighters Ser.: No. 31). (C). 1992. 28.00 (*81-7041-526-8*, Pub. by Anmol) S Asia.

***Madam C.J. Walker: Self-Made Businesswoman.** Della A. Yannuzzi. LC 99-16447. (African-American Biographies Ser.). (Illus.). 112p. (gr. 6 up). 2000. lib. bdg. 20.95 (*0-7660-1204-2*) Enslow Pubs.

Madam de Stael, Novelist: The Emergence of the Artist As Woman. fac. ed. Madelyn Gutwirth. LC 78-5836. (Illus.). 336p. 1994. pap. 104.20 (*0-7837-7625-X*, 204737700007) Bks Demand.

Madam Dragonfly. Jane Hayter-Hames. 207p. (C). 1989. text 59.00 (*1-872795-20-X*, Pub. by Pentland Pr) St Mut.

Madam Fate. Marcia Douglas. LC 98-20395. 272p. 1998. 24.00 (*1-56947-134-7*, Pub. by Soho Press) FS&G.

Madam Felix's Gold: The Story of the Madam Felix Mining District, Calaveras County, California. Willard P. Fuller, Jr. et al. (Illus.). 162p. (Orig.). 1996. pap. 21.91 (*0-9655090-0-1*) Foothill Res.

Madam Guyon's Spiritual Letters see Guyon Speaks Again

Madam How & Lady Why: First Lessons in Earth Lore for Children. Charles Kingsley. 1977. text 22.95 (*0-8369-8163-4*, 8303) Ayer.

Madam I'm Adam: And Other Palindromes. William B. Irvine. (Illus.). 80p. 1988. pap. 5.95 (*0-684-18850-3*, Scribners Ref) Mac Lib Ref.

Madam Kitty. Peter Norden. 1978. mass mkt. 1.50 (*0-345-28191-8*) Ballantine Pub Grp.

***Madam President.** William G. Salomone. 319p. 2000. pap. 12.95 (*1-58721-812-7*) First Bks Lib.

***Madam President: Shattering the Last Glass Ceiling.** Eleanor Clift & Tom Brazaitis. LC 00-36565. (Illus.). 352p. 2000. 25.00 (*0-684-85619-0*) Scribner.

Madam Sarah, 2 vols., Set. large type ed. Cornelia Otis Skinner. reprint ed. 10.00 (*0-318-65670-1*) NAVH.

Madam Secretary. Blood. 320p. 1999. pap. 16.95 (*0-312-19505-2*) St Martin.

Madam Secretary: A Biography of Madeleine Albright. Thomas Blood. LC 97-16521. (Illus.). 320p. 1997. text 24.95 (*0-312-17180-3*) St Martin.

Madam Secretary: The Story of Madeleine Albright. Jeremy Byman. LC 97-38397. (Notable Americans Ser.). (Illus.). 96p. (YA). (gr. 5 up). 1998. lib. bdg. 18.95 (*1-883846-23-4*) M Reynolds.

Madam Wongs Guide to Men & Other Difficulties. Eliza Bussey. 128p. (Orig.). 1996. pap. 13.00 (*0-9652626-1-8*) Orge Blossom.

Madam, Your Daughter Is Molting. Lisa Davidson. 74p. (Orig.). 1994. pap. 7.00 (*0-944920-10-1*) Bellowing Ark Pr.

Madama Butterfly. Daniel S. Brink. (Black Dog Opera Library). 144p. 1998. 19.98 (*1-57912-019-9*) Blck Dog & Leventhal.

***Madama Butterfly.** Hal Leonard Publishing Company Staff. 484p. 2000. pap. 24.95 (*0-634-01944-9*) H Leonard.

Madama Butterfly: Vocal Score. Giacomo Puccini. (ENG & ITA.). 1986. pap. 19.95 (*0-7935-5388-1*); pap. 24.95 (*0-7935-4416-5*, 50338200) H Leonard.

Madama Butterfly in Full Score. Giacomo Puccini. 496p. 1990. pap. 19.95 (*0-486-26345-2*) Dover.

Madama Butterfly Libretto. Giacomo Puccini. 64p. 1986. pap. 4.95 (*0-7935-2614-0*, 50340150) H Leonard.

***Madame.** Antoni Libera. Tr. by Agniewska Kolakowska from POL. LC 99-49705. 288p. 2000. 24.00 (*0-374-20006-8*) FS&G.

***Madame Alexande: Collector's Dolls Price Guide.** 25th ed. Linda Crowsey. (Illus.). 96p. 2000. pap. 9.95 (*1-57432-172-2*) Collector Bks.

***Madame Alexander Dolls: An American Legend.** Stephanie Finnegan. LC 98-67943. (Illus.). 240p. 1999. 60.00 (*0-942620-22-4*) Portfolio Pr.

Madame Alexander "Little People" Marjorie I. Biggs. Ed. by Cliff Biggs. LC 79-66461. (Ser. I). (Illus.). 1979. 35.00 (*0-9603218-0-2*) M Biggs.

***Madame Alexander Store Exclusives & Limited Editions: Identification & Values.** Linda Crowsey. (Illus.). 144p. 2000. pap. 24.95 (*1-57432-173-0*) Collector Bks.

Madame Audrey's Guide to Mostly Cheap but Good Reference Books for Small & Rural Libraries. Audrey Lewis. LC 98-30767. 352p. 1998. 45.00 (*0-8389-0733-4*) ALA.

Madame Bidet & Other Fixtures: Poems. Lawrence P. Spingarn. (Illus.). 29p. (Orig.). 1968. pap. 7.95 (*0-912288-00-0*) Perivale Pr.

Madame Blavatsky's Baboon: A History of the Mystics, Mediums, & Misfits Who Brought Spiritualism to America. Peter Washington. (Illus.). 480p. 1996. pap. 14.00 (*0-8052-1024-5*) Schocken.

Madame Boskey's Fortune-Telling Kit: A Book & Card Set. Kirsten Hall & Amy Christensen. LC 97-149482. (Illus.). 64p. (J). (gr. 3-9), 1996. pap., boxed set 12.95 (*0-8118-1460-2*) Chronicle Bks.

***Madame Bovary.** 1999. 9.95 (*1-58130-574-5*) Novel Units.

***Madame Bovary.** 1999. 11.95 (*1-58130-575-3*) Novel Units.

Madame Bovary. Gustave Flaubert. Tr. by Lowell Bair. 448p. 1982. mass mkt. 5.95 (*0-553-21341-5*, Bantam Classics) Bantam.

Madame Bovary. Gustave Flaubert. (Barron's Book Notes Ser.). 1985. pap. 3.95 (*0-8120-3524-0*) Barron.

Madame Bovary. Gustave Flaubert. Tr. by Mildred Marmur. LC 96-36797. (New York Public Library Collector's Edition Ser.). (Illus.). 384p. 1997. 18.50 (*0-385-48719-3*) Doubleday.

Madame Bovary. Gustave Flaubert. Tr. by Francis Steegmuller. LC 92-54294. 1993. 17.00 (*0-679-42031-2*) Everymns Lib.

Madame Bovary. Gustave Flaubert. (Coll. GF). (FRE.). pap. 9.95 (*0-685-34900-4*) Fr & Eur.

Madame Bovary. Gustave Flaubert. Ed. by Gothot-Mesch. (Coll. Prestige). (FRE.). 49.95 (*0-685-34899-7*) Fr & Eur.

Madame Bovary. Gustave Flaubert. Ed. by Gothot-Mesch. (FRE.). 1961. pap. 11.95 (*0-8288-9748-4*, 2266033581) Fr & Eur.

Madame Bovary, 001. Gustave Flaubert. Ed. by Germaine Bree. Tr. by Merloyd Lawrence. (C). 1969. pap. 13.96 (*0-395-05210-6*, RivEd) HM.

Madame Bovary. Gustave Flaubert. Ed. by Thomas Hardy. (Cloth Bound Pocket Ser.). (Illus.). 1999. 7.95 (*3-8290-3006-1*) Konemann.

Madame Bovary. Gustave Flaubert. 396p. (C). 1982. pap. 8.44 (*0-07-554378-8*) McGraw.

Madame Bovary. Gustave Flaubert. Tr. by Mildred Marmur. (Illus.). 1964. mass mkt. 5.95 (*0-451-52387-3*, Sig Classics) NAL.

Madame Bovary. Gustave Flaubert. (FRE.). (C). 1972. pap. 13.95 (*0-8442-1758-1*, VF1758-1) NTC Contemp Pub Co.

Madame Bovary. Gustave Flaubert. (Illus.). (C). 1965. pap. text 14.75 (*0-393-09608-4*) Norton.

Madame Bovary. Gustave Flaubert. Tr. by Gerard Manley Hopkins from FRE. LC 99-462502. (Oxford World's Classics Hardcovers Ser.). 400p. 1999. 15.00 (*0-19-210025-4*) OUP.

Madame Bovary. Gustave Flaubert. Tr. by Francis Steegmuller. (Modern Library College Editions). 396p. (C). 1982. pap. text 4.00 (*0-685-04267-7*) Random.

Madame Bovary. Gustave Flaubert. (Folio Ser.: No. 804). (FRE.). 1976. pap. 10.95 (*2-07-036804-1*) Schoenhof.

Madame Bovary. Gustave Flaubert. Ed. by Victor Brombert. LC 85-10284. (ENG & FRE.). 440p. 1985. 6.95 (*0-88332-467-9*) Schoenhof.

Madame Bovary. Gustave Flaubert. 1964. 11.05 (*0-606-00911-6*, Pub. by Turtleback) Demco.

Madame Bovary. Gustave Flaubert. Tr. & Intro. by Geoffrey Wall. 320p. 1993. pap. 8.95 (*0-14-044526-9*, Penguin Classics) Viking Penguin.

Madame Bovary. Gustave Flaubert. Tr. by Francis Steegmuller. 1991. pap. 12.00 (*0-679-73636-0*) Vin Bks.

Madame Bovary. Gustave Flaubert. (Classics Library). 275p. 1998. pap. 3.95 (*1-85326-078-9*, 0789WW, Pub. by Wrdsworth Edits) NTC Contemp Pub Co.

Madame Bovary. Rosemary Lloyd. (Unwin Critical Library). 336p. 1989. 44.95 (*0-04-800084-1*) Routledge.

***Madame Bovary.** large type ed. Gustave Flaubert. 544p. 2000. pap. 22.00 (*0-06-095695-X*, HarpCollins) HarperTrade.

Madame Bovary. Gustave Flaubert. 320p. 1983. reprint ed. lib. bdg. 27.95 (*0-89966-324-9*) Buccaneer Bks.

Madame Bovary. unabridged ed. Gustave Flaubert. LC 96-11835. (Thrift Editions Ser.). 256p. 1996. reprint ed. pap. text 2.00 (*0-486-29257-6*) Dover.

Madame Bovary. unabridged ed. Gustave Flaubert. (FRE.). pap. 7.95 (*2-87714-130-6*, Pub. by Bookking Intl) Distribks Inc.

Madame Bovary: Life in a Country Town. Gustave Flaubert. Tr. by Gerard Manley Hopkins. (Oxford World's Classics Ser.). 390p. 1998. pap. 7.95 (*0-19-283399-5*) OUP.

Madame Bovary: Representations of the Masculine. Mary Orr. (Romanticism & after in France/Le Romantisme et apres en France Ser.: Vol. 3). 229p. 1999. pap. text 37.95 (*0-8204-4247-X*) P Lang Pubng.

Madame Bovary: The End of Romance. Eric Gans. (Masterwork Studies: No. 23). 152p. (C). 1989. 29.00 (*0-8057-7984-1*, TMWS 23, Twayne) Mac Lib Ref.

***Madame Bovary -- Representations of the Masculine.** Mary Orr. Ed. by Allan W. Raitt. (Romanticism & after in France Ser.). 229p. 1999. pap. 37.95 (*3-906762-90-4*, Pub. by P Lang) P Lang Pubng.

Madame Bovary & the Trial of Flaubert. Gustave Flaubert. 1976. 23.95 (*0-8488-1002-3*) Amereon Ltd.

An Asterisk (*) at the beginning of an entry indicates that the title is appearing for the first time.

Madame Bovary Notes. James L. Roberts. (Cliffs Notes Ser.). 80p. 1964. pap. 4.95 (*0-8220-0780-0*, Cliff) IDG Bks.

Madame Butterfly. (Penguin Readers Level 2). 1979. write for info. (*0-201-43890-9*) Addison-Wesley.

***Madame Butterfly.** David Henry Hwang. 1998. pap. 5.33 (*0-452-27259-9*) Addson-Wesley Educ.

Madame Butterfly. David Henry Hwang. (C). 1997. pap. text. write for info. (*0-8013-3142-0*) Longman.

Madame Butterfly. John L. Long. 1997. pap. 14.95 (*0-9666591-0-4*) Seconda Donna.

Madame Butterfly. John L. Long. 1972. reprint ed. lib. bdg. 27.00 (*0-8422-8092-8*) Irvington.

***Madame Butterfly: Japonisme, Puccini, & the Search for the Real Cho-Cho-San.** Jan Van Rij. (Illus.). 192p. 2000. pap. 24.95 (*1-880656-52-3*) Stone Bridge Pr.

Madame C. J. Walker: Entrepreneur. Cookie Lommel. (Black American Ser.). (Illus.). 192p. (YA). 1993. mass mkt. 3.95 (*0-87067-597-4*, Melrose Sq) Holloway.

Madame C. J. Walker: Pioneer Businesswoman. Marian W. Taylor. LC 93-14653. (Junior Black Americans of Achievement Ser.). (Illus.). 76p. (J). (gr. 3-6). 1993. lib. bdg. 15.95 (*0-7910-2039-8*) Chelsea Hse.

Madame Campan: Educator of Women, Confidante of Queens. Millicent S. Mali. LC 78-65428. 1978. pap. text 23.00 (*0-8191-0662-3*) U Pr of Amer.

Madame Childs: The Lady & the Legend. Elva B. McLin. 220p. 1992. 20.00 (*0-9629883-1-6*) Athens State.

Madame Cleo's Girls. Lucianne Goldberg. 1993. mass mkt. 5.99 (*0-671-70145-2*) PB.

Madame Crowl's Ghost & Other Tales of Mystery. Joseph Sheridan Le Fanu. Ed. by Montague R. James. LC 72-167459. (Short Story Index Reprint Ser.). 1977. reprint ed. 18.95 (*0-8369-3985-9*) Ayer.

Madame Curie. Eva Curie. (FRE.). 1985. pap. 12.95 (*0-7859-2194-X*, 207031068X) Fr & Eur.

Madame Curie. Eve Curie. Tr. by Vincent Sheean. (Illus.). 394p. 1986. pap. 14.95 (*0-306-80281-3*) Da Capo.

Madame Curie - Albert Einstein. Naunerle C. Farr. (Pendulum Illustrated Biography Ser.). (Illus.). (J). (gr. 4-12). 1979. pap. text 2.95 (*0-88301-356-8*) Pendulum Pr.

Madame Curie - Albert Einstein. Naunerle N. Farr. (Pendulum Illustrated Biography Ser.). (Illus.). (J). (gr. 4-12). 1979. student ed. 1.25 (*0-88301-380-0*) Pendulum Pr.

Madame Curie Daughter of Poland. Robert Woznicki. LC 83-73378. (Illus.). 175p. 1984. 12.50 (*1-881284-07-7*) Am Inst Polish.

Madame De. Louise De Vilmorin. Tr. by Duff Cooper from FRE. 64p. 1998. pap. 12.95 (*1-885983-27-1*, Helen Mx) Turtle Point Pr.

Madame de Charriere et la Revolution des Idees, Vol. 12. Medha N. Karmarkar. (The/Age of Revolution & Romanticism Ser.). (FRE.). 241p. (C). 1996. text 48.95 (*0-8204-2660-1*) P Lang Pubng.

Madame de la Fayette's The Princess of Cleves: A New Translation. Michael G. Paulson & Tamara Alvarez-Detrell. 204p. (Orig.). (C). 1994. pap. text 35.00 (*0-8191-9732-7*) U Pr of Amer.

Madame de Lafayette. Stirling Haig. LC 71-79207. (Twayne's World Authors Ser.). 1970. lib. bdg. 17.95 (*0-8057-2508-3*) Irvington.

Madame de Lambert (1647-1733) ou le Feminisme Moral. Marie-Jose Fassiotto. LC 84-47692. (American University Studies: Romance Languages & Literature: Ser. II, Vol. 7). 149p. (Orig.). (C). 1984. text 20.30 (*0-8204-0131-5*) P Lang Pubng.

Madame de Mauves see Works of Henry James Jr.: Collected Works

***Madame de Pompadour: Sex, Culture & the Power Game.** Margaret Crosland. 2001. 29.95 (*0-7509-2338-5*, Pub. by Sutton Publng) Intl Pubs Mktg.

Madame de Pontivy: Christel. Charles-Augustin Sainte-Beuve. (FRE.). 156p. 1920. pap. 11.95 (*0-7859-1541-9*, 2711682099) Fr & Eur.

Madame de Sevigne. Gaston Boissier. Tr. by Henry L. Williams. LC 79-38341. (Select Bibliographies Reprint Ser.). 1977. 17.95 (*0-8369-6794-1*) Ayer.

Madame de Sevigne. Anne I. Ritchie. LC 77-37716. reprint ed. 29.50 (*0-404-56809-2*) AMS Pr.

Madame de Sevigne: A Life & Letters. Frances Mossiker. LC 85-4096. 560p. 1985. reprint ed. pap. text 27.00 (*0-231-06153-6*) Col U Pr.

Madame de Sevigne: A Portrait in Letters. Harriet R. Allentuch. LC 78-16378. 219p. 1978. reprint ed. lib. bdg. 59.50 (*0-313-20537-X*, ALMS, Greenwood Pr) Greenwood.

Madame de Sevigne: A Seventeenth-Century Life. Jeanne A. Ojala & William T. Ojala. LC 89-37007. (Women's Ser.). 234p. 1990. 19.50 (*0-85496-169-0*) Berg Pubs.

Madame de Sevigny. Gerard-Gailly. 15.50 (*0-685-34031-7*) Fr & Eur.

Madame de Stael. Olga G. Von Taxis-Bordogna. 382p. reprint ed. write for info. (*0-318-71474-4*) G Olms Pubs.

Madame de Stael - Charles de Villers - Benjamin Constant: Correspondance. Ed. by Kurt Kloocke. 338p. 1993. 55.80 (*3-631-46107-0*) P Lang Pubng.

Madame de Stael et l'Europe: Colloque, Deuxieme Centenaire de la Naissance de Madame de Stael, 1766-1966. 17.50 (*0-685-35006-1*) Fr & Eur.

Madame de Toucainville's Magnificent Hat. Sue Bland. (Northern Lights Books for Children Ser.). (Illus.). 32p. (J). (ps-4). 1994. text 12.95 (*0-88995-115-2*, Pub. by Red Deer) Genl Dist Srvs.

Madame de Treymes. Edith Wharton. Ed. by Denise Kohn. (Masterworks of Literature Ser.). pap. 13.95 (*0-8084-0486-5*) NCUP.

Madame de Treymes. Edith Wharton. (Collected Works of Edith Wharton). 146p. 1998. reprint ed. lib. bdg. 88.00 (*1-58201-986-X*) Classic Bks.

Madame de Treymes & Others. Edith Wharton. LC 73-100130. 1981. 20.00 (*0-684-17283-6*, SL419, Scribners Ref) Mac Lib Ref.

Madame de Treymes & Three Novellas. Edith Wharton. 400p. 1995. per. 10.00 (*0-684-80684-3*, Scribner Pap Fic) S&S Trade Pap.

Madame Delphine. George W. Cable. LC 04-22066. 1986. 11.50 (*0-403-00039-4*) Scholarly.

Madame Delphine see Collected Works of George W. Cable

Madame Delphine. George W. Cable. (Works of George Cable). 1988. reprint ed. 59.00 (*0-685-48943-4*) Rprt Serv.

***Madame Deluxe.** Tenaya Darlington. 96p. 2000. pap. 13.95 (*1-56689-105-1*, Pub. by Coffee Hse) Consort Bk Sales.

Madame D'Epinay, Lettres a Mon Fils, Essais sur l'Education, et Morceaux Choisis. Ed. by Ruth P. Weinreb. (FRE., Illus.). 144p. (YA). (gr. 10-12). 1989. pap. text 6.67 (*1-877653-01-2*) Wayside Pub.

Madame Dorion. Jerome Peltier. 44p. 1981. pap. 6.95 (*0-87770-240-3*) Ye Galleon.

Madame du Chatelet. Esther Ehrman. (Women's Ser.). (Illus.). 98p. (C). 1987. 25.00 (*0-907582-90-7*) Berg Pubs.

Madame Ex. Herve Bazin. (FRE.). 1977. pap. 12.95 (*0-7859-3081-7*) Fr & Eur.

Madame Gervaisais. Edmond De Goncourt & Jules De Goncourt. (Folio Ser.: No. 1347). (FRE.). pap. 9.95 (*2-07-037347-9*) Schoenhof.

Madame Gervaisais. Edmond E. Goncourt. (FRE.). 1982. pap. 11.95 (*0-7859-2455-8*, 2070373479) Fr & Eur.

Madame Guyon. Jan Johnson. (Women of Faith Ser.). 176p. 1999. mass mkt. 4.99 (*0-7642-2175-2*) Bethany Hse.

Madame Jazz: Contemporary Women Instrumentalists. Leslie Gourse. (Illus.). 304p. 1996. pap. 14.95 (*0-19-510647-4*) OUP.

Madame Jeanne Guyon: Child of Another World. Dorothy Coslet. 219p. 1992. pap. 6.99 (*0-87508-144-4*) Chr Lit.

***Madame Joy: The Story of Human Drug Use & the Politics of Its Regulation.** Monique Berkhout & Francesca Robinson. 2000. pap. 12.95 (*0-7322-6506-1*) HarpC.

Madame Junek-1928 Targa Florio & Rogue of the Peking to Paris Race. James T. Crow. (Illus.). 1983. 37.50 (*0-938237-01-2*) Gold Stein Pr.

Madame Knipper's Journey to Eastern Prussia. Jean-Luc Lagarce. Tr. by Paul Antal from FRE. 92p. (Orig.). 1984. pap. text 8.95 (*0-913745-10-3*) Ubu Repertory.

***Madame La Mort & Other Plays.** Rachilde et al. Ed. & Tr. by Kiki Gounaridou & Frazer Lively from FRE. LC 97-26493. (PAJ Bks.). 136p. 1998. text 35.00 (*0-8018-5761-9*); pap. text 15.95 (*0-8018-5762-7*) Johns Hopkins.

Madame le Professeur: Women Educators in the Third Republic. Jo B. Margadant. LC 89-70243. 370p. 1990. reprint ed. pap. 114.70 (*0-608-02558-5*, 206320300004) Bks Demand.

Madame Macadam Travelling Theatre. Thomas Kilroy. 96p. (C). 1992. pap. 11.95 (*0-413-66310-8*, A0616, Methuen Drama) Methn.

Madame Maigret's Own Case. Georges Simenon. 182p. (C). 1991. pap. 6.00 (*0-15-655106-3*, Harvest Bks) Harcourt.

Madame Mao: The White-Boned Demon. Ross Terrill. (Illus.). 448p. 1992. pap. 13.00 (*0-671-74484-4*, Touchstone) S&S Trade Pap.

Madame Mao: The White-Boned Demon. rev. ed. Ross Terrill. LC 98-45872. (Illus.). 466p. 1997. pap. 17.95 (*0-8047-2922-0*) Stanford U Pr.

Madame Modjeska, Countess Bozenta: Polish-American Actress & American Poets. LC 93-10547. (C). 1993. 15.00 (*0-924197-14-5*) SUNYB Coun Intl Studies.

Madame Nak's Horn of Plenty 1999. SPG Inc. Staff & Calvin P. Kline. (Illus.). 69p. 1998. pap. 4.95 (*0-944149-10-3*) Sneaky Pete.

***Madame Nelson's French Verb Book with All the Answers.** Mary D. Nelson. (FRE & ENG.). 332p. 1999. 25.00 (*0-8425-2463-0*) Brigham.

Madame of the Heights. Marianne Hancock. Ed. by Jane Weinberger. LC 98-60227. 240p. 1998. 25.00 (*1-883650-54-2*); pap. 15.00 (*1-883650-49-6*) Windswept Hse.

Madame Piquedru. Beatrix Potter. (FRE., Illus.). 58p. (J). 1990. 9.95 (*0-7859-3623-8*, 2070560686) Fr & Eur.

Madame Piquedru. Beatrix Potter. (Gallimard Ser.). (FRE.). 58p. (J). 1990. 10.95 (*2-07-056068-6*) Schoenhof.

Madame President. R. B. Mawhiney. 80p. 1984. mass mkt. 7.95 (*0-931764-04-1*) Roberts Pub Co.

Madame President. Eugene McCreary. 501p. 1998. pap. 14.95 (*0-9659308-0-7*) Erica Hse.

Madame Saint-Huberty d'Apres Sa Correspondence et Ses Papiers de Famille. Edmond L. De Goncourt. 319p. 1990. reprint ed. lib. bdg. 79.00 (*0-7812-9104-6*) Rprt Serv.

Madame Sarah. May Agate. LC 73-82817. 1972. reprint ed. 20.95 (*0-405-08197-9*, Pub. by Blom Pubns) Ayer.

Madame Sourdis. Emile Zola. 4.95 (*0-686-55788-3*) Fr & Eur.

Madame Trotte-Menu. Beatrix Potter. (FRE., Illus.). 58p. (J). 1990. 9.95 (*0-7859-3634-3*, 2070561054) Fr & Eur.

Madame Trotte-Menu. Beatrix Potter. (Gallimard Ser.). (FRE.). 59p. (J). 1990. 10.95 (*2-07-056105-4*) Schoenhof.

Madame Tussaud in England: Career Woman Extraordinary. Pauline Chapman. 1992. 30.00 (*1-870948-79-3*, Pub. by Quiller Pr) St Mut.

Madame Tussauds. Lionel Lambourne. 1999. pap. 19.95 (*0-525-48425-6*) NAL.

Madame Vestris & Her Times. Charles E. Pearce. LC 70-77975. (Illus.). 314p. 1972. 26.95 (*0-405-08845-0*, Pub. by Blom Pubns) Ayer.

Madame Wrinkleski Predicts: A Women's Guide to Getting Older. Illus. by Rick Stromoski & Trisar, Inc., Staff. 32p. 1995. 4.50 (*1-886386-52-8*) Trisar.

Madame Yevonde. Robin Gibson & Pam Roberts. (Illus.). 120p. 1990. pap. 35.00 (*1-85514-024-1*, Pub. by Natl Port Gall) Antique Collect.

Madams of San Francisco. Curt Gentry. 1977. pap. text 3.95 (*0-89174-015-5*) Comstock Edns.

Madams of San Francisco. Curt Gentry. 320p. 1996. reprint ed. pap. 8.95 (*0-89174-064-3*) Comstock Edns.

Madan Mohan Malaviya the Man & His Ideology. S. R. Bakshi. (C). 1991. 45.00 (*81-7041-429-6*, Pub. by Anmol) S Asia.

Madbury, Its People & Places. Eloi A. Adams. (Illus.). 152p. 1998. reprint ed. pap. 22.50 (*0-8328-9723-X*); reprint ed. lib. bdg. 29.50 (*0-8328-9722-1*) Higginson Bk Co.

Madcap Bumper Book of Horrors--Things That Go Bump. Gyles Brandreth. (Illus.). 288p. (J). (gr. 1-6). 1998. pap. 6.95 (*0-233-99084-4*, Pub. by Andre Deutsch) Trafalgar.

Madcap Bumper Book of Magic. Gyles Brandreth. (Illus.). 288p. (J). (gr. 1-6). 1998. pap. 6.95 (*0-233-99296-0*, Pub. by Andre Deutsch) Trafalgar.

Madcap Heiress. Carrie Alexander. 1996. per. 3.50 (*0-373-44008-1*, 1-44008-0) Harlequin Bks.

Madcaps, Screwballs & Con Women: The Female Trickster in American Culture. Lori Landay. LC 97-32805. (Illus.). 272p. (C). 1998. text 45.00 (*0-8122-3435-9*) U of Pa Pr.

Madcaps, Screwballs, & Con Women: The Female Trickster in American Culture. Lori Landay. LC 97-32805. (Feminist Cultural Studies, the Media, & Political Culture). (Illus.). 272p. 1998. pap. 22.50 (*0-8122-1651-2*) U of Pa Pr.

***Madchild Running: A Young Native American Man Encounters an Amazing Variety of People.** Keith Egawa. LC 99-50154. (Literature Ser.). 223p. 1999. 23.95 (*1-878610-72-4*, Pub. by Red Crane Bks) Consort Bk Sales.

Maddalena Licheri: Italian Essays. Giovanni Pibiri. 126p. 1986. pap. 15.00 (*0-89304-579-9*) Cross-Cultrl NY.

Maddalena Sirmen: Three Violin Concertos. Maddalena L. Sirmen. Ed. by Jane L. Berdes. (Recent Researches in Music of the Classic Era Ser.: Vol. RRC38). (Illus.). xx, 97p. 1991. pap. 40.00 (*0-89579-262-1*) A-R Eds.

Madden Ballads. 385p. (C). 1989. pap. text 100.00 (*0-89235-119-5*) Primary Srce Media.

***Madden NFL 2000: Official Strategy Guide.** Prima Development Staff. 1999. pap. 12.99 (*0-7615-2293-X*, Prima Games) Prima Pub.

Maddening Model: (Hazards, Inc.) Suzanne Simms. (Desire Ser.). 1995. per. 3.25 (*0-373-05923-X*, 1-05923-7) Silhouette.

Madder. David Constantine. LC 87-73052. 80p. (Orig.). 1988. pap. 11.95 (*1-85224-039-3*, Pub. by Bloodaxe Bks) Dufour.

Madder Ghost. Martyn Crucefix. LC 97-208586. 80p. 1997. pap. 17.95 (*1-900564-10-6*, Pub. by Enitha Pr) Dufour.

***Madder Music Stronger Wine: The Life of Ernest Dowson Poet & Deca.** Jad Adams. 2000. text 29.50 (*1-86064-470-8*) I B T.

Madderlake's Trade Secrets: Finding & Arranging Flowers Naturally. Tom Pritchard. 1994. 27.50 (*0-517-88158-6*, Crown) Crown Pub Group.

Maddest Idea. James L. Nelson. LC 96-42484. 432p. 1997. per. 14.00 (*0-671-51925-5*) PB.

Maddie. Brian Caswell. (Storybridge Ser.). (J). 1995. pap. 9.95 (*0-7022-2735-8*, Pub. by Univ Queensland Pr) Intl Spec Bk.

Maddie Goes to Paris. Louise Leblanc. (First Novels Ser.). (Illus.). 61p. (J). (gr. 1-4). 1995. mass mkt. 3.99 (*0-88780-278-8*, Pub. by Formac Publ Co); bds. 14.95 (*0-88780-279-6*, Pub. by Formac Publ Co) Formac Dist Ltd.

Maddie in Danger. Louise Leblanc. (First Novels Ser.). (Illus.). 62p. (J). (gr. 1-4). 1995. mass mkt. 3.99 (*0-88780-306-7*, Pub. by Formac Publ Co); bds. 14.95 (*0-88780-307-5*, Pub. by Formac Publ Co) Formac Dist Ltd.

Maddie in Goal. Louise Leblanc. (First Novels Ser.). (Illus.). 62p. (J). (gr. 1-4). 1995. mass mkt. 3.99 (*0-88780-202-8*, Pub. by Formac Publ Co); bds. 14.95 (*0-88780-203-6*, Pub. by Formac Publ Co) Formac Dist Ltd.

Maddie in Hospital. Louise Leblanc. (First Novels). (Illus.). 58p. (J). 1996. bds. 14.95 (*0-88780-375-X*, Pub. by Formac Publ Co) Formac Dist Ltd.

Maddie in Hospital. Louise Leblanc. Tr. by Sarah Cummins. (First Novels Ser.). (Illus.). 58p. (J). 1996. mass mkt. 3.99 (*0-88780-374-1*, Pub. by Formac Publ Co) Formac Dist Ltd.

Maddie in Trouble. Louise LeBlanc. (First Novels). 58p. (J). (gr. 1-4). 1998. text 3.99 (*0-88780-428-4*, Pub. by Formac Publ Co) Formac Dist Ltd.

***Maddie in Trouble.** Louise LeBlanc. (First Novels). (Illus.). 58p. (J). 1998. bds. 14.95 (*0-88780-429-2*, Pub. by Formac Publ Co) Formac Dist Ltd.

***Maddie Retta Lauren: Sandersville, Georgia, 1864.** Kathleen Duey. (American Diaries Ser.: No. 15). (Illus.). (J). (gr. 4-6). 2000. pap. 4.50 (*0-689-83377-6*) Aladdin.

***Maddie Retta Lauren, Sandersville, Georgia, C.S.A., 1864.** Kathleen Duey. (American Diaries Ser.: Vol. 15). 2000. 9.85 (*0-606-17902-X*) Turtleback.

***Maddie Tries to Be Good.** Louise Leblanc. (Illus.). 64p. (J). (gr. 1-4). 1999. mass mkt. 3.99 (*0-88780-482-9*) Formac Publ Co.

***Maddie Tries to Be Good.** Louise LeBlanc & Sarah Cummins. (First Novels). (Illus.). 62p. (J). 2000. bds. write for info. (*0-88780-483-7*, Pub. by Formac Publ Co) Formac Dist Ltd.

Maddie Wants Music! Louise Leblanc. (First Novels Ser.). (Illus.). 61p. (J). (gr. 1-4). 1995. mass mkt. 3.99 (*0-88780-219-2*, Pub. by Formac Publ Co); bds. 14.95 (*0-88780-220-6*, Pub. by Formac Publ Co) Formac Dist Ltd.

***Maddie's Justice.** Leslie LaFoy. 304p. 2000. mass mkt. 5.50 (*0-553-58045-0*) Bantam.

Maddie's Love-Child. Miranda Lee. (From Here to Paternity Ser.). 1997. per. 3.50 (*0-373-11884-8*, 1-11884-3) Harlequin Bks.

Maddie's Love-Child. large type ed. Miranda Lee. (Harlequin Romance Ser.). 1997. 20.95 (*0-263-15066-6*) Thorndike Pr.

Madding of Daniel O'Hooligan. Peter Wear. 1991. 16.95 (*0-7022-2341-7*, Pub. by Univ Queensland Pr) Intl Spec Bk.

Maddon's Rock. large type ed. Hammond Innes. 1971. 27.99 (*0-85456-052-1*) Ulverscroft.

***Maddox.** Darin Thomas. 80p. 1999. 16.95 (*1-929072-54-6*) Deep South Pubng.

Maddy - Us Maddys: An Account of the Family in England & the Descendants of William Maddy of Fairfax of Fairfax County, Virginia, & James Maddy of Fairfax & Orange County. Olive Maddy. (Illus.). 280p. 1994. reprint ed. pap. 44.00 (*0-8328-4036-X*); reprint ed. lib. bdg. 54.00 (*0-8328-4035-1*) Higginson Bk Co.

Maddy Lawrence's Big Adventure. Linda Turner. (Intimate Moments Ser.). 1996. per. 3.99 (*0-373-07709-2*, 1-07709-8) Silhouette.

Made According to Pattern. Charles W. Slemming. 1999. pap. text 5.99 (*0-87508-565-2*) Chr Lit.

Made by Cartier: One Hundred Fifty Years of Tradition & Innovation. Franco Cologni & Ettore Moccheti. (Illus.). 256p. 1993. 75.00 (*1-55859-599-6*) Abbeville Pr.

Made by Hong Kong. Ed. by Suzanne Berger & Richard K. Lester. LC 97-189765. (Illus.). 392p. (C). 1997. text 32.00 (*0-19-590358-7*) OUP.

Made by Machine: A Catalogue of the Machinery Collection at the Hanford Mills Museum. Scott Stevens & Keith Bott. (Illus.). 50p. (Orig.). 1990. pap. 6.95 (*1-879444-00-3*) Hanford Mills Museum.

Made Fit for God in That Affliction. Robert M. Claytor. LC 96-232541. (Illus.). 155p. (Orig.). 1996. pap. 10.95 (*0-9653186-0-5*) Bedewrite Pr.

***Made for Each Other.** Doreen Owens Malek. (Intimate Moments Ser.: Bk. 1041). 2000. mass mkt. 4.50 (*0-373-27111-5*, 1-27111-3) Silhouette.

Made for Each Other. Niqui Stanhope. (Arabesque Ser.). 1999. mass mkt. 4.99 (*1-58314-014-X*) BET Bks.

Made for Each Other. William Steig. LC 99-26425. (Illus.). 48p. (YA). (gr. 9 up). 2000. 13.95 (*0-06-028512-5*) HarpC.

Made for Each Other. William Steig. LC 99-26425. (Illus.). 48p. (YA). (ps-3). 2000. lib. bdg. 13.89 (*0-06-028513-3*) HarpC Child Bks.

Made for Each Other. Steig William. LC 99-26425. 48p. (J). pap. 4.95 (*0-06-443592-X*) HarpC Child Bks.

Made for Each Other: A Symbiosis of Birds & Pines. Ronald M. Lanner. (Illus.). 180p. 1996. 29.95 (*0-19-508902-2*); pap. 15.95 (*0-19-508903-0*) OUP.

Made for Each Other: Devotions for Newly Married Couples. Roy G. Gesch. 112p. 1987. pap. 8.99 (*0-570-04453-7*, 12-3059) Concordia.

Made for Each Other - Ravished, 2 bks. in 1. Parris A. Bonds. 304p. 1993. mass mkt. 4.99 (*0-505-51915-1*, Love Spell) Dorchester Pub Co.

Made for Giving: Gifts from the Garden. Pamela Westland. (Illus.). 128p. 1998. 18.95 (*0-7621-0067-2*, Pub. by RD Assn) Penguin Putnam.

Made for His Pleasure: Experiencing Our Father's Pleasure As We Glorify Him. Alistair Begg. LC 96-200721. 12.99 (*0-8024-7138-2*, 212) Moody.

Made for Life. C. Turner. mass mkt. 13.95 (*0-340-72887-6*, Pub. by Hodder & Stought Ltd) Trafalgar.

An Asterisk (*) at the beginning of an entry indicates that the title is appearing for the first time.

Made for One Another. Thomas Ulrich. Tr. by Howard Fine from GER. LC 97-37736. 144p. 1998. pap. 12.95 (*1-885394-26-8*) Bluestar Communs.

Made for Television: Euston Films Limited. Manuel Alvarado & John Stewart. 228p. (Orig.). (C). 1988. pap. text 11.95 (*0-685-63002-1*, A0159) Heinemann.

Made for the Country. Robert Kimber. 224p. 1991. 17.95 (*1-55821-103-9*) Lyons Pr.

Made for the Outdoors. Len McDougall. (Illus.). 224p. 1995. pap. 12.95 (*1-55821-329-5*) Lyons Pr.

Made for the Shade. Judy Glattstein. LC 98-20098. (Illus.). 160p. 1998. pap. 19.95 (*0-7641-0512-4*) Barron.

Made for the Shade. Judy Glattstein. 1996. pap. write for info. (*0-316-31592-3*) Little.

***Made from Scratch: A Recipe for Success.** Ornella Curatolo. 1999. pap. 17.95 (*0-9660092-3-1*) Puget Sound.

Made from Scratch: A Report on Cooking, Crafts, Etc. Center for Self-Sufficiency, Research Division Sta. LC 83-90712. 50p. 1985. ring bd. 25.95 (*0-910811-07-5*) Ctr Self Suff.

Made from Stardust: Exploring the Place of Human Beings Within Creation. Denis Edwards. (Illus.). 1992. pap. 9.00 (*1-86371-037-X*) Harper SF.

Made from This Earth: American Women & Nature. Vera Norwood. LC 92-22562. (Gender & American Culture Ser.). (Illus.). xxiv, 368p. (C). 1993. 49.95 (*0-8078-2062-8*); pap. 19.95 (*0-8078-4396-2*) U of NC Pr.

Made in Africa: Learning from Carpentry Hand Tool Projects. Janet Leek et al. 72p. 1993. pap. 12.00 (*1-85339-209-X*, Pub. by Intermed Tech) Stylus Pub VA.

Made in Alabama: A State Legacy. Ed. by E. Bryding Adams. LC 95-37694. (Illus.). 232p. 1990. pap. 40.00 (*0-931394-40-6*) U of Ala Pr.

Made in America. Heard. 1990. pap. 40.00 (*0-673-46493-8*) Addson-Wesley Educ.

Made in America. Laurie Olsen. 1997. 25.00 (*1-56584-400-9*, Pub. by New Press NY) Norton.

Made in America. Lisa M. Steinman. LC 86-26550. 256p. 1987. 14.00 (*0-300-03810-0*) Yale U Pr.

Made in America: An Informal History of the English Language in the United States. Bill Bryson. 432p. 1996. pap. 12.50 (*0-380-71381-0*, Avon Bks) Morrow Avon.

Made in America: Immigrant Students in Our Public Schools. Laurie Olsen. 288p. 1998. pap. 14.95 (*1-56584-471-8*, Pub. by New Press NY) Norton.

Made in America: Printmaking, 1760-1860. Ed. by Stephanie A. Munsing. LC 73-161317. (Illus.). 59p. (Orig.). 1973. pap. 5.00 (*0-914076-52-3*) Lib Co Phila.

Made in America: Regaining the Productive Edge. Michael L. Dertouzos et al. 248p. 1989. 35.00 (*0-262-04100-6*) MIT Pr.

Made in America: Self-Styled Success from Horatio Alger to Oprah Winfrey. Jeffrey L. Decker. LC 97-19568. 1997. pap. 17.95 (*0-8166-3021-6*); text 44.95 (*0-8166-3020-8*) U of Minn Pr.

Made in America: The Business of Apparel & Sewn Products Manufacturing. 2nd rev. ed. Sue Pekarsky Gary & Connie Ulasewicz. LC 98-93596. Orig. Title: Made in America: A Handbook for Design Based Manufacturing of Apparel & Sewn Products. (Illus.). 154p. 1998. pap. 24.95 (*0-9662009-2-6*) GarmentoSpeak.

Made in America: The Total Business Concept. Peter L. Grieco, Jr. & Michael W. Gozzo. LC 88-107799. (Illus.). 302p. 1988. 29.95 (*0-945456-00-X*) PT Pubns.

Made in America: A Handbook for Design Based Manufacturing of Apparel & Sewn Products see Made in America: The Business of Apparel & Sewn Products Manufacturing

Made in Beverly Hills. Ronn Kaiser. 288p. 1986. pap. 3.95 (*0-380-75225-5*, Avon Bks) Morrow Avon.

Made in Brooklyn: A Visual Diary. Peter Arnell. (Illus.). 134p. 1996. write for info. (*0-9631817-9-3*) Sidney Pr.

***Made in California: Art, Image, & Identity, 1900-2000.** Stephanie Barron et al. (Illus.). 344p. 2000. 65.00 (*0-520-22764-6*); pap. 34.95 (*0-520-22765-4*) U CA Pr.

Made in China: Ideas & Inventions from Ancient China. Suzanne Williams. LC 96-69368. (Illus.). 48p. (J). (gr. 5-8). 1996. lib. bdg. 18.95 (*1-881896-14-5*) Pacific View Pr.

***Made in China: Voices of the New Economic Revolution.** Robert Lawrence Kuhn. 256p. 2000. 25.00 (*1-57500-134-9*, Pub. by TV Bks) HarpC.

Made in Czechoslovakia. Ruth A. Forsythe. (Illus.). 72p. 1982. pap. 21.95 (*0-915410-82-6*, 4040) Antique Pubns.

Made in Czechoslovakia, Bk. 2. Ruth A. Forsythe. (Illus.). 96p. 1993. 37.95 (*0-915410-99-0*, 4055); pap. 29.95 (*0-915410-98-2*, 4054) Antique Pubns.

Made in France. Henry C. Bunner. LC 71-94707. (Short Story Index Reprint Ser.). (Illus.). 1977. 17.95 (*0-8369-3085-1*) Ayer.

Made in France: Recit. Pierre Daninos. 247p. 14.95 (*0-686-55566-X*) Fr & Eur.

Made in Goatswood: New Tales of Horror in the Severn Valley. Ramsey Campbell et al. Ed. by Scott D. Aniolowski. (Call of Cthulhu Fiction Ser.). (Illus.). 288p. (Orig.). 1995. pap. 10.95 (*1-56882-046-1*, 6009) Chaosium.

Made in God's Image. Del Olsen. 128p. (Orig.). 1985. pap. 3.70 (*0-310-46381-5*, 18382P) Zondervan.

Made in God's Image? Eve & Adam in the Genesis Mosaics at San Marco, Venice. Penny H. Jolly. LC 96-28461. (California Studies in the History of Art). 127p. 1997. 45.00 (*0-520-20537-5*, Pub. by U CA Pr) Cal Prin Full Svc.

Made in God's Image: The Catholic Vision of Human Dignity. Ed. by Regis Duffy & Angelus Gambatese. LC 98-40531. 192p. 1999. 14.95 (*0-8091-3850-6*) Paulist Pr.

Made in Hawaii. Jane F. Abernethy & Suelyn C. Tune. LC 83-4895. (Illus.). 140p. (J). (gr. 3-12). 1983. pap. 8.95 (*0-8248-0870-3*, Kolowalu Bk) UH Pr.

Made in Heaven see Desde el Cielo: Guia del Matrimonio Judio

Made in Heaven. Perf. by Queen. 60p. 1996. pap. 16.95 (*0-7935-6475-1*) H Leonard.

Made in Heaven. Amberlina Wicker. 256p. 1995. mass mkt. 4.99 (*0-8217-0116-9*, Zebra Kensgtn); mass mkt. 4.99 (*0-7860-0116-X*, Pinncle Kensgtn) Kensgtn Pub Corp.

Made in Heaven: A Jewish Wedding Guide. Aryeh Kaplan. 234p. 1983. 20.00 (*0-940118-11-4*) Moznaim.

Made in Hungary: Hungarian Contributions to Universal Culture. unabridged ed. Andrew L. Simon. LC 98-96916. 460p. 1999. 42.00 (*0-9665734-2-0*) Simon Publns.

Made in Italy, Vol. 10. 2nd rev. ed. Maria Ardizzi. Tr. by Anna Maria Castrilli from ITA. 246p. 1999. pap. 8.00 (*1-55071-054-0*) Guernica Editions.

Made in Italy: A Shopper's Guide to Florence, Milan, Rome & Venice. Annie Brody & Patricia Schultz. LC 86-40544. (Illus.). 560p. (Orig.). 1987. pap. 14.95 (*0-89480-305-0*, 1305) Workman Pub.

Made in Italy: Small-Scale Industrialization & Its Consequences. Michael L. Blim. LC 89-16338. 304p. 1990. 65.00 (*0-275-93101-3*, C3101, Greenwood Pr) Greenwood.

Made in Japan. Boye L. De Mente. 192p. 1991. 17.95 (*0-8442-8506-4*, Passprt Bks) NTC Contemp Pub Co.

Made in Japan. Japan Commission on Industrial Performance Staff. LC 97-26637. (Illus.). 500p. 1998. 42.00 (*0-262-10060-6*) MIT Pr.

Made in Japan: Akio Morita & Sony. Akio Morita et al. 1989. pap. 9.95 (*0-317-02806-5*) NAL.

Made in Japan & Other Japanese 'Business Novels' Tr. by Tamae K. Prindle from JPN. LC 89-4218. 200p. (C). (gr. 13). 1990. 53.95 (*0-87332-529-X*, East Gate Bk); pap. 27.50 (*0-87332-772-1*, East Gate Bk) M E Sharpe.

Made in Japan Ceramics Bk. 3: Identification & Values. Carole B. White. LC 94-182382. (Collector's Guide to Ser.). 1998. pap. text 19.95 (*1-57432-051-3*, 5048) Collector Bks.

Made in Japan Ceramics, 1921-1941. Barbara A. Ifert. LC 94-65618. (Illus.). 160p. (Orig.). 1994. pap. text 16.95 (*0-88740-613-0*) Schiffer.

***Made in Korea: Chung Ju Yung & the Rise of Hyundai.** Richard M. Steers. LC 98-30135. (Illus.). 256p. 1999. 29.95 (*0-415-92050-7*) Routledge.

Made in L. A. The Prints of Cirrus Editions. Bruce Davis. (Illus.). 368p. 65.00 (*0-87587-173-9*) LA Co Art Mus.

Made in Lancashire: A History of Regional Industrialisation. Steve Timmins. LC 98-19957. (Illus.). 240p. 1998. text 79.95 (*0-7190-4539-8*, Pub. by Manchester Univ Pr) St Martin.

Made in Managua: A Nonfiction Account of One Journalist's Trip Through a Telling Place & Time. Lawrence J. Maushard. (Illus.). 162p. (Orig.). 1990. pap. 5.95 (*0-9626912-0-8*) Quimby Archives.

Made in Manitoba: An Anthology of Short Fiction. Ed. by Wayne Tefs. 1997. pap. 5.95 (*0-88801-145-8*, Pub. by Turnstone Pr) Genl Dist Srvs.

***Made in Mexico.** Illus. by Peter Laufer & Susan L. Roth. LC 99-38220. 32p. (J). 2000. 16.95 (*0-7922-7118-1*) Natl Geog.

Made in Milwaukee: Editions from John Gruenwald, Printmaker. Janet Treacy. (Illus.). 20p. 1992. pap. 4.95 (*0-944110-67-3*) Milwauk Art Mus.

***Made in Our Image: The Fallacy of the User-Friendly God.** Steven J. Lawson. LC 00-8519. 220p. 2000. pap. 10.99 (*1-57673-610-5*, Pub. by Multnomah Pubs) GL Services.

Made in Paradise: Hollywood's Films of Hawai'i & the South Seas. Luis I. Reyes. (Illus.). 320p. (Orig.). 1995. 45.00 (*1-56647-089-7*) Mutual Pub HI.

Made in Philadelphia, No. 7. Judith Tannenbaum. 44p. (Orig.). 1987. pap. text 10.00 (*0-88454-044-8*) U of Pa Contemp Art.

Made in Philadelphia VI. Ned Rifkin. (Illus.). 38p. 1984. pap. 7.00 (*0-88454-035-9*) U of Pa Contemp Art.

Made in Russia: The Holocaust. Ed. by Carlos W. Porter. 415p. 1988. pap. 7.50 (*0-939484-30-7*, 0695, Inst Hist Rev) Legion Survival.

Made in Scotland: An Anthology of New Scottish Plays. Ed. by Ian Brown & Mark Fisher. LC 95-223551. (Methuen Anthologies Ser.). 256p. 1995. pap. 19.95 (*0-413-69180-2*, A0745) Heinemann.

Made in Sweden: Art Handicrafts Design. Anja Notini. (Illus.). 185p. 1988. 45.00 (*0-88736-300-8*) Mecklermedia.

Made in the Ives Shops. Turner Publishing Company Staff & Gerald A. Robinson. LC 90-70005. 136p. 1990. 34.95 (*0-938021-83-4*) Turner Pub KY.

Made in the Shade: A Collection of Recipes by the Junior League of Greater Ft. Lauderdale. Junior League of Greater Ft. Lauderdale Staff. LC 98-66544. (Illus.). 192p. 1998. 22.95 (*0-9604158-1-5*) Jr League Ft Lauderdale.

Made in the Shade: Sunkissed Cuisine from the Junior League of Greater Fort Lauderdale. Photos by Andrew Itkoff. (Illus.). 292p. 1998. 21.95 (*0-9660194-9-0*) Jr League Lauder.

Made in U. S. A. An Americanization of Modern Art in the '50s & '60s. Sidra Stich. (Illus.). 265p. 1987. pap. 34.95 (*0-520-05757-0*, Pub. by U CA Pr) Cal Prin Full Svc.

Made in U. S. A. Estudio en Naturalezas Muertas. Silvio M. Palau. (SPA.). 167p. 1985. pap. 9.50 (*0-910061-27-0*, 1116) Ediciones Norte.

***Made in U. S. A. Poets Celebrate 20th Century American Art.** Jan Greenberg. LC 99-462335. 2000. write for info. (*0-8109-4386-7*) Abrams.

Made in Virginia: Furniture from the 1830's to the Present. Diana L. Blanchard Gross & D. Thomas Wessells. (Illus.). 24p. 1998. pap. 3.00 (*1-886845-04-2*) Penin Fine Arts.

Made in Whose Image? Genetic Engineering & Christian Ethics. Thomas A. Shannon. LC 97-11086. (Society/Religion - Religion/Society Ser.). 136p. 1998. 45.00 (*0-391-04054-5*); pap. 15.00 (*0-391-04055-3*) Humanities.

***Made in Whose Image? Genetic Engineering & Christian Ethics.** Thomas A. Shannon. LC 99-45066. 131p. 2000. 44.95 (*1-57392-632-9*, Humanity Bks); pap. 17.95 (*1-57392-631-0*, Humanity Bks) Prometheus Bks.

Made in York: A Survey of the Agricultural & Industrial Heritage of York County, Pennsylvania. Georg R. Sheets. 500p. 1991. text 24.95 (*0-9629635-0-X*) Agri Indust Mus.

Made into Movies: From Literature to Films. Stuart Y. McDougal. 528p. (C). 1985. pap. text 43.50 (*0-03-063804-6*, Pub. by Harcourt Coll Pubs) Harcourt.

***Made Kindred by the Spirit.** Ronald J. Philips. 2000. pap. 12.99 (*0-87148-609-1*) Pathway Pr.

***Made Not Born: The Brave New World of Biotechnology.** Ed. by Casey Walker. LC 00-30104. 192p. 2000. pap. 16.00 (*1-57805-059-6*) Sierra.

Made of Mud: Stoneware Potteries in Central Pennsylvania, 1831-1929. Jeannette Lasansky. LC 79-2708. (Illus.). 1979. pap. 12.50 (*0-271-00228-X*, Keystone Bks) Pa St U Pr.

Made of Stone: An Illustrated History of Stone Houses in America. Lawrence Grow. (Illus.). 160p. 1991. 24.95 (*0-8069-7426-5*) Sterling.

Made on Staten Island: Agriculture, Industry, & Suburban Living in the City. Charles L. Sachs. (Artisans & the Arts Ser.). (Illus.). 120p. 1988. pap. text 24.25 (*0-9606756-1-2*); lib. bdg. 36.50 (*0-9606756-0-4*) Staten Island.

Made-Over Chelsea. Hilda Stahl. LC 94-123102. (Best Friends Ser.: Vol. 7). 160p. (J). (gr. 4-7). 1992. pap. 4.99 (*0-89107-683-2*) Crossway Bks.

Made Possible By ... The Death of Public Broadcasting in the United States. James Ledbetter. LC 97-38229. 280p. 1997. 25.00 (*1-85984-904-0*, Pub. by Verso) Norton.

Made Possible By . . . The Death of Public Broadcasting in the United States. James Ledbetter. 288p. 1998. pap. 15.00 (*1-85984-029-9*, Pub. by Verso) Norton.

Ideal Made Real, or Applied Metaphysics for Beginners (1912) Christian D. Larson. 264p. 1998. reprint ed. pap. 19.95 (*0-7661-0348-X*) Kessinger Pub.

***Made Thing: An Anthology of Contemporary Southern Poetry.** 2nd ed. Ed. by Leon Stokesbury. LC 99-43633. 2000. 38.00 (*1-55728-578-0*); pap. text 22.00 (*1-55728-579-9*) U of Ark Pr.

Made to Be Loved: Enjoying Spiritual Intimacy with God & Your Spouse. Steve Bell & Valerie Bell. 192p. 1999. pap. 11.99 (*0-8024-3399-5*) Moody.

***Made to Last: Historic Preservation in Seattle & King County.** Lawrence Kreisman. LC 99-36928. (Illus.). 225p. 1999. pap. text 29.95 (*0-295-97846-5*) U of Wash Pr.

Made to Measure: New Materials for the 21st Century. Philip Ball. LC 97-4027. 445p. 1997. 29.95 (*0-691-02733-1*, Pub. by Princeton U Pr) Cal Prin Full Svc.

***Made to Measure: New Materials for the 21st Century.** Philip Ball. 1999. pap. 17.95 (*0-691-00975-9*, Pub. by Princeton U Pr) Cal Prin Full Svc.

Made-to-Measure Problem-Solving Victor Newman. LC 98-163867. xi, 139p. 1998. pap. 26.95 (*0-566-08006-0*) Ashgate Pub Co.

Made to Order: Charting the Course Beyond Mass Customization. Bart Victor & Andrew C. Boynton. LC 97-38480. 242p. 1998. 29.95 (*0-87584-798-6*) Harvard Busn.

Made to Order: The Myth of Reproductive & Genetic Progress. Ed. by Patricia Spallone & Deborah L. Steinberg. (Athene Ser.). 256p. 1987. text 50.00 (*0-08-034954-4*, Pergamon Pr); pap. text 19.95 (*0-08-034953-6*, Pergamon Pr) Elsevier.

Made to Order: The Myth of Reproductive & Genetic Progress. Ed. by Patricia Spallone & Deborah L. Steinberg. (Athene Ser.). 270p. (C). 1987. pap. text 19.95 (*0-8077-6226-1*) Tchrs Coll.

Made-to-Person Therapy for Ulcer Disease. F. Di Mario et al. (Advances in Gastroenterology Ser.: No. 6). 216p. 1993. text 32.00 (*1-57235-022-9*) Piccin Nuova.

Made-to-Person Therapy for Ulcer Disease. F. Di Mario et al. (Advances in Gastroenterology Ser.: Vol. 6). (Illus.). 216p. 1993. text 36.00 (*88-299-1124-0*, Pub. by Piccin Nuova) Gordon & Breach.

Made to Play House: Dolls & the Commercialization of American Girlhood, 1830-1930. Miriam Formanek-Brunell. LC 98-27077. 233p. 1998. pap. text 15.95 (*0-8018-6062-8*) Johns Hopkins.

Made to Play House: The History of Dolls & the Contest for Girlhood, 1830-1930. Miriam Formanek-Brunell. LC 93-1993. (Illus.). 256p. 1993. 32.50 (*0-300-05072-0*) Yale U Pr.

Made to Seem. Rae Armantrout. (New American Poetry Ser.: No. 20). 64p. 1995. pap. 9.95 (*1-55713-220-8*) Sun & Moon CA.

Made to Wear: Contemporary Jewellery Design. Janice West. (Illus.). 128p. 1998. 50.00 (*0-85331-727-5*, Pub. by Lund Humphries) Antique Collect.

Made-Up Minds: A Constructivist Approach to AI. Gary L. Drescher. (Artificial Intelligence - Bobrow, Brady & Davis Ser.). 240p. 1991. 35.00 (*0-262-04120-0*) MIT Pr.

Made Visible. Natalie Safir. 64p. 1998. pap. 8.50 (*1-880286-40-8*) Singular Speech Pr.

Made Whole Through Our Marriage to God. Helen M. Wright. LC 96-230256. 347p. 1996. pap. text 18.20 (*1-886505-04-7*) H M Wright.

Made with Lace: 40 Exquisite Lace Garments & Accessories. Ginny Barnston. 128p. 1997. pap. 19.95 (*0-8019-8939-6*) Krause Pubns.

Made with Passion: The Hemphill Folk Art Collection in the National Museum of American Art. Lynda R. Hartigan. 256p. 1990. 55.00 (*0-87474-293-5*) Smithsonian.

Made with Words: A Prose Miscellany. May Swenson. Ed. by Gardner McFall. LC 97-39284. 264p. (C). 1998. 34.50 (*0-472-09658-3*, 09658) U of Mich Pr.

***Made You Look: Who Do You Look Like? Denise Bella Vlasis. 360p. (C). 2000. 59.95 (*1-928739-00-8*, Pub. by Thrillennium Bks) ACCESS Pubs Network.**
Makes a great gift idea. Featuring more than 101 TOP PROFESSIONAL CELEBRITY IMPERSONATORS, MADE YOU LOOK is the definitive guide to the Celebrity Impersonator Industry. For those curious about who, how & where these unique actors perform, this book will take you behind the scenes into their world of illusion. Made You Look is filled with the biographies, contact information & over 200 photographs of the impersonations. It also includes a "How To" Section. e-mail: madeyoulook_2000hotmail.com *Publisher Paid Annotation.*

M

***Madeira.** Ed. by Berlitz Publishing Staff. (Pocket Guides Ser.). (Illus.). 2001. pap. 8.95 (*2-8315-7699-7*) Berlitz.

Madeira. Christopher Catling. LC 94-68478. (Illustrated Travel Guides from Thomas Cook Ser.). (Illus.). 192p. (Orig.). 1994. pap. 12.95 (*0-8442-9071-8*, Passprt Bks) NTC Contemp Pub Co.

Madeira. Insight Guides Staff. (Insight Guides). 1998. pap. text 7.95 (*0-88729-542-8*); pap. text 22.95 (*0-88729-705-6*) Langenscheidt.

Madeira. Alex Liddel. 272p. 1998. pap. 21.95 (*0-571-19097-9*) Faber & Faber.

Madeira. Alex Liddell. (Faber Books on Wine). (Illus.). 297p. 1998. 37.95 (*0-571-19096-0*) Faber & Faber.

Madeira 2nd ed. 2nd ed. Rod Bolt. (Orig.). 1999. pap. text 14.95 (*1-86011-901-8*) Cadgn Bks.

Madeira Applique by Machine: Plus Heirloom Sewing from A to Z. Martha Pullen. LC 97-65222. (Marth'a Sewing Room Ser.). (Illus.). 107p. (Orig.). 1997. text 19.95 (*1-878048-12-0*) M Pullen.

Madeira Pocket Guide, 1998. rev. ed. Berlitz Editors. (Pocket Guides Ser.). (Illus.). 1998. pap. 8.95 (*2-8315-6472-7*) Berlitz.

Madelaine. Joseph Louis. 1987. pap. 2.95 (*0-317-54101-3*) Bantam.

Madeleine see Noor-un-Nisa Inayat Khan (Madeleine): George Cross MBE, Croix de Guerre with Gold Star

***Madeleine.** Rhodes. (J). 2000. pap. 10.95 (*0-552-13309-4*, Pub. by Transworld Publishers Ltd) Trafalgar.

Madeleine. large type ed. Bernard Taylor. 1989. 11.50 (*0-7089-2064-0*) Ulverscroft.

Madeleine. Ed. by Annette K. Baxter. LC 79-8767. (Signal Lives Ser.). 1980. reprint ed. lib. bdg. 37.95 (*0-405-12817-7*) Ayer.

Madeleine. Bernard Taylor. 368p. 1993. reprint ed. pap. text, mass mkt. 4.50 (*0-8439-3404-2*) Dorchester Pub Co.

Madeleine: An Autobiography. Ed. by Marcia Carlisle. 364p. 1986. reprint ed. 9.95 (*0-89255-108-9*) Persea Bks.

Madeleine Albright. Michael Burgan. LC 98-6880. 144p. (J). (gr. 7 up). 1998. 24.90 (*0-7613-0367-7*, Copper Beech Bks) Millbrook Pr.

***Madeleine Albright.** Judy L. Hasday. (Women of Achievement Ser.). (Illus.). (J). 1999. 14.35 (*0-606-18035-4*) Turtleback.

Madeleine Albright. Megan Howard. LC 97-27450. (Biography Ser.). (Illus.). 128p. (J). (gr. 6-9). 1998. 25.26 (*0-8225-4935-2*, Lerner Publctns) Lerner Pub.

Madeleine Albright. Jill C. Wheeler. LC 98-27393. (Women of the World Ser.). (J). 2002. lib. bdg. 21.35 (*1-57765-316-5*) ABDO Pub Co.

***Madeleine Albright: A Twentieth-Century Odussey, Vol. 1.** Michael Dobbs. 2000. pap. 16.00 (*0-8050-5660-2*, Owl) H Holt & Co.

Madeleine Albright: Against All Odds. Michael Dobbs. LC 98-53592. (Illus.). 464p. 1999. 27.50 (*0-8050-5659-9*) H Holt & Co.

***Madeleine Albright: First Woman Secretary of State.** Barbara Kramer. LC 99-21294. (People to Know Ser.). (Illus.). 112p. (J). (gr. 6 up). 2000. lib. bdg. 20.95 (*0-7660-1143-7*) Enslow Pubs.

Madeleine Albright: She Speaks for America. Suzanne Freedman. LC 97-13840. (Book Report Biography Ser.). (J). 1998. 22.00 (*0-531-11454-6*) Watts.

Madeleine Albright: Stateswoman see Women of Distinction: Hardcover

Madeleine Albright: Stateswoman see Women of Distinction: Paperback

Madeleine Albright: U. S. Secretary of State. Rose Blue & Corrine J. Nadan. LC 98-13723. (Library of Famous Women). (Illus.). 64p. (J). (gr. 4-7). 1998. lib. bdg. 17.95 (*1-56711-253-6*) Blackbirch.

***Madeleine Albright & the New American Diplomacy.** Thomas W. Lippman. LC 00-27464. 288p. 2000. 27.00 (*0-8133-9767-7*, Pub. by Westview) HarpC.

Madeleine & Andre Gide: The Platonic Marriage of Saint & Homosexual. Jean Schlumberger. Tr. by Richard H. Akeroyd. (Illus.). 1981. 20.00 (*0-916620-45-X*) Portals Pr.

Madeleine Cooks. Madeleine Kamman. LC 85-62641. (Illus.). 256p. 1986. 22.95 (*0-688-06203-2*, Wm Morrow) Morrow Avon.

Madeleine de Scudery: Her Romantic Life & Death. Dorothy McDougall. LC 72-80149. (Illus.). 1972. reprint ed. 26.95 (*0-405-08764-0*, Pub. by Blom Pubns) Ayer.

Madeleine Delbrel: A Life Beyond Boundaries. Charles F. Mann. LC 95-67111. 208p. 1996. pap. 12.95 (*0-9645600-9-7*) New Wrld Pr.

Madeleine Delbrel: A Life Beyond Boundaries. 2nd expanded rev. ed. Charles F. Mann. LC 97-75546. (Illus.). 232p. 1998. pap. 12.95 (*0-9645600-6-2*, 0-9645600) New Wrld Pr.

Madeleine Leininger: Cultural Care Diversity & Universality Theory. Cheryl L. Reynolds & Madeleine Leininger. (Notes on Nursing Theories Ser.: Vol. 8). (Illus.). 64p. (C). 1993. text 22.95 (*0-8039-5097-7*); pap. text 9.95 (*0-8039-5098-5*) Sage.

Madeleine L'Engle: Author of "A Wrinkle in Time" Doreen Gonzales. LC 91-3883. (People in Focus Ser.). (Illus.). 112p. (J). (gr. 4-6). 1991. lib. bdg. 13.95 (*0-87518-485-5*, Dillon Silver Burdett) Silver Burdett Pr.

***Madeleine Sophie Barat: A Life.** Phil Kilroy. 2000. 34.95 (*0-8091-0526-8*) Paulist Pr.

***Madeleine Sophie Barat, 1779-1865: A Biography.** Phil Kilroy. LC 00-22738. 2000. write for info. (*1-85918-114-7*, Pub. by Cork Univ) Stylus Pub VA.

Madeleine Takes Command. Ethel C. Brill. LC 96-83472. (Living History Library). (Illus.). 208p. (YA). (gr. 6 up). 1996. reprint ed. pap. 11.95 (*1-883937-17-5*, 17-5) Bethlehem ND.

Madeleine Vionnet. Betty Kirke. LC 98-36380. (Illus.). 244p. 1998. 100.00 (*0-8118-1997-3*) Chronicle Bks.

Madeleine's Cowboy. Kristine Rolofson. (Temptation Ser.). 1994. per. 2.99 (*0-373-25578-0*, 1-25578-5) Harlequin Bks.

Madeleine's Cowboy. Kristine Rolofson. (Bestselling Authors Ser.). 1998. mass mkt. 1.99 (*0-373-83360-1*, 1-83360-7) Harlequin Bks.

Madeleine's Ghost: A Novel of New York, New Orleans & the Next World. Robert Girardi. 368p. 1996. pap. 11.95 (*0-385-31636-4*, Delta Trade) Dell.

Madeleines Song: A Sinner Saved by Grace. Madeleine Stires. LC 97-77324. 1997. mass mkt., per. 12.95 (*1-889131-22-9*) CasAnanda.

***Madeleine's World: A Child's Journey from Birth to Age Three.** Brian Hall. 262p. 2000. reprint ed. text 20.00 (*0-7881-6905-X*) DIANE Pub.

Madelein's Marriage. Emma Goldrick. 1989. per. 2.50 (*0-373-11208-4*) Harlequin Bks.

Madeleva: A Biography. Gail P. Mandell. LC 96-36300. (Illus.). 303p. (C). 1997. text 54.50 (*0-7914-3439-7*); pap. text 19.95 (*0-7914-3440-0*) State U NY Pr.

Madeleva, 1994: One Woman's Life. Gail P. Mandell. LC 94-5932. (Madeleva Lectures). 64p. (Orig.). 1994. pap. 4.95 (*0-8091-3499-3*) Paulist Pr.

Madeline. Ludwig Bemelmans. LC 39-21791. (Madeline Ser.). (Illus.). 46p. (J). (ps-3). 1977. pap. 5.99 (*0-14-050198-3*, PuffinBks) Peng Put Young Read.

Madeline. Ludwig Bemelmans. LC 92-44867. (Madeline Ser.). (Illus.). 32p. (J). (ps-3). 1993. pap. 19.99 (*0-14-054845-9*, PuffinBks) Peng Put Young Read.

Madeline. Ludwig Bemelmans. Tr. by Ernesto L. Grosman from ENG. LC 93-18716. (Madeline Ser.). (SPA., Illus.). 64p. (J). (ps-3). 1993. 16.99 (*0-670-85154-X*, Viking Child) Peng Put Young Read.

Madeline. Ludwig Bemelmans. (Madeline Ser.). (Illus.). (J). (ps-3). 1993. pap. 8.99 incl. audio (*0-14-095121-0*) Peng Put Young Read.

Madeline. Ludwig Bemelmans. (Madeline Ser.). (Illus.). 48p. (J). (ps-3). 2000. pap. 6.99 (*0-14-056439-X*, PuffinBks) Peng Put Young Read.

Madeline. Ludwig Bemelmans. LC 76-50664. (Madeline Ser.). (J). (ps-3). 1977. 10.19 (*0-606-03874-4*, Pub. by Turtleback) Demco.

Madeline. Ludwig Bemelmans. (Madeline Ser.). (J). (ps-3). 1996. 10.19 (*0-606-08812-1*, Pub. by Turtleback) Demco.

***Madeline.** Ludwig Bemelmans. (Madeline Ser.). (Illus.). (J). (ps-3). 2000. 12.44 (*0-606-18426-0*) Turtleback.

Madeline. Ludwig Bemelmans. Tr. by Ernesto L. Grosman from ENG. (Madeline Ser.). (SPA., Illus.). 32p. (J). (ps-3). 1996. pap. 5.99 (*0-14-055761-X*) Viking Penguin.

Madeline. Cynthia Holzschuher. (Literature Unit Ser.). (Illus.). 48p. 1995. pap., teacher ed. 7.95 (*1-55734-538-4*) Tchr Create Mat.

Madeline. Ludwig Bemelmans. (Madeline Ser.). (J). (ps-3). 1995. reprint ed. lib. bdg. 25.95 (*1-56849-657-5*) Buccaneer Bks.

Madeline. unabridged ed. Ludwig Bemelmans. (Madeline Ser.). (SPA.). (J). (ps-3). 1997. 24.95 incl. audio (*0-87499-409-8*); pap. 15.95 incl. audio (*0-87499-408-X*) Live Oak Media.

Madeline, 4 vols., Set. Ludwig Bemelmans. (Madeline Ser.). (SPA.). (J). (ps-3). 1997. pap., teacher ed. 31.95 incl. audio (*0-87499-410-1*) Live Oak Media.

***Madeline, 2 vols., Set.** unabridged ed. Ludwig Bemelmans. Tr. by Ernesto Livon Grosman from ENG. (Madeline Ser.). (SPA.). (J). (ps-3). 1999. pap. 29.95 incl. audio (*0-87499-570-1*) Live Oak Media.

Madeline: A Study Guide. Garrett Christopher. Ed. by J. Friedland & R. Kessler. (Little Novel-Ties Ser.). (J). (gr. k-2). 1992. pap. text 14.95 (*0-88122-735-8*) Lrn Links.

Madeline: A Study Guide. Marina Petralia. Ed. by J. Friedland & R. Kessler. (Spanish Little Novel-Ties Ser.). (SPA.). (J). (gr. k-2). 1996. pap. text 14.95 (*1-56982-726-5*) Lrn Links.

Madeline: After the Fall of Usher. Marie Kiraly. 416p. (Orig.). 1996. mass mkt. 5.99 (*0-425-15573-0*) Berkley Pub.

Madeline A Pop-up Book. Ludwig Bemelmans. LC 86-51634. (Madeline Ser.). (Illus.). (J). (ps-3). 1987. 16.99 (*0-670-81667-1*, Viking Child) Peng Put Young Read.

Madeline & the Bad Hat. Ludwig Bemelmans. LC 77-1976. (Madeline Ser.). (Illus.). (J). (ps-3). 1957. 16.99 (*0-670-44614-9*, Viking Child) Peng Put Young Read.

Madeline & the Bad Hat. Ludwig Bemelmans. LC 57-62. (Madeline Ser.). (Illus.). (J). (ps-3). 1977. pap. 5.99 (*0-14-050206-8*, PuffinBks) Peng Put Young Read.

***Madeline & the Bad Hat.** Ludwig Bemelmans. (Madeline Ser.). (Illus.). 64p. (J). (ps-3). 2000. pap. 6.99 (*0-14-056648-1*, PuffinBks) Peng Put Young Read.

***Madeline & the Bad Hat.** Ludwig Bemelmans. (Madeline Ser.). (Illus.). (J). (ps-3). 2000. 12.44 (*0-606-18427-9*) Turtleback.

Madeline & the Gypsies. Ludwig Bemelmans. LC 77-23792. (Madeline Ser.). (Illus.). (J). (ps-3). 1959. 16.99 (*0-670-44682-3*, Viking Child) Peng Put Young Read.

Madeline & the Gypsies. Ludwig Bemelmans. (Madeline Ser.). (Illus.). 59p. (J). (ps-3). 1977. pap. 5.99 (*0-14-050261-0*, PuffinBks) Peng Put Young Read.

***Madeline & the Gypsies.** Ludwig Bemelmans. (Madeline Ser.). (Illus.). 64p. (J). (ps-3). 2000. pap. 6.99 (*0-14-056647-3*, PuffinBks) Peng Put Young Read.

Madeline & the Gypsies. Ludwig Bemelmans. (Madeline Ser.). (J). (ps-3). 1959. 10.19 (*0-606-01010-6*, Pub. by Turtleback) Demco.

***Madeline & the Gypsies.** Ludwig Bemelmans. (Madeline Ser.). (Illus.). (J). (ps-3). 2000. 12.44 (*0-606-18428-7*) Turtleback.

Madeline Book & Toy Box. Ludwig Bemelmans. (Madeline Ser.). (J). (ps-3). 1991. pap. 24.99 (*0-14-034880-8*, PuffinBks) Peng Put Young Read.

Madeline in America & Other Holiday Tales. Ludwig Bemelmans. LC 98-45089. (Madeline Ser.). (Illus.). 111p. (J). (ps-3). 1999. 19.95 (*0-590-03910-5*, Pub. by Scholastic Inc) Penguin Putnam.

***Madeline in America & Other Holiday Tales.** deluxe ed. Ludwig Bemelmans. (Madeline Ser.). (J). (ps-3). 1999. 125.00 (*0-439-09633-2*) Scholastic Inc.

Madeline in London. Ludwig Bemelmans. LC 76-54807. (Madeline Ser.). (Illus.). (J). (ps-3). 1961. 16.99 (*0-670-44648-3*, Viking Child) Peng Put Young Read.

Madeline in London. Ludwig Bemelmans. (Madeline Ser.). (Illus.). 56p. (J). (ps-3). 1977. pap. 5.99 (*0-14-050199-1*, PuffinBks) Peng Put Young Read.

***Madeline in London.** Ludwig Bemelmans. (Madeline Ser.). (Illus.). 64p. (J). (ps-3). 2000. pap. 6.99 (*0-14-056649-X*, PuffinBks) Peng Put Young Read.

Madeline in London. Ludwig Bemelmans. (Madeline Ser.). (J). (ps-3). 1978. 10.19 (*0-606-03875-2*, Pub. by Turtleback) Demco.

***Madeline in London.** Ludwig Bemelmans. (Madeline Ser.). (Illus.). (J). (ps-3). 2000. 12.44 (*0-606-18429-5*) Turtleback.

Madeline in London. unabridged ed. Ludwig Bemelmans. (Madeline Ser.). (J). (ps-3). 1995. pap. 15.95 incl. audio (*0-670-44655-6*) Live Oak Media.

Madeline Island & the Chequamegon Region. John O. Holzhueter. LC 74-20919. (Illus.). 62p. 1974. pap. 4.95 (*0-87020-146-8*, MAIS) State Hist Soc Wis.

Madeline Murphy Speaks. Madeline W. Murphy. LC 88-63313. (Illus.). 388p. (Orig.). 1988. pap. 15.95 (*0-935132-12-0*) C H Fairfax.

Madeline Paper Dolls. Jody Wheeler. (Madeline Ser.). (Illus.). (J). (ps-3). 1994. pap. 6.99 (*0-670-85601-0*) Viking Penguin.

Madeline Playtime Activity Book. Ludwig Bemelmans. (Madeline Ser.). (Illus.). 16p. (J). (ps-3). 1997. pap. 6.99 (*0-670-87464-7*) Viking Penguin.

Madeline the Mermaid: And Other Fishy Tales. Anna Fienberg. 48p. (J). (gr. 1-5). 1996. 12.95 (*1-86373-838-X*) IPG Chicago.

***Madeline's Birthday Activity Book.** Jody Wheeler. (J). 1999. pap. 7.99 (*0-670-88767-6*, Viking Child) Peng Put Young Read.

Madeline's Christmas. Ludwig Bemelmans. (Madeline Ser.). (Illus.). (J). (ps-3). 1993. pap. 9.99 incl. audio (*0-14-095108-3*, PuffinBks) Peng Put Young Read.

***Madeline's Christmas.** Ludwig Bemelmans. (Madeline Ser.). (Illus.). 32p. (J). (ps-3). 2000. pap. 6.99 (*0-14-056650-3*, PuffinBks) Peng Put Young Read.

Madeline's Christmas. Ludwig Bemelmans. (Madeline Ser.). (J). (ps-3). 1984. 10.19 (*0-606-03983-X*, Pub. by Turtleback) Demco.

Madeline's House: Madeline; Madeline's Rescue; Madeline & the Bad Hat. Ludwig Bemelmans. (Madeline Ser.). (Illus.). (J). (ps-3). 1989. pap. 12.99 (*0-14-095028-1*, PuffinBks) Peng Put Young Read.

***Madeline's Rescue.** (J). 1999. 9.95 (*1-56137-473-3*) Novel Units.

Madeline's Rescue. Ludwig Bemelmans. LC 53-8709. (Madeline Ser.). (Illus.). 56p. (J). (ps-3). 1953. 16.99 (*0-670-44716-1*, Viking Child) Peng Put Young Read.

Madeline's Rescue. Ludwig Bemelmans. (Madeline Ser.). (Illus.). (J). (ps-3). 1993. pap. 8.99 incl. audio (*0-14-095122-9*, PuffinBks) Peng Put Young Read.

***Madeline's Rescue.** Ludwig Bemelmans. (Madeline Ser.). (Illus.). 64p. (J). (ps-3). 2000. pap. 6.99 (*0-14-056651-1*, PuffinBks) Peng Put Young Read.

Madeline's Rescue. Ludwig Bemelmans. LC 77-2573. (Madeline Ser.). (J). (ps-3). 1977. 10.19 (*0-606-03876-0*, Pub. by Turtleback) Demco.

Madeline's Rescue: A Study Guide. Merrily Hansen. Ed. by J. Friedland & R. Kessler. (Little Novel-Ties Ser.). (J). (gr. k-2). 1996. pap. text 14.95 (*1-56982-683-8*) Lrn Links.

Madeline's Velcro. Ludwig Bemelmans. (Madeline Ser.). (J). (ps-3). 1997. pap. 14.98 (*0-670-78126-6*) NAL.

Madelon de l'An 40. large type ed. Georges Coulonges. 1996. pap. 25.99 (*2-84011-145-4*) Ulverscroft.

Madelyn Whiting's Soul Food. Madelyn Whiting. 52p. 1994. pap. 8.95 (*0-9646091-0-X*) Joyful Living Inst.

Mademoiselle Bambu, Filles et Ports d'Europe-Pere Barbancon. Pierre M. Orlan. (FRE.). 1982. pap. 10.95 (*0-7859-4163-0*) Fr & Eur.

Mademoiselle Colombe see Jean Anouilh: Five Plays

Mademoiselle de Maupin. Theophile Gautier. Ed. by Boschot. pap. 8.95 (*0-685-11302-7*) Fr & Eur.

Mademoiselle de Maupin. Theophile Gautier. (FRE.). 1991. reprint ed. pap. 12.95 (*0-7859-4672-1*) Fr & Eur.

Mademoiselle de Maupin. unabridged ed. Theophile Gautier. (FRE.). Date not set. reprint ed. pap. 8.95 (*2-87714-347-3*, Pub. by Bookking Intl) Distribks Inc.

Mademoiselle de Scudery & the Looking-Glass Self. Joanne Davis. LC 92-8710. (Currents in Comparative Romance Languages & Literatures Ser.: Vol. 7). 135p. (C). 1994. text 39.95 (*0-8204-1904-4*) P Lang Pubng.

Mademoiselle Fifi. Guy de Maupassant. (FRE.). 1977. 10.95 (*0-8288-9618-6*, M12713) Fr & Eur.

Mademoiselle Fifi. Guy de Maupassant. (Folio Ser.: No. 945). 1960. pap. 8.95 (*2-07-036945-5*, 583) Schoenhof.

Mademoiselle Fifi & Other Stories. Guy de Maupassant. Tr. & Intro. by David Coward. LC 92-10105. (World's Classics Ser.). 288p. 1993. pap. 8.95 (*0-19-282923-8*) OUP.

***Mademoiselle Fifi & Other Stories.** Guy de Maupassant. (Oxford World's Classics Ser.). 288p. 1999. pap. 9.95 (*0-19-283752-4*) OUP.

Mademoiselle Fifi & Other Stories. Guy de Maupassant. 1993. reprint ed. lib. bdg. 22.95 (*1-56849-174-3*) Buccaneer Bks.

Mademoiselle Fifi & Other Stories Vol. 2: Collected Novels & Stories. Guy de Maupassant. Ed. by Ernest A. Boyd. LC 77-157789. (Short Story Index Reprint Ser.). 1977. reprint ed. 18.95 (*0-8369-3901-8*) Ayer.

Mademoiselle Irnois & Other Stories. Arthur J. De Gobineau. Ed. & Tr. by Annette Smith. Ed. by David Smith. 1988. 50.00 (*0-520-05946-8*, Pub. by U CA Pr) Cal Prin Full Svc.

Mademoiselle Irnois-Les Conseils de Rabelais. Arthur D. Gobineau. (FRE.). 380p. 1985. pap. 13.95 (*0-7859-2502-3*, 2070376400) Fr & Eur.

Mademoiselle la Quintinie. George Sand. (FRE.). 370p. 1979. pap. 45.00 (*0-7859-5395-7*) Fr & Eur.

Mademoiselle Mitoufle. Beatrix Potter. (FRE., Illus.). 58p. (J). 1990. 9.95 (*0-7859-3633-5*, 2070561046) Fr & Eur.

Mademoiselle Mitoufle. Beatrix Potter. (Gallimard Ser.). (FRE.). 37p. (J). 1990. 10.95 (*2-07-056104-6*) Schoenhof.

Mademoiselle Moon. Marie-Louise Gay. LC 93-111725. 32p. (ps-3). 1996. 12.95 (*0-7737-2653-5*) Stoddart Publ.

Madera para 'Esculpir la Imagen de una Santa: Rasgos Biograficos, Revelaciones, Profecias, Confidencias con la Santissima Virgen de El Buen Suceso, de la Venerable Madre Mariana de Jesue Torres y Berriochoa. Luis E. Y Almeida & Jose L. De Zayas y Arancibia. LC 87-81079. (SPA., Illus.). 190p. (Orig.). (C). 1987. pap. 13.95 (*1-877905-08-9*) Am Soc Defense TFP.

Maderati. Richard Greenberg. 1987. pap. 5.25 (*0-8222-0713-3*) Dramatists Play.

Madha Khasira al-Alam bi-Inhtat al-Muslimin see Islam & the World

Madhakkirat Yasu' Al-Nasiry, Vol. 1. Dahesh. (ARA & ENG., Illus.). 150p. 1991. 40.00 (*0-935359-11-7*) Daheshist.

***Madhava Kandali Ramayana, Pt. I.** Tr. by Shanti Lal Nagar. 2000. 68.50 (*81-215-0936-X*, Pub. by M Manoharial) S Asia.

Madhhab Ibn Adam al-Awwal: Muskilat al-'Unf fi al-'Alam al-Islami. Jawdat Sa'id. (Taghyir al-Nafs wa-al-Mujtama Ser.). 240p. 1993. pap. 3.95 (*1-57547-045-4*) Dar Al-Fikr.

Madhist Faith & Sudanic Tradition: History of Dar Mahalist, 1870-1930. Lidwien Kapteijns. 366p. 1985. 69.50 (*0-7103-0090-5*) Routledge.

Madhouse in Goa: A Play Martin Sherman. LC 98-234624. 108 p. 1998. write for info. (*0-573-62291-4*) S French Trade.

Madhouse Nudes. Robert Schultz. LC 96-38619. 1997. 21.50 (*0-684-83262-3*) S&S Trade.

***Madhouse Nudes.** Robert Schultz. 2000. pap. 14.00 (*0-931209-90-0*) Mid-Prairie Bks.

Madhubala: Her Life Her Films. Khatija Akbar. LC 97-901433. (C). 1997. pap. 14.00 (*81-7476-153-5*, Pub. by UBS Pubs Dist) S Asia.

Madhubani Painting. Mulk-Raj Anand. (Illus.). 60p. 1982. 37.95 (*0-318-36343-7*) Asia Bk Corp.

Madhubani Paintings: Indian Native. Norio Osaki. (Arts Collection Ser.: Vol. 120). (Illus.). 256p. 1998. pap. 14.95 (*4-7636-1620-X*, Pub. by Kyoto Shoin) Bks Nippan.

***Madhumalati: An Indian Sufi Romance.** Ed. by Aditya Behl & Simon Weightman. (Oxford World's Classics Ser.). 240p. 2001. 10.95 (*0-19-284037-1*) OUP.

Madhur Jaffrey's Flavors of India. Madhur Jaffrey. LC 98-36922. (Great Food Ser.). (Illus.). 320p. 1998. pap. 21.95 (*1-884656-06-4*) W One Hund Seventy Five.

Madhur Jaffrey's Flavours of India. Madhur Jaffrey. LC 98-194334. 320 p. 1995. write for info. (*0-563-37074-2*) BBC Bks.

Madhur Jaffrey's Indian Cooking. Madhur Jaffrey. LC 95-9793. 224p. 1995. 24.00 (*0-8120-6548-4*) Barron.

Madhur Jaffrey's Quick & Easy Indian Cooking. Madhur Jaffrey. LC 95-31296. (Illus.). 144p. 1996. pap. 15.95 (*0-8118-1183-2*) Chronicle Bks.

Madhur Jaffrey's World-of-the-East Vegetarian Cooking. Madhur Jaffrey. (Illus.). 460p. 1981. pap. 25.00 (*0-394-74867-0*) Knopf.

Madhur Jaffrey's World Vegetarian: More Than 750 Meatless Recipes from Around the Globe. Madhur Jaffrey. LC 98-30318. (Illus.). 760p. 1999. 40.00 (*0-517-59632-6*) C Potter.

Madhusudan Saraswati on the Bhagavaddita. S. K. Gupta. 1977. 19.95 (*0-89684-246-0*, Pub. by Motilal Bnarsidass) S Asia.

Madhusudana Saraswati Bhagavad Gita. Tr. by Swami Gambhirananda from SAN. LC 98-909935. 1038p. 1998. 19.95 (*81-7505-194-9*, Pub. by Advaita Ashrama) Vedanta Pr.

Madhyamaka Schools in India: A Study of the Madhyamaka Philosophy & of the Division of the System into the Prasangika & Svarantrika. Peter D. Santina. xxiii, 242p. 1986. 17.50 (*81-208-0153-9*, Pub. by Motilal Bnarsidass) S Asia.

Madhyamaka Thought in China. Ming-Wood Liu. LC 94-953. (Sinica Leidensia Ser.: Vol. 30). 1994. 126.00 (*90-04-09984-0*) Brill Academic Pubs.

Madhyamakasastram of Nagarjuna, Vol. 1. Raghunath Pandeya. (C). 1988. 58.00 (*81-208-0554-2*, Pub. by Motilal Bnarsidass) S Asia.

Madhyamakasastram of Nagarjuna, Vol. 2. Ed. by Raghunath Pandeya. (C). 1989. 48.50 (*81-208-0555-0*, Pub. by Motilal Bnarsidass) S Asia.

Madhyamika & Yogacara: A Study of Mahayana Philosophies. Gadjin M. Nagao. Ed. by Leslie S. Kawamura. LC 89-4278. (SUNY Series in Buddhist Studies). 318p. 1991. text 21.50 (*0-7914-0186-3*) State U NY Pr.

Madhyastham Adhiniyam Arbitration Act. I. J. Malhotra. (HIN.). (C). 1990. text 70.00 (*0-89771-488-1*) St Mut.

Madibaland. Denis Beckett. LC 98-137586. 211p. 1998. write for info. (*0-14-027456-1*, Penguin Bks) Viking Penguin.

Madiera at Sundown: A Raj Trilogy. Eric Prabhakar. (C). 1990. 23.00 (*81-7001-071-3*, Pub. by Chanakya) S Asia.

Madigal. Beverly MacDonald. LC 97-221126. 410 p. 1995. write for info. (*0-330-35644-5*) Pan.

Madigan. R. Howard Trembly. LC 98-88649. 290p. 1999. pap. 14.95 (*0-88739-198-2*) Creat Arts Bk.

Madinan Society at the Time of the Prophet Vol. 1: Its Characteristics & Organization. An Attempt to Apply the Rules of the Muhaddithun in the Criticism of Historical Reports. Akram Diya' al Umari. Tr. by Huda Khattab from ARA. LC 89-2185. 250p. (C). 1991. text 19.95 (*0-912463-36-8*); pap. text 10.95 (*0-912463-37-6*) IIIT VA.

Madinan Society at the Time of the Prophet Vol. 2: The Jihad Against the Mushrikun. An Attempt to Apply the Rules of the Muhaddithun in the Criticism of Historical Reports. Akram Diya' al Umari. Tr. by Huda Khattab from ARA. LC 89-2185. 250p. (C). 1991. pap. 10.95 (*0-912463-39-2*); text 19.95 (*0-912463-38-4*) IIIT VA.

Madison. John Cunningham. (Images of America Ser.). 1998. pap. 16.99 (*0-7524-0837-2*) Arcadia Publng.

***Madison.** Brent Nicastro. LC 99-32507. (ENG, GER & SPA., Illus.). 112p. 1999. 14.95 (*1-879483-63-7*) Prairie Oak Pr.

Madison. Rand McNally Staff. LC 98-682865. (Easy Finder Plus Ser.). 1996. 9.95 (*0-528-97091-7*) Rand McNally.

***Madison: Character in Time: The U. S. Presidents.** R. David Cox. 40p. 1998. 5.95 (*1-929403-10-0*) History Proj.

Madison: Meeting the 21st Century. Doug Moe. 1990. 29.95 (*0-89781-313-8*) Am Historical Pr.

Madison - God's Beautiful Farm: The E. A. Sutherland Story. Ira Gish & Harry M. Christman. (Pioneer Classics Ser.). 192p. 1989. reprint ed. pap. 7.95 (*0-945460-09-0*) Upward Way.

Madison Avenue. Mathias Braschler. 1999. 45.00 (*3-905328-16-X*) Scalo Pubs.

Madison Avenue in Asia: Politics & Transnational Advertising. Michael H. Anderson. LC 81-69078. (Illus.). 380p. 1984. 45.00 (*0-8386-3101-0*) Fairleigh Dickinson.

Madison Avenue Murder. Liza Bennett. 224p. (Orig.). 1989. spiral bd. 3.50 (*0-373-26016-4*) Harlequin Bks.

Madison Avenue, U. S. A. Martin Mayer. (NTC's Business Classics Ser.). (Illus.). 304p. 1994. pap. 11.95 (*0-8442-3247-5*, NTC Business Bks) NTC Contemp Pub Co.

Madison Catalogue of 2786 Stars for the Epoch 1910 from Meridian Observations. Albert S. Flint. Ed. by Arthur J. Roy. LC 39-33947. (Carnegie Institution of Washington Publication Ser.: No. 515). 77p. reprint ed. pap. 30.00 (*0-608-10155-9*, 200790600066) Bks Demand.

Madison Conference, 1957 see Research Opportunities in Renaissance Drama: The Reports of the Modern Language Association Conferences

Madison Connection: Voices from the Heartland. 9th rev. ed. Ed. by Harvest Staff. (Illus.). 240p. 1999. 35.99 (*0-939074-09-5*, 0146-5414) Harvest Pubns.

Madison County Cookbook: With Stories & Traditions. St. Joseph's Catholic Church, Winterset, Iowa Staf. (Illus.). 516p. 1995. pap. 17.95 (*0-8065-1733-6*, Citadel Pr) Carol Pub Group.

Madison County Cookbook with Stories & Traditions. St. Joseph Church Committee Staff. Ed. by Teresa Hoffelmeyer & Frank S. Palmer. (Illus.). 512p. 1994. 21.95 (*0-9644705-0-0*) St Joseph Ch.

Madison County Folklore. Bonnie F. Bolinger. Ed. & Intro. by Burr E. Fancher. 80p. (Orig.). (J). (gr. 4 up). 1995. pap. 5.00 (*1-887335-00-5*) Fancher & Assocs.

Madison County History, Vol. 2. Ed. by Madison Historical Comm. Staff. (Illus.). 280p. 1997. 79.50 (*0-9660880-5-0*) Madison Cty Hist.

***Madison County, Kentucky Court Order Bk. B: 1791-1801.** Jackie Couture. 319p. 2000. pap. 28.00 (*0-7884-1463-1*, 1463) Heritage Bk.

Madison County, Kentucky, Court Order Book A, 1787-1791. Jackie Couture. v, 152p. (Orig.). 1996. pap. 20.00 (*0-7884-0594-2*, C587) Heritage Bk.

Madison County, Kentucky Taxpayers, 1787-1799. T.L.C. Genealogy Staff. LC 92-60553. 119p. (Orig.). 1992. pap., spiral bd. 10.00 (*1-886633-08-8*) TLC Genealogy.

Madison County, Mississippi Will Abstracts. Betty C. Wiltshire. 133p. 1999. pap. 15.00 (*1-885480-33-4*) Pioneer Pubng.

Madison County, Virginia Marriages, 1792-1850. John Vogt & T. William Kethley, Jr. 156p. 1984. pap. 12.95 (*0-935931-08-2*) Iberian Pub.

Madison During the Civil War Era: A Portfolio of Rare Photographs by John S. Fuller, 1860-1863 , 1. John O. Holzhueter. 1998. pap. 4.95 (*0-87020-301-0*) State Hist Soc Wis.

***Madison Entertainment, 2000.** (Illus.). 646p. 1999. pap. 30.00 (*1-58553-037-9*, 0049) Enter Pubns.

Madison Finds a Line. Sunny Warner. LC 99-20696. (Illus.). 32p. (J). (ps-2). 1999. 15.00 (*0-395-88508-6*) HM.

Madison in the Twentieth Century. Madison Historical Society Staff. LC 98-86604. (Images of America Ser.). (Illus.). 128p. 1998. pap. 16.99 (*0-7524-0940-9*) Arcadia Publng.

Madison, Monroe, & Quincy Adams. Michael Weber. LC 95-30060. (Complete History of Our Presidents Ser.: Vol. 2). (J). 1996. write for info. (*0-86593-407-X*) Rourke Corp.

Madison, Norridgewock & Smithfield. Frank H. Sleeper. (Images of America Ser.). (Illus.). 128p. 1998. pap. 16.99 (*0-7524-0956-5*) Arcadia Publng.

Madison on the "General Welfare" of America: His Consistent Constitutional Vision of Limited Government. Leonard R. Sorenson. 224p. (C). 1995. text 62.00 (*0-8476-8064-9*); pap. text 22.95 (*0-8476-8065-7*) Rowman.

Madison Poems & Collages. D. A. Levy. 1980. 12.00 (*0-685-04199-9*) Quixote.

Madison Register, 1903 (Town History & Directory) Compiled by Mitchell & Randall. 137p. 1997. reprint ed. pap. 21.00 (*0-8328-5870-6*) Higginson Bk Co.

Madison Retro. Larry W. Phillips. Ed. by Marv Balousek. 222p. (Orig.). 1994. pap. 12.95 (*1-878569-22-8*) Badger Bks Inc.

Madison River, MT. John Holt & Jeff Findley. (River Journal Ser.: Vol. 1, No. 1). (Illus.). 48p. (Orig.). 1992. pap. 15.95 (*1-878175-26-2*) F Amato Pubns.

Madison Station. Guy A. Bockmon. LC 97-74195. (Illus.). 192p. 1997. 29.95 (*1-57736-057-5*, Hillsboro Pr) Providence Hse.

Madison Symposium on Complex Analysis: (Proceedings of the Symposium on Complex Analysis Held June 2-7, 1991 at the University of Wisconsin-Madison) Ed. by Alexander Nagel & Edgar L. Stout. LC 92-23702. (Contemporary Mathematics Ser.: Vol. 137). 478p. 1992. pap. 49.00 (*0-8218-5147-0*, CONM/137) Am Math.

Madison's "Advice to My Country" Adrienne Koch. LC 66-12878. (Whig-Clio Bicentennial Lectures). 236p. 1966. reprint ed. pap. 73.20 (*0-8357-6547-4*, 203591100097) Bks Demand.

Madkhal Ila Al-Dahishiyyah. Ghazi Brax. (ARA & ENG.). 135p. 1992. 15.00 (*0-935359-12-5*) Daheshist.

Madkhal ila Fahm al-Judhur Man Ana? Wa Limadha? Wa-ila-Ayn? Muhammad Sa id Ramadan al-Buti. (Hadha Huwa al-Islam Ser.). 128p. 1991. pap. 1.95 (*1-57547-016-0*) Dar Al-Fikr.

Madkhal ila Islamiyat al Ma'rifah: Ma'a Mukhattat Muqtarah li-Islamiyat 'Ilm al Tarikh - (Introduction to the Islamization of Knowledge & History) 2nd ed. Imad D. Khalil. LC 91-6493. (Silsilat Islamiyat al Ma'rifah Ser.: No. 9). (ARA.). 103p. 1991. pap. 5.00 (*0-912463-60-0*) IIIT VA.

Madlands. J. Allen Kirsch & Marv Balousek. 335p. 1993. pap. 12.95 (*1-878569-18-X*) Badger Bks Inc.

***Madlenka.** Peter Sis. LC 99-57730. (Illus.). 48p. (ps-3). 2000. pap. 17.00 (*0-374-39969-7*) FS&G.

Madly in Love. Aliki Barnstone. LC 96-83430. 80p. 1997. pap. 11.95 (*0-88748-248-1*) Carnegie-Mellon.

Madly Singing in the Mountains: An Appreciation & Anthology of Arthur Waley. Ed. by Ivan Morris. 404p. 1981. reprint ed. pap. 9.95 (*0-916870-35-9*) Creat Arts Bk.

Madman, No. 1. Michael D. Allred. (Illus.). 48p. (J). (gr. 4 up). 1994. reprint ed. pap. 3.95 (*0-87816-275-5*) Kitchen Sink.

Madman Adventures, No. 3. Michael D. Allred. (Illus.). 48p. 1993. pap. 2.95 (*1-56862-026-8*) Kitchen Sink.

Madman Adventures Collection. Michael D. Allred. Ed. by Philip Amara. (Illus.). 112p. (YA). 1994. pap. 14.95 (*0-87816-314-X*) Kitchen Sink.

Madman & the Medusa. Tchicaya U. Tam'si. Tr. by Sonja H. Smith & William J. Smith. LC 88-26086. 264p. reprint ed. pap. 81.90 (*0-608-10480-9*, 207109800008) Bks Demand.

Madman & the Nun & the Crazy Locomotive: Three Plays (Including "The Water Hen") Stanislaw I. Witkiewicz. Ed. by Daniel Gerould & C. S. Durer. 128p. 1988. pap. 10.95 (*0-936839-83-X*) Applause Theatre Bk Pubs.

Madman Boogaloo. pap. 8.95 (*1-56971-404-5*, Pub. by Dark Horse Comics) Penguin Putnam.

Madman Comics, Vol. 1. 1998. pap. 17.95 (*1-56971-091-0*) Dark Horse Comics.

Madman Comics: The Complete, Vol. 2. 1998. pap. 17.95 (*1-56971-186-0*) Dark Horse Comics.

Madman of Chu: The Chinese Myth of Loyalty & Dissent. Laurence A. Schneider. LC 78-54800. (Illus.). 282p. reprint ed. pap. 87.50 (*0-7837-4681-4*, 204442800003) Bks Demand.

Madman of Mount Everest. Ann Livesay. 326p. per. 12.95 (*0-9662817-2-1*) Silver River.

Madman on Lakeshore Drive. Dalian Moore. LC 94-71400. 32p. 1994. pap. text 9.95 (*1-885206-00-3*, Iliad Pr) Cader Pubng.

Madman Richard Stahlman. Richard R. Sayell. 178p. 1984. 6.95 (*0-89697-138-4*) Intl Univ Pr.

Madman, the Kite & the Island. Felix Leclerc. 153p. 1983. pap. 3.95 (*0-7736-7054-8*) Genl Dist Srvs.

***Madman's Mailbox: The Voice of Dementia.** Brandon Cornett. LC 99-43. 118p. 1999. spiral bd. 14.75 (*1-55212-294-8*) Trafford Pub.

***Madman's Will.** large type ed. John Newton Chance. 240p. 1999. pap. 18.99 (*0-7089-5605-X*, Linford) Ulverscroft.

***Madness.** Claudio Edinger. 1998. 29.00 (*85-7234-074-2*) Empresa Artes.

Madness: The Price of Poetry. Jeremy Reed. LC 90-80803. 208p. 1990. 36.00 (*0-7206-0744-2*) Dufour.

Madness & a Bit of Hope. Safiya Henderson-Holmes. 120p. 1991. pap. 9.95 (*0-86316-136-7*) Writers & Readers.

Madness & a Bit of Hope. Safiya Henderson-Holmes. 120p. 1991. 19.95 (*0-86316-135-9*) Writers & Readers.

Madness & Art: The Life & Works of Adolf Wolfli. Walter Morgenthaler. Tr. & Intro. by Aaron H. Esman. LC 91-46761. (Texts & Contexts Ser.). (Illus.). xviii, 156p. 1992. text 60.00 (*0-8032-3156-3*) U of Nebr Pr.

Madness & Blake's Myth. Paul Youngquist. LC 88-43441. 224p. 1990. lib. bdg. 35.00 (*0-271-00669-2*) Pa St U Pr.

Madness & Civilization: A History of Insanity in the Age of Reason. Michel Foucault. 1988. reprint ed. pap. 13.00 (*0-679-72110-X*) Vin Bks.

Madness & Cure. Robert J. Langs. 296p. (C). 1995. text 38.95 (*0-89876-218-9*) Gardner Pr.

Madness & Democracy. Marcel Gauchet & Gladys Swain. Tr. by Catherine Porter from FRE. LC 98-45014. 368p. 1999. 29.95 (*0-691-03372-2*, Pub. by Princeton U Pr) Cal Prin Full Svc.

Madness & Matt Lamb. Donald Kuspit. (Illus.). 30p. (Orig.). 1996. pap. 12.00 (*0-9652065-0-5*) Fassbender Gallery.

Madness & Modernism: Insanity in the Light of Modern Art, Literature, & Thought. Louis A. Sass. (Illus.). 607p. 1994. pap. text 21.95 (*0-674-54137-5*, SASMAX) HUP.

Madness & Reason. Jennifer Radden. (Studies in Applied Philosophy). 176p. 1985. text 55.00 (*0-04-170034-1*); pap. text 16.95 (*0-04-170035-X*) Routledge.

Madness & Revolution: The Lives & Legends of Theroigne de Mericourt. Elisabeth Roudinesco. Tr. by Martin Thom. (Illus.). 296p. (gr. 13). 1992. pap. 20.00 (*0-86091-597-2*, A9770, Pub. by Verso) Norton.

Madness & Sexual Politics in the Feminist Novel: Studies in Bronte, Woolf, Lessing & Atwood. Barbara H. Rigney. LC 78-53291. 158p. reprint ed. pap. 49.00 (*0-608-09922-8*, 206926000003) Bks Demand.

Madness & Social Representations: Living with the Mad in One French Community. Denise Jodelet. Ed. by Gerard Duveen. Tr. by Tim Pownall. (Medicine & Society Ser.: No. 5). 316p. 1992. 60.00 (*0-520-07865-9*, Pub. by U CA Pr); pap. 16.00 (*0-520-07866-7*, Pub. by U CA Pr) Cal Prin Full Svc.

***Madness & Society in Eighteenth-Century Scotland.** R. A. Houston. LC 99-31585. (Oxford Studies in Social History). (Illus.). 464p. 2000. text 90.00 (*0-19-820787-5*) OUP.

Madness & the Criminal Law. Norval Morris. LC 82-13435. (Studies in Crime & Justice). 168p. (C). 1995. pap. text 8.95 (*0-226-53908-3*) U Ch Pr.

Madness & the Criminal Law. Norval Morris. LC 82-13435. (Studies in Crime & Justice). 237p. (C). 1998. lib. bdg. 24.00 (*0-226-53907-5*) U Ch Pr.

***Madness Cannabis & Colonialism: The Native Only Lunatic Asylums.** James Mills. 2000. text 65.00 (*0-312-23359-0*) St Martin.

Madness, Chaos, & Violence: Therapy with Families at the Brink. John Brendler et al. 220p. (C). 1998. text 20.00 (*0-7881-5667-5*) DIANE Pub.

Madness, Heresy, & the Rumor of Angels: The Revolt Against the Mental Health System. Seth Farber. LC 93-1276. 286p. 1993. 49.95 (*0-8126-9199-7*); pap. 18.95 (*0-8126-9200-4*) Open Court.

Madness in America: Cultural & Medical Perceptions of Mental Illness Before 1914. Lynn Gamwell & Nancy Tomes. (Studies in the History of Psychiatry). (Illus.). 182p. 1995. text 42.50 (*0-8014-3161-1*) Cornell U Pr.

Madness in Its Place: Narratives of Severalls Hospital, 1913-1997. Diana Gittins. LC 97-39489. (Illus.). 256p. (C). 1998. 85.00 (*0-415-16786-8*); pap. 25.99 (*0-415-18388-X*) Routledge.

Madness in Late Imperial China: From Illness to Deviance. Vivien W. Ng. LC 90-50237. 208p. 1990. 35.00 (*0-8061-2297-8*) U of Okla Pr.

Madness in Literature. Lillian Feder. LC 79-3206. 347p. reprint ed. pap. 107.60 (*0-8357-6198-3*, 203465400090) Bks Demand.

Madness in My Country & the Welfare of Children. Betty Williams. Ed. by David H. Darst. (International Albert Schweitzer Lecture Ser. at Yale University). (Illus.). 12p. (Orig.). pap. text 3.50 (*1-885007-03-5*) A Schweitzer.

Madness in Society: Chapters in the Historical Sociology of Mental Illness. George Rosen. LC 68-13112. 348p. 1998. pap. text 14.95 (*0-226-72642-8*, P913) U Ch Pr.

Madness in the Family. William Saroyan. Ed. by Leo Hamalian. LC 87-28268. 160p. 1988. 9.95 (*0-8112-1064-2*, Pub. by New Directions) Norton.

Madness in the Making: The Triumphant Rise & Untimely Fall of America's Show Inventors. David Lindsay. LC 97-39617. (Illus.). 384p. 1997. 27.00 (*1-56836-203-X*) Kodansha.

***Madness in the Morning: Life & Death in the Early Morning Ratings War.** Richard Hack. 304p. 1999. pap. 22.95 (*1-893224-01-5*) New Millenn Enter.

Madness in the Streets. Dana Landers. 293p. mass mkt. 7.99 (*1-55197-005-8*) Picasso Publ.

Madness in Valencia & the Witless Lady. Lope de Vega. 144p. 1996. pap. text 14.95 (*0-948230-66-5*) Theatre Comm.

Madness, Masks & Laughter: An Essay on Comedy. R. D. Glasgow. LC 94-21586. 1995. 49.50 (*0-8386-3559-8*) Fairleigh Dickinson.

Madness, Melancholy & the Limits of the Self. Ed. by Andrew D. Weiner et al. (Graven Images: Vol. 3). (Illus.). 248p. 1996. pap. 25.00 (*0-9655464-0-3*) U of Wis Law.

Madness Network News Reader. Ed. by Sherry Hirsch et al. (Illus.). 192p. (Orig.). 1974. pap. 14.00 (*0-912078-35-9*) L R Frank.

Madness of a Seduced Woman. Susan F. Schaeffer. 592p. 1991. pap. 16.95 (*0-452-26709-9*, Plume) Dutton Plume.

Madness of Art: A Guide to Living & Working in Chicago. Adam Langer. LC 96-15362. 268p. (Orig.). 1996. pap. 12.95 (*1-55652-268-1*) Chicago Review.

Madness of Epic: Reading Insanity from Homer to Statius. Debra Hershkowitz. (Oxford Classical Monographs). 360p. 1998. text 80.00 (*0-19-815245-0*) OUP.

Madness of George III. Alan Bennett. 94p. (Orig.). 1993. pap. 11.95 (*0-571-16749-7*) Faber & Faber.

Madness of King George. Alan Bennett. 1995. pap. 10.00 (*0-679-76871-8*) Random.

***Madness of King Nebuchadnezzar: The Ancient Near Eastern Origins & Early History of Interpretation of Daniel 4** Matthias Henze. LC 99-36633. (Supplements to the Journal for the Study of Judaism Ser.). 1999. write for info. (*90-04-11421-1*) Brill Academic Pubs.

Madness of Lady Bright see Rimers of Eldritch & Other Plays

Madness of Nietzsche. E. Podach. 1973. 250.00 (*0-87968-179-9*) Gordon Pr.

Madness of Philip & Other Tales of Childhood. Josephine D. Bacon. LC 75-98557. (Short Story Index Reprint Ser.). 1977. 19.95 (*0-8369-3131-9*) Ayer.

Madness of Prince Hamlet: And Other Delusions & Extraordinary States of Mind. Robert Youngson. 352p. 1999. pap. 12.95 (*0-7867-0624-4*) Carroll & Graf.

Madness of the Saints: Ecstatic Religion in Bengal. June McDaniel. LC 88-35657. (Illus.). 346p. 1989. pap. text 19.95 (*0-226-55723-5*) U Ch Pr.

Madness of the Saints: Ecstatic Religion in Bengal. June McDaniel. LC 88-35657. (Illus.). 352p. 1996. lib. bdg. 54.00 (*0-226-55722-7*) U Ch Pr.

Madness of Things Peruvian: Democracy under Siege. Alvaro Vargas Llosa. LC 93-12632. 230p. (C). 1994. text 39.95 (*1-56000-114-3*) Transaction Pubs.

Madness of Ushers: Coping with Vision & Hearing Loss (Usher Syndrome Type II) Dorothy H. Stiefel. 92p. 1991. 10.00 (*1-879518-06-6*) Busn Living Pubns.

Madness on the Couch: Blaming the Victim in the Heyday of Psychoanalysis. Edward Dolnick. LC 98-23737. (Illus.). 352p. 1998. 25.00 (*0-684-82497-3*) Simon & Schuster.

Madness Season. C. S. Friedman. 1990. mass mkt. 6.99 (*0-88677-444-6*, Pub. by DAW Bks) Penguin Putnam.

Madoc: A Mystery. Paul Muldoon. 1991. 19.95 (*0-374-19557-9*) FS&G.

Madoc: A Mystery. Paul Muldoon. 272p. 1992. pap. 12.00 (*0-374-52344-4*) FS&G.

Madonna see Pop Culture Legends

Madonna. (Illus.). 64p. 1984. 20.45 (*0-86683-827-9*, 8467) Harper SF.

Madonna. Ivan Arguelles. LC 98-213529. 23p. 1998. pap. 5.00 (*1-57141-043-0*) Runaway Spoon.

Madonna. Thomas Kinsella. 24p. 1991. pap. 11.95 (*1-873790-11-2*) Dufour.

Madonna. Gordon Matthews. Ed. by Diane Arico. LC 85-10587. (Hot Rock Ser.). (Illus.). 64p. (YA). (gr. 8-12). 1985. pap. 3.50 (*0-685-10385-4*) S&S Trade.

Madonna. Keith E. Greenberg. (Illus.). 40p. (YA). (gr. 7-12). 1999. reprint ed. text 15.00 (*0-7881-6439-2*) DIANE Pub.

***Madonna: An Anthology of Verse & Prose.** Ed. by Barry Leonard. (Illus.). 64p. 1999. text 20.00 (*0-7881-6567-4*) DIANE Pub.

Madonna: Bawdy & Soul. Karlene Faith. LC 98-103001. 256p. 1997. pap. 19.95 (*0-8020-8063-4*); text 45.00 (*0-8020-4208-2*) U of Toronto Pr.

Madonna: Bedtime Stories. Ed. by Jeannette DeLisa. (Illus.). 60p. (Orig.). 1995. pap. text 18.95 (*0-89724-505-9*, PF9507) Wrner Bros.

***Madonna: Blonde Ambition.** expanded ed. Mark Bego. (Illus.). 2000. pap. 18.95 (*0-8154-1051-4*) Cooper Sq.

Madonna: In Her Own Words. Mick St. Michael. (In Their Own Words Ser.). (Illus.). 94p. pap. 15.95 (*0-7119-2139-3*, OP 45814) Omnibus NY.

***Madonna: Mary in the Catholic Tradition.** Frederic M. Jelly. 228p. (Orig.). 1998. pap. 22.00 (*1-57910-195-X*) Wipf & Stock.

***Madonna: New Style Book.** Debbie Voller. (Illus.). 126p. 1999. pap. 24.95 (*0-7119-7511-6*, OP48105) Omnibus NY.

Madonna: The Early Days. deluxe ed. Michael McKenzie. 96p. 1993. pap. text 19.95 (*0-9638519-3-4*) Wrldwide Televid.

Madonna - Erotica. Ed. by Carol Cuellar. 116p. (Orig.). (C). 1992. pap. text 18.95 (*0-7692-0702-2*, VF1911) Wrner Bros.

Madonna - Like a Prayer. Ed. by Carol Cuellar. 76p. (Orig.). (C). 1989. pap. text 14.95 (*0-7692-0698-0*, VF1571) Wrner Bros.

Madonna - Something to Remember. Ed. by Carol Cuellar. 76p. (Orig.). (C). 1996. pap. text 18.95 (*0-7692-0694-8*, PF9555) Wrner Bros.

Madonna & Child. Nancy Linn. (Illus.). 160p. 1984. pap. 5.00 (*0-9613812-1-3*) A White Pub.

Madonna & Child: The Development of Christian Symbolism. Lois S. Jones. Ed. by Preston Jones. (Development of Christian Symbolism Ser.: Vol. I). (Illus.). 52p. 1992. pap. 5.00 (*1-882238-02-8*) Swan-Jones Prod.

Madonna & the Coming Light. Earlyne C. Chaney. LC 93-70271. 174p. (Orig.). 1993. pap. text 15.95 (*0-918936-27-6*) Astara.

Madonna Anno Domini. Joshua Clover. LC 96-45285. 64p. 1997. pap. 11.95 (*0-8071-2148-7*); text 19.95 (*0-8071-2147-9*) La State U Pr.

***Madonna Complex.** Norman Bogner. 352p. 2000. 25.95 (*0-312-87519-3*, Pub. by Forge NYC) St Martin.

Madonna Confessions. Arthur Geis. (Orig.). pap. text 4.95 (*0-9621575-0-3*) Artisan IL.

Madonna Diaries. Cimino Publishing Group Staff. 1997. pap. text 24.95 (*1-901674-03-7*, Pub. by Arrowhead) Cimino Pub Grp.

Madonna of 115th Street: Faith & Community in Italian Harlem, 1880-1950. Robert A. Orsi. LC 85-10799. 366p. (C). 1988. reprint ed. pap. 17.00 (*0-300-04264-7*) Yale U Pr.

Madonna of the Future see Works of Henry James Jr.: Collected Works

Madonna of the Tubs. Elizabeth S. Ward. LC 74-85688. (American Fiction Reprint Ser.). 1977. 18.95 (*0-8369-7017-9*) Ayer.

Madonna on Her Back. Alyson Hagy. LC 85-50089. 150p. 1986. 15.00 (*0-913773-19-0*) S Wright.

Madonna Revealed. Douglas Thompson. 1991. pap. 12.95 (*1-55972-099-9*, Birch Ln Pr) Carol Pub Group.

Madonna Scrapbook. Lee Randall. (Illus.). 224p. 1992. pap. 15.95 (*0-8065-1297-0*, Citadel Pr) Carol Pub Group.

Madonna Scrapbook. Lee Randall. (Illus.). 224p. 1998. pap. text 16.00 (*0-7881-5568-7*) DIANE Pub.

Madonna Superstar: Photographs. Karl Lagerfeld. 1991. pap. 10.95 (*0-393-30766-2*) Norton.

Madonna Swan: A Lakota Woman's Story. Mark St. Pierre. LC 91-50306. (Illus.). 224p. 1994. pap. 11.95 (*0-8061-2676-0*) U of Okla Pr.

Madonna und Ihre Griechischen Tochter. Harald Haarmann. (GER.). 1996. write for info. (*3-487-10163-7*) G Olms Pubs.

Madonnas & Magdalens: The Origins & Development of Victorian Sexual Attitudes. Eric Trudgill. LC 75-31829. 323p. 1976. 39.95 (*0-8419-0241-0*) Holmes & Meier.

Madonnas & Maidens: Sexual Confusion in Lawrence & Gide. Richard T. Driskill. LC 96-32147. (Sexuality & Literature Ser.: Vol. 6). VIII, 303p. (C). 1999. text 55.95 (*0-8204-3493-0*) P Lang Pubng.

Madonnas & Martyrs: Militarism & Violence in the Philippines. Anne-Marie Hilsdon. 240p. 1996. pap. 24.95 (*1-86373-890-8*, Pub. by Allen & Unwin Pty) Paul & Co Pubs.

Madonnas by Donatello & His Circle. Anna Jolly. (European University Studies: No. 28, Vol. 319). (Illus.). 360p. 1998. pap. 56.95 (*3-631-32623-8*) P Lang Pubng.

Madonnas by Donatello & His Circle. Anna Jolly. LC 98-13054. (European University Studies: Series 28, Vol. 319). (Illus.). 360p. (C). 1998. pap. text 56.95 (*0-8204-3538-4*) P Lang Pubng.

Madonnas that Maim: Popular Catholicism in Italy since the Fifteenth Century. Michael P. Carroll. (Illus.). 256p. 1992. text 39.95 (*0-8018-4299-9*) Johns Hopkins.

Madonna/The Immaculate Collection. Ed. by Carol Cuellar. 112p. 1990. pap. text 17.95 (*0-7692-1502-5*, VF1697) Wrner Bros.

Madonnica: The Woman & the Icon from A to Z. Matthew Rettenmund. LC 94-48309. 1995. pap. 16.95 (*0-312-11782-5*) St Martin.

Madonny. O. Waclaw Chabrowski. 46p. 1965. 2.50 (*0-940962-13-6*) Polish Inst Art & Sci.

Madopar HBS. Ed. by C. David Marsden et al. (Journal: European Neurology: Vol. 27, Suppl. 1). (Illus.). vi, 142p. 1987. pap. 45.25 (*3-8055-4692-0*) S Karger.

Madoulina. Joe Eoueme Bognmo. LC 99-61826. 32p. (J). (gr. k-3). 1999. pap. 6.95 (*1-56397-822-9*) Boyds Mills Pr.

Madoulina. Joe Eoueme Bognmo. LC 99-61826. 32p. (J). (ps-3). 1999. 14.95 (*1-56397-769-9*) Boyds Mills Pr.

Madras House. unabridged ed. Granville Barker. Ed. by William-Alan Landes. LC 99-50101. 88p. 1999. pap. 7.00 (*0-88734-722-3*) Players Pr.

Madras in the Olden Time. J. Talboys Wheeler. (C). 1994. 48.00 (*81-206-0553-5*, Pub. by Asian Educ Servs) S Asia.

Madras Tercenternary Celebration Committee Commemoration Volume. Tercentenary Madras Staff. (C). 1994. 88.00 (*81-206-0537-3*, Pub. by Asian Educ Servs) S Asia.

Madre: Life & Spirituality. Obbard. 1996. pap. text 11.95 (*0-8189-9468-1*) Alba.

Madre: The Life & Spirituality of Teresa of Avila. Elizabeth R. Obbard. 160p. 1996. pap. 39.95 (*0-85439-468-0*, Pub. by St Paul Pubns) St Mut.

Madre: The Woman & the Priest. 2nd ed. Grazia Deledda. Ed. by D. M. Lawrence & Eric Lane. Tr. by M. G. Steegman from ITA. (European Classics). 224p. 1999. reprint ed. pap. 9.99 (*0-946626-20-0*, Pub. by Dedalus) Hippocrene Bks.

Madre Cabrini. rev. ed. (SPA.). 211p. 1989. reprint ed. pap. text 7.00 (*0-9619397-2-9*) MSSH.

Madre Secreta. Lee Wilkinson. 1999. per. 3.50 (*0-373-33515-6*, 1335157) Harlequin Bks.

Madre Teresa de Calcuta. Jose Luis Gonzalez-Balado. 1998. pap. 20.95 (*84-7880-558-3*) Planeta.

***Madre Teresa de los Pobres.** J. L. Gonzales. (SPA.). 1999. 21.95 (*84-08-02298-9*) Planeta Edit.

Madre y el Aprendizaje del Nino: La Experiencia Urbana Puertorriquena. Carlos I. Guevara & Myrna Sesman. LC 77-9261. 150p. 1978. pap. 4.50 (*0-8477-2739-4*) U of PR Pr.

M

An Asterisk (*) at the beginning of an entry indicates that the title is appearing for the first time.

Madregale V: 6 & Mehrstimmige Madregale aus verschiedenen Drucken. Orlando di Lasso. (Samtliche Werke (Alte Reihe) Ser.: Vol. 10). (Illus.). 1973. reprint ed. pap. 85.00 (0-8450-1910-4) Broude.
Madres de la Patria y las Bellas Mentiras: La Imagene de la Mujer en el Discurso Literario de la Republica Dominica, 1844-1899. Catharina Vallejo. LC 98-89964. (Coleccion Polymita Ser.). (SPA.). 335p. 1999. pap. 29.00 (0-89729-890-X) Ediciones.
***Madres Del Verbo.** Nina M. Scott. LC 99-37410. 1999. pap. 24.95 (0-8263-2144-5) U of NM Pr.
Madres Que Trabajan - Working Moms. M. Nelt. (SPA.). 150p. 1995. write for info. (1-56063-524-X) Editorial Unilit.
Madrich/RCA. 19.99 (0-89906-587-2, MADH) Mesorah Pubns.
Madrid. 64p. pap. text 9.95 (88-7009-543-6, Pub. by Bonechi) Eiron.
Madrid. (Insight Compact Guides Ser.). 1996. pap. 12.95 (0-614-12816-1, Insight Trvl Guides) HM.
Madrid. (New Essential Guides Ser.). 1996. pap. 7.95 (0-614-97910-2) NTC Contemp Pub Co.
Madrid. (Baedeker's Ser.). (Illus.). 144p. 1992. pap. 17.00 (0-13-063603-7, P-H Travel) Prntice Hall Bks.
Madrid. Annie Bennett. (Blue Guide Ser.). (Illus.). 256p. (Orig.). 1997. pap. 18.95 (0-393-31345-X, Norton Paperbks) Norton.
Madrid. Hugh Broughton. (Architecture Guides Ser.). (Illus.). 320p. 1998. pap. 5.95 (3-89508-640-1, 520203) Konemann.
Madrid. Tom Burns. (Everything under the Sun Ser.). (Illus.). 192p. 1994. pap. 6.95 (0-8442-9208-7, Passprt Bks) NTC Contemp Pub Co.
Madrid. D K Publishing Staff. LC 98-32197. (Eyewitness Travel Guides Ser.). 224p. (Orig.). 1999. pap. 22.95 (0-7894-4179-9) DK Pub Inc.
***Madrid.** DK Publishing Staff. (Eyewitness City Maps Ser.). 2000. pap. 7.95 (0-7894-5640-0) DK Pub Inc.
***Madrid.** Dana Facaros. 288p. 1999. pap. text 17.95 (1-86011-950-6, Pub. by Cadgn Bks) Globe Pequot.
***Madrid.** Fodor's Staff. 96p. (Orig.). 2000. pap. 12.00 (0-679-00641-9) Random.
Madrid. Insight Guides Staff. (Insight Guides). 1998. pap. text 21.95 (0-88729-706-4) Langenscheidt.
Madrid. Deborah Kent. (Cities of the World Ser.). 1999. lib. bdg. 9.95 (0-516-26462-1) Childrens.
Madrid. Deborah Kent. LC 98-45242. (Cities of the World Ser.). 64p. (YA). (gr. 4-9). 1999. 26.00 (0-516-20783-0) Childrens.
Madrid. Michelin Staff. 1999. pap. text 9.95 (2-06-660901-3) Michelin.
Madrid. Graham J. Shields. LC 98-115328. (World Bibliographical Ser.). 292p. 1996. lib. bdg. 84.00 (1-85109-250-1) ABC-CLIO.
***Madrid.** Damien Simonis. 2000. pap. 14.99 (1-86450-123-5) Lonely Planet.
***Madrid.** 2nd ed. Annie Bennett. (Blue Guide Ser.). (Illus.). (Orig.). 2000. pap. 19.95 (0-393-32011-1) Norton.
***Madrid.** 2nd ed. Insight Guides Staff. (Insight Guides). 1998. pap. text 12.95 (0-88729-896-6) Langenscheidt.
Madrid. 2nd ed. Insight Guides Staff. 2000. pap. 22.95 (0-88729-039-6, Insight Guides) Langenscheidt.
***Madrid.** 2nd ed. Rough Guides Staff. (Miniguides Ser.). (Illus.). 2000. pap. 9.95 (1-85828-535-6, Pub. by Rough Guides) Penguin Putnam.
Madrid & Castile. Catherine Clancy. (Crowood Travel Guides Ser.). (Illus.). 352p. 1991. pap. 24.95 (1-85223-468-7, Pub. by Crowood) Trafalgar.
***Madrid Atlas.** Michelin Travel Publication Staff. (Illus.). 2000. pap. 12.95 (2-06-204200-0) Michelin.
Madrid, Barcelona, Seville & Granada. Reg Butler. (Illus.). 100p. 1996. pap. 6.95 (1-872876-46-3, Pub. by Settle Pr) Assoc Pubs Grp.
Madrid for Less. (For Less Compact Guides Ser.). 1999. pap. 9.95 (1-901811-16-6) IPG Chicago.
Madrid in Your Pocket Guide. (In Your Pocket Guides Ser.). 1997. per. 9.95 (2-06-651201-X, 6512) Michelin.
Madrid, 1900: The Capital As Cradle of Literature & Culture. Michael Ugarte. LC 95-41931. (Studies in Romance Literatures). 1996. 35.00 (0-271-01559-4) Pa St U Pr.
Madrid, 1937: Letters of the Abraham Lincoln Brigade from the Spanish Civil War. Ed. by Cary Nelson & Jefferson Hendricks. LC 98-138978. (Illus.). 624p. (C). 1996. 45.00 (0-415-91408-6) Routledge.
Madrid Observed. 3rd ed. Michael Jacobs. (Illus.). 286p. 1998. pap. text 14.95 (1-873429-24-X, Pub. by Pallas Athene) Cimino Pub Grp.
Madrid Plenary Meeting of the Trilateral Commission, 1986. Ed. by Charles B. Heck & Michael M. Yoshitsu. (Trialogue Ser.: No. T38). (Illus.). 52p. (Orig.). 1986. pap. 6.00 (0-930503-11-2) Trilateral Comm.
***Madrid Pocket Guide.** rev. ed. Berlitz Editors. (Illus.). 144p. 2000. pap. 8.95 (2-8315-7700-4) Berlitz.
***Madrid Pocket Guide: Spanish ed.** 1999. pap. 8.95 (2-8315-7033-6) Berlitz.
Madrid Revisited: Life & Labor in a New Mexican Mining Camp in the Great Depression. 2nd ed. Richard Melzer. (Illus.). 64p. 1997. reprint ed. pap. 9.95 (1-58096-000-6) Ancient City Pr.
***Madrid Seville Barcelona.** Dana Facaros. (Cadgn Bks). (Illus.). 2000. pap. 14.95 (1-86011-942-5) Cadgn Bks.
Madrid Street Map with Index. 1997. 12.95 (2-06-700042-X, 42) Michelin.
Madridwalks: Four Intimate Walking Tours of Madrid. George Semler. (Walks Ser.). (Illus.). 88p. 1995. pap. 14.95 (0-8050-2254-6, Owl) H Holt & Co.
Madrigal at Ferrara, 1579-1597, 2 vols., Vol. 1. Anthony Newcomb. LC 78-573. (Princeton Studies in Music: No. 7). 318p. reprint ed. pap. 98.60 (0-8357-4646-1, 203757700001) Bks Demand.
Madrigal at Ferrara, 1579-1597, 2 vols., Vol. 2. Anthony Newcomb. LC 78-573. (Princeton Studies in Music: No. 7). 230p. reprint ed. pap. 71.30 (0-8357-4647-X, 203757700002) Bks Demand.
Madrigal Singing. Charles K. Scott. LC 77-109634. (Select Bibliographies Reprint Ser.). 1977. 18.95 (0-8369-5243-X) Ayer.
Madrigal Sonata: For Flute-Violin-Piano. B. Martinu. 1987. pap. 22.00 (0-7935-5568-X) H Leonard.
Madrigale IV: 4 & 5-Stimmige Madrigale aus Verschiedenen Drucken. Orlando di Lasso. (Samtliche Werke (Alte Reihe) Ser.: Vol. 8). (Illus.). 1973. reprint ed. pap. 85.00 (0-8450-1908-2) Broude.
Madrigale I: Das 1 & 2 Buch 5-Stimmiger Madrigale (1555 & 1557) Orlando di Lasso. (Samtliche Werke (Alte Reihe) Ser.: Vol. 2). (Illus.). 1973. reprint ed. pap. 85.00 (0-8450-1902-3) Broude.
Madrigale III: Die Beiden Madrigalsammlungen (1585 & 1587) Orlando di Lasso. (Samtliche Werke (Alte Reihe) Ser.: Vol. 6). (Illus.). 1973. reprint ed. pap. 85.00 (0-8450-1906-6) Broude.
Madrigale II: Das 3 & 4, Buch 5-Stimmiger Madrigale (1562 & 1567) Orlando di Lasso. (Samtliche Werke (Alte Reihe) Ser.: Vol. 4). (Illus.). 1973. reprint ed. pap. 85.00 (0-8450-1904-X) Broude.
Madrigali A Quattro Cinque E Sei Voci, Libro Primo, 1588. Luca Marenzio. Ed. by Steven Ledbetter. (Secular Works: Vol. 7). (Illus.). xxvi, 167p. 1977. pap. 50.00 (0-8450-7107-6) Broude.
Madrigali Spirituali a Cinque Voci, Libro Primo, 1584. Luca Marenzio. (Secular Works: Vol. 17). 1991. pap. 50.00 (0-8450-7117-3) Broude.
Madrigalium Spiritualium Liber Primus cum Sex Vocibus see Complete Works of Philippe De Monte
Madrigals. Mark Dunster. 27p. (Orig.). 1996. pap. 5.00 (0-89642-318-2) Linden Pubs.
Madrigals, Bk. 8. Claudio Monteverdi. 384p. 1991. pap. 19.95 (0-486-26739-3) Dover.
Madrigals, Bks. 4-5. Claudio Monteverdi. 256p. 1986. pap. 12.95 (0-486-25102-0) Dover.
***Madrigals & Mistletoe.** Hayley Ann Solomon. (Regency Romance Ser.). 1999. mass mkt. 4.99 (0-8217-6306-7, Zebra Kensgtn) Kensgtn Pub Corp.
Madrigals, Madrigals, Madrigals. Contrib. by Koulman. 1971. 5.00 (0-913334-09-X, CM1011) Consort Music.
Madrigal's Magic Key to Spanish. Margarita Madrigal. (Illus.). 512p. 1989. pap. 11.95 (0-385-41095-6) Doubleday.
Madrigals Michelangelo Rossi. Mann. 1998. lib. bdg. 150.00 (0-226-50338-0) U Ch Pr.
Madrikhim Handbook. Samuel Joseph. 197p. (YA). (gr. 10-12). 1990. pap. text 4.95 (0-933873-52-2) Torah Aura.
Madrona Murders. Frederick Mugler. LC 98-85385. 325p. 1998. 25.00 (0-9663501-5-4); pap. 15.00 (0-7388-0023-6) Xlibris Corp.
Madrono: A West American Journal of Botany, an Eighty Year Index Vols. 1-43, 1916-1996: A Publication of the California Botanical Society. Ed. & Compiled by R. John Little. LC 97-62196. 202p. (Orig.). 1997. pap. 45.00 (0-9661882-0-9) Sycamore CA.
Madrugada. David May. (Orig.). 1997. mass mkt. 6.95 (1-56333-574-3, Badboy) Masquerade.
Madrugada. Antonio B. Vallejo. Ed. by Donald W. Bleznick & Martha T. Halsey. (SPA.). 111p. 1982. reprint ed. pap. text 9.95 (0-8290-0895-0) Irvington.
Madrugada: A Libretto for Toru/Takemitsu. Barry Gifford. (Illus.). 60p. (Orig.). 2000. pap. 12.00 (0-88739-105-2) Creat Arts Bk.
Mad's Creature Presentation. Duck Edwing. 192p. (Orig.). 1993. mass mkt. 3.99 (0-446-36454-1, Pub. by Warner Bks) Little.
Mad's Fast Look at Fast Living. Stan Hart & Paul Coker. 1987. mass mkt. 3.95 (0-446-34970-4, Pub. by Warner Bks) Little.
Mad's How to Be a Successful Dog. Spot. LC 99-31143. 1999. pap. 7.95 (1-55853-784-8) Rutledge Hill Pr.
Mad's Sergio Aragones on Parade. Sergio Aragones. (Illus.). 160p. (Orig.). 1982. mass mkt. 6.95 (0-446-37369-9) Warner Bks.
Madselin's Choice. Elizabeth Henshall. (Historical Ser.: No. 14). 1999. mass mkt. 4.99 (0-373-30323-8, 1-30323-9) Harlequin Bks.
Madselin's Choice. large type ed. Elizabeth Henshall. (Mills & Boon Large Print Ser.). 350p. 1997. 23.99 (0-263-15181-6, Pub. by Mills & Boon) Ulverscroft.
Madstones & Twisters. Ed. by Mody C. Boatright et al. LC 58-9269. (Texas Folklore Society Publications: No. 28). 169p. 1958. 12.95 (0-87074-017-2) UNTX Pr.
Madtail Miniwhale & Other Shape Poems. Wes Magee. (Illus.). 1991. pap. 9.95 (0-14-034031-9, Pub. by Pnguin Bks Ltd) Trafalgar.
***Madumo: A Man Bewitched.** Adam Ashforth. LC 99-57325. 248p. 1999. 20.00 (0-226-02971-9) U Ch Pr.
Madura Country: A Manual. Compiled by J. H. Nelson. (Illus.). (C). 1989. reprint ed. 62.50 (81-206-0424-5, Pub. by Asian Educ Servs) S Asia.
Maduracion Osea. M. Sempe & C. Pavia. (SPA.). 147p. 1994. pap. 38.75 (84-7978-154-8, Pub. by Ediciones Diaz) IBD Ltd.
Madurese Phonology & Morphology. Alan M. Stevens. (American Oriental Ser.: Vol. 52). vii, 215p. 1968. pap. 8.00 (0-940490-52-8) Am Orient Soc.
Madurez de la Sra. Eliot. Angus Wilson. Tr. by Maribel De Juan. (Nueva Austral Ser.: No. 24). (SPA.). 1991. pap. text 29.95 (84-239-1824-6) Elliots Bks.
Maduros en Cristo. Warren W. Wiersbe. Ed. by Gary Hilliker. (New Testament Ser.). (SPA.). 166p. 1992. 7.95 (1-879892-12-X) Editorial Bautista.
Madwives: Schizophrenic Women in the 1950s. Carol A. Warren. LC 86-14620. 283p. (C). 1991. pap. text 17.00 (0-8135-1689-7) Rutgers U Pr.
Madwoman Can't Speak: or Why Insanity Is Not Subversive. Marta Caminero-Santangelo. LC 98-4027. (Reading Women Writing Ser.). (Illus.). 224p. 1998. 39.95 (0-8014-3514-5); pap. text 14.95 (0-8014-8514-2) Cornell U Pr.
Madwoman in the Attic: A Study of Women & the Literary Imagination in the Nineteenth Century. Sandra M. Gilbert & Susan Gubar. LC 78-20792. (Illus.). 733p. 1979. pap. 22.00 (0-300-02596-3) Yale U Pr.
***Madwoman in the Attic: The Woman Writer & the Nineteenth-Century Literary Imagination.** 2nd ed. Sandra M. Gilbert & Susan Gubar. LC 99-86038. 770p. 2000. pap. 19.95 (0-300-08458-7) Yale U Pr.
Madwoman of Chaillot. adapted ed. Jean Giraudoux. 1950. pap. 5.25 (0-8222-0714-1) Dramatists Play.
Madwoman of the Sacred Heart. Alexandro Jodorowsky & Jean M. Giraud. 144p. 1996. pap. 12.95 (1-56971-136-4) Dark Horse Comics.
Madwoman's Reason: The Concept of the Appropriate in Ethical Thought. Nancy J. Holland. LC 97-33170. 1998. 30.00 (0-271-01770-8); pap. 14.95 (0-271-01771-6) Pa St U Pr.
Madwoman's Underclothes: Essays & Occasional Writings. Germaine Greer. LC 87-11475. 1989. pap. 12.95 (0-87113-308-3, Atlntc Mnthly) Grove-Atltic.
***Madworld: The Battle Game.** Paul A. Lidbert. (Illus.). 20p. (J). 1998. 4.95 (1-929332-07-6, CFE0201) Crunchy Frog.
Mae C. Jemison: First Black Female Astronaut. Ebraska D. Ceasor. Ed. by Charlotte T. Durant & Ethel Pye. (Illus.). 40p. (Orig.). (J). (ps-1). 1992. pap. 4.00 (0-913678-22-8) New Day Pr.
Mae Franking's My Chinese Marriage: An Annotated Edition. Katherine Anne Porter. Ed. by Holly Franking. LC 91-12698. (Illus.). 159p. 1991. 16.95 (0-292-75132-X) U of Tex Pr.
***Mae Jemison.** Sonia W. Black. 64p. (J). (gr. 3-7). 2000. pap. 3.95 (1-57255-801-6) Mondo Pubng.
Mae Jemison. Liza Burby. LC 96-37466. (Making Their Mark Ser.). (J). (gr. 2-4). 1997. lib. bdg. 15.93 (0-8239-5027-1, PowerKids) Rosen Group.
Mae Jemison: A Space Biography. Della A. Yannuzzi. LC 97-34159. (Countdown to Space Ser.). (Illus.). 48p. (J). (gr. 4-10). 1998. lib. bdg. 18.95 (0-89490-813-8) Enslow Pubs.
Mae Jemison, Astronaut. Garnet N. Jackson. (Illus.). (J). (gr. 1-4). 1994. pap. 4.95 (0-8136-5245-6); lib. bdg. 9.95 (0-8136-5239-1) Modern Curr.
Mae West. deluxe limited ed. Tim Malachosky & James Greene. (Illus.). 350p. 1993. 85.00 (0-9637169-4-8) Empire Pub CA.
Mae West: A Bio-Bibliography. Carol M. Ward. LC 88-24649. (Popular Culture Bio-Bibliographies Ser.). 241p. 1989. lib. bdg. 49.95 (0-313-24716-1, WMA/, Greenwood Pr) Greenwood.
Mae West: Empress of Sex. Maurice Leonard. (Illus.). 424p. 1992. 22.50 (1-55972-151-0, Birch Ln Pr) Carol Pub Group.
Mae West: She Who Laughs, Lasts. June Sochen. Ed. by Alan M. Kraut & Jon L. Wakelyn. (American Biographical History Ser.). (Illus.). 128p. 1992. pap. text 11.95 (0-88295-891-7) Harlan Davidson.
Mae West Is Dead: Recent Lesbian & Gay Fiction. 2nd ed. Ed. by Adam Mars-Jones. 320p. 1987. pap. 11.95 (0-571-14898-0) Faber & Faber.
Maebelle's Suitcase. Tricia Tusa. (Reading Rainbow Bks.). 1991. 11.19 (0-606-12407-1, Pub. by Turtleback) Demco.
Maebelle's Suitcase. Tricia Tusa. LC 90-40678. (Illus.). 32p. (J). (gr. k-3). 1991. reprint ed. mass mkt. 5.99 (0-689-71444-0) Aladdin.
Maechte Des Guten und Boesen: Vorstellungen Um 12 und 13. (Miscellanea Mediaevalia Ser.: Vol.11). (C). 1977. 219.25 (3-11-007261-0) De Gruyter.
***Maeda @ Media.** John Maeda. (Illus.). 480p. 2000. 75.00 (0-8478-2295-8) Rizzoli Intl.
Maedi-Visna & Related Diseases. Ed. by G. Petursson. (Developments in Veterinary Virology Ser.). (C). 1989. text 191.50 (0-7923-0481-0) Kluwer Academic.
***Maekawa Kunio & the Emergence of the Japanese Modernist Architecture.** Jonathan M. Reynolds. LC 00-37406. 2001. write for info. (0-520-21495-1) U CA Pr.
Maelduin of Arran. Nellie McCaslin. LC 96-32005. 55p. (Orig.). (YA). (gr. 6-12). 1996. pap. 5.00 (0-88734-480-1) Players Pr.
Maelstrom. Keith Douglass. (Carrier Ser.: No. 5). 336p. (Orig.). 1993. mass mkt. 5.99 (0-515-11080-9, Jove) Berkley Pub.
Maelstrom. Sam Llewellyn. 1996. mass mkt. 5.99 (0-671-78997-X, PB Trade Paper) PB.
***Maelstrom: Poltergeist.** Matthew J. Costello. (Legacy Ser.). (Illus.). (J). 2000. mass mkt. 5.99 (0-441-00711-2) Ace Bks.
Maelstrom: The United States, Southern Europe, & the Challenges of the Mediterranean. Ed. by John W. Holmes. 251p. (C). 1995. 42.95 (0-8157-3718-1); pap. 18.95 (0-8157-3717-3) Brookings.
Maelzel's Chess Player: Sigmund Freud & the Rhetoric of Deceit. Robert Wilcocks. 360p. (Orig.). (C). 1993. pap. text 26.95 (0-8476-7810-5); lib. bdg. 69.50 (0-8476-7809-1) Rowman.
***Mae'n Braf Allan.** Childs Play Inc. Staff. 1999. pap. text 2.99 (0-85953-652-1) Childs Play.
Maenad: Mary's Song. Katrina A. Oosting. LC 97-68875. 208p. 1998. 13.95 (1-887750-73-8) Rutledge Bks.
Mae's Night Flight. Fran B. Innes. (Illus.). 32p. 1993. 7.95 (1-895387-29-9) Creative Bk Pub.
***Maes Promise.** Melody Walcott. 325p. 1999. pap. text 8.95 (1-885478-95-X, Pub. by Genesis Press) BookWorld.
Maestra Normal. Manuel Galvez. LC 90-83956. (SPA.). 299p. (Orig.). 1991. pap. 19.95 (0-89729-580-3) Ediciones.
Maestro. John Gardner. LC 93-19364. 280p. 1993. 23.00 (1-883402-24-7) S&S Trade.
***Maestro.** Sam Milano. (Nexus Ser.). 2000. mass mkt. 10.95 (0-352-33511-4) Virgin Bks.
Maestro. Tim Wynne-Jones. LC 96-13454. 240p. (YA). (gr. 5 up). 1996. 16.95 (0-531-09544-4); lib. bdg. 17.99 (0-531-08894-4) Orchard Bks Watts.
Maestro. Tim Wynne-Jones. LC 97-28227. 240p. (J). (gr. 4-7). 1998. pap. 4.99 (0-14-038705-6, PuffinBks) Peng Put Young Read.
Maestro. Tim Wynne-Jones. (J). 1998. 10.09 (0-606-13587-1, Pub. by Turtleback) Demco.
***Maestro, Vol. 4.** Prod. by Life Publishers International Staff. (Vida Nueva Ser.). (SPA., Illus.). 207p. 2001. teacher ed., boxed set. write for info. (0-7361-0191-8); pap., teacher ed. write for info. (0-7361-0192-6) Life Pubs Intl.
Maestro: The Life of Arturo Toscanini. H. Howard Taubman. LC 76-57171. 342p. 1977. reprint ed. lib. bdg. 47.50 (0-8371-9434-2, TAMA, Greenwood Pr) Greenwood.
***Maestro Tomo 2: March to August 2000.** (SPA., Illus.). 207p. 1999. teacher ed. write for info. (0-7361-0123-3); pap., teacher ed. write for info. (0-7361-0122-5) Life Pubs Intl.
Maestro Chronicles. Harry C. Pellow. 1984p. per. 19.50 (0-941210-08-1) HCP Res.
***Maestro de Esgrima.** Arturo Perez-Reverte. 356p. 1999. pap. 4.95 (84-204-4198-8) Santillana.
Maestro De la Palabra. Carlos Brassel Morales. 1997. pap. text 10.98 (968-409-956-8) Edamex.
Maestro in the Kitchen Vol. 1: Orchestrating Memorable Occassions. Brent Marmo. Ed. by Bette Jack & R. Craig Beonar. (Illus.). 240p. 1998. 29.95 (0-9661034-0-8) Wamso MN Orch.
Maestro Myth: Great Conductors in Pursuit of Power. Norman Lebrecht. (Illus.). 402p. 1999. reprint ed. 42.95 (0-7351-0093-4) Replica Bks.
Maestro Myth: Great Conductors in Pursuit of Power. rev. ed. Norman Lebrecht. (Illus.). 400p. 1999. pap. 15.95 (0-8065-2088-4, Citadel Pr) Carol Pub Group.
Maestro Myth: Great Conductors in the Pursuit of Power. Norman Lebrecht. (Illus.). 384p. 1992. 22.50 (1-55972-108-1, Birch Ln Pr) Carol Pub Group.
Maestro Myth: Great Conductors in the Pursuit of Power. Norman Lebrecht. (Illus.). 384p. 1993. pap. 15.95 (0-8065-1450-7, Citadel Pr) Carol Pub Group.
Maestro Plays. Martin. 101. 13.95 (0-15-200259-6) Harcourt.
Maestro Plays. Bill Martin, Jr. (J). 1995. 15.95 (0-8050-1746-1, Bks Young Read) H Holt & Co.
Maestro Plays. Bill Martin, Jr. LC 95-49126. (Illus.). 48p. (J). (ps-3). 1996. reprint ed. pap. 6.00 (0-15-201217-6, Voyager Bks) Harcourt.
Maestro, Please! Cartoons by Ed Fisher. Ed Fisher. (Illus.). 128p. 1992. pap. 7.95 (1-55783-108-4) Applause Theatre Bk Pubs.
Maestro, Sep. 1999-Feb. 2000, Tomo 1. Life Publishers International Staff. (SPA.). 112p. 1999. teacher ed. write for info. (0-7361-0075-X) Life Pubs Intl.
Maestro, Sep. 1999-Feb. 2000, Tomo 1. Life Publishers International Staff. (SPA., Illus.). 1999. pap., teacher ed. write for info. (0-7361-0074-1) Life Pubs Intl.
***Maestro, Sept. 2000 to Feb. 2001, Tomo 3.** Prod. by Life Publishers International Staff. (SPA., Illus.). 207p. 2000. teacher ed. write for info. (0-7361-0151-9); pap., boxed set. write for info. (0-7361-0150-0) Life Pubs Intl.
Maestro y la Forma de la Verdad. Humberto Perez.Tr. of Teacher & the Truth. (SPA.). 240p. 1995. 12.99 (0-89922-493-8, C091-4938) Caribe Betania.
Maestros de Instuccion Publica de Puerto Rico: Perfiles Sociologicos y Profesionales. Luis N. Falcon & Patria C. De Crespo. 169p. (C). 1975. pap. 3.00 (0-8477-2711-4) U of PR Pr.
Maestros, Dilettantes, & Philistines: The Musician in the Victorian Novel. Emily Auerbach. (American University Studies: English Language & Literature: Ser. IV, Vol. 103). 213p. (C). 1989. text 38.95 (0-8204-0926-X) P Lang Pubng.
Maestros Hispanicos del Siglo Viente. Levine Rodriguez. (SPA.). 194p. (C). 1979. pap. text. write for info. (0-318-69171-X) Harcourt Coll Pubs.
Maestro's Newsletter. Harry C. Pellow. 200p. (Orig.). 1989. 19.95 (0-941210-12-X) HCP Res.
Maestros of the Pen: A History of Classical Music Criticism in America. Mark N. Grant. Ed. by Eric Friedheim. LC 98-28959. (Illus.). 416p. 1998. text 37.50 (1-55553-363-9) NE U Pr.
Maestro's Spec Book & Emergency Breakdown Procedures. Harry C. Pellow. 1984. per. 19.95 (0-941210-09-X) HCP Res.
Maeterlinck. Auguste Baily. LC 74-6385. (Studies in French Literature: No. 45). 1974. lib. bdg. 75.00 (0-8383-1877-0) M S G Haskell Hse.
***Maeterlinck: Pelleas et Melisande: With Les Aveugles, l'Intruse & Interieur.** M. Maeterlinck. Ed. by Leighton Hodson. (FRE.). 140p. (C). 1999. pap. text 18.95 (1-85399-551-7, Pub. by Brist Class Pr) Focus Pub-R Pullins.
Maeterlinck's Plays in Performance. Katharine J. Worth. (Theatre in Focus Ser.). (Illus.). 124p. 1985. pap. write for info. incl. sl. (0-85964-155-4) Chadwyck-Healey.
***Maeve & the Long Arm Folly.** Mary Arrigan. 144p. 2000. pap. 8.95 (1-901737-20-9, Pub. by Anvil Books Ltd) Dufour.
Maeve, 1 Girl, 4 Women. Terry Hooper & David Gordon. pap. 12.95 (1-56097-248-3, Pub. by Fantagraph Bks) Seven Hills Bk.

An Asterisk (*) at the beginning of an entry indicates that the title is appearing for the first time.

Maezenatentum in Berlin: Buergersinn & Kulturelle Kompetenz unter sich Veraendernden Bedingungen. Ed. by Guenter Braun & Waldtraut Braun. (GER., Illus.). 258p. (C). 1993. lib. bdg. 44.65 (*3-11-013788-7*) De Gruyter.

Mafeking Diary. Solomon T. Plaatje. Ed. by John Comaroff. LC 89-22784. (Illus.). 190p. 1990. pap. 12.95 (*0-8214-0945-X*); text 24.95 (*0-8214-0944-1*) Ohio U Pr.

Mafeking Memories. Frederick S. Saunders. Ed. by Phillip T. Smith. LC 95-10947. 144p. 1995. 29.50 (*0-8386-3635-7*) Fairleigh Dickinson.

Maffeo Pantaleoni. Mario Baldassarri. LC 96-38023. 212p. 1997. text 79.95 (*0-312-17358-X*) St Martin.

***Maffetone Method: The Holistic, Low-Stress, No-Pain Way to Exceptional Fitness.** Philip Maffetone. LC 99-22495. 208p. 1999. pap. 14.95 (*0-07-134331-8*) McGraw.

Mafhum al-Taghyir. Jawdat Sa id. (Majalis Bi'r 'Ajam Ser.). 1995. pap. 3.95 (*1-57547-197-3*) Dar Al-Fikr.

Mafia. Joe Dorigo. 1992. 17.98 (*1-55521-788-5*) Bk Sales Inc.

Mafia. Time-Life Books Editors. LC 92-42181. (True Crime Ser.). (Illus.). 192p. 1993. lib. bdg. 17.45 (*0-7835-0009-2*) Time-Life.

Mafia. Time-Life Books Editors. LC 92-42181. (True Crime Ser.). (Illus.). 192p. (gr. 11). 1999. 14.95 (*0-7835-0008-4*) Time-Life.

Mafia: Money & Politics in Sicily, 1950-1997. Rene Seindal. LC 99-222923. 200p. 1998. 30.00 (*87-7289-455-5*, Pub. by Mus Tusculanum) Paul & Co Pubs.

Mafia & Clientelism: Roads to Rome in Post-War Calabria. James Walstom. 192p. 1988. lib. bdg. 67.50 (*0-415-00368-7*) Routledge.

Mafia & Mafiosi: Origin, Power, & Myth. Henner Hess. LC 98-12809. 1998. text 45.00 (*0-8147-3588-6*); pap. text 19.00 (*0-8147-3589-4*) NYU Pr.

Mafia Cookbook. Joseph Iannuzzi. LC 93-13520. (Illus.). 160p. 1993. 14.50 (*0-671-86925-6*) S&S Trade.

Mafia Cop: The Story of an Honest Cop Whose Family Was the Mob. Lou Eppolito & Bob Drury. Ed. by Julie Rubinstein. 328p. 1993. mass mkt. 5.99 (*0-671-74222-1*) PB.

Mafia Dynasty: The Rise & Fall of the Gambino Crime Family. John H. Davis. LC 92-53366. 544p. 1994. mass mkt. 6.99 (*0-06-109184-7*, Harp PBks) HarpC.

Mafia Encyclopedia. Carl Sifakis. (Illus.). 367p. 1988. pap. 19.95 (*0-8160-1856-1*) Facts on File.

Mafia Encyclopedia. 2nd ed. Carl Sifakis. LC 98-42297. (Illus.). 400p. 1999. pap. 19.95 (*0-8160-3857-0*) Facts on File.

Mafia Encyclopedia. 2nd ed. Carl Sifakis. LC 98-42297. (Illus.). 414p. 1999. 40.00 (*0-8160-3856-2*) Facts on File.

***Mafia Just Moved in Next Door & They're Dropping by for Dinner Cookbook: Easy Italian Recipes.** Ed. by Lagoon Books Staff. 64p. 2000. 5.95 (*1-902813-15-4*, Pub. by Lagoon Bks) Midpt Trade.

Mafia Lesbian. Vladimir Kek. 199p. 1999. pap. 14.95 (*0-7414-0014-6*) Buy Books.

Mafia Manager. 1997. pap. 7.95 (*0-312-15574-3*) St Martin.

Mafia Manager: A Guide to Success. Lee Wallek. LC 91-72880. (Illus.). 160p. 1991. pap. 20.00 (*0-913204-27-7*) December Pr.

Mafia Marriage: My Story. Rosalie Bonanno & Beverly Donofrio. 240p. 1991. mass mkt. 4.99 (*0-380-70536-2*, Avon Bks) Morrow Avon.

Mafia of a Sicilian Village, 1860-1960: A Study of Violent Peasant Entrepreneurs. Anton Blok. (Illus.). 293p. (C). 1988. reprint ed. pap. text 13.95 (*0-88133-325-5*) Waveland Pr.

Mafia Princess: Growing Up in Sam Giancana's Family. Antoinette Giancana & Thomas C. Renner. 408p. 1985. mass mkt. 5.50 (*0-380-69849-8*, Avon Bks) Morrow Avon.

Mafia Puppets. Arthur W. Bourassa. 1994. 16.95 (*0-533-10720-2*) Vantage.

Mafia-Syndicate = Organized Crime: The Government Within the Government. A. Yards. LC 76-23355. 202p. 1977. reprint ed. pap. 4.95 (*0-9603108-0-0*) A Yards.

Mafia Through the Eyes of a Child: A Closer Look at the New York Mafia. G. L. Sundance. Ed. by Gloria D. Ladd & James E. Gilliland. LC 98-122302. (Illus.). 270p. 1998. 29.95 (*1-890668-06-0*) Electronic Books.

Mafia/Syndicate = Organized Crime: The Government Within the Government. 2nd ed. (Illus.). 202p. 1977. reprint ed. write for info. (*0-614-30253-6*) A Yards.

Mafic Dykes & Emplacement Mechanisms: Proceedings of the Second International Conference, Adelaide, South Australia, 12 - 15 September 1990. Ed. by A. J. Parker et al. (Illus.). 560p. (C). 1990. text 123.00 (*90-6191-158-3*, Pub. by A A Balkema) Ashgate Pub Co.

***Mafioso, Big Business & the Financial Crisis: The State-Business Relations in South Korea & Japan.** Ingyu Oh. 218p. 2000. text 65.95 (*0-7546-1089-6*, Pub. by Ashgate Pub) Ashgate Pub Co.

Mafouz & Idris: Studies in Arabic Short Fiction. Mona N. Mikhail. 272p. (C). 1992. text 45.00 (*0-8147-5474-0*) NYU Pr.

Mafteach Maamorim Sichos Umichtovim, Vol. 1. Yosef Y. Shagalow. (HEB.). 256p. 1980. 12.00 (*0-8266-0525-7*) Kehot Pubn Soc.

Mafteach Maamorim V'Sichos, 5740-5745, Vol. 2. Yosef Y. Shagalow. LC 79-93328. (HEB.). 80p. (Orig.). 1985. pap. 3.00 (*0-8266-0526-5*) Kehot Pubn Soc.

Mafteach Maamorim V'Sichos, 5745-5750, Vol. 3. Yosef Y. Shagalow. LC 79-93328. (HEB.). 94p. (Orig.). 1990. pap. 3.00 (*0-8266-0527-3*) Kehot Pubn Soc.

Mafteach Maamorim V'Sichos, 5750-5751, Vol. 4. Yosef Y. Shagalow. LC 79-93328. (HEB.). 40p. (Orig.). 1991. pap. 3.00 (*0-8266-0524-9*) Kehot Pubn Soc.

Maftehoth Hatalmud: Keys to the Talmud, 2 vols., Set. 55.00 (*0-910218-89-7*) Bennet Pub.

Mafteiach Bivrei Horambam Shebelikkutei Sichos, Vol. 1. (HEB.). 92p. (Orig.). 1985. pap. 5.00 (*0-8266-5309-X*) Kehot Pubn Soc.

Mafteiach Bivrei Horambam Shebelikkutei Sichos, Vol. 2. (HEB.). 96p. (Orig.). 1986. pap. 5.00 (*0-8266-5310-3*) Kehot Pubn Soc.

Mafteichos Admur Hatzemach Tzedek Vol. 2: Meluyim. Yitchok Gansbourgh. (HEB.). 80p. (Orig.). 1982. pap. 3.00 (*0-8266-5323-5*) Kehot Pubn Soc.

Mafteichos Likkutie Sichos, 29 vols., Set. (HEB.). 811p. reprint ed. 30.00 (*0-8266-5861-X*) Kehot Pubn Soc.

Mafteichos Lisifre: Rabbi Shalom Dov Baer Schneersohn. 647p. 1982. reprint ed. 17.00 (*0-8266-5329-4*) Kehot Pubn Soc.

Mafulu Mountain People of British New Guinea. Robert W. Williamson. LC 75-35168. reprint ed. 47.50 (*0-404-14182-X*) AMS Pr.

***Mag Bay Fishing Chart & Guide.** (Illus.). 1999. 14.95 (*1-929394-10-1*, B010) Baja Directions.

Mag Force, No. 2. Margaret Weis. 384p. 1999. mass mkt. 6.99 (*0-451-45543-6*, ROC) NAL.

Mag Force, No. 3. Margaret Weis. 1998. mass mkt. 6.99 (*0-451-45618-1*, ROC) NAL.

Mag. Johannis Hus Tractatus Responsiyus. Jan Hus. LC 78-63201. (Heresies of the Early Christian & Medieval Era Ser.: Second Ser.). reprint ed. 42.50 (*0-404-16229-0*) AMS Pr.

***Mag-Marjorie & Won Over: Two Novels.** Charlotte Perkins Gilman. LC 99-71485. 272p. 1999. pap. 16.95 (*0-9655309-4-9*) Ironweed Pr.

MAG, '95: Magnetic Bearings, Magnetic Drives & Dry Gas Seals International Conference. Ed. by Paul Allaire. LC 95-61419. 380p. 1995. pap. text 89.95 (*1-56676-364-9*) Technomic.

MAG, '93: Magnetic Bearings, Magnetic Drives & Dry Gas Seals International Conference & Exhibition. Ed. by Paul E. Allaire. LC 93-60809. 275p. 1993. pap. text 79.95 (*1-56676-085-2*) Technomic.

MAG-24: Marine Air Group 24. Turner Publishing Company Staff. (Illus.). 96p. Date not set. 49.95 (*1-56311-269-8*) Turner Pub KY.

Magadan Oblast: Economy, Industry, Government, Business. 2nd rev. ed. Russian Information & Business Center, Inc. Staff. (Russian Regional Business Directories Ser.). (Illus.). 200p. 1997. pap. 99.00 (*1-57751-397-5*) Intl Business Pubns.

***Magadan Oblast Regional Investment & Business Guide.** Global Investment & Business Center, Inc. Staff. (Russian Regional Investment & Business Guides Ser.: Vol. 44). (Illus.). 350p. 1999. pap. 99.00 (*0-7397-0848-1*) Intl Business Pubns.

***Magadan Oblast Regional Investment & Business Guide.** Contrib. by Global Investment & Business Center, Inc. Staff. (Russian Regional Investment & Business Guides Ser.: Vol. 28). (Illus.). 350p. 2000. pap. 99.95 (*0-7397-2992-6*) Intl Business Pubns.

Magadhan Literature. Haraprasad Sastri. (Bibliotheca Indo-Buddhica Ser.: No. 28). 133p. (C). 1986. reprint ed. 15.00 (*81-7030-010-X*) S Asia.

Magali/Magali: An Aztec Legend about Good Fortune (Una Ieyenja Azteca Sobre La Buena Fortuna) Patricia Petersen. LC 98-14834. (Cuentos en Dos Idiomas (Tales in Two Languages) Ser.). (Illus.). 32p. (J). (gr. 3-6). 1998. 16.95 (*1-56492-250-2*) Laredo.

Magana Hausa: Native Literature or Proverbs, Tales, Fables & Historical Fragments in the Haussa Language. Jacob F. Schon. (B. E. Ser.: No. 37). (ENG & HAU.). 1885. 40.00 (*0-8115-2988-6*) Periodicals Srv.

Magamese Redox Enzymes. Ed. by V. L. Pecoraro. 290p. 1992. 155.00 (*0-471-18743-7*, Wiley-VCH) Wiley.

***Magarity Dealerships' Tribute to Philadelphia Scholastic Basketball.** (Illus.). 154p. 2000. pap. 14.95 (*0-615-11366-4*) T Silary.

Magarodidae (Insecta: Hemiptera) see Fauna of New Zealand Series

Magasin D'Antiquites: Barnabe Rudge. Charles Dickens. (FRE.). 1962. 99.50 (*0-8288-3428-8*, F77005) Fr & Eur.

Magasin de l'Univers - The Dutch Republic As the Centre of the European Book Trade. Ed. by Christiane Berkvens-Stevelinck et al. (Brill's Studies in Intellectual History: Vol. 31). (ENG & FRE., Illus.). x, 319p. 1991. 107.00 (*90-04-09493-8*) Brill Academic Pubs.

***Magazine.** James Mallon. LC 99-70723. 256p. 2000. 22.95 (*1-57197-181-5*) Pentland Pr.

Magazine: Blackline Masters. (FRE.). (C). 1987. 22.50 (*0-8442-1370-5*, VF1370-5) NTC Contemp Pub Co.

Magazine: Everthing You Need to Know to Make It in the Magazine Business. 4th rev. ed. Leonard Mogel. LC 98-70934. (Illus.). 224p. 1998. pap. text 40.00 (*0-88362-223-8*, 15404) GATFPress.

Magazine Advertising Graphics. Ed. by Pie Editorial Staff. 1998. 69.95 (*4-89444-082-2*, Pub. by Pie Bks) Bks Nippan.

Magazine & Feature Writing. Hiley Ward. LC 92-15674. xiii, 367p. (C). 1993. pap. text 44.95 (*1-55934-086-X*, 1086) Mayfield Pub.

Magazine Article: How to Think It, Plan It, Write It. Peter P. Jacobi. LC 96-47073. 256p. 1997. pap. 14.95 (*0-253-21111-5*) Ind U Pr.

Magazine Article: How To Think It, Plan It, Write It. Peter P. Jacobi. LC 96-47073. 1997. 29.95 (*0-253-33265-6*) Ind U Pr.

Magazine Article Writing. 2nd ed. Betsy P. Graham. 248p. (C). 1993. pap. text 49.00 (*0-03-075009-1*, Pub. by Harcourt Coll Pubs) Harcourt.

Magazine Beach. Lewis Nett. 1996. 23.00 (*0-614-96943-3*, HarperPrism) HarpC.

Magazine Careers Directory. 5th ed. Bradley J. Morgan. Ed. by Diane Dupuis. (Career Advisor Ser.). 1993. 17.95 (*0-8103-9440-5*, 089143) Visible Ink Pr.

Magazine Design. Chris Foges. (Pro-Graphics Ser.). 160p. 1999. pap. 37.50 (*2-88046-450-1*) Watsn-Guptill.

Magazine Design. William Owen. 272p. (C). 1991. text. write for info. (*0-697-14791-6*) Brown & Benchmark.

Magazine Design William Owen. LC 91-199134. 240p. 1991. write for info. (*1-85669-003-2*) L King Pubng.

Magazine Design: A Hands-On Guide. R. Walker. (Illus.). 176p. 1992. 44.95 (*0-948905-66-2*) Chapman & Hall.

***Magazine Design 2.** Ed. by B. Martin Pedersen. (Illus.). 256p. 2000. 70.00 (*1-888001-91-7*, Pub. by Graphis US) Watsn-Guptill.

Magazine Dimensions, '98. Ed Papazian. 366p. 1997. pap. 205.00 (*0-9621947-8-6*) Media Dynamics.

Magazine Dimensions '99. Ed Papazian. 390p. 1998. pap. 225.00 (*1-892605-02-3*) Media Dynamics.

Magazine Dimensions, '97. Ed Papazian. 364p. 1996. pap. 185.00 (*0-9621947-6-X*) Media Dynamics.

Magazine Editing. John Morrish. LC 96-7410. (Illus.). 288p. (C). 1996. 100.00 (*0-415-15263-1*); pap. 29.99 (*0-415-13672-5*) Routledge.

Magazine Editing & Production. 6th ed. J. William Click & Russell N. Baird. LC 91-22489. 336p. (C). 1993. text 40.50 (*0-697-13930-1*) Brown & Benchmark.

Magazine Editors Talk to Writers. Judy Mandell. LC 95-52686. 208p. 1996. pap. 14.95 (*0-471-11991-1*) Wiley.

Magazine Feature Writing. Richard A. Wilber. 418p. 1994. pap. text 49.95 (*0-312-07262-7*) St Martin.

***Magazine from Cover to Cover: Inside a Dynamic Industry.** Sammye Johnson & Patricia Prijatel. LC 99-16450. 376p. 2000. pap. 19.95 (*0-658-00229-5*, 002295) NTC Contemp Pub Co.

Magazine Fundamentals. 3rd ed. Ed. by John W. Cutsinger, Jr. (Illus.). 24p. 1984. pap. text 8.50 (*0-916084-15-9*) Columbia Scholastic.

Magazine Journalism Today. Davis. 260p. 1988. pap. 46.95 (*0-7506-0728-9*) Buttrwrth-Heinemann.

Magazine Law: Practical Guide. Peter Mason & Derrick Smith. LC 97-42921. (Blueprint Ser.). 216p. (C). 1998. 85.00 (*0-415-15141-4*); pap. 27.99 (*0-415-15142-2*) Routledge.

Magazine-Made America: The Cultural Transformation of the Postwar Periodical. David Abrahamson. Ed. by Lee Becker. (Communication Ser.). 128p. (Orig.). (C). 1996. text 42.50 (*1-57273-008-0*); pap. text 18.95 (*1-57273-009-9*) Hampton Pr NJ.

Magazine Marketing: How to Use Traditional Methods & Explore Creative Models. Cook Communications Ministries International Staff. (Interlit Imprint Ser.: Vol. 12). 40p. 1995. pap. text 6.00 (*1-884752-17-9*, 44156) Cook Min Intl.

***Magazine Newcomer Video Guide.** Vikki Wells. 1998. 10.00 (*0-7872-5108-9*) Kendall-Hunt.

Magazine Novels of Pauline Hopkins Including Hagar's Daughter, & Of One Blood. Pauline E. Hopkins. (Schomburg Library of Nineteenth-Century Black Women Writers). (Illus.). 672p. 1988. text 49.95 (*0-19-505248-X*) OUP.

Magazine Novels of Pauline Hopkins Including Hagar's Daughter, Winona, & Of One Blood. Pauline E. Hopkins. (Schomburg Library of Nineteenth-Century Black Women Writers). 672p. 1990. reprint ed. pap. text 16.95 (*0-19-506325-2*) OUP.

Magazine of "Fantasy & Science Fiction," April 1965. Ed. by Edward L. Ferman. (Alternatives Ser.). (Illus.). 176p. 1981. 18.95 (*0-8093-1007-4*) S Ill U Pr.

Magazine of Her Own? Domesticity & Desire in the Woman's Magazine, 1800-1914. Margaret Beetham. (Illus.). 256p. (C). 1996. pap. 29.99 (*0-415-14112-5*) Routledge.

Magazine Photo Collage: A Multicultural Assessment & Treatment Technique. Helen Landgarten. LC 93-16792. (Illus.). 224p. 1993. text 31.95 (*0-87630-706-3*) Brunner-Mazel.

Magazine Publishing. Sammye Johnson & Patricia Prijatel. LC 99-21757. 360p. 1999. 44.95 (*0-8442-3356-0*) NTC Contemp Pub Co.

Magazine Publishing Industry. Charles P. Daly et al. LC 96-32138. 310p. 1996. pap. text 26.00 (*0-205-16612-1*) Allyn.

Magazine Selection: How to Build a Community-Oriented Collection. William A. Katz. LC 72-171066. 168p. 1971. reprint ed. pap. 52.10 (*0-608-11194-5*, 201759000007) Bks Demand.

Magazine U. S. A. Edwin T. Cornelius, Jr. et al. (Illus.). 160p. 1984. pap. text 6.95 (*0-89209-269-6*); audio 75.00 (*0-89209-270-X*) Pace Grp Intl.

Magazine Writer's Handbook. Franklynn Peterson & Judi Kesselman-Turkel. 263p. 1983. 17.95 (*0-13-543751-2*) P-H.

Magazine Writing & the New Literature. Henry M. Alden. LC 70-175686. (Select Bibliographies Reprint Ser.). (C). 1977. reprint ed. 23.95 (*0-8369-5030-5*) Ayer.

Magazine Writing That Sells. Don McKinney. 240p. 1994. 16.99 (*0-89879-642-3*, Wrtrs Digest Bks) F & W Pubns Inc.

Magazines: A Bibliography for Their Analysis with Annotations & Study Guide. Fred K. Paine & Nancy E. Paine. LC 86-29825. 698p. 1987. 66.00 (*0-8108-1975-9*) Scarecrow.

Magazines: Inside & Out. Steven Heller & Teresa Fernandes. LC 95-36552. (Illus.). 160p. 1996. 34.95 (*0-86636-380-7*) PBC Intl Inc.

Magazines & Masks: Caras y Caretas As a Reflection of Buenos Aires, 1898-1908. Howard M. Fraser. LC 86-32670. (Illus.). 257p. 1987. pap. 39.95 (*0-87918-063-3*) ASU Lat Am St.

Magazines Career Directory: A Practical One-Stop Guide to Getting a Job in Public Relations. 5th ed. Ed. by Bradley J. Morgan. (Career Advisor Ser.). 300p. 1993. 39.00 (*0-8103-5610-4*, 101582) Gale.

Magazines for Children. Ed. by Donald R. Stoll. LC 90-219822. 48p. reprint ed. pap. 30.00 (*0-7837-4584-2*, 204430300002) Bks Demand.

Magazines for Children: A Guide for Parents, Teachers, & Librarians. 2nd ed. Ed. by Selma K. Richardson. LC 90-45152. 139p. (C). 1991. pap. text 25.00 (*0-8389-0552-8*, 0552-8) ALA.

Magazines for Kids & Teens. rev. ed. Ed. by Donald R. Stoll. LC 97-139394. 118p. 1996. pap. 15.95 (*0-87207-243-6*, 243) Intl Reading.

Magazines for Libraries. 9th ed. Ed. by Bill Katz & Linda Sternberg Katz. 1350p. 1997. 170.00 (*0-8352-3907-1*) Bowker.

M

Magazines for the Millions: Gender & Commerce in the Ladies' Home Journal & the Saturday Evening Post, 1880-1910. Helen Damon-Moore. LC 93-33767. (Illus.). 263p. (C). 1994. text 59.50 (*0-7914-2057-4*); pap. text 19.95 (*0-7914-2058-2*) State U NY Pr.

***Magazines Handbook.** Jenny McKay. LC 00-28186. (Media Practice Ser.). 2000. pap. write for info. (*0-415-17035-4*) Routledge.

Magazines in the Twentieth Century. 2nd ed. Theodore B. Peterson. LC 64-18668. (Illus.). 498p. reprint ed. pap. 154.40 (*0-8357-6199-1*, 203445800090) Bks Demand.

Magazines of the American South. Sam G. Riley. LC 85-8012. (Historical Guides to the World's Periodicals & Newspapers Ser.). 359p. 1986. lib. bdg. 65.00 (*0-313-24337-9*, RPA/, Greenwood Pr) Greenwood.

Magazn Good Idea Book. Ed. by Steven E. Miller. (Lotus Magazine Ser.). 1988. pap. 19.95 (*0-201-15664-4*) Addison-Wesley.

Magd des Herrn see Handmaid of the Lord

Magda Portal's Truth & Hope: A XX Century Feminist of Latin America. Daniel Reedy & Cecilia Bustamante. (Seagreen Ser.). (Illus.). 200p. (C). 1989. pap. 12.95 (*0-685-30777-8*) Extramares Edit.

Magda Rose. large type ed. Paul Luria. LC 98-74551. 150p. (J). (gr. 4-5). 1999. pap. 12.95 (*0-943864-98-4*) Davenport.

Magdalen Metaphysicals: Idealism & Orthodoxy at Oxford, 1901-1945. James Patrick. LC 84-20751. xl, 192p. 1985. 18.95 (*0-86554-145-0*, MUP/H135) Mercer Univ Pr.

Magdalena. Sarah Aldridge. 336p. 1995. reprint ed. pap. 9.95 (*0-9646648-1-X*) A&M Bks.

Magdalena: International Women's Experimental Theatre. Compiled & Intro. by Susan Bassnett. LC 89-31863. (Illus.). 136p. 1990. 19.95 (*0-85496-016-3*) Berg Pubs.

Magdalena Abakanowicz. Barbara Rose. LC 93-26843. (Illus.). 224p. 1994. 49.50 (*0-8109-1947-8*, Pub. by Abrams) Time Warner.

Magdalena Abakanowicz: Recent Sculpture. Michael Brenson. LC 93-79991. (Illus.). 68p. 1993. pap. 15.00 (*0-911517-61-8*) Mus of Art RI.

Magdalena & Balthasar: An Intimate Portrait of Life in Sixteenth-Century Europe Revealed in the Letters of a Nuremberg Husband & Wife. Steven Ozment. LC 86-15545. (Illus.). 192p. (C). 1989. pap. 14.00 (*0-300-04378-3*) Yale U Pr.

Magdalena Jetelova. Rosy Greenless. 1996. 35.00 (*3-89322-813-6*, Pub. by Edition Cantz) Dist Art Pubs.

Magdalene. B. J. Guttmann. LC 98-123939. 231 p. 1996. write for info. (*1-85863-742-2*, Pub. by Minerva Pr) Unity Dist.

Magdalene. Michael Johnson. 44p. 1996. pap. 3.50 (*0-87129-635-7*, M69) Dramatic Pub.

An Asterisk (*) at the beginning of an entry indicates that the title is appearing for the first time.

Magdalene Legacy: A Presbyterian Minister Examines the Wounded Icon of Sexuality. Sandra M. Rushing. LC 93-40160. 240p. 1994. 59.95 (0-89789-388-3, Bergin & Garvey) Greenwood.

Magdalene Sermon & Earlier Poems. Eilean N. Chuilleanain. LC 90-72090. 64p. 1991. pap. 8.95 (0-916390-43-8) Wake Forest.

Magdalens: Islands of Sand. George Fischer. (Illus.). 88p. 1992. 24.95 (1-55109-018-X) Nimbus Publ.

Mage: La Boule de Cristal, Vol. 1. Guy Des Cars. (FRE.). 190p. 1974. 6.95 (0-8288-9567-8, M5736) Fr & Eur.

***Mage: The Ascension.** Dierdre Brooks. 2000. 29.95 (1-56504-405-3); 69.95 (1-56504-438-X) White Wolf.

Mage: The Ascension. 2nd ed. Phil Brucato et al. (Mage). 1995. 28.00 (1-56504-400-2, 4300) White Wolf.

Mage: The Hero Defined. Matt Wagner. (Illus.). 96p. 1998. pap. 9.95 (1-58240-012-1) Image Comics.

Mage: The Hero Discovered: Collected Edition, No. 1. Matt Wagner. (Illus.). 56p. 1998. pap. 5.95 (1-58240-052-0) Image Comics.

Mage: The Hero Discovered: Collected Edition, No. 2. Matt Wagner. (Illus.). 56p. 1998. pap. 5.95 (1-58240-051-2) Image Comics.

Mage: The Hero Discovered: Collected Edition, No. 3. Matt Wagner. (Illus.). 56p. 1999. pap. 5.95 (1-58240-053-9) Image Comics.

Mage: The Sorcerer's Crusade. Phil Brucato & Brian Campbell. (Mage Ser.). (Illus.). 1998. 28.00 (1-56504-489-4, 4800) White Wolf.

Mage Chronicles, Vol. 1. Phil Brucato et al. (Mage Ser.). (Illus.). 200p. 1997. pap. 22.00 (1-56504-415-0, 4013) White Wolf.

Mage Chronicles, Vol. 2. Therese Neilsen & David Martin. (Werewolf Ser.). (Illus.). (Orig.). 1997. pap. 20.00 (1-56504-443-6, 4015) White Wolf.

***Mage Chronicles, Vol. 3.** Chris Hind. 2000. pap. text 17.95 (1-56504-444-4) White Wolf.

Mage et les Signes de la Main. Guy Des Cars. (FRE.). 240p. 1976. 13.95 (0-7859-1166-9, 2080608800) Fr & Eur.

Mage Heart. Jane Routley. 480p. 2000. reprint ed. mass mkt. 5.99 (0-380-78127-1, Avon Bks) Morrow Avon.

Mage in the Iron Mask. Brian Thomsen. 1996. pap. 5.99 (0-7869-0506-9, Pub. by TSR Inc) Random.

Mage Quest. C. Dale Brittain. 368p. (Orig.). 1993. mass mkt. 4.99 (0-671-72169-0) Baen Bks.

***Mage Storytellers Companion.** Jackie Cassada. (Mage Storyteller's Guide Ser.). 2000. pap. 14.95 (1-56504-406-1) White Wolf.

Mage Tarot Deck. Wolf White Wolf Publishing Staff. (Mage Ser.). (Illus.). 1995. boxed set 25.00 (1-56504-433-9, 4020) White Wolf.

Mageborn Traitor. Melanie Rawn. LC 97-143884. 688p. 1997. pap. 23.95 (0-88677-730-5, Pub. by DAW Bks) Penguin Putnam.

Mageborn Traitor: Exiles, Vol. 2. Melanie Rawn. Vol. 2. 842p. 1998. pap. 6.99 (0-88677-731-3, Pub. by DAW Bks) Penguin Putnam.

***Magehound.** Elaine Cunningham. (Forgotten Realms Ser.: Bk. I). (Illus.). 320p. 2000. mass mkt. 5.99 (0-7869-1561-7) TSR Inc.

Magellan. Tim Joyner. 365p. 1994. pap. 16.95 (0-87742-263-X) Intl Marine.

Magellan: A Voyage around the World. Fiona MacDonald. (Expedition Ser.). (Illus.). 32p. (J). (gr. 2-9). 1998. pap. 7.95 (0-531-15341-X) Watts.

Magellan & Da Gama. Clint Twist. LC 93-19303. (Beyond the Horizons Ser.). 48p. (J). 1994. lib. bdg. 24.26 (0-8114-7254-X) Raintree Steck-V.

Magellan & the Exploration of South America. Barron's Educational Editors. (Great Explorers Ser.). (Illus.). 32p. (J). (gr. 5). 1998. pap. 5.95 (0-7641-0531-0) Barron.

Magellan Heart. Donald A. Sears. LC 81-85192. (Selected Poems Ser.). 109p. 1982. pap. 9.95 (0-911906-24-X); text 15.95 (0-911906-25-8) Harian Creative Bks.

Magellanic Clouds. Ed. by Raymond Haynes & Douglas Milne. (C). 1991. lib. bdg. 169.00 (0-7923-1110-8) Kluwer Academic.

Magellanic Clouds. Bengt E. Westerlund. (Cambridge Astrophysics Ser.: No. 29). (Illus.). 294p. (C). 1997. text 74.95 (0-521-48070-1) Cambridge U Pr.

Magellanic Clouds: Proceedings of the Symposium, Santiago De Chile, March 1969. Magellanic Clouds Symposium Staff. Ed. by A. B. Muller. LC 73-154743. (Astrophysics & Space Science Library: No.23). 189p. 1971. text 94.00 (90-277-0205-5) Kluwer Academic.

Magellan's Voyage: A Narrative Account of the First Circumnavigation. Antonio Pigafetta. (Illus.). 208p. 1994. reprint ed. pap. 8.95 (0-486-28099-3) Dover.

Magelord: House of Bairn, Vol. 3. Thomas K. Martin. (Magelord Trilogy Ser.). 1999. mass mkt. 5.99 (0-441-00623-X) Ace Bks.

Magelord: The Awakening. Thomas K. Martin. (Magelord Trilogy Ser.). 288p. 1997. mass mkt. 5.99 (0-441-00435-0) Ace Bks.

Magelord: Time of Madness. Thomas K. Martin. (Magelord Trilogy Ser.: Vol. 2). 256p. 1998. mass mkt. 5.99 (0-441-00533-0) Ace Bks.

Magen David: How the Six-Pointed Star Became the Emblem of the Jewish People. Gunther Plaut. (Illus.). 114p. 1990. 22.50 (0-910250-16-2) Bnai Brith Intl.

Magen David: How the Six-Pointed Star Became the Emblem of the Jewish People. W. Gunther Plaut. (Illus.). 114p. 1990. pap. 12.95 (0-910250-17-0) Bnai Brith Intl.

***Magenta & Me: My First Preschool Ready to Read Pre-Level 1.** Deborah Reber. LC 99-46900. Vol. 2. (Illus.). 24p. (J). (ps-3). 2000. pap. 3.99 (0-689-83123-4, Simon Spot) Litle Simon.

Magenta Moth. John Patrick. 1983. pap. 5.25 (0-8222-0716-8) Dramatists Play.

Magenta or Cyan. Bruce Braunstein. (Orig.). 1986. 19.95 (0-685-14660-X) Tetragrammaton.

Magenta's Tartan Socks. Nikki Johnston. LC 93-18047. (Illus.). (J). 1994. write for info. (0-383-03700-X) SRA McGraw.

Magenta's Visit. Michael T. Smith & Alice Wilder. (Illus.). 24p. (J). (gr. k-3). 1999. mass mkt. 3.50 (0-689-82443-2, 076714003507, Simon Spot) Litle Simon.

Mager Six-Pack, 6 vols. Robert F. Mager. Incl. Analyzing Performance Problems: Or You Really Oughta Wanna. 3rd rev. ed. Peter Pipe. LC 96-72446. (Illus.). 187p. 1997. pap. 19.95 (1-879618-17-6, 404); Goal Analysis: How to Clarify Your Goals So You Can Actually Achieve Them. 3rd rev. ed. LC 96-72445. (Illus.). 170p. 1997. pap. 19.95 (1-879618-04-4, 405); How to Turn Learners on... Without Turning Them Off: Ways to Ignite Interest in Learning. 3rd rev. ed. LC 96-72444. (Illus.). 161p. 1997. pap. 19.95 (1-879618-18-4, 406); Making Instruction Work: A Step-by-Step Guide to Designing & Developing Instruction That Works. 2nd rev. ed. LC 96-72447. (Illus.). 288p. 1997. pap. 19.95 (1-879618-02-8, 407); Measuring Instructional Results: How to Find Out If Your Instructional Objectives Have Been Achieved. 3rd rev. ed. LC 96-72448. (Illus.). 192p. 1997. pap. 19.95 (1-879618-16-8, 403); Preparing Instructional Objectives: A Critical Tool in the Development of Effective Instruction. 3rd rev. ed. LC 96-72449. (Illus.). 202p. 1997. pap. 19.95 (1-879618-03-6, 402); 95.00 (1-879618-15-X) Ctr Effect Perf.

Mage's Blood & Old Bones: A Tunnels & Trolls Anthology. Elizabeth Danforth et al. (Illus.). 180p. (Orig.). 1992. pap. 7.95 (0-940244-66-7) Flying Buffalo.

Mages Hellenises: Zoroastre, Ostanes & Hystaspe d'Apres la Tradition Grecque, 2 vols. Joseph Bidez & Franz Cumont. LC 75-10629. (Ancient Religion & Mythology Ser.). (FRE & GRE.). 1976. reprint ed. 58.95 (0-405-07005-5) Ayer.

Magestone. Andre Norton & Mary H. Schaub. (Secrets of the Witch World Ser.: Vol. 2). 288p. (Orig.). 1996. reprint ed. mass mkt. 5.99 (0-446-60222-1, Pub. by Warner Bks) Little.

Maggee & the Lake Minder. Richard Thompson. (Illus.). 32p. (J). (gr. k-3). 1991. pap. 4.95 (1-55037-152-5, Pub. by Annick); lib. bdg. 14.95 (1-55037-154-1, Pub. by Annick) Firefly Bks Ltd.

Maggi: Three Faces of Poetry. Maggi H. Meyer. 176p. 1988. per. 10.00 (0-915727-11-0) im-Press.

Maggi Hambling: An Eye Through a Decade, 1981-1991. Contrib. by Mel Gooding & George Melly. LC 91-75249. (Illus.). 72p. (Orig.). 1991. pap. 14.95 (0-930606-66-3) Yale Ctr Brit Art.

Maggid of Dubno & His Parables. rev. ed. Benno Heineman. 1978. 20.95 (0-87306-156-X) Feldheim.

Maggid of Mezritch. Yitzchak Dorfman. 133p. 1989. 13.95 (0-944070-16-7) Targum Pr.

Maggid Speaks: Favorite Stories & Parables of Rabbi Sholom Schwadron. Paysach J. Krohn. (ArtScroll Ser.). (Illus.). 272p. 1987. 21.99 (0-89906-230-X); pap. 18.99 (0-89906-231-8) Mesorah Pubns.

Maggie. Stephen Crane. (Classics Library). 1998. pap. 3.95 (1-85326-559-4, 5594WW, Pub. by Wrdsworth Edits) NTC Contemp Pub Co.

Maggie. Ann M. Martin. (California Diaries: Vol. 3). 160p. (YA). (gr. 4-8). 1997. pap. text 3.99 (0-590-29837-2) Scholastic Inc.

Maggie. Ann M. Martin. (California Diaries). (YA). (gr. 6-8). 1997. 9.09 (0-606-11181-6, Pub. by Turtleback) Demco.

***Maggie: A Girl of the Streets.** Stephen Crane. (Norton Critical Editions Ser.). (C). 1999. pap. text 30.00 (0-393-98960-7) Norton.

***Maggie: A Girl of the Streets: And Other Tales of New York.** Stephen Crane. (Penguin Classics Ser.). 2000. pap. 8.95 (0-14-043797-5) Viking Penguin.

***Maggie: Diary Three.** Ann M. Martin. (California Diaries: Vol. 13). 144p. (gr. 6-8). 1999. mass mkt. 4.99 (0-439-09547-6) Scholastic Inc.

***Maggie: Diary Three.** Ann Matthews Martin. (Illus.). (J). 1999. 9.34 (0-606-18524-0) Turtleback.

Maggie: Diary Two. Ann M. Martin. (California Diaries: Vol. 8). (J). (gr. 6-8). 1998. pap. text 3.99 (0-590-02383-7) Scholastic Inc.

***Maggie: Diary Two.** Ann M. Martin. (California Diaries). (YA). (gr. 6-8). 1998. 9.09 (0-606-13239-2, Pub. by Turtleback) Demco.

Maggie: Her Marriage. Taylor Caldwell. 204p. reprint ed. lib. bdg. 21.95 (0-88411-169-5) Amereon Ltd.

Maggie - Woman of Roberts County. Char Jarman. 132p. 1999. pap. write for info. (1-57579-148-X) Pine Hill Pr.

Maggie, a Girl of the Streets. Stephen Crane. 166p. 1985. mass mkt. 5.99 (0-449-30024-2, Prem) Fawcett.

Maggie, a Girl of the Streets. Stephen Crane. Ed. by Thomas A. Gullason. (Critical Editions Ser.). (C). 1979. pap. text 12.50 (0-393-95024-7) Norton.

Maggie, a Girl of the Streets. Stephen Crane. LC 95-9642. (Literary Classics Ser.). 90p. 1995. pap. 5.95 (1-57392-037-1) Prometheus Bks.

Maggie, a Girl of the Streets. Stephen Crane. LC 98-86156. xvii, 374p. 1999. pap. 11.95 (0-312-15266-3) St Martin.

Maggie, a Girl of the Streets. Stephen Crane. 1989. pap. 6.50 (0-685-26534-X) Vin Bks.

Maggie, a Girl of the Streets. Stephen Crane. (Works of Stephen Crane). 1990. reprint ed. lib. bdg. 79.00 (0-685-44763-4) Rprt Serv.

Maggie, a Girl of the Streets: A Story of New York. Stephen Crane. Ed. by Kevin J. Hayes. LC 98-86156. 384p. 1999. text 39.95 (0-312-21824-9) St Martin.

Maggie, a Girl of the Streets: A Story of New York. Stephen Crane. LC 66-20867. 192p. 1978. reprint ed. 50.00 (0-8201-1268-2) Schol Facsimiles.

Maggie, a Girl of the Streets: And Selected Stories. Stephen Crane. Ed. by Alfred Kazin. 224p. 1991. mass mkt. 4.95 (0-451-52552-3, Sig Classics) NAL.

Maggie, a Girl of the Streets & George's Mother: Two Novels. Stephen Crane. 1983. 11.09 (0-606-02532-4, Pub. by Turtleback) Demco.

Maggie, a Girl of the Streets & Other Short Fiction. Stephen Crane. 208p. 1986. mass mkt. 4.95 (0-553-21355-5, Bantam Classics) Bantam.

Maggie Adams, Dancer. Karen S. Dean. 1980. pap. 1.75 (0-380-75366-9, Avon Bks) Morrow Avon.

Maggie Adams, Dancer. Karen S. Dean. 176p. (YA). (gr. 5 up). 1982. pap. 2.50 (0-380-80200-7, Avon Bks) Morrow Avon.

Maggie among the Seneca. rev. ed. Robin Moore. LC 89-77110. 112p. (J). (gr. 4-7). 1990. 13.95 (0-397-32455-3); lib. bdg. 14.89 (0-397-32456-1) HarpC Child Bks.

Maggie & a Horse Named Devildust. Judy Alter. LC 88-22815. (Illus.). 160p. (J). (gr. 3-10). 1989. pap. 5.95 (0-936650-08-7, Pub. by E C Temple) Sunbelt Media.

Maggie & Devildust Ridin' High. Judy Alter. LC 89-2683. (Illus.). 160p. (Orig.). (J). (gr. 3-10). 1990. pap. 5.95 (0-936650-10-9, Pub. by E C Temple) Sunbelt Media.

Maggie & Her Colonel. Merline Lovelace. (Great Escapes Ser.). 1994. pap. 1.99 (0-373-83273-7, 1-83273-2) Harlequin Bks.

***Maggie & Keisha - Best Friends: Complete Patterns for Two Cloth Dolls & Their Wardrobes.** Paulette Morrissey. (Illus.). 39p. 1999. spiral bd. 13.95 (1-893502-09-0) Morrissey Co.

Maggie & Me. Ted Stanton. 1999. pap. 3.99 (0-14-034363-6, Viking) Viking Penguin.

Maggie & Other Stories. Stephen Crane. (Airmont Classics Ser.). (YA). (gr. 11 up). 1968. mass mkt. 3.25 (0-8049-0166-X, CL-166) Airmont.

Maggie & Other Stories. Stephen Crane. 26.95 (0-88411-572-0) Amereon Ltd.

Maggie & Ruby. Jane Resh Thomas. (J). 1999. write for info. (0-7868-0188-3) Hyperion.

***Maggie & Shine.** Luanne Armstrong & Dorothy Woodend. 90p. (J). (gr. 4-6). 1999. pap. 6.95 (1-895836-67-0, Tesseract) Bk Collective.

Maggie & Silky. Amy Ehrlich. 1999. pap. 4.99 (0-14-054274-4) NAL.

***Maggie & the Ferocious Beast: The Big Scare.** Betty Paraskevas. LC 98-35946. (Illus.). 40p. (J). (ps-1). 1999. per. 15.00 (0-689-82489-0) S&S Bks Yung.

Maggie & the Gambler. Ann Carberry. 384p. (Orig.). 1995. mass mkt. 4.99 (0-380-77880-7, Avon Bks) Morrow Avon.

Maggie & the Maverick. Laurie Grant. (Historical Ser.: No. 461). 1999. per. 4.99 (0-373-29061-6, 1-29061-8) Harlequin Bks.

Maggie & the Monster. Elizabeth Winthrop. LC 86-19593. (Illus.). 32p. (J). (ps-3). 1987. lib. bdg. 15.95 (0-8234-0639-3) Holiday.

Maggie & the Monster. Elizabeth Winthrop. LC 86-19593. (Illus.). 32p. (J). (ps-3). 1987. pap. 5.95 (0-8234-0698-9) Holiday.

Maggie & the Pirate. Ezra Jack Keats. 40p. (J). (ps-3). 1992. pap. 4.95 (0-590-44852-8, Blue Ribbon Bks) Scholastic Inc.

Maggie & the Pirate. Ezra Jack Keats. (Illus.). (J). 1979. 10.15 (0-606-04471-X, Pub. by Turtleback) Demco.

Maggie & the Search for Devildust. Judy Alter. LC 88-8019. (Illus.). 160p. (J). (gr. 3-10). 1989. pap. 5.95 (0-936650-09-5, Pub. by E C Temple) Sunbelt Media.

Maggie B. Irene Haas. LC 74-18183. (Illus.). 32p. (J). 1997. mass mkt. 5.99 (0-689-81507-7) Atheneum Yung Read.

Maggie B. Irene Haas. LC 74-18183. (Illus.). 32p. (J). (ps-2). 1975. 16.00 (0-689-50021-1) McElderry Bks.

Maggie B. Irene Haas. (Illus.). 32p. (J). (ps-2). 1997. 16.00 (0-689-81588-3) S&S Childrens.

Maggie Can Count: A Counting Tweeter Book. Salina Yoon. 10p. (J). (gr. k). 1999. pap. 7.95 (1-58117-056-4) Intervisual Bks.

Maggie Cassidy. Jack Kerouac. LC 93-247893. 202p. 1993. pap. 12.95 (0-14-017906-2, Penguin Bks) Viking Penguin.

***Maggie Celebrates Ayybam-I-Hba.** Patti Rae Tomarelli & Wendy Cowper-Thomas. LC 99-34977. (Illus.). (J). 1999. write for info. (0-87743-276-7) Bahai.

***Maggie Colvin's Fabulous Fakes.** Maggie Colvin. (Illus.). 2000. 27.95 (0-7153-0920-X, Pub. by D & C Pub) Sterling.

Maggie Craig. Marie Joseph. 3.50 (0-09-925390-9) Arrow Bks.

***Maggie Davis: The Poetry of Falling: Works on Paper.** Genevieve Linneham. (Illus.). 2000. pap. 1.00 (0-9619219-8-6) Polk Mus Art.

Maggie Forevermore. Joan Lowery Nixon. LC 86-20135. 112p. (J). (gr. 3-7). 1987. 13.95 (0-15-250345-5) Harcourt.

Maggie Greeno: The Life of Margaret Ann Wallace Greeno. George McDow, Jr. LC 95-215243. (Illus.). 272p. (Orig.). 1995. pap. 18.95 (0-938373-15-3) Lahontan Images.

Maggie Jordan. large type ed. Emma Blair. (Charnwood Ser.). 720p. 1994. 27.99 (0-7089-8757-5, Charnwood) Ulverscroft.

Maggie Lynn & Her Perpetual State of Fulfillment in Johnstown, Ohio: A Novella by Brad James. Jennifer Bosveld. (Illus.). 60p. 1996. pap. 7.95 (0-944754-37-6) Pudding Hse Pubns.

Maggie Marmelstein fo President. Marjorie Weinman Sharmat. LC 75-6300. (Trophy Bk.). (Illus.). 128p. (J). (gr. 4-7). 1976. mass mkt. 4.95 (0-06-440079-4, HarpTrophy) HarpC Child Bks.

Maggie Marmelstein for President. Marjorie Weinman Sharmat. (J). 1975. 10.05 (0-606-00724-5, Pub. by Turtleback) Demco.

Maggie Marmelstein for President: A Study Guide. Joyce Friedland & Rikki Kessler. (Novel-Ties Ser.). (J). (gr. 3-5). 1982. pap. text, teacher ed., student ed. 15.95 (0-88122-006-X) Lrn Links.

***Maggie May's Diary, 1.** Thomas E. Coughlin. LC 98-73598. 1998. pap. 13.95 (0-9666202-0-8) Fitzgerald & LaChapelle.

Maggie, Medworth & Me: How to Cook for Pets. Thomas E. Croel. 84p. 1984. write for info. (0-318-58345-3) G Whittell Mem.

Maggie Poor. Illus. by Maggie Poor. 24p. 1999. pap. 12.00 (0-933519-38-9) D W Bell Gallery.

Maggie Rose. Linda H. Lee. LC 96-95475. 192p. 1997. 18.95 (0-8034-9226-X, Avalon Bks) Bouregy.

Maggie Rowan. Catherine Cookson. 384p. (Orig.). 1995. mass mkt. 7.99 (0-552-14081-3) Bantam.

Maggie Simpson's Alphabet Book. Matt Groening & Maggie Groening. LC 91-2867. (Illus.). 32p. (J). (ps-1). 1991. 2.95 (0-694-00318-2) HarpC Child Bks.

Maggie Simpson's Alphabet Book. Matt Groening & Maggie Groening. LC 91-2867. (Illus.). 32p. (J). (ps-1). 1991. lib. bdg. 11.89 (0-06-020236-X) HarpC Child Bks.

Maggie Simpson's Book of Animals. Matt Groening & Maggie Groening. LC 91-2866. (Illus.). 32p. (J). (ps-1). 1991. 2.95 (0-694-00321-2) HarpC Child Bks.

Maggie Simpson's Book of Animals. Matt Groening & Maggie Groening. LC 91-2866. (Illus.). 32p. (J). (ps-1). 1991. lib. bdg. 11.89 (0-06-020237-8) HarpC Child Bks.

Maggie Simpson's Book of Colors & Shapes. Matt Groening & Maggie Groening. LC 91-2864. (Illus.). 32p. (J). (ps-1). 1991. 2.95 (0-694-00320-4) HarpC Child Bks.

Maggie Simpson's Book of Colors & Shapes. Matt Groening & Maggie Groening. LC 91-2864. (Illus.). 32p. (J). (ps-1). 1991. lib. bdg. 11.89 (0-06-020235-1) HarpC Child Bks.

Maggie Simpson's Counting Book. Matt Groening & Maggie Groening. LC 91-2865. (Illus.). 32p. (J). (ps-1). 1991. 2.95 (0-694-00319-0) HarpC Child Bks.

Maggie Simpson's Counting Book. Matt Groening & Maggie Groening. LC 91-2865. (Illus.). 32p. (J). (ps-1). 1991. lib. bdg. 11.89 (0-06-020238-6) HarpC Child Bks.

Maggie Suzanne, Star of Christmas. Marilyn Goss. (Illus.). 36p. (J). (gr. 3 up). 1988. 15.95 (0-9620766-0-0) Art Room Pubns.

Maggie, the Dog of My Life. Patricia J. Hollingworth. 1981. 25.00 (0-7223-1445-0, Pub. by A H S Ltd) St Mut.

Maggie the Freak. Eve Bunting. (FastBack Romance Ser.). 1984. 11.27 (0-606-00339-8, Pub. by Turtleback) Demco.

Maggie, Too. Joan Lowery Nixon. LC 84-19766. 101p. (J). (gr. 3-7). 1985. 11.95 (0-15-250350-1, Harcourt Child Bks) Harcourt.

Maggie Valley, North Carolina . . . Then & Now. Scottie D. Andrews. (Illus.). xii, 108p. 1998. reprint ed. pap. 12.95 (0-9664996-2-X) Broguin.

Maggie Walker, Business Leader. Garnet N. Jackson. (Illus.). (J). (gr. 1-4). 1994. pap. 4.95 (0-8136-5248-0); lib. bdg. 9.95 (0-8136-5242-1) Modern Curr.

***Maggie Way.** Andrews. (J). 2000. pap. 8.95 (0-552-14036-8, Pub. by Transworld Publishers Ltd) Trafalgar.

Maggie's American Dream: The Life & Times of a Black Family. James P. Comer. (Illus.). 352p. 1989. pap. 13.95 (0-452-26318-2, Dutt) Dutton Plume.

***Maggie's Baby, 35.** Colleen Faulkner. (Bouquet Ser.). 2000. mass mkt. 3.99 (0-8217-6487-X, Zebra Kensgtn) Kensgtn Pub Corp.

Maggie's Boy. large type ed. Beryl Kingston. 605p. 1995. 27.99 (0-7505-0758-6, Pub. by Mgna Lrg Print) Ulverscroft.

***Maggie's Choice: Jonathan Edwards & the Great Awakening.** Norma Jean Lutz. (American Adventure Ser.: No. 8). (J). (gr. 3-6). 1998. pap. 3.97 (1-57748-145-3) Barbour Pub.

Maggie's Choice: Jonathan Edwards & the Great Awakening. Norma Jean Lutz. LC 98-17241. (American Adventure Ser.: No. 8). (Illus.). 144p. (J). (gr. 4-7). 1999. lib. bdg. 15.95 (0-7910-5048-3) Chelsea Hse.

Maggie's Colorful Garden: A Touchy, Feely Lift-the-Flap Colors Book. Salina Yoon. 10p. (J). (gr. k). 1999. pap. 7.95 (1-58117-057-2) Intervisual Bks.

Maggie's Dad 1000 Book Celebration. Diana Palmer. 1995. per. 3.75 (0-373-09991-6, 1-09991-0) Silhouette.

Maggie's Farm. John Sherry. LC 83-63238. 246p. 1986. 22.00 (0-932966-50-0) Permanent Pr.

***Maggie's Heart & Other Stories.** George M. Flynn. LC 99-96626. 124p. 1999. pap. 8.99 (0-9675355-0-6) G Flynn NJ.

***Maggie's Holiday.** Jill Dow. (Windy Edge Farm Ser.). (Illus.). (J). (ps-2). 1999. pap. text 7.99 (0-7112-0852-2) F Lincoln.

Maggie's Man. Alicia Scott. 1997. per. 3.99 (0-373-07776-9, 1-07776-7) Silhouette.

Maggie's Mountain. Dell Dean. pap. 6.00 (0-88734-259-0) Players Pr.

***Maggie's Musings.** Margaret Koepplinger. 1999. pap. write for info. (1-58235-295-X) Watermrk Pr.

Maggie's Pride. Deborah Wood. 295p. (Orig.). 1996. mass mkt. 5.50 (0-515-11830-3, Jove) Berkley Pub.

Maggie's Rags. unabridged ed. Sheila Evans. LC 96-83788. 186p. (Orig.). 1996. pap. 9.95 (1-888934-10-7) Central OR Coast.

***Maggie's Way: Observations from below Your Knees.** Bill Stanton. 2000. pap. 14.95 (0-7407-1216-0) Andrews & McMeel.

Maggie's Weaning. Mary J. Deutschbein. 27p. (J). 1994. pap. 6.95 (1-885678-08-8) Moon Gold.

Maggie's Weaning. 2nd ed. Mary J. Deutschbein. LC 99-63807. (Illus.). 24p. (J). (ps-1). 1999. pap. 6.95 (0-912500-58-1) La Leche.

An Asterisk (*) at the beginning of an entry indicates that the title is appearing for the first time.

Maggody Militia. Joan Hess. 272p. 1998. mass mkt. 5.99 (0-451-40726-1, Onyx) NAL.

Maggot. John Fowles. 464p. 1998. pap. 13.95 (0-316-29049-1) Little.

***Maggots.** Brian Chippendale. 2000. pap. 16.95 (0-9700858-3-4) Highwater Bks.

Maggy's Child. Karen Robards. 416p. 1994. mass mkt. 6.99 (0-440-20830-0) Dell.

Maggy's Child. large type ed. Karen Robards. LC 93-47353. 1994. 25.95 (1-56895-057-8) Wheeler Pub.

Magheen. Louise Gherasim. LC 97-6765. 347p. (Orig.). 1997. pap. 26.95 (1-880664-24-0) E M Pr.

***Maghreb.** Anthony G. Pazzanita. LC 99-219147. Vol. 208. 368p. 1998. lib. bdg. 85.00 (1-85109-310-9) ABC-CLIO.

***Maghrebian Mosaic: A Literature in Transition.** Ed. by Mildred Mortimer. 320p. 2000. lib. bdg. 59.95 (0-89410-888-3, Three Contnts) L Rienner.

Maghrib in Question: Essays in History & Historiography. Ed. by Michel Le Gall & Kenneth J. Perkins. LC 96-44825. (Illus.). 304p. 1997. 40.00 (0-292-76576-2) U of Tex Pr.

***Magi.** Adrian Gilbert. 1999. pap. 13.00 (0-7475-3100-5, Pub. by Blmsbury Pub) Trafalgar.

Magi. Susan Lustig. 16p. (Orig.). 1995. pap. 2.50 (1-57514-178-7, 3052) Encore Perform Pub.

***Magi: From Zoroaster to the "Three Wise Men"** Ken R. Vincent. LC 99-50567. 1999. 16.95 (0-941037-88-6, BIBAL Press) D & F Scott.

Magi Astrology: The Key to Success in Love & Money. Magi Society Staff. LC 98-46503. (Illus.). 448p. (Orig.). 1999. pap. 14.95 (1-56170-128-9, 168) Hay House.

Magi at Christmas: A Winter Love Story. G. W. Kroeker. 175p. 1997. pap. 9.95 (0-9659308-7-4) Erica Hse.

Magi Society Ephemeris. Magi Society Staff. LC 96-19651. 752p. 1996. 30.00 (1-56170-331-1, 150) Hay House.

Magia d'Amore. Murray Pomerance. (Classics Ser.: No. 139). 136p. (Orig.). 1998. pap. 12.95 (1-55713-308-5, Pub. by Sun & Moon CA) Consort Bk Sales.

Magia de la Isla - Island Enchantment. Robyn Donald. (Bianca Ser.: No. 367). 1996. per. 3.50 (0-373-33367-6, 1-33367-3) Harlequin Bks.

Magia de la Palabra. Washington Llorens. LC 80-19972. (Coleccion Mente y Palabra). (SPA.). x, 171p. 1981. 6.00 (0-8477-0576-5); pap. 5.00 (0-8477-0577-3) U of PR Pr.

Magia de la Sonrisa. Boling Dutch. (SPA.). 1997. pap. text 9.98 (968-403-340-0) Selector.

Magia de las Piedra y los Cristales. Migene Gonzalez-Wippler. 1989. 9.95 (0-942272-19-6) Original Pubns.

Magia de las Piedras y los Cristales: Y Como Usarla Mejorar Tu Vida. Migene Gonzalez-Wippler. LC 96-163660.Tr. of Release the Power of Crystals & Stones. (SPA.). 160p. 1999. pap. 6.95 (1-56718-331-X) Llewellyn Pubns.

Magia de un Regalo Excepcional. Patron Lujan Roger. (SPA.). 1997. pap. text 19.98 (968-409-984-3) Edamex.

Magia del Amor-Calypso's Enchantment. Kate Walker. 1996. per. 3.50 (0-373-33356-0) Harlequin Bks.

Magia del Mar. David Doubilet. (SPA.). 1997. 38.99 (3-8228-8533-9) Benedikt Taschen.

Magia del Multinivel: Como Cualquier Persona Puede Lograr un Negocio Colosal de Ventas de Multinivel a Par de Cero. Venus C. Andrecht. (SPA.). 290p. (Orig.). 1994. pap. 18.95 (0-941903-08-7) Ransom Hill.

Magia del Sexo. Miriam Stoppard. (SPA., Illus.). 1997. 60.00 (968-13-2346-7) Edit Diana.

Magia e Historia en los "Cuentos Negros", "Por Que" y "Ayapa" de Lydia Cabrera. Sara Soto. LC 87-81464. (Coleccion Ebano y Canela). (SPA.). 164p. (Orig.). 1988. pap. 12.00 (0-89729-444-0) Ediciones.

Magia Hecha en Casa. Diurny Rizzo. 1994. pap. 5.95 (0-942272-38-2) Original Pubns.

Magia Olvidada: A Forgotten Magic. Kathleen O'Brien. (Bianca Ser.: Vol. 128). (SPA.). 1998. per. 3.50 (0-373-33478-8, 1-33478-8) Harlequin Bks.

Magia Peligrosa. Jennifer Greene. Orig. Title: Single Dad. (SPA.). 1996. per. 3.50 (0-373-35134-8) Harlequin Bks.

Magia y Brujeria en Mexico. B. Schefler. (SPA.). 1997. pap. 10.50 (968-38-0098-X) Edit Diana.

Magia y Tu. Migene Gonzalez-Wippler.Tr. of Magic & You. (SPA.). 160p. 1999. pap. 6.95 (1-56718-332-8) Llewellyn Pubns.

Magian Gospel of Brother Yeshua. Charles C. Wise, Jr. LC 79-84277. (Illus.). 306p. 1979. 11.95 (0-917023-05-6); pap. 5.95 (0-917023-06-4) Magian Pr.

Magic. Illus. by Pam Adams. LC 90-46518. (Imagination Ser.). 32p. (Orig.). (J). (ps-2). 1978. 9.99 (0-85953-104-X, Pub. by Childs Play); pap. 3.99 (0-85953-081-7, Pub. by Childs Play) Random House.

Magic. Illus. by Pam Adams. (Imagination Ser.). (SPA.). (Orig.). (J). 1978. pap. 6.99 (0-85953-971-7) Childs Play.

Magic. Kimberly Cates. 328p. 1998. per. 6.50 (0-671-01494-3) PB.

Magic. D K Publishing Staff. (Funpax Ser.). 1999. 4.95 (0-7894-4315-5) DK Pub Inc.

Magic. Peter Eldin. LC 97-1424. (Illus.). 64p. (J). (gr. 3-7). 1997. 16.95 (0-7534-5084-4) LKC.

***Magic.** Robin L. Hatcher. 448p. 1999. mass mkt. 5.99 (0-8439-4661-X, Pub. by Dorchester Pub Co) CMG.

Magic. Tami Hoag. 336p. 1991. mass mkt. 6.99 (0-553-29053-3) Bantam.

Magic: A Pictoral History of Conjurers in the Theater. David L. Price. LC 81-68623. 544p. 1985. 60.00 (0-8453-4738-1, Cornwall Bks) Assoc Univ Prs.

Magic: A Reference Guide. Earle J. Coleman. LC 86-29611. (American Popular Culture Ser.). 214p. 1987. lib. bdg. 47.95 (0-313-23397-7, CMA/) Greenwood.

Magic: A Treatise on Esoteric Ethics. Manly P. Hall. pap. 4.95 (0-89314-384-7) Philos Res.

Magic! Against the Odds. Howard Blatt. LC 97-134542. (J). 1996. mass mkt. 4.50 (0-671-00301-1) PB.

Magic: An Introduction. Houghton Mifflin Company Staff. (Literature Experience 1993 Ser.). (J). (gr. 3). 1992. pap. 9.48 (0-395-61785-5) HM.

Magic: Earvin Johnson. Bill Morgan. 136p. (J). (gr. 4-6). 1992. 2.95 (0-590-46050-1, 063) Scholastic Inc.

Magic: Its Rites & History. Maurice Bouisson. Tr. by G. Almayrac from FRE. LC 79-8094. (Satanism Ser.). (Illus.). 1985. reprint ed. 36.00 (0-404-18405-7) AMS Pr.

Magic: Stage Illusions & Scientific Diversions. Albert A. Hopkins. LC 67-12462. (Illus.). 570p. 1972. 33.95 (0-405-08635-0, Pub. by Blom Pubns) Ayer.

Magic: Stage Illusions Special Effects & Trick Photography. Albert A. Hopkins. (Illus.). 556p. 1990. pap. 13.95 (0-486-26561-7) Dover.

Magic: The Cookbook of the Junior League of Birmingham. 5th ed. Illus. by Olive G. Arant. LC 81-85953. 348p. 1982. 14.95 (0-9607810-0-5) Jr League Birm.

Magic: The Final Fantasy Collection. Isaac Asimov. 275p. 1998. text 22.00 (0-7881-5367-6) DIANE Pub.

Magic: The Final Fantasy Collection. Isaac Asimov. 1997. mass mkt. 5.99 (0-614-27749-3, HarperPrism) HarpC.

Magic: The Gathering. Richard Garfield. 36p. 1993. 7.95 (1-880992-22-2); 2.45 (1-880992-23-X) Wizards Coast.

Magic: The Gathering. Mike Grell. 1999. pap. text 12.95 (1-56971-403-7) Dark Horse Comics.

***Magic: The Gathering - Official Encyclopedia; The Complete Card Guide, 1.** Beth Moursund. (Illus.). 224p. 2000. pap. 23.95 (1-56025-214-6, Thunders Mouth) Avalon NY.

***Magic: The Gathering - Official Encyclopedia; The Complete Card Guide, 2.** Beth Moursund. (Illus.). 144p. 2000. pap. 23.95 (1-56025-221-9, Thunders Mouth) Avalon NY.

Magic: The Gathering Adventurers Guide. Bradygames Staff. 167p. 1997. pap. text 19.99 (1-56686-579-4) Brady Pub.

Magic: The Gathering, Distant. Ed. by Kathy Ice. 384p. 1997. mass mkt. 5.99 (0-06-105765-7, HarperPrism) HarpC.

***Magic: The Untold Story of U. S. Intelligence & the Evacuation of...** David B. Lowman. (Illus.). 2000. pap. 24.95 (0-9602736-1-1) Athena Pr.

***Magic Vol. 4: The Gathering - Official Encyclopedia.** Beth Moursund. (Illus.). 192p. 1999. pap. 23.95 (1-56025-211-1, Thunders Mouth) Avalon NY.

Magic . . . Naturally! Science Entertainments & Amusements. Vicki Cobb. LC 76-13179. (Illus.). (J). (gr. 5-7). 1976. 12.95 (0-397-31631-3) HarpC Child Bks.

Magic . . . Naturally! Science Entertainments & Amusements. Vicki Cobb. LC 90-21829. (Illus.). 160p. (J). (gr. 4 up). 1993. lib. bdg. 16.89 (0-06-022475-4) HarpC Child Bks.

Magic - The Gathering: The Official Encyclopedia - The Complete Card Guide. Kathryn Haines. (Illus.). 224p. 1996. pap. 19.95 (1-56025-140-9, Thunders Mouth) Avalon NY.

Magic, a Pictorial History. Milbourne Christopher. (Illus.). 224p. 1991. pap. 14.95 (0-486-26373-8) Dover.

Magic Act. Laurence Klavan. 1989. pap. 5.25 (0-8222-0715-X) Dramatists Play.

***Magic Adventures of Mumfie.** Britt Allcroft. (Illus.). (J). 2000. 5.99 (0-375-80097-2, Pub. by Random Bks Yng Read) Random.

Magic Amber. Charles Reasoner. LC 93-43180. (Legends of the World Ser.). (Illus.). 32p. (J). (gr. 2-5). 1994. pap. 4.95 (0-8167-3408-9) Troll Communs.

Magic Amber. Charles Reasoner. LC 93-43180. (Legends of the World Ser.). (Illus.). 32p. (J). (gr. 2-5). 1997. lib. bdg. 18.60 (0-8167-3407-0) Troll Communs.

Magic Amber: A Korean Legend. Charles Reasoner. LC 93-43180. (Legends of the World Ser.). 1994. 9.15 (0-606-06550-4, Pub. by Turtleback) Demco.

***Magic & Craft of Media Writing.** Carl Sessions Stepp. LC 99-56108. 320p. 2000. pap. 14.95 (0-658-00874-9, 008749, Teach Yrslf) NTC Contemp Pub Co.

Magic & Divination at the Courts of Burgundy & France: Text & Context of Laurens Pignon's Contre les Devineurs (1411) Jan R. Veenstra. LC 97-35526. (Studies in Intellectual History: No. 83). 410p. 1997. 132.00 (90-04-10925-0) Brill Academic Pubs.

Magic & Divination in Ancient Palestine & Syria. Ann Jeffers. LC 95-49418. (Studies in the History of the Ancient Near East: Vol. 8). 1996. 100.50 (90-04-10513-1) Brill Academic Pubs.

Magic & Divination in the Middle Ages: Texts & Techniques in the Islamic & Christian Worlds. Charles Burnett. LC 96-30650. (Collected Studies: Vol. CS557). 384p. 1996. 109.95 (0-86078-615-3, Pub. by Variorum) Ashgate Pub Co.

Magic & Loss. Greg R. Lampman. LC 95-131071. 184p. (Orig.). 1994. 18.95 (1-57174-017-1); pap. 9.95 (1-57174-015-5) Hampton Roads Pub Co.

Magic & Madness in the Library: Protagonists among the Stacks. Ray Bradbury. Ed. & Intro. by Eric Graeber. 160p. 1998. pap. 19.00 (0-913559-36-9) Birch Brook Pr.

Magic & Madness in the Library: Protagonists among the Stacks. aut. limited num. ed. Ray Bradbury. Ed. & Intro. by Eric Graeber. 160p. 1998. 60.00 (0-913559-37-7) Birch Brook Pr.

Magic & Magicians see Unexplained

Magic & Medicine of Plants. Reader's Digest Editors. LC 85-30101. (Illus.). 464p. 1986. 27.95 (0-89577-221-3, Pub. by RD Assn) Penguin Putnam.

Magic & Medicine of Plants. Storey Publishing Staff. 1997. 28.00 (0-676-57141-7) Random.

Magic & Mischief: Tales from Cornwall. Illus. by Anthony Bacon Venti. LC 97-34091. 144p. (J). (gr. 2-7). 1999. 17.00 (0-395-86968-4, Clarion Bks) HM.

Magic & Moonbeams. Margot Dalton. (Superromance Ser.: No. 431). 1990. per. 2.95 (0-373-70431-3) Harlequin Bks.

Magic & Moonbeams. Margot Dalton. (Men at Work Ser.: Vol. 15). 1998. mass mkt. 4.50 (0-373-81027-X, 1-81027-4) Harlequin Bks.

Magic & Moonlight, 1. Sharon Pisacreta. (Love Spell Ser.). 368p. 1999. mass mkt. 5.50 (0-8439-4541-9) Dorchester Pub Co.

Magic & Moonlight: Quick & Easy Projects for the Modern Home. Patricia Meehan. (Patricia Meehan's Stencil Classics Ser.). (Illus.). 32p. 1999. pap. 12.95 (1-85585-667-0, Pub. by Collins & Br) Sterling.

Magic & Music of Perfumes. Eduard Maurer & R. Christopher Abel. 1996. reprint ed. pap. 4.95 (1-55818-351-5, Sure Fire) Holmes Pub.

Magic & Mysteries of Mexico: The Arcane Secrets & Occult Lore of the Ancient Mexicans &... Lewis Spence. 1994. pap. 14.95 (0-87877-193-X) Newcastle Pub.

***Magic & Mystery in Ancient Egypt.** Christian Jacq. 2000. pap. 14.95 (0-285-63462-3, Pub. by Souvenir Pr Ltd) IPG Chicago.

Magic & Mystery in Tibet. Alexandra David-Neel. (Illus.). 321p. 1971. pap. 8.95 (0-486-22682-4) Dover.

Magic & Mystery in Tibet. Alexandra David-Neel. LC 93-38172. (Collector's Library of the Unknown). (Illus.). 320p. 1994. reprint ed. write for info. (0-8094-8406-4) Time-Life.

***Magic & Mystery of Trees: A Beginner's Guide.** Teresa Moorey. (Headway Guides for Beginners Ser.). (Illus.). 96p. 2000. pap. 11.95 (0-340-77204-2, Pub. by Headway) Trafalgar.

Magic & Mystery of Trees: A Beginner's Guide. Teresa Moorey. (Beginner's Guide Ser.). (Illus.). 86p. 1998. pap. 11.95 (0-340-70494-2, Pub. by Hodder & Stought Ltd) Trafalgar.

Magic & Mystery of Westville. William W. Winn & Mike Haskey. LC 98-55429. 1998. write for info. (0-9666090-0-X) Westville Hist Hand.

Magic & Mysticism: Studies in Bygone Beliefs. H. Stanley Redgrove. 1970. 7.95 (0-8216-0111-3) Carol Pub Group.

Magic & Mystics of Java. Nina Epton. 212p. 1974. 26.00 (0-900860-39-1, Pub. by Octagon Pr) ISHK.

Magic & Myth of the Movies. Parker Tyler. LC 82-49240. (Cinema Classics Ser.). 209p. 1985. lib. bdg. 11.00 (0-8240-5783-X) Garland.

Magic & Perception: The Art & Science of Fooling the Senses. Robert Friedhoffer. (Illus.). 48p. (J). (gr. 6-8). 1996. lib. bdg. 24.00 (0-531-11254-3) Watts.

Magic & Perception: The Art & Science of Fooling the Senses. Robert Friedhoffer. (Illus.). 96p. (J). (gr. 6-8). 1996. pap. 6.95 (0-531-15803-9) Watts.

Magic & Power of Lavender. Maggie Tisserand & Monika Juenemann. 133p. (Orig.). 1994. pap. 9.95 (0-941524-88-4) Lotus Pr.

Magic & Religion. Andrew Lang. LC 76-137255. reprint ed. 29.50 (0-404-03857-3) AMS Pr.

Magic & Religion. Andrew Lang. LC 69-13964. 316p. 1969. reprint ed. lib. bdg. 65.00 (0-8371-0933-7, LAMR) Greenwood.

Magic & Romance of Art Dolls. Stephanie Farago. LC 85-80880. (Illus.). 224p. (C). 1986. 49.95 (0-935363-00-9) Farago Pubns.

Magic & Science of Jewels & Stones, Vol. I. Isidore Kozminsky. 176p. 1988. 9.95 (0-9615875-6-3) Cassandra Pr.

Magic & Science of Jewels & Stones, Vol. II. Isidore Kozminsky. 168p. 1988. 9.95 (0-9615875-9-8) Cassandra Pr.

***Magic & Showmanship: A Handbook for Conjurers.** Henning Nelms. LC 99-52791. 2000. pap. 8.95 (0-486-41087-0) Dover.

Magic & Sorcery Dingbats Book. Carole Marsh. (Carole Marsh Dingbats Bks.). (Illus.). (J). (gr. 3-12). 1994. pap. 19.95 (0-7933-5378-5); lib. bdg. 29.95 (0-7933-5377-7); disk 29.95 (0-7933-5379-3) Gallopade Intl.

Magic & Sorcery in France: Sorcerers of Bygone. Robert Blanchard. 155p. (Orig.). 1994. 45.00 (1-57179-038-1) Intern Guild ASRS.

Magic & Spells. Hugh Kenner. (Chapbooks in Literature Ser.). (Illus.). 29p. 1987. pap. text 5.00 (0-9614940-8-5) Bennington Coll.

Magic & the Healing. Nick O'Donohoe. 352p. (Orig.). 1994. pap. text 4.99 (0-441-00053-3) Ace Bks.

Magic & the Law: Keeping Your Organization Out of Trouble & How to Defeat a Wage Garnishment, Etc. Nelson H. White. LC 80-50273. (Magick & the Law Ser.: Vol. 4). (Illus.). 75p. (Orig.). 1982. pap. 20.00 (0-939856-25-5) Tech Group.

Magic & the Law: or Getting What You Want from the Government, the Courts, & Private Persons, Inc. & Protecting What You Write & Say, Bk. 3, Pts. I-IV. Nelson H. White. LC 80-50273. (Illus.). 125p. 1980. pap. 25.00 (0-939856-09-3) Tech Group.

Magic & the Law: or How to Keep What You've Got & How to Protect Yourself from Assorted Crooks & Nuts. Nelson H. White. LC 80-50273. (Magick & the Law Ser.: Vol. 2). (Illus.). 100p. (Orig.). 1980. pap. 20.00 (0-939856-08-5) Tech Group.

Magic & the Law: or How to Organize & Operate Your Own Occult Church, Coven or Lodge. rev. ed. Nelson H. White. LC 76-7197. (Magick & the Law Ser.: Vol. 1). (Illus.). 48p. (Orig.). 1976. pap. 18.00 (0-939856-02-6) Tech Group.

Magic & the Law: or How to Set-Up & Operate Your Own Occult Shop. Nelson H. White. LC 80-50273. (Magick & the Law Ser.: Vol. 5). (Illus.). 85p. (Orig.). 1982. pap. 25.00 (0-939856-31-X) Tech Group.

Magic & The Pain. Fran C. Goodman. 225p. 1994. 10.95 (0-9643473-0-X) Francie PR.

Magic & the Tarot: Using Tarot to Manipulate the Unseen Powers of the Universe. Tony Willis. (Illus.). 272p. (Orig.). 1987. pap. 12.95 (0-85030-625-6, Pub. by Aqrn Pr) HarpC.

Magic & the Texan. Martha Hix. 320p. 1998. mass mkt. 4.99 (0-8217-5822-5, Zebra Kensgtn) Kensgtn Pub Corp.

Magic & the Western Mind: Ancient Knowledge & the Transformation of Consciousness. Gareth Knight. LC 90-27860. (Llewellyn's Western Magick Historical Ser.). (Illus.). 240p. 1991. pap. 12.95 (0-87542-374-4) Llewellyn Pubns.

Magic & Witchcraft in the Dark Ages. Eugene D. Dukes. LC 95-39869. 322p. (C). 1996. pap. text 29.00 (0-7618-0148-0); lib. bdg. 44.00 (0-7618-0147-2) U Pr of Amer.

Magic & You see Magia y Tu

Magic Animals of Japan. Davis Pratt. LC 67-17483. (Illus.). (J). (gr. 1-4). 1967. lib. bdg. 5.88 (0-87466-020-3) HM.

Magic Apostrophe. 2nd ed. Jenny Sullivan. 213p. (J). (gr. 4). 1996. reprint ed. pap. 15.95 (0-8464-4843-2) Beekman Pubs.

Magic Apple House. Cuteco. (DA - Computer Education Ser.). (J). (gr. k-8). 1996. pap., suppl. ed. 7.95 (0-538-66385-5); pap., suppl. ed. 24.95 (0-538-66386-3) S-W Pub.

Magic Apple House. Cuteco. (DA - Computer Education Ser.). (J). (gr. k-8). 1996. pap. 7.95 (0-538-66389-8); pap., suppl. ed. 7.95 (0-538-66387-1); pap., suppl. ed. 24.95 (0-538-66388-X); pap., suppl. ed. 24.95 (0-538-66390-1) S-W Pub.

***Magic Apple House: Grade K-2 Basic Skills Builder.** McGraw-Hill Staff. 1999. pap. 19.95 (1-57768-302-1) MG-Hill OH.

Magic Apple Tree: A Country Year. large type ed. Susan Hill. 1983. 15.95 (0-7089-0987-6) Ulverscroft.

Magic Ark. Peggy Wang. 90p. (Orig.). (J). pap., pap. text 9.95 incl. audio (0-88710-143-7) Yale Far Eastern Pubns.

Magic Ark. Peggy Wang. 90p. (Orig.). 1986. 18.90 incl. audio (0-685-12386-3) Yale Far Eastern Pubns.

Magic Arts in Celtic Britain. Lewis Spence. (Illus.). 208p. (C). 1995. reprint ed. pap. 22.50 (0-89341-763-7) Hollowbrook.

Magic Arts in Celtic Britain. Lewis Spence. 211p. 1996. reprint ed. pap. 13.95 (1-56459-517-X) Kessinger Pub.

Magic Arts in Celtic Britain. unabridged ed. Lewis Spence. LC 98-37461. 198p. 1999. pap. 7.95 (0-486-40447-1) Dover.

Magic Arts in Celtic Britain. 2nd ed. Lewis Spence. (Illus.). 1996. reprint ed. pap. 14.95 (0-87877-233-2) Newcastle Pub.

Magic at Our Hand. Nancy R. Exeter. (Illus.). 234p. (Orig.). 1988. pap. 11.95 (0-935427-15-5) Foundation Hse.

Magic Attic Club Series Boxed Set: Alison on the Trail; Keisha the Fairy Queen; Cowgirl Megan; Heather, Belle of the Ball, 4 vols., Set. Trisha Magraw & Sheri Cooper Sinykin. (Magic Attic Club Ser.). (Illus.). (J). (gr. 2-6). 1995. boxed set 22.95 (1-57513-030-0) Magic Attic.

Magic Attic Club Series Boxed Set: Alison Saves the Wedding; Heather Takes the Reins; Keisha Leads the Way; Downhill Megan, 4 vols., Set. Trisha Magraw & Sheri Cooper Sinykin. (Magic Attic Club Ser.). (Illus.). (J). (gr. 2-6). 1996. boxed set 22.95 (1-57513-033-5) Magic Attic.

Magic Attic Club Series Boxed Set: Cheyenne Rose; Rose Faces the Music; Rose's Magic Touch; Trapped Beyond the Magic Attic; The Secret of the Attic, 5 vols., Set. Incl. Cheyenne Rose. Laura E. Williams. Ed. by Susan Korman. LC 97-27256. (Illus.). 80p. (J). (gr. 2-6). 1997. pap. 5.95 (1-57513-103-X); Rose Faces the Music. L. E. Williams & Nina Alexander. Ed. by Susan Korman. LC 97-27263. (Illus.). 72p. (J). (gr. 2-6). 1997. pap. 5.95 (1-57513-107-2); Rose's Magic Touch. Nina Alexander & Laura E. Williams. Ed. by Susan Korman. LC 97-28008. (Illus.). 72p. (J). (gr. 2-6). 1997. pap. 5.95 (1-57513-105-6); Secret of the Attic. Sheri Cooper Sinykin. (Illus.). 80p. (J). (gr. 2-6). 1995. 12.95 (1-57513-000-9); Trapped Beyond the Magic Attic. Sheri Cooper Sinykin. Ed. by Judith Bodnar. LC 97-28005. (Illus.). 72p. (J). (gr. 2-6). 1997. pap. 5.95 (1-57513-101-3); (Magic Attic Club Ser.). (J). (gr. 2-6). Set pap. 22.95 (1-57513-110-2) Magic Attic.

Magic Attic Club Series Boxed Set: Cheyenne Rose; Rose Faces the Music; Rose's Magic Touch; Trapped Beyond the Magic Attic; The Secret of the Attic, 5 vols., Set. L. E. Williams et al. (Magic Attic Club Ser.). 80p. (J). (gr. 3-6). 1999. 49.95 (1-57513-111-0, Pendant Press) Magic Attic.

Magic Attic Club Series Boxed Set: The Secret of the Attic; Three Cheers for Keisha; Alison Goes for the Gold; Princess Megan; Heather at the Barre, 5 vols., Set. Trisha Magraw & Sheri Cooper Sinykin. (Magic Attic Club Ser.). (Illus.). (J). (gr. 2-6). 1995. pap., boxed set 22.95 (1-57513-029-7) Magic Attic.

Magic Babushka. Phyllis L. Tildes. LC 97-14274. (Illus.). 32p. (J). (ps-3). 1998. 15.95 (0-88106-840-3, Talewinds) Charlesbridge Pub.

Magic Background of Modern Anti-Semitism: An Analysis of the German-Jewish Relationship. Adolf Leschnitzer. LC 55-6501. 246p. reprint ed. pap. 76.30 (0-608-11737-4, 201043700070) Bks Demand.

Magic Badge. Norman Friedman. 48p. (Orig.). 1984. pap. 4.50 (0-941720-16-0) Slough Pr TX.

Magic Badgerkettle & A Spouse for A Mouse. LC 94-46335. 1995. 17.00 (4-7700-1941-6) Kodansha.

***Magic Barrel.** Bernard Malamud. 224p. 1999. pap. 12.00 (0-374-52586-2) FS&G.

M

*__Magic Barrel.__ large type ed. Bernard Malamud. LC 00-24297. 267p. 2000. 27.95 (*0-7838-9010-9*, G K Hall Lrg Type) Mac Lib Ref.

Magic Bat. Geoffrey Griffin. LC 94-40434. (Publish-a-Book Ser.). (Illus.). (J). (gr. 1-6). 1995. lib. bdg. 22.83 (*0-8114-7270-1*) Raintree Steck-V.

Magic Bean Tree: A Legend from Argentina. Nancy Van Laan. LC 96-38632. (Illus.). 32p. (J). (gr. k-5). 1998. 15.00 (*0-395-82746-9*) HM.

Magic Beans. Margaret Hillert. (Illus.). (J). (ps). 1966. pap. 5.10 (*0-8136-5553-6*, TK2339); lib. bdg. 7.95 (*0-8136-5053-4*, TK2338) Modern Curr.

Magic Beans: 150 Delicious Recipes Featuring Nature's Low Fat, Nutrient-Rich, Disease-Fighting. Patti Bazel Geil. 208p. 1996. pap. 12.95 (*0-471-34747-7*) Wiley.

Magic Beans: 150 Delicious Recipes Featuring Nature's Low Fat, Nutrient-Rich, Disease-Fighting. Patti B. Geil. 1996. pap. 12.95 (*1-56561-077-6*) Wiley.

Magic Behind the Tribbles. Erdmann. 1999. per. write for info. (*0-671-01943-0*) S&S Trade.

Magic Bicycle. John Bibee. LC 83-240. (Spirit Flyer Ser.: Vol. 1). (Illus.). 215p. (Orig.). (J). (gr. 4-9). 1983. pap. 6.99 (*0-87784-348-1*, 348) InterVarsity.

Magic Bicycle. William Hill. LC 97-66907. 323p. (YA). (gr. 7-12). 1998. pap. 13.95 (*1-890611-00-X*, 00-X) Otter Crk Pr.

Magic Bicycle. William Hill. LC 97-66907. 328p. (gr. 3-10). 1998. 22.95 (*1-890611-07-7*, 07-7) Otter Crk Pr.

Magic Bird. Elizabeth Ballinger. (Illus.). 64p. (J). (gr. 3-5). 1994. pap. 6.95 (*1-879331-45-4*, Classc Pub) Marciel Pub & Print.

Magic Bishop: Hugo Ball, Dada Poet. Erdmute W. White. LC 98-21817. (Studies in German Literature, Linguistics & Culture). 180p. 1998. 55.00 (*1-57113-128-0*) Camden Hse.

Magic, Black & White, Charmes & Counter Charmes, Divination & Demonology among the Hindus, Hebrews, Arabs & Egyptians. T. Witton Davies. 130p. 1972. reprint ed. spiral bd. 13.50 (*0-7873-0239-2*) Hlth Research.

Magic Blanket That Made All Dreams Happy! Nancy E. Johnson. (Illus.). 42p. (J). (ps-1). 1994. lib. bdg. 10.95 (*0-614-08417-2*); lib. bdg. 29.95 (*0-9642307-0-4*) TotTales.

Magic Bones. Abhijit Sen & Papri S. Raman. 264p. (YA). (gr. 9-10). 1992. 14.95 (*0-932377-49-1*) Facet Bks.

Magic Book. Ed. by Lydia Darbyshire. (Illus.). 224p. 1997. 19.98 (*0-7858-0791-8*) Bk Sales Inc.

*__Magic Book: Divine Ways to Live Your Life Wisely.__ Nicole Sommesous. 2000. 10.95 (*0-7225-3898-7*) Thorsons PA.

Magic Bookshelf: A Parents' Guide to Showing Growing Minds the Path to the Best Children's Literature. Janie Jarvis & Richard Jarvis. LC 98-96291. 155p. 1999. pap. 16.95 (*0-9665111-0-7*) Lorica.

Magic Boot. Remy Simard. (Illus.). 24p. (J). (ps-2). 1995. pap. 5.95 (*1-55037-410-9*, Pub. by Annick); text 16.95 (*1-55037-411-7*, Pub. by Annick) Firefly Bks Ltd.

Magic Boots. Scott Emerson. (Illus.). 32p. (J). (ps-3). 1999. reprint ed. pap. 6.95 (*0-87905-874-9*) Gibbs Smith Pub.

Magic Bow & Silver Flute. Chen Li. (Asian Folk Tales Ser.). (Illus.). 24p. (J). 1995. 9.95 (*983-9808-67-2*, Pub. by Delta Edits) Weatherhill.

Magic Box see Three Magic Flip Books

Magic Box see Bank Street Ready-to-Read Books: Levels 1, 2 & 3

Magic Box. (ARA., Illus.). 100p. (YA). pap. 5.95 (*0-86685-743-5*, LDL946, Pub. by Librairie du Liban) Intl Bk Ctr.

Magic Box. Dale Bulla. (Illus.). 24p. (J). (gr. 2-6). 1993. 14.95 (*1-884197-00-0*) N Horizon Educ.

Magic Box. Dale Bulla. (Illus.). 24p. (J). (gr. 2-6). 1994. pap. 6.95 (*1-884197-04-3*) N Horizon Educ.

Magic Box. Olga Cossi. LC 89-8461. 192p. (YA). 1990. pap. 12.95 (*1-56554-381-5*) Pelican.

Magic Box. Olga Cossi. LC 89-8461. 192p. (YA). (gr. 12). 1990. 12.95 (*0-88289-748-9*) Pelican.

Magic Box. Helena Miller. Ed. by Joel Lurie Grishaver. (Illus.). (Orig.). (J). (gr. k up). 1996. pap. text 18.95 (*0-933873-92-1*) Torah Aura.

Magic Boxes: Children & Black English. Marilyn S. Rosenthal. LC PE3102.N42R6. (CAL-ERIC - CLL Series on Languages & Linguistics: No. 43). 79p. reprint ed. pap. 30.00 (*0-8357-3360-2*, 203959800013) Bks Demand.

Magic Boy & Girlfriend. James Kochalka. (Illus.). 144p. 1998. pap. 8.95 (*1-891830-03-1*) Top Shelf Prodns.

Magic Braid. Rina Singh. (Illus.). (J). Date not set. pap. write for info. (*0-920813-25-9*) Sister Vis Pr.

Magic Bubble Trip. Ingrid Schubert & Dieter Schubert. LC 84-25071.Tr. of Helemaal Verkikkerd. (Illus.). 32p. (J). (ps-3). 1985. 11.95 (*0-916291-02-2*); pap. 6.95 (*0-916291-03-0*) Kane-Miller Bk.

Magic Bullet. large type ed. Harry Stein. LC 94-49409. 544p. 1995. lib. bdg. 24.95 (*0-7838-1226-4*, G K Hall Lrg Type) Mac Lib Ref.

Magic Bullets, Friendly Fire & the Umbrella Man. Carl Sifakis. 1996. 25.00 (*0-8050-4791-3*) H Holt & Co.

*__Magic by Daylight.__ Lynn Bailey. (Magical Love Ser.). 1999. mass mkt. 5.99 (*0-515-12701-9*, Jove) Berkley Pub.

Magic by Gosh: The Life Times of Albert Goshman. Patrick Page & Albert Goshman. Ed. by Kathy Diamond. LC 85-90956. (Illus.). 160p. 1985. 49.95 (*0-318-19317-5*) Magic By Gosh.

Magic by the Bay: How the San Francisco Giants & Oakland Athletics Captured the Baseball World. John Shea & John Hickey. LC 90-31854. (Illus.). 334p. (Orig.). 1990. pap. 12.95 (*1-55643-086-8*) North Atlantic.

*__Magic by the Lake.__ Edward Eager. LC 85-7654. (Illus.). 208p. (J). 1999. 17.00 (*0-15-202077-2*, Harcourt Child Bks); pap. 6.00 (*0-15-202076-4*, Harcourt Child Bks) Harcourt.

*__Magic Camera.__ Ed. by Brent Thomas. LC 00-102513. (The Magic Camera: 1). (J). (gr. 4-7). 2000. pap. 11.95 (*0-9666919-3-8*) Independent Spirit.

*__Magic Can Be Murder.__ Vivian Vande Velde. LC 00-8595. (Illus.). 192p. (J). (gr. 8-12). 2000. 17.00 (*0-15-202665-7*, Harcourt Child Bks) Harcourt.

Magic Candle. Charmaine Dey. 62p. 1982. pap. 4.95 (*0-942272-00-5*) Original Pubns.

Magic Cantina. Robert L. Leach. 128p. 1999. pap. 9.95 (*0-9668580-0-X*) Vast Sky.

Magic Cap. Lisa W. Gilbert & Flavia M. Weedn. LC 94-32814. (Flavia's Dream Maker Stories Ser.: No. 5). (Illus.). 48p. (J). (ps-3). 1995. 10.95 (*0-7868-0119-0*, Pub. by Hyprn Child) Time Warner.

Magic Cap Companion. Danny Goodman. 1996. pap. write for info. (*0-201-40794-9*) Addison-Wesley.

Magic Cap Complete: The Official Guide to All the Capabilities of Magic Cap Communicators. General Magic, Inc. Staff. 608p. 1995. pap. 29.95 (*0-201-48948-1*) Addison-Wesley.

Magic Cap Programmer's Cookbook. Barry Boone. 384p. 1995. pap. 44.95 (*0-201-40953-4*) Addison-Wesley.

Magic Cap Programming. Andrew Novobiliski. 1996. pap. write for info. (*0-201-40954-2*) Addison-Wesley.

Magic Card Tricks. Jack Mingo. (Illus.). 96p. 1995. pap. 14.95 (*0-8092-3446-7*, 344670, Contemporary Bks) NTC Contemp Pub Co.

Magic Cards Simplified: For Player Parents & Beginning Players of Magic, the Gathering. George Baxter & Russell A. Stultz. LC 96-41000. viii, 125 p. 1997. pap. 7.95 (*1-55622-522-9*) Wordware Pub.

*__Magic Carousel Pony.__ Jerry Smath. (Jewel Sticker Stories Ser.). (Illus.). 24p. (J). (ps-2). 1999. pap. 3.99 (*0-448-41959-9*, G & D) Peng Put Young Read.

Magic Carpet: Aleppo in Flatbush: The Story of a Unique Ethnic Jewish Community. 4th ed. Joseph A. Sutton. LC 79-65516. (Illus.). 336p. 1991. text 24.95 (*0-686-27080-0*) Thayer-Jacoby.

Magic Carpet & Other Tales. Illus. by Walter Anderson. LC 87-10434. 186p. (J). (ps up). 1997. reprint ed. 50.00 (*0-87805-327-1*) U Pr of Miss.

Magic Carpet Ride. Jerry Smath. LC 99-208996. (Jewel Sticker Stories Ser.). (Illus.). 24p. 1998. pap. text 3.99 (*0-448-41835-5*, G & D) Peng Put Young Read.

Magic Carpet Ride: Integrating Technology into the K-12 Classroom. Annette Lamb. (Illus.). 211p. (C). 1997. pap. text 23.95 (*0-9641581-5-9*) Vision to Action.

Magic Carpet Ride: Integrating Technology into the K-12 Classroom. 2nd ed. Annette Lamb. 211p. (C). 1998. pap. 28.95 (*0-9641581-8-3*) Vision to Action.

Magic Carpetry: Flying Your Car with Your Mind. Jo Claire. LC 90-85490. (Orig.). 1991. pap. 9.50 (*0-9628554-0-5*) Eureka Bks.

Magic Carpets. Nick Bantock. 1999. pap. 18.95 (*0-670-85589-8*) Viking Penguin.

Magic Carpets. Lucy Keane. (Romance Ser.: No. 178). 1992. per. 2.79 (*0-373-03178-5*, 1-03178-0) Harlequin Bks.

Magic Casement. Dave Duncan. (The Wizards of Fantasy Promotion: Pt. 1). 320p. (Orig.). 1990. mass mkt. 4.95 (*0-345-36628-X*, Del Rey) Ballantine Pub Grp.

Magic Casements: The Use of Poetry in the Expanding of Consciousness. 2nd ed. George Trevelyab. 64p. 1996. pap. write for info. (*1-85860-047-2*) ACCESS Pubs Network.

Magic Castle. Carole Smith. LC 97-36513. 288p. 1998. text 23.95 (*0-312-17196-X*) St Martin.

Magic Castle. Carole Smith. 1999. mass mkt. 6.99 (*0-312-96820-5*) St Martin.

Magic Caterpillar. Bernice Brown. Ed. by Jeff Eberspacher. (Illus.). 48p. (J). (gr. k-3). 1992. pap. 6.95 (*1-877740-20-9*); lib. bdg., boxed set 11.95 (*1-877740-19-5*) Nel-Mar Pub.

Magic Cauldron: Witchcraft for Good & Evil. Margaret O'Connell. LC 75-26757. (Illus.). 256p. (J). (gr. 9-12). 1975. 38.95 (*0-87599-187-4*) S G Phillips.

Magic Cellar. Colene Copeland. (Illus.). 94p. (J). (gr. 1-7). 1995. 8.95 (*0-938810-17-0*) Jordan Valley.

*__Magic Charms from A to Z.__ 1999. pap. 12.95 (*1-881098-12-5*, Pub. by Witches Almanac) Consort Bk Sales.

Magic Chest: Where You Are, Where You've Been, Where You're Going. Cornelia H. Eulert. LC 97-43841. 160p. 1998. pap. 25.95 (*1-56032-738-3*) Hemisp Pub.

Magic Chest of Oz. Donald Abbott. (Illus.). 119p. (J). (gr. 3 up). 1993. pap. 9.95 (*0-929605-20-9*) Books of Wonder.

Magic Child. Kit Basom. 272p. (C). 1992. pap. write for info. (*1-874640-15-7*, Pub. by Argyll Pubng) St Mut.

Magic Child: All about Love & Power from the Inside Out. Jane Meyers. LC 98-74025. (Illus.). 332p. 1999. pap. 19.95 (*1-58151-020-9*) BookPartners.

Magic Chopsticks. large type ed. Patricia P. Pyne. (Illus.). 24p. (J). (gr. 1-8). 1996. lib. bdg. 14.95 (*0-9655465-9-4*) Pelican Pub.

Magic Christian. Terry Southern. 160p. 1996. reprint ed. pap. 11.00 (*0-8021-3465-3*, Grove) Grove-Atltic.

Magic Christmas. Created by Francine Pascal. (Sweet Valley Twins Magna Edition Ser.: No. 1). 256p. (J). (gr. 3-7). 1992. pap. 3.99 (*0-553-48051-0*) Bantam.

Magic Christmas: A Play for Children in One Act. Faye Julian. (Illus.). 28p. (J). (gr. k-12). 1983. pap. 3.00 (*0-88680-121-4*) I E Clark.

Magic Christmas Pony. Regina F. Cooley. LC 91-76342. (Illus.). 36p. (J). (gr. 1-5). 1991. 19.95 (*1-880450-04-6*) Capstone Pub.

Magic Christmas Stocking. Louise B. Egan. (Illus.). 52p. (J). 1994. 16.95 (*0-8362-4510-5*) Andrews & McMeel.

*__Magic Christmas Tree.__ Carolyn Irby. 16p. (J). (gr. k-3). 1999. pap. 7.00 (*0-8059-4642-X*) Dorrance.

Magic Circle. Donna J. Napoli. (Illus.). 128p. (YA). (gr. 7 up). 1995. pap. 4.99 (*0-14-037439-6*, PuffinBks) Peng Put Young Read.

Magic Circle. Donna Jo Napoli. 1995. 9.60 (*0-606-07818-5*, Pub. by Turtleback) Demco.

Magic Circle. Katherine Neville. 1999. mass mkt. 7.99 (*0-345-42313-5*) Ballantine Pub Grp.

Magic Circle: Preschool & Kindergarten Activity Guide. Gerry Dunne & George Hadley. (Illus.). 117p. (J). 1996. spiral bd. 21.95 (*1-56499-031-1*, IP9031) Innerchoice Pub.

Magic City. Yusef Komunyakaa. LC 92-53863. (Wesleyan Poetry Ser.). 68p. 1992. pap. 12.95 (*0-8195-1208-7*, Wesleyan Univ Pr); text 25.00 (*0-8195-2205-8*, Wesleyan Univ Pr) U Pr of New Eng.

*__Magic City.__ E. Nesbit. (Illus.). (J). 2000. 14.95 (*1-58717-024-8*) SeaStar.

*__Magic City.__ E. Nesbit & H. R. Millar. LC 00-25204. (Illus.). (J). 2000. pap. write for info. (*1-58717-025-6*) SeaStar.

Magic City. James W. Buel. LC 74-15728. (Popular Culture in America Ser.). (Illus.). 294p. 1975. reprint ed. 87.95 (*0-405-06364-4*) Ayer.

Magic City. Edith Nesbit. (Illus.). 224p. (J). (gr. 3 up). 1996. reprint ed. 24.95 (*0-929605-62-4*); reprint ed. pap. 12.95 (*0-929605-53-5*) Books of Wonder.

Magic City: A Novel. Jewell P. Rhodes. 288p. 1998. pap. 13.00 (*0-06-092907-3*) HarpC.

Magic City: Unemployment in a Working-Class Community. Gregory Pappas. LC 88-47935. (Anthropology of Contemporary Issues Ser.). (Illus.). 232p. 1989. 39.95 (*0-8014-2277-9*) Cornell U Pr.

Magic City: Unemployment in a Working-Class Community. Gregory Pappas. LC 88-47935. (Anthropology of Contemporary Issues Ser.). (Illus.). 224p. reprint ed. pap. 69.50 (*0-608-20094-8*, 207136600011) Bks Demand.

Magic Cloud. (Teletubbies 11x11 Coloring Activity Bks.: Vol. 2). (Illus.). 24p. (J). 1998. pap. write for info. (*0-7666-0260-5*, Honey Bear Bks) Modern Pub NYC.

Magic Code: The Use of Magical Patterns in Fantasy for Children. Maria Nikolajeva. (Studies Published by the Swedish Institute for Children's Books). 163p. (Orig.). 1988. pap. 46.00 (*91-22-01200-1*) Coronet Bks.

Magic Corn. Holli C. Persall. (Illus.). 24p. (J). (gr. k-4). 1990. 10.95 (*0-9628486-0-3*) Rhyme Time.

Magic Cornfield. Barbara Willard. LC 96-24850. (Illus.). 48p. (J). 1997. 16.00 (*0-15-201428-4*) Harcourt.

Magic Crayon. Tony Palazzo. (Illus.). (J). (gr. k-2). 1967. lib. bdg. 12.95 (*0-87460-089-8*) Lion Bks.

Magic Crayon. Molly Piper. (Illus.). 32p. (J). (gr. k-5). 1997. pap. 5.95 (*1-891360-00-0*) Little Deer.

Magic Crocodile & Other Folktales from Indonesia. Illus. by Charlene K. Smoyer. LC 94-10876. 144p. (J). (gr. 5-9). 1994. 16.95 (*0-8248-1654-4*, Kolowalu Bk) UH Pr.

Magic Crossbow: Beginning Through Intermediate. (Bilingual Readers in Vietnamese & English Ser.). (ENG & VIE., Illus.). 1998. pap. 8.40 (*0-8442-6111-4*, E6111-4) NTC Contemp Pub Co.

*__Magic Crystal?__ Louis Sachar. (Marvin Redpost Ser.: Vol. 8). (Illus.). 80p. (J). (ps-3). 2000. pap. 3.99 (*0-679-89002-5*) Random.

*__Magic Crystal?__ Louis Sachar. (Marvin Redpost Ser.: Vol. 8). (Illus.). 80p. (J). (ps-3). 2000. 11.99 (*0-679-99002-X*) Random Bks Yng Read.

Magic Crystal. Heather Maisner. LC 95-39346. (Candlewick Gamebook Ser.). (Illus.). 32p. (J). (gr. 3-6). 1997. reprint ed. pap. 7.99 (*0-7636-0140-3*) Candlewick Pr.

Magic Crystal: A Wildlife Adventure Game. Heather Maisner. LC 95-39346. (Illus.). 32p. (J). (gr. 4-7). 1996. pap. 14.99 (*1-56402-867-4*) Candlewick Pr.

Magic Cubes: New Recreations, 2 pts., Set. William H. Benson & Oswald Jacoby. (Illus.). 96p. (Orig.). 1982. pap. 5.95 (*0-486-24140-8*) Dover.

Magic Cures & Incantations. John L. Heatwole. (Virginia & West Virginia Mountain & Valley Folklife Ser.). (Illus.). 32p. 1997. pap. 6.00 (*1-893934-00-4*) Mt Folklife Series.

Magic Cylinder Book: Hidden Pictures to Color & Discover. Ivan Moscovich. (J). 1991. pap. 7.95 (*0-906212-67-7*, Pub. by Tarquin Pubns) Parkwest Pubns.

Magic Dance: The Display of the Self-Nature of the Five Wisdom Dakinis. Thinley Norbu. LC 98-20349. (Orig.). 1998. pap. 14.00 (*0-87773-885-8*, Pub. by Shambhala Pubns) Random.

Magic Daughter: A Memoir of Living with Multiple Personality Disorder. Jane Phillips. 238p. 1999. reprint ed. text 23.00 (*0-7881-5682-9*) DIANE Pub.

Magic Detectives: Join Them in Solving Strange Mysteries. Joe Nickell. LC 89-62787. (Young Readers Ser.). (Illus.). 115p. (J). (gr. 4-9). 1989. pap. 9.95 (*0-87975-547-4*) Prometheus Bks.

Magic Disc. Janie S. Gill. 23p. (J). 1999. 5.95 (*0-89868-492-7*); pap. 3.95 (*0-89868-491-9*); lib. bdg. 10.95 (*0-89868-490-0*) ARO Pub.

Magic Dishpan of Oz. Jeff Freedman. (Illus.). 120p. (J). (gr. 2 up). 1995. 34.95 (*0-929605-36-5*); pap. 9.95 (*0-929605-35-7*) Books of Wonder.

Magic, Divination & Demonology among the Hebrews & Their Neighbors. Thomas W. Davies. 1970. 15.00 (*0-87068-051-X*) Ktav.

Magic, Divination & Demonology among the Hebrews & Their Neighbors, 1898. T. Witton Davies. 150p. 1993. reprint ed. pap. 14.75 (*1-56459-412-2*) Kessinger Pub.

Magic Dog: And Other Stories. Antonio B. Rojo. Ed. by Frank Janney. 261p. 1990. 26.00 (*0-685-46973-5*); pap. 14.00 (*0-685-46974-3*) Ediciones Norte.

Magic Dogs of the Volcanoes. Manlio Argueta. 1995. 13.00 (*0-606-09582-9*, Pub. by Turtleback) Demco.

Magic Dogs of the Volcanoes (Los Perros Magicos de los Volcanes) Manlio Argueta. (ENG & SPA., Illus.). 32p. (J). (gr. 1 up). 1995. pap. 7.95 (*0-89239-129-4*) Childrens Book Pr.

Magic Dogs of the Volcanoes (Los Perros Magicos de los Volcanes) Manlio Argueta et al. LC 90-2254. (ENG & SPA., Illus.). 32p. (YA). (ps-3). 1990. 14.95 (*0-89239-064-6*) Childrens Book Pr.

Magic Dreidels: A Hanukkah Story. Eric A. Kimmel. LC 96-2405. (Illus.). 32p. (J). (gr. k-3). 1996. lib. bdg. 16.95 (*0-8234-1256-3*) Holiday.

Magic Dreidels: A Hanukkah Story. Eric A. Kimmel. LC 96-2405. (Illus.). 32p. (J). (ps-3). 1997. reprint ed. pap. 6.95 (*0-8234-1274-1*) Holiday.

Magic Drum: Stories from Africa's Savannah, Sea, & Skies. Robin Miranda. LC 95-981891. 1995. 12.95 (*9966-884-05-X*) Nocturnal Sun.

Magic Dulcimer. Lorraine Lee. LC 83-17125. (Illus.). 130p. 1983. pap. 12.95 (*0-938756-09-5*) Yellow Moon.

Magic Dwells: A Poetic & Psychological Study of the Navaho Emergence Myth. Sheila Moon. LC 85-12620. 206p. 1985. pap. 7.95 (*0-917479-06-8*) Guild Psy.

Magic Easter Egg. Ellen Patrick. LC 96-145410. (Easter Ornament Bks.). (Illus.). 8p. (J). (ps-3). 1996. 2.95 (*0-689-80784-8*) S&S Childrens.

Magic Egg & Other Stories. Frank R. Stockton. LC 75-132126. (Short Story Index Reprint Ser.). 1977. 18.95 (*0-8369-3683-3*) Ayer.

Magic Egg & Other Tales from Ukraine. Barbara J. Suwyn. Ed. by Natalie O. Kononenko. LC 97-6734. (Illus.). 210p. 1997. 29.50 (*1-56308-425-2*) Libs Unl.

Magic Elizabeth. Norma Kassirer. LC 98-45084. (Illus.). 176p. (J). (gr. 3-7). 1999. pap. 4.95 (*0-06-440748-9*, HarpTrophy) HarpC Child Bks.

Magic Engineer. L. E. Modesitt, Jr. (Saga of Recluce Ser.). 617p. 1995. mass mkt. 5.99 (*0-8125-3405-0*, Pub. by Tor Bks) St Martin.

Magic Everywhere: How to Perform Amazing Magic Using Everyday Household Objects. Mathew Costello. LC 98-40677. 144p. 1999. pap. 10.00 (*0-609-80357-3*) Crown Pub Group.

Magic Eye. N. E. Thing Enterprises Staff.Tr. of Oeil Magique. (FRE., Illus.). (J). pap. 7.99 (*0-590-24505-8*) Scholastic Inc.

Magic Eye: A New Bag of Tricks. N. E. Thing Enterprises Staff. (Illus.). 32p. 1995. 12.95 (*0-8362-0768-8*) Andrews & McMeel.

Magic Eye: The 3D Guide. N.E. Thing Enterprises Staff et al. (Illus.). 64p. 1995. 10.95 (*0-8362-0467-0*) Andrews & McMeel.

Magic Eye Gallery: A Showing of 88 Images. N. E. Thing Enterprises Staff. (Illus.). 96p. 1995. 12.95 (*0-8362-7044-4*) Andrews & McMeel.

Magic Eye Poster Book: A Book of Posters. N. E. Thing Enterprises Staff. 1994. pap. 12.95 (*0-8362-3203-8*) Andrews & McMeel.

Magic Eye III, Vol. III. N. E. Thing Enterprises Staff.Tr. of Oeil Magique III. (FRE., Illus.). (J). pap. 7.99 (*0-590-24610-0*) Scholastic Inc.

Magic Eyes: Scenes from an Andean Girlhood. Wendy Ewald. LC 92-53269. (Illus.). 180p. (Orig.). 1992. pap. 18.95 (*0-941920-21-6*) Bay Pr.

Magic, Faith & Healing: Studies in Primitive Psychiatry. Ed. by Ari Kiev. 496p. 1996. pap. 60.00 (*1-56821-809-5*) Aronson.

Magic Fan. Keith Baker. LC 88-18727. (Illus.). 32p. (J). (gr. k-3). 1989. 14.95 (*0-15-250750-7*) Harcourt.

Magic Fan. Keith Baker. (Illus.). 32p. (J). (gr. k-5). 1997. pap. 7.00 (*0-15-200983-3*, Voyager Bks) Harcourt.

Magic Fan. Keith Baker. 1997. 12.20 (*0-606-12408-X*, Pub. by Turtleback) Demco.

Magic Fan. 93rd ed. Keith Baker. 1993. pap. text 17.10 (*0-15-300334-0*, Harcourt Child Bks) Harcourt.

Magic Feather: A Jamaican Legend. Ed. by Lisa Rojany. LC 95-9982. (Legends of the World Ser.). (Illus.). 32p. (J). (gr. 2-6). 1997. lib. bdg. 18.60 (*0-8167-3751-7*) Troll Communs.

Magic Feather: A Jamaican Legend. Ed. by Lisa Rojany. LC 95-9982. (Illus.). 32p. (J). (gr. 2-6). 1998. pap. 4.95 (*0-8167-3752-5*) Troll Communs.

Magic Feather: A Jamaican Legend. Lisa Rojany. (Legends of the World Ser.). 1995. 9.15 (*0-606-07819-3*, Pub. by Turtleback) Demco.

Magic Finger. Roald Dahl. LC 66-18657. (Illus.). 46p. (J). (gr. 3-6). 1966. 15.00 (*0-06-021381-7*) HarpC Child Bks.

Magic Finger. Roald Dahl. LC 66-18657. (Trophy Picture Bk.). (Illus.). 48p. (J). (gr. 3-6). 1983. pap. 3.95 (*0-06-443045-6*, HarpTrophy) HarpC Child Bks.

Magic Finger. Roald Dahl. (Illus.). 64p. (J). (ps-12). 1996. 16.99 (*0-670-85252-X*, Viking Child) Peng Put Young Read.

Magic Finger. Roald Dahl. LC 96-45417. (Illus.). 63p. (J). (gr. 2-6). 1998. pap. 4.99 (*0-14-130229-1*, PuffinBks) Peng Put Young Read.

Magic Finger. Roald Dahl. LC 96-45417. 1997. 9.19 (*0-606-11588-9*, Pub. by Turtleback) Demco.

Magic Finger of Dahl. Roald Dahl. 64p. 1997. pap. write for info. (*0-14-037158-3*) Viking Penguin.

Magic Fingers. (J). (gr. 3-6). 1995. pap. 7.95 (*0-9647538-0-4*) Mulcahy Pubns.

Magic Fire. Judson Harriss. LC 86-25174. 1986. pap. 7.50 (*0-89314-421-5*) Philos Res.

Magic Fire. Christopher Pike, pseud. (YA). 1999. per. 4.50 (*0-671-02057-9*, Archway) PB.

Magic Fire. Christopher Pike, pseud. 1998. 9.60 (*0-606-13588-X*, Pub. by Turtleback) Demco.

Magic Fish. Freya Littledale. LC 86-189345. (Easy-to-Read Folktales Ser.). (Illus.). 32p. (J). (ps-3). 1986. pap. 2.99 (*0-590-41100-4*) Scholastic Inc.

An Asterisk (*) at the beginning of an entry indicates that the title is appearing for the first time.

Magic Fish. Freya Littledale. (Easy-to-Read Folktale Ser.). (J). 1985. 8.19 (*0-606-01145-5*, Pub. by Turtleback) Demco.

Magic Fish Rap. Jon Chardiet. 32p. (J). (gr. k-3). 1993. pap. 5.95 incl. audio (*0-590-66152-3*) Scholastic Inc.

Magic Fishbone. Charles Dickens. LC 96-53972. (Illus.). (J). 2000. 17.00 (*0-15-201080-7*, Harcourt Child Bks) Harcourt.

Magic Flight. **S. Bernadine Riske. LC 98-93138. (Illus.). 20p. (J). (gr. 5-12). 1998. pap. 9.95 (*1-885981-18-X*, Brisk Pubns) Brisk Pubng.**

Molly Mouse & Ollie Owl lived in the famous Shobird Theater until Molly Mouse heard people talking about moving the theater to make room for a shopping mall. Molly called out to Ollie Owl in the rafters in the theater, "They want to move our house:. What can we do? Molly mouse called a meeting with her friends in the park & Ollie came up with a plan to move their theater home. They caught a big balloon on the roof of the Shobird & tied it to the theater. The balloon rose into the skies with Mollie, Ollie & their friends, birds & animals, dogs & cats riding in a basket with the balloon that flew them out to sea where they saw many strange creatures. The west wind finally blew the balloon & its menagerie back to its home on land in Minnesota. The story based on current interest in balloons & present remodeling early historic theaters with popular appeal for children & adults, grades K - 12, all ages. Poetry. ***Publisher Paid Annotation.***

Magic Flower. Florence Baccus. 30p. (J). (ps-8). 1991. 12.95 (*0-9649059-0-6*) LilliBooks.

Magic Flower. Ida Vinson. 1999. pap. text 9.95 (*1-56492-272-3*) Laredo.

Magic Flute. David Foil. (Black Dog Opera Library).Tr. of Zauberflote. (Illus.). 142p. 1996. 19.98 (*1-884822-82-7*) Blck Dog & Leventhal.

Magic Flute. Ed. & Tr. by Nicholas John from GER. Tr. by Anthony Beasch from GER. (English National Opera Guide Series: Bilingual Libretto, Articles: No. 3).Tr. of Zauberflote. (Illus.). 1980. pap. 9.95 (*0-7145-3768-3*) Riverrun NY.

***Magic Flute.** Keith D. Jones. LC 99-91037. 214p. 1999. pap. 11.95 (*0-9674994-0-2*) Stormsdream.

Magic Flute. Wolfgang Amadeus Mozart. LC 97-1348. (Illus.). 40p. (YA). (gr. 3 up). 1997. 17.95 (*0-8118-1003-8*) Chronicle Bks.

***Magic Flute.** Wolfgang Amadeus Mozart & Emanuel Schikaneder. LC 00-25259.Tr. of Zauberflote. (Illus.). 2000. 50.00 incl. cd-rom (*0-7892-0645-5*) Abbeville Pr.

Magic Flute. June W. Rogers. 1976. pap. 5.25 (*0-87129-078-2*, M10) Dramatic Pub.

Magic Flute. Linda Rogers. 36p. 1992. pap. write for info. (*0-88984-129-2*) Porcup Quill.

Magic Flute: Easy Piano Picture Book. Amanda Holden. (Illus.). 48p. 1992. pap. 9.95 (*0-571-51112-0*) Faber & Faber.

Magic Flute: Libretto. Composed by Wolfgang Amadeus Mozart.Tr. of Zauberflaute. 56p. 1986. pap. 4.95 (*0-7935-2864-X*, 50340050) H Leonard.

Magic Flute: 1791 Libretto by Emanuel Schikaneder. Wolfgang Amadeus Mozart. Tr. & Intro. by Judith A. Eckelmeyer. LC 79-67268. xxix, 65p. 1980. lib. bdg. 39.95 (*0-88946-955-5*) E Mellen.

Magic Flute & Other Children's Stories. (J). (gr. 5 up). 1981. pap. 4.95 (*0-8351-0850-3*) China Bks.

Magic Flute Solos. 1990. 9.95 (*0-685-32112-6*, M386) Hansen Ed Mus.

Magic Flute Unveiled: Esoteric Symbolism in Mozart's Masonic Opera. Jacques Chailley. (Illus.). 368p. (Orig.). 1992. pap. 14.95 (*0-89281-358-X*) Inner Tradit.

Magic Flutes. Eva Ibbotson. 264p. 1986. mass mkt. 2.95 (*0-446-30081-0*, Pub. by Warner Bks) Little.

Magic for All Ages. Walter B. Gibson. 1980. pap. 10.00 (*0-87980-389-4*) Wilshire.

Magic for Beginners. Harry Baron. LC 90-48770. (Illus.). 176p. 1991. pap. 9.95 (*1-55958-089-5*) Prima Pub.

Magic for Beginners. Harry Baron. (Illus.). 154p. 1998. reprint ed. pap. 11.95 (*0-947533-58-3*, Pub. by Breese Bks) Firebird Dist.

Magic for Beginners: The Power to Change Your World. J.H. Brennan. LC 97-48970. (Llewellyn's for Beginners Ser.). (Illus.). 317p. (Orig.). 1998. pap. 9.95 (*1-56718-086-8*) Llewellyn Pubns.

Magic for Beginners No. 2: Card Tricks & Other Close-up Illusions, Vol. 2. Harry Baron. LC 95-3352. (Illus.). 160p. 1995. pap. 9.95 (*0-7615-0017-0*) Prima Pub.

Magic for Dummies. David Pogue. LC GV1547.P73 1998. (For Dummies Ser.). (Illus.). 408p. 1998. pap. 19.99 (*0-7645-5101-9*) IDG Bks.

***Magic for Grandparents.** Peter Sosna. 116p. 1999. 21.95 (*0-7351-0170-1*) Replica Bks.

***Magic for Joy.** Holly Fuhrmann. 2000. pap. 8.50 (*1-893896-19-6*) Ima Jinn.

***Magic for Kids.** Fay Presto. LC 99-12753. 72p. 1999. pap. 10.95 (*0-7534-5210-3*) LKC.

Magic for Lovers. Keith Morgan. (Orig.). 1995. pap. 7.95 (*1-872189-07-5*, Pub. by Mandrake Pr) Holmes Pub.

Magic for Lovers: How to Use Magical & Astrological Techniques to Locate Your Ideal Lover. Kathleen McCormack. (Illus.). 176p. 1987. pap. 6.95 (*0-85030-468-7*) Aqrn Pr.

Magic for Marigold. L. M. Montgomery. 284p. (J). 1976. 23.95 (*0-8488-1102-X*) Amereon Ltd.

Magic for Marigold. L. M. Montgomery. 288p. (J). 1988. mass mkt. 3.99 (*0-7704-2233-0*) Bantam.

Magic for Marigold. L. M. Montgomery. 288p. (YA). 1989. mass mkt. 4.50 (*0-553-28046-5*) Bantam.

Magic for the Aquarian Age. Green. 1987. 9.95 (*0-85030-318-4*, Pub. by Aqrn Pr) Harper SF.

Magic Forest. Stewart E. White. 19.95 (*0-8488-1510-6*) Amereon Ltd.

Magic Forest. Stewart E. White. 1976. lib. bdg. 9.95 (*0-89968-126-3*, Lghtyr Pr) Buccaneer Bks.

Magic Forest. Stewart E. White. 146p. 1990. reprint ed. lib. bdg. 19.95 (*0-89966-663-9*) Buccaneer Bks.

Magic Forest, 2 vols., Set. unabridged ed. Michele Hemenway & Sara A. Buchanan. Ed. by David Dobson. LC 98-206255. 72p. (J). (ps-6). 1998. pap. 24.95 incl. audio (*1-57895-022-8*, Bridge Res) Curriculm Presbytrn KY.

Magic Frog. F. I. Rejab. (Illus.). 40p. (J). 1995. 9.95 (*983-9808-14-1*, Pub. by Delta Edits) Weatherhill.

***Magic from the Mountain.** Pat Williams. 2001. 16.99 (*0-8007-1779-1*) Revell.

Magic Frontiers Adventure Guide. Brian Wyant & Eric Wyant. Ed. by Judith Hancock. (Illus.). 128p. 1998. pap. 18.00 (*1-883788-57-9*) Event Horzn.

Magic Frontiers Book of Adventures. Brian Wyant & Eric Wyant. (Illus.). 128p. 1997. pap. 9.95 (*1-883788-02-1*) Event Horzn.

Magic Frontiers Explorer Edition Roleplaying Game. Brian Wyant & Eric Wyant. Ed. by Judith Hancock. (Illus.). 208p. 1998. pap. 28.00 (*1-883788-56-0*) Event Horzn.

Magic Frontiers Universal Handbook. Brian Wyant & Eric Wyant. (Illus.). 520p. 1997. pap. 39.95 (*1-883788-05-6*) Event Horzn.

Magic Garden. Christopher Carrie. (Crayola Coloring Storybks.). (Illus.). 32p. (J). (ps). 1991. 1.99 (*0-86696-313-8*) Binney & Smith.

Magic Garden. Irene Corey. (J). (gr. k-3). 2000. pap. 7.00 (*0-87602-376-6*) Anchorage.

Magic Garden. Gene S. Porter. 1990. reprint ed. lib. bdg. 27.95 (*0-89968-544-7*) Buccaneer Bks.

Magic Garden. Gene Stratton-Porter. 1976. reprint ed. lib. bdg. 21.95 (*0-89190-942-7*, Rivercity Pr) Amereon Ltd.

Magic Garden Explained: The Internals of UNIX System V Release 4, an Open-Systems Design. Berny Goodheart & James Cox. LC 93-23385. 500p. (C). 1994. pap. text 53.00 (*0-13-098138-9*) Prntice Hall Bks.

Magic Gardens. Corinne Heline. (Illus.). 126p. (Orig.). 1987. reprint ed. pap. text 14.00 (*0-933963-17-3*) New Age Bible.

Magic Garment: Principles of Costume Design. Rebecca Cunningham. (Illus.). 395p. (C). 1994. reprint ed. pap. text 32.95 (*0-88133-762-5*) Waveland Pr.

Magic Gem: A Story Coloring Book. Baba Hari Dass. LC 76-10032. (Illus.). 32p. (Orig.). (J). (ps-2). 1976. pap. 3.50 (*0-918100-07-0*) Sri Rama.

Magic Glass: The Individual & Society as Seen in the Gams of Herman Melville's Moby-Dick. Hilda U. Stubbings. LC 91-67127. xvi, 148p. (Orig.). (C). 1992. 37.50 (*1-880622-01-7*); pap. 24.95 (*1-880622-00-9*) Rubena Pr.

Magic Glasses. Yogesh Patel. (Early Reading Ser.). (Illus.). (J). 1995. pap. 4.99 (*0-85953-945-8*) Childs Play.

Magic Glasses. Yogesh Patel. (Children's Stories Published in Other Lands Ser.). (Illus.). 32p. (J). (gr. k-3). 1996. lib. bdg. 12.95 (*1-56674-146-7*, HTS Bks) Forest Hse.

Magic Glasses: Professional Edition. Rachmiel Tobesman. (Illus.). 55p. 1996. 24.95 (*0-9677266-1-1*) Child Access Ctr MD.

***Magic Glasses: Stories & Other Activities for Children of Separation & Divorce.** Rachmiel Tobesman. (Illus.). 38p. (J). (ps-12). 1998. 9.95 (*0-9677266-0-3*) Child Access Ctr MD.

Magic Globe: An Around-the-World Adventure Gamebook. Heather Maisner. LC 94-15164. (Illus.). (J). (gr. 3-6). 1995. 12.95 (*1-56402-445-8*) Candlewick Pr.

Magic Globe: An Around-the-World Adventure Gamebook. Heather Maisner. LC 94-15164. (Candlewick Gamebks.). (Illus.). 32p. (J). (gr. 4-7). 1996. reprint ed. pap. 7.99 (*1-56402-853-4*) Candlewick Pr.

Magic Goes Away. Larry Niven. 224p. 1985. mass mkt. 4.99 (*0-441-51554-1*) Ace Bks.

Magic Goose. Daniel Pinkwater. 80p. (J). (gr. 2-5). 1997. pap. text 3.50 (*0-590-31349-5*) Scholastic Inc.

Magic Goose. Daniel Pinkwater. 1997. 8.70 (*0-606-11589-7*, Pub. by Turtleback) Demco.

Magic Gourd. (Butterfly Collection). 1989. 9.95 (*0-86685-490-8*, LDL46E, Pub. by Librairie du Liban) Intl Bk Ctr.

Magic Gourd. Christine Skilton. (J). 1991. 9.95 (*0-86685-568-8*) Intl Bk Ctr.

Magic Grandfather. Doris M. Disney. 224p. 1989. mass mkt. 2.95 (*0-8217-2584-X*, Zebra Kensgtn) Kensgtn Pub Corp.

Magic Grandfather. Doris M. Disney. reprint ed. lib. bdg. 20.95 (*0-88411-842-8*) Amereon Ltd.

Magic Guitar Chord Chart 96: Chord Diagrams & Movable. B. Stein. 4p. 1986. pap. 1.75 (*0-7935-5520-5*, 50394200) H Leonard.

Magic Handbook. Peter Eldin. (Illus.). 192p. (J). (gr. 4-6). 1985. per. 8.99 (*0-671-55039-X*) S&S Trade.

Magic Happens! Laurie F. Huck. LC 96-21009. (J). 1996. pap. text 5.95 (*0-8348-0375-5*) Weatherhill.

Magic Hare. Lynne Reid Banks. LC 92-10585. (Illus.). 64p. (J). 1993. 15.00 (*0-688-10895-4*, Wm Morrow) Morrow Avon.

Magic Hare. Lynne Reid Banks. LC 92-10585. 64p. (J). (gr. 4-7). 1994. mass mkt. 5.99 (*0-380-71562-7*, Avon Bks) Morrow Avon.

Magic Hare. Lynne Reid Banks. LC 92-10585. 1993. 11.19 (*0-606-06551-2*, Pub. by Turtleback) Demco.

Magic Harvest: Food, Folklore & Society. Piero Camporesi. Tr. by Joan Hall. 260p. 1994. 55.95 (*0-7456-0835-3*) Blackwell Pubs.

Magic Harvest: Food, Folkore & Society. Piero Camporesi. Tr. by Joan Hall. 253p. 1999. reprint ed. pap. 22.95 (*0-7456-2196-1*) Blackwell Pubs.

Magic Hat see Three Magic Flip Books

***Magic Hat.** Scholastic Books Staff. (Teletubbies Ser.). (Illus.). 24p. (J). (ps-k). 2000. mass mkt. 3.50 (*0-439-13855-8*) Scholastic Inc.

Magic Hat. 2nd ed. Kim W. Chapman. LC 76-20842. (Illus.). 46p. (J). (gr. k up). 1976. 5.00 (*0-914996-10-X*) Lollipop Power.

Magic Hat & Other Danish Fairy Tales. Clara Stroebe & Marty Noble. LC 99-25113. (Children's Thrift Classics). (Illus.). 80p. (J). 1999. pap. 1.00 (*0-486-40792-6*) Dover.

Magic Hat of Mortimer Wintergreen. Myron Levoy. LC 87-45292. (Charlotte Zolotow Bk.). (Illus.). 224p. (J). (gr. 3-7). 1988. 11.95 (*0-06-023841-0*) HarpC Child Bks.

Magic Herbs: More Than 200 Delicious & Healthy Recipes That Are Naturally Low-Fat & Fat-Free. Julie M. Cull. 240p. 1996. pap. 12.95 (*1-56561-087-3*) Wiley.

Magic Herbs: More Than 200 Delicious & Healthy Recipes That Are Naturally Low-Fat & Fat-Free. Julie Metcalf Cull. 240p. 1996. pap. 12.95 (*0-471-34748-5*) Wiley.

Magic Herbs for Arthritis, Rheumatism & Related Ailments. Richard M. Lucas. LC 80-22346. 248p. 1981. 14.95 (*0-13-543900-0*, Parker Publishing Co); 4.95 (*0-685-03916-1*, Parker Publishing Co) P-H.

***Magic Hill.** A. A. Milne, pseud. LC 99-42773. (Illus.). 32p. (J). 2000. 14.99 (*0-525-46147-7*, Dutton Child) Peng Put Young Read.

Magic Hockey Skates. Allen Morgan. 32p. (J). (ps-3). 1994. pap. 6.95 (*0-19-540851-9*) OUP.

Magic Hockey Skates. unabridged ed. Allen Morgan. LC 98-226123. (Illus.). 32p. (J). (gr. k-3). 1996. pap. 8.95 (*0-7737-5697-3*) STDK.

Magic Hockey Stick. Peter Maloney & Felicia Zekauskas. Ed. by Diane Arico. LC 99-17201. (Illus.). 40p. (J). (ps-3). 1999. 12.99 (*0-8037-2476-4*, Dial Yng Read) Peng Put Young Read.

Magic Hole in the Sky. Karen Derman. (Illus.). 48p. (Orig.). (J). 1995. pap. 14.95 (*0-9630026-0-0*); pap. 9.95 (*0-9630026-1-9*); pap. 24.95 incl. audio (*0-9630026-2-7*) Childlight Pr.

***Magic Holiday: Storybook, Necklace & Gift Box Mini Craft Kit.** Rita Balducci. (Barbie Ser.). (Illus.). 16p. (J). (gr. 1-4). 2000. bds. 6.99 (*1-57584-449-4*, Pub. by Rdrs Digest) S&S Trade.

Magic Horn. Diane MacLaurin. Ed. by Pamela Karcher. (Illus.). 75p. (Orig.). (YA). (gr. 6 up). 1993. pap. write for info. (*0-934549-01-X*) Laurin Hse.

Magic Horn. Anne Nicholson & Charlotte B. Chorpenning. 69p. 1954. reprint ed. pap. 3.50 (*0-87129-051-0*, M75) Dramatic Pub.

Magic Horse. Idries Shah. LC 97-5086. (Illus.). 40p. (J). (gr. 4-7). 1998. 17.00 (*1-883536-11-1*, Hoopoe Books) ISHK.

Magic Hour. Susan Isaacs. 496p. 1998. mass mkt. 6.99 (*0-06-109948-1*, Harp PBks) HarpC.

Magic Hourglass: A Time-Travel Adventure Gamebook. Heather Maisner. LC 94-10404. (Candlewick Gamebks.). (Illus.). 32p. (J). (gr. 2-5). 1996. reprint ed. pap. 7.99 (*1-56402-854-2*) Candlewick Pr.

Magic House & His Mad Dash. Jennifer G. Welch & Darryl Price. 1980. pap. 7.95 (*0-318-04458-7*) Pudding Hse Pubns.

Magic Hummingbird: A Hopi Folktale. Tr. by Ekkehart Malotki. LC 95-80961. (Illus.). 40p. (J). (gr. k-7). 1996. 15.95 (*1-885772-04-1*) Kiva Pubng.

Magic in Action. rev. ed. Richard Bandler. LC 84-61646. 1985. 22.95 (*0-916990-14-1*) META Pubns.

Magic in Ancient Egypt. Geraldine Pinch. (Illus.). 192p. (Orig.). 1995. pap. 19.95 (*0-292-76559-2*) U of Tex Pr.

***Magic in Boiardo & Ariosto.** Julia M. Kisacky. LC 98-30521. (Studies in Italian Culture: No. 25). 200p. 2000. text 46.95 (*0-8204-4252-6*) P Lang Pubng.

Magic in Ithkar IV, No. 4. Ed. by Robert Adams & Andre Norton. (Illus.). 288p. (Orig.). 1987. pap. 3.50 (*0-8125-4719-5*, Pub. by Tor Bks) St Martin.

Magic in Ithkar I. Andre Norton & Robert Adams. 320p. 1988. pap. 3.95 (*0-8125-4715-2*) Tor Bks.

Magic in Ithkar III, No. 3. Andre Norton & Robert Adams. (Illus.). 320p. 1989. pap. 3.95 (*0-8125-4709-8*) Tor Bks.

Magic in Names & Other Things. Edward Clodd. 246p. 1997. reprint ed. pap. 19.95 (*0-7661-0077-4*) Kessinger Pub.

Magic in the Ancient World. Fritz Graf. Tr. by Franklin Philip from GRE. LC 97-20985. (Revealing Antiquity Ser.: No. 10). 272p. 1998. 36.50 (*0-674-54151-0*) HUP.

Magic in the Ancient World. Fritz Graf. 1999. pap. 16.95 (*0-674-54153-7*) HUP.

***Magic in the Ancient World.** Fritz Graf & Franklin Philip. 319p. 1999. pap. text 16.95 (*0-674-54150-2*) HUP.

Magic in the Dark: A Young Viewer's History of the Movies. Nicholas E. Meyer. LC 85-13004. (Illus.). 284p. reprint ed. pap. 88.10 (*0-7837-5335-7*, 204507500005) Bks Demand.

Magic in the Middle Ages. Richard Kieckhefer. (Cambridge Medieval Textbooks Ser.). (Illus.). 230p. (C). 1990. pap. text 15.95 (*0-521-31202-7*) Cambridge U Pr.

***Magic in the Middle Ages.** Richard Kieckhefer. (Canto Book Ser.). (Illus.). 240p. 2000. pap. 13.95 (*0-521-78576-6*) Cambridge U Pr.

Magic in the Mirror. H. McKay. (Illus.). (J). mass mkt. 7.95 (*0-340-72289-4*, Pub. by Hodder & Stought Ltd) Trafalgar.

Magic in the Mist. Margaret M. Kimmel. LC 74-18186. (Illus.). 32p. (J). (gr. k-4). 1975. 15.00 (*0-689-50026-2*) McElderry Bks.

Magic in the Mountains, the Yakima Shaman: Power & Practice. Donald M. Hines. LC 93-78220. (Illus.). 254p. (Orig.). 1993. pap. 17.95 (*0-9629539-3-8*) Great Eagle Pub.

Magic in the Mud. Gerald Crawford. (Illus.). 48p. (J). (gr. 1-4). Date not set. 14.95 (*0-9672996-0-8*) Red Mud Pr.

***Magic in the Pool of Making.** Webb. 1998. pap. 7.50 (*0-7459-2234-1*, Pub. by Lion Pubng) Trafalgar.

Magic in the Rain. large type ed. Paula Lindsay. (Linford Romance Library). 304p. 1993. pap. 16.99 (*0-7089-7337-X*, Linford) Ulverscroft.

Magic in the Shadows. FASA Corp. Staff. (Shadowrun Ser.). (Illus.). 176p. 1998. pap. 20.00 (*1-55560-358-0*, 03580F, Pub. by FASA Corp) NTC Contemp Pub Co.

Magic in the Streets. Francine Witte. 28p. 1994. pap. 7.00 (*0-937669-51-2*) Owl Creek Pr.

Magic in the Web: Action & Language in Othello. Robert B. Heilman. LC 77-21918. 298p. 1977. reprint ed. lib. bdg. 69.50 (*0-8371-9784-8*, HEMW, Greenwood Pr) Greenwood.

Magic in Theory & Practice. Aleister Crowley. 1973. lib. bdg. 300.00 (*0-87968-128-4*) Krishna Pr.

Magic in Vienna. large type ed. Betty A. Neels. LC 94-3361. 253p. 1994. lib. bdg. 16.95 (*0-8161-7455-5*, G K Hall Lrg Type) Mac Lib Ref.

Magic in Your Mind. Uell S. Andersen. 1976. pap. 15.00 (*0-87980-089-5*) Wilshire.

Magic Ink & Other Stories. William Black. LC 79-37537. (Short Story Index Reprint Ser.). 1977. reprint ed. 21.95 (*0-8369-4096-2*) Ayer.

***Magic Interactive Encyclopedia.** 1999. cd-rom. write for info. (*0-7869-1511-0*) TSR Inc.

Magic Island. William Buehler & W. B. Seabrook. (Illus.). 336p. 1994. pap. 10.95 (*1-56924-949-0*) Marlowe & Co.

Magic Islands: A Treasure-Trove of San Juan Islands Lore. rev. ed. David Richardson. (Illus.). 96p. 1995. reprint ed. pap. 4.95 (*0-945742-08-8*) Orcas Pub.

Magic Jack O Lantern. Sandra Heath. 1999. mass mkt. 4.99 (*0-451-19840-9*, Sig) NAL.

Magic Johnson. Neil Cohen. (J). 1992. pap. write for info. (*0-316-15050-9*) Little.

Magic Johnson. Steven Frank. LC 94-5778. (Basketball Legends Ser.). (Illus.). 64p. (J). (gr. 3 up). 1994. lib. bdg. 15.95 (*0-7910-2430-X*) Chelsea Hse.

Magic Johnson. Bob Italia. Ed. by Rosemary Wallner. LC 92-19754. 32p. (J). 1992. lib. bdg. 13.98 (*1-56239-120-8*) ABDO Pub Co.

Magic Johnson. James R. Rothaus. (Sports Superstars Ser.). (Illus.). 32p. (J). (gr. 2-6). 1991. lib. bdg. 21.36 (*0-89565-732-5*) Childs World.

Magic Johnson. Quincy Troupe. (Illus.). 32p. 2000. lib. bdg. 15.49 (*0-7868-0510-2*, Pub. by Hyprn Ppbks) Little.

Magic Johnson, 6 bks., Set I, Reading Level 8. Laurie Rozakis et al. (Winning Spirit Ser.). (Illus.). 48p. (J). (gr. 4-8). 1988. lib. bdg. 21.27 (*0-86592-025-7*) Rourke Enter.

Magic Johnson: Basketball Great. Sean Dolan. Ed. by Nathan I. Huggins. LC 92-21378. (Black Americans of Achievement Ser.). (Illus.). 124p. (YA). (gr. 5 up). 1992. lib. bdg. 19.95 (*0-7910-1975-6*) Chelsea Hse.

Magic Johnson: Basketball's Smiling Superstar. Rick L. Johnson. LC 92-3175. (Taking Part Ser.). (Illus.). 64p. (J). (gr. 3 up). 1992. lib. bdg. 13.95 (*0-87518-553-3*, Dillon Silver Burdett) Silver Burdett Pr.

Magic Johnson: Champion with a Cause. Keith E. Greenberg. (Sports Achievers Ser.). (Illus.). 64p. (J). (gr. 4-9). 1992. lib. bdg. 18.60 (*0-8225-0546-0*, Lerner Publctns) Lerner Pub.

Magic Johnson: Champion with a Cause. Keith E. Greenberg. (Illus.). 64p. (J). (gr. 4-9). 1992. pap. 4.95 (*0-8225-9612-1*, Lerner Publctns) Lerner Pub.

Magic Johnson: Hero on & off Court. Bill Gutman. (J). (gr. 4-7). 1992. pap. 4.80 (*0-395-64546-8*) HM.

Magic Johnson: Hero on & off Court. Bill Gutman. LC 92-5002. (Sports World Ser.). (Illus.). 48p. (J). (gr. 3-6). 1992. pap. 5.95 (*1-56294-821-0*) Millbrook Pr.

Magic Johnson: The Rookie Year. Joseph Nazel. 1990. pap. 3.95 (*0-87067-844-2*) Holloway.

Magic Journey. Ilse Klipper. (Illus.). 83p. (Orig.). (J). (gr. k-5). 1983. pap. 5.95 (*0-9605022-1-1*) Pathways Pr CA.

Magic Journey. John Nichols. 546p. 1983. mass mkt. 5.99 (*0-345-31049-7*, Ballantine) Ballantine Pub Grp.

Magic Journey. John Nichols. 1996. pap. 12.95 (*0-345-41033-5*) Ballantine Pub Grp.

Magic Journey. John Nichols. LC 99-42425. 540p. 2000. pap. 14.00 (*0-8050-6339-0*, Owl) H Holt & Co.

Magic Kerchief. Kirby Larson. LC 99-18846. (Illus.). 32p. (J). (ps-3). 2000. 15.95 (*0-8234-1473-6*) Holiday.

Magic Key: A Story for Mothers & Children. Else Fleissner. Ed. by Robert F. Fleissner. (Illus.). 64p. (gr. 3-6). 1999. pap. 15.00 (*1-887196-05-6*) Wells Col Pr.

Magic Key: Bible Symbolism for Children. Joyce Fekete. (Illus.). 32p. (Orig.). 1993. pap. text 2.50 (*0-917426-09-6*) Am New Church Sunday.

***Magic Kingdom.** Stanley Elkin & Rick Moody. 317p. 2000. pap. 12.95 (*1-56478-259-X*) Dalkey Arch.

Magic Kingdom: Walt Disney & the American Way of Life. Steven Watts. LC 97-18301. 608p. 1998. 30.00 (*0-395-83587-9*) HM.

Magic Kingdom for Sale - Sold! Terry Brooks. 324p. 1986. 16.95 (*0-345-31757-2*, Ballantine) Ballantine Pub Grp.

Magic Kingdom for Sale - Sold! Terry Brooks. 320p. 1987. mass mkt. 6.99 (*0-345-31758-0*, Ballantine) Ballantine Pub Grp.

M

Magic Kingdom for Sale - Sold! Terry Brooks. 1986. 12.09 (*0-606-02550-2*, Pub. by Turtleback) Demco.

*__Magic Kingdom of God: Christianity & Global Culture Industries.__ Michael Budde. 192p. 1998. pap. text 22.00 (*0-8133-3076-9*, Pub. by Westview) HarpC.

Magic Kits: Meaningful Activities for the Gifted in the Classroom Through Knowledge, Interests, Training & Stimulation. Janet Heuer et al. (Illus.). 56p. 1980. pap. 14.95 (*0-936386-11-8*) Creative Learning.

Magic Knight Rayearth. Clamp. Vol. 1. (Illus.). 192p. (YA). (gr. 3 up). 1999. pap. 11.95 (*1-892213-00-1*) Mixx Enter Inc.

*__Magic Knight Rayearth, No. 2__ Clamp. (YA). (gr. 4 up). 1999. pap. 11.95 (*1-892213-08-7*, Mixx Manga) Mixx Enter Inc.

Magic Knight Rayearth, Vol. 3. Clamp. (Illus.). 208p. (YA). (gr. 4 up). 1999. pap. 11.95 (*1-892213-16-8*, Mixx Manga) Mixx Enter Inc.

*__Magic Knight Rayearth, Vol. 4.__ Clamp. (Illus.). 2000. pap. 11.95 (*1-892213-43-5*) Mixx Enter Inc.

*__Magic Knight Rayearth, Vol. 5.__ Clamp. (Illus.). (J). 2000. pap. 11.95 (*1-892213-52-4*) Talisman Hse.

Magic Knitting Needles of Mary Walker Phillips. Ed. by Goldstein Gallery Staff. 13p. 1987. pap. 2.00 (*0-939719-02-9*) UMN Goldstein Gall.

Magic Labyrinth see Philip Jose Farmer: The Complete Riverworld Novels

Magic Labyrinth. Philip Jose Farmer. LC PS3556.A72M66 1998. 1998. pap. 12.95 (*0-345-41970-7*, Del Rey) Ballantine Pub Grp.

Magic Labyrinth of Philip Jose Farmer. Edgar L. Chapman. LC 81-21603. (Milford Series: Popular Writers of Today: Popular Writers of Today: Vol. 38). 96p. 1984. pap. 15.00 (*0-89370-258-7*) Millefleurs.

Magic Lake: A Mystical Healing Lake of the Cherokee. Thomas B. Underwood. (Illus.). 20p. (J). (gr. 1-3). 1982. 4.00 (*0-935741-08-9*) Cherokee Pubns.

Magic Lamp. (Scheherezade Children's Stories Ser.). (Illus.). 16p. (J). 1997. 4.95 (*1-873938-92-6*, Pub. by Garnet-Ithaca) LPC InBook.

Magic Lamp. Inis I. Hurd. LC 87-30728. (Illus.). 140p. (J). (gr. 4-7). 1989. lib. bdg. 14.50 (*0-944517-00-5*) Christian Center.

Magic Lamp: Goal Setting for People Who Hate Setting Goals. rev. ed. Keith Ellis. LC 97-44336. 1998. pap. 13.00 (*0-609-80166-X*) Crown Pub Group.

Magic Land: Designing Your Own Enchanted Garden. Julie M. Messervy. LC 97-31531. (Illus.). 160p. 1998. 19.95 (*0-02-862091-7*) Macmillan Gen Ref.

Magic Lands: Western Cityscapes & American Culture after 1940. John M. Findlay. (Illus.). 1992. 50.00 (*0-520-07703-2*, Pub. by U CA Pr); pap. 18.95 (*0-520-08435-7*, Pub. by U CA Pr) Cal Prin Full Svc.

Magic Lantern. Timothy Garton Ash. 176p. 1993. pap. 12.00 (*0-679-74048-1*) McKay.

Magic Lantern. Edward Hays. LC 91-75961. (Illus.). 223p. 1991. pap. 10.95 (*0-939516-15-2*) Forest Peace.

*__Magic Lantern: A Fable about Leadership, Personal Excellence & Empowerment.__ Joe Rubino. (Illus.). 170p. 2000. pap. 14.95 (*0-9678529-0-0*) Vision Works.

*__Magic Lantern: Having a Ball & Christmas Eve.__ Jose Tomas de Cuellar. Ed. by Margo Glantz. Tr. by Margaret A. Carson. LC 99-59209. (Library of Latin America). 208p. 2000. 30.00 (*0-19-511502-3*) OUP.

*__Magic Lantern: Having A Ball & Christmas Eve.__ Jose Tomas de Cuellar. Ed. by Margo Glantz. Tr. by Margaret A. Carson. LC 99-59209. (Library of Latin America). 208p. 2000. pap. 14.95 (*0-19-511503-1*) OUP.

Magic Lanterns. Derek Greenacre. (Album Ser.: No. 169). (Illus.). 32p. pap. 6.25 (*0-85263-791-8*, Pub. by Shire Pubns) Parkwest Pubns.

Magic Lens: A Sprial Tour Through the Human Ideas of Grammar, Vol. I. rev. ed. Michael Thompson. (YA). (gr. 8-12). 1995. pap., student ed. 14.99 (*0-88092-210-9*) Royal Fireworks.

Magic Lens: A Sprial Tour Through the Human Ideas of Grammar, Vol. II. rev. ed. Michael Thompson. (YA). (gr. 8-12). 1995. pap., student ed. 14.99 (*0-88092-211-7*) Royal Fireworks.

Magic Lens: A Sprial Tour Through the Human Ideas of Grammar, Vols. I & II. Michael Thompson. (YA). (gr. 8-12). 1995. pap., teacher ed. 15.00 (*0-88092-212-5*) Royal Fireworks.

Magic Life: A Novel Philosophy. Ace Starry. LC 98-86217. 264p. 1999. 19.95 (*0-9665281-6-6*) Rare Bird.

Magic Links: Manual. Jackie Kiraithe. Ed. by Linda Gonzales. 200p. (J). 48.00 (*0-942787-95-1*) Binet Intl.

Magic Links Big Book. Jackie Kiraithe & Linda Gonzales. (Illus.). 36p. (J). 1992. 48.00 (*0-942787-94-3*) Binet Intl.

Magic Links Manual. Linda Gonzales. 200p. 1992. write for info. (*0-942787-49-8*) Binet Intl.

Magic Listening Cap. Yoshiko Uchida. (Illus.). 160p. (Orig.). (J). 1987. reprint ed. pap. 8.95 (*0-88739-016-1*) Creat Arts Bk.

Magic Little Friend: (This Book Really Talks to You) Dezra-Lehr Guthrie. 110p. 1999. pap. 6.95 (*1-881542-45-9*) Blue Star Prodns.

Magic Locket. Elizabeth Koda-Callan. LC 88-5508. (Magic Charm Bks.). (Illus.). 48p. (J). (ps-3). 1988. bds. 12.95 (*0-89480-602-5*, 1602) Workman Pub.

Magic-Lover's Treasury of the Fantastic. Ed. by Margaret Weis. LC 97-12855. 432p. (Orig.). 1998. mass mkt. 13.99 (*0-446-67284-X*, Pub. by Warner Bks) Little.

Magic Machine: A Musical. Sidney Berger & Rob Landes. 38p. (J). 1995. pap. 4.00 (*1-57514-147-7*, 0087) Encore Perform Pub.

*__Magic Magnetic Letters.__ rev. ed. Sally Lloyd Jones. 24p. (J). (gr. k-2). 2000. boxed set. write for info. (*1-57584-697-7*, Pub. by Rdrs Digest) S&S Trade.

*__Magic Magnetic Numbers.__ rev. ed. Sally Lloyd Jones. (Illus.). 24p. (J). 2000. boxed set. write for info. (*1-57584-698-5*, Pub. by Rdrs Digest) S&S Trade.

Magic Maguey. Tony Johnston. LC 94-32660. (Illus.). 32p. (J). (ps-3). 1996. 15.00 (*0-15-250988-7*) Harcourt.

Magic Mail: How to Use Only Internet E-Mail to Do Fascinating, Fabulous, Fantastic & Fun Stuff on the Internet & You Don't Have to be a Rocket Scientist to Understand This Book (Although You Can Be One-We Wouldn't Be at All Offended at That; Some of Our Best Friends. Ned B. Johnson. 136p. (Orig.). 1994. pap. 14.95 (*0-9636381-9-X*) Whyte Rose Pr.

Magic Makeover: Tricks for Looking Thinner, Younger, & More Confident - Instantly! Lynda Millner. LC 97-3655. (Illus.). 176p. (Orig.). 1997. pap. 14.95 (*1-56474-222-9*) Fithian Pr.

Magic Man: Peter of Mystic Mountain. Friends of Peter. Ed. by Jaya Brand. (Illus.). 126p. (Orig.). 1991. pap. 13.00 (*1-878682-00-8*) Roaring Lion Pub.

Magic Man: The Life & Films of Steven Spielberg. William Schoell. LC 97-40181. (J). 1998. 18.95 (*0-936389-57-5*) Tudor Pubs.

Magic Mandala Coloring Book: Sacred Geometry for Awakening & Healing. Martha Bartfeld. (Illus.). 216p. 1998. spiral bd. 19.95 (*0-9662285-0-2*) Mandalart Creations.

*__Magic Mat.__ Sharon Gaskin. (Illus.). 24p. (J). 2000. pap. 7.00 (*0-8059-4856-2*) Dorrance.

Magic Maui Cookbook. pap. 9.95 (*0-9637637-9-2*) Cleall Pubng.

Magic May Return. Ed. by Larry Niven. 256p. 1983. mass mkt. 4.99 (*0-441-51549-5*) Ace Bks.

Magic Mean Machine. Beatrice Gormley. (Illus.). 128p. (Orig.). (YA). (gr. 5 up). 1989. pap. 2.95 (*0-380-75519-X*, Avon Bks) Morrow Avon.

Magic Meatloaf Menus. Sarah Shockley. (Magic Menu Ser.). (Illus.). 200p. (Orig.). 1987. pap. 12.95 (*0-941661-00-8*) Magic Menus OK.

Magic Menorah. (J). 2000. write for info. (*0-689-82606-0*) S&S Bks Yung.

Magic Menu. Ellen H. Robertson. (Illus.). (Orig.). 1954. pap. 2.00 (*0-87505-136-7*) Borden.

Magic Menus. American Diabetes Association Staff. LC 96-42081. 256p. 1996. pap. 14.95 (*0-945448-72-4*, 4707-01, Pub. by Am Diabetes) NTC Contemp Pub Co.

Magic Merlin Preschool. Suzanne Michaels. LC 96-70796. (Illus.). xx, 324p. (Orig.). 1997. pap. 24.95 (*0-9654779-1-6*) A-Parent Love.

Magic Message Book. Dezra-Lehr Guthrie. 100p. 1999. pap. 6.95 (*1-881542-44-0*) Blue Star Prodns.

Magic Messages for Pulpit, Pew & Pint Sized People. Arnold C. Westphal. 1987. per. 4.95 (*0-915398-27-3*) Visual Evangels.

Magic Methods of Screenwriting. 2nd ed. D. Lee. (C). 1995. pap. text 52.00 (*0-07-037097-4*) McGraw.

Magic Middletown. Dwight W. Hoover. LC 84-43152. (Illus.). 181p. 1986. reprint ed. pap. 56.20 (*0-7837-9653-6*, 205928600005) Bks Demand.

Magic Mind Power: Make It Work for You! 2nd ed. Leslie M. LeCron. 176p. 1982. reprint ed. pap. 8.95 (*0-87516-496-X*) DeVorss.

*__Magic Mineral to Killer Dust: Turner & Newall & the Asbestos Hazard.__ Geoffrey Tweedale et al. LC 99-54994. 320p. 2000. write for info. (*0-19-829690-8*) OUP.

Magic Minutes: Quick Read-Alouds for Every Day. Pat Nelson. LC 92-35887. (Illus.). 151p. 1993. pap. text 18.50 (*0-87287-996-8*) Libs Unl.

Magic Mirror. Orson Scott Card. LC 99-27497. (Illus.). 32p. 1999. 15.95 (*0-87905-876-5*) Gibbs Smith Pub.

Magic Mirror. Jade. Ed. by Judith D. Vosburg. (Illus.). 10p. (Orig.). 1990. pap. text 2.50 (*0-9619008-5-7*) Eye Cat.

Magic Mirror. Linda L. Moffit. LC 89-50125. (Illus.). 80p. (Orig.). (J). (gr. k-7). 1989. pap. 9.95 (*0-87516-615-6*) DeVorss.

Magic Mirror. large type ed. Mickey Friedman. (General Ser.). 354p. 1990. lib. bdg. 18.95 (*0-8161-4823-6*, G K Hall Lrg Type) Mac Lib Ref.

Magic Mirror. Elsie Singmaster. 1993. reprint ed. lib. bdg. 89.00 (*0-7812-5831-6*) Rprt Serv.

Magic Mirror: Law in American History. Kermit L. Hall. 416p. 1989. pap. text 25.95 (*0-19-504460-6*) OUP.

Magic Mirror: Movies & Modernity in Russia, 1908-1918. Denise J. Youngblood. LC 98-48706. (Studies in Film). 1999. 19.95 (*0-299-16234-6*); 49.95 (*0-299-16230-3*) U of Wis Pr.

Magic Mirror: Myth's Abiding Power. Elizabeth M. Baeten. LC 96-27863. (SUNY Series in the Philosophy of the Social Sciences). 245p. (C). 1996. text 65.50 (*0-7914-3091-X*); pap. text 21.95 (*0-7914-3092-8*) State U NY Pr.

Magic Mirror: Violetta Books' Second Annual Poetry Anthology. Ed. by Kathleen Gilbert. (Violetta Books Annual Poetry Anthologies). (Illus.). 27p. (Orig.). 1986. pap. 3.00 (*0-915913-07-0*) Violetta Bks.

Magic Mirror, an Antique Optical Toy. 81st ed. McLoughlin Bros. Staff. 1980. pap. 3.95 (*0-486-23847-4*) Dover.

Magic Mirror of M. C. Escher. Bruno Ernst. (Taschen Special Ser.). (Illus.). 111p. 1995. pap. 14.99 (*1-886155-00-3*) Taschen Amer.

Magic Mixtures. Jean Stangl. 1986. pap. 8.99 (*0-8224-4377-5*) Fearon Teacher Aids.

Magic Molecules: How Drugs Work. Susan Aldridge. LC 98-21346. (Illus.). 282p. (C). 1998. 24.95 (*0-521-58414-0*) Cambridge U Pr.

Magic Moment: Bach & Beyond. Laurie Efrein. (Illus.). 353p. (Orig.). 1984. pap. 17.00 (*0-917573-00-5*) CAO Times.

*__Magic Moments.__ Yvette Pompa. (Barbie Mini Craft Ser.). (Illus.). 16p. (J). (gr. k-3). 2000. 6.99 (*1-57584-412-5*, Pub. by Rdrs Digest) S&S Trade.

Magic Moments: The Busy Woman's Guide to Forgotten Pleasures. Kim Goad. LC 97-12432. 288p. (Orig.). 1997. pap. 9.95 (*1-881394-10-7*) Commune-A-Key.

Magic Moments: 100 Seasons of Spartan Basketball. Jack Ebling & John Farina. LC 98-34924. (Illus.). 248p. 1998. 39.95 (*1-886947-41-4*) Sleepng Bear.

Magic Moments of a Poet. 2nd ed. Bobby L. Jackson. LC 83-50265. (YA). (gr. 10 up). 1994. reprint ed. pap. 7.95 (*0-9634932-7-2*) Multicult Pubns.

Magic Monastery. Idries Shah. 208p. 1972. 25.00 (*0-900860-89-8*, Pub. by Octagon Pr) ISHK.

Magic Monastery. Idries Shah. 208p. 1992. reprint ed. pap. 15.00 (*0-86304-058-6*, Pub. by Octagon Pr) ISHK.

Magic Money. David A. Adler. (First Stepping Stone Bks.). 1997. 9.19 (*0-606-11590-0*, Pub. by Turtleback) Demco.

Magic Money Box, Vol. 3738. Rozanne L. Williams. (Emergent Reader Bks.). (Illus.). 16p. (J). (gr. k-2). 1995. pap. 2.75 (*1-57471-009-5*) Creat Teach Pr.

Magic Money Box, Vol. 3981. Rozanne L. Williams. (Emergent Reader Big Bks.). (Illus.). 16p. (J). (gr. k-2). 1996. pap. 12.98 (*1-57471-119-9*) Creat Teach Pr.

Magic Monster. Joseph A. Uphoff, Jr. (Halloween Ser.: No. 9). 38p. 1992. pap. text 2.00 (*0-943123-24-0*) Arjuna Lib Pr.

Magic Moon Machine. Jane Belk Moncure. LC 87-30959. (Magic Castle Readers Ser.). (Illus.). 32p. (J). (ps-2). 1988. lib. bdg. 21.36 (*0-89565-410-5*) Childs World.

Magic Motors, 1930. Brooks Brierley. (Illus.). 160p. (C). 1996. 34.95 (*0-9615791-2-9*) Garrett & String.

Magic Motif Crochet. Maggy Ramsay. LC 87-5381. (Illus.). 160p. 1987. 16.95 (*0-87131-519-X*) M Evans.

Magic Mountain. Gross. 1998. 23.95 (*0-8057-9151-5*, Twyne) Mac Lib Ref.

Magic Mountain. Gross. 1999. per. 13.95 (*0-8057-9152-3*) Mac Lib Ref.

Magic Mountain. Thomas Mann. 1976. 33.95 (*0-8488-0576-3*) Amereon Ltd.

Magic Mountain. Thomas Mann. Tr. by Helen T. Lowe-Porter. (C). 1967. pap. text 6.75 (*0-07-553665-X*, 30993) McGraw.

Magic Mountain. Thomas Mann. 1996. pap. 17.00 (*0-679-77287-1*) McKay.

Magic Mountain. Thomas Mann. 340p. 1983. reprint ed. lib. bdg. 28.95 (*0-89966-454-7*) Buccaneer Bks.

Magic Mountain. Thomas Mann. Tr. by John E. Woods. 700p. 1995. reprint ed. 50.00 (*0-679-44183-2*) Knopf.

*__Magic Mountain: A Guide to Defining & Using a Budget Surplus.__ Kevin A. Hassett & R. Glenn Hubbard. 39p. 1999. pap. 9.95 (*0-8447-7127-9*, Pub. by Am Enterprise) Pub Resources Inc.

Magic Mountains. Rennie McOwan. (Illus.). 160p. 1996. 29.95 (*1-85158-707-1*, Pub. by Mainstream Pubng) Trafalgar.

Magic Mountains: Hill Stations & the British Raj. Dane Kennedy. LC 95-14014. (Illus.). 265p. (C). 1996. 42.50 (*0-520-20188-4*, Pub. by U CA Pr) Cal Prin Full Svc.

*__Magic Mouse.__ John Cast. 1999. pap. text 3.99 (*0-85953-568-1*) Childs Play.

*__Magic Movie Moments: Classic Scenes from Cinema.__ George Perry. (Illus.). 176p. 2000. 30.00 (*0-670-88932-6*, Viking Studio) Studio Bks.

Magic Moving Alphabet. Frank Moore. (Illus.). 32p. 1978. pap. 3.95 (*0-486-23593-9*) Dover.

Magic Moving Picture Book. Bliss, Sands & Co. Staff. Orig. Title: The Motograph Moving Picture Book. 32p. (J). (gr. 4 up). 1975. reprint ed. pap. 3.95 (*0-486-23224-7*) Dover.

Magic Mud & Other Great Experiments: The Best of Dr. Zed's Brilliant Science Activities. Gordon Penrose. (Illus.). 48p. (YA). (gr. 3 up). 1994. pap. 8.95 (*0-920775-18-7*, Pub. by Owl Bks) Firefly Bks Ltd.

Magic Mushrooms Around the World: A Scientific Journey Across Cultures & Time. Jochen Gartz. Ed. & Tr. by Claudia Taake from GER. LC 96-77598.Tr. of Narrenshwamme: Psychotrope Pilze in Europa: Herausforderung au Forschung und Wertsystem. (Illus.). 136p. 1996. pap. 22.95 (*0-9653399-0-4*, LIS Publns) Luna Info.

Magic Mushrooms of the Pacific Northwest. John W. Allen. (Ethnomycological Journals Sacred Mushroom Studies: No. 4). (Illus.). 1996. pap. 12.00 (*1-58214-026-X*) Mltilingl Bks.

Magic Music. (Read with Me Key Words to Reading Ser.: No. 9010-10). (Illus.). (J). (ps-2). 1990. teacher ed. 3.95 (*0-317-04034-0*, Ladybrd) Penguin Putnam.

Magic Music. Ladybird Books Staff. (Read with Me Key Words to Reading Ser.: No. 9010-10). (Illus.). (J). (ps-2). 1990. 3.50 (*0-7214-1323-4*, Ladybrd) Penguin Putnam.

Magic Music from the Telharmonium. Reynold H. Weidenaar. LC 94-24901. (Illus.). 436p. 1995. 66.00 (*0-8108-2692-5*) Scarecrow.

*__Magic Music from the Telharmonium: Storyboard Script.__ Reynold Weidenaar. (Illus.). i, 80p. 1998. ring bd. 10.00 (*1-930696-51-5*) Magnetic Msc Co.

*__Magic Mustache.__ Gary Barwin. (Illus.). 32p. (J). (gr. k-3). 1999. text 17.95 (*1-55037-607-1*, Pub. by Annick Pr) Firefly Bks Ltd.

Magic Mustache. Gary Barwin & Stephane Jorisch. (Illus.). 32p. (J). (gr. k-3). 1999. pap. 6.95 (*1-55037-606-3*, Pub. by Annick Pr) Firefly Bks Ltd.

Magic, Mystery, & Monsters. Sybil Downing & Jane V. Barker. (Colorado Heritage Ser.). (Illus.). 47p. (J). reprint ed. pap. 7.95 (*1-878611-06-2*) Silver Rim Pr.

Magic, Myth & Medicine. Donald T. Atkinson. LC 72-8510. (Essay Index Reprint Ser.). 1977. reprint ed. 21.95 (*0-8369-7316-X*) Ayer.

Magic Nesting Doll. Jacqueline K. Ogburn. LC 98-34397. 2000. lib. bdg. 16.01 (*0-8037-2428-4*, Dial Yng Read) Peng Put Young Read.

Magic Nesting Doll. Jacqueline K. Ogburn. LC 98-34397. (Illus.). 32p. (ps-3). 2000. 16.99 (*0-8037-2414-4*, Dial Yng Read) Peng Put Young Read.

Magic Nuggets: Making Magic Happen in Every Area of Life. Lee Wotherspoon. 104p. 1997. pap. 12.95 (*0-9620664-5-1*, 00123) S A G E.

Magic Numbers: Baseball's Best Single-Season Hitters, Decade-by-Decade. Mel R. Freese. LC 97-51614. 320p. 1998. pap. 35.00 (*0-7864-0298-9*) McFarland & Co.

Magic Numbers of Dr. Matrix. rev. ed. Martin Gardner. LC 84-43183. (Illus.). 332p. 1985. pap. 20.95 (*0-87975-282-3*) Prometheus Bks.

Magic Nutcracker. M. Hillert. (Illus.). (J). 4.95 (*0-87895-667-0*) Modern Curr.

Magic Nutcracker. Margaret Hillert. (Illus.). (J). (ps). 1981. pap. 5.10 (*0-8136-5574-9*, TK2341); lib. bdg. 7.95 (*0-8136-5074-7*, TK2340) Modern Curr.

Magic Oak: A Potawatomi Fable. Jack Wooldridge. (Potawatomi Fables Ser.). (Illus.). 21p. (Orig.). (J). (gr. 2-5). 1997. pap. 7.00 (*1-887963-08-1*) Pota Pr.

Magic of a Common Language: Jakobson, Mathesius, Trubetzkoy & the Prague Linguistic Circle. Jindrich Toman. (Current Studies in Linguistics: Vol. 26). (Illus.). 400p. 1995. 44.50 (*0-262-20096-1*) MIT Pr.

*__Magic of a Million, 1.__ David M. Schwartz & David Whitin. 80p. 1998. pap. 10.95 (*0-590-70133-9*) Scholastic Bk Fairs.

*__Magic of a Name: The Rolls-Royce Story (the First Forty Years)__ Peter Pugh. 320p. 2000. 50.00 (*1-84046-151-9*) Totem Bks.

Magic of a Symbol. Florence Farr. Ed. by Darcy Kuntz. (Golden Dawn Studies: Vol. 6). (Orig.). 1995. pap. 8.95 (*1-55818-337-X*) Holmes Pub.

Magic of Acrylic Painting with Brenda Harris, Series 1. Toby Willis-Camp. (Illus.). 100p. 1991. pap. text. write for info. (*1-883576-21-0*) Alexander Art.

Magic of Acrylic Painting with Brenda Harris, Series 2. Toby Willis-Camp. (Illus.). 100p. 1992. pap. text. write for info. (*1-883576-22-9*) Alexander Art.

Magic of Acrylic Painting with Brenda Harris, Series 3. Shirley Tucker. (Illus.). 44p. 1993. pap. text. write for info. (*1-883576-37-7*, BK-604) Alexander Art.

Magic of Acrylic Painting with Brenda Harris, Series 3. Shirley Tucker. Ed. by John Hartman. (Illus.). 44p. 1993. pap. text. write for info. (*1-883576-36-9*, BK-603); pap. text. write for info. (*1-883576-38-5*, BK-605) Alexander Art.

Magic of Aromatherapy: The Use of Scent for Healing Body, Mind, & Spirit. Gwydion O'Hara. LC 97-32117. (Illus.). 320p. 1999. pap. 14.95 (*1-56718-348-4*) Llewellyn Pubns.

*__Magic of Asia.__ Ed. by Lorenz Books Staff. (Illus.). 2000. pap. 24.95 (*0-7548-0239-6*, Lorenz Bks) Anness Pub.

*__Magic of Balboa Park.__ Mardi Snow. LC 99-70669. (Illus.). 112p. 2000. 35.00 (*0-9653087-6-6*, Pub. by Photosecrets); pap. 19.95 (*0-9653087-9-0*, Pub. by Photosecrets) Natl Bk Netwk.

Magic of Bandelier. David E. Stuart. LC 88-72050. (Illus.). 132p. 1989. pap. 11.95 (*0-941270-56-4*) Ancient City Pr.

*__Magic of Believing.__ Ted Andrews. Ed. by Pagyn Alexander-Harding & Diane Haugen. LC 00-100043. 220p. 2000. 17.95 (*1-888767-43-X*, Pub. by Dragonhawk Pubg) Partners Pubs Grp.

Magic of Believing. Claude M. Bristol. 1991. per. 5.99 (*0-671-74521-2*) PB.

Magic of Believing. Claude M. Bristol. 180p. 1991. pap. 10.00 (*0-671-76412-8*, Fireside) S&S Trade Pap.

*__Magic of Big Game: Original Essays on Hunting Big Game Around the World.__ Terry Wieland. (Illus.). 324p. 1999. 39.00 (*0-924357-77-0*) Countrysport Pr.

Magic of Blood. Dagoberto Gilb. LC 94-4315. 304p. 1994. pap. 12.00 (*0-8021-3399-1*, Grove) Grove-Atltic.

Magic of Blood. Dagoberto Gilb. LC 93-13195. 289p. 1993. reprint ed. 10.95 (*0-8263-1436-8*) U of NM Pr.

Magic of Blue. Neysa Griffith. (Illus.). 32p. (J). (ps-3). 1995. 6.95 (*1-56844-029-4*) Enchante Pub.

Magic of Candle Burning. Gerina Dunwich. (Citadel Library of the Mystic Arts). 195p. 1989. pap. 6.95 (*0-8065-1141-9*, Citadel Pr) Carol Pub Group.

Magic of Ceramics. David W. Richerson. LC 99-56648. (Illus.). 250p. 2000. 45.00 (*1-57498-050-5*, G041) Am Ceramic.

*__Magic of Change: The Illusion... The Excitement... The Reward.__ Tom Britton & Kent Cummins. LC 00-90420. 192p. 2000. 21.95 (*0-9651376-5-1*, Pub. by Bullion Bks) Midpt Trade.

Magic of Chant-O-Matics. Raymond Buckland. 232p. (C). 1982. pap. text 9.95 (*0-13-545079-9*) P-H.

Magic of Character Doll. Sabine Reinelt. LC 95-146721. (Illus.). 96p. 1999. 29.95 (*0-87588-414-8*) Hobby Hse.

Magic of Chef Aldo: His "True Taste of Italy" Favorites. Aldo Ottavianni & Lawrence Fanale. (Illus.). 94p. (Orig.). 1996. pap. 21.95 (*0-9629299-1-3*) B A Perry & Assocs.

*__Magic of Chia: Revival of an Ancient Wonder Food.__ James Scheer. 200p. 2000. pap. 12.95 (*1-55643-367-0*) North Atlantic.

Magic of Children: A Celebration of Life, Love & Happiness. Mark Freed. (Illus.). 160p. 1998. 12.95 (*1-890114-49-9*) Physicians Pr.

Magic of Chording, 3 vols. unabridged ed. Phyllis Chvostal. (Illus.). 28p. (Orig.). (J). 1998. pap. 6.00 (*0-9631050-7-8*) Safe Harbour.

Magic of Christmas. Emma Craig et al. 400p. 1998. mass mkt. 5.99 (*0-505-52283-7*, Love Spell) Dorchester Pub Co.

Magic of Christmas. Andrea Edwards. (Special Edition Ser.). 1993. per. 3.50 (*0-373-09856-1*, 5-09856-1) Silhouette.

Magic of Christmas. Beverly Lloyd. 16p. (J). 1996. pap. 3.95 (*0-87718-051-2*, 12007E) Willis Music Co.

Magic of Christmas: A Collection of Stories, Poems, Essays, & Traditions by Favorite LDS Authors. LC 92-24376. 100p. 1992. 9.95 (*0-87579-652-4*) Deseret Bk.

Magic of Christmas: Big Note Piano Edition. Ed. by Carol Cuellar. 32p. (Orig.). (YA). (gr. 9-12). 1994. pap. text 4.50 (*0-89898-982-5*, F3439P3X) Wrner Bros.

An Asterisk (*) at the beginning of an entry indicates that the title is appearing for the first time.

Magic of Christmas: Easy Piano Duets Edition. Ed. by Carol Cuellar. 32p. (Orig.). (YA). (gr. 9-12). 1994. pap. text 4.50 (*0-89898-985-X*, F3442P8X) Wrner Bros.

Magic of Christmas: Easy Piano Edition. Ed. by Carol Cuellar. 32p. (Orig.). (YA). (gr. 9-12). 1994. pap. text 4.50 (*0-89898-981-7*, F3438P2X) Wrner Bros.

Magic of Christmas: Intermediate - Advanced Piano Edition. Ed. by Carol Cuellar. 32p. (Orig.). (YA). (gr. 9-12). 1994. pap. text 4.50 (*0-89898-983-3*, F3440P1X) Wrner Bros.

Magic of Christmas - Alto Sax Edition: Popular Songs & Traditional Carols. rev. ed. Ed. by Carol Cuellar. 32p. (Orig.). (YA). (gr. 9-12). 1994. pap. text 4.50 (*0-89724-738-8*, F3445ASA) Wrner Bros.

Magic of Christmas - Easy Organ Edition: Popular Songs & Traditional Carols. Ed. by Carol Cuellar. 32p. (Orig.). (YA). (gr. 9-12). 1994. pap. text 4.50 (*0-910957-45-2*, F3451EOX) Wrner Bros.

Magic of Christmas - Five Finger Piano Edition: Popular Songs & Traditional Carols. Ed. by Carol Cuellar. 32p. (Orig.). (YA). (gr. 9-12). 1994. pap. text 4.50 (*0-89898-984-1*, F3441PFX) Wrner Bros.

Magic of Christmas - French Horn Edition: Popular Songs & Traditional Carols. Ed. by Carol Cuellar. 32p. (Orig.). (YA). (gr. 9-12). 1994. pap. text 4.50 (*0-910957-48-7*, F3454FHX) Wrner Bros.

Magic of Christmas - Guitar Edition: Popular Songs & Traditional Carols. Ed. by Carol Cuellar. 32p. (Orig.). (YA). (gr. 9-12). 1994. pap. text 4.50 (*0-910957-42-8*, F3448GTX) Wrner Bros.

Magic of Christmas - Harmonica Edition: Popular Songs & Traditional Carols. Ed. by Carol Cuellar. 32p. (Orig.). (YA). (gr. 9-12). 1994. pap. text 4.50 (*0-910957-47-9*, F3453HAX) Wrner Bros.

Magic of Christmas - Piano-Vocal-Chords: Popular Favorites. Ed. by Carol Cuellar. 32p. (Orig.). (YA). (gr. 9-12). 1994. pap. 4.50 (*0-89898-977-9*, F3436SMX) Wrner Bros.

Magic of Christmas - Piano-Vocal-Chords: Traditional Favorites. Ed. by Carol Cuellar. 32p. (Orig.). (YA). (gr. 9-12). 1994. pap. text 4.50 (*0-89898-978-7*, F3437SMX) Wrner Bros.

Magic of Christmas - Recorder Edition: Popular Songs & Traditional Carols. Ed. by Carol Cuellar. 32p. (Orig.). (YA). (gr. 9-12). 1994. pap. text 4.50 (*0-910957-43-6*, F3449REX) Wrner Bros.

Magic of Christmas - Violin Edition: Popular Songs & Traditional Carols. Ed. by Carol Cuellar. 32p. (Orig.). (YA). (gr. 9-12). 1994. pap. text 4.50 (*0-910957-46-0*, F3452V1X) Wrner Bros.

Magic of Christmas Bass Clef. 32p. (YA). 1994. pap. 4.50 (*0-910957-44-4*, F3450BCX) Wrner Bros.

Magic of Christmas Miracles: An All-New Collection of Inspiring True Stories. Ed. by Jamie C. Miller et al. LC 98-23939. 192p. 1998. 15.00 (*0-688-16456-0*, Wm Morrow) Morrow Avon.

Magic of Christmas, Tenor Sax. 32p. (YA). 1994. pap. 4.50 (*0-910957-40-1*, F3446TSX) Wrner Bros.

***Magic Of Conflict.** Crum. 1998. per. 14.00 (*0-684-85448-1*) S&S Trade.

Magic of Conflict: Personal Guidance System, Set. Thomas F. Crum. 1989. pap. text, student ed. 74.95 incl. audio (*1-877803-03-0*) Aiki Works.

Magic of Conflict: Turning a Life of Work into a Work of Art. Thomas F. Crum. (Illus.). 256p. 1988. pap. 14.00 (*0-671-66836-6*, Touchstone) S&S Trade Pap.

Magic of Conflict Video Seminar. Thomas Crum. Ed. by Judith Warner. pap. 124.95 incl. audio, VHS (*1-877803-07-3*) Aiki Works.

Magic of Conflict Workbook: Your Personal Guidance System. rev. ed. Thomas F. Crum. Ed. by Judith Warner. (Illus.). 92p. 1997. pap. text 10.00 (*1-877803-02-2*) Aiki Works.

***Magic of Crazy Quilting: A Complete Resource for Embellished Quilting.** J. Marsha Michler. LC 98-84098. (Illus.). 144p. 1998. pap. 21.95 (*0-87341-622-8*, MCQ) Krause Pubns.

Magic of Crystals. Bean Jones. 1996. pap. 16.00 (*0-7322-5708-5*) Harper Hse.

Magic of Crystals: A Look at Earth's Natural Wonders. Wendy Jones. 128p. 1996. pap. 16.00 (*0-207-19027-5*) Harper SF.

***Magic of Dialogue: Transforming Conflict into Cooperation.** Daniel Yankelovitch. LC 99-22116. 240p. 1999. 23.50 (*0-684-85457-0*) Simon & Schuster.

Magic of Disney. 88p. 1997. pap. 9.95 (*0-7935-8353-5*) H Leonard.

Magic of Dogs: Bonding with, Training, & Caring for Your Dog from Puppyhood to Adulthood. Bill Tarrant. (Illus.). 272p. 1995. 22.95 (*1-55821-365-1*) Lyons Pr.

Magic of Drawing. Robert R. Dvorak. (Illus.). 160p. (Orig.). (YA). (gr. 5 up). 1993. pap. 16.95 (*0-945625-03-0*) Inkwell Pr.

Magic of Drawing & the Artist's Drawing Pad. 2nd ed. R. R. Dvorak. (Illus.). 150p. 1993. pap. 16.95 (*0-945625-04-9*) Inkwell Pr.

***Magic of Dreams & Spirit Guides: A Spiritual Journey.** Robin James. 203p. 1999. pap. 9.95 (*0-9675484-0-3*) Shining Hand.

Magic of Duplication: Leverage Your Time & Multiply Your Profits. Greg Roy. 160p. 1997. 18.95 (*0-9651638-6-5*) Nehemiah Sol.

Magic of Egypt: The Foundation of the Eqyptian Religions; with the Magical Rituals & Spells Described. E. A. Wallis Budge. 1995. pap. 6.95 (*1-55818-313-2*) Holmes Pub.

"Magic" of Electricity. rev. ed. Cary I. Sneider et al. Ed. by Kay Fairwell. (Great Explorations in Math & Science (GEMS) Ser.). (Illus.). 64p. (Orig.). (J). (gr. 3-6). 1993. reprint ed. pap., teacher ed. 16.00 (*0-912511-52-4*, GEMS) Lawrence Science.

Magic of Fat-Free Cooking. Trudy Monti & Harry Monti. 176p. (Orig.). 1996. pap. 12.95 (*0-9649321-5-6*) Tiger Press.

Magic of Fat Loss: Lose Fat & Double Your Energy for Life! Robert Kennedy & Dwayne Hines, II. (Illus.). 64p. 1997. pap. 10.50 (*1-55210-006-5*, Pub. by MuscleMag Intl) BookWorld.

Magic of Film Editing. Joseph F. Robertson. (Illus.). 352p. (Orig.). 1984. pap. 16.50 (*0-8306-1267-X*, 1267P) McGraw-Hill Prof.

Magic of Flamingos. Pamela Haigh. 16p. 1986. pap. 30.00 (*0-7223-1978-9*, Pub. by A H S Ltd) St Mut.

Magic of Floral Painting II. Gary Jenkins. 52p. 1989. reprint ed. pap. 12.50 (*0-924639-02-4*) Bob Ross Inc.

***Magic of Folk Wisdom: A Source Book from the Ages.** Patricia Telesco. (Illus.). 2000. 9.99 (*0-7858-1205-9*) Bk Sales Inc.

Magic of Free Machine Embroidery. Doreen Curran. 112p. 1994. pap. 24.00 (*0-916896-58-7*) Lacis Pubns.

Magic of Galaxies & Stars. L. A. Gurevich. 200p. (C). 1987. 30.00 (*0-7855-6302-4*, Pub. by Collets) St Mut.

Magic of Getting What You Want. David J. Schwartz. 276p. 1987. pap. 12.00 (*0-425-10391-9*) Berkley Pub.

Magic of Grandparenting. Charmaine L. Ciardi et al. LC 95-7659. 1995. pap. 9.95 (*0-8050-4075-7*) H Holt & Co.

Magic of Green. Neysa Griffith. LC 93-34811. (Illus.). 32p. (J). 1995. 6.95 (*1-56844-028-6*) Enchante Pub.

Magic of Herbs. H. Gamache. 1991. lib. bdg. 69.95 (*0-8490-4968-7*) Gordon Pr.

Magic of Herbs. Henri Gamache. 1984. pap. 4.95 (*0-942272-10-2*) Original Pubns.

Magic of Herbs. Henri Gamache. 7.95 (*0-685-22021-4*) Wehman.

Magic of Herbs. Henri Gamache. 88p. 1972. reprint ed. spiral bd. 9.00 (*0-7873-0341-0*) Hlth Research.

Magic of Hildie. Carol A. Vercz. 6.95 (*0-910119-44-9*) SOCO Pubns.

***Magic of Horses: Activity Book.** Kim Marie Wood. LC 00-101728. (Illus.). 64p. (YA). (gr. 2-12). 2000. pap. 14.95 (*0-9671978-3-X*) Syncopated Pr.

Magic of Horses: Horses As Healers. Sharon Janus. LC 97-66587. 160p. (Orig.). 1997. pap. 16.00 (*1-888604-06-9*) SunShine CO.

Magic of Humor in Caregiving. James R. Sherman. (Illus.). 80p. 1995. pap. 9.95 (*0-935538-19-4*) Pathway Bks.

Magic of Irises. Barbara P. Lawton. LC 97-40543. (Illus.). 192p. 1998. 39.95 (*1-55591-267-2*) Fulcrum Pub.

Magic of Isha Swift. C. J. Murray. 86p. 1998. pap. 13.95 (*1-57502-884-0*, PO2158) Morris Pubng.

Magic of Italy. (In Classical Mood Ser.: Vol. 8). (Illus.). 1997. write for info. incl. cd-rom (*1-886614-30-X*) Intl Masters Pub.

Magic of Jewels & Charms. George F. Kunz. LC 97-20117. (Illus.). 494p. 1997. reprint ed. pap. text 12.95 (*0-486-29671-7*) Dover.

Magic of JuJu: An Appreciation of the Black Arts Movement. Kalamu Ya Salaam. 300p. pap. 17.95 (*0-88378-196-4*) Third World.

Magic of JuJu: An Appreciation of the Black Arts Movement. Kalamu Ya Salaam. 300p. 1998. 29.95 (*0-88378-191-3*) Third World.

Magic of Kefir Vol. 1: An Ancient Food for Modern Maladis. Donna Gates & Linda Schatz. 50p. 1996. 5.95 (*0-9638458-0-2*) Omega Nutri.

Magic of Kew. Photos by James Bartholomew. LC 88-5296. (Illus.). 128p. (C). 1988. 25.00 (*0-941533-23-9*, NAB); pap. 18.95 (*0-941533-24-7*, NAB) I R Dee.

***Magic of Kokopelli.** Ed. by Stephen W. Hill. 2000. pap. 12.95 (*1-885772-12-2*) Kiva Pubng.

***Magic of Kol Nidre: A Yom Kippur Story.** Bruce Siegel. LC 97-19314. (Illus.). 32p. (YA). (gr. k up). 1998. 16.95 (*1-58013-003-8*); pap. 6.95 (*1-58013-002-X*) Kar-Ben.

Magic of Krynn. Ed. by Tracy Hickman. LC 86-51591. (DragonLance Tales Ser.: Vol. 1). (Illus.). 352p. (Orig.). 1987. pap. 5.99 (*0-88038-454-9*, Pub. by TSR Inc) Random.

***Magic of Lasting Love: The Step-By-Step Program to Help You Make Love Last.** Joel D. Block. 252p. 2000. pap. 12.95 (*1-58741-027-3*) Wellness Inst.

Magic of Lionel Trains. 14.95 (*0-937522-52-X*, Pub. by TM Bks Video) Motorbooks Intl.

Magic of Lionel Trains, No. 2. 14.95 (*0-937522-59-7*, Pub. by TM Bks Video) Motorbooks Intl.

Magic of Lionel Trains, No. 3. 14.95 (*0-937522-71-6*, Pub. by TM Bks Video) Motorbooks Intl.

Magic of Lionel Trains, No. 4. 14.95 (*0-937522-60-0*, Pub. by TM Bks Video) Motorbooks Intl.

Magic of Living. Betty A. Neels. 1998. pap. 3.99 (*0-373-83393-8*, 1-83393-8) Harlequin Bks.

Magic of Losing Weight. Mark McHale. (Illus.). iii, 130p. 1998. pap. 19.95 (*0-9664458-0-5*) BAM Enter.

Magic of Love. Reginald C. Armor. LC 67-14304. 120p. (Orig.). 1992. pap. 10.95 (*0-917849-14-0*, 0500) Sci of Mind.

Magic of Love. Barbara Cartland. 19.95 (*0-89190-898-6*) Amereon Ltd.

Magic of Love. Tracy L. Knecht. LC 94-72732. (Illus.). 32p. (Orig.). (J). (gr. 3-5). 1995. pap. 7.95 (*1-884242-97-9*) Multicult Pubns.

Magic of Love. Alyssa Logan. LC 96-45316. (Janet Dailey's Love Scenes Ser.). 1997. pap. 3.50 (*1-56853-031-5*, Signal Hill) New Readers.

Magic of Love. large type ed. Newlyn Nash. (Linford Romance Library). 1989. pap. 16.99 (*0-7089-6784-1*, Linford) Ulverscroft.

***Magic of M. C. Escher.** J. L. Locher. (Illus.). 200p. 2000. 39.95 (*0-8109-6720-0*, Pub. by Abrams) Time Warner.

Magic of Magic: A How-To Guide for Using Magic in Affective Education. rev. ed. Rich Campbell. (Illus.). 148p. 1990. pap., spiral bd. 23.95 (*0-9633284-1-7*); ring bd. 28.95 (*0-9633284-0-9*) Brougham Pr.

Magic of Mathematics: Discovering the Spell of Mathematics. Theoni Pappas. LC 94-11653. 224p. 1994. pap. 10.95 (*0-933174-99-3*) Wide World-Tetra.

Magic of Matsumoto: The Suzuki Method of Education. Carolyn M. Barrett. LC 94-39778. vii, 156p. 1995. 19.95 (*0-88280-126-0*) ETC Pubns.

Magic of Melatonin. Alex Duarte. 41p. 1994. pap. text 6.00 (*1-891036-03-3*) Nutri Tapes.

***Magic of Merlin.** Stephanie Spinner. LC 99-34415. (Road to Reading Ser.). 48p. 2000. 10.99 (*0-307-46403-2*) Gldn Bks Pub Co.

***Magic of Merlin.** Stephanie Spinner & Valerie Sokolova. LC 99-34415. (Road to Reading Ser.). (Illus.). 48p. (J). (ps-3). 2000. 3.99 (*0-307-26403-3*) Gldn Bks Pub Co.

***Magic of Mess Painting: The Creativity Mobilization Technique.** Virginia B. Goldstein. Ed. by Kathy Goss. LC 99-61323. (Illus.). 224p. 1999. pap. 17.95 (*0-9657825-4-9*) Trans Hyper.

Magic of Method Selling. Ed. by Lodie Bunce. (Illus.). 163p. 1994. per. write for info. (*0-9641729-0-9*) eDreampubng.

Magic of Mexican Shamans. IGOOS Staff. (Illus.). 105p. 1994. 15.00 (*1-883147-81-6*) Intern Guild ASRS.

Magic of Mexican Shamaws. IGOOS Staff. (Illus.). 105p. 1994. 15.00 (*1-883147-80-8*) Intern Guild ASRS.

Magic of Micah Lasher. Micah Lasher. 256p. 1996. pap. 15.00 (*0-684-81390-4*) S&S Trade.

Magic of Mickey, Vol. 24. 48p. 1970. pap. 6.95 (*0-7935-5395-4*, 00100480) H Leonard.

Magic of Mind Power: Awareness Techniques for the Creative Mind. Duncan McColl. 177p. 1999. reprint ed. pap. 14.50 (*1-899836-29-2*, Pub. by Crown Hse) LPC Group.

Magic of Minerals. Page Bryant. 64p. 1987. pap. 7.50 (*0-89540-162-2*, SB-162) Sun Pub.

Magic of Minerals. O. Medenbach & H. Wilk. Tr. by J. S. White from GER. (Illus.). 204p. 1989. 95.95 (*0-387-15730-1*) Spr-Verlag.

Magic of Modula, No. 2. Keith Hopper. (C). 1991. pap. text 29.95 (*0-201-50993-8*) Addison-Wesley.

***Magic of Morocco.** Tahar B. Jalloun. (Illus.). 2000. 45.00 (*2-84576-010-8*) Vilo Intl.

Magic of Motivation: Quotations to Empower Dreams for the Road to Success. Career Press. LC 98-28303. 128p. 1998. pap. 7.99 (*1-56414-385-6*) Career Pr Inc.

Magic of Movement. Laura Mitchell. 96p. (C). 1988. 35.00 (*0-86242-076-8*, Pub. by Age Concern Eng) St Mut.

Magic of Moving Averages. Scot Lowry. 240p. 1998. pap. 29.95 (*0-934380-43-0*, 1287) Traders Pr.

Magic of Music. Cherry Lane Music Staff. 1999. pap. text 19.95 (*1-57560-106-0*, Pub. by Cherry Lane) H Leonard.

Magic of Music, Bk. 1. Dennis Alexander. 24p. 1998. pap. 5.95 (*0-7390-0331-3*, 18110) Alfred Pub.

Magic of Music, Bk. 2. Dennis Alexander. 24p. 1998. pap. 5.95 (*0-7390-0330-5*, 18111) Alfred Pub.

***Magic of Music: Book 3, Bk. 3.** Dennis Alexander. 24p. 1999. pap. 5.95 (*0-7390-0681-9*, 18112) Alfred Pub.

Magic of Music - Children's Song: Piano - Vocal. Ed. by Milton Okun. (Illus.). 80p. (Orig.). (J). 1988. pap. text 9.95 (*0-89524-372-5*) Cherry Lane.

Magic of Music - Christmas Songs: Piano - Vocal. Ed. by Milton Okun. (Illus.). 56p. (Orig.). 1988. pap. text 9.95 (*0-89524-457-8*) Cherry Lane.

Magic of Music - Holiday Songs: Piano - Vocal. Ed. by Milton Okun. (Illus.). 63p. (Orig.). 1990. pap. text 7.95 (*0-89524-380-6*) Cherry Lane.

Magic of Mustards. Richard M. Gauerke. 108p. 1993. pap. 5.95 (*0-934860-98-X*) Adventure Pubns.

Magic of Mutual Funds. George Hartman. 208p. 1995. pap. 12.95 (*0-7737-5679-5*) Stoddart Publ.

Magic of Mythical Creatures. Colleayn Mastin. LC 96-910711. (Illus.). 32p. (J). (gr. 1 up). 1997. 17.95 (*1-895910-45-5*) Grasshopper Bks.

Magic of Mythical Creatures. Colleayn O. Mastin. (Illus.). 32p. (J). (gr. 1). 1999. pap. 9.95 (*1-895910-43-9*, Pub. by Grasshopr Bks) Orca Bk Pubs.

Magic of Myths: Stories of Superstitions, Legends, & Folklore. Julie C. Heather. LC 89-51352. (Illus.). 176p. (Orig.). 1989. pap. 8.95 (*0-934616-42-6*) Valkyrie Pub Hse.

Magic of New Ishtar Power. Al G. Manning. LC 77-4502. 229p. 1986. reprint ed. pap. 9.95 (*0-941698-13-0*) Pan Ishtar.

***Magic of New Zealand.** Holger Leue & Graeme Lay. (Panoramic Ser.). (Illus.). 128p. 1999. 24.95 (*1-86436-471-8*, Pub. by New Holland) BHB Intl.

Magic of NLP Demystified: A Pragmatic Guide to Communication & Change. rev. ed. Byron A. Lewis & Frank Pucelik. LC 90-5742. (Positive Change Guide Ser.). (Illus.). 176p. 1990. pap. 9.95 (*1-55552-017-0*) Metamorphous Pr.

Magic of Numbers. Eric T. Bell. (Illus.). 425p. 1991. reprint ed. pap. 9.95 (*0-486-26788-1*) Dover.

Magic of Numbers: Learning Center. rev. ed. Irene Handberg. 8p. 1995. teacher ed. 24.95 (*1-56831-011-0*) Lrning Connect.

Magic of Numbers: Learning Center, Set. rev. ed. Irene Handberg. 90p. 1999. pap. 59.95 (*1-56831-000-5*) Lrning Connect.

Magic of Numbers: Supplementary Text for High Schools. Paul C. Emekwulu. LC 89-91024. 173p. (Orig.). (YA). (gr. 9-12). 1993. pap. text 19.95 (*0-9623353-0-4*) Novelty Bks.

Magic of Numbers & Motion: The Scientific Career of Rene Descartes. William R. Shea. LC 89-10813. (Illus.). 416p. (C). 1990. 54.95 (*0-88135-098-2*, Sci Hist) Watson Pub Intl.

Magic of Numbers & Motion: The Scientific Career of Rene Descartes. William R. Shea. LC 89-10813. (Illus.). 416p. 1993. pap. text 18.95 (*0-88135-183-0*, Sci Hist) Watson Pub Intl.

Magic of Numbers with Joy & Fun. Lalbhai D. Patel. 168p. (YA). (gr. 8-12). 1998. pap. 14.95 (*1-884962-19-X*) BookWorld.

Magic of Oil Painting, No. 1. William Alexander. (How to Draw & Paint Ser.). (Illus.). 32p. 1989. pap. 6.95 (*0-929261-37-2*, HT162) W Foster Pub.

Magic of Oil Painting, No. 2. William Alexander. (How to Draw & Paint Ser.). (Illus.). 32p. 1989. pap. 6.95 (*0-929261-60-7*, HT208) W Foster Pub.

Magic of Oil Painting with Buck Paulson, Series 1. Toby Willis-Camp. (Illus.). 104p. 1991. pap. text. write for info. (*1-883576-18-0*) Alexander Art.

Magic of Opera. J. Merrill Knapp. LC 81-22173. (Music Reprint Ser.). 387p. 1983. reprint ed. lib. bdg. 35.00 (*0-306-76148-3*) Da Capo.

Magic of Opera. J. Merrill Knapp. (Quality Paperbacks Ser.). (Illus.). viii, 381p. 1985. reprint ed. pap. 14.95 (*0-306-80251-1*) Da Capo.

Magic of Orange. Neysa Griffith. LC 93-35439. (Illus.). 32p. (J). 1995. 6.95 (*1-56844-026-X*) Enchante Pub.

Magic of Origami. Alice Gray et al. LC 77-74654. (Illus.). 132p. 1985. pap. 15.00 (*0-87040-624-8*) Japan Pubns USA.

Magic of Our Universe: Beyond the Facts. Kent Davis Moberg. 359p. 1999. pap. 14.95 (*0-9663797-2-1*) Camelot Prodns.

Magic of Oz. L. Frank Baum. (J). 20.95 (*0-8488-0787-1*) Amereon Ltd.

Magic of Oz. L. Frank Baum. (Illus.). 256p. (J). 1985. mass mkt. 4.95 (*0-345-33288-1*, Del Rey) Ballantine Pub Grp.

Magic of Oz. L. Frank Baum. LC 97-48701. (Illus.). 288p. (J). 1998. pap. 7.95 (*0-486-40019-0*) Dover.

Magic of Oz. Peter Glassman. LC 98-74774. (Illus.). 272p. (J). (gr. 4-7). 1999. 22.00 (*0-688-14977-4*, Wm Morrow) Morrow Avon.

Magic of Paper Sculpture: 16 Exciting & Creative Projects. David Swinton. (Illus.). 128p. 1997. pap. 16.95 (*0-304-34887-2*, Pub. by Cassell) Sterling.

Magic of Past Life Therapy. Richard A. Greene. ("Magic Of" Ser.: Vol. 2). 165p. (Orig.). 1992. pap. 14.95 (*0-942783-03-4*) Next Step Pubns.

Magic of Patience. LC 88-33442. (Jataka Tales Ser.). (Illus.). 32p. (Orig.). (J). (gr. 1-5). 1989. 16.95 (*0-89800-188-9*) Dharma Pub.

Magic of Patience. LC 88-33442. (Jataka Tales Ser.). (Illus.). 32p. (Orig.). (J). (ps-4). 1989. pap. 7.95 (*0-89800-189-7*) Dharma Pub.

Magic of Physics. Davies. (C). 1998. write for info. (*0-201-62608-X*) Addison-Wesley.

Magic of Physics. R. J. Weiss. 70p. 1987. 8.00 (*0-685-52037-4*, X20) SPIE.

Magic of Pomme. Ilse Sondheimer. LC 86-62731. (Illus.). (J). (gr. k-4). 1990. pap. 4.95 (*0-943156-03-3*); lib. bdg. 13.95 (*0-943156-02-5*) Rainbow Pr NY.

***Magic of Provence: Pleasures of Southern France.** Yvonne Lenard. LC 99-51797. 324p. 2000. 22.00 (*0-87127-212-1*) Princeton Bk Co.

Magic of Psychic Healing. Richard A. Greene. ("Magic Of" Ser.: Vol. 1). 189p. (Orig.). 1992. pap. 14.95 (*0-942783-02-6*) Next Step Pubns.

Magic of Purple. Neysa Griffith. (Illus.). 32p. (J). (ps-3). 1995. 6.95 (*1-56844-031-6*) Enchante Pub.

Magic of Rapport. Jerry Richardson. LC 87-63211. 1988. 16.95 (*0-916990-20-6*) META Pubns.

Magic of Recluce. L. E. Modesitt, Jr. (Saga of Recluce Ser.). 501p. 1992. mass mkt. 5.99 (*0-8125-0518-2*, Pub. by Tor Bks) St Martin.

Magic of Red. Neysa Griffith. LC 93-34813. (Illus.). 32p. (J). 1995. 6.95 (*1-56844-025-1*) Enchante Pub.

Magic of Ribbons. Kay Anderson. (Illus.). 158p. (Orig.). 1998. pap. 29.50 (*1-85486-186-7*) Nexus Special Interests.

Magic of Salt Dough. Brigitte Casagranda. (Illus.). 96p. (Orig.). 1997. pap. 17.95 (*0-85532-830-4*, Pub. by Srch Pr) A Schwartz & Co.

Magic of Sea Shells. rev. ed. Fredlee. LC 76-12931. (Illus.). 36p. (Orig.). (J). (gr. 1-3). 1985. pap. 4.50 (*0-89317-010-0*) Windward Pub.

Magic of Self-Confidence. Daniel Meacham. 1985. pap. 5.95 (*0-671-54193-5*, Fireside) S&S Trade Pap.

Magic of Self-Respect. 53p. 1983. 5.25 (*0-318-18187-8*) Newspaper Guild.

Magic of Sex. Miriam Stoppard. LC 91-29292. (Illus.). 256p. 1992. 29.95 (*1-56458-015-6*) DK Pub Inc.

Magic of Shabbos: An Introductory Guide. Mordechai Rhine. Ed. by Bonnie Goldman. 224p. 1998. 13.95 (*1-880582-25-2*); pap. 9.95 (*1-880582-26-0*) Judaica Pr.

***Magic of Shapeshifting.** Rosalyn Greene. LC 00-26121. (Illus.). 288p. 2000. pap. 16.95 (*1-57863-171-8*) Weiser.

***Magic of Soy: Healthy Cooking with Soy Protein Isolates.** Ed. by Genisoy Incorporated Staff. LC 00-20295. (Illus.). 128p. 2000. pap. 9.95 (*1-57067-090-0*) Book Pub Co.

***Magic of Spider Woman.** Lois Duncan. (Illus.). (J). 2000. pap. 5.99 (*0-590-46156-7*) Scholastic Inc.

Magic of Spider Women. Lois Duncan. LC 95-17366. (Illus.). (J). 1996. write for info. (*0-590-46095-1*) Scholastic Inc.

Magic of Star Dieting. David R. Ware. LC 87-72047. (Illus.). 180p. (Orig.). 1987. pap. 12.00 (*0-9618477-0-0*) PATH.

Magic of Stories: Literature-Based Language Intervention. C. Strong & K. Hoggan-North. 350p. 1995. pap. text 42.00 (*0-930599-36-5*) Thinking Pubns.

Magic of Teamwork: Proven Principles for Building a Winning Team. Pat Williams. LC 97-1497. 288p. 1997. 22.99 (*0-7852-7584-3*) Nelson.

Magic of the Black Mirror. Ruth Chew. 128p. (J). (gr. 4-7). 1990. pap. 2.99 (*0-590-43186-2*) Scholastic Inc.

M

M

Magic of the Book. William D. Orcutt. LC 79-107730. (Essay Index Reprint Ser.). 1977. 36.95 (*0-8369-2009-0*) Ayer.

Magic of the Cotswold Way. Mollie Harris. (Illus.). 160p. 1996. pap. 15.95 (*0-7509-1189-1*, Pub. by Sutton Pub Ltd) Intl Pubs Mktg.

Magic of the Crystals. Francisco Bostrom. 126p. 1998. pap. 14.95 (*1-886708-00-2*) Merrill-West Pub.

Magic of the Demon Ewaz. Robert Morga. Ed. by Thorguard Templar. (Illus.). 110p. 1994. spiral bd. 8.00 (*1-883147-86-7*) Intern Guild ASRS.

Magic of the Duck Pond. Susan Donahoe. (J). (gr. k-3). 1999. pap. 6.95 (*0-533-12747-5*) Vantage.

Magic of the Glits. C. S. Adler. 96p. (J). 1987. pap. 2.50 (*0-380-70403-X*, Avon Bks) Morrow Avon.

Magic of the Gods & Goddesses: How to Invoke Their Powers. D. J. Conway. LC 97-17438. (Illus.). 448p. 1999. pap. 17.95 (*1-56718-179-1*) Llewellyn Pubns.

Magic of the Heart: Reflections on Divine Love. Swami Chidvilasananda. LC 96-70628. 256p. (Orig.). 1996. pap. 12.95 (*0-911307-43-5*) SYDA Found.

*__Magic of the Many: Josiah Quincy & the Rise of Mass Politics in Boston, 1800-1830.__ Matthew H. Crocker. LC 99-15158. 280p. 2000. text 35.00 (*1-55849-222-4*) U of Mass Pr.

Magic of the Medals. Ed. by Currey Copple. 160p. (Orig.). 1996. pap. 12.95 (*0-9650432-0-7*) KatMar.

Magic of the Mind: An Exposition of the Kalakarama Sutta. Bhikkhu Nanananda. 90p. 1997. 7.20 (*955-24-0135-6*, Pub. by Buddhist Pub Soc) Vipassana Res Pubns.

Magic of the Mind: How to Do What You Want with Your Life. Louise Berlay. 1983. reprint ed. pap. 10.00 (*0-9617296-0-0*) Berle Bks.

Magic of the Minimum Dose. Shepherd. 1996. 15.95 (*0-85207-298-8*, Pub. by C W Daniel) Natl Bk Netwk.

Magic of the Minimum Dose. Dorothy Shepherd. 1964. 15.95 (*0-85032-112-3*) Formur Intl.

Magic of the Moon. large type ed. Joan E. Pickart. (Nightingale Series Large Print Bks.). 211p. 1992. pap. 14.95 (*0-8161-5301-9*, G K Hall Lrg Type) Mac Lib Ref.

Magic of the Mountains: Memories from California's Sequoia National Forest, 1919-1926. Norman L. Norris. Ed. by Eleanor Norris. LC 98-96795. (Illus.). 183p. 1998. pap. 20.00 (*0-9667922-0-3*) Tule Rvr Cntry.

*__Magic of the Musicals.__ 80p. 1999. otabind 10.95 (*0-634-00046-2*) H Leonard.

*__Magic of the Senses: A Guide for Personal Enrichment.__ Jean Champagne. (Illus.). 100p. 1999. pap. 11.95 (*0-7414-0311-0*) Buy Books.

Magic of the State. Michael Taussig. LC 96-13469. (Illus.). 232p. (C). 1997. 75.00 (*0-415-91790-5*); pap. 19.99 (*0-415-91791-3*) Routledge.

Magic of the Swatchways: Cameos of Cruising in Small Yachts. Maurice Griffiths. (Illus.). 240p. 1997. pap. 16.50 (*1-57409-042-9*) Sheridan.

Magic of the Word. May Rowland. LC 73-180756. 182p. 1972. 3.48 (*0-87159-094-8*) Unity Bks.

Magic of Thelema: A Handbook of the Rituals of Aleister Crowley. Lon M. DuQuette. LC 93-10004. (Illus.). 288p. (Orig.). 1993. pap. 15.95 (*0-87728-778-3*) Weiser.

Magic of Thinking Big. David J. Schwartz. 260p. 1990. 16.95 (*0-13-547134-6*, Busn); pap. 6.95 (*0-13-547118-4*, Busn) P-H.

Magic of Thinking Big. David J. Schwartz. 1986. audio 12.00 (*0-671-61860-1*, Sound Ideas) S&S Audio.

Magic of Thinking Big. David J. Schwartz. 192p. 1987. per. 11.00 (*0-671-64678-8*) S&S Trade Pap.

Magic of Thinking Big in Selling. Jon Doherty & Robert G. Hoehn. 224p. 1983. pap. 7.95 (*0-13-545210-4*) P-H.

Magic of Thinking Success. David J. Schwartz. 1987. pap. 10.00 (*0-87980-420-3*) Wilshire.

Magic of Three A. M. James O. Page. Ed. by Keith Griffiths. LC 86-82551. 177p. 1986. text 14.95 (*0-936174-02-1*) Jems Comm.

Magic of Trees. Ed. by Beyeler Foundation Staff. (Illus.). 148p. 1999. 45.00 (*3-7757-0798-0*, Pub. by Gerd Hatje) Dist Art Pubs.

Magic of Two. Saranne Dawson. (Love Spell Ser.). 368p. 1999. mass mkt. 5.50 (*0-505-52308-6*, Love Spell) Dorchester Pub Co.

Magic of Unknowing: An East-West Soliloquy. Mervyn Sprung. 160p. 1987. pap. 19.95 (*0-921149-08-5*) Broadview Pr.

Magic of Vowels. Ray Barsch. Ed. by Betty Lou Kratoville. (Orig.). (J). (gr. 1-4). 1997. pap. text, wbk. ed. 14.00 (*1-57128-079-0*, 8079-0) High Noon Bks.

*__Magic of Water: Reflection & Transparency at the Water's Edge.__ Ted Hochschwender. LC 00-29437. 2000. write for info. (*1-881529-62-2*) Custom & Limited.

*__Magic of Wine: A Book of Quotations.__ Jacqueline L. Quillen & George Boynton, Sr. LC 99-55747. 2000. 16.95 (*0-87833-173-5*) Taylor Pub.

Magic of Winning Proposals, Vol. 1. Laura Ricci. Ed. by George Wilkerson. LC 98-93370. 100p. 1998. ring bd. 250.00 (*0-9657399-1-0*) RThree.

Magic of Yellow. Neysa Griffith. LC 93-34812. (Illus.). 32p. (J). 1995. 6.95 (*1-56844-027-8*) Enchante Pub.

Magic of You. large type ed. Johanna Lindsey. LC 96-17262. (Romc-Hall Ser.). 366p. 1997. 26.95 (*0-7838-1839-4*, G K Hall Lrg Type) Mac Lib Ref.

Magic of You. large type ed. Johanna Lindsey. LC 92-97517. 416p. 1993. mass mkt. 6.99 (*0-380-75629-3*, Avon Bks) Morrow Avon.

Magic of Zen. Inez Stein. LC 96-22210. (Illus.). 134p. (Orig.). 1996. lib. bdg. 26.95 (*0-89334-263-7*) Humanics Ltd.

Magic on Ice: Figure Skating Stars, Tips & Facts. Patty Cranston. (Illus.). 48p. (J). (gr. 4-8). 1998. pap. 6.95 (*1-55074-455-0*, Pub. by Kids Can Pr) Genl Dist Srvs.

Magic 100. Al Lenski. 112p. Date not set. 24.95 (*1-56311-222-1*) Turner Pub KY.

Magic 1,000-Foot Circle: Eighth Air Force Precision Bombing, Mission No. 113 of 9 October 1943. Robert H. Hodges. (World War II Monograph: Vol. 24). (Illus.). 28p. 1997. 15.95 (*1-57638-101-3*, M24H); pap. 5.95 (*1-57638-100-5*, M24S) Merriam Pr.

Magic or Medicine? An Investigation of Healing & Healers. Robert Buckman & Karl Sabbagh. LC 94-42853. 261p. 1995. 27.95 (*0-87975-948-8*) Prometheus Bks.

Magic or Not? Eager. LC 99-22566. 208p. 1999. 17.00 (*0-15-202081-0*, Odyssey) Harcourt.

Magic or Not? Eager. LC 99-22566. 208p. 1999. pap. 6.00 (*0-15-202080-2*, Odyssey) Harcourt.

Magic Orange Tree: And Other Haitian Folktales. Ed. by Diane Wolkstein. LC 97-118784. 1997. pap. 14.00 (*0-8052-1077-6*) Schocken.

Magic Paintbrush. Robin Muller. 32p. (J). 1992. pap. 7.95 (*0-385-25373-7*) Doubleday.

Magic Paintbrush. Laurence Yep. LC 99-34959. (Illus.). 96p. (J). (gr. 3-7). mass mkt. write for info. (*0-06-440852-3*) HarpC.

Magic Paintbrush. Laurence Yep. LC 99-34959. (Illus.). 96p. (J). (gr. 2-5). 2000. lib. bdg. 13.89 (*0-06-028200-2*) HarpC Child Bks.

Magic Paintbrush. Laurence Yep. LC 99-34959. (Illus.). 96p. (J). (gr. 3-7). 2000. 13.95 (*0-06-028199-5*) HarpC Child Bks.

Magic Peach: A Story from Japan. Janet Palazzo-Craig. LC 96-131603. (First-Start Legends Ser.). (Illus.). 32p. (Orig.). (J). (gr. k-2). 1996. pap. 4.95 (*0-8167-3996-X*) Troll Communs.

Magic Peach: A Story from Japan. enl. ed. Janet Palazzo-Craig. 1999. pap. text 18.95 (*0-8167-3997-8*) Troll Communs.

Magic Peasant. Henry Brewis. (Illus.). 128p. 1986. pap. 8.95 (*0-85236-162-9*, Pub. by Farming Pr) Diamond Farm Bk.

Magic Pen Five. (J). 1991. pap. 1.97 (*1-56297-109-3*, MP-5) Lee Pubns KY.

Magic Pen Four. (J). 1991. pap. 1.97 (*1-56297-108-5*, MP-4) Lee Pubns KY.

Magic Pen of Joseph Clement Coll. 2nd ed. Walt Reed. (Illus.). 176p. 1994. reprint ed. pap. 30.00 (*0-9627642-0-5*) Illustration Hse.

Magic Pen One. (J). (gr. 3 up). 1991. pap. 1.97 (*1-56297-105-0*, MP-1) Lee Pubns KY.

Magic Pen Three. (J). 1991. pap. 1.97 (*1-56297-107-7*, MP-3) Lee Pubns KY.

Magic Pen Two. (J). 1991. pap. 1.97 (*1-56297-106-9*, MP-2) Lee Pubns KY.

Magic Pencil: Teaching Children Creative Writing Exercises & Activities for Children, Their Parents, & Their Teachers. rev. ed. Eve Shelnutt. LC 94-2861. (Illus.). 128p. 1993. reprint ed. pap. 8.95 (*1-56145-045-6*) Peachtree Pubs.

Magic Penny Big Book: Black & White Nellie Edge I Can Read & Sing Big Book. Malvina Reynolds. (Illus.). (J). (ps-2). 1988. pap. text 21.00 (*0-922053-19-7*) N Edge Res.

Magic People. Arland Ussher. 12.95 (*0-8159-6200-2*) Devin.

*__Magic Phrase: Critical Essays on Christina Stead.__ Ed. by Margaret Harris. 2000. pap. 32.95 (*0-7022-2506-1*, Pub. by Univ Queensland Pr) Intl Spec Bk.

Magic Picture see Three Magic Flip Books

Magic Place. Lemieux. LC 98-29378. (Fairy Lair Ser.: 3). 160p. (J). (gr. 4-6). 1998. mass mkt. 3.99 (*0-689-81727-4*) S&S Childrens.

Magic Pocket. Michio Mado. Tr. by U. Michiko. LC 97-75774. (Illus.). 32p. (J). (ps-3). 1998. per. 16.00 (*0-689-82137-9*) S&S Childrens.

Magic Poems. Ed. by John Foster. (Illus.). 32p. (J). (gr. k up). 1997. pap. 7.95 (*0-19-276153-6*) OUP.

Magic Pool. Gaele Mogwe. (Junior African Writers Ser.). (Illus.). 80p. (J). (gr. 3 up). 1992. pap. 3.88 (*0-7910-2910-7*) Chelsea Hse.

*__Magic Porridge Pot.__ (First Favourite Tales Ser.). 32p. (J). 1999. text 4.95 (*0-7214-9742-X*, Ladybrd) Penguin Putnam.

Magic Porridge Pot, 001. Paul Galdone. LC 76-3531. (Illus.). 32p. (J). (ps-3). 1979. 16.00 (*0-395-28805-3*, Clarion Bks) HM.

Magic Porridge Pot. Harriet Ziefert. (Illus.). (J). (ps-2). 1997. pap. 3.99 (*0-14-038189-9*) Viking Penguin.

Magic Porridge Pot: Children's Story Written in Arabic. (ARA., Illus.). (J). (gr. 3-5). 1987. 4.95 (*0-86685-205-0*) Intl Bk Ctr.

Magic Pouch. Claire Jones & Bob Varga. 38p. (J). (gr. k-5). 1995. mass mkt. 4.00 (*1-58193-166-2*) Brown Bag Prods.

Magic Power of Healing: Learn to Heal Yourself. Beverly C. Jaegers. (Illus.). 110p. 1979. pap. text 6.00 (*0-910035-01-6*) Aries Prod.

Magic Power of Self-Image. Maxwell Maltz. 1989. mass mkt. 5.99 (*0-671-70461-3*) PB.

Magic Power of White Witchcraft. rev. ed. Gavin Frost & Yvonne Frost. LC 99-24054. 224p. 1999. pap. 12.00 (*0-7352-0093-9*) PH Pr.

Magic Power of Your Mind. Walter M. Germain. 320p. 1966. pap. 10.00 (*0-87980-093-3*) Wilshire.

Magic Prague. Angelo M. Ripellino. Tr. by David N. Marinelli from ITA. LC 92-11065. 1993. 40.00 (*0-520-07352-5*, Pub. by U CA Pr) Cal Prin Full Svc.

Magic Presence. Godfre R. King. LC 84-50382. (Saint Germain Ser.: Vol. 2). (Illus.). 400p. 1935. 26.00 (*1-878891-06-5*); pap. 18.00 (*1-878891-07-3*) St Germain Press Inc.

Magic Pretzel. James Magorian. LC 88-71603. (Illus.). 32p. (J). (gr. 2-5). 1988. pap. 3.00 (*0-930674-28-6*) Black Oak.

*__Magic Pretzel.__ Daniel Pinkwater. LC 00-21993. (Werewolf Club Ser.: Vol. 1). (Illus.). 78p. (J). (gr. 2-5). 2000. pap. 3.99 (*0-689-83790-9*) Aladdin.

*__Magic Pretzel.__ Daniel Pinkwater. (Werewolf Club Ser.). (Illus.). (J). (gr. 4-6). 2000. 15.00 (*0-689-83800-X*) Atheneum Yung Read.

Magic Principality: A Pocket Guide to Monaco-Monte Carlo. LC 94-2632. (Eringer Travel Guide Ser.). 112p. 1994. pap. 8.95 (*0-910155-30-5*) Bartleby Pr.

Magic Pumpkin. Bill Martin, Jr. LC 89-11162. (Illus.). 32p. (J). (ps-2). 1996. pap. 5.95 (*0-8050-4904-5*, B Martin BYR) H Holt & Co.

Magic Pumpkin. Bill Martin, Jr. & John Archambault. LC 89-11162. (Illus.). 32p. (J). (ps-2). 1995. 14.95 (*0-8050-1134-X*, Bks Young Read) H Holt & Co.

*__Magic Pumpkin.__ Scholastic Books Staff. (Teletubbies Ser.). (Illus.). 12p. (ps-k). 2000. 5.99 (*0-439-15514-2*) Scholastic Inc.

Magic Puppets. Molly Mia Stewart. (Sweet Valley Kids Ser.: No. 53). (J). (gr. 1-3). 1994. 8.70 (*0-606-07106-7*, Pub. by Turtleback) Demco.

Magic Purse. Yoshiko Uchida. LC 92-30132. (Illus.). 32p. (J). (gr. 1-4). 1993. 15.95 (*0-689-50559-0*) McElderry Bks.

Magic Quilt. Clair Thompson. (Illus.). (J). (gr. k-2). 1995. pap. 8.95 incl. audio (*0-7608-0493-1*); pap. 4.95 (*1-56801-786-3*) Sundance Pub.

Magic Quilt, Big bk. Blair Thompson. (Illus.). (J). (gr. k-2). 1995. pap. 17.95 (*1-56801-785-5*) Sundance Pub.

Magic Quilted Mandalas: Circle Medallions Made Easy. Sheila Finklestein. LC 98-87363. (Illus.). 128p. 1999. per. 18.95 (*0-87341-635-X*) Krause Pubns.

Magic Quilts. Charles E. Fager. (Illus.). 100p. (J). (gr. 3-6). 1990. pap. 12.95 (*0-945177-03-8*) Kimo Pr.

Magic Reader, 5 bks., Bk. 1. Louise Guhl. 51p. 1989. 4.95 (*0-8497-9380-7*, WP190) Kjos.

Magic Reader, 5 bks., Bk. 2. Louise Guhl. 50p. 1989. 4.95 (*0-8497-9381-5*, WP191) Kjos.

Magic Reader, 5 bks., Bk. 3. Louise Guhl. 47p. 1989. 4.95 (*0-8497-9382-3*, WP192) Kjos.

Magic Reader, 5 bks., Bk. 4. Louise Guhl. 52p. 1991. 4.95 (*0-8497-9429-3*, WP318) Kjos.

Magic Reader, 5 bks., Bk. 5. Louise Guhl. 48p. 1991. 4.95 (*0-8497-9430-7*, WP319) Kjos.

*__Magic Realism.__ Joan Mellen. (Literary Topics Ser.: Vol. 5). (Illus.). 179p. 2000. 49.95 (*0-7876-3972-9*) Gale.

Magic Realism: Social Context & Discourse. Maria-Elena Angulo. LC 94-35674. (Latin American Studies: Vol. 5). (Illus.). 144p. 1995. text 35.00 (*0-8153-1183-4*, H1675) Garland.

Magic Realism & the Legacy of the Holocaust. Ori Z. Soltes. (Illus.). (Orig.). 1997. pap. write for info. (*1-881456-37-4*) B B K Natl Jew Mus.

Magic, Rhetoric, & Literacy: An Eccentric History of the Composing Imagination. William A. Covino. LC 93-41344. (SUNY Series, Literacy, Culture, & Learning: Theory & Practice). 189p. (C). 1994. pap. text 16.95 (*0-7914-2084-1*) State U NY Pr.

Magic, Rhetoric, & Literacy: An Eccentric History of the Composing Imagination. William A. Covino. LC 93-41344. (SUNY Series, Literacy, Culture, & Learning: Theory & Practice). 189p. (C). 1994. text 49.50 (*0-7914-2083-3*) State U NY Pr.

Magic Ride in Foozbah Land: An Inside Look at Diabetes. Jean Betschart. 48p. 1995. pap. 12.95 (*0-471-34755-8*) Wiley.

Magic Ring: Interconnected Stories. Jonathan Gillman. LC 98-83090. 208p. 2000. pap. 13.95 (*0-88739-235-0*) Creat Arts Bk.

Magic Ringlet. Konstantin Paustovsky. pap. 5.00 (*0-201-09277-8*) Addison-Wesley.

Magic Rocking Chair. Anne Carabis. (Illus.). 28p. (Orig.). (J). (ps-3). 1980. pap. 3.50 (*0-9605802-0-4*) Carabis.

Magic Saddle. Cristobel Mattingley. LC 95-72230. (Illus.). 40p. (J). (ps-3). 1996. 16.00 (*0-689-80959-X*) S&S Bks Yung.

*__Magic Salsa.__ Woods. 176p. 1998. pap. 14.95 (*0-471-34672-1*) Wiley.

Magic Salsa: 125 Naturally Low-Fat Bold & Brassy Sauces to Add Flavor to Any Meal. David Woods. LC 98-231252. 176p. 1998. pap. 14.95 (*1-56561-147-0*) Wiley.

Magic School & Other Stories see Escuela de Magia y Otros Cuentos

Magic School Bis Gets Ants in Its Pants see Autobus Magico Siente un Inquietante Hormigueo

Magic School Bus: Hello Out There. Joanna Cole. 24p. (J). (gr. k-2). 1995. pap. 3.50 (*0-590-52792-4*) Scholastic Inc.

Magic School Bus All Dried Up see Autobus Magico Se Reseca

Magic School Bus All Dried Up: A Book about Deserts. Joanna Cole. (Magic School Bus Ser.). (J). (ps-3). 1996. pap. 2.99 (*0-590-50831-8*) Scholastic Inc.

Magic School Bus All Dried Up: A Book about Deserts. Suzanne Weyn. (Magic School Bus Ser.). (J). (gr. k-2). 1996. 8.19 (*0-606-09583-7*, Pub. by Turtleback) Demco.

Magic School Bus All Dried up: A Book about Deserts see L'Autobus Magique Se Fait RtTir: Un Livre Sur les Deserts

Magic School Bus & the Electric Field Trip. Illus. by Bruce Degen. LC 97-2080. (Magic School Bus Ser.). 56p. (J). (gr. 1-4). 1997. 15.95 (*0-590-44682-7*); pap. 4.99 (*0-590-44683-5*) Scholastic Inc.

*__Magic School Bus & the Electric Field Trip.__ Illus. by Bruce Degen. (Magic School Bus Ser.). (J). (gr. k-4). 1999. pap. text 39.92 (*0-439-04356-5*) Scholastic Inc.

*__Magic School Bus & the Electric Field Trip: Literature Unit.__ Ruth M. Young. (Illus.). 48p. 1999. pap., teacher ed. 7.95 (*1-57690-082-7*, TCM2082) Tchr Create Mat.

Magic School Bus Answers Questions: A Book of Questions & Answers. Joanna Cole. (Magic School Bus Ser.). (Illus.). 32p. (J). (gr. k-2). 1999. mass mkt. 3.50 (*0-439-04332-8*) Scholastic Inc.

Magic School Bus Ant Farm Package. Joanna Cole. (Illus.). (J). (ps-3). 1996. pap. 9.99 (*0-590-56621-0*) Scholastic Inc.

Magic School Bus at the Waterworks. Joanna Cole. (Magic School Bus Ser.). (FRE., Illus.). (J). (gr. 1-4). pap. 6.99 (*0-590-71792-8*); pap. 13.99 incl. audio (*0-590-73932-8*) Scholastic Inc.

Magic School Bus at the Waterworks. Joanna Cole. (Magic School Bus Ser.). (Illus.). 56p. (J). (ps-3). 1986. 14.95 (*0-590-43739-9*, Scholastic Hardcover) Scholastic Inc.

Magic School Bus at the Waterworks. Joanna Cole. LC 86-6672. (Magic School Bus Ser.). (Illus.). 40p. (J). (gr. 1-4). 1988. pap. 4.95 (*0-590-40360-5*, Scholastic Hardcover) Scholastic Inc.

Magic School Bus at the Waterworks. Joanna Cole. (Magic School Bus Ser.). (Illus.). (J). (gr. 1-4). 1995. 14.95 (*0-614-03341-1*) Scholastic Inc.

Magic School Bus at the Waterworks. Joanna Cole. (Magic School Bus Ser.). (J). (gr. 1-4). 1986. 10.15 (*0-606-03611-3*, Pub. by Turtleback) Demco.

Magic School Bus at the Waterworks. large type ed. Joanna Cole. (Magic School Bus Ser.). (J). (ps-3). 1989. 19.95 (*0-590-72488-6*) Scholastic Inc.

Magic School Bus at the Waterworks, Big Bk. large type ed. Joanna Cole. (Magic School Bus Ser.). (FRE., Illus.). (J). (gr. 1-4). 35.99 (*0-590-73528-4*) Scholastic Inc.

Magic School Bus at the Waterworks: Teacher's Edition. Greg Young. (Science/Literature Unit Ser.). (Illus.). 48p. (J). 1996. pap., teacher ed. 7.95 (*1-57690-088-6*, TCM2088) Tchr Create Mat.

Magic School Bus Beehive Activity. Joanna Cole. 1996. pap. write for info. (*0-590-94832-6*, Scholastic Hardcover) Scholastic Inc.

Magic School Bus Blows Its Top see Autobus Magico Explota

*__Magic School Bus Blows Its Top: A Book about Volcanoes.__ Gail Herman. (Magic School Bus Ser.). (Illus.). (J). (ps-3). 1999. pap. 10.55 (*0-7857-7533-1*) Econo-Clad Bks.

Magic School Bus Blows Its Top: A Book about Volcanoes. Gail Herman. Tr. by Lucie Duchesne. (Magic School Bus Ser.). (FRE., Illus.). 32p. (J). (gr. k-2). 1996. pap. 5.99 (*0-590-16046-X*) Scholastic Inc.

Magic School Bus Blows Its Top: A Book about Volcanoes. Gail Herman. LC 96-181115. (Magic School Bus Ser.). (Illus.). 32p. (J). (ps-3). 1996. pap. 2.99 (*0-590-50835-0*) Scholastic Inc.

Magic School Bus Blows Its Top: A Book about Volcanoes. Gail Herman. (Magic School Bus Ser.). (Illus.). (J). (gr. k-2). 1996. 8.19 (*0-606-09584-5*, Pub. by Turtleback) Demco.

Magic School Bus Briefcase, 5 bks., Set. Joanna Cole. (Magic School Bus Ser.). (Illus.). (J). (ps-3). 1995. pap. 24.75 (*0-590-22300-3*) Scholastic Inc.

Magic School Bus Butterfly & the Bog Beast: A Book about Butterfly Camouflage. Nancy E. Krulik. (Magic School Bus Ser.). (Illus.). (J). (ps-3). 1996. pap. 2.99 (*0-590-50834-2*) Scholastic Inc.

Magic School Bus Butterfly & the Bog Beast: A Book about Butterfly Camouflage. Nancy E. Krulik. (Magic School Bus Ser.). (Illus.). (J). (gr. k-2). 1996. 8.19 (*0-606-09585-3*, Pub. by Turtleback) Demco.

Magic School Bus Explorations, No. C. Scholastic, Inc. Staff. Vol. C. 64p. (J). (ps-3). 1995. pap. 3.95 (*0-590-25759-5*) Scholastic Inc.

Magic School Bus Explorations, No. A. Scholastic, Inc. Staff. Vol. A. 64p. (J). (gr. k-3). 1995. pap. 3.95 (*0-590-25757-9*) Scholastic Inc.

Magic School Bus Explores the Senses. Joanna Cole. LC 98-18662. (Magic School Bus Ser.). (Illus.). 47p. (J). (gr. 1-4). 1999. 15.95 (*0-590-44697-5*); 159.50 (*0-439-05987-9*) Scholastic Inc.

*__Magic School Bus Gets a Bright Idea: A Book about Light.__ Nancy White. (Magic School Bus Ser.). (Illus.). 32p. (J). (gr. k-2). 1999. mass mkt. 3.50 (*0-439-10274-X*) Scholastic Inc.

*__Magic School Bus Gets Ants in Its Pants: A Book about Ants.__ Linda Beech. (Magic School Bus Ser.). (Illus.). (J). (ps-3). 1999. pap. 9.95 (*0-7857-7531-5*) Econo-Clad Bks.

Magic School Bus Gets Ants in Its Pants: A Book about Ants. Linda Beech. Tr. by Lucie Duchesne. (Magic School Bus Ser.). (FRE., Illus.). (J). (gr. k-2). 1996. pap. 5.99 (*0-590-16037-0*) Scholastic Inc.

Magic School Bus Gets Ants in Its Pants: A Book about Ants. Linda Beech. (Magic School Bus Ser.). (Illus.). (J). (ps-3). 1996. pap. 2.99 (*0-590-40024-X*) Scholastic Inc.

Magic School Bus Gets Ants in Its Pants: A Book about Ants. Linda Beech. (Magic School Bus Ser.). (Illus.). (J). (gr. k-2). 1996. 8.19 (*0-606-09586-1*, Pub. by Turtleback) Demco.

*__Magic School Bus Gets Baked in a Cake: A Book about Kitchen Chemistry.__ Linda Beech. (Magic School Bus Ser.). (Illus.). (J). (ps-3). 1999. pap. 10.55 (*0-7857-5622-1*) Econo-Clad Bks.

Magic School Bus Gets Baked in a Cake: A Book about Kitchen Chemistry. Linda Beech. Tr. by Lucie Duchesne from ENG. (Magic School Bus Ser.). (FRE., Illus.). 32p. (J). (gr. k-2). pap. 5.99 (*0-590-24660-7*) Scholastic Inc.

Magic School Bus Gets Baked in a Cake: A Book about Kitchen Chemistry. Linda Beech. LC 94-38834. (Magic School Bus Ser.). (Illus.). 32p. (J). (ps-3). 1995. pap. 2.99 (*0-590-22295-3*) Scholastic Inc.

An Asterisk (*) at the beginning of an entry indicates that the title is appearing for the first time.

Magic School Bus Gets Baked in a Cake: A Book about Kitchen Chemistry. Linda Beech. (Magic School Bus Ser.). (Illus.). (J). (gr. k-2). 1995. 8.19 (*0-606-07820-7*, Pub. by Turtleback) Demco.

Magic School Bus Gets Cold Feet: A Book about Warm & Cold Blooded Animals. Tracey West. (Magic School Bus Ser.). (Illus.). (J). (gr. k-2). 1998. 8.19 (*0-606-13589-8*, Pub. by Turtleback) Demco.

Magic School Bus Gets Cold Feet: A Book about Warm & Cold Blooded Animals. Tracy West. (Magic School Bus Ser.). 32p. (J). (gr. k-2). 1998. pap. text 2.99 (*0-590-39724-9*) Scholastic Inc.

Magic School Bus Gets Eaten see Autobus Magico es Devorado

***Magic School Bus Gets Eaten: A Book about Food Chains.** Patricia Relf. (Magic School Bus Ser.). (Illus.). (J). (gr. k-2). 1999. pap. 10.55 (*0-7857-7530-7*) Econo-Clad Bks.

Magic School Bus Gets Eaten: A Book about Food Chains. Patricia Relf. Tr. by Lucie Duchesne. (Magic School Bus Ser.). (FRE., Illus.). 32p. (J). (gr. k-2). 1996. pap. 5.99 (*0-590-16038-9*) Scholastic Inc.

Magic School Bus Gets Eaten: A Book about Food Chains. Patricia Relf. LC 96-181116. (Magic School Bus Ser.). (Illus.). (J). (ps-3). 1996. pap. 2.99 (*0-590-48414-1*) Scholastic Inc.

Magic School Bus Gets Eaten: A Book about Food Chains. Patricia Relf. (Magic School Bus Ser.). (Illus.). (J). (gr. k-2). 1996. 8.19 (*0-606-09587-X*, Pub. by Turtleback) Demco.

Magic School Bus Gets Planted: A Book about Photosynthesis. Illus. by Bruce Degen. (Magic School Bus Ser.). (J). (gr. k-2). 1997. pap. 2.99 (*0-614-29015-5*) Scholastic Inc.

Magic School Bus Gets Planted: A Book about Photosynthesis. Illus. by Bruce Degen. (Magic School Bus Ser.). (J). (gr. k-2). 1997. mass mkt. 2.99 (*0-590-92246-7*) Scholastic Inc.

Magic School Bus Gets Planted: A Book about Photosynthesis, Incl. planting pkg. Joanna Cole. (Magic School Bus Ser.). (Illus.). (J). (gr. k-2). 1997. pap. text 9.99 (*0-590-33117-5*) Scholastic Inc.

Magic School Bus Gets Planted: A Book about Photosynthesis see Autobus Magico Se Queda Plantado: Un Libro Sobre la Fotosintesis

***Magic School Bus Gets Programmed: A Book About Computers, Vol. 1.** Nancy White. (Magic School Bus Ser.). (Illus.). 32p. (J). (gr. k-2). 1999. mass mkt. 3.50 (*0-590-18731-7*) Scholastic Inc.

***Magic School Bus Goes Upstream: A Book about Salmon Migration.** Nancy E. Krulik. (Magic School Bus Ser.). (Illus.). (J). (ps-3). 1999. pap. 10.55 (*0-613-02738-8*) Econo-Clad Bks.

Magic School Bus Goes Upstream: A Book about Salmon Migration. Nancy E. Krulik. (Magic School Bus Ser.). (Illus.). (J). (gr. k-2). 1997. pap. 2.99 (*0-614-29016-3*) Scholastic Inc.

Magic School Bus Goes Upstream: A Book about Salmon Migration. Nancy E. Krulik. (Magic School Bus Ser.). (Illus.). (J). (gr. k-2). 1997. pap. 2.99 (*0-590-92232-7*) Scholastic Inc.

Magic School Bus Goes Upstream: A Book about Salmon Migration. Nancy E. Krulik. (Magic School Bus Ser.). (Illus.). (J). (gr. k-2). 1997. 8.19 (*0-606-11591-9*, Pub. by Turtleback) Demco.

Magic School Bus Going Batty see Autobus Magico Vuelo Nocturno

Magic School Bus Going Batty: A Book about Bats. Nancy E. Krulik. LC 49-243550. (Magic School Bus Ser.). (Illus.). 32p. (J). (ps-3). 1996. pap. text 2.99 (*0-590-73872-0*) Scholastic Inc.

***Magic School Bus Going Batty: A Book about Bats.** Nancy E. Krulik. (Magic School Bus Ser.). (Illus.). (J). (ps-3). 1999. pap. 10.55 (*0-613-00274-1*) Econo-Clad Bks.

Magic School Bus Going Batty: A Book about Bats. Nancy E. Krulik. (Magic School Bus Ser.). (Illus.). (J). (gr. k-2). 1996. 8.19 (*0-606-10864-5*, Pub. by Turtleback) Demco.

Magic School Bus Hello Out There: A Sticker Book about the Solar System. Joanna Cole. LC 96-143571. 16p. (J). (ps-3). 1995. pap. 3.50 (*0-590-88129-9*, Scholastic Hardcover) Scholastic Inc.

Magic School Bus Hops Home: A Book about Animal Habitats. Patricia Relf. LC 94-25969. (Magic School Bus Ser.). (Illus.). 32p. (J). (ps-3). 1995. pap. 2.50 (*0-590-48413-3*) Scholastic Inc.

Magic School Bus Hops Home: A Book about Animal Habitats. Patricia Relf. (Magic School Bus Ser.). (Illus.). (J). (gr. k-2). 1995. 8.19 (*0-606-07821-5*, Pub. by Turtleback) Demco.

Magic School Bus in a Pickle see Autobus Magico se Descompone

Magic School Bus in a Pickle: A Book about Microbes. Nancy E. Krulik. LC 98-141285. (Magic School Bus Ser.). (Illus.). 32p. (J). (gr. k-2). 1998. pap. text 2.99 (*0-590-39377-4*) Scholastic Inc.

Magic School Bus in a Pickle: A Book about Microbes. Nancy E. Krulik. (Magic School Bus Ser.). (Illus.). (J). (gr. k-2). 1998. 8.19 (*0-606-13590-1*, Pub. by Turtleback) Demco.

Magic School Bus in a Sticky Situation: A Sticker Activity Book. Scholastic, Inc. Staff. 32p. (gr. k-2). 1997. pap. text 3.50 (*0-590-92250-5*) Scholastic Inc.

Magic School Bus in the Arctic: A Book about Heat. Joanna Cole. LC QC256.S32 1998. (Magic School Bus Ser.). (Illus.). 32p. (J). (gr. k-2). 1998. pap. 2.99 (*0-590-18724-4*, Pub. by Scholastic Inc) Penguin Putnam.

Magic School Bus in the Arctic: A Book about Heat see Autobus Magico en el Artico: Un Libro Sobre el Calor

***Magic School Bus in the Haunted Museum: A Book about Sound.** Linda Beech. (Magic School Bus Ser.). (Illus.). (J). (ps-3). 1999. pap. 10.55 (*0-7857-5623-X*) Econo-Clad Bks.

Magic School Bus in the Haunted Museum: A Book about Sound. Linda Beech. Tr. by Lucie Duchesne. (Magic School Bus Ser.). (FRE., Illus.). 32p. (J). (gr. k-2). pap. 5.99 (*0-590-24657-7*) Scholastic Inc.

Magic School Bus in the Haunted Museum: A Book about Sound. Linda Beech. LC 94-25970. (Magic School Bus Ser.). (Illus.). 32p. (J). (gr. k-2). 1995. pap. 2.50 (*0-590-48412-5*) Scholastic Inc.

Magic School Bus in the Haunted Museum: A Book about Sound. Linda Beech. (Magic School Bus Ser.). (Illus.). (J). (gr. k-2). 1995. 7.70 (*0-606-07822-3*, Pub. by Turtleback) Demco.

Magic School Bus in the Rain Forest: A Book about Rainforest Ecology. Joanna Cole. LC 99-158336. (Magic School Bus Ser.). (Illus.). 32p. (J). (gr. k-2). 1998. pap. 8.95 (*0-590-81837-6*, Pub. by Scholastic Inc) Penguin Putnam.

Magic School Bus in the Solar System see Autobus Magico En El Sistema Solar

Magic School Bus in the Time of the Dinosaurs see Autobus Magico en Tiempos de los Dinosauros

Magic School Bus in the Time of the Dinosaurs. Illus. by Bruce Degen. (Magic School Bus Ser.). (FRE.). (J). (gr. 1-4). pap. 6.99 (*0-590-24641-0*) Scholastic Inc.

Magic School Bus in the Time of the Dinosaurs. Illus. by Bruce Degen. LC 93-5753. (Magic School Bus Ser.). 56p. (J). (ps-3). 1994. 15.95 (*0-590-44688-6*) Scholastic Inc.

Magic School Bus in the Time of the Dinosaurs. Illus. by Bruce Degen. (Magic School Bus Ser.). 56p. (J). (gr. 1-4). 1995. pap. 4.95 (*0-590-44689-4*) Scholastic Inc.

Magic School Bus in the Time of the Dinosaurs. Illus. by Bruce Degen. (Magic School Bus Ser.). (J). (gr. 1-4). 1995. 9.90 (*0-606-07823-1*, Pub. by Turtleback) Demco.

Magic School Bus in the Time of the Dinosaurs: Teacher's Edition. Ruth Young. (Science/Literature Unit Ser.). (Illus.). 48p. (J). 1996. pap., teacher ed. 7.95 (*1-57690-087-8*, TCM2087) Tchr Create Mat.

Magic School Bus Inside a Beehive. Joanna Cole. (Magic School Bus Ser.). (SPA., Illus.). 56p. (J). (gr. 1-4). pap. 4.95 (*0-590-37042-1*); pap. 4.95 (*0-590-44685-1*) Scholastic Inc.

Magic School Bus Inside a Beehive. Joanna Cole. LC 95-38288. (Magic School Bus Ser.). (Illus.). 56p. (J). (ps-3). 1996. 15.95 (*0-590-44684-3*) Scholastic Inc.

Magic School Bus Inside a Beehive. Joanna Cole. (Magic School Bus Ser.). (Illus.). (J). (ps-3). 1998. pap. text 4.95 (*0-590-25721-8*) Scholastic Inc.

Magic School Bus Inside a Beehive. Joanna Cole. (Magic School Bus Ser.). (Illus.). (J). (gr. 1-4). 1997. 10.15 (*0-606-12881-6*, Pub. by Turtleback) Demco.

Magic School Bus Inside a Beehive. Joanna Cole. (Magic School Bus Ser.). (Illus.). (J). (gr. 1-4). 1998. 10.15 (*0-606-12989-8*, Pub. by Turtleback) Demco.

Magic School Bus Inside a Beehive. Ruth Young. (Science/Literature Unit Ser.). (Illus.). 48p. (J). (gr. 3-5). 1997. pap., teacher ed. 7.95 (*1-57690-137-8*, TCM2137) Tchr Create Mat.

Magic School Bus Inside a Hurricane see Autobus Magico Dentro De Un Huracan

Magic School Bus Inside a Hurricane. Joanna Cole. LC 94-34703. (Magic School Bus Ser.). (Illus.). 48p. (J). (gr. 1-4). 1996. pap. 4.95 (*0-590-44687-8*) Scholastic Inc.

Magic School Bus Inside a Hurricane. Joanna Cole. (Magic School Bus Ser.). (J). (gr. 1-4). 1995. 10.15 (*0-606-09588-8*, Pub. by Turtleback) Demco.

Magic School Bus Inside a Hurricane. Illus. by Bruce Degen. LC 94-34703. (Magic School Bus Ser.). 56p. (J). (ps-3). 1995. 14.95 (*0-590-44686-X*, Scholastic Hardcover) Scholastic Inc.

Magic School Bus Inside a Hurricane. Greg Young. (Science/Literature Unit Ser.). (Illus.). 48p. (J). 1997. pap., teacher ed. 7.95 (*1-57690-089-4*, TCM2089) Tchr Create Mat.

Magic School Bus Inside Ralphie: A Book about Germs. Beth Nadler. Tr. by Lucie Duchesne. (Magic School Bus Ser.). (FRE., Illus.). 32p. (J). (gr. k-2). pap. 5.99 (*0-590-24658-5*) Scholastic Inc.

Magic School Bus Inside Ralphie: A Book about Germs. Beth Nadler. LC 94-44655. (Magic School Bus Ser.). (Illus.). 32p. (J). (ps-3). 1995. pap. 2.99 (*0-590-40025-8*) Scholastic Inc.

Magic School Bus Inside Ralphie: A Book about Germs. Beth Nadler. (Magic School Bus Ser.). (Illus.). (J). (gr. k-2). 1995. 8.19 (*0-606-07824-X*, Pub. by Turtleback) Demco.

Magic School Bus Inside the Earth. Joanna Cole. LC 87-4563. (Magic School Bus Ser.). (Illus.). 56p. (J). (ps-3). 1987. 15.95 (*0-590-40759-7*, Scholastic Hardcover) Scholastic Inc.

Magic School Bus Inside the Earth. Joanna Cole. (Magic School Bus Ser.). (Illus.). 56p. (J). (gr. 1-4). 1989. pap. 4.95 (*0-590-40760-0*, Scholastic Hardcover) Scholastic Inc.

Magic School Bus Inside the Earth. Joanna Cole. (Magic School Bus Ser.). (Illus.). (J). (gr. 1-4). 1989. 9.90 (*0-606-04012-9*, Pub. by Turtleback) Demco.

Magic School Bus Inside the Earth: Teacher's Edition. Ruth Young. (Science/Literature Unit Ser.). (Illus.). 48p. 1995. pap., teacher ed. 7.95 (*1-55734-544-9*) Tchr Create Mat.

Magic School Bus Inside the Human Body. Joanna Cole. LC 88-3070. (Magic School Bus Ser.). (Illus.). 56p. (J). (gr. 1-4). 1990. pap. 4.95 (*0-590-41427-5*, Scholastic Hardcover) Scholastic Inc.

Magic School Bus Inside the Human Body. Joanna Cole. (Magic School Bus Ser.). (Illus.). (J). (gr. 1-4). 1992. pap. 3.95 (*0-685-53602-5*) Scholastic Inc.

Magic School Bus Inside the Human Body. Joanna Cole. (Magic School Bus Ser.). (J). (ps-3). 1993. 19.95 (*0-590-72633-1*) Scholastic Inc.

Magic School Bus Inside the Human Body. Joanna Cole. (Magic School Bus Ser.). (Illus.). (J). (gr. 1-4). 1990. 9.90 (*0-606-04736-0*, Pub. by Turtleback) Demco.

Magic School Bus Inside the Human Body. Joanna Cole & Bruce Degen. LC 88-3070. (Magic School Bus Ser.). (Illus.). 56p. (J). (ps-3). 1989. 14.95 (*0-590-41426-7*, Scholastic Hardcover) Scholastic Inc.

Magic School Bus Inside the Human Body. Young. (Literature/Science Unit Ser.). 48p. (J). 1996. pap., wbk. ed. 7.95 (*1-55734-815-4*) Tchr Create Mat.

***Magic School Bus Kicks Up a Storm: A Book about Weather.** Nancy White. (Magic School Bus Ser.). (Illus.). 32p. (J). (gr. k-2). 2000. pap. 4.50 (*0-439-10275-8*) Scholastic Inc.

Magic School Bus Lost in the Solar System. Joanna Cole. LC 89-10185. (Magic School Bus Ser.). (Illus.). 56p. (J). (ps-3). 1990. 15.95 (*0-590-41428-3*, Scholastic Hardcover) Scholastic Inc.

Magic School Bus Lost in the Solar System. Joanna Cole. LC 89-10185. (Magic School Bus Ser.). (Illus.). 40p. (J). (gr. 1-4). 1992. pap. 4.95 (*0-590-41429-1*, Scholastic Hardcover) Scholastic Inc.

Magic School Bus Lost in the Solar System. Joanna Cole. (Magic School Bus Ser.). (J). (ps-3). 1993. 19.95 (*0-590-72599-8*) Scholastic Inc.

Magic School Bus Lost in the Solar System. Joanna Cole. (Magic School Bus Ser.). (SPA., Illus.). 56p. (J). (gr. 1-4). 1994. pap. 4.95 (*0-590-46429-9*) Scholastic Inc.

Magic School Bus Lost in the Solar System. Joanna Cole. (Magic School Bus Ser.). (Illus.). (J). (gr. 1-4). 1990. 10.15 (*0-606-00583-8*, Pub. by Turtleback) Demco.

Magic School Bus Lost in the Solar System: Teacher's Edition. Ruth Young. (Science/Literature Unit Ser.). (Illus.). 48p. (J). 1996. pap., teacher ed. 7.95 (*1-57690-086-X*, TCM2086) Tchr Create Mat.

Magic School Bus Makes a Rainbow: A Book about Color. Joanna Cole. (Magic School Bus Ser.). (Illus.). 32p. (J). (gr. k-2). 1997. pap. text 2.99 (*0-590-92251-3*) Scholastic Inc.

Magic School Bus Makes a Rainbow: A Book about Color. Joanna Cole. (Magic School Bus Ser.). (Illus.). (J). (gr. k-2). 1997. 8.95 (*0-606-12763-1*) Turtleback.

***Magic School Bus Meets the Rot Squad: A Book about Decomposition.** Linda Beech. (Magic School Bus Ser.). (Illus.). (J). (ps-3). 1999. pap. text 10.55 (*0-7857-7509-9*) Econo-Clad Bks.

Magic School Bus Meets the Rot Squad: A Book about Decomposition. Linda Beech. LC 94-44652. (Magic School Bus Ser.). (Illus.). 32p. (J). (ps-3). 1995. pap. 2.50 (*0-590-40023-1*) Scholastic Inc.

Magic School Bus Meets the Rot Squad: A Book about Decomposition. Linda Beech. Tr. by Lucie Duchesne. (Magic School Bus Ser.). (FRE., Illus.). 32p. (J). (gr. k-2). 1996. pap. 5.99 (*0-590-16036-2*) Scholastic Inc.

Magic School Bus Meets the Rot Squad: A Book about Decompostion. Linda Beech. (Magic School Bus Ser.). (Illus.). (J). (gr. k-2). 1995. 8.19 (*0-606-07825-8*, Pub. by Turtleback) Demco.

Magic School Bus on the Ocean Floor. Joanna Cole. (Magic School Bus Ser.). (FRE., Illus.). (J). (gr. 1-4). pap. 6.99 (*0-590-24318-7*) Scholastic Inc.

Magic School Bus on the Ocean Floor. Joanna Cole. LC 91-17695. (Magic School Bus Ser.). (Illus.). 56p. (J). (ps-3). 1992. 15.95 (*0-590-41430-5*, 003, Scholastic Hardcover) Scholastic Inc.

Magic School Bus on the Ocean Floor. Joanna Cole. (Magic School Bus Ser.). (Illus.). (J). (ps-3). 1993. 19.95 (*0-590-72836-9*) Scholastic Inc.

Magic School Bus on the Ocean Floor. Joanna Cole. LC 91-17695. (Magic School Bus Ser.). (Illus.). 56p. (J). (gr. 1-4). 1994. pap. 4.95 (*0-590-41431-3*) Scholastic Inc.

Magic School Bus on the Ocean Floor. Joanna Cole. (Magic School Bus Ser.). (SPA., Illus.). 56p. (J). (ps-3). 1994. pap. 4.95 (*0-590-47506-1*) Scholastic Inc.

Magic School Bus on the Ocean Floor. Joanna Cole. (Magic School Bus Ser.). (Illus.). (J). (gr. 1-4). 1994. 9.90 (*0-606-06552-0*, Pub. by Turtleback) Demco.

Magic School Bus on the Ocean Floor. Ruth Young. (Science/Literature Unit Ser.). (Illus.). 48p. (J). 1996. pap., teacher ed. 7.95 (*1-57690-085-1*, TCM2085) Tchr Create Mat.

Magic School Bus Out of This World see Autobus Magico Ve las Estrella

***Magic School Bus Out of This World: A Book about Space Rocks.** Jackie Posner. (Magic School Bus Ser.). (Illus.). (J). (ps-3). 1999. pap. 10.55 (*0-613-00275-X*) Econo-Clad Bks.

Magic School Bus Out of This World: A Book about Space Rocks. Jackie Posner. LC 49-243560. (Magic School Bus Ser.). (Illus.). 32p. (J). (gr. k-2). 1996. pap. text 2.99 (*0-590-92156-8*) Scholastic Inc.

Magic School Bus Out of This World: A Book about Space Rocks. Jackie Posner. (Magic School Bus Ser.). (Illus.). (J). (gr. k-2). 1996. 8.19 (*0-606-10865-3*, Pub. by Turtleback) Demco.

***Magic School Bus Plants Seeds: A Book about How Living Things Grow.** Patricia Relf. (Magic School Bus Ser.). (Illus.). (J). (ps-3). 1999. pap. 10.55 (*0-7857-5621-3*) Econo-Clad Bks.

Magic School Bus Plants Seeds: A Book about How Living Things Grow. Patricia Relf. LC 94-38345. (Magic School Bus Ser.). (Illus.). 32p. (J). (ps-3). 1995. pap. 2.99 (*0-590-22296-1*) Scholastic Inc.

Magic School Bus Plants Seeds: A Book about How Living Things Grow. Patricia Relf. (Magic School Bus Ser.). (Illus.). (J). (gr. k-2). 1995. 8.19 (*0-606-07826-6*, Pub. by Turtleback) Demco.

Magic School Bus Plays Ball: A Book about Forces. Joanna Cole. (Magic School Bus Ser.). (Illus.). 32p. (J). (gr. k-2). 1998. pap. 2.99 (*0-590-92240-8*) Scholastic Inc.

Magic School Bus Plays Ball: A Book about Forces. Joanna Cole. (Magic School Bus Ser.). (Illus.). (J). (gr. k-2). 1998. 8.19 (*0-606-13591-X*, Pub. by Turtleback) Demco.

Magic School Bus Science Explorations - A. Scholastic, Inc. Staff. 1995. pap. 3.95 (*0-590-48766-3*) Scholastic Inc.

Magic School Bus Science Explorations - B. Scholastic, Inc. Staff. 64p. (J). (ps-3). 1995. pap. 3.95 (*0-590-25758-7*) Scholastic Inc.

Magic School Bus Science Explorations - C. Scholastic, Inc. Staff. 1995. pap. 3.95 (*0-590-48770-1*) Scholastic Inc.

Magic School Bus Sees Stars: A Book About Stars. Joanna Cole. (Magic School Bus Ser.). (Illus.). (J). (gr. k-2). 1999. pap. 3.50 (*0-590-52102-0*) Scholastic Inc.

Magic School Bus Sees Stars: A Book About Stars. Joanna Cole. (Magic School Bus Ser.). (Illus.). (J). (ps-3). 1999. pap. text 3.50 (*0-590-18732-5*) Scholastic Inc.

Magic School Bus Shows & Tells: A Book about Archaeology. Jackie Posner. LC 49-243570. (Magic School Bus Ser.). (J). (gr. k-2). 1997. pap. text 2.99 (*0-590-92242-4*) Scholastic Inc.

Magic School Bus Shows & Tells: A Book about Archaeology. Jackie Posner. (Magic School Bus Ser.). (J). (gr. k-2). 1997. pap. 2.99 (*0-614-29013-9*) Scholastic Inc.

Magic School Bus Shows & Tells: A Book about Archaeology. Jackie Posner. (Magic School Bus Ser.). (J). (gr. k-2). 1997. 8.19 (*0-606-10866-1*, Pub. by Turtleback) Demco.

Magic School Bus Shows & Tells: A Book about Archaeology see Autobus Magico Muestra Y Cuenta: Un Libro Sobre Arqueologia

Magic School Bus Spins a Web: A Book about Spiders. Joanna Cole. (Magic School Bus Ser.). (Illus.). 32p. (J). (gr. k-2). 1997. pap. text 2.99 (*0-590-92234-3*) Scholastic Inc.

Magic School Bus Spins a Web: A Book about Spiders. Joanna Cole. (Magic School Bus Ser.). (Illus.). (J). (gr. k-2). 1997. 8.95 (*0-606-12764-X*) Turtleback.

Magic School Bus Super Fun Pack. (ps-3). 1996. pap. 8.99 (*0-590-87907-3*) Scholastic Inc.

Magic School Bus Takes a Dive: A Book about Coral Reefs. Joanna Cole. LC QH541.5.C7W48 1998. (Magic School Bus Ser.). (Illus.). 32p. (J). (gr. k-2). 1998. pap. 2.99 (*0-590-18723-6*, Pub. by Scholastic Inc) Penguin Putnam.

Magic School Bus Takes a Dive: A Book about Coral Reefs see Autobus Magico Se Zambulle: Un Libro Sobre los Arrecifes de Coral

***Magic School Bus Takes Flight: A Book about Flight.** Joanna Cole. (Magic School Bus Ser.). (Illus.). (J). (ps-3). 1999. pap. 10.55 (*0-613-03342-6*) Econo-Clad Bks.

Magic School Bus Takes Flight: A Book about Flight. Joanna Cole. (Magic School Bus Ser.). (J). (gr. k-2). 1997. pap. text 2.99 (*0-590-73871-2*) Scholastic Inc.

Magic School Bus Takes Flight: A Book about Flight. Joanna Cole. (Magic School Bus Ser.). (Illus.). (J). (gr. k-2). 1997. 8.95 (*0-606-11592-7*) Turtleback.

Magic School Bus Ups & Downs see Autobus Magico Sube Y Baja: Un Libro Sobre Como Flotar Y Hundirse

Magic School Bus Ups & Downs: A Book about Floating & Sinking. Jane B. Mason. LC 49-243580. (Magic School Bus Ser.). (Illus.). 32p. (J). (gr. k-2). 1997. pap. 2.99 (*0-590-92158-4*) Scholastic Inc.

Magic School Bus Ups & Downs: A Book about Floating & Sinking. Jane B. Mason. (Magic School Bus Ser.). (J). (gr. k-2). 1997. 8.19 (*0-606-10867-X*, Pub. by Turtleback) Demco.

***Magic School Bus Ups & Downs: A Book about Sinking & Floating.** Jane B. Mason. (Magic School Bus Ser.). (Illus.). (J). (ps-3). 1999. pap. 10.65 (*0-613-00533-3*) Econo-Clad Bks.

Magic School Bus Ups & Downs: A Book about Sinking & Floating. Jane B. Mason. (Magic School Bus Ser.). (J). (gr. k-2). 1997. pap. 2.99 (*0-614-29014-7*) Scholastic Inc.

Magic School Bus Wet All Over: A Book about the Water Cycle. Patricia Relf. (Magic School Bus Ser.). (Illus.). (J). (ps-3). 1996. pap. 2.99 (*0-590-50833-4*) Scholastic Inc.

Magic School Bus Wet All Over: A Book about the Water Cycle. Patricia Relf. (Magic School Bus Ser.). (Illus.). (J). (gr. k-2). 1996. 8.19 (*0-606-09589-6*, Pub. by Turtleback) Demco.

Magic Science: 50 Jaw-Dropping, Mind-Boggling, Head-Scratching Activities for Kids. Jim Wiese. LC 97-29444. 120p. (J). 1998. pap. 12.95 (*0-471-18239-7*) Wiley.

Magic, Science, & Health. Anderson. (C). 1995. pap. text 50.00 (*0-15-500828-5*, Pub. by Harcourt Coll Pubs); pap. text, teacher ed. 26.75 (*0-15-503183-X*) Harcourt Coll Pubs.

Magic, Science & Religion & Other Essays. Bronislaw Malinowski. LC 84-19290. 274p. 1984. reprint ed. lib. bdg. 65.00 (*0-313-24687-4*, MMSR, Greenwood Pr) Greenwood.

Magic, Science & Religion & Other Essays. Bronislaw Malinowski. (Illus.). 274p. (C). 1992. reprint ed. pap. text 12.95 (*0-88133-657-2*) Waveland Pr.

Magic, Science & Religion & the Scope of Rationality. Stanley J. Tambiah. (Lewis Henry Morgan Lectures). (Illus.). 199p. (C). 1990. pap. text 17.95 (*0-521-37631-9*) Cambridge U Pr.

M

An Asterisk (*) at the beginning of an entry indicates that the title is appearing for the first time.

Magic Secrets. Rose Wyler. LC 67-4229. (I Can Read Bks.). (Illus.). 64p. (J). (gr. 2-4). 1967. lib. bdg. 10.89 (*0-06-020069-3*) HarpC Child Bks.

Magic Secrets. Gerald Ames & Rose Wyler. (I Can Read Bks.). (Illus.). 64p. (J). (gr. 2-4). 1978. reprint ed. pap. 3.50 (*0-06-444007-9*, HarpTrophy) HarpC Child Bks.

Magic Secrets. rev. ed. Rose Wyler & Gerald Ames. (I Can Read Bks.). (Illus.). 64p. (J). (gr. 2-4). 1990. 14.95 (*0-06-026646-5*) HarpC Child Bks.

Magic Secrets. rev. ed. Rose Wyler & Gerald Ames. LC 89-35841. (I Can Read Bks.). (Illus.). 64p. (J). (gr. 2-4). 1990. lib. bdg. 14.89 (*0-06-026647-3*) HarpC Child Bks.

Magic Secrets. rev. ed. Rose Wyler & Gerald Ames. LC 89-35841. (I Can Read Bks.). (Illus.). 64p. (J). (ps-3). 1991. pap. 3.95 (*0-06-444153-9*, HarpTrophy) HarpC Child Bks.

Magic Seesaw. Mary D. Thomas. 160p. 1992. pap. 10.50 (*0-9634826-0-2*) New Hope AL.

Magic Seven. Lida A. Churchill. 90p. 1996. reprint ed. spiral bd. 10.00 (*0-7873-1131-6*) Hlth Research.

Magic 7: Tools for Building Your Multiple Intelligences. Nancy Margulies. (Interactive Comics Ser.: Vol. 2). (Illus.). 36p. 1995. 16.00 (*1-56976-022-5*, 1056-F3) Zephyr Pr AZ.

Magic Seven, 1901. Lida A. Churchill. 88p. 1996. reprint ed. pap. 8.95 (*1-56459-964-7*) Kessinger Pub.

Magic Sewing Machine. Sunny Warner. LC 96-42221. (Illus.). 32p. (J). (ps-3). 1997. 16.00 (*0-395-82747-7*) HM.

Magic Shadow Show: Four Stories - Four Plays, 2 bks. Tracey Williamson. (Illus.). 24p. (J). (gr. k-4). 1999. pap. 17.95 (*0-525-44765-2*, Dutton Child) Peng Put Young Read.

Magic Shell see Regalo Magico (The Magic Shell)

Magic Shell. Nicholasa Mohr. LC 93-30403. (Illus.). 64p. (J). (gr. 2-5). 1995. 13.95 (*0-590-47110-4*, Scholastic Hardcover) Scholastic Inc.

Magic Ship. Sandra Paretti. Tr. by Ruth Hein from GER. LC 98-46493.Tr. of Das Zauberschiff. 320p. 1999. reprint ed. pap. 16.95 (*0-89272-463-3*) Down East.

Magic Ships: The Life Story of Colin Archer. Lorna McDonald. (Illus.). xi, 175p. 1997. pap. 24.95 (*1-875998-26-8*, Pub. by Central Queensland) Accents Pubns.

Magic Shoelaces. Pam Adams. (FRE., Illus.). 32p. (J). 1989. pap. 3.99 (*0-85953-471-5*); pap. 3.99 (*0-85953-820-6*); pap. 3.99 (*0-85953-572-X*) Childs Play.

Magic Shoelaces. Audrey Wood. LC 90-49097. (Illus.). 32p. (J). (ps-2). 1989. 7.99 (*0-85953-109-0*); pap. 3.99 (*0-85953-321-2*) Childs Play.

Magic Shoelaces. Audrey Wood. (J). 1996. lib. bdg. 11.95 (*0-85953-899-0*) Childs Play.

Magic Shoes. Christiane Renauld. (Child's World Library). (Illus.). 32p. (J). (gr. k-5). 1992. lib. bdg. 18.50 (*0-89565-753-8*) Childs World.

Magic Shop: Healing with the Imagination. Helen Graham. LC 92-44083. 240p. (Orig.). 1993. pap. 10.95 (*0-87728-770-8*) Weiser.

***Magic Show.** Mark Setteducati & Anne Benkovitz. (Illus.). 22p. 1999. pap. 18.95 (*0-7611-1595-1*) Workman Pub.

***Magic Show Book & Kit.** Henry Gordon. (Illus.). 48p. (J). (gr. 3-7). 1999. reprint ed. pap. 12.99 (*1-58184-054-3*) Somerville Hse.

Magic Show Mystery. Illus. by Daniel M. Duffy. LC 98-30605. (Adventures of Benny & Watch: No. 4). 32p. (J). (gr. 1-3). 1998. pap. 3.95 (*0-8075-4939-8*) A Whitman.

Magic Shows. David Graham. (CSU Poetry Ser.: Vol. XX). 92p. (Orig.). 1986. pap. 6.00 (*0-914946-58-7*) Cleveland St Univ Poetry Ctr.

Magic Shufflepoof: (An Original Story for Reading & Language Arts Education in Grades K-6) Flora Joy. (Storytelling in Education Funbooks Ser.). (Illus.). 48p. (Orig.). 1994. pap. text 7.00 (*1-884624-00-6*) Storytelling Wrld Pr.

Magic Sign: The Electric Art - Architecture of Las Vegas. Charles F. Barnard. (Illus.). 323p. 1993. 25.00 (*0-911380-91-4*) ST Pubns.

Magic Skateboard. Enid Richemont. LC 92-53010. (Illus.). 80p. (J). (gr. 3-6). 1993. 14.95 (*1-56402-132-7*) Candlewick Pr.

***Magic Skates. Mary Henke. (Illus.). 32p. (Orig.). 1999. pap. 6.95 (*0-87012-602-4*) McClain.**

An inspirational & motivational Christmas Story. In our fast paced world of instant gratification, parents have a difficult time telling children that they cannot always have what they want immediately. This story shows how one young girl named Mary learned that through Love & Trust, Dreams can come true.

Publisher Paid Annotation.

Magic Slippers. Barbara Boswell et al. 1996. mass mkt. 5.99 (*0-380-78370-3*, Avon Bks) Morrow Avon.

Magic Spectacles. Gordon J. Rowe. LC 98-85756. (Illus.). 32p. (J). 1998. pap. 8.95 (*1-56167-444-3*) Am Literary Pr.

Magic Spells. Christy Yorke. 368p. 1999. mass mkt. 5.99 (*0-553-57842-1*) Bantam.

***Magic Spells.** large type ed. Christy Yorke. LC 00-29579. (Core Ser.). 497p. 2000. write for info. (*0-7838-9028-1*, G K Hall Lrg Type) Mac Lib Ref.

Magic Spells & Formulas: Aramaic Incantations of Late Antiquity. S. Shaked & Joseph Naveh. (Illus.). 296p. 1993. text 28.00 (*965-223-841-4*, Pub. by Magnes Pr) Eisenbrauns.

Magic Spells & Formulas: The Prophetical Stories: The Narratives about the Prophets in the Hebrew Bible, Their Literary Types & History. Alexander Rofe. 218p. 1988. text 20.00 (*965-223-685-3*, Pub. by Magnes Pr) Eisenbrauns.

Magic Spices: 200 Healthy Recipes Featuring Common Spices. Donna L. Weihofen. LC 98-231251. 256p. 1998. pap. 14.95 (*1-56561-162-4*) Wiley.

***Magic Spices: 200 Healthy Recipes Featuring Common Spices.** Donna L. Weihofen. 256p. 1998. pap. 14.95 (*0-471-34683-7*) Wiley.

Magic Spoon Cookbook. Suzanne Gooding. (Illus.). 68p. (J). (gr. k up). 1997. spiral bd. 14.95 (*1-57054-085-3*) Klutz.

Magic Spring. Nami Rhee. (Whitebird Bks.). (Illus.). 32p. (J). (ps-3). 1993. lib. bdg. 15.95 (*0-399-22420-3*, G P Putnam) Peng Put Young Read.

Magic Squad & the Dog of Great Potential. Mary Quattlebaum. (Illus.). 128p. (J). (gr. 2-5). 1998. pap. 3.99 (*0-440-41279-X*, YB BDD) BDD Bks Young Read.

***Magic Squad & the Dog of Great Potential.** Mary Quattlebaum. 1998. 9.09 (*0-606-13592-8*, Pub. by Turtleback) Demco.

Magic Square: Cities in Ancient China. Alfred Schinz. (Illus.). 428p. 1997. 216.00 (*3-930698-02-1*) Edition A Menges.

Magic Squares & Cubes. W. S. Andrews et al. 419p. 1960. pap. 9.95 (*0-486-20658-0*) Dover.

Magic Stack-n-Whack Quilts. Bethany S. Reynolds. LC 97-46322. 1998. pap. text 19.95 (*1-57432-704-6*, 4995, Am Quilters Soc) Collector Bks.

Magic Staff: An Autobiography of Andrew Jackson Davis. 5th ed. Andrew J. Davis. 552p. 1998. reprint ed. pap. 24.50 (*0-7873-0241-4*) Hlth Research.

Magic Star - 6 Inspirations. Mace B. McEligot. (Illus.). 22p. (Orig.). 1995. pap. 10.00 (*0-9647921-0-9*) Mace Motif.

Magic Star 8 Innovations. Mace B. McEligot. (Illus.). 52p. 1997. reprint ed. pap. 16.95 (*0-9647921-1-7*) Mace Motif.

Magic Step. John Dranow. 128p. (Orig.). 1991. pap. text 11.95 (*0-913123-35-8*) Galileo.

Magic, Step-by-Step. Tom Russell. LC 96-3019. (Illus.). 80p. (J). 1997. 17.95 (*0-8069-9533-5*) Sterling.

Magic Step-by-Step. Tom Russell. (J). (gr. 3-7). 1997. 17.95 (*0-614-29117-8*) Sterling.

Magic Step by Step. Tom Russell. (Illus.). 80p. 1998. 6.95 (*0-8069-9548-3*, Chapelle) Sterling.

***Magic Steps.** Tamora Pierce. LC 99-31943. (Circle Opens Ser.: Vol. 1). (Illus.). 288p. (J). (gr. 4-7). 2000. 16.95 (*0-590-39588-2*, Scholastic Ref) Scholastic Inc.

Magic Stick. Barbara Shook Hazen. (Whole-Language Big Bks.). 16p. (J). (ps-2). 1992. pap. 14.95 (*1-56784-053-1*) Newbridge Educ.

***Magic Still Dwells: Comparative Religion in the Postmodern Age.** Ed. by Patton & Sally J. Patton. LC 99-31468. 250p. 2000. 45.00 (*0-520-21971-6*, Pub. by U CA Pr) Cal Prin Full Svc.

Magic Still Dwells: Comparative Religion in the Postmodern Age. Ed. by Patton & Benjamin C. Ray. LC 99-31468. 250p. 2000. pap. 17.95 (*0-520-22105-2*, Pub. by U CA Pr) Cal Prin Full Svc.

Magic Stopwatch. Heather Maisner. LC 97-6311. (Illus.). 32p. (J). (gr. 3-6). 1997. 14.99 (*0-7636-0302-3*) Candlewick Pr.

Magic Story. Frederic V. Dey. 1928. pap. 4.50 (*0-87516-020-4*) DeVorss.

Magic Story. J. McDonald. 1984. pap. 6.95 (*0-912576-09-X*) R Collier.

Magic Story. Frederic Van Rensselaer Dey. 63p. 1996. reprint ed. spiral bd. 11.00 (*0-7873-0907-9*) Hlth Research.

Magic Story Starters: Grade 1 to 3. Linda Polon. (Illus.). 44p. (Orig.). 1986. pap. 6.95 (*0-673-18561-3*, GoodYrBooks) Addson-Wesley Educ.

Magic String. Francene Sabin. LC 81-4076. (Illus.). 32p. (J). (gr. k-2). 1981. lib. bdg. 17.25 (*0-89375-547-8*) Troll Communs.

Magic String. Francene Sabin. LC 81-4076. (Illus.). 32p. (J). (gr. k-2). 1996. pap. 3.95 (*0-89375-548-6*) Troll Communs.

Magic Summer. Stanley Cohen. (Illus.). 319p. 1989. pap. 8.95 (*0-15-655117-9*) Harcourt.

Magic Summer: The '69 Mets. Photos by Stanley Cohen. LC 87-33362. (Illus.). 352p. 1988. 16.95 (*0-15-155096-4*) Harcourt.

Magic, Superstitions & Folklore: Index of Authors & Subjects. rev. ed. Sally M. Frost. LC 92-34792. 129p. 1992. 47.50 (*1-55914-894-2*); pap. 44.50 (*1-55914-895-0*) ABBE Pubs Assn.

Magic Surprises. (J). (gr. 3 up). 1991. pap. 2.68 (*1-56297-103-4*, KNMS) Lee Pubns KY.

Magic Swap Shop. rev. ed. Fay Welch. (J). (gr. 3-12). 1985. pap. 6.00 (*0-88734-509-3*) Players Pr.

Magic Tales Beauty. Robin Lawrie. (J). Date not set. pap. 3.95 (*0-448-11255-8*) Putnam Pub Group.

Magic Tales Jack. Robin Lawrie. Date not set. pap. 3.95 (*0-448-11253-1*) Putnam Pub Group.

Magic Tales Rumpel. Robin Lawrie. (J). Date not set. pap. 3.95 (*0-448-11254-X*) Putnam Pub Group.

Magic Tales Snow. Robin Lawrie. (J). Date not set. pap. 3.95 (*0-448-11252-3*) Putnam Pub Group.

Magic Tales Wild. Robin Lawrie. (J). Date not set. pap. 3.95 (*0-448-11251-5*) Putnam Pub Group.

***Magic Tanach & Other Short Plays.** Gabrielle Suzanne Kaplan. LC 99-77394. (YA). (gr. 1-12). 1999. pap. 11.95 (*0-86705-044-6*) A R E Pub.

Magic Tapestry: A Chinese Folktale. Illus. & Retold by Hitz Demi. LC 93-11426. (J). 1995. 17.95 (*0-8050-2810-2*) H Holt & Co.

***Magic Telescope.** (Illus.). 12p. (ps-k). 1999. bds. 8.99 (*0-590-98335-0*) Scholastic Inc.

Magic Telescope. Richard Paul. (Illus.). 32p. (Orig.). (J). (gr. k-3). 1996. pap. 9.95 (*0-9653238-0-3*) Twilght Pr.

Magic Temple. Hilton Hotema. 142p. 1998. reprint ed. pap. 15.00 (*0-7873-0428-X*) Hlth Research.

***Magic Terror: Seven Tales.** Peter Straub. LC 99-53216. 352p. 2000. 24.95 (*0-375-50393-5*) Random.

Magic That Works: John W. Campbell & the American Response to Technology. Albert I. Berger. Ed. by Mary A. Burgess. LC 84-373. (Milford Series: Popular Writers of Today: Popular Writers of Today: Vol. 46). 232p. 1993. pap. 25.00 (*0-89370-275-7*, 10404305) Millefleurs.

Magic the Gathering: Battlemage: The Official Strategy Guide. Mark Walker. LC 96-72644. 240p. 1997. per. 19.99 (*0-7615-1061-3*) Prima Pub.

Magic, the Gathering: Pocket Players' Guide. Wizards of the Coast Inc. Staff. LC 95-137115. 242 p. 1994. write for info. (*1-880992-29-9*) Wizards Coast.

Magic: The Gathering: The Official Advanced Strategy Guide. Beth Moursund & Mark Justice. (Magic Ser.). (Illus.). 128p. 1998. pap. 17.95 (*1-56025-199-9*, Thunders Mouth) Avalon NY.

Magic: The Gathering: The Official Deckbuilders' Guide. Tim Dedopulos. (Illus.). 144p. 1998. pap. text 13.95 (*1-56025-156-5*, Thunders Mouth) Avalon NY.

Magic: The Gathering: The Official Guide to Portal - Cards, Strategies & Techniques. Beth Moursund. LC 98-156057. (Illus.). 64p. 1997. pap. text 10.95 (*1-56025-152-2*, Thunders Mouth) Avalon NY.

Magic: The Gathering: The Official Guide to Portal Second Age Guide - Cards, Strategies & Techniques. Wizards of the Coast Staff. (Illus.). 72p. 1998. pap. 10.95 (*1-56025-198-0*, Thunders Mouth) Avalon NY.

Magic: The Gathering: The Official Guide to Tempest - Cards, Strategies & Techniques. Beth Moursund. (Illus.). 124p. 1998. pap. 16.95 (*1-56025-157-3*, Thunders Mouth) Avalon NY.

Magic: The Gathering: The Official Strategy Guide - The Color Illustrated Guide to Winning Play. Beth Moursund. (Illus.). 126p. (Orig.). 1997. pap. 16.95 (*1-56025-149-2*, Thunders Mouth) Avalon NY.

Magic: The Gathering Vol. 2: The Official Encyclopedia. 5th ed. Magazine Duelist. LC 96-61056. (Illus.). 144p. 1997. pap. text 21.95 (*1-56025-150-6*, Thunders Mouth) Avalon NY.

Magic: The Gathering Vol. 3: The Official Encyclopedia. Beth Moursund. (Magic Ser.: Vol. 3). (Illus.). 128p. 1998. pap. 22.95 (*1-56025-189-1*, Thunders Mouth) Avalon NY.

***Magic: The Gathering - Official Encyclopedia Vol. 5: The Complete Card Guide.** Cory Herndon. (Illus.). 176p. 2000. pap. 23.95 (*1-56025-271-5*, Thunders Mouth) Avalon NY.

Magic Theatre. pap. 30.00 (*1-56997-097-1*) Knowldge Adv.

Magic Theatre I Children's Musical Revue. Saundra Mathews-Deacon. (J). 1977. pap. 5.50 (*0-87129-230-0*, M12) Dramatic Pub.

Magic Theatre II Children's Musical Revue. Saundra Mathews-Deacon. 1981. 5.50 (*0-87129-396-X*, M45) Dramatic Pub.

Magic Thread: Astrological Chart Interpretation Using Depth Psychology. Richard Idemon. (Illus.). 272p. (Orig.). 1996. pap. 14.95 (*0-87728-864-X*) Weiser.

***Magic Time.** Barbara Hambly. 2000. 24.00 (*0-06-105068-7*, HarperPrism) HarpC.

Magic Time: A Guide to the Real Martha's Vineyard. Susan Spence & Rick Glassberg. LC 96-84801. (Illus.). 290p. (Orig.). 1996. pap. 19.95 (*0-9651451-0-7*) Dauntless Oyster.

Magic Tools for Raising Kids. Elizabeth Crary. (Tools for Everyday Parenting Ser.). (Illus.). 128p. (Orig.). 1995. pap. 9.95 (*0-943990-77-7*); lib. bdg. 18.95 (*0-943990-78-5*) Parenting Pr.

Magic Touch. Gila Manolson. 1992. pap. 11.95 (*1-56871-185-9*) Feldheim.

Magic Touch: Two Hand Rock Technique. Dave Celentano. 48p. 1986. pap. text 14.95 incl. audio (*0-931759-16-1*) Centerstream Pub.

Magic Toy Box. Rodney Peppe. LC 95-26136. (Illus.). 32p. (J). (ps-k). 1996. 15.99 (*0-7636-0010-5*) Candlewick Pr.

Magic Toy Shop. (Favorite Christmas Tales Ser.). (Illus.). 24p. (J). 1993. 4.98 (*0-7853-0274-3*) Pubns Intl Ltd.

Magic Toy Shop: Memories to Cherish. Jean Daugherty. (Illus.). 48p. 1998. pap. 14.95 (*0-9654732-2-8*) Signature NY.

Magic Toyshop. Angela Carter. LC 95-26415. 200p. 1996. pap. 11.95 (*0-14-025640-7*, Penguin Bks) Viking Penguin.

Magic Toyshop. Phil Roxbee-Cox & Jenny Tyler. (Young Puzzles Ser.). (Illus.). 32p. (J). (gr. k up). 1998. lib. bdg. 14.95 (*1-58086-122-9*, Usborne) EDC.

Magic Toyshop. Phil Roxbee-Cox & Jenny Tyler. (Young Puzzles Ser.). (Illus.). 32p. (J). (ps up). 1998. pap. 6.95 (*0-7460-2847-4*, Usborne) EDC.

Magic Toyshop - Musical. Patricia C. Clapp et al. 1995. 5.95 (*0-87129-505-9*, M07) Dramatic Pub.

Magic Trail Fish. Shasha. (J). 1995. pap. 14.00 (*0-689-80070-3*) S&S Bks Yung.

Magic Treble Tree. Jessian L. Rhoton. Vol. I. (Illus.). 48p. (J). 1989. lib. bdg. write for info. (*0-318-65826-7*) Happy Music Pub.

Magic Treble Tree. Jessian L. Rhoton. (All about the Magic of Music Ser.). (Illus.). 48p. (J). 1990. write for info. (*0-9624162-9-0*) Happy Music Pub.

Magic Tree. Gerald McDermott. (J). 1995. 15.95 (*0-8050-3080-8*) H Holt & Co.

***Magic Tree: A Folktale from Nigeria.** T. Obinkaram Echewa. LC 91-19770. (Illus.). 32p. (J). 1999. 15.89 (*0-688-16232-0*, Wm Morrow) Morrow Avon.

Magic Tree: A Folktale from Nigeria. T. Obinkaram Echewa. LC 91-19770. (Illus.). 32p. (YA). (ps-3). 1999. 16.00 (*0-688-16231-2*, Wm Morrow) Morrow Avon.

Magic Tree: A Tale from the Congo. Gerald McDermott. LC 72-76567. 41p. 1973. write for info. (*0-03-086716-9*) Holt R&W.

Magic Tree House Collection: Dinosaurs Before Dark; Knight at Dawn; Mummies in the Morning; Pirates Past Noon. Mary Pope Osborne. (Magic Tree House Ser.: No. 1-4). (J). (gr. k-3). 1996. boxed set 4.00 (*0-679-88389-4*, Pub. by Random Bks Yng Read) Random.

***Magic Treehouse Bundle.** Mary Pope Osborne. (J). (ps-3). 1999. pap. 15.96 (*0-641-01436-8*) Random.

Magic Treehouse Goes to Am Rev. Mary Pope Osborne. (J). 1999. pap. write for info. (*0-679-88608-7*, Bullseye Bks) Random Bks Yng Read.

Magic Treehouse Visits America. Mary Pope Osborne. (J). 1998. lib. bdg. 14.99 (*0-679-98542-5*, Pub. by Random Bks Yng Read) Random.

Magic Trees of the Mind: How to Nurture Your Child's Intelligence, Creativity, & Healthy Emotions from Birth through Adolescence. Marian Diamond. LC 97-36971. 1998. 26.95 (*0-525-94308-0*) NAL.

Magic Trees of the Mind: How to Nurture Your Child's Intelligence, Creativity & Healthy Emotions from Birth Through Adolescence. Marian Diamond. 480p. 1999. pap. 13.95 (*0-452-27830-9*, Plume) Dutton Plume.

Magic Tricks. Keith Fields. (Illus.). 80p. 1995. 16.95 (*1-57215-100-5*) World Pubns.

Magic Tricks. Ray Miller. (Illus.). 8p. (J). 1997. pap. 6.95 (*1-880592-70-3*, Pub. by Pace Prods) Andrews & McMeel.

Magic Tricks: The Master's Secrets. Ian Adair. 1995. 14.95 (*0-7858-0497-8*) Bk Sales Inc.

Magic Tricks & Card Tricks. Wilfrid Jonson. (Illus.). 196p. 1954. pap. 4.95 (*0-486-20909-1*) Dover.

Magic Tricks & More Anita Higman. LC 98-207708. (Cover-to-Cover Chapter Bks.). 56 p. 1997. write for info. (*0-7891-2004-6*) Perfection Learn.

Magic Tricks, Card Shuffling, & Dynamic Computer Memories. S. Brent Morris. LC 97-74358. (Spectrum Ser.). (Illus.). 150p. 1998. pap. text 28.95 (*0-88385-527-5*, CARDS/JR) Math Assn.

Magic Tricks for Children. Len Collis. (Illus.). 96p. (J). (gr. 3 up). 1989. pap. 6.95 (*0-8120-4289-1*) Barron.

Magic Tricks for Children. Len Collis. (J). 1989. 12.05 (*0-606-04472-8*, Pub. by Turtleback) Demco.

Magic Tricks for Kids Vol. 1: Everyday Objects. Daniel J. Morlock. (My Favorite Ser.). (J). 1995. 14.99 (*0-9649646-0-0*) Morlock Assocs.

Magic Tricks, Science Facts. Robert Friedhoffer. (J). 1990. pap. 6.95 (*0-531-15186-7*) Watts.

Magic Trumpet. Victor Cowie & Victor Davies. (J). 1997. pap. 4.95 (*0-88801-094-X*, Pub. by Turnstone Pr) Genl Dist Srvs.

Magic-Users & Illusionists. TSR Hobbies Staff. 1983. 10.00 (*0-394-53612-6*) Random.

Magic Valley. Margaret B. Houston. 1993. reprint ed. lib. bdg. 75.00 (*0-7812-5937-1*) Rprt Serv.

Magic Valley Travellers: Welsh Stories of Fantasy & Horror. Peter Haining. LC 74-186559. (Illus.). 256p. (J). 1974. write for info. (*0-575-01686-8*) V Gollancz.

Magic Village (Guatemala) Reading Level 2. (Fitting In Ser.). 1993. 2.95 (*0-88336-994-X*); audio 6.95 (*0-88336-770-X*) New Readers.

***Magic Wand.** School Zone Publishing Staff. (Illus.). (J). 2000. bds. 4.99 (*0-88743-809-1*) Sch Zone Pub Co.

Magic Wand. Hilton Hotema. 48p. 1998. reprint ed. spiral bd. 11.00 (*0-7873-1273-8*) Hlth Research.

Magic Wand: Short Course in Photography. London & Jones Staff. (C). 1997. text 9.00 (*0-673-97304-2*) Addson-Wesley Educ.

Magic Wand & Other Bright Experiments on Light & Color. Paul Dorothy et al. (Exploratorium Science Snackbook Ser.). 144p. (YA). (gr. 5 up). 1995. pap. 10.95 (*0-471-11515-0*) Wiley.

Magic Washing Machine: A Diary of a Single Motherhood. Beverly Slapin. LC 83-22547. (Woman in History Ser.: Vol. 75). 80p. 1983. lib. bdg. 40.00 (*0-86663-049-X*) Ide Hse.

Magic Weaver of Rugs. Jerrie Oughten. LC 93-4850. (Illus.). 32p. (J). 1994. 16.00 (*0-395-66140-4*) HM.

Magic Well: A One-Act Comedy. Hermann Ammann. (Illus.). 37p. (J). (gr. k up). 1972. pap. 3.25 (*0-88680-122-2*) I E Clark.

Magic Well: Director's Script. Hermann Ammann. (Illus.). 37p. (J). (gr. k up). 1972. pap. 7.50 (*0-88680-123-0*) I E Clark.

Magic Wheel. Brian Birchall. LC 93-18048. (Illus.). (J). 1994. pap. write for info. (*0-383-03701-8*) SRA McGraw.

Magic Whistle Blows. Henderson. 1999. pap. 9.95 (*0-312-24532-7*) St Martin.

Magic, White & Black. Franz Hartmann. LC 34-13669. 298p. 1980. reprint ed. pap. 14.00 (*1-878683-09-8*) TAT Found.

Magic, White & Black: The Science of Finite & Infinite Life. Franz Hartman. 292p. 1992. reprint ed. pap. 21.50 (*1-56459-132-8*) Kessinger Pub.

Magic White & Black: or The Science of Finite & Infinite Life. 4th ed. Franz Hartmann. 166p. 1998. reprint ed. pap. 18.50 (*0-7873-0375-5*) Hlth Research.

Magic Whorehouse. Thomas Tolnay. LC 79-63343. (Illus.). 1979. pap. 12.50 (*0-912292-57-1*) Smith.

Magic Whorehouse. limited ed. Thomas Tolnay. LC 79-63343. (Illus.). 1979. 75.00 (*1-882986-02-4*) Smith.

Magic Whorehouse: Etching Edition. deluxe limited ed. Thomas Tolnay. LC 79-63343. (Illus.). (Orig.). 1979. 200.00 (*1-882986-03-2*) Smith.

Magic Windows ABCs. Chuck Murphy. (Illus.). 14p. (J). (ps-2). 1997. per. 14.95 (*0-689-81286-8*) S&S Childrens.

An Asterisk (*) at the beginning of an entry indicates that the title is appearing for the first time.

Magic Windows (Ventanas Magicas) Carmen Lomas Garza et al. LC 98-38379. (ENG & SPA., Illus.). 32p. (J). (gr. 1-4). 1999. 15.95 (*0-89239-157-X*) Childrens Book Pr.

Magic, Witchcraft, & Paganism in America: A Bibliography. 2nd ed. J. Gordon Melton & Isotta Poggi. LC 91-45867. (Religious Information Systems Ser.: Vol. 3). 422p. 1992. text 30.00 (*0-8153-0499-4*, SS#723) Garland.

Magic, Witchcraft, & Religion: An Anthropological Study of the Supernatural. 4th rev. ed. Ed. by Arthur C. Lehmann & James E. Myers. LC 96-19789. xii, 474p. (C). 1996. pap. text 46.95 (*1-55934-688-4*, 1688) Mayfield Pub.

***Magic, Witchcraft & Religion: An Anthropological Study of the Supernatural.** 5th ed. Arthur C. Lehmann & James E. Myers. LC 00-26306. 2000. write for info. (*0-7674-1692-9*) Mayfield Pub.

Magic with Everyday Objects. George Schindler. 2000. pap. 16.95 (*0-8128-8565-1*, Scrbrough Hse) Madison Bks UPA.

Magic with Incense & Powders. Anna Riva. 128p. (Orig.). 1985. pap. 4.95 (*0-943832-11-X*) Intl Imports.

Magic with Rope, Ribbon, & String see Bill Severn's Magic with Rope, Ribbon, & String

Magic with Sand: A History of AFG Industries. Billy M. Jones. (Illus.). 172p. 1984. 10.00 (*0-685-10136-3*) Wichita Ctr Entrep SBM.

Magic Within: An Anthology. Ed. by Emily Alward et al. LC 94-60709. 208p. 1994. pap. 9.95 (*0-9641438-9-5*) WorldEdge Pr.

***Magic Wool: Creative Activities with Natural Sheep's Wool.** Dagmar Schmidt. (Illus.). 2000. pap. 12.95 (*0-86315-313-5*) Floris Bks.

Magic Word. W. D. Gann. (Illus.). 1950. pap. 23.00 (*0-939093-06-5*) Lambert Gann Pub.

Magic Word Is Photosynthesis. Lynne Hudgins. (Nature's Natives Ser.). 24p. (J). (gr. 3-6). 1996. text 3.50 (*1-889203-00-9*) L Hudgins.

Magic Word Is Photosynthesis. Lynne Hudgins. (Illus.). 32p. (J). (gr. 3-6). 1996. text 5.50 (*1-889203-07-6*) L Hudgins.

Magic Words. Judy Mullican. (HRL Little Bks.). (Illus.). 8p. (Orig.). (J). (ps up). 1997. pap. text 10.95 (*1-57332-053-6*) HighReach Lrning.

Magic Words. large type ed. Judy Mullican. (HRL Big Bks.). (Illus.). 8p. (Orig.). (J). (ps-k). 1998. pap. text 10.95 (*1-57332-112-5*) HighReach Lrning.

Magic Words: Poems. Edward Field & Knud Rasmussen. LC 96-20465. (Illus.). 32p. (J). (ps-3). 1998. 17.00 (*0-15-201498-5*) Harcourt.

Magic Words That Bring You Riche$ Ted Nicholas. 1998. pap. 19.95 (*1-887741-00-3*) Nicholas Direct.

Magic Workbook. Donald J. Klein. 1999. pap. 17.95 (*0-87013-504-X*) Mich St U Pr.

Magic World. Edith Nesbit. (Illus.). (YA). (gr. 5 up). 1996. pap. 4.99 (*0-14-036765-9*) Viking Penguin.

Magic World: American Indian Songs & Poems. William Brandon. LC 90-47852. 168p. (C). 1992. pap. 12.95 (*0-8214-0991-3*) Ohio U Pr.

Magic World: American Indian Songs & Poems. Intro. & Pref. by William Brandon. LC 90-47852. 168p. (C). 1992. reprint ed. 26.95 (*0-8214-0981-6*) Ohio U Pr.

Magic World: Magicalism. Hilton Hotema. (Illus.). 73p. 1998. reprint ed. pap. 12.50 (*0-7873-1316-5*) Hlth Research.

Magic World & Ninety-One Other Stories. Regina Pagoulatou. LC 83-72497. (GRE.). 275p. 1983. 10.00 (*0-317-39604-8*, Anthe Pubns) Pella Pub.

Magic World Behind the Curtain: Andrei Serban in the American Theatre. 2nd ed. Ed Menta. LC 94-22375. (Artists & Issues in the Theatre Ser.: Vol. 5). (Illus.). XIV, 208p. (C). 1997. reprint ed. pap. 22.95 (*0-8204-3728-X*) P Lang Pubng.

Magic World of Amazing Randi. James Randi. 168p. 1989. pap. 10.95 (*1-55850-982-8*) Adams Media.

Magic World of Orson Welles. James Naremore. LC 89-42895. (Illus.). 328p. 1989. reprint ed. pap. 14.95 (*0-87074-299-X*) SMU Press.

Magic Years. Selma Fraiberg. 320p. 1981. 40.00 (*0-684-16849-9*, Scribners Ref) Mac Lib Ref.

Magic Years. Selma Fraiberg. 320p. 1996. per. 12.00 (*0-684-82550-3*) S&S Trade.

Magic Years: Understanding & Handling the Problems of Early Childhood. Selma Fraiberg. LC 59-6073. 320p. 1966. pap. 11.00 (*0-684-71768-9*, Scribners Ref) Mac Lib Ref.

Magic Yosemite Winters: A Century of Winter Sports. Gene Rose. Ed. by Robert Frohlich & Laurel H. Lippert. LC 99-72749. (Illus.). 160p. 1999. 40.00 (*1-893057-00-3*) Coldstream Pr.

Magica Inocencia (Magical Innocence), No. 134. Susan Carroll. (Harlequin Deseo Ser.). (SPA.). 1998. mass mkt. 3.50 (*0-373-35264-6*, 1-35264-0) Harlequin Bks.

Magica Sexualis: Mystic Love Book. Igoos Staff. 225p. (Orig.). 1994. 45.00 (*1-883147-79-4*) Intern Guild ASRS.

Magica Sexualis: Mystic Love Book. Igoos Staff. (Illus.). 225p. (Orig.). 1994. 45.00 (*1-883147-49-2*) Intern Guild ASRS.

Magical A-Life Avatars: A New Paradigm for the Internet. Peter Small. LC 98-34252. 337p. 1998. pap. 38.95 (*1-884777-58-9*) Manning Pubns.

***Magical Acts, Hypercubes & Pie: Meanderings Through Science, Medicine & Mathematics.** Beverly Orndorff. Ed. by Walter R. T. Witschey. 180p. 1999. write for info. (*0-9674451-0-8*) Science Mus VA.

Magical Adventures of Pretty Pearl. Virginia Hamilton. LC 82-48629. (Charlotte Zolotow Bk.). 320p. (J). (gr. 6 up). 1986. pap. 7.95 (*0-06-440178-2*, HarpTrophy) HarpC Child Bks.

***Magical Adventures of Pretty Pearl.** Virginia Hamilton. (J). (gr. 5 up). 1999. 20.75 (*0-8446-6998-9*) Peter Smith.

Magical Adventures of Pretty Pearl. Virginia Hamilton. (J). 1986. 11.05 (*0-606-03253-3*, Pub. by Turtleback) Demco.

Magical Adventures of Sun Beams. Karen Mack. (Illus.). 32p. (J). (ps-4). 1992. pap. 5.95 (*0-9631644-0-6*) Shooting Star.

Magical Alphabets. Nigel Pennick. LC 92-7859. (Illus.). 256p. 1992. pap. 14.95 (*0-87728-747-3*) Weiser.

Magical Amulet Bag. Sigrid Wynne-Evans. Ed. & Illus. by Lori S. Berry. 72p. (Orig.). 1996. pap. 10.95 (*0-9648360-1-7*) Beaded Bear.

Magical Amulet Bag, Vol. 2. Sigrid Wynne-Evans. Ed. & Illus. by Lori Berry. 72p. (Orig.). 1997. pap. 11.95 (*0-9648360-2-5*) Beaded Bear.

Magical & Mystical Sites: Europe & the British Isles. Elizabeth Pepper & John Wilcock. LC 92-28748. (Illus.). 304p. 2000. reprint ed. pap. 16.95 (*0-933999-44-5*) Phanes Pr.

Magical & Ritual Use of Aphrodisiacs. Richard A. Miller. LC 92-7672. (Illus.). 176p. (Orig.). 1992. pap. 10.95 (*0-89281-402-0*, Destiny Bks) Inner Tradit.

Magical & Ritual Use of Herbs. Richard A. Miller. LC 92-4925. (Illus.). 128p. 1992. pap. 10.95 (*0-89281-401-2*, Destiny Bks) Inner Tradit.

Magical & Ritual Use of Perfumes. Richard A. Miller & Iona Miller. LC 88-32020. (Illus.). 183p. 1990. pap. 12.95 (*0-89281-210-9*, Destiny Bks) Inner Tradit.

Magical & the Monstrous: Two Faces of the Child-Figure in the Fiction of Julio Cortazar & Jose Donoso. Sarah E. King. LC 92-25653. (Harvard Dissertations in Romance Languages Ser.). 136p. 1992. text 15.00 (*0-8153-0607-5*) Garland.

Magical Approach: Seth Speaks about the Art of Creative Living. Jane Roberts. (Seth Bk.). 192p. 1995. pap. 12.95 (*1-878424-09-2*) Amber-Allen Pub.

Magical Aromatherapy: The Power of Scent. Scott Cunningham. LC 89-38755. (New Age Ser.). (Illus.). 224p. (Orig.). 1989. mass mkt. 3.95 (*0-87542-129-6*) Llewellyn Pubns.

Magical Arrows: The Maori, the Greeks, & the Folklore of the Universe. Gregory Schrempp. LC 91-33076. (New Directions in Anthropological Writing Ser.). 238p. (C). 1992. pap. text 17.95 (*0-299-13234-X*) U of Wis Pr.

Magical Art. Heyoehkah Merrifield. LC 87-401423. (Illus.). (Orig.). (C). 1986. pap. 12.95 (*0-945122-00-4*) Rain Bird Pubs.

Magical Art of Solomon; Being Ars Notoria: A Grimoire. Ed. by Dracy Kuntz. (Kabbalistic-Grimoire Ser.: No. 3). (Illus.). (Orig.). 1995. pap. 9.95 (*1-55818-372-8*) Holmes Pub.

Magical Arts. Time-Life Books Editors. (Mysteries of the Unknown Ser.). (Illus.). 144p. 1990. lib. bdg. write for info. (*0-8094-6381-4*) Time-Life.

Magical Beaded Medicine Bag Book: Techniques for Beadlovers. Wendy Simpson Conner. LC 95-95202. (Beading Bks.). (Illus.). 52p. 1996. 11.95 (*0-9645957-2-9*) Interstell Pub.

The concept of the "prayer pouch" (or medicine bag) is as old as time itself. There is a special magic in making one's own bag, & filling it with the amulets that symbolize the meaning of one's own life. This book has many styles of medicine bags to make - Chinese finger weaving, Peyote Stitch, beading on leather, plus much more; all shown with easy-to-follow step-by-step illustrations & beautiful full color photos. The projects help the reader to focus on positive energy, & taking control of one's life through the realization of one's own power. Make your own magic! The author is a third-generation bead artist - her grandmother designed beaded gowns & jewelry for the Ziegfeld Follies. Wendy is the author of the immensely popular Best Little Beading Book. *Publisher Paid Annotation.*

Magical Beginning, Enchanted Land. Deepak Chopra. 2001. 23.00 (*0-517-70220-7*) Crown Pub Group.

Magical Big Top Counting Book. 12p. (J). (ps). 1997. 37.50 (*1-888074-56-6*) Pckts Lrning.

Magical Body: Power, Fame & Meaning in a Melanesian Society. Richard Eves. (Studies in Anthropology & History: Vol. 23). 324p. 1998. text 56.00 (*90-5702-305-9*, Harwood Acad Pubs) Gordon & Breach.

Magical Bond. Robert D. Smith et al. LC 98-83071. 1999. 16.95 (*0-9669660-0-7*) Smith Garrity.

Magical Calendar: A Synthesis of Magical Symbolism from the Seventeenth Centry Renaissance of Medieval Occultism. Ed. by Adam McLean. (Magnum Opus Hermetic Sourceworks Ser.: No. 1). (Illus.). 135p. (Orig.). 1993. pap. 18.00 (*0-933999-33-X*) Phanes Pr.

Magical Carousel & Commentaries. Patrizia Norelli-Bachelet. (Illus.). 153p. 1979. text 27.00 (*0-945747-30-6*) Aeon Bks.

Magical Chance. Dallas L. Sharp. LC 73-117842. (Essay Index Reprint Ser.). 1977. 17.95 (*0-8369-2133-X*) Ayer.

Magical Chango: An Enchanting Book on Manners & Friendship. Diana Lewis. Ed. by Jeri D. Widmer. (Illus.). 24p. (J). (ps-4). 1997. pap. 9.95 (*0-9659901-3-3*) DiLee Publ.

Magical Child. Carol DiMarco. (Illus.). 25p. (Orig.). (J). (gr. k-3). 1997. pap. 10.95 (*1-886383-19-7*) Pride & Imprints.

Magical Child: Rediscovering Nature's Plan for Our Children. Joseph C. Pearce. 276p. 1992. pap. 13.95 (*0-452-26789-7*, Plume) Dutton Plume.

Magical Child Magical Adult, Set. Joseph C. Pearce. 142p. 1995. 16.95 incl. audio (*1-879323-24-9*) Sound Horizons AV.

Magical Child Within You. Bruce Davis. LC 82-84601. 128p. (Orig.). 1995. reprint ed. pap. 7.95 (*0-89087-422-0*) Celestial Arts.

Magical Christmas. Kathryn M. Bailey. LC 98-72924. (Adventures of Andria Ser.). (Illus.). 35 p. 1998. write for info. (*0-9659689-1-X*) Huckleberry Hollow.

Magical Christmas. Heather Graham. 1997. mass mkt. 6.99 (*0-451-40796-2*, Onyx) NAL.

Magical Christmas Dream. Mary E. Padron. LC 95-92595. (Illus.). 32p. (Orig.). (J). (ps-2). 1996. pap. 12.95 (*0-9648284-0-5*) Pink Hse Pr.

Magical Circle. rev. ed. Ramslove. (Illus.). 96p. 1985. pap., spiral bd. 24.95 (*0-9614605-0-4*) Trout Gulch Pr.

Magical Circus Train. Ron Kidd. (Illus.). 16p. (J). (ps up). text 19.95 (*0-9627001-5-0*) Futech Educ Prods.

Magical Classroom. Michael Strauss. 1997. pap. 13.95 (*0-614-27631-4*) Heinemann.

Magical Classroom: Exploring Science, Language & Perception with Children. Michael Strauss. LC 96-49474. 1997. pap. 15.95 (*0-435-08145-4*, 08145) Heinemann.

Magical Control of the Body: The Treatment of Eating Disorders Through Art Therapy. Mary Levens. LC 94-23957. (Illus.). 160p. (C). 1995. 65.00 (*0-415-12216-3*, C0393) Routledge.

Magical Control of the Body: The Treatment of Eating Disorders Through Art Therapy. Mary Levens. LC 94-23957. (Illus.). 160p. (C). (gr. 13). 1995. pap. 24.99 (*0-415-12217-1*, RC552) Routledge.

***Magical Creatures.** Ed. by Witches Almanac Staff. (Illus.). 2000. pap. 12.95 (*1-881098-14-1*) Witches Almanac.

***Magical Dead.** Peter Garrison. (Changeling Saga Ser.: Bk. 3). 352p. 2000. pap. 13.00 (*0-441-00683-3*) Ace Bks.

Magical Desert. Helena Weiss-Meyer. LC 97-68998. 112p. 1998. pap. 13.50 (*0-88739-169-9*) Creat Arts Bk.

Magical Diaries of Aleister Crowley: Tunisia, 1923. Aleister Crowley. Ed. by Stephen Skinner. LC 95-50923. 272p. 1999. reprint ed. pap. 14.95 (*0-87728-856-9*) Weiser.

Magical Diary: A Personal Ritual Journal. Donald M. Kraig. 240p. (Orig.). 1990. otabind 9.95 (*0-87542-322-1*) Llewellyn Pubns.

Magical Display: The Art of Photomicrography. Michael Davidson. (Illus.). 128p. 1998. pap. 24.95 (*0-945798-83-0*) Amber Lotus.

Magical East. Philip Wilkinson & Michael Pollard. LC 94-43884. (Mysterious Places Ser.). (Illus.). 96p. (YA). (gr. 5 up). 1994. lib. bdg. 19.95 (*0-7910-2754-6*) Chelsea Hse.

Magical Effects of Color. Joen Wolfrom. Ed. by Harold Nadel. LC 92-53800. (Illus.). 128p. 1995. pap. 20.95 (*0-914881-53-1*, 10064) C & T Pub.

Magical Enchantress's Test of Virtue: An Exciting 66 Fairy Tale Journey. deluxe ed. Miranda M. Noble. LC 97-69820. (Illus.). 200p. (J). (gr. 2-12). 1998. vinyl bd. 23.50 (*1-886197-22-9*) Joy Books.

Magical Encounter. Alma F. Ada. 1994. pap. 15.50 (*0-88272-838-5*) Santillana.

Magical Essence of Being: Human & Divine Imagenetics & Humanology in Motion. Jeanie Lemaire & Corinn Codye. LC 98-71299. (Illus.). 224p. 1998. pap. 17.95 (*0-9648540-1-5*) Balancing Arts.

Magical Fabric Art: Spellwork & Wishcraft Through Patchwork, Quilting & Sewing. Sandra M. Scarpa. LC 98-3384. (Illus.). 224p. 1998. pap. 15.95 (*1-56718-653-X*) Llewellyn Pubns.

***Magical First Day.** Julie Mayfield. LC 98-35734. (Illus.). (J). 1998. write for info. (*1-56763-336-6*); pap. write for info. (*1-56763-337-4*) Ozark Pub.

Magical Fountain of Love. Dorothy E. Mittoo-Walker. (Illus.). 48p. 1994. 10.00 (*0-912444-33-9*) DARE Bks.

***Magical Garden: Spells, Charms & Lore for Magical Gardens & the Curious Gardeners Who Tend Them.** Sophia & Denny Sargent. LC 99-55087. (Illus.). 2000. 10.95 (*0-7407-0500-8*) Andrews & McMeel.

Magical Gardens: Myth, Mulch, & Marigolds. Patricia Monaghan. LC 97-27784. (Illus.). 192p. (Orig.). 1997. pap. 17.95 (*1-56718-466-9*, K466-9) Llewellyn Pubns.

Magical Gateways. Alan Richardson. LC 92-17844. (New Age Ser.). (Illus.). 208p. 1992. mass mkt. 4.95 (*0-87542-681-6*) Llewellyn Pubns.

Magical Gemstones Christmas. Amye Rosenberg. (Illus.). 16p. (J). (ps-2). 1999. pap. 9.99 (*0-689-82439-4*) Litle Simon.

Magical Gift of Kindness. Joy Haney. 1997. pap. 9.95 (*1-880969-28-9*) Schl Prophet.

Magical Girl Pretty Sammy: No Need for Tenchi. Hitoshi Okuda. (Illus.). 184p. 1998. pap. 15.95 (*1-56931-288-5*, Cadence Bks) Viz Commns Inc.

***Magical Golf.** Bobby McGee. (Illus.). 170p. 2000. 21.95 (*1-930499-03-5*) Bobbysez Pub.

Magical Guardians: Exploring the Nature & Spirit of Trees. Philip Heselton. (Illus.). 1998. pap. 24.95 (*1-86163-057-3*, Pub. by Capall Bann Pubng) Holmes Pub.

Magical Hands. Marjorie Barker. LC 89-31373. (Illus.). 28p. (J). (ps up). 1991. 16.00 (*0-88708-103-7*, Picture Book Studio) S&S Childrens.

Magical Hearth: Home for the Modern Pagan. Janet Thompson. LC 95-17611. 144p. 1995. pap. text 9.95 (*0-87728-824-0*) Weiser.

Magical Herbal Baths of Santeria. Carlos Montenegro. 1997. pap. 5.95 (*0-942272-45-5*) Original Pubns.

Magical Herbalism: The Secret Craft of the Wise. 2nd ed. Scott Cunningham. LC 83-80172. (Practical Magick Ser.). (Illus.). 2604p. 1983. pap. 9.95 (*0-87542-120-2*) Llewellyn Pubns.

***Magical History of the Horse.** Janet Farrar & Virginia Russell. (Illus.). 1998. pap. 24.95 (*1-86163-033-6*, Pub. by Capall Bann Pubng) Holmes Pub.

Magical Household see Casa Magica: Fortalezca su Hogar con Amor Salud y Felicidad

Magical Household: Empower Your Home with Love Protection, Health & Happiness. Scott Cunningham & David Harrington. LC 87-45740. (Practical Magick Ser.). (Illus.). 208p. (Orig.). 1987. pap. 9.95 (*0-87542-124-5*) Llewellyn Pubns.

***Magical I Ching.** J. H. Brennan. LC 00-24132. (Illus.). 264p. 2000. pap. 14.95 (*1-56718-087-6*) Llewellyn Pubns.

Magical Images & the Magical Imagination: A Practical Handbook for Self Transformation Using the Techniques of Creative Visualization & Meditation. Gareth Knight. (Illus.). 94p. 1998. pap. 9.95 (*0-9650839-3-4*) Sun Chalice.

Magical Incenses & Perfumes. Jan Brodie. (Orig.). 1999. pap. 22.95 (*1-898307-59-8*, Pub. by Capall Bann Pubng) Holmes Pub.

Magical Journey with Carlos Castaneda. Margaret Runyan Castaneda. (Illus.). 204p. 1996. pap. write for info. (*0-9696960-1-9*) Mil2enia Pr.

***Magical Kittens.** Donna Bell. (Regency Romance Ser.). 2000. mass mkt. 4.99 (*0-8217-6691-0*, Zebra Kensgtn) Kensgtn Pub Corp.

Magical Land of Noom. Peter Glassman. LC 97-39518. (Illus.). 192p. (J). (gr. 3-7). 1998. reprint ed. 22.00 (*0-688-14117-X*, Wm Morrow) Morrow Avon.

Magical Lands: Color & Find Hidden Pictures. Jack Keely. (Troubador Color-&-Find Hidden Pictures Ser.). (Illus.). 48p. (J). (ps-3). 1998. pap. 2.99 (*0-8431-7829-9*, Price Stern) Peng Put Young Read.

Magical Letter of Roger Bacon. Roger Bacon. 1988. pap. 6.95 (*1-55818-102-4*, Sure Fire) Holmes Pub.

***Magical Life.** Bobby McGee. (Illus.). 170p. 2000. pap. 15.95 (*1-930499-07-8*) Bobbysez Pub.

Magical Life of Dion Fortune: Priestess of the Twentieth Century. Alan Richardson. (Illus.). 256p. 1991. pap. 14.00 (*1-85538-051-X*, Pub. by Aqrn Pr) Harper SF.

***Magical Life Workbook.** Bobby McGee. (Illus.). 50p. 2000. pap., wbk. ed. 13.95 (*1-930499-08-6*) Bobbysez Pub.

Magical Lore of Animals. Yvonne Aburrow. (Orig.). 1997. pap. 23.95 (*1-898307-80-6*, Pub. by Capall Bann Pubng) Holmes Pub.

Magical Lore of Cats. Marion Davies. (Illus.). (Orig.). 1995. pap. 21.95 (*1-898307-66-0*, Pub. by Capall Bann Pubng) Holmes Pub.

Magical Lore of Herbs. Marion Davis. 1994. pap. 22.95 (*1-898307-14-8*, Pub. by Capall Bann Pubng) Holmes Pub.

Magical Math Book. Longe. (Illus.). 96p. (J). (gr. 3-7). 1998. pap. 5.95 (*0-8069-9990-X*) Sterling.

Magical Math Book. Bob Longe. LC 97-33100. (Illus.). 96p. (J). (gr. 3-7). 1997. 14.95 (*0-8069-9989-6*) Sterling.

Magical Maze: Seeing the World Through Mathematical Eyes. Ian Stewart. LC 98-13185. 268p. 1998. 24.95 (*0-471-19297-X*) Wiley.

Magical Maze: Seeing the World Through Mathematical Eyes. Ian Stewart. 268p. 1999. pap. 16.95 (*0-471-35065-6*) Wiley.

***Magical Mazes.** Juliet Snape & Charles Snape. (Illus.). 32p. (J). (gr. k-2). 1999. pap. 12.95 (*0-8109-2926-0*, Pub. by Abrams) Time Warner.

Magical Melons. Carol R. Brink. (J). 1990. 9.05 (*0-606-04473-6*, Pub. by Turtleback) Demco.

Magical Melons. Carol R. Brink. LC 90-144. (Illus.). 208p. (J). (gr. 4-6). 1990. reprint ed. mass mkt. 3.95 (*0-689-71416-5*) Aladdin.

Magical Memories. Disney Enterprises, Inc. Staff & Pixar Animation Studios Staff. (Disney-Pixar's "A Bug's Life" Library: Vol. 12). (Illus.). 44p. (J). (gr. 1-6). 1998. 3.99 (*1-57973-028-0*) Advance Pubs.

***Magical Memories.** Donna Fletcher. (Magical Love Ser.). 2000. mass mkt. 5.99 (*0-515-12886-4*) Berkley Pub.

Magical Message According to Ioannes. James M. Pryse. 230p. 1996. reprint ed. spiral bd. 15.50 (*0-7873-0685-1*) Hlth Research.

Magical Message According to Ioannes St. John. James M. Pryse. 240p. 1993. reprint ed. pap. 14.95 (*1-56459-337-1*) Kessinger Pub.

Magical Mimics in Oz. Jack Snow. (Illus.). 243p. (J). (gr. 3 up). 1991. pap. 12.95 (*0-929605-09-8*) Books of Wonder.

Magical Moment. Barbara Cartland. (Camfield Novel of Love Ser.: 140). 176p. (Orig.). 1995. mass mkt. 3.99 (*0-515-11594-0*, Jove) Berkley Pub.

Magical Moment. Monica Jackson. 256p. 1999. mass mkt. 4.99 (*1-58314-021-2*) BET Bks.

Magical Moments. (J). (gr. 3 up). 1991. pap. 1.97 (*1-56297-119-0*, WD-180M) Lee Pubns KY.

***Magical Moments.** Donna Fletcher. 1999. mass mkt. 5.99 (*0-515-12681-0*, Jove) Berkley Pub.

Magical Moments: A New Mother's Journal. Mari M. Robeson. (Illus.). 140p. 1998. spiral bd. 15.95 (*0-9670065-0-3*, LS-1-J) Le Sol Studio.

***Magical Moments: Stories form the Heart.** Jeayn P. Fahey. 107p. 2000. pap. 12.95 (*0-9700214-0-2*) J P Fahey.

Magical Monarch of Mo. L. Frank Baum. (Illus.). (J). (gr. 4-8). 1982. 22.50 (*0-8446-1609-5*) Peter Smith.

Magical Money Tricks: The Incredible Magic Money Maker & Other Cool Tricks with Cash. Michael J. Searls. (Illus.). 48p. (J). (gr. 2-9). 1997. spiral bd. 14.95 (*1-889692-02-6*) Summit Finan.

Magical Moonballs. Laura L. Seeley. LC 92-16698. (Illus.). (J). (ps-3). 1992. 16.95 (*1-56145-063-4*) Peachtree Pubs.

Magical Moonballs. Laura L. Seeley. (Illus.). 48p. (J). (ps-3). 1998. reprint ed. pap. 7.95 (*1-56145-189-4*) Peachtree Pubs.

M

M

Magical Muriel. Mary Buckman. LC 90-60453. (One in a Series of Predictable Books). (Illus.). (Orig.). (J). (gr. k-2). 1991. pap. text 12.95 (1-879414-07-4) Mary Bee Creat.

Magical Mushrooms, Mischievous Molds. George W. Hudler. LC 98-10163. 272p. 1998. 29.95 (0-691-02873-7, Pub. by Princeton U Pr) Cal Prin Full Svc.

***Magical Mushrooms, Mischievous Molds.** George W. Hudler. (Illus.). 272p. 2000. pap. 14.95 (0-691-07016-4) Princeton U Pr.

Magical Musical Celebration/Kwanzaa. Aremu & Steifel. 1997. pap. 19.95 (0-936073-26-8) Gumbs & Thomas.

Magical Musical Spiraled Seashell, & Friends. Dick Bozung. (Illus.). 160p. (Orig.). (YA). 1989. pap. 20.00 (0-9622341-1-7); audio. write for info. (0-9622341-5-X) Seven Arrows.

Magical, Mysterious Meteorites. Madelyn W. Carlisle. LC 92-12776. (Let's Investigate Ser.). (Illus.). 32p. (J). (gr. 2-6). 1996. lib. bdg. 14.45 (1-56674-132-7) Forest Hse.

Magical, Mysterious Meteorites. Madelyn Wood Carlisle. (Let's Investigate Ser.). 1992. 10.15 (0-606-01638-4, Pub. by Turtleback) Demco.

Magical, Mystical, Marvelous Coat. Catherine Ann Cullen. 2001. write for info. (0-316-16334-1) Little.

Magical Needlework. Dorothy Morrison. LC 97-52214. (Illus.). 244p. (Orig.). 1998. pap. 17.95 (1-56718-470-7) Llewellyn Pubns.

Magical Objects. Laurie Dolphin. 1999. 15.99 (0-525-45904-9) NAL.

Magical Pantheons: A Golden Dawn Journal. Ed. by Sandra T. Cicero et al. (Golden Dawn Journal Ser.: Vol. 4). 348p. (Orig.). 1999. pap. 14.95 (1-56718-861-3) Llewellyn Pubns.

Magical Passes: Practical Wisdom of the Shamans of Ancient Mexico. Carlos Castaneda. LC 97-26884. (Illus.). 240p. 1998. 25.00 (0-06-017584-2) HarpC.

Magical Passes: The Practical Wisdom of the Shamans of Ancient Mexico. Carlos Castaneda. (Illus.). 240p. (Orig.). 1999. pap. 14.00 (0-06-092882-4) HarpC.

Magical Pencil. Radhika Kaula. LC 96-90890. (Illus.). 20p. (Orig.). (J). (ps-6). 1996. pap. 4.99 (0-9653862-0-1) Transnatl Computing.

Magical Pencil Coloring & Exploring Book. Radhika Kaula. (Illus.). 32p. (Orig.). (J). (ps-3). 1997. pap. 4.05 (0-9653862-1-X) Transnatl Computing.

Magical Piece of Sand. J. S. Hills. (Illus.). 32p. (J). (ps-2). 1989. pap. 6.95 (0-923889-27-2) Inquisitors Pub.

Magical Pine Ring: Culture & the Imagination in Armenian-American Literature. Margaret Bedrosian. LC 91-17264. 256p. 1991. 34.95 (0-8143-2339-1) Wayne St U Pr.

Magical Place: Poems, Paintings & Photographs of Martha's Vineyard. Brooks Robards. (Illus.). 80p. 1998. pap. 19.95 (0-9645250-2-X) Smmrst Pr.

***Magical Pokemon Journey: Journey One, Party with Pikachu.** Yumi Tsukirino. (Illus.). (YA). 2000. pap. 13.95 (1-56931-506-X, Viz Comics) Viz Commns Inc.

Magical Power of Suru. Nobuo Sato. 196p. 1995. pap. 12.95 (0-8048-2025-2) Tuttle Pubng.

Magical Power of the Saints: Evocations & Candle Rituals. Ray T. Malbrough. LC 98-19622. (Illus.). 240p. 1998. pap. 7.95 (1-56718-456-1) Llewellyn Pubns.

***Magical Quest: Creating Career Success.** Tarin Frances. 185p. (C). 1998. pap. 15.00 (0-9674449-0-X) Love Seeker Pr.

Magical Rainbow Man. Shahastra. LC 81-90690. (Magical Rainbow Ser.). (Illus.). 64p. (J). (ps-7). 1982. pap. 8.95 (0-911281-00-2) Magical Rainbow.

Magical Rainbow Man & the Journey of Love. Shahastra. 48p. (J). (ps-3). Date not set. 4.95 (0-9615079-9-3) Merrill-West Pub.

***Magical Rainbow Sponge: Tips & Techniques.** Dee Gruenig. Ed. by Anne Generas. 38p. 2000. mass mkt. 9.99 (0-9676461-1-1) Ranger.

Magical Realism: Theory, History, Community. Ed. by Lois P. Zamora & Wendy B. Faris. LC 94-47223. (Illus.). 592p. 1995. text 64.95 (0-8223-1611-0); pap. text 22.95 (0-8223-1640-4) Duke.

Magical Realism in West African Fiction: Seeing with a Third Eye. Brenda Cooper. LC 97-35008. (Routledge Research in Postcolonial Studies). 264p. (C). 1998. 75.00 (0-415-18239-5) Routledge.

Magical Realism of Alyce Frank. Joseph Dispenza. Ed. by Emily S. Drabanski. (New Mexico Magazine Distinguished Artists Ser.: Vol. III). (Illus.). 76p. 1999. 38.95 (0-937206-57-1) New Mexico Mag.

***Magical Realism of Alyce Frank.** limited ed. Joseph Dispenza. Ed. by Emily S. Drabanski. (New Mexico Magazine Distinguished Artists Ser.: Vol. III). (Illus.). 76p. 1999. 195.00 (0-937206-60-1) New Mexico Mag.

Magical Realist Fiction: An Anthology. Ed. by David Young & Keith Hollaman. LC 83-19974. 519p. (C). pap. 20.00 (0-582-28452-X) Oberlin Coll Pr.

Magical Realm: An Irish Childhood. Kathleen Coyle. (Illus.). 272p. (J). (gr. 4-7). 1998. pap. 14.95 (0-86327-548-6, Pub. by Wolfhound Press) Irish Amer Bk.

***Magical Reels: A History of Cinema in Latin America.** John King, III. (Illus.). 320p. 2000. pap. 20.00 (1-85984-233-X, Pub. by Verso) Norton.

Magical Religion & Modern Witchcraft. Ed. by James R. Lewis. LC 95-42351. 423p. (C). 1996. text 59.50 (0-7914-2889-3); pap. text 24.95 (0-7914-2890-7) State U NY Pr.

Magical Rites from the Crystal Well. 3rd ed. Intro. by Ed Fitch. LC 83-80134. (Illus.). 160p. 1984. pap. 9.95 (0-87542-230-6) Llewellyn Pubns.

Magical Ritual Methods. William G. Gray. (Illus.). 301p. 1980. pap. 16.95 (0-87728-498-9) Weiser.

Magical Ritual of the Sanctum Regnum. Eliphas Levi. Ed. by Joseph Bouleur & W. Wynn Westcott. 1992. reprint ed. pap. 8.95 (1-55818-184-9, Sure Fire) Holmes Pub.

Magical Ritual of the Sanctum Regnum. Eliphas Levi. Ed. by W. Wynn Westcott. 108p. 1992. reprint ed. pap. 7.95 (0-922802-95-5) Kessinger Pub.

***Magical Running.** Bobby McGee. (Illus.). 170p. 2000. pap. 15.95 (1-930499-00-0) Bobbysez Pub.

***Magical Running Workbook.** Bobby McGee. (Illus.). 50p. 2000. pap., wbk. ed. 13.95 (1-930499-01-9) Bobbysez Pub.

Magical Science. rev. ed. Eric Ladizinsky. (Illus.). 80p. (J). (gr. 3-6). 1998. pap. 6.95 (1-56565-980-5, 09805W, Pub. by Lowell Hse Juvenile) NTC Contemp Pub Co.

Magical Sites: Women Travelers in 19th Century Latin America. Ed. by Marjorie Agosin & Julie H. Levison. LC 99-11291. 256p. 1998. pap. 17.00 (1-877727-94-6, Pub. by White Pine) Consort Bk Sales.

Magical Spree of Katie McGee. Nancy J. Hill. (Illus.). 32p. (J). (ps-k). 1999. pap. 10.95 (0-9669436-0-0) Serenity Press.

Magical Staff: The Vitalist Tradition in Western Medicine. Matthew Wood. (Illus.). 223p. (Orig.). 1992. pap. 14.95 (1-55643-127-9) North Atlantic.

Magical Starfruit Tree. Rosalind C. Wang. Ed. by Julie Livingston. (Illus.). 32p. (J). (gr. k-2). 1994. 14.95 (0-941831-89-2) Beyond Words Pub.

Magical State: Nature, Money & Modernity in Venezuela. Fernando Coronil. LC 97-8000. 1997. pap. text 20.00 (0-226-11602-6); lib. bdg. 50.00 (0-226-11601-8) U Ch Pr.

Magical Tale: Color Plus Fun with Magic Wand. Golden Books Staff. 56p. 1999. pap. text 3.99 (0-307-27616-3) Gldn Bks Pub Co.

Magical Tales. R. J. Stewart. 1990. pap. 12.95 (0-85030-876-3, Pub. by Aqrn Pr) Harper SF.

Magical Tales: The Story-Telling Tradition, 1. R. J. Stewart. LC 99-179330. (Illus.). 192p. 1998. reprint ed. pap. text 12.95 (1-892137-02-X) Mercury NC.

Magical Tales about Willie the Wizard. Urban R. Coombs. (Illus.). 216p. (YA). 1994. pap. 12.95 (1-57087-081-0) Prof Pr NC.

Magical Tales from Many Lands. Illus. by Jane Ray. LC 93-12164. 128p. (J). 1993. 22.99 (0-525-45017-3, Dutton Child) Peng Put Young Read.

Magical Tattwa Cards: A Complete System of Self-Development, Incl. 26 cards. Jonn Mumford. LC 97-2899. (Illus.). 288p. 1999. 29.95 (1-56718-472-3) Llewellyn Pubns.

***Magical Thoughts of Grieving Children: Treating Children with Complicated Mourning & Advice for Parents.** James A. Fogarty. Ed. by John D. Morgan. LC 99-46201. (Death, Value & Meaning Ser.). (Illus.). 184p. 2000. 38.95 (0-89503-205-8); pap. 25.95 (0-89503-206-6) Baywood Pub.

Magical Tree. Destini Lavranos & Sheri Ritchie. (Illus.). 2p. (J). (ps). 1993. 14.95 (0-9638393-0-6) Bedtime Bks.

Magical Universe: The Best of Magical Blend Magazine. Ed. by Michael Langevin & Jerry Snider. LC 96-46576. 284p. 1996. pap. 15.95 (1-893183-22-X, Swan Raven) Granite Pub.

Magical Universe: The Best of Magical Blend Magazine. Jerry Snider & Michael Langevin. LC 96-46576. 302p. 1996. per. 16.95 (0-926524-39-9) Blue Wtr Pubng.

***Magical Urbanism: Latinos Reinvent the U. S. Big City.** Mike Davis. 128p. 2000. 19.00 (1-85984-771-4, Pub. by Verso) Norton.

***Magical Wish.** Betty G. Moody. LC 98-174991. (Illus.). (J). 1998. 15.95 (0-9663522-1-1) Character Lines.

***Magical Woman.** Audrey Savage. LC 99-65318. 192p. 2000. pap. 11.95 (1-56315-210-X, Pub. by SterlingHse) Natl Bk Netwk.

***Magical Work.** Bobby McGee. (Illus.). 170p. 2000. 19.95 (1-930499-05-1) Bobbysez Pub.

***Magical Work: The Workbook.** Bobby McGee. (Illus.). 50p. 2000. pap., wbk. ed. 13.95 (1-930499-06-X) Bobbysez Pub.

Magical World of the Tarot: Four-Fold Mirror of the Universe. Gareth Knight. (Illus.). 192p. (Orig.). 1991. pap. 14.00 (0-85030-940-9, Pub. by Aqrn Pr) Harper SF.

Magical World of the Tarot: Fourfold Mirror of the Universe. Gareth Knight. LC 96-22675. (Illus.). 224p. 1996. pap. 14.95 (0-87728-873-9) Weiser.

Magical World of Unicorns. Michael Hague. LC 98-31792. (Illus.). 40p. (J). (gr. 3-4). 1999. 16.00 (0-689-82849-7) S&S Bks Yung.

Magical World of X-Mas: Piano 4H. pap. 8.95 (0-7692-1151-8, PF0630) Wrner Bros.

Magical Writings of Thomas Vaughan. Arthur E. Waite. 160p. 1974. reprint ed. spiral bd. 14.50 (0-7873-0920-6) Hlth Research.

Magical Writings of Thomas Vaughan (Eugenius Philalethes) A Verbatim Reprint of His First Four Treatises; Anthroposophia Theomagica; Anima Magica Abscondita, Magia Adamica, & the True Coecum Terrae. Arthur E. Waite. 194p. 1992. reprint ed. pap. 13.95 (1-56459-241-3) Kessinger Pub.

***Magical Years: A Boyhood Remembrance.** Walter W. Benjamin. LC 98-87263. 1998. 24.95 (1-890676-29-2, Pub. by Beavers Pond) Bookman Bks.

Magicardstory: Little Joe & the Joker. Victor H. Van Maren, Jr. LC 93-94195. (Illus.). 36p. (YA). (gr. 6-12). 1993. reprint ed. pap. text 7.00 (0-9639397-1-8) Key Thoughts.

Magicardstory: The Wizard of Wishes. unabridged ed. Victor H. Van Maren, Jr. (Illus.). 48p. (Orig.). (YA). (gr. 6-12). 1997. pap. 15.00 (0-9639397-2-6) Key Thoughts.

***Magician.** W. Somerset Maugham. 288p. 1999. 26.95 (0-7351-0175-2) Replica Bks.

Magician. W. Somerset Maugham. 208p. 1992. pap. 12.95 (0-14-018595-X, Viking) Viking Penguin.

Magician. J. R. Roberts. (Gunsmith Ser.: No. 155). 192p. (Orig.). 1994. mass mkt. 3.99 (0-515-11495-2, Jove) Berkley Pub.

Magician. W. Somerset Maugham. 233p. 1974. reprint ed. spiral bd. 11.50 (0-7873-0589-8) Hlth Research.

***Magician.** rev. ed. Ivan Bulloch. (I Want to Be Ser.). (Illus.). (J). 2000. 9.95 (1-58728-084-1); pap. 5.95 (1-58728-090-6) Two Can Pub.

Magician. 2nd ed. Sol Stein. 272p. 1991. reprint ed. 19.95 (0-9628587-0-6) Colophon NY.

Magician: Apprentice. Raymond E. Feist. LC 92-13250. Vol. 1. 512p. 1985. mass mkt. 6.99 (0-553-56494-3, Spectra) Bantam.

Magician: Apprentice. Raymond E. Feist. LC 92-13250. 528p. 1986. mass mkt. 6.99 (0-553-56493-5, Spectra) Bantam.

Magician - His Training & Work. W. E. Butler. 175p. 1979. pap. 7.00 (0-87980-212-X) Wilshire.

Magician among the Spirits. Harry Houdini. (Illus.). 294p. 1972. 18.95 (0-405-02801-6) Arno Press.

Magician of Lublin. Isaac Bashevis Singer. 175p. 1992. reprint ed. lib. bdg. 14.95 (0-89966-156-4) Buccaneer Bks.

Magician Out of Manchuria. Charles G. Finney. (Illus.). 1989. 25.00 (0-937986-92-5) D M Grant.

Magician, the Witch & the Law. Edward Peters. LC 78-51341. (Middle Ages Ser.). 216p. 1982. pap. text 16.95 (0-8122-1101-4) U of Pa Pr.

Magician Within: Accessing the Shaman in the Male Psyche. Robert Moore & Douglas Gillette. 304p. 1994. reprint ed. pap. 12.50 (0-380-72070-1, Avon Bks) Morrow Avon.

Magicians. J. B. Priestley. LC 90-43613. 160p. 1996. 17.95 (0-913720-73-9) Beil.

Magicians: A Novel of Transformation & Co-Creation. Honora Finkelstein. 208p. 1994. pap. 12.00 (1-885776-00-4) Sunweavers.

Magicians & Fairies. Robert R. Ingpen & Molly Perham. (Mystery & Magic Ser.). 96p. (J). (gr. 5-12). 1996. lib. bdg. 19.95 (0-7910-3929-3) Chelsea Hse.

***Magicians & Illusionists.** Adam Woog. LC 99-32345. (History Makers Ser.). (Illus.). 144p. (YA). (gr. 6-9). 2000. lib. bdg. 23.70 (1-56006-573-7) Lucent Bks.

Magician's Apprentice. Sidney Rosen & Dorothy Rosen. LC 93-10781. (J). (gr. 4-7). 1993. lib. bdg. 19.95 (0-87614-809-7, Carolrhoda) Lerner Pub.

Magician's Assistant. Ann Patchett. LC 97-2139. 357p. 1997. 23.00 (0-15-100263-0) Harcourt.

Magician's Assistant. Ann Patchett. 357p. (C). 1998. pap. 13.00 (0-15-600621-9, Harvest Bks) Harcourt.

Magician's Castle Fantasy. Mary Laycock & Peggy McLean. Ed. by Margaret Smart. (Illus.). 80p. (Orig.). (J). (gr. 5-10). 1996. pap. 9.95 (1-882293-05-3, A-1700) Activity Resources.

Magician's Companion: A Practical & Encyclopedic Guide to Magical & Religious Symbolism. Bill Whitcomb. LC 92-13331. (Llewellyn's Sourcebook Ser.). (Illus.). 608p. 1998. pap. 24.95 (0-87542-868-1) Llewellyn Pubns.

Magician's Doubts: Nabakov & the Risks of Fiction. Michael Wood. LC 95-8394. 264p. 1995. text 35.00 (0-691-00632-6, Pub. by Princeton U Pr) Cal Prin Full Svc.

Magician's Doubts: Nabokov & the Risks of Fiction. Michael Wood. (Readers' Subscription Book Club). 260p. 1995. pap. text 14.95 (0-691-04830-4, Pub. by Princeton U Pr) Cal Prin Full Svc.

Magician's Gambit. David Eddings. (Belgariad Ser.: Bk. 3). 320p. 1986. mass mkt. 6.99 (0-345-33545-7, Del Rey) Ballantine Pub Grp.

Magician's Gambit. David Eddings. (Belgariad Ser.). 1983. 12.09 (0-606-01241-9, Pub. by Turtleback) Demco.

Magician's Girl. Doris Grumbach. 200p. 1993. pap. 8.95 (0-393-31091-4) Norton.

Magician's Lover. Flora Speer. 400p. 1998. mass mkt. 5.99 (0-505-52263-2, Love Spell) Dorchester Pub Co.

Magician's Nephew. C. S. Lewis. 1984. 5.95 (0-87129-541-5, M57) Dramatic Pub.

Magician's Nephew. C. S. Lewis. LC 93-14301. (Chronicles of Narnia Ser.: Bk. 6). (Illus.). 208p. (J). (gr. 3 up). 1994. 16.95 (0-06-023497-0) HarpC Child Bks.

Magician's Nephew. C. S. Lewis. LC 93-14301. (Chronicles of Narnia Ser.: Bk. 6). (Illus.). 208p. (J). (gr. 4-7). 1994. pap. 6.95 (0-06-440505-2, HarpTrophy); pap. 4.95 (0-06-447110-1, HarpTrophy) HarpC Child Bks.

Magician's Nephew. C. S. Lewis. LC 93-14301. (Chronicles of Narnia Ser.: Bk. 6). (J). (gr. 4-8). 1994. 12.05 (0-606-06553-9, Pub. by Turtleback); 10.05 (0-606-06554-7, Pub. by Turtleback) Demco.

Magician's Nephew. abr. ed. C. S. Lewis. (Chronicles of Narnia Ser.). (J). (gr. 4-7). 1997. audio 18.00 (0-553-47768-4) BDD Aud Pub.

Magician's Nephew. abr. ed. C. S. Lewis & Robin Lawrie. LC 98-24263. (Chronicles of Narnia Ser.: Bk. 6). (Illus.). 64p. (J). (gr. 3-7). 1999. pap. 10.95 (0-06-443515-6, HarpTrophy) HarpC Child Bks.

***Magician's Nephew.** large type ed. C. S. Lewis. LC 99-49183. (Chronicles of Narnia Ser.: Bk. 6). 210p. (J). (gr. 4-7). 2000. 21.95 (0-7862-2231-X) Silhouette.

***Magician's Nephew: Full-Color Collector's Edition.** C. S. Lewis. LC 93-14301. (Chronicles of Narnia Ser.: Bk. 6). (Illus.). 208p. (J). (gr. 4-7). 2000. mass mkt. 7.95 (0-06-440943-0, HarpTrophy) HarpC Child Bks.

Magician's Nephew: One-Act. C. S. Lewis. 1985. pap. 5.95 (0-87129-368-4, M86) Dramatic Pub.

Magician's Nephew Study Guide. Andrew Clausen. 62p. (J). (gr. 5-7). 1997. student ed., ring bd. 12.99 (1-58609-149-2) Progeny Pr WI.

Magicians of Caprona. Diana Wynne Jones. LC 99-219891. 224p. (gr. 5-9). 1999. mass mkt. 5.95 (0-688-16613-X, Wm Morrow) Morrow Avon.

Magicians of Erianne. James R. Berry. LC 85-45833. 256p. (YA). (gr. 7 up). 1988. 13.95 (0-06-020556-3) HarpC Child Bks.

Magicians of Light: Photographs from the Collection of the National Gallery of Canada. Ed. by James Borcoman. (Illus.). 316p. 1996. pap. 24.95 (0-88884-627-4, Pub. by Natl Gallery) U Ch Pr.

Magicians of the Emptiness. Liviu Pendofunda. 148p. (C). 1997. pap. write for info. (0-9623183-5-3) Moonfall Pr VA.

***Magicians of the Millennium: Traveling the Rainbow Bridge.** large type ed. JoShanna Bush & Diane Virbick. (Illus.). 168p. 1999. pap. 12.95 (0-9672888-0-0) Souls Sng.

Magicians of the Soul: Exploring the World of Paranormal & Mystical Experience. Ted L. Orcutt. LC 95-94237. 264p. 1995. 35.00 (0-9623434-4-7) Global Village.

Magician's Quest. Claire Delacroix. LC 96-345. (Historical Ser.). 299p. 1995. per. 4.50 (0-373-28881-6, 1-28881-0) Harlequin Bks.

Magician's Reflection: A Complete Guide to Creating Personal Magical Symbols & Systems. Bill Whitcomb. (Illus.). 400p. 1999. 24.95 (1-56718-814-1) Llewellyn Pubns.

Magicians, Seers, & Mystics: Apollonius of Tyana; The Unknown Master of the Albigeneses; Christian Rosenkreutz & the Rosicrucians; Mystery of the Templars; Nicholas Flamen & the Philosophers Stone; Saint-German the Immortal; Madame Blavatsky & the Theosophists. Reginald Merton. Tr. by Maurice Magre. 287p. 1994. reprint ed. pap. 19.95 (1-56459-432-7) Kessinger Pub.

Magician's Tale. David Hunt, pseud. 1998. reprint ed. mass mkt. 7.50 (0-425-16482-9) Berkley Pub.

Magicians, Theologicans, & Doctors: Studies in Folk Medicine & Folklore As Reflected in the Rabbinical Responsa. H. J. Zimmels. LC 96-41934. 304p. 1997. pap. 40.00 (0-7657-5971-3) Aronson.

Magician's Visit: A Passover Tale. Barbara Diamond Goldin. 1995. 10.19 (0-606-07827-4, Pub. by Turtleback) Demco.

Magician's Ward. Patricia C. Wrede. LC 97-14690. 320p. 1997. 22.95 (0-312-85369-6, Pub. by Tor Bks) St Martin.

Magician's Ward. Patricia C. Wrede. 1998. mass mkt. 5.99 (0-8125-2085-8, Pub. by Tor Bks) St Martin.

Magicians Wife. James M. Cain. 1986. pap. 9.95 (0-88748-018-7) Carnegie-Mellon.

Magician's Wife. Brian Moore. LC 97-34064. 240p. 1999. pap. 12.95 (0-452-27959-3, Plume) Dutton Plume.

Magician's Wife. Brian Moore. LC 97-931173. 300p. (J). 1997. 28.01 (0-676-97090-7) Random.

***Magician's Wife** Brian Moore. LC 97-50372. 358 p. 1998. write for info. (0-7540-1142-9) Chivers N Amer.

Magician's Wife. large type ed. Brian Moore. LC 97-50372. (Basic Ser.). 1998. 27.95 (0-7862-1388-4) Thorndike Pr.

Magician's Workbook: A Modern Grimoire. Steve Savedow. LC 94-49077. (Illus.). 288p. (Orig.). 1995. reprint ed. pap. 14.95 (0-87728-823-2) Weiser.

Magicien des Bayous. Karen Leabo. (Rouge Passion Ser.). (FRE.). 1994. pap. 3.50 (0-373-37292-2, 1-37292-9) Harlequin Bks.

Magicienne - Wait & See. Robert Munsch. (Droles D'Histories Ser.). (FRE., Illus.). 24p. (J). (ps up). 1994. pap. 6.95 (2-89021-214-9, Pub. by La Courte Ech) Firefly Bks Ltd.

Magicienne Trahie & L'ile des mers gelees see Thorgal: The Sorceress Betrayed

Magiciennes. Boileau-Narcejac. (FRE.). 192p. 1972. pap. 10.95 (0-7859-1708-X, 2070361780) Fr & Eur.

Magick Bk. 4: Liber ABA. 2nd rev. ed. Aleister Crowley. LC 97-37399. Vol. 4. (Illus.). 926p. 1997. 60.00 (0-87728-919-0) Weiser.

Magick Made Easy: Charms, Spells, Potions & Power. Patricia Telesco. LC BF1611.T45 1999. 269p. 1999. pap. 16.00 (0-06-251630-2) HarpC.

Magick Portions: HOQ to Prepare & Use Homemade Aphrodisiacs, Oils, Brews & Much More. Gerina Dunwich. LC 97-51860. 176p. 1998. pap. text 10.95 (0-8065-1982-7, Citadel Pr) Carol Pub Group.

Magick Without Peers. Ariadne Rainbird & David Rankine. (Orig.). 1997. pap. 22.95 (1-898307-99-7, Pub. by Capall Bann Pubng) Holmes Pub.

Magick Without Tears. rev. ed. Aleister Crowley. LC 82-83310. 560p. 1991. pap. 19.95 (1-56184-018-1) New Falcon Pubns.

***Magickal Astrology: Understanding Your Place in the Cosmos.** Skye Alexander. 224p. 2000. pap. 12.99 (1-56414-479-8, New Page Bks) Career Pr Inc.

Magickal Dance: Your Body As an Instrument of Power. Ted Andrews. LC 92-18981. (Practical Guide to Personal Power Ser.). (Illus.). 240p. 1993. pap. 9.95 (0-87542-004-4) Llewellyn Pubns.

Magickal, Mythical, Mystical Beasts: How to Invite Them into Your Life. D. J. Conway. LC 96-9051. (Illus.). 272p. (Orig.). 1999. pap. 14.95 (1-56718-176-7) Llewellyn Pubns.

Magickal Places A Wiccan Guide to Sacred Sites & Spiritual Centers. Patricia Telesco. LC 99-39698. 1999. pap. text 14.00 (0-8065-2138-4) Carol Pub Group.

Magickal Qaballah. Frater Zarathustra. LC 86-50965. (Illus.). 75p. (Orig.). 1986. pap. 25.00 (0-939856-63-8) Tech Group.

Magickal Record. Keith Morgan. (Orig.). 1994. pap. 7.95 (1-872189-35-0, Pub. by Mandrake Pr) Holmes Pub.

Magickal Year: Sourcing Our Pagan Past. Diana Ferguson. LC 96-973. (Illus.). 224p. 1996. 29.95 (0-87728-882-8) Weiser.

Magickian: A Study in Effective Magick. Phillip Cooper. LC 93-18793. (Illus.). 240p. (Orig.). 1993. pap. 12.95 (0-87728-777-5) Weiser.

An Asterisk (*) at the beginning of an entry indicates that the title is appearing for the first time.

Magicnet. John DeChancie. 1993. 18.00 (*0-688-12759-2*, Wm Morrow) Morrow Avon.

Magicnet. John DeChancie. 240p. 1994. mass mkt. 4.99 (*0-380-77394-5*, Avon Bks) Morrow Avon.

Magicnet. John DeChancie. 2000. 18.00 (*0-380-97230-1*, Avon Bks) Morrow Avon.

Magico De Salermo Pedro De Vayalarde: Primera y Segunda Partes. Juan Salvo y Vela. Ed. by Donald C. Buck. LC 94-72491. (Coleccion Teatro). (SPA.). 207p. (Orig.). 1995. pap. 19.00 (*0-89729-750-4*) Ediciones.

Magico Prodigioso. Pedro Calderon de la Barca. Ed. by Bernard Sese. (Nueva Austral Ser.: Vol. 88). (SPA.). 1991. pap. text 12.95 (*84-239-1888-2*) Elliots Bks.

Magico Prodigioso. 9th ed. Pedro Calderon de la Barca. (SPA.). 160p. 1989. pap. write for info. (*0-7859-5133-4*) Fr & Eur.

Magico Prodigioso: A Composite Edition & Study of the Manuscript & Printed Versions. Pedro Calderon de la Barca. Ed. by Melveena McKendrick. (Illus.). 288p. 1992. text 79.00 (*0-19-815867-X*) OUP.

Magic's Greatest Gimmick. Daniel Waldron. (Orig.). 1996. pap. 5.00 (*0-941543-12-9*) Sun Dog Pr.

Magic's Pawn. Mercedes Lackey. (Last Herald-Mage Ser.: Bk. 1). 352p. 1989. mass mkt. 5.99 (*0-88677-352-0*, Pub. by DAW Bks) Penguin Putnam.

Magic's Price. Mercedes Lackey. (Last Herald-Mage Ser.: Bk. 3). 352p. 1990. mass mkt. 6.99 (*0-88677-426-8*, Pub. by DAW Bks) Penguin Putnam.

Magic's Promise. Mercedes Lackey. (Last Herald-Mage Ser.: Bk. 2). 320p. 1990. mass mkt. 5.99 (*0-88677-401-2*, Pub. by DAW Bks) Penguin Putnam.

Magic's Touch: From Fast Break to Fundamentals with Basketball's Most Exciting Player. Earvin "Magic" Johnson & Roy S. Johnson. 1989. 17.95 (*0-685-26629-X*) Addison-Wesley.

Magic's Touch: From Fast Break to Fundamentals with Basketball's Most Exciting Player. 3rd ed. Earvin "Magic" Johnson & Roy S. Johnson. (Illus.). 208p. 1992. pap. 8.95 (*0-201-63222-5*) Addison-Wesley.

Magid Fasts for Ramadan. Mary Matthews. LC 95-10452. (Illus.). 48p. (J). (ps-3). 1996. 15.95 (*0-395-66589-2*, Clarion Bks) HM.

***Magid Fasts for Ramadan.** Mary Matthews. (Illus.). 48p. (J). (gr. 1-5). 2000. pap. 6.95 (*0-618-04035-8*, Clarion Bks) HM.

Magie Chez les Chaldeensis see Chaldean Magic: Its Origin & Development

Magie du Subconscient. Bernard S. Nagy. 222p. 1985. 18.50 (*2-920083-08-2*) Edns Roseau.

Magie Et l'Astrologie Dans l'Antiquite et au Moyen-Age. Louis F. Maury. (Volkskundliche Quellen Ser.: Reihe II). iv, 484p. 1980. reprint ed. write for info. (*3-487-06956-3*) G Olms Pubs.

Magie, Mystik, Messianismus. R. J. Werblowsky. Ed. by Gary Smith et al. (Haskala Ser.: Bd. 19). (Illus.). 272p. Date not set. 63.00 (*3-487-10318-4*) G Olms Pubs.

Magii from the Blue Star: The Spiritual Drama & Mystical Heritage of Elvis Aaron Presley. Maia C. Shamayyim. (Illus.). 169p. 1989. spiral bd. 22.95 (*1-888420-00-6*) Johannine Grove.

Magii from the Blue Star: The Spiritual Drama & Mystical Heritage of Elvis Aaron Presley. 2nd ed. Maia C. Shamayyim. Ed. by Simeon Nartoomid. (Illus.). Date not set. pap. write for info. (*1-888420-07-3*) Johannine Grove.

***Magi'i of Cyador.** L. E. Modesitt, Jr. LC 99-55274. 544p. 2000. 25.95 (*0-312-87226-7*, Pub. by Tor Bks) St Martin.

Magika Hiera: Ancient Greek Magic & Religion. Ed. by Christopher A. Faraone & Dirk Obbink. 312p. 1997. reprint ed. pap. 17.95 (*0-19-511140-0*) OUP.

Magilloth & Rashi, Linear. Avraham Schwartzbaum. 1998. 19.95 (*0-9610558-0-4*) Feldheim.

***Magill's Cinema Annual.** 725p. 2000. 95.00 (*0-7876-2903-0*, UXL) Gale.

Magill's Cinema Annual: A Retrospective of the Films of 1996. (Illus.). 695p. 1997. pap. 39.95 (*1-57859-043-4*) Visible Ink Pr.

Magill's Cinema Annual: A Retrospective of the Films of 1997. Visible Ink Press Staff. 695p. 1998. text 39.95 (*1-57859-056-6*) Visible Ink Pr.

***Magill's Cinema Annual: 1999 Edition.** Gale Group Staff. 725p. 1999. 90.00 (*0-7876-2902-2*) Gale.

Magill's Cinema Annual, 1997. 750p. 1997. 90.00 (*0-7876-1155-7*, 00156279) Gale.

Magill's Cinema Annual, 1998. 1998. 90.00 (*0-7876-1156-5*, 00156280) Gale.

Magill's Cinema Annual, 1996. 15th ed. Fhaner & Scanlon. 699p. 1996. 83.00 (*0-7876-0762-2*) Visible Ink Pr.

Magill's Cinema Annual, 1995. 95th ed. Ed. by Shawn Brennan. (Magill's Cinema Annual Ser.). 700p. 1995. 90.00 (*0-7876-0732-0*, 109885) Gale.

Magill's Guide to Science Fiction & Fantasy Literature, 4 vols. Ed. by T. A. Shippey. 1216p. 1996. lib. bdg. 300.00 (*0-89356-906-2*) Salem Pr.

***Magill's Legal Guide, 3 vols., Vol. 1.** Ed. by Timothy Hall. LC 99-35385. (Illus.). 1080p. (C). (gr. 7 up). 1999. lib. bdg. 315.00 (*0-89356-165-7*) Salem Pr.

Magill's Literary Annual, 1981: Books of 1980, 2 vols., Set. Ed. by Frank N. Magill. LC 77-99209. 950p. 1981. lib. bdg. 55.00 (*0-89356-281-5*) Salem Pr.

Magill's Literary Annual, 1982: Books of 1981, 2 vols., Set. Ed. by Frank N. Magill. LC 77-99209. 1007p. 1982. lib. bdg. 55.00 (*0-89356-282-3*) Salem Pr.

Magill's Literary Annual, 1983: Books of 1982, 2 vols., Set. Ed. by Frank N. Magill. LC 77-99209. 938p. 1983. lib. bdg. 55.00 (*0-89356-283-1*) Salem Pr.

Magill's Literary Annual, 1984: Books of 1983, 2 vols. Frank N. Magill. LC 77-99209. 996p. 1984. lib. bdg. 55.00 (*0-89356-284-X*) Salem Pr.

Magill's Literary Annual, 1985: Books of 1984, 2 vols., Set. Ed. by Frank N. Magill. LC 77-99209. 1067p. 1985. lib. bdg. 60.00 (*0-89356-285-8*) Salem Pr.

Magill's Literary Annual, 1986: Books of 1985, 2 vols., Set. Ed. by Frank N. Magill. LC 77-99209. 988p. 1986. lib. bdg. 60.00 (*0-89356-286-6*) Salem Pr.

Magill's Literary Annual, 1987: Books of 1986, 2 vols., Set. Ed. by Frank N. Magill. LC 77-99209. 1026p. 1987. lib. bdg. 65.00 (*0-89356-287-4*) Salem Pr.

Magill's Literary Annual, 1988: Books of 1987, 2 vols., Set. Ed. by Frank N. Magill. LC 77-99209. 1013p. 1988. lib. bdg. 65.00 (*0-89356-288-2*) Salem Pr.

Magill's Literary Annual, 1989: Books of 1988, 2 vols., Set. Ed. by Frank N. Magill. LC 79-99209. 938p. 1989. lib. bdg. 65.00 (*0-89356-289-0*) Salem Pr.

Magill's Literary Annual, 1978, 2 vols., Set. Ed. by Frank N. Magill. LC 77-99209. 946p. 1978. lib. bdg. 55.00 (*0-89356-278-5*) Salem Pr.

Magill's Literary Annual, 1990: Books of 1989, 2 vols., Set. Ed. by Frank N. Magill. LC 77-99209. 933p. 1990. lib. bdg. 70.00 (*0-89356-290-4*) Salem Pr.

Magill's Literary Annual, 1991: Books of 1990, 2 vols., Set. Ed. by Frank N. Magill. LC 77-99209. 924p. 1991. lib. bdg. 70.00 (*0-89356-291-2*) Salem Pr.

Magill's Literary Annual, 1992: Books of 1991, 2 vols., Set. Ed. by Frank N. Magill. LC 77-99209. 937p. 1992. lib. bdg. 70.00 (*0-89356-292-0*) Salem Pr.

Magill's Literary Annual, 1993: Books of 1992, 2 vols., Set. Ed. by Frank N. Magill. LC 77-99209. 899p. 1993. lib. bdg. 70.00 (*0-89356-293-9*) Salem Pr.

Magill's Literary Annual, 1994: Books of 1993, 2 vols., Set. Ed. by Frank N. Magill. LC 77-99209. 876p. 1994. lib. bdg. 70.00 (*0-89356-294-7*) Salem Pr.

Magill's Literary Annual, 1995: Books of 1994, 2 vols., Set. Ed. by Frank N. Magill. LC 77-99209. 1067p. 1995. lib. bdg. 75.00 (*0-89356-295-5*) Salem Pr.

Magill's Literary Annual, 1996: Books of 1995. Ed. by Salem Press Editors. 950p. 1996. lib. bdg. 75.00 (*0-89356-296-3*) Salem Pr.

Magill's Literary Annual, 1997: Books of 1996, 2 vols., Vol. 1. Salem Press Editors. Ed. by Frank N. Magill. 1000p. 1997. lib. bdg. 75.00 (*0-89356-297-1*) Salem Pr.

***Magill's Literary Annual, 1998: Books of 1997.** Salem Press Editors. 1000p. (YA). (gr. 9-12). 1998. lib. bdg. 75.00 (*0-89356-298-X*) Salem Pr.

Magill's Literary Annual, 1999: The Books of 1998, 2 vols. annuals Salem Press Editors. 1000p. 1999. lib. bdg. 75.00 (*0-89356-299-8*) Salem Pr.

Magill's Literary Annual, 1977, 2 vols., Set. Ed. by Frank N. Magill et al. LC 77-99209. 960p. 1977. lib. bdg. 55.00 (*0-89356-077-4*) Salem Pr.

Magill's Literary Annual, 1979: Books of 1978, 2 vols., Set. Ed. by Frank N. Magill. LC 77-99209. 926p. 1979. lib. bdg. 55.00 (*0-89356-279-3*) Salem Pr.

***Magill's Literary Annual 2000, 2 Vols.** Ed. by John D. Wilson. 950p. 2000. 75.00 (*0-89356-274-2*) Salem Pr.

***Magill's Medical Guide, Revised Edition, 1998.** rev. ed. Salem Press Editors. LC 98-27251. (Illus.). 2077p. (YA). (gr. 9-12). 1998. lib. bdg. 310.00 (*0-89356-937-2*) Salem Pr.

Magill's Survey of American Literature, 6 vols., Set. Ed. by Frank N. Magill. LC 91-28113. (Illus.). 2160p. 1991. lib. bdg. 542.79 (*1-85435-437-X*) Marshall Cavendish.

Magill's Survey of Science: Applied Science, 6 vols., Set. Ed. by Frank N. Magill. LC 92-35688. 3107p. 1991. lib. bdg. 475.00 (*0-89356-705-1*) Salem Pr.

Magill's Survey of Science: Life Science, 6 vols., Set. Ed. by Frank N. Magill. 2964p. 1991. lib. bdg. 475.00 (*0-89356-612-8*) Salem Pr.

Magill's Survey of Science: Physical Science, 6 vols., Set. Ed. by Frank N. Magill. LC 91-32962. 2981p. 1992. lib. bdg. 475.00 (*0-89356-618-7*) Salem Pr.

***Magill's Survey of Science, Applied Science Supplement (1998) Applied Science Supplement.** Ed. by Frank N. Magill et al. (Applied Science Series, Supplement). 448p. (YA). (gr. 9 up). 1998. lib. bdg., suppl. ed. 90.00 (*0-89356-934-8*) Salem Pr.

***Magill's Survey of Science, Earth Science Supplement (1998) Earth Science Supplement.** Ed. by Frank N. Magill et al. (Earth Science Series, Supplement). 448p. (YA). (gr. 9 up). 1998. lib. bdg., suppl. ed. 90.00 (*0-89356-933-X*) Salem Pr.

***Magill's Survey of Science, Life Science Supplement (1998) Life Science Supplement.** Ed. by Frank N. Magill et al. (Life Science Series, Supplement). 448p. (gr. 9 up). 1998. lib. bdg., suppl. ed. 90.00 (*0-89356-936-4*) Salem Pr.

***Magill's Survey of Science, Physical Science Supplement (1998) Physical Science Supplement.** Ed. by Frank N. Magill et al. (Physical Science Series, Supplement). 448p. (YA). (gr. 9 up). 1998. lib. bdg., suppl. ed. 90.00 (*0-89356-935-6*) Salem Pr.

Magill's Survey of World Literature, 6 vols. Ed. by Frank N. Magill. LC 92-11198. 1992. 389.95 (*1-85435-482-5*) Marshall Cavendish.

Maginn: A Verse Play for Voices. Frank Fagan. LC 92-71509. (Orig.). 1993. pap. 9.95 (*0-9632732-1-3*) Dendron Pr.

Maginot Imitations: Major Fortifications of Germany & Neighboring Countries. J. E. Kaufmann & H. W. Kaufmann. LC 96-38170. 200p. 1997. 55.00 (*0-275-95720-9*, Praeger Pubs) Greenwood.

Maginot Line: None Shall Pass. J. E. Kaufmann & H. W. Kaufmann. LC 96-38170. 192p. 1997. 57.95 (*0-275-95719-5*, Praeger Pubs) Greenwood.

Magischen Kanale. Marshall McLuhan. 540p. 1995. text 13.00 (*3-364-00308-4*) Gordon & Breach.

***Magislerio Symbolorium.** Enrique Denzinger. (SPA.). 1998. pap. 24.95 (*0-8245-2154-4*) Crossroad NY.

Magister. TSR Staff. (Forgotten Realms Ser.). (Illus.). 128p. 1999. pap. 19.95 (*0-7869-1430-0*) TSR Inc.

Magister Ludens, der Erzahler in Henrich Wittenweilers Ring. Christa W. Cross. LC 83-16926. (University of North Carolina Studies in the Germanic Languages & Literatures: No. 102). (GER.). 127p. reprint ed. pap. 39.40 (*0-608-20059-X*, 207133100011) Bks Demand.

Magister Paulus Niavis . . . Epistole Breues . . . Epistole Mediocres . . . Epistole Longiores. Rand Johnson. 1995. boxed set 35.00 (*1-879288-51-6*) Medieval Inst.

Magister Regis: Studies in Honor of Robert Earl Kaske. Ed. by Arthur Groos et al. LC 86-80020. 302p. reprint ed. pap. 93.70 (*0-7837-5602-X*, 204550800005) Bks Demand.

Magisterial Imagination: Six Masters of the Human Sciences. Max Lerner. LC 93-39856. 212p. (C). 1994. 34.95 (*1-56000-168-2*) Transaction Pubs.

Magisterial Tribunals in Victoria. Maurice W. Gerkens. xv, 146p. 1988. pap. 40.50 (*0-455-20820-4*, Pub. by LawBk Co) Gaunt.

Magisterium: Teaching Authority in the Catholic Church. Francis A. Sullivan. 1984. pap. 14.95 (*0-8091-2577-3*) Paulist Pr.

Magistracy Rediscovered: Connecticut, 1636-1818. Everett C. Goodwin. Ed. by Robert Berkhofer. LC 80-28681. (Studies in American History & Culture: No. 24). 193p. 1981. reprint ed. pap. 59.90 (*0-8357-1160-9*, 207009600064) Bks Demand.

Magistrate As Chairman. 2nd ed. Lady Ralphs & Geoffrey Norman. 234p. 1992. pap. 24.00 (*0-406-00118-9*, UK, MICHIE) LEXIS Pub.

Magistrates at Work: Sentencing & Social Structure. Sheila Brown. 176p. 1991. 113.00 (*0-335-09651-4*); pap. 33.95 (*0-335-09650-6*) OpUniv Pr.

Magistrates Court. 2nd ed. Julie O'Malley. (Cavendish Practice Notes Ser.). 1996. pap. 32.00 (*1-85941-301-3*, Pub. by Cavendish Pubng) Gaunt.

Magistrates' Court & European Law: A Practical Guide. Richard Powell. 220p. 1997. pap. 59.50 (*1-85811-160-9*, Pub. by CLT Prof) Gaunt.

Magistrates of the Roman Republic. T. Robert Broughton. (American Philological Association Philological Monographs). 578p. 1974. 67.95 (*0-89130-706-0*, 40 00 15) OUP.

Magistrates of the Roman Republic, Vol. III: Supplement. T. Robert Broughton. (American Philological Association Philological Monographs). 294p. 1974. 44.95 (*0-89130-811-3*, 40-00-15) OUP.

Magistrates of the Sacred: Parish Priests & Indian Parishioners in Eighteenth-Century Mexico. William B. Taylor. 1999. pap. text 34.95 (*0-8047-3659-6*) Stanford U Pr.

Magistrates of the Sacred: Priests & Parishioners in Eighteenth-Century Mexico. William B. Taylor. LC 95-22982. 984p. 1996. 75.00 (*0-8047-2456-3*) Stanford U Pr.

Magistrate's Tale. Nora Naish. 1996. pap. 9.99 (*0-7493-2415-5*) Buttrwrth-Heinemann.

Magistrats du Parlement de Paris, 1770-90 Dictionnaire Biographique et Genealogique. Joel Felix. (FRE.). 239p. 1990. pap. 95.00 (*0-7859-8226-4*, 2904177140) Fr & Eur.

Magistri Petri de Ybernia Exposito. E. Peters. 1998. 68.75 (*90-6831-819-5*, Pub. by Peeters Pub) Bks Intl VA.

Magli: Storia E Immagini Di una Dinastia. Samuele Mazza. (ENG & ITA., Illus.). 112p. 1997. 80.00 (*88-7813-739-1*, Pub. by Art Bks Intl) Partners Pubs Grp.

Magma: The Indestructible. Henry W. Crosby. LC 94-61513. (Illus.). 1994. pap. 9.95 (*0-936029-36-6*) Western Bk Journ.

Magmas, Rocks & Planetary Development: A Survey of Magma/Igneous Rock Systems. Eric A. Middlemost. 288p. (C). 1997. pap. text 42.19 (*0-582-23089-6*, Drumbeat) Longman.

Magmatic Processes: Physicochemical Principles. Ed. by B. O. Mysen. LC 86-83155. (Special Publication: No. 1). 490p. 1987. 65.00 (*0-941809-00-5*) Geochemical Soc.

Magmatic Processes & Plate Tectonics. Ed. by H. M. Prichard et al. (Geological Society Special Publication Classic Ser.: No. 76). (Illus.). 536p. 1997. pap. 40.00 (*1-897799-87-X*, Pub. by Geol Soc Pub Hse) AAPG.

Magmatic Systems. Ed. by Michael P. Ryan. (International Geophysics Ser.: No. 57). (Illus.). 401p. 1994. text 73.00 (*0-12-605070-8*) Acad Pr.

Magmatism: In Relation to Diverse Tectonic Settings. Ed. by Rajesh K. Srivastava & R. Chandra. (Illus.). 475p. (C). 1996. text 110.00 (*90-5410-275-6*, Pub. by A A Balkema) Ashgate Pub Co.

***Magmatism & Geodynamics: Terrestrial Magmatism Throughout the Earth's History.** Ed. by O. A. Bogatikov. 536p. 2000. text 175.00 (*90-5699-168-X*, G & B Science) Gordon & Breach.

Magmatism & the Causes of Continental Break-Up. Ed. by B. C. Storey et al. (Geological Society Special Publications: No. 68). (Illus.). viii, 408p. 1992. 108.00 (*0-903317-83-4*, 281, Pub. by Geol Soc Pub Hse) AAPG.

Magmatism & Transformation of Active Areas of the Earth's Crust. T. I. Frolova et al. Tr. by R. Chakravarty from RUS. (Illus.). 283p. (C). 1993. text 91.00 (*90-6191-499-X*, Pub. by A A Balkema) Ashgate Pub Co.

Magmatism in Extensional Structural Settings: The Phanerozoic African Plate. Ed. by A. B. Kampunzu & R. T. Lubala. (Illus.). 664p. 1991. 293.95 (*0-387-50136-3*) Spr-Verlag.

***Magna Brava: Magnum's Women Photographers.** Sara Stevenson et al. (Illus.). 240p. 1999. 65.00 (*3-7913-2160-9*, Pub. by Prestel) te Neues.

Magna Carta. Ed. & Compiled by John Langdon-Davies. 39.00 (*1-56696-062-2*) Jackdaw.

Magna Carta. 2nd ed. James C. Holt. (Illus.). 575p. (C). 1992. pap. text 29.95 (*0-521-27778-7*) Cambridge U Pr.

***Magna Carta: A Commentary on the Great Charter of King John.** William S. McKechnie. LC 99-38731. 2000. write for info. (*1-58477-031-7*) Lawbk Exchange.

***Magna Carta: Complete Text Edition.** King John of England. 1999. reprint ed. pap. 3.95 (*0-89979-114-X*) British Am Bks.

Magna Carta: Text & Commentary. A. Dick Howard. LC 64-66214. (Illus.). 64p. (C). 1997. reprint ed. pap. text 7.50 (*0-8139-0121-9*) U Pr of Va.

Magna Carta & Medieval Government. J. C. Holt. 310p. (C). 1985. 55.00 (*0-907628-38-9*) Hambledon Press.

Magna Carta & Other Addresses. William D. Guthrie. LC 74-84309. (Essay Index Reprint Ser.). 1977. 18.95 (*0-8369-1082-6*) Ayer.

Magna Carta & Other Addresses. William D. Guthrie. LC 74-84309. (Essay Index Reprint Ser.). 282p. reprint ed. lib. bdg. 16.25 (*0-8290-0471-8*) Irvington.

Magna Carta & Other Great Charters of England: With an Historical Treatise & Copious Explanatory Notes. Boyd C. Barrington. 342p. 1993. reprint ed. 45.00 (*0-8377-1955-0*, Rothman) W S Hein.

Magna Carta & the Idea of Liberty. James C. Holt et al. LC 82-4. 196p. 1982. reprint ed. pap. 9.50 (*0-89874-471-7*) Krieger.

Magna Carta & the Tradition of Liberty. 1984. lib. bdg. 250.00 (*0-87700-623-7*) Revisionist Pr.

Magna Carta Barons & Their American Descendants: Together with the Pedigrees of the Founders of the Order of Runnemede Deduced from the Sureties for the Enforcement of the Statues of the Magna Carta of King John. Charles H. Browning. 463p. 1998. reprint ed. lib. bdg. 45.00 (*0-8328-7009-9*) Higginson Bk Co.

Magna Carta for the Nuclear Age. David Krieger & Robert Woetzel. LC 94-15529. 1994. 12.00 (*1-880831-12-0*); pap. 8.00 (*1-880831-11-2*) Aletheia Pr.

Magna Carta in the Seventeenth Century. Maurice Ashley. LC 65-23456. (Magna Carta Essays Ser.). 76p. (Orig.). reprint ed. pap. 30.00 (*0-8357-3733-0*, 203645900003) Bks Demand.

Magna Carta Latina: The Privilege of Singing, Articulating & Reading a Language & Keeping It Alive. 2nd ed. Eugen Rosenstock-Huessy & Ford L. Battles. LC 75-23378. (Pittsburgh Reprint Ser.: No. 1). 296p. 1997. reprint ed. pap. text 19.00 (*0-915138-07-7*) Argo Bks.

Magna Carta of Child Rearing: Mold Them & Not Make Them. Ulysses Tuff. 56p. 1994. pap. text 4.95 (*1-885657-00-5*) The Way The Truth.

Magna Carta of the Christian Church. Karl F. Althoff. Tr. by Werner Grimm from GER. 19p. 1982. pap. 3.00 (*0-919924-15-8*, Pub. by Steiner Book Centre) Anthroposophic.

Magna Charta. James Daugherty. (Illus.). 181p. (YA). (gr. 5 up). 1998. reprint ed. pap. 10.95 (*0-9643803-5-8*) Beautiful Feet.

Magna Charta Barons & Their American Descendants (1898) Together with the Pedigrees of the Founders of the Order of Runnemede. Charles H. Browning. LC 73-77634. (Illus.). 463p. 2000. reprint ed. 18.50 (*0-8063-0055-8*) Genealog Pub.

Magna Charta for America. Jack P. Greene et al. LC 84-45900. (Memoirs Ser.: Vol. 165). 1986. 35.00 (*0-87169-165-5*, M165-GRJ) Am Philos.

***Magna Charta Sureties, 1215: The Barons Named in the Magna Charta, 1215, & Some of Their Descendants Who Settled in America During the Early Colonial Years.** 5th ed. Frederick L. Weis & William R. Beall. 236p. 1999. 20.00 (*0-8063-1609-8*) Genealog Pub.

Magna Vita Sancti Hugonis: The Life of St. Hugh of Lincoln, I. Ed. by Decima L. Douie & David H. Farmer. (Oxford Medieval Texts Ser.). (Illus.). 190p. 1985. text 85.00 (*0-19-822207-6*) OUP.

Magna Vita Sancti Hugonis: The Life of St. Hugh of Lincoln, II. Ed. by Decima L. Douie & David H. Farmer. (Oxford Medieval Texts Ser.). (Illus.). 256p. 1985. text 75.00 (*0-19-822208-4*) OUP.

Magnalia Christi Americana, Bks. I & II. Cotton Mather. Ed. by Kenneth B. Murdock & Elizabeth W. Miller. LC 73-76383. (John Harvard Library). (Illus.). 512p. reprint ed. pap. 158.80 (*0-7837-2496-9*, 205745900005) Bks Demand.

Magnalia Christi Americana: America's Literary Old Testament. Michael J. Mages. LC 98-48854. (Illus.). 415p. 1999. 89.95 (*1-57309-358-0*) Intl Scholars.

Magnalia Christi Americana or: The Ecclesiastical History of New England from Its First Planting. Cotton Mather. (Notable American Authors Ser.). 1999. reprint ed. lib. bdg. 125.00 (*0-7812-3960-5*) Rprt Serv.

Magnalia Christi Americana, or the Ecclesiastical History of New-England from the Year 1620, Unto the Year 1698, 7 bks., Set. Cotton Mather. LC 74-141092. (Research Library of Colonial Americana). (Illus.). 1972. reprint ed. 63.95 (*0-405-03297-8*) Ayer.

***Magnaway: The Ultimate Transportation.** large type ed. Terence S. Kirk. Ed. by Pauline Jones. LC 99-93413. (Illus.). 83p. 2000. 14.95 (*0-944531-02-4*, 8814) Owl Wise Pub.

Magnel Laboratory for Reinforced Concrete. (PCI Journal Reprints Ser.). 4p. 1980. pap. 6.00 (*0-686-40137-9*, JR233) P-PCI.

Magnesite: Geology, Mineralogy, Geochemistry, Formation of Mg-Carbonates. Ed. by Peter Moeller. (Monograph Series on Mineral Deposits: No. 28). (Illus.). viii, 300p. 1989. 52.00 (*3-443-12028-8*, Pub. by Gebruder Borntraeger) Balogh.

Magnesium. Alan Gaby. 48p. 1993. pap. 3.95 (*0-87983-602-4*, 36024K, Keats Publng) NTC Contemp Pub Co.

Magnesium. Colin Uttley. LC 98-53200. (Elements Ser.: Vol. 2). 32p. (J). (gr. 3-5). 2000. lib. bdg. 22.79 (*0-7614-0889-4*, Benchmark NY) Marshall Cavendish.

M

An Asterisk (*) at the beginning of an entry indicates that the title is appearing for the first time.

Magnesium: Current Status & New Developments Theoretical, Biologicial & Medical Aspects. Ed. by Theophile Theophanides & Jane Anastassopoulou. LC 97-41298. 436p. 1997. text 214.00 (0-7923-4821-4) Kluwer Academic.

Magnesium: Its Biologic Significance. Jerry K. Aikawa. 144p. 1981. 99.00 (0-8493-5871-X, QP535) CRC Pr.

Magnesium: Miracle Mineral. 1996. lib. bdg. 251.99 (0-8490-5872-4) Gordon Pr.

Magnesium Alloys AMS Handbook. 1997. 89.00 (0-7680-0086-6) Soc Auto Engineers.

***Magnesium Alloys & Their Applications.** K. U. Kainer. Ed. by B. L. Mordike. 750p. 1999. 298.00 (3-527-29936-X) Wiley.

Magnesium & Magnesium Compounds. (Metals & Minerals Ser.). 1993. lib. bdg. 250.95 (0-8490-8939-5) Gordon Pr.

Magnesium & Man. Warren E. Wacker. LC 80-14189. (Commonwealth Fund Publications). (Illus.). 171p. 1980. 33.95 (0-674-54225-8) HUP.

Magnesium & the Cardiovascular System Journal Vol. 4, Nos. 5-6: Magnesium. Ed. by J. Durlach & B. M. Altura. (Illus.). vi, 134p. 1986. pap. 62.75 (3-8055-4282-8) S Karger.

Magnesium & the Cell. Ed. by Nicholas J. Birch. (Illus.). 289p. 1993. text 104.00 (0-12-099620-0) Acad Pr.

Magnesium Casting Technology. Arthur William Brace & F. A. Allen. LC 58-821. (Illus.). 174p. reprint ed. pap. 54.00 (0-608-11701-3, 205132500095) Bks Demand.

Magnesium Deficiency. Ed. by M. J. Halpern & J. Durlach. (Illus.). viii, 248p. 1985. 162.75 (3-8055-3979-7) S Karger.

Magnesium Deficiency in the Pathogenesis of Disease: Early Roots of Cardiovascular, & Renal Abnormalities. Ed. by Mildred S. Seelig. LC 78-27742. (Topics in Bone & Mineral Disorders Ser.). 504p. 1980. 95.00 (0-306-40202-5, Kluwer Plenum) Kluwer Academic.

Magnesium, Diabetes & Carbohydrate Metabolism Journal: Magnesium, Vol. 2, Nos. 4-6. Ed. by J. Durlach & B. M. Altura. (Illus.). iv, 172p. 1984. pap. 85.25 (3-8055-3865-0) S Karger.

Magnesium from China, Russia, & Ukraine: An International Trade Investigation. (Illus.). 140p. (Orig.). (C). 1995. pap. text 40.00 (0-7881-1936-2) DIANE Pub.

Magnesium from the People's Republic of China, Russia, & Ukraine: An International Trade Investigation. (Illus.). 157p. (Orig.). (C). 1994. pap. text 50.00 (0-7881-0742-9) DIANE Pub.

Magnesium Homeostasis. Ed. by G. A. Quamme. (Journal: Mineral & Electrolyte Metabolism Ser.: Vol. 19, Nos. 4-5, 1993). (Illus.). 132p. 1993. pap. 81.00 (3-8055-5881-3) S Karger.

Magnesium in Automotive Components: 1996 International Congress & Exposition. LC 96-207890. (Special Publications). 53p. 1996. pap. 30.00 (1-56091-793-8, SP-1163) Soc Auto Engineers.

Magnesium in Biological Systems Environmental & Biological Aspects: Environmental & Biomedical Aspects. Bela Fazekastamas-Selmeczi & Pal Stefanovits. Ed. by T. Fazekas et al. LC 95-149500. 350p. 1994. pap. 395.00 (963-05-6681-8, Pub. by Akade Kiado) St Mut.

Magnesium in Cellular Processes & Medicine. Ed. by B. M. Altura et al. iv, 244p. 1987. 172.25 (3-8055-4369-7) S Karger.

Magnesium in Clinical Medicine & Therapeutics Journal: Magnesium & Trace Elements, Vol. 10, Nos. 2-4, 1991-92. Ed. by M. Burton. (Illus.). 252p. 1993. pap. 35.75 (3-8055-5696-9) S Karger.

Magnesium Products Design. Robert S. Busk. (Mechanical Engineering Ser.: Vol. 53). (Illus.). 560p. 1986. text 199.00 (0-8247-7576-7) Dekker.

Magnesium, Stress & the Cardiovascular System. Ed. by B. M. Altura. (Journal: Magnesium: Vol. 5, No. 3-4, 1986). (Illus.). 120p. 1986. pap. 55.00 (3-8055-4355-7) S Karger.

Magnesium Technology 2000. Ed. by Howard I. Kaplan et al. (Illus.). 262p. 113.00 (0-87339-466-6) Minerals Metals.

Magnet Board Fun: For Everyday, Seasons, & Holidays. Liz Wilems & Dick Wilmes. (Illus.). 224p. 1998. pap. 16.95 (0-943452-28-7) Building Blocks.

Magnet Book. Levine. (Illus.). 80p. (J). (gr. 3-7). 1998. pap. 10.95 (0-8069-9944-6) Sterling.

Magnet Book. Shar Levine & Leslie Johnstone. LC 97-13987. (Illus.). 80p. (J). 1997. 19.95 (0-8069-9943-8) Sterling.

Magnet Dowsing: or The Magnet Study of Life. B. Bhattacharyya. 150p. 1998. reprint ed. pap. 16.50 (0-7873-1152-9) Hlth Research.

Magnet Effect. Jesse Berst. 240p. 2000. 24.95 (0-07-134803-4) McGraw.

Magnet Effect: Designing Outreach Events That Draw Kids to Christ. Barry St. Clair & Jim Burns. LC 95-100165. (Love/Sex/Dating Series). 192p. (Orig.). 1994. pap. 9.99 (1-56476-352-8, 6-3352, Victor Bks) Chariot Victor.

Magnet Fun. Instructional Fair Staff. (Book Box Ser.). 1998. 7.95 (1-56822-768-X) Instruct Fair.

Magnet Hospitals: Attraction & Retention of Professional Nurses. Margaret L. McClure et al. 150p. (Orig.). (C). 1983. pap. 16.25 (1-55810-070-9, G-160, Am Acad Nurses) Am Nurses Pub.

Magnet Investing: Build a Portfolio & Pick Winning Stocks Using Your Home Computer. Jordan L. Kimmel. LC 98-68587. (Illus.). 239p. 1999. pap. 24.95 (0-9626003-6-9) Next Decade.

***Magnet Investing: Build a Portfolio & Pick Winning Stocks Using Your Home Computer.** 2nd rev. ed. Jordan L. Kimmel. (Illus.). 250p. 2000. pap. 24.95 (0-9626003-8-5, Pub. by Next Decade) IPG Chicago.

Magnet Magic. (Illus.). (J). (ps-2). 1991. pap. 5.10 (0-8136-5693-1); lib. bdg. 7.95 (0-8136-5193-X) Modern Curr.

Magnet Magic. Raintree Steck-Vaughn Publishing Staff. (Read All about It - Science & Social Studies). (Illus.). 32p. (J). (gr. k-3). 1997. pap. 4.95 (0-8114-3770-1) Raintree Steck-V.

Magnet Magic Etc. Marie A. Hoyt. (Illus.). 12p. (J). (gr. 2-8). 1983. pap. text 3.00 (0-914911-01-5) Educ Serv Pr.

Magnet Schools Pockets of Excellence in a Sea of Diversity. Bradley Scott & Anna DeLuna. 100p. (Orig.). 1995. pap. text 25.00 (1-878550-54-3) Inter Dev Res Assn.

Magnet Science. Glen Vecchione. (Illus.). 128p. (J). (gr. 5-9). 1996. pap. 5.95 (0-8069-0889-0) Sterling.

Magnet Therapy: Balancing Your Body's Energy Flow for Self-Healing. Holger Hannemann. LC 90-36927. (Illus.). 128p. (Orig.). 1990. pap. 10.95 (0-8069-7378-1) Sterling.

Magnet Therapy: The Gentle & Effective Way to Balance Body Systems. Ghanshyam Singh Birla. LC 99-37558. (Illus.). 160p. 1999. pap. 12.95 (0-89281-841-7) Inner Tradit.

Magnet Therapy: The Pain Cure Alternative. Ronald Lawrence & Paul J. Rosch. LC 98-12167. 272p. 1998. per. 15.00 (0-7615-1547-X) Prima Pub.

Magnetic - Opto-Magnetic Storage: Media & Materials. 1992. 2650.00 (0-89336-921-7, GB-160) BCC.

Magnetic Altitude Control of Low Earth Orbit Satellites. Rafal Wisniewski. LC 98-41451. 1998. 54.95 (3-540-76247-7) Spr-Verlag.

Magnetic & Electromagnetic Shielding. Tsuneji Rikitake. 1987. text 206.50 (90-277-2406-7) Kluwer Academic.

Magnetic & Electron Structures of Transition Metals & Alloys. Ed. by V. G. Veselago & L. I. Vinokurova. (Proceedings of the Institute of General Physics of the Academy of Sciences of the U. S. S. R. Ser.: Vol. 3). 216p. (C). 1988. text 165.00 (0-941743-14-4) Nova Sci Pubs.

Magnetic & Gravity Anomalies in the Great Valley & Western Sierra Nevada Metamorphic Belt, California. John W. Cady. LC 75-19540. (Geological Society of America, Special Paper: No. 168). 80p. reprint ed. pap. 30.00 (0-608-14462-2, 202503100041) Bks Demand.

Magnetic & Inelastic Scattering of Neutrons by Metals. Ed. by T. J. Rowland & Paul A. Beck. LC 67-29670. (Metallurgical Society Conference Ser.: Vol. 43). 239p. reprint ed. pap. 74.10 (0-608-11352-2, 200153200079) Bks Demand.

Magnetic & Other Properties of Oxides & Related Compounds see Nuclear Particles & Physics: Group I

Magnetic & Other Properties of Oxides & Related Compounds: Hexagonal Ferrites - Special Lanthanide & Actinide Compounds see Crystal & Solid State Physics: Group III

Magnetic & Other Properties of Oxides & Related Compounds: Spinels, Fe Oxides & Fe- Me-O-Compounds see Crystal & Solid State Physics: Group III

Magnetic & Velocity Fields of Solar Active Regions. Ed. by G. Ai et al. (ASP Conference Series Proceedings: Vol. 46). xxxviii, 562 p. 1993. 34.00 (0-937707-65-1) Astron Soc Pacific.

Magnetic Atoms & Molecules. William Weltner. 436p. 1989. pap. 9.95 (0-486-66140-7) Dover.

Magnetic Bearings. Ed. by G. E. Schweitzer. (Illus.). xi, 394p. 1988. 152.95 (0-387-50426-5) Spr-Verlag.

Magnetic Beef Gourmet. Sterling Staff. (Magnet Gourmet Ser.). (Illus.). 10p. 1997. pap. 5.95 (0-8069-9857-1) Sterling.

Magnetic Blueprint of Life. 2nd ed. Albert R. Davis & Walter C. Rawls, Jr. (Illus.). 150p. 1988. reprint ed. pap. 15.00 (0-911311-15-7) Acres USA.

Magnetic Bond. Wilbur F. Kalinke. viii, 152p. 1997. pap. 6.95 (1-891346-02-4, 0003) Kalinke Bks.

Magnetic Bread Gourmet. (Magnet Gourmet Ser.). (Illus.). 10p. 1998. pap. 4.95 (0-8069-1857-8) Sterling.

Magnetic Bubble Theory. 2nd rev. ed. A. H. Eschenfelder. (Solo Motets from the Seventeenth Century Ser.: Vol. 14). (Illus.). 364p. 1981. 56.95 (0-387-10790-8) Spr-Verlag.

Magnetic Ceramics. Ed. by Bhaskar B. Ghate & John J. Simmins. (Ceramic Transactions Ser.: Vol. 47). 1995. 88.00 (0-944904-81-5, CT047) Am Ceramic.

Magnetic Ceramics. Raul Valenzuela. LC 93-43325. (Chemistry of Solid State Materials Ser.: No. 4). (Illus.). 332p. (C). 1994. text 90.00 (0-521-36485-X) Cambridge U Pr.

Magnetic Circuit. Heinz Rieger. LC TK0454.4.M3R. (Siemens Programmed Instruction Ser.: 4). 69p. reprint ed. pap. 30.00 (0-608-12360-9, 205208100033) Bks Demand.

Magnetic Compass Deviation & Correction. W. Denne. (C). 1987. 100.00 (0-85174-332-3) St Mut.

Magnetic Connections. Barbara Perry. (Illus.). 198p. (Orig.). 1985. pap. 12.50 (0-9616312-0-1, TXV-101-598) Arkbridge Assn.

Magnetic Control of Industrial Motors: D-C Motors Controllers, Pt. 3. Gerhart W. Heumann. LC 61-11593. 313p. reprint ed. 97.10 (0-8357-9925-5, 201262400082) Bks Demand.

Magnetic Cookie Gourmet. Sterling Staff. (Magnet Gourmet Ser.). (Illus.). 10p. 1997. pap. 5.95 (0-8069-9856-3) Sterling.

Magnetic Cooling. Charles G. Garrett. LC 53-10474. (Harvard Monographs in Applied Science: No. 4). 124p. reprint ed. pap. 38.50 (0-608-10271-7, 200156200079) Bks Demand.

Magnetic Core Selection for Transformers & Inductors: A User's Guide to Practice & Specification, Vol. 102. 2nd ed. William T. McLyman. LC 97-1909. (Electrical Engineering & Electronics Ser.). (Illus.). 672p. 1997. text 99.75 (0-8247-9841-4) Dekker.

Magnetic Critical Scattering. Malcolm F. Collins. (Oxford Series on Neutron Scattering in Condensed Matter). (Illus.). 200p. 1989. text 65.00 (0-19-504600-5) OUP.

Magnetic Current. Edward Leedskalnin. 26p. 1997. reprint ed. pap. 11.50 (0-7873-0549-9) Hlth Research.

***Magnetic Dichroism in Core-Level Photoemission.** Kai Starke. LC 99-47500. (Tracts in Modern Physics Ser.: Vol. 159). (Illus.). x, 136p. 2000. 84.00 (3-540-66268-5) Spr-Verlag.

Magnetic Domains: The Analysis of Magnetic Microstructures. A. Hubert & R. Schafer. LC 98-16905. (Illus.). 720p. 1998. 119.00 (3-540-64108-4) Spr-Verlag.

Magnetic Effect. 6th ed. Albert R. Davis & Walter C. Rawls, Jr. (Illus.). 128p. 1990. reprint ed. pap. 15.00 (0-911311-17-3) Acres USA.

***Magnetic, Electrical & Optical Properties, & Applications of Intermetallic Compounds, Vol. 4.** J. H. Westbrook & R. L. Fleischer. LC 99-52443. 276p. 2000. pap. 115.00 (0-471-61261-8) Wiley.

Magnetic Energy Conversion: Proceedings of Symposium 13 of the COSPAR 27th Plenary Meeting Held in Espoo, Finland, 18-29 July, 1988. Ed. by G. E. Brueckner & Boris V. Somov. (Advances in Space Research Ser.: Vol. 10). (Illus.). 208p. 1990. pap. 97.00 (0-08-040169-4, Pergamon Pr) Elsevier.

Magnetic Excitations & Fluctuations. Ed. by Stephen W. Lovesey et al. (Solid-State Sciences Ser.: Vol. 54). (Illus.). 240p. 1984. 69.95 (0-387-13789-0) Spr-Verlag.

Magnetic Field. Johannes G. Lang. LC QC0754.2.M3M. (Siemens Programmed Instruction Ser.: No. 3). 67p. reprint ed. pap. 30.00 (0-608-12362-5, 205208000033) Bks Demand.

Magnetic Field Computation with R-Functions. Amalia Ivanyi. LC 99-188297. 248p. 1999. 52.00 (963-05-7562-0, Pub. by Akade Kiado) Intl Spec Bk.

Magnetic Field of the Earth. Merrill. (C). 1998. pap. text 54.95 (0-12-491246-X) Acad Pr.

Magnetic Field of the Earth's Lithosphere: The Satellite Perspective. R. A. Langel & W. J. Hinze. LC 97-51319. (Illus.). 400p. (C). 1998. text 100.00 (0-521-47333-0) Cambridge U Pr.

Magnetic Field Therapy Handbook: Balancing Your Energy Field. R. Allen Walls. (Illus.). 107p. 1995. pap. 9.95 (0-9621790-3-5) Inner Search Found.

Magnetic Fields. WHO Staff. (Environmental Health Criteria Ser.: No. 69). 197p. 1987. 26.00 (92-4-154269-1) World Health.

***Magnetic Fields: Theory & Applications.** Heinz E. Knoepfel. LC 99-58796. 636p. 2000. 160.00 (0-471-32205-9) Wiley.

Magnetic Fields & Cancer in People Residing Near Swedish High Voltage Power Lines. Maria Feychting & Anders Ahlbom. (Illus.). 100p. (Orig.). (C). 1994. pap. text 35.00 (0-7881-0772-0) DIANE Pub.

Magnetic Fields Health & Safety Guide. WHO Staff. (Health & Safety Guides: No. 27). 24p. 1989. 5.00 (92-4-154348-5) World Health.

Magnetic Fields in Astrophysics, Vol. 3. Ya B. Zeldovich et al. xvi, 366p. 1983. text 322.00 (0-677-06380-6) Gordon & Breach.

Magnetic Fields in Galaxies. Ed. by F. Krause. 176p. 1990. pap. text 580.00 (0-677-26020-2) Gordon & Breach.

Magnetic Fields of Celestial Bodies. Shih-Hui Yeh. LC 94-29057. (Astrophysics & Space Science Library: Vol. 198). 1994. text 204.50 (0-7923-3028-5) Kluwer Academic.

Magnetic Fields of Galaxies. A. A. Ruzmailin et al. (C). 1988. text 215.00 (90-277-2450-4) Kluwer Academic.

Magnetic Fluids. Elmar S. Blums et al. LC 96-47046. xii, 416p. (C). 1996. lib. bdg. 280.00 (3-11-014390-9) De Gruyter.

Magnetic Fluids & Applications Handbook. Ed. by Boris M. Berkovski. (UNESCO Series of Learning Materials). 1996. write for info. (1-56700-053-3) Begell Hse.

Magnetic Fluids & Applications Handbook & Database. Ed. by Boris M. Berkovsky. 851p. 1996. 165.00 (1-56700-062-2) Begell Hse.

Magnetic Hamburger Gourmet. (Magnet Gourmet Ser.). (Illus.). 10p. 1998. pap. 4.95 (0-8069-1851-9) Sterling.

Magnetic Healer's Guide: or Personal Experiences in Magnetic & Suggestive Healing. J. O. Crone. 1996. reprint ed. spiral bd. 14.00 (0-7873-1035-2) Hlth Research.

Magnetic Healer's Guide: or Personal Experiences in Magnetic & Suggestive Healing (1903) J. O. Crone. 127p. 1996. reprint ed. pap. 13.50 (1-56459-766-0) Kessinger Pub.

Magnetic Healing. Burl Payne. (Illus.). 200p. (Orig.). 1997. pap. 19.95 (1-56550-051-2) Vis Bks Intl.

Magnetic Healing: Advanced Techniques for the Application of Magnetic Forces. Buryl Payne. LC 98-67862. 234p. 1998. pap. 15.95 (0-914955-42-X) Lotus Pr.

Magnetic Healing & Meditation. Larry Johnson. LC 88-51529. (Illus.). 157p. (Orig.). (C). 1989. pap. text 12.95 (0-924071-00-1) White Elephant.

***Magnetic Helicity in Space & Laboratory Plasmas.** Michael R. Brown et al. LC 99-26374. (Geophysical Monograph Ser.: Vol. 111). 11p. 1999. 69.00 (0-87590-094-1) Am Geophysical.

Magnetic Hysteresis. Edward Della Torre. LC 98-46940. 224p. 1999. 59.95 (0-7803-4719-6) IEEE Standards.

Magnetic Hysteresis in Novel Magnetic Materials: Proceedings of the NATO Advanced Study Institute on Magnetic Hysteresis Held in Mykonos, Greece, 1996. Ed. by George C. Hadjipanayis. LC 97-20241. (NATO ASI Series: Series E: Applied Sciences: Vol. 338). 905p. 1997. text 465.00 (0-7923-4604-1) Kluwer Academic.

Magnetic Ice Cream Gourmet. (Magnet Gourmet Ser.). (Illus.). 10p. 1998. pap. 4.95 (0-8069-1859-4) Sterling.

Magnetic Image Resonance in Food Science. Brian Hills. LC 97-37413. 352p. 1998. 99.95 (0-471-17087-9, Wiley-Interscience) Wiley.

***Magnetic Imaging & Its Applications to Materials.** Marc de Graef. (Experimental Methods in the Physical Sciences Ser.: Vol. 36). 300p. 2000. 155.00 (0-12-475983-1) Acad Pr.

Magnetic Information Storage Technology. Shan X. Wang & Alex Taratorin. LC 98-24797. (Illus.). 22p. (C). 1999. 79.95 (0-12-734570-1) Acad Pr.

Magnetic Ions in Crystals. K. W. Stevens. LC 96-33485. 264p. 1997. text 85.00 (0-691-02693-9, Pub. by Princeton U Pr); pap. text 29.95 (0-691-02692-0, Pub. by Princeton U Pr) Cal Prin Full Svc.

Magnetic Isotope Effect in Radical Reactions: An Introduction. Kev M. Salikhov. LC 95-45887. (Illus.). 160p. 1996. text, student ed. 75.00 (3-211-82784-6) Spr-Verlag.

Magnetic Los Angeles: Planning the Twentieth-Century Metropolis. Greg Hise. LC 96-50423. (Creating the North American Landscape Ser.). (Illus.). 256p. 1997. text 35.95 (0-8018-5543-8) Johns Hopkins.

Magnetic Los Angeles: Planning the Twentieth-Century Metropolis. Greg Hise. LC 96-50423. (Creating the North American Landscape Ser.). (Illus.). 294p. 1999. pap. 18.95 (0-8018-6255-8) Johns Hopkins.

Magnetic Magic. Paul Doherty & John Cassidy. 68p. 1994. 11.95 (1-878257-86-2) Klutz.

Magnetic Materials. D. J. Craik & Robert S. Tebble. LC 71-80119. 740p. reprint ed. pap. 200.00 (0-608-10028-5, 205124500005) Bks Demand.

Magnetic Materials - Microstructure & Properties Vol. 232: Materials Research Society Symposium Proceedings. Ed. by Y. Sugita et al. 347p. 1991. text 70.00 (1-55899-126-3) Materials Res.

Magnetic Materials, Processes & Devices: 4th International Symposium. Ed. by L. T. Romankiw & D. A. Herman, Jr. LC 95-61591. (Proceedings Ser.: Vol. 95-18). (Illus.). 802p. 1996. 92.00 (1-56677-113-7) Electrochem Soc.

***Magnetic Materials, Processes & Devices V: Applications to Storage & Microelectromechanical Systems (MEMS)** International Symposium on Magnetic Materials, Processes, and Devices et al. LC 99-62243. 706p. 1999. 93.00 (1-56677-214-1, PV 98-20) Electrochem Soc.

***Magnetic Materials, Structures & Processing for Information Storage: Materials Research Society Symposium Proceedings, Vol. 614.** Ed. by B. J. Daniels et al. 2000. text 73.00 (1-55899-522-6) Materials Res.

Magnetic Materials to Mutagenic Agents see Ullmann's Encyclopedia of Industrial Chemistry

***Magnetic Miracles: Your Guide to the Use of Magnetics for Radiant Health.** Catherine J. Norris. (Illus.). 192p. 2000. pap. 14.99 (0-9678931-0-0) Energy Essentials.

Magnetic Molecular Materials. Ed. by Dante Gatteschi et al. (C). 1991. text 219.50 (0-7923-1243-0) Kluwer Academic.

Magnetic Monopoles: Selected Reprints. Ed. by Alfred S. Goldhaber & W. Peter Trower. (Illus.). 140p. (C). 1991. per. 17.00 (0-917853-41-5, RB-57) Am Assn Physics.

Magnetic Motor Stimulation. W. J. Levy et al. (Supplements to Electroencephalography & Clinical Neurophysiology Ser.: Vol. 43). 394p. 1991. 218.00 (0-444-81351-9) Elsevier.

Magnetic Mountain: Stalinism As a Civilization. Stephen Kotkin. LC 94-11839. (Illus.). 1997. pap. 24.95 (0-520-20823-4, Pub. by U CA Pr) Cal Prin Full Svc.

Magnetic Multilayers. L. H. Bennett & R. E. Watson. 300p. 1994. text 99.00 (981-02-1767-6) World Scientific Pub.

***Magnetic Multilayers & Giant Magnetoresistance: Fundamentals & Industrial Applications.** Ed. by Ursula Hartmann. LC 99-55326. (Series in Surface Sciences: Vol. 37). (Illus.). 335p. 2000. 89.95 (3-540-65568-9) Spr-Verlag.

Magnetic Mushroom Gourmet. Sterling Staff. (Magnet Gourmet Ser.). (Illus.). 10p. 1997. pap. text 5.95 (0-8069-9860-1) Sterling.

Magnetic Music Ministry: Ten Productive Goals. Bill Owens. Ed. by Herb Miller. (Effective Church Ser.). 144p. (Orig.). 1996. pap. 12.95 (0-687-00731-3) Abingdon.

Magnetic Neutron Scattering: Proceedings of the 3rd Summer School on Neutron Scattering. A. Furrer. 250p. 1995. text 78.00 (981-02-2353-6) World Scientific Pub.

Magnetic North. Elizabeth Robins. LC 72-96893. reprint ed. lib. bdg. 22.50 (0-8398-1760-6) Irvington.

***Magnetic North: Canadian Steam in Twilight.** Karl Zimmermann & Roger Cook. 160p. 1999. 40.00 (1-55046-306-3) Bomporto.

Magnetic North Pole: White Days, White Nights. Preety Sengupta. (C). 1993. 20.00 (81-7031-325-2, Pub. by Arnold Pubs) S Asia.

Magnetic Onion Gourmet. Sterling Staff. (Magnet Gourmet Ser.). (Illus.). 10p. 1997. pap. 5.95 (0-8069-9861-X) Sterling.

Magnetic Orientation in Animals. R. Wiltschko et al. Ed. by Sydney D. Bradshaw et al. LC 95-24610. (Zoophysiology Ser.: Vol. 33). (Illus.). 336p. 1995. 163.95 (3-540-59257-1) Spr-Verlag.

An Asterisk (*) at the beginning of an entry indicates that the title is appearing for the first time.

Magnetic Oxides, 2 pts., Pt. 1. Ed. by Derek J. Craik. LC 73-14378. 504p. 1975. reprint ed. pap. 156.30 (*0-608-08263-5*, 202667300001) Bks Demand.

Magnetic Oxides, 2 pts., Pt. 2. William Drake. Ed. by Derek J. Craik. LC 73-14378. 337p. reprint ed. pap. 104.50 (*0-608-08264-3*, 202667300002) Bks Demand.

Magnetic Particle Inspection of Fixed Offshore Structures: Inspector-Diver Training. Lawrence Goldberg. (Illus.). 94p. (C). 1993. pap. 45.00 (*0-931403-12-X*, 435) Am Soc Nondestructive.

Magnetic Particle Testing Programmed Instruction Book. (Self-Study Instruction Handbook Ser.). 410p. 1977. pap. 32.25 (*0-318-17227-5*, 1503) Am Soc Nondestructive.

Magnetic Phase Transitions. Ed. by M Ausloos & R. J. Elliot. (Solid-State Sciences Ser.: Vol. 48). (Illus.). 269p. 1984. 73.95 (*0-387-12842-5*) Spr-Verlag.

Magnetic Phenomena. Ed. by A. P. Maclin et al. (Lecture Notes in Physics Ser.: Vol. 337). vi, 142p. 1989. 41.00 (*0-387-51428-7*) Spr-Verlag.

Magnetic Poetry Book of Poetry. Dave Kapell. LC 97-22179. (Illus.). 160p. 1997. 13.95 (*0-7611-0737-1*) Workman Pub.

Magnetic Pork Gourmet. Sterling Staff. (Magnet Gourmet Ser.). (Illus.). 10p. 1997. pap. 5.95 (*0-8069-9858-X*) Sterling.

Magnetic Potato Gourmet. (Magnet Gourmet Ser.). (Illus.). 10p. 1998. pap. 4.95 (*0-8069-1861-6*) Sterling.

Magnetic Properties of Coordination & Organometallic Transition Metal Compounds see Atomic & Molecular Physics: Group II

Magnetic Properties of Coordination & Organometallic Transition Metal Compounds, 1964-1968, Suppl. 1 see Atomic & Molecular Physics: Group II

Magnetic Properties of Coordination & Organometallic Transition Metal Compounds, 1971-1972 see Atomic & Molecular Physics: Group II

Magnetic Properties of Free Radicals see Atomic & Molecular Physics: Group II

Magnetic Properties of Free Radicals: Organic Anion Radicals see Atomic & Molecular Physics: Group II

Magnetic Properties of Free Radicals: Organic Cation Radicals & Polyradicals see Atomic & Molecular Physics: Group II

Magnetic Properties of Layered Transition Metal Compounds. Ed. by L. J. De Jongh. (C). 1989. text 268.50 (*0-7923-0238-9*) Kluwer Academic.

Magnetic Properties of Low-Dimensional Systems No. 2: New Developments. Ed. by L. M. Falicov et al. (Proceedings in Physics Ser.: Vol. 50). (Illus.). ix, 247p. 1990. 71.95 (*0-387-52353-7*) Spr-Verlag.

Magnetic Properties of Matter. LC 96-226129. 272p. 1996. lib. bdg. 39.00 (*981-02-2812-0*) World Scientific Pub.

Magnetic Properties of Matter. Ed. by G. Asti et al. 500p. (C). 1991. text 137.00 (*981-02-0530-9*) World Scientific Pub.

Magnetic Properties of Matter: Proceedings of the Italian National School on Condensed Matter. Ed. by F. Borsa & V. Tognetti. 556p. (C). 1988. pap. 54.00 (*9971-5-0371-9*); text 138.00 (*9971-5-0368-9*) World Scientific Pub.

Magnetic Properties of Metals. 1990. 1331.95 (*0-387-51288-8*) Spr-Verlag.

Magnetic Properties of Metals. Ed. by H. P. Wijn. 400p. 1993. 1281.95 (*0-387-55114-X*) Spr-Verlag.

Magnetic Properties of Metals: D-Elements, Alloys & Compounds. Ed. by H. P. Wijn. (Data in Science & Technology Ser.). 200p. 1991. 64.95 (*0-387-53485-7*) Spr-Verlag.

Magnetic Properties of Metals: Supplement to Volume 19: Subvolume A: 3d, 4d, 5d Elements, Alloys & Compounds. H. P. Wijn. 400p. 1997. 1707.00 (*3-540-60334-4*) Spr-Verlag.

Magnetic Properties of Metals, Subvol. I, Magnetic Alloys for Technical Applications see Crystal & Solid State Physics: Group III

Magnetic Properties of Metals, Subvol. H, Liquid-Quenched Alloys see Crystal & Solid State Physics: Group III

***Magnetic Properties of Metals: Supplement to Volume 19 Pt. B: Alloys & Compounds of d-Elements with Main Group Elements, Pt. 1.** Ed. by W. Martienssen & H. P. J. Wijn. (Landolt-Boernstein Numerical Data & Functional Relationships in Science & Technology - New Series: Vol. 32). (Illus.). xiv, 348p. 1999. 2402.00 incl. cd-rom (*3-540-62472-4*) Spr-Verlag.

Magnetic Properties of Non-Metallic Inorganic Compounds Based on Transition Elements. Ed. by H. P. Wijn et al. (Solid-State Physics Ser.: Vol. 27). 335p. 1994. 1320.95 (*0-387-57770-X*) Spr-Verlag.

Magnetic Properties of Non-Metallic Inorganic Compounds Based on Transition Elements: Part b: Pnictides & Chalcogenides II, Part 2: Lanthanide Monochalcogenides. Landolt-Bornstein. viii, 459p. 1999. 1092.00 (*3-540-63268-9*) Spr-Verlag.

Magnetic Properties of Non-Metallic Inorganic Compounds Based on Transition Elements: Pnictides & Chalcogenides II Lanthanide Monopnictides. Ed. by H. P. Wijn & W. Martienssen. (Numerical Data & Functional Relationships in Science & Technology Ser.: Group III, Vol. 27). vii, 453p. 1998. 1963.00 (*3-540-56066-1*) Spr-Verlag.

Magnetic Properties of Non-Metallic Inorganic Compounds Based on Transition Elements, Subvol. D, Oxy-Spinels see Crystal & Solid State Physics: Group III

Magnetic Properties of Non-Metallic Inorganic Compounds Based on Transition Elements, Subvol. F2, Perovskite-Type Layered Cuprates see Crystal & Solid State Physics: Group III

Magnetic Properties of Non-Metallic Inorganic Compounds Based on Transition Elements, Subvol. G, Various Other Oxides see Crystal & Solid State Physics: Group III

Magnetic Properties of Non-Metallic Inorganic Compounds Based on Transition Elements, Subvol. H, Boron Containing Oxides see Crystal & Solid State Physics: Group III

Magnetic Properties of Non-Metallic Inorganic Compounds Based on Transition Elements, Subvol. J1, Halides I see Crystal & Solid State Physics: Group III

Magnetic Properties of Non-Metallic Inorganic Compounds Based on Transition Elements, Subvol. J2, Halides see Crystal & Solid State Physics: Group III

Magnetic Properties of Non-Metallic Inorganic Compounds Based on Transition Elements, Binary Actinide Oxides, Pt. 2. Ed. by H. P. Wijn. (Numerical Data & Functional Relationships in Science & Technology Ser.: Vol. 27). (Illus.). viii, 249p. 1999. write for info. incl. cd-rom (*3-540-63272-7*) Spr-Verlag.

***Magnetic Properties of Organic Materials** Paul M. Lahti. LC 99-26161. (Illus.). 752p. 1999. text 195.00 (*0-8247-1976-X*) Dekker.

***Magnetic Reconnection: MHD Theory & Applications.** Eric Priest & Terry Forbes. LC 99-14939. (Illus.). 451p. (C). 2000. 85.00 (*0-521-48179-1*) Cambridge U Pr.

***Magnetic Reconnection in Plasmas.** Dieter Biskamp. LC 99-87680. (Cambridge Monographs on Plasma Physics: Vol. 3). (Illus.). 496p. 2000. write for info. (*0-521-58288-1*) Cambridge U Pr.

Magnetic Reconnection in the Solar Atmosphere, Vol. 111. Ed. by R. D. Bentley & J. T. Mariska. (ASP Conference Series Proceedings). 436p. 1996. 52.00 (*1-886733-31-7*) Astron Soc Pacific.

Magnetic Recording: The First 100 Years. Ed. by Eric D. Daniel et al. LC 98-8207. 360p. 1998. pap. 49.95 (*0-7803-4709-9*) Inst Electrical.

Magnetic Recording Handbook. 2nd ed. C. Denis Mee & Eric D. Daniel. LC 96-19057. (Illus.). 624p. 1996. 89.50 (*0-07-041275-8*) McGraw.

Magnetic Recording Technology. 2nd ed. C. D. Mee. LC 95-44642. 704p. 1996. 65.00 (*0-07-041276-6*) McGraw.

Magnetic Refrigeration: A Survey on Technology & Markets. Richard K. Miller & Terri C. Walker. LC 88-80922. (Survey on Technology & Markets Ser.: No. 38). 50p. 1989. pap. text 200.00 (*1-55865-037-7*) Future Tech Surveys.

Magnetic Resonance. Nicholas A. Matwiyoff. LC 89-10774. (Illus.). 134p. reprint ed. pap., wbk. ed. 41.60 (*0-608-07189-7*, 206741400009) Bks Demand.

Magnetic Resonance: Bioeffects, Safety & Patient Management. 2nd ed. Frank G. Shellock & Emanuel Kanal. LC 96-46644. 360p. 1996. pap. text 47.00 (*0-397-58437-7*) Lppncott W & W.

Magnetic Resonance: Current Trends. Ed. by C. L. Khetrapal & G. Govil. 430p. 1992. 139.95 (*0-387-54271-X*) Spr-Verlag.

Magnetic Resonance: Introduction, Advanced Topics & Applications to Fossil Energy. Ed. by Leonidas Petrakis & Jacques P. Fraissard. 1984. text 326.50 (*90-277-1752-4*) Kluwer Academic.

Magnetic Resonance: Symposium, Utrech, April 1985. Ed. by William Penn. (Journal: Diagnostic Imaging in Clinical Medicine: Vol. 55, No. 1-2, 1986). (Illus.). 108p. (Orig.). 1986. pap. 76.75 (*3-8055-4259-3*) S Karger.

Magnetic Resonance Angiography. Ed. by Ingolf P. Arlart et al. LC 95-31126. (Medical Radiology Ser.). 1995. (*3-540-56896-4*) Spr-Verlag.

Magnetic Resonance Angiography. Ed. by Ingolf P. Arlart et al. (Medical Radiology, Diagnostic Imaging & Radiation Oncology Ser.). (Illus.). 440p. 1995. 239.00 (*0-387-56896-4*) Spr-Verlag.

Magnetic Resonance Angiography: A Practical Approach. Ed. by B. Kent Yucel. (Illus.). 225p. 1994. text 79.00 (*0-07-072695-7*) McGraw-Hill HPD.

Magnetic Resonance Annual, 1988. fac. ed. Magnetic Resonance Annual Staff. Ed. by Herbert Y. Kressel. LC 85-646023. (Illus.). 357p. pap. 110.70 (*0-7837-7223-8*, 204707500005) Bks Demand.

Magnetic Resonance Annual, 1986. Ed. by Herbert Y. Kressel. LC 85-646023. 267p. 1986. reprint ed. pap. 82.80 (*0-608-00394-8*, 206110800007) Bks Demand.

Magnetic Resonance Annual, 1987. Ed. by Herbert Y. Kressel. LC 85-646023. (Illus.). 349p. 1987. reprint ed. pap. 108.20 (*0-608-00671-8*, 206125800007) Bks Demand.

Magnetic Resonance Annual, 1985. Magnetic Resonance Annual Staff. LC 85-646023. 334p. 1985. reprint ed. pap. 103.60 (*0-608-00365-4*, 206108200007) Bks Demand.

Magnetic Resonance at High Pressure. G. B. Benedek. LC 63-18561. (Interscience Tracts on Physics & Astronomy Ser.: Vol. 24). 109p. reprint ed. pap. 33.80 (*0-608-10048-X*, 205513000008) Bks Demand.

***Magnetic Resonance Cholangiopancreatography: Early Diagnosis of Pancreatobiliary Diseases.** J. Sai & J. Ariyama. (Illus.). 145p. 2000. 85.00 (*4-431-70273-3*) Spr-Verlag.

Magnetic Resonance Image Techniques. Ajay M. Parikh. (Illus.). 349p. (C). 1991. pap. text 65.00 (*0-8385-6084-9*, A6084-6, Apple Lange Med) McGraw.

***Magnetic Resonance Imaging.** V. Kuperman. 200p. (C). 1999. text 95.00 (*0-12-429150-3*) Acad Pr.

Magnetic Resonance Imaging. R. Sigal. (Illus.). 115p. 1988. 59.95 (*0-387-18424-4*) Spr-Verlag.

Magnetic Resonance Imaging. 3rd ed. David D. Stark & Walter G. Bradley. LC 98-36686. (Illus.). 2800p. (C). (gr. 13). 1998. text 399.00 (*0-8151-8518-9*, 28607) Mosby Inc.

Magnetic Resonance Imaging: Atlas of the Head, Neck & Spine. Catherine M. Mills et al. LC 87-29344. 305p. reprint ed. pap. 94.60 (*0-7837-2728-3*, 204310800006) Bks Demand.

Magnetic Resonance Imaging: Basic Principles. Stuart W. Young. LC 86-42889. 298p. 1988. reprint ed. pap. 92.40 (*0-608-03462-2*, 206416300008) Bks Demand.

Magnetic Resonance Imaging: Clinical Principles. Ed. by Val M. Runge. LC 91-35577. (Illus.). 439p. 1992. reprint ed. pap. 136.10 (*0-608-05878-5*, 205984400007) Bks Demand.

Magnetic Resonance Imaging: Mathematical Foundations, & Applications. Walter Schempp. LC 97-48760. 288p. 1998. 99.95 (*0-471-16736-3*) Wiley.

Magnetic Resonance Imaging: Physical & Biological Principles. 2nd ed. Stewart C. Bushong. LC 95-3071. (Illus.). 512p. (C). (gr. 13). 1995. text 56.00 (*0-8151-1342-0*, 24166) Mosby Inc.

Magnetic Resonance Imaging: Physical Principles & Sequence Design. E. Mark Haacke et al. LC 99-22880. 914p. 1999. 144.95 (*0-471-35128-8*) Wiley.

***Magnetic Resonance Imaging: Principles, Methods & Techniques.** Perry Sprawls. LC 00-34862. 2000. write for info. (*0-944838-97-9*) Med Physics Pub.

Magnetic Resonance Imaging: Theory & Practice. Marinus T. Vlaardingerbroek & Jacques A. Den Boer. LC 95-39241. (Illus.). 383p. 1996. text 98.50 (*3-540-60080-9*) Spr-Verlag.

***Magnetic Resonance Imaging: Theory & Practice.** 2nd ed. Marinus T. Vlaardingerbroek & J. A. de Boer. LC 99-36438. xxiii, 481p. 1999. 109.00 (*3-540-64877-1*) Spr-Verlag.

Magnetic Resonance Imaging & Computed Tomography: Clinical Neuro-Orbital Anatomy. Jonathan D. Wirtschafter et al. LC 92-49178. 1992. write for info. (*1-56055-010-4*) Am Acad Ophthal.

Magnetic Resonance Imaging & Computed Tomography of the Head & Spine. 2nd ed. C. Barrie Grossman. (Illus.). 488p. 1989. 125.00 (*0-683-03768-4*) Lppncott W & W.

Magnetic Resonance Imaging & Computed Tomography of the Head & Spine. 2nd ed. C. Barrie Grossman. (Illus.). 828p. 1996. 139.00 (*0-683-03769-2*) Lppncott W & W.

Magnetic Resonance Imaging & Spectroscopy. fac. ed. Fred A. Mettler et al. LC 86-13620. (Illus.). 331p. 1986. reprint ed. pap. 102.70 (*0-7837-7823-6*, 204757900008) Bks Demand.

Magnetic Resonance Imaging & Spectroscopy in Sports Medicine. Ed. by M. Osteaux & K. Meirleir. (Illus.). 216p. 1991. 123.00 (*0-387-52548-3*) Spr-Verlag.

Magnetic Resonance Imaging & the Kidney: Metabolic Studies/Clinical Research. Z. H. Endre. Date not set. write for info. (*0-8247-9488-5*) Dekker.

Magnetic Resonance Imaging Atlas of the Extremities. Kang & Donald Resnick. 400p. 1990. text 205.00 (*0-7216-3071-5*, W B Saunders Co) Harcrt Hlth Sci Grp.

Magnetic Resonance Imaging for Food Research & Technology. Michael J. McCarthy. LC 92-34008. 1992. text 69.95 (*0-442-01021-4*) Chapman & Hall.

Magnetic Resonance Imaging in Coronary Artery Disease. Ed. by Ernst E. Van Der Wall & Albert De Roos. (C). 1991. text 233.50 (*0-7923-0940-5*) Kluwer Academic.

Magnetic Resonance Imaging in Multiple Sclerosis. Kesselrin. 72.00 (*0-86577-334-3*) Thieme Med Pubs.

Magnetic Resonance Imaging in Orthopaedics & Rheumatology. David W. Stoller et al. (Illus.). 404p. 1988. text 125.00 (*0-397-50958-8*) Lppncott W & W.

Magnetic Resonance Imaging in Orthopaedics & Sports Medicine. 2nd ed. David W. Stoller. 1408p. 1996. text 411.00 (*0-397-58475-X*) Lppncott W & W.

Magnetic Resonance Imaging in Orthopaedics & Sports Medicine. 2nd ed. David W. Stoller et al. 1300p. 1996. text 261.00 (*0-397-51542-1*) Lppncott W & W.

Magnetic Resonance Imaging of Bone & Soft Tissue Tumors & Their Mimics. A. M. De Schepper. (Series in Radiology - A Clinical Atlas). (C). 1989. text 160.00 (*0-7923-0343-1*) Kluwer Academic.

Magnetic Resonance Imaging of Carcinoma of the Urinary Bladder. Jelle O. Barentsz. (Series in Radiology). (C). 1990. text 206.50 (*0-7923-0838-7*) Kluwer Academic.

Magnetic Resonance Imaging of Central Nervous System Diseases. W. J. Huk et al. (Illus.). 530p. 1991. 415.00 (*0-387-17641-1*) Spr-Verlag.

Magnetic Resonance Imaging of CNS Disease: A Teaching File. Douglas H. Yock. LC 95-154083. (Illus.). 752p. (C). (gr. 13). 1994. text 143.00 (*0-8016-8098-0*, 08098) Mosby Inc.

Magnetic Resonance Imaging of Orthopedic Trauma. Stephen J. Eustace et al. LC 98-27271. 267p. 1999. 115.00 (*0-412-15211-8*) Chapman & Hall.

Magnetic Resonance Imaging of the Body. Jeffrey C. Weinreb & Helen C. Redman. (Advanced Exercises in Diagnostic Radiology Ser.). (Illus.). 272p. 1987. pap. text 45.00 (*0-7216-2059-0*, W B Saunders Co) Harcrt Hlth Sci Grp.

Magnetic Resonance Imaging of the Body. 3rd ed. Charles B. Higgins et al. LC 96-36164. 1616p. 1996. text 261.00 (*0-397-51711-4*) Lppncott W & W.

Magnetic Resonance Imaging of the Brain & Spine. 2nd ed. Ed. by Scott W. Atlas. LC 95-6253. (Illus.). 1675p. 1995. text 270.00 (*0-7817-0282-8*) Lppncott W & W.

Magnetic Resonance Imaging of the Central Nervous System. Ed. by Michael Brant-Zawadzki & David Norman. LC 86-15476. (Illus.). 416p. 1987. reprint ed. pap. 129.00 (*0-608-05840-8*, 205980600007) Bks Demand.

Magnetic Resonance Imaging of the Elbow. Ed. by Russell C. Fritz. (Illus.). 150p. 1999. text 95.00 (*0-7817-0286-0*) Lppncott W & W.

Magnetic Resonance Imaging of the Knee. Jerrold H. Mink et al. LC 86-43229. (Illus.). 192p. reprint ed. pap. 59.60 (*0-7837-7122-3*, 204695100004) Bks Demand.

Magnetic Resonance Imaging of the Pediatric Brain: An Anatomical Atlas. G. Salamon et al. 368p. 1990. text 116.50 (*0-88167-612-8*) Lppncott W & W.

Magnetic Resonance Imaging of the Pediatric Brain: An Anatomical Atlas. G. Salamon et al. LC 90-8325. (Illus.). 364p. reprint ed. pap. 112.90 (*0-608-09745-4*, 206991400007) Bks Demand.

Magnetic Resonance Imaging of the Spine. Val M. Runge et al. (Illus.). 550p. 1994. text 150.00 (*0-397-51290-2*) Lppncott W & W.

Magnetic Resonance Imaging of the Thorax. Miriam Sperber & Marc C. Kaiser. (Illus.). 264p. (C). 1987. 65.00 (*0-87527-375-0*) Green.

Magnetic Resonance Imaging Physics: Physical Principles & Sequence Design. E. Mark Haacke & Robert W. Brown. LC 98-26974. (Illus.). 928p. 1998. 98.00 (*0-387-94694-2*) Spr-Verlag.

Magnetic Resonance Imaging Technologist (MRI) Rudman. (Admission Test Ser.: ATS-115). pap. 49.95 (*0-8373-5815-9*) Nat Learn.

Magnetic Resonance in Chemistry & Biology: Based on Lectures at the Ampere International Summer School on Magnetic Resonance in Chemistry & Biology, Basko Polje, Yugoslavia, June 1971. Ed. by Janko N. Herak & Kresimir J. Adamic. LC 73-90726. (Illus.). 569p. reprint ed. pap. 176.40 (*0-7837-0873-4*, 204118100019) Bks Demand.

Magnetic Resonance in Colloid & Interface Science. Ed. by Jacques P. Fraissard & Henry A. Resing. (NATO Advanced Study Institutes Series C, Mathematical & Physical Sciences: No. 61). 710p. 1980. text 226.00 (*90-277-1153-4*) Kluwer Academic.

Magnetic Resonance in Epilepsy. Ruben I. Kuzniecky & Graeme D. Jackson. LC 94-25557. (Illus.). 345p. 1994. text 120.00 (*0-7817-0227-5*) Lppncott W & W.

Magnetic Resonance in Experimental & Clinical Oncology. Ed. by Jeffrey L. Evelhoch et al. (Developments in Oncology Ser.). (C). 1990. text 157.00 (*0-7923-0935-9*) Kluwer Academic.

Magnetic Resonance in Food Science. Ed. by P. S. Belton. 292p. 1995. 129.00 (*0-85404-725-5*) CRC Pr.

Magnetic Resonance in Medicine. 3rd ed. Peter A. Rinck. 256p. 1993. 95.00 (*0-632-03781-4*) Blackwell Sci.

Magnetic Resonance in Medicine & Biology. M. A. Hopf & F. W. Smith. (Progress in Nuclear Medicine Ser.: Vol. 8). (Illus.). viii, 180p. 1984. 142.75 (*3-8055-3868-5*) S Karger.

Magnetic Resonance in Multiple Sclerosis. David H. Miller et al. LC 96-21044. (Illus.). 210p. (C). 1997. text 90.00 (*0-521-47325-X*) Cambridge U Pr.

Magnetic Resonance in Nephrourology: Clinical & Experimental Applications. Ed. by S. Pomer & W. E. Hull. LC 93-9946. 1993. 132.00 (*0-387-56450-0*) Spr-Verlag.

Magnetic Resonance Neuroimaging. Walter Kucharczyk. 496p. 1993. lib. bdg. 135.00 (*0-8493-4719-X*, RC349) CRC Pr.

Magnetic Resonance Neuroimaging. 2nd ed. John Kucharczyk & Michael Moseley. 1998. 130.00 (*0-8493-7607-6*) CRC Pr.

Magnetic Resonance (NMR) Imaging, 2 vols., 1. 2nd ed. C. Leon Partain et al. (Illus.). 1988. text 250.00 (*0-7216-2516-9*, W B Saunders Co) Harcrt Hlth Sci Grp.

Magnetic Resonance (NMR) Imaging, 2 vols., 2. 2nd ed. C. Leon Partain et al. (Illus.). 1988. text 315.00 (*0-7216-2517-7*, W B Saunders Co) Harcrt Hlth Sci Grp.

Magnetic Resonance (NMR) Imaging, 2 vols., Set. 2nd ed. C. Leon Partain et al. (Illus.). 1988. text 555.00 (*0-7216-1340-3*, W B Saunders Co) Harcrt Hlth Sci Grp.

Magnetic Resonance of Biomolecules: An Introduction to the Theory & Practice of NMR & ESR in Biological Systems. P. F. Knowles et al. LC 75-4872. 357p. reprint ed. pap. 110.70 (*0-8357-8941-1*, 203361800086) Bks Demand.

Magnetic Resonance of Carbonaceous Solids: Developed by a Symposium Sponsored by the 1989 International Chemical Congress of Pacific Basin Societies, Honolulu, Hawaii, December 17-22, 1989. Ed. by Robert E. Botto & Yuzo Sanada. LC 92-36495. (Advances in Chemistry Ser.: No. 229). (Illus.). 678p. 1993. 165.00 (*0-8412-1866-8*, Pub. by Am Chemical) OUP.

Magnetic Resonance of Carbonaceous Solids: Developed from a Symposium Sponsored by the International Chemical Congress of the Pacific Basin Societies. Ed. by Robert E. Botto & Yuzo Sanada. LC 92-36495. (Advances in Chemistry Ser.: No. 229). (Illus.). 680p. 1993. reprint ed. pap. 200.00 (*0-608-06801-2*, 206699800009) Bks Demand.

Magnetic Resonance of Myelin, Myelination, & Myelin Disorders, Vol. XII. 2nd rev. ed. M. S. Van der Knaap & J. Valk. (Illus.). 569p. 1996. 298.00 (*3-540-59277-6*) Spr-Verlag.

Magnetic Resonance of the Brain, Head & Neck. Val M. Runge. LC 93-24586. (Illus.). 608p. 1993. text 189.00 (*0-397-51244-9*) Lppncott W & W.

Magnetic Resonance of the Heart & Great Vessels: Clinical Applications. Ed. by J. Bogaert et al. LC 98-24570. (Medical Radiology Ser.). (Illus.). 433p. 1999. 189.00 (*3-540-63448-7*) Spr-Verlag.

***Magnetic Resonance of the Heart & Great Vessels: Clinical Applications.** Ed. by J. Bogaert et al. (Medical Radiology Ser.). (Illus.). xii, 286p. 2000. 75.00 (*3-540-67217-6*) Spr-Verlag.

Magnetic Resonance of the Reproductive System. Shirley McCarthy & Florence P. Haseltine. 180p. 1986. 68.95 (*0-316-55374-3*, Little Brwn Med Div) Lppncott W & W.

M

Magnetic Resonance of the Temporomandibular Joint. E. Palacios et al. (Illus.). 135p. 1990. text 85.00 (*0-86577-363-7*) Thieme Med Pubs.

Magnetic Resonance Scanning & Epilepsy. Ed. by Frederick Andermann et al. (NATO ASI Ser.: Vol. 264). (Illus.). 334p. (C). 1994. text 105.00 (*0-306-44735-5*, Kluwer Plenum) Kluwer Academic.

Magnetic Resonance Spectroscopy & Imaging in Neurochemistry. Ed. by Herman Bachelard. LC 97-15443. (Advances in Neurochemistry Ser.: Vol. 8). (Illus.). 436p. (C). 1997. text 115.00 (*0-306-45520-X*, Kluwer Plenum) Kluwer Academic.

*__Magnetic Resonance Spectroscopy Diagnosis of Neurological Diseases.__ Else Rubaek&Danielsen Staff. LC 98-44756. (Illus.). 344p. 1999. text 165.00 (*0-8247-0238-7*) Dekker.

Magnetic Resonance Spectroscopy of Biofluids: A New Tool in Clinical Biology. J. D. De Certaines. 292p. 1989. text 104.00 (*981-02-0062-5*) World Scientific Pub.

Magnetic Resonance Techniques in Clinical Trials in Multiple Sclerosis. M. Filippi et al. LC 98-51407. (Topics in Neuroscience Ser.). x, 192p. 1999. 119.00 (*88-470-0041-6*, Pub. by Spr-Verlag) Spr-Verlag.

Magnetic Resonance Test & Syllabus, Vol. 31. William G. Bradley, Jr. et al. (Professional Self-Evaluation & Continuing Education Program Ser.). (Illus.). 800p. 1991. 190.00 (*1-55903-031-3*) Am Coll Radiology.

Magnetic Sensors. Richard Boll & K. J. Overshott. LC 89-25053. (Sensors Ser.). xii, 513p. 1989. pap. write for info. (*0-89573-677-2*, Wiley-VCH) Wiley.

Magnetic Soup Gourmet. (Magnet Gourmet Ser.). (Illus.). 10p. 1998. pap. 4.95 (*0-8069-1855-1*) Sterling.

Magnetic Stimulation in Clinical Neurophysiology. Sudhansu Chokroverty. 308p. 1989. text 75.00 (*0-409-90151-2*) Buttrwrth-Heinemann.

*__Magnetic Stimulation of the Human Nervous System.__ K. R. Mills. LC 99-20411. (Illus.). 336p. 2000. text 59.50 (*0-19-262986-7*) OUP.

Magnetic Storms. Ed. by Bruce T. Tsurutani et al. LC 97-11445. (Geophysical Monographs: Vol. 98). 1997. 70.00 (*0-87590-080-1*) Am Geophysical.

Magnetic Superconductors: Recent Developments. K. P. Sinha & S. L. Kakani. (Illus.). 219p. (C). 1989. text 175.00 (*0-941743-62-4*) Nova Sci Pubs.

Magnetic Susceptibility of Superconductors & Other Spin Systems. R. A. Hein et al. (Illus.). 636p. (C). 1992. text 149.50 (*0-306-44197-7*, Kluwer Plenum) Kluwer Academic.

Magnetic Systems with Competing Interactions. H. T. Diep. 350p. 1994. text 99.00 (*981-02-1715-3*) World Scientific Pub.

Magnetic Tape Librarian. Jack Rudman. (Career Examination Ser.: C-2872). 1994. pap. 27.95 (*0-8373-2872-1*) Nat Learn.

Magnetic Tape Recording for the Eighties. 1986. lib. bdg. 250.00 (*0-8490-3772-7*) Gordon Pr.

Magnetic Tape Storage & Handling: A Guide for Libraries & Archives. John W. Van Bogart. 34p. 1995. pap. 10.00 (*1-887334-40-8*) Coun Lib & Info.

Magnetic Teaching: Making God's Word Stick in the Lives of Your Teens. Rick Bundschuh. Ed. by Leslie Durden & Dale Reeves. LC 98-5818. (Empowered Youth Products Ser.). (Illus.). 112p. 1998. pap. 9.99 (*0-7847-0824-X*, 26-23330) Standard Pub.

Magnetic Therapy. Abbot G. Burke. LC 80-22941. 92p. 1987. reprint ed. pap. 8.95 (*0-87516-588-5*) DeVorss.

Magnetic Therapy in Eastern Europe: A Review of 30 Years of Research. Jiri Jerabek & William Pawluk. (Illus.). 161p. 1998. pap. 34.95 (*0-9664227-0-8*) W Pawluk.

*__Magnetic Travel Fun.__ Jess Brallier. (Illus.). 48p. (J). 2000. 14.99 (*0-448-44086-5*, Plat & Munk) Peng Put Young Read.

Magnetic Ultra Thin Films, Multilayers & Surfaces: Proceedings of Symposium E of the 1996 E-MRS Spring Conference, Strasbourg, France, June 4-7, 1996. F. Petroff & M. A. Gijs. LC 98-149214. 550p. 1997. 327.00 (*0-444-20503-9*) Elsevier.

Magnetic Ultrathin Films - Multilayers & Surfaces, 1997: Materials Research Society Symposium Proceedings, Vol. 475. Ed. by D. D. Chambliss et al. LC 97-39818. 630p. 1997. text 75.00 (*1-55899-379-7*) Materials Res.

Magnetic Ultrathin Films, Multilayers & Surfaces. Ed. by A. Fert et al. (Symposium Proceedings Ser.: Vol. 384). 553p. 1995. text 83.00 (*1-55899-287-1*) Materials Res.

*__Magnetic Venture: The Story of Oxford Instruments.__ Audrey Wood. (Illus.). 320p. 2000. text 45.00 (*0-19-924108-2*) OUP.

Magnetics Engineering Fundamentals & Computer-Aided Design Solutions. Fred M. Lilienstein. LC 92-26751. 1993. text 115.95 (*0-442-00738-8*, VNR) Wiley.

Magneticstratigraphy. N. D. Opdyke & J. G. Channell. LC 96-5925. (International Geophysics Ser.: Vol. 64). (Illus.). 349p. 1996. text 99.00 (*0-12-527470-X*) Acad Pr.

Magnetism. Jason Cooper. LC 92-8807. (Science Secrets Ser.). (J). 1992. 8.95 (*0-685-59294-4*) Rourke Corp.

Magnetism. Ron Marson. (Task Cards Ser.: No. 19). (Illus.). 88p. 1991. teacher ed. 16.00 (*0-941008-90-8*) Tops Learning.

*__Magnetism.__ Ron Marson. (Science with Simple Things Ser.: No. 33). (Illus.). 64p. 2000. teacher ed. 15.00 (*0-941008-54-1*) Tops Learning.

Magnetism. Peter Riley. (Straightforward Science Ser.). 1999. pap. text 6.95 (*0-531-15372-X*) Watts.

Magnetism. Peter D. Riley. LC 98-18300. (Straightforward Science Ser.). (J). 1999. 19.00 (*0-531-14506-9*) Watts.

Magnetism. Daniel J. Spero. (Science Mini-Unit Intermediate Ser.: Vol. 1). (Illus.). 16p. (J). (gr. 3-6). 1994. pap. text 5.95 (*1-55799-292-4*, EMC832) Evan-Moor Edu Pubs.

Magnetism. John Woodruff. LC 97-24645. (Science Projects Ser.). (Illus.). 1998. 24.26 (*0-8172-4946-X*) Raintree Steck-V.

Magnetism. Ed. by Alan D. Boardman. LC 80-40124. (Physics Programs Ser.: Vol. 2). (Illus.). 104p. reprint ed. pap. 32.30 (*0-608-17605-2*, 203045500069) Bks Demand.

Magnetism see Encyclopedia of Physics

Magnetism: An Introductory Survey. E. W. Lee. (Illus.). 281p. 1984. reprint ed. pap. 8.95 (*0-486-24689-2*) Dover.

Magnetism: Principles & Applications. Derek J. Craik. LC 93-38155. (Illus.). 467p. 1995. reprint ed. pap. 144.80 (*0-608-03998-5*, 206473500011) Bks Demand.

Magnetism: Principles & Applications. 3rd ed. Derek Craik. LC 93-38155. 468p. 1995. pap. 74.95 (*0-471-95417-9*) Wiley.

Magnetism - A Supramolecular Function: Proceedings of the NATO Advanced Research Workshop, Carcans-Maubuisson, France, September 16-20, 1995. Ed. by Olivier Kahn. LC 96-28676. (NATO Advanced Science Institutes Series C). 672p. (C). 1996. text 327.50 (*0-7923-4153-8*) Kluwer Academic.

Magnetism & Electricity. (Jump Ser.). (Illus.). 32p. (J). (gr. 2-7). pap. write for info. (*1-882210-27-1*) Action Pub.

Magnetism & Electricity. Mel Feigen. (Hands-On Minds-On Science Ser.). (Illus.). 96p. 1994. pap., teacher ed. 11.95 (*1-55734-646-1*) Tchr Create Mat.

Magnetism & Electricity. Mel Feigen. (Hands-On Minds-On Science Ser.). (Illus.). 96p. 1994. pap., teacher ed. 11.95 (*1-55734-643-7*) Tchr Create Mat.

Magnetism & Electricity. Daniel J. Spero. Ed. by Marilyn Evans & Jill Norris. (Science Ser.). (Illus.). 33p. (J). (gr. 4-6). Date not set. pap., wbk. ed. 3.50 (*1-58610-125-0*) Learn Horizon.

Magnetism & Electricity: A Unified Text. D. J. Craik. LC 98-27221. 324p. 1999. 185.00 (*0-471-98639-9*) Wiley.

Magnetism & Electromagnetism, Vol. 20. Lab-Volt Systems, Inc. Staff. (F.A.C.E.T. Ser.). (Illus.). 86p. (Orig.). (C). 1993. pap. text. write for info. (*0-86657-064-0*, TM90879-00) Lab-Volt.

Magnetism & Electromagnetism, Vol. 20. Lab-Volt Systems, Inc. Staff. (F.A.C.E.T. Ser.). (Illus.). 20p. (Orig.). (C). 1993. pap. text, teacher ed. write for info. (*0-86657-093-4*, TM90879-10) Lab-Volt.

Magnetism & Electronic Correlations in Local-Moment Systems: Rare-Earth Elements & Compounds: Proceedings of the Workshop Berlin, Germany. Ed. by M. Donath et al. 400p. 1998. 84.00 (*981-02-3538-0*) World Scientific Pub.

Magnetism & Its Effects on the Living System. 9th ed. Albert R. Davis & Walter C. Rawls, Jr. LC 74-84423. (Illus.). 132p. 1988. reprint ed. pap. 15.00 (*0-911311-14-9*) Acres USA.

Magnetism & Magnetic Materials. 2nd ed. J. P. Jakubovics. 175p. 1994. pap. 50.00 (*0-901716-54-5*) Ashgate Pub Co.

Magnetism & Magnetic Materials: Chicago, 1971, 2 pts. American Institute of Physics. Ed. by C. D. Graham, Jr. & J. J. Rhyne. LC 59-2468. (AIP Conference Proceedings Ser.: No. 5). 1573p. 1972. 22.00 (*0-88318-104-5*) Am Inst Physics.

Magnetism & Magnetic Materials: Denver, Co., 1972, 2 pts. American Institute of Physics. Ed. by C. D. Graham, Jr. & J. J. Rhyne. LC 72-623469. (AIP Conference Proceedings Ser.: No. 10). 1714p. 1973. 24.00 (*0-88318-109-6*) Am Inst Physics.

Magnetism & Magnetic Materials: Proceedings of the Annual Conference on Magnetic Materials, 22nd, Pittsburgh, June 15-18, 1976. Annual Conference on Magnetic Materials. LC 76-47106. (AIP Conference Proceedings Ser.: No. 34). 1976. 19.50 (*0-88318-133-9*) Am Inst Physics.

Magnetism & Magnetic Materials: Proceedings of the 7th Conference. Conference on Magnetism & Magnetic Materials Staff. Ed. by J. A. Osborn. LC 72-623469. 383p. reprint ed. pap. 118.80 (*0-608-30791-2*, 201938900011) Bks Demand.

Magnetism & Magnetic Materials: Proceedings, 1973, 2 pts. American Institute of Physics. Ed. by C. D. Graham, Jr. & J. J. Rhyne. LC 52-2468. (AIP Conference Proceedings Ser.: No. 18). 1974. 25.00 (*0-88318-117-7*) Am Inst Physics.

Magnetism & Magnetic Materials: Proceedings, 1974. Conference on Magnetism & Magnetic Materials 20th,. Ed. by C. D. Graham, Jr. et al. LC 75-2647. (AIP Conference Proceedings Ser.: No. 24). 792p. 1975. 30.00 (*0-88318-123-1*) Am Inst Physics.

Magnetism & Magnetic Materials: Proceedings, 1975. Ed. by J. J . Becker et al. LC 76-10931. (AIP Conference Proceedings Ser.: No. 29). 693p. 1976. 30.00 (*0-88318-128-2*) Am Inst Physics.

Magnetism & Magnetic Resonance in Solids. Alberto P. Guimaraes. LC 97-35865. 297p. 1998. 74.95 (*0-471-19774-2*, Wiley-Interscience) Wiley.

*__Magnetism & Magnets.__ Jon Richards. LC 99-31624. (Science Factory Ser.). (Illus.). 32p. (J). (gr. 1-4). 1999. 21.90 (*0-7613-3257-X*, Copper Beech Bks) Millbrook Pr.

Magnetism & Metallurgy of Soft Magnetic Materials. Chih-Wen Chen. (Illus.). 592p. 1986. reprint ed. pap. 16.95 (*0-486-64997-0*) Dover.

Magnetism & Structure in Systems of Reduced Dimension. R. F. Farrow et al. (NATO ASI Ser.: Vol. 309). (Illus.). 522p. (C). 1993. text 145.00 (*0-306-44529-8*, Kluwer Plenum) Kluwer Academic.

*__Magnetism & Superconductivity.__ Laurent-Patrick Levy. LC 99-56699. (Texts & Monographs in Physics). (Illus.). xi, 461p. (C). 2000. 58.95 (*3-540-66688-5*) Spr-Verlag.

*__Magnetism Beyond 2000.__ Ed. by A. J. Freeman & S. D. Bader. 820p. 1999. 213.00 (*0-444-50337-4*, North Holland) Elsevier.

Magnetism in Disorder. Trevor J. Hicks. (Oxford Series on Neutron Scattering in Condensed Matter: Vol. 11). (Illus.). 162p. 1995. text 85.00 (*0-19-851016-0*) OUP.

Magnetism in Medicine. Wilfried Andra. 512p. 1998. 205.00 (*3-527-40221-7*, Wiley-VCH) Wiley.

Magnetism in Solids: Some Current Topics. A. P. Cracknell & R. A. Vaughan. (Scottish Universities Summer School in Physics, a NATO Advanced Study Institute Ser.: No. 22). (Illus.). 490p. 1981. 189.00 (*0-905945-05-0*) IOP Pub.

*__Magnetism, Magnetic Materials & Their Applications: Proceedings: Latin American Workshop on Magnetism, Magnetic Materials & Their Applications (4th: 1998: Sao Paulo, Brazil)__ 499p. 1999. 174.00 (*0-87849-827-3*, Pub. by Trans T Pub) Enfield Pubs NH.

Magnetism, Magnetic Materials & Their Applications: Proceedings of the International Workshop, La Habana, Cuba, 21-29 May 1991. J. L. Sanchez-Llamazares. (Illus.). 356p. 1992. 161.00 (*0-7503-0189-9*) IOP Pub.

Magnetism, Magnetic Materials & Their Applications III: Proceedings of the III Latin American Workshop. LC 97-129750. 382p. 1996. lib. bdg. 61.00 (*981-02-2733-7*) World Scientific Pub.

Magnetism of Amorphous Metals & Alloys. J. A. Fernandez Baca & W. Y. Ching. 400p. 1995. text 109.00 (*981-02-1033-7*) World Scientific Pub.

Magnetism, Planetary Rotation, & Convention in the Solar System: Retrospect & Prospect, Vol. 7. Ed. by W. O'Reilly. (Geophysical Surveys Ser.: Nos. 1, 2 & 3). 1985. text 171.50 (*90-277-2050-9*) Kluwer Academic.

Magnetismo de Jose Marti. Fidel Aguirre. LC 84-82243. (Coleccion Cuba y sus Jueces). (SPA., Illus.). 207p. (Orig.). 1985. pap. 9.95 (*0-89729-361-4*) Ediciones.

Magnetite Biomineralization & Magnetoreception in Organisms: A New Biomagnetism. J. L. Kirschvink et al. LC 85-17037. (Topics in Geobiology Ser.: Vol. 5). (Illus.). 704p. (C). 1985. 159.50 (*0-306-41993-9*, Plenum Trade) Perseus Pubng.

Magnetite Dense Medium, Its Rheology Effect on Separation Efficiency. J. Laskowski. 109p. 1990. text 384.00 (*2-88124-473-4*) Gordon & Breach.

Magnetization, Oscillations & Waves. A. G. Gurevich & G. A. Melkov. LC 96-34577. (Illus.). 464p. 1996. boxed set 159.95 (*0-8493-9460-0*) CRC Pr.

Magneto & Iono Plas: ASR Vo514 Proceedings of Symposium Nine & the COSPAR Interdisciplinary Scientific Commission D of the COSPAR Twenty-fifth Plenary Meeting Held in Graz, Austria, 25 June-7 July 1984. Ed. by E. R. Schmerling et al. LC 83-645550. (Illus.). 434p. 1985. pap. 54.00 (*0-08-033193-9*, Pub. by PPL) Elsevier.

Magneto-Fluid & Plasma Dynamics. Symposium in Applied Mathematics Staff. LC 66-20436. (Proceedings of Symposia in Applied Mathematics Ser.: No. 18). 301p. 1967. pap. 93.40 (*0-608-05174-8*, 205259500001) Bks Demand.

Magneto-Fluid & Plasma Dynamics: Proceedings. Applied Mathematics Symposium Staff. Ed. by H. Grad. LC 66-20436. (Proceedings of Symposia in Applied Mathematics Ser.: Vol. 18). 293p. 1967. pap. 34.00 (*0-8218-1318-8*, PSAPM/18) Am Math.

Magneto Hydrodynamics in Binary Stars. 1997. lib. bdg. 250.00 (*0-7923-3023-4*) Kluwer Academic.

Magneto-Ionic Theory & Its Applications to the Ionosphere: A Monograph. John A. Ratcliffe. LC 59-896. 216p. reprint ed. pap. 61.60 (*0-608-11666-1*, 2050747) Bks Demand.

*__Magneto-Optical Recording Materials.__ Richard J. Gambino. Ed. by Takao Suzuki. LC 99-27335. 464p. 1999. 99.95 (*0-7803-1009-8*) Inst Electrical.

*__Magneto-Optics.__ Ed. by Satoru Sugano & N. Kojima. LC 99-50348. (Series in Solid-State Sciences: Vol. 128). (Illus.). ix, 334p. 2000. 82.00 (*3-540-65961-7*) Spr-Verlag.

Magneto-Optics under Conditions of the Integer & Factional Quantum Hall Effects in Si Mosfet, Vol. 11. I. V. Kukushkin & V. B. Timofeev. (Soviet Scientific Reviews Ser.: Vol. 11, Pt. 1). ii, 106p. 1989. pap. text 117.00 (*3-7186-4902-0*) Gordon & Breach.

Magneto-Resistive Heads: Fundamentals & Applications. John C. Mallinson. (Electromagnetism Ser.). (Illus.). 133p. 1995. text 49.95 (*0-12-466630-2*) Acad Pr.

Magneto-Solid Mechanics. Francis C. Moon. LC 83-23372. (Wiley-Interscience Publications). 448p. reprint ed. pap. 138.90 (*0-7837-2403-9*, 204008800006) Bks Demand.

Magneto-Structural Correlations in Exchange Coupled Systems. Ed. by R. D. Willett et al. 1984. text 278.00 (*90-277-1876-8*) Kluwer Academic.

*__Magnetoacoustic Polarization Phenomena in Solids.__ V. P. Gudkov & V. Gavenda. (Illus.). 200p. 2000. 64.00 (*0-387-95023-0*) Spr-Verlag.

Magnetochemistry. R. L. Carlin. (Illus.). 350p. 1985. 130.95 (*0-387-15816-2*) Spr-Verlag.

Magnetocumulative Generators. Larry L. Altgilbers et al. LC 99-13257. (High Pressure Shock Compression of Condensed Matter Ser.). 500p. 1999. 99.00 (*0-387-98786-X*) Spr-Verlag.

Magnetodynamic Phenomena in the Solar Atmosphere: Prototypes of Stellar Magnetic Activity:Proceedings of the 153Rd Colloquium of the International Astronomical Union, Held in Makuhari, Near Tokyo, May 22-27, 1995. International Astronomical Union Staff et al. Ed. by Y. Uchida et al. LC 96-30322. 636p. 1996. text 265.00 (*0-7923-4176-7*) Kluwer Academic.

Magnetoelectric Devices: Transducers, Transformers, & Machines. Gordon R. Slemon. LC 66-21039. (Illus.). 556p. reprint ed. pap. 172.40 (*0-608-10055-2*, 201261500082) Bks Demand.

Magnetogasdynamics & Plasma Dynamics. Pai Shih-I. (Illus.). 1962. 39.95 (*0-387-80608-3*) Spr-Verlag.

Magnetohydrodynamic Electrical Power Generation. Hugo K. Messerle. LC 94-18580. (Energy Engineering Learning Package Ser.). 210p. 1995. pap. 79.95 (*0-471-94252-9*) Wiley.

Magnetohydrodynamic Equilibrium & Stability of Stellarators. F. L. Bauer et al. (Illus.). x, 196p. 1984. 79.95 (*0-387-90966-4*) Spr-Verlag.

Magnetohydrodynamics. R. Moreau. (C). 1990. text 182.50 (*0-7923-0937-5*) Kluwer Academic.

Magnetohydrodynamics: Proceedings of Magnethydrodynamics Conference, Northwestern University, Evanston, Ill. Ed. by Ali B. Cambel & Thomas P. Anderson. LC TK2970.N6. 403p. reprint ed. pap. 125.00 (*0-608-11020-5*, 200637400058) Bks Demand.

Magnetohydrodynamics: Waves & Shock Waves in Curved Space-Time. Andre Lichnerowicz. (Mathematical Physics Studies). 292p. (C). 1994. text 140.00 (*0-7923-2805-1*) Kluwer Academic.

Magnetohydrodynamics & Spectral Theory. Alexander E. Lifschitz. (C). 1989. text 329.00 (*90-247-3713-3*) Kluwer Academic.

Magnetohydrodynamics in Binary Stars. C. G. Campbell. LC 97-20159. (Astrophysiics & Space Science Library). 306p. 1997. lib. bdg. 148.00 (*0-7923-4606-8*) Kluwer Academic.

Magnetohydrodynamics in Process Metallurgy: Proceedings of a Symposium Sponsored by TMS Extraction & Processing Division, TMS Light Metals Division & the Iron & Steel Society, Held During the 1992 TMS Annual Meeting, San Diego, California, March 1-5, 1992. Minerals, Metals & Matrials Society Staff. Ed. by J. Szekely et al. LC 91-51129. (Illus.). 316p. 1991. reprint ed. pap. 98.00 (*0-7837-9129-1*, 204992900004) Bks Demand.

Magnetohydrodynamics of Plasma Relaxation. S. Ortolani & D. D. Schnack. 200p. 1993. text 61.00 (*981-02-0860-X*) World Scientific Pub.

Magnetomechanics in Magnetic Fusion Reactor Technology. K. Miya. (Series in Theoretical & Applied Mechanics: Vol. 7). 400p. (C). 1993. text 64.00 (*9971-5-0726-9*) World Scientific Pub.

Magnetooptics & Spectroscopy of Antiferromagnets. V. V. Eremenko et al. (Illus.). 296p. 1992. 144.95 (*0-387-97701-5*) Spr-Verlag.

*__Magnetoresistive Oxides & Related Materials Vol. 602: Materials Research Society Symposium Proceedings.__ Ed. by M. Rzchowski et al. 2000. text 93.00 (*1-55899-510-2*) Materials Res.

Magnetosheath: Proceedings of the Topical Meeting of the COSPAR Interdisciplinary Scientific Commission D (Meeting D6) of the COSPAR 29th Plenary Meeting Held in Washington, D. C., U. S. A., 28 August-5 September, 1992. Ed. by C. T. Russell. (Advances in Space Research Ser.: Vol. 14). (Illus.). 142p. 1994. pap. 165.00 (*0-08-042484-8*) Elsevier.

Magnetosphere-Ionosphere Coupling. Y. Kamide & W. Baumjohann. LC 92-36356. (Physics & Chemistry in Space Ser.: Vol. 23). 1993. 174.95 (*0-387-55983-3*) Spr-Verlag.

Magnetospheres of the Earth & Jupiter: Proceedings of the Neil Brice Memorial Symposium, Frascati, Italy, May 28 - June 1, 1974. Ed. by V. Formisano. LC 75-4587. (Astrophysics & Space Science Library: No. 52). 481p. 1975. lib. bdg. 222.50 (*90-277-0564-X*) Kluwer Academic.

*__Magnetospheric Current Systems.__ Ed. by Shin-ichi Ohtani et al. (Geophysical Monograph Ser.: Vol. 118). 2000. write for info. (*0-87590-976-0*) Am Geophysical.

Magnetospheric Currents. Ed. by T. A. Potemra. (Geophysical Monograph Ser.: Vol. 28). (Illus.). 357p. 1983. 33.00 (*0-87590-055-0*) Am Geophysical.

Magnetospheric Particles & Fields. Ed. by Billy M. McCormac. (Astrophysics & Space Science Library: No. 58). 1976. lib. bdg. 141.50 (*90-277-0702-2*) Kluwer Academic.

Magnetospheric Phenomena in Astrophysics. Ed. by Richard I. Epstein & Feldman C. William. LC 86-71149. (AIP Conference Proceedings Ser.: No. 144). 355p. 1986. lib. bdg. 65.00 (*0-88318-343-9*) Am Inst Physics.

Magnetospheric Physics: Achievements & Prospects. Ed. by B. Hultqvist & Carl-Gunne Falthammer. LC 90-21579. (Illus.). 208p. (C). 1990. text 102.00 (*0-306-43804-6*, Kluwer Plenum) Kluwer Academic.

Magnetospheric Physics: Proceedings of the Advanced Summer Institute, Sheffield, England, 13-12 August, 1973. Advanced Summer Institute Staff. Ed. by Billy M. McCormac. LC 74-76472. (Astrophysics & Space Science Library: No. 44). 370p. 1974. lib. bdg. 165.00 (*90-277-0454-6*) Kluwer Academic.

Magnetospheric Plasma Physics. Ed. by A. Nishida. 364p. 1982. text 191.50 (*90-277-1345-6*) Kluwer Academic.

*__Magnetospheric Plasma Sources & Losses: Final Report of the ISSI Study Project on Source & Loss Processes of Magnetospheric Plasma.__ Bengt Hultqvist. LC 99-32646. (Space Sciences Ser.). 482p. 1999. write for info. (*0-7923-5846-5*) Kluwer Academic.

Magnetospheric Research with Advanced Techniques. Ed. by R. L. Xu & A. T. Y. Lui. LC 99-163020. (COSPAR Colloquia Ser.: Vol. 9). 222p. 1998. write for info. (*0-08-043330-8*, Pergamon Pr) Elsevier.

Magnetospheric Substorms. Ed. by T. A. Potemra. (Geophysical Monograph Ser.: Vol. 64). 488p. 1991. 70.00 (*0-87590-030-5*, GM0640305) Am Geophysical.

Magnetostriction: Theory & Applications - Magnetoelasticity. E. DuTremolet deLacheisseri. 432p. 1993. lib. bdg. 149.00 (*0-8493-6934-7*, QC754) CRC Pr.

Magnetotail Physics. Ed. by Anthony T. Lui. LC 86-27614. (Johns Hopkins Studies in Earth & Planetary Sciences Ser.). (Illus.). 404p. 1987. text 70.00 (*0-8018-3496-1*) Johns Hopkins.

An Asterisk (*) at the beginning of an entry indicates that the title is appearing for the first time.

Magnetresonanztomographie Von Tumoren des HNO-Gebiets: Hypopharynx und Larynx. P. Held & H. Pickrahn. (Illus.). viii, 56p. 1995. pap. 28.00 (*3-8055-6023-0*) S Karger.

Magnetresonanztomographie von Tumoren des HNO-Gebiets, Nasopharynx, Oropharynx, Mundhohle und-Boden. P. Held et al. (Illus.). viii, 64p. 1997. pap. 28.00 (*3-8055-6495-3*) S Karger.

Magnets see Young Scientist Concepts & Projects

Magnets see Imanes

***Magnets.** Karen Bryant-Mole. LC 97-41943. (Science All Around Me Ser.). (Illus.). 24p. (J). (gr. k-2). 1998. 12.95 (*1-57572-629-7*) Heinemann Lib.

Magnets. Margie Burton et al. Ed. by Susan Evento. (Early Connections Ser.). 16p. (J). (gr. k-2). 1998. pap. 4.25 (*1-892393-57-3*) Benchmark Educ.

Magnets. Cindy Christianson. (Hands-On Minds-On Science Ser.). (Illus.). 96p. 1995. pap., teacher ed. 11.95 (*1-55734-612-7*) Tchr Create Mat.

Magnets. Jason Cooper. LC 92-8807. (Science Secrets Discovery Library). 24p. (J). (gr. k-4). 1992. lib. bdg. 10.95 (*0-86593-165-8*) Rourke Corp.

Magnets. Steve Parker. (Learn about Ser.). (Illus.). 64p. (J). (gr. 3-7). 1997. 7.95 (*1-85967-179-9*, Lorenz Bks) Anness Pub.

Magnets. Brenda Parkes. Ed. by Jennifer DiGregorio. (Guided Reading Ser.). 8p. (J). (gr. k). 1997. pap. text 3.95 (*1-56784-926-1*) Newbridge Educ.

***Magnets.** Josie Stewart & Lynn Salem. (Illus.). 8p. (J). (gr. k-2). 2000. pap. 3.75 (*1-58323-007-6*) Seedling Pubns.

Magnets: Detective Files. Richard Walker. (Illus.). 32p. (J). (gr. 2-6). 1998. 19.95 (*1-57145-323-7*, Silver Dolph) Advantage Pubs.

***Magnets: Hands on Elementary School Science.** 2nd ed. (Illus.). 50p. 2000. teacher ed. 35.00 (*1-883410-45-2*) L Poore.

***Magnets: Thematic Unit.** Jennifer Overend Prior. Ed. by Janet A. Hale. (Illus.). 80p. (J). 1999. pap., teacher ed. 9.95 (*1-57690-377-X*, TCM2377) Tchr Create Mat.

***Magnets & Magnetism: Student Science Journal.** Peter R. Bergethon. (Illus.). 96p. (J). (gr. 4-6). 1999. pap. text. write for info. (*1-58447-015-1*) Symmetry Lrng.

***Magnets & Magnetism: Teacher Manual.** Peter R. Bergethon. (Illus.). xix, 96p. 1999. pap. text, teacher ed. write for info. (*1-58447-014-3*) Symmetry Lrng.

Magnets & Motors: Complete Unit. National Science Resources Center Staff. (Science & Technology for Children Ser.). (Illus.). (Orig.). (YA). (gr. 6 up). 1991. pap. text. write for info. (*0-89278-691-4*) Carolina Biological.

Magnets & Motors Student Activity Book. National Science Resources Center Staff. (Science & Technology for Children Ser.). (Illus.). 61p. (YA). (gr. 6 up). 1991. pap. text, student ed. write for info. (*0-89278-693-0*) Carolina Biological.

Magnets & Motors Teacher's Guide. National Science Resources Center Staff. (Science & Technology for Children Ser.). (Illus.). 136p. (YA). (gr. 6 up). 1991. pap. text, teacher ed. write for info. (*0-89278-692-2*) Carolina Biological.

Magnets & Sparks. Wendy Madgwick. LC 98-14618. (Science Starters Ser.). (J). 1999. 22.83 (*0-8172-5328-9*) Raintree Steck-V.

Magnets, Bulbs, Batteries. (ARA., Illus.). (J). (gr. 5-12). 1987. 4.95 (*0-86685-206-9*) Intl Bk Ctr.

***Magnets for Health: A Practical Guide.** Jose Luis Hinojosa. LC 00-39108. (Illus.). 112p. 2000. pap. 19.95 (*1-56072-808-6*, Nova Kroshka Bks) Nova Sci Pubs.

***Magnets for Misery: Trailer Parks & America's Dark Heart of Whiteness.** Mark Van de Walle. 2000. pap. 19.99 (*1-890451-08-8*, Juno Books) pwerHse Cultrl.

Magnets, Magnets, Magnets. Donna Snipes. LC 85-90366. 1985. 3.98 (*0-916809-03-X*) Scott Pubns MI.

Magnevist. 2nd rev. ed. Roland Felix et al. (Illus.). 250p. 1997. 115.00 (*0-632-04184-6*) Blackwell Sci.

***Magnifica.** Johann Sebastian Bach. (Music Scores Ser.). (Illus.). 1998. pap. text 7.98 (*963-9059-21-8*) Kone Music.

***Magnificant Maryland Coloring Book.** Carole Marsh. (Maryland Experience! Ser.). (Illus.). (J). (gr. k-5). 2000. pap. 3.95 (*0-7933-9615-8*) Gallopade Intl.

Magnificant Mendez. Jane W. Hickman & Delon Lyren. 177p. 1994. pap. text 22.99 (*1-887210-01-6*) Summit Records.

***Magnificant Michigan Coloring Book.** Carole Marsh. (Michigan Experience! Ser.). (Illus.). (J). (gr. k-5). 2000. pap. 3.95 (*0-7933-9567-4*) Gallopade Intl.

***Magnificant Missouri Coloring Book.** Carole Marsh. (Missouri Experience! Ser.). (Illus.). (J). (gr. k-5). 2000. pap. 3.95 (*0-7933-9575-5*) Gallopade Intl.

Magnificant Obsession. large type ed. Lloyd C. Douglas. 1994. 65.95 (*0-7862-9981-9*, G K Hall Lrg Type) Mac Lib Ref.

Magnificat. deluxe ed. Edgar Galeano Dominguez. Ed. by Carol Shepherd. Tr. by Adrian Dokmecian. LC 92-62928. (ENG & SPA., Illus.). 70p. 1996. reprint ed. 35.00 (*1-882759-00-1*, GALEDG96001) Palladium MI.

Magnificat, Vol. 3. Julian May. 1997. mass mkt. 6.99 (*0-345-36249-7*, Del Rey) Ballantine Pub Grp.

Magnificat: Homilies in Praise of the Blessed Virgin Mary. Bernard of Clairvaux & Amadeus of Lausanne. (Cistercian Fathers Ser.: No. 18). 1993. pap. 7.95 (*0-87907-148-6*) Cistercian Pubns.

Magnificat: Mary's & Ours. Betty L. Schwab. 1996. pap. 6.25 (*1-55673-653-3*) CSS OH.

Magnificat: Musicians as Biblical Interpreters. Samuel Terrien. LC 94-34748. 1995. pap. 9.95 (*0-8091-3485-3*) Paulist Pr.

Magnificat: Poems. Marilyn N. Waniek. LC 94-6066. 64p. 1994. pap. 8.95 (*0-8071-1922-9*); text 15.95 (*0-8071-1921-0*) La State U Pr.

Magnificat: The Life & Times of Timothy Cardinal Manning. Francis J. Weber. LC 98-8179. 1998. write for info. (*0-87461-914-9*) McNally & Loftin.

Magnificat: Vocal Score Chorus. C. P. Bach. (ENG & LAT.). 128p. 1986. per. 7.95 (*0-7935-1129-1*, 50324490) H Leonard.

Magnificat in C. Score for Orchestral Accompaniment. Johann Pachelbel. Ed. by Henry Woodward. LC M 2020.P3. 148p. reprint ed. pap. 45.90 (*0-608-10793-X*, 200345000030) Bks Demand.

Magnificat in D the Six Motets in Full Score. Johann Sebastian Bach. 208p. 1995. text 13.95 (*0-486-28804-8*) Dover.

Magnificat, Opus One Hundred Eight, Score & Eight Parts, (Trumpet, Trombone, Bass Tuba, Kettle Drum, Cymbals) Flor Peeters. LC M 1528.M3. 45p. reprint ed. pap. 30.00 (*0-608-10722-0*, 200438900058) Bks Demand.

***Magnificat Pilgrim's Guide to the Great Jubilee: A Spiritual Manual.** Ed. by Peter J. Cameron & Romanus Cessario. (Illus.). 304p. 1999. lib. bdg. 4.50 (*0-9676186-1-4*) Magnificat.

***Magnificat Pilgrim's Guide to the Great Jubilee: Boston Archdiocese.** Ed. by Peter J. Cameron & Romanus Cessario. (Illus.). 304p. 1999. lib. bdg. 4.50 (*0-9676186-4-9*) Magnificat.

***Magnificat Pilgrim's Guide to the Great Jubilee: Brooklyn Diocese.** Ed. by Peter J. Cameron & Romanus Cessario. (Illus.). 304p. 1999. lib. bdg. 4.50 (*0-9676186-3-0*) Magnificat.

***Magnificat Pilgrim's Guide to the Great Jubilee: New York Archdiocese.** Ed. by Peter J. Cameron & Romanus Cessario. (Illus.). 340p. 1999. 0.85 (*0-9676186-0-6*) Magnificat.

***Magnificat Pilgrim's Guide to the Great Jubilee: Norwich Diocese.** Ed. by Peter J. Cameron & Romanus Cessario. (Illus.). 304p. 1999. lib. bdg. 4.50 (*0-9676186-2-2*) Magnificat.

***Magnificat Pilgrim's Guide to the Great Jubilee: Washington Archdiocese.** Ed. by Peter J. Cameron & Romanus Cessario. (Illus.). 304p. 1999. lib. bdg. 4.50 (*0-9676186-6-5*) Magnificat.

Magnificence. John Skelton. LC 73-133739. (Tudor Facsimile Texts. Old English Plays Ser.: No. 11). reprint ed. 59.50 (*0-404-53311-6*) AMS Pr.

Magnificence. John Skelton. Ed. by Paula Neuss. LC 79-3125. (Revels Plays Ser.). 245p. reprint ed. pap. 76.00 (*0-8357-4032-3*, 203672400005) Bks Demand.

Magnificence: A Play. Howard Brenton. 71p. (C). 1988. pap. write for info. (*0-413-46750-3*, A0163, Methuen Drama) Methn.

Magnificence of Man & Truth--and More. Russell M. Nelson. LC 97-78187. 58 p. 1998. write for info. (*0-87579-985-X*) Deseret Bk.

Magnificent. Gail Smith. 1995. pap. 8.99 (*0-8341-9431-7*, MB-718) Nazarene.

***Magnificent Activist: The Writings of Thomas Wentworth Higginson (1823-1911)** Ed. by Howard N. Meyer. 600p. 2000. pap. text 22.50 (*0-306-80954-0*) Da Capo.

Magnificent Addiction: Discovering Addiction as Gateway to Healing. Philip R. Kavanaugh. LC 91-41755. 240p. (Orig.). 1992. pap. 14.95 (*0-944031-36-6*) Aslan Pub.

***Magnificent Ambersons.** V. F. Perkins. 1999. pap. 10.95 (*0-85170-373-9*) British Film Inst.

Magnificent Ambersons. Booth Tarkington. 24.95 (*0-88411-700-6*) Amereon Ltd.

Magnificent Ambersons. Booth Tarkington. LC 89-45565. (Library of Indiana Classics). (Illus.). 536p. 1989. 25.00 (*0-253-35875-2*); pap. 14.95 (*0-253-20546-8*, MB-546) Ind U Pr.

Magnificent Ambersons. large type ed. Booth Tarkington. LC 94-42124. 446p. 1995. 21.95 (*0-7838-1223-X*, G K Hall Lrg Type) Mac Lib Ref.

Magnificent Ambersons. Booth Tarkington. (Works of Booth Tarkington). 516p. 1999. reprint ed. lib. bdg. 128.00 (*1-58201-861-8*) Classic Bks.

Magnificent Ambersons. 98th ed. Booth Tarkington. LC 98-19552. (Modern Library Ser.). 1998. pap. 11.95 (*0-375-75250-1*) Modern Lib NY.

Magnificent Ambersons: A Reconstruction. Robert L. Carringer. 318p. 1993. 42.50 (*0-520-07857-8*, Pub. by U CA Pr) Cal Prin Full Svc.

***Magnificent Australia.** Robert Coupe. 1998. 49.95 (*1-86436-221-9*) New Holland.

Magnificent Barbarians: Little-Told Tales of the TX Revolution. Bill Walraven & Marjorie K. Walraven. (Illus.). 224p. (C). 1995. pap. 16.95 (*1-57168-045-4*) Sunbelt Media.

Magnificent Book of Kites: Explorations in Design, Construction, Enjoyment & Flight. Maxwell Eden. LC 98-9880. 480p. 1998. 17.98 (*1-57912-025-3*) Blck Dog & Leventhal.

***Magnificent Book of Kites: Explorations in Design, Construction, Enjoyment & Flight.** Maxwell Eden. (Illus.). 464p. 2000. pap. 14.95 (*0-8069-4990-2*) Sterling.

Magnificent Century. Thomas B. Costain. 1994. reprint ed. lib. bdg. 41.95 (*1-56849-371-1*) Buccaneer Bks.

Magnificent Churches on the Prairie: A Story of Immigrant Priests, Builders & Homesteaders. James Coomber. LC 97-76915. (Illus.). 102p. 1996. pap. 29.95 (*0-911042-45-8*) NDSU Inst Reg.

Magnificent Collie. Patricia Starkweather. Ed. by Luana Luther. LC 97-65309. (Pure Breds Ser.). (Illus.). 320p. 1997. 28.50 (*0-944875-34-3*) Doral Pub.

***Magnificent Colorado.** Todd Caudle. (Colorado Souvenir Ser.). (Illus.). 64p. 1998. pap. 9.95 (*1-888845-06-6*) Skyline Pr.

Magnificent Corpses: Searching Through Europe for St. Peter's Head, St. Claire's Heart, St. Stephen's Hand, & Other Saintly Relics. Anneli Rufus. LC 99-15317. (Illus.). 320p. 1999. pap. 14.95 (*1-56924-687-4*) Marlowe & Co.

Magnificent Deception. Said Salah. (Arabian Story Masterpiece Ser.). 71p. 1990. 8.00 (*1-887584-26-9*) Intl Prom Art.

Magnificent Defeat. Frederick Buechner. LC 84-48764. 144p. 1985. pap. 11.00 (*0-06-061174-X*, Pub. by Harper SF) HarpC.

Magnificent Entertainments: Fancy Dress Balls of Canada's Governors General, 1876-1898. Cynthia Cooper. LC 98-151437. (Illus.). 185p. 1997. 36.95 (*0-86492-187-X*, Pub. by Goose Ln Edits) Genl Dist Srvs.

Magnificent Face of Nature. Mary A. Simon. 1997. pap. write for info. (*1-57553-699-4*) Watermrk Pr.

Magnificent Failure: The Story of Father Solanus Casey. David R. Collins. LC 99-19049. 66p. (YA). (gr. 6-9). 1999. pap. 3.95 (*0-8198-4800-X*) Pauline Bks.

Magnificent Farce & Other Diversions of a Book-Collector. Alfred E. Newton. LC 73-121492. (Essay Index Reprint Ser.). 1977. 30.95 (*0-8369-1767-7*) Ayer.

Magnificent Fight: Marines in the Battle for Wake Island. Robert J. Cressman. (Illus.). 37p. (C). 1996. reprint ed. pap. text 25.00 (*0-7881-3523-6*) DIANE Pub.

Magnificent Fight: The Battle for Wake Island. Robert J. Cressman. LC 94-32013. (Illus.). 352p. 1995. 32.95 (*1-55750-140-8*) Naval Inst Pr.

Magnificent Horses of the World, 6 bks. Photos by Tomas Micek. Incl. Andalusian Horses. LC 95-16322. (Illus.). (J). (gr. 3 up). 1995. lib. bdg. 23.93 (*0-8368-1366-9*); Arabian Horses. LC 95-16321. (Illus.). 48p. (J). (gr. 3 up). 1995. lib. bdg. 23.93 (*0-8368-1367-7*); Friesian Horses. LC 95-16320. (Illus.). 48p. (J). (gr. 3 up). 1995. lib. bdg. 23.93 (*0-8368-1368-5*); Icelandic Ponies. LC 95-16315. (Illus.). 48p. (J). (gr. 3 up). 1995. lib. bdg. 23.93 (*0-8368-1370-7*); Lipizzaner Horses. Photos by Elisabeth Kellner. LC 95-16313. (Illus.). 48p. (J). (gr. 3 up). 1995. lib. bdg. 23.93 (*0-8368-1371-5*); Palimino Horses: Austria's Haflingers. Photos by Elisabeth Kellner. LC 95-16336. (Illus.). (J). (gr. 3 up). 1995. lib. bdg. 23.93 (*0-8368-1369-3*); (Illus.). (J). 1995. Set lib. bdg. 143.60 (*0-8368-1365-0*) Gareth Stevens Inc.

Magnificent Illusions. Lloyd K. Ulery. 96p. 1987. 7.95 (*0-930984-06-4*) Psychic Bks.

Magnificent Jadeite Jewellery: Christie's Auction, Hong Kong, May 1, 1995. Ed. by David Warren. (Illus.). 180p. 1999. reprint ed. text 45.00 (*0-7881-6445-7*) DIANE Pub.

Magnificent Mainers. Jeff Hollingsworth. (Illus.). 256p. (Orig.). 1995. pap. 14.95 (*0-924771-11-9*, Covered Brdge Pr) Douglas Charles Ltd.

Magnificent Man: Created in God's Image. Deborah Bass. Ed. by Samuel Bass. 64p. 1999. pap. 6.00 (*0-9671417-0-2*) BibleScope.

Magnificent Marriage. Barbara Cartland. 20.95 (*0-88411-247-0*) Amereon Ltd.

Magnificent Masquerade. large type ed. Elizabeth Mansfield. LC 90-35643. 393p. 1990. reprint ed. lib. bdg. 18.95 (*1-56054-009-5*) Thorndike Pr.

Magnificent Maya see Lost Civilizations Series

Magnificent Maya. Ed. by Dale Brown. (Lost Civilizations Ser.). (Illus.). 168p. 1993. lib. bdg. 25.93 (*0-8094-9880-4*) Time-Life.

***Magnificent M. D.** Carol Grace. (Desire Ser.). 2000. mass mkt. 3.99 (*0-373-76277-1*) Silhouette.

***Magnificent Mesquite.** Ken E. Rogers. LC 99-50890. (Corrie Herring Hooks Ser.: Vol. 46). (Illus.). 200p. 2000. 24.95 (*0-292-77105-3*) U of Tex Pr.

Magnificent Metric System: A Magical Guide to the Marvels of Metrics. Don Berggren. LC 76-40527. (Illus.). (Orig.). 1976. 2.95 (*0-912800-34-8*) Woodbridge Pr.

Magnificent Microworld Adventures: Microscopic Topics. Mike Wood. (J). (gr. 4-9). 1995. 16.95 (*1-881431-53-3*, 1312) AIMS Educ Fnd.

Magnificent Mile: A History of Hillsboro Beach. Carmen R. McGarry. (Illus.). 248p. 1997. 24.95 (*0-9641216-3-8*) RitAmelia Pr.

***Magnificent Mind Listens Mindfully.** Ellen Arnold. (Illus.). 32p. 2000. pap. 10.00 (*1-56976-112-4*, 1141) Zephyr Pr AZ.

***Magnificent Mind Magnifies Meaning When Reading.** Ellen Arnold. (Illus.). 32p. 2000. pap. 10.00 (*1-56976-114-0*) Zephyr Pr AZ.

***Magnificent Mind Masters Multiplication.** Ellen Arnold. (Illus.). 32p. 2000. pap. 10.00 (*1-56976-116-7*, 1145) Zephyr Pr AZ.

***Magnificent Mississippi Coloring Book.** Carole Marsh. (Mississippi Experience! Ser.). (Illus.). (J). (gr. k-5). 2000. pap. 3.95 (*0-7933-9559-3*) Gallopade Intl.

Magnificent Mitscher. Theodore Taylor. LC 91-14412. (Illus.). 416p. 1991. 29.95 (*1-55750-800-3*) Naval Inst Pr.

Magnificent Mittens: The Beauty of Warm Hands. Anne Zilborg. Ed. by Elaine Rowley. (Illus.). 144p. 1998. 29.95 (*0-9646391-3-0*) XRX Inc.

Magnificent Mobiles. Melanie Williams. 1994. 10.98 (*0-7858-0151-0*) Bk Sales Inc.

Magnificent Moisants: Champions of Early Flight. Doris Rich. LC 98-6876. 264p. 1998. 24.95 (*1-56098-860-6*) Smithsonian.

***Magnificent Molas: The Art of the Kuna Indians.** Michel Perrin. (Illus.). 208p. 2000. text 45.00 (*2-08-013674-7*, Pub. by Flammarion) Abbeville Pr.

Magnificent Moments: The World's Greatest Wildlife Photographs. Ed. by George H. Harrison. LC 95-7008. (Illus.). 144p. 1995. 35.00 (*1-57223-023-1*, 0231) Willow Creek Pr.

***Magnificent Monarchs.** Linda Glaser. LC 99-86640. (Illus.). 2000. lib. bdg. write for info. (*0-7613-1700-7*) Millbrook Pr.

Magnificent Monologues for Kids. Chambers Stevens. Ed. by Renee Rolle-Whatley. LC 98-75015. 80p. (J). (gr. k-8). 1999. pap. 13.95 (*1-883995-08-6*) Sandcastle Pub.

Magnificent Montez. Horace Wyndham. LC 70-91592. (Illus.). 1972. 26.95 (*0-405-09109-5*) Ayer.

Magnificent Mountain Women: Adventures in the Colorado Rockies. Janet Robertson. LC 89-14717. (Illus.). xxiii, 274p. 1990. pap. 12.00 (*0-8032-8933-2*, Bison Books) U of Nebr Pr.

Magnificent Mummies. Tony Bradman. (Blue Bananas Ser.). (Illus.). 1997. pap. text 4.99 (*0-7497-2767-5*) London Brdge.

Magnificent Mummy Maker. Elvira Woodruff. 160p. (J). (gr. 4-7). 1995. pap. 3.50 (*0-590-45743-8*) Scholastic Inc.

Magnificent Mummy Maker. Elvira Woodruff. (J). 1994. 9.09 (*0-606-07828-2*, Pub. by Turtleback) Demco.

Magnificent Muslims. Marguerite Brown. LC 81-80056. 98p. 1981. 8.00 (*0-911026-10-X*) New World Press NY.

Magnificent Myths. Clifford. 1992. mass mkt. 10.95 (*0-8359-0207-2*) P-H.

Magnificent 92 Indiana Courthouses. rev. ed. I. Wilmer Counts & Jon Dilts. LC 99-28355. 1999. write for info. (*0-253-33638-4*) Ind U Pr.

Magnificent Numbers of the Great Pyramid & Stonehenge. Bonnie Gaunt. LC 85-91026. (Illus.). 216p. (Orig.). 1985. pap. 10.00 (*0-9602688-1-2*) Adventures Unltd.

Magnificent Obsession. Lloyd C. Douglas. 1976. 23.95 (*0-8488-0479-1*) Amereon Ltd.

Magnificent Obsession. Lloyd C. Douglas. 1982. lib. bdg. 27.95 (*0-89966-387-7*) Buccaneer Bks.

Magnificent Obsession. Lloyd C. Douglas. LC 99-20071. 1999. pap. 12.00 (*0-395-95774-5*) HM.

Magnificent Obsession. large type ed. Lloyd C. Douglas. LC 91-39205. 424p. 1992. reprint ed. lib. bdg. 19.95 (*1-56054-311-6*) Thorndike Pr.

Magnificent Obsession: The Autobiography of William Ragsdale Cannon. William R. Cannon. LC 98-55936. 400p. 1999. 25.00 (*0-687-08575-6*) Abingdon.

Magnificent Obsessions: A Photo Novel. Lesley Choyce. (Illus.). 144p. 1991. pap. 14.95 (*1-55082-020-6*, Pub. by Quarry Pr) LPC InBook.

Magnificent Obsessions: Twenty Remarkable Collectors in Pursuit of Their Dreams. Mitch Tuchman. (Illus.). 143p. 1999. reprint ed. pap. 20.00 (*0-7881-6110-5*) DIANE Pub.

Magnificent Peninsula: The Comprehensible Guidebook to Mexico's Baja California. 6th rev. ed. Jack Williams. LC 97-62453. (Illus.). 288p. 1998. pap. 18.95 (*1-891275-00-3*) H J Williams.

Magnificent Percheron. Edna C. Nelson. (Illus.). 1963. pap. 8.95 (*0-87505-115-4*) Borden.

Magnificent Places: Oregon Coast. Jack McGowan. (Illus.). 95p. 1996. pap. text 19.95 (*1-55868-250-3*) Gr Arts Ctr Pub.

Magnificent Places: Oregon Coast. Jack McGowan. 1997. 27.95 (*1-55868-291-0*) Gr Arts Ctr Pub.

Magnificent Poet. Hardie W. Daniel. LC 85-70859. (Illus.). 112p. 1986. 10.00 (*0-942172-01-9*) Endeavor Pub.

Magnificent Ponderosa. Rose Houk. (Plateau Ser.). 32p. 1993. pap. 5.95 (*0-89734-115-5*) Mus Northern Ariz.

Magnificent Prayers of Saint Bridget of Sweden. Bridget. (Illus.). 19p. 1994. reprint ed. pap. 2.00 (*0-89555-220-5*) TAN Bks Pubs.

Magnificent Recycling Machine Adventure: With Buffalo Biff & Farley's Raiders. unabridged ed. Joe Loesch. Ed. by Cheryl J. Hutchinson. (Backyard Adventure Ser.: Vol. 3). (Illus.). 56p. (J). (gr. 1-5). 1996. pap. 14.95 incl. audio (*1-887729-04-6*) Toy Box Prods.

Magnificent Recycling Machine Adventure: With Buffalo Biff & Farley's Raiders. unabridged ed. Joe Loesch. Ed. by Cheryl J. Hutchinson. (Backyard Adventure Ser.: Vol. 3). (Illus.). 56p. (J). (gr. 1-6). 1996. pap. 16.95 incl. audio compact disk (*1-887729-05-4*) Toy Box Prods.

Magnificent Ride: The First Reformation in Hussite Bohemia. Thomas A. Fudge. LC 97-39853. (St. Andrews Studies in Reformation History). (Illus.). 315p. 1998. text 87.95 (*1-85928-372-1*, Pub. by Ashgate Pub) Ashgate Pub Co.

Magnificent Rocks: The Story of Mining, Men, & Minerals at Franklin & Sterling Hill, N. J. 2nd rev. ed. Susan B. Cooper & Pete J. Dunn. 74p. (J). (gr. 4-8). 1997. pap. text 15.00 (*0-9662132-0-3*) S Cooper.

Magnificent Rogue. Iris Johansen. LC 94-116582. 416p. 1993. mass mkt. 6.99 (*0-553-29944-1*) Bantam.

Magnificent Rogues of San Francisco: A Galley of Fakers & Frauds, Rascals & Robber Barons, Scoundrels & Scalawags. Charles F. Adams. LC 97-36488. (Illus.). 352p. 1998. 27.95 (*0-87015-262-9*) Pacific Bks.

Magnificent Savages. Fred M. Stewart. 1997. mass mkt. 6.99 (*0-614-27743-4*) Forge NYC.

Magnificent Savages. large type ed. Fred M. Stewart. LC 96-21106. 1996. 26.95 (*0-7838-1901-3*, G K Hall Lrg Type) Mac Lib Ref.

Magnificent 7, Teacher's Handbook. Mary K. Beall & John Carter. 48p. 1995. pap. 19.95 (*0-7390-0097-7*, 11695) Alfred Pub.

***Magnificent 7.** Lois Fiftal et al. 1999. pap., teacher ed. 44.95 incl. audio compact disk (*0-7390-0099-3*, 18749) Alfred Pub.

Magnificent Seven: Great Composers in Song. John Carter & Mary Kay Beall. 1995. pap., student ed. 22.50 (*0-7390-0696-7*, 11694) Alfred Pub.

Magnificent Seven: The Authorized Story of American Gold. Amy Chow. (Illus.). 112p. (YA). (gr. 6 up). 1996. 19.95 (*0-553-09774-1*) Bantam.

M

An Asterisk (*) at the beginning of an entry indicates that the title is appearing for the first time.

Magnificent 7: The Sequel Teacher's Handbook: Great Composers in Song. John Carter & Mary K. Beall. 48p. 1999. pap., teacher ed. 19.95 (*0-7390-0081-0*, 18734) Alfred Pub.
Magnificent 7: The Sequel Teacher's Kit: Great Composers in Song. John Carter & Mary K. Beall. 1999. pap. 44.95 incl. audio compact disk (*0-7390-0080-2*, 18737) Alfred Pub.
Magnificent Siberian. large type ed. Louis Charbonneau. (Ulverscroft Large Print Ser.). 592p. 1997. 27.99 (*0-7089-3787-X*) Ulverscroft.
Magnificent Society & the Democracy Amendments: How to Free Your Congressmen from the Control of the Special Interests. John Reid. LC 80-85474. 220p. 1981. 11.95 (*0-939428-00-8*); pap. 8.95 (*0-939428-01-6*) Pony X Pr.
Magnificent South Africa. BHB International Staff & Robert T. Teske. 1997. pap. text 49.95 (*1-86825-976-5*, Pub. by New5 Holland) BHB Intl.
Magnificent Spinster. May Sarton. 384p. 1995. pap. 11.00 (*0-393-31249-6*) Norton.
*__Magnificent Transition.__ Alan Halverson. 288p. 1999. pap. 12.95 (*1-56167-535-0*) Am Literary Pr.
Magnificent Trickster: The Story of Milarepa. Molly MacGregor. LC 88-92347. 1992. pap. 9.99 (*0-929929-01-2*) MM Pr.
*__Magnificent Universe.__ Ken Croswell. LC 99-23875. (Illus.). 192p. 1999. 60.00 (*0-684-84594-6*) S&S Trade.
Magnificent Visions: Interiors from New York, Barcelona, Milan, Mexico City, Paris, West Berlin, London & Los Angeles. Elizabeth Heyert. (Illus.). 1989. 40.00 (*0-318-42510-6*) Viking Penguin.
Magnificent Voyage of Emily Carr. Jovette Marchessault. Tr. by Linda Gaboriau. 104p. (Orig.). 1992. pap. 11.95 (*0-88922-314-9*, Pub. by Talonbks) Genl Dist Srvs.
Magnificent Wilf. Gordon Rupert Dickson. 320p. 1995. 21.00 (*0-671-87664-3*) Baen Bks.
Magnificent Wilf. Gordon Rupert Dickson. 304p. 1996. mass mkt. 5.99 (*0-671-87719-4*) Baen Bks.
Magnificient Cosmos Magazine. Sasi. 1998. write for info. (*0-7167-3381-1*) W H Freeman.
Magnificient Helmets. Harry Knill. (J). (gr. 1-9). 1992. pap. 6.95 (*0-88388-167-5*) Bellerophon Bks.
Magnificient Meditations of Assurance, Peace, & Wisdom. Armen Z. Mesrobian. LC 97-95009. (Illus.). 238p. 1998. per. 14.00 (*0-9632735-2-3*) EPS Excel Pub.
*__Magnificooks: Recipes of Celebrations from the Choir, Congregation & Clergy.__ Ed. by Christ Church Cathedral Staff. 121p. 2000. pap. 12.00 (*0-615-11221-8*) Ch Church Cath.
Magnified Be Thy Name: Prayers & Thoughts for Children from the Baha'i Holy Writings. Compiled by Child Education Committee of the National Spiritua. 64p. (J). 1983. 7.50 (*0-900125-35-7*) Bahai.
Magnify Him. 1991. pap. 1.35 (*0-8341-9561-5*) Lillenas.
Magnify the Lord. Compiled by Ken Bible. 125p. 1986. ring bd. 7.99 (*0-8341-9254-3*, MB-559) Lillenas.
Magnify the Lord. Jane Landreth. 20p. 1994. 1.50 (*1-885022-00-X*) Precious Gems.
Magnify the Lord, Vols. 1 & 2. Compiled by Ken Bible. 1986. audio 19.99 (*0-685-68425-3*, TA-9077B) Lillenas.
Magnify the Lord with Me. large type ed. George E. Weaver. 160p. 1997. pap. 10.00 (*1-885066-37-6*) Four-G Pubs.
*__Magnify Your Vision for the Small Church, 1.__ John Rowell. 1998. pap. 14.99 (*0-9668853-0-9*) Northside Comm.
Magnifying God's Word. George L. Glass, Sr. LC 92-11978. 164p. (Orig.). 1992. pap. 3.99 (*0-932581-49-8*) Word Aflame.
Magnifying Mirrors: Women, Surrealism, & Partnership. Renee R. Hubert. LC 93-17640. (Illus.). xii, 425p. 1994. text 90.00 (*0-8032-2370-6*) U of Nebr Pr.
Magnifying Priesthood Power. Robert Millett. LC 89-85213. 187p. 1980. reprint ed. 14.98 (*0-88290-037-4*) Horizon Utah.
Magnifying Your Aaronic Priesthood Calling. Shane R. Barker. 1995. pap. 7.95 (*0-88494-977-X*) Bookcraft Inc.
Magnin & Co. A California Legacy. Devin T. Frick. Ed. by Jean Walsh. 1998. 29.95 (*0-9663493-1-8*) Park Place.
Magnitude & Delay: Approximation of 1-D & 2-D Digital Filters. B. A. Shenoi. Ed. by A. Lacroix & A. N. Venetsanopoulos. LC 99-23433. (Digital Signal Processing Ser.). (Illus.). 250p. 1999. 95.00 (*3-540-64161-0*) Spr-Verlag.
Magnitude 8: Earthquakes & Life along the San Andreas Fault. Philip L. Fradkin. LC 98-12685. (Illus.). 325p. 1998. 27.50 (*0-8050-4696-8*) H Holt & Co.
Magnitude of Life. Susan M. Davis. 1998. pap. write for info. (*1-58235-000-0*) Watermrk Pr.
Magnitude Scaling. Milton Lodge. (Quantitative Applications in the Social Sciences Ser.: Vol. 25). 88p. 1981. pap. 10.95 (*0-8039-1747-3*) Sage.
Magnitude 8 Earthquakes & Life along the San Andreas Fault Philip L. Fradkin. LC 99-18476. 348p. 1999. pap. 15.95 (*0-520-22119-2*, Pub. by U CA Pr) Cal Prin Full Svc.
Magnitudes: Poems from Hollywood. Mark Dunster. 11p. 1998. pap. 5.00 (*0-89642-507-X*) Linden Pubs.
*__Magnolia.__ Ginny Aiken. LC 99-57970. 280p. 2000. pap. 8.99 (*0-8423-3559-5*) Tyndale Hse.
Magnolia. Philip Callow. LC 97-11589. 208p. (Orig.). 1996. pap. write for info. (*0-7490-0168-2*) Allison & Busby.
Magnolia: A Care Manual. Graham Rankin. LC 98-56391. (Care Manual Ser.: Vol. 6). (Illus.). 128p. 1999. 19.95 (*1-57145-638-4*, Laurel Glen Pub) Advantage Pubs.
Magnolia: Botanicals Lined. 160p. 1995. text 14.95 (*1-55156-007-0*) Paperblank.
*__Magnolia: The Shooting Script.__ Paul Thomas Anderson. LC 99-59360. 224p. 2000. 32.95 (*1-55704-409-0*, Pub. by Newmarket); pap. text 22.95 (*1-55704-406-6*, Pub. by Newmarket) Norton.
Magnolia Bakery Cookbook: Baking the Old-Fashioned Way. Jennifer Appelt & Allysa Torey. LC 99-37070. (Illus.). 128p. 1999. 24.50 (*0-684-85910-6*) S&S Trade.
Magnolia Blossom. Lorena Diemer. 88p. 1997. pap. 10.95 (*1-878406-11-6*, Paintbrsh) Parker Dstb.
Magnolia Club. Robert H. Neill. 1990. 25.00 (*0-9617591-7-8*) MS River Pub.
Magnolia Collection. Gene Westbrook. Ed. by Isabelle Hanson. LC 84-52524. (Illus.). 256p. 1985. spiral bd. 14.95 (*0-9614247-0-2*) Gene Westbrook.
*__Magnolia Convalescent Center.__ William I. Riddle. LC 00-190927. 2000. 25.00 (*0-7388-2112-8*); pap. 18.00 (*0-7388-2113-6*) Xlibris Corp.
Magnolia Dawn: Blossoms of the South. Erica Spindler. (Special Edition Ser.). 1993. per. 3.50 (*0-373-09857-X*, 5-09857-9) Silhouette.
Magnolia Dreams. Harriet Segal. 544p. 1992. mass mkt. 4.99 (*0-380-71457-4*, Avon Bks) Morrow Avon.
Magnolia Garden. C. R. Gibson Company Staff. 1997. 6.00 (*0-7852-3730-5*) Gibson.
*__Magnolia Hall.__ Errol Miller. Ed. by David Baratier. 72p. 2000. pap. 8.00 (*1-886350-51-5*, Pub. by Pavement Saw) SPD-Small Pr Dist.
Magnolia Leaves: Poems. Mary W. Fordham. LC 71-168122. reprint ed. 27.50 (*0-404-00050-9*) AMS Pr.
Magnolia Reich: An American Holocaust. David Squvainmid. 306p. 1997. mass mkt. 4.99 (*1-55197-315-4*) Picasso Publ.
Magnolia Street. Louis Golding. 608p. 1997. pap. 10.95 (*0-575-60041-1*, Pub. by V Gollancz) Trafalgar.
Magnolia Tree. Martha Kirkland. 304p. 1998. mass mkt. 5.99 (*0-515-12361-7*, Jove) Berkley Pub.
*__Magnolias.__ large type ed. Julie Ellis. LC 99-41968. (Romance Ser.). 1999. 27.95 (*0-7838-8769-8*, G K Hall & Co) Mac Lib Ref.
*__Magnolias: A Gardener's Guide.__ J. M. Gardiner. LC 99-57402. (Illus.). 330p. 2000. 39.95 (*0-88192-446-6*) Timber.
*__Magnolias & Mayhem.__ Jeffrey Marks. 2000. 24.50 (*1-57072-112-2*); pap. 15.00 (*1-57072-128-9*) Overmountain Pr.
Magnolias & Such. Margaret K. Biggs. (Illus.). 1982. 2.50 (*0-943696-00-3*) Red Key Pr.
Magnolias Southern Cuisine. Donald Barickman. LC 95-12066. (Illus.). 152p. 1995. 19.95 (*0-941711-31-5*) Wyrick & Co.
Magnum: Fifty Years at the Front Line of History. Russell Miller. LC 97-49040. (Illus.). 336p. 1998. 26.00 (*0-8021-1631-0*, Grove) Grove-Atltic.
Magnum: Fifty Years at the Front Lines of History. Russell Miller. (Illus.). 336p. 1999. pap. 15.00 (*0-8021-3653-2*, Grove) Grove-Atltic.
Magnum Cinema: Photographs from 50 Years of Movie-Making. Alain Bergala. (Illus.). 360p. (C). 1995. 69.95 (*0-7148-3375-4*, Pub. by Phaidon Press) Phaidon Pr.
Magnum Cinema: Photographs from 50 Years of Movie-Making. Alain Bergala. (Illus.). 360p. 1998. pap. 29.95 (*0-7148-3772-5*, Pub. by Phaidon Press) Phaidon Pr.
*__Magnum Degrees.__ Magnum Photographers Staff. (Illus.). 535p. 2000. 69.95 (*0-7148-3821-7*) Phaidon Pr.
Magnum Fault. Raboo Rodgers. 192p. (J). (gr. 5 up). 1984. 11.95 (*0-685-07882-5*, 5-95260) HM.
Magnum in Parvo. William Halfpenny & John Halfpenny. LC 68-8318. (Illus.). 56p. 1972. reprint ed. 19.95 (*0-405-08589-3*, Pub. by Blom Pubns) Ayer.
Magnum Landscape. Frwd. by Ian Jeffrey. 184p. 1997. 19.95 (*0-7148-3642-7*, Pub. by Phaidon Press) Phaidon Pr.
Magnum Libre d'Escrime: Big Book of Fencing. 2nd ed. Rudy Volkman. (Illus.). 271p. 1997. spiral bd. 25.00 (*0-9668038-0-9*) R Volkmann.
Magnum Opus: My Own Journal. Roberta Rubly-Burggraff. (Illus.). 72p. (Orig.). (YA). (gr. 7-12). 1999. pap. 5.95 (*0-937997-14-5*) Hi-Time Pflaum.
Magnum Opus: Studies in the Narrative Fiction of Thomas Mann. Ernest M. Wolf. Ed. by Peter D. Brown. (Studies in Modern German Literature: Vol. 25). X, 288p. 1989. 39.95 (*0-8204-0710-0*) P Lang Pubng.
Magnum Opus Musicum VIII: Motetten zu 6 Stimmen (Nr. 374-418) Orlando di Lasso. (Samtliche Werke (Alte Reihe) Ser.: Vol. 15). (Illus.). 1973. reprint ed. pap. 85.00 (*0-8450-1915-5*) Broude.
Magnum Opus Musicum XI: Motetten fur 8, 9, 10 & 12 Stimmen (Nr. 493-516) Orlando di Lasso. (Samtliche Werke (Alte Reihe) Ser.: Vol. 21). (Illus.). 1973. reprint ed. pap. 85.00 (*0-8450-1921-X*) Broude.
Magnum Opus Musicum V: Motetten fur 5 Stimmen (Nr. 249-289) Orlando di Lasso. (Samtliche Werke (Alte Reihe) Ser.: Vol. 9). (Illus.). 1973. reprint ed. pap. 85.00 (*0-8450-1909-0*) Broude.
Magnum Opus Musicum IV: Motetten fur 5 Stimmen (Nr. 212-248) Orlando di Lasso. (Samtliche Werke (Alte Reihe) Ser.: Vol. 7). 1973. reprint ed. pap. 85.00 (*0-8450-1907-4*) Broude.
Magnum Opus Musicum IX: Motetten fur 6 Stimmen (Nr. 419-456) Orlando di Lasso. (Samtliche Werke (Alte Reihe) Ser.: Vol. 17). (Illus.). 1973. reprint ed. pap. 85.00 (*0-8450-1917-1*) Broude.
Magnum Opus Musicum I: Motetten fur 2, 3 & 4 Stimmen (Nr. 1-90) Orlando di Lasso. (Samtliche Werke (Alte Reihe) Ser.: Vol. 1). (Illus.). 1973. reprint ed. pap. 85.00 (*0-8450-1901-5*) Broude.
Magnum Opus Musicum VII: Motetten zu 6 Stimmen (Nr. 336-373) Orlando di Lasso. (Samtliche Werke (Alte Reihe) Ser.: Vol. 13). (Illus.). 1973. reprint ed. pap. 85.00 (*0-8450-1913-9*) Broude.
Magnum Opus Musicum VI: Motetten zu 5 & 6 Stimmen (Nr. 290-335) Orlando di Lasso. (Samtliche Werke (Alte Reihe) Ser.: Vol. 11). (Illus.). 1973. reprint ed. pap. 85.00 (*0-8450-1911-2*) Broude.
Magnum Opus Musicum X: Motetten fur 6, 7 & 8 Stimmen (Nr. 457-492) Orlando di Lasso. (Samtliche Werke (Alte Reihe) Ser.: Vol. 19). (Illus.). 1973. reprint ed. pap. 85.00 (*0-8450-1919-8*) Broude.
Magnum Opus Musicum III: Motetten fur 5 Stimmen (Nr. 161-211) Orlando di Lasso. (Samtliche Werke (Alte Reihe) Ser.: Vol. 5). (Illus.). 1973. reprint ed. pap. 85.00 (*0-8450-1905-8*) Broude.
Magnum Opus Musicum II: Motetten fur 4 & 5 Stimmen (Nr. 91-160) Orlando di Lasso. (Samtliche Werke (Alte Reihe) Ser.: Vol. 3). (Illus.). 1973. reprint ed. pap. 85.00 (*0-8450-1903-1*) Broude.
Magnum Opus: or The Great Work: The Complete Ritual Work of Scottish Rite Freemasonry. Albert Pike. 650p. 1992. reprint ed. pap. 45.00 (*1-56459-245-6*) Kessinger Pub.
Magnum-68 in the World. Marc Weltzmann. 368p. (C). 1998. pap. 59.95 (*2-85025-559-9*) Dist Art Pubs.
Magnus. 1994. write for info. (*1-56476-900-3*, Victor Bks) Chariot Victor.
Magnus. Sigmund Brouwer. LC 94-13611. (Illus.). 500p. 1994. pap. 11.99 (*1-56476-296-3*, 6-3296, Victor Bks) Chariot Victor.
Magnus. George M. Brown. 1999. pap. 11.95 (*0-86241-814-3*, Pub. by Canongate Books) Interlink Pub.
Magnus Felix Ennodius. Stefanie A. Kennell. (Illus.). 232p. (C). text 42.50 (*0-472-10917-0*, 10917) U of Mich Pr.
Magnus Machina: The Great Machine, (New Maps of the Inner Terrain of Modern Ma n) enl. rev. ed. Jan. 216p. 1981. 20.00 (*0-936380-05-5*) Chan Shal Imi.
Magnus Merriman. Eric Linklater. (Classics Ser.). 308p. 1995. pap. 9.95 (*0-86241-313-3*, Pub. by Canongate Books) Interlink Pub.
Mago de Oz. L. Frank Baum. 1987. 15.05 (*0-606-10414-3*, Pub. by Turtleback) Demco.
Mago Desinventor (The Magic Dis-inventor) Marco T. Cost. Tr. by Monica Mansour. (SPA., Illus.). (J). (gr. 5-6). 1994. pap. 5.99 (*968-16-4240-6*, Pub. by Fondo) Continental Bk.
Magog, 1982 Cancelled: Did Israel Prevent the Third World War? David A. Lewis. LC 82-62079. 144p. 1982. pap. 4.95 (*0-89221-103-2*) New Leaf.
Magomero: Portrait of an African Village. Landeg White. (Illus.). 288p. (C). 1989. pap. text 22.95 (*0-521-38909-7*) Cambridge U Pr.
Magpie in the Tower. Helen Pereira. 128p. 1990. pap. 6.35 (*0-920021-74-3*) Creative Bk Pub.
Magpie Magic: A Tale of Colorful Mischief. April Wilson. Ed. by Skip Skwarek. LC 97-37647. (Illus.). 40p. (J). (ps-3). 1999. 14.99 (*0-8037-2354-7*, Dial Yng Read) Peng Put Young Read.
Magpie on the Gallows. Madeline DeFrees. 82p. 1982. 12.00 (*0-914742-66-3*) Copper Canyon.
Magpie on the Gallows. Madeline DeFrees. 84p. 1982. pap. 6.00 (*0-914742-65-5*) Copper Canyon.
Magpie Reveries: Iconographic Mandalas. James Koehnline. 50p. Date not set. 10.00 (*0-936756-91-8*) Autonomedia.
Magpie Rising: Sketches from the Great Plains. Michael K. Gilfillan & Merrill Gilfillan. (Profiles Ser.). 196p. 1998. pap. 13.95 (*1-889097-26-8*, Pub. by Hard Pr MA) Consort Bk Sales.
Magpies: The Ecology & Behavior of Black-Billed & Yellow-Billed Magpies. Tim R. Birkhead. (Poyser Popular Bird Bks.). (Illus.). 270p. 1991. text 39.00 (*0-85661-067-4*, 784667) Acad Pr.
Magpies, Monkeys & Morals: What Philosophers Say about Animal Liberation. Angus Taylor. 200p. 1999. pap. 16.95 (*1-55111-202-7*) Broadview Pr.
Magpies' Nest. Illus. by Julie Downing. LC 94-1773. 32p. (J). (ps-3). 1995. 15.95 (*0-395-62155-0*, Clarion Bks) HM.
Magpie's Story. 28p. (J). 1988. 4.99 (*0-310-55820-4*, 19091) Zondervan.
Magritte. Andre Breton. (Illus.). 1964. pap. 10.00 (*0-914412-24-8*, Inst Arts Catalogues) Menil Found.
Magritte. Ed. by Jose M. Faerna. (Great Modern Masters Cameo Bks.). (Illus.). 64p. (J). (gr. 6). 1996. pap. 11.98 (*0-8109-4680-7*, Pub. by Abrams) Time Warner.
*__Magritte.__ Siegfried Gohr. 112p. 2000. 24.95 (*0-8109-6700-6*, Pub. by Abrams) Time Warner.
Magritte. A. M. Hammacher. (Masters of Art Ser.). (Illus.). 128p. 1986. 24.95 (*0-8109-1419-0*, Pub. by Abrams) Time Warner.
Magritte. Jacques Meuris. Tr. by J. A. Underwood. (Illus.). 236p. 1990. 85.00 (*0-87951-409-4*, Pub. by Overlook Pr) Penguin Putnam.
Magritte. Jacques Meuris. 1994. pap. 19.99 (*3-8228-0546-7*) Taschen Amer.
Magritte. Jacques Meuris. (SPA.). 1996. pap. 19.99 (*3-8228-0666-8*) Taschen Amer.
Magritte. Jacques Meuris. (Big Art Ser.). 1998. 19.99 (*3-8228-7215-6*) Taschen Amer.
*__Magritte.__ Jacques Meuris. 1999. 19.99 (*3-8228-7368-3*) Taschen Amer.
Magritte. Bernard Noel. (Illus.). 1995. pap. 12.00 (*0-517-88414-3*) Random.
Magritte. Marcel Pacquet. 1994. pap. 9.99 (*3-8228-9648-9*) Taschen Amer.
Magritte, 11 vols. Marcel Paquet. (Thunder Bay Artists Ser.). (Illus.). 96p. 1997. pap. text 4.99 (*1-57145-126-9*, Thunder Bay) Advantage Pubs.
Magritte. Marcel Paquet. (SPA.). 1996. pap. 9.99 (*3-8228-0684-6*) Taschen Amer.
Magritte. Taschen Staff. (SPA.). (J). 1998. 39.99 (*3-8228-8029-9*, Pub. by Benedikt Taschen) Bks Nippan.
Magritte. Taschen Staff. 1998. 29.99 (*3-8228-7750-6*) Taschen Amer.
Magritte. Richard Calvocoressi. (Color Library). (Illus.). 128p. (C). 1993. reprint ed. pap. 14.95 (*0-7148-2760-6*, Pub. by Phaidon Press) Phaidon Pr.
Magritte. rev. ed. Suzi Gablik. LC 84-51498. (World of Art Ser.). (Illus.). 228p. (C). 1985. pap. 14.95 (*0-500-20199-4*, Pub. by Thames Hudson) Norton.
*__Magritte, 1898-1998.__ Contrib. by Sarah Whitfield et al. LC 98-156454. (Illus.). 335p. 1998. 60.00 (*0-8109-6359-0*) Abrams.
Magruders American Government. W. McClenaghan. 1993. 36.47 (*0-13-544560-4*) P-H.
Magsaysay & the Philippine Peasantry: The Agrarian Impact on Philippine Politics, 1953-1956. Frances L. Sterner. LC 61-63199. (University of California Publications in Social Welfare: Vol. 10). 304p. reprint ed. pap. 94.30 (*0-608-11693-9*, 202145500022) Bks Demand.
Maguey Utilization in Highland Central Mexico: An Archaeological Ethnography. Jeffrey R. Parsons & Mary H. Parsons. LC 90-34597. (Anthropological Papers Ser.: No. 82). (Illus.). xvi, 388p. (Orig.). 1990. pap. 22.00 (*0-915703-20-3*) U Mich Mus Anthro.
Maguey y Sus Usos en Guatemala: An Ch'ech, Sajchi' o ki' Jose B. Camposeco. (SPA., Illus.). 54p. (Orig.). 1995. pap. 3.75 (*1-886502-00-5*, Ediciones Yax Te) Yax Te Found.
*__Magus.__ John Fowles. 640p. 2001. pap. 15.95 (*0-316-29619-8*, Back Bay) Little.
Magus. John Fowles. LC 97-39455. 1998. 23.95 (*0-679-60283-6*) Modern Lib NY.
Magus. John Fowles. LC 97-189578. 1997. write for info. (*0-09-974391-4*) Trafalgar.
Magus. rev. ed. John Fowles. 672p. 1985. mass mkt. 7.50 (*0-440-35162-6*) Dell.
*__Magus: A Complete System of Occult Philosophy.__ fac. ed. Francis Barrett. LC 99-49429. (Illus.). 432p. 2000. pap. 19.95 (*0-87728-942-5*) Weiser.
*__Magus: A Complete System of Occult Philosophy.__ limited ed. Francis Barrett. LC 99-49429. 432p. 2000. 85.00 (*0-87728-943-3*) Weiser.
Magus: A Complete System of Occult Philosophy. Francis Barrett. 228p. 1975. reprint ed. pap. 18.95 (*0-8065-0462-5*, Citadel Pr) Carol Pub Group.
*__Magus of Java: Teachings of an Authentic Taoist Immortal.__ Kosta Danaos. (Illus.). 208p. 2000. pap. 14.95 (*0-89281-813-1*, Inner Trad) Inner Tradit.
Magus of Strovolos. Kyriacos C. Markides. 236p. 1989. pap. 13.95 (*0-14-019034-1*, Penguin Bks) Viking Penguin.
Magus the Lollipop Man. Michael Mullen. (YA). 1997. pap. 4.95 (*0-86327-017-4*, Pub. by Wolfhound Press) Irish Amer Bk.
Magy la Magnifica. Don Clark. 1994. pap. 19.95 (*1-884321-02-X*); disk 9.95 (*1-884321-03-8*) Big Sky Orig.
Magyar Chambers-English Dictionary for Speakers of Hungarian. C. M. Schwarz & M. a. Seaton. 950p. (C). 1992. 65.00 (*963-05-6312-6*, Pub. by Akade Kiado) St Mut.
Magyar Culture in Socialist Romania. Radu R. Florescu. (Ethnology Ser.: No. 1). (Illus.). 1976. pap. 5.00 (*0-89304-005-3*, CCC103) Cross-Cultrl NY.
Magyar Demokraciaert (For Hungarian Democracy) Sandor Kiss. LC 83-80075. (Tanuk Korukrol Ser.). 88p. 1983. 6.00 (*0-910539-03-0*) Hungarian Alumni.
Magyar Kulpolitika Hungarista Utja see Hungarista: Ways of Hungarian Foreign Politics
*__Magyar Mozaik III.__ Rita Hegedus & Beatrix Oszko. 350 150p. 1999. pap. 52.00 (*963-05-7580-9*) Intl Spec Bk.
Magyar Nep Vedelmeben: Vitairatok es beszedek, 1955-1956. Ed. by Imre Nagy & Bela K. Kiraly. xix, 265p. (Orig.). 1984. pap. 10.00 (*0-930888-27-8*, Pub. by Dialogues Europeennes) Puski-Corvin.
Magyarorszag see Hungary
*__Magyars: Their Life & Civilization.__ Gyula Laszlo. 128p. 1999. 48.00 (*963-13-4807-5*, Pub. by Corvina Bks); pap. 21.00 (*963-13-4226-3*, Pub. by Corvina Bks) St Mut.
Magyars in the Ninth Century. Carlile A. Macartney. LC 31-19298. 253p. reprint ed. pap. 72.20 (*0-608-12055-3*, 2024496) Bks Demand.
Mah & Family Values. Morris Peavey. LC 98-170607. 128p. 1998. pap. 14.00 (*0-8059-4252-1*) Dorrance.
Mah Jong: One Step at a Time. Alain Gelbman. (Illus.). 50p. 1991. pap. 4.95 (*0-923891-35-8*, S5) Ishi Pr Intl.
Mah Jong: The Rules for Playing the Chinese Game. 2nd ed. Tze-Chung Li. 79p. 1991. pap. 12.95 (*0-937256-02-1*) Chinese Cult Serv.
Mah Jong, Anyone: A Manual of Modern Play. Kitty Strauser & Lucille Evans. LC 64-16009. (Illus.). 60p. 1964. bds. 12.95 (*0-8048-0390-0*) Tuttle Pubng.
Mah Jong for Beginners. rev. ed. Shozo Kanai & Margaret Farrell. LC 58-12108. (Illus.). 64p. 1955. bds. 10.95 (*0-8048-0391-9*) Tuttle Pubng.
Mah Jong Handbook: How to Play, Score, & Win the Modern Game. Eleanor N. Whitney. LC 64-17162. (Illus.). 176p. 1964. 16.95 (*0-8048-0392-7*) Tuttle Pubng.
Mah Jong Player's Companion. Patricia A. Thompson. 1998. pap. 12.95 (*0-86417-891-3*, Pub. by Kangaroo Pr) Seven Hills Bk.
Mah Jong Unlimited. Tong S. Tjoa. (Illus.). 168p. 1998. pap. 14.00 (*0-8059-4367-6*) Dorrance.
Mah-Jongg. Dieter Kohnen. LC 98-21164. (Illus.). 64p. 1998. 7.95 (*0-8069-0752-5*) Sterling.
Mah la'Asot: What Should I Do?: A Book of Ethical Problems & Jewish Responses. Janis Alper & Joel Lurie Grishaver. (Illus.). 64p. (Orig.). (J). (gr. 4-8). 1992. pap. text 5.50 (*0-933873-69-7*) Torah Aura.
Maha Bodhi Tree in Anuradhapura, Sri Lanka: The Oldest Historical Tree in the World. H. S. Nissanka. (C). 1994. 32.00 (*0-7069-7063-2*, Pub. by Vikas) S Asia.

M

An Asterisk (*) at the beginning of an entry indicates that the title is appearing for the first time.

Maha Calisa Samgraha: An Anthology of Calisas & Aratis Forming Part of the Hindu Religious Poetry & Public Worship Text in Nagari & Roman Scripts with Hindi & English Translation. Ed. by R. C. Prasad. Tr. by Atma R. Sharma. (C). 1994. 14.00 (*81-208-1199-2*, Pub. by Motilal Bnarsidass) S Asia.

Maha Kaccana: Master of Doctrinal Exposition. Bhikkhu Bodhi. 56p. 1995. 3.75 (*955-24-0138-0*, Pub. by Buddhist Pub Soc) Vipassana Res Pubns.

Maha Kala in the Center. Roberto Valenza. (Illus.). 48p. 1994. pap. 7.00 (*1-878888-17-X*) Nine Muses Books.

Maha-Vairocana-Abhisambodhi Tantra: With Buddhaguhya's Commentary. Stephen Hodge. (Studies in Tantric Traditions). 388p. (C). 1999. text 65.00 (*0-7007-1183-X*, Pub. by Curzon Pr Ltd) UH Pr.

Mahabharata. William Buck. (Illus.). 1973. pap. 17.95 (*0-520-04393-6*, Pub. by U CA Pr) Cal Prin Full Svc.

Mahabharata. Chakravarti Rajagopalachari. 1979. pap. 7.95 (*0-89744-929-0*) Auromere.

***Mahabharata.** Illus. by Shirley Triest. 451p. 2000. pap. 17.95 (*0-520-22704-2*) U CA Pr.

Mahabharata. Virendra Verma & K. K. Mohindroo. 202p. (C). 1997. pap. 80.00 (*81-209-0031-6*, Pub. by Pitambar Pub) St Mut.

Mahabharata. Virendra Verma & Paresh Saxena. 202p. (C). 1997. 150.00 (*81-209-0732-9*, Pub. by Pitambar Pub) St Mut.

Mahabharata. John Murdoch. 160p. 1986. reprint ed. 14.00 (*0-8364-1762-3*, Pub. by Manohar) S Asia.

Mahabharata. R. K. Narayan. (C). 1989. reprint ed. 8.00 (*81-7094-001-X*, Pub. by Vision) S Asia.

Mahabharata, Bks. 6 & 7. Gitomer. 1995. lib. bdg. 34.95 (*0-226-25247-7*) U Ch Pr.

Mahabharata, Set. Ed. & Tr. by J. A. Van Buitenen from SAN. LC 72-97802. 1999. lib. bdg. 40.00 (*0-226-84650-4*) U Ch Pr.

Mahabharata, 2 bks., Set, Bks. 2 & 3. Ed. & Tr. by J. A. Van Buitenen. LC 75-5067. 880p. 1981. pap. text 32.50 (*0-226-84664-4*) U Ch Pr.

Mahabharata: A Literary Study. Krishna Chaitanya. 462p. 1993. 39.95 (*81-85120-04-8*) Asia Bk Corp.

***Mahabharata: A Shortened Modern Prose Version of the Indian Epic.** R. K. Narayan. LC 00-33776. 2000. pap. write for info. (*0-226-56822-9*) U Ch Pr.

***Mahabharata: An English Version Based on Selected Verses.** C. V. Narasimhan et al. LC 98-148375. (Illus.). 1998. text 16.50 (*0-231-02624-2*) Col U Pr.

Mahabharata: An English Version Based on Selected Verses. rev. ed. Chakravarthi V. Narasimhan. LC 98-148375. 254p. 1997. pap. 18.50 (*0-231-11055-3*) Col U Pr.

Mahabharata: Bhagvat-Geeta. Intro. by George Hendrick. LC 59-6527. 174p. 1972. reprint ed. 50.00 (*0-8201-1109-0*) Schol Facsimiles.

Mahabharata: The Book of the Beginning, Vol. 1, Bk. 1. J. A. Van Buitenen. LC 72-97802. (Illus.). lii, 544p. 1980. pap. text 24.95 (*0-226-84663-6*, P879) U Ch Pr.

Mahabharata: The Book of Virata & the Book of Effort, Vol. 3, Bks. 4 & 5. J. A. Van Buitenen. LC 72-97802. (Illus.). x, 582p. (C). 1983. pap. text 29.00 (*0-226-84665-2*) U Ch Pr.

***Mahabharata: The Condensed Version of the World's Greatest Epic.** abr. ed. Krishna Dharma. (Illus.). 288p. 2000. 19.95 (*1-887089-25-X*, Pub. by Torchlght Pub) Natl Bk Netwk.

Mahabharata: The Fifth Veda. Purnaprajna Das. Ed. by Nityananda Das. 752p. 1998. pap. 17.95 (*0-923519-08-4*) New Jaipur.

Mahabharata: The Greatest Spiritual Epic of All Time. Krishna Dharma. LC 98-50280. (Illus.). 960p. 1999. 39.95 (*1-887089-17-9*) Torchlght Pub.

Mahabharata: The Story of the Great War. Annie W. Besant. 1992. pap. 12.50 (*81-7059-183-X*, 7605, Quest) Theos Pub Hse.

Mahabharata: The Tharu Barka Naach. Kurt W. Meyer. Tr. by Ashok Tharu & Dinesh Rai. (Illus.). 124p. 1998. 18.00 (*0-9666742-2-7*); pap. 10.00 (*0-9666742-0-0*) Rusca Pr.

Mahabharata Vol. I: The Stories of the Great Epic. Swami Satyeswarananda Giri Babaji. LC 93-84705. (Illus.). 528p. 1993. pap. text 20.00 (*1-877854-24-7*) Sanskrit Classics.

Mahabharata Vol. 2: Spiritual Interpretation. Swami Satyeswarananda Giri. (Illus.). 421p. (Orig.). 1986. pap. 20.00 (*1-877854-09-3*) Sanskrit Classics.

Mahabharata, An English Abridgement with Introduction, Notes & Review. Ed. by John Murdoch. 1987. reprint ed. 12.00 (*0-8364-2042-X*, Pub. by Usha) S Asia.

Mahabharata Is Believable. Subash Mazumdar. LC 97-66792. 128p. 1997. 14.95 (*1-887750-60-6*) Rutledge Bks.

Mahabharata of Krishna-Dwaipayana Vyasa, 12 vols., Set. Kisari M. Ganguly. 1988. reprint ed. 275.00 (*81-215-0094-X*, Pub. by M Manoharial) Coronet Bks.

Mahabharata of Vyasa. P. Lal. 400p. 1980. 15.95 (*0-7069-1033-8*); 29.95 (*0-318-37171-5*) Asia Bk Corp.

Mahabhasya of Patanjali. Surendranath Dasgupta. (C). 1991. 20.00 (*81-215-0530-5*, Pub. by M Manoharial) Coronet Bks.

Mahabohdi: or The Great Buddhist Temple under the Bohdl Tree at Buddha-Gaya. Alexander Cunningham. LC 78-72402. reprint ed. 28.00 (*0-404-17264-4*) AMS Pr.

Mahabone: or The Grand Lodge Door Opened Wherein Is Discovered the Whole Secrets of Freemasonry Both Ancient & Modern. 66p. 1996. reprint ed. pap. 14.95 (*1-56459-994-9*) Kessinger Pub.

MaHaBote Families. Eric Solibakke. 140p. 1997. pap. 18.00 (*0-86690-472-7*, s3688-014) Am Fed Astrologers.

Mahadev Govind Ranade. Ed. by Verinder Grover. (C). 1991. 52.00 (*81-7100-245-5*, Pub. by Deep & Deep Pubns) S Asia.

Mahadev Govind Ranade: Socio-Economic Ideology. S. R. Bakshi. (Indian Freedom Fighters Ser.: No. 41). 1993. 34.00 (*81-7041-605-1*, Pub. by Anmol) S Asia.

Mahadevi Varma & the Chhayavad Age of Modern Hindi Poetry. Karine Schomer. (Illus.). 350p. 1998. pap. text 16.95 (*0-19-564450-6*) OUP.

Mahakam. Robert Meijn. LC 98-85360. 192p. 1999. pap. 11.95 (*1-56315-193-6*, Pub. by SterlingHse) Natl Bk Netwk.

Mahakassapa: Father of the Sangha. Hellmuth Hecker. 40p. 1987. 1.50 (*955-24-0026-0*, Pub. by Buddhist Pub Soc) Vipassana Res Pubns.

***Mahale: A Photographic Encounter with Chimpanzees.** Angelika Hofer et al. 2000. 24.95 (*0-8069-5889-8*) Sterling.

Mahalia Jackson: Born to Sing Gospel Music. Evelyn Witter. (Sower Ser.). (Illus.). 128p. (J). (gr. 5-9). 1985. pap. 7.99 (*0-88062-045-5*) Mott Media.

Mahalia Jackson: Gospel Singer see Women of Achievement

Mahalia Jackson: Gospel Singer. Darlene Donloe. (Black American Ser.). (Illus.). 192p. (YA). 1992. mass mkt. 4.95 (*0-87067-893-0*, Melrose Sq) Holloway.

Mahalia Jackson: The Queen of Gospel Song. Leslie Gourse. (Impact Biographies Ser.). (Illus.). (YA). (gr. 10-12). 1996. lib. bdg. 23.60 (*0-531-11228-4*) Watts.

Mahalia Jackson, Young Gospel Singer. Montrew Dunham. (Childhood of Famous Americans Ser.). (J). 1995. 10.05 (*0-606-07829-0*) Turtleback.

Mahamudra: Boundless Joy & Freedom. Ole Nydahl. Tr. by Hannah Nydahl from TIB. LC 91-26450. (Illus.). 96p. (Orig.). 1991. pap. 9.95 (*0-931892-69-4*) B Dolphin Pub.

Mahamudra Teachings of the Supreme Siddhas: The Eighth Situpa, Tanpa' Nyinchay on "The Aspiration Prayer on Mahamudra of Definitive Meaning" by the Third Karmapa, Rangjung Dorje. Tr. by Lama S. Dorje. LC 93-40280. 208p. 1995. pap. 15.95 (*1-55939-025-5*) Snow Lion Pubns.

Mahan Is Not Enough: The Proceedings of a Conference on the Works of Sir Julian Corbett & Admiral Sir Herbert Richmond. Ed. by John B. Hattendorf & James Goldrick. LC 93-32581. (Historical Monographs: No. 10). 416p. (Orig.). 1993. pap. 10.00 (*0-9637973-1-X*) Naval War Coll.

Mahan on Naval Warface: Selections from the Writings of Rear Admiral Alfred T. Mahan. Alfred Thayer Mahan. LC 99-30216. 416p. 1999. pap. text 13.95 (*0-486-40729-2*) Dover.

Mahanabi Sharanika. Ahmad Nawaz. LC 98-70821. (BEN.). xiv, 84p. 1998. pap. 10.00 (*1-58225-138-X*) Ananta Prakashani.

Mahanarayana Upanisad. Tr. by Swami Vimalananda from SAN. 1979. pap. 8.95 (*81-7120-331-0*) Vedanta Pr.

Mahanga: Pacific Poems. Vernice W. Pere. 40p. (C). 1978. pap. 4.50 (*0-939154-02-1*) Inst Polynesian.

Mahanirvana Tantra with the Commentary of Hariharananda Bharati. Arthur Avalon, pseud. (C). 1989. 27.00 (*81-208-0541-0*, Pub. by Motilal Bnarsidass) S Asia.

Maharaj: A Biography of Shriman Tapasviji Maharaj, a Mahatma Who Lived for 185 Years, 1767-1952. rev. ed. T. S. Murthy. 246p. 1986. pap. 8.95 (*0-913922-17-X*) Dawn Horse Pr.

***Maharajas' Jewels.** Katherine Prior & John Adamson. (Illus.). 208p. 2000. 67.50 (*0-86565-218-X*) Vendome.

Maharajas' Palaces: European Style in Imperial India. Sylvie Raulet. LC 97-5250. (Illus.). 297p. 1997. text 85.00 (*0-86565-989-3*) Vendome.

Maharal: The Story of Rabbi Yehudah Loew. Yaacor D. Shulman. LC 92-73906. 236p. (J). (gr. 5-9). 1992. 17.95 (*1-56062-168-0*) CIS Comm.

Maharashta Purana: An Eighteenth Century Bengali Historical Text. Gangarama. Tr. by Edward C. Dimock, Jr. & Pratul C. Gupta. LC 64-63437. 115p. reprint ed. pap. 35.70 (*0-608-11617-3*, 200135400076) Bks Demand.

Maharashtra Shabadakosh. Datta Karve et al. 1988. reprint ed. 85.00 (*81-206-0375-3*, Pub. by Asian Educ Servs) S Asia.

***Maharashtrian Cuisine.** S. Marathe. 1998. pap. 50.00 (*81-86982-12-4*, Pub. by Business Pubns) St Mut.

Maharishi: The Biography of the Man Who Gave Transcendental Meditation to the West. P. Mason. 1994. pap. 24.95 (*1-85230-571-1*, Pub. by Element MA) Penguin Putnam.

Maharishi Ayur-Veda Global Campaign to Create a Disease-Free Society in Every Country. LC 91-71302. (Illus.). 1991. write for info. (*0-89186-054-1*) Age Enlight Pr.

Maharishi Effect - Creating Coherence in World Consciousness: Promoting Positive & Evolutionary Trends Throughout the World. LC 90-61981. (Illus.). 90p. 1990. pap. 8.00 (*0-923569-08-1*, B-08) Maharishi U Mgmt Pr.

Maharishi Forum of Natural Law & National Law for Doctors: Perfect Health for Everyone Disease-Free Society. 2nd rev. ed. Maharishi M. Yogi. 480p. 1995. pap. 15.00 (*81-7523-003-7*, A15) Maharishi U Mgmt Pr.

Maharishi Gandharva-Ved, Creating Balance in Nature & Harmony in World Consciousness. LC 90-56341. (Global Achievements Ser.). (Illus.). 212p. (Orig.). 1991. pap. 19.95 (*0-89186-053-3*) Age Enlight Pr.

Maharishi International University: Scholarly Exchange with the Universities of China. (Illus.). 212p. 1985. pap. 12.50 (*0-948804-00-9*, C06) Maharishi U Mgmt Pr.

***Maharishi Mahesh Yogi: A Living Saint for the New Millennium.** Theresa Olson. 1999. pap. text. write for info. (*1-57582-040-4*) Samhita Enterprises.

Maharishi Mahesh Yogi on the Bhagavad-Gita: A New Translation & Commentary, Chapters 1-6. Tr. by Mahesh Yogi. 496p. 1990. pap. 14.95 (*0-14-019247-6*, Arkana) Viking Penguin.

Maharishi Technology of the Unified Field: The Neurophysiology of Enlightenment. Robert K. Wallace. LC 86-61345. 368p. (Orig.). 1986. pap. 11.95 (*0-9616944-0-8*) MIU Neurosci Pr.

Maharishi University of Management: Wholeness on the Move. Maharishi M. Yogi. Orig. Title: Maharishi's Absolute Theory of Management. (Illus.). 352p. 1995. pap. 15.00 (*81-7523-001-0*, A17) Maharishi U Mgmt Pr.

Maharishi Vedic University - Introduction: Vedic Knowledge for Everyone. 2nd ed. Maharishi M. Yogi. 362p. 1994. pap. 15.00 (*90-71750-17-5*, A19) Maharishi U Mgmt Pr.

Maharishi's Absolute Theory of Government: Automation in Administration. 2nd ed. Maharishi M. Yogi. 567p. 1995. reprint ed. pap. 15.00 (*81-7523-002-9*) Maharishi U Mgmt Pr.

Maharishi's Absolute Theory of Management see Maharishi University of Management: Wholeness on the Move

Maharishi's Programme to Create World Peace: Global Inauguration Demonstrating the Mechanics to Create Coherence in World Consciousness, the Basis of World Peace. LC 86-32102. (Illus.). 573p. 1987. pap. 16.95 (*0-89186-052-5*) Age Enlight Pr.

Mahasatipatthana Sutta: The Great Discourse on the Establishing of Awareness. rev. ed. Ed. by Vipassana Research Institute Staff. LC 96-22631. 96p. 1996. pap. text 6.95 (*0-9649484-0-0*) Vipassana Res Pubns.

Mahaska County (Iowa), A Story of the Early Days. Semira A. Phillips. 383p. 1993. reprint ed. lib. bdg. 42.00 (*0-8328-3520-X*) Higginson Bk Co.

Mahasutras: Great Discourses of the Buddha. Tr. by Peter Skilling. (PLI, SAN & TIB.). 951p. (C). 1994. 68.50 (*0-86013-319-2*) Wisdom MA.

Mahatma, 8 vols., Set. D. G. Tendulkar. 2850p. 1983. 150.00 (*0-934676-44-5*) Greenlf Bks.

Mahatma - Life of Mohandas Karamchand Gandhi, 8 vols., Set. D. G. Tendulkar. 1963. 160.00 (*0-318-36658-4*) Asia Bk Corp.

Mahatma & the Hare: A Dream Story. H. Rider Haggard. Ed. by R. Reginald & Douglas Melville. LC 77-92411. (Lost Race & Adult Fantasy Ser.). (Illus.). 1978. reprint ed. lib. bdg. 19.95 (*0-405-11021-9*) Ayer.

Mahatma & the Millionaire: A Study in Gandhi-Birla Relations. M. M. Juneja. (C). 1993. text 25.00 (*0-8364-2836-6*, Pub. by Manohar) S Asia.

Mahatma & the Netaji: 2 Men of Destiny of India. Samar Guha. 244p. 1986. 31.95 (*0-318-36614-2*) Asia Bk Corp.

Mahatma & the Poet: Letters & Debates Between Gandhi & Tagore, 1915-1941. Ed. by Sabyasachi Bhattacharya. 1997. reprint ed. pap. 5.00 (*81-237-2202-8*, Pub. by Natl Bk Trust) S Asia.

Mahatma Gandhi. Sankar Ghose. (C). 1991. 22.50 (*81-7023-205-8*, Pub. by Allied Pubs) S Asia.

Mahatma Gandhi. Caroline Lazo. LC 92-14314. (Peacemakers Ser.). (Illus.). 64p. (J). (gr. 4 up). 1993. lib. bdg. 13.95 (*0-87518-526-6*, Dillon Silver Burdett) Silver Burdett Pr.

Mahatma Gandhi. Romain Rolland. Tr. by Catherine Groth from FRE. 132p. (C). 1994. 10.00 (*0-934676-81-X*) Greenlf Bks.

Mahatma Gandhi, 10 vols., Set. Pyarelal. Incl. Vol. I. Early Phase, 1869-1896. 875p. 1983. 40.00 (*0-934676-41-0*); Vol. II. Discovery of Satyagraha, 1896-1902. 445p. 1983. 65.00 (*0-934676-42-9*); Vol. III. Birth of Satyagraha, 1902-1906. 648p. 1983. 40.00 (*0-934676-73-9*); Vol. IX. Last Phase, 1944-7 (Part One) (Illus.). 742p. 1983. 75.00 (*0-934676-43-7*); (Illus.), 7200p. 1983. 585.00 (*0-934676-86-0*) Greenlf Bks.

Mahatma Gandhi: A Bibliography, 2. April Carter. LC 94-46929. (Bibliographies of World Leaders Ser.: No. 2). 184p. 1995. lib. bdg. 65.00 (*0-313-28296-X*, Greenwood Pr) Greenwood.

Mahatma Gandhi: A Biography. B. R. Nanda. 541p. 1989. 34.95 (*0-318-36657-6*) Asia Bk Corp.

Mahatma Gandhi: A Biography: Complete. unabridged ed. B. R. Nanda. (Oxford India Paperbacks Ser.). (Illus.). 542p. (C). 1996. pap. 18.95 (*0-19-563855-7*) OUP.

Mahatma Gandhi: A Great Life in Brief. Vincent Sheean. 187p. 1990. 12.95 (*0-318-36650-9*) Asia Bk Corp.

Mahatma Gandhi: A Revaluation. Ed. by Mohit Chakrabarti. (C). 1994. 17.50 (*81-7024-635-0*, Pub. by Ashish Pub Hse) S Asia.

Mahatma Gandhi: A Study of His Message of Non-Violence. V. P. Gaur. 145p. 1977. 9.95 (*0-940500-60-4*, Pub. by Sterling) Asia Bk Corp.

Mahatma Gandhi: An East German Marxist Interpretation. Herbert Fischer. 125p. 1984. 14.00 (*0-934676-66-6*) Greenlf Bks.

Mahatma Gandhi: Congress & Its Leadership. S. R. Bakshi. (C). 1990. text 26.00 (*81-7041-256-0*, Pub. by Anmol) S Asia.

Mahatma Gandhi: Nonviolent Power in Action. Dennis Dalton. 279p. 1995. pap. 18.50 (*0-231-08119-7*) Col U Pr.

***Mahatma Gandhi: Nonviolent Power in Action.** Dennis Dalton. 2000. reprint ed. pap. 18.50 (*0-231-12237-3*) Col U Pr.

Mahatma Gandhi: Prophet of Freedom. J. Bosco. 1989. pap. 15.00 (*0-86217-266-7*, Pub. by Veritas Pubns) St Mut.

Mahatma Gandhi: The Father of Modern India. H. S. Polak et al. 1986. 49.95 (*0-318-36651-7*) Asia Bk Corp.

Mahatma Gandhi & Christianity. B. Srinivasa Murthy. 100p. (Orig.). 1998. pap. 18.95 (*0-941910-06-7*) Long Beach Pubns.

Mahatma Gandhi & Comparative Religion. rev. ed. K. L. Rao. 1990. 15.00 (*81-208-0755-3*, Pub. by Motilal Bnarsidass) S Asia.

Mahatma Gandhi & His Apostles. Ved Mehta. LC 92-83709. 28p. (C). 1993. reprint ed. pap. 17.00 (*0-300-05539-0*) Yale U Pr.

***Mahatma Gandhi & India's Independence in World History.** Ann Malaspina. LC 99-50570. (In World History Ser.). (Illus.). 128p. (YA). (gr. 5 up). 2000. lib. bdg. 20.95 (*0-7660-1398-7*) Enslow Pubs.

Mahatma Gandhi & Jawaharlal Nehru, Vol. IV. Ed. by Madhu Limaye. (C). 1991. 40.00 (*0-685-49094-7*, Pub. by BR Pub) S Asia.

Mahatma Gandhi & Jawaharlal Nehru: A Historic Partnership since 1916-1948, Vol. II. Madhu Limaye. 1989. 62.00 (*0-685-34763-X*, Pub. by BR Pub) S Asia.

Mahatma Gandhi & Jawaharlal Nehru: A Historic Partnership, 1916-1948, Vol. 3. Madhu Limaye. 1990. 50.00 (*81-7018-583-1*, Pub. by BR Pub) S Asia.

Mahatma Gandhi & Jawaharlal Nehru Vol. I: A Historic Partnership, 1916-1948. Madhu Limaye. (C). 1989. 27.50 (*81-7018-548-3*) S Asia.

Mahatma Gandhi & Jawaharlal Nehru Vol. 3: A Historic Partnership, Set. Madhu Limaye. (C). 1990. text 50.00 (*81-7018-547-5*, Pub. by BR Pub) S Asia.

***Mahatma Gandhi & Martin Luther King Jr. The Power of Nonviolent Action.** 546p. 1999. 59.00 (*92-3-103431-6*, U3431, Pub. by UNESCO) Bernan Associates.

Mahatma Gandhi & Teacher's Guide. (YA). (gr. 10). pap. text 4.95 (*1-878099-17-5*) Vidya Bks.

Mahatma Gandhi As a Linguistic Nationalist. Peter Brock. (C). 1995. pap. 9.00 (*0-945921-30-6*, Pub. by S Asia Pubs) S Asia.

Mahatma Gandhi at Work: His Own Story Continued. Mahatma Gandhi. Ed. by C. F. Andrews. LC 75-37343. (Select Bibliographies Reprint Ser.). 1977. reprint ed. 25.95 (*0-8369-6690-2*) Ayer.

Mahatma Gandhi in a Cadillac. Gerald Rosen. LC 95-18529. 275p. (Orig.). 1995. 21.95 (*1-883319-35-8*) Frog Ltd CA.

Mahatma Gandhi in a Cadillac. Gerald Rosen. LC 95-18529. 275p. (Orig.). 1995. pap. 12.95 (*1-883319-36-6*) North Atlantic.

Mahatma Gandhi the Beloved Patient. Dinshh Mehta. (Illus.). 180p. (Orig.). 1996. pap. 22.00 (*0-934676-85-2*) Greenlf Bks.

Mahatma Gandhi the Journalist. Sailendra N. Bhattacharyya. LC 84-595. (Illus.). 195p. 1984. reprint ed. lib. bdg. 55.00 (*0-313-24461-8*, BHMG, Greenwood Pr) Greenwood.

Mahatma Gandhi, 125 Years: Remembering Gandhi, Understanding Gandhi, Relevance of Gandhi. B. R. Nanda. LC 95-903287. (C). 1995. 56.00 (*81-224-0723-4*, Pub. by Wiley Estrn) Franklin.

***Mahatma Jotirao Phooley: Father of the Indian Social Revolution.** Dhananjay V. Keer. 1998. 24.00 (*81-7154-066-X*, Pub. by Popular Prakashan) S Asia.

Mahatma Letters to A. P. Sinnett. 2nd ed. Compiled by A. Trevor Barker. LC 75-10574. 590p. 1993. reprint ed. 24.95 (*0-911500-20-0*); reprint ed. pap. 16.95 (*0-911500-21-9*) Theos U Pr.

***Mahatma Letters to A. P. Sinnett: In Chronological Sequence.** Ed. by Vicente Hao Chin, Jr. 600p. 1998. pap. 26.95 (*81-7059-273-9*, Pub. by Theos Pub Hse) Natl Bk Netwk.

Mahatma I & II. Brian Grattan. 328p. (Orig.). 1994. pap. 19.95 (*0-929385-77-2*) Light Tech Pubng.

Mahatmas & Genuine Occultism. rev. ed. G. De Purucker. Ed. by Emmett Small & Helen Todd. Orig. Title: The Masters & the Path of Occultism. (Illus.). 100p. 1972. pap. 5.00 (*0-913004-07-3*) Point Loma Pub.

Mahatmas & Their Letters. Geoffrey Barborka. 1989. 24.95 (*0-8356-7062-7*) Theos Pub Hse.

Mahavairocana-Sutra. Chikyo Yamamoto. 1990. 70.00 (*81-85179-46-8*, Pub. by Aditya Prakashan) S Asia.

Mahavamsa: The Great Chronicle of Sri Lanka. Douglas Bullis & Mahanama. LC 98-12597. 480p. 1999. 70.00 (*0-89581-943-0*) Asian Humanities.

Mahavamsa: or The Great Chronicle of Ceylon. Wilhelm Geiger. 1986. reprint ed. 23.00 (*0-8364-1845-X*, Pub. by KP Bagchi) S Asia.

Mahavansi. the Raja-Ratnacari. & the Raja-Vali, Forming the Sacred & Historical Books of Ceylon, 3 vols., Set. Edward Upham. LC 78-70132. reprint ed. 115.00 (*0-404-17670-4*) AMS Pr.

Mahavastu, 3 vols., Set. Tr. by J. J. Jones from SAN. (C). 1956. 122.50 (*0-86013-261-7*) Wisdom MA.

Mahavastu, Vol. 1. Tr. by J. J. Jones from SAN. (C). 1956. 42.50 (*0-86013-041-X*) Wisdom MA.

Mahavastu, Vol. 2. Tr. by J. J. Jones from SAN. (C). 1956. 45.00 (*0-86013-042-8*) Wisdom MA.

Mahavastu, Vol. 3. Tr. by J. J. Jones from SAN. (C). 1956. 45.00 (*0-86013-043-6*) Wisdom MA.

Mahayana Buddhism. Nalinaksha Dutt. 1976. reprint ed. 11.00 (*0-8364-0430-0*) S Asia.

Mahayana Buddhism. rev. ed. Nalinaksha Dutt. 1978. 22.00 (*0-89684-032-8*, Pub. by Motilal Bnarsidass) S Asia.

Mahayana Buddhism: An Approach to Its Essence. Yoshifumi Ueda. Ed. by Masao Kodani. Tr. by Taitetsu Unno from JPN. 80p. (Orig.). (C). 1989. pap. 8.00 (*1-877604-02-X*) Pure Land.

Mahayana Buddhism: The Doctrinal Foundations. Paul Williams. 272p. 1989. 55.00 (*0-415-02536-2*) Routledge.

Mahayana Buddhism: The Doctrinal Foundations. Paul Williams. 272p. (C). 1989. pap. 25.99 (*0-415-02537-0*) Routledge.

Mahayana Buddhist Meditation: Theory & Practice. Ed. by Minoru Kiyota. 1991. reprint ed. text 19.50 (*81-208-0760-X*, Pub. by Motilal Bnarsidass) S Asia.

M

An Asterisk (*) at the beginning of an entry indicates that the title is appearing for the first time.

***Mahayana Buddhist Texts from Nepal: Narratives & Rituals of Newar Buddhism.** Todd T. Lewis. LC 99-45350. (C). 2000. text 59.50 (*0-7914-4611-5*) State U NY Pr.

***Mahayana Buddhist Texts from Nepal: Popular Buddhist Texts from Nepal.** Todd T. Lewis. LC 99-45350. (C). 2000. pap. text 19.95 (*0-7914-4612-3*) State U NY Pr.

Mahayana Way to Buddhahood. Susumu Yamaguchi. Tr. by Buddhist Books International from JPN. LC 82-4416. 1982. 14.95 (*0-914910-11-6*) Buddhist Bks.

Mahayanasutralamkara by 'Asanga' Tr. by Surekha V. Limaye. (Bibliotheca Indo-Buddhica Ser.: No. 94). (C). 1992. 54.00 (*81-7030-347-8*) S Asia.

Mahdi. large type ed. A. J. Quinnell. (Adventure Suspense Ser.). 416p. 1982. 27.99 (*0-7089-8081-3*, Charnwood) Ulverscroft.

Mahdi: A Millennium Thriller. Margo Dockendorf. LC 98-74708. 440p. 1999. 24.95 (*1-879384-35-3*) Cypress Hse.

Mahdi: The Last Refuge of Human Beings. H. Feridouni. 32p. (Orig.). 1989. pap. text 2.25 (*1-871031-18-4*) Abjad Bk.

Mahdi of Allah: The Story of the Dervish, Mohammed Ahmed. Richard A. Bermann. Tr. by Robin John. LC 80-1935. reprint ed. 36.00 (*0-404-18955-5*) AMS Pr.

Mahdiism & Egyptian Sudan. 2nd ed. F. R. Wingate. (Illus.). 618p. 1993. reprint ed. 55.00 (*0-7146-1738-5*, Pub. by F Cass Pubs) Intl Spec Bk.

Mahdism in West Africa: The Ijebu Mahdiyya Movement. Peter B. Clarke. 224p. 1996. 35.00 (*1-898942-06-4*, Pub. by Luzac Oriental) Weatherhill.

Mahealani & the King of Hawaii. Rianna M. Williams. (Illus.). 104p. (J). (gr. 4-9). 1997. write for info. (*0-9658621-0-0*) Ka Mea.

Maher, Waller & Derham: Legal Process: Commentary & Materials. 5th ed. M. D. Smith & K. S. Pose. xxx, 593p. 1988. pap. 63.00 (*0-455-20783-6*, Pub. by LawBk Co) Gaunt.

Maher, Waller & Derham: Legal Process: Commentary & Materials. 5th ed. Malcom D. Smith & K. S. Pose. xxx, 593p. 1988. 85.00 (*0-455-20784-4*, Pub. by LawBk Co) Gaunt.

Maher, Waller & Derham: Legal Process: Commentary & Materials. 6th ed. Malcolm D. Smith et al. 640p. 1994. pap. 72.00 (*0-455-21228-7*, Pub. by LawBk Co) Gaunt.

Mahilaka: An Archaeological Investigation of an Early Town in Northwestern Madagascar. Marie de Chantal Radimilahy. LC 99-159010. 293p. 1998. write for info. (*91-506-1313-8*) Uppsala Universitet.

Mahimnastavae: or Mahimna Stotra. W. Norman Brown. 1983. reprint ed. 20.00 (*0-8364-1001-7*, Pub. by Motilal Bnarsidass) S Asia.

Mahina Tiare, Pacific Passages. Barbara Marrett & John Neal. LC 92-91094. (Illus.). 306p. 1993. 27.95 (*0-918074-05-3*) Pacific Intl.

Mahina Tiare, Pacific Passages. Barbara Marrett & John Neal. LC 92-91094. (Illus.). 306p. 1994. pap. 19.95 (*0-918074-04-5*) Pacific Intl.

Mahi's Story. Gohar Kordi. 134p. 1997. pap. 11.95 (*0-7043-4373-8*, Pub. by Womens Press) Trafalgar.

Mahisasura in Art & Thought. Upendra N. Dhal. (Illus.). 95p. (C). 1991. 24.00 (*81-85133-47-6*, Pub. by Eastern Bk Linkers) Nataraj Bks.

Mahishasuramardini in Indian Art. Shanti L. Nagar. (C). 1988. 74.00 (*81-85179-09-3*, Pub. by Aditya Prakashan) S Asia.

Mahlen Oder Malen? (Duden-Taschenbuch Ser.: No. 13). 191p. 1971. 12.25 (*3-411-01143-2*, Pub. by Bibliogr Inst Brockhaus) Langenscheidt.

Mahler. Edward Seckerson. (Illustrated Lives of the Great Composers Ser.). (Illus.). 150p. 1996. 17.95 (*0-7119-0259-3*, OP 42456) Omnibus NY.

Mahler: A Biography. Jonathan Carr. LC 97-9520. (Illus.). 272p. 1997. 29.95 (*0-87951-802-2*, Pub. by Overlook Pr) Penguin Putnam.

Mahler: A Biography. Jonathan Carr. 254p. 1999. pap. 16.95 (*0-87951-887-1*, Pub. by Overlook Pr) Penguin Putnam.

Mahler: A Musical Physiognomy. Theodor W. Adorno. Tr. by Edmund Jephcott. LC 88-14248. 192p. 1992. 30.00 (*0-226-00768-5*) U Ch Pr.

Mahler: A Musical Physiognomy. Theodor W. Adorno. 178p. (C). 1996. reprint ed. pap. text 14.00 (*0-226-00769-3*) U Ch Pr.

***Mahler: Das Lied von der Erde.** Stephen E. Hefling. (Cambridge Music Handbooks Ser.). (Illus.). 128p. (C). 2000. 44.95 (*0-521-47534-1*); pap. 15.95 (*0-521-47558-9*) Cambridge U Pr.

***Mahler: His Life, Work & World.** Kurt Blaukopf & Herta Blaukopf. LC 91-65994. (Illus.). 256p. 2000. pap. 27.50 (*0-500-28197-1*, Pub. by Thames Hudson) Norton.

Mahler: "Symphony, No. 3" Peter Franklin. (Cambridge Music Handbooks Ser.). (Illus.). 141p. (C). 1991. text 39.95 (*0-521-37071-X*); pap. text 12.95 (*0-521-37947-4*) Cambridge U Pr.

Mahler & Kohut: Perspectives on Development, Psychopathology, & Technique. Ed. by Selma Kramer & Salman Akhtar. LC 93-38650. 200p. 1994. 40.00 (*1-56821-156-2*) Aronson.

Mahler Companion. Ed. by Donald Mitchell & Andrew Nicholson. LC 98-45827. (Illus.). 656p. 1999. text 75.00 (*0-19-816376-2*) OUP.

Mahler, Consciousness & Temporality. David B. Greene. x, 314p. 1984. text 33.00 (*0-677-06160-9*) Gordon & Breach.

Mahler der Sitten, Bd. 2. Ed. by Johann J. Bodmer & Johann J. Breitinger. (GER.). 1285p. 1972. reprint ed. write for info. (*3-487-04242-8*) G Olms Pubs.

Mahler Functions & Transcendence. Kumiko Nishioka. LC 96-33383. (Lecture Notes in Mathematics Ser.: Vol. 153). 185p. 1996. pap. 35.00 (*3-540-61472-9*) Spr-Verlag.

***Mahler Remembered.** Norman Lebrecht. (Illus.). 336p. 2001. pap. 16.00 (*0-571-14692-9*) Faber & Faber.

Mahler Studies. Ed. by Stephen E. Hefling. LC 96-10284. (Illus.). 322p. (C). 1997. text 64.95 (*0-521-47165-6*) Cambridge U Pr.

***Mahler's Fourth Symphony.** James L. Zychowicz. (Illus.). 288p. 2000. text 65.00 (*0-19-816206-5*) OUP.

Mahler's Problem in Metric Number Theory. V. G. Sprindzuk. Tr. by B. Volkmann. LC 73-86327. (Translations of Mathematical Monographs: Vol. 25). 192p. 1969. text 35.00 (*0-8218-1575-X*, MMONO/25) Am Math.

Mahler's 7th Symphony: A Symposium. Henry L. De La Grange & Herta Blaukopf. Ed. by James L. Zychowicz. 148p. 1991. pap. 15.95 (*0-89579-391-1*) A-R Eds.

Mahler's 6th Symphony: A Study. Norman R. Del Mar. (Eulenburg Music Ser.). (Illus.). 153p. 1982. reprint ed. pap. 22.50 (*0-903873-29-X*) Da Capo.

Mahler's 6th Symphony: A Study in Musical Semiotics. Robert Samuels. (Studies in Music Theory & Analysis: No. 6). 191p. (C). 1996. text 54.95 (*0-521-48166-X*) Cambridge U Pr.

Mahmood of Ghazni. Fazl Ahmad. (Heroes of Islam Ser.: Bk. 8). 120p. (Orig.). (YA). (gr. 7-12). 1984. pap. 3.50 (*1-56744-246-3*) Kazi Pubns.

Mahmud Shabistari The Secret Garden. Johnson Pasha. 1999. 17.00 (*0-86304-019-5*) Octagon Pr.

Mahmud Shaltut & Islamic Modernism. Kate Zebiri. 204p. 1996. 45.00 (*0-614-21201-4*, 749) Kazi Pubns.

Mahmud's Diary: The Diary of Mirza Mahmud-i-Zarqani - Chronicling Abdu'l-Baha's Journey to America. Mahmud-i-Zarqani. Tr. by Mohi Sobhani & Shirley Macias from PER. (Illus.). 600p. 1998. 39.95 (*0-85398-418-2*) G Ronald Pub.

Mahnke Grammar. Dan Mahnke. Date not set. pap. text 13.77 (*0-395-94523-2*); pap. text 13.77 (*0-395-94525-9*) HM.

Mahnke Grammar: Level 1. Dan Mahnke. Date not set. pap. text 23.67 incl. audio (*0-395-94520-8*) HM.

Mahnke Grammar Links. Dan Mahnke. Date not set. pap. text 19.77 (*0-395-82884-8*); pap. text 9.87 (*0-395-82885-6*); pap. text 9.87 (*0-395-82886-4*) HM.

Mahogany & Other Stories. Boris Pilnyak. Tr. by Vera T. Reck & Michael Green. (RUS.). 302p. 1993. pap. 16.95 (*0-87501-104-7*) Ardis Pubs.

Mahogany Ship Relic or Legend? Bill Potter. 130p. 1987. pap. 30.00 (*0-949759-09-0*, Pub. by Deakin Univ) St Mut.

Mahoma. Juan Vernet. (Nueva Austral Ser.: No. 2). (SPA.). 1991. pap. text 24.95 (*84-239-1802-5*) Elliots Bks.

Mahomed: Ghazals Erbe. Carl-Heinz Domken. (GER.). 104p. 1986. write for info. (*3-487-08338-8*) G Olms Pubs.

Mahomet & His Successors, Vol. 1. Washington Irving. 368p. 1985. 240.00 (*1-85077-045-X*, Pub. by Darf Pubs Ltd) St Mut.

Mahomet & His Successors, Vol. 2. Washington Irving. 512p. 1985. 300.00 (*1-85077-046-8*, Pub. by Darf Pubs Ltd) St Mut.

Mahomet & Islam. W. Muir. 256p. 1986. 220.00 (*1-85077-085-9*, Pub. by Darf Pubs Ltd) St Mut.

Mahommedan Law, 2 vols. Ed. by Syed A. Ali. (C). 1985. 900.00 (*0-7855-6734-8*, Pub. by Himalayan Bks); 450.00 (*81-7002-013-1*, Pub. by Himalayan Bks); write for info. (*81-7002-012-3*, Pub. by Himalayan Bks) St Mut.

Mahoning. A. F. Moritz. LC 95-123824. (Illus.). 112p. 1994. pap. 11.95 (*0-919626-73-4*, Pub. by Brick Bks) Genl Dist Srvs.

Mahoning Memories: A History of Youngstown & Mahoning County. Frederick J. Blue et al. 1995. write for info. (*0-89865-944-2*) Donning Co.

Mahoning Valley Poetry. Ed. by Julie Brown & Robert Brown. (Illus.). 150p. (Orig.). 1993. pap. 8.00 (*0-9637849-3-5*) Bacchae Pr.

Mahonri M. Young. Frank J. Mather, Jr. (Illus.). 59p. (Orig.). 1940. pap. write for info. (*1-879886-05-7*) Addison Gallery.

Mahonri Young: His Life & Art. Thomas E. Toone. LC 96-21198. (Illus.). 220p. 1997. 75.00 (*1-56085-055-8*) Signature Bks.

Mahorun Badlai Gayun (Gujerati) large type ed. Gulshan Nanda. (Charnwood Large Print Ser.). 1990. 27.99 (*0-7089-2271-6*, Charnwood) Ulverscroft.

Mahrajan Alijja. Sonia Beiruti. Ed. by Ramzi Kaliffe. (Silsilat Daliluki Sayidati (Woman's Guide) Ser.: No. 6).Tr. of Omelets. (ARA., Illus.). 40p. 1990. pap. 8.50 (*1-58311-029-1*) Eastern Corp.

Mahseer in the Rivers of Nepal Disrupted by Dams & Ranching Strategies. Tej K. Shrestha. 1997. pap. 114.00 (*0-7855-7432-8*, Pub. by Ratna Pustak Bhandar) St Mut.

Mahsuri: The Legend of Langkawi. F. I. Rejab. (Illus.). 40p. (J). 1995. 9.95 (*983-9808-24-9*, Pub. by Delta Edits) Weatherhill.

Mahu: or The Material. Robert Pinget. Tr. by Alan Sheridan-Smith from FRE. 144p. (Orig.). (C). 1985. pap. 8.95 (*0-7145-0354-1*) Riverrun NY.

Mahua: The Tree of the Poor. Ram Prasas. 87p. 1993. pap. 100.00 (*81-7089-168-X*, Pub. by Intl Bk Distr) St Mut.

Mahuts & Annwm Aval: 2 Full-Length Video Theatre Plays. David Seals. Tr. by Arthwyr A. Meurig & Pierre Jakez-Helias from CHY. (7 Council Fires of Sweet Medicine Ser.: Acts 4 & 5). (Illus.). (C). 1996. audio 17.00 (*1-887786-31-7*); audio 17.00 (*1-887786-30-9*) Sky & Sage Bks.

Mahuts & Annwm Aval: 2 Full-Length Video Theatre Plays. David Seals. Tr. by Arthwyr A. Meurig & Pierre Jakez-Helias from CHY. (7 Council Fires of Sweet Medicine Ser.: Acts 4 & 5). (Illus.). 250p. (C). 1996. 20.00 (*1-887786-14-7*) Sky & Sage Bks.

Mahzor Hadash: A New High Holiday Prayer Book. deluxe rev. ed. Sidney Greenberg & Jonathan D. Levine. 17.50 (*0-317-56071-9*) Prayer Bk.

Mahzor Hadash: A New High Holiday Prayer Book. rev. ed. Sidney Greenberg & Jonathan D. Levine. 15.95 (*0-87677-075-8*) Prayer Bk.

Mahzor Hashalem: High Holiday Prayer Book, Vol. 1, Rosh Hashahah. Philip Birnbaum. 646p. 1988. 24.00 (*0-88482-246-X*) Hebrew Pub.

Mahzor Hashalem: High Holyday Prayer Book, 5 vols. Philip Birnbaum. 1971. 98.00 (*0-88482-169-2*) Hebrew Pub.

Mahzor Hashalem: High Holyday Prayer Book. Philip Birnbaum. 1042p. 1979. 27.00 (*0-88482-240-0*) Hebrew Pub.

Mahzor Hashalem: High Holyday Prayer Book, 2 vols. Philip Birnbaum. 1988. 44.00 (*0-88482-170-6*) Hebrew Pub.

Mahzor Hashalem: Prayer Book for Pesah, Vol. 4. Philip Birnbaum. 459p. 1971. 20.00 (*0-88482-172-2*) Hebrew Pub.

Mahzor Hashalem: Prayer Book for Shavuot, Vol. 5. Philip Birnbaum. 358p. 1971. 20.00 (*0-88482-173-0*) Hebrew Pub.

Mahzor Hashalem: Prayer Book for Sukkot, Vol. 3. Philip Birnbaum. 478p. 1971. 20.00 (*0-88482-174-9*) Hebrew Pub.

Mahzor Hashalem High Holiday Prayer Book Vol. 2: Yom Kippur. Philip Birnbaum. 770p. 1988. 24.00 (*0-88482-247-8*) Hebrew Pub.

Mahzor Leshalosh Regalim: Prayer Book for Three Festivals. Philip Birnbaum. 641p. 1971. 24.50 (*0-88482-149-8*) Hebrew Pub.

Mai. Marina Carr. LC 95-182206. 72p. 1997. pap. 14.95 (*1-85235-161-6*) Dufour.

Mai. Marina Carr. LC 95-182206. 72p. 1997. 24.95 (*1-85235-162-4*, Pub. by Gallery Pr) Dufour.

Mai: The Multilateral Agreement on Investment & the Threat to American Democracy. Maude Barlow & Tony Clarke. LC 98-232312. 120p. 1998. pap. 9.95 (*0-7737-5979-4*) Stoddart Publ.

***Mai Affair: A Story & Its Lessons.** David Henderson. 2000. pap. 16.95 (*1-86203-039-1*) Royal Inst Intl Affairs.

***Mai Am un Singur Dor: Simpozion Ocazional de Aniversarea a 145 Ani de la Nasterea Luceafarului: Poezie - Romanesti.** 2nd ed. Theodor Damian et al. (RUM., Illus.). 52p. 1998. pap. write for info. (*1-888067-05-5*) Romanian Inst.

Mai am un Singur Dor: Simpozion Occazional de Aniversarea a 145 ani de la Nasterea Luceafarului Poeziel Romanesti. Mihail Eminescu et al. 56p. 1996. pap. 3.00 (*1-888067-02-0*) Romanian Inst.

Mai Chanuka. Menachem M. Schneerson. (HEB.). 36p. 1994. pap. 3.00 (*0-8266-5275-1*) Kehot Pubn Soc.

Mai I Rangiatea: Maori Wellbeing & Development. Ed. by Pania T. Whaiti et al. 250p. 1998. pap. 29.95 (*1-86940-135-2*, Pub. by Auckland Univ) Paul & Co Pubs.

Mai Jing see Pulse Classic: A Translation of the Mai Jing

Mai-Li's Surprise see Sorpresa de Mai-Li

Mai-Li's Surprise. Marjorie Jackson. (Books for Young Learners). (Illus.). 16p. (J). (gr. k-2). 1996. pap. text 5.00 (*1-57274-020-5*, A2470) R Owen Pubs.

Mai, 1935 a Fevrier 1942 see Carnets

Mai, the Psychic Girl, Vol. 1. Kazuya Kudo & Ryoichi Ikegami. Ed. by Seiji Horibuchi. Tr. by Satoru Fujii & James D. Hudnall from JPN. (Illus.). 292p. (Orig.). 1989. pap. 16.95 (*0-929279-25-5*) Viz Commns Inc.

Mai, the Psychic Girl, Vol. 2. Kazuya Kudo & Ryoichi Ikegami. Ed. by Seiji Horibuchi. Tr. by Satoru Fujii & James D. Hudnall. (Illus.). 266p. (Orig.). 1989. pap. 16.95 (*0-929279-24-7*) Viz Commns Inc.

Mai, the Psychic Girl, Vol. 3. Kazuya Kudo & Ryoichi Ikegami. Ed. by Seiji Horibuchi. Tr. by Satoru Fujii & James D. Hudnall. (Illus.). 258p. (Orig.). 1989. pap. 16.95 (*0-929279-27-1*) Viz Commns Inc.

Mai, the Psychic Girl, Vol. 4. Kazuya Kudo & Ryoichi Ikegami. Ed. by Seiji Horibuchi. Tr. by Satoru Fujii & James D. Hudnall. (Illus.). 282p. (Orig.). 1989. pap. 16.95 (*0-929279-28-X*) Viz Commns Inc.

Mai the Psychic Girl Perfect Collection, Vol. 1. Kazuya Kudo. (Illus.). 368p. 1996. pap. 19.95 (*1-56931-070-X*) Viz Commns Inc.

Mai the Psychic Girl Perfect Collection, Vol. 2. Kazuya Kudo. (Illus.). 360p. 1996. pap. 19.95 (*1-56931-066-1*) Viz Commns Inc.

Mai the Psychic Girl Perfect Collection, Vol. 3. Kazuya Kudo. (Illus.). 360p. 1996. pap. 19.95 (*1-56931-059-9*) Viz Commns Inc.

Mai Weini - A Small Village in the Highlands of Eritrea: A Study of the People, Their Livelihood, & Land Tenure During the Times of Turbulence. Kjetil Tronvoll. LC 98-11533. (Illus.). 363p. 1997. 79.95 (*1-56902-058-2*) Red Sea Pr.

Mai Weini - A Small Village in the Highlands of Eritrea: A Study of the People, Their Livelihood & Land Tenure During the Times of Turbulence. Kjetil Tronvoll. LC 98-11533. (Illus.). xvi, 311p. 1998. pap. 21.95 (*1-56902-059-0*) Red Sea Pr.

Maia: A Dinosaur Grows Up. anniversary ed. John R. Horner & James Gorman. Ed. by Jeri D. Walton & Terrance L. Blumer. (Illus.). 56p. (YA). 1998. reprint ed. 14.95 (*0-933819-02-1*) Museum Rockies.

Maias. Eca de Queiros. LC 99-228033. 640p. 1999. pap. 15.95 (*0-14-044694-X*, PuffinBks) Peng Put Young Read.

Maiasaura: The Good Mother Dinosaur. Elizabeth Sandell. Ed. by Marjorie Oelerich & Harlan S. Hansen. LC 88-39799. (Dinosaur Discovery Era Ser.). (Illus.). 32p. (J). (gr. k-5). 1989. pap. text 5.95 (*0-944280-23-4*); lib. bdg. 12.95 (*0-944280-17-X*) Bancroft-Sage.

Maiasaura (Cretaceous Period) see New Dinosaur Collection

Maiba. Russell Soaba. LC 83-50511. (Illus.). 115p. (Orig.). 1979. pap. 10.95 (*0-89410-414-4*, Three Contnts) L Rienner.

Maid & Mistress: Feminine Solidarity & Class Difference in the Private Sphere. Susan A. Yates. LC 90-13327. (Age of Revolution & Romanticism Ser.: Vol. 1). 204p. (C). 1992. text 39.95 (*0-8204-1248-1*) P Lang Pubng.

Maid & the Mouse & the Odd-Shaped House: A Story in Rhyme. Paul O. Zelinsky. (Picture Puffin Ser.). (Illus.). (J). 1993. 10.19 (*0-606-05448-0*, Pub. by Turtleback) Demco.

Maid for Marriage. Peters. 1993. per. 2.99 (*0-373-17159-5*) Harlequin Bks.

Maid for Marriage. large type ed. Sue Peters. 1992. reprint ed. lib. bdg. 18.95 (*0-263-13134-3*) Mac Lib Ref.

Maid for the Part. Katherine Frayn. (Rainbow Romances Ser.: No. 891). 160p. 1994. 14.95 (*0-7090-4938-2*) Parkwest Pubns.

Maid in the Shade. Jacqueline Turner-Banks. (Illus.). 159p. (J). 1998. 13.00 (*0-9639147-3-1*) ReGeJe Press.

Maid in the U. S. A. Mary Romero. (Perspectives on Gender Ser.). 256p. (C). (gr. 13). 1992. 70.00 (*0-415-90611-3*, A7362); pap. 19.99 (*0-415-90612-1*, A7366) Routledge.

***Maid Margaret.** S. R. Crockett. 252p. 2000. pap. 9.95 (*0-594-00477-2*) Eightn Hundrd.

Maid Marian & Her Merry Men. Robinson. 1992. pap. text. write for info. (*0-582-09554-9*, Pub. by Addison-Wesley) Longman.

Maid Mary Anne. Ann M. Martin. (Baby-Sitters Club Ser.: No. 66). 192p. (J). (gr. 3-7). 1993. pap. 3.50 (*0-590-47004-3*) Scholastic Inc.

Maid Mary Anne. Ann M. Martin. (Baby-Sitters Club Ser.: No. 66). (J). 1993. 8.60 (*0-606-05138-4*, Pub. by Turtleback) Demco.

Maid of Killeena & Other Stories. William Black. LC 71-152936. (Short Story Index Reprint Ser.). 1977. reprint ed. 20.95 (*0-8369-3794-5*) Ayer.

***Maid of Maiden Lane.** Amelia E. Barr. 252p. 2000. pap. 9.95 (*0-594-00678-3*) Eightn Hundrd.

***Maid of Midnight.** Ana Seymour. (Historical Ser.). 2000. mass mkt. 4.99 (*0-373-29140-X*, 1291400) Harlequin Bks.

***Maid of Orleans.** unabridged ed. Friedrich Von Schiller. 72p. (Orig.). 1999. pap. 7.00 (*0-88734-814-9*) Players Pr.

Maid of the Mountain. Jackson Gregory. 1976. reprint ed. lib. bdg. 25.95 (*0-88411-283-7*) Amereon Ltd.

Maid of the North: Feminist Folk Tales from Around the World. Ethel J. Phelps. LC 80-21500. (Illus.). 192p. 1995. pap. 9.95 (*0-8050-0679-6*, Owl) H Holt & Co.

Maid of the North: Feminist Folk Tales from Around the World. Ethel J. Phelps. 1981. 15.05 (*0-606-01826-3*, Pub. by Turtleback) Demco.

Maid of the Stones. limited ed. John Hankins. (Illus.). 86p. 1999. pap. 16.95 (*1-889260-03-7*) Writers Bk Club.

Maid to Marry see Killer & Other Plays

***Maid to Murder, 1 vol.** Kate Kingsbury. (Pennyfoot Hotel Mystery Ser.: Vol.12). 214p. 1999. mass mkt. 5.99 (*0-425-16967-7*) Berkley Pub.

Maid to Order in Hong Kong: Stories of Filipina Workers. Nicole Constable. LC 96-48241. (Illus.). 256p. 1996. text 39.95 (*0-8014-3331-2*); pap. text 16.95 (*0-8014-8382-4*) Cornell U Pr.

Maida Heatter's Best Dessert Book Ever. Maida Heatter. (Illus.). 1990. 27.50 (*0-394-57832-5*) Random.

Maida Heatter's Book of Great Chocolate. Maida Heatter. LC 99-234817. (Illus.). 432p. 1995. pap. 15.00 (*0-679-76533-6*) Random.

Maida Heatter's Book of Great Desserts. Maida Heatter. LC 98-45993. (Illus.). 528p. 1999. 24.95 (*0-8362-7861-5*) Andrews & McMeel.

Maida Heatter's Book of Great Desserts. rev. ed. Maida Heatter. (Illus.). 448p. 1991. 30.45 (*0-679-40509-7*) Random.

Maida Heatter's Brand-New Book of Great Cookies. Maida Heatter. LC 95-5250. 272p. 1995. 25.00 (*0-679-43874-2*) Random.

***Maida Herman Solomon: Mental Health Pioneer.** Anne Sugarman Evans. LC 99-23603. (Illus.). 125p. 2000. write for info. (*0-930395-31-X*, Pub. by Biblio NY); pap. write for info. (*0-930395-30-1*, Pub. by Biblio NY) Holmes & Meier.

***Maida Springer: Pan-Africanist & International Labor Leader.** Yevette Richards. (Biography Ser.). (Illus.). 350p. 2000. 29.95 (*0-8229-4139-2*) U of Pittsburgh Pr.

Maida's Little House. Inez Irwin. 1976. 18.95 (*0-8488-1383-9*) Amereon Ltd.

Maiden. Jude Deveraux. 1991. mass mkt. 7.50 (*0-671-74379-1*) PB.

Maiden. Timothy S. Arthur. (Works of Timothy Shay Arthur). 1989. reprint ed. lib. bdg. 79.00 (*0-7812-1799-7*) Rprt Serv.

***Maiden: A Novel.** Cynthia Buchanan. LC 99-26438. 224p. 1999. reprint ed. pap. 12.00 (*0-688-16789-6*, Wm Morrow) Morrow Avon.

Maiden & Married Life of Mary Powell, Afterwards Mistress Milton, 2 vols., 1 bk. Anne Manning. LC 79-8166. reprint ed. 44.50 (*0-404-62021-3*) AMS Pr.

***Maiden & Mother: Devotions to the Blessed Virgin Mary Throughout the Year.** R. Margaret Miles. 208p. 2000. pap. 14.95 (*0-89870-780-3*, Pub. by Ignatius Pr) Midpt Trade.

Maiden & the Unicorn. Isolde Martyn. 448p. 1999. reprint ed. mass mkt. 5.99 (*0-553-58168-6*) Bantam.

Maiden & the Warrior. Jacqueline Navin. (Historical Ser.). 1998. per. 4.99 (*0-373-29003-9*, 1-29003-0) Harlequin Bks.

***Maiden Bride.** Cindy Harris. 320p. (Orig.). 1999. mass mkt. 4.99 (*0-8439-4650-4*, Leisure Bks) Dorchester Pub Co.

An Asterisk (*) at the beginning of an entry indicates that the title is appearing for the first time.

***Maiden Bride.** Linda Needham. LC 99-96443. 384p. 2000. mass mkt. 5.99 (*0-380-79636-8*, Avon Bks) Morrow Avon.

Maiden Bride. Deborah Simmons. (Historical Ser.). 1996. per. 4.99 (*0-373-28932-4*, 1-28932-1) Harlequin Bks.

Maiden Bride, Vol. 1. 4th ed. Rexanne Becnel. 336p. 1996. mass mkt. 5.99 (*0-312-95978-8*) St Martin.

Maiden Castle. John Cowper Powys. 496p. 1994. pap. 19.95 (*0-912568-18-6*) Colgate U Pr.

Maiden Czar. Robert Bly. 1999. pap. write for info. (*0-679-76856-4*) Knopf.

Maiden King: The Reunion of Masculine & Feminine. Robert Bly. 1999. pap. 12.95 (*0-8050-5778-1*, Owl) H Holt & Co.

Maiden King: The Reunion of Masculine & Feminine. Robert Bly & Marion Woodman. LC 98-21706. 256p. 1998. 24.00 (*0-8050-5777-3*) H Holt & Co.

Maiden, Mother, Crone: The Myth & Reality of the Triple Goddess. D. J. Conway. LC 94-6807. (Illus.). 240p. 1999. pap. 12.95 (*0-87542-171-7*) Llewellyn Pubns.

Maiden of Galilee see Doncella de Galilea

Maiden of Inverness. Arnette Lamb. Ed. by Carolyn Tolley. 339p. (Orig.). 1995. mass mkt. write for info. (*0-671-88220-1*) PB.

Maiden of Northland: A Hero Tale of Finland. Aaron Shepard. LC 95-78300. (Illus.). 40p. (J). (gr. 3-7). 1996. 16.00 (*0-689-80485-7*) Atheneum Yung Read.

Maiden of Orleans. 2nd rev. ed. Friedrich Schiller. Tr. by John T. Krumpelmann. LC 63-62703. (North Carolina. University. Studies in the Germanic Languages & Literatures: No. 37). reprint ed. 27.00 (*0-404-50937-1*) AMS Pr.

Maiden Serenade. Richard Hurowitz. LC 95-74701. 231p. 1997. 19.95 (*0-9648479-0-6*) Puppy Hse.

Maiden Speech. Eleanor Brown. LC 96-210361. 64p. 1996. pap. 15.95 (*1-85224-351-1*, Pub. by Bloodaxe Bks) Dufour.

Maiden Stone. Rona Munro. 96p. 1996. pap. text 14.95 (*1-85459-243-2*, Pub. by N Hern Bks) Theatre Comm.

Maiden Voyage. Tania Aebi. LC 96-96662. 1996. pap. 10.00 (*0-345-41012-2*) Ballantine Pub Grp.

Maiden Voyage. Cynthia Bass. 304p. 1998. mass mkt. 5.99 (*0-553-58063-9*) Bantam.

Maiden Voyage. Giovanni. Ed. by John P. Schumake. (Orig.). (J). (gr. 4-6). 1992. pap. 9.95 (*0-9616789-5-X*) Earnest Pubns.

***Maiden Voyage.** Ann L. McLaughlin. LC 99-21330. (Illus.). 352p. 1999. pap. 14.95 (*1-880284-38-3*) J Daniel.

Maiden Voyage. Kathleen Thompson Norris. 1976. 17.95 (*0-89190-305-4*) Amereon Ltd.

Maiden Voyage. Judith O'Brien. 368p. 1997. per. 5.99 (*0-671-50219-0*) PB.

Maiden Voyage. Denton Welch. 274p. 1999. pap. 15.95 (*1-878972-28-6*, Pub. by Exact Change) SPD-Small Pr Dist.

Maiden Voyage. Geoffrey Marcus. (Illus.). 340p. 1991. reprint ed. lib. bdg. 45.95 (*0-89966-792-9*) Buccaneer Bks.

Maiden Voyages. Mary Morris. 1993. pap. 14.00 (*0-679-74030-9*) McKay.

Maiden Voyages & Infant Colonies: Two Women's Travel Narratives of the 1790s. Deidre Coleman. (Literature of Travel, Exploration & Empire Ser.). (Illus.). 224p. 1998. 75.00 (*0-7185-0149-7*, Pub. by Leicester U Pr) Cassell & Continuum.

Maiden Voyages & Infant Colonies: Two Women's Travel Narratives of the 1790s. Deirdre Coleman. (Literature of Travel, Exploration & Empire Ser.). (Illus.). 224p. 1998. pap. 24.95 (*0-7185-0150-0*) Bks Intl VA.

Maiden Wheat. Tracy Nickels. 1999. pap. write for info. (*1-928727-02-6*) Get n Even.

Maiden Widow. E.D.E.N. Southworth. (Notable American Authors Ser.). 1999. reprint ed. lib. bdg. 125.00 (*0-7812-8903-3*) Rprt Serv.

Maidenhome. Xiaoqi Ding. Tr. by Chris Berry & Cathy Silber. LC 94-15414. 224p. 1994. pap. 8.95 (*1-879960-36-2*) Aunt Lute Bks.

Maidenhome. Xiaoqi Ding. Tr. by Chris Berry & Cathy Silber. 224p. 1996. 24.95 (*0-908569-77-7*, Pub. by Univ Otago Pr) Intl Spec Bk.

***Maidens & Love.** Sulamith Wulfing. (Illus.). 58p. 2000. 9.95 (*1-885394-41-1*, Pub. by Bluestar Communs) ACCESS Pubs Network.

Maiden's Bequest. George MacDonald. Ed. by Michael Phillips. LC 85-4024. 288p. (Orig.). 1985. pap. 8.99 (*0-87123-823-3*) Bethany Hse.

Maiden's Bequest; The Minister's Restoration; The Laird's Inheitance. George MacDonald. Ed. by Michael Phillips. (George MacDonald Collection). 672p. 1998. text 12.99 (*0-7642-2148-5*) Bethany Hse.

Maiden's Grave. Jeffery Deaver. 419p. 1996. mass mkt. 7.50 (*0-451-18848-9*, Sig) NAL.

Maiden's Heart. Julie Beard. 352p. 1999. mass mkt. 6.50 (*0-515-12515-6*, Jove) Berkley Pub.

Maiden's Honour. (Mongolia Society Occasional Papers: No. 15). 1990. pap. 15.00 (*0-910980-55-1*) Mongolia.

Maidens, Meal & Money. Ed. by Claude Meillassoux. Tr. by Felicity Edholm from FRE. LC 79-52834. (Themes in the Social Sciences Ser.). 200p. 1981. pap. text 24.95 (*0-521-29708-7*) Cambridge U Pr.

Maiden's Oath. James Lawson. (Notable American Authors Ser.). 1999. reprint ed. lib. bdg. 125.00 (*0-7812-3762-9*) Rprt Serv.

Maiden's Prayer. Nicky Silver. 1998. pap. 5.25 (*0-8222-1684-1*) Dramatists Play.

Maiden's Prayer. large type ed. Joan Fleming. 352p. 1998. pap. 17.99 (*0-7089-5383-2*, Linford) Ulverscroft.

Maiden's Sword, 2. Ethel Herr. LC 97-33839. (Seekers Ser.). 32p. 1997. pap. 9.99 (*1-55661-747-X*) Bethany Hse.

***Maiden's Tale.** Margaret Frazer. 245p. 1998. mass mkt. 5.99 (*0-425-16407-1*, Prime Crime) Berkley Pub.

Maidens Trip. Emma Smith. 224p. (C). 1989. 50.00 (*0-947712-05-4*, Pub. by S A Baldwin) St Mut.

Maides Tragedy. Francis Beaumont & John Fletcher. LC 70-38151. (English Experience Ser.: No. 431). 82p. 1972. reprint ed. 25.00 (*90-221-0431-1*) Walter J Johnson.

***M'aidez.** George A. Reynolds. LC 99-74761. 192p. 2000. pap. 13.95 (*1-57197-196-3*, Pub. by Pentland Pr) Assoc Pubs Grp.

Maids. Jean Genet. Tr. by Bernard Frechtman from FRE. 1988. pap. 8.95 (*0-394-17390-2*) Grove-Atltic.

Maids & Deathwatch. Jean Genet. Tr. by Bernard Frechtman from FRE. LC 53-7149. 168p. 1988. pap. 11.00 (*0-8021-5056-X*, Grove) Grove-Atltic.

Maids & Mistresses, Cousins & Queens: Women's Alliances in Early Modern England. Ed. by Susan Frye & Karen Robertson. LC 98-3448. (Illus.). 368p. 1999. pap. 19.95 (*0-19-511735-2*); text 60.00 (*0-19-511734-4*) OUP.

Maids in Heaven. S. Austen. mass mkt. 6.95 (*0-7472-4663-7*, Pub. by Headline Bk Pub) Trafalgar.

Maid's Metamorphosis. LC 72-133701. (Tudor Facsimile Texts. Old English Plays Ser.: No. 88). reprint ed. 49.50 (*0-404-53388-4*) AMS Pr.

Maid's Tale. Kathleen Ferguson. 204p. 1994. 29.95 (*1-898142-04-1*) Dufour.

Maid's Tale. Kathleen Ferguson. 202p. 1995. pap. 12.95 (*1-85371-262-0*) Dufour.

Maid's Tragedy. Francis Beaumont & John Fletcher. Ed. by T. W. Craik. (Revels Plays Ser.). 210p. 1990. pap. 17.95 (*0-7190-1636-3*, Pub. by Manchester Univ Pr) St Martin.

***Maid's Tragedy: Francis Beaumont & John Fletcher.** Ed. by T. W. Craik. (Revels Plays Ser.). 212p. 1999. pap. 19.95 (*0-7190-3098-6*, Pub. by Manchester Univ Pr) St Martin.

Maidstone Past & Present. Richard Stutely. 96p. 1987. pap. 50.00 (*0-905392-74-4*) St Mut.

Maidu Indian Myths & Stories of Hanc'ibyjim. Ed. by William Shipley. LC 91-70319. 192p. (Orig.). 1991. pap. 12.95 (*0-930588-52-5*) Heyday Bks.

Maidu Texts. Roland B. Dixon. LC 73-3539. (American Ethnological Society Publications: No. 4). reprint ed. 39.50 (*0-404-58154-4*) AMS Pr.

Maigret a l'Ecole see Maigret Goes to School

Maigret a l'Ecole. Georges Simenon. (FRE.). pap. 8.95 (*0-685-11305-1*) Fr & Eur.

Maigret a New York. Georges Simenon. (FRE.). pap. 8.95 (*0-685-11304-3*) Fr & Eur.

Maigret a Peur. Georges Simenon. (FRE.). pap. 8.95 (*0-685-11306-X*) Fr & Eur.

Maigret a Vichy. Georges Simenon. (FRE.). pap. 8.95 (*0-685-36573-5*) Fr & Eur.

Maigret Afraid. Georges Simenon. Tr. by Margaret Duff. LC 82-23233. (Helen & Kurt Wolff Bk.). 170p. 1996. pap. 6.00 (*0-15-655142-X*, Harvest Bks) Harcourt.

Maigret & the Apparition. Georges Simenon. LC 80-14212. 176p. 1991. pap. 6.00 (*0-15-655127-6*, Harvest Bks) Harcourt.

Maigret & the Bum. Georges Simenon. 1995. pap. 6.00 (*0-15-600249-3*) Harcourt.

Maigret & the Burglar's Wife. large type ed. Georges Simenon. Tr. by J. Maclaren-Ross. LC 93-17773. (ENG & FRE.). 219p. 1993. lib. bdg. 20.95 (*1-56054-530-5*) Thorndike Pr.

Maigret & the Calame Report. Georges Simenon. Tr. by Moura Budberg. 192p. 1996. pap. 6.00 (*0-15-655153-5*, Harvest Bks) Harcourt.

Maigret & the Death of a Harbor-Master. Georges Simenon. Tr. by Stuart Gilbert. 182p. 1989. pap. 5.95 (*0-15-655161-6*) Harcourt.

Maigret & the Gangsters. Georges Simenon. Tr. by Louise Varese from FRE. 162p. 1986. 14.95 (*0-15-155565-6*) Harcourt.

Maigret & the Gangsters. Georges Simenon. Tr. by Louise Varese. 160p. 1988. pap. 3.50 (*0-380-70414-5*, Avon Bks) Morrow Avon.

Maigret & the Headless Corpse. Georges Simenon. Tr. by Eileen Ellenbogen. LC 84-25228. (Helen & Kurt Wolff Bk.). 196p. (C). 1985. pap. 6.00 (*0-15-655144-6*, Harvest Bks) Harcourt.

Maigret & the Hotel Majestic. Georges Simenon. Tr. by Caroline Hillier. LC 77-84398. 182p. 1991. pap. 6.00 (*0-15-655133-0*, Harvest Bks) Harcourt.

Maigret & the Informer. Georges Simenon. lib. bdg. 18.95 (*0-8488-2033-9*) Amereon Ltd.

Maigret & the Killer. Georges Simenon. lib. bdg. 19.95 (*0-8488-2034-7*) Amereon Ltd.

Maigret & the Loner. Georges Simenon. 166p. 19.95 (*0-89190-429-8*) Amereon Ltd.

Maigret & the Madwoman. large type ed. Georges Simenon. Tr. by Eileen Ellenbogen from FRE. LC 93-22858. 231p. 1994. reprint ed. lib. bdg. 20.95 (*1-56054-533-X*) Thorndike Pr.

Maigret & the Nahour Case. Georges Simenon. Tr. by Alastair Hamilton. LC 82-47661. 168p. 1993. pap. 5.95 (*0-15-655149-7*, Harvest Bks) Harcourt.

Maigret & the Pickpocket. Georges Simenon. Tr. by Nigel Ryan from FRE. LC 85-8740. (Helen & Kurt Wolff Bk.). 156p. 1995. pap. 6.00 (*0-15-655145-4*, Harvest Bks) Harcourt.

Maigret & the Saturday Caller. Georges Simenon. Tr. by Tony White. 1991. 17.95 (*0-15-155566-4*) Harcourt.

Maigret & the Spinster. Georges Simenon. Tr. by Eileen Ellenbogen. LC 76-27416. 168p. (C). 1996. pap. 6.00 (*0-15-655129-2*, Harvest Bks) Harcourt.

Maigret & the Tavern by the Seine. Georges Simenon. Tr. by Geoffrey Sainsbury. 182p. 1990. pap. 6.00 (*0-15-655164-0*, Harvest Bks) Harcourt.

Maigret & the Toy Village. Georges Simenon. Tr. by Eileen Ellenbogen. LC 93-49682. 1994. pap. 5.95 (*0-15-655154-3*, Harvest Bks) Harcourt.

Maigret & the Wine Merchant. Georges Simenon. Tr. by Eileen Ellenbogen. LC 79-26173. 187p. 1993. pap. 6.00 (*0-15-655125-X*, Harvest Bks) Harcourt.

Maigret & the Yellow Dog. Georges Simenon. (Helen & Kurt Wolff Bk.). 140p. 1995. pap. 6.00 (*0-15-655157-8*) Harcourt.

Maigret at the Gai-Moulin. Georges Simenon. Tr. by Geoffrey Sainsbury.Tr. of La/Danseuse du Gai-Moulin. 1991. 17.95 (*0-15-155568-0*) Harcourt.

Maigret at the Gai-Moulin. large type ed. Georges Simenon. Tr. by Geoffrey Sainsbury. LC 92-9650.Tr. of La/Danseuse du Gai-Moulin. 208p. 1992. reprint ed. lib. bdg. 19.95 (*1-56054-415-5*) Thorndike Pr.

Maigret au Picratt's. Georges Simenon. (FRE.). pap. 3.95 (*0-685-11307-8*) Fr & Eur.

Maigret aux Assises. Georges Simenon. (FRE.). pap. 3.95 (*0-685-11308-6*) Fr & Eur.

Maigret Bides His Time. Georges Simenon. Tr. by Alastair Hamilton. LC 84-25134. 160p. 1992. pap. 5.95 (*0-15-655151-9*, Harvest Bks) Harcourt.

Maigret Bides His Time. large type ed. Georges Simenon. Tr. by Alastair Hamilton from FRE. LC 93-14176. 1993. lib. bdg. 20.95 (*1-56054-531-3*) Thorndike Pr.

Maigret Chez le Coroner. Georges Simenon. (FRE.). pap. 3.95 (*0-685-11309-4*) Fr & Eur.

Maigret Chez le Ministre. Georges Simenon. (FRE.). pap. 3.95 (*0-685-11310-8*) Fr & Eur.

Maigret et la Grande Perche. Georges Simenon. (FRE.). pap. 3.95 (*0-685-11311-6*) Fr & Eur.

Maigret et la Jeune Morte. Georges Simenon. (FRE.). pap. 3.95 (*0-685-11312-4*) Fr & Eur.

Maigret et la Vielle Dame. Georges Simenon. (FRE.). pap. 3.95 (*0-685-11313-2*) Fr & Eur.

Maigret et l'Affaire Nahour. Georges Simenon. (FRE.). pap. 3.95 (*0-685-36571-9*) Fr & Eur.

Maigret et le Client Du Samedi. Georges Simenon. (FRE.). pap. 3.95 (*0-685-11314-0*) Fr & Eur.

Maigret et le Clochard. Georges Simenon. (FRE.). pap. 3.95 (*0-685-11315-9*) Fr & Eur.

Maigret et le Clochard: Level B. Georges Simenon. text 8.95 (*0-88436-047-4*) EMC-Paradigm.

Maigret et le Corps Sans Tete. Georges Simenon. (FRE.). 1992. pap. 11.95 (*0-7859-3257-7*, 2266051032) Fr & Eur.

Maigret et le Corps Sans Tete, La Boule Noire, Maigret Tend un Piege, Les Complices, En Cas de Malheur, Un Echec de Maigret, Le Petit Homme d'Arkhangelsh, Maigret S'Amuse. Georges Simenon. (FRE.). 1989. 49.95 (*0-7859-0482-4*, 2258027977) Fr & Eur.

Maigret et le Fantome. Georges Simenon. (FRE.). pap. 3.95 (*0-685-36568-9*) Fr & Eur.

Maigret et le Fantome: B Level. Georges Simenon. 8.95 (*0-8219-1470-7*) EMC-Paradigm.

Maigret et le Fueur. Georges Simenon. (FRE.). pap. 3.95 (*0-685-36575-1*) Fr & Eur.

Maigret et le Voleur Paresseux. Georges Simenon. (FRE.). pap. 3.95 (*0-685-11317-5*) Fr & Eur.

Maigret et les Braves Gens. Georges Simenon. (FRE.). pap. 3.95 (*0-685-11318-3*) Fr & Eur.

Maigret et les Petit Cochons. Georges Simenon. (FRE.). pap. 3.95 (*0-685-11319-1*) Fr & Eur.

Maigret et les Temoins Recalcitrants. Georges Simenon. (FRE.). pap. 3.95 (*0-685-11320-5*) Fr & Eur.

Maigret et les Temoins Recalcitrants, La Vielle, L'Ours en Peluche, Une Confidence de Maigret, Le Veuf, Maigret aux Assises, Maigret et les Viellards, Betty. Georges Simenon. (FRE.). 830p. 1990. 49.95 (*0-7859-0483-2*, 2258031532) Fr & Eur.

Maigret et les Viellards. Georges Simenon. (FRE.). pap. 3.95 (*0-685-11321-3*) Fr & Eur.

Maigret et l'Homme Du Banc. Georges Simenon. (FRE.). pap. 3.95 (*0-685-11322-1*) Fr & Eur.

Maigret et l'Homme Tout Seul. Georges Simenon. (FRE.). pap. 3.95 (*0-685-36578-6*) Fr & Eur.

Maigret et l'Inspecteur Maigrecieux, la Passager Clandestin, le Temoignage De l'Enfant Du Choeur, le Client le Plus Obstine Du Monde, On Ne Tue Pas les Pauvres Types, la Jument Perdue, Maigret et Son Mort, Pedigree. Georges Simenon. (FRE.). 1988. 49.95 (*0-7859-0477-8*, 2258021154) Fr & Eur.

Maigret et l'Inspecteur Malgracieux. Georges Simenon. (FRE.). pap. 3.95 (*0-685-11323-X*) Fr & Eur.

Maigret et Son Mort. Georges Simenon. (FRE.). pap. 3.95 (*0-685-11324-8*) Fr & Eur.

Maigret Goes Home. Georges Simenon. Tr. by Robert Baldick. 1989. 16.95 (*0-15-155150-2*) Harcourt.

Maigret Goes to School. large type ed. Georges Simenon. Tr. by Daphne Woodward from FRE. LC 93-23967.Tr. of Maigret a l'Ecole. 205p. 1994. lib. bdg. 20.95 (*1-56054-532-1*) Thorndike Pr.

Maigret Has Doubts. Georges Simenon. 160p. 1988. pap. 3.50 (*0-380-70410-2*, Avon Bks) Morrow Avon.

Maigret Has Scruples. Georges Simenon. 1995. pap. 6.00 (*0-15-600247-7*) Harcourt.

Maigret Has Scruples. Georges Simenon. Tr. by Robert Eglesfield. (Helen & Kurt Wolff Bk.). 192p. 1996. pap. 6.00 (*0-15-655160-8*) Harcourt.

Maigret Hesitates. Georges Simenon. Tr. by Lyn Moir. 182p. 1993. pap. 5.95 (*0-15-655152-7*, Harvest Bks) Harcourt.

Maigret in Court. Georges Simenon. Tr. by Robert Brain. 160p. 1988. pap. 3.50 (*0-380-70411-0*, Avon Bks) Morrow Avon.

Maigret in Exile. Georges Simenon. Tr. by Eileen Ellenbogen from FRE. LC 78-13771. (Helen & Kurt Wolff Bk.). 168p. 1994. pap. 5.95 (*0-15-655136-5*, Harvest Bks) Harcourt.

Maigret in Holland. Georges Simenon. 176p. 1994. pap. 5.95 (*0-15-600084-9*) Harcourt.

Maigret in Montmartre. Georges Simenon. Tr. by Daphne Woodward. 202p. 1989. pap. 6.00 (*0-15-655162-4*) Harcourt.

Maigret in Vichy. Georges Simenon. Tr. by Eileen Ellenbogen. 182p. 1995. pap. 6.00 (*0-15-655140-3*, Harvest Bks) Harcourt.

Maigret, Lognon et les Gangsters. Georges Simenon. (FRE.). pap. 3.95 (*0-685-11325-6*) Fr & Eur.

Maigret Loses His Temper. Georges Simenon. Tr. by Robert Eglesfield. LC 80-14212. (Helen & Kurt Wolff Bk.). 144p. 1993. pap. 5.95 (*0-15-655128-4*, Harvest Bks) Harcourt.

Maigret on the Defensive. Georges Simenon. 160p. 1987. pap. 3.50 (*0-380-70409-9*, Avon Bks) Morrow Avon.

Maigret on the Riviera. Georges Simenon. 140p. 1989. pap. 5.95 (*0-15-655158-6*) Harcourt.

Maigret S'Amuse. Georges Simenon. (FRE.). pap. 3.95 (*0-685-11326-4*) Fr & Eur.

Maigret Se Trompe. Georges Simenon. (FRE.). pap. 3.95 (*0-685-11327-2*) Fr & Eur.

Maigret Se Trompe, Crime Impuni, Maigret a l'Ecole, Maigret et la Jeun Morte. Georges Simenon. (FRE.). 860p. 1990. 49.95 (*0-7859-0480-8*, 2258025966) Fr & Eur.

M

Maigret Sets a Trap. Georges Simenon. 20.95 (*0-89190-427-1*) Amereon Ltd.

Maigret Sets a Trap. Georges Simenon. Tr. by Daphne Woodward. LC 78-13655. (Helen & Kurt Wolff Bk.). 182p. 1992. pap. 5.95 (*0-15-655126-8*, Harvest Bks) Harcourt.

Maigret Tend un Piege. Georges Simenon. (FRE.). pap. 3.95 (*0-685-11328-0*) Fr & Eur.

Maigret Trio: Maigret's Failure, Maigret in Society, & Maigret & the Lazy Burglar. Georges Simenon. 23.95 (*0-89190-425-5*) Amereon Ltd.

Maigret Trio: Maigret's Failure, Maigret in Society, & Maigret & the Lazy Burglar. Georges Simenon. Tr. by Daphne Woodward & Robert Eglesfield. LC 83-8381. 288p. 1994. pap. 10.00 (*0-15-655137-3*, Harvest Bks) Harcourt.

Maigret Voyage. Georges Simenon. (FRE.). pap. 3.95 (*0-685-11329-9*) Fr & Eur.

Maigret's Boyhood Friend. Georges Simenon. 19.95 (*0-89190-426-3*) Amereon Ltd.

Maigret's Boyhood Friend. Georges Simenon. Tr. by Eileen Ellenbogen. LC 80-25139. 192p. 1996. pap. 6.00 (*0-15-655131-4*, Harvest Bks) Harcourt.

Maigret's Christmas: 9 Stories. Georges Simenon. Tr. by Jean Stewart. LC 77-1724. (Helen & Kurt Wolff Bk.). 336p. 1992. pap. 10.00 (*0-15-655132-2*, Harvest Bks) Harcourt.

Maigret's Memoirs. Georges Simenon. Tr. by Jean Stewart from FRE. LC 85-8591. (Helen & Kurt Wolff Bk.). 160p. 1985. reprint ed. 13.95 (*0-15-155148-0*) Harcourt.

Maigret's Memoirs. Georges Simenon. Tr. by Jean Stewart. 144p. 1989. reprint ed. pap. 3.50 (*0-380-70412-9*, Avon Bks) Morrow Avon.

Maigret's Mistake. Georges Simenon. Tr. by Alan Hodge. 188p. 1988. pap. 6.00 (*0-15-655155-1*) Harcourt.

Maigret's Pipe. Georges Simenon. Tr. by Jean Stewart from FRE. (Helen & Kurt Wolff Bk.). 336p. 1994. pap. 11.00 (*0-15-655146-2*, Harvest Bks) Harcourt.

Maigret's Revolver. Georges Simenon. Tr. by Nigel Ryan. LC 84-4634. (Helen & Kurt Wolff Bk.). (FRE.). 176p. 1984. 12.95 (*0-15-155562-1*) Harcourt.

Maigret's Revolver. large type ed. Georges Simenon. Tr. by Nigel Ryan from FRE. LC 92-18389. (Nightingale Ser.). 241p. 1992. pap. 14.95 (*0-8161-5316-7*, G K Hall Lrg Type) Mac Lib Ref.

Maigret's Rival. Georges Simenon. Tr. by Helen Thomson. LC 83-33697. 182p. 1994. pap. 5.95 (*0-15-655141-1*, Harvest Bks) Harcourt.

Maigret's War of Nerves. Georges Simenon. Tr. by Geoffrey Sainsbury. LC 85-24749. (Helen & Kurt Wolff Bk.). 180p. 1986. 13.95 (*0-15-155570-2*) Harcourt.

Maigret's War of Nerves. Georges Simenon. Tr. by Geoffrey Sainsbury. 160p. 1989. pap. 3.50 (*0-380-70413-7*, Avon Bks) Morrow Avon.

Maija Grotell: Works Which Grow from Belief. Jeff Schlanger & Toshiko Takaezu. Ed. by Gerry Williams. (Studio Potter Monographs). (Illus.). 96p. (Orig.). 1996. pap. 30.00 (*0-9652176-2-0*) Studio Potter.

Mail. Peggy Burns. (Stepping Through History Ser.). (Illus.). 32p. (J). 1994. lib. bdg. 5.00 (*1-56847-249-8*) Raintree Steck-V.

Mail. Mameve Medwed. 320p. 1998. reprint ed. mass mkt. 11.99 (*0-446-67375-7*, Pub. by Warner Bks) Little.

Mail & Electronic Surveys: The Tailored Design Method. 2nd ed. Don A. Dillman. LC 99-38738. 464p. 1999. 47.50 (*0-471-32354-3*) Wiley.

***Mail & Grow Rich: How to Get Rich in Mail Order in the Information Age.** Ted Ciuba. 224p. 2000. pap. 19.97 (*0-9672414-0-5*, Pub. by Parthenon Mktg) ACCESS Pubs Network.

Mail & Mystery, Family & Friends: Drama Curriculum for Second & Third Grades. Helen Landalf & Pamela Gerke. LC 99-25288. 268p. 1999. pap. 19.95 (*1-57525-188-4*) Smith & Kraus.

Mail & Supply Clerk. Jack Rudman. (Career Examination Ser.: C-3162). 1994. pap. 23.95 (*0-8373-3162-5*) Nat Learn.

Mail Art: An Annotated Bibliography. John Held, Jr. LC 91-18332. (Illus.). 582p. 1991. 60.50 (*0-8108-2455-8*) Scarecrow.

Mail Art Anno Klimt: Postcard Art of the Wiener Werkstatte. Otto Breicha & Sigrun Loos. 320p. pap. 39.95 (*3-201-01320-X*) Moyer Bell.

Mail Art International. (Illus.). 318p. (C). 1997. pap. 45.00 (*3-86106-021-3*) Dist Art Pubs.

An Asterisk (*) at the beginning of an entry indicates that the title is appearing for the first time.

***Mail by the Pail.** Colin Bergel. (Illus.). 32p. 2000. 16.95 (*0-8143-2890-3*, Great Lks Bks) Wayne St U Pr.

***Mail by the Pail.** Colin Bergel. LC 00-9687. (Illus.). (J). 2000. pap. write for info. (*0-8143-2891-1*) Wayne St U Pr.

Mail Call! The History of the U. S. Mail Service. Nancy O'Keefe Bolick. LC 94-49. (First Bks.). (Illus.). 64p. (J). (gr. 4-6). 1994. lib. bdg. 22.00 (*0-531-20170-8*) Watts.

Mail Carrier Spider: I'm a Book with Wheels. Rita Balducci & Reader's Digest Editors. (Pull-Back 'n Go Ser.: No. 3). (Illus.). 10p. (J). (gr. k-3). 1998. bds. 7.99 (*1-57584-213-0*, Pub. by Rdrs Digest) Random.

Mail Carriers see Community Helpers Series

Mail Carriers. Dee Ready. (Community Helpers Ser.). (Illus.). 24p. (J). (gr. k-3). 1997. lib. bdg. 14.00 (*0-516-20878-0*) Childrens.

***Mail Center Management Report 2000 Yearbook.** annuals Laime Vaitkus. (Illus.). 200p. 2000. pap. 199.00 (*1-58673-022-3*) IOMA.

Mail Clerk. Jack Rudman. (Career Examination Ser.: C-2280). 1994. reprint ed. pap. 19.95 (*0-8373-2280-4*) Nat Learn.

Mail Course of Instruction in Magnetic Healing. Sidney A. Weltmer. 77p. 1996. reprint ed. spiral bd. 15.00 (*0-7873-0949-4*) Hlth Research.

Mail Division Supervisor. Jack Rudman. (Career Examination Ser.: C-2624). 1994. pap. 29.95 (*0-8373-2624-9*) Nat Learn.

Mail Drops. 2nd ed. CWL. (Security & Survival Ser.). 48p. (Orig.). 1987. pap. 18.00 (*0-939856-76-X*) Tech Group.

Mail for Husher Town. Mary L. Cuneo. 2000. lib. bdg. write for info. (*0-688-16526-5*, Grenwillow Bks) HarpC Child Bks.

Mail for Husher Town. Mary Louise Cuneo. LC 98-52877. (Illus.). 24p. (J). (ps-3). 2000. 15.95 (*0-688-16525-7*, Grenwillow Bks) HarpC Child Bks.

***Mail from Jail: A Glimpse into a Mother's Nightmare.** Sitamon M. Youssef & Adam Youssef. LC 00-90690. 96p. 2000. pap. 12.95 (*0-9678224-0-8*) T S Commns.

Mail Handler: U. S. Postal Service. 8th ed. LC 84-16729. 1985. 8.00 (*0-317-56563-X*, Arco) Macmillan Gen Ref.

Mail Handler - Mail Processor: U. S. Postal Service. 11th ed. E. P. Steinberg. 288p. 1994. per. 11.00 (*0-671-84642-6*, Arco) Macmillan Gen Ref.

Mail Handler (U. S. P. S.) Jack Rudman. (Career Examination Ser.: C-462). 1994. pap. 19.95 (*0-8373-0462-8*) Nat Learn.

Mail It! High Impact Business Mail: From Design to Delivery. Alice P. McElhone & Edward B. Butler. (Pitney Bowes Best Practices Guide Ser.). (Illus.). 250p. (Orig.). 1996. pap. 29.95 (*0-9647121-0-5*) Benchmark CT.

***Mail Must Go Through - A Canyon Adventure.** Ron Swisher. (Illus.). 32p. (J). (gr. k-6). 1999. 16.95 (*0-9677729-0-7*) TRB Pubng.

Mail Myself to You see Enviarme a Ti

Mail Myself to You. 2nd ed. Woody Guthrie. (Let Me Read Ser.). (Illus.). 8p. (J). (ps-1). 1994. text 2.95 (*0-673-36196-9*, GoodYrBooks) Addson-Wesley Educ.

Mail Nudes: Postcard Book. Taschen, Benedikt Staff. 1997. pap. 5.99 (*3-8228-8087-6*) Taschen Amer.

Mail on the Move. James H. Bruns. LC 92-22587. (Illus.). 224p. 1992. pap. 37.00 (*0-933449-15-1*) Transport Trails.

***Mail-Order Bride.** Sandra Donovan. (Splendor Historical Romances Ser.). 1999. mass mkt. 4.99 (*0-8217-6468-3*, Zebra Kensgtn) Kensgtn Pub Corp.

***Mail-Order Bride.** Maureen McKade. 384p. 2000. mass mkt. 5.99 (*0-380-80285-6*, Avon Bks) Morrow Avon.

Mail Order Bride. large type ed. Frank Fields. (Linford Western Large Print Ser.). 256p. 1998. pap. 17.99 (*0-7089-5275-5*, Linford) Ulverscroft.

Mail-Order Bridegroom. Day Leclaire. LC 95-7056. (Romance Ser.). 185p. 1995. per. 2.99 (*0-373-03361-3*, 1-03361-2) Harlequin Bks.

Mail-Order Bridegroom. Day Leclaire. (Promo Ser.). 1999. per. 4.50 (*0-373-21968-7*) Harlequin Bks.

Mail-Order Brides: Women for Sale. Mila Glodava & Richard Onizuka. LC 94-71444. 150p. (Orig.). 1994. pap. 19.95 (*1-880293-03-X*) Alaken.

Mail-Order Brood. Arlene James. (Silhouette Romance Ser.). 1994. per. 2.75 (*0-373-19024-7*, 1-19024-8) Harlequin Bks.

Mail-Order Brother. Suzanne Weyn. (Full House Stephanie Ser.). (J). (gr. 4-6). 1998. pap. 3.99 (*0-671-01726-8*, Minstrel Bks) PB.

Mail Order Business. Williams (Geo) Staff et al. 160p. 1991. spiral bd. 22.95 (*0-8403-7174-8*) Kendall-Hunt.

***Mail Order Business Directory.** 19th ed. Barry Klein. 500p. 2001. pap. 95.00 (*0-915344-92-0*) Todd Pubns.

Mail Order Business Directory, 1994. 17th ed. 85.00 (*0-87340-014-3*) B Klein Pubns.

***Mail Order Business (Personal Imports) in Japan: A Strategic Entry Report, 1996.** Compiled by Icon Group International Staff. (Illus.). 162p. 1999. ring bd. 1620.00 incl. audio compact disk (*0-7418-1253-3*) Icon Grp.

Mail Order Cat. Alan Benjamin & Barbara Blitzer. 1985. 12.95 (*0-671-54619-8*, Fireside) S&S Trade Pap.

***Mail-Order Cinderella.** Kathryn Jensen. (Desire Ser.: Vol. 1318). 2000. mass mkt. 3.99 (*0-373-76318-2*, 1-76318-4) Harlequin Bks.

Mail Order! Clip Art from the 40s, 50s & 60s. Jerry Jankowski. (Illus.). 120p. 1999. pap. 16.95 (*0-88108-218-X*) Art Dir.

Mail Order Cowboy. Pamela Bauer. (American Romance Ser.). 1998. per. 3.99 (*0-373-16718-0*, 1-16718-8) Harlequin Bks.

Mail Order Cowboy. large type ed. Patricia Coughlin. (Silhouette Romance Ser.). 1995. 18.95 (*0-373-59639-1*) Harlequin Bks.

Mail Order Dealer Questions & Answers. Alfred Stern. 48p. 1987. pap. 12.00 (*0-915665-15-8*) Premier Publishers.

Mail Order Dealer's Advertising Rate Manual. Owen Bates. 110p. 1994. pap. 15.00 (*0-915665-30-1*) Premier Publishers.

Mail Order for Fun & Profit. (For Fun & Profit Ser.). (Illus.). 350p. (Orig.). Date not set. pap. 24.95 (*1-56559-922-5*) HGI-Over Fifty.

Mail Order Foreign Bargains Directory. 1987. lib. bdg. 150.00 (*0-8490-3908-8*) Gordon Pr.

Mail-Order Grooms: Holding Out for a Hero; Mail-Order Bridegroom, 2 bks. Vickie Lewis Thompson & Day Leclaire. (By Request 2's Ser.). 2000. mass mkt. 4.99 (*0-373-21711-0*, 1-21711-6) Harlequin Bks.

***Mail Order in Germany: A Strategic Entry Report, 1998.** Compiled by Icon Group International Staff. (Country Industry Report). (Illus.). 96p. 1999. ring bd. 960.00 incl. audio compact disk (*0-7418-0081-0*) Icon Grp.

Mail Order Laws & Regulations. 1987. lib. bdg. 150.00 (*0-8490-3867-7*) Gordon Pr.

Mail Order Legal Guide. 400p. 1993. 65.00 (*0-317-55685-1*) B Klein Pubns.

Mail Order Legal Guide. 2nd ed. Erwin J. Keup. LC 93-29534. (Illus.). 310p. 1998. pap. 29.95 (*1-55571-190-1*, Oasis Pr) PSI Resch.

Mail Order Made Easy. J. Frank Brumbaugh. 1982. pap. 20.00 (*0-87980-394-0*) Wilshire.

Mail-Order Male. Carol Grace. (Romance Ser.). 1993. per. 2.75 (*0-373-08955-4*, 5-08955-2) Silhouette.

***Mail Order Marriage.** large type ed. Margaret Way. (Thorndike Harlequin Romance Ser.). 2000. 22.95 (*0-263-16356-3*) Mills & Boon.

Mail-Order Marriage: 50th Anniversary. anniversary ed. Margaret Way. (Romance Ser.: No. 3551). 1999. per. 3.50 (*0-373-03551-9*, 1-03551-8) Harlequin Bks.

Mail-Order Marriage: 50th Anniversary. anniversary large type ed. Margaret Way. (Romance Ser.: No. 3551). 1999. per. 3.50 (*0-373-15797-5*, 1-15797-3) Harlequin Bks.

Mail-Order Marriages. Debbie Macomber. Vol. 1. 384p. 2000. per. 5.99 (*0-373-83434-9*) Harlequin Bks.

Mail-Order Matty. Emilie Richards. (Special Edition Ser.: No. 1113). 1997. per. 3.99 (*0-373-24113-5*, 1-24113-2) Silhouette.

***Mail-Order Matty.** large type ed. Emilie Richards. (Romance Ser.). 2000. 22.95 (*0-373-59721-5*) Silhouette.

Mail Order Millions: It Worked for Me . . . It Will Work for You. L. Lawrence Baird. 1995. 15.95 (*0-9623724-2-0*) Baird-Hedges Pub.

Mail-Order Mix-Up. Pamela Toth. (Special Edition Ser.). 1998. per. 4.25 (*0-373-24197-6*, 1-24196-7) Silhouette.

Mail Order Moonlighting. 2nd rev. ed. Cecil C. Hoge, Sr. LC 87-17953. 359p. 1988. pap. 19.95 (*0-89815-222-4*) Ten Speed Pr.

Mail-Order Mother. Kate Denton. (Romance Ser.). 1998. per. 3.50 (*0-373-03510-1*, 1-03510-4) Harlequin Bks.

Mail-Order Mother. large type ed. Kate Denton. (Larger Print Ser.). 1998. per. 3.50 (*0-373-15756-8*, 1-15756-9) Harlequin Bks.

Mail-order Murder see Mistletoe Murder

Mail Order Murder. Leslie Meier. 1999. pap. 5.95 (*0-14-015832-4*, Viking) Viking Penguin.

Mail Order Murder. Patricia Springer. 1999. mass mkt. 5.99 (*0-7860-0640-4*) Kensgtn Pub Corp.

Mail Order on the Kitchen Table: This Book Is for the Beginner Who Wants to Make Money in Mail Order Satisfaction Guaranteed. Marilyn S. Schultz. (Illus.). 192p. (C). 1988. 19.95 (*0-9620482-0-8*) Tribute Inc.

Mail Order Product Guide. 250p. 1989. 35.00 (*0-915344-12-2*) B Klein Pubns.

Mail Order Product Guide. 2nd ed. Ed. by Barry T. Klein. 275p. 2001. pap. 50.00 (*0-915344-51-3*) Todd Pubns.

Mail Order Riches Success Kit. 9th ed. Tyler Gregory Hicks. 600p. 1998. pap. 99.50 (*1-56150-204-9*) Intl Wealth.

Mail Order Riches Success Kit. 10th ed. Tyler Gregory Hicks. 600p. 1999. pap. 99.50 (*1-56150-255-3*) Intl Wealth.

***Mail Order Riches Success Kit.** 11th ed. Tyler G. Hicks. 600p. 2000. pap. 99.50 (*1-56150-315-0*) Intl Wealth.

Mail Order Selling: How to Market Almost Anything by Mail. 3rd ed. Irving Burstiner. LC 94-48372. (Small Business Editions Ser.). 292p. 1995. 79.95 (*0-471-09791-8*); pap. 19.95 (*0-471-09759-4*) Wiley.

Mail Order Success Secrets: How to Create a $1,000,000-a-Year Business Starting from Scratch. 2nd rev. ed. Tyler Hicks. LC 98-15805. 336p. 1998. per. 14.95 (*0-7615-1441-4*) Prima Pub.

Mail Order Treasure in Your Library: How to Find It. Faith W. Crown. (Illus.). x, 39p. 1993. reprint ed. pap. 6.00 (*0-9632462-0-8*) Juniper H Pubns.

Mail Order Wife. Phyllis Halldorson. (Romance Ser.). 1996. per. 3.25 (*0-373-19133-2*, 1-19133-7) Silhouette.

Mail-Order Wings. Beatrice Gormley. (Illus.). 164p. (J). (gr. 3-7). 1984. pap. 2.95 (*0-380-67421-1*, Avon Bks) Morrow Avon.

Mail Processing Equipment Operator. Jack Rudman. (Career Examination Ser.: C-3460). 1994. pap. 27.95 (*0-8373-3460-8*) Nat Learn.

Mail Royal. Nigel Tranter. mass mkt. 11.95 (*0-340-53539-3*, Pub. by Hodder & Stought Ltd) Trafalgar.

Mail Surveys. Thomas W. Mangione. (Applied Social Research Methods Ser.: Vol. 40). 132p. 1995. 42.00 (*0-8039-4662-7*); pap. 18.95 (*0-8039-4663-5*) Sage.

***Mailbox Magic.** Nancy Poydar. LC 99-51776. (Illus.). 32p. (J). (ps-3). 2000. 15.95 (*0-8234-1525-2*) Holiday.

Mailbox Mania. Beverly Lewis. (Cul-de-Sac Kids Ser.). 80p. (J). (gr. 2-5). 1996. pap. 3.99 (*1-55661-729-1*) Bethany Hse.

Mailbox Mice Mystery. Graham Percy. (J). 1999. 12.99 (*0-679-88603-6*, Pub. by Random Bks Yng Read) Random.

Mailbox, 1995-1996 Intermediate Yearbook. Ed. by Becky Andrews. (Illus.). 320p. 1996. 29.95 (*1-56234-138-3*) Educ Ctr.

Mailbox, 1995-1996 Primary Yearbook. Ed. by Diane Badden. (Illus.). 320p. 1996. 29.95 (*1-56234-137-5*) Educ Ctr.

Mailbox, 1995-1996 Preschool Yearbook. Ed. by Jayne M. Gammons. (Illus.). 320p. 1996. 29.95 (*1-56234-135-9*) Educ Ctr.

Mailbox, 1995-1996 Kindergarten Yearbook. Ed. by Jan Trautman. (Illus.). 320p. 1996. 29.95 (*1-56234-136-7*) Educ Ctr.

Mailbox, 1996-1997 Intermediate Yearbook. Ed. by Becky Andrews. (Illus.). 320p. 1997. 29.95 (*1-56234-167-7*) Educ Ctr.

Mailbox, 1996-1997 Primary Yearbook. Ed. by Diane Badden. 320p. 1997. 29.95 (*1-56234-166-9*) Educ Ctr.

Mailbox, 1996-1997 Kindergarten Yearbook. Ed. by Jan Trautman. (Illus.). 320p. 1997. 29.95 (*1-56234-165-0*) Educ Ctr.

Mailbox Preschool Yearbook. Ed. by Jayne M. Gammons. (Illus.). 320p. 1997. 29.95 (*1-56234-164-2*) Educ Ctr.

Mailbox Superbook: Your Complete Resource for an Entire Year of Fourth-Grade Success! Becky S. Andrews. LC 97-44710. (J). (gr. 4). 1997. pap. write for info. (*1-56234-177-4*) Educ Ctr.

Mailbox Superbook: Your Complete Resource for an Entire Year of Preschool Success! Ada H. Goren & Barbara Backer. LC 98-5940. 1998. pap. 28.00 (*1-56234-195-2*) Educ Center.

Mailbox Superbook: Your Complete Resource for an Entire Year of Third-Grade Success! Grade 3. Cynthia Holcomb & Thad H. McLaurin. LC 97-32811. 1998. write for info. (*1-56234-199-5*) Educ Ctr.

Mailbox Superbook, Grade 4: Your Complete Resource for an Entire Year of Fourth-Grade Success! Becky S. Andrews. LC 97-44710. 1997. pap. 29.95 (*1-56234-200-2*) Educ Ctr.

Mailbox Superbook, Grade 1: Your Complete Resource for an Entire Year of First-Grade Success! Sharon Murphy. LC 97-47383. 1997. 29.95 (*1-56234-197-9*) Educ Ctr.

Mailbox Superbook, Grade 2: Your Complete Resource for an Entire Year of Second-Grade Success! Cynthia Holcomb et al. LC 98-5187. 1998. pap. 41.60 (*1-56234-198-7*) Education Concepts.

Mailbox Superbook, Kindergarten: Your Complete Resource for an Entire Year of Kindergarten Success! Ada H. Goren & Kimberli Carrier. LC 98-9418. 1998. pap. 41.60 (*1-56234-196-0*) Education Concepts.

Mailboxes. Ed. by Glenn Novak. LC 97-23280. (Illus.). 136p. (Orig.). 1997. pap. 14.95 (*0-88266-970-2*) Storey Bks.

Mail.dat GCA Standard 130-1995, Version 96-1. 2nd rev. ed. Ed. by Dan Minnick. (Illus.). 75p. 1996. pap. 48.00 (*0-933505-32-9*) Graph Comm Assn.

***Mailer: A Biography.** Mary V. Dearborn. LC 99-32214. (Illus.). 448p. 1999. 30.00 (*0-395-73655-2*) HM.

Mailer: A Biography Hilary Mills. LC 83-24852. 477 p. 1984. write for info. (*0-07-042423-3*) McGraw.

***Mailer Leaves Ham.** John M. Bennett. 159p. 1999. pap. 9.95 (*1-880766-19-1*, Pub. by Pantograph Pr) SPD-Small Pr Dist.

Mailer's America. Joseph Wenke. LC 86-40389. 271p. 1987. reprint ed. pap. 84.10 (*0-608-02297-7*, 206293800004) Bks Demand.

Mailing & Other Tyneside Pottery. R. C. Bell. (Album Ser.: No. 170). (Illus.). 32p. 1989. pap. 4.75 (*0-85263-792-6*, Pub. by Shire Pubns) Parkwest Pubns.

Mailing May. Michael O. Tunnell. LC 96-35259. (Illus.). 32p. (J). (ps-3). 1997. lib. bdg. 15.89 (*0-688-12879-3*, Grenwillow Bks) HarpC Child Bks.

Mailing May. Michael O. Tunnell. LC 96-35259. (Illus.). 32p. (J). (ps up). 1997. 16.00 (*0-688-12878-5*, Grenwillow Bks) HarpC Child Bks.

***Mailing May.** Michael O. Tunnell. LC 93-35259. (Illus.). 32p. (J). (ps-3). 2000. mass mkt. 5.95 (*0-06-443724-8*) Morrow Avon.

Maillard Reaction: Consequences for the Chemical & Life Sciences. Ed. by Raphael Ikan. 228p. 1996. 225.00 (*0-471-96300-3*) Wiley.

Maillard Reaction in Food Processing, Human Nutrition & Physiology. Ed. by P. A. Finot et al. (Advances in Life Sciences Ser.). 500p. 1990. 117.50 (*0-8176-2354-X*) Birkhauser.

Maillard Reaction in Foods & Nutrition. Ed. by George R. Waller & Milton S. Feather. LC 83-3852. (ACS Symposium Ser.: No. 215). 596p. 1983. lib. bdg. 65.95 (*0-8412-0769-0*) Am Chemical.

Maillard Reaction in Foods & Nutrition. Ed. by George R. Waller & Milton S. Feather. LC 83-3852. (ACS Symposium Ser.: No. 215). (Illus.). 598p. 1983. reprint ed. pap. 185.40 (*0-608-03207-7*, 206372600007) Bks Demand.

Maillard Reactions in Chemistry, Food, & Health: Proceedings of the Fifth International Symposium on the Maillard Reaction, Held at the University of Minnesota, 1993. Ed. by Theodore P. Labuza et al. 458p. 1994. 157.00 (*0-85186-802-9*, R6802) CRC Pr.

Maillard Reactions in Food: Proceedings of the International Symposium, Uddevalla, Sweden, September 1979. C. Ericksson. (Progress in Food & Nutrition Science Ser.: Vol. 5). (Illus.). 500p. 1982. 170.00 (*0-08-025496-9*, Pergamon Pr) Elsevier.

Maillard Reactions in Foods & Medicine. Ed. by J. O'Brien et al. (Special Publication Ser.: Vol. 223). 480p. 1998. 145.00 (*0-85404-733-6*) Spr-Verlag.

Maillol. Bertrand Lorquin. LC 94-61693. (Illus.). 200p. 1995. 40.00 (*0-500-97417-9*, Pub. by Thames Hudson) Norton.

Maillol Nudes: Thirty-Five Lithographs by Aristide Maillol. Aristide Maillol. (Dover Art Library). Orig. Title: The Dialogues of the Courtesans. (Illus.). 32p. 1980. pap. 4.95 (*0-486-24000-2*) Dover.

Mailman. Patrick Brady. 164p. (Orig.). 1995. pap. 10.95 (*1-886935-31-9*) New Prdigm Pr.

Mailman Would Not Kill. Henry Madere. 226p. (Orig.). 1997. pap. 11.95 (*0-9656529-0-4*) Madere Ent.

MailMaster Pro User's Guide. Gary Tanin. (Pro Software Ser.). (Illus.). 188p. (C). 1990. ring bd., boxed set 35.00 (*1-878835-00-9*, VP0290A1) Bran-Tan Alley Soft.

Maimed by the Sea - Erosion along the Coasts of Oregon & Washington - A Documentary. Bert Webber. (Illus.). 126p. 1983. 12.95 (*0-87770-288-8*) Ye Galleon.

Maimie Papers: Letters from an Ex-Prostitute. Maimie Pinzer. Ed. by Sue Davidson & Ruth C. Rosen. LC 77-21693. 528p. 1997. pap. text 19.95 (*1-55861-143-6*) Feminist Pr.

Maimonidean Studies, Vol. 1. Ed. by Arthur Hyman. 1994. 35.00 (*0-88125-358-8*) Ktav.

Maimonidean Studies, Vol. II. Ed. by Arthur Hyman. 1995. 35.00 (*0-88125-427-4*) Ktav.

Maimonidean Studies, Vol. 3. Ed. by Arthur Hyman. 1995. 35.00 (*0-88125-497-5*) Ktav.

Maimonidean Studies, Vol. 4. Arthur Hyman. 2000. 35.00 (*0-88125-622-6*) Ktav.

Maimonides: A Collection of Critical Essays. Ed. by Joseph A. Buijs. LC 87-40617. 336p. (C). 1990. pap. text 17.50 (*0-268-01368-3*) U of Notre Dame Pr.

Maimonides: A Guide for Today's Perplexed. Kenneth Seeskin. 141p. (Orig.). 1991. pap. 12.95 (*0-87441-509-8*) Behrman.

Maimonides: His Nature, Histroy & Messianic Beliefs. Amos Funkenstein. 1998. pap. text 14.95 (*965-05-0909-7*, Pub. by Israel Ministry Def) Gefen Bks.

Maimonides: His Wisdom for Our Time. large type ed. Ed. by Gilbert S. Rosenthal. (Large Print Jewish Classics Ser.). 120p. 1991. pap. 9.95 (*0-8027-2646-1*) Walker & Co.

Maimonides: Selected Essays, Original Anthology. Ed. by Steven Katz. LC 79-7176. (Jewish Philosophy, Mysticism & History of Ideas Ser.). 1980. lib. bdg. 56.95 (*0-405-12234-9*) Ayer.

Maimonides & Abrabanel on Prophecy. Isaac Abravanel & Alvin J. Reines. LC 73-119106. 321p. reprint ed. pap. 99.60 (*0-7837-0156-X*, 204045200017) Bks Demand.

Maimonides & Aquinas: A Contemporary Appraisal. Jacob Haberman. 29.50 (*0-87068-685-2*) Ktav.

***Maimonides & Medieval Jewish.** Frank. 2000. pap. 21.00 (*0-8133-9124-5*, Pub. by Westview) HarpC.

Maimonides & Palamas on God. George C. Papademetriou. LC 93-50531. 127p. (Orig.). (C). 1994. pap. text 9.95 (*0-916586-68-5*, Pub. by Holy Cross Orthodox) BookWorld.

Maimonides & Philosophy. Ed. by Y. Yovel & Shlomo Pines. 296p. (C). 1986. lib. bdg. 132.50 (*90-247-3439-8*, Pub. by M Nijhoff) Kluwer Academic.

Maimonides & St. Thomas on the Limits of Reason. Idit Dobbs-Weinstein. LC 94-3369. (SUNY Series in Philosophy). 278p. (C). 1995. text 64.50 (*0-7914-2415-4*); pap. text 21.95 (*0-7914-2416-2*) State U NY Pr.

Maimonides' Commentary on Avoth. Paul Forchheimer. pap. 11.95 (*0-87306-332-5*) Feldheim.

Maimonides' Commentary on Mishnah Sanhedrin. Tr. by Fred Rosner from HEB. LC 81-51800. 224p. 1981. 17.00 (*0-87203-099-7*) Hermon.

***Maimonides' Empire of Light: Popular Enlightenment in an Age of Belief.** Ralph Lerner & Maimonides. LC 00-21360. 1999. 35.00 (*0-226-47313-9*) U Ch Pr.

Maimonides' Ethics: The Encounter of Philosophic & Religious Morality. Raymond L. Weiss. 234p. 1991. 34.50 (*0-226-89152-6*) U Ch Pr.

Maimonides' Introduction to His Commentary on the Mishnah. Tr. & Anno. by Fred Rosner. LC 94-14644. 256p. 1995. 35.00 (*1-56821-241-0*) Aronson.

Maimonides' Introduction to the Talmud: A Translation of Maimonides Introduction to His Commentary on the Mishna with Complete Original Hebrew Text. 3rd rev. ed. Anno. by Tzvi Lampel. 288p. 1998. pap. 15.95 (*1-880582-28-7*) Judaica Pr.

Maimonides' Mishneh Torah, a Collection of Manuscripts from the Library of the Jewish Theological Seminary of America: An Index to the Microfilm Collection, Reels 1-9. University Microfilms International Staff. LC 80-23113. 1980. pap. 15.00 (*0-8357-0530-7*) Univ Microfilms.

Maimonides Octocentennial Series, No. I[00ad]IV. Asher Hirsch Ginzberg et al. (Jewish People; History, Religion, Literature Ser.). 1973. reprint ed. 18.95 (*0-405-05278-2*) Ayer.

Maimonides on Judaism & the Jewish People. Menachem M. Kellner. LC 90-44128. (SUNY Series in Jewish Philosophy). 180p. (C). 1991. text 21.50 (*0-7914-0691-1*) State U NY Pr.

Maimonides on the "Decline of the Generations" & the Nature of Rabbinic Authority. Menachem M. Kellner. LC 95-19975. (SUNY Series in Jewish Philosophy). 224p. (C). 1996. pap. text 17.95 (*0-7914-2922-9*) State U NY Pr.

Maimonides on the "Decline of the Generations" & the Nature of Rabbinic Authority. Menachem M. Kellner. LC 95-19975. (SUNY Series in Jewish Philosophy). 224p. (C). 1996. text 54.50 (*0-7914-2921-0*) State U NY Pr.

Maimonides' Political Thought: Studies in Ethics, Law, & the Human Ideal. Howard Kreisel. LC 99-13651. (SUNY Series in Jewish Philosophy). 360p. (C). 1999. pap. text 24.95 (*0-7914-4190-3*) State U NY Pr.

An Asterisk (*) at the beginning of an entry indicates that the title is appearing for the first time.

Maimonides' Political Thought: Studies in Ethics, Law, & the Human Ideal. Howard Kreisel. LC 99-13651. (SUNY Series in Jewish Philosophy). 416p. (C). 1999. text 73.50 (*0-7914-4189-X*) State U NY Pr.

Maimonides Reader. Ed. & Intro. by Isadore Twersky. LC 76-160818. pap. 19.95 (*0-87441-206-4*) Behrman.

Maimonides-Torah & Philosophic Quest. David Hartman. LC 76-6305. 288p. 1977. pap. 14.95 (*0-8276-0255-3*) JPS Phila.

Main. Trevanian. 336p. 1987. mass mkt. 5.99 (*0-515-09272-X*, Jove) Berkley Pub.

Main Advantages of Non-Involute Spur Gears. J. Hlebanja. (Nineteen Ninety-Two Fall Technical Meeting Ser.: Vol. 92FTM5). (Illus.). 6p. 1992. pap. text 30.00 (*1-55589-585-9*) AGMA.

Main Agreement of the National Industrial Council for the Motor Industry. Ed. by National Industrial Council Staff & B. G. Du Preez. 1989. ring bd. write for info. (*0-7021-2263-7*, Pub. by Juta & Co) Gaunt.

Main Attraction. Jayne Ann Krentz. 1994. mass mkt. 4.50 (*0-373-83267-2*, 1-83267-4); per. 4.99 (*0-373-83317-2*) Harlequin Bks.

Main Battle Tanks. John Nicholaus. (Army Library). (Illus.). 48p. (J). (gr. 3-8). 1989. 13.95 (*0-685-58576-X*) Rourke Corp.

Main Battle Tanks. John Nicholaus. (Army Library). (Illus.). 48p. (J). (gr. 3-8). 1989. lib. bdg. 23.93 (*0-86592-420-1*) Rourke Enter.

Main Battle Tanks: Developments in Design since 1945. Rolf Hilmes. Tr. by Richard E. Simpkin. (Illus.). 130p. 1987. 53.00 (*0-08-034756-8*, Pergamon Pr) Elsevier.

Main Bitch. Bob George. 224p. 1995. pap. write for info. (*0-7490-0257-3*) Allison & Busby.

Main Brides. Gail Scott. 234p. 1993. pap. 16.95 (*0-88910-456-5*, Pub. by CHP) SPD-Small Pr Dist.

Main Chapters in American Labor History: From Origins to the Present. David Brody. LC 92-42134. 272p. 1993. text 57.95 (*0-19-506790-8*); pap. text 21.95 (*0-19-506791-6*) OUP.

Main Corpse. large type ed. Diane Mott Davidson. LC 96-49135. (Large Print Bks.). 1997. 25.95 (*1-56895-409-3*) Wheeler Pub.

Main Corpse. Diane Mott Davidson. 384p. 1997. reprint ed. mass mkt. 6.50 (*0-553-57463-9*, Crimeline) Bantam.

Main Coupee. Blaise Cendrars. (FRE.). 448p. 1975. pap. 11.95 (*0-7859-1792-6*, 2070366197) Fr & Eur.

Main Course: Heritage & Hope Cookbook. Ed. by Bettye H. Carpenter. (Illus.). 304p. 1988. pap. 12.95 (*0-317-91270-4*) S Main Baptist Ch.

Main Course Salads. (Popular Brands Cookbooks Ser.). (Illus.). 24p. 1995. pap. write for info. (*1-56144-670-X*) Modern Pub NYC.

Main Course Salads. Ray Overton. LC 99-60107. (Illus.). 122p. 1999. 15.95 (*1-56352-512-7*) Longstreet.

Main Course Salads: Creative Salads That Satisfy. Donna Rodnitzky. LC 99-15219. (Illus.). 255p. 1999. pap. 14.95 (*0-89529-928-3*, Avery) Penguin Putnam.

***Main-Course Sandwiches.** Ray Overton. LC 99-61760. (Illus.). 128p. 1999. 15.95 (*1-56352-576-3*) Longstreet.

Main-Course Soups. Ray Overton. LC 97-73570. (Illus.). 124p. 1998. 15.95 (*1-56352-445-7*) Longstreet.

Main-Course Vegetarian Pleasures. Jeanne Lemlin. LC 94-23966. 272p. 1998. pap. 17.00 (*0-06-095022-6*) HarpC.

***Main Courses.** Anness Publishing Staff. 2000. pap. 12.95 (*0-7548-0472-0*) Anness Pub.

Main Currents in American Legal Thought. Bernard Schwartz. LC 92-74821. 678p. 1993. 49.95 (*0-89089-532-5*) Carolina Acad Pr.

Main Currents in American Thought, 3 vols., Set. Vernon L. Parrington. 1993. reprint ed. lib. bdg. 225.00 (*0-7812-5283-0*) Rprt Serv.

Main Currents in American Thought, Vol. II. Vernon L. Parrington. LC 87-6028. 516p. 1987. pap. 21.95 (*0-8061-2081-9*) U of Okla Pr.

Main Currents in Caribbean Thought: The Historical Evolution of Caribbean Society in Its Ideological Aspects, 1492-1900. Gordon K. Lewis. LC 82-17128. (Johns Hopkins Studies in Atlantic History & Culture). 391p. reprint ed. pap. 121.30 (*0-608-06104-2*, 206643600008) Bks Demand.

Main Currents in Contemporary German, British, & American Philosophy. enl. rev. ed. W. Stegmueller. 584p. 1969. text 155.50 (*90-277-0011-7*) Kluwer Academic.

Main Currents in Modern Economics. Ben Seligman. 950p. 1989. pap. 34.95 (*0-88738-811-6*) Transaction Pubs.

Main Currents in Nineteenth Century Literature, 6 vols., Set. George Brandes. LC 72-3577. (Studies in European Literature: No. 56). 1972. reprint ed. lib. bdg. 375.00 (*0-8383-1574-7*) M S G Haskell Hse.

Main Currents in Sociological Thought: Durkheim, Pareto, Weber. Raymond Aron. 360p. 1998. pap. text 24.95 (*0-7658-0436-0*) Transaction Pubs.

Main Currents in Sociological Thought Vol. 1: Montesquieu, Comte, Marx, Tocqueville, & the Sociologists & the Revolution of 1848. Raymond Aron. LC 97-30354. 374p. 1998. pap. 24.95 (*0-7658-0401-8*) Transaction Pubs.

Main Currents in the History of American Journalism. Willard G. Bleyer. LC 70-77720. (American Scene Ser.). (Illus.). v, 464p. 1973. reprint ed. lib. bdg. 59.50 (*0-306-71358-6*) Da Capo.

Main Currents in Twentieth Century Literary Criticism: A Critical Survey. Yiannis Stamiris. LC 82-50402. xvi, 320p. 1986. 49.00 (*0-87875-254-4*) Whitston Pub.

Main Currents Mass Communications Edition. 2nd ed. Phillip H. Agee et al. 384p. (C). 1997. pap. text 44.00 (*0-06-040185-0*) Addson-Wesley Educ.

Main Currents of Critical Psychology. M. H. Van Ijzendoorn et al. Tr. by M. Schoen. 250p. 1984. text 32.50 (*0-8290-1517-5*); pap. text 16.95 (*0-8290-1518-3*) Irvington.

Main Currents of Modern French Drama. Hugh A. Smith. LC 68-22946. (Essay Index Reprint Ser.). 1977. 23.95 (*0-8369-0883-X*) Ayer.

Main Currents of Scientific Thought see History of the Sciences

Main Currents of Spanish Literature. Jeremiah D. Ford. LC 68-13689. 1968. reprint ed. 30.00 (*0-8196-0213-2*) Biblo.

Main Currents of Western Thought: Readings in Western European Intellectual History from the Middle Ages to the Present. 4th ed. Franklin L. Baumer. LC 77-90945. 806p. 1978. reprint ed. pap. 25.00 (*0-300-02233-6*) Yale U Pr.

Main Dish Salads. Norman Kolpas. LC 97-38728. (Illus.). 128p. 1998. 24.95 (*0-7621-0000-1*, Pub. by RD Assn) Penguin Putnam.

Main-Dish Salads. Time-Life Books Editors. Ed. by Catherine Hackett. LC 96-49782. (Great Taste - Low Fat Ser.). (Illus.). 160p. (J). (gr. 7). 1999. spiral bd. 14.95 (*0-7835-4566-5*) Time-Life.

***Main Dish Soups.** Frederica Langeland. LC 99-47394. (Illus.). 2000. 19.95 (*0-7621-0266-7*, Pub. by RD Assn) Penguin Putnam.

Main Dish Soups & Stews . . . And Breads: A Family Primer. Narda Butler & Barbara Beckman. (Family Primer Ser.). 56p. 1995. pap. text 4.95 (*0-9648494-2-9*) Dreamspnnrs.

Main Dishes. Louise Stoltzfus. LC 94-14899. (Best of Favorite Recipes from Quilters Ser.). (Illus.). 64p. 1994. 7.95 (*1-56148-114-9*) Good Bks PA.

Main Dishes: With over 140 Complete Menus. 3rd ed. Sue Gregg. (Eating Better Cookbooks: Vol. 1). (Illus.). 294p. 1997. spiral bd. 20.00 (*1-878272-13-6*) S Gregg Cookbks.

Main-d'oeuvre: Poemes, 1913-1949. Pierre Reverdy. (FRE.). 548p. 1989. pap. 49.95 (*0-7859-1542-7*, 2715215819) Fr & Eur.

Main-d'Oeuvre Potentielle et Emploi Regional en Union Sovietique. C. Beaucourt. (Economies et Societes Series G: No. 24). 1966. pap. 34.00 (*0-8115-0715-7*) Periodicals Srv.

Main Economic Indicators: Sources & Definitions. OECD Staff. 160p. 1997. pap. 32.00 (*92-64-15602-X*, 31-97-17-1, Pub. by Org for Econ) OECD.

Main Economic Indicators Sources & Methods: Interest Rates & Share Price Indices. OECD Staff. LC 98-157133. 68p. 1998. pap. 18.00 (*92-64-16036-1*, 31-98-14-1, Pub. by Org for Econ) OECD.

Main Economic Indicators Sources & Methods: Mexico. 74p. (Orig.). 1997. pap. 19.00 (*92-64-15453-1*, 31-97-13-1, Pub. by Org for Econ) OECD.

Main Economic Policy Areas of the EC after 1992. 4th ed. Ed. by Peter Coffey. LC 93-24818. (International Studies in Economics & Econometrics: Vol. 30). 1993. lib. bdg. 138.50 (*0-7923-2375-0*) Kluwer Academic.

Main Economic Policy Areas of the EEC. Peter Coffey. 1983. lib. bdg. 94.00 (*90-247-2793-6*) Kluwer Academic.

Main Economic Policy Areas of the EEC - Toward 1992: The Challenge to the Community's Economic Policies When the "Real" Common Market Is Created by the End of 1992. 3rd rev. ed. Ed. by Peter Coffey. (C). 1990. lib. bdg. 120.00 (*0-7923-0810-7*) Kluwer Academic.

Main Elements of Microeconomics. 2nd ed. Date not set. pap. text, teacher ed. write for info. (*0-8299-0442-5*) West Pub.

***Main Event.** (World Championship Wrestling - New World Order Colossal Sticker Activity Book Ser.). (Illus.). 240p. 1999. pap. write for info. (*0-7666-0449-7*, Honey Bear Bks) Modern Pub NYC.

Main Events & Developments on the Electronic Information Services Market 1991-1992: Commission of the European Communities. 100p. (Orig.). (C). 1995. pap. text 30.00 (*0-7881-1976-1*) DIANE Pub.

Main Features & Trends in Petroleum & Mining Agreements: A Technical Paper. 129p. 1983. pap. 13.50 (*92-1-104057-4*, E.83.II.A.9) UN.

Main Gauche. Guy de Maupassant. 9.95 (*0-686-54795-0*) Fr & Eur.

Main Gauche. Guy de Maupassant. (FRE.). 1978. pap. 10.95 (*0-7859-2972-X*, 2080703005) Fr & Eur.

***Main Group Chemistry.** 2nd ed. Massey. LC 99-56863. 2000. text. write for info. (*0-471-49037-7*) Wiley.

***Main Group Chemistry** 2nd ed. Massey. LC 99-56863. 2000. pap. text. write for info. (*0-471-49039-3*) Wiley.

Main Group Elements & Their Compounds. K. V. Das. 525p. 1997. 139.00 (*3-540-61425-7*) Spr-Verlag.

Main Idea. Linda Ward-Beech et al. (Comprehension Skills Ser.). 1997. pap., student ed. 8.20 (*0-8114-7830-0*); pap., student ed. 8.20 (*0-8114-7836-X*); pap., student ed. 8.20 (*0-8114-7842-4*); pap., student ed. 8.20 (*0-8114-7848-3*); pap., student ed. 8.20 (*0-8114-7854-8*) Raintree Steck-V.

Main Idea, Levels 8-12. 8th ed. Tank. (Comprehension Skills Ser.). 1998. pap. text 6.33 (*0-89061-345-1*) NTC Contemp Pub Co.

Main Idea: Reading Level 10-J. 10th ed. Pauk. (Single Skills Ser.). 1993. pap. 5.65 (*0-89061-382-6*, Jamestwn Pub) NTC Contemp Pub Co.

Main Idea: Reading Level 11-K. 11th ed. Pauk. (Single Skills Ser.). 1993. pap. 5.65 (*0-89061-388-5*, Jamestwn Pub) NTC Contemp Pub Co.

Main Idea: Reading Level 12-L. (Single Skills Ser.). (Orig.). 1993. pap. 5.65 (*0-89070-394-9*, Jamestwn Pub) NTC Contemp Pub Co.

Main Idea: Reading Level 3-C. 3rd ed. Pauk. (Single Skills Ser.). 1993. pap. 5.65 (*0-89061-365-6*, Jamestwn Pub) NTC Contemp Pub Co.

Main Idea: Reading Level 4-D. 4th ed. Pauk. (Single Skills Ser.). 1993. pap. 5.65 (*0-89061-371-0*, Jamestwn Pub) NTC Contemp Pub Co.

Main Idea: Reading Level 5-E. 5th ed. Pauk. (Single Skills Ser.). 1993. pap. 5.65 (*0-89061-327-3*, Jamestwn Pub) NTC Contemp Pub Co.

Main Idea: Reading Level 6-F. 6th ed. Pauk. (Single Skills Ser.). 1993. pap. 5.65 (*0-89061-333-8*, Jamestwn Pub) NTC Contemp Pub Co.

Main Idea: Reading Level 9-I. 9th ed. Pauk. (Single Skills Ser.). 1993. pap. 5.65 (*0-89061-376-1*, Jamestwn Pub) NTC Contemp Pub Co.

Main Idea: Reading to Learn. 2nd ed. Myrna B. Skidell & Sidney G. Becker. LC 98-15220. 453p. 1998. pap. 40.00 (*0-205-28322-5*) Allyn.

Main Idea 1. Donna Townsend et al. (Comprehension Skills Ser.). 1997. pap., student ed. 8.76 (*0-8114-1954-1*) Raintree Steck-V.

Main Idea Prep. Donna Townsend. (Comprehension Skills Ser.). 1997. pap., student ed. 8.76 (*0-8114-1966-5*) Raintree Steck-V.

Main Institutions of Jewish Law, 2 vols., Set. rev. ed. Isaac Herzog. 737p. 1980. pap. 16.95 (*0-900689-14-5*) Bloch.

Main Institutions of Roman Private Law. William W. Buckland. LC 93-79708. 434p. 1994. reprint ed. 115.00 (*1-56169-066-X*) Gaunt.

Main Issues in Bioethics. Andrew C. Varga. LC 80-82084. 348p. (Orig.). (C). 1984. pap. 14.95 (*0-8091-2327-4*) Paulist Pr.

Main Issues in Bioethics. Andrew C. Varga. LC 80-82084. 235p. (Orig.). reprint ed. pap. 72.90 (*0-608-14653-6*, 202078000018) Bks Demand.

***Main Issues in Mental Health & Race.** Ed. by David Ndegwa & D. Olajide. 278p. 2000. 74.95 (*1-84014-812-8*) Ashgate Pub Co.

Main Justice: The Men & Women Who Enforce the Nation's Criminal Laws & Guard Its Liberties. James McGee & Brian Duffy. 384p. 1996. 25.00 (*0-684-81135-9*) Simon & Schuster.

Main Lectures: Proceedings of the International Congress of Logopedics & Phoniatrics, 17th, Copenhagen, August, 1977, 94175 +P +C +013Vol. 29, No. 1 +059 +91164 +P +C + International Congress of Logopedics & Phoniatrics. Ed. by E. Loebell et al. (Folia Phoniatrics Ser.: Vol. 29, No. 1). (Illus.). 1977. 28.75 (*3-8055-2780-2*) S Karger.

Main Line FUN-ics: Vernaculaire Extraordinaire on the Main Line. Michael L. Ellis, 3rd. (Illus.). (Orig.). 1994. pap. text 3.50 (*0-929178-50-5*) Valley Forge Pub.

Main Line Is Murder. Donna Huston Murray. 1995. mass mkt. 5.99 (*0-312-95637-1*) St Martin.

Main Line King's Indian. John Nunn. 288p. 1996. pap. 29.00 (*0-87447-719-0*) H Holt & Co.

Main Line Wasp. W. Thacher Longstreth. 1990. 21.95 (*0-393-02780-5*) Norton.

Main Man. Tim C. Leedom & Harry W. Carpenter. 449p. 1999. mass mkt. 9.95 (*0-939040-17-4*) Truth Seeker.

Main Papers see European Nutrition Conference: Proceedings, 2nd, Munich, 1976

Main Philosophical Writings & the Novel Allwill. Friedrich H. Jacobi. Ed. & Tr. by George Di Giovanni. (McGill-Queen's Studies in the History of Religion Ser.). 704p. 1995. 95.00 (*0-7735-1018-4*, Pub. by McG-Queens Univ Pr) CUP Services.

Main Principles of the German Basic Law. Ed. by Christian Starck. 149p. 1983. pap. 44.00 (*3-7890-0922-9*, Pub. by Nomos Verlags) Intl Bk Import.

Main Problems in American History, Vol. 1. 4th ed. Ed. by Howard H. Quint et al. 367p. (C). 1978. pap. text. write for info. (*0-534-11247-1*) Wadsworth Pub.

Main Problems in American History Vol. 1: Reconstruction: The Nation's Unfinished Business Black Life after Reconstruction, 1877-1910. abr. ed. Henry F. Bedford & Thomas C. Colt. (PaperBook Series in History). (Illus.). 128p. (C). 1996. pap. text 2.25 (*1-877891-32-0*) Paperbook Pr Inc.

Main Problems in American History Vol. 2: The Impact of Industrialization on American Society Labor's Response to Modern Industrialism. abr. ed. Sigmund Diamond & Herbert G. Gutman. (PaperBook Series in History). (Illus.). 128p. (C). 1996. pap. text 2.25 (*1-877891-33-9*) Paperbook Pr Inc.

Main Problems in American History Vol. 3: American Imperialism & Progressivism: Coping with Social Change. abr. ed. Norman A. Graebner & James T. Patterson. (PaperBook Series in History). (Illus.). 128p. (C). 1996. pap. text 2.25 (*1-877891-34-7*) Paperbook Pr Inc.

Main Problems in American History Vol. 4: The Emergence of the "New Woman," 1870-1920 & New Women: From the 1920s to the Present. abr. ed. Nancy S. Dye & Nancy Woloch. (PaperBook Series in History). (Illus.). 128p. (C). 1996. pap. text 2.25 (*1-877891-35-5*) Paperbook Pr Inc.

Main Problems in American History Vol. 5: The New Deal & President Roosevelt an American Foreign Policy. abr. ed. Dean Albertson & Robert H. Ferrell. (PaperBook Series in History). (Illus.). 128p. (C). 1996. pap. text 2.25 (*1-877891-36-3*) Paperbook Pr Inc.

Main Problems in American History Vol. 6: The United States & the Cold War & the Military-Industrial Complex. abr. ed. Richard J. Barnet & Peter D. Jones. (PaperBook Series in History). (Illus.). 128p. (C). 1996. pap. text 2.25 (*1-877891-37-1*) Paperbook Pr Inc.

Main Problems in American History Vol. 7: The Fifties. abr. ed. Blanche Wiesen Cook & Gerald Markowitz. (PaperBook Series in History). (Illus.). 128p. (C). 1996. pap. text 2.25 (*1-877891-38-X*) Paperbook Pr Inc.

Main Problems in American History Vol. 8: American Political History, 1960-1987 & American Social History, 1960-1987. abr. ed. William H. Chafe & Maurice Isserman. (PaperBook Series in History). (Illus.). 128p. (C). 1996. pap. text 2.25 (*1-877891-39-8*) Paperbook Pr Inc.

Main Progressions in Eidetic Analysis. Laurie Purcell. (Orig.). 1990. pap. 11.00 (*0-913412-29-5*) Brandon Hse.

Main Report see Water & Power Resources of West Pakistan, a Study in Sector Planning

Main Report: Proceedings of the International Association of Logopedics & Phoniatrics 18th Congress, Washington, D. C., August 1980. International Association of Logopedics & Phoniatr. Ed. by B. Fritzell et al. (Journal: Folia Phoniatrica: Vol. 32, No. 2). (Illus.). 72p. 1980. pap. 28.75 (*3-8055-1235-X*) S Karger.

Main Ridge Community at Lost City: Virgin Anasazi Architecture, Ceramics, & Burials. Margaret M. Lyneis. LC 92-53608. (Anthropological Papers: No. 117). (Illus.). 120p. 1992. pap. 25.00 (*0-87480-411-6*) U of Utah Pr.

Main Road. 1980. pap. 2.00 (*0-935350-01-2*) Luna Bisonte.

Main Road. deluxe limited ed. 1980. pap. 6.00 (*0-935350-77-2*) Luna Bisonte.

***Main Rooster & Other Short Stories.** Marlin D. Tucker. LC 00-131041. (Illus.). 382p. (YA). 2000. pap. 14.95 (*1-56883-077-7*, 1-56883-077-7) Colonial Pr AL.

Main Source: Learning from Television News. John P. Robinson & Mark R. Levy. LC 85-22195. (People & Communication Ser.: No. 17). (Illus.). 272p. (Orig.). 1986. reprint ed. pap. 84.40 (*0-7837-4559-1*, 204408700003) Bks Demand.

Main Springs of Western Civilization. Abdul H. Siddiqui. 160p. 1993. 12.50 (*1-56744-127-0*) Kazi Pubns.

Main Stalk: A Synthesis of Navajo Philosophy. John R. Farella. LC 84-8803. 221p. 1990. reprint ed. pap. 16.95 (*0-8165-1210-8*) U of Ariz Pr.

Main Stream. Stuart P. Sherman. (BCL1-PS American Literature Ser.). 239p. 1992. reprint ed. lib. bdg. 79.00 (*0-7812-6623-8*) Rprt Serv.

Main Stream of Mathematics: From the Earliest Beginnings to the Age of Relativity. Edna E. Kramer. (Illus.). 334p. (C). 1988. reprint ed. pap. text 12.95 (*0-945726-01-5*); reprint ed. lib. bdg. 35.00 (*0-945726-00-7*) Scholars Bookshelf.

Main Stream of Music & Other Essays. Donald F. Tovey. LC 76-29391. reprint ed. 50.00 (*0-404-15355-0*) AMS Pr.

Main Street. Sinclair Lewis. 544p. 1996. mass mkt. 5.95 (*0-553-21451-9*) Bantam.

Main Street. Sinclair Lewis. 1920. 11.05 (*0-606-01015-7*, Pub. by Turtleback) Demco.

Main Street. Sinclair Lewis. LC 95-16373. 448p. 1995. pap. 9.95 (*0-14-018901-7*, Penguin Classics) Viking Penguin.

Main Street. Peter Viney & Karen Viney. 122p. 1996. pap. text, teacher ed. 16.95 (*0-19-434525-4*) OUP.

Main Street. Sinclair Lewis. 297p. 1984. reprint ed. lib. bdg. 31.95 (*0-89966-495-4*) Buccaneer Bks.

Main Street. Sinclair Lewis. (Collected Works of Sinclair Lewis). 451p. 1998. reprint ed. lib. bdg. 108.00 (*1-58201-673-9*) Classic Bks.

Main Street. unabridged ed. Sinclair Lewis. LC 99-11770. 384p. 1999. pap. text 2.50 (*0-486-40655-5*) Dover.

Main Street, No. 2. Peter Viney et al. (Illus.). 62p. 1993. pap. text, wbk. ed. 6.95 (*0-19-434478-9*) OUP.

Main Street, No. 3. Peter Viney et al. (Illus.). 70p. 1994. pap. text, wbk. ed. 6.95 (*0-19-434482-7*) OUP.

Main Street, No. 4. Peter Viney et al. (Illus.). 74p. 1994. pap. text, wbk. ed. 6.95 (*0-19-434518-1*) OUP.

Main Street, No. 5. Peter Viney et al. (Illus.). 102p. 1995. pap. text, student ed. 10.95 (*0-19-434520-3*); pap. text, wbk. ed. 6.95 (*0-19-434522-X*) OUP.

Main Street, No. 6. Peter Viney & Karen Viney. (Illus.). 100p. 1995. pap. text, student ed. 10.95 (*0-19-434524-6*); pap. text, wbk. ed. 6.95 (*0-19-434526-2*) OUP.

Main Street: Home for Christmas, Bk. 2. Susan E. Kirby. 128p. (Orig.). (J). 1994. pap. 3.50 (*0-380-77407-0*, Avon Bks) Morrow Avon.

Main Street: Lemonade Days, Bk. 1. Susan E. Kirby. 128p. (Orig.). (J). 1994. pap. 3.50 (*0-380-77406-2*, Avon Bks) Morrow Avon.

Main Street: One of Modern Library's 100 Best Novels. Sinclair Lewis. 1976. 25.95 (*0-8488-0828-2*) Amereon Ltd.

Main Street: One of Modern Library's 100 Best Novels. Sinclair Lewis. 496p. 1996. pap. 10.95 (*0-7867-0325-3*) Carroll & Graf.

Main Street: One of Modern Library's 100 Best Novels. Sinclair Lewis. LC 98-31439. 1999. pap. 9.95 (*0-375-75314-1*) Modern Lib NY.

Main Street: One of Modern Library's 100 Best Novels. Sinclair Lewis. (Signet Classics Ser.). 440p. 1998. mass mkt. 5.95 (*0-451-52682-1*, Sig) NAL.

Main Street: One of Modern Library's 100 Best Novels. Sinclair Lewis. LC 96-4005. 463p. 1996. pap. text 8.95 (*1-57392-048-7*) Prometheus Bks.

Main Street: Student Book 1. Peter Viney et al. (Illus.). 94p. 1993. pap. text, student ed. 10.95 (*0-19-434472-X*) OUP.

Main Street: Student Book 2. Peter Viney et al. (Illus.). 94p. 1993. pap. text, student ed. 10.95 (*0-19-434476-2*) OUP.

Main Street: Student Book 3. Peter Viney et al. (Illus.). 96p. 1994. pap. text, student ed. 10.95 (*0-19-434480-0*) OUP.

Main Street: Teacher's Book 1. Peter Viney et al. (Illus.). 118p. 1993. pap. text, teacher ed. 16.95 (*0-19-434473-8*) OUP.

Main Street: Teacher's Book 2. Peter Viney et al. (Illus.). 118p. 1994. teacher ed., spiral bd. 16.95 (0-19-434477-0) OUP.
Main Street: Teacher's Book 3. Peter Viney et al. (Illus.). 120p. 1994. pap. text, teacher ed. 16.95 (0-19-434481-9) OUP.
Main Street: Teacher's Book 4. Peter Viney et al. (Illus.). 124p. 1995. pap. text, teacher ed. 16.95 (0-19-434486-X) OUP.
Main Street: Teacher's Book 5. Peter Viney et al. (Illus.). 126p. 1995. pap. text, teacher ed. 16.95 (0-19-434521-1) OUP.
Main Street: The Revolt of Carol Kennicott. Martin Bucco. LC 93-7659. (Twayne's Masterwork Studies). 160p. 1993. 23.95 (0-8057-8373-3, Twyne); pap. 13.95 (0-8057-8377-6, Twayne) Mac Lib Ref.
Main Street: Workbook 1. Peter Viney et al. (Illus.). 62p. 1993. pap. text, wbk. ed. 6.95 (0-19-434474-6) OUP.
Main Street America. Reader's Digest Editors. LC 98-5245. (Explore America Ser.). 1998. write for info. (0-7621-0077-X) RD Assn.
Main Street America & the Third World. rev. ed. John M. Hamilton. LC 88-30653. 220p. (Orig.). 1989. pap. 10.95 (0-932020-64-X) Seven Locks Pr.
Main Street Amusement: Movies & Commercials Entertainment in a Southern City, 1896-1930. Gregory A. Waller. LC 94-43157. (Illus.). 320p. 1995. text 49.00 (1-56098-504-6); pap. text 19.95 (1-56098-547-X) Smithsonian.
Main Street & Babbitt. Sinclair Lewis. Ed. by John Hersey. 898p. 1992. 40.00 (0-940450-61-5, Pub. by Library of America) Penguin Putnam.
Main Street, & Other Poems. Joyce Kilmer. (Collected Works of Joyce Kilmer). 78p. 1998. reprint ed. lib. bdg. 88.00 (1-58201-664-X) Classic Bks.
Main Street & Wall Street. William Z. Ripley. LC 73-2531. (Big Business; Economic Power in a Free Society Ser.). 1973. reprint ed. 26.95 (0-405-05109-3) Ayer.
Main Street & Wall Street. William Z. Ripley. LC 72-93640. 1973. reprint ed. text 30.00 (0-914348-07-8) Scholars Bk.
Main Street Beats Wall Street: How the Top Investment Clubs Are Outperforming the Investment. Richard J. Maturi. 200p. 1994. text 24.95 (1-55738-804-0) Twntyfirst Cent Pubs.
Main Street Blues: The Decline of Small-Town America. Richard O. Davies. LC 97-51225. (Urban Life & Landscape Ser.). 248p. 1998. text 50.00 (0-8142-0781-2, DAVMAI); pap. text 21.95 (0-8142-0782-0, DAVMAX) Ohio St U Pr.
***Main Street Diners: Where Hoosiers Begin the Day.** Wendell Trogdon. (Illus.). 200p. 2000. pap. 14.95 (0-9642371-7-2) Backroads Pr.
Main Street Festivals: The National Trust Traveler's Guide to Traditional & Unique Events on America's Main Streets. National Trust for Historic Preservation Staff. LC 97-33058. (Illus.). 240p. 1998. pap. 16.95 (0-471-19290-2) Wiley.
***Main Street, Florida: In Old Picture Postcards.** Donald D. Spencer. LC 00-26679. (Illus.). 2000. write for info. (0-89218-336-5) Camelot Pub.
Main Street in Crisis: The Great Depression & the Old Middle Class on the Northern Plains. Catherine M. Stock. LC 91-32613. (Illus.). xiv, 306p. 1992. 39.95 (0-8078-2011-3) U of NC Pr.
Main Street in Crisis: The Great Depression & the Old Middle Class on the Northern Plains. Catherine M. Stock. 320p. 1997. pap. 16.95 (0-8078-4689-9) U of NC Pr.
Main Street Lawyer. Joseph T. Karcher. (American Biography Ser.). 189p. 1991. reprint ed. lib. bdg. 59.00 (0-7812-8225-X) Rprt Serv.
Main Street Memories. Lighten Up Enterprises Staff. (Places of the Heart Ser.). 366p. 1994. spiral bd. 8.50 (1-879127-33-4) Lighten Up Enter.
Main Street Musings, Vol. 1. Mary M. Marshall. (Illus.). v, 70p. (Orig.). 1996. pap. 7.25 (0-9651379-0-2) M M Marshall.
***Main Street, North Dakota Vol. 1: In Vintage Postcards.** Geneva Roth Olstad. (Postcard History Ser.). (Illus.). 128p. 2000. pap. 18.99 (0-7385-0726-1) Arcadia Publng.
***Main Street, North Dakota Vol. 2: In Vintage Postcards.** Geneva Roth Olstad. (Postcard History Ser.). (Illus.). 128p. 2000. pap. 18.99 (0-7385-0760-1) Arcadia Publng.
Main Street, Not Wall Street: Investing Close to Home, the Smart Way to Make More Money. John Rubino. LC 97-47694. 320p. 1998. 25.00 (0-688-15421-2, Wm Morrow) Morrow Avon.
Main Street Notes. Salibelle Royster. (Cliffs Notes Ser.). 64p. 1965. pap. 4.95 (0-8220-0798-3, Cliff) IDG Bks.
Main Street of America Cookbook. Marian Clark. LC 97-28528. 308p. (Orig.). 1997. pap. 14.95 (1-57178-024-6) Coun Oak Bks.
***Main Street Renewal: A Handbook for Public Officials & Citizens.** Roger L. Kemp. 440p. 2000. lib. bdg. 65.00 (0-7864-0812-X) McFarland & Co.
Main Street Revisited: Time, Space, & Image Building in Small-Town America. Richard V. Francaviglia. LC 95-47773. (American Land & Life Ser.). (Illus.). 256p. 1996. pap. 17.95 (0-87745-543-0); text 39.95 (0-87745-542-2) U of Iowa Pr.
Main Street, Siberia. Dale M. Heckman. LC 98-94062. 1999. pap. 14.95 (0-533-12967-2) Vantage.
Main Street Student Book. Peter Viney et al. LC 92-22748. (Illus.). 96p. (YA). 1994. pap. text, student ed. 10.95 (0-19-434485-1) OUP.
Main Street to Miracle Mile: American Roadside Architecture. Chester H. Liebs. LC 95-14226. (Illus.). 262p. 1995. pap. 24.95 (0-8018-5095-9) Johns Hopkins.
Main Street U. S. A., in Early Photographs: 113 Detroit Publishing Co. Views. Cynthia Read-Miller. (Illus.). 128p. 1988. pap. 12.95 (0-486-25841-6) Dover.
Main Street's New Neighbors. Melvin K. Whiteleather. LC 72-13183. (Essay Index Reprint Ser.). 1977. reprint ed. 19.95 (0-8369-8180-4) Ayer.
Main Tendue. Philippe Heriat. (FRE.). 320p. 1973. pap. 10.95 (0-7859-2327-6, 2070365018) Fr & Eur.
Main Teste. Eugene Labiche. 9.95 (0-686-54230-4) Fr & Eur.
Main Theme: C, Bolling's California Suite for Flute-Jazz Piano-Bass & Drums. C. Bolling. 1990. 10.00 (0-685-32228-9, SHAT60) Hansen Ed Mus.
Main Themes in the Debate over Property Rights see Property Rights in American History: From the Colonial Era to the Present
Main Thing: A New Look at Ecclesiastes. Gary Holloway. LC 97-71322. 160p. 1997. pap. 12.95 (0-89112-023-8) Abilene Christ U.
Main Thing . . . Is to Keep the Main Thing the Main Thing: Wit, Wisdom, Quotations, & Illustrations. T. F. Tenney. LC 93-27899. (Illus.). 300p. (Orig.). 1993. pap. 9.99 (1-56722-013-4) Word Aflame.
Main-Travelled Roads. Hamlin Garland. LC 95-34866. xxi, 247p. 1995. pap. 12.00 (0-8032-7058-5, Bison Books) U of Nebr Pr.
Main Travelled Roads see Collected Works of Hamlin Garland
Main Travelled Roads. Hamlin Garland. (Collected Works of Hamlin Garland). 1988. reprint ed. lib. bdg. 59.00 (0-7812-1215-4) Rprt Serv.
Main-Travelled Roads. Hamlin Garland. (J). 1987. reprint ed. lib. bdg. 27.95 (0-89966-555-1) Buccaneer Bks.
Main Trends in Aesthetics & the Sciences of Art. Ed. by Mikel Dufrenne. LC 79-12758. (Main Trends in the Social & Human Sciences Ser.). 418p. (C). 1979. pap. 26.50 (0-8419-0507-X) Holmes & Meier.
Main Trends in History. rev. ed. Geoffrey Barraclough. 1991. 45.00 (0-8419-1287-4); pap. 19.95 (0-8419-1062-6) Holmes & Meier.
Main Types of Geological Maps: Purpose, Use & Preparation. Editions Technip Staff. 360p. 1997. 475.00 (2-7108-0622-3, Pub. by Edits Technip) Enfield Pubs NH.
***Man with St. Vitus' Dance.** Bart Baxter. 44p. 2000. pap. 10.00 (0-9647199-9-1) Floating Bridge Pr.
Main Works: Writings in the Social Philosophy & Ethics, Vol. 3. Paul Johannes Tillich. Ed. by Erdmann Sturm. LC 97-50310. Orig. Title: Hauptwerke - Sozialphilosophische und Ethische Schriften. 712p. 1997. text 121.00 (3-11-011537-9) De Gruyter.
Main Works Vol. 6: Theological Writings. Paul Johannes Tillich. xiv, 446p. (C). 1992. lib. bdg. 135.40 (3-11-011540-9); lib. bdg. 135.40 (3-11-011539-5) De Gruyter.
Main Works - Hauptwerke Vol. 2, Bd. 2: Writings in the Philosophy of Culture - Kullturphilosophische Schriften. Paul Johannes Tillich. 1990. 103.10 (3-11-011536-0) De Gruyter.
Main Works in Six Volumes (Hauptwerke in 6 Banden) Vol. 2: Writings in the Philosophy of Culture (Kulturphilosophische Schriften) Paul Johannes Tillich. Ed. by Michael Palmer & Carl H. Ratschow. xiv, 380p. (C). 1990. lib. bdg. 106.15 (3-11-011535-2); lib. bdg. write for info. (0-318-67997-3) De Gruyter.
Maine see From Sea to Shining Sea
Maine see One Nation Series
***Maine.** (Switched on Schoolhouse Ser.). (Illus.). (J). 2000. pap. 24.95 (0-7403-0271-X) Alpha AZ.
Maine. Earl Bechlin. (Adventure Guide Ser.). (Illus.). 360p. (Orig.). 1999. pap. 16.95 (1-55650-860-3) Hunter NJ.
Maine. Capstone Press, Geography Department Staff. (One Nation Ser.). (Illus.). 48p. (J). (gr. 3-7). 1997. lib. bdg. 19.00 (0-516-20927-2) Childrens.
***Maine.** LeeAnne Engfer. 72p. 1999. pap. text 5.95 (0-8225-9787-X) Lerner.
Maine. LeeAnne Engfer. (Hello U. S. A. Ser.). (Illus.). 72p. (J). (gr. 3-6). 1991. lib. bdg. 19.93 (0-8225-2701-4, Lerner Publctns) Lerner Pub.
Maine. Charles Feil. LC 96-24516. (View from Above Ser.: Vol. 1). (Illus.). 96p. 1999. pap. 15.95 (0-89272-462-5) Down East.
Maine. Paul Joseph. LC 97-10498. (United States Ser.). (Illus.). 32p. (J). 1998. lib. bdg. 19.93 (1-56239-861-X, Checkerboard Library) ABDO Pub Co.
Maine. Kathleen Thompson. LC 85-9975. (Portrait of America Library). 48p. (J). (gr. 4-8). 1996. pap. 5.95 (0-8114-7444-5) Raintree Steck-V.
Maine. Kathleen Thompson. LC 85-9975. (Portrait of America Library). (Illus.). 48p. (YA). (gr. 3-6). 1996. lib. bdg. 22.83 (0-8114-7339-2) Raintree Steck-V.
Maine. 2nd ed. Deborah Kent. LC 98-33878. (America the Beautiful Second Ser.). 144p. (YA). (gr. 5-8). 1999. 32.00 (0-516-20994-9) Childrens.
Maine: A Coastal Portrait. Photos by Richard Procopic. (Illus.). 32p. 1996. pap. 9.95 (1-881535-20-7) New Eng Pr VT.
Maine: A Guide down East. Federal Writers' Project Staff. (American Guidebook Ser.). 476p. 1936. reprint ed. 89.00 (0-403-02170-7) Somerset Pub.
Maine: A Guide down East. Federal Writers' Project Staff & Writers Program-WPA Staff. (American Guide Ser.). 1989. reprint ed. lib. bdg. 79.00 (0-7812-1018-6, 1018) Rprt Serv.
Maine: A Narrative History. Neil Rolde. (Illus.). 368p. (Orig.). 1990. pap. 19.95 (0-88448-069-0) Tilbury Hse.
Maine: Acadia National Park. Appalachian Mountain Club Book Staff. (AMC Trail Maps Ser.). Date not set. pap. text 3.95 (1-878239-23-6) AMC Books.
Maine: An Explorer's Guide. 9th rev. ed. Christina Tree & Elizabeth Roundy. LC 98-56010. (An Explorer's Guide Ser.). (Illus.). 524p. 1999. pap. 18.95 (0-88150-460-2, Pub. by Countryman) Norton.
Maine: Cobb's America Guyed Books. Irvin S. Cobb. (Collected Works of Irvin S. Cobb). 55p. 1998. reprint ed. lib. bdg. 88.00 (1-58201-599-6) Classic Bks.
Maine: Cruising the Coast by Car. Arthur Layton. LC 94-40886. (Illus.). 180p. (Orig.). 1994. pap. 9.95 (1-56626-087-6, Cntry Rds Pr) NTC Contemp Pub Co.
Maine: Cruising the Coast by Car. 2nd rev. ed. Arthur Layton. LC 97-2221. (Illus.). 140p. (Orig.). 1997. pap. 10.95 (1-56626-182-1, Cntry Rds Pr) NTC Contemp Pub Co.
***Maine: Off the Beaten Path.** 4th ed. Wayne Curtis. (Off the Beaten Path Ser.). (Illus.). 208p. (Orig.). 2000. pap. 12.95 (0-7627-0644-9) Globe Pequot.
Maine: Off the Beaten Path: A Guide to Unique Places. 3rd ed. Wayne Curtis. LC 98-17469. (Off the Beaten Path Ser.). (Illus.). 256p. (Orig.). 1998. pap. 12.95 (0-7627-0190-0) Globe Pequot.
Maine: The Pine Tree State from Prehistory to the Present. Ed. by Richard W. Judd et al. (Illus.). 586p. (C). 1995. 30.00 (0-89101-082-3); text 49.95 (0-89101-081-5) U Maine Pr.
***Maine: The Spirit of America.** Edgar Allen Beem. LC 99-55231. (Illus.). 96p. 2000. 12.95 (0-8109-5570-9, Pub. by Abrams) Time Warner.
Maine: 9 Poems. Ira Sadoff. 13p. 1981. pap. 5.00 (0-913219-28-2); 10.00 (0-913219-29-0) Pym-Rand Pr.
Maine - Collected Works of Federal Writers Project. Federal Writers' Project Staff. 1991. reprint ed. lib. bdg. 98.00 (0-7812-5603-8) Rprt Serv.
Maine, a Peopled Landscape: Salt Documentary Photography, 1978-1995. Stewart Dory et al. Ed. by Hugh T. French. LC 95-5471. (Illus.). 170p. 1995. pap. 22.95 (0-87451-717-6) U Pr of New Eng.
Maine, a View from Above. Charles Feil. LC 96-24516. (Illus.). 96p. 1996. 30.00 (0-89272-381-5) Down East.
***Maine Amphibians & Reptiles.** Ed. by Malcolm L. Hunter, Jr. et al. (Illus.). 272p. 1999. pap. 19.95 (0-89101-096-3) U Maine Pr.
Maine & Other State Greats (Biographies) Carole Marsh. (Carole Marsh Maine Bks.). (Illus.). (J). (gr. 3-8). 1994. pap. 19.95 (1-55609-615-1); lib. bdg. 29.95 (1-55609-614-3); disk 29.95 (1-55609-616-X) Gallopade Intl.
***Maine & the Modern Spirit.** Susan C. Larsen. (Illus.). 36p. 2000. 12.00 (0-915171-55-4) Katonah Gal.
Maine Animals. North Country Press Staff. (Maine Nature Ser.). 64p. 1997. pap. text 4.50 (0-945980-25-6) Nrth Country Pr.
Maine at Gettysburg: Report of Maine Commissioners. Contrib. by Executive Committee Staff. (Illus.). 602p. 1996. reprint ed. lib. bdg. 65.00 (0-8328-5175-2) Higginson Bk Co.
Maine at Gettysburg: Report of the Maine Monuments Commission. Maine Commissioners Staff. (Illus.). 602p. 1994. 45.00 (1-879664-23-2) Stan Clark Military.
Maine at Work in 1861. 1999. 39.50 (0-8328-9857-0) Higginson Bk Co.
Maine at Work in 1861: Directory of 17,000 Maine Residents & Their Occupations & Businesses. Robert M. Jackson, Jr. 334p. 1999. 47.50 (0-8328-9856-2) Higginson Bk Co.
Maine Atlantic Salmon: A National Treasure. Ed Baum. LC 97-94393. (Illus.). 240p. 1997. 49.95 (0-9660496-9-1) Atlan Salmon.
***Maine Atlas & Gazetteer.** 23rd ed. DeLorme Mapping Co. Staff. (Illus.). 2000. pap. 19.95 (0-89933-282-X) DeLorme Map.
Maine Bandits, Bushwackers, Outlaws, Crooks, Devils, Ghosts, Desperadoes & Other Assorted & Sundry Characters! Carole Marsh. (Carole Marsh Maine Bks.). (Illus.). (J). (gr. 3-8). 1994. pap. 19.95 (0-7933-0526-8); lib. bdg. 29.95 (0-7933-0527-6); disk 29.95 (0-7933-0528-4) Gallopade Intl.
Maine Bar Directory, 2000: Listing of Maine Bar Lawyers & Legal Community. Tower Pub. Staff. 800p. 2000. pap. text 45.00 (1-881758-66-4) Tower Pub ME.
Maine Bicentennial Atlas: An Historical Survey. Maine Historical Society Staff. (Illus.). 1976. pap. 10.00 (0-685-03278-7); pap. write for info. (0-915592-23-1) Maine Hist.
Maine "BIO" Bingo! 24 Must Know State People for Kids to Learn about While Having Fun! Carole Marsh. (Bingo! Ser.). (Illus.). (J). (gr. 2-8). 1998. pap. 14.95 (0-7933-8579-2) Gallopade Intl.
Maine Birds. James Kavanagh. (Pocket Naturalist Ser.). (Illus.). 1997. 5.95 (1-889903-37-X, Pub. by Waterford WA) Falcon Pub Inc.
Maine Bookstore Book: A Surprising Guide to Our State's Bookstores & Their Specialties for Students, Teachers, Writers & Publishers. Carole Marsh. (Carole Marsh Maine Bks.). (Illus.). 1994. pap. 19.95 (0-7933-2913-2); lib. bdg. 29.95 (0-7933-2912-4); disk 29.95 (0-7933-2914-0) Gallopade Intl.
***Maine Business Directory, 1999.** American Business Directories Staff. 704p. 1999. boxed set 375.00 incl. cd-rom (0-7687-0131-7, 1048-7115) Am Busn Direct.
***Maine Business Directory (2000)** American Business Directories Staff et al. 704p. 2000. boxed set 375.00 incl. cd-rom (0-7687-0216-X) Am Busn Direct.
Maine Captured in Color. rev. ed. Mary Calvert. (Illus.). 1983. 16.95 (0-9609914-1-7) M Calvert.
Maine Census Index 1890 Union Vets. (Illus.). lib. bdg. 97.00 (0-89593-362-4, Accel Indexing) Genealogical Srvcs.
Maine Census Index, 1870 (Portland, Cumberland Counties) (Illus.). 1991. lib. bdg. 190.00 (0-89593-360-8, Accel Indexing) Genealogical Srvcs.
Maine Central in Color. Jeremy F. Plant & George F. Melvin. LC 98-65132. (Illus.). 1998. write for info. (1-878887-97-1) Morning NJ.
Maine Central in Color, Vol. 1. Jeremy F. Plant. (Illus.). 128p. 1998. 49.95 (1-878887-96-3) Morning NJ.
***Maine Central in Color, Vol. 2.** Plant & Melvin. (Illus.). 128p. 1999. 54.95 (1-58248-030-3) Morning NJ.
Maine Charm String. Elinor Graham. (American Autobiography Ser.). 231p. 1995. reprint ed. lib. bdg. 79.00 (0-7812-8537-2) Rprt Serv.
Maine City & Town Atlas. 118p. (Orig.). pap. 11.95 (0-9619656-4-9) Hart Hse Map.
Maine Civil Remedies. rev. ed. Andrew M. Horton & Peggy L. McGehee. 500p. 1993. suppl. ed. 35.00 (0-318-69465-4, MICHIE) LEXIS Pub.
Maine Civil Remedies. rev. ed. Andrew M. Horton & Peggy L. McGehee. 500p. 1994. spiral bd. 115.00 (1-56257-314-4, MICHIE) LEXIS Pub.
Maine Civil Remedies. 3rd ed. Andrew M. Horton & Peggy L. McGehee. 613p. 95.00 (1-55834-403-9) LEXIS Pub.
Maine Civil Remedies, 1998 Supplement. Horton & McGeehee. 90p. 1998. suppl. ed. 40.00 (0-327-00340-5, 8161112) LEXIS Pub.
Maine Classic Christmas Trivia: Stories, Recipes, Activities, Legends, Lore & More! Carole Marsh. (Carole Marsh Maine Bks.). (Illus.). (J). (gr. 3-8). 1994. pap. 19.95 (0-7933-0529-2); lib. bdg. 29.95 (0-7933-0530-6); disk 29.95 (0-7933-0531-4) Gallopade Intl.
Maine Coast. George Putz. (Illus.). 175p. 1997. 15.98 (0-89009-882-4) Bk Sales Inc.
Maine Coast Guide for Small Boats: Casco Bay. Curtis Rindlaub. (Maine Coast Guide for Small Boats Ser.: Vol. 2). (Illus.). 288p. (Orig.). 1999. pap. write for info. (0-9649246-2-5) Diamond Pass.
***Maine Coast Postcards.** Joyce K. Bibber. (Postcard History Ser.). 128p. 1999. pap. 18.99 (0-7524-1338-4) Arcadia Publng.
Maine Coastales! Carole Marsh. (Carole Marsh Maine Bks.). (J). 1994. lib. bdg. 29.95 (0-7933-7284-4) Gallopade Intl.
Maine Coastales! Carole Marsh. (Carole Marsh Maine Bks.). (Illus.). (J). (gr. 3-8). 1994. pap. 19.95 (1-55609-609-7); lib. bdg. 29.95 (1-55609-608-9); disk 29.95 (1-55609-610-0) Gallopade Intl.
Maine Collection. Portland Museum of Art Staff. LC 92-85255. 254p. 1993. 12.95 (0-9635386-0-8) Portland Mus.
Maine Consumer Law Guide. 2nd ed. Maine Attorney General. 445p. 1998. pap. text, per. 19.95 (1-881758-41-9) Tower Pub ME.
Maine Cooking - Old Time Secrets: Mainstays of Maine. Robert P. Coffin & Ruth P. Coffin. (Illus.). 159p. 1991. reprint ed. pap. 8.95 (0-9621570-6-6) North Lights.
Maine Coon Cat. Stuart A. Kallen. LC 95-12656. (Illus.). 24p. (J). (ps-4). 1995. lib. bdg. 13.98 (1-56239-448-7) ABDO Pub Co.
***Maine Coon Cat.** Joanne Mattern. (Learning about Cats Ser.). 48p. (YA). (gr. 5 up). 2000. lib. bdg. 21.26 (0-7368-0565-6, Capstone Bks) Capstone Pr.
***Maine Coon Cats.** Contrib. by Lynn M. Stone. LC 99-27277. (Read All About Cats Ser.). 24p. 1999. lib. bdg. write for info. (0-86593-553-X) Rourke Corp.
Maine Coon Cats: Everything about Purchase, Care, Nutrition, Reproduction, Diseases & Behavior. Carol H. Daly. LC 95-14958. (Complete Pet Owner's Manual Ser.). (Illus.). 1995. pap. 6.95 (0-8120-9038-1) Barron.
***Maine Coon Cats: Everything about Purchase, Care, Nutrition, Reproduction, Diseases & Behavior.** Jennifer Quasha. LC 99-53565. (Kid's Cat Library). 24p. (J). 1999. 18.60 (0-8239-5510-9, PowerKids) Rosen Group.
Maine Corporation Law & Practice. James B. Zimpritch. (National Corporation Law Ser.). 1992. ring bd. 126.00 (0-13-109315-0) Aspen Law.
***Maine Crime in Perspective 2000.** Ed. by Kathleen O'Leary Morgan & Scott E. Morgan. 22p. 2000. spiral bd. 19.00 (0-7401-0318-0) Morgan Quitno Corp.
Maine Crime Perspective, 1998. Ed. by Kathleen O'Leary Morgan & Scott E. Morgan. 20p. 1998. pap. 19.00 (1-56692-918-0) Morgan Quitno Corp.
Maine Crime Perspectives, 1999. Kathleen O'Leary Morgan. 22p. 1999. spiral bd. 19.00 (0-7401-0118-8) Morgan Quitno Corp.
Maine Criminal Practice. 1945. ring bd., suppl. ed. 49.00 LEXIS Pub.
Maine Criminal Practice, 3 vols., Set. 2nd ed. David P. Cluchey & Michael D. Seitzinger. 1500p. 1994. spiral bd. 185.00 (1-56257-317-9, 81615-10, MICHIE) LEXIS Pub.
Maine "Crinkum-Crankum" A Funny Word Book about Our State. Carole Marsh. (Carole Marsh Maine Bks.). (Illus.). (J). 1994. pap. 19.95 (0-7933-4866-8); lib. bdg. 29.95 (0-7933-4865-X); disk 29.95 (0-7933-4867-6) Gallopade Intl.
***Maine Dictionary.** John McDonald. (Illus.). 128p. (C). 2000. pap. 12.95 (1-58066-057-6, Covered Brdge Pr) Douglas Charles Ltd.
Maine Dingbats! Bk. 1: A Fun Book of Games, Stories, Activities & More about Our State That's All in Code! for You to Decipher. Carole Marsh. (Carole Marsh Maine Bks.). (Illus.). (J). (gr. 3-12). 1994. pap. 19.95 (0-7933-3831-X); lib. bdg. 29.95 (0-7933-3830-1); disk 29.95 (0-7933-3832-8) Gallopade Intl.
Maine District Court: A Quarter Century of Progress. Harriet P. Henry. 80p. 1987. boxed set 39.50 (0-89442-038-0, MICHIE); boxed set 39.50 (0-614-05982-8, MICHIE) LEXIS Pub.
Maine Early Census, Vol. 1. Ronald V. Jackson. (Illus.). lib. bdg. 30.00 (0-89593-725-5, Accel Indexing) Genealogical Srvcs.
***Maine Environmental & Land Use Statutes Deskbook.** Chip Ahrens & Daniel Boxer. 700p. 1999. pap. text 95.00 (1-881758-58-3) Tower Pub ME.

An Asterisk (*) at the beginning of an entry indicates that the title is appearing for the first time.

Maine Environmental & Land Use Statutes Deskbook, 1994. Pierce Atwood Environmental Department Staff et al. 670p. 1994. 67.50 (*1-56257-346-2*, MICHIE) LEXIS Pub.

Maine Environmental & Land Use Statutes Deskbook, 1995. Pierce Atwood Environmental Department Staff et al. Ed. by Philip F. Ahrens. 670p. 1994. pap. 70.00 (*0-88063-755-2*, MICHIE) LEXIS Pub.

Maine Environmental Law Handbook. Verrill & Dana Staff. (State Environmental Law Ser.). 373p. 1990. pap. text 79.00 (*0-86587-225-2*) Gov Insts.

Maine Evidence. John Tetso. (Illus.). 128p. 1993. ring bd., suppl. ed. 39.50 (*0-614-03134-6*, MICHIE) LEXIS Pub.

Maine Evidence. 3rd ed. Peter L. Murray & Richard H. Field. 670p. 1994. spiral bd. 115.00 (*1-56257-198-2*, MICHIE) LEXIS Pub.

***Maine Evidence.** 5th ed. A. Field & Murray. 650p. 1999. write for info. (*0-327-04911-1*, 8163512) LEXIS Pub.

Maine Evidence: 2000 Edition. Peter L. Murray & Richard H. Field. 626p. pap. 85.00 (*0-327-12512-8*) LEXIS Pub.

Maine Facts & Factivities. Carole Marsh. (Carole Marsh State Bks.). (Illus.). (J). (gr. 4-7). 1996. pap., teacher ed. 19.95 (*0-7933-7885-0*, C Marsh) Gallopade Intl.

***Maine Facts & Symbols.** Emily McAuliffe. LC 99-25111. (States & Their Symbols Ser.). 1999. 14.60 (*0-7368-0376-9*) Capstone Pr.

Maine Facts & Symbols. Emily McAuliffe. (States & Their Symbols Ser.). 1999. 15.00 (*0-531-12002-3*) Watts.

Maine Families in 1790, Vol. 1. Ed. by Ruth Gray. LC 88-62540. 384p. 1989. 35.00 (*0-929539-05-2*, 1105) Picton Pr.

Maine Families in 1790, Vol. 2. Ed. by Ruth Gray & Alice M. Long. LC 88-62540. 416p. 1990. 35.00 (*0-929539-72-9*, 1172) Picton Pr.

Maine Families in 1790, Vol. 3. Ed. by Ruth Gray & Joseph C. Anderson. LC 88-62540. 416p. 1992. 35.00 (*0-929539-80-X*, 1399) Picton Pr.

Maine Families in 1790, Vol. 4. Ed. by Joseph C. Anderson & Lois Thurston. LC 88-62540. 416p. 1994. 35.00 (*0-89725-126-1*, 1439) Picton Pr.

Maine Families in 1790, Vol. 5. Ed. by Joseph C. Anderson, II. 402p. 1996. 35.00 (*0-89725-255-1*, 1726) Picton Pr.

Maine Families in 1790 No. 31, Vol. 6: Maine Genealogical Society Special Publication. Joseph C. Anderson. LC 88-62540. 608p. 1998. 45.00 (*0-89725-361-2*, 1895) Picton Pr.

Maine Family Law: Divorce, Separation & Annulment, 2000 Edition. Jon D. Levy. 808p. pap. 105.00 (*0-327-12448-2*) LEXIS Pub.

***Maine Family Law: 1999 Edition.** Levy. 700p. 1999. write for info. (*0-327-04993-6*, 8164013) LEXIS Pub.

Maine Family Law Forms. 2nd ed. Dana E. Prescott. LC 98-89024. 700p. 1998. 149.00 (*0-327-00637-4*, 8164511); disk. write for info. (*0-327-00638-2*, 8164511) LEXIS Pub.

Maine Family Law Forms: Discovery, Trial & Settlement. Harold Horwood. 1994. ring bd., suppl. ed. 65.00 (*0-614-03136-2*, MICHIE) LEXIS Pub.

Maine Family Law Forms: Discovery, Trial & Settlement, 2 vols., Set. Dana E. Prescott. LC 93-23910. 750p. 1994. spiral bd. 205.00 (*0-250-40712-4*, 81645-10, MICHIE) LEXIS Pub.

Maine Family Law, 1988-1991: Divorce, Separation & Annulment. Jon D. Levy. 380p. 1994. spiral bd. 85.00 (*0-89442-076-3*, MICHIE) LEXIS Pub.

Maine Family Law, 1998 Supplement. Jon Levy. 150p. 1998. pap., suppl. ed. write for info. (*0-327-00716-8*, 8164310) LEXIS Pub.

Maine Family Law, 1997. 2nd ed. Peter L. Murray & Jon D. Levy. LC 97-70182. 636p. 1997. pap. text 75.00 (*1-55834-464-0*, 81640-12, MICHIE) LEXIS Pub.

Maine Farmer: Marriage Notices from the Maine Farmer 1833-1852. LC 96-127119. 487p. (Orig.). 1996. pap. 37.00 (*0-7884-0373-7*, Y591) Heritage Bk.

Maine Federal Census Index, 1880 (Excluding Cumberland County) (Illus.). lib. bdg. write for info. (*0-89593-361-6*, Accel Indexing) Genealogical Srvcs.

Maine Federal Census Index, 1850. Ronald V. Jackson. LC 77-85952. (Illus.). lib. bdg. 92.00 (*0-89593-059-5*, Accel Indexing) Genealogical Srvcs.

Maine Federal Census Index, 1840. Ronald V. Jackson. LC 77-85951. (Illus.). 1978. lib. bdg. 67.00 (*0-89593-058-7*, Accel Indexing) Genealogical Srvcs.

Maine Federal Census Index, 1800 (Enumerations) Ronald V. Jackson. LC 77-85944. (Illus.). 1979. lib. bdg. 46.00 (*0-89593-054-4*, Accel Indexing) Genealogical Srvcs.

Maine Federal Census Index, 1860 (Excluding Portland), 3 vols., Set. Ed. by Ronald Vern Jackson. LC 99-197473. 1991. lib. bdg. 500.00 (*0-89593-359-4*, Accel Indexing) Genealogical Srvcs.

Maine Federal Census Index, 1810. Ronald V. Jackson. LC 77-85947. (Illus.). 1976. lib. bdg. 46.00 (*0-89593-055-2*, Accel Indexing) Genealogical Srvcs.

Maine Federal Census Index, 1830. Ronald V. Jackson. LC 77-85949. (Illus.). 1977. lib. bdg. 62.00 (*0-89593-057-9*, Accel Indexing) Genealogical Srvcs.

Maine Federal Census Index, 1820. Ronald V. Jackson. LC 77-85948. (Illus.). 1976. lib. bdg. 46.00 (*0-89593-056-0*, Accel Indexing) Genealogical Srvcs.

Maine Federal Census Index, 1790, (1908) Ronald V. Jackson. (Illus.). 1978. lib. bdg. 46.00 (*0-89593-672-0*, Accel Indexing) Genealogical Srvcs.

Maine Festival Fun for Kids! Carole Marsh. (Carole Marsh Maine Bks.). (Illus.). (YA). (gr. 3-12). 1994. pap. 19.95 (*0-7933-3984-7*); lib. bdg. 29.95 (*0-7933-3983-9*); disk 29.95 (*0-7933-3985-5*) Gallopade Intl.

***Maine Fishing Map Book, Vol. 2.** annuals 2000th ed. 2000. pap. 10.95 (*0-89933-170-X*) DeLorme Map.

***Maine Fishing Maps Vol. 1: Lakes & Ponds, 2.** 2000th ed. Charlton Swasey & Donald Wilson. (Illus.). 87p. 2000. reprint ed. per. 10.95 (*0-89933-169-6*) DeLorme Map.

Maine Food & Fun Guide. annuals Filomena T. Day & Jack Milo. 250p. (Orig.). 1995. pap. 24.95 (*0-9635054-0-8*) Better Day Vent.

Maine Food & Fun Guide: The Restaurant & Recreation Bible. 5th rev. ed. (Illus.). 200 20p. 1996. pap. 24.95 (*0-614-13294-0*) Better Day Vent.

Maine Forever: A Guide to Nature Conservancy Preserves in Maine, Vol. II. 2nd rev. ed. Ruth A. Hill. (Illus.). 128p. 1990. pap. 17.95 (*0-9614136-1-1*) Nature Cnsrvncy ME Chap.

Maine Forts. William Linz & Mary Linz. LC 97-60844. (Illus.). 58p. (Orig.). 1997. pap. 5.00 (*1-883650-41-0*) Windswept Hse.

Maine Genealogist & Biographer, Vol. 1. 135p. 1986. reprint ed. pap. 14.50 (*0-935207-44-9*) Danbury Hse Bks.

Maine Genealogist & Biographer, Vol. 2. 148p. 1986. reprint ed. pap. 16.00 (*0-935207-49-X*) Danbury Hse Bks.

Maine Genealogist & Biographer, Vol. 3. 168p. 1986. reprint ed. pap. 18.00 (*0-935207-54-6*) Danbury Hse Bks.

Maine Genealogy: A Bibliographical Guide. 2nd rev. ed. John E. Frost. 1985. pap. 4.00 (*0-915592-33-9*) Maine Hist.

Maine "GEO" Bingo! 38 Must Know State Geography Facts for Kids to Learn While Having Fun! Carole Marsh. (Bingo! Ser.). (Illus.). (J). (gr. 2-8). 1998. pap. 14.95 (*0-7933-8580-6*) Gallopade Intl.

***Maine Geographic Calendar.** (Illus.). 14p. 2001. spiral bd. 9.95 (*0-89933-168-8*) DeLorme Map.

Maine Ghosts & Legends: Twenty-Six Encounters with the Supernatural. Thomas A. Verde. LC 89-50567. 144p. (Orig.). 1989. pap. 8.95 (*0-89272-273-8*) Down East.

Maine Government! The Cornerstone of Everyday Life in Our State! Carole Marsh. (Carole Marsh Maine Bks.). (Illus.). (J). (gr. 3-12). 1996. pap. 19.95 (*0-7933-6239-3*); pap. 19.95 (*0-7933-6263-6*); lib. bdg. 29.95 (*0-7933-6238-5*); lib. bdg. 29.95 (*0-7933-6262-8*); disk 29.95 (*0-7933-6240-7*); disk 29.95 (*0-7933-6264-4*) Gallopade Intl.

Maine Governments Performance Standards, 1990. Ed. by Greg Michels. (Governments Performance Standards Ser.). (Illus.). 150p. 1990. text 125.00 (*1-55507-487-1*) Municipal Analysis.

***Maine Hamlet.** Lura Beam. (Illus.). 256p. 2000. pap. 14.95 (*0-88448-221-9*) Tilbury Hse.

Maine, Heads of Families at the First Census of the U. S. Taken in 1790. 105p. 1987. reprint ed. pap. 11.50 (*0-935207-10-4*) Danbury Hse Bks.

***Maine Health Care in Perspective 2000.** Ed. by Kathleen O'Leary Morgan & Scott E. Morgan. 21p. 2000. spiral bd. 19.00 (*0-7401-0218-4*) Morgan Quitno Corp.

Maine Health Care Perspective, 1998. Ed. by Kathleen O'Leary Morgan & Scott E. Morgan. 20p. 1998. pap. 19.00 (*1-56692-818-4*) Morgan Quitno Corp.

Maine Health Care Perspective 1999. Ed. by Kathleen O'Leary Morgan. 21p. 1999. spiral bd. 19.00 (*0-7401-0068-8*) Morgan Quitno Corp.

Maine "HISTO" Bingo! 42 Must Know State History Facts for Kids to Learn While Having Fun! Carole Marsh. (Bingo! Ser.). (Illus.). (J). (gr. 2-8). 1998. pap. 14.95 (*0-7933-8581-4*) Gallopade Intl.

Maine Historical & Biographical Index, Vol. 1. Ronald V. Jackson. LC 78-53701. (Illus.). 1984. lib. bdg. 30.00 (*0-89593-184-2*, Accel Indexing) Genealogical Srvcs.

Maine Historical & Genealogical Recorder, Vol. 1. 57p. 1986. reprint ed. pap. 7.00 (*0-935207-11-2*) Danbury Hse Bks.

Maine Historical & Genealogical Recorder, Vol. 2. 69p. 1986. reprint ed. pap. 8.00 (*0-935207-13-9*) Danbury Hse Bks.

Maine Historical & Genealogical Recorder, Vol. 3. 77p. 1986. reprint ed. pap. 9.00 (*0-935207-21-X*) Danbury Hse Bks.

Maine Historical & Genealogical Recorder, Vol. 4. 80p. 1986. reprint ed. pap. 9.00 (*0-935207-23-6*) Danbury Hse Bks.

Maine Historical & Genealogical Recorder, Vol. 5. 65p. 1986. reprint ed. pap. 7.50 (*0-935207-26-0*) Danbury Hse Bks.

Maine Historical & Genealogical Recorder, Vol. 6. 69p. 1986. reprint ed. pap. 8.00 (*0-935207-27-9*) Danbury Hse Bks.

Maine Historical & Genealogical Recorder, Vol. 7. 62p. 1986. reprint ed. pap. 7.50 (*0-935207-28-7*) Danbury Hse Bks.

Maine Historical & Genealogical Recorder, Vol. 8. 67p. 1986. reprint ed. pap. 8.00 (*0-935207-29-5*) Danbury Hse Bks.

Maine Historical & Genealogical Recorder, Vol. 9. 101p. 1986. reprint ed. pap. 11.00 (*0-935207-30-9*) Danbury Hse Bks.

Maine Historical & Genealogical Recorder, Vols. 1-9. 647p. 1986. reprint ed. pap. 65.00 (*0-935207-32-5*) Danbury Hse Bks.

***Maine Historical Sketches.** Augustus F. Moulton. (Illus.). 313p. 2000. pap. 24.00 (*0-7884-1490-9*, 1490) Heritage Bk.

Maine History! Surprising Secrets about Our State's Founding Mothers, Fathers & Kids! Carole Marsh. (Carole Marsh Maine Bks.). (Illus.). (J). (gr. 3-12). 1996. pap. 19.95 (*0-7933-6086-2*); lib. bdg. 29.95 (*0-7933-6085-4*); disk 29.95 (*0-7933-6087-0*) Gallopade Intl.

Maine Hot Air Balloon Mystery. Carole Marsh. (Carole Marsh Maine Bks.). (Illus.). (J). (gr. 2-9). 1994. 29.95 (*0-7933-2489-0*); pap. 19.95 (*0-7933-2490-4*); disk 29.95 (*0-7933-2491-2*) Gallopade Intl.

Maine Hot Zones! Viruses, Diseases, & Epidemics in Our State's History. Carole Marsh. (Hot Zones! Ser.). (Illus.). (J). (gr. 3-12). 1998. pap. 19.95 (*0-7933-8886-4*); lib. bdg. 29.95 (*0-7933-8885-6*) Gallopade Intl.

Maine in America: American Art at the Farnsworth Art Museum. Pamela J. Belanger. (Illus.). 256p. 1999. 55.00 (*0-918749-08-5*) U Pr of New Eng.

Maine in Perspective, 1998. Ed. by Kathleen O'Leary Morgan & Scott E. Morgan. 24p. 1998. pap. 19.00 (*1-56692-868-0*) Morgan Quitno Corp.

***Maine in Perspective, 1999.** Ed. by Kathleen O'Leary Morgan. 26p. 1999. spiral bd. 19.00 (*1-56692-968-7*) Morgan Quitno Corp.

***Maine In Perspective 2000.** Ed. by Kathleen O'Leary Morgan & Scott E. Morgan. 26p. 2000. spiral bd. 19.00 (*0-7401-0268-0*) Morgan Quitno Corp.

Maine in the Age of Discovery: Christopher Levett's Voyage, 1623-1624 & a Guide to Sources. Ed. by Emerson W. Baker, Jr. 1988. pap. 14.00 (*0-318-42474-6*) Maine Hist.

Maine in the Making of the Nation, 1783-1870. Elizabeth Ring. (Illus.). 384p. 1991. pap. text. write for info. (*0-933858-13-2*) Kennebec River.

Maine Indian Dictionary for Kids! Carole Marsh. (Carole Marsh State Bks.). (J). (gr. 2-9). 1996. 29.95 (*0-7933-7701-3*, C Marsh); pap. 19.95 (*0-7933-7702-1*, C Marsh) Gallopade Intl.

Maine Ingredients: Fresh & Fabulous Recipes from the Junior League of Portland, Maine. Junior League of Portland, ME, Inc. Staff. 320p. 1995. 18.95 (*0-9644691-0-3*) Jr League Portland ME.

***Maine Investment & Business Guide: Business, Investment, Export-Import Opportunities, 50 vols., Vol. 19.** Global Investment Center, USA Staff. (U. S. Regional Investment & Business Library-99: Vol. 19). (Illus.). 350p. (Orig.). 1999. pap. 59.95 (*0-7397-1118-0*) Intl Business Pubns.

Maine Island Classics: Living & Knitting on a Maine Island. Chellie Pingree & Debby Anderson. (Illus.). 80p. 1992. pap. 15.95 (*0-89272-315-7*) Down East.

Maine Island Kids: Sweaters & Stories from Offshore. Chellie Pingree & Debby Anderson. (Illus.). 80p. (Orig.). 1992. pap. 15.95 (*0-89272-316-5*) Down East.

Maine Islands. Dorothy Simpson. 1987. pap. 10.95 (*0-942396-51-0*) Blackberry ME.

Maine Jeopardy! Answers & Questions about Our State! Carole Marsh. (Carole Marsh Maine Bks.). (Illus.). (J). (gr. 3-12). 1994. pap. 19.95 (*0-7933-4137-X*); lib. bdg. 29.95 (*0-7933-4136-1*); disk 29.95 (*0-7933-4138-8*) Gallopade Intl.

Maine "Jography" A Fun Run Thru Our State! Carole Marsh. (Carole Marsh Maine Bks.). (Illus.). (J). (gr. 3-8). 1994. pap. 19.95 (*1-55609-597-X*); lib. bdg. 29.95 (*1-55609-596-1*); disk 29.95 (*1-55609-598-8*) Gallopade Intl.

Maine Jury Instruction Manual. 3rd ed. Donald G. Alexander. 95.00 (*0-327-12449-0*) LEXIS Pub.

Maine Jury Instruction Manual, Issue 3. Alexander. 150p. 1999. ring bd. write for info. (*0-327-01261-7*, 8165714) LEXIS Pub.

Maine Jury Instruction Manual, 1990-1992. 2nd ed. Donald G. Alexander. 280p. 1993. ring bd., suppl. ed. 37.00 (*1-56257-250-4*, MICHIE) LEXIS Pub.

Maine Jury Instruction Manual, 1990-1992. 2nd ed. Donald G. Alexander. 280p. 1994. spiral bd. 115.00 (*0-89442-108-5*, MICHIE) LEXIS Pub.

Maine Jury Instructions Manual. 2nd ed. Maine Trial Lawyers Association Staff. 1996. ring bd. write for info. (*1-894421-08-6*, 81655-10, MICHIE) LEXIS Pub.

Maine Jury Instructions Manual, Issue 1. 3rd ed. Maine Trial Lawyers Association Staff. 1997. ring bd. 45.00 (*1-55834-352-0*, 81657-12, MICHIE) LEXIS Pub.

Maine Kid's Cookbook: Recipes, How-To, History, Lore & More! Carole Marsh. (Carole Marsh Maine Bks.). (Illus.). (J). (gr. 3-8). 1994. pap. 19.95 (*0-7933-0538-1*); lib. bdg. 29.95 (*0-7933-0539-X*); disk 29.95 (*0-7933-0540-3*) Gallopade Intl.

Maine Land Use & Zoning Control: Case Law Perspectives on Planning & Growth. Orlando E. Delogu. 870p. 1992. pap. 75.00 (*0-88063-324-7*, MICHIE) LEXIS Pub.

Maine Library Book: A Surprising Guide to the Unusual Special Collections in Libraries Across Our State for Students, Teachers, Writers & Publishers - Includes Reproducible Mailing Labels Plus Activities for Young People! Carole Marsh. (Carole Marsh Maine Bks.). (Illus.). 1994. pap. 19.95 (*0-7933-3063-7*); lib. bdg. 29.95 (*0-7933-3062-9*); disk 29.95 (*0-7933-3064-5*) Gallopade Intl.

Maine Life at the Turn of the Century. Jack Barnes & Diane Barnes. LC 95-237757. (Images of America Ser.). 1995. pap. 16.99 (*0-7524-0240-4*) Arcadia Publng.

Maine Lighthouses: A Pictorial Guide. 2nd rev. ed. Courtney Thompson. LC 97-95350. (Illus.). 128p. 1998. 24.95 (*0-9651786-4-1*, Pub. by Catnap Publns); pap. 19.95 (*0-9651786-3-3*, Pub. by Catnap Publns) Magazines Inc.

Maine Lighthouses in Watercolor. Ed. by Heritage Printing Staff. (Illus.). 128p. 1995. write for info. (*0-9644127-0-5*) W Long.

Maine Lines: Poems, Serious & Otherwise, about Maine. Harris B. Stewart, Jr. & John C. Holden. LC 98-60898. 111p. 1998. write for info. (*1-881539-21-0*) Tabby Hse Bks.

Maine Lobsterboats: Builders & Lobstermen Speak of Their Craft. Virginia L. Thorndike. LC 98-3275. (Illus.). 256p. 1998. pap. 16.95 (*0-89272-403-X*) Down East.

Maine Made Guns & Their Makers. rev. ed. Dwight B. Demeritt, Jr. LC 96-78221. (Illus.). 438p. 1997. 55.00 (*0-913764-30-2*) Maine St Mus.

Maine Man: (By the Year 2000: Marriage) Ellen James. (Harlequin Super Romance Ser.: Series Vol. 822). 1999. mass mkt. 4.25 (*0-373-70822-X*, Harlequin) Harlequin Bks.

Maine Manual on Professional Responsibility. 1993. ring bd., suppl. ed. 27.50 (*0-614-03138-9*, MICHIE) LEXIS Pub.

Maine Manual on Professional Responsibility. rev. ed. Maine Board of Overseers of the Bar Staff. 300p. 1994. ring bd. 65.00 (*0-89442-082-8*, MICHIE) LEXIS Pub.

Maine Manual on Professional Responsibility. 2nd rev. ed. Maine Board of Overseers Staff. 500p. 1997. pap. 125.00 (*1-881758-37-0*) Tower Pub ME.

Maine Manual on Professional Responsibility, Vol. 2. rev. ed. Maine Board of Overseers of the Bar Staff. 370p. 1994. ring bd. 65.00 (*1-56257-301-2*, MICHIE) LEXIS Pub.

Maine Manufacturers Register. rev. ed. Ed. by Frank Lambing. 1998. 55.00 (*1-58202-074-4*) Manufacturers.

***Maine Map & Guide 2000.** Delmore Staff. 2000. pap. 2.95 (*0-89933-082-7*) DeLorme Map.

Maine Massacre. Janwillem Van de Wetering. LC 96-20635. (Soho Crime Ser.). 231p. 1996. pap. 12.00 (*1-56947-064-2*) Soho Press.

Maine Math! How It All Adds up in Our State. Carole Marsh. (Carole Marsh Maine Bks.). (Illus.). (YA). (gr. 3-12). 1996. pap. 19.95 (*0-7933-6545-7*); lib. bdg. 29.95 (*0-7933-6544-9*) Gallopade Intl.

Maine Media Book: A Surprising Guide to the Amazing Print, Broadcast & Online Media of Our State for Students, Teachers, Writers & Publishers - Includes Reproducible Mailing Labels Plus Activities for Young People! Carole Marsh. (Carole Marsh Maine Bks.). (Illus.). 1994. pap. 19.95 (*0-7933-3219-2*); lib. bdg. 29.95 (*0-7933-3218-4*); disk 29.95 (*0-7933-3220-6*) Gallopade Intl.

Maine Media Law Guide. Maine State Bar Association Staff. (State Law Ser.). 140p. (Orig.). 1993. pap. text 14.95 (*0-913507-42-3*) New Forums.

Maine Mining Adventures. C. J. Stevens. LC 94-60304. (Illus.). 1994. pap. 10.00 (*1-882425-03-0*) J Wade.

Maine Mining Adventures. C. J. Stevens. LC 94-60304. (Illus.). 1994. 20.00 (*1-882425-02-2*) J Wade.

Maine Mountain Guide. 8th rev. ed. Appalachian Mountain Club Staff. LC 99-21954. (Illus.). 1999. pap. 18.95 (*1-878239-74-0*) AMC Books.

Maine Mystery Van Takes Off! Bk. 1: Handicapped Maine Kids Sneak off on a Big Adventure. Carole Marsh. (Carole Marsh Maine Bks.). (Illus.). (J). (gr. 3-12). 1994. 29.95 (*0-7933-5018-2*); pap. 19.95 (*0-7933-5019-0*); disk 29.95 (*0-7933-5020-4*) Gallopade Intl.

Maine, New Hampshire & Vermont Pocket Guides. Edward Soomre. 186p. 1995. pap. 13.95 (*0-939430-23-1*) Scanner Master.

***Maine, New Hampshire, Rhode Island & Vermont Limited Liability Company: Forms & Practice Manual, 2 vols.** Michael B. Piesner et al. LC 99-37730. 938p. 1999. ring bd. 295.00 (*1-57400-042-X*) Data Trace Pubng.

Maine-New Hampshire-Vermont Automotive Directory. Ed. by T. L. Spelman. 1985. 24.95 (*1-55527-016-6*) Auto Contact Inc.

***Maine, New Hampshire, Vermont, Massachusetts, Rhode Island, Connecticut.** Cynthia Mascott. (Rails-to-Trails Ser.). (Illus.). 256p. 2000. pap. 14.95 (*0-7627-0449-7*) Globe Pequot.

Maine 1970 Census: Heads of Families. pap. 16.50 (*1-877677-45-0*) Herit Quest.

Maine Objections at Trial. Carlson & Bright. 190p. 1991. pap. text 39.50 (*0-327-03911-6*, 81660-10, MICHIE) LEXIS Pub.

Maine Objections at Trial. Ronald L. Carlson. 190p. 1991. pap. 39.50 (*0-614-05889-9*, MICHIE) LEXIS Pub.

Maine Objections at Trial. Ronald L. Carlson & Myron H. Bright. 200p. 1991. pap. 39.50 (*0-88063-321-2*, MICHIE) LEXIS Pub.

Maine Odyssey: Good Times & Hard Times, Bath, 1936-1986. Kenneth R. Martin & Ralph L. Snow. LC 88-61039. (Illus.). 320p. 1988. 30.00 (*0-9620401-0-X*) Patten Free Lib.

Maine One Hundred Years Ago. Nichols & Pashard. (Historical Ser.). (Illus.). 1977. pap. 3.50 (*0-89540-049-9*, SB-049) Sun Pub.

Maine Picture Country Inns. Stonehouse Publishing Company Staff. (Illus.). pap. 14.95 (*0-921128-36-3*) StHse.

***Maine Poems.** Leo Connellan. 132p. 1999. pap. 10.95 (*0-942396-83-9*) Blackberry ME.

Maine Politics & Government. Kenneth T. Palmer et al. LC 92-6080. (Politics & Governments of the American States Ser.). (Illus.). xxviii, 240p. 1992. pap. text 22.00 (*0-8032-8718-6*) U of Nebr Pr.

Maine Politics & Government. Kenneth T. Palmer et al. LC 92-6080. (Politics & Governments of the American States Ser.). (Illus.). xxviii, 240p. 1992. text 45.00 (*0-8032-3680-8*) U of Nebr Pr.

Maine (Portland & Cumberland Co.) Federal Census, 1860. 1991. 155.00 (*0-89593-614-3*, Accel Indexing) Genealogical Srvcs.

Maine Postal History & Postmarks. Sterling T. Dow. LC 75-1790. (Illus.). 256p. 1976. reprint ed. 35.00 (*0-88000-065-1*) Quarterman.

Maine Probate Abstracts, 2 vols., Set. Ed. by John E. Frost. LC 90-63577. 1501p. 1991. 125.00 (*0-929539-60-5*, 1160) Picton Pr.

Maine Probate Forms. rev. ed. Butterworth Staff. 290p. 1991. suppl. ed. 20.00 (*0-685-59038-0*, MICHIE) LEXIS Pub.

Maine Probate Forms. rev. ed. Compiled by Michie Company Editorial Staff. 290p. 1991. ring bd. 55.00 (*0-89442-116-6*, 81670, MICHIE) LEXIS Pub.

Maine Probate Forms. rev. ed. Michie Editors Staff. 1991. ring bd. 55.00 (*0-327-00985-3*, 81670, MICHIE) LEXIS Pub.

Maine Probate Forms, Issue 5. Professional Publications Staff. 30p. 1998. ring bd. 43.00 (*0-327-00525-4*, 8167215) LEXIS Pub.

Maine Probate Law. rev. ed. Philip C. Hunt. 1993. suppl. ed. 35.00 (*0-685-74264-4*, MICHIE) LEXIS Pub.

Maine Probate Law. 2nd rev. ed. Philip C. Hunt. 500p. 1994. spiral bd. 95.00 (*0-88063-431-6*, MICHIE) LEXIS Pub.

Maine Probate Law, Issue 7. Philip C. Hunt. LC 91-2003. 75p. 1998. ring bd. write for info. (*0-327-00554-8*, 8166713) LEXIS Pub.

Maine Probate Procedure. Patricia Ainslie. Ed. by Beth Duthie. (Illus.). 72p. 1993. ring bd., suppl. ed. 27.00 (*0-614-03139-7*, MICHIE) LEXIS Pub.

Maine Probate Procedure. Mitchell & Hunt. 1991. ring bd. 115.00 (*0-327-01045-2*, 81675-10, MICHIE) LEXIS Pub.

Maine Probate Procedure. 2nd rev. ed. James E. Mitchell. 650p. 1994. spiral bd. 115.00 (*1-56257-303-9*, MICHIE) LEXIS Pub.

Maine Probate Procedure, Issue 6. James E. Mitchell & Philip C. Hunt. LC 91-43264. 30p. 1998. ring bd. write for info. (*0-327-00555-6*, 8167616) LEXIS Pub.

Maine Probate Series, 3 vols. Hunt et al. 1991. ring bd. 195.00 (*0-327-01036-3*, 81680, MICHIE) LEXIS Pub.

Maine Probate Series, 3 vols., Set. Butterworth Staff. 1991. ring bd. 195.00 (*0-250-40780-9*, MICHIE) LEXIS Pub.

Maine Probate Series, 3 vols., Set. 5th rev. ed. American Academy of Orthopaedic Surgeons Staff. 1991. ring bd. 195.00 (*0-614-05891-0*, MICHIE) LEXIS Pub.

Maine Province & Court Records, Vol. 1. 1991. reprint ed. 50.00 (*0-685-41038-2*) Maine Hist.

Maine Quiz Bowl Crash Course! Carole Marsh. (Carole Marsh Maine Bks.). (Illus.). (J). (gr. 3-8). 1994. pap. 19.95 (*1-55609-612-7*); lib. bdg. 29.95 (*1-55609-611-9*); disk 29.95 (*1-55609-613-5*) Gallopade Intl.

Maine Reader: The Down East Experience from 1614 to the Present. Ed. by Charles Shain & Samuella Shain. LC 97-71856. (Illus.). 576p. 1997. pap. 19.95 (*1-56792-078-0*) Godine.

Maine Real Estate. 4th ed. Ralph Palmer & Elaine Richer. LC 97-22040. 363p. (C). 1997. pap. text 35.40 (*0-13-899642-3*) P-H.

Maine Register 1822. 144p. 1972. reprint ed. text 9.95 (*0-317-46936-3*) Tower Pub ME.

*__Maine Related Regulations.__ NILS Publishing Company. LC 98-66834. (Illus.). 1999. write for info. (*0-89246-501-8*) NILS Pub.

Maine Reports, 1820-1955, 77 vols., Set. 1976. 1750.00 (*1-57588-327-9*, 302710) W S Hein.

Maine Retirement & Relocation Guide. large type ed. (Retirement & Relocation Guides Ser.). (Illus.). 350p. Date not set. pap. 24.95 (*1-56559-143-7*) HGI-Over Fifty.

Maine Rivers. North Country Press Staff. (Maine Nature Ser.). 64p. 1997. pap. text 4.50 (*0-945980-12-4*) Nrth Country Pr.

Maine Road Encyclopedia. Ian Penney. 208p. 1996. pap. 17.95 (*1-85158-710-1*, Pub. by Mainstream Pubng) Trafalgar.

Maine Rollercoasters! Carole Marsh. (Carole Marsh Maine Bks.). (Illus.). (YA). (gr. 3-12). 1994. pap. 19.95 (*0-7933-5282-7*); lib. bdg. 29.95 (*0-7933-5281-9*); disk 29.95 (*0-7933-5283-5*) Gallopade Intl.

Maine Roots: Growing up Poor in the Kennebec Valley. Mark Walker. (Illus.). 196p. 1994. 19.50 (*0-89725-170-9*, 1517) Picton Pr.

Maine Rubison: Downeast Settlers During the American Revolution. John H. Ahlin. LC 66-29480. (Illus.). 224p. 1966. reprint ed. pap. 19.50 (*0-89725-320-5*, 1846) Picton Pr.

Maine Sampler: A Collection of Maine Humor. Bill Sawyer. (Illus.). 32p. 1988. pap. 4.95 (*0-89272-215-0*) Down East.

Maine Scenes & Seasons. Photos by Richard Procopio. LC 92-81160. (Illus.). 80p. (Orig.). 1992. pap. 14.95 (*0-933050-95-X*) New Eng Pr VT.

Maine Scenic Spendor: The Play of Color, Light & Shadow. Paul A. Knaut, Jr. LC 95-70151. (Illus.). 80p. (Orig.). 1995. pap. write for info. (*0-940188-34-1*) M Roberts CA.

Maine School Trivia: An Amazing & Fascinating Look at Our State's Teachers, Schools & Students! Carole Marsh. (Carole Marsh Maine Bks.). (Illus.). (J). (gr. 3-8). 1994. pap. 19.95 (*0-7933-0535-7*); lib. bdg. 29.95 (*0-7933-0536-5*); disk 29.95 (*0-7933-0537-3*) Gallopade Intl.

Maine Sea Fisheries: The Rise & Fall of a Native Industry, 1830-1890. Wayne M. O'Leary. LC 96-17724. (Illus.). 448p. 1996. text 55.00 (*1-55553-280-2*) NE U Pr.

Maine Sea Fisheries: The Rise & Fall of a Native Industry, 1830-1890. Wayne N. O'Leary. LC 96-17724. (Illus.). 448p. 1996. pap. text 24.95 (*1-55553-281-0*) NE U Pr.

Maine Silly Basketball Sportsmysteries, Vol. I. Carole Marsh. (Carole Marsh Maine Bks.). (Illus.). (J). (gr. 3-8). 1994. pap. 19.95 (*0-7933-0532-2*); lib. bdg. 29.95 (*0-7933-0533-0*); disk 29.95 (*0-7933-0534-9*) Gallopade Intl.

Maine Silly Basketball Sportsmysteries, Vol. II. Carole Marsh. (Carole Marsh Maine Bks.). (Illus.). (J). (gr. 3-8). 1994. pap. 19.95 (*0-7933-1685-5*); lib. bdg. 29.95 (*0-7933-1684-7*); disk 29.95 (*0-7933-1686-3*) Gallopade Intl.

Maine Silly Football Sportsmysteries, Vol. I. Carole Marsh. (Carole Marsh Maine Bks.). (Illus.). (J). (gr. 3-8). 1994. pap. 19.95 (*1-55609-604-6*); lib. bdg. 29.95 (*1-55609-602-X*); disk 29.95 (*1-55609-606-2*) Gallopade Intl.

Maine Silly Football Sportsmysteries, Vol. II. Carole Marsh. (Carole Marsh Maine Bks.). (Illus.). (J). (gr. 3-8). 1994. pap. 19.95 (*1-55609-605-4*); lib. bdg. 29.95 (*1-55609-603-8*); disk 29.95 (*1-55609-607-0*) Gallopade Intl.

Maine Silly Trivia! Carole Marsh. (Carole Marsh Maine Bks.). (Illus.). (J). (gr. 3-8). 1994. pap. 19.95 (*1-55609-594-5*); lib. bdg. 29.95 (*1-55609-593-7*); disk 29.95 (*1-55609-595-3*) Gallopade Intl.

Maine Speaks: An Anthology of Maine Literature. Ed. by Maine Literature Project Staff. LC 89-60344. (Illus.). 466p. (gr. 7-12). 1989. 29.95 (*0-9618592-1-0*); pap. 19.95 (*0-9618592-2-9*) Maine Writers.

Maine Spelling Bee! Score Big by Correctly Spelling Our State's Unique Names. Carole Marsh. (Carole Marsh Maine Bks.). (Illus.). (YA). (gr. 3-12). 1996. pap. 19.95 (*0-7933-6698-4*); pap. 19.95 (*0-7933-6722-0*); lib. bdg. 29.95 (*0-7933-6697-6*); lib. bdg. 29.95 (*0-7933-6721-2*) Gallopade Intl.

Maine Spring & Other Poems. Elsie H. Boynton. 61p. (Orig.). 1993. pap. text 6.95 (*0-9639352-0-8*) E H Boynton.

Maine State Constitution: A Reference Guide, 9. Marshall J. Tinkle. LC 92-14612. (Reference Guides to the State Constitutions of the United States Ser.: No. 9). 224p. 1992. lib. bdg. 69.50 (*0-313-26618-2*, TKS, Greenwood Pr) Greenwood.

Maine State Parks. Barbara McCaig & Boyce. (Illus.). 100p. (Orig.). 1989. pap. text 5.95 (*0-935201-64-5*) Affordable Adven.

Maine Summer Mahogany. Janet Dailey. (Janet Dailey Americana Ser.: No. 19). 1991. per. 3.59 (*0-373-89869-X*) Harlequin Bks.

Maine Timeline: A Chronology of Maine History, Mystery, Trivia, Legend, Lore & More. Carole Marsh. (Carole Marsh Maine Bks.). (Illus.). (J). (gr. 3-12). 1994. pap. 19.95 (*0-7933-5933-3*); lib. bdg. 29.95 (*0-7933-5932-5*); disk 29.95 (*0-7933-5934-1*) Gallopade Intl.

Maine to the Wilderness. Roderick M. Engert. (Illus.). 108p. 1993. 15.95 (*0-614-29613-7*) North South Trader.

Maine Tort Law. Donald M. Zillman. 750p. 1994. spiral bd. 90.00 (*1-56257-215-6*, MICHIE) LEXIS Pub.

Maine Tort Law. Donald M. Zillman et al. 1997. ring bd. 95.00 (*0-327-00924-1*, 81590-10, MICHIE) LEXIS Pub.

Maine Tort Law, No. 4. Donald M. Zillman et al. LC 94-4435. 250p. 1998. ring bd. write for info. (*0-327-00316-2*, 81692-14) LEXIS Pub.

Maine Tort Law, No. 5. Donald M. Zillman et al. LC 94-4435. 150p. 1998. ring bd. write for info. (*0-327-00317-0*, 81692-15) LEXIS Pub.

*__Maine Tort Law, 1999 Edition.__ Donald N. Zillman et al. 1000p. 1999. 115.00 (*0-327-04952-9*, 8169011) LEXIS Pub.

Maine Towns & Counties. Michael J. Denis. (New England Towns & Counties Ser.). 73p. (Orig.). 1981. pap. 8.50 (*0-935207-02-3*) Danbury Hse Bks.

Maine Trivia. John Cole. LC 98-2977. 192p. 1998. pap. 6.95 (*1-55853-603-5*) Rutledge Hill Pr.

Maine Two-Footers. Linwood Moody. Ed. by Robert Jones. LC 97-78044. 250p. 1998. 44.95 (*0-911581-47-2*) Heimburger Hse Pub.

Maine 2000! Coming Soon to a Calendar Near You - The 21st Century! - Complete Set of AL 2000 Items. Carole Marsh. (Two Thousand! Ser.). (Illus.). (J). (gr. 3-12). 1998. pap. 75.00 (*0-7933-9347-7*); lib. bdg. 85.00 (*0-7933-9348-5*) Gallopade Intl.

Maine 2000! Coming Soon to a Calendar Near You-The 21st Century! Carole Marsh. (Two Thousand! Ser.). (Illus.). (J). (gr. 3-12). 1998. pap. 19.95 (*0-7933-8733-7*); lib. bdg. 29.95 (*0-7933-8732-9*) Gallopade Intl.

Maine UFO's & Extraterrestrials! A Look at the Sightings & Science in Our State. Carole Marsh. (Carole Marsh Maine Bks.). (Illus.). (J). (gr. 3-12). 1997. pap. 19.95 (*0-7933-6392-6*); lib. bdg. 29.95 (*0-7933-6391-8*) Gallopade Intl.

Fodor Maine, Vt., New Hampshire 2000: Expert Advice & Smart Choices, Where to Stay, Eat & Explore on & off the Beaten Path. 5th ed. Fodors Travel Publications, Inc. Staff. (2000 Ser.). (Illus.). 1999. pap. 14.00 (*0-679-00411-4*) Fodors Travel.

*__Maine, Vermont, New Hampshire 2001.__ Fodors Travel Publications, Inc. Staff. 2000. pap. 14.00 (*0-679-00663-X*, Pub. by Fodors Travel) Random House.

Maine Wills, 1640-1760. William M. Sargent. 953p. 1996. reprint ed. pap. 60.00 (*0-8063-0516-9*, 5150) Clearfield Co.

Maine Wills, 1640-1760, 2 vols. William M. Sargent. 1993. reprint ed. pap. text 50.00 (*1-55613-689-7*) Heritage Bk.

Maine Woods see **Writings of Henry D. Thoreau**

Maine Woods. Henry David Thoreau. 30.95 (*0-8488-0643-3*) Amereon Ltd.

Maine Woods. Henry David Thoreau. (Penguin Nature Classics Ser.). 1988. 18.05 (*0-606-07830-4*, Pub. by Turtleback) Demco.

Maine Woods. Henry David Thoreau. 480p. 1988. pap. 13.95 (*0-14-017013-8*, Penguin Bks) Viking Penguin.

Maine Woods. Henry David Thoreau. 1990. reprint ed. lib. bdg. 21.95 (*0-89966-653-1*) Buccaneer Bks.

Maine Workers' Compensation Act, 2 vols., Set. 4th rev. ed. Charles D. Devoe. 790p. 1992. ring bd. 135.00 (*1-56257-315-2*, MICHIE) LEXIS Pub.

Maine Workers' Compensation Commission: Appellate Division Decisions, 1982-1992. Ed. by Charles D. Devoe. 1994. ring bd. 475.00 (*0-614-05892-9*, MICHIE) LEXIS Pub.

Maine Workers' Compensation Commission: Appellate Division Decisions, 1982-1993. Ed. by Charles D. Devoe. 900p. 1994. suppl. ed. 120.00 (*0-685-74265-2*, MICHIE) LEXIS Pub.

Maine Workers' Compensation Commission: Appellate Division Decisions, 1982-1993, Set. Ed. by Charles D. Devoe. 900p. 1993. 475.00 (*0-685-46118-1*, MICHIE) LEXIS Pub.

Maine Workplace Resource Guide to Discrimination & Harassment. Kelley M. Hashey. (Illus.). 100p. (Orig.). 1993. pap. 12.95 (*0-9638687-0-5*) KH Intl.

Maineland Use Control Law: Cases, Notes, Comments. 2nd ed. Orlando E. Delogu. LC 97-13537. 972p. (C). 1997. lib. bdg. 85.00 (*1-881758-34-6*) Tower Pub ME.

*__Maine/New Hampshire/Vermont State Credit Directory, 2000 Edition.__ rev. ed. American Business Directories Staff. 384p. 1999. boxed set 115.00 incl. cd-rom (*0-7687-0305-0*) Am Busn Direct.

*__Maine's Achieving Women: Conversations with Entrepreneurs.__ Mary Lyons. (Illus.). 176p. 2000. pap. 11.95 (*0-9678276-0-4*) Lilac River.

Maine's Golden Road: A Memoir. John Gould. (Illus.). 300p. 1995. 21.00 (*0-393-03806-8*) Norton.

Maine's Golden Road: A Memoir. John Gould. 192p. 1996. pap. 12.95 (*0-940160-68-4*) Parnassus Imprints.

Maine's Hall of Fame, Vol. 1. John E. Cayford. (Illus.). 208p. (Orig.). 1987. pap. 9.95 (*0-941216-22-5*) Cay-Bel.

Maine's Hall of Fame, Vol. 2. John E. Cayford. LC 88-62792. (Illus.). 214p. (Orig.). (YA). (gr. 6 up). 1995. pap. 9.95 (*0-941216-43-8*, 0-941216-43-8) Cay-Bel.

Maine's (Most Devastating!) Disasters & (Most Calamitous!) Catastrophies! Carole Marsh. (Carole Marsh Maine Bks.). (Illus.). (J). (gr. 3-8). 1994. pap. 19.95 (*0-7933-0523-3*); lib. bdg. 29.95 (*0-7933-0524-1*, 0-7933-0525-X) Gallopade Intl.

Maine's (Most Devastating!) Disasters & (Most Calamitous!) Catastrophies! Carole Marsh. (Carole Marsh Maine Bks.). (Illus.). (J). (gr. 3-8). 1997. disk 29.95 (*0-7933-0525-X*) Gallopade Intl.

Maine's Most Scenic Roads: Twenty-Five Routes off the Beaten Path. John Gibson. LC 98-28623. (Illus.). 176p. 1998. pap. 12.95 (*0-89272-422-6*) Down East.

Maine's Natural Heritage: Rare Species & Unique Natural Features. Dean B. Bennett. LC 86-50855. (Illus.). 285p. 1988. 39.95 (*0-89272-228-2*) Down East.

Maine's Unsolved Mysteries (And Their "Solutions") Includes Scientific Information & Other Activities for Students. Carole Marsh. (Carole Marsh Maine Bks.). (Illus.). (J). (gr. 3-12). 1994. pap. 19.95 (*0-7933-5780-2*); lib. bdg. 29.95 (*0-7933-5779-9*); disk 29.95 (*0-7933-5781-0*) Gallopade Intl.

Maineville, Ohio, History: 100 Years As an Incorporated Town, 1850-1950. Robert Brenner. (Illus.). 216p. 1997. reprint ed. lib. bdg. 27.50 (*0-8328-7153-2*) Higginson Bk Co.

Mainframe Assembler Programming. William Qualls. LC 97-31763. 576p. 1998. pap. 49.99 incl. disk (*0-471-24993-9*) Wiley.

Mainframe to Client/Server Migration: Strategic Planning Issues & Techniques. Janet G. Butler. LC 96-14045. (Illus.). 210p. 1996. pap. 290.00 (*1-56607-967-5*) Comput Tech Res.

Mainfranken und Rhoen. 3rd rev. ed. Erwin Rutte & Norbert Wilczewski. (Sammlung Geologischer Fuehrer Ser.: Band 74). (GER., Illus.). viii, 232p. 1982. spiral bd. 29.00 (*3-443-15067-5*, Pub. by Gebruder Borntraeger) Balogh.

Maingot's Abdominal Operations, 2 vols. 10th ed. Michael J. Zinner. 1997. text 115.00 (*0-8385-6118-7*) Appleton & Lange.

Maingot's Abdominal Operations, Vol. I. 10th ed. Rodney Maingot & Michael J. Zinner. LC 96-28893. (C). 1998. pap. text 175.00 (*0-8385-6104-7*, A-6104-2, Apple Lange Med) McGraw.

Maingot's Abdominal Operations, Vol. II. 10th ed. Rodney Maingot & Michael J. Zinner. LC 96-28893. (C). 1998. pap. text 175.00 (*0-8385-6105-5*, A6105-9, Apple Lange Med) McGraw.

Maingot's Abdominal Operations, 2 vols., Vols. I & II. 10th ed. Rodney Maingot & Michael J. Zinner. LC 96-28893. 2150p. (C). 1997. 325.00 (*0-8385-6106-3*, A6106-7, Apple Lange Med) McGraw.

Mainie Jellett & the Modern Movement in Ireland. Bruce Arnold. (Illus.). 244p. (C). 1992. 70.00 (*0-300-05463-7*) Yale U Pr.

Mainland. Gordon Hoban. LC 89-92323. 133p. (Orig.). 1990. pap. 10.95 (*0-944204-10-4*) Omniun.

Mainland China Organizations of Higher Learning in Science & Technology & Their Publications, a Selected Guide. U. S. Library of Congress, Science & Technology Di. LC 77-38090. (China Classic & Contemporary Works in Reprint Ser.). reprint ed. 32.50 (*0-404-56963-3*) AMS Pr.

Mainland Greece. NTC Publishing Group Staff. (Passport Essential Guide Ser.). (Illus.). 128p. 1998. pap. 8.95 (*0-8442-0136-7*, 01367, Passprt Bks) NTC Contemp Pub Co.

Mainland Haole: The White Experience in Hawaii. Elvi Whittaker. LC 85-454. 272p. 1986. text 52.50 (*0-231-05316-9*) Col U Pr.

Mainland Luau: How to Capture the Flavor of Hawaii in Your Own Backyard. 2nd rev. ed. Patricia L. Fry. (Illus.). 80p. 1997. reprint ed. pap. 9.95 (*0-9612642-3-3*) Matilija Pr.

Mainline see **Northwest's Own Railway - Spokane, Portland & Seattle Railway & Its Subsidiaries**

Mainline. Deborah Christian. 1997. mass mkt. 5.99 (*0-614-27808-2*); mass mkt. 5.99 (*0-8125-4908-2*, Pub. by Tor Bks) St Martin.

Mainline Farming for Century Twenty-One. Dan Skow & Charles Walters, Jr. LC 90-86048. 206p. 1991. pap. 19.00 (*0-911311-27-0*) Acres USA.

Mainline Free Zones, Mediterranean, Gulf, Indian Subcontinent. Ed. by Richard L. Bolin. LC 95-185882. 101p. (C). 1995. pap. text 40.00 (*0-945951-11-6*) Flagstaff Inst.

Mainline Steam Revival. Ron Ziel. 41.95 (*0-8488-0863-0*) Amereon Ltd.

*__Mainline to the Future: Congregations for the Twenty-First Century.__ Jackson W. Carroll. 2000. pap. text 16.95 (*0-664-50122-2*) Westminster John Knox.

*__Mainline to the Future: Congregations for the 21st Century.__ Jackson W. Carroll. 220p. 2000. pap. 16.95 (*0-664-22253-6*, Pub. by Westminster John Knox) Presbyterian Pub.

Mainly on the Air. Max Beerbohm. LC 72-287. (Essay Index Reprint Ser.). 1977. reprint ed. 19.95 (*0-8369-2785-0*) Ayer.

Mainly Victorian. Stewart M. Ellis. LC 75-99692. (Essay Index Reprint Ser.). 1977. 30.95 (*0-8369-1407-4*) Ayer.

Mains Sales. Jean-Paul Sartre. 1951. write for info. (*0-318-63483-X*) Fr & Eur.

Mains Sales. Jean-Paul Sartre. (FRE.). 1976. pap. 10.95 (*0-8288-3747-3*, F131510) Fr & Eur.

Mains Sales. Jean-Paul Sartre. (Folio Ser.: No. 806). 1951. 8.95 (*2-07-036806-8*) Schoenhof.

Mains Sales. Jean-Paul Sartre. (FRE.). (C). 1948. pap. 9.95 (*0-8442-1760-3*, VF1760-3) NTC Contemp Pub Co.

Mains Sales de Sartre. Marc Buffat. (FRE.). 247p. 1991. pap. 14.95 (*0-7859-2182-6*, 2070384411) Fr & Eur.

Mains Sales, Satre: Critical Monographs in English. Paul Reed. 64p. 1993. pap. 32.00 (*0-85261-247-8*, Pub. by Univ of Glasgow) St Mut.

Mains Simplifiees: Lexique Chiromancie. Claire Savard. (FRE.). 1998. 49.95 (*0-320-00156-3*) Fr & Eur.

Mainsail to the Wind: A Book of Sailing Quotations. William Galvani. LC 99-31027. 160p. 1999. 22.95 (*1-57409-069-0*); pap. 14.95 (*1-57409-067-4*) Sheridan.

Mainspring o Human Progress. 3rd ed. Henry G. Weaver. LC 97-60571. 253p. 1997. pap. 12.95 (*1-57246-064-4*) Foun Econ Ed.

Mainspring of Human Progress. 3rd ed. Henry G. Weaver. 287p. 1997. pap. text 5.95 (*0-910614-02-4*) Foun Econ Ed.

Mainsprings of Civilization. Ellsworth Huntington. LC 72-4278. (World Affairs Ser.: National & International Viewpoints). 660p. 1972. reprint ed. 39.95 (*0-405-04572-7*) Ayer.

Mainsprings of Indian & Pakistani Foreign Policies. S. M. Burke. LC 74-78992. 318p. reprint ed. pap. 98.60 (*0-608-16068-7*, 203320800084) Bks Demand.

Mainsprings of the German Revival, Vol. 5--5. Henry C. Wallich. LC 76-25963. (Yale Studies in Economics: No. 5). 401p. 1976. reprint ed. lib. bdg. 38.50 (*0-8371-9017-7*, WAMG, Greenwood Pr) Greenwood.

Mainstay: For the Spouse of the Chronically Ill-a Moving Personal Account & a Companion Guide. Maggie Strong. 352p. 1988. 17.95 (*0-316-81923-9*) Little.

Mainstay: For the Well Spouse of the Chronically Ill. 3rd rev. ed. Maggie Strong. LC 97-93088. xvi, 480p. 1997. pap. 15.00 (*0-9657179-0-9*) Brdford Bks.

Mainstream. Hamilton Basso. LC 73-106406. (Essay Index Reprint Ser.). 1977. 21.95 (*0-8369-1444-9*) Ayer.

Mainstream. James Simmons. 112p. 1996. pap. 15.95 (*1-897648-27-8*, Pub. by Poolbeg Pr) Dufour.

Mainstream. 6th ed. Isaacs. (C). 1993. pap. text, student ed. 18.50 (*0-15-501564-8*, Pub. by Harcourt Coll Pubs) Harcourt.

Mainstream: Test Manual. 6th ed. Raiford. (C). 1994. pap. text, teacher ed., suppl. ed. 40.00 (*0-15-501565-6*, Pub. by Harcourt Coll Pubs) Harcourt.

Mainstream America Vol. 1: Life & Thought Today. Joseph A. Wytrwal. (Illus.). 700p. Date not set. 15.00 (*0-910552-13-4*) Endurance.

Mainstream & Margins: Jews, Blacks, & Other Americans. Peter I. Rose. LC 83-4693. 241p. 1983. 39.95 (*0-87855-473-4*) Transaction Pubs.

Mainstream Civilization to 1500. 6th ed. Chodoro. (C). 1994. pap. text 15.95 (*0-15-501198-7*) Harcourt Coll Pubs.

Mainstream Companion of Scottish Literature. T. Royle. text 29.95 (*1-85158-583-4*, Pub. by Mainstream Pubng) Trafalgar.

Mainstream Ethics. Tato Laviera. LC 88-6377. 64p. (Orig.). 1988. pap. 7.00 (*0-934770-90-5*) Arte Publico.

*__Mainstream Mathematical Economics in the 20th Century.__ P. C. Nicola. (Illus.). xx, 521p. 2000. 92.00 (*3-540-67084-X*) Spr-Verlag.

Mainstream Music of Early Twentieth Century America: The Composers, Their Times, & Their Works, 28. Nicholas E. Tawa. LC 92-10676. (Contributions to the Study of Music & Dance Ser.: No. 28). 224p. 1992. 55.00 (*0-313-28563-2*, TMR/, Greenwood Pr) Greenwood.

Mainstream of Civilization. 2nd ed. Joseph R. Strayer. (Illus.). (C). 1989. write for info. (*0-318-52969-6*) Harcourt Coll Pubs.

Mainstream of Civilization, 4 vols. 5th ed. Stanley Chodorow et al. (C). 1989. trans. write for info. (*0-318-65020-7*) Harcourt Coll Pubs.

Mainstream of Civilization. 6th ed. Stanley Chodorow et al. (Illus.). 120p. (C). 1994. text 26.95 (*0-15-501197-9*) Harcourt.

Mainstream of Civilization since 1500. 6th ed. Stanley Chodorow et al. (Illus.). 650p. (C). 1994. pap. text 17.95 (*0-15-501199-5*) Harcourt Coll Pubs.

Mainstream of Civilization to 1715. 6th ed. Stanley Chodorow et al. (Illus.). 630p. (C). 1994. pap. text 17.95 (*0-15-501201-0*) Harcourt Coll Pubs.

Mainstream of Western Political Thought. Judith A. Best. LC 80-11042. 149p. 1980. pap. text 23.95 (*0-87705-243-3*, Kluwer Acad Hman Sci) Kluwer Academic.

An Asterisk (*) at the beginning of an entry indicates that the title is appearing for the first time.

Mainstream of Western Political Thought. Judith A. Best. LC 97-13010. 152p. 1997. pap. 24.50 (*0-7618-0770-5*) U Pr of Amer.

Mainstream or Special? Educating Students with Disabilities. Josephine C. Jenkinson. LC 96-21562. 248p. (C). 1996. 75.00 (*0-415-12835-8*); pap. 24.99 (*0-415-12836-6*) Routledge.

Mainstream Protestant "Decline" The Presbyterian Pattern. Ed. by Milton J. Coalter et al. (Presbyterian Presence Ser.). 168p. (Orig.). 1990. pap. 19.95 (*0-664-25150-1*) Westminster John Knox.

***Mainstream PSI: Psychic Abilities in the Real World.** Stanford Burberick. 1999. 22.95 (*1-57174-133-X*) Hampton Roads Pub Co.

Mainstream Slaughter: 12 Poems. Dave Wright. 16p. 1995. pap. 5.00 (*1-884185-11-8*) O Zone.

Mainstream Videoconferencing: A Developers Guide to Distance Media. Charles Sauer & Joe Duran. LC 96-44237. 304p. (C). 1997. pap. text 39.95 (*0-201-84747-7*) Addison-Wesley.

Mainstreaming: A Practical Guide. James L. Paul et al. (C). 1977. 29.95 (*0-8156-0136-0*) Syracuse U Pr.

Mainstreaming: Feminist Research for Teaching Religious Studies. Ed. by Arlene Swidler & Walter E. Conn. 96p. (Orig.). 1985. pap. text 14.00 (*0-8191-4725-7*); lib. bdg. 39.00 (*0-8191-4724-9*) U Pr of Amer.

Mainstreaming: Learners & Their Environment. Martin Kaufman et al. (Illus.). 531p. 1986. pap. text 25.95 (*0-914797-21-2*) Brookline Bks.

Mainstreaming - Inclusion: A Program Designed for Students with a Variety of Handicapping Conditions. Doris Robinson & Wendy Mopsik. LC 93-79191. (Special Student Book). 30p. (J). (gr. 3-8). 1993. 7.95 (*1-884063-07-1*) Mar Co Prods.

Mainstreaming African-American Studies: A Resource Guide for Middle & High School Teachers. Clarissa Myrick-Harris et al. 240p. (Orig.). 1990. pap. text. write for info. (*1-878531-02-6*) Black Res Ctr.

Mainstreaming & the American Dream: Sociological Perspectives on Parental Coping with Blind & Visually Impaired Children. Howard L. Nixon, II. LC 91-6866. 256p. 1992. pap. 34.95 (*0-89128-191-6*) Am Foun Blind.

Mainstreaming Biodiversity in Agricultural Development: Toward Good Practice. Stefano Pagiola et al. LC 97-994. (Environment Papers: No. 15). 50p. 1997. pap. 22.00 (*0-8213-3884-6*, 13884) World Bank.

Mainstreaming Emotionally Disturbed Children. Ed. by A. J. Pappanikou & James L. Paul. (Special Education & Rehabilitation Monograph Ser.: No. 10). (C). 1981. pap. 18.95 (*0-8156-2246-5*) Syracuse U Pr.

Mainstreaming Equality in the European Union. Teresa L. Rees. LC 97-17427. (Illus.). 280p. (C). 1998. 75.00 (*0-415-11533-7*); pap. 24.99 (*0-415-11534-5*) Routledge.

Mainstreaming ESL: Case-Studies in Integrating ESL Students into the Mainstream Curriculum. Ed. by John Clegg. LC 96-11904. 239p. 1996. 99.00 (*1-85359-349-4*, Pub. by Multilingual Matters); pap. 34.95 (*1-85359-348-6*, Pub. by Multilingual Matters) Taylor & Francis.

Mainstreaming Exceptional Students: A Guide for Classroom Teachers. 4th ed. Jane Schultz. 464p. 1994. pap. text 64.00 (*0-205-15724-6*) Allyn.

Mainstreaming Exceptional Students: A Guide for Classroom Teachers. 4th ed. Jane B. Schulz & C. Dale Carpenter. (C). 1994. pap., teacher ed. write for info. (*0-205-16405-6*, H6405-8) Allyn.

Mainstreaming Gender & Development in the World Bank: Progress & Recommendations. Carolin O. N. Moser et al. LC 98-39050. (Environmentally & Socially Sustainable Development: Social Development Ser.). 48p. 1999. pap. 22.00 (*0-8213-4262-2*, 14262) World Bank.

***Mainstreaming Handbook: Legal Guidance & Classroom Strategies.** Deborah Coughlin. LC 99-55088. 144p. 2000. pap. text 15.00 (*0-325-00226-6*) Heinemann.

Mainstreaming Handicapped Children: Outcomes, Controversies, & New Directions. Ed. by C. Julius Meisel. 312p. (C). 1986. text 59.95 (*0-89859-582-7*) L Erlbaum Assocs.

Mainstreaming in the Social Studies. Ed. by John Herlihy & Myra T. Herlihy. LC 80-81636. (National Council for the Social Studies Bulletin: No. 62). 104p. reprint ed. pap. 32.30 (*0-608-16970-6*, 202773000056) Bks Demand.

Mainstreaming of New Age. Manuel Vasquez. Ed. by Kenneth R. Wade. LC 98-156066. 222p. 1998. pap. 10.99 (*0-8163-1653-8*) Pacific Pr Pub Assn.

Mainstreaming Outsiders: The Production of Black Professionals. James E. Blackwell. LC 81-82121. (Illus.). 345p. (C). 1981. 39.95 (*0-930390-39-3*) Gen Hall.

Mainstreaming Outsiders: The Production of Black Professionals. 2nd ed. James E. Blackwell. LC 87-80426. (Illus.). 400p. (C). 1987. text 44.95 (*0-930390-76-8*) Gen Hall.

Mainstreaming Retardation Delinquency. Ed. by Richard Greene. LC 90-71602. 215p. 1990. pap. 24.95 (*0-87762-735-5*) Scarecrow.

Mainstreaming the Environment: The World Bank Group & the Environment since the Rio Earth Summit--Fiscal 1995. 316p. 1995. pap. 22.00 (*0-8213-3290-2*, 13290) World Bank.

Mainstreaming the Environment: The World Bank Group & the Environment since the Rio Earth Summit--Fiscal 1995. (SPA.). 80p. 1995. pap. 22.00 (*0-8213-3292-9*, 13292) World Bank.

Mainstreaming the Environment: The World Bank Group & the Environment since the Rio Earth Summit--Fiscal 1995. 64p. 1996. pap. 22.00 (*0-8213-3481-6*, 13481) World Bank.

Mainstreaming the Exceptional Child: A Bibliography. Mary C. Clarkson. LC 81-84656. (Checklists in the Humanities & Education Ser.: No. 6). 250p. reprint ed. pap. 77.50 (*0-8357-6348-X*, 203562200096) Bks Demand.

Mainstreaming the Handicapped: A Design Guide. Uriel Cohen et al. (Publications in Architecture & Urban Planning: No. R79-5). (Illus.). vi, 64p. 1992. reprint ed. per. 11.00 (*0-938744-05-4*) U of Wis Ctr Arch-Urban.

Mainstream(s) & Margins: Cultural Politics in the 90s, 367. Ed. by Michael Morgan & Susan Leggett. LC 95-37339. (Contributions in Political Science Ser.: No. 367). 264p. 1996. 65.00 (*0-313-29796-7*, Greenwood Pr) Greenwood.

Mainstreams in American Aesthetics: A Marxist Analysis. Willis Truitt. 154p. 1991. 55.00 (*0-614-13739-X*) Haven Pubns.

Mainstreams in Industrial Organization. Ed. by William G. Shepherd & Henry W. De Jong. (C). 1988. lib. bdg. 234.00 (*90-247-3363-4*) Kluwer Academic.

Mainstreams of American Media: A Narrative & Intellectual History of American Journalism. Hiley H. Ward. LC 96-30900. 542p. 1996. pap. text 67.00 (*0-205-14922-7*) Allyn.

Mainstreams of Modern Art. 2nd ed. John Canaday. (C). 1981. pap. text 69.50 (*0-03-057638-5*, Pub. by Harcourt Coll Pubs) Harcourt.

Mainstreet: A Portrait of Small-Town Michigan. 2nd ed. Manny Crisostomo. (Illus.). 205p. 1986. 28.95 (*0-9614344-4-9*) Historical Soc MI.

Maintain & Repair Your Computer Printer & Save a Bundle. Stephen J. Bigelow. 240p. 1991. 26.95 (*0-8306-2563-1*) McGraw-Hill Prof.

Maintain & Repair Your Notebook, Palmtop, & Pen Computers: A Technician's Guide. Stephen J. Bigelow. 1994. 27.00 (*0-07-005275-1*) McGraw-Hill Prof.

Maintain & Repair Your Notebook, Palmtop, or Pen Computer. Stephen J. Bigelow. LC 93-28420. 300p. 1993. 27.00 (*0-8306-4454-7*, Windcrest) TAB Bks.

Maintain Your Yard the Lazy Way. Judith Larner Lowry. 304p. 1999. pap. text. write for info. (*0-02-863012-2*) Macmillan.

Maintainability: A Key to Effective Serviceability & Maintenance Management. Benjamin S. Blanchard et al. LC 94-13474. 560p. 1995. 120.00 (*0-471-59132-7*) Wiley.

Maintainability & Maintenance Management. 2nd enl. fac. rev. ed. Joseph D. Patton. LC 88-13043. (Illus.). 460p. 1994. pap. 142.60 (*0-7837-7633-0*, 204738600007) Bks Demand.

Maintainability & Maintenance Management. 3rd ed. Joseph D. Patton, Jr. LC 94-50673. 452p. 1994. 76.00 (*1-55617-510-8*) ISA.

***Maintainability of Digital Systems: Technical Basis & Human Factors Review.** W. F. Stubler. 144p. 2000. per. 15.00 (*0-16-059209-7*) USGPO.

Maintainer's Helper - Group A. Jack Rudman. (Career Examination Ser.: C-465). 1994. pap. 23.95 (*0-8373-0465-2*) Nat Learn.

Maintainer's Helper - Group B. Jack Rudman. (Career Examination Ser.: C-466). 1994. pap. 23.95 (*0-8373-0466-0*) Nat Learn.

Maintainer's Helper - Group C. Jack Rudman. (Career Examination Ser.: C-467). 1994. pap. 23.95 (*0-8373-0467-9*) Nat Learn.

Maintainer's Helper - Group D. Jack Rudman. (Career Examination Ser.: C-468). 1994. pap. 23.95 (*0-8373-0468-7*) Nat Learn.

Maintainer's Helper - Group E. Jack Rudman. (Career Examination Ser.: C-469). 1994. pap. 23.95 (*0-8373-0469-5*) Nat Learn.

***Maintaining a Balance: The Economic, Environmental & Social Impacts of Shrimp Farming in Latin America.** James A. Tobey et al. (Coastal Resources Center - Coastal Management Reports: No. 2202). (Illus.). 62p. 1998. pap. write for info. (*1-885454-04-X*) Coastal Res.

Maintaining a Competitive Workforce: Employer-Based Training in the Canadian Economy. Derek Hum et al. Ed. by Stephen T. Easton. 109p. 1996. pap. 15.95 (*0-88645-160-4*, Pub. by Inst Res Pub) Ashgate Pub Co.

Maintaining a Drug-Free Workplace: The Management Primer on the Major Legal Issues Surrounding Drugs & Alcohol in the Workplace. Robert A. Naeve. Ed. by Margaret L. Johnson. 199p. (Orig.). 1990. pap. 38.00 (*0-932823-03-3*) Am Somerset.

Maintaining a Lead Safe Home: A Do-It-Yourself Manual for Homeowners & Property Managers. Dennis Livingston. LC 97-94481. (Illus.). 79p. 1997. pap. 14.95 (*0-9659833-0-7*) Commun Res Projs.

Maintaining a Sense of Place: A Citizen's Guide to Community Preservation. John C. Waters. LC 83-12810. 110p. (Orig.). 1983. pap. 6.50 (*0-911847-00-6*) U GA Inst Community.

Maintaining a Sound Tax System: 1998-1999 Budget. LC 98-187698. 45 p. 1998. write for info. (*2-550-32702-0*) Gvt Quebec.

Maintaining a Spirit Filled Life. Buddy Harrison. 1985. pap. 1.00 (*0-89274-383-2*) Harrison Hse.

Maintaining & Enriching Your EAP. 50p. (Orig.). 1984. pap. text 5.95 (*0-9610026-3-8*) Perf Resource Pr.

Maintaining & Operating Finished Water Storage Facilities. Gregory J. Kirmeyer. LC 98-47148. 1999. write for info. (*0-89867-983-4*) Am Water Wks Assn.

Maintaining & Repairing VCRs. 2nd ed. Robert L. Goodman. 356p. 1989. pap. 18.95 (*0-07-155501-3*) McGraw.

Maintaining & Repairing VCRs. 2nd ed. Robert L. Goodman. (Illus.). 320p. 1989. 27.95 (*0-8306-9003-4*, 3103); pap. 18.95 (*0-8306-9103-0*, 3103) McGraw-Hill Prof.

Maintaining & Repairing VCRs. 3rd ed. Robert L. Goodman. (Illus.). 544p. 1992. 29.95 (*0-8306-4079-7*, 4204); pap. 19.95 (*0-8306-4080-0*, 4204) McGraw-Hill Prof.

Maintaining & Repairing VCRs. 4th ed. Robert L. Goodman. LC 95-22901. (Illus.). 544p. 1995. 44.95 (*0-07-024199-6*); pap. 24.95 (*0-07-024200-3*) McGraw-Hill Prof.

***Maintaining & Repairing VCRs & Camcorders.** Robert L. Goodman. LC 99-25562. 1999. pap. 34.95 (*0-07-024834-6*) McGraw-Hill Pubng.

Maintaining & Repairing VCRs & Camcorders. 2nd ed. Bob Goodman. LC 99-18444. 650p. 1999. pap. text 34.95 (*0-07-024828-1*) McGraw.

Maintaining & Repairing Your Scale Model Trains. Jim Volhard. LC 99-218934. 1999. pap. text 5.95 (*0-89024-324-7*) Kalmbach.

Maintaining & Troubleshooting Electric Motors. Tel-A-Train, Inc. Staff. 1989. student ed. 17.50 (*1-56355-085-7*) Tel-A-Train.

Maintaining & Troubleshooting Electrical Equipment. Terry Wireman & Roy Parks. LC 87-4234. (Illus.). 179p. 1987. 24.95 (*0-8311-1164-X*) Indus Pr.

Maintaining & Troubleshooting HPLC Systems: A Users Guide. Dennis J. Runser. LC 80-25444. 184p. 1981. 89.95 (*0-471-06479-3*) Wiley.

Maintaining & Troubleshooting Industrial Motor Controls. Tel-A-Train, Inc. Staff. 1991. student ed. 17.50 (*1-56355-272-8*) Tel-A-Train.

Maintaining Balance. Dick Iverson. 166p. 1989. pap. 10.99 (*0-914936-80-8*) City Bible Pub.

Maintaining Bearings. Tel-A-Train, Inc. Staff. 1987. student ed. 6.50 (*1-56355-005-9*) Tel-A-Train.

Maintaining Biodiversity in Forest Ecosystems. Ed. by Malcolm L. Hunter, Jr. LC 98-40458. 550p. 1999. pap. text 44.95 (*0-521-63768-6*) Cambridge U Pr.

Maintaining Biodiversity in Forest Ecosystems. Ed. by Malcolm L. Hunter, Jr. LC 98-40458. (Illus.). 550p. (C). 1999. text 100.00 (*0-521-63104-1*) Cambridge U Pr.

Maintaining Brakes & Clutches. Tel-A-Train, Inc. Staff. 1987. student ed. 6.50 (*1-56366-008-3*) Tel-A-Train.

***Maintaining Budgetary Discipline: Spending & Revenue Options.** Ed. by Sherry Snyder. (Illus.). 284p. 1999. pap. text 40.00 (*0-7881-8128-9*) DIANE Pub.

***Maintaining Budgetary Discipline: Spending & Revenue Options.** United States Congressional Budget Office. LC 99-205597. (Illus.). 304p. 1999. write for info. (*0-16-050016-8*) USGPO.

Maintaining Centrifugal Pumps. Tel-A-Train, Inc. Staff. 1987. student ed. 6.50 (*1-56355-015-6*) Tel-A-Train.

***Maintaining Children in School: The Contribution of Social Services Departments.** Jeni Vernon & Ruth Sinclair. 64p. 1999. pap. 18.95 (*1-900990-43-1*, Pub. by Natl Childrens Bur) Paul & Co Pubs.

Maintaining Communication with Persons with Dementia: An Educational Program for Nursing Home Staff & Family Members. Ronald W. Toseland & Phillip McCallion. LC 97-43904. 1998. 125.00 (*0-8261-1207-2*) Springer Pub.

***Maintaining Communication with Persons with Dementia: An Educational Program for Nursing Home Staff & Family Members.** Ronald W. Toseland & Phillip McCallion. LC 97-43904. 1998. 29.95 (*0-8261-1229-3*) Springer Pub.

Maintaining Competitiveness with High Wages. Alan S. Blinder. 20p. 1992. pap. 9.95 (*1-55815-171-0*) ICS Pr.

Maintaining Cultures for Biotechnology & Industry. Ed. by Jennie C. Hunter-Cevera & Angela Belt. (Illus.). 320p. 1996. pap. text 39.95 (*0-12-361946-7*) Acad Pr.

Maintaining Dating Purity. David W. Merck. LC 96-42567. 1996. 3.75 (*1-889520-01-2*) Truth for Eternity.

Maintaining Distribution-System Water Quality. 88p. 1986. pap. 33.00 (*0-89867-347-X*, 20231) Am Water Wks Assn.

Maintaining Diversity in Higher Education. Robert Birnbaum. LC 83-48156. (Jossey-Bass Higher Education Ser.). 227p. reprint ed. pap. 70.40 (*0-7837-0162-4*, 204045900017) Bks Demand.

Maintaining Downtown's Curb Appeal. Delores P. Palma & Doyle G. Hyett. (Publications Ser.). (Illus.). ii, 36p. 1995. pap. 21.00 (*1-893312-07-0*) HyettPalma Pubns.

Maintaining Electronic Systems. Whitaker. 470p. 1991. boxed set 99.95 (*0-8493-7411-1*, QA) CRC Pr.

Maintaining Energy Security in a Global Context. William F. Martin et al. Ed. by Charles B. Heck. (Triangle Papers: Vol. 48). 142p. (Orig.). 1996. pap. 12.00 (*0-930503-73-2*) Trilateral Comm.

Maintaining Faculty Excellence. Ed. by Keith Kroll. LC 85-644753. (New Directions for Community Colleges Ser.: No. CC 79). 140p. 1993. pap. 22.00 (*1-55542-730-8*) Jossey-Bass.

Maintaining Family Ties: Inclusive Practice in Foster Care. Sally E. Palmer. LC 95-185858. 1995. pap. 9.95 (*0-87868-599-5*) Child Welfare.

***Maintaining Flexible Pavements: The Long Term Pavement Performance Experiment SPS-3, 5-Year Data Analysis.** D. A. Morian et al. (Illus.). 223p. (C). 1999. pap. text 35.00 (*0-7881-7588-2*) DIANE Pub.

Maintaining Function in Older Adults. Linda A. Newman. LC 95-13936. (Illus.). 141p. 1995. pap. text 29.00 (*0-7506-9568-4*) Buttrwrth-Heinemann.

Maintaining Future Military Aircraft Design Capability. Jeffrey A. Drezner et al. LC 92-15886. 1992. pap. 7.50 (*0-8330-1254-1*, R-4199-AF) Rand Corp.

Maintaining High Level Wellness in Older Years. Southern Conference on Gerontology Staff. Ed. by Lois N. Knowles. LC 72-190141. (Institute of Gerontology Ser.: No. 14). 110p. reprint ed. pap. 34.10 (*0-7837-4927-9*, 204459300004) Bks Demand.

Maintaining High Safety Standards in the Turbulent '90s: Proceedings of the 4th Annual European Corporate & Regional Aircraft Operators Safety Seminar, March 10-12, 1992, Brussels, Belgium. Flight Safety Foundation Staff. LC 91-657078. (Flight Safety Digest Ser. Special Supplement: Vol. 11, No. 7, July 1992). 135p. reprint ed. pap. 41.90 (*0-7837-7029-4*, 204684400004) Bks Demand.

Maintaining Morale: A Guide to Assessing the Morale of Midlevel Administrators & Faculty Members. Linda K. Johnsrud. LC 95-83564. 148p. (Orig.). 1996. pap. 35.00 (*1-878240-47-1*) Coll & U Personnel.

Maintaining Neighborhood Watch. Ed. by Jean O'Neil. 4p. 1986. pap. 3.95 (*0-934513-23-6*, R1A) Natl Crime DC.

Maintaining Nuclear Stability in South Asia. Neil Joeck. (Adelphi Papers: No. 312). 90p. 1998. pap. text 28.95 (*0-19-829406-9*) OUP.

Maintaining Outer Space for Peaceful Uses. 333p. 20.00 (*92-808-0537-1*) UN.

Maintaining Perspective. Dennis Black. LC 96-32404. (Orig.). 1996. pap. 37.95 (*0-912150-39-4*) Atwood Pub LLC.

Maintaining Perspective: A Decade of Collegiate Legal Challenges. Dennis Black. 294p. 1997. pap. text 37.95 (*1-891859-11-0*) Atwood Pub LLC.

Maintaining Prosperity in an Ageing Society. OECD Staff. LC 98-186025. 128p. 1998. pap. 20.00 (*92-64-16093-0*, Pub. by Org for Econ) OECD.

Maintaining Radiation Protection Records. Intro. by Charles B. Meinhold. LC 92-49562. (Report Ser.: No. 114). 86p. (Orig.). 1992. pap. text 30.00 (*0-929600-27-4*) NCRP Pubns.

M

Maintaining Sanity in the Classroom: Classroom Management Techniques. 2nd ed. Rudolf Dreikurs et al. LC 97-43852. 1998. pap. write for info. (*1-56032-727-8*) Hemisp Pub.

Maintaining Shift Continuity: The Principles of Shift Turnover. H. C. Howlett, 2nd. (Illus.). 11p. 1994. pap. 5.50 (*1-57614-012-1*) TECHSTAR.

Maintaining the Delicate Balance in Christian Living. Jay Edward Adams. 115p. 1998. pap. 9.95 (*1-889032-11-5*) Timeless Texts.

Maintaining the Longterm Productivity of Pacific Northwest Forest Ecosystems. Ed. by David A. Perry. LC 89-20168. (Illus.). 256p. 1989. text 44.95 (*0-88192-144-0*) Timber.

Maintaining the Miracle Vol. 1: An Owner's Manual for the Human Body. Ted D. Adams et al. (Illus.). 246p. reprint ed. pap. 17.95 (*0-9638937-7-7*) Capp Pubng.

Maintaining the Momentum of Beijung: The Contribution of African Gender NGOs. Ed. by Nana A. Apt et al. LC 98-72625. (University of North London Voices in Development Management Ser.). 234p. 1998. text 59.95 (*1-85972-483-3*, Pub. by Avebry) Ashgate Pub Co.

Maintaining the Privacy of Library Records: A Handbook & Guide. Arlene C. Bielefield & Lawrence Cheeseman. LC 94-7153. 203p. 1994. 49.95 (*1-55570-066-7*) Neal-Schuman.

Maintaining the Profession: A Fieldbook for Clinical Supervisors. William R. Olcott. 238p. 1996. 19.95 (*1-889346-00-4*) Rainmaker Pr.

Maintaining the Safety Net: Income Redistribution Programs in the Reagan Administration. Ed. by John C. Weicher. LC 84-9259. (AEI Studies: No. 401). 224p. reprint ed. pap. 69.50 (*0-8357-4502-3*, 203735800008) Bks Demand.

Maintaining the Self in Communication: Concept & Guidebook. Harold Barrett. LC 97-72960. xiii, 305p. (Orig.). 1998. pap. text 19.95 (*0-9658440-5-6*) Alpha & Omega.

***Maintaining the Sublime: Heidegger & Adorno.** Jan Rosiek. LC 99-59289. 529p. 2000. 42.95 (*3-906763-22-6*); pap. 42.95 (*0-8204-4612-2*) P Lang Pubng.

Maintaining U. S. Leadership in Aeronautics: Breakthrough Technologies to Meet Future Air & Space Transportation Needs & Goals. National Research Council Staff. LC 98-226157. 148p. 1998. pap. text 27.75 (*0-309-06226-8*) Natl Acad Pr.

Maintaining V-Belts. Tel-A-Train, Inc. Staff. 1987. student ed. 6.50 (*1-56355-034-2*) Tel-A-Train.

Maintaining Working Relationships. Learning Business Staff. 1997. 26.95 (*0-7506-3151-1*) Buttrwrth-Heinemann.

Maintaining Your Deliverance: A Practical Guide for Victorious Christian Living. Lorenzo Irving. 64p. (Orig.). 1996. pap. 5.95 (*0-9651710-0-0*) Life Ctr Mnstries.

***Maintaining Your Gains: COPE Program for Depression.** John H. Greist et al. (Illus.). 9p. 1999. pap. write for info. (*0-9702974-7-5*) Healthcare Sys.

Maintaining Your Old House in Cambridge. Charles Sullivan et al. (Illus.). 75p. 1988. pap. 9.95 (*0-9620072-0-X*) Cambridge Historical.

Maintaining Your Quality Edge. Joint Commission on Accreditation of Healthcare Organizations. (Illus.). 420p. 1997. 220.00 (*0-86688-474-2*, M-971) Joint Comm Hlthcare.

Maintenace Mechanic's-Machinist's Toolbox Manual. John D. Bies. 380p. 1998. pap. text 9.95 (*0-13-545666-5*) P-H.

Maintenance & Loss of Minority Languages. Ed. by Willem Fase et al. LC 92-9267. (Studies in Bilingualism: No. 1). xii, 403p. 1992. 89.00 (*1-55619-344-0*); pap. 29.95 (*1-55619-348-3*) J Benjamins Pubng Co.

Maintenance & Operation of Bulk Grain Stores. D. B. Williams & A. D. Gracey. (Agricultural Services Bulletin Ser.: No. 113). 166p. 1995. pap. 25.00 (*92-5-103489-3*, F34893, Pub. by FAO) Bernan Associates.

Maintenance & Operations of Buildings & Grounds, Pt. II. 576p. 1997. pap. 65.00 (*0-913359-99-8*) APPA VA.

Maintenance & Repair of Architectural Cast Iron. John G. Waite. 14p. 1992. pap. 1.00 (*0-16-061648-4*) USGPO.

Maintenance & Repair of Laboratory, Diagnostic Imaging, & Hospital Equipment. LC 96-127663. (CHI, ENG, FRE & SPA.). vi, 158p. 1994. pap. text 39.00 (*92-4-154463-5*, 1150423) World Health.
Maintenance & Repair Operations Reprints. LC 87-71967. 66p. 1987. pap. text 10.00 (*0-935406-93-X*) Am Prod & Inventory.
Maintenance & Repairs, Vol. III. Ed. by Practical Sailor Staff. (Practical Sailor Library). (Illus.). 1995. pap. 14.95 (*1-879620-34-0*) Belvoir Pubns.
Maintenance & Transmission of Ethnic Identity: A Study of Four Ethnic Groups of Religious Jews in Israel. Linda B. Soroff. LC 95-17243. 260p. (C). 1995. 44.00 (*0-8191-9964-8*) U Pr of Amer.
Maintenance & Utility Costs: Results of a Survey. M. H. Smith. 1991. pap. 40.00 (*0-86022-280-2*, Pub. by Build Servs Info Assn) St Mut.
Maintenance Behavior & Communication in the Brown Pelican. Ralph W. Schreiber. viii, 78p. 1977. 6.00 (*0-318-12920-5*) Am Ornithologists.
Maintenance Carpenter. Jack Rudman. (Career Examination Ser.: C-1349). 1994. pap. 23.95 (*0-8373-1349-X*) Nat Learn.
Maintenance Carpenter Foreman. Jack Rudman. (Career Examination Ser.: C-1350). 1994. pap. 29.95 (*0-8373-1350-3*) Nat Learn.
***Maintenance Compendium: The Ongoing Reference for Building Operations.** rev. ed. 250p. 1999. ring bd. 24.95 (*1-57203-047-X*) Inst Real Estate.
Maintenance Computerization Handbook. K. L. Petrocelly. LC 92-40191. 186p. 1993. 74.00 (*0-88173-150-1*) Fairmont Pr.
Maintenance Contracts for Building Engineering Services. 2nd ed. 1989. 120.00 (*0-7855-7031-4*, Pub. by Build Servs Info Assn) St Mut.
Maintenance Contracts for Building Engineering Services. 2nd ed. M. H. Smith. (C). 1992. 129.00 (*0-7855-2666-8*, Pub. by Build Servs Info Assn) St Mut.
Maintenance Crew Chief. Jack Rudman. (Career Examination Ser.: C-3461). 1994. pap. 34.95 (*0-8373-3461-6*) Nat Learn.
Maintenance, Custodial Branch Initial-Level Supervisor Examination (U. S. P. S.) Jack Rudman. (Career Examination Ser.: C-1775). 1994. pap. 34.95 (*0-8373-1775-4*) Nat Learn.
Maintenance Development Program Aptitude Test USPS. Jack Rudman. (Career Examination Ser.: C-3609). 1994. pap. 34.95 (*0-8373-3609-0*) Nat Learn.
Maintenance Electrician. Jack Rudman. (Career Examination Ser.: C-1351). 1994. pap. 27.95 (*0-8373-1351-1*) Nat Learn.
Maintenance Electrician Foreman. Jack Rudman. (Career Examination Ser.: C-1352). 1994. pap. 29.95 (*0-8373-1352-X*) Nat Learn.
Maintenance Engineering Handbook. 5th ed. Lindley R. Higgins. 1280p. 1994. 125.00 (*0-07-028811-9*) McGraw.
***Maintenance Fundamentals.** R. Keith Mobley. LC 98-53101. 360p. 1999. 59.95 (*0-7506-7151-3*) Buttrwrth-Heinemann.
Maintenance Locksmith. Jack Rudman. (Career Examination Ser.: C-1353). 1994. pap. 23.95 (*0-8373-1353-8*) Nat Learn.
Maintenance Log. Weems & Plath Staff. (Illus.). 98p. (Orig.). 1991. pap. 15.95 (*1-878797-10-7*) Weems & Plath.
Maintenance Machinist. Jack Rudman. (Career Examination Ser.: C-1354). 1994. pap. 23.95 (*0-8373-1354-6*) Nat Learn.
***Maintenance Man.** Michael Baisden. Ed. by Chandra Sparks. LC 94-12045. (Illus.). 320p. 1999. 22.95 (*0-9643675-3-X*) Legacy Publng.
***Maintenance Man: A Novel.** Michael Baisden. 2000. pap. 12.00 (*0-7432-0478-6*, Scribner Pap Fic) S&S Trade Pap.
Maintenance Man Trainee. Jack Rudman. (Career Examination Ser.: C-464). 1994. pap. 23.95 (*0-8373-0464-4*) Nat Learn.
Maintenance Man (Worker) Jack Rudman. (Career Examination Ser.: C-463). 1994. pap. 23.95 (*0-8373-0463-6*) Nat Learn.
Maintenance Management. James K. Jordan. 112p. 1990. pap. 36.00 (*0-89867-526-X*, 20252) Am Water Wks Assn.
Maintenance Management. Harold Roffman. 187p. 1997. ring bd. 44.50 (*0-929442-05-9*, 2210pp) Prof Prnting & Pub.
Maintenance Management. Paul D. Tomlingson. 160p. 1995. pap. text, spiral bd., wbk. ed. 24.95 (*0-7872-1514-7*) Kendall-Hunt.
Maintenance Management: Results of a Survey. J. Armstrong. (C). 1981. pap. 25.00 (*0-86022-130-X*, Pub. by Build Servs Info Assn) St Mut.
Maintenance Management & Technology Handbook. Derek Stoneham. LC 97-44025. 392p. 1998. 204.00 (*1-85617-315-1*) Elsevier.
Maintenance Management & Terotechnology. Husband. 1976. 72.95 (*0-566-00146-2*) Ashgate Pub Co.
Maintenance Management Audit: A Step by Step Workbook to Better Your Facility's Bottom Line. Harvey H. Kaiser et al. 1991. spiral bd. 64.95 (*0-87629-287-2*, 67299) R S Means.
Maintenance Management for Health Care Facilities. 2nd ed. W. Thomas Schipper. (Illus.). 278p. (Orig.). 1990. 100.00 (*0-87258-548-4*, 055854); 150.00 incl. disk (*0-87258-659-6*, 055852) Am Hospital.
Maintenance Management for Medical Equipment. American Hospital Association Staff. (Illus.). 270p. (Orig.). 1994. pap. 100.00 (*0-685-72235-X*, 055855) Am Hospital.
Maintenance Management for Quality Production. Ed. by John L. Winter & Richard S. Zakrzewski. LC 83-51535. (Manufacturing Update Ser.). 294p. reprint ed. pap. 91.20 (*0-608-14866-0*, 202616000048) Bks Demand.
Maintenance Management Manual with Special Reference to Developing Countries. LC 95-210771. (UNIDO General Studies). 334p. 42.00 (*92-1-106292-6*) UN.
Maintenance Management of Street & Highway Signs. (National Cooperative Highway Research Program Report Ser.: No. 157). 134p. 1990. 12.00 (*0-309-04910-5*) Transport Res Bd.
Maintenance Management, Traffic Safety, & Roadsides. Ed. by Norman Solomon. (Transportation Research Record Ser.: No. TRR1409). (Illus.). 112p. 1993. pap. text 25.00 (*0-309-05556-3*) Transport Res Bd.
Maintenance Management, Traffic Safety, & Snow Removal. LC 92-30100. (Transportation Research Record Ser.: No. 1352). 82p. 1992. 21.00 (*0-309-05216-5*) Transport Res Bd.
Maintenance Manager's Standard Manual. 2nd ed. Thomas A. Westerkamp. LC 96-51120. 640p. (C). 1997. text 79.95 (*0-13-243734-1*) P-H.
Maintenance Mason. Jack Rudman. (Career Examination Ser.: C-1355). 1994. pap. 23.95 (*0-8373-1355-4*) Nat Learn.
Maintenance Mason Foreman. Jack Rudman. (Career Examination Ser.: C-1356). 1994. pap. 29.95 (*0-8373-1356-2*) Nat Learn.
Maintenance Mechanic. Jack Rudman. (Career Examination Ser.: C-1357). 1994. pap. 23.95 (*0-8373-1357-0*) Nat Learn.
Maintenance Mechanic (Automated Mail Processing Equipment) (A.M.P.E) (U.S.P.S.) Jack Rudman. (Career Examination Ser.: C-1606). 1994. pap. 27.95 (*0-8373-1606-5*) Nat Learn.
Maintenance Mechanics Qualification Program. 2nd ed. Clint C. Bell. LC 80-85404. 78p. 1989. reprint ed. pap. 30.00 (*0-608-00685-8*, 203560400096) Bks Demand.
Maintenance Minimization for Competitive Advantage: A Life-Cycle Approach for Product Manufacturers & End-Users. Hans Reiche. LC 92-46257. 208p. 1994. text 68.00 (*2-88124-589-7*) Gordon & Breach.
***Maintenance of Animal/Human & Plant Pathogen Vectors: A Methods Manual.** Ed. by Karl Maramorosch & Farida Mahmood. LC 99-48243. 340p. 1999. 85.00 (*1-57808-049-5*) Science Pubs.
Maintenance of Brick & Stone Masonry Structures. Ed. by A. M. Sowden. 350p. 1987. mass mkt. 114.50 (*0-419-14930-9*, A3829, E & FN Spon) Routledge.
Maintenance of Capital: Financial vs. Physical. Ed. by Robert R. Sterling & Kenneth W. Lemke. LC 82-16847. 323p. (C). 1982. 30.00 (*0-914348-32-9*) Scholars Bk.
Maintenance of Factory Services, No. 1. 1982. 52.00 (*0-7855-2888-1*) St Mut.
Maintenance of Factory Services, 2 vols., No. 2. 1982. 125.00 (*0-85083-077-X*) St Mut.
Maintenance of Fluid & Electrolyte Balance see Principles of Applied Clinical Chemistry: Chemical Background & Medical Applications
Maintenance of Free Trade: According to the Three Essential Parts of Traffic. Gerard De Malynes. LC 73-115927. (Reprints of Economic Classics Ser.). 105p. 1971. reprint ed. lib. bdg. 29.50 (*0-678-00644-X*) Kelley.
Maintenance of Highway Structures. LC 92-23519. (Transportation Research Record Ser.: No. 1347). 87p. 1992. 21.00 (*0-309-05213-0*) Transport Res Bd.
Maintenance of Instruments & Systems. L. D. Goettsche & R. H. Zielske. LC 94-6671. (Practical Guide Ser.). 1994. 145.00 (*1-55617-512-4*) ISA.
Maintenance of Knowledge-Based Systems: Theory, Techniques & Tools. Frans Coenen & Trevor Bench-Capon. (APIC Ser.). (Illus.). 352p. 1993. text 88.00 (*0-12-178120-8*) Acad Pr.
Maintenance of Microorganisms, & Cultured Cells: A Manual of Laboratory Methods. 2nd ed. Ed. by A. E. Doyle & A. Doyle. (Illus.). 308p. 1991. 58.00 (*0-12-410351-0*) Acad Pr.
Maintenance of Numerically Controlled Machine Tools, 2 vols. 1983. 125.00 (*0-7855-2883-0*) St Mut.
Maintenance of Pavements & Roadsides. LC 92-21953. (Transportation Research Record Ser.: No. 1334). 64p. 1992. 17.00 (*0-309-05202-5*) Transport Res Bd.
Maintenance of Process Plant. 2nd ed. Ed. by Arthur Townsend. 66p. 1992. pap. 25.00 (*0-85295-292-9*, 9CH5) Gulf Pub.
Maintenance of Rattlesnakes in Captivity. James B. Murphy & Barry L. Armstrong. (Special Publications: No.3). (Illus.). 40p. 1978. pap. 3.00 (*0-89338-006-7*) U KS Nat Hist Mus.
Maintenance of Roadway Pavement & Structures (TRR 1392) Ed. by Susan E. Brown. (Transportation Research Record Ser.). (Illus.). 160p. 1993. pap. text 31.00 (*0-309-05464-8*) Transport Res Bd.
Maintenance Organization & Systems. Anthony Kelly. LC 97-29516. 320p. 2000. text 74.95 (*0-7506-3603-3*) Buttrwrth-Heinemann.
Maintenance Painter. Jack Rudman. (Career Examination Ser.: C-1358). 1994. pap. 23.95 (*0-8373-1358-9*) Nat Learn.
Maintenance Painter Foreman. Jack Rudman. (Career Examination Ser.: C-1359). 1994. pap. 29.95 (*0-8373-1359-7*) Nat Learn.
Maintenance Painting Program for Maximum Return on Investment. Ed. by Lawrence T. Coker & Robert S. Gaddis. (Press Reports). 58p. 1982. 15.00 (*0-89852-395-8*, 0101R095) TAPPI.
***Maintenance Pharmacotherapies for Neuropsychiatric Disorders.** Stephanie Richards & Samuel Gershon. LC 98-45218. 390p. 1999. text 59.95 (*0-87630-894-9*) Brunner-Mazel.
Maintenance Planning: Methods & Mathematics. P. Lyonnet. (Illus.). 224p. (C). (gr. 13). 1991. text 48.96 (*0-412-37680-6*, Chap & Hall NY) Chapman & Hall.
***Maintenance Planning & Scheduling Manual.** Richard D. Palmer. 1999. 79.95 (*0-07-048264-0*) McGraw.
Maintenance Plumber. Jack Rudman. (Career Examination Ser.: C-1360). 1994. pap. 27.95 (*0-8373-1360-0*) Nat Learn.
Maintenance Plumber Foreman. Jack Rudman. (Career Examination Ser.: C-1361). 1994. pap. 29.95 (*0-8373-1361-9*) Nat Learn.
***Maintenance Programme Set-Up.** M. Smith & A. Tate. 69p. 1998. pap. 80.00 (*0-86022-491-0*, Pub. by Build Servs Info Assn) St Mut.
Maintenance Resource Management: Adapting Materials Requirements Planning. Ed. by Dinesh Shenoy & Bikash Bhadury. LC 98-140985. 256p. 1997. pap. 64.95 (*0-7484-0648-4*, Pub. by Tay Francis Ltd) Taylor & Francis.
***Maintenance Scheduling in Restructured Power Systems.** M. Shahidehpour & M. Marwali. LC 00-31338. (International Series In Engineering & Computer Science). 2000. write for info. (*0-7923-7872-5*) Kluwer Academic.
Maintenance Standardization for Capital Assets: A Cost-Productivity Approach. M. S. Srinivasan & S. Srinivasan. LC 86-9320. (Illus.). 320p. 1986. 65.00 (*0-275-92193-X*, C2193, Praeger Pubs) Greenwood.
Maintenance Strategy. Anthony Kelly. LC 97-15499. 272p. 2000. text 75.95 (*0-7506-2417-5*) Buttrwrth-Heinemann.
Maintenance Supervisor. Jack Rudman. (Career Examination Ser.: C-2044). 1994. pap. 29.95 (*0-8373-2044-5*) Nat Learn.
Maintenance Supervisor (Plant & Equipment) (Career Examimation Ser.). 1997. pap. 29.95 (*0-8373-3787-9*, C3787) Nat Learn.
Maintenance Supervisor (Revenue) (Career Examination Ser.: C-3665). pap. 29.95 (*0-8373-3665-1*) Nat Learn.
Maintenance Supervisor (Track Equipment) Jack Rudman. (Career Examination Ser.: C-3546-9). 1994. pap. 29.95 (*0-8373-3546-9*) Nat Learn.
Maintenance Supervisor's Handbook. Ed. by Frank L. Evans. LC 62-21195. 377p. reprint ed. pap. 116.90 (*0-608-11400-6*, 205198400023) Bks Demand.
Maintenance Systems Life-Cycle Management. M. Taylor. 1996. pap. 145.00 (*1-85953-043-5*, Pub. by Tech Comm) St Mut.
Maintenance Techniques for Interior Plants. rev. ed. David L. Hamilton. Ed. by Patricia A. Hamilton. (Illus.). 60p. 1997. pap. 12.00 (*1-877809-57-8*) Park Pl Pubns.
Maintenance Technologies. 1996. 30.00 (*1-56091-839-X*, SP-1188) Soc Auto Engineers.
Maintenance Time Management. John W. Criswell. 132p. 1991. 57.00 (*0-88173-116-1*) Fairmont Pr.
Maintenance Welder. Jack Rudman. (Career Examination Ser.: C-1362). 1994. pap. 23.95 (*0-8373-1362-7*) Nat Learn.
Maintenance Work Zone Safety Devices Development & Evaluation. Dale Stout et al. 193p. (C). 1993. pap. text 15.00 (*0-309-05255-6*, SHRP-H-371) SHRP.
Maintenance Worker. 4th ed. Hy Hammer. 240p. 1985. per. 14.95 (*0-671-87941-3*, Arc) IDG Bks.
Maintien De L'ordre see Law & Order
Mainu & the Prince of Bakara. Reed Yarrow. LC 99-60680. (Illus.). 205p. (J). (gr. 3-7). 1999. 14.95 (*1-893731-04-9*) Mandolin Hse.
Mainz Meeting: Proceedings of the Seventh International Conference on Turkish Linguistics, August 3-6, 1994. International Conference on Turkish Linguistics Staff et al. LC 98-218051. (Turcologica Ser.). 1998. write for info. (*3-447-03864-0*) Harrassowitz.
Mainzer Becken. Karlheinz Rothausen & Volker Sonne. (Sammlung Geologischer Fuehrer Ser.: Band 79). (GER., Illus.). xii, 203p. 1984. spiral bd. 23.00 (*3-443-15043-8*, Pub. by Gebruder Borntraeger) Balogh.
Mainzer Becken und Seine Randgebiete: Eine Einfuehrung In die Geologie des Gebietes Zwischen Hunsrueck, Taunus, Vogelsberg, Spessart und Odenwald. Wilhelm Wenz. (GER., Illus.). 351p. 1971. reprint ed. 42.50 (*3-87429-004-2*, 013913, Pub. by Koeltz Sci Bks) Lubrecht & Cramer.
Maiolica. Timothy Wilson. (Illus.). 80p. 1995. 19.95 (*1-85444-041-1*, 903, Pub. by Ashmolean Mus); pap. 12.95 (*0-907849-90-3*, 903P, Pub. by Ashmolean Mus) A Schwartz & Co.
***Maiolica in the Making: The Gentili Barnabei Archive.** Catherine Hess. LC 98-45718. (Bibliographies & Dossiers Ser.). (Illus.). 192p. 1999. pap. 35.00 (*0-89236-500-5*, Pub. by J P Getty Trust) OUP.
***Maire, a Novel.** Linda Windsor. (Fires of Glennmara Ser.: No. 1). 2000. pap. 11.99 (*1-57673-625-3*) Multnomah Pubs.
Maire de Casterbridge. Thomas Hardy. (FRE.). 480p. 1984. pap. 16.95 (*0-7859-2497-3*, 2070376036) Fr & Eur.
Mairead Corrigan & Betty Williams: Making Peace in Northern Ireland. Bettina Ling & Sarah Buscher. LC 98-774. 112p. (YA). (gr. 7 up). 1999. 19.95 (*1-55861-200-9*, Pub. by Feminist Pr); pap. 9.95 (*1-55861-201-7*, Pub. by Feminist Pr) Consort Bk Sales.
Mairi. Wendy MacIntyre. 236p. 1992. pap. text 12.95 (*0-88982-122-4*, Pub. by Oolichan Bks) Genl Dist Srvs.
Mais Aimons-Nous Ceux Que Nous Aimons? Henry De Montherlant. (FRE.). 240p. 1973. 19.95 (*0-7859-0111-6*, M3789) Fr & Eur.
Mais Ils Epousent les Brunes. Anita Loos. (FRE.). 192p. 1982. pap. 8.95 (*0-7859-4172-X*, 2070373967) Fr & Eur.
Mais, Ou Est Donc Gah-Ning? Robert Munsch. (FRE., Illus.). 32p. (Orig.). (J). (ps-1). 1994. pap. 4.95 (*1-55037-984-4*, Pub. by Annick) Firefly Bks Ltd.
Mais Oui! Chantal P. Thompson & Elaine M. Phillips. (FRE.). (C). 1996. teacher ed. 18.76 (*0-669-35356-6*); text 61.16 incl. audio (*0-669-35349-3*); pap. text, wbk. ed., lab manual ed. 34.36 (*0-669-34959-3*) HM Trade Div.
Mais Oui! annot. ed. Chantal P. Thompson & Elaine M. Phillips. (FRE.). (C). 1996. text, teacher ed. 62.36 incl. audio (*0-669-35350-7*) HM Trade Div.
***Mais Oui! Book of French Wit & Wisdom.** Living Language Staff. (Living Language Ser.). 2000. 4.95 (*0-609-60619-0*) Liv Lang.
Mais Oui, Marie Creole Cookin: Life & Flavor in the Creole Tradition. Marie Lastrapes. (Illus.). 60p. 1999. pap. 9.95 (*0-9672043-0-5*) Maries Catering.
Mais Papa, Pourquoi. Michelle Graham. Tr. by Sylvie Pichot.Tr. of But Daddy, Why?. (Illus.). 96p. (J). (gr. k-5). 1997. pap. 5.00 (*0-9658766-2-4*) Rays of Hope.
Mais Que Fait Donc Dieu Sur Terre? Le Conflit De Satan Avec Dieu. (FRE.). 112p. 1999. pap. write for info. (*0-9671955-0-0*) Para Pubns Min.
Mais Qui Va Trouver le Tresor? Sylvie Desrosiers. (Novels in the Roman Jeunesse Ser.). (FRE.). 96p. (J). (gr. 4-7). 1992. pap. 8.95 (*2-89021-175-4*, Pub. by La Courte Ech) Firefly Bks Ltd.
Maisie. Alice Schertle. LC 91-27549. (Illus.). 32p. (J). (gr. k up). 1995. 16.00 (*0-688-09310-8*) Lothrop.
Maisie & the Dolphin. Rabley. Date not set. pap. text. write for info. (*0-582-03148-6*, Pub. by Addison-Wesley) Longman.
***Maisie Goes to a Wedding.** Aileen Paterson. (Illus.). 32p. (J). (gr. 1-3). 2000. pap. write for info. (*1-871512-54-9*) Glowworm Bks.
Maisie's Way. Grace Thompson. (Pendragon Island Ser.: Vol. 4). 256p. 1998. 25.00 (*0-7278-5392-9*) Severn Hse.
***Maisie's Way.** large type ed. Grace Thompson. 384p. 1999. 31.99 (*0-7089-4164-8*) Ulverscroft.
Maison a Vapeur. Jules Verne. 8.95 (*0-686-55929-0*) Fr & Eur.
Maison apres Vent: Recits Noels. Charles Dickens. (FRE.). 1979. 110.00 (*0-8288-3429-6*, F77240) Fr & Eur.
Maison Assassinee. Pierre Magnan. (FRE.). 1985. pap. 13.95 (*0-7859-4224-6*) Fr & Eur.
Maison au Bout de la Mer. Laird Koenig. (FRE.). 344p. 1987. pap. 11.95 (*0-7859-2541-4*, 2070378438) Fr & Eur.
Maison Basse. Marcel Ayme. (FRE.). 248p. 1978. pap. 10.95 (*0-7859-1870-1*, 2070370194) Fr & Eur.
Maison Curutchet. Alejandro Lapunzina. LC 97-4043. (Illus.). 176p. (Orig.). 1997. pap. 19.95 (*1-56898-095-7*) Princeton Arch.
Maison dans la Baleine. Marie-Francine Hebert. (Novels in the Premier Roman Ser.). (FRE., Illus.). 64p. (J). (gr. 2-5). 1995. pap. 8.95 (*2-89021-240-8*, Pub. by La Courte Ech) Firefly Bks Ltd.
Maison de Bernarda Alba Suivi de Noces de Sang. Federico Garcia Lorca. (FRE.). 256p. 1973. pap. 10.95 (*0-7859-2296-2*, 2070362825) Fr & Eur.
Maison de Claudine. Sidonie-Gabrielle Colette. (FRE.). 158p. 1990. pap. 10.95 (*0-7859-4721-3*) Fr & Eur.
Maison de la Rue du Cerisier: La Terreur see Terreur, Bk. 2, The Horror
Maison de la Rue du Cerisier: Le Dernier Cauchemar see Dernier Cauchemar, Bk. 3, The Final Nightmare
Maison de la Rue du Cerisier: L'Ensorcellement see L'Ensorcellement, Bk. 1, The Haunting
Maison de l'Inceste. Anais Nin. (POR.). 24.95 incl. audio (*0-318-36212-0*) Fr & Eur.
Maison de Papier. Francoise Mallet-Joris. (FRE.). 272p. 1970. 10.95 (*0-8288-9910-X*, F140728); pap. 3.95 (*0-686-56308-5*) Fr & Eur.
Maison de Rendez-Vous: Roman. Alain Robbe-Grillet. (FRE.). 192p. 1980. pap. 13.95 (*0-7859-1514-1*, 2707303151) Fr & Eur.
Maison des Atlantes. Angelo Rinaldi. (FRE.). 1973. pap. 15.95 (*0-7859-4013-8*) Fr & Eur.
Maison du Chat-qui-pelote. Pierre-Georges Castex. Ed. by Castex. Incl. Bal de Sceaux. Vendetta. (Class. Garnier Ser.). Set pap. 29.95 (*0-685-23883-0*) Fr & Eur.
Maison du Chat-Qui-Pelote: Avec: La Vendetta, la Bourse, le Bal de Sceaux. Honore de Balzac. write for info. (*0-318-63484-8*) Fr & Eur.
Maison du Chat-Qui-Pelote & la Vendetta, la Bourse & le Bal de Sceaux. Honore de Balzac. (Folio Ser.: No. 1441). (FRE.). pap. 12.95 (*2-07-037441-6*) Schoenhof.
Maison du Chat-Qui Pelote & le Bal de Sceaux & la Vendetta. Honore de Balzac. (FRE.). 1985. pap. 16.95 (*0-7859-1969-4*, 2070374416) Fr & Eur.
Maison Ikkoku: Bedside Manners. Rumiko Takahashi. (Illus.). 200p. 1997. pap. text 15.95 (*1-56931-179-X*, Viz Comics) Viz Commns Inc.
Maison Ikkoku: Dogged Pursuit. Rumiko Takahashi. (Illus.). 280p. 1998. pap. 17.95 (*1-56931-285-0*) Viz Commns Inc.
Maison Ikkoku: Domestic Dispute. Rumiko Takahashi. (Maison Ikkoku Ser.). (Illus.). 232p. 1998. pap. 16.95 (*1-56931-241-9*) Viz Commns Inc.
***Maison Ikkoku: Game, Set, Match, Vol. 13.** Rumiko Takahashi. (Maison Ikkoku Ser.). (Illus.). 256p. 1999. pap. text 16.95 (*1-56931-435-7*, Pub. by Viz Commns Inc) Publishers Group.
Maison Ikkoku: Good Housekeeping. Rumiko Takahashi. (Illus.). 204p. 1996. pap. text 15.95 (*1-56931-134-X*) Viz Commns Inc.
Maison Ikkoku: Intensive Care. Rumiko Takahashi. (Illus.). 184p. 1997. pap. text 15.95 (*1-56931-201-X*, Viz Comics) Viz Commns Inc.
Maison Ikkoku: Learning Curves. Rumiko Takahashi. (Illus.). 232p. 1998. pap. text 16.95 (*1-56931-256-7*, Viz Comics) Viz Commns Inc.
Maison Ikkoku: Student Affairs. Rumiko Takahashi. (Illus.). 264p. 1999. pap. 16.95 (*1-56931-352-0*) Viz Commns Inc.

M

An Asterisk (*) at the beginning of an entry indicates that the title is appearing for the first time.

Maison Ikkoku Family Affairs. Rumiko Takahashi. (Illus.). 224p. 1995. pap. text 16.95 (*1-56931-040-8*) Viz Commns Inc.

Maison Ikkoku-Home Sweet Home. Rumiko Takahashi. (Illus.). 264p. 1995. pap. 16.95 (*1-56931-086-6*) Viz Commns Inc.

Maison Jennie. large type ed. Julie Ellis. LC 95-2659. 641p. 1995. 23.95 (*0-7862-0428-1*) Thorndike Pr.

Maison Nucingen & Melmoth Reconcilie. Honore de Balzac. (Folio Ser.: No. 1957). (FRE.). (Orig.). pap. 10.95 (*2-07-038052-1*) Schoenhof.

Maison Philibert. Jean Lorrain. Ed. by Michel Desbrueres. (FRE., Illus.). 368p. 1995. pap. 74.95 (*2-86808-067-7*) Intl Scholars.

Maison, Prison et Folle Evasion. Sonia Sarfati. (Premier Roman Ser.). (FRE., Illus.). 64p. (J). (gr. 2 up). 1996. pap. 8.95 (*2-89021-257-2*, Pub. by La Courte Ech) Firefly Bks Ltd.

Maison Qui S'Envole. Claude Roy. (Folio - Junior Ser.: No. 1). (FRE., Illus.). 90p. (J). (gr. 5-10). 1977. pap. 7.95 (*2-07-033001-X*) Schoenhof.

Maison sans racines see Return to Beirut

***Maison System Bk. I: Games.** Karen M. Maison. (J). (gr. k). 1999. write for info. (*0-9671421-3-X*) K M Maison.

Maison System Bk. I: Music Fundamentals for Beginners, 3 vols. Karen M. Maison. (Illus.). 60p. (J). (gr. k-6). 1996. spiral bd. write for info. (*0-9671421-0-5*) K M Maison.

***Maison System Bk. II: Games.** Karen M. Maison. (J). (gr. k-6). 1999. write for info. (*0-9671421-4-8*) K M Maison.

Maison System Bk. II: Music Fundamentals for Beginners, 3 vols. Karen M. Maison. (Illus.). 60p. (J). (gr. k-6). 1996. spiral bd. write for info. (*0-9671421-1-3*) K M Maison.

***Maison System Bk. III: Games.** Karen M. Maison. (J). (gr. k-6). 1999. write for info. (*0-9671421-5-6*) K M Maison.

Maison System Bk. III: Music Fundamentals for Beginners, 3 vols. Karen M. Maison. (Illus.). 64p. (J). (gr. k-6). 1996. spiral bd. write for info. (*0-9671421-2-1*) K M Maison.

Maison Tellier. Guy de Maupassant. (FRE.). 254p. 1978. pap. 11.95 (*0-7859-4689-6*) Fr & Eur.

Maison Tellier: Une Partie de Campagne. (FRE.). 330p. pap. 28.95 (*0-7859-4693-4*) Fr & Eur.

Maison Tellier: Une Partie de Campagne. Guy de Maupassant. (FRE.). 1980. pap. 10.95 (*0-7859-3088-4*) Fr & Eur.

Maisons d'Adobe: Habitations Amerindiennes: le Sud-Ouest. Bonnie Shemie. (Native Dwellings Ser.). (FRE., Illus.). 24p. 1996. 13.95 (*0-88776-331-6*) Tundra Bks.

Maisons De Bois: The Northwest Coast. Illus. by Bonnie Shemie. (Native Dwellings Ser.). (FRE.). 24p. (J). 1996. 13.95 (*0-88776-289-1*) Tundra Bks.

Maisons d'Hotes de Charme en France (Bed & Breakfast a la Francaise) 648p. 1997. 49.95 (*0-7859-9472-6*) Fr & Eur.

Maistre Studies. Ed. & Tr. by Richard A. Lebrun. LC 88-26147. 318p. (C). 1988. lib. bdg. 49.00 (*0-8191-7201-4*) U Pr of Amer.

Maisy & Her Friends. Lucy Cousins. 1999. pap. text. write for info. (*0-7636-0821-1*) Candlewick Pr.

Maisy at the Farm. Lucy Cousins. LC 97-92360. (Maisy Bks.). (Illus.). 16p. (J). (ps). 1998. 12.99 (*0-7636-0576-X*) Candlewick Pr.

***Maisy en la Granja.** Lucy Cousins. (Maisy Bks.). (Illus.). (J). (ps). 1999. 16.95 (*84-88061-97-8*) SL Ed Serres.

Maisy Dresses Up. Lucy Cousins. LC 98-43219. (Maisy Bks.). (Illus.). 24p. (J). (ps). 1999. 10.99 (*0-7636-0885-8*) Candlewick Pr.

***Maisy Dresses Up.** Lucy Cousins. LC 98-43219. (Maisy Bks.). (Illus.). 24p. (J). (ps). 1999. pap. 3.29 (*0-7636-0909-9*) Candlewick Pr.

***Maisy Drives the Bus.** Lucy Cousins. LC 99-54075. (Maisy Bks.). (Illus.). 24p. (J). (ps). 2000. 3.29 (*0-7636-1085-2*) Candlewick Pr.

***Maisy Drives the Bus.** Lucy Cousins. LC 99-54075. (Maisy Bks.). (Illus.). 24p. (J). (ps-k). 2000. 9.99 (*0-7636-1083-6*) Candlewick Pr.

Maisy Goes Swimming. Lucy Cousins. (Maisy Bks.). 14p. (J). (ps). 1990. 13.95 (*0-316-15834-8*) Little.

Maisy Goes to Bed. Lucy Cousins. LC 89-43577. (Maisy Bks.). (Illus.). 14p. (J). (ps). 1990. 13.95 (*0-316-15832-1*) Little.

Maisy Goes to School. Lucy Cousins. LC 91-58743. (Maisy Bks.). (Illus.). 16p. (J). (ps). 1992. 12.95 (*1-56402-085-1*) Candlewick Pr.

Maisy Goes to the Playground. Lucy Cousins. LC 91-58742. (Maisy Bks.). (Illus.). 16p. (J). (ps). 1992. 12.95 (*1-56402-084-3*) Candlewick Pr.

Maisy Se Va al Parque. Lucy Cousins. (Maisy Bks.). (SPA., Illus.). (J). (ps). 1997. 16.95 (*84-88061-45-5*) SL Ed Serres.

Maisy Makes Gingerbread. Lucy Cousins. LC 98-53909. (Maisy Bks.). (Illus.). 24p. (J). (ps). 1999. 10.99 (*0-7636-0887-4*) Candlewick Pr.

***Maisy Makes Gingerbread.** Lucy Cousins. LC 98-53909. (Maisy Bks.). (Illus.). 24p. (J). (ps). 1999. pap. 3.29 (*0-7636-0910-2*) Candlewick Pr.

***Maisy Takes a Bath.** Lucy Cousins. LC 99-53240. (Maisy Bks.). (Illus.). 24p. (J). (ps). 2000. 9.99 (*0-7636-1082-8*); pap. 3.29 (*0-7636-1084-4*) Candlewick Pr.

***Maisy y Sus Amigos.** Lucy Cousins. (SPA., Illus.). (J). (ps-k). 1999. 16.95 (*84-95040-02-6*) SL Ed Serres.

Maisy's Bedtime. Lucy Cousins. LC 98-49555. (Maisy Bks.). (Illus.). 24p. (J). (ps). 1999. 10.99 (*0-7636-0884-X*); pap. 3.29 (*0-7636-0908-0*) Candlewick Pr.

***Maisy's Busy Book.** Lucy Cousins. (Maisy Bks.). (Illus.). (J). (ps). 1999. pap. text 4.99 (*0-7636-0927-7*) Candlewick Pr.

Maisy's Colors. Lucy Cousins. LC 96-85451. (Maisy Bks.). (Illus.). 24p. (J). (ps). 1997. 8.99 (*0-7636-0159-4*) Candlewick Pr.

Maisy's Colors. 2nd ed. Lucy Cousins. LC 96-85451. (Maisy Bks.). (Illus.). 24p. (J). (ps). 1999. bds. 5.99 (*0-7636-0237-X*, Pub. by Candlewick Pr) Penguin Putnam.

Maisy's Day. Lucy Cousins. (Illus.). (ps-k). 1999. pap. text 3.99 (*0-7636-0750-9*) Candlewick Pr.

Maisy's Favorite Things. Lucy Cousins. (Illus.). 24p. (ps-1). 1999. pap. text 1.49 (*0-7636-0820-3*) Candlewick Pr.

Maisy's Mix-and-Match Mousewear. Lucy Cousins. LC 00-265158. (Maisy Bks.). (Illus.). 12p. (J). (ps). 1999. 6.99 (*0-7636-0751-7*) Candlewick Pr.

Maisy's Party Book. Lucy Cousins. (Maisy Bks.). (Illus.). 16p. (J). (ps). 1999. pap. text 4.99 (*0-7636-0926-9*) Candlewick Pr.

Maisy's Pool. Lucy Cousins. LC 99-14585. (Maisy Bks.). (Illus.). 24p. (J). (ps). 1999. 10.99 (*0-7636-0886-6*); pap. 9.99 (*0-7636-0907-2*) Candlewick Pr.

Maisy's Pop-Up Playhouse. Lucy Cousins. LC 96-124605. (Maisy Bks.). (Illus.). (J). (ps). 1995. 19.99 (*1-56402-635-3*) Candlewick Pr.

Maitake: King of Mushrooms. Shari Lieberman & Ken Babal. LC 98-222773. pap. 3.95 (*0-87983-882-5*, 38825K, Keats Publng) NTC Contemp Pub Co.

Maite. Dolores R. Attias. (SPA.). 280p. 1994. pap. 12.95 (*0-9628328-5-5*) Starlite Inc.

***Maithunian Trilogy.** Willa C. Chew. LC 97-91123. 1999. 22.95 (*0-533-12564-2*) Vantage.

***Maitland Concept of Manipulative Therapy.** 6th ed. Kevin Banks & G. D. Maitland. (Illus.). 352p. 2000. pap. text 65.00 (*0-7506-3911-3*) Buttrwrth-Heinemann.

Maitlands Vertibal Manipulation. Maitland. 400p. Date not set. pap. 80.00 (*0-7506-2447-7*) Buttrwrth-Heinemann.

Maitrayaniya Upanisad: A Critical Essay with Text, Translation & Commentary. J. A. Van Buitenen. (Disputationes Rheno-Trajectinae: No. 6). 1962. pap. 44.65 (*90-279-0032-9*) Mouton.

Maitre see Theatre

Maitre a Danser. fac. ed. Pierre Rameau. (Monuments of Music & Music Literature in Facsimile, II Ser.: Vol. 45). (Illus.). 1967. lib. bdg. 45.00 (*0-8450-2245-8*) Broude.

Maitre de Clavecin. fac. ed. Michel Corrette. (Monuments of Music & Music Literature in Facsimile Ser., Series II: Vol. 13). 1976. lib. bdg. 45.00 (*0-8450-2213-X*) Broude.

Maitre de Clavecin pour l'Accompagnement, Methode Theoretique et Pratique. Michel Corrette. vi, 90p. 1974. reprint ed. 52.00 (*3-487-05431-0*) G Olms Pubs.

Maitre de la Parole - Kouma Lafolo Kouma. Camara Laye. (FRE.). 1980. pap. 11.95 (*0-7859-3231-3*, 2266033891) Fr & Eur.

Maitre de Milan. Jacques Audiberti. 264p. 1950. 9.95 (*0-7859-0362-3*, F83780) Fr & Eur.

Maitre de Santiago. Henry De Montherlant. 160p. 1972. write for info. (*0-318-63485-6*) Fr & Eur.

Maitre de Santiago. Henry De Montherlant. (FRE.). 1972. pap. 10.95 (*0-8288-3722-8*, F115750) Fr & Eur.

Maitre de Santiago. Henry De Montherlant. (Folio Ser.: No. 142). (FRE.). 160p. 1972. 6.95 (*2-07-036142-X*) Schoenhof.

Maitre D'Heure. Claude Faraggi. (FRE.). 177p. 1977. pap. 10.95 (*0-7859-2398-5*, 2070369900) Fr & Eur.

Maitre du Monde. Jules Verne. 8.95 (*0-686-55930-4*) Fr & Eur.

Maitres see Chronique des Pasquier

Maitres. Georges Duhamel. (Chronique Des Pasquier Ser.: Vol. VI). (FRE.). 256p. 1974. pap. 10.95 (*0-7859-1770-5*, 2070365255) Fr & Eur.

Maitres Anciens. Thomas Bernhard. (FRE.). 253p. 1991. pap. 10.95 (*0-7859-2165-6*, 2070383903) Fr & Eur.

Maitres de la Lumiere. Jean Rollet. (FRE., Illus.). 301p. 1980. lib. bdg. 75.00 (*2-04-010496-8*) Hacker.

Maitres des Maisons Astrologiques: Guide d'Interpretation des Maitres des Maisons. Michel Groleau. LC 96-941412. (FRE.). 1997. 14.95 (*2-89466-006-5*) Edns Roseau.

Maitres Musiciens de la Renaissance Francaise, 23 vols. Ed. by Henry Expert. Incl. Chansonnettes Mesurees de Ian-Antoine de Baif. Jacques Mauduit. (Illus.). 1952. reprint ed. pap. 37.50 (*0-8450-1210-X*); Chansons. Clement Janequin. 1952. reprint ed. pap. 37.50 (*0-8450-1207-X*); Danceries: Premier Volume. Claude Gervaise & Estienne Du Terte. 1952. reprint ed. pap. 37.50 (*0-8450-1223-1*); Deuxieme Fascicule des 150 Psaumes. Claude Goudimel. 1952. reprint ed. pap. 37.50 (*0-8450-1204-5*); Dodecacorde, Premier Fascicule. Claude LeJeune. (Illus.). 1952. reprint ed. pap. 37.50 (*0-8450-1211-8*); Liber Quindecim Missarum Pt. 1: Brumel: "Missa De Beata Virgine;" de la Rue: "Missa Ave Maria" Antoine Brumel & Pierre De la Rue. 1952. reprint ed. pap. 37.50 (*0-8450-1208-8*); Liber Quindecim Missarum Pt. 2: Io. Mouton: Missa Alma redemtoris; Fevin: Missa Mente tota. J. Mouton & A. de Fevin. 1952. reprint ed. pap. 37.50 (*0-8450-1209-6*); Melanges Premier Fascicule. Claude LeJeune. (Illus.). 1952. reprint ed. pap. 37.50 (*0-8450-1216-9*); Melanges, Premier Fascicule. Eustache Du Caurroy. 1952. reprint ed. pap. 37.50 (*0-8450-1217-7*); Musique, Deuxieme Fascicule. Guillaume Costeley. 1952. reprint ed. pap. 37.50 (*0-8450-1218-5*); Musique, Premier Fascicule. Guillaume Costeley. 1952. reprint ed. pap. 37.50 (*0-8450-1203-7*); Musique, Troiseme Fascicule. Guillaume Costeley. 1952. reprint ed. pap. 37.50 (*0-8450-1219-3*); Poesies de P. de Ronsard et Autres Poetes. Francois Regnard. 1952. pap. 37.50 (*0-8450-1215-0*); Premier Fascicule des Melanges. Orlando di Lasso. 1952. reprint ed. pap. 37.50 (*0-8450-1201-0*); Premier Fascicule des 150 Psaumes. Claude Goudimel. 1952. reprint ed. pap. 37.50 (*0-8450-1202-9*); Pseaumes en Vers Mezurez, Deuxieme Fascicule. Claude LeJeune. (Illus.). 1952. reprint ed. pap. 37.50 (*0-8450-1221-5*); Pseaumes en Vers Mezurez, Premier Fascicule. Claude LeJeune. 1952. reprint ed. pap. 37.50 (*0-8450-1220-7*); Pseaumes en Vers Vezurez, Troisieme Fascicule. Claude LeJeune. (Illus.). 1952. reprint ed. pap. 37.50 (*0-8450-1222-3*); Trente et une Chansons Musicales: Claude de Sermisy, Clement Janequin et al. Ed. by Pierre Attaingnant. 1952. reprint ed. pap. 37.50 (*0-8450-1205-3*); Troisieme Fascicule des 150 Psaumes. Claude Goudimel. 1952. reprint ed. pap. 37.50 (*0-8450-1206-1*); (Illus.). 1952. reprint ed. Set pap. 675.00 (*0-8450-1200-2*) Broude.

Maitres Sonneurs. George Sand. (Folio Ser.: No. 1139). (FRE.). pap. 12.95 (*2-07-037139-5*) Schoenhof.

Maitres Sonneurs. George Sand. (FRE.). 1979. pap. 16.95 (*0-7859-2895-2*) Fr & Eur.

Maitres Sonneurs. unabridged ed. George Sand. (FRE.). Date not set. reprint ed. pap. 8.95 (*2-87714-340-6*, Pub. by Bookking Intl) Distribks Inc.

Maitresse see Oeuvres

Maitresse see Oeuvres

Maitresse du Jeu. Sidney Sheldon. (FRE.). 576p. 1988. pap. 20.95 (*0-7859-4298-X*, 2070380459) Fr & Eur.

Maitreya see Miroku - Maitreya

Maitreya. Severo Sarduy. 100p. 1987. pap. 9.50 (*0-910061-31-9*, 1205) Ediciones Norte.

Maitreya's Mission, Vol. 1. 3rd ed. Benjamin Creme. LC 97-222727. 411p. (Orig.). 1993. pap. 13.00 (*90-71484-08-4*) Share Intl.

Maitreya's Mission, Vol. 2. Benjamin Creme. LC 97-222727. (Illus.). 718p. (Orig.). 1993. pap. 18.00 (*90-71484-11-4*) Share Intl.

Maitreyasamiti Texts in Tocharian A. Ji Xianlin. LC 98-38369. (Trends in Linguistics Ser.). 320p. 1998. 124.00 (*3-11-014904-4*) De Gruyter.

Maitri Upanisat. Tr. by Srisa C. Vidyarnava & Mohan L. Sandal. LC 73-3827. (Sacred Books of the Hindus: No. 31, Pt. 2). reprint ed. 18.00 (*0-404-57832-2*) AMS Pr.

***Maiz y Coca-Cola: Adventures, Scrapes, & Shamanism in the Amazon & Andes.** Diane Terezakis. LC 00-190386. 355p. 2000. 25.00 (*0-7388-1768-6*); pap. 18.00 (*0-7388-1769-4*) Xlibris Corp.

Maize. Ed. by Y. P. S. Bajaj. (Biotechnology in Agriculture & Forestry Ser.: No. 25). 608p. 1994. 398.95 (*0-387-56392-X*) Spr-Verlag.

Maize & Blue: The Michigan Wolverines Story. Neal Bernards. LC 98-30934. (College Sports Today Ser.). (Illus.). 32p. (YA). (gr. 4 up). 1999. lib. bdg. 21.30 (*0-88682-979-8*, Creat Educ) Creative Co.

Maize Diseases: A Reference Source for Seed Technologists. Denis C. McGee. LC 88-70647. (Illus.). 160p. (Orig.). 1988. pap. text 34.00 (*0-89054-090-X*) Am Phytopathol Soc.

Maize Genetics & Breeding in the 20th Century. LC 98-38059. 150p. 1998. lib. bdg. 27.00 (*981-02-2866-X*) World Scientific Pub.

Maize Genome Mapping: Bibliography. Ed. by Andrew Kalinski. 48p. (Orig.). (C). 1996. pap. text 25.00 (*0-7881-2695-4*) DIANE Pub.

Maize Handbook. Ed. by M. Freeling & Virginia Walbot. (Illus.). 759p. 1996. pap. 42.95 (*0-387-94735-3*) Spr-Verlag.

Maize Handbook. Ed. by Michael Freeling & Virginia Walbot. LC 92-32462. (Illus.). 759p. 1993. 86.95 (*0-387-97826-7*) Spr-Verlag.

Maize in Human Nutrition. (Food & Nutrition Ser.: No. 25). 168p. 1993. 25.00 (*92-5-103013-8*, F0138, Pub. by FAO) Bernan Associates.

Maize in Tropical Africa. Marvin P. Miracle. LC 66-11805. (Illus.). 348p. 1966. reprint ed. pap. 107.90 (*0-7837-9789-3*, 206051800005) Bks Demand.

Maize Science. R. K. Maiti & Pedro Wesche-Ebeling. (Illus.). 542p. 1998. 85.00 (*1-57808-019-3*) Science Pubs.

Maize Seed Industries in Developing Countries. Ed. by Michael L. Morris. LC 97-40583. 404p. 1998. pap. text 29.95 (*1-55587-790-7*); lib. bdg. 59.95 (*1-55587-789-3*) L Rienner.

Maize Technology Development & Transfer: A GIS Application for Research Planning in Kenya. Rashid M. Hassan. LC 98-14961. (CAB International Publication). 250p. 1998. 85.00 (*0-85199-287-0*) OUP.

Maizie. Linda O. High. LC 94-22370. 192p. (J). (gr. 4-6). 1995. 14.95 (*0-8234-1161-3*) Holiday.

Maizon at Blue Hill. Jacqueline Woodson. (J). 1992. 9.09 (*0-606-05918-0*, Pub. by Turtleback) Demco.

Maj Canton's Reference Guide to Movies & Miniseries for TV & Cable, 1984-1994. Maj Canton. LC 94-78089. 410p. (Orig.). 1994. pap. 115.00 (*1-883422-44-2*) Adams-Blake.

Majah: Indigenous Peoples & the Law. Ed. by Greta Bird et al. 298p. 1996. pap. 39.00 (*1-86287-197-3*, Pub. by Federation Pr) Gaunt.

Majakovski: Bilingual Edition. Adriano Spatola. Tr. by Paul Vangelisti. 1975. per. 2.50 (*0-88031-019-7*) Invisible-Red Hill.

Majatnik. 2nd ed. Mikhail Armalinskii, pseud. LC 84-90582. (RUS.). 130p. (Orig.). 1984. pap. 4.00 (*0-916201-01-5*) M I P Co.

M

***Majestic Big Game: The Ultimate Tribute to North America's Greatest Game Animals.** Voyageur Press Editors. Ed. by Danielle Ibister. LC 99-14624. (Majestic Wildlife Library). (Illus.). 160p. 2000. 35.00 (*0-89658-439-9*) Voyageur Pr.

Majestic Blue Horses. Jeanie Figler. LC 99-11491. (Illus.). (J). 1999. 9.95 (*1-56492-273-1*) Laredo.

***Majestic Discus.** Manfred Goebel. (Aqualog Special Ser.: Vol. 6). (Illus.). 48p. 1999. 25.00 (*3-931702-43-X*, Pub. by Verlag ACS) Hollywood.

Majestic Elk. Todd R. Berger. LC 98-11499. (Illus.). 160p. 1998. 35.00 (*0-89658-384-8*) Voyageur Pr.

Majestic Failure: The Fall of the Shah. Marvin Zonis. LC 90-46355. (Illus.). 360p. 1998. 29.95 (*0-226-98928-3*) U Ch Pr.

Majestic Honor: Biblical Perspectives in Black History. Ernest C. Sargent. (Illus.). 1993. pap. 9.00 (*1-883435-00-5*) Insight Pubns.

Majestic Hymns of the Church. James A. Stewart. 1966. pap. 2.49 (*1-56632-042-9*) Revival Lit.

Majestic in His Wrath: A Pictoral Life of Frederick Douglass. Frederick S. Voss. LC 94-23940. (Illus.). 144p. 1995. pap. 15.95 (*1-56098-522-4*) Smithsonian.

Majestic Is Your Name. rev. ed. David Hazard. (Rekindling the Inner Fire Ser.: Vol. 5). 176p. 1993. pap. 8.99 (*1-55661-336-9*) Bethany Hse.

Majestic Journey: Coronado's Inland Empire. Stewart L. Udall. (Illus.). 176p. 1995. pap. 19.95 (*0-89013-285-2*) Museum NM Pr.

Majestic Kid. Mark Medoff. 1986. pap. 5.25 (*0-8222-0717-6*) Dramatists Play.

Majestic Lights: The Aurora in Science, History & the Arts. Robert Eather. (Illus.). 324p. 1980. 49.00 (*0-87590-215-4*) Am Geophysical.

Majestic Molokai: A Nature Lover's Guide. Cameron B. Kepler & Angela K. Kepler. (Illus.). 144p. 1992. pap. 14.95 (*0-935180-73-7*) Mutual Pub HI.

***Majestic Mountains.** Reader's Digest Editors. LC 99-22010. (Earth, Its Wonders, Its Secrets Ser.). 1999. write for info. (*0-7621-0136-9*) RD Assn.

Majestic Mule Deer: The Ultimate Tribute to the Most Popular Game Animal of the West. Voyageur Press Editors. LC 98-46017. (Majestic Wildlife Library). (Illus.). 17p. 1999. 35.00 (*0-89658-413-5*) Voyageur Pr.

Majestic Praise. Contrib. by Dennis R. Johnson. 1985. 9.99 (*0-685-68341-9*, MB-541) Lillenas.

***Majestic Secret.** Michelle McGriff. 197p. 1999. pap. 14.95 (*0-7414-0333-1*) Buy Books.

Majestic Splendor: Portraits of the Rocky Mountains. Shiro Shirahata. 1997. 80.00 (*0-8118-1867-5*) Chronicle Bks.

***Majestic Universe: Views from Here to Infinity...** Serge Brunier. Tr. by Storm Dunlop. (Illus.). 216p. 2000. 39.95 (*0-521-66307-5*) Cambridge U Pr.

Majestic Whitetails: The Ultimate Tribute to North America's Most Popular Game Animal. Ed. by Voyageur Press Editors. LC 97-424. (Illus.). 160p. 1997. 35.00 (*0-89658-337-6*) Voyageur Pr.

***Majestic Whitetails Calendar 2001.** Text by Voyageur Press Editors. (Illus.). 26p. 2000. pap. 10.95 (*0-89658-472-0*) Voyageur Pr.

***Majesty: Prima's Official Strategy Guide.** Joe Minton. LC 99-69667. (Official Strategy Guides Ser.). (Illus.). 268p. (YA). 2000. pap. 19.99 (*0-7615-2772-9*) Prima Pub.

Majesty: The Exceptional Trees of Hawaii. Jodi P. Belknap. Ed. by Momi Cazimero. LC 82-60598. (Illus.). 72p. 1982. 12.95 (*0-686-38728-7*) Outdoor Circle.

Majesty & Mystery of the Sea. Ed. by John Sammis. (Illus.). 96p. 1994. 16.95 (*1-884506-14-3*) Third Story.

***Majesty of Beaufort.** Nancy E. White. LC 00-38527. 2000. pap. write for info. (*1-56554-720-9*) Pelican.

Majesty of Charleston. Photos & Text by Peter Beney. LC 93-10099. (Illus.). 96p. 1993. 15.95 (*0-88289-955-4*) Pelican.

Majesty of Colonial Williamsburg. Peter Beney. LC 96-41796. (Illus.). 160p. 1997. 29.95 (*0-88289-993-7*); pap. text 19.95 (*1-56554-249-5*) Pelican.

Majesty of Colonial Williamsburg. Peter Beney. (Majesty Architecture Ser.). 1997. 29.95 (*0-614-28059-1*) Pelican Publishing Co.

***Majesty of Colonial Williamsburg Postcard Book.** Peter Beney. 2000. pap. text 9.95 (*1-56554-761-6*) Pelican.

Majesty of Man. H. Leibowitz. 1992. 19.99 (*0-89906-542-2*); pap. 16.99 (*0-89906-543-0*) Mesorah Pubns.

Majesty of Man: The Dignity of Being Human. rev. ed. Ronald B. Allen. LC 98-15296. 218p. 1998. pap. text 11.99 (0-8254-2139-X) Kregel.

Majesty of Natchez. 2nd ed. Photos & Text by Steven Brooke. LC 98-48354. (Majesty Architecture Ser.). (Illus.). 96p. 1999. pap. 16.95 (1-56554-158-8) Pelican.

***Majesty of Natchez Postcard Book.** Steven Brooke. (Illus.). 1998. pap. 9.95 (1-56554-340-8) Pelican.

Majesty of Savannah. Peter Beney. LC 92-10968. (Illus.). 96p. 1992. 15.95 (0-88289-906-6) Pelican.

Majesty of Snowy Whiteness. Frank W. Sandford. 39p. 1963. pap. 1.50 (0-910840-10-5) Kingdom.

Majesty of the Felicianas. Paul Malone & Lee Malone. LC 88-29072. (Illus.). 96p. 1989. 15.95 (0-88289-712-8) Pelican.

***Majesty of the French Quarter.** Kerri W. McCaffety. LC 99-40865. (Illus.). 192p. 1999. 39.95 (1-56554-414-5) Pelican.

***Majesty of the French Quarter Postcard Book.** Kerri W. McCaffety. (Illus.). 2000. pap. text 9.95 (1-56554-739-X) Pelican.

***Majesty of the Garden District Postcard Book.** Paul Malone. 1999. pap. 9.95 (1-56554-640-7) Pelican.

Majesty of the Grand Canyon: 150 Years in Art. Joni L. Kinsey. (Illus.). 160p. 1998. 19.95 (1-885440-31-6) First Glance.

Majesty of the Law: The Court Houses of Allegheny County. James D. Van Trump. LC 88-61708. (Illus.). 188p. 1988. 19.95 (0-916670-12-0) Pitt Hist & Landmks Found.

Majesty of the River Road. Paul Malone & Lee Malone. LC 87-31160. (Illus.). 96p. 1988. 15.95 (0-88289-674-1) Pelican.

Majesty's Rancho. Zane Grey. 1976. 24.95 (0-88411-661-1) Amereon Ltd.

***Majic Man.** Max Allan Collins. (Nathan Heller Novels Ser.). 2000. mass mkt. 8.99 (0-451-19945-6, Pub. by Signet) Penguin Books.

***Majic Man.** large type ed. Max A. Collins. (Basic Ser.). 512p. 2000. 28.95 (0-7862-2529-7) Thorndike Pr.

Majic Man: A Nathan Heller Novel. Max A. Collins. LC 99-13679. 304p. 1999. 23.95 (0-525-94515-6) NAL.

Majid's Dream. 2nd ed. Melody Ghandchi. (Illus.). 62p. (J). (gr. 1-2). 1996. reprint ed. 16.00 (1-879402-38-6) Tahrike Tarsile Quran.

Majipoor Chronicles: Majipoor Chronicles. Robert Silverberg. Vol. 3. 400p. 1996. mass mkt. 5.99 (0-06-105485-2, HarperPrism) HarpC.

Majnun: The Madman in Medieval Islamic Society. Michael W. Dois. 514p. 1996. 125.00 (0-614-21552-8, 751) Kazi Pubns.

Majolica. C. R. Gibson Company Staff. 1997. 6.00 (0-7667-2212-0) Gibson.

Majolica. rev. ed. Mike Schneider. LC 89-64084. (Illus.). 144p. 1990. pap. 14.95 (0-88740-769-2) Schiffer.

Majolica. 3rd rev. ed. Mike Schneider. LC 99-60371. (Illus.). 144p. 1999. pap. 14.95 (0-7643-0825-4) Schiffer.

Majolica: A Complete History & Illustrated Survey. Marilyn G. Karmason & Joan B. Stacke. (Illus.). 240p. 1989. 75.00 (0-8109-1534-0, Pub. by Abrams) Time Warner.

Majolica: European & American Wares. Jeffrey B. Snyder & Leslie Bockol. LC 93-87062. (Illus.). 160p. 1994. pap. text 29.95 (0-88740-561-4) Schiffer.

Majolica Figures. Helen Cunningham. LC 96-71097. (Illus.). 176p. 1997. 34.95 (0-7643-0214-0) Schiffer.

***Major.** Rick Shelley. 1999. mass mkt. 5.99 (0-441-00680-9) Ace Bks.

***Major: A Political Life.** Anthony Seldon. 1998. pap. 13.95 (0-7538-0145-0, Pub. by Orion Pubng Grp) Trafalgar.

Major: A Political Life. Anthony Seldon. LC 97-223819. (Illus.). 856p. 50.00 (0-297-81607-1, Pub. by Weidenfeld & Nicolson) Trafalgar.

Major Abolitionist Poems of Castro Alves. Ed. by James J. Wilhelm. Tr. by Amy A. Peterson from POR. LC 89-23406. (Library of World Literature in Translation: Vol. 5). 188p. 1990. text 15.00 (0-8240-2991-7) Garland.

Major Accident Reporting System: Lessons Learned from Accidents Notified. G. Drogaris. LC 93-29726. 254p. 1993. 193.00 (0-444-81665-8) Elsevier.

***Major Account Sales Strategies: An Easy-to-Use Guide to Winning Large Sales.** Alan L. Shifflett. LC 00-39042. 296p. 2000. boxed set. write for info. (1-57444-288-0) St Lucie Pr.

Major Account Sales Strategy. Neil Rackham. 218p. 1989. 24.95 (0-07-051114-4) McGraw.

Major Acquisitions of the Pierpont Morgan Library, 1924-1974, 4 vols. Pierpont Morgan Library Curators Staff. Incl. Vol. 1. Autograph Letters & Manuscripts. 1974. (0-87598-043-0); (Illus.). 1974. Set pap. (0-686-86598-7) Pierpont Morgan.

Major Airline Cargo Series. Ed. by Becky Dean et al. 48p. 1998. pap. 14.95 (1-891726-18-8, AIR Inc) Aviation Info.

Major American Short Stories. 3rd ed. A. Walton Litz. (Illus.). 896p. (C). 1994. pap. text 34.95 (0-19-507899-3) OUP.

Major & Minor Approach-Depart Aspects. Sakoian & Louis S. Acker. 38p. 1974. 8.00 (0-86690-194-9, S1428-014) Am Fed Astrologers.

Major & Minor Keys: Critical Essays on Philippine Fiction & Poetry. Ricaredo Demetillo. 180p. (Orig.). 1987. pap. 15.00 (971-10-0287-6, Pub. by New Day Pub) Cellar.

Major & Mrs. Holt's Battlefield Guide to the Normandy Landings. Toni Holt. 1999. pap. text 24.95 (0-85052-662-0) Leo Cooper.

Major & Mrs. Holt's Battlefield Guide to the Ypres Salient. Tonie Holt & Valmai Holt. (Illus.). 272p. 1999. pap. 24.95 (0-85052-551-9, Pub. by Leo Cooper) Combined Pub.

***Major & Mrs. Holt's Guide to Gallipoli.** Tonie Holt & Valmai Holt. 2000. pap. 24.95 (0-85052-638-8, Pub. by Pen & Sword) Combined Pub.

Major & the Librarian. Nikki Benjamin. 1999. per. 4.25 (0-373-24228-X, Harlequin) Harlequin Bks.

Major Anders Lindgren's Teaching Exercises: A Manual for Instructors & Riders. Anders Lindgren. LC 98-31462. (Illus.). 160p. 1998. 24.95 (0-939481-53-7) Half Halt Pr.

Major Andre. Anthony Bailey. LC 86-29577. 192p. 1987. 15.95 (0-374-19917-5) FS&G.

Major Andre's Journal: Eyewitness Accounts of the American Revolution. John Andre. LC 67-29031. 128p. reprint ed. pap. 18.95 (0-405-01103-2) Ayer.

Major Andrew Henry in Idaho. Margaret H. Lindsley. Tr. by Lawrence Lindsley & Bruce Campbell. (Illus.). 24p. 1985. pap. 4.00 (1-890535-03-6) H & J Spec.

Major Appliance Service National Price Guide: MASPG. Steve Walker & Dean Landers. 123p. 169.95 (1-930797-09-5) Appliance Univ.

Major Appliances. (Fix-It-Yourself Ser.). (Illus.). 144p. 1987. lib. bdg. 23.27 (0-8094-6205-2) Time-Life.

Major Appliances. Time-Life Books Editors. LC 98-4231. (How to Fix It Ser.: Vol. 2). (Illus.). 144p. 1998. 16.99 (0-7835-5651-9) Time-Life.

Major Appliances. Time Life Staff. (Fix-It-Yourself Ser.). (Illus.). 144p. 1987. 17.27 (0-8094-6204-4) Time-Life.

Major Appliances: Operation, Maintenance, Troubleshooting & Repair. Billy C. Langley. 547p. 1993. 51.80 (0-13-544834-4) P-H.

Major Arthropod Pests & Weeds of Agriculture in Southeast Asia: Distribution, Importance & Origin. D. F. Waterhouse. 141p. (Orig.). 1993. pap. 72.00 (1-86320-077-0) St Mut.

Major Attraction. Roz D. Fox. LC 95-13686. (Superromance Ser.). 299p. 1995. per. 3.75 (0-373-70649-9, 1-70649-8) Harlequin Bks.

***Major Attraction.** Roz D. Fox. 2000. mass mkt. 4.50 (0-373-82241-3, 1-82241-0) Harlequin Bks.

Major Authors & Illustrated Children, Vol. 5. Joyce Nakamura. 1992. write for info. (0-8103-8495-7, 101444) Gale.

Major Authors & Illustrators Children & Young Adults Supplement. Joyce Nakamura. LC 99-159523. 652p. 1997. 95.00 (0-7876-1704-0) Gale.

Major Authors & Illustrators for Children & Young Adults: A Selection of Sketches from Something about the Author, 6 vols., Set. Ed. by Laurie Collier & Joyce Nakamura. LC 92-73849. (Illus.). 2609p. 1992. 299.00 (0-8103-7702-0, 007290-M94800) Gale.

Major Automotive Items & Combinations, WW II: ORD 3 SNL G-1. Department of the Army Staff. (Illus.). 168p. 1988. reprint ed. pap. 20.00 (0-910667-15-2) Victory WW Two.

Major Award Decisionmaking at the National Science Foundation. National Academy of Sciences Panel on Decisionmaki et al. LC 94-66065. 174p. (Orig.). (C). 1994. pap. text 35.00 (0-309-05029-4) Natl Acad Pr.

Major Barbara. George Bernard Shaw. Ed. by Elizabeth T. Forter. (Crofts Classics). 192p. 1971. pap. 4.95 (0-88295-088-6) Harlan Davidson.

Major Barbara. George Bernard Shaw. 160p. 1989. pap. 7.95 (0-14-045018-1) Viking Penguin.

***Major Barbara.** George Bernard Shaw. 1998. lib. bdg. 17.95 (1-56723-089-X) Yestermorrow.

Major Barbara. unabridged ed. George Bernard Shaw. Ed. by William-Alan Landes. LC 97-27716. 84p. 1997. pap. 7.00 (0-88734-703-7) Players Pr.

Major Battles & Campaigns, Vol. 1 see Defeat of Imperial Germany, 1917-1918

Major Bible Prophecies see Grandes Profecias de la Biblia

Major Bible Prophecies. John F. Walvoord. 1996. 5.99 (0-310-21487-4) Zondervan.

Major Bible Prophecies: Thirty-Seven Crucial Prophecies That Affect You Today. John F. Walvoord. 352p. 1991. pap. write for info. (0-310-54129-8) Zondervan.

***Major Bible Prophecies: 37 Crucial Prophecies That Affect You Today.** John F. Walvoord. 2000. pap. 16.99 (0-310-23467-0) Zondervan.

***Major Bible Prophecies: 37 Crucial Prophecies That Affect You Today.** John F. Walvoord. 2000. pap. text 44.99 (0-310-23422-0) Zondervan.

Major Bible Themes Revised Edition. rev. ed. John F. Walvoord. 384p. 1974. 22.99 (0-310-22390-3, 6303) Zondervan.

Major Biological Processes in European Tidal Estuaries. Ed. by C. H. Heip & P. M. Herman. LC 95-40164. (Developments in Hydrobiology Ser.: Vol. 110). 276p. (C). 1995. text 184.00 (0-7923-3699-2) Kluwer Academic.

Major Black American Writers Through the Harlem Renaissance see Writers of English: Lives & Works

Major Blues Tunes in All Twelve Keys. J. Ruwe. 64p. 1997. pap. 12.95 (0-7935-8662-3) H Leonard.

Major Butler's Legacy: Five Generations of a Slaveholding Family. Malcolm Bell, Jr. LC 86-11353. (Illus.). 702p. 1987. 40.00 (0-8203-0897-8) U of Ga Pr.

Major Butler's Legacy: Five Generations of a Slaveholding Family. Malcolm Bell, Jr. LC 86-11353. (Brown Thrasher Bks.). (Illus.). 702p. 1989. pap. text 22.95 (0-8203-1177-4) U of Ga Pr.

Major Canadian Authors: A Critical Introduction to Canadian Literature in English. 2nd rev. ed. David Stouck. LC 87-38089. (Illus.). xiv, 330p. 1988. pap. text 12.95 (0-8032-9188-4, Bison Books) U of Nebr Pr.

Major Carbon Industries in India. Ed. by P. K. Jain. 216p. (C). 1982. text 136.00 (90-6191-400-0, Pub. by A A Balkema) Ashgate Pub Co.

Major Challenges to Philanthropy. Robert L. Payton. 127p. 1984. 10.00 (0-318-37631-8) Ind Sector.

Major Changes & Crisis: The Impact on Women in Latin America & the Caribbean. 279p. 20.00 (92-1-121177-8, E.90.II.G.13) UN.

Major Characters in American Fiction. Ed. by Jack Salzman. 960p. 1995. 60.00 (0-8050-3060-3) H Holt & Co.

Major Chemical & Petrochemical Companies of Europe, 1989-1990. Ed. by R. M. Whiteside. (C). 1989. lib. bdg. 254.50 (1-85333-376-X, Pub. by Graham & Trotman) Kluwer Academic.

Major Chemical & Petrochemical Companies of Europe, 1990, 5 Vols. 4th ed. 300p. 1994. text 159.00 (0-8103-9822-2, 070333-M99406) Gale.

***Major Chemical & Petrochemical Companies of Europe, 2000.** 1999. 495.00 (1-86099-172-6, Pub. by G & W) Am Educ Systs.

***Major Chemical & Petrochemical Companies of the Far East & Australasia, 2000.** (Orig.). 1999. pap. text 450.00 (1-86099-178-5, Pub. by G & W) Am Educ Systs.

***Major Chemical & Petrochemical Companies of the World, 2000.** 2000. pap. 855.00 (1-86099-192-0, Pub. by G & W) Am Educ Systs.

Major Chemical Companies of the World, 1999, 2 vols., Set. Ed. by V. Bentley et al. 2020p. 1999. pap. 855.00 (1-86099-135-1, Pub. by G & W) Am Educ Systs.

Major Chemical Hazards. Victor C. Marshall. LC 86-27611. (Corrosion & Its Prevention Ser.). 587p. 1987. text 118.00 (0-470-20813-9) P-H.

Major Chemical Hazards: A Systematic Approach to Safety & Reliability in Industrial Operations, 7 vols. Institution of Chemical Engineers Staff. 1996. 149.00 (0-85295-367-4, 53674, Pub. by IChemE) Gulf Pub.

Major Cities & Their Peripheries. (Local & Regional Authorities in Europe Ser.: No. 51). 1993. 12.00 (92-871-2394-2, Pub. by Council of Europe) Manhattan Pub Co.

Major Cities of Europe. 1998. pap. 14.95 (1-86315-107-9) Little Hills.

Major Clinical Trials on Thrombolysis for Acute Myocardial Infarction. Ed. by Peter Sleight & Luigi Tavazzi. LC 92-17095. (Illus.). 93p. 1992. reprint ed. pap. 30.00 (0-608-05767-3, 205973100007) Bks Demand.

***Major Comes to Texas,** K. N. Casper. (Superromance Ser.: Vol. 915). 2000. mass mkt. 4.50 (0-373-70915-3) Harlequin Bks.

***Major Companies of Africa South of the Sahara, 1999.** 4th ed. 900p. 1999. 530.00 (1-86099-141-6, Pub. by G & W) Gale.

***Major Companies of Central & Eastern Europe & the Commonwealth of Independent States 2000.** 9th ed. 1350p. 1999. 1070.00 (1-86099-175-0, Pub. by G & W) Gale.

Major Companies of Europe, 1991-1992 Vols. 1-3, Set. Ed. by R. M. Whiteside & J. Forsyth. (C). 1991. lib. bdg. 1030.00 (1-85333-080-9, Pub. by Graham & Trotman) Kluwer Academic.

Major Companies of Europe 1991 & Medium Companies of Europe 1991-92, 6 vols., Set, Vols. 1-3. Ed. by R. M. Whiteside & J. Forsyth. (C). 1991. lib. bdg. 999.00 (1-85333-609-2) G & T Inc.

***Major Companies of Europe 2000.** 19th ed. Vol. 2. 1999. 560.00 (1-86099-162-9, Pub. by G & W) Gale.

***Major Companies of Europe 2000, Vol. 3.** 19th ed. 1999. 560.00 (1-86099-163-7, Pub. by G & W) Gale.

***Major Companies of Europe 2000, Vol. 4.** 19th ed. 1999. 560.00 (1-86099-164-5, Pub. by G & W) Gale.

***Major Companies of Europe 2000: Major Companies of Europe Two Thousand.** 19th ed. Vol. 1. 1999. 560.00 (1-86099-161-0, Pub. by G & W) Gale.

***Major Companies of Latin America & the Caribbean, 1999.** 4th ed. 1300p. 1999. 765.00 (1-86099-134-3, GML00299-113491, Pub. by G & W) Gale.

***Major Companies of Scandinavia 2000.** 5th ed. J. Bradley. 1999. pap. text 560.00 (1-86099-171-8, Pub. by G & W) Am Educ Systs.

***Major Companies of South West Asia, 1999.** 3rd rev. ed. 841p. 1999. (1-86099-140-8) G & W.

Major Companies of South West Asia. 620p. Date not set. 395.00 (1-86099-041-X, GML00198-110955, Pub. by Art Trade Pr) Gale.

***Major Companies of the Arab World 2000.** 23rd ed. Graham & Whiteside Ltd. Staff. 1294p. 1999. pap. 890.00 (1-86099-160-2, Pub. by G & W) Gale.

Major Companies of the Far East & Australasia 2000. 16th ed. 575.00 (1-86099-166-1, Pub. by G & W) Gale.

Major Companies of the Far East & Australasia 2000, Vol. 2. 16th ed. 575.00 (1-86099-167-X, Pub. by G & W) Gale.

Major Companies of the Far East & Australasia 2000, Vol. 3. 16th ed. 390.00 (1-86099-168-8, Pub. by G & W) Gale.

Major Conservation Issues of the 1990s: Results of the World Conservation Congress Workshops, Montreal, Canada, 13-23 October 1996. World Conservation Congress Staff & Jeffrey A. McNeely. LC 98-179194. vii, 203 p. 1998. write for info. (2-8317-0433-2) IUCN.

Major Construction Works. Keith Potts. 328p. (C). 1996. pap. text 48.95 (0-582-10298-7) Addison-Wesley.

Major Counting of Nonintersecting Lattice Paths & Generating Functions for Tableaux. C. Krattenthaler. LC 95-3815. (Memoirs of the American Mathematical Society Ser: No. 552). 109p. 1995. pap. 35.00 (0-8218-2613-1, MEMO/115/552) Am Math.

Major Criminal Justice Systems: A Comparative Survey. 2nd ed. Ed. by George F. Cole et al. LC 87-23232. (Sage Focus Editions Ser.: Vol. 32). 288p. 1987. reprint ed. pap. 89.30 (0-608-03565-3, 205965000009) Bks Demand.

Major Crises in Contemporary American Foreign Policy: A Documentary History. Russell D. Buhite. LC 96-32415. (Primary Documents in American History & Contemporary Issues Ser.). 520p. 1997. 65.00 (0-313-29468-2) Greenwood.

Major Crisis? The Politics of Economic Policy in Britain in the 1990s. Werner Bonefeld et al. LC 95-19398. (Illus.). 256p. 1995. pap. 29.95 (1-85521-550-0, Pub. by Dartmth Pub); text 82.95 (1-85521-544-6, Pub. by Dartmth Pub) Ashgate Pub Co.

Major Critical Essays. George Bernard Shaw. 1988. reprint ed. lib. bdg. 79.00 (0-7812-0175-6) Rprt Serv.

Major Critical Essays. George Bernard Shaw. LC 74-145292. 1971. reprint ed. 49.00 (0-403-01205-8) Scholarly.

Major Critics: The Development of English Literary Criticism. Ed. by Charles S. Holmes et al. LC 83-45783. reprint ed. 29.00 (0-404-20123-7) AMS Pr.

Major Dad. Shelley Cooper. (Intimate Moments Ser.). 1998. per. 4.25 (0-373-07876-5, 1-07876-5) Silhouette.

Major Decisions: A Guide to College Majors. LC 97-139557. 159p. 1997. 20.00 (1-878172-70-0, 397MD, Wintergreen-Orchard) Riverside Pub Co.

Major Decisions: A Guide to College Majors. 2nd ed. Richard Blumenthal & Joseph Despres. 168p. (Orig.). (YA). (gr. 12). 1992. pap. 15.00 (1-878172-20-4, Wintergreen-Orchard) Riverside Pub Co.

***Major Demographic Shifts Occurring in California, Vol. 5.** Elias Lopez. 11p. 1999. pap. write for info. (1-58703-114-0, CRB Note 6) CA St Libry.

Major Depression: Prevention & Treatment. Michael R. Lowry. 136p. 1984. 15.00 (0-87527-186-3) Green.

Major Depressive Disorder: The Latest Assessment & Treatment Strategies. Anton O. Tolman. LC 95-70155. (Condensed Reviews for Professionals Ser.). 96p. (Orig.). (C). 1995. pap. 14.95 (1-887537-10-4) Compact Clinicals.

Major Determinants Affecting the Demand & Supply of Energy Resources: An Analysis of the Petroleum Market. Angelos Pagoulatos. Ed. by Stuart Bruchey. LC 78-22704. (Energy in the American Economy Ser.). (Illus.). 1979. lib. bdg. 23.95 (0-405-12006-0) Ayer.

Major Development & Transportation Projects: Public-Private Partnerships. Ed. by B. Kent Lall & Daniel L. Jones, Jr. LC 90-980. 381p. 1990. pap. text 6.00 (0-87262-764-0) Am Soc Civil Eng.

Major Dictionary Afrikaans-English-Afrikaans. 13th ed. M. S. Kritzinger. (AFR & ENG.). 1410p. 1986. 150.00 (0-8288-0540-7, F55120) Fr & Eur.

Major Disasters see It's a Fact!

Major Display Materials: Markets, Technologies. Robert Moran. LC 98-124883. 174p. 1997. 3250.00 (1-56965-456-5, GB-203) BCC.

Major Distractions. Leslie D. Guccione. (Desire Ser.). 1994. per. 2.99 (0-373-05870-5, 1-05870-0) Silhouette.

Major Donors: The Key to Successful Fundraising. unabridged ed. Robert M. Zimmerman. 16p. 1998. pap. 1295.00 (0-9665259-1-4) Zmmrmn Lhmn.

Major Donors, 1995. 3rd ed. Mark W. Scott. 1994. 185.00 (1-56995-057-1) Taft Group.

Major Donors, 1994: A Listing of More Than 16,000 Individuals Who Have Recently Donated Major Gifts to America's Largest Non-Profit Organizations. 2nd ed. Ed. by Mark W. Scott. 1000p. 1993. 180.00 (1-879784-78-5, 600446) Taft Group.

Major Donors, 1997. 5th ed. Mark W. Scott. 180.00 (1-56995-059-8) Taft Group.

Major Donors, 1996. 4th ed. Mark W. Scott. 1995. 180.00 (1-56995-058-X) Taft Group.

Major Donors, 1993: A Listing of More Than 8000 Individuals Who Have Recently Donated Major Gifts to America's Largest Nonprofit Organizations. Ed. by Mark W. Scott. (Who Gives in America Ser.). 530p. 1992. 175.00 (1-879784-35-1, 600352) Taft Group.

Major Economic Factors in Metropolitan Growth & Arrangement, Vol. 1. (Metropolitan America Ser.). 144p. 1974. 18.95 (0-405-05414-9) Ayer.

Major Edmund Bradford: U. S. Army & Confederate States Army. Ed. by Calvert W. Tazewell. LC 90-81466. 1991. pap. write for info. (1-878515-51-9) W S Dawson.

Major Egyptian Forgeries: The Fabrication of Ra-Hotep - Nofret & Nefertiti. Manu Ampim. (Illus.). 1995. pap. write for info. (0-9636447-6-9) Advan The Res.

Major Elements. Ed. by J. Benton Jones, Jr. (Plant Nutrition Ser.: Vol. 2). 1994. VHS 104.95 (1-884015-26-3) CRC Pr.

Major Employers of Europe 1999: The Job Finders Directory. Ed. by R. Crawford. 1100p. 1999. 270.00 (1-86099-155-6, Pub. by G & W) Gale.

***Major Employers of Europe, 2001: The Job Finder's Directory.** 2000. pap. 270.00 (1-86099-210-2, Pub. by G & W) Am Educ Systs.

Major Employment Law Principles Established by the EEOC, the OFCCP & the Courts. Howard J. Anderson. LC 80-607842. 117p. reprint ed. pap. 36.30 (0-608-12747-7, 202434000036) Bks Demand.

***Major Energy Companies of Europe, 2000.** (Orig.). 1999. pap. text 460.00 (1-86099-173-4, Pub. by G & W) Am Educ Systs.

***Major Energy Companies of the Far East & Australasia, 2000.** 1999. pap. text 450.00 (1-86099-179-3, Pub. by G & W) Am Educ Systs.

Major Energy Companies of the World, 1999. Ed. by V. Bentley et al. 300p. 1999. pap. 855.00 (1-86099-136-X) Am Educ Systs.

***Major Energy Companies of the World, 2000.** 2000. pap. text 855.00 (1-86099-194-7, Pub. by G & W) Am Educ Systs.

Major Enquiry. Laurence Henderson. 192p. 1986. reprint ed. pap. 5.95 (0-89733-199-0) Academy Chi Pubs.

An Asterisk (*) at the beginning of an entry indicates that the title is appearing for the first time.

Major European Governments. 9th ed. Jorgen S. Rasmussen & Joel C. Moses. LC 94-17290. 710p. (C). 1995. pap. text 75.00 (*0-534-22212-9*) Harcourt.

Major European Governments. 10th ed. Rasmussen. (C). Date not set. pap. text. write for info. (*0-15-507864-X*) Harcourt Coll Pubs.

Major Events in the History of Life. J. William Schopf. 1991. pap. 41.25 (*0-86720-268-8*) Jones & Bartlett.

Major Evolutionary Radiations. Ed. by P. D. Taylor & G. P. Larwood. (Systematics Association Special Volume Ser.: Vol. 42). (Illus.). 456p. 1991. 145.00 (*0-19-857718-4*) OUP.

***Major Factors Affecting America's Cities.** 30p. 1998. pap. 10.00 (*1-886152-53-5*, 3544) Natl League Cities.

Major Figures of Austrian Literature: The Interwar Years, 1918-1938. Ed. & Intro. by Donald G. Daviau. LC 95-1998. (Studies in Austrian Literature, Culture, & Thought). 588p. 1995. 59.95 (*0-929497-60-0*) Ariadne CA.

Major Figures of Modern Austrian Literature. Ed. & Intro. by Donald G. Daviau. (Studies in Austrian Literature, Culture, & Thought). 481p. 1988. 39.95 (*0-929497-00-7*) Ariadne CA.

Major Figures of Nineteenth-Century Austrian Literature. Ed. by Donald G. Daviau. LC 97-43722. (Studies in Austrian Literature, Culture & Thought). 572p. 1998. 59.95 (*1-57241-047-7*) Ariadne CA.

Major Figures of Turn-of-the-Century Austrian Literature. Ed. & Intro. by Donald G. Daviau. LC 90-893. (Studies in Austrian Literature, Culture & Thought). lx, 488p. 1990. 45.00 (*0-929497-30-9*) Ariadne CA.

Major Film Directors of the American & British Cinema. Gene D. Phillips. LC 88-46163. (Illus.). 288p. 1990. 49.50 (*0-934223-08-4*) Lehigh Univ Pr.

Major Film Directors of the American & British Cinema. rev. ed. Gene D. Phillips. LC 98-31914. 320p. 1999. 46.50 (*0-934223-59-9*) Lehigh Univ Pr.

Major Film Theories: An Introduction. Dudley Andrew. (Illus.). 288p. (Orig.). 1976. pap. text 13.95 (*0-19-501991-1*) OUP.

Major Financial Institutions of Continental Europe, 1989-90. Ed. by R. M. Whiteside. (C). 1990. lib. bdg. 326.00 (*1-85333-361-1*, Pub. by Graham & Trotman) Kluwer Academic.

Major Financial Institutions of Europe, 1991-1992. Ed. by R. M. Whiteside. (Major Companies Ser.). 264p. (C). 1991. text 350.00 (*1-85333-618-1*, Pub. by Graham & Trotman) Kluwer Academic.

***Major Financial Institutions of Europe, 2000.** 1999. pap. text 495.00 (*1-86099-174-2*, Pub. by G & W) Am Educ Systs.

***Major Financial Institutions of the Arab World, 2000.** 1999. 485.00 (*1-86099-170-X*, Pub. by G & W) Am Educ Systs.

***Major Financial Institutions of the Arab World, 2000.** 2000. pap. 485.00 (*1-86099-215-3*, Pub. by G & W) Am Educ Systs.

***Major Financial Institutions of the Far East & Australasia, 2000.** 1999. pap. text 505.00 (*1-86099-180-7*, Pub. by G & W) Am Educ Systs.

Major Financial Institutions of the World, 1999. Ed. by C. Oddy et al. 865p. 1999. pap. 935.00 (*1-86099-137-8*) Am Educ Systs.

***Major Financial Institutions of the World, 2000.** 2000. pap. text 855.00 (*1-86099-195-5*, Pub. by G & W) Am Educ Systs.

Major Flaps in the Head & Neck. 3rd rev. ed. Pactick J. Gullane et al. LC 98-37604. (Self-Instructional Package Ser.). (Illus.). 1999. pap. text 25.00 (*1-56772-069-2*) AAO-HNS.

***Major Food & Drink Companies of Europe, 2000.** 1999. pap. text 485.00 (*1-86099-176-9*, Pub. by G & W) Am Educ Systs.

***Major Food & Drink Companies of the Far East & Australasia, 2000.** 1999. 465.00 (*1-86099-181-5*, Pub. by G & W) Am Educ Systs.

Major Food & Drink Companies of the World, 1999. Ed. by V. Bentley et al. 2315p. 1999. pap. 855.00 (*1-86099-138-6*) Am Educ Systs.

***Major Food & Drink Companies of the World, 2000.** 2000. pap. text 855.00 (*1-86099-196-3*, Pub. by G & W) Am Educ Systs.

Major Forms of Crime. Ed. by Robert F. Meier. (Criminal Justice System Annuals Ser.: Vol. 21). 320p. (Orig.). (C). 1984. pap. text 26.00 (*0-8039-2095-4*) Sage.

Major Forms of Crime. Ed. by Robert F. Meier. LC 84-15953. (Sage Criminal Justice System Annuals Ser.: Vol. 21). 247p. (Orig.). 1984. reprint ed. pap. 76.60 (*0-608-02790-1*, 206385700007) Bks Demand.

Major Fractures of the Pilon, the Talus, & the Calcaneus: Current Concepts of Treatment. Ed. by Joseph Schatzker & H. Tscherne. LC 92-49465. 1994. 155.00 (*0-387-55837-3*) Spr-Verlag.

Major French Milton Critics of the Nineteenth Century. Harry Redman, Jr. LC 93-39661. (Duquesne Studies: Language & Literature Ser.: Vol. 14). 404p. (C). 1994. text 48.00 (*0-8207-0249-8*) Duquesne.

Major General Adam Stephen & the Cause of American Liberty. Harry M. Ward. LC 89-30959. (Illus.). 262p. 1989. text 35.00 (*0-8139-1227-X*) U Pr of Va.

***Major-General Darius Nash Couch: Enigmatic Valor.** A. M. Gambone. (Army of the Potomac Ser.: Vol. 25). (Illus.). 335p. 2000. 35.00 (*0-935523-75-8*) Butternut & Blue.

Major General George Henry Thomas: The Dependable General. Frank A. Palumbo. LC 83-17261. (Illus.). 465p. 1983. 35.00 (*0-89029-311-2*) Morningside Bkshop.

Major General Henry Knox & the Last Heirs to Montpelier. 2nd ed. Thomas M. Griffiths. Ed. by Arthur M. Griffiths. LC 90-63843. (Illus.). 160p. 1991. 17.95 (*0-9628001-0-4*) Monmouth Pr.

Major General John Alexander McClernand: Politician in Uniform. Richard L. Kiper. LC 99-22750. 352p. 1999. text 35.00 (*0-87338-636-1*) Kent St U Pr.

Major-General John Frederick Hartranft: Citizen Soldier & Pennsylvania Statesman. A. M. Gambone. (Army of the Potomac Ser.). (Illus.). 369p. 1995. 30.00 (*0-935523-46-4*) Butternut & Blue.

***Major General John S. Marmaduke, C. S. A.** Jerry Ponder. Ed. by Lois G. Webb. LC 99-70227. (Illus.). 259p. (gr. 7 up). 1999. pap. 17.95 (*0-9623922-8-6*) Ponder Bks.

Major General Orde Charles Wingate & the Development of Long-Range Penetration. L. Rossetto. 492p. 1982. pap. text 61.95 (*0-89126-107-9*) MA-AH Pub.

Major General Thomas Maley Harris. H. E. Matheny. 296p. 1963. reprint ed. pap. 14.95 (*0-87012-003-4*) McClain.

MAJOR GENERAL THOMAS MALEY HARRIS...a member of the Military Commission that tried the President Abraham Lincoln assassination conspirators...& Roster of the 10th West Virginia Volunteer Infantry Regiment, 1861-1865. Reprinted, 1996. *Publisher Paid Annotation.*

Major Gentl & the Achimoto Wars. Kojo Laing. (African Writers Ser.). 185p. (C). 1992. pap. 8.95 (*0-435-90978-9*, 90978) Heinemann.

Major Gift Programs: Practical Implementation. Gough, Jr. 200p. 1997. 59.00 (*0-8342-0934-9*, 09349) Aspen Pub.

Major Gifts: Solicitation Strategies. Richard E. Matheny. LC 95-119607. 167p. 1994. per. 41.50 (*0-89964-309-4*, 25302) Coun Adv & Supp Ed.

Major Gods of Ancient Yucatan. Karl A. Taube. LC 92-5435. (Studies in Pre-Columbian Art & Archaeology: No. 32). (Illus.). 168p. 1992. pap. 18.00 (*0-88402-204-8*, TAMGP) Dumbarton Oaks.

***Major Hazard Control: A Practical Manual.** Ed. by G. R. Kliesch. (Illus.). 296p. 1999. pap. text 50.00 (*0-7881-8194-7*) DIANE Pub.

Major Hazard Control: A Practical Manual, ILO Contribution to the International Programme on Chemical Safety of UNEP, ILO, WHO (IPCS) x, 296p. (Orig.). 1993. reprint ed. pap. 40.50 (*92-2-106432-8*) Intl Labour Office.

Major Hazards & Their Management. Geoff Wells. 180p. 1997. 42.00 (*0-85295-368-2*, 53682, Pub. by IChemE) Gulf Pub.

Major Hazards Onshore & Offshore. Ed. by N. Gibson. 275p. 1992. 203.00 (*1-56032-259-4*) Hemisp Pub.

***Major Histocompatibility Complex.** Ed. by M. Kasahara. (Illus.). xxiv, 561p. 2000. 239.00 (*4-431-70276-8*) Spr-Verlag.

Major Histocompatibility Complex Region of Domestic Animal Species. Ed. by Lawrence B. Schook & Susan J. Lamont. 336p. 1996. boxed set 104.95 (*0-8493-8032-4*, 8032) CRC Pr.

Major Home Appliances: A Common Sense Repair Manual. Darell L. Rains. (Illus.). 160p. (Orig.). 1987. pap. 15.95 (*0-8306-2747-2*) McGraw-Hill Prof.

Major Ideologies: An Interpretative Survey of Democracy, Socialism & Nationalism. 2nd ed. Alexander J. Groth. LC 82-18755. 268p. (C). 1983. pap. 17.50 (*0-89874-579-9*) Krieger.

***Major Impacts & Plate Tectonics: A Model for the Phanerzoic Evolution of the Earth's Lithosphere.** Neville J. Price. LC 00-37717. (Illus.). 2000. pap. write for info. (*0-7484-0850-9*) Taylor & Francis.

***Major in Success: Make College Easier, Beat the System & Get a Very Cool Job.** 3rd ed. Patrick Combs. 2000. pap. 11.95 (*1-58008-209-2*) Ten Speed Pr.

Major Incident. large type ed. Nicholas Rhea. (Dales Large Print Ser.). 288p. 1998. pap. 19.99 (*1-85389-785-X*, Dales) Ulverscroft.

Major Incident Medical Management & Support: The Practical Approach. Advanced Life Support Group. 205p. 1995. pap. text 43.00 (*0-7279-0928-2*, Pub. by BMJ Pub) Login Brothers Bk Co.

Major Indian Novelists. K. Venkata Reddy. 1991. text 22.50 (*81-85218-29-3*, Pub. by Prestige) Advent Bks Div.

Major Indicators for the Asiatic & European RSFSR. Fyodor I. Kushnirsky. (Analysis with Estimates Ser.). 158p. (Orig.). 1983. pap. text 100.00 (*1-55831-059-2*) Delphic Associates.

Major Inflations in History. Ed. by Forrest H. Capie. (International Library of Macroeconomic & Financial History: Vol. 1). 688p. 1991. text 265.00 (*1-85278-402-4*) E Elgar.

Major Information Technology Companies of the World 1999. Ed. by D. Shave. 1200p. 1999. pap. 855.00 (*1-86099-153-X*, Pub. by G & W) Am Educ Systs.

***Major Infrastructure Projects in Indonesia: A Strategic Entry Report, 1999.** Compiled by Icon Group International. (Illus.). 189p. 1999. ring bd. 1890.00 incl. audio compact disk (*0-7418-1883-3*) Icon Grp.

***Major International Treaties of the 20th Century, 2 vols.** J. A. S. Grenville & Bernard Wasserstein. LC 00-32833. 2000. write for info. (*0-415-23799-8*) Routledge.

Major International Treaties since 1945: A History & Guide with Texts. J. A. Grenville & Bernard Wasserstein. LC 87-11250. 400p. 1988. 85.00 (*0-416-38080-8*) Routledge.

Major Interpretations of the American Past. Ed. by Richard L. Rapson. LC 72-149210. (Literature of History Ser.). (Orig.). (C). 1971. 32.50 (*0-89197-284-6*); pap. text 9.95 (*0-89197-285-4*) Irvington.

***Major Issues in Gereontological Nursing.** 4th rev. ed. Ed. by John Lantz. (Illus.). 143p. 1999. pap. write for info. (*1-57801-037-3*) Western Schls.

Major Issues in Gerontological Nursing. 3rd rev. ed. John Lantz. Ed. by Barbara Halliburton. 127p. 1996. pap. 29.95 (*1-57801-009-8*) Western Schls.

Major Issues in the Life & Work of C. G. Jung. Ed. by William Schoenl. LC 96-32905. 104p. (Orig.). 1996. pap. text 19.50 (*0-7618-0470-6*); lib. bdg. 34.50 (*0-7618-0469-2*) U Pr of Amer.

Major John Andre: A Gallant in Spy's Clothing. Robert M. Hatch. (Illus.). 332p. 1986. 17.95 (*0-685-11808-8*) HM.

Major Jones's Scenes in Georgia. William T. Thompson. LC 76-91094. (Illus.). 196p. 1969. reprint ed. lib. bdg. 22.75 (*0-8398-1956-0*) Irvington.

Major Knesset Debates, 1948-1981 Series, 6 vols., Set. 1993. 350.00 (*0-8191-8341-5*) U Pr of Amer.

Major Knesset Debates, 1948-1981 Vol. 1: Peoples Council & Provisional Council of State, 1948-1949. Ed. by Netanel Lorch. 364p. (C). 1992. lib. bdg. 69.50 (*0-8191-8342-3*) U Pr of Amer.

Major Knesset Debates, 1948-1981 Vol. 2: The Constituent Assembly - First Knesset (1949-1951) Ed. by Natanel Lorch. 360p. (C). 1991. lib. bdg. 69.50 (*0-8191-8343-1*) U Pr of Amer.

Major Knesset Debates, 1948-1981 Vol. 3: Second Knesset (1951-1955), Third Knesset (1955-1959) Ed. by Netanel Lorch. 432p. (C). 1992. lib. bdg. 69.50 (*0-8191-8344-X*) U Pr of Amer.

Major Knesset Debates, 1948-1981 Vol. 4: Fourth Knesset (1949-1961), Fifth Knesset (1961-1965), Sixth Knesset (1965-1969) Ed. by Netanel Lorch. 574p. (C). 1992. lib. bdg. 89.50 (*0-8191-8345-8*) U Pr of Amer.

Major Knesset Debates, 1948-1981 Vol. 5: Seventh Knesset (1969-1973), Eighth Knesset (1974-1977) Ed. by Netanel Lorch. 405p. (C). 1991. lib. bdg. 69.50 (*0-8191-8346-6*) U Pr of Amer.

Major Knesset Debates, 1948-1981 Vol. 6: Ninth Knesset (1977-1981) Ed. by Netanel Lorch. 445p. (C). 1992. lib. bdg. 69.50 (*0-8191-8347-4*) U Pr of Amer.

Major Latin Poems of Jacopo Sannazaro. Jacopo Sannazaro. Tr. by Ralph Nash from LAT. (Illus.). 254p. (C). 1996. 44.95 (*0-8143-2549-1*); pap. 19.95 (*0-8143-2576-9*) Wayne St U Pr.

***Major League Baseball's Best Shots: The Greatest Baseball Photography of All Time.** Kindersley Dorling. (Illus.). 2000. 30.00 (*0-7894-6119-6*) DK Pub Inc.

Major League Dad. Tim Burke et al. LC 94-3069. 200p. 1994. 16.99 (*1-56179-212-8*) Focus Family.

Major League Dads. Molly Wigand. LC PZ7.W6375Maj 1999. (Ready to Read). (Illus.). 32p. (J). (ps-3). 1999. pap. 3.99 (*0-689-82630-3*, 076714003996, Simon Spot) Litle Simon.

Major League Handbook. 10th ed. STATS Publishing Staff & Bill James. (Illus.). 400p. 1998. pap. 19.95 (*1-884064-56-6*) STATS.

Major League Losers: The Real Cost of Sports & Who's Paying for It. Mark S. Rosentraub. LC 96-26446. (Illus.). 528p. 1997. 30.00 (*0-465-08317-X*, Pub. by Basic) HarpC.

***Major League Losers: The Real Cost of Sports & Who's Paying for It.** rev. ed. Mark S. Rosentraub. 496p. 1999. pap. 16.00 (*0-465-07143-0*) HarpC.

Major League Mystery. Rebecca Price-Janney. LC 93-45633. (Heather Reed Mystery Ser.: Vol. 5). (J). 1994. 5.99 (*0-8499-3535-0*) Word Pub.

Major League Trouble. Laura O'Neil. (Full House Michelle Ser.). 96p. (J). (gr. 4-7). 1996. per. 3.99 (*0-671-53575-7*, PB Trade Paper) PB.

Major Legal Systems in the World Today: An Introduction to the Comparative Study of Law. 2nd ed. Rene David & John E. Brierly. LC 78-67751. 1978. reprint ed. pap. 24.95 (*0-02-907610-2*) Free Pr.

Major Literary Characters, 20 bks. Incl. Brett Ashley. Ed. by Harold Bloom. 200p. 1991. lib. bdg. 29.95 (*0-7910-0951-3*); Caliban. Ed. by Harold Bloom. 200p. (C). 1992. lib. bdg. 34.95 (*0-7910-0914-9*); Gatsby. Ed. by Harold Bloom. 200p. 1991. lib. bdg. 34.95 (*0-7910-0958-0*); Hamlet. William Shakespeare. LC 89-31353. 200p. 1990. lib. bdg. 34.95 (*0-7910-0919-X*); Hester Prynne. Intro. by Harold Bloom. 200p. 1989. lib. bdg. 34.95 (*0-7910-0945-9*); Holden Caulfield. Ed. by Harold Bloom. LC 90-1678. 200p. 1991. lib. bdg. 34.95 (*0-7910-0953-X*); Huck Finn. Intro. by Harold Bloom. 200p. 1989. lib. bdg. 34.95 (*0-7910-0940-8*); Isabel Archer. Ed. by Harold Bloom. 200p. (C). 1992. lib. bdg. 29.95 (*0-7910-0934-3*); Joan of Arc. Ed. by Harold Bloom. 200p. (C). 1992. lib. bdg. 29.95 (*0-7910-0960-2*); Julius Caesar. William Shakespeare. LC 92-35489. (Illus.). 200p. 1993. lib. bdg. 29.95 (*0-7910-0921-1*); Lolita. Ed. by Harold Bloom. 200p. (C). 1996. 29.95 (*0-7910-0961-0*); Macbeth. Ed. by Harold Bloom & William Golding. LC 90-2459. 200p. 1991. lib. bdg. 34.95 (*0-7910-0923-8*); Marlow. Ed. by Harold Bloom. 200p. (C). 1992. lib. bdg. 29.95 (*0-7910-0963-7*); Rosalind. Ed. by Harold Bloom. 200p. 1992. lib. bdg. 29.95 (*0-7910-0927-0*); Willy Loman. Ed. by Harold Bloom. 200p. 1991. lib. bdg. 29.95 (*0-7910-0962-9*); 1992. Set pap. text 699.00 (*0-7910-2580-2*) Chelsea Hse.

Major Local Tobacco Control Ordinances in the U. S. Ed. by Mark Pertschuk. (Illus.). 139p. (Orig.). (C). 1994. pap. text 30.00 (*0-7881-1457-3*) DIANE Pub.

***Major Market Share Companies: Asia-Pacific.** 500p. 2000. 1000.00 (*0-86338-887-6*, Pub. by Euromonitor PLC) Gale.

***Major Market Share Companies: Europe.** 500p. 2000. 1000.00 (*0-86338-888-4*, Pub. by Euromonitor PLC) Gale.

***Major Market Share Companies: The Americas.** 500p. 2000. 1000.00 (*0-86338-886-8*, Pub. by Euromonitor PLC) Gale.

***Major Marketing Campaigns 1998.** annuals Gale Group Staff. 525p. 1999. 130.00 (*0-7876-3815-3*) Gale.

***Major Mass Markets, 1999.** Ed. by Keith Caiedo et al. 802p. 1999. 179.95 (*0-87228-128-0*, Salesmn Gde) Douglas Pubns.

***Major McKinley: William McKinley & the Civil War.** William H. Armstrong. LC 99-48531. 248p. 2000. 18.00 (*0-87338-657-4*) Kent St U Pr.

Major Medicinal Plants: Botany, Culture & Uses. fac. ed. Julia F. Morton. (Illus.). 448p. 1977. 99.95 (*0-398-03673-X*) C C Thomas.

***Major Meltdown.** K. S. Rodriguez. (Dawson's Creek Ser.: No. 4). (YA). (gr. 8 up). 1999. per. 4.99 (*0-671-02477-9*) PB.

Major Mental Handicap: Methods & Costs of Prevention. CIBA Foundation Staff. LC 78-15495. (CIBA Foundation Symposium: New Ser.: No. 59). 234p. reprint ed. pap. 72.60 (*0-608-14301-4*, 202218300024) Bks Demand.

Major Minor Finder. CFKR Career Materials Staff. 16p. (YA). (gr. 7 up). 1995. pap. 4.20 (*0-934783-08-X*) CFKR Career.

Major, Modern & Contemporary Theologies: A Handbook of Digests. Howard A. Slaatte. LC 96-35447. 80p. 1996. pap. 14.00 (*0-7618-0577-X*) U Pr of Amer.

Major Modern Black American Writers see Writers of English: Lives & Works

Major Modern Essayists. 2nd ed. Ed. by Gilbert H. Miller & Alan F. Crooks. LC 93-20970. 487p. 1994. pap. text 38.80 (*0-13-497983-4*) P-H.

Major Monuments of Western Art: An Introduction to the Visual Arts. Bruce Cole. 176p. 2000. 30.00 (*0-06-430907-X*, Icon Edns) HarpC.

Major Ned H. Roberts & the Schuetzen Rifle. Gerald O. Kelver. 1995. pap. 13.95 (*1-877704-22-9*) Pioneer Pr.

Major Neuroses & Behavior Disorders in Children. Melitta Sperling. LC 73-17747. 464p. 1994. pap. 60.00 (*1-56821-248-8*) Aronson.

Major Noah. Isaac Goldberg. LC 74-39475. (Select Bibliographies Reprint Ser.). 1977. reprint ed. 21.95 (*0-8369-9908-8*) Ayer.

Major Operations of the Navies in the War American Independence. Alfred Thayer Mahan. (Notable American Authors Ser.). 1999. reprint ed. lib. bdg. 125.00 (*0-7812-3932-X*) Rprt Serv.

Major Operations of the Navies in the War of American Independence. Alfred Thayer Mahan. LC 69-10128. (Illus.). 280p. 1969. reprint ed. lib. bdg. 35.00 (*0-8371-1002-5*, MAWI, Greenwood Pr) Greenwood.

Major Operations of the Navies in the War of American Independence. Alfred Thayer Mahan. (BCL1 - U. S. History Ser.). 280p. 1991. reprint ed. lib. bdg. 79.00 (*0-7812-6119-8*) Rprt Serv.

Major Orchestral Works in Full Score. Felix Mendelssohn. 406p. 1975. pap. 18.95 (*0-486-23184-4*) Dover.

Major Papers on Early Primates, Compiled from the Publications of the American Museum of Natural History, 1982-1948. Henry F. Osborn et al. LC 78-72712. 1980. 55.50 (*0-404-18282-8*) AMS Pr.

Major Pentatonic Scales for Guitar see Pentatonicas Mayores Escalas para Guitarra

Major Pharmaceutical Companies of the World 1999. Ed. by S. E. Hoernig. 1100p. 1999. pap. 855.00 (*1-86099-154-8*, Pub. by G & W) Am Educ Systs.

***Major Pharmaceutical Companies of the World, 2000.** (Orig.). 2000. pap. 855.00 (*1-86099-199-8*, Pub. by G & W) Am Educ Systs.

Major Phase see Henry Adams

Major Philosophers of Jewish Prayer in the Twentieth Century. Jack J. Cohen. LC 99-49432. 227p. 2000. pap. 19.95 (*0-8232-1957-7*, Pub. by Fordham) BookMasters.

Major Plays of Chikamatsu. Donald Keene. 1990. pap. text 21.50 (*0-231-07415-8*) Col U Pr.

Major Plays of Nikolai Erdman: The Warrant & the Suicide. Ed. & Tr. by John Freedman. (Russian Theatre Archive Ser.: Vol. 1). 160p. 1995. text 30.00 (*3-7186-5582-9*, ECU40, Harwood Acad Pubs); pap. text 15.00 (*3-7186-5583-7*, ECU18, Harwood Acad Pubs) Gordon & Breach.

Major Poems, 5 vols. in 1. Timothy Dwight. LC 68-24207. 574p. 1969. 75.00 (*0-8201-1059-0*) Schol Facsimiles.

Major Poems of the Hebrew Bible at the Interface of Hermeneutics & Structural Analysis Vol. 1: Ex. 15, Deut. 32 & Job 3. J. P. Fokkelman. LC 98-208780. vii, 206p. 1998. text 69.00 (*90-232-3367-0*, Pub. by Van Gorcum) Eisenbrauns.

Major Poetical Upanisads. Swami Gabhivananda. 180p. pap. 5.95 (*0-87481-587-8*, Pub. by Ramakrishna Math) Vedanta Pr.

Major Policies & Actions: IEA the First 20 Years. Richard Scott. 394p. (Orig.). 1995. pap. 65.00 (*92-64-14337-8*, Pub. by Org for Econ) OECD.

Major Political Events in Indochina, 1945-1990. Darren Sagar. (Major Political Events Ser.). 256p. 1991. lib. bdg. 29.95 (*0-8160-2308-5*) Facts on File.

Major Political Events in South Africa, 1948-1990. Eileen Riley. LC 90-22490. 256p. 1991. reprint ed. pap. 79.40 (*0-608-02861-4*, 206392500007) Bks Demand.

Major Powers at a Crossroads: Economic Interdependence & an Asian Pacific Security Community. Ming Zhang. LC 95-2153. 223p. 1995. lib. bdg. 49.95 (*1-55587-593-9*) L Rienner.

M

Major Powers in Northeast Asia: Seeking Peace & Security. Ed. by Tae-Hwan Kwak & Edward A. Olsen. LC 96-12043. 250p. 1996. lib. bdg. 52.00 (1-55587-566-1) L Rienner.

Major Powers in Northeast Asian Security. Ralph A. Cossa. (Illus.). 75p. (Orig.). (C). 1997. pap. text 25.00 (0-7881-3647-X) DIANE Pub.

Major Powers in Northeast Asian Security. Ralph A. Cossa. 77p. 1996. per. 4.50 (0-16-061188-1) USGPO.

Major Premiership 1990-1997. Dorey. LC 98-38458. 1999. text 65.00 (0-312-21839-7) St Martin.

Major Principles of Media Law. Overbeck. (C). 1998. pap. text 56.00 (0-15-507293-5, Pub. by Harcourt Coll Pubs) Harcourt.

Major Problems in American Colonial History: Documents & Essays. Ed. by Karen O. Kupperman. (Major Problems in American History Ser.). 580p. (C). 1993. pap. text 29.16 (0-669-19922-2) HM Trade Div.

Major Problems in American Constitutional History: Documents & Essays, 2 vols., Vol. 1: The Colonial Era Through Reconstruction. Ed. by Kermit L. Hall. (Major Problems in American History Ser.). 645p. (C). 1992. pap. text 29.16 (0-669-21209-1) HM Trade Div.

Major Problems in American Constitutional History: Documents & Essays, 2 vols., Vol. 2: From Circa 1870 to the Present. Ed. by Kermit L. Hall. (Major Problems in American History Ser.). 578p. (C). 1992. pap. text 29.16 (0-669-21210-5) HM Trade Div.

Major Problems in American Environmental History: Documents & Essays. Ed. by Carolyn Merchant. (Major Problems in American History Ser.). 544p. (C). 1993. pap. text 29.16 (0-669-24993-9) HM Trade Div.

Major Problems in American Foreign Policy, 2 Vols. 2nd ed. Thomas G. Paterson. (C). 1984. pap. text 29.16 (0-669-06449-1) HM Trade Div.

Major Problems in American Foreign Policy: Documents & Essays, 2 vols., Vol. II. 3rd ed. Ed. by Thomas G. Paterson. LC 88-80720. (Major Problems in American History Ser.). 721p. (C). 1990. pap. text 29.16 (0-669-15857-7) HM Trade Div.

Major Problems in American Foreign Relations Vol. I: To 1920: Documents & Essays, 2 vols., Vol. I. 4th ed. Thomas G. Paterson & Dennis J. Merrill. LC 94-77213. (Major Problems in American History Ser.). 592p. (C). 1995. pap. text 29.16 (0-669-35077-X) HM Trade Div.

Major Problems in American Foreign Relations Vol. 2: Documents & Essays Since 1914, 2 vols., Vol. II. 4th ed. Thomas G. Paterson & Dennis J. Merrill. LC 94-77213. (Major Problems in American History Ser.). 592p. (C). 1995. pap. text 29.16 (0-669-35078-8) HM Trade Div.

Major Problems in American History since 1945: Documents & Essays. Ed. by Robert Griffith. (Major Problems in American History Ser.). 727p. (C). 1992. pap. text 29.16 (0-669-19625-8) HM Trade Div.

Major Problems in American History, 1920-1945: Documents & Essays. Colin Gordon. LC 98-72031. (American History Ser.). 451 p. 1999. pap. text 31.56 (0-395-87074-7) HM.

Major Problems in American Indian History: Documents & Essays. Albert L. Hurtado & Peter J. Iverson. LC 93-71043. (Major Problems in American History Ser.). 570p. (C). 1994. pap. text 29.16 (0-669-27049-0) HM Trade Div.

***Major Problems in American Military History: Documents & Essays.** John W. Chambers & G. Kurt Piehler. LC 98-72009. (Major Problems in American History Ser.). xx, 488p. (C). 1999. write for info. (0-669-33538-X) HM Trade Div.

Major Problems in American Sport History. Steven A. Riess. LC 96-76951. (Major Problems in American History Ser.). 512p. (C). 1996. pap. text 29.16 (0-669-35380-9) HM Trade Div.

Major Problems in American Urban History: Documents & Essays. 3rd ed. Howard P. Chudacoff. 476p. (C). 1994. pap. text 29.16 (0-669-24376-0) HM Trade Div.

Major Problems in American Women's History: Documents & Essays. 2nd ed. Mary B. Norton & Ruth M. Alexander. 530p. (C). 1996. pap. text 29.16 (0-669-35390-6) HM Trade Div.

Major Problems in California History. Sucheng Chan & Spencer C. Olin. 512p. (C). 1996. pap. text 29.16 (0-669-27588-3) HM Trade Div.

Major Problems in China's Foreign Relations since 1840. Joseph D. Lowe. (Illus.). xxxii, 180p. 1994. pap. 52.00 (0-930325-30-3) Lowe Pub.

Major Problems in Early Modern Russian History. A. Dallin. Ed. by Nancy S. Kollmann. LC 91-46584. (Articles on Russian & Soviet History, 1500-1991 Ser.: Vol. 1). 472p. 1992. reprint ed. text 25.00 (0-8153-0558-3) Garland.

***Major Problems in Mexican American History: Documents & Essays.** Zaragosa Vargas. LC 98-72090. (Major Problems in American History Ser.). xvii, 483p. 1999. write for info. (0-395-84555-6) HM.

Major Problems in State Constitutional Revision. Pi Sigma Alpha Committee on Publications. Ed. by W. Brooke Graves. LC 78-779. 306p. 1978. reprint ed. lib. bdg. 59.75 (0-313-20266-4, PSAM, Greenwood Pr) Greenwood.

Major Problems in Texas. Haynes. (C). Date not set. pap. write for info. (0-395-85833-X) HM.

Major Problems in the Civil War & Reconstruction: Documents & Essays. Ed. by Michael Perman. LC 90-81121. (Major Problems in American History Ser.). 598p. (C). 1991. pap. text 29.16 (0-669-20148-0) HM Trade Div.

***Major Problems in the Civil War & Reconstruction: Documents & Essays.** 2nd ed. Michael Perman. LC 97-72533. (Major Problems in American History Ser.). 1998. 31.56 (0-395-86849-1) HM.

Major Problems in the Early Republic, 1787-1848: Documents & Essays. Ed. by Sean Wilentz. (Major Problems in American History Ser.). 568p. (C). 1992. pap. text 29.16 (0-669-24332-9) HM Trade Div.

Major Problems in the Era of the American Revolution, 1760-1791: Documents & Essays. Ed. by Richard D. Brown. (Major Problems in American History Ser.). 620p. (C). 1992. pap. text 29.16 (0-669-19755-6) HM Trade Div.

Major Problems in the Gilded Age & the Progressive Era: Documents & Essays. 3rd ed. Ed. by Leon Fink. (Major Problems in American History Ser.). 592p. (C). 1993. pap. text 29.16 (0-669-21680-1) HM Trade Div.

Major Problems in the History of American Workers: Documents & Essays. Ed. by Eileen Boris & Nelson Lichtenstein. LC 90-82495. (Major Problems in American History Ser.). 681p. (C). 1991. pap. text 29.16 (0-669-19925-7) HM Trade Div.

Major Problems in the History of Imperial Russia. Ed. by James Cracraft. LC 93-70549. 661p. (C). 1994. pap. text 29.96 (0-669-21497-3) HM Trade Div.

Major Problems in the History of the American South: Documents & Essays, 2 vols. Ed. by Paul D. Escott & David R. Goldfield. LC 89-85075. (Major Problems in American History Ser.). (C). 1990. pap. text 15.00 (0-685-74208-3) HM Trade Div.

Major Problems in the History of the American South: Documents & Essays, 2 vols., Vol. I. Ed. by Paul D. Escott & David R. Goldfield. LC 89-85075. (Major Problems in American History Ser.). 597p. (C). 1990. pap. text 29.16 (0-669-13157-1) HM Trade Div.

Major Problems in the History of the American South: Documents & Essays, 2 vols., Vol. II. Ed. by Paul D. Escott & David R. Goldfield. LC 89-85075. (Major Problems in American History Ser.). 673p. (C). 1990. pap. text 29.96 (0-669-19924-9) HM Trade Div.

Major Problems in the History of the American West. 2nd ed. Clyde A. Milner, II et al. 550p. (C). 1997. pap. text 23.67 (0-669-41580-4) HM Trade Div.

Major Problems in the History of the American West: Documents & Essays. Clyde A. Milner, II. LC 88-80718. (Major Problems in American History Ser.). 681p. (C). 1989. pap. text 29.16 (0-669-15134-3) HM Trade Div.

Major Problems in the History of the Italian Renaissance. Benjamin G. Kohl & Alison A. Smith. 464p. (C). 1995. pap. text 30.76 (0-669-28002-X) HM Trade Div.

Major Problems in the History of the Vietnam War. 2nd ed. Robert J. McMahon. LC 94-77794. (Major Problems in American History Ser.). 576p. (C). 1995. pap. text 29.16 (0-669-35252-7) HM Trade Div.

Major Problems in the History of the Vietnam War: Documents & Essays. Ed. by Robert J. McMahon. (Major Problems in American History Ser.). 635p. (C). 1990. pap. text 29.16 (0-669-18013-0) HM Trade Div.

Major Process Equipment & Repair. 2nd ed. Heinz P. Bloch & Fred K. Geitner. (Practical Machinery Management for Process Plants Ser.: Vol. 4). 720p. 1997. 95.00 (0-88415-663-X, 5663) Gulf Pub.

Major Prophets: Teacher's Guide. Mark Grubbs. 1980. 6.50 (0-8100-0399-6, 22N0828) WELS Board.

Major Prophets of To-Day. Edwin E. Slosson. LC 68-8493. (Essay Index Reprint Ser.). 1977. 23.95 (0-8369-0882-1) Ayer.

Major Prose of Thomas Henry Huxley. Ed. by Alan P. Barr. LC 96-13712. (Humanities Center Series on Science & the Humanities). (C). 1997. 50.00 (0-8203-1864-7) U of Ga Pr.

Major Psychological Assessment Instruments. 2nd ed. Ed. by Charles S. Newmark. LC 95-40858. 480p. (C). 1996. 68.00 (0-205-16869-8) Allyn.

Major Psychological Assessment Instruments, Vol. I. Charles S. Newmark. 430p. 1985. text 97.00 (0-205-08457-5, H84577, Longwood Div) Allyn.

Major Purchases see Compras Mayores

Major Recessions: Britain & the World, 1920-1995. Christopher Dow. LC 98-36848. (Illus.). 490p. 1999. text 98.00 (0-19-828858-1) OUP.

***Major Recessions: Britain & the World 1920-1995.** Christopher Dow. 496p. 2000. pap. 24.95 (0-19-924123-6) OUP.

Major Religions of the World. Marcus Bach. 128p. 1984. reprint ed. pap. 5.95 (0-87516-543-5) DeVorss.

Major Research Topics in Combustion. Ed. by M. Yousuff Hussaini et al. (ICASE - NASA LaRC Ser.). (Illus.). xvi, 650p. 1992. 144.95 (0-387-97752-X) Spr-Verlag.

Major Robert Farmar of Mobile. Robert R. Rea. LC 90-32562. 200p. 1990. 34.95 (0-8173-0505-X) U of Ala Pr.

Major Short Stories of D. H. Lawrence: A Handbook. Martin F. Kearney. LC 97-35670. (Garland Reference Library of the Humanities). 264p. 1997. text 54.00 (0-8153-2135-X, H1948) Garland.

Major Shorter Works: Solo Piano. 19.95 (0-7935-4304-5, 5042379) H Leonard.

Major Sins in Islam. Muhammad bin Uthman Adh-Shahabi. 550p. 1993. text 35.00 (1-56744-489-X) Kazi Pubns.

Major Sins in Islam. M. I. Siddiqui. 1988. pap. 7.50 (1-56744-128-9) Kazi Pubns.

Major Soils & Soil Regions in the Netherlands. H. De Bakker. (Illus.). 1978. text 148.50 (90-6193-590-3) Kluwer Academic.

Major Spanish Searches in Eastern North America. Ed. & Comment by David B. Quinn. (Illus.). xxiv, 594p. 1979. 65.95 (0-405-10761-7) Arno Press.

Major Speeches & Debates of Senator McCarthy. Joseph R. McCarthy. 1975. 250.00 (0-87968-308-2) Gordon Pr.

Major Stages & Steps in Energy Manpower Analysis: A Practical Framework. viii, 80p. (Orig.). 1986. pap. 13.50 (92-2-105246-X) Intl Labour Office.

Major State Aids & Taxes: A Comparative Analysis. 214p. pap. text 40.00 (0-7881-4224-0) DIANE Pub.

***Major State Aids & Taxes (In Minnesota) A Comparative Analysis (1997 Update)** Karen Baker & Nina Manzi. (Illus.). 230p. 1999. pap. text 35.00 (0-7881-8160-2) DIANE Pub.

Major State Health Care Policies: Fifty State Profiles, 1997. 6th ed. Health Policy Tracking Service Staff. LC 98-228420. vi, 294 p. 1998. write for info. (1-55516-819-1) Natl Conf State Legis.

Major Stories & Essays. Henry James. LC 99-20130. (Library of America College Editions Ser.). (C). 1999. pap. 11.95 (1-883011-75-2, Pub. by Library of America) Penguin Putnam.

Major Strategies in Twentieth-Century Drama: Apocalyptic Vision, Allegory & Open Form. Estelle M. Raben. (American University Studies: English Language & Literature: Ser. IV, Vol. 67). 164p. (C). 1989. text 21.50 (0-8204-0567-1) P Lang Pubng.

Major Styles of Art, 1800-1900. (Shorewood Art Programs for Education Ser.). 20p. 1974. teacher ed. 131.75 (0-88185-067-5); 176.75 (0-685-07242-8) Shorewood Fine Art.

Major Styles of Art, 1400-1800. (Shorewood Art Programs for Education Ser.). 20p. 1974. teacher ed. 131.75 (0-88185-066-7); 176.75 (0-685-07241-X) Shorewood Fine Art.

Major Styles of Modern Art. (Shorewood Art Programs for Education Ser.). 24p. 1975. teacher ed. 131.75 (0-88185-068-3); 176.75 (0-685-07243-6) Shorewood Fine Art.

Major Suit Raises. Michael Lawrence. 86p. (Orig.). 1987. pap. 4.95 (0-9628297-1-4) C & T Bridge.

Major Tax Planning--university Of Southern California's Annual Institute on Federal Taxation. text 345.00 (0-8205-4286-5) Bender.

Major Taylor: The Extraordinary Career of a Champion Bicycle Racer. Andrew Ritchie. LC 95-44486. (Illus.). 336p. (C). 1996. reprint ed. pap. 15.95 (0-8018-5303-6) Johns Hopkins.

Major Technological Risk: An Assessment of Industrial Disasters. Patrick Lagadec. (Illus.). 536p. 1982. 235.00 (0-08-028913-4, Pub. by Pergamon Repr) Franklin.

***Major Telecommunications Companies of Europe, 2000.** 1999. pap. text 485.00 (1-86099-177-7, Pub. by G & W) Am Educ Systs.

***Major Telecommunications Companies of the Far East & Australasia, 2000.** 1999. pap. text 465.00 (1-86099-182-3, Pub. by G & W) Am Educ Systs.

Major Telecommunications Companies of the World, 1999. Ed. by V. Bentley et al. 1999. pap. 855.00 (1-86099-139-4) Am Educ Systs.

***Major Telecommunications Companies of the World, 2000.** 2000. pap. text 855.00 (1-86099-197-1, Pub. by G & W) Am Educ Systs.

Major Temples & Famous Statues of Deities. Robert G. Wilhelm. (Ancient Greek & Roman Resource Ser.). (Illus.). 100p. 24.95 (1-56696-129-7) Jackdaw.

Major, the Poacher & the Wonderful One-Trout River. Dayton O. Hyde. LC 97-70991. 160p. (J). 1998. pap. 9.95 (1-56397-691-9) Boyds Mills Pr.

Major Themes from the Minor Prophets. Gerald H. Twombly. (Adult Study Guide Ser.). 144p. (Orig.). 1981. pap. 7.99 (0-88469-132-2) BMH Bks.

Major Themes in Modern Arabic Thought: An Anthology. Ed. by Trevor J. LeGassick. (ARA.). 225p. (C). 1997. reprint ed. pap. text 30.00 (0-7881-3937-1) DIANE Pub.

Major Themes in Modern Philosophies of Judaism. Eliezer Berkovits. 1974. 25.00 (0-87068-264-4) Ktav.

Major Themes in the Reformed Tradition. Donald McKim. 470p. 1998. pap. 37.00 (1-57910-104-6) Wipf & Stock.

Major Themes in the Reformed Tradition. fac. ed. Ed. by Donald K. McKim. LC 91-36867. 467p. 1992. reprint ed. pap., per. 144.80 (0-7837-7964-X, 204772000008) Bks Demand.

Major Themes of the Bible. Foster H. Shannon. LC 90-81387. (Biblical Theology Ser.). 192p. 1990. pap. 12.95 (0-938462-14-8) Green Leaf CA.

Major Themes of the Qur'an. Fazlur Rahman. 190p. 1996. pap. 19.95 (0-614-21060-7, 1534) Kazi Pubns.

Major Themes of the Qur'an. 2nd ed. Fazlur Rahman. LC 79-54189. 1994. 25.00 (0-88297-051-8); pap. 16.00 (0-88297-046-1) Bibliotheca.

Major Theories of Personality Disorder. Ed. by John F. Clarkin & Mark F. Lenzenweger. LC 95-53935. 402p. 1996. lib. bdg. 46.00 (1-57230-082-5) Guilford Pubns.

***Major 300 World Furniture Manufacturers.** Stefan Wille & Aktrin Research Institute Staff. 2000. write for info. (1-894330-15-3) AKTRIN.

Major Timber Trees of Guyana: A Field Guide. A. M. Polak. (Tropenbos Technical Ser.: No. 2). (Illus.). 272p. 1992. pap. 65.00 (90-5113-013-9, Pub. by Backhuys Pubs) Balogh.

Major Timber Trees of Guyana: A Lens Key. M. Brunner et al. (Tropenbos Technical Ser.: No. 10). (Illus.). 184p. 1994. pap. 65.00 incl. disk (90-5113-022-8, Pub. by Backhuys Pubs) Balogh.

Major Timber Trees of Guyana: Timber Characteristics & Utilization. J. Gerard et al. (Tropenbos Technical Ser.: No. 15). (Illus.). 224p. 1996. pap. 40.00 (90-5113-027-9, Pub. by Backhuys Pubs) Balogh.

Major Topics on China & Japan: A Handbook for Teachers. Ed. by Harold C. Hinton & Marius B. Jansen. LC 78-10673. (Illus.). 326p. 1979. reprint ed. lib. bdg. 69.50 (0-313-20657-0, HIMT, Greenwood Pr) Greenwood.

Major Transitions in Evolution. John Maynard-Smith & Eors Szathmary. (Illus.). 360p. 1998. pap. text 29.95 (0-19-850294-X) OUP.

Major Transportation Companies of the Arab World, 1987-1988. Ed. by G. C. Bricault. (C). 1987. pap. text 146.50 (0-86010-737-X, Pub. by Graham & Trotman) Kluwer Academic.

Major Trends & Issues in Early Childhood Education: Challenges, Controversies & Insights. Ed. by Joan P. Isenberg & Mary Jalongo. LC 96-50440. (Early Childhood Education Ser.: Vol. 62). 240p. (C). 1997. text 54.00 (0-8077-3623-6) Tchrs Coll.

Major Trends & Issues in Early Childhood Education: Challenges, Controversies & Insights. Ed. by Joan P. Isenberg & Mary Jalongo. LC 96-50440. (Early Childhood Education Ser.: Vol. 62). 240p. (C). 1997. pap. text 25.95 (0-8077-3622-8) Tchrs Coll.

Major Trends Characterizing Human Settlements Development in the ECE Region. Ed. by Economic Commission for Europe Staff. LC 99-170199. 80p. 1998. 20.00 (92-1-116695-0) UN.

Major Trends in Jewish Mysticism. Gershom Scholem. 480p. 1995. pap. 16.00 (0-8052-1042-3) Schocken.

Major Trends in Mexican Philosophy. Universidad Nacional Autonoma de Mexico, Consejo T et al. LC 66-14624. 338p. reprint ed. pap. 104.80 (0-608-18678-3, 203191000077) Bks Demand.

Major Trends in Modern Hebrew Fiction. Isaiah Rabinovich. Tr. by M. Roston from HEB. LC 68-15035. 300p. reprint ed. pap. 93.00 (0-608-11050-7, 202014900016) Bks Demand.

Major Tricolore: Redecouverte de la France et des Francais par le Major W. Marmaduke Thompson. Pierre Daninos. (FRE., Illus.). 192p. 1968. pap. 19.95 (0-7859-5239-X) Fr & Eur.

Major Tricolore: Redecouverte de la France et des Francais par le Major W. Marmaduke Thompson. Pierre Daninos. (FRE., Illus.). 160p. 1971. 10.95 (0-8288-9172-9, F97941) Fr & Eur.

Major Tricolore, Comment Peut-On Etre Francais. Pierre Daninos. 11.50 (0-685-37286-3) Fr & Eur.

Major Tudor Authors: A Bio-Bibliographical Critical Sourcebook. Alan Hager. LC 96-25008. 528p. 1997. lib. bdg. 99.50 (0-313-29436-4, Greenwood Pr) Greenwood.

Major 20th-Century Writers: A Selection of Sketches from Contemporary Authors, 4 vols. Ed. by Bryan Ryan. 3300p. 1990. 295.00 (0-8103-7766-7) Gale.

Major Twentieth-Century Writers: A Selection of Sketches from Contemporary Authors, 5 vols. 2nd ed. Ed. by Bryan Ryan. LC 98-39995. 3124p. 1998. 315.00 (0-8103-8450-7) Gale.

Major 20th Century Writers: A Selection of Sketches from Contemporary Authors. 2nd ed. Kathleen Wilson & Bryan Ryan. LC 98-39995. 1998. write for info. (0-7876-2958-8); pap. write for info. (0-8103-8453-1) Gale.

Major U. S. Statistical Series: Definitions, Publications, Limitations. Jean S. Stratford & Juri Stratford. LC 92-16746. 150p. (C). 1992. pap. text 35.00 (0-8389-0600-1) ALA.

Major United Methodist Beliefs. rev. ed. Mack B. Stokes. (Orig.). 5.00 (0-687-08212-9) Abingdon.

Major United Methodist Beliefs. rev. ed. Mark B. Stokes. 1991. pap. text 4.95 (0-687-22924-3) Abingdon.

Major Unsolved Crimes. Phelan Powell. LC 99-24140. (Crime, Justice, & Punishment Ser.). (Illus.). (YA). (gr. 8 up). 1999. lib. bdg. 19.95 (0-7910-4277-4) Chelsea Hse.

***Major Vices.** Mary R. Daheim. 256p. (Orig.). 2000. mass mkt. 6.50 (0-380-77491-7, Avon Bks) Morrow Avon.

Major Victorian Poets, 001. Ed. by William E. Buckler. LC 72-5645. 650p. (Orig.). (C). 1973. pap. 13.96 (0-395-14024-2, RivEd) HM.

Major Violation: The Unbalanced Priorities in Athletics & Academics. Gary D. Funk. LC 90-20653. (Illus.). 192p. (Orig.). 1991. 17.95 (0-88011-441-X, PFUN0441) Human Kinetics.

Major William Boarman (1630-1709) Charles County, Maryland: His Descendants. Mary L. Donnelly. (Boarman - Bowman & Allied Families Ser.). (Illus.). 452p. 1991. 50.00 (0-939142-11-2) M L Donnelly.

Major Women Writers of Seventeenth-Century England. Ed. by James Fitzmaurice et al. LC 96-49138. 408p. (Orig.). 1997. text 52.50 (0-472-09609-5, 09609); pap. text 29.95 (0-472-06609-9, 06609) U of Mich Pr.

Major Works. Thomas Browne. Ed. & Intro. by C. A. Patrides. 560p. 1977. pap. 15.95 (0-14-043109-8, Penguin Classics) Viking Penguin.

Major Works of R. N. Elliott. Sarah E. Hutchinson & Stacey Sawyer. 1994. text 45.00 (0-07-413179-6, Irwn McGrw-H) McGrw-H Hghr Educ.

Major Works of Sri Aurobindo, 20 vols. Sri Aurobindo. 12500p. 1989. 250.00 (0-89071-336-7, Pub. by SAA) Acrpls Bks CO.

Major Works of Sri Aurobindo. Sri Aurobindo. 13200p. 1996. 300.00 (81-7058-469-8, Pub. by SAA) E-W Cultural Ctr.

Major Works of Sri Aurobindo, 10 vols., Set. Sri Aurobindo. (Life Companion Library). 1983. 125.00 (0-685-59363-0, Pub. by Madanlal Himatsinghka) MMC.

Major Works of Sri Aurobindo, 22 vols., Set. Sri Aurobindo. 1990. 300.00 (0-685-59362-2, Pub. by Sri Aurob Ashram Trust) Acrpls Bks CO.

Major World Nations. (Illus.). 94-144p. (J). (gr. 5). 1998. 1256.85 (0-7910-4788-1) Chelsea Hse.

Major Writers of Early American Literature: Introductions to Nine Major Writers. Ed. by Everett H. Emerson. LC 72-1378. 310p. 1972. pap. 16.95 (0-299-06194-9) U of Wis Pr.

Major Writers of Short Fiction: Stories & Commentaries. Ann Charters. LC 92-52525. 1461p. (C). 1993. pap. text 46.95 (0-312-07944-3) St Martin.

Major Writers of Short Fiction: Stories & Commentaries - Instructor's Manual. Ann Charters. 1993. teacher ed. 6.66 (0-312-08369-6) St Martin.

Major Writings of Germaine de Stael. Germaine De Stael. Tr. & Intro. by Vivian Folkenflik. 411p. (C). 1992. pap. text 21.00 (0-231-05587-0) Col U Pr.

M

An Asterisk (*) at the beginning of an entry indicates that the title is appearing for the first time.

Majorca: The Art of Living. Lanning Aldrich. 208p. 1998. 50.00 (*1-55670-847-5*) Stewart Tabori & Chang.

Majorcan Food & Cookery. Elizabeth Carter. (Illus.). 228p. (Orig.). 1989. pap. 18.00 (*0-907325-43-2*, Pub. by Prospect) Food Words.

Majorelle: An Artist in Morocco. Pierre Berge & Madison Cox. LC 99-30840. (Small Books of Great Gardens Ser.). 79p. 1999. text 18.95 (*0-86565-210-4*) Vendome.

Majoring in Engineering: How to Get from Your Freshman Year to Your First Job. John Garcia. LC 95-6749. 138p. 1995. pap. 10.00 (*0-374-52441-6*, Noonday) FS&G.

Majoring in High School: Survival Tips for Students. Carol Carter. LC 94-41603. 224p. (Orig.). (gr. 7-12). 1995. pap. 10.00 (*0-374-52430-0*, Noonday) FS&G.

Majoring in Law: How to Get from Your Freshman Year to Your First Job. Stefan Underhill. LC 95-11395. 134p. 1995. pap. 11.00 (*0-374-52442-4*, Noonday) FS&G.

Majoring in Nursing: From Prerequisites to Postgraduate Study & Beyond. Janet R. Katz. Ed. by Carol Carter. LC 98-15168. 144p. 1999. pap. 11.00 (*0-374-52567-6*, Noonday) FS&G.

Majoring in Psychology: Career Options for Undergraduates. Betsy Levonian Morgan & Ann J. Korschgen. LC 98-125166. 128p. (C). 1997. pap. text 9.00 (*0-205-27525-7*) Allyn.

***Majoring in Success: Building Your Career While Still in College.** Anthony Arcieri & Marianne Green. 128p. 1999. pap. 8.00 (*1-57509-046-5*) Octameron Assocs.

***Majoring in the Minors: A Glimpse of Baseball in a Small Town.** John G. Hall. 432p. 2000. reprint ed. text 60.00 (*1-882336-09-7*) OK Bylines.

Majoring in the Rest of Your Life. Ed. by Carol Carter. LC 99-15634. (Illus.). 332p. (C). 1999. pap. text 30.67 (*0-13-013154-7*) P-H.

Majoring in the Rest of Your Life: Career Secrets for College Students. rev. ed. Carol Carter. LC 95-8346. 244p. 1995. pap. 10.00 (*0-374-52451-3*) FS&G.

***Majoring in the Rest of Your Life: Career Secrets for College Students.** 3rd rev. ed. Carol Carter. LC 98-46504. (Illus.). 288p. 1999. pap. text 13.00 (*0-374-52602-8*) FS&G.

Majoritarian Solution: Re-Establishing America's Purpose. James Hufferd. 232p. (Orig.). (C). 1990. pap. text 22.50 (*0-8191-7749-0*); lib. bdg. 40.00 (*0-8191-7748-2*) U Pr of Amer.

Majorities & Minorities. Ed. by John W. Chapman & Alan Wertheimer. (Nomos Ser.: Vol. 32). (C). 1990. text 45.00 (*0-8147-1433-1*) NYU Pr.

Majority & Minority: The Dynamics of Race & Ethnicity in American Life. 6th ed. Norman R. Yetman. LC 98-20954. 592p. 1998. pap. 44.00 (*0-205-14569-8*) Allyn.

Majority Finds Its Past: Placing Women in History. Gerda Lerner. 250p. 1981. pap. 9.95 (*0-19-502899-6*) OUP.

Majority Leadership in the U. S. House. Barbara Sinclair. LC 83-278. 283p. 1983. reprint ed. pap. 87.80 (*0-608-07387-3*, 206761400009) Bks Demand.

Majority Minority Relationships. 4th ed. John E. Farley. LC 99-19735. 594p. 1999. 65.33 (*0-13-948860-X*, Pub. by P-H) S&S Trade.

Majority Motions: A Pocket Guide to Parliamentary Decision-Making (Majority Rules) Hermon W. Farwell. 1989. pap. 3.50 (*0-9604216-4-5*) High Pubs.

Majority of Scoundrels. Don Berry. LC 61-10198. 1990. reprint ed. pap. 7.95 (*0-89174-028-7*) Comstock Edns.

Majority Rule. Elaine Spitz. LC 83-23151. (Chatham House Series on Change in American Politics). 256p. (Orig.). reprint ed. pap. 79.40 (*0-8357-3453-6*, 203971400013) Bks Demand.

Majority Rule & the Judiciary. William L. Ransom. LC 78-166099. (American Constitutional & Legal History Ser). 1971. reprint ed. lib. bdg. 22.50 (*0-306-70205-3*) Da Capo.

Majority Rule or Minority Will: Adherence to Precedence on the U. S. Supreme Court. Harold J. Spaeth & Jeffrey A. Segal. LC 98-35793. (Illus.). 368p. (C). 1999. text 59.95 (*0-521-62424-X*) Cambridge U Pr.

Majority Rules: A Manual of Procedure for Most Groups. 2nd ed. Hermon W. Farwell. LC 88-91195. 120p. 1988. pap. 8.50 (*0-9604216-2-9*) High Pubs.

Majority Text: Essays & Reviews in the Continuing Debate. Intro. by Theodore P. Letis. 210p. (Orig.). (C). 1987. pap. 10.95 (*0-944355-00-5*) IBTS.

Majorization & the Lorenz Order: Brief Introduction. Barry C. Arnold. (Lecture Notes in Statistics Ser.: Vol. 43). vi, 122p. 1987. 42.95 (*0-387-96592-0*) Spr-Verlag.

***Majors: In Pursuit of Golf's Holy Grail.** John Feinstein. LC 99-11390. (Illus.). 480p. (gr. 8). 1999. 25.00 (*0-316-27971-4*) Little.

***Majors: In Pursuit of Golf's Holy Grail.** John Feinstein. 512p. 2000. pap. 14.95 (*0-316-27795-9*, Back Bay) Little.

Majors & Minors. Paul Laurence Dunbar. LC 76-83918. (Black Heritage Library Collection). 1977. 35.95 (*0-8369-8563-X*) Ayer.

Majors & Minors. Paul Laurence Dunbar. 1991. reprint ed. pap. 22.95 (*0-88143-123-0*) Ayer.

Majors & Minors. Paul Laurence Dunbar. (Notable American Authors Ser.). 1992. reprint ed. lib. bdg. 75.00 (*0-7812-2708-9*) Rprt Serv.

Majors Exploration: A Search & Find Guide for College & Career Direction. Diane L. Reeves & Bradbury. LC 98-47211. 234p. 1998. ring bd. 22.60 (*0-13-011379-4*) P-H.

Major's Jacobite. large type ed. Janis Coles. 1995. 27.99 (*0-7089-3290-8*) Ulverscroft.

***Major's Mistake.** Andrea Pickens. (Regency Romance Ser.). 2000. mass mkt. 4.99 (*0-451-20096-9*) Signet.

Major's Muslin. Marie-Louise Hall. 1998. pap. 4.99 (*0-373-30314-9*, 1-30314-8) Harlequin Bks.

Major's Muslin. large type ed. Marie-Louise Hall. (Mills & Boon Large Print Ser.). 350p. 1997. 23.99 (*0-263-15091-7*) Ulverscroft.

Majorski's Ghost: A Marty Fenton Novel. Robert Cohen. LC 95-12322. 1995. pap. 14.95 (*0-925168-39-4*) North Country.

Majuba, 1881. Ian Castle. (Illus.). 96p. 1996. pap. 14.95 (*1-85532-503-9*, Pub. by Ospry) Stackpole.

Majuro, a Village in the Marshall Islands. Alexander Spoehr. (Field Museum of Natural History Ser.: Vol. 39). (Illus.). 1949. 25.00 (*0-527-01895-3*) Periodicals Srv.

Majyk by Design. Esther Friesner. 256p. (Orig.). 1994. mass mkt. 4.99 (*0-441-00116-5*) Ace Bks.

MAK Architecture Guide. R. M. Schindler. Ed. by Peter Noever. (Museum Guides Ser.). (Illus.). 114p. 1997. pap. 14.95 (*3-7913-1675-3*, Pub. by Prestel) te Neues.

MAK Architecture Guide: RM Schindler. (Illus.). 114p. (Orig.). 1996. pap. 14.95 (*3-7913-1575-7*, Pub. by Prestel) te Neues.

MAK-Austrian Museum of Applied Arts, Vienna. Ed. by Peter Noever. (Museum Guides Ser.). (Illus.). 176p. (Orig.). 1996. pap. 14.95 (*3-7913-1472-6*, Pub. by Prestel) te Neues.

***Makah.** Jeanne M. Eder. LC 99-23350. (Indian Nations Ser.). (Illus.). 48p. (ps-3). 1999. 25.69 (*0-8172-5459-5*) Raintree Steck-V.

Makah Indians. Elizabeth Colson. LC 73-15051. (Illus.). 308p. 1974. reprint ed. lib. bdg. 35.00 (*0-8371-7153-9*, COMI, Greenwood Pr) Greenwood.

***Makai.** Kathleen Tyau. 296p. 2000. pap. 14.00 (*0-8070-8345-3*) Beacon Pr.

***Makai.** Kathleen Tyau. LC 99-14576. 256p. 1999. text 23.00 (*0-374-20000-9*) FS&G.

Makalienski's Bones. large type ed. Jan Webster. 416p. 1996. 27.99 (*0-7089-3621-0*) Ulverscroft.

Makam: The Modal Practice in Turkish Art Music. Karl Signell. (Music Reprint Ser.). 220p. 1985. reprint ed. 27.50 (*0-306-76248-X*) Da Capo.

Makamat of Al Hariri. Al Hariri. 528p. 1986. 350.00 (*1-85077-141-3*, Pub. by Darf Pubs Ltd) St Mut.

Makana Aloha: Gift of Love. Barbara S. McDonagh. LC TXU 635-646. 24p. (J). (gr. k-8). 1994. 12.95 (*0-9643781-0-8*) Liko Pubng.

***Makao Government & Business Contacts Handbook: Strategic Government & Business Contacts for Conducting Succesful Business, Export-Import & Investment Activity.** International Business Publications, USA Staff & Global Investment Center, USA Staff. (World Export-Import & Business Library: 130). (Illus.). 250p. 2000. pap. 99.95 (*0-7397-6145-5*) Intl Business Pubns.

***Makarie und Mercurius: Goethes Wilhelm Meisters Wanderjahre Als Hermetischer Roman.** Diethelm Bruggemann. Ed. by Katharina Mommsen. (Germanic Studies in America), 158p. 1999. 30.95 (*3-906763-44-7*, Pub. by P Lang) P Lang Pubng.

Makarim Al-Akhlag: A Treatise on Alishir Navar. Khavandmir. (Gibb Memorial New Ser.: Vol. 27). 1979. 29.00 (*0-906094-11-9*, Pub. by Aris & Phillips) David Brown.

***Makars: An Anthology.** Ed. & Intro. by Jackie Tasioulas. 600p. 1999. pap. 16.00 (*0-86241-820-8*, Pub. by Canongate Books) Interlink Pub.

Makar's Dream, & Other Stories. Vladimir G. Korolenko. Tr. by Marian Fell from RUS. LC 74-163037. (Short Story Index Reprint Ser.). 1977. reprint ed. 19.95 (*0-8369-3951-4*) Ayer.

Makashe's African Village. Christie Spell. Ed. by Kali Sichen. LC 89-64456. (Illus.). (J). (gr. k-8). 1989. pap. 9.95 (*0-916299-14-7*) North Scale Co.

Makashe's Chicken. Christie Spell. Ed. by Kali Sichen. (Illus.). (J). (gr. k-8). 1994. pap. 9.95 (*0-916299-15-5*) North Scale Co.

Makawehi Dunes & Sinkhole. Faith M. Roelofs. (Exploring Kauai: Field Site Guides for Teachers Ser.). 1993. pap. write for info. (*1-882163-11-7*) Moanalua Grdns Fnd.

Makbara. Juan Goytisolo. (Masks Ser.). 270p. 1994. pap. 14.99 (*1-85242-266-1*) Serpents Tail.

Makbeth: An Update of Shakespeare. Richard Schechner. (Illus.). 54p. 1978. pap. 4.00 (*0-88680-124-9*) I E Clark.

Makbeth: An Update of Shakespeare. Richard Schechner. (Illus.). 54p. 1978. pap. 7.50 (*0-88680-125-7*) I E Clark.

Make . . . Repeats. Skillman C. Hunter. 1992. pap. write for info. (*1-882351-00-2*) Acrobytes Sftware.

Make-a-Bible-Verse Acrostics. Peggy Cupp & Virginia Mueller. Ed. by Pat Fittro. 48p. 1996. pap. 1.49 (*0-7847-0496-1*, 02596) Standard Pub.

***Make a Book: Six Different Books to Make, Write & Illustrate.** Deborah Jaffe. (Illus.). 32p. (J). (gr. 3 up). 2000. pap. 14.99 (*0-525-46446-8*, Dutton Child) Peng Put Young Read.

Make a Calendar: Early Learning Workbooks. Peter M. Spizzirri. Ed. by Linda Spizzirri. (Illus.). 32p. (J). (ps-2). 1997. pap. 2.95 (*0-86545-234-2*) Spizzirri.

Make A Castle. Sterling Publishing Staff. (J). 1999. pap. text 5.95 (*0-8069-1945-0*) Sterling.

***Make a Change Opposites.** Margot Thompson. 2000. 8.95 (*0-7613-1043-6*) Millbrook Pr.

Make a Deal with the IRS: 1997 Edition. rev. ed. Harry Charles. (Illus.). 148p. (Orig.). 1996. pap. 12.95 (*0-9645776-1-5*) Cairo Busn Pr.

Make a Difference. Henry W. Foster. LC 96-48006. 1997. 22.50 (*0-684-82685-2*) S&S Trade.

Make a Difference: A Directory of Youth Opportunities. Michael Groth. 82p. (YA). 1998. pap. 4.50 (*1-887418-05-9*) United Way MN.

***Make a Difference: How One Man Helped to Solve America's Poverty Problem.** Gary MacDougal. LC 99-55710. 368p. 2000. text 29.95 (*0-312-25223-4*, Thomas Dunne) St Martin.

***Make a Difference: Songbook.** Composed by Steve Angrisano. 104p. 1998. pap. 8.95 (*1-57992-001-2*) OR Catholic.

Make a Doll House. Balloon Books Staff. 1999. pap. text 5.95 (*0-8069-3792-0*) Sterling.

***Make a Doll's Shop: Press Out & Play.** Ed. by Sterling Publishing Staff. (Illus.). (J). 2000. pap. 5.95 (*0-8069-2669-4*) Sterling.

Make-a-Face. Jane Byrne Stevenson. (Illus.). 64p. (J). (gr. 1-5). 1998. pap. 16.95 (*1-895897-58-0*) Somerville Hse.

Make-a-Face: Face & Body Painting Kit for Kids of All Ages. Sharon E. McKay & Jane B. Stevenson. (Illus.). 64p. (J). (gr. k up). 1996. spiral bd. 15.95 (*0-8362-1074-3*) Andrews & McMeel.

Make a Family - Make Their Wardrobe. Paulette Morrissey. (Illus.). 1999. spiral bd. 15.95 (*1-893502-10-4*) Morrissey Co.

Make a Glad Sound. Herbert Rothgarber. 1974. 5.00 (*0-913334-17-0*, CM1021) Consort Music.

***Make a Joyful Noise.** Bobby Jones & Lesley Sussman. LC 00-40254. (Illus.). 224p. 2000. 22.95 (*0-312-25258-7*) St Martin.

Make a Joyful Noise. Frank Von Christierson. LC 87-61196. 152p. 1987. pap. 8.00 (*0-936609-05-2*) QED Ft Bragg.

Make a Joyful Noise: A Pop-Up Book of Christmas Carols. Francesca Crespi. (Illus.). 5p. (J). (ps up). 1997. per. 14.95 (*0-689-81526-3*) Aladdin.

Make a Joyful Noise: A Pop-Up Book of Christmas Carols. Francesca Crespi. (J). 1997. write for info. (*0-614-29304-9*) Litle Simon.

Make a Joyful Noise unto the Lord. Magrate Yap. 1990. spiral bd. 15.95 (*0-89985-300-5*) Christ for the Nations.

Make a Joyful Sound: Poems for Children by African-American Poets. Ed. by Deborah Slier. LC 90-26284. 112p. (J). 1991. 12.95 (*1-56288-000-4*) Checkerboard.

Make a Joyful Sound: Poems for Children by African-American Poets. Ed. by Deborah Slier. LC 95-24413. (Illus.). 112p. (J). (ps-3). 1996. 13.95 (*0-590-67432-3*, Cartwheel) Scholastic Inc.

Make a Joyful Table: A Healthy Exchanges Cookbook. JoAnna M. Lund et al. LC 99-17055. (Illus.). 336p. 1999. 22.95 (*0-399-14527-3*, G P Putnam) Peng Put Young Read.

Make a Kite! Peter Murray. LC 93-49604. (Umbrella Bks.). (Illus.). 24p. (J). (gr. 2-6). 1998. lib. bdg. 21.36 (*1-56766-083-5*) Childs World.

***Make a Life, Not Just a Living.** 2000. pap. text 8.99 (*0-8054-1984-5*) Broadman.

Make a Mil-Yen: Teaching English in Japan. Don Best. LC 93-44380. 176p. (Orig.). 1994. pap. 14.95 (*1-880656-11-6*) Stone Bridge Pr.

Make-a-Mix. expanded rev. ed. Karine Eliason et al. LC 95-36622. (Illus.). 332p. 1995. pap. 17.95 (*1-55561-073-0*) Fisher Bks.

Make-A-Mix Cookery: How to Make Your Own Mixes. Karine Eliason. 1978. write for info. (*0-89586-008-2*) Berkley Pub.

***Make a Name for Yourself.** Robin Fisher Roffer. LC 00-36040. 2000. write for info. (*0-7679-0492-3*) Broadway BDD.

***Make a Name for Yourself: Eight Steps for Creating an Unforgettable Personal Brand of Success.** Robin Fisher Roffer. 272p. 2000. 23.95 (*0-7679-0491-5*) Broadway BDD.

Make a New Sound. George Self. 1976. pap. 25.00 (*0-900938-46-3*, UE26909) Eur-Am Music.

Make a Note of It: Wit & Wisdom from Fund Raisers for Fund Raisers. William A. Olcott. LC 97-51685. 138p. 1998. 24.95 (*1-56625-102-8*) Bonus Books.

Make-a-Play. Russell Field et al. (NHL Coolest Books on Earth Ser.). 32p. (J). (gr. 3 up). 1999. pap. 9.99 (*1-58184-038-1*) Somerville Hse.

Make a Quilt in a Day Log Cabin. 20th rev. ed. Eleanor Burns. (Illus.). 96p. 1998. pap. 18.95 (*0-922705-98-4*) Quilt Day.

Make a Rainbow & 15 Inspirations. 88p. (Orig.). 1993. pap. 10.95 (*0-7692-1040-6*, VF1969) Wrner Bros.

Make a Rainbow & 9 EP Coates: Easy Piano. 47p. 1993. pap. 8.95 (*0-7692-1152-6*, PF0854) Wrner Bros.

Make a Salad Face. David Drew. LC 92-34335. (Illus.). (J). 1993. 2.50 (*0-383-03640-2*) SRA McGraw.

***Make-a-Saurus: My Life with Raptors & Other Dinosaurs.** Brian Cooley & Mary Ann Wilson. (Illus.). 64p. (J). (gr. 3-6). 2000. lib. bdg. 24.95 (*1-55037-645-4*, Pub. by Annick Pr); per. 14.95 (*1-55037-644-6*, Pub. by Annick Pr) Firefly Bks Ltd.

Make a Scrapbook see Hacen un Album de Recortes

Make a Scrapbook. Derek Prime. (Sarah & Paul Ser.). (J). 3.99 (*1-871676-35-5*, Pub. by Christian Focus) Spring Arbor Dist.

Make a Shield from Wisdom: Selected Verses from Nasir-i Khusraw's Divan. Tr. & Intro. by Annemarie Schimmel. LC 92-19645. (Islamic Texts & Contexts Ser.). (ENG & PER.). 100p. 1993. 49.95 (*0-7103-0455-2*, B0086) Routledge.

Make a Small House. Sterling Publishing Staff. (Illus.). 8p. (J). (gr. k-1). 1999. pap. text 2.95 (*0-8069-1947-7*) Sterling.

Make a Small Treehouse. Sterling Publishing Staff. (Balloon Books). 1999. pap. text 2.95 (*0-8069-1949-3*) Strlng Pub CA.

Make a Splash, NO. 2. Janet Garman. LC 97-47764. (Home Run Rudy Ser.). 128p. (J). (gr. 3-7). 1998. 4.99 (*0-7814-3018-6*, Chariot Bks) Chariot Victor.

Make a Splash! Care about the Ocean. Thompson Yardley. LC 91-22963. (Lighter Look Bk.). (Illus.). 40p. (J). (gr. 2-6). 1992. lib. bdg. 20.90 (*1-56294-147-X*) Millbrook Pr.

Make a Splash: Swimming Holes & Waterfalls of the Green Mountains. Ascanio Condivi. LC 98-91299. (Travel Guide Ser.). 112 p. 1998. write for info. (*0-9663556-0-1*) Master Studios.

Make a Treat with Wheat. 3rd ed. Hazel Richards. 67p. 1968. reprint ed. spiral bd. 6.95 (*0-9670776-0-5*) L G Richards.

Make a Way Somehow: African-American Life in a Northern Community, 1790-1965. Kathryn Grover. (Illus.). 344p. 1994. text 45.00 (*0-8156-2626-6*); pap. text 19.95 (*0-8156-2627-4*) Syracuse U Pr.

Make a Way Somehow: African Americans in Geneva, New York 1790-1965. Kathryn Grover. LC 91-72024. (Illus.). (Orig.). 1991. pap. 9.00 (*0-9613821-4-7*) Geneva Hist Soc Mus.

Make a Windsor Chair with Michael Dunbar. Michael Dunbar. LC 83-50681. (Illus.). 176p. 1985. pap. 19.95 (*0-918804-21-3*) Taunton.

***Make a Wish for Me.** Lenora Mattingly Weber. (Beany Malone Ser.). 286p. (J). 1999. reprint ed. pap. 12.95 (*0-9639607-8-4*) Image Cascade.

***Make a Wish, Honey Bear!** Marcus Pfister. (Illus.). 32p. (J). (gr. k-3). 1999. lib. bdg. 15.88 (*0-7358-1244-6*, Pub. by North-South Bks NYC) Chronicle Bks.

***Make a Wish, Honey Bear!** Marcus Pfister. Tr. by Sibylle Kazeroid. (Illus.). 32p. (J). (ps-k). 1999. 15.95 (*0-7358-1243-8*, Pub. by North-South Bks NYC) Chronicle Bks.

Make a Wish, Molly. Barbara Cohen. (J). 1994. pap. 4.50 (*0-440-91018-8*) BDD Bks Young Read.

Make a Wish, Molly. Barbara Cohen. 48p. (J). (gr. 4-7). 1995. pap. 3.50 (*0-440-41058-4*) Dell.

Make a Wish, Molly. Barbara Cohen. (J). 1995. 8.95 (*0-606-07831-2*) Turtleback.

Make a Zine! A Guide to Self-Publishing Disguised As a Book on How to Produce a Zine. Bill Brent. LC 97-70048. (Illus.). 192p. (Orig.). 1997. pap. 10.00 (*0-9637401-4-8*) Black Books.

Make-Ahead Salads. Jean Pare. 80p. 1998. pap. 7.99 (*1-896891-22-5*) Companys Coming.

Make Alike Recipes Book see Secret Make Alike Recipes

Make All America a School: Mind Extension University, the Education Network. Glenn R. Jones. 75p. 1990. pap. 9.95 (*0-945373-01-5*) Jones Twenty-First Century Ltd.

Make an Appointment with Yourself: Simple Steps to Positive Self-Esteem. Maida Berenblatt & Alena J. Berenblatt. LC 94-31966. 120p. (Orig.). 1994. pap. 7.95 (*1-55874-319-7*, 3197) Health Comm.

Make an Interactive Science Museum: Hands-On Exhibits. Robert Gardner. LC 95-22078. (J). 1995. text. write for info. (*0-07-022866-3*) McGraw-Hill Prof.

Make an Interactive Science Museum: Hands-On Exhibits. Robert Gardner. LC 95-22078. (Illus.). 128p. (J). (gr. 4-8). 1995. pap. 16.95 (*0-07-022867-1*) McGraw-Hill Prof.

Make & Break. Michael Frayn. 104p. (C). 1988. pap. write for info. (*0-413-47790-8*, A0164, Methuen Drama) Methn.

Make & Color Halloween Decoration. Jill E. Osborne. (J). (ps-3). 1989. pap. 1.95 (*0-89375-644-X*) Troll Communs.

Make & Take Technology. Marsha Lifter & Marian E. Adams. LC 98-170771. 223 p. 1997. write for info. (*1-57369-096-1*) Visions Tech.

Make Anger Your Ally. Neil C. Warren. LC 93-19663. 1993. pap. 10.99 (*1-56179-121-0*) Focus Family.

Make Anger Your Ally. Neil Clark Warren. 1999. mass mkt. 6.99 (*1-56179-707-3*) Focus Family.

Make Any Block, Any Size: Easy Drawing Method, Unlimited Pattern Possibilities, Sensational Quilt Designs. Joen Wolfrom. Ed. by Liz Aieloski & Joyce Lytle. LC 98-37242. 144p. 1999. pap. 27.95 (*1-57120-068-1*, 10185) C & T Pub.

Make Audits Pay: Leveraging the Audit into Consulting Services. Ed. by Linda C. Delahanty. (AICPA Practice Aid Series). 245p. 1999. pap. 50.00 (*0-87051-247-1*, 006704) Am Inst CPA.

Make Barrettes & More: 16 Projects for Creating Beautiful Jewelry. Jo Moody. (Make Jewelry Ser.). (Illus.). 96p. 1997. pap. 15.99 (*1-56496-285-7*, Quarry Bks) Rockport Pubs.

Make Beliefs: A Gift for Your Imagination. 2nd ed. Bill Zimmerman. Tr. by Teodorina B. Zimmerman. LC 86-80832. (ENG & SPA., Illus.). 128p. (Orig.). (YA). 1994. pap. text 8.50 (*0-935966-03-X*) Guarionex Pr.

Make Beliefs for Kids. Bill Zimmerman. (Illus.). 96p. (Orig.). (J). (gr. k). 1996. pap. 9.95 (*0-8362-1048-4*) Andrews & McMeel.

Make Beliefs for Kids of All Ages. 2nd ed. Bill Zimmerman. (Illus.). 106p. (J). (gr. 7-9). 1998. reprint ed. pap., wbk. ed. 8.50 (*0-935966-10-2*) Guarionex Pr.

Make Beliefs for Kids of All Ages. 2nd ed. Bill Zimmerman. (Illus.). 96p. 1999. reprint ed. pap. 8.50 (*0-935966-13-7*) Guarionex Pr.

Make Believe. Chanie Flam. (Goldie Gold Board Book Ser.: Vol. 3). (Illus.). (J). (ps-1). bds. 4.95 (*1-58330-027-9*) Feldheim.

Make Believe. Susan Beth Pfeffer. 144p. (J). (gr. 4-7). 1995. 14.95 (*0-8050-1754-2*, Bks Young Read) H Holt & Co.

***Make Believe.** Joanna Scott. LC 99-31277. 272p. (gr. 8). 2000. 23.95 (*0-316-77616-5*) Little.

Make Believe. Teresa Warfield. 336p. (Orig.). 1995. mass mkt. 4.99 (*0-515-11610-6*, Jove) Berkley Pub.

Make-Believe. large type ed. Faith Baldwin. LC 90-44506. 371p. 1990. reprint ed. lib. bdg. 19.95 (*1-56054-053-2*) Thorndike Pr.

Make Believe. Ed. & Illus. by Better Homes & Gardens. (Max the Dragon Project Book Ser.). 32p. (J). (gr. k-3). 1991. reprint ed. lib. bdg. 12.95 (*1-878363-32-8*) Forest Hse.

M

M

*Make Believe: A Novel. Joanna Scott. (Illus.). 272p. 2001. pap. 13.95 (0-316-77666-1, Back Bay) Little.
*Make Believe: A Novel. Joanna Scott. LC 00-39637. 2000. pap. write for info. (0-7838-9086-9, G K Hall & Co) Mac Lib Ref.
Make Believe: A True Story. Diana Athill. LC 93-47421. 130p. 1994. 18.00 (1-883642-21-3) Steerforth Pr.
Make-Believe: The Broadway Musical in the 1920s. Ethan Mordden. LC 96-40962. 272p. 1997. 30.00 (0-19-510594-X) OUP.
Make-Believe Ball Player. Alfred Slote. LC 89-30598. (Illus.). 112p. (J). (gr. 2-5). 1989. 13.00 (0-397-32285-2); lib. bdg. 12.89 (0-397-32286-0) HarpC Child Bks.
Make-Believe Ball Player. Alfred Slote. LC 89-30598. (Trophy Bk.). 112p. (J). (gr. 4-7). 1992. pap. 4.95 (0-06-440425-0, HarpTrophy) HarpC Child Bks.
Make-Believe Ball Player. Alfred Slote. 1992. 9.05 (0-606-01073-4, Pub. by Turtleback) Demco.
Make-believe Ballrooms. Peter J. Smith. LC 88-39292. 1990. pap. 9.95 (0-87113-367-9, Atlntc Mnthly) Grove-Atltic.
Make-Believe Bride. Alaina Hawthorne. (Romance Ser.: No. 1164). 1996. per. 3.25 (0-373-19164-2, 1-19164-2) Silhouette.
Make Believe Engagement (Bride's Bay) Day Leclaire. LC 96-2363. (Romance Ser.). 185p. 1996. per. 3.25 (0-373-03404-0, 1-03404-0) Harlequin Bks.
Make-Believe Face: Growing up "Born-Again" Inside the Religious Right. unabridged ed. L. L. Morton. 250p. (Orig.). 1993. pap. 7.95 (0-9634673-0-1) Indep-Hse Pr.
Make-Believe Family. large type ed. Elizabeth Duke. 288p. 1996. 23.99 (0-263-14383-X, Pub. by Mills & Boon) Ulverscroft.
*Make-Believe Games & Activities for Imaginative Play: A Book for Parents, Teachers & the Young Children in Their Lives. Dorothy G. Singer & Jerome L. Singer. LC 00-28444. (Illus.). 180p. 2000. pap. 19.95 (1-55798-717-3, 441-7173, Magination Press) Am Psychol.
Make-Believe Honeymoon. Kristine Rolofson. LC 95-22322. 219p. 1995. mass mkt. 3.25 (0-373-25660-4, 1-25660-1) Harlequin Bks.
Make-Believe Husband. 20th ed. Linda Varner. (Romance Ser.). 1998. per. 3.50 (0-373-19310-6, 1-19310-1) Silhouette.
Make-Believe Marriage. Renee Roszel. LC 95-13537. (Romance Ser.). 184p. 1995. per. 2.99 (0-373-03370-2, 1-03370-3) Harlequin Bks.
Make-Believe Marriage. Renee Roszel. (Promo Ser.). 1999. per. 4.50 (0-373-21982-2, 1-21982-3) Harlequin Bks.
Make-Believe Media: The Politics of Entertainment. 4th ed. Michael J. Parenti. LC 90-63541. 241p. (Orig.). (C). 1991. pap. text 24.95 (0-312-05603-6) St Martin.
Make-Believe Mom. Muriel Jensen. (American Romance Ser.). 1994. per. 3.50 (0-373-16534-X) Harlequin Bks.
Make-Believe Mom. Muriel Jensen. (Promo Ser.). 1999. per. 4.50 (0-373-21953-9, 1-21953-4) Harlequin Bks.
Make-Believe Mom. Elizabeth Sites. (Romance Ser.). 1996. per. 3.25 (0-373-19136-7, 1-19136-0) Silhouette.
Make-Believe Mother. large type ed. Pamela Bauer & Judy Kaye. Vol. 432. 250p. 1999. per. 3.50 (0-373-15832-7, 1-15832-8, Mira Bks) Harlequin Bks.
Make-Believe Mother: Kids & Kisses. Pamela Bauer & Judy Kaye. (Kids & Kisses Ser.). 1998. per. 3.50 (0-373-03538-1, 1-03538-5, Mira Bks) Harlequin Bks.
Make-Believe Mother: Kids & Kisses. large type ed. Pamela Bauer & Judy Kaye. (Larger Print Ser.). 1999. per. 3.50 (0-373-15784-3, 1-15784-1) Harlequin Bks.
*Make Believe Mystery. Carolyn Keene. (Nancy Drew Notebooks: No. 36). 80p. (J). (gr. 2-4). 2000. per. 3.99 (0-671-04267-X, Minstrel Bks) PB.
Make-Believe Songs. Don Williams et al. LC 98-171653. (Disney Babies Ser.). (J). 1998. write for info. (0-7853-2722-3) Pubns Intl Ltd.
Make Believe with Barney. Linda C. Dowdy. LC 96-83767. (Barney Ser.). (Illus.). 14p. (J). (ps-3). 1996. bds. 7.95 (1-57064-094-7) Lyrick Pub.
Make Believe World of Maxfield Parrish. Alma Gilbert. LC 97-14112. (Illus.). 84p. (Orig.). 1997. pap. 17.95 (0-89815-936-9) Ten Speed Pr.
Make-Believers. Berry Fleming. LC 87-62813. 428p. 1988. 24.95 (0-933256-71-X) Second Chance.
Make Better Home Videos. David Owen. 192p. (Orig.). 1993. pap. 12.95 (0-572-01933-5, Pub. by W Foulsham) Trans-Atl Phila.
Make Better Videos with Your Camcorder. Erwin K. Thomas. 192p. 1991. 21.95 (0-8306-2183-0); pap. 12.95 (0-8306-2182-2) McGraw-Hill Prof.
Make Bold to Be Ashamed. Eugen Rosenstock-Huessy. (Eugen Rosenstock-Huessy Lectures: Vol. 7). 37p. 1997. pap. 18.00 incl. audio (0-912148-26-8) Argo Bks.
Make Bracelets: 16 Projects for Creating Beautiful Jewelry. Jo Moody. (Make Jewelry Ser.). (Illus.). 96p. 1997. pap. 15.99 (1-56496-272-5, Quarry Bks) Rockport Pubs.
Make Cards! Kim Solga. (Art & Activities for Kids Ser.). (Illus.). 48p. (J). (gr. 4-7). 1992. 11.99 (0-89134-481-0, 30425, North Lght Bks) F & W Pubns Inc.
Make Clothes Fun! Kim Solga. (Art & Activities for Kids Ser.). (Illus.). 48p. (J). (gr. 1-6). 1992. 11.95 (0-89134-421-7, 30377, North Lght Bks) F & W Pubns Inc.
Make Cloud Shades, Yes You Can! Claira Dobry. (Illus.). 126p. 1985. spiral bd. 19.95 (0-9615218-1-3); per. 19.95 (0-9615218-0-5) Dobry Enter.
Make Costumes! for Creative Play. Priscilla Hershberger. (Art & Activities for Kids Ser.). (Illus.). 48p. (J). (gr. 4-7). 1992. 11.99 (0-89134-450-0, 30424, North Lght Bks) F & W Pubns Inc.
Make Custom Drapery, Yes You Can! Claira Dobry. (Illus.). 195p. 1982. spiral bd. 19.95 (0-9615218-3-X); per. 19.95 (0-9615218-2-1) Dobry Enter.
Make Death Love Me. Ruth Rendell. lib. bdg. 19.95 (0-8488-2018-5) Amereon Ltd.
Make Death Love Me. Ruth Rendell. 1998. lib. bdg. 23.95 (1-56723-150-0, 159) Yestermorrow.
*Make Disciples! Reaching the Postmodern World for Christ. Terry A. Bowland. LC 99-49164. 1999. pap. write for info. (0-89900-856-9) College Pr Pub.
Make Doll Shoes: Workbook One, Vol. I. Lyn Alexander. LC 90-179616. Vol. I. (Illus.). 40p. (C). 1985. pap. text 5.95 (0-87588-335-4) Hobby Hse.
Make Doll Shoes: Workbook Two, Vol. II. Lyn Alexander. Vol. II. (Illus.). 40p. (C). 1985. pap. text 5.95 (0-87588-336-2) Hobby Hse.
Make Dollars with Your Computer. 195p. (Orig.). 1993. pap. 14.95 (1-57327-003-2, M Pr CA) Busn Concepts.
Make Earrings: 16 Projects for Creating Beautiful Jewelry. Jo Moody. (Make Jewelry Ser.). (Illus.). 96p. 1997. pap. 15.99 (1-56496-273-3, Quarry Bks) Rockport Pubs.
Make 'Em Pay. George Hayduke. 224p. 1986, reprint ed. pap. 7.95 (0-8184-0421-3) Carol Pub Group.
Make 'Em Pay: Ultimate Revenge Techniques from the Master Trickster. George Hayduke. 224p. 1986. text 19.95 (0-87364-351-8) Paladin Pr.
Make 'Em Talk: Principles of Military Interrogation. Patrick McDonald. 80p. 1993. pap. 16.00 (0-87364-728-9) Paladin Pr.
*Make Every Minute Count: 750 Tips & Strategies to Revolutionize How You Manage Your Time. Harlan Lane & Christian Wayser. (Illus.). 2000. pap. 14.95 (1-56924-613-0) Marlowe & Co.
Make Family Time Prime Time: Fun Ways to Build Faith in Your Family. Denise C. Yribarren & DeAnn L. Koestner. LC 96-61095. 112p. 1997. pap. 12.95 (0-89622-712-X) Twenty-Third.
Make Fantastic Home Videos: How Anyone Can Shoot Great Videos! John Fuller. (Illus.). 96p. 1996. pap. 12.95 (0-936262-37-0) Amherst Media.
Make Fashion Magic. Shell Kepler. LC 96-69674. (Illus.). 128p. 1996. pap. 14.95 (0-8487-1553-5) Oxmoor Hse.
Make Fax-on-Demand Dollars: With a Low Cost, Automated, Information Sales Profit Center & Robot Receptionist. unabridged ed. Gary Yasumura. 80p. 1997. pap. 18.95 (0-9660299-1-7, PB2) CyberInk.
Make Five Bible Models. Charlotte Stowell & Gordon Stowell. (Illus.). 32p. (J). 1997. pap. 13.95 (0-8192-1678-X) Morehouse Pub.
Make Four Million Dollars by Next Thursday! Stephen Manes. (Illus.). 96p. (J). 1996. pap. 4.50 (0-440-41370-2) BDD Bks Young Read.
Make Four Million Dollars by Next Thursday! Stephen Manes. 1996. 9.19 (0-606-00584-6, Pub. by Turtleback) Demco.
Make Friends with Mother Goose: Black & White Nellie Edge I Can Read & Sing Big Book, Vol. II. Illus. by Melissa Saylor. (J). (ps-2). 1991. pap. text 22.00 (0-922053-24-3) N Edge Res.
Make Friends with Mother Goose Big Book: Black & White Nellie Edge I Can Read & Sing Big Book, Vol. I. Illus. by Melissa Saylor. (J). (ps-2). 1988. pap. text 22.00 (0-922053-11-1) N Edge Res.
Make Friends with Your Feelings. 2nd rev. ed. Martha B. Beveridge. Ed. by Terrisa Bruce-Phipps. 20p. 1994. pap. 3.50 (1-889237-09-4) Options Now.
Make Friends with Your Shadow: How to Accept & Use Positively the Negative Side of Your Personality. William A. Miller. LC 80-67793. 144p. (Orig.). 1981. pap. 12.99 (0-8066-1855-8, 10-4238, Augsburg) Augsburg Fortress.
Make Friends, Zachary! Muriel Blaustein. LC 88-6308. (Illus.). 32p. (J). (ps-2). 1990. 12.95 (0-06-020545-8) HarpC Child Bks.
Make Gentle the Life of This World: The Vision of Robert F. Kennedy. Robert F. Kennedy. Ed. & Intro. by Maxwell Taylor Kennedy. LC 98-55988. 208p. 1999. pap. 11.00 (0-7679-0371-4) Broadway BDD.
Make Gentle the Life of This World: The Vision of Robert F. Kennedy. Robert F. Kennedy. Ed. by Maxwell Taylor Kennedy. LC 97-45018. (Illus.). 192p. (C). 1998. 20.00 (0-15-100356-4) Harcourt.
*Make Girls Count in School-to-Work Programs. Gina Salazar. 88p. 1998. pap. text 35.00 (1-929573-01-4) Girls Count.
Make Haste, My Beloved. Frances J. Roberts. 1978. 11.99 (0-932814-25-5); pap. 8.50 (0-932814-26-3) Kings Farspan.
Make Haste Slowly: Moderates, Conservatives, & School Desegregation in Houston. William H. Kellar. LC 98-35020. (Centennial Series of the Association of Former Students, Texas A&M University: Vol. 80). (Illus.). 256p. 1999. 38.95 (0-89096-818-7) Tex A&M Univ Pr.
Make His Praise Glorious. J. Kip Givens. 1994. pap. 4.95 (0-9641158-0-8) Redemp Fellowship.
*Make History: Ancient Egypt. Nancy Fister & Charlene Olexiewicz. (Illus.). 32p. (J). (gr. 2-6). 1999. pap. 9.95 (0-7373-0153-8, 01538W) NTC Contemp Pub Co.
Make-in-a-Minute Messages. Jill Eckhardt & Janet Skiles. 112p. teacher ed. 12.99 (0-86653-746-5, GA1461) Good Apple.
*Make It! Engineering the Manufacturing Solution. John Garside. LC 99-30644. 273p. 1999. text 54.95 (0-7506-4569-5) Buttrwrth-Heinemann.
Make It - II: An Index to Projects & Materials, 1974-1987. Mary E. Heim. LC 88-11503. 552p. 1989. 52.00 (0-8108-2125-7) Scarecrow.
Make It a Merry Christmas! Nancy Jensen. (Illus.). (J). (gr. 2-6). 1997. pap. 9.99 (1-57584-177-0, RD Childrens) Rdrs Digest.
Make It a Winning Life: Success Strategies for Life, Love & Business. Wolf J. Rinke. LC 91-75609. 283p. 1992. 24.95 (0-9627913-8-5) Achvmnt Pubs.
Make It Accurate: Get the Maximum Performance from Your Hunting Rifle. Craig Boddington. (Illus.). 224p. Date not set. 24.95 (1-57157-150-7) Safari Pr.
Make It & Fly It. Watermill Press Staff. (J). (gr. 4-7). 1997. pap. 5.95 (0-8167-2848-8) Troll Communs.
Make It Balance. David Evans & Claudette Williams. (Let's Explore Science Ser.). (Illus.). (J). 1995. 287.28 (0-590-74510-7) Scholastic Inc.
*Make It Better. Lilly Barnes. (Life Skills for Little Ones Ser.). (Illus.). 24p. (J). (ps-k). 1998. pap. 12.95 (1-895897-29-7) Somerville Hse.
Make It Big in the $100 Billion Outsource Contracting Industry: Turn Your Knowledge Experience & Commitment into Lifetime Strategic Partnerships. Robert W. Jennings. Ed. by John Passaro. LC 96-90573. 227p. 1997. 49.95 (0-9654311-0-X) Westfield Pr.
Make It, Break It. Elizabeth McDonald. 1999. pap. 3.95 (0-14-054278-7) NAL.
Make It Change. David Evans & Claudette Williams. (Let's Explore Science Ser.). (Illus.). (J). 12.95 (0-590-74511-5) Scholastic Inc.
Make It Count: How to Generate a Legacy That Gives Meaning in Your Life. John Kotre. LC 99-25231. 256p. 1999. 23.50 (0-684-83513-4) Free Pr.
Make It Easy in Your Kitchen. Laurie B. Grad. 1985. pap. 9.95 (0-685-09889-3) HM.
Make It Easy, Make It Light: More Than 200 Quick Recipes for Tasty, Healthful Dishes. Laurie B. Grad. 368p. 1997. 10.99 (0-88365-984-0) Galahad Bks.
Make It Easy, Make It Quick Cookbook. Laurie B. Grad. 1991. 9.98 (0-88365-773-2) Galahad Bks.
*Make It Fresh: More Than 150 Recipes for a Healthy You. Weight Watchers Staff. (Weight Watchers Ser.). 2000. pap. 9.95 (0-8487-2355-4) Oxmoor Hse.
*Make It Funky. (Roots of Rhythm Ser.: Vol. 19). (Illus.). 30p. 2000. write for info. (1-892207-97-4) Intl Masters Pub.
Make It Go! Godfrey Hall. (Funstations Ser.). (Illus.). 48p. (YA). (gr. 3-7). 1997. pap. 21.99 (0-8431-7970-8, Price Stern) Peng Put Young Read.
Make It Go Right! Rych McCain. 14p. 1990. 3.00 (0-9611904-2-6) Street Wise Pubns.
Make It Great - With Oat Bran. VeraLee Wiggins. 32p. (Orig.). 1990. pap. 0.89 (0-8280-0582-6) Review & Herald.
*Make It Happen! SNAPP Your Way to Success in Business & in Life. Tresa Eyres & Ron Biagi. LC 00-132417. 288p. 2000. pap. 24.95 (0-9677773-0-5) Its How.
Make It Happen! Spiritual Principles for Christian Achievement. Sheila M. Norman. 220p. (Orig.). 1997. pap. 12.95 (0-9657718-0-6) Joy Pubns CA.
*Make It Happen Before Lunch: 50 Cut-to-the-Chase Strategies for Getting the Business Results You Want. Stephan Schiffman. 176p. 2000. 16.95 (0-07-136071-9) McGraw.
*Make It Home Before Dark: God's Call to Holiness in Our Walk with Him. Crawford W. Loritts. 224p. 2000. 16.99 (0-8024-5437-2) Moody.
Make It in Clay: A Beginner's Guide to Ceramics. Charlotte F. Speight & John Toki. LC 96-29176. 169p. 1997. pap. text 28.95 (1-55934-632-9, 1632) Mayfield Pub.
Make It in Paper: Creative Three-Dimensional Paper Projects. Michael Grater. (Illus.). 93p. (J). (gr. 5 up). 1983. reprint ed. pap. 4.95 (0-486-24468-7) Dover.
Make It Italian. (Illus.). 1998. write for info. (1-886614-75-X) Intl Masters Pub.
Make It Legal: Copyright, Trademark, & Libel Law: Privacy & Publicity Rights. Lee Wilson. LC 90-80448. 272p. 1990. pap. 18.95 (0-927629-08-9) Allworth Pr.
*Make It Memorable: Writing & Packaging TV News with Style. Bob Dotson. 225p. 2000. 29.95 (1-56625-158-3) Bonus Books.
Make It Merry: A Medley of Christmas Crafts. Creative Publishing International Staff & Crafts Magazine Staff. LC 99-23412. 176p. 1999. 24.95 (0-86573-175-6) Creat Pub Intl.
Make it Merry: A Medley of Christmas Crafts. Creative Publishing International Staff & Crafts Magazine Staff. LC 99-23412. (Illus.). 176p. 1999. pap. 19.95 (0-86573-176-4) Creat Pub Intl.
Make It Merry in Plastic Canvas: Over 65 All New Projects, Bk. 5. LC 94-74355. 96p. 1996. pap. text 15.95 (0-942237-69-2) Oxmoor Hse.
Make It Metric. Thomas Camilli. (Illus.). 72p. (Orig.). 1982. pap. text 9.95 (0-9607366-7-0, KP111) Kino Pubns.
Make It Metric. Thomas Camilli. 66p. (Orig.). 1982. pap. 9.99 (0-89824-421-8) Trillium Pr.
Make It Move. Susan Canizares. LC 98-53313. 1999. pap. 10.01 (0-439-08121-1) Scholastic Inc.
Make It Move! Thomas-Cochran. (What a Wonderful World Intro Ser.). 1993. pap. text. write for info. (0-582-91075-7, Pub. by Addison-Wesley) Longman.
Make It New. 1987. 34.95 (0-387-17597-0) Spr-Verlag.
Make It New: Essays. Ezra Pound. 1988. reprint ed. lib. bdg. 79.00 (0-7812-0195-0) Rprt Serv.
Make It New: Essays. Ezra Pound. LC 71-145243. 1971. reprint ed. 59.00 (0-403-01158-2) Scholarly.
Make It or Break It: The Crucial Decision in Your Relationship. Robert Walzer & Rhoda Daum. 220p. 1990. 19.95 (0-8290-2226-0) Irvington.
Make It Pay Gold Dredge No. 4: Klondike, Yukon, Canada. abr. ed. David Neufeld & Patrick Habiluk. LC 94-66660. (Illus.). 64p. 1994. pap. 7.95 (0-929521-88-9) Pictorial Hist.
*Make It Simple Recipe Collection. (Illus.). 240p. 2000. 24.95 (0-696-20972-1, Better Homes) Meredith Bks.
Make It Simpler: A Practical Guide to Problem Solving in Mathematics. Carol Meyer. 1983. text 19.95 (0-201-20036-8) Addison-Wesley.
Make It So: Leadership for the Next Generation. Wess Roberts & Bill Ross. 1996. pap. 12.00 (0-614-12596-0, PB Trade Paper) PB.
Make It So: Leadership Lessons from Star Trek: The Next Generation. Wess Roberts & Bill Ross. 256p. 1996. pap. 12.00 (0-671-52098-9) S&S Trade.
*Make It So You Don't Have to Fake It! 55 Fast-Acting Strategies for Long-Lasting Success. Patricia Fripp. LC 99-65363. 122p. 2000. pap. 11.95 (0-937539-41-4) Executive Bks.
*Make It Special! Craft Kit. Judy Kayschke. (Illus.). 16p. (J). (gr. 1-3). 2000. bds. 11.99 (1-57584-407-9) Rdrs Digest.
*Make It Take It! Creating Movement Challenge Kits for Play at Home or School. Lynn Cox & Terry Lubbers. LC 99-64342. (Illus.). 159p. 2000. pap. 19.99 (0-9664413-4-6) Tekna Bks.
Make It Tasty Spice Blend & Food Business Cookbook. Alpha Pyramis Research Division Staff. (Illus.). 78p. (C). 1993. ring bd. 49.95 (0-913597-09-0) Prosperity & Profits.
Make It Tasty Spice Blends No Salt Cookbook. (Illus.). 72p. 1993. ring bd. 19.95 (0-911569-96-0) Prosperity & Profits.
Make It Tasty Spice Recipe Greetings to Duplicate & Use. Lamp Light Press Staff. 60p. 1993. ring bd. 29.95 (0-917593-29-4, Lamp Light Pr) Prosperity & Profits.
Make It Today for Pre-K Play: Easy to Make Equipment for Motor Development. Joyce Hamman. Ed. by Linda Milliken. (Illus.). 80p. 1993. pap. 7.95 (1-56472-014-4) Edupress Inc.
Make It Unanimous: The Finest Hour for Equity, Opportunity & the Free Market System. Harry Hill & Fred Stainken. Ed. by JoAnne Stoddard & Barbara Anderson. LC 98-72344. xii, 190p. 1999. pap. 24.95 (0-9664561-0-6) American Publ Aff & Publ.
Make It with Balloons. Watermill Press Staff. (J). (gr. 4-7). 1992. pap. 5.95 (0-8167-2849-6) Troll Communs.
Make It with Boxes. Joan Irvine. (Illus.). 96p. (J). 1991. pap. text 9.95 (1-55074-056-3) Kids Can Pr.
Make It with Paper. Susan Tollard. 1992. 17.98 (1-55521-803-2) Bk Sales Inc.
Make It with Style. Donna Lang. 1997. pap. write for info. (0-517-88238-8) C Potter.
Make It with Style: Baby Access. Donna Lang. 1996. pap. write for info. (0-517-88731-2) C Potter.
Make It with Style: Draperies & Swags. Donna Lang & Judy Petersen. LC 97-6641. 1997. pap. 18.00 (0-517-88716-9) Crown Pub Group.
Make It with Style: Window Shades & Blinds: Creating Roman, Balloon & Austrian Shades. Donna Lang & Judy Petersen. LC 96-49687. 1997. pap. 18.00 (0-517-88237-X) Crown Pub Group.
Make It with Style - Slipcovers: With Instructions for More Than 30 Designer Looks. Donna Lang. LC 97-42918. 1998. pap. 18.00 (0-517-88241-8) C Potter.
*Make it Work! Geography, 4 vols. Andrew Haslam. 192p. (J). (gr. 3-8). 1999. write for info. (0-7166-5121-1) World Bk.
*Make It Your Business. abr. ed. Stephan Schiffman. 1998. audio 12.00 (0-671-04305-6) S&S New Media.
Make It Your Business: The Definitive Guide for Launching & Succeeding in Your Business. Stephan Schiffman. LC 99-163542. 260p. 1998. 24.00 (0-671-02178-8) S&S Trade.
Make It Your Business: The Definitive Guide to Launching, Managing & Succeeding in Your Own Business. Stephen Schiffman. 272p. 1999. per. 14.00 (0-671-02179-6, PB Trade Paper) PB.
Make it Your Own: Personalizing Patterns for Creative Design. Lori Bottom & Ronda Chaney. LC 94-1491. (Illus.). 160p. 1994. pap. 18.95 (0-8019-8380-0) Krause Pubns.
Make it Your Own: Personalizing Patterns for Creative Design. Lori Bottom & Ronda Chaney. (Illus.). 168p. 1999. reprint ed. pap. text 19.00 (0-7881-6018-4) DIANE Pub.
Make It Yourself. Hal Danby. (Illus.). 127p. 1974. 19.00 (0-8464-1187-3) Beekman Pubs.
Make-It-Yourself Barrier Activities. Nancy L. McKinley & Linda Schwartz. 210p. (J). (gr. k-12). 1987. pap. 37.00 (0-930599-16-0) Thinking Pubns.
Make It Yourself Gift Book: Gifts to Make at Home for All Your Family & Friends. Reader's Digest Editors. LC 97-40456. 1998. 27.95 (0-7621-0021-4, Pub. by RD Assn) Penguin Putnam.
Make Known His Deeds: Among the People. Debbie S. Russell. 190p. (Orig.). 1996. pap. 7.95 (1-57502-373-3, P01193) Morris Pubng.
Make Landscaping Your Business. Laurence W. Price. LC 97-71227. (Illus.). 136p. (Orig.). 1997. pap. 9.95 (0-9611966-2-9) Botany Bks.
Make Lemonade. (Assessment Packs Ser.). 15p. 1998. pap. text 15.95 (1-58303-049-2) Pthways Pubng.
Make Lemonade. Virginia E. Wolff. LC 92-41182. 208p. (J). (gr. 6-9). 1995. 15.95 (0-8050-2228-7, Bks Young Read) H Holt & Co.
Make Lemonade. Virginia E. Wolff. LC 92-41182. 208p. (J). (gr. 7-12). 1994. pap. 3.95 (0-590-48141-X) Scholastic Inc.
Make Lemonade. Virginia E. Wolff. (Point Signature Ser.). (J). 1993. 9.05 (0-606-06555-5, Pub. by Turtleback) Demco.
Make Lemonade. large type ed. Virginia E. Wolff. LC 93-21003. (Teen Scene Ser.). (YA). (gr. 9-12). 1993. 16.95 (0-7862-0056-1) Thorndike Pr.
Make Like a Tree & Leave. Paula Danziger. 126p. (J). (gr. 4-7). 1998. pap. 4.99 (0-698-11686-0, PapStar) Peng Put Young Read.

Make Like a Tree & Leave. Paula Danziger. 1998. 10.09 (*0-606-13593-6*, Pub. by Turtleback) Demco.

Make Love, Not War: The Sexual Revolution: An Unfettered History. David Allyn. 2000. write for info. (*0-316-03916-0*) Little.

***Make Love, Not War: The Sexual Revolution: An Unfettered History.** David Allyn. LC 99-33784. (Illus.). 432p. (gr. 8). 2000. 26.95 (*0-316-03930-6*) Little.

Make Love with Life Journal: An Inspirational Interactive Self-Help Resource, Vol. 3. Ken Vegotsky. Ed. by Stephanie Vegotsky. LC 97-18582. (Love Living & Live Loving Ser.). (Illus.). 112p. 1997. pap. 7.95 (*1-886508-02-X*) Adi Gaia Esalen.

Make Love Your Aim. Eugenia Price. 160p. 1989. mass mkt. 3.95 (*0-515-10039-0*, Jove) Berkley Pub.

Make Man Talk True: Nigerian Drama in English since 1970. Chris Dunton. (New Perspectives on African Literature Ser.: No. 5). 226p. 1992. lib. bdg. 85.00 (*0-905450-87-6*, Pub. by H Zell Pubs) Seven Hills Bk.

Make Me a Lie. Nancy E. Valmus. Ed. by Rand Hall. (Pocket Poetry Ser.). 60p. 1989. pap. 9.50 (*0-937025-01-1*) Shadowood Pubns.

Make Me a Map of the Valley: The Civil War Journal of Stonewall Jackson's Topographer. Jedediah Hotchkiss. Ed. by Archie P. McDonald. LC 73-82036. (Illus.). 392p. 1989. reprint ed. pap. 12.95 (*0-87074-270-1*) SMU Press.

Make-Me-a-Match. Illus. by Diana Lederman. (ENG, FRE & HEB.). (J). 1992. spiral bd. 4.95 (*965-229-025-4*, Pub. by Gefen Pub Hse) Gefen Bks.

Make-Me-a-Match - Hanukah. Diana Lederman. (ENG, FRE & HEB.). 1994. spiral bd. 4.95 (*965-229-118-8*, Pub. by Gefen Pub Hse) Gefen Bks.

Make-Me-a-Match - Israel. Diana Lederman. (ENG, FRE & HEB., Illus.). 1994. spiral bd. 4.95 (*965-229-120-X*, Pub. by Gefen Pub Hse) Gefen Bks.

Make-Me-a-Match - Les Fetes des Tishri. Diana Lederman. (ENG, FRE & HEB., Illus.). 1994. spiral bd. 4.95 (*965-229-119-6*, Pub. by Gefen Pub Hse) Gefen Bks.

Make-Me-a-Match - Pesach. Diana Lederman. (ENG, FRE & HEB., Illus.). 1994. spiral bd. 4.95 (*965-229-116-1*, Pub. by Gefen Pub Hse) Gefen Bks.

Make-Me-a-Match - Purim. Diana Lederman. (ENG, FRE & HEB., Illus.). 1994. spiral bd. 4.95 (*965-229-117-X*, Pub. by Gefen Pub Hse) Gefen Bks.

Make-Me-a-Match - Shabbat. Diana Lederman. (ENG, FRE & HEB., Illus.). 1994. spiral bd. 4.95 (*965-229-115-3*, Pub. by Gefen Pub Hse) Gefen Bks.

***Make Me a Miracle.** Charles Tazewell. (Illus.). 256p. 2000. 21.95 (*1-58029-108-2*, Celebrity Bks) Hambleton-Hill.

Make Me a Peanut Butter Sandwich & a Glass of Milk. Ken Robbins. (Illus.). 32p. (J). (ps up). 1992. 14.95 (*0-590-43550-7*, 023, Scholastic Hardcover) Scholastic Inc.

Make Me a Sabbath of Your Heart: Call to Discipleship. 2nd ed. David M. Knight. (Spiritual Growth Through Matthew's Gospel Ser.: Vol. 3). 192p. 1988. reprint ed. pap. 10.00 (*0-942971-05-1*) His Way.

Make Me a Zoo. Dorothy Cowan. (Illus.). 64p. (Orig.). (J). (ps-1). 1991. pap. text 8.95 (*0-86530-177-8*, IP 194-5) Incentive Pubns.

***Make Me an Instrument.** Stephen D. Hower. 2000. pap. 14.99 (*0-570-05253-X*) Concordia.

***Make Me an Instrument of Your Peace: Living in the Spirit of the Prayer of Saint Francis.** Kent Nerburn. LC 98-43675. 1999. pap. write for info. (*0-06-251582-9*) Harper SF.

Make Me an Instrument of Your Peace: Living in the Spirit of the Prayer of Saint Francis. Kent Nerburn. LC 98-43675. 144p. 1999. 16.00 (*0-06-251581-0*, Pub. by Harper SF) HarpC.

Make Me Disappear. Cameron Kent. 126p. 1994. pap. 9.99 (*0-88092-100-5*) Royal Fireworks.

Make Me Disappear. Cameron Kent. 126p. (J). (gr. 4-6). 1994. lib. bdg. 15.00 (*0-88092-101-3*) Royal Fireworks.

Make Me Don't Break Me. Moshe Gans. 18.99 (*0-89906-113-3*, MAKH); pap. 15.99 (*0-89906-114-1*, MAKP) Mesorah Pubns.

Make Me Feel Important. Joe Gilbert. LC 93-86380. 284p. 1993. 24.95 (*1-56091-458-0*, M114) Soc Auto Engineers.

Make Me Musical. 2nd rev. ed. David Harp. (Illus.). 64p. (J). (ps-4). 1989. pap. 14.95 incl. audio (*0-918321-15-8*) Musical I Pr.

Make Me Pele for a Day. Ted Sod. 1994. 5.50 (*0-87129-465-6*, M11) Dramatic Pub.

Make Me Work. Ralph Lombreglia. LC 93-26485. 1994. 20.00 (*0-374-20004-1*) FS&G.

***Make Millions from Your Kitchen Table.** Martha Ivery. 2000. pap. 12.95 (*1-57532-264-1*) Press-Tige Pub.

Make Mine Ice Cream. Melvin Berger. Ed. by Natalie Lunis. (Early Science Big Bks.). (Illus.). 16p. (J). (ps-2). 1993. pap. 16.95 (*1-56784-007-8*) Newbridge Educ.

Make Mine Ice Cream: Mini Book. Melvin Berger. Ed. by Natalie Lunis. (Early Science Big Bks.). (Illus.). 16p. (J). (ps-2). 1993. pap. 3.95 (*1-56784-032-9*) Newbridge Educ.

Make Mine Ice Cream Theme Pack. Melvin Berger. Ed. by Susan Evento. (Macmillan Early Science Big Bks.). (Illus.). (J). (ps-2). 1995. pap. 49.95 (*1-56784-139-2*) Newbridge Educ.

Make Mine Low-fat & Tasty, Too! LC 98-217942. ii, 82 p. 1995. write for info. (*0-934474-72-9*) Cookbook Pubs.

Make Mine to Go. Elizabeth Craft. (@Cafe Ser.: No. 3). (YA). 1998. per. 3.99 (*0-671-00447-6*, Archway) PB.

Make Money at Home: 101 Home Based Business Ideas. Mike Nix. 160p. (Orig.). 1995. pap. text 9.95 (*0-9646277-0-1*) B&T Prodns.

Make Money Entertaining Kids: No Experience Necessary. Keith Johnson. (Illus.). 144p. 1997. pap. 15.00 (*1-890833-05-3*) KMJ Educ.

Make Money Freelance News Writing. Ian McCrone. 1997. pap. text 15.95 (*0-86417-788-7*) Seven Hills Bk.

***Make Money in MLM: Full Time, Part Time, Any Time for a Lifetime.** Bob Powers. LC 00-131114. (Illus.). 192p. 2000. pap. 15.95 (*0-9673451-0-3*) Life Long Pubg.

Make Money Make Money - A Simple Guide to Investing. Roger A. Wynkoop. LC 83-60735. (Orig.). 1983. pap. 9.95 (*0-912545-00-3*) Success Now.

Make Money Moonlighting! The Four Best Ways to Earn Money with Your Computer & the Four Traps to Avoid. John R. Mortz. 121p. 1989. pap. 9.95 (*0-9623722-2-6*) Amer Inst Comput Tech.

Make Money Owning Your Car (And Enjoy Every Minute) rev. ed. John R. Olson. (Illus.). 184p. 1976. 9.95 (*0-686-09315-1*) Electronic Flea.

Make Money Reading Books: How to Start & Operate Your Own Home-Based Freelance Reading Service. Bruce Fife. LC 92-26184. 144p. 1993. pap. 15.00 (*0-941599-20-5*, Pub. by Piccadilly Bks) Empire Pub Srvs.

Make Money Trading Mortgages. Delbert M. Ashby. LC 94-61113. 160p. 1994. pap. 49.95 (*0-9642690-0-7*) Wellington Co.

Make Money with Horses: You Can Do It! Don Blazer. LC 97-92440. (Illus.). 142p. 1998. pap. 19.95 (*0-9660127-0-4*) Success is Easy.

Make Money with S & P 500 Options: Using Grandmill's Option Tables. William Grandmill. 1990. pap. 44.95 (*0-930233-40-9*) Windsor.

Make Money with Your Camera. David Arndt. (Illus.). 128p. 1999. pap. 29.95 (*0-936262-84-2*) Amherst Media.

Make More Money Now: Dramatic New 21-Day Money Making System Guaranteed to Make Everything You Say & Write Powerful, Influential, Convincing & Instantly Lucrative. Alvin G. Donovan, III & Meg Northcroft. 200p. 1997. 19.95 (*0-9657077-0-9*) Pavillion.

Make Moving Patterns: How to Make Optical Illusions of Your Own. Tim Armstrong. (Illus.). pap. 12.95 (*0-906212-26-X*, Pub. by Tarquin Pubns) Parkwest Pubns.

Make Muzzleloader Accessories Top. R. H. McCrory. 1971. 6.00 (*0-913150-67-3*) Pioneer Pr.

***Make My Baby Jump.** Clint Brown. Ed. by Gerald Doggett. 138p. 1998. 10.00 (*0-9672114-0-9*, BK MMBJ 4000) Tribe Music.

Make My Day. Patrick Oliphant. (Illus.). 160p. 1992. pap. 8.95 (*0-8362-2072-2*) Andrews & McMeel.

Make My Day! Hayduke's Best Revenge Techniques for the Punks in Your Life. George Hayduke. 224p. 1987. text 19.95 (*0-87364-436-0*) Paladin Pr.

Make My Day! Hayduke's Best Revenge Techniques for the Punks in Your Life. George Hayduke. 224p. 1988. reprint ed. pap. 7.95 (*0-8184-0464-7*) Carol Pub Group.

Make My Day Law: Colorado's Experiment in Home Protection. William Wilbanks. 396p. (Orig.). (C). 1990. pap. text 29.50 (*0-8191-7776-8*); lib. bdg. 59.00 (*0-8191-7775-X*) U Pr of Amer.

Make My Joy Complete: Philippians. Eleanor M. Loewen. Ed. by Maynard Shelly. LC 87-83120. (Bible Studies). 80p. 1988. pap. 1.95 (*0-87303-123-7*) Faith & Life.

***Make My Life a Prayer: Devotions from the Personal Journals of Keith Green.** Keith Green. 200p. 2001. 12.99 (*0-7369-0360-7*) Harvest Hse.

Make My Own Book Kit - Alphabet. Linda P. Silbert & Alvin J. Silbert. (Little Twirps Preschool Ser.). (J). (ps-2). 1984. student ed. 5.98 (*0-89544-319-8*) Silbert Bress.

Make My Own Book Kit - Animals. Linda P. Silbert & Alvin J. Silbert. (Little Twirps Preschool Ser.). (J). (ps-2). 1984. student ed. 5.98 (*0-89544-316-3*) Silbert Bress.

Make My Own Book Kit - I Am Special. Linda P. Silbert & Alvin J. Silbert. (Strong Kids Early Childhood Program Ser.). 1993. 5.98 (*0-89544-321-X*) Silbert Bress.

Make My Own Book Kit - Numbers. Linda P. Silbert & Alvin J. Silbert. (Little Twirps Preschool Ser.). (J). (ps-2). 1984. student ed. 5.98 (*0-89544-318-X*) Silbert Bress.

Make My Own Book Kit - Say No to Drugs. Linda P. Silbert & Alvin J. Silbert. (Strong Kids Early Childhood Program Ser.). 1993. 5.98 (*0-89544-323-6*) Silbert Bress.

Make My Own Book Kit - Say No to Strangers. Linda P. Silbert & Alvin J. Silbert. (Strong Kids Early Childhood Program Ser.). 1993. 5.98 (*0-89544-322-8*) Silbert Bress.

Make My Own Book Kit - Shapes. Linda P. Silbert & Alvin J. Silbert. (Little Twirps Preschool Ser.). (J). (ps-2). 1984. student ed. 5.98 (*0-89544-317-1*) Silbert Bress.

Make Necklaces: 16 Projects for Creating Beautiful Jewelry. Jo Moody. (Make Jewelry Ser.). (Illus.). 96p. 1997. pap. 15.99 (*1-56496-271-7*, Quarry Bks) Rockport Pubs.

Make New Friends. Shirley Backels. (Friendship Unit Ser.). 22p. 1992. pap. text 4.99 (*1-57156-023-8*) Wild Goose UT.

Make News & Make Noise! How to Get Publicity for Your Book. Shelly Roberts. LC 93-87210. 64p. (Orig.). 1994. pap. 5.95 (*1-882587-03-0*) Paradigm San Diego.

Make No Bones. Aaron J. Elkins. 240p. 1993. mass mkt. 5.99 (*0-446-40308-3*, Pub. by Warner Bks) Little.

Make No Law: The Sullivan Case & the First Amendment. Anthony Lewis. LC 92-50104. 368p. 1992. pap. 14.00 (*0-679-73939-4*) Vin Bks.

Make No Mistake. Carolyn Keene. Ed. by Ann Greenberg. (Nancy Drew Files: No. 56). 160p. (YA). (gr. 6 up). 1991. per. 3.50 (*0-671-70033-2*, Archway) PB.

Make No Mistake. Carolyn Keene. (Nancy Drew Files: No. 56). (YA). (gr. 6 up). 1991. 8.60 (*0-606-04737-9*, Pub. by Turtleback) Demco.

Make No Small Plans: A Cooperative Revival for Rural America. Lee Egerstrom. LC 94-72991. (Illus.). 294p. (Orig.). 1995. pap. 19.95 (*1-883477-04-2*) Lone Oak MN.

Make or Break Spring. Janet McNaughton. LC 98-168564. 192p. 1999. pap. 9.95 (*1-895387-93-0*) Creative Bk Pub.

Make-or-Buy Decision. Anthony J. Gambino. 128p. 1980. pap. 20.00 (*0-86641-000-7*, 80120) Inst Mgmt Account.

Make-or-Buy Decisions in Tooling for Mass Production. William A. Paton & Robert L. Dixon. LC 61-63325. (Michigan Business Studies: No. 35). 40p. reprint ed. pap. 30.00 (*0-608-13526-7*, 202209100024) Bks Demand.

Make Pins: 16 Projects for Creating Beautiful Jewelry. Jo Moody. (Make Jewelry Ser.). (Illus.). 96p. 1997. pap. 15.99 (*1-56496-274-1*, Quarry Bks) Rockport Pubs.

Make Prayers to the Raven: A Koyukon View of the Northern Forest. Richard K. Nelson. LC 82-8441. xvi, 320p. 1986. pap. 15.00 (*0-226-57163-7*) U Ch Pr.

Make Presentations with Confidence. 2nd rev. ed. Vivian Buchan. LC 97-10352. (Barron's Business Success Ser.). (Orig.). 1997. pap. text 6.95 (*0-8120-9892-7*) Barron.

Make Room for Baby. Kristin Morgan. (Romance Ser.). 1995. per. 2.99 (*0-373-19084-0*, 1-19084-2) Silhouette.

Make Room for Baby: (Accidental Dads) Cathy G. Thacker. (American Romance Ser.: Vol. 747). 1998. per. 3.99 (*0-373-16747-4*, 1-16747-7) Harlequin Bks.

Make Room for Daddy. Emily Dalton. LC 95-13559. (American Romance Ser.). 249p. 1995. per. 3.50 (*0-373-16586-2*, 1-16586-9) Harlequin Bks.

Make Room for Danny. Aquinas, Thomas, Saint. 1992. pap. 15.95 (*1-55927-187-6*) Audio Renaissance.

Make Room for Dreams: Spiritual Challenges to Zionism, 39. Haim Gordon. LC 88-34716. (Contributions in Philosophy Ser.: No. 39). 188p. 1989. 45.00 (*0-313-26054-0*, GNM/, Greenwood Pr) Greenwood.

Make Room for Elisa. Johanna Hurwitz. LC 92-45864. (Illus.). 80p. (J). (gr. k up). 1993. 15.00 (*0-688-12404-6*, Wm Morrow) Morrow Avon.

Make Room for Elisa. Johanna Hurwitz. (Young Puffin Ser.). (J). 1995. 9.19 (*0-606-07832-0*, Pub. by Turtleback) Demco.

***Make Room for Jesus in Your Inn.** Gwendolyn Adele Bancroft. (Illus.). 180p. 1999. pap. write for info. (*0-7392-0460-2*, PO3770) Morris Pubng.

***Make Room for Joy: Finding Magical Moments in Your Everyday Life.** Susan L. Colantuono. Ed. by Nancy Brooks. 142p. 2000. pap. 14.95 (*0-9673129-0-6*) Interlude Prodns.

Make Room for Mommy. Suzanne McMinn. 1996. per. 3.25 (*0-373-19191-X*, 1-19191-5) Silhouette.

Make Room for Quilts: Beautiful Decorating Ideas from Nancy J. Martin. 2nd rev. ed. Nancy J. Martin. (Illus.). 216p. 1998. 27.95 (*1-56477-221-7*, B167R, That Patchwrk Pl) Martingale & Co.

Make Room for Rodney: Manuscript Edition. Marion Holbrook. 1946. pap. 3.00 (*0-8222-0718-4*) Dramatists Play.

Make Room for Sentiment: A Physician's Story. Theodore E. Woodward et al. LC 98-15858. (Illus.). 278p. 1998. 23.80 (*0-9619119-1-3*) Medical Alumni Association of Univ.

Make Room for the Hollyhocks & Where the Birds Don't Sing. Lorraine H. Hare. Ed. by Shannon Johnson et al. 160p. (YA). (gr. 4 up). 1999. pap. 12.99 (*1-893053-00-8*) PaceSetter.

Make Room for the Mystery of God. John Paul, II, pseud. 96p. 1995. pap. 2.95 (*0-8198-4783-6*) Pauline Bks.

Make Room for TV: Television & the Family Ideal in Postwar America. Lynn Spigel. LC 91-32770. (Illus.). 246p. 1992. pap. text 18.00 (*0-226-76967-4*) U Ch Pr.

Make Room for TV: Television & the Family Ideal in Postwar America. Lynn Spigel. LC 91-32770. (Illus.). 246p. 1992. lib. bdg. 48.50 (*0-226-76966-6*) U Ch Pr.

Make Sculptures! Kim Solga. (Art & Activities for Kids Ser.). (Illus.). 48p. (J). (gr. 1-6). 1992. 11.99 (*0-89134-420-9*, 30378, North Lght Bks) F & W Pubns Inc.

Make Sense of Your Dreams: An Illustrated Guide to Dream Interpretation. Susan G. Ellis. LC 88-60683. (Illus.). 256p. 1988. 24.95 (*0-9619831-2-4*) Sudavel Pub.

Make Sense Who May: Essays on Samuel Beckett's Later Works. Ed. by Robin J. Davis & Lance S. Butler. (Irish Literary Studies: No. 30). (C). 1988. 53.00 (*0-389-20791-8*, N8349) B&N Imports.

Make Shapes 1: 19 Mathematical Models to Cut Out & Decorate. Gerald Jenkins & Anne Wild. (Tarquin Make Mathematical Shapes Ser.). (Illus.). 24p. (Orig.). (J). (gr. 4 up). Date not set. reprint ed. pap. 6.95 (*0-906212-00-6*, Pub. by Tarquin Pubns) Parkwest Pubns.

Make Shapes 3. Gerald Jenkins & Anne Wild. (Tarquin Make Mathematical Shapes Ser.). 24p. (Orig.). (J). (gr. 4 up). 1985. pap. 4.95 (*0-906212-02-2*, Pub. by Tarquin Pubns) Parkwest Pubns.

Make Shapes 2: 8 Mathematical Models to Cut Out, Give & Decorate. Gerald Jenkins & Anne Wild. (Tarquin Make Mathematical Shapes Ser.). (Illus.). 24p. (Orig.). (J). (gr. 4 up). Date not set. reprint ed. pap. 6.95 (*0-906212-01-4*, Pub. by Tarquin Pubns) Parkwest Pubns.

***Make Some Noise: 101 Great Things to Do in a Nightclub or a Bar.** Charles Graudins & Chuck Fresh. (Illus.). 35p. 1999. pap. 29.99 (*1-929554-01-X*, MSN001) Modern Rock.

***Make Someone Happy.** unabridged ed. Bob Wendorf. 1999. pap. 12.95 (*0-9677943-0-7*) Psych Savvy.

Make Someone Smile & 40 More Ways to Be a Peaceful Person. Judy Lalli. LC 95-39198. (Illus.). 80p. (J). (gr. k up). 1996. pap. 9.95 (*0-915793-99-7*) Free Spirit Pub.

Make Something Ugly... For a Change! The Definitive Guide to Papier & Cloth Mache. Dan Reeder. LC 99-17217. (Illus.). 80p. 1999. pap. 17.95 (*0-87905-907-9*) Gibbs Smith Pub.

***Make Success Measurable! A Mindbook-Workbook for Setting Goals & Taking Action.** Smith. LC 98-44988. 244p. 1999. 29.95 (*0-471-29559-0*) Wiley.

Make Sure You Do Not Have Breast Cancer. Philip Strax. 1991. pap. 8.95 (*0-312-05441-6*) St Martin.

Make Swags & Jabots, Yes You Can! Claira Dobry. (Illus.). 118p. 1986. spiral bd. 19.95 (*0-9615218-5-6*); per. 19.95 (*0-9615218-4-8*) Dobry Enter.

Make Take Games see Table & Floor Games: Easy to Make - Fun to Play

Make That Change! Tools & Techniques for Facilitating Change. Kogan Page Staff. Ed. by Steve Smith. (How to Be Better Ser.). 1998. pap. text 14.95 (*0-7494-2485-0*) Kogan Page Ltd.

Make That Scene: A Writer's Guide to Setting, Mood & Atmosphere. William Noble. 224p. 1988. 17.95 (*0-8397-5708-5*, Pub. by Eriksson) IPG Chicago.

Make the Bible Live. Glenn O'Neal. pap. 3.50 (*0-88469-020-2*) BMH Bks.

Make the Big Time Where You Are. Frosty Westering. 140p. 1990. 14.95 (*0-9629400-0-3*) Big Five Prodns.

Make the Change to Customer Driven Sales. Phil Kline. LC 97-183493. 1996. pap. text 24.95 (*0-87425-403-5*) HRD Press.

Make the Circle Bigger: We Need Each Other. Rickie Moore. LC 90-4065. (Illus.). 128p. (Orig.). 1990. pap. 19.95 (*0-89334-133-9*) Humanics Ltd.

Make the Circle Bigger: We Need Each Other. Rickie Moore. LC 90-4065. (Illus.). 128p. (Orig.). 1990. lib. bdg. 29.95 (*0-89334-193-2*, 193-2) Humanics Ltd.

Make the Connection: Ten Steps to a Better Body & a Better Life. Bob Greene & Oprah Winfrey. (J). 1997. 18.95 (*0-316-35367-1*) Little.

Make the Connection: Ten Steps to a Better Body & a Better Life. rev. ed. Bob Greene & Oprah Winfrey. (Illus.). 240p. (J). 1999. pap. 9.95 (*0-7868-8298-0*, Pub. by Hyperion) Time Warner.

Make the Connection: The Cancon Method of Dog Training. unabridged ed. (Illus.). 180p. 1997. pap. 24.00 (*0-9662713-3-5*) Canine Connect.

Make the Fur Fly: A History of a Union Volunteer Division in the American Civil War. Timothy B. Mudgett. LC 97-26247. 188p. 1997. 24.95 (*1-57249-084-5*, Burd St Pr) White Mane Pub.

Make the Future Work: Appropriate Technology Guide. Budgett-Meakin. 1993. pap. text. write for info. (*0-582-08838-0*, Pub. by Addison-Wesley) Longman.

Make the Jerk Pay: Tracking down a Deadbeat Dad/And Getting Child Support. Louis J. Rose & Roy Malone. Ed. by Fred W. Lindecke. LC 98-93329. (Illus.). xiv, 188p. 1999. pap. 14.95 (*0-9606846-3-8*) Albion Pr.

Make the Most of Carriage Driving. Vivian Ellis et al. 1995. pap. 39.00 (*0-85131-602-6*, Pub. by J A Allen) Trafalgar.

Make the Most of Your Mind. Tony Buzan. 1986. 11.00 incl. audio (*0-671-61856-3*) S&S Bks Yung.

Make the Most of Your Mind. Tony Buzan. 157p. 1984. per. 11.00 (*0-671-49519-4*) S&S Trade.

Make the Music Go Bang. Ed. by Don Snowden. LC 97-19851. (Illus.). 256p. 1997. pap. 17.95 (*0-312-16912-4*) St Martin.

***Make the Noise Quack Quack.** (J). 1999. 4.99 (*0-7214-2734-0*, Ladybrd) Penguin Putnam.

Make the Old Testament Live: From Curriculum to Classroom. Ed. by Richard S. Hess & Gordon J. Wenham. LC 98-35494. 176p. 1998. pap. text 15.00 (*0-8028-4427-8*) Eerdmans.

Make the Path Clear, Vol. 1. 4.95 (*0-685-10124-X*) Cooper & Cooper Pub.

Make the Right Call. Drew Bledsoe & Greg Brown. LC 98-38629. (Illus.). 40p. (J). (gr. 2-7). 1998. 14.95 (*0-87833-215-4*) Taylor Pub.

***Make the Right Call! Football.** 3rd ed. National Football League Staff. 1999. pap. 14.95 (*1-57243-342-6*) Triumph Bks.

Make the Right Call! Major League Baseball's Official Rules & Interpretations Plus League Umpire's Guide & Instructions. 3rd ed. (Illus.). 228p. (Orig.). 1996. pap. 13.95 (*1-57243-112-1*) Triumph Bks.

Make the Right Career Moves. Deborah P. Bloch. LC 99-13607. (Here's How Ser.). 160p. 1999. pap. 12.95 (*0-8442-2076-0*, 20760, Natl Textbk Co) NTC Contemp Pub Co.

Make the Right Choice. Dottie Waddell & Phil Clanton. (J). (gr. k-4). 1989. 10.95 incl. audio (*0-937124-32-X*, KIM 9114C) Kimbo Educ.

Make the Right Move: The Smart Way to Buy a House. Richard Krebs. LC 92-80756. 96p. (Orig.). 1992. pap. 12.95 (*0-9632619-0-8*) Sigma South.

Make the Sale! How to Sell Media with Marketing. M. A. Shaver. LC 95-92489. 295p. (Orig.). (C). 1994. pap. 24.95 (*0-9621415-6-9*, Pub. by Copy Wrkshp) Natl Bk Netwk.

Make Thee an Ark. Theda Hagan. 164p. 1999. pap. 9.99 (*0-7392-0199-9*, PO3195) T Hagan.

***Make Their Days: Activities for Residents in Long-Term Care.** Enid J. Portnoy. LC 99-11374. 112p. 1999. pap. text 18.95 (*0-398-06943-3*) C C Thomas.

***Make Their Furnishings - Make Their Home: A Complete House & all the Furnishings for the "Make a Family" Set of Dolls.** Paulette Morrissey. (Illus.). 1999. spiral bd. 15.95 (*1-893502-13-9*) Morrissey Co.

Make Them Choose You: The Executive Selection Process. James D. Kohlmann. (Replacing Mystery With Strategy Ser.). 144p. 1987. 20.50 (*0-13-547878-2*) P-H.

***Make Them Hunters.** expanded rev. ed. Illus. by Maurya M. Reid et al. (Adirondack Reidings Ser.: Vol. I). x, 137p. 1998. pap. 9.95 (*1-890072-01-X*) Reid Pubns.

M

*Make Things Fly Poems About The Wind: Poems about the Wind. Dorothy M. Kennedy. LC 97-13028. (Illus.). 32p. (J). (gr. 4-7). 1998. pap. 16.00 (0-689-81544-1) McElderry Bks.

*Make Things Happen. John J. Doubt. 126p. 1999. pap. write for info. (0-7392-0494-7, PO3855) Morris Pubng.

Make Things Happen! Tools & Techniques for Project Management. Kogan Page Staff. (How to Be Better Ser.). 1998. pap. text 14.95 (0-7494-2484-2) Kogan Page Ltd.

Make Things Without Needles. Morrow. Date not set. pap. text. write for info. (0-582-05852-X, Pub. by Addison-Wesley) Longman.

*Make This Castle. rev. ed. I. Ashman. (Cut-Out Models Ser.). (Illus.). 32p. (YA). (gr. 4-7). 2000. pap. 9.95 (0-7460-3303-6, Pub. by Usbrne Pbng UK) EDC.

Make This Egyptian Mummy. Iain Ashman. (Cut-Out Models Ser.). (Illus.). 32p. (J). (gr. 2-7). 1995. pap. 9.95 (0-7460-1988-2, Usborne) EDC.

Make This Egyptian Temple. Iain Ashman. (Cut-Out Models Ser.). (Illus.). 32p. (J). (gr. 4 up). 1990. pap. 9.95 (0-7460-0461-3) EDC.

Make This Egyptian Temple. Iain Ashman. (Usborne Cut-Out Models Ser.). 1999. pap. 9.95 (0-7460-3781-3, Usborne) EDC.

Make This Election Count! The Aims of Communists in '72. Gus Hall. 48p. 1972. pap. 0.60 (0-87898-093-8) New Outlook.

Make This Medieval Castle. I. Ashman. (gr. 2-7). 1998. pap. text 9.95 (0-7460-3292-7, Usborne) EDC.

Make This Medieval Town. Iain Ashman. (Usborne Cut-Out Models Ser.). 1999. pap. 9.95 (0-7460-3302-8, Usborne) EDC.

Make This Model American Fort. Ed. by Iain Ashman. (Cut-Out Models Ser.). (Illus.). 32p. (YA). (gr. 4 up). 1999. pap. text 9.95 (0-7460-3439-3, Usborne) EDC.

Make This Model Castle. Iain Ashman. 32p. (J). (gr. 4 up). 1988. pap. 9.95 (0-86020-578-9, Usborne) EDC.

Make This Model Crusader Castle. Iain Ashman. (Cut-Out Models Ser.). (Illus.). 32p. (YA). (gr. 4-7). 1996. pap. 9.95 (0-7460-2435-5, Usborne) EDC.

Make This Model Doll's House. Iain Ashman. (Cut-Out Models Ser.). (Illus.). 32p. (J). (gr. 2-7). 1993. pap. 9.95 (0-7460-1316-7, Usborne) EDC.

Make This Model Greek Temple. Ian Ashman. (Cut-Out Models Ser.). (Illus.). 32p. (J). (gr. 4 up). 1998. pap. 9.95 (0-7460-3314-1, Usborne) EDC.

Make This Model Haunted House. Iain Ashman. (Cut-Out Models Ser.). (Illus.). 32p. (J). (gr. 4-7). 1991. pap. 9.95 (0-7460-0647-0, Usborne) EDC.

Make This Model Lost Temple. Iain Ashman. (Cut-Out Models Ser.). 32p. (YA). (gr. 2-7). 1992. pap. 9.95 (0-7460-1211-X, Usborne) EDC.

Make This Model Medieval Port Cut Out Model. Iain Ashman. (Cut-Out Models Ser.). (Illus.). 32p. (J). (gr. 2-7). 1994. text 9.95 (0-7460-1844-4, Usborne) EDC.

Make This Model Village. Iain Ashman. (Cut-Out Models Ser.). (Illus.). 32p. (J). (gr. 4-7). 1988. pap. 9.95 (0-86020-579-7) EDC.

Make This Model Wizards Castle. Iain Ashman. (Cut-Out Models Ser.). (Illus.). 32p. (J). (gr. 2-7). 1991. pap. 9.95 (0-7460-0607-1, Usborne) EDC.

Make This Roman Fort. Iain Ashman. (Cut-Out Models Ser.). (Illus.). 32p. (J). (gr. 4 up). 1989. pap. 9.95 (0-7460-0256-4) EDC.

Make This Roman Villa. Iain Ashman. (Cut-Out Models Ser.). (Illus.). 32p. (J). (gr. 4 up). 1990. pap. 9.95 (0-7460-0462-1) EDC.

Make This Roman Villa. Iain Ashman. (Usborne Cut-Out Models Ser.). 1999. pap. 9.95 (0-7460-3690-6, Usborne) EDC.

Make This Viking Settlement. Iain Ashman. (Cut-Out Models Ser.). (Illus.). 32p. (J). (gr. 4 up). 1989. pap. 9.95 (0-7460-0257-2) EDC.

Make This Viking Settlement. Iain Ashman. 1999. pap. 9.95 (0-7460-3692-2, Usborne) EDC.

Make Time for This. Neva Biggs et al. 70p. 1985. 10.00 (0-911051-23-6) Plain View.

Make Time Work for You. unabridged ed. Merrill E. Douglass. 23p. pap. 12.95 incl. audio (0-88432-177-0, S13050) Audio-Forum.

*Make Toys. rev. ed. Ivan Bulloch. (Let's Ser.). (Illus.). (J). 2000. 9.95 (1-58728-028-0); pap. 4.95 (1-58728-032-9) Two Can Pub.

Make Training Worth Every Penny: On-Target Evaluation. Jane Holcomb. 155p. 1994. pap. 19.95 (1-56912-099-4) Wharton Pub.

Make 22 Herbal Gifts for the Holidays. Compiled by Rachael Kelly. LC 95-36943. (Storey Publishing Bulletin Ser.: No. A-149). 1995. pap. 2.95 (0-88266-012-8, Storey Pub) Storey Bks.

Make Uncle Sam an Offer . . . Or Someone Else Will. Janis Huffman. (Orig.). 1989. pap. 15.00 (0-685-25975-7) Post Intl Pubns.

Make-Up. Felicity Everett. (Practical Guides Ser.). (Illus.). 32p. (YA). (gr. 6 up). 1987. lib. bdg. 14.95 (0-88110-242-3) EDC.

Make-Up. Felicity Everett. (Practical Guides Ser.). (Illus.). 32p. (YA). (gr. 6 up). 1987. pap. 6.95 (0-7460-0075-8) EDC.

Make-Up. rev. ed. John Baird. 132p. 1941. 5.00 (0-573-69031-6) French.

Make up Artist's Manual: A Hoomestudy Course to Become a Certified Makeup Artist. Bernice Kentner. 200p. 1990. ring bd. 17.50 (0-941522-10-5) Ken Kra Pubs.

*Make-Up Book. Joy Terri. 96p. 1999. 24.95 (1-85368-987-4) New Holland.

Make up, Don't Break up. Bonnie E. Weil. LC 99-36903. 288p. 1999. 22.95 (1-58062-163-5) Adams Media.

*Make Up, Don't Break Up: Finding & Keeping Love for Singles & Couples. Bonnie Eaker Weil. 384p. 2000. pap. 6.95 (1-58062-407-3) Adams Media.

Make-Up Magic: A Complete Guide to a Beautiful New You. Debra Reece. Ed. by Trudy Settel. (Illus.). 64p. (Orig.). 1987. pap. 3.95 (0-932523-01-3) Briarcliff Pr.

Make-Up Stories. Eric C. Waldemar, Jr. 59p. 1996. pap. 5.60 (0-87129-616-0, M94) Dramatic Pub.

*Make-Up Techniques for Photography: Step by Step. Cliff Hollenbeck. (Illus.). 120p. 2000. pap. 29.95 (1-58428-037-9, Pub. by Amherst Media) IPG Chicago.

Make-Up Types & Styles. Margaret Rogers. 128p. 1995. pap. text 24.50 (0-572-02142-9, Pub. by W Foulsham) Trans-Atl Phila.

*Make Up Your Life: Every Woman's Guide to the Power of Makeup. Victoria Jackson & Andrea Cagan. 240p. 2000. 27.50 (0-06-019639-4, Cliff Street) HarperTrade.

Make up Your Mind: Entrepreneurs Talk about Decision Making. Ann G. Ehringer. LC 94-73597. 374p. 1995. pap. 19.95 (1-56343-101-7) Silver Lake.

Make up Your Mind, Marsha! A Brownie Girl Scout Book. Jane O'Connor. LC 92-45880. (Here Comes the Brownies Ser.: No. 3). (Illus.). 64p. (J). (gr. 1-4). 1993. pap. 4.95 (0-448-40164-9, G & D) Peng Put Young Read.

Make Us One. Arranged by Clydesdale. 1995. pap. 6.95 (3-10-051301-0) Word Enter.

Make Us One: Celebrating Spiritual Unity in the Midst of Cultural Diversity: Removing Barriers, Building Bridges. Delbert W. Baker. Ed. by Jerry D. Thomas. LC 95-18148. 284p. 1995. pap. 5.97 (0-8163-1267-2) Pacific Pr Pub Assn.

Make vs. Buy Decisions. Vincent C. Guess. Ed. by Martin P. Edelman. LC 88-83819. (Illus.). 73p. 1988. 40.00 (1-55822-014-3) Am Prod & Inventory.

Make Way for August. Mamie Moore. Ed. by Literacy Volunteers of New York City Staff. (New Writers' Voices Ser.). (Illus.). 64p. (Orig.). 1991. pap. text 3.50 (0-929631-36-6, Signal Hill) New Readers.

*Make Way for Babies! So Many Babies. 2000. per. 4.50 (0-373-24317-0) S&S Trade.

Make Way for Ducklings. Robert McCloskey. (Illus.). (J). (gr. k-3). 1941. 16.99 (0-670-45149-5, Viking Child) Peng Put Young Read.

*Make Way for Ducklings. Robert McCloskey. 76p. (J). (ps-3). 1999. pap. 6.99 (0-14-056434-9, PuffinBks) Peng Put Young Read.

Make Way for Ducklings. Robert McCloskey. (Picture Puffin Ser.). (J). 1976. 10.19 (0-606-03886-8, Pub. by Turtleback) Demco.

Make Way for Ducklings. Robert McClosky. (Illus.). (J). 1993. pap. 9.99 incl. audio (0-14-095118-0, PuffinBks) Peng Put Young Read.

Make Way for Ducklings: A Study Guide. Garrett Christopher. Ed. by Joyce Friedland & Rikki Kessler. (Little Novel-Ties Ser.). (J). (gr. k-2). 1991. pap. text 14.95 (0-88122-593-2) Lrn Links.

Make Way for Ducklings Literature Mini-Unit. Janet Lovelady. (Illus.). 32p. (J). (gr. 2-4). 1989. student ed. 4.95 (1-56096-006-X) Mari.

Make Way for Dumb Bunnies. Sue Denim. LC 95-15311. (Dumb Bunnies Ser.). (Illus.). 32p. (J). (ps-3). 1996. 12.95 (0-590-58286-0, Blue Sky Press) Scholastic Inc.

Make Way for Dumb Bunnies. Sue Denim. (Illus.). 32p. (J). (ps-3). 1998. pap. 4.99 (0-590-58288-7) Scholastic Inc.

Make Way for Learning. (Captain Kangaroo Fun-to-Learn Activity Bks.: Vol. 3). (J). 1998. pap. write for info. (0-7666-0217-6, Honey Bear Bks) Modern Pub NYC.

Make Way for Love: A Story to Open Your Heart. Lency Spezzano. LC 94-69093. 163p. (Orig.). 1995. text 22.00 (0-9643435-1-7); pap. text 12.00 (0-9643435-0-9) Psychol Vision Pr.

Make Way for Mommy (Mommy & Me) Muriel Jensen. LC 95-22333. 249p. 1995. per. 3.50 (0-373-16606-0) Harlequin Bks.

Make Way for Sam Houston. Jean Fritz. LC 85-25601. (Illus.). 109p. (J). (gr. 4-6). 1986. pap. 7.95 (0-399-21304-X, G P Putnam) Peng Put Young Read.

Make Way for Sam Houston. Jean Fritz. 112p. (YA). (gr. 5 up). 1998. pap. 5.99 (0-698-11646-1, PapStar) Peng Put Young Read.

Make Way for Sam Houston. Jean Fritz. 1986. 13.15 (0-606-00921-3, Pub. by Turtleback) Demco.

Make Way for the Automobile: The History of the Maine Automobile Association, 1910-1997. Jill Cournoyer et al. LC 98-30596. (Illus.). 96p. 1998. pap. write for info. (1-892168-00-6) Custom Communs.

Make Way for the King of the Jungle: A Peanuts Collection. Charles M. Schulz. (Illus.). 128p. 1995. pap. 8.95 (0-8362-1788-8) Andrews & McMeel.

Make Way for Tooth Decay. Bobbi Katz. LC 98-22397. (Hello Readers! Ser.). (Illus.). (J). 1999. write for info. (0-590-52290-6) Scholastic Inc.

Make Way for Triplets. Fran Bevington. LC 91-66575. 1992. pap. 7.95 (0-9630697-5-6) Triple Treat.

*Make Wire Beads. Lisa Van Herik. Ed. by Edward Van Herik. (Illus.). 64p. 2000. spiral bd. 17.95 (0-9675725-0-9) BeaDifferent Pr.

Make Your Airplane Last Forever. Nicholas E. Silitch. (Illus.). 160p. 1982. pap. 12.95 (0-8306-2328-0, 2328) McGraw-Hill Prof.

Make Your Beds, Bananaheads. Mike Thaler. (Illus.). 32p. (J). (ps-3). 1997. pap. 3.50 (0-8167-4356-8, Whistlstop) Troll Communs.

Make Your Bets: How to Win at Gambling. Picton Publishing (Chippenham) Ltd. Staff. (C). 1987. pap. 22.00 (0-948251-49-2, Pub. by Picton) St Mut.

Make Your Business Grow: Take a Strategic Approach. David Irwin. LC 98-208383. (ITBP PROFESSIONAL). 204p. 1998. pap. 19.99 (1-86152-204-5) Thomson Learn.

Make Your Child Smart. Stanley H. Freeman & Rebecca A. Freeman. LC 86-72225. 106p. 1987. pap. 15.00 (0-939961-00-8, 1500A) Axis Bks.

Make Your Community Work for Older People. 6p. 1987. write for info. (1-55672-024-6) US HHS.

*Make Your Day. Tess Marcin. 671p. 1999. pap. 25.95 (0-7414-0237-8) Buy Books.

Make Your Dream Come True. Charles R. Swindoll. 80p. 1990. pap. 3.99 (0-8423-7007-2, 727007-2) Tyndale Hse.

Make Your Dreams Come True: Simple Steps for Changing the Beliefs That Limit You. Pamala Oslie. LC 98-15626. 176p. 1998. pap. 12.95 (1-878424-33-5) Amber-Allen Pub.

Make Your Events Special: How to Plan & Organize Successful Special Events Programs for Nonprofit Organizations. 2nd ed. Ted Geier. 123p. 1992. reprint ed. 24.95 (0-685-66425-2) Cause Effect.

Make Your Events Special: How to Produce Successful Special Events for Nonprofit Organizations. Ted Geier. ii, 127p. (Orig.). 1986. pap. 24.95 (0-9619425-0-9) Cause Effect.

Make Your Family What You Want It to Be. Myron C. Severson. LC 85-13111. (Illus.). 112p. (Orig.). 1985. pap. 7.95 (0-9614948-7-5) Frontier Pubns.

Make Your Harmonica Play Well. Douglas Tate. (Illus.). 46p. 1998. pap. 9.95 (1-57424-062-5) Centerstream Pub.

Make Your Home Beautiful. Jimmie B. Marshall. 1997. 4.95 (0-9625557-7-0) Excelsior Cee.

Make Your Home into Your Castle: The Complete Do-It-Yourself Book of Home Security. Dan M. Bowers. LC 94-96523. 264p. 1994. 15.00 (0-9643804-0-4) D M Bowers.

Make Your House Do the Housework. rev. ed. Don Aslett & Laura A. Simons. (Illus.). 208p. (Orig.). 1995. pap. 14.99 (1-55870-384-5, Betrwy Bks) F & W Pubns Inc.

Make Your House Radon Free. Carl Giles & Barbara Giles. (Illus.). 128p. 1989. 15.95 (0-8306-9291-6); pap. 9.95 (0-8306-3291-3) McGraw-Hill Prof.

Make Your Job Interview a Success. 4th ed. Jacob I. Biegeleisen. 240p. 1994. per. 12.95 (0-671-87070-X, Arc) IDG Bks.

Make Your Juicer Your Drug Store. Laura Newman. LC 66-125414. (Illus.). 192p. 1998. pap. 4.95 (0-87904-001-7) Lust.

Make Your Kid Rich: A Financial Guide for the Whole Family. Gene Balliett. 201p. (Orig.). 1993. pap. 12.95 (0-9636537-0-9) PCI-Prof Comm.

Make Your Life Worthwhile. annuals Emmet Fox. LC 83-48456. 256p. 1984. pap. 13.00 (0-06-062913-4, RD 508, Pub. by Harper SF) HarpC.

Make Your Living Playing Craps. Larry Edell. LC 95-82225. 58p. (Orig.). 1996. pap. 19.95 (1-885516-02-9) SD Writs Mnthly.

Make Your Mark! Influencing Across Your Organization. Sue Craig. LC 97-9738. (Illus.). 254p. 1998. pap. 19.95 (0-07-709159-0) McGraw.

Make Your Mark in Food Service. (Make Your Mark Ser.). 128p. teacher ed. 3.95 (0-8092-0833-4) NTC Contemp Pub Co.

Make Your Mark in Health Services. (Make Your Mark Ser.). 128p. teacher ed. 3.95 (0-8092-0831-8) NTC Contemp Pub Co.

Make Your Mark in Retail Jobs. (Make Your Mark Ser.). 128p. teacher ed. 3.95 (0-8092-0832-6) NTC Contemp Pub Co.

Make Your Mark in the Hotel Industry. (Make Your Mark Ser.). 128p. teacher ed. 3.95 (0-8092-0834-2) NTC Contemp Pub Co.

Make Your Medicine Safe: How to Prevent Side Effects from the Drugs You Take. Jay S. Cohen. LC 98-92458. 1998. mass mkt. 7.50 (0-380-79075-0, Avon Bks) Morrow Avon.

Make Your Mind Work for You. Joan Minninger & Eleanor Dugan. Ed. by Sally Peters. 256p. 1990. reprint ed. mass mkt. 4.95 (0-671-68474-4) PB.

*Make Your Mission Statement Effective: How to Identify & Promote the Values of Your Organisation. Marianne Talbot. 144p. 2000. pap. 14.95 (1-85703-557-7, Pub. by How To Bks) Midpt Trade.

Make Your Own Adventure Story. Cherry Denman. 24p. (J). (gr. k-3). 1999. pap. 9.95 (0-316-85563-4) Little.

Make Your Own Animal Masks. Sterling Publishing Company, Inc. Staff. (Balloon Bks.). (Illus.). 18p. (J). 1997. 7.95 (0-8069-0503-4) Sterling.

Make Your Own Aquarium Sticker Activity Book. Cathy Beylon. (J). pap. text 1.00 (0-486-28603-7) Dover.

Make Your Own Artist's Tools & Materials. Vance Studley. LC 92-10293. Orig. Title: Making Artist's Tools. (Illus.). 144p. 1992. reprint ed. pap. text 10.95 (0-486-27246-X) Dover.

Make Your Own Beads & Jewelry. (Illus.). 64p. 1993. 5.98 (0-7853-0283-2, 3616700) Pubns Intl Ltd.

Make Your Own Book. Matt Liddle. LC 93-83466. (Discovery Kit Ser.). (Illus.). 64p. (Orig.). (J). (gr. 3 up). 1993. 18.95 (1-56138-337-6) Running Pr.

Make Your Own Booklet. John Dumpleton. LC 79-3815. (Illus.). 1980. pap. 2.95 (0-8008-5058-0) Taplinger.

Make Your Own Breaks: Become an Entrepreneur & Create Your Own Future. Jim Lang. 224p. 1994. pap. 15.95 (1-880030-25-X) DBM Pub.

Make-Your-Own-Button Book. Andrea Wayne-Von Konigslow & Linda Granfield. LC 93-15230. (Illus.). 40p. (J). (gr. 3-7). 1994. pap. 12.95 (1-56282-486-4, Pub. by Hyprn Child) Little.

*Make-Your-Own-Button Book. Andrea Wayne-Von Konigslow & Linda Granfield. (Illus.). 32p. 1998. pap. 12.95 (0-921051-89-1) Somerville Hse.

Make Your Own Calendar 1997, Vol. 1. Illus. by Sue Dennen. 24p. 1996. 6.95 (0-316-18107-2) Little.

*Make Your Own Calendar 2001. Sue Dennen. (Illus.). 24p. (J). (gr. 1-5). 2000. 6.95 (0-316-19210-4) Little.

*Make Your Own Calendar 2000. Ed. by Sue Dennen. (Illus.). 24p. 1999. pap. 6.95 (0-316-18888-3) Little.

Make Your Own Christm. Anne V. Brady. (J Hook Ser.). 1995. mass mkt. 4.99 (0-425-15058-5) Berkley Pub.

Make Your Own Christmas. Anne V. Brady. 144p. (Orig.). 1996. mass mkt. write for info. (0-614-17549-6) Berkley Pub.

Make Your Own Christmas Cards. Tomie De Paola. (Illus.). 32p. (J). (ps-2). 1998. pap. 8.99 (0-8431-7444-7) Putnam Pub Group.

*Make Your Own Christmas Cards. Roger Generazzo. 16p. 1999. 6.99 (0-307-33700-6, Goldn Books) Gldn Bks Pub Co.

Make Your Own Christmas Sticker Postcards: Eight Blank Cards & 73 Colorful Stickers. Crystal Collins-Sterling. (Illus.). (J). (gr. k-3). 1993. pap. 4.95 (0-486-27538-8) Dover.

*Make Your Own Circular Slide Rule. Mark A. McMenamin & Amy L. McMenamin. (Technology Quest Ser.: No. 2). (Illus.). 12p. 2000. pap. 10.00 (0-9651136-8-X, 108) Meanma Pr.

Make Your Own Contract see Simple Contracts for Personal Use

Make Your Own Cool Crafts. Kate Mason. (J). (gr. 4-7). 1994. pap. 5.95 (0-8167-3226-4) Troll Communs.

Make Your Own Cosmetics. Neal's Yard Remedies Staff & Susan Curtis. (Illus.). 144p. (Orig.). 1997. pap. 14.95 (1-85410-469-1, Pub. by Aurum Pr) London Brdge.

Make Your Own Creepy Spooky Horrors. 1997. pap. 1.95 (0-8167-2249-8) Troll Communs.

Make Your Own Curtains & Blinds. Lani Van Reenen. LC 94-1410. (Illus.). 72p. 1994. 18.95 (0-88266-865-X, Storey Pub) Storey Bks.

Make Your Own Cushions & Covers. Lani Van Reenen. LC 94-1411. (Illus.). 72p. 1994. 18.95 (0-88266-875-7, Storey Pub) Storey Bks.

Make Your Own Decorative Boxes with Easy-to-Use Patterns. Karen K. Larsen. LC 94-44866. (Illus.). 32p. 1995. reprint ed. pap. text 3.50 (0-486-27814-X) Dover.

Make Your Own Dinosaur out of Chicken Bones: Foolproof Instructions for Budding Paleontologists. Christopher McGowan. LC 97-186864. (Illus.). 160p. (J). (gr. 4-7). 1997. pap. 13.00 (0-06-095226-1) HarpC.

Make Your Own Doll's House Furniture. Maurice Harper. (Illus.). 176p. 1995. pap. 15.95 (0-946819-59-9, Pub. by Guild Master) Sterling.

Make Your Own Egyptian Mummy Case. Museum Press British. (gr. 4-7). 1999. pap. text 6.95 (0-7141-1785-4) Brimax Bks.

*Make Your Own Egyptian Pyramid. James Putnam. 24p. 1999. pap. 9.95 (0-688-17019-6, Wm Morrow) Morrow Avon.

Make Your Own Electric Guitar. Melvyn Hiscock. (Illus.). 160p. 1986. pap. 16.95 (0-7137-1706-8, Pub. by Blandford Pr) Sterling.

Make Your Own Fairy Tale. Reed Books. 24p. (J). (gr. k-3). 1999. pap. 9.95 (0-316-85564-2) Little.

Make-Your-Own Fort & Playhouse: With Paper Linx. Philip Poissant & Dede Sinclair. (Illus.). 56p. (J). pap. 29.95 (1-895897-15-7) Somerville Hse.

Make Your Own Friendship Bracelets (with String in Five Colors) (J). (gr. 4-7). 1997. pap. 6.95 (0-8167-3112-8) Troll Communs.

Make Your Own Games Workshop. Craig Pearson. (Crafts Workshop Ser.). (J). (gr. 3-8). 1982. pap. 11.99 (0-8224-9782-4) Fearon Teacher Aids.

Make Your Own Great Earrings: Beads, Wire, Polymer Clay, Fabric, Found Objects. Jane LaFerla. LC 97-26423. (Illus.). 128p. 1998. 24.95 (1-57990-031-3); pap. 14.95 (1-57990-014-3, Pub. by Lark Books) Random.

Make Your Own Great Vests: 90 Ways to Jazz up Your Wardrobe. Carol Parks. (Illus.). 160p. 1996. pap. 14.95 (0-8069-0973-0) Sterling.

Make Your Own Groceries. Daphne M. Hartwig. LC 79-2453. (Illus.). 1979. pap. write for info. (0-672-52279-9) Macmillan.

Make Your Own Handcrafted Doors & Windows. John Birchard. LC 87-33701. (Illus.). 296p. (Orig.). 1988. pap. 19.95 (0-8069-6544-4) Sterling.

Make Your Own Haunted House. Cathy Beylon. (Illus.). 1995. pap. 1.00 (0-486-28604-5) Dover.

Make Your Own Horse Clothing. Jean Perry. 112p. (C). 1990. pap. 21.00 (0-85131-383-3, Pub. by J A Allen) Trafalgar.

Make Your Own Horse Equipment. Jean Perry. 111p. (C). 1990. pap. 35.00 (0-85131-393-0, Pub. by J A Allen) Trafalgar.

Make Your Own Incredible Jewelry with Friendly Plastic: A Book & Kit. Luann Columbo. (Illus.). 32p. (Orig.). (J). 1996. pap. 9.95 (0-8362-2228-8) Andrews & McMeel.

Make Your Own Insulated Window. E. A. Prouxl. 1983. pap. 2.95 (0-88266-294-5, Storey Pub) Storey Bks.

Make Your Own Japanese Clothes: Patterns & Ideas for Modern Wear. John Marshall. LC 87-82861. (Illus.). 136p. 1988. pap. 25.00 (0-87011-865-X) Kodansha.

Make Your Own Jewelry Book & Box Set. Barbara Feldman. (Make Your Own Jewelry Ser.). (Illus.). 64p. (J). (gr. 4-6). 1994. boxed set 16.95 (0-89577-636-7) Rdrs Digest.

Make Your Own Jewish Calendar Coloring Book. Chaya Burstein. (J). 1995. pap. 2.50 (0-486-28630-4) Dover.

Make Your Own Jigs & Woodshop Furniture. Jeff Greef. LC 94-14764. (Illus.). 144p. 1994. 24.99 (1-55870-340-3, Betrwy Bks) F & W Pubns Inc.

Make Your Own Kite. John W. Jordan. (Illus.). 96p. (Orig.). 1981. 7.95 (0-918464-35-8); pap. 4.95 (0-918464-34-X) D Armstrong.

*Make Your Own Little Blue Car. (Illus.). 5p. (J). (ps-k). 2000. 4.98 (0-7651-1748-7) Smithmark.

Make Your Own Little Golden Book. Golden Books Staff. 1999. pap. text 9.99 (*0-307-16287-7*) Gldn Bks Pub Co.
***Make Your Own Little Red Plane.** (Illus.). 5p. (J). (ps-k). 2000. 4.98 (*0-7651-1749-5*) Smithmark.
Make Your Own Living Trust. large type ed. Denis Clifford. LC 93-45047. 1994. 24.95 (*0-7862-0136-3*) Thorndike Pr.
Make Your Own Living Trust. 3rd rev. ed. Denis Clifford. Ed. by Mary Randolph. LC 97-34274. (Illus.). 336p. 1998. pap. 34.95 (*0-87337-429-0*) Nolo com.
***Make Your Own Living Trust.** 4th ed. Denis Clifford. LC 99-45009. (Illus.). 335p. 2000. pap. 34.95 (*0-87337-556-4*) Nolo com.
Make Your Own Megillah. Judyth Groner & Madeline Wikler. (Illus.). 32p. (J). (ps-2). pap. 4.95 (*1-58013-013-5*) Kar-Ben.
Make Your Own Mixes & Prepared Foods. Ben Howard. LC 93-11724. 188p. 1994. pap. 14.95 (*1-56825-007-X*) Rainbow Books.
***Make Your Own Mummy.** Mirly Starke. (Illus.). 16p. (J). (gr. 3-7). 2000. pap. 8.95 (*0-8167-6607-X*) Troll Communs.
Make Your Own Museum: An Activity Kit for Children. Andrea P. Belloli. (Getty Trust Publications). (Illus.). 44p. 1999. boxed set 19.95 (*0-89236-297-9*) OUP.
Make Your Own Newspaper. Chris Harris & Ray Harris. 48p. 1993. pap. 9.95 (*1-55850-219-X*) Adams Media.
Make Your Own Noah's Ark with Twenty-Three Stickers Book. Lynn Adams. (Little Activity Bks.). (Illus.). (J). 1995. pap. 1.00 (*0-486-28928-1*) Dover.
Make Your Own Old Fashioned Cl. Claire Bryant. 80p. 1990. pap. 5.95 (*0-486-26361-4*) Dover.
***Make Your Own Ornaments: Inspired by Medieval Stained Glass.** Metropolitan Museum of Art Staff. (Illus.). 32p. (J). (ps-3). 2000. 16.99 (*0-670-89367-6*, Viking Child) Peng Put Young Read.
Make Your Own Outdoor Flags & Banners. Marsha McCloskey & Linda Moore. LC 97-119603. (Illus.). 24p. (Orig.). 1999. pap. 6.95 (*0-9635422-5-7*, FSP6) Feathered Star.
Make Your Own Patterns: An Easy Step-by-Step Guide to Making over 60 Patterns. Rene Bergh. (Illus.). 128p. 1997. pap. 17.95 (*1-85368-702-2*, Pub. by New5 Holland) Sterling.
Make Your Own Performing Puppets. Teddy C. Long. LC 94-35536. (Illus.). 96p. (J). (gr. 4-7). 1995. 19.95 (*1-895569-32-X*, Pub. by Tamos Bks) Sterling.
***Make Your Own Riding Clothes.** Perry. 2000. pap. 14.95 (*0-85131-718-9*, Pub. by J A Allen) Trafalgar.
***Make Your Own Roman Villa.** Pat Sheehan. 24p. 1999. pap. 9.95 (*0-688-17020-X*, Wm Morrow) Morrow Avon.
Make-Your-Own-Soap Kit. Marily Starke. (Illus.). 8p. (J). (gr. 2-7). 1998. pap. 8.95 (*0-8167-4548-X*) Troll Communs.
Make Your Own Solar System. Karen Farrington. (Illus.). 24p. (J). (gr. 1 up). 1998. pap. 7.95 (*0-688-16330-0*, Wm Morrow) Morrow Avon.
Make Your Own Southern Belle Cloth Doll & Her Wardrobe. Claire Bryant. LC 99-23441. (Illus.). 80p. 1999. pap. text 6.95 (*0-486-40483-8*) Dover.
Make Your Own Space Machines. Karen Farrington. (Illus.). 24p. (J). (gr. 1 up). 1998. pap. 7.95 (*0-688-16329-7*, Wm Morrow) Morrow Avon.
Make Your Own Space Story. Cherry Denman. (Illus.). 24p. (J). (gr. 2-5). 1998. pap. 8.95 (*0-316-85561-8*) Little.
Make Your Own Spanish Category Pictionary: Thematic Skillbuilder. Linda Milliken. (Illus.). 64p. (J). (gr. k-2). 1994. pap., student ed. 6.95 (*1-56472-030-6*) Edupress Inc.
Make Your Own Spooky Story. Cherry Denman. 24p. (J). (gr. k-3). 1998. pap. 8.95 (*0-316-85562-6*) Little.
Make Your Own Starship: Klingon Battle Cruiser. Ruth Wickings. (Illus.). 12p. (J). (gr. 2-6). 1996. pap. 5.99 (*0-689-80920-4*) S&S Childrens.
Make Your Own Starship: USS Enterprise: The Next Generation. Ruth Wickings. (Illus.). 12p. (J). (ps up). 1996. 5.99 (*0-689-80919-0*) S&S Trade.
Make Your Own Sticker Calendar. Cathy Beylon. 1999. pap. text 4.50 (*0-486-40583-4*) Dover.
***Make Your Own Tattoo: From Temptu, the Creators of the Original Temporary Tattoo.** Roy Zuckerman & Jean-Chris Miller. LC 99-39194. (Illus.). 144p. 1999. 17.98 (*1-57912-080-6*, Pub. by Blck Dog & Leventhal) Workman Pub.
***Make Your Own Teddy Bear & Bear Clothes.** Jodie Davis. (Quick Starts for Kids! Ser.). (Illus.). 64p. (J). (gr. 3 up). 2000. pap. 8.95 (*1-885593-75-9*) Williamson Pub Co.
Make Your Own Teddy Bear Book & Kit: Everything You Need to Create Your Very Own Bear. Alicia Merrett. LC 94-67766. (Illus.). 48p. 1995. pap. 9.95 (*1-56138-541-7*) Running Pr.
Make Your Own Teddy Bear Calendar Coloring Book, Vol. 181. Theodore Menten. (Illus.). (J). 1991. pap. 2.50 (*0-486-26911-6*) Dover.
Make Your Own Teddy Bears: Instructions & Full-Size Patterns for Jointed & Unjointed Bears & Their Clothing. Doris King. 64p. (Orig.). 1986. pap. 4.95 (*0-486-24942-5*) Dover.
Make Your Own Time Capsule. Steven Caney. LC 89-40725. (Steven Caney's Kids' America Kits Ser.). (Illus.). 64p. (Orig.). (J). (gr. 2-6). 1991. pap. 14.95 (*0-89480-418-9*, 1418) Workman Pub.
Make Your Own Time Capsule. Mary Packard. (Illus.). (J). (gr. 2-7). 1999. pap. 6.95 (*0-8167-4976-0*) Troll Communs.
Make Your Own Valentine Cards. (J). (ps-3). 1992. pap. 2.95 (*0-8167-1613-7*) Troll Communs.
Make Your Own Valentine Sticker Postcard. Crystal Collins-Sterling. (Illus.). 1996. pap. text 4.95 (*0-486-28814-5*) Dover.
Make Your Own Valentines! Felicia Bond. (Illus.). 32p. (J). (ps-3). 1999. 9.95 (*0-694-01259-9*) HarpC Child Bks.
Make Your Own Valentines. Disney. 40p. 1999. 7.99 (*0-7364-0100-8*, Pub. by Mouse Works) Time Warner.
***Make Your Own Valentine's Day Cards.** (Illus.). (J). 1999. pap. text. write for info. (*0-307-33701-4*) Gldn Bks Pub Co.
Make Your Own Viking Ship. Museum British Press. 1999. pap. text 6.95 (*0-7141-1786-2*) Brimax Bks.
Make Your Own Web Page: A Guide for Kids. Ted Pedersen. LC 98-30511. (Illus.). 96p. (J). (gr. 8 up). 1998. pap. 4.99 (*0-8431-7459-5*) Putnam Pub Group.
Make Your Own Will: A Guide to Making a Michigan Statutory Will Without a Lawyer. Michael Maran. (Illus.). 96p. (Orig.). 1990. pap. 4.95 (*0-936343-04-4*) Grand River.
Make Your Own Wooden Kitchen Utensils. 56th ed. Vance Studley. LC 92-41040. Orig. Title: The Woodworker's Book of Wooden Kitchen Utensils. (Illus.). 128p. 1993. reprint ed. pap. 6.95 (*0-486-27561-2*) Dover.
Make Your Own Working Camera. Adrian Thornton. 16p. (Orig.). 1988. pap. 14.95 (*0-944845-00-2*) STAT Pub.
Make Your Own Working Paper Clock. James S. Rudolph. LC 83-47570. 40p. 1983. pap. 14.00 (*0-06-091066-6*, CN1066, Perennial) HarperTrade.
Make Your Own World of Christmas. Claude Kailer & Rosemary Lowndes. LC 73-22563. (Illus.). 107p. 1974. pap. 5.95 (*0-672-51981-X*, Bobbs) Macmillan.
Make Your Paycheck Last. 4th rev. ed. Harold Moe. (Illus.). 128p. 1997. pap. 11.95 (*0-9612310-7-6*) Harsand Pr.
Make Your Paycheck Last: The Complete Step by Step Guide to Financial Success. expanded rev. ed. Harold R. Moe. Ed. by Jeanne Choutka. (Illus.). 116p. 1994. student ed. 14.95 (*0-9612310-5-X*) Harsand Pr.
Make Your Paycheck Last: The Complete Step by Step Guide to Financial Success. 2nd rev. ed. Harold R. Moe. Ed. by Jeanne Choutka. (Illus.). 120p. 1994. pap. 7.95 (*0-9612310-2-5*) Harsand Pr.
Make Your Point! Currid, Cheryl, & Company Staff. LC 93-34367. 304p. 1995. boxed set 24.95 (*1-55958-414-9*) Prima Pub.
***Make Your Point.** Anna Kournikova. 2000. 14.95 (*0-87833-252-9*) Taylor Pub.
Make Your Quilting Pay for Itself. Sylvia Landman. LC 97-23573. (Illus.). 144p. 1997. pap. 18.99 (*1-55870-446-9*, Betrwy Bks) F & W Pubns Inc.
Make Your Scanner a Great Design & Production Tool. rev. ed. Michael Sullivan. LC 97-34611. (Illus.). 160p. 1998. pap. 28.99 (*0-89134-841-7*, North Lght Bks) F & W Pubns Inc.
Make Your Team a Winner! Tips & Techniques for Success in Today's Work Teams. Ed. by Dartnell Corporation Editors. 184p. Date not set. pap. 14.95 (*0-85013-341-6*) Dartnell Corp.
Make Your Training Results Last: A Practical Guide to Tracking Training Follow-Through. Gloria E. Bader. 1995. pap. 14.95 (*1-883553-39-3*) R Chang Assocs.
Make Your Training Results Last: A Practical Guide to Tracking Training Follow-Through. Gloria E. Bader & Audrey E. Bloom. (High Impact Training Ser.). (Illus.). 120p. 1994. pap. 14.95 (*0-7879-5093-9*) R Chang Assocs.
Make Your Voice Heard: An Actor's Guide to Increased Dramatic Range Through Vocal Training. Chuck Jones. 144p. 1996. pap. text 16.95 (*0-8230-8333-0*) Watsn-Guptill.
***Make Your Walls Tumble: How to Change Your Impossible to Difficult, Then Achieve Success.** John Clements. 2000. pap. 19.95 (*0-910882-16-9*) Lexngton Hse.
***Make Your Website Work for You: How to Convert Your Online Content into Profits.** Jeff Cannon. 208p. 1999. pap. 19.95 (*0-07-135241-4*) McGraw.
Make Your Woodworking Pay for Itself. rev. ed. Jack Neff. (Illus.). 128p. 1996. pap. 18.99 (*1-55870-418-3*, Betrwy Bks) F & W Pubns Inc.
***Make Yours a Winning Team.** John C. Maxwell. 2000. 9.99 (*0-88486-281-X*, Inspirational Pr) Arrowood Pr.
***Make Yourself a Monster: Aliens.** Ross. LC 98-50751. 1999. 22.90 (*0-7613-1556-X*) Millbrook Pr.
Make Yourself a Monster: Aliens. Kathy Ross. LC 98-50751. (Books for Halloween & Thanksgiving Ser.). (Illus.). 48p. (J). (gr. k-3). 1999. pap. 6.95 (*0-7613-1049-5*, Copper Beech Bks) Millbrook Pr.
Make Yourself at Home. Bo Niles. 192p. 1995. mass mkt. 4.99 (*0-425-14536-0*); mass mkt. 4.99 (*0-425-14539-5*) Berkley Pub.
Make Yourself Ready: Preparing to Meet the King. Harland W. Miller. LC 96-79609. 224p. (Orig.). 1998. pap. 11.99 (*0-933451-36-9*) Prescott Pr.
Make Yourself Ready: Study Guide. Harland Miller. 214p. 1997. spiral bd. 12.95 (*0-9661146-0-4*) Eternal Hope.
Make Your Own Calendar CB P 181. 1981. pap. text 2.50 (*0-486-24193-9*) Dover.
Makedonen, Ihre Sprache und Ihr Volkstum. Otto Hoffmann. v, 284p. 1974. reprint ed. write for info. (*3-487-05292-X*) G Olms Pubs.
Makedonika. Eugene N. Borza. Ed. by Carol G. Thomas. LC 95-8423. 270p. 1995. 37.95 (*0-941690-64-4*); pap. 18.95 (*0-941690-65-2*) Regina Bks.
Make'em Laugh. Steve Allen. LC 92-20700. (Illus.). 339p. 1993. 25.95 (*0-87975-837-6*) Prometheus Bks.
Makeover. Marcia Biederman. (Academy First Mystery Ser.). 240p. 1984. pap. 5.95 (*0-89733-226-1*) Academy Chi Pubs.
Makeover Campaign. Suzanne Weyn. 160p. 1990. pap. 2.95 (*0-380-75850-4*, Avon Bks) Morrow Avon.
Makeover Club. Suzanne Weyn. 128p. (YA). (gr. 7 up). 1986. pap. 2.50 (*0-380-75007-4*, Avon Bks) Morrow Avon.
Makeover Manual: From Color Me Beautiful. Mary Spillane. (Illus.). 192p. 1999. pap. 23.95 (*0-330-37350-1*) Trans-Atl Phila.
Makeover Summer. Suzanne Weyn. 128p. (YA). (gr. 7 up). 1988. pap. 2.95 (*0-380-75521-1*, Avon Bks) Morrow Avon.
Makepeace: A Spirit of Adventure in Craft & Design. Jeremy Myerson. (Illus.). 192p. 1995. 45.00 (*0-7892-0067-8*, Cross Riv Pr) Abbeville Pr.
Makepeace Experiment. Abram Tertz, pseud. 191p. 1989. reprint ed. pap. 13.95 (*0-8101-0838-0*) Northwestern U Pr.
Maker & Craftsman: The Story of Dorothy L. Sayers. Alzina S. Dale. LC 92-23960. (Wheaton Literary Ser.). 172p. 1992. pap. 11.99 (*0-87788-523-0*, H Shaw Pubs) Waterbrook Pr.
Maker & Takers: How Wealth & Progress Are Made - & How They Are Taken Away or Prevented. Edmund Contoski. LC 96-78787. 480p. (Orig.). 1997. pap. 24.95 (*0-9655007-4-8*) Am Liberty Pubs.
Maker, Lover & Keeper. James McDermott. 112p. (C). 1988. 35.00 (*0-85597-454-0*, Pub. by McCrimmon Pub) St Mut.
Maker of Heaven & Earth: The Christian Doctrine of Creation in the Light of Modern Knowledge. Langdon Gilkey. 392p. 1986. reprint ed. pap. text 32.00 (*0-8191-4976-4*) U Pr of Amer.
Maker of Modern Arabia. Ameen F. Rihani. LC 83-1485. (Illus.). 370p. 1983. reprint ed. lib. bdg. 92.50 (*0-313-23854-5*, RIMA, Greenwood Pr) Greenwood.
Maker of Modern Japan: The Life of Shogun Tokugawa Ieyasu. Arthur L. Sadler. LC 75-41238. reprint ed. 47.50 (*0-404-14595-7*) AMS Pr.
Maker of Modern Mexico: Porfirio Diaz. E. Tweedie. (Mexico Ser.). 1979. lib. bdg. 250.00 (*0-8490-2968-6*) Gordon Pr.
Maker of Moons. Robert W. Chambers. LC 75-98565. (Short Story Index Reprint Ser.). 1977. 24.95 (*0-8369-3139-4*) Ayer.
Maker of Rainbows, & Other Fairy-Tales & Fables. Richard Le Gallienne. LC 77-167460. (Short Story Index Reprint Ser.). (Illus.). 1977. reprint ed. 18.95 (*0-8369-3986-7*) Ayer.
Maker of Saints. Thulani Davis. 256p. 1996. 21.50 (*0-684-81225-8*) S&S Trade.
Maker of Shadows. Jack Mann. 1977. 6.50 (*0-685-88837-1*) Bookfinger.
Maker of Shadows. Charles E. Vivan. Ed. by R. Reginald & Douglas A. Menville. LC 75-46310. (Supernatural & Occult Fiction Ser.). 1976. reprint ed. lib. bdg. 23.95 (*0-405-08172-3*) Ayer.
Maker of Signs. Whit Burnett. LC 79-106252. (Short Story Index Reprint Ser.). 1977. 20.95 (*0-8369-3289-7*) Ayer.
Maker of the New Orient: Samuel Robbins Brown. William E. Griffis. (Notable American Authors Ser.). 1992. reprint ed. lib. bdg. 75.00 (*0-7812-2966-9*) Rprt Serv.
Maker of Universes. Philip Jose Farmer. 1993. reprint ed. lib. bdg. 18.95 (*0-89968-397-5*, Lghtyr Pr) Buccaneer Bks.
Maker of Universes. rev. ed. Philip Jose Farmer. (World of Tiers Ser.: No. 1). 224p. 1980. reprint ed. 15.00 (*0-932096-07-7*) Phantasia Pr.
Makeready on the Sheetfed Offset Press. Robert J. Schneider, Jr. (Illus.). 1990. pap. text, teacher ed. 8.00 (*0-88362-151-7*, 0681) GATFPress.
Makeready on the Sheetfed Offset Press. Robert J. Schneider, Jr. (Illus.). 50p. 1990. pap. text 20.00 (*0-88362-150-9*) GATFPress.
Makers & Markets: The Wright Collection of Twentieth-Century Native American Art. Penelope B. Drooker & Martine Maurel. LC 98-65658. (Peabody Museum Press Ser.). (Illus.). 184p. 1998. pap. 30.00 (*0-87365-825-6*, PRMAKE) Peabody Harvard.
***Makers & Users: American Decorative Arts, 1620-1830, from the Chipstone Collection.** Ann S. Martin. LC 99-38249. (Illus.). 72p. 1999. pap. 19.95 (*0-932900-46-1*) Elvejhem Mus.
Maker's Instructions. Johnston. 1998. pap. 5.99 (*1-85792-369-3*, Pub. by Christian Focus) Spring Arbor Dist.
Makers of a New Nation. John S. Bassett. 1928. 100.00 (*0-686-83612-X*) Elliots Bks.
Makers of a New Nation. John S. Bassett. (BCL1 - U. S. History Ser.). 344p. 1991. reprint ed. lib. bdg. 89.00 (*0-7812-6035-3*) Rprt Serv.
Makers of American Machinist Tools. Kenneth L. Cope. (Illus.). 320p. (Orig.). 1994. pap. 27.50 (*1-879335-55-7*) Astragal Pr.
Makers of American Thought: An Introduction to Seven American Writers. Ed. by Ralph G. Ross. LC 74-78993. (Minnesota Library on American Writers). 307p. reprint ed. pap. 95.20 (*0-608-15981-6*, 203328900084) Bks Demand.
Makers of Cajun Music see Cajun & Creole Music Makers: Musiciens Cadiens et Creoles
Makers of Canada Series, 12 vols., Set. W. L. Grant. (BCL1 - History - Canada Ser.). 1991. reprint ed. lib. bdg. 900.00 (*0-7812-6348-4*) Rprt Serv.
Makers of Christian Theology in America: A Handbook. Ed. by Mark G. Toulouse & James O. Duke. LC 97-18743. (ARE Membership Ser.). 560p. 1997. pap. 34.95 (*0-687-00766-6*) Abingdon.
Makers of Christianity. LC 92-38185. 1993. 10.00 (*0-19-283105-4*) OUP.
***Makers of Classical Archaeology: A Reference Work.** Linda M. Medwid. LC 99-462362. 320p. 2000. 99.95 (*1-57392-826-7*, Humanity Bks) Prometheus Bks.
Makers of Democracy in Latin America. Harold E. Davis. LC 68-56190. reprint ed. 53.00 (*0-8154-0272-4*) Cooper Sq.
Makers of English Fiction. 3rd ed. William J. Dawson. LC 74-142617. (Essay Index Reprint Ser.). 1977. 20.95 (*0-8369-2043-0*) Ayer.
Makers of Europe: Dickinson College, James Henry Morgan Lectures, 1930. Robert S. Conway. LC 67-28748. (Essay Index Reprint Ser.). 1977. 16.95 (*0-8369-0330-7*) Ayer.
Makers of Freedom. George S. Eddy & Kirby Page. LC 79-117786. (Essay Index Reprint Ser.). 1977. 23.95 (*0-8369-1803-7*) Ayer.
Makers of Hebrew Books in Italy. David Amram. 418p. (C). 1988. 150.00 (*0-900470-46-1*, Pub. by New5 Holland) St Mut.
Makers of Hebrew Books in Italy. David W. Amram. 350p. 1983. 45.00 (*0-87556-013-X*) Saifer.
Makers of History. Annie H. Foster. LC 76-38544. (Biography Index Reprint Ser.). 1977. reprint ed. 18.95 (*0-8369-8121-9*) Ayer.
Makers of India. Hugh G. Rawlinson. LC 77-134126. (Essay Index Reprints - Living Names Ser.). 1977. reprint ed. 15.95 (*0-8369-2251-4*) Ayer.
Makers of Literature: Being Essays on Shelley, Landor, Browning, Byron, Arnold, Coleridge, Lowell, Whittier & Others. George E. Woodberry. LC 67-30237. (Essay Index Reprint Ser.). 1977. 29.95 (*0-8369-1588-7*) Ayer.
Makers of Mathematics. Stuart H. Hollingdale. 1991. pap. 14.95 (*0-14-014922-8*) Viking Penguin.
***Makers of Miracles: The Cast of the Federation Story.** Ed. by David Headon & John Williams. (Illus.). 275p. 2000. pap. 34.95 (*0-522-84858-3*, Pub. by Melbourne Univ Pr) Paul & Co Pubs.
Makers of Modern Culture: Five Twentieth-Century Thinkers. Roland N. Stromberg. (Illus.). 150p. (C). 1991. pap. text 9.95 (*0-88295-875-5*) Harlan Davidson.
***Makers of Modern Economics.** Ed. by Arnold Heertje. LC 92-29859. 174p. 1999. 80.00 (*1-85898-787-3*) E Elgar.
Makers of Modern Economics, Vol. II. Ed. by Arnold Heertje. LC 92-29859. 192p. 1995. 80.00 (*1-85898-237-5*) E Elgar.
Makers of Modern Economics, Vol. III. Ed. by Arnold Heertje. 160p. 1997. 75.00 (*1-85898-546-3*) E Elgar.
Makers of Modern Europe. Carlo Sforza. LC 68-57338. (Essay Index Reprint Ser.). 1977. 28.95 (*0-8369-1064-8*) Ayer.
Makers of Modern Italy: Napoleon to Mussolini. John A. Marriott. LC 74-30842. (Illus.). 228p. 1975. reprint ed. lib. bdg. 65.00 (*0-8371-7936-X*, MAMA, Greenwood Pr) Greenwood.
Makers of Modern Medicine. James J. Walsh. LC 70-107741. (Essay Index Reprint Ser.). 1977. 22.95 (*0-8369-1538-0*) Ayer.
Makers of Modern Orissa. J. K. Samal & P. K. Nayak. LC 96-906113. (C). 1997. 27.50 (*81-7017-322-1*, Pub. by Abhinav) S Asia.
Makers of Modern Strategy from Machiavelli to the Nuclear Age. Ed. by Peter Paret et al. LC 85-17029. (Illus.). 944p. 1986. pap. text 24.95 (*0-691-02764-1*, Pub. by Princeton U Pr) Cal Prin Full Svc.
Makers of Music: Biographical Sketches of the Great Composers. Robert F. Sharp. LC 72-5562. (Essay Index Reprint Ser.). 1977. reprint ed. 24.95 (*0-8369-7278-3*) Ayer.
Makers of Naval Tradition. Carroll S. Alden & Ralph Earle. LC 76-167303. (Essay Index Reprint Ser.). 1977. reprint ed. 30.95 (*0-8369-2733-8*) Ayer.
Makers of Nineteenth Century Culture: A Biographical Dictionary. Ed. by Justin Wintle. 734p. 1983. 49.95 (*0-7100-9295-4*, Routledge Thoemms) Routledge.
Makers of Nineteenth Century Europe. Ralph Flenley. LC 77-108637. (Essay Index Reprint Ser.). 1977. 18.95 (*0-8369-1571-2*) Ayer.
Makers of Psychology: The Personal Factor. Harvey Mindess. 182p. 1988. 35.95 (*0-89885-371-0*, Kluwer Acad Hman Sci); pap. 20.95 (*0-89885-380-X*, Kluwer Acad Hman Sci) Kluwer Academic.
Makers of Rome: Nine Lives by Plutarch. Plutarch. Tr. & Intro. by Ian Scott-Kilvert. (Classics Ser.). 368p. 1965. pap. 12.95 (*0-14-044158-1*, Penguin Classics) Viking Penguin.
Makers of Science. Ivor B. Hart. LC 68-8469. (Essay Index Reprint Ser.). 1977. 20.95 (*0-8369-0076-6*) Ayer.
Makers of the American Mind. Robert C. Whittemore. 497p. 1977. 27.95 (*0-8369-2431-2*) Ayer.
Makers of the City. Lewis Fried. LC 89-5201. 256p. (C). 1990. lib. bdg. 30.00 (*0-87023-693-8*) U of Mass Pr.
Makers of the Empire see British Empire
Makers of the Harpischord & Clavichord, 1440-1840. 3rd ed. Donald H. Boalch. Ed. by Charles Mould. (Illus.). 820p. 1995. text 160.00 (*0-19-318429-X*) OUP.
Makers of the Media Mind: Journalism Educators & Their Ideas. Ed. by W. David Sloan. 376p. (C). 1990. pap. 49.95 (*0-8058-0699-7*); text 99.95 (*0-8058-0698-9*) L Erlbaum Assocs.
***Makers of the Modern World: The Lives of Ninety-Two Writers, Artists.** Louis Untermeyer. 832p. 1999. 39.95 (*0-7351-0144-2*) Replica Bks.
***Makers of the Piano, 1820-1860, Vol. 2.** Martha N. Clinkscale. (Illus.). 506p. 1999. text 130.00 (*0-19-816625-7*) OUP.
Makers of the Piano, 1700-1820. Martha N. Clinkscale. LC 93-16320. 418p. 1993. text 85.00 (*0-19-816323-1*) OUP.
Makers of the Twentieth-Century Novel. Ed. by Harry R. Garvin. LC 74-4975. 322p. 1976. 37.50 (*0-8387-1522-2*) Bucknell U Pr.
Makers of the United States Air Force. John L. Frisbee. 347p. 1988. pap. 21.00 (*0-912799-41-2*) AFH & MP.
Makers of the United States Air Force. John L. Frisbee. 363p. 1996. per. 21.00 (*0-16-048757-9*) USGPO.

An Asterisk (*) at the beginning of an entry indicates that the title is appearing for the first time.

Makers of the Unwritten Constitution: The Fred Morgan Kirby Lectures Delivered at Lafayette College, 1929. William B. Munro. (Fred Morgan Kirby Lectures, Lafayette College, 1929 Ser.). 156p. 1982. reprint ed. 35.00 (*0-8377-0842-7*, Rothman) W S Hein.

Makers of the Western Tradition, Vol. 1. 7th ed. J. Kelley Sowards. LC 96-86790. 1997. pap. text 32.95 (*0-312-14252-8*) St Martin.

Makers of the Western Tradition, Vol. 2. 7th ed. J. Kelley Sowards. LC 96-86790. 1997. pap. text 32.95 (*0-312-14251-X*) St Martin.

Makers of the World: Caste, Craft & Mind of South Indian Artisans. Jan Brouwer. (Illus.). 626p. 1995. text 55.00 (*0-19-563091-2*) OUP.

Makers of 20th-Century Modern Architecture. Ed. by Donald L. Johnson & Donald Langmead. (Illus.). 1997. lib. bdg. 95.00 (*1-884964-93-1*) Fitzroy Dearborn.

Makers of 20th-Century Modernist Architecture: A Bio-Critical Sourcebook. Donald L. Johnson & Donald Langmead. LC 95-46055. 512p. 1997. lib. bdg. 89.50 (*0-313-29353-8*, Greenwood Pr) Greenwood.

Makers of Venice: Doges, Conquerors, Painters & Men of Letters. Margaret O. Oliphant. LC 77-173809. (Illus.). reprint ed. 39.50 (*0-404-04815-3*) AMS Pr.

Makers of War. Francis Neilson. 1971. 250.00 (*0-87700-002-6*) Revisionist Pr.

Makers of World History, Vol. 1. 2nd ed. J. Kelley Sowards. 333p. 1994. pap. text 35.95 (*0-312-09650-X*) St Martin.

Makers of World History, Vol. 2. 2nd ed. J. Kelley Sowards. 319p. 1994. pap. text 35.95 (*0-312-09651-8*) St Martin.

Makes Me Wanna Holler: A Young Black Man in America. Nathan McCall. 1995. 12.00 (*0-614-32215-4*) Vin Bks.

Makes Me Wanna Holler: A Young Black Man in America. Nathan McCall. LC 93-30654. 416p. 1995. pap. 13.00 (*0-679-74070-8*) Vin Bks.

Makeshift Husband. Hilda Stahl. (Prairie Ser.: Bk. 3). 172p. 1993. pap. 6.99 (*0-934998-48-5*) Evangel Indiana.

Maketing Tofu Second Generation Products: Varieties & Okara Products (1977-1985) Labels, Ads, Posters & Other Graphics. Ed. by Akiko Aoyagi. 205p. 1988. spiral bd. 82.00 (*0-933332-31-9*) Soyfoods Center.

Makeup. rev. ed. Felicity Everett. (Fashion Guide Ser.). (Illus.). 32p. (J). (gr. 6 up). 1998. pap. 6.95 (*0-7460-3111-4*, Usborne); lib. bdg. 14.95 (*1-58086-035-4*, Usborne) EDC.

Makeup Artist. Kathryn A. Quinlan. LC 98-45187. (Careers Without College Ser.). (J). (gr. 3-4). 1999. write for info. (*0-7368-0175-8*) Capstone Pr.

*__Makeup Artist.__ Kathryn A. Quinlan. 1999. 19.93 (*0-516-21773-9*) Capstone Pr.

Makeup for Photography. 3rd ed. Elliot De Picciotto. (Illus.). 35p. 1993. reprint ed. pap. 17.50 (*0-934420-15-7*) Studio Pr NE.

Makeup for Theatre, Film & Television: A Step by Step Photographic Guide. Lee Baygan. LC 81-1911. (Illus.). 208p. 1982. spiral bd. 29.95 (*0-89676-093-6*, Drama Pubs) QSMG Ltd.

Makewehi Dunes & Sinkhole Field Site Guide for Teachers. Faith M. Roelofs. (Exploring the Islands Ser.). 1993. teacher ed. write for info. (*1-882163-22-2*) Moanalua Grdns Fnd.

*__Makhail Bakhtin & Biblical Scholarship: An Introduction.__ Barbara Green. LC 00-36572. (Society of Biblical Literature Semeia Studies). 2000. pap. write for info. (*0-88414-020-2*) Soc Biblical Lit.

Makiawisug: The Gift of the Little People. Melissa J. Fawcett & Joseph Bruchac. (Illus.). 28p. (J). (gr. 2-4). 1997. 19.95 (*0-9656933-2-5*) Lttle People.

Makiguchi the Value Creator: Revolutionary Japanese Educator & Founder of Soka Gakkai. Dayle M. Bethel. (Illus.). 68p. (Orig.). 1994. pap. 14.95 (*0-8348-0318-6*) Weatherhill.

Makiko's Diary: A Merchant Wife in 1910 Kyoto. Tr. by Nakano Makiko from JPN. LC 94-39864.Tr. of Meiji Yonjusannen Kyoto. (ENG & JPN., Illus.). 304p. 1995. 45.00 (*0-8047-2440-7*); pap. 14.95 (*0-8047-2441-5*) Stanford U Pr.

Makimba's Animal World. Bobby L. Jackson. Ed. by April Gordon. LC 93-79595. (Illus.). 32p. (Orig.). (J). (gr. k-4). 1994. 15.95 (*0-9634932-9-9*); pap. 7.95 (*0-9634932-8-0*) Multicult Pubns.

Makin' Buckskin Clothes. Roberta Moss. 1982. 7.50 (*0-913150-48-7*) Pioneer Pr.

Makin' Do in Illinois. Phyliss Ellett et al. (Illus.). 180p. 1993. pap. 9.95 (*1-878488-64-3*) Quixote Pr IA.

Makin' Do in South Dakota. Marilyn Fitzgerald et al. (Illus.). 167p. (Orig.). 1991. pap. 9.95 (*1-878488-54-6*) Quixote Pr IA.

Makin' Muffins. Susan Devins. (Illus.). (J). (gr. 1-5). 1998. pap. 12.99 (*0-525-46002-0*, Dutton Child) Peng Put Young Read.

Makin' Muffins. Susan Devins. (Illus.). 32p. (J). (gr. 1 up). 1998. pap. 12.99 (*1-894042-22-0*) Somerville Hse.

Makin Music! Chris Patella & Eileen Oddo. (Illus.). 75p. (Orig.). (J). (gr. k-2). 1989. audio, lp. write for info. (*0-318-64483-5*) Musical Munchkins.

Makin' Music. Chris Patella & Eileen Oddo. (Musical Munchkins Are...Ser.). (Illus.). 75p. (J). (gr. k-2). 1989. teacher ed. 9.95 incl. audio (*0-944333-02-8*) Musical Munchkins.

Makin' Numbers: Howard Aiken & the Computer. Ed. by I. Bernard Cohen & Gregory W. Welch. LC 98-43964. (Illus.). 320p. 1999. 40.00 (*0-262-03263-5*) MIT Pr.

*__Makin' Waves: Fun with Kids in the Tub.__ Created by Melcher, Inc. Staff. (Soapdish Editions Ser.). 2000. 7.95 (*0-8118-2971-5*) Chronicle Bks.

Making: The Proper Habit of Our Being. Marion Montgomery. LC 99-19017. 344p. 1999. 37.50 (*1-890318-39-6*) St Augustines Pr.

*__Making a Baby: Everything You Need to Know to Get Pregnant.__ Debra Fulghum Bruce & Samuel Thatcher. 416p. (Orig.). 2000. pap. 14.00 (*0-345-43543-5*) Ballantine Pub Grp.

Making a Baby in Union Park, Chicago. Layle Silbert. 77p. 1983. pap. 5.00 (*0-917402-19-7*) Downtown Poets.

Making a Better Confession: A Deeper Examination of Conscience. Con O'Connell. 1997. pap. text 1.95 (*0-89243-863-0*) Liguori Pubns.

Making a Broadway Musical: Making It Run, an Anatomy of Entrepreneurship. John D. Mitchell. (Illus.). 131p. 1989. 25.00 (*0-87359-050-3*) Northwood Univ.

Making a Business from Biomass in Energy Environment, Chemicals, Fibres & Materials. Overend. LC 97-221334. 1770p. 1997. 400.00 (*0-08-042996-3*, Pergamon Pr) Elsevier.

Making a Change from City Living to Country Living & from Country Living to City Living: A Report. Center for Self-Sufficiency, Research Division Sta. LC 83-90713. 55p. 1985. ring bd. 39.95 (*0-910811-05-9*) Ctr Self Suff.

Making a Choice: A Practical Guide for Surviving the Streets & Accomplishing Your Dreams. Mark G. Harden. (Illus.). 134p. (Orig.). (YA). (gr. 8-12). 1995. pap. text 10.95 (*0-8187-0214-1*) Harlo Pr.

Making a Church from Scratch. Troy Benitone. 1998. pap. 14.95 (*1-885224-18-4*) Bristol Hse.

Making a Claim for Disability Benefits: A Qualitative Study Amongst People with Disabilities. A. Hedges & A. Thomas. (DSS Research Report Ser.). 1994. 30.00 (*0-11-762162-5*, HM21625, Pub. by Statnry Office) Bernan Associates.

Making a Claim under a Title Insurance Policy: Fall, 1992, Action Guide. Davida S. Tussman & Charles A. Hansen. Ed. by Ellen C. Lester. 62p. 1992. pap. text 47.00 (*0-88124-564-X*, RE-11452) Cont Ed Bar-CA.

Making a Clock-Accurate Sundial: Timepiece & Teacher. Sam Muller. LC 97-8226. (Illus.). 48p. (Orig.). 1997. pap. 8.95 (*0-87961-246-0*) Naturegraph.

Making a Complaint Against the Police. NCCL Staff. (URD.). (C). 1988. 30.00 (*0-7855-6067-X*, Pub. by NCCL) St Mut.

*__Making a Complex Decisions: Facilitator Guide.__ John Hopkins University Staff. (Illus.). 2000. pap. 35.00 (*0-538-69825-X*) Sth-Wstrn College.

Making a Difference. Michael Edwards & David Hulme. 1991. 30.00 (*1-85383-144-1*, Pub. by Escan Pubns) Island Pr.

Making a Difference. Ed. by Gayle Greene & Coppelia Kahn. 288p. (Orig.). (C). 1985. pap. 18.99 (*0-415-01011-X*, 4069) Routledge.

Making a Difference. Ed. by Gayle Greene & Coppelia Kahn. 288p. (Orig.). 1985. 14.95 (*0-416-37470-0*, 4147) Routledge.

Making a Difference. Smoke. (C). 1993. pap., teacher ed. 5.96 (*0-395-63683-3*); pap. text 29.56 (*0-395-63682-5*) HM.

Making a Difference: A Directory of Northwest Environmental Non-Profit Organizations. Ed. by Rhea M. Connors. Date not set. pap. 7.00 (*0-9665952-1-1*) Sugar Mtn Press.

Making a Difference: A Fifty-Year History of Kansas-Nebraska Southern Baptists. Marjorie Stith. LC 95-33630. 352p. 1995. pap. 19.95 (*1-881576-61-2*) Providence Hse.

Making a Difference: A Guide to Fundraising & Nonprofit Management. unabridged ed. Olaf Engvig & Mona Engvig. Ed. by Ann Krilanovich. LC 98-90053. 100p. 1998. pap. text. write for info. (*0-9655451-1-3*) Craft Pr CA.

Making A Difference: Canadian Multicultural Literature. Ed. by Smaro Kamboureli. 456p. (C). 1996. pap. text 29.75 (*0-19-541078-5*) OUP.

Making a Difference: Effective Citizenship. Maryrose Eannace. (Illus.). 150p. 1992. text 35.00 (*0-936826-38-X*) PS Assocs Croton.

Making a Difference: Innovations in Adult Education. Ed. by Werner Mauch & Uta Papen. LC 97-26319. 216p. 1997. 19.95 (*3-631-32038-8*) P Lang Pubng.

Making a Difference: Lessons from Teach for America Classrooms, Vol. 1. Compiled by Julie Pier Brodie. LC 97-212062. (Illus.). 1997. write for info. (*0-7622-0594-6*) Creative Pubns.

Making a Difference: Listening, Loving & Serving. Colleen Rockers. Ed. by Kathy Coffey. (Crossings : Vol. 2). 80p. (YA). 1998. pap. 3.95 (*1-889108-28-6*) Liv Good News.

Making a Difference: Measuring the Impact of Information on Development: Proceedings of a Workshop Held in Ottawa, Canada 10-12 July 1995. Ed. by Paul McConnell. LC 97-701287. iv, 254p. 1995. pap. 19.95 (*0-88936-783-3*, Pub. by IDRC Bks) Stylus Pub VA.

Making a Difference: Outcomes of a Decade of Assessment in Higher Education. Trudy Banta & Associates Staff. LC 93-19501. 430p. (C). 1993. text 36.95 (*1-55542-578-X*) Jossey-Bass.

Making a Difference: Personal Essays by Today's College Teachers. 1997. pap. text 3.00 (*0-944210-99-6*) Townsend NJ.

Making a Difference: Psychology & the Construction of Gender. Rachel T. Hare-Mustin. 226p. (C). 1992. pap. 16.00 (*0-300-05222-7*) Yale U Pr.

Making a Difference: Selected Writings of Dorothy Watson. Sandra Wilde. LC 96-11839. 300p. 1996. text 65.00 (*0-435-07211-0*) Heinemann.

Making a Difference: Selected Writings of Dorothy Watson. Ed. by Sandra Wilde. LC 96-11839. 300p. 1996. pap. text 27.00 (*0-435-08873-4*) Heinemann.

Making a Difference? Social Work after Hillsborough. Tim Newburn. 1993. pap. 35.00 (*0-902789-81-3*, Pub. by Natl Inst Soc Work) St Mut.

*__Making a Difference: Stories by & about Lawyers Who Have.__ Ed. by Norma Ann Dawson. 76p. 1999. pap. 10.95 (*0-7414-0008-1*) Buy Books.

Making a Difference: The Fire Officer's Role. OnGuard Inc. Staff. 232p. 1988. pap. text, student ed. 14.95 (*1-56916-110-0*); teacher ed., ring bd. 35.95 (*1-56916-111-9*) OnGuard.

*__Making a Difference: The Kennedy Family & the History of Mental Retardation.__ Edward Shorter. (Illus.). 240p. 2000. 74.50 (*1-56639-782-0*); pap. 22.95 (*1-56639-783-9*) Temple U Pr.

Making a Difference: The Practice of Sociology. Irwin Deutscher. LC 98-8590. 468p. 1998. text 49.95 (*1-56000-359-6*) Transaction Pubs.

Making a Difference: Twelve Qualities That Make You a Leader. Shelia M. Bethel. 1990. pap. 12.95 (*0-425-12309-X*) Berkley Pub.

Making a Difference: Young People in Community Crime Prevention. National Crime Prevention Council Staff. LC 85-61344. (Illus.). 132p. (Orig.). 1985. pap. 11.95 (*0-934513-00-7*, M2B) Natl Crime DC.

Making a Difference College & Graduate Guide: Outstanding Colleges to Help You Make a Better World. 6th rev. ed. Ed. by Miriam Weinstein. (Illus.). 350p. 1999. pap. 13.00 (*0-9634618-4-2*) SageWorks Pr.

*__Making a Difference College & Graduate Guide: Outstanding Colleges to Help You Make a Better World.__ 7th ed. Ed. by Miriam Weinstein. 432p. 2000. pap. 19.95 (*0-86571-412-6*, Pub. by New Soc Pubs) Consort Bk Sales.

Making a Difference College Guide: Outstanding Colleges to Help You Make a Better World. 4th rev. ed. Miriam Weinstein. (Illus.). 300p. (YA). (gr. 11-12). 1995. pap. 16.00 (*0-9634618-3-4*) SageWorks Pr.

Making a Difference for Students at Risk: Trends & Alternatives. Ed. by Margaret C. Wang & Maynard C. Reynolds. LC 94-32842. 240p. 1994. 61.95 (*0-8039-6188-X*) Corwin Pr.

Making a Difference for Students at Risk: Trends & Alternatives. Ed. by Margaret C. Wang & Maynard C. Reynolds. LC 94-32842. 240p. 1994. pap. 24.95 (*0-8039-6189-8*) Corwin Pr.

Making a Difference in College Admission: A Step-by-Step Guide for the Secondary School Counselor. Kenneth Hitchner & Anne Tifft-Hitchner. LC 89-710. 296p. 1989. pap. text 29.95 (*0-87628-549-3*) Ctr Appl Res.

Making a Difference in Preaching. Haddon W. Robinson. LC 99-37518. 160p. 1999. 16.99 (*0-8010-9092-X*) Baker Bks.

*__Making a Difference in the World.__ Lynne Cherry. (Meet the Author Ser.). (Illus.). 32p. (YA). (gr. 7-10). 2000. 14.95 (*1-57274-373-5*) R Owen Pubs.

Making a Difference in Your World see Don't Let 'Em Crumble Your Cookies: It's Your Life!

Making a Difference Scholarships. Ed. by Miriam Weinstein. 200p. (YA). (gr. 10 up). 1999. pap. 13.00 (*0-9634618-5-0*) SageWorks Pr.

*__Making a Difference Scholarships for a Better World: Fellowships, Social Entrepreneur Funds, Community Service Awards.__ 2nd ed. Ed. by Miriam Weinstein. 240p. 2000. pap. 15.95 (*0-86571-415-0*) New Soc Pubs.

Making a Difference While You're Making a Living. David Bertrand & J. Mark Bertrand. LC 98-87460. 212p. 1998. pap. 12.95 (*0-9666773-0-7*) New Paradigm TX.

Making a Digital Book: Art, Computers, Design & the Production of the Great Central Valley, California's Heartland. Stephen Johnson. Ed. by David M. Hamilton. (Illus.). 52p. 1993. pap. 15.00 (*0-931095-04-2*) Live Oak.

Making a Dream Come True. Dave Leapard. (C). 1993. student ed. 14.00 (*1-881592-33-2*) Hayden-McNeil.

Making a Financial Case. Nebsm. 96p. pap. text. write for info. (*0-7506-3308-5*) Buttrwrth-Heinemann.

Making a Fortune Quickly in Fix-Up Properties. Andrew J. McLean. LC 95-22784. 368p. 1997. pap. 14.95 (*0-8092-4839-5*, 483950, Contemporary Bks) NTC Contemp Pub Co.

Making a Friend in Youth: Developmental Theory & Pair Therapy. Robert L. Selman & Lynn H. Schultz. LC 89-20362. (Illus.). 374p. 1996. 35.95 (*0-226-74790-5*) U Ch Pr.

Making a Friend in Youth: Developmental Theory & Pair Therapy. Robert S. Selman & Lynn Schultz. LC 97-43304. 373p. 1998. reprint ed. pap. text 25.95 (*0-202-30605-4*); reprint ed. lib. bdg. 49.95 (*0-202-30606-2*) Aldine de Gruyter.

Making a Garden. 1996. 35.00 (*0-02-860373-7*) Macmillan.

Making a Garden: Reliable Techniques, Outstanding Plants & Honest Advice. Rita Buchanan & Steve Buchanan. LC 98-28215. (Illus.). 160p. 1998. 35.00 (*0-395-89753-X*) HM.

Making a Goal Writer Great: A Creativity Workbook for Screenwriters. Linda Seger. LC 99-33998. 220p. 1999. pap. 14.95 (*1-879505-49-5*, Pub. by Silman James Pr) SCB Distributors.

Making a Good Layout. Lori Siebert & Lisa Ballard. (Graphic Design Basics Ser.). (Illus.). 128p. 1992. 24.99 (*0-89134-423-3*, North Lght Bks) F & W Pubns Inc.

*__Making a Good Move: Opening the Door to a Successful Pastorate.__ 144p. 1999. pap. text 15.00 (*0-687-08133-5*) Abingdon.

Making a Good Script Great. Linda Seger. LC 89-19906. 1989. 17.50 (*0-573-60691-9*) S French Trade.

Making a Good Script Great. 2nd ed. Linda Seger. LC 94-32338. 242p. 1994. pap. 12.95 (*0-573-69921-6*) S French Trade.

Making a Grass Basket see Mingqiileg

Making a Grass Basket see Mingqiller Tapernarneg

Making a Grass Basket. large type ed. Kelly J. Lincoln. (Illus.). 16p. (J). (gr. k-3). 1999. pap. text 21.00 (*1-58084-062-0*) Lower Kuskokwim.

*__Making a Habit of Success.__ Mack R. Douglas. 464p. 1999. 19.90 (*1-57866-071-8*) Galahad Bks.

Making a Healthy World: Agencies Actors & Policies in International Health. Meri Koivusalo. LC 97-36972. (C). 1998. pap. 25.00 (*1-85649-494-2*, Pub. by Zed Books); text 65.00 (*1-85649-493-4*) Zed Books.

*__Making a Heart for God: A Week Inside a Catholic Monastery.__ Dianne Aprile. 2000. 21.95 (*1-893361-14-4*) SkyLight Paths.

Making A Herb Garden. Storey Publishing Staff. 1997. 24.95 (*0-676-57228-6*) Random.

Making a Historical Culture: Historiography in Norway. Ed. by William H. Hubbard et al. 340p. 1995. 43.00 (*82-00-22699-9*) Scandnvan Univ Pr.

Making a Home in Stillwater. Peggy McCormick. LC 88-83680. (Illus.). 96p. 1989. pap. 14.95 (*0-934188-28-9*) Evans Pubns.

Making a Japanese Garden. Herb L. Gustafson. LC 98-40923. 1998. 24.95 (*0-8069-0963-3*) Sterling.

Making a Just Peace: Human Rights & Domination Systems. C. Dale White. 176p. 1998. pap. 10.95 (*0-687-03133-8*) Abingdon.

Making a Killing: A New Play. John Nassivera. LC 87-460823. 88 p. 1986. write for info. (*0-573-60847-4*) S French Trade.

Making a Killing: A Smoking Satire on Selling Cigarettes. Gordon B. Lindsay. 304p. 1997. pap. 19.98 (*0-88290-609-7*, 1982) Horizon Utah.

Making a Killing: An End of the World Black Comedy. William M. Johnson. 382p. 1996. 42.50 (*1-85776-080-8*, Pub. by Book Guild Ltd) Trans-Atl Phila.

Making a Killing: HMOs & the Threat to Your Health. Jamie Court & Francis Smith. LC 99-37783. 1999. 29.95 (*1-56751-169-4*) Common Courage.

Making a Killing: HMOs & the Threat to Your Health. Jamie Court & Francis Smith. LC 99-37783. 224p. 1999. pap. 12.71 (*1-56751-168-6*, Pub. by Common Courage) SPD-Small Pr Dist.

Making a Killing: The Business of Guns in America. Tom Diaz. LC 98-34227. 256p. 1999. 25.00 (*1-56584-470-X*, Pub. by New Press NY) Norton.

*__Making a Killing: The Business of Guns in America.__ Tom Diaz. 2000. pap. 14.95 (*1-56584-567-6*, Pub. by New Press NY) Norton.

Making a Landscape of Continuity: The Practice of Innocenti & Webel. Ed. by Gary R. Hilderbrand. (Illus.). 128p. 1997. 45.00 (*1-56898-122-8*) Princeton Arch.

Making a Leap: Theatre of Empowerment: A Practical Handbook for Drama & Theatre Work with Youn. Sara Clifford. LC 99-159338. 10p. 1998. pap. text 26.95 (*1-85302-632-8*) Jessica Kingsley.

Making a Life, Building a Community: A History of the Jews of Hartford. David G. Dalin & Jonathan Rosenbaum. LC 97-19875. (New Perspectives Ser.). (Illus.). 330p. 1997. 49.95 (*0-8419-1374-9*); pap. 24.95 (*0-8419-1375-7*) Holmes & Meier.

*__Making a Life in Yorkville: Experience & Meaning in the Life-course Narrative of an Urban Working-class Man, 130.__ Gerald Handel. LC 99-49048. (Contributions in Sociology Ser.). 176p. 2000. write for info. (*0-313-31307-5*, Greenwood Pr) Greenwood.

Making a Life, Making a Living: Reclaiming Your Purpose & Passion in Business & in Life. Mark Albion. LC 99-30166. 256p. 2000. 23.95 (*0-446-52404-2*, Pub. by Warner Bks) Little.

*__Making a Life, Making a Living: Reclaiming Your Purpose & Passion in Business & in Life.__ Mark Albion. 2000. pap. 13.95 (*0-446-67651-9*) Warner Bks.

Making a Life, Not Just a Living. Ron Jenson. LC 97-40913. 224p. 1998. reprint ed. pap. 12.99 (*0-8054-1196-8*) Broadman.

Making a Living. James A. Newman. (Illus.). 120p. (Orig.). (J). (gr. 2-8). 1991. pap. 7.95 (*0-9642980-0-7*) J A Newman.

Making a Living As an Artist. Art Calenders Editors. LC 98-10803. (Art Calendar Guide Ser.). 1998. pap. 17.95 (*1-55821-729-0*) Lyons Pr.

Making a Living As an Artist: A Guide to Navigating the Art Marketplace. Drew Steis et al. Ed. by Carolyn Blakeslee. (Illus.). 220p. (Orig.). 1993. pap. 17.95 (*0-945388-01-2*, BOAC) Art Calendar.

Making a Living in Conservation: A Guide to Outdoor Careers. Albert M. Day. LC 70-162449. 96p. 1971. write for info. (*0-8117-0964-7*) Stackpole.

Making a Living in Europe: Human Geographies of Economic Change. Alan R. Townsend. LC 96-38677. (Illus.). 288p. (C). 1997. 75.00 (*0-415-14479-5*); pap. 25.99 (*0-415-14480-9*) Routledge.

Making a Living in Rural Sudan: Production of Women, Labour Migration of Men, & Policies for Peasants' Needs. Grawert. LC 97-28034. 256p. 1998. text 69.95 (*0-312-21006-X*) St Martin.

Making a Living in the Stock Market. Robert Eldridge. 180p. 1999. boxed set 24.95 (*0-910019-99-1*, Pub. by Lghthse Pub Gp) Origin Bk Sales.

Making a Living in Your Local Music Market: How to Survive & Prosper. 2nd ed. Dick Weissman. 304p. 1999. per. 14.95 (*0-7935-9562-2*) H Leonard.

Making a Living While Making a Difference: The Expanded Guide to Creating Careers with a Conscience. rev. ed. Melissa Everett. 240p. 1999. pap. 17.95 (*0-86571-400-2*, Pub. by New Soc Pubs) Consort Bk Sales.

Making a Living Without a Job: Winning Ways for Creating Work that You Love. Barbara Winter. LC 93-9450. 272p. 1993. pap. 13.95 (*0-553-37165-7*) Bantam.

An Asterisk (*) at the beginning of an entry indicates that the title is appearing for the first time.

Making a Lottery of Good Causes: The National Lottery & the Politicisation of Charity. Roger Cummins & Robert Whelan. LC 96-164286. (Choice in Welfare Ser.: No. 25). 28p. 1995. pap. 7.95 (*0-255-36362-1*, Pub. by Inst Economic Affairs) Coronet Bks.

Making a Love That Lasts: How to Find Love Without Settling for Sex. 2nd rev. ed. Jacob Aranza. LC 96-43157. 140p. (YA). 1996. pap. 9.99 (*1-56955-019-0*, Vine Bks) Servant.

Making a Market: The Institutional Transformation of an African Society. Jean Ensminger. LC 92-15498. (Political Economy of Institutions & Decisions Ser.). (Illus.). 230p. (C). 1992. text 59.95 (*0-521-42060-1*) Cambridge U Pr.

Making a Market: The Institutional Transformation of an African Society. Jean Ensminger. (Political Economy of Institutions & Decisions Ser.). 230p. 1996. pap. text 19.95 (*0-521-57426-9*) Cambridge U Pr.

Making a Match: Courtship in Shakespeare & His Society. Ann J. Cook. ix, 273p. 1991. text 47.50 (*0-691-06842-9*, Pub. by Princeton U Pr) Cal Prin Full Svc.

Making a Medical Living: Doctors & Patients in the English Market for Medicine, 1720-1911. Anne Digby. (Cambridge Studies in Population, Economy & Society in Past Time: No. 24). (Illus.). 369p. (C). 1994. text 69.95 (*0-521-34526-X*) Cambridge U Pr.

Making a Middle Class: Student Life in English Canada during the Thirties. Paul Axelrod. 304p. (C). 1990. text 55.00 (*0-7735-0753-1*, Pub. by McG-Queens Univ Pr) CUP Services.

Making a Middle Landscape. Peter G. Rowe. (Illus.). 336p. 2000. reprint ed. pap. text 29.95 (*0-262-68077-7*) MIT Pr.

Making a Miracle. Hunter Tylo. LC 99-57477. (Illus.). 352p. 2000. 24.95 (*0-671-02778-6*, PB Hardcover) PB.

Making a Modern Classic: The Architecture of the Philadelphia Museum of Art. David B. Brownlee. LC 97-7682. (Illus.). 126p. 1997. 32.00 (*0-87633-112-6*); pap. 22.00 (*0-87633-111-8*) Phila Mus Art.

Making a Necessity of Virtue: Aristotle & Kant on Virtue. Nancy Sherman. 404p. 1997. text 59.95 (*0-521-56383-6*); pap. text 21.95 (*0-521-56487-5*) Cambridge U Pr.

Making a New Deal: Industrial Workers in Chicago, 1919-1939. Lizabeth Cohen. (Illus.). 544p. (C). 1991. pap. text 17.95 (*0-521-42838-6*) Cambridge U Pr.

Making a New Nation: The Formation of Slovenia. Ed. by Danica Fink-Hafner & John Robbins. LC 96-43128. 334p. 1997. text 78.95 (*1-85521-656-6*, Pub. by Dartmth Pub) Ashgate Pub Co.

*__Making a Place for Kids with Disabilities.__ Dale Borman Fink. LC 99-37526. 224p. 2000. 65.00 (*0-275-96565-1*, Praeger Pubs) Greenwood.

Making a Place for Ourselves: The Black Hospital Movement, 1920-1945. Vanessa N. Gamble. (Illus.). 296p. 1995. text 55.00 (*0-19-507889-6*) OUP.

Making a Place for Pleasure in Early Childhood Education. Joseph J. Tobin. LC 96-41890. 240p. 1997. 32.00 (*0-300-06968-5*) Yale U Pr.

Making a Place in the Faculty Rewards System for Work with K-12: A Project Report of Four Universities. Ed. by Crystal J. Gips & Carol F. Stoel. 120p. 1999. pap. 16.00 (*1-56377-046-6*, SC9901) Am Assn Higher Ed.

*__Making a Prince's Museum: Drawings for the Late-Eighteenth-Century Redecoration of the Villa Borghese.__ Carole Paul et al. LC 99-58367. (Illus.). 180p. 2000. 24.95 (*0-89236-539-0*, Getty Res Inst) J P Getty Trust.

Making a Real Killing: Rocky Flats & the Nuclear West. Len Ackland. LC 99-6500. 296p. 1999. 34.95 (*0-8263-1877-0*) U of NM Pr.

Making a Republic. Jon Silkin. (SAP Title Ser.). 88p. 1997. pap. 11.50 (*1-85075-816-6*, Pub. by Sheffield Acad) CUP Services.

Making a Sacrifice Like Art. Sam Silva. (Dog River Review Poetry Ser.: Ser. 18). 20p. (Orig.). 1995. pap. 3.00 (*0-916155-31-5*) Trout Creek.

Making a Sampler Quilt: Twenty Traditional Patchwork Blocks with Both Hand & Quick Machine Techniques. Lynne Edwards. LC 96-26591. (Illus.). 144p. 1997. 24.95 (*0-89577-911-0*, Pub. by RD Assn) Penguin Putnam.

Making a Scene: The Contemporary Drama of Jewish-American Women. Ed. & Intro. by Sarah B. Cohen. LC 96-21140. 436p. 1996. 45.00 (*0-8156-2713-0*, COMS); pap. 19.95 (*0-8156-0404-1*, COMSP) Syracuse U Pr.

Making a Social Body: British Cultural Formation, 1830-1864. Mary Poovey. LC 95-4153. 266p. 1995. pap. text 12.95 (*0-226-67524-6*); lib. bdg. 34.00 (*0-226-67523-8*) U Ch Pr.

Making a Soul: Human Destiny & the Debt of Our Existence. John G. Bennett. (Spiritual Classics Edition Ser.). 128p. (Orig.). 1995. pap. 14.00 (*1-881408-00-0*) Bennett Bks.

Making a Spectacle: Feminist Essays on Contemporary Women's Theatre. Ed. by Lynda Hart. (Women & Culture Ser.). 368p. 1988. text 44.50 (*0-472-09389-4*, 09389); pap. text 18.95 (*0-472-06389-8*, 06389) U of Mich Pr.

Making a Statement with Song. Phyllis R. Emert. (Perspectives on History Ser.: Pt. III). 1998. pap. 6.95 (*1-57960-022-0*) Disc Enter Ltd.

Making a Stenciled ABC Quilt: With Full-Size Patterns. Marie M. Sturmer. (Illus.). 48p. (Orig.). 1991. pap. 3.95 (*0-486-26939-6*) Dover.

*__Making a Technical Presentation.__ John Hopkins University Staff. 2000. pap. 59.50 incl. cd-rom (*0-538-69807-1*); pap. 10.50 (*0-538-69808-X*) Sth-Wstrn College.

*__Making a Technical Presentation: Facilitator Guide.__ John Hopkins University Staff. 2000. pap. 35.00 (*0-538-69809-8*) Sth-Wstrn College.

Making a Traditional Applique Sampler Quilt: Full-Size Templates & Complete Instructions for 12 Quilt Blocks. Andrea Shedletsky. 48p. (Orig.). 1986. pap. 4.95 (*0-486-24999-9*) Dover.

Making a Trail. Joyce Thompson. (Illus.). 1982. 9.60 (*0-9607488-0-6*); pap. 7.65 (*0-9607488-1-4*) TX Womans U Pr.

*__Making a Voice.__ Kirk. 1999. 28.00 (*0-8133-3797-6*, Pub. by Westview) HarpC.

Making a Voice: African Resistance to Segregation in South Africa. Joyce E. Kirk. LC 97-30476. 342p. 1997. pap. 79.00 (*0-8133-2769-5*, Pub. by Westview) HarpC.

Making a Way to Freedom: A History of African Americans on Long Island. Lynda R. Day. LC 97-40816. 1997. write for info. (*1-55787-149-3*) Hrt of the Lakes.

Making a Winning Short. Edmond Levy. 1995. pap. 14.95 (*0-8050-2680-0*) H Holt & Co.

Making a World of Difference: A Multifaith Resource Book for Primary Teachers. Elizabeth Hughes. (Education Ser.). (Illus.). 128p. 1994. pap., spiral bd. 45.00 (*0-304-32657-7*) Continuum.

Making a Writing Program Work. Thomas L. Hilgers & Joy Marsella. (Illus.). 280p. (C). 1992. 48.00 (*0-8039-4574-4*); pap. 24.95 (*0-8039-4575-2*) Sage.

Making Abortion Rare: A Healing Strategy for a Divided Nation. David C. Reardon. LC 95-81057. 224p. (Orig.). 1996. 24.95 (*0-9648957-7-3*) Acorn Books.

Making Accounting Decisions. George Staubus. LC 77-73906. 1978. text 35.00 (*0-914348-19-1*) Scholars Bk.

Making Accounting Policy: The Quest for Credibility in Financial Reporting. David Solomons. (Wharton Executive Library). (Illus.). 262p. 1986. text 30.00 (*0-19-503701-4*) OUP.

Making Acquisitions Work: Learning from Companies' Successes & Failures. (Research Reports: No. P516). 1996. 545.00 (*0-85058-863-4*) Economist Intell.

Making Administration Public: Decolonizing Bureaucracy in Namibia. Tor Sellstrom et al. (Illus.). 1997. pap. text 26.95 (*91-7106-404-4*) Transaction Pubs.

Making Adorable Teddy Bears: From Anita Louise's Bearlace Cottage. Anita L. Crane. (Illus.). 144p. (Orig.). 1996. pap. 14.95 (*0-8069-0993-5*, Chapelle) Sterling.

Making Ads Pay. John Caples. 1966. pap. 6.95 (*0-486-21575-X*) Dover.

Making Advanced Grammar Work: Grammar in Context for ESL Students. Kristan Cavina. LC 98-92677. xiv, 322p. 1998. pap. 24.00 (*1-889850-06-3*) De Anza Pr.

Making Advanced Grammar Work: Instructor's Manual. Kristan Cavina. 52p. 1997. pap. text, teacher ed. write for info. (*1-889850-07-1*) De Anza Pr.

Making Advances: What You Can Do about Sexual Harassment at Work. Liz Curtis. (Illus.). 122p. 1995. pap. 9.95 (*0-563-36960-4*, Pub. by BBC) Parkwest Pubns.

Making Adverts. Davies. 1991. pap. text. write for info. (*0-582-05943-7*, Pub. by Addison-Wesley) Longman.

Making Affirmative Action Work in Higher Education: Analysis of Institutional & Federal Policies with Recommendations: A Report of the Carnegie Council. Carnegie Council on Policy Studies in Higher Educa. LC 75-27205. (Carnegie Council Ser.). 298p. reprint ed. pap. 92.40 (*0-608-14787-7*, 202565100045) Bks Demand.

*__Making Aging in Place Work.__ Ed. by Leon A. Pastalan. LC 99-31598. (Journal of Housing for the Elderly: Vol. 16, No. 4). 130p. (C). 1999. 39.95 (*0-7890-0753-3*) Haworth Pr.

*__Making Aid Work: Innovative Approaches for Africa at the Turn of the Century.__ Ed. by Peter H. Koehn & Olatunde J. Ojo. LC 99-35031. 224p. 1999. 52.00 (*0-7618-1457-4*); pap. 29.50 (*0-7618-1458-2*) U Pr of Amer.

Making Aid Work: Lessons from Successful Technical Cooperation in the Former Soviet Bloc. Raymond J. Struyk. 225p. 1996. 52.50 (*0-87766-657-1*); pap. 23.50 (*0-87766-658-X*) U Pr of Amer.

Making All the Difference: Inclusion, Exclusion & American Law. Martha Minow. LC 90-1754. 424p. 1990. 39.95 (*0-8014-2446-1*) Cornell U Pr.

Making All the Difference: Inclusion, Exclusion & American Law. Martha Minow. LC 90-1754. 424p. 1991. reprint ed. pap. text 16.95 (*0-8014-9977-1*) Cornell U Pr.

Making All Things New. large type ed. Henri J. M. Nouwen. 96p. 1986. pap. 7.95 (*0-8027-2560-0*) Walker & Co.

Making All Things New: Dialogue, Pluralism, & Evangelization. Michael Amaladoss. LC 90-40483. 216p. 1990. reprint ed. pap. 67.00 (*0-7837-9847-4*, 206057600005) Bks Demand.

Making All Things New - Reissue. Henri J. M. Nouwen. LC 80-8897. 96p. 1998. 16.00 (*0-06-066326-X*, Pub. by Harper SF) HarpC.

Making Alternative Histories. Ed. by Peter R. Schmidt & Thomas C. Patterson. (School of American Research Advanced Seminar Book Ser.). (Illus.). 312p. 1996. text 50.00 (*0-933452-92-6*); pap. text 24.95 (*0-933452-93-4*) Schol Am Res.

Making America. (C). 1995. pap., teacher ed. 11.96 (*0-395-71436-2*) HM.

Making America. Carol Berkin. (C). 1995. pap. text, student ed. 19.56 (*0-395-50249-7*) HM.

Making America. Carol Berkin. (C). 1995. pap., teacher ed., suppl. ed. 11.96 (*0-395-71438-9*) HM.

Making America, No. 2. Carol Berkin. (C). 1995. pap. text, student ed. 19.56 (*0-395-50250-0*) HM.

Making America, Vol. 1. Berkin. (C). Date not set. pap. text 48.36 (*0-395-50252-7*) HM.

Making America, Vol. 2. Berkin. (C). Date not set. pap. text 48.36 (*0-395-50253-5*) HM.

Making America: A History of the United States, Vol. I. annot. ed. Carol Berkin et al. (C). 1994. text, teacher ed. 49.56 (*0-395-71883-X*) HM.

Making America: A History of the United States, Vol. II. annot. ed. Carol Berkin et al. (C). 1994. text, teacher ed. 49.56 (*0-395-71884-8*) HM.

Making America: A History of the United States, Brief Edition. Carol Berkin et al. (C). 1996. text, teacher ed. 11.96 (*0-395-83776-6*); pap. text 27.96 (*0-395-83645-X*) HM.

Making America: A History of the United States, Brief Edition. annot. ed. Carol Berkin et al. (C). 1996. text, teacher ed. 40.36 (*0-395-83846-0*) HM.

Making America: A History of the United States, Brief Edition, Vol. I. Carol Berkin et al. (C). 1996. pap. text, student ed. 19.56 (*0-395-83777-4*) HM.

Making America: A History of the United States, Brief Edition, Vol. II. Carol Berkin et al. (C). 1997. pap. text, student ed. 19.56 (*0-395-83778-2*) HM.

Making America: A History of the United States Since 1865 : Brief Edition. Carol Berkin et al. 384p. (C). 1996. pap. text 27.96 (*0-395-83646-8*) HM.

Making America: The Society & Culture of the United States. Ed. by Luther S. Luedtke. LC 91-50786. (Illus.). xii, 570p. (C). 1992. pap. 19.95 (*0-8078-4370-9*) U of NC Pr.

Making America Vol. I: A History of the United States: To 1877. Carol Berkin et al. 500p. (C). 1994. pap. text 48.36 (*0-395-71880-5*) HM.

Making America Vol. B: A History of the United States, Since 1865. Carol Berkin et al. 600p. (C). 1994. pap. text 48.36 (*0-395-71881-3*) HM.

Making America Competitive: Policies for a Global Future. Marcia L. Whicker & Raymond A. Moore. LC 88-5889. 225p. 1988. 55.00 (*0-275-93056-4*, C3056, Praeger Pubs) Greenwood.

Making America Complete. Berkin. (C). Date not set. text 63.16 (*0-395-50251-9*) HM.

Making America Complete. Carol Berkin. (C). 1996. pap. text 39.16 (*0-395-77442-X*) HM.

Making America Corporate, 1870-1920. Olivier Zunz. LC 90-31028. (Illus.). 278p. 1992. pap. text 13.95 (*0-226-99460-0*) U Ch Pr.

Making America Corporate, 1870-1920. Olivier Zunz. LC 90-31028. (Illus.). x, 278p. 1998. 29.95 (*0-226-99459-7*) U Ch Pr.

Making America Orthodox. Peter E. Gillquist. 32p. 1985. pap. 2.00 (*0-917651-08-1*) Holy Cross Orthodox.

Making America Safer: What Citizens & Their State & Local Officials Can Do to Combat Crime. Ed. by Edwin Meese, 3rd & Robert E. Moffit. 206p. 1997. pap. 19.95 (*0-89195-069-9*) Heritage Found.

Making American Foreign Policy. John T. Rourke et al. LC 93-73227. (Illus.). 512p. (C). 1994. text 34.95 (*1-56134-116-9*, Dshkn McG-Hill) McGrw-H Hghr Educ.

Making American Foreign Policy. 2nd ed. John T. Rourke & Ralph G. Carter. 614p. (C). 1996. text. write for info. (*0-697-32682-9*) Brown & Benchmark.

Making American Foreign Policy: President - Congress Relations from the Second World War to the Post-Cold War Era. 2nd ed. Philip J. Briggs. LC 94-16780. 251p. 1994. reprint ed. pap. 24.95 (*0-8476-7946-2*); reprint ed. lib. bdg. 62.50 (*0-8476-7945-4*) Rowman.

Making American Foreign Policy: President - Congress Relations from the Second World War to Vietnam. Philip J. Briggs. 292p. (Orig.). (C). 1991. pap. text 28.00 (*0-8191-8113-7*); lib. bdg. 48.00 (*0-8191-8112-9*) U Pr of Amer.

Making American Government Work: A Proposal to Reinvigorate Federalism. Garry K. Ottosen. 191p. (Orig.). (C). 1992. pap. text 26.00 (*0-8191-8793-3*); lib. bdg. 49.00 (*0-8191-8792-5*) U Pr of Amer.

Making American Industry Safe for Democracy: Comparative Perspectives on the State & Employee Representation in the Era of World War I. LC 96-45881. 272p. 1997. pap. text 21.95 (*0-252-06628-6*) U of Ill Pr.

Making American Industry Safe for Democracy: Comparative Perspectives on the State & Employee Representation in the Era of World War I. Jeffrey Haydu. LC 96-45881. 272p. 1997. text 49.95 (*0-252-02289-0*) U of Ill Pr.

Making American Tradition: Visions & Revisions from Ben Franklin to Alice Walker. Cushing Strout. 272p. (C). 1990. pap. text 17.00 (*0-8135-1517-3*) Rutgers U Pr.

Making Americans: An Essay on Individualism & Money. Quentin Anderson. LC 92-8693. 1992. 21.95 (*0-15-155941-4*) Harcourt.

Making Americans, Remaking America: Immigration & Immigrant Policy. Louis DeSipio & Rodolfo O. De la Garza. LC 98-10675. (Dilemmas in American Politics Ser.). 168p. (C). 1998. pap. 17.00 (*0-8133-1944-7*, Pub. by Westview) HarpC.

Making America's Budget Policy: From the 1980s to the 1990s. Joseph J. Minarik. LC 89-27503. 248p. (C). (gr. 13). 1990. 66.95 (*0-87332-573-7*) M E Sharpe.

Making America's Budget Policy: From the 1980s to the 1990s. Joseph J. Minarik. LC 89-27503. 248p. (C). (gr. 13). 1990. pap. 34.95 (*0-87332-621-0*) M E Sharpe.

*__Making an after Dinner Speech: How to Make a Speech That Has Them Rolling in the Aisles.__ John Bowden. (Illus.). 144p. 1999. pap. 19.95 (*1-85703-478-3*, Pub. by How To Bks) Trans-Atl Phila.

*__Making an Angel.__ Antony Gormley. 2000. pap. 24.95 (*1-86154-063-9*) Booth-Clibborn.

Making an Angel. Walter J. Miller. LC 77-4747. 64p. (Orig.). 1977. pap. 3.95 (*0-918524-01-6*) Lintel.

Making an Archtop Guitar. Robert Benedetto. (Illus.). 264p. 1996. reprint ed. pap. 39.95 (*1-57424-000-5*) Centerstream Pub.

Making an Evangelical Latin Mission see Hacia una Misionologia Evangelical Latino

Making an Exceptional Difference: Enhancing the Impact of Microcomputer Technology on Children with Disabilities. Ed. by Harvey Pressman. 320p. (Orig.). 1987. pap. text 24.95 (*0-930958-03-9*) Excptnl Parent.

*__Making an Exhibition of Myself: The Autobiography of Peter Hall.__ Peter Hall. (Oberon Bks.). 2000. pap. 25.95 (*1-84002-115-2*) Theatre Comm.

*__Making An Exit.__ Elinor Fuchs. 2001. text (*0-8050-6317-X*) H Holt & Co.

*__Making An Exit.__ Elinor Fuchs. 2002. pap. (*0-8050-6318-8*) H Holt & Co.

Making an Herb Garden: Beautiful Designs, Plantings & Ornamentation. Catherine Mason. LC 97-60005. (Illus.). 96p. 1997. 24.95 (*1-57076-089-6*, Trafalgar Sq Pub) Trafalgar.

Making an Impact: A Guide to EIA Law & Policy. William Sheate. (Environmental Law Ser.). 270p. 1994. 115.00 (*1-874698-50-3*, Pub. by Cameron May) Gaunt.

Making an Impact: A Handbook on Counselor Advocacy. Karen Eriksen. LC 96-31393. 200p. 1996. pap. 19.95 (*1-56032-544-5*) Taylor & Francis.

*__Making an Impact - Children & Domestic Violence: A Reader.__ Marianne Hester et al. LC 99-41639. 194p. 1999. 29.95 (*1-85302-844-4*) Jessica Kingsley.

Making an Impact in Therapy: How the Master Clinicians Intervene. Len Bergantino. LC 93-38140. 300p. 1994. pap. 50.00 (*1-56821-162-7*) Aronson.

Making an Issue of Child Abuse: Political Agenda Setting for Social Problems. Barbara J. Nelson. LC 83-18044. xiv, 184p. 1986. pap. text 13.00 (*0-226-57201-3*) U Ch Pr.

Making an Old-Fashioned Patchwork Sampler Quilt on the Sewing Machine: Full-Size Templates & Complete Instructions for 24 Quilt Blocks. Andrea Shedletsky. (Crafts Ser.). 80p. (Orig.). 1984. pap. 5.95 (*0-486-24588-8*) Dover.

Making & Adjusting Single Reeds. Phillip Rehfeldt. 1991. 11.00 (*0-933251-02-5*) Mill Creek Pubns.

Making & Breaking Families. Jill Curtis. 200p. 1998. 55.00 (*1-85343-411-6*, Pub. by Free Assoc Bks); pap. 23.50 (*1-85343-412-4*) Free Assoc Bks.

Making & Breaking Governments: Cabinets & Legislatures in Parliamentary Democracies. Kenneth A. Shepsle. (Political Economy of Institutions & Decisions Ser.). (Illus.). 315p. (C). 1996. pap. text 19.95 (*0-521-43836-5*) Cambridge U Pr.

Making & Breaking Governments: Cabinets & Legislatures in Parliamentary Democracies. Kenneth A. Shepsle & Michael J. Laver. (Political Economy of Institutions & Decisions Ser.). (Illus.). 315p. (C). 1996. text 59.95 (*0-521-43245-6*) Cambridge U Pr.

Making & Breaking of Affectional Bonds. John Bowlby. 192p. 1979. pap. 13.95 (*0-685-03350-3*, NO. 2052) Routledge.

Making & Breaking of Affectional Bonds. John Bowlby. 192p. (C). 1979. pap. 20.99 (*0-415-04326-3*, NO. 2051) Routledge.

Making & Coating Photographic Emulsions. Vitalii L. Zelikman & S. M. Levi. LC 65-2520. (Focal Library). (Illus.). 312p. reprint ed. pap. 96.80 (*0-608-30110-8*, 205161900098) Bks Demand.

Making & Decorating Your Own Paper: Innovative Techniques & Original Projects. Kathy Blake & Bill Milne. LC 93-45440. (Illus.). 144p. 1994. 27.95 (*0-8069-0544-1*) Sterling.

Making & Decorating Your Own Paper: Innovative Techniques & Original Projects. Kathy Blake & Bill Milne. (Illus.). 144p. 1995. pap. 14.95 (*0-8069-0545-X*) Sterling.

Making & Dressing Dolls' House Dolls in One Twelfth Scale. Sue Atkinson. (Illus.). 192p. 1993. 29.95 (*0-7153-9909-8*, Pub. by D & C Pub) Sterling.

Making & Dressing Dolls' House Dolls in 1/12 Scale. Sue Atkinson. (Illus.). 192p. pap. 19.95 (*0-7153-0788-6*, Pub. by D & C Pub) Sterling.

*__Making & Dressing Traditional Teddy Bears.__ Brian Gibbs & Donna Gibbs. 2000. 27.95 (*0-7153-0970-6*, Pub. by D & C Pub) Sterling.

Making & Enjoying Telescopes: 6 Complete Projects & a Stargazer's Guide. Robert Miller & Kenneth Wilson. (Illus.). 160p. 1997. pap. 14.95 (*0-8069-1278-2*) Sterling.

Making & Flying Stunt Kites. Wolfgang Schimmelpfennig. LC 95-20180. (Illus.). 80p. (J). 1995. 19.95 (*0-8069-0870-X*) Sterling.

Making & Flying Stunt Kites & One-Liners. Wolfgang Schimmelpfennig. 80p. 1996. pap. 12.95 (*0-8069-0871-8*) Sterling.

Making & Keeping Friends: Ready-to-Use Lessons, Stories, & Activities for Building Relationships (Grades 4-8) John J. Schmidt. LC 97-16948. 1997. pap. text 28.95 (*0-87628-553-1*) Ctr Appl Res.

Making & Managing High-Quality Workplaces: An Organizational Ecology. Fritz Steele. (Organizational Psychology Ser.). 222p. (C). 1986. pap. text 18.95 (*0-8077-2812-8*) Tchrs Coll.

Making & Managing Money. Howard A. Chatterton & Margaret Chatterton. 125p. 1994. 34.95 (*0-912212-32-2*) Fire Eng.

Making & Managing Policy: Formulation, Analysis, Evaluation. Ed. by G. Ronald Gilbert. LC 84-1867. (Public Administration & Public Policy Ser.: No. 2). 375p. 1984. reprint ed. pap. 116.30 (*0-608-01320-X*, 206206400001) Bks Demand.

M

Making & Marketing Arms: The French Experience & Its Implications for the International System. Edward A. Kolodziej. LC 86-30567. (Illus.). 545p. reprint ed. pap. 169.00 (0-608-06338-X, 206669900008) Bks Demand.

Making & Marketing Music: The Musician's Guide to Financing, Distributing & Promoting Albums. Jodi Summers. LC 98-72765. (Illus.). 208p. (Orig.). 1999. pap. 18.95 (1-58115-015-6) Allworth Pr.

Making & Mastering Wood Planes. Finck. 2000. pap. write for info. (0-8069-6163-5) Sterling.

Making & Meaning: The Young Michelangelo, the Artist in Rome, 1496-1501. Michael Hirst & Jill Dunkerton. (National Gallery Publications). (Illus.). 144p. 1994. 30.00 (0-300-06135-8) Yale U Pr.

Making & Meaning of Hospital Policy in the United States & Canada. Terry Boychuk. LC 98-58120. 200p. (C). 1999. text 42.50 (0-472-10928-6, 10928) U of Mich Pr.

Making & Metaphor: A Discussion of Meaning in Contemporary Craft. Ed. by Gloria A. Hickey. (Mercury Ser.: CCFCS No. 66). (Illus.). 178p. 1994. pap. 19.95 (0-660-14028-4, Pub. by CN Mus Civilization) U of Wash Pr.

Making & Molding Identity in Schools: Student Narratives on Race, Gender, & Academic Engagement. Ann L. Davidson. LC 95-47050. (SUNY Series in Power, Social Identity, & Education). 257p. (C). 1996. pap. text 19.95 (0-7914-3082-0) State U NY Pr.

Making (And Occasional Unraveling) of a Sports Car Buff. Harry I. Phillips. Ed. by Bruce Thurber. (Illus.). 132p. (Orig.). 1991. pap. 6.00 (0-9629911-0-4) H I Phillips.

*__Making & Opposing a Summary Judgment Motion, Spring 1998 Action Guide.__ Victoria B. Henley & Henry E. Needham, Jr. Ed. by Linda W. Russell. 88p. 1998. pap. 58.00 (0-7626-0222-8, CP-11045) Cont Ed Bar-CA.

Making & Painting Victorian Birdhouses. Joyce Rice. LC 98-40475. (Illus.). 128p. 1999. pap. 24.99 (0-89134-881-6, 31359, North Lght Bks) F & W Pubns Inc.

Making & Remaking Asian America Through Immigration Policy, 1850-1990. Bill Ong Hing. LC 92-25507. (Asian America Ser.). 354p. 1994. 55.00 (0-8047-2118-1) Stanford U Pr.

Making & Remaking Asian America Through Immigration Policy, 1850-1990. Bill Ong Hing. xvi, 340p. 1994. pap. 16.95 (0-8047-2360-5) Stanford U Pr.

Making & Remaking of Christian Theology: Essays in Honour of Maurice Wiles. Ed. by Sarah Coakley & David A. Pailin. LC 92-42790. (Illus.). 304p. 1993. text 49.95 (0-19-826739-8) OUP.

Making & Remaking of the British Constitution. Nolan & Stephen Sedley. LC 98-151840. (Law in Its Social Setting Ser.). 142p. 1997. pap. 44.00 (1-85431-704-0, Pub. by Blackstone Pr) Gaunt.

*__Making & Remaking Pennsylvania's Civil War.__ William Alan Blair & William Pencak. LC 00-37330. (Illus.). 2000. write for info. (0-271-02079-2) Pa St U Pr.

Making & Repairing Wooden Clock Cases. V. J. Taylor & H. A. Babb. (Illus.). 192p. 1994. pap. 19.95 (0-7153-0286-8, Pub. by D & C Pub) Sterling.

Making & Selling Culture. Ed. by Richard Ohmann. LC 96-22546. 278p. 1996. pap. 22.95 (0-8195-5301-8, Wesleyan Univ Pr) U Pr of New Eng.

Making & Selling Herbal Crafts: Tips, Techniques, Projects. Alyce Nadeau. (Illus.). 128p. 1996. pap. 14.95 (0-8069-3176-0) Sterling.

Making & Setting a Fishnet. Mildred Jacobson. (Alaska Ser.: Vol. 8). 23p. 1977. reprint ed. pap. 4.95 (1-878051-03-2, CP042) Circumpolar Pr.

Making & Spending Money along the Bosporus: The Lysimachi Coinages Minted by Byzantium & Chalcedon. Constantin Marinescu. (Illus.). 300p. Date not set. text 59.50 (0-472-11052-7, 11052) U of Mich Pr.

Making & Taking Decisions. 96p. pap. text. write for info. (0-7506-3333-6) Buttrwrth-Heinemann.

Making & the Ministry of a Prophetess. 1999. pap. 10.00 (1-885858-05-1) KILN Bks.

Making & Thinking: A Study of Intelligent Activities. Andrew Harrison. LC 78-56369. 216p. (C). 1978. text 32.95 (0-915144-55-7) Hackett Pub.

*__Making & Unmaking of a University Museum: The McCord, 1921-1996.__ Brian Young. (Illus.). 208p. 2000. 65.00 (0-7735-2049-X, Pub. by McG-Queens Univ Pr); pap. 24.95 (0-7735-2050-3, Pub. by McG-Queens Univ Pr) CUP Services.

Making & Unmaking of an Evangelical Mind: The Case of Edward Carnell. Rudolph Nelson. 272p. 1988. text 69.95 (0-521-34263-5) Cambridge U Pr.

Making & Unmaking of Local Self-Government. Nirmala Rao. 272p. 1994. text 72.95 (1-85521-635-3, Pub. by Dartmth Pub) Ashgate Pub Co.

Making & Unmaking of the Haya Lived World: Consumption, Commoditization, & Everyday Practice. Brad Weiss. LC 95-37842. (Body, Commodity, Text Ser.). (Illus.). 264p. 1996. text 49.95 (0-8223-1725-7); pap. text 17.95 (0-8223-1722-2) Duke.

Making & Unmaking of Urban Communities. (C). 2001. pap. 37.33 (0-205-29614-9, Longwood Div) Allyn.

Making & Unmaking the Prospects for Rhetoric: Selected Papers from the 1996 Rhetoric Society of America Conference. Ed. by Theresa Enos & Richard McNabb. LC 96-45595. 250p. 1996. pap. 24.95 (0-8058-2015-9); text 49.95 (0-8058-2014-0) L Erlbaum Assocs.

Making & Use of the Geometrical Instrument Called a SECTOR. Thomas Hood. LC 73-6147. (English Experience Ser.: No. 610). (Illus.). 1973. reprint ed. 30.00 (90-221-0610-1) Walter J Johnson.

*__Making & Using a Flower Press.__ Deborah Tukua. LC 99-14636. 1999. pap. 3.95 (1-58017-204-0) Random.

Making & Using Dried Foods. Phyllis Hobson. LC 93-33376. (Illus.). 192p. 1994. pap. 14.95 (0-88266-615-0, Storey Pub) Storey Bks.

Making & Using Flavored Oils & Vinegars. Glenn Andrews. 1989. pap. 2.95 (0-88266-556-1, Garden Way Pub) Storey Bks.

Making & Using Mustards. Claire Hopley. Ed. by Kim Foster & Connie Parkinson. (Country Wisdom Bulletin Ser.). (Illus.). 32p. 1991. 2.95 (0-88266-697-5, Storey Pub) Storey Bks.

Making & Using of Index Numbers. Wesley C. Mitchell. LC 65-19653. (Reprints of Economic Classics Ser.). 114p. 1965. reprint ed. 29.50 (0-678-00098-0) Kelley.

Making & Using Scientific Equipment. David E. Newton. LC 92-38039. (Experimental Science Book Ser.). (Illus.). 160p. (YA). (gr. 9-12). 1993. lib. bdg. 24.00 (0-531-11176-8) Watts.

Making & Using the Dry Fly. Paul H. Young. (Illus.). 96p. 1992. reprint ed. 18.95 (0-9629439-8-3) Centenn Pubns.

Making & Using Visible Absorption Measurements. Norman E. Griswold & M. L. Gillette. Ed. by C. L. Stanitski. (Modular Laboratory Program in Chemistry Ser.). 12p. (C). 1997. pap. text 1.50 (0-87540-488-X) Chem Educ Res.

*__Making & Writing Words: 74 Lessons & Worksheets.__ (Illus.). 160p. (J). 2000. pap. 14.99 (0-88724-560-9, CD-2600) Carson-Dellos.

*__Making Animal Babies.__ Illus. by Sneed B. Collard, III & Steve Jenkins. LC 99-35797. 32p. (J). 2000. 16.00 (0-395-95317-0) HM.

*__Making Animal Characters with Polymer Clay.__ Sherian Frey. LC 00-29215. (Illus.). 128p. 2000. write for info. (1-58180-041-X) North Lght.

Making Animal Pulltoys. Ed Sibbett, Jr. 44p. 1990. pap. 3.50 (0-486-26249-9) Dover.

Making Animal Quilts: Patterns & Projects. Willow A. Soltow. LC 86-81231. 192p. 1986. pap. 12.95 (0-934672-39-3) Good Bks PA.

Making Animated Whirligigs. 2nd unabridged ed. Anders S. Lunde. LC 98-4576. Orig. Title: More Whirligigs. (Illus.). 160p. 1998. pap. 9.95 (0-486-40049-2) Dover.

Making Antique Furniture. Ed. by Vic Taylor. (Illus.). 160p. 1988. 25.95 (0-8306-0356-5, 3056) McGraw-Hill Prof.

Making Antique Furniture Reproductions: Instructions & Measured Drawings for 40 Classic Projects. Franklin H. Gottshall. LC 93-48643. Orig. Title: Reproducing Antique Furniture. (Illus.). 256p. 1994. reprint ed. pap. 14.95 (0-486-27976-6) Dover.

Making Anything Possible: Excellence in Self-Accountability, Credit & Blame. Al Marino. 176p. 1996. reprint ed. pap. 12.95 (1-890295-00-0) Ldrship Resources.

Making Apple Pies & Crusts. Phyllis Hobson. LC 75-20773. (Country Kitchen Library). (Illus.). 60p. 1984. pap. 3.95 (0-88266-075-6, Garden Way Pub) Storey Bks.

Making Architecture: The Getty Center. Pref. by Harold M. Williams. LC 97-20564. (Illus.). 178p. 1997. pap. 50.00 (0-89236-463-7, Pub. by J P Getty Trust) OUP.

Making Aristocracy Work: The Peerage & the Political System in Britain, 1884-1914. Andrew Adonis. LC 92-40926. (Oxford Historical Monographs). (Illus.). 324p. (C). 1993. text 57.00 (0-19-820389-6, Clarendon Pr) OUP.

Making Arms in the Machine Age: Philadelphia's Frankford Arsenal, 1816-1870. James J. Farley. LC 93-19126. (Illus.). 160p. (C). 1993. 35.00 (0-271-01000-2) Pa St U Pr.

Making Arrangements. Matt Simpson. 1982. pap. 12.95 (0-906427-40-1, Pub. by Bloodaxe Bks) Dufour.

Making Arrows the Old Way!! Douglas Spotted-Eagle. Ed. by Monte Smith. (Illus.). 32p. 1989. pap. 4.50 (0-943604-22-2, BOO/19) Eagles View.

Making Art Safely: Alternative Methods & Materials in Drawing, Painting, Graphic Design, & Photography. Merle Spandorfer. (Design & Graphic Design Ser.). (Illus.). 272p. 1996. pap. 34.95 (0-442-02131-3, VNR) Wiley.

Making Art Safely: Alternative Methods & Materials in Drawing, Painting, Graphic Design, & Photography. Merle Spandorfer et al. 255p. 1992. 54.95 (0-471-28884-5, VNR) Wiley.

Making Art Safely: Alternative Methods & Materials in Drawing, Painting, Graphic Design, & Photography. Merle Spandorfer et al. (Design & Graphic Design Ser.). 255p. 1995. pap. 34.95 (0-471-28728-8, VNR) Wiley.

Making Art Safely: Alternatives in Drawing, Painting, Printmaking, Graphic Design, & Photography. Merle Spandorfer et al. LC 92-4841. 1993. text 54.95 (0-442-23489-9, VNR) Wiley.

Making Artist's Tools see Make Your Own Artist's Tools & Materials

Making A's in College: The Handbook. Sandra U. Gibson & James Gibson. 1994. pap., per. 11.95 (0-915849-23-2) Workbks Pr.

Making A's in College: The Video Workshop, 2 cass.; set. Sandra U. Gibson. 96p. (YA). 1994. pap. 87.00 incl. VHS (0-915849-22-4) Workbks Pr.

Making Assessment Elementary. Kathleen Strickland & James Strickland. LC 99-33237. 1999. pap. text 27.00 (0-325-00200-2) Heinemann.

Making Australian Art, 1916-1946: Sydney Ure Smith - Patron & Publisher. Nancy Underhill. (Illus.). 320p. 1992. text 45.00 (0-19-553237-6) OUP.

Making Authentic Country Furniture: With Measured Drawings of Museum Classics. John G. Shea. (Illus.). 240p. 1994. reprint ed. pap. text 12.95 (0-486-27774-7) Dover.

Making Authentic Craftsman Furniture: Instructions & Plans for 50 Projects. Ed. by Gustav Stickley. 128p. 1986. reprint ed. pap. 8.95 (0-486-25000-8) Dover.

Making Authentic Pennsylvania Dutch Furniture: With Measured Drawings of Museum Classics. unabridged ed. John G. Shea. LC 92-13621. Orig. Title: The Pennsylvania Dutch & Their Furniture. (Illus.). 240p. 1992. reprint ed. pap. text 14.95 (0-486-27227-3) Dover.

Making Authentic Shaker Furniture: With Measured Drawings of Museum Classics. John G. Shea. Orig. Title: The American Shakers & Their Furniture with Measured Drawings of Museum Classics. (Illus.). 224p. 1992. reprint ed. pap. 11.95 (0-486-27003-3) Dover.

Making Automation Work: Successful Strategies for Managing New Technology. rev. ed. J. R. McDaniel. LC 92-27799. (Series in Entrepreneurship). 232p. 1992. text 20.00 (0-8153-0997-X) Garland.

Making Babies, 3 vols. Assorted. LC 96-308. 634p. 1995. per. 5.50 (0-373-20115-X) Harlequin Bks.

*__Making Babies.__ Arienne Noble. 2001. write for info. (0-688-17644-5, Wm Morrow) Morrow Avon.

Making Babies. Sara B. Stein. LC 73-15267. (Open Family Ser.). (Illus.). 48p. (J). (gr. 1 up). 1974. 10.95 (0-8027-6171-2) Walker & Co.

Making Babies. Sara B. Stein. LC 73-15267. (Open Family Ser.). (Illus.). 48p. (J). (ps-8). 1984. pap. 7.95 (0-8027-7221-8) Walker & Co.

Making Babies: Biomedical Technologies, Reproductive Ethics, & Public Policy. Melo-Mart In, Inmaculada De Staff. LC 98-20219. 1998. write for info. (0-7923-5116-9) Kluwer Academic.

Making Backyard Birdhouses: Attracting, Feeding & Housing Your Favorite Birds. Sandy Cortright & Will Pokriots. (Illus.). 128p. 1997. pap. 14.95 (0-8069-0893-9) Sterling.

Making Baskets. Maryanne Gillooly. (Illus.). 32p. 1986. pap. 2.95 (0-88266-341-0, Garden Way Pub) Storey Bks.

*__Making Bead & Wire Jewelry: Simple Techniques, Stunning Designs.__ Dawn Cusick. LC 99-55035. (Illus.). 128p. 2000. 27.95 (1-57990-148-4, Pub. by Lark Books) Sterling.

Making Beautiful Banners. Barbara Webster. (Illus.). 128p. 1998. 14.95 (0-8069-4897-3, Chapelle) Sterling.

*__Making Beautiful Hemp & Bead Jewelry.__ Mickey Baskett. (Illus.). 96p. 1999. pap. 12.95 (0-8069-6275-5) Sterling.

Making Beautiful Wax Dolls. Judy Meier. LC 89-61679. (Orig.). 1989. pap. text 15.95 (0-916809-32-3) Scott Pubns MI.

Making Beer. 2nd ed. William J. Mares. 208p. 1994. pap. 17.00 (0-679-75502-0) Knopf.

Making Being Here Enough: Installations, 1980-1995. Roni Horn. LC 97-207162. (Illus.). 104p. 45.00 (3-7965-9901-X, 530035) Dist Art Pubs.

Making Believe: Philosophical Reflections on Fiction, 25. C. G. Prado. LC 83-5693. (Contributions in Philosophy Ser.: No. 25). 169p. 1984. 52.95 (0-313-24013-2, PMB/, Greenwood Pr) Greenwood.

Making Benefit-Cost Analysis Work. Lewis & Brod. 59.95 (1-85972-247-4) Ashgate Pub Co.

Making Bent Willow Furniture. Brenda Cameron & Brian Cameron. LC 98-12990. (Rustic Home Ser.). (Illus.). 139p. 1998. pap. 19.95 (1-58017-048-X) Storey Bks.

Making Bentwood Trellises, Arbors, Gates & Fences. Jim Long. LC 98-11781. (Rustic Home Ser.). (Illus.). 156p. 1998. pap. 19.95 (1-58017-051-X) Storey Bks.

*__Making Better Capital Investment Decisions.__ Louis C. Gapenski. LC 00-36206. 2000. write for info. (1-56793-137-5) Health Admin Pr.

Making Better Career Choices. Derk Glover. 130p. 1995. ring bd. 65.00 (0-7494-1687-4, Kogan Pg Educ) Stylus Pub VA.

Making Better Citizens: Housing Reform & the Community Development Strategy in Cincinnati, 1890-1960. Robert B. Fairbanks. (Greater Cincinnati Bicentennial History Ser.). 256p. 1988. text 24.95 (0-252-01554-1) U of Ill Pr.

Making Better Decisions about School Problems: How Administrators Use Evaluation to Find Solutions. Naftaly S. Glasman. LC 93-37725. 192p. 1994. pap. 24.95 (0-8039-6125-1) Corwin Pr.

*__Making Better Environmental Decisions: An Alternative to Risk Assessment.__ Mary O'Brien. LC 99-56868. (Illus.). 352p. 2000. 55.00 (0-262-15051-4) MIT Pr.

*__Making Better Environmental Decisions: An Alternative to Risk Assessment.__ Mary O'Brien. LC 99-56868. (Illus.). 352p. 2000. pap. 22.95 (0-262-65053-3) MIT Pr.

*__Making Better International Law: The International Law Commission at 50: Proceedings of the United Nations Colloquium on Progressive Development & Codification of International Law = Pour un Meilleur Droit International: La Commission du Droit International a 50 Ans: Actes du Colloque des Nations Unies sur le Developpement Progressif et la Codification du Droit International.__ United Nations Colloquium on Progressive Development & Codification of International Law Staff. LC 98-221832. xi, 451p. 1998. write for info. (92-1-033076-5) UN.

Making Better Use of School Buildings. LC 96-185720. 35p. 1996. 12.00 (92-64-14880-9, 95-96-04-1, Pub. by Org for Econ) OECD.

Making Big Books A to Z. Gasquet. (Illus.). 96p. (J). (ps-2). 1996. pap., wbk. ed. 11.95 (1-55734-049-8) Tchr Create Mat.

Making Big Books with Children, Vol. 1. Joy Evans et al. (Illus.). 64p. (J). (gr. k-2). 1989. pap. 11.95 (1-55799-165-0, EMC 303) Evan-Moor Edu Pubs.

Making Big Books with Children, Vol. 2. Joy Evans & Jo E. Moore. (Illus.). 64p. (J). (gr. k-2). 1994. pap. text 11.95 (1-55799-285-8, EMC387) Evan-Moor Edu Pubs.

*__Making Big Bucks Selling Real Estate: Learn the Secrets of Selling Homes & Land from the Master Sales Trainer.__ Terry L. Weaver. LC 99-58942. 221p. 2000. pap. 19.95 (1-58151-065-9, Pub. by BookPartners) Midpt Trade.

Making Big Money in 1600: The Life & Times of Isma'il Abu Taqiyya, Egyptian Merchant. Nelly Hanna. LC 97-5469. (Middle East Studies Beyond Dominant Paradigms). 224p. 1997. 44.95 (0-8156-2749-1); pap. 19.95 (0-8156-2763-7) Syracuse U Pr.

*__Making Big Money! Marketing Your Own Web Site Business.__ Steven Rogers. (Illus.). 56p. 1998. spiral bd. (0-9677963-0-X) S R Rogers Enter.

Making Big Profits in Real Estate Investing. Jack W. Strickland, Jr. 49p. (Orig.). 1991. pap. write for info. (0-9630577-0-7) Strickland Invest.

Making Big Words: Multilevel, Hands-On Spelling & Phonics Activities. Patricia M. Cunningham & Dorothy P. Hall. (Illus.). 160p. 1994. 14.99 (0-86653-807-0) Good Apple.

Making Birdhouses: Practical Projects for Decorative Houses, Tables & Feeders. Andre Newton-Cox. 64p. 1998. pap. text 7.95 (1-85967-673-1, Lorenz Bks) Anness Pub.

Making Birdhouses & Bird Feeders, 2 vols., Set. Scott D. Campbell. (Illus.). 1989. pap. 5.45 (0-486-25917-X) Dover.

Making Birdhouses & Feeders. Charles R. Seif. LC 85-8654. (Illus.). 128p. (Orig.). (YA). (gr. 10-12). 1985. pap. 10.95 (0-8069-6244-5) Sterling.

Making Bits & Pieces Mosaics: Creative Projects for Home & Garden. Marlene H. Marshall. LC 97-31831. 1998. 24.95 (1-58017-015-3) Storey Bks.

*__Making Bits & Pieces Mosaics: Creative Projects for Home & Garden.__ Marlene Hurley Marshall. (Illus.). 96p. 2000. pap. 16.95 (1-58017-307-1, 67307) Storey Bks.

Making Boards Effective: The Dynamics of Nonprofit Governing Boards. Alvin Zander. LC 93-19577. (Nonprofit Sector-Management Ser.). 189p. 1993. text 30.95 (1-55542-580-1) Jossey-Bass.

Making Bodies, Making History: Feminism & German Identity. Leslie A. Adelson. LC 92-37873. (Modern German Culture & Literature Ser.). xvi, 197p. (C). 1993. text 40.00 (0-8032-1036-1) U of Nebr Pr.

*__Making Bodybrain-Compatible Education a Reality: Coaching for the ITI Model.__ Karen D. Olsen. 214p. 1999. spiral bd. 24.95 (0-9624475-8-7) Bks Educators.

Making Bonsai Landscapes: The Art of Saikei. Herb L. Gustafson. (Illus.). 192p. 1999. pap. 19.95 (0-8069-1879-9) Sterling.

Making Book. Teresa Nielsen Hayden. Ed. by Patrick Nielsen Hayden. LC 93-87492. (Boskone Bks.). 160p. 1994. pap. 11.00 (0-915368-55-2) New Eng SF Assoc.

Making Books. Deri Robins & Charlotte Stowell. LC 93-48560. (Illus.). (J). 1994. pap. 7.95 (1-85697-518-5) LKC.

Making Books: A Step-by-Step Guide to Your Own Publishing. Gillean Chapman. 1992. pap. 4.95 (0-395-94619-0) HM.

Making Books: A Step-by-Step Guide to Your Own Publishing. Gillian Chapman & Pam Robson. (Illus.). 32p. (J). (gr. 3-6). 1992. 13.45 (1-56294-169-0); pap. 6.95 (1-56294-840-7); lib. bdg. 19.90 (1-56294-154-2) Millbrook Pr.

*__Making Books: Designs in British Publishing since 1945.__ Alan Bartram. LC 99-29885. (Illus.). 160p. 1999. 39.95 (1-884718-93-0, 55471) Oak Knoll.

Making Books Across the Curriculum: Pop Ups, Flaps, Shapes, Wheels & Many More. Natalie Walsh. LC 94-232192. 112p. 1994. pap. 14.95 (0-590-49647-6) Scholastic Inc.

Making Books & Journals: 20 Great Weekend Projects. Constance Richards. LC 98-45006. (Weekend Crafter Ser.). (Illus.). 80p. 1999. pap. 14.95 (1-57990-092-5) Lark Books.

*__Making Books by Hand: A Step-by-Step Guide.__ Mary McCarthy. 2000. pap. text 16.99 (1-56496-675-5) Rockport Pubs.

Making Books by Hand: A Step-by-Step Guide. Mary McCarthy & Philip Manna. (Illus.). 108p. 1997. 24.99 (1-56496-328-4, Quarry Bks) Rockport Pubs.

Making Books That Fly, Fold, Wrap, Hide, Pop Up, Twist, & Turn: Books for Kids to Make. Gwen Diehn. LC 97-41037. (Illus.). 96p. (J). (gr. 4-7). 1998. 19.95 (1-57990-023-2, Pub. by Lark Books) Random.

*__Making Books with Pockets--April.__ Michelle Noble Barnett et al. Ed. by Marilyn Evans. (Making Books with Pockets : Vol. 4). (Illus.). 96p. (J). (gr. 1-3). 1999. pap., teacher ed. 10.95 (1-55799-701-2, 587) Evan-Moor Edu Pubs.

*__Making Books with Pockets--August.__ Michelle Noble Barnett et al. Ed. by Marilyn Evans. (Making Books with Pockets : Vol. 8). (Illus.). 96p. (J). (gr. 1-3). 1999. pap., teacher ed. 10.95 (1-55799-705-5, 591) Evan-Moor Edu Pubs.

*__Making Books with Pockets--February.__ Michelle Noble Barnett et al. Ed. by Marilyn Evans. (Making Books with Pockets : Vol. 2). (Illus.). 96p. (J). (gr. 1-3). 1999. pap., teacher ed. 10.95 (1-55799-699-7, 585) Evan-Moor Edu Pubs.

*__Making Books with Pockets--January.__ Michelle Noble Barnett et al. Ed. by Marilyn Evans. (Making Books with Pockets : Vol. 1). (Illus.). 96p. (J). (gr. 1-3). 1999. pap., teacher ed. 10.95 (1-55799-698-9, 584) Evan-Moor Edu Pubs.

*__Making Books with Pockets--July.__ Michelle Noble Barnett et al. Ed. by Marilyn Evans. (Making Books with Pockets : Vol. 7). (Illus.). 96p. (J). (gr. 1-3). 1999. pap., teacher ed. 10.95 (1-55799-704-7, 590) Evan-Moor Edu Pubs.

*__Making Books with Pockets--June.__ Michelle Noble Barnett et al. Ed. by Marilyn Evans. (Making Books with Pockets : Vol. 6). (Illus.). 96p. (J). (gr. 1-3). 1999. pap., teacher ed. 10.95 (1-55799-703-9, 589) Evan-Moor Edu Pubs.

An Asterisk (*) at the beginning of an entry indicates that the title is appearing for the first time.

*__Making Books with Pockets--March.__ Michelle Noble Barnett et al. Ed. by Marilyn Evans. (Making Books with Pockets : Vol. 3). (Illus.). 96p. (J). (gr. 1-3). 1999. pap., teacher ed. 10.95 (*1-55799-700-4*, 586) Evan-Moor Edu Pubs.

*__Making Books with Pockets--May.__ Michelle Noble Barnett et al. Ed. by Marilyn Evans. (Making Books with Pockets : Vol. 5). (Illus.). 96p. (J). (gr. 1-3). 1999. pap., teacher ed. 10.95 (*1-55799-702-0*, 588) Evan-Moor Edu Pubs.

*__Making Books with Pockets--November.__ Michelle Noble Barnett et al. Ed. by Marilyn Evans. (Making Books with Pockets : Vol. 11). (Illus.). 96p. (J). (gr. 1-3). 1999. pap., teacher ed. 10.95 (*1-55799-708-X*, 594) Evan-Moor Edu Pubs.

*__Making Books with Pockets--October.__ Michelle Noble Barnett et al. Ed. by Marilyn Evans. (Making Books with Pockets : Vol. 10). (Illus.). 96p. (J). (gr. 1-3). 1999. pap., teacher ed. 10.95 (*1-55799-707-1*, 593) Evan-Moor Edu Pubs.

*__Making Books with Pockets--September.__ Michelle Noble Barnett et al. Ed. by Marilyn Evans. (Making Books with Pockets : Vol. 9). (Illus.). 96p. (J). (gr. 1-3). 1999. pap., teacher ed. 10.95 (*1-55799-706-3*, 592) Evan-Moor Edu Pubs.

*__Making Books with Pockets-December.__ Michelle Noble Barnett et al. Ed. by Marilyn Evans. (Making Books with Pockets : Vol. 12). (Illus.). 96p. (J). (gr. 1-3). 1999. pap., teacher ed. 10.95 (*1-55799-709-8*, 595) Evan-Moor Edu Pubs.

Making Boxes & Chests. Reader's Digest Editors. (Workshop Companion Ser.). 128p. 1999. pap. text 19.95 (*0-7621-0202-0*, Pub. by RD Assn) Penguin Putnam.

Making Bread at Midnight. Sheryl St. Germain. 100p. (Orig.). (C). 1992. pap. 9.95 (*0-941720-87-X*) Slough Pr TX.

*__Making, Breaking Codes: Introduction to Cryptology.__ Paul Garrett. 550p. 2000. 66.67 (*0-13-030369-0*, Prentice Hall) P-H.

Making Bricks Without Straw: Nathaniel Greene's Southern Campaign & Mao Tse-Tung's Mobile War. John M. Dederer. (Illus.). 98p. 1983. pap. text 12.00 (*0-89745-049-3*) Sunflower U Pr.

Making Building Blocks with the CINVA-Ram Block Press. 26p. 1966. 6.25 (*0-86619-012-0*) Vols Tech Asst.

Making Buildings Safer for People During Hurricanes, Earthquakes, & Fires. Andrzej S. Nowak. 200p. (C). (gr. 13). 1990. text 57.95 (*0-442-26473-9*) Chapman & Hall.

Making Built-In Cabinets. Reader's Digest Editors. (Workshop Companion (Reader's Digest) Ser.). (Illus.). 1999. 19.95 (*0-7621-0203-9*, Pub. by RD Assn) Penguin Putnam.

Making Bureaucracies Think: The Environmental Impact Statement Strategy of Administrative Reform. Serge Taylor. LC 81-84456. 424p. 1984. 52.50 (*0-8047-1152-6*) Stanford U Pr.

Making Bureaucracies Work. Carol H. Weiss. Ed. by Allen H. Barton. LC 80-12774. (Sage Focus Editions Ser.: No. 22). 309p. 1980. reprint ed. pap. 95.80 (*0-608-01167-3*, 205946700001) Bks Demand.

Making Business Decisions: Real Cases from Real Companies. Frances Boyd. 176p. (C). 1994. pap. text 25.65 (*0-201-59281-9*) Addison-Wesley.

Making Business Decisions: Real Cases from Real Companies. Frances Boyd. LC 93-34169. 1994. pap. text. write for info. (*0-8013-0821-6*) Longman.

Making Business French Work: Models, Materials, Methodologies. Ed. by Steven J. Loughrin-Sacco & Jayne Abrate. LC 97-62140. 250p. 1997. pap. text 25.00 (*1-891611-00-3*) SDSU Ciber Pr.

Making Buying Decisions: Using the Computer as a Tool. Richard Clodfelter & Peter Dublin. (General Business & Business Education Ser.). (C). 1995. mass mkt. 43.95 (*0-8273-6797-X*) Delmar.

Making Buying Decisions: Using the Computer as a Tool. Richard Clodfelter & Peter Dublin. (General Business & Business Education Ser.). 32p. 1996. text, teacher ed. 10.00 (*0-8273-6798-8*, VNR) Wiley.

Making Byzantine Vestments: How to Design & Sew Byzantine Vestments. 7th ed. Ronald Golini. (Illus.). 1997. reprint ed. pap. 8.95 (*1-880971-29-1*) Light&Life Pub Co MN.

Making Cabinets & Built-Ins: Techniques & Plans. Sam Allen. Ed. by Laurel Ornitz. LC 86-5997. (Illus.). 384p. (Orig.). 1986. pap. 19.95 (*0-8069-6330-1*) Sterling.

Making CAD-CAM Data Transfer Work: IGES & Other Solutions (a Hands-On Guide) Ralph Mayer. Ed. by Jonathan Linden. (Illus.). 250p. 1987. 295.00 (*0-932007-13-9*) Mgmt Roundtable.

Making Campaigns Count: Leadership & Coalition-Building in 1980, 110. Darrell M. West. LC 83-13021. (Contributions in Political Science Ser.: No. 110). 198p. 1984. 57.95 (*0-313-24235-6*, WCC/, Greenwood Pr) Greenwood.

Making Canadian Indian Policy: The Hidden Agenda, 1968-1970. Sally M. Weaver. (Studies in the Structure of Power). 352p. 1980. pap. text 13.95 (*0-8020-6403-5*) U of Toronto Pr.

Making Candles. Judy A. Sadler. (Kids Can Do It Ser.). (Illus.). 40p. (J). (gr. 3 up). 1998. pap. 5.95 (*1-55074-501-8*, Pub. by Kids Can Pr) Genl Dist Srvs.

*__Making Candles & Potpourri: Illuminate & Infuse Your Home.__ Catherine Bardey. LC 99-41225. (Illus.). 192p. 1999. pap. text 10.98 (*1-57912-076-8*, Pub. by Blck Dog & Leventhal) Workman Pub.

*__Making Capital Budgeting Decisions: Maximizing the Value of the Firm, Vol. 1.__ Hazel Johnson. (Corporate Finance Manuals Ser.). (Illus.). 256p. 1999. pap. text 34.95 (*0-273-63879-3*, Pub. by F T P-H) Natl Bk Netwk.

Making Capital from Culture: The Corporate Form of Capitalist Cultural Production. Bill Ryan. (Studies in Organization: No. 35). xii, 290p. (C). 1991. lib. bdg. 54.95 (*3-11-012548-X*, 236-91) De Gruyter.

Making Capitalism: The Social & Cultural Construction of a South Korean Conglomerate. Roger L. Janelli. 288p. (C). 1995. pap. 14.95 (*0-8047-2524-1*) Stanford U Pr.

Making Capitalism: The Social & Cultural Construction of a South Korean Conglomerate. Roger L. Janelli & Dawnhee Yim. LC 92-18093. 296p. 1993. 39.50 (*0-8047-1609-9*) Stanford U Pr.

Making Capitalism in China: The Taiwan Connection. You-tien Hsing. LC 96-26627. (Illus.). 264p. 1998. 35.00 (*0-19-510324-6*) OUP.

Making Capitalism Without Capitalists: The New Ruling Elites in Eastern Europe. Gil Eyal et al. LC 98-30214. (Illus.). 240p. 1999. 35.00 (*1-85984-819-2*, Pub. by Verso) Norton.

*__Making Capitalism Without Capitalists: The New Ruling Elites in Eastern Europe.__ Gil Eyal et al. 288p. 2001. pap. 20.00 (*1-85984-312-3*, Pub. by Verso) Norton.

Making Capitalism Work. Leonard Silk et al. LC 96-25257. 256p. (C). 1996. text 27.50 (*0-8147-8064-4*) NYU Pr.

Making Capitation Work: Clinical Operations in an Integrated Delivery System. Ed. by Gloria G. Mayer et al. Date not set. ring bd. 189.00 (*0-8342-0677-3*, S178) Aspen Pub.

Making Cards. Penny King. LC 96-37357. (Illus.). 24p. 1997. lib. bdg. 17.27 (*1-57505-205-9*, Carolrhoda) Lerner Pub.

Making Cards. Charlotte Stowell. LC 94-47818. (Step-by-Step Ser.). (Illus.). 40p. (J). (gr. 3-6). 1995. pap. 7.95 (*1-85697-590-8*) LKC.

Making Career Decisions That Count: A Practical Guide. Luzz. 148p. (C). 1996. pap. text 26.60 (*0-13-777731-0*) P-H.

Making Career Transitions: Ensuring a Successful Career Change. Jane Ballbach & Jan Slater. (Personal Growth & Development Collection). (Illus.). 106p. 1996. pap. 14.95 (*1-883553-79-2*) R Chang Assocs.

Making Cars. Dodds. (Scotland's Past in Action Ser.). (Illus.). 88p. (Orig.). Date not set. pap. 6.95 (*0-948636-81-5*, 6815, Pub. by Natl Mus Scotland) A Schwartz & Co.

Making CBT Happen: Prescriptions for Successful Implementation of Computer-Based Training in Your Organization. Gloria J. Gery. LC 86-51671. (Illus.). 226p. (Orig.). 1987. reprint ed. pap. 39.95 (*0-9617968-0-4*) Ziff Inst.

Making Cents Out of Signs. 2nd rev. ed. Sherry Peters. (Illus.). 160p. 1997. pap. 12.95 (*0-9659990-0-9*) Ein Gavar Pub.

*__Making Ceramic Sculptural: Techniques, Projects, Inspirations.__ Raul Acero. Ed. by Deborah Morgenthal. (Illus.). 160p. 2000. write for info. (*1-57990-175-1*, Pub. by Lark Books) Sterling.

Making Certain It Goes On: Poems. Richard Hugo. 1991. pap. 14.95 (*0-393-30784-0*) Norton.

Making Certain It Goes On: The Collected Poems of Richard Hugo. Richard Hugo. 1984. 25.00 (*0-393-01784-2*) Norton.

Making Chair Seats from Cane, Rush & Other Natural Materials. rev. ed. Ruth B. Comstock. (Illus.). 48p. 1988. reprint ed. pap. 3.95 (*0-486-25693-6*) Dover.

Making Chairs. Vic Taylor. (Illus.). 100p. (Orig.). 1989. pap. 17.95 (*1-85486-007-0*) Nexus Special Interests.

Making Chairs & Tables. Guild of Mastercraftsman Staff. LC 97-222407. (Illus.). 128p. 1997. pap. text 14.95 (*1-86108-053-0*, Pub. by Guild Master) Sterling.

Making Change. Neale S. Godfrey. LC 97-685. 1997. 21.50 (*0-684-83202-X*) S&S Trade.

Making Change: A Woman's Guide to Designing Her Financial Future. Neale S. Godfrey & Tad Richards. 283p. 1999. pap. 12.00 (*0-684-84610-1*, Fireside) S&S Trade Pap.

Making Change: Even Still More Observations of a Chiropractic Advocate. William D. Esteb. 240p. (Orig.). 1995. pap. text 24.95 (*0-9631711-4-3*) Back Talk Systs.

Making Change: Three Educators Join the Battle for Better Schools. Maureen H. Holland. LC 97-31509. 240p. 1998. pap. 24.95 (*0-435-08152-7*) Heinemann.

Making Change Happen? fac. ed. Ed. by Dale Mann. LC 78-21849. (Policy Analysis & Education Ser.). 363p. 1978. reprint ed. pap. 112.60 (*0-7837-8645-X*, 204794300009) Bks Demand.

Making Change Happen: A Step by Step Guide. Graham Wilson. 256p. 1993. 105.00 (*0-273-60359-0*) St Mut.

Making Change Happen: Practical Planning for School Leaders. Jerry J. Herman & Janice L. Herman. LC 93-27064. 168p. 1993. pap. 22.95 (*0-8039-6097-2*) Corwin Pr.

Making Change Happen: Practical Planning for School Leaders. Jerry J. Herman & Janice L. Herman. LC 93-27064. 168p. 1994. 51.95 (*0-8039-6096-4*) Corwin Pr.

*__Making Change Happen One Person at a Time: Assessing Change Capacity Within Your Organization.__ Charles H. Bishop, Jr. LC 00-29965. 2000. 27.95 (*0-8144-0528-2*) AMACOM.

Making Change in Education: Preparing Schools for the Future. Jamieson A. McKenzie. LC 86-40485. 150p. 1987. 22.95 (*0-915253-11-9*) Wilkerson Pub Co.

*__Making Change in Mathematics Education: Learning from the Field.__ Ed. by Joan Ferrini-Mundy et al. LC 98-46363. (Illus.). 148 p. 1998. pap. 13.95 (*0-87353-442-5*) NCTM.

Making Change Irresistible: Overcoming Resistance to Change in Your Organization. Ken Hultman. LC 98-18575. 224p. 1998. 27.95 (*0-89106-121-5*, 7791, Pub. by Consulting Psychol) Natl Bk Netwk.

Making Change Pay. T. Lambert. 1996. pap. 129.00 (*1-85953-041-9*, Pub. by Tech Comm) St Mut.

Making Change Work for You! Richard S. Deems. Ed. by Dave Kirchner. LC 95-75608. (AMI How-to Ser.). 108p. 1995. per. 12.95 (*1-884926-38-X*, CHANG) Amer Media.

Making Change Work for You in Health Care. Richard S. Deems & K. C. Warner. Ed. by Karen M. Miller. LC 98-70378. (How-To Book Ser.). 93p. 1998. pap. 14.95 (*1-884926-85-1*, CHANH) Amer Media.

Making Changes: A Guide to Future Oriented Education. John W. Thomas. (Education Futures Ser.: No. 6). (Illus.). 1981. teacher ed. 19.95 (*0-88280-082-5*); pap. text, student ed. 15.95 (*0-88280-081-7*) ETC Pubns.

Making Changes: A Practical Guide to Vernacular Harmony. E. Salzman & Michael Sahl. 224p. 1986. pap. 13.50 (*0-7935-5569-8*, 50335290) H Leonard.

Making Changes: Family Voices on Living with Disabilities. Ed. by Jan Spiegle & Richard A. Van Den Pol. LC 93-23937. 216p. 1993. pap. 16.95 (*0-914797-93-X*) Brookline Bks.

Making Changes: Guidebook for Managing Life's Challenges. J. Colleen Breen. 192p. 1994. pap. 12.95 (*0-925190-33-0*) Fairview Press.

Making Changes for Good: A Cognitive Behavioral Approach for Sex Offender Relapse Prevention. Gregory L. Little & Kenneth D. Robinson. 58p. 1998. pap. 18.00 (*0-940829-22-3*) Eagle Wing Bks.

Making Chaplaincy Work: Practical Approaches. Ed. by Laurel A. Burton. LC 88-541. (Journal of Health Care Chaplaincy: Vol. 1, No. 2). (Illus.). 98p. 1988. text 29.95 (*0-86656-743-7*) Haworth Pr.

*__Making Character Bears.__ Valerie Tyler. 192p. 1999. pap. text 17.95 (*1-86108-069-7*) Guild Master.

Making Character Dolls' Houses in 1-12 Scale. Brian Nickolls. (Illus.). 192p. 1995. 29.95 (*0-7153-0200-0*, Pub. by D & C Pub) Sterling.

*__Making Character Dolls' Houses in 1/2 Scale.__ Brian Nickolls. (Illus.). 2000. pap. 19.95 (*0-7153-0854-8*) D & C Pub.

Making Charcoal: The Retort Method. 28p. 1979. 7.25 (*0-86619-071-6*) Vols Tech Asst.

Making Charcoal & Coke. 1996. lib. bdg. 250.95 (*0-8490-8295-1*) Gordon Pr.

Making Charisma: The Social Construction of Paul's Public Image. Anthony J. Blasi. 170p. (C). 1991. 39.95 (*0-88738-400-5*) Transaction Pubs.

Making Charities Effective: A Guide for Charities & Voluntary Bodies. Peter L. George. 1989. pap. 19.95 (*1-85302-019-2*, Pub. by Jessica Kingsley) Taylor & Francis.

Making Cheese & Butter. Phyllis Hobson. (Country Kitchen Library). (Illus.). 45p. 1984. pap. 3.95 (*0-88266-019-5*, Garden Way Pub) Storey Bks.

Making Cheese, Butter & Yogurt. P. Hobson. (Storey Publishing Bulletin Ser.: Vol. A-57). 1983. pap. 2.95 (*0-88266-232-5*) Storey Bks.

Making Childcare Choices. Gail Sagel & Lori Berke. LC 99-23372. 304p. 1999. pap. 12.95 (*1-58062-182-1*) Adams Media.

Making Children Mind Without Losing Yours. Kevin Leman. 192p. 1987. pap. 10.95 (*0-440-55184-6*) Dell.

Making Children Mind Without Losing Yours. Kevin Leman. 192p. (gr. 10). 1994. pap. 10.99 (*0-8007-5256-2*) Revell.

*__Making Children Mind Without Losing Yours.__ 2nd ed. Kevin Leman. 272p. 2000. pap., student ed. 12.99 (*0-8007-5731-9*) Chosen Bks.

Making Chinese Papercuts. Robert Borja & Corinne Borja. Ed. by Kathleen Tucker. LC 79-18358. 40p. (J). (gr. 3-8). 1980. lib. bdg. 14.95 (*0-8075-4948-7*) A Whitman.

Making Choice Theory Work in the Quality Classroom. Sally Berman. 110p. 1997. pap. 25.95 (*1-57517-040-X*) SkyLght.

*__Making Choices.__ Peter Galassi et al. (Illus.). 328p. 2000. 55.00 (*0-8109-6213-6*, Pub. by Abrams) Time Warner.

Making Choices. Wayne Harrel. 1995. 3.50 (*0-87129-549-0*, M55) Dramatic Pub.

Making Choices: A New Perspective on the History of Domestic Life in Illinois. Ed. by Janice T. Wass. (Illus.). 76p. (Orig.). 1995. pap. 10.00 (*0-89792-149-6*) Ill St Museum.

Making Choices: A Personal Look at Alcohol & Drug Use. 2nd ed. Marjorie E. Scaffa et al. 176p. (C). 1999. pap. write for info. (*0-697-22323-X*) Brown & Benchmark.

Making Choices: A Personal Look at Alcohol & Drugs. Marjorie E. Scaffa et al. 176p. (C). 1991. text. write for info. (*0-697-13944-1*) Brown & Benchmark.

Making Choices: A Program for Youth. 2nd ed. Linda Schoyer & Chery Duray. (Illus.). 174p. (J). (gr. 4-10). 1997. pap. 39.95 (*0-9622766-7-7*) Pittsburgh Peace.

Making Choices: A Recasting of Decision Theory. Frederic Schick. 169p. 1997. text 54.95 (*0-521-58181-8*); pap. text 16.95 (*0-521-58840-5*) Cambridge U Pr.

Making Choices: How to Prevent Alcohol & Other Drug Problems at Work. Carole Remboldt. 1994. wbk. ed. 27.50 (*1-56246-097-8*, 328810, HazeldenJohnson Inst) Hazelden.

Making Choices: Practical Wisdom for Everyday Moral Decisions. Peter Kreeft. 210p. (Orig.). (C). 1990. pap. 10.99 (*0-89283-638-5*) Servant.

Making Choices: The Joy of a Courageous Life. Alexandra Stoddard. LC 93-23921. 1994. 22.00 (*0-688-10935-7*, Wm Morrow) Morrow Avon.

*__Making Choices: 1929 - 1939 - 1948 - 1955.__ Peter Galassi et al. (Illus.). 2000. 55.00 (*0-87070-030-8*); pap. 34.95 (*0-87070-029-4*) Mus of Modern Art.

Making Choices Co. Alexandra Stoddard. LC 93-23921. 224p. 1995. pap. 14.00 (*0-380-71625-9*, Avon Bks) Morrow Avon.

Making Choices about Conflict, Security & Peacemaking Pt. 1: Personal Perspectives. Carol M. Lieber. (Illus.). 399p. (Orig.). 1994. pap. 28.00 (*0-942349-08-3*) Eductrs Soc Respons.

Making Choices Curriculum: Life Skills for Adolelscents. Barbara F. Lang & Mary Halter. 1995. teacher ed., student ed., ring bd. 89.95 (*0-911655-49-2*) Advocacy Pr.

Making Choices for Health Care. Frank Honigsbaum et al. LC 97-5361. 1997. write for info. (*1-85775-251-1*, Radcliffe Med Pr) Scovill Paterson.

Making Choices for Multicultural Education: Five Approaches to Race, Class, & Gender. 3rd ed. Christine E. Sleeter. 256p. 1999. pap. 42.95 (*0-471-36477-0*) Wiley.

*__Making Choices for Multicultural Education: Five Approaches to Race, Class, Etc.__ Christine E. Sleeter. 1999. pap. text 83.90 (*0-471-37543-8*) Wiley.

Making Choices in Sexuality: Research & Application with InfoTrac. McCammon & Knox. (Psychology Ser.). 1998. pap. 28.00 incl. cd-rom (*0-534-36353-9*) Brooks-Cole.

Making Choices in Sexuality: Research & Applications. Susan McCammon et al. LC 97-41780. 1997. pap. 30.25 (*0-534-35595-1*) Brooks-Cole.

Making Choices Workbook: Life Skills for Adolescents. Barbara F. Lang & Mary Halter. 1994. pap., student ed. 8.95 (*0-911655-37-9*) Advocacy Pr.

M

Making Christ Known: Historic Mission Documents from the Lausanne Movement, 1974-1989. Ed. by John R. Stott. LC 97-14961. 288p. 1997. pap. 30.00 (*0-8028-4315-8*) Eerdmans.

Making Christians: Clement of Alexandria & the Rhetoric of Legitimacy. Denise Kimber Buell. LC 98-34873. 1999. 39.50 (*0-691-05980-2*, Pub. by Princeton U Pr) Cal Prin Full Svc.

Making Christmas Jewelry in Polymer Clay. Photos & Text by Jeffrey B. Snyder. LC 95-16319. (Illus.). 64p. (Orig.). 1995. pap. 12.95 (*0-88740-832-X*) Schiffer.

Making Christology Relevant to the Third World: Applying Christopraxis to Local Struggle. Daniel L. Lukito. LC 98-20867. (European University Studies: Series 23, Vol. 630). 266p. (C). 1998. pap. 41.95 (*0-8204-3442-6*) P Lang Pubng.

Making Christology Relevant to the Third World Vol. 630: Applying Christopraxis to Local Struggle, Vol. 630. Daniel L. Lukito. (European University Studies: No. 23). 266p. 1998. 41.95 (*3-906760-27-8*) P Lang Pubng.

Making Christ's Peace a Part of Your Life. Dietrich Von Hildebrand. LC 98-34832. 126p. 1998. pap. 9.95 (*0-918477-80-8*) Sophia Inst Pr.

*__Making Church Relevant, 2.__ Dale E. Galloway. LC 99-32617. (Beeson Pastoral Ser.). 160p. 1999. text 19.99 (*0-8341-1822-X*) Beacon Hill.

Making Cider. Jo Deal. (Illus.). 92p. (Orig.). 1993. reprint ed. pap. 10.95 (*0-9619072-1-5*) G W Kent.

Making Cities Livable: Wege Zur Menschlichen Stadt. Ed. by Suzanne H. Lennard et al. (ENG & GER., Illus.). 460p. 1997. 49.00 (*0-935824-07-3*); pap. 38.00 (*0-935824-08-1*) Gondolier.

Making Cities Work: How Two People Mobilized a Community to Meet Its Needs. rev. ed. Basil Entwistle. LC 89-38023. (Illus.). 198p. 1992. pap. 12.95 (*0-932727-52-2*) Hope Pub Hse.

Making Cities Work: How Two People Mobilized a Community to Meet Its Needs. rev. ed. Basil Entwistle. LC 89-38023. (Illus.). 200p. 1993. lib. bdg. 19.95 (*0-932727-53-0*) Hope Pub Hse.

*__Making Citizen Soldiers: ROTC & the Ideology of American Military Service.__ Michael S. Neiberg. LC 99-44354. 288p. 2000. 39.95 (*0-674-54312-2*) HUP.

Making Civil Rights Law: Thurgood Marshall & the Supreme Court, 1936-1961. Mark V. Tushnet. LC 93-397. 416p. 1994. text 60.00 (*0-19-508412-8*) OUP.

Making Civil Rights Law: Thurgood Marshall & the Supreme Court, 1936-1961. Mark V. Tushnet. 416p. 1996. pap. 21.00 (*0-19-510468-4*) OUP.

Making Classic & Modern Wooden Lamps: Easy to Master Techniques to Create Your Own Lamps. Edward R. Turner. (Illus.). 256p. 2000. pap. 24.95 (*0-88179-164-4*, Pub. by Hartley & Marks) Publishers Group.

*__Making Classic Cakes.__ Emma Summer. (Illus.). 2000. 11.95 (*0-7548-0564-6*, Lorenz Bks) Anness Pub.

Making Classic Carved Furniture: The Queen Anne Stool. Ron Clarkson & Tom Heller. LC 93-87051. (Illus.). 96p. (Orig.). 1994. pap., per. 18.95 (*0-88740-588-6*) Schiffer.

Making Classic Chairs: A Craftsman's Chippendale Reference. Ron Clarkson. (Illus.). 158p. 1997. pap. 24.95 (*1-56523-081-7*) Fox Chapel Pub.

Making Climate Forecasts Matter. Paul C. Stern et al. LC 99-6247. 1999. 34.00 (*0-309-06475-9*) Natl Acad Pr.

*__Making Clocks.__ Laurie Penman. (Illus.). 122p. 1999. pap. 35.00 (*0-907868-71-1*) Clockwks Pr.

*__Making Collaboration Work: Lessons from Innovation in Natural Resource Management.__ Julia M. Wondolleck & Steven L. Yaffee. LC 00-8858. 280p. 2000. 50.00 (*1-55963-461-8*); pap. 25.00 (*1-55963-462-6*) Island Pr.

Making Collaborative Connections with Medical Providers: A Guide for Mental Health Professionals. L. Kevin Hamberger et al. LC 99-10456. 160p. 1999. pap. 32.95 (*0-8261-1258-7*) Springer Pub.

Making Collectible Santas & Christmas Ornaments in Wood: 40 Classic Christmas Patterns. 2nd ed. Jim Maxwell & Margie Maxwell. (Illus.). 36p. 1996. pap. 6.95 (*1-56523-034-5*) Fox Chapel Pub.

Making Collector Plates on Your Scroll Saw. Jery Boohe & Judy G. Roberts. (Illus.). 50p. (Orig.). 1994. pap. 12.95 (*1-56523-050-7*) Fox Chapel Pub.

An Asterisk (*) at the beginning of an entry indicates that the title is appearing for the first time.

Making College Count: A Real World Look at How to Succeed in & after College. Patrick O'Brian. LC 96-94706. (Illus.). 176p. (Orig.). (YA). (gr. 11-12). 1996. pap. 14.95 (*0-9633678-3-8*) Graphic Mngmt.

Making Colonial Furniture: Instructions & Diagrams for 24 Projects. James M. O'Neill. LC 97-137. (Illus.). 142p. 1997. reprint ed. pap. text 9.95 (*0-486-29666-0*) Dover.

Making Colonial Furniture Reproductions: Over 100 Projects with Measured Drawings. unabridged ed. John G. Shea. LC 94-16487. (Illus.). 224p. 1994. pap. text 13.95 (*0-486-28262-7*) Dover.

Making Color Sing. Jeanne Dobie. (Illus.). 160p. 1986. 27.50 (*0-8230-2993-X*) Watsn-Guptill.

***Making Color Sing.** Jeanne Dobie. (Illus.). 160p. 2000. pap. 19.95 (*0-8230-2992-1*) Watsn-Guptill.

Making Colours. (C). 1977. write for info. (*0-201-13840-9*) Addison-Wesley.

Making Commercial Law: Essays in Honour of Roy Goode. Ed. by Ross Cranston. LC 97-7395. (Illus.). 616p. 1997. text 115.00 (*0-19-826081-4*) OUP.

Making Commissions Work: A Handbook for Parish Religious Education Boards/Commissions. Ed. by Maria T. McClain. 104p. (Orig.). 1996. pap. 15.00 (*1-55833-151-4*) Natl Cath Educ.

***Making Common Ground: Public/Private Partnerships in Land for Housing.** Geoffrey K. Payne. 256p. 1999. pap. 25.00 (*1-85339-479-3*) Intermed Tech.

Making Common Sense: Leadership As Meaning-Making in a Community of Practice. Wilfred H. Drath & Charles J. Palus. LC 94-17583. 27p. 1994. pap. text 15.00 (*0-912879-97-1*) Ctr Creat Leader.

Making Common Sense a Common Practice: Proceedings of the Constraint Management Symposium. 148p. (Orig.). 1995. pap. 25.00 (*1-55822-121-2*) Am Prod & Inventory.

Making Common Sense a Common Practice: Proceedings of the 1996 Constraints Management Symposium. LC 97-144555. 168p. (Orig.). 1996. pap. 25.00 (*1-55822-151-4*) Am Prod & Inventory.

Making Common Sense Common Practice: A Leaders Guide to Using What You Already Know. V. R. Buzzotta et al. LC 96-71404. (Illus.). 230p. 1996. 24.95 (*1-886710-01-5*) New Leaders.

Making Common Sense Common Practice: A Leader's Guide to Using What You Already Know. V. R. Buzzotta & Alan Cheney. (Illus.). 175p. 1996. write for info. (*0-614-13045-X*) Psy Assocs.

Making Common Sense Common Practice: Achieving High Performance Using What You Already Know. V. R. Buzzotta et al. LC 97-29039. 230p. 1997. reprint ed. lib. bdg. 24.95 (*1-57444-194-9*) CRC Pr.

***Making Common Sense Common Practice: Models for Manufacturing Excellence.** Ron Moore. 1999. write for info. (*0-08-815899-3*) Elsevier.

Making Common Sense Common Practice: Models for Manufacturing Excellence. Ron Moore. LC 98-54948. 352p. 1999. 29.95 (*0-88415-899-3*, 5899, Cashman Dud) Gulf Pub.

Making Common Sense of Japan. Steven R. Reed. LC 93-12871. (Policy & Institutional Studies). 208p. (C). 1993. pap. 15.95 (*0-8229-5510-5*); text 49.95 (*0-8229-3757-3*) U of Pittsburgh Pr.

Making Communicative. Lee. 1995. pap., wbk. ed. 22.19 (*0-07-037694-8*) McGraw.

Making Community Meetings Work: Ten Tips for Successful Public Events. Debra Stein. 31p. 1996. pap. text 14.95 (*0-87420-783-5*, C06) Urban Land.

***Making Complex Decisions.** John Hopkins University Staff. 2000. pap. 59.50 (*0-538-69823-3*); pap. 10.50 (*0-538-69824-1*) Sth-Wstrn College.

Making Computers More Human. R. Hicks & James Essinger. 158p. 1991. 140.00 (*1-85617-057-8*, Pub. by Elsvr Adv Tech) Elsevier.

Making Computers People-Literate. Elaine Weiss. LC 93-41613. (Jossey-Bass Management Ser.). (Illus.). 307p. 1994. pap. 43.95 (*1-55542-622-0*) Jossey-Bass.

Making Computers Work for Administrators. Ed. by Kenneth C. Green & Steven W. Gilbert. LC 85-644752. (New Directions for Higher Education Ser.: No. HE 62). 1988. pap. 22.00 (*1-55542-919-X*) Jossey-Bass.

Making Connection: Poems of Exile. Bahman Sholevar. LC 79-129145. (Literature-Poetry Ser.). (Illus.). 103p. (Orig.). 1979. 8.95 (*0-911323-01-5*); pap. 3.95 (*0-911323-02-3*) Concourse Pr.

***Making Connections.** (C). 1999. lab manual ed. 12.90 (*0-536-60049-X*) Pearson Custom.

Making Connections. Alison. (C). 1995. pap. 31.16 (*0-395-72044-3*) HM.

Making Connections. Ed. by Tanya Szrajber. 123p. 1996. pap. text 22.00 (*3-7186-5850-X*, Harwood Acad Pubs) Gordon & Breach.

Making Connections. Valeri-Gold. (Adaptable Courseware-Softside Ser.). Date not set. pap. 15.00 (*0-534-16052-2*) Wadsworth Pub.

***Making Connections: A Practical Guide for Bringing the World of Voice Output Communication to Students with Severe Disabilities.** Peggy Locke & Jackie Levin. (Illus.). 111p. 1998. pap. 27.00 (*0-9666667-1-2*) AbleNet Inc.

Making Connections: Adult Day Health Care for People with AIDS. Leah Mason. LC 92-44741. (Practical Guide Ser.). 1993. 10.00 (*1-881277-14-3*) United Hosp Fund.

Making Connections: An Interactive Approach to Academic Reading. Kenneth J. Pakenham. 384p. (C). 1994. pap. text 21.95 (*0-521-65762-8*) Cambridge U Pr.

Making Connections: An Interactive Approach to Academic Reading: Instructor's Manual. Kenneth J. Pakenham. 96p. (C). 1994. pap., teacher ed. 6.00 (*0-521-65716-4*) Cambridge U Pr.

Making Connections: Arts & Sciences 1111. Oklahoma State Staff. 126p. (C). 1997. per. 10.95 (*0-7872-4187-3*, 41418701) Kendall-Hunt.

***Making Connections: Arts & Sciences 1111.** 2nd ed. (Webb) Oklahoma State Staff. 136p. (C). 1999. per. 16.95 (*0-7872-5992-6*, 41599201) Kendall-Hunt.

Making Connections: Building Support Networks for Families Living with Hiv. Josie Thomas et al. (Illus.). 74p. 1996. pap. 8.00 (*0-9642014-2-9*) Inst Fmly Ctr.

Making Connections: Case Discussions for Student-Centered Classroom Assessment. 2nd ed. Kathy Busick & Richard J. Stiggins. LC 96-79211. (Illus.). 160p. (Orig.). 1996. pap. text 16.00 (*0-9655101-0-7*) Assessmnt Trning.

***Making Connections: Citizens & Their Government.** 65p. 1998. pap. 15.00 (*1-886152-48-9*, 3543) Natl League Cities.

Making Connections: Essays in French Culture & Society in Honour of Philip Thody. Ed. by James Dolamore. 283p. 1999. 44.95 (*3-906760-69-3*, Pub. by P Lang) P Lang Pubng.

Making Connections: Essays in French Culture & Society in Honour of Philip Thody. Ed. by James Dolamore. (Illus.). 283p. 1998. pap. text 44.95 (*0-8204-4206-2*) P Lang Pubng.

Making Connections: Facilitated Communicating in an Inclusive Classroom. Karen Strandt-Conroy & Laural A. Sabin. (Movin' On Ser.). 58p. 1993. pap. text 8.00 (*1-886928-05-3*) DRI Pr.

Making Connections: Integrating Art into the Classroom: a Handbook of Lesson Plans for Kindergarten Through Grade Five. Sheri Castelnuovo & Sandy Rodgers. (Illus.). 1995. pap. write for info. (*0-913883-22-0*) Madison Art.

Making Connections: Interdisciplinary Art Activities. Barbara Mickelsen Ervin. LC 98-233160. 1998. write for info. (*0-8251-3733-0*) J W Walch.

Making Connections: Michigan & the Wider World. James Killoran et al. (Illus.). 98p. (YA). (gr. 4 up). 1997. pap. text 6.95 (*1-882422-39-2*) Jarrett Pub.

Making Connections: Multicultural Music & the National Standards. Ed. by William M. Anderson & Marvelene C. Moore. 128p. 1998. 30.00 incl. audio compact disk (*1-56545-108-2*) MENC.

Making Connections: Multicultural Music & the National Standards. Ed. by William M. Anderson & Marvelene C. Moore. 144p. 1998. pap. 20.00 incl. audio compact disk (*1-56545-106-6*, 1510) MENC.

***Making Connections: Readings in Relational Communication.** 2nd ed. Ed. by Kathleen Galvin & Pamela Cooper. LC 98-46496. 330p. (C). 1999. pap. text. write for info. (*1-891487-21-3*) Roxbury Pub Co.

Making Connections: Teaching & the Human Brain. fac. ed. Renate N. Caine & Geoffrey Caine. LC 91-7631. (Illus.). 203p. (Orig.). 1991. reprint ed. pap. 63.00 (*0-608-01024-3*, 2082500) Bks Demand.

***Making Connections: Technological Learning & Regional Economic Change.** Ed. by Edward J. Malecki & Paivi Oinas. LC 98-45773. (Organization of Industrial Space Ser.). 298p. 1999. text 69.95 (*1-84014-550-1*, Pub. by Ashgate Pub) Ashgate Pub Co.

***Making Connections: The Long-Distance Bus Industry in the United States.** (Illus.). 256p. 2000. 69.95 (*0-7546-0207-9*, Pub. by Ashgate Pub) Ashgate Pub Co.

Making Connections: The Minister As Practical Theologian. Osmer et al. 192p. 1997. pap. 16.95 (*0-687-01729-7*) Abingdon.

Making Connections: The Relational Worlds of Adolescent Girls at Emma Willard School. Ed. by Carol Gilligan et al. 352p. 1990. pap. text 15.50 (*0-674-54041-7*) HUP.

Making Connections: Total Body Integration Through Bartenieff Fundamentals. Peggy Hackney. (Illus.). 264p. 1998. pap. 45.00 (*90-5699-592-8*) Gordon & Breach.

Making Connections: Total Body Integration Through Bartenieff Fundamentals. Peggy Hackney. 272p. 1998. text 29.00 (*90-5699-591-X*) Gordon & Breach.

Making Connections: Women's Studies, Women's Movements, Women's Lives. Ed. by Mary Kennedy et al. LC 93-25525. (Gender & Society Ser.). 210p. 1993. 89.95 (*0-7484-0097-4*); pap. 29.95 (*0-7484-0098-2*) Taylor & Francis.

***Making Connections, Achieving Success, Understanding Others.** 2nd ed. Joseph Bocchi et al. 368p. (C). 1999. per. 32.95 (*0-7872-6351-6*, 41635101) Kendall-Hunt.

Making Connections Across the Curriculum: Reading for Analysis. Chittenden & Malcolm Kiniry. 1986. pap. text 18.50 (*0-312-50666-X*) St Martin.

Making Connections Between Multicultural & Global Education Teacher Educators & Teacher Education. Merry M. Merryfield. 1996. 25.00 (*0-89333-134-1*) AACTE.

Making Connections for Africa: Report from a Constituency Builders' Dialogue. Imani Countess et al. LC 97-37593. 94p. 1997. pap. 8.95 (*0-9634238-4-3*) Africa Policy Info.

Making Connections in Practice Teaching. David T. Sawdon et al. (C). 1986. 65.00 (*0-7855-4023-7*, Pub. by Natl Inst Soc Work) St Mut.

Making Connections in Practice Teaching: A Student Unit Perspective on Social Work Education & Community Work. David T. Sawdon. (C). 1986. 49.00 (*0-7855-3737-6*, Pub. by Natl Inst Soc Work); 70.00 (*0-7855-5901-9*, Pub. by Natl Inst Soc Work); 95.00 (*0-7855-0081-2*, Pub. by Natl Inst Soc Work) St Mut.

Making Connections in Practice Teaching: A Student Unit Perspective on Social Work Education & Community Work. Ed. by David T. Sawdon. (C). 1986. pap. 30.00 (*0-902789-36-8*, Pub. by Natl Inst Soc Work) St Mut.

Making Connections L1. Carolyn Kessler et al. (Secondary ESL). (J). 1993. mass mkt. 24.95 (*0-8384-3828-8*) Heinle & Heinle.

Making Connections 1: 1996 Version, No. 1. McCloskey. (Adult ESL Ser.). 168p. (Orig.). (J). 1996. mass mkt., student ed. 31.95 (*0-8384-7008-4*); mass mkt., wbk. ed. 7.50 (*0-8384-7000-9*) Heinle & Heinle.

Making Connections 3. Carolyn Kessler et al. (Secondary ESL Ser.). (J). 1995. mass mkt., suppl. ed. 65.95 (*0-8384-3842-3*) Heinle & Heinle.

Making Connections 3. McCloskey. (Secondary ESL Ser.). (J). 1995. mass mkt., suppl. ed. 104.95 (*0-8384-3844-X*) Heinle & Heinle.

Making Connections 3. McCloskey. (Adult ESL Ser.). (J). 1996. mass mkt., student ed. 24.95 (*0-8384-7010-6*) Heinle & Heinle.

Making Connections 3. McCloskey & Lydia Stack. (Secondary ESL Ser.). (J). 1995. suppl. ed. 18.00 incl. audio (*0-8384-3843-1*) Heinle & Heinle.

Making Connections 3, No. 3. McCloskey. (Secondary ESL Ser.). (J). 1995. mass mkt., teacher ed. 29.95 (*0-8384-3845-8*); mass mkt., wbk. ed. 8.50 (*0-8384-4243-9*) Heinle & Heinle.

Making Connections 3: Activity Masters. McCloskey. (Secondary ESL Ser.). (J). 1995. mass mkt., suppl. ed. 25.95 (*0-8384-4342-7*) Heinle & Heinle.

Making Connections 3: Text, No. 3. McClsokey et al. (Secondary ESL Ser.). 160p. (J). 1995. mass mkt. 31.95 (*0-8384-3841-5*) Heinle & Heinle.

Making Connections Through Reading & Writing. Maria Valeri-Gold & Mary P. Deming. 304p. 1993. 26.75 (*0-534-21498-3*) Wadsworth Pub.

Making Connections Thru Reading & Writing. 2nd ed. Valeri-Gold. (Developmental Study/Study Skill Ser.). 2000. pap. 25.75 (*0-534-50928-2*) Wadsworth Pub.

Making Connections 2. Carolyn Kessler et al. (Secondary ESL). (J). 1993. mass mkt. 24.95 (*0-8384-3835-0*) Heinle & Heinle.

Making Connections 2. McCloskey. (Secondary ESL Ser.). (J). 1994. suppl. ed. 25.95 incl. audio (*0-8384-3838-5*) Heinle & Heinle.

Making Connections 2. McCloskey. (Adult ESL Ser.). (J). 1996. mass mkt., student ed. 24.95 (*0-8384-7011-4*) Heinle & Heinle.

Making Connections 2: Activity Masters. McCloskey. (Secondary ESL Ser.). (J). 1994. pap., suppl. ed. 11.75 (*0-8384-4341-9*) Heinle & Heinle.

Making Connections 2: 1996 Version, Bk. 2. McCloskey. (Adult ESL Ser.). (J). 1996. mass mkt., wbk. ed. 7.50 (*0-8384-7040-8*) Heinle & Heinle.

Making Connections 2: 1996 Version, No. 2. McCloskey. (Adult ESL Ser.). (J). 1996. mass mkt., teacher ed. 29.95 (*0-8384-7041-6*) Heinle & Heinle.

Making Connections 2: 1996 Version, No. 2. McCloskey. (Adult ESL Ser.). 184p. (J). 1997. pap., student ed. 31.95 (*0-8384-7012-2*) Heinle & Heinle.

Making Connections with Mathematics. John Egsgard et al. (Illus.). 102p. (YA). (gr. 9 up). 1989. pap. 19.95 (*0-939765-27-6*, G116) Janson Pubns.

Making Connections with Others: A Handbook on Interpersonal Practice. Deborah Davidson & Suzanne Peloquin. 168p. 1998. pap. text 35.00 (*1-56900-100-6*, 1142) Am Occup Therapy.

Making Connections with Writing: An Expressive Writing Model in Japanese Schools. Mary M. Kitagawa & Chisato Kitagawa. LC 86-29406. 186p. (Orig.). (C). 1987. pap. text 24.00 (*0-435-08437-2*, 08437) Heinemann.

Making Connections 1-student Text Paper. McCloskey. (Adult ESL). (J). 1996. mass mkt., student ed. 24.95 (*0-8384-7009-2*) Heinle & Heinle.

Making Connections 1-workbook. McCloskey. (Secondary ESL). (J). 1994. text, wbk. ed. 8.95 (*0-8384-3831-8*) Heinle & Heinle.

Making Connections 2-workbook. McCloskey. (Secondary ESL). (J). 1994. mass mkt., wbk. ed. 8.95 (*0-8384-3840-7*) Heinle & Heinle.

Making Connections '97. 4th ed. Cochran. 1997. 21.50 (*0-07-292886-7*) McGraw.

Making Constitutional Law: Thurgood Marshall & the Supreme Court, 1961-1991. Mark V. Tushnet. 256p. 1997. 35.00 (*0-19-509314-3*) OUP.

Making Contact. Joyce Pope. (Curious Creatures Ser.). (Illus.). 48p. (J). 1992. lib. bdg. 5.00 (*0-8114-3155-X*) Raintree Steck-V.

Making Contact. Virginia M. Satir. LC 75-28768. (Illus.). 96p. 1995. pap. 7.95 (*0-89087-119-1*) Celestial Arts.

Making Contact. Carol J. Verburg. 1997. pap. text 2.55 (*0-312-15004-0*); pap. text 5.00 (*0-312-15005-9*) St Martin.

Making Contact: A Serious Handbook for Locating & Communicating with Extraterrestrials. Ed. by Bill Fawcett. LC 97-1653. (Illus.). 356p. 1997. 23.00 (*0-688-14486-1*, Wm Morrow) Morrow Avon.

Making Contact: A Serious Handbook for Locating & Communicating with Extraterrestrials. Bill Fawcett. (SPA.). 448p. 1998. mass mkt. 6.99 (*0-380-73154-1*, Avon Bks) Morrow Avon.

Making Contact: Readings from Home & Abroad. 4th ed. Carol J. Verburg. LC 96-86782. 792p. 1997. pap. 38.95 (*0-312-13350-2*) St Martin.

Making Contact: Uses of Language in Psychotherapy. Leston L. Havens. 215p. 1986. reprint ed. pap. text 13.50 (*0-674-54316-5*) HUP.

Making Contact & Rules for Writting, Vol. 1. Verburg. 1997. pap. text 31.75 (*0-312-18799-8*) St Martin.

Making Contact Book. O'Driscoll. 1991. pap. text. write for info. (*0-582-06447-3*, Pub. by Addison-Wesley) Longman.

Making Contact with Human Sexuality. Joan Atwood. (Illus.). 96p. (Orig.). pap. 6.95 (*0-942494-66-0*) Coleman Pub.

***Making Contemporary Wooden Tables: 18 Elegant Projects from Designer/Craftsmen.** Thomas W. Stender. LC 00-27457. (Illus.). 128p. 2000. pap. 19.95 (*1-57990-167-0*, Pub. by Lark Books) Sterling.

Making Contracting Work Better & Cost Less. 1994. lib. bdg. 252.75 (*0-8490-5833-3*) Gordon Pr.

Making Contributions: An Historical Overview of Women's Roles in Physics. Ed. by Barbara Lotze. (Occasional Publications). 132p. 1984. per. 12.50 (*0-917853-09-1*, OP-52) Am Assn Physics.

Making Conversation. Mark Larson. LC 97-3498. 126p. 1997. pap. text 18.50 (*0-86709-424-9*, 0424) Heinemann.

Making Cool Crafts & Awesome Art! A Kids' Treasure Trove of Fabulous Fun. Roberta Gould. Ed. by Susan Williamson. LC 96-51658. (Kids Can Ser.). (Illus.). 160p. (Orig.). (J). (gr. 2-5). 1997. pap. 12.95 (*1-885593-11-2*) Williamson Pub Co.

Making Cooperative Learning Work: Student Teams in K-12 Classrooms. Paul J. Vermette. LC 96-53392. 240p. 1997. pap. text 33.00 (*0-13-206392-1*) P-H.

Making Corrections: Punishment American-Style. (C). Date not set. write for info. (*0-13-010900-2*) P-H.

Making Country Furniture. George Buchanan. LC 97-34430. 1998. 22.95 (*1-56158-262-X*) Taunton.

Making Country Rustic Wood Projects. Patrick Spielman & Sherri S. Valitchka. LC 89-22018. (Illus.). 164p. (Orig.). 1990. pap. 14.95 (*0-8069-7258-0*) Sterling.

Making Country Style Curtains. Casey. (Country Wisdom Bulletin Ser.: Vol. A-98). 1988. pap. 2.95 (*0-88266-487-5*) Storey Bks.

Making Creativity Accountable: How Successful Advertisers Manage Their Television & Print. Ron Harding. LC 91-8651. 208p. 1991. 52.95 (*0-89930-337-4*, HTV/, Quorum Bks) Greenwood.

Making Crime Pay. Harold S. Long. LC 88-81589. 88p. (Orig.). 1988. pap. text 9.95 (*0-915179-83-0*) Loompanics.

Making Crime Pay: How to Locate Hidden Assets. Association of Certified Fraud Examiners Staff. LC 98-5403. 315p. 1998. wbk. ed. 199.00 (*1-889277-15-0*) Assn Certified Fraud.

***Making Crime Pay: Law & Order in Contemporary American Politics.** Katherine Beckett. (Studies in Crime & Public Policy). (Illus.). 168p. 1999. pap. 14.95 (*0-19-513626-8*) OUP.

Making Cult Connections. Rye. 1994. pap. text, teacher ed. 2.09 (*0-312-08072-7*) St Martin.

Making Culture: English-Canadian Institutions & the Arts Before the Massey Commission. Maria Tippett. 254p. 1990. text 40.00 (*0-8020-2743-1*); pap. text 17.95 (*0-8020-6784-0*) U of Toronto Pr.

Making Customer Satisfaction Happen. Chapman & Hall Staff. pap. text 48.00 (*0-412-78630-3*) Chapman & Hall.

Making Customer Satisfaction Happen. Roderick M. McNealy. 208p. 1994. 29.95 (*0-412-58920-6*, Chap & Hall NY) Chapman & Hall.

Making Dance Special. Melanie Peter. LC 98-153340. 160p. 1997. pap. 160.00 (*1-85346-434-1*, Pub. by David Fulton) Taylor & Francis.

Making Day Care Better: Training, Evaluation & the Process of Change. Ed. by James T. Greenman & Robert W. Fuqua. LC 83-18261. (Early Childhood Education Ser.). 285p. (Orig.). reprint ed. pap. 88.40 (*0-8357-3458-7*, 203972000013) Bks Demand.

Making Dead Oysters Talk: Techniques for Analyzing Oysters from Archaeological Sites. rev. ed. Bretton W. Kent. Ed. by Richard B. Hughes et al. LC 92-20097. (Illus.). 76p. (C). 1992. student ed., spiral bd. 10.00 (*1-878399-54-3*) Div Hist Cult Progs.

Making Deals: The Business of Negotiating. Marvin Gottlieb & William J. Healey. 1990. 29.95 (*0-317-03943-1*) NY Inst Finance.

Making Deals: The Business of Negotiating. 2nd ed. Marvin Gottlieb & William J. Healy. (Illus.). xiii, 194p. 1998. reprint ed. pap. 30.00 (*0-9664133-0-X*) Commun Project.

Making Decisions. (Open Learning For Supervisory Management). 1986. pap. text 19.50 (*0-08-034164-0*, Pergamon Pr) Elsevier.

Making Decisions. Lynn Blinn. LC 79-54910. (C). 1980. teacher ed. 8.00 (*0-8273-1711-5*) Delmar.

Making Decisions. Maggie W. Brown. Ed. by Thomas Zanzig. (Discovering Program Ser.). (Illus.). 37p. (J). 1990. teacher ed. 6.00 (*0-88489-201-8*); text 3.00 (*0-88489-200-X*) St Marys.

Making Decisions. Robert Heller & Tim Hindle. LC 98-18011. (Essential Managers Handbks.). (Illus.). 72p. 1999. pap. 6.95 (*0-7894-2889-X*) DK Pub Inc.

Making Decisions. Dennis V. Lindley. 220p. 1991. pap. 89.95 (*0-471-90808-8*) Wiley.

Making Decisions: A Multi-Disciplinary Introduction. Percy C. Hill et al. 264p. (C). 1986. reprint ed. pap. text 24.00 (*0-8191-5388-5*) U Pr of Amer.

Making Decisions: A Multi-Disciplinary Introduction. 2nd ed. Percy H. Hill et al. 1980. pap. text. write for info. (*0-201-03103-5*) Addison-Wesley.

Making Decisions: How to Develop Effective Skills for Making Good Decisions. Dean Juniper. 144p. 2000. pap. 14.95 (*1-85703-296-9*, Pub. by How To Bks) Midpt Trade.

Making Decisions: Learning to Take Control of Your Life. J. Michael Farr & Susan Christophersen. Ed. by Greg Croy. (Career & Life Skills Ser.). (Illus.). 58p. 1991. pap. 5.95 (*0-942784-57-X*, MG) JIST Works.

Making Decisions about Children: Psychological Questions & Answers. 2nd ed. H. Rudolph Schaffer. LC 97-37882. 256p. 1998. pap. 26.95 (*0-631-20259-5*) Blackwell Pubs.

***Making Decisions about Diverse Learners: A Guide for Educators.** Fern Aefksy. LC 00-22350. 2000. write for info. (*1-883001-94-3*) Eye On Educ.

An Asterisk (*) at the beginning of an entry indicates that the title is appearing for the first time.

Making Decisions about Liability & Insurance. Ed. by Colin Camerer. 144p. (C). 1993. lib. bdg. 134.00 (*0-7923-9393-7*) Kluwer Academic.
Making Decisions & Forming Opinions. Susan B. Annand. 1997. 6.95 (*1-55708-591-9*, MCC941) McDonald Pub Co.
Making Decisions on Cumulative Environmental Impacts: A Conceptual Framework. Frances H. Irwin & Barbara Rodes. LC 91-41132. (Illus.). 62p. (Orig.). (C). 1992. pap. 9.00 (*0-89164-134-3*) World Wildlife Fund.
Making Decisions under Stress: Implications for Individual & Team Training. Ed. by Janis A. Cannon-Bowers. LC 98-25041. (Illus.). 447p. 1998. 49.95 (*1-55798-525-1*) Am Psychol.
Making Decorative Fabric-Covered Boxes. Mary J. Hiney. (Illus.). 128p. 1997. pap. 14.95 (*0-8069-1297-9*, Chapelle) Sterling.
Making Decorative Lawn Ornaments & Patio Containers. Edie Stockstill. LC 94-49353. (Illus.). 144p. 1995. 27.95 (*0-8069-1290-1*, Chapelle) Sterling.
Making Decorative Lawn Ornaments & Patio Containers. Edie Stockstill. (Illus.). 144p. 1996. pap. 14.95 (*0-8069-1291-X*) Sterling.
Making Decorative Mirrors & Shelves. Holly Jorgensen. LC 97-33684. (Illus.). 128p. 1998. 27.95 (*0-8069-9339-1*) Sterling.
Making Decorative Mirrors & Shelves. Holly Jorgensen. (Illus.). 128p. 1999. pap. text 14.95 (*0-8069-9338-3*) Sterling.
Making Decoys: The Century-Old Way. Grayson Chesser & Curtis J. Badger. LC 88-16085. (Illus.). 176p. 1989. 29.95 (*0-8117-0986-8*) Stackpole.
Making Democracy in Spain: Grass-Roots Struggle in the South, 1955-1975. Joe Foweraker. 304p. (C). 1989. text 85.00 (*0-521-35406-4*) Cambridge U Pr.
Making Democracy Work: A Framework for Macroeconomic Policy in South Africa. MERG Policy Group. 348p. 1994. pap. 18.95 (*1-86808-183-4*) OUP.
Making Democracy Work: Civic Traditions in Modern Italy. Robert D. Putnam. 258p. 1992. pap. text 16.95 (*0-691-03738-8*, Pub. by Princeton U Pr) Cal Prin Full Svc.
Making Democracy Work: Swedish Experiences & Peruvian Options. Ed. by David Wirmark. (Institute of Latin American Studies: No. 29). (Illus.). 188p. 1996. pap. 72.50 (*91-85894-49-4*, Pub. by Almqvist Wiksell) Coronet Bks.
Making Democracy Work: The Life & Letters of Luther Halsey Gulick, 1892-1993. Lyle C. Fitch. LC 96-28063. (Illus.). 436p. 1996. pap. 21.95 (*0-87772-371-0*) UCB IGS.
***Making Democracy Work Better: Mediating Structures, Social Capital, & the Democratic Prospect: Mediating Structures, Social Capital, & the Democratic Prospect.** Richard A. Couto. LC 98-53439. (Illus.). 384p. 1999. 49.95 (*0-8078-2488-7*); pap. 19.95 (*0-8078-4824-7*) U of NC Pr.
Making Designer Furniture for Children, the Home & Garden. Hans-Werner Bastian. (Illus.). 80p. (Orig.). 1994. pap. 23.50 (*1-85486-111-5*, Pub. by Nexus Special Interests) Trans-Atl Phila.
Making Desks & Bookcases. Reader's Digest Editors. (Workshop Companion Ser.). 128p. 1999. 19.95 (*0-7621-0204-7*, Pub. by RD Assn) Penguin Putnam.
Making Development Sustainable: From Concepts to Action. Ismail Serageldin. LC 94-30977. (Environmentally Sustainable Development Proceedings Ser.: 2). 48p. 1994. pap. 22.00 (*0-8213-3042-X*, 13042) World Bank.
Making Development Sustainable: Redefining Institutions, Policy, & Economics. Ed. by Johan Holmberg. LC 92-16882. 362p. 1992. reprint ed. text 50.00 (*1-55963-213-5*) Island Pr.
Making Development Work: Legislative Reform for Institutional Transformation & Good Governance. Ann W. Seidman et al. LC 98-55764. 1999. 129.00 (*90-411-9708-7*) Kluwer Law Intl.
Making Diagnosis Meaningful: Enhancing Evaluation & Treatment of Psychological Disorders. Ed. by James W. Barron. LC 98-12803. 363p. 1998. 39.95 (*1-55798-496-4*) Am Psychol.
Making Difficulties: Research & the Construction of SEN. Ed. by Peter Clough & Len Barton. 192p. 1995. pap. 24.95 (*1-85396-294-5*, Pub. by P Chapman) Taylor & Francis.

Making Digital Negatives for Contact Printing: A Step-by-Step Guide to Affordable Enlarged Negatives for Platinum, Silver, & Other Printing Processes. 2nd rev. ed. Dan Burkholder. (Illus.). 350p. 1999. pap. 34.95 (0-9649638-6-8) Bladed Iris.
Completely revised & updated in this 1999 second edition, Dan Burkholder's award-winning book is a step-by-step guide to making affordable enlarged negatives for contact printing on silver, platinum, palladium & other contact printing processes. Exciting new techniques for making negatives with desktop printers are now included, as well as tips for using the latest imaging software. Photo Eye, the world's largest distributor of photography books, called it a "revolutionary book on this innovative & affordable technique." Jerry Uelsmann said of the book, "Making Digital Negatives is indispensable. It is clear, concise & insightful." In addition to the easy to follow text, illustrations & photographs, Burkholder's book includes a CD-ROM with calibration utilities, test images & demo software (both Mac & PC) & a separate color calibration print. Photographers wishing to combine the power & precision of digital imaging with the beauty & permanence of traditional photographic printing will find this book invaluable. Contact Bladed Iris Press, PO Box 111877, Carrollton, TX 75011-1877; phone 972-242-9819, fax: 972-242-9651; e/mail: bladediris@aol.com: www.danburkholder.com.
Publisher Paid Annotation.

Making Direct Mail Work: How to Boost Your Profits with Effective Direct Mail Promotion. Peter Arnold. (Illus.). 144p. 1999. pap. 19.95 (*1-85703-297-7*, Pub. by How To Bks) Trans-Atl Phila.
Making Disability: Exploring the Social Transformation of Human Variation. Paul C. Higgins. 302p. 1992. pap. 37.95 (*0-398-06392-3*) C C Thomas.
Making Disability: Exploring the Social Transformation of Human Variation. Paul C. Higgins. 302p. (C). 1992. text 54.95 (*0-398-05769-9*) C C Thomas.
Making Disciples: A Comprehensive Catechesis for the RCIA Catechumenate. M. Jane Carew. 1997. spiral bd. 32.95 (*0-87973-363-2*) Our Sunday Visitor.
Making Disciples: A Handbook of Christian Moral Formation. Timothy E. O'Connell. LC 97-37558. 192p. 1998. pap. 19.95 (*0-8245-1727-X*, Herdr & Herdr) Crossroad NY.
***Making Disciples: Faith Formation in the Wesleyan Tradition.** Sondra Higgins Matthaei. LC 00-38578. 2000. write for info. (*0-687-02475-7*) Abingdon.
Making Disciples: Following Jesus' Model. Michael T. Flynn. LC 97-90020. iii, 64p. (Orig.). 1997. pap. 5.00 (*0-9656897-1-9*) FreshWind Minist.
Making Disciples in the Congregation: A Guide to Christian Formation Through the Process of Mentoring & the Experience of Congregational Worship. Paul Versluis, III. (Occasional Papers: No. 17). 98p. 1995. pap. 10.00 (*0-936273-23-2*) Inst Mennonite.
Making Disclosure: Ideas & Interests in Ontario Securities Regulation. Mary G. Condon. LC 99-188396. (Illus.). 384p. 1997. text 60.00 (*0-8020-2982-5*) U of Toronto Pr.
Making Discoveries in Knots. Ham Gerber. LC 89-81890. (Illus.). 64p. (Orig.). 1990. pap. 8.00 (*0-8323-0475-1*) Binford Mort.
Making Discovery Work: A Handbook for Lawyers & Judges. William Schwarzner. 1985. 55.00 (*0-317-29434-2*, #H43988) Harcourt.
Making Diversity Happen: Controversies & Solutions. Ed. by Ann M. Morrison et al. LC 93-40166. (Special Reports: No. 320G). 127p. 1993. pap. text 20.00 (*0-912879-72-6*) Ctr Creat Leader.
Making Diversity Meaningful in the Boardroom. John Carver & Miriam M. Carver. LC 97-4566. (CarverGuide Ser.: No. CG 09). 26p. 1997. pap. 10.95 (*0-7879-0835-5*) Jossey-Bass.
***Making Do: Women, Family & Home in Montreal During the Great Depression.** Denyse Baillargeon. Tr. by Yvonne Klein. 200p. 1999. pap. 29.95 (*0-88920-326-1*) W Laurier U Pr.
Making Do or Making Art: A Study of American Recycling. Verni Greenfield. LC 85-20963. (American Material Culture & Folklife Ser.). (Illus.). 152p. reprint ed. pap. 47.20 (*0-8357-1702-X*, 207049700097) Bks Demand.
***Making Do Out of Doo Doo: Lessons in Life for Hardiness, Health & Fitness.** JoAnne Owens-Navslar & Wes Sime. Ed. by Linda J. Dageforde. LC 99-25909. 100p. 1999. pap. 12.95 (*1-886225-44-3*, 5000) Dageforde Pub.
Making Doctors. Simon Sinclair. LC 98-115314. 1997. 49.50 (*1-85973-950-4*, Pub. by Berg Pubs); pap. 19.50 (*1-85973-955-5*, Pub. by Berg Pubs) NYU Pr.
Making Documentaries & Reality Videos. Barry Hampe. 320p. 1995. pap. 16.95 (*0-8050-4451-5*) H Holt & Co.
Making $$$ at Home. Darla Sims. Ed. by Rodney Charles. LC 95-72374. 625p. (Orig.). (YA). (gr. 9). 1996. pap. 25.00 (*1-887472-02-9*) Sunstar Pubng.
Making Dollars for Your Team, Club, Organization. Bill Foster. Date not set. write for info. (*0-614-30299-4*) B F Pub.
Making Dollars with Pennies: How the Small Investor Can Beat the Wizards on Wall Street. R. Max Bowser. LC 97-74045. (Illus.). 200p. 1998. pap. 19.95 (*0-915216-98-1*) Marathon Intl Bk.
Making Dollhouses & Dioramas. Robert Schleicher. (Illus.). 192p. 1990. pap. 10.95 (*0-486-26335-5*) Dover.
Making Dolls. Sunnhild Reinckens. Tr. by Donald Maclean. (GER., Illus.). 56p. (J). (ps-3). 1989. reprint ed. pap. 10.95 (*0-86315-093-4*, Pub. by Floris Bks) Gryphon Hse.
Making Dolls' House Furniture. Patricia King. (Illus.). 176p. 1993. pap. 15.95 (*0-946819-24-6*, Pub. by Guild Master) Sterling.
Making Dolls' House Interiors in 1/12 Scale. Carol Lodder. (Illus.). 192p. 1997. pap. 19.95 (*0-7153-0615-4*) Sterling.
Making Doll's House Miniatures with Polymer Clay. Sue Heaser. LC 98-134291. (Illus.). 128p. 1998. 27.95 (*0-7063-7590-4*, Pub. by WrLock) Sterling.
Making Dolls' Houses in 1/12 Scale. Brian Nickolls. LC 98-137931. (Illus.). 192p. 1996. pap. 19.95 (*0-7153-0480-1*, Pub. by D & C Pub) Sterling.
Making Drama. Burton. 1995. pap. text. write for info. (*0-582-80356-X*, Pub. by Addison-Wesley) Longman.
Making Drama Special: Developing Drama Practice for Special Educational Needs. Melanie Peter. 176p. 1995. pap. 24.95 (*1-85346-316-7*, Pub. by David Fulton) Taylor & Francis.
***Making Dream Ice Cream: Easy Ices & Sorbets for Every Season.** (Illus.). 64p. 2000. 11.95 (*1-85967-782-7*, Lorenz Bks) Anness Pub.
Making Dried Flower Arrangements. Barbara Coates. (Illus.). 72p. (Orig.). 1994. pap. 15.95 (*0-86417-579-5*) Seven Hills Bk.
Making Drugs in Puerto Rico: Tax Benefits for the Pharmaceutical Industry in the 1980s. (Illus.). 37p. (Orig.). (C). 1992. pap. text 20.00 (*1-56806-014-9*) DIANE Pub.
Making Each & Every Farmer Count - Participation in Agricultural Engineering Projects. FAO Staff. 64p. 1998. pap. 11.00 (*92-5-104069-9*, F40699) FAO.
Making Each Minute Count: Time-Savers, Tips, & Kid-Tested Strategies for the Music Class. Cheryl Lavender. Ed. by Emily Crocker. 240p. (Orig.). 1991. per. 19.95 (*0-7935-0348-5*, HL44223055) H Leonard.
Making Early American & Country Furniture. unabridged ed. Franklin H. Gottshall. LC 95-16671. (Illus.). 160p. 1995. reprint ed. pap. text 11.95 (*0-486-28807-2*) Dover.
Making Early Histories in Museums. Nick Merriman. LC 98-37092. (Making Histories in Museums Ser.). 1999. 89.50 (*0-7185-0110-1*, Pub. by Leicester U Pr) Cassell & Continuum.
Making Early Stringed Instruments. R. Zachary Taylor. 111p. 1991. reprint ed. pap. 24.95 (*0-85442-051-7*, I436, Pub. by Stobart Davies) Bold Strummer Ltd.
Making Earth Ready for Life: Earth Started as a Hot Rock. Ima Kook. LC 98-96235. (As Dreamed by Itsy Ser.). (Illus.). 44p. (J). (gr. k-3). 2000. 14.95 (*1-892298-08-2*) Abique.
Making Economic & Environmental Sense: How Green Technology Works Better, Costs Less. Karen Flagstad. (Illus.). 48p. (Orig.). (C). 1994. pap. text 25.00 (*0-7881-1551-0*) DIANE Pub.
Making Economic Sense. Murray N. Rothbard. LC 95-78335. 439p. (Orig.). 1995. pap. 19.95 (*0-945466-18-8*) Ludwig von Mises.
Making Educated Decisions: A Landscape Preservation Bibliography. Ed. by Charles A. Birnbaum et al. LC 94-41041. (NPS Reading List Ser.). 1994. per. 5.50 (*0-16-045145-0*, 024-005-01142-1) USGPO.
Making Educated Decisions: A Landscape Preservation Bibliography. Ed. by Charles A. Birnbaum & Cheryl Wagner. (Illus.). 160p. 1998. pap. text 30.00 (*0-7881-7158-5*) DIANE Pub.
Making Education Count: Developing & Using International Indicators. LC 95-160314. (Orig.). 1994. pap. 58.00 (*92-64-14050-6*) OECD.
Making Educational History: A Feminist Perspective. Jill Blackmore. 117p. 1992. pap. 60.00 (*0-7300-1361-8*, ESA846, Pub. by Deakin Univ) St Mut.
Making Effective Decisions. Velocity Inc. Staff. (Illus.). 20p. 1999. pap. text 11.95 (*1-58099-013-4*) Velocity Busn.
Making Effective Presentations. LIDSTONE. 1985. 78.95 (*0-566-02382-2*) Ashgate Pub Co.
Making Effective Referrals. Sharon Cheston. 1991. text 29.95 (*0-89876-170-0*) Gardner Pr.
Making Effective Speeches. John Bowden. 144p. 1998. pap. 19.95 (*1-85703-291-8*, Pub. by How To Bks) Trans-Atl Phila.
Making Electronic Manuscripts. Michael Barnard. (Blueprint Ser.). 32p. (C). 1990. pap. 13.95 (*0-948905-38-7*) Chapman & Hall.
Making Emu Happen: Problems & Proposals: A Symposium. Peter B. Kenen. LC 96-21195. (Essays in International Finance Ser.). 1996. write for info. (*0-88165-106-0*) Princeton U Pr.
Making End-of-Life Decisions. Lee E. Norrgard & Jo DeMars. LC 92-28781. (Choices & Challenges Ser.). 200p. 1992. lib. bdg. 45.00 (*0-87436-613-5*) ABC-CLIO.
Making Ends Meet. Henry Felder. LC 94-231791. 192p. Date not set. pap. 10.99 (*0-8280-0789-6*) Review & Herald.
Making Ends Meet: Congressional Budgeting in the Age of Deficits. Daniel P. Franklin. LC 92-33123. 254p. 1992. pap. 23.95 (*0-87187-656-6*) Congr Quarterly.
Making Ends Meet: How Single Mothers Survive Welfare & Low-Wage Work. Kathryn Edin & Laura Lein. LC 96-40379. 320p. (C). 1997. text 42.50 (*0-87154-229-3*); pap. text 19.95 (*0-87154-234-X*) Russell Sage.
Making Ends Meet: How to Budget When You Don't Have Enough Money! Steven J. Schoeneck. 14p. 1995. pap. text 3.49 (*0-9648735-1-6*) PUP Pubng.
Making English Accessible: Using Electronic Networks for Interaction in the Classroom. Joy K. Peyton & Martha French. Ed. by Shawn Mahshie. (Illus.). 96p. (J). 1996. pap. text, teacher ed. 13.95 (*0-88095-206-7*) Gallaudet U Pre Coll.
Making English Work for You. Hoyt. (PS - Communication/English Ser.). (C). 1992. mass mkt. 23.50 (*0-538-70701-1*) S-W Pub.
Making Environmental Laws Work: Law & Policy in the UK & USA. William Wilson. LC 99-495109. 256p. 1999. 40.00 (*1-901362-79-5*, Pub. by Hart Pub) Intl Spec Bk.
Making Environmental Policy: An Introductory Analysis. Daniel J. Fiorino. LC 94-28832. 1995. pap. 17.95 (*0-520-08918-9*, Pub. by U CA Pr) Cal Prin Full Svc.
Making Equity Planning Work: Leadership in the Public Sector. Norman Krumholz & John Forester. (Illus.). 288p. 1990. 44.95 (*0-87722-700-4*); pap. text 22.95 (*0-87722-701-2*) Temple U Pr.
Making Ethical Choices: A Guide for Staff. Mark A. Henry. LC 98-55709. 35p. 1999. pap. 29.95 (*1-56991-111-8*) Am Correctional.
Making Ethical Choices, Resolving Ethical Dilemmas. Gini G. Scott. LC 98-14547. 368p. 1998. pap. text 16.95 (*1-55778-754-9*) Paragon Hse.
Making Ethical Decisions: A Casebook. Louis B. Weeks. LC 87-14703. 118p. (C). 1987. pap. 14.95 (*0-664-24064-X*) Westminster John Knox.
Making Ethnic Choices: California's Punjabi Mexican Americans. Karen I. Leonard. (Asian American History & Culture Ser.). 368p. (C). 1992. 59.95 (*0-87722-890-6*) Temple U Pr.
Making Ethnic Choices: California's Punjabi Mexican Americans. Karen I. Leonard. (Asian American History & Culture Ser.). 368p. (C). 1994. pap. 22.95 (*1-56639-202-0*) Temple U Pr.
Making Ethnic Ways: Communities & the Transformations in Taita, Kenya, 1800-1950. Bill Bravman. (Social History of Africa Ser.). 304p. 1998. 24.95 (*0-325-00104-9*); 65.00 (*0-325-00105-7*) Greenwood.
Making Eu Foreign Policy. Smith. LC 98-23464. 264p. 1999. text 65.00 (*0-312-21582-7*) St Martin.
Making Eucharistic Vestments on a Limited Budget. 2nd ed. Linda B. Hall. Ed. & Intro. by James E. Barrett. (Illus.). 48p. 1985. reprint ed. pap. text 10.50 (*0-942466-07-1*) Hymnary Pr.
Making Europe Accessible for Tourists with Disabilities: Handbook for the Tourism Industry. European Commission. LC 97-168795. 119 p. 1996. 16.00 (*92-827-7300-0*, Pub. by Comm Europ Commun) Bernan Associates.
Making Europe Work: Intergovernmental Conference, 1996. Richard E. Baldwin. 134p. 1995. pap. text 14.95 (*1-898128-23-5*, Pub. by Ctr Econ Policy Res) Brookings.
Making European Breads. Glenn Andrews. LC 97-13175. 1997. pap. 2.95 (*0-88266-998-2*, Storey Pub) Storey Bks.
Making European Policies Work: Comparative Syntheses, Vol. 1. Ed. by Heinrich Siedentopf & Jaques Ziller. (European Institute of Public Administration Ser.). 256p. (C). 1989. text 35.00 (*0-8039-8137-6*) Sage.
Making European Policies Work: National Reports, Vol. 2. Ed. by Heinrich Siedentopf & Jaques Ziller. (European Institute of Public Administration Ser.). 320p. (C). 1989. text 55.00 (*0-8039-8138-4*) Sage.
Making Evaluation Meaningful. Richard Curwin & Tim Timmerman. (Series in Education). 1988. pap. 12.95 (*0-8290-1078-5*); text 22.50 (*0-8290-0555-2*) Irvington.
Making Every Day Count: Daily Readings for Young People on Solving Problems, Setting Goals, & Feeling Good about Yourself. Pamela Espeland & Elizabeth Verdick. 392p. (YA). (gr. 5 up). 1998. pap. 9.95 (*1-57542-047-3*) Free Spirit Pub.
Making Every Minute Count: Time Management for Librarians. Ann Nauman & Marvene Dearman. (Illus.). 100p. (C). 1991. 19.50 (*0-931315-06-9*) Lib Learn Res.
Making Every Vote Count: Nonpartisan Election Monitoring in Asia. LC 96-6445. 104p. (Orig.). 1996. pap. 9.95 (*1-880134-25-X*) Natl Demo Inst.
Making Every Vote Count: Reassessing Canada's Election System. Ed. by Henry Milner. 200p. 1999. pap. 19.95 (*1-55111-256-6*) Broadview Pr.
Making Fabulous Pincushions: 93 Designs for Spectacular & Unusual Projects. Jo Packam. (Illus.). 144p. 1996. pap. 14.95 (*0-8069-0995-1*, Chapelle) Sterling.
Making Face, Making Soul - Haciendo Caras: Creative & Critical Perspectives by Feminists of Color. Ed. by Gloria Anzaldua. LC 90-9428. 448p. 1990. lib. bdg. 25.95 (*1-879960-11-7*) Aunt Lute Bks.
Making Face, Making Soul - Haciendo Caras: Creative & Critical Perspectives by Feminists of Color. Ed. by Gloria Anzaldua. LC 90-9428. 448p. 1990. pap. 17.95 (*1-879960-10-9*) Aunt Lute Bks.
Making Faces. Kevyn Aucoin. LC 97-12658. (Illus.). 160p. (gr. 8). 1997. 29.95 (*0-316-28686-9*) Little.
Making Faces. Kevyn Aucoin. 1998. write for info. (*0-316-28641-9*) Little.
***Making Faces.** Kevyn Aucoin. 160p. 1999. pap. 20.00 (*0-316-28685-0*) Little.
Making Faces. Norman Messenger. 11.95 (*0-394-22354-3*) Beginner.
Making Faces. Norman Messenger. LC 92-52807. (Illus.). 20p. (J). 1993. 14.95 (*1-56458-111-X*) DK Pub Inc.
Making Faces: Memoirs of a Caricaturist. Aline Fruhauf. LC 90-2793. 288p. 1990. reprint ed. pap. 10.95 (*0-936784-85-7*) J Daniel.
Making Faces: Self-Portraits by Alex Katz. John W. Coffey. LC 90-60420. (Illus.). 32p. (Orig.). 1990. pap. 10.95 (*0-88259-958-5*) NCMA.
Making Faces: Using Forensic & Archaeological Evidence. John Prag & Richard Neave. LC 97-18786. (Texas A&M Anthropology Ser.: No. 1). (Illus.). 256p. 1997. 39.95 (*0-89096-784-9*) Tex A&M Univ Pr.
Making Faces Book & Kit. Jacqueline Russon. (Illus.). 48p. 1995. 19.95 (*0-8069-4351-3*) Sterling.
Making Faces (Relist Kit) Jacqueline Russon. (Illus.). 48p. (J). 1996. pap. 9.95 (*0-8069-0932-3*) Sterling.
Making Facts Come Alive: Choosing Quality Nonfiction Literature K-8. Ed. by Rosemary Bamford & Janice V. Kristo. LC 97-69085. (Illus.). 384p. (J). (gr. k-8). 1998. pap. text, teacher ed. 39.95 (*0-926842-67-6*) CG Pubs Inc.
Making Facts Matter: Reading Non-Fiction 5-11. Margaret Mallett. 160p. 1992. pap. 27.00 (*1-85396-165-5*, Pub. by P Chapman) Taylor & Francis.
Making Faith - Sense: Theological Reflection in Everyday Life. Robert L. Kinast. LC 98-46238. 89p. 1999. pap. 8.95 (*0-8146-2513-4*) Liturgical Pr.
Making Faith-Sense: Theological Reflection in Everyday Life. Robert L. Kinast. 1999. write for info. (*0-08-146251-4*) Elsevier.
Making Families Work & What to Do When They Don't: Thirty Guides for Imperfect Parents of Imperfect Children. Bill Borcherdt. LC 96-14633. 1996. pap. 19.95 (*0-7890-0127-6*) Haworth Pr.

M

An Asterisk (*) at the beginning of an entry indicates that the title is appearing for the first time.

Making Families Work & What to Do When They Don't: Thirty Guides for Imperfect Parents of Imperfect Children. Bill Borcherdt. 232p. 1996. lib. bdg. 39.95 (0-7890-0073-3) Haworth Pr.

Making Fancy Birdhouses & Feeders. Charles R. Self. LC 88-19215. (Illus.). 128p. 1988. pap. 12.95 (0-8069-6690-4) Sterling.

Making Farmer's Co-Operative Work: Design, Governance & Management. Tushaar Shah. LC 95-23270. 248p. (C). 1996. 32.00 (0-8039-9259-9) Sage.

Making Fast Food: From the Frying Pan into the Fryer. Ester Reiter. 224p. (C). 1991. 65.00 (0-7735-0843-0) McG-Queens Univ Pr.

Making Fast Food: From the Frying Pan into the Fryer. Ester Reiter. 224p. 1992. pap. 9.95 (0-7735-0947-X, Pub. by McG-Queens Univ Pr) CUP Services.

Making Fast Food: From the Frying Pan into the Fryer. 2nd ed. Ester Reiter. (Illus.). 224p. (C). 1995. pap. 19.95 (0-7735-1387-6, Pub. by McG-Queens Univ Pr) CUP Services.

Making Fathers Pay: The Enforcement of Child Support. David L. Chambers. LC 79-11953. 380p. 1979. 39.00 (0-226-10077-4) U Ch Pr.

Making Federalism Work: A Study of Program Coordination at the Community Level. James L. Sundquist. LC 78-104334. 293p. 1969. pap. 14.95 (0-8157-8217-9) Brookings.

Making Feedback Work: Turning Feedback from Employee Surveys into Change. Joe Folkman. (Illus.). 128p. 1998. pap. 9.95 (1-890009-42-3) Exec Excell.

Making Feminist History: The Literary Scholarship of Sandra M. Gilbert & Susan Gubar. William E. Cain. LC 93-3787. (Wellesley Studies in Critical Theory, Literary History & Culture: Vol. 1). li, 325p. 1994. text 25.00 (0-8153-1467-1) Garland.

M

***Making Fiscal Policy in Japan: Economic Effects & Institutional Settings.** Hiromitsu Ishi. (Illus.). 416p. 2000. text 85.00 (0-19-924071-X) OUP.

Making Fitness Fun. Becky Tirabassi. (Thoroughly Fit Ser.). 1994. 19.99 incl. VHS (0-310-24678-4) Zondervan.

Making Flawless Cabinets & Built-Ins. Reader's Digest Editors. (Woodworking Ser.). 128p. 1999. 19.95 (0-7621-0186-5, Pub. by RD Assn) Penguin Putnam.

***Making Fleece Crafts.** Judy Ann Sadler & June Bradford. (Kids Can Do It Ser.). (Illus.). 40p. (YA). 2000. pap. 5.95 (1-55074-739-8, Pub. by Kids Can Press) Genl Dist Srvs.

***Making Fleece Crafts.** Judy Ann Sadler & June Bradford. (Kids Can Do It Ser.). (Illus.). 40p. (YA). (gr. 3 up). 2000. 12.95 (1-55074-847-5, Pub. by Kids Can Press) Genl Dist Srvs.

Making Flutes. William Marsh. 40p. 1998. 7.00 (0-937013-85-4, Pub. by Potes Poets) SPD-Small Pr Dist.

Making Food Healthy & Safe for Children: How to Meet the National Health & Safety Performance Standards--Guidelines for Out-of-Home Child Care Programs. National Center for Education in Maternal and Child Health (U.S.). LC 96-67628. (Illus.). 896p. 1997. write for info. (1-57285-030-2) Nat Ctr Educ.

Making for Planet Alice: New Women Poets. Ed. by Maura Dooley. LC 97-171758. (Illus.). 176p. 1997. pap. 19.95 (1-85224-398-8, Pub. by Bloodaxe Bks) Dufour.

Making Foreign Economic Policy. I. M. Destler. LC 79-5119. 244p. 1980. 34.95 (0-8157-1822-5); pap. 14.95 (0-8157-1821-7) Brookings.

Making Foreign People Pay. Ali C. Budak. LC 98-16967. (Studies in Modern Law & Policy: Vol. 5). (Illus.). 8p. 1998. text 74.95 (1-84014-436-X, K1370.B83, Pub. by Ashgate Pub Co) Ashgate Pub Co.

Making Foreign Policy. Kegley. pap. text. write for info. (0-312-00318-8, St Martins Paperbacks) St Martin.

Making 4-Track Music. 3rd rev. ed. John Peel. (Illus.). 114p. 1989. pap. 12.95 (0-933224-51-6, T033) Bold Strummer Ltd.

Making Fractions. Andrew King. LC 97-41603. (Math for Fun Ser.). (Illus.). 32p. (J). (gr. 2-4). 1998. pap. 5.95 (0-7613-0732-X, Copper Beech Bks); lib. bdg. 20.90 (0-7613-0723-0, Copper Beech Bks) Millbrook Pr.

Making Free Trade Work: The Canada - U. S. Agreement. Ed. by Peter Morici. LC 89-71317. 198p. 1990. reprint ed. pap. 61.40 (0-608-02006-0, 206266200003) Bks Demand.

Making Freedom Pay: North Carolina Freedpeople Working for Themselves, 1865-1900. Sharon Ann Holt. LC 99-38381. 184p. 1999. 30.00 (0-8203-2170-2) U of Ga Pr.

Making Friends. Sarah Levete. LC 97-41646. (How Do I Feel About... Ser.). (Illus.). 24p. (J). (gr. k-4). 1998. lib. bdg. 19.90 (0-7613-0808-3, Copper Beech Bks) Millbrook Pr.

Making Friends. Margaret Mahy. LC 89-13246. (Illus.). 32p. (J). (gr. k-3). 1990. 13.95 (0-689-50498-5) McElderry Bks.

Making Friends. Andrew Matthews. (Illus.). 144p. 1991. pap. 14.95 (0-8431-2969-7, Price Stern) Peng Put Young Read.

Making Friends. Kate Petty. LC 91-14193. (Playground Ser.). (Illus.). 24p. (J). (ps-3). 1991. pap. 5.95 (0-8120-4660-9) Barron.

Making Friends. Fred Rogers. (Illus.). 32p. (J). (ps-1). 1996. pap. 6.99 (0-698-11409-4, PapStar) Peng Put Young Read.

Making Friends. William Schulz. (Options Ser.). 64p. (Orig.). (gr. 1-8). 1989. pap., teacher ed. 8.00 (0-920541-53-4) Peguis Pubs Ltd.

***Making Friends: Face Facts, Sky, , Vol. 3.** Kate Andrews. (Making Friends Ser.: No. 3). 128p. (J). (gr. 3-7). 1999. mass mkt. 3.99 (0-380-80932-X, Avon Bks) Morrow Avon.

***Making Friends: Grow Up, Amy, Vol. 4.** Kate Andrews. (Making Friends Ser.: No. 4). 128p. (J). (gr. 3-7). 1999. mass mkt. 3.99 (0-380-80933-8, Avon Bks) Morrow Avon.

Making Friends: The Influences of Culture & Development. Luanna H. Meyer. LC 97-29475. (Children, Youth & Change Ser.). 425p. 1997. 48.95 (1-55766-301-7) P H Brookes.

Making Friends: Training Your Dog Positively. Linda Colflesh. (Illus.). 224p. 1990. 19.95 (0-87605-687-7) Howell Bks.

Making Friends & Making Them Count. Em Griffin. LC 87-2619. (Illus.). 223p. (Orig.). 1987. pap. 12.99 (0-87784-996-X, 996) InterVarsity.

Making Friends in School: Promoting Peer Relationships in Early Childhood. Patricia Ramsey. (Early Childhood Education Ser.: Vol. 32). 256p. 1991. text 42.00 (0-8077-3128-5) Tchrs Coll.

Making Friends in School: Promoting Peer Relationships in Early Childhood. Patricia G. Ramsey. (Early Childhood Education Ser.: Vol. 32). 256p. 1991. pap. text 18.95 (0-8077-3127-7) Tchrs Coll.

Making Friends with Books Series Collection 1: Preprimer, Primer, First Reader, 15 vols. 2nd ed. Alvin Granowsky. Ed. by Morton Botel & John Dawkins. Orig. Title: Bookshop A. (Illus.). (J). (gr. 1-3). 1998. reprint ed. pap. 60.00 (1-891564-09-9) M Botel Assocs.

Making Friends with Books Series Collection 2: Beginning Second, High Second, 16 vols. 2nd ed. Alvin Granowsky. Ed. by Morton Botel & John Dawkins. Orig. Title: Bookshop B. (Illus.). (J). (gr. 2-5). 1998. reprint ed. pap. 70.00 (1-891564-10-2) M Botel Assocs.

Making Friends with Books Series Collection 3: Beginning Third, High Third, 16 vols. 2nd ed. Alvin Granowsky. Ed. by Morton Botel & John Dawkins. Orig. Title: Bookshop C. (Illus.). (J). (gr. 3-8). 1998. reprint ed. pap. 70.00 (1-891564-11-0) M Botel Assocs.

Making Friends with Frankenstein: A Book of Monstrous Poems & Pictures. Colin McNaughton. LC 93-20027. (Illus.). 96p. (J). (ps up). 1994. 19.99 (1-56402-308-7) Candlewick Pr.

Making Friends with Frankenstein: A Book of Monstrous Poems & Pictures. Colin McNaughton. LC 93-20027. 1996. 15.19 (0-606-10258-2, Pub. by Turtleback) Demco.

Making Friends with Frankenstein: A Book of Monstrous Poems & Pictures. Colin McNaughton. LC 93-20027. (Illus.). 96p. (J). (gr. 1-6). 1996. reprint ed. pap. 9.99 (1-56402-962-X) Candlewick Pr.

***Making Friends with My Ostomy.** Katy Hirsch. LC 99-91160. (Illus.). 32p. (J). (gr. k-5). 1999. pap. 11.95 (0-9674418-0-3) Hirsch & Assocs.

Making Friends with Pain: Learning to Live Well with Chronic Illness. Elizabeth Flora. LC 99-90431. (Illus.). 160p. 1999. pap. 11.95 (0-9671641-2-5) Sadie Bks.

Making Friends with the Bible. Elouise R. Fraser & Louis A. Kilgore. LC 94-3953. 168p. (Orig.). 1994. pap. 9.99 (0-8361-3666-7) Herald Pr.

***Making Friends with Time.** Tracy D. Sarriugarte & Peggy R. Ward. Ed. by Jean Terra & Diane Ronayne. 200p. 1999. pap. 13.95 (0-9673303-0-0) PBJ Pubng.

Making Friends with Your Father: A Book for Daughters. Kay M. Strom. 160p. 1992. pap. 9.99 (0-310-54891-8) Zondervan.

Making Friends with Your Mother: A Book for Daughters. Kay M. Strom. 160p. 1991. pap. 9.99 (0-310-53251-5) Zondervan.

Making Friends with Your Three-Year Old, Vol. 1. Janet Poland. (Magical Years Ser.: No. 3). 1995. mass mkt. 4.99 (0-312-95627-4) St Martin.

Making Friends with Your Unconscious: The User Friendly Guide. Patricia O. Hudson. 153p. (Orig.). 1993. pap. 9.95 (0-9634886-1-9) Ctr Pr TX.

Making Friends with Yourself: Christian Growth & Acceptance. Leo P. Rock. 144p. 1990. pap. 7.95 (0-8091-3155-2) Paulist Pr.

Making Friends with Yourself: Christian Growth & Self-Acceptance. Leo P. Rock. 144p. (C). 1996. pap. 39.95 (0-85439-333-1, Pub. by St Paul Pubns) St Mut.

Making Friendship Bands. Lynette Silver. LC 97-199175. (Illus.). 40p. 1995. pap. 5.95 (1-86351-135-0, Pub. by Sally Milner) Sterling.

Making Full Proof of Our Ministry. 5th ed. Ralph Reynolds. 152p. (C). 1989. pap. 5.95 (1-877917-07-9) Alpha Bible Pubns.

Making Furniture in Preindustrial America: The Social Economy of Newtown & Woodbury, Conn. Edward S. Cooke, Jr. LC 95-52689. (Johns Hopkins Studies in Industry & Society: Vol. 10). (Illus.). 304p. (C). 1996. text 45.00 (0-8018-5253-6) Johns Hopkins.

Making Furniture Masterpieces: 30 Projects with Measured Drawings. unabridged ed. Franklin H. Gottshall. LC 96-26466. (Illus.). 224p. 1996. reprint ed. pap. text 13.95 (0-486-29338-6) Dover.

Making Game: An Essay on Woodcock. 2nd ed. Guy De la Valdene. LC 88-63675. (Illus.). 192p. 1990. 24.95 (0-944439-14-4) Clark City Pr.

Making Garden Furniture. Chris Graham. (Illus.). 128p. 1997. 35.00 (1-85223-987-5, Pub. by Cro1wood) Trafalgar.

***Making Garden Ornaments.** Simona Hill. 64p. 2000. 11.95 (0-7548-0461-5) Anness Pub.

Making Gardens: An Essential Guide to Planning & Planting. Patrick Taylor. LC 97-42040. (Illus.). 224p. 1998. 29.95 (0-88192-420-2) Timber.

***Making Gears: By the Single-Toothed Hob Method.** Eugene E. Petersen. (Illus.). 172p. 2000. pap. 15.00 (0-9642614-5-6) Knoll Pubs.

Making Gender: The Politics & Erotics of Culture. Sherry B. Ortner. LC 96-12293. 288p. 1997. pap. 18.00 (0-8070-4633-7) Beacon Pr.

Making Gender Work: Managing Equal Opportunities. Ed. by Jenny Shaw & Diane Perrons. LC 95-15678. 256p. 1995. 114.00 (0-335-19366-8); pap. 33.95 (0-335-19365-X) OpUniv Pr.

Making Ghostbusters. Ed. by Don Shay. (Illus.). 224p. (Orig.). 1985. pap. 14.95 (0-918432-68-5) Baseline Bks.

***Making Gift Boxes.** Linda Hendry. (Kids Can Do It Ser.). 40p. (J). (gr. 3). 1999. 5.95 (1-55074-503-4) Kids Can Pr.

Making Gifts with Woodworker: Another Selection from over 90 Years of the World's Best Woodworking Magazine. Ed. by Zachary Taylor. (Illus.). 160p. (Orig.). 1994. pap. 36.00 (1-85486-110-7, Pub. by Nexus Special Interests) Trans-Atl Phila.

Making Gingerbread Houses. Hart. LC 96-8967. (Storey Publishing Bulletin Ser.: Vol. A-154). 1996. 16.95 (0-88266-493-X) Storey Bks.

Making Gingerbread Houses & Cookies. Lauren Jarrett. 1998. pap. 16.95 (1-58017-074-9) Storey Bks.

Making GIS Work for Your Business. 104p. 1995. pap. 85.00 (0-11-330673-3, HM06733, Pub. by Statnry Office) Bernan Associates.

Making Glass Beads. Cindy Jenkins. Ed. by Leslie Dierks. LC 96-49598. (Illus.). 112p. 1997. 21.95 (1-887374-16-7, Pub. by Lark Books) Random.

Making Global Connections in the Middle School: Lessons on the Environment, Development & Equity. Ed. by William Luderer. 87p. (Orig.). 1994. pap. text 12.00 (0-928630-02-1) Global Learning.

Making Global Deals: What Every Executive Should Know about Negotiating Abroad. Jeswald W. Salacuse. LC 92-9273. 193p. 1992. pap. 15.00 (0-8129-2090-2, Times Bks) Crown Pub Group.

Making Glorious Gifts from Your Garden. Marie Browning. (Illus.). 128p. 1999. 27.95 (0-8069-2479-9) Sterling.

Making God. Stefan Petrucha. LC 97-77706. 159p. 1998. pap. 12.50 (0-9661593-0-6) Between Lines.

***Making God Known: Offering the Gift of Life.** With A Mission Youth with a Mission Staff. 96p. 1999. pap. 6.99 (0-310-22703-8) Zondervan.

Making God Real in the Orthodox Christian Home. Anthony M. Coniaris. 1977. pap. 11.95 (0-937032-07-7) Light&Life Pub Co MN.

Making God Real to Your Children see Que Los Ninos Vengan a Mi

Making God Real to Your Children. Sally Leman Chall. 192p. (Orig.). (gr. 11). 1995. mass mkt. 5.99 (0-8007-8630-0, Spire) Revell.

Making God's Good News Known. T. M. Moore. (Orig.). 1985. pap. text 4.95 (0-934688-18-4); pap. text, teacher ed. 3.95 (0-934688-19-2) Great Comm Pubns.

Making God's Word Stick. Emmett Cooper & Steve Wamberg. 168p. 1996. pap. 9.99 (0-7852-7506-1) Nelson.

Making Good: Law & Moral Regulation in Canada, 1867-1939. Carolyn Strange & Tina Loo. LC 97-180929. (Themes in Canadian Social History Ser.). 170p. 1997. text 45.00 (0-8020-0884-4, KF345) U of Toronto Pr.

Making Good Career & Life Decisions. Jist Staff. 1997. mass mkt. 13.82 (1-56370-293-2) JIST Works.

Making Good Decisions. Terence Duniho. 1989. pap. 2.50 (1-878287-28-1) Type & Temperament.

Making Good Decisions. rev. ed. James C. Campbell. (Skill Centered Leadership Ser.). 12p. 1997. pap., wbk. ed. 12.95 incl. audio (1-891160-61-1) ClamShell Pub.

Making Good Decisions: Decision-Making Techniques for Your Career & Your Life. rev. ed. JIST Works, Inc. Staff & Northern Virginia Community College Staff. (Career Emphasis Ser.). (Illus.). 73p. 1990. pap. text 5.95 (0-942784-10-3, CE12) JIST Works.

Making Good Decisions about Kinship Care. June Mickens et al. LC 96-39922. 1997. 19.95 (1-57073-380-5) Amer Bar Assn.

Making Good on Our Promises: Moving Beyond Rhetoric to Action. AACC Commission to Improve Minority Education Staff. 41p. 1993. pap. 15.00 (0-87117-258-5, 1356) Comm Coll Pr Am Assn Comm Coll.

Making Good Preaching Better: A Step-by-Step Guide to Scripture-Based People-Centered Preaching. Alvin Rueter. LC 96-42563. 280p. 1997. pap. 19.95 (0-8146-2215-1) Liturgical Pr.

***Making Good Sense: Process Improvement Approach to Logistics Financial Management.** Marygail K. Brauner. LC 00-40306. (J). 2000. write for info. (0-8330-2854-5) Rand Corp.

Making Gospel Sense: To a Troubled Church. James W. McClendon, Jr. LC 95-180872. 176p. 1995. pap. 14.95 (0-8298-1072-2) Pilgrim OH.

Making Gourd Musical Instruments. Ginger Summit & Jim Widess. LC 99-11128. (Illus.). 144p. 1999. 27.95 (0-8069-1369-X) Sterling.

Making Governance Work: TQE for School Boards. William K. Poston, Jr. LC 93-47928. (Total Quality Education Ser.: Vol. 8). 144p. 1994. pap. 18.95 (0-8039-6144-8) Corwin Pr.

Making Government Work. 121p. 1978. 1.50 (0-914389-05-X) Common Cause.

Making Government Work: A Conservative Agenda for the States. Ted Lezar. LC 93-47055. 1993. pap. 15.95 (0-89526-730-6) Regnery Pub.

Making Government Work: Electronic Delivery of Federal Services. (Illus.). 178p. (Orig.). (C). 1994. pap. text 35.00 (0-7881-0444-6) DIANE Pub.

Making Government Work: Electronic Delivery of Federal Services. (Orig.). 1994. lib. bdg. 250.00 (0-8490-8580-2) Gordon Pr.

***Making Government Work: Lessons from America's Governors & Mayors.** Ed. by Paul J. Andrisani et al. LC 00-20507. 352p. 2000. 35.00 (0-8476-9972-2) Rowman.

Making Government Work for Your City's Kids: Getting Through the Intergovernmental Maze of Programs for Children & Families. 60p. 1992. 30.00 (0-933729-71-5, No. 8010) Natl League Cities.

Making Governments Plan: State Experiments in Managing Land Use. Raymond J. Burby et al. LC 97-2189. (Illus.). 200p. 1997. text 32.50 (0-8018-5623-X) Johns Hopkins.

Making Grapevine Wreaths. Gayle O'Donnell. LC 96-1982. (Illus.). 1996. pap. 2.95 (0-88266-445-X, Storey Pub) Storey Bks.

Making Gray Gold: Narratives of Nursing Home Care. Timothy Diamond. 296p. 1995. pap. text 13.95 (0-226-14474-7) U Ch Pr.

Making Gray Gold: Narratives of Nursing Home Care. Timothy Diamond. LC 91-45755. (Women in Culture & Society Ser.). 296p. 1998. 24.95 (0-226-14473-9) U Ch Pr.

Making Great Cheese: 30 Simple Recipes from Cheddar to Chevre, Plus 18 Scrumptious Dishes. Barbara Ciletti. LC 98-53253. (Illus.). 144p. 1999. 24.95 (1-57990-109-3, Pub. by Lark Books) Random.

Making Great Gingerbread Houses: Delicious Designs from Cabins to Castles, from Lighthouses to Treehouses. Aaron Morgan. Ed. by Paige G. Blomgren. LC 99-29333. (Illus.). 128p. 1999. 24.95 (1-57990-136-0, Pub. by Lark Books) Random.

Making Great Lamps: 50 Illuminating Projects, Techniques & Ideas. Deborah Morgenthal. LC 98-21475. (Illus.). 144p. 1998. 26.95 (1-57990-057-7, Pub. by Lark Books) Random.

Making Great Power Late. Geoffrey Holmes. LC 92-13685. (Foundations of Modern Britain Ser.). 464p. (C). 1993. text 77.95 (0-582-48438-3, Pub. by Addison-Wesley) Longman.

***Making Great Presentations.** Ghassan Hasbani. (Essentials Ser.). 78p. 2000. pap. 9.95 (1-85703-509-7, Pub. by How To Bks) Midpt Trade.

Making Great Sausage: 25 Savory Links from Around the World. Chris Kobler. Ed. by Jane LaFerla. LC 99-25466. (Illus.). 128p. 1999. 24.95 (1-57990-131-X, Pub. by Lark Books) Sterling.

Making Green Revolution: The Politics of Agricultural Development in China. Benedict Stavis. (Monograph: No. 1). 287p. 1974. 6.50 (0-86731-000-6) Cornell CIS RDC.

Making Greeting Cards with Rubber Stamps. Mary Jo McGraw. LC 96-32192. (Illus.). 128p. 1997. pap. 21.99 (0-89134-713-5, North Lght Bks) F & W Pubns Inc.

Making Groups Effective. 2nd ed. Alvin Zander. LC 94-18129. (Management Ser.). 289p. 1994. text 32.95 (0-7879-0009-5) Jossey-Bass.

Making Groups Work: Rethinking Practice. Joan Benjamin et al. LC 98-197584. 208p. 1998. pap. 24.95 (1-86448-304-0, Pub. by Allen & Unwin Pty) Paul & Co Pubs.

Making Growth Happen: Learning from Successful First-Generation Entrepreneurs. S. Phansalkar. LC 98-37063. 1998. write for info. (0-7619-9293-6); pap. write for info. (0-7619-9294-4) Sage.

Making Gypsy Willow Furniture. Bim Willow. LC 97-80806. (Illus.). 64p. 1998. pap. 14.95 (0-7643-0407-0) Schiffer.

Making Halleluwjah Hats! Crafts & Activities Based on Bible Stories. Mary Doerfler-Dall. LC 98-197303. (Illus.). 160p. (J). (ps-3). 1998. pap. 14.95 (0-8091-3788-7, 3788-7) Paulist Pr.

***Making Hand-Dipped Candles.** Betty Oppenheimer. LC 99-14635. 1999. pap. 3.95 (1-58017-205-9) Storey Bks.

***Making Hand-Sewn Boxes: Techniques & Projects.** Jackie Woolsey. 144p. 1999. pap. text 17.95 (1-86108-085-9) Guild Master.

Making Handbags & Purses: 50 Patterns & Designs from Casual to Corporate. Carol Parks. LC 97-31147. (Illus.). 128p. 1997. 24.95 (1-57990-012-7, Pub. by Lark Books) Random.

***Making Handbags & Purses: 50 Patterns & Designs from Casual to Corporate.** Carol Parks. (Illus.). 2000. pap. 16.95 (1-57990-194-8) Lark Books.

Making Handsome Bookcases & Desks. Nick Engler. (Secrets of Successful Woodworking Ser.). 128p. 1999. pap. text 19.95 (0-7621-0187-3, Pub. by RD Assn) Penguin Putnam.

Making Handsome Bookcases & Desks: Secrets of Successful Woodworking. Nick Engler & Sue Hausmann. (Illus.). 128p. 1958. text 19.95 (0-87596-819-8) Rodale Pr Inc.

Making Hard Decisions: An Introduction to Decision Analysis. Robert T. Clemen. 557p. (C). 1991. text 47.75 (0-534-92336-4) Wadsworth Pub.

Making Hard Decisions: An Introduction to Decision Analysis. 2nd ed. Robert T. Clemen. 752p. (C). 1997. pap. 94.95 (0-534-26034-9) Wadsworth Pub.

***Making Hard Decisions with Decisiontools.** 2nd rev. ed. Robert T. Clemen & Terence Reilly. LC 00-31451. 2001. write for info. (0-534-36597-3) Wadsworth Pub.

Making Haste Slowly: The Troubled History of Higher Education in Mississippi. David G. Sansing. LC 90-37004. 384p. 1990. text 45.00 (0-87805-458-8) U Pr of Miss.

Making Hay. Verlyn Klinkenborg. LC 97-224913. (Illus.). 320p. 1997. pap. text 14.95 (1-55821-611-1) Lyons Pr.

Making Headway: Talking in Pairs Intermediate. Tania Bastow & Ceri Jones. (Illus.). 80p. 1999. pap. text 9.95 (0-19-435555-1) OUP.

Making Headway: Talking in Pairs Pre-Intermediate. Tania Bastow & Ceri Jones. (Illus.). 80p. 1999. pap. text 9.95 (0-19-435548-9) OUP.

Making Health Care Decisions: Your Right to Decide - Advance Directives - Living Wills - Powers of Attorney. 32p. 1992. pap. 5.00 (*0-685-67154-2*, 4704) CCH INC.

Making Health Care Equipment: Ideas for Local Design & Production. Adam Platt & Nicola Carter. (Illus.). 96p. 1990. pap. 15.00 (*1-85339-067-4*, Pub. by Intermed Tech) Stylus Pub VA.

Making Health Care Reform Work: How the New Law Affects You & Your Employer. Peter M. Berkery. pap. 9.95 (*0-7863-0344-1*, Irwn Prfssnl) McGraw-Hill Prof.

Making Health Certain. R. S. Clymer. 192p. 1921. 15.00 (*0-916285-51-0*) Humanitarian.

Making Health Certain (1921) R. Swinburne Clymer. 190p. 1998. reprint ed. pap. 14.95 (*0-7661-0503-2*) Kessinger Pub.

Making Health Communication Programs Work: A Planner's Guide. (Illus.). 131p. (Orig.). (C). 1993. pap. text 40.00 (*0-7881-0080-7*) DIANE Pub.

Making Health Decisions. 2nd ed. B. Gmur. 1975. 24.48 (*0-13-547927-4*); student ed. 26.80 (*0-685-03879-3*) P-H.

Making Health Education Work: Health Education in Health Program Development, with Primary Attention on Programming for Low-Income & Minority Groups. Jeannette Simmons. LC 76-26205. 168p. reprint ed. pap. 52.10 (*0-608-16630-8*, 202665600050) Bks Demand.

Making Health Reform Work: The View from the States. Ed. by John J. DiIulio, Jr. & Richard P. Nathan. 179p. (C). 1994. 34.95 (*0-8157-1852-7*) Brookings.

Making Health Reform Work: The View from the States. Ed. by John J. DiIulio, Jr. & Richard P. Nathan. 179p. (C). 1994. pap. 14.95 (*0-8157-1851-9*) Brookings.

Making Health Work: Human Growth in Modern Japan. Carl Mosk. (Studies in Demography: Vol. 8). (Illus.). 174p. (C). 1996. 48.00 (*0-520-08315-6*, Pub. by U CA Pr) Cal Prin Full Svc.

Making Healthy Decisions. BSCS Staff. (Injury Prevention Ser.: Vol. 1). 80p. 1996. ring bd. 7.90 (*0-7872-1218-0*) Kendall-Hunt.

Making Healthy Decisions, No. 1. BSCS Staff. (Injury Prevention Ser.: Vol. 1). 176p. 1996. teacher ed., ring bd. 22.90 (*0-7872-1219-9*) Kendall-Hunt.

Making Healthy Decisions Fitness, No. 1. BSCS Staff. 172p. 1996. teacher ed., spiral bd. 22.90 (*0-7872-1223-7*) Kendall-Hunt.

Making Healthy Decisions Fitness, No. 2. BSCS Staff. 166p. 1996. teacher ed., spiral bd. 22.90 (*0-7872-1225-3*) Kendall-Hunt.

Making Healthy Decisions Fitness, Unit 1. BSCS Staff. 86p. 1996. spiral bd. 7.90 (*0-7872-1222-9*) Kendall-Hunt.

Making Healthy Decisions Fitness, Unit 2. BSCS Staff. 82p. 1996. spiral bd. 7.90 (*0-7872-1224-5*) Kendall-Hunt.

Making Healthy Decisions Nutrition, Unit 1. BSCS Staff. 200p. 1996. teacher ed., spiral bd. 22.90 (*0-7872-1207-5*) Kendall-Hunt.

***Making Healthy Families.** Gayle Peterson. 2000. 23.95 (*0-9625231-5-1*) Shadow & Light.

Making Healthy Food Choices. 20p. 1993. pap. 10.00 (*1-57979-049-6*) DIANE Pub.

Making Healthy Food Choices. 16p. 1998. pap. 2.75 (*0-16-049809-0*, Agriculture Dept) USGPO.

Making Healthy Tomorrows: Cardiac Fitness & a Healthier Lifestyle. Barry Franklin. 208p. 1993. pap. 12.95 (*1-881139-07-7*) Glovebox Guidebks.

Making Heirloom Toys. Jim Makowicki. LC 96-17860. 160p. 1996. pap. 19.95 (*1-56158-112-7*) Taunton.

Making Her Rights a Reality: Women's Human Rights & Development. Ed. by Gillian Moon. LC 97-123679. 120p. 1997. pap. 15.95 (*1-875870-24-5*, Pub. by Oxfam Pub) Stylus Pub VA.

Making Herbal Dream Pillows. Jim Long. LC 98-14498. (Spirit of Aromatherapy Ser.). (Illus.). 64p. 1998. 14.95 (*1-58017-075-7*) Storey Bks.

Making Heroes of Scholars: The Honor Society of Phi Kappa Phi, 1971-1983. Neal O'Steen. (Illus.). 142p. 1985. 10.00 (*0-9614651-0-7*); pap. 6.00 (*0-9614651-1-5*) Honor Soc P K P.

Making High School Work: Lessons from the Open School. Tom Gregory. 288p. (C). 1993. text 44.00 (*0-8077-3294-X*); pap. text 19.95 (*0-8077-3293-1*) Tchrs Coll.

Making His Heart Glad. Marie Chapian. (Heart for God Ser.: VOL 3). (Illus.). 176p. 1989. text 11.99 (*1-55661-083-1*) Bethany Hse.

Making His Mark. Horatio Alger, Jr. (Illus.). 307p. 1979. reprint ed. 30.00 (*0-686-35753-1*) G K Westgard.

Making His Mark. Horatio Alger, Jr. (Works of Horatio Alger Jr.). 1989. reprint ed. lib. bdg. 79.00 (*0-685-27600-7*) Rprt Serv.

Making His Mind My Mind. J. J. Turner. Ed. by B. H. Banks. (Illus.). 96p. (Orig.). 1989. pap. 4.50 (*0-89315-400-8*) Lambert Bk.

Making His Way. Horatio Alger, Jr. (Works of Horatio Alger Jr.). 1989. reprint ed. lib. bdg. 79.00 (*0-685-27579-5*) Rprt Serv.

Making His Way: Frank Courtney's Struggle Upward. Horatio Alger, Jr. LC 74-15724. (Popular Culture in America Ser.). 290p. 1975. reprint ed. 26.95 (*0-405-06361-X*) Ayer.

Making Historic Properties Accessible. Thomas C. Jester. 14p. 1993. pap. 1.50 (*0-16-061660-3*) USGPO.

Making Histories in Museums. Ed. by Gaynor Kavanagh. LC 96-33747. 224p. (C). 1996. text 99.50 (*0-7185-0007-5*) Bks Intl VA.

***Making Histories in Museums.** Gaynor Kavanagh. (Illus.). 2000. pap. text 26.95 (*0-7185-0008-3*) Leicester U Pr.

Making History. Stephen Fry. LC 98-31946. 400p. 1999. pap. 13.00 (*1-56947-150-9*) Soho Press.

Making History. David Reynolds. 1998. write for info. (*0-679-45743-7*) Random.

Making History: A Social Studies Curriculum in the Participation Series. Sheldon Berman. 90p. (Orig.). 1984. pap. 19.00 (*0-614-18084-8*) Eductrs Soc Respons.

Making History: Agency, Structure, & Change in Social Theory. Alex Callinicos. LC 87-47766. 276p. 1988. text 49.95 (*0-8014-2121-7*) Cornell U Pr.

***Making History: Interviews with Four Generals of Cuba's Revolutionary Armed Forces.** Ed. by Mary-Alice Waters. (Illus.). 193p. 1999. pap. text 15.95 (*0-87348-902-0*); lib. bdg. 50.00 (*0-87348-903-9*) Pathfinder NY.

Making History: The American Left & the American Mind. Richard Flacks. 376p. 1989. pap. text 19.50 (*0-231-04833-5*) Col U Pr.

***Making History: The Biographical Narratives of Robert Penn Warren.** Jonathan S. Cullick. LC 99-57982. (Southern Literary Studies). 192p. 2000. 45.00 (*0-8071-2558-X*); pap. 18.95 (*0-8071-2603-9*) La State U Pr.

Making History: The Normans & Their Historians in Eleventh-Century Italy. Kenneth B. Wolf. LC 94-44633. (Middle Ages Ser.). 192p. 1995. 32.50 (*0-8122-3298-4*) U of Pa Pr.

***Making History: The Story of Canada in the 20th Century.** 2000. write for info. (*0-13-032008-0*) P-H.

Making History: Writings on History & Culture. E. P. Thompson. LC 94-29225. 384p. 1994. 30.00 (*1-56584-216-2*, Pub. by New Press NY); pap. 17.00 (*1-56584-217-0*, Pub. by New Press NY) Norton.

Making History Vol. 42, No. 1: Textuality & the Forms of Eighteenth-Century Culture (Bucknell Review) Ed. by Greg Clingham. (Illus.). 160p. 1998. 24.00 (*0-8387-5384-1*) Bucknell U Pr.

Making History Come Alive. James Howard & Thomas Mendenhall. 97p. (C). 1982. pap. 5.50 (*0-931989-09-4*) Coun Basic Educ.

Making History for Stalin: The Story of the Belomor Canal. Cynthia A. Ruder. LC 97-24059. 192p. 1998. 49.95 (*0-8130-1567-7*) U Press Fla.

Making History in Twentieth-Century Quebec. Ronald Rudin. LC 98-150395. (Illus.). 270p. 1997. text 50.00 (*0-8020-0853-4*); pap. text 18.95 (*0-8020-7838-9*) U of Toronto Pr.

Making History in Vermont: The Election of a Socialist to Congress. Steven Rosenfeld. LC 91-34055. 500p. (C). 1992. text 35.00 (*0-89341-698-3*); pap. text 17.50 (*0-89341-699-1*) Hollowbrook.

Making History Matter. Robert Dawidoff. LC 99-17037. (Illus.). 304p. 2000. 64.50 (*1-56639-748-0*); pap. 22.95 (*1-56639-749-9*) Temple U Pr.

***Making Hole.** 3rd rev. ed. (Rotary Drilling Ser.: Unit II, Lesson 1). (Illus.). 136p. (Orig.). 2000. pap. text 16.00 (*0-88698-190-5*) PETEX.

Making Holy the Day: A Commentary in the Liturgy of the Hours. Charles E. Miller. 1976. 1.50 (*0-89942-410-4*, 410/04) Catholic Bk Pub.

Making Home Accessories. Jo Finnis. 1995. 7.98 (*0-7858-0129-4*) Bk Sales Inc.

Making Home Happy. 202p. Date not set. pap. 7.95 (*1-881545-13-X*) Angelas Bkshelf.

Making Home Peaceful. 227p. 1997. pap. 7.95 (*1-881545-75-X*) Angelas Bkshelf.

Making Home-School Work. Mhemooda Malek. 54p. 1997. spiral bd. 15.00 (*1-874579-96-2*, Pub. by Natl Childrens Bur) Paul & Co Pubs.

Making Homemade Candy. Glenn Andrews. 1989. pap. 2.95 (*0-88266-568-5*, Garden Way Pub) Storey Bks.

***Making Hope Happen: A Workbook for Turning Possibilities into Reality.** Diane McDermott & C. R. Snyder. 168p. 1999. pap. 14.95 (*1-57224-167-5*) New Harbinger.

Making Housing Affordable: Breaking down Regulatory Barriers: A Self-Assessment Guide for States. 91p. (Orig.). (C). 1995. pap. text 25.00 (*0-7881-1974-5*) DIANE Pub.

Making Humour Work: Taking Your Job Seriously & Yourself Lightly. Michael G. Crisp & Terry Paulson. LC 88-72262. (Fifty-Minute Ser.). (Illus.). 77p. (Orig.). 1989. pap. 10.95 (*0-931961-61-0*) Crisp Pubns.

Making Hypermedia Work: A User's Guide to HyTime. Steven J. DeRose & David G. Durand. LC 94-16201. 408p. (C). 1994. text 95.50 (*0-7923-9432-1*) Kluwer Academic.

Making Ice Cream & Frozen Yogurt. Maggie Oster. LC 95-30536. (Storey Publishing Bulletin Ser.: Vol. A-142). 1995. pap. 2.95 (*0-88266-414-X*) Storey Bks.

Making Ice Creams, Ices, & Sherbets. Phyllis Hobson. LC 77-4714. (Country Kitchen Library). (Illus.). 76p. 1984. pap. 3.95 (*0-88266-105-1*, Garden Way Pub) Storey Bks.

Making Images Move: Photographs & the Avant-Garde Cinema. Jan-Christopher Horak. Ed. by Charles Musser. LC 97-17444. (Smithsonian Studies in the History of Film & Television). (Illus.). 320p. 1995. text 36.95 (*1-56098-744-8*) Smithsonian.

***Making iMovies.** Scott Smith. (Illus.). 200p. 2000. pap. text 39.99 (*0-201-70489-7*, Pub. by Peachpit Pr) Addison-Wesley.

***Making Inclusion Work: Video & Facilitator's Guide.** Anne M. Beninghof. 56p. 1999. 39.50 incl. VHS (*1-57035-206-2*) Sopris.

***Making Independent Films: Advice from the Filmmakers.** Liz Stubbs & Richard Rodriguez. 224p. 2000. pap. 16.95 (*1-58115-057-1*, Pub. by Allworth Pr) Watsn-Guptill.

Making Indian Bows & Arrows... The Old Way. Douglas Spotted-Eagle. Ed. by Monte Smith. (Illus.). 105p. 1988. per. 12.95 (*0-943604-21-4*, BOO/18) Eagles View.

Making Indonesia. Ed. by Daniel S. Lev & Ruth T. McVey. (Studies on Southeast Asia: SOSEA 20). 201p. (Orig.). 1996. pap. 18.00 (*0-87727-719-2*, SOSEA 20) Cornell SE Asia.

Making Inferences: Advanced Level. (Comprehension Skills Ser.). 60p. (YA). (gr. 8-12). 1993. pap. 8.45 (*0-89061-619-1*, Jamestwn Pub) NTC Contemp Pub Co.

Making Inferences: Intermediate Level. (Comprehension Skills Ser.). 60p. (YA). (gr. 6-12). 1993. pap. 8.31 (*0-89061-639-6*, Jamestwn Pub) NTC Contemp Pub Co.

Making Inferences: Introductory Level. (Comprehension Skills Ser.). 60p. (YA). (gr. 6-12). 1993. pap. 7.91 (*0-89061-659-0*, Jamestwn Pub) NTC Contemp Pub Co.

Making Infill Projects Work. Eric Smart. LC 85-51153. 128p. (Orig.). reprint ed. pap. 39.70 (*0-7837-1006-2*, 204131600020) Bks Demand.

***Making Information Available in Digital Format: Perspectives from Practitioners.** Ed. by Terry Coppock. (Illus.). vii, 168p. 1999. 30.00 (*0-11-497276-1*, Pub. by Statnry Office) Balogh.

Making Information Technology Work. Shivraj Kanungo. LC 99-23168. 430p. 1999. 59.95 (*0-7619-9331-2*) Sage.

Making Information Work: Conference Proceedings January 18-23, 1992, Washington, D. C. Ed. by Karen Glass & Mark Miller. 345p. (Orig.). 1992. pap. text 20.00 (*1-55877-141-7*) Natl Governor.

***Making Informed Medical Decisions: Where to Look & How to Use What You Find.** Nancy Oster et al. 280p. 2000. pap. 17.95 (*1-56592-459-2*, Patient-Centered) OReilly & Assocs.

Making Innovation Happen: Concept Management Through Integration. Gerhard J. Plenert & Shozo Hibino. LC 97-37096. 200p. 1997. lib. bdg. 39.95 (*1-57444-090-X*) St Lucie Pr.

Making Inquiries into Alleged Child Abuse & Neglect: Partnership with Families. Ed. by Dendy Platt & David Shemmings. 302p. 1998. pap. 54.95 (*0-471-97222-3*) Wiley.

Making Instruction Work. Robert F. Mager. 1988. pap. 17.95 (*1-56103-467-3*) Ctr Effect Perf.

Making Instruction Work: A Step-by-Step Guide to Designing & Developing Instruction That Works see Mager Six-Pack

Making Instructional Design Decisions. 2nd ed. Barbara Seels & Zita Glasgow. LC 97-13742. 342p. 1997. pap. 62.00 (*0-13-520602-2*) P-H.

Making Instruments Count: Essays on Historical Scientific Instruments Presented to Gerard L'Estrange Turner. R. G. Anderson et al. 512p. 1993. 111.95 (*0-86078-394-4*, Pub. by Variorum) Ashgate Pub Co.

Making Integrated Curriculum Work: Teachers, Students, & the Quest for Coherent Curriculum. P. Elizabeth Pate et al. LC 96-42444. 1996. 34.00 (*0-8077-3598-1*); pap. 16.95 (*0-8077-3597-3*) Tchrs Coll.

Making Integrated Health Care Work: Case Studies, 2 vols. Dean C. Coddington et al. (Health Ser.). (Illus.). 250p. (Orig.). (C). 1996. pap. 42.00 (*1-56829-011-X*, 4829) Med Group Mgmt.

Making Integrated Health Care Work: The Analysis, 2 vols. Dean C. Coddington et al. (Health Ser.). 300p. (C). 1996. 51.00 (*1-56829-010-1*, 4828) Med Group Mgmt.

Making Integrated Health Care Work & Making Integrated Health Care Work: Case Studies, 2 vols., Vol. 1 & 2. Dean C. Coddington et al. 1996. text 75.00 (*1-56829-014-4*) Med Group Mgmt.

Making Interfaith Marriage Work: A Nonjudgmental Guide to Coping with the Spiritual, Emotional, & Psychological Issues. Steven C. Reuben. LC 93-48111. 256p. 1994. pap. 12.95 (*1-55958-506-4*) Prima Pub.

Making Interior Models. Susumu Kurabayashi. (Illus.). 144p. 1994. pap. 34.95 (*4-7661-0798-5*, Pub. by Graphic-Sha) Bks Nippan.

Making Intermediate Grammar Work: Grammar in Context for ESL Students. Kristan Cavina. LC 97-91562. 264p. (Orig.). 1997. pap. text 22.00 (*1-889850-04-7*) De Anza Pr.

Making Intermediate Grammar Work: Instructor's Manual. Kristan Cavina. 52p. 1997. pap. text, teacher ed. write for info. (*1-889850-05-5*) De Anza Pr.

***Making Intimate Connections: Seven Guidelines for Better Couple Communication.** Albert Ellis & Ted Crawford. 160p. 2000. pap. 15.95 (*1-886230-33-1*) Impact Pubs CA.

Making Invisible Latino Adolescents Visible: A Critical Approach for Building Upon Latino Diversity. Ed. by Martha Montero-Sieburth & Francisco Villarruel. LC 99-35516. (MSU Series on Children, Youth & Families). 350p. 1999. 60.00 (*0-8153-2344-1*, SS1103) Garland.

Making Invisible Theatre: Community Theatre in Practice. Chris Johnston. (Illus.). 240p. (C). 1998. 65.00 (*0-415-10880-2*) Routledge.

Making Iron & Steel: Independent Mills in Pittsburgh, 1820-1920. John N. Ingham. LC 91-11199. (Historical Perspectives on Business Enterprise Ser.). 297p. 1991. text 55.00 (*0-8142-0542-9*) Ohio St U Pr.

***Making Iron on the Bald Eagle: Roland Curtin's Ironworks & Workers' Community.** Gerald G. Eggert. LC 99-39502. 189p. 1999. 22.50 (*0-271-01946-8*) Pa St U Pr.

Making It. Jo A. Mills. 1986. pap. 6.95 (*0-89137-439-6*) Quality Pubns.

Making It. Leonard Mogel. 76p. 1999. pap. text 12.00 (*0-536-02265-8*) P-H.

Making It. Ira Skutch. 256p. 1999. 24.95 (*0-947993-84-3*, Pub. by Mlvrn Pubg Co) Brit Bk Co Inc.

Making It. Elise Title. (Temptation Ser.: No. 340). 1991. per. 2.95 (*0-373-25440-7*) Harlequin Bks.

Making It. Joann Wheeler. (Illus.). 46p. (Orig.). 1988. teacher ed. 7.95 (*0-916177-38-6*); student ed. 10.95 (*0-916177-39-4*); write for info. (*0-318-68789-5*); 5.95 (*0-685-50629-0*) Am Eng Pubns.

Making It. rev. ed. Barbara Heiner. 288p. 1995. pap. 21.95 (*0-385-25514-4*) Doubleday.

Making It, Set. Joann Wheeler. (Illus.). (Orig.). 1988. 29.95 (*0-916177-42-4*) Am Eng Pubns.

Making It! A Play in 3-Acts. Hindi Brooks. 60p. 1984. pap. 4.00 (*0-88680-216-4*) I E Clark.

Making It: A Primer for Establishing & Operating a Profitable Small Business. Charles A. Horne. 75p. (C). 1994. pap. 15.95 (*1-884985-00-9*) Tri Star Intl.

***Making it: Tips for Teachers from a Successful Adult with Learning Disabilities.** Christopher Lee & Rosemary Jackson. 2001. pap. text. write for info. (*0-86709-474-5*, Pub. by Boynton Cook Pubs) Heinemann.

Making It - Migration & Adaptation among Haitian Boat People in the United States. Rose-Marie Cassagnol Chierici. (Immigrant Communities & Ethnic Minorities in the U. S. & Canada Ser.: No. 70). 1990. 49.50 (*0-404-19480-X*) AMS Pr.

Making It, a Guide to Cross-Country Sking, Snowshoeing & Winter Survival. John C. Hitchcock & Charles K. Fox. LC 73-17340. (Illus.). 1973. 4.95 (*0-915180-18-9*) Harrowood Bks.

Making It & Breaking It: The Fate of Public Interest Commitment During Law School. Robert V. Stover. LC 88-12100. 176p. 1989. text 19.95 (*0-252-01557-6*) U of Ill Pr.

Making It As a Couple: Prescription for a Quality Relationship. rev. ed. Allen Fay. LC 97-61526. 226p. 1998. pap. 12.95 (*0-9659818-0-0*) FMC.

Making It As a Sports Official. M. C. O'Bryant. (Illus.). 90p. (Orig.). 1991. pap. text 12.00 (*0-88314-520-0*) AAHPERD.

Making It As a Stepparent. Claire Berman. LC 85-45177. 224p. 1986. reprint ed. pap. 12.00 (*0-06-097019-7*, PL 7019, Perennial) HarperTrade.

Making It Better: Activities for Children in a Stressful World. Barbara Oehlberg. LC 96-41338. (Illus.). 144p. (Orig.). 1996. pap. 16.95 (*1-884834-26-4*, 3044) Redleaf Pr.

***Making It Better: Expanding Information Technology Research to Meet Society's Needs.** LC 00-9738. 2000. write for info. (*0-309-06991-2*) Natl Acad Pr.

Making It Big: Sex Stars, Porn Films & Me. ChiChi LaRue & John Erich. LC 97-23969. 250p. (Orig.). 1997. pap. 12.95 (*1-55583-392-6*) Alyson Pubns.

Making It Big: The Diary of a Broadway Musical. Barbara Isenberg. LC 96-43721. (Illus.). 240p. (YA). 1996. 25.00 (*0-87910-088-5*) Limelight Edns.

Making It Big in America: A Self-Made Millionaire Tells How Anyone Can Get Ahead in Business & Life. Andrew Wood. LC 95-3304. 272p. 1995. pap. 15.95 (*0-7615-0018-9*) Prima Pub.

Making It Click see Business of Studio Photography: How to Start & Run a Successful Photography Studio

Making It Click! Starting a Successful Photography Studio. Edward R. Lilley. 348p. 29.95 (*0-614-07445-2*) SOS Pubng.

Making It Count: The Improvement of Social Research & Theory. Stanley Lieberson. 1985. pap. 16.95 (*0-520-06037-7*, Pub. by U CA Pr) Cal Prin Full Svc.

Making It Count: The Improvement of Social Research & Theory. Stanley Lieberson. LC 84-25285. 271p. reprint ed. pap. 84.10 (*0-7837-4843-4*, 204449000003) Bks Demand.

Making It Crazy: An Ethnography of Psychiatric Clients in an American Community. Sue E. Estroff. LC 79-64660. 338p. 1981. pap. 16.95 (*0-520-05451-2*, Pub. by U CA Pr) Cal Prin Full Svc.

Making It Easy... Southwest Desserts. Pete Nolasco. 1998. pap. text 18.95 (*1-55622-650-0*, Rep of TX Pr) Wordware Pub.

Making It Explicit: Reasoning, Representing & Discursive Commitment. Robert B. Brandom. LC 93-50631. 752p. 1994. text 57.50 (*0-674-54319-X*, BRAMAK) HUP.

Making It Explicit: Reasoning, Representing & Discursive Commitment. Robert B. Brandom. 768p. 1998. pap. text 24.95 (*0-674-54330-0*) HUP.

***Making It Happen.** Jean O'Neil. Ed. by Judy Kirby. 12p. 1999. pap. 5.95 (*0-934513-90-2*) Natl Crime DC.

Making It Happen: A Non-Technical Guide To Project Management. Kyle MacKenzie. 256p. 1998. pap. 29.95 (*0-471-64234-7*) Wiley.

Making It Happen: A Positive Guide to the Future. Ed. by John M. Richardson. 232p. 1982. 9.95 (*0-942718-00-3*) Roundtable Pr.

Making It Happen: Designing Research with Implementation in Mind. Milton D. Hakel. LC 82-10726. (Studying Organizations Ser.: No. 3). 152p. 1982. reprint ed. pap. 47.20 (*0-608-01168-1*, 205946800001) Bks Demand.

Making It Happen: Exploring the Creative Process Through the Sculptures of David Adickes. Linda Wiley. LC 96-94360. (Illus.). 160p. 1996. 42.95 (*1-888775-06-8*); pap. 19.95 (*1-888775-07-6*) My Own Bckyrd.

Making It Happen: Interaction in the Second Language Classroom. Patricia A. Richard-Amato. 1988. pap. text 44.00 (*0-8013-0027-4*, 75692) Longman.

Making It Happen: Interaction in the Second Language Classroom: from Theory to Practice. 2nd ed. Patricia A. Richard-Amato. LC 95-15297. 496p. 1995. pap. text 44.10 (*0-201-42018-X*) Addison-Wesley.

Making It Happen: Report of the Secretary's Conference on Educational Technology. 60p. (Orig.). (C). 1996. pap. text 20.00 (*0-7881-3170-2*) DIANE Pub.

***Making It Happen: Stories from Inside the New Workplace.** Contrib. by Systems Thinker Newsletter Editors. LC 98-48877. (Illus.). 96p. 1999. pap. 24.95 (*1-883823-32-3*) Pegasus Comm.

M

Making It Happen: Student Involvement in Education Planning, Decision Making, & Instruction. Michael L. Wehmeyer & Deanna J. Sands. LC 97-41736. 1998. 36.95 (*1-55766-330-0*) P H Brookes.

Making It Happen: Student Involvement in Educational Planning, Decision Making, & Instruction. Michael L. Wehmeyer & Deanna J. Sands. LC 97-41736. 1998. 36.95 (*1-55766-329-7*) P H Brookes.

Making It Happen in the Real Estate Profession. Gregory C. Hill. LC 76-49275. (Salesman Hill Edition Ser.). 160p. 1976. 12.95 (*0-917224-02-7*) Gregory Pubns.

Making It Home: Memoir - Diary - Countrylife. Lars Nordstrom. LC 97-1278. (Illus.). 150p. 1997. pap. 15.00 (*0-915986-27-2*) Prescott St Pr.

Making It in Advertising: An Inside's Guide to Career Opportunities. Leonard Mogel. LC 92-32051. 193p. 1993. pap. 10.00 (*0-02-034552-6*) Macmillan.

Making It in America. Jerry Jasinowski & Robert Hamrin. 352p. 1996. pap. 14.00 (*0-684-82473-6*, Fireside) S&S Trade Pap.

***Making It in America: A Biographical Sourcebook of Eminent Ethnic Americans.** Elliott R. Barkan. 2001. lib. bdg. 65.00 (*1-57607-098-0*) ABC-CLIO.

Making It in America: The Role of Ethnicity in Business Enterprise, Education & Work Choices. 16.00 (*0-614-14846-4*) Balch Inst Ethnic Studies.

Making It in America: The Role of Ethnicity in Business, Enterprise, Education & Work Choices. M. Mark Stolarik & Murray Friedman. LC 84-46100. 143p. 1987. 20.00 (*0-614-32306-1*) Balch IES Pr.

Making It in America: The Role of Ethnicity in Education, Business Enterprise & Work Choices. Ed. by M. Mark Stolarik & Murray Friedman. LC 84-46100. 144p. 1986. 28.50 (*0-8387-5092-3*) Bucknell U Pr.

***Making It in America: What Immigrants Know & Americans Have Forgotten.** Marcia A. Steele. 176p. 2000. 19.99 (*1-893232-07-7*) Steele Success.

Making It in Book Publishing. Leonard Mogel. LC 95-34430. 256p. 1996. pap. 16.95 (*0-02-860593-4*) Macmillan Info.

Making It in Country Music: An Insiders Guide to Launching or Advancing Your Career. Scott Faragher. (Illus.). 224p. 1995. pap. 9.95 (*0-8065-1710-7*, Citadel Pr) Carol Pub Group.

Making It in Japan. Mark Gauthier. (Illus.). 232p. (Orig.). (C). 1994. pap. text 40.00 (*0-7881-1058-6*) DIANE Pub.

Making It in Japan. Mark Gauthier. 232p. (Orig.). 1997. pap. 16.95 (*4-385-35476-6*, Pub. by Vac Wrk Pubns) Seven Hills Bk.

Making It in Japan: Work, Life, Leisure & Beyond. Mark Gauthier. Ed. by Forbes Benning. (Illus.). 254p. 1993. 45.00 (*1-57979-211-1*, 2118) DIANE Pub.

Making It in Mink. Albert Woodley. LC 92-90668. (Illus.). 241p. (Orig.). 1992. pap. 20.00 (*0-9638004-0-X*) A Woodley.

Making It in Publishing: An Insider's Guide to Career Opportunities. Leonard Mogel. LC 93-9012. 1994. write for info. (*0-02-034533-X*) Macmillan.

Making It in Radio: Your Future in the Modern Medium. Dan Blume. LC 83-71022. (Illus.). 176p. (Orig.). 1983. pap. 9.95 (*0-912349-00-X*) Continent Media.

Making It in the Business: Overcoming Obstacles & Reaching Your Goals in the Entertainment Industry. Andrea Hill. pap. 13.95 (*1-889198-07-2*) Ctr Pr CA.

Making It in the Construction Business: The Contractor's Survival Guide. Robert A. Baldwin. 1993. pap. 19.95 (*0-8306-3991-8*) McGraw-Hill Prof.

***Making it in the Free World: Women in Transition from Prison.** Patricia O'Brien. LC 00-36566. (C). 2001. pap. text 18.95 (*0-7914-4862-1*) State U NY Pr.

***Making it in the Free World: Women in Transition from Prison.** Patricia O'Brien. LC 00-36566. (C). 2001. text 57.50 (*0-7914-4861-4*) State U NY Pr.

Making It in the Music Business: The Business & Legal Guide for Songwriters & Performers. rev. ed. Lee Wilson. LC 99-47535. 288p. 1999. pap. 18.95 (*1-58115-036-9*) Allworth Pr.

Making It Last. 224p. 1991. 15.95 (*1-56062-076-5*); pap. 12.95 (*1-56062-077-3*) CIS Comm.

Making It Macintosh. Apple Computer, Inc. Staff. (C). 1993. pap. 39.95 incl. cd-rom (*0-201-62626-8*) Addison-Wesley.

***Making It Magnetic: How to Promote Your Website.** Rebecca Hart. 25p. 2000. pap. 9.95 (*0-9701324-3-3*) Broadripple.

Making It National: Nationalism & Australian Popular Culture. Graeme Turner. 208p. 1995. pap. 19.95 (*1-86373-722-7*, Pub. by Allen & Unwin Pty) Paul & Co Pubs.

Making It New: Collected Essays & Writings of Henry Geldzahler. Henry Geldzahler. LC 93-85297. 280p. (C). 1994. 21.95 (*0-9627987-6-2*) Turtle Point Pr.

Making It New: Essays, Interviews, & Talks. Henry Geldzahler. 384p. 1996. pap. 16.00 (*0-15-600439-9*, Harvest Bks) Harcourt.

Making It New: Modernism in Malahalam, Marathi & Hindi Poetry. E. V. Ramkrishnan. (C). 1995. 29.50 (*81-85952-26-4*, Pub. by M Manoharial) S Asia.

Making It New: The Avant Garde in Exhibition. Bruce Altschuler. LC 93-34281. (Illus.). 288p. 1994. 49.50 (*0-8109-3637-2*, Pub. by Abrams) Time Warner.

Making It on Your Own see Secrets of Self-Employment: Surviving & Thriving on the Ups & Downs at Being Your Own Boss

Making it Ours: Queering the Canon Mark D. Hawthorne. LC 98-60103. 193 p. 1998. write for info. (*1-889431-29-X*) Univ Pr South.

Making It Real. Vik Muniz. 1997. pap. text 22.95 (*0-916365-49-2*) Ind Curators.

Making It Right. Clairece B. Feagin. 1990. pap. 6.06 (*0-8092-4139-0*) NTC Contemp Pub Co.

Making It So. Robert Van Laarhoven. Ed. & Illus. by Dana Danielson. Illus. by Yvette Edwards. 1997. 14.95 (*0-9661255-0-9*) V Commun.

Making It Their Own: Severn Ojibwe Communicative Practices. Lisa P. Valentine. (Anthropological Horizons Ser.). (Illus.). 272p. 1995. text 55.00 (*0-8020-0643-4*); pap. text 19.95 (*0-8020-7596-7*) U of Toronto Pr.

Making It Through. Loretta Petit. (Illus.). 40p. 1996. pap. write for info. (*0-9653573-0-9*) Frstfruit Pubng.

Making It Through College: The Multicultural Guide for Success & Surviving the Real Deal. Rajen Persaud. 182p. (Orig.). (YA). (gr. 9-12). 1995. pap. 7.95 (*0-9642713-8-9*) D & R Pub CA.

Making It Through College: Your Passport to the Information Age. rev. ed. Rajen Persaud. LC 96-86248. (Illus.). 290p. 1996. pap. 19.95 (*0-9642713-6-2*) D & R Pub CA.

Making It up As We Go Along: The Story of the (Albany) Free School. Chris Mercogliano. LC 97-51792. 1998. pap. 21.00 (*0-325-00043-3*, Pub. by Boynton Cook Pubs) Heinemann.

Making It Whole: A Victorian Circle & the Shape of Their World. Diana Postlethwaite. LC 84-20677. 302p. reprint ed. pap. 93.70 (*0-608-09867-1*, 206983200006) Bks Demand.

Making It Work: Effective Administration in the Small Church. Douglas A. Walrath. 112p. 1994. pap. 12.00 (*0-8170-1211-7*) Judson.

Making It Work: The Prostitutes' Rights Movement in Perspective. Valerie Jenness. LC 92-43845. (Social Problems & Social Issues Ser.). 164p. 1993. pap. text 21.95 (*0-202-30464-7*); lib. bdg. 43.95 (*0-202-30463-9*) Aldine de Gruyter.

Making It Work: Turning Strategies into Action Throughout Your Organization. Alan Weiss. 256p. 1990. 24.95 (*0-88730-412-5*, HarpBusn) HarpInfo.

Making It Your Business: The Personal Transition from Employee to Entrepreneur. Melvin J. Gravely, II. LC 96-5515. 224p. (Orig.). 1997. pap. 16.95 (*0-9656194-1-9*) Impact Grp.

Making Its Mark: Proceedings of the 7th ECMWF Workshop on the Use of Parallel Processors in Meteorology Reading, U. K. 2-6 December, 1996. Ed. by Geerd-R Hoffmann & Norbert Kreitz. LC 98-163360. 450p. 1998. 108.00 (*981-02-3350-7*) World Scientific Pub.

Making Jesus Lord, Bk. 3. Barry St. Clair. (Moving Toward Maturity Ser.). 132p. (YA). 1991. pap. 6.50 (*0-89693-293-1*, 6-1293) Chariot Victor.

Making Jesus Lord: The Dynamic Power of Laying down Your Rights. Loren Cunningham. Orig. Title: Winning God's Way. 160p. 1997. pap. 8.99 (*1-57658-012-1*) YWAM Pub.

Making Jewelry. Sara Grisewood. LC 94-44862. (Step-by-Step Ser.). (Illus.). 40p. (J). (gr. 3-7). 1995. 13.90 (*1-85697-589-4*, Kingfisher) LKC.

Making Jewelry. Sara Grisewood. LC 94-44862. (Step-by-Step Ser.). (Illus.). (J). (gr. 4-8). 1995. pap. 7.95 (*1-85697-588-6*, Kingfisher) LKC.

Making Jigs & Fixtures: Techniques for Better Woodworking. Nick Engler. LC 99-19191. (Workshop Companion Ser.). (Illus.). 128p. 1999. pap. 12.95 (*0-7621-0206-3*, Pub. by RD Assn) Penguin Putnam.

Making Joint Decisions: Preventing & Relieving Arthritis Pain. Anne E. Hunt. Ed. by Eric A. Mein. (Natural Remedies for Common Ailments & Conditions Ser.). 83p. (Orig.). 1991. pap. 4.95 (*0-87604-279-5*, 364) ARE Pr.

Making Joints. Reader's Digest Editors. (Woodworking Ser.). 120p. 1999. 21.95 (*0-7621-0176-8*, Pub. by RD Assn) Penguin Putnam.

***Making Journals by Hand: 20 Creative Projects for Keeping Your Thought,** Jason Thompson. 2000. pap. text 21.99 (*1-56496-676-3*) Rockport Pubs.

Making Judaism Meaningful: Ambivalence & Tradition in a Havurah Community. Chava Weissler. LC 88-35118. (Immigrant Communities & Ethnic Minorities in the U. S. & Canada Ser.: No. 35). 1989. 67.50 (*0-404-19445-1*) AMS Pr.

Making Judgements: Advanced Level. (Comprehension Skills Series). 60p. (YA). (gr. 8-12). 1993. pap. 8.45 (*0-89061-613-2*, Jamestwn Pub) NTC Contemp Pub Co.

Making Judgements: Intermediate Level. (Comprehension Skills Ser.). 60p. (YA). (gr. 6-12). 1993. pap. 8.31 (*0-89061-633-7*, Jamestwn Pub) NTC Contemp Pub Co.

Making Judgements: Introductory Level. (Comprehension Skills Ser.). 60p. (YA). (gr. 6-12). 1993. pap. 7.91 (*0-89061-653-1*, Jamestwn Pub) NTC Contemp Pub Co.

Making Judgments. rev. ed. Rev. by Beth Bridgman. (Horizons Concepts Ser.: Level 1). (Illus.). 24p. (J). (gr. 4-9). 1998. pap. 5.95 (*1-58086-047-8*, Usborne) EDC.

Making Judgments. rev. ed. Rev. by Beth Bridgman. (Horizons Concepts Ser.: Level 2). (Illus.). 24p. (J). (gr. 4-9). 1998. pap. 5.95 (*1-58086-057-5*, Usborne) EDC.

***Making Justice Our Project: Teachers Working Toward Critical Whole Language Practice.** Carole Edelsky. LC 99-41266. 382p. 1999. pap. 24.95 (*0-8141-3044-5*) NCTE.

Making Kallitypes: A Definitive Guide. Dick Stevens. (Illus.). 233p. 1993. pap. text 44.95 (*0-240-80181-4*, Focal) Buttrwrth-Heinemann.

Making Kids Smarter: A Guide For Developing & Teaching Children Successfully. Pedro R Portes. 192p. (Orig.). 1998. pap. text 19.89 (*1-884532-28-4*) Butler Bks.

Making Kitchen Cabinets: A Foolproof System for the Home Workshop. Paul Levine. LC 87-51674. (Illus.). 192p. 1988. pap. 19.95 (*0-918804-94-9*, 070067) Taunton.

Making Kitchen Cabinets with Paul Levine: A Foolproof System for the Home Workshop. Paul Levine. LC 87-51674. (Illus.). 192p. 1988. 19.95 incl. VHS (*0-918804-95-7*) Taunton.

Making Kites. David Jefferis. LC 92-42913. (Step-by-Step Ser.). (Illus.). 40p. (J). (gr. 3-7). 1993. pap. 7.95 (*1-85697-922-9*, Kingfisher) LKC.

Making Kites. Robert Wilkens. 1993. 12.98 (*1-55521-840-7*) Bk Sales Inc.

Making Kites. Robert Wilkins et al. (Crafts for Children Ser.). (Illus.). 32p. (YA). (gr. 3 up). 1997. pap. 4.95 (*1-56010-216-0*, CC06) W Foster Pub.

Making Knowledge Count: Advocacy & Social Science. Ed. by Peter Harries-Jones. 272p. (C). 1991. text 65.00 (*0-7735-0819-8*, Pub. by McG-Queens Univ Pr) CUP Services.

Making Labour Law in Australia: Industrial Relations, Politics & Law. Laura Bennett. 1994. pap. write for info. (*0-455-21212-0*, Pub. by LawBk Co) Gaunt.

Making Language: Thirty-Fifth Anniversary Issue. Ed. by Francine Ringold. 144p. 1992. pap. 6.90 (*0-685-62341-6*) Art & Human Council Tulsa.

Making Law: The State, the Law, & Structural Contradictions. Ed. by William J. Chambliss & Marjorie S. Zatz. LC 93-16103. 464p. 1993. 41.95 (*0-253-31338-4*); pap. 19.95 (*0-253-20834-3*) Ind U Pr.

Making Law Bind: Essays Legal & Philosophical. Tony Honore. LC 86-16142. 288p. 1987. text 79.00 (*0-19-825467-9*, Clarendon Pr) OUP.

Making Law, Order, & Authority in British Columbia, 1821-1871. Tina Loo. (Social History of Canada Ser.). (Illus.). 352p. (C). 1994. text 45.00 (*0-8020-2961-2*); pap. text 18.95 (*0-8020-7784-6*) U of Toronto Pr.

Making Lawn Ornaments in Wood: Complete Building Techniques & Patterns. Paul Meisel. 130p. (Orig.). 1998. pap. 14.95 (*1-56523-104-X*) Fox Chapel Pub.

Making Laws & Making News: Media Strategies in the U. S. House of Representatives. Timothy Cook. 240p. 1989. 34.95 (*0-8157-1558-7*); pap. 14.95 (*0-8157-1557-9*) Brookings.

***Making Learning Happen.** Jeffrey N. Golub. LC 99-42070. 2000. pap. text 14.00 (*0-86709-493-1*, Pub. by Boynton Cook Pubs) Heinemann.

Making Legal Aid Pay. J. J. Dirks. (Waterlow Practitioner's Library). 112p. 1989. pap. 19.95 (*0-08-036918-9*, Pergamon Pr) Elsevier.

Making Leisure Provision for People with Profound Learning & Multiple Disabilities. J. Hogg & J. Cavet. LC 94-72669. 267p. 1995. pap. 47.75 (*0-412-41150-4*) Chapman & Hall.

Making Leisure Provision for People with Profound Learning & Multiple Disabilities. Ed. by J. Hogg & J. Cavet. (Illus.). 278p. 1994. pap. text 49.95 (*1-56593-125-4*, 0437) Thomson Learn.

Making Less Garbage: A Planning Guide for Communities. Bette K. Fishbein & Caroline Gelb. LC 92-27072. 192p. (Orig.). 1993. pap. 30.00 (*0-918780-58-6*) INFORM NY.

Making Life a Masterpiece. Orison S. Marden. 329p. 1998. pap. 28.00 (*0-89540-365-X*) Sun Pub.

Making Life a Prayer: Selected Writings of John Cassian see Upper Room Spiritual Classics: Series 1

Making Life Choices: Heal. expanded rev. ed. Sizer & Whitney. (HA - Social Studies). (C). 1997. mass mkt. 69.95 (*0-314-22602-8*) S-W Pub.

Making Life Choices: Health Skills & Concepts. Frances S. Sizer & Eleanor N. Whitney. LC 92-39251. 1993. mass mkt., student ed. 61.50 (*0-314-01686-4*) West Pub.

Making Life Choices: Health Skills & Concepts. expanded ed. Frances S. Sizer & Eleanor N. Whitney. LC 92-39251. 1993. mass mkt. 61.50 (*0-314-01158-7*) West Pub.

***Making Life Choices: Health Skills & Concepts for Teachers.** 2nd ed. Sizer-Webb et al. (Health & Fitness Ser.). (C). 1999. text 225.00 (*0-538-43004-4*); text 225.00 (*0-538-43005-2*) Sth-Wstrn College.

Making Life Choices: Health/Skills/Concepts. rev. ed. Sizer & Whitney. 1996. pap. 55.00 (*0-314-21320-1*) Thomson Learn.

***Making Life Count! 50 Ways to Great Days.** Julie Alexander. 185p. 2000. pap. 11.95 (*0-9659310-1-3*, Pub. by Great Days) Herveys Bklink.

Making Life Make Sense: Answers to Hard Questions about God & You. Jay Kesler & Tim Stafford. 176p. (J). 1991. pap. 8.99 (*0-310-71191-6*) Zondervan.

Making Life More Livable. large type ed. Irving R. Dickman. LC 83-6412. (Illus.). 96p. 1983. pap. 19.95 (*0-89128-115-0*) Am Foun Blind.

Making Life Rich Without Any Money. Phil Callaway. LC 98-15495. 160p. 1998. pap. 8.99 (*1-56507-899-3*) Harvest Hse.

Making Life Story Books. T. Ryan & R. Walker. (C). 1989. 65.00 (*0-903534-60-6*, Pub. by Brit Ag for Adopt & Fost) St Mut.

***Making Life Work: Daily Words of Encouragement & Faith.** Paul Faulkner. LC 00-102073. 370p. 2000. pap. 10.95 (*0-89112-439-X*) Abilene Christ U.

Making Life Work: Putting God's Wisdom into Action. Bill Hybels. LC 98-28371. 204p. 2000. 15.99 (*0-8308-1789-1*, 1789) InterVarsity.

Making Life Work: Putting God's Wisdom into Action. Bill Hybels & Lynne Hybels. LC 98-28371. 204p. 1998. pap. 10.99 (*0-8308-1788-3*, 1788) InterVarsity.

Making Lifelong Learning Work: Learning Cities for a Learning Century. Norman Longworth. LC 99-235662. 240p. pap. 29.95 (*0-7494-2727-2*, Kogan Pg Educ) Stylus Pub VA.

***Making Light: Wit & Humor in Photography.** Joel Smith. (Illus.). 32p. 2000. pap. 4.99 (*0-9644263-4-X*) F L Loeb Art Ctr.

Making Light of It. James Broughton. (Illus.). 124p. (Orig.). 1992. pap. 7.95 (*0-87286-265-8*) City Lights.

Making Light Work: Advances in Near Infrared Spectroscopy: the 4th International Conference on Near Infrared Spectroscopy, August 19-23, 1991, Aberdeen, Scotland. Ed. by Ian Murray & Ian A. Cowe. LC 92-11232. 652p. 1992. 325.00 (*3-527-28498-2*, Wiley-VCH) Wiley.

Making Light Work: The Science of Optics. David Darling. LC 91-3999. (Experiment! Ser.). (Illus.). 60p. (J). (gr. 4-6). 1991. lib. bdg. 13.95 (*0-87518-476-6*, Dillon Silver Burdett) Silver Burdett Pr.

Making Liqueurs at Home. Carmen Patrick. 74p. (Orig.). 1989. pap. 9.95 (*0-919574-76-9*) Gordon Soules Bk.

Making Liqueurs for Gifts. Mimi Freid. 1988. pap. 2.95 (*0-88266-499-9*, Garden Way Pub) Storey Bks.

Making Literacy Work: The Specific Literacy Approach. Stephen Anzalone & Stephen McLaughlin. (Illus.). 73p. 1983. pap. 4.00 (*0-932288-73-1*) Ctr Intl Ed U of MA.

Making Literature Matter. John Schilb. 1999. pap. text 43.95 (*0-312-09726-3*) St Martin.

Making Little Boxes from Wood. John Bennett. (Illus.). 148p. 1993. pap. 14.95 (*0-946819-39-4*, Pub. by Guild Master) Sterling.

Making Local News. Phyllis Kaniss. LC 90-21587. (Illus.). 270p. 1991. 29.95 (*0-226-42347-6*) U Ch Pr.

Making Local News. Phyllis Kaniss. (Illus.). x, 260p. 1997. lib. bdg. 14.95 (*0-226-42348-4*) U Ch Pr.

***Making Loss Matter: Creating Meaning in Difficult Times.** David Wolpe. 240p. 2000. pap. 13.95 (*1-57322-820-6*, Riverhd Trade) Berkley Pub.

Making Loss Matter: Creating Meaning in Difficult Times. David J. Wolpe. LC 99-20677. 224p. 1999. 23.95 (*1-57322-141-4*, Riverhead Books) Putnam Pub Group.

Making Love: How to Be Your Own Sex Therapist. Patricia E. Raley. 288p. 1980. pap. 12.95 (*0-380-48819-1*, Avon Bks) Morrow Avon.

Making Love: Poems. Karen Alkalay. 24p. 1980. 15.00 (*0-89304-062-2*); pap. 5.00 (*0-89304-063-0*) Cross-Cultrl NY.

Making Love: Sexual Love the Divine Way. Barry Long. Ed. by Clive Tempest. LC 98-91353. 128p. 1999. pap. 12.95 (*1-899324-14-3*) B Long Bks.

Making Love Again: Regaining Sexual Potency Through the New Injection Treatment. J. Francois Eid & Carol A. Pearce. LC 93-5918. (Illus.). 144p. 1993. pap. 15.95 (*0-87630-722-5*) Brunner-Mazel.

Making Love Better Than Ever: Reaching New Heights of Passion & Pleasure after 40. Barbara Keesling. LC 98-20725. 1998. 24.95 (*0-89793-230-7*) Hunter Hse.

Making Love Better Than Ever: Reaching New Heights of Passion & Pleasure after 40. Barbara Keesling. LC 98-20725. (Illus.). 208p. 1998. pap. 13.95 (*0-89793-231-5*) Hunter Hse.

Making Love Happen. Mary-Katherine MacDougall. Ed. by Alex Liepa. 236p. 1980. 8.95 (*0-940175-02-9*) Now Comns.

Making Love Happen. Rebecca Sydnor. 240p. 1991. mass mkt. 4.99 (*0-380-71401-9*, Avon Bks) Morrow Avon.

Making Love Last Forever see Para Que el Amor No Se Apague

Making Love Last Forever. Gary Smalley. 224p. 1996. pap. text, wbk. ed. 12.95 (*0-8054-9791-9*, LifeWy Press) LifeWay Christian.

Making Love Last Forever. Gary Smalley. 320p. 1996. 21.99 (*0-8499-1194-X*) Word Pub.

Making Love Last Forever. Gary Smalley. 240p. (C). 1997. pap. 12.99 (*0-8499-4086-9*) Word Pub.

Making Love Modern: The Intimate Public Worlds of New York's Literary Women. Nina Miller. LC 97-44487. 304p. 1999. pap. 18.95 (*0-19-511605-4*) OUP.

Making Love Stay: Everything You Ever Knew about Love but Forget. Peggy Vaughan & James Vaughan. 234p. 1997. pap. 15.00 (*0-936390-13-1*) Dialog Pr.

Making Love to Roget's Wife: Poems New & Selected. Ronald Koertge. LC 96-33030. 1997. 26.00 (*1-55728-462-8*); pap. 16.00 (*1-55728-461-X*) U of Ark Pr.

Making Love to the Minor Poets of Chicago. James Conrad. LC 99-55719. 496p. 2000. text 25.95 (*0-312-20472-8*) St Martin.

Making Loveable Teddy Bears & Their Clothes. Marion Thielmann. (Illus.). 144p. 1998. pap. 14.95 (*0-8069-9713-3*) Sterling.

Making Loving Memories: A Gentle Guide to What You Can Do When Your Baby Dies. Mary L. Eddy & Linda Raydo. Ed. by Joy Johnson. (Illus.). 12p. (Orig.). 1990. pap. 2.00 (*1-56123-003-0*, MLMC) Centering Corp.

Making Macros & Much, Much More: Comprehensive Customization of Solid Works Using Visual Basic. Jerry Winters. (Illus.). 350p. 1998. pap., spiral bd. 39.95 (*1-892131-02-1*, MMMMM-SW) VB CAD.

Making Magic. (Magical Library). (Illus.). (YA). (gr. 5 up). 24.95 (*0-614-21963-9*) Random.

Making Magic. Karen Van Der Zee. LC 95-4583. (Presents Ser.). 186p. 1995. per. 3.25 (*0-373-11729-9*, 1-11729-0) Harlequin Bks.

***Making Magic Windows: Creating Papel Picado - Cut Paper Art with Carmen Lomas Garza.** Carmen Lopez Garza. LC 98-38518. (SPA., Illus.). 64p. (J). (gr. 4-7). 1999. pap. 9.95 (*0-89239-159-6*) Childrens Book Pr.

***Making Magic Work Inspiring Confidence & Motivating Your Staff.** Philip Deaver. 208p. 2001. 15.95 (*0-7868-5306-9*, Pub. by Disney Pr) Time Warner.

Making Magick: What It Is & How It Works. Edain McCoy. LC 97-20979. (Illus.). 336p. (Orig.). 1997. pap. 14.95 (*1-56718-670-X*, K670-X) Llewellyn Pubns.

Making Magickal Incense & Ritual Perfumes. Keith Morgan. (Orig.). 1993. pap. 9.95 (*1-872189-02-4*, Pub. by Mandrake Pr) Holmes Pub.

Making Magickal Tools & Ritual Equipment. Keith Morgan. (Orig.). 1994. pap. 9.95 (*1-872189-45-8*, Pub. by Mandrake Pr) Holmes Pub.

An Asterisk (*) at the beginning of an entry indicates that the title is appearing for the first time.

***Making Magnificent Machines: Fun with Math, Science & Engineering.** Carolyn McBride. LC 99-34584. 1999. 22.00 (*1-56976-102-7*) Zephyr Pr AZ.

Making Major Financial Decisions: Money Management. Ransbottom. (YA - Adult Education Ser.). 1993. pap., wbk. ed. 5.95 (*0-538-70841-7*) S-W Pub.

Making Majorities: Constituting the Nation in Japan, Korea, China, Malaysia, Fiji, Turkey & the United States. Dru C. Gladney. LC 97-42928. (East-West Center Series on Contemporary Issues in Asia & the Pacific). 1998. write for info. (*0-8047-4656-7*); 55.00 (*0-8047-3047-4*); pap. 19.95 (*0-8047-3048-2*) Stanford U Pr.

Making Make-Believe: Fun Props, Costumes & Creative Play Ideas. MaryAnn F. Kohl. LC 99-18613. (Illus.). 192p. (J). (gr. 1-3). 1999. pap. 14.95 (*0-87659-198-5*, Pub. by Gryphon Hse) Consort Bk Sales.

Making Malcolm: The Myth & Meaning of Malcolm X. Michael E. Dyson. 256p. 1996. reprint ed. pap. 10.95 (*0-19-510285-1*) OUP.

Making Managed Care Work for You. Ed. by Joseph L. Bruneni. (Illus.). 1997. 48.00 (*1-886308-01-2*) Optical Lab.

Making Managed Care Work for You: Strategies for Local Market Dominance. Genie James. LC 96-20990. 336p. 1996. text 45.00 (*0-7863-1012-X*, Irwn Prfssnl) McGraw-Hill Prof.

Making Managed Health Care Work for Kids in Foster Care: A Guide to Purchasing Services. Ellen S. Battistelli. 80p. 1996. pap. 7.95 (*0-87868-683-5*) Child Welfare.

Making Managed Healthcare Work: A Practical Guide to Strategies & Solutions. Peter Boland. 620p. 1992. 99.00 (*0-8342-0391-X*) Aspen Pub.

Making Management Decisions. 2nd ed. Steve Cooke & Nigel Slack. LC 90-20450. 1992. write for info. (*0-13-543406-8*) P-H.

***Making Managers in Universities & Colleges.** Craig Prichard. LC 99-41464. 2000. pap. 34.95 (*0-335-20485-6*) OpUniv Pr.

Making Manufacturing Cells Work. Lee R. Nyman. 387p. 1994. 60.00 (*0-07-047977-1*) McGraw.

Making Manufacturing Cells Work. Ed. by Lee R. Nyman. (Illus.). 388p. 1992. 75.00 (*0-87263-419-1*) SME.

***Making Many Glad: The Life & Labours of Daniel Baker.** William M. Baker. 2000. pap. 10.99 (*0-85151-781-1*) Banner of Truth.

Making Maple Syrup. N. Perrin. 1983. pap. 2.95 (*0-88266-226-0*, Storey Pub) Storey Bks.

Making Marble-Action Games, Gadgets, Mazes, & Contraptions: Designs for 10 Outlandish, Ingenious, & Intricate Woodworking Projects. Alan Bridgewater & Gill Bridgewater. LC 99-11796. (Illus.). 144p. 1999. pap. 19.95 (*0-8117-2855-2*) Stackpole.

Making Mark Twain Work in the Classroom. James S. Leonard. LC 98-42358. 1999. write for info. (*0-8223-2278-1*); pap. 17.95 (*0-8223-2297-8*) Duke.

Making Markets: An Interdisciplinary Perspective on Economic Exchange, 135. Robin Cantor et al. LC 91-42731. (Contributions in Economics & Economic History Ser.: No. 135). 208p. 1992. 55.00 (*0-313-26821-5*, CME/, Greenwood Pr) Greenwood.

Making Markets: Opportunism & Restraint on Wall Street. Mitchel Y. Abolafia. LC 96-20665. (Illus.). 240p. 1996. 32.50 (*0-674-54324-6*) HUP.

Making Marks: Drawing in the 20th Century from Picasso to Kiefer. Russell Bowman. 72p. 1998. pap. 19.95 (*0-944110-59-2*) Milwauk Art Mus.

Making Marriage Magnificent: 365 Ways to Happiness. Reed Markham & Lorena Markham. 128p. 1997. pap. 6.98 (*0-88290-613-5*) Horizon Utah.

Making Marriage Meaningful. Brent A. Barlow. viii, 117p. (C). 1980. pap. text 2.95 (*0-8425-1828-2*, Friends of the Library) Brigham.

Making Marriage Successful. Henry E. White, Jr. LC 82-15270. (Illus.). 430p. 1983. text 42.50 (*0-8290-1261-3*); pap. text 22.95 (*0-8290-1348-2*) Irvington.

Making Marriage Work. Bishops' Committee for Pastoral Research Staff & Practices National Conference of Catholic Bishops. (Marriage Is a Sacrament Ser.). 48p. (Orig.). (C). 1990. pap. 2.95 (*1-55586-355-8*) US Catholic.

Making Marriage Work: Meditations on I Corinthians 13. Norman W. Goodacre. (Illus.). 135p. (Orig.). 1996. pap. 7.95 (*1-85311-129-5*, 847, Pub. by Canterbury Press Norwich) Morehouse Pub.

***Making Marriage Work for Dummies.** Steven Simring & Sue Klavans Simring. 384p. 1999. pap. 19.99 (*0-7645-5173-6*) IDG Bks.

Making Marvelous Music Boxes. Sharon Ganskee. (Illus.). 128p. 1997. pap. text 14.95 (*0-8069-4282-7*, Chapelle) Sterling.

Making Masks. Vivian Frank & Deborah Jaffe. (Crafts for Children Ser.). (Illus.). 32p. (YA). (gr. 3 up). 1997. pap. 4.95 (*1-56010-218-7*, CC08) W Foster Pub.

Making Masks. Vivien Frank. 1992. 12.98 (*1-55521-780-X*) Bk Sales Inc.

Making Masks. Helen McNiven & Peter McNiven. (First Arts & Crafts Ser.). (Illus.). 32p. (J). (gr. 1-6). 1994. lib. bdg. 21.40 (*1-56847-212-9*) Raintree Steck-V.

Making Master Guitars. Ray Courtnail. (Illus.). 1993. 124.95 (*0-7090-4809-2*, I330) Bold Strummer Ltd.

Making Materials: Teacher's Guide. (Pathways Through Science Ser.). 1993. pap. text. write for info. (*0-582-09463-1*, Pub. by Addison-Wesley) Longman.

Making Materials-Based Learning Work. Derek Rowntree. 144p. 1997. pap. 25.00 (*0-7494-2240-8*, Kogan Pg Educ) Stylus Pub VA.

Making Materials Source Book. (Pathways Through Science Ser.). 1993. pap. text. write for info. (*0-582-09423-2*, Pub. by Addison-Wesley) Longman.

Making Math Matter: A Math Resource - Book for Middle & Secondary Teachers. John Mudore. LC 93-77825. 144p. (Orig.). 1994. pap. 20.00 (*0-9636514-8-X*) Infinity Pubs.

Making Mead: A Complete Guide to the Making of Sweet & Dry Mead, Melomel, Metheglin, Hippocras, Pyment & Cyser. Bryan Acton & Peter Duncan. 68p. pap. 10.95 (*0-9619072-8-2*) G W Kent.

Making Mead (Honey Wine) History, Recipes, Methods & Equipment. Roger A. Morse. (Illus.). 128p. 1992. reprint ed. pap. text 10.95 (*1-878075-04-7*) Wicwas Pr.

Making Meals with Mary: Recepies Based on Scientific Nutritional Information. Mary Hughen. LC 98-73871. 125p. 1998. pap. 8.95 (*1-890683-02-7*) CJH Ent.

Making Meaning: A Guide for Passing the Regents' Essay. 3rd ed. Sarah Larson. 196p. (C). 1998. per. 29.95 (*0-7872-5063-5*, 41506301) Kendall-Hunt.

Making Meaning: Inference & Rhetoric in the Interpretation of Cinema. David Bordwell. LC 89-30324. (Harvard Film Studies). (Illus.). 348p. 1989. 40.00 (*0-674-54335-1*) HUP.

Making Meaning: Inference & Rhetoric in the Interpretation of Cinema. David Bordwell. (Harvard Film Studies). 352p. (C). 1991. pap. 21.50 (*0-674-54336-X*) HUP.

***Making Meaning in Indian Cinema.** Ed. by Ravi S. Vasudevan. (Illus.). 272p. 2000. text 24.95 (*0-19-564545-6*) OUP.

Making Meaning, Making Change: Participatory Curriculum Development for Adult ESL Literacy. Elsa R. Auerback. Ed. by Fran Keenan. (Language in Education Ser.). (Illus.). 140p. (Orig.). 1992. pap. text 16.50 (*0-937354-79-1*) Delta Systems.

Making Meaning of Community in an American High School. Kathleen K. Abowitz. LC 99-34834. (Understanding Education & Policy Ser.). 224p. (C). 1999. 42.50 (*1-57273-206-7*) Hampton Pr NJ.

***Making Meaning of Community in an American High School.** Kathleen K. Abowitz. LC 99-34834. (Understanding Education & Policy Ser.). 224p. (C). 1999. pap. 19.95 (*1-57273-207-5*) Hampton Pr NJ.

***Making Meaning of Narratives.** Ed. by Ruthellen Josselson & Amia Lieblich. LC 98-40298. (Narrative Study of Lives Ser.: Vol. 6). 282p. 1999. 69.95 (*0-7619-0326-7*) Sage.

Making Meaning of Whiteness: Exploring Racial Identity with White Teachers. Alice McIntyre. LC 96-45473. (SUNY Series, the Social Context of Education). (Illus.). 193p. (C). 1997. text 57.50 (*0-7914-3495-8*); pap. text 18.95 (*0-7914-3496-6*) State U NY Pr.

Making "Meanwhile" Meaningful. John H. Hampsch. 16p. 1997. pap. 1.25 (*1-57918-025-6*, 7106) Queenship Pub.

Making Mechanical Marvels in Wood. Raymond Levy. LC 91-9634. (Illus.). 200p. 1991. pap. 14.95 (*0-8069-7358-7*) Sterling.

Making Medical Decisions: An Approach to Clinical Decision Making for the Practicing Physician. Richard A. Gross. LC 98-29289. 120p. (C). 1999. pap. text 18.00 (*0-943126-75-4*) Amer Coll Phys.

Making Medical Doctors: Science & Medicine at Vanderbilt since Flexner. Timothy C. Jacobson. LC 86-6991. (History of American Science & Technology Ser.). (Illus.). 366p. reprint ed. pap. 113.50 (*0-608-09229-0*, 205273300005) Bks Demand.

Making Medical History: The Life & Times of Henry E. Sigerist. Ed. by Elizabeth Fee & Theodore M. Brown. LC 96-8862. (Illus.). 400p. 1997. text 39.95 (*0-8018-5355-9*) Johns Hopkins.

Making Medical Spending Decisions: The Law, Ethics & Economics of Rationing Mechanisms. Mark A. Hall. LC 96-24738. 312p. 1996. text 35.00 (*0-19-509219-8*) OUP.

Making Meetings Productive. Mescon Group Staff. (Performance Through Participation Ser.). 1996. text, teacher ed. 23.95 (*0-538-84945-2*); text, suppl. ed. 14.95 (*0-538-84944-4*) S-W Pub.

***Making Meetings Work.** Julie-Ann Amos. 64p. 2000. pap. 9.95 (*1-85703-622-0*, Pub. by How To Bks) Midpt Trade.

***Making Meetings Work.** Patrick Forsyth. 96p. 2000. pap. 17.95 (*0-8464-5106-9*) Beekman Pubs.

Making Meetings Work. Patrick Forsyth. 1996. pap. 25.00 (*0-85292-637-5*, Pub. by IPM Hse) St Mut.

Making Meetings Work: Achieving High Quality Group Decisions. John E. Tropman. 192p. 1995. 42.00 (*0-8039-7358-6*); pap. 19.50 (*0-8039-7359-4*) Sage.

Making Melody. Jane B. Gillespie. LC 83-22461. 1983. pap. 8.95 (*0-87233-073-7*) Bauhan.

Making Melody Song Book: Popular Choruses & Hymns That Bless, Endure & Honor the Lord. rev. ed. Compiled by N. A. Woychuk. 352p. (Orig.). 1978. pap. 10.00 (*1-880960-03-6*) Script Memory FI.

Making Membership Meaningful. John L. McCreight. LC 93-73487. 1994. pap. 6.95 (*1-55673-582-0*, 7981) CSS OH.

Making Memoirs. James Lord. (Illus.). 19p. 1995. 145.00 (*0-9640399-4-X*); pap. 45.00 (*0-9640399-3-1*) Elysium Pr.

***Making Memories.** Penny Boylan. 2000. 16.95 (*0-7548-0486-0*, Lorenz Bks) Anness Pub.

Making Memories. Janette Oke. LC 99-6737. 32p. 1999. 14.99 (*0-7642-2190-6*) Bethany Hse.

Making Memories. Ann H. White. 1996. per. 3.99 (*0-373-24067-8*, 1-24067-0) Silhouette.

Making Memories: A Parent Home Portfolio. Sally Walker & Lori Whitman. (Illus.). 208p. 1996. pap. 4.95 (*1-880505-22-3*, CLC0193) Pieces of Lrning.

Making Memories: Ideas for Family Missions Involvement. Mary Ann Appling. Ed. by Karen Gross. 91p. (Orig.). 1993. pap. text 6.95 (*1-56309-077-5*, N934109, New Hope) Womans Mission Union.

Making Memories: Martha's Sewing Room Series 600. Martha C. Pullen. LC 96-71614. (Illus.). 276p. (Orig.). 1997. pap. text 19.95 (*1-878048-11-2*) M Pullen.

***Making Memories: Reflections on Parenting from the Head of a Psychoanalyst & the Heart of a Father.** David W. Krueger. LC 99-91586. 1999. 25.00 (*0-7388-0912-8*); pap. 18.00 (*0-7388-0913-6*) Xlibris Corp.

Making Memories: With Fabric, Photos, & Family Keepsakes. Margaret Sindelar. LC 98-19047. (Illus.). 128p. 1998. pap. 27.95 (*1-56477-234-9*, DB350) Martingale & Co.

Making Memories That Count: Nurturing Your Child in Christian Values. Debra F. Bruce. 176p. (Orig.). 1994. pap. 7.99 (*0-88243-345-8*, 02-0345) Gospel Pub.

Making Memory Books. Amanda Lewis & Esperanca Melo. LC 99-63007. (Kids Can Do It Ser.). 40p. (J). (gr. 3-7). 1999. 5.95 (*1-55074-567-0*) Kids Can Pr.

Making Memory Books by Hand: Memories to Keep & Share. Kristina Feliciano. 128p. 1999. pap. 21.99 (*1-56496-585-6*) Rockport Pubs.

***Making Memory Boxes: Box Projects to Make, Give & Keep.** Barbara Mauriello. 2000. pap. 22.00 (*1-56496-711-5*) Rockport Pubs.

Making Men: Gender, Literary Authority & Women's Writing in Caribbean Narrative. Belinda Edmondson. LC 98-22005. 1999. write for info. (*0-8223-2131-9*); pap. 17.95 (*0-8223-2263-3*) Duke.

Making Men: Rugby & Masculine Identity. Ed. by John Nauright & Timothy J. Chandler. LC 95-35435. (Illus.). 260p. 1996. 52.50 (*0-7146-4637-7*, Pub. by F Cass Pubs); pap. 26.50 (*0-7146-4156-1*, Pub. by F Cass Pubs) Intl Spec Bk.

Making Men: Sophists & Self-Presentation in Ancient Rome. Maud Gleason. LC 94-9443. 256p. 1995. text 35.00 (*0-691-04800-2*, Pub. by Princeton U Pr) Cal Prin Full Svc.

Making Men Moral. Nancy K. Bristow. 1998. pap. text 19.50 (*0-8147-1308-4*) NYU Pr.

Making Men Moral: Civil Liberties & Public Morality. Robert P. George. 258p. 1995. pap. text 21.00 (*0-19-826024-5*) OUP.

Making Men Moral: Social Engineering During the Great War. Nancy K. Bristow. (American Social Experience Ser.). (Illus.). 298p. (C). 1996. text 45.00 (*0-8147-1220-7*) NYU Pr.

***Making Mentoring Happen: A Simple & Effective Guide to Implementing a Successful Mentoring Program.** Kathy Lacey. 2000. pap. text 14.95 (*1-875680-68-3*) Woodslane.

***Making Merry with My Friends.** Allen Adams. (Illus.). (J). 1999. mass mkt. 10.95 (*0-7880-0998-2*) CSS OH.

Making MG's. John P. Williams. (Illus.). 96p. 1995. 19.95 (*1-874105-53-7*, Pub. by Vloce Pub) Motorbooks Intl.

Making Michigan's Constitution. James K. Pollock. 1963. pap. 12.50 (*0-911586-25-3*) Wahr.

Making Microchips: Policy, Globalization, & Economic Restructuring in the Semiconductor Industry. Jan Mazurek. LC 98-35601. (Urban & Industrial Environment Ser.). (Illus.). 261p. 1998. 30.00 (*0-262-13345-8*) MIT Pr.

Making Microplans: A Community Based Process in Programming & Development. R. Goethert et al. 166p. 1988. pap. 25.00 (*1-85339-085-2*, Pub. by Intermed Tech) Stylus Pub VA.

Making Microsoft Office Work. Ralph Soucie. Ed. by Jeff Pepper. 512p. 1994. pap. text 24.95 (*0-07-881188-0*) Osborne-McGraw.

Making Middle Schools Work. fac. ed. Jon W. Wiles & Joseph W. Bondi. LC 86-71816. (Illus.). 103p. 1986. reprint ed. pap. 32.00 (*0-608-01036-7*, 208251200011) Bks Demand.

Making Midi Work - By Someone Who Does. David Grigger. (C). 1987. pap. 9.98 (*0-939067-49-8*) Alexander Pub.

Making Midwives Legal: Childbirth, Medicine, & the Law. Raymond G. DeVries. LC 96-6312. (Women & Health Ser.). Orig. Title: Regulating Birth. 232p. 1996. reprint ed. pap. text 19.95 (*0-8142-0703-0*) Ohio St U Pr.

Making Millions in the Export-Import Market, 2 vols., Set. 1992. lib. bdg. 250.00 (*0-8490-5471-0*) Gordon Pr.

Making Millions with Legal Con Games & Pyramid Schemes. William W. Walter. (Illus.). 213p. (Orig.). 1991. pap. 10.95 (*0-9629922-1-6*) Walston Pub.

***Making Minestrone.** Stella Blackstone. (Illus.). 32p. (J). (ps-3). 2000. 15.99 (*1-84148-211-0*) Barefoot Bks NY.

Making Miniature Dolls with Polymer Clay: How to Create & Dress Period Dolls in 1/12 Scale. Sue Heaser. LC 99-198146. 128p. 1999. 27.95 (*0-7063-7750-8*, Pub. by WrLock) Sterling.

Making Miniature Flowers with Polymer Clay. Barbara Quast. LC 98-10111. (Illus.). 128p. 1998. pap. 22.99 (*0-89134-821-2*, North Lght Bks) F & W Pubns Inc.

Making Miniature Furniture. Richard A. Lyons. LC 99-48937. 128p. 1999. pap. text 7.95 (*0-486-40719-5*) Dover.

Making Miniature Furniture. Richard A. Lyons & Elizabeth G. Lyons. 240p. 1988. pap. 14.95 (*0-13-547258-X*) P-H.

Making Miniature Gardens. Freida Gray. (Illus.). 192p. 1999. pap. 19.95 (*1-86108-058-1*, Pub. by Guild Master) Sterling.

Making Miniature Oriental Rugs & Carpets. Ian McNaughton. (Illus.). 102p. 1998. pap. 12.95 (*1-86108-066-2*, Pub. by Guild Master) Sterling.

***Making Miniature Villages in Polymer Clay.** Gail Ritchey. LC 99-36221. (Illus.). 128p. 2000. pap. 22.99 (*0-89134-956-1*, 31422, North Lght Bks) F & W Pubns Inc.

Making Miniatures: Dolls' House Projects in One-Twelfth Scale. Venus Dodge & Martin Dodge. (Illus.). 192p. 1993. pap. 19.95 (*0-7153-9963-2*, Pub. by D & C Pub) Sterling.

Making Miniatures in Polymer Clay. Mary Kaliski. LC 97-62345. (Illus.). 84p. 1998. pap. 15.95 (*0-916809-24-2*) Scott Pubns MI.

Making Minnesota Territory, 1849-1858. Marilyn F. Ziebarth. Ed. by Anne R. Kaplan. LC 98-51071. 112p. 1999. pap. 15.95 (*0-87351-373-8*, Borealis Book) Minn Hist.

***Making Minty Malone.** Isabel Wolff. 2000. mass mkt. 6.99 (*0-451-40925-6*, Onyx) NAL.

Making Minutes Count Even More. David Johnson. 1997. pap. text 8.95 (*0-86651-303-5*) Seymour Pubns.

Making Miracles: Exploration into the Dynamics of Self-Healing. Paul C. Roud. 1990. pap. 9.95 (*0-446-39118-2*) Warner Bks.

Making Miracles: Finding Meaning in Life's Chaos. Paul P. Pearsall. 320p. 1993. reprint ed. pap. 10.00 (*0-380-71948-7*, Avon Bks) Morrow Avon.

Making Mischief: Dada Invades New York. Francis M. Naumann & Beth Venn. (Illus.). 256p. 1996. 49.50 (*0-8109-6821-5*, Pub. by Abrams) Time Warner.

Making Mischief: Dada Invades New York. Francis M. Naumann et al. LC 96-9890. 1996. write for info. (*0-87427-105-3*) Whitney Mus.

M

Making Miss Right. Charnes. (C). 1999. write for info. (*0-415-06009-5*); pap. write for info. (*0-415-06010-9*) Routledge.

Making Mobiles. Guy R. Williams. (Illus.). (J). (gr. 7 up). 1969. 12.95 (*0-87523-167-5*) Emerson.

Making Model Aircraft. Bryan Philpott. 1990. pap. 12.95 (*1-85260-192-2*, Pub. by P Stephens) Haynes Manuals.

Making Models. Diana Craig. (Crafts for Children Ser.). (Illus.). 32p. (YA). (gr. 3 up). 1997. pap. 4.95 (*1-56010-217-9*, CC07) W Foster Pub.

Making Models. R. Gibson. (How to Make Ser.). (Illus.). 32p. (J). (gr. 3-7). 1995. text 6.95 (*0-7460-2077-5*, Usborne); lib. bdg. 14.95 (*0-88110-755-7*, Usborne) EDC.

Making Models: Three-D Creations from Paper & Clay. Diana Craig. LC 92-18413. (First Guide Ser.). (Illus.). 96p. (J). (gr. 3-6). 1993. pap. 9.95 (*1-56294-710-9*) Millbrook Pr.

Making Models in 3D Studio R4: Interactive CD-Rom for Windows 3.1 & 95. Autodesk Press Staff. (Illus.). 56.95 incl. cd-rom (*0-7668-0085-7*, Pub. by Delmar) Thomson Learn.

Making Modernism: Picasso & the Creation of the Market for Modern Art. Michael C. Fitzgerald. LC 94-14062. 320p. 1995. text 27.50 (*0-374-10611-8*) FS&G.

Making Modernism: Picasso & the Creation of the Market for Twentieth-Century Art. Michael C. Fitzgerald. (Illus.). 324p. 1996. pap. 17.95 (*0-520-20653-3*, Pub. by U CA Pr) Cal Prin Full Svc.

Making Molehills Out of Mountains: Reclaiming Your Personal Power in Your Relationships. Steve Frisch. 250p. 1998. pap. 18.95 (*0-9651511-5-8*) Alive & Well.

Making Mondragon: The Growth & Dynamics of the Worker Cooperative Complex. 2nd rev. ed. William F. Whyte & Kathleen K. Whyte. 352p. 1991. pap. text 19.95 (*0-87546-182-4*, ILR Press) Cornell U Pr.

Making Money. Henry Hills. LC 86-61581. (Segue Bks.). (Illus.). 72p. (Orig.). 1986. pap. 7.50 (*0-937804-25-8*) Segue NYC.

Making Money at the Races. David Barr. 1980. pap. 10.00 (*0-87980-268-5*) Wilshire.

Making Money by Finding Money in the 25 Billion Dollar Conspiracy. Lou S. Gattis, III. (Illus.). 20p. (Orig.). 1987. spiral bd. 10.00 (*0-936241-06-3*) Cheetah Pub.

Making Money (Counterfeiting) Rogues & Rascals Who Made Their Own. Edward C. Rochette. LC 86-22120. (Illus.). 150p. (Orig.). 1987. pap. 10.00 (*0-939650-25-8*) S J Durst.

Making Money for Yourself. Russ Von Hoelscher & George F. Sterne. 310p. 1991. pap. write for info. (*0-940398-18-4*) Profit Ideas.

Making Money from Writing: How to Become a Freelance Writer. Carole Baldock. 144p. 1998. pap. 19.95 (*1-85703-244-6*, Pub. by How To Bks) Trans-Atl Phila.

Making Money in a Health Service Business on Your Home-Based PC. 2nd ed. Rick Benzel. LC 96-29742. (Illus.). 316p. 1997. pap. text 34.95 incl. cd-rom (*0-07-913139-5*) McGraw.

Making Money in Cellular Phone Audety. Date not set. pap. write for info. (*1-884350-70-4*) Alpha Pubng.

Making Money in China: All You Need to Know about Doing Business Internationally. Ed. by Patrick W. Nee. (Making Money Internationally Ser.). (Illus.). 200p. 1998. pap. 24.95 (*1-891382-01-2*) Intrntnlst.

Making Money in Commercial Real Estate. unabridged ed. John Vivian. 79p. 1998. pap. text, wbk. ed. 49.50 (*0-9666993-0-0*) Assoc Res Consultants.

***Making Money in Commercial Real Estate.** 2nd rev. ed. John Vivian. 117p. 1999. pap. text 49.50 (*0-9666993-1-9*) Assoc Res Consultants.

***Making Money in Commercial Real Estate - Acreage & Lots.** John Vivan. 121p. 1999. pap. text 49.50 (*0-9666993-3-5*) Assoc Res Consultants.

Making Money in Cyberspace: The Inside Information You Need to Start or Take Your Own Business On-Line. Paul Edwards et al. LC 98-4004. (Illus.). 282p. 1998. 15.95 (*0-87477-884-0*, Tarcher Putnam) Putnam Pub Group.

Making Money in Direct Response Sales. Date not set. pap. write for info. (*1-884350-67-4*) Alpha Pubng.

An Asterisk (*) at the beginning of an entry indicates that the title is appearing for the first time.

M

Making Money in Film & Video: A Freelancer's Handbook. 2nd ed. Raul DeSilva. LC 92-13908. 192p. 1992. pap. 34.95 (0-240-80144-X, Focal) Buttrwrth-Heinemann.

Making Money in Mexico: All You Need to Know about Doing Business Internationally. Ed. by Patrick W. Nee. (Making Money Internationally Ser.). (Illus.). 200p. 1998. pap. 24.95 (1-891382-00-4); pap. 24.95 (1-891382-02-0) Intrntnlst.

Making Money in Real Estate: How to Build Financial Independence with Residential & Commerical Property. Carolyn Janik. 280p. 1999. 27.95 (0-938721-69-0) Kiplinger Bks.

Making Money in South America: All You Need to Know about Doing Business Internationally. Ed. by Patrick W. Nee. (Making Money Internationally Ser.). (Illus.). 200p. 1998. pap. 24.95 (1-891382-03-9) Intrntnlst.

Making Money in the Fitness Business: If I Knew the Fitness Business Was This Hard, I'd Have Gotten a "Real Job"! Thomas G. Plummer. (Illus.). 352p. (Orig.). 1998. pap. 59.00 (0-9652432-1-4, Fitness Mgmt Bks) Fitness Mgmt.

Making Money in the '90s: Drive Yourself to Success. Timothy Johnson. LC 91-77164. 208p. (Orig.). 1992. pap. 17.95 (1-880782-07-3) Spirit Dance.

Making Money in the Novelty Telegram Business. Thomas Antion. 1990. 49.95 (0-926395-02-5) Anchor Maryland.

Making Money in Voice-Overs: Winning Strategies to a Successful Career in Commercials, Cartoons & Radio. Terri Apple. LC 98-45809. 225p. 1998. pap. 16.95 (1-58065-011-2, Pub. by Lone Eagle Pub) Natl Bk Netwk.

Making Money Last. Bennett Financial Advisors Staff. 320p. 1995. pap. text 21.95 (0-7872-0962-7) Kendall-Hunt.

Making Money Last: Financial Clarity for the Surviving Spouse. limited ed. Richard Demetriou. 316p. 1996. pap. text 22.95 (0-7872-2322-0) Kendall-Hunt.

Making Money Making Furniture. Blair Howard. LC 99-17163. (Illus.). 128p. 1999. pap. 19.99 (1-55870-500-7, 70423, Popular Woodwkng Bks) F & W Pubns Inc.

Making Money Matter: Financing America's Schools. National Research Council Staff. Ed. by Helen F. Ladd & Janet S. Hansen. 368p. 1999. 49.95 (0-309-06528-3, Joseph Henry Pr) Natl Acad Pr.

Making Money Teaching Music. Barbara Newsam & David Newsam. (Illus.). 240p. (Orig.). 1995. pap. 18.99 (0-89879-657-1, Wrtrs Digest Bks) F & W Pubns Inc.

Making Money the Old-Fashioned Way: A Story of Black Entrepreneurship. Aaron A. Bocage & George E. Waters, Jr. (Illus.). iii, 110p. 1997. pap. text 13.95 (0-9661712-0-9) EDTEC.

Making Money Through Intuition. Alpha Development Group Staff & Nancy Rosanoff. (Complete Idiot's Guide Ser.). (Illus.). 371p. 1999. pap. 17.95 (0-02-862740-7) Macmillan Gen Ref.

Making Money While Making a Difference: How to Profit with a Nonprofit Partner. Richard Steckel et al. LC 99-71802. 248p. 1999. pap. 14.95 (0-9653744-9-1) High Tide Pr.

Making Money with Baseball Cards: A Handbook of Insider Secrets & Strategies. Donn Pearlman & Paul Green. (Illus.). 214p. 1989. pap. 7.95 (0-933893-77-9) Bonus Books.

Making Money with Boats. Fred Edwards. LC 96-9328. 215p. 1996. pap. 19.95 (0-87033-482-4) Cornell Maritime.

Making Money with Boats. Fred Edwards. 1996. pap. 19.95 (0-07-021880-3) McGraw-Hill Prof.

Making Money with Classified Ads. Melvin Powers. 1995. pap. 20.00 (0-87980-435-1) Wilshire.

Making Money with Online Entertainment: How to Create & Profit from Online Content. Jessica M. Mulligan. (Illus.). 320p. 1997. pap., pap. text 39.95 incl. cd-rom (0-07-913177-8) McGraw.

Making Money with the Telephone: The Complete Handbook of Telephone Marketing. M. T. Brown. LC 77-89655. 1977. 12.95 (0-930490-01-0) Future Shop.

Making Money with Vending Machine. Billy Mason. 1995. pap. 7.00 (0-942140-06-0) Kelso.

Making Money with Your Computer. Paul Bocij. (Orig.). 1996. pap. 29.95 (1-898307-29-6, Pub. by Capall Bann Pubng) Holmes Pub.

Making Money with Your Computer at Home. 2nd rev. ed. Paul Edwards & Sarah Edwards. LC 97-19612. (Working from Home Ser.). 320p. 1997. pap. 15.95 (0-87477-898-0, Tarcher Putnam) Putnam Pub Group.

Making Money with Your Creative Paint Finishes. Lynette Harris. LC 98-19910. 160p. 1998. pap. 18.99 (0-89134-824-7, North Lght Bks) F & W Pubns Inc.

Making Money Writing Newsletters: From Moonlighting to Full-Time Work, How to Set up & Run a Newsletter Production Service. Elaine Floyd. LC 93-22547. (Illus.). 132p. (Orig.). 1994. pap. 29.95 (0-9630222-1-0) EFG Inc MO.

*Making Monsters. Edward J. Ingebretsen. 2000. 30.00 (0-226-38006-8) U Ch Pr.

Making Monsters: False Memories, Psychotherapy, & Sexual Hysteria. Richard Ofshe & Ethan Watters. 340p. 1998. text 23.00 (0-7881-5931-3) DIANE Pub.

Making Monsters: False Memories, Psychotherapy, & Sexual Hysteria. Richard Ofshe & Ethan Watters. 340p. 1994. 23.00 (0-684-19698-0) S&S Trade.

Making Monsters: False Memories, Psychotherapy, & Sexual Hysteria. Richard Ofshe & Ethan Watters. LC 95-49014. 352p. (C). 1996. pap. 15.95 (0-520-20583-9, Pub. by U CA Pr) Cal Prin Full Svc.

Making Monsters: History of Homophobia. Byrne Fone. Date not set. pap. write for info. (0-8050-4560-0) H Holt & Co.

Making Moral Choices: An Introduction. Mark Miller. LC 95-61146. 96p. (Orig.). 1995. pap. 9.95 (0-89622-666-2) Twenty-Third.

Making Moral Decisions. Ed. by Jean Holm & John Bowker. LC 94-15114. (Themes in Religious Studies). 1994. 45.00 (1-85567-096-8); pap. 16.95 (1-85567-097-6) St Martin.

Making Moral Decisions. J. Philip Wogaman. 1991. pap. 1.80 (0-687-12654-1) Abingdon.

Making Moral Decisions: A Christian Approach to Personal & Social Ethics. Paul T. Jersild. LC 90-44766. 128p. (Orig.). 1991. pap. 14.00 (0-8006-2471-8, 1-2471, Fortress Pr) Augsburg Fortress.

***Making Moral Sense: Beyond Habermas & Gauthier.** Logi Gunnarsson. LC 99-86800. (Illus.). 326p. 2000. write for info. (0-521-78023-3) Cambridge U Pr.

Making More Changes: Editor's Choice. Ed. by Mary L. Santovec. LC 95-9383. 250p. 1995. pap. 39.95 (0-912150-37-8) Atwood Pub LLC.

Making More Changes: Editor's Choice. Ed. by Mary Lou Santovec. 250p. 1996. pap. text 39.95 (1-891859-12-9) Atwood Pub LLC.

Making More Money on the Internet. 2nd ed. Alfred Glossbrenner & Emily Glossbrenner. LC 96-25433. (Illus.). 336p. 1996. 29.95 (0-07-024300-X); pap. 19.95 (0-07-024447-2) McGraw.

Making More Money Retailing: Low Cost Ideas for Successful Merchandising & Boosting Profits from Your Retail Store. Barbara Lambeis & Susan Ratliff. 140p. 1994. pap. 10.95 (0-9624798-8-8) Mktg Methods Pr.

***Making More Plants: The Science, Art & Joy of Propagation.** Ken Druse. (Illus.). 256p. 2000. 45.00 (0-517-70787-X) C Potter.

Making More Waves: New Writing by Asian American Women. Ed. by Elaine H. Kim et al. LC 96-52670. 340p. 1997. pap. 18.00 (0-8070-5913-7) Beacon Pr.

***Making More Wooden Mechanical Models.** Alan Bridgewater & Gill Bridgewater. LC 99-21732. (Illus.). 128p. 1999. pap. 24.99 (1-55870-508-2, 70444, Popular Woodwkng Bks) F & W Pubns Inc.

***Making More Words: Multilevel, Hands-On Phonics & Spelling Activities.** Patricia M. Cunningham. (Illus.). (J). 2000. pap. 17.99 (1-56417-900-1) Good Apple.

Making Mortal Choices: Three Exercises in Moral Casuistry. Hugo A. Bedau. 136p. 1997. pap. 15.95 (0-19-510878-7); text 39.95 (0-19-510877-9) OUP.

Making Mortise-&-Tenon Joints. Perf. by Frank Klausz. text 19.95 incl. VHS (0-918804-57-4, 60021) Taunton.

***Making Mosaics: Designs, Techniques & Projects.** Leslie Dierks. 96p. 2000. 19.95 (0-86573-168-3) Creat Pub Intl.

Making Mosaics: Designs, Techniques & Projects. Leslie Dierks. LC 96-31470. (Illus.). 128p. 1997. 24.95 (0-8069-4872-8) Sterling.

Making Most of Kitchens. Gilly Love. LC 97-65577. (Illus.). 80p. 1997. 19.95 (0-8478-2031-9, Pub. by Rizzoli Intl) St Martin.

Making Most of Outdoor Spaces. Love. LC 98-65892. 80p. 1999. 19.95 (0-8478-2135-8, Pub. by Rizzoli Intl) St Martin.

***Making Most of Your Buffalo State Experiences.** 376p. (C). 1998. text 25.75 (0-536-01514-7) Pearson Custom.

Making Motherhood Safe. Anne Tinker & Marjorie A. Koblinsky. LC 93-19573. (Discussion Paper Ser.: Vol. 202). 161p. 1993. pap. 22.00 (0-8213-2468-3, 12468) World Bank.

Making Motherhood Safe. Anne Tinker et al. (Discussion Paper Ser.: No. 202). (SPA.). 108p. 1994. pap. 22.00 (0-8213-2973-1, 12973) World Bank.

Making Movies. Sidney Lumet. 1996. pap. 12.00 (0-679-75660-4) Random.

Making Movies. Phillip Turner. LC 97-221752. 256p. 1997. write for info. (1-84024-004-0) Summers.

Making Movies: The Inside Guide to Independent Movie Production. John A. Russo. 320p. 1989. pap. 15.95 (0-440-50046-X) Dell.

Making Movies on Your Own: Practical Talk from Independent Filmmakers. Kevin J. Linden. LC 98-16263. (Illus.). 200p. 1998. pap. 35.00 (0-7864-0517-1) McFarland & Co.

Making Movies with Your PC. Robert Hone & Margy Kuntz. 480p. (Orig.). 1994. pap. 24.95 (1-55958-389-4) Prima Pub.

Making Movies Work: Thinking Like a Filmmaker. Jon Boorstin. (Illus.). 228p. (Orig.). 1995. pap. 19.95 (1-879505-27-4) Silman James Pr.

***Making Moving Toys: 30 Quick & Easy Projects to Make.** Pippa Howes. LC 99-494993. 128p. 1999. pap. text 19.95 (1-85585-453-8) Collins & Br.

Making Mr. Right. Val Daniels. 1999. per. 3.50 (0-373-15809-2, 1-15809-6) Harlequin Bks.

Making Mr. Right. Val Daniels. 1999. per. 3.50 (0-373-03563-2, 1-03563-3) Harlequin Bks.

Making MS-DOS & PC-DOS Work for You. Human Connection Staff. 1984. pap. 16.95 (0-8306-1848-1) McGraw-Hill Prof.

Making Mud Pies for Beaver. Richard E. Faler, Jr. (Illus.). 20p. (Orig.). 1994. pap. 3.95 (1-881399-14-1) Beaver Pond P&P.

Making Multicandidate Elections More Democratic. Samuel Merrill. LC 87-25856. (Illus.). 150p. 1988. reprint ed. pap. 46.50 (0-608-06487-4, 206678400009) Bks Demand.

Making Multicultural Education Work. Stephen May. LC 94-9690. (Language & Education Library: Vol. 7). 1994. 74.95 (1-85359-237-4, Pub. by Multilingual Matters) Taylor & Francis.

Making Multicultural Education Work. Stephen May. LC 94-9690. (Language & Education Library: Vol. 7). 223p. 1994. pap. 29.95 (1-85359-236-6) Taylor & Francis.

Making Multimedia Work. Michael Goodwin. 360p. 1995. pap. 19.99 (1-56884-468-9) IDG Bks.

Making Multiplication Easy. Scholastic, Inc. Staff. 1991. pap. 9.95 (0-590-49140-7) Scholastic Inc.

***Making Music.** Susan Bonners. 2002. text (0-374-34732-8) FS&G.

Making Music. Eloise Franco & Johan Franco. (Illus.). (J). (gr. 1-5). 1976. pap. 4.95 (0-87516-212-6) DeVorss.

Making Music: Improvisation for Organists. Jan Overduin. LC 97-46196. (Illus.). 224p. 1998. pap. text 29.95 (0-19-386075-9) OUP.

***Making Music for Folk Harp: Beginning Level.** Susan Raimond. 32p. 1999. pap. 14.95 incl. audio compact disk (0-7866-2967-3, 96704BCD) Mel Bay.

Making Music for the Joy of It. Stephanie Judy. 288p. 1990. pap. 16.95 (0-87477-593-0, Tarcher Putnam) Putnam Pub Group.

Making Music in Looking Glass Land: Guide to Survival & Business Skills for the Classical Musician. 3rd ed. Helen Highstein. 1997. 17.95 (0-9629075-9-6) Concert Artists.

Making Music in the Classroom: Ages 3 - 7. Elizabeth L. Mayer. (Making Music with John Langstaff Ser.). 24p. (J). (ps-2). 1994. pap., per. 4.95 (1-886380-07-4) Langstaff Vid.

Making Music in the Classroom: Ages 7-11. Elizabeth L. Mayer. (Making Music with John Langstaff Ser.). 24p. (J). (gr. 2-6). 1994. pap. 4.95 (1-886380-08-2) Langstaff Vid.

***Making Music Modern: New York in the 1920s.** Carol J. Oja. LC 99-52604. 512p. 2000. 45.00 (0-19-505849-6) OUP.

Making Music on the Organ. rev. ed. Peter Hurford. (Illus.). 176p. 1990. pap. text 24.95 (0-19-816207-3) OUP.

Making Music on Your PC. Victoria Camp. LC 97-11569. 1997. 29.95 incl. cd-rom (1-55755-327-0) Abacus MI.

Making Music Special: Practical Ways to Create Music. John Childs. LC 96-214420. 176p. 1996. pap. text 24.95 (1-85346-417-1, Pub. by David Fulton) Taylor & Francis.

***Making Music Together: An Interactionist Perspective on Small-Group Performance in Jazz.** Peter Reinholdsson. LC 98-215452. (Studia Musicologica Upsaliensia Nova Ser.: Vol. 14). 440 p. 1998. pap. 97.50 (91-554-4243-9, Pub. by Almqvist Wiksell) Coronet Bks.

***Making Music with Charlie Chaplin.** Eric James. (Filmmakers Ser.: No. 171). (Illus.). 160p. 2000. 24.95 (0-8108-3741-2) Scarecrow.

Making Music with Children: Ages 3-7. Elizabeth L. Mayer. (Making Music with John Langstaff Ser.). 24p. (J). (ps-2). 1994. pap. 4.95 (1-886380-05-8) Langstaff Vid.

Making Music with Children: Ages 7-11. Elizabeth L. Mayer. (Making Music with John Langstaff Ser.). 24p. (J). (gr. 2-7). 1994. pap. 4.95 (1-886380-06-6) Langstaff Vid.

Making Music with Children Bk. I: Why It Matters, Bk. I. Elizabeth L. Mayer. (Music Makes a Difference Ser.). 12p. 1994. pap. text, per. 1.95 (1-886380-00-7) Langstaff Vid.

Making Music with Digital Audio: Direct-to-Disk on the PC. Ian Waugh. (Illus.). 160p. 1997. pap. 17.95 (1-878427-56-3, XC8029) Cimino Pub Grp.

Making Music with John Langstaff Series. Elizabeth L. Mayer. 96p. (J). (ps). 1994. pap. 10.95 (1-886380-09-0) Langstaff Vid.

Making Music with Pleasure, Vol. 2. Orley R. Herron. 80p. 1996. write for info. (1-889555-07-X) Stephen Aubry.

Making Music with the Young Child with Special Needs: A Guide for Parents. Elaine Streeter. 64p. 1993. pap. 14.95 (1-85302-187-3) Taylor & Francis.

***Making Music with Your Computer.** 2nd ed. Brent Edstrom. 2000. pap. 39.95 (0-87288-744-8) Intertec Pub.

Making Music with Your PC Vol. 1: A Beginner's Guide. Warren Sirota. (Illus.). 350p. 1994. pap. 19.95 (1-55958-595-1) Prima Pub.

Making Music Your Business: A Guide for Young Musicians. David Ellefson. LC 97-9673. (Illus.). 144p. 1997. pap. 14.95 (0-87930-460-X) Miller Freeman.

Making Musical Instruments: Banjo, Snare Drum, Dulicmer Tambourine Hardanger Fiddle the Dolmetsch Recorder. Irving Sloane. (Illus.). 160p. 1992. reprint ed. pap. 29.95 (0-933224-60-5, T027) Bold Strummer Ltd.

Making Musical Instruments Made by Hand: Featuring 75 Exotic Musical Instruments. Jay Havighurst. (Illus.). 108p. 1999. pap. text 24.99 (1-56496-352-7, Quarry Bks) Rockport Pubs.

Making Musicals: An Informal Introduction to the World of Musical Theatre. Tom Jones. LC 97-13033. (Illus.). 224p. (Orig.). 1997. pap. 16.95 (0-87910-095-8) Limelight Edns.

***Making Musics: Contemporary Collaborations Between Poets & Composers.** Joseph Duemer & David Rakowski. (Border Crossings Ser.: 8). 340p. 2000. 75.00 (0-8153-2504-5) Garland.

Making Muslim Space in North America & Europe. Ed. by Barbara D. Metcalf. LC 95-43429. (Comparative Studies on Muslim Societies: Vol. 22). (Illus.). 263p. (C). 1996. 55.00 (0-520-20403-4, Pub. by U CA Pr); pap. 22.50 (0-520-20404-2, Pub. by U CA Pr) Cal Prin Full Svc.

Making My Name: Poems. Joseph A. Soldati. LC 92-22961. 60p. 1992. pap. 14.95 (0-7734-9525-8, Mellen Poetry Pr) E Mellen.

Making My Room Special: Creative Ways to Decorate Your Room. Emilie Barnes. LC 98-38010. (Illus.). 32p. (YA). 1999. 14.99 (0-7369-0044-6) Harvest Hse.

Making My Way: Memories of a Boyhood along the Skipanon River. Rudolph T. Shappee. LC 98-75227. (Illus.). 205p. (YA). 1999. pap. 11.95 (0-9669637-0-9) South Jetty.

Making NAFTA Work: U. S. Firms & the New North American Business Environment. Ed. by Stephen Blank & Jerry Haar. LC 98-5602. 112p. 1997. 16.95 (1-57454-047-5) U Miami N-S Ctr.

Making National Energy Policy. Ed. by Hans H. Landsberg. 151p. 1993. pap. 22.50 (0-915707-70-5) Resources Future.

Making National Vocational Qualifications Work for Social Care. Des Kelly et al. (C). 1989. 35.00 (0-7855-6304-0, Pub. by Natl Inst Soc Work) St Mut.

Making National Vocational Qualifications Work for Social Care. Des Kelly et al. (C). 1990. 30.00 (0-7855-5900-0, Pub. by Natl Inst Soc Work); 35.00 (0-7855-0076-6, Pub. by Natl Inst Soc Work); pap. 21.00 (0-902789-66-X, Pub. by Natl Inst Soc Work) St Mut.

Making Native American Pottery. Michael Simpson. LC 90-5836. (Illus.). 148p. 1989. pap. 7.95 (0-87961-191-X) Naturegraph.

Making Natural Knowledge: Constructivism & the History of Science. Jan Golinski. LC 97-24028. (History of Science Ser.). (Illus.). 240p. (C). 1998. text 54.95 (0-521-44471-3); pap. text 16.95 (0-521-44913-8) Cambridge U Pr.

***Making Natural Liquid Soaps.** Catherine Failor. LC 99-57462. (Illus.). 144p. 2000. pap. 18.95 (1-58017-243-1) Storey Bks.

***Making Natural Milk Soap.** Casey Makela. LC 99-34998. 1999. pap. 3.95 (1-58017-220-2) Random.

Making Nature, Shaping Culture: Plant Biodiversity in Global Context. Lawrence Busch et al. LC 95-10244. (Our Sustainable Future Ser.). (Illus.). xv, 261p. 1995. text 50.00 (0-8032-1256-9) U of Nebr Pr.

***Making New Discoveries.** Charles R. Swindoll. 63p. 1998. pap., student ed. 5.95 (1-57972-190-7) Insight Living.

Making New Discoveries. Charles R. Swindoll. (Swindoll Bible Study Guide Ser.). 80p. 1995. pap. 5.99 (0-8499-8630-3) Word Pub.

Making New Friends. (Happy Endings Padded Storybooks Ser.). (Illus.). 32p. (J). (ps-1). 1998. pap. write for info. (0-7666-0159-5, Honey Bear Bks) Modern Pub NYC.

Making New Friends: People Who Look Different. Wayne H. Miller. Ed. by Denise M. Smith. (Sandy Dallas Series of Books for Children, Parents, & Teachers). (Illus.). 100p. (Orig.). (YA). (gr. 6-12). 1995. pap. text 4.95 (0-9634735-8-1) Hiram Charles.

Making New Materials. Snape & Rowlands. (Science at Work Ser.). 1992. pap. text. write for info. (0-582-07428-2, Pub. by Addison-Wesley) Longman.

Making New York's City Government Serve Our Communities: A CSS Citizen's Guide to the New York City Council. Walter A. Fields, Jr. LC 92-195799. (SPA.). 30p. 1991. pap. 5.00 (0-88156-119-3) Comm Serv Soc NY.

Making News: A Study in the Construction of Reality. Gaye Tuchman. LC 78-53075. (Illus.). 1980. pap. 14.95 (0-02-932960-4) Free Pr.

Making News: How to Get News Coverage for Disability Rights Issues. Tari S. Hartman & Mary Johnson. 165p. 1993. pap. 10.95 (0-9627064-3-4) Advocado Pr.

Making News: Revised & Updated Edition. Harvard Business Review Staff. 340p. 1993. pap. 16.95 (0-07-103389-0) McGraw.

***Making News of Police Violence: A Comparative Study of Toronto & New York City.** Jeffery Ian Ross. LC 99-54878. 224p. 2000. 64.00 (0-275-96825-1, C6825, Praeger Pubs) Greenwood.

Making Nightmares Pay. rev. ed. Anthony Dubetz & Willard Gellis. 1987. 6.00 (0-917455-03-7) Big Foot NY.

Making Noise: Creating Sounds on Your PC. Richard Leinecker. LC 94-26301. 1994. pap. 24.95 incl. disk (1-55851-386-8, M&T Bks) IDG Bks.

Making Noise Quietly. Robert Holman. 40p. (C). 1988. pap. write for info. (0-413-15250-2, A0166, Methuen Drama) Methn.

***Making Noise Quietly.** Robert Holman. (Nick Hern Bks.). 2000. pap. 14.95 (1-85459-452-4) Theatre Comm.

Making Nosew Jackets & Vests. Patrick Lose. (Illus.). 144p. 1998. 14.95 (0-8069-1299-5, Chapelle) Sterling.

Making Not Breaking. Cherry Hill. (Illus.). 244p. 1992. 27.95 (0-914327-43-7) Breakthrgh NY.

Making Notes. Billy Joel & Anthony Rudel. (Illus.). 304p. 1998. 23.95 (1-57322-119-8, Riverhead Books) Putnam Pub Group.

Making Numbers Make Sense: A Sourcebook for Developing Numeracy in Grades K-8. 1993. write for info. (0-201-96664-6) Addison-Wesley.

Making Numbers Make Sense: A Sourcebook for Developing Numeracy in Grades K-8. Ronald E. Ritchart. 1993. pap. 15.00 (0-201-81749-7) Addison-Wesley.

Making of a Baltimore Album Quilt. Frances Benton. (Illus.). 64p. 1995. 16.95 (1-881320-45-6, Black Belt) Black Belt Communs.

***Making of a Bestseller: From Author to Reader.** Arthur T. Vanderbilt, 2nd. LC 99-12074. 240p. 1999. pap. 28.50 (0-7864-0663-1) McFarland & Co.

***Making of a Bible.** American Bible Society Staff. 2000. pap. 4.95 (5-550-01012-7) Nairi.

Making of a Black Bishop. Quintin E. Primo. (Illus.). xvii, 172p. 1998. pap. 18.95 (1-892142-02-3, 110) Cedar Tree Bks.

Making of a Blockbuster: How Wayne Huizenga Built a Sports & Entertainment Empire from Trash, Grit, & Videotape. Gail DeGeorge. LC 95-41880. 354p. 1995. 24.95 (0-471-12269-6); pap. 5.99 (0-471-19172-8) Wiley.

An Asterisk (*) at the beginning of an entry indicates that the title is appearing for the first time.

Making of a Blockbuster: How Wayne Huizenga Built a Sports & Entertainment Empire from Trash, Grit & Videotape. Gail Degeorge. 354p. 1997. pap. 14.95 (*0-471-15903-4*) Wiley.

Making of a Chef: Mastering Heat at the Culinary Institute of America. Michael Ruhlman. LC 97-30078. 305p. 1997. 27.50 (*0-8050-4674-7*) H Holt & Co.

***Making of a Chef: Mastering Heat at the Culinary Institute of America.** Michael Ruhlman. 320p. 1999. pap. text 15.00 (*0-8050-6173-8*) H Holt & Co.

Making of a Chicano Militant: Lessons from Cristal. Jose A. Gutierrez. LC 98-13866. (Studies in American Autobiography). xiii, 334 p. 1999. pap. 19.95 (*0-299-15984-1*) U of Wis Pr.

Making of a Chicano Militant: Lessons from Cristal. Jose Angel Gutierrez. LC 98-13866. (Studies in American Autobiography). 368p. 1999. 50.00 (*0-299-15980-9*) U of Wis Pr.

Making of a Chinese City: History & Historiography in Harbin. soren Clausen & Stig Thogersen. LC 94-30519. (Studies on Modern China Ser.). (Illus.). 252p. (C). (gr. 13). 1995. text 81.95 (*1-56324-475-6*, East Gate Bk) M E Sharpe.

Making of a Chinese City: History & Historiography in Harbin. Soren Clausen & Stig Thogersen. LC 94-30519. (Studies on Modern China). (Illus.). 252p. (C). (gr. 13). 1995. pap. text 36.95 (*1-56324-476-4*, East Gate Bk) M E Sharpe.

Making of a Choreographer: Ninette de Valois & Bar aux Folies-Bergere. Beth Genne. LC 96-69521. (Studies in Dance History: Vol. 12). (Illus.). 155p. (Orig.). 1996. pap. 21.95 (*0-9653519-1-2*, Pub. by Soc Dance Hist) U Pr of New Eng.

***Making of A Christian Empire: Lactantius & Rome.** Elizabeth Depalma Digeser. LC 99-16168. 1999. 39.95 (*0-8014-3594-3*) Cornell U Pr.

Making of a Christian Leader see Lider No Nace, Se Hace

Making of a Christian Leader. 214p. 1978. pap. 10.99 (*0-310-24221-5*, 9573P) Zondervan.

Making of a Conservative Environmentalist: With Reflections on Government, Industry, Scientists, the Media, Education, Economic Growth, the Public, the Great Lakes, Activists, & the Sunsetting of Toxic Chemicals. Gordon K. Durnil. LC 94-24989. 216p. 1995. text 19.95 (*0-253-32873-X*) Ind U Pr.

Making of a Cook. Madeleine Kamman. 1994. pap. 24.95 (*0-02-560658-1*) S&S Trade.

Making of a Cop. Harvey Rachlin. Ed. by Elaine Pfefferblit. 320p. (Orig.). 1991. reprint ed. mass mkt. 4.99 (*0-671-74740-1*) PB.

Making of a Counter Culture: Reflections on the Technocratic Society & Its Youthful Opposition. Theodore Roszak. LC 94-34092. 310p. (C). 1996. pap. 15.95 (*0-520-20122-1*, Pub. by U CA Pr) Cal Prin Full Svc.

Making of a Country Lawyer. Gerry Spence. (Illus.). 448p. 1997. pap. 14.95 (*0-312-16914-0*) St Martin.

***Making of a Country Lawyer: An Autobiography.** Gerry Spence. (Illus.). 437p. 1998. pap. 15.00 (*0-7881-5958-5*) DIANE Pub.

Making of a Cowman. G. Marshall Hartman. Ed. by G. Gail Gesell. (Illus.). 248p. 1993. write for info. (*0-942078-43-8*) R Tanner Assocs Inc.

Making of a Critic. Irving Howe. (Chapbooks in Literature Ser.). 28p. 1982. pap. text 5.00 (*1-878603-01-9*) Bennington Coll.

Making of a Dissident. Goldfarb. 1989. 19.95 (*0-684-18992-5*, Scribners Ref) Mac Lib Ref.

Making of a Doctor: Medical Education in Theory & Practice. R. S. Downie et al. LC 92-13057. (Oxford Medical Publications). (Illus.). 224p. 1992. 49.95 (*0-19-262136-X*) OUP.

Making of a Doctor, Early Memoirs of Mavis Kelsey, Sr., 1912-1949. Mavis P. Kelsey, Sr. 250p. 1995. 65.00 (*0-9613308-5-6*) Kelsey-Seybold Found.

Making of a Feminist: Early Journals & Letters of M. Carey Thomas. Ed. by Marjorie H. Dobkin. LC 79-88605. 314p. 1980. pap. 19.95 (*0-87338-237-4*) New Mark Pr.

Making of a Fly: The Genetics of Animal Design. Peter A. Lawrence. (Illus.). 242p. 1992. pap. 49.95 (*0-632-03048-8*) Blackwell Sci.

Making of a Fringe Candidate, 1992. Lenora B. Fulani. LC 92-76223. (Illus.). 241p. 1993. pap. 11.95 (*0-9628621-3-4*) Castillo Intl.

Making of a Garden Gertrude Jekyll. Gertrude Jekyll. Ed. by Cherry Lewis. (Illus.). 172p. 1984. 49.50 (*0-907462-52-9*) Antique Collect.

Making of a Genius. Aaron Stern. LC 70-181866. 171p. 1971. 14.95 (*0-916560-02-3*) Renaiss Pubs.

Making of a Godly Man A Guide to Help Men Live Out the Seven Promises, 1. John T. Trent. LC 98-55366. 1999. pap. text 12.99 (*0-8499-3754-X*) Word Pub.

Making of a Government: Political Leaders in Modern Mexico. Roderic A. Camp. LC 84-8811. 237p. 1984. 34.00 (*0-8165-0871-2*) U of Ariz Pr.

Making of a Great Canadian Railway. Frederick A. Talbot. Ed. by Stuart Bruchey. LC 80-1347. (Railroads Ser.). (Illus.). 1981. reprint ed. lib. bdg. 44.95 (*0-405-13818-0*) Ayer.

Making of a Gymnast. Jean Boulogne et al. LC 77-95185. 96 p. 1978. 8.95 (*0-8015-4803-9*) NAL.

Making of a Happy Family: A Workbook for Parents. Larry Koenig. 47p. 1992. pap. 12.00 (*1-886901-00-7*) Up With Youth.

Making of a Heretic: Gender, Authority, & the Priscillianist Controversy. Virginia Burrus. LC 94-33270. (Transformation of the Classical Heritage Ser.: Vol. XXIV). 319p. 1995. 52.50 (*0-520-08997-9*, Pub. by U CA Pr) Cal Prin Full Svc.

Making of a Hero. Disney Staff. (Mulan Ser.). (Illus.). (J). 1998. pap. text 2.99 (*0-307-25703-7*, 25703, Goldn Books) Gldn Bks Pub Co.

Making of a Hinterland: State, Society, & Economy in Inland North China, 1853-1937. Kenneth Pomeranz. LC 92-17008. 1993. 48.00 (*0-520-08051-3*, Pub. by U CA Pr) Cal Prin Full Svc.

Making of a History: Walter Prescott Webb & The Great Plains. Gregory M. Tobin. LC 76-3120. 204p. reprint ed. pap. 63.30 (*0-8357-7766-9*, 203612500002) Bks Demand.

Making of a Japanese Periphery, 1750-1920. Karen Wigen. LC 93-36270. 1994. 50.00 (*0-520-08420-9*, Pub. by U CA Pr) Cal Prin Full Svc.

Making of a Journalist. William S. White. LC 86-5628. (Illus.). 264p. 1986. 32.50 (*0-8131-1603-1*) U Pr of Ky.

Making of a Knight: How Sir James Earned His Armor. Patrick O'Brien. LC 97-36867. (Illus.). 32p. (J). (gr. 1-4). 1998. 15.95 (*0-88106-354-1*) Charlesbridge Pub.

Making of a Knight: How Sir James Earned His Armor. Patrick O'Brien. LC 97-36867. (Illus.). (J). (ps-3). 1998. pap. 6.95 (*0-88106-355-X*) Charlesbridge Pub.

Making of a Land Surveyor. Michael J. Schmitz. Ed. by Roy Minnick. (Illus.). 223p. (C). 1978. pap. 49.00 (*0-910845-03-4*, 715) Landmark Ent.

Making of a Leader. Frank Damazio. 332p. 1988. pap. 21.99 (*0-914936-84-0*) City Bible Pub.

Making of a Leader: Recognizing the Stages of Leadership Development. J. Robert Clinton. LC 88-61777. 272p. (Orig.). 1988. pap. 11.00 (*0-89109-192-0*) NavPress.

Making of a Leader Study Guide. Frank Damazio. 50p. 1991. pap., student ed. 6.99 (*0-914936-57-3*) City Bible Pub.

Making of a Man. Orison S. Marden. 307p. 1998. pap. 26.00 (*0-89540-408-7*, SB-408) Sun Pub.

Making of a Man: A Sexual Fantasy. Audrey Savage. Ed. by Charlotte Wright. 214p. (Orig.). 1992. pap. 10.00 (*0-929698-02-9*) Bk Weaver Pub.

Making of a Man of God. Mark T. Barclay. 80p. (Orig.). (C). pap. 5.00 (*0-944802-19-2*) M Barclay Pubns.

Making of a Man of God: Studies in I & II Timothy. Dean Fetterhoff. pap. 5.99 (*0-88469-030-X*) BMH Bks.

Making of a Man of God: Studies in the Life of David. Alan Redpath. LC 62-10731. (Alan Redpath Library). 256p. (gr. 10). 1994. reprint ed. pap. 11.99 (*0-8007-5516-2*) Revell.

Making of a Martial Artist. Sang K. Shim. (Illus.). 1980. 20.00 (*0-685-06224-4*); pap. 9.95 (*0-685-06225-2*) S K Shim Pub.

Making of a Martial Artist. Shim. 1991. pap. 6.95 (*0-942062-02-7*) S K Shim Pub.

***Making of a Mediator: Developing Artistry in Practice.** Michael D. Lang & Alison Taylor. LC 99-50521. 240p. 2000. 34.95 (*0-7879-4992-2*, Pfffr & Co) Jossey-Bass.

Making of a Metropolis: Planning & Growth of Dehli. A. K. Jain. 1990. 72.00 (*81-85135-47-9*, Pub. by Natl Bk Orgn) S Asia.

Making of a Mexican American Mayor. Mario Garcia. LC 97-60855. 197p. 1998. pap. 12.50 (*0-87404-276-3*) U of Tex Pr.

Making of a Mining District: Keweenaw Native Copper, 1500-1870. David J. Krause. LC 92-14640. (Great Lakes Bks.). (Illus.). 302p. (C). 1992. pap. 19.95 (*0-8143-2407-X*, Great Lks Bks); text 39.95 (*0-8143-2406-1*, Great Lks Bks) Wayne St U Pr.

Making of a Minister: From Village Pietism to Global Pluralism. O. Walter Wagner. LC 93-90563. (Studies in Ministry & Parish Life). viii, 287p. 1993. 24.95 (*0-913552-53-4*) Exploration Pr.

Making of a Missile Crisis, October, 1962. Herbert S. Dinerstein. LC 75-36943. 320p. reprint ed. pap. 99.20 (*0-608-18408-X*, 203057200069) Bks Demand.

Making of a Missionary: De Vez en Cuando: From Time to Time. Rick Johnson. (Illus.). 128p. (Orig.). 1996. pap. 8.95 (*0-9648163-0-X*) Intl Action Minst Pr.

Making of a Modern Gay World, 1935-1975. George Chauncey. 448p. Date not set. pap. write for info. (*0-465-04303-8*) Basic.

Making of a Modern Gay World, 1935-1975. George Chauncey. 448p. 1998. 25.00 (*0-465-04302-X*, Pub. by Basic) HarpC.

Making of a Modern Japanese Architecture, 1868 to Present. David B. Stewart. LC 87-81685. (Illus.). 304p. 1988. 60.00 (*0-87011-844-7*) Kodansha.

Making of a Modern Quaker: Roger Cowan Wilson 1906-1991. Fred Brown. 1996. pap. 36.00 (*0-7162-0502-5*) Epworth Pr.

Making of a Moonie. Barker. 1993. 69.95 (*0-7512-0136-7*) Ashgate Pub Co.

Making of a Mormon Apostle: A Biography of Rudger Clawson. David S. Hoopes & Roy Hoopes. (Illus.). 370p. 1989. 24.95 (*0-8191-7298-7*) Madison Bks UPA.

Making of a Mystic: Seasons in the Life of Teresa of Avila. Francis L. Gross, Jr. & Toni P. Gross. LC 92-12040. 285p. (C). 1993. text 21.50 (*0-7914-1411-6*) State U NY Pr.

Making of a Myth: The United States & China, 1897-1912. Paul A. Varg. LC 79-25619. 184p. 1980. reprint ed. lib. bdg. 38.50 (*0-313-22125-1*, VAMA, Greenwood Pr) Greenwood.

Making of a New Eastern Question: British Palestine Policy & the Origins of Israel, 1917-1925. D. Edward Knox. LC 80-21879. 225p. reprint ed. pap. 69.80 (*0-608-17271-5*, 202951900061) Bks Demand.

Making of a New Environmental Consciousness: A Comparative Study of the Environmental Movements in Sweden, Denmark, & the Netherlands. Andrew Jamison et al. (Environment, Politics, & Society Ser.). 224p. 1993. pap. 28.00 (*0-7486-0235-6*, Pub. by Edinburgh U Pr) Col U Pr.

Making of a New Europe: R. W. Seton-Watson & the Last Years of Austria-Hungary. Hugh Seton-Watson & Christopher Seton-Watson. 470p. 1981. 50.00 (*0-295-95792-1*) U of Wash Pr.

***Making of a New Racial Order.** Seidman & Winant. 2000. 28.00 (*0-465-04340-2*, Pub. by Basic) HarpC.

Making of a Ninja: Ashida Kim's Training Camp. (Illus.). 172p. 1987. reprint ed. pap. 7.95 (*0-8065-1035-8*, Citadel Pr) Carol Pub Group.

Making of a Pagan. Maighread Medbh. 66p. (Orig.). 1990. pap. 11.95 (*0-85640-455-1*, Pub. by Blackstaff Pr) Dufour.

Making of a Para. Rory Bridson. (Illus.). 192p. 1995. 19.95 (*1-85367-222-X*, Pub. by Greenhill Bks) Stackpole.

Making of a Pariah State: The Adventurist Politics of Mummar Quaddafi. Martin Sicker. LC 86-30543. 147p. 1987. 47.95 (*0-275-92667-2*, C2667, Praeger Pubs) Greenwood.

Making of a Pastoral Person. 2nd expanded rev. ed. Gerald R. Niklas. LC 96-11427. 229p. (Orig.). 1996. pap. 12.95 (*0-8189-0761-4*) Alba.

Making of a Pastry Chef: Recipes & Inspirations from America's Best Pastry Chefs. Andrew MacLauchlan. LC 99-13033. 352p. 1999. pap. 29.95 (*0-471-29320-2*) Wiley.

Making of a Periphery: Economic Development & Cultural Encounters in Southern Tanzania. Ed. by Pekka Seppala & Bertha Koda. 344p. 1998. pap. 28.95 (*91-7106-416-8*) Transaction Pubs.

***Making of a Poem: A Norton Anthology of Poetic Forms.** Mark Strand & Eavan Boland. LC 99-55233. 448p. 2000. 27.50 (*0-393-04916-7*) Norton.

Making of a Preacher & Fallen from Grace. George B. Kulp & C. F. Wimberly. 1986. pap. 3.99 (*0-88019-203-8*) Schmul Pub Co.

Making of a Primary: The Illinois Presidential Primary, 1912-1992. John S. Jackson, III et al. LC 96-10244. 98p. 1996. text 7.50 (*0-938943-11-1*) U IL Spgfld Pub Affrs.

Making of a Profession: A Century of Electrical Engineering in America. M. McMahon. LC 83-22325. 320p. 1984. 39.95 (*0-87942-173-8*, PC01677) Inst Electrical.

Making of a Professional: Manton S. Eddy, U.S.A, 185. Henry Gerard Philips. LC 99-15456. 185. 280p. 2000. 65.00 (*0-313-31183-8*, Greenwood Pr) Greenwood.

Making of a Psychotherapist. N. Symington. 240p. 1997. pap. 32.00 (*1-85575-139-9*, Pub. by H Karnac Bks Ltd) Other Pr LLC.

Making of a Psychotherapist. Neville Symington. LC 96-43136. 240p. 1997. 37.50 (*0-8236-3083-8*, BN03083) Intl Univs Pr.

Making of a Public Profession. Frances K. Zemans & Victor G. Rosenblum. LC 80-71013. xvi, 247p. 1980. 22.50 (*0-910058-97-0*, 304960); pap. 20.00 (*0-910058-88-1*, 304960) W S Hein.

Making of a Quagmire: America & Vietnam During the Kennedy Era. David Halberstam. Ed. by Daniel J. Singal. 224p. (C). 1987. pap. 18.75 (*0-07-555092-X*) McGraw.

Making of a Race Car. Richard Huff. LC 98-19230. (Race Car Legends Ser.). (Illus.). 64p. (YA). (gr. 3 up). 1999. lib. bdg. 16.95 (*0-7910-5020-3*) Chelsea Hse.

Making of a Racist State: British Imperialism & the Union of South Africa. Bernard M. Magubane. 474p. 1995. pap. text 19.95 (*0-86543-241-4*) Africa World.

Making of a Racist State: British Imperialism & the Union of South Africa, 1875-1910. Bernard M. Magubane. 474p. 1995. 69.95 (*0-86543-240-6*) Africa World.

Making of a Radical: A Political Autobiography. Scott Nearing. (Good Life Ser.). 316p. pap. 16.95 (*1-890132-59-4*) Chelsea Green Pub.

Making of a Radical: A Political Autobiography. Scott Nearing. LC 78-180725. 1972. pap. 11.95 (*0-911394-07-9*) Good Life Ctr.

Making of a Radical: A Political Autobiography. Scott Nearing. LC 78-180725. 308p. 1976. 16.95 (*0-911394-06-0*) Good Life Ctr.

Making of a Railway. L. T. C. Rolt. (Illus.). 160p. 1997. pap. 22.95 (*0-7509-1354-1*, Pub. by Sutton Pub Ltd) Intl Pubs Mktg.

Making of a Reader. Marilyn Cochran-Smith. Ed. by Cynthia Wallat & Judith Green. LC 83-25795. (Language & Learning for Human Service Professions Ser.: Vol. 2). 256p. 1984. pap. 39.50 (*0-89391-219-0*); text 73.25 (*0-89391-187-9*) Ablx Pub.

Making of a Sailor: or Sea Life Aboard a Yankee Square-Rigger. Frederick P. Harlow. (Illus.). 416p. 1988. reprint ed. pap. 9.95 (*0-486-25613-8*) Dover.

Making of a Saint: A Romance of Mediaeval Italy. W. Somerset Maugham. LC 75-30388. (Works of W. Somerset Maugham). 1977. reprint ed. 26.95 (*0-405-07815-3*) Ayer.

Making of a Scientist. Anne Roe. LC 73-15059. 244p. 1974. reprint ed. lib. bdg. 65.00 (*0-8371-7151-2*, ROMS, Greenwood Pr) Greenwood.

Making of a Seaman. 3rd ed. Rowan O'Neill. (Illus.). 164p. 1982. pap. 2.95 (*0-933704-45-3*) Dawn Pr.

Making of a Seaman. 4th ed. Rowan O'Neill. (Illus.). 164p. 1988. pap. 5.95 (*0-933704-53-4*) Dawn Pr.

Making of a Secret Agent. Frank Pickersgill. Ed. by George H. Ford. (Illus.). 274p. 1978. mass mkt. 5.95 (*0-88780-123-4*, Pub. by Formac Publ Co) Formac Dist Ltd.

Making of a Senator: Dan Quayle. Richard F. Fenno, Jr. 180p. 1988. 33.95 (*0-87187-511-X*); pap. 21.95 (*0-87187-506-3*) Congr Quarterly.

Making of a Senator, 1974: A Biography of Richard S. Schweiker. Burton R. Landes. LC 75-7003. 120p. 1974. 2.50 (*0-614-13003-4*) B R Landes.

Making of a Serial Killer: The Real Story of the Gainsville Student Murders in the Killer's Own Words. Danny Rolling & Sondra London. LC 98-134716. (Illus.). 250p. (Orig.). 1996. pap. 12.95 (*0-922915-40-7*) Feral Hse.

Making of a Sino-Marxist World View: Perceptions & Interpretations of World History in the People's Republic of China. Dorothea A. Martin. LC 89-49161. (Studies on Contemporary China). 160p. (gr. 13). 1990. text 79.95 (*0-87332-656-3*, East Gate Bk) M E Sharpe.

Making of a Social Disease: Tuberculosis in Nineteenth-Century France. David S. Barnes. LC 94-15230. 1995. 50.00 (*0-520-08772-0*, Pub. by U CA Pr) Cal Prin Full Svc.

Making of a Southerner. Katharine D. Lumpkin. LC 91-26583. (Brown Thrasher Bks.). 280p. 1991. reprint ed. pap. 15.95 (*0-8203-1385-8*) U of Ga Pr.

Making of a Soviet Scientist. Roald Z. Sagdeev. Ed. by Susan Eisenhower. 339p. 1994. 24.95 (*0-471-02031-1*) Wiley.

Making of a Soviet Scientist: My Adventures in Nuclear Fusion & Space from Stalin to Star Wars. Roald Z. Sagdeev. LC 93-40709. 339p. 1995. pap. 17.95 (*0-471-12929-1*) Wiley.

Making of a Spiritual Movement: The Untold Story of Paul Twitchell & Eckankar. rev. ed. David C. Lane. (Understanding Cults & Spiritual Movements Ser.). 211p. 1994. pap. 15.00 (*0-9611124-6-8*) Del Mar Pr.

Making of a Spiritual Movement: The Untold Story of Paul Twitchell & Eckankar. 4th rev. ed. David C. Lane. (Understanding Cults & Spiritual Movements Ser.: No. 1). (Illus.). 171p. 1989. pap. 19.95 (*0-685-26797-0*) Del Mar Pr.

Making of a Spiritual Warrior: A Woman's Guide to Daily Victory. Quin Sherrer & Ruthanne Garlock. LC 98-37328. 1999. 9.99 (*1-56955-111-1*) Servant.

Making of a Statesman. Joel Chandler Harris. (Notable American Authors Ser.). 1992. reprint ed. lib. bdg. 75.00 (*0-7812-3023-3*) Rprt Serv.

Making of a Statesman & Other Stories. Joel Chandler Harris. LC 79-113665. (Short Story Index Reprint Ser.). 1977. 20.95 (*0-8369-3394-X*) Ayer.

Making of a Stockbroker. Edwin Lefevre. LC 75-2645. (Wall Street & the Security Market Ser.). 1975. reprint ed. 28.95 (*0-405-06970-7*) Ayer.

Making of a Stockbroker. Edwin Lefevre. LC 84-80693. 341p. 1999. reprint ed. pap. 16.00 (*0-87034-072-7*) Fraser Pub Co.

Making of a Strike: Mexican Silver Workers' Struggles in Real del Monte, 1766-1775. Doris M. Ladd. LC 87-5897. 215p. 1988. reprint ed. pap. 66.70 (*0-608-03485-1*, 206419900008) Bks Demand.

Making of a Sugar Giant: Tate & Lyle, 1859-1989. P. Chalmin. xviii, 782p. 1990. text 160.00 (*3-7186-0434-5*) Gordon & Breach.

Making of a Surgeon. William A. Nolen. 269p. 1990. reprint ed. pap. 16.00 (*0-922811-46-6*, Pub. by Mid-List) SPD-Small Pr Dist.

Making of a Surgeon. 2nd ed. William A. Nolen. 288p. 1990. reprint ed. 17.95 (*0-922811-05-9*) Mid-List.

Making of a Teacher: Conversations with Eknath Easwaran. Timothy Flinders & Carol L. Flinders. LC 88-37467. (Illus.). 192p. (Orig.). 1989. 22.00 (*0-915132-55-9*); pap. 12.00 (*0-915132-54-0*) Nilgiri Pr.

Making of a Teacher: Fifty Years in Social Work. Alice T. Davis. LC 88-17807. (Illus.). 208p. reprint ed. pap. 64.50 (*0-7837-5364-0*, 204512800005) Bks Demand.

Making of a Teacher: Teacher Knowledge & Teacher Education. Pamela Grossman. (Series on School Reform). 200p. (C). 1990. text 38.95 (*0-8077-3048-3*); pap. text 18.95 (*0-8077-3047-5*) Tchrs Coll.

Making of a Theologian. Martin H. Scharlemann. 182p. 1984. pap. 6.50 (*0-911770-54-2*) Concordia Seminary.

Making of a Transnational Community: Migration, Development & Cultural Change in the Dominican Republic. Eugenia Georges. 280p. 1990. text 52.50 (*0-231-07096-9*) Col U Pr.

Making of a Vampire: Vlad the Impaler, Paracelsus, Rabbi Loew, St. Gernmain, Dracula. Alexander Sendrea. LC 82-70967. 1982. 8.00 (*0-917944-04-6*) Am Inst Writing Res.

Making of a Warrior: The Champ. Rodney D. Walker. (Illus.). 70p. 1998. pap. text 11.99 (*0-9659275-1-2*) Shekinah.

Making of a Winner. David E. Moe. (Illus.). 110p. (Orig.). 1987. pap. 6.95 (*0-9615797-1-4*); lib. bdg. 12.95 (*0-9615797-2-2*) Moe-Tavation.

Making of a Winner: The Porsche 917. Larry Pihera. LC 72-7354. 183p. 1972. write for info. (*0-397-00807-4*, Lippnctt) Lppncott W & W.

***Making of a World Power: War & the Military Revolution in 17th Century England.** James Scott Wheeler. 1999. 36.95 (*0-7509-2025-4*) A Sutton.

Making of Adolf Hitler: The Birth & Rise of Nazism. Eugene Davidson. LC 96-37316. (Illus.). 448p. 1997. pap. 19.95 (*0-8262-1117-8*) U of Mo Pr.

***Making of America.** Ed. by Raintree Steck-Vaughn Publishing Staff. (Illus.). 2000. 114.20 (*0-7398-2814-2*) Raintree Steck-V.

Making of America: Industry & Finance. Ed. by Robert M. La Follette. LC 73-2516. (Big Business; Economic Power in a Free Society Ser.). 1973. reprint ed. 34.95 (*0-405-05096-8*) Ayer.

Making of America: Labor. Ed. by Robert M. LaFollette. LC 72-89744. (American Labor, from Conspiracy to Collective Bargaining Ser., No. 1). 433p. 1970. reprint ed. 34.95 (*0-405-02132-1*) Ayer.

Making of America: The Substance & Meaning of the Constitution. W. Cleon Skousen. LC 85-8875. 932p. 1985. 26.95 (*0-88080-017-8*) Natl Ctr Constit.

M

An Asterisk (*) at the beginning of an entry indicates that the title is appearing for the first time.

***Making of American Audiences: From Stage to Television, 1750-1990.** Richard Butsch. (Cambridge Studies in the History of Mass Communications). (Illus.). 448p. (C). 2000. 64.95 (*0-521-66253-2*); pap. 24.95 (*0-521-66483-7*) Cambridge U Pr.

Making of American Exceptionalism: The Knights of Labor & Class Formation in the Nineteenth Century. Kim Voss. 312p. 1993. text 45.00 (*0-8014-2882-3*); pap. text 17.95 (*0-8014-8119-8*) Cornell U Pr.

Making of American Politics, 1750-1850. M. J. Heale. LC 77-24250. 271p. reprint ed. pap. 84.10 (*0-608-30063-2*, 201631800003) Bks Demand.

***Making of American Resorts: Saratoga Springs, Ballston Spa & Lake George.** Theodore Corbett. LC 00-28074. (Illus.). 288p. (C). 2001. text 59.00 (*0-8135-2841-0*); pap. text 28.00 (*0-8135-2842-9*) Rutgers U Pr.

Making of Americans. Gertrude Stein. LC 95-16357. 925p. 1995. pap. 16.95 (*1-56478-088-0*) Dalkey Arch.

Making of Americans: An Opera & a Play from the Novel by Gertrude Stein. Leon Katz. LC 76-76850. 1973. pap. 10.00 (*0-87110-110-6*) Ultramarine Pub.

Making of America's Homeless: From Skid Row to New Poor, 1945-1984. Kim Hopper & Jill Hamberg. LC 85-672771. 91p. (Orig.). 1984. pap. 7.50 (*0-88156-033-2*) Comm Serv Soc NY.

Making of America's Soviet Policy. Ed. by Joseph S. Nye. LC 83-51295. 379p. 1984. pap. 117.50 (*0-7837-8651-4*, 208231400009) Bks Demand.

Making of an Adult Educator: An Autobiographical Journey. Malcolm S. Knowles. LC 89-11121. (Higher Education-Adult & Continuing Education Ser.). 236p. 1989. text 36.95 (*1-55542-169-5*) Jossey-Bass.

Making of an African King: Patrilineal & Matrilineal Struggle among the Effutu of Ghana. Anthony Ephirim-Donkor. LC 98-37137. 226p. 1998. 69.95 (*0-86543-716-5*); pap. 19.95 (*0-86543-717-3*) Africa World.

Making of an Afro American: Martin Robison Delany. Dorothy Sterling. LC 96-7781. (Illus.). 368p. (Orig.). 1996. reprint ed. pap. 14.95 (*0-306-80721-1*) Da Capo.

Making of an Alienated Generation: The Political Socialization of Secondary School Students in Transitional Hong Kong. Sai-Wing Leung. LC 97-73878. (Illus.). 344p. 1997. text 83.95 (*1-84014-159-X*, Pub. by Ashgate Pub) Ashgate Pub Co.

Making of an American. Jacob A. Riis. (Illus.). Date not set. reprint ed. 35.00 (*0-87556-811-4*) Saifer.

Making of an American: An Adaptation of Memorable Tales by Charles Sealsfield. Ulrich S. Carrington. LC 74-77736. (Bicentennial Series in American Studies: No. 2). 223p. reprint ed. pap. 69.20 (*0-8357-8942-X*, 203343800086) Bks Demand.

Making of an American Community: A Case Study of Democracy in a Frontier County. Merle E. Curti. vii, 483p. 1959. 57.50 (*0-8047-0534-8*) Stanford U Pr.

Making of an American Community: A Case Study of Democracy in a Frontier County. Merle E. Curti et al. LC 59-5051. 495p. 1959. reprint ed. pap. 30.00 (*0-7837-5129-X*, 204485700004) Bks Demand.

Making of an American High School: The Credentials Market & Central High School of Philadelphia. David F. Labaree. LC 87-10595. 272p. (C). 1988. 42.50 (*0-300-04091-1*) Yale U Pr.

Making of an American High School: The Credentials Market & the Central High School of Philadelphia, 1838-1939. David F. Labaree. 222p. (C). 1992. reprint ed. pap. 19.00 (*0-300-05469-6*) Yale U Pr.

Making of an American, 1902. Jacob A. Riis. (Illus.). 443p. 1992. pap. 35.00 (*0-87556-121-7*) Saifer.

Making of an American Pluralism: Buffalo, New York, 1825-60. David A. Gerber. (Statue of Liberty-Ellis Island Centennial Ser.). (Illus.). 560p. 1989. text 34.95 (*0-252-01595-9*) U of Ill Pr.

Making of an American Senate: Reconstitutive Change in Congress, 1787. Elaine K. Swift. 264p. (C). 1996. text 42.50 (*0-472-10702-X*, 10702) U of Mich Pr.

Making of an American Thinking Class: Intellectuals & Intelligentsia in Puritan Massachusetts. Darren Staloff. LC 96-53600. 296p. 1997. text 19.95 (*0-19-511352-7*) OUP.

Making of an Arab Nationalist: Ottomanism & Arabism in the Life & Thought of Sati Al-Husri. William L. Cleveland. LC 78-155961. (Princeton Studies on the Near East). 227p. 1971. reprint ed. pap. 70.40 (*0-608-03762-1*, 206458500009) Bks Demand.

Making of an Army "Old China Hand" A Memoir of Colonel David D. Barrett. John N. Hart. LC 85-60379. (China Research Monographs: No. 27). xii, 109p. (Orig.). 1985. pap. 12.00 (*0-912966-75-0*) IEAS.

Making of an Artist: Gautier's Voyage en Espagne. Kathleen Bulgin. LC 88-61673. (ENG & FRE.). 113p. 1988. lib. bdg. 18.95 (*0-917786-64-5*) Summa Pubns.

Making of an Assassin. Henry J. Howley. 160p. 1992. pap. 9.95 (*0-9633061-0-3*) Dart Pubns.

Making of an Atlantic Ruling Class. Kees Van der Pijl. 331p. (C). 1985. pap. 20.00 (*0-86091-801-7*, Pub. by Verso) Norton.

Making of an Avant-Garde: Tel Quel. Niilo Kauppi. LC 93-39605. (Approaches to Semiotics Ser.: No. 1123). (Illus.). xix, 515p. (C). 1994. lib. bdg. 160.00 (*3-11-013952-9*) Mouton.

Making of an Economic Vision: John Paul II's on Social Concern. Ed. by Oliver F. Williams & John W. Houck. 394p. (C). 1991. pap. text 35.50 (*0-8191-8253-2*); lib. bdg. 63.00 (*0-8191-8252-4*) U Pr of Amer.

Making of an Efficient Physician. Sherry A. Delio & George Hein. 110p. 1987. 7.00 (*0-89970-042-X*, OP653895WE) AMA.

Making of an Efficient Physician. Sherry A. Delio & George Hein. 100p. 1995. 52.50 (*1-56829-042-X*, 4694) Med Group Mgmt.

Making of an Egyptian Arab Nationalist: The Early Years of Azzam Pasha, 1893-1936. Ralph M. Coury. 250p. 1998. 45.00 (*0-86372-233-4*, Pub. by Garnet-Ithaca) LPC InBook.

Making of an Engineer. Lawrence P. Grayson. 304p. 1993. text 46.95 (*0-471-59799-6*) Wiley.

Making of an English Country Garden. Deborah Kellaway. 1989. 17.95 (*0-7011-3292-2*) Random.

Making of an English Revolutionary: The Early Parliamentary Career of John Pym. William W. Macdonald. LC 80-65867. 208p. 1982. 32.50 (*0-8386-3018-9*) Fairleigh Dickinson.

Making of an English 'Underclass'? The Social Divisions of Welfare & Labour. Kirk Mann. 192p. 1991. pap. 34.95 (*0-335-09718-9*) OpUniv Pr.

Making of an Enterprise: The Society of Jesus in Portugal, Its Empire, & Beyond--1540-1750. Dauril Alden. LC 94-4820. 1995. 75.00 (*0-8047-2271-4*) Stanford U Pr.

Making of an Immigrant City: Ethnic & Cultural Conflict in Jersey City, New Jersey, 1850-1877. Douglas V. Shaw. LC 76-6366. (Irish Americans Ser.). 1976. 23.95 (*0-405-09358-6*) Ayer.

Making of an Industrial Society: Whickham, 1560-1765. David A. Levine & Keith Wrightson. (Oxford Studies in Social History). (Illus.). 478p. 1991. text 120.00 (*0-19-820066-8*) OUP.

Making of an Inmate. Ann Cordilia. 133p. 1983. 22.95 (*0-87073-722-8*); pap. 13.95 (*0-87073-723-6*) Schenkman Bks Inc.

Making of an Insurgent: An Autobiography, 1882-1919. Fiorello H. LaGuardia. LC 85-24782. (Illus.). 222p. 1986. reprint ed. lib. bdg. 59.50 (*0-313-22769-1*, LAMI, Greenwood Pr) Greenwood.

Making of an Insurrection: Parisian Sections & the Gironde. Morris Slavin. LC 86-4847. (Illus.). 256p. 1986. text 43.50 (*0-674-54328-9*) HUP.

Making of an Islamic Political Leader: Conversations with Hasan Al-Turabi. Mohamed E. Hamdi. LC 98-5352. 144p. (C). 1998. 49.00 (*0-8133-3512-4*, Pub. by Westview) HarpC.

Making of Angels. Virginia L. Kroll. LC 98-140529. (Illus.). 64p. (J). (gr. k-2). 1998. pap. text 7.95 (*1-889108-41-3*) Liv Good News.

Making of Anti-Sexist Men. Harry Christian. LC 93-39857. (Male Orders Ser.). 224p. (C). 1994. pap. 24.99 (*0-415-09762-2*, B4219) Routledge.

Making of Apartheid, 1948-1961: Conflict & Compromise. Deborah Posel. (Illus.). 310p. 1997. pap. text 32.00 (*0-19-571515-2*) OUP.

Making of Armageddon. Mark Cotta Vaz. 176p. (J). 1998. pap. 19.45 (*0-7868-8347-2*, Pub. by Hyperion) Time Warner.

Making of Bamana Sculpture: Creativity & Gender. Sarah C. Brett-Smith. (RES Monographs on Anthropology & Aesthetics). (Illus.). 376p. (C). 1995. text 105.00 (*0-521-44484-5*) Cambridge U Pr.

Making of Beaubourg: A Building Biography of the Centre Pompidou Paris. Nathan Silver. LC 93-45768. (Illus.). 220p. 1994. 28.00 (*0-262-19348-5*) MIT Pr.

Making of Beaubourg: A Building Biography of the Centre Pompidou Paris. Nathan Silver. (Illus.). 220p. 1997. reprint ed. pap. 14.00 (*0-262-69197-3*) MIT Pr.

Making of Belize: Globalization in the Margins. Anne Sutherland. LC 97-48627. 224p. 1998. 59.95 (*0-89789-579-7*, Bergin & Garvey); pap. 19.95 (*0-89789-583-5*, Bergin & Garvey) Greenwood.

Making of Black Revolutionaries. James Forman. LC 97-22031. (Illus.). xxiii, 568p. 1997. pap. 22.50 (*0-295-97659-4*) U of Wash Pr.

Making of Blind Men. Robert A. Scott. LC 80-20558. 145p. (C). 1991. pap. 24.95 (*0-87855-687-7*) Transaction Pubs.

Making of Bourgeois Europe. Colin Mooers. 192p. (C). 1991. pap. 19.00 (*0-86091-507-7*, A4510, Pub. by Verso) Norton.

Making of Brazil: Portuguese Roots, 1500-1822. N. P. MacDonald. LC 97-121666. (Illus.). 520p. 1996. 62.50 (*1-85776-068-9*, Pub. by Book Guild Ltd) Trans-Atl Phila.

Making of British Colonial Development Policy, 1914-1940. Stephen Constantine. (Illus.). 340p. 1984. text 47.50 (*0-7146-3204-X*, BHA-03204, Pub. by F Cass Pubs) Intl Spec Bk.

Making of Byzantine History: Studies Dedicated to Donald M. Nicol on His Seventieth Birthday. Ed. by Roderick Beaton & Charlotte Roueche. (Center for Hellenic Studies). 232p. 1993. 77.95 (*0-86078-385-5*, Pub. by Variorum) Ashgate Pub Co.

Making of Byzantium, 600-1025. Mark Whittow. LC 95-44924. (Illus.). 480p. 1996. pap. 19.95 (*0-520-20497-2*, Pub. by U CA Pr) Cal Prin Full Svc.

***Making of C S Forester's Horatio Hornblower.** Tom McGregor. 136p. 1999. pap. 22.00 (*0-06-107357-1*) HarpC.

Making of Canadian Food Aid Policy. Mark W. Charlton. 256p. (Orig.). 1992. 65.00 (*0-7735-0937-2*, Pub. by McG-Queens Univ Pr); pap. 27.95 (*0-7735-0938-0*, Pub. by McG-Queens Univ Pr) CUP Services.

Making of Channel 4. Peter Catterall. LC 98-29722. 160p. 1999. 22.50 (*0-7146-4485-4*, Pub. by F Cass Pubs); 45.00 (*0-7146-4926-0*, Pub. by F Cass Pubs) Intl Spec Bk.

Making of Chassidim: A Letter Written by the Previous Lubavitcher Rebbe Rabbi Yosef Yitzchak Schneersohn. Tr. by Shimon Neubort from YID. LC 97-124335. 224p. 1996. 18.00 (*1-881400-19-0*) S I E.

Making of Chaucer's English: A Study of Words. Christopher Cannon. LC 97-35262. (Cambridge Studies in Medieval Literature: No. 39). (Illus.). xiii, 435p. (C). 1998. 64.95 (*0-521-59274-7*) Cambridge U Pr.

Making of Citizen & Subject in Contemporary Africa. Mahmood Mamdani. LC 95-25318. (Princeton Studies in Culture, Power & History). 344p. 1996. text 57.50 (*0-691-01107-9*, Pub. by Princeton U Pr) Cal Prin Full Svc.

Making of Citizen Kane. rev. ed. Robert L. Carringer. LC 84-8777. 185p. (C). 1996. pap. 16.95 (*0-520-20567-7*, Pub. by U CA Pr) Cal Prin Full Svc.

Making of Citizens. write for info. (*0-340-65264-0*, Pub. by E A) Routldge.

Making of Citizens: Cities of Peasants Revisited. Bryan Roberts. (Arnold Publications). (Illus.). 272p. 1995. pap. text 39.95 (*0-340-60478-6*, B4020) OUP.

***Making of Citizens: Young People, News & Politics.** David Buckingham. 2000. pap. 22.99 (*0-415-21461-0*) Routledge.

***Making of Citizens: Young People, News & Politics.** David Buckingham. (Media, Education & Culture Ser.). (Illus.). 288p. 2000. 75.00 (*0-415-21460-2*) Routledge.

Making of Citizens Young People, Television News & the Limits of Politics, 1. David Buckingham. 1999. pap. text 22.95 (*0-8153-3412-5*) Garland.

Making of Classical Edinburgh. A. J. Youngson. (Illus.). 448p. 1989. pap. 30.00 (*0-85224-576-9*, Pub. by Edinburgh U Pr) Col U Pr.

Making of Cognitive Science: Essays in Honor of George A. Miller. Ed. by William Hirst. (Illus.). 296p. 1988. text 47.95 (*0-521-34255-4*) Cambridge U Pr.

Making of Colonial Lucknow, 1856-1877. Veena T. Oldenburg. LC 83-16008. 314p. 1984. reprint ed. pap. 97.40 (*0-7837-9407-X*, 206015200004) Bks Demand.

Making of Community Work. David N. Thomas. (Orig.). 1983. 46.25 (*0-7855-0841-4*, Pub. by Natl Inst Soc Work) St Mut.

Making of Conair: And Some History of Auxiliary Equipment for Plastic Processors. John Reib. LC 95-62105. 144p. 1996. text 34.95 (*1-56676-356-8*) Technomic.

Making of Connersville & Fayette County Vol. II: Stories about Its People, Places, & Events. H. Max Walters. Ed. by David N. Walters. LC 88-80563. 290p. (Orig.). 1989. pap. 14.00 (*0-945374-01-1*) LTJ Pubs.

Making of Contemporary Africa: Development of African Society since 1800. 2nd ed. Bill Freund. LC 97-46029. 352p. 1998. 55.00 (*1-55587-805-9*); pap. 19.95 (*1-55587-806-7*) L Rienner.

Making of Contemporary Europe. R. Ben Jones. LC 79-11619. 225p. (C). 1981. 39.95 (*0-8419-0668-8*); pap. 19.50 (*0-8419-0669-6*) Holmes & Meier.

Making of Curriculum: Collected Essays. Ivor F. Goodson. LC 94-36910. (Studies in Curriculum History Ser.: 21). 236p. 1995. 85.00 (*0-7507-0320-2*, Falmer Pr) Taylor & Francis.

Making of Curriculum: Collected Essays. 2nd ed. Ivor F. Goodson. LC 94-36910. (Studies in Curriculum History Ser.: 21). 236p. 1995. pap. 27.95 (*0-7507-0321-0*, Falmer Pr) Taylor & Francis.

Making of Detente: Soviet-American Relations in the Shadow of Vietnam. Keith L. Nelson. LC 94-34423. 248p. 1995. text 35.00 (*0-8018-4883-0*) Johns Hopkins.

Making of Disintegration. Dave Thompson. 1997. pap. 7.95 (*1-896522-24-6*) CN06.

***Making of Disney's Animal Kingdom Theme Park.** Melody Malmberg. LC 98-200587. 160p. (J). 1998. 24.95 (*0-7868-6402-8*, Pub. by Hyperion) Time Warner.

Making of Doctor Who. Terrance Dicks. 1976. 17.95 (*0-8488-0262-4*) Amereon Ltd.

Making of Domesday Book. Vivian H. Galbraith. LC 80-2224. 1981. reprint ed. 36.50 (*0-404-18761-7*) AMS Pr.

Making of Dragonheart. Jody Duncan. 160p. 1996. pap. 16.00 (*1-57297-109-6*) Blvd Books.

***Making of Dungeons & Dragons: The Movie.** John Baxter. 2000. pap. 19.95 (*0-7869-1751-2*) Wizards Coast.

Making of Early Medieval India. B. D. Chattopadhyaya. 284p. 1994. 24.00 (*0-19-563415-2*) OUP.

Making of Early Medieval India. Brajadulal Chattopadhyaya. (Illus.). 282p. 1997. reprint ed. pap. text 15.95 (*0-19-564076-4*) OUP.

Making of Eastern Europe. 2nd ed. Philip Longworth. LC 97-1346. 320p. 1997. pap. 19.95 (*0-312-17445-4*) St Martin.

Making of Eastern Europe: From Prehistory to Postcommunism. 2nd ed. Philip Longworth. LC 97-1346. 320p. 1997. text 55.00 (*0-312-17444-6*) St Martin.

Making of Eastern Europe: From the Earliest Times to 1815. David Turnock. 416p. (C). 1988. lib. bdg. 62.50 (*0-415-01267-8*) Routledge.

Making of Economic Policy. Steven M. Sheffrin. (Macroeconomics & Finance Ser.). (C). 1991. pap. 26.95 (*1-55786-294-X*) Blackwell Pubs.

Making of Economic Policy: A Transaction Cost Politics Perspective. Avinash K. Dixit. (Munich Lectures). (Illus.). 210p. 1996. 25.50 (*0-262-04155-3*) MIT Pr.

Making of Economic Policy: A Transaction Cost Politics Perspective. Avinosh K. Dixit. (Munich Lectures). (Illus.). 216p. 1998. pap. text 12.50 (*0-262-54098-3*) MIT Pr.

Making of Economic Policy: Theory & Evidence from Britain & the United States since 1945. Paul Mosley. LC 83-40518. 240p. 1984. text 29.95 (*0-312-50688-0*) St Martin.

Making of Economic Policy in Africa. Ravi Gulhati. (EDI Seminar Ser.). 119p. 1990. 7.95 (*0-8213-1341-X*, 11341) World Bank.

Making of Economic Reform in Eastern Europe: Conversations with Leading Reformers in Poland, Hungary & the Czech Republic. Ed. by Mario I. Blejer & Fabrizio Coricelli. (Studies of Communism in Transition). 168p. 1995. 80.00 (*1-85898-150-6*) E Elgar.

Making of Economic Society. 10th ed. Robert L. Heilbroner & William Milberg. LC 97-19483. 190p. (C). 1997. pap. text 39.93 (*0-13-874736-9*) P-H.

Making of Economics. Canterbury. 1976. pap. 10.50 (*0-534-00429-6*) Thomson Learn.

***Making of Education Policy in South Africa.** K. B. Hartshorne. LC 99-457109. 1999. write for info. (*0-19-571500-4*) OUP.

Making of Elizabethan Foreign Policy, 1558-1603. R. B. Wernham. (Una's Lectures: No. 3). (Illus.). 120p. 1980. pap. 16.95 (*0-520-03974-2*, Pub. by U CA Pr) Cal Prin Full Svc.

Making of Energy & Telecommunications Policy. Georgia A. Persons. LC 94-34318. 208p. 1995. 59.95 (*0-275-95039-5*, Praeger Pubs) Greenwood.

Making of England, AD 600-700. Ed. by Leslie Webster & Janet Backhouse. (Illus.). 288p. 1992. pap. 35.00 (*0-8020-7721-8*) U of Toronto Pr.

Making of England of Elizabeth. A. B. Hinds. 152p. (C). 1984. reprint ed. pap. text 20.00 (*0-87556-388-0*) Saifer.

Making of England, 55 B. C. to 1399. 7th ed. C. Warren Hollister. 363p. (C). 1996. pap. text 26.36 (*0-669-39716-4*) HM Trade Div.

Making of English Law - King Alfred to the Twelfth Century Vol. 1: Legislation & It's Limits. Patrick Wormald. LC 98-50476. 528p. 1999. 99.95 (*0-631-13496-4*) Blackwell Pubs.

Making of English Reading Audiences, 1790-1832. Jon P. Klancher. LC 86-22443. 223p. reprint ed. pap. 69.20 (*0-608-20447-1*, 207170000002) Bks Demand.

Making of English Teachers. Robert Protherough & Judith Atkinson. (English, Language & Education Ser.). 176p. 1991. pap. 31.95 (*0-335-09374-4*) OpUniv Pr.

Making of English Towns. David W. Lloyd. (Illus.). 290p. 1998. pap. 35.00 (*0-575-06576-1*, Pub. by V Gollancz) Trafalgar.

Making of Enter the Dragon. Robert Clouse. LC 87-81257. 240p. (Orig.). 1987. pap. 13.95 (*0-86568-098-1*, 145) Unique Pubns.

Making of Equal Opportunities: Policies in Universities. S. Neal. LC 97-12934. 176p. 1997. pap. 37.95 (*0-335-19807-4*) OpUniv Pr.

Making of Europe: Conquest, Colonization, & Cultural Change, 950-1350. Robert Bartlett. 447p. 1993. text 55.00 (*0-691-03298-X*, Pub. by Princeton U Pr) Cal Prin Full Svc.

Making of Europe: Conquest, Colonization & Cultural Change, 950-1350. Robert Bartlett. LC 93-195830. 432p. 1993. write for info. (*0-7139-9074-0*, A Lane) Viking Penguin.

Making of Europe: Conquest, Colonization, & Cultural Change, 9500-1350. Robert Bartlett. 447p. 1993. pap. text 19.95 (*0-691-03780-9*, Pub. by Princeton U Pr) Cal Prin Full Svc.

Making of European Environmental Policy: The Netherlands, the EU & Acid Rain. J. Duncan Liefferink. LC 96-28199. (Issues in Environmental Politics Ser.). 216p. 1997. text 69.95 (*0-7190-4924-5*, Pub. by Manchester Univ Pr) St Martin.

Making of Exile Cultures: Iranian Television in Los Angeles. Hamid Naficy. LC 93-13428. 302p. 1993. pap. 19.95 (*0-8166-2087-3*); text 49.95 (*0-8166-2084-9*) U of Minn Pr.

Making of Fascism. Dahlia S. Elazar. LC 97-40884. 1999. 56.00 (*0-275-95864-7*, Praeger Pubs) Greenwood.

Making of Federal Coal Policy. Robert H. Nelson. LC 83-7155. (Duke Press Policy Studies). (Illus.). xi, 261p. (C). 1983. text 46.95 (*0-8223-0497-X*) Duke.

Making of Fianna Fail Power in Ireland, 1923-1948. Richard Dunphy. 356p. 1995. text 75.00 (*0-19-820474-4*) OUP.

Making of Foreign Policy. Andrew Berding. LC 66-14226. (U. S. A. Survey Ser.). 102p. 1966. 4.95 (*0-87107-002-2*) Potomac.

Making of Frederick the Great. Edith Simon. LC 76-51768. (Illus.). 296p. 1977. reprint ed. lib. bdg. 65.00 (*0-8371-9440-7*, SIMF, Greenwood Pr) Greenwood.

Making of Geology: Earth Science in Britain, 1660-1815. Roy Porter. LC 76-56220. 300p. reprint ed. pap. 85.50 (*0-608-13048-6*, 2024515) Bks Demand.

Making of Global Enterprises. Ed. by Geoffrey Jones. LC 93-5942. 205p. 1994. 45.00 (*0-7146-4554-0*, Pub. by F Cass Pubs); pap. 19.50 (*0-7146-4103-0*, Pub. by F Cass Pubs) Intl Spec Bk.

Making of Go down, Moses. James Early. LC 72-80404. 140p. 1972. 12.95 (*0-87074-003-2*) SMU Press.

Making of God's Little Barber & Life in the Barber Shop. Russell L. Carrithers. Ed. by John S. Rodman. (Illus.). 303p. 1998. pap. 12.95 (*0-9664085-0-0*) Barber-Shop.

Making of Goodnight Moon: A 50th Anniversary Retrospective. Leonard S. Marcus. LC 97-126836. (Trophy Nonfiction Bk.). (Illus.). 32p. (J). 1997. pap. 5.95 (*0-06-446192-0*, HarpTrophy) HarpC Child Bks.

Making of Great Men: Male Domination & Power among the New Guinea Baruya. Maurice Godelier. (Cambridge Studies in Social & Cultural Anthropology: No. 56). (Illus.). 275p. 1986. pap. text 25.95 (*0-521-31212-4*) Cambridge U Pr.

Making of Haiti: The Saint Domingue Revolution from Below. Carolyn E. Fick. LC 90-30956. 376p. 1990. pap. text 21.50 (*0-87049-667-0*) U of Tenn Pr.

Making of Harcourt General: A History of Growth Through Diversification, 1922-1992. Harvard Business Review Staff. 320p. 1994. 39.95 (*0-07-103589-3*) McGraw.

Making of Harcourt General: A History of Growth Through Diversification, 1922-1992. Bettye H. Pruitt. LC 93-50567. 320p. 1994. 35.00 (*0-87584-509-6*) Harvard Busn.

An Asterisk (*) at the beginning of an entry indicates that the title is appearing for the first time.

Making of Hawaii: A Study in Social Evolution. 2nd ed. William F. Blackman. LC 75-35175. 37.50 (*0-404-14204-4*) AMS Pr.

Making of Hibernian. Alan Lugton. 300p. 1996. 45.00 (*0-85976-424-9*, Pub. by J Donald) St Mut.

*__Making of Hibernian.__ Alan Lugton. 228p. 2000. pap. 25.95 (*0-85976-509-1*, Pub. by J Donald) Dufour.

Making of Hibernian, Vol. 3. Alan Lugton. 280p. 1998. pap. 47.85 (*0-85976-498-2*, Pub. by J Donald) St Mut.

Making of High Performance Athletes: Discipline, Diversity, & Ethics. Debra Shogun. LC 99-189646. 160p. 1999. text 40.00 (*0-8020-4395-X*); pap. text 14.95 (*0-8020-8201-7*) U of Toronto Pr.

Making of History: A Study of the Literary Forgeries of James Macpherson & Thomas Chatterton in Relation to Eighteenth Century Ideas of History & Fiction. Ian Haywood. LC 85-45753. 232p. 1987. 38.50 (*0-8386-3261-0*) Fairleigh Dickinson.

Making of Homeric Verse: The Collected Papers of Milman Parry. Milman Parry. Ed. by Adam M. Parry. (Illus.). 552p. 1987. pap. text 35.00 (*0-19-520560-X*) OUP.

Making of Homeric Verse: The Collected Papers of Milman Parry. Ed. by Adam M. Parry & Richard M. Dorson. LC 80-747. (Folklore of the World Ser.). (Illus.). 1981. reprint ed. lib. bdg. 63.95 (*0-405-13321-9*) Ayer.

Making of Hong Kong Society: The Studies of Class Formation in Early Hong Kong. Wellington K. Chan. (Illus.). 272p. 1991. 65.00 (*0-19-827320-7*) OUP.

Making of Hunting Decoys. William Veasey. LC 86-62452. (Illus.). 256p. 1986. 45.00 (*0-88740-073-6*) Schiffer.

Making of India: A Historical Survey. Ranbir Vohra. LC 96-43435. 344p. (C). 1997. pap. text 30.95 (*1-56324-695-3*) M E Sharpe.

Making of India: A Historical Survey. Ranbir Vohra. LC 96-43435. 344p. (C). (gr. 13-13). 1997. text 74.95 (*1-56324-694-5*) M E Sharpe.

*__Making of India: A Historical Survey.__ 2nd ed. Ranbir Vohra. 368p. 2000. text 72.95 (*0-7656-0711-5*) M E Sharpe.

Making of India & Indian Traditions. Jacob Pandian. LC 94-16912. 304p. 1994. pap. text 34.40 (*0-13-124421-3*) P-H.

Making of India & Pakistan: Selected Documents, 6 vols. S. R. Bakshi. 4100p. 1997. 4000.00 (*81-7100-913-1*, Pub. by Print Hse) St Mut.

Making of Indian Literature: A Consolidated Report of Workshops on Literary Translation, 1986-88. Ed. by Ayyappa Paniker. (C). 1991. 17.50 (*81-7201-115-6*, Pub. by Indian Pubs) S Asia.

Making of India's Constitution. H. R. Khanna. (C). 1989. 40.00 (*0-89771-755-4*, Pub. by Eastern Book) St Mut.

Making of India's Foreign Policy. Jayantanuja Bandyopadhyaya. 362p. 1991. 19.95 (*0-940500-35-3*) Asia Bk Corp.

*__Making of Indo-Persian Culture: Indian & French Studies.__ Ed. by Muzaffar Alam. 2000. 58.00 (*81-7304-210-1*, Pub. by Manohar) S Asia.

Making of Industrial Relations: The Ahmedabad Textile Industry, 1918-1939. Sujata Patel. 172p. 1988. 18.95 (*0-19-562064-X*) OUP.

*__Making of Intelligence.__ Ken Richardson. 2000. 24.95 (*0-231-12004-4*) Col U Pr.

Making of Iran's Islamic Revolution: From Monarchy to Islamic Republic. 2nd ed. Mohsen M. Milani. LC 94-14600. 268p. (C). 1994. pap. 29.00 (*0-8133-8476-1*, Pub. by Westview) HarpC.

Making of Iraq, 1900-1963: Capital, Power & Ideology. Samira Haj. LC 96-7618. (SUNY Series in the Social & Economic History of the Middle East). 215p. (C). 1997. text 57.50 (*0-7914-3241-6*); pap. text 18.95 (*0-7914-3242-4*) State U NY Pr.

Making of Ireland: A History. James F. Lydon. LC 98-13707. 432p. 1998. pap. 22.99 (*0-415-01348-8*) Routledge.

Making of Ireland: A History. James F. Lydon. LC 98-13707. 432p. (C). 1998. 75.00 (*0-415-01347-X*) Routledge.

Making of Ireland: Landscapes in Geology. Michael Williams & David Harper. (Illus.). 98p. 1999. 48.00 (*1-898162-06-9*, Pub. by IMMEL Pubng) Trans-Atl Phila.

Making of Ireland & Its Undoing, 1200-1600. Alice S. Green. LC 75-37883. (Select Bibliographies Reprint Ser.). 1977. reprint ed. 30.95 (*0-8369-6720-8*) Ayer.

Making of Israeli Militarism. Uri Ben-Eliezer. LC 97-46020. 320p. Date not set. 35.00 (*0-253-33387-3*) Ind U Pr.

Making of Jacobean Culture: James I & the Renegotiation of Elizabethan Literary Practice. Curtis Perry. (Illus.). 296p. (C). 1997. text 59.95 (*0-521-57406-4*) Cambridge U Pr.

*__Making of Japanese Manchuria, 1904-1932.__ Yoshihisa Tak Matsusaka. (Illus.). 475p. 2000. 49.50 (*0-674-00369-1*) HUP.

Making of Japan's China Policy. Lalima Varma. ix, 186p. 1991. 18.00 (*81-85163-23-5*, Pub. by Kalinga) Nataraj Bks.

Making of Jewish & Christian Worship. Ed. by Paul F. Bradshaw & Lawrence A. Hoffman. LC 90-70856. (Two Liturgical Traditions Ser.: Vol. 1). (C). 1992. pap. text 14.00 (*0-268-01208-3*) U of Notre Dame Pr.

Making of Johnson's Dictionary, 1746-1773. 2nd ed. Allen Reddick. LC 96-151729. (Studies in Publishing & Printing History). (Illus.). 274p. (C). 1996. pap. text 19.95 (*0-521-56838-2*) Cambridge U Pr.

Making of Judge Dredd. David Chute et al. LC 99-233628. (Illus.). 192p. (J). 1995. pap. 15.95 (*0-7868-8106-2*, Pub. by Hyperion) Time Warner.

*__Making of Kind of Blue: Miles Davis & His Masterpiece.__ Eric Nisenson. 2000. 22.95 (*0-312-26617-0*) St Martin.

*__Making of Kingdoms.__ Ed. by Tania Dickinson & David Griffiths. (Anglo-Saxon Studies in Archaeology & History: Vol. 10). (Illus.). 224p. 1999. pap. 60.00 (*0-947816-93-3*, Pub. by Oxford Univ Comm Arch) David Brown.

Making of King's Lynn: A Documentary Survey. Dorothy M. Owen. (Records of Social & Economic History Ser.: Vol. IX). 1984. 69.00 (*0-19-726027-6*) OUP.

Making of Knowledge in Composition: Portrait of an Emerging Field. Stephen M. North. LC 87-5141. 403p. (C). 1987. pap. text 27.50 (*0-86709-151-7*, 0151, Pub. by Boynton Cook Pubs) Heinemann.

Making of Labour Law in Europe: A Comparative Study of Nine Countries up to 1945. B. Hepple. Ed. by Paul O'Higgins. (Studies in Labour & Social Law). 428p. 1986. text 130.00 (*0-7201-1697-X*) Continuum.

Making of Landscape Photographs: A Practical Guide to the Art & Techniques. Charlie Waite. (Illus.). 160p. 1993. pap. 19.95 (*1-85585-149-0*, Pub. by Collins & Br) Trafalgar.

Making of Language. Mike Beaken. 208p. 1996. pap. 19.50 (*0-7486-0717-X*, Pub. by Edinburgh U Pr) Col U Pr.

Making of Late Antiquity. Peter Brown. (Jackson Lectures). 152p. (C). 1993. pap. 13.50 (*0-674-54321-1*) HUP.

Making of Latin: An Introduction to Latin, Greek & English Etymology. R. S. Conway. 1983. 32.50 (*0-89241-335-2*) Caratzas.

Making of Latin: An Introduction to Latin, Greek & English Etymology. R. S. Conway. 1995. pap. 18.00 (*0-89241-341-7*) Caratzas.

*__Making of Latin America.__ 2000. write for info. (*0-582-09234-5*) Pearson Educ.

*__Making of Latin London: Salsa Music, Place & Identity.__ Patria Roman-Velazquez. LC 99-72849. 167p. 1999. 61.95 (*1-84014-881-0*, Pub. by Ashgate Pub) Ashgate Pub Co.

Making of Legends: More True Stories of Frontier America. Mark Dugan. LC 97-4096. (Illus.). 300p. 1997. pap. 19.95 (*0-8040-0996-1*); text 36.95 (*0-8040-0995-3*) Swallow.

Making of Luke - Acts. Henry J. Cadbury. 386p. 1999. pap. 24.95 (*1-56563-453-5*) Hendrickson MA.

Making of Malcolm Lowry's "Under the Volcano" Frederick Asals. LC 96-2221. x, 476p. 1996. 85.00 (*0-8203-1826-4*) U of Ga Pr.

Making of Man-Midwifery: Childbirth in England, 1660-1770. Adrian Wilson. (Illus.). 256p. (C). 1995. 39.50 (*0-674-54323-8*) HUP.

Making of Man-Midwifery: Childbirth in England, 1660-1770. Adrian Wilson. 288p. 1995. 75.00 (*1-85728-292-2*, Pub. by UCL Pr Ltd) Taylor & Francis.

*__Making of Manchester Jewelry.__ Bill Williams. (Parkes-Wiener Series on Jewish Studies). 332p. 1999. pap. (*0-85303-375-7*) Intl Spec Bk.

*__Making of Manchester Jewelry.__ Bill Williams. (Parkes-Wiener Series on Jewish Studies). (Illus.). 332p. 1999. 47.50 (*0-85303-368-4*) Intl Spec Bk.

Making of Manchester Jewry, 1740-1875. Bill Williams. LC 75-43635. (Illus.). 400p. 1976. 49.50 (*0-8419-0252-6*) Holmes & Meier.

Making of Mark. A. Q. Morton. LC 95-32755. (Biblical Press Ser.: Vol. 41). 112p. 1996. text 59.95 (*0-7734-2393-1*, Mellen Biblical Pr) E Mellen.

Making of Mark: An Exploration. Harold Riley. LC 89-37902. 275p. (C). 1989. 25.00 (*0-86554-359-3*, MUP/H297) Mercer Univ Pr.

Making of Martin Luther King & the Civil Rights Movement. Ed. by Brian Ward & Tony Badger. 336p. (C). 1996. text 55.00 (*0-8147-9295-2*) NYU Pr.

Making of Martin Luther King & the Civil Rights Movement. Ed. by Brian Ward & Tony Badger. 336p. (C). 1996. pap. text 19.50 (*0-8147-9296-0*) NYU Pr.

Making of Marx's Capital, Vol. 1. Roman Rosdolsky. 452p. (C). 1992. pap. 22.95 (*0-86104-915-2*, Pub. by Pluto GBR) Stylus Pub VA.

Making of Marx's "Capital", Vol. 2. Roman Rosdolsky. (C). pap. 22.95 (*0-86104-305-7*, Pub. by Pluto GBR) Stylus Pub VA.

Making of Marx's Critical Theory: A Bibliographical Analysis. Allen Oakley. LC 83-9732. 143p. (Orig.). 1983. pap. 9.95 (*0-7100-9570-8*, Routledge Thoemms) Routledge.

Making of Masculinities: The New Men's Studies. Ed. by Harry Brod. LC 86-28796. 304p. 1987. text 44.95 (*0-04-497035-8*); pap. text 22.95 (*0-04-497036-6*) Routledge.

Making of McPaper: The Inside Story of U. S. A. Today. Peter Prichard. 1989. mass mkt. 5.95 (*0-312-91168-8*) St Martin.

Making of McPaper: The Inside Story of U. S. A. Today. Peter Prichard. 1989. pap. 5.95 (*0-318-42582-3*) St Martin.

Making of Meaning: Metaphors, Models, & Maxims for Writing Teachers. Ann E. Berthoff. LC 81-9948. 208p. (Orig.). (C). 1981. pap. text 22.00 (*0-86709-003-0*, 0003, Pub. by Boynton Cook Pubs) Heinemann.

*__Making of Memory.__ Steven Rose. 2000. pap. 14.95 (*0-553-40748-1*, Pub. by Transworld Publishers Ltd) Trafalgar.

Making of Men: Masculinities, Sexualities & Schooling. Mairtin Mac an Ghaill. LC 93-37338. 1994. pap. 32.95 (*0-335-15781-5*) OpUniv Pr.

Making of Methodism. Barrie Tabraham. 1996. pap. 18.00 (*0-7162-0499-1*) TPI PA.

*__Making of Miami Beach, 1933-1941: The Architecture of Lawrence Murray Dixon.__ Jean-Francois Lejeune & Allan T. Shulman. (Illus.). 240p. 2000. text 50.00 (*0-8478-2280-X*) Rizzoli Intl.

Making of Michigan, 1820-1860: A Pioneer Anthology. Ed. by Justin L. Kestenbaum. LC 89-5457. (Great Lakes Bks.). 422p. 1990. pap. 19.95 (*0-8143-1919-X*) Wayne St U Pr.

Making of Microsoft: How Bill Gates & His Team Created the World's Most Successful Software Company. Daniel Ichbiah & Susan L. Knepper. 320p. 1992. pap. 12.95 (*1-55958-225-1*) Prima Pub.

Making of Middle English, 1765-1910 David Matthews. LC 98-53478. (Medieval Cultures Ser.). 1999. write for info. (*0-8166-3186-7*) U of Minn Pr.

*__Making of Middle English, 1765-1910.__ David Matthews. LC 98-53478. 1999. 39.95 (*0-8166-3185-9*) U of Minn Pr.

Making of Middlebrow Culture. Joan S. Rubin. LC 91-22241. (Illus.). xxii, 416p. (C). 1992. pap. 19.95 (*0-8078-4354-7*) U of NC Pr.

*__Making of Milwaukee.__ John Gurda. 1999. 24.95 (*0-938076-14-0*) Milwaukee Cty Hist Soc.

Making of Mind: A Personal Account of Soviet Psychology. Aleksandr R. Luria. Ed. by Michael Cole & Sheila Cole. (Illus.). 234p. 1979. pap. 17.50 (*0-674-54327-0*) HUP.

Making of Mind: A Personal Account of Soviet Psychology. Aleksandr R. Luria. Ed. by Michael Cole & Sheila Cole. (Illus.). 234p. (C). 1979. 30.00 (*0-674-54326-2*) HUP.

Making of Ministry. Timothy F. Sedgwick. LC 93-22815. 119p. 1993. pap. 10.95 (*1-56101-082-0*) Cowley Pubns.

Making of Mizoram: Role of Laldenga, 2 vols. Suhas Chatterjee. 445p. (C). 1994. pap. 325.00 (*81-85880-38-7*, Pub. by Print Hse) St Mut.

Making of Modern Africa: A Guide to Archives. Chris Cook. 224p. 1995. 35.00 (*0-8160-2071-X*) Facts on File.

Making of Modern Alabama: State History & Geography. (Illus.). 256p. (YA). (gr. 9). 1993. 24.95 (*1-882700-01-5*) Yellowhammer.

Making of Modern Belize: Politics, Society & British Colonialism in Central America. Cedric H. Grant. LC 75-36022. (Cambridge Commonwealth Ser.). 416p. reprint ed. pap. 118.60 (*0-608-15729-5*, 2031661) Bks Demand.

Making of Modern British Politics, 1867-1939. 2nd ed. Martin Pugh. LC 92-22093. 344p. 1993. pap. 32.95 (*0-631-17928-3*) Blackwell Pubs.

Making of Modern Cameroon: A History of Substate Nationalism & Disparate Union, 1914-1961. Emmanuel Chiabi. LC 97-33470. 304p. (C). 1997. 42.50 (*0-7618-0896-5*) U Pr of Amer.

Making of Modern Colombia: A Nation in Spite of Itself. David Bushnell. 384p. 1994. pap. 22.50 (*0-520-08289-3*, Pub. by U CA Pr) Cal Prin Full Svc.

Making of Modern Drama. Richard Gilman. 1987. pap. 10.95 (*0-306-80293-7*) Da Capo.

*__Making of Modern Drama: A Study of Bhuchner, Ibsen, Strindberg, Chekhov, Pirandello, Brecht, Handke.__ Richard Gilman. LC 99-45334. 320p. 2000. pap. 18.00 (*0-300-07902-8*) Yale U Pr.

*__Making of Modern Economics: The Lives & Ideas of the Great Thinkers.__ Mark Skousen. (Illus.). 384p. 1999. 74.95 (*0-7656-0479-5*) M E Sharpe.

Making of Modern Ethiopia, 1896-1974. Teshale Tibebu. LC 94-42814. 276p. (C). 1994. 49.95 (*1-56902-000-0*); pap. 16.95 (*1-56902-001-9*) Red Sea Pr.

Making of Modern Europe 1648 to 1780. Geoffrey Treasure. (Illus.). 700p. (Orig.). 1985. pap. 16.95 (*0-416-72370-5*, 9521) Routledge.

Making of Modern India: Rammohun Roy to Gandhi & Nehru. G. N. Raghavan. (C). 1988. 24.00 (*81-212-0112-8*, Pub. by Gian Publng Hse) S Asia.

Making of Modern Intellectual Property Law: The British Experience, 1760-1911. Brad Sherman & Lionel Bently. 240p. (C). 1999. text 69.95 (*0-521-56363-1*) Cambridge U Pr.

Making of Modern Irish History. D. George Boyce. 272p. (C). 1996. pap. 22.99 (*0-415-12171-X*) Routledge.

Making of Modern Irish History: Revisionism & the Revisionist Controversy. Alan O'Day. Ed. by D. George Boyce. LC 95-36523. 272p. (C). 1996. 70.00 (*0-415-09819-X*) Routledge.

*__Making of Modern Japan.__ Marius B. Jansen. (Illus.). 896p. 2000. 35.00 (*0-674-00334-9*) HUP.

Making of Modern Japan. John H. Gubbins. LC 73-169760. (Select Bibliographies Reprint Ser.). 1977. reprint ed. 25.95 (*0-8369-5980-9*) Ayer.

Making of Modern Japan. John H. Gubbins. LC 72-82095. (Japan Library). (Illus.). 1973. reprint ed. lib. bdg. 32.00 (*0-8420-1390-3*) Scholarly Res Inc.

Making of Modern Japan. 2nd ed. Kenneth B. Pyle. 240p. (C). 1995. pap. text 27.96 (*0-669-20020-4*) HM Trade Div.

Making of Modern Japan: A Reader. Ed. & Intro. by Tim Megarry. 619p. (C). 1996. pap. 39.00 (*1-874529-35-3*, Pub. by Greenwich Univ Pr) NYU Pr.

Making of Modern Libya: State Formation, Colonization, & Resistance, 1830-1932. Ali A. Ahmida. LC 93-18526. (SUNY Series in the Social & Economic History of the Middle East). 222p. (C). 1994. text 22.50 (*0-7914-1761-1*) State U NY Pr.

Making of Modern Marriage: Matrimonial Control & the Rise of Sentiment in Neuchatel, 1550-1800. Jeffrey R. Watt. LC 92-52775. (Illus.). 320p. 1993. text 45.00 (*0-8014-2493-3*) Cornell U Pr.

Making of Modern Memphis. John Branston & Kenneth Neill. (Illus.). 196p. 1996. reprint ed. pap. 7.50 (*0-9649821-1-0*) Contemp Media.

Making of Modern Nepal: A Study of History, Art & Culture of the Principalities of Western Nepal. Ram N. Pandey. 1997. pap. 106.00 (*0-7855-7436-0*, Pub. by Ratna Pustak Bhandar) St Mut.

Making of Modern New Guinea. Stephen W. Reed. LC 75-30077. (Institute of Pacific Relations Ser.). (Illus.). 352p. 1982. reprint ed. 47.50 (*0-404-59554-5*) AMS Pr.

Making of Modern New Guinea-with Special Reference to Culture Contact in the Mandated Territory. W. S. Read. LC 43-7044. (American Philosophical Society, Memoirs Ser.: Vol. 18). 353p. reprint ed. pap. 109.50 (*0-608-11769-2*, 200036400025) Bks Demand.

*__Making of Modern Russia.__ 3rd ed. Lionel Kochan. LC 98-161236. 544p. 1998. pap. 15.95 (*0-14-015715-8*) Viking Penguin.

*__Making of Modern Sindh: British Policy & Social Change in the Nineteenth Century.__ Hamida Khuhro. (Illus.). 384p. 1999. text 45.00 (*0-19-579008-1*) OUP.

Making of Modern South Africa: Conquest, Segregation & Apartheid. 2nd ed. Nigel Worden. (Historical Association Studies). (Illus.). 192p. (C). 1995. pap. 16.95 (*0-631-19882-2*) Blackwell Pubs.

*__Making of Modern South Africa: Conquest, Segregation & Apartheid.__ 3rd ed. Nigel Worden. LC 99-56506. (Historical Association Studies). (Illus.). 224p. 2000. text 54.95 (*0-631-21716-9*); pap. text 22.95 (*0-631-21661-8*) Blackwell Pubs.

*__Making of Modern Switzerland, 1848-1998.__ Michael Butler et al. LC 00-27824. 2000. write for info. (*0-312-23459-7*) St Martin.

Making of Modern Tapestry: My Voyage of Discovery. Silvia Heyden. (Illus.). 208p. 1998. pap. 29.90 (*0-9663450-1-0*) S Heyden.

Making of Modern Tibet. A. Tom Grunfeld. LC 86-29840. 288p. (C). (gr. 13). 1988. pap. text 38.95 (*0-87332-503-6*) M E Sharpe.

Making of Modern Tibet. rev. ed. A. Tom Grunfeld. LC 96-11504. 370p. (C). (gr. 13). 1996. text 80.95 (*1-56324-713-5*, East Gate Bk); pap. text 27.95 (*1-56324-714-3*, East Gate Bk) M E Sharpe.

Making of Modern Turkey. Feroz Ahmad. LC 93-20425. (Making of the Modern Middle East Ser.). 240p. (C). 1993. pap. 25.99 (*0-415-07836-9*, B0275) Routledge.

Making of Modern Turkey. Feroz Ahmad. LC 93-20425. (Making of the Modern Middle East Ser.). 240p. 1993. 55.00 (*0-415-07835-0*, B0271) Routledge.

Making of Modern Uganda. Kenneth Ingham. LC 83-1698. 303p. (C). 1983. reprint ed. lib. bdg. 41.50 (*0-313-23114-1*, INMU, Greenwood Pr) Greenwood.

Making of Moll Flanders. Anthony Hayward. (Illus.). 96p. 1998. 24.95 (*0-7472-7742-7*, Pub. by Headline Bk Pub) Trafalgar.

Making of Molly March. large type ed. Juliet Dymoke. (Ulverscroft Large Print Ser.). 528p. 1997. 27.99 (*0-7089-3734-9*) Ulverscroft.

Making of Monetary Union. David Begg. 1994. pap. text, student ed. 14.95 (*1-898128-05-7*, Pub. by Ctr Econ Policy Res) Brookings.

Making of Monkey King. Robert Kraus & Debby Chen. Tr. by Nguyen N. Ngan. LC 97-80532. (Adventures of Monkey King Ser.: No. 1). (Illus.). 34p. (J). (gr. 2-5). 1998. 16.95 (*1-57227-043-8*) Pan Asian Pubns.

Making of Monkey King. Robert Kraus & Debby Chen. Tr. by Pauling Kobylinski. (Adventures of Monkey King Ser.: No. 1). (ENG & SPA., Illus.). 32p. (J). (gr. 3-6). 1998. 16.95 (*1-57227-044-6*) Pan Asian Pubns.

Making of Monkey King. Robert Kraus & Debby Chen. Tr. by Nguyen N. Ngan. (Adventures of Monkey King Ser.: No. 1). (CHI & ENG., Illus.). 34p. (J). (gr. 3-6). 1998. 16.95 (*1-57227-045-4*); 16.95 (*1-57227-046-2*) Pan Asian Pubns.

Making of Monkey King: English/Hmong. Robert Kraus & Debby Chen. Tr. by Xe Susane Moua. (Adventures of Monkey King Ser.). (Illus.). 34p. (J). (gr. 3-6). 1998. 16.95 (*1-57227-047-0*) Pan Asian Pubns.

Making of Moral Theology: A Study of the Roman Catholic Tradition (Martin D'Arcy Memorial Lectures 1981-1982) John Mahoney. (Illus.). 382p. 1989. pap. text 23.00 (*0-19-826730-4*) OUP.

Making of Music. Ralph Vaughan Williams. LC 76-1009. (Illus.). 61p. 1976. reprint ed. lib. bdg. 49.50 (*0-8371-8771-0*, WIMM, Greenwood Pr) Greenwood.

Making of Musical Instruments. Thomas C. Young. LC 79-90698. (Essay Index Reprint Ser.). 1977. 23.95 (*0-8369-1317-5*) Ayer.

Making of My Fair Lady. Keith Garebian. (Illus.). 135p. (Orig.). 1993. pap. 9.95 (*1-55022-161-2*, Pub. by ECW) LPC InBook.

Making of My Special Hand: Madison's Story. Jamee R. Heelan. LC 98-18086. (Rehabilitation Institute of Chicago Learning Book Ser.). (Illus.). 32p. (J). (gr. 1-5). 2000. 14.95 (*1-56145-186-X*) Peachtree Pubs.

*__Making of NAFTA: How the Deal Was Done.__ Maxwell A. Cameron & Brian W. Tomlin. LC 00-8915. 2000. write for info. (*0-8014-3800-4*) Cornell U Pr.

Making of Neo-Palladianism: Lord Burlington's House & Garden. John Harris. LC 93-49024. (Illus.). 224p. 1994. 55.00 (*0-300-05983-3*) Yale U Pr.

Making of Neoclassical Economics. John F. Henry. 256p. (C). (gr. 13). 1990. text 74.95 (*0-04-445664-6*) Routledge.

Making of New Deal Democrats: Voting Behavior & Realignment in Boston, 1920-1940. Gerald H. Gamm. LC 89-32478. (Illus.). 296p. 1990. pap. text 26.00 (*0-226-28061-6*); lib. bdg. 49.95 (*0-226-28060-8*) U Ch Pr.

Making of New Germany, 2 Vols., Set. Philip Scheidemann. Tr. by J. E. Michell. (Select Bibliographies Reprint Ser.). 1977. 51.95 (*0-8369-5615-X*) Ayer.

Making of New World Slavery: From the Baroque to the Modern, 1492-1800. Robin Blackburn. LC 96-45603. 496p. 1997. 65.00 (*1-85984-890-7*, Pub. by Verso) Norton.

Making of New World Slavery: From the Baroque to the Modern, 1492-1800. Robin Blackburn. 608p. 1998. pap. 25.00 (*1-85984-195-3*, Pub. by Verso) Norton.

M

Making of Nicholas Longworth: Annals of an American Family. Clara L. De Chambrun. (Select Bibliographies Reprint Ser.). 1977. reprint ed. 29.95 (*0-8369-5882-9*) Ayer.
Making of Northern Nigeria. C. W. Orr. 320p. 1986. 250.00 (*1-85077-138-3*, Pub. by Darf Pubs Ltd) St Mut.
Making of Orcadia: Narrative Identity in the Prose Work of George Mackay Brown. Berthold Schoene. LC 95-17799. (Anglo-Amerikanische Studien Ser.: Vol. 6). 296p. 1995. pap. 52.95 (*3-631-48770-3*) P Lang Pubng.
Making of Oregon: A Study in Historical Geography. Samuel N. Dicken & Emily F. Dicken. LC 79-89087. (Two Centuries of Oregon Geography Ser.: Vol. 1). (Illus.). 222p. 17.95 (*0-87595-081-7*) Oregon Hist.
Making of Our Middle Schools. Elmer E. Brown. LC 77-89153. (American Education: Its Men, Institutions, & Ideas. Series 1). 1977. reprint ed. 35.95 (*0-405-01391-4*) Ayer.
Making of Paul Klee's Career, 1914-1920. Otto K. Werckmeister. LC 88-27423. (Illus.). 368p. 1989. 54.00 (*0-226-89358-8*) U Ch Pr.
Making of Pennsylvania. Sydney G. Fisher. 1993. reprint ed. lib. bdg. 89.00 (*0-7812-5453-1*) Rprt Serv.
Making of Percy's Reliques. Nick Groom. 304p. 1999. 75.00 (*0-19-818459-X*) OUP.
*__Making of Peter Grimes: Essays.__ Ed. by Paul Banks. (Aldeburgh Studies in Music). (Illus.). 298p. 2000. pap. 35.00 (*0-85115-791-2*) Boydell & Brewer.
Making of Peter Grimes: The Facsimile of Britten's Composition Draft. Ed. by Paul Banks. 256p. (C). 1996. 170.00 (*0-85115-632-0*) Boydell & Brewer.
Making of Piers Plowman. Malcolm Godden. 1989. text 56.95 (*0-582-05924-0*, Pub. by Addison-Wesley) Longman.
Making of Piers Plowman. Malcolm Godden. LC 89-37583. 227p. 1990. reprint ed. pap. 70.40 (*0-608-03588-2*, 206441100009) Bks Demand.
Making of Planning Applications. RICS Staff. (C). 1991. text 90.00 (*0-85406-497-4*, Pub. by R-I-C-S Bks) St Mut.
Making of Plowshares. Vernelle B. Allen. 77p. (Orig.). 1994. pap. write for info. (*1-885984-14-6*) Wings of Healing.
Making of Political Identities. Ernesto Laclau. LC 93-50722. (Phronesis Ser.). 320p. (C). 1994. pap. 20.00 (*0-86091-663-4*, Pub. by Verso) Norton.
Making of Portuguese Democracy. Kenneth Maxwell. 264p. (C). 1995. text 59.95 (*0-521-46077-8*) Cambridge U Pr.
Making of Portuguese Democracy. Kenneth Maxwell. 264p. 1997. pap. text 19.95 (*0-521-58596-1*) Cambridge U Pr.
*__Making of Post-Protestant Christianity.__ Ben M. Carter. LC 00-9578. 2000. pap. write for info. (*0-941037-87-8*, BIBAL Press) D & F Scott.
Making of Post-War Canada. Peter S. Li. 200p. 1997. pap. text 24.00 (*0-19-540920-5*) OUP.
Making of Pretty Hate Machine & the Downward Spiral. Alan Cross. 1997. pap. 7.95 (*1-896522-31-9*) CN06.
Making of Pride & Predjudice. Birtwistle. 1995. pap. 20.95 (*0-14-025157-X*, Pub. by Pnguin Bks Ltd) Trafalgar.
Making of Quantum Leap. Scott Nance. 208p. 1996. 5.50 (*0-06-105438-0*, HarperPrism) HarpC.
Making of Rehabilitation: A Political Economy of Medical Specialization, 1890-1980. Glenn Gritzer & Arnold Arluke. LC 84-28008. (Comparative Studies of Health Systems & Medical Care: Vol. 15). 1985. pap. 15.95 (*0-520-06604-9*, Pub. by U CA Pr) Cal Prin Full Svc.
Making of Religion. Andrew Lang. LC 68-59286. reprint ed. 51.50 (*0-404-03854-9*) AMS Pr.
Making of Rhodes. Fliss Coombs. (Illus.). 128p. 1997. pap. 17.95 (*0-563-38785-8*, BBC-Parkwest) Parkwest Pubns.
*__Making of Robert E. Lee.__ Michael Fellman. LC 99-44062. (Illus.). 2000. 29.95 (*0-679-45650-3*) Random.
Making of Roumania: A Study of an International Problem, 1856-1866. T. W. Riker. LC 70-135830. (Eastern Europe Collection). 1971. reprint ed. 35.95 (*0-405-02772-9*) Ayer.
Making of Rubens. Svetlana Alpers. LC 94-30637. (Illus.). 186p. 1995. 40.00 (*0-300-06010-6*) Yale U Pr.
Making of Rubens. Svetlana Alpers. (Illus.). 186p. 1996. pap. 25.00 (*0-300-06744-5*) Yale U Pr.
Making of Russian Absolutism, 1613-1801. 2nd ed. Paul Dukes. (History of Russia Ser.). 256p. (C). 1990. pap. 44.00 (*0-582-00324-5*, 78647) Longman.
Making of Sacagawea: A Euro-American Legend. Donna J. Kessler. LC 95-12834. (FRE & LAT., Illus.). 258p. (C). 1996. text 34.95 (*0-8173-0777-X*) U of Ala Pr.
Making of Sacagawea: A Euro-American Legend. Donna J. Kessler. 258p. 1998. pap. text 19.95 (*0-8173-0928-4*) U of Ala Pr.
Making of Schindler's List: Behind the Scenes of an Epic Film. Franciszek Palowski. LC 97-41443. (Illus.). 196p. 1998. 21.95 (*1-55972-445-5*) Carol Pub Group.
Making of Scientific Management, 2 vols., Set. E. F. Brech. 438p. 1996. 150.00 (*1-85506-354-9*) Bks Intl VA.
Making of Scotland: Nation, Culture & Social Change. Ed. by Stephen Kendrick & David Mccrone. 256p. 1989. 45.00 (*0-85224-631-5*, Pub. by Edinburgh U Pr) Col U Pr.
Making of Scottish Educational Policy: Government & Secondary Schooling Since 1945. Andrew McPherson & Charles Raab. 352p. 1988. 60.00 (*0-85224-515-7*, Pub. by Edinburgh U Pr) Col U Pr.
Making of Shakespeare's Dramatic Poetry. G. R. Hibbard. 184p. 1981. pap. 11.95 (*0-8020-6424-8*); text 30.00 (*0-8020-2400-9*) U of Toronto Pr.
Making of Silicon Valley: A One Hundred Year Renaissance. LC 95-72050. 133p. 1996. pap. 24.95 (*0-9649217-5-8*, 68598) Snta Clara Valley.
Making of Sir Philip Sidney. Edward Berry. (Illus.). 256p. 1998. text 45.00 (*0-8020-4288-0*) U of Toronto Pr.
Making of Social Movements in Latin America: Identity, Strategy & Democracy. Ed. by Arturo Escobar & Sonia E. Alvarez. 400p. (C). 1992. pap. 35.00 (*0-8133-1207-8*, Pub. by Westview) HarpC.
Making of Social Policy in Britain, 1830-1990. 2nd ed. Kathleen Jones. 285p. (C). 1994. pap. 29.95 (*0-485-12104-2*, Pub. by Athlone Pr) Humanities.
Making of Spanish Democracy, Vol. 1. Donald Share. LC 86-515. (Democracy in the World Ser.). 248p. 1986. 55.00 (*0-275-92125-5*, C2125, Praeger Pubs) Greenwood.
Making of Spawn. (Illus.). 1997. pap. 9.99 (*0-934551-22-7*) Starlog Grp Inc.
Making of Star Trek. Stephen E. Whitfield & Gene Roddenberry. (Illus.). 480p. 1986. mass mkt. 5.99 (*0-345-34019-1*, Del Rey) Ballantine Pub Grp.
Making of Star Trek: Prime Dective. Terry Erdmann. (s). (Illus.). 192p. 1998. pap. 18.00 (*0-671-02494-9*) S&S Trade.
Making of Star Wars: Episode I: The Phantom Menace. Laurent Bouzereau & Jody Duncan. LC 99-90347. 1999. 39.95 (*0-345-43111-1*, Del Rey) Ballantine Pub Grp.
Making of Starship Troopers. Paul M. Sammon. LC 97-224834. 144p. 1997. pap. 15.00 (*1-57297-252-1*) Blvd Books.
Making of Statisticians. J. Gani. (Illus.). 263p. 1982. 65.95 (*0-387-90684-3*) Spr-Verlag.
Making of Stonehenge. Rodney Castleden. LC 93-12736. 320p. (C). (gr. 13). 1994. 65.00 (*0-415-08513-6*) Routledge.
Making of Strategy: Rules, States & War. Ed. by Williamson Murray et al. (Illus.). 696p. (C). 1994. text 54.95 (*0-521-45389-5*) Cambridge U Pr.
Making of Strategy: Rules, States & War. Ed. by Williamson Murray et al. (Illus.). 704p. 1996. pap. text 20.95 (*0-521-56627-4*) Cambridge U Pr.
Making of Strawberry. deluxe ed. Jana Paulson. (Set 1 Ser.: Vol. 1). (Illus.). 20p. (J). (ps-3). 1997. pap. 2.50 (*1-890567-00-0*) Berry Bks Ltd.
Making of Technological Man: The Social Origins of French Engineering Education. John H. Weiss. 384p. 1982. 42.00 (*0-262-23112-3*) MIT Pr.
Making of Telecommunication Policy. Dick W. Olufs, 3rd. LC 98-7499. (Explorations in Public Policy Ser.). 214p. 1998. 49.95 (*1-55587-707-9*) L Rienner.
Making of Terrorism. Michel Wieviorka. Tr. by David G. White. (Illus.). 386p. 1993. pap. text 19.95 (*0-226-89652-8*); lib. bdg. 52.95 (*0-226-89650-1*) U Ch Pr.
Making of Tests for Index Numbers: Mathematical Methods of Descriptive Statistics. A. Vogt & J. Barta. (Illus.). xiv, 220p. 1997. 63.00 (*3-7908-1011-8*) Spr-Verlag.
Making of Textual Culture: "Grammatica" & Literary Theory, 350-1100. Martin Irvine. (Cambridge Studies in Medieval Literature: No. 19). (Illus.). 624p. (C). 1994. text 85.00 (*0-521-41447-4*) Cambridge U Pr.
Making of the Aborogines. Bain Attwood. 240p. (C). 1990. pap. text 19.95 (*0-04-370185-X*) Routledge.
Making of the Alice Books: Lewis Carroll's Uses of Earlier Children's Literature. Ronald Reichertz. LC 98-219961. 264p. 1997. text 55.00 (*0-7735-1625-5*, Pub. by McG-Queens Univ Pr) CUP Services.
*__Making of the Alice Books: Lewis Carroll's Uses of Earlier Children's Literature.__ Ronald Reichertz. 256p. 2000. pap. 22.95 (*0-7735-2081-3*, Pub. by McG-Queens Univ Pr) CUP Services.
Making of the American Constitution. Merrill Jensen. LC 79-4386. (Anvil Ser.). 192p. 1979. reprint ed. pap. 11.50 (*0-88275-904-3*) Krieger.
Making of the American Landscape. Ed. by Michael P. Conzen. LC 89-20047. (Illus.). 449p. (C). 1990. pap. 36.99 (*0-415-91178-8*) Routledge.
Making of the American Landscape. Ed. by Michael P. Conzen. 256p. 1990. pap. text 20.95 (*0-04-917010-4*) Routledge.
Making of the American Nation: or The Rise & Decline of Oligarchy in the West. J. Arthur Partridge. 1977. 27.95 (*0-8369-9192-3*, 9061) Ayer.
Making of the Arab-Israeli Conflict, 1947-1951. Ilan Pappe. 320p. 1992. text 69.50 (*1-85043-357-7*, Pub. by I B T) St Martin.
Making of the Arab-Israeli Conflict, 1947-1951. Ilan Pappe. 336p. 1994. text 24.95 (*1-85043-819-6*, Pub. by I B T) St Martin.
*__Making of the Atom Bomb.__ Victoria Sherrow. LC 99-42640. (World History Ser.). 96-128p. (J). 2000. 23.70 (*1-56006-585-0*) Lucent Bks.
Making of the Atomic Bomb. Richard Rhodes. 928p. 1995. per. 17.00 (*0-684-81378-5*, Touchstone) S&S Trade Pap.
Making of the Australian National University, 1946-1996. S. G. Foster & Margaret M. Varghese. LC 96-204685. xi, 464 p. 1996. write for info. (*1-86448-083-1*, Pub. by Allen & Unwin Pty) Paul & Co Pubs.
Making of the Australian Workers Union, 1886-1911. John Merritt. (Illus.). 340p. 1986. 38.00 (*0-19-554667-9*) OUP.
Making of the Backward Pupil in Education in England, 1870-1914. Ian C. Copeland. Ed. by Peter Gordon. LC 98-30483. (Education Ser.). 256p. 1999. 57.50 (*0-7130-0216-6*, Pub. by Woburn Pr); pap. 27.50 (*0-7130-4037-8*, Pub. by Woburn Pr) Intl Spec Bk.
Making of the Bahamas. Cash & Maples. Date not set. pap. text. write for info. (*0-582-02805-1*, Pub. by Addison-Wesley) Longman.
Making of the Balkan States. William S. Murray. LC 10-17934. (Columbia University. Studies in the Social Sciences: No. 102). reprint ed. 24.50 (*0-404-51102-3*) AMS Pr.
Making of the Bible. William Barclay. 106p. (C). 1992. pap. 35.00 (*0-7855-6828-X*, Pub. by St Andrew) St Mut.
Making of the Bible. William Barclay. 106p. 1993. pap. 30.00 (*0-7152-0420-3*, Pub. by St Andrew) St Mut.
*__Making of the Bibles Moralisees, 2 vols.__ John Lowden. Incl. Book of Ruth. LC 98-46494. (Illus.). 320p. 2000. 85.00 (*0-271-01919-0*); Vol. 1. Making of the Bibles Moralisees. LC 98-46494. (Illus.). 352p. 2000. 85.00 (*0-271-01909-3*); (Illus.). 2000. 160.00 Pa St U Pr.
Making of the Bibles Moralisees see Making of the Bibles Moralisees
Making of the Book. A. J Cox. Ed. by Paul S. Koda. LC 85-28384. (History of the Book: Vol. 3). 88p. 1986. reprint ed. 25.00 (*0-938768-10-7*) Oak Knoll.
Making of the British Middle Class? Studies of Regional & Cultural Diversity Since the 18th C. Alan J. Kidd. LC 99-194758. 1999. 92.00 (*0-7509-1780-6*) A Sutton.
Making of the Chemist. Ed. by David Knight & Helge Kragh. LC 97-43009. (Illus.). 400p. (C). 1998. 80.00 (*0-521-58351-9*) Cambridge U Pr.
Making of the Civil Law. Alan Watson. LC 80-27591. 209p. (C). 1981. 42.50 (*0-674-54310-6*) HUP.
Making of the Civilized Mind, Vol. 4. Seymour W. Itzkoff. LC 89-12733. 309p. (C). 1990. text 57.95 (*0-8204-1154-X*) P Lang Pubng.
Making of the Common Law. Paul Brand. LC 92-25671. 504p. 1992. 70.00 (*1-85285-070-1*) Hambledon Press.
Making of the Constitution. Gordon S. Wood. LC 87-73124. (Charles Edmondson Historical Lectures). 41p. (Orig.). 1987. pap. 5.95 (*0-918954-49-5*) Baylor Univ Pr.
Making of the Constitution. Charles Warren. xii, 832p. 1993. reprint ed. 75.00 (*0-8377-2721-9*, Rothman) W S Hein.
Making of the Creeds. Frances M. Young. LC 90-44767. 128p. (Orig.). (C). 1991. pap. 13.00 (*0-334-02488-9*) TPI PA.
Making of the Cretan Landscape. Oliver Rackham & Jennifer Moody. LC 93-49016. 272p. 1997. text 79.95 (*0-7190-3646-1*); text 29.95 (*0-7190-3647-X*) Manchester Univ Pr.
Making of the Crofting Community. James Hunter. 350p. 1996. pap. 39.00 (*0-85976-406-0*, Pub. by J Donald) St Mut.
*__Making of the Crow.__ Bridget Baiss. 2000. 25.00 (*1-870048-54-7*, Pub. by Making Crow Inc) Making of the Crow.
Making of the Dentiste, 1650-1760. Roger King. LC 98-27420. (History of Medicine in Context Ser.). 288p. 1998. 84.95 (*1-84014-653-2*) Ashgate Pub Co.
*__Making of the Dutch Republic.__ 2000. write for info. (*0-582-06384-1*) Pearson Educ.
Making of the Earth: Geological Forces That Shape Our Planet. Jon Erickson. (Living Earth Ser.). Date not set. 40.00 (*0-8160-4276-4*) Facts on File.
Making of the Empire State. Jacques W. Redway. 263p. 1993. reprint ed. lib. bdg. 79.00 (*0-7812-5196-6*) Rprt Serv.
Making of the English Country House, 1500-1640 Malcolm Airs. LC 76-379881. viii, 208 p. 1975. write for info. (*0-85139-378-0*) Arch Pr Bks.
Making of the English Landscape. W. G. Hoskins. 1992. pap. 22.95 (*0-14-015410-8*, Pub. by Pnguin Bks Ltd) Trafalgar.
Making of the English Literary Canon: From the Middle Ages to the Late Eighteenth Century. Trevor Ross. 408p. 1998. text 65.00 (*0-7735-1683-2*, Pub. by McG-Queens Univ Pr) CUP Services.
*__Making of the English Literary Canon: From the Middle Ages to the Late Eighteenth Century.__ Trevor Ross. 408p. 2000. pap. 24.95 (*0-7735-2080-5*, Pub. by McG-Queens Univ Pr) CUP Services.
Making of the English Middle Class: Business, Society & Family Life in London 1660-1730. Peter Earle. 1989. 55.00 (*0-520-06826-2*, Pub. by U CA Pr) Cal Prin Full Svc.
*__Making of the English Working Class.__ E. P. Thompson. 1999. 31.50 (*0-8446-6993-8*) Peter Smith.
Making of the English Working Class. Edward P. Thompson. 1966. pap. 25.00 (*0-394-70322-7*) Vin Bks.
*__Making of the Filipino Nation & Republic: From Barangays, Tribes, Sultanates & Colony (Ang Pagbubuo Ng Bansa at Republika Ng Pilipinas: Mula sa Mga Barangay, Tribu, Sultanato at Kolonya.__ Jose V. Abueva. LC 98-947826. (Pamana Ser.). (TAG & ENG.). 1078p. 1999. pap. text 120.00 (*971-542-215-2*, Pub. by U of Philippines Pr) UH Pr.
Making of the French Episcopate, 1589-1661. Joseph Bergin. LC 96-18336. 752p. 1996. 57.00 (*0-300-06751-8*) Yale U Pr.
Making of the Georgian Nation. 2nd ed. Ronald G. Suny. LC 94-6592. 448p. 1994. 39.95 (*0-253-35579-6*); pap. 17.95 (*0-253-20915-3*) Ind U Pr.
Making of the Gulf War: Origins of Kuwait's Long-Standing Territorial Dispute with Iraq. D. H. Rahman. 1998. 45.00 (*0-86372-207-5*, Pub. by Garnet-Ithaca) LPC InBook.
Making of the Hapsburg Monarchy, 1550-1700. R. J. Evans. 556p. 1984. pap. text 29.95 (*0-19-873085-3*) OUP.
Making of the Hawthorne Subject. Alison Easton. 328p. (C). 1996. 49.95 (*0-8262-1040-6*) U of Mo Pr.
*__Making of the Indian Atomic Bomb.__ Abraham. LC 98-27616. 180p. 1998. text 55.00 (*1-85649-629-5*, Pub. by Zed Books) St Martin.
Making of the Indian Atomic Bomb. Agraham. LC 98-27616. 2000. pap. text 19.95 (*1-85649-630-9*, Pub. by Zed Books) St Martin.
Making of the Indian Working Class: The Case of the Tata Iron & Steel Company, 1880-1946. Vinay Bahl. LC 94-32846. 432p. (C). 1995. text 49.95 (*0-8039-9187-8*) Sage.
Making of the Iranian Community in America: A Case Study of Dual Marginality, Continuity & Change. Maboud Ansari. 185p. 1992. 45.00 (*0-9632600-0-6*) Pardis Pr.
Making of the Jewish Middle Class: Women, Family & Identity in Imperial Germany. Marion A. Kaplan. (Studies in Jewish History). (Illus.). 368p. 1994. reprint ed. pap. text 19.95 (*0-19-509396-8*) OUP.
Making of the Labor Bureaucrat: Union Leadership in the United States, 1870-1920. Warren R. Van Tine. LC 73-79508. 246p. 1973. 30.00 (*0-87023-146-4*) U of Mass Pr.
Making of the Labor Party in New South Wales, 1880-1990. Raymond Markey. 328p. 1989. 27.95 (*0-86840-370-9*, Pub. by New South Wales Univ Pr) Intl Spec Bk.
Making of the Labour Movement: The Formation of the Transport & General Workers' Union, 1870-1922. Ken Coates & Tony Topham. LC 95-161500. (Illus.). xxxv, 909p. 1994. pap. 37.50 (*0-85124-565-X*, Pub. by Spkesman) Coronet Bks.
Making of the Lebanese Merchant Republic. Carolyn Gates. LC 96-60436. 180p. 1998. text 59.50 (*1-86064-047-8*, Pub. by I B T) St Martin.
*__Making of the Magdalen: Preaching & Popular Devotion in the Later Middle Ages.__ Katherine Ludwig Jansen. LC 99-45174. (Illus.). 332p. 1999. text 39.50 (*0-691-05850-4*, Pub. by Princeton U Pr) Cal Prin Full Svc.
Making of the Masters: Clifford Roberts, Augusta National & Golf's Most Prestigious Tournament. David Owen. LC 98-55532. (Illus.). 277p. 1999. 25.00 (*0-684-85729-4*) S&S Trade.
Making of the Meiji Constitution: The Oligarchs & the Constitutional Development of Japan, 1868-1891. George M. Beckmann. LC 72-7963. 158p. 1975. reprint ed. lib. bdg. 38.50 (*0-8371-6553-9*, BEMC, Greenwood Pr) Greenwood.
Making of the Messiah: Christianity & Resentment. Robert Sheaffer. LC 91-27091. 192p. 1991. 25.95 (*0-87975-691-8*) Prometheus Bks.
Making of the Mexican Mind: A Study in Recent Mexican Thought. Patrick Romanell. LC 76-86778. (Essay Index Reprint Ser.). 1977. 18.95 (*0-8369-1189-X*) Ayer.
Making of the Middle Ages. Richard W. Southern. (Illus.). (C). 1961. pap. 14.00 (*0-300-00230-0*, Y46) Yale U Pr.
Making of the Miskitu People of Nicaragua: The Social Construction of Ethnic Identity. Claudia Garcia. LC 97-114820. (Studia Sociologica Upsaliensia: Vol. 41). 175p. (Orig.). 1996. pap. 42.50 (*91-554-3684-6*) Coronet Bks.
*__Making of the Modern Architect & Engineer: Origins & Development of an Occupation.__ Ulrich Pfammatter. (Illus.). 328p. 2000. pap. 38.00 (*3-7643-6217-0*) Birkhauser.
Making of the Modern Body: Sexuality & Society in the Nineteenth-Century. Ed. by Catherine Gallagher & Thomas Laqueur. (Representation Bks.: No. 1). 1987. pap. 18.95 (*0-520-05961-1*, Pub. by U CA Pr) Cal Prin Full Svc.
Making of the Modern Canon: Genesis & Crisis of a Literary Idea. Jan Gorak. LC 90-39034. (Vision, Division & Revision). 309p. (C). 1991. text 60.00 (*0-485-11388-0*, Pub. by Athlone Pr) Humanities.
*__Making of the Modern Christmas.__ J. M. Golby. 2000. reprint ed. pap. 15.95 (*0-7509-2136-6*, Pub. by Sutton Publng) Intl Pubs Mktg.
Making of the Modern Christmas. John M. Golby & A. W. Purdue. LC 86-7083. (Illus.). 152p. 1986. reprint ed. pap. 47.20 (*0-7837-9757-5*, 206048500005) Bks Demand.
*__Making of the Modern English State, 1460-1660.__ Philip Edwards. LC 00-30888. (British Studies). 2000. pap. write for info. (*0-312-23614-X*) St Martin.
Making of the Modern Gulf States: Kuwait, Bahrain, Qatar, the United Arab Emirates & Oman, 1. Rosemarie Said Zahlan. 1999. pap. text 25.00 (*0-86372-229-6*) Garnet-Ithaca.
Making of the Modern Gulf States: Kuwait, Bahrain, Qatar, United Arab Emirates, Oman. Rosemarie S. Zahlan. 250p. 1989. pap. text 16.95 (*0-04-445293-4*) Routledge.
Making of the Modern Homosexual. Ed. by Kenneth Plummer. 280p. 1981. 56.00 (*0-389-20159-6*, N6929) B&N Imports.
Making of the Modern Jew. Milton Steinberg. (Brown Classics in Judaica Ser.). 318p. (C). 1987. reprint ed. pap. text 26.50 (*0-8191-4492-4*) U Pr of Amer.
Making of the Modern Mind: A Survey of the Intellectual Background of the Present Age. John H. Randall, Jr. LC 76-20740. 720p. 1976. reprint ed. pap. text 34.50 (*0-231-04143-8*) Col U Pr.
Making of the Modern Near East, 1792-1923. M. E. Yapp. LC 87-2068. 404p. (C). 1989. pap. 49.00 (*0-582-49380-3*, 73592) Longman.
Making of the Modern University: Intellectual Transformation & the Marginalization of Morality. Julie A. Reuben. 376p. 1996. pap. text 18.95 (*0-226-71020-3*) U Ch Pr.
Making of the Modern University: Intellectual Transformation & the Marginalization of Morality. Julie A. Reuben. 376p. 1996. lib. bdg. 55.00 (*0-226-71018-1*) U Ch Pr.
Making of the Modern World. Douglas Johnson. LC 70-26009. 1971. write for info. (*0-389-04128-9*) B&N Imports.
Making of the Modern World. 2nd ed. Robert W. Strayer. 515p. 1995. pap. text 50.95 (*0-312-05017-8*) St Martin.
Making of the Monroe Doctrine. Ernest R. May. (Illus.). 328p. (C). 1992. pap. 14.95 (*0-674-54341-6*) Belknap Pr.

An Asterisk (*) at the beginning of an entry indicates that the title is appearing for the first time.

Making of the Mosaic: A History of Canadian Immigration Policy. Ninette Kelley & Michael J. Trebilcock. LC 99-185777. (Illus.). 704p. 1998. text 75.00 (*0-8020-4323-2*) U of Toronto Pr.

***Making of the Mosaic: A History of Canadian Immigration Policy.** Ninette Kelley & Michael J. Trebilcock. LC 99-185777. (Illus.). 704p. 1998. pap. text 29.95 (*0-8020-8146-0*) U of Toronto Pr.

Making of the National Labor Relations Board: A Study in Economics, Politics, & the Law, 1933-1937. James A. Gross. LC 74-5284. (Illus.). 265p. (C). 1974. text 34.50 (*0-87395-270-7*) State U NY Pr.

Making of the National Poet: Shakespeare, Adaptation & Authorship, 1660-1769. Michael Dobson. (Illus.). 276p. 1995. reprint ed. pap. text 22.00 (*0-19-818323-2*) OUP.

Making of the Neville Family in England, 1166-1400 A.D. Charles R. Young. (Illus.). 192p. 1996. 60.00 (*0-85115-668-1*) Boydell & Brewer.

Making of the New Deal: The Insiders Speak. Ed. by Katie Louchheim. (Illus.). 392p. 1983. pap. text 10.95 (*0-674-54346-7*) HUP.

Making of the New Poor Law: The Politics of Inquiry, Enactment, & Implementation, 1832-1839. Anthony Brundage. LC 77-20881. 219p. reprint ed. pap. 67.90 (*0-7837-5895-2*, 205908300006) Bks Demand.

Making of the New Testament: Origin, Collection, Text & Canon. Arthur G. Patzia. LC 94-45403. 208p. (Orig.). 1995. pap. text 14.99 (*0-8308-1859-6*, 1859) InterVarsity.

Making of the New Testament Documents. E. Earle Ellis. LC 99-19912. (Biblical Interpretation Ser.). 432p. 1999. 118.00 (*90-04-11332-0*) Brill Academic Pubs.

Making of the 1944 Education Act. Michael Barber. LC 93-42667. (Education Ser.). 144p. 1995. 90.00 (*0-304-32659-3*) Continuum.

Making of the 1944 Education Act. Michael Barber. LC 93-42667. (Education Ser.). 144p. 1995. pap. 29.95 (*0-304-32661-5*) Continuum.

***Making of the 1996 Farm Act.** Lyle Schertz & Otto C. Doering. LC 99-28326. (Illus.). 206p. 1999. text 44.95 (*0-8138-2608-X*) Iowa St U Pr.

Making of the NIV. Ed. by Kenneth L. Barker. 192p. (gr. 12). 1997. reprint ed. pap. 12.99 (*0-8010-5742-6*) Baker Bks.

***Making of the Pacemaker: Celebrating a Life-Saving Invention.** Wilson Greatbatch. LC 00-23296. (Illus.). 290p. 2000. 32.95 (*1-57392-806-2*) Prometheus Bks.

Making of the Pentateuch: A Methodological Study. R. N. Whybray. (Journal for the Study of the Old Testament Supplement Ser.: Vol. 53). 263p. 1987. pap. 29.95 (*1-85075-063-7*, Pub. by Sheffield Acad) CUP Services.

Making of the Pope. Andrew M. Greeley. 1999. write for info. (*0-316-32560-0*) Little.

***Making of the Pope of the Millennium: Kalendarium of the Life of Karol Wojtyla.** Adam Boniecki. LC 00-102005. (Illus.). 938p. 2000. 45.00 (*0-944203-49-3*) Marian Pr.

Making of the President, 1960. Theodore H. White. 1993. reprint ed. lib. bdg. 45.95 (*1-56849-143-3*) Buccaneer Bks.

***Making of the President 1789: The Unauthorized Campaign Biography.** Marvin Kitman. (Illus.). 2000. pap. 14.00 (*0-8021-3735-0*, Grove) Grove-Atltic.

Making of the Professional Actor. Adrian Cairns. 224p. 1996. 45.00 (*0-7206-1002-8*, Pub. by P Owen Ltd) Dufour.

***Making of the Republican Citizen: Political Ceremonies & Symbols in China, 1911-1929.** Henrietta Harrison. LC 99-41111. (Illus.). 388p. 2000. text 82.00 (*0-19-829519-7*) OUP.

Making of the Roman Army: From Republic to Empire. Lawrence Keppie. LC 97-30610. (Illus.). 272p. 1998. pap. 19.95 (*0-8061-3014-8*) U of Okla Pr.

Making of the Roman Catholic Church in Ireland, 1850-1860. Emmet J. Larkin. LC 79-19560. (Illus.). 544p. reprint ed. pap. 168.70 (*0-7837-6857-5*, 204668600003) Bks Demand.

Making of the Rugrats Movie: Behind the Scences at Klasky Csupo. Jan Breslauer. (Rugrats Ser.). (Illus.). 144p. (J). (ps-3). 1998. 25.00 (*0-671-02809-X*, PB Hardcover) PB.

Making of the SAS & the World's Elite Forces. Terry White. 192p. 1994. 19.95 (*1-85367-184-3*, 5420) Stackpole.

Making of the Scottish Rural Landscape. David Turnock. LC 94-44740. 329p. 1995. 86.95 (*1-85928-027-7*, Pub. by Scolar Pr) Ashgate Pub Co.

Making of the Second Reform Bill. F. B. Smith. (Modern Revivals in History Ser.). 320p. 1993. 63.95 (*0-7512-0113-8*, Pub. by Gregg Pub) Ashgate Pub Co.

Making of the Second World War. 2nd ed. Anthony P. Adamthwaite. (Historical Problems: Studies & Documents). (Illus.). 1977. pap. text 19.95 (*0-04-940057-6*) Routledge.

Making of the Second World War. 2nd ed. Anthony P. Adamthwaite. 240p. (C). 1989. pap. 23.99 (*0-415-90716-0*) Routledge.

Making of the Shelley Myth: An Annotated Bibliography of Criticism of Percy Bysshe Shelley, 1822-1860. Karsten Engelberg. 468p. 1988. lib. bdg. 89.50 (*0-313-27670-6*) Greenwood.

Making of the Soviet System: Essays in the Social History of Interwar Russia. Moshe Lewin. 368p. 1994. pap. 16.95 (*1-56584-125-5*, Pub. by New Press NY) Norton.

Making of the Soviet Union. 2nd ed. Joan Hasler. 1989. pap. text 17.20 (*0-582-22505-1*, 78427) Longman.

Making of the State Reader: Social & Aesthetic Contexts of the Reception of Soviet Literature. E. A. Dobrenko. Tr. by Jesse M. Savage from RUS. LC 97-12325. 382p. 1997. 49.50 (*0-8047-2854-2*) Stanford U Pr.

***Making of the Taiwan Relations Act: Twenty Years in Retrospect.** David Tawei Lee. (Studies on Contemporary Taiwan). 228p. 2000. text 45.00 (*0-19-592209-3*) OUP.

Making of the Trek Films. Edward Gross et al. (History of Trek Ser.: Vol. 2). (Illus.). 200p. (Orig.). 1991. pap. 14.95 (*0-685-50335-6*) Retro Vision.

Making of the Tudor Dynasty. Ralph A. Griffiths & Roger S. Thomas. 210p. 1993. pap. 19.95 (*0-312-10358-1*) St Martin.

Making of the Unborn Patient: A Social Anatomy of Fetal Surgery. Monica J. Casper. LC 97-39331. (Illus.). 267p. (C). 1998. text 50.00 (*0-8135-2515-2*); pap. text 20.00 (*0-8135-2516-0*) Rutgers U Pr.

Making of the University of Michigan 1817-1992. Howard H. Peckham. (Illus.). 416p. (C). 1994. text 34.95 (*0-472-09594-3*) U of Mich Pr.

Making of the University of Michigan, 1817-1992. Howard Peckham. 416p. 1994. pap. text 16.95 (*0-472-06594-7*, 06594) U of Mich Pr.

Making of the Urban Landscape. J. W. Whitehand. (IBG Special Publications). (Illus.). 256p. (C). 1993. pap. text 30.95 (*0-631-19198-4*) Blackwell Pubs.

***Making of the Victorian Organ.** Nicholas Thistlethwaite. (Musical Texts & Monographs). (Illus.). 584p. (C). 1999. pap. 34.95 (*0-521-66364-4*) Cambridge U Pr.

***Making of the White Man.** Paul Lawrence Guthrie. 200p. 1999. pap. 10.00 (*1-930097-06-9*) Lushena Bks.

Making of the Whiteman: History, Tradition & the Teachings of Elijah Muhammad. Paul L. Guthrie. 104p. (Orig.). 1997. pap. 10.00 (*1-56411-122-9*) Untd Bros & Sis.

Making of the Wizard of Oz: Movie Magic & Studio Power in the Prime of MGM - And the Miracle of Production #1060. Aljean Harmetz. (Illus.). 352p. (J). 1998. pap. 14.95 (*0-7868-8352-9*, Pub. by Hyperion) Time Warner.

Making of the Wren Library, Trinity College, Cambridge: From the Seventeenth to the Nineteenth Century. Ed. by David McKitterick. (Illus.). 171p. (C). 1995. text 90.00 (*0-521-44305-9*) Cambridge U Pr.

Making of Theatre: From Drama to Performance. Robert W. Corrigan. LC 80-19046. 352p. reprint ed. pap. 109.20 (*0-7837-3952-4*, 204378100011) Bks Demand.

Making of "This Side of Paradise" James L. W. West, III. LC 82-40487. (Illus.). 136p. 1983. 28.95 (*0-8122-7867-4*) U of Pa Pr.

Making of Three Russian Revolutionaries: Voices from the Menshevik Past. Leopold Haimson et al. (Illus.). 528p. 1988. text 89.95 (*0-521-26325-5*) Cambridge U Pr.

***Making of Tocqueville's Democracy in America.** James T. Schleifer. LC 99-25721. 2000. 20.00 (*0-86597-204-4*) Liberty Fund.

Making of Tocqueville's Democracy in America. 2nd ed. James T. Schleifer. LC 99-25721. 2000. pap. 10.00 (*0-86597-205-2*) Liberty Fund.

***Making of 2001: A Space Odyssey: Testimony & Commentary by Stanley Kubrick, Arthur C. Clarke, Jeremy Bernstein, Jerome Agel, Keir Dullea, & Others.** Stanley Kubrick. Ed. by Stephanie Schwan & Martin Scorsese. LC 99-55776. (Modern Library Movies Ser.). 2000. pap. 15.95 (*0-375-75528-4*) Modern Lib NY.

Making of U. S. China Policy: From Normalization to the Post-Cold War Era. Tan Qingshan. LC 92-41402. 190p. 1992. pap. text 16.95 (*1-55587-314-6*) L Rienner.

Making of U. S. China Policy: From Normalization to the Post-Cold War Era. Tan Qingshan. LC 92-41402. 190p. 1992. lib. bdg. 37.00 (*1-55587-336-7*) L Rienner.

Making of United Kingdom. (Sense of History Ser.). 1992. pap. text. write for info. (*0-582-20737-1*, Pub. by Addison-Wesley) Longman.

Making of United Nations Security Council Resolution 242: Centerpiece of Arab-Israeli Negotiations. David A. Korn. (Pew Case Studies in International Affairs). 50p. (C). 1992. pap. text 3.50 (*1-56927-450-9*) Geo U Inst Dplmcy.

**Making of United States International Economic Policy
 Principles, Problems & Proposals for Reform.** 5th ed. Stephen D. Cohen. LC 99-34427. 328p. 2000. 69.50 (*0-275-96503-1*) Greenwood.

**Making of United States International Economic Policy
 Principles, Problems & Proposals of Reform.** 5th ed. Stephen D. Cohen. LC 99-34427. 328p. 2000. pap. 29.95 (*0-275-96504-X*) Greenwood.

Making of Urban America. 2nd rev. ed. Ed. by Raymond A. Mohl. LC 97-2493. 368p. (C). 1997. 50.00 (*0-8420-2637-1*, SR Bks); pap. 21.95 (*0-8420-2639-8*, SR Bks) Scholarly Res Inc.

Making of Urban America: A History of City Planning in the United States. John W. Reps. (Illus.). 590p. 1965. pap. text 45.00 (*0-691-00618-0*, Pub. by Princeton U Pr) Cal Prin Full Svc.

Making of Urban Europe, 1000-1950. Paul M. Hohenberg & Lynn H. Lees. (Studies in Urban History). (Illus.). 416p. 1985. 44.50 (*0-674-54360-2*) HUP.

Making of Urban Europe, 1000-1950. Paul M. Hohenberg & Lynn H. Lees. LC 84-25333. (Studies in Urban History). (Illus.). 416p. 1990. pap. 15.95 (*0-674-54361-0*) HUP.

Making of Urban Europe, 1000-1994. rev. ed. Paul M. Hohenberg & Lynn H. Lees. LC 95-9303. Orig. Title: Making of Urban Europe, 1000-1950. (Illus.). 448p. (Orig.). (C). 1995. pap. text 21.50 (*0-674-54362-9*) HUP.

Making of Urban Europe, 1000-1950 see Making of Urban Europe, 1000-1994

Making of Urban Revolution in China: The CCP-GMD Struggle for Beiping-Tianjin, 1945-1949. Joseph K. Yick. LC 95-5921. (Studies on Contemporary China). (Illus.). 260p. (C). 1995. text 81.95 (*1-56324-605-8*, East Gate Bk) M E Sharpe.

Making of Urban Revolution in China: The CCP-GMD Struggle for Beiping-Tianjin, 1945-1949. Joseph K. Yick. LC 95-5921. (Studies on Contemporary China). (Illus.). 260p. (C). (gr. 13). 1995. pap. text 36.95 (*1-56324-606-6*, East Gate Bk) M E Sharpe.

Making of Vedant. T. G. Mainkar. 170p. 1980. 15.95 (*0-318-37172-3*) Asia Bk Corp.

Making of Victorian Sexuality. Michael Mason. (Illus.). 348p. 1995. pap. 15.95 (*0-19-285312-0*) OUP.

Making of Victorian Sexuality: Sexual Behaviour & Its Understanding. Michael Mason. LC 93-28824. (Illus.). 348p. 1994. 30.00 (*0-19-812247-0*, Clarendon Pr) OUP.

Making of Virginia Architecture. Charles E. Brownell et al. Ed. by Monica S. Rumsey. (Illus.). 472p. (Orig.). (C). 1992. 50.00 (*0-917046-34-X*); pap. 24.95 (*0-917046-33-1*) Va Mus Arts.

Making of Walden: With the Text of the First Version. J. Lyndon Shanley. (Midway Reprint Ser.). 1974. reprint ed. pap. text 12.00 (*0-226-74956-8*) U Ch Pr.

Making of Walden: With the Text of the First Version. James L. Shanley. LC 57-6990. (Midway Reprint Ser.). 216p. reprint ed. pap. 67.00 (*0-608-09529-X*, 205433100005) Bks Demand.

Making of Wales. John Davies. 1999. pap. text 22.95 (*0-7509-2176-5*) A Sutton.

Making of Waterworld. Janine Pourroy. (Illus.). 160p. (Orig.). 1995. pap. 15.00 (*1-57297-005-7*) Blvd Books.

Making of Western Labor Radicalism: Denver's Organized Workers, 1878-1905. David Brundage. LC 93-34180. (Working Class in American History Ser.). (Illus.). 224p. 1994. text 26.95 (*0-252-02075-8*) U of Ill Pr.

Making of William Penn. Mabel R. Brailsford. LC 77-124227. (Select Bibliographies Reprint Ser.). 1977. 24.95 (*0-8369-5416-5*) Ayer.

Making of William Penn. Mabel R. Brailsford. 1993. reprint ed. lib. bdg. 89.00 (*0-7812-5433-7*) Rprt Serv.

Making of Womanhood: Gender Relations in the Mahabharata. Shalini Shah. (C). 1995. 28.00 (*81-7304-098-2*, Pub. by Manohar) S Asia.

Making of Wordsworth's Poetry, 1785-1798. Paul D. Sheats. LC 72-90645. 323p. reprint ed. pap. 100.20 (*0-7837-2332-6*, 205742000004) Bks Demand.

Making of Yeats' "A Vision" A Study of the Automatic Script, Vol. I. George M. Harper. LC 86-11888. 318p. 1987. text 36.95 (*0-8093-1342-1*) S Ill U Pr.

Making of Yeats' "A Vision" A Study of the Automatic Script, Vol. II. George M. Harper. LC 86-11888. 480p. 1987. text 34.95 (*0-8093-1343-X*) S Ill U Pr.

Making of Zimbabwe: Decolonization in the Context of Regional & International Politics. Mordechai Tamarkin. 326p. 1990. text 45.00 (*0-7146-3355-0*, Pub. by F Cass Pubs) Intl Spec Bk.

Making Original & Portrait Dolls in Cernit. Rotraut Schrott. LC 93-159281. (Illus.). 110p. 1993. 29.95 (*0-87588-394-X*) Hobby Hse.

***Making our High Schools Better.** Anne Wescott Dodd. 304p. 2000. pap. 16.95 (*0-312-23346-9*) St Martin.

Making Our High Schools Better: How Parents & Teachers Can Work Together. 2nd ed. Ann W. Dodd & Jean L. Konzal. LC 98-46121. (Illus.). 304p. 1999. text 26.95 (*0-312-21335-2*) St Martin.

***Making Our Lives Work: Strategies to Lessen Stress & Build Self-Esteem.** 2nd rev. ed. Shirley A. Mahood. LC 99-72942. xiv, 146p. 1999. pap. 12.95 (*1-887322-14-0*) Emprise NY.

Making Ourselves at Home: Women Builders & Designers. Janice Goldfrank. LC 95-7215. (Illus.). 240p. 1995. pap. 20.00 (*0-918949-26-2*) Goldfrank.

Making Out: The Book of Lesbian Sex & Sexuality. Zoe Schramm-Evans & Nina Rapi. (Illus.). 160p. 1995. pap. 24.00 (*0-04-440932-X*) NYU Pr.

Making Out in Chinese. Ray Daniels. (CHI & ENG.). 104p. 1998. pap. 6.95 (*4-900737-13-5*, Pub. by Yen Bks) Tuttle Pubng.

Making Out in Indonesian. Peter Constantine. (IND.). 228p. (Orig.). 1994. pap. 6.95 (*4-900737-02-X*) Tuttle Pubng.

Making Out in Japan. Todd Geers & Erika Geers. (JPN & ENG.). 24p. 1992. pap. 14.95 incl. audio (*0-8048-1713-8*) Tuttle Pubng.

Making Out in Japanese. Todd Geers & Erika Geers. 104p. (Orig.). 6.95 (*4-900737-09-7*, Pub. by Yen Bks) Tuttle Pubng.

Making Out in Korean. Peter Constantine. (ENG & KOR., Illus.). 104p. (Orig.). 1995. pap. 6.95 (*4-900737-33-X*) Tuttle Pubng.

Making Out in Thai. John Clewley. LC 95-174525. (THA.). 104p. (Orig.). 1994. pap. 6.95 (*4-900737-01-1*) Tuttle Pubng.

Making Out in Vietnamese. Peter Constantine. 104p. 1998. pap. 6.95 (*4-900737-48-8*) Tuttle Pubng.

Making Outreach Visible: A Guide to Documenting Professional Service & Outreach. Ed. by Amy Driscoll & Ernest Lynton. 244p. 1999. pap. 19.00 (*1-56377-045-8*, FR9901) Am Assn Higher Ed.

Making Paper & Fabric Rubbings: Capturing Designs from Brasses, Gravestones, Carved Doors, Coins & More. Cecily Barth Firestein. LC 98-37318. (Illus.). 112p. 1999. 19.95 (*1-57990-104-2*, Pub. by Lark Books) Random.

Making Parish Meetings Work: Planning, Leading, Listening, Running, Evaluating. Medard Laz. LC 96-52317. 128p. 1997. pap. 5.95 (*0-87793-597-1*) Ave Maria.

Making Parish Policy: A Workbook on Sacramental Policies. Ronald J. Lewinski. 264p. 1996. pap. 19.00 (*1-56854-116-3*, PARPOL) Liturgy Tr Pubns.

Making Participatory Management Work. David R. Powers & Mary F. Powers. LC 82-49282. (Jossey-Bass Higher Education Ser.). 267p. reprint ed. pap. 82.80 (*0-8357-4916-9*, 203784600009) Bks Demand.

Making Partner: A Guide for Law Firm Associates. LC 91-76632. 120p. 1992. 19.95 (*0-89707-730-X*, 511-0303) Amer Bar Assn.

Making Partnerships Work: Importance of Written Agreement for Capital Accounting & Distributive Shore Items. 2nd rev. ed. Holmes F. Crouch. Ed. by Irma J. Crouch. LC 98-70247. (Series 200 Tax Guides: Vol. 204). (Illus.). 224p. 1998. pap. 19.95 (*0-944817-52-1*) Allyear Tax.

Making Paths & Walkways: Creative Ideas & Simple Techniques Stone, Brick, Bark, Pebbles, Grass & More. Paige Blomgren. LC 99-12166. (Illus.). 144p. 1999. 24.95 (*1-57990-108-5*, Pub. by Lark Books) Random.

Making Pavement Maintenance More Effective: Training Supplement. 15p. (C). 1994. pap. text 10.00 (*0-309-05757-4*, SHRP-H-380) SHRP.

Making PCR: A Story of Biotechnology. Paul Rabinow. LC 95-49103. (Illus.). 208p. (C). 1996. 22.50 (*0-226-70146-8*) U Ch Pr.

Making PCR: A Story of Biotechnology. Paul Rabinow. LC 95-49103. 200p. (C). 1997. pap. 13.00 (*0-226-70147-6*) U Ch Pr.

***Making Peace.** George Mitchell. LC 99-86633. 220p. 2000. pap. text 16.95 (*0-520-22523-6*, Pub. by U CA Pr) Cal Prin Full Svc.

Making Peace. George J. Mitchell. LC 99-61004. (Illus.). 191p. 1999. 24.00 (*0-375-40606-9*) Knopf.

M

***Making Peace: A First Hand Account of the Arab-Israeli Peace Process.** Eytan Bentsur. 2000. write for info. (*0-275-96876-6*, Praeger Pubs) Greenwood.

Making Peace: A Reading/Writing/Thinking Text on Global Community. Elaine Brooks & Len Fox. 295p. (C). 1995. pap. text 19.95 (*0-521-65780-6*) Cambridge U Pr.

Making Peace: A Reading/Writing/Thinking Text on Global Community: Instructor's Manual. Elaine Brooks & Len Fox. 26p. (C). 1995. pap., teacher ed. 6.00 (*0-521-65779-2*) Cambridge U Pr.

Making Peace: One Woman's Journey Around The World. Jan Phillips. 1990. pap. 12.95 (*0-377-00200-3*) Friendship Pr.

Making Peace: Resolving Personal Conflicts. Anne Hummel. (Beatitudes Ser.). 48p. 1993. mass mkt. 5.99 (*0-310-59653-X*) Zondervan.

Making Peace: The Legacy of Hiroshima & Nagasaki. Ed. by Chizu Iiyama. (Illus.). 40p. (Orig.). (J). (gr. 4-12). 1995. teacher ed. 10.00 (*1-881506-07-X*) Natl Japnse Am HS.

Making Peace: The Reconstruction of Gender in Interwar Britain. Susan K. Kent. LC 93-18776. 200p. (C). 1993. text 32.50 (*0-691-03140-1*, Pub. by Princeton U Pr) Cal Prin Full Svc.

Making Peace at Mayfield: A Whole School Approach to Conflict Resolution. Colleen Breheney et al. LC 97-101760. 81p. 1996. pap. text 18.00 (*0-435-07229-3*, 07229) Heinemann.

Making Peace in Your Stepfamily: Surviving & Thriving As Parents & Stepparents. Harold H. Bloomfield & Robert B. Kory. LC 92-35074. 304p. 1993. 19.45 (*1-56282-885-1*, Pub. by Hyperion) Time Warner.

Making Peace Possible: The Promise of Economic Conversion. Lloyd J. Dumas & Marek Thee. (Illus.). 208p. 1999. 150.00 (*0-08-037252-X*, Pub. by Pergamon Repr) Franklin.

Making Peace Prayers in Pictures. Marjorie Anne. 32p. 1986. pap. 30.00 (*0-7223-1991-6*, Pub. by A H S Ltd) St Mut.

***Making Peace Prevail: Preventing Violent Conflict in Macedonia.** Alice Ackermann. 272p. 1999. 45.00 (*0-8156-2812-9*); pap. text 24.95 (*0-8156-0602-8*) Syracuse U Pr.

Making Peace with Chronic Pain: A Whole-Life Strategy. Marlene Hunter. 192p. 1996. pap. 18.95 (*0-87630-821-3*) Brunner-Mazel.

Making Peace with Cochise: The 1872 Journal of Captain Joseph Alton Sladen. Ed. by Edwin R. Sweeney. LC 97-14203. (Illus.). 204p. 1997. 24.95 (*0-8061-2973-5*) U of Okla Pr.

Making Peace with Conflict: Practical Skills for Conflict Transformation. Ed. by Carolyn Schrock-Shenk & Lawrence Ressler. LC 99-22053. 200p. 1999. pap. 14.99 (*0-8361-9127-7*) Herald Pr.

Making Peace With Food: Freeing Yourself From the Diet/Weight Obsession. rev. ed. Susan Kano. LC 88-45561. (Illus.). 272p. 1989. reprint ed. pap. 15.00 (*0-06-096328-X*, PL 6328, Perennial) HarperTrade.

Making Peace with Germany, 1918: The Pre-Armistice Negotiations. Robert Randle. (Pew Case Studies in International Affairs). 50p. (C). 1993. pap. text 3.50 (*1-56927-435-5*) Geo U Inst Dplmcy.

***Making Peace with Money.** Jerrold J. Mundis. LC 99-18925. 288p. 1999. 14.95 (*0-7407-0040-5*) Andrews & McMeel.

Making Peace with My Mother. Sylvia B. Grossman. 210p. 1992. pap. 14.95 (*1-879198-07-X*) Knwldg Ideas & Trnds.

Making Peace with the Future: The United Nations & World Security - 30th U. N. of the Next Decade Conference 1995. 40p. (Orig.). (C). 1995. pap. text 25.00 (*0-7881-2623-7*) DIANE Pub.

Making Peace with the Planet. Barry Commoner. 304p. 1992. pap. 11.95 (*1-56584-012-7*, Pub. by New Press NY) Norton.

Making Peace with the Planet. Barry Commoner. 1993. 24.00 (*0-8446-6701-3*) Peter Smith.

Making Peace with the PLO: The Rabin's Government Road to the Oslo Accord. David Makovsky. LC 95-39631. 239p. 1995. pap. 8.00 (*0-944029-60-4*) Wash Inst NEP.

M

Making Peace with the '60s. David Burner. LC 96-3336. 286p. 1996. text 34.50 (*0-691-02660-2*, Pub. by Princeton U Pr) Cal Prin Full Svc.

Making Peace with the '60s. David Burner. 304p. 1987. reprint ed. pap. text 16.50 (*1-881089-21-5*) Brandywine Press.

Making Peace with the 60s. David Burner. (Illus.). 302p. (C). 1996. pap. text 14.95 (*0-691-05953-5*, Pub. by Princeton U Pr) Cal Prin Full Svc.

Making Peace with Your Adult Children. S. L. Smith. LC 91-7157. (Illus.). 398p. (C). 1991. 23.95 (*0-306-43767-8*, Plenum Trade) Perseus Pubng.

Making Peace with Your Parents. Harold H. Bloomfield. LC 96-96684. 1996. pap. 10.00 (*0-345-41047-5*) Ballantine Pub Grp.

Making Peace With your Past H. Bloomfield. 13.00 (*0-06-093314-3*) HarpC.

Making Peace with Your Past. abr. ed. Norman Wright. 176p. 1997. mass mkt. 5.99 (*0-8007-8645-9*, Spire) Revell.

Making Peace with Your Past. 2nd rev. ed. Martha B. Beveridge. Ed. by Terrisa Bruce-Phipps. 17p. 1994. pap. 3.50 (*1-889237-07-8*) Options Now.

Making Peace with Your Past: The 6 Essential Steps to Enjoying a Great Future. Harold H. Bloomfield. LC 99-89719. 288p. 2000. 24.00 (*0-06-019528-2*, HarpCollins) HarperTrade.

Making Peace with Your Teenager: The Rest Strategy. Kevin Huggins & Phil Landrum. LC 93-24752. 224p. (Orig.). 1993. pap. 12.99 (*0-929239-71-7*) Discovery Hse Pubs.

Making Peace with Yourself. Harold H. Bloomfield. LC 96-96696. (Orig.). 1996. pap. 10.00 (*0-345-41011-4*) Ballantine Pub Grp.

Making Peace Work: The Role of the International Development Community. Nicole Ball & Tammy Halevy. LC 96-33786. (Overseas Development Council Ser.: Vol. 18). 132p. (Orig.). 1996. pap. text 13.95 (*1-56517-022-9*) Overseas Dev Council.

***Making Peasants Backward: Managing Populations in Russian Agricultural Cooperatives, 1861-1914.** Yanni Kotsonis. LC 98-55363. 272p. 1999. text 65.00 (*0-312-22099-5*) St Martin.

Making People Disappear: An Amazing Chronicle of Photographic Deception. A. Jaubert. (Intelligence & National Security Library). (Illus.). 192p. 1989. pap. 32.95 (*0-08-037430-1*, 3714M) Brasseys.

Making People Friendly Towns. Tibbalds. 1992. text. write for info. (*0-582-09384-8*, Pub. by Addison-Wesley) Longman.

Making People Respond. Primo Angeli. (Illus.). 144p. 1997. pap. 34.95 (*0-942604-59-8*) Madison Square.

Making People Respond: Design for Marketing & Communication. Ed. by Dan Imhoff. (Illus.). 144p. 39.95 (*0-8230-3004-0*) Madison Square.

Making People Respond: Design for Marketing & Communication. Angeli Primo. LC 97-214110. (Illus.). 144p. 1997. pap. text 34.95 (*0-8230-2966-2*) Watsn-Guptill.

Making Peoples: A History of the New Zealanders: From Polynesian Settlement to the End of the Nineteenth Century. James Belich. 484p. 1996. text 34.00 (*0-8248-1890-3*) UH Pr.

Making People's Music: Moe Asch & Folkways Records. Peter D. Goldsmith. LC 97-33293. (Illus.). 468p. 1998. 34.95 (*1-56098-812-6*) Smithsonian.

***Making People's Music: Moe Asch & Folkways Records.** Peter D. Goldsmith. 468p. 2000. pap. 19.95 (*1-56098-370-1*) Smithsonian.

***Making Perfect Landings in Light Airplanes.** Ron Fowler. LC 99-59178. (Illus.). 144p. 2000. pap. 21.95 (*0-8138-0438-8*) Iowa St U Pr.

Making Perfect Takeoffs in Light Airplanes. Ron Fowler. LC 91-15181. (Illus.). 156p. 1991. 21.95 (*0-8138-0949-5*) Iowa St U Pr.

Making Period Dolls' House Accessories. Andrea Barham. (Illus.). 176p. 1997. pap. 17.95 (*1-86108-014-X*, Pub. by Guild Master) Sterling.

***Making Pet Palaces: Princely Homes & Furnishings to Pamper Your Pets.** Leslie Dierks. (Illus.). 128p. 2000. reprint ed. text 25.00 (*0-7881-6912-2*) DIANE Pub.

Making Phonology Functional: What Do I Do First? Shelley L. Velleman. LC 97-52015. 215p. 1998. text 46.00 (*0-7506-9525-0*) Buttrwrth-Heinemann.

Making Physics: A Biography of Brookhaven National Laboratory, 1946-1972. Robert P. Crease. LC 98-30327. 1999. 38.00 (*0-226-12017-1*) U Ch Pr.

Making Physics: A Biography of Brookhaven National Laboratory, 1946-1972. Robert P. Crease. LC 98-30327. (Illus.). 434p. 2000. pap. text 22.50 (*0-226-12019-8*) U Ch Pr.

Making Picture Frames. unabridged ed. Linda Hendry & Lisa Rebnord. (Kids Can Do It Ser.). (Illus.). 40p. (J). (gr. 3-7). 1999. pap. 5.95 (*1-55074-505-0*, Pub. by Kids Can Pr) Genl Dist Srvs.

Making Picture Frames in Wood. Manly Banister. LC 81-50985. (Home Craftsman Bks.). (Illus.). 128p. (YA). (gr. 10-12). 1982. pap. 10.95 (*0-8069-7542-3*) Sterling.

***Making "pictures in Our Heads" Government Advertising in Canada.** Jonathan W. Rose. LC 99-46404. (Praeger Series in Political Communication). 272p. 2000. write for info. (*0-275-96842-1*, Praeger Pubs) Greenwood.

Making Pigeons Pay. rev. ed. Wendell M. Levi. 1984. reprint ed. 20.00 (*0-910876-03-7*) Levi Pub.

Making Places in the Prehistoric World. Johanna Bruch. 1999. pap. text 29.95 (*1-85728-753-3*) UCL Pr Ltd.

***Making Plant Medicine.** Richard A. Cech. (Illus.). 296p. 2000. pap. 14.98 (*0-9700312-0-3*) Horizon Herbs.

Making Plant Places: Original Craft Projects for Making Containers, Hangers, Boxes, Baskets & Stands. Susan McDiarmid. LC 99-50033. (Illus.). 314p. 2000. pap. 24.95 (*0-88179-172-5*, Pub. by Hartley & Marks) Andrews & McMeel.

Making Plastic-Laminate Countertops. Herrick Kimball. LC 96-9014. (Illus.). 144p. 1997. pap. 19.95 (*1-56158-135-6*, 070262) Taunton.

Making Plays. Theresa Sullivan. 1992. pap. text 9.32 (*0-582-07876-8*) Longman.

***Making Plays: Interviews with Contemporary British Dramatist Directors.** Duncan Wu. LC 00-35266. (Illus.). 272p. 2000. pap. 18.95 (*0-312-23372-8*) St Martin.

Making Plays: Interviews with Contemporary British Dramatists Directors. Duncan Wu. text. write for info. (*0-312-23371-X*) St Martin.

Making Plays: The Writer-Director Relationship in the Theater Today. Richard Nelson & David Jones. Ed. by Colin Chambers. 165p. 1995. pap. 13.95 (*0-571-16354-8*) Faber & Faber.

Making Plum Jam. John Stewig. 32p. (J). Date not set. 14.99 (*0-7868-0460-2*, Pub. by Hyprn Child) Little.

Making Plum Jam. John Stewig. (Illus.). 32p. (J). Date not set. lib. bdg. 15.49 (*0-7868-2402-6*, Pub. by Hyprn Child) Little.

Making Poems. Ebborn & Alcorn. 1991. pap. text. write for info. (*0-582-05940-2*, Pub. by Addison-Wesley) Longman.

Making Policies for Children: A Study of the Federal Process. Cheryl D. Hayes. LC 82-2218. 281p. reprint ed. pap. 87.20 (*0-7837-1264-2*, 204140300020) Bks Demand.

Making Policy in Europe. Ed. by Svein S. Anderson & Kjell A. Eliassen. 1993. text 62.00 (*0-8039-8969-5*); pap. text 22.95 (*0-8039-8970-9*) Sage.

***Making Policy, Making Change: How Communities are Taking Law into Their Own Hands.** Makani Themba. 196p. 1999. pap. 28.00 (*1-890759-07-4*) Chardon Pr.

Making Policy Not Tea: Women in Parliament. Ed. by Arthur Baysting et al. (Illus.). 212p. 1994. 32.00 (*0-19-558275-6*) OUP.

Making Polymer Clay Jewellery. Sue Heaser. (Illus.). 128p. 1998. pap. text 16.95 (*0-304-35030-3*) Continuum.

***Making Popular Music: Musicians, Creativity & Institutions.** Jason Toynbee. 224p. 2000. text 65.00 (*0-340-65224-1*); pap. text 24.95 (*0-340-65223-3*) OUP.

Making Portfolio Assessment Easy: Reproducible Forms & Checklists & Strategies for Using... Mary Sullivan. 1996. pap. text 13.56 (*0-590-24507-4*) Scholastic Inc.

Making Portfolios, Products, & Performances Meaningful & Manageable for Students & Teachers: Instructional Strategies & Thematic Activities. Imogene Forte & Sandra Schurr. Ed. by Leslie Britt & Karla Westerman. (Illus.). 144p. (Orig.). (J). (gr. 4-8). 1995. pap. text 14.95 (*0-86530-313-4*, IP313-4) Incentive Pubns.

Making Positive Change: An Interactive Training Program. Marcella M. Murray. 88p. 1993. teacher ed. 2400.00 (*0-9630252-1-X*) Ctr Human Work.

Making Positive Choices: Career Development for Women in Social Care. What Women Can Do - What Organisations Can Do. Gayle Foster & Julia Phillipson. 1994. pap. 30.00 (*0-902789-95-3*, Pub. by Natl Inst Soc Work) St Mut.

Making Positive Choices: Career Development for Women in Social Care. What Women Can Do/What Organisations Can Do. Ed. by Gayle Foster & Julia Phillipson. 1994. pap. 50.00 (*0-902789-96-1*) Natl Inst Soc Work.

Making Positive Moves: Developing Short Term Fostering Services. Ed. by Judith Stone. 168p. 1995. pap. 30.00 (*1-873868-18-9*) BAAF.

Making Potpourri. Madeleine H. Siegler. Ed. by Kim Foster & Connie Parkinson. (Country Wisdom Bulletin Ser.). (Illus.). 32p. 1991. 2.95 (*0-88266-698-3*, Garden Way Pub) Storey Bks.

Making Potpourri. D. Webb. 1991. 18.95 (*0-8306-5307-4*) McGraw-Hill Prof.

Making Potpourri, Colognes & Soaps: 102 Natural Recipes. David A. Webb. (Illus.). 144p. 1988. 14.95 (*0-8306-9018-2*); pap. 10.95 (*0-8306-2918-1*) McGraw-Hill Prof.

Making Potpourri, Colognes & Soaps: 102 Two Natural Recipes. David A. Webb. 176p. 1988. pap. 12.95 (*0-07-155961-2*) McGraw.

Making Powder Horns, Bk. II. Robert D. Byerly. (Illus.). iv, 88p. (Orig.). 1996. mass mkt. 7.50 (*0-9653364-0-9*) Making Powder.

Making Prayer Work. Robert R. Leichtman & Carl Japikse. 144p. 1996. pap. 9.95 (*0-89804-828-1*, Enthea Pr) Ariel GA.

Making Presentations. DK Publishing Staff. LC 97-38907. (Essential Managers Handbks.). (Illus.). 72p. 1999. pap. 6.95 (*0-7894-2449-5*) DK Pub Inc.

Making Presentations. Jane Westberg & Hilliard Jason. 89p. (Orig.). (C). 1991. pap. text 15.00 (*0-938540-13-0*) CIS.

Making Presents. Ray Gibson. (How to Make Ser.). (Illus.). 64p. (J). (gr. 3-7). 1996. pap. 9.95 (*0-7460-2319-7*, Usborne); lib. bdg. 17.95 (*0-88110-795-6*, Usborne) EDC.

Making Presents. Penny King. LC 96-37356. (Illus.). 24p. 1997. lib. bdg. 17.27 (*1-57505-206-7*, Carolrhoda) Lerner Pub.

Making Pressed Flower Pictures. Scott Kennedy. (Illus.). 120p. 1982. reprint ed. pap. 9.95 (*0-486-24422-9*) Dover.

Making Printed Circuit Boards. Janet L. Axelson. 352p. 1993. pap. 22.95 (*0-07-002799-4*) McGraw.

Making Printed Circuit Boards. Janet L. Axelson. LC 93-9149. 1993. text 29.95 (*0-8306-3950-0*); pap. text 19.95 (*0-8306-3951-9*) McGraw-Hill Prof.

Making Prints from Nature. L. Bethmann. LC 97-50633. 1998. pap. 2.95 (*1-58017-013-7*) Storey Bks.

Making Problems, Creating Solutions: Challenging Young Mathematicians. Jill Ostrow. LC 98-26806. 176p. 1998. pap. text 19.50 (*1-57110-041-5*) Stenhse Pubs.

Making Process of God's Leaders. John Tetsola. 141p. (Orig.). 1994. pap. 9.99 (*0-9634306-3-7*) End-Time Wave.

Making Professional Development Schools Work: Politics, Policy & Practice. Ed. by Marsha Levine & Roberta Trachman. LC 97-1604. (School Reform Ser.). 272p. (C). 1997. text 50.00 (*0-8077-3634-1*); pap. text 22.95 (*0-8077-3633-3*) Tchrs Coll.

Making Profits Out of Seafood Wastes: Proceedings of the International Conference on Fish By-Products. Ed. by Sue Keller. (Alaska Sea Grant Report: No. 90-07). (Illus.). 239p. (Orig.). 1991. 10.00 (*1-56612-007-1*) AK Sea Grant CP.

Making Profits with Dairy Cows & Quotas. Gordon Throup. 300p. 1994. text 36.95 (*0-85236-281-1*, Pub. by Farming Pr) Diamond Farm Bk.

Making Progress. Ellen A. Knodt. 400p. (C). 1997. pap. text 53.00 (*0-673-38332-6*) Addson-Wesley Educ.

Making Progress: Education & Culture in New Times. Dennis Carlson. 168p. (C). 1996. 45.00 (*0-8077-3577-9*); pap. text 19.95 (*0-8077-3576-0*) Tchrs Coll.

Making Progress in English. Eve Bearne. LC 97-32907. 376p. (C). 1998. pap. 39.99 (*0-415-15996-2*) Routledge.

Making Progress in English: Grammar & Composition. Patricia R. Furey & Lionel Menasche. LC 89-16602. (Pitt Series in English As a Second Language). 232p. 1990. pap. text 15.95 (*0-472-08109-8*, 08109) U of Mich Pr.

Making Progress in Russian. Patricia A. Davis & Donald V. Oprendek. LC 71-170354. 327p. (C). 1988. pap., student ed. 33.95 (*0-471-60290-6*) Wiley.

Making Progress in Russian. Sloane & Bronstein. 224p. 1997. pap. text 34.95 (*0-471-14115-1*) Wiley.

Making Progress in Russian: A Second Year Course. 2nd ed. Arna Bronstein. LC 96-29535. (RUS.). 584p. 1996. pap. 80.95 (*0-471-14810-5*) Wiley.

Making Project Control Systems Work: Proceedings of a Session Sponsored by the Construction Division. Ed. by Paul M. Teicholz. 42p. 1985. 3.00 (*0-87262-504-4*) Am Soc Civil Eng.

Making Punk a Threat Again: Profane Existence: Best Cuts 1989-1993. Ed. by Daniel Siskind. (Illus.). 140p. 1997. pap. 10.00 (*0-9662035-0-X*) Profane Exist.

Making Puppets Come Alive: How to Learn & Teach Hand Puppetry. unabridged ed. Larry Engler & Carol Fijan. LC 96-44552. (Illus.). 192p. 1997. reprint ed. pap. text 8.95 (*0-486-29378-5*) Dover.

Making Quality Critical. Wilkinson. 1994. pap. 20.99 (*1-86152-389-0*, Pub. by ITBP) Thomson Learn.

Making Quality Critical: New Perspectives on Organizational Change. 2nd ed. Ed. by Adrian Wilkinson & Hugh Willmott. LC 94-10912. (Critical Perspectives on Work & Organization Ser.). 224p. (C). 1994. pap. 29.95 (*0-415-11754-2*, B4743) Thomson Learn.

Making Quality Work: A Leadership Guide for the Results-Driven Manager. Y. S. Chang et al. LC 92-53330. 320p. 1993. 25.00 (*0-88730-582-2*, HarpBusn) HarpInfo.

Making Quality Work: A Leadership Guide for the Results-Driven Manager. George Labivitz et al. 208p. 1995. pap. 18.95 (*0-471-13211-X*) Wiley.

Making Quality Work: A Leadership Guide for the Results-Driven Manager. George Labovitz et al. LC 93-61340. 200p. (C). 1993. pap. 16.00 (*0-939246-54-6*) Wiley.

Making Quick Breads. Barbara Karoff. Ed. by Kim Foster & Connie Parkinson. (Country Wisdom Bulletin Ser.). (Illus.). 32p. 1992. 2.95 (*0-88266-760-2*, Garden Way Pub) Storey Bks.

Making Quick, Simple & Effective Overheads (for Public Speaking) Danton O'Day. (Illus.). 8p. (Orig.). 1996. pap. 2.50 (*1-884241-68-9*, SPS0023) Energeia Pub.

Making Race: The Politics & Economics of Colored Identity in South Africa. Ian Goldin. 352p. (C). 1988. pap. text 27.95 (*0-582-01979-6*, 70432) Longman.

Making Race & Nation: A Comparison of the United States, South Africa & Brazil. Anthony W. Marx. LC 97-20437. (Cambridge Studies in Comparative Politics). (Illus.). 408p. (C). 1997. 29.95 (*0-521-58455-8*) Cambridge U Pr.

Making Race & Nation: A Comparison of the United States, South Africa & Brazil. Anthony W. Marx. LC 99-162515. (Cambridge Studies in Comparative Politics). 416p. (C). 1998. pap. 18.95 (*0-521-58590-2*) Cambridge U Pr.

***Making Racial Inequality.** Oliver. 2000. 25.00 (*0-465-05200-2*, Pub. by Basic); pap. 18.00 (*0-465-05201-0*, Pub. by Basic) HarpC.

Making Rag Dolls. unabridged ed. Juanita Clarke. LC 95-1027. (Illus.). 80p. 1995. reprint ed. pap. text 12.95 (*0-486-28684-3*) Dover.

Making Reading Possible Through Effective Classroom Management. Ed. by Diane K. Lapp. LC 80-10444. 248p. reprint ed. pap. 76.90 (*0-608-15488-1*, 202972700064) Bks Demand.

Making Real Friends in a Phony World. Jim Conway. Orig. Title: Friendship. 208p. 1991. pap. 8.95 (*0-310-54251-0*) Zondervan.

Making Real Friends in a Phony World. Jim Conway. Orig. Title: Friendship. 208p. 1991. reprint ed. pap. 8.99 (*0-310-54841-1*) Zondervan.

Making Real Money in Rental Properties: A Street Smart Guide to Finding Money-Making Opportunities in ANY Market. Susan J. Underhill & Ken Upshaw. 200p. 1992. pap. 16.95 (*1-55738-253-0*, Irwn Prfssnl) McGraw-Hill Prof.

Making Redundancy Work for You. Michael Bretherton & Chris Dunn. (C). 1988. 510.00 (*0-7855-4551-4*) St Mut.

Making Relationships: Gender in the Forming of Academic Community. Kathleen Dixon. LC 95-53029. (Studies in Composition & Rhetoric: No. 2). VIII, 172p. (C). 1997. text 41.95 (*0-8204-3123-0*) P Lang Pubng.

Making Representations: Museums in the Post-Colonial Era. Moira G. Simpson. LC 96-11517. (Illus.). 304p. (C). 1996. 85.00 (*0-415-06785-5*) Routledge.

Making Research Relevant. Poindexter. 1999. pap. text 53.95 (*0-312-19162-6*) St Martin.

Making Research Work: Promoting Child Care Policy & Practice. Dorota Iwaniec & John Pinkerton. LC 98-5759. 302p. 1998. pap. 54.95 (*0-471-97952-X*) Wiley.

Making Residential Care Work: Structure & Culture in Children's Homes. Elizabeth Brown et al. LC 98-70907. (Dartington Social Research Ser.: No. 1). (Illus.). 200p. 1998. pap. 16.95 (*1-84014-457-2*) Ashgate Pub Co.

Making Ridge Till Work for You. 1995. 9.95 (*0-944079-17-2*) Lessiter Pubns.

Making Rights Work. Penny Smith. LC 99-11977. xiii, 240p. 1999. 68.95 (*1-84014-784-9*, Pub. by Ashgate Pub) Ashgate Pub Co.

Making Ritual with Motherpeace Cards: Multicultural, Woman-Centered Practices for Spiritual Growth. Vicki Noble. LC 98-3527. (Illus.). 224p. 1998. pap. 14.00 (*0-609-80208-9*) Harmony Bks.

***Making Robots Smarter: Combining Sensing & Action Through Robot Learning.** Katharina Morik et al. LC 99-32645. 269p. 1999. write for info. (*0-7923-8562-4*) Kluwer Academic.

Making Romantic Fabric Covered Boxes. Mary Jo Hiney. LC 97-51571. (Illus.). 128p. 1998. 27.95 (*0-8069-9995-0*, Chapelle) Sterling.

Making Room. Phoebe Koehler. LC 91-41356. (Illus.). 48p. (J). (ps-3). 1993. lib. bdg. 14.95 (*0-02-750875-7*, Bradbury S&S) S&S Childrens.

Making Room. Sheila Fischman. Tr. by Michel Tremblay from FRE. 256p. 1990. reprint ed. pap. text 12.95 (*1-85242-162-2*) Serpents Tail.

Making Room: Recovering Hospitality As a Christian Tradition. Christine D. Pohl. LC 99-31765. 214p. 1999. pap. 15.00 (*0-8028-4431-6*) Eerdmans.

Making Room: The Economics of Homelessness. Brendan O'Flaherty. (Illus.). 352p. 1996. 44.50 (*0-674-54342-4*) HUP.

Making Room: The Economics of Homelessness. Brendan O'Flaherty. (Illus.). 368p. 1998. pap. text 17.95 (*0-674-54343-2*) HUP.

***Making Room at the Table: An Invitation to Multicultural Worship.** Brian K. Blount. 176p. 2000. pap. 15.95 (*0-664-22202-1*) Westminster John Knox.

Making Room for Katherine. Philippa G. Mulford. LC 93-32268. 160p. (J). (gr. 5-9). 1994. mass mkt. 14.95 (*0-02-767652-8*, Mac Bks Young Read) S&S Childrens.

Making Room for Making Art: A Thoughtful & Practical Guide to Bringing the Pleasure of Artistic Expression Back into Your Life. Sally Warner. LC 93-40774. (Illus.). 224p. (Orig.). 1994. pap. 12.95 (*1-55652-212-6*) Chicago Review.

Making Room for Students: Sharing Teacher Authority in Room 104. Celia Oyler. 192p. (C). 1996. text 40.00 (*0-8077-3546-9*); pap. text 18.95 (*0-8077-3545-0*) Tchrs Coll.

Making Room to Pray. Terry Teykl. 129p. 1993. pap., student ed. 11.95 (*0-917851-66-8*) Bristol Hse.

Making Room to Pray. Terry Teykl. 1998. 13.00 (*1-57892-046-9*) Prayer Pt Pr.

Making Roses Behave. A. E. Albera. (Illus.). 1960. spiral bd. 4.95 (*0-87505-244-4*) Borden.

Making Rules in the Uruguay Round of the GATT: A Study of International Leadership. Jarrod Wiener. LC 95-19400. (Illus.). 256p. 1995. text 79.95 (*1-85521-673-6*, Pub. by Dartmth Pub) Ashgate Pub Co.

Making Rural Australia: An Economic History of Technical & Institutional Creativity, 1788-1860. Geoffrey Raby. (Illus.). 240p. 1997. pap. text 38.00 (*0-19-553420-4*) OUP.

***Making Russian Democracy Work: Social Capital, Economic Development & Democratization.** Christopher Marsh. LC 00-29227. (Studies in Russian History: Vol. 4). 202p. 2000. lib. bdg. 89.95 (*0-7734-7803-5*) E Mellen.

Making Rustic Furniture: The Tradition, Spirit & Technique with Dozens of Project Ideas. Daniel Mack. LC 90-4517. (Illus.). 160p. 1992. pap. 19.95 (*1-887374-12-4*, Pub. by Lark Books) Sterling.

Making Rustic Originals: Turning Furniture Finds into Folk Art. Abby Ruoff. LC 98-35415. (Illus.). 216p. 1999. pap. 24.95 (*0-88179-155-5*) Hartley & Marks.

***Making Sabbath Special: Simple Traditions to Make the Sabbath a Delight.** Celeste P. Walker. Ed. by Jerry D. Thomas. LC 98-45168. 127p. 1999. pap. 9.99 (*0-8163-1706-2*) Pacific Pr Pub Assn.

Making Safe Food: A Management Guide for Microbiological Quality. W. F. Harrigan & R. W. Park. (Illus.). 160p. 1991. pap. text 37.00 (*0-12-326045-0*) Acad Pr.

Making Safety Work: Getting Management Commitment to Occupational Health & Safety. Andrew Hopkins. 224p. 1996. pap. 24.95 (*1-86373-869-X*, Pub. by Allen & Unwin Pty) Paul & Co Pubs.

Making Saints: Religion & the Public Image of the British Army, 1809-1885. Kenneth E. Hendrickson, 3rd. LC 97-14917. 200p. 1998. 36.00 (*0-8386-3729-9*) Fairleigh Dickinson.

Making Salads: Making Salads. Deni Bown. (101 Essential Tips Ser.). 72p. 1996. pap. 4.95 (*0-7894-0563-6*) DK Pub Inc.

Making Sales Manager: All You Need to Know to Lead & Succeed. Robert Nesbit & Arthur Miller. 225p. 1992. 24.95 (*1-55738-400-2*, Irwn Prfssnl) McGraw-Hill Prof.

***Making Salmon: An Environmental History of the Northwest Fisheries Crisis.** Joseph E. Taylor, III. LC 99-35414. (Illus.). 488p. 1999. 34.95 (*0-295-97840-6*) U of Wash Pr.

Making Samplers: 20 Complete Charted Projects from Today's Best Designers. Embroiderers Guild Staff. (Illus.). 144p. 1997. pap. 17.95 (*0-7153-0483-6*) Sterling.

Making Santas with Katie Redd. Katie Redd. LC 97-61776. (Illus.). 92p. 1997. pap. 14.95 (*0-916809-94-3*) Scott Pubns MI.

Making Sauerkraut & Pickled Vegetables at Home see Cultured Cabbage: Rediscovering the Art of Making Sauerkraut

Making School a Place of Peace. Theresa M. Bey & Gwendolyn Y. Turner. LC 95-22884. (Illus.). 184p. 1995. 55.95 (*0-8039-6192-8*); pap. 24.95 (*0-8039-6193-6*) Corwin Pr.

Making School & Community Recreation Fun for Everyone: Places & Ways to Integrate. Ed. by M. Sherril Moon. LC 94-28438. 256p. 1994. pap. 32.00 (*1-55766-155-3*) P H Brookes.

Making School by Hand: Developing a Meaning-Centered Curriculum from Everyday Life. Mary K. Glover. LC 96-39059. (Illus.). 138p. (Orig.). 1997. pap. 19.95 (*0-8141-3037-2*) NCTE.

***Making School Count: Promoting Urban Student Motivation & Success.** Karen Manheim Teel & Andrea DeBruin-Parecki. LC 00-32179. 2000. pap. write for info. (*0-415-23055-1*) Routledge.

Making School Inclusion Work: A Guide to Everyday Practices. Katie Blenk & Doris L. Fine. LC 94-38275. 254p. 1994. pap. 24.95 (*0-914797-96-4*) Brookline Bks.

Making School Reform Happen see Keepers of the Dream: The Triumph of Effective Schools

Making Schools Effective. Brighouse. (C). Date not set. write for info. (*0-415-10587-0*); pap. text. write for info. (*0-415-10588-9*) Routledge.

Making Schools More Effective. Barry McGaw. (C). 1993. pap. 70.00 (*0-86431-135-4*, Pub. by Aust Council Educ Res) Stylus Pub VA.

Making Schools Multicultural: Campus & Classroom. Carl A. Grant & Mary L. Gomez. 430p. (C). 1995. pap. text 39.00 (*0-02-345601-9*, Macmillan Coll) P-H.

Making Schools Safe for Students: Creating a Proactive School Safety Plan. Peter D. Blauvelt. LC 99-6377. (One-Off Ser.). (Illus.). 192p. 1999. pap. 59.95 (*0-8039-6888-4*) Corwin Pr.

Making Schools Smarter: A System for Monitoring School & District Progress. Kenneth Leithwood & Robert Aitken. (Illus.). 216p. 1995. pap. 34.95 (*0-8039-6292-4*) Corwin Pr.

***Making Schools Smarter: A System for Monitoring School & District Progress.** 2nd ed. Kenneth A. Leithwood et al. LC 00-29536. 2000. pap. write for info. (*0-7619-7505-5*) Corwin Pr.

Making Schools Work: Improving Performance & Controlling Costs. Eric A. Hanushek. LC 94-283225. (Orig.). (C). 1994. pap. 14.95 (*0-8157-3425-5*) Brookings.

Making Schools Work: Improving Performance & Controlling Costs. Eric A. Hanushek. LC 94-283225. 195p. (Orig.). (C). 1994. 34.95 (*0-8157-3426-3*) Brookings.

Making Schools Work: Practical Management of Support Operations. William K. Poston, Jr. et al. LC 92-3073. 208p. 1992. pap. 21.95 (*0-8039-6016-6*) Corwin Pr.

Making Schools Work for Underachieving Minority Students: Next Steps for Research, Policy, & Practice, 36. Ed. by Josie G. Bain & Joan L. Herman. LC 89-48904. (Contributions to the Study of Education Ser.: No. 36). 320p. 1990. 59.95 (*0-313-26889-4*, BMH/) Greenwood.

Making Science: Between Nature & Society. Stephen Cole. (Illus.). 304p. (Orig.). 1992. text 49.95 (*0-674-54347-5*) HUP.

Making Science: Between Nature & Society. Stephen Cole. (Illus.). 304p. (Orig.). (C). 1995. pap. text 16.95 (*0-614-07250-6*) HUP.

Making Science: Between Nature & Society. Stephen Cole & Linda Gordon. (Illus.). 304p. (Orig.). (C). 1995. pap. text 18.50 (*0-674-54344-0*) HUP.

Making Science Our Own: Public Images of Science, 1910-1955. Marcel C. LaFollette. LC 89-20555. (Illus.). 312p. 1995. pap. text 19.95 (*0-226-46779-1*) U Ch Pr.

Making Science Our Own: Public Images of Science, 1910-1955. Marcel C. LaFollette. LC 89-20555. (Illus.). 312p. 1995. lib. bdg. 54.00 (*0-226-46778-3*) U Ch Pr.

Making Science Pay: Economics of Agricultural R & D Policy. Julian M. Alston & Philip G. Pardey. (Studies in Agricultural Policy). 324p. 1995. 29.95 (*0-8447-3900-6*) Am Enterprise.

Making Scientific Comparisons. Bob De Weese. (Science Mini-Unit Intermediate Ser.: Vol. 7). (Illus.). 16p. (J). (gr. 3-6). 1994. pap. text 5.95 (*1-55799-298-3*, EMC838) Evan-Moor Edu Pubs.

***Making Scrapbooks: Complete Guide to Preserving Your Treasured Memories.** Vanessa-Ann. LC 97-33672. (Illus.). 128p. 1998. 24.95 (*0-8069-9900-4*) Sterling.

***Making Scripture Memorable: Over 150 Fun Bible Memory Activities for Families at Home or Church.** Susan L. Lingo. (Illus.). 128p. 2000. pap. text 14.99 (*0-7847-1110-0*, 02826) Standard Pub.

Making Scripture Memory Fun: 52 Unforgettable Bible Verse Adventures for Children. Ed. by Beth Wolf. LC 98-14148. (Illus.). 128p. 1998. per. 15.99 (*0-7644-2065-8*, Vital Ministry) Group Pub.

Making Scripture Stick: 52 Unforgettable Bible Verse Adventures for Children. Lisa Flinn & Barbara Younger. 108p. (J). 1992. pap. 14.99 (*1-55945-093-2*) Group Pub.

Making SCSI Work Vol. 1: A Practical Users Guide. Paralan Staff. Ed. by Marc D. Brooks et al. (Illus.). 140p. (Orig.). 1999. pap. 19.95 (*0-9657465-0-X*) Paralan Corp.

Making Seasonal Big Books with Children. Jo E. Moore et al. (Illus.). 64p. (J). (gr. k-2). 1990. pap. 11.95 (*1-55799-194-4*, EMC304) Evan-Moor Edu Pubs.

Making Second Ghetto. Arnold R. Hirsch. LC 97-50586. 362p. 1998. pap. text 17.00 (*0-226-34244-1*) U Ch Pr.

Making Security Social. Greg Eghigian. (Social History, Popular Culture & Politics in Germany Ser.). (Illus.). 400p. (C). text 59.50 (*0-472-11122-1*, 11122) U of Mich Pr.

Making Self-Publishing Pay: Profiles of Successful Small Presses. Suzanne P. Thomas. 256p. 2000. pap. 18.95 (*0-9664691-2-7*) Gemstone Hse.

Making Sense. Ed. by Jerome S. Bruner & Helen Haste. 260p. 1988. 65.00 (*0-416-38240-1*); pap. 15.95 (*0-416-92490-5*) Routledge.

Making Sense. Anne Chapman. 1994. pap. 15.00 (*0-87447-470-1*) College Bd.

***Making Sense: A Theory of Interpretation.** Paul Thom. LC 99-48748. 128p. 2000. pap. 17.95 (*0-8476-9783-5*); text 59.95 (*0-8476-9782-7*) Rowman.

Making Sense: Animal Perception & Communication. Bruce Brooks. LC 93-10474. (Knowing Nature Ser.). 80p. (J). 1993. 17.00 (*0-374-34742-5*) FS&G.

***Making Sense: Ellen Gallagher, Christian Marclay & Liliana Porter, 4 vols.** Contemporary Museum Staff & Adam Lerner. (Illus.). 2000. pap. 25.00 (*0-9700986-0-X*) Contemp Mus.

Making Sense: Modula 2. E. Tatham. 1994. pap. write for info. (*1-85032-278-3*) Thomson Learn.

Making Sense: Reading Comprehension Improved Through Categorizing. Christian Gerhard. Ed. by Helen J. James. LC 75-37706. 175p. reprint ed. pap. 54.30 (*0-608-18368-7*, 203510000092) Bks Demand.

***Making Sense: The Meaning of a Life.** Joseph B. Fabry. LC 00-34444. 2000. write for info. (*1-55896-406-1*, Skinner Hse Bks) Unitarian Univ.

Making Sense As a School Principal: Persisting Questions, Creative Opportunities. Richard Ackerman et al. (Education Ser.). 207p. 1995. 29.95 (*0-7879-0164-4*) Jossey-Bass.

Making Sense in English. Ruth Pierson & Susan Vik. Ed. by Kathleen Sands-Boehmer. 304p. (Orig.). (C). 1987. pap. text 24.91 (*0-201-14585-5*) Addison-Wesley.

***Making Sense in Geography & Environmental Studies: A Student's Guide to Research, Writing, & Style.** 2nd ed. Margot Northey & David B. Knight. (Illus.). 224p. 2000. pap. 13.95 (*0-19-541527-2*) OUP.

Making Sense in Life & Literature. Hans U. Gumbrecht. Tr. by Glen Burns from GER. (Theory & History of Literature Ser.: Vol. 79). 416p. (C). 1992. pap. 19.95 (*0-8166-1954-9*); text 49.95 (*0-8166-1952-2*) U of Minn Pr.

Making Sense of a Changing Economy: Technology, Markets, & Morals. Edward J. Nell. 240p. (C). 1996. pap. 22.99 (*0-415-13640-7*) Routledge.

Making Sense of a New World: Learning to Read in a Second Language. Eve Gregory. LC 96-215973. (One-Off Ser.). (Illus.). 208p. 1996. pap. (*1-85396-263-5*) Corwin Pr.

Making Sense of a Primary Care Led Health Service. Peter Littlejohns & Christina R. Victor. LC 96-25406. 1996. write for info. (*1-85775-048-9*, Radcliffe Med Pr) Scovill Paterson.

Making Sense of Academic Life: Academics, Universities & Change. Peter G. Taylor. LC 99-12582. 167p. 1999. pap. 34.95 (*0-335-20184-9*, Pub. by OpUniv Pr) Taylor & Francis.

Making Sense of Adolescence: How to Parent from the Heart. 2nd ed. John Crudele & Richard Erickson. 271p. 1999. reprint ed. 22.95 (*0-9669924-0-7*); reprint ed. pap. 13.95 (*0-9669924-1-5*) J Crudele.

Making Sense of Adoption: A Parent's Guide. Lois R. Melina. LC 89-45106. 288p. (Orig.). 1989. pap. 13.00 (*0-06-096319-0*, PL 6319, Perennial) HarperTrade.

Making Sense of Advance Directives. Nancy King. 240p. (C). 1991. lib. bdg. 118.00 (*0-7923-1163-9*, Pub. by Kluwer Academic) Kluwer Academic.

Making Sense of Advance Directives. rev. ed. Nancy M. King. LC 95-42746. (Clinical Medical Ethics Ser.). 286p. 1996. pap. 19.95 (*0-87840-605-0*) Georgetown U Pr.

Making Sense of Algebra: Cognitive Processes: Influencing Comprehension. M. E. McGregor. 139p. (C). 1991. pap. 100.00 (*0-7300-1282-4*, ECT403, Pub. by Deakin Univ) St Mut.

Making Sense of America: Sociological Analyses & Essays. Herbert J. Gans. LC 98-36860. (Legacies of Social Thought Ser.: No. 124). 384p. 1998. pap. 27.95 (*0-8476-9041-5*) Rowman.

Making Sense of America: Sociological Analysis & Essays. Herbert J. Gans. LC 98-36860. (Legacies of Social Thought Ser.: No. 124). 384p. 1998. text 65.00 (*0-8476-9040-7*) Rowman.

Making Sense of Astrology. Ronny Martens & Tim Trachet. LC 98-3528. (Illus.). 250p. 1998. 23.95 (*1-57392-218-8*) Prometheus Bks.

***Making Sense of Attention Deficit/Hyperactivity Disorder** Carol R. Lensch. LC 99-36508. 168p. 2000. 55.00 (*0-89789-700-5*, Bergin & Garvey) Greenwood.

Making Sense of Audit. 2nd ed. Donald Irvine & Sally Irvine. LC 97-5656. (Business Side of General Practice Ser.). 1997. write for info. (*1-85775-119-1*, Radcliffe Med Pr) Scovill Paterson.

Making Sense of Behavior: The Meaning of Control. William T. Powers. Ed. by Dag Forssell. LC 99-216013. 186p. (C). 1998. pap. 14.95 (*0-9647121-5-6*) Benchmark CT.

Making Sense of College Grades. Ohmer Milton et al. LC 85-45910. (Jossey-Bass Higher Education Ser.). (Illus.). 309p. reprint ed. pap. 95.80 (*0-7837-6519-3*, 204563100007) Bks Demand.

Making Sense of Data. Mary M. Lindquist et al. LC 92-41881. (Curriculum & Evaluation Standards for School Mathematics Addenda Ser.: Grades K-6). (Illus.). 48p. 1992. pap. 12.95 (*0-87353-318-6*) NCTM.

Making Sense of Data: A Self-Instruction Manual on the Interpretation of Epidemiological Data. 2nd ed. J. H. Abramson. LC 93-36497. (Illus.). 416p. (C). 1994. pap. text 36.50 (*0-19-508969-3*) OUP.

Making Sense of Dental Practice Management: The Business Side of General Dental Practice. Raj Rattan. LC 95-52760. 237p. 1996. pap. 29.95 (*1-85775-017-9*, Radcliffe Med Pr) Scovill Paterson.

Making Sense of Development: An Introduction to Classical & Contemporary Theories of Development & Their Application to Southeast Asia. P. W. Preston. 304p. 1987. text 49.95 (*0-7102-0813-8*, Routledge Thoemms) Routledge.

Making Sense of Developmentally & Culturally Appropriate Practice (DCAP) in Early Childhood Education. Eunsook Hyun. (Rethinking Childhood Ser.: Vol. 6). XVI, 176p. (C). 1998. pap. text 29.95 (*0-8204-3765-4*) P Lang Pubng.

Making Sense of Drama: A Guide to Classroom Practice. Jonothan Neelands. 122p. (Orig.). (C). 1985. pap. text 19.50 (*0-435-18658-2*, 18658) Heinemann.

***Making Sense of Elementary Algebra: Data, Equations, & Graphs, Preliminary Edition.** Elaine A. Kasimatis & Cindy L. Erickson. 560p. 1999. pap. text 65.00 (*0-201-85900-9*) Addison-Wesley.

Making Sense of Ethnomethodology. Eric Livingston. 160p. (C). 1988. pap. write for info. (*0-7102-1262-3*, Routledge Thoemms); text 55.00 (*0-7102-1261-5*, Routledge Thoemms) Routledge.

Making Sense of Experiential Learning: Diversity in Theory & Practice. Ed. by Susan W. Weil & Ian McGill. 304p. 1990. pap. 41.95 (*0-335-09713-8*) OpUniv Pr.

Making Sense of Faith: An Introduction to Theology. R. Charles Hill. 192p. 1995. pap. 9.95 (*0-85574-150-3*, Pub. by E J Dwyer) Morehouse Pub.

Making Sense of Federal Dollars: A Funding Guide for Social Service Providers. Madelyn DeWoody. LC 94-214548. (Orig.). 1994. pap. 9.95 (*0-87868-505-7*) Child Welfare.

Making Sense of Federal Dollars: A Guide to Understanding Allocation Formulas. 2nd ed. Paula Duggan. 75p. 1996. pap. text 21.00 (*1-882061-63-2*) Northeast-Midwest.

Making Sense of Federal Employment & Training Policy for Youth & Adults Vol. II: Expert Recommendations to Create a Comprehensive & Unified System. Kristina M. Moore & Alan S. Zuckerman. 54p. 1995. pap. text. write for info. (*1-887031-51-0*) Am Youth Policy.

Making Sense of Federal Manpower Policy. 2nd ed. Sar A. Levitan & Garth L. Mangum. (Policy Papers in Human Resources & Industrial Relations Ser.: No. 2). (Orig.). (C). 1973. pap. 5.00 (*0-87736-102-9*) U of Mich Inst Labor.

Making Sense of Fibromyalgia. Daniel J. Wallace & Janice Wallace. LC 98-28531. (Illus.). 256p. 1999. 25.00 (*0-19-511611-9*) OUP.

Making Sense of Futures Options. 32p. 1994. pap. 3.50 (*0-915513-43-9*) Ctr Futures Ed.

Making Sense of Hierarchy: Cognition as Social Process in Fiji. Christian Toren. LC 90-37699. (Monographs on Social Anthropology: Vol. 61). (Illus.). 256p. (C). 1990. text 70.00 (*0-485-19561-5*, Pub. by Athlone Pr) Humanities.

Making Sense of Humanity: And Other Philosophical Essays, 1982-1993. Bernard Williams. 263p. (C). 1995. pap. text 18.95 (*0-521-47868-5*) Cambridge U Pr.

Making Sense of Humanity: And Other Philosophical Essays, 1982-1993. Bernard Williams. 263p. (C). 1995. text 59.95 (*0-521-47279-2*) Cambridge U Pr.

Making Sense of Humor: How to Add Joy to Your Life. Lila Green. LC 94-5527. (Illus.). 130p. 1994. pap. 10.00 (*1-879198-12-6*) Knwldg Ideas & Trnds.

Making Sense of Illness: Science, Society & Disease. Robert A. Aronowitz. (Studies in the History of Medicine Ser). 283p. (C). 1999. pap. text 17.95 (*0-521-55825-5*) Cambridge U Pr.

Making Sense of Illness: Studies in Twentieth Century Medical Thought. Robert A. Aronowitz. LC 97-9805. (Studies in the History of Medicine). 282p. (C). 1998. 29.95 (*0-521-55234-6*) Cambridge U Pr.

Making Sense of Illness: The Social Psychology of Health & Disease. Alan Radley. 256p. 1995. text 45.00 (*0-8039-8908-3*); pap. text 15.99 (*0-8039-8909-1*) Sage.

***Making Sense of Integrated Science: A Guide for High Schools.** Biological Sciences Curriculum Study Staff. (Illus.). xii, 243p. 2000. pap. text 24.00 (*1-929614-03-9*) Biological Sciences.

Making Sense of it All. Lund. LC 98-33536. 190p. 1998. pap. text 27.80 (*0-13-924002-0*) P-H.

Making Sense of It All: Pascal & the Meaning of Life. Thomas V. Morris. 224p. (Orig.). 1992. pap. 14.00 (*0-8028-0652-X*) Eerdmans.

Making Sense of Japanese: What the Textbooks Don't Tell You. Jay Rubin. (Power Japanese Ser.). 1998. pap. text 13.00 (*4-7700-2310-3*, Pub. by Kodansha Intl) Kodansha.

Making Sense of Java: A Guide for Managers & the Rest of Us. Bruce Simpson. 180p. (C). 1996. pap. text 29.95 (*0-13-263294-2*) P-H.

Making Sense of Journals in the Life Sciences: From Specialty Origins to Contemporary Assortment. Ed. by Tony Stankus. LC 92-4085. (Serials Librarian Ser.: Suppl. No. 8). (Illus.). 261p. 1992. 49.95 (*1-56024-181-0*) Haworth Pr.

Making Sense of Journals in the Life Sciences: From Specialty Origins to Contemporary Assortment. Tony Stankus. LC 92-4085. (Serials Librarian Ser.: Suppl. No. 8). 261p. 1996. pap. 19.95 (*0-7890-0080-6*) Haworth Pr.

Making Sense of Journals in the Physical Sciences: From Specialty Origins to Contemporary Assortment. Ed. by Tony Stankus. LC 92-4092. (Serials Librarian Ser.: Suppl. No. 7). (Illus.). 239p. 1992. 49.95 (*1-56024-180-2*) Haworth Pr.

Making Sense of Journals in the Physical Sciences: From Specialty Origins to Contemporary Assortment. Tony Stankus. LC 92-4092. (Serials Librarian Ser.: Suppl. No. 7). 239p. 1996. pap. 19.95 (*0-7890-0079-2*) Haworth Pr.

Making Sense of Law Firms: Strategy, Structure & Ownership. Stephen Mayson. LC 98-128322. 566p. 1997. 84.00 (*1-85431-700-8*, Pub. by Blackstone Pr) Gaunt.

Making Sense of Literature. John Reichert. LC 77-24455. 234p. 1978. lib. bdg. 10.00 (*0-226-70769-5*) U Ch Pr.

Making Sense of MacIntyre. Michael Fuller. LC 97-78319. (Avebury Series in Philosophy). 158p. 1998. text 59.95 (*1-84014-173-5*, Pub. by Ashgate Pub) Ashgate Pub Co.

Making Sense of Managed Care Vol. I: Building Blocks & Fundamentals. Ed. by Kimball Miller & Elaine Miller. LC 97-70473. 141p. 1997. 32.00 (*0-924674-51-2*) Am Coll Phys Execs.

Making Sense of Managed Care Vol. II: Strategic Positioning. Ed. by Kimball Miller & Elaine Miller. LC 97-70473. 185p. 1997. 32.00 (*0-924674-52-0*) Am Coll Phys Execs.

Making Sense of Managed Care Vol. III: Operational Issues & Practical Answers. Ed. by Kimball Miller & Elaine Miller. LC 97-70473. 199p. 1997. 32.00 (*0-924674-53-9*) Am Coll Phys Execs.

Making Sense of Management: A Critical Introduction. Mats Alvesson & Hugh Willmott. LC 96-68525. 272p. 1996. 79.95 (*0-8039-8388-3*); pap. 27.50 (*0-8039-8389-1*) Sage.

Making Sense of Management Jargon. J. M. Harries & R. Woodgate. 146p. (C). 1986. 70.00 (*0-86236-027-7*, Pub. by Granary); pap. 60.00 (*0-7855-2250-6*, Pub. by Granary) St Mut.

Making Sense of Managing Culture. David Cray & Geoffrey R. Mallory. (Illus.). 224p. 1997. mass mkt. 29.95 (*0-415-07382-0*) Routledge.

Making Sense of Managing Culture. David Cray & Geoffrey R. Mallory. LC 98-164549. 224p. 1998. pap. 40.00 (*1-86152-177-4*) Thomson Learn.

Making Sense of Managing Culture. David Cray & Geoffrey R. Mallory. LC 98-164549. (Illus.). 224p. 1998. pap. 13.99 (*1-86152-178-2*) Thomson Learn.

Making Sense of Menopause: Over One Hundred Fifty Women & Experts Share Their Wisdom, Experience & Common Sense Advice. Faye K. Cone. LC 93-2526. 384p. 1993. per. 13.00 (*0-671-78638-5*, Fireside) S&S Trade Pap.

Making Sense of Metric. M. C. Malcolm. 64p. (Orig.). 1989. pap. 9.95 (*0-8464-1390-6*) Beekman Pubs.

Making Sense of Modern Times: Peter L. Berger & the Vision of Interpretive Sociology. Ed. by James D. Hunter & Stephen C. Ainley. 256p. 1986. pap. 15.95 (*0-7102-0745-X*, 0745, Routledge Thoemms) Routledge.

Making Sense of Modernity: Religion & Public Life, Vol. 28. Ed. by Paul Gottfried. 118p. (C). 1994. pap. 21.50 (*1-56000-726-5*) Transaction Pubs.

Making Sense of Modula-2. E. Tatham. 1994. mass mkt. 34.95 (*0-412-57290-7*, Chap & Hall NY) Chapman & Hall.

Making Sense of Money: Using Money & Manipulatives. Beth M. Kobett & Kay Sammons. Ed. by Meg Stillman. (Illus.). 64p. 1997. pap., teacher ed. 7.99 (*0-7916-0619-8*, W-MM9624) WORLD CLASS Lrning.

Making Sense of Music: Foundations for Music Education. Colin Durrant & Graham Welch. (Cassell Education Ser.). (Illus.). 192p. 1995. 80.00 (*0-304-33084-1*); pap. 29.95 (*0-304-33082-5*) Continuum.

***Making Sense of My World.** Ann Sharp & Laurance Splitter. 1999. pap. 22.50 (*0-86431-321-7*, Pub. by Aust Council Educ Res) Stylus Pub VA.

Making Sense of NHS Complaints & Disciplinary Procedures. David Pickersgill & Tony Stanton. LC 97-1119. 1997. write for info. (*1-85775-163-9*, Radcliffe Med Pr) Scovill Paterson.

Making Sense of Nietzsche: Reflections Timely & Untimely. Richard Schacht. LC 94-1914. (International Nietzsche Studies). 304p. 1994. pap. text 17.95 (*0-252-06412-7*) U of Ill Pr.

Making Sense of Nietzsche: Reflections Timely & Untimely. Richard Schacht. LC 94-1914. (International Nietzsche Studies). 304p. 1995. text 49.95 (*0-252-02125-8*) U of Ill Pr.

Making Sense of OSHA Compliance. Jeffrey Vincoli. LC 97-11924. 269p. 1997. text 59.00 (*0-86587-535-9*) Gov Insts.

Making Sense of Pain & Struggle: Finding the Strength to Go On. Neva Coyle. (Devotional Daybook Ser.). 16p. (Orig.). 1992. pap. 8.99 (*1-55661-276-1*) Bethany Hse.

M

An Asterisk (*) at the beginning of an entry indicates that the title is appearing for the first time.

Making Sense of Paul: A Basic Introduction to Pauline Theology. Virginia Wiles. LC 99-98001. 2000. pap. 16.95 (*1-56563-117-X*) Hendrickson MA.
Making Sense of Pensions & Retirement. Ed. by John Lindsay & Norman Ellis. LC 95-14243. 1995. write for info. (*1-85775-090-X*, Radcliffe Med Pr) Scovill Paterson.
***Making Sense of Performance Measurement in the Nonprofit Sector.** Diane E. Yoder & James M. Ferris. 18p. 1999. pap. 10.00 (*0-929556-19-4*) Ind Sector.
Making Sense of Personnel Management. 2nd ed. Sally Irvine & Hilary Haman. LC 97-5360. (Business Side of General Practice Ser.). 1997. write for info. (*1-85775-124-8*, Radcliffe Med Pr) Scovill Paterson.
Making Sense of Place: Children's Understanding of Large-Scale Environments. M. H. Matthews. (Illus.). 352p. (C). 1992. text 68.00 (*0-389-20987-2*) B&N Imports.
Making Sense of Politics. Arthur B. Sanders. LC 90-33581. 225p. 1990. reprint ed. pap. 69.80 (*0-608-00112-0*, 206087700006) Bks Demand.
Making Sense of Primary Inspection. Ian Sandbrook. LC 96-12681. 148p. 1996. 87.95 (*0-335-19665-9*); pap. 29.95 (*0-335-19664-0*) OpUniv Pr.
Making Sense of Psychiatric Cases. George I. Szmukler et al. (Illus.). 175p. 1986. pap. 28.95 (*0-19-261437-1*) OUP.
Making Sense of Qualitative Data: Complimentary Research Strategies. Amanda Coffey & Paul Atkinson. LC 95-41813. 220p. (C). 1996. 44.00 (*0-8039-7052-8*); pap. 18.50 (*0-8039-7053-6*) Sage.
Making Sense of Religion. Donald Reeves. (Illus.). 157p. 1992. pap. 7.95 (*0-563-20759-0*, BBC-Parkwest) Parkwest Pubns.
Making Sense of Research & Development. Ed. by Mark R. Baker & Simon Kirk. 1995. write for info. (*1-85775-094-2*, Radcliffe Med Pr) Scovill Paterson.
Making Sense of Secondary Science: Research into Children's Ideas. Ed. by Rosalind Driver et al. 176p. (C). 1993. pap. 22.99 (*0-415-09765-7*, B2450) Routledge.
Making Sense of Sentencing. Ed. by Julian V. Roberts & David P. Cole. 432p. 1999. pap. 27.95 (*0-8020-7644-0*); text 65.00 (*0-8020-0686-8*) U of Toronto Pr.
Making Sense of Sex: How Genes & Gender Influence Our Relationships. David P. Barash & Judith E. Lipton. LC 97-25746. 240p. 1997. 24.95 (*1-55963-452-9*) Island Pr.
***Making Sense of Shakespeare.** Charles H. Frey. LC 99-30591. 216p. 1999. 38.00 (*0-8386-3831-7*) Fairleigh Dickinson.
Making Sense of Social Development. Ed. by Karen Littleton et al. LC 98-25642. (Illus.). vi, 278p. (C). (gr. 13). 1999. pap. 22.99 (*0-415-17374-4*, D6390) Routledge.
***Making Sense of Social Security Reform.** Daniel N. Shaviro. LC 00-21709. 1999. 25.00 (*0-226-75116-3*) U Ch Pr.
Making Sense of Space: The History of Norwegian Space Activities. Ed. by John P. Collett. 1995. 48.00 (*82-00-22692-1*) Scandnvan Univ Pr.
Making Sense of Spelling & Pronunciation. Christine Digby & John Myers. LC 92-23301. 1993. 9.00 (*0-13-554205-7*) P-H.
Making Sense of Sport. 2nd ed. Ellis Cashmore. LC 95-25971. 304p. (C). 1996. 80.00 (*0-415-13306-8*); pap. 24.99 (*0-415-13307-6*) Routledge.
***Making Sense of Standards & Technologies for Serials Management: A Guide.** Rosemary Russell. 192p. 2000. pap. 85.00 (*1-85604-338-X*, LAP338X, Pub. by Library Association) Bernan Associates.
Making Sense of Statistics: A Conceptual Overview. Fred Pyrczak. 128p. (C). 1995. pap. text 19.95 (*1-884585-00-0*) Pyrczak Pub.
Making Sense of Statistics in Psychology: A Second-Level Course. B. S. Everitt. (Illus.). 368p. 1996. 90.00 (*0-19-852366-1*); pap. text 45.00 (*0-19-852365-3*) OUP.
Making Sense of Subsidiarity: How Much Centralization for Europe? David Begg et al. 192p. (C). 1994. pap. 14.95 (*1-898128-03-0*) Brookings.
Making Sense of Suffering: The Healing Confrontation with Your Own Past. rev. ed. J. Konrad Stettenbacher. LC 93-8157. 1994. pap. 11.95 (*0-452-01159-0*, Mer) NAL.
Making Sense of Suicide: An In-Depth Look at Why People Kill Themselves. Ed. by David Lester. LC 97-10780. 208p. (Orig.). 1997. pap. text 22.95 (*0-914783-82-3*) Charles.
***Making Sense of Taste: Food & Philosophy.** Carolyn Korsmeyer. LC 99-16165. 1999. 29.95 (*0-8014-3698-2*) Cornell U Pr.
Making Sense of Teaching. Sally Brown & Donald McIntyre. LC 92-17382. (Developing Teachers & Teaching Ser.). 1993. pap. 34.95 (*0-335-15795-5*) OpUniv Pr.
Making Sense of Television: The Psychology of Audience Interpretation. Sonia M. Livingstone. (International Series in Experimental Social Psychology). (Illus.). 226p. 1990. 54.00 (*0-08-036760-7*, 2605; 2704, Prgamon Press) Buttrwrth-Heinemann.
Making Sense of Television: The Psychology of Audience Interpretation. Sonia M. Livingstone. 226p. 1996. pap. 31.95 (*0-7506-2744-1*) Buttrwrth-Heinemann.
Making Sense of Television: The Psychology of Audience Interpretation. 2nd ed. Sonia M. Livingstone. LC 97-51630. (International Series in Social Psychology). 224p. (C). 1998. pap. 25.99 (*0-415-18536-X*) Routledge.
Making Sense of Television: The Psychology of Audience Interpretation. 2nd ed. Sonia M. Livingstone. LC 97-51630. (International Series in Social Psychology). (Illus.). 224p. (C). 1998. 85.00 (*0-415-18623-4*) Routledge.
Making Sense of Testing & Assessment. American Association of School Administrators Staf. 28p. 1993. pap. 2.50 (*0-87652-190-1*) Am Assn Sch Admin.
Making Sense of the Children Act: A Guide for the Social & Welfare Services. Nick Allen. LC 97-38899. 298p. 1998. pap. 54.95 (*0-471-97831-0*) Wiley.
Making Sense of the Dollars: The Costs & Uses of Faculty Compensation. Kathryn M. Moore & Marilyn J. Amey. Ed. & Frwd. by Jonathan D. Fife. (ASHE-ERIC Higher Education Reports: No. 94-5). 111p. (Orig.). 1994. pap. 24.00 (*1-878380-26-5*) GWU Grad Schl E&HD.
Making Sense of the ECG. Andrew Houghton & David Gray. (Illus.). 288p. 1997. pap. text 27.95 (*0-340-67657-4*, Pub. by E A) OUP.
Making Sense of the Economy. Ed. by Roger Martin-Fagg. LC 96-38882. (Self-Development for Managers Ser.). 144p. 1996. pap. 17.95 (*0-415-10318-5*, Pub. by ITBP) Thomson Learn.
Making Sense Of The Economy. Roger Martin-Fagg. 1996. pap. text 12.99 (*1-86152-521-4*) Thomson Learn.
Making Sense of the Episcopal Church: Leader's Guide. Ken Clark & Charlie Steen. 33p. (Orig.). 1996. pap., teacher ed. 10.95 (*0-8192-1667-4*) Morehouse Pub.
Making Sense of the Internet: A Guide for Small Voluntary Organisation. Mark Watson. 1998. pap. 50.00 (*1-899942-23-8*, Pub. by Natl Inst Soc Work) St Mut.
Making Sense of the Jonestown Suicides: A Sociological History of Peoples Temple. Judith M. Weightman. LC 83-21999. (Studies in Religion & Society: Vol. 7). 240p. 1984. lib. bdg. 89.95 (*0-88946-871-0*) E Mellen.
Making Sense of the Media: A Handbook of Popular Education Techniques. Eleonora C. Ferreira & Joao P. Ferreira. LC 93-24487. 128p. (Orig.). (C). 1996. pap. text 17.00 (*0-85345-880-4*, Pub. by Monthly Rev) NYU Pr.
Making Sense of the Molly Maguires. Kevin Kenny. (Illus.). 336p. 1998. pap. 19.95 (*0-19-511631-3*) OUP.
Making Sense of the New NHS White Paper. Mark Baker. LC 98-195926. 143 p. 1998. write for info. (*1-85775-239-2*) Scovill Paterson.
Making Sense of the Old Testament: 3 Crucial Questions. Tremper Longman, III. LC 98-30481. (3 Crucial Questions Ser.). 160p. (C). (gr. 13). 1998. pap. 11.99 (*0-8010-5828-7*) Baker Bks.
Making Sense of the Red Book. 3rd ed. Norman Ellis & John Chisholm. LC 97-22326. (Business Side of General Practice Ser.). 1997. write for info. (*1-85775-291-0*, Radcliffe Med Pr) Scovill Paterson.
***Making Sense of the Revelation: A Clear Message of Hope.** William L. Turner. LC 99-56448. 160p. 2000. pap. 16.00 (*1-57312-268-8*) Smyth & Helwys.
***Making Sense of the Trinity: 3 Crucial Questions.** Millard J. Erickson. LC 99-52525. 112p. 2000. pap. 11.99 (*0-8010-6287-X*) Baker Bks.
***Making Sense of War: The Second World War & the Fate of the Bolshevik Revolution.** Amir Weiner. (Illus.). 368p. 2000. 39.50 (*0-691-05702-8*) Princeton U Pr.
***Making Sense of Women's Lives: An Introduction to Women's Studies.** Ed. by Michele Plott & Lauri Umanski. 2000. pap. text 38.75 (*0-939693-53-4*) Collegiate Pr.
***Making Sense of Word Problems.** Lieven Verschaffel. 2000. 67.00 (*90-265-1628-2*) Swets.
Making Sense of Your Dollars: A Biblical Approach to Wealth. Ian Hodge. 192p. 1995. pap. text. write for info. (*1-879998-08-4*) Ross Hse Bks.
Making Sense of Your Freedom: Philosophy for the Perplexed. James W. Felt. LC 93-40065. (Illus.). 128p. 1994. text 29.95 (*0-8014-2908-0*); pap. text 9.95 (*0-8014-8191-0*) Cornell U Pr.
Making Sense of Your Kids. Joyce Sibley & Jerry Aldridge. (Illus.). 233p. 1998. 14.00 (*1-58107-003-9*) New Forums.
Making Sense of Your Teenager. Lawrence Kutner. (Parent & Child Ser.). 224p. 1998. reprint ed. pap. 11.00 (*0-380-71355-1*, Avon Bks) Morrow Avon.
Making Sense of Your World: A Biblical Worldview. W. Gary Phillips & William E. Brown. 291p. (C). 1996. pap. text 15.50 (*1-879215-32-2*) Sheffield WI.
Making Sense Out of Sorrow: A Journey of Faith. Foster R. McCurley & Alan Weitzman. LC 95-6281. 96p. (Orig.). 1995. pap. 8.00 (*1-56338-113-3*) TPI PA.
Making Sense Out of Suffering. Peter Kreeft. 196p. (Orig.). 1986. pap. 10.99 (*0-89283-219-3*) Servant.
Making Sense out of Suffering. large type ed. Peter Kreeft. 1988. pap. 14.95 (*0-8027-2596-1*) Walker & Co.
Making-Sense-Out-of-Suffering Therapy. Jack Wintz. LC 96-85000. (Illus.). 88p. (Orig.). 1996. pap. 4.95 (*0-87029-296-X*, 20156) Abbey.
Making Sense, Shaping Meaning: Writing in the Context of a Capacity-Based Approach to Learning. Pat D'Arcy. LC 89-31481. 163p. (Orig.). (YA). (gr. 11). 1989. pap. text 21.50 (*0-86709-245-9*, 0245, Pub. by Boynton Cook Pubs) Heinemann.
Making Sense Society. Ian Marsh et al. 640p. (C). 1996. pap. text 32.75 (*0-582-22895-6*, Pub. by Addison-Wesley) Longman.
***Making Sense with Offenders: Personal Constructs, Therapy & Change.** Julia Houston. LC 97-33472. (Series in Offender Rehabilitation). 292p. 1998. pap. 65.95 (*0-471-96627-4*) Wiley.
Making Sentences. Lynn H. Ruppard. (Basic Skills Ser.). (Illus.). 32p. (J). (gr. 3). 1997. pap. text 4.95 (*0-88724-417-3*, CD-2117) Carson-Dellos.
Making Sentences. Danielle Schultz. (Basic Skills Ser.). (Illus.). 32p. (J). (gr. 1). 1997. pap. text 4.95 (*0-88724-407-6*, CD-2107) Carson-Dellos.
Making Sentences. Danielle Schultz. (Basic Skills Ser.). (Illus.). 32p. (J). (gr. 2). 1997. pap. text 4.95 (*0-88724-412-2*, CD-2112) Carson-Dellos.
Making Seventy Thousand Dollars a Year As a Self-Employed Manufacturer's Representative. rev. ed. Leigh Silliphant et al. 190p. 1988. pap. 9.95 (*0-89815-241-0*) Ten Speed Pr.
Making Sex: Body & Gender from the Greeks to Freud. Thomas Laqueur. (Illus.). 352p. 1990. text 42.00 (*0-674-54349-1*) HUP.
Making Sex: Body & Gender from the Greeks to Freud. Thomas Laqueur. (Illus.). 336p. 1992. pap. text 17.50 (*0-674-54355-6*) HUP.
***Making Sexual History.** Jeffrey Weeks. LC 99-36411. 272p. 1999. pap. 24.95 (*0-7456-2115-5*) Blackwell Pubs.
***Making Sexual History.** Jeffrey Weeks. LC 99-36411. 272p. 1999. 59.95 (*0-7456-2114-7*, Pub. by Polity Pr) Blackwell Pubs.
Making Shaker Woodenware. Kerry Pierce. LC 98-39310. (Illus.). 128p. 1998. pap. 17.95 (*0-8069-3178-7*) Sterling.
Making Shaped Books. Gillian Chapman & Pam Robson. LC 94-44661. (Illus.). 32p. (J). (gr. k-3). 1995. lib. bdg. 19.90 (*1-56294-560-2*) Millbrook Pr.
Making Shaped Books. Gillian Chapman & Pam Robson. LC 94-44661. (Illus.). 32p. (J). (gr. k-3). 1996. pap. 7.95 (*0-7613-0139-9*) Millbrook Pr.
Making Shapes. Gary Gibson. (Science for Fun Ser.). (Illus.). 32p. (J). (gr. 2-4). 1996. lib. bdg. 20.90 (*1-56294-631-5*, Copper Beech Bks) Millbrook Pr.
Making Shapes. Gary Gibson. (Science for Fun Ser.). 1995. 10.15 (*0-606-09826-7*, Pub. by Turtleback) Demco.
Making, Shaping & Treating of Steel. 10th ed. AISE Staff et al. LC 84-81539. (Illus.). 1572p. 1985. text 125.00 (*0-930767-00-4*, 6357Z) Assn Iron & Steel.
***Making, Shaping & Treating of Steel.** 11th ed. R. J. Fruehan & AISE Steel Foundation Staff. LC 98-73477. xxvi, 767 p. 1998. write for info. (*0-930767-02-0*) Assn Iron & Steel.
Making Shiftwork Tolerable. Timothy H. Monk & Simon Folkard. 101p. 1992. pap. 25.00 (*0-85066-822-0*, Pub. by Tay Francis Ltd) Taylor & Francis.
Making Ships in Bottles: Beginners to Advanced. Leon Labistour. 1995. pap. 17.95 (*0-8128-8558-9*, Scrbrough Hse) Madison Bks UPA.
***Making Shoji.** Toshio Odate. LC 99-49812. (Illus.). 128p. 2000. pap. 21.95 (*0-941936-47-3*, Pub. by Linden Pub Fresno) IPG Chicago.
Making Sibling Teams Work: The Next Generation. Craig E. Aronoff & John L. Ward. (Family Business Leadership Ser.: Vol. 10). (Illus.). 72p. 1997. pap. 14.95 (*1-891652-00-1*) Busn Owner Res.
***Making Silence Speak: Women's Voices in Greek Literature & Society.** A. P. Lardinois & Laura McClure. LC 00-33648. 2001. pap. write for info. (*0-691-00466-8*) Princeton U Pr.
***Making Silver Chains: Simple Techniques, Beautiful Designs.** Glen Waszek. Ed. by Cindy Burda. (Illus.). 112p. 2000. write for info. (*1-57990-183-2*, Pub. by Lark Books) Sterling.
Making Simple Musical Instruments: A Melodious Collection of Strings, Winds, Drums & More. Bart Hopkin. Ed. by Deborah Morgenthal. LC 94-3543. (Illus.). 144p. (Orig.). (YA). 1995. 24.95 (*0-937274-80-1*, Pub. by Lark Books) Random.
Making Simple Musical Instruments: Melodious Collection of Strings, Winds, Drums, & More. Bart Hopkin. LC 94-3543. (Illus.). 144p. 1999. pap. 18.95 (*1-57990-048-8*, Pub. by Lark Books) Random.
***Making Skin-on-Frame Boats.** Robert Morris. (Illus.). 320p. 2000. pap. 24.95 (*0-88179-191-1*, Pub. by Hartley & Marks) Andrews & McMeel.
***Making Small Business Work for You.** 2nd ed. 1998. write for info. (*0-7248-1072-2*) P-H.
Making Small Workshop Tools. Stan Bray. (Workshop Practice Ser.: No. 14). (Illus.). 96p. (Orig.). 1987. pap. 18.50 (*0-85242-886-3*, Pub. by Nexus Special Interests) Trans-Atl Phila.
Making Smart Choices about Drugs. 60p. (J). (gr. 4 up). 1991. 6.95 (*0-88679-263-0*) Educ Insights.
Making Smart Choices about Your Future. 69p. (J). 1989. 5.95 (*0-88679-393-9*); 6.95 (*0-88679-808-6*) Educ Insights.
Making Snowshoes. Kathleen Lynch. (Alaska Ser.: Vol. 9). 46p. (Orig.). 1974. pap. 4.95 (*1-878051-06-7*, CP053) Circumpolar Pr.
Making Soap for Fun & Profit. Linda C. Inlow. Ed. by Kathyrn Doll. LC 98-91683. (Illus.). 80p. 1999. pap., wbk. ed. 14.95 (*0-9619634-2-5*) Kopacetic Ink.
Making Soaps & Candles. Phyllis Hobson. LC 74-75461. (Country Kitchen Library). (Illus.). 46p. 1984. pap. 3.95 (*0-88266-026-8*, Garden Way Pub) Storey Bks.
***Making Soaps & Scents: Perfumes, Soaps, Splashes & Shampos That You Can Make at Home.** Catherine Bardey. LC 99-40548. (Life's Litte Luxuries Ser.: Vol. 2). (Illus.). 192p. 1999. pap. 10.98 (*1-57912-059-8*) Blck Dog & Leventhal.
Making Social Policy: The Mechanisms of Government & Politics, & How to Investigate Them. Peter Levin. LC 95-50905. 256p. (C). 1996. pap. 28.95 (*0-335-19084-7*) OpUniv Pr.
Making Social Policy: The Mechanisms of Government & Politics, & How to Investigate Them. Peter J. Levin. LC 95-50905. 256p. (C). 1996. 94.00 (*0-335-19085-5*) OpUniv Pr.
Making Social Policy in Australia: An Introduction. Tony Dalton et al. LC 96-127321. 272p. 1996. pap. 29.95 (*1-86448-023-8*, Pub. by Allen & Unwin Pty) Paul & Co Pubs.
Making Social Studies Come Alive: 65 Classroom-Tested Activities & Projects. Scholastic, Inc. Staff. LC 97-145034. 1997. pap. 9.95 (*0-590-96381-3*) Scholastic Inc.
Making Software Development Visible: Effective Project Control. David P. Youll. LC 90-42922. (Wiley Series in Softwear Engineering Practice). (Illus.). 177p. 1990. reprint ed. pap. 54.90 (*0-608-05899-8*, 206623400007) Bks Demand.
Making Software Measurement Work: Building an Effective Measurement Program. Bill Hetzel. 304p. 1993. 74.99 (*0-471-56568-7*) Wiley.
Making Software More Accessible for People with Disabilities: A White Paper on the Design of Software Application Programs to Increase Their Accessibility for People with Disabilities. George C. Vanderheiden. (Illus.). 74p. (Orig.). (C). 1994. pap. text 30.00 (*0-7881-1050-0*) DIANE Pub.
Making Solidarity Work: The Norwegian Labour Market Model in Transition. Ed. by Arild H. Steen & Jon E. Dolvik. (Illus.). 377p. (C). 1997. text 41.00 (*82-00-37679-6*) Scandnvan Univ Pr.
Making Soliders in the Public Schools: An Analysis of the Army JROTC Curriculum. Catherine Lutz & Lesley Bartlett. (Illus.). 40p. (Orig.). (C). 1995. pap. text 20.00 (*0-7881-1895-1*) DIANE Pub.
***Making Some Noise Todays Modern Christian Rock.** 88p. 1998. otabind 14.95 (*0-7935-8382-9*) H Leonard.
Making Something of Ourselves: On Culture & Politics in the United States. Richard M. Merelman. LC 83-5959. 200p. (C). 1984. pap. 12.95 (*0-520-04915-2*, Pub. by U CA Pr) Cal Prin Full Svc.
Making Sound Credit Policy Decisions. Frederick C. Scherr. Ed. by Teresa Donohue. 200p. (Orig.). 1996. pap. 22.00 (*0-934914-99-0*) NACM.
Making Sounds. Julian Rowe. (Illus.). 32p. (J). (gr. 3-6). 1994. pap. 4.95 (*0-516-48136-3*) Childrens.
Making Space: Design for Compact Living. Rick Ball. LC 88-22431. (Illus.). 136p. 1990. pap. 15.95 (*0-87951-365-9*, Pub. by Overlook Pr) Penguin Putnam.
Making Space: Remodeling for More Living Area. Ernie Bryant. 240p. 1992. 22.95 (*0-8306-3932-2*, 2803); pap. 12.60 (*0-8306-3931-4*, 2803) McGraw-Hill Prof.
***Making Space: The Development of Spatial Representation & Reasoning.** Nora S. Newcombe & Janellen Huttenlocher. LC 99-87408. (Illus.). 280p. 2000. 37.50 (*0-262-14069-1*) MIT Pr.
Making Space for Science: Territorial Themes in the Shaping of Knowledge. Ed. by Crosbie Smith et al. LC 97-28072. 376p. 1998. text 75.00 (*0-312-21053-1*) St Martin.
Making Space for the Mormons. Richard L. Bushman. (Leonard J. Arrington Mormon History Lecture Ser.: Vol. 2). 40p. (Orig.). 1997. pap. 5.95 (*0-87421-230-8*) Utah St U Pr.
Making Sparkling Wines. 2nd ed. John Restall & Donald Hebbs. (Illus.). 144p. (Orig.). 1995. pap. 14.95 (*1-85486-119-0*, Pub. by Nexus Special Interests) Trans-Atl Phila.
Making Special Events Fit in the 21st Century. 2nd ed. Robert L. Jackson. (Illus.). 156p. 1997. pap. 26.95 (*1-57167-033-5*) Sagamore Pub.
Making Special Schools Ordinary: Models for the Developing Special School, Vol. 1. Derek Baker & Keith Bovair. 260p. 1989. 79.95 (*1-85000-436-6*, Falmer Pr); pap. 37.95 (*1-85000-437-4*, Falmer Pr) Taylor & Francis.
Making Special Schools Ordinary Vol. 2: Practitioners Changing Special Education. Ed. by Derek Baker & Keith Bovair. 220p. 1990. pap. 37.95 (*1-85000-439-0*, Falmer Pr) Taylor & Francis.
Making Standards Work: How to Implement Standards-Based Assessments in the Classroom, School & District. Douglas B. Reeves. (Illus.). xviii, 226p. 1997. ring bd. 34.95 (*0-9644955-2-X*) Adv Learn.
Making Statistics Fun: The Easy-to-Understand Guide to SPC & Data Analysis. H. J. Harrington et al. LC 97-38124. 1997. write for info. (*0-07-027056-2*) McGraw.
Making Stories. Irene Watts. 96p. (C). 1992. pap. text 16.50 (*0-435-08614-6*, 08614) Heinemann.
Making Stories, Making Selves: Feminist Reflections on the Holocaust. R. Ruth Linden. LC 92-20410. (Helen Hooven Santmyer Prize in Women's Studies). 191p. (C). 1993. pap. text 16.95 (*0-8142-0584-4*) Ohio St U Pr.
Making Strategic Planning Work in Practice. Ed. by Basil W. Denning. LC 89-8826. (Best of Long Range Planning Ser.: Vol. 3). 130p. 1989. 72.00 (*0-08-037121-3*, 2905, Pub. by Pergamon Repr) Franklin.
Making Strategic Spatial Plans. Healey. LC 97-198778. 288p. 1996. pap. 27.95 (*1-85728-664-2*, Pub. by UCL Pr Ltd) Taylor & Francis.
Making Strategic Spatial Plans. Ed. by Patsy Healey et al. LC 97-198778. 288p. 1996. 90.00 (*1-85728-663-4*, Pub. by UCL Pr Ltd) Taylor & Francis.
Making Strategy: An Introduction to National Security Processes & Problems. Dennis M. Drew & Donald M. Snow. (Illus.). 1988. pap. 10.00 (*1-58566-021-3*) Air Univ.
***Making Strategy: The Journey of Strategic Management.** Colin Eden & Fran Ackermann. LC 98-61376. 384p. 1998. 82.00 (*0-7619-5224-1*); pap. 27.95 (*0-7619-5225-X*) Sage.
Making Strategy Happen: Transforming Plans into Reality. Arnold S. Judson. 250p. 1990. 34.95 (*0-912841-33-8*) Planning Forum.
Making Strategy Work: How Senior Managers Produce Results. Richard G. Hamermesh. LC 85-12456. (Management Series on Problem Solving, Decision Making & Strategic Thinking). 245p. 1986. 34.95 (*0-471-80319-7*) Wiley.
Making Strategy Work: Turning Strategic Plans into Tangible Results. Timothy J. Galpin. LC 97-24231. 240p. 1997. 28.95 (*0-7879-1001-5*) Jossey-Bass.

An Asterisk (*) at the beginning of an entry indicates that the title is appearing for the first time.

Making Stress Work for You. Helen Graham. LC 98-24645. 224p. 1998. pap. 14.95 (*0-89594-948-2*) Crossing Pr.

***Making Student Teaching Work: Creating a Partnership.** Mary A. Lowenhaupt & Corinne E. Stephanik. (Fastback Ser.). 46p. 1999. pap. 3.00 (*0-87367-647-5*, FB447) Phi Delta Kappa.

Making Successful Presentations: A Self-Teaching Guide. 2nd ed. Terry C. Smith. LC 90-35306. (Self-Teaching Guides Ser.). 224p. 1991. 37.95 (*0-471-52849-8*); pap. 19.95 (*0-471-52848-X*) Wiley.

Making Sure We Are True to Our Founders: The Association of the Bar of the City of New York, 1970-95. Jeffrey B. Morris & George W. Martin. LC 96-53943. 1997. 30.00 (*0-8232-1738-8*) Fordham.

Making Table Wine at Home. George M. Cooke & J. T. Lapsley. LC 87-71575. (Illus.). 48p. 1988. pap. 5.00 (*0-931876-80-X*, 21434) ANR Pubns CA.

Making Tables & Chairs. Reader's Digest Editors. (Workshop Companion (Reader's Digest) Ser.). (Illus.). 1999. 19.95 (*0-7621-0207-1*, Pub. by RD Assn) Penguin Putnam.

Making Tales: The Poetics of Wordsworth's Narrative Experiments. Don H. Bialostosky. LC 83-5069. 208p. 1984. pap. text 12.50 (*0-226-04576-5*) U Ch Pr.

Making Tales: The Poetics of Wordsworth's Narrative Experiments. Don H. Bialostosky. LC 83-5069. 208p. 1984. lib. bdg. 25.00 (*0-226-04575-7*) U Ch Pr.

Making Tales: The Poetics of Wordsworth's Narrative Experiments. Don H. Bialostosky. LC 83-5069. 220p. Date not set. reprint ed. pap. 68.20 (*0-608-20666-0*, 207210300003) Bks Demand.

Making Tariff in the United States. Thomas W. Page. (Brookings Institution Reprint Ser.). reprint ed. lib. bdg. 40.50 (*0-685-70237-5*) Irvington.

Making Taxes Pay You: The Practical Guide to Property Tax Sales. Roger K. Brown. write for info. (*0-8187-0104-8*) Harlo Press.

Making Teacher Education More Relevant. Ed. by Ayers Bagley. (NSCTE Monographs). 1970. 10.00 (*0-933669-03-8*) Soc Profs Ed.

Making Teaching Community Property: A Menu for Peer Collaboration & Peer Review. Pat Hutchings. 128p. 1996. pap. 25.00 (*1-56377-031-8*, TI9601) Am Assn Higher Ed.

Making Teams Work: A Guide to Creating & Managing Teams. ODI Staff. 142p. 1993. write for info. (*0-9636723-0-4*) ODI.

Making Teams Work Module 3: Managing for the Future. Deborah Ancona et al. (GI - Organizational Behavior Ser.). 1995. pap. 7.95 (*0-538-85875-3*) S-W Pub.

Making Technology Masculine: Men, Women & Modern Machines in America, 1870-1945. Ruth Oldenziel. LC 99-496066. 1999. pap. 24.95 (*90-5356-381-4*, Pub. by Amsterdam U Pr) U of Mich Pr.

Making Technology Our Own? Domesticating Technology into Everyday Life. Ed. by Merete Lie & Knut Sorensen. 232p. (C). 1996. text 36.00 (*82-00-22758-8*) Scandnvan Univ Pr.

Making Technology Work. Neal Swernofsky. (Tech & Industrial Education Ser.). 1989. pap. 24.95 (*0-8273-3318-8*) Delmar.

Making Technology Work: Sustainable Development in Practice. ITDG Staff. 16p. (Orig.). 1992. pap. 5.00 (*1-85339-176-X*, Pub. by Intermed Tech) Stylus Pub VA.

Making Teddy Bears. Joyce Luckin. LC 95-45368. (Illus.). 128p. 1996. pap. 14.95 (*0-486-29209-6*) Dover.

Making Teddy Bears in Miniature. Angela Bullock. LC 98-186640. (Illus.). 96p. (Orig.). 1997. pap. 19.95 (*0-87588-497-0*, H5382) Hobby Hse.

Making Telecommuting Happen: A Guide for Telemanagers & Telecommuters. Jack M. Nilles. 196p. 1994. pap. 25.95 (*0-442-01857-6*, VNR) Wiley.

Making Television: A Video Production Guide for Teachers. John LeBaron. LC 81-703. (Illus.). 352p. (Orig.). reprint ed. pap. 109.20 (*0-7837-0989-7*, 204129500020) Bks Demand.

Making Television: Authorship & the Production Process. Ed. by Robert J. Thompson & Gary Burns. LC 89-48746. (Media & Society Ser.). 224p. 1990. 55.00 (*0-275-92746-6*, C2746, Greenwood Pr) Greenwood.

Making TeX Work. Norman Walsh. Ed. by Deborah Russell. (Computer Science). (Illus.). 522p. (Orig.). 1994. pap. 29.95 (*1-56592-051-1*) Thomson Learn.

Making Textbooks Work for You. Carol K. Ingall. 1996. pap. text. write for info. (*0-87441-576-4*) Behrman.

Making the Abolition of War a Realistic Goal. Gene Sharp. 16p. 1991. 2.00 (*1-880813-03-3*) A Einstein Inst.

Making the Alphabet Dance: Recreational Word Play. Ross Eckler. (Illus.). 279p. (C). 1999. text 24.00 (*0-7881-5893-7*) DIANE Pub.

Making the Amalgamated: Gender, Ethnicity & Class in the Baltimore Clothing Industry, 1899-1939. Jo Anne Argersinger. LC 98-9922. (Studies in Industry & Society). 248p. 1999. 39.95 (*0-8018-5989-1*) Johns Hopkins.

Making the American Home: Middle-Class Women & Domestic Material Culture, 1840-1940. Ed. by Marilyn F. Motz & Pat Browne. LC 88-70387. (Illus.). 212p. (C). 1988. 33.95 (*0-87972-433-1*); pap. 16.95 (*0-87972-434-X*) Bowling Green Univ Popular Press.

Making the American Self: Jonathan Edwards to Abraham Lincoln. Daniel W. Howe. LC 96-34982. (Studies in Cultural History). 352p. 1997. 41.50 (*0-674-16551-1*) HUP.

Making the American Team: Sport, Culture, & the Olympic Experience. Mark Dyreson. LC 97-4663. (Sport & Society Ser.). 296p. 1997. 18.95 (*0-252-06654-5*); text 44.95 (*0-252-02349-8*) U of Ill Pr.

Making the Australian Chartered Accountant. Chris Poullaos. LC 94-2646. (New Works in Accounting History). 368p. 1994. reprint ed. text 20.00 (*0-8153-1717-4*) Garland.

Making the Automatic Decision see Pocket Printer Series

***Making the Band.** 2000. per. 11.95 (*0-7434-1701-1*) S&S Trade.

Making the Basketball Team: Get off the Bench & into the Game. Lane Czaplinski. (Illus.). 144p. (YA). (gr. 7 up). 1996. pap. 12.00 (*1-885758-08-1*) Quality Sports.

Making the Best Apple Cider. E. A. Proulx. 1983. pap. 2.95 (*0-88266-222-8*, Storey Pub) Storey Bks.

***Making the Best Man's Speech.** John Bowden. (Essentials Ser.). 77p. 2000. pap. 9.95 (*1-85703-527-5*, Pub. by How To Bks) Midpt Trade.

Making the Best Medical Records & Documentation. (Illus.). 200p. 1999. pap. 45.00 (*1-58383-041-3*, RECORD9) Robert D Keene.

Making the Best of Basics: Family Preparedness Handbook. 10th expanded rev. ed. James Talmidge Stevens. LC 96-7076. (Illus.). 336p. 1997. pap. 22.95 (*1-882723-25-2*, Pub. by Gold Leaf Pr) Origin Bk Sales.

Making the Best of Schools: A Handbook for Parents, Teachers, & Policymakers. Jeannie Oakes & Martin Lipton. LC 89-39035. 336p. (C). 1990. 37.00 (*0-300-04650-2*) Yale U Pr.

Making the Best of Schools: A Handbook for Parents, Teachers, & Policymakers. Jeannie Oakes & Martin Lipton. 336p. (C). 1991. reprint ed. pap. 15.00 (*0-300-05123-9*) Yale U Pr.

Making the Best of Second Best: A Guide to Positive Stepparenting. Kathleen Fox. LC 98-93251. 179p. 1998. pap. 11.95 (*0-9665543-0-2*) FoxCraft Inc.

Making the Best of Stress: How Life's Hassles Can Form the Fruit of the Spirit. Mark R. McMinn. LC 95-49667. 182p. (Orig.). 1996. pap. 10.99 (*0-8308-1981-9*) InterVarsity.

Making the Best Use of Time. Barbara L. McCombs & Linda Brannan. (Skills for Job Success Ser.). (Illus.). 32p. (Orig.). 1990. teacher ed. 1.95 (*1-56119-030-6*); disk 39.95 (*1-56119-115-9*) Educ Pr MD.

Making the Best Use of Time. Barbara L. McCombs & Linda Brannan. (Skills for Job Success Ser.). (Illus.). 32p. (Orig.). 1990. pap., student ed. 5.95 (*1-56119-029-2*) Educ Pr MD.

Making the Best Use of Time, Set. Barbara L. McCombs & Linda Brannan. (Skills for Job Success Ser.). (Illus.). 32p. (Orig.). 1990. teacher ed., student ed. 54.95 (*1-56119-073-X*) Educ Pr MD.

Making the Bible Our Own. George Drew. 65p. 1985. pap. 7.95 (*0-940754-29-0*) Ed Ministries.

Making the Bible Yours. 13th ed. Earl C. Wolf. 104p. 1984. reprint ed. pap. 7.99 (*0-8341-0892-5*) Beacon Hill.

Making the Big Move: How to Transform Relocation into a Creative Life Transition. Cathy Goodwin. LC 98-68751. 192p. 1999. pap. 13.95 (*1-57224-135-7*) New Harbinger.

***Making the Black Atlantic: Britain & the African Diaspora.** James Walvin. LC 99-27606. 256p. 1999. pap. 19.95 (*0-304-70217-X*) Continuum.

Making the Body Beautiful: A Cultural History of Aesthetic Surgery. Sander L. Gilman. LC 98-48423. (Illus.). 544p. 1999. 29.95 (*0-691-02672-6*, Pub. by Princeton U Pr) Cal Prin Full Svc.

***Making the Body Beautiful: A Cultural History of Aesthetic Surgery.** Sander L. Gilman. (Illus.). 544p. 2001. pap. 16.95 (*0-691-07053-9*) Princeton U Pr.

Making the Brain/Body Connection: A Playful Guide to Releasing Mental, Physical & Emotional Blocks to Success. Sharon Promislow. LC 97-901126. (Illus.). 1998. 15.95 (*0-9681066-2-5*) Kinetic Pub.

***Making the Brain/Body Connection: A Playful Guide to Releasing Mental, Physical & Emotional Blocks to Success.** Sharon Promislow. 2000. pap. 15.95 (*0-9681066-3-3*) Kinetic Pub.

Making the Break. Patt Perkins & Marcia Hootman. LC 82-6324. (Illus.). 130p. 1982. pap. 5.95 (*0-943172-00-4*) New Wave.

***Making the Bridegroom's Speech.** John Bowden. (Essentials Ser.). (Illus.). 64p. 2000. pap. 9.95 (*1-85703-567-4*, Pub. by How To Bks) Midpt Trade.

Making the Case: Measuring the Impact of Youth Development Programs. Dale A. Blyth et al. (Illus.). 28p. (Orig.). 1996. pap. 6.95 (*1-57482-721-9*) Search Inst.

Making the Case for Family Support. LC 96-7943. 1996. write for info. (*1-885429-13-4*) Family Resource.

Making the Case for Professional Service. Ernest A. Lynton. 120p. 1995. pap. 12.00 (*1-56377-033-4*, FR9501) Am Assn Higher Ed.

***Making the Case for Your Library: A How-to-Do-It Manual.** (How-to-Do-It Manuals for Librarians Ser.). 2000p. 2000. pap. 45.00 (*1-55570-399-2*) Neal-Schuman.

Making the Case for Yourself: A Diet Book for Smart Women. Susan Estrich. 208p. 1999. reprint ed. pap. 12.00 (*1-57322-713-7*, Riverhd Trade) Berkley Pub.

Making the Chemotherapy Decision. David Drum. 288p. 1996. 27.00 (*1-56565-445-5*) Lowell Hse.

***Making the Chemotherapy Decision.** 3rd ed. David Drum. 352p. 2000. pap. 16.95 (*0-7373-0383-2*, 03832W, Pub. by Lowell Hse) NTC Contemp Pub Co.

Making the Church Work: Converting the Church for the 21st Century. Edward H. Hammett. LC 97-11345. 128p. 1997. pap. 12.00 (*1-57312-157-6*) Smyth & Helwys.

***Making the Church Work: Converting the Church for the 21st Century.** 2nd ed. Edward H. Hammett. LC 00-41023. 2000. write for info. (*1-57312-320-X*) Smyth & Helwys.

***Making the Cisco Connection: The Story Behind the Real Internet Superpower.** David Bunnell & Adam Brate. 240p. 2000. text 24.95 (*0-471-35711-1*) Wiley.

Making the Commons Work: Theory, Practice, & Policy. William A. Blomquist. Ed. by Daniel W. Bromley. LC 92-24880. 339p. 1992. pap. 21.95 (*1-55815-217-2*) ICS Pr.

Making the Commons Work: Theory, Practice, & Policy. Ed. by Daniel W. Bromley. LC 92-24880. 339p. 1992. 44.95 (*1-55815-198-2*) ICS Pr.

***Making the Conncections: Using Internal Communications to Turn Strategy into Action.** Bill Quirke. LC 99-46262. 320p. 2000. 79.95 (*0-566-08175-X*, Pub. by Ashgate Pub) Ashgate Pub Co.

Making the Connection. John W. Crawford. Ed. by Patricia Schultz. LC 89-12527. (Poetry Ser.: Vol. 2). 64p. 1989. pap. 12.95 (*0-88946-887-7*) E Mellen.

Making the Connection. Steffee. 1997. 15.95 (*0-538-71777-7*) Thomson Learn.

Making the Connection: A Comparison of Dance in the Concert Versus Worship Setting. Diane Smagatz-Rawlinson. Ed. by Doug Adams. 1989. pap. 3.00 (*0-941500-51-9*) Sharing Co.

***Making the Connection: A Personal Guide to Help You Through the Detours of Life.** Ed. by Linda MacKillop. 1999. 19.95 (*0-9675839-0-X*); pap. 14.95 (*0-9675839-1-8*) Creative Pr Pubng.

Making the Connection: Getting Work to Work. Jane A. Petrick. LC 98-87262. 79p. 1998. pap. 19.95 (*0-9664670-0-0*) ID Publ.

Making the Connection: Integrated Activities to Build Business Skills. LC 96-40950. 1996. write for info. (*0-538-71783-1*) S-W Pub.

Making the Connection: Keys to Quality Customer Service in Health Care. Pennie Myers & Don W. Nance. 60p. 1997. spiral bd., wbk. ed. 29.00 (*0-9620723-7-0*) MAS.

Making the Connection: Language & Academic Achievement Among African American Students Proceedings Of A Conference Of The Coalition On Language Diversity In Education / Carolyn T. Adger et al. LC 98-52017. (Language in Education Ser.). 1999. write for info. (*1-887744-42-8*) Delta Systems.

Making the Connection Vol. 1: Learning Skills Through Literature: K-2. Patricia Pavelka. Ed. by Deborah Sumner. (Illus.). 136p. 1995. pap., teacher ed. 17.95 (*1-884548-03-2*) Soc Dev Educ.

Making the Connection Vol. 2: Learning Skills Through Literature (3-6) Patricia Pavelka. Ed. by Aldene Fredenburg. LC 95-71328. (Illus.). 132p. (Orig.). 1997. pap., teacher ed. 17.95 (*1-884548-11-3*, 5022) Soc Dev Educ.

Making the Connection Between Grammar & Composition - With Forbidden Words. rev. ed. Jackie Mallis. 244p. 1997. pap., per. 25.00 (*0-86617-057-X*) Multi Media TX.

Making the Connections: Essays in Feminist Social Ethics. Beverly W. Harrison. Ed. by Carol S. Robb. LC 84-45718. 336p. 1986. reprint ed. pap. 18.50 (*0-8070-1515-6*) Beacon Pr.

Making the Connections: Proceedings of the 20th Biennial Conference on Ground Water. Ed. by Johannes J. DeVries & Jeff Woled. 197p. 1996. pap. text. write for info. (*1-887192-03-4*) U Cal CWWR.

Making the Connections: Women, Work, & Abuse. Patricia Murphy. LC 92-75487. 280p. 1993. per. 41.95 (*1-878205-65-X*) St Lucie Pr.

Making the Contact. Robert A. Russell. 90p. 1980. reprint ed. pap. 6.95 (*0-87516-391-2*) DeVorss.

Making the Corn Belt: A Geographical History of Middle-Western Agriculture. John C. Hudson. LC 93-35723. (Midwestern History & Culture Ser.). 1994. 35.00 (*0-253-32832-2*) Ind U Pr.

***Making the Corporate Connection: A Step-by-Step Guide to Sponsorship.** Corliss M. Tillman. (C). 1999. 39.95 (*0-9641819-2-4*) M Systs Pubng.

***Making the Corps.** Thomas E. Ricks. (Illus.). 320p. 1998. pap. 13.00 (*0-684-84817-1*, Touchstone) S&S Trade Pap.

***Making the Corps.** Thomas E. Ricks. (Illus.). 320p. 2000. reprint ed. text 24.00 (*0-7881-6994-7*) DIANE Pub.

Making the Corps: 61 Men Came to Paris Island to Become Marines, Not All of Them Made It. Thomas E. Ricks. LC 97-25174. 320p. 1997. 24.00 (*0-684-83109-0*) S&S Trade.

Making the Curriculum Work. OECD Staff. LC 99-176975. 128p. 1998. pap. 20.00 (*92-64-16141-4*, 9698061P) OECD.

***Making the Dawn Welcome: Essays on Everyday Possibilities.** Helen Hills. LC 99-55352. (Illus.). 132p. 1999. 18.95 (*1-884540-51-1*) Haleys.

***Making the Dawn Welcome: Essays on Everyday Possibilities.** Helen Hills & Brian Wiprud. LC 99-55352. (Illus.). 132p. 1999. pap. 12.95 (*1-884540-50-3*) Haleys.

Making the Deal: Quick Tips for Successful Negotiating. George M. Hartman. LC 91-41086. 128p. 1992. pap. 12.95 (*0-471-54379-9*) Wiley.

Making the Dean's List. Edmond C. Hallberg & Rochelle Aschieris. (Illus.). 322p. (C). 1999. pap. text 32.00 (*0-930175-06-9*, Legal Bks) Omb.

***Making the Difference.** ATA Foundation Staff. 29p. 1998. pap. 25.00 (*0-88711-388-5*) Am Trucking Assns.

Making the Difference. Margaret Hinchey. 48p. 1998. pap. 10.99 (*0-570-01554-5*) Concordia.

Making the Difference: Gender, Personhood & Theology. Elaine L. Graham. LC 95-14881. 288p. 1996. pap. 22.00 (*0-8006-2960-4*, 1-2960, Fortress Pr) Augsburg Fortress.

Making the Difference: Journal Writing for at-Risk Youth. David Boers. 80p. (J). (gr. k-12). 1993. pap. text 10.00 (*1-886790-01-9*) WISC Publ.

Making the Difference: Schools, Families & Social Division. R. W. Connell et al. 224p. 1982. pap. 14.95 (*0-86861-132-8*, Pub. by Allen & Unwin Pty) Paul & Co Pubs.

Making the Difference for Teachers: The Field Experience in Actual Practice. Gloria A. Slick. LC 95-6675. (Illus.). 176p. 1995. pap. 22.95 (*0-8039-6211-8*) Corwin Pr.

Making the Difference for Teachers: The Field Experience in Actual Practice. Ed. by Gloria A. Slick. LC 95-6675. (Illus.). 176p. 1995. 51.95 (*0-8039-6210-X*) Corwin Pr.

***Making the E-Business Transformation.** Peter A. Gloor. LC 00-25095. vi, 178p. 2000. pap. 34.95 (*1-85233-265-4*) Spr-Verlag.

Making the Economy Work. Jon Shields & Employment Institute. LC 90-148435. xiv, 290 p. 1989. write for info. (*0-333-47133-4*) Macmillan.

Making the Empire Work: London & American Interest Groups, 1690-1790. Alison G. Olson. 272p. 1992. 51.95 (*0-674-54318-1*) HUP.

Making the English Canon: Print-Capitalism & the Cultural Past, 1700-1770. Jonathan B. Kramnick. LC 98-21089. 296p. (C). 1999. text 54.95 (*0-521-64127-6*) Cambridge U Pr.

***Making the Environment Count: Selected Essays of Alan Randall.** Alan Randall. LC 99-17604. (New Horizons in Environmental Economics Ser.). 256p. (C). 1999. 90.00 (*1-84064-086-3*) E Elgar.

Making the Estrogen Decision. Susan M. Lark. Ed. by Phyllis Herman. (Good Health Guides Ser.). 48p. 1996. pap. 3.95 (*0-87983-696-2*, 36962K, Keats Publng) NTC Contemp Pub Co.

***Making the Eucharist Matter.** Frank Andersen. LC 99-37728. 144p. 1999. pap. 12.95 (*0-87793-695-1*) Ave Maria.

Making the Exceptional Normal Without Reengineering. Dale Furtwengler. LC 97-97108. 128p. 1997. pap. 11.95 (*0-9661478-0-4*) Peregrine Press.

Making the Fascist Self: The Political Culture of Interwar Italy. Mabel Berezin. LC 96-53410. (Wilder House Series in Politics, History, & Culture). (Illus.). 296p. 1996. pap. text 18.95 (*0-8014-8420-0*) Cornell U Pr.

Making the Fascist Self: The Political Culture of Interwar Italy. Mabel Berezin. LC 96-53410. (Wilder House Series in Politics, History, & Culture). (Illus.). 296p. 1997. text 45.00 (*0-8014-3202-2*) Cornell U Pr.

Making the Fast Track Pay. Andrew Dalton. LC 99-488015. 112p. 1998. pap. 41.00 (*1-85811-193-5*, Pub. by CLT Prof) Gaunt.

***Making the Father of the Bride's Speech.** John Bowden. (Essentials Ser.). (Illus.). 64p. 2000. pap. 9.95 (*1-85703-568-2*, Pub. by How To Bks) Midpt Trade.

Making the Federal Government Accountable: Enforcing the Mandate for Effective Financial Management. Dan Burton. 51p. (C). 1999. text 20.00 (*0-7881-7658-7*) DIANE Pub.

Making the Federal Government User Friendly: Hearing Before the Subcommittee on Government Programs & Oversight of the Committee on Small Business, House of Representatives, One Hundred Fifth Congress, First Session, Federick, Md, November 20, 1997. United States Staff. LC 98-160804. iii, 115 p. 1998. write for info. (*0-16-056187-6*) USGPO.

Making the Future Work. R. Genof. xviii, 254p. 1993. pap. write for info. (*1-86373-526-7*, Pub. by Allen & Unwin Pty) IPG Chicago.

***Making the Games Happen: Profiles of Sport Management Professionals.** Matthew J. Robinson. LC 00-40605. 2000. write for info. (*0-8342-1796-1*) Aspen Pub.

Making the Gods in New York: The Yoruba Religion in the African American Community. rev. ed. Mary C. Curry. LC 97-8411. (Studies in African American History & Culture). (Illus.). 216p. 1997. text 53.00 (*0-8153-2919-9*) Garland.

Making the Gods Work for You: The Astrological Language of the Psyche. Caroline W. Casey. LC 98-6090. 272p. 1998. 23.00 (*0-609-60058-3*) Harmony Bks.

Making the Gospel Plain: The Writings of Bishop Reverdy C. Ransom. Anthony B. Pinn. LC 99-13076. 304p. 1999. pap. 20.00 (*1-56338-264-4*) TPI PA.

Making the Grade. W. Royce Adams. (C). 1997. pap. text, teacher ed. 37.96 (*0-669-35508-9*) HM Trade Div.

Making the Grade. C Bosch. LC 90-62674. (Decision Is Yours Ser.). (Illus.). 64p. (Orig.). (J). (gr. 3-6). 1991. pap. 5.95 (*0-943990-48-3*) Parenting Pr.

Making the Grade. Carl W. Bosch. LC 90-62674. (Decision Is Yours Ser.). (Illus.). 64p. (J). (gr. 3-6). 1991. lib. bdg. 16.95 (*0-943990-49-1*) Parenting Pr.

Making the Grade? Ted Kowalski. (C). 1994. pap. text. write for info. (*0-8013-1359-7*) Longman.

Making the Grade. 2nd ed. W. Royce Adams. 480p. (C). 1997. pap. text 38.76 (*0-669-35507-0*); pap. text, student ed. 19.16 (*0-669-35509-7*) HM Trade Div.

Making the Grade: A Guide to School Drug Prevention Programs. Drug Strategies Staff. (Illus.). 36p. 1996. pap. 12.95 (*0-9665342-0-4*) Drug Strtgies.

Making the Grade: A Self-Worth Perspective on Motivation & School Reform. Martin V. Covington. (Illus.). 361p. (C). 1992. text 64.95 (*0-521-34261-9*); pap. text 21.95 (*0-521-34803-X*) Cambridge U Pr.

Making the Grade: An Adolescent's Struggle with ADD. Roberta N. Parker & Harvey C. Parker. Tr. by Richard DiMatteo. (Illus.). 48p. (Orig.). (J). (gr. 5-10). 1992. pap. 11.00 (*0-9621629-1-4*) Spec Pr FL.

Making the Grade: Grades 3-4. Kaplan Staff. LC 97-3407. 320p. (J). (gr. 3-4). 1997. 15.00 (*0-684-83693-9*) Kaplan.

Making the Grade: How to Help Your Elementary School Child Have a Happy & Successful School Experience. Ginger E. Black. 1989. pap. 8.95 (*0-8184-0501-5*) Carol Pub Group.

Making the Grade: Learning Adventures for Your Family. Kaplan Staff. 352p. (J). (gr. 1-2). 1998. 15.00 (*0-684-84847-3*) S&S Trade.

Making the Grade: Raising Your GPA by Studying Smarter, Not Harder. 2nd rev. ed. Meredith D. Gall & Joyce P. Gall. (Illus.). 224p. 1988. pap. 10.95 (*1-55958-232-4*) Prima Pub.

M

An Asterisk (*) at the beginning of an entry indicates that the title is appearing for the first time.

M

Making the Grade: Reflections on Being Learning Disabled. Dayle A. Upham & Virginia H. Trumbull. LC 97-25950. 128p. 1997. pap. text 15.95 (*0-435-08150-0*) Heinemann.
Making the Grade: Strategies for Reading in the Social Sciences, Sciences, & Humanities. W. Royce Adams. 462p. (C). 1992. pap. text 36.76 (*0-669-21379-9*); teacher ed. 37.96 (*0-669-28157-3*); 19.16 (*0-669-28158-1*) HM Trade Div.
Making the Grade: The Academic Side of College Life. Howard S. Becker et al. LC 94-41458. 1995. pap. 21.95 (*1-56000-807-5*) Transaction Pubs.
Making the Grade: The Benefits of Law Enforcement Accreditation. Gerald L. Williams. 48p. (Orig.). 1989. pap. 2.50 (*1-878734-08-3*) Police Exec Res.
Making the Grade: The Teen's Guide to Homework Success. Janice E. Gabe. (Illus.). 80p. (YA). pap. text 7.95 (*0-9639023-1-8*) Prof Resource.
Making the Grade in Graduate School: Survival Strategy 101. Contrib. by Howard G. Adams. (C). 1993. 5.00 (*1-887284-02-8*) Natl Consortium.
Making the Grade Seminars Student Notes. Steve Douglass & Al Janssen. (Illus.). 42p. (C). Date not set. pap. 49.00 (*1-57902-008-9*) Integrtd Res.
Making the Grades: How You Can Achieve Greater Success with Less Stress in School & Beyond. Frederick Hageman. LC 94-68681. 165p. (YA). (gr. 7-12). 1995. pap. 14.95 (*0-9643040-9-0*) Rising Crescent.
Making the Grant Process Work. 2nd ed. 1994. 73.00 (*1-56925-013-8*, MGP2) Capitol Publns.
Making the Grass Greener on Your Side: A CEO's Journey to Leading by Serving. Ken Melrose. LC 95-34423. (Illus.). 250p. 1995. 24.95 (*1-881052-21-4*) Berrett-Koehler.
*__Making the Heartland Quilt.__ Douglas K. Meyer. LC 99-41235. (Illus.). 384p. 2000. 49.95 (*0-8093-2289-7*) S Ill U Pr.
Making the Holy Spirit Your Partner: Discovering His Plan, Purpose, & Power. Michael S. Pitts. 71p. 1992. pap. 7.00 (*0-9633583-0-8*) Present Trth.
Making the House Fall Down. Beatrice Hawley. LC 77-82222. 64p. 1977. pap. 3.95 (*0-914086-19-7*) Alice James Bks.
*__Making the Impossible Possible: Think It! Act It! Become It!__ Jason Boreyko. LC 99-60931. 256p. 1999. 22.95 (*0-9670400-0-0*, Pub. by J Boreyko) BookWorld.
Making the International Connection: How Canada's Approach to International Science & Technology Can Help Small & Medium-Sized Enterprises. Monique Frize. 52p. (Orig.). (C). 1994. pap. text 35.00 (*0-7881-1550-2*) DIANE Pub.
Making the Internet Family Friendly. Bill Wilson & Brian Lang. LC 98-46106. 180p. 1999. pap. 12.99 (*0-7852-7568-1*) Nelson.
Making the Invisible Visible: A Multicultural Planning History. Leonie Sandercock. LC 97-16212. (California Studies in Critical Human Geography: Vol. 2). 268p. 1998. 45.00 (*0-520-20734-3*, Pub. by U CA Pr); pap. 15.95 (*0-520-20735-1*, Pub. by U CA Pr) Cal Prin Full Svc.
Making the Invisible Woman Visible. Anne F. Scott. LC 82-8563. 416p. 1984. 15.95 (*0-252-01123-6*); text 34.95 (*0-252-01110-4*) U of Ill Pr.
*__Making the Journey: Being & Becoming a Teacher of English Language Arts.__ 2nd ed. Leila Christenbury. LC 99-87970. 336p. 2000. pap. text 24.00 (*0-86709-476-1*, Pub. by Boynton Cook Pubs) Heinemann.
Making the Journey with Christ: The Way of the Cross. Judy Sardello. (Illus.). 53p. 1993. pap. 0.95 (*0-8199-0965-3*) Franciscan Pr.
Making the Law. Saywell & Vegh. 1991. pap. text. write for info. (*0-7730-5098-1*) Addison-Wesley.
Making the Light Come: The Poetry of Gerald Stern. Ed. by Jane Somerville. LC 89-70498. 140p. (C). 1990. text 29.95 (*0-8143-2238-7*) Wayne St U Pr.
Making the Light Come: The Poetry of Gerald Stern. Jane Somerville. LC 89-70498. 139p. reprint ed. pap. 43.10 (*0-608-10586-4*, 2071207) Bks Demand.
Making the Link: Teacher Professional Development on the Internet. Ronald D. Owston. LC 97-50314. 174p. 1998. pap. 24.00 (*0-325-00077-8*) Heinemann.
Making the Local News: Sources & Resources for Local Journalism. Bob Franklin & David Murphy. LC 97-32618. (Illus.). 288p. (C). 1998. 85.00 (*0-415-16802-3*); pap. 24.99 (*0-415-16803-1*) Routledge.
Making the Majors: The Transformation of Team Sports in America. Eric M. Leifer. LC 95-13469. (Illus.). 400p. (C). 1996. 56.00 (*0-674-54322-X*) HUP.
Making the Majors: The Transformation of Team Sports in America. Eric M. Leifer. (Illus.). 400p. 1998. pap. text 22.95 (*0-674-54331-9*) HUP.
Making the Managerial Presidency: Comprehensive Reorganization Planning, 1905-1996. 2nd ed. Peri E. Arnold. LC 97-52290. (Studies in Government & Public Policy). 456p. 1998. 50.00 (*0-7006-0893-1*); pap. 25.00 (*0-7006-0894-X*) U Pr of KS.
Making the Market Right for the Efficient Use of Energy. Ed. by Behram N. Kursunoglu. 303p. (C). 1993. 145.00 (*1-56072-084-0*) Nova Sci Pubs.
*__Making the Mass Come Alive.__ John Hampsch. 35p. 2000. pap. 2.95 (*1-57918-130-9*) Queenship Pub.
*__Making the Masters: Clifford Roberts Augusta National & Golfs Most Prestigious Tournament.__ 288p. 1999. 24.50 (*0-684-86721-4*) S&S Trade.
Making the Mature Years Count. 1991. pap. text 1.35 (*0-8474-0831-0*) Back to Bible.
Making the Medieval Book: Techniques of Production. Ed. by Linda L. Brownrigg. (Proceedings of the Seminar in the History of the Book to 1500 Ser.). (Illus.). xvi, 248p. (C). 1995. 98.00 (*0-9626372-2-X*) Anderson-Lovelace Pubs.
Making the Medieval Book: Techniques of Production. Ed. by Linda L. Brownrigg. (Proceedings of the Seminar in the History of the Book to 1500 Ser.). (Illus.). xvi, 248p. (C). 1995. pap. 55.00 (*0-9626372-3-8*) Anderson-Lovelace Pubs.
Making the Message Clear: How to Master the Business Communication Tools That Direct Productivity, Excellence & Power. James P. Eicher. LC 87-80283. 123p. (C). 1987. 14.95 (*0-929514-00-9*) Grinder Delozier.
Making the Message Mine. Marlo Morgan. Ed. by Jeannette Grimme. (Illus.). 115p. (Orig.). (YA). Date not set. pap. text. write for info. (*1-883473-01-2*) M M Co.
Making the MIRV: A Study of Defense Decision Making. Ted Greenwood. 256p. (C). 1988. reprint ed. pap. text 25.00 (*0-8191-7077-1*) U Pr of Amer.
Making the Missouri Synod Functional Again. Waldo J. Werning. 338p. 1992. pap. 10.95 (*0-9632650-0-8*) Biblical Renew.
Making the Modern: Industry, Art & Design in America. Terry Smith. LC 92-935. (Illus.). 528p. (C). 1993. 55.00 (*0-226-76346-3*) U Ch Pr.
Making the Modern: Industry, Art & Design in America. Terry Smith. xvi, 528p. 1994. pap. text 34.95 (*0-226-76347-1*) U Ch Pr.
Making the Modern Reader: Cultural Mediation in Early Modern Literary Anthologies. Barbara M. Benedict. LC 95-53313. 264p. (C). 1996. text 39.50 (*0-691-02578-9*, Pub. by Princeton U Pr) Cal Prin Full Svc.
Making the Moments Count: Leisure Activities for Caregiving Relationships. Joanne A. Decker. LC 97-12488. xii, 192 p. 1997. pap. 14.95 (*0-8018-5700-7*); text 29.95 (*0-8018-5699-X*) Johns Hopkins.
Making the Money Last: Financial Clarity for the Surviving Spouse. limited ed. BFA Staff et al. 288p. 1996. pap. text, per. 29.95 (*0-7872-2172-4*) Kendall-Hunt.
*__Making the Money Sing: Private Wealth & Public Power in the Search for Peace.__ John Tirman. 160p. 2000. 27.50 (*0-8476-9922-6*) Rowman.
*__Making the Most of a Small Garden.__ Peter McHoy. 160p. 2000. pap. 14.95 (*1-84215-051-0*) Anness Pub.
Making the Most of Action Learning. Scott Inglis. LC 94-9706. 256p. 1994. 67.95 (*0-566-07452-4*, Pub. by Gower) Ashgate Pub Co.
Making the Most of Bathrooms. Catherine Haig. LC 96-67705. (Illus.). 80p. 1996. 19.95 (*0-8478-1975-2*, Pub. by Rizzoli Intl) St Martin.
Making the Most of Bedrooms. Karen Howes. LC 96-71509. (Illus.). 80p. 19.95 (*0-8478-2016-5*, Pub. by Rizzoli Intl) St Martin.
Making the Most of Being Mentored: How to Grow from a Mentoring Partnership. Gordon F. Shea. LC 99-72374. (Crisp 50-Minute Bks.). (Illus.). 96p. 1999. pap. 10.95 (*1-56052-546-0*, Pub. by Crisp Pubns) Natl Bk Netwk.
Making the Most of Change: When Change Is Making the Most of You. Roz Turner. LC 95-80407. 126p. 1995. pap. 6.95 (*1-883697-39-5*) Hara Pub.
Making the Most of Conifers & Heathers. 2nd ed. Adrian Bloom. (Illus.). 78p. 1989. pap. 12.95 (*0-903001-61-6*, Pub. by Burall Floraprint) J Markham Assocs.
Making the Most of Fieldwork Education: A Practical Approach. A. Alsop & S. Ryan. LC 96-84232. (Illus.). 240p. (Orig.). (C). 1996. pap. text 45.00 (*1-56593-439-3*, 1108) Singular Publishing.
*__Making the Most of HACCP: Learning from Others' Experience.__ Tony Mayes & Sara Mortimore. 320p. 2000. text 108.00 (*1-85573-504-0*, Pub. by Woodhead Pubng) Am Educ Systs.
Making the Most of Living Rooms. Amanda Evans. LC 98-65891. (Illus.). 80p. 1998. 19.95 (*0-8478-2128-5*, Pub. by Rizzoli Intl) St Martin.
Making the Most of Marin. Patricia Arrigoni. 1990. pap. 15.95 (*0-9625468-9-5*) Trvl Pubs Intl.
*__Making the Most of Marin: A Northern California Guide.__ 3rd rev. ed. Patricia Arrigoni. Ed. by Carroll Dana. (Illus.). 400p. 2000. pap. 19.95 (*0-9625468-7-9*, Pub. by Trvl Pubs Intl) Sunbelt Pubns.
*__Making the Most of Media Exposure for Global Change Versus Our Experience with the Media.__ Gabriel of Sedona & Niann Emerson Chase. 72p. 1998. ring bd. 6.06 (*0-9647357-5-X*, Pub. by Starseed & Uran) Aquarian Concpts.
Making the Most of Middle Age. large type ed. Brice Pitt. 119p. 1991. 17.95 (*1-85089-170-2*, Pub. by ISIS Lrg Prnt) Transaction Pubs.
Making the Most of New Technology: A How-to-Do-It Manual for Librarians. Kathleen R. Imhoff. (How-to-Do-It Manuals Ser.). 127p. 1996. pap. 45.00 (*1-55570-232-5*) Neal-Schuman.
Making the Most of Rhododendrons Azaleas. Christopher Fairweather. (Illus.). 112p. 1993. pap. 17.95 (*0-903001-66-7*, Pub. by Burall Floraprint) J Markham Assocs.
Making the Most of Small Spaces. Anoof Parikh. 80p. 1994. 19.95 (*0-8478-1801-2*, Pub. by Rizzoli Intl) St Martin.
Making the Most of Sonoma County: A California Guide. 2nd rev. ed. Don Edwards. (Illus.). 307p. 1986. reprint ed. pap. 12.95 (*0-9615030-0-9*) Valley of Moon Pr.
Making the Most of Storage. Debora Robertson. LC 95-71192. (Illus.). 80p. 1996. 19.95 (*0-8478-1937-X*, Pub. by Rizzoli Intl) St Martin.
Making the Most of Student Performance Data. Leslie J. Farlow & Martha E. Snell. LC 94-16009. (Innovations Ser.: No. 3). 1994. 21.95 (*0-940898-36-5*) Am Assn Mental.
*__Making the Most of Summer School: A Meta-Analytic & Narrative Review.__ Harris Cooper. (Monographs of the Society for Research in Children Development). 120p. 2000. pap. 32.95 (*0-631-22152-2*) Blackwell Pubs.
Making the Most of "The American Promise" A Study Guide, Vol. I. John Moretta & David Wilcox. 1998. pap. text, student ed. 23.95 (*0-312-11198-3*) St Martin.
Making the Most of the Best of Your Life. Kathryn Grant & Penny R. Giesbrecht. 176p. (Orig.). 1990. pap. 9.95 (*0-929292-15-4*) Hannibal Bks.
Making the Most of the Least: Alternative Ways to Development. Ed. by Leonard Berry & Robert W. Kates. LC 79-11619. 282p. 1980. 44.95 (*0-8419-0434-0*) Holmes & Meier.
Making the Most of the Second Half of SHRP: Proceedings of the SHRP Midcourse Assessment Meeting. (SHRP Working Papers: No. 001G). 88p. 1990. 5.00 (*0-685-41021-8*) Transport Res Bd.
Making the Most of Today: Daily Readings for Young People on Self-Awareness, Creativity, & Self-Esteem. Pamela Espeland & Rosemary Wallner. LC 91-14494. (Self-Help for Kids Ser.). 392p. (YA). (gr. 5 up). 1991. pap. 9.95 (*0-915793-33-4*) Free Spirit Pub.
Making the Most of Work Spaces. Loffie Mack. LC 95-67264. (Illus.). 80p. 1995. 19.95 (*0-8478-1897-7*, Pub. by Rizzoli Intl) St Martin.
Making the Most of Your Appraisal: Career & Professional Development Planning for Lecturers. Graham Webb. LC 94-28207. (Teaching & Learning in Higher Education Ser.). 160p. 1994. pap. 29.95 (*0-7494-1256-9*, Kogan Pg Educ) Stylus Pub VA.
Making the Most of Your College Education. Marianne Ragins. 88p. (Orig.). 1995. pap. 10.95 (*0-8050-4404-3*, Owl) H Holt & Co.
*__Making the Most of Your Corporate Brand.__ Nicholas Ind. (Management Briefings Ser.). 95p. 1998. pap. 142.50 (*0-273-63384-8*, Pub. by Pitman Pbg) Trans-Atl Phila.
Making the Most of Your Inspection: Primary. David Clegg & Shirley Billington. LC 93-50646. 144p. 1994. write for info. (*0-7507-0246-X*, Falmer Pr) Taylor & Francis.
Making the Most of Your Inspection: Secondary. David Clegg & Shirley Billington. LC 93-50131. 144p. 1994. write for info. (*0-7507-0248-6*, Falmer Pr); pap. 29.95 (*0-7507-0249-4*, Falmer Pr) Taylor & Francis.
Making the Most of Your Life. John J. Morgan & Ewing T. Webb. LC 70-152199. (Essay Index Reprint Ser.). 1977. reprint ed. 23.95 (*0-8369-2248-4*) Ayer.
Making the Most of Your Llama: An Owner's Manual. 2nd rev. ed. Linda C. Beattie. Ed. by Kathryn Doll. LC 98-67195. (Illus.). 89p. (Orig.). 1998. pap. text 17.95 (*0-9619634-1-7*) Kopacetic Ink.
Making the Most of Your Medical Deductions. 32p. 1983. 2.50 (*0-685-07390-4*) P-H.
Making the Most of Your Memory: Practical Memory Exercises for All Ages. George Singer & Lisl Singer. LC 95-186756. 1994. pap. 7.95 (*1-86324-018-7*, Pub. by LaTrobe Univ) Intl Spec Bk.
Making the Most of Your Mission. John D. Whetten. LC 81-66421. 83p. 1990. reprint ed. pap. 6.95 (*0-87579-347-9*) Deseret Bk.
Making the Most of Your Money: Completely Revised & Updated for the Twenty-First Century. Jane Bryant Quinn. LC 97-23183. 944p. 1997. 29.50 (*0-684-81176-6*) Simon & Schuster.
Making the Most of Your Money: How to Develop a Personal Financial Strategy for Maximum Impact. Ray Linder. 180p. 1995. pap. 10.99 (*1-56476-389-7*, 6-3389, Victor Bks) Chariot Victor.
Making the Most of Your Own Backyard. Sunset Books Editors. LC 96-67825. (Illus.). 320p. 1996. pap. 24.95 (*0-376-03078-X*, 203078, Pub. by Sunset Books) Leisure AR.
*__Making the Most of Your Relationships: How to Find Satisfaction & Intimacy with Family & Friends.__ William Stewart. 144p. 2000. 14.95 (*1-85703-576-3*, Pub. by How To Bks) Midpt Trade.
Making the Most of Your Sewing Machine & Serger Accessories. Joanne Pugh-Gannon. LC 98-50985. 1999. 27.95 (*0-8069-8453-8*) Sterling.
Making the Most of Your Southern Experience. Linda L. Arthur & Michael T. Mills. 208p. (C). 1996. text 28.20 (*0-536-59277-2*) Pearson Custom.
Making the Most of Your Teenage Years. David Burrows. (YA). 1995. pap. 6.99 (*1-56229-456-3*) Pneuma Life Pub.
*__Making the Most of Your Time.__ Julie-Ann Amos. (Essentials Ser.). 64p. 2000. pap. 9.95 (*1-85703-519-4*, Pub. by How To Bks) Midpt Trade.
Making the Move: A Practical Guide to Senior Residential Communities. Lettice Stuart. LC 96-47039. 256p. 1997. pap. 12.00 (*0-380-78981-7*, Avon Bks) Morrow Avon.
Making the Move to Visual Basic 4 from Cobol. Mike Stanley & Steve Wilent. LC 96-24288. (Special Reports). 1996. write for info. (*1-880935-47-3*) Pinnacle WA.
Making the Music Decision. Jack R. Christianson. LC 95-77390. 1995. pap. 8.95 (*0-88494-990-7*) Bookcraft Inc.
*__Making the New Baskets: Alternative Materials, Simple Techniques.__ Jane LaFerla. (Illus.). 128p. 2000. 27.95 (*1-57990-151-4*, Pub. by Lark Books) Sterling.
Making the New Commonwealth. R. J. Moore. (Illus.). 224p. 1987. text 59.00 (*0-19-820112-5*) OUP.
Making the New Europe. M. L. Smith & Peter M. Stirk. 256p. 1990. text 39.00 (*0-86187-777-2*, Pub. by P P Pubs) Cassell & Continuum.
Making the New Europe: European Unity & the Second World War. Ed. by M. L. Smith & Peter M. Stirk. 208p. 1993. pap. 17.95 (*1-85567-177-8*, Pub. by P P Pubs) Cassell & Continuum.
Making the News. Peter Golding & Philip Elliott. LC 78-41006. 253p. reprint ed. pap. 78.50 (*0-608-18737-2*, 203033400068) Bks Demand.
Making the News: A Guide for Nonprofits & Activists. Jason Salzman. LC 98-9517. 320p. (C). 1998. pap. 19.95 (*0-8133-6898-7*, Pub. by Westview) HarpC.
Making the News: An Anthology of the Newsbooks of Revolutionary England, 1641-1660. Ed. by Joad Raymond. LC 93-1629. 1993. text 49.95 (*0-312-10093-0*) St Martin.
Making the News: Modernity & the Mass Press in Nineteenth-Century France. Ed. by Dean De la Motte & Jeannene M. Przyblyski. LC 98-38552. (Studies in Print Culture & the History of the Book). (Illus.). 400p. 1999. 70.00 (*1-55849-176-7*); pap. 22.95 (*1-55849-177-5*) U of Mass Pr.
Making the Newsmakers: International Handbook on Journalism Training. Philip Gaunt. LC 92-10618. 256p. 1992. lib. bdg. 59.95 (*0-313-27984-5*, GNK/, Greenwood Pr) Greenwood.
Making the Non-Profit Organization Work: A Legal & Accounting Guide for Administrators. Ed. by Arnold J. Olenick & Phil Olenick. LC 83-12885. 416p. 1983. 49.95 (*0-87624-354-5*, Inst Busn Plan) P-H.
Making the Nonprofit Sector in the U. S. Hammack. pap. 19.95 (*0-253-21410-6*) Ind U Pr.
Making the Nonprofit Sector in the United States: A Reader. Ed. & Intro. by David C. Hammack. LC 98-7117. (Philanthropic Studies). 592p. 1998. 39.95 (*0-253-33489-6*) Ind U Pr.
Making the Numbers Count: The Management Accountant As Change Agent on the World Class Team. Brian H. Maskell. (Illus.). 150p. 1996. 29.00 (*1-56327-070-6*) Productivity Inc.
Making the Ordinary Schools Special. Tony Dessent. 192p. 1987. pap. 34.95 (*1-85000-236-3*, Falmer Pr) Taylor & Francis.
Making the Path While You Walk. Craig Van Riper. 27p. (Orig.). (C). 1993. pap. 15.00 (*0-9631985-1-3*) Sagittarius Pr.
Making the Patient Your Partner: Communication Skills for Doctors & Other Caregivers. Thomas S. Gordon & W. Edwards. LC 94-42698. 240p. 1997. pap. 21.95 (*0-86569-273-4*, Auburn Hse) Greenwood.
Making the Peace: A 15-Session Violence Prevention Curriculum for Young People. Paul Kivel et al. LC 96-34103. (Making the Peace Program Ser.: Vol. 1). (Illus.). viii, 180p. 1997. pap. text 24.95 (*0-89793-205-6*) Hunter Hse.
Making the Peace: Public Order & Public Security in Modern Britain. Charles Townshend. 274p. 1993. text 32.00 (*0-19-822978-X*) OUP.
Making the Physician Network Work: Leadership, Design & Incentives. Lisa K. Rolfe & Paul Wehner. LC 95-11325. 116p. 1995. pap. 56.50 (*1-55648-142-X*, 164101) AHPI.
Making the Piece Fit. 2nd ed. (C). 1996. write for info. (*0-8087-7191-4*) Pearson Custom.
Making the Playground. Eileen Adams. 56p. 1993. pap. 10.00 (*0-948080-92-2*, Trentham Bks) Stylus Pub VA.
Making the Poor Poorer: The Welfare State after the Fowler Reviews. Michael Meacher & Margaret Beckett. 1986. 40.00 (*0-85124-425-4*); pap. 40.00 (*0-85124-435-1*) St Mut.
Making the Prostate Therapy Decision. Jeff Baggish. 208p. 1995. 22.95 (*1-56565-207-X*) Lowell Hse.
Making the Prostate Therapy Decision. Jeff Baggish. (Illus.). 208p. 1996. pap. 16.00 (*1-56565-433-1*) Lowell Hse.
*__Making the Prostate Therapy Decision.__ 2nd rev. ed. Jeff Baggish. 240p. 1998. pap. 16.00 (*1-56565-869-8*, 08698W, Pub. by Lowell Hse) NTC Contemp Pub Co.
Making the Prozac Decision. 3rd rev. ed. Carol Turkington & Eliot F. Kaplan. LC 98-231517. 272p. 1997. pap. 15.00 (*1-56565-803-5*, 08035W, Pub. by Lowell Hse) NTC Contemp Pub Co.
Making the Prozac Decision: A Guide to Anti-Depressants. Carol Turkington & Eliot F. Kaplan. 240p. 1995. pap. 15.00 (*1-56565-332-7*) Lowell Hse.
Making the Radiation Therapy Decision. David J. Brenner & Eric J. Hall. (Illus.). 216p. 1996. 27.00 (*1-56565-333-5*) Lowell Hse.
Making the Right Connections: A Guide for Nature Writers. James Heintzman. Ed. by Michael Gross & Ronald Zimmerman. (Interpreter's Handbook Ser.). (Illus.). 54p. (C). 1988. pap. text 7.00 (*0-932310-07-9*) U of Wis-Stevens Point.
Making the Right Decision: Ethics for Managers. William D. Hall & Arthur Andersen. 272p. 1993. pap. 14.95 (*0-471-58633-1*) Wiley.
Making the Right Things Happen. Carl Japikse. 304p. 2000. pap. 17.95 (*0-89804-046-9*, Pub. by Ariel GA) Alliance Bk Co.
*__Making the Rugby World: Race, Gender, Commerce.__ Ed. by Timothy J. L. Chandler & John Nauright. LC 99-27732. (Sport in the Global Society Ser.: No. 10). 256p. 1999. 59.50 (*0-7146-4853-1*); pap. 24.50 (*0-7146-4411-0*) F Cass Pubs.
Making the Rules for Small Business Success: Secrets for Doing Business in the 21st Century. Jeanie Swisher. ix, 100p. 1999. pap. 19.95 (*1-890066-20-6*) Spectrm Pubs.
Making the Scene: Setting the Stage for Success. Michael Gallina. (Illus.). 140p. (Orig.). 1992. pap. 19.95 (*0-8256-6050-5*, M723) Shawnee Pr.
*__Making the Skeleton Dance.__ Patricia Garfinkel. 2000. 22.50 (*0-8076-1464-5*) Braziller.
Making the Small Church Effective. Carl S. Dudley. LC 78-2221. 1978. pap. 11.95 (*0-687-23044-6*) Abingdon.
Making the Small Machinist Shop Profitable. 1996. lib. bdg. 251.95 (*0-8490-8313-3*) Gordon Pr.

An Asterisk (*) at the beginning of an entry indicates that the title is appearing for the first time.

Making the Spirit Dance Within: Native Students & the Joe Duquette High School. Celia Haig-Brown et al. LC 98-151718. (Our Schools/Our Selves Ser.). 189p. 1997. pap. 19.95 (*1-55028-566-1*, Pub. by J Lorimer) Formac Dist Ltd.

Making the Surface Transportation System More Secure: A Research & Development Strategy to Improve the Surface Transportation System. National Academy Press Staff. 1999. 44.95 (*0-309-06529-1*) Natl Acad Pr.

Making the Team. Nancy Carlson. (Nancy Carlson's Neighborhood Ser.). (Illus.). 32p. (J). (ps-3). 1994. pap. 4.95 (*0-87614-855-0*, First Ave Edns); lib. bdg. 17.27 (*0-87614-281-1*, First Ave Edns) Lerner Pub.

*__Making the Team: A Guide for Managers__ Leigh L. Thompson. LC 99-35844. (Executive Education Ser.). 318p. 1999. pap. 39.20 (*0-13-014363-4*) P-H.

Making the Team: Field Guide for Managers. (C). 2000. pap. write for info. (*0-13-016408-9*) P-H.

*__Making the Team: Field Guide for Managers.__ (C). 2000. text. write for info. (*0-13-016564-6*) P-H.

Making the Team: The Cultural Work of Baseball Fiction. Timothy Morris. LC 96-10131. 208p. 1997. text 34.95 (*0-252-02294-7*) U of Ill Pr.

Making The Team: The Cultural Work Of Baseball Fiction. Timothy Morris. LC 96-10131. 208p. 1997. 13.95 (*0-252-06597-2*) U of Ill Pr.

*__Making the Technical Sale: A Handbook for Technical Sales Professionals.__ James F. Milbery & Richard E. Greenwald. 2000. pap. text 34.95 (*0-9662889-9-8*) Muska Lipman.

Making the "Terrible" Twos Terrific! John K. Rosemond. 194p. 1993. pap. 8.95 (*0-8362-2811-1*) Andrews & McMeel.

Making the Timeless Timely: Thoughts & Reflections of a Contemporary Reform Rabbi. Samuel M. Stahl. 382p. 1993. 21.95 (*0-89015-931-9*) Sunbelt Media.

*__Making the Town: Ga State & Society in Early Colonial Accra.__ John Parker. LC 00-25969. 325p. 2000. 25.00 (*0-325-00190-1*, E00190); write for info. (*0-325-00191-X*) Greenwood.

Making the Transition to a Macrobiotic Diet: A Beginner's Guide to the Natural Way of Health. Carolyn Heidenry. LC 86-32291. (Illus.). 112p. pap. 6.95 (*0-89529-363-3*, Avery) Penguin Putnam.

Making the Transition to Home Health Nursing: A Practical Guide. Denise Lovejoy. LC 97-16428. 200p. 1997. 32.95 (*0-8261-9740-X*) Springer Pub.

Making the Transition to Managed Behavioral Health Care: A Guide for Agencies & Practitioners. Anna Scheyett. LC 97-36711. 165p. 1997. pap. 21.95 (*0-87304-300-6*) Manticore Pubs.

Making the Ultimate Demo. 2nd ed. GINO ROBAIR. LC 99-62486. 180p. 1999. pap. text 29.95 (*0-87288-728-6*) Intertec Pub.

Making the Weather. Alexander G. McAdie. LC 77-10233. reprint ed. 29.50 (*0-404-16213-4*) AMS Pr.

Making the Wiseguys Weep: The Jimmy Roselli Story. David Evanier. LC 98-11739. (Illus.). 256p. 1998. 24.00 (*0-374-19927-2*) FS&G.

Making the World. Douglas Wood. LC 97-23472. (Illus.). 40p. (J). (ps-2). 1998. per. 16.00 (*0-689-81358-9*) S&S Childrens.

Making the World Less Safe: The Unhealthy Trend in Health, Safety & Environmental Regulation. Richard L. Stroup & John C. Goodman. 1989. pap. 10.00 (*0-943802-27-X*, 137) Natl Ctr Pol.

Making The World Safe for Democracy: A Century of Wilsonianism & Its Totalitarian Challengers. Amos Perlmutter. LC 97-9883. 216p. (C). (gr. 13). 1997. 34.95 (*0-8078-2365-1*) U of NC Pr.

Making the World Safe for Existence: Celebration of the Saints among the Sierra Nahuat of Chignautla, Mexico. Doren L. Slade. LC 91-43631. 312p. (C). 1992. text 52.50 (*0-472-10289-3*, 10289) U of Mich Pr.

Making the Writing & Research Connection with the I-Search Process: A How-to-Do-It Manual for Teachers & School Librarians. Marilyn Z. Joyce & Julie I. Tallman. LC 95-47717. (How-to-Do-It Manuals Ser.: No. 62). 150p. 1997. pap. 45.00 (*1-55570-252-X*) Neal-Schuman.

Making the Writing Process Work: Strategies for Composition & Self-Regulation. 2nd ed. Karen R. Harris & Steven Graham. LC 95-20777. (Cognitive Strategy Training Ser.). 240p. 1995. pap. 24.95 (*1-57129-010-9*) Brookline Bks.

Making Theater: Developing Plays with Young People. Herbert R. Kohl. (Illus.). 150p. 1988. 21.95 (*0-915924-16-1*); pap. 13.95 (*0-915924-17-X*) Tchrs & Writers Coll.

*__Making Their Mark: Central School of Art Staff & Students 1896-1966.__ Sylvia Backmeyer. 160p. 2000. pap. 29.95 (*0-7136-5261-6*, Pub. by A & C Blk) Midpt Trade.

Making Their Mark: Educating African-American Children. Israel Tribble, Jr. 124p. 12.95 (*0-931761-30-1*) Beckham Pubns.

Making Their Mark: Women Artists Move into the Mainstream, 1970-85. Randy Rosen et al. Ed. by Catherine Brawer. (Illus.). 300p. 1991. pap. 35.00 (*1-55859-161-3*) Abbeville Pr.

Making Their Own Way: Southern Blacks' Migration to Pittsburgh, 1916-1930. Peter Gottlieb. LC 86-7041. (Blacks in the New World Ser.). (Illus.). 280p. (C). 1987. text 29.95 (*0-252-01354-9*) U of Ill Pr.

Making Their Own Way: Southern Blacks' Migration to Pittsburgh, 1916-30. Peter Gottlieb. LC 97-139535. 272p. pap. text 15.95 (*0-252-06617-0*) U of Ill Pr.

Making Their Way. Ashton & Lowe. 240p. 1990. 69.00 (*0-335-09392-2*) U of Toronto Pr.

Making Their Way. Ashton & Lowe. 1990. pap. 25.00 (*0-335-09391-4*) U of Toronto Pr.

Making Their Way: Education, Training, & the Labour Market in Canada & Britain. Ed. by David Ashton & Graham S. Lowe. 256p. 1990. text 60.00 (*0-8020-2773-3*); pap. text 22.95 (*0-8020-6823-5*) U of Toronto Pr.

Making Them Like Us: Peace Corps Volunteers in the 1960's. Fritz Fischer. LC 98-16158. 256p. 1998. 27.95 (*1-56098-889-4*) Smithsonian.

*__Making Them Like Us: Peace Corps Volunteers in the 1960s.__ Fritz Fischer. (Illus.). 237p. 2000. pap. 15.95 (*1-56098-671-9*) Smithsonian.

Making Them Move. Badler. 1998. 88.95 incl. VHS (*1-55860-951-2*) Morgan Kaufmann.

Making Them Move: Mechanics, Control & Animation of Articulated Figures. Ed. by Norman Badler et al. (Computer Graphics & Geometric Modeling Ser.). (Illus.). 348p. 1998. pap. text 57.95 (*1-55860-106-6*) Morgan Kaufmann.

Making Them Move: Mechanics, Control & Animation of Articulated Figures. Ed. by Norman Badler et al. (Computer Graphics & Geometric Modeling Ser.). (Illus.). 1998. VHS 36.95 (*1-55860-154-6*) Morgan Kaufmann.

Making Them Move: Mechanics, Control & Animation of Articulated Figures. Ed. by Norman I. Badler et al. (Computer Graphics & Geometric Modeling Ser.). (Illus.). 348p. 1990. text 85.95 incl. VHS (*1-55860-155-4*) Morgan Kaufmann.

Making Themes Work. Anne Davies et al. (Building Connections Ser.). 88p. (Orig.). 1993. pap., teacher ed. 14.00 (*1-895411-60-2*) Peguis Pubs Ltd.

Making Theory - Constructing Art: On the Authority of the Avant-Garde. Daniel Herwitz. (Illus.). 376p. (C). 1993. 38.50 (*0-226-32891-0*) U Ch Pr.

Making Theory - Constructing Art: On the Authority of the Avant-Garde. Daniel Herwitz. (Illus.). 354p. 1996. reprint ed. pap. text 22.50 (*0-226-32892-9*) U Ch Pr.

Making Things: The Hand Book of Creative Discovery. Ann S. Wiseman. 1997. 12.95 (*0-614-28843-6*) Little.

Making Things: The Handbook of Creative Discovery. rev. ed. Ann S. Wiseman. LC 96-7070. (Illus.). 176p. (J). (gr. k-3). 1997. pap. 14.70 (*0-316-94756-3*) Little.

Making Things Better: Competing in Manufacturing. (Illus.). 241p. (C). 1993. pap. text 50.00 (*1-56806-376-8*) DIANE Pub.

Making Things Change. Gary Gibson. LC 95-10820. (Science for Fun Ser.). (Illus.). 32p. (J). (gr. 2-4). 1995. lib. bdg. 20.90 (*1-56294-645-5*, Copper Beech Bks) Millbrook Pr.

Making Things Change. Gary Gibson. (Science for Fun Ser.). (Illus.). 32p. (J). (gr. 2-4). 1996. pap. 4.95 (*0-7613-0464-9*, Copper Beech Bks) Millbrook Pr.

Making Things Change. Gary Gibson. (Science for Fun Ser.). 1995. 10.15 (*0-606-09827-5*, Pub. by Turtleback) Demco.

Making Things Float & Sink. Gary Gibson. (Science for Fun Ser.). 1995. 10.15 (*0-606-09828-3*, Pub. by Turtleback) Demco.

Making Things Float & Sink: With Easy-to-Make Scientific Projects. Gary Gibson. (Science for Fun Ser.). (Illus.). 32p. (J). (gr. 2-4). 1995. lib. bdg. 20.90 (*1-56294-617-X*, Copper Beech Bks) Millbrook Pr.

Making Things Float & Sink: With Easy-to-Make Scientific Projects. Gary Gibson. (Science for Fun Ser.). (Illus.). 32p. (J). (gr. 2-4). 1995. pap. 4.95 (*1-56294-635-8*, Copper Beech Bks) Millbrook Pr.

Making Things Greener: Motivations & Influences in the Greening of Manufacturing. Mardie Townsend. LC 98-70992. (Studies in Green Research). (Illus.). 216p. 1998. text 59.95 (*1-84014-385-1*, Pub. by Ashgate Pub) Ashgate Pub Co.

Making Things Grow: The Story of Mississippi Chemical Corporation. Jo G. Prichard. (Illus.). 260p. 1998. 40.00 (*1-57806-109-1*) U Pr of Miss.

Making Things Happen: Getting it Done-1997 Project Achievement Report Europe & the CIS. 152p. 25.00 (*92-1-126111-2*) UN.

Making Things in South Asia: The Role of Artist & Craftsman. Pref. by Michael W. Meister. (Proceedings of the South Asia Seminar Ser.: No. 4), (Illus.). 216p. (Orig.). 1988. pap. 10.00 (*0-936115-03-3*) U Penn South Asia.

Making Things Perfectly Queer: Interpreting Mass Culture. Alexander Doty. LC 92-40036. 168p. 1993. pap. 15.95 (*0-8166-2245-0*); text 39.95 (*0-8166-2244-2*) U of Minn Pr.

Making Things Right: The Sacrament of Reconciliation. Jeannine T. Leichner. (Illus.). 62p. (J). (gr. 2-4). 1980. pap. 5.95 (*0-87973-351-9*, 351) Our Sunday Visitor.

Making Things Right: The Sacrament of Reconciliation. Jeannine T. Leichner. (SPA., Illus.). 62p. (J). (gr. 2-4). 1980. pap. 5.95 (*0-87973-349-7*, 349) Our Sunday Visitor.

Making Things Right When Things Go Wrong: Ten Proven Ways to Put Your Life in Order. Paul Faulkner. LC 96-152032. 245p. 1995. pap., student ed. 10.99 (*1-878990-49-7*) Howard Pub LA.

Making Things Work: Russian-American Economic Relations, 1900-1930. (Illus.). 126p. 1993. pap. 19.95 (*0-8179-9242-1*) Hoover Inst Pr.

Making Things Work: Transportation & Trade Expansion in Western North America. Profiles of Western U. S.-Canada Border Crossings. (Illus.). 506p. (Orig.). (C). 1994. pap. text 95.00 (*0-7881-1158-2*) DIANE Pub.

Making Thirteen Colonies. Joy Hakim. (History of US Ser.: Vol. 2). (Illus.). 160p. (YA). (gr. 5 up). 1993. text 14.95 (*0-19-507747-4*) OUP.

Making Thirteen Colonies. Joy Hakim. (History of Us Ser.). 1993. 16.05 (*0-606-09417-2*, Pub. by Turtleback) Demco.

Making Thirteen Colonies (1600 - 1740) see History of U. S.

Making Thoughts Become: A Handbook for Teachers & Adults. Betty B. Taylor. (Illus.). 1978. pap. 4.25 (*0-933198-00-0*) Cac Pubns.

Making Time. Ed. by Frank A. Dubinskas. LC 87-28411. 238p. (C). 1988. 34.95 (*0-87722-535-4*) Temple U Pr.

*__Making Time: Considering Time as a Material in Contemporary Video & Film.__ Amy Cappellazzo. 2000. pap. 25.00 (*0-9676480-0-9*) Palm Bch Inst.

*__Making Time for Me: A Practical Guide to Getting Priorities Right.__ Penelope Ody. 1999. pap. 13.95 (*1-85626-331-2*, Pub. by Cathie Kyle) Trafalgar.

Making Time for Quality: How to Delegate Responsibility While Retaining Accountability. Harold S. Haller. (Illus.). 145p. 1999. pap. 25.00 (*1-893796-00-0*) H S Haller.

Making Timeless Toys in Wood: Quality Strom Toys & Plans. Janet A. Strombeck & Richard H. Strombeck. (Illus.). 96p. (Orig.). (YA). (gr. 10-12). 1986. pap. 10.95 (*0-912355-05-0*) Sun Designs.

Making Touch. Gary Elder. (Illus.). 40p. 1981. reprint ed. pap. 5.00 (*0-914974-28-9*) Holmgangers.

*__Making Tough Decisions.__ Robert Wandberg. LC 00-27290. (Life Skills Ser.). 64p. (YA). (gr. 7-12). 2000. lib. bdg. 22.60 (*0-7368-0697-0*, LifeMatters Bks) Capstone Pr.

Making Tough Decisions: Tactics for Improving Managerial Decision Making. Paul C. Nutt. LC 88-46079. (Management-Leadership & Management Development Ser.). 648p. 1989. text 48.95 (*1-55542-138-5*) Jossey-Bass.

Making Toys: Heirloom Cars & Trucks in Wood. Sam Martin & Roger Schroeder. (Illus.). 103p. 1997. pap. 17.95 (*1-56523-079-5*) Fox Chapel Pub.

Making TQM Work: Quality Tools for Human Service Organizations. John Gunther & Frank Hawkins. LC 98-56533. (Social Work Ser.). 144p. 1999. pap. 31.95 (*0-8261-1187-4*) Springer Pub.

Making TQM Work: The Human Factor, 1993. teacher ed., student ed. 695.00 incl. VHS (*0-685-72117-5*, PB60) Soc Human Resc Mgmt.

Making Track. Stack Sutton. 168p. 1992. 19.95 (*0-8027-4131-2*) Walker & Co.

Making Track. large type ed. Stack Sutton. LC 94-8815. 259p. 1994. lib. bdg. 18.95 (*0-7862-0215-7*) Thorndike Pr.

Making Tracks. David Hawcock. LC 93-79584. (Illus.). 16p. (J). (ps-3). 1994. 12.95 (*0-7868-0000-3*, Pub. by Hyprn Child) Little.

Making Tracks. Steve Parker. LC 96-38759. (Supersmarts Ser.). (Illus.). 24p. (J). (gr. 2-5). 1998. pap. text 4.99 (*0-7636-0628-6*) Candlewick Pr.

*__Making Tracks.__ Adrienne Wolfert. (Adventures in America Ser.). (Illus.). 96p. (J). 2000. lib. bdg. 14.95 (*1-893110-16-8*) Silver Moon.

Making Tracks: An American Rail Odyssey. Terry Pindell. (Illus.). 88p. 1995. pap. 14.95 (*0-8050-1740-2*, Owl) H Holt & Co.

Making Tracks: An Introduction to Cross-Country Skiing. Dave Wicks. LC 94-43251. (Illus.). 104p. 1995. pap. 14.95 (*0-87108-849-5*) Pruett.

Making Tracks: Land Machines. Steve Parker. LC 96-38759. (SuperSmarts Ser.). 24p. (J). (gr. 2-5). 1997. 11.99 (*0-7636-0129-2*) Candlewick Pr.

Making Tracks: Poems in Scots, English & Gaelic with Translation. William Neill. 96p. (C). 1989. 45.00 (*0-903065-65-7*, Pub. by G Wright Pub) St Mut.

*__Making Tracks: The Politics of Local Rail Transport.__ Iain Docherty. 324p. 1999. text 87.95 (*1-84014-765-2*, Pub. by Ashgate Pub) Ashgate Pub Co.

Making Tracks: The Rise of Blondie. Debbie Harry. Ed. by Victor Bockris. LC 98-21876. (Illus.). 192p. 1998. reprint ed. pap. 19.95 (*0-306-80858-7*) Da Capo.

Making Trade Talks Work: Lessons from Recent History. American Chamber of Commerce in Japan Staff. 188p. 1997. pap. 30.00 (*4-915682-08-0*) Tuttle Pubng.

Making Trademarks Work. Inglis. pap. write for info. (*0-471-96670-3*) Wiley.

Making Traditional Pull-Along Toys in Wood. Alan Bridgewater & Gill Bridgewater. (Illus.). 159p. 1998. pap. text 13.00 (*0-7881-5898-8*) DIANE Pub.

Making Traditional Teddy Bears: Featuring 12 Collectible Designs. Brian Gibbs. LC 97-192070. (Illus.). 128p. 1997. 24.95 (*0-7153-0431-3*) Sterling.

Making Traditional Wooden Planes. unabridged ed. John M. Whelan. LC 96-83120. (Illus.). 128p. (Orig.). 1996. pap. 19.95 (*1-879335-69-7*) Astragal Pr.

*__Making Training Pay.__ 2000. boxed set 150.00 (*0-8464-5107-7*) Beekman Pubs.

Making Training Stick: A Collection of Techniques to Follow-up Training. Dora B. Johnson & Barbara Carnes. LC 88-72288. (Illus.). 149p. 1992. ring bd. 44.95 (*0-923285-01-6*) Baldwin Ctr.

Making Training Work: How to Achieve Bottom Line Results & Lasting Success. Berton H. Gunter. 152p. 1996. pap. 27.00 (*0-87389-340-9*, H0894) ASQ Qual Pr.

Making Transatlantic Defense Cooperation Work: Findings & Recommendations of the CSIS Atlantic Partnership Project. Geoffrey Pattie et al. LC 96-14000. (CSIS Panel Reports). (C). 1996. pap. text 14.95 (*0-89206-286-X*) CSIS.

Making Transitions Work. Elisbeth Donaldson. 1980. pap. 19.95 (*1-55059-168-1*) Detselig Ents.

Making Transnationals Accountable: A Significant Step for Britain. David Bailey et al. LC 93-38033. (Illus.). 240p. (C). 1994. pap. 25.99 (*0-415-06871-1*, B3709) Routledge.

*__Making Transparent Soap: The Art of Crafting, Molding, Scenting & Coloring.__ Catherine Failor. LC 99-55700. (Illus.). 144p. 2000. pap. 18.95 (*1-58017-244-X*) Storey Bks.

Making Trifles of Terrors: Redistributing Complicities in Shakespeare. Harry Berger, Jr. Ed. & Intro. by Peter Erickson. LC 96-17085. 1997. write for info. (*0-8047-2732-5*); pap. 19.95 (*0-8047-2852-6*) Stanford U Pr.

Making Trouble: Cultural Constructions of Crime, Deviance & Control. Ed. by Jeff Ferrell & Neil Websdale. LC 99-13732. (Social Problems & Social Issues Ser.). 392p. 1999. lib. bdg. 50.95 (*0-202-30617-8*) Aldine de Gruyter.

*__Making Trouble: Cultural Constructions of Crime, Deviance & Control.__ Ed. by Jeff Ferrell & Neil Websdale. LC 99-13732. (Social Problems & Social Issues Ser.). 392p. 1999. pap. text 25.95 (*0-202-30618-6*) Aldine de Gruyter.

Making Trouble: Essays on Gay History, Politics, & the University. John D'Emilio. LC 92-10049. 336p. (C). 1992. pap. 23.99 (*0-415-90510-9*, A6487) Routledge.

Making Turkey Callers in the Gobbler's Shop: The Gobbler's Shop. Neil D. Cost et al. LC 99-90184. (Illus.). 132p. 1999. write for info. (*0-9671259-0-1*) B Berryhill.

Making Twenty Thousand Dollars a Month at Home. Yuri Kononenko. Ed. by Laurie Collister. (Illus.). 125p. (Orig.). 1988. pap. 14.95 (*0-9618404-1-2*) Progress Pub.

Making Twig Furniture & Household Things. 3rd rev. ed. Abby Ruoff. LC 99-43782. (Illus.). 320p. 2000. pap. 24.95 (*0-88179-185-7*, Pub. by Hartley & Marks) Andrews & McMeel.

Making Twig Garden Furniture. Abby Ruoff. LC 96-52936. (Illus.). 208p. 1997. pap. 24.95 (*0-88179-144-X*) Hartley & Marks.

*__Making Twig Garden Furniture.__ 2nd ed. Abby Ruoff. (Illus.). 2000. 24.95 (*0-88179-186-5*) Hartley & Marks.

Making Twig Mosaic Rustic Furniture. Larry Hawkins & Douglas Congdon-Martin. LC 96-71786. (Illus.). 64p. 1997. pap. 14.95 (*0-7643-0242-6*) Schiffer.

Making Two Plus Two Equal Five see Making 2+2=5: 22 Action Steps Leaders Take to Boost Productivity

Making 2+2=5: 22 Action Steps Leaders Take to Boost Productivity. John H. Zenger. Orig. Title: Making Two Plus Two Equal Five. 160p. 1996. text 22.95 (*0-7863-1094-4*, Irwn Prfssnl) McGraw-Hill Prof.

Making Two Worlds One & the Story of All-American Indian Days. Hila Gilbert. (Illus.). 60p. 1986. pap. 8.00 (*0-9617748-0-0*) Connections Pr WY.

Making Unemployment Insurance Work: Reforming Unemployment Insurance: Toward Greater Employment. Oren M. Levin-Waldman. (Public Policy Brief Ser.: Vol. 26). 54p. (Orig.). 1996. pap. text 3.00 (*0-941276-17-1*) J Levy.

Making Unions Unnecessary. 2nd ed. Charles L. Hughes. 1989. pap. 24.95 (*1-55840-453-8*) Exec Ent Pubns.

Making Unions Unnecessary. 2nd ed. Charles L. Hughes. 184p. 1994. pap. 70.95 (*0-471-11276-3*) Wiley.

*__Making Unions Unnecessary: 21st Century Edition.__ Charles L. Hughes. 2000. 25.00 (*0-9662687-1-7*) Ctr For Values.

Making Universal Service Policy: Enhancing the Process Through Multidisciplinary Perspective. Ed. by Barbara A. Cherry et al. LC 98-7805. (LEA's Telecommunications Ser.). 272p. 1999. 59.95 (*0-8058-2456-1*); pap. 24.50 (*0-8058-2457-X*) L Erlbaum Assocs.

Making UNIX & Windows NT Talk: Object-Oriented Inter-Platform Communications. Mark Nadelson & Thomas Hagan. 512p. 1999. pap. 44.95 incl. disk (*0-87930-584-3*) C M P Books.

Making Up: Beauty for Every Age, Every Woman. Rex Hilverdink & Diana L. Jewell. (Illus.). 132p. 1988. pap. 22.50 (*0-517-56955-8*) C Potter.

Making up a Society: The Novels of George Eliot. Philip Fisher. LC 81-4909. 254p. 1981. reprint ed. pap. 78.80 (*0-608-00904-0*, 206169800010) Bks Demand.

Making up Accountants: The Organizational & Professional Socialization of Trainee Charted Accountants. Ed. by Fiona Anderson-Gough et al. (Institute of Charted Accountants Ser.). 147p. 1998. text 55.95 (*1-84014-539-0*, Pub. by Ashgate Pub) Ashgate Pub Co.

Making up for Lost Time. Karin Kallmaker. LC 97-51649. 288p. (Orig.). 1998. pap. 11.95 (*1-56280-196-1*) Naiad Pr.

Making up for Lost Time. Adriane G. Berg. 272p. 1995. reprint ed. mass mkt. 5.99 (*0-380-72490-1*, Avon Bks) Morrow Avon.

Making Up in Jesus Foundation: How to Dress in the Foundation of Jesus Christ's Make Up. 1999. pap. text 5.00 (*0-9665035-2-X*) V Thomas.

Making up Megaboy. Virginia Walter. (Illus.). 64p. (YA). 1999. pap. 8.95 (*0-385-32686-6*) Bantam.

Making up Megaboy. Virginia Walter. LC 97-36073. (Illus.). 62p. (J). 1998. 16.95 (*0-7894-2488-6*) DK Pub Inc.

Making Us Crazy: DSM: The Psychiatric Bible & the Creation of Mental Disorders. Herb Kutchins & Stuart A. Kirk. LC 97-22228. 320p. 1997. 27.00 (*0-684-82280-6*) Free Pr.

*__Making Use: Scenario-Based Design of Human-Computer Interactions.__ John M. Carroll. LC 00-21621. (Illus.). 376p. 2000. 39.95 (*0-262-03279-1*) MIT Pr.

Making Use of Clinical Audit: A Guide to Practice in the Health Professions. Maurice Kogan & Sally J. Redfern. LC 95-10765. 192p. 1995. 114.95 (*0-335-19543-1*) OpUniv Pr.

Making Use of Clinical Audit: A Guide to Practice in the Health Professions. Maurice Kogan & Sally J. Redfern. LC 95-10765. 192p. 1995. pap. 33.95 (*0-335-19542-3*) Taylor & Francis.

*__Making Use of the Census.__ 2nd rev. ed. Susan Lumas. 117p. 1999. pap. 9.95 (*1-873162-43-X*) PRO Pubns.

M

An Asterisk (*) at the beginning of an entry indicates that the title is appearing for the first time.

Making Value Judgements: Principles of Sound Reasoning. Elliot D. Cohen. LC 84-28874. 180p. (C). 1985. pap. text 9.50 (*0-89874-802-X*) Krieger.

Making Vancouver, 1863-1913. Robert A. McDonald. LC 96-162574. (Illus.). 336p. 1996. 49.95 (*0-7748-0555-2*, F1089) U of Wash Pr.

Making Vancouver, 1863-1913. Robert A. McDonald. (Illus.). 336p. 1997. pap. 25.95 (*0-7748-0570-6*, F1087) U of Wash Pr.

Making Victorian Dolls' House Furniture. Patricia King. (Illus.). 160p. 1996. pap. 19.95 (*0-946819-56-4*, Pub. by Guild Master) Sterling.

Making Videos for Money. Barry Hampe. LC 97-33173. 320p. 1998. pap. 17.95 (*0-8050-5441-3*) H Holt & Co.

Making Villains, Making Heroes: Joseph R. McCarthy, Martin Luther King, Jr. & the Politics of American Memory. Gary Daynes. Ed. by Stuart Bruchey et al. LC 97-38427. (Studies in American Popular History & Culture). 284p. 1997. text 63.00 (*0-8153-2992-X*) Garland.

Making Violence Part of the Game. John C. Bridges. LC 97-40873. 259p. 1998. pap. 35.00 (*1-56072-506-0*, Nova Kroshka Bks) Nova Sci Pubs.

Making Violence Sexy: Feminist Views on Pornography. Ed. by Diana E. Russell. 320p. 1993. pap. 2.00 (*0-335-19200-9*) OpUniv Pr.

Making Violence Sexy: Feminist Views on Pornography. Ed. by Diana E. Russell. LC 92-41999. (Athene Ser.). 320p. (C). 1993. text 46.00 (*0-8077-6269-5*); pap. text 19.95 (*0-8077-6268-7*) Tchrs Coll.

Making Visible the Invisible: An Anthology of Original Essays on Film Acting. Ed. by Carole Zucker. LC 89-36466. (Illus.). 438p. 1990. 45.00 (*0-8108-2220-2*) Scarecrow.

Making Visible the Invisible: An Anthology of Original Essays on Film Acting. Ed. by Carole Zucker. LC 89-36466. (Illus.). 438p. 1993. reprint ed. pap. 23.50 (*0-8108-2687-9*) Scarecrow.

Making Vision Happen: A Communities of Joy Workbook. Leonard M. Young & Gary W. Logan. 75p. (Orig.). 1995. pap. text 12.00 (*0-8309-0717-3*) Herald Pub Hse.

Making Visitors Mindful: Principles for Creating Sustainable Visitor Experience Through. Gianna Moscardo. (Advances in Tourism Applications Ser.: Vol. 2). (Illus.). 224p. 1999. pap. 16.95 (*1-57167-259-1*) Sagamore Pub.

Making Vocational Choices: A Theory of Vocational Personalities & Work Environments. 3rd rev. ed. John L. Holland. LC 97-8435. 312p. 1997. 31.00 (*0-911907-27-0*) Psych Assess.

Making Votes Count: Strategic Coordination in the World's Electoral System. Gary W. Cox. (Political Economy of Institutions & Decisions Ser.). 354p. 1997. text 59.95 (*0-521-58516-3*); pap. text 18.95 (*0-521-58527-9*) Cambridge U Pr.

Making War: The President & Congress from Barbary to Baghdad. John F. Lehman. 320p. 1992. text 24.00 (*0-684-19239-X*, Scribners Ref) Mac Lib Ref.

Making War & Making Peace: Why Some Christians Fight & Some Don't. Dennis Byler. LC 89-2222. (Peace & Justice Ser.: Vol. 8). 104p. (Orig.). 1989. pap. 6.99 (*0-8361-3497-4*) Herald Pr.

Making War in the Heavenlies: A Different Look at Spiritual Warfare. Bill Randles. (Illus.). 193p. (Orig.). 1994. pap. 10.00 (*0-9646626-0-4*) B Randles.

*__Making War Not Love.__ Draitser. LC 99-19094. 336p. 1999. text 45.00 (*0-312-22129-0*) St Martin.

*__Making Washington Work: Tales of Innovation in the Federal Government.__ Ed. by John D. Donahue. LC 99-6552. 1999. pap. 18.95 (*0-8157-1895-0*) Brookings.

Making Waves. Carolyn Keene. Ed. by Ann Greenberg. (Nancy Drew Files: No. 81). 160p. (J). (gr. 6 up). 1993. mass mkt. 3.99 (*0-671-73085-1*, Archway) PB.

Making Waves. Carolyn Keene. (Nancy Drew Files: No. 81). (YA). (gr. 6 up). 1993. 9.09 (*0-606-02803-X*, Pub. by Turtleback) Demco.

Making Waves. Catherine Todd. 352p. 1997. mass mkt. 5.99 (*0-380-78773-3*, Avon Bks) Morrow Avon.

Making Waves. Charles H. Townes. LC 94-28606. (Masters of Modern Physics Ser.). 1994. 29.95 (*1-56396-381-7*) Spr-Verlag.

Making Waves. Charles H. Townes. (AIP Masters of Modern Physics Ser.). 320p. (C). 1995. 34.95 (*1-56396-334-5*, AIP Pr) Spr-Verlag.

*__Making Waves.__ Barbara Williams. LC 99-57832. (Illus.). 224p. (J). (gr. 4-8). 2000. 17.99 (*0-8037-2515-9*, Dial Yng Read) Peng Put Young Read.

Making Waves, 1, 4. Stephanie Doyon. (On the Road Ser.: No. 4). 224p. (gr. 7 up). 1999. per. 3.99 (*0-689-82110-7*, 076714004504) S&S Childrens.

Making Waves: A History of Feminism in Western Society. Marlene LeGates. 397p. (C). 1996. text 25.95 (*0-7730-5483-9*) Addison-Wes.

Making Waves: An Anthology of Writings by & about Asian American Women. Ed. by Asian Women United of California Staff. LC 88-47661. (Illus.). 480p. (YA). (gr. 9-12). 1989. pap. 22.00 (*0-8070-5905-6*) Beacon Pr.

Making Waves: Bold Exposes from Talk Radio's Number One Night Time Host. Michael Reagan. LC 96-15763. 304p. 1996. 22.99 (*0-7852-7588-6*) Nelson.

Making Waves: Engineering, Politics & the Social Management of Technology. Edward Wenk, Jr. LC 94-21212. 1995. pap. text. write for info. (*0-252-06448-8*) U of Ill Pr.

Making Waves: Engineering, Politics & the Social Management of Technology. Edward Wenk, Jr. LC 94-21212. 288p. 1995. 26.95 (*0-252-02149-5*) U of Ill Pr.

Making Waves: Essays. Mario Vargas Llosa. Ed. & Tr. by John King, III from SPA. LC 97-267. 338p. 1997. 27.50 (*0-374-20038-6*) FS&G.

Making Waves: Essays. Mario Vargas Llosa. 368p. 1998. pap. 14.95 (*0-14-027556-8*) Viking Penguin.

Making Waves: Finding Out about Rhythmic Motion. Bernie Zubrowski. (Boston Children's Museum Activity Book). (Illus.). 96p. (J). (gr. 3 up). 1994. 14.93 (*0-688-11787-2*, Wm Morrow) Morrow Avon.

Making Waves: Finding Out about Rhythmic Motion. Bernie Zubrowski. LC 93-35455. (Boston Children's Museum Activity Book). (Illus.). 96p. (J). (gr. 5 up). 1994. pap. 6.95 (*0-688-11788-0*, Wm Morrow) Morrow Avon.

Making Waves: Finding Out about Rhythmic Motion. Bernie Zubrowski. (Boston Children's Museum Activity Bks.). (J). 1994. 12.15 (*0-606-06556-3*, Pub. by Turtleback) Demco.

*__Making Waves: Stories from My Life.__ Yakov L. Alpert. LC 00-35918. (Illus.). 288p. 2000. 30.00 (*0-300-07821-8*) Yale U Pr.

Making Waves: The Inside Story of Managing & Motivating the First Women's Team to Compete for the America's Cup. Anna S. Huntington. 282p. 1996. 19.95 (*1-56530-191-9*) Summit TX.

*__Making Waves: The Origins & Future of Greenpeace.__ Jim Bohlen. 235p. 2000. 48.99 (*1-55164-167-4*); pap. 19.99 (*1-55164-166-6*) Black Rose.

Making Weapons, Talking Peace: A Physicist's Odyssey from Hiroshima to Geneva. 2nd ed. Herbert F. York. (Illus.). 359p. 1997. reprint ed. pap. 17.20 (*0-934637-44-X*) U of CA Inst Global.

Making Weight: Healing Men's Conflicts with Food, Weight & Shape. Arnold Andersen et al. LC 00-8779. 256p. 1999. pap. 14.95 (*0-936077-35-2*, Pub. by Gurze Bks) Publishers Group.

Making Welfare Work: Reconstructing Welfare for the Millennium. Frank Field. LC 99-87302. 197p. 2000. pap. 24.95 (*0-7658-0626-6*) Transaction Pubs.

Making Wheels: A Technical Manual on Wheel Manufacture. R. A. Dennis. (Illus.). 160p. 1992. pap. 29.50 (*1-85339-141-7*, Pub. by Intermed Tech) Stylus Pub VA.

Making Whiteness: The Culture of Segregation in the South, 1890-1940. Grace E. Hale. LC 97-40906. 448p. 1998. 30.00 (*0-679-44263-4*) Pantheon.

Making Whiteness: The Culture of Segregation in the South, 1890-1940. Grace E. Hale. (Illus.). 448p. 1999. pap. 15.00 (*0-679-77620-6*) Vin Bks.

Making Whole Grain Breads. Phyllis Hobson. LC 84-21240. (Country Kitchen Library). (Illus.). 44p. 1984. pap. 3.95 (*0-88266-032-2*, Garden Way Pub) Storey Bks.

Making Wild Wines & Meads. Pattie Vargas & Rich Gulling. LC 99-23137. 1999. pap. 16.95 (*1-58017-182-6*) Storey Bks.

Making Windows Applications Work Together. Robert Krumm. LC 94-19592. 1994. pap. 34.95 incl. disk (*1-55851-385-X*, M&T Bks) IDG Bks.

*__Making Windows 2000 Professional Work for You.__ (Illus.). 128p. 2000. pap. 8.99 (*0-7645-8634-3*, CPG Pr) IDG Bks.

*__Making Windows 98 Work for You.__ Brian Underdahl. (Cliffs Technology Extension Ser.). 128p. 1999. 8.99 (*0-7645-8532-0*) IDG Bks.

Making Wine at Home the Professional Way. Lance Cutler. 50p. (Orig.). 1996. pap. 11.95 (*0-9637438-3-X*) Wine Patrol Pr.

Making Wines, Beers, & Soft Drinks. Phyllis Hobson. (Country Kitchen Library). (Illus.). 60p. 1984. pap. 3.95 (*0-88266-063-2*, Garden Way Pub) Storey Bks.

Making Winning Presentations: How to Carry the Day with Confidence & Success. 2nd ed. Ghassan Hasbani. (Business & Management Ser.). (Illus.). 154p. 1999. pap. 19.95 (*1-85703-497-X*, Pub. by How To Bks) Trans-Atl Phila.

Making Wire Jewelry: 60 Easy Projects in Silver, Copper, & Brass. Helen Clegg & Mary Larom. LC 97-17291. (Illus.). 112p. (Orig.). 1997. pap. 18.95 (*1-57990-002-X*, Pub. by Lark Books) Random.

Making Wire Jewelry Book & Kit. Lark Books Staff. (Illus.). 1998. 50.00 (*1-57990-033-X*, Pub. by Lark Books) Random.

Making Wise Choices. Linda K. Sibley. LC 97-204438. (Ministry of Confident Kids). (Illus.). 416p. 1997. teacher ed. 39.99 (*0-7847-0641-7*, 42051) Standard Pub.

Making Wise Choices: A Guide for Women. Charlotte E. Thompson. 140p. (Orig.). 1993. pap. 12.95 (*0-8283-1972-3*) Branden Bks.

Making Wise Choices: Helping Children Understand Social & Moral Issues. Gayle Leininger et al. Ed. by Jennifer Law. 58p. (Orig.). (gr. 4). 1995. pap. text 6.95 (*1-56309-130-5*, N957102, New Hope) Womans Mission Union.

Making Wise Medical Decisions: How to Get the Information You Need. Resources for Rehabilitation Staff. LC 98-23960. 219p. 1998. pap. 39.95 (*0-929718-21-6*) Resc Rehab.

Making Women Matter: The Role of the United Nations. 3rd ed. Hilkka Pietila & Jeanne Vickers. (Illus.). 224p. 1996. text 19.95 (*1-85649-458-6*) Zed Books.

Making Women Pay: The Hidden Costs of Fetal Rights. Rachel Roth. LC 99-44982. 1999. 29.95 (*0-8014-3607-9*) Cornell U Pr.

Making Wood Boxes & Coal Bins. L. Seddon. 1997. pap. 2.95 (*0-88266-292-9*) Storey Bks.

Making Wood Decoys. Patrick Spielman. LC 82-50556. (Illus.). 164p. 1982. pap. 14.95 (*0-8069-7660-8*) Sterling.

Making Wood Folk Instruments. Dennis Waring. LC 90-37056. (Illus.). 160p. (Orig.). 1990. pap. 14.95 (*0-8069-7482-6*) Sterling.

Making Wood Signs. Patrick Spielman. LC 80-54342. (Home Craftsman Bks.). (Illus.). 148p. (YA). (gr. 10-12). 1981. pap. 10.95 (*0-8069-8984-X*) Sterling.

Making Wood Work: Value Added Policies & Programs. Helen Birss. 92p. (Orig.). (YA). (gr. 12 up). 1994. pap. text 30.00 (*0-7881-0843-3*) DIANE Pub.

Making Wooden Baskets on Your Scroll Saw. John Nelson & William Guimond. (Illus.). 60p. 1998. pap. 9.95 (*1-56523-099-X*) Fox Chapel Pub.

Making Wooden Boxes with Dale Power. Dale Power. LC 99-60109. (Illus.). 64p. 1999. pap. 14.95 (*0-7643-0848-3*) Schiffer.

Making Wooden Dinosaurs: Plans & Instructions with Notes on Each Species. Richard D. Pougher. LC 97-13866. (Illus.). 224p. 1997. pap. 19.95 (*0-8117-2992-3*) Stackpole.

Making Wooden Jigsaw Puzzles. Evan J. Kern. LC 96-3963. (Illus.). 128p. 1996. pap. 16.95 (*0-8117-2555-3*) Stackpole.

Making Wooden Mechanical Models: 15 Designs with Visible Wheels, Cranks, Pistons, Cogs & Cams. Alan Bridgewater & Gill Bridgewater. LC 95-14143. (Illus.). 144p. (Orig.). 1995. pap. 21.99 (*1-55870-381-0*, Betrwy Bks) F & W Pubns Inc.

Making Wooden Toys. Richard Blizzard. (Illus.). 64p. (Orig.). 1994. pap. 15.95 (*0-7195-5296-6*, Pub. by John Murray) Trafalgar.

Making Wooden Toys: Twelve Easy-to-Do Projects with Full-Size Templates. James T. Stasio. 48p. (Orig.). 1986. pap. 3.95 (*0-486-25112-8*) Dover.

*__Making Woodwork Aids & Devices.__ rev. ed. Robert Wearing. (Illus.). (Orig.). 2000. pap. 12.95 (*1-86108-129-4*) Guild Master.

Making Words: Early Learning Workbooks. Peter M. Spizzirri. Ed. by Linda Spizzirri. (Illus.). 32p. (J). (ps-2). 1997. pap. 2.95 (*0-86545-235-0*) Spizzirri.

Making Words: Multilevel, Hands-On, Developmentally Appropriate Spelling & Phonics Activities. Patricia M. Cunningham & Dorothy P. Hall. (Illus.). 192p. (J). (gr. 1-3). 1994. 15.99 (*0-86653-806-2*, GA1498) Good Apple.

Making Work: Self-Created Jobs in Participatory Organizations. W. Ronco & Lisa Peattie. LC 83-9527. (Environment, Development, & Public Policy: Public Policy & Social Services Ser.). (Illus.). 224p. 1983. 49.50 (*0-306-41230-6*, Plenum Trade) Perseus Pubng.

Making Work, Making Trouble: Prostitution as a Social Problem. Deborah R. Brock. LC 98-219071. 224p. 1998. text 45.00 (*0-8020-0976-X*); pap. text 18.95 (*0-8020-7935-0*) U of Toronto Pr.

Making Work Pay: Taxation, Benefits, Employment & Unemployment. OECD Staff. LC 98-100529. (Jobs Study Ser.). 100p. 1997. pap. 19.00 (*92-64-15666-6*, 21-97-09-1, Pub. by Org for Econ) OECD.

Making Work Pay: Wage Insurance for the Working Poor. Barry Bluestone & Teresa Ghilarducci. (Public Policy Briefs Ser.: Vol. 28). (Illus.). 40p. (Orig.). 1996. pap. text 3.00 (*0-941276-20-1*) J Levy.

Making Work Pay in the Child Care Industry: Promising Practices for Improving Compensation. Dan Bellm & National Center for the Early Childhood Work Force Staff. LC 98-169363. 64 p. 1997. write for info. (*1-889956-11-2*) Natl Ctr EC.

Making Workbenches: Planning, Building, Outfitting. Sam Allen. LC 95-4875. (Illus.). 160p. 1995. pap. 14.95 (*0-8069-0535-2*) Sterling.

Making Workers Soviet: Power, Class, & Identity. Ed. by Lewis H. Siegelbaum & Ronald G. Suny. (Illus.). 416p. 1995. text 52.50 (*0-8014-3022-4*); pap. text 21.95 (*0-8014-8211-9*) Cornell U Pr.

Making Workfare a Success: Alternative Work Experience Program; Two Year Report. JoAnne Schneider. (Illus.). 103p. (Orig.). 1996. pap. text 15.00 (*0-7881-3189-3*) DIANE Pub.

*__Making Working Wooden Locks: Complete Plans for 5 Working Wooden Locks.__ Tim Detweiler. (Illus.). 96p. 2000. pap. 21.95 (*0-941936-60-0*, Pub. by Linden Pub Fresno) IPG Chicago.

Making Workshops Work. Jeana McKinney. 33p. 1994. pap. text 12.00 (*0-912207-29-9*) NAFSA Washington.

Making Worlds: Gender, Metaphor, Materiality. Susan Hardy Aiken & Pinano. LC 97-21106. (C). 1994. 35.00 (*0-8165-1779-7*) U of Ariz Pr.

Making Worlds: Gender, Metaphor, Materiality. Susan Hardy Aiken & Pinano. LC 97-21106. (C). 1997. pap. 17.95 (*0-8165-1780-0*) U of Ariz Pr.

Making Wreaths. Barbara R. Rogers. 128p. 1994. pap. 9.95 (*1-56799-026-6*, Friedman-Fairfax) M Friedman Pub Grp Inc.

Making Wreaths. Storey Publishing Staff. 1997. pap. 9.95 (*0-676-57047-X*) Random.

Making Wreaths. Pamela Westland. 1992. 12.98 (*1-55521-769-9*) Bk Sales Inc.

Making Yo Yos see Ciumek Tungliakun

Making Your AR-15 into a Legal Pistol. Duncan Long. (Illus.). 88p. 1991. 14.00 (*0-87364-622-3*) Paladin Pr.

*__Making Your Bad Back Better with the O'Connor Technique: How You Can Become Your Own Chiropractor.__ 2nd rev. ed. William T. O'Connor. (Illus.). 402p. 2000. pap. 37.95 (*0-9664991-1-5*, 002) Aegis Genomics.

Making Your Case: Critical Thinking & the Argumentative Essay. Brooke Noel Moore. LC 94-38160. x, 246p. (C). 1995. pap. text 25.95 (*1-55934-331-1*, 1331) Mayfield Pub.

Making Your Church Grow: The Role of Leadership in Church Growth. Richard K. Smith. (Orig.). 1993. pap. 8.95 (*1-55673-446-8*) CSS OH.

Making Your Church More Inviting: A Step-by-Step Guide for In-Church Training. Roy M. Oswald. LC 92-72456. (Orig.). 1992. pap. 14.95 (*1-56699-055-6*, AL134) Alban Inst.

Making Your Dreams Come True: Find Your Passion with America's Dream Coach. Marcia Wieder. LC 99-31657. 224p. 1999. 20.00 (*0-609-60608-5*, Crown) Crown Pub Group.

Making Your Family Work. Mary G. Durkin. 176p. (Orig.). 1990. mass mkt. 4.50 (*0-446-35835-5*, Pub. by Warner Bks) Little.

Making Your Husband Feel Loved. Betty Malz. LC 97-48824. (Orig.). 1998. pap. 12.99 (*0-88419-534-1*) Creation House.

Making Your Life a Ministry: The Priscilla Principle. Jo Berry. 176p. 1984. pap. 6.95 (*0-310-42631-6*, 11218P) Zondervan.

Making Your Living from the Stockmarket: A How-To Book for the Novice Investor. Tom Luzmeier & Jesse Taylor. LC 93-74997. 184p. (Orig.). pap. 24.95 (*0-9639975-0-5*) Blue Walrus.

Making Your Love Last Forever: A Book for Couples. Norman Wright. 1999. 12.99 (*0-88486-240-2*) Arrowood Pr.

Making Your Mark. 5th rev. ed. Lisa Fraser. (Illus.). 48p. (YA). (gr. 9-13). 1996. pap. 6.95 (*0-9696427-6-8*) L D F Pub Inc.

Making Your Mark: Establishing Unique Corporate Identities with Graphic Design. Supon Design Group Staff. 1998. 19.95 (*1-889491-08-X*, Pub. by Design Ed) Bks Nippan.

Making Your Mark: How to Develop a Personal Marketing Plan for Becoming More Visible & More Appreciated at Work. Deborah Shouse. Ed. by Kelly Scanlon & Jane D. Guthrie. LC 95-69805. (Illus.). 78p. (Orig.). 1995. pap. 12.95 (*1-878542-98-2*, 12-0022) SkillPath Pubns.

Making Your Mark: That's Marketing (8 Step Checklist for Marketing Right) Alyce P. Cornyn-Selby. (Illus.). 74p. (Orig.). 1988. pap. 8.95 (*0-941383-05-9*) Beynch Pr.

Making Your Mark Health in Service Jobs. Pogrund. 128p. 1996. pap. 11.93 (*0-8092-0915-2*) NTC Contemp Pub Co.

Making Your Mark in Retail Jobs. Pogrund. 128p. 1996. pap. 11.93 (*0-8092-0910-1*) NTC Contemp Pub Co.

Making Your Marriage Last. Joan W. Anderson. 32p. 1998. pap. 1.95 (*0-7648-0147-3*) Liguori Pubns.

Making Your Marriage Magnificent. Joy R. Martin. (Joyful Living Ser.). 31p. 1983. pap. 2.50 (*0-912623-01-2*) Joyful Woman.

Making Your Marriage Work. Mary Ann Diorio. 1998. pap. 5.00 (*0-930037-05-7*, MYMW) Daystar Comm.

*__Making Your Money Grow: Balance Risks & Rewards - Control Your Own Finances - Watch Your Money Grow.__ John Whiteley. (Essentials Ser.). (Illus.). 64p. 1999. pap. 9.95 (*1-85703-524-0*, Pub. by How To Bks) Trans-Atl Phila.

Making Your Money Work for You: How to Use Simple Investment Principles to Increase Your Wealth. Simon Collins. (Personal Finance Ser.). (Illus.). 144p. 1999. pap. 19.95 (*1-85703-462-7*, Pub. by How To Bks) Trans-Atl Phila.

Making Your Office Work for You. 2nd rev. ed. Jan Yager. LC 98-73526. 226p. 2000. pap. 22.95 (*1-889262-24-2*) Hannacroix.

Making Your Office Work for You. 2nd rev. ed. Jan Yager. LC 98-73526. 226p. 2001. 31.95 (*1-889262-55-2*) Hannacroix.

Making Your Own Biscotti & Dunking Cookies. Dona Z. Meilach. LC 96-226673. 1996. 14.00 (*0-517-70495-1*) Random.

Making Your Own Cards: Creative Designs for Special Occasions. Lynda Watts. LC 95-216341. (Illus.). 96p. 1995. pap. 12.95 (*1-85368-239-X*, Pub. by New5 Holland) Sterling.

Making Your Own Cross Stitch Gifts: Creative Ideas for Giving. Sheila Coulson. LC 94-23178. (Illus.). 96p. 1995. pap. 16.95 (*0-88266-892-7*, Storey Pub) Storey Bks.

Making Your Own Days. Kenneth Koch. LC 98-15810. 320p. 1998. 27.50 (*0-684-83992-X*) S&S Trade.

Making Your Own Days: The Pleasures of Reading & Writing Poetry. Kenneth Koch. 320p. 1999. per. 14.00 (*0-684-82438-8*) S&S Trade.

Making Your Own Gourmet Coffee Drinks: Espressos, Cappuccinos, Lattes, Mochas, & More! Matthew Tekulsky. (Illus.). 96p. 1993. 12.00 (*0-517-58824-2*, Crown) Crown Pub Group.

Making Your Own Jewelry: Creative Designs to Make & Wear. Wendy H. Milne. Ed. by Deborah Balmuth. LC 94-4909. (Illus.). 96p. 1994. 18.95 (*0-88266-883-8*, Storey Pub) Storey Bks.

Making Your Own Jumps. Mary G. Watson. (Threshold Picture Guides Ser.). (Illus.). 24p. (Orig.). (J). (gr. 3 up). 1988. pap. 12.00 (*0-901366-76-5*) Half Halt Pr.

Making Your Own Paper: An Introduction to Creative Paper-Making. Marianne Saddington. Ed. by Pam Art. LC 91-41503. (Illus.). 96p. 1992. pap. 18.95 (*0-88266-784-X*, Garden Way Pub) Storey Bks.

Making Your Own Papercrafts Gifts: Creative Designs from Paper. Melanie Williams. (Illus.). 96p. 1996. pap. 12.95 (*1-85368-523-2*, Pub. by New5 Holland) Sterling.

Making Your Own Papier Mache: Creative Ideas for Beautiful Designs. Melanie Williams. (Illus.). 96p. 1996. pap. 12.95 (*1-85368-325-6*, Pub. by New5 Holland) Sterling.

Making Your Own Telescope. rev. ed. Allyn J. Thompson. (Illus.). 224p. 1981. 14.95 (*0-933346-12-3*) Sky Pub.

Making Your Patient Your Partner: Communication Skills for Doctors & Other Caregivers. Thomas Gordon & W. Sterling Edwards. LC 94-42698. 240p. 1995. 55.00 (*0-86569-255-6*, Auburn Hse) Greenwood.

Making Your Sales Team Number 1. Thomas L. Quick. 192p. 1992. pap. 19.95 (*0-8144-7741-0*) AMACOM.

An Asterisk (*) at the beginning of an entry indicates that the title is appearing for the first time.

Making Your Second Marriage a First-Class Success: A Couple's Guide. Doug Moseley & Naomi Moseley. LC 98-22822. 256p. 1998. per. 15.95 (*0-7615-1424-4*) Prima Pub.

Making Your Small Farm Profitable: 20 Guiding Principles, New Crops & New Markets, Maximize Net Profits Per Acre. Ron Macher. LC 99-16219. (Illus.). 288p. 1999. pap. 19.95 (*1-58017-161-3*) Storey Bks.

Making Your Voice Heard: An Advocacy Manual for Board Members & Staff of Programs & Services for Older Americans. 53p. 1993. pap. 10.00 (*0-910883-67-X*, 4191) Natl Coun Aging.

Making Your Way: A Practical Guide to Life. Paul A. Reilly. 97p. (Orig.). 1996. pap. 12.00 (*0-9655159-0-7*) Expanding Awareness.

Making Your Way to an Access in Mathematics. Russell Baker. 38p. (C). 1994. text 9.40 (*0-536-58619-5*) Pearson Custom.

***Making Your Workplace Drug Free: A Kit for Employers.** Ed. by Joan White Quinlan. (Illus.). 107p. (C). 1999. pap. text 35.00 (*0-7881-8322-2*) DIANE Pub.

Making Yourself. Orison S. Marden. 320p. 1998. pap. 28.00 (*0-89540-413-3*, SB-413) Sun Pub.

Making Yourself Even More Beautiful, Vol. I, No. 1. S. Jill Miller-Lewis. (Illus.). 46p. (Orig.). 1987. pap. 8.00 (*0-934155-03-8*) Miller Des.

Making Yourself Ready, No. 1. P. Hobson. 1991. pap. text 8.95 (*0-947252-00-2*) Impact Christian.

Makings for Meditation: A Collection of Parapoems, Reverent & Irreverent. Elsa Gidlow. (Illus.). 48p. 1973. reprint ed. pap. 5.00 (*0-912932-05-8*) Booklegger Pubng.

Makings of a Health Food Nut. Cobb Young. LC 93-33693. (Illus.). 112p. 1995. pap. 9.95 (*0-942963-44-X*) Distinctive Pub.

Makings of Dr. Charcot's Hysteria Shows: Research Through Performance. Ed. by Dianne Hunter. LC 98-12031. (Studies in Theatre Arts: Vol. 4). 156p. 1998. text 79.95 (*0-7734-8499-X*) E Mellen.

Makings of Happiness. Ronald Wallace. LC 90-21292. (Pitt Poetry Ser.). 73p. 1991. pap. 30.00 (*0-7837-8549-6*, 204936400011) Bks Demand.

Makings of Maleness: Men, Women, & the Flight of Daedalus. Peter Tatham. 304p. (C). 1992. text 45.00 (*0-8147-8203-5*); pap. text 18.50 (*0-8147-8204-3*) NYU Pr.

Makings of the Medieval Hebrew Book. Malachi Beit-Arie. (Studies in Palaeography & Codicology). (Illus.). 284p. 1993. 40.00 (*965-223-804-X*, Pub. by Magnes Pr) Gefen Bks.

Makinig of Mizoram: Role of Laldenga, 2 vols. Suhas Chatterjes. LC 95-901189. 445p. 1995. pap. 138.00 (*81-85880-72-7*, Pub. by Print Hse) St Mut.

Makin's of a Cowboy: The Making of a Man. Bob Kahla. Ed. by Johnny Lee. (Illus.). 148p. 1995. 19.95 (*1-882820-02-9*) Cracked Egg.

Makioka Sisters. Jun'ichiro Tanizaki. LC 92-55051. 1993. 20.00 (*0-679-42452-0*) Everymns Lib.

Makioka Sisters. Jun'ichiro Tanizaki. 544p. 1995. pap. 15.00 (*0-679-76164-0*) Random.

***Makirallemni.** large type ed. Agnes Kairaiuak et al.Tr. of When I Went on the Tundra. (ESK., Illus.). 8p. (J). (gr. k-3). 2000. pap. text 6.00 (*1-58084-195-3*) Lower Kuskokwim.

Makkah a Hundred Years Ago. Ed. by Angelo Pesce. 128p. (C). 1995. 66.00 (*0-907151-36-1*, Pub. by IMMEL Pubng); 66.00 (*0-907151-44-2*, Pub. by IMMEL Pubng) St Mut.

Makkoth. (ENG & HEB.). 15.00 (*0-910218-76-5*) Bennet Pub.

***Mako Shark.** Brad Burnham. LC 00-25483. (Underwater World of Sharks Ser.). (Illus.). (J). 2000. write for info. (*0-8239-5585-0*, PowerKids) Rosen Group.

Mako Sharks see Animals & the Environment

Mako Sharks see Tiburones Makos

Mako Sharks. Anne Welsbacher. (Sharks Ser.). (Illus.). 48p. (J). (gr. 3-7). 1995. lib. bdg. 19.00 (*0-516-35272-5*) Childrens.

Makonde. John Stoner. LC 96-7893. (Heritage Library of African Peoples). (Illus.). 64p. (YA). (gr. 7-12). 1996. lib. bdg. 16.95 (*0-8239-2016-X*) Rosen Group.

Makos. Christopher Makos. LC 96-47566. (Illus.). 96p. 1997. text 13.00 (*0-312-15291-4*, Stonewall Inn) St Martin.

Makos Men - Sewn Photos. Photos by Christopher Makos. (Illus.). 96p. 1996. pap. 35.00 (*0-9642009-3-7*) Pohlmann Pr.

Makoto Fujimura, New York Works. Robert Kushner & Eric Walstedt. Ed. by Valerie Dillon. (Illus.). 48p. 1996. write for info. (*0-9648340-1-4*) Dillon Gallery.

Makoto Sei Watanabe: Conceiving the City. Makoto S. Watanabe. LC 99-174999. (Talenti Ser.). 20p. (FRE, ITA & KOR., Illus.). 144p. 1998. pap. 39.99 (*88-7838-038-5*) Rockport Pubs.

Ma'Koulat Bahriya. Sonia Beiruti. Ed. by Ramzi Kaliffe. (Silsilat Daliluki Sayidati (Woman's Guide) Ser.: No. 17).Tr. of Seafood Appetizers. (ARA., Illus.). 40p. 1990. pap. 8.50 (*1-58311-040-2*) Eastern Corp.

Makrokosmos und Mikosmos. Seelenfragen, Lebensfragen, Geistesfragen see Macrocosm & Microcosm

Makrookonomik. 2nd ed. 1995. 25.00 (*0-387-58385-8*) Spr-Verlag.

Maksim Gorky: A Reference Guide. Edith W. Clowes. (Reference Bks.). 248p. 1987. 45.00 (*0-8161-8722-3*, Hall Reference) Macmillan.

Makso's Farm: Makso (Bilingual English, Haitian Creole) Maude Heurtelor. Ed. by Fequiere Vilsaint. 20p. (J). (gr. 1-3). Date not set. pap. 12.00 (*1-881839-68-0*) Educa Vision.

Makua Laiana: Story of Lorenzo Lyons. Lorenzo Lyons. (American Autobiography Ser.). 278p. 1995. reprint ed. lib. bdg. 79.00 (*0-7812-8583-6*) Rprt Serv.

Makuna: Portrait of an Amazonian People. Kaj Arhem. LC 98-13898. 192p. 1998. 34.95 (*1-56098-874-6*) Smithsonian.

Mal. Francois Mauriac. Ed. by Jean Aufort. (FRE.). 1952. 14.95 (*0-8288-9753-0*, F100590) Fr & Eur.

Mal-Aimes. Francois Mauriac. (FRE.). 1945. pap. 15.95 (*0-7859-5488-0*) Fr & Eur.

Mal d'Afrique. Jarda Cervenka. LC 94-67069. (Minnesota Voices Project Ser.: Vol. 66). 120p. 1995. pap. 11.95 (*0-89823-158-2*) New Rivers Pr.

Mal de Amores. Angeles Mastretta. 1998. pap. 15.00 (*0-375-70200-8*) Vin Bks.

Mal de Piedra see Blood Relations

Mal Etrange. Paul De Grosbois. (Novels in the Roman Plus Ser.). (FRE.). 160p. (YA). (gr. 8 up). 1991. pap. 8.95 (*2-89021-167-3*, Pub. by La Courte Ech) Firefly Bks Ltd.

***Mal-Tempo.** William Russo. LC 99-90728. 160p. 1999. pap. 15.95 (*1-892183-13-7*) DTTN.

Mal Vikraya (Sale of Goods) 2nd ed. Avtar Singh. (HIN.). (C). 1978. 60.00 (*0-7855-5130-1*) St Mut.

Mala. Gita Wolf. (FRE., Illus.). 32p. (J). (gr. k-3). 1996. lib. bdg. 16.95 (*1-55037-501-6*, Pub. by Annick) Firefly Bks Ltd.

Mala. Gita Wolf. (Illus.). 32p. (J). (ps-3). 1996. 16.95 (*1-55037-491-5*, Pub. by Annick); pap. 6.95 (*1-55037-490-7*, Pub. by Annick) Firefly Bks Ltd.

Mala Hora. Gabriel Garcia Marquez. (SPA.). 187p. 1979. 10.00 (*0-8288-8587-7*) Fr & Eur.

Mala Hora. Gabriel Garcia Marquez. (SPA.). pap. 11.50 (*968-411-202-5*, Pub. by Edicnes Era) Continental Bk.

Mala Jugada. Armando De Armas. Ed. by Angel De Fana. (SPA., Illus.). 130p. 1996. pap. 15.00 (*1-890829-07-2*) DFana Editions.

Mala Meditation for Physical, Mental & Spiritual Prosperity. Guru K. Khalsa. Ed. by Edith Cracchiolo. (Illus.). 20p. (Orig.). 1995. pap. text 6.50 (*0-9646830-7-5*) Sacred Gems.

Mala Noche: And Other "Illegal" Adventures. Walt Curtis.Tr. of Bad Night. (Illus.). 224p. 1997. pap. 14.95 (*0-9623683-4-2*) BridgeCity Bks.

***Mala Onda.** Alberto Fuguet. (SPA.). 2000. pap. 14.95 (*956-239-018-7*) Santillana.

Mala Reputacion: Yesterday's Outlas. Raye Morgan. (Deseo Ser.). (SPA.). 1996. per. 3.50 (*0-373-35169-0*, 1-35169-1) Harlequin Bks.

Mala Suerte, Level 1. Helena Gonzalez Vela & Antonio Orefudo. (Leer en Espanol Ser.). (SPA.). (C). 1998. pap. 5.95 (*84-294-4045-3*) Santillana.

Mala Yerba y Esa Sangre (Bad Weed & This Blood) Mariano Azuela. (SPA.). 226p. 1958. pap. 8.99 (*968-16-0910-7*, Pub. by Fondo) Continental Bk.

Malabar & Its Folk. T. K. Panikkar. 288p. 1986. reprint ed. 12.00 (*0-8364-1730-5*, Pub. by Manohar) S Asia.

Malabar Farm. Louis Bromfield. 1976. reprint ed. lib. bdg. 28.95 (*0-88411-506-2*) Amereon Ltd.

Malabar Farm. Louis Bromfield. LC 98-33594. (Illus.). 375p. 1999. reprint ed. pap. 14.00 (*1-888683-84-8*) Wooster Bk.

Malabar in Asian Trade, 1740-1800. Ashin Das Gupta. LC 66-44074. (Cambridge South Asian Studies). 216p. reprint ed. pap. 61.60 (*0-608-12224-6*, 2024446) Bks Demand.

Malabsorption in Coeliac Sprue. O. J. Cluysenaer & J. H. Van Tongeren. 1977. pap. text 141.50 (*90-247-2000-1*) Kluwer Academic.

Malacca: A Study of Tourism Potential. 65p. 1989. pap. 35.00 (*1-882866-53-3*) Pac Asia Trvl.

Malacca-Singapore Straits: Guide to Planned Passages for Deep Draught Vessels. ICS Staff & OCIMF Staff. 1987. 36.00 (*0-7855-1771-5*, Pub. by Witherby & Co) St Mut.

Malacca-Singapore Straits: Guide to Planned Transits by Deep Draught Vessels. ICS-OCIMF Staff. (C). 1990. 195.00 (*0-7855-4683-9*, Pub. by Witherby & Co) St Mut.

Malacca-Singapore Straits - Guide to Planned Passages for Deep Draught Vessels. ICS Staff & OCIMF Staff. (C). 1981. 55.00 (*0-900886-62-5*, Pub. by Witherby & Co) St Mut.

Malachi. J. Vernon McGee. (Thru the Bible Commentary Ser.: Vol. 33). 1997. pap. 6.97 (*0-7852-0623-X*) Nelson.

Malachi: A New Translation with Introduction & Commentary. Ed. by Andrew E. Hill. LC 96-50480. (Anchor Bible Reference Library Ser.). (Illus.). 480p. 1998. pap. 37.95 (*0-385-46892-X*) Doubleday.

Malachi: Messenger of Divine Love. Thomas J. Delaughter. LC 75-40410. 160p. (Orig.). 1976. 6.00 (*0-914520-08-3*); pap. text 6.00 (*0-914520-07-5*) Insight Pr.

Malachi: Messenger of Rebuke & Renewal. David M. Levy. 1992. pap. 8.95 (*0-915540-20-7*) Frnds Israel.

***Malachi's Message for Today.** G. Campbell Morgan. 131p. 1998. pap. 14.00 (*1-57910-176-3*) Wipf & Stock.

Malachite. Ruth Langan. (Historical Ser.). 1998. per. 4.99 (*0-373-29007-1*, 1-29007-1) Harlequin Bks.

Malachite & Agate 1: Lesbian Poetry. Ed. by Marianne Milton. 106p. (Orig.). 1997. pap. 9.95 (*0-9657478-0-8*) Clove Pr.

Malachite Palace. Alma F. Ada. Tr. by Rosa Zubizarreta from SPA. LC 95-44676. 32p. (J). (ps-3). 1998. 16.00 (*0-689-31972-X*) Atheneum Yung Read.

Malacofauna of Hong Kong & Southern China II, 2 vols. Ed. by Brian Morton. 700p. (C). 1985. pap. text 127.50 (*962-209-120-2*, Pub. by HK Univ Pr) Coronet Bks.

Malacofauna of Hong Kong & Southern China III. Ed. by Brian Morton. 524p. 1994. pap. 87.50 (*962-209-365-5*, Pub. by HK Univ Pr) Coronet Bks.

Malacwi: Wildlife, Parks & Reserves Judy Carter. LC 89-161327. 176 p. 1987. write for info. (*0-333-43349-1*) Trans-Atl Phila.

Maladapted Mind: Classic Readings in Evolutionary Psychopathology. Ed. by Simon Baron-Cohen. LC 97-199891. 304p. 1997. 69.95 (*0-86377-460-1*) L Erlbaum Assocs.

Malade Age en Pratique Medicale. Ed. by W. Meier-Ruge. (Geriatrie en Pratique Quotidienne Ser.: Vol. 1). viii, 256p. 1990. pap. 31.50 (*3-8055-5292-0*) S Karger.

Malade Imaginaire. Moliere. (Coll. Class. du Theatre). (FRE., Illus.). 1964. pap. 7.95 (*0-8288-9941-X*, F39998) Fr & Eur.

Malades D'Hier, Malades D'Aujourd'Hui see Illness & Self in Society

Maladie du Sachs see Case of Doctor Sachs: A Novel

Maladie Humaine. Ferdinando Camon. (FRE.). 215p. 1987. pap. 10.95 (*0-7859-2062-5*, 2070378306) Fr & Eur.

Maladies des Cucurbitacees see Colour Atlas of Cucurbit Diseases: Observation, Identification & Control

Maladies of Marcel Proust. Bernard Straus. LC 80-11204. 175p. 1980. 39.95 (*0-8419-0546-0*) Holmes & Meier.

Maladies Systemiques. 2nd ed. M. F. Kahn & A. P. Peltier. (FRE., Illus.). 950p. 1985. 125.00 (*2-257-12299-2*) S M P F Inc.

Malady of Death. Marguerite Duras. Tr. by Barbara Bray from FRE. LC 83-49427.Tr. of La/Maladie de la Mort. 64p. 1988. pap. 7.95 (*0-8021-3036-4*, Grove) Grove-Atltic.

Malaeska: The Indian Wife of the White Hunter. Anna S. Stephens. LC 75-175875. 1972. reprint ed. 19.95 (*0-405-09000-5*, Pub. by Blom Pubns) Ayer.

Malaga Burning: An American Woman's Eyewitness Account of the Spanish Civil War. unabridged ed. Gamel Woolsey. LC 96-70662. Orig. Title: Death's Other Kingdom. (Illus.). 208p. 1998. 22.00 (*0-9648736-1-3*) Pythia Pr.

***Malagasy-English/English Malagasy Dictionary & Phrasebook.** Janie Rasoloson. 180p. 2000. pap. 11.95 (*0-7818-0843-X*) Hippocrene Bks.

Malagasy Newspaper Reader. Lucien Randrianarivelo & Tom Jedele. LC 96-84386. 250p. 1997. write for info. (*1-881265-31-5*) Dunwoody Pr.

Malagasy Textiles. John Mack. (Ethnography Ser.: No. 14). (Illus.). 60p. 1989. pap. 10.50 (*0-7478-0015-4*, Pub. by Shire Pubns) Parkwest Pubns.

Malaina & the Magic Agate. Bridget A. Leighton. LC 95-94588. (Illus.). 32p. (Orig.). (J). (gr. 1-6). 1995. pap. 8.95 (*0-9647549-9-1*) B A Leighton.

Malaise of the Spirit: A Case Study. Paris Finley. Ed. by Judith Kleinfeld. (Teaching Cases in Cross-Cultural Education Ser.). 74p. (C). 1989. pap. text 7.50 (*1-877962-07-4*) Univ AK Ctr CCS.

Malama: Hawaiian Land & Water. Ed. by Dana N. Hall. LC 85-72888. (Bamboo Ridge Ser.: No. 29). (Illus.). 156p. (Orig.). 1985. pap. 8.00 (*0-910043-12-4*) Bamboo Ridge Pr.

***Malama I Na Kahawai.** Mahele Kumuwaiwai Kai. Ed. by Kawika Burgess & Keao NeSmith. (Illus.). (YA). (gr. 7-12). 1999. write for info. (*0-9665331-0-0*) UHH Hale Kuamoo.

***MalaMala: Pathway to an African Eden.** Laura Hurwitz. Ed. by Emily McGalliard. x, 170p. 1999. pap. 35.00 (*0-9662257-2-4*) Vista Pubns CT.

***MalaMala: Pathway to an African Eden.** Laura Hurwitz. Ed. by Emily McGalliard. (Illus.). x, 170p. 1999. 45.00 (*0-9662257-1-6*) Vista Pubns CT.

Malamalama: A History of the University of Hawaii. Robert M. Kamins & Robert E. Potter. LC 97-50348. (Illus.). 336p. 1998. text 35.00 (*0-8248-2006-1*) UH Pr.

Malan on Bills of Exchange, Cheques & Promissory Notes in South African Law. 2nd rev. ed. F. R. Malan et al. 570p. 1995. pap. write for info. (*0-409-04105-X*, MICHIE) LEXIS Pub.

Malan on Bills of Exchange, Cheques, & Promissory Notes in South African Law. 3rd ed. F. R. Malan & J. T. Pretorius. LC 98-189422. 573p. 1997. write for info. (*0-409-04106-8*) Buttrwrth-Heinemann.

Malandre. Henri Troyat. (Eygletiere Ser.: No. 3). 1971. pap. 11.95 (*0-7859-3273-9*, 2277123463) Fr & Eur.

Malaparte: A House Like Me. Michael Mcdonough. LC 99-24603. 200p. 1999. 50.00 (*0-609-60378-7*) Crown Pub Group.

Malaparte in Jassy. Samuel Astrachan. LC 89-30755. 156p. (C). 1989. 24.95 (*0-8143-2162-3*) Wayne St U Pr.

Malaparte in Jassy. Samuel Astrachan. LC 89-30755. 155p. reprint ed. pap. 48.10 (*0-608-10587-2*, 2071208) Bks Demand.

Malaquias Montoya, 1997: Adaline Kent Award. Joseph Zirker. LC 97-67255. (Illus.). 28p. (Orig.). 1997. pap. 5.00 (*0-930495-30-6*) San Fran Art Inst.

Malaria: A Layman's Guide. Martine Maurel. 120p. pap. 12.95 (*1-86812-534-3*) Menasha Ridge.

Malaria: A Survey of Existing Legislation. WHO Staff. (International Digest of Health Legislation Offprints: Vol. 7, No. 4). 32p. 1956. 3.00 (*92-4-169074-7*) World Health.

Malaria: Host Responses to Infection. Ed. by Mary M. Stevenson. 208p. 1989. lib. bdg. 159.00 (*0-8493-4745-9*, RC159) CRC Pr.

***Malaria: Molecular & Clinical Aspects.** Ed. by Mats Wahlgren & Peter Perlmann. 578p. 1999. text 120.00 (*90-5702-446-2*, Harwood Acad Pubs) Gordon & Breach.

Malaria: Obstacles & Opportunities. Institute of Medicine Staff. Ed. by Stanley C. Oaks, Jr. et al. 328p. 1991. text 39.95 (*0-309-04527-4*) Natl Acad Pr.

Malaria: Parasite Biology, Pathogenesis, & Protection. Ed. by Irwin W. Sherman. LC 98-8261. (Illus.). 500p. 1998. 99.95 (*1-55581-131-0*) ASM Pr.

Malaria: Waiting for the Vaccine. G. Targett. LC 91-40008. 236p. 1992. 314.50 (*0-471-93100-4*, Wiley-Liss) Wiley.

Malaria - That Remains a Killer. N. L. Pal. 1994. pap. 100.00 (*0-7855-2755-9*, Pub. by Scientific Pubs) St Mut.

Malaria & Barbesiosis. Ed. by Miodrag Ristic et al. (New Perspectives in Clinical Microbiology Ser.). 1984. text 225.00 (*0-89838-675-6*) Kluwer Academic.

Malaria & Development, Vol. 17. Brown. 124p. 1997. pap. text 28.00 (*90-5699-603-7*) Gordon & Breach.

Malaria & Greek History. William H. Jones. LC 75-23729. reprint ed. 35.00 (*0-404-13287-1*) AMS Pr.

Malaria Capers: Tales of Parasites & People. Robert S. Desowitz. 288p. 1993. pap. 13.95 (*0-393-31008-6*) Norton.

Malaria Control & National Health Goals. (Technical Report Ser.: No. 680). 68p. 1982. pap. text 6.00 (*92-4-120680-2*) World Health.

Malaria Control As Part of Primary Health Care: Report of a WHO Study Group, 1984. WHO Staff. (Technical Report Ser.: No. 712). 73p. 1984. 8.00 (*92-4-120712-4*) World Health.

Malaria Dreams: An African Adventure. Stuart Stevens. LC 89-6842. 256p. 1990. pap. 12.00 (*0-87113-361-X*, Atlntc Mnthly) Grove-Atltic.

Malaria Immunology. Ed. by P. Pearlmann & Hans Wigzell. (Progress in Allergy Ser.: Vol. 41). (Illus.). x, 374p. 1988. 228.00 (*3-8055-4672-6*) S Karger.

Malaria-Immunology & Immunopathology. Ed. by Dan T. Spira & Charles L. Greenblatt. 1978. pap. 51.50 (*3-8055-2940-6*) S Karger.

Malaria in Panama. James S. Simmons. 1979. 30.95 (*0-405-10628-9*) Ayer.

Malaria in the Interior Valley of North America: A Selection from a Treatise, Historical, Etiological, & Practical, on the Principal Diseases of the Interior Valley of North America As They Appear in the Caucasian, African, Indian, & Esquimaux Varieties of Its Population. Daniel Drake. Ed. by Norman D. Levine. LC 64-14806. (Facsimile Reprints in the History of Science Ser.: No. 3). 306p. reprint ed. pap. 94.90 (*0-8357-9687-6*, 201113700074) Bks Demand.

Malaria in the Upper Mississippi Valley, 1760-1900. Erwin H. Ackerknecht. Ed. by Barbara G. Rosenkrantz. LC 76-25650. (Public Health in America Ser.). (Illus.). 1977. reprint ed. lib. bdg. 18.95 (*0-405-09805-7*) Ayer.

***Malaria Methods & Protocols.** Ed. by Denise L. Doolan. 375p. 2000. 99.50 (*0-89603-823-8*) Humana.

***Malaria Shots Not Included: A Guide to Surviving Life after College.** Marcia Wallace. LC 00-190330. 2000. 25.00 (*0-7388-1728-7*); pap. 18.00 (*0-7388-1729-5*) Xlibris Corp.

Malaria Vaccine Development: A Multi-Immune Response Approach. Ed. by Stephen L. Hoffman. 1996. 75.00 (*1-55581-111-6*) ASM Pr.

Malaria Vaccine Development: Pre-Erythrocytic Stages Proceedings of a Conference Held in Bethesda, Maryland, U. S. A. Ed. by S. L. Hoffmann & L. J. Martinez. (Bulletin of WHO Ser.: Suppl. to Vol. 68, 1990). 196p. 1990. pap. text 35.00 (*92-4-068680-0*, 1036801) World Health.

Malariology, with Special Reference to Malaya. A. A. Sandosham & V. Thomas. (Illus.). 408p. (Orig.). 1983. pap. 47.50 (*9971-69-052-7*, Pub. by Sngapore Univ Pr) Coronet Bks.

Malarkey. Sheila Simonson. (WWL Mystery Ser.). 1998. per. 4.99 (*0-373-26275-2*, 1-26275-7, Wrldwide Lib) Harlequin Bks.

Malarkey. Sheila Simonson. LC 96-44923. 288p. 1996. 23.95 (*0-312-15168-3*, Thomas Dunne) St Martin.

Malas Hierbas, Diccionario Clasificatorio Ilustrado. Francisco Guell. (LAT & SPA.). 224p. 1970. pap. 29.95 (*0-7859-0878-1*, S-50018) Fr & Eur.

Malatesta. Henry De Montherlant. 1973. write for info. (*0-318-63486-4*); pap. 10.95 (*0-8288-3723-6*, M3790) Fr & Eur.

Malatesta. Henry De Montherlant. (Folio Ser.: No. 305). (FRE.). 1973. 6.95 (*2-07-036305-8*) Schoenhof.

Malatesta: Life & Ideas. Errico Malatesta. Ed. by Vernon Richards. 309p. 1965. pap. 10.00 (*0-900384-15-8*) Left Bank.

Malathion: Toxic Time Bomb. Betsy Russell-Manning. LC 90-85143. (Illus.). 265p. 1991. spiral bd. 19.95 (*0-930165-49-7*) Greensward Pr.

Malatimadhava. Bhavabhuti. Ed. by Michael Coulson. 344p. 1990. 29.95 (*0-19-562354-1*) OUP.

Malavikagnimitram of Kalidasa. Tr. by M. R. Kale. (C). 1987. reprint ed. pap. 11.50 (*0-8364-2630-4*, Pub. by Motilal Bnarsidass) S Asia.

Malawi. Robert B. Boeder. (Profiles of Africa Ser.). 1996. text 26.50 (*0-86531-777-1*) Westview.

Malawi. Karen L. Niesen & Christine Onaga. LC 95-22633. (Country Guide Series Report from the AACRAO-AID Project). 1998. 22.00 (*0-929851-51-X*) Am Assn Coll Registrars.

Malawi. 2nd rev. ed. Samuel Decalo. LC 96-192626. (World Bibliographical Ser.). 220p. 1995. lib. bdg. 62.00 (*1-85109-238-2*) ABC-CLIO.

***Malawi: A Country Study Guide.** Global Investment & Business Center, Inc. Staff. (World Country Study Guides Library: Vol. 104). (Illus.). 350p. 2000. pap. 59.00 (*0-7397-2402-9*) Intl Business Pubns.

Malawi: Democratic Theory & Public Policy. Mekki Mtewa. 137p. 1986. 18.95 (*0-87047-004-3*); pap. 13.95 (*0-87047-005-1*) Schenkman Bks Inc.

Malawi: Strengthening Democratic Institutions, Final Activity Report, May 31, 1995. Laurie Cooper. ii, 144p. 1996. pap. text 16.00 (*1-879720-01-9*) Intl Fndt Elect.

Malawi: The Bradt Travel Guide. 2nd ed. Philip Briggs. LC 99-18956. (Illus.). 272p. 1999. pap. 17.95 (*1-898323-84-4*, Pub. by Bradt Pubns) Globe Pequot.

Malawi: The History of the Nation. Bridglal Pachai. LC 73-173415. (Illus.). 336p. reprint ed. pap. 104.20 (*0-8357-6200-9*, 203447200090) Bks Demand.

M

An Asterisk (*) at the beginning of an entry indicates that the title is appearing for the first time.

Malawi - A Country Study Guide: Basic Information for Research & Pleasure. Global Investment Center, USA Staff. (World Country Study Guide Library: Vol. 104). (Illus.). 350p. 1999. pap. 59.00 (*0-7397-1501-1*) Intl Business Pubns.

***Malawi Business Intelligence Report, 190 vols.** Global Investment & Business Center, Inc. Staff. (World Business Intelligence Library: Vol. 104). (Illus.). 350p. 2000. pap. 99.95 (*0-7397-2602-1*) Intl Business Pubns.

***Malawi Business Law Handbook, 190 vols.** Global Investment & Business Center, Inc. Staff. (Global Business Law Handbooks Library: Vol. 104). (Illus.). 350p. 2000. pap. 99.95 (*0-7397-2002-3*) Intl Business Pubns.

***Malawi Business Opportunity Yearbook.** Global Investment & Business Center, Inc. Staff. (Global Business Opportunity Yearbooks Library: Vol. 104). (Illus.). 2000. pap. 99.95 (*0-7397-2202-6*) Intl Business Pubns.

***Malawi Business Opportunity Yearbook: Export-Import, Investment & Business Opportunities.** International Business Publications, U. S. A. Staff & Global Investment Center, U. S. A. Staff. (Global Business Opportunity Yearbooks Library: Vol. 104). (Illus.). 350p. 1999. pap. 99.95 (*0-7397-1302-7*) Intl Business Pubns.

M

Malawi Cichlids: Keeping & Breeding Them in Captivity. David Boruchowitz. (Illus.). 64p. 1997. pap. 6.95 (*0-7938-0359-4*, RE-610) TFH Pubns.

Malawi Cichlids: MBUNA. Mary E. Sweeney. (Illus.). 64p. 1997. 12.95 (*0-7938-0115-X*, WW-031) TFH Pubns.

***Malawi Country Review 2000.** Robert C. Kelly et al. (Illus.). 60p. 1999. pap. 39.95 (*1-58310-528-X*) CountryWatch.

Malawi Efter Banda: Forandringar i Landet Dar Tystnad Radde. Anna Grauers et al. (Afrikafakta Ser.: Nr. 5). 43p. 1997. write for info. (*91-7106-409-5*, Pub. by Nordic Africa) Transaction Pubs.

***Malawi Foreign Policy & Government Guide.** Global Investment & Business Center, Inc. Staff. (World Foreign Policy & Government Library: Vol. 100). (Illus.). 350p. 1999. pap. 99.00 (*0-7397-3598-5*) Intl Business Pubns.

***Malawi Foreign Policy & Government Guide.** Global Investment & Business Center, Inc. Staff. (World Foreign Policy & Government Library: Vol. 100). (Illus.). 350p. 2000. pap. 99.95 (*0-7397-3802-X*) Intl Business Pubns.

Malawi in Pictures. Department of Geography, Lerner Publications. (Visual Geography Ser.). (Illus.). 64p. (YA). (gr. 6-9). 1989. lib. bdg. 19.93 (*0-8225-1842-2*, Lerner Publctns) Lerner Pub.

***Malawi Investment & Business Guide.** Global Investment & Business Center, Inc. Staff. (Global Investment & Business Guide Library: Vol. 104). (Illus.). 2000. pap. 99.95 (*0-7397-1802-9*) Intl Business Pubns.

***Malawi Investment & Business Guide: Export-Import, Investment & Business Opportunities.** International Business Publications, USA Staff & Global Investment Center, USA Staff. (World Investment & Business Guide Library-99: Vol. 104). (Illus.). 350p. 1999. pap. 99.95 (*0-7397-0299-8*) Intl Business Pubns.

Malay: Language Survival Kit. Anita Ramly. (Illus.). 130p. 1996. pap. 5.95 (*0-86442-463-9*) Lonely Planet.

***Malay Archipelago.** Alfred Russel Wallace. 2000. pap. 19.95 (*962-593-645-9*, Pub. by Periplus) Tuttle Pubng.

Malay Archipelago: The Land of Orange Utan & the Bird of Paradise. Alfred R. Wallace. (Illus.). 668p. 1990. pap. text 32.00 (*0-19-588955-X*) OUP.

Malay Customs & Traditions. Alwi Bin Alhady. LC 77-87477. (Illus.). reprint ed. 42.50 (*0-404-16789-6*) AMS Pr.

Malay-English - English-Malay Standard Dictionary. A. E. Coope. 631p. (Orig.). 1993. pap. 16.95 (*0-7818-0103-6*) Hippocrene Bks.

Malay-English Dictionary. William Marsden. (ENG & MAY.). 1977. reprint ed. 101.95 (*0-518-19003-X*) Ayer.

Malay Frontier: Unity & Duality in a Sumatran Kingdom. Jane Drakard. (Studies on Southeast Asia: No. 7). (Illus.). 215p. (Orig.). (C). 1990. pap. text 15.00 (*0-87727-706-0*) Cornell SE Asia.

Malay Magic. Walter W. Skeat. (Illus.). 1984. reprint ed. 55.00 (*0-19-582598-5*) OUP.

Malay Magic: An Introduction to the Folklore & Popular Religion of the Malay Peninsula. Walter W. Skeat. (Illus.). 685p. 1965. reprint ed. 45.00 (*0-7146-2026-2*, Pub. by F Cass Pubs) Intl Spec Bk.

Malay Magic: Being an Introduction to the Folklore & Popular Religion of the Malay Peninsula. Walter W. Skeat. LC 70-174437. (Illus.). 1972. reprint ed. lib. bdg. 30.95 (*0-405-08980-5*) Ayer.

Malay Poisons & Charm Cures. 2nd ed. John D. Gimlette. LC 77-87027. reprint ed. 37.50 (*0-404-16821-3*) AMS Pr.

Malay Politics in Sarawak, 1946-1966: The Search for Unity & Political Ascendancy. Said Sanib. (Illus.). 1985. 38.00 (*0-19-582572-1*) OUP.

Malay Society in the Late Nineteenth Century: The Beginnings of Change. J. M. Gullick. (South-East Asian Historical Monographs). (Illus.). 428p. 1987. reprint ed. 55.00 (*0-19-588850-2*) OUP.

Malay Society in the Late Nineteenth Century: The Beginnings of Change. J. M. Gullick. (South-East Asian Historical Monographs). (Illus.). 428p. 1990. reprint ed. pap. 18.95 (*0-19-588952-5*) OUP.

Malay Survival. 56p. 1993. pap. 55.00 incl. audio (*0-88432-617-9*, AFMA20) Audio-Forum.

Malay, Survival, Set. unabridged ed. (MAY.). 56p. pap. 55.00 incl. audio (*0-88432-608-X*, AFMA20) Audio-Forum.

Malay Village & Malaysia: Social Values & Rural Development. Peter J. Wilson. LC 66-27877. (Monographs). 181p. 1968. pap. 10.00 (*0-87536-322-9*) HRAFP.

Malaya: Communist or Free? Victor W. Purcell. LC 75-30076. (Institute of Pacific Relations Ser.). reprint ed. 32.50 (*0-404-59553-7*) AMS Pr.

Malaya Pt. I: The Malayan Union Experiment, 1942-1948. A. J. Stockwell. (British Documents on the End of the Empire Ser.: Series B, Vol. 3). xciv, 392p. 1995. pap. 125.00 (*0-11-290540-4*, HM05404, Pub. by Statnry Office) Balogh.

Malaya Pt. II: The Communist Insurrection, 1948-1953. A. J. Stockwell. (British Documents on the End of the Empire Ser.: Series B, Vol. 3). xxx, 486p. 1995. pap. 125.00 (*0-11-290541-2*, HM05412, Pub. by Statnry Office) Balogh.

Malaya Pt. III: The Alliance Route to Independence 1953-1957. A. J. Stockwell. (British Documents on the End of the Empire Ser.: Series B, Vol. 3). xxxii, 458p. 1995. pap. 125.00 (*0-11-290542-0*, HM05420, Pub. by Statnry Office) Balogh.

Malaya, Indonesia, Borneo & the Philippines: A Geographical, Economic, & Political Description of Malaya, the East Indies, the Philippines. Charles Robequain. Tr. by E. D. Laborde. LC 75-30078. reprint ed. 37.00 (*0-404-59555-3*) AMS Pr.

Malayalam. R. E. Asher & T. C. Kumari. LC 97-3094. (Descriptive Grammars Ser.). 520p. (C). 1997. 190.00 (*0-415-02242-8*) Routledge.

Malayalam: A University Course & Reference Grammar. 3rd rev. ed. Rodney F. Moag. 625p. 1994. pap. text 33.60 (*0-89148-046-3*) Ctr S&SE Asian.

Malayalam Dictionary. 3rd ed. Collins1. (MAL.). 544p. 1918. 75.00 (*0-7859-9817-9*) Fr & Eur.

Malayalam-English Dictionary. H. Gundert. 1116p. 1982. 75.00 (*0-8288-1770-7*, M14098) Fr & Eur.

Malayalam-English Dictionary. H. Gundert. (ENG & MAL.). 1116p. 1989. reprint ed. 38.00 (*81-206-0066-5*, Pub. by Asian Educ Servs) S Asia.

Malayalam Grammar. 2nd ed. H. Gundert. (MAL.). 448p. 1968. 49.95 (*0-7859-9818-7*) Fr & Eur.

Malayalam Short Stories. Ed. by K. A. Panikar. 152p. 1981. 16.95 (*0-318-36917-6*) Asia Bk Corp.

Malayan Campaign, 1948-60. John Scurr. (Men-at-Arms Ser.: No. 132). (Illus.). 48p. pap. 11.95 (*0-85045-476-X*, 9064, Pub. by Ospry) Stackpole.

Malayan Cases, Vol. IV. Shah. 1967. 132.00 (*9971-70-009-3*, MICHIE) LEXIS Pub.

Malayan Emergency: The Domino That Stood Still. Donald Mackay. LC 97-25794. (Illus.). 174p. 1997. 29.95 (*1-85753-118-3*, Pub. by Brasseys) Brasseys.

Malayan Fern Allies: Handbook to the Determination of the Fern Allies of the Malayan Island. V. A. Rosenburgh. 261p. (C). 1985. text 175.00 (*0-89771-649-3*, Pub. by Intl Bk Distr) St Mut.

Malayan Fern Allies: Handbook to the Determination of the Fern Allies of the Malayan Islands. V. A. Rosenburgh. 261p. (C). 1985. reprint ed. 175.00 (*81-7089-033-0*, Pub. by Intl Bk Distr) St Mut.

Malayan Law Journal: Consolidated Subject Index, General Index & Table of Cases Reported, 1932-1991, 1992-1994, 3 vols. Malayan Law Journal Editors. 1995. write for info. (*0-409-99660-2*, MICHIE) LEXIS Pub.

Malayan Law Journal Words & Phrases Judicially Defined. 1990. 380.00 (*9971-70-073-5*, MICHIE) LEXIS Pub.

Malayan Railway: Keretapi Tanah Melayu. J. A. Stanistreet. 64p. (C). 1985. 50.00 (*0-85361-132-7*) St Mut.

Malayan Tin Industry to 1914, with Reference to the States of Perak, Selangor, Negri, Sembilan, & Pahang. fac. ed. Wong Lin Ken. LC 64-17266. (Association for Asian Studies, Monographs & Papers: No. 14). 314p. 1994. pap. 97.40 (*0-7837-7671-3*, 204742400007) Bks Demand.

Malayan Union Controversy, 1942-1948. Albert Lau. (South-East Asian Historical Monographs). 340p. 1991. 45.00 (*0-19-588964-9*) OUP.

Malaysia see Cultures of the World - Group 1

Malaysia see Markets of Asia-Pacific

Malaysia. Christine Osborne. (Essential Guides Ser.). (Illus.). 128p. 1994. 7.95 (*0-8442-8921-3*, 89213) NTC Contemp Pub Co.

Malaysia. Jonathan Rowell. LC 96-17968. (Economically Developing Countries Ser.). (J). 1997. lib. bdg. 24.26 (*0-8172-4531-6*) Raintree Steck-V.

Malaysia. Joann B. Stedman. LC 86-17286. (World Education Ser.). (Illus.). 184p. 1986. pap. text 20.00 (*0-910054-85-1*) Am Assn Coll Registrars.

Malaysia. Joann B. Stedman. (Pelham Guides Ser.). 53p. (C). 1996. 22.00 (*0-929851-89-7*) Am Assn Coll Registrars.

Malaysia. Nelles Verlag. (Nelles Guides Ser.). 1994. pap. 14.95 (*3-88618-375-0*, Pub. by Nelles Verlag) Seven Hills Bk.

***Malaysia.** Neil Wilson. (AAA Essential Guides Ser.). (Illus.). 2000. pap. 8.95 (*0-8442-0132-4*, Passprt Bks) NTC Contemp Pub Co.

***Malaysia.** rev. ed. (Periplus Travel Maps Ser.). 2000. pap. 7.95 (*962-593-777-3*) Tuttle Pubng.

Malaysia. 11th ed. Insight Guides Staff. (Insight Guides). 1998. pap. text 22.95 (*0-88729-707-2*) Langenscheidt.

Malaysia. 17th ed. Insight Guides Staff. 2000. pap. 23.95 (*0-88729-040-X*, Insight Guides) Langenscheidt.

Malaysia: A Complete Guide. Passport Books Staff. 1992. pap. 12.95 (*0-8442-9719-4*, Passprt Bks) NTC Contemp Pub Co.

***Malaysia: A Country Study Guide.** Global Investment & Business Center, Inc. Staff. (World Country Study Guides Library: Vol. 105). (Illus.). 350p. 2000. pap. 59.00 (*0-7397-2403-7*) Intl Business Pubns.

Malaysia: A Kick Start Guide for Business Travelers. Guy Brooks & Victoria Brooks. 160p. 1995. pap. 9.95 (*0-88908-845-4*) Self-Counsel Pr.

Malaysia: Enterprise Training, Technology, & Productivity. (Country Study Ser.). 144p. 1997. pap. 22.00 (*0-8213-4059-X*, 14059) World Bank.

Malaysia: Growth & Equity in a Multiracial Society. Kevin Young et al. LC 79-3677. (World Bank Country Economic Report). 365p. reprint ed. pap. 113.20 (*0-7837-4245-2*, 204393500012) Bks Demand.

Malaysia: Growth, Equity & Structural Transformation. Ismail Salleh & Saha D. Mayanathan. LC 93-23261. (Lessons of East Asia Ser.). 66p. 1993. pap. 22.00 (*0-8213-2610-4*, 12610) World Bank.

Malaysia: Malaysia. (Case Studies in Population Policy). 44p. pap. 7.50 (*92-1-151212-3*, 90.XIII.26) UN.

Malaysia: New States in a New Nation. R. S. Milne & K. J. Ratnam. (Studies in Commonwealth Politics & History: No. 2). 512p. 1973. 45.00 (*0-7146-2988-X*, Pub. by F Cass Pubs) Intl Spec Bk.

Malaysia: Selected Historical Readings. 2nd ed. Ed. by Robin W. Winks. 1990. reprint ed. 70.00 (*3-262-01215-7*) Periodicals Srv.

Malaysia: The Heart of Southeastern Asia. Gavin Young. (Seven Days Photography Ser.). 1997. 39.95 (*981-00-2733-8*, Pub. by Select Bks) Weatherhill.

Malaysia - A Country Study Guide: Basic Information for Research & Pleasure. Global Investment Center, USA Staff. (World Country Study Guide Library: Vol. 105). (Illus.). 350p. 1999. pap. 59.00 (*0-7397-1502-X*) Intl Business Pubns.

Malaysia - A Foreigners' Guide. Lynn Witham. (Illus.). 450p. (Orig.). 1988. pap. 24.95 (*0-945908-00-8*) Hornbill Bks.

Malaysia - Singapore - Brunei. 2nd rev. ed. Nelles Verlag Staff. (Nelles Guides Ser.). (Illus.). 256p. 1999. pap. 15.95 (*3-88618-902-3*) Hunter NJ.

Malaysia & Singapore Handbook. 5th rev. ed. Ed. by Joshua Eliot. (Footprint Handbks.). (Illus.). 704p. 1996. 21.95 (*0-8442-4909-2*, Passprt Bks) NTC Contemp Pub Co.

***Malaysia & Singapore 98-99.** 2nd ed. Sean Sheehan & Wendy Hutton. (Traveler's Companion Ser.). 1998. pap. text 22.95 (*0-7627-0239-7*) Globe Pequot.

Malaysia & the "Original People" A Case Study of the Impact of Development on Indigenous Peoples. Robert K. Dentan et al. LC 98-122138. 175p. 1996. pap. text 20.00 (*0-205-19817-1*) Allyn.

Malaysia & UNCED Vol. IELP: An Analysis of Diplomatic Process: 1989-1992. Fauziah M. Taib. LC 97-223545. (International Environmental Law & Policy Ser.: No. 44). 352p. 1997. 109.00 (*90-411-0683-9*) Kluwer Academic.

Malaysia Business & Investment Opportunities Yearbook-98: Business, Investment, Export-Import. Contrib. by Russian Information & Business Center, Inc. Staff. (Business & Investment Opportunity Library-98). (Illus.). 350p. 1998. pap. 99.00 (*1-57751-977-9*) Intl Business Pubns.

***Malaysia Business Intelligence Report, 190 vols.** Global Investment & Business Center, Inc. Staff. (World Business Intelligence Library: Vol. 105). (Illus.). 350p. 2000. pap. 99.95 (*0-7397-2603-X*) Intl Business Pubns.

***Malaysia Business Law Handbook, 190 vols.** Global Investment & Business Center, Inc. Staff. (Global Business Law Handbooks Library: Vol. 105). (Illus.). 350p. 2000. pap. 99.95 (*0-7397-2003-1*) Intl Business Pubns.

***Malaysia Business Opportunity Yearbook.** Global Investment & Business Center, Inc. Staff. (Global Business Opportunity Yearbooks Library: Vol. 105). (Illus.). 2000. pap. 99.95 (*0-7397-2203-4*) Intl Business Pubns.

***Malaysia Business Opportunity Yearbook: Export-Import, Investment & Business Opportunities.** International Business Publications, U. S. A. Staff & Global Investment Center, U. S. A. Staff. (Global Business Opportunity Yearbooks Library: Vol. 105). (Illus.). 350p. 1999. pap. 99.95 (*0-7397-1303-5*) Intl Business Pubns.

***Malaysia Country Review 2000.** Robert C. Kelly et al. (Illus.). 60p. 1999. pap. 39.95 (*1-58310-529-8*) CountryWatch.

Malaysia Diving Guide. Andrea Ferrari & Antonella Ferrari. LC 98-945542. 167 p. 1997. write for info. (*962-593-170-8*) Periplus.

***Malaysia Foreign Policy & Government Guide.** Contrib. by Global Investment & Business Center, Inc. Staff. (World Foreign Policy & Government Library: Vol. 101). (Illus.). 350p. 1999. pap. 99.00 (*0-7397-3599-3*) Intl Business Pubns.

***Malaysia Foreign Policy & Government Guide.** Global Investment & Business Center, Inc. Staff. (World Foreign Policy & Government Library: Vol. 101). (Illus.). 350p. 2000. pap. 99.95 (*0-7397-3803-8*) Intl Business Pubns.

***Malaysia Government & Business Contacts Handbook: Strategic Government & Business Contacts for Conducting Succesful Business , Export-Import & Investment Activity.** International Business Publications, USA Staff & Global Investment Center, USA Staff. (World Export-Import & Business Library: 131). (Illus.). 250p. 2000. pap. 99.95 (*0-7397-6146-3*) Intl Business Pubns.

Malaysia in Pictures. rev. ed. Ed. by Lerner Publications, Department of Geography Staff. (Visual Geography Ser.). (Illus.). 64p. (YA). (gr. 6-9). 1997. lib. bdg. 19.93 (*0-8225-1854-6*, Lerner Publctns) Lerner Pub.

***Malaysia Investment & Business Guide.** Global Investment & Business Center, Inc. Staff. (Global Investment & Business Guide Library: Vol. 105). (Illus.). 2000. pap. 99.95 (*0-7397-1803-7*) Intl Business Pubns.

Malaysia Investment & Business Guide: Economy, Export-Import, Business & Investment Climate, Business Contacts. Contrib. by Russian Information & Business Center, Inc. Staff. (Russia, NIS & Emerging Markets Investment & Business Library-98). (Illus.). 350p. 1998. pap. 99.00 (*1-57751-873-X*) Intl Business Pubns.

***Malaysia Investment & Business Guide: Export-Import, Investment & Business Opportunities.** International Business Publications, USA Staff & Global Investment Center, USA Staff. (World Investment & Business Guide Library-99: Vol. 105). (Illus.). 350p. 1999. pap. 99.95 (*0-7397-0300-5*) Intl Business Pubns.

Malaysia, No Problem Lah! Richard Yates & Maria Yates. LC 94-90263. (Illus.). 275p. 1994. 19.95 (*0-87012-523-0*) McClain.

This book is based on the authors' diaries & letters written during their four years of living in Malaysia & traveling throughout Southeast Asia, & compares life in Malaysia from 1987-1993. The diaries provide insight into the struggle between old & new value systems. The text contains numerous anecdotes chosen to give insight into the joys & frustrations of life & travel in Malaysia & beyond. The 118 photos have been selected to offer readers some visual experience of the authors' adventures. *Publisher Paid Annotation.*

Malaysia, Singapore,& Brunei: The Rough Guide. Charles De Ledesman et al. LC 97-216133. 645p. 1997. pap. 18.95 (*1-85828-232-2*) Viking Penguin.

***Malaysia Tax Guide.** Global Investment & Business Center, Inc. Staff. (World Tax Guide Library: Vol. 5). (Illus.). 350p. 1999. pap. 99.00 (*0-7397-0179-7*) Intl Business Pubns.

Malaysia the Beautiful. Jennifer Rodrigo. 1999. 49.95 (*1-85368-744-8*) New5 Holland.

Malaysia to 2003: From Redistribution to Growth. LC 95-237472. (Research Reports: M216). 1994. 395.00 (*0-85058-764-6*) Economist Intell.

Malaysia 2020. Alan Robinson. (Euromoney Country Guide Ser.). 219p. 1997. 170.00 (*1-85564-595-5*, Pub. by Euromoney) Am Educ Systs.

***Malaysia with Map.** (Illus.). 128p. 2000. pap. 14.95 (*1-85974-245-9*) New5 Holland.

Malaysia ,1997: Country Travel Map. Periplus Editions. 1997. 7.95 (*962-593-043-4*) Periplus.

Malaysian & Singapore Company & Securities Law Reports, 5 vols. Ed. by Walter Woon. 1994. write for info. (*0-409-99695-5*, ASIA, MICHIE) LEXIS Pub.

Malaysian Court Forms in Civil Proceedings, Vol. 1, Issue 0. Ed. by Edgar Joseph, Jr. et al. 1995. ring bd. write for info. (*0-409-99752-8*, MICHIE) LEXIS Pub.

Malaysian Democracy: An Indian Perspective (1982) Shiv Lal. 432p. 1986. 120.00 (*0-7855-1820-7*, Pub. by Archives Pubs) St Mut.

Malaysian Economy: Pacific Connections. Mohamed Ariff. (South-East Asian Social Science Monographs). (Illus.). 236p. 1991. text 45.00 (*0-19-588564-3*) OUP.

Malaysian Favorites. Lee M. Yoong & Yoong S. Ying. (Illus.). 196p. 1995. 19.95 (*983-9808-03-6*, Pub. by Delta Edits) Weatherhill.

Malaysian Law of Sale of Goods - Cases & Materials. E. R. Ivamy & Vincent Powell-Smith. xxx, 306p. 1995. pap. write for info. (*0-409-99786-2*, MICHIE) LEXIS Pub.

Malaysian Legal Essays. M. B. Hooker. 456p. 1986. 110.00 (*9971-70-047-6*, MICHIE) LEXIS Pub.

Malaysian Politics: The Second Generation. Gordon P. Means. (South-East Asian Social Science Monographs). (Illus.). 388p. 1991. 65.00 (*0-19-588983-5*) OUP.

Malaysian Politics under Mahathir. R. S. Milne. (Politics in Asia Ser.). 1999. pap. 24.99 (*0-415-17143-1*) Routledge.

***Malaysian Politics under Mahathir.** R. S. Milne & Diane K. Mauzy. LC 99-222809. 1999. write for info. (*0-415-17142-3*) Routledge.

Malaysian Standard Form of Building Contract. Powell-Smith. 171p. 1990. boxed set 60.00 (*0-409-99592-4*, MICHIE) LEXIS Pub.

Malaysia's Defence & Foreign Policies. Abdul R. Baginda et al. LC 95-940736. 137 p. 1995. write for info. (*967-978-512-2*, Pub. by Pelanduk) Weatherhill.

Malaysia's Forests: A Resource Without a Future? Rachel Berger. 216p. (C). 1991. text 125.00 (*0-906527-32-5*, Pub. by Surrey Beatty & Sons) St Mut.

Malaysia's National Language Policy & the Legal System. Richard Mead. LC 87-50360. (Monographs: No. 30). ix, 118p. 1988. pap. 13.00 (*0-938692-30-5*) Yale U SE Asia.

Malaysia's Political Economy: Politics, Patronage & Profits. Edmund T. Gomez & K. S. Jomo. LC 97-3763. (Illus.). 227p. (C). 1997. text 64.95 (*0-521-59007-8*); pap. text 19.95 (*0-521-59996-2*) Cambridge U Pr.

***Malaysia's Political Economy: Politics, Patronage & Profits.** 2nd ed. Terence Gomez & K. S. Jome. LC 99-30801. (Illus.). 272p. (C). 1999. pap. 22.95 (*0-521-66368-7*) Cambridge U Pr.

***Malaysis.** 2nd ed. Helen Oon. (Globetrotter Travel Guides Ser.). (Illus.). 128p. 2000. pap. 10.95 (*1-85974-435-4*) New5 Holland.

Malbim Esther. Jonathan Taub. 206p. 1998. 17.95 (*1-56871-135-2*, Pub. by Targum Pr) Feldheim.

An Asterisk (*) at the beginning of an entry indicates that the title is appearing for the first time.

Malbim Haggadah. Ed. & Tr. by Yisroel Shaw. Tr. & Adapted by Jonathan Taub. 320p. 1993. 19.95 (*1-56871-007-0*, Pub. by Targum Pr) Feldheim.

Malbim on Mishle. Tr. by Avivah Gottleib-Zornberg & Charles Wengrov. 328p. 1993. 8.95 (*0-87306-280-9*) Feldheim.

***Malbim on Ruth.** Tr. by Shmuel Kurtz. 1999. 9.95 (*1-58330-366-9*) Feldheim.

Malbone. Thomas W. Higginson. (Notable American Authors Ser.). 1992. reprint ed. lib. bdg. 75.00 (*0-7812-3117-5*) Rprt Serv.

Malbone Street Wreck. Brian J. Cudahy. LC 99-25764. 144p. 1999. 32.50 (*0-8232-1931-3*, Pub. by Fordham); pap. 19.95 (*0-8232-1932-1*, Pub. by Fordham) BookMasters.

Malcev-Admissible Algebras. Hyo C. Myung. (Progress in Mathematics Ser.: Vol. 64). 376p. 1986. 84.00 (*0-8176-3345-6*) Birkhauser.

Malchus. 1990. pap. 6.95 (*0-9618197-2-3*) Crushed Grapes.

Malcolm. James Purdy. LC 94-28945. 196p. 1995. pap. 12.99 (*1-85242-368-4*) Serpents Tail.

Malcolm. adapted ed. James Purdy. 1966. pap. 5.25 (*0-8222-0719-2*) Dramatists Play.

Malcolm. deluxe ed. George MacDonald. 1988. 27.50 (*0-940652-53-6*) Sunrise Bks.

Malcolm. George MacDonald. (George MacDonald Original Works Ser.: Series V). 450p. 1995. reprint ed. 22.00 (*1-881084-31-0*) Johannesen.

Malcolm: The Life of the Man Who Changed Black America. Bruce Perry. (Illus.). 560p. 1991. 24.95 (*0-88268-103-6*) Station Hill Pr.

Malcolm & Me: Life in the Litterbox. William J. Thomas. (Illus.). 128p. 1993. 19.95 (*0-7737-2741-8*) Genl Dist Srvs.

Malcolm & Me: Life in the Litterbox. William J. Thomas. 128p. 1996. pap. 14.95 (*0-7737-5790-2*) Stoddart Publ.

Malcolm & the Amazing Technicolor. Brande. 1996. pap. 7.50 (*0-7459-3170-7*, Pub. by Lion Pubng) Trafalgar.

Malcolm & the Cross: The Nation of Islam, Malcolm X, & Christianity. Louis A. DeCaro, Jr. LC 98-19687. 282p. 1998. 29.95 (*0-8147-1860-4*) NYU Pr.

Malcolm & the Cross: The Nation of Islam, Malcolm X, & Christianity. Louis A. Decaro. pap. text 18.50 (*0-8147-1932-5*) NYU Pr.

Malcolm Baldridge National Quality Award: A Yardstick for Quality Growth. Maureen S. Heaphy. (Engineering Process Improvement). 464p. (C). 1995. pap. 37.00 (*0-201-63368-X*) Addison-Wesley.

***Malcolm Cochran Collection: (Re) Collections.** Kristin Chambers & Jan Riley. (Illus.). 48p. 1999. pap. 20.00 (*1-880353-10-5*) Cleveland Ctr.

Malcolm Forbes: The Man Who Had Everything. Christopher Winans. 227p. 1991. 33.00 (*0-7206-0808-2*, Pub. by P Owen Ltd) Dufour.

Malcolm Hillier's Christmas. Storey Publishing Staff. 1997. pap. 16.95 (*0-676-57025-9*) Random.

Malcolm Hillier's Container Gardening Through the Year. Malcolm Hillier. LC 94-26717. (Illus.). 160p. 1995. 24.95 (*1-56458-869-6*) DK Pub Inc.

Malcolm Hillier's Herb Garden. Storey Publishing Staff. 1997. 24.95 (*0-676-57026-7*) Random.

Malcolm Hillier's Wreaths & Garland. Storey Publishing Staff. 1997. 22.95 (*0-676-57027-5*) Random.

Malcolm Lowry. Daniel B. Dodson. LC 70-126542. (Columbia Essays on Modern Writers Ser.: No. 51). 48p. (Orig.). 1971. pap. text 12.00 (*0-231-03244-7*) Col U Pr.

Malcolm Lowry: A Preface to His Fiction. Richard K. Cross. LC 79-16091. (C). 1994. lib. bdg. 12.50 (*0-226-12125-9*) U Ch Pr.

Malcolm Lowry: A Preface to His Fiction. Richard K. Cross. LC 79-16091. (C). 1994. pap. 5.95 (*0-226-12126-7*) U Ch Pr.

Malcolm Lowry, a Bibliography. J. Howard Woolmer. LC 82-50810. (Illus.). 197p. 1983. 30.00 (*0-913506-12-5*, 50294, Pub. by Woolmer-Brotherson) Oak Knoll.

Malcolm Lowry's "La Mordida" Ed. by Patrick A. McCarthy. LC 95-12606. xxiii, 400p. 1996. 75.00 (*0-8203-1763-2*) U of Ga Pr.

Malcolm MacDonald: Bringing an End to Empire. Clyde Sanger. LC 96-132147. (Illus.). 528p. 1995. 49.95 (*0-7735-1303-5*, Pub. by McG-Queens Univ Pr) CUP Services.

Malcolm St. Clair: His Films, 1919-1945. Ruth A. Dwyer. LC 94-15371. (Filmmakers Ser.: No. 38). (Illus.). xxvii, 250p. 1997. 42.00 (*0-8108-2709-3*) Scarecrow.

Malcolm Then & Now. Nelson George. (J). 1995. 14.95 (*0-8050-2387-9*) H Holt & Co.

Malcolm X see Read-&-Discover Photo-Illustrated Biographies Series

Malcolm X. Arnold Adoff. LC 99-21527. (Illus.). 64p. (J). (gr. 2-5). 2000. pap. 4.25 (*0-06-442118-X*) HarpC.

Malcolm X. Lucile Davis. (Read-&-Discover Biographies Ser.). (Illus.). 24p. (J). (gr. k-3). 1997. lib. bdg. 13.75 (*0-516-20901-9*) Childrens.

Malcolm X. Mark Falstein. (Illus.). 1994. mass mkt. 6.55 (*0-8224-3224-2*) Fearon Teacher Aids.

Malcolm X. Kibibi V. Mack-Williams. LC 92-46767. (Pioneers Ser.). 112p. (J). 1993. lib. bdg. 25.27 (*0-86625-493-5*) Rourke Pubns.

Malcolm X. Miriam Sagan. LC 96-43227. (Mysterious Deaths Ser.). (Illus.). (YA). 1997. lib. bdg. 22.45 (*1-56006-264-9*) Lucent Bks.

Malcolm X. Sande Smith. 1993. 12.98 (*1-55521-863-6*) Bk Sales Inc.

Malcolm X: A Fire Burning Brightly. Walter Dean Myers. LC 99-21527. (Illus.). 40p. (J). (gr. k-3). 2000. 15.95 (*0-06-027707-6*) HarpC.

***Malcolm X: A Fire Burning Brightly.** Walter Dean Myers. LC 99-21527. (Illus.). 40p. (J). (gr. k-3). 2000. lib. bdg. 15.89 (*0-06-027708-4*) HarpC Child Bks.

Malcolm X: A Selected Bibliography. Compiled by Lenwood G. Davis & Marsha L. Moore. LC 83-18329. 146p. 1984. lib. bdg. 55.00 (*0-313-23061-7*, DAM/, Greenwood Pr) Greenwood.

Malcolm X: Another Side of the Movement. Mark Davies. Ed. by Richard Gallin. (History of the Civil Rights Movement Ser.). (Illus.). 128p. (J). (gr. 5 up). 1990. lib. bdg. 12.95 (*0-382-09925-7*) Silver Burdett Pr.

Malcolm X: Another Side of the Movement. Mark Davies. Ed. by Richard Gallin. (History of the Civil Rights Movement Ser.). (Illus.). 128p. (YA). (gr. 5 up). 1990. pap. 7.95 (*0-382-24063-4*) Silver Burdett Pr.

Malcolm X: Another Side of the Movement. Mark Davies. (History of the Civil Rights Movement Ser.). (J). 1990. 13.15 (*0-606-04739-5*, Pub. by Turtleback) Demco.

Malcolm X: As They Knew Him. David Gallen. 320p. 1992. 21.95 (*0-88184-851-4*) Carroll & Graf.

Malcolm X: As They Knew Him. Ed. by David Gallen. 320p. 1992. pap. 11.95 (*0-88184-850-6*) Carroll & Graf.

Malcolm X: Biography of Black Civil Rights Leader. Jack Rummel. (Black American Ser.). (Illus.). 192p. (YA). 1990. mass mkt. 3.95 (*0-87067-554-0*, Melrose Sq) Holloway.

Malcolm X: Black Rage. David R. Collins. LC 91-39951. (People in Focus Ser.). (Illus.). 104p. (YA). (gr. 5 up). 1992. lib. bdg. 13.95 (*0-87518-498-7*, Dillon Silver Burdett) Silver Burdett Pr.

Malcolm X: By Any Means Necessary. Walter Dean Myers. 224p. (J). (gr. 7-9). 1993. 13.95 (*0-590-46484-1*) Scholastic Inc.

Malcolm X: By Any Means Necessary. Walter Dean Myers. LC 92-13480. 224p. (J). (gr. 5 up). 1994. pap. 4.50 (*0-590-48109-6*) Scholastic Inc.

Malcolm X: By Any Means Necessary. Walter Dean Myers. (Illus.). 224p. (J). 1998. pap. 5.99 (*0-590-29912-3*) Scholastic Inc.

Malcolm X: By Any Means Necessary. Walter Dean Myers. 1999. pap. 5.99 (*0-590-98759-3*) Scholastic Inc.

Malcolm X: By Any Means Necessary. Walter Dean Myers. (YA). (gr. 5-8). 1999. mass mkt. 4.99 (*0-590-66221-X*) Scholastic Inc.

Malcolm X: By Any Means Necessary: A Biography. Walter Dean Myers. (J). 1993. 9.60 (*0-606-05919-9*, Pub. by Turtleback) Demco.

Malcolm X: Developing Self-Esteem, Self-Love, & Self-Dignity. AESOP Enterprises, Inc. Staff & Gwendolyn J. Crenshaw. (Heroes & Sheroes Ser.). 27p. (J). (gr. 3-12). 1991. pap. write for info. incl. audio (*1-880771-00-4*) AESOP Enter.

Malcolm X: His Life & Legacy. Kevin Brown. LC 94-5381. (Illus.). 112p. (YA). (gr. 7 up). 1995. lib. bdg. 27.40 (*1-56294-500-9*) Millbrook Pr.

Malcolm X: Justice Seeker. Ed. by James B. Gwynne. (Illus.). 112p. 1993. pap. 10.00 (*0-935821-01-5*) Steppngstones.

Malcolm X: Militant Black Leader. Jack Rummel. Ed. by Nathan I. Huggins. (Black Americans of Achievement Ser.). (Illus.). 124p. (YA). (gr. 5 up). 1989. lib. bdg. 19.95 (*1-55546-600-1*) Chelsea Hse.

Malcolm X: Militant Black Leader. Jack Rummel. Ed. by Nathan I. Huggins. (Black Americans of Achievement Ser.). (Illus.). 124p. (YA). (gr. 5 up). 1989. pap. 9.95 (*0-7910-0227-6*) Chelsea Hse.

Malcolm X: Racial Spokesman. David Shirley. LC 93-17700. (Junior Black Americans of Achievement Ser.). (Illus.). 76p. (J). (gr. 3-6). 1993. lib. bdg. 15.95 (*0-7910-2106-8*) Chelsea Hse.

Malcolm X: Racial Spokesman. David Shirley. LC 93-17700. (Junior Black Americans of Achievement Ser.). (Illus.). 76p. (J). (gr. 3-6). 1994. pap. 4.95 (*0-7910-2112-2*) Chelsea Hse.

Malcolm X: Speeches at Harvard. Archie Epps. (Illus.). 191p. 1994. pap. 10.95 (*1-56924-975-X*) Marlowe & Co.

Malcolm X: The FBI File. Clayborne Carson. 1995. mass mkt. 6.99 (*0-345-40009-7*) Ballantine Pub Grp.

Malcolm X: The FBI File. Clayborne Carson. (Illus.). 512p. 1991. pap. 13.95 (*0-88184-758-5*) Carroll & Graf.

Malcolm X: The Last Speeches. Malcolm X. Ed. by Bruce Perry. LC 89-61591. (Illus.). 188p. (Orig.). (C). 1989. reprint ed. pap. 16.95 (*0-87348-543-2*) Pathfinder NY.

Malcolm X: The Man & His Times. Ed. by John Henrik Clarke. LC 90-84761. 1991. reprint ed. 35.00 (*0-86543-200-7*); reprint ed. pap. 14.95 (*0-86543-201-5*) Africa World.

Malcolm X: The Man in Context. Ed. by N.O.B.O. Staff. 200p. Date not set. 14.95 (*0-86543-495-6*) Africa World.

Malcolm X & Black Pride. Robert Cwiklik. LC 92-23687. (Gateway Civil Rights Ser.). (Illus.). 32p. (J). (gr. 2-4). 1991. pap. 5.95 (*1-878841-73-4*); lib. bdg. 20.90 (*1-56294-042-2*) Millbrook Pr.

Malcolm X & Black Pride. Robert Cwiklik. (Gateway Civil Rights Ser.). (J). 1991. 10.15 (*0-606-01450-0*, Pub. by Turtleback) Demco.

Malcolm X As Cultural Hero & Other Afrocentric Essays. Molefi K. Asante. LC 93-21330. 185p. 1993. 39.95 (*0-86543-401-8*); pap. 12.95 (*0-86543-402-6*) Africa World.

Malcolm X for Beginners. Aboul Alkalimat. (Documentary Comic Bks.). (Illus.). 64p. (Orig.). 1990. pap. 4.95 (*0-86316-143-X*) Writers & Readers.

Malcolm X for Beginners. Bernard A. Doctor. (Illus.). 192p. (Orig.). 1992. 19.95 (*0-86316-145-6*); pap. 9.95 (*0-86316-146-4*) Writers & Readers.

Malcolm X Great Nubian Quiz. Al I. Obaba. (Great Nubian Quiz Bks.). (Illus.). 43p. (YA). 1988. pap. 5.95 (*0-916157-16-4*) African Islam Miss Pubns.

Malcolm X on Afro-American History. 3rd ed. Malcolm X. LC 72-103696. (Illus.). 92p. 1990. pap. 10.95 (*0-87348-592-0*) Pathfinder NY.

Malcolm X Speaks. 2nd ed. Malcolm X. LC 90-64058. (Illus.). 233p. 1989. reprint ed. lib. bdg. 17.95 (*0-87348-546-7*) Pathfinder NY.

Malcolm X Speaks: Selected Speeches & Statements. Malcolm X. Ed. by George Breitman. LC 90-300551. (Illus.). 240p. 1990. pap. 9.95 (*0-8021-3213-8*, Grove) Grove-Atltic.

Malcolm X Talks to Young People. Malcolm X. LC 90-64197. (Illus.). 110p. (Orig.). 1990. reprint ed. pap. 10.95 (*0-87348-628-5*) Pathfinder NY.

Malcolm X Talks to Young People. Malcolm X. LC 90-64197. (Illus.). 110p. (Orig.). 1991. reprint ed. lib. bdg. 35.00 (*0-87348-631-5*) Pathfinder NY.

***Malcolm's Honor, Vol. 519.** Jillian Hart. (Historical Ser.). 2000. mass mkt. 4.99 (*0-373-29119-1*, 1-29119-4) Harlequin Bks.

Malcontent see Jacobean Drama: An Anthology

Malcontent. Mark Dunster. 21p. (Orig.). 1994. pap. 4.00 (*0-89642-246-1*) Linden Pubs.

Malcontent. John Marston. 1976. 18.95 (*0-89190-098-5*) Amereon Ltd.

Malcontent. John Marston. Ed. by Simon Trussler. (Student Editions of Minor Jacobean Masterpieces Ser.). 192p. (C). 1988. pap. write for info. (*0-413-16290-7*, A0167, Methuen Drama) Methn.

Malcontent. John Marston. Ed. by George K. Hunter. (Revels Plays Ser.). (Illus.). 171p. 1999. pap. 19.95 (*0-7190-3094-3*) St Martin.

Malcontent. John Marston. Ed. by M. L. Wine. LC 64-17228. (Regents Renaissance Drama Ser.). 151p. reprint ed. pap. 46.90 (*0-608-16436-4*, 202671000051) Bks Demand.

Malcontent. 2nd ed. Marston. (New Mermaids Ser.). (C). 1999. pap. 8.00 (*0-393-90089-4*) Norton.

Malcontent & Other Plays. John Marston. Ed. & Notes by Keith Sturgess. LC 96-48198. (The World's Classics Ser). 428p. 1997. pap. 12.95 (*0-19-282250-0*) OUP.

Malcontent & Other Plays. John Marston. 544p. pap. 15.95 (*0-14-043635-9*, Pub. by Pnguin Bks Ltd) Trafalgar.

***Malcontenta.** Barry Maitland. 2000. 24.95 (*1-55970-527-2*, Pub. by Arcade Pub Inc) Time Warner.

Malcove Collection. Sheila D. Campbell. (Illus.). 440p. 1998. reprint ed. pap. 39.95 (*0-8020-8169-X*) U of Toronto Pr.

***Malden: Massachusetts.** Malden Historical Society Staff. LC 99-69233. (Images of America Ser.). (Illus.). 128p. 2000. pap. 18.99 (*0-7385-0405-X*) Arcadia Publng.

Maldescensus Testis. Ed. by A. Kelami & J. P. Pryor. (Progress in Reproductive Biology & Medicine Ser.: Vol. 10). (Illus.). viii, 176p. 1984. 144.50 (*3-8055-3791-3*) S Karger.

Maldicion de La Momia. R. L. Stine, pseud. (Escalofrios Ser.: No. 5).Tr. of Curse of the Mummy's Tomb. 1996. 9.09 (*0-606-10441-0*, Pub. by Turtleback) Demco.

Maldicion de la Momia. R. L. Stine, pseud. LC 49-125480. (Escalofrios Ser.: No. 5).Tr. of Curse of the Mummy's Tomb. (SPA.). (J). (gr. 3-7). 1996. mass mkt. 3.99 (*0-590-94004-X*) Scholastic Inc.

Maldiciones Sin Quebrantar. Rebecca Brown & Daniel Yoder. LC 97-7480.Tr. of Unbroken Curses. (SPA.). 175p. 1996. pap. 10.99 (*0-88368-399-7*) Whitaker Hse.

Maldito Amor. Rosario Ferre. 1998. pap. 13.00 (*0-375-70063-3*) Vin Bks.

Malditos Amores. Vega De Rosario. (Romance Real Ser.). (SPA.). 192p. 1981. pap. 1.50 (*0-88025-006-2*) Roca Pub.

Maldive Islands Money. T. Browder. (Illus.). 1997. lib. bdg. 8.00 (*0-932106-06-4*) S J Durst.

Maldives. 64p. pap. text 9.95 (*88-8029-180-7*, Pub. by Bonechi) Eiron.

Maldives, 1. 1993. 19.95 (*1-55650-312-1*) Hunter NJ.

Maldives. Andrew D. Forbes. LC 94-187470. (World Bibliographical Ser.). 116p. 1993. lib. bdg. 59.00 (*1-85109-076-2*) ABC-CLIO.

Maldives. Insight Guides Staff. (Insight Guides). 1998. pap. text 12.95 (*0-88729-326-3*) Langenscheidt.

***Maldives.** Verlag Nelles. (Nelles Guides Ser.). (Illus.). 256p. 1999. pap. 15.95 (*3-88618-139-1*) Hunter NJ.

***Maldives.** Roseline Ngcheong-Lum. (Cultures of the World Ser.). (Illus.). (J). 2000. 35.64 (*0-7614-1157-7*, Benchmark NY) Marshall Cavendish.

***Maldives.** 2nd ed. Stafania Lamberti. (Globetrotter Travel Guides Ser.). (Illus.). 128p. 2000. pap. 10.95 (*1-85974-364-1*) New5 Holland.

Maldives. 3rd ed. Kirsten Ellis. pap. 21.95 (*962-217-613-5*) China Guides.

***Maldives: A Country Study Guide.** Global Investment & Business Center, Inc. Staff. (World Country Study Guides Library: Vol. 106). (Illus.). 350p. 2000. pap. 59.00 (*0-7397-2404-5*) Intl Business Pubns.

Maldives: Globetrotter Travel Guide. Ed. by Globetrotter Staff. (Globe Trotter Travel Guides Ser.). (Illus.). 128p. 1997. pap. 10.95 (*1-85368-568-2*, Pub. by New5 Holland) Globe Pequot.

***Maldives: The Bradt Travel Guide.** 2nd ed. Royston Ellis. LC 99-57731. (Illus.). 272p. 1999. pap. 17.95 (*1-898323-74-7*, Pub. by Bradt Pubns) Globe Pequot.

Maldives - A Country Study Guide: Basic Information for Research & Pleasure. Global Investment Center, USA Staff. (World Country Study Guide Library: Vol. 106). (Illus.). 350p. 1999. pap. 59.00 (*0-7397-1503-8*) Intl Business Pubns.

***Maldives Business Intelligence Report, 190 vols.** Global Investment & Business Center, Inc. Staff. (World Business Intelligence Library: Vol. 106). (Illus.). 350p. 2000. pap. 99.95 (*0-7397-2604-8*) Intl Business Pubns.

***Maldives Business Law Handbook, 190 vols.** Global Investment & Business Center, Inc. Staff. (Global Business Law Handbooks Library: Vol. 106). (Illus.). 350p. 2000. pap. 99.95 (*0-7397-2004-X*) Intl Business Pubns.

***Maldives Business Opportunity Yearbook.** Global Investment & Business Center, Inc. Staff. (Global Business Opportunity Yearbooks Library: Vol. 106). (Illus.). 2000. pap. 99.95 (*0-7397-2204-2*) Intl Business Pubns.

***Maldives Business Opportunity Yearbook: Export-Import, Investment & Business Opportunities.** International Business Publications, U. S. A. Staff & Global Investment Center, U. S. A. Staff. (Global Business Opportunity Yearbooks Library: Vol. 106). (Illus.). 350p. 1999. pap. 99.95 (*0-7397-1304-3*) Intl Business Pubns.

***Maldives Country Review 2000.** Robert C. Kelly et al. (Illus.). 60p. 1999. pap. 39.95 (*1-58310-530-1*) CountryWatch.

***Maldives Foreign Policy & Government Guide.** Contrib. by Global Investment & Business Center, Inc. Staff. (World Foreign Policy & Government Library: Vol. 102). (Illus.). 350p. 1999. pap. 99.00 (*0-7397-3600-0*) Intl Business Pubns.

***Maldives Foreign Policy & Government Guide.** Global Investment & Business Center, Inc. Staff. (World Foreign Policy & Government Library: Vol. 102). (Illus.). 350p. 2000. pap. 99.95 (*0-7397-3804-6*) Intl Business Pubns.

***Maldives Investment & Business Guide.** Global Investment & Business Center, Inc. Staff. (Global Investment & Business Guide Library: Vol. 106). (Illus.). 2000. pap. 99.95 (*0-7397-1804-5*) Intl Business Pubns.

***Maldives Investment & Business Guide: Export-Import, Investment & Business Opportunities.** International Business Publications, USA Staff & Global Investment Center, USA Staff. (World Investment & Business Guide Library-99: Vol. 106). (Illus.). 350p. 1999. pap. 99.95 (*0-7397-0301-3*) Intl Business Pubns.

Maldonado Miracle. Theodore Taylor. 1986. 9.60 (*0-606-12410-1*, Pub. by Turtleback) Demco.

Maldonado Miracle. Theodore Taylor. 128p. (gr. 4-7). 1986. mass mkt. 4.50 (*0-380-70023-9*, Avon Bks) Morrow Avon.

Maldonado Miracle: A Study Guide. Estelle Kleinman. Ed. by J. Friedland & R. Kessler. (Novel-Ties Ser.). (J). (gr. 4-6). 1996. pap. text 15.95 (*1-56982-637-4*) Lrn Links.

Maldoror. Comte De Lautreamont. Tr. by Guy Wernham. LC 66-12289. 1965. pap. 12.95 (*0-8112-0082-5*, NDP207, Pub. by New Directions) Norton.

Maldoror & Poems. Comte De Lautreamont. Tr. & Intro. by Paul Knight. 288p. 1988. pap. 11.95 (*0-14-044342-8*, Penguin Classics) Viking Penguin.

Maldoror & the Complete Works. Comte De Lautreamont. Tr. by Alexis Lykiard from FRE. 352p. 1998. pap. 15.95 (*1-878972-12-X*) Exact Change.

Male - Female Continuum: Paths to Colleagueship. 2nd ed. Carol Pierce et al. LC 88-92431. (Illus.). 82p. 1998. pap. 14.00 (*0-929767-02-0*) New Dynam Pubns.

Male - Female Language: With a Comprehensive Bibliography. 2nd ed. Mary R. Key. 1996. 36.00 (*0-8108-3083-3*) Scarecrow.

Male - Female Roles: Opposing Viewpoints. Ed. by Jonathan S. Petrikin. LC 94-4975. (Opposing Viewpoints Ser.). (Illus.). 312p. (YA). (gr. 10 up). 1995. pap. text 16.20 (*1-56510-175-8*); lib. bdg. 26.20 (*1-56510-174-X*) Greenhaven.

Male Aesthetic Surgery. Ed. by Daniel Marchac et al. (Illus.). 418p. 1996. text 99.95 (*0-7506-9277-4*) Buttrwrth-Heinemann.

Male Almanac: Essential New Information about Sex, Fitness, Health & Life. Ed. by Michael LaFavore. LC 95-37601. 320p. 1996. pap. 9.95 (*0-87596-345-5*) Rodale Pr Inc.

Male & Female. Ezergailis. 1975. pap. text 99.50 (*90-247-1704-3*, Pub. by M Nijhoff) Kluwer Academic.

Male & Female: A Study of the Sexes in a Changing World. Margaret Mead. 1996. pap. 12.00 (*0-688-14676-7*, Quil) HarperTrade.

Male & Female: The Classic Study of the Sexes. Margaret Mead. Date not set. pap. 12.00 (*0-614-97758-4*, Harvest Bks) Harcourt.

Male & Female - He Created Them. Charles Gallagher. (Celebrate Love Ser.). 70p. (Orig.). 1990. pap. text 3.95 (*0-911905-35-9*) Past & Mat Rene Ctr.

***Male & Female Circumcision: Medical, Legal & Ethical Considerations in Pediatric Practice.** Ed. by George C. Denniston et al. LC 99-37490. 547p. (C). 1999. text 155.00 (*0-306-46131-5*, Kluwer Plenum) Kluwer Academic.

Male & Female Costume. George B. Brummell. Ed. by Eleanor Parker. LC 71-177521. (Illus.). 334p. 1978. reprint ed. 27.95 (*0-405-08314-9*, Pub. by Blom Pubns) Ayer.

Male & Female Created He Them. Kharalambos Ansell. Date not set. pap. 6.00 (*1-879038-84-6*, 9054) Synaxis Pr.

Male & Female Energies: The Balancing Act. Mary Ellen Flora. LC 97-68786. (Energy Ser.). (Illus.). 224p. 1997. pap. 15.00 (*1-886983-02-X*) CDM Pubns.

Male & Female, Feminine & Masculine. U. Dieckmann et al. 1974. pap. 3.00 (*0-317-13546-5*) C G Jung Frisco.

Male & Female Figure in Motion: Sixty Classic Photographic Sequences. Eadweard Muybridge. (Illus.). vi, 121p. 1984. pap. 10.95 (*0-486-24745-7*) Dover.

Male & Female He Created Them: A Guide to Classical Torah Commentary on the Roles & Natures of Men & Women. Yisrael B. Reuven. 222p. 1996. 17.95 (*1-56871-096-8*) Targum Pr.

Male & Female Homosexuality: Psychological Approaches. Louis Diamant. (Clinical & Community Psychology Ser.). 292p. 1987. 63.95 (*0-89116-449-9*) Hemisp Pub.

M

An Asterisk (*) at the beginning of an entry indicates that the title is appearing for the first time.

Male & Female in Developing South-East Asia. Ed. by Wazir J. Karim et al. LC 94-46165. (Cross-Cultural Perspectives on Women Ser.). 224p. 1995. 39.50 (*0-85496-905-5*, Pub. by Berg Pubs); pap. 19.50 (*1-85973-027-2*, Pub. by Berg Pubs) NYU Pr.

Male & Female Nudes. Elte Shuppan Staff. (Pose File Ser.: Vol. 6). (Illus.). 160p. 1994. pap. 49.95 (*4-87199-041-9*, Pub. by Erute-Shuppan) Bks Nippan.

Male & Female Realities: Understanding the Opposite Sex. Joe Tanenbaum. reprint ed. 18.95 (*0-9634522-1-5*); reprint ed. pap. 12.95 (*0-9634522-0-7*) Tanenbaum Assocs.

Male & Female Roles in the Eighteenth Century: The Challenge to Replacement & Displacement in the Novels of Isabelle de Charriere. Kathleen M. Jaeger. LC 94-4388. (Age of Revolution & Romanticism Ser.: Vol. 6). XI, 241p. (C). 1994. text 45.95 (*0-8204-2179-0*) P Lang Pubng.

Male Animal see Best Plays of the Modern American Theatre: Second Series, 1939-1946

Male Animal. Suzanne Carey. (Silhouette Romance Ser.). 1994. per. 2.75 (*0-373-19025-5*, 1-19025-5) Harlequin Bks.

Male Anxiety & Female Chastity: A Comparative Study of Chinese Ethical Values in Ming-Ch'ing Times. Ju-K'ang T'ien. Ed. by Jacques Gernet & Erik J. Zurcher. (T'oung Pao Monographies: Vol. XIV). (Illus.). (Orig.). 1988. pap. 54.50 (*90-04-08361-8*) Brill Academic Pubs.

Male Attitudes Toward Family Planning: A Study of St. Lucian Men. Nesha Z. Haniff. 82p. 1989. pap. 5.00 (*0-916683-23-0*) Intl Plan Parent.

Male Authors, Female Readers: Representation & Subjectivity in Middle English Devotional Literature. Anne C. Bartlett. 208p. 1995. text 35.00 (*0-8014-3038-0*) Cornell U Pr.

Male Bashing: Women's Favorite Pastime. Jan B. King. Ed. by Cliff Carle. 64p. 1994. pap. 5.95 (*0-918259-72-X*) CCC Pubns.

Male Batterer: A Treatment Approach. Daniel J. Sonkin et al. 272p. 1985. 32.95 (*0-8261-5090-X*) Springer Pub.

Male Birth Control Pill. (Landmark Ser.). 1979. 25.50 (*0-8422-4110-8*) Irvington.

***Male Bodies: Health, Culture & Identity.** D. Watson. LC 99-29672. 170p. 2000. 85.00 (*0-335-19786-8*, Pub. by OpUniv Pr) Taylor & Francis.

***Male Bodies: Health, Culture & Identity.** D. Watson. 2000. pap. 25.95 (*0-335-19785-X*) OpUniv Pr.

***Male Body: A New Look at Men in Public & in Private.** Susan Bordo. LC 99-25386. (Illus.). 368p. 1999. text 25.00 (*0-374-28065-7*) FS&G.

***Male Body: A New Look at Men in Public & in Private.** Susan Bordo. (Illus.). 368p. 2000. pap. 14.00 (*0-374-52732-6*) FS&G.

Male Body: A Physician's Guide to What Every Man Should Know About His Sexual Health. Abraham Morgentaler. LC 93-18035. 192p. 1993. pap. 10.00 (*0-671-86426-2*) S&S Trade.

Male Body: An Owner's Manual: The Ultimate Guide to Staying Healthy & Fit for Life. K. Winston Caine & Perry Garfinkel. Ed. by Men's Health Books Staff. LC 96-18195. (Illus.). 432p. 1996. pap. 19.95 (*0-87596-401-X*); text 31.95 (*0-87596-297-1*) St Martin.

Male Body: Features, Exploits, Conclusions. Ed. by Laurence Goldstein. LC 94-24555. (Illus.). 344p. 1994. pap. 16.95 (*0-472-06597-1*, 06597) U of Mich Pr.

Male Body: Features, Exploits, Conclusions. Ed. by Laurence Goldstein. LC 94-24555. 344p. 1995. text 44.50 (*0-472-09597-8*, 09597) U of Mich Pr.

Male Bonding. 2nd ed. Ed. by David A. Sprigle. (Foto Factory Anthology Ser.). (Illus.). 124p. 1998. reprint ed. 40.00 (*1-883923-24-7*, FF 100) FotoFactory.

Male Bonding, Vol. 1. Ed. by David Sprigle. (FotoFactory Anthology Ser.: Vol. 4). (Illus.). 140p. 1998. 40.00 (*1-883923-15-8*, FF100) FotoFactory.

Male Bonding Volume 2. Ed. by David A. Sprigle. (FotoFactory Anthology Ser.: Vol. 4, Pt. 2). (Illus.). 140p. 1998. 49.95 (*1-883923-32-8*, FF400) FotoFactory.

Male Call: Becoming Jack London. Jonathan Auerbach. LC 96-14682. (New Americanists Ser.). (Illus.). 296p. 1996. text 49.95 (*0-8223-1827-X*); pap. text 17.95 (*0-8223-1820-2*) Duke.

Male Care Matters: Harold Almon's Guide to: Things Someone Will Tell a Son. rev. ed. Ed. by Harold Almon. (Illus.). 93p. 1996. spiral bd. 19.95 (*0-917921-12-7*) Bee At Ease Pr.

Male Chauvinist Pigs' Guide to Women: Every Day is Halloween. Male Chauvinist Pigs of America, Staff. LC 95-81190. (Illus.). 104p. (Orig.). 1996. pap. 9.95 (*0-9648853-1-X*) Male Chauvinist.

Male Code: Rules Men Live & Love By. Twyman L. Towery. LC 91-77118. 233p. 1992. 19.95 (*0-944435-17-3*) Glenbridge Pub.

Male Colors: The Construction of Homosexuality in Tokugawa Japan. Gary P. Leupp. LC 94-40395. (Illus.). 317p. 1996. 45.00 (*0-520-08627-9*, Pub. by U CA Pr) Cal Prin Full Svc.

Male Colors: The Construction of Homosexuality in Tokugawa Japan. Gary P. Leupp. LC 94-40395. (Illus.). 1997. pap. 19.95 (*0-520-20900-1*, Pub. by U CA Pr) Cal Prin Full Svc.

Male Continence. John H. Noyes. 1975. 250.00 (*0-87968-231-0*) Gordon Pr.

Male Continence, 4 vols. in 1. John H. Noyes. Incl. Dixon & His Copyists, a Criticism of the Accounts of the Oneida Community in "New America," "Spiritual Wives," & Kindred Publications. 2nd ed. LC 72-2975. Essay on Scientific Propagation. LC 72-2975. Salvation from Sin, the End of Christian Faith. LC 72-2975. LC 72-2975. reprint ed. 37.50 (*0-404-10739-7*) AMS Pr.

Male Continence. John H. Noyes. (Notable American Authors Ser.). 1999. reprint ed. lib. bdg. 125.00 (*0-7812-4648-2*) Rprt Serv.

Male Couple: How Relationships Develop. David P. McWhirter & Andrew M. Mattison. xv, 341 p. 1985. 18.95 (*0-13-547661-5*, Busn) P-H.

***Male Couple's Guide: Finding a Man, Making a Home, Building a Life.** 3rd ed. Eric Marcus. LC 98-44944. 320p. 1999. pap. 17.00 (*0-06-095275-X*) HarpC.

Male Criminal Activity from Childhood Through Youth. Marcel Le Blanc & M. Frechette. (Research in Criminology Ser.). (Illus.). xi, 228p. 1989. 123.95 (*0-387-96859-8*) Spr-Verlag.

Male Cross-Dresser Support Group. Tama Janowitz. LC 93-26215. 320p. 1994. per. 12.00 (*0-671-87150-1*, WSP) PB.

Male Dancer: Bodies, Spectacle, Sexualities. Ramsey Burt. LC 94-32793. (Illus.). 240p. (C). (gr. 13). 1995. 85.00 (*0-415-08899-2*, C0334); pap. 25.99 (*0-415-08900-X*, C0335) Routledge.

Male Daughters, Female Husbands: Gender & Sex in an African Society. Ifi Amadiume. (C). 1987. pap. 22.50 (*0-86232-595-1*, Pub. by St Martin) St Martin.

Male Daughters, Female Husbands: Gender & Sex in an African Society. Ifi Amadiume. (C). 1987. text 49.95 (*0-86232-594-3*, Pub. by Zed Books) St Martin.

***Male Depression & Alcoholism: Pocketbook Edition.** Salloum. 2000. 14.95 (*1-85317-894-2*, Pub. by Martin Dunitz) Blackwell Sci.

Male Dominance & Female Autonomy: Domestic Authority in Matrilineal Societies. Alice Schlegel. LC 72-78401. (Comparative Studies). 224p. 1972. 15.00 (*0-87536-327-X*) HRAFP.

Male Envy: The Logic of Malice in Literature & Culture. Mervyn Nicholson. LC 99-10347. 249p. 1999. 65.00 (*0-7391-0062-9*) Lxngtn Bks.

***Male Erotic Massage: A Guide to Sex & Spirit.** Kenneth Ray Stubbs. 168p. 1999. pap. 17.95 (*0-939263-16-5*, Pub. by Secret Garden) ACCESS Pubs Network.

***Male Escort's Handbook: Your Guide to Getting Rich the Hard Way.** Aaron Lawrence. 250p. 2000. pap. 14.95 (*0-9667691-1-2*) Late Night Pr.

Male Experience. 3rd ed. James A. Doyle. 368p. (C). 1994. text. write for info. (*0-697-10458-3*) Brown & Benchmark.

Male Experience. 4th ed. Doyle. 2001. 23.00 (*0-697-25284-1*, WCB McGr Hill) McGrw-H Hghr Educ.

Male Factor in Human Infertility. Ed. by W. M. Thompson et al. (Studies in Fertility & Sterility). 1984. lib. bdg. 174.50 (*0-85200-810-4*) Kluwer Academic.

Male Fantasies Vol. 1: Women, Floods, Bodies, History. Klaus Theweleit. Tr. by Stephen Conway et al from GER. LC 86-25057. (Theory & History of Literature Ser.: Vol. 22). (Illus.). 539p. 1987. pap. 19.95 (*0-8166-1449-0*) U of Minn Pr.

Male Fantasies Vol. 2: The Male Body: Psychoanalyzing the White Terror. Klaus Theweleit. Tr. by Erica Carter & Chris Turner from GER. (Theory & History of Literature Ser.: Vol. 23).Tr. of Mannerphantasien, Vol. 2. (Illus.). 480p. (Orig.). 1989. pap. 19.95 (*0-8166-1451-2*) U of Minn Pr.

Male, Female: The Evolution of Human Sex Differences. David C. Geary. LC 98-26961. 410p. 1998. 49.95 (*1-55798-527-8*) Am Psychol.

Male-Female - Female-Male Dictionary. Jenny L. Bader & Bill Brazell. (Orig.). 1996. pap. write for info. (*0-446-67187-8*) Warner Bks.

Male-Female Careers - The First Decade: A Study of MBA's. Mary A. Devanna. 1984. pap. 17.50 (*0-317-11513-8*) CU Ctr Career Res.

Male-Female Comedy Teams in American Vaudeville, 1865-1932. Shirley Staples. Ed. by Bernard Beckerman. LC 83-24253. (Theater & Dramatic Studies: No. 16). 336p. reprint ed. 104.20 (*0-8357-1520-5*, 207046100093) Bks Demand.

Male-Female Differences: A Bio-Cultural Perspective. Roberta L. Hall et al. LC 85-16924. 320p. 1985. 37.50 (*0-275-91335-X*, C1335, Praeger Pubs) Greenwood.

***Male, Female, Email: The Struggle for Relatedness in a Paranoid Society.** Michael A. Civin. LC 99-43547. 240p. 2000. 25.95 (*1-892746-30-1*) Other Pr LLC.

Male Femaling: A Grounded Approach to Cross-Dressing & Sex-Changing. Richard Ekins. LC 96-16356. (Illus.). 200p. (C). 1997. 80.00 (*0-415-10624-9*); pap. 24.99 (*0-415-10625-7*) Routledge.

Male Fertility & Infertility. Ed. by T. D. Glover & C. L. Barratt. LC 98-55696. (Illus.). 260p. (C). 1999. text 74.95 (*0-521-62375-8*) Cambridge U Pr.

Male Fertility & It's Regulation. T. J. Lobl & E. S. Hafez. (Advances in Reproductive Health Care Ser.). 1985. text 322.00 (*0-85200-805-8*) Kluwer Academic.

Male Fitness Stars of TV & the Movies. Susan Zannos. (Legends of Health & Fitness Ser.). (Illus.). 128p. (YA). (gr. 6-12). 2000. lib. bdg. 24.95 (*1-58415-016-5*) M Lane Pubs.

Male for Christmas. Lynsey Stevens. (Australians Ser.: No. 6). 1998. per. 4.50 (*0-373-82578-1*, 1-82578-5) Harlequin Bks.

Male for Sale. Tiffany White. (Yours Truly Ser.: Vol. 3). 1995. per. 3.50 (*0-373-52003-4*) Harlequin Bks.

Male G-Spot Vol. 1: Advanced Techniques for Liberated Lovers. (Sex Masters Collection). (Illus.). 86p. (Orig.). 1997. pap. write for info. (*1-890677-00-0*) Delphi Pr.

Male Genital System see International Classification of Rodent Tumours, Pt. I, The Rat

Male Herbal: Health Care for Men & Boys. James Green. 278p. 1991. pap. 14.95 (*0-89594-458-8*) Crossing Pr.

Male Heterosexual. Larry A. Morris. 272p. 1996. 45.00 (*0-8039-5639-8*); pap. 19.95 (*0-8039-5640-1*) Sage.

Male Homemaker's Handbook. unabridged ed. Tom Pinnock. Ed. by Dick Richmond. LC 96-61715. 108p. 1997. pap. 10.00 (*1-882467-15-9*) Wildstone Media.

Male Homosexual Behavior & the Effects of AIDS Education: A Study of Behavior & Safer Sex in New Zealand & South Australia. B. R. Rosser. LC 91-4626. 264p. 1991. 69.50 (*0-275-93809-3*, C3809, Praeger Pubs) Greenwood.

Male Homosexuality: A Contemporary Psychoanalytic Perspective. Richard C. Friedman. 1990. pap. 19.00 (*0-300-04745-2*) Yale U Pr.

Male Homosexuality in Central & South America. Ed. by Stephen O. Murray. 202p. 1987. pap. 10.95 (*0-942777-58-1*) Floating Lotus.

Male Homosexuality in Four Societies: Brazil, Guatemala, the Philippines, & the United States. Frederick L. Whitman & Robin M. Mathy. LC 85-16752. 241p. 1985. 55.00 (*0-275-90037-1*, C0037, Praeger Pubs) Greenwood.

Male Image. Pettifer. LC 99-12112. 204p. 1999. text 65.00 (*0-312-22246-7*) St Martin.

Male Impersonators: Gay Men Performing Masculinity. Mark Simpson. 224p. (C). (gr. 13). 1994. pap. 18.99 (*0-415-90991-0*, Pub. by Tavistock) Routldge.

Male in Crisis. Karl Bednarik. Tr. by Helen Sebba from GER. LC 81-7122. 194p. 1981. reprint ed. lib. bdg. 45.50 (*0-313-22713-6*, BEMS, Greenwood Pr) Greenwood.

Male in Farm Animal Reproduction. Ed. by M. Courot. (Current Topics in Veterinary Medicine & Animal Science Ser.). 1984. text 247.50 (*0-89838-682-9*) Kluwer Academic.

Male Infertility. Ed. by T. B. Hargreave. (Clinical Practice in Urology Ser.). (Illus.). 300p. 1983. 94.00 (*0-387-12055-6*) Spr-Verlag.

Male Infertility. 2nd ed. Ed. by T. B. Hargreave. LC 94-10499. 1994. write for info. (*3-540-19840-7*) Spr-Verlag.

Male Infertility. 2nd ed. Ed. by T. B. Hargreave. LC 94-10499. 1994. 184.00 (*0-387-19840-7*) Spr-Verlag.

Male Infertility. 2nd ed. Ed. by Timothy B. Hargreave. LC 97-39625. (Illus.). xi, 466p. 1997. pap. 69.00 (*3-540-76216-7*) Spr-Verlag.

***Male Infertility: A Guide for the Clinician.** Anne M. Jequier. LC 99-16293. (Illus.). 384p. 2000. 159.00 (*0-632-05129-9*) Blackwell Sci.

Male Infertility: Men Talking. Mary-Claire Mason. LC 93-11986. 224p. (C). 1993. text 69.95 (*0-415-07289-1*, B2423) Routledge.

Male Infertility - From A-Z: A Concise Encyclopedia. J. M. Hollanders et al. LC 96-23150. (Studies in Profertility Ser.: Vol. 4). 198p. 1996. 65.00 (*1-85070-758-8*) Prthnon Pub.

Male Infertility & Sexual Dysfunction. Ed. by Wayne J. Hellstrom. LC 96-3247. (Illus.). 624p. 1997. 149.00 (*0-387-94859-7*) Spr-Verlag.

Male Intergenerational Intimacy. Theo Sanfort. 1990. pap. 19.95 (*0-918393-78-7*, Harrington Park) Haworth Pr.

Male Intergenerational Intimacy: Historical, Socio-Psychological, & Legal Perspectives. Ed. by Theo G. Sandfort et al. 325p. 1991. 9.95 (*1-56024-000-8*) Haworth Pr.

Male Journey in Japanese Prints. Roger S. Keyes. 190p. (C). 1989. 85.00 (*0-520-06512-3*, Pub. by U CA Pr) Cal Prin Full Svc.

***Male Lust: Power, Pleasure & Transformation.** Ed. by Kerwin Kay et al. LC 99-39462. 372p. 2000. pap. 24.95 (*1-56023-982-4*, Harrington Park); lib. bdg. 49.95 (*1-56023-981-6*, Harrington Park) Haworth Pr.

Male Malady: Fictions of Impotence in the French Romantic Novel. Margaret Waller. LC 92-13863. 269p. (C). 1993. 48.00 (*0-8135-1908-X*) Rutgers U Pr.

Male Masochism: Modern Revisions of the Story of Love. Carol Siegel. LC 94-15404. 222p. reprint ed. pap. 68.90 (*0-608-09363-7*, 205410900002) Bks Demand.

Male Matters: Masculinity, Anxiety & the Male Body on the Line. Calvin Thomas. LC 95-17447. 288p. 1996. 24.95 (*0-252-02202-5*) U of Ill Pr.

Male Matters: Masculinity, Anxiety & the Male Body on the Line. Calvin Thomas. LC 95-17447. 264p. 1996. 16.95 (*0-252-06500-X*) U of Ill Pr.

Male-Mediated Developmental Toxicity. Ed. by D. R. Mattison & A. F. Olshan. (Reproductive Biology Ser.). (Illus.). 418p. (C). 1994. text 125.00 (*0-306-44815-7*, Kluwer Plenum) Kluwer Academic.

Male Member: Being a Compendium of Fact, Figures, Foibles & Anecdotes about the Male Sexual Organ in Man & Beast. Kit Schwartz. 192p. 1985. pap. 11.95 (*0-312-50933-2*) St Martin.

Male Menopause. Jed Diamond. LC 97-26509. 384p. 1997. 22.95 (*1-57071-143-7*) Sourcebks.

Male Menopause. Jed Diamond. 432p. 1998. reprint ed. pap. 14.95 (*1-57071-397-9*) Sourcebks.

***Male Menopaws: The Silent Howl.** Marty Sacks. LC 98-27374. (Illus.). 64p. 1998. pap. 9.95 (*0-89815-945-8*) Ten Speed Pr.

***Male Mid-Life Crisis: Psychological Dynamics, Theological Issues, & Pastoral Interventions.** Justin K. Lim. 184p. 2000. 46.00 (*0-7618-1766-2*); pap. 26.50 (*0-7618-1767-0*) U Pr of Amer.

Male Middle Age. Georges Duby. 224p. 1993. 37.50 (*0-226-16773-9*) U Ch Pr.

Male-Midwife & the Female Doctor. Charles E. Rosenberg & Carroll-Smith Rosenberg. LC 73-20642. (Sex, Marriage & Society Ser.). (Illus.). 224p. 1979. reprint ed. 28.95 (*0-405-05810-1*) Ayer.

***Male Mind at Work: A Woman's Guide to Winning at Working with Men.** Deborah J. Swiss. 304p. 2000. text 25.00 (*0-7382-0327-0*, Pub. by Perseus Pubng) HarpC.

Male Modeling. Ruth Tolman & Jeffery McFarland. 130p. 1981. pap. 99.50 (*0-685-11675-1*) World Modeling.

Male Multiple Orgasm Vol. 3: Advanced Techniques for Liberated Lovers. (Sex Masters Collection). 86p. (Orig.). 1997. pap. write for info. (*1-890677-02-7*) Delphi Pr.

Male Myths & Icons: Masculinity in Popular Culture. Roger Horrocks. LC 95-7737. 1995. pap. 19.95 (*0-312-12623-9*) St Martin.

Male Nude. David Leddick. (Klotz Ser.). (Illus.). 1998. pap. 29.99 (*3-8228-7966-5*) Taschen Amer.

***Male Nude.** David Leddick. 1998. 38.99 (*3-8228-7655-0*) Benedikt Taschen.

Male Nude: A Male View. Ed. by Peter Weiermair. 152p. 1995. 49.95 (*3-905514-43-5*) Dist Art Pubs.

Male Nude in Contemporary Photography. Melody D. Davis. (Visual Studies). (Illus.). 184p. 1991. 59.95 (*0-87722-839-6*) Temple U Pr.

Male Nude in Contemporary Photography. Melody D. Davis. (Visual Studies). (Illus.). 184p. (C). 1994. pap. 24.95 (*1-56639-198-9*) Temple U Pr.

Male Nudes by Women: An Anthology. Peter Weiermair. (Illus.). 154p. 49.95 (*3-905514-67-2*) Dist Art Pubs.

Male of the Species. Ed. by David Sprigle. (Illus.). 166p. 1999. 60.00 (*1-883923-40-9*, FF9100) FotoFactory.

***Male Olympic Champions.** Michael V. Uschan. LC 99-40332. (History Makers Ser.). (Illus.). 144p. (YA). (gr. 6-9). 2000. lib. bdg. 23.70 (*1-56006-614-8*) Lucent Bks.

Male on Male Rape: The Hidden Toll of Stigma & Shame. Michael Scarce. LC 97-25772. (Illus.). 334p. (C). 1997. 27.95 (*0-306-45627-3*, Plen Insight) Perseus Pubng.

Male or Female? A Methodological Study of Grave Gifts As Sex-Indicators in Iron Age Burials from Athens. Agneta Stromberg. (Studies in Mediterranean Archaeology & Literature: No. 123). (Illus.). 217p. (Orig.). 1993. pap. 52.50 (*91-7081-076-1*, Pub. by P Astroms) Coronet Bks.

***Male Order.** A. Amory. 1998. mass mkt. 6.95 (*0-7472-5838-4*, Pub. by Headline Bk Pub) Trafalgar.

Male Order: Life Stories from Boys Who Sell Sex. Barbara Gibson. (Sexual Politics Ser.). 1997. pap. 19.95 (*0-304-33287-9*) Continuum.

Male Order: Unwrapping Masculinity. Ed. by Rutherford. (C). 1988. pap. 19.50 (*0-85315-690-5*, Pub. by Lawrence & Wishart) NYU Pr.

Male Ordered Health Care: The Inequities of Women. Shirlee Pasau-Buck & Edward M. Jones. LC 94-65426. 184p. 1994. pap. 9.95 (*0-9627246-2-9*) Power NY.

Male Out Migration & Matri-Weighted Households: A Case Study of a Junjab Village in Pakistan. Naveedi Rahat. (C). 1990. text 26.00 (*81-7075-015-6*, Pub. by Hindustan) S Asia.

Male Plague. Martin Wray. 310p. 1999. 17.95 (*0-7541-0547-4*, Pub. by Minerva Pr) Unity Dist.

***Male Potency: A Man's Guide to Optimal Sexual Health.** L. B. Johnson. 1999. pap. 3.95 (*1-58054-060-0*) Woodland UT.

Male Pretense: A Gender Study of Sir Philip Sidney's Life & Texts. Katrina Bachinger. LC 94-39589. (Salzburger Studien Ser.). 164p. 1995. text 79.95 (*0-7734-1270-0*) E Mellen.

Male Prostitution. D. J. West. LC 92-40327. 1993. 49.95 (*1-56024-368-6*) Haworth Pr.

Male Prostitution. D. J. West. LC 92-40327. 1993. pap. 19.95 (*1-56023-022-3*, Harrington Park) Haworth Pr.

***Male Rain: Selected Poems.** Cal E. Rollins. LC 99-462195. 64p. 2000. pap. 14.95 (*1-890688-05-3*) Kalimat.

Male Rape: A Casebook of Sexual Aggressions. Ed. by Anthony M. Scacco, Jr. LC 81-667777. (Studies in Modern Society: Political & Social Issues: No. 15). (Illus.). 352p. 1982. 32.50 (*0-404-61621-6*); pap. 12.95 (*0-404-61622-4*) AMS Pr.

Male Reproduction & Fertility. Ed. by Andres Negro-Vilar. LC 81-40374. 406p. 1983. reprint ed. pap. 125.90 (*0-608-00446-4*, 206116100007) Bks Demand.

***Male Reproductive Function.** Christina Wang. LC 99-24999. (Endocrine Updates Ser.). 1999. write for info. (*0-7923-8520-9*) Kluwer Academic.

Male Reproductive Function & Semen. T. Mann & C. Lutwak-Mann. (Illus.). 498p. 1981. 142.00 (*0-387-10383-X*) Spr-Verlag.

Male Sexual Abuse: A Trilogy of Intervention Strategies. John C. Gonsiorek et al. LC 93-39292. 1994. 58.00 (*0-8039-3716-4*); pap. 26.00 (*0-8039-3717-2*) Sage.

Male Sexual Armor: Erotic Fantasies & Sexual Realities of the Cop on the Beat & the Man in the Street. Patrick Suraci. LC 92-1138. 1992. 19.95 (*0-8290-2467-0*) Irvington.

Male Sexual Awareness: Increasing Sexual Satisfaction. Barry McCarthy & Emily McCarthy. LC 97-45907. (Illus.). 304p. 1998. pap. 12.95 (*0-7867-0473-X*) Carroll & Graf.

Male Sexual Dysfunction. Bruce Goldberg. 1987. 12.00 incl. audio (*1-885577-36-2*) B Goldberg.

***Male Sexual Dysfunction.** Ed. by Robert J. Krane et al. (Illus.). 352p. 1998. write for info. (*0-443-07848-3*) Church.

Male Sexual Dysfunction. Robert J. Krane & Michael B. Siroky. 1983. 86.95 (*0-316-50331-2*) Little.

Male Sexual Endurance: A Man's Book about Ejaculatory Control. Robert W. Birch. 190p. 1997. 19.95 (*1-57074-349-5*) PEC.

Male Sexual Fitness. Eric Braverman. (Good Health Guides Ser.). 48p. (Orig.). 1998. pap. 3.95 (*0-87983-762-4*, 37624K, Keats Publng) NTC Contemp Pub Co.

Male Sexual Machine: An Owner's Manual. Kenneth Purvis. (Illus.). 210p. 1998. pap. text 11.00 (*0-7881-5449-4*) DIANE Pub.

Male Sexual Vitality. Michael T. Murray. LC 93-29270. (Getting Well Naturally Ser.). (Illus.). 160p. 1994. pap. 9.95 (*1-55958-428-9*) Prima Pub.

An Asterisk (*) at the beginning of an entry indicates that the title is appearing for the first time.

Male Sexuality. Fiona Giles. 1999. pap. write for info. (*0-375-75118-1*) Villard Books.

Male-Specific Coliphages As Indicators of Viral Contamination of Drinking Water. Mark D. Sobsey et al. LC 95-167332. (Illus.). 170p. 1995. pap. 53.00 (*0-89867-798-X*, 90684) Am Water Wks Assn.

Male Sports Stars. Chelsea House Publishing Staff. 1998. 83.74 (*0-7910-4592-7*) Chelsea Hse.

Male Sterility for Motility Disorders: Etiological Factors & Treatment. S. Hamamah & R. Mieusset. Ed. by F. Oliviennes & Rene Frydman. (Illus.). 314p. 1999. 140.00 (*0-387-98673-1*) Spr-Verlag.

Male Sterility in Higher Plants. M. L. Kaul. (Monographs on Theoretical & Applied Genetics: Vol. 10). (Illus.). 960p. 1988. 351.95 (*0-387-17952-6*) Spr-Verlag.

Male Stress Syndrome: How to Survive Stress in the '90s. 2nd ed. Georgia Witkin. LC 94-27468. 240p. 1994. 23.00 (*1-55704-206-3*, Pub. by Newmarket); pap. 12.95 (*1-55704-205-5*, Pub. by Newmarket) Norton.

Male Subjectivity at the Margins. Kaja Silverman. (Illus.). 368p. (C). 1992. pap. 25.99 (*0-415-90419-6*, A5732) Routledge.

Male Survivor: The Impact of Sexual Abuse. Matthew P. Mendel. 264p. 1994. 46.00 (*0-8039-5441-7*); pap. 21.00 (*0-8039-5442-5*) Sage.

Male Survivors Dictionary. Steven Jacobsen. 45p. 1998. pap. 5.00 (*0-9667182-0-8*) Mens Resource Ctr.

Male to Female: La Cage aux Folles. Photos by Vivienne Maricevic. (Illus.). 140p. 39.95 (*3-905514-86-9*) Dist Art Pubs.

Male-to-Female Dictionary. Susan Shapiro. LC 96-174557. (Illus.). 160p. 1996. pap. 7.99 (*1-57297-116-9*) Blvd Books.

***Male to Female Dictionary: The Handy Guide to the Babble of the Sexes.** Susan Shapiro. 1998. pap. 7.99 (*0-425-16743-7*) Blvd Books.

***Male to Male: Sexual Feelings Across the Boundaries of Identity.** Edward J. Tejirian. LC 00-27137. 408p. 2000. 49.95 (*1-56023-975-1*, Harrington Park); pap. text 24.95 (*1-56023-976-X*, Harrington Park) Haworth Pr.

Male Trouble. Ed. by Constance Penley & Sharon Willis. LC 92-25407. (Camera Obscura Bks.: Vol. 3). 336p. (C). 1993. pap. 18.95 (*0-8166-2172-1*) U of Minn Pr.

Male Trouble: A Crisis in Representation: French Art in the Age of Neoclassicism. Abigail Solomon-Godeau. LC 96-61191. (Illus.). 264p. 1997. 29.95 (*0-500-01765-4*, Pub. by Thames Hudson) Norton.

Male Trouble: A Crisis in Representation: French Art in the Age of Neoclassicism. Abigail Solomon-Godeau. LC 96-61191. (Interplay Ser.). (Illus.). 264p. 1999. pap. 24.95 (*0-500-28037-1*, Pub. by Thames Hudson) Norton.

***Male Victims of Sexual Assault.** 2nd ed. Ed. by Gillian C. Mezey & Michael King. 176p. 2000. text 39.95 (*0-19-262932-8*) OUP.

Male Violence. Ed. by John Archer. 352p. (C). 1993. pap. 27.99 (*0-415-08962-X*) Routledge.

Male Writers. Ed. by Richard S. Rennert. (Profiles of Great Black Americans Ser.). (Illus.). 64p. (J). (gr. 3 up). 1993. lib. bdg. 14.95 (*0-7910-2061-4*) Chelsea Hse.

Male Writers. Richard S. Rennert. (Profiles of Great Black Americans Ser.). (Illus.). 64p. (J). (gr. 3 up). 1994. pap. 5.95 (*0-7910-2062-2*) Chelsea Hse.

Male Writers. Richard Scott Rennert. (Profiles of Great Black Americans Ser.). (J). 1994. 12.40 (*0-606-07833-9*) Turtleback.

Malebranche's First & Last Critics: Simon Foucher & Dortous de Mairan. Tr. by Richard A. Watson & Marjorie Grene. LC 94-29320. (Journal of the History of Philosophy Monographs). 148p. (C). 1995. pap. 36.95 (*0-8093-1972-1*) S Ill U Pr.

Malebranche's Theory of the Soul: A Cartesian Interpretation. Tad Schmaltz. 320p. 1996. text 65.00 (*0-19-510344-0*) OUP.

Maledicta 8 (1984-85) The International Journal of Verbal Aggression. Ed. by Reinhold Aman. LC 77-649633. (Maledicta: International Journal of Verbal Aggression Ser.: Vol. 8). (Illus.). 320p. 1985. pap. 25.00 (*0-916500-28-4*) Maledicta.

Maledicta 11 (1990-95) The International Journal of Verbal Aggression. Ed. by Reinhold Aman. LC 77-649633. (Illus.). 160p. 1995. pap. 12.50 (*0-916500-31-4*) Maledicta.

Maledicta 4, (1980) The International Journal of Verbal Aggression. Ed. by Reinhold Aman. LC 77-649633. (Maledicta: International Journal of Verbal Aggression Ser.: Vol. 4, No. 1 & 2). (Illus.). 320p. 1980. pap. 25.00 (*0-916500-55-1*) Maledicta.

Maledicta 14 (2000) The International Journal of Verbal Aggression. Ed. by Reinhold Aman. LC 77-649633. (Illus.). 160p. 2000. pap. 15.00 (*0-916500-34-9*) Maledicta.

Maledicta 9 (1986-87) Lillian Mermin Feinsilver Festschrift. Ed. by Reinhold Aman. LC 77-649633. (Maledicta: International Journal of Verbal Aggression Ser.: Vol. 9). (Illus.). 320p. 1988. pap. 25.00 (*0-916500-29-2*) Maledicta.

Maledicta 10, (1988-1989) The International Journal of Verbal Aggression. Ed. by Reinhold Aman. LC 77-649633. (Illus.). 320p. 1990. pap. 25.00 (*0-916500-30-6*) Maledicta.

Maledicta 5, (1981) Elias Petropoulos Festschrift. Ed. by Reinhold Aman. LC 77-649633. (Maledicta: International Journal of Verbal Aggression Ser.: Vol. 5, Nos. 1 & 2). (Illus.). 352p. (C). 1982. pap. 25.00 (*0-916500-25-X*) Maledicta.

Maledicta 7, (1983) Peter Tamony Festschrift. Ed. by Reinhold Aman. LC 77-649633. (Maledicta: International Journal of Verbal Aggression Ser.: Vol. 7). (Illus.). 320p. 1984. pap. 25.00 (*0-916500-27-6*) Maledicta.

Maledicta 1, (1977) G. Legman Festschrift. Ed. by Reinhold Aman. LC 76-649633. (Maledicta: International Journal of Verbal Aggression Ser.: Vol. 1 No. 1 & 2). (C). 1978. pap. 25.00 (*0-916500-50-0*) Maledicta.

Maledicta 6, (1982) The International Journal of Verbal Aggression. Ed. by Reinhold Aman. LC 77-649633. (Maledicta: International Journal of Verbal Aggression Ser.: Vol. 6, Nos. 1 & 2). (Illus.). 320p. 1983. pap. 25.00 (*0-916500-26-8*) Maledicta.

Maledicta 13 (1997-99) The International Journal of Verbal Aggression. Ed. by Reinhold Aman. LC 77-649633. (Illus.). 160p. 2000. pap. 15.00 (*0-916500-33-0*) Maledicta.

Maledicta 3 (1979) Ernest Borneman Festschrift. Ed. by Reinhold Aman. LC 77-649633. (Maledicta: International Journal of Verbal Aggression Ser.: Vol. 3). (Illus.). 1979. reprint ed. pap. 25.00 (*0-916500-48-9*) Maledicta.

Maledicta 12 (1996) The International Journal of Verbal Aggression. Ed. by Reinhold Aman. (Illus.). 160p. (Orig.). 1996. pap. 12.50 (*0-916500-32-2*) Maledicta.

Maledicta 2 (1978) The International Journal of Verbal Aggression. Ed. by Reinhold Aman. LC 77-649633. (Maledicta: International Journal of Verbal Aggression Ser.: Vol. 2, No. 1-2). (Illus.). (C). 1979. pap. 25.00 (*0-916500-52-7*) Maledicta.

Male/Female. Vince Aletti. 1999. 29.95 (*0-89381-881-X*) Aperture.

***Male/Female Roles.** Laura K. Egendorf. LC 99-25743. (Opposing Viewpoints Ser.). 312p. (YA). (gr. 9-12). 2000. pap. 17.45 (*0-7377-0130-7*); lib. bdg. 27.45 (*0-7377-0131-5*) Greenhaven.

Malefic. Luis Royo. (Illus.). 80p. 1997. pap. 18.95 (*1-56163-181-7*) NBM.

Malefices. Boileau-Narcejac. (FRE.). 213p. 1985. pap. 11.95 (*0-7859-2016-1*, 2070376621) Fr & Eur.

Maleficus. James Toland. Ed. by William Chapin. 210p. 1999. pap. 9.95 (*0-7392-0258-8*, P03322) Morris Pubng.

Maleic Anhydride. B. C. Trivedi & B. M. Culbertson. LC 82-9126. (Illus.). 887p. 1982. reprint ed. pap. 200.00 (*0-608-09366-1*, 205411100002) Bks Demand.

***Maleness of God.** Brenda J. Baker. 240p. 1999. pap. 14.95 (*1-55050-158-5*, Pub. by Coteau) Genl Dist Srvs.

Malen'Kaya Tereza. Dmitri S. Merezhkovsky. LC 84-22518. 208p. 1989. pap. 9.50 (*0-938920-43-X*) Hermitage Pubs.

Malentendu see Caligula

Malentendu. Incl. Caligula. write for info. (*0-318-63487-2*) Fr & Eur.

Malentendu. Albert Camus. (Coll. Soleil Ser.). 6.95 (*0-685-37267-7*) Schoenhof.

M'Aleph V'ad Tav: Spirit Duplicating Reading Primer. Avivia Langsam. (Illus.). 1997. pap., teacher ed. 18.00 (*0-915152-02-9*, A040) Langsam Publishing Co.

Maler Des Lichts: Nordische Kunst Auf Skagen. Knud Voss. Tr. by Barbara Leonhardt & Albrecht Leonhardt from DAN. (GER., Illus.). 260p. (C). 1995. 58.00 (*3-8170-2026-0*, Pub. by Knstvrlag Weingrtn) Intl Bk Import.

Maler Muller-Bibliographie. Friedrich Meyer. viii, 175p. 1974. reprint ed. write for info. (*3-487-05286-5*) G Olms Pubs.

Malerei - Grafik - Lichtkinetik. Franz Kumher. (Veroffentlichungen Des Sudostdeutscshen Kulturwerks. Reihe A: Kultur und Dichtung: Bd. 33). (GER.). 76p. 1992. write for info. (*3-487-09615-3*) G Olms Pubs.

Malerei am Hofe der Este. Katja Conradi. (Studien Zur Kunstgeschichte: Bd. 110). (Illus.). 207p. 1997. 54.00 (*3-487-10246-3*) G Olms Pubs.

Malerei des Nationalsozialismus: Der Maler Werner Peiner (1897-1984) Anja Hesse. (Studien Zur Kunstgeschichte Ser.: Vol. 94). (GER.). x, 430p. 1995. write for info. (*3-487-09978-0*) G Olms Pubs.

Malerei des 19.Jahrhunderts. Karin Volland. (GER., Illus.). 128p. 1996. text 31.00 (*90-5705-052-8*, Verlag Kunst) Gordon & Breach.

Malerei im Film - Peter Greenaway. Michael Schuster. (Szene Ser.: Bd. 1). 210p. 1997. 45.00 (*3-487-10316-8*) G Olms Pubs.

Malerei, 1970-1995. Michael Venezia. 1997. 35.00 (*3-928762-60-5*, Pub. by Richter Verlag) Dist Art Pubs.

Maleri Im Film: Peter Greenaway. Michael Schuster. (GER.). 178p. 1998. write for info. (*3-487-10663-9*) G Olms Pubs.

Males at Risk: The Other Side of Child Sexual Abuse. Frank G. Bolton, Jr. et al. 224p. (C). 1989. text 52.00 (*0-8039-3236-7*) Sage.

Males, Females & Behavior: Toward Biological Understanding. Ed. by Lee Ellis & Linda Ebertz. LC 97-32949. 344p. 1998. 69.50 (*0-275-95941-4*, Praeger Pubs) Greenwood.

Male's Honour & Female's Shame: Gender & Ethnic Identity Constructions among Turkish Divorcees in the Migration Context. Aylin Akpinar. LC 98-139457. 172p. 1998. write for info. (*91-506-1261-1*) Uppsala Universitet.

Males with Eating Disorders. Ed. by Arnold E. Andersen. LC 89-23909. (Eating Disorders Monographs: No. 4). (Illus.). 274p. 1990. text 39.95 (*0-87630-556-7*) Brunner-Mazel.

Maleshop: Men, Consumerism & Shopping Culture. Ed. by Cook. 1995. pap. 22.50 (*0-85315-805-3*, Pub. by Lawrence & Wishart) NYU Pr.

Maleshop: Men, Consumerism & Shopping Culture. Ed. by David Cook. 256p. (C). 1996. pap. 22.50 (*0-85315-821-5*, Pub. by Lawrence & Wishart) NYU Pr.

Malesian Seed Plants Vol. 1: Spot-Characters. M. M. Van Balgooy. 154p. 1998. pap. 28.00 (*90-71236-31-5*, Pub. by Rijksherbarium) Balogh.

Malesian Seed Plants Vol. 2: Portraits of Tree Families. (Illus.). 307p. 1998. pap. 56.00 (*90-71236-36-6*, Pub. by Rijksherbarium) Balogh.

Malevich. Ed. by Jose M. Faerna. LC 96-84006. (Great Modern Masters Ser.). (Illus.). 64p. 1996. pap. 11.98 (*0-8109-4691-2*, Pub. by Abrams) Time Warner.

Malevich. Serge Fauchereau. (Grandes Monografias). (SPA., Illus.). 224p. 1993. 200.00 (*84-343-0673-5*) Elliots Bks.

Malevich: Exhibition Leningrad-Moscow-Amsterdam, 1989. V. Volboudt. (C). 1990. pap. 220.00 (*0-7855-4460-7*, Pub. by Collets) St Mut.

Malevil. Robert Merle. (FRE.). 1983. pap. 19.95 (*0-7859-4179-7*) Fr & Eur.

Malevolence. Thomas Lashley. 184p. 1997. 19.95 (*1-56315-080-8*) SterlingHse.

Malevolent Eye: An Essay on the Evil Eye, Fertility & the Concept of Mana. Pierre B. Gravel. LC 94-37744. (American University Studies: Series XI, Vol. 64). XXXIII, 212p. (C). 1995. pap. text 49.95 (*0-8204-2275-4*) P Lang Pubng.

Malevolent Insemination & Other Essays on Clarin. Ed. by Noel Valis. LC 81-50963. (Michigan Romance Studies: Vol. 10). 220p. 1990. pap. 15.00 (*0-939730-09-X*) Mich Romance.

Malevolent Leader: Political Socialization in an American Sub-Culture. Dean Jaros et al. (Reprint Series in Political Science). (C). 1993. reprint ed. pap. text 5.00 (*0-8290-3422-6*, PS-488) Irvington.

Malevolent Neutrality: The United States, Great Britain, & the Origins of the Spanish Civil War. Douglas Little. LC 84-19930. 288p. (C). 1985. 37.50 (*0-8014-1769-4*) Cornell U Pr.

Malevolent Nurture: Witch-Hunting & Maternal Power in Early Modern England. Deborah Willis. LC 95-16429. (Illus.). 280p. 1995. text 42.50 (*0-8014-3004-6*); pap. text 17.95 (*0-8014-8194-5*) Cornell U Pr.

Malevolent Silence & Poems for Sandy. Ronin. 88p. 1998. pap. 10.00 (*1-57502-909-X*, PO2505) Morris Pubng.

Malfaiteur. Julien Green. (FRE.). 1987. pap. 16.95 (*0-7859-2710-7*) Fr & Eur.

Malfeasance. Murray, Keith, Publishing Staff & Alan Bold. 1990. pap. text 40.00 (*1-870978-27-7*, Pub. by K Murray Pub) St Mut.

Malformation Syndromes. Ed. by Daniel Bergsma. (March of Dimes Ser.: Vol. 10, No. 7). 1974. 12.95 (*0-686-10017-4*) March of Dimes.

Malformations see Handbook of Clinical Neurology

Malformations see Encyclopedia of Urology

Malformations of the External Genitalia. Ed. by M. Westenfelder. (Monographs in Pediatrics: Vol. 12). (Illus.). xiii, 112p. 1981. pap. 55.75 (*3-8055-1509-X*) S Karger.

Malformed Fetus & Stillbirth: A Diagnostic Approach. Robin M. Winter et al. 324p. 1988. 720.00 (*0-471-90946-7*) Wiley.

Malformed Infant & Child: An Illustrated Guide. Richard M. Goodman & Robert J. Gorlin. (Illus.). 464p. (C). 1983. pap. text 52.50 (*0-19-503255-1*) OUP.

Malgudi Days. R. K. Narayan. 256p. 1995. pap. 11.95 (*0-14-018543-7*, Penguin Classics) Viking Penguin.

Malgudi Days II. R. K. Narayan. 1999. pap. write for info. (*0-670-80632-3*) Viking Penguin.

Malguk Quliaqtuak (Two Stories) H. Kaveolook. (ESK.). 15p. 1974. pap. 2.00 (*0-933769-42-3*) Alaska Native.

Malhadado Vol. 8: Complete Plays 8. Manuel P. Garcia. 98p. 1998. 4.95 (*1-885901-58-5*, Liberts) Presbyters Peartree.

Malhamat al-Harafish see Harafish

Malheur d'Aimer. Claude Roy. (FRE.). 1974. pap. 10.95 (*0-7859-4029-4*) Fr & Eur.

Malheur Indifferent. Peter Handke. (FRE.). 122p. 1977. pap. 10.95 (*0-7859-2396-9*, 2070369765) Fr & Eur.

Malheurs de Sophie. Illus. by Anne Cote.Tr. of Sophie's Misfortune. (FRE.). 1998. boxed set 12.95 incl. audio (*2-921997-47-9*, Pub. by Coffragants) Penton Overseas.

***Malheurs de Sophie.** Illus. by Anne Cote.Tr. of Sophie's Misfortune. (FRE.). 1998. pap., boxed set 16.95 incl. audio compact disk (*2-921997-46-0*, Pub. by Coffragants) Penton Overseas.

Malheurs de Sophie. C. Segur. (Folio - Junior Ser: No. 496). (FRE., Illus.). 220p. 1988. pap. 9.95 (*2-07-033496-1*) Schoenhof.

Malheurs de Sophie - Petites Filles Modeles. unabridged ed. Comtesse de Segur. (FRE.). pap. 7.95 (*2-87714-289-2*, Pub. by Bookking Intl) Distribks Inc.

Mali. Rheal Drisdelle. LC 98-131254. (Country Profiles Ser.). (Illus.). 64p. (C). 1997. pap. 9.95 (*0-85598-334-5*, Pub. by Oxfam Pub) Stylus Pub VA.

Mali. Andrea L. Stamm. 207. 366p. 1998. lib. bdg. 90.00 (*1-85109-166-1*) ABC-CLIO.

***Mali: A Country Study Guide.** Global Investment & Business Center, Inc. Staff. (World Country Study Guides Library: Vol. 107). (Illus.). 350p. 2000. pap. 59.00 (*0-7397-2405-3*) Intl Business Pubns.

Mali: Crossroads of Africa. Philip Koslow. LC 94-26193. (Kingdoms of Africa Ser.). (Illus.). 72p. (J). (gr. 3 up). 1995. lib. bdg. 17.95 (*0-7910-3127-6*) Chelsea Hse.

***Mali: The Bradt Travel Guide.** Ross Velton. (Illus.). 320p. 1999. pap. 18.95 (*1-898323-93-3*, Pub. by Bradt Pubns) Globe Pequot.

Mali - A Country Study Guide: Basic Information for Research & Pleasure. Global Investment Center, USA Staff. (World Country Study Guide Library: Vol. 107). (Illus.). 350p. 1999. pap. 59.00 (*0-7397-1504-6*) Intl Business Pubns.

***Mali Business Intelligence Report, 190 vols.** Global Investment & Business Center, Inc. Staff. (World Business Intelligence Library: Vol. 107). (Illus.). 350p. 2000. pap. 99.95 (*0-7397-2605-6*) Intl Business Pubns.

***Mali Business Law Handbook, 190 vols.** Global Investment & Business Center, Inc. Staff. (Global Business Law Handbooks Library: Vol. 107). (Illus.). 350p. 2000. pap. 99.95 (*0-7397-2005-8*) Intl Business Pubns.

***Mali Business Opportunity Yearbook.** Global Investment & Business Center, Inc. Staff. (Global Business Opportunity Yearbooks Library: Vol. 107). (Illus.). 2000. pap. 99.95 (*0-7397-2205-0*) Intl Business Pubns.

***Mali Business Opportunity Yearbook: Export-Import, Investment & Business Opportunities.** International Business Publications, U. S. A. Staff & Global Investment Center, U. S. A. Staff. (Global Business Opportunity Yearbooks Library: Vol. 107). (Illus.). 350p. 1999. pap. 99.95 (*0-7397-1305-1*) Intl Business Pubns.

***Mali Country Review 2000.** Robert C. Kelly et al. (Illus.). 60p. 1999. pap. 39.95 (*1-58310-531-X*) CountryWatch.

***Mali Foreign Policy & Government Guide.** Global Investment & Business Center, Inc. Staff. (World Foreign Policy & Government Library: Vol. 103). (Illus.). 350p. 2000. pap. 99.95 (*0-7397-3805-4*) Intl Business Pubns.

***Mali Foreign Policy & Government Guide: World Foreign Policy & Government Library.** Contrib. by Global Investment & Business Center, Inc. Staff. (World Foreign Policy & Government Library: Vol. 103). (Illus.). 350p. 1999. pap. 99.00 (*0-7397-3601-9*) Intl Business Pubns.

Mali in Pictures. rev. ed. Ed. by Lerner Publications, Department of Geography Staff. (Visual Geography Ser.). (Illus.). 64p. (YA). (gr. 6-9). 1996. lib. bdg. 19.93 (*0-8225-1869-4*, Lerner Publctns) Lerner Pub.

***Mali Investment & Business Guide.** Global Investment & Business Center, Inc. Staff. (Global Investment & Business Guide Library: Vol. 107). (Illus.). 2000. pap. 99.95 (*0-7397-1805-3*) Intl Business Pubns.

***Mali Investment & Business Guide: Export-Import, Investment & Business Opportunities.** International Business Publications, USA Staff & Global Investment Center, USA Staff. (World Investment & Business Guide Library-99: Vol. 107). (Illus.). 350p. 1999. pap. 99.95 (*0-7397-0302-1*) Intl Business Pubns.

Mali Leksikon Mikroracunarskih Izraza: Multilingual Computer Dictionary (Serbo-German-English) Dusan Petkovic. (CRO, ENG, GER & SER.). 268p. 1990. pap. 95.00 (*0-8288-3924-7*, F101450) Fr & Eur.

Malibu. Michael Banks. LC 91-33456. 160p. (Orig.). 1992. pap. 6.95 (*1-56474-014-5*) Fithian Pr.

Malibu Million Dollar Rock. Stefani B. Ninman. LC 79-53369. (Illus.). 36p. 1979. pap. 4.00 (*0-930422-21-X*) Dennis-Landman.

Malibu Stories. Donald Rawley. LC 91-2465. 68p. (Orig.). 1991. pap. 12.50 (*0-941749-23-1*) Black Tie Pr.

Malibu Summer. Jane C. Miner. 360p. (gr. 7-9). 1995. mass mkt. 3.99 (*0-590-20354-1*) Scholastic Inc.

Malibu's Cooking Again. Ed. by Cathy Rogers. (Illus.). 126p. (Orig.). 1995. pap. 19.95 (*0-9644695-0-2*) Image Maker Pub.

***Malic Acid & Magnesium for Fibromyalgia & Chronic Pain Syndrome.** 7th rev. ed. Billie J. Sahley & Katherine M. Birkner. (Illus.). 36p. 1999. pap. write for info. (*1-889391-15-8*) Pain & Stress.

Malice. Kate Jennings. 32p. 1988. pap. 5.00 (*1-889806-01-3*) Devils Millhopper.

Malice. Danielle Steel. LC 94-43652. 360p. 1996. 24.95 (*0-385-30604-0*) Delacorte.

Malice. Danielle Steel. 416p. 1997. mass mkt. 7.50 (*0-440-22323-7*) Dell.

***Malice.** large type ed. Danielle Steel. 384p. 1999. 31.99 (*0-7089-9072-X*) Ulverscroft.

Malice. limited ed. Danielle Steel. 408p. 1996. 200.00 (*0-385-31520-1*) Doubleday.

Malice Aforethought. large type ed. Francis Iles. 444p. 1980. 27.99 (*0-7089-0477-7*) Ulverscroft.

Malice Defeated & the Matchless Rogue. Elizabeth Cellier. LC 92-22035. (Augustan Reprints Ser.: Nos. 249-250). 1988. reprint ed. 21.50 (*0-404-70249-X*) AMS Pr.

Malice Domestic. Ed. by Sara Woods. 1986. pap. 3.50 (*0-380-69861-7*, Avon Bks) Morrow Avon.

Malice Domestic: An Anthology of Original Traditional Mystery Stories. Rae Foley. LC 98-41390. 261p. 1998. write for info. (*0-7540-3570-0*) Chivers N Amer.

Malice Domestic: An Anthology of Original Traditional Mystery Stories. large type ed. Ed. by Rae Foley. LC 98-41390. 1998. 25.95 (*0-7838-0385-0*, G K Hall & Co) Mac Lib Ref.

Malice Domestic No. 2: An Anthology of Original Traditional Mystery Stories. Ed. by Mary Higgins Clark et al. 272p. 1993. per. 5.99 (*0-671-73827-5*) PB.

Malice Domestic No. 5: An Anthology of Original Traditional Mystery Stories. Ed. by Martin H. Greenberg & Phyllis A. Whitney. 1996. mass mkt. 5.99 (*0-671-89632-6*, PB Trade Paper) PB.

Malice Domestic Vol. 3: An Anthology of Original Traditional Mystery Stories. Ed. by Nancy Pickard et al. 288p. 1994. mass mkt. 4.99 (*0-671-73828-3*) PB.

Malice Domestic Vol. 6: An Anthology of Original Traditional Mystery Stories. 6th ed. Ed. by Anne Perry. 1997. per. 5.99 (*0-671-89633-4*) PB.

Malice Domestic Vol. 7: An Anthology of Original Traditional Mystery Stories. Ed. by Sharyn McCrumb. 256p. 1998. mass mkt. 5.99 (*0-380-79406-3*, Avon Bks) Morrow Avon.

***Malice for Aforethought.** J M Gregson. 1999. 25.00 (*0-7278-5454-2*, Pub. by Severn Hse) Chivers N Amer.

Malice in Cornwall. Graham Thomas. LC 97-95353. Vol. 2. 230p. 1998. mass mkt. 5.99 (*0-8041-1656-3*) Ivy Books.

***Malice in London: An Erskine Powell Mystery.** Graham Thomas. 240p. 2000. mass mkt. 6.50 (*0-8041-1840-X*) Fawcett.

Malice in Maggody: An Ozarks Murder Mystery. Joan Hess. 192p. 1987. 13.95 (*0-317-53413-0*) St Martin.

***Malice in Miniature: A Dorothy Martin Mystery.** Jeanne M. Dams. 272p. 2000. mass mkt. 5.99 (*0-06-101345-5*) HarpC.

M

Malice in Miniature: A Dorothy Martin Mystery. Jeanne M. Dams. LC 98-24415. (Dorothy Martin Mystery Ser.). (Illus.). 220p. (gr. 8). 1998. 22.95 (*0-8027-3322-0*) Walker & Co.

Malice in the Highlands. Graham Thomas. 1998. mass mkt. 5.50 (*0-8041-1657-1*) Ivy Books.

***Malice in the Highlands.** Graham Thomas. 312p. 2000. 31.99 (*0-7089-4291-1*) Ulverscroft.

Malice in Wonderland. John Perkins. 1993. pap. 15.00 (*0-9636328-0-9*) ProMotion Pub.

Malice Intended. Ron Handberg. 608p. 1997. mass mkt. 6.50 (*0-06-101246-7*, Harp PBks) HarpC.

Malice on the Moors. Graham Thomas. 1999. mass mkt. 5.99 (*0-8041-1839-6*) Ivy Books.

Malicious Intent: A Hollywood Fable. Mike Walker. 1999. 24.00 (*1-890862-05-3*) Bancroft MD.

Malicious Intent: A Writer's Guide to How Murderers, Robbers, Rapists & Other Criminals Think. Sean P. Mactire. (Howdunit Ser.). 240p. 1995. pap. 16.99 (*0-89879-648-2*, Wrtrs Digest Bks) F & W Pubns Inc.

***Malicious Mobile Code.** Roger Grimes. Ed. by Sue Miller. (Illus.). 300p. 2000. pap. 34.95 (*1-56592-682-X*) OReilly & Assocs.

Malicious Resplendence. Robert Williams. LC 98-204414. 1997. 79.95 (*1-56097-278-5*) Fantagraph Bks.

Malicious Resplendence. Robert Williams. (Illus.). 300p. 1999. pap. 49.95 (*1-56097-366-8*, Pub. by Fantagraph Bks) Seven Hills Bk.

M

Malick Sidibe. Ed. by Andre Magnin. (Illus.). 256p. 1998. 49.95 (*3-931141-93-4*, Pub. by Scalo Pubs) Dist Art Pubs.

Malicroix. Henri Bosco. (FRE.). 1973. pap. 11.95 (*0-7859-2202-4*, 207036397X) Fr & Eur.

Malidittu la Lingua: Damned Language. Vincenzo Ancona. Tr. by Gaetano Cipolla. 212p. 1991. pap. 16.00 incl. audio (*0-921252-14-5*) LEGAS.

Malign Masters 20th Century. Harry Redner. LC 96-37665. 240p. 1997. text 55.00 (*0-312-17324-5*) St Martin.

Malign Neglect: Race, Crime, & Punishment in America. Michael H. Tonry. (Illus.). 256p. 1996. pap. 13.95 (*0-19-510469-2*) OUP.

Malign Neglect: Race, Crime & Punishment in America. Michael H. Tonry. (Illus.). 248p. 1995. 27.50 (*0-19-507720-2*) OUP.

Malignancies of the Genitourinary Tract. Ed. by A. Ackermann & V. Diehl. LC 92-49944. 1993. write for info. (*3-540-54433-X*) Spr-Verlag.

Malignancies of the Vulva. Ed. by P. G. Knapstein et al. (Illus.). 189p. 1991. 112.00 (*0-86577-389-0*) Thieme Med Pubs.

Malignancy & Chronic Inflammation in the Gastrointestinal Tract: New Concepts: Proceedings of the 81st Falk Symposium, Held in Berlin, Germany, November 3-5, 1994. Ed. by E. O. Riecken et al. LC 95-35759. 1995. text 73.50 (*0-7923-8889-5*) Kluwer Academic.

Malignancy & the Hemostatic System. Ed. by Maria B. Donati et al. LC 80-39949. (Monographs of the Mario Negri Institute for Pharmacological Research). 148p. 1981. reprint ed. pap. 45.90 (*0-608-00425-1*, 206114000007) Bks Demand.

***Malignant Bone Tumors.** Allan W. Yasko. (ACS Atlas of Clinical Oncology Ser.). 448p. 2000. boxed set 99.95 incl. cd-rom (*1-55009-136-0*) DEKR.

Malignant Brain Tumors. Ed. by David G. Thomas & David I. Graham. 1994. 175.00 (*0-387-19689-7*); 180.00 (*3-540-19689-7*) Spr-Verlag.

Malignant Catarrhal Fever in Asian Livestock. Ed. by P. W. Daniels & Purnomo Ronohardjo. 127p. (Orig.). 1988. pap. 100.50 (*0-949511-71-4*) St Mut.

Malignant Cell Secretion. Ed. by V. Krsmanovic & J. F. Whitfield. 320p. 1990. 177.00 (*0-8493-6936-3*, RC268, CRC Reprint) Franklin.

Malignant Diseases of Infancy, Childhood & Adolescence. 2nd ed. Arnold Altman & Allen D. Schwartz. (Major Problems in Clinical Pediatrics Ser.: Vol. 18). 1983. text 160.00 (*0-7216-1211-3*, W B Saunders Co) Harcrt Hlth Sci Grp.

Malignant Effusions: A Multimodal Approach to Cytologic Diagnosis. Carlos Bedrossian. LC 91-7105. (Illus.). 288p. 1994. 145.00 (*0-89640-196-0*) Igaku-Shoin.

Malignant Heritage: Yankee Progressives & the Negro Question, 1901-1914. David W. Southern. LC 68-20410. 126p. reprint ed. 39.10 (*0-8357-9429-6*, 201506700092) Bks Demand.

Malignant Hyperthermia. Ed. by Beverly A. Britt. (C). 1987. text 147.50 (*0-89838-960-7*) Kluwer Academic.

Malignant Hyperthermia: Current Concepts. Ed. by Nalda Felipe et al. (Illus.). 220p. (C). 1989. 32.00 (*0-926592-00-9*) Normed Verlag.

Malignant Hyperthermia: Proceedings of the 3rd International Symposium on Malignant Hyperthermia, 1994. Ed. by M. Morio et al. (Illus.). xvi, 272p. 1996. 165.00 (*4-431-70171-0*) Spr-Verlag.

Malignant Hyperthermia Membrane-Linked Diseases, Vol. III. S. Tsuyoshi Ohnishi. 352p. 1993. lib. bdg. 160.00 (*0-8493-8093-6*, RD82) CRC Pr.

Malignant Hyperthermias. Ed. by M. Aubert et al. 1993. 38.00 (*0-926592-11-4*) Normed Verlag.

Malignant Liver Tumors: Current & Emerging Therapies. Pierre-Alain Clavien & Kim Lyerly. LC 98-49184. (Illus.). 1999. 125.00 (*0-632-04406-3*) Blackwell Sci.

Malignant Lymphoma: Biology, Natural History & Treatments. Alan C. Aisenberg. LC 90-13686. (Illus.). 395p. 1991. text 54.50 (*0-8121-1382-9*) Lppncott W & W.

Malignant Lymphoma: Diagnosis, Biology & Treatment. Wendy N. Erber. 1991. text 117.00 (*3-7186-5058-4*, Harwood Acad Pubs) Gordon & Breach.

Malignant Lymphomas: Biology & Treatment, Vol. VIII. Ed. by Gerassimos A. Pangalis. LC 95-33049. (ESO Monographs). (Illus.). 189p. 1995. 137.00 (*3-540-60122-8*) Spr-Verlag.

Malignant Lymphomas & Hodgkin's Disease: Experimental & Therapeutic Advances. Ed. by F. Cavalli et al. (Developments in Oncology Ser.). 1986. text 253.50 (*0-89838-727-2*) Kluwer Academic.

Malignant Lymphomas, Including Hodgkin's Disease: Diagnosis, Management, & Special Problems, No. 66. Ed. by Bruce W. Dana. LC 93-127. (Cancer Treatment & Research Ser.). 192p. (C). 1993. text 175.50 (*0-7923-2171-5*) Kluwer Academic.

Malignant Lymphoproliferative Diseases. Ed. by J. G. Van der Tweel et al. (Boerhaave Series for Postgraduate Medical Education: No. 17). (Illus.). 520p. 1980. text 226.00 (*90-6021-451-X*) Kluwer Academic.

Malignant Melanoma. Kirkman. 1998. text 99.95 (*0-443-05063-5*, W B Saunders Co) Harcrt Hlth Sci Grp.

Malignant Melanoma. Ed. by Rona M. Mackie. (Pigment Cell Ser.: Vol. 6). (Illus.). viii, 204p. 1983. 121.00 (*3-8055-3690-9*) S Karger.

Malignant Melanoma: Biology, Diagnosis, & Therapy. Ed. by Larry Nathanson. (Cancer Treatment & Research Ser.). (C). 1988. text 150.00 (*0-89838-384-6*) Kluwer Academic.

Malignant Melanoma: Clinical & Histological Diagnosis. Vincent J. McGovern. LC 76-3793. (Wiley Medical Publications). 192p. reprint ed. pap. 59.60 (*0-608-13853-3*, 205598800042) Bks Demand.

Malignant Melanoma & Other Melanocytic Neoplasms. Ed. by A. Bernard Ackerman. (Illus.). 352p. 1984. 53.50 (*0-685-24940-9*, MA1091) Mosby Inc.

Malignant Mesothelioma. Ed. by Douglas W. Henderson. 390p. 1991. 120.00 (*0-89116-977-6*) Hemisp Pub.

Malignant Neoplasms in Childhood & Adolescence. Ed. by H. Riehm. (Monographs in Pediatrics: Vol. 18). (Illus.). viii, 396p. 1986. 130.50 (*3-8055-4206-2*) S Karger.

***Malignant Sadness: The Anatomy of Depression.** Lewis Wolpert. LC 99-45815. 208p. 2000. 23.00 (*0-684-87058-4*) Free Pr.

***Malignant Self Love: Narcissism Revisited.** Samuel Vaknin. Ed. by Lidija Rangelovska. LC 99-181758. 438p. 1999. pap. 49.95 (*80-238-3384-7*) Narcissus Pubns.

Malignant Skin Tumours. 2nd ed. Anthony J. Emmett. Ed. by Michael G. O'Rourke. (Illus.). 425p. 1991. text 185.00 (*0-443-04089-3*) Church.

Malignant Tales. Clemente Palma. Tr. by Guillermo I. Castillo-Feliu from SPA. LC 87-35997. (C). 1988. lib. bdg. 25.50 (*0-8191-6879-3*) U Pr of Amer.

Malignant Tumors of the Ear, Nose, & Throat. V. S. Pogosov & V. F. Antoniv. (Illus.). 600p. 1984. 70.00 (*0-8236-3082-X*) Intl Univs Pr.

Malignant Tumors of the Skin. Ed. by A. C. Chu & R. L. Edelson. (Illus.). 464p. 1999. text 175.00 (*0-340-74086-8*) OUP.

Malignant Tumors of the Thyroid: Clinical Concepts & Controversies. Ed. by R. H. Cobin & D. K. Sirota. (Illus.). 232p. 1992. 160.00 (*0-387-97570-5*) Spr-Verlag.

Malignant Tumours of the Mouth, Jaw & Salivary Glands. Ed. by J. D. Langdon & J. M. Henk. 288p. 1995. text 145.00 (*0-340-55794-X*, Pub. by E A) OUP.

Maligned Master: The Real Story of Antonio Salieri. Volkmar Braunbehrens. Tr. by Eveline L. Kanes from GER. LC 92-28067. (Illus.). 264p. 1993. 25.00 (*0-88064-140-1*) Fromm Intl Pub.

Maligned Master: The Real Story of Antonio Salieri. Volkmar Braunbehrens. Tr. by Eveline L. Kanes from GER. (Illus.). 264p. 1994. pap. 15.95 (*0-88064-155-X*) Fromm Intl Pub.

Malignent Tumor. Langdon. 1995. 85.00 (*0-340-44794-X*, Pub. by E A) Routldge.

Malik: The History the Legend the Myth (the Story of Malcolm X) Maxine Sprott. (Illus.). 66p. (Orig.). (J). (gr. 5). 1991. pap. 8.00 (*0-9629982-9-X*) Vital Edits.

Malik & the Magnificent Glowing Light. Vincent L. Johnson. LC 97-92998. (Illus.). 32p. (J). (ps-3). 1997. pap. 7.95 (*0-9657033-0-4*) Marzetta Bks.

Maliki School of Law: Spread & Domination in North & West Africa, 8th-14th Centuries. Mansour H. Mansour. 197p. 1995. 64.95 (*1-880921-81-2*); pap. 44.95 (*1-880921-80-4*) Austin & Winfield.

Malikitisches Verfahrensrecht. Peter Scholz. XLVII, 598p. 1997. 95.95 (*3-631-32217-8*) P Lang Pubng.

Malim Sahib's Hindustani. C. T. Willson. (C). 1987. 50.00 (*0-85174-187-8*) St Mut.

Malina. Ingeborg Bachmann. Tr. by Philip Boehm from GER. LC 90-4953. (Modern German Voices Ser.). 256p. 1991. 27.50 (*0-8419-1192-4*) Holmes & Meier.

Malina. Ingeborg Bachmann. Tr. by Philip Boehm. (Portico Paperbacks Ser.). 1999. pap. 15.95 (*0-8419-1189-4*) Holmes & Meier.

Malinche in Mexican Literature: From History to Myth. Sandra M. Cypress. LC 91-15702. (Texas Pan American Ser.). (Illus.). 255p. (C). 1991. pap. 15.95 (*0-292-75134-6*); text 27.50 (*0-292-75131-1*) U of Tex Pr.

***Malinche's Conquest.** Anna Lanyon. 2000. pap. 14.95 (*1-86448-780-1*, Pub. by Allen & Unwin Pty) IPG Chicago.

Malinda Martha & Her Skipping Stones. Marcia Trimble. LC 98-94131. (Illus.). 32p. (J). (ps-3). 1999. 15.95 (*1-891577-72-7*); pap. 15.95 (*1-891577-73-5*) Images Press.

A pocketful of stones turns an ordinary day at the beach into an extraordinary day of self-discovery. Malinda Martha learns a new skill that outlasts her creations on the shifting sand at the edge of Nantucket Harbor. After the waves wash over her sandcastle & her sandfaces, she learns to skip stones. As the "skippin' stones spin shapes that shimmer" she experiences the joy that comes from making something happen for the first time...discovers her own ability to create that joy. In her lifelike, spirited watercolor paintings, Susi Grell sends the stones skimming across the water, enticing kids of all ages to "spin rings on the sea." A jingle & a touch of tongue twisting offer readers the fun of playing with words. Marcia Trimble introduces her favorite character, Malinda Martha, in MALINDA MARTHA & HER SKIPPING STONES. Says the author, "My daughter, Malinda & I spent many hours skipping stones at the beach on Nantucket Harbor so Malinda Martha very naturally skipped right into the pages of my book. It's an opportunity that came along to leave a legacy to my daughter. How could a writer pass that up?" To order: Images Press, tel: 650-948-8251, FAX: 650-941-6114. E-mail: Bugsmom2@aol.com. Also available for booksellers & libraries through Baker & Taylor, Ingram Books & Quality Books, Inc. & on the internet through amazon.com. *Publisher Paid Annotation.*

Malinda Martha Meets Mariposa: A Star Is Born. Marcia Trimble. LC 98-94132. (Illus.). 32p. (J). (gr. k-5). 1999. 15.95 (*1-891577-57-3*) Images Press.

A lot can happen in five weeks. A whole life cycle! Nature's miracle of metamorphosis! In MALINDA MARTHA MEETS MARIPOSA, Malinda Martha imagines this miracle of nature happening in her own backyard. When, on the first day back to school, Malinda Martha is faced with writing about her summer vacation, images of the sunflowers that she grew in her summer garden pop into her head & fall as a curtain of sunflower faces before her...whereupon a stage appears & she imagines herself producing & directing a show featuring the metamorphosis of a Monarch butterfly. What Malinda Martha really shares with the class is pleasantly open to the reader's imagination. John Lund brings together imagination & reality with his charming illustrations of Malinda Martha's theatrical production & his true-to-life images in the stages of the life cycle of the Monarch...subtly painted into a decorative border for children to find as they follow the continuous cycle of text & illustration. MALINDA MARTHA MEETS MARIPOSA offers children the enjoyment that comes from active learning...the chance to act out the life-cycle of the Monarch. To order: Images Press, tel: 650-948-8251, FAX: 650-941-6114. E-mail: Bugsmom2@aol.com. Also available for booksellers & libraries through Baker & Taylor, Ingram Books & Quality Books, Inc. & on the internet through amazon.com. *Publisher Paid Annotation.*

Malinda Martha Meets Mariposa: A Star Is Born. Marcia Trimble. LC 98-94132. (Illus.). 32p. (J). (gr. k-5). 2000. pap. 7.95 (*1-891577-58-1*) Images Press.

A lot can happen in five weeks. A whole life cycle! Nature's miracle of metamorphosis! In MALINDA MARTHA MEETS MARIPOSA, Malinda Martha imagines this miracle of nature happening in her own backyard. When, on the first day back to school, Malinda Martha is faced with writing about her summer vacation, images of the sunflowers that she grew in her summer garden pop into her head & fall as a curtain of sunflower faces before her...whereupon a stage appears & she imagines herself producing & directing a show featuring the metamorphosis of a Monarch butterfly. What Malinda Martha really shares with the class is pleasantly open to the reader's imagination. John Lund brings together imagination & reality with his charming illustrations of Malinda Martha's theatrical production & his true-to-life images in the stages of the life cycle of the Monarch...subtly painted into a decorative border for children to find as they follow the continuous cycle of text & illustration. MALINDA MARTHA MEETS MARIPOSA offers children the enjoyment that comes from active learning...the chance to act out the life-cycle of the Monarch. To order: Images Press, tel: 650-948-8251, FAX: 650-941-6114. E-mail: Bugsmom2@aol.com. Also available for booksellers & libraries through Baker & Taylor, Ingram Books & Quality Books, Inc. & on the internet through amazon.com. *Publisher Paid Annotation.*

Malingering & Deception in Adolescents: Assessing Credibility in Clinical & Forensic Settings. Joseph T. McCann. LC 97-37671. 243p. 1997. 34.95 (*1-55798-460-3*, 431-7990) Am Psychol.

Malinke, 14 vols. C. O. Nwanunibu. (Heritage Library of African Peoples). (Illus.). 64p. (YA). (gr. 7-12). 1996. lib. bdg. 16.95 (*0-8239-1979-X*) Rosen Group.

Malinois. Jan Kaldenbach. LC 97-910025. (Illus.). 128p. (Orig.). 1997. pap. write for info. (*1-55059-151-7*) Detselig Ents.

Malinowski among the Magi: The Natives of Mailu. Bronislaw Malinowski. Ed. by Michael Young. 250p. (C). 1988. lib. bdg. 57.50 (*0-415-00249-4*) Routledge.

Malinowski & the Work of Myth. Ivan Strenski. 228p. 1992. text 49.50 (*0-691-07414-3*, Pub. by Princeton U Pr); pap. text 16.95 (*0-691-02077-9*, Pub. by Princeton U Pr) Cal Prin Full Svc.

Malinowski in Mexico: The Economics of a Mexican Market System. Bronislaw Malinowski & Julio De La Fuente. Ed. by Susan Drucker-Brown. (International Library of Anthropology). 246p. 1985. pap. 13.95 (*0-7102-0584-8*, Routledge Thoemms) Routledge.

Malinowski, Rivers, Benedict, & Others: Essays on Culture & Personality, Vol. 4. George W. Stocking, Jr. LC 86-40061. (History of Anthropology Ser.: No. 4). (Illus.). 240p. 1997. pap. 18.95 (*0-299-10734-5*) U of Wis Pr.

Malinowskis Kiriwina: Fieldwork Photography 1915-1918. Michael W. Young. LC 98-23064. (Illus.). 312p. 1999. 40.00 (*0-226-87650-0*) U Ch Pr.

Malin's Clinical Diabetes. 2nd ed. Malcolm Nattrass. (Illus.). 432p. 1996. text 75.00 (*0-412-30860-6*, Pub. by E A) OUP.

***Maliy Bizness (puti K uspehu)** Valeriy Yusim. 1999. text. write for info. (*0-9673753-1-2*) Gelany.

Malkeh & Her Children: A Novel. Marjorie Edelson. 704p. (Orig.). 1992. pap. 12.00 (*0-345-37971-3*) Ballantine Pub Grp.

Malkin. Sophie Masson. LC 00-8079. (J). pap. write for info. (*0-88489-669-2*) St Marys.

Mall. Richie T. Cusick. Ed. by Patricia MacDonald. 224p. (Orig.). (YA). (gr. 7 up). 1992. mass mkt. 3.99 (*0-671-70958-5*, Archway) PB.

Mall. Gail W. Starr. Ed. by John Graves. (Orig.). 1980. pap. text 6.95 (*0-686-30560-4*) Envision Comm.

***Mall: A Novel.** Eric Bogosian. 256p. 2000. 22.50 (*0-684-85727-8*) S&S Trade.

Mall, Mayhem & Magic. Holly Lisle & Chris Guin. 1995. per. 5.99 (*0-671-87678-3*) Baen Bks.

Mall Naturalism & Criticism. 1976. pap. text 65.00 (*90-247-1739-6*) Kluwer Academic.

Mall of America: Reflections of a Virtual Community. Eric Nelson. LC 97-45765. 272p. 1998. pap. 14.95 (*1-880090-58-9*) Galde Pr.

Mall Purchase Night. Rick Cook. 352p. 1993. per. 4.99 (*0-671-72198-4*) Baen Bks.

Mall Rats: A Stick Foster Mystery. Kevin Robinson. 202p. 1992. 19.95 (*0-8027-3215-1*) Walker & Co.

Mall Time. Chaz Brenchley. 320p. 1992. text 24.95 (*0-340-52827-3*, Pub. by Hodder & Stought Ltd) Trafalgar.

Mall Walking in San Diego County. William Carroll. LC 90-86355. (Explore San Diego County Ser.). (Illus.). 144p. (Orig.). 1990. pap. 10.00 (*0-910390-31-2*) Coda Publications.

Mallaig Line Steam. Picton Publishing Staff. (Illus.). (C). 1987. 22.00 (*0-7855-2192-5*, Pub. by Picton) St Mut.

Mallal's Digest, 3. 4th rev. ed. Butterworth Staff. 805p. 1994. 400.00 (*0-409-99679-3*, MICHIE) LEXIS Pub.

Mallal's Digest, 5 vols., Vol. 1. 4th ed. 1990. 400.00 (*0-409-99589-4*, MICHIE) LEXIS Pub.

Mallal's Digest, 5 vols., Vol. 2. 4th ed. 1991. 400.00 (*0-409-99596-7*, MICHIE) LEXIS Pub.

Mallal's Digest, Vol. 2. 4th ed. Butterworth Staff. 1133p. 1994. write for info. (*0-409-99717-X*, MICHIE) LEXIS Pub.

Mallal's Digest, 5 vols., Vol. 3. 4th ed. 1991. 400.00 (*0-409-99603-3*, MICHIE) LEXIS Pub.

Mallal's Digest, 5 vols., Vol. 4. 4th ed. 1991. 400.00 (*0-409-99606-8*, MICHIE) LEXIS Pub.

Mallal's Digest, 5 vols., Vol. 5. 4th ed. 1991. 400.00 (*0-409-99610-6*, MICHIE) LEXIS Pub.

Mallal's Digest, Vol. 5. 4th ed. Ed. by Butterworth Staff. 703p. 1994. write for info. (*0-409-99716-1*, SI, MICHIE) LEXIS Pub.

Mallal's Digest Case & Legislation Citator, 1932 to 1991, 2 vols., Set. Butterworth Staff. 1994. write for info. (*0-409-99739-0*, ASIA, MICHIE) LEXIS Pub.

Mallal's Digest Case & Legislation Citator, 1932 to 1991: Case Citator. Butterworth Staff. 647p. 1994. write for info. (*0-409-99696-3*, ASIA, MICHIE) LEXIS Pub.

Mallal's Digest Case & Legislation Citator, 1932 to 1991: Legislation Citator. Butterworth Staff. 211p. 1994. write for info. (*0-409-99738-2*, ASIA, MICHIE) LEXIS Pub.

Mallal's Digest 1989. anniversary ed. Butterworths Editors. ix, 393p. 1992. suppl. ed. write for info. (*0-409-99626-2*, MICHIE) LEXIS Pub.

Mallal's Digest, 1990. 1991. 250.00 (*0-409-99604-1*, MICHIE) LEXIS Pub.

Mallal's Digest 1995. annuals 4th ed. Butterworths Editors. xliv, 632p. 1996. suppl. ed. write for info. (*0-409-99825-7*, MICHIE) LEXIS Pub.

Mallal's Digest 1991. annuals Butterworths Editors. ix, 539p. 1993. suppl. ed. write for info. (*0-409-99623-8*, MICHIE) LEXIS Pub.

An Asterisk (*) at the beginning of an entry indicates that the title is appearing for the first time.

Mallal's Digest, 1993. Ed. by Malayan Law Journal Staff. 1994. write for info. (0-409-99694-7, ASIA, MICHIE) LEXIS Pub.

Mallal's Digest 1993. anniversary ed. Butterworths Editors. ix, 578p. 1994. suppl. ed. write for info. (0-409-99711-0, MICHIE) LEXIS Pub.

Mallal's Digest 1992. annuals Butterworths Editors. ix, 543p. 1993. suppl. ed. write for info. (0-409-99647-5, MICHIE) LEXIS Pub.

Mallards: A Pictorial Study. Tricia Veasey. LC 87-62513. (Illus.). 128p. (Orig.). 1987. pap. 9.95 (0-88740-116-3) Schiffer.

Mallarme. Wallace Fowlie. LC 53-9931. (Illus.). 1962. pap. 2.45 (0-226-25881-5, P93) U Ch Pr.

Mallarme: La Lucidite et sa Face d'Ombre. Jean-Paul Sartre. (Gallimard Ser.). (FRE.). 171p. 1986. pap. 13.95 (2-07-070686-9) Schoenhof.

Mallarme: Poem in Prose. Stephen Ratcliffe. LC 98-60130. xii, 100p. 1998. pap. 12.95 (0-9655497-1-2) SB Review Pubns.

***Mallarme: The Poet & His Circle.** Rosemary Lloyd. LC 99-35644. 296p. 1999. 35.00 (0-8014-3662-1) Cornell U Pr.

Mallarme & the Sublime. Louis W. Marvick. LC 85-27750. (SUNY Series, Intersections). 211p. (C). 1986. text 64.50 (0-88706-278-4); pap. text 21.95 (0-88706-279-2) State U NY Pr.

Mallarme & the Symbolist Drama. Haskell M. Block. LC 63-9302. (Wayne State University Studies: Language & Literature: No. 14). 173p. reprint ed. pap. 49.40 (0-7837-3818-8, 2043638) Bks Demand.

Mallarme & the Symbolist Drama, No. 14. Language and Literature--14. Haskell M. Block. LC 77-9242. (Wayne State University Study of Language & Literature: No. 14). 164p. 1977. reprint ed. lib. bdg. 38.50 (0-8371-9706-6, BLMS, Greenwood Pr) Greenwood.

Mallarme in Italy: Literary Influence & Critical Response. Olga Ragusa. 1957. 15.00 (0-913298-34-4) S F Vanni.

***Mallarme in Prose.** Stephane Mallarme. Ed. & Tr. by Mary Ann Caws from FRE. Tr. by Jill Anderson et al from FRE. 2001. pap. 14.95 (0-8112-1451-6, Pub. by New Directions) Norton.

Mallarme in the Twentieth Century. Ed. by Robert G. Cohn & Gerald E. Gillespie. LC 98-2933. 304p. 1998. 43.50 (0-8386-3795-7) Fairleigh Dickinson.

Mallarme, or the Poet of Nothingness. Jean-Paul Sartre. Tr. & Intro. by Ernest Sturm. LC 86-43027. (FRE.). 182p. 1988. 25.00 (0-271-00498-3) Pa St U Pr.

Mallarme, or the Poet of Nothingness. Jean-Paul Sartre. Tr. & Intro. by Ernest Sturm. 150p. 1991. pap. 14.95 (0-271-00755-9) Pa St U Pr.

Mallarme par un des Siens. Edouard Dujardin. LC 77-10259. reprint ed. 39.50 (0-404-16314-9) AMS Pr.

***Mallarme's Children: Symbolism & the Renewal of Experience.** Richard C. Smith. LC 98-43751. 395p. 2000. 45.00 (0-520-21828-0, Pub. by U CA Pr) Cal Prin Full Svc.

Mallarme's Divagations: A Guide & Commentary. Robert G. Cohn. LC 89-13832. (American University Studies: Romance Languages & Literature: Ser. II, Vol. 144). X, 411p. (C). 1991. text 55.95 (0-8204-1313-5) P Lang Pubng.

Mallarme's "Divine Transportation" Real & Apparent Sources of Literary Value. Peter Dayan. (Oxford Modern Languages & Literature Monographs). 288p. 1987. 55.00 (0-19-815841-6) OUP.

Mallarme's Masterpiece: New Findings. Robert G. Cohn, Jr. (De Proprietatibus Litterarum, Ser. Practica: No. 1). 1966. pap. text 24.65 (90-279-0089-2) Mouton.

Mallarme's Masterwork. Cohn. (Coll. De Proprietatibus Litterarum, Series Practica). 22.50 (0-685-34939-X, F67500) Fr & Eur.

Mallarme's un Coup de Des: An Exegesis. Robert G. Cohn. LC 77-10256. reprint ed. 34.50 (0-404-16311-4) AMS Pr.

Mallcops, Ducks, & Fenderheads. Kevin Fagan. (Drabble Ser.). (Illus.). 128p. (J). 1998. pap. 9.95 (1-56163-216-3) NBM.

Malleable. unabridged ed. George Maguire. LC 96-90282. 250p. (Orig.). 1996. pap. 5.99 (0-9652611-0-7, Sound Fiction) Wee Howf.

Malleable Cast. Spencer Selby. (Chapbook Ser.). (Orig.). 1995. pap. text, per. 10.00 (0-945112-20-3) Generator Pr.

Malleable Matter/Stretchable Space: Interweaving Art, Math & Nature in N-Dimensions. Rochelle Newman. (Illus.). 400p. (C). 2000. text 53.95 (0-9614504-5-2) Pythagorean Pr.

Malled. Mary L. Deans. Ed. by Rosa M. Leonard. 180p. (Orig.). 1990. pap. 7.95 (0-9624388-1-2) Flatrock Bks.

Mallen Girl. Catherine Cookson. 288p. 1988. mass mkt. 6.99 (0-552-09896-5) Bantam.

Mallen Girl. large type ed. Catherine Cookson. LC 99-38129. (Thorndike Romance Ser.). 411p. 2000. 28.95 (0-7862-2140-2) Thorndike Pr.

Mallen Litter. Catherine Cookson. 320p. 1988. mass mkt. 6.99 (0-552-10151-6) Bantam.

Mallen Litter. Catherine Cookson. LC 99-38128. 2000. pap. 30.00 (0-7862-2139-9) Mac Lib Ref.

Mallen Streak. Catherine Cookson. 256p. 1984. mass mkt. 6.99 (0-552-09720-9) Bantam.

***Mallen Streak.** Catherine Cookson. (J). 2000. pap. 12.95 (0-552-14699-4) Transworld Publishers Ltd.

Mallen Streak. large type ed. Catherine Cookson. LC 99-16641. (Thorndike Romance Ser.). 1999. 27.95 (0-7862-2141-0) Thorndike Pr.

Mallet: John Mallet, the Huguenot, & His Descendants, 1694-1894. A. S. Mallett. 342p. 1992. reprint ed. pap. 43.00 (0-8328-2208-6); reprint ed. lib. bdg. 53.00 (0-8328-2207-8) Higginson Bk Co.

Mallet Control for the Xylophone. George L. Stone. (Illus.). 56p. 1998. pap. text 9.00 (1-892764-05-9) G B Stone.

***Mallet Duets for the Student & Teacher.** Karen E. Pershing. 40p. 1999. pap. 7.95 (0-7390-0531-6, 17325) Alfred Pub.

***Mallet Mayhem.** Voyce McGinley. 64p. 1999. pap. 9.95 (0-7866-0566-9, 95498) Mel Bay.

Mallets on the Mendocino Coast: Caspar Lumber Company, Railroads & Steamships. 3rd ed. Ted Wurm. (Illus.). 134p. 1999. reprint ed. 34.95 (0-9650213-4-3) TimberTimes.

***Mallett Millennium: Fine Antique Furniture & Works of Art.** Lanto Synge. (Illus.). 350p. 2000. 89.50 (1-85149-329-8) Antique Collect.

Malleus Maleficarum. Ed. & Tr. by Montague Summers. LC 68-57193. 323p. 1972. reprint ed. 30.95 (0-405-09016-1, Pub. by Blom Pubns) Ayer.

Malleus Maleficarum. Montague Summers. 278p. 1971. reprint ed. pap. 12.95 (0-486-22802-9) Dover.

Malleus Maleficarum: Heinrich Kramer & James Sprenger. Heinrich Kramer & James Sprenger. Tr. by Montague Summers. 1990. 25.75 (0-8446-0169-1) Peter Smith.

Malleus Maleficarum, 1487: (With Bulle & Approbatio) Heinrich Kramer. (Rechtsgeschichte, Zivilisationsprozess, Psychohistorie - Quellen und Studien Ser.: Bd. 1). (GER.). 314p. 1992. lib. bdg. write for info. (3-487-09379-0) G Olms Pubs.

Malliavin Calculus & Related Topics. David Nualart. LC 94-48195. (Probability & Its Applications Ser.). 1995. 54.95 (0-387-94432-X) Spr-Verlag.

Malliavin Calculus for Processes with Jumps. K. Bichteler et al. (Stochastics Monographs: Theory & Applications of Stochastic Processes: Vol. 2). x, 158p. 1987. text 101.00 (2-88124-185-9) Gordon & Breach.

Mallinckrodt E. H. & S. Reference Manual. Date not set. ring bd. write for info. (0-88061-177-4) Intl Loss Cntrl.

Mallinckrodt E. H. & S. Working Copy. Date not set. spiral bd. write for info. (0-88061-178-2) Intl Loss Cntrl.

Mallinckrodt 125th Anniversary Publication. History Factory Staff. (Illus.). 150p. (Orig.). 1992. write for info. (1-882771-00-1) Hist Factory.

Mallinckrodt Small Site E. H. & S. Working Copy. Date not set. write for info. (0-88061-179-0) Intl Loss Cntrl.

***Mallinford.** Love. 2000. pap. 12.95 (0-552-99771-4, Pub. by Transworld Publishers Ltd) Trafalgar.

Mallion's Pride. large type ed. Carola Salisbury. 1977. 12.00 (0-85456-528-0) Ulverscroft.

Mallorca. (Arte & Arquitectura Ser.). (Illus.). 440p. 2000. 29.95 (3-8290-2598-X, 540584) Konemann.

Mallorca. David Hewson. LC 90-202847. (Travels in Spain Ser.). 1990. pap. write for info. (1-85391-035-X) Sterling.

Mallorca. Insight Guides Staff. (Insight Guides). 1998. pap. text 7.95 (0-88729-543-6) Langenscheidt.

***Mallorca.** Insight Guides Staff. 1999. pap. 12.95 (0-88729-499-5) Langenscheidt.

***Mallorca.** Konemann Inc. Staff. (Illus.). 504p. 2000. 19.95 (3-8290-2597-1) Konemann.

Mallorca. Nigel Tisdall. (Illustrated Travel Guides from Thomas Cook Ser.). (Illus.). 192p. (Orig.). 1994. pap. 12.95 (0-8442-9091-2, Passprt Bks) NTC Contemp Pub Co.

Mallorca. 2nd ed. (Insight Guides Ser.). (Illus.). 1999. pap. 21.95 (0-88729-181-3) Langenscheidt.

Mallorca & Menorca. 2nd ed. Rough Guides Staff. 304p. 1999. pap. 16.95 (1-85828-408-2, Pub. by Rough Guides) Penguin Putnam.

Mallorca & Menorca: Globetrotter Travel Guide. Globetrotter Staff. (Illus.). 128p. 1997. pap. 17.95 (1-85368-428-7, Pub. by New5 Holland) Globe Pequot.

***Mallorca & Menorca Pocket Guide.** Berlitz Editors. (Illus.). 192p. 2000. pap. 8.95 (2-8315-7168-5) Berlitz.

Mallorcan Affair. large type ed. Priscilla Page. (Linford Romance Library). 256p. 1993. pap. 16.99 (0-7089-7472-4, Linford) Ulverscroft.

Mallords & Their Neighbors. Neil W. Northey. (Illus.). 181p. 1998. pap. 6.95 (1-881545-82-2) Angelas Bkshelf.

Malloreon: Guardians of the West, King of the Murgos, Demon Lord of Karanda, Sorceress of Darshiva, & Seeress of Kell, Set. D. Eddings. 1992. mass mkt., boxed set 29.87 (0-345-37988-8) Ballantine Pub Grp.

Mallory & McCall's Irish Pub Songbook. Janna M. Geller & Mallory Geller. 136p. 1998. pap. 17.95 (0-7866-3369-7, 97047) Mel Bay.

Mallory & the Dream Horse. Ann M. Martin. LC 94-135668. (Baby-Sitters Club Ser.: No. 54). 192p. (J). (gr. 3-7). 1992. pap. 3.25 (0-590-44965-6) Scholastic Inc.

Mallory & the Dream Horse. Ann M. Martin. (Baby-Sitters Club Ser.: No. 54). (J). 1992. 8.35 (0-606-01896-4, Pub. by Turtleback) Demco.

Mallory & the Ghost Cat. Ann M. Martin. (Baby-Sitters Club Mystery Ser.: No. 3). 160p. (J). 1992. pap. 3.25 (0-590-44799-8) Scholastic Inc.

Mallory & the Ghost Cat. Ann M. Martin. (Baby-Sitters Club Mystery Ser.: No. 3). (J). 1992. 8.35 (0-606-02501-4, Pub. by Turtleback) Demco.

Mallory & the Mystery Diary. Ann M. Martin. (Baby-Sitters Club Ser.: No. 29). (gr. 3-7). 1989. pap. 3.99 (0-590-67397-1) Scholastic Inc.

Mallory & the Mystery Diary. Ann M. Martin. (Baby-Sitters Club Ser.: No. 29). 192p. (J). (gr. 4-6). 1989. pap. 3.50 (0-590-42500-5, Apple Paperbacks) Scholastic Inc.

Mallory & the Mystery Diary. Ann M. Martin. (Baby-Sitters Club Ser.: No. 29). (J). 1989. 9.09 (0-606-01845-X, Pub. by Turtleback) Demco.

Mallory & the Trouble with Twins. Ann M. Martin. (Baby-Sitters Club Ser.: No. 21). (J). 1989. pap. 3.50 (0-590-43507-8) Scholastic Inc.

Mallory & the Trouble with Twins. Ann M. Martin. (Baby-Sitters Club Ser.: No. 21). (J). (gr. 3-7). 1997. pap. text 3.99 (0-590-67389-0) Scholastic Inc.

Mallory & the Trouble with Twins. Ann M. Martin. (Baby-Sitters Club Ser.: No. 21). (J). 1989. 9.09 (0-606-04089-7, Pub. by Turtleback) Demco.

Mallory Hates Boys (& Gym) Ann M. Martin. (Baby-Sitters Club Ser.: No. 59). 192p. (J). (gr. 4-6). 1992. 3.50 (0-590-45660-1) Scholastic Inc.

Mallory Keep. Aileen Armitage. 288p. 1998. 24.00 (0-7278-5308-2) Severn Hse.

Mallory on Strike. Ann M. Martin. LC 96-15686. (Baby-Sitters Club Ser.: No. 47). 144p. (J). (gr. 4 up). 1996. lib. bdg. 21.27 (0-8368-1571-8) Gareth Stevens Inc.

Mallory on Strike. Ann M. Martin. (Baby-Sitters Club Ser.: No. 47). 192p. (J). (gr. 4-6). 1991. pap. 3.25 (0-590-44971-0) Scholastic Inc.

Mallory on Strike. Ann M. Martin. (Baby-Sitters Club Ser.: No. 47). (J). 1991. 8.35 (0-606-00586-2, Pub. by Turtleback) Demco.

Mallory Pike, #1 Fan. Ann M. Martin. (Baby-Sitters Club Ser.: No. 80). 192p. (J). (gr. 3-7). 1994. pap. 3.99 (0-590-48224-6) Scholastic Inc.

Mallory Pike, #1 Fan. Ann M. Martin. (Baby-Sitters Club Ser.: No. 80). (J). 1994. 9.09 (0-606-06920-8, Pub. by Turtleback) Demco.

Mallory y El Gato Fantasma. Ann M. Martin. 1995. 15.05 (0-606-10396-1, Pub. by Turtleback) Demco.

Mallory's Christmas Wish. Ann M. Martin. (Baby-Sitters Club Ser.: No. 92). (J). 1995. pap. 3.50 (0-590-22876-5) Scholastic Inc.

Mallory's Christmas Wish. Ann M. Martin. (Baby-Sitters Club Ser.: No. 92). (J). 1995. 8.60 (0-606-08481-9, Pub. by Turtleback) Demco.

Mallory's Moving & Her Monkey Is Missing. Bill Fried. (Illus.). 24p. (J). (ps-3). 1995. reprint ed. mass mkt. 5.95 (0-9645463-0-2) ECV.

Mallorys of Mystic: Six Generations in American Maritime Enterprise. James P. Baughman. LC 70-184363. (American Maritime Library: No. 4). (Illus.). 549p. reprint ed. pap. 170.20 (0-7837-6147-3, 204454800009) Bks Demand.

Mallory's Oracle. Carol O'Connell. 329p. 1995. mass mkt. 5.99 (0-515-11647-5, Jove) Berkley Pub.

Mallory's Oracle. large type ed. Carol O'Connell. LC 95-21030. 330p. 1995. lib. bdg. 23.95 (1-57490-024-2, Beeler LP Bks) T T Beeler.

Mallos, Megarsos, Antioche du Pyramos. F. W. Imhoof-Blumer. (FRE.). 37p. 1979. reprint ed. pap. 5.00 (0-916710-58-0) Obol Intl.

Malloy: Treaties, Conventions, International Acts, Protocols & Agreements Between the United States & Other Powers. 800.00 (1-57588-394-5) W S Hein.

Malloy's GMDSS: A Technical Approach. E. Michael Malloy. Ed. by Jane Johnson. (Illus.). 300p. 1995. spiral bd. write for info. (0-9673944-0-6) Malloy Comm.

Malloy's Sports Collectibles Value Guide. Roderick A. Malloy. LC 92-50673. (Illus.). 448p. 1993. pap. 17.95 (0-87069-689-0, Wllce-Homestd) Krause Pubns.

***Malls: The Sound of "M"** Cynthia Fitterer Klingel & Peg Ballard. LC 99-20957. (Wonder Books Ser.). (Illus.). 24p. (J). 1999. lib. bdg. 21.41 (1-56766-686-8) Childs World.

Mallwalker Wisdom: It's Good for Your Heart. Nancy H. Phillips. LC 97-94494. 240p. 1997. pap. 7.95 (0-9660466-1-7) A&R Assocs.

Malmedy Trial: A Report Based on Documents & Personal Experiences. 2nd ed. Dietrich Ziemssen. (World War II Monograph Ser.: Vol. 105). (Illus.). 48p. 1998. pap. 12.95 (1-57638-116-1, M105) Merriam Pr.

***Malmedy Trial: A Report Based on Documents & Personal Experiences.** 2nd rev. ed. Dietrich Ziemssen. (World War II Historical Society Monograph Ser.: Vol. 105). (Illus.). 48p. 1998. 22.95 (1-57638-117-X, M105) Merriam Pr.

Malmond. Ivan Laszlo. LC 94-78724. 216p. (Orig.). 1995. pap. 12.95 (1-882897-00-5) Lost Coast.

Malmsteen Yngwie Odyssey Tab: Guitar Personality Book. (Orig.). 1997. pap. 27.95 (0-7692-0570-4, 00660001) Wrner Bros.

Malmsteen Yngwie Trilogy Tab: Guitar Personality Book. (Orig.). 1997. pap. 27.95 (0-7692-0572-0, 00694757) Wrner Bros.

Malnourished Child. Ed. by Robert M. Suskind & Leslie Lewinter-Suskind. LC 89-70284. (Nestle Nutrition Workshop Ser.: No. 19). (Illus.). 431p. 1990. reprint ed. pap. 133.70 (0-608-05882-3, 205984800007) Bks Demand.

Malnourished Children of the Rural Poor: The Web of Food, Health, Education, Fertility, & Agricultural Production. Judith Balderston et al. LC 81-3483. 223p. 1981. 24.95 (0-86569-071-5, Auburn Hse) Greenwood.

Malnutrition - A Problem of Industrial Societies? Ed. by J. C. Somogyi. (Bibliotheca Nutritio et Dieta Ser.: No. 42). (Illus.). x, 118p. 1988. 100.00 (3-8055-4811-7) S Karger.

Malnutrition & Poverty: Magnitude & Policy Options. Shlomo Reutlinger & Marcelo Selowsky. LC 76-17240. (World Bank Staff Occasional Papers: No. 23). 96p. reprint ed. pap. 30.00 (0-7837-5384-5, 204514800005) Bks Demand.

Malnutrition & the Infantile Brain. Irene Sjogren et al. 63p. 1972. write for info. (91-7106-056-1, Pub. by Nordic Africa) Transaction Pubs.

Malnutrition, Environment, & Behavior: New Perspectives. David A. Levitsky. LC 78-58016. (Illus.). 299p. reprint ed. pap. 92.70 (0-608-08540-5, 206906300002) Bks Demand.

***Malnutrition in the Elderly.** Ed. by O. Seiler & H. B. Staehelin. 140p. 1999. 45.00 (3-7985-1166-7, Pub. by D Steinkopff) Spr-Verlag.

Malnutrition in the Elderly: A National Crisis. 1997. lib. bdg. 250.95 (0-8490-8207-2) Gordon Pr.

Malnutrition in the Elderly: A National Crisis: A Focus on the Problems, Causes, Consequences, & Solutions. Kathy Cope. (Illus.). 77p. 1998. pap. text 20.00 (0-7881-4814-1) DIANE Pub.

Malnutrition in the Elderly, a National Crisis. Kathy Cope. 95p. 1996. pap. 9.00 (0-16-061595-X) USGPO.

Malo Tupou: An Oral History. Tupou P. Fanua & Lois W. Webster. (Illus.). 200p. 1997. pap. text 25.00 (0-908597-26-6) UH Pr.

Malocclusion & the Periodontium. Ed. by James A. McNamara, Jr. & Katherine A. Ribbens. LC RK0523.. (Craniofacial Growth Monographs: No. 15). (Illus.). 280p. reprint ed. pap. 86.80 (0-8357-8667-6, 205231000091) Bks Demand.

Maloche - Nicht Mildtatigkeit. Ludger Heid. (Haskala - Wissenschaftliche Abhandlungen Ser.: Vol. 12). (GER.). 648p. 1995. write for info. (3-487-09975-6) G Olms Pubs.

Malolos: The Crisis of the Republic. Teodoro A. Agoncillo. LC 97-947310. xviii, 700 p. 1997. write for info. (971-542-096-6) U of Philippines Pr.

Malone: Jeremiah Dumas Malone, a Genealogical Outline. E. E. Malone. (Illus.). 159p. 1993. reprint ed. pap. 25.00 (0-8328-3714-8); reprint ed. lib. bdg. 35.00 (0-8328-3713-X) Higginson Bk Co.

Malone Meurt. Samuel Beckett. (FRE.). 208p. 1947. write for info. (0-318-72557-6) Fr & Eur.

Malone Meurt. Samuel Beckett. (FRE.). 224p. 1951. pap. 28.95 (0-7859-0922-2, F86041) Fr & Eur.

Malone Society Collections, Vol. I, Pt. III. (Malone Society Ser.). (Illus.). 79p. (C). 1965. text 59.00 (0-19-729004-3) OUP.

Malone Society Collections, Vol. IV. (Malone Society Ser.). (Illus.). 79p. 1956. text 59.00 (0-19-729008-6) OUP.

Malone Society Collections, Vol. V. (Malone Society Ser.). (Illus.). 110p. 1959. text 59.00 (0-19-729009-4) OUP.

Malone Society Collections, Vol. IX. (Malone Society Ser.). (Illus.). 79p. 1971. text 59.00 (0-19-729012-4) OUP.

Malone Society Collections: Jacobean & Caroline Revels Accounts, 1603-1642, Vol. 13. Ed. by W. L. Streitberg. (Malone Society Ser.). 224p. 1986. 55.00 (0-19-729023-X) OUP.

Malone Society Collections Vol. 10: The Dramatic Records in the Declared Accounts of the Office of Works, 1560-1640, Vol. 10. Ed. by F. P. Wilson. (Malone Society Ser.). 83p. 1975. text 55.00 (0-19-729013-2) OUP.

Malone Society Collections Vol. 14: Jacobean Academic Plays. Ed. by Susanne Gossett & Thomas L. Berger. (Malone Society Ser.). (Illus.). 156p. 1988. text 65.00 (0-19-729025-6) OUP.

Malone's of Glendine, County Clare Ireland Cookbook. John S. Malone. 1999. pap. 25.00 (0-9657105-2-1) J S Malone.

Maloney's Antiques & Collectibles Resource Directory. 5th ed. David J. Maloney, Jr. 672p. 1999. pap. 29.95 (1-58221-016-0) Krause Pubns.

Maloof: The Ghassani Legacy. George H. Malouf. (Illus.). 608p. 1992. text 150.00 (0-9632681-0-4) Malouf Prods.

Malory. Marylyn Parins. (Critical Heritage Ser.). 420p. 1988. text 75.00 (0-415-00223-0) Routledge.

Malory. Eugene Vinaver. (BCL1-PR English Literature Ser.). 208p. 1992. reprint ed. lib. bdg. 79.00 (0-7812-7188-6) Rprt Serv.

Malory: Style & Vision in La Morte d'Arthur. Mark Lambert. LC 74-29727. (Yale Studies in English: No. 186). 241p. reprint ed. pap. 74.80 (0-8357-8213-1, 203379300087) Bks Demand.

Malory: Text & Sources. P. J. Field. LC 98-38487. (Arthurian Studies). 328p. 1998. 90.00 (0-85991-536-0) Boydell & Brewer.

Malory Works. 2nd ed. Thomas Malory. Ed. by Eugene Vinaver. (Oxford Standard Authors Ser.). 828p. 1977. pap. text 25.95 (0-19-281217-3) OUP.

Malory's Book of Arms: The Narrative of Combat in Le Morte D'Arthur. Andrew Lynch. LC 96-47724. (Arthurian Studies: Vol. 39). 192p. 1997. 60.00 (0-85991-511-5) Boydell & Brewer.

Malory's Grail Quest: Invention & Adaptation in Medieval Prose Romance. Sandra N. Ihle. LC 82-70554. (Illus.). 213p. 1983. reprint ed. pap. 66.10 (0-608-07447-0, 206767400009) Bks Demand.

***Malory's Grail Seekers & Fifteenth-Century English Hagiography.** Alfred Robert Kraemer. LC 98-18008. (Studies in the Humanities: Vol. 44). 129p. (C). 1999. text 40.95 (0-8204-4123-6) P Lang Pubng.

Malory's Le Morte D'Arthur: King Arthur & the Legends of the Round Table. Keith Baines. (J). 1962. 13.09 (0-606-03433-1, Pub. by Turtleback) Demco.

Malory's Morte D'Arthur: Remarking Arthurian Tradition. Catherine Battistone. text. write for info. (0-312-22998-4) St Martin.

Malory's Originality: A Critical Study of Le Morte D'Arthur. Robert M. Lumiansky. LC 78-19255. 1979. 28.95 (0-405-10612-2) Ayer.

***Malos Presagios.** Gunter Grass. 267p. 1999. pap. 17.95 (84-204-2697-0) Santillana.

Malpais Gold. H. Glenn Carson. (Illus.). 148p. 1978. pap. 3.50 (0-941620-09-3) Carson Ent.

Malpais, Mt. Taylor & Zuni Mountains: A Hiking Guide & History. S. Robinson. LC 94-18694. (Coyote Bks.). (Illus.). 276p. 1994. pap. 13.95 (0-8263-1527-5) U of NM Pr.

Malparto: A Book for Parents Experiencing a Miscarriage. Joy Johnson & Marv Johnson. (SPA., Illus.). 24p. 1981. pap. text 3.50 (1-56123-058-8, MALC) Centering Corp.

Malpighiaceae of India. R. C. Srivastava. (C). 1993. 175.00 (81-7136-011-4, Pub. by Periodical Expert) St Mut.

Malpractice: A Trial Lawyer's Advice for Physicians. Walter G. Alton, Jr. 1977. 21.50 (0-316-03500-9, Little Brwn Med Div) Lppncott W & W.

M

An Asterisk (*) at the beginning of an entry indicates that the title is appearing for the first time.

Malpractice: What They Don't Teach You in Dental School. Jeffrey J. Tonner. LC 95-39879. 1995. 69.95 (*0-87814-460-9*) PennWell Bks.

Malpractice & Contact Lenses. 2nd ed. Harvey M. Rosenwasser. (Illus.). 136p. 1991. text 42.00 (*0-7506-9192-1*) Buttrwrth-Heinemann.

Malpractice & Contact Lenses: A Guide to Limiting Liability in Contact Lens Practice. Harvey M. Rosenwasser. 96p. (Orig.). (C). 1988. pap. 15.00 (*0-9620349-0-8*) Gillman-Marcuse.

Malpractice & Liability in Clinical Obstetrical Nursing. Sara D. Cohn. LC 89-18588. (Aspen Ser. in Obstetrical & Gynecological Nursing). 244p. 1990. pap. 72.00 (*0-8342-0141-0*, 20141) Aspen Pub.

Malpractice Epidemic: A Layman's Guide to Medical Malpractice. Bernard L. Remakus. Ed. by Cara O'Donnell. LC 89-17582. 1990. 22.95 (*0-87949-295-3*) Ashley Bks.

Malpractice in Health Occupations: Index of New Information. Gerald D. MacFarland. 150p. 1994. 47.50 (*0-7883-0050-4*); pap. 44.50 (*0-7883-0051-2*) ABBE Pubs Assn.

Malpractice in the Emergency Room, 1992. (Litigation & Administrative Practice Course Handbook, 1983-84 Ser.). 185p. 1992. pap. 35.00 (*0-685-69464-X*) PLI.

Malpractice Issues in Librarianship. 85p. 1992. 27.00 (*0-87111-397-X*) SLA.

Malpractice Issues in Radiology. Leonard Berlin et al. LC 98-6639. (Illus.). 154p. 1998. write for info. (*1-890705-00-4*) Am Roentgen.

Malpractice Liability in the Business Professions: A Survey Guide for Attorneys & Clients. Warren Freedman. LC 94-38535. 304p. 1995. 89.50 (*0-89930-874-0*, Quorum Bks) Greenwood.

Malpractice Liability in the Helping & Healing Professions: A Survey Guide for Attorneys & Clients. Warren Freedman. LC 94-40461. 280p. 1995. 72.95 (*0-89930-908-9*, Quorum Bks) Greenwood.

Malpractice Prevention & Liability Control for Hospitals. James E. Orlikoff & William R. Fifer. LC 85-4063. vii, 146p. 1981. 24.75 (*0-939450-62-3*) AHPI.

Malpractice Risk Management in Psychiatry: A Comprehensive Guide. Frederic F. Flach. LC 97-36799. (Hatherleigh CME Bk.). 384p. 1998. pap. 39.95 (*1-57826-013-2*, Pub. by Hatherleigh) Norton.

Malpractice Suit: A Survival Guide for Physicians & their Families. Ed. by Graham Chedd et al. 123p. 1989. 295.00 incl. VHS (*0-9624044-0-3*) Eidetics.

Malraux: An Essay in Political Criticism. David O. Wilkinson. LC 67-22875. 240p. reprint ed. pap. 74.40 (*0-7837-4466-8*, 204417400001) Bks Demand.

Malraux, Sartre, & Aragon As Political Novelists. Catharine S. Brosman. LC 65-63876. (University of Florida Humanities Monographs: No. 17). 71p. reprint ed. pap. 30.00 (*0-7837-5829-4*, 204554800006) Bks Demand.

Malraux, the Absolute Agnostic: or Metamorphosis As Universal Law. Claude Tannery. Tr. by Teresa L. Fagan. 3385p. 1991. 43.50 (*0-226-78962-4*) U Ch Pr.

Malstria - Malena: Medals & Motifs in Etruscan Mirror Craft. Ingela M. Wiman. (Studies in Mediterranean Archaeology: Vol. XCI). (Illus.). 263p. (Orig.). 1990. pap. 125.00 (*91-7081-018-4*, Pub. by P Astroms) Coronet Bks.

***Malt Whisky.** Helen Arthur. (Evergreens Ser.). 1998. 16.99 (*3-8228-7572-4*) Benedikt Taschen.

Malt Whisky. Charles Maclean. (Illus.). 176p. 1997. 40.00 (*1-85732-683-0*, Pub. by Millers Pubns) Antique Collect.

Malt Whisky Almanac. 6th rev. ed. Wallace Milroy. (Illus.). 160p. 1996. 14.95 (*1-897784-26-0*, Pub. by N Wilson Pubng) Interlink Pub.

***Malt Whisky Cellar Book.** Neil Wilson. 2000. 22.95 (*1-897784-56-2*, Pub. by N Wilson Pubng) Interlink Pub.

Malt Whisky File. 2nd ed. John Lamond & Robin Tucek. LC 98-123552. (Illus.). 256p. 1998. 24.95 (*1-55821-669-3*) Lyons Pr.

Malt Whisky File: The Connoisseur's Guide to Malt Whiskies & Distilleries. John Lamond & Robin Tucek. (Illus.). 225p. 1997. 19.95 (*0-932664-93-8*, 6830) Wine Appreciation.

Malta. Roger Balm. LC 95-42380. (American Geographical Society Around the World Program Ser.). 1996. 18.95 (*0-939923-58-0*); pap. 13.95 (*0-939923-57-2*) M & W Pub Co.

***Malta.** Ed. by Berlitz Publishing Staff. (Pocket Guides Ser.). (Illus.). 2001. pap. 8.95 (*2-8315-7701-2*) Berlitz.

Malta. Susie Boulton. (Illustrated Travel Guides from Thomas Cook Ser.). (Illus.). 192p. 1994. pap. 12.95 (*0-8442-9069-6*, Passprt Bks) NTC Contemp Pub Co.

Malta. Insight Guides Staff. (Insight Guides). 1998. pap. text 7.95 (*0-88729-544-4*) Langenscheidt.

Malta. Michelin Staff. 1999. pap. text 9.95 (*2-06-652601-0*) Michelin.

Malta. Ruth Weed Roerig. (Images of America Ser.). 1997. pap. 16.99 (*0-7524-0972-7*) Arcadia Publng.

Malta. John R. Thackrah. (World Bibliographical Ser.: No. 64). 163p. 1985. lib. bdg. 50.00 (*1-85109-007-X*) ABC-CLIO.

Malta. 2nd ed. (Insight Guides Ser.). (Illus.). 1999. pap. 21.95 (*0-88729-177-5*) Langenscheidt.

Malta. 2nd ed. Susie Boulton. (Passport's Illustrated Travel Guides Ser.). (Illus.). 192p. 1998. pap. 14.95 (*0-8442-4824-X*, 4824X, Passprt Bks) NTC Contemp Pub Co.

***Malta.** 2nd ed. Leo Braack. (Globetrotter Travel Guides Ser.). (Illus.). 2001. pap. 10.95 (*1-85974-594-6*) New5 Holland.

***Malta.** 2nd ed. Ed. by New Holland Publishing Staff. (Globetrotter Travel Packs Ser.). (Illus.). 2001. pap. 14.95 (*1-85974-596-2*) New5 Holland.

Malta. 2nd rev. ed. David M. Boswell & Brian W. Beeley. 304p. 1998. lib. bdg. 79.00 (*1-85109-269-2*) ABC-CLIO.

***Malta, 6 vols. , Set.** Sean Sheehan. LC 99-53436. (Cultures of the World Ser.: Vol. 20). (Illus.). 128p. (YA). (gr. 4-7). 2000. lib. bdg. 35.64 (*0-7614-0993-9*) Marshall Cavendish.

***Malta: A Country Study Guide.** Global Investment & Business Center, Inc. Staff. (World Country Study Guides Library: Vol. 108). (Illus.). 350p. 2000. pap. 59.00 (*0-7397-2406-1*) Intl Business Pubns.

Malta: Globetrotter Travel Guide. Globetrotter Staff. (Illus.). 128p. 1996. pap. text 17.95 (*1-85368-431-7*, Pub. by New5 Holland) Globe Pequot.

Malta: The Spitfire Year, 1942. Christopher Shores et al. (Illus.). 500p. 1991. 55.00 (*0-948817-16-X*, Pub. by Grub St) Seven Hills Bk.

Malta - A Country Study Guide: Basic Information for Research & Pleasure. Global Investment Center, USA Staff. (World Country Study Guide Library: Vol. 108). (Illus.). 350p. 1999. pap. 59.00 (*0-7397-1505-4*) Intl Business Pubns.

***Malta & Gozo.** 2nd ed. (Illus.). 2000. per. 8.95 (*1-85368-967-X*) New5 Holland.

***Malta & Gozo.** 3rd ed. Susie Boulton. (Illustrated Travel Guides Ser.). (Illus.). 2000. pap. 14.95 (*0-658-00507-3*, Passprt Bks) NTC Contemp Pub Co.

Malta & Gozo. 4th ed. Peter M. Eadie. (Blue Guide Ser.). (Illus.). 160p. 1995. pap. 16.95 (*0-393-31272-0*, Norton Paperbks) Norton.

Malta & the Maltese: A Study in Nineteenth Century Migration. Charles A. Price. LC 77-87724. reprint ed. 32.50 (*0-404-16516-8*) AMS Pr.

Malta, Britain, & the European Powers, 1793-1815. Desmond Gregory. LC 95-12552. (Illus.). 368p. 1995. 55.00 (*0-8386-3590-3*) Fairleigh Dickinson.

Malta Business & Investment Opportunities Yearbook-98: Business, Investment, Export-Import. Contrib. by Russian Information & Business Center, Inc. Staff. (Business & Investment Opportunity Library-98). (Illus.). 350p. 1998. pap. 99.00 (*1-57751-961-2*) Intl Business Pubns.

***Malta Business Intelligence Report, 190 vols.** Global Investment & Business Center, Inc. Staff. (World Business Intelligence Library: Vol. 108). (Illus.). 350p. 2000. pap. 99.95 (*0-7397-2606-4*) Intl Business Pubns.

***Malta Business Law Handbook, 190 vols.** Global Investment & Business Center, Inc. Staff. (Global Business Law Handbooks Library: Vol. 108). (Illus.). 350p. 2000. pap. 99.95 (*0-7397-2006-6*) Intl Business Pubns.

***Malta Business Opportunity Yearbook.** Global Investment & Business Center, Inc. Staff. (Global Business Opportunity Yearbooks Library: Vol. 108). (Illus.). 2000. pap. 99.95 (*0-7397-2206-9*) Intl Business Pubns.

***Malta Business Opportunity Yearbook: Export-Import, Investment & Business Opportunities.** International Business Publications, U. S. A. Staff & Global Investment Center, U. S. A. Staff. (Global Business Opportunity Yearbooks Library: Vol. 108). (Illus.). 350p. 1999. pap. 99.95 (*0-7397-1306-X*) Intl Business Pubns.

***Malta Concerto: The History of Malta.** Michael J. Kearney. Ed. by Laurel Strand. (Illus.). 960p. 2000. pap. 48.00 (*0-944958-47-8*, Pub. by Elfin Cove Pr) Koen Pacific.

***Malta Convoys.** David A. Thomas. 2000. 36.95 (*0-85052-663-9*, Pub. by Pen & Sword) Combined Pub.

***Malta Country Review 2000.** Robert C. Kelly et al. (Illus.). 60p. 1999. pap. 39.95 (*1-58310-532-8*) CountryWatch.

Malta, 1565. Tim Pickles. (Campaign Ser.: No. 50). (Illus.). 96p. 1998. pap. 16.95 (*1-85532-603-5*, Pub. by Osprey) Stackpole.

***Malta Foreign Policy & Government Guide.** Contrib. by Global Investment & Business Center, Inc. Staff. (World Foreign Policy & Government Library: Vol. 104). (Illus.). 350p. 1999. pap. 99.00 (*0-7397-3602-7*) Intl Business Pubns.

***Malta Foreign Policy & Government Guide.** Global Investment & Business Center, Inc. Staff. (World Foreign Policy & Government Library: Vol. 104). (Illus.). 350p. 2000. pap. 99.95 (*0-7397-3806-2*) Intl Business Pubns.

***Malta Investment & Business Guide.** Global Investment & Business Center, Inc. Staff. (Global Investment & Business Guide Library: Vol. 108). (Illus.). 2000. pap. 99.95 (*0-7397-1806-1*) Intl Business Pubns.

Malta Investment & Business Guide: Economy, Export-Import, Business & Investment Climate, Business Contacts. Contrib. by Russian Information & Business Center, Inc. Staff. (Russia, NIS & Emerging Markets Investment & Business Library-98). (Illus.). 350p. 1998. pap. 99.00 (*1-57751-927-2*) Intl Business Pubns.

***Malta Investment & Business Guide: Export-Import, Investment & Business Opportunities.** International Business Publications, USA Staff & Global Investment Center, USA Staff. (World Investment & Business Guide Library-99: Vol. 108). (Illus.). 350p. 1999. pap. 99.95 (*0-7397-0303-X*) Intl Business Pubns.

Malta of the Knights. Elizabeth W. Schermerhorn. LC 76-29838. reprint ed. 57.50 (*0-404-15429-8*) AMS Pr.

Malta on the Brink: From Western Democracy to Libyan Satellite. Enzo Rossi. (C). 1986. 35.00 (*0-907967-79-5*, Pub. by Inst Euro Def & Strat) St Mut.

Malta Pocket Guide, 1998. rev. ed. Berlitz Editors. (Pocket Guides Ser.). (Illus.). 136p. 1998. pap. 8.95 (*2-8315-6313-5*) Berlitz.

***Malta Tax Guide.** Global Investment & Business Center, Inc. Staff. (World Tax Guide Library: Vol. 18). (Illus.). 350p. 1999. pap. 99.00 (*0-7397-0192-4*) Intl Business Pubns.

***Malta with Map.** Globetrotter Staff. (Illus.). 128p. 1999. pap. 14.95 (*1-85974-126-6*) New5 Holland.

Malta 1565, 50. Osprey Staff. 1999. pap. text 17.95 (*1-85532-830-5*) Osprey.

Malta's Ancient Temples & Ruts. Rowland Parker & Michael Rubinstein. (Institute for Cultural Research Monograph: No. 26). (Illus.). 70p. (Orig.). 1988. pap. 10.00 (*0-904674-14-2*, Pub. by Octagon Pr) ISHK.

Malta's Road to Independence. Edith Dobie. LC 67-15591. 308p. reprint ed. pap. 95.50 (*0-8357-9733-3*, 201621000002) Bks Demand.

Maltaverne. Francois Mauriac. 22.50 (*0-685-34296-4*) Fr & Eur.

Maltby Family of Massachusetts. Art Reierson. (Illus.). 374p. 1998. pap. 58.00 (*0-8328-9467-2*); lib. bdg. 68.00 (*0-8328-9466-4*) Higginson Bk Co.

Maltby-Maltbie Family History. D. M. Verril. (Illus.). 435p. 1993. reprint ed. pap. 68.00 (*0-8328-3048-8*); reprint ed. lib. bdg. 78.00 (*0-8328-3047-X*) Higginson Bk Co.

Maltby-Morehouse Family: A List of Pedigrees with Genealogical Notes. Ed. by G. L. Morehouse. 157p. 1994. reprint ed. pap. 25.00 (*0-8328-4344-X*); reprint ed. lib. bdg. 35.00 (*0-8328-4343-1*) Higginson Bk Co.

***Maltese.** Vicki Abbott. (Best of the Breed Library). (Illus.). 2000. write for info. (*1-58245-160-5*) Howell Bks.

Maltese. Albert Borg & Marie Azzopardi-Alexander. LC 96-13272. (Descriptive Grammars Ser.). 416p. (C). 1996. 180.00 (*0-415-02243-6*) Routledge.

Maltese. Kathy Digiacomo. 1997. pap. 9.95 (*0-7938-2384-6*, KW-111S) TFH Pubns.

Maltese. Bobbie Linden. LC 98-22378. (Owner's Guide to a Happy, Healthy Pet Ser.). (Illus.). 160p. 1998. 12.95 (*0-87605-237-5*) Howell Bks.

Maltese. Anna K. Nicholas. (Illus.). 288p. 1984. 23.95 (*0-87666-569-5*, PS-803) TFH Pubns.

Maltese: Everything about Purchase, Care, Nutrition, Breeding, Behavior, & Training. Joe Fulda. LC 95-17374. (Complete Pet Owner's Manual Ser.). (Illus.). 1995. pap. 6.95 (*0-8120-9332-1*) Barron.

Maltese Angel: A Novel. Catherine Cookson. 528p. 1994. mass mkt. 6.99 (*0-552-13684-0*) Bantam.

Maltese Angel: A Novel. large type ed. Catherine Cookson. LC 94-42977. 739p. 1995. 24.95 (*0-7862-0386-2*) Thorndike Pr.

Maltese Anthology. Arthur J. Arberry. LC 75-8831. 280p. 1975. reprint ed. lib. bdg. 39.75 (*0-8371-8112-7*, ARMA, Greenwood Pr) Greenwood.

Maltese Boyhood: Stories. Philip Ward. 1976. pap. 5.95 (*0-902675-41-9*) Oleander Pr.

Maltese Cat. Rudyard Kipling. LC 92-60477. (Illus.). 54p. (YA). 1992. reprint ed. 17.95 (*0-932433-93-6*) Windswept Hse.

Maltese Champions, 1952-1990. Camino E. E. & Bk. Co. Staff. (Illus.). 200p. 1992. pap. 36.95 (*1-55893-012-4*) Camino E E & Bk.

Maltese Champions, 1990-1994. Camino E. E. & Bk. Co. Staff. (Illus.). 130p. 1995. pap. 36.95 (*1-55893-040-X*) Camino E E & Bk.

Maltese Complete Course, 2 cass. J. Aquilina. (Teach Yourself Ser.). 240p. 1977. pap. 25.95 incl. audio (*0-8442-3866-X*, 686189) NTC Contemp Pub Co.

Maltese Dog. Lyrick Publishing Staff. (Wishbone Mysteries Ser.). 144p. (J). 1998. pap. 1.99 (*1-57064-486-1*) Lyrick Pub.

Maltese Dog see Wishbone Mysteries

Maltese Dog Scrapbook, Vol. I. J. P. Antonelli. (Illus.). 168p. 1998. 32.00 (*0-8059-4253-X*) Dorrance.

Maltese-English - English-Maltese Dictionary & Phrasebook. Grazio Falzon. LC 97-41115. (ENG & MLT.). 175p. (Orig.). 1997. pap. 11.95 (*0-7818-0565-1*) Hippocrene Bks.

Maltese Falcon. Dashiell Hammett. 148p. Date not set. 18.95 (*0-8488-2436-9*) Amereon Ltd.

Maltese Falcon. Dashiell Hammett. 1992. pap. 9.00 (*0-679-74094-5*) Random.

Maltese Falcon. Dashiell Hammett. 736p. 1991. Not sold separately (*0-614-32012-7*) Random Hse Value.

Maltese Falcon. Dashiell Hammett. (Vintage Crime Ser.). 1989. 15.10 (*0-606-12411-X*, Pub. by Turtleback) Demco.

Maltese Falcon. Dashiell Hammett. (Vintage Crime Ser.). 217p. 1989. pap. 10.00 (*0-679-72264-5*) Vin Bks.

Maltese Falcon. Dashiell Hammett. 1992. pap. 9.00 (*0-394-23903-2*) Vin Bks.

***Maltese Falcon.** Richard Layman. Ed. by Gale Group Publishing Staff. (Literary Masterpieces Ser.: Vol. 3). (Illus.). 192p. 2000. 49.95 (*0-7876-3965-6*) Gale.

Maltese Falcon, Set. large type ed. Dashiell Hammett. (YA). (gr. 10 up). reprint ed. 10.00 (*0-89064-044-0*) NAVH.

Maltese Falcon: John Huston, Director. John Huston. Ed. by William Luhr. LC 95-15172. (Films in Print Ser.: Vol. 22). (Illus.). 280p. (C). 1995. text 48.00 (*0-8135-2236-6*); pap. text 17.00 (*0-8135-2237-4*) Rutgers U Pr.

***Maltese Falcon, the Thin Man, Red Harvest.** Dashiell Hammett. 672p. 2000. 20.00 (*0-375-41125-9*) Knopf.

Maltese Goddess: An Archaeological Mystery. Lyn Hamilton. 256p. 1998. mass mkt. 5.99 (*0-425-16240-0*, Prime Crime) Berkley Pub.

Maltese Puppy. Melissa Cleary. 256p. (Orig.). 1995. mass mkt. 4.99 (*0-425-14721-5*, Prime Crime) Berkley Pub.

Maltese Today. Vicki Henrieff. (Illus.). 160p. 1996. 25.95 (*0-87605-231-6*) Macmillan.

***Malteserkreuz und Preu & Beta; Enadler: Ein Beitrag Zur Grundungsgeschichte der Genossenschaft der Rheinisch-westfalischen Malteser-Devotionsritter.** Urs Buhlmann. (Beitrage zur Kirchen- und Kulturgeschichte Ser.). 298p. 1999. 48.95 (*3-631-35575-0*) P Lang Pubng.

Malthey, Robert Dedication. Ed. by Martine Jotterand-Bellomo & H. P. Klinger. (Cytogenetics & Cell Genetics Ser.: Vol. 34, Nos. 1-2). (Illus.). vi, 192p. 1982. pap. 139.25 (*3-8055-3650-X*) S Karger.

Malthus. William Petersen. LC 78-31479. 312p. reprint ed. pap. 96.80 (*0-7837-2311-3*, 205739900004) Bks Demand.

Malthus: Critical Responses, 4 vols. Geoffrey Gilbert. LC 97-10392. 1600p. (C). 1998. 580.00 (*0-415-14011-0*) Routledge.

Malthus: Founder of Modern Demography. William Petersen. LC 98-19058. 332p. 1998. pap. 29.95 (*0-7658-0481-6*) Transaction Pubs.

Malthus & the Population Controversy, 1803-1830, 10 vols., Set. (History of British Economic Thought Ser.). 3940p. (C). (gr. 13). 1994. text, boxed set 1070.00 (*0-415-10503-X*, B3787) Routledge.

Malthus' Essay on Population, 11 vols. 6th ed. Ed. by Samuel Hollander. 5970p. (C). 1996. 1565.00 (*0-415-14304-7*) Routledge.

Malthus Factor. Eric B. Ross. LC 98-29913. 1998. pap. 25.00 (*1-85649-564-7*) Zed Books.

Malthus Factor. Eric B. Ross. LC 98-29913. 1998. text 65.00 (*1-85649-563-9*) Zed Books.

Malthus Library Catalogue: The Personal Collection of Thomas Robert Malthus at Jesus College, Cambridge University. Thomas Robert Malthus et al. 150p. 1983. 46.00 (*0-08-029386-7*, Pergamon Pr) Elsevier.

Malthuscritical Responses, Vol. 1. 216p. (C). Date not set. write for info. (*0-415-14013-7*) Routledge.

Malthuscritical Responses, Vol. 2. 232p. (C). Date not set. write for info. (*0-415-14015-3*) Routledge.

Malthuscritical Responses, Vol. 3. 216p. (C). Date not set. write for info. (*0-415-14012-9*) Routledge.

Malthuscritical Responses, Vol. 4. 232p. (C). Date not set. write for info. (*0-415-14014-5*) Routledge.

Malthusian Worlds: U. S. Leadership & the Governing of the Population Crisis. Ronald Greene. LC 99-21202. 304p. 1999. 65.00 (*0-8133-9073-7*, Pub. by Westview) HarpC.

Malting & Brewing Science, Vol. 2. D. E. Briggs & Tom W. Young. 536p. 1982. 135.00 (*0-8342-1684-1*) Aspen Pub.

Maltrato y Abuso Sexual de Ninos. Simari. (Serie Actualidades - Actualities Ser.).Tr. of Mistreatment & Sexual Abuse of Children. (SPA.). 2.29 (*1-56063-661-0*, 496252) Editorial Unilit.

Maltreated Child: The Maltreatment Syndrome in Children; a Medical, Legal, & Social Guide. 5th ed. Vincent J. Fontana & Douglas J. Besharov. LC 95-30664. (Illus.). 174p. 1995. pap. 31.95 (*0-398-06548-9*); text 40.95 (*0-398-06547-0*) C C Thomas.

Maltreated Children: Experience, Brain Development, & the Next Generation. Bruce D. Perry. 240p. 1998. 29.00 (*0-393-70212-X*) Norton.

Maltreatment & the School-Age Child: Developmental Outcomes & System Issues. Phyllis T. Howing et al. 177p. 1993. pap. 8.95 (*1-56024-292-2*) Haworth Pr.

Maltreatment & the School-Age Child: Developmental Outcomes & System Issues. Phyllis T. Howing et al. LC 92-1205. (Illus.). 180p. 1993. lib. bdg. 39.95 (*1-56024-291-4*) Haworth Pr.

***Maltreatment in Early Childhood: Tools for Research-Based Intervention.** Ed. by Kathleen Coulborn Faller. LC 99-87450. 258p. 2000. 49.95 (*0-7890-0784-3*, Maltreatment & Trauma Pr); pap. text 24.95 (*0-7890-0819-X*, Maltreatment & Trauma Pr) Haworth Pr.

Maltreatment of Children in Global Perspective. Human Relations Staff. 1996. 25.00 (*0-8161-7387-7*, Hall Reference) Macmillan.

Maltreatment of Children in Global Perspective. large type ed. Hraf. 1994. 14.95 (*0-8161-1602-4*, G K Hall Lrg Type) Mac Lib Ref.

Maluka: A Novel , 2 pts. Sadhu S. Dhami. LC 98-908045. 345p. 1997. write for info. (*81-7380-402-8*, Pub. by Pubn Bureau) S Asia.

Maluku. Ed. by Kal Muller. 176p. 1991. pap. 37.50 (*0-945971-33-8*) Periplus.

Maluku: De Molukken. Kal Muller. Ed. by David Pickell. Tr. by Maureen Pattiruhu from ENG. (Indonesie Reisbibliotheek Ser.). (DUT.). 175p. 1991. pap. 19.95 (*0-945971-18-4*) Periplus.

Maluku, Sea-Lands of Bounty for Trade Investment & Tourism. (Illus.). 200p. 1997. 45.00 (*0-9638417-3-4*) Eriako Assocs.

Mal'uocchiu: Ambiguity, Evil Eye & the Language of Distress. Sam Migliore. LC 97-169892. (Anthropological Horizons Ser.). (Illus.). 144p. 1997. pap. text 16.95 (*0-8020-7922-9*) U of Toronto Pr.

Mal'Uocchiu: Ambiguity, Evil Eye, & the Languages of Distress. Sam Migliore. (Anthropological Horizons Ser.: No. 10). (Illus.). 40.00p. 1997. text 40.00 (*0-8020-0959-X*) U of Toronto Pr.

Malu's Wolf. Ruth Craig. LC 95-6031. 192p. (J). (gr. 3-7). 1995. 15.95 (*0-531-09484-7*); lib. bdg. 16.99 (*0-531-08784-0*) Orchard Bks Watts.

Malvaceae. Paul A. Frytell. Ed. by Dennis E. Breedlove. (Flora of Chiapas Ser.: Pt. 3). (Illus.). 90p. (Orig.). 1990. pap. 10.00 (*0-940228-22-X*) Calif Acad Sci.

Malvaceae of Mexico. Paul A. Fryxell. Ed. by Christiane Anderson. (Systematic Botany Monographs: Vol. 25). (Illus.). 522p. 1988. boxed set 40.00 (*0-912861-25-8*) Am Soc Plant.

Malvales, Parietales, Myrtiflorae. Tr. by Israel Program for Scientific Translations Staff from RUS. (Flora of the U. S. S. R. (Flora SSSR) Ser.: Vol. 15). (Illus.). xxiii, 565p. 1987. reprint ed. 231.00 (*3-87429-235-5*, 003936, Pub. by Koeltz Sci Bks) Lubrecht & Cramer.

Malvaloca - Dona Clarines. Alvarez Quinteros. (SPA.). 148p. 1966. 9.95 (*0-8288-7106-X*) Fr & Eur.

Malvano Immunoenzymatic Essay. Malvano. 1980. lib. bdg. 141.50 (*90-247-2314-0*, Pub. by M Nijhoff) Kluwer Academic.

An Asterisk (*) at the beginning of an entry indicates that the title is appearing for the first time.

***Malvasia's Life of the Carracci: Commentary & Translation.** Carlo C. Malvasia & Anne Summerscale. LC 99-36322. 2000. 85.00 (*0-271-01899-2*) Pa St U Pr.

Malvina Reynolds Songbook. 4th enl. ed. Malvina Reynolds. LC 74-20175. (Illus.). 112p. 1984. pap. 7.00 (*0-915620-07-3*) Schroder Music.

Malwa in Transition or a Century of Anarchy: The First Phase, 1698-1765. Raghubir Sinh. (C). 1993. reprint ed. 30.00 (*81-206-0750-3*, Pub. by Asian Educ Servs) S Asia.

***Malyasia.** 2nd rev. ed. Ooi Keat Gin. Vol. 12. 435p. 1999. lib. bdg. 81.00 (*1-85109-311-7*) ABC-CLIO.

Mama. Ruby J. Jensen. 1983. mass mkt. 3.50 (*0-8217-1247-0*, Zebra Kensgtn) Kensgtn Pub Corp.

Mama. Terry McMillan. Ed. by Jane Rosenman. 260p. 1991. pap. 14.00 (*0-671-74523-9*, WSP) PB.

Mama. Terry McMillan. 320p. 1994. per. 6.99 (*0-671-88448-4*, Pocket Star Bks) PB.

***Mama.** Eleanor Schick. LC 99-16373. (Illus.). 32p. (J). (gr. k-3). 2000. 15.95 (*0-7614-5060-2*, Cav Child Bks) Marshall Cavendish.

***Mama.** Weeks. 32p. (J). (ps-2). 2001. 15.95 (*0-06-027507-3*) HarpC Child Bks.

Mama. abr. ed. Terry McMillan. 1994. 16.00 incl. audio (*0-453-00865-8*, Pub. by Penguin-HghBrdg) Penguin Putnam.

Mama, Across the Sea. Alex Godard & George Wendt. LC 99-10098. 48p. 1999. 16.95 (*0-8050-6161-4*) H Holt & Co.

Mama & Daddy Bear's Divorce. Cornelia M. Spelman. LC 98-9299. (Illus.). 32p. (J). (ps-1). 1998. lib. bdg. 13.95 (*0-8075-5221-6*) A Whitman.

Mama & Her Boys. Lee B. Hopkins. LC 99-60225. 160p. (J). 2000. pap. 8.95 (*1-56397-814-8*) Boyds Mills Pr.

***Mama & Her Boys.** Lee B. Hopkins. LC 99-60224. 96p. (J). 2000. pap. 8.95 (*1-56397-813-X*) Boyds Mills Pr.

Mama & Her Boys. Lee B. Hopkins. LC 81-47445. 192p. (J). (gr. 4-7). 1981. 12.95 (*0-06-022578-5*) HarpC Child Bks.

Mama & Her Chilluns. Ruth L. Frazier. 103p. (Orig.). (YA). 1993. pap. 12.95 (*0-9649881-0-0*) Frazier Bks.

***Mama & Me Adrift in America: Learning to Get Rich in Real Estate.** Lola Hoffman. 2000. pap. 12.50 (*1-892614-23-5*) Briarwood VA.

Mama & Me & the Model T. Faye Gibbons. LC 98-31518. 40p. (J). (gr. k-2). 1999. 16.00 (*0-688-15298-8*, Wm Morrow) Morrow Avon.

***Mama & Me & the Model T.** Faye Gibbons. LC 98-31518. 40p. (J). (gr. k-2). 1999. lib. bdg. 15.93 (*0-688-15299-6*, Wm Morrow) Morrow Avon.

***Mama & Other Tragedies.** Frances Trevino-Benavides. 29p. 1999. pap. 8.00 (*1-877603-63-5*) Pecan Grove.

Mama Bangia's Magic Kitchen. B. Bangia. (Illus.). 48p. (Orig.). 1994. pap. 6.95 (*0-9637255-2-1*) Dancing Unicorn.

Mama Black Widow. Iceberg Slim. LC 98-12906. 288p. (Orig.). 1998. pap. 13.00 (*0-393-31765-X*) Norton.

Mama Black Widow. Iceberg Slim & Robert Beck. 320p. (Orig.). 1996. mass mkt. 6.99 (*0-87067-975-9*, BH975-9) Holloway.

Mama Blanca's Memoirs. Teresa De la Parra. Tr. by Harriet De Onis. (Latin American Literature Ser.). 216p. (C). 1992. pap. 14.95 (*0-8229-5910-0*); text 49.95 (*0-8229-3835-9*) U of Pittsburgh Pr.

Mama, Busca el Martillo! Hay una Mosca en la Cabeza de Papa. Tr. of Mama Get the Hammer! There's a Fly. (ENG & SPA.). 1995. pap. text 8.99 (*0-88113-352-3*) Caribe Betania.

Mama, Buy Me a China Doll. Launa D. Morphew. LC 96-42012. 1997. write for info. (*1-56763-314-5*); pap. write for info. (*1-56763-315-3*) Ozark Pub.

Mama Can't Remember Anymore: Care Management of Aging Parents & Loved Ones. 2nd rev. ed. Nancy Wexler. 1997. pap. text 14.95 (*0-9629358-2-4*) Wein & Wein.

***Mama! Can't You Hear My Cry? One Teen's Desperate Call for Help.** 168p. 1999. pap. 21.95 (*0-9672898-0-7*) Triple Oak.

Mama Cat Has Three Kittens. Denise Fleming. LC 98-12249. (J). (ps-1). 1998. 15.95 (*0-8050-5745-5*) H Holt & Co.

Mama Collection: Six Plays for the 1990s. Ed. by Liz Jones. 1997. pap. 24.95 (*0-86819-532-4*, Pub. by Currency Pr) Accents Pubns.

Mama Come Home. Jennie Phillips. 60p. 1996. pap. 8.00 (*1-885857-18-7*) Four Wnds Pubng.

Mama, Coming & Going. Judith Caseley. LC 92-29402. (Illus.). 32p. (J). (ps-3). 1994. 14.00 (*0-688-11441-5*, Grenwillow Bks) HarpC Child Bks.

Mama Cooks a Day Ahead. Toni Reifel & Bette Woodward. (Illus.). 260p. 1990. write for info. (*0-9628049-0-8*) Mama Cooks.

Mama Cooks a Day Ahead. Toni Reifel & Bette Woodward. (Illus.). 260p. 1991. reprint ed. write for info. (*0-9628049-1-6*) Mama Cooks.

Mama Cooks a Day Ahead. Toni Reifel & Bette Woodward. (Illus.). 260p. 1993. reprint ed. write for info. (*0-9628049-4-0*) Mama Cooks.

Mama Cooks California Style: New Twists on Jewish Classics. Jewish Home for the Aging Staff. LC 96-80095. 1997. 23.95 (*0-9654802-0-8*) Jewish Home Aging.

Mama Cooks for Christmas. Toni Reifel & Bette Woodward. (Illus.). 190p. 1991. 7.95 (*0-9628049-2-4*) Mama Cooks.

Mama Cooks with Kids in the Kitchen. Toni Reifel & Bette Woodward. Ed. & Illus. by Suzanne Jamieson. 108p. 1992. write for info. (*0-9628049-3-2*) Mama Cooks.

Mama, Daddy, Baby & Me. Lisa Gewing. LC 88-35483. (Illus.). 30p. (J). (ps). 1989. 14.95 (*0-944296-04-1*) Spirit Pr.

Mama Day. Gloria Naylor. 320p. 1988. 17.95 (*0-89919-716-7*, Pub. by Ticknor & Fields) HM.

Mama Day. Gloria Naylor. (Contemporaries Ser.). 320p. 1993. pap. 13.00 (*0-679-72181-9*) Vin Bks.

Mama Day. Gloria Naylor. 1993. pap. 10.00 (*0-394-25625-5*) Vin Bks.

Mama Dear. Monique Guilmore et al. 384p. 1997. mass mkt. 4.99 (*0-7860-0397-9*, Pinncle Kensgtn) Kensgtn Pub Corp.

Mama Dip's Kitchen. Mildred Council. LC 99-19973. (Illus.). 230p. 1999. 27.50 (*0-8078-2508-5*); pap. 15.95 (*0-8078-4790-9*) U of NC Pr.

Mama, Do You Love Me? Barbara M. Joosse. (Illus.). 32p. (J). (ps-1). 1991. 14.95 (*0-87701-759-X*) Chronicle Bks.

Mama, Do You Love Me? Barbara M. Joosse. (Illus.). 24p. 1998. bds. 6.95 (*0-8118-2131-5*) Chronicle Bks.

Mama Don't Allow. Thacher Hurd. LC 83-47703. (Illus.). 40p. (J). (ps-3). 1984. 16.00 (*0-06-022689-7*) HarpC Child Bks.

Mama Don't Allow. Thacher Hurd. LC 83-47703. (Trophy Picture Bk.). (Illus.). 40p. (J). (ps-3). 1985. pap. 5.95 (*0-06-443078-2*, HarpTrophy) HarpC Child Bks.

Mama Dont Allow. Thacher Hurd. LC 83-47703. (Illus.). 32p. (J). (ps-3). 1984. lib. bdg. 15.89 (*0-06-022690-0*) HarpC Child Bks.

Mama Don't Allow: Starring Miles & the Swamp Band. Thacher Hurd. 1985. 10.15 (*0-606-00832-2*, Pub. by Turtleback) Demco.

Mama Drama: Making Your Peace With the One Woman Who Can Push Your Buttons, Make You Cry & Drive You Crazy. Denise McGregor. LC 98-12781. 224p. 1998. text 21.95 (*0-312-18627-4*) St Martin.

Mama Drama: Making Your Peace With the One Woman Who Can Push Your Buttons, Make You Cry & Drive You Crazy. Denise McGregor. 1999. pap. 12.95 (*0-312-20421-3*, St Martins Paperbacks) St Martin.

***Mama Elizabeti.** Stephanie Stuve-Bodeen. LC 99-47890. (Illus.). 32p. (YA). (ps up). 2000. 15.95 (*1-58430-002-7*, Pub. by Lee & Low Bks) Publishers Group.

Mama Eres Increible! Linda Weber.Tr. of Mom, You're Incredible!. (SPA.). 196p. 1995. pap. 7.99 (*1-56063-974-1*) Editorial Unilit.

Mama Fanelli's Secret Italian Recipes. Joan L. Craig. (Illus.). 105p. (Orig.). 1992. pap. text 11.95 (*0-9632570-1-3*) J&W Craig Ent.

***Mama Flora's Family: A Novel.** Alex Haley & David Stephens. 454p. 1999. mass mkt. 6.99 (*0-440-23543-X*) Dell.

Mama Flora's Family: A Novel. Alex Haley & David Stevens. LC 98-5389. 394p. 1998. 25.00 (*0-684-83471-5*) Scribner.

***Mama Gansa.** Michael Hague. 2000. 14.50 (*84-241-3347-1*) Everest SP.

Mama, Get the Hammer: There's a Fly on Papa's Head. Barbara Johnson. LC 94-21895. 179p. 1994. pap. 10.99 (*0-8499-3417-6*) Word Pub.

Mama Get the Hammer! There's a Fly see Mama, Busca el Martillo! Hay una Mosca en la Cabeza de Papa

Mama God, Papa God: A Caribbean Tale. Richardo Keens-Douglas. LC 98-38628. (Illus.). (J). 1999. 15.95 (*1-56656-307-0*, Pub. by Interlink Pub) Kane-Miller Bk.

Mama Goes to School. Claudette C. Mitchell et al. (Visions: African-American Experiences: Vol. 9). (Illus.). 8p. (Orig.). (J). (gr. k-1). 1996. pap. text 3.00 (*1-57518-051-0*) Arborlake.

Mama Goose Un-coloring Book. Marji Gold-Vukson. (J). (ps-3). 1994. pap. text 9.97 (*0-937659-91-6*) GCT.

Mama, I Want to Sing. Vy Higginsen & Tonya Bolden. 192p. (YA). (gr. 7-9). 1995. pap. 3.25 (*0-590-44202-3*) Scholastic Inc.

Mama, I Want to Sing: Libretto. 1995. pap. 6.95 (*0-88145-115-0*) Broadway Play.

Mama, Ia Zhulika Liubliu. Natallia Medvedeva. (RUS.). 170p. (Orig.). 1988. pap. 15.00 (*0-89830-114-9*) Russica Pubs.

Mama, If You Had a Wish. Jeanne Modesitt. LC 91-31354. (Illus.). 40p. (J). (ps-1). 1993. pap. 15.00 (*0-671-75437-8*, Green Tiger S&S) S&S Childrens.

Mama If You Had a Wish. Jeanne Modesitt. LC 91-31354. 40p. (J). 1999. per. 5.99 (*0-689-82412-2*) Aladdin.

Mama Is a Miner. George E. Lyon. LC 93-49398. (Illus.). 32p. (J). (gr. k-3). 1994. 15.95 (*0-531-06853-6*); lib. bdg. 16.99 (*0-531-08703-4*) Orchard Bks Watts.

Mama Is Hapai. large type ed. Chaika P. Hale. (Illus.). 32p. (J). (gr. 1-6). 1998. 14.00 (*0-9653971-2-2*) Anoai Pr.

Mama, It Ain't Over 'Til the Pink Marble Comes! Sandee Williams & Jeanne Todd. 186p. 1994. pap. text 9.95 (*0-929292-77-4*) Hannibal Bks.

Mama Jean's Book of Wisdom: With 20 Racial No-No's. Jean C. Taylor. 65p. 1998. pap. 14.95 (*1-55630-839-6*) Brentwood Comm.

Mama John: The Lifelong Missionary Service of Mary Saunders. Nina Ellison. Ed. by Susan Hansen. 144p. (Orig.). 1996. pap. text 9.95 (*1-56309-171-2*, N964107, New Hope) Womans Mission Union.

Mama Knows. Tracie Foreman. Ed. by Linda J. Dageforde. LC 96-70908. (Illus.). 116p. (Orig.). 1996. pap. 9.95 (*1-886225-18-4*, 1000) Dageforde Pub.

Mama Leah's Jewish Kitchen. Leah L. Fischer & Maria P. Robbins. LC 93-32919. 320p. 1994. pap. 12.95 (*0-02-002650-1*) Macmillan.

Mama Leah's Jewish Kitchen. Leah Fischer & Maria P. Robbins. Ed. by Philip Turner. 320p. 1990. 23.00 (*0-02-538461-9*) Hafner.

Mama, Let's Dance. Patricia Hermes. 176p. (J). (gr. 4-7). 1993. pap. 2.99 (*0-590-46633-X*) Scholastic Inc.

Mama, Let's Dance: A Novel. Patricia Hermes. (J). 1991. 8.09 (*0-606-05449-9*, Pub. by Turtleback) Demco.

Mama Lola: A Vodou Priestess in Brooklyn. Karen M. Brown. LC 90-40070. (Comparative Studies in Religion & Society: No. 4). (Illus.). 432p. 1991. 48.00 (*0-520-07073-9*, Pub. by U CA Pr) Cal Prin Full Svc.

Mama Lola: A Vodou Priestess in Brooklyn. Karen M. Brown. (Illus.). 1992. reprint ed. pap. 17.95 (*0-520-07780-6*, Pub. by U CA Pr) Cal Prin Full Svc.

Mama Loves. Lisa McCue. LC 98-23375. (J). 1999. 7.99 (*0-679-89462-4*); lib. bdg. 11.99 (*0-679-99462-9*) Random.

Mama Makes up Her Mind. Bailey White. 12.16 incl. audio (*0-201-40657-8*) Addison-Wesley.

Mama Makes up Her Mind: And Other Dangers of Southern Living. Bailey White. LC 92-47059. 1993. 17.95 (*0-201-63295-0*) Addison-Wesley.

Mama Makes up Her Mind: And Other Dangers of Southern Living. Bailey White. 1994. pap. 11.00 (*0-679-75160-2*) Vin Bks.

***Mama, Mama.** Jean Marzollo. (Illus.). 16p. (J). (ps-k). 1999. 5.95 (*0-694-01245-9*) HarpC Child Bks.

Mama Might Be Better off Dead: The Failure of Health Care in Urban America. Laurie K. Abraham. LC 93-15514. 304p. 1993. 22.50 (*0-226-00138-5*) U Ch Pr.

Mama Might Be Better off Dead: The Failure of Health Care in Urban America. Laurie K. Abraham. xii, 302p. 1994. pap. 13.00 (*0-226-00139-3*) U Ch Pr.

Mama 'n 'Em: An Oral History of Thomaston. Ed. by Kathryn Friday & Alan Brown. LC 94-79512. 64p. (Orig.). 1994. pap. 5.00 (*0-942979-24-9*) Livingston U Pr.

Mama Ndiyalila: Stories Mothobi Mutloatse. LC 82-237433. (Staffrider Ser.). 163 p. 1982. write for info. (*0-86975-134-4*, Pub. by Ravan Pr) Ohio U Pr.

Mama One, Mama Two. Patricia MacLachlan. LC 81-47795. (Charlotte Zolotow Bk.). (Illus.). 32p. (J). (ps-3). 1982. lib. bdg. 15.89 (*0-06-024082-2*) HarpC Child Bks.

Mama 1 Mama 2. Patricia MacLachlan. LC 81-47795. (Charlotte Zolotow Bk.). (Illus.). 32p. (J). (gr. 1-3). 1982. 13.00 (*0-06-024081-4*) HarpC Child Bks.

Mama, Papa & Baby Joe. Niki Daly. (Illus.). 32p. (J). 1999. pap. 4.99 (*0-14-054969-2*, PuffinBks) Peng Put Young Read.

Mama Pays the Grocery Bill. Rosemary Williamson. 334p. Date not set. pap. 10.00 (*1-887150-08-0*) Millennia Bks.

Mama Poc: An Ecologist's Account of the Extinction of a Species. Anne LaBastille. (Illus.). 320p. 1991. pap. 10.95 (*0-393-30800-6*) Norton.

Mama por Estapas Revisada. Beatrice De Zapata Espinoza. (SPA.). 1998. pap. 6.99 (*0-8297-1215-1*) Vida Pubs.

Mama Provi & the Pot of Rice. Casanova S. Rosa. LC 95-44677. (Illus.). 32p. (J). (gr. k-3). 1997. 16.00 (*0-689-31932-0*) Atheneum Yung Read.

***Mama Pursues Murderous Shadows.** Nora DeLoach. 192p. 2000. mass mkt. 5.99 (*0-553-57722-0*) Bantam.

Mama Rocks, Papa Sings. Nancy Van Laan. LC 93-39225. (Illus.). 40p. (J). (ps-2). 1995. 15.00 (*0-679-84016-8*, Pub. by Knopf Bks Yng Read) Random.

Mama Rocks the Empty Cradle. Nora DeLoach. 208p. 1999. mass mkt. 5.99 (*0-553-57720-4*) Bantam.

Mama Rose: A Novel. Bernadene H. Coleman. 292p. 1998. pap. 12.95 (*1-881524-35-3*) Milligan Bks.

Mama Ros's Texican Libro de Cocina. Henry A. Harris. Ed. by Sandra Chatfield. 80p. (Orig.). pap. 9.95 (*1-886084-09-2*) Last Pubng.

***Mama Said.** Edmund F. Benson & Susan Benson. (Illus.). 16p. (J). (gr. 3-4). 1999. pap. text 2.95 (*1-58614-095-7*) Arise Found.

***Mama Said, "Get in the House" Embracing the Wisdom of Mama & God.** Theresa C. Allen. Ed. by Pamela Brooks. LC 99-98137. xi, 129p. 2000. pap. 13.00 (*0-9676710-0-0*) Allens Ink.

***Mama Sana, Bebe Sano: Una Guia en Espanol E ingles Sobre el Embarazo la Atencion Prenatal, el Nacimiento y el Cuidado.** Aliza A. Lifshitz. (ENG & SPA., Illus.). 464p. 1999. pap. 15.00 (*0-380-79245-1*, Avon Bks) Morrow Avon.

Mama Saves a Victim. Nora DeLoach. (Mama Mystery Ser.: No. 4). 156p. (YA). (gr. 9 up). 1998. pap. 10.95 (*0-87067-874-4*) Holloway.

Mama, Say I Do: (A Whisper in God's Ear), a 3-Act Comedy. Sam Birnkrant. (Illus.). 58p. 1970. pap. 4.00 (*0-88680-126-5*) I E Clark.

Mama Says . . . Dee Grayson. LC 91-71162. 128p. (Orig.). 1991. 2.95 (*1-879821-00-1*) Greetings Alien.

***Mama Says: Inspiration, Prayers, Wit & Wisdom from the Mothers in Our Lives.** Loyola Press Staff. LC 99-37630. 273p. 2000. pap. 10.95 (*0-8294-1342-1*) Loyola Pr.

Mama, Sing Old Shep. Charlene Jones. LC 95-71411. 384p. 1996. pap. 12.95 (*1-888101-07-5*) Red Springs.

Mama Solves a Murder. Nora L. Deloach. (Mama Mystery Ser.: No. 1). 192p. 1994. mass mkt. 4.95 (*0-87067-969-4*) Holloway.

Mama Stalks the Past. Nora DeLoach. LC 97-10117. 208p. 1997. 21.95 (*0-553-10662-7*) Bantam.

Mama Stalks the Past. Nora DeLoach. 272p. 1998. mass mkt. 5.99 (*0-553-57721-2*) Bantam.

Mama Stands Accused. Nora DeLoach. (Mama Mystery Ser.: No. 3). 156p. 1998. pap. 10.95 (*0-87067-873-6*, BH 873-6) Holloway.

Mama Stories. Lolette Kuby. (Illus.). 64p. (Orig.). 1995. pap. 9.95 (*0-933087-36-5*) Bottom Dog Pr.

Mama Susan's Dixie Cooking. Susan W. Kelly. Ed. by Jon Hildreth. (Illus.). 224p. 1991. 18.00 (*0-9630735-3-2*) Toad Hall.

Mama Talks Too Much. Marisabina Russo. LC 98-17695. (J). 1999. lib. bdg. write for info. (*0-688-16412-9*, Grenwillow Bks) HarpC Child Bks.

Mama Talks Too Much. Marisabina Russo. LC 98-17695. (Illus.). 32p. (YA). (ps-3). 1999. 16.00 (*0-688-16411-0*, Grenwillow Bks) HarpC Child Bks.

Mama, te Agradezco por Tu Gran Amor: Anthology. Ed. by Susan Polis Schutz. LC 93-19833.Tr. of Mother, Thank You for All Your Love. (SPA & ENG.). 64p. 1993. pap. 7.95 (*0-88396-369-8*) Blue Mtn Art.

***Mama Tiger, Baba Tiger.** Juli Mahr. LC 99-53519. (Share-a-Story Ser.). (Illus.). (J). 2000. write for info. (*0-7894-5615-X*) DK Pub Inc.

***Mama Tina.** large type unabridged ed. Christina Noble. 1999. 25.95 (*0-7531-5709-8*, 157098, Pub. by ISIS Lrg Prnt) ISIS Pub.

***Mama Toscana: The Authentic Tuscan Cookbook.** Alvaro Maccioni. (Illus.). 224p. 2000. 45.00 (*1-86205-174-7*, Pub. by Pavilion Bks Ltd) Trafalgar.

Mama Traps a Killer. Nora DeLoach. (Mama Mystery Ser.: No. 2). 192p. 1995. mass mkt. 4.95 (*0-87067-747-0*) Holloway.

Mama Was a Preacher. deluxe ed. Author22 Publishing Staff. LC 98-96141. 460p. 1999. pap. 19.95 (*1-892183-02-1*) DTTN.

Mama, Watch Out - I'm Growing Up. Adrienne V. Sealy. (Illus.). (J). (gr. 2-5). 1978. lib. bdg. 4.95 (*0-9602670-1-8*) Assn Family Living.

***Mama Went to Jail for the Vote.** Kathleen Karr. 32p. (J). 2000. 14.99 (*0-7868-0593-5*, Pub. by Hyperion); pap. 4.99 (*0-7868-1435-7*, Pub. by Hyperion); lib. bdg. 15.49 (*0-7868-2509-X*, Pub. by Hyperion) Little.

Mama, Were You Ever Young? John Hay. (J). 1998. 13.95 (*0-671-75219-7*) S&S Bks Yung.

Mama, Were You Ever Young? John Hay. (Illus.). 32p. (J). (gr. k-4). 1991. 13.95 (*0-88138-134-9*, Green Tiger S&S) S&S Childrens.

Mama! Why Did You Kill Us? Domenico Mondrone. LC 67-62523. 49p. 1998. pap. 2.00 (*0-89555-616-2*, 1541) TAN Bks Pubs.

Mama Yetta & Other Poems. Hermine Pinson. viii, 54p. 1999. pap. 12.00 (*0-930324-39-0*) Wings Pr.

Mama, Your Slip is Showing! A How-It-Is Prescription Guide for Caregivers on Aging. Janet Riesen & Eloise Grall. 36p. (Orig.). 1990. pap. 5.95 (*0-9626993-0-6*) Armadillo Niche.

Mama Zooms. Jane Cowen-Fletcher. (J). (ps-3). 1993. 19.95 (*0-590-72848-2*) Scholastic Inc.

Mama Zooms. Jane Cowen-Fletcher. 32p. (J). (ps-3). 1994. pap. 3.95 (*0-590-45775-6*) Scholastic Inc.

Mama Zooms. Jane Cowen-Fletcher. 1995. 10.19 (*0-606-11593-5*, Pub. by Turtleback) Demco.

Mamaarim Yiddush. Joseph I. Schneersohn. (YID.). 234p. reprint ed. 10.00 (*0-8266-5706-0*) Kehot Pubn Soc.

Mamainde Stress: The Need for Strata. David Eberhard. LC 95-67930. (Publications in Linguistics: Vol. 122). 176p. 1995. pap. 25.00 (*1-55671-003-8*) S I L Intl.

Mamaka Kaiao: Modern Hawaiian Vocabulary Listing. Hawaiian Lexicon Committee. Ed. by Hokulani Cleeland. (ENG & HAW.). 232p. (C). 1996. pap. 10.00 (*0-9645646-3-7*) Aha Punana Leo.

***Mamaka Kaiao 1998.** Hawaiian Lexicon Committee. (ENG & HAW.). 311p. (YA). (gr. 10 up). 1998. pap. 9.95 (*1-58191-005-3*) Aha Punana Leo.

Maman, Je T'Adore. William Saroyan. (FRE.). 1983. pap. 11.95 (*0-7859-4191-6*) Fr & Eur.

Maman, l'Ecole a Ete Inondee! (Mom, the School Flooded) Ken Rivard. (FRE., Illus.). 32p. (J). (ps-2). 1996. pap. 4.95 (*1-55037-478-8*, Pub. by Annick); lib. bdg. 15.95 (*1-55037-479-6*, Pub. by Annick) Firefly Bks Ltd.

Maman Sabouleux. Eugene Labiche. 9.95 (*0-686-54231-2*) Fr & Eur.

Mamarazza. Mariann Sayn-Wittgenstein-Sayn. 2000. 125.00 (*3-88243-641-7*, Pub. by Steidl) Dist Art Pubs.

Mamas & the Papas. (Piano-Vocal-Guitar Ser.). 72p. 1991. per. 14.95 (*0-7935-0836-3*, 00120843) H Leonard.

Mamas & the Papas, No. 291. 48p. 1992. pap. 5.95 (*0-7935-1291-3*, 00243506) H Leonard.

Mamas & the Papas: California Dreamin' Doug Hall. (Illus.). 192p. 1998. pap. 15.95 (*1-55082-216-0*, Pub. by Quarry Pr) LPC InBook.

Mamas & the Papas: 16 of Their Greatest Hits, No. 303. 48p. 1992. pap. 6.95 (*0-7935-1287-5*, 00102215) H Leonard.

***Mama's Baby (Papa's Maybe) New Welsh Short Fiction.** Ed. by Lewis Davies & Arthur Smith. 500p. 2000. pap. 15.95 (*1-902638-03-4*, Pub. by Parthian) Dufour.

Mama's Bank Account. Kathryn Forbes. 154p. 1968. reprint ed. pap. 9.00 (*0-15-656377-0*, Harvest Bks) Harcourt.

Mama's Boy. Bev Arthur & Martin Arthur. LC 86-14348. (Illus.). 216p. (Orig.). 1986. pap. 9.95 (*0-89407-054-1*) Strawberry Hill.

Mama's Boy. Richard T. Pienciak. 1997. mass mkt. 6.99 (*0-451-40748-2*, Onyx) NAL.

Mama's Boy. Charles King. 448p. 1993. reprint ed. mass mkt. 5.50 (*0-671-74470-4*) PB.

***Mama's Boy: Gay Men Write about Their Mothers.** Ed. by Dean Kostos & Eugene Grygo. 2000. pap. 15.00 (*1-891305-20-4*) Painted Leaf.

Mama's Boyz: As American As Sweet Potato Pie. Jerry Craft. LC 97-94046. (Illus.). 96p. (Orig.). 1997. pap. 9.95 (*0-9656967-0-7*) American Pub Co.

Mama's Cookin' John B. Harris. LC 96-95243. (Illus.). 160p. 1997. 15.95 (*0-9641614-1-9*) Harris Farms.

***Mamas Day.** (J). (gr. k-3). 2002. per. write for info. (*0-689-83475-6*) S&S Childrens.

Mama's Decision. Edith Bajema. (Open Door Bks.). (Illus.). 69p. 1992. pap. text 3.95 (*1-56212-014-X*, 1740-2150) CRC Pubns.

Mamas, Don't Let Your Cowboys Grow up to Be Babies. Dallas Williams. (Illus.). 96p. 1998. pap. 8.95 (*1-55022-359-3*, Pub. by ECW) Genl Dist Srvs.

Mama's Garden. Barbara S. Berry. (Illus.). 195p. 1998. 25.00 (*1-887905-10-3*) Pkway Pubs.

Mama's Girl. Veronica Chambers. 208p. 1997. pap. 12.00 (*1-57322-599-1*, Riverhd Trade) Berkley Pub.

Mama's Girl: Playscript. Dell Dean. LC 93-5664. 20p. (Orig.). 1995. pap. 5.00 (*0-88734-342-2*) Players Pr.

M

An Asterisk (*) at the beginning of an entry indicates that the title is appearing for the first time.

Mama's Homemade Love: A Southern Woman Leaves a Legacy. Barbara M. Sims. 225p. 1999. 12.99 (*1-57748-578-5*) Barbour Pub.

Mama's Little Baby: The Black Woman's Guide to Pregnancy, Childbirth, & Baby's First Year. Dennis Brown & Pamela A. Toussaint. 512p. 1998. pap. 16.95 (*0-452-27419-2*, Plume) Dutton Plume.

***Mama's Little Matchmaker.** Alice Holden. (Zebra Regency Romance Ser.). 2000. mass mkt. 4.99 (*0-8217-6584-1*, Zebra Kensgtn) Kensgtn Pub Corp.

Mama's Little One. 2nd rev. ed. Kristina Heath. (Illus.). 28p. (J). (ps up). 1998. mass mkt. 10.00 (*0-935790-05-5*) Muh-He-Con-Neew.

Mama's Morning. Kate Sternberg. LC 97-41105. (Illus.). 32p. (J). (ps-2). 1997. pap. 9.95 (*0-9660366-0-3*) Advantage Books.

***Mama's Perfect Present.** Diane Goode. (J). (ps-3). 1999. pap. 5.99 (*0-14-056549-3*, PuffinBks) Peng Put Young Read.

Mama's Promises: Poems. Marilyn N. Waniek. LC 85-5258. 49p. 1985. pap. 11.95 (*0-8071-1250-X*) La State U Pr.

Mama's Psychiatry: Advice Freely Given in Spite of Sassy Comebacks from Papa's Kids. Cleo N. Taylor. 118p. (Orig.). 1993. pap. 4.95 (*0-9636386-0-2*) Bluebonnet Bks.

Mama's Rules for Livin' Mamie McCullough. LC 95-838606. (Illus.). 160p. 1996. pap. 6.99 (*1-56292-085-5*, HB-085) Honor Bks OK.

Mama's Special Plate. Alex N. Holland et al. (Illus.). 16p. (J). (gr. k-6). 1997. pap. 10.26 (*1-56606-043-5*) Bradley Mann.

Mama's Tea Cakes: 101 Delicious Soul Food Desserts. Wilbert Jones. LC 98-4654. (Illus.). x, 122p. 1998. 14.95 (*1-55972-464-1*, Birch Ln Pr) Carol Pub Group.

Mama's Way. Helen Ketteman. (J). 2000. lib. bdg. 13.01 (*0-8037-2423-3*, Dial Yng Read) Peng Put Young Read.

Mama's Way. Thyra F. Bjorn. 220p. 1986. reprint ed. lib. bdg. 35.95 (*0-89966-569-1*) Buccaneer Bks.

Mamaw. Susan Dodd. LC 87-40661. 1988. 18.95 (*0-670-82180-2*) Grossman.

Mamaw. Susan Dodd. 1988. 18.95 (*0-318-37677-6*) Viking Penguin.

***Mamaw: A Novel of an Outlaw Mother.** Susan Dodd. LC 99-36178. 368p. 1999. reprint ed. pap. 13.00 (*0-688-17001-3*, Wm Morrow) Morrow Avon.

Mambas. Sherie Bargar & L. Johnson. (J). 1997. pap. 2.50 (*0-8167-1259-X*) Troll Communs.

Mambas. Sherie Bargar & Linda Johnson. (Culebras Ser.). 24p. (J). (gr. k-4). Date not set. lib. bdg. 10.95 (*0-86593-331-6*) Rourke Corp.

Mambas. Sherie Bargar & Linda Johnson. (Snake Discovery Library: Set I). (Illus.). 24p. (J). (gr. k-4). 1986. lib. bdg. 14.60 (*0-86592-960-2*) Rourke Enter.

Mambas, Reading Level 2. Linda Johnson. (Snake Discovery Library: Set I). (Illus.). 24p. (J). (gr. k-5). 1986. 8.95 (*0-685-58805-X*) Rourke Corp.

Mamba's Daughters. DeBose Heyward. 24.95 (*0-89190-749-1*) Amereon Ltd.

Mamba's Daughters: A Novel of Charleston. DeBose Heyward. LC 94-35503. 334p. 1995. pap. 16.95 (*1-57003-042-1*) U of SC Pr.

Mambo. Earl Atkinson. (Ballroom Dance Ser.). 1986. lib. bdg. 250.00 (*0-8490-3627-5*) Gordon Pr.

Mambo: For One Piano, Four Hands. Ed. by Carole Flatau. (Keyboard Ensemble Ser.). 12p. (Orig.). (C). 1997. pap. text 4.50 (*0-7692-0102-4*, PA9702) Wrner Bros.

Mambo Combinations. Earl Atkinson. (Ballroom Dance Ser.). 1983. lib. bdg. 250.00 (*0-87700-475-7*) Revisionist Pr.

Mambo Hips & Make Believe: A Novel. Wanda Coleman. LC 99-43143. 403p. 1999. 25.00 (*1-57423-095-6*); pap. 16.00 (*1-57423-094-8*) Black Sparrow.

Mambo Kings Play Songs of Love. Oscar Hijuelos. LC 89-46348. 384p. 1994. pap. 13.00 (*0-06-097327-7*, Perennial) HarperTrade.

***Mambo Kings Play Songs of Love: A Novel,** Oscar Hijuelos. LC 99-53997. (Perennial Classics Ser.). 464p. 2000. pap. 14.00 (*0-06-095545-7*, Perennial) HarperTrade.

***Mambos! Sambas! Rhumbas!** (LAT.). 112p. 2000. otabind 12.95 (*0-634-01347-5*) H Leonard.

Mambroru: History & Structure in a Domain of Northwestern Sumba. Rodney Needham. LC 86-18061. (Illus.). 320p. 1987. text 55.00 (*0-19-823400-7*) OUP.

***Mambru.** Alma Flor Ada. 1999. pap. text 7.95 (*1-58105-405-X*) Santillana.

Mambu: A Melanesian Millennium. Kenelm O. Burridge. LC 94-42499. (Mythos Ser.). 296p. 1995. text 55.00 (*0-691-04388-4*, Pub. by Princeton U Pr); pap. text 16.95 (*0-691-00166-9*, Pub. by Princeton U Pr) Cal Prin Full Svc.

Mame. (Vocal Score Ser.). 232p. 1987. per. 45.00 (*0-88188-573-8*, 00384224) H Leonard.

Mame: Vocal Selections. (Illus.). 48p. 1982. pap. 8.95 (*0-88188-095-7*, 00384226) H Leonard.

Mamechiasautus. (Microfaxc Ser.). (J). 1997. pap. text 0.99 (*0-7894-2128-3*) DK Pub Inc.

Mameluke: or Slave Dynasty of Egypt, 1260-1517. William Muir. LC 71-180367. reprint ed. 32.00 (*0-404-56307-4*) AMS Pr.

Mametz Wood: Somme. Michael Renshall. (Battleground Europe Ser.). 1999. pap. text 16.95 (*0-85052-664-7*) Leo Cooper.

Mamgu-Portrait of a Puritan. David Walters. 144p. (C). 1989. pap. 29.00 (*0-7855-6863-8*, Pub. by D Brown & Sons Ltd) St Mut.

Ma'mi. Okniba Launko. (Junior African Writers Ser.). (Illus.). 80p. (J). (gr. 3 up). 1995. pap. 4.95 (*0-7910-3164-0*) Chelsea Hse.

***Mami Amor's Little Stories.** Rebecca Padilla. Ed. by Felix Padilla. (Illus.). 34p. 1999. 16.00 (*0-9675413-2-8*) Libros Latin Treas.

Mami! Cuanto te Quiero! P. Fernando Lopez. LC 83-80417. (Coleccion Espejo de Paciencia). (SPA., Illus.). 91p. (Orig.). 1983. pap. 6.00 (*0-89729-329-0*) Ediciones.

Mami, Papi, de Donde Vienen los Bebes? Graciela Ayad & Richard Panzer. Ed. by Nancy Makowski. LC 96-72340. (Maravilloso Mundo del Amor Verdadero Ser.). (ENG & SPA., Illus.). 24p. (Orig.). (J). (gr. k-3). 1997. pap. 12.95 (*1-888933-08-9*) Ctr Educ Media.

Mamie D. Eisenhower, Wife, Mother, First Lady: Her Impact & Influence on Her Time. Edith P. Mayo et al. LC 98-70448. (Eisenhower Seminar Ser.: No. 1). (Illus.). 1998. pap. 5.95 (*0-9663741-0-X*) Eisenhower Natl.

***Mamie Doud Eisenhower, 1896-1979: Mamie Diud Eisenhower, Eighteen Ninety.** Susan Sinnott. LC 99-16785. (Encyclopedia of First Ladies Ser.). (J). 2000. 33.00 (*0-516-20599-4*) Childrens.

Mamie's Children: Three Generations of Prairie Women. Judy Schultz. (Illus.). 248p. 1998. pap. 14.95 (*0-88995-167-5*, Pub. by Red Deer) Genl Dist Srvs.

Mamiferos. Steve Parker. (SPA.). Date not set. 14.95 (*84-372-3714-9*) Santillana.

Mamiferos. Planeta Staff. 1998. 109.95 (*84-88720-30-0*) Planeta.

Mamiferos de Colombia: Sus Nombres Comunes e Indigenas. Jose V. Rodriguez Mahetha et al. (Occasional Papers in Conservation Biology: No. 3). (SPA.). 55p. (Orig.). (C). 1996. pap. text 10.00 (*1-881173-16-X*) Conser Intl.

Mamiferos del Oceano. Arthur Morton. Tr. by Angelita L. Aguilar. (SPA.). (J). (gr. k-3). 1994. 12.50 (*1-57842-066-0*) Delmas Creat.

Mamiferos Dominan la Tierra see Mammals Dominate the Earth

Mamiferos Dominan la Tierra. Chelsea House Publishing Staff et al. (SPA., Illus.). 32p. (YA). (gr. 3 up). 1996. lib. bdg. 15.95 (*0-7910-4038-0*) Chelsea Hse.

Mamillia, Pts. 1 & 2; Anatomie of Flatterie, 1583-1593 see Life & Complete Works in Prose & Verse of Robert Greene

***Mamis: Famous Latino Authors Remember Their Mothers.** Ed. by Esmeralda Santiago & Joie Davidow. LC 99-47102. (Illus.). 208p. 2000. 20.00 (*0-375-40879-7*) Knopf.

Mamleuk Military Society. David Ayalon. LC 81-464204. (Collected Studies). 364 p. 1979. 22.00 (*0-86078-049-X*) Variorum.

Mamluk Economics: A Study & Translation of Al-Maqrizi's Igathah. Adel Allouche. 176p. (C). 1994. 35.00 (*0-87480-431-0*) U of Utah Pr.

Mamluks in Egyptian Politics & Society. Ed. by Thomas Philipp & Ulrich Haarmann. LC 97-9821. (Studies in Islamic Civilization). 320p. (C). 1998. text 59.95 (*0-521-59115-5*) Cambridge U Pr.

Mamluks, 1250-1517. David Nicolle. (Men-at-Arms Ser.). (Illus.). 48p. 1993. pap. 11.95 (*1-85532-314-1*, 9230, Pub. by Ospry) Stackpole.

***Mamma Used to Say: Pearls of Wisdom from the World of Yiddish.** Rarhel Rozmarin. LC 00-39303. 2000. write for info. (*1-58330-423-1*) Feldheim.

***Mammal.** Steve Parker. (Eyewitness Books). (Illus.). (J). (gr. 4-7). 2000. 19.99 (*0-7894-6560-4*) DK Pub Inc.

***Mammal.** Steve Parker. (Eyewitness Books). (J). (gr. 4-7). 2000. 15.95 (*0-7894-5818-7*) DK Pub Inc.

Mammal Collection Management. Ed. by Hugh H. Genoways et al. LC 87-50996. (C). 1987. 40.00 (*0-89672-157-4*); pap. 24.00 (*0-89672-156-6*) Tex Tech Univ Pr.

Mammal Collectors' Manual. D. W. Nagorsen & R. L. Peterson. (Illus.). 80p. pap. 16.57 (*0-88854-255-0*) Brill Academic Pubs.

Mammal Footprints: Facts & Fun Books. Peter M. Spizzirri. Ed. by Linda Spizzirri. (Illus.). 32p. (J). (ps-2). 1997. pap. 1.25 (*0-86545-284-9*) Spizzirri.

Mammal in the Mirror: Understanding Our Place in the Natural World. David P. Barash & Ilona A. Barash. LC QP34.5.B34 1999. 336p. 1999. text 24.95 (*0-7167-3391-9*, Sci Am Lib) W H Freeman.

***Mammal in the Mirror: Understanding Our Place in the Natural World.** David P. Barash & Ilona A. Barash. 2000. pap. 14.95 (*0-7167-4166-0*) W H Freeman.

Mammal Mazes: An Educational-Activity Coloring Book. Spizzirri Publishing Co. Staff. Ed. by Linda Spizzirri. (Illus.). 32p. (J). (gr. 1-8). 1989. pap. 1.25 (*0-86545-144-3*) Spizzirri.

Mammal Phylogeny, 2 vols., Set. 1993. 180.95 (*0-387-97676-0*) Spr-Verlag.

Mammal Phylogeny: Mesozoic Differentiation, Multituberculates, Monotremes, Early Therians & Marsupials. Frederick S. Szalay et al. LC 91-29232. 249p. 1993. 95.95 (*0-387-97854-2*) Spr-Verlag.

Mammal Phylogeny: Placentals. Ed. by Frederick S. Szalay et al. LC 91-29232. 321p. 1993. 107.95 (*0-387-97853-4*) Spr-Verlag.

Mammal Remains from Archaeological Sites Pt. 1: Southeastern & Southwestern United States. Stanley J. Olsen. LC 85-176642. (Papers of the Peabody Museum of Archaeology & Ethnology: Vol. 56, No. 1). (Illus.). 176p. (C). 1996. reprint ed. pap. 35.00 (*0-87365-162-6*, P56-1) Peabody Harvard.

Mammal Species of the World: A Taxonomic & Geographic Reference. 2nd ed. Ed. by Don E. Wilson & DeeAnn M. Reeder. LC 92-22703. 1312p. (C). 1993. text 75.00 (*1-56098-217-9*) Smithsonian.

Mammal Study. Boy Scouts of America. (Illus.). 48p. (YA). (gr. 6-12). 1972. pap. 2.90 (*0-8395-3271-7*, 33271) BSA.

Mammalabilia. Douglas Florian. LC 99-10702. 48p. (J). 2000. 16.00 (*0-15-202167-1*, Harcourt Child Bks) Harcourt.

***Mammalabilia.** Douglas Florian. (J). 2000. 24.26 (*0-7398-2199-7*) Raintree Steck-V.

Mammalia see Text-Book of Palaeontology

Mammalia: Carnivora Families Herpesidae Canidae Ursidae Ailuropodidae, Vol. 2. (Fauna of British India Ser.). xii, 504p. 1985. 50.00 (*1-55528-039-0*, Pub. by Today Tomorrow) Scholarly Pubns.

Mammalia: Primates Carnivora Families Felidae & Viveridae, Vol. 1. R. I. Pocock. (Fauna of British India Ser.). xxxiv, 464p. 1985. reprint ed. 50.00 (*1-55528-038-2*, Pub. by Today Tomorrow) Scholarly Pubns.

Mammalian Amino Acid Transport: Mechanisms & Control. M. S. Kilberg & D. Haussinger. LC 92-37711. (Illus.). 328p. (C). 1992. text 110.00 (*0-306-44359-7*, Kluwer Plenum) Kluwer Academic.

Mammalian Anatomy: The Cat. Dale W. Fishbeck & Aurora Sebastiani. (Illus.). 190p. 1998. pap. text 18.95 (*0-89582-364-0*) Morton Pub.

Mammalian Auditory Pathway: Neuroanatomy. Ed. by Arthur N. Popper et al. (Handbook of Auditory Research Ser.: Vol. 1). (Illus.). 448p. 1992. 89.95 (*0-387-97678-7*) Spr-Verlag.

Mammalian Auditory Pathway: Neuroanatomy. Ed. by Arthur N. Popper et al. (Handbook of Auditory Research Ser.: Vol. 1). (Illus.). 448p. 1995. 49.95 (*0-387-97800-3*) Spr-Verlag.

Mammalian Auditory Pathway: Neurophysiology. Ed. by Arthur N. Popper & Richard R. Fay. (Handbook of Auditory Research Ser.: Vol. 2). (Illus.). 368p. 1992. 89.95 (*0-387-97690-6*) Spr-Verlag.

Mammalian Auditory Pathway: Neurophysiology. Ed. by Arthur N. Popper & Richard R. Fay. (Handbook of Auditory Research Ser.: Vol. 2). (Illus.). 368p. 1995. 49.95 (*0-387-97801-1*) Spr-Verlag.

Mammalian Behavior: The Theory & the Science. John P. Smith. LC 90-80105. 420p. 1990. pap. text 29.50 (*0-9627194-0-4*) Bench Mark Bks.

Mammalian Cell As a Microorganism: Genetic & Biochemical Studies in Vitro. Theodore T. Puck. LC 73-188127. 219p. (C). 1972. 28.95 (*0-8162-6980-7*); pap. text 26.95 (*0-8162-6970-X*) Holden-Day.

Mammalian Cell Biotechnology: A Practical Approach. Ed. by M. Butler. (Practical Approach Ser.). (Illus.). 264p. 1991. pap. text 45.00 (*0-19-963209-X*) OUP.

Mammalian Cell Biotechnology in Protein Production. Ed. by Hansjoerg Hauser & Roland Wagner. 480p. (C). 1997. text 146.70 (*3-11-013403-9*) De Gruyter.

Mammalian Cell Culture: The Use of Serum-Free Hormone-Supplemented Media. Ed. by Jennie P. Mather. LC 84-1985. 312p. 1984. 79.50 (*0-306-41584-4*, Plenum Trade) Perseus Pubng.

Mammalian Cell-Derived Recombinant Human Growth Hormone: Pharmacology, Metabolism & Clinical Results. Ed. by N. Stahnke & M. Zachmann. (Journal: Hormone Research Ser.: Vol. 37, Suppl. 2, 1992). (Illus.). iv, 56p. 1992. pap. 26.25 (*3-8055-5743-4*) S Karger.

Mammalian Cell Membranes. G. A. Jamieson & D. M. Robinson. LC 75-33317. 1976. write for info. (*0-408-70722-4*) Buttrwrth-Heinemann.

Mammalian Cell Mutagenesis. Ed. by Martha M. Moore et al. LC 87-21784. (Banbury Reports: No. 28). (Illus.). 280p. 1988. text 77.00 (*0-87969-228-6*) Cold Spring Harbor.

Mammalian Cell Mutagenesis: The Maturation of Test Systems. Ed. by Abraham W. Hsie et al. LC 79-21186. (Banbury Report: Vol. 2). 538p. 1979. reprint ed. pap. 166.80 (*0-608-01800-7*, 206245300003) Bks Demand.

Mammalian Cell Transformation: Mechanisms of Carcinogenesis & Assays for Carcinogens. Ed. by J. Carl Barrett & Raymond W. Tennant. LC 85-14616. (Carcinogenesis - A Comprehensive Survey Ser.: No. 9). (Illus.). 479p. 1985. reprint ed. pap. 148.50 (*0-608-00674-2*, 206126100007) Bks Demand.

Mammalian Cell Transformation by Chemical Carcinogens. Nawin C. Mishra & Myron A. Mehlman. LC 82-51185. (Advances in Modern Environmental Toxicology Ser.: Vol. 1). (Illus.). 504p. 1981. text 58.00 (*0-911131-01-9*) Specialist Journals.

Mammalian Cell Transformation Protocols. Remy A. Aubin. (Methods in Molecular Biology Ser.). (Illus.). 1999. 74.50 (*0-89603-442-9*) Humana.

Mammalian Cells: Probes & Problems, Proceedings. Ed. by C. R. Richmond et al. LC 75-600009. (ERDA Symposium Ser.). 324p. 1975. pap. 16.00 (*0-685-01478-9*, CONF-731007); fiche 6.50 (*0-87079-267-9*, CONF-731007) DOE.

Mammalian Cochlear Nuclei: Organization & Function. M. A. Merchan et al. (NATO ASI Ser.: Vol. 239). (Illus.). 532p. (C). 1993. text 145.00 (*0-306-44406-2*, Kluwer Plenum) Kluwer Academic.

Mammalian Cytochromes P-450, 2 vols., Vol. I. Ed. by F. Peter Guengerich. 240p. 1987. 329.90 (*0-8493-6673-9*, QP671) CRC Pr.

Mammalian Cytochromes P-450, Vol. I. F. Peter Guengerich. LC 86-17640. 1987. 126.00 (*0-8493-6674-7*, CRC Reprint) Franklin.

Mammalian Cytochromes P-450, 2 vols., Vol. II. Ed. by F. Peter Guengerich. LC 86-17640. 244p. 1987. 123.00 (*0-8493-6675-5*, CRC Reprint) Franklin.

Mammalian Development. Ed. by Peter Lonai. 432p. 1996. text 114.00 (*3-7186-5862-3*, Harwood Acad Pubs); pap. text 39.00 (*3-7186-5920-4*, Harwood Acad Pubs) Gordon & Breach.

Mammalian Diseases & Arachnids, Vol. I. Ed. by William B. Nutting. LC 83-20998. 288p. 1984. 163.00 (*0-8493-6562-7*, RA641, CRC Reprint) Franklin.

Mammalian Diseases & Arachnids, Vol. II. William B. Nutting. LC 83-20998. 304p. 1984. 165.00 (*0-8493-6563-5*, RA641, CRC Reprint) Franklin.

Mammalian Dispersal Patterns: The Effect of Social Structure on Population Genetics. Ed. by Diane B. Chepko-Sade & Zuleyma T. Halpin. LC 87-6026. (Illus.). 352p. (Orig.). 1987. pap. text 22.95 (*0-226-10268-8*) U Ch Pr.

Mammalian Dispersal Patterns: The Effect of Social Structure on Population Genetics. Ed. by Diane B. Chepko-Sade & Zuleyma T. Halpin. LC 87-6026. (Illus.). 360p. (Orig.). 1996. lib. bdg. 66.00 (*0-226-10266-1*) U Ch Pr.

Mammalian Egg Coat. Ed. by J. Dietl. (Illus.). 190p. 1989. 101.00 (*0-387-50272-6*) Spr-Verlag.

Mammalian Egg Transfer. Ed. by Cyril E. Adams. 256p. 1982. 145.00 (*0-8493-6140-0*, QL739, CRC Reprint) Franklin.

Mammalian Energetics: Interdisciplinary Views of Metabolism & Reproduction. Ed. by Thomas E. Tomasi & Teresa H. Horton. LC 91-55568. (Illus.). 288p. 1992. text 49.95 (*0-8014-2659-6*) Cornell U Pr.

Mammalian Evolution & Environmental Change in the Neogene of Europe Vol. 1: Hominoid Evolution & Climatic Change in Europe. Ed. by Jorge Agusti et al. LC 98-49430. (Illus.). 392p. 1999. 100.00 (*0-521-64097-0*) Cambridge U Pr.

Mammalian Fauna of the Judith River Formation, Late Cretaceous, Judithian, Northcentral Montana. Marisol Montellano. (Publications in Geological Sciences: Vol. 136). (C). 1992. pap. 18.95 (*0-520-09768-8*, Pub. by U CA Pr) Cal Prin Full Svc.

Mammalian Faunal Butchering Practices at an Inland La Jollan Site (CA-SDI-6153) Lynne E. Christenson. viii, 115p. (C). 1985. reprint ed. pap. text 13.75 (*1-55567-015-6*) Coyote Press.

Mammalian Fetus: Physiological Aspects of Development. Cold Spring Harbor Symposia on Quantitative Biolog. LC 34-8174. (Cold Spring Harbor Symposia on Quantitative Biology Ser.: Vol. 19). (Illus.). 238p. 1954. pap. 73.80 (*0-7837-8975-0*, 204975600003) Bks Demand.

***Mammalian Models for Biomedical Research.** rev. ed. Intro. by Leo A. Whitehair. 82p. (C). 2000. reprint ed. pap. text 20.00 (*0-7881-8514-4*) DIANE Pub.

Mammalian Names: Chinese/English/Latin. W. Sung. (CHI, ENG & LAT.). 285p. 1994. 95.00 (*0-320-00580-1*) Fr & Eur.

Mammalian Names (Latin, Chinese & English) Wang Sung. 1994. 24.95 (*7-03-001965-2*) Sci Pr.

Mammalian Neuroendocrinology. Paul V. Malven. 272p. (C). 1993. boxed set 89.95 (*0-8493-8757-4*, QP356) CRC Pr.

Mammalian Osteology. B. Miles Gilbert. (Special Publications: No. 3). (Illus.). 428p. (Orig.). 1990. reprint ed. pap. 30.00 (*0-943414-71-7*) MO Arch Soc.

Mammalian Osteology, rev. ed. B. Miles Gilbert. LC 80-84455. (Illus.). 428p. (Orig.). 1980. reprint ed. pap. 25.00 (*0-9611174-0-0*) Bone Bks.

Mammalian Paleofaunas of the World. Donald E. Savage & Donald E. Russell. LC 82-13764. (Evolutionary Biology Ser.). (Illus.). 432p. 1983. write for info. (*0-201-06494-4*) Addison-Wesley.

***Mammalian Physiology.** 3rd ed. (C). 1998. lab manual ed. write for info. (*0-8087-5697-4*) Pearson Custom.

Mammalian Preimplantation Embryo: Regulation of Growth & Differentiation In Vitro. Ed. by Barry D. Bavister. LC 87-13986. (Illus.). 398p. (C). 1987. text 132.00 (*0-306-42595-5*, Kluwer Plenum) Kluwer Academic.

Mammalian Proteases Vol. 1: A Glossary & Bibliography: Endopeptidases. Alan J. Barrett & J. Ken McDonald. 1980. text 104.00 (*0-12-079501-9*) Acad Pr.

Mammalian Proteases Vol. 2: A Glossary & Bibliography: Exopeptidases. Alan J. Barrett. Ed. by J. K. McDonald. 377p. 1986. text 104.00 (*0-12-079502-7*) Acad Pr.

Mammalian Radiations: An Analysis of Trends in Evolution, Adaption & Behavior. John F. Eisenberg. LC 80-27940. (Illus.). 620p. 1982. lib. bdg. 72.00 (*0-226-19537-6*) U Ch Pr.

Mammalian Radiations: An Analysis of Trends in Evolution, Adaption & Behavior. John F. Eisenberg. LC 80-27940. (Illus.). 610p. 1983. pap. text 25.00 (*0-226-19538-4*) U Ch Pr.

Mammalian Reproductive Biology. F. H. Bronson. (Illus.). 336p. 1989. pap. text 22.00 (*0-226-07559-1*) U Ch Pr.

Mammalian Reproductive Biology. F. H. Bronson. (Illus.). 336p. 1992. lib. bdg. 45.00 (*0-226-07558-3*) U Ch Pr.

Mammalian Semiochemistry: The Investigation of Chemical Signals Between Mammals. Eric S. Albone. LC 83-10231. 372p. 1984. 411.00 (*0-471-10253-9*) Halsted Pr.

Mammalian Sex Chromosomes & Sex-Determining Genes. Ed. by Ken C. Reed & Jennifer A. Graves. LC 92-1483. xviii, 410p. 1993. text 131.00 (*3-7186-5276-5*) Gordon & Breach.

***Mammalian Social Learning: Comparative & Ecological Perspectives.** Ed. by Hilary Box & Kathleen Gibson. LC 98-41965. (Symposia of the Zoological Society of London Ser.: No. 72). (Illus.). 432p. (C). 1999. 95.00 (*0-521-63263-3*) Cambridge U Pr.

Mammalian Telencephalon: Surface Morphology & Cerebral Cortex. The Vertebrate Neuraxis As a Whole. Subject & Authors Index to Vols. 1-5 see Central Nervous System of Vertebrates: A General Survey of Its Comparative Anatomy with an Introduction to Pertinent Fundamental Biologic & Logical Concepts

Mammalian Thermogenesis. Ed. by Lucien Girardier & Michael J. Stock. LC 83-1929. (Illus.). 300p. 1983. 88.00 (*0-412-23550-1*, NO. 6822) Chapman & Hall.

Mammalian Tumor Cell Heterogeneity. Ed. by John T. Leith & Daniel L. Dexter. 160p. 1986. 94.00 (*0-8493-6162-1*, RC267, CRC Reprint) Franklin.

An Asterisk (*) at the beginning of an entry indicates that the title is appearing for the first time.

Mammalian Zoogeography of a Rocky Mountain - Great Plains Interface in New Mexico, Oklahoma, & Texas. Ed. by Walter W. Dalquest et al. (Special Publications: No. 34). 1990. pap. 14.00 (*0-89672-230-9*) Tex Tech Univ Pr.

Mammalla of India. Robert A. Sterndale. 540p. (C). 1983. 150.00 (*81-7002-010-7*, Pub. by Himalayan Bks) St Mut.

Mammalogy. Feldhamer. LC 98-12994. 576p. 1998. 74.38 (*0-697-16733-X*) McGraw.

Mammalogy. 2nd ed. Feldhamer. 2002. 60.74 (*0-07-290948-X*) McGraw.

Mammalogy. 3rd ed. Martin. 352p. 2000. spiral bd. 28.13 (*0-697-00643-3*) McGraw.

Mammalogy. 3rd ed. Terry A. Vaughan. LC 77-2111. 576p. (C). 1986. text 91.00 (*0-03-058474-4*) SCP.

Mammalogy. 4th ed. Vaughan. (C). 1999. text 92.00 (*0-03-025034-X*) Harcourt Coll Pubs.

Mammals see Wonderful World of Animals

Mammals. Deni Bown. LC 92-54312. (Eyewitness Explorers Ser.). (Illus.). 64p. (J). (gr. 4-7). 1998. pap. 5.95 (*0-7894-2983-7*) DK Pub Inc.

Mammals. Ed. by Martyn Bramwell. LC 93-4336. (Picturepedia Ser.). 48p. (J). (gr. k-3). 1993. 12.95 (*1-56458-386-4*) DK Pub Inc.

Mammals. M. Barbara Brownell. LC 93-19467. (Nature Library). (J). (gr. 1-3). 1994. 10.50 (*0-87044-890-0*) Natl Geog.

Mammals. David Burnie. LC 92-54312. (Eyewitness Explorers Ser.). (Illus.). 64p. (J). (gr. 4-7). 1993. 9.95 (*1-56458-228-0*) DK Pub Inc.

Mammals. Carson Creagh & Discoveries Library Staff. LC 95-32820. (Nature Company Discoveries Library). (Illus.). 64p. (J). (gr. 4-7). 1999. 16.00 (*0-8094-9372-1*) Time-Life.

***Mammals.** Vicky Franchino. (Simply Science Ser.). (Illus.). 32p. (J). (gr. 1-2). 2000. write for info. (*0-7565-0032-X*) Compass Point.

Mammals. Michael George. (Nature Books Ser.). (Illus.). 32p. (J). (gr. 2-6). 1992. lib. bdg. 22.79 (*0-89565-846-1*) Childs World.

***Mammals.** Ernestine Gierecke. LC 98-6361. (Outside My Window Ser.). 24p. (J). 1999. 19.92 (*1-57572-681-5*) Heinemann Lib.

***Mammals.** George McKay. LC 99-36486. (The/Little Guides Ser.). 320p. 1999. pap. 14.95 (*1-875137-59-9*) Weldon Owen.

Mammals. Moore & Jepson. (Illus.). 32p. (J). (gr. 2-3). 1996. pap., teacher ed. 2.95 (*1-55799-506-0*, 4108) Evan-Moor Edu Pubs.

Mammals. National Audubon Society Staff & John Grassy. LC 98-2939. (Audubon Society First Field Guide Ser.). (Illus.). 160p. (YA). (gr. 3-7). 1998. 17.95 (*0-590-05471-6*, Pub. by Scholastic Inc); vinyl bd. 10.95 (*0-590-05489-9*, Pub. by Scholastic Inc) Penguin Putnam.

Mammals. Judy Nayer. (At Your Fingertips Ser.). (Illus.). 12p. (J). (ps-3). 1993. bds. 6.95 (*1-56293-337-X*, McClanahan Book) Learn Horizon.

Mammals. Joy Richardson. LC 92-32913. (Picture Science Ser.). 32p. (J). 1993. lib. bdg. 20.00 (*0-531-14253-1*) Watts.

Mammals. Marc Robinson. LC 95-50116. (Nature Company 2-in-1 Poster Pack Ser.). (Illus.). 14p. (gr. k-7). 1999. pap. 9.95 (*0-7835-4795-1*) Time-Life.

Mammals, 11 vols. Angela Royston. LC 94-27458. (Science Nature Guides Ser.). (Illus.). 80p. (J). (gr. 1-8). 1995. 12.95 (*1-57145-016-5*, Silver Dolph) Advantage Pubs.

Mammals. Stephen Savage. (What's the Difference? Ser.). 48p. (J). (gr. k-3). 1999. pap. 7.95 (*0-7398-1476-1*) Raintree Steck-V.

***Mammals.** Stephen Savage. LC 99-13021. (What's the Difference? Ser.). 32p. (J). 2000. lib. bdg. 25.69 (*0-7398-1354-4*) Raintree Steck-V.

***Mammals** Stephen Savage. LC 99-13021. (What's the Difference? Ser.). (Illus.). (J). 2000. write for info. (*0-07-398135-4*) McGraw.

Mammals. L. M. Stone. LC 98-6329. (Animals in Disguise Ser.). (J). 1998. (*0-86593-485-1*) Rourke Corp.

Mammals. Lynn M. Stone. LC 97-16381. (Desert Animals Discovery Library). 24p. (J). (gr. k-4). 1997. lib. bdg. 15.93 (*0-86625-628-8*) Rourke Pubns.

***Mammals.** Barbara Taylor. LC 99-176668. (DK Pockets Ser.). 128p. (J). 1998. pap. 6.95 (*0-7894-3417-2*) DK Pub Inc.

Mammals. Rod Theodorou. LC 99-17397. 1999. write for info. (*1-57572-883-4*) Heinemann Lib.

Mammals. Time-Life Books Editors. Ed. by Karin Kinney. LC 97-28565. (Student Library). (Illus.). 128p. (J). (gr. 3-8). 1999. 14.99 (*0-7835-1351-8*) Time-Life.

Mammals. Hugh Westrup. LC 95-1960. (Prehistoric North America Ser.). (Illus.). 48p. (J). (gr. 2-4). 1996. lib. bdg. 21.90 (*1-56294-546-7*) Millbrook Pr.

Mammals. 4th ed. Ernest Booth et al. (Pictured Key Nature Ser.). 208p. (C). 1982. text. write for info. (*0-697-04781-4*, WCB McGr Hill) McGrw-H Hghr Educ.

Mammals, 10 bks., Set. P. Copeland. (Smithsonian Coloring Bks.). (Illus.). 32p. (J). (ps-8). 1984. pap. 29.50 (*0-87474-335-4*) Smithsonian.

Mammals: An Artistic Approach:Power Carving, Woodburning, Texturing, Painting. Desiree Hajny. LC 96-10170. (Artistic Approach to Woodcarving Ser.: Bk. 1). (Illus.). 154p. 1994. pap. 19.95 (*1-56523-036-1*) Fox Chapel Pub.

Mammals: An Educational Coloring Book. Spizzirri Publishing Co. Staff. Ed. by Linda Spizzirri. (Illus.). 32p. (J). (gr. 1-8). 1981. pap. 1.99 (*0-86545-027-7*) Spizzirri.

***Mammals: An Explore Your World Handbook.** Discovery Books Staff & Philip Meyers. LC 00-27287. (Illus.). 192p. (J). 2000. pap. 14.95 (*1-56331-838-5*, Pub. by Discovery) Random.

Mammals: Notes for a Short Course Organized by P. D. Gingerich & C. E. Badgley. Ed. by T. W. Broadhead. (Studies in Geology). (Illus.). 234p. (C). 1984. pap. 12.00 (*0-910249-07-5*) U of Tenn Geo.

Mammals: Our Living World. Jenny E. Tesar. (J). 1993. 22.60 (*0-516-09334-7*) Childrens.

Mammals: The Small Plant-Eaters. Linda Losito et al. (Encyclopedia of the Animal World Ser.). (Illus.). 96p. (J). (gr. 4-9). 1989. 19.95 (*0-8160-1958-4*) Facts on File.

Mammals: Whales, Panthers, Rats & Bats: The Characteristics of Mammals from Around the World. Gallimard Jeunesse. LC 96-31736. (Scholastic Voyages of Discovery Ser.; Natural History). 48p. (J). (gr. 3 up). 1997. 19.95 (*0-590-47654-8*) Scholastic Inc.

Mammals, a Guide to Familiar American Species: 218 Animals in Full Color. Herbert Spencer Zim. (Golden Guide Ser.). 1987. 11.05 (*0-606-11594-3*, Pub. by Turtleback) Demco.

***Mammals & Ocean Life.** School Zone Publishing Staff. (Illus.). (J). 2000. pap. 3.79 (*0-88743-863-6*) Sch Zone Pub Co.

Mammals As Predators: The Proceedings of a Symposium Held by the Zoological Society of London & the Mammal Society, London, 22-23 November 1991. Ed. by N. Dunstone & M. L. Gorman. LC 92-39591. (Illus.). 508p. (C). 1993. text 125.00 (*0-19-854067-1*, Clarendon Pr) OUP.

Mammals Dominate the Earth. Andreu Llamas. LC 95-3966. (Edades de la Tierra Ser.).Tr. of Mamiferos Dominan la Tierra. (ENG & SPA., Illus.). 32p. (J). (gr. 3-12). 1996. lib. bdg. 15.95 (*0-7910-3456-9*) Chelsea Hse.

Mammals Found at the Awatovi Site. Barbara Lawrence. (HU PMP Ser.: Vol. 35, No. 3). (Illus.). 1951. pap. 25.00 (*0-527-01290-4*) Periodicals Srv.

Mammals from Pouches & Eggs. Marshall. Ed. by Jennifer A. Graves et al. (C). 1990. 60.00 (*0-643-05020-5*, Pub. by CSIRO) Accents Pubns.

Mammals from the Mexican State of Sinaloa Pt. II: Chiroptera. J. Knox Jones, Jr. et al. (Occasional Papers: No. 6). 29p. 1972. pap. 1.00 (*0-686-80301-9*) U KS Nat Hist Mus.

Mammals in Hawai'i: A Synopsis & Notational Bibliography. rev. ed. P. Quentin Tomich. (Illus.). 375p. 1986. pap. 24.50 (*0-930897-10-2*, SP76) Bishop Mus.

Mammals in Kansas. James W. Bee et al. (Public Education Ser.: No. 7). (Illus.). x, 302p. 1981. pap. 12.95 (*0-89338-014-8*) U KS Nat Hist Mus.

Mammals in Kansas. James W. Bee et al. Ed. by Joseph T. Collins. (Public Education Ser.: No. 7). (Illus.). x, 302p. 1981. 17.95 (*0-89338-015-6*) U KS Nat Hist Mus.

Mammals in the Seas Vol. 3: General Papers & Large Cetaceans (FAO/UNEP) (Fisheries Reports: No. 5). 504p. 1981. 85.00 (*92-5-100513-3*, F2319, Pub. by FAO) Bernan Associates.

Mammals in Wyoming. Tim W. Clark & Mark R. Stromberg. Ed. by Joseph T. Collins. (Public Education Ser.: No. 10). (Illus.). xii, 308p. 1987. 25.00 (*0-89338-026-1*) U KS Nat Hist Mus.

Mammals in Wyoming. Tim W. Clark & Mark R. Stromberg. Ed. by Joseph T. Collins. (Public Education Ser.: No. 10). (Illus.). xii, 308p. 1987. pap. 12.95 (*0-89338-025-3*) U KS Nat Hist Mus.

Mammal's Notebook: Collected Writings of Erik Satie. Erik Satie. Ed. by Ornella Volta. Tr. by Anthony Melville from FRE. (Atlas Arkhive Ser.: Vol. 5). (Illus.). 208p. (Orig.). 1996. pap. 22.99 (*0-947757-92-9*) Serpents Tail.

Mammals of Africa: An Identification Manual. Ed. by J. Meester & H. W. Setzer. LC 70-169904. 505p. reprint ed. pap. 156.60 (*0-608-17752-0*, 205649600069) Bks Demand.

Mammals of Alaska. Ed. by Penny Rennick. (Alaska Geographic Guides Ser.). (Illus.). 176p. (Orig.). 1996. pap. 17.95 (*1-56661-034-6*) Alaska Geog Soc.

***Mammals of Alberta.** Don Pattie & Chris Fisher. 240p. 1999. pap. 19.95 (*1-55105-209-1*) Lone Pine.

Mammals of Ancient Egypt. Dale J. Osborn. (Natural History of Egypt Ser.). 224p. 1998. pap. 75.00 (*0-85668-510-0*, Pub. by Aris & Phillips) David Brown.

Mammals of Ancient Egypt. Dale J. Osborn. (Natural History of Egypt Ser.). (Illus.). 224p. 1998. 95.00 (*0-85668-522-4*, Pub. by Aris & Phillips) David Brown.

Mammals of Antarctica. Lynn M. Stone. LC 95-5993. (Antarctica Discovery Library). 24p. (J). (gr. k-4). 1995. lib. bdg. 15.93 (*1-55916-140-X*) Rourke Bk Co.

Mammals of Arizona. Donald F. Hoffmeister. LC 85-24621. (Illus.). 602p. 1986. 68.00 (*0-8165-0873-9*) U of Ariz Pr.

Mammals of Arizona. rev. ed. Dick Nelson & Sharon Nelson. (Easy Field Guide Ser.). (Illus.). 32p. (J). 1994. pap. 1.50 (*0-935810-16-1*) R H Pub.

Mammals of Australia. Ronald Straham. (Illus.). 756p. 1996. 75.00 (*1-56098-673-5*) Smithsonian.

Mammals of Big Bend Ranch State Park, Texas. Franklin D. Yancey. (Special Publications: No. 39). 210p. 1997. pap. text 19.95 (*0-9640188-5-3*) Mus TX Tech.

Mammals of California & Nevada. E. Lendell Cockrum & Yar Petryszyn. (Illus.). 178p. 1994. pap. 9.95 (*0-918080-34-7*) Treas Chest Bks.

Mammals of Canada. A. F. Banfield. LC 73-92298. (Illus.). 1974. text 47.50 (*0-8020-2137-9*) U of Toronto Pr.

Mammals of Colorado. James P. Fitzgerald et al. LC 94-1626. (Illus.). 488p. 1994. 59.95 (*0-87081-333-1*) Univ Pr Colo.

Mammals of Delight: Poems, 1972-1977. Mary N. Korte. 1978. 4.00 (*0-685-50206-6*) Oyez.

Mammals of Delight: Poems, 1972-1977. deluxe ed. Mary N. Korte. 1978. 12.50 (*0-685-50205-8*) Oyez.

Mammals of Denali. rev. ed. Adolph Murie. LC 94-14061. 1994. 9.95 (*0-930931-12-2*) Alaska Natural.

Mammals of El Salvador. William Henry Burt & Ruben A. Stirton. LC 61-64173. (University of Michigan, Museum of Zoology, Miscellaneous Publications: No. 117). 69p. reprint ed. pap. 30.00 (*0-608-07032-7*, 206723900009) Bks Demand.

Mammals of Florida. Larry N. Brown. (Illus.). 224p. 1997. pap. 22.95 (*0-89317-042-9*) Windward Pub.

Mammals of Georgia: A Study of Their Distribution & Functional Role in the Ecosystem. Frank B. Golley. LC 62-22075. 230p. reprint ed. pap. 71.30 (*0-608-15794-5*, 203104200073) Bks Demand.

Mammals of Great Smoky Mountains National Park. Donald W. Linzey. (Illus.). 152p. (Orig.). 1995. pap. text 14.95 (*0-939923-48-3*) M & W Pub Co.

Mammals of Great Smoky Mountains National Park. Alicia V. Linzey & Donald W. Linzey. LC 74-111048. 148p. (Orig.). reprint ed. pap. 45.90 (*0-608-15466-0*, 202937700060) Bks Demand.

Mammals of Indiana. Marcus W. Lyon, Jr. LC 73-17829. (Natural Sciences in America Ser.). (Illus.). 388p. 1974. reprint ed. 33.95 (*0-405-05747-4*) Ayer.

Mammals of Keewatin. Francis Harper. (Miscellaneous Publications: No. 12). 94p. 1956. pap. 5.00 (*0-686-80292-6*) U KS Nat Hist Mus.

Mammals of Kentucky. Roger W. Barbour & Wayne H. Davis. LC 74-7870. (Illus.). 368p. 1974. 29.00 (*0-8131-1314-8*) U Pr of Ky.

Mammals of Lacreek National Wildlife Refuge, South Dakota. R. B. Wilhelm et al. (Special Publications: No. 17). (Illus.). 39p. (Orig.). 1981. pap. 4.00 (*0-89672-091-8*) Tex Tech Univ Pr.

Mammals of Lake Tahoe. Robert T. Orr. (Illus.). 127p. 1949. 7.50 (*0-940228-07-6*) Calif Acad Sci.

Mammals of Los Angeles County, California. Charles A. McLaughlin. (Science Ser.: No. 21). (Illus.). 34p. 1959. pap. 8.00 (*0-938644-02-5*) Nat Hist Mus.

Mammals of Louisiana & Its Adjacent Waters. George H. Lowery, Jr. LC 73-89662. (Illus.). xxiv, 565p. 1974. 29.95 (*0-8071-0609-7*) La State U Pr.

***Mammals of Madagascar.** Nick Garbutt. LC 98-86267. (Illus.). 224p. 1998. 37.50 (*0-300-07751-3*) Yale U Pr.

Mammals of Mesa Verde National Park, Colorado. Sydney Anderson. (Museum Ser.: Vol. 14, No. 3). 39p. 1961. pap. 2.25 (*0-317-04937-2*) U KS Nat Hist Mus.

Mammals of Minnesota. Evan B. Hazard. LC 82-2706. (Illus.). 285p. 1982. pap. 21.95 (*0-8166-0952-7*) U of Minn Pr.

Mammals of Nepal - With Reference to Those of India, Bangladesh, Bhutan & Pakistan. Tej K. Shrestha. 1997. pap. 106.00 (*0-7855-7437-9*, Pub. by Ratna Pustak Bhandar) St Mut.

Mammals of Nevada. E. Raymond Hall. (Illus.). 734p. 1995. text 55.00 (*0-87417-261-6*) U of Nev Pr.

Mammals of New Guinea. rev. ed. Tim Flannery. (Comstock Bk.). (Illus.). 464p. 1995. text 85.00 (*0-8014-3149-2*) Cornell U Pr.

Mammals of New Mexico. rev. ed. Dick Nelson & Sharon Nelson. (Easy Field Guide Ser.). (Illus.). 32p. (J). 1985. pap. 1.50 (*0-935810-22-6*) R H Pub.

Mammals of Nigeria. D. C. Happold. (Illus.). 420p. 1987. 135.00 (*0-19-857565-3*) OUP.

***Mammals of North America: Temperate & Arctic Regions.** Adrian Forsyth. (Illus.). 352p. 1999. 40.00 (*1-55209-409-X*) Firefly Bks Ltd.

Mammals of North America: The Descriptions of Species Based Chiefly on the Collections in the Museum of the Smithsonian Institution. Spencer F. Baird. LC 73-17797. (Natural Sciences in America Ser.). (Illus.). 844p. 1974. reprint ed. 64.95 (*0-405-05710-5*) Ayer.

Mammals of North-Central Texas. Walter W. Dalquest & Norman V. Horner. (Illus.). 261p. 1984. 15.00 (*0-915323-01-X*) Midwestern St U Pr.

Mammals of Northwestern South Dakota. Kenneth W. Andersen & J. Knox Jones, Jr. (Museum Ser.: Vol. 19, No. 5). 33p. 1971. pap. 1.75 (*0-317-04914-3*) U KS Nat Hist Mus.

Mammals of Pakistan. T. J. Roberts. LC 97-930912. (Illus.). 1997. write for info. (*0-19-577852-9*) OUP.

***Mammals of Southern Africa.** 2nd rev. ed. Chris Stuart & Tilde Stuart. LC 99-74801. (Illus.). 272p. 2000. pap. 32.50 (*0-88359-047-6*, Pub. by R Curtis Pubng) Chelsea Green Pub.

Mammals of Texas. rev. ed. William B. Davis & David J. Schmidly. (Illus.). 328p. 1995. pap. 17.95 (*1-885696-00-0*) TX Prks & Wldlife.

Mammals of the Adirondack Region, Northwestern New York: Introductory Chapter Treating of the Location & Boundaries of the Region, Its Geological History, Topography, Climate, General Features, Botany & Faunal Position. Clinton H. Merriam. LC 73-17832. (Natural Sciences of America Ser.). 320p. 1974. reprint ed. 23.95 (*0-405-05750-4*) Ayer.

Mammals of the Adirondacks: A Field Guide. William K. Chapman & Dennis Aprill. 160p. 1991. pap. 13.95 (*0-932052-61-4*) North Country.

Mammals of the Canyon Country. D. Armstrong. (Illus.). 263p. 2.95 (*0-614-05154-1*) Canyonlands.

Mammals of the Canyon Country. David M. Armstrong. (Illus.). 263p. (Orig.). (C). 1982. pap. 3.95 (*0-937407-01-1*) Canyonlands.

Mammals of the Carolinas, Virginia, & Maryland. William D. Webster et al. LC 85-1171. (Illus.). xii, 255p. 1985. 29.95 (*0-8078-1663-9*) U of NC Pr.

Mammals of the Eastern United States. 3rd ed. John O. Whitaker, Jr. & W. J. Hamilton, Jr. LC 98-11962. (Illus.). 608p. 1998. 50.00 (*0-8014-3475-0*, Comstock Pub) Cornell U Pr.

Mammals of the Edwards Plateau, TX. Jim R. Goetze. (Special Publications). (Illus.). 270p. 1998. pap. text 19.95 (*0-9640188-7-X*) Mus TX Tech.

Mammals of the Grand Mesa, Colorado. Sydney Anderson. (Museum Ser.: Vol. 9, No. 16). 10p. 1959. pap. 1.00 (*0-317-04923-2*) U KS Nat Hist Mus.

Mammals of the Great Lakes Region. rev. ed. Allen Kurta. LC 94-26780. (Illus.). 392p. (C). 1995. pap. 17.95 (*0-472-06497-5*, 06497) U of Mich Pr.

Mammals of the Holy Land. Mazin B. Qumsiyeh. LC 96-33969. 352p. 1996. 35.00 (*0-89672-364-X*) Tex Tech Univ Pr.

Mammals of the Indo-Malayan Region: A Systematic Review. G. B. Corbet & J. E. Hill. (Illus.). 496p. 1992. text 125.00 (*0-19-854693-9*) OUP.

Mammals of the Intermountain West. Samuel B. Zeveloff. LC 88-20462. (Illus.). 352p. 1988. pap. 14.95 (*0-87480-327-6*) U of Utah Pr.

Mammals of the Kelley-Roosevelts & Delacour Asiatic Expeditions. Wilfred H. Osgood. LC 33-22124. (Field Museum of Natural History, Publication 1362 Ser. : Vol. 18, No. 10). 149p. reprint ed. pap. 46.20 (*0-608-03780-X*, 206462700009) Bks Demand.

Mammals of the Llano Estacado. Larry L. Choate. (Special Publications). (Illus.). 240p. Date not set. pap. text 19.95 (*0-9640188-6-1*) Mus TX Tech.

Mammals of the Mexican Boundary of the United States Pt. 1: Catalogue of the Species of Mammals Occurring in That Region, Families Didelphildae to Muridae. Edgar A. Mearns. LC 73-18787. (Natural Sciences in America Ser.). 576p. 1974. reprint ed. 44.95 (*0-405-05777-6*) Ayer.

Mammals of the National Parks. Richard G. Van Gelder. LC 81-17162. (Illus.). 336p. 1982. pap. 10.95 (*0-8018-2689-6*) Johns Hopkins.

Mammals of the Neotropics Vol. 1: The Northern Neotropics: Panama, Colombia, Venezuela, Guyana, Suriname, French Guinana. John F. Eisenberg. LC 88-27479. (Illus.). 549p. 1989. pap. text 45.00 (*0-226-19540-6*) U Ch Pr.

Mammals of the Neotropics Vol. 1: The Northern Neotropics: Panama, Colombia, Venezuela, Guyana, Suriname, French Guinana. John F. Eisenberg. LC 88-27479. (Illus.). 550p. 1995. lib. bdg. 100.00 (*0-226-19539-2*) U Ch Pr.

Mammals of the Neotropics Vol. 2: The Southern Cone: Chile, Argentina, Uruguay, & Paraguay. Kent H. Redford & John F. Eisenberg. (Illus.). 460p. 1992. pap. text 48.00 (*0-226-70682-6*); lib. bdg. 110.00 (*0-226-70681-8*) U Ch Pr.

***Mammals of the Neotropics Vol. 3: The Central Neotropics; Ecuador, Peru, Bolivia, Brazil.** John F. Eisenberg. (Illus.). 2000. pap. text 40.00 (*0-226-19542-2*) U Ch Pr.

Mammals of the Northeast. John Whitaker, Jr. & Randall R. Reeves. Ed. by Winston Williams & Tim Ohr. (Northeast Nature Ser.). (Illus.). 128p. 1998. pap. 16.95 (*0-911977-17-1*) Wrld Tampa.

Mammals of the Northern Great Plains. J. Knox Jones, Jr. et al. LC 82-2693. (Illus.). 391p. 1983. reprint ed. pap. 121.30 (*0-608-02676-X*, 206332900004) Bks Demand.

Mammals of the Northern Rockies. Tom J. Ulrich. LC 86-8759. (Illus.). 160p. (Orig.). 1986. pap. 12.00 (*0-87842-200-5*) Mountain Pr.

Mammals of the Northwest: Washington, Oregon, Idaho, & British Columbia. Earl J. Larrison. LC 73-94501. (Trailside Ser.). (Illus.). 1976. pap. 8.95 (*0-914516-04-3*) Seattle Audubon Soc.

Mammals of the Pacific Northwest: From the Coast to the High Cascades. Chris Maser. LC 98-7570. (Illus.). 512p. 1998. pap. 26.95 (*0-87071-438-4*) Oreg St U Pr.

Mammals of the Pacific States: California, Oregon, Washington. Lloyd G. Ingles. (Illus.). xii, 506p. 1965. pap. 19.95 (*0-8047-1843-1*) Stanford U Pr.

***Mammals of the Rocky Mountains.** Don Pattie et al. (Illus.). 296p. 2000. pap. 18.95 (*1-55105-211-3*) Lone Pine.

Mammals of the San Francisco Bay Region. William D. Berry & Elizabeth Berry. LC 59-6052. (California Natural History Guides Ser.: No. 2). (Illus.). 80p. reprint ed. pap. 30.00 (*0-608-17993-0*, 202903900058) Bks Demand.

Mammals of the San Gabriel Mountains of California. Terry A. Vaughan. (Museum Ser.: Vol. 7, No. 9). 70p. 1954. pap. 3.75 (*0-317-04962-3*) U KS Nat Hist Mus.

Mammals of the South-West Pacific & Moluccan Islands. Tim Flannery. (Comstock Bk.). (Illus.). 464p. 1995. text 85.00 (*0-8014-3150-6*) Cornell U Pr.

Mammals of the Southwest. E. Lendell Cockrum. LC 81-21834. (Illus.). 176p. reprint ed. pap. 54.60 (*0-7837-5044-7*, 204472200004) Bks Demand.

Mammals of the Southwest Desert. rev. ed. George Olin. Ed. by Rose Houk et al. LC 81-86094. (Illus.). 100p. 1982. pap. 5.95 (*0-911408-60-6*) SW Pks Mnmts.

Mammals of the Southwestern United States & Northwestern Mexico. rev. ed. E. Lendell Cockrum & Yar Petryszyn. (Illus.). 187p. 1993. reprint ed. pap. 9.95 (*0-918080-66-5*, 20988) Treas Chest Bks.

Mammals of the Soviet Union, Vol. 2, Pt. 3. Ed. by V. G. Heptner. 1000p. 1996. lib. bdg. 225.00 (*1-886106-67-3*) Science Pubs.

Mammals of the Soviet Union Vol. II, Pt. 1A: Sinenia & Carnivora (Cows, Wolves & Bears) Ed. by V. G. Heptner. 733p. 1998. 150.00 (*1-886106-81-9*) Science Pubs.

Mammals of the Thar Desert. Ishwar Prakash. 114p. 1995. 100.00 (*81-7233-078-2*, Pub. by Scientific Pubs) St Mut.

Mammals of the Wild Northwest. Gary Twesten. (Illus.). 73p. 1988. pap. 20.00 (*0-9602428-5-6*) G Twesten.

Mammals of the Wolf Ranch Local Fauna, Pliocene of the San Pedro Valley, Arizona. Jessica A. Harrison. (Occasional Papers: No. 73). 18p. 1978. pap. 1.00 (*0-686-79818-X*) U KS Nat Hist Mus.

Mammals of the World on Stamps. (Illus.). 76p. 1973. 5.00 (*0-318-13302-4*) Am Topical Assn.

Mammals of Tucuman: Mamiferos de Tucuman. Ruben M. Barquez et al. (ENG & SPA., Illus.). 282p. (Orig.). 1991. pap. 15.00 (*1-883090-03-2*) OK Museum.

Mammals of Utah: Taxonomy & Distribution. Stephen D. Durrant. (Museum Ser.: Vol. 6). 549p. 1952. 15.00 (*0-686-80278-0*) U KS Nat Hist Mus.

Mammals of Victoria: Distribution, Ecology & Conservation. Ed. by Peter Menkhorst. (Illus.). 290p. 1996. pap. text 50.00 (*0-19-554016-6*) OUP.

Mammals of Virginia. Donald W. Linzey. (Illus.). 500p. 1998. 59.95 (*0-939923-36-X*) M & W Pub Co.

Mammals of Wisconsin. Hartley H. Jackson. (Illus.). 518p. 1961. 64.95 (*0-299-02150-5*) U of Wis Pr.

Mammals' Size & Climate. LeGendre. 1996. pap. text 19.95 (*0-226-47066-0*); lib. bdg. 54.50 (*0-226-47065-2*) U Ch Pr.

***Mammals Structure & Function.** (C). 2000. write for info. (*0-8087-7592-8*) Pearson Custom.

Mammary Development & Cancer. Ed. by S. Rudland et al. LC 98-110810. (Biochemical Society Symposium Ser.: Vol. 63). (Illus.). 319p. (C). 1997. text 95.00 (*1-85578-087-9*, Pub. by Portland Pr Ltd) Ashgate Pub Co.

Mammary Gland: Development, Regulation & Function. M. C. Neville & C. W. Daniel. LC 87-18606. (Illus.). 648p. (C). 1987. text 135.00 (*0-306-42641-2*, Kluwer Plenum) Kluwer Academic.

Mammary Gland Transgenesis: Therapeutic Protein Production. Fidel O. Castro. LC 97-44557. (Biotechnology Intelligence Unit (SV) Ser.). 192p. 1997. 129.00 (*1-57059-518-6*) Landes Bioscience.

Mammary Gland Transgenesis: Therapeutic Protein Production. Ed. by Fidel O. Castro. LC 97-44557. (Biotechnology Intelligence Unit (SV) Ser.). 192p. 1998. 129.00 (*3-540-63712-5*) Spr-Verlag.

Mammary Plays: Two Plays. Paula Vogel. LC 97-40169. 176p. 1998. pap. text 13.95 (*1-55936-144-1*) Theatre Comm.

Mammary Tumor Cell Cycle, Differentiation, & Metastasis: Advances in Cellular & Molecular Biology of Breast Cancer. Ed. by Robert B. Dickson & Marc E. Lippman. LC 96-4654. 448p. 1996. text 345.00 (*0-7923-3905-3*) Kluwer Academic.

Mammary Tumorigenesis & Malignant Progression: Advances in Cellular & Molecular Biology of Breast Cancer. Ed. by Robert B. Dickson & Marc E. Lippman. LC 93-40375. (Cancer Treatment & Research Ser.: Vol. 71). 384p. (C). 1994. text 290.00 (*0-7923-2647-4*) Kluwer Academic.

Mammatocumulus. Josephine Clare. LC 76-58627. (Poetry Ser.). 1977. pap. 4.50 (*0-685-75802-8*) Ocotillo.

Mamme Dear: A Turn-of-the-Century Collection of Model Yiddish Letters. Tr. & Intro. by Lewis Glinert. LC 96-45382. 240p. 1997. 30.00 (*0-7657-5982-9*) Aronson.

Mammies No More: The Changing Image of Black Women on Stage & Screen. Lisa M. Anderson. LC 97-9782. (Illus.). 160p. 1997. 22.95 (*0-8476-8419-9*) Rowman.

Mammographic Appearances. A. Willemin. (Illus.). 1973. 126.25 (*3-8055-1584-7*) S Karger.

Mammographic Imaging: A Practical Guide. Valerie Fink-Andoline et al. (Illus.). 272p. 1992. text 59.00 (*0-397-51096-9*) Lppncott W & W.

Mammographic Imaging: A Practical Guide. 2nd ed. Valerie F. Andolina et al. 416p. text 56.00 (*0-7817-1696-9*) Lppncott W & W.

Mammographic Interpretation: A Practical Approach. 2nd ed. Marc J. Homer. LC 96-43895. (Illus.). 402p. 1996. text 98.00 (*0-07-029720-7*) McGraw-Hill HPD.

Mammography. P. Haehnel & C. Kleitz. (Illus.). vi, 137p. 1988. 38.95 (*0-387-15328-4*) Spr-Verlag.

Mammography. Heinlein. 2000. text 59.00 (*0-323-00407-5*) Mosby Inc.

Mammography. Luz A. Venta. 400p. 1999. text. write for info. (*0-7817-1663-2*) Lppncott W & W.

Mammography: Hearings Before a Subcommittee of the Committee on Appropriations, United States Senate, One Hundred Fifth Congress, First Session, Special Hearings, February 5, 1997-Washington, DC; February 20, 1997-Philadelphia, PA; February 24, 1997-Pittsburgh, PA; March 3, 1997-Hershey, PA. USGPO Staff. LC 98-167856. (S. Hrg. Ser.). v, 198 p. 1998. write for info. (*0-16-056448-4*) USGPO.

Mammography: Self-Assessment & Review. Linda Lefave. LC 93-3913. (Pretest Specialty Level Ser.). (Illus.). 160p. 1993. pap. text 25.00 (*0-07-052017-8*) McGraw-Hill HPD.

Mammography: The Requisites. Rubin. (Illus.). 384p. (C). (gr. 13). 2000. text 79.00 (*0-8151-7481-0*, 27477) Mosby Inc.

Mammography Exam Review. Philipot. 224p. 1992. pap. text 28.95 (*0-397-55019-7*) Lppncott W & W.

Mammography for Radiologic Technologists. 2nd ed. Gini Wentz & Ward C. Parsons. (Illus.). 210p. 1996. pap. 42.00 (*0-07-105845-1*) McGraw-Hill HPD.

Mammography Image Analysis. Ralph Highnam & Michael Brady. LC 99-10452. 22p. 1999. write for info. (*0-7923-5620-9*) Kluwer Academic.

Mammography in Health & Medicine: Research Subject Analysis with Reference Bibliography. Wilson R. Koebetz. LC 85-48098. 150p. 1987. 47.50 (*0-88164-468-4*); pap. 44.50 (*0-88164-469-2*) ABBE Pubs Assn.

Mammography of the Breast: Index of New Information. Lizabeth L. Holtzer. LC 95-16306. 1995. 47.50 (*0-7883-0703-7*); pap. 44.50 (*0-7883-0704-5*) ABBE Pubs Assn.

Mammography Quality Control: The Why & How Book. Calvin P. Myers. (Illus.). 41p. 1997. pap. text 19.95 (*0-944838-83-9*) Med Physics Pub.

Mammolina: A Story about Maria Montessori. Barbara O'Connor. LC 92-415. (Creative Minds Ser.). (J). (gr. 3-6). 1993. pap. 2.98 (*0-87614-602-7*, Carolrhoda); lib. bdg. 19.95 (*0-87614-743-0*, Carolrhoda) Lerner Pub.

Mammon. Grant Sutherland. 198p. (C). 1990. 30.00 (*0-7316-3788-7*, Pub. by Pascoe Pub) St Mut.

Mammon & Manon in Early New Orleans: The First Slave Society in the Deep South, 1718-1819. Thomas N. Ingersoll. LC 98-25313. (Illus.). 520p. 1999. pap. 25.00 (*1-57233-024-4*); text 60.00 (*1-57233-023-6*) U of Tenn Pr.

Mammon & the Pursuit of Empire: The Political Economy of British Imperialism, 1860-1912. Lance E. Davis & Robert A. Huttenback. (Interdisciplinary Perspectives on Modern History Ser.). (Illus.). 414p. 1987. text 89.95 (*0-521-23611-8*) Cambridge U Pr.

Mammon of Unrighteousness. Hjalmar H. Boyesen. LC 78-104421. 386p. reprint ed. lib. bdg. 29.00 (*0-8290-2395-X*) Irvington.

Mammon of Unrighteousness. Hjalmar H. Boyesen. 386p. (C). 1987. reprint ed. pap. text 8.95 (*0-8290-2378-X*) Irvington.

Mammoth. Barbara Hehner. (Ice Age Bones & Book Ser.). (Illus.). 64p. (J). (gr. 1-7). 1998. pap. 15.99 (*1-58184-003-9*) Somerville Hse.

Mammoth. Barbara Hehner. (Ice Age Bones & Book Ser.: No. 1). (Illus.). 64p. (J). (gr. 1-7). 1998. pap. 15.99 (*1-894042-19-0*) Somerville Hse.

Mammoth & the Mouse: Microhistory & Morphology. Florike Egmond & Peter Mason. LC 96-47416. (Illus.). 264p. 1997. text 45.00 (*0-8018-5477-6*); pap. text 15.95 (*0-8018-5478-4*) Johns Hopkins.

Mammoth Area Rock Climbs. 2nd rev. ed. Marty Lewis & John Moynier. (Eastern Sierra Climbing Guides Ser.: Vol. 2). (Illus.). 96p. 1996. pap. 12.00 (*0-9676116-3-6*) Maximus Pr.

***Mammoth Book Encyclopedia of the Unsolved.** Colin Wilson. 624p. 2000. pap. 12.95 (*0-7867-0793-3*, Pub. by Carroll & Graf) Publishers Group.

Mammoth Book of Armchair Crimes, Detectives & Thrillers. Ed. by Peter Haining. (Mammoth Book Ser.). 416p. 1998. pap. 10.95 (*0-7867-0584-1*) Carroll & Graf.

Mammoth Book of Arthurian Legends. Ed. by Mike Ashley. LC 98-16798. (Mammoth Book Ser.). x, 566p. 1998. pap. 10.95 (*0-7867-0532-9*) Carroll & Graf.

Mammoth Book of Astounding Puzzles. Ed. by Victor Serebriakoff. (Mammoth Book Ser.). 512p. 1992. pap. 10.95 (*0-88184-856-5*) Carroll & Graf.

Mammoth Book of Astounding Word Games. Ed. by Peter Newby. (Mammoth Book Ser.). 512p. 1995. pap. 10.95 (*0-7867-0213-3*) Carroll & Graf.

***Mammoth Book of Battles.** Ed. by Jon E. Lewis. (Mammoth Book Ser.). (Illus.). 512p. 1999. pap. text 10.95 (*0-7867-0689-9*) Carroll & Graf.

Mammoth Book of Best New Horror, 7 vols., No. 7. 7th ed. Ed. by Stephen Jones. 512p. 1996. pap. 10.95 (*0-7867-0372-5*) Carroll & Graf.

Mammoth Book of Best New Horror, No. 8. Ed. by Stephen Jones. 513p. 1997. pap. 10.95 (*0-7867-0474-8*) Carroll & Graf.

Mammoth Book of Best New Horror, No. 9. Ed. by Stephen Jones. (Mammoth Book Ser.). 512p. 1998. pap. 10.95 (*0-7867-0585-X*) Carroll & Graf.

***Mammoth Book of Best New Horror, No. 10.** Ed. by Stephen Jones. (Mammoth Book Ser.). 512p. 1999. pap. text 10.95 (*0-7867-0690-2*) Carroll & Graf.

***Mammoth Book of Best New Horror, No. 11.** Stephen Jones. 512p. 2000. pap. 11.95 (*0-7867-0792-5*, Pub. by Carroll & Graf) Publishers Group.

Mammoth Book of Brainstorming Puzzles. David J. Bodycombe. (Mammoth Book Ser.). (Illus.). 560p. 1996. pap. 10.95 (*0-7867-0299-0*) Carroll & Graf.

***Mammoth Book of Bridge.** Ed. by Mark Horton. (Mammoth Book Ser.). 512p. 2000. pap. text 10.95 (*0-7867-0691-0*) Carroll & Graf.

***Mammoth Book of British Kings & Queens.** Ed. by Mike Ashley. (Mammoth Book Ser.). (Illus.). 832p. 1999. pap. text 18.95 (*0-7867-0692-9*) Carroll & Graf.

Mammoth Book of British Kings & Queens of Britain & Ireland. Ed. by Mike Ashley. (Mammoth Book Ser.). (Illus.). 544p. 1998. 29.95 (*0-7867-0405-5*) Carroll & Graf.

Mammoth Book of Cats. Ed. by Mark Bryant. (Mammoth Book Ser.). 512p. 1999. pap. text 10.95 (*0-7867-0651-1*) Carroll & Graf.

Mammoth Book of Chess. Graham Burgess. LC 97-12079. (Mammoth Book Ser.). (Illus.). 5454p. 1997. pap. 11.95 (*0-7867-0431-4*) Carroll & Graf.

***Mammoth Book of Chess: Featuring Internet & Computer Games.** Graham Burgess. (Illus.). 512p. 2000. pap. 11.95 (*0-7867-0725-9*, Pub. by Carroll & Graf) Publishers Group.

Mammoth Book of Classic Science Fiction: Short Novels of the 1930's. Ed. by Isaac Asimov et al. 572p. 1988. pap. 8.95 (*0-88184-410-1*) Carroll & Graf.

Mammoth Book of Comic Fantasy. Ed. by Michael Ashley. LC 98-6915. (Mammoth Book Ser.). xv, 524 p. 1998. pap. 10.95 (*0-7867-0533-7*) Carroll & Graf.

Mammoth Book of Comic Fantasy II. Ed. by Michael Ashley. (Mammoth Book Ser.). 544p. 1999. pap. text 10.95 (*0-7867-0694-5*) Carroll & Graf.

Mammoth Book of Crossword Puzzles. Richard B. Manchester. 416p. 1989. pap. 12.95 (*0-88486-030-2*) Arrowood Pr.

Mammoth Book of Dinosaurs. (Dinosaur Bindups II Ser.). (Illus.). 240p. (J). (gr. 2-5). 1996. write for info. (*1-56144-776-5*, Honey Bear Bks) Modern Pub NYC.

Mammoth Book of Dogs: A Collection of Stories, Verse & Prose. Ed. & Pref. by Frank Jackson. (Mammoth Book Ser.). (Illus.). 533p. 1999. pap. 10.95 (*0-7867-0605-8*) Carroll & Graf.

Mammoth Book of Dracula. Ed. by Stephen Jones. LC 97-9797. (Mammoth Book Ser.). 512p. 1997. pap. 10.95 (*0-7867-0428-4*) Carroll & Graf.

Mammoth Book of Dreams. Ed. by Pierre Daco. 544p. 1995. pap. 9.95 (*0-7867-0215-X*) Carroll & Graf.

***Mammoth Book of Endurance & Adventure.** Ed. by Jon E. Lewis. 512p. 2000. pap. 11.95 (*0-7867-0788-7*, Pub. by Carroll & Graf) Publishers Group.

Mammoth Book of Erotica. Ed. by Maxim Jakubowski. (Mammoth Book Ser.). 600p. 1994. pap. 10.95 (*0-7867-0158-7*) Carroll & Graf.

***Mammoth Book of Erotica.** Ed. by Maxim Jakubowski. 624p. 2000. reprint ed. pap. 11.95 (*0-7867-0787-9*, Pub. by Carroll & Graf) Publishers Group.

***Mammoth Book of Eyewitness History 2000.** Ed. by Jon E. Lewis. 608p. 2000. pap. 12.95 (*0-7867-0747-X*, Pub. by Carroll & Graf) Publishers Group.

Mammoth Book of Fairy Tales. Ed. by Mike Ashley. LC 97-34051. (Mammoth Book Ser.). (Illus.). 544p. 1997. pap. 10.95 (*0-7867-0475-6*) Carroll & Graf.

Mammoth Book of Fantastic Science Fiction: Short Novels of the 1970s. Ed. by Isaac Asimov et al. (Mammoth Book Ser.). 512p. 1992. pap. 9.95 (*0-88184-795-X*) Carroll & Graf.

Mammoth Book of Fortune Telling. Celestine. LC 97-20113. (Illus.). 512p. 1997. pap. 10.95 (*0-7867-0429-2*) Carroll & Graf.

Mammoth Book of Fun & Games. Richard B. Manchester. 416p. 1991. pap. 12.95 (*0-88486-044-2*) Arrowood Pr.

Mammoth Book of Gay Erotica. Ed. by Lawrence Schimel. (Mammoth Book Ser.). 544p. 1998. pap. 10.95 (*0-7867-0476-4*) Carroll & Graf.

Mammoth Book of Gay Short Stories. Ed. by Peter Burton. LC 97-28172. (Mammoth Book Ser.). 512p. 1997. pap. 10.95 (*0-7867-0430-6*) Carroll & Graf.

Mammoth Book of Ghost Stories. Ed. by Richard Dalby. 600p. 1990. pap. 9.95 (*0-88184-590-6*) Carroll & Graf.

Mammoth Book of Golden Age Detective Stories. Intro. by Marie Smith. 544p. 1994. pap. 9.95 (*0-7867-0088-2*) Carroll & Graf.

Mammoth Book of Golden Age Science Fiction: Short Novels of the 1940s. Ed. by Isaac Asimov et al. 512p. 1989. pap. 8.95 (*0-88184-480-2*) Carroll & Graf.

Mammoth Book of Great Detective Stories. Ed. by Herbert Van Thal. 640p. 1989. pap. 9.95 (*0-88184-530-2*) Carroll & Graf.

***Mammoth Book of Haunted House Stories.** Ed. by Peter Haining. 512p. 2000. pap. 11.95 (*0-7867-0791-7*, Pub. by Carroll & Graf) Publishers Group.

***Mammoth Book of Heroic & Outrageous Women.** Ed. by Gemma Alexander. (Mammoth Book Ser.). 512p. 1999. pap. text 10.95 (*0-7867-0695-3*) Carroll & Graf.

Mammoth Book of Historical Detectives. Ed. by Mike Ashley. (Mammoth Book Ser.). 544p. 1995. pap. 9.95 (*0-7867-0214-1*) Carroll & Graf.

Mammoth Book of Historical Erotica. Ed. by Maxim Jakubowski. (Mammoth Book Ser.). 512p. 1998. pap. 10.95 (*0-7867-0586-8*) Carroll & Graf.

Mammoth Book of Historical Whodunnits. Ed. by Mike Ashley. (Mammoth Book Ser.). 512p. 1993. pap. 9.95 (*0-7867-0024-6*) Carroll & Graf.

***Mammoth Book of Humor.** Ed. by Geoff Tibballs. 512p. 2000. pap. 11.95 (*0-7867-0783-6*, Pub. by Carroll & Graf) Publishers Group.

Mammoth Book of International Erotica. Ed. by Maxim Jakubowski. (Mammoth Book Ser.). 544p. 1996. pap. 11.95 (*0-7867-0373-3*) Carroll & Graf.

Mammoth Book of Jack the Ripper. Ed. by Maxim Jakubowski & Nathan Braund. (Mammoth Book Ser.). 1999. pap. 11.95 (*0-7867-0626-0*) Carroll & Graf.

Mammoth Book of Killer Women. Ed. by Richard Glyn Jones. (Mammoth Book Ser.). 560p. 1993. pap. 9.95 (*0-88184-882-4*) Carroll & Graf.

***Mammoth Book of Lesbian Erotica.** Ed. by Rose Collis. 512p. 2000. pap. 11.95 (*0-7867-0726-7*, Pub. by Carroll & Graf) Publishers Group.

Mammoth Book of Lesbian Short Stories. Ed. by Emma Donoghue. (Mammoth Book Ser.). 624p. 1999. pap. 10.95 (*0-7867-0627-9*) Carroll & Graf.

***Mammoth Book of Life Before the Mast: Sailors Eyewitness Stories from the Age of Fighting Ships.** Ed. by Jon E. Lewis. 512p. 2001. pap. 11.95 (*0-7867-0811-5*, Pub. by Carroll & Graf) Publishers Group.

***Mammoth Book of Locked-Room Mysteries & Impossible Crimes.** Ed. by Mike Ashley. 512p. 2000. pap. 11.95 (*0-7867-0790-9*, Pub. by Carroll & Graf) Publishers Group.

Mammoth Book of Love & Sensuality. Caroline Rey. LC 96-40924. (Mammoth Book Ser.). (Illus.). 512p. 1997. pap. 11.95 (*0-7867-0374-1*) Carroll & Graf.

***Mammoth Book of Men O'War.** Ed. by Mike Ashley. (Mammoth Book Ser.). 512p. 1999. pap. text 11.95 (*0-7867-0696-1*) Carroll & Graf.

Mammoth Book of Mindbending Puzzles. Victor Serebriakoff. (Mammoth Book Ser.). 544p. 1995. pap. 10.95 (*0-7867-0280-X*) Carroll & Graf.

Mammoth Book of Modern Science Fiction: Short Novels of the 1980s. Ed. by Isaac Asimov et al. (Illus.). 544p. 1993. pap. 9.95 (*0-88184-959-6*) Carroll & Graf.

Mammoth Book of Modern War Stories. Ed. by Jon E. Lewis. 544p. 1993. pap. 9.95 (*0-88184-958-8*) Carroll & Graf.

***Mammoth Book of Murder & Science.** Roger Wilkes. 512p. 2000. pap. 11.95 (*0-7867-0789-5*, Pub. by Carroll & Graf) Publishers Group.

Mammoth Book of New Erotica. Ed. by Maxim Jakubowski. (Mammoth Book Ser.). 533p. 1998. pap. 11.95 (*0-7867-0535-3*) Carroll & Graf.

Mammoth Book of New Sherlock Holmes Adventures. George Sand. Ed. by Mike Ashley. LC 97-34047. (Mammoth Book Ser.). 512p. 1997. pap. 10.95 (*0-7867-0477-2*) Carroll & Graf.

Mammoth Book of New World Science Fiction: Short Novels of the 1960s. Ed. by Isaac Asimov et al. 512p. 1991. pap. 9.95 (*0-88184-702-X*) Carroll & Graf.

Mammoth Book of Nostradamus & Other Prophets. Ed. by Damon Wilson. (Mammoth Book Ser.). 512p. 1999. pap. 11.95 (*0-7867-0628-7*) Carroll & Graf.

***Mammoth Book of Oddballs & Eccentrics.** Karl Shaw. 512p. 2000. pap. 11.95 (*0-7867-0724-0*, Pub. by Carroll & Graf) Publishers Group.

Mammoth Book of Oddities. Frank O'Neil. LC 96-38173. 512p. 1996. pap. 8.95 (*0-7867-0375-X*) Carroll & Graf.

Mammoth Book of 1001 Great Lives. Jonathan Law. LC 96-152774. (Mammoth Book Ser.). 512p. 1996. pap. 9.95 (*0-7867-0298-2*) Carroll & Graf.

***Mammoth Book of Private Lives.** Ed. by Jon E. Lewis. 512p. 2000. pap. 11.95 (*0-7867-0748-8*, Pub. by Carroll & Graf) Publishers Group.

Mammoth Book of Pulp Fiction. Ed. by Maxim Jakubowski. LC 96-18818. (Mammoth Book Ser.). 512p. 1996. pap. 10.95 (*0-7867-0300-8*) Carroll & Graf.

Mammoth Book of Seek-a-Word Puzzles. Richard B. Manchester. 400p. 1996. pap. text 12.95 (*0-88486-146-5*, Bristol Park Bks) Arrowood Pr.

***Mammoth Book of Short Erotic Novels.** Ed. by Maxim Jakubowski & Michael Hemmingson. (Mammoth Book Ser.). 487p. 2000. pap. 11.95 (*0-7867-0713-5*) Carroll & Graf.

***Mammoth Book of Sword & Honor.** Ed. by Mike Ashley. 512p. 2000. pap. 11.95 (*0-7867-0727-5*, Pub. by Carroll & Graf) Publishers Group.

Mammoth Book of Tasteless Lists. Karl Shaw. LC 98-6958. (Mammoth Book Ser.). 512p. 1998. pap. 10.95 (*0-7867-0537-X*) Carroll & Graf.

Mammoth Book of Terror. Ed. by Stephen Jones. (Mammoth Book Ser.). 648p. 1991. pap. 10.95 (*0-88184-622-8*) Carroll & Graf.

***Mammoth Book of the History of Murder.** Ed. by Colin Wilson. (Mammoth Book Ser.). 512p. 2000. pap. 11.95 (*0-7867-0714-3*) Carroll & Graf.

Mammoth Book of the Supernatural. Colin Wilson. 576p. 1991. pap. 9.95 (*0-88184-734-8*) Carroll & Graf.

Mammoth Book of the Third Reich at War. Ed. by Michael Veranov. (Illus.). 688p. 1997. pap. 10.95 (*0-7867-0478-0*) Carroll & Graf.

Mammoth Book of the West. Ed. by Jon E. Lewis. (Mammoth Book Ser.). (Illus.). 512p. 1996. pap. 11.95 (*0-7867-0376-8*) Carroll & Graf.

Mammoth Book of the World's Greatest Chess Games. Graham Burgess et al. (Mammoth Book Ser.). (Illus.). 512p. 1998. pap. 10.95 (*0-7867-0587-6*) Carroll & Graf.

Mammoth Book of True Crime: A New Edition. rev. ed. Colin Wilson. (Mammoth Book Ser.). 608p. 1998. pap. 11.95 (*0-7867-0536-1*) Carroll & Graf.

Mammoth Book of True War Stories. Ed. by Jon E. Lewis. (Mammoth Book Ser.). 1999. pap. 11.95 (*0-7867-0629-5*) Carroll & Graf.

Mammoth Book of 20th Century Ghost Stories. Ed. by Peter Haining. (Mammoth Book Ser.). 496p. 1998. pap. 11.95 (*0-7867-0583-3*) Carroll & Graf.

Mammoth Book of Unsolved Crime. Ed. by Roger Wilkes. (Mammoth Book Ser.). 512p. 1998. pap. 10.95 (*0-7867-0588-4*) Carroll & Graf.

Mammoth Book of Vampires. Ed. by Stephen Jones. (Mammoth Book Ser.). 512p. 1992. pap. 9.95 (*0-88184-796-8*) Carroll & Graf.

Mammoth Book of Victorian & Edwardian Ghost Stories. Ed. by Richard Dalby. LC 96-154348. 544p. 1995. pap. 10.95 (*0-7867-0279-6*) Carroll & Graf.

Mammoth Book of Vintage Science Fiction: Short Novels of the 1950s. Ed. by Isaac Asimov et al. (Mammoth Book Ser.). 512p. 1990. pap. 8.95 (*0-88184-621-X*) Carroll & Graf.

Mammoth Book of War Diaries & Letters: A Collection of Letters & Diaries from the Battlefield. Ed. by Jon E. Lewis. (Mammoth Book Ser.). 512p. 1999. pap. 10.95 (*0-7867-0589-2*) Carroll & Graf.

Mammoth Book of Werewolves. Ed. by Stephen Jones. 544p. 1994. pap. 9.95 (*0-7867-0087-4*) Carroll & Graf.

Mammoth Book of Word Games. Richard B. Manchester. 416p. 1990. pap. 12.95 (*0-88486-031-0*) Arrowood Pr.

Mammoth Book of World Sports: Every Sport Ever Played. Ed. by Noam Friedlander. (Mammoth Book Ser.). 1999. pap. 11.95 (*0-7867-0625-2*) Carroll & Graf.

Mammoth Book of Zombies. Stephen Jones. 512p. 1993. pap. 9.95 (*0-7867-0023-8*) Carroll & Graf.

Mammoth Cave. John J. Wagoner & Lewis D. Cutliff. LC 84-62868. (Illus.). 52p. (Orig.). 1985. pap. 6.95 (*0-936478-08-X*) Interpretive Pubns.

Mammoth Cave: The Story Behind the Scenery. Joy M. Lyons. LC 91-60037. (Illus.). 48p. (Orig.). 1991. 7.95 (*0-88714-050-5*) KC Pubns.

Mammoth Cave National Park, KY. (Illus.). 1996. 8.99 (*1-56695-004-X*) Trails Illustrated.

Mammoth Dictionary of Symbols. Nadia Julien. LC 96-19281. (Mammoth Book Ser.). (Illus.). 512p. 1996. pap. 9.95 (*0-7867-0301-6*) Carroll & Graf.

Mammoth Gold: The Ghost Towns of Lake District. Gary Caldwell. LC 89-26340. (Illus.). 174p. (Orig.). 1990. pap. 8.95 (*0-931378-12-5*) Live Oak.

Mammoth Hunt: In Search of the Giant Elephants of Nepal. R. Lenska. 1996. pap. 219.00 (*0-7855-7434-4*, Pub. by Ratna Pustak Bhandar) St Mut.

Mammoth Hunters. Jean M. Auel. (Earth's Children Ser.: No. 3). 752p. 1986. mass mkt. 7.99 (*0-553-28094-5*, Bantam Classics) Bantam.

Mammoth Hunters. Jean M. Auel. LC 85-17503. (Earth's Children Ser.). 656p. 1985. 19.95 (*0-517-55627-8*, Crown) Crown Pub Group.

An Asterisk (*) at the beginning of an entry indicates that the title is appearing for the first time.

Mammoth Hunters. Jean M. Auel. (Earth's Children Ser.). (J). 1985. 12.60 (*0-606-03115-4*, Pub. by Turtleback) Demco.

Mammoth Hunters. large type ed. Jean M. Auel. LC 86-4284. 1211p. 1991. pap. 17.95 (*1-56054-981-5*) Thorndike Pr.

Mammoth Incident. George R. Harker. LC 95-92087. 132p. (Orig.). 1995. 29.95 (*0-9638802-8-4*) Dr Leisure.

Mammoth Incident. George R. Harker. LC 95-92087. 202p. (Orig.). 1995. pap. 4.99 (*0-9638802-7-6*) Dr Leisure.

Mammoth Lakes. John Moynier. (Twelve Short Hikes Ser.). (Illus.). 32p. 1997. pap. 4.95 (*1-57540-091-X*) Falcon Pub Inc.

Mammoth Lakes Sierra: A Handbook for Roadside & Trail. 6th ed. Dean Rinehart et al. Ed. by Genny Smith. LC 93-1250. (Illus.). 220p. 1993. pap. 14.95 (*0-931378-13-3*) Live Oak.

Mammoth Magic. Shelley R. Gill. (Illus.). 36p. (J). (gr. k-6). 1986. 15.95 (*0-934007-06-3*); pap. 8.95 (*0-934007-01-2*) Paws Four Pub.

Mammoth Mix-Up. Elizabeth Levy. LC 94-47960. (Brian & Pea Brain Mystery Ser.). (Illus.). 96p. (J). (gr. 2-5). 1995. lib. bdg. 12.89 (*0-06-024815-7*) HarpC Child Bks.

Mammoth Mix-Up. Elizabeth Levy. LC 94-47960. (Brian & Pea Brain Mystery Ser.). (Illus.). 96p. (J). (gr. 2-5). 1996. pap. 3.95 (*0-06-442043-4*, HarpTrophy) HarpC Child Bks.

Mammoth Mix-Up: Starring Brian & Pea Brain. Elizabeth Levy. 1996. 9.15 (*0-606-09590-X*, Pub. by Turtleback) Demco.

Mammoth Puzzle Carnival. David J. Bodycombe. LC 97-18975. (Mammoth Book Ser.). (Illus.). 512p. 1997. pap. 10.95 (*0-7867-0427-6*) Carroll & Graf.

***Mammoth Sails Tonight!** Adrian Mitchell. 88p. 2000. pap. 13.95 (*1-84002-134-9*) Theatre Comm.

Mammoth Trees of Calaveras: Scene of Wonder & Curiosity in California, 1872. J. M. Hutchings. Ed. by William R. Jones. (Illus.). 32p. 1978. reprint ed. pap. 2.00 (*0-89646-050-9*) Vistabooks.

Mammoths see Extinct Species Collection

Mammoths. Adrian Lister & Paul Bahn. (Illus.). 168p. 1994. pap. 30.00 (*0-02-572985-3*) P-H.

Mammoths. Dick Mol et al. 1993. pap. 5.95 (*0-9624750-2-5*) L Agenbroad.

Mammoths, Mastodonts, & Elephants: Biology, Behavior, & the Fossil Record. Gary Haynes. (Illus.). 427p. (C). 1993. pap. text 37.95 (*0-521-45691-6*) Cambridge U Pr.

***Mammy.** Brendan O'Carroll. LC 98-50381. 174p. 1999. pap. 10.95 (*0-452-28103-2*) NAL.

Mammy. Brendan O'Carroll. LC 95-123591. 174 p. 1994. write for info. (*0-86278-372-0*) OBrien Pr.

***Mammy.** large type ed. Brendan O'Carroll. 225p. 2000. lib. bdg. 26.95 (*1-58547-037-6*) Ctr Point Pubg.

Mammy: An Appeal to the Heart of the South; &, The Correct Thing to Do--to Say--to Wear. Charlotte H. Brown. LC 94-42137. (African American Women Writers, 1910-1940 Ser.). 1995. 25.00 (*0-8161-1632-6*, G K Hall & Co) Mac Lib Ref.

Mammy: An Appeal to the Heart of the South; &, The Correct Thing to Do--to Say--to Wear. Charlotte H. Brown. Ed. by Henry Louis Gates, Jr. LC 94-42137. (African American Women Writers 1910-1940 Ser.). 149p. 1995. 15.95 (*0-7838-1395-3*, Hall Reference) Macmillan.

Mammy & Uncle Mose: Black Collectibles & American Stereotyping. Kenneth Goings. LC 93-41305. (Blacks in the Diaspora Ser.). 176p. 1994. 39.95 (*0-253-32592-7*); pap. 17.95 (*0-253-20881-5*) Ind U Pr.

Mammy Rosie. Albert M. Bagby. LC 71-38638. (Black Heritage Library Collection). 1977. reprint ed. 20.95 (*0-8369-8996-1*) Ayer.

Mammy Tittleback & Her Family. Helen H. Jackson. 1976. lib. bdg. 8.50 (*0-89968-052-6*, Lghtyr Pr) Buccaneer Bks.

Mammy's Cracklin' Bread. Theodore H. Shackelford. LC 77-38023. (Black Heritage Library Collection). 1977. reprint ed. 15.95 (*0-8369-8989-9*) Ayer.

***Mamnaging Vocational Training Systems: A Handbook for Senior Administrators.** Vladimir Gasskov. 112p. 2000. pap. 19.95 (*92-2-110867-8*, Pub. by ILO) ILO Pubns Ctr.

Mamphela Ramphele: Challenging Apartheid in South Africa. Judith Harlan. LC 99-39674. 2000. 19.95 (*1-55861-227-0*); pap. text 9.95 (*1-55861-226-2*) Feminist Pr.

Mamuka. Gitel Greenhut. LC 91-61769. 200p. (C). 1991. 18.95 (*1-56062-072-2*) CIS Comm.

Mamur & the Girl in the Nile. Michael Pearce. 1995. pap. write for info. (*0-446-40316-4*, Mysterious Paperbk) Warner Bks.

Mamur Zapt & the Donkey-Vous. Michael Pearce. 272p. 1992. 17.95 (*0-89296-486-3*) Mysterious Pr.

Mamur Zapt & the Donkey-Vous. Michael Pearce. 272p. 1993. mass mkt. 4.99 (*0-446-40181-1*, Pub. by Warner Bks) Little.

Mamur Zapt & the Men Behind. Michael Pearce. 240p. 1994. mass mkt. 5.50 (*0-446-40183-8*, Pub. by Warner Bks) Little.

***Mamzelle Dragonfly.** Raphael Confiant. Tr. by Linda Coverdale from FRE. LC 99-57740. 224p. 2000. 23.00 (*0-374-19932-9*) FS&G.

***Man.** Irving Wallace. 1999. per. 19.99 (*0-671-03894-X*) S&S Trade.

***Man: A Country Study Guide, 110 vols.** International Business Publications, USA Staff & Global Investment Center, USA Staff. (World Country Study Guides Library Ser.: Vol. 211). (Illus.). 350p. 2000. pap. 69.95 (*0-7397-1034-6*) Intl Business Pubns.

***Man: Bible Study.** Lyle L. Luchterband. (People's Bible Teachings Ser.). 1999. 37.99 (*0-8100-0878-5*) Northwest Pub.

Man: Christian Anthropology in the Conflicts of the Present. Jurgen Moltmann. LC 73-88350. 136p. (Orig.). reprint ed. pap. 42.20 (*0-608-16308-2*, 202687200053) Bks Demand.

Man: Computer, Ape or Angel? Larry Azar. LC 88-71528. 1989. 19.95 (*0-8158-0452-0*) Chris Mass.

Man: Fragments of a Forgotten History. Theosophical Society Staff. 192p. 1996. reprint ed. pap. 17.95 (*1-56459-533-1*) Kessinger Pub.

Man: From Glory to Ashes & Back. Lyle L. Luckterhand. LC 97-69964. (People's Bible Teachings Ser.). 181p. 1998. pap. text 9.99 (*0-8100-0799-1*, 15N0609) Northwest Pub.

Man: His Nature & Place in the World. Arnold Gehlen. Tr. by Clare McMillan & Karl A. Pillemer. (European Perspectives Ser.). (Illus.). 480p. 1988. text 87.50 (*0-231-05218-9*) Col U Pr.

Man: His True Nature & Ministry. Louis-Claude De Saint-Martin. (Illus.). 512p. 1993. reprint ed. pap. 27.00 (*1-56459-299-5*) Kessinger Pub.

Man: King of Mind, Body & Circumstance. James Allen. 55p. 1992. pap. 6.00 (*0-89540-212-2*, SB-212) Sun Pub.

Man: Manuscript Edition. Mel Dinelli. 1950. pap. 13.00 (*0-8222-0721-4*) Dramatists Play.

***Man: Photographs of the Male Nude.** Trevor Watson et al. (Illus.). 160p. 2000. 40.00 (*0-312-26430-5*) St Martin.

Man: The Bridge Between Two Worlds. Franz E. Winkler. LC 80-82064. 268p. 1980. reprint ed. pap. 4.95 (*0-913098-32-9*) Orion Society.

Man: The Broken Image. Carol R. Murphy. LC 68-30960. (Orig.). 1968. pap. 1.00 (*0-87574-158-4*) Pendle Hill.

Man: The Perennial Question. Morris A. Inch. LC 98-48618. (Studies in Theological Anthropology). 208p. 1998. pap. 24.50 (*0-7618-1303-9*) U Pr of Amer.

Man: The Social Creator. Henry D. Lloyd. (Notable American Authors Ser.). 1999. reprint ed. lib. bdg. 125.00 (*0-7812-3804-8*) Rprt Serv.

Man - The Dwelling Place of God. A. W. Tozer. LC 89-60632. 174p. 1996. pap. 9.99 (*0-87509-415-5*) Chr Pubns.

Man - The Human Feelings Dimension: Poetry, Music & Freedom, & Other Lectures. unabridged ed. 84p. 1996. 36.50 incl. audio (*1-889954-52-7*); pap. 22.00 incl. audio (*1-889954-53-5*) J Cassidy Prodns.

Man - The Moral Dimension: Moral Prejudice in Human Opinion & Judgment & Other Lectures. unabridged ed. 56p. 1996. 34.00 incl. audio (*1-889954-50-0*); pap. 19.50 incl. audio (*1-889954-51-9*) J Cassidy Prodns.

Man - The Regenerative Evolutionary Spirit. Ruth E. Norman. 345p. (C). 1988. 18.00 (*0-932642-95-0*) Unarius Acad Sci.

Man - Women. Michael Rothenberg & Joanne Kyger. (Illus.). 48p. 1988. 65.00 (*1-878471-06-6*) Big Bridge Pr.

Man a Machine: Man a Plant. Julien O. De La Mettrie. Tr. by Richard Watson & Maya Rybalka from FRE. LC 94-29259. (Hackett Classics Ser.). 96p. (C). 1994. pap. text 8.95 (*0-87220-194-5*); lib. bdg. 29.95 (*0-87220-195-3*) Hackett Pub.

Man, a Woman & a Dream. Hod Payne. 290p. (Orig.). 1994. pap. 11.95 (*0-9641574-0-3*) Ski-Lak.

Man about the House: Man Talk. Alison Kelly. (Presents Ser.: Vol. 1975). 1998. per. 3.75 (*0-373-11975-5*, 1-11975-9) Harlequin Bks.

Man about Town. Loyal Kolbreck. 92p. 1980. per. 3.50 (*0-614-24764-0*) Tesseract SD.

Man about Town: Frank Lloyd Wright in New York City. Herbert Muschamp. (Illus.). 224p. 1985. reprint ed. pap. text 9.95 (*0-262-63100-8*) MIT Pr.

***Man about Town: The Letters of James Graham, Victorian Entrepreneur, 1854-1864.** Ed. by Sally Graham. 452p. 1999. 29.95 (*0-522-84821-4*, Pub. by Melbourne Univ Pr) Paul & Co Pubs.

Man after God's Heart. Luis Palau. LC 97-51672. Orig. Title: Heart after God. 160p. 1998. pap. 12.99 (*1-57293-030-6*) Discovery Hse Pubs.

Man Against Aging. Robert S. Ropp. Ed. by Robert J. Kastenbaum. LC 78-22216. (Aging & Old Age Ser.). 1979. reprint ed. lib. bdg. 28.95 (*0-405-11829-5*) Ayer.

Man Against Cancer: The Story of Cancer Research. Isaac Berenblum. LC 52-13023. 196p. reprint ed. pap. 60.80 (*0-608-30502-2*, 200383000037) Bks Demand.

***Man Against Nature: Firsthand Accounts of Adventure & Exploration.** Charles Neider. (Illus.). 2000. pap. write for info. (*0-8154-1040-9*) Cooper Sq.

Man Ahead of His Times: Butrus Al-Bustani, 1819-1883. Yusuf K. Khoury. 240p. 1995. pap. 25.00 (*0-88206-211-5*) Caravan Bks.

Man Alive! Greg Leichner. LC 97-91692. (Illus.). 220p. 1997. pap. 10.00 (*0-9661936-8-7*) Speed Light NM.

Man Alone. Andre Choraqui. 284p. 1970. 39.95 (*0-87855-180-8*) Transaction Pubs.

Man Alone. William C. Gault. 200p. 1995. pap. 15.00 (*0-936071-43-5*) Gryphon Pubns.

***Man Alone.** Lindsay McKenna. (Special Edition Ser.: Bk. 1357). 2000. mass mkt. 4.50 (*0-373-24357-X*, 1-24357-5) Silhouette.

Man Alone: Meditations on the Seven Last Words of Jesus on the Cross. Alan Falconer. (Illus.). 96p. (Orig.). 1993. pap. 7.95 (*1-85607-096-4*, Pub. by Columba Press) Whitecap Bks.

***Man Alone Cook Book.** Don Tibbenham. 160p. 2000. pap. 7.95 (*0-7160-2009-2*, Pub. by Elliot RW Bks) Midpt Trade.

Man & a Country: And Other Stories. Hakob Karapents. LC 94-9971. (ARM.). 250p. 1994. pap. 20.00 (*0-9628715-7-5*) Blue Crane Bks.

***Man & a Map.** Scott Nitzel. 380p. 2000. pap. 14.95 (*0-9679618-0-7*) October Turtles.

Man & a Million. Jackie Merritt. 1995. per. 3.75 (*0-373-09988-6*, 1-09988-6) Silhouette.

Man & a Woman: Includes Original French Lyrics. 1985. pap. 6.95 (*0-7935-1055-4*, 00123036) H Leonard.

Man & Animals: Living, Working & Changing Together. (Illus.). 80p. 1984. pap. 9.95 (*0-934718-68-7*) U Museum Pubns.

Man & Beast. Phyllis Bottome. LC 79-122689. (Short Story Index Reprint Ser.). (Illus.). 1977. 15.95 (*0-8369-3523-3*) Ayer.

Man & Beast. C. W. Hume. 222p. 1982. pap. 32.00 (*0-900767-28-6*, Pub. by Univs Fed Animal Welfare) St Mut.

Man & Beast in American Comic Legend. Richard M. Dorson. LC 81-48622. 206p. 1982. reprint ed. pap. 63.90 (*0-7837-3696-7*, 205787400009) Bks Demand.

Man & Biologically Active Substances: Introduction to the Pharmacology of Health. 2nd ed. I. I. Brekhman. 90p. 1980. 46.00 (*0-08-023169-1*, Pub. by Pergamon Repr) Franklin.

Man & Boy. Terence Rattigan. 101p. 1964. 16.95 (*0-910278-42-3*) Boulevard.

Man & Cat: The Benefits of Cat Ownership. Reinhold Bergler. (Illus.). 120p. 1991. 42.95 (*0-632-03157-3*) Blackwell Sci.

Man & Child. Arthur Adamov. Tr. by Jo Levy from FRE. LC 91-2145. 160p. 1991. 19.95 (*0-7145-4165-6*) Riverrun NY.

Man & Citizen (De Homine & de Cive) Thomas Hobbes. Ed. by Bernard Gert. LC 90-36836. (Hackett Classics Ser.). 392p. (C). 1991. reprint ed. pap. text 10.95 (*0-87220-111-2*); reprint ed. lib. bdg. 32.95 (*0-87220-112-0*) Hackett Pub.

Man & Computer: Proceedings of the International Conference, 1st, Bordeaux, 1970. International Conference on Man & Computer Staff. Ed. by M. Marois. (Illus.). 400p. 1972. 126.25 (*3-8055-1418-2*) S Karger.

Man & Cultural Heritage: Papers in Honor of Fred B. Kniffen. Ed. by William G. Haag & H. Jesse Walker. (Geoscience & Man Ser.: Vol. 5). (Illus.). 244p. 1974. pap. 12.50 (*0-938909-04-5*) Geosci Pubns LSU.

Man & Earth: Contemporary Paintings from Taiwan. 2nd ed. Tr. by Chang Tzong-Zurg. (Illus.). 80p. 1994. pap. 28.00 (*0-9640498-1-3*) Asian Art Coord.

Man & Environment. W. Manshard & O. E. Fischnich. 108p. (C). 1975. pap. 23.00 (*0-08-019673-X*, Pergamon Pr) Elsevier.

***Man & Environment.** 5th ed. (C). 2000. lab manual ed. write for info. (*0-8087-0192-4*) Pearson Custom.

Man & Environment in the Great Basin. Ed. by David B. Madsen & James F. O'Connell. (SAA Papers: No. 2). 248p. 1982. pap. 25.00 (*0-932839-02-9*) Soc Am Arch.

Man & Environment in the Lower Mississippi Valley. Ed. by Sam B. Hilliard. LC 79-107134. (Geoscience & Man Ser.: Vol. 19). (Illus.). 174p. 1978. pap. 12.00 (*0-938909-18-5*) Geosci Pubns LSU.

Man & Environmental Processes. Ed. by K. J. Gregory & D. E. Walling. (Studies in Physical Geography). 224p. 1980. text 45.00 (*0-89158-696-2*); pap. text 19.90 (*0-89158-865-5*) Westview.

Man & Fisheries of an Amazon Frontier. Michael Goulding. (Developments in Hydrobiology Ser.: Vol. 4). 140p. 1981. text 126.50 (*90-6193-755-8*) Kluwer Academic.

Man & Forest: A New Dimension in the Himalaya. K. M. Gupta & Desh Bandhu. 329p. 1983. pap. 175.00 (*0-7855-0377-3*, Pub. by Intl Bks & Periodicals) St Mut.

Man & Forest: A New Dimension in the Himalaya. 2nd ed. K. M. Gupta. 338p. 1988. reprint ed. write for info. (*1-55528-216-4*, Pub. by Today Tomorrow) Scholarly Pubns.

Man & God. Lois Degler. LC 74-28943. (Illus.). 1975. pap. 3.00 (*0-930422-04-X*) Dennis-Landman.

Man & His Ancestors. Alan H. Brodrick. LC 74-502456. (Radius Book Ser.). ix, 238 p. 1971. write for info. (*0-09-107690-0*) Hutchinson.

Man & His Becoming. Rene Guenon. (C). 1981. 15.00 (*0-8364-2351-8*, Pub. by M Manoharial) S Asia.

Man & His Becoming. Philip H. Phenix. LC 64-8264. (Brown & Haley Lectures). 125p. reprint ed. pap. 38.80 (*0-608-30587-1*, 205062500087) Bks Demand.

***Man & His Becoming: According to the Vedanta.** Rene Guenon. Tr. by Richard C. Nicholson. 168p. 1999. 28.50 (*81-215-0901-7*, Pub. by M Manoharial) Coronet Bks.

Man & His Bodies. 12th ed. Annie W. Besant. 1990. 4.95 (*81-7059-153-8*, 7083, Quest) Theos Pub Hse.

Man & His Camel. Jo Bertini. (Illus.). 32p. (J). 1996. pap. 14.95 (*0-7022-2739-0*, Pub. by Univ Queensland Pr) Intl Spec Bk.

Man & His Deities. Karl R. Bakk. LC 89-91059. (Orig.). 1989. pap. 9.95 (*0-922958-15-7*) H W Parker.

Man & His Destiny. rev. ed. Murtaza Mutahheri. Tr. by Islamic Seminary Staff from PER.Tr. of Insan wa Sarnawisht. 124p. (C). 1985. reprint ed. pap. 4.00 (*0-941724-39-5*) Islamic Seminary.

Man & His Destiny - The Release of the Human Mind: A Study of Citta in Relation to Dhamma in some Ancient Indian Texts. Jan Ergardt. (Studia Orientalia Lundensia: No. 3). x, 162p. 1986. 46.00 (*90-04-07878-9*) Brill Academic Pubs.

Man & His Environment. Harry G. Johnson. LC 96-225060. 48p. 1990. pap. text 8.00 (*0-902594-50-8*, BN-OP 6) Natl Planning.

Man & His Environment: Proceedings 1st Banff Conference Pollution, Banff Canada 05-68. University of Calgary Staff & M. Ward. LC 70-113396. 1970. 98.00 (*0-08-015763-7*, Pub. by Pergamon Repr) Franklin.

Man & His Geologic Environment. 2nd ed. David N. Cargo & Bob F. Mallory. LC 76-7655. (C). 1977. text. write for info. (*0-201-00894-7*) Addison-Wesley.

Man & His God. Denis Lane. 1981. pap. 4.99 (*0-85234-155-5*, Pub. by Evangelical Pr) P & R Pubng.

Man & His House in the Himalayas. Ed. by Girad Toffin. (C). 1991. text 80.00 (*0-7855-0149-5*, Pub. by Ratna Pustak Bhandar) St Mut.

Man & His Mind. Swami Nihsreyasananda. 343p. pap. 6.95 (*81-7120-643-3*) Vedanta Pr.

Man & His Mission. Claude Guild. 188p. (Orig.). 1990. pap. 6.95 (*0-940999-53-6*, C-2143) Star Bible.

***Man & His Mother: An Adopted Son's Search.** Tim Green. (Illus.). 225p. 2000. text 23.00 (*0-7881-9015-6*) DIANE Pub.

Man & His Music, 2 vols., Set. Alec Harmen & Mell Harmen. 1988. reprint ed. lib. bdg. 150.00 (*0-7812-0229-9*) Rprt Serv.

Man & His Nature, Vol. 3. rev. ed. John G. Bennett. (Dramatic Universe Ser.). 315p. 1987. 20.00 (*0-934254-19-2*, Pub. by Coombe Springs Pr); pap. 14.95 (*0-934254-18-4*, Pub. by Coombe Springs Pr) Claymont Comm.

Man & His Pan: If You Can't Cook It in a Non-Stick Skillet, It's Not Worth Cooking! John Boswell. LC 99-24099. 251p. 1999. pap. 16.95 (*0-8362-7854-2*) Andrews & McMeel.

Man & His Physical Environment: Readings in Environmental Geology. Ed. by Garry D. McKenzie & Russell O. Utgard. LC 79-187012. 350p. reprint ed. pap. 108.50 (*0-608-11750-1*, 201587000097) Bks Demand.

Man & His Relationships: Creation to Eternity. C. D. Whitfield. (Illus.). 88p. 1997. pap. 5.95 (*1-892084-13-9*) Vineyard Pub.

Man & His Secrets see Hombre y Sus Secretos

Man & His Seven Principles. Robson. 1986. 10.95 (*0-8356-7309-X*) Theos Pub Hse.

Man & His Seven Principles: An Ancient Basis for a New Psychology. L. L. Wright. Ed. by Emmett Small & Helen Todd. (Theosophical Manual Ser.: No. 4). 1975. pap. 5.00 (*0-913004-21-9*) Point Loma Pub.

Man & His Ship: Peter Minuit & the Kalmar Nyckel. C. A. Weslager. 20.00 (*0-9625563-0-0*); pap. 9.95 (*0-9625563-1-9*) Kalmar Nyckel Found.

Man & His Symbols. C. G. Jung. 432p. 1968. mass mkt. 7.99 (*0-440-35183-9*, LE) Dell.

Man & His Symbols. C. G. Jung. LC 64-18631. (Illus.). 320p. 1969. 30.00 (*0-385-05221-9*) Doubleday.

Man & His Work. Ed. by A. G. Zdravomyslov et al. Tr. by Stephen P. Dunn. LC 72-77457. Orig. Title: Chelovek: Ego Rabota. 406p. reprint ed. pap. 125.90 (*0-8357-9437-7*, 201613500098) Bks Demand.

Man & His World. Clark Blaise. 144p. 1993. per. write for info. (*0-88984-148-9*) Porcup Quill.

Man & Inner Security. Harry L. Heckel. LC 97-40507. 178p. 2000. lib. bdg. 27.00 (*1-56072-483-8*, Nova Kroshka Bks) Nova Sci Pubs.

Man & Islam. Ali Shariati. Tr. by Fathollah Marjani from PER. 150p. (Orig.). 1981. 17.95 (*0-941722-02-3*); pap. 6.95 (*0-941722-00-7*) Book Dist Ctr.

Man & Land in Chinese History: An Economic Analysis. Kang Chao. LC 84-51715. 288p. 1986. 42.50 (*0-8047-1271-9*) Stanford U Pr.

Man & Learning in Modern Society. Charles E. Odegaard et al. LC 59-15076. (Illus.). 203p. 1959. 20.00 (*0-295-73835-9*) U of Wash Pr.

Man & Machine; Cyberware, 1. FASA Corp. Staff. 1999. pap. text 20.00 (*1-55560-363-7*) FASA Corp.

Man & Machines. R. Page. 1975. pap. 3.55 (*0-08-016889-2*, Pergamon Pr) Elsevier.

Man & Mask: Forty Years in the Life of a Singer. Fedor I. Shaliapin. 1988. reprint ed. lib. bdg. 49.00 (*0-7812-0789-4*) Rprt Serv.

Man & Mask: Forty Years in the Life of a Singer. Fedor I. Shaliapin. LC 73-181256. 358p. 1932. reprint ed. 39.00 (*0-403-01679-7*) Scholarly.

Man & Materialism. Fred Hoyle. LC 70-167358. (Essay Index Reprints - World Perspectives Ser.: Vol. 8). 1977. reprint ed. 18.95 (*0-8369-2653-6*) Ayer.

***Man & Medicine.** F. E. Udwadia. (Illus.). 640p. 2001. 39.95 (*0-19-565457-9*) OUP.

Man & Medicine: An Introduction to Medical Knowledge. Henry E. Sigerist. 1982. 25.95 (*0-8434-0156-7*) McGrath NH.

Man & Message: A Guide to Meaning-Based Text Analysis. Kathleen Callow. LC 98-6629. 400p. (C). 1998. 64.00 (*0-7618-1127-3*); pap. 44.50 (*0-7618-1128-1*) U Pr of Amer.

Man & Metals: A History of Mining in Relation to the Development of Civilization, 2 vols. Thomas A. Rickard. LC 74-358. (Gold Ser.: Vol. 16). (Illus.). 1974. reprint ed. 81.95 (*0-405-05919-1*) Ayer.

Man & Microbes. Arno Karlen. 272p. 1996. per. 13.00 (*0-684-82270-9*, Touchstone) S&S Trade Pap.

Man & Mind. Jeanne Lampl-de Groot. ix, 441p. 1985. 65.00 (*0-8236-3087-0*) Intl Univs Pr.

Man & Mission: E. B. Gaston & the Origins of the Fairhope Single-Tax Colony. Paul M. Gaston. LC 93-7774. 161p. 1993. 20.00 (*1-881320-10-3*, Black Belt) Black Belt Communs.

Man & Modern Society: Philosophical Essays. Homer T. Rosenberger. LC 72-85861. (Horizons of the Humanities Ser.: Vol. 1). 272p. 1972. lib. bdg. 8.00 (*0-917264-05-3*) Rose Hill.

Man & Mouse: Animals in Medical Research. 2nd ed. William Paton. (Illus.). 304p. 1993. pap. 16.95 (*0-19-286146-8*) OUP.

Man & Mu: The Cradle of Becoming & Unbecoming: Desiderata for Human Science. Stacey B. Day. LC 97-72905. (Illus.). 200p. (Orig.). (C). 1998. lib. bdg. 39.50 (*0-934314-00-4*) Intl Found Biosocial Dev.

Man & Music in India. Ed. by Roshmi Goshwami. (C). 1992. 12.00 (*81-215-0557-7*, Pub. by M Manoharial) Coronet Bks.

Man & Mustang. George Ancona. LC 91-29513. (Illus.). 48p. (J). (gr. 3-7). 1992. lib. bdg. 15.95 (*0-02-700802-9*, Mac Bks Young Read) S&S Childrens.

M

Man & Nature. George P. Marsh. Ed. by David Lowenthal. LC 65-11591. (John Harvard Library). 496p. 1965. pap. 19.50 (*0-674-54452-8*) HUP.

Man & Nature. Intro. by Hans F. Sennholz. (Freeman Classics Ser.). 225p. (Orig.). 1993. pap. 12.95 (*0-910614-88-1*) Foun Econ Ed.

Man & Nature: The Chinese Tradition & the Future. Ed. by Tang Yi-Jie et al. LC 89-30881. (Cultural Heritage & Contemporary Life Series I. Culture & Values: Vol. 1). 236p. (Orig.). 1989. 45.00 (*0-8191-7412-2*); pap. 17.50 (*0-8191-7413-0*) Coun Res Values.

Man & Nature: The Ecological Crisis & Social Progress. Evgeni K. Fedorov. LC 80-202. 176p. reprint ed. pap. 54.60 (*0-608-17702-4*, 203004200067) Bks Demand.

Man & Nature: The Spiritual Crisis in Modern Man. Seyyed Hossein Nasr. 150p. 1996. pap. 12.95 (*0-614-21440-8*, 1483) Kazi Pubns.

Man & Nature: The Spiritual Crisis of Modern Man. Seyyed Hossein Nasr. 156p. (C). 1997. pap. 12.95 (*1-871031-65-6*) Kazi Pubns.

Man & Nature in the Philosophical Thought of Wang Fu-Chih. Alison H. Black. 346p. 1987. 30.00 (*0-295-96338-7*) U of Wash Pr.

Man & Nature in the Renaissance. Allen G. Debus. LC 77-91085. (Cambridge History of Science Ser.). (Illus.). 180p. 1978. pap. text 17.95 (*0-521-29328-6*) Cambridge U Pr.

Man & Picture: Papers from the First International Symposium for Ethnological Research. Ed. by Nils-Arvid Bringeus. (Illus.). 264p. (Orig.). 1986. pap. text 52.00 (*91-22-00794-6*) Coronet Bks.

***Man & River Systems: The Functioning of River Systems at the Basin Scale.** Josette Garnier & J. M. Mouchel. LC 99-88827. (Developments in Hydrobiology Ser.). (Illus.). 408p. 2000. write for info. (*0-7923-6159-8*) Kluwer Academic.

Man & Running. Vladimir Volkov & Evgeny C. Milner. Tr. by Daniel C. Drew from RUS. (Illus.). 136p. (Orig.). 1992. pap. 25.00 (*0-88314-527-8*) AAHPERD.

Man & Sea in the Mesolithic. Ed. by Anders Fischer. (Oxbow Monographs in Archaeology: No. 53). (Illus.). 440p. 1996. 75.00 (*0-946897-96-4*, Pub. by Oxbow Bks) David Brown.

Man & Settlement in the Upper Santa Ana River Drainage: A Cultural Resources Overview. Jeffrey Altschul et al. (Statistical Research Technical Ser.: No. 1). (Illus.). 137p. 1984. spiral bd. 10.00 (*1-879442-00-0*) Stats Res.

Man & Settlement in the Upper Santa Ana River Drainage: A Cultural Resources Overview. fac. ed. Jeffrey Altschul et al. (Illus.). 144p. 1984. reprint ed. pap. text 15.63 (*1-55567-566-2*) Coyote Press.

Man & Sin. Charles H. Shofstahl. 1985. pap. 1.99 (*1-56632-014-3*) Revival Lit.

Man & Society in Africa: An Introduction to Sociology. Theophilus O. Odetola et al. LC 82-23975. (Illus.). 176p. reprint ed. pap. 54.60 (*0-8357-2967-2*, 203922900011) Bks Demand.

Man & Society in an Age of Reconstruction. Intro. by Bryan Turner. (Karl Mannheim Ser.: Vol. 2). (C). 1998. 100.00 (*0-415-13674-1*) Routledge.

Man & Society in Calamity: The Effects of War, Revolution, Famine, Pestilence Upon Human Mind, Behavior, Social Organization & Cultural Life. Pitirim A. Sorokin. LC 69-10157. (Illus.). 352p. 1968. reprint ed. lib. bdg. 65.00 (*0-8371-0236-7*, SOMS) Greenwood.

Man & Structures. Jens Wilhelmsen. 1977. 3.25 (*0-901269-25-5*) Grosvenor USA.

Man & Superman. George Bernard Shaw. 20.95 (*0-89190-969-9*) Amereon Ltd.

Man & Superman. George Bernard Shaw. 272p. 1989. pap. 9.95 (*0-14-045019-X*) Viking Penguin.

Man & System: Foundations for the Study of Human Relations. Harry H. Turney-High. LC 68-16216. (Illus.). (C). 1968. 52.50 (*0-89197-547-0*) Irvington.

Man & Talent: Search for the Unknown. Shin'ichi Suzuki. Tr. by Kyoko I. Selden from JPN. LC 89-69847. 110p. (Orig.). 1990. pap. 14.95 (*0-9621416-1-5*) Shar Prods.

Man & the Artist: Essays on Ivo Andric. Zelimir B. Juricic. LC 85-15822. (Illus.). 142p. (Orig.). (C). 1986. pap. text 19.50 (*0-8191-4908-X*); lib. bdg. 44.50 (*0-8191-4907-1*) U Pr of Amer.

Man & the Biosphere: Toward a Coevolutionary Political Economy. Kenneth M. Stokes. LC 91-31580. (Illus.). 336p. (gr. 13). 1992. text 77.95 (*1-56324-023-8*) M E Sharpe.

Man & the Biosphere: Toward a Coevolutionary Political Economy. Kenneth M. Stokes. LC 91-31580. (Illus.). 336p. (gr. 13). 1994. pap. text 38.95 (*1-56324-024-6*) M E Sharpe.

Man & the Church see Theological Investigations

Man & the Cosmos. Lars Thunberg. LC 84-22157. 184p. 1985. pap. text 10.95 (*0-88141-019-5*) St Vladimirs.

Man & the Machine Interface. Cronly-Dillon. 1991. 137.00 (*0-8493-7515-0*, QP474) CRC Pr.

Man & the Marine Environment. Ed. by Robert A. Ragotzkie. 200p. 1983. 112.00 (*0-8493-5759-4*, GC21, CRC Reprint) Franklin.

Man & the Maritime Environment. Ed. by Harold Edward Fisher. (Illus.). 264p. 1995. pap. text 24.95 (*0-85989-393-6*, Pub. by Univ Exeter Pr) Northwestern U Pr.

Man & the Mountain: Sydney Laurence's Mt. McKinley. Cyrus P. Francisco. 1990. 9.95 (*0-9626029-0-6*) L F Casella Commns.

Man & the Movies. Ed. by William R. Robinson. LC 67-24549. (Illus.). 387p. reprint ed. 120.00 (*0-8357-9389-3*, 205166000004) Bks Demand.

Man & the Myths. Michael Ackland. (Miegunyah Press Ser.: 2:2). 368p. 1995. 49.95 (*0-522-84650-5*, Pub. by Melbourne Univ Pr) Paul & Co Pubs.

Man & the Natural World: Changing Attitudes in England, 1500-1800. Keith Thomas. 1983. 26.75 (*0-8446-6911-3*) Peter Smith.

Man & the Natural World: Changing Attitudes in England, 1500-1800. Keith Thomas. (Illus.). 332p. 1996. reprint ed. pap. 15.95 (*0-19-511122-2*) OUP.

Man & the Sea. rev. ed. B. L. Gordon. LC 76-116208. (Illus.). xxvi, 498p. 1994. reprint ed. pap. 20.00 (*0-910258-06-6*) Book & Tackle.

Man & the State. Jacques Maritain. LC 51-555. 1995. pap. text 11.95 (*0-226-50552-9*, P5) U Ch Pr.

Man & the State. Jacques Maritain. LC 97-41522. 224p. 1998. reprint ed. pap. 19.95 (*0-8132-0905-6*) Cath U Pr.

Man & the Two Trees. 18p. 1993. pap. 0.75 (*1-57593-985-1*, 18-008-001) Living Stream Ministry.

Man & the Universe (1908) Oliver Lodge. 306p. 1998. reprint ed. pap. 24.95 (*0-7661-0560-1*) Kessinger Pub.

Man & the World of the Stars: The Spiritual Communion of Mankind. 2nd ed. Rudolf Steiner. Tr. by Dorothy S. Osmond from GER. 197p. 1982. pap. 8.95 (*0-88010-008-7*) Anthroposophic.

Man & Time see Papers from Eranos Yearbooks

Man & Transformation see Papers from Eranos Yearbooks

Man & Universe: Mugaddamai Bar Jahan Bin'i Islami. rev. ed. Murtaza Mutahheri. Tr. by Islamic Seminary Staff from PER. 663p. (C). reprint ed. text 18.00 (*0-941724-52-2*) Islamic Seminary.

Man & Value. Roman Ingarden. (Philosophia Resources Library). 184p. 1984. lib. bdg. 66.00 (*3-88405-042-7*) Philosophia Pr.

Man & Value: Essays in Honor of William H. Werkmeister. William H. Werkmeister. LC 80-27314. 341p. reprint ed. pap. 105.80 (*0-608-11082-5*, 202260600028) Bks Demand.

Man & Vegetation see Alinsan Walnabat

Man & Wife. Wilkie Collins. Ed. & Intro. by Norman Page. (Oxford World's Classics Ser.). 688p. 1999. pap. 13.95 (*0-19-283696-X*) OUP.

Man & Wife: A Novel see Works of Wilkie Collins

Man & Wife for Life. Joseph Kanzlemar. LC 90-70125. 160p. 1990. pap. 7.95 (*0-914984-23-3*) Starburst.

***Man & Wife in America: A History.** Hendrik Hartog. LC 99-56466. 416p. 2000. pap. text 29.95 (*0-674-00262-8*) HUP.

Man & Wife, Pt. 2: Incl. the Short Stories: Miss or Mrs.?; The Frozen Deep see Works of Wilkie Collins

Man & Wildfowl. Janet Kear. (Illus.). 288p. 1990. text (*0-85661-055-0*, 784655) Poyser.

Man & Wolf. Ed. by H. Frank. (Perspectives in Vertebrate Science Ser.). 1987. lib. bdg. 333.00 (*90-6193-614-4*) Kluwer Academic.

Man & Woman. Havelock Ellis. LC 73-20621. (Sex, Marriage & Society Ser.). (Illus.). 430p. 1974. reprint ed. 30.95 (*0-405-05826-8*) Ayer.

Man & Woman. Dietrich Von Hildebrand. LC 65-25840. 103p. reprint ed. pap. 32.00 (*0-608-13429-5*, 202257500028) Bks Demand.

Man & Woman, & Child. Harold W. Percival. LC 52-6126. 1992. reprint ed. pap. 9.95 (*0-911650-08-3*) Word Foun.

Man & Woman, Boy & Girl: Differentiation & Dimorphism of Gender Identity from Conception to Maturity. John Money & Anke A. Ehrhardt. LC 72-4012. (Illus.). 327p. (Orig.). reprint ed. pap. 101.40 (*0-7837-3394-1*, 204335200008) Bks Demand.

Man & Woman Manifesto: Let the Revolution Begin. Christopher A. Anderson. LC 93-74322. (Illus.). 167p. (Orig.). 1994. pap. 12.50 (*0-931353-33-5*) Andersons Pubns.

Man & Woman Relationship: A New Center for the Universe. Christopher A. Anderson. LC 85-71216. (Illus.). 235p. 1985. 18.00 (*0-931353-00-9*) Andersons Pubns.

Man & Woman, War & Peace: The Strategist's Companion. Anthony Wilden. 328p. 1987. 27.50 (*0-7100-9867-7*, 98677, Routledge Thoemms) Routledge.

Man & Yosemite: A Photographer's View of the Early Years. Ted N. Orland. (Illus.). 96p. (Orig.). 1985. 19.95 (*0-9614547-0-9*); pap. 10.95 (*0-9614547-1-7*) Image Continuum.

Man Answers Death. Ed. by Corliss Lamont. LC 79-99031. (Granger Index Reprint Ser.). 1977. 23.95 (*0-8369-6106-4*) Ayer.

Man Apart. large type ed. Jane Donnelly. 329p. 1982. 27.99 (*0-7089-0803-9*) Ulverscroft.

***Man Apart: A Family Bond.** Ginna Gray. (Special Edition Ser.: Bk. 1330). 2000. per. 4.50 (*0-373-24330-8*, 1-24330-2) Silhouette.

Man As a Being of Sense & Perception. Rudolf Steiner. Tr. by Dorothy Lenn from GER. 53p. 1981. pap. 6.00 (*0-919924-11-5*, Pub. by Steiner Book Centre) Anthroposophic.

Man As a Picture of the Living Spirit. Rudolf Steiner. Tr. by George Adams from GER. 31p. (Orig.). 1972. pap. 4.95 (*0-85440-253-5*, Pub. by R Steiner Pr) Anthroposophic.

Man As God: The Word of Faith Movement. Curtis I. Crenshaw. 450p. (Orig.). 1994. pap. 14.95 (*1-877818-11-9*) Footstool Pubns.

***Man as Hero: The Human Figure in Western Art.** Pierce Rice. (Illus.). 160p. 2000. pap. text 15.95 (*0-393-73056-5*) Norton.

Man As Infinite Spirit. James H. Robb. LC 74-76084. (Aquinas Lectures). 1974. 15.00 (*0-87462-139-9*) Marquette.

Man As Male & Female: A Study in Sexual Relationships from a Theological Point of View. Paul K. Jewett. 200p. 1999. reprint ed. pap. 20.00 (*1-881266-06-0*) Fuller Seminary.

Man As Male & Female: Study in Sexual Relationships from a Theological Point of View. fac. ed. Paul K. Jewett. LC 74-32471. 200p. reprint ed. pap. 62.00 (*0-7837-7960-7*, 204771600008) Bks Demand.

Man As Man: The Science & Art of Ethics. Thomas J. Higgins. LC 92-60679. 585p. (C). 1992. reprint ed. 30.00 (*0-89555-461-5*) TAN Bks Pubs.

Man As Sign: Essays on the Philosophy of Language. Augusto Ponzio. (Approaches to Semiotics Ser.: No. 89). xii, 412p. (C). 1990. lib. bdg. 129.25 (*3-11-012167-0*) Mouton.

Man As Symphony of the Creative Word. rev. ed. Rudolf Steiner. 192p. 1991. pap. 20.95 (*1-85584-125-8*, Pub. by R Steiner Pr) Anthroposophic.

Man As the Measure: The Crossroads. Ed. by Daniel Adelson. LC 77-184153. (Community Psychology Ser.: Vol. I). 146p. 1972. 35.95 (*0-87705-058-9*, Kluwer Acad Hman Sci) Kluwer Academic.

Man-at-a-Typewriter Journalism: Fifty Years Reporting Pacific Northwest Business. Elliot Marple. LC 99-93056. (Illus.). 176p. (Orig.). 1999. pap. 12.95 (*0-9670261-0-5*) E Marple.

Man at Arms, 15-Year Index, 1979-1993. Man at Arms Magazine Staff. LC 94-78248. (Illus.). 117p. 1994. pap. 20.00 (*0-917218-66-3*) A Mowbray.

Man at Fourteen. Don Schultz. 174p. 1993. pap. 9.95 (*0-9635625-0-9*) Doess Pubs.

Man at Home. Michael Heffernan. LC 88-10597. 71p. 1988. pap. 16.00 (*1-55728-042-8*) U of Ark Pr.

Man at Home in the Universe: A Study of the Great Evolutionary Cycle: the "Globes", the "Rounds", "Races", "Root-Races" & "Sub-Races" Elsie Benjamin. (Study Ser.: No. 8). 36p. 1981. pap. 5.00 (*0-913004-43-X*) Point Loma Pub.

Man at Kambala. large type ed. Kay Thorpe. (Linford Romance Library). 286p. 1984. pap. 16.99 (*0-7089-6035-9*, Linford) Ulverscroft.

Man at the Limit. Valeri Povolayev. (Dramatised Eyewitness Reports Ser.). 272p. 1984. 22.00 (*0-7855-1226-8*, Pub. by Collets) St Mut.

Man at the Wheel. Michael Kenyon. 192p. 1988. pap. 3.50 (*0-380-70381-5*, Avon Bks) Morrow Avon.

Man Before His Time: J. C. Ruppenthal. Mary L. James. (Saga Ser.). 192p. 1988. 14.95 (*0-929160-00-2*) Farwest Pr.

Man Before Others: Rudolf Steiner Remembered. 2nd ed. 220p. 1995. 24.95 (*1-85584-007-3*, Pub. by R Steiner Pr) Anthroposophic.

Man Behind Macbeth: And Other Studies. James Fergusson. 188p. (C). 1986. 39.00 (*0-7855-2153-4*) St Mut.

Man Behind Magic. Richard C. Barret. 1999. pap. 4.99 (*0-14-032738-X*, Viking) Viking Penguin.

***Man Behind the Badge.** Dawn Stewardson. (Superromance Ser.: Bk. 947). 2000. mass mkt. 4.50 (*0-373-70947-1*, 1-70947-6) Harlequin Bks.

Man Behind the Badge (March Madness) Vickie Taylor. (Intimate Moments Ser.: No. 916). 1999. per. 4.25 (*0-373-07916-8*, 1-07916-9) Harlequin Bks.

Man Behind the Camera. Ed. by Hermit Bernsheim et al. LC 76-24683. (Sources of Modern Photography Ser.). (Illus.). 1979. reprint ed. lib. bdg. 15.95 (*0-405-09655-0*) Ayer.

Man Behind the Gun. Edward G. Longacre. 294p. 1977. 20.00 (*0-942211-99-5*) Olde Soldier Bks.

Man Behind the Iron Mask, Vol. 1. John Noone. 320p. 1994. pap. 16.95 (*0-312-12345-0*) St Martin.

Man Behind the Magic. Kristina Logan. (Romance Ser.). 1993. per. 2.75 (*0-373-08950-3*, 5-08950-3) Silhouette.

Man Behind the Magic: The Story of Walt Disney. Katherine Greene. 1998. pap. 14.99 (*0-670-88476-6*) Viking Penguin.

Man Behind the Mill: The Life & Stories of L. J. Maasdam. Constance S. Kramer. LC 96-94123. 173p. (Orig.). 1996. pap. 9.95 (*0-9643179-0-7*) Kramer Pubng.

***Man Behind the Miracle.** Madeline Hartmann. LC 99-59803. 224p. 2000. pap. 12.95 (*1-882897-40-4*) Lost Coast.

Man Behind the Myth: Seeing Jesus as He Really is. Rodney M. Howard-Browne. 358p. 1999. 19.99 (*1-57778-102-3*) Albury Pub.

Man Behind the Smile: Tony Blair & the Politics of Perversion. Leo Abse. LC 97-122345. (Illus.). 1997. 28.95 (*1-86105-078-X*, Robson-Parkwest) Parkwest Pubns.

Man Behind the Sound-Bite: The Real Story of Reverend Al Sharpton. Michael Klein. LC 91-74101. (Illus.). 294p. (Orig.). 1991. pap. 9.95 (*0-9628621-1-8*) Castillo Intl.

Man Behind the Syndrome. Peter Beighton & Greta Beighton. 240p. 1986. 54.95 (*3-540-16218-6*) Spr-Verlag.

Man Behind the Syndrome. Peter H. Beighton & G. J. Beighton. (Illus.). 250p. 1991. reprint ed. 60.95 (*0-387-16218-6*) Spr-Verlag.

***Man Behind the Voice, Vol. 835.** Lisa Bingham. (American Romance Ser.). 2000. mass mkt. 4.25 (*0-373-16835-7*, 1-16835-0) Harlequin Bks.

Man Betrayed. J. V. Jones. (Book of Words Ser.: Bk. 2). 608p. 1996. mass mkt. 6.99 (*0-446-60351-1*, Pub. by Warner Bks) Little.

Man Between Past & Future. Brunetto Chiarelli. (Mankind Quarterly Monographs: No. 7). 132p. 1996. pap. 16.50 (*0-941694-50-X*) Inst Study Man.

Man, Bird, & Beast. Ed. by J. Frank Dobie. LC 33-1132. (Texas Folklore Society Publications: No. 8). (Illus.). 185p. 1965. reprint ed. 12.95 (*0-87074-131-4*) UNTX Pr.

Man Bites Town: Notes of a Man Who Doesn't Take Notes. Harry Shearer. 236p. 1999. reprint ed. text 19.00 (*0-7881-6223-3*) DIANE Pub.

Man Born to Be King. Dorothy L. Sayers. LC 90-82158. 338p. (YA). (gr. 9). 1990. pap. text 14.95 (*0-89870-307-7*) Ignatius Pr.

***Man Business & Investment Opportunities Yearbook: Investment, Export-Import & Other Opportunities & Contacts, 110 vols.** International Business Publications, USA Staff & Global Investment Center, USA Staff. (World Business Opportunities Library Ser.: Vol. 200). (Illus.). 350p. 2000. pap. 99.95 (*0-7397-1070-2*) Intl Business Pubns.

***Man Business Law Handbook: Basic Business Legislation & Regulations Affecting Business & Investment Activites, 110 vols.** International Business Publications, USA Staff & Global Investment Center, USA Staff. (World Law Handbooks Library: Vol. 200). (Illus.). 2000. pap. 99.95 (*0-7397-1083-4*) Intl Business Pubns.

Man Called Abe. large type ed. Jim Bowden. (Linford Western Library). 224p. 1994. pap. 16.99 (*0-7089-7580-1*, Linford) Ulverscroft.

Man Called Brazos. large type ed. Theodore V. Olsen. (Linford Western Library). 1991. pap. 16.99 (*0-7089-7015-X*, Linford) Ulverscroft.

Man Called Daddy. Hugh O'Neill. LC 95-26787. 223p. 1996. 12.95 (*1-55853-393-1*) Rutledge Hill Pr.

***Man Called Daws.** Robert A. Stephens. 178p. 1999. pap. 12.95 (*0-9672799-0-9*) R Stephens.

Man Called Hughes. Thomas Morrissey. 512p. 1989. 75.00 (*1-85390-138-5*, Pub. by Veritas Pubns) St Mut.

***Man Called Intrepid: The Incredible WWII Narrative of the Hero Whose Spy Netwok & Secret Diplomacy Changed the Course of History.** William Stevenson. (Illus.). 512p. 2000. pap. 18.95 (*1-58574-154-X*) Lyons Pr.

Man Called Jesse: Love That Man! K. N. Casper. (Superromance Ser.). 1998. per. 4.25 (*0-373-70806-8*, 1-70806-4) Harlequin Bks.

Man Called Jesus. Jean-Noel Bezancon. 144p. (C). 1990. 45.00 (*0-85439-334-X*, Pub. by St Paul Pubns) St Mut.

Man Called Khushwant Singh. Rohini Singh. (C). 1996. 21.00 (*81-7476-080-6*, Pub. by UBS Pubs Dist) S Asia.

Man Called Khushwant Singh. Ed. by Rohini Singh. 1996. reprint ed. pap. 11.50 (*81-7476-079-2*) UBS Pubs.

Man Called Lion. P. Capstick. (Illus.). 275p. 1994. 24.95 (*1-57157-011-X*) Safari Pr.

Man Called Midas. Leonard Siegelman. 225p. 1997. pap. 11.95 (*0-9660482-0-2*) Shaker Pub Co.

Man Called Mike: The Inspiring Story of a Shy Christopher Hilton. Christopher Hilton. (Illus.). 256p. 1995. pap. 19.95 (*0-947981-92-6*, Pub. by Motor Racing) Motorbooks Intl.

Man Called Mr. Pentecost. David DuPlessis & Bob Slosser. LC 76-53322. 247p. 1977. pap. 7.99 (*0-88270-184-3*) Bridge-Logos.

Man Called Noon. Louis L'Amour. 192p. 1984. mass mkt. 4.50 (*0-553-24753-0*) Bantam.

Man Called Noon. large type ed. Louis L'Amour. (Special Ser.). 271p. 1993. reprint ed. 18.95 (*1-56054-645-X*) Thorndike Pr.

Man Called Norman, 1. 1999. mass mkt. 5.99 (*1-56179-714-6*) Focus Family.

Man Called Norman. Mike Adkins. 178p. 1989. pap. 9.99 (*0-929608-25-9*) Focus Family.

Man Called Peter. Catherine Marshall. 93p. 1955. pap. 5.50 (*0-87129-693-4*, M14) Dramatic Pub.

Man Called Peter. Catherine Marshall. 1976. mass mkt. 4.95 (*0-380-00894-7*, Avon Bks) Morrow Avon.

Man Called Peter. Catherine Marshall. 352p. 1994. pap. 9.00 (*0-380-72204-6*, Avon Bks) Morrow Avon.

Man Called Peter: The Story of Peter Marshall. 2nd anniversary ed. Catherine Marshall. 384p. 1999. 18.99 (*0-8007-9264-5*) Chosen Bks.

Man Called Peter & the Prayers of Peter Marshall: A Spiritual Life. Catherine Marshall. 512p. 1996. 14.99 (*0-88486-149-X*, Inspirational Pr) Arrowood Pr.

Man Called Raleigh. W. Horace Carter. LC 87-83704. (Illus.). 264p. (Orig.). 1988. pap. 9.95 (*0-937866-15-6*) Atlantic Pub Co.

Man Called Raven. Richard Van Camp. (Illus.). (J). 1997. lib. bdg. 21.20 (*0-516-20546-3*) Childrens.

Man Called Raven. Richard Van Camp. LC 96-31905. (Illus.). (J). (gr. 5-7). 1997. 15.95 (*0-89239-144-8*) Childrens Book Pr.

***Man Called Ryker.** Ray Hogan. LC 99-27124. 1999. 19.95 (*0-7862-2026-0*) Thorndike Pr.

***Man Called Ryker.** Ray Hogan. 1999. 19.00 (*0-7540-8079-X*) Chivers N Amer.

Man Called Sampson, 1580-1989: The Ancestry & Progeny of Sampson, a Mashantucket Pequot Indian. Will Ottery & Rudi Ottery. 432p. 1989. 150.00 (*0-929539-51-6*, 1151) Picton Pr.

***Man Called Shiloh.** James Milton Hanna. LC 99-97800. 228p. 2000. pap. 12.95 (*0-9640458-7-7*) Cherokee Bks DE.

Man Called Sparrow. Ralph H. Allen, Jr. (Illus.). 157p. (Orig.). 1997. pap. 5.95 (*0-945277-02-4*) New Creation Bks.

Man Called Trouble. Jeffrey A. Poston. 192p. 1991. mass mkt. 3.50 (*0-87067-369-6*) Holloway.

Man Called White: A Biography by Walter White. Walter White. LC 94-33641. 408p. 1995. reprint ed. pap. 17.95 (*0-8203-1698-9*) U of Ga Pr.

Man Called White: American Negro. Walter F. White. LC 69-18561. (His History & Literature Ser.: No. 2). 1980. reprint ed. 35.95 (*0-405-01906-8*) Ayer.

Man Cannot Speak for Her: A Critical Study of Early Feminist Rhetoric, 2 vols. Karlyn K. Campbell. (Contributions in Women's Studies). 1989. 104.95 (*0-313-26668-9*, CMK/, Greenwood Pr) Greenwood.

An Asterisk (*) at the beginning of an entry indicates that the title is appearing for the first time.

Man Cannot Speak for Her: A Critical Study of Early Feminist Rhetoric, Vol. 1. Karlyn K. Campbell. LC 88-37438. 224p. 1989. pap. 21.95 (*0-275-93269-9*, B32661, Praeger Pubs) Greenwood.

Man Cannot Speak for Her: A Critical Study of Early Feminist Rhetoric, Vol. 1. Karlyn K. Campbell. LC 88-32825. (Contributions in Women's Studies: No. 101). 220p. 1989. 49.95 (*0-313-25649-7*, CMK01, Greenwood Pr) Greenwood.

Man Cannot Speak for Her: A Critical Study of Early Feminist Rhetoric, Vol. 2. Karlyn K. Campbell. LC 88-37378. (Contributions in Women's Studies: No. 102). 587p. 1989. 65.00 (*0-313-25650-0*, CMK02, Greenwood Pr) Greenwood.

Man Cannot Speak for Her: A Critical Study of Early Feminist Rhetoric, Vol. 2. Compiled by Karlyn K. Campbell. LC 88-37438. 587p. 1989. pap. 27.95 (*0-275-93267-2*, B32662, Praeger Pubs) Greenwood.

Man Caught by a Fish: Book of Jonah. M. M. Brem. (Arch Bks.: Set 4). 1970. pap. 1.99 (*0-570-06025-7*, 59-1136) Concordia.

Man Chain. Robert Gillespie. LC 79-12276. 75p. 1979. 4.00 (*0-87886-102-5*, Greenfld Rev Pr) Greenfld Rev Lit.

Man Changes the World. David Burnie et al. LC 98-25947. (Earth, Its Wonders, Its Secrets Ser.). 1999. write for info. (*0-7621-0115-6*) RD Assn.

Man Charles Dickens, a Victorian Portrait. Edward C. Wagenknecht. (BCL1-PR English Literature Ser.). 364p. 1992. reprint ed. lib. bdg. 89.00 (*0-7812-7515-6*) Rprt Serv.

Man Christ Jesus. G. T. Bustin. 1987. pap. 9.99 (*0-88019-226-7*) Schmul Pub Co.

Man, Climate & Architecture. 2nd ed. B. Givoni. vii, 175p. 1976. 66.75 (*0-85334-678-X*); pap. 114.95 (*0-85334-108-7*) Elsevier.

***Man Climbs Out of Manhole.** David Hernandez. 48p. 2000. pap. 8.00 (*1-888219-15-7*) Pearl Edit.

Man Comes to America. Harold Coy. LC 76-189260. x, 150p. 1973. write for info. (*0-316-15906-9*) Little.

Man Condemned. large type ed. Peter Alding. (Dales Mystery Ser.). 192p. 1992. pap. 18.99 (*1-85389-302-1*, Dales) Ulverscroft.

Man Corn: Cannibalism & Violence in the American Southwest & Mexico. Christy Turner, II & Jacqueline A. Turner. LC 98-8856. 547p. 1999. 65.00 (*0-87480-566-X*) U of Utah Pr.

Man Crazy: A Novel. Joyce Carol Oates. 288p. 1998. pap. 12.95 (*0-452-27724-8*, Plume) Dutton Plume.

Man Crazy: A Novel. large type ed. Joyce Carol Oates. LC 97-41717. 1997. 26.95 (*0-7862-1273-X*) Thorndike Pr.

Man Cures, God Heals: Religion & Medical Practice among the Akans of Ghana. Kofi Appiah-Kubi. LC DT0510.43.A5. (Illus.). 189p. 1981. reprint ed. pap. 58.60 (*0-608-00248-8*, 206075100006) Bks Demand.

Man Dangling: Three Short Plays. Murray Schisgal. 1988. pap. 5.25 (*0-8222-0722-2*) Dramatists Play.

Man, Decisions, Society, Vol. 10. Tom R. Burns & Baumgartner. (Studies in Cybernetics). xiv, 342p. 1986. text 106.00 (*2-88124-004-6*); pap. text 46.00 (*2-88124-026-7*) Gordon & Breach.

Man Deep in Mendip: The Caving Diaries of Harry Savory, 1910-1921. Ed. by John Savory. 192p. (C). 1990. 26.95 (*0-8093-1623-4*) S Ill U Pr.

Man Defined. Allen Campbell. (Illus.). 286p. (Orig.). 1992. pap. text 10.00 (*0-9634502-0-4*) RACY Pub.

Man Descending: Selected Stories. Guy Vanderhaeghe. 230p. 1992. pap. 5.95 (*0-7736-7367-9*) Genl Dist Srvs.

Man, Development & Environment. R. S. Doria et al. 1990. 47.50 (*81-7024-288-6*, Pub. by Ashish Pub Hse) S Asia.

Man Discovers God. George S. Eddy. LC 68-24849. (Essay Index Reprint Ser.). 1977. reprint ed. 20.95 (*0-8369-0401-X*) Ayer.

Man Discovers the Galaxies. Richard Berendzen. LC 84-1770. 1984. pap. text 21.00 (*0-231-05827-6*) Col U Pr.

Man Discovers the Galaxies. Richard Berendzen. 1976. text 15.95 (*0-07-004845-2*) McGraw.

Man-Eater of Jassapur. large type ed. Duff Hart-Davis. 464p. 1986. 27.99 (*0-7089-1531-0*) Ulverscroft.

Man-Eater of Malgudi. R. K. Narayan. 176p. 1993. pap. 16.99 (*0-14-018548-8*, Penguin Classics) Viking Penguin.

Man-Eaters. Jim Corbett, pseud. (Adventure Library: Vol. 11). (Illus.). 288p. 1997. lib. bdg. 35.00 (*1-885283-11-3*) Advent Library.

***Man Eaters: An Enthralling Study of the Animals That Prey on People.** Michael Bright. (Illus.). 2000. 24.95 (*1-58574-197-3*) Lyons Pr.

Man-Eaters & Blood Suckers. Kristy Murray. (True Stories Ser.). (Illus.). 100p. (J). (gr. 2-3). 1998. pap. 6.95 (*1-86448-630-9*) IPG Chicago.

Man-Eaters of Kumaon. Jim Corbett, pseud. Date not set. lib. bdg. 21.95 (*0-8488-1967-5*) Amereon Ltd.

Man-Eaters of Kumaon. Jim Corbett, pseud. (Oxford India Paperbacks Ser.). (Illus.). 228p. (C). 1993. pap. 8.95 (*0-19-562255-3*) OUP.

Man-Eaters of Kumaon. Jim Corbett, pseud. 238p. 1985. reprint ed. lib. bdg. 31.95 (*0-89966-574-8*) Buccaneer Bks.

Man-Eaters of Tsavo. 2nd ed. J. H. Patterson. (Peter Capstick Library). (Illus.). 384p. 1985. text 22.95 (*0-312-51010-1*) St Martin.

Man Eating Bugs. Peter Menzel & Faith D'Aluisio. 1998. text 24.95 (*1-58008-051-0*) Ten Speed Pr.

Man Eating Bugs. Peter Menzel & Faith D'Aluisio. LC 98-4411. (Illus.). 192p. 1998. pap. 19.95 (*1-58008-022-7*) Ten Speed Pr.

Man-Eating Leopard of Rudraprayag. Jim Corbett, pseud. (Illus.). 198p. 1989. pap. 9.95 (*0-19-562256-1*) OUP.

Man-Eating Leopard of Rudraprayag. Jim Corbett, pseud. 200p. 1991. reprint ed. lib. bdg. 19.95 (*0-89966-798-8*) Buccaneer Bks.

Man-Eating Myth: Anthropology & Anthropophagy. W. Arens. (Illus.). 220p. 1980. pap. text 13.95 (*0-19-502793-0*) OUP.

Man, Economy & State: A Treatise on Economic Principles. 2nd rev. ed. Murray N. Rothbard. 987p. (C). 1993. reprint ed. pap. text 24.95 (*0-945466-15-3*) Ludwig von Mises.

Man Enough: Embodying Masculinities. Victor J. Seidler. LC 97-68533. 240p. 1997. 79.95 (*0-7619-5407-4*); pap. 29.95 (*0-7619-5408-2*) Sage.

Man Enough to Be a Woman: The Autobiography of Jayne County. Jane County & Rupert Smith. LC 95-68386. (Illus.). 184p. (Orig.). 1996. pap. 17.99 (*1-85242-338-2*) Serpents Tail.

Man-Environment Processes. David Drew. (Processes in Physical Geography Ser.: No. 6). (Illus.). 152p. 1983. pap. text 16.95 (*0-04-551063-6*) Routledge.

***Man Equals Man & The Elephant Calf.** Bertolt Brecht. Ed. by John Willett & Ralph Manheim. Tr. by Gerald Nellhaus from GER. LC 99-59183. 160p. 2000. pap. 10.95 (*1-55970-501-9*, Pub. by Arcade Pub Inc) Time Warner.

Man Everybody Was Afraid Of. Joseph Hansen. LC 78-4190. (Rinehart Suspense Novel Ser.). 192p. 1995. pap. 5.95 (*0-8050-0723-7*, Owl) H Holt & Co.

Man Farthest Down: A Record of Observation & Study in Europe. Booker T. Washington et al. LC 82-19593. (Social Science Classics, Black Classics Ser.). 455p. 1983. pap. 24.95 (*0-87855-933-7*) Transaction Pubs.

Man, Fishes, & the Amazon. Nigel J. Smith. 176p. 1981. text 57.50 (*0-231-05156-5*) Col U Pr.

Man Flies: The Story of Alberto Santos-Dumont, Master of the Balloon. unabridged ed. Nancy Winters. LC 98-16442. (Illus.). 160p. 1998. 23.00 (*0-88001-636-1*) HarpC.

Man, Food & Agriculture in the Middle East. Ed. by Thomas S. Stickley et al. 1969. 25.00 (*0-8156-6015-4*, Pub. by Am U Beirut); pap. 25.00 (*0-8156-6093-6*, Pub. by Am U Beirut) Syracuse U Pr.

Man for All Connections: Raoul Wallenberg & the Hungarian State Apparatus, 1944-1945. Andrew Handler. LC 95-4291. 144p. 1996. 52.95 (*0-275-95214-2*, Praeger Pubs) Greenwood.

Man for All Nations: The Story of Clyde & Ruth Taylor. Carolyn Curtis. 30p. 1998. pap. 3.99 (*0-87509-776-6*) Chr Pubns.

Man for All Nations: The Story of Clyde & Ruth Taylor. Carolyn Curtis. Vol. 20. (Illus.). 195p. (gr. 4-7). 1998. pap. 9.99 (*0-87509-768-5*) Chr Pubns.

Man for All Seasons. rev. ed. Robert Bolt. 1999. pap. 5.95 (*0-333-58052-4*) St Martin.

Man for All Seasons: A Curriculum Unit. Center for Learning Network Staff & Robert Bolt. (Drama Ser.). 105p. (YA). (gr. 9-12). 1990. spiral bd. 18.95 (*1-56077-118-6*) Ctr Learning.

Man for All Seasons: A Play in Two Acts. Robert Bolt. 1962. 14.10 (*0-606-01664-3*, Pub. by Turtleback) Demco.

Man for All Seasons: A Play in Two Acts. Robert Bolt. LC 89-40518. (Vintage International Ser.). 95p. 1990. pap. 9.00 (*0-679-72822-8*) Vin Bks.

Man for All Seasons: A Unit Plan. Mary B. Collins. 70p. 1992. teacher ed., ring bd. 16.95 (*1-58337-119-2*) Teachers Pet Pubns.

***Man for All Seasons: Reproducible Teaching Unit.** James Scott. 74p. (YA). (gr. 7-12). 2000. pap. 29.50i (*1-58049-228-2*, TU141) Prestwick Hse.

Man for All Seasons: Toward Christian Manhood. (Illus.). 20p. (YA). (gr. 9-12). 1996. pap. text 3.95 (*0-913717-10-X*, 2333) Hewitt Res Fnd.

Man for All Time. Rebecca Winters. LC 96-613. (Superromance Ser.). 296p. 1995. per. 3.75 (*0-373-70650-2*, 1-70650-6) Harlequin Bks.

Man for Always. large type ed. Nancy John. 352p. pap. 18.99 (*0-7089-5438-3*) Ulverscroft.

Man for Arkansas: Sid McMath & the Southern Reform Tradition. Jim Lester. (Illus.). 303p. 1976. 19.95 (*0-914546-11-2*) J W Bell.

Man for Christmas. Annabel Murray. 1993. per. 2.99 (*0-373-11613-6*, 1-11613-6) Harlequin Bks.

Man for Easter. Stella Cameron. (American Romance Ser.: No. 433). 1992. per. 3.39 (*0-373-16433-5*, 1-16433-4) Harlequin Bks.

Man for Her. Ann Evans. 1997. per. 3.99 (*0-373-70752-5*, 1-70752-0) Harlequin Bks.

Man for Himself. Erich Fromm. LC 47-12365. 1995. pap. 14.95 (*0-8050-1403-9*, Owl) H Holt & Co.

Man for Me. large type ed. Theresa Charles. 464p. 1986. 27.99 (*0-7089-1500-0*) Ulverscroft.

Man for Megan: The Ultimate. Darlene Scalera. 1999. per. 3.99 (*0-373-16762-8*, Harlequin) Harlequin Bks.

Man for Mom. Sherry Lewis. (Superromance Ser.: No. 826). 1999. per. 4.25 (*0-373-70826-2*, 1-70826-2) Harlequin Bks.

Man for Mom: (That Special Woman!) Gina F. Wilkins. (Special Edition Ser.). 1995. per. 3.75 (*0-373-09955-X*, 1-09955-5) Silhouette.

Man for Others. Patricia Treece. 198p. pap. 7.95 (*0-913382-58-2*, 102-297) Marytown Pr.

Man Freud & Monotheism. Moshe Ater. 278p. pap. 19.00 (*965-223-808-2*) Gefen Bks.

Man from Archangel & Other Tales of Adventure. Arthur Conan Doyle. LC 73-101801. (Short Story Index Reprint Ser.). 1977. 19.95 (*0-8369-3189-0*) Ayer.

Man from Atlantis: Spellbound. Judith McWilliams. 1995. per. 3.25 (*0-373-05954-X*) Harlequin Bks.

Man from Babel. Eugene Jolas. Ed. by Andreas Kramer & Rainer Rumold. LC 98-6674. (Henry McBride Series in Modernism & Modernity). (Illus.). 326p. 1998. 30.00 (*0-300-07536-7*) Yale U Pr.

Man from Bar Twenty. Clarence Mulford. (Hopalong Cassidy Ser.). 1976. reprint ed. lib. bdg. 24.95 (*0-88411-229-2*) Amereon Ltd.

Man from Blue River (Home on the Ranch) Judith Bowen. (Superromance Ser.). 1996. per. 3.99 (*0-373-70689-8*, 1-70689-4) Harlequin Bks.

Man from Briondo. large type ed. Dudley Dean. (Linford Western Library). 288p. 1988. pap. 16.99 (*0-7089-6600-4*, Linford) Ulverscroft.

***Man from Butte City.** large type ed. Lauran Paine. (Paperback Ser.). 2000. pap. 23.95 (*0-7838-8927-5*, G K Hall Lrg Type) Mac Lib Ref.

Man from Clare. John B. Keane. 1992. pap. 12.95 (*0-85342-092-0*) Dufour.

Man from Clay County. large type ed. Elliot Conway. (Dales Large Print Ser.). 224p. 1998. pap. 19.99 (*1-85389-821-X*, Dales) Ulverscroft.

Man from Colorado. large type ed. Louis Trimble. (Linford Western Library). 240p. 1988. pap. 16.99 (*0-7089-6603-9*, Linford) Ulverscroft.

Man from Cougar Pass. Barbara McCauley. (Desire Ser.: No. 698). 1992. per. 2.89 (*0-373-05698-2*, 5-05698-1) Harlequin Bks.

***Man from Coyanosa.** large type ed. Lauran Paine. 224p. 1999. pap. 20.99 (*1-85389-938-0*, Dales) Ulverscroft.

Man from Enterprise: The Biography of John Amos, Founder of A, Incorporated. Seymour Shubin. LC 98-35590. 1998. 29.95 (*0-86554-615-0*, H463) Mercer Univ Pr.

Man from Forever. Vella Munn. (Intimate Moments Ser.). 1996. per. 3.99 (*0-373-07695-9*, 1-07695-9) Silhouette.

Man from Galilee. Daniel H. Bloom. (Illus.). 32p. 1987. 9.95 (*0-915361-90-6*) Lambda Pubs.

Man from Galilee: Sermons & Orders for Lent & Easter. Tom Pilgrim. 1997. pap. text 9.50 (*0-7880-1134-0*) CSS OH.

Man from Galilee: Sermons & Orders of Worship for Lent & Easter. Thomas A. Pilgrim. LC 97-26626. 94p. 1997. pap. 9.50 (*0-7880-1131-6*) CSS OH.

Man from Glengarry. Ralph Connor. 1976. lib. bdg. 19.50 (*0-89968-017-8*, Lghtyr Pr) Buccaneer Bks.

Man from Glengarry. Ralph Connor. 392p. 1996. pap. 7.95 (*0-7710-9890-1*) McCland & Stewart.

Man from God Knows Where. Dennis Carroll. 286p. 1997. 74.95 (*1-85607-221-5*, Pub. by Columba Press); pap. 54.95 (*1-85607-130-8*, Pub. by Columba Press) Intl Scholars.

Man from Guyana. Edward R. Asregadoo. LC 89-91456. 1990. 18.95 (*0-87212-231-X*) Libra.

Man from Halifax: Sir John Thompson, Prime Minister. P. B. Waite. 576p. 1986. pap. 19.95 (*0-8020-6624-0*); text 40.00 (*0-8020-5659-8*) U of Toronto Pr.

Man from High Mountain. Kay David. (Superromance Ser.: Bk. 848). 1999. per. 4.25 (*0-373-70848-3*, 1-70848-6) Harlequin Bks.

***Man from Home.** Booth Tarkington. (Works of Booth Tarkington). 175p. 1999. reprint ed. lib. bdg. 88.00 (*1-58201-862-6*) Classic Bks.

Man from Home: A Novel by Henry Leon Wilson Founded on the Play by N. Booth Tarkington & Harry Leon Wilson. Harry Leon Wilson. (Collected Works of Harry Leon Wilson). 307p. 1999. reprint ed. lib. bdg. 98.00 (*1-58201-879-0*) Classic Bks.

Man from Internal Affairs. Nat Hentoff. 224p. 1985. 15.95 (*0-89296-141-4*, Pub. by Mysterious Pr) Little.

Man from Internal Affairs. Nat Hentoff. 224p. 1986. mass mkt. 3.95 (*0-445-40509-0*, Pub. by Mysterious Pr) Little.

Man from Kanpur. large type ed. Nara Lake. (Linford Romance Library). 368p. 1996. pap. 16.99 (*0-7089-7966-1*, Linford) Ulverscroft.

Man from Lamb Hill. large type ed. Margaret Allan. (Dales Large Print Ser.). 238p. 1996. pap. 18.99 (*1-85389-595-4*, Dales) Ulverscroft.

Man from Maine. Edward Bok. 1993. reprint ed. lib. bdg. 89.00 (*0-7812-5429-9*) Rprt Serv.

Man from Mundania. Piers Anthony. 352p. 1989. mass mkt. 5.99 (*0-380-75289-1*, Avon Bks) Morrow Avon.

Man from Natchez. Elizabeth August. (Romance Ser.: No. 790). 1991. per. 2.50 (*0-373-08790-X*) Silhouette.

Man from Nazareth: Life of Christ - From the Annunciation to the Resurrection. Diane H. Balay. 128p. 1997. spiral bd. 11.95 (*0-687-05318-8*) Abingdon.

***Man from Nowhere.** large type ed. T. T. Flynn. LC 00-25942. (Paperback Ser.). 241p. 2000. pap. 23.95 (*0-7838-9025-7*, G K Hall Lrg Type) Mac Lib Ref.

Man from Nowhere. large type ed. Theodore V. Olsen. (Linford Western Library). 1990. pap. 16.99 (*0-7089-6946-1*, Linford) Ulverscroft.

Man from Oklahoma. Lisa Harris. 1996. per. 3.50 (*0-373-25710-4*, 1-25710-4) Harlequin Bks.

Man from Outback. Lucy Walker. 1981. mass mkt. 1.75 (*0-345-29500-5*) Ballantine Pub Grp.

Man from Outback. Lucy Walker. 1974. mass mkt. 0.75 (*0-345-20477-8*) Ballantine Pub Grp.

***Man from Peculiar, Vol. 216.** J R Roberts. (Gunsmith Ser.). 1999. mass mkt. 4.99 (*0-515-12708-6*, Jove) Berkley Pub.

Man from Porklock: Engagements, 1944-1981. Theodore R. Weiss. LC 82-47622. (Princeton Series of Collected Essays). 329p. 1982. reprint ed. pap. 102.00 (*0-7837-9476-2*, 206021800004) Bks Demand.

Man from Right Field. Lynn Burgmaier. LC 98-90372. 1998. 19.95 (*0-533-12770-X*) Vantage.

Man from Robber's Roost. Peter Field. 176p. 1989. pap. 2.75 (*0-380-70425-0*, Avon Bks) Morrow Avon.

Man from St. Petersburg. Ken Follett. 360p. 1983. mass mkt. 7.99 (*0-451-16351-6*) NAL.

Man from Scottsboro: Clarence Norris & the Infamous 1931 Alabama Rape Trial, in His Own Words 1997. Kwando M. Kinshasa. LC 96-45530. (Illus.). 239p. 1997. lib. bdg. 32.50 (*0-7864-0276-8*) McFarland & Co.

Man from Shadow Ridge. Brock Thoene & Bodie Thoene. LC 89-18467. (Saga of the Sierras Ser.: No. 1). 24p. (Orig.). 1990. pap. 8.99 (*1-55661-098-X*) Bethany Hse.

Man from Shadow Valley: (Secret Fantasies) Regan Forest. LC 95-13565. (Temptation Ser.). 216p. 1995. per. 3.25 (*0-373-25638-8*, 1-25638-7) Harlequin Bks.

Man from Skibbereen. Louis L'Amour. 192p. (Orig.). 1983. mass mkt. 4.50 (*0-553-24906-1*) Bantam.

Man from Snowy River & Other Verses. Banjo Paterson. 262p. Date not set. 22.95 (*0-8488-2534-9*) Amereon Ltd.

Man from Snowy River & Other Verses. A. B. Paterson. 198p. 1989. reprint ed. lib. bdg. 31.95 (*0-89966-589-6*) Buccaneer Bks.

***Man from Snowy River & Other Verses: Australia's Best Loved Poetry Collection.** Paterson. 2000. pap. 15.95 (*0-207-19173-5*) Collins Angus & Robertson Pubs.

Man from Snowy River & 29 PS. 96p. 1992. pap. 12.95 (*0-7692-1153-4*, PF0801) Wrner Bros.

***Man from Socorro.** large type ed. Curt Longbow. 224p. 1999. pap. 18.99 (*0-7089-5539-8*, Linford) Ulverscroft.

Man from the Bar-20. Clarence Mulford. 1995. pap. 4.99 (*0-8125-5050-1*, Pub. by Forge NYC) St Martin.

Man from the Broken Hills. Louis L'Amour. 224p. 1996. reprint ed. mass mkt. 4.50 (*0-553-27679-4*) Bantam.

Man from the Ciguri. unabridged ed. Jean Moebius. (Illus.). 80p. (Orig.). (YA). (gr. 11 up). 1996. pap. 7.95 (*1-56971-135-6*) Dark Horse Comics.

Man from the Desert. large type ed. Luke Short. LC 92-37235. (Western Ser.). 269p. 1993. reprint ed. lib. bdg. 19.95 (*1-56054-230-6*) Thorndike Pr.

***Man From the East.** Tom Reiss. 2000. 25.00 (*0-06-019765-X*) HarpC.

***Man from the East.** Tom Reiss. 2000. pap. 14.00 (*0-06-095704-2*) HarpC.

Man from the Mercury: A Charles Angoff Memorial Reader. Intro. by Thomas Yoseloff. LC 85-20754. 320p. 1986. 29.50 (*0-8386-3280-7*) Fairleigh Dickinson.

Man from the North. Arnold Bennett. LC 74-17023. (Collected Works of Arnold Bennett: Vol. 51). 1977. reprint ed. 25.95 (*0-518-19132-X*) Ayer.

***Man from the North Country.** Laurie Paige. 2000. mass mkt. 4.50 (*0-373-82221-9*, 1-82221-2) Harlequin Bks.

Man from the Other Side. Uri Orlev. Tr. by Hillel Halkin. LC 90-47898. 144p. (J). (gr. 5 up). 1991. 16.00 (*0-395-53808-4*) HM.

Man from the Other Side. Uri Orlev. Tr. by Hillel Halkin. LC 94-30189. (Illus.). 192p. (J). (gr. 1-8). 1995. pap. 4.99 (*0-14-037088-9*, PuffinBks) Peng Put Young Read.

Man from the Other Side. Uri Orlev. 1995. 9.09 (*0-606-07834-7*, Pub. by Turtleback) Demco.

Man from the Past. 2nd ed. Roy C. Higby. (Illus.). 1994. reprint ed. pap. 9.25 (*0-914692-02-X*) Big Moose.

Man from the Sky. Avi. Ed. by ALC Staff. LC 92-389. (Illus.). 96p. (YA). (gr. 5 up). 1992. mass mkt. 4.95 (*0-688-11897-6*, Wm Morrow) Morrow Avon.

Man from the Sky. Avi. (J). 1992. 9.05 (*0-606-01381-4*, Pub. by Turtleback) Demco.

Man from the Sky. large type ed. Avi. (Illus.). (J). 1993. 33.50 (*0-614-09840-8*, L-34110-00) Am Printing Hse.

Man from the Sky. 94th ed. Cullinan. (J). 1994. text 17.40 (*0-15-302201-9*, Harcourt Child Bks) Harcourt.

***Man from the Staked Plains.** large type ed. Jack Sheriff. 264p. 1999. pap. 18.99 (*0-7089-5564-9*, Linford) Ulverscroft.

Man from the U. S. S. R. & Other Plays. Vladimir Nabokov. Tr. by Dmitri Nabokov. 342p. 1986. 75.60 (*0-317-40746-5*) St Mut.

Man from the Valley: Memoirs of a Twentieth Century Virginian. Francis P. Miller. LC 71-132255. (Illus.). 280p. reprint ed. pap. 86.80 (*0-8357-3867-1*, 203659900004) Bks Demand.

Man from Tibet. Clyde B. Clason. 224p. 1998. pap. 14.00 (*0-915230-17-8*) Rue Morgue.

Man from Two Rivers. large type ed. Luke Short. LC 95-32169. 175p. 1996. lib. bdg. 20.95 (*0-7838-1466-6*, G K Hall Lrg Type) Mac Lib Ref.

Man from U. N. C. L. E. Doomsday Affair. Harry Whittington. 18.95 (*0-8488-0666-2*) Amereon Ltd.

Man from U. N. C. L. E. Book. Jon Heitland. (Illus.). 256p. 1987. pap. 13.95 (*0-312-00052-9*) St Martin.

Man from Wells Fargo. large type ed. Will Comstock. LC 97-40849. 1998. 18.95 (*0-7862-0680-2*, G K Hall Lrg Type) Mac Lib Ref.

***Man From Wells Fargo: Breyfogel's Gold.** Nye. 1998. 20.00 (*0-7862-0990-9*) Mac Lib Ref.

Man from Whom God Nothing Hid. Meister Eckhart. Ed. by Ursula Fleming. 160p. 1990. pap. 11.95 (*0-87243-176-2*) Templegate.

***Man from Wyoming.** (Western Trio). (Illus.). 2000. 30.00 (*0-7862-2115-1*) Mac Lib Ref.

***Man Gave Names to All the Animals.** Bob Dylan. LC 98-28826. (Illus.). 32p. (J). (ps-2). 1999. 16.00 (*0-15-202005-5*, Harcourt Child Bks) Harcourt.

Man, God & Civilization. John G. Jackson. 352p. 1972. pap. 10.95 (*0-8065-0858-2*, Citadel Pr) Carol Pub Group.

Man, God & Civilization. John G. Jackson. 338p. 1999. reprint ed. lib. bdg. 34.95 (*0-7351-0103-5*) Replica Bks.

Man, God & Immortality: Thoughts on Human Progress (1927) James George Frazer. 438p. 1998. reprint ed. pap. 29.95 (*0-7661-0188-6*) Kessinger Pub.

Man, God, & Nature in the Enlightenment. Ed. by Donald C. Mell, Jr. et al. LC 87-51123. (Medieval Studies : No. 2). 247p. 1988. 39.95 (*0-937191-03-5*); pap. 14.95 (*0-937191-13-2*) Mich St U Pr.

M

An Asterisk (*) at the beginning of an entry indicates that the title is appearing for the first time.

Man, God & the Universe. I. K. Taimni. LC 74-4167. (Illus.). 447p. 1974. reprint ed. pap. 8.95 (*0-8356-0447-0*, Quest) Theos Pub Hse.

Man God Loved. Deborah Bacon. LC 87-60005. (Illus.). 315p. (Orig.). 1987. pap. 13.95 (*0-9606498-2-4*) Candlebeam Pr.

Man-god or Sense of Life. Luc Ferry. 1996. pap. text 10.95 (*0-226-24485-7*); lib. bdg. 27.50 (*0-226-24484-9*) U Ch Pr.

***Man God Uses.** Henry Blackaby & Tom Blackaby. LC 99-37776. 224p. 1999. 15.99 (*0-8054-2145-9*) Broadman.

Man, Gods, & Nature. Michael K. Dudley. pap. 12.95 (*1-878751-15-8*) Na Kane O Ka Malo.

Man-Gods in the Mexican Highlands: Indian Power & Colonial Society, 1520-1800. Serge Gruzinski. Tr. by Eileen Corrigan from FRE. LC 88-39838. 240p. 1989. 37.50 (*0-8047-1513-0*) Stanford U Pr.

Man, God's Robot. James S. Prothro. 1998. pap. text 19.95 (*0-9662919-0-5*) Robot Pubg.

***Man, God's Robot Workbook.** James S. Prothro. Ed. by Rosalynn A. Curry. 51p. 1999. pap. 9.95 (*0-9662919-8-0*) Robot Pubg.

Man, Grand Symbol of the Mysteries. Manly P. Hall. pap. 17.95 (*0-89314-389-8*) Philos Res.

Man, Grand Symbol of the Mysteries. Manly P. Hall. (Illus.). 254p. 1999. 21.95 (*0-89314-513-0*) Philos Res.

Man Handling: How to Handle Any Man, Any Time. Susan Thomas. 110p. 1994. pap. 13.95 (*0-9635026-8-9*) Picasso Publ.

Man Has a Need to Love. (Shorewood Art Programs for Education Ser.). 8p. 1974. teacher ed. 107.00 (*0-88185-034-9*); 143.00 (*0-685-07223-1*) Shorewood Fine Art.

Man, His First Two Million Years: A Brief Introduction to Anthropology. Ashley Montagu. LC 80-15749. (Illus.). 262p. 1980. reprint ed. lib. bdg. 35.00 (*0-313-22600-8*, MOMH, Greenwood Pr) Greenwood.

Man, His Nature & Destiny. Cornelius R. Stam. 219p. 1961. 14.00 (*1-893874-08-7*) Berean Bibl Soc.

Man-Hour Standards see Means Productivity Standards

Man Hungry. Gary Bowen. (Orig.). 1996. mass mkt. 5.95 (*1-56333-374-0*, Badboy) Masquerade.

Man Hunt. Sonia Caulton. Ed. by Ginger Whitaker. 1997. pap. 12.95 (*0-9655545-0-3*) SistahGirl Pub.

Man, Husband, Father. Buddy Harrison. LC 96-108638. 1995. pap. 8.99 (*0-89274-792-7*, HH-792) Harrison Hse.

Man I Am Watching. Mark Linenthal. 1987. pap. 5.95 (*0-938979-02-7*) EG Bksellers.

Man, I Need a Job! Finding Employment with a Criminal History. 2nd ed. Ned Rollo. (Information Ser.). 76p. (Orig.). 1993. pap. 5.95 (*1-878436-15-5*) OPEN TX.

Man I Never Wanted to Be. John J. Clayton. LC 97-36395. 230p. 1998. 24.00 (*1-57962-014-0*) Permanent Pr.

***Man I Never Wanted to Be.** John J. Clayton. 232p. 1999. pap. 16.00 (*1-57962-057-4*) Permanent Pr.

Man I Used to Know: Love That Man. Margot Dalton. (Superromance Ser.: No. 831). 1999. per. 4.25 (*0-373-70831-9*, 1-70831-2, Harlequin) Harlequin Bks.

Man in a Country Boy. Helene B. Davidson. (Illus.). 185p. (Orig.). 1997. per. 14.95 (*0-9656698-0-7*) H B Davidson.

Man in a Hurry. James A. Stewart. 1968. 3.99 (*1-56632-063-1*) Revival Lit.

Man in a Million. Darlene Scalera. (American Romance Ser.: Bk. 807). 2000. per. 3.99 (*0-373-16807-1*, 1-16807-9) Harlequin Bks.

Man in a Motel Room. Michael Dudley. (Chapbks.: No. 18). 40p. (Orig.). 1986. pap. 3.50 (*0-913719-84-6*, High Coo Pr) Brooks Books.

Man in a Net. William Butler. 160p. 1971. 16.95 (*0-8464-0586-5*) Beekman Pubs.

Man in Adaptation Vol. 2: Cultural Present. 2nd ed. Yehudi A. Cohen. 615p. 1974. pap. text 34.95 (*0-202-01110-0*) Aldine de Gruyter.

***Man in Black.** Thomson. 1998. text 22.95 (*1-85375-284-3*, Pub. by Prion) Trafalgar.

***Man in Charge: A Novel.** Morris H. Philipson. LC 00-37790. (Phoenix Fiction Ser.). 2000. pap. write for info. (*0-226-66751-0*) U Ch Pr.

Man in Competition with the Spruce Budworm. Philip M. Tuchinsky. 60p. 1981. pap. text 9.95 (*0-8176-3047-3*) Birkhauser.

Man in Dark Times (Uddhivasta Dharmashala) G. P. Deshpande. (C). 1990. pap. 10.00 (*81-7046-036-0*, Pub. by Seagull Bks) S Asia.

Man in Demand. Cheryl A. Porter. (Love & Laughter Ser.: No. 21). 1997. per. 3.50 (*0-373-44021-9*, 1-44021-3) Harlequin Bks.

Man in Demand. rev. ed. Emily Hunter & Wayne Hunter. (Illus.). 224p. 1975. reprint ed. pap., teacher ed. 9.99 (*0-89081-511-9*); reprint ed. pap. text, student ed. 7.99 (*0-89081-510-0*) Harvest Hse.

Man in Essence: Folk Tales & Photographs from Irian Jaya, Indonesia. Laurens Hillhouse. LC 90-83582. (Illus.). 96p. (Orig.). 1990. pap. 9.95 (*0-9627359-0-6*) Hillhse Pubns.

Man in Estrangement: A Comparison of the Thought of Paul Tillich & Erich Fromm. Guyton B. Hammond. LC 65-18546. 206p. reprint ed. pap. 63.90 (*0-8357-3256-8*, 203947700013) Bks Demand.

Man in Evolution. 2nd rev. ed. G. De Purucker. Ed. by Grace F. Knoche. LC 76-45503. 377p. 1977. pap. 14.95 (*0-911500-55-3*) Theos U Pr.

Man in Evolutionary Perspective. Ed. by C. Loring Brace & James F. Metress. LC 72-14184. 486p. (C). reprint ed. 150.70 (*0-8357-9926-3*, 201261800082) Bks Demand.

***Man in Flames.** Serge Filippini. Tr. by Liz Nash from FRE. (Dedalus Europe 1999 Ser.).Tr. of Homme Encendie. 367p. 1999. pap. 16.99 (*1-873982-24-0*, Pub. by Dedalus) Subterranean Co.

Man in Full: A Novel. Tom Wolfe. LC 98-29842. 800p. 1999. mass mkt. 8.50 (*0-553-58093-0*) Bantam.

Man in Full: A Novel. Tom Wolfe. LC 98-29842. 742p. 1998. 28.95 (*0-374-27032-5*) FS&G.

Man in Full: A Novel. aut. limited ed. Tom Wolfe. 1998. 200.00 (*0-374-27030-9*) FS&G.

***Man in Full: A Novel.** large type ed. Tom Wolfe. LC 98-48925. 1998. 32.95 (*1-56895-694-0*) Wheeler Pub.

Man in God's World: The Biblical Idea of Office. Paul G. Schrontenboer. (Jubilee Perspectives Ser.: No. 1). 32p. (Orig.). 1989. reprint ed. pap. 2.95 (*0-9621880-0-X*) Shiloh Pubns.

Man in Gray. Eleanor Smith. 310p. Date not set. 24.95 (*0-8488-2665-5*) Amereon Ltd.

Man in Green. Patrick Doud. 64p. (Orig.). 1996. pap. 10.00 (*1-889960-00-4*) First Intensity.

***Man in His Original Dignity: Legal Ethics in France.** 146p. 2000. 74.95 (*0-7546-2110-3*) Ashgate Pub Co.

Man in His Right Mind. Harold W. Darling. 158p. 1977. reprint ed. text 9.50 (*0-85364-097-1*) Attic Pr.

Man in Love. Richard Daley Outram. (Illus.). 64p. 1985. pap. write for info. (*0-88984-069-5*, Pub. by Porcup Quill) Genl Dist Srvs.

Man in Lower Ten. Mary Roberts Rinehart. 19.95 (*0-8488-0839-8*) Amereon Ltd.

Man in Lower Ten. Mary Roberts Rinehart. 1976. lib. bdg. 19.95 (*0-89968-180-8*, Lghtyr Pr) Buccaneer Bks.

Man in My Basement. Walter Mosley. 2000. write for info. (*0-316-57082-6*) Little.

Man in Nature: America Before the Days of the Whiteman. Carl Ortwin Sauer. (New World Writing Ser.). (Illus.). 1975. 17.50 (*0-913666-28-9*); pap. 10.95 (*0-913666-01-7*) Turtle Isl Foun.

Man in Northeastern North America. Ed. by Frederick Johnson. LC 76-43756. (Papers of the Robert S. Peabody Foundation for Archaeology: Vol. 3). reprint ed. 64.50 (*0-404-15597-9*) AMS Pr.

Man in Place. Michael Hannon & Jack Curtis. (Illus.). 36p. 1982. 75.00 (*0-918824-33-8*) Turkey Pr.

Man in Revolt. A. Niel. 109p. 1973. 4.95 (*0-318-37033-6*) Asia Bk Corp.

Man in Search of Immortality: Testimonials from the Hindu Scriptures. Swami Nikhilananda. LC 68-101793. 112p. 1992. pap. 10.50 (*0-911206-27-2*) Ramakrishna.

Man in Society: A Biosocial View. Pierre L. Van den Berghe. LC 78-1393. 349p. 1981. lib. bdg. 27.95 (*0-444-99051-8*, VMI/) Greenwood.

Man in Sport. Ed. by Robert Riger. (Illus.). 1967. pap. 3.50 (*0-912298-10-3*) Baltimore Mus.

Man in Systems. Ed. by Milton D. Rubin. (Illus.). xii, 496p. (C). 1971. text 323.00 (*0-677-14060-6*) Gordon & Breach.

Man in the Amazon. Ed. by Charles Wagley. LC 74-10857. (Illus.). xvi, 330p. 1974. 20.00 (*0-8130-0501-9*) U Press Fla.

Man in the Amazon. Latin American Conference Staff. Ed. by Charles Wagley. LC 74-10857. (Illus.). 346p. reprint ed. pap. 107.30 (*0-7837-5011-0*, 204467800004) Bks Demand.

Man in the Arena. Harold L. Oshry & Kate Winters. 250p. 1995. write for info. (*1-888069-05-8*) Biography For Everyone.

Man in the Arena: The Life & Times of A. C. Sutphin. unabridged ed. George Condon. Ed. by Jeffrey Leitch. (Illus.). 256p. 1996. 22.95 (*0-9649900-0-8*); pap. 18.50 (*0-9649900-1-6*) A C Sutphin.

Man in the Bamboo Cage. Nigel Cawthorne. (Illus.). 1991. 30.95 (*0-85052-148-3*) Leo Cooper.

Man in the Black Chevrolet. Todd Moore. LC 76-29870. 1976. pap. 1.50 (*0-916918-04-1*) Duck Down.

Man in the Black Coat: Russia's Literature of the Absurd. Daniil Kherms & Alexander Vredensky. Ed. by George Gibian. 258p. 1987. reprint ed. pap. 15.95 (*0-8101-0735-X*) Northwestern U Pr.

Man in the Black Coat Turns. Robert Bly. LC 88-45108. 80p. 1991. reprint ed. pap. 10.00 (*0-06-097186-X*, PL 7186, Perennial) HarperTrade.

Man in the Blue Truck. Russ Sheetz. Ed. by Shirley Warren. (Illus.). 12p. (Orig.). (J). (ps). 1990. pap. 3.95 (*1-877801-06-2*) Still Waters.

Man in the Bowler Hat: His History & Iconography. Fred M. Robinson. LC 92-37188. (Illus.). xvi, 199p. (C). 1993. 29.95 (*0-8078-2073-3*) U of NC Pr.

Man in the Bowler Hat: His History & Iconography. Fred M. Robinson. LC 92-37188. 215p. reprint ed. pap. 66.70 (*0-608-08615-0*, 206913800003) Bks Demand.

Man in the Box. Thomas Moran. 272p. 1998. pap. 12.00 (*1-57322-649-1*, Riverhd Trade) Berkley Pub.

Man in the Box. Thomas Moran. LC 96-41042. 272p. 1997. 21.95 (*1-57322-060-4*, Riverhead Books) Putnam Pub Group.

Man in the Box. large type ed. Thomas Moran. LC 97-1888. (Core Ser.). 344p. 1997. 26.95 (*0-7838-8123-1*, G K Hall Lrg Type) Mac Lib Ref.

Man in the Box: A Story from Vietnam. Marylois Dunn. Ed. by Jerri S. Richards. (Illus.). 104p. (Orig.). (YA). (gr. 6-12). 1997. pap. 12.50 (*1-887303-16-2*) Blu Lantern Pub.

Man in the Brown Suit. Agatha Christie. 240p. 1984. mass mkt. 5.99 (*0-425-06786-6*) Berkley Pub.

Man in the Brown Suit. Agatha Christie. 1984. 10.60 (*0-606-00964-7*, Pub. by Turtleback) Demco.

Man in the Brown Suit. Agatha Christie. 1998. lib. bdg. 19.95 (*1-56723-032-6*) Yestermorrow.

***Man in the Brown Suit, Set.** unabridged ed. Agatha Christie. 1999. 35.95 incl. audio (*1-55685-595-8*) Audio Bk Con.

Man in the Buick: & Other Stories. Kathleen George. LC 99-19247. 192p. (Orig.). 1999. pap. 14.95 (*1-886157-20-0*) BkMk.

Man in the Cardboard Mask. Alvin Greenberg. LC 84-15533. 128p. (Orig.). 1985. pap. 8.95 (*0-918273-02-1*) Coffee Hse.

Man in the Ceiling. Jules Feiffer. LC 92-59953. (Michael di Capua Bks.). (Illus.). 32p. (J). (gr. 4-7). 1993. 15.95 (*0-06-205035-4*) HarpC Child Bks.

Man in the Ceiling. Jules Feiffer. LC 92-59953. (Trophy Bk.). (Illus.). 192p. (J). (gr. 3-7). 1995. pap. 6.95 (*0-06-205907-6*, HarpTrophy) HarpC Child Bks.

Man in the Ceiling. Jules Feiffer. 1995. 12.30 (*0-606-07835-5*) Turtleback.

Man in the Cosmic Ocean. Edmond B. Szekely. (Illus.). 56p. 1970. pap. 4.50 (*0-89564-054-6*) IBS Intl.

Man in the Crowd: The Uneasy Streets of Garry Winogrand. Fran Lebowitz & Ben Lifson. Ed. by Jeffrey Fraenkel. 168p. 1999. 45.00 (*1-881337-05-7*) Fraenkel Gal.

Man in the Dog Suit. adapted ed. Edwin Corle. Ed. by William H. Wright. 1959. pap. 5.25 (*0-8222-0723-0*) Dramatists Play.

Man in the Dugout: Baseball's Top Managers & How They Got That Way. 2nd expanded ed. Leonard Koppett. LC 99-41177. (Illus.). 424p. 2000. 29.50 (*1-56639-745-6*) Temple U Pr.

Man in the Dugout: Fifteen Big League Managers Speak Their Minds. Donald Honig. LC 94-42714. (Illus.). xiii, 343p. 1995. pap. 14.95 (*0-8032-7270-7*, Bison Books) U of Nebr Pr.

Man in the Everglades: 2000 Years of Human History in the Everglades National Park. Charlton W. Tebeau. LC 68-17768. 1968. 20.00 (*0-87024-073-0*) U of Miami Pr.

Man in the Gray Flannel Suit. Sloan Wilson. 20.95 (*0-8488-1512-2*) Amereon Ltd.

Man in the Gray Flannel Suit. Sloan Wilson. LC 79-18970. 1980. reprint ed. lib. bdg. 16.00 (*0-8376-0448-6*) Bentley Pubs.

Man in the Gray Flannel Suit. Sloan Wilson. 250p. 1991. reprint ed. lib. bdg. 35.95 (*0-89966-862-3*) Buccaneer Bks.

Man in the Green Chevy. Susan R. Cooper. 1991. reprint ed. per. 3.50 (*0-373-26071-7*) Harlequin Bks.

Man in the Green Coat. Carola Dunn. 192p. 1987. 16.95 (*0-8027-0937-0*) Walker & Co.

Man in the High Castle. Philip K. Dick. 1992. pap. 12.00 (*0-679-74067-8*) Vin Bks.

Man in the Holocene: A Story. Max Frisch. Tr. by Geoffrey Skelton. LC 79-3351. (Helen & Kurt Wolff Bk.). (Illus.). 128p. 1994. pap. 6.95 (*0-15-656952-3*, Harvest Bks) Harcourt.

Man in the Ice. Konard Spindler. 352p. 1995. 34.95 (*0-385-25462-8*) Doubleday.

Man in the Ice: His Times & Environment. Ed. by H. Seidler et al. 200p. 1996. 48.00 (*3-211-82799-4*) Spr-Verlag.

Man in the Iron Lung: Poems by Mark O'Brien. Mark O'Brien. 48p. 1997. pap. 8.00 (*1-891420-03-8*) Lemonade Factory.

Man in the Iron Mask. Alexandre Dumas. (Classics Illustrated Study Guides Ser.). (Illus.). 1997. mass mkt. 4.99 (*1-57840-037-6*, Pub. by Acclaim Bks) Penguin Putnam.

Man in the Iron Mask. Alexandre Dumas. (Illustrated Classics Collection 4). 64'p. 1994. pap. 4.95 (*0-7854-0750-2*, 40503) Am Guidance.

Man in the Iron Mask. Alexandre Dumas. 1976. 27.95 (*0-8488-1293-X*) Amereon Ltd.

Man in the Iron Mask. Alexandre Dumas. 1976. lib. bdg. 35.95 (*0-89968-146-8*, Lghtyr Pr) Buccaneer Bks.

Man in the Iron Mask. Alexandre Dumas. Ed. & Intro. by David Coward. (Oxford World's Classics Ser.). 654p. 1998. pap. 11.95 (*0-19-283842-3*) OUP.

Man in the Iron Mask. Alexandre Dumas. Ed. by Naunerle C. Farr. (Now Age Illustrated IV Ser.). (Illus.). (J). (gr. 4-12). 1978. student ed. 1.25 (*0-88301-340-1*); pap. text 2.95 (*0-88301-316-9*) Pendulum Pr.

Man in the Iron Mask. Alexandre Dumas. LC 98-65626. (Illus.). (J). (gr. 4-7). 1998. pap. 3.99 (*0-679-89433-0*, Pub. by Random Bks Yng Read) Random.

Man in the Iron Mask. Alexandre Dumas. LC 98-47663. 448p. 1998. pap. 14.95 (*0-89526-348-3*, Pub. by Regnery Pub) Natl Bk Netwk.

Man in the Iron Mask. Alexandre Dumas. 592p. 1998. pap. 4.99 (*0-8125-6499-5*, Pub. by Tor Bks) St Martin.

***Man in the Iron Mask.** Alexandre Dumas. 1998. 10.09 (*0-606-13594-4*, Pub. by Turtleback) Demco.

***Man in the Iron Mask.** Paul Mantell. (Bullseye Step into Classics Ser.). (J). 1998. 9.09 (*0-606-13965-6*, Pub. by Turtleback) Demco.

Man in the Iron Mask. rev. ed. Alexandre Dumas. Tr. by Jacqueline Rogers. 464p. 1992. mass mkt. 6.95 (*0-451-52564-7*, Sig Classics) NAL.

Man in the Iron Mask. rev. ed. Alexandre Dumas. 496p. 1998. mass mkt. 6.99 (*0-451-19700-3*, Sig) NAL.

Man in the Iron Mask Readalong. Alexandre Dumas. (Illustrated Classics Collection 4). 64p. 1994. pap. 14.95 incl. audio (*0-7854-0766-9*, 40505) Am Guidance.

Man in the Ivory Tower: F. Cyril James of McGill. Stanley B. Frost. (Illus.). 344p. (C). 1991. text 65.00 (*0-7735-0803-1*, Pub. by McG-Queens Univ Pr) CUP Services.

***Man in the Kitchen: A Man's Macrobiotic Guide to Preparing Meals & a Guide for Women to Prepare Meals That Men Like.** Warren S. Wepman. (Illus.). 160p. 2000. pap. 12.95 (*1-882984-41-2*) One Peaceful World.

Man in the Kitchen Texas Style! Daisy E. O'Neal. 150p. (Orig.). 1990. pap. 9.95 (*0-9626482-0-5*) Star-Daze Prodns.

Man in the Light of Occultism, Theosophy & Philosophy. rev. ed. Rudolf Steiner. LC 88-92553. 216p. 1989. lib. bdg. 16.00 (*0-89345-057-X*, Spir Sci Lib) Garber Comm.

Man in the Living Environment: Report. University of Wisconsin, Workshop on Global Ecolog. LC 77-187506. (Illus.). 312p. reprint ed. pap. 89.00 (*0-8357-6785-X*, 2035462) Bks Demand.

Man in the Making: What You Need to Know As You're Becoming a Man. Greg Johnson. LC 96-32722. 144p. 1996. pap. 7.99 (*0-8054-5395-4*, 4253-95) Broadman.

Man in the Mangroves: The Socio-Economic Situation of Human Settlements in Mangrove Forests. 117p. pap. 15.00 (*92-808-0607-6*, E.86.III.A.7) UN.

Man in the Middle. Gregory Djanikian. LC 84-70176. (Poetry Ser.). 79p. 1984. pap. 11.95 (*0-88748-002-0*) Carnegie-Mellon.

Man in the Mirror. David Ignatius. 1996. write for info. (*0-614-18295-6*) Random.

Man in the Mirror: John Howard Griffin & the Story of "Black Like Me" Robert Bonazzi. LC 97-18711. (Illus.). 180p. (Orig.). 1997. pap. 14.00 (*1-57075-118-8*) Orbis Bks.

Man in the Mirror: Solving the 24 Problems Men Face. Patrick Morley. LC 97-21288. 320p. 1997. pap. 12.99 (*0-310-21768-7*) Zondervan.

***Man in the Mirror: Solving the 24 Problems Men Face.** Patrick Morley. 2000. mass mkt. 7.99 (*0-310-23493-X*) Zondervan.

Man in the Mirror: William Marion Reedy & His Magazine. Max Putzel. LC 97-46994. 376p. 1998. pap. 19.95 (*0-8262-1178-X*) U of Mo Pr.

Man in the Mirror of the Book: A Life of Jorge Luis Borges. James Woodall. (Illus.). 333p. 1996. pap. text 18.00 (*0-340-67226-9*, Pub. by Hodder & Stought Ltd) Lubrecht & Cramer.

Man in the Modern Age. Karl Jaspers. LC 75-41155. reprint ed. 42.00 (*0-404-14558-2*) AMS Pr.

***Man in the Moon.** Diane Brookes. 32p. 1998. pap. 7.95 (*0-9683234-0-5*) RRP.

Man in the Moon. Alan Cullen. (J). 1964. 6.00 (*0-87602-153-4*) Anchorage.

Man in the Moon. Henny Wenkart. (Teaching Jonny's Sister to Read Ser.: Vol. 2). (Illus.). 23p. (J). (gr. k-3). 1961. pap. 2.95 (*0-911612-02-5*) Wenkart.

Man in the Moon & His Flying Balloon. Lou Alpert. (Illus.). 32p. (J). (ps-8). 1991. lib. bdg. 12.95 (*1-879085-05-4*, Whispering Coyote) Charlesbridge Pub.

Man in the Moon Must Die. Jeff Bredenberg. 208p. (Orig.). 1993. mass mkt. 4.50 (*0-380-76914-X*, Avon Bks) Morrow Avon.

Man in the Moon: or A Discourse of a Voyage Thither by D. Gonsales. Francis Godwin. Tr. by E. Mabon. LC 77-38188. (English Experience Ser.: No. 459). 136p. 1972. reprint ed. 30.00 (*90-221-0459-1*) Walter J Johnson.

Man in the Moone: An Anthology of Antique Science Fiction & Fantasy. Faith K. Pizor & T. Allan Comp. LC 72-190276. xx, 230p. (J). 1971. write for info. (*0-283-97815-5*, Pub. by S1 & J) Trafalgar.

Man in the Past, the Present & the Future: The Sun-Initiation of the Druid Priest & the Moon-Science. Rudolf Steiner. Tr. by E. Goodard from GER. 82p. 1982. pap. 8.95 (*0-85440-403-1*, Pub. by R Steiner Pr) Anthroposophic.

Man in the Pulpit (Questions for a Father) Ruth Rehmann. Tr. by Christoph Lohmann & Pamela Lohmann from GER. LC 96-13097. (European Women Writers Ser.). xviii, 215p. 1997. pap. 15.00 (*0-8032-8960-X*, Bison Books); text 40.00 (*0-8032-3917-3*) U of Nebr Pr.

Man in the Queue. Josephine Tey. LC 79-28589. 256p. 1995. per. 9.00 (*0-684-81502-8*) S&S Trade.

Man in the Queue. Josephine Tey. LC 79-28589. 1981. reprint ed. lib. bdg. 16.00 (*0-8376-0450-8*) Bentley Pubs.

***Man in the Red Truck: Indiscretions of an Older Woman.** large type ed. G. J. Foy. 160p. 1999. pap. 9.95 (*1-893362-13-2*) Jean Hse.

Man in the Red Velvet Dress: Inside the World of Cross Dressing. J. J. Allen. (Illus.). 288p. 1996. 21.95 (*1-55972-338-6*, Birch Ln Pr) Carol Pub Group.

Man in the Roman Street. Harold B. Mattingly. 1966. pap. 7.95 (*0-393-00337-X*) Norton.

Man in the Sea, Vol. I. Ed. by Yu-Chong Lin & Kathleen K. Shida. (Illus.). 330p. 1990. text 35.50 (*0-941332-12-8*, D312) Best Pub Co.

Man in the Sea, Vol. II. Ed. by Yu-Chong Lin & Kathleen K. Shida. (Illus.). 232p. 1990. text 33.00 (*0-941332-13-6*, D313) Best Pub Co.

Man in the Shadow. large type ed. Rae Foley. LC 94-1084. 283p. 1994. lib. bdg. 17.95 (*0-7862-0190-8*) Thorndike Pr.

Man in the Shadows: Fred Coe & the Golden Age of Television. Jon Krampner. LC 96-8339. (Illus.). 272p. (C). 1997. 32.95 (*0-8135-2359-1*) Rutgers U Pr.

Man in the Street. Thomas A. Bailey. (History - United States Ser.). 334p. 1993. reprint ed. lib. bdg. 89.00 (*0-7812-4837-X*) Rprt Serv.

Man in the Street: The Impact of American Public Opinion on Foreign Policy. Thomas A. Bailey. 1964. 16.50 (*0-8446-0015-6*) Peter Smith.

Man in the Sycamore Tree: The Good Life & Hard Times of Thomas Merton. Edward Rice. LC 84-22490. (Illus.). 192p. 1985. pap. 6.95 (*0-15-656960-4*, Harvest Bks) Harcourt.

Man in the Universe. Clyde E. Daniels. 73p. (Orig.). 1991. pap. 7.95 (*0-9634437-0-4*) Hall-Ware Pub.

Man in the Universe. Fred Hoyle. LC 66-17067. (Bampton Lectures in America: No. 17). 89p. reprint ed. pap. 30.00 (*0-608-30023-3*, 202224100025) Bks Demand.

Man in the Wall: Poems. James Laughlin. LC 92-45790. 128p. 1993. 19.95 (*0-8112-1236-X*, Pub. by New Directions) Norton.

Man in the Wall: Poems. James Laughlin. LC 92-45790. Vol. 759. 128p. 1993. pap. 9.95 (*0-8112-1237-8*, NDP759, Pub. by New Directions) Norton.

M

An Asterisk (*) at the beginning of an entry indicates that the title is appearing for the first time.

Man in the Wheatfield. Robert Laxalt. LC 87-10774. 192p. 1987. reprint ed. 18.00 (*0-87417-130-X*) U of Nev Pr.
Man in the White House: His Powers & Duties. Wilfred E. Binkley. LC JK0516.B49. (Johns Hopkins Paperbacks Ser.). 320p. reprint ed. pap. 99.20 (*0-608-10154-0*, 202075900018) Bks Demand.
***Man in the White Suit.** Nick Drake. 64p. 1999. pap. (*1-85224-488-7*, Pub. by Bloodaxe Bks) Dufour.
Man in the Window. Jon Cohen. 256p. 1993. mass mkt. 5.99 (*0-446-36402-9*, Pub. by Warner Bks) Little.
***Man in the Woods.** Rosemary Wells. (Illus.). 224p. (J). (gr. 5-9). 2000. pap. 5.99 (*0-14-130972-5*, PuffinBks) Peng Put Young Read.
Man in the Woods. Rosemary Wells. (YA). 1985. pap. 2.95 (*0-590-43732-1*) Scholastic Inc.
Man in the World: The Political Theology of Johannes Baptist Metz. Roger D. Johns. LC 76-26491. (American Academy of Religion. Dissertation Ser.: No. 16). 220p. reprint ed. pap. 68.20 (*0-7837-5466-3*, 204523100005) Bks Demand.
Man in the Yellow Gloves. David St. John. 1985. pap. 25.00 (*0-686-40384-3*) Penumbra Press.
Man in the Yellow Hat: Theology & Psychoanalysis in Child Therapy. Dorothy Martyn. (American Academy of Religion Academy Ser.). 197p. (C). 1992. 24.95 (*1-55540-630-0*, 010176); pap. 15.95 (*1-55540-631-9*) OUP.
Man in Three Worlds. Andre N. Chouraqui. Tr. by Kenton Kilmer from FRE. LC 84-15338. (Illus.). 246p. (Orig.). 1985. lib. bdg. 44.50 (*0-8191-4242-5*) U Pr of Amer.
Man in Transition . . . His Role As Father, Son, Friend & Lover. Kenneth Byers. 216p. (gr. 9 up). 1990. pap. 9.95 (*0-9619040-3-8*) Journeys Together.
Man in Uniform. Cynthis Rooy. 1997. mass mkt. 1.78 (*0-8217-5776-8*) Kensgtn Pub Corp.
Man in Universe. Reinhold Ebertin. 104p. 1973. 9.50 (*0-86690-092-6*, E1098-024) Am Fed Astrologers.
Man in White Is Always Right: Cricket & the Law. David Fraser. (Institute of Criminology Monographs: No. 4). xii, 274p. 1993. pap. 33.95 (*0-86758-696-6*) Gaunt.
Man-Induced Land Subsidence. Ed. by Thomas L. Holzer. LC 84-16881. (Reviews in Engineering Geology Ser.: Vol. 6). (Illus.). 232p. 1984. reprint ed. pap. 72.00 (*0-608-07763-1*, 206785100010) Bks Demand.
***Man Inside.** W. Watts Biggers. 150p. 1999. 14.00 (*0-917453-37-9*, Pub. by Bamberger) SPD-Small Pr Dist.
***Man Investment & Business Guide: Investment, Export-Import, Foreign Economic Assistance Projects, Contacts & More.** International Business Publications, USA Staff & Global Investment Center, USA Staff. (World Investment Guides Library Ser.: Vol. 204). (Illus.). 350p. 2000. pap. 99.95 (*0-7397-1082-6*) Intl Business Pubns.
Man Is a Cause: Political Consciousness & the Fiction of Ghassan Kanafani. Muhammad Siddiq. LC 84-7320. (Near Eastern Studies: No. 2). 128p. (Orig.). 1984. pap. 9.95 (*0-295-96154-6*) U of Wash Pr.
Man Is a Man: Hooker Family Saga. Marguariete Overholser. LC 93-70835. (Illus.). 344p. 1993. pap. 19.95 (*0-8323-0500-6*) Binford Mort.
Man Is Born Perfect. Charles L. Ellington. LC 88-91063. 112p. 1988. 22.00 (*0-317-91084-1*) CLE Investment Grp Inc.
Man Is Culture. Ousmane Sembene. (Hans Wolff Memorial Lectures). (ENG & FRE.). 24p. (Orig.). 1979. pap. text 2.50 (*0-941934-14-4*) Indiana Africa.
Man Is Dead. Derek Lamar. 250p. 1999. pap. 14.95 (*1-893075-00-1*) Spirit Pr OR.
Man Is His Faith: Ivan Kireyevsky & Orthodox Christianity. Alexey Young. 68p. (Orig.). 1980. pap. 3.50 (*0-9504257-1-0*, Y001) St John Kronstadt.
Man Is Not Alone: A Philosophy of Religion. Abraham Joshua Heschel. 320p. 1976. pap. 14.00 (*0-374-51328-7*) FS&G.
Man Is Risen. Harold S. Cober. (Illus.). 100p. (Orig.). (C). 1994. pap. 5.95 (*1-877633-22-4*) Luthers.
Man Is the Measure. Reuben Abel. 320p. 1997. pap. 16.95 (*0-684-83636-X*) Free Pr.
Man Is the Measure: A Cordial Invitation to the Central Problems of Philosophy. Reuben Abel. LC 75-16646. (Illus.). 1976. pap. 16.95 (*0-02-900110-2*) Free Pr.
Man Is Wolf to Man: A Story of Survival. Janusz Bardach & Kathleen Gleeson. LC 98-5402. 397p. 1998. 29.95 (*0-520-21352-1*, Pub. by U CA Pr) Cal Prin Full Svc.
Man is Wolf to Man: Surviving the Gulag. Janusz Bardach & Kathleen Gleeson. LC 98-5402. 397p. 1999. pap. 17.95 (*0-520-22152-4*, Pub. by U CA Pr) Cal Prin Full Svc.
Man Jesus. Mary H. Austin. (Collected Works of Mary Hunter Austin). 214p. 1998. reprint ed. lib. bdg. 88.00 (*1-58201-526-0*) Classic Bks.
Man Jump's Out of an Airplane. Barry Yourgrau. LC 98-54262. (Orig.). 1999. pap. text 10.95 (*1-55970-486-1*, Pub. by Arcade Pub Inc) Time Warner.
Man Kann Ruhig Darnbersprechen: Level A. Heinrich Spoerl. text 7.95 (*0-88436-743-6*) EMC-Paradigm.
Man Kidnapped by UFO for Third Time. Ray Miller. Ed. by Robert Bixby. 39p. 1994. pap. text 6.00 (*0-9624453-6-3*) March Street Pr.
Man Kills Woman. D. L. Flusfeder. LC 93-21735. 1993. 21.00 (*0-374-20162-5*) FS&G.
Man Kok Tsui: Archaeological Site 30, Lantau Island, Hong Kong. Sydney G. Davis & Mary Tregear. LC DS0796.H47D3. 54p. reprint ed. pap. 30.00 (*0-608-11791-9*, 201769700007) Bks Demand.
Man-Kzin Wars. Larry Niven et al. 304p. 1991. reprint ed. per. 6.99 (*0-671-72076-7*) Baen Bks.
Man-Kzin Wars V. Larry Niven. 336p. 1992. mass mkt. 5.99 (*0-671-72137-2*) Baen Bks.
Man-Kzin Wars VII. Created by Larry Niven. 352p. 1995. mass mkt. 5.99 (*0-671-87670-8*) Baen Bks.
Man-Kzin Wars VI. Created by Larry Niven. 416p. (Orig.). 1994. mass mkt. 5.99 (*0-671-87607-4*) Baen Bks.
Man-Kzin Wars III. Larry Niven et al. 320p. 1990. mass mkt. 5.99 (*0-671-72008-2*) Baen Bks.
Man-Kzin Wars II. Larry Niven et al. 320p. 1990. mass mkt. 5.99 (*0-671-72036-8*) Baen Bks.
Man, Land & Food. Lester R. Brown. LC 75-26299. (World Food Supply Ser.). (Illus.). 1976. reprint ed. 17.95 (*0-405-07771-8*) Ayer.
Man, Language & Society: Contributions to the Sociology of Language. Ed. by Samir K. Ghosh. (Janua Linguarum, Ser. Minor: No. 109). 1972. pap. text 41.55 (*90-279-2120-2*) Mouton.
Man, Law, & Modern Forms of Life. International Asssociation for Philosophy of Law &. Ed. by I. Niiniluoto et al. LC 85-11749. (Law & Philosophy Library). 336p. 1985. text 182.50 (*90-277-1869-5*, D Reidel) Kluwer Academic.
Man Lay Dead. Ngaio Marsh. lib. bdg. 20.95 (*0-8488-2104-1*) Amereon Ltd.
Man Lay Dead. Ngaio Marsh. (Dead Letter Mysteries Ser.). 192p. 1997. mass mkt. 5.50 (*0-312-96358-0*) St Martin.
Man Lay Dead. Ngaio Marsh. 1976. reprint ed. lib. bdg. 21.95 (*0-88411-488-0*) Amereon Ltd.
Man Like Cade. Barbara McCauley. (Desire Ser.). 1994. per. 2.99 (*0-373-05832-2*, 5-05832-6) Silhouette.
Man Like Jake. Kristina Logan. (Romance Ser.). 1994. per. 2.75 (*0-373-08998-8*, 5-08998-2) Silhouette.
***Man Like Mac.** Fay Robinson. (Superromance Ser.: Bk. 911). 2000. per. 4.50 (*0-373-70911-0*, 1-70911-2) Harlequin Bks.
Man Like Matthew. large type ed. Mary Mackie. (Linford Romance Library). 1991. pap. 16.99 (*0-7089-7118-0*) Ulverscroft.
Man Like Morgan Kane. Beverly Barton. 1997. per. 3.99 (*0-373-07819-6*, 1-07819-5) Silhouette.
***Man Like O'Rourke.** large type ed. Jeanne Whitmee. LC 99-15671. 1999. pap. 19.95 (*0-7838-8654-3*, G K Hall & Co) Mac Lib Ref.
Man Like Smith: (Southern Knights) Marilyn Pappano. (Intimate Moments Ser.). 1995. per. 3.75 (*0-373-07626-6*, 1-07626-4) Silhouette.
Man Limitless (1906) Floyd B. Wilson. 230p. 1998. reprint ed. pap. 19.95 (*0-7661-0354-4*) Kessinger Pub.
Man Liszt. Ernest Newman. (Music Book Index Ser.). 313p. 1992. reprint ed. lib. bdg. 89.00 (*0-7812-9484-3*) Rprt Serv.
Man Living on a Side Creek & Other Poems. Stephan Torre. LC 93-48473. 94p. (C). 1993. pap. 12.95 (*0-8147-8208-6*); text 25.00 (*0-8147-8207-8*) NYU Pr.
***Man Loves the Wine She Serves Through Her Body: An Erotic Encounter with the Divine Feminine.** David Bryen. (Illus.). 100p. 1999. pap. 21.95 (*0-9674947-0-2*) West Hills.
Man Lowell Remembered: Andre Garin OMI, 1822-1895. Gaston Carriere. Ed. & Tr. by Lucien Sawyer from FRE. Orig. Title: L'Inoubliable Fondateur. (Illus.). vii, 107p. 1998. pap. 10.00 (*0-9665255-0-7*) Mssnry Oblates Mry Immac.
Man-Machine Interfaces for Industrial Control: Proceedings of the 6th Annual Advanced Control Conference. Ed. by Edward J. Kompass & Theodore J. Williams. 152p. 1983. reprint ed. 18.00 (*0-914331-05-1*, Control Engrng) Cahners Busn Des Plaines.
Man Machine Simulation Models: Psychosocial & Performance Interaction. A. I. Siegel & J. J. Wolf. LC 70-84967. 191p. reprint ed. pap. 59.30 (*0-8357-9377-X*, 205513100008) Bks Demand.
Man-Machine System Experiments. Henry M. Parsons. LC 71-166483. (Illus.). 648p. reprint ed. pap. 200.00 (*0-608-06181-6*, 206651300008) Bks Demand.
Man-Machine Systems - Inventions, Models, Devices, Performance & Control: Index of New Information. John S. Newbury. 160p. 1997. 47.50 (*0-7883-1776-8*); pap. 44.50 (*0-7883-1777-6*) ABBE Pubs Assn.
***Man Made.** Ken Baker. 2001. 18.95 (*1-58542-083-2*, Tarcher Putnam) Putnam Pub Group.
***Man Made: Thomas Eakins & the Construction of Gilded Age Manhood.** Martin A. Berger. LC 00-22764. (Men & Masculinity Ser.: Vol. 6). (Illus.). 181p. 2000. pap. 19.95 (*0-520-22209-1*, Pub. by U CA Pr) Cal Prin Full Svc.
***Man Made: Thomas Eakins & the Construction of Gilded-Age Manhood.** Martin A. Berger. LC 00-22764. (Men & Masculinity Ser.: Vol. 6). (Illus.). 181p. 2000. 50.00 (*0-520-22208-3*) U CA Pr.
Man Made Catastrophes: From the Burning of Rome to the Lockerbie Crash. Lee A. Davis. (Encyclopedia of Disasters Ser.). (Illus.). 320p. 1993. lib. bdg. 40.00 (*0-8160-2035-3*) Facts on File.
Man-Made City: The Land-Use Confidence Game in Chicago. Gerald D. Suttles. LC 89-20161. (Illus.). 326p. 1990. 29.95 (*0-226-78193-3*) U Ch Pr.
Man-Made Climate Change: Economic Aspects & Policy Options. Ed. by O. Hohmeyer et al. LC 98-46825. (ZEW Economic Studies). (Illus.). viii, 401p. 1999. pap. 89.00 (*3-7908-1146-7*) Spr-Verlag.
Man-Made Disasters. Barry A. Turner. (Wykeham Science Ser.: No. 53). 210p. 1978. 18.00 (*0-85109-750-2*) Taylor & Francis.
Man-Made Disasters. Barry A. Turner. LC 78-11425. (Wykeham Science Ser.: No. 53). 254p. (C). 1979. pap. 18.00 (*0-8448-1372-9*, Crane Russak) Taylor & Francis.
Man-Made Disasters. 2nd ed. Barry A. Turner & Nick F. Pidgeon. LC 96-39979. 200p. 1997. pap. text 56.95 (*0-7506-2087-0*) Buttrwrth-Heinemann.
Man Made Fibres in the European Community: Proportion of Imports Expected to Exceed 10 Percent of Market by 1997. Market Intelligence Staff. 248p. 1993. 4500.00 (*1-56753-556-9*) Frost & Sullivan.
Man-Made Lakes: Their Problems & Environmental Effects. Ed. by William C. Ackermann et al. LC 73-86486. (Geophysical Monograph Ser.: Vol. 17). (Illus.). 847p. 1973. 35.00 (*0-87590-017-8*) Am Geophysical.
Man-Made Landscape. Ed. by W. Tietze. 100p. (C). 1975. pap. 23.00 (*0-08-019667-5*, Pergamon Pr) Elsevier.
Man-Made Language. Dale Spender. LC 99-198018. 256p. 1990. pap. 23.50 (*0-86358-401-2*, Pub. by Rivers Oram) NYU Pr.
Man Made Language. 2nd ed. Dale Spender. 1985. pap. 13.95 (*0-7102-0315-2*, Routledge Thoemms) Routledge.
Man-Made Man: The Genome Project: The Faustian Dream Come True? Ed. by Peter Doherty & Agneta Sutton. LC 98-120476. 128p. 1997. pap. 25.00 (*1-85182-278-X*, Pub. by Four Cts Pr) Intl Spec Bk.
Man-Made Medicine: Women's Health, Public Policy & Reform. Ed. by Kary L. Moss. LC 96-21855. 304p. 1996. text 49.95 (*0-8223-1811-3*); pap. text 15.95 (*0-8223-1816-4*) Duke.
Man-Made Minds: The Promise of Artificial Intelligence. M. Mitchell Waldrop. LC 86-22370. (Illus.). 288p. 1987. 22.95 (*0-8027-0899-4*); pap. 14.95 (*0-8027-7297-8*) Walker & Co.
Man-Made Mineral Fibres. WHO Staff. (Environmental Health Criteria Ser.: No. 77). 165p. 1988. 30.00 (*92-4-154277-2*) World Health.
Man-Made Mineral Fibres & Radon: The Evaluation of Carcinogenic Risks to Humans. (IARC Monographs). 300p. 1988. text 72.00 (*92-832-1243-6*) World Health.
Man Made of Rain, 1. Brendan Kennelly. LC 98-189159. 1999. 35.00 (*1-85224-454-2*); pap. text 18.95 (*1-85224-455-0*) Bloodaxe Bks.
Man Made of Words: Essays, Stories, Passages. N. Scott Momaday. LC 96-46492. 1997. text 22.95 (*0-312-15581-6*) St Martin.
Man Made of Words: Essays, Stories, Passages. N. Scott Momaday. (Illus.). 224p. 1998. pap. 12.95 (*0-312-18742-4*) St Martin.
Man-Made UFOs, 1944-1994. Renato Vesco & David Hatcher Childress. (Illus.). 372p. (Orig.). 1994. pap. 18.95 (*0-932813-23-2*) Adventures Unltd.
Man-Made Wonders Series, 6 bks., Set. Jason Cooper. (J). 1991. lib. bdg. 87.60 (*0-86592-626-3*) Rourke Enter.
Man, Magic & Fantasy: The Domestication of Imagination. Marc E. Jones. 215p. 1978. 16.00 (*0-87878-016-5*) Sabian Pub.
Man Management & Rig Management. Ed. by Jean Pietrobono. (Rotary Drilling Ser.: Unit IV). (Illus.). 75p. (Orig.). 1987. pap. text 25.00 (*0-88698-128-X*, 2.40000) PETEX.
Man Master of His Destiny. Omraam M. Aivanhov. (Izvor Collection: Vol. 202). 194p. 1989. pap. 7.95 (*0-911857-01-X*) Prosveta USA.
Man, Master of His Destiny. Omraam M. Aivanhov. 194p. 1982. mass mkt. 7.95 (*2-85566-377-6*, Pub. by Prosveta) Prosveta USA.
Man May Fish. T. C. Moore. (Illus.). 226p. 1985. reprint ed. 35.00 (*0-86140-024-0*, Pub. by Smyth) Dufour.
***Man, Meaning & Mystery: 100 Years of History of Religions in Norway: The Heritage of W. Brede Kristensen.** Sigurd Helde. LC 00-31150. (Numen Book Ser.). 2000. write for info. (*90-04-11497-1*) Brill Academic Pubs.
Man Meets Dog. Konrad Lorenz. Tr. by Marjorie K. Wilson from GER. Orig. Title: So Kam der Mensch auf den Hund. (Illus.). 211p. (C). 1998. reprint ed. pap. text 15.00 (*0-7881-5861-9*) DIANE Pub.
Man Meets Dog. Konrad Lorenz. Tr. by Marjorie K. Wilson. LC 94-33112. Orig. Title: So Kam der Mensch auf den Hund. (Illus.). 240p. 1994. reprint ed. pap. 12.00 (*1-56836-051-7*) Kodansha.
Man Meets Microbes. 2nd ed. Jamison. 1984. write for info. (*0-409-10721-2*) Buttrwrth-Heinemann.
Man Mencken: A Biographical & Critical Survey. Isaac Goldberg. LC 68-54271. reprint ed. 32.50 (*0-404-02857-8*) AMS Pr.
***Man... Mercenary... Monarch.** Joan Elliott Pickart. (Special Edition Ser.: Vol. 130). 248p. 2000. per. 4.50 (*0-373-24303-0*) Silhouette.
Man, Metals, & Modern Magic. James Gordon Parr. LC 77-25186. 238p. 1978. reprint ed. lib. bdg. 65.00 (*0-313-20122-6*, PAMM, Greenwood Pr) Greenwood.
Man, Mind, & Land: A Theory of Resource Use. Walter I. Firey. LC 77-12902. 256p. 1978. reprint ed. lib. bdg. 49.75 (*0-8371-9834-8*, FIMM, Greenwood Pr) Greenwood.
Man, Mind & Music. Frank S. Howes. LC 70-128878. (Select Bibliographies Reprint Ser.). 1977. reprint ed. 18.95 (*0-8369-5498-X*) Ayer.
Man, Mind & Music: Music Book Index. Frank S. Howes. 184p. 1993. reprint ed. lib. bdg. 69.00 (*0-7812-9652-8*) Rprt Serv.
Man, Minerals, & Masters. Charles W. Littlefield. (Illus.). 172p. 1980. pap. 9.50 (*0-89540-059-6*, SB-059) Sun Pub.
Man, Minerals, & Masters. Charles W. Littlefield. (Illus.). 175p. 1996. reprint ed. pap. 9.00 (*1-56459-571-4*) Kessinger Pub.
Man Missing. Mignon G. Eberhart. 192p. 1988. pap. 2.95 (*0-446-32737-9*) Warner Bks.
Man, Models, & Management: An Overview of the Arizona Strip & the Management of Its Cultural Resources. Jeffrey H. Altschul & Helen C. Fairley. 400p. 1989. write for info. (*0-318-70191-X*) US BLM.
Man, Morals & Education. Frederick Mayer. 1962. 16.95 (*0-8084-0206-4*) NCUP.
Man, Morals & Society. J. C. Flugel. 328p. 1970. 60.00 (*0-8236-3085-4*); pap. 24.95 (*0-8236-8139-4*, 23085) Intl Univs Pr.
Man, Music & Cosmos: A Goethean Study of Music. Anny Von Lange. 354p. 1992. 49.95 (*1-85584-160-6*, Pub. by R Steiner Pr) Anthroposophic.
Man Must Eat. William K. Slater. LC 64-13951. 124p. reprint ed. pap. 38.50 (*0-608-12090-1*, 202412600035) Bks Demand.
Man Must Stand Up: The Autobiography of a Gentle Activist. John E. Reinecke. Ed. by Alice M. Beechert & Edward D. Beechert. (Biography Monograph/Pacific & Asian Personal Papers). 96p. (Orig.). 1993. pap. text 12.00 (*0-8248-1517-3*) UH Pr.
Man Must Teach - 1959. Eugen Rosenstock-Huessy. (Eugen Rosenstock-Huessy Lectures: Vol. 21). 20p. 1997. pap. 10.00 incl. audio (*0-912148-40-3*) Argo Bks.
Man Must Work. Hans F. Sennholz. 8p. 1991. pap. 2.00 (*0-910884-36-6*) Libertarian Press.
Man, Myth, & Deity. Arthur Fleisig. 400p. (Orig.). 1996. pap. write for info. (*0-9651922-1-0*) Nordel Pubng.
Man, Myth & Magic: The Illustrated Encyclopedia of Mythology, Religion & the Unknown, 21 vols. rev. ed. Ed. by Richard Cavendish. LC 94-10784. (Illus.). 2976p. 1994. lib. bdg. 714.21 (*1-85435-731-X*) Marshall Cavendish.
Man Named Dave: A Story of Triumph & Forgiveness. Dave Pelzer. LC 99-38433. 288p. 1999. 19.95 (*0-525-94521-0*, Dutt) Dutton Plume.
***Man Named Dave: A Story of Triumph & Forgiveness.** large type ed. Dave Pelzer. LC 99-86695. 2000. 26.95 (*1-56895-842-0*) Wheeler Pub.
***Man Named Dave: A Story of Triumph & Forgiveness.** Dave Pelzer. 2000. reprint ed. pap. 11.00 (*0-452-28190-3*) Penguin Books.
Man Named Paul: Touched by the Light. Irene Sherrod. 170p. (Orig.). 1988. pap. 9.95 (*0-940999-31-5*, C-2143) Star Bible.
Man Named Thoreau. Robert Burleigh. LC 85-7947. (Illus.). 48p. (J). (gr. 3 up). 1985. 15.00 (*0-689-31122-2*) Atheneum Yung Read.
Man Naturally: Photos by Sherwin Carlquist. Sherwin Carlquist. LC 96-228854. (Illus.). 224p. 1996. 39.00 (*0-9648861-0-3*) Pinecone Press.
Man, Nature & The Nature of Man, Set. unabridged ed. Alan Watts. 1991. 11.95 incl. audio (*1-55927-121-3*) Audio Renaissance.
Man Next Door. Ellen James. (Superromance Ser.). 1996. per. 3.99 (*0-373-70708-8*, 1-70708-2) Harlequin Bks.
Man Next Door. Bernadette Pruitt. LC 98-96612. 192p. 1998. 18.95 (*0-8034-9323-1*, Avalon Bks) Bouregy.
Man Nobody Knows. Bruce Barton. 1998. pap. 7.95 (*0-9652894-1-9*) GA Publng.
***Man Nobody Knows.** Bruce Barton. 128p. 2000. pap. text 12.95 (*1-56663-294-3*, Pub. by I R Dee) Natl Bk Netwk.
Man Nobody Knows. Bruce Barton. 240p. 1992. reprint ed. lib. bdg. 29.95 (*0-89966-949-2*) Buccaneer Bks.
Man Nobody Knows - His Method. Bruce Barton. Ed. by Raul G. Fonseca. 48p. (Orig.). 1987. pap. 1.00 (*0-940999-28-5*, C-2134) Star Bible.
Man O' War. Walter Farley. LC 62-9000. (Black Stallion Ser.). (Illus.). 352p. (J). (gr. 4-6). 1983. pap. 4.99 (*0-394-86015-2*, Pub. by Knopf Bks Yng Read) Random.
Man O' War. Walter Farley. (Black Stallion Ser.). (J). (gr. 6-9). 1962. 10.09 (*0-606-02742-4*, Pub. by Turtleback) Demco.
Man O' War. William Shatner. 320p. 1997. mass mkt. 6.99 (*0-441-00454-7*) Ace Bks.
***Man O' War: Thoroughbred Legends.** Edward L. Bowen. 2000. 24.95 (*1-58150-040-8*) Blood-Horse.
Man of Affairs, 1 vol. Anne Barbour. (Signet Regency Romance Ser.). 224p. 1999. mass mkt. 4.99 (*0-451-19693-7*) NAL.
Man of Africa. Samuel Y. Ntara. Tr. by T. Cullen Young from NYA. (B. E. Ser.: No. 101). 1934. 25.00 (*0-8115-3033-7*) Periodicals Srv.
Man of All Passions: The Conflicting Drives & Complex Desires of a Man of God. Robert Hicks. LC 95-22513. 1995. 16.00 (*0-89109-791-0*) NavPress.
Man of Amazing Grace: In Memoriam, Frank H. Wardlaw, 1913-1989. Nicholas G. Malavis. (Illus.). 46p. 1990. pap. 12.50 (*0-89096-456-4*) Tex A&M Univ Pr.
Man of Amman: The Life of Dai Davies. Phil Melling. LC 94-239037. 135p. 1994. pap. 24.00 (*1-85902-083-6*, Pub. by Gomer Pr) St Mut.
Man of Ashes. Salomon Isacovici et al. Tr. & Intro. by Dick Gerdes. LC \\. (Texts & Contexts Ser.). (Illus.). xvi, 244p. 1999. text 29.95 (*0-8032-2501-6*) U of Nebr Pr.
Man of Blood. large type ed. Margaret Duffy. (Dales Mystery Ser.). 492p. 1994. pap. 18.99 (*1-85389-421-4*, Dales) Ulverscroft.
***Man of Bones: Exceptional Riddles for Adults & Kids.** Emmanuel Williams. LC 00-100652. (Illus.). 68p. 2000. pap. 9.95 (*1-885003-50-1*, Pub. by R D Reed Pubs) Midpt Trade.
"Man of Books & a Man of the People" E. Y. Mullins & the Crisis Moderate Southern Baptist Leadership. William E. Ellis. LC 85-13738. xi, 228p. 1985. text 18.95 (*0-86554-175-2*, MUP-H165) Mercer Univ Pr.
***Man of Character.** Paola Capriolo. 192p. 2000. pap. 15.00 (*1-85242-605-5*) Serpents Tail.
Man of Chivalry. large type ed. Jacqui Bennett. (Linford Romance Library). 304p. 1989. pap. 16.99 (*0-7089-6690-X*, Linford) Ulverscroft.
Man of Circumstance & Selected Yellow Mountain Poems, 1946-1996. limited large type ed. Albert Stewart. LC 96-27310. 68p. 1996. pap. 8.00 (*0-9647515-4-2*) Ltd Edits.
Man of Color. John Somerville. (American Autobiography Ser.). 170p. 1995. reprint ed. lib. bdg. 69.00 (*0-7812-8641-7*) Rprt Serv.

M

Man of Confidence: A Greek POW in World War II. Anastasios Aslanis. (Illus.). 259p. 1995. pap. 24.95 (*0-89745-183-X*) Sunflower U Pr.

Man of Contrasts. Hee I. Cho. (Illus.). 224p. (Orig.). 1977. pap. 16.95 (*0-86568-039-6*, 508) Unique Pubns.

Man of Courage: The Life & Career of Tommy Farr. Bob Lonkhurst. (Illus.). 367p. 1998. pap. 27.50 (*1-85776-373-4*, Pub. by Book Guild Ltd) Trans-Atl Phila.

Man of Destiny. Martin Gross. LC 96-47657. 384p. 1997. mass mkt. 24.00 (*0-380-97417-7*, Avon Bks) Morrow Avon.

Man of Destiny. George Bernard Shaw. Ed. by William-Alan Landes. LC 91-52543. 60p. (Orig.). 1992. pap. 7.00 (*0-88734-234-5*) Players Pr.

Man of Destiny: A Novel. Martin L. Gross. 480p. 1998. mass mkt. 6.99 (*0-380-79011-4*, Avon Bks) Morrow Avon.

Man of Distinction among Them: Alexander Mckee & British-Indian Affairs along the Ohio Country Frontier, 1754-1799. Larry L. Nelson. LC 98-43050. (Illus.). 280p. 1999. text 35.00 (*0-87338-620-5*) Kent St U Pr.

Man of Fashion: Peacock Males & Perfect Gentlemen. Colin McDowell. LC 97-60245. (Illus.). 208p. 1997. 50.00 (*0-500-01797-2*, Pub. by Thames Hudson) Norton.

Man of Feeling. Henry Mackenzie. (C). 1958. pap. 12.50 (*0-393-00214-4*) Norton.

Man of Feeling see Novels of Henry Mackenzie

Man of God. Eugene P. Vedder. (Orig.). 1987. pap. 0.95 (*0-88172-129-8*) Believers Bkshelf.

Man of God: Essays on the Life & Work of the Preacher. Ed. by Shawn D. Mathis. 256p. 1996. pap. 12.99 (*0-89225-459-9*, G54599) Gospel Advocate.

Man of God, St. John of Shanghai & San Francisco. Compiled by Peter Perekrestov. 254p. 12.95 (*1-879066-06-8*) Conciliar Pr.

Man of Her Dream. Briony Shilton. 1993. mass mkt. 5.95 (*1-56201-047-6*) Blue Moon Bks.

Man of Her Dreams see Hombre de Sus Suenos: (The Man of Her Dreams)

Man of His Counsel. Effie M. Williams. 112p. pap. 3.00 (*0-686-29156-5*) Faith Pub Hse.

Man of His Word: A Biography of John A. Toews. Elfrieda T. Nafziger. (Illus.). 200p. (Orig.). 1992. pap. 11.50 (*1-895432-18-9*) Kindred Prods.

Man of His Word: Home on the Ranch. Merline Lovelace. (Intimate Moments Ser.: Bk. 938). 1999. per. 4.25 (*0-373-07938-9*, 1-07938-3) Silhouette.

Man of Holiness. Vaughn J. Featherstone. LC 97-50234. 1998. 16.95 (*1-57345-354-4*) Deseret Bk.

Man of Honor. George C. Eggleston. (American Fiction Reprint Ser.). 1977. 20.95 (*0-8369-7027-6*) Ayer.

Man of Honor. George C. Eggleston. (Notable American Authors Ser.). 1992. reprint ed. lib. bdg. 75.00 (*0-7812-2776-3*) Rprt Serv.

***Man of Honor: A Crookseye Canyon Story, Vol. 576.** Tina Leonard. (Intrigue Ser.). 2000. mass mkt. 4.25 (*0-373-22576-8*, 1-22576-2) Harlequin Bks.

Man of Honor: Living the Life of Godly Character. Ray Pritchard. LC 96-10520. 1996. pap. 12.99 (*0-89107-899-1*) Crossway Bks.

Man of Honor: The Autobiography of Joseph Bonanno. Joseph Bonanno & Sergio Lalli. 1999. reprint ed. 49.95 (*1-56849-722-9*) Buccaneer Bks.

Man of Honour. large type ed. Caroline Anderson. 1995. 11.50 (*0-7505-0819-1*, Pub. by Mgna Lrg Print) Ulverscroft.

Man of Honour. large type ed. Lys Holland. 1990. pap. 16.99 (*0-7089-6916-X*, Linford) Ulverscroft.

Man of Honour: Adam Czartoryski As a Statesman of Russia & Poland, 1795-1831. W. H. Zawadzki. (Illus.). 392p. 1993. text 90.00 (*0-19-820303-9*) OUP.

Man of Ice. Diana Palmer. (Desire Ser.). 1996. per. 3.50 (*0-373-76000-0*, 1-76000-8) Silhouette.

***Man of Ice.** large type ed. Diana Palmer. (Silhouette Romance Ser.). 2000. 22.95 (*0-373-59685-5*) Harlequin Bks.

Man of Independence. Jonathan Daniels. LC 98-22079. (Give 'Em Hell Harry Ser.). 384p. 1998. pap. 22.50 (*0-8262-1190-9*) U of Mo Pr.

Man of Jasmine & Other Texts: Impressions from a Mental Illness. Unica Zurn. Tr. by Malcolm Green from GER. 192p. 1994. reprint ed. pap. 14.99 (*0-947757-80-5*, Pub. by Atlas Pr) Serpents Tail.

Man of La Mancha. Joe Darion & Dale Wasserman. 1966. pap. 9.95 (*0-394-40619-2*) Random.

Man of La Mancha: Complete Vocal Score. Mitch Leigh & Joe Darion. (Illus.). 150p. pap. 40.00 (*0-89524-265-6*, 3709) Cherry Lane.

Man of La Mancha: Vocal Score. Mitch Leigh & Joe Darion. Ed. by Ludwig Flato. (Illus.). 150p. (Orig.). 1990. pap. text 40.00 (*0-89524-558-2*, Pub. by Cherry Lane) H Leonard.

Man of Labrador. Benjamin W. Powell. 234p. 1993. pap. write for info. (*1-883704-00-6*) Cleaveland.

Man of Last Resort. Melville D. Post. 284p. 1980. reprint ed. lib. bdg. 14.25 (*0-89968-198-0*, Lghtyr Pr) Buccaneer Bks.

Man of Letters. Taha Husayn. Tr. by Mona El-Zayyat. 160p. 1995. 25.00 (*977-424-344-7*, Pub. by Am Univ Cairo Pr) Col U Pr.

Man of Letters. Ed. by C. H. Layman. 1991. text 60.00 (*0-7486-0164-3*, Pub. by Edinburgh U Pr) Col U Pr.

Man of Letters: Census of H. L. Mencken's Correspondence. Compiled by Betty Adler. (Orig.). 1969. 7.00 (*0-910556-03-2*) Enoch Pratt.

Man of Letters: Montgomery Remembered. Ed. by Laura M. Petersen & Thea S. Lowry. LC 93-71932. 125p. (Orig.). 1993. pap. 15.00 (*0-918704-03-0*) Fels & Firn.

Man of Letters: The Early Life & Love-Letters of Robert Chambers. Ed. by C. H. Layman. (Illus.). 204p. 1994. pap. 22.00 (*0-7486-0193-7*, Pub. by Edinburgh U Pr) Col U Pr.

Man of Light in Iranian Sufism. Henri Corbin. 174p. 1996. pap. 14.00 (*0-614-21308-8*, 1428) Kazi Pubns.

Man of Light in Irenian Sufism. 2nd ed. Henry Corbin. Tr. by Nancy Pearson from FRE. 174p. 1999. reprint ed. pap. 14.00 (*0-930872-48-7*) Omega Pubns NY.

Man of Magic & Mystery: A Guide to the Work of Walter B. Gibson. J. Randolph Cox. LC 88-31917. (Illus.). 416p. 1989. 41.50 (*0-8108-2192-3*) Scarecrow.

Man of Mana: Marius Barbeau, a Biography. abr. ed. Laurence Nowry. LC 96-134745. (Illus.). 448p. 1998. 27.95 (*1-55021-100-5*, Pub. by NC Ltd) U of Toronto Pr.

Man of Manners. Erasmus Jones. 72p. 1993. reprint ed. pap. 7.95 (*1-877984-19-1*) Hendricksn Group.

***Man of Many Devices, Who Wandered Full Many Ways: Festschrift in Honor of Janos M. Bak.** Ed. by Balazs Nagy & Marcell Sebok. 600p. (C). 1999. 69.95 (*963-9116-67-X*) Ctrl Europ Univ.

Man of Many Frontiers: The Diaries of "Billy the Bear" Iaeger. Ed. by Allen L. Shepherd et al. LC 95-149513. (Illus.). 540p. (Orig.). 1994. pap. 25.00 (*0-9631699-3-9*) Making Hist.

Man of Many Letters: The Mam Letters, 1911-1921. Lilburn Kingsbury. LC 90-84353. (Illus.). 209p. (Orig.). 1990. pap. 9.95 (*1-879046-00-8*) Jacaranda AZ.

Man of Many Minds. E. Everett Evans. 1976. reprint ed. lib. bdg. 20.95 (*0-88411-982-3*) Amereon Ltd.

***Man of Maybe Half-a-Dozen Faces.** Ray Vukcevich. LC 99-54814. 256p. 2000. text 22.95 (*0-312-24652-8*) St Martin.

Man of Means. Lori Soard. 165p. 1999. pap. 5.00 (*1-58365-019-9*) BT Pub.

***Man of Means & Fools Fall in Love, 2 bks. in 1.** Lori Soard. 400p. 2001. pap. 7.99 (*1-58582-006-7*, Serenade Double Features) Brk Tree Bks.

Man of Mode see Restoration Plays

Man of Mode see Six Restoration Plays

Man of Mode. George Etherege. 62p. (C). 1989. pap. write for info. (*0-413-19070-6*, AO327, Methuen Drama) Methn.

Man of Mode. George Etherege. Ed. by John Barnard. (New Mermaids Ser.). (C). 1979. pap. text 11.25 (*0-393-90041-X*) Norton.

Man of Mode. George Etherege. Ed. by W. B. Carnochan. LC 66-17766. (Regents Restoration Drama Ser.). xxii, 158p. 1966. pap. text 10.95 (*0-8032-5356-7*, BB 256) U of Nebr Pr.

Man of Mt. Moriah (1898) Clarence M. Boutelle. 386p. 1999. reprint ed. pap. 19.95 (*0-7661-0815-5*) Kessinger Pub.

Man of My Dreams. Margot Dalton. LC 96-336. 298p. 1995. per. 3.75 (*0-373-70664-2*, 1-70664-7) Harlequin Bks.

Man of My Dreams. Johanna Lindsey. 432p. 1992. mass mkt. 6.99 (*0-380-75626-9*, Avon Bks) Morrow Avon.

Man of My Dreams. Johanna Lindsey. 405p. 1999. 26.00 (*0-7278-2214-4*, Pub. by Severn Hse) Chivers N Amer.

Man of My Dreams. Evelyn D. Seitz. 80p. 1999. pap. 9.00 (*0-8059-4721-3*) Dorrance.

Man of My Dreams: Provocative Writing on Men Loving Men. Ed. by Christopher Navratil. LC 96-26172. 192p. 1996. pap. 14.95 (*0-8118-1396-7*) Chronicle Bks.

Man of Orn & Other Fanciful Tales. Frank Stockton. (Notable American Authors Ser.). 1999. reprint ed. lib. bdg. 125.00 (*0-7812-8927-0*) Rprt Serv.

***Man of Passion.** Lindsay McKenna. (Special Edition Ser.: Bk. 1334). 2000. mass mkt. 4.50 (*0-373-24334-0*, 1-24334-4) Silhouette.

Man of Peace - Casimir Michael Cypher: His Meaning in Life Was Found in Death. Anselm W. Romb. (Illus.). 67p. (Orig.). 1985. pap. 3.75 (*0-913382-17-5*, 105-42) Marytown Pr.

Man of Principle. large type ed. Dawn Stacey. (Dales Romance Ser.). 175p. 1993. pap. 18.99 (*1-85389-364-1*, Dales) Ulverscroft.

Man of Principle: Essays in Honor of Hans F. Sennholz. Ed. by John W. Robbins & Mark Spangler. 571p. (C). 1992. 30.00 (*0-9631818-0-7*) Grove City Coll.

Man of Promise: Lord Rosebery. E. T. Raymond. LC 72-1276. (Select Bibliographies Reprint Ser.). 1977. reprint ed. 18.95 (*0-8369-6834-4*) Ayer.

Man of Reason: "Male" & "Female" in Western Philosophy. 2nd ed. Genevieve Lloyd. LC 93-17468. 166p. 1993. pap. 13.95 (*0-8166-2414-3*) U of Minn Pr.

Man of Secrets. Amanda Stevens. 1996. per. 3.75 (*0-373-22397-8*, 1-22397-3) Harlequin Bks.

Man of Smoke. Aldo Palazzeschi. Tr. by Nicholas J. Perella & Ruggero Stefanini from ITA. LC 92-1240. 272p. (Orig.). 1992. pap. 14.95 (*0-934977-26-7*) Italica Pr.

Man of Sorrow: The Life, Letters & Times of the Reverend Patrick Bronte. John Lock & Canon Dixon. 566p. 1979. reprint ed. lib. bdg. 93.50 (*0-313-27686-2*) Greenwood.

Man of Sorrows. limited ed. Joe Coleman. (Illus.). 32p. 1993. 40.00 (*0-9638129-0-4*) Gates of Heck.

Man of Steel. John Byrne & Dick Giordano. (Illus.). 152p. 1991. mass mkt. 7.50 (*0-930289-28-5*, Pub. by Warner Bks) Little.

Man of Steel: (Into the Heartland) Kathleen Creighton. 1995. mass mkt. 3.75 (*0-373-07677-0*, 1-07677-7) Silhouette.

Man of Steel & Velvet. Aubrey P. Andelin. 301p. 1994. mass mkt. 5.99 (*0-911094-23-7*) Pacific Santa Barbara.

Man of Stone. James Forte. 62p. (Orig.). 1992. pap. 16.00 (*1-889560-05-7*) Wildflower Pub.

Man of Straw. Heinrich Mann. 304p. 1992. pap. 11.95 (*0-14-018137-7*, Penguin Classics) Viking Penguin.

Man of Taste: Occasion'd by an Epistle of Mr. Pope's on That Subject. James Bramston. (Augustan Reprints Ser.: No. 171). 1975. reprint ed. 14.50 (*0-404-70171-X*) AMS Pr.

Man of Texas. large type ed. Amy Sadler. (Western Ser.). 1994. pap. 16.99 (*0-7089-7595-X*, Linford) Ulverscroft.

Man of the Beatitudes: Piergiorgio Frassoti. Luciana Frassati. 192p. (C). 1990. text 39.00 (*0-85439-286-6*, Pub. by St Paul Pubns) St Mut.

Man of the Canyon: An Old Indian Remembers His Life. Richard G. Emerick & Mark Hanna. LC 92-62434. (Illus.). 192p. (Orig.). (C). 1993. 27.95 (*1-880811-06-5*); pap. 12.95 (*1-880811-07-3*) North Lights.

Man of the Century. James Thayer. LC 96-49457. 352p. 1997. pap. 24.95 (*1-55611-512-1*, Pub. by D I Fine) Penguin Putnam.

Man of the Century: The Life & Times of Pope John Paul II. Jonathan Kwitny. LC 97-6532. 1995. 30.00 (*0-8050-2688-6*) H Holt & Co.

Man of the Clan: Little People of the Ozark Mountains. Gary Hutchison. 128p. 1995. pap. 10.95 (*1-885631-14-6*) G F Hutchison.

Man of the Crowd. unabridged ed. Edgar Allan Poe. 1994. lib. bdg. 18.95 incl. audio (*1-883049-44-X*) Sound Room.

Man of the Crowd, Set. unabridged ed. Edgar Allan Poe. (Poe Ser.). 1994. 16.95 incl. audio (*1-883049-38-5*, 391134, Pub. by Sound Room) Lndmrk Audiobks.

Man of the Desert. Grace Livingston Hill. (Grace Livingston Hill Ser.: Vol. 63). 1991. pap. 4.99 (*0-8423-3955-8*) Tyndale Hse.

Man of the Desert. Grace Livingston Hill. 289p. 1975. reprint ed. lib. bdg. 25.95 (*0-89190-015-2*, Rivercity Pr) Amereon Ltd.

Man of the Family. Andrea Edwards. 1993. per. 3.39 (*0-373-09809-X*, 5-09809-0) Silhouette.

***Man of the Family.** Kathleen Karr. LC 99-26051. (Illus.). 178p. (YA). (gr. 5-9). 1999. 16.00 (*0-374-34764-6*) FS&G.

Man of the Family. Ralph Moody. (J). 1976. 26.95 (*0-8488-1436-3*) Amereon Ltd.

Man of the Family. Ralph Moody. LC 92-37787. (Illus.). 272p. (C). 1993. pap. 10.95 (*0-8032-8195-1*, Bison Books) U of Nebr Pr.

Man of the Family. Ralph Moody. 1986. reprint ed. lib. bdg. 29.95 (*0-89966-564-0*) Buccaneer Bks.

Man of the Forest. Zane Grey. 1976. 26.95 (*0-8488-1025-2*) Amereon Ltd.

***Man of the Forest.** Zane Grey. 352p. 2000. mass mkt. 4.99 (*0-8125-9036-8*) Tor Bks.

Man of the Forest: The Authorized Edition. Zane Grey. LC 96-21514. (Illus.). ix, 385p. 1996. pap. 15.00 (*0-8032-7062-3*, Bison Books) U of Nebr Pr.

Man of the Hour. Peter Blauner. LC 98-31801. 432p. (gr. 8). 1999. 24.00 (*0-316-03817-2*) Little.

***Man of the Hour.** Peter Blauner. 496p. 2000. mass mkt. 7.99 (*0-446-60541-7*, Pub. by Warner Bks) Little.

Man of the Hour. Alice French. Ed. by Elizabeth Hardwick. LC 76-51666. (Rediscovered Fiction by American Women Ser.). (Illus.). 1977. reprint ed. lib. bdg. 33.95 (*0-405-10045-0*) Ayer.

Man of the House. Adrianne Byrd et al. 384p. 1998. pap. 4.99 (*0-7860-0524-6*) Kensgtn Pub Corp.

Man of the House. Joan Fassler. LC 73-80122. (Illus.). 32p. (J). (ps-3). 1975. 16.95 (*0-87705-010-4*, Kluwer Acad Hman Sci) Kluwer Academic.

Man of the House. Joan Jonker. 416p. 1995. mass mkt. 9.95 (*0-7472-4660-2*, Pub. by Headline Bk Pub) Trafalgar.

Man of the House. Stephen McCauley. 1996. per. 14.00 (*0-671-00225-2*) PB.

Man of the House: A Novel. Stephen McCauley. 320p. 1996. 22.00 (*0-684-81053-0*) S&S Trade.

Man of the House at Huffington Row: A Christmas Story. Mary B. Barrett. LC 97-2212. (Illus.). 32p. (C). (gr. 1-3). 1998. 16.00 (*0-15-201580-9*) Harcourt.

Man of the Land. Carol Devine. (Desire Ser.). 1995. per. 3.25 (*0-373-05909-4*, 1-05909-6) Silhouette.

Man of the Light. Michel Vovelle. Tr. by Lydia G. Cochrane. LC 96-48853. 456p. 1997. pap. text 18.95 (*0-226-86570-3*); lib. bdg. 57.00 (*0-226-86568-1*) U Ch Pr.

Man of the Midnight Sun. Jean Barrett. (Intrigue Ser.). 1996. per. 3.75 (*0-373-22384-6*, 1-22384-1) Harlequin Bks.

Man of the Mist. Elizabeth Mayne. (Historical Ser.). 1996. per. 4.50 (*0-373-28913-8*, 1-28913-1) Harlequin Bks.

Man of the Moment. Jackie Weger. (American Romance Ser.: No. 435). 1992. per. 3.39 (*0-373-16435-1*, 1-16435-9) Harlequin Bks.

Man of the Mountain. Christine Rimmer. 1994. mass mkt. 3.50 (*0-373-09886-3*) Silhouette.

Man of the People. Chinua Achebe. LC 66-22929. 160p. 1981. pap. 10.95 (*0-385-08616-4*, Anchor NY) Doubleday.

Man of the People: A Life of Harry S. Truman. Alonzo L. Hamby. LC 94-43806. (Illus.). 800p. 1995. 35.00 (*0-19-504546-7*) OUP.

Man of the People: A Life of Harry S. Truman. Alonzo L. Hamby. (Illus.). 784p. 1998. reprint ed. pap. 21.50 (*0-19-512497-9*) OUP.

Man of the Plains: Recollections of Luther North, 1856-1882. Luther H. North. Ed. by Donald F. Danker. LC 61-6409. (Pioneer Heritage Ser.: No. 4). 371p. reprint ed. pap. 115.10 (*0-7837-7045-6*, 204685600004) Bks Demand.

Man of the River: Memoir of a Brown Water Sailor in Vietnam, 1968-1969. Jimmy R. Bryant. Ed. by Pia S. Seagrave. LC 98-25602. (Illus.). 160p. 1998. pap. 6.95 (*1-887901-23-X*) Sergeant Kirk.

Man of the Trees: Selected Writings of Richard St. Barbe Baker. Richard S. Baker. (Illus.). 144p. (Orig.). 1989. 17.50 (*0-9600772-0-0*); pap. 12.50 (*0-9600772-1-9*) Ecology Action.

Man of the Twentieth Century: Recollections of Warren V. Keller as Told to Rosemarie Keller Skaine & James C. Skaine. Warren V. Keller et al. LC 99-90634. (Illus.). xvi, 144p. 1999. pap. 14.95 (*0-9672240-0-4*) Authors Castle.

***Man of the World.** Antwone Quinton Fisher. 2000. write for info. (*0-688-17699-2*, Wm Morrow) Morrow Avon.

Man of the World see Novels of Henry Mackenzie

Man of the World: Memoirs of Europe, Asia & North America (1930s to 1980s) Klaus H. Pringsheim & Victor Bosen. (Illus.). 180p. 1995. pap. 18.95 (*0-88962-584-0*) Mosaic.

Man of Truth & Peace. Yoel Schwartz. 1997. 11.95 (*0-87306-783-5*) Feldheim.

Man of Two Tribes. Arthur W. Upfield. (Napoleon Bonaparte Mysteries Ser.). Date not set. lib. bdg. 20.95 (*0-8488-2170-X*) Amereon Ltd.

Man of Two Tribes. Arthur W. Upfield. 224p. 1986. pap. 6.00 (*0-02-025950-6*) Macmillan.

***Man of Two Worlds: My Life in Science Fiction & Comics.** Julius Schwartz. (Illus.). 224p. 2000. pap. 14.00 (*0-380-81051-4*) HarpC.

Man of Vision: Saint Alphonsus Liguori. Alphonsus Liguori & Redemptorist Pastoral Publication Staff. 48p. 1997. pap. 2.95 (*0-85231-157-5*) Liguori Pubns.

Man of Vision: The Story of Paul Pinsky. George K. Engebretson. LC 97-71041. (Illus.). viii, 100p. 1997. write for info. (*0-9631154-5-6*) Watermark.

Man of Vision, Francis H. McLean, 1869-1945. Ralph Ormsby. LC 75-99972. 158p. reprint ed. pap. 49.00 (*0-608-18325-3*, 203160100075) Bks Demand.

Man-of-War. Richard Platt & Stephen Biesty. (Illus.). (J). 21.95 (*0-590-74610-3*) Scholastic Inc.

Man-of-War Life. Charles Nordhoff. LC 85-4935. (Classics of Naval Literature Ser.). 290p. 1985. reprint ed. 32.95 (*0-87021-349-0*) Naval Inst Pr.

Man-of-War Life. Charles Nordhoff. (Notable American Authors Ser.). 1999. reprint ed. lib. bdg. 125.00 (*0-7812-4635-0*) Rprt Serv.

Man of War, Man of Peace: The Unauthorised Biography of Gerry Adams. David Sharrock & Mark Devenport. LC 99-224497. (Illus.). 520p. 1998. pap. 19.95 (*0-330-35396-9*, Pub. by Picador) Trans-Atl Phila.

Man of Zen: The Recorded Sayings of Layman P'ang. Ruth F. Sasaki & Yoshitaka Triya. LC 92-19901. (Illus.). 136p. 1992. reprint ed. pap. 7.95 (*0-8348-0258-9*, Inklings Edits) Weatherhill.

Man Offbeat. A. Rhett Stuart. 60p. (Orig.). 1989. pap. 8.95 (*0-9625153-0-2*) Freedom Voices Pubns.

Man, Oh, Man, You Have Fallen Too. John K. Seagrove. LC 95-94825. 221p. (Orig.). (YA). 1998. per. 15.00 (*0-9647633-1-1*) Kendall Pubng.

Man on a Mission with a Message. Fay B. Engstrom. LC 99-167419. (Illus.). 200p. (Orig.). 1997. pap. 25.00 (*0-9659520-0-2*) Delmay Pubs.

Man on a Mountain. Joe Barnes. LC 68-58686. 1969. 6.95 (*0-87651-200-7*); pap. 3.50 (*0-87651-201-5*) Southern U Pr.

***Man on a Red Horse.** Fred Grove. 272p. 2000. pap. 4.50 (*0-8439-4771-3*, Leisure Bks) Dorchester Pub Co.

Man on A Red Horse: A Western Story. Fred Grove. LC 98-2607. 1998. 18.95 (*0-7862-1157-1*) Thorndike Pr.

Man on a Red Horse: A Western Story. large type ed. Fred Grove. LC 99-11209. 1999. 20.95 (*0-7862-1169-5*) Thorndike Pr.

Man on a Trestle. Ken Kennedy. 285p. (Orig.). 1982. pap. 3.50 (*0-9608864-0-0*) Saguaro.

Man on Fire see Saint Paul the Apostle: The Story of the Apostle to the Gentiles

Man on Fire. large type ed. A. J. Quinnell. (Adventure Suspense Ser.). 422p. 1982. 11.50 (*0-7089-8045-7*, Charnwood) Ulverscroft.

Man on Fire: John Brown & the Cause of Liberty. Jules Abels. LC 72-117961. 464p. reprint ed. pap. 143.90 (*0-608-13758-8*, 205168000001) Bks Demand.

Man on Spikes. Eliot Asinof. LC 97-43204. 1998. 75.00 (*0-8093-2200-5*); pap. 14.95 (*0-8093-2190-4*) S Ill U Pr.

Man on Stage: Play Stories. Stephen Dixon. LC 96-76625. (Illus.). 96p. 1996. pap. 12.00 (*1-57650-053-5*) Hi Jinx Pr.

Man on the Assembly Line. Charles R. Walker & Robert H. Guest. Ed. by Lewis A. Coser & Walter W. Powell. LC 79-7027. (Perennial Works in Sociology). (Illus.). 1980. reprint ed. lib. bdg. 19.95 (*0-405-12126-1*) Ayer.

Man on the Balcony. Maj Sjowall & Per Wahloo. Date not set. lib. bdg. 18.95 (*0-8488-2163-7*) Amereon Ltd.

Man on the Balcony: The Story of a Crime. Maj Sjowall & Per Wahloo. Tr. by Alan Blair. LC 92-50693. (Vintage Crime - Black Lizard Ser.). 1993. pap. 10.00 (*0-679-74596-3*) Vin Bks.

Man on the Box. Harold MacGrath. LC 70-124776. reprint ed. 29.50 (*0-404-04130-2*) AMS Pr.

Man on the Box. Harold MacGrath. LC 78-145155. 361p. 1972. reprint ed. 16.00 (*0-403-01083-7*) Scholarly.

Man on the Buckskin. large type ed. Peter Dawson. LC 95-13844. 269p. 1995. 18.95 (*0-7862-0479-6*) Thorndike Pr.

***Man on the Cross.** Big Guy Books Staff. (Illus.). (J). 2001. 16.95 (*1-929945-06-X*) Big Guy Books.

Man on the Flying Trapeze: The Life & Times of W. C. Fields. Simon Louvish. LC 97-23731. 576p. 1997. 29.95 (*0-393-04127-1*) Norton.

Man on the Flying Trapeze: The Life & Times of W. C. Fields. Simon Louvish. (Illus.). 574p. 1999. pap. 18.00 (*0-393-31840-0*, Norton Paperbks) Norton.

Man on the Grassy Knoll. John R. Craig & Phillip A. Rogers. 312p. (Orig.). 1992. mass mkt. 4.50 (*0-380-77127-6*, Avon Bks) Morrow Avon.

An Asterisk (*) at the beginning of an entry indicates that the title is appearing for the first time.

Man on the Ice Cap: The Life of August Courtauld. Nicholas Wollaston. LC 81-456286. 282p. reprint ed. pap. 87.50 (*0-608-15468-7*, 202938500060) Bks Demand.

Man on the Kafue: The Archaeology & History of the Itezhitezhi Area of Zambia. Robin Derricourt. LC 84-6293. (Illus.). 272p. 1985. text 37.50 (*0-936508-10-8*) Barber Pr.

Man on the Mat. H. Scrimshire. (J). 1995. bds. 3.99 (*1-85792-083-X*, Pub. by Christian Focus) Spring Arbor Dist.

Man on the Moon. Anastasia Suen. LC 97-2628. (Illus.). 32p. (J). (ps up). 1997. 15.99 (*0-670-87393-4*) Viking Penguin.

***Man on the Moon , 3 Vols., Set.** Andrew Chaiken. (YA). (gr. 7). 1999. 99.95 (*0-7835-5679-9*) Little.

Man on the Moon: The Change of the Century. Tom Fallon. LC 87-90496. 192p. (Orig.). 1988. pap. 9.00 (*0-9616146-3-3*) Small-Small Pr.

Man on the Moon: The Shooting Script. Scott Alexander & Larry Karaszewski. LC 99-51519. (Shooting Script Ser.). (Illus.). 224p. 1999. pap. 16.95 (*1-55704-400-7*, Pub. by Newmarket) Norton.

Man on the Moon: The Voyages of the Apollo Astronauts. Andrew Chaikin. 704p. 1998. pap. 15.95 (*0-14-027201-1*) Viking Penguin.

***Man on the Moon Vol. 1: One Giant Leap.** Andrew Chaikin. Ed. by Lee Hassig. LC 99-15449. (Illus.). 368p. 1999. write for info. (*0-7835-5675-6*) Time-Life.

***Man on the Moon Vol. 2: The Odyssey Continues.** Andrew Chaikin. Ed. by Lee Hassig. LC 99-15449. (Illus.), 256p. 1999. write for info. (*0-7835-5676-4*) Time-Life.

Man on the Moon Vol. 3: Lunar Explorers. Andrew Chaikin. Ed. by Lee Hassig. LC 99-15449. (Illus.). 336p. 1999. write for info. (*0-7835-5677-2*) Time-Life.

Man on the Spot: Essays on British Empire History, 31. Roger D. Long. LC 95-9667. (Contributions in Comparative Colonial Studies: Vol. 31). 256p. 1995. 59.95 (*0-313-29524-7*, Greenwood Pr) Greenwood.

Man on the Tower. Charles Rafferty. LC 94-37208. (Poetry Award Ser.). 64p. 1995. pap. 12.00 (*1-55728-340-0*) U of Ark Pr.

Man on the Tower. Charles Rafferty. LC 94-37208. (Poetry Award Ser.). 64p. 1995. 18.00 (*1-55728-339-7*) U of Ark Pr.

Man on the Train. W . J . Chaput. 1988. pap. 4.50 (*0-373-97064-1*) Harlequin Bks.

Man or Mango? A Lament. Lucy Ellmann. LC 97-51544. 224p. 1998. 22.00 (*0-374-20228-1*) FS&G.

Man or Mango? A Lament. Lucy Ellmann. LC 99-19809. 224p. 1999. pap. 12.00 (*0-312-20967-3*, Picador USA) St Martin.

Man or Mankind: Was Adam a "Man" or Humankind. Edward F. Halpin. 80p. 1997. pap. 7.95 (*0-8059-4035-9*) Dorrance.

Man or Matter. Ernst Lehrs. pap. 24.00 (*0-85440-430-9*, 1027, Pub. by R Steiner Pr) Anthroposophic.

Man Out at First. Matt Christopher. (Peach Street Mudders Story). (J). 1993. 9.40 (*0-606-07836-3*) Turtleback.

Man Out at First: A Peach Street Mudders Story. Matt Christopher. (Illus.). 64p. (J). (gr. 2-4). 1995. pap. 3.95 (*0-316-14122-4*) Little.

Man Out There. large type ed. Lee F. Gregson. 224p. 1992. pap. 16.99 (*0-7089-7255-1*, Linford) Ulverscroft.

Man Outside. rev. ed. Wolfgang Borchert. Tr. by A. D. Porter from GER. LC 76-145929. 1971. pap. 11.95 (*0-8112-0011-6*, NDP319, Pub. by New Directions) Norton.

Man over Money: The Southern Populist Critique of American Capitalism. Bruce Palmer. LC 79-24698. (Fred W. Morrison Series in Southern Studies). 329p. reprint ed. pap. 102.00 (*0-608-06000-3*, 206632800008) Bks Demand.

Man Overboard. Karen Leabo. (Desire Ser.). 1995. per. 3.25 (*0-373-05946-9*, 1-05946-8) Silhouette.

Man Overboard. Brad Strickland & Barbara Strickland. (Mystery Files of Shelby Woo Ser.: Vol. 13). (J). (gr. 4-6). 1999. pap. 3.99 (*0-671-02697-6*) PB.

Man Overboard. Francis M. Crawford. (Works of Francis Marion Crawford). 1990. reprint ed. lib. bdg. 79.00 (*0-7812-2554-X*) Rprt Serv.

***Man Overboard, an Old Testament Rhyme Based on the Book of Jonah: Full Score Scripture Musical.** 2000. pap. 14.95 (*5-550-01676-1*) Nairi.

***Man Overboard, an Old Testament Rhyme Based on the Book of Jonah: Scripture Musical.** 2000. pap., student ed. 2.50 (*5-550-01677-X*) Nairi.

Man Peo Man. 5th ed. Ellwood. 1995. pap. text. write for info. (*0-13-207069-3*) Allyn.

Man Pleaser. Jel D. Lewis. 200p. (Orig.). 1996. pap. 12.95 (*0-9639917-3-6*) Writers Unltd.

Man Plus Woman: God's Design. R. P. Daniels. 76p. pap. 4.95 (*0-88172-180-8*) Believers Bkshelf.

Man Possessed. Donna Baker. 192p. 1996. 22.00 (*0-7278-5175-6*) Severn Hse.

Man Possessed. large type ed. Donna Baker. LC 96-52558. 318p. 1997. pap. 20.95 (*0-7862-1021-4*) Thorndike Pr.

Man Power: The Call for the Spiritual Revival of Men in America. Edwin L. Cole. LC 96-46548. 1997. pap. 10.99 (*0-7852-7347-6*) Nelson.

Man Program: Self-Help Counseling for Child Molesters. Jerry M. Goffman. LC 86-73818. 60p. 1986. pap. text 12.95 (*0-9612754-2-1*) Batterers Anon.

***Man Pursued.** large type ed. James Gordon White. 264p. 1999. pap. 18.99 (*0-7089-5567-3*, Linford) Ulverscroft.

Man Question: Visions of Subjectivity in Feminist Theory. Kathy E. Ferguson. 222p. 1994. 48.00 (*0-520-07939-6*, Pub. by U CA Pr); pap. 16.95 (*0-520-07991-4*, Pub. by U CA Pr) Cal Prin Full Svc.

"Man Question" in International Relations. Ed. by Marysia Zalewski & Jane Parpart. LC 97-25242. 232p. (C). 1997. pap. 21.00 (*0-8133-2396-7*, Pub. by Westview) HarpC.

Man Ray. Marina Vanci-Perahim. LC 97-77351. (Great Modern Masters Ser.). (Illus.). 64p. 1998. 11.98 (*0-8109-4672-6*, Pub. by Abrams) Time Warner.

***Man Ray.** Kate Ware. (Illus.). 252p. 2000. 39.99 (*3-8228-7185-0*) Taschen Amer.

Man Ray. 2nd ed. Jed Perl. (Masters of Photography Ser.). (Illus.). 96p. (Orig.). 1997. reprint ed. 18.95 (*0-89381-743-0*) Aperture.

***Man Ray, 6 vols., Vol. 3.** Alexander Games. (Reveries Ser.). (Illus.). 120p. 1999. 14.95 (*1-85995-579-7*, Pub. by Parkstone Pr) Bks Intl VA.

Man Ray: American Artist. Neil Baldwin. (Quality Paperbacks Ser.). (Illus.). 449p. 1991. reprint ed. pap. 16.95 (*0-306-80423-9*) Da Capo.

Man Ray: Paris/L. A. Text by Dickran Tashijian. LC 96-69015. (Illus.). 128p. 1996. 60.00 (*1-889195-00-6*); pap. 30.00 (*0-9646426-8-9*, 620111) Smart Art Pr.

Man Ray: Photographs. Jean-Hubert Martin. LC 81-53058. (Illus.). 256p. 1997. reprint ed. pap. 34.95 (*0-500-27473-8*, Pub. by Thames Hudson) Norton.

Man Ray: Photographs, Paintings, Objects. Schirmer's Visual Library Staff. 120p. (C). 1997. pap. 11.95 (*0-393-31624-6*) Norton.

***Man Ray: Photography & Its Double.** Emmanuelle De l'Ecotais. Ed. by Herbert Lottmann. (Illus.). 260p. 1998. 65.00 (*3-927258-66-0*) Gingko Press.

Man Ray, 1890-1976. Man Ray & Andre Breton. LC 95-5561. (Illus.). 352p. 1995. 65.00 (*0-8109-4277-1*) Abrams.

Man Ray's Celebrity Portrait Photographs. Man Ray. (Illus.). 80p. 1995. reprint ed. pap. text 9.95 (*0-486-28811-0*) Dover.

Man Ray's Graphic Work: Catalogue Raisonne, 2 vols., Set, Vols. 1 & 2. Luciano Anselmino & Bianca Pilat. (ITA., Illus.). 1984. 250.00 (*1-55660-087-9*) A Wofsy Fine Arts.

Man Ray's Paris Portraits, 1921-39. rev. ed. Timothy Baum. (Illus.). 132p. 1997. 19.95 (*0-9660353-0-5*) S Dali Mus.

Man, Religion & Science: A Functional View. William Bailey. LC 80-65860. (Illus.). 242p. (Orig.). 1981. pap. 1150.00 (*0-9604196-0-8*) W Bailey Pub.

Man, Robot & Society. Masanao Toda. 224p. 1981. lib. bdg. 67.00 (*0-89838-060-X*) Kluwer Academic.

Man-S-Laughter. Ellen Frith. LC 95-196612. 268p. 1995. pap. 14.95 (*0-88982-147-X*) Oolichan Bks.

Man Seen Afar. Wellesley Pole. 186p. 1983. pap. 7.95 (*0-85435-085-3*, Pub. by C W Daniel) Natl Bk Netwk.

Man Seen Afar. Wellesley T. Pole & Rosamond Lehmann. 128p. (Orig.). pap. 11.95 (*0-8464-4248-5*) Beekman Pubs.

Man Sent by God. 2nd ed. Paul Aronica. 32p. 1988. reprint ed. pap. 1.50 (*0-89944-134-3*, 134-3) Salesiana Pubs.

Man She Almost Married. Maggie Price. (Intimate Moments Ser.: No. 838). 1998. per. 4.25 (*0-373-07838-2*, 1-07838-5) Silhouette.

Man She Left Behind. Janice Carter. (Temptation Ser.). 1998. per. 4.25 (*0-373-70779-7*, 1-70779-3) Harlequin Bks.

Man She Married. Dani Sinclair. (Intrigue Ser.: No. 507). 1999. per. 3.99 (*0-373-22507-5*, 1-22507-7) Harlequin Bks.

Man She Married: Wilderness Child, The Wedding, Mystery Wife, 3 bks. in 1. Ann Major et al. (By Request Ser.). 1999. per. 6.99 (*0-373-20161-3*, 1-20161-5) Harlequin Bks.

Man Shy. large type ed. Valerie Parv. 232p. 1990. 19.95 (*0-7451-1167-X*, G K Hall Lrg Type) Mac Lib Ref.

Man Sitting in the Corridor. Marguerite Duras. Tr. by Barbara Bray. 48p. 1991. pap. 5.95 (*1-56201-006-9*) FoxRock.

Man-Size. large type ed. William M. Raine. LC 93-21817. 363p. 1993. lib. bdg. 18.95 (*1-56054-582-8*) Thorndike Pr.

Man Size in Marble. E. Nesbit. LC 99-214309. 64p. 1997. pap. 5.95 (*0-929605-72-1*) Books of Wonder.

Man-Size in Marble. E. Nesbit. (Classic Frights Ser.). 1997. 11.05 (*0-606-13595-2*, Pub. by Turtleback) Demco.

Man Smiles at Death with Half a Face. Jose Rodrigues Migueis. Tr. & Intro. by George Monteiro. LC 90-38976. 109p. 1990. reprint ed. pap. 33.80 (*0-608-02325-6*, 206296600004) Bks Demand.

Man, Society & Nature. Ed. by P. Banerjee & S. K. Gupta. (C). 1988. 21.50 (*81-208-0566-6*, Pub. by Motilal Bnarsidass) S Asia.

Man, Son of Man: In the Stanzas of Dzyan. Sri Madhava Ashish. LC 79-98267. 1970. 14.95 (*0-8356-0011-4*) Theos Pub Hse.

Man-Song. John G. Neihardt. LC 91-19103. (Landmark Edition Ser.). viii, 117p. 1991. text 45.00 (*0-8032-3332-9*) U of Nebr Pr.

Man-Song. John G. Neihardt. (Collected Works of John G. Neihardt). 124p. 1999. reprint ed. lib. bdg. 88.00 (*1-58201-785-9*) Classic Bks.

Man, Soul & Body: Essays in Ancient Thoughts from Plato to Dionysius. John M. Rist. (Collected Studies: No. CS549). 320p. 1996. 98.95 (*0-86078-547-5*, Pub. by Variorum) Ashgate Pub Co.

Man Spirit. Palmanteer & Rogers. 1979. 4.00 (*0-912678-38-0*, Greenfld Rev Pr) Greenfld Rev Lit.

Man Stands Alone. Julian S. Huxley. LC 72-128265. (Essay Index Reprint Ser.). 1977. 24.95 (*0-8369-1961-0*) Ayer.

Man Story see Collected Works of E. W. Howe

Man Survives. Vladimir Maksimov. Tr. by Anselm Hollo from RUS. LC 75-15657. 106p. 1975. reprint ed. lib. bdg. 49.50 (*0-8371-8217-4*, MAMSU, Greenwood Pr) Greenwood.

Man Sword. Larry Townsend. 1994. mass mkt. 4.95 (*1-56333-188-8*, Badboy) Masquerade.

***Man That Corrupted Hadleyburg.** Adapted by James Glossman. 56p. 1999. pap. 3.50 (*0-87129-949-6*, MB7) Dramatic Pub.

Man That Corrupted Hadleyburg. Mark Twain, pseud. (Classics Library). pap. 3.95 (*1-85326-561-6*, 5616WW, Pub. by Wrdsworth Edits) NTC Contemp Pub Co.

Man That Corrupted Hadleyburg. ed. Mark Twain, pseud. 1.43 (*1-929120-69-9*) Electric Umb OR.

Man That Corrupted Hadleyburg. Mark Twain, pseud. (Works of Mark Twain). 1988. reprint ed. lib. bdg. 59.00 (*0-7812-1128-X*) Rprt Serv.

Man That Corrupted Hadleyburg & Other Stories & Essays (1900) Ed. by Shelley F. Fishkin. (Oxford Mark Twain). (Illus.). 528p. 1997. text 25.00 (*0-19-511420-5*) OUP.

Man That Corrupted Hadleyburg & Other Stories & Essays (1900) Mark Twain, pseud. Ed. by Shelley F. Fishkin. (Oxford Mark Twain Stories Ser.). (Illus.). 528p. 1996. 19.95 (*0-19-510150-2*) OUP.

Man That Got Away. Harper Allen. (Intrigue Ser.). 1998. per. 3.99 (*0-373-22468-0*, 1-22468-2) Harlequin Bks.

Man That Rum Made. 254p. 1995. pap. 6.95 (*1-881545-05-9*) Angelas Bkshelf.

Man the Artist. J. Slater. 1970. 3.35 (*0-08-006899-5*, Pergamon Pr) Elsevier.

Man, the False Prophet & the Harlot: The Identity of the Antichrist Finally Revealed. Anthony M. Giliberti. 280p. (Orig.). 1991. pap. 15.00 (*0-9628419-0-0*) This Is The Gnrtion.

Man, the Fox & the Skunk see Garside Readers

Man, the Hat, & the Cat. Illus. by Toni D. Stewaart. 13p. (Orig.). (J). (gr. k-2). 1999. pap. 2.50 (*1-889658-02-2*) New Canaan Pub.

Man the Hunter. Ed. by Richard B. Lee & Irven DeVore. LC 67-17603. 431p. 1968. pap. text 31.95 (*0-202-33032-X*) Aldine de Gruyter.

Man the Master. I. S. Kapil. 194p. 1985. 11.95 (*0-318-37150-2*) Asia Bk Corp.

Man, the Measure of All Things: In the Stanzas of Dzyan. Sri K. Prem & Sri Madhava Ashish. LC 74-87256. 1969. 16.95 (*0-8356-0006-8*, Quest) Theos Pub Hse.

Man, the Moon & the Marriage Vow. Christine Rimmer. 1996. per. 3.99 (*0-373-24010-4*, 1-24010-0) Silhouette.

Man the Nazis Couldn't Catch. John Laffin. (Illus.). 224p. (Orig.). 1997. pap. 17.95 (*0-7509-1442-4*, Pub. by Sutton Pub Ltd) Intl Pubs Mktg.

***Man, the Ring & the Wedding: With These Rings, No. 141.** Patricia Thayer. (Romance Ser.). 1999. mass mkt. 3.50 (*0-373-19412-9*) Silhouette.

Man the Saint see Saints in the World

Man, the State & War: A Theoretical Analysis. Kenneth N. Waltz. LC 59-11482. (Institute of War & Peace Studies). (C). 1965. pap. text 20.50 (*0-231-08564-8*) Col U Pr.

Man, the Tool-Maker. 6th ed. Kenneth P. Oakley. LC 50-13440. viii, 102p. 1992. reprint ed. pap. text 1.95 (*0-226-61270-8*, P20) U Ch Pr.

Man, the Triune God (1932) Geoffrey Hodson. 84p. 1998. reprint ed. pap. 14.95 (*0-7661-0240-8*) Kessinger Pub.

Man the Worlds Rejected. Gordon Rupert Dickson. 256p. (Orig.). 1986. pap. 2.95 (*0-8125-3572-3*, Pub. by Tor Bks) St Martin.

Man Things: Equal Time for Men. Lauran Paine, Jr. LC 97-67125. 160p. (Orig.). 1997. 12.95 (*0-9657607-3-1*) Cascade Publng.

Man to Cross Rivers With. Richard Davis. LC 99-61619. (Illus.). 272p. 1999. pap. 12.95 (*1-890437-09-3*) Western Reflections.

Man to Die For. Suzanne Brockmann. 1995. per. 3.75 (*0-373-07681-9*, 1-07681-9) Silhouette.

Man to Die For. Eileen Dreyer. 480p. 1997. mass mkt. 5.50 (*0-06-104055-X*, Harp PBks) HarpC.

Man to Heal Differences: Essays & Talks on St. Frances de Sales. Elisabeth Stopp. LC 96-68191. 1997. pap. 21.95 (*0-916101-22-3*) St Joseph.

Man to Man. Serendipity House Staff. (Focus Ser.). 1994. pap. text 4.95 (*1-883419-95-6*) Serendipity Hse.

Man to Man. Jackson Gregory. 1976. reprint ed. lib. bdg. 26.95 (*0-88411-284-5*) Amereon Ltd.

Man to Man: A Guide for Men in Abusive Relationships. rev. ed. Edward W. Gondolf & David M. Russell. (Illus.). 53p. (Orig.). 1994. pap. 4.95 (*0-945819-61-7*) Sulzburger & Graham Pub.

Man to Man: Chuck Swindoll Selects His Most Significant Writings for Men. Charles R. Swindoll. 368p. 1996. 19.99 (*0-310-21056-9*) Zondervan.

Man to Man: Chuck Swindoll Selects His Most Significant Writings for Men. Charles R. Swindoll. 384p. 1998. pap. 12.99 (*0-310-21943-4*) Zondervan.

Man to Man: Surviving Prostate Cancer. Michael Korda. 1997. pap. 12.00 (*0-679-78123-4*) Vin Bks.

Man to Man: Surviving Prostate Cancer. large type ed. Michael Korda. 1996. 23.95 (*0-7862-0825-2*) Thorndike Pr.

Man-to-Man: When Your Partner Says No - Pressured Sex & Date Rape. S. A. Johnson. Ed. by Euan Bear et al. LC 98-129284. 40p. (Orig.). 1992. pap. 6.50 (*1-884444-32-6*) Safer Soc.

Man to Man Daybreak. Charles R. Swindoll. 1996. 9.99 (*0-310-96860-7*) Zondervan.

***Man-to-Man Defense.** Ed. by Bob Murrey. 160p. 1999. pap. 16.95 (*1-57167-429-2*) Coaches Choice.

***Man to Marry.** Carole Mortimer. (Presents Ser.). 2000. mass mkt. 3.99 (*0-373-12086-9*) Harlequin Bks.

***Man to Marry.** large type ed. Carole Mortimer. (Thorndike Harlequin Romance Ser.). 2000. 22.95 (*0-263-16286-9*) Mills & Boon.

Man to Match the Mountain: Overcoming the Obstacles of Life. David Roper. LC 96-33524. 288p. (Orig.). 1996. pap. 10.99 (*1-57293-013-6*) Discovery Hse Pubs.

Man to Send Rain Clouds: Contemporary Stories by American Indians. Intro. by Kenneth H. Rosen. 192p. 1992. reprint ed. pap. 12.95 (*0-14-017317-X*, Penguin Bks) Viking Penguin.

Man to Slay a Dragon. Meagan McKinney. 1996. pap. 21.95 (*0-8217-5221-9*) NAL.

Man to Slay Dragons. Meagan McKinney. 416p. 1996. mass mkt. 5.99 (*0-8217-5345-2*, Zebra Kensgtn) Kensgtn Pub Corp.

Man to Slay Dragons. large type ed. Meagan McKinney. LC 96-18366. 440p. 1996. lib. bdg. 23.95 (*1-57490-063-3*, Beeler LP Bks) T T Beeler.

Man to Trust. Justine Davis. 1997. per. 3.99 (*0-373-07805-6*, 1-078054) Silhouette.

Man Too White. Gyorgy Sebestyen. Tr. & Afterword by Michael Mitchell. LC 92-11111. (Studies in Austrian Literature, Culture, & Thought). 1993. pap. 12.50 (*0-929497-27-9*) Ariadne CA.

***Man-Trackers & Dog Handlers in Search & Rescue: Basic Guidelines & Information.** Greg Fuller et al. LC 00-25788. (Illus.). 98p. 2000. 25.00 (*1-879471-30-2*); pap. 9.95 (*1-879471-31-0*) DBS Prodns.

Man Tracks: A Rite-of-Passage Program for Christian Men. Ellis Hackler. LC 96-61874. 208p. 1997. pap. 9.99 (*1-883893-92-5*) WinePress Pub.

Man, Transportation Interface Specialty Conference: Papers. LC 78-322836. 381p. reprint ed. pap. 118.20 (*0-608-16424-0*, 202656200050) Bks Demand.

Man Trap. Liz Ireland. 1993. per. 2.75 (*0-373-08963-5*, 5-08963-6) Silhouette.

***Man Triumphant.** Annalee Skarin. 253p. 1999. reprint ed. pap. 8.95 (*1-891265-03-2*) M A P.

Man Trouble. J. D. Rage. 73p. 1989. pap., per. 5.00 (*1-886206-01-5*) Venom Pr.

Man under a Pear Tree. Keith Ratzlaff. LC 97-70025. (Anhinga Prize for Poetry - 1996 Ser.). 96p. (Orig.). 1997. 18.95 (*0-938078-51-8*); pap. 10.00 (*0-938078-50-X*) Anhinga Pr.

Man Under Authority. Samuel Leith. 9.99 (*1-85792-016-3*, Pub. by Christian Focus) Spring Arbor Dist.

Man under Stress. Ed. by A. T. Welford. LC 74-5440. (Illus.). 144p. 1974. 36.00 (*0-85066-073-4*) Taylor & Francis.

Man under the Mistletoe. Debra Carroll. LC 96-3377. 217p. 1995. per. 3.25 (*0-373-25668-X*, 1-25668-4) Harlequin Bks.

Man Verdi. Frank Walker. LC 82-2755. (Phoenix Ser.). xviii, 526p. (C). 1995. reprint ed. pap. 11.95 (*0-226-87132-0*) U Ch Pr.

Man Visible & Invisible: Examples of Different Types of Men As Seen by Means of Trained Clairvoyance (1909) C. W. Leadbeater. 144p. 1998. reprint ed. pap. 17.95 (*0-7661-0255-6*) Kessinger Pub.

Man vs. Machine: Kasparov vs. Deep Blue. David Goodman & Raymond Keene. LC 97-220049. (Illus.). 128p. (Orig.). 1997. pap. 14.95 (*1-888281-06-5*) HThree.

Man vs. the State: With Six Essays on Government, Society, & Freedom. Herbert Spencer & Eric Mack. LC 81-17214. (C). 1982. reprint ed. 14.00 (*0-913966-97-5*); reprint ed. pap. 7.50 (*0-913966-98-3*) Liberty Fund.

Man Walking on Eggshells. Herbert Simmons. LC 97-5673. 221p. 1997. pap. 11.00 (*0-393-31618-1*) Norton.

Man Wanders Sometimes. Kent Baker. 228p. 1989. 22.95 (*0-7737-2296-3*) Genl Dist Srvs.

***Man Was Made for Tranquility.** Lester Sumrall. 1999. pap. 2.95 (*0-937580-62-7*) Sumrall Pubng.

Man Was Not Born to Cry. Joel S. Goldsmith. LC 98-7112. 210p. 1998. reprint ed. 21.95 (*1-889051-31-4*); reprint ed. pap. 13.95 (*1-889051-32-2*) Acrpls Bks CO.

Man Was Not Born to Cry. Joel S. Goldsmith. 224p. 1984. reprint ed. pap. 7.95 (*0-8065-0915-5*, Citadel Pr) Carol Pub Group.

Man We Serve. Paul Kim. 1977. pap. 20.50 (*0-8191-0080-3*) U Pr of Amer.

Man, Whence, How & Whither. abr. ed. D. L. Besant et al. 540p. 1997. reprint ed. pap. 25.00 (*0-7873-1068-9*) Hlth Research.

Man Who Ate Everything: And Other Gastronomic Feats, Disputes, & Pleasurable Pursuits. Jeffrey Steingarten. LC 97-2815. 512p. 1997. 30.00 (*0-679-43088-1*) Knopf.

Man Who Ate Everything: And Other Gastronomic Feats, Disputes, & Pleasurable Pursuits. Jeffrey Steingarten. LC 97-2815. 528p. 1998. pap. 14.00 (*0-375-70202-4*) Vin Bks.

***Man Who Ate the 747.** Ben Sherwood. 272p. 2000. 19.95 (*0-553-80182-1*) Bantam.

***Man Who Ate the 747.** Ben Sherwood. LC 00-23713. 2000. write for info. (*0-385-33533-4*) Delacorte.

***Man Who Ate Toronto: Memoirs of a Food Critic.** James Chatto. 360p. 2000. pap. 18.95 (*1-55199-050-4*) MW&R.

***Man Who Became Caravaggio.** Peter Robb. LC 99-43576. (Illus.). 570p. 2000. 30.00 (*0-8050-6356-0*, J Macrae Bks) H Holt & Co.

***Man Who Brought Me Roses.** Margaret Rogers Baker. LC 00-190445. 2000. 25.00 (*0-7388-1750-3*); pap. 18.00 (*0-7388-1751-1*) Xlibris Corp.

Man Who Built Washington: A Life of John McShain. Carl M. Brauer. (Illus.). 300p. 1996. 49.50 (*0-914650-31-9*) Hagley Museum.

Man Who Burned Money. deluxe ed. Barbara Unger. 1980. 7.50 (*0-317-39742-7*) Bellevue Pr.

Man Who Burned the White House: The Story of Admiral of the Fleet Sir George Cockburn (1772-1853) (Maritime) A. J. Pack. 288p. 1987. 65.00 (*0-85937-332-0*, Pub. by K Mason Pubns Ltd) St Mut.

Man Who Called Himself Devlin. William M. Green. 1978. write for info. (*0-672-52514-3*, Bobbs) Macmillan.

***Man Who Called It Love.** Blum. 2000. pap. 27.00 (*0-7382-0278-9*, Pub. by Perseus Pubng) HarpC.

An Asterisk (*) at the beginning of an entry indicates that the title is appearing for the first time.

Man Who Came for Christmas: Back to the Ranch. Bethany Campbell. (Romance Ser.). 1993. per. 2.99 (*0-373-03293-5*, 1-03293-7) Harlequin Bks.

Man Who Came in from the Back of Beyond. Biyi Bandele-Thomas. (African Writers Ser.). 140p. (C). 1992. pap. 9.95 (*0-435-90587-2*, 90587) Heinemann.

Man Who Came to Dinner see Best Plays of the Modern American Theatre: Second Series, 1939-1946

Man Who Came to Dinner see Six Modern American Plays

Man Who Came to Dinner. George S. Kaufman & Moss Hart. 1939. pap. 5.25 (*0-8222-0725-7*) Dramatists Play.

Man Who Carried the Cross for Jesus: Luke 23:26; Mark 15:21. Constance Head. (Arch Bks.). (Illus.). (J). (gr. k-4). 1979. pap. 1.99 (*0-570-06124-5*, 59-1242) Concordia.

Man Who Cast Two Shadows. Carol O'Connell. 336p. 1996. mass mkt. 6.99 (*0-515-11890-7*, Jove) Berkley Pub.

Man Who Cast Two Shadows. large type ed. Carol O'Connell. 1995. pap. 20.95 (*1-56895-258-9*, Compass) Wheeler Pub.

***Man Who Caught Fish.** Walter L. Krudop. LC 98-49493. 32p. (J). 2000. 16.00 (*0-374-34786-7*) FS&G.

Man Who Caught the Weather & Other Stories. Bess S. Aldrich. 293p. 1975. reprint ed. lib. bdg. 23.95 (*0-88411-258-6*) Amereon Ltd.

M

Man Who Changed Everything. Elizabeth Sites. (Romance Ser.). 1995. per. 2.75 (*0-373-19059-X*, 1-19059-4) Silhouette.

Man Who Changed the Future: The Extra-Ordinary Discovery of Robert Leaton Cook Rodriguez. Lynden Herbert & Robert Cook. (Illus.). 192p. (Orig.). 1995. pap. 19.95 (*1-887397-00-0*) CIP Pr.

Man Who Climbed the Mountain. Lisa T. Melton. 360p. 1989. 25.00 (*0-9623449-0-7*) M Okada Assn.

Man Who Climbed the Pecan Trees. Horton Foote. 1989. pap. 3.25 (*0-8222-0724-9*) Dramatists Play.

***Man Who Could Be King.** Chuck Young. LC 00-190855. 249p. 2000. 25.00 (*0-7388-2036-9*); pap. 18.00 (*0-7388-2037-7*) Xlibris Corp.

Man Who Could Call down Owls. Eve Bunting. LC 83-17568. (Illus.). 32p. (J). (gr. k-3). 1984. lib. bdg. 16.00 (*0-02-715380-0*, Mac Bks Young Read) S&S Childrens.

Man Who Could Fly: The Bob Beamon Story. Bob Beamon. LC 99-226244. 175p. 1999. 18.95 (*1-885478-89-5*, Pub. by Genesis Press) BookWorld.

Man Who Could Not Kill Enough: The Secret Murders of Milwaukee's Jeffrey Dahmer. Anne E. Schwartz. (Illus.). 224p. 1992. 17.95 (*1-55972-117-0*, Birch Ln Pr) Carol Pub Group.

Man Who Could Not Shudder. John Dickson Carr. 1986. mass mkt. 3.50 (*0-8217-1703-0*, Zebra Kensgtn) Kensgtn Pub Corp.

Man Who Couldn't be Killed: An Incredible Story of Faith & Courage During China's Cultural Revolution. Stanley M. Maxwell. LC 94-26486. 222p. 1995. pap. 10.99 (*0-8163-1235-4*) Pacific Pr Pub Assn.

Man Who Couldn't Pay. R. Woodman. (Look 'N See Ser.). (J). 1995. 0.60 (*1-85792-174-7*, Pub. by Christian Focus) Spring Arbor Dist.

Man Who Couldn't See Himself: A Love Story. Richard Torregrossa. LC 99-18574. (Illus.). 111p. 1999. pap. 7.95 (*1-55874-678-1*) Health Comm.

***Man Who Couldn't Speak.** Concordia Publishing Staff. (Arch Books Ser.). (Illus.). 16p. (J). (gr. k-4). 1999. pap. 1.99 (*0-570-07560-2*) Concordia.

Man Who Counted: A Head-Crackling Collection of Mathematical Adventures. Malba Tahan. 224p. 1993. pap. 14.95 (*0-393-30934-7*) Norton.

Man Who Cried. Catherine Cookson. mass mkt. 6.95 (*0-552-11350-6*, Pub. by Transworld Publishers Ltd) Trafalgar.

Man Who Cried Genocide. William L. Patterson. LC 91-18360. 232p. 1991. pap. 7.95 (*0-7178-0685-5*) Intl Pubs Co.

Man Who Cried I Am. John A. Williams. LC 99-205163. 400p. 1985. reprint ed. pap. 12.95 (*0-938410-24-5*, Thunders Mouth) Avalon NY.

***Man Who Cried Rain Drops.** Carter Hall. Ed. by Elizabeth Gold. (Illus.). 51p. 1999. pap. 14.95 (*0-9671029-0-1*) Rickard Pubg.

Man Who Cures Cancer. William K. Eidem. 304p. 1996. 26.95 (*0-9651968-0-1*) Am Educ Systs.

Man Who Didn't Fly. Margot Bennett. 200p. 1994. 19.50 (*0-7451-8624-6*, Black Dagger) Chivers N Amer.

Man Who Died: A Story. D. H. Lawrence. LC 93-39307. (Illus.). 1994. 21.00 (*0-88001-353-2*) HarpC.

Man Who Died: A Story. D. H. Lawrence. (Illus.). 112p. 1995. pap. 12.00 (*0-88001-429-6*) HarpC.

Man Who Died & Went to Heaven. John O'Brien. 32p. (YA). (gr. 10 up). 1980. pap. 3.50 (*0-87129-788-4*, M47) Dramatic Pub.

Man Who Died En Route. Nell Altizer. LC 88-7581. 72p. 1989. 17.50 (*0-87023-645-8*) U of Mass Pr.

Man Who Died Twice. Samuel Peeples. 252p. 1984. pap. 6.00 (*0-89733-121-4*) Academy Chi Pubs.

Man Who Discovered Quality: How W. Edwards Deming Brought the Quality Revolution to America - The Stories of Ford, Xerox & GM. Andrea Gabor. (Illus.). 326p. 1992. pap. 13.95 (*0-14-016528-2*, Penguin Bks) Viking Penguin.

Man Who Does Not Exist: The Irish Peasant in the Works of W. B. Yeats & J. M. Synge. Deborah Fleming. LC 95-4346. 240p. 1995. text 47.50 (*0-472-10581-7*, 10581) U of Mich Pr.

Man Who Drank a Thousand Beers. Steve Heller. LC 84-4245. 109p. 1984. pap. 10.00 (*0-933428-03-0*) Chariton Review.

Man Who Elected Lincoln. James Monaghan. LC 73-7310. (Illus.). 334p. 1973. reprint ed. lib. bdg. 35.00 (*0-8371-6920-8*, MOMW, Greenwood Pr) Greenwood.

Man Who Fell in Love with a Chicken. David B. Axelrod. Ed. by Stanley H. Barkan. (Cross-Cultural Review Chapbook Ser.: No. 2). 16p. 1980. 15.00 (*0-89304-825-9*, CCC127); pap. 5.00 (*0-89304-801-1*); audio 10.00 (*0-89304-826-7*) Cross-Cultrl NY.

Man Who Fell In Love With The Moon. Tom Spanbauer. LC 92-52624. 368p. 1992. pap. 14.00 (*0-06-097497-4*, Perennial) HarperTrade.

***Man Who Fell in Love with the Moon: A Novel.** Tom Spanbauer. 368p. 2000. pap. 13.00 (*0-8021-3663-X*, Grove) Grove-Atltic.

***Man Who Fell to Earth.** Walter Tevis. (Del Rey Impact Ser.). 209p. 1999. pap. 11.00 (*0-345-43161-8*, Del Rey) Ballantine Pub Grp.

Man Who Fell to Earth. Walter Tevis. 1993. reprint ed. 29.95 (*0-89968-374-6*, Lghtyr Pr) Buccaneer Bks.

Man Who Fenced the West. Glen Coleman. Ed. by Shirley Schoonover. (Illus.). 104p. 1984. 20.00 (*0-9614346-0-0*) Osthoff-Thalden.

Man Who Folded Himself. David Gerrold. 1976. reprint ed. lib. bdg. 19.95 (*0-88411-191-1*) Amereon Ltd.

Man Who Folded Himself. David Gerrold. 1993. reprint ed. lib. bdg. 25.95 (*1-56849-200-6*) Buccaneer Bks.

Man Who Found the Loch Ness Monster: And Other Fables for Grown-Ups. Joseph F. Littell. LC 91-90212. (Illus.). 128p. 1991. 12.95 (*1-880243-00-8*) New World.

Man Who Found the Missing Link: Eugene Dubois & His Lifelong Quest to Prove Darwin Right. Shipman. 28.00 (*0-684-85581-X*) S&S Trade.

Man Who Found the Money: John Stewart Kennedy & the Financing of the Western Railroads. Saul Engelbourg & Leonard Bushkoff. 230p. 1996. 34.95 (*0-87013-414-0*) Mich St U Pr.

Man Who Founded a Town. Esther H. Mumford. (Washington Biography Ser.). (Illus.). 32p. (Orig.). (J). (gr. 2-5). 1990. 8.95 (*0-9605670-2-X*); pap. 4.95 (*0-9605670-3-8*) Ananse Pr.

Man Who Gained the Whole World. Frank Yancy. (Illus.). 263p. (Orig.). pap. 10.00 (*1-56411-127-X*) Untd Bros & Sis.

Man Who Got Capone. Frank Spiering. 1977. write for info. (*0-672-52231-4*) Sams.

***Man Who Got Lost in Duty Free & Other Video-Illustrated Case Studies for Examinations.** Andrew Levy. LC 99-24400. (Video Casebook Ser.: Vol. II). (Illus.). 1999. pap. 29.95 incl. cd-rom (*0-632-05382-8*) Blackwell Sci.

Man Who Had Everything. Louis Bromfield. 278p. reprint ed. lib. bdg. 22.95 (*0-88411-510-0*) Amereon Ltd.

Man Who Had His Hair Cut. Thiery. LC 75-5001. 224p. 1976. reprint ed. lib. bdg. 65.00 (*0-8371-7426-0*, THMW, Greenwood Pr) Greenwood.

Man Who Hated Banks & Other Mysteries. Michael Gilbert. LC 98-114046. 256p. 1997. pap. 16.00 (*1-885941-17-X*) Crippen & Landru.

Man Who Heard Too Much. Bill Granger. 1990. mass mkt. 4.95 (*0-446-36086-4*, Pub. by Warner Bks) Little.

Man Who Invented Florida. Randy Wayne White. 1997. mass mkt. 5.99 (*0-614-27784-1*) St Martin.

Man Who Invented Florida. Randy Wayne White. 1997. mass mkt. 5.99 (*0-312-95398-4*, Pub. by Tor Bks) St Martin.

Man Who Invented Genocide: The Public Career & Consequences of Raphael Lemkin. James J. Martin. LC 84-6682. 360p. 1984. 13.95 (*0-939484-17-X*, 0954, Inst Hist Rev); pap. 7.98 (*0-939484-14-5*, 0953, Inst Hist Rev) Legion Survival.

Man Who Invented Sin. Sean O'Faolain. (Illus.). 1974. reprint ed. 12.95 (*0-8159-6212-6*) Devin.

Man Who Kept His Heart in a Bucket. Sonia Levitin. (Baby-Sitters Club Ser.). (J). 1995. 11.19 (*0-606-07837-1*) Turtleback.

Man Who Kept House. Peter C. Asbjornsen & J. E. Moe. LC 91-37599. (Illus.). 32p. (J). (ps-3). 1992. 13.95 (*0-689-50560-4*) McElderry Bks.

Man Who Kept House. Kathleen Hague. LC 80-26258. (Illus.). 32p. (J). (ps-3). 1988. pap. 4.95 (*0-15-251699-9*, Voyager Bks) Harcourt.

Man Who Kept House. Kathleen Hague. (J). 1981. 10.15 (*0-606-01849-2*, Pub. by Turtleback) Demco.

Man Who Kept House. Kathleen Hague & Michael Hague. LC 80-26258. (Illus.). 32p. (J). (ps-3). 1981. 12.95 (*0-15-251698-0*, Harcourt Child Bks) Harcourt.

Man Who Killed Belle Starr. Peter Matthiessen. (International Ser.). 432p. 2000. pap. 14.00 (*0-375-70181-8*) Vin Bks.

Man Who Killed Himself. large type ed. Julian Symons. LC 99-18824. 1999. 19.95 (*0-7838-8586-5*) Mac Lib Ref.

Man Who Killed Rasputin: Prince Youssoupov & the Murder That Helped Bring down the Russian Empire. Greg King. (Illus.). 320p. 1995. 24.95 (*1-55972-295-9*, Birch Ln Pr) Carol Pub Group.

Man Who Killed Rasputin: Prince Youssoupov & the Murder That Helped Bring Down the Russian Empire. Greg King. LC 97-48713. (Illus.). 320p. 1998. pap. text 16.95 (*0-8065-1971-1*, Citadel Pr) Carol Pub Group.

Man Who Killed the Deer. Frank Waters. 224p. 1984. per. 5.99 (*0-671-55502-2*, WSP) PB.

Man Who Killed the Deer. Frank Waters. LC 73-149327. 266p. 1995. pap. 11.95 (*0-8040-0194-4*) Swallow.

Man Who Killed Time. Arthur Fauquez. (J). 1964. 6.00 (*0-87602-154-2*) Anchorage.

Man Who Killed too Soon. large type ed. Michael Underwood. (Linford Mystery Library). 416p. 1997. pap. 16.99 (*0-7089-5075-2*, Linford) Ulverscroft.

Man Who Knew. Ralph W. Trine. 230p. 1996. pap. 20.00 (*0-89540-267-X*, SB-267) Sun Pub.

***Man Who Knew Charlie Chaplin.** Eric Koch. 2000. pap. 14.00 (*0-88962-718-5*) Mosaic.

Man Who Knew Coolidge: Being the Soul of Lowell Schmaltz, Constructive & Nordic Citizen. Sinclair Lewis. LC 79-157784. (Short Story Index Reprint Ser.). 1980. reprint ed. 23.95 (*0-8369-3896-8*) Ayer.

Man Who Knew Infinity. Robert Kanigel. 464p. 1992. per. 14.00 (*0-671-75061-5*, WSP) PB.

***Man Who Knew to Much, Tales of the Long Bow, The Return of Don Quixote, Vol. 8.** G. K. Chesterton. 1999. pap. text 29.95 (*0-89870-675-0*) Ignatius Pr.

Man Who Knew Too Much. G. K. Chesterton. 1976. 20.95 (*0-8488-0350-7*) Amereon Ltd.

Man Who Knew Trees. James Girard. (American Autobiography Ser.). 35p. 1995. reprint ed. lib. bdg. 69.00 (*0-7812-8530-5*) Rprt Serv.

Man Who Knows. Emmanuel Bove. Tr. by Janet Louth from FRE. LC 99-14136. 136p. 1999. pap. 15.95 (*0-8101-6057-9*, Marlboro) Northwestern U Pr.

Man Who Laid the Egg: The Life of Desiderius Erasmus. Louise A. Vernon. 130p. (J). (gr. 4-8). 1995. pap. 7.95 (*1-882514-15-7*) Greenleaf TN.

Man Who Laughs. 1994. 14.95 (*1-882931-08-4*) Heavy Metal Magazine.

Man Who Laughs. Victor Hugo. (Illus.). 250p. 1998. reprint ed. pap. 18.95 (*0-9665458-3-4*) Virtual Ink.

Man Who Learned to Walk in Shoes That Pinch: Contemporary Fables by Margaret Harmon. Margaret Harmon. LC 92-72656. 160p. 1993. 15.00 (*0-9628423-1-1*) Abyss Pubns.

Man Who Liked Couscous. large type ed. Jane Wallace. 320p. 1987. 27.99 (*0-7089-1606-6*) Ulverscroft.

Man Who Liked Slow Tomatoes. K. C. Constantine. (Mario Balzic Detective Novel Ser.). 192p. 1993. pap. 5.95 (*0-87923-953-0*) Godine.

Man Who Likes Mexico. W. Gillpatrick. 1976. lib. bdg. 59.95 (*0-8490-2201-0*) Gordon Pr.

Man Who Listens to Horses. Monty Roberts. 1999. mass mkt. 6.99 (*0-345-42705-X*) Ballantine Pub Grp.

Man Who Listens to Horses. Monty Roberts. 1998. mass mkt. write for info. (*0-449-00384-1*, Crest) Fawcett.

Man Who Listens to Horses. Monty Roberts. 304p. 1997. 23.00 (*0-679-45689-9*) Random.

Man Who Listens to Horses. Monty Roberts. 304p. 1997. 23.00 (*0-09-180206-7*) Random.

Man Who Listens to Horses. Monty Roberts & Lucy Grealy. LC 97-17318. 258p. 1997. 23.00 (*0-679-45658-9*) Random.

Man Who Listens to Horses. large type ed. Monty Roberts. LC 97-32699. 464p. 1998. 32.00 (*0-7862-1302-7*) Mac Lib Ref.

Man Who Lived Alone. Donald Hall. (Illus.). 36p. (J). (gr. 3-5). 1998. pap. 11.95 (*1-56792-050-0*) Godine.

Man Who Lived in a Shoe. Henry J. Forman. LC 98-85543. 276p. 1998. reprint ed. pap. 12.00 (*1-892323-06-0*) Vivisphere.

Man Who Lived in Sorcy Wood. Brendan McNamee. 62p. 1987. pap. 7.95 (*1-85186-026-6*) Dufour.

Man Who Lived Twice: A Father Risks All for His Family's Freedom. Stanley M. Maxwell. LC 96-35460. 1997. pap. 10.99 (*0-8163-1372-5*) Pacific Pr Pub Assn.

Man Who Lives in Paradise: Autobiography of A. C. Gilbert. A. C. Gilbert. LC 54-9126. 400p. 1990. 24.95 (*0-911581-20-0*) Heimburger Hse Pub.

Man Who Lost Everything. Paul Kuttner. LC 76-17142. 352p. 1976. 8.95 (*0-8069-0152-7*) Sterling.

Man Who Lost Himself. Osbert Sitwell. 1971. reprint ed. 39.00 (*0-403-00721-6*) Scholarly.

Man Who Lost His Shadow. Fathy Ghanem. 352p. 1995. 40.00 (*977-424-347-1*, Pub. by Am Univ Cairo Pr) Col U Pr.

Man Who Lost His Shadow. Fathy Ghanem. Tr. by Desmond Stewart from ARA. 352p. 1980. reprint ed. pap. 12.95 (*0-89410-207-9*, Three Contnts) L Rienner.

Man Who Lost His Wife. large type ed. Julian Symons. (Keating's Choice Ser.). 296p. 1992. 21.95 (*1-85089-372-1*, Pub. by ISIS Lrg Prnt) Transaction Pubs.

Man Who Lost the River. Bernard Sabath. 1963. pap. 5.50 (*0-87129-135-5*, M81) Dramatic Pub.

Man Who Loved Attending Funerals. Frank Collymore. (Caribbean Writers Ser.). 192p. 1993. pap. 9.95 (*0-435-98931-6*, 98931) Heinemann.

Man Who Loved Balloons. Dianna Shaffer. (Illus.). 32p. (J). (ps-8). 1989. pap. text 4.95 (*1-877995-02-9*) Koala Pub Co.

Man Who Loved Buffalo. Joseph Bruchac. LC 95-35358. (Illus.). (J). 1998. 16.00 (*0-15-200044-5*) Harcourt.

Man Who Loved Children. Christina Stead. 1995. pap. 14.95 (*0-8050-0499-8*, Owl) H Holt & Co.

Man Who Loved Children. Christina Stead. 1995. 22.00 (*0-679-44364-9*) Knopf.

***Man Who Loved Christmas: America's Bravest, No. 877.** Kathryn Shay. (Superromance Ser.). 1999. mass mkt. 4.25 (*0-373-70877-7*) Harlequin Bks.

Man Who Loved Clowns. June R. Wood. (J). 1995. pap. write for info. (*0-7868-1123-4*, Pub. by Hyprn Child) Little.

Man Who Loved Clowns. June R. Wood. LC 95-9688. 224p. (J). (gr. 3-7). 1995. pap. 4.95 (*0-7868-1084-X*, Pub. by Hyprn Ppbks) Little.

Man Who Loved Clowns. June R. Wood. 192p. (J). (gr. 5-9). 1992. 15.95 (*0-399-21888-2*, G P Putnam) Peng Put Young Read.

Man Who Loved Clowns. June R. Wood. 1995. 10.05 (*0-606-08814-8*, Pub. by Turtleback) Demco.

Man Who Loved God. William X. Kienzle. LC 96-34604. (Father Koesler Mystery Ser.: No. 19). 274p. 1997. 19.95 (*0-8362-2754-9*) Andrews & McMeel.

Man Who Loved God. William X. Kienzle. (Father Koesler Mystery Ser.: No. 19). 1998. mass mkt. 6.99 (*0-345-40290-1*) Ballantine Pub Grp.

Man Who Loved His Wife. large type ed. Vera Caspary. 496p. 1986. 27.99 (*0-7089-1400-4*) Ulverscroft.

Man Who Loved Levittown. W. D. Wetherell. 128p. 1987. pap. 3.95 (*0-380-70112-X*, Avon Bks) Morrow Avon.

Man Who Loved Levittown. W. D. Wetherell. LC 85-1172. (Drue Heinz Literature Prize Ser.). 145p. 1985. 22.50 (*0-8229-3520-1*) U of Pittsburgh Pr.

Man Who Loved Only Numbers: The Story of Paul Erdos & the Search for Mathematical Truth. Paul Hoffman. LC 98-14027. (Illus.). 302p. (J). 1998. 22.95 (*0-7868-6362-5*, Pub. by Hyperion) Time Warner.

***Man Who Loved Only Numbers: The Story of Paul Erdos & the Search for Mathematical Truth.** Paul Hoffman. (Illus.). 336p. 1999. reprint ed. pap. 12.95 (*0-7868-8406-1*, Pub. by Hyperion) Time Warner.

Man Who Loved the Flag. Idella F. Bodie. LC 96-41692. (Illus.). 48p. (Orig.). (J). (gr. 3-5). 1997. pap. 5.95 (*0-87844-135-2*) Sandlapper Pub Co.

Man Who Loved the Stars: The Autobiography of John A. Brashear. John A. Brashear. LC 87-25190. (Illus.). 224p. 1988. reprint ed. pap. 69.50 (*0-608-00899-0*, 206169300010) Bks Demand.

Man Who Loved to Draw Horses: James Howe, 1780-1836. Ed. by Andrew Cameron. 96p. 1986. pap. text 10.00 (*0-08-032466-5*, Pub. by Aberdeen U Pr) Macmillan.

Man Who Loves Salmon. Sherman Alexie. LC 98-197517. 36p. 1998. pap. 25.00 (*0-931659-39-6*) Limberlost Pr.

Man Who Loves Salmon. limited ed. Sherman Alexie. LC 98-197517. 36p. 1998. 125.00 (*0-931659-40-X*) Limberlost Pr.

Man Who Made Diamonds. Loader. (Longman Originals Ser.). 1995. pap. text. write for info. (*0-582-08144-0*, Pub. by Addison-Wesley) Longman.

Man Who Made Husbands Jealous. Jilly Cooper. 736p. 1994. mass mkt. 7.99 (*0-552-13895-9*) Bantam.

Man Who Made Littlewoods: The Story of John Moores. Barbara Clegg. (Illus.). 224p. 1994. 45.00 (*0-340-57479-8*, Pub. by Hodder & Stought Ltd) Trafalgar.

Man Who Made Models & Other Stories. R. A. Lafferty. (Booklet Ser.: No. 18). 51p. (Orig.). 1984. pap. 2.50 (*0-936055-16-2*) C Drumm Bks.

***Man Who Made Paris... Paris: The Illustrated Biography of Georges-Eugene Haussmann.** Willet Weeks. (Illus.). 160p. 2000. 25.00 (*1-902809-33-5*, Pub. by Allison & Busby) Intl Pubs Mktg.

***Man Who Made Parks: The Story of Parkbuilder Frederick Law Olmsted.** Frieda Wishinsky. LC 98-75029. (Illus.). 32p. (J). 1999. 15.95 (*0-88776-435-5*) Tundra Bks.

Man Who Married the Moon & Other Pueblo Indian Folk Stories. Charles F. Lummis. LC 74-7989. (Illus.). reprint ed. 37.50 (*0-404-11877-1*) AMS Pr.

Man Who Mastered Time. Ray Cummings. LC 74-15960. (Science Fiction Ser.). 362p. 1975. reprint ed. 29.95 (*0-405-06284-2*) Ayer.

Man Who Met God in a Bar: The Gospel According to Marvin: A Novel. Robert F. Capon. LC 89-78168. 143p. 1990. 15.95 (*0-911519-22-X*) Richelieu Court.

Man Who Met the Train. Harold Adams. LC 87-73206. (Carl Wilcox Mystery Ser.: No. 7). 240p. 1988. 15.95 (*0-89296-251-8*) Mysterious Pr.

Man Who Missed the Party: A Carol Wilcox Mystery. Harold Adams. 192p. 1989. 16.95 (*0-89296-252-6*, Pub. by Mysterious Pr) Little.

***Man Who Mistook His Job for a Life: More Musings & Meditations For Men Who Do Too Much.** 176p. 2005. per. 12.00 (*0-684-85793-6*) S&S Trade.

Man Who Mistook His Wife for a Hat: And Other Clinical Tales. Oliver W. Sacks. LC 98-4723. (Illus.). 256p. 1998. per. 13.00 (*0-684-85394-9*, Touchstone) S&S Trade Pap.

Man Who Moved a Mountain. Richard C. Davids. LC 75-99609. (Illus.). 272p. 1972. pap. 12.99 (*0-8006-1237-X*, 1-1237, Fortress Pr) Augsburg Fortress.

Man Who Moved the World: The Life & Work of Mohamed Amin. Bob Smith & Salim Amin. (Illus.). 1999. 29.95 (*1-874041-99-7*) Interlink Pub.

Man Who Murdered Himself. Richard Fliegel. Ed. by Jane Chelius. 288p. (Orig.). 1994. mass mkt. 4.99 (*0-671-74451-8*) PB.

Man Who Never Comes Back. William O. Boggs. 40p. (Orig.). 1992. pap. 5.00 (*0-9628478-3-6*) North Star OH.

Man Who Never Died: Manuscript Edition. Barrie Stavis. 1959. pap. 13.00 (*0-8222-0727-3*) Dramatists Play.

Man Who Never Laughed. Illus. by Mary Glutterbuck. (J). 1987. 9.95 (*0-86685-567-X*) Intl Bk Ctr.

Man Who Never Missed. Steve Perry. (Matador Trilogy Ser.: No. 1). 1986. mass mkt. 4.99 (*0-441-51918-0*) Ace Bks.

Man Who Never Was. Illus. by David Levine & Almada Negreiros. LC 81-83226. 195p. (Orig.). 1982. pap. 7.50 (*0-943722-08-X*); text 17.50 (*0-943722-07-1*) Gavea-Brown.

Man Who Never Was: Freudian Tales of Women & Their Men. Janet Sayers. 236p. 1999. text 24.00 (*0-7881-6378-7*) DIANE Pub.

Man Who Once Played Catch with Nellie Fox. John Manderino. LC 98-2824. 280p. 1998. 22.50 (*0-89733-448-5*) Academy Chi Pubs.

Man Who Once Was & Now Is. Terry Bennett. pap. write for info. (*0-9667720-1-6*) Emmanuel Found.

Man Who Once Was Whizzer White. Dennis J. Hutchinson. LC 97-47302. (Illus.). 577p. 1998. 30.00 (*0-684-82794-8*) Free Pr.

An Asterisk (*) at the beginning of an entry indicates that the title is appearing for the first time.

***Man Who Outlived Himself: An Appreciation of John Donne: A Dozen of His Best Poems.** Ed. by Al Purdy & Doug Beardsley. 109p. 2000. pap. 14.95 (*1-55017-219-0*) Harbour Pub Co.

Man Who Owned Charley. Duane A. Smith. Ed. by William T. Hickman. 384p. (Orig.). 1993. pap. text 5.95 (*0-9636756-0-5*) Agape P&WS.

Man Who Owned the Hogs. Leonard P. Dugger. LC 92-43933. 208p. 1993. boxed set 21.95 (*1-879384-18-3*) Cypress Hse.

Man Who Owned the Pistols. Helene C. Phelan. (Illus.). 336p. (Orig.). 1981. pap. 8.50 (*0-9605836-0-2*) Phelan.

Man Who Owned Vermont. Bret Lott. LC PS3562.O784M3. 224p. 1988. mass mkt. 5.95 (*0-671-64587-0*, WSP) PB.

Man Who Owned Vermont. Bret Lott. LC PS3562.O784M3. 231p. 1999. pap. 12.00 (*0-671-03820-6*) PB.

Man Who Painted Indians, George Catlin see Benchmark Biographies - Group 1

Man Who Painted Roses: The Story of Pierre-Joseph Redoute. large type ed. Antonia Ridge. 1976. 27.99 (*0-85456-496-9*) Ulverscroft.

Man Who Paints Nature. Thomas Locker. LC 98-21666. (Meet the Author Ser.). (Illus.). 32p. (J). (gr. 2-5). 1999. 14.95 (*1-57274-328-X*, 722) R Owen Pubs.

Man Who Passed History By: The Family & Times of Gov. Littleton Waller Tazewell. Littleton W. Tazewell & Lynda R. Heaton. LC 90-80458. 250p. (Orig.). 1991. pap. write for info. (*1-878515-20-9*) W S Dawson.

Man Who Planted Trees. Jean Giono.Tr. of Homme Qui Plantait des Arbres. (Illus.). (J). boxed set 21.95 incl. audio (*0-930031-35-0*) Chelsea Green Pub.

Man Who Planted Trees. Jean Giono. LC 85-9925.Tr. of Homme Qui Plantait des Arbres. (Illus.). 56p. 1985. 16.95 (*0-930031-02-4*) Chelsea Green Pub.

Man Who Planted Trees. Jean Giono. Tr. by Jean Roberts from FRE.Tr. of Homme Qui Plantait des Arbres. (Illus.). 56p. (J). (gr. k-12). 1996. pap. 16.95 (*0-7737-5733-3*) Direct Cinema.

Man Who Planted Trees. Jean Giono.Tr. of Homme Qui Plantait des Arbres. (Illus.). 96p. (J). 1996. 14.00 (*1-86046-293-6*) Harvill Press.

Man Who Planted Trees. Jean Giono. LC 99-37198.Tr. of Homme Qui Plantait des Arbres. 96p. (J). 2000. pap. 6.00 (*1-57062-538-7*, Pub. by Shambhala Pubns) Random.

Man Who Planted Trees. Jean Giono. LC 85-9925.Tr. of Homme Qui Plantait des Arbres. (Illus.). 56p. 1987. reprint ed. pap. 7.95 (*0-930031-06-7*) Chelsea Green Pub.

Man Who Played with Fire. Janet Lorimer. (Ten-Minute Thrillers Ser.). 32p. (YA). (gr. 6-12). 1995. pap. 2.95 (*0-7854-1067-8*, 40811) Am Guidance.

Man Who Played with Fire Readalong. Janet Lorimer. (Ten-Minute Thrillers Ser.). 32p. (YA). (gr. 6-12). 1995. pap. 12.95 incl. audio (*0-7854-1078-3*, 40813) Am Guidance.

Man Who Ran: Jonah. Maclean. 1996. mass mkt. 2.99 (*1-85792-228-X*, Pub. by Christian Focus) Spring Arbor Dist.

Man Who Rocked the Earth. Arthur C. Train & Robert W. Wood. LC 74-16523. (Science Fiction Ser.). (Illus.). 234p. 1975. reprint ed. 20.95 (*0-405-06315-6*) Ayer.

Man Who Rode Midnight. Elmer Kelton. LC 89-48853. (Texas Tradition Ser.: No. 14). 270p. 1990. reprint ed. 19.95 (*0-87565-047-3*); reprint ed. pap. 11.95 (*0-87565-048-1*) Tex Christian.

Man Who Rode the Tiger: The Life & Times of Judge Sammuel Seabury. 2nd ed. Herbert Mitgang. xxiv, 380p. 1996. reprint ed. pap. 17.00 (*0-8232-1722-1*) Fordham.

Man Who Rode the Tiger: The Life & Times of Judge Samuel Seabury. 2nd ed. Herbert Mitgang. LC 96-24906. xxiv, 380p. 1996. reprint ed. 30.00 (*0-8232-1721-3*) Fordham.

Man Who Rode with Eliyahu Hanavi. Leibel Estrin. (Illus.). 32p. (J). (ps-3). 1990. 9.95 (*0-922613-23-0*); pap. 7.95 (*0-922613-24-9*) Hachai Pubng.

Man Who Ruled in Hell. Grant Stockbridge & Will Murray. (Spider Ser.: No. 46). (Illus.). 96p. 1998. per. 10.00 (*1-891729-03-9*, S-46) Pulp Advents.

Man Who Sacked Rome: Charles de Bourbon, Constable of France, 1490-1527. Vincent J. Pitts. LC 93-18629. (American University Studies: Vol. 142). (Illus.). X, 614p. 1994. 89.95 (*0-8204-2456-0*) P Lang Pubng.

Man Who Sang the Sillies. John Ciardi. LC 61-11734. (Illus.). (J). (gr. 4-6). 1961. lib. bdg. 11.89 (*0-397-30569-9*) HarpC Child Bks.

Man Who Saved Christmas. Marisa Carroll. 1996. per. 3.99 (*0-373-70718-5*, 1-70718-1) Harlequin Bks.

Man Who Saved Forty-Two Lives in the Layland Mine Explosion. Dennis Deitz. (Illus.). 18p. (C). 1992. pap. 4.00 (*0-938985-09-4*) Mntn Memories Bks.

Man Who Saw Through Time. Loren S. Eiseley. LC 72-12150. 128p. 1973. pap. 10.95 (*0-684-13285-0*, SL 429, Scribners Ref) Mac Lib Ref.

Man Who Shorted Out the Electric Chair. Mitchell Symons. 256p. (Orig.). 1996. mass mkt. 5.99 (*0-380-77444-5*, Avon Bks) Morrow Avon.

***Man Who Shot Dan McGrew.** Emil F. Rasmussen. LC 99-91970. 2000. 25.00 (*0-7388-1450-4*); pap. 18.00 (*0-7388-1451-2*) Xlibris Corp.

Man Who Sold the Milky Way: A Biography of Bart Bok. David H. Levy. LC 93-4039. (Illus.). 246p. 1993. 38.00 (*0-8165-1149-7*) U of Ariz Pr.

Man Who Sold the Milky Way: A Biography of Bart Bok. David H. Levy. LC 93-4039. (Illus.). 246p. 1995. pap. 15.95 (*0-8165-1524-7*) U of Ariz Pr.

Man Who Sold the Moon. Robert A. Heinlein. 1999. lib. bdg. 19.95 (*1-56723-155-1*) Yestermorrow.

***Man Who Sold the Moon.** Robert A. Heinlein. 320p. 2000. reprint ed. per. 5.99 (*0-671-57863-4*) Baen Bks.

***Man Who Squeezed the Buffalo off the Nickel.** Danny C. Myers. (Illus.). ii, 24p. 1999. pap. 5.00 (*0-9700701-0-1*) D C Myers.

Man Who Stayed Behind. Sidney Rittenberg & Amanda Bennett. LC 93-6541. (Illus.). 512p. 1993. 25.00 (*0-671-73595-0*) S&S Trade.

Man Who Stole the Mona Lisa. Robert Noah. LC 97-36510. 1998. text 22.95 (*0-312-16916-7*) St Martin.

***Man Who Stopped the Trains to Auschwitz: George Mantello, El Salvador & Switzerland's Finest Hour.** David Kranzler. LC 00-29158. 352p. 2000. pap. 19.95 (*0-8156-0644-3*) Syracuse U Pr.

***Man Who Stopped the Trains to Auschwitz: George Mantello, El Salvador, & Switzerland's Finest Hour.** David Kranzler. 352p. 2000. 45.00 (*0-8156-2873-0*) Syracuse U Pr.

Man Who Stopped Time. Judith A. Green. (Adult Basic Learner Ser.). (Illus.). 189p. (Orig.). 1979. pap. text 8.98 (*0-89061-173-4*, 201, Jamestwn Pub) NTC Contemp Pub Co.

Man Who Stopped Time - ALS. Ed. by Jamestown Publishers Staff. 1979. pap. 9.00 (*0-8092-0020-1*, Jamestwn Pub) NTC Contemp Pub Co.

Man Who Talks with the Flowers. Glenn Clark. pap. 4.95 (*0-910924-09-0*) Macalester.

Man Who Tamed Mallory. large type ed. J. D. Kincaid. (Linford Western Large Print Service). 256p. 1996. pap. 16.99 (*0-7089-7814-2*, Linford) Ulverscroft.

Man Who Tapped the Secrets of Creative Power: The Spiritual Journey of Glenda Clark. Miles Clark. 170p. (Orig.). pap. write for info. (*0-9619579-0-5*) Lorkot Pr.

Man Who Tapped the Secrets of the Universe. Glenn Clark. pap. 4.95 (*0-910924-10-4*) Macalester.

Man Who Tapped the Secrets of the Universe. Glenn Clark. (Illus.). 61p. 1999. reprint ed. 5.00 (*1-879605-07-4*) U Sci & Philos.

Man Who Tasted Shapes. Richard E. Cytowic. LC 97-38214. (Illus.). 252p. 1998. pap. text 16.00 (*0-262-53152-6*, Bradford Bks) MIT Pr.

Man Who Tasted Shapes: A Bizarre Medical Mystery Offers Revolutionary Insights into Emotions, Reasoning & Consciousness. Richard E. Cytowic. 272p. 1995. mass mkt. 11.99 (*0-446-67068-5*, Pub. by Warner Bks) Little.

Man Who Thought He Was Messiah. Curt Leviant. 226p. 1990. 9.95 (*0-8276-0371-1*) JPS Phila.

Man Who Took a Bite Out of His Wife & Other Stories. Bev Jafek. LC 92-36789. 224p. 1993. 21.95 (*0-87951-499-X*, Pub. by Overlook Pr) Penguin Putnam.

Man Who Took a Bite Out of His Wife & Other Stories. Bev Jafek. 224p. 1995. pap. 10.95 (*0-87951-607-0*, Pub. by Overlook Pr) Penguin Putnam.

Man Who Travelled on Motorways. Trevor Hoyle. 280p. (Orig.). 1982. pap. 11.95 (*0-7145-3790-X*) Riverrun NY.

Man Who Tricked a Ghost. Laurence Yep. LC 93-22202. (Illus.). 32p. (J). (gr. k-4). 1997. 15.95 (*0-8167-3030-X*) BrdgeWater.

Man Who Tricked a Ghost. Laurence Yep. LC 93-22202. (Illus.). 32p. (J). (gr. k-4). 1995. pap. 4.95 (*0-8167-3031-8*, Troll Medallion) Troll Communs.

Man Who Tricked a Ghost. Laurence Yep. (J). 1993. 10.15 (*0-606-07838-X*) Turtleback.

Man Who Tried to Burn New York. Nat Brandt. LC 86-5833. (York State Book Ser.). (Illus.). 308p. 1986. reprint ed. pap. 95.50 (*0-608-07597-3*, 205991200010) Bks Demand.

***Man Who Tried to Cheat Death: Romanian Scary Stories Anthology.** Gabriel Stanescu. Ed. & Tr. by Mac L. Ricketts. (Illus.). 65p. 2000. lib. bdg. 10.00 (*1-887304-12-6*) Criterion GA.

Man Who Tried to Save the World: The Dangerous Life & Mysterious Disappearance of Fred Cuny. Scott Anderson. LC 98-43936. 384p. 1999. 24.95 (*0-385-48665-0*) Doubleday.

***Man Who Tried to Save the World: The Dangerous Life & Mysterious Disappearance of Fred Cuny.** Scott Anderson. 400p. 2000. pap. 14.00 (*0-385-48666-9*, Anchor NY) Doubleday.

Man Who Turned Back the Clock & Other Short Stories. Steve Allen. LC 95-20054. 348p. 1995. 25.95 (*1-57392-002-9*) Prometheus Bks.

Man Who Turned into Himself: A Novel. David P. Ambrose. LC 95-16220. 208p. 1995. pap. 10.00 (*0-312-13119-4*) St Martin.

Man Who Understood Cats. Michael A. Dymmoch. 224p. 1995. mass mkt. 4.99 (*0-380-72265-8*, Avon Bks) Morrow Avon.

Man Who Vanished. Amy Keyishian. (J). 1996. pap. 4.75 (*0-553-54268-0*) BDD Bks Young Read.

Man Who Vanished. Amy Keyishian. (Ghostwriter Ser.). 1996. 8.60 (*0-606-09325-7*, Pub. by Turtleback) Demco.

Man Who Walked Through Time. Colin Fletcher. 1989. pap. 13.00 (*0-679-72306-4*) Vin Bks.

Man Who Walked to the Moon. Howard McCord. LC 97-15513. 128p. 1997. 18.00 (*0-929701-51-8*) McPherson & Co.

Man Who Wanted Seven Wives: The Greenbrier Ghost & the Famous Murder Mystery of 1897. 2nd ed. Katie Letcher Lyle. LC 99-61240. (Illus.). 227p. 1999. 22.95 (*1-891852-04-3*) Quarrier Pr.

***Man Who Wanted Seven Wives: The Greenbrier Ghost & the Famous Murder Mystery of 1897.** 2nd rev. ed. Katie Letcher Lyle. LC 99-61240. (Illus.). 170p. 1999. pap. 12.95 (*1-891852-05-1*) Quarrier Pr.

Man Who Wanted to Be Guilty. Henrik Stangerup. Tr. by David Gress-Wright from DAN. 140p. 1991. reprint ed. pap. 12.95 (*0-7145-2930-3*) M Boyars Pubs.

Man Who Was Chesterton. G. K. Chesterton. LC 79-128221. (Essay Index Reprint Ser.). 1977. 46.95 (*0-8369-1908-4*) Ayer.

Man Who Was Different see Hombre Diferente

Man Who Was Dorian Gray. Jerusha H. McCormack. text 24.95 (*0-312-23278-0*) St Martin.

Man Who Was Frankenstein Peter Haining. LC 80-477823. 166p. 1979. write for info. (*0-584-10356-5*) F Muller.

Man Who Was Horse. Julius Lester. LC 97-25210. (Illus.). 40p. (J). (gr. k-3). 1998. 16.99 (*0-8037-1787-3*, Dial Yng Read) Peng Put Young Read.

Man Who Was It. George Pavloff. (Illus.). 72p. (J). (gr. 1 up). 1990. 12.95 (*0-931474-39-6*) TBW Bks.

Man Who Was Late. Louis Begley. 256p. 1994. pap. 10.00 (*0-449-90911-5*, Columbine) Fawcett.

Man Who Was Marked by Winter. Paula Meehan. 66p. 1994. pap. 12.00 (*0-910055-14-9*) East Wash Univ.

Man Who Was Marked by Winter. Paula Meehan. 66p. 1994. reprint ed. 21.00 (*0-910055-13-0*) East Wash Univ.

Man Who Was Not Tall Enough. Jennifer Rees Larcombe. LC 98-51208. (Best Bible Stories Ser.). (Illus.). 24p. (J). (ps-3). 1999. pap. 2.99 (*1-58134-052-4*) Crossway Bks.

Man Who Was Poe. Avi. LC 89-42537. 224p. (YA). (gr. 7 up). 1991. mass mkt. 4.99 (*0-380-71192-3*, Avon Bks) Morrow Avon.

Man Who Was Poe. Avi. 1997. mass mkt. 4.99 (*0-380-73022-7*, Avon Bks) Morrow Avon.

Man Who Was Poe. Avi. (J). 1989. 9.60 (*0-606-04970-3*, Pub. by Turtleback) Demco.

***Man Who Was Poe.** Stacie Champlin Dreibrodt. Ed. by Dawn Michelle Robbins. (YA). 1999. 11.95 (*1-58130-617-2*); 9.95 (*1-58130-616-4*) Novel Units.

Man Who Was Poe: A Spine-Chilling Tale of Mystery & Murder. Avi. (J). 1997. 9.60 (*0-606-11595-1*, Pub. by Turtleback) Demco.

Man Who Was Shakespeare. Eva T. Clark. LC 75-113577. reprint ed. 24.00 (*0-404-01549-2*) AMS Pr.

Man Who Was Shakespeare: A Summary of the Case Unfolded in "The Mysterious William Shakespeare, the Myth & the Reality" Charlton Ogburn. LC 95-21081. 96p. 1995. pap. 5.95 (*0-939009-90-0*) EPM Pubns.

Man Who Was Taller Than God. Harold Adams. (Carl Wilcox Mystery Ser.). 1998. pap. 7.95 (*0-8027-7554-3*) Walker & Co.

Man Who Was Taller Than God: A Carl Wilcox Mystery. Harold Adams. LC 92-13260. 156p. 1992. 18.95 (*0-8027-1239-8*) Walker & Co.

Man Who Was Thursday. G. K. Chesterton. (Classics Ser.). 192p. 1990. pap. 12.99 (*0-14-018388-4*, Penguin Classics) Viking Penguin.

Man Who Was Thursday. G. K. Chesterton. (Classics Library). 184p. 1998. pap. 3.95 (*1-85326-236-6*, 2366WW, Pub. by Wrdsworth Edits) NTC Contemp Pub Co.

Man Who Was Thursday. large type ed. G. K. Chesterton. LC 98-52504. 288p. 1999. 24.95 (*1-56000-492-4*) Transaction Pubs.

Man Who Was Thursday. G. K. Chesterton. reprint ed. lib. bdg. 20.95 (*0-89190-577-4*, Rivercity Pr) Amereon Ltd.

Man Who Was Thursday. G. K. Chesterton. 1990. reprint ed. lib. bdg. 16.95 (*0-89968-495-5*) Buccaneer Bks.

Man Who Was Thursday. G. K. Chesterton. (Illus.). 128p. 1986. reprint ed. pap. 3.95 (*0-486-25121-7*) Dover.

Man Who Was William Shakespeare. Peter Sammartino. LC 89-43010. (Illus.). 136p. 1990. 14.50 (*0-8453-4827-2*, Cornwall Bks) Assoc Univ Prs.

Man Who Wasn't Maigret. large type ed. Patrick Marnham. (Illus.). 560p. 1993. 27.99 (*0-7089-8712-5*, Charnwood) Ulverscroft.

Man Who Wasn't Maigret: A Portrait of Georges Simenon. Patrick Marnham. LC 92-16351. 1993. 25.00 (*0-374-20171-4*) FS&G.

Man Who Wasn't There. large type ed. John Wainwright. (Mystery Ser.). 336p. 1992. 27.99 (*0-7089-2671-1*) Ulverscroft.

Man Who Went Away. Harold Bell Wright. 1998. lib. bdg. 47.95 (*1-56723-110-1*) Yestermorrow.

Man Who Went Out for Cigarettes. Adrian Blevins-Church. Ed. by Bertha Rogers. (Award Chapbook Ser.). 26p. (Orig.). 1996. pap. 5.00 (*0-9646844-2-X*) Bright Hill.

Man Who Went up in Smoke. Maj Sjowall & Per Wahloo. Date not set. lib. bdg. 18.95 (*0-8488-2164-5*) Amereon Ltd.

Man Who Went up in Smoke. Maj Sjowall & Per Wahloo. Tr. by Joan Tate from SWE. LC 92-50694. (Vintage Crime - Black Lizard Ser.). 1993. pap. 10.00 (*0-679-74597-1*) Vin Bks.

Man Who Whispered. Rick Boyer. 266p. 1998. mass mkt. 5.99 (*0-8041-1044-1*) Ivy Books.

Man Who Wins see Collected Works of Robert Herrick

Man Who Wins. Robert Herrick. (Collected Works of Robert Herrick). 1988. reprint ed. lib. bdg. 59.00 (*0-7812-1260-X*) Rprt Serv.

Man Who Wore Layers of Clothing in the Winter. James Magorian. LC 94-71880. 121p. (Orig.). 1994. pap. 6.00 (*0-930674-40-5*) Black Oak.

Man Who Worked for Collister. Mary T. Earle. LC 71-101806. (Short Story Index Reprint Ser.). 1977. 20.95 (*0-8369-3194-7*) Ayer.

Man Who Works . . . Esther M. Letellier. 154p. 1984. per. 10.00 (*0-614-24794-2*) Tesseract SD.

Man Who Would Be Daddy. Marie Ferrarella. (Romance Ser.). 1996. per. 3.25 (*0-373-19175-8*, 1-19175-8) Silhouette.

Man Who Would Be God. Paul Ruffin. LC 93-5225. (Southwest Life & Letters Ser.). 168p. (Orig.). 1993. pap. 10.95 (*0-87074-363-5*) SMU Press.

Man Who Would Be God: Stories. Paul Ruffin. LC 93-5225. (Southwest Life & Letters Ser.). 168p. 1993. 22.50 (*0-87074-354-6*) SMU Press.

Man Who Would Be King. Rudyard Kipling. reprint ed. lib. bdg. 22.95 (*0-88411-995-5*) Amereon Ltd.

Man Who Would Be King. Rudyard Kipling. 1990. reprint ed. lib. bdg. 18.95 (*0-89968-536-6*) Buccaneer Bks.

Man Who Would Be King: And Other Stories. Rudyard Kipling. (Classics Library). 212p. 1998. pap. 3.95 (*1-85326-209-9*, 2099WW, Pub. by Wrdsworth Edits) NTC Contemp Pub Co.

***Man Who Would Be King: The Life of Philippe d' Orleans, Regent of France.** Christine Pevitt. LC 99-26991. (Illus.). 384p. 1999. reprint ed. pap. 15.00 (*0-688-16983-X*, Wm Morrow) Morrow Avon.

***Man Who Would Be King & Other Stories.** Rudyard Kipling. 352p. 1999. pap. 8.95 (*0-19-283629-3*) OUP.

Man Who Would Be King, & Other Stories. Rudyard Kipling. LC 93-42876. 128p. 1994. pap. 1.50 (*0-486-28051-9*) Dover.

Man Who Would Be Messiah: A Biographical Novel. W. Gunther Plaut. 258p. 1990. pap. 12.95 (*0-88962-400-3*) Mosaic.

Man Who Would Dam the Amazon & Other Accounts from Afield. John G. Mitchell. LC 89-78517. 382p. 1990. reprint ed. pap. 118.50 (*0-7837-8907-6*, 204961800001) Bks Demand.

Man Who Wrote Dracula. large type ed. Daniel Farson. 480p. 1996. 27.99 (*0-7089-3497-8*) Ulverscroft.

***Man Who Wrote the Book: A Novel.** Erik Tarloff. LC 99-57839. 288p. 2000. 23.00 (*0-609-60468-6*, Crown) Crown Pub Group.

Man Whom Women Loved. Aschan. mass mkt. write for info. (*0-312-90055-4*) Tor Bks.

Man, Wife & Little Wonder. Robin Nicholas. 1998. per. 3.50 (*0-373-19301-7*, 1-19301-0) Silhouette.

Man with a Broken Heart. Jim Brancaleone. (Orig.). 1977. pap. 5.95 (*0-9601186-1-6*) Brancaleone Educ.

Man with a Bull-Tongue Plow. Jesse Stuart. LC 83-45891. reprint ed. 32.00 (*0-404-20248-9*, PS3537) AMS Pr.

Man with a Dream: The Story of Saint John Bosco. Peter M. Rinaldi. (Illus.). 162p. 1978. reprint ed. pap. 5.00 (*0-89944-035-5*, 035-5) Salesiana Pubs.

Man with a Maid. 216p. 1996. mass mkt. 7.95 (*1-56201-024-7*) Blue Moon Bks.

***Man with a Maid.** 224p. 2000. mass mkt. 7.95 (*1-56201-181-2*, Pub. by Blue Moon Bks) Publishers Group.

Man with a Maid. LC 08-27284. 1968. pap. 4.50 (*0-8021-3113-1*, Grove) Grove-Atltic.

Man with a Maid. 2nd ed. James Jennings. 1995. mass mkt. 4.95 (*1-56333-307-4*) Masquerade.

Man with a Maid: And Other Entertainments. 672p. 1998. mass mkt. 7.95 (*0-7867-0549-3*) Carroll & Graf.

Man with a Mission. Suzanne Barclay. (Intimate Moments Ser.). 1993. mass mkt. 3.39 (*0-373-07483-2*, 5-07483-6) Silhouette.

***Man with a Mission: Mel Trotter & His Legacy for the Rescue Mission Movement.** Leona Hertel. LC 99-57355. 2000. pap. text 10.99 (*0-8254-2799-1*) Kregel.

Man with a Nose, & the Other Uncollected Stories of H. G. Wells. H. G. Wells. Ed. by J. R. Hammond. LC 84-14624. 248p. (C). 1984. text 19.95 (*0-485-11247-7*, Pub. by Athlone Pr) Humanities.

Man with a Past. Celeste Hamilton. (Montana Mavericks Ser.). 1995. mass mkt. 3.99 (*0-373-50175-7*, 1-50175-8) Harlequin Bks.

***Man with a Past.** Jayne Ann Krentz. 2001. mass mkt. 6.99 (*1-55166-624-3*, 1-66624-7, Mira Bks) Harlequin Bks.

Man with a Past, No. 239. Jayne Ann Krentz. 1991. per. 4.59 (*0-373-83239-7*) Harlequin Bks.

Man with a Patient Heart. Olive Schneider. LC 93-71140. 349p. 1993. pap. 7.95 (*0-916035-59-X*) Evangel Indiana.

Man with a Shattered World: The History of a Brain Wound. Aleksandr R. Luria. LC 86-31866. 168p. 1987. pap. 14.95 (*0-674-54625-3*) HUP.

Man with a Squirrel. Nicholas Kilmer. 88p. 1995. 22.50 (*0-8050-3666-0*) H Holt & Co.

***Man with a Squirrel, Vol. 22.** Nicholas Kilmer. (Missing Mysteries Ser.: Vol. 22). 2000. pap. 14.95 (*1-890208-39-6*) Poisoned Pen.

Man with a Thousand Eyes. Steven She. 96p. (Orig.). 1989. pap. 9.95 (*0-940584-17-4*) Gull Bks.

Man with a Vision. Kenneth Haney. 1997. pap. 12.95 (*1-880969-27-0*) Schl Prophet.

Man with an Axe: A Detective Sergeant Mulheisen Mystery. Jon A. Jackson. (Detective Sergeant Mulheisen Mysteries Ser.). 234p. 1999. reprint ed. pap. text 12.00 (*0-8021-3603-6*, Grove) Grove-Atltic.

***Man with Bogart's Face.** Andrew J. Fenady. 88p. 2000. pap. 5.60 (*0-87129-999-2*, MB9) Dramatic Pub.

***Man with My Cat.** Paul Engleman. LC 99-55740. 272p. 2000. text 23.95 (*0-312-24651-X*, Minotaur) St Martin.

Man with Night Sweats: Poems. Thom Gunn. 96p. 1993. pap. 8.00 (*0-374-52381-9*, Noonday) FS&G.

Man with No Face. Peter Turnbull. LC 98-35163. 240p. 1998. text 21.95 (*0-312-19298-3*) St Martin.

***Man with No Face.** Peter Turnbull. 416p. 2000. 31.99 (*0-7089-4287-3*) Ulverscroft.

Man with No Name: Turn Lemons into Lemonade. Wally Amos. 142p. (Orig.). 1994. 16.95 incl. audio (*1-879323-37-0*) Sound Horizons AV.

Man with No Time. Timothy Hallinan. 336p. 1995. mass mkt. 4.99 (*0-380-71371-3*, Avon Bks) Morrow Avon.

***Man with PSI: A Historical Novel of a High-Tech Espionage.** Alan Eagle. LC 99-93645. 1999. 21.50 (*0-533-13074-3*) Vantage.

Man with the Baton. David Ewen. LC 68-57316. (Essay Index Reprint Ser.). 1977. 22.95 (*0-8369-0433-8*) Ayer.

Man with the Bird on His Head: The Amazing Fulfillment of a Mysterious Island Prophecy. John Rush & Abbe Anderson. (International Adventures Ser.). 192p. 1997. pap. 8.99 (*1-57658-005-9*) YWAM Pub.

An Asterisk (*) at the beginning of an entry indicates that the title is appearing for the first time.

Man with the Black Coat: Russia's Literature of the Absurd. Daniil Kharms & Aleksandr I. Vvedenskii. Tr. by George Gibian. LC 97-17494. 1997. 14.95 (*0-8101-1573-5*) Northwestern U Pr.

*****Man with the Black Glove.** Ursel Scheffler. (Illus.). 62p. (J). (gr. 2-3). 1999. 13.95 (*0-7358-1178-4*, Pub. by North-South Bks NYC); lib. bdg. 13.88 (*0-7358-1179-2*, Pub. by North-South Bks NYC) Chronicle Bks.

Man with the Black Mouth. R. G. Vliet. (Illus.). 1970. pap. 10.00 (*0-87711-010-7*) Story Line.

Man with the Book. 2nd ed. Henry Einspruch. 1976. pap. 1.25 (*1-880226-14-6*) M J Pubs.

Man with the Broken Ear. Edmond About. Tr. by Henry Holt. LC 74-15941. (Science Fiction Ser.). 258p. 1975. reprint ed. 23.95 (*0-405-06271-0*) Ayer.

Man with the Buzzer in His Throat. Jim Pritchard. (Chapbook Ser.). (Illus.). 6p. 1995. pap. 10.00 (*0-9652505-2-0*) Synaesthesia.

*****Man with the Getaway Face.** Richard Stark. LC 98-6630. 224p. 1998. mass mkt. 12.00 (*0-446-67466-4*, Pub. by Warner Bks) Little.

Man with the Giant Stride: The Story of Ken Witt. Joe Swatek. 168p. 1998. pap. 15.95 (*1-886225-38-9*, 1000) Dageforde Pub.

Man with the Golden Arm. Nelson Algren. LC 89-71471. 348p. 1990. pap. 10.95 (*1-888363-18-5*) Seven Stories.

Man with the Golden Arm. 50th anniversary ed. Nelson Algren. Ed. by William J. Savage, Jr. & Daniel Simon. LC 99-41331. (Illus.). 454p. 1999. text 35.00 (*1-58322-007-0*, Pub. by Seven Stories); pap. text 14.95 (*1-58322-008-9*, Pub. by Seven Stories) Publishers Group.

Man with the Golden Gun. Ian Fleming. (FRE.). 9.95 (*0-685-11338-8*); pap. 9.95 (*0-685-11339-6*) Fr & Eur.

*****Man with the Golden Gun.** Ian Fleming. LC 99-40376. 190p. 1999. pap. 24.95 (*0-7658-0654-1*) Transaction Pubs.

Man with the Hoe. limited ed. Lois Rather. (Illus.). 1977. 35.00 (*0-686-20513-8*) Rather Pr.

Man with the Key Is Not Here: A Key to What They Really Mean in China. Karin Malmstrom & Nancy Nash. Ed. by Shann Davies. (Illus.). (Orig.). 1990. pap. text 5.95 (*0-9626164-0-0*) Pacific Venture.

Man with the Little Dog. Georges Simenon. Tr. by Jean Stewart. 176p. 1989. 16.95 (*0-15-156933-9*) Harcourt.

Man with the Long Shadow. Clara H. Stuart. LC 96-61789. 384p. (Orig.). 1997. pap. 16.95 (*1-883893-89-5*) WinePress Pub.

Man with the Miraculous Hands. Joseph Kessel. Tr. by Helen Weaver & Leo Raditsa. LC 70-160922. (Biography Index Reprint Ser.). 1977. reprint ed. 18.95 (*0-8369-8085-9*) Ayer.

Man with the $100,000 Breasts. Michael Konik. 240p. Date not set. 24.95 (*0-929712-72-2*) Huntington Pr.

*****Man with the $100,000 Breasts: And Other Gambling Stories.** Michael Konik. LC 99-45642. 256p. 1999. pap. 12.00 (*0-7679-0445-1*) Broadway BDD.

Man with the Red Umbrella. A. P. Miceli. 1974. 22.95 (*0-87511-603-5*) Claitors.

Man with the Scar. Judith A. Green. (Adult Basic Learner Ser.). (Illus.). 203p. (Orig.). 1979. pap. text 8.98 (*0-89061-153-X*, 202, Jamestwn Pub) NTC Contemp Pub Co.

Man with the Steel Guitar: A Portrait of Ambition, Desperation, & Crime. Norman Greenberg. LC 79-63084. 181p. reprint ed. 56.20 (*0-608-16631-6*, 202753100055) Bks Demand.

Man with the Thorn in His Flesh. A. C. Archer. pap. 4.99 (*0-88019-146-5*) Schmul Pub Co.

Man with the White Liver. 2nd ed. Angela Jackson. Ed. by Maurice Kenny & Josh Gosciak. LC 87-9240. (Illus.). 24p. (C). 1987. pap. 3.00 (*0-936556-16-1*) Contact Two.

Man with Three Fingers. Date not set. pap. text. write for info. (*0-17-556558-9*) Addison-Wesley.

Man with Two Heads. large type ed. John N. Chance. 240p. pap. 18.99 (*0-7089-5420-0*) Ulverscroft.

Man with Two Left Feet: And Other Stories. P. G. Wodehouse. 224p. 1991. pap. 8.95 (*0-14-001601-5*) Viking Penguin.

Man Within. Graham Greene. 224p. 1994. pap. 11.95 (*0-14-018530-5*, Penguin Classics) Viking Penguin.

Man Within His Life-World: Contributions to Phenomenology by Scholars from East-Central Europe. Anna-Teresa Tymieniecka. 804p. (C). 1989. text 373.50 (*90-277-2767-8*) Kluwer Academic.

Man Without a Badge. Dani Sinclair. 1997. per. 3.75 (*0-373-22401-X*, 1-22401-3) Silhouette.

Man Without a Country. Edward E. Hale. 1976. lib. bdg. 18.95 (*0-89968-152-2*, Lghtyr Pr) Buccaneer Bks.

Man Without a Country: And It's History. Edward E. Hale. 80p. 1994. pap. 9.95 (*0-939218-03-8*) Chapman Billies.

Man Without a Country & Other Stories. Hale. (Classics Library). 1998. pap. 3.95 (*1-85326-558-6*, 5586WW, Pub. by Wrdsworth Edits) NTC Contemp Pub Co.

Man Without a Country & Other Stories. Edward E. Hale. 1976. 19.95 (*0-8488-1355-3*) Amereon Ltd.

Man Without a Country & Other Tales. Edward E. Hale. 1998. lib. bdg. 19.95 (*1-56723-043-1*) Yestermorrow.

Man Without a Country & Other Tales. Edward E. Hale. LC 74-152942. (Short Story Index Reprint Ser.). 1977. reprint ed. 18.95 (*0-8369-3801-1*) Ayer.

Man Without a Face. Isabelle Holland. LC 71-37736. (Trophy Keypoint Bk.). 160p. (J). (gr. 7 up). 1987. reprint ed. mass mkt. 4.95 (*0-06-447028-8*, HarpTrophy) HarpC Child Bks.

*****Man Without a Face: The Autobiography of Communism's Greatest Spymaster.** Markus Wolf & Anne McElvoy. LC DD287.7.W65A3 1999. 464p. 1999. pap. text 14.00 (*1-891620-12-6*, Pub. by PublicAffairs NY) HarpC.

Man Without a Gun: One Diplomat's Secret Struggle to Free the Hostages, Fight Terrorism, & End a War. Giandomenico Picco. (Illus.). 352p. 1999. 27.50 (*0-8129-2910-1*, Times Bks) Crown Pub Group.

Man Without a Haven. Beverly Bird. (Intimate Moments Ser.). 1995. mass mkt. 3.75 (*0-373-07641-X*, 1-07641-3) Silhouette.

Man Without a Mate Cookbook: The Successful Lifestyle Cookbook for the Unmarried Man. Bob Lunt. LC 91-66424. (Successful Life Alone Cookbook Ser.). (Illus.). 135p. 1991. 10.95 (*0-9630296-3-0*) SKM Pub.

Man Without a Memory. Maura Seger. 1995. per. 3.75 (*0-373-07675-4*, 1-07675-1) Silhouette.

Man Without a Wife. Beverly Bird. (Intimate Moments Ser.). 1995. per. 3.75 (*0-373-07652-5*, 1-07652-0) Silhouette.

*****Man Without a World: A Silent Film with English Subtitles Supposedly Made in 1928 by the Imaginary Film Director Yevgeny Antinov.** Eleanor Antin. 76p. 2000. pap. 10.95 (*1-892295-81-4*) Green Integer.

*****Man Without a Yesterday.** large type ed. Mark Bannerman. 256p. 1999. pap. 18.99 (*0-7089-5515-0*, Linford) Ulverscroft.

Man Without Content. Giorgio Agamben. Tr. by Georgia Albert from ITA. LC 99-21526. (Meridian: Crossing Aesthetics Ser.). 130p. 1999. pap. 14.95 (*0-8047-3554-9*) Stanford U Pr.

Man Without Equal see Hombre Sin Igual

Man Without Equal: Jesus, the Man Who Changed the World. Bill Bright. LC 91-28459. (Uniqueness of Jesus Ser.: Bk. 1). 128p. 1992. mass mkt. 4.99 (*1-56399-012-1*) NewLife Pubns.

Man Without Love: (Wounded Warriors) Beverly Bird. (Wounded Warriors Ser.). 1995. per. 3.75 (*0-373-07630-4*, 1-07630-6) Silhouette.

*****Man Without Medicine.** Cynthia Haseloff. 240p. 1999. mass mkt. 4.50 (*0-8439-4581-8*, Pub. by Dorchester Pub Co) CMG.

Man Without Medicine. large type ed. Cynthia Haseloff. 1999. 20.00 (*0-7838-1675-8*, G K Hall Lrg Type) Mac Lib Ref.

Man Without Medicine: A Western Story. Cynthia Haseloff. LC 96-7764. 1996. 16.95 (*0-7862-0664-0*) Five Star.

Man Without Medicine: A Western Story. large type ed. Cynthia Haseloff. LC 97-28188. (Western Ser.). 309p. 1997. lib. bdg. 19.95 (*0-7862-1192-X*) Thorndike Pr.

Man Without Memory: Stories. Richard Burgin. LC 88-20854. (Illinois Short Fiction Ser.). 136p. 1989. 14.95 (*0-252-01602-5*) U of Ill Pr.

Man Without Qualities. Robert Musil. 1965. pap. 12.00 (*0-399-50152-5*, Perigee Bks) Berkley Pub.

Man Without Qualities, Vol. 1. Robert Musil. Tr. by Sophie Wilkins & Burton Pike. 1996. pap. 20.00 (*0-679-76787-8*) Vin Bks.

Man Without Qualities, Vol. 2. Robert Musil. Tr. by Sophie Wilkins & Burton Pike. 1996. pap. 24.00 (*0-679-76802-5*) Vin Bks.

Man Without Words. Susan Schaller. LC 95-3438. 210p. 1995. pap. 12.95 (*0-520-20265-1*, Pub. by U CA Pr) Cal Prin Full Svc.

Man-Wolf, & Other Tales. Emile Erckmann & Alexandre Erckmann. Ed. by R. Reginald & Douglas A. Menville. LC 75-46268. (Supernatural & Occult Fiction Ser.). 1976. reprint ed. lib. bdg. 21.95 (*0-405-08126-X*) Ayer.

Man, Woman & Child. Bobby Hutchinson. (Superromance Ser.). 1993. per. 3.50 (*0-373-70556-5*, 1-70556-5) Harlequin Bks.

Man, Woman & Child. Erich Segal. 224p. 1993. mass mkt. 7.50 (*0-553-56235-5*) Bantam.

Man, Woman, & God. Christopher A. Anderson. LC 93-74323. (Illus.). 514p. (Orig.). 1994. pap. 18.00 (*0-931353-34-3*) Andersons Pubns.

Man, Woman, & God. Vincent Fecher. LC 93-14036. 102p. (Orig.). 1993. pap. 6.95 (*0-8189-0672-3*) Alba.

Man Woman Book: How We Are. J. Bruce Evans. LC 89-42867. (Illus.). 112p. 1988. 9.95 (*0-937552-26-7*, QRP Bks) Quail Ridge.

Man-Woman Book: The Transformation of Love. Ron Smothermon. 1985. pap. 15.00 (*0-932654-09-6*) Context Pubns.

Man, Woman, Earth. Gerzon. 22.00 (*0-06-251145-9*) HarpC.

Man Worth Knowing. Sue M. Vinson. 138p. (Orig.). 1998. pap. 10.00 (*0-916067-09-2*) Elec Media Pub.

Man Worth Marrying. Phyllis Halldorson. (Romance Ser.: No. 1395). 1999. mass mkt. 3.50 (*0-373-19395-5*, 1-19395-2) Silhouette.

Man Worth Waiting For. large type ed. Helen Brooks. 1998. 21.95 (*0-263-15590-0*, G K Hall & Co) Mac Lib Ref.

Man You Loved to Hate see Von: The Life & Films of Erich von Stroheim

Man You'll Marry. Debbie Macomber. (Romance Ser.: No. 196). 1992. per. 2.89 (*0-373-03196-3*, 1-03196-2) Harlequin Bks.

Ma'na Al-Iman Wa-al-Islam. Al-Izz I. Abd-al-Salam. (Writings of Al-'Izz ibn 'Abd-al-Salam Ser.). (ARA.). 32p. (Orig.). 1995. pap. 1.95 (*1-57547-225-2*) Dar Al-Fikr.

Mana Cards see Mana Karten: Verbinde Dich Mit der Kraft Uralter Hawaiianischer Weisheit

Mana Cards: The Power of Hawaiian Wisdom. Catherine Kalama Becker. LC 97-76453. (Illus.). 44p. 1998. pap. 36.50 (*0-9660142-0-0*) Radiance Netwk.

Mana Karten: Verbinde Dich Mit der Kraft Uralter Hawaiianischer Weisheit. Catherine Becker. Tr. by Tara Lamontagne.Tr. of Mana Cards. (GER., Illus.). 100p. 1998. pap. 30.50 (*0-9660142-1-9*) Radiance Netwk.

Mana Magic see Huna Magic - Empowers You to Create Health, Wealth & Relationships: Learn the Secret Within the Secret

Mana: or Vital Force. 5th ed. Max F. Long. 125p. 1976. pap. 4.00 (*0-910764-04-2*) Huna Res Inc.

Mana Tangata: Draft Declaration on the Rights of Indigenous Peoples 1993: Background & Discussion on Key Issues: An Explanatory Document. United Nations Staff. LC 95-111445. 52p. 1994. write for info. (*0-478-04329-5*, Pub. by Manaaki Whenua) Balogh.

Manabendra Nath Roy: An Annotated Bibliography. S. M. Ganguly. (C). 1993. 18.00 (*81-7074-124-6*, Pub. by KP Bagchi) S Asia.

Manage a Trois. Owen Hill et al. (Took Modern Poetry in English Ser.: No. 49). 29p. 1998. 3.00 (*1-879457-56-3*) Norton Coker Pr.

*****Manage for the Long Term Present: A Framework for Sustainable Growth.** Michael G. Coleman & Sandra B. Austin. (Illus.). 320p. 1999. 29.95 (*1-929733-04-6*) MicroPress.

Manage Globally, Sell Locally: The Art of Strategic Account Management. A. Lee Blackstone. LC 94-11218. 216p. 1994. text 27.50 (*0-7863-0330-1*, Irwn Prfssnl) McGraw-Hill Prof.

Manage It! Exploiting Information Systems for Effective Management. Mike Wright & David Rhodes. LC 85-28114. 208p. 1986. 49.95 (*0-275-90047-9*, C0047, Praeger Pubs) Greenwood.

Manage IT (Information Technology) Managing the Small Computer or Department Network. Mary Kelly. (Illus.). 201p. 1998. pap. 89.00 (*1-883422-07-8*) Adams-Blake.

Manage Like You Own It. Mack Hanan. 160p. 1994. 21.95 (*0-8144-5112-8*) AMACOM.

*****Manage or Perish: The Challenges of Managed Mental Health Care in Europe.** Jose Guimon & Norman Sartorius. 620p. 2000. 225.00 (*0-306-46210-9*, Kluwer Plenum) Kluwer Academic.

Manage People Not Personnel. 300p. 1990. 32.50 (*0-07-103274-6*) McGraw.

Manage to the Individual, If You Want to Know How, Ask! A Story about the Belief System of Motivation & Performance. Thad Green & Bill Barkley. 300p. (Orig.). 1995. pap. 14.95 (*1-887395-03-2*) Belief Syst Inst.

*****Manage Your Anger: Adams,&Polly.** abr. ed. Gael Lindenfield. 1998. audio 9.95 (*0-694-51910-3*, CPN10135) HarperAudio.

*****Manage Your Career.** Brian Sutton. 1998. pap. 13.95 (*0-09-927228-8*, Pub. by Random) Trafalgar.

*****Manage Your College Experience.** 3rd ed. Ed. by Lee. 180p. 1999. pap. text 18.70 (*0-536-02623-8*) P-H.

Manage Your Fears, Manage Your Anger: A Psychiatrist Speaks. Abraham A. Low. LC 95-60989. 472p. 1995. 20.00 (*0-915005-05-0*) Willett Pub Co.

Manage Your Life, 4 vols. 4th ed. Williams. (C). 1990. pap. text, teacher ed. 1.96 (*0-395-57223-1*) HM.

Manage Your Life, 4 vols. 4th ed. Robert Williams & James Long. (C). 1990. pap. text. write for info. (*0-395-35972-4*) HM Soft Schl Col Div.

Manage Your Own Financial Future. Vesmark Inc Staff. 1997. pap. text 19.95 (*0-9650293-0-1*) Vesmark.

Manage Your Own Home Renovation. Carl Heldmann. LC 86-45714. (Illus.). 176p. 1987. pap. 8.95 (*0-88266-442-5*, Garden Way Pub) Storey Bks.

Manage Your Plant for Profit & Your Promotion. Richard W. Ogden. LC 78-2540. 204p. reprint ed. pap. 63.30 (*0-608-12147-9*, 202390500034) Bks Demand.

Manage Your Stress! 1995. pap. 149.00 incl. audio, VHS (*1-56052-342-5*) Crisp Pubns.

Manage Your Stress. 100p. 1995. pap. 24.95 incl. audio (*1-56052-347-6*) Crisp Pubns.

Manage Your Time! 1995. pap. 149.00 incl. audio, VHS (*1-56052-341-7*) Crisp Pubns.

Manage Your Time. 80p. 1995. pap. 24.95 incl. audio (*1-56052-346-8*) Crisp Pubns.

Manage Your Time. Tim Hindle. LC 97-38909. (Essential Managers Handbks.). (Illus.). 72p. 1999. pap. 6.95 (*0-7894-2446-0*) DK Pub Inc.

Manage Your Time. 2nd ed. Ron Fry. LC 94-5492. (How to Study Ser.). 128p. (C). 1994. pap. 6.95 (*1-56414-078-4*) Career Pr Inc.

Manage Your Time, Your Work, Yourself. 2nd rev. ed. Merrill E. Douglass & Donna N. Douglass. LC 92-37820. 176p. 1993. pap. 15.95 (*0-8144-7825-5*) AMACOM.

Manage Your Time/Market Your Business: The Time-Marketing Equation. Ruth Klein. 192p. 1995. 21.95 (*0-8144-0280-1*) AMACOM.

Manageable Windows 2000: Hands-on Messaging Administration, Microsoft Exchange Ed. Thomas Henderson. 736p. 1999. pap. text 49.99 (*0-471-33314-X*) Wiley.

Managed Behavioral Health Care: An Industry Perspective. Sharon A. Shueman et al. LC 93-34578. (Illus.). 290p. 1994. pap. 41.95 (*0-398-06425-3*) C C Thomas.

Managed Behavioral Health Care: An Industry Perspective. Sharon A. Shueman et al. LC 93-34578. (Illus.). 290p. (C). 1994. text 60.95 (*0-398-05897-0*) C C Thomas.

Managed Behavioral Health Market Share in the United States, 1998-1999. 5th rev. ed. Monica E. Oss & John H. Clary. (Illus.). 50p. 1998. spiral bd. 65.00 (*1-878586-15-7*, DR-1) Open Minds PA.

Managed Behavioral Health Readiness Audit Tool. Monica E. Oss & John H. Clary. 38p. 1998. spiral bd. 39.00 (*1-878586-29-7*, M-2) Open Minds PA.

Managed Behavioral Health Services: An Annotated Bibliography: 1989-1994. Ed. by Jane Kramer & Saul Feldman. 76p. 1999. pap. text 20.00 (*0-7881-7651-X*) DIANE Pub.

Managed Behavioral Healthcare: History, Models, Strategic Challenges, & Future Course. Tom Trabin & Michael Freeman. (Managed Behavioral Healthcare Library). 1995. pap. 35.00 (*1-887452-01-X*) CentraLink.

Managed Behavioral Healthcare: Provider Training & Development. American Board of Certified Managed Care Providers. Ed. by Alex D'Alessandro. LC 92-48824. 1992. pap. 95.00 (*0-935255-77-X*) Of Course Pubns.

Managed Behavioral Healthcare Manual. Margaret D. Bischel. 275p. 1997. ring bd. 225.00 (*1-893826-02-3*) Apollo Managed.

Managed Care: A Sourcebook for Occupational Therapy. Ed. by AOTA Staff. LC 96-227563. 160p. (Orig.). 1996. pap. text 35.00 (*1-56900-046-8*, 1161) Am Occup Therapy.

Managed Care: Advances in Financing. Ed. by Linda F. Wolf. (Illus.). 306p. (C). 1998. pap. text 45.00 (*0-7881-4988-1*) DIANE Pub.

Managed Care: An Agency Guide to Surviving & Thriving. David Emenhiser et al. 1995. pap. text 9.95 (*0-87868-597-9*) Child Welfare.

Managed Care: An Agent's Door to the Samll Group Market. Dearborn Financial Institute Staff. LC 98-38592. 131p. 1998. 34.00 (*0-7931-2849-8*, Real Estate Ed) Dearborn.

*****Managed Care: Anatomy of a Mass Medical Movement.** Richard D. Smith. (Illus.). 425p. 2000. pap. text 40.00 (*1-55605-294-4*) Wyndham Hall.

Managed Care: Financial, Legal & Ethical Issues. Ed. by David A. Bennahum. LC 98-50328. (Pilgrim Library of Ethics). 224p. 1999. pap. 23.95 (*0-8298-1274-1*) Pilgrim OH.

*****Managed Care: Good But Not Perfect.** 2000. write for info. (*0-8013-3032-7*) Addison-Wesley.

Managed Care: Integrating the Delivery & Financing of Health Care, Pt. A. Ed. by HIAA Staff. LC 97-125731. 251p. 1995. pap. 30.00 (*1-879143-26-7*) Health Ins Assn Am.

Managed Care: Integrating the Delivery & Financing of Health Care, Pt. B. Ed. by Jane Stein. 226p. 1996. pap. text 30.00 (*1-879143-29-1*) Health Ins Assn Am.

Managed Care: Integrating the Delivery & Financing of Health Care Study Manual, Pt. A. HIAA Staff. 64p. 1995. pap. 10.00 (*1-879143-27-5*) Health Ins Assn Am.

Managed Care: Integrating the Delivery & Financing of Health Care Study Manual, Pt. B. HIAA Staff. 64p. 1996. pap. 10.00 (*1-879143-30-5*) Health Ins Assn Am.

Managed Care: Made in America. Arnold Birenbaum. LC 97-5578. 208p. 1997. 39.95 (*0-275-95916-3*, Praeger Pubs) Greenwood.

Managed Care: Managing the Process. Mary E. Reres. 238p. 1996. pap. text 30.00 (*0-9660741-0-6*) Natl Prof Educ.

Managed Care: Practice & Progress. Robert Royce. LC 96-29999. 1997. write for info. (*1-85775-280-5*, Radcliffe Med Pr) Scovill Paterson.

Managed Care: Practice Strategies for Nursing. Margaret M. Conger. LC 98-40281. 290p. 1999. 55.00 (*0-7619-0964-8*) Sage.

Managed Care: Practice Strategies for Nursing. Marge Conger. LC 98-40281. 1999. 24.95 (*0-7619-0965-6*) Sage.

Managed Care: Serving the Needs of Women? 116 Recommended Consumer Protections. Belinda Rochelle et al. 74p. 1998. pap. 10.00 (*1-877966-40-1*) Ctr Women Policy.

Managed Care: Strategies, Networks & Management. Montague Brown. (HCMR Ser.). 272p. 1993. 41.00 (*0-8342-0504-1*, 20504) Aspen Pub.

Managed Care: What It Is & How It Works. Wendy Knight. LC 98-35906. 160p. 1998. 29.00 (*0-8342-1089-4*, 10894) Aspen Pub.

Managed Care Pt. C: Integrating the Delivery & Financing of Health Care. Andrew Alcorn et al. Ed. by Julie Hopkins. (HIAA Insurance Education Ser.). (Illus.). 233p. 1998. pap. text 30.00 (*1-879143-46-1*) Health Ins Assn Am.

Managed Care Pt. C: Integrating the Delivery & Financing of Health Care Study Manual. Health Insurance Association of America Staff. (HIAA Insurance Education Ser.). 76p. 1998. pap., student ed. 10.00 (*1-879143-47-X*) Health Ins Assn Am.

*****Managed Care Acquisition Report, 1999.** Irving Levin Associates, Inc. Staff. (Illus.). v, 180p. 1999. pap. 495.00 (*1-930625-07-3*) I Levin.

Managed Care & Antitrust: The PPO Experience. 132p. 1990. pap. 40.00 (*0-89707-553-6*, 503-0086) Amer Bar Assn.

Managed Care & Capitation: Issues in Nursing. Teri Britt et al. LC 98-3607. 30p. 1998. pap. 15.95 (*1-55810-141-1*) Am Nurses Pub.

Managed Care & Capitation Contracting for Home Health Agencies. Ino. LC 96-7927. 1996. 175.00 (*0-8342-0614-5*) Aspen Pub.

Managed Care & Changing Health Care Markets. Michael Morrisey. LC 97-43998. 1998. 39.95 (*0-8447-4038-1*); pap. 16.95 (*0-8447-4039-X*) Am Enterprise.

Managed Care & Children with Special Health Care Needs. American Academy of Pediatrics Staff. 197p. 1997. pap. 29.95 (*0-910761-80-9*) Am Acad Pediat.

Managed Care & Chronic Illness: Challenges & Opportunities. Peter D. Fox & Teresa Fama. 368p. 1996. 59.00 (*0-8342-0844-X*, 20844) Aspen Pub.

Managed Care & Contracting: A Guide for the Practicing Ophthalmologist. 3rd rev. ed. Preferred Health Strategies Staff. (Illus.). 1994. pap. write for info. (*1-929196-03-2*) Am Opthlmc Admin.

An Asterisk (*) at the beginning of an entry indicates that the title is appearing for the first time.

***Managed Care & Developmental Disabilities: Reconciling the Realities of Managed Care with the Individual Needs of Persons with Disabilities.** Dale Mitchell. LC 99-62954. 200p. 2000. pap. 19.95 (1-892696-07-X, Pub. by High Tide Pr) IPG Chicago.

Managed Care & Medical Cost Containment in Workers' Compensation: A National Inventory, 1995-1996. Stacey M. Eccleston. LC 95-39458. 320p. (Orig.). 1995. pap. 250.00 (0-935149-54-6, WC-95-4) Workers Comp Res Inst.

Managed Care & Medical Cost Containment in Worker's Compensation: A National Inventory, 1997-1998. Stacey M. Eccleston & Carter M. Yeager. LC 97-45627. 300p. 1997. pap. 250.00 (0-935149-71-6, WC-97-6) Workers Comp Res Inst.

***Managed Care & Pain.** unabridged ed. Stephen D. Lande & Ronald J. Kulich. 180p. 2000. pap. write for info. (0-9677735-0-4) Amer Pain IL.

***Managed Care & Privatization Child Welfare Tracking Project.** Charlotte McCullough. 1999. pap. 14.95 (0-87868-773-4, CWLA Pr) Child Welfare.

Managed Care & Public Health. Paul K. Halverson et al. LC 97-26357. 400p. 49.00 (0-8342-0897-0, 20897) Aspen Pub.

Managed Care & the Cardiac Patient. Ed. by Richard Ott et al. LC 94-40714. (Illus.). 334p. 1995. text 54.00 (1-56053-122-3) Hanley & Belfus.

***Managed Care & the Evaluation & Adoption of Emerging Medical Technologies.** Steven Garber et al. xvii, 70p. 2000. pap. 12.00 (0-8330-2831-6, MR-1195-NIMA) Rand Corp.

***Managed Care & the Evaluation & Adoption of Emerging Medical Technologies.** Steven Garber et al. (C). 2000. pap. 8.00 (0-8330-2849-9, MR-1195/1) Rand Corp.

Managed Care & the Law: Liability & Risk Management. Charles G. Benda & Fay A. Rozovsky. 506p. ring bd. 145.00 (0-316-17408-4, 74084) Aspen Law.

Managed Care & You: The Consumer Guide to Managing Your Health Care. 2nd ed. Michael E. Cafferky. (Illus.). 224p. (Orig.). 1995. pap. 14.95 (0-07-600759-6, ME104) Practice Mgmt Info.

Managed Care & You: The Consumer Guide to Managing Your Healthcare. 3rd rev. ed. Michael Cafferky. LC 98-113154. 234p. 1997. pap. 12.95 (1-885987-04-8, ME083, Health Info Pr) Practice Mgmt Info.

Managed Care Answer Book. annuals Sheryl T. Dacso & Clifford C. Dacso. 536p. 1994. 118.00 (1-56706-127-3, S154) Panel Pubs.

Managed Care Answer Book. 2nd ed. Sherly T. Dacso. LC 97-122155. 536p. 1996. 125.00 (1-56706-357-8) Panel Pubs.

Managed Care Answer Book. annuals 2nd ed. Sheryl T. Dacso. 536p. boxed set 125.00 (1-56706-398-5, S154) Panel Pubs.

***Managed Care Answer Book, 1.** 4th ed. Clifford C. Dacso. 1128p. 1999. boxed set 136.00 (0-7355-0464-4) Panel Pubs.

Managed Care Answer Book: Forms & Checklists. annuals Sheryl T. Dacso & Clifford C. Dacso. 400p. Date not set. pap. 96.00 incl. disk (1-56706-407-8, 64078) Panel Pubs.

Managed Care Answer Book: Forms & Checklists, 1. 2nd ed. Donald R. Levy et al. LC 99-171120. (Panel Answer Book Ser.). 560p. 1998. pap. 96.00 (1-56706-968-1) Panel Pubs.

Managed Care Answer Book for Mental Health Professionals. Gayle M. Tuttle & Dianne R. Woods. LC 97-13571. 152p. 1997. pap. 19.95 (0-87630-848-5) Brunner-Mazel.

Managed Care Blues & How to Cure Them. Walter A. Zelman & Robert A. Berenson. LC 98-16018. 192p. 1998. 45.00 (0-87840-679-4); pap. 17.95 (0-87840-680-8) Georgetown U Pr.

Managed Care Challenge for Nurse Executives. American Organization of Nurse Executives Staff. LC 96-24117. (AONE Leadership Ser.). (Illus.). 124p. (Orig.). 1996. pap. 40.00 (1-55648-164-0, 154154) AHPI.

Managed Care Concepts. D. Cole & F. Vogenberg. (Orig.). 1996. pap. text 49.46 (1-56870-226-4) RonJon Pub.

Managed Care Contract Reference Guide. MediSphere Health Partner Staff. 65p. 1998. pap. 30.50 (1-56829-091-8) Med Group Mgmt.

Managed Care Contracting: A Guide for Health Care Professionals. Wendy Knight. LC 97-12838. 288p. 1997. 59.00 (0-8342-0883-0, 20883) Aspen Pub.

***Managed Care Contracting: A Practical Guide for Health Care Executives.** Thomas M. Reardon. LC 98-43360. 1999. 45.95 (0-7879-4581-1) Jossey-Bass.

Managed Care Contracting: Advising the Managed Care Organization. Maureen E. Corcoran. (BNA's Health Law & Business Ser.: No. 1700). 1996. 125.00 (1-55871-332-8) BNA.

Managed Care Contracting: Concepts & Applications for the Health Care Executive. Douglas Conrad et al. LC 96-3242. (Management Ser.). 146p. 1996. 20.00 (1-56793-042-5, 0979) Health Admin Pr.

***Managed Care Contracting: Successful Negotiation Strategies.** Reed Tinsley. LC 99-40899. (Illus.). 150p. 1999. 45.00 (1-57947-005-X) AMA.

***Managed Care Contracting & Capitation Strategies.** Ed. by AIS Editorial Staff. 37p. 1998. spiral bd. 9.00 (0-929156-40-4) Atlantic Info Services Inc.

Managed Care Contracting Handbook: Planning & Negotiating the Managed Care Relationship. Maria Todd. 240p. 1996. per. 65.00 (0-7863-0999-7, Irwn McGrw-H) McGrw-H Hghr Educ.

Managed Care Contracting Manual. 1994. 275.00 (0-937925-68-3, MCC) Capitol Publns.

Managed Care Contracts Manual. Robert W. McAdams, Jr. et al. LC 95-47265. 492p. Date not set. ring bd. 269.00 (0-8342-0813-X) Aspen Pub.

Managed Care Coordinator. (Career Examination Ser.: C-3686). pap. 34.95 (0-8373-3686-4) Nat Learn.

Managed Care Course: The Easy Way to Learn What You Can't Afford Not to Know. Alice Jane Lippner. (Illus.). 304p. 1997. pap. 65.00 (0-9662096-0-5) Infobriefings.

Managed Care CPT Guidebook. Ed. by Michael Grambo. 150p. (C). Date not set. 395.00 (1-56329-325-0) St Anthony Pub.

Managed Care Curriculum for Baccalaureate Nursing Programs. Ed. by Sylvia E. Hart. 42p. (Orig.). 1995. pap. text 25.95 (1-55810-118-7, MCC-1) Am Nurses Pub.

Managed Care Desk Reference, 1996-1997. 2nd ed. Sarah E. Hutchinson & Glen Coulthard. 1996. text 79.00 (0-07-413105-2, Irwn McGrw-H) McGrw-H Hghr Educ.

Managed Care Desk Reference, 1997-1998: The Complete Guide to Managed Care Terminology. 3rd rev. ed. Marianne Fazen. 360p. (Orig.). 1997. pap. 65.00 (0-614-29573-4) HCS Pubns.

Managed Care Desk Reference, 1994: The Complete Guide to Terminology & Resources. Marianne F. Fazen. LC 94-172104. 352p. (Orig.). 1994. pap. 65.00 (0-9639835-0-4) HCS Pubns.

Managed Care Desk Reference, 1996-1997: The Complete Guide to Terminology & Resources. 2nd rev. ed. Marianne F. Fazen. Ed. by Jay Lechtman. 200p. (C). Date not set. 79.00 (1-56329-322-6) St Anthony Pub.

***Managed Care Essentials: A Book of Readings.** Health Administration Press Staff. LC 99-43249. 1999. pap. 42.00 (1-56793-112-X) Health Admin Pr.

Managed Care Ethics: Essays on the Impact of Managed Care on Traditional Medical Ethics. John LaPuma. LC 97-41350. (Hatherleigh CME Book Ser.). 224p. 1998. pap. 39.95 (1-57826-012-4, Pub. by Hatherleigh) Norton.

***Managed Care Facts, Trends & Data, 1999-2000.** 4th rev. ed. Ed. by Phoebe Eliopoulos. 305p. 1999. pap. 275.00 (0-929156-65-X) Atlantic Info Services Inc.

Managed Care 1500, 1996-97 Edition: A Complete Guide to the Most Influential Managed Care Leaders & Organizations. Ed. by Richard Sorian. 200p. (Orig.). 1996. pap. 195.00 (1-881393-65-8) Faulkner & Gray.

Managed Care Handbook: How to Prepare Your Medical Practice for the Managed Care Revolution. 2nd ed. James R. Lyle & Hoyt W. Torras. Ed. by Kathryn Swanson & Maureen Lynch. LC 96-21217. 428p. (Orig.). 1996. pap. 49.95 (1-57066-055-7, ME074) Practice Mgmt Info.

Managed Care in a Time of Transition Proceedings. 1998. pap. 35.00 (0-938959-56-5) Soc Actuaries.

***Managed Care in American Indian & Alaska Native Communities** Mim Dixon. LC 98-74063. ix, 195 p. 1998. write for info. (0-87553-238-1) Am Pub Health.

Managed Care in Cincinnati: Implications for Health Care Reform. 60p. 1994. 95.00 (1-55871-306-9) BNA PLUS.

Managed Care in Dentistry. Bryan Quattlebaum. LC 94-23729. 1994. 44.95 (0-87814-432-3) PennWell Bks.

Managed Care in Human Services. Stephen P. Wernet. LC 99-19943. 240p. 1999. pap. text 39.95 (0-925065-30-7) Lyceum IL.

Managed Care in Medicaid: Lessons for Policy & Program Design. Robert E. Hurley et al. LC 92-48437. 215p. 1993. pap. text 20.00 (0-910701-95-4, 0930) Health Admin Pr.

Managed Care in the Inner Cities: Programs & Strategies for Providers, Plans & Communities. Dennis P. Andrulis. LC 98-56051. 1999. 41.95 (0-7879-4623-0) Jossey-Bass.

Managed Care Law Manual. Aspen Health Law Center Staff. Ed. by Cynthia Conner. LC 93-44768. 1996. ring bd. 279.00 (0-8342-0523-8) Aspen Pub.

Managed Care Law Manual. Aspen Health Law Center Staff. 1996. disk 323.00 (0-8342-0848-2) Aspen Pub.

Managed Care Law Manual. Aspen Health Law Center Staff et al. 1996. 279.00 (0-8342-0541-6) Aspen Pub.

Managed Care Legal Issues: A Practical Guide for Health Care Decision-Makers. Bruce A. Johnson & Gerald A. Niederman. LC 97-185721. 260p. (Orig.). 1996. pap. 25.00 (1-56829-076-4, 4906) Med Group Mgmt.

Managed Care Liability: Examining Risks & Responsibilities in a Changing Health Care System. Ed. by David L. Leitner. LC 96-80429. 488p. 1997. pap. 74.95 (1-57073-393-7) Amer Bar Assn.

Managed Care Library on CD-ROM. Aspen Health Law Center Staff & Peter R. Kongstvedt. 1997. 199.00 (0-8342-1063-0) Aspen Pub.

Managed Care Made Easy: Survival of the HMO Era. Vikram Khanna. LC 97-28567. 256p. 1997. pap. text 14.95 (1-882606-26-4) Peoples Med Soc.

Managed Care Made Simple. Robert A. Baldor. LC 95-9515. 1995. pap. 21.95 (0-86542-474-8) Blackwell Sci.

***Managed Care Made Simple.** 2nd ed. Robert A. Baldor. LC 97-43321. (Illus.). 1998. pap. 23.95 (0-632-04378-4) Blackwell Sci.

Managed Care Manual. Becker. LC 99-182082. 1998. pap. text 39.95 (0-323-00077-0) Mosby Inc.

Managed Care Manual. Evelyn Eskin et al. Ed. by David B. Wash. (Illus.). xii, 252p. (Orig.). 1996. spiral bd. 54.95 (1-890045-00-4) T L C Med Pub.

Managed Care Manual: Medicaid & State Health Reform. Larry S. Gage & H. E. Von Oehsen. (Health Law Ser.). 1995. pap. write for info. (0-614-06270-5) West Group.

Managed Care Manual: Medicaid & State Health Reform. Larry S. Gage & William H. Von Oehsen. LC 95-214970. (Health Law Ser.). 1995. write for info. (0-87632-294-1) West Group.

Managed Care Manual: Medicaid, Medicare & State Health Reform. Larry S. Gage & William H. Von Oehsen. LC 97-169042. (Health Law Ser.). 1996. write for info. (0-8366-1071-7) West Group.

Managed Care Monograph. National Hospice Organization, Commercial Reimburs. 37p. 1993. 10.50 (0-931207-21-5) Natl Hospice.

Managed Care on Trial: Recapturing Trust, Integrity, & Accountability in Healthcare. Dennis Robbins. LC 98-15938. (Illus.). 225p. 1998. 40.00 (0-07-053099-8) McGraw.

Managed Care Operational Strategies: A Medical Office Survival Guide. Thomas Prince & Edward Mayberry. LC 97-204049. 500p. (C). 1997. 169.00 (1-56329-404-4) St Anthony Pub.

Managed Care Organizations: Practical Implications for Medical Practices & other Providers. Colodia Owens. 185p. 1996. pap. text 44.95 (1-57066-094-8) Practice Mgmt Info.

Managed Care, Outcomes, & Quality: A Practical Guide. Steven Isenberg. LC 97-17252. (Illus.). 352p. 1997. pap. 59.00 (0-86577-687-3) Thieme Med Pubs.

Managed Care, Outcomes, & Quality: A Practical Guide. Steven F. Isenberg. LC 97-17252. 1997. write for info. (3-13-109941-0) Thieme Med Pubs.

Managed Care Pharmacy: Principles & Practice. Ed. by Albert I. Wertheimer & Robert Navarro. LC 98-33388. (Illus.). 412p. 1999. pap. text 49.95 (0-7890-0639-1) Haworth Pr.

***Managed Care Pharmacy Practice.** Robert Navarro. LC 99-29131. 656p. 1999. write for info. (0-8342-1205-6) Aspen Pub.

Managed Care Plan for Medical Assistance, General Assistance Medical Care & Minnesota Care: A Report to the Minnesota Legislature. (Illus.). 95p. (Orig.). (C). 1994. pap. text 35.00 (0-7881-0621-X) DIANE Pub.

Managed Care Primer, Monograph 1. (Cardiovascular Specialist's Guide to Managed Care Ser.). (Illus.). 78p. (Orig.). 1993. pap. text. write for info. (1-882764-02-1) Am Coll Cardiology.

***Managed Care Provider's Toolbox.** Margaret D. Bischel. (Illus.). 415p. 1998. ring bd. write for info. (1-893826-04-X) Apollo Managed.

Managed Care Quality: A Practical Guide. Al Assaf & Robyn Assaf. LC 97-35083. 296p. 1997. boxed set 59.95 (1-57444-073-X) St Lucie Pr.

***Managed Care Readiness Assessment Tool for Child & Family Serving Agencies.** Henry Yennie. (Illus.). 60p. 1999. spiral bd. 39.00 (1-878586-30-0, M-3) Open Minds PA.

Managed Care Referral: Development & Management Strategies - How to Develop a Systematic Plan for Building Your Referral Business in Today's Healthcare Environment. John F. O'Malley. LC 96-3675. 288p. 1996. text 45.00 (0-7863-0878-8, Irwn Prfssnl) McGraw-Hill Prof.

Managed Care Register. Contrib. by Russell Perkins. 700p. 1999. pap. 45.00 (1-880874-56-3) Dorland Hlthcare.

Managed Care Resource Guide - Agency Settings. Ed. by Vivian H. Jackson. (Managed Care Resource Guides Ser.). 124p. (Orig.). (C). 1995. 50.00 (0-87101-245-6, 2456) Natl Assn Soc Wkrs.

Managed Care Resource Guide - Private Practice. Ed. by Vivian H. Jackson. LC 96-20270. (Managed Care Resource Guides Ser.). 121p. (Orig.). (C). 1996. 50.00 (0-87101-247-2, 247-2) Natl Assn Soc Wkrs.

Managed Care Risk: Reducing Risk While Increasing Patient Satisfaction. James W. Saxton & Thomas L. Leaman. LC 98-9985. 224p. 1998. 49.00 (0-8342-1023-1, 10231) Aspen Pub.

***Managed Care Services: Policy, Programs & Research.** Nancy W. Veeder et al. (Illus.). 304p. (C). 2000. text 49.00 (0-19-513429-X) OUP.

***Managed Care Services: Policy, Programs, & Research.** Nancy W. Veeder et al. (Illus.). 304p. (C). 2000. pap. text 29.95 (0-19-513430-3) OUP.

Managed Care Strategies: A Physician Practice Desk Reference. George B. Moseley & George B. Moseley, III. LC 98-32278. 609p. 1999. 79.00 (0-8342-0735-4, 07354) Aspen Pub.

Managed Care Strategies: A Strategy Guide for Healthcare Organizations. Jeff Rogers. (Illus.). 186p. 1996. wbk. ed. 49.00 (0-923680-08-X, 4203) Amer ComVision Inc.

Managed Care Survival Manual: The Rehabilitation Therapist's Guide to Capitation & Per-Case Payment. Brian Rasmussen. 122p. (Orig.). 1996. pap. 69.95 (1-887759-02-6, P-118) Am Phys Therapy Assn.

***Managed Care Systems & Emerging Infections: Challenges & Opportunities for Strengthening Surveillance.** Institute of Medicine Staff. 128p. 2000. pap. 25.00 (0-309-06828-2) Natl Acad Pr.

***Managed Care Tracking System: State Profiles on Public Sector Managed Behavioral Health Care & Other Reforms.** Ed. by Gail K. Robinson. (Illus.). 280p. 1999. pap. text 45.00 (0-7881-8175-0) DIANE Pub.

***Managed Care Yearbook.** 4th ed. Ed. by Melanie A. Matthews. 478p. 1998. per. 253.50 (1-882364-26-0, Amer Busn Pub) Hlth Res Pub.

Managed Casualty: The Japanese-American Family in World War II. Leonard Broom & John Kitsuse. LC 57-9006. (University of California Publications in Social Welfare: Vol. 6). 232p. reprint ed. pap. 72.00 (0-608-13941-6, 202139400022) Bks Demand.

Managed Community Long-Term Care in Texas: Planning for the 21st Century. Jacqueline L. Angel. LC 97-73906. (Policy Research Project Report Ser.). 163p. 1997. pap. 16.00 (0-89940-732-3) LBJ Sch Pub Aff.

Managed Competition: A Health Care System for Pennsylvania. 120p. (Orig.). (C). 1993. pap. text 35.00 (0-7881-0026-2) DIANE Pub.

Managed Competition & Its Potential to Reduce Health Spending. (Illus.). 43p. (C). 1993. pap. text 25.00 (1-56806-421-7) DIANE Pub.

Managed Competition & Its Potential to Reduce Health Spending. 1995. lib. bdg. 250.95 (0-8490-7588-2) Gordon Pr.

Managed Competition & Pharmaceutical Care: A Challenge for the Profession. Ed. by Dev S. Pathak & Alan Escovitz. LC 96-10194. (Journal of Research in Pharmaceutical Economics: Vol. 7, Nos. 1/2). 169p. (C). 1996. 49.95 (1-56024-821-1, Pharmctl Prods) Haworth Pr.

Managed Competition & Pharmaceutical Care: A Challenge for the Profession. Ed. by Dev S. Pathak & Alan Escovitz. LC 96-10194. (Journal of Research in Pharmaceutical Economics: Vol. 7, Nos. 1/2). 169p. (C). 1997. pap. 19.95 (0-7890-0211-6, Pharmctl Prods) Haworth Pr.

Managed Dental Care: A Guide to Dental HMOs. Donald S. Mayes. Ed. by Mary Brennan. LC 93-78068. 248p. (Orig.). 1993. pap. 40.00 (0-89154-464-X) Intl Found Employ.

***Managed Dying: HMO Survival Guide.** Barbara Johanna Janesick & Karon L. Goldsmith. LC 00-190657. 164p. 2000. 25.00 (0-7388-1910-7); pap. 18.00 (0-7388-1911-5) Xlibris Corp.

Managed Economy. Michael D. Reagan. LC 81-13262. 288p. 1982. reprint ed. lib. bdg. 65.00 (0-313-23154-0, REME, Greenwood Pr) Greenwood.

Managed Economy: Essays in British Economic Policy & Performance Since 1929. Charles H. Feinstein. 1983. text 45.00 (0-19-828289-3) OUP.

Managed Economy: Essays in British Economic Policy & Performance Since 1929. Charles H. Feinstein. (Illus.). 292p. 1983. pap. text 19.95 (0-19-828290-7) OUP.

Managed Futures: Performance, Evaluation & Analysis of Commodity Funds, Pools & Accounts. Ed. by Carl C. Peters. 400p. (Orig.). 1992. text 65.00 (1-55738-291-3, Irwn Prfssnl) McGraw-Hill Prof.

Managed Futures in the Institutional Portfolio. Charles B. Epstein. LC 91-33347. (Finance Editions Ser.). 336p. 1992. 59.50 (0-471-52983-4) Wiley.

Managed Grasslands: Analytical Studies. Ed. by R. W. Snaydon. (Ecosystems of the World Ser.: No. 17B). 286p. 1987. 273.00 (0-444-42565-9) Elsevier.

Managed Grasslands: Regional Studies. Ed. by Alicia I. Breymeyer. (Ecosystems of the World Ser.: No. 17A). xii,388p. 1991. 262.50 (0-444-42998-0) Elsevier.

Managed Health Care: A Teaching Syllabus. Compiled by SFTM Task Force on Managed Health Care Staff. 112p. 1990. 12.00 (0-942295-19-6, 57) Soc Tchrs Fam Med.

Managed Health Care: Effect on Employers' Costs Difficult to Measure. (Illus.). 43p. (Orig.). (C). 1994. pap. text 25.00 (0-7881-0706-2) DIANE Pub.

Managed Health Care - Problems & Promises: Summary from 21st NCSL's Annual Meeting, July 1995. 12p. 1995. 15.00 (1-55516-398-X, 7302-2012) Natl Conf State Legis.

Managed Health Care Dictionary. 2nd ed. Richard Rognehaugh. LC 98-3103. 240p. 1998. 19.95 (0-8342-1144-0, 11440) Aspen Pub.

Managed Health Care Guide for Caseworkers & Foster Parents. Ellen S. Battistelli. LC 97-19976. 1997. pap. 9.95 (0-87868-682-7, CWLA Pr) Child Welfare.

Managed Health Care Handbook. 3rd ed. Kongstvedt. 1997. 115.50 (0-7616-1753-1) Morgan Kaufmann.

Managed Health Care Handbook. 3rd ed. Peter R. Kongstvedt. LC 96-13500. 750p. 1996. 99.00 (0-8342-0733-8, 20733) Aspen Pub.

Managed Health Care in the Lab: Reengineering, Leadership & Best Value. Paul Bozzo. LC 98-21036. 208p. 1998. text 75.00 (0-397-58773-2) Lppncott W & W.

***Managed Health Care Medicine Handbook.** 4th ed. Kongstvedt. 2000. 110.00 (0-8342-1726-0) Aspen Pub.

Managed Health Care, 1989. 320p. 1989. 17.50 (0-317-99784-X, A4-4272) PLI.

***Managed Health Care Simplified: A Glossary of Terms.** Austrin. 176p. (C). 2000. text 17.95 (0-7668-2050-5) Delmar.

***Managed Health Care Simplified: A Glossary of Terms.** Michael S. Austrin. LC 99-56122. (Illus.). 1999. write for info. (0-7668-2078-5) Delmar.

Managed Healthcare Fellowship Leading Integration Forward: What Is Pharmacy's Role? 24p. (Orig.). 1996. pap. write for info. (1-884033-13-X) Bimark.

Managed Healthcare U. S. Evidence: U. S. Evidence & Lessons for the National Health Service. Robinson. LC 97-13906. (State of Health Ser.). 206p. 1997. 105.00 (0-335-19949-6); pap. 29.95 (0-335-19948-8) OpUniv Pr.

Managed Heart: Commercialization of Human Feeling. Arlie Russell Hochschild. LC 83-1399. 307p. (C). 1983. pap. 16.95 (0-520-05454-7, Pub. by U CA Pr) Cal Prin Full Svc.

Managed Heart: Commercialization of Human Feeling. Arlie Russell Hochschild. LC 83-1399. 307p. reprint ed. pap. 95.20 (0-7837-4825-6, 204447200003) Bks Demand.

***Managed Home Care Market Report.** Loretta De Rosa. 18p. 1998. spiral bd. 47.00 (0-929156-52-8) Atlantic Info Services Inc.

***Managed Home Healthcare: A Guide to Integrating Home Care Services into Managed Care.** Carol Schaffer. 140p. 1999. pap. 93.00 (0-929156-61-7) Atlantic Info Services Inc.

***Managed in Hong Kong: Adaptive Systems, Entrepreneurship & Human Resources.** Ed. by Chris Rowley & Robert Fitzgerald. LC 99-57241. (Studies in

M

Asia Pacific Business Ser.: Vol. 8). (Illus.). 144p. 2000. 57.50 (*0-7146-5026-9*, Pub. by F Cass Pubs); pap. 24.50 (*0-7146-8082-6*, Pub. by F Cass Pubs) Intl Spec Bk.

***Managed Medicare & Medicaid Factbook: 1999.** 3rd rev. ed. 563p. 1999. pap. 292.00 (*0-929156-60-9*) Atlantic Info Services Inc.

Managed Mental Health Care. Ed. by William Goldman & Saul Feldman. LC 87-646993. (New Directions for Mental Health Services Ser.: No. MHS 59). 111p. (Orig.). 1993. pap. 25.00 (*1-55542-676-X*) Jossey-Bass.

Managed Mental Health Care: A Guide for Practitioners, Employers, & Hospital Administrators. Thomas R. Giles. LC 92-49082. (Practitioner Guidebook Ser.). 192p. (C). 1993. 48.00 (*0-205-14838-7*, Longwood Div) Allyn.

Managed Mental Health Care: Major Diagnostic & Treatment Approaches Handbook for Providers. Ed. by S. Richard Sauber. LC 97-1084. (Mental Health Practice under Managed Care Ser.: No. 8). 352p. 1997. pap. 37.95 (*0-87630-812-4*) Brunner-Mazel.

Managed Mental Health Care: The Bradman Approach. Leo H. Bradman. 177p. 1992. pap. write for info. (*1-883945-01-1*) UniPsych Pr.

Managed Mental Health Care in the Public Sector: A Survival Manual. Ed. by Kenneth Minkoff & David Pollack. (Chronic Mental Illness Ser.: Vol. 4). 410p. 1997. text 44.00 (*90-5702-536-1*, Harwood Acad Pubs) Gordon & Breach.

Managed Mental Health Care in the Public Sector: A Survival Manual, Vol. 4. Ed. by Kenneth Minkoff & David Pollack. LC 98-168725. 410p. 1997. pap. text 23.00 (*90-5702-537-X*, Harwood Acad Pubs) Gordon & Breach.

Managed Mental Health Services. Saul Feldman. (Illus.). 326p. 1992. pap. 39.95 (*0-398-06115-7*) C C Thomas.

Managed Mental Health Services. Saul Feldman. (Illus.). 326p. (C). 1992. text 54.95 (*0-398-05759-1*) C C Thomas.

Managed Mental Healthcare Video Resource Manual. 86p. 1991. student ed. 30.00 (*1-883066-03-4*); VHS 195.00 (*1-883066-02-6*) Natl Comm Mental.

Managed Money at the Crossroads: The European Experience. Melchior Palyi. LC 57-11375. 206p. reprint ed. pap. 63.90 (*0-608-15040-1*, 202594500047) Bks Demand.

Managed Mosaic: Ancient Maya Agriculture & Resource Use. Ed. by Scott L. Fedick. (Illus.). 360p. 1996. text 60.00 (*0-87480-519-8*) U of Utah Pr.

***Managed Pharmacy Benefit Market.** Michael Deskin. 22p. 1998. spiral bd. 47.00 (*0-929156-49-8*) Atlantic Info Services Inc.

Managed Physical/Occupational Therapy & Rehabilitation Care Manual. Margaret D. Bischel. (Illus.). 275p. 1996. ring bd. 225.00 (*1-893826-01-5*) Apollo Managed.

Managed Professionals: Unionized Faculty & Restructuring Academic Labor. Gary Rhoades. LC 97-22368. (SUNY Series, Frontiers in Education). 320p. (C). 1998. text 73.50 (*0-7914-3715-9*); pap. text 24.95 (*0-7914-3716-7*) State U NY Pr.

Managed Service Restructuring in Health Care: A Strategic Approach in a Competitive Environment. Robert L. Goldman & Sanjib K. Mukherjee. LC 93-43876. 105p. 1995. lib. bdg. 39.95 (*1-56024-896-3*) Haworth Pr.

Managed Trade: The Case Against Import Targets. Douglas A. Irwin. LC 94-19846. 100p. 1994. 29.95 (*0-8447-3878-6*) Am Enterprise.

Managed Trade: The Case Against Import Targets. Douglas A. Irwin. LC 94-19846. 100p. 1995. pap. 14.95 (*0-8447-3879-4*) Am Enterprise.

Managed Trade: The New Competition Between Nations. Raymond J. Waldmann. LC 86-17231. 224p. 1986. 34.95 (*0-88730-143-6*, HarpBusn) HarpInfo.

Managed Trade & Economic Sovereignty. Robert Kuttner. LC 89-85885. 50p. 1989. 12.00 (*0-944826-17-2*) Economic Policy Inst.

Managed Trading: The Myths & Truths. Jack D. Schwager. LC 96-10256. 318p. 1996. 55.00 (*0-471-02057-5*) Wiley.

Managed Vision Benefits. 2nd ed. Jesse Rosenthal & Mort Soroka. LC 98-70020. 198p. 1998. pap. 40.00 (*0-89154-524-7*) Intl Found Employ.

***Managed Workers' Compensation Market.** Patrick Gallagher & Christine Morgan. 18p. 1998. spiral bd. 47.00 (*0-929156-51-X*) Atlantic Info Services Inc.

Management. (Quick Study Academic Ser.). 4p. pap. 3.95 (*1-57222-230-1*) Barcharts.

Management. (Best Practices Ser.: No. 1768). 1993. 175.00 (*0-614-12668-1*) Economist Intell.

Management, 3 vols. (C). 1989. write for info. (*0-395-52922-0*) HM.

Management. Ramon J. Aldag & Timothy M. Stearns. (SWC-Management). (C). 1987. mass mkt. 47.00 (*0-538-07702-6*, G70) S-W Pub.

Management. Harold Babson. (C). 1993. pap. text, student ed. 25.00 (*0-07-006836-4*) McGraw.

***Management.** Christos M. Cotsakos. 2001. write for info. (*0-06-662008-2*, HarpBusn) HarpInfo.

Management. Liz Croft. 390p. 1990. pap. 125.00 (*0-85297-358-6*, Pub. by Chartered Bank) St Mut.

***Management.** Peter F. Drucker. 1999. 20.00 (*0-06-662021-X*) HarpC.

Management. Dunham & Pierce. (C). 1989. pap., student ed. 23.33 (*0-673-39802-1*) Addson-Wesley Educ.

Management. Robert D. Gatewood et al. 288p. (C). 1995. text, student ed. 18.75 (*0-256-18485-2*, Irwn McGrw-H) McGrw-H Hghr Educ.

Management, 5 vols. Griffin. (C). 1995. pap., teacher ed., suppl. ed. 11.96 (*0-395-74870-4*) HM.

Management. Hunt. (C). Date not set. pap., student ed. write for info. (*0-395-41257-9*); text. write for info. (*0-395-35696-2*) HM.

Management. John M. Ivancevich & Peter Lorenzi. 296p. (C). 1993. text, student ed. 24.70 (*0-256-14473-7*, Irwn McGrw-H) McGrw-H Hghr Educ.

Management. Kinicki. 2000. 52.00 (*0-07-230181-3*) McGraw.

Management, 6 vols. Kreitner. (C). Date not set. pap., teacher ed., suppl. ed. 11.96 (*0-395-72120-2*) HM.

Management, 6 vols. Kreitner. (C). 1994. pap., teacher ed., suppl. ed. 11.96 (*0-395-72121-0*) HM.

Management, 6 vols. Kreitner. (C). 1995. pap., student ed. write for info. (*0-395-77078-5*) HM.

Management, 7 vols. Kreitner. (C). 1997. pap. 11.96 (*0-395-87191-3*) HM.

Management. Patrick Montana. (Barron's EZ-101 Study Keys Ser.). 144p. 1991. pap. 5.95 (*0-8120-4606-4*) Barron.

***Management.** Pierce/University of Minnesota Staff. 2001. pap. 60.00 (*0-324-04958-7*) Thomson Learn.

Management. Peter P. Schoderbek et al. 650p. (C). 1988. 16.00 (*0-318-62947-X*) Harcourt Coll Pubs.

Management. Ian Whyte & John Plenderleith. 321p. 1990. pap. 125.00 (*0-85297-344-6*, Pub. by Chartered Bank) St Mut.

Management. Williams. (GC - Principles of Management Ser.). 1999. mass mkt., student ed. 14.00 (*0-538-86164-9*) S-W Pub.

Management. rev. ed. Albanese et al. 1997. 74.95 (*0-87393-330-3*) Dame Pubns.

Management. 2nd ed. Kathryn M. Bartol & David C. Martin. LC 93-26387. (Series in Management). (C). 1993. text 71.00 (*0-07-005078-3*) McGraw.

Management. 2nd ed. Kathryn M. Bartol & David C. Martin. (C). 1993. pap. text, student ed. 22.50 (*0-07-005116-X*) McGraw.

Management. 2nd ed. Louis E. Boone et al. Ed. by Paul S. Donnelly. (C). 1984. text. write for info. (*0-318-57307-5*) Random.

Management. 2nd ed. Richard M. Hodgetts. 624p. (C). 1988. 3.30 (*0-15-554653-8*) Harcourt Coll Pubs.

Management. 2nd ed. Ivancevich. 1997. pap., student ed. 27.50 (*0-07-292408-X*) McGraw.

Management. 2nd ed. Patrick Montana & Bruce Charnov. LC 92-27960. (Barron's Business Review Ser.). 492p. 1993. pap. 13.95 (*0-8120-1549-5*) Barron.

***Management** 2nd ed. Bucklin Smith. 382p. 2000. 29.95 (*0-471-38062-8*) Wiley.

Management, 3 vols. 3rd ed. (C). 1989. pap. text 5.96 (*0-395-52342-7*) HM.

Management, 3 vols. 3rd ed. (C). 1990. 170.76 (*0-395-52890-9*) HM.

Management, 3 vols. 3rd ed. (C). 1990. VHS. write for info. (*0-395-52891-7*) HM.

Management, 3 vols. 3rd ed. (C). 1990. pap. text, teacher ed. 2.76 (*0-395-52935-2*) HM.

Management. 3rd ed. Kathryn M. Bartol & David C. Martin. LC 96-46735. 848p. (C). 1997. 81.88 (*0-07-005722-2*) McGraw.

Management. 3rd ed. Thomas S. Bateman & Scott A. Snell. 264p. (C). 1995. text, student ed. 24.37 (*0-256-19717-2*, Irwn McGrw-H) McGrw-H Hghr Educ.

Management. 3rd ed. Roger Bennett. 404p. 1997. pap. 47.50 (*0-7121-1068-2*, Pub. by Pitman Pub) Trans-Atl Phila.

Management, 3vols. 3rd ed. Griffin. (C). 1989. pap. text 5.56 (*0-395-52346-X*); pap. text 3.96 (*0-395-52892-5*) HM.

Management, 3 vols. 3rd ed. Griffin. (C). 1990. pap. text 3.96 (*0-395-52345-1*); pap. text 4.36 (*0-395-52340-0*) HM.

Management. 3rd ed. Richard M. Hodgetts & Donald F. Kuratko. 650p. (C). 1990. text 91.00 (*0-15-554631-7*) Dryden Pr.

Management. 3rd ed. Koch. (C). 1995. pap. text, teacher ed. 77.50 (*0-03-011018-1*) Harcourt.

Management. 3rd ed. Maidment. 1994. 12.74 (*1-56134-281-5*) McGraw.

***Management.** 3rd ed. Patrick J. Montana & Bruce H. Charnov. LC 99-16327. (Business Review Ser.). 2000. 14.95 (*0-7641-1276-7*) Barron.

Management. 4th ed. Axelrod et al. (C). 1986. student ed. write for info. (*0-318-60299-7*) Addison-Wesley.

Management. 4th ed. Bateman-Snell. 720p. 1998. 81.88 (*0-256-26142-3*) McGraw.

Management. 4th ed. Louis E. Boone & David L. Kurtz. (C). 1992. pap. text, student ed. 22.50 (*0-07-006577-2*) McGraw.

Management. 4th ed. Richard L. Daft. (C). 1996. text 89.00 (*0-03-017989-0*, Pub. by Harcourt Coll Pubs) Harcourt.

Management. 4th ed. Richard L. Daft. (C). 1996. pap. text, teacher ed. 49.50 (*0-03-017994-7*); pap. text, teacher ed. 82.00 (*0-03-017999-8*, Pub. by Harcourt Coll Pubs); audio compact disk 246.00 (*0-03-017992-0*, Pub. by Harcourt Coll Pubs) Harcourt.

Management. 4th ed. Don Hellriegel & John W. Slocum. LC 85-1113. (Business Ser.). (C). 1986. text. write for info. (*0-201-11542-5*); student ed. write for info. (*0-318-60298-9*); 80.00 (*0-201-11546-8*) Addison-Wesley.

Management. 4th ed. Robert Kreitner. 750p. 1988. teacher ed. write for info. (*0-318-63317-5*); write for info. (*0-318-63316-7*); trans. write for info. (*0-318-63318-3*) HM.

Management. 5th ed. Armstrong. 144p. (C). 1997. pap. text 20.63 (*0-673-98021-9*) Addison-Wesley Educ.

Management. 5th ed. Richard L. Daft. (C). 1999. pap. text, student ed. Price not set. (*0-03-026511-8*) Harcourt Coll Pubs.

***Management.** 5th ed. Richard L. Daft. LC 99-12430. (Illus.). 2000. text. write for info. (*0-03-025967-3*) Harcourt Coll Pubs.

Management, 5 vols. 5th ed. Griffin. (C). 1995. text 75.96 (*0-395-73110-0*) HM.

Management, 5 vols. 5th ed. Griffin. (C). 1995. pap. text, student ed. 20.36 (*0-395-74868-2*) HM.

Management. 5th ed. Don Hellriegel. (Business Ser.). (Illus.). 864p. (C). 1989. text 38.36 (*0-201-17890-7*) Addison-Wesley.

Management, 5 vols. 5th ed. Kreitner. (C). 1992. pap. text, teacher ed., suppl. ed. 5.56 (*0-395-59251-8*) HM.

Management. 5th ed. Makay. (C). Date not set. write for info. (*0-395-77771-2*) HM.

Management. 5th ed. Leslie W. Rue & Betsy C. Byars. (C). 1989. student ed. 18.95 (*0-256-07568-9*, Irwn McGrw-H) McGrw-H Hghr Educ.

Management. 5th ed. Leslie W. Rue & Lloyd L. Byars. (C). 1989. text 54.95 (*0-256-06896-8*, Irwn McGrw-H) McGrw-H Hghr Educ.

Management, 5 vols. 5th annot. ed. Ricky W. Griffin. (C). 1995. text, teacher ed. 56.76 (*0-395-74869-0*) HM.

Management. 6th ed. (C). 1998. write for info. (*0-13-921669-3*, Macmillan Coll) P-H.

Management. 6th ed. David R. Griffin. LC 98-72034. 1998. text 64.47 (*0-395-89351-8*) HM.

Management, 6 vols. 6th ed. Kreitner. (C). 1994. pap. text, student ed. 20.76 (*0-395-72122-9*) HM.

Management, 6 vols. 6th ed. Robert Kreitner. 768p. (C). 1995. text 72.36 (*0-395-71046-4*) HM.

Management. 6th ed. Stephen P. Robbins & Mary K. Coulter. LC 98-10502. 645p. 1998. text 80.00 (*0-13-921503-4*) P-H.

Management. 6th ed. John J. Schermerhorn. LC 98-24485. 624p. 1998. 97.95 incl. cd-rom (*0-471-24113-X*) Wiley.

Management. 7th ed. Lloyd L. Byars & Leslie W. Rue. 312p. (C). 1995. text, student ed. 23.12 (*0-256-14483-4*, Irwn McGrw-H) McGrw-H Hghr Educ.

Management. 7th ed. Hellriegel. (GC - Principles of Management Ser.). (C). 1995. pap., student ed. 20.95 (*0-538-84079-X*) S-W Pub.

Management. 8th ed. Hellreigel. (GC - Principles of Management Ser.). 1998. pap., student ed. 15.25 (*0-538-87683-2*) S-W Pub.

Management. 8th ed. Hellreigel & Slocum. LC 98-23041. (GC - Principles of Management Ser.). 1998. pap. 95.95 (*0-538-87672-7*) S-W Pub.

***Management.** 9th ed. Hellriegal. (SWC-General Business Ser.). 2001. pap. 63.00 (*0-324-05558-7*); pap., student ed. 15.00 (*0-324-05559-5*) Sth-Wstrn College.

Management. 9th ed. Rue. LC 99-26770. 496p. 1999. pap. 52.50 (*0-07-228885-X*) McGraw.

Management see Radio Book

Management: A Basic Handbook. W. Coventry & Irving Burstinger. 1977. 12.95 (*0-13-549188-6*, Spectrum IN) Macmillan Gen Ref.

Management: A Biblical Approach. Myron D. Rush. 240p. 1983. pap. 10.99 (*0-88207-607-8*, 6-2607, Victor Bks) Chariot Victor.

Management: A Global Perspective. 10th ed. Heinz Wilhrich et al. LC 92-14916. (McGraw-Hill Series in Management). 784p. (C). 1993. 82.81 (*0-07-069170-3*) McGraw.

Management: A Sociological Introduction. Keith Grint. LC 95-30834. 275p. (C). 1995. write for info. (*0-7456-1148-6*, Pub. by Polity Pr); pap. text 35.95 (*0-7456-1149-4*, Pub. by Polity Pr) Blackwell Pubs.

Management: A Study of Industrial Organization. John H. Lee, Jr. Ed. by Alfred D. Chandler. LC 79-7550. (History of Management Thought & Practice Ser.). 1980. reprint ed. lib. bdg. 15.95 (*0-405-12334-5*) Ayer.

Management: A Total Quality Perspective. Gregory M. Bounds et al. LC 94-33898. (C). 1994. mass mkt. 87.95 (*0-538-84344-6*) S-W Pub.

Management: Account (Accounting) abr. ed. Intro. by Luanna C. Blagrove. (AMERCE Management Ser.). (Illus.). 250p. 1988. 24.95 (*0-939776-04-9*) Blagrove Pubns.

Management: An International Approach. Jennifer George. (C). 1996. pap. text. write for info. (*0-201-82135-4*) Addison-Wesley.

Management: An International Perspective. R. Hal Mason & Robert Spich. 256p. (C). 1987. pap. text 15.95 (*0-256-05631-5*, Irwn McGrw-H) McGrw-H Hghr Educ.

Management: An Introduction. David Boddy & Rob Paton. LC 97-32792. 1998. 39.99 (*0-13-257098-X*) P-H.

Management: Applications & Skill Development. Robert N. Lussier. LC 96-15162. (GC - Principles of Management Ser.). 1996. mass mkt. 84.95 (*0-538-85126-0*) S-W Pub.

Management: Building Competitive Advantage. 3rd ed. Thomas S. Bateman & Scott A. Snell. 704p. (C). 1995. text 68.95 (*0-256-14053-7*, Irwn Prfssnl) McGraw-Hill Prof.

Management: Building Competitive Advantage. 4th ed. Thomas S. Bateman & Scott Snell. LC 98-8256. 1998. 96.59 (*0-07-304025-8*) McGraw.

Management: Case Approach. Lawrence R. Jauch. (C). 1993. pap. text, teacher ed. 10.75 (*0-03-098025-9*) Harcourt Coll Pubs.

Management: Challenges in the 21st Century. Pamela S. Lewis et al. LC 94-22667. (SWC-General Business). 724p. (C). 1994. mass mkt. 58.25 (*0-314-04568-6*) West Pub.

Management: Challenges in the 21st Century. 3rd ed. Lewis & Goodman. (SWC-Management Ser.). 2000. pap. 46.75 (*0-324-00993-3*); pap., student ed. 16.00 (*0-324-01200-4*) Thomson Learn.

Management: Challenges in 21st Century. 2nd ed. Lewis & Goodman. LC 97-20809. (SWC-Management Ser.). 1997. pap. 76.95 (*0-538-87899-1*) S-W Pub.

Management: Competencies & Incompetencies. William P. Anthony. LC 79-25171. 604p. (C). 1981. text. write for info. (*0-201-00085-7*) Addison-Wesley.

Management: Comprehension, Analysis & Application. Robert D. Gatewood et al. LC 94-31969. 800p. (C). 1995. text 68.95 (*0-256-13784-6*, Irwn Prfssnl) McGraw-Hill Prof.

Management: Concepts & Applications. Burt K. Scanlan. 480p. (C). 1990. pap. text 98.00 (*0-536-57742-0*) Pearson Custom.

Management: Concepts & Practice. Ed. by Fred R. Brown. LC 77-84858. 1977. 18.95 (*0-912338-15-6*); fiche 7.95 (*0-912338-16-4*) Lomond.

Management: Concepts & Practices. 2nd ed. Tim Hannagan. 640p. 1998. pap. 59.50 (*0-273-63103-9*, Pub. by Pitman Pub) Trans-Atl Phila.

***Management: Concepts, Practices & Skills.** 8th ed. Premeaux Mondy. (SWC-General Business Ser.). 1999. 39.95 (*0-324-03309-5*) Sth-Wstrn College.

Management: Covenants, Contracts. abr. ed. Intro. by Luanna C. Blagrove. (AMERCE Management Ser.). (Illus.). 250p. 1988. 24.95 (*0-939776-02-2*) Blagrove Pubns.

Management: Critical Success Factors. Chung. 784p. 1986. student ed. 18.00 (*0-685-17394-1*, H03262); write for info. (*0-318-61498-7*, H03254) P-H.

Management: Embracing the 21st Century. 3rd ed. Trewatha et al. 1997. 74.95 (*0-87393-310-9*) Dame Pubns.

Management: Embracing the 21st Century (Study Guide) 3rd ed. Trewatha et al. 1997. pap., student ed. 25.95 (*0-87393-311-7*) Dame Pubns.

Management: Expert Approach. 3rd ed. Lawrence R. Jauch. (C). 1993. pap. text, teacher ed., suppl. ed. 10.75 (*0-03-098024-0*) Harcourt Coll Pubs.

Management: Function & Strategy. Thomas P. Bateman & Carl P. Zeithaml. 796p. (C). 1989. text 64.95 (*0-256-05733-8*, Irwn McGrw-H) McGrw-H Hghr Educ.

Management: Function & Strategy. 2nd annot. ed. Thomas S. Bateman & Carl P. Zeithaml. LC 92-22184. 752p. (C). 1992. teacher ed. write for info. (*0-256-11780-2*, Irwn McGrw-H) McGrw-H Hghr Educ.

Management: Ideas & Actions. W. Jack Duncan. LC 98-15512. 288p. (C). 1999. text 65.00 (*0-19-511846-4*); pap. text 39.95 (*0-19-511847-2*) OUP.

Management: Leadership Action. 4th ed. (C). 1997. 177.00 (*0-673-55996-3*) PH School.

Management: Leadership in Action. 5th ed. Daruty. LC 95-8641. Orig. Title: Management: Concepts & Applications. (C). 1996. pap. text, student ed. 27.19 (*0-673-98020-0*) Addson-Wesley Educ.

Management: Leadership in Action. 5th ed. Donald C. Mosley et al. LC 95-8641. Orig. Title: Management: Concepts & Applications. (Illus.). 672p. (C). 1997. text 87.00 (*0-673-99264-0*) Addson-Wesley Educ.

***Management: Leadg People & Org In 21ST Cent: On Location Videos.** 2nd ed. 2000. VHS. write for info. (*0-13-031346-7*) P-H.

***Management: Leading & Organizing in the 21st Century.** Dessler & Starke. 2000. 113.27 (*0-13-016348-1*) Prntice Hall Bks.

***Management: Leading People & Organizations in the 21st Century.** 400p. 2000. write for info. (*0-13-018619-8*); teacher ed. write for info. (*0-13-018618-X*) P-H.

Management: Leading People & Organizations in the 21st Century. Gary Dessler. LC 97-32116. 703p. (C). 1997. 96.00 (*0-13-862970-6*) P-H.

***Management: Leading People & Organizations in the 21st Century.** 2nd ed. 2000. write for info. (*0-13-018362-8*); student ed. write for info. (*0-13-018365-2*) P-H.

***Management: Leading People & Organizations in the 21st Century.** 2nd ed. Gary Dessler. 608p. 2000. 86.67 (*0-13-017780-6*, Prentice Hall) P-H.

Management: Leading People & Organizations in the 21st Century D-CART. Dessler. 1999. 76.00 (*0-13-011086-8*) P-H.

Management: Manage Mensurate. Intro. by Luanna C. Blagrove. (AMERCE Management Ser.). (Illus.). 250p. 1988. 24.95 (*0-939776-05-7*) Blagrove Pubns.

Management: Management Integration Book 2. 368p. (C). 2000. text 46.00 (*0-536-59867-3*) Pearson Custom.

Management: Meeting & Exceeding Customer Expectations. 6th ed. Plunkett. (GC - Principles of Management Ser.). 1997. mass mkt., student ed. 21.95 (*0-538-85659-9*); mass mkt., suppl. ed. 21.95 (*0-538-86311-0*) S-W Pub.

Management: Meeting & Exceeding Customer Expectations. 6th ed. Plunkett. LC 96-37322. (GC - Principles of Management Ser.). (C). 1997. mass mkt. 94.95 (*0-538-84496-5*) S-W Pub.

Management: Meeting & Exceeding Customer Expectations. 7th ed. Attner & Allen. 2001. pap. text 65.25 (*0-324-02725-7*) Thomson Learn.

***Management: Meeting New Challenges.** (C). 1999. pap. text 0.00 (*0-321-04659-5*) Addison-Wesley.

***Management: Meeting New Challenges.** (C). 1999. pap. text. write for info. (*0-321-07599-4*) Addison-Wesley.

***Management: Meeting New Challenges.** 344p. (C). 1999. pap. text. write for info. (*0-321-04657-9*) Addson-Wesley Educ.

***Management: Meeting New Challenges.** (C). 1999. pap. text. write for info. (*0-321-07598-6*) Addson-Wesley Educ.

***Management: Meeting New Challenges.** (C). 2000. pap. text 0.00 (*0-321-04658-7*) HEPC Inc.

***Management: Meeting New Challenges.** (C). 1999. write for info. (*0-13-026180-7*) PH School.

***Management: Meeting New Challenges.** (C). 2000. ring bd. write for info. (*0-13-017288-X*) PH School.

Management: Meeting New Challenges. Ed. by Black. LC 99-26073. 648p. (C). 1999. 96.00 (*0-321-01407-3*, Prentice Hall) P-H.

An Asterisk (*) at the beginning of an entry indicates that the title is appearing for the first time.

Management: Meeting New Challenges. Stewart Black. 656p. (C). 1999. pap. write for info. (*0-321-04655-2*) Addison-Wesley Educ.

Management: Paper Version. Williams. 1999. pap. 43.00 (*0-324-02216-6*) Thomson Learn.

Management: Past & Present: A Casebook on the History of American Business. Alfred D. Chandler et al. 1995. mass mkt. 102.95 (*0-538-85412-X*) S-W Pub.

Management: Principles, Theory & Practice. Francis J. Bridges & Libby L. Roquemore. (Illus.). 480p. (C). 1996. pap. text. write for info. (*0-9623126-4-9*) ESM Bks.

Management: Processes & Paradigms for the Twenty-First Century. Benjamin F. Findley, Jr. LC 98-96300. (Illus.). xv, 212p. 1998. pap. 17.95 (*0-9618129-3-1*) Prof Mgmt Resces.

Management: Quality & Competitiveness. John M. Ivancevich et al. LC 93-30802. 688p. (C). 1993. text 68.95 (*0-256-12453-1*, Irwn McGrw-H) McGrw-H Hghr Educ.

Management: Quality & Competitiveness. 2nd ed. John W. Ivancevich et al. 672p. (C). 1996. text 68.95 (*0-256-18939-0*, Irwn McGrw-H) McGrw-H Hghr Educ.

Management: Responsibility for Performance. Peter Hess & Julie Siciliano. LC 95-16946. (Management Ser.). (C). 1995. pap. text 36.00 (*0-07-028457-1*) McGraw.

Management: Skills & App/Career Handbook/Bu. 7th ed. Rue & Hjorth-Pkg. 1996. 60.00 (*0-256-22694-6*) McGraw.

Management: Skills & Application. 6th ed. Leslie W. Rue & Lloyd L. Byars. 608p. (C). 1991. text 39.95 (*0-256-08702-4*, Irwn McGrw-H) McGrw-H Hghr Educ.

Management: Skills & Application. 8th ed. Leslie W. Rue. LC 96-45341. 576p. (C). 1996. per. 39.95 (*0-256-22737-3*, Irwn McGrw-H) McGrw-H Hghr Educ.

Management: Skills, Functions & Organization Performance. 2nd ed. Anderson. 1988. student ed. 18.00 (*0-205-11435-0*, H1435-0) Allyn.

Management: Skills, Functions & Organization Performance. 2nd ed. Carl R. Anderson. 1988. teacher ed. write for info. (*0-205-11437-7*, H1437-6); write for info. (*0-205-11438-5*, H1438-4); trans. write for info. (*0-205-11439-3*, H1439-2) Allyn.

Management: Strategies for Success in the 21st Century. Raymond C. Shea. (C). 1996. 62.00 (*0-02-409781-0*, Macmillan Coll) P-H.

Management: Student Learning Guide. 4th ed. Leon C. Megginson. (C). 1992. pap. 23.50 (*0-06-500695-X*) Addison-Wesley Educ.

Management: Study Guide. rev. ed. Kirk et al. 1997. pap. 25.95 (*0-87393-425-3*) Dame Pubns.

Management: Tasks, Practices, Responsibilities. Peter F. Drucker. LC 84-48157. 864p. 1993. reprint ed. pap. 20.00 (*0-88730-615-2*, HarpBusn) HarpInfo.

Management: The Competitive Edge. 2nd ed. Edmund R. Gray & Larry R. Smeltzer. 516p. (C). 1996. pap. text, per. 65.95 (*0-7872-2022-1*) Kendall-Hunt.

Management: The Managerial Ethos & the Future of Planet Earth. Thomas Berry. (Teilhard Studies: No. 3). 1980. pap. 3.50 (*0-89012-016-1*) Am Teilhard.

Management: Theory, Process & Practice. 4th ed. Richard M. Hodgetts. 738p. (C). 1988. trans. 22.75 (*0-15-554656-2*) Harcourt Coll Pubs.

Management: Theory, Process & Practice. 5th ed. Richard M. Hodgetts. 780p. (C). 1989. VHS, disk. write for info. (*0-318-67133-6*) Dryden Pr.

Management: Total Quality in a Global Environment. Michael J. Stahl. LC 94-15348. (Illus.). 800p. (C). 1994. 38.95 (*1-55786-610-4*) Blackwell Pubs.

***Management: Update 2001 Edition.** 6th ed. John R. Schermerhorn. 647p. (C). 2000. write for info. incl. cd-rom (*0-471-38755-X*) Wiley.

Management: A Biblical Approach - Christ Life see Administracion: Un Enfoque Biblico - Vida Cristiana

***Management Account: Strategic Approach.** 2nd ed. Morse/Davis/Hartgraves. 1999. pap., student ed. 21.25 (*0-324-00804-X*) Thomson Learn.

Management Accountants: Responding to Change. Donald L. Madden & James R. Holmes. Ed. by Claire Barth. 63p. (Orig.). 1990. pap. 20.00 (*0-86641-185-2*, 90246) Inst Mgmt Account.

Management Accountants' Handbook. 4th ed. Donald E. Keller et al. LC 91-35066. 926p. 1992. 180.00 (*0-471-51408-X*) Wiley.

Management Accounting 366p. (C). 1995. text 45.00 (*0-536-59189-X*) Pearson Custom.

Management Accounting. Peter Atrill & Eddie McLaney. (Illus.). 512p. (C). 1994. pap. 47.95 (*0-631-19538-6*) Blackwell Pubs.

Management Accounting. Raiborn Barfield. (Miscellaneous/Catalogs Ser.). 1993. text, teacher ed. write for info. (*0-314-01273-7*) S-W Pub.

Management Accounting. Leslie Chadwick. Ed. by David Weir. LC 92-23921. (Elements of Business Ser.). (Illus.). 288p. 1993. pap. 64.95 (*0-415-07084-8*) Thomson Learn.

Management Accounting. Leslie Chadwick. Ed. by David Weir. LC 92-23921. (Elements of Business Ser.). (Illus.). 128p. (C). 1993. pap. 26.95 (*0-415-07085-6*, B0106) Thomson Learn.

Management Accounting. Dafashy. 364p. 2000. pap. text 20.50 (*0-536-01630-5*) Pearson Custom.

Management Accounting. Wayne J. Morse et al. (C). 1986. pap. text. write for info. (*0-201-15870-1*) Addison-Wesley.

Management Accounting. David Wright. LC 95-50909. (Modular Texts in Business & Economics Ser.). 1996. pap. write for info. (*0-582-26253-4*, Pub. by Addison-Wesley) Longman.

Management Accounting. 2nd ed. Orig. Title: Cost Accountant. (C). 1989. write for info. (*0-201-15776-4*) Addison-Wesley.

Management Accounting. 2nd ed. Rajiv D. Banker. Ed. by Anthony A. Atkinson. LC 96-34705. 741p. (C). 1996. 93.00 (*0-13-255761-4*) P-H.

Management Accounting. 3rd ed. Hansen. (AB - Accounting Principles Ser.). (C). 1994. pap. text, student ed. 18.00 (*0-538-82960-5*) S-W Pub.

Management Accounting. 3rd ed. Hilton. 1997. text 68.74 (*0-07-031039-4*) McGraw.

Management Accounting. 3rd ed. Wayne J. Morse et al. (Illus.). 896p. (C). 1991. text 61.25 (*0-201-52827-4*) Addison-Wesley.

Management Accounting. 4th ed. Hansen. LC 95-26788. (AQ - Managerial Accounting Ser.). 1996. mass mkt. 71.95 (*0-538-85630-0*); mass mkt., student ed. 20.00 (*0-538-85631-9*) S-W Pub.

Management Accounting. 4th ed. Hansen. (AQ - Managerial Accounting Ser.). 1997. text, student ed. 10.95 (*0-538-86109-6*) S-W Pub.

Management Accounting. 4th ed. Hansen et al. 1996. text 12.50 (*0-538-86110-X*) Sth-Wstrn College.

Management Accounting. 5th ed. Don R. Hansen. (SWC-Accounting). 1999. pap., student ed. 23.25 (*0-324-01230-6*) Thomson Learn.

Management Accounting. 5th ed. Donald B. Hansen. LC 99-14476. (SWC-Accounting). 1999. text 98.95 (*0-324-00226-2*) S-W Pub.

***Management Accounting, Vol. 1.** 2nd ed. Chadwick. (ITBP Textbooks Ser.). 1998. pap. 16.99 (*1-86152-260-6*) Thomson Learn.

Management Accounting, Vols. I & II. Ed. by Richard M. Wilson. LC 97-37086. (International Library of Management). 880p. 1997. text 379.95 (*1-85521-574-8*, Pub. by Ashgate Pub) Ashgate Pub Co.

Management Accounting: A Conceptual Approach. Lloyd R. Amev & Don A. Egginton. LC 73-86099. (Longman Business Ser.). 696p. reprint ed. pap. 200.00 (*0-608-13119-9*, 202522400043) Bks Demand.

***Management Accounting: A Road of Discovery.** James T. Mackey & Michael F. Thomas. LC 99-24166. (SWC-Accounting Ser.). 561p. 1999. pap. 67.95 (*0-538-87189-X*) S-W Pub.

Management Accounting: A Spreadsheet Approach. Neil Marriott & Roy Chandler. LC 92-40486. 1993. 35.90 (*0-13-555152-8*) P-H.

Management Accounting: A Strategic Approach. Al J. Hartgraves et al. LC 95-18158. (C). 1995. mass mkt. 80.95 (*0-538-84435-3*) S-W Pub.

Management Accounting: A Strategic Approach. Morse & Davis. (AB - Accounting Principles Ser.). (C). 1995. mass mkt., student ed. 21.95 (*0-538-84491-4*) S-W Pub.

Management Accounting: A Strategic Approach. Morse & Davis. (AQ - Managerial Accounting Ser.). 1996. text 5.95 (*0-538-86265-3*) S-W Pub.

***Management Accounting: A Strategic Approach.** 2nd ed. Davis Morse. LC 99-29552. (SWC-Accounting Ser.). 704p. 1999. 106.95 (*0-538-87889-4*) Thomson Learn.

Management Accounting: An Annotated Manual. Hai Yap Teoh. 612p. 1992. pap. 55.00 (*0-409-30358-5*, NZ, MICHIE) LEXIS Pub.

Management Accounting: An Introduction. Pauline Weetman. 385p. (Orig.). 1996. pap. 57.50 (*0-273-62362-1*, Pub. by Pitman Pub) Trans-Atl Phila.

***Management Accounting: An Introduction.** 2nd ed. Pauline Weetman. 416p. (Orig.). 1999. pap. 57.50 (*0-273-63838-6*, Pub. by F T P-H) Trans-Atl Phila.

Management Accounting: Check Figures. 2nd ed. Hansen. 1991. 5.00 (*0-538-82167-1*) Sth-Wstrn College.

Management Accounting: Concepts & Applications. 7th ed. W. Steve Albrecht & K. Fred Skousen. (SWC-Accounting). 1998. pap., student ed. 19.00 (*0-538-87627-1*) S-W Pub.

Management Accounting Custom Edition. 176p. (C). 1996. text 23.60 (*0-536-59617-4*) Pearson Custom.

Management Accounting: European Perspectives. Ed. by Alnoor Bhimani. LC 97-121421. (Illus.). 274p. (C). 1996. text 69.00 (*0-19-828966-9*) OUP.

Management Accounting: Strategy & Control. Charles H. Brandon & Ralph E. Drtina. 906p. (C). 1996. 89.69 (*0-07-017853-4*) McGraw.

Management Accounting & Cases. 2nd ed. Atkinson & Banker. 1996. pap. text, student ed. 33.40 (*0-13-262965-8*) P-H.

Management Accounting & Control Systems: Organisational & Behavioural Approach. Norman B. Macintosh. LC 94-31614. 281p. 1995. 115.00 (*0-471-94409-2*) Wiley.

Management Accounting & Control Systems: Organisational & Behavioural Approach. Norman B. Macintosh. LC 94-31614. 294p. 1995. pap. 79.00 (*0-471-94411-4*) Wiley.

Management Accounting for Business Decisions. Colin Drury. LC 97-21927. 1997. pap. 20.99 (*1-86152-102-2*) Thomson Learn.

Management Accounting for Financial Decisions. Keith Ward et al. 352p. 1991. pap. text 49.95 (*0-7506-0067-5*) Buttrwrth-Heinemann.

Management Accounting for Financial Institutions: The Complete Desktop Reference. 2nd rev. ed. Leonard P. Cole. (C). 1994. text 60.00 (*1-55738-738-9*, Irwn Prfssnl) McGraw-Hill Prof.

Management Accounting for Food Service Skillbook. Educational Foundation of the National Restaurant. (Management Skills Program Ser.). 76p. (Orig.). 1992. pap. text 10.95 (*0-915452-95-2*) Educ Found.

Management Accounting for Healthcare Organizations. 5th rev. ed. Bruce R. Neumann & Keith E. Boles. LC 97-75989. 745p. 1998. 65.00 (*0-944496-60-1*) Teach-em.

Management Accounting for Hospitality & Tourism. 3rd ed. Kotas. (ITBP Textbooks Ser.). 1999. pap. 22.99 (*1-86152-490-0*) Thomson Learn.

Management Accounting for Non-Specialists. Peter Atrill & Eddie McLaney. LC 95-17923. 1995. write for info. (*0-13-376724-8*) Prntice Hall Bks.

Management Accounting for Non-Specialists 2nd ed. Peter Atrill & E. J. McLaney. LC 98-50053. 1998. write for info. (*0-13-982927-X*) P-H.

Management Accounting for the Hospitality Industry. Deborah Adams. LC 98-119244. 1997. pap. text 33.95 (*0-304-32906-1*) Continuum.

Management Accounting for the Lending Banker. M. A. Pitcher. 176p. 1979. 55.00 (*0-85297-050-1*, Pub. by Chartered Bank); pap. 44.00 (*0-85297-047-1*, Pub. by Chartered Bank) St Mut.

Management Accounting in Support of Manufacturing Excellence: Profiles of Shingo Prize-Winning Organizations. Richard L. Jenson et al. Ed. by Claire Barth. (Illus.). 143p. (Orig.). 1996. pap. 40.00 (*0-86641-248-4*, 96311) Inst Mgmt Account.

Management Accounting Issues in Cellular Manufacturing & Focused-Factory Systems. Dileep Dhavale. Ed. by Claire Barth. (Illus.). 268p. (Orig.). 1995. pap. 60.00 (*0-86641-247-6*, 96310) Inst Mgmt Account.

Management-Accounting Simulation: An Integrative Approach to Cost Analysis & Profit Planning. 2nd rev. ed. Kenneth R. Goosen. 240p. (C). 1988. pap. text 15.00 (*0-317-93369-8*) Micro Accounting.

Management Accounting Systems & Records. Bob Grimsley. 1972. pap. 20.95 (*0-8464-0588-1*) Beekman Pubs.

Management Accounting Systems & Records. 2nd ed. Bob Grimsley. 132p. 1982. text 49.95 (*0-566-02349-0*) Ashgate Pub Co.

Management Accounting with Sap R/3. Francon Bonnafy. (C). 2000. 52.95 (*0-201-61912-1*) Addison-Wesley.

Management Accounts: How to Use Them to Control Your Business. Tony Skone. LC 94-42507. (Managerial Accounting Ser.). 1995. 61.95 (*0-566-07483-4*, Pub. by Gower) Ashgate Pub Co.

Management Activities Manual. Hunt. (C). Date not set. pap. write for info. (*0-395-41262-5*) HM.

Management, Analysis & Display of Geoscience Data: Proceedings of the First Annual Conference, Golden, CO, January 27-29, 1982. Ed. by Daniel F. Merriam. 60p. 1983. pap. 57.00 (*0-08-030248-3*, Pergamon Pr) Elsevier.

Management Analysis in Public Organizations: History, Concepts, & Techniques. Ray C. Oman et al. LC 91-25533. 224p. 1992. 59.95 (*0-89930-403-6*, OMA, Quorum Bks) Greenwood.

Management Analysis Trainee. Jack Rudman. (Career Examination Ser.: C-470). 1994. pap. 27.95 (*0-8373-0470-9*) Nat Learn.

Management Analyst. Jack Rudman. (Career Examination Ser.: C-1061). 1994. pap. 34.95 (*0-8373-1061-X*) Nat Learn.

Management Analyst Aide. Jack Rudman. (Career Examination Ser.: C-1721). 1994. reprint ed. pap. 29.95 (*0-8373-1721-5*) Nat Learn.

Management & Administrative Skills for Mental Health Professionals. O'Donohue. 450p. (C). 1999. 39.95 (*0-12-524195-X*) Acad Pr.

Management & Allison Industries. 7th ed. Charles S. White et al. (C). 1995. text 73.95 (*0-256-17758-9*, Irwn McGrw-H) McGrw-H Hghr Educ.

Management & Automation in the Petroleum Industry: Proceedings of the Institute of Petroleum Summer Meeting, held at Bath, Somerset 2-5 June, 1970. Ed. by Peter Hepple. LC 72-183034. 295p. reprint ed. pap. 91.50 (*0-608-13901-7*, 202368800033) Bks Demand.

Management & Avoidance of Derivatives Litigation, 1995. (Corporate Law & Practice Course Handbook, 1985-86 Ser.). 560p. 1994. pap. 99.00 (*0-614-17190-3*, B4-7110) PLI.

Management & Avoidance of Derivatives Litigation, 1996. (Corporate Law & Practice Course Handbook, 1985-86 Ser.). Date not set. pap. 99.00 (*0-614-17215-2*, B4-7137) PLI.

Management & Biology of Carcinoma in Situ & Cancer of the Testis. Ed. by N. E. Skakkebaek et al. (Journal: European Urology: Vol. 23, No. 1, 1993). (Illus.). iv, 256p. 1993. reprint ed. 78.50 (*3-8055-5768-X*) S Karger.

Management & Business. Nigel J. Roome. LC 94-33847. (Environmental Agenda Ser.). 80p. (C). 1994. pap. 8.95 (*0-7453-0925-9*, Pub. by Pluto GBR) Stylus Pub VA.

Management & Business Ethics: Violations of the Public Trust. 5th ed. Schermerhorn. 855p. 1995. pap. text 134.90 (*0-471-15420-2*) Wiley.

Management & Business in Britain & France: The Age of the Corporate Economy (1850-1990) Ed. by Youssef Cassis et al. (Illus.). 254p. 1995. text 49.95 (*0-19-828940-5*) OUP.

Management & Business Skills in the Built Environment. Mike Waterhouse & Geoff Crook. LC 95-67589. (Built Environment Series of Textbooks). (Illus.). 216p. (Orig.). (C). 1995. pap. 32.99 (*0-419-19540-8*, E & FN Spon) Routledge.

Management & Care of the Elderly: Psychosocial Perspectives. Ed. by Mary S. Harper. 400p. (C). 1991. 55.00 (*0-8039-4044-0*) Sage.

Management & Care of the Elderly: Psychosocial Perspectives. Ed. by Mary S. Harper. LC 90-9250. 375p. reprint ed. pap. 116.30 (*0-608-09787-X*, 206996100007) Bks Demand.

Management & Case Supplement. 5th ed. Schermerhorn. 502p. 1995. pap. text 58.00 (*0-471-14733-8*) Wiley.

Management & Clinical Engineering. Ed. by Cesar A. Caceres et al. LC 80-69068. (Artech Medical Library). 494p. reprint ed. pap. 153.20 (*0-8357-4187-7*, 203696500006) Bks Demand.

Management & Competition in the NHS. 2nd ed. Christopher Ham. LC 97-17065. 1997. write for info. (*1-85775-104-3*, Radcliffe Med Pr) Scovill Paterson.

Management & Complex Organizations in Comparative Perspective, 36. Ed. by Raj P. Mohan. LC 78-22133. (Contributions in Sociology Ser.: No. 36). (Illus.). 273p. 1979. 69.50 (*0-313-20752-6*, MMA/, Greenwood Pr) Greenwood.

Management & Computer Applications. (Illus.). 256p. 1996. text. write for info. (*0-412-73050-2*, Chap & Hall NY) Chapman & Hall.

Management & Conservation of Small Populations. Tim W. Clark & John H. Seebeck. 316p. (Orig.). 1990. pap. text 12.00 (*0-913934-16-X*) Chicago Zoo.

Management & Control of Foreign Exchange Risk. Laurent L. Jacque. 400p. (C). 1996. lib. bdg. 119.95 (*0-7923-9682-0*) Kluwer Academic.

Management & Control of Foreign Exchange Risk. Laurent L. Jacque. 400p. 1997. pap. 66.00 (*0-7923-8088-6*) Kluwer Academic.

Management & Control of Growth: Issues, Techniques, Problems, Trends, 5 vols., Vol. 1. Urban Land Institute Staff. LC 74-83560. 607p. 1975. reprint ed. pap. 188.20 (*0-608-08265-1*, 202981600001) Bks Demand.

Management & Control of Growth: Issues, Techniques, Problems, Trends, 5 vols., Vol. 2. Urban Land Institute Staff. LC 74-83560. 608p. 1975. reprint ed. pap. 188.50 (*0-608-08266-X*, 202981600002) Bks Demand.

M

Management & Control of Growth: Issues, Techniques, Problems, Trends, 5 vols., Vol. 3. Urban Land Institute Staff. LC 74-83560. 606p. 1975. reprint ed. pap. 187.90 (*0-608-08267-8*, 202981600003) Bks Demand.

Management & Control of Growth: Issues, Techniques, Problems, Trends, 5 vols., Vol. 4. Urban Land Institute Staff. LC 74-83560. 351p. 1975. reprint ed. pap. 108.90 (*0-608-08268-6*, 202981600004) Bks Demand.

Management & Control of Growth: Issues, Techniques, Problems, Trends, 5 vols., Vol. 5. Urban Land Institute Staff. LC 74-83560. 352p. 1975. reprint ed. pap. 109.20 (*0-608-08269-4*, 202981600005) Bks Demand.

***Management & Control of Production & Logistics (MCPL '97) A Proceedings Volume from the IFAC IFIP Conference, Campinas, SP, Brazil, 31 August-3 September, 1997.** Z. Binder et al. LC 98-24451. 1998. 166.50 (*0-08-043036-8*, Pergamon Pr) Elsevier.

Management & Control of Quality. 2nd ed. James R. Evans & William M. Lindsay. Ed. by Smith. LC 92-16910. (SWC-Management). 550p. (C). 1992. mass mkt. 48.00 (*0-314-00864-0*) West Pub.

Management & Control of Quality. 3rd ed. James R. Evans & William M. Lindsay. LC 95-21956. 700p. (C). 1995. pap. 67.50 (*0-314-06215-7*) West Pub.

Management & Control of Quality. 4th ed. Evans. LC 98-3009. (Principles of Management Ser.). 1998. pap. 96.95 (*0-538-88242-5*) S-W Pub.

Management & Control of Quality. 4th ed. James R. Evans & William M. Lindsay. LC 98-3009. 1998. write for info. (*0-324-00045-6*) Sth-Wstrn College.

Management & Control of Stickies. Mahendra R. Doshi & Jeffrey M. Dyer. LC 98-195027. (Illus.). 43p. 1998. pap. 40.00 (*0-9657447-2-8*) Doshi & Assocs.

Management & Control of Viral Haemorrhagic Fevers. B. R. Bannister. xii, 65p. 1996. 22.00 (*0-11-321860-5*, Pub. by Statnry Office) Balogh.

Management & Control Theory. Ed. by A. J. Berry et al. LC 97-45889. (History of Management Thought Ser.). 497p. 1998. text 179.95 (*1-84014-013-5*, Pub. by Ashgate Pub) Ashgate Pub Co.

Management & Corporations, 1985. Ed. by Melvin Anshen & George L. Bach. LC 75-4938. 253p. 1975. reprint ed. lib. bdg. 65.00 (*0-8371-8051-1*, ANMC, Greenwood Pr) Greenwood.

Management & Cost Accounting. Charles T. Horngren. LC 98-33960. 1998. write for info. (*0-13-080547-5*) P-H.

Management & Cost Accounting. 3rd ed. Colin Drury. (Illus.). 308p. (C). 1994. pap. text, student ed. 22.00 (*0-412-46400-4*, Chap & Hall NY) Chapman & Hall.

Management & Cost Accounting. 4th ed. Colin Drury. 900p. 1996. pap., student ed. 26.95 (*1-86152-002-6*, Pub. by ITBP) Thomson Learn.

Management & Cost Accounting. 4th rev. ed. Drury. (ITBP Textbooks Ser.). 1996. pap., student ed. 15.99 (*1-86152-510-9*) Thomson Learn.

***Management & Cost Accounting.** 5th ed. Cohn Drury. (ITBP Textbooks Ser.). 2000. pap., student ed. 39.95 (*1-86152-537-0*) Thomson Learn.

***Management & Cost Accounting.** 5th ed. Colin Drury. (ITBP Textbooks Ser.). 2000. write for info. (*1-86152-596-6*, Pub. by ITBP); write for info. (*1-86152-597-4*, Pub. by ITBP) Thomson Learn.

***Management & Cost Accounting.** 5th ed. Colin Drury. (ITBP Textbooks Ser.). 2000. pap. 26.99 (*1-86152-536-2*) Thomson Learn.

Management & Cost Accounting: Spreadsheet Applications Manual. 3rd ed. Alicia M. Gazely. LC 92-42398. 256p. 1993. mass mkt. 44.95 (*0-412-46430-6*) Chapman & Hall.

Management & Cultural Values The Indigenization of Organizations in Asia Henry S. Kao et al. LC 99-17242. 1999. write for info. (*0-7619-9319-3*) Sage.

Management & Delivery of Social Care Services. Taylor Vigars. 190p. 1993. pap. 36.95 (*0-582-20962-5*) Ashgate Pub Co.

Management & Design of Long-Life Systems, Apr. 24-26, 1973, Denver, CO. Ed. by Harris M. Schurmeier. (Science & Technology Ser.: Vol. 34). (Illus.). 198p. 1974. 20.00 (*0-87703-069-3*, Am Astronaut Soc) Univelt Inc.

Management & Development of Major Rivers. Ed. by Aly M. Shady et al. LC 96-902102. (Water Resources Management Ser.: No. 3). (Illus.). 500p. 1996. text 34.95 (*0-19-563470-5*) OUP.

An Asterisk (*) at the beginning of an entry indicates that the title is appearing for the first time.

Management & Diseases of Sheep. British Council Staff. 467p. 1980. 75.00 (*0-85198-451-7*) OUP.

Management & Disposition of Excess Weapons Plutonium. Committee on International Security & Arms Control. 288p. (Orig.). (C). 1994. pap. text 39.00 (*0-309-05042-1*) Natl Acad Pr.

Management & Disposition of Excess Weapons Plutonium: Reactor-Related Options. National Research Council Staff & Panel on Reactor-Related Options for Dispositioin. 436p. (Orig.). (C). 1995. pap. text 45.00 (*0-309-05145-2*) Natl Acad Pr.

Management & Ecology of Freshwater Plants: Proceedings of the 9th International Symposium on Aquatic Weeds, European Weed Research Society, Dublin, Ireland, 1994. Ed. by J. M. Caffrey et al. LC 96-54609. (Development in Hydrobiology Ser.: Vol. 120). 354p. 1997. text 234.00 (*0-7923-4433-2*) Kluwer Academic.

Management & Engineering of Fire Safety & Loss Prevention: Onshore & Offshore - Proceedings of the Third Internat. Conf., 18-20 Feb., 1991, Aberdeen, Scotland, U. K. Ed. by BHR Group Ltd. Staff. 358p. 1991. mass mkt. 164.95 (*1-85166-676-1*) Elsevier.

Management & Financing of Road Maintenance Report ESCAP/World Bank Seminar (1966, Bangkok) Economic Commission for Europe. 73p. 1997. pap. 10.00 (*92-1-119822-4*) UN.

M

Management & Financing of Roads: An Agenda for Reform. Ian G. Heggie. LC 95-2089. (World Bank Technical Papers: No. 275). 172p. 1995. pap. 22.00 (*0-8213-3143-4*, 13143) World Bank.

Management & Gender: Issues & Attitudes. Margaret F. Karsten. LC 93-4225. 288p. 1993. 65.00 (*0-89930-812-0*, Quorum Bks); pap. 22.95 (*0-275-94501-4*, Quorum Bks) Greenwood.

Management & Health of Farmed Deer. Ed. by H. W. Reid. (Current Topics in Veterinary Medicine & Animal Science Ser.). (C). 1988. text 137.50 (*0-89838-408-7*) Kluwer Academic.

Management & Industrial Structure in Japan. Naoto Sasaki. (Illus.). 160p. 1981. text 41.00 (*0-08-024056-9*, Pergamon Pr); pap. text 19.25 (*0-08-024057-7*, Pergamon Pr) Elsevier.

Management & Industry in China. Ed. by C. Carl Pegels. LC 86-25260. 294p. 1986. 65.00 (*0-275-92553-6*, C2553, Praeger Pubs) Greenwood.

Management & Industry in Russia: Formal & Informal Relations in the Period of Transition. Ed. by Simon Clarke. LC 95-4048. (Management & Industry in Russia Ser.). 1995. 90.00 (*1-85898-062-3*) E Elgar.

Management & Law for Water Resources. Luis V. Cunha et al. LC 77-76111. 1977. 40.00 (*0-918334-20-9*) WRP.

Management & Leadership for Nurse Managers. Russell C. Swansburg. 576p. 1990. pap. 41.25 (*0-86720-439-7*) Jones & Bartlett.

Management & Leadership in Higher Education. Chester O. McCorkle & Sandra O. Archibald. LC 82-48073. (Jossey-Bass Series in Higher Education). (Illus.). 264p. reprint ed. pap. 81.90 (*0-8357-4908-8*, 203783800009) Bks Demand.

Management & Leadership in Nursing. Warren F. Stevens. (Illus.). 1978. text 27.00 (*0-07-061260-9*) McGraw.

Management & Leadership Nurse Manager. 2nd ed. Russell C. Swansburg. (Nursing Ser.). 680p. (C). 1996. pap. text 48.75 (*0-86720-734-5*) Jones & Bartlett.

Management & Leadership Nurse Managers. 2nd ed. Russell C. Swansburg. (Nursing Ser.). 208p. 1996. pap., teacher ed. 10.00 (*0-7637-0180-7*) Jones & Bartlett.

Management & Machiavelli. Antony Jay. 308p. (C). 1996. pap. text 14.95 (*0-13-602608-7*) P-H.

Management & Machiavelli: Discovering a New Science of Management in the Timeless Principles of Statecraft. Antony Jay. LC 94-5605. 288p. 1996. pap. text 14.95 (*0-89384-260-5*, Pfiffr & Co) Jossey-Bass.

Management & Maintenance Needs & Problems in the Omaha Housing Authority's Four Family Developments. Joan V. Holley. 55p. 1982. pap. 4.00 (*1-55719-021-6*) U NE CPAR.

Management & Management Mistakes & Successes. 4th ed. Schermerhorn. 957p. 1995. pap. text 131.90 (*0-471-15421-0*) Wiley.

Management & Managing Business Ethics Set. 5th ed. John R. Schermerhorn. 877p. 1995. pap. text 134.90 (*0-471-15423-7*) Wiley.

Management & Marketing Dictionary English-German. W. Schafer. (ENG & GER.). 513p. 1995. pap. 25.00 (*3-423-05815-3*, Pub. by CH Beck Verlag) IBD Ltd.

Management & Marketing Dictionary, English-German. W. Schafer. (ENG & GER.). 1995. 25.00 (*0-7859-9731-8*) Fr & Eur.

Management & Marketing Dictionary German-English. W. Schafer. (ENG & GER.). 506p. 1995. pap. 25.00 (*3-423-05816-1*, Pub. by CH Beck Verlag) IBD Ltd.

Management & Marketing Encyclopedic Dictionary, English-German. Wolfgang Koschnick. (ENG & GER.). 859p. 1998. 295.00 (*0-7859-9668-0*) Fr & Eur.

Management & Marketing of Services. Peter Mudie & Angela Cottam. 250p. 1993. pap. text 44.95 (*0-7506-0789-0*) Buttrwrth-Heinemann.

Management & Marketing of Services. 2nd ed. Mudie & Cottom. LC 99-461880. 306p. 1999. pap. text 34.95 (*0-7506-3594-0*) Buttrwrth-Heinemann.

Management & Marketing/Management und Marketing: Encyclopedic Dictionary. Wolfgang J. Koschnick. LC 97-23231. (ENG & GER.). 944p. (C). 1997. text 124.00 (*3-11-015197-9*) De Gruyter.

Management & Measurement of Software Quality. Mike Kelly. (UNICOM Applied Information Technology Ser.). 224p. 1993. 105.95 (*0-291-39801-4*, Pub. by Avebury Technical) Ashgate Pub Co.

Management & Monitoring of Resident & Migratory Birds & Their Habitats in Latin America & the Caribbean: An Interamerican Perspective. Ed. by Frank F. Rivera-Milan et al. (ENG & SPA.). 48p. (C). 1997. reprint ed. pap. text 30.00 (*0-7881-4288-7*) DIANE Pub.

Management & Morale. Fritz J. Roethlisberger. LC 41-4302. 317p. reprint ed. pap. 98.30 (*0-608-10747-6*, 200158700079) Bks Demand.

Management & Morality: A Developmental Perspective. Patrick Maclagan. LC 97-62444. vi, 212p. 1998. pap. write for info. (*0-8039-7680-1*) Sage.

Management & Natural Enviroment Module. 3rd ed. Mark Starik. 52p. (C). 1994. pap. text 17.00 (*0-03-003034-X*) Dryden Pr.

Management & Office Information Systems. Ed. by Shi-Kuo Chang. LC 83-26875. (Management & Information Systems Ser.). 492p. 1984. 110.00 (*0-306-41447-3*, Plenum Trade) Perseus Pubng.

***Management & Operations of Intelligent Transportation Systems: An ITE Recommended Practice.** ITE Committee Staff & Walter H. Kraft. LC 99-58530. 64p. 1999. pap. text 25.00 (*0-935403-39-6*, RP-030A) Inst Trans Eng.

Management & Operations of the Oklahoma-Arkansas IRS District: Hearing Before the Subcommittee on Taxation & IRS Oversight of the Committee on Finance, United States Senate, One Hundred Fifth Congress, First Session ... December 3, 1997. United States. LC 98-153715. (S. Hrg. Ser.). iii, 131p. 1998. write for info. (*0-16-056289-9*) USGPO.

***Management & Operations of Traffic Control Systems.** James M. Giblin & Walter H. Kraft. LC 00-37039. (Illus.). 478p. 2000. text 50.00 (*0-935403-40-X*) Inst Trans Eng.

Management & Organisation: Relational Alternatives to Individualism. Ed. by Dian-Marie Mosking. 256p. 1995. 78.95 (*1-85972-167-2*, Pub. by Avebury) Ashgate Pub Co.

***Management & Organisational Behavior.** 5th ed. Laurie J. Mullins. (Illus.). 864p. 1999. pap. 59.50 (*0-273-63552-2*) F T P H.

Management & Organisational Behaviour. I. J. Mullins. 546p. (C). 1989. 195.00 (*0-7855-5691-5*, Pub. by Inst Pur & Supply) St Mut.

Management & Organisational Behaviour: A Student Workbook. 2nd ed. Karen Meudell & Tony Callen. 224p. 1995. pap. 34.50 (*0-273-61929-2*) F T P-H.

Management & Organization. Brian Stone. 332p. 1996. pap. 120.00 (*0-85297-412-4*, Pub. by Chartered Bank) St Mut.

Management & Organization. 2nd ed. Dubrin & Ireland. 1999. 59.25 (*0-538-83621-0*) Sth-Wstrn College.

Management & Organization. 5th ed. J. Clifton Williams et al. (Thomson Executive Press). 1985. pap. 39.50 (*0-538-07440-X*, G44) S-W Pub.

Management & Organization of the Acquisitions Department. Ed. by Twyla Racz & Rosina Tammany. LC 94-28265. (Acquisitions Librarian Ser.). (Illus.). 131p. 1994. lib. bdg. 39.95 (*1-56024-583-2*) Haworth Pr.

Management & Organizational Behavior. Robert Coffey & Curtis Cook. (C). 1994. text 66.25 (*0-256-18239-6*, Irwn McGrw-H) McGrw-H Hghr Educ.

Management & Organizational Behavior. Robert E. Coffey et al. LC 93-36578. 672p. (C). 1993. text 68.95 (*0-256-11685-7*, Irwn Prfssnl) McGraw-Hill Prof.

Management & Organizational Behavior. Robert Coffey et al. 168p. (C). 1994. text, student ed. 26.87 (*0-256-16655-2*, Irwn McGrw-H) McGrw-H Hghr Educ.

Management & Organizational Behavior. McKee. (C). 1997. text 69.50 (*0-03-003698-4*, Pub. by Harcourt Coll Pubs) Harcourt.

Management & Organizational Behavior. R. Wayne Mondy et al. 720p. 1989. student ed. 18.00 (*0-685-29837-X*, H20621) Allyn.

Management & Organizational Behavior. R. Wayne Mondy et al. 720p. 1989. teacher ed. write for info. (*0-318-66379-1*, H20571); write for info. (*0-318-66380-5*, H20597); write for info. (*0-318-66382-1*, H23948); trans. write for info. (*0-318-66381-3*, H20605); VHS. write for info. (*0-318-66383-X*, H26131) P-H.

Management & Organizational Behavior. 2nd ed. Cook. 1996. 43.75 (*0-256-26372-8*, WCB McGr Hill) McGrw-H Hghr Educ.

Management & Organizational Behavior. 2nd ed. Curtis Cook et al. LC 96-44030. 640p. (C). 1996. text 68.95 (*0-256-20807-7*, Irwn McGrw-H) McGrw-H Hghr Educ.

Management & Organizational Behavior. 2nd ed. Bernard Keys & Burt K. Scanlan. LC 87-17035. 682p. (C). 1988. reprint ed. lib. bdg. 57.50 (*0-89464-246-4*) Krieger.

Management & Organizational Behavior. 3rd ed. Schuh. (C). 1994. pap. text. write for info. (*0-07-057067-1*) McGraw.

Management & Organizational Behavior: Course Packet. 2nd ed. 180p. (C). 1994. text 15.60 (*0-536-58582-2*) Pearson Custom.

Management & Organizational Behavior: Course Packet. 3rd ed. 180p. (C). 1994. text 16.00 (*0-536-58738-8*) Pearson Custom.

Management & Organizational Behavior Classics. 6th ed. Ed. by Michael T. Matteson & John M. Ivancevich. LC 94-49391. 480p. (C). 1995. text 37.25 (*0-256-16204-2*, Irwn McGrw-H) McGrw-H Hghr Educ.

Management & Organizational Behavior Classics. 7th ed. Michael T. Matteson & John M. Joinvancevich. LC 98-23853. 1998. 45.03 (*0-256-26457-0*, Irwn Prfssnl) McGraw-Hill Prof.

Management & Organizational Behavior Essentials. John R. Schermerhorn. LC 95-37720. 321p. 1995. pap. 46.95 (*0-471-13308-6*) Wiley.

Management & Organizational Behaviour. L. J. Mullins. 546p. (C). 1989. 175.00 (*0-7855-4622-7*, Pub. by Inst Pur & Supply) St Mut.

Management & Organizational Theory: Structural & Behavioral Systems. Charles S. Telly. 706p. (C). 1990. pap. 105.00 (*0-536-57865-6*) Pearson Custom.

***Management & Organizations.** J. T. Lie. LC 99-41116. 2000. text 69.95 (*0-312-22841-4*) St Martin.

Management & People in Banking. 2nd ed. Bryan Livy. 1985. 75.00 (*0-85297-143-5*, Pub. by Chartered Bank) St Mut.

Management & Performance. 3rd ed. Szylagyi. (C). 1988. pap., student ed. 21.00 (*0-673-16682-1*) Addson-Wesley Educ.

Management & Planning, Vol. 1. Ed. by Jill Muehrcke. (Leadership Ser.). 123p. 1990. spiral bd. 20.00 (*0-614-07100-3*) Soc Nonprofit Org.

Management & Planning, Vol. 2. Ed. by Jill Muehrcke. (Leadership Ser.). 130p. 1993. spiral bd. 20.00 (*0-614-07101-1*) Soc Nonprofit Org.

Management & Practice of Low Visual Acuity. Albert Dowie. (C). 1989. 85.00 (*0-900099-24-0*, Pub. by Assn Brit Dispen Opticians) St Mut.

Management & Practices for the Health Professional. M. Cronin. 176p. (C). 1994. spiral bd. write for info. (*0-933195-64-8*) CA College Health Sci.

Management & Prevention of Diarrhea: Practical Guidelines. 3rd ed. Ed. by World Health Organization Staff. (CHI, ENG, FRE & SPA.). v, 50p. 1993. pap. text 12.00 (*92-4-154454-6*, 1153230) World Health.

Management & Processing of Complex Data Structures: Third Workshop on Information Systems & Artificial Intelligence, Hamburg, Germany, February 28-March 2, 1994: Proceedings. Ed. by Kai von Luck & Heinz Marburger. LC 94-1559. (Lecture Notes in Computer Science Ser.: Vol. 777). v, 220p. 1994. 39.95 (*0-387-57802-1*) Spr-Verlag.

Management & Quality. 3rd ed. Evans. Date not set. pap. text, teacher ed. write for info. (*0-314-07148-2*) West Pub.

Management & Recrafting America. 7th ed. Lloyd L. Byars et al. (C). 1999. text 66.25 (*0-256-17860-7*, Irwn McGrw-H) McGrw-H Hghr Educ.

Management & Regional Science for Economic Development. Manas Chatterji. 1982. lib. bdg. 119.00 (*0-89838-108-8*) Kluwer Academic.

Management & Regulation of Coastal Zones. Eric J. Fitch. ring bd. 49.95 (*1-56670-473-1*) Lewis Pubs.

Management & Supervision. Walter Berthelsen & Joseph T. Straub. 394p. (C). 1992. pap. text 42.69 (*1-56226-102-9*) CAT Pub.

Management & Supervision. Brent Bombard et al. 278p. (C). 1991. pap. text 35.42 (*1-56226-060-X*) CAT Pub.

Management & Supervision. Byrne et al. 414p. (C). 1995. pap. text 49.95 (*1-56226-247-5*) CAT Pub.

Management & Supervision. Joseph T. Straub. 446p. (C). 1990. pap. text 40.45 (*1-56226-024-3*) CAT Pub.

Management & Supervision: A Study Guide. Joseph T. Straub. 230p. (C). 1991. pap. text 21.61 (*1-56226-038-3*) CAT Pub.

Management & Supervision for Working Professionals, Vol. I. 3rd ed. Herman Koren. 256p. 1995. lib. bdg. 65.00 (*1-56670-203-8*, L1203) Lewis Pubs.

Management & Supervision for Working Professionals, Vol. II. 3rd ed. Herman Koren. 272p. 1995. lib. bdg. 65.00 (*1-56670-204-6*, L1204) Lewis Pubs.

Management & Supervision in Law Enforcement. Wayne W. Bennett & Karen M. Hess. Ed. by Jucha. 645p. (C). 1992. text 54.75 (*0-314-91105-7*) West Pub.

Management & Supervision in Law Enforcement. 2nd ed. Wayne W. Bennett & Karen Hess. LC 95-37730. 650p. (C). 1996. 83.95 (*0-314-06751-5*) West Pub.

Management & Supervision in Law Enforcement. 3rd ed. Hess Bennett. 2000. 4975.00 (*0-534-55431-8*) Thomson Learn.

Management & Supervision Instructor's Manual. Walter Berthelsen & Joseph T. Straub. 354p. 1992. pap. text. write for info. (*1-56226-124-X*) CAT Pub.

Management & Supervision Instructor's Manual & Test Bank. Joseph T. Straub. 460p. 1990. pap. write for info. (*1-56226-026-X*) CAT Pub.

Management & Supervision of Jail Inmates with Mental Disorders. Martin Drapkin & William C. Collins. 300p. 1999. ring bd. 133.50 (*1-887554-08-4*) Civic Res Inst.

Management & Supervision of Law Enforcement Personnel. Frank A. Lombardo et al. 500p. 1995. pap. 34.95 (*0-87526-428-X*) Gould.

Management & Technological Changes to Improve Competitiveness: Case Studies of Small to Medium Sized Apparel Industries. Karlene M. Crawford & James F. Cox. 50p. 1988. pap. text 16.00 (*1-55822-002-X*) Am Prod & Inventory.

Management & the Arts. William J. Byrnes. 210p. 1992. pap. text 44.95 (*0-240-80131-8*, Focal) Buttrwrth-Heinemann.

Management & the Arts. 2nd ed. Byrnes. LC 98-31726. 336p. 1999. pap. text 44.95 (*0-240-80334-5*, Focal) Buttrwrth-Heinemann.

Management & the Worker: An Account of a Research Program Conducted by the Western Electric Co, Hawthorne Works, Chicago. Fritz J. Roethlisberger & William J. Dickson. 639p. 1939. 52.50 (*0-674-54676-8*) HUP.

Management & Therapy of Sickle Cell Disease. 1990. lib. bdg. 250.00 (*0-87700-885-X*) Revisionist Pr.

Management & Therapy of Sickle Cell Disease. 3rd rev. ed. Ed. by Clarice D. Reid et al. (Illus.). 114p. 1997. pap. text 40.00 (*0-7881-3853-7*) DIANE Pub.

Management & Treatment of Benign Cutaneous Vascular Lesions. Oon T. Tan. (Illus.). 225p. 1992. text 98.50 (*0-8121-1489-2*) Lppncott W & W.

Management & Utilization of Arid Land Plants: Symposium Proceedings. rev. ed. Ed. by David R. Patton et al. 124p. 1997. 20.60 (*0-89904-656-8*, Bear Meadows Resrch Grp); pap. 15.60 (*0-89904-657-6*, Bear Meadows Resrch Grp) Crumb Elbow Pub.

***Management & Welfare of Farm Animals: The UFAW Farm Handbook.** 4th ed. Ed. by R. Ewbank et al. 308p. 1999. pap. 160.00 (*1-900630-00-1*, Pub. by Univs Fed Animal Welfare) St Mut.

Management & Welfare of Farm Animals: The UFAW Handbook. 3rd ed. Ed. by P. K. Ray. 260p. 1994. reprint ed. pap. 175.00 (*0-900767-87-1*, Pub. by Univs Fed Animal Welfare) St Mut.

Management Application of Value Engineering: For Business & Government. Donald E. Parker. LC 94-76015. (Illus.). 204p. (C). 1994. text 44.95 (*0-9641052-0-9*) L D Miles.

***Management Aptitude of Entrepreneurs** Daniel J. Knutson. LC 99-30494. (Studies in Entrepreneurship). 1999. write for info. (*0-8153-3503-2*) Garland.

Management Assessment of Energy from Biomass & Wastes Executive Conference, January 1979. (Biomass Ser.). 197p. 1980. pap. 25.00 (*0-910091-26-9*) Inst Gas Tech.

Management Assessment of Peat As an Energy Resource Executive Conference, July 1979. (Synthetic Fuels Ser.). 331p. 1980. pap. 40.00 (*0-910091-27-7*) Inst Gas Tech.

Management Assistance Services for Nonprofit Organizations: A Planning Manual. Carol L. Barbeito. 110p. 1998. pap. 39.95 (*1-893014-00-2*) Applied Resrch & Dev.

Management Audit Manual. 57p. 1988. 11.00 (*0-317-01708-X*) NARUC.

Management Audit Manual, Vol. II. 301p. 1992. 37.50 (*0-317-05194-6*) NARUC.

Management Auditing As a Regulatory Tool: The New York State Experience. Howard H. Greenbaum. LC 86-21207. 367p. 1986. 75.00 (*0-275-92473-4*, C2473, Praeger Pubs) Greenwood.

Management Auditor. Jack Rudman. (Career Examination Ser.: C-3217). 1994. pap. 34.95 (*0-8373-3217-6*) Nat Learn.

Management Auditor Trainee. Jack Rudman. (Career Examination Ser.: C-3285). 1994. pap. 29.95 (*0-8373-3285-0*) Nat Learn.

Management Audits: The Assesment of Quality Management Systems. 3rd rev. ed. Allan J. Sayle. 667p. 1997. 48.00 (*0-9511739-0-1*, P659) A Sayle Assocs.

Management Audits of Branch Claims Offices of National Insurance Companies. John H. Roush, Jr. LC 74-31546. 197p. 1975. pap. 21.00 (*0-9600830-1-4*) J H Roush.

Management Basics: The How-To Guide for Managers. John Payne & Shirley Payne. LC 98-17612. 304p. 1998. pap. 9.95 (*1-58062-023-X*) Adams Media.

***Management Basics for Information Professionals.** Bendik Rugaas et al. LC 99-86970. 560p. 2000. pap. 55.00 (*1-55570-370-4*) Neal-Schuman.

Management Buy-Ins: Entrepreneurship, Active Investors, & Corporate Restructuring. Ken Robbie & Mike Wright. LC 95-4959. (Studies in Finance). 330p. 1996. text 79.95 (*0-7190-4281-X*) Manchester Univ Pr.

Management Buy-Outs. Ed. by Mike Wright. (International Library of Management). 708p. 1994. 296.95 (*1-85521-392-3*, Pub. by Dartmth Pub) Ashgate Pub Co.

Management Buy-Outs. 2nd ed. Ian Webb. 100p. 1990. text 74.95 (*0-566-02810-7*, Pub. by Gower) Ashgate Pub Co.

Management Buy-Outs & Venture Capital: Into the Next Millennium. Ed. by Mike Wright & Ken Robbie. LC 98-27890. 368p. 1999. 110.00 (*1-85898-999-X*) E Elgar.

Management by Filipino Values: A Sequel to Understanding Filipino Values. Tomas D. Andres. vi, 276p. (Orig.). 1985. pap. 15.75 (*971-10-0209-4*, Pub. by New Day Pub) Cellar.

Management by Inspiration: Leadership Through Self-Understanding. Allan E. Flood. Ed. by Caroline Hall-Otis. LC 91-66692. 105p. (Orig.). 1991. pap. 9.95 (*0-9630873-0-4*) Pugrose Pub.

Management by Involvement: An Action Guide. Gene F. Brady. LC 87-26052. (Insight Book Ser.). 166p. 1989. 35.95 (*0-89885-409-1*, Kluwer Acad Hman Sci); pap. 20.95 (*0-89885-410-5*, Kluwer Acad Hman Sci) Kluwer Academic.

Management by Japanese Systems. Sang M. Lee. Ed. by Gary Schwendiman. LC 82-7612. 562p. 1982. 105.00 (*0-275-91710-X*, C1710, Praeger Pubs) Greenwood.

Management by Menu. Lendal H. Kotschevar. LC 75-5732. (Illus.). 381p. 1975. text 19.95 (*0-915452-20-0*); student ed. 32.50 (*0-915452-22-7*) Educ Found.

Management by Menu. 3rd ed. Educational Foundation of the National Restaurant. 84p. (Orig.). 1993. student ed., boxed set. write for info. (*0-915452-73-1*) Educ Found.

Management by Objectives. Didactic Systems Staff. (Simulation Game Ser.). (POR.). 1970. pap. 35.00 (*0-89401-053-0*) Didactic Syst.

Management by Objectives. David E. Olsson. LC 67-21207. (Illus.). xiv, 112p. 1968. 15.95 (*0-87015-168-1*) Pacific Bks.

Management by Objectives. 2nd ed. Didactic Systems Staff. 1978. pap. 26.25 (*0-89401-142-1*) Didactic Syst.

Management by Objectives: A Handbook for Governmental Managers & Supervisors. Peter Thomas. 1978. 8.95 (*0-912164-11-5*) Masterco Pr.

Management by Objectives: A Japanese Experience. Takanobu Hongo. (Illus.). 86p. 1980. text 14.00 (*92-833-1057-8*, 310575); pap. text 10.25 (*92-833-1058-6*, 310583) Productivity Inc.

Management by Objectives for Insurance Companies. Didactic Systems Staff. (Simulation Game Ser.). 1972. pap. 26.25 (*0-89401-054-9*) Didactic Syst.

An Asterisk (*) at the beginning of an entry indicates that the title is appearing for the first time.

Management by Objectives in Mental Health Services. Vernon R. Wiehe. 1974. 8.95 (*0-912164-10-7*) Masterco Pr.

Management by One-Liners. Bill F. Stewart & Gerre Brenneman. 1988. 33.00 (*0-87117-178-3*, 1107) Comm Coll Pr Am Assn Comm Coll.

Management by Projects: Achieving Success in a Changing World. Albert Hamilton. 449p. 1997. 114.00 (*0-7277-2632-3*, 2632, Pub. by T Telford) RCH.

Management by Proverbs: Applying Timeless Wisdom in the Workplace. Michael A. Zigarelli. 286p. 1999. 14.99 (*0-8024-6194-8*) Moody.

Management by Responsibility. G. Michael Durst. (Illus.). 206p. 1987. pap. 24.00 (*0-9602552-1-4*) Train Sys.

Management by Slime & Grime. Gerhard Flemming. Ed. by Diane Parker & Brigitte Hall. LC 91-60283. 150p. (Orig.). 1991. pap. 7.95 (*0-9629268-0-9*) Gerhard Flemming.

Management by Task Forces: A Manual on the Operation of Interdisciplinary Teams. Lawrence W. Bass. LC 74-82702. 197p. 1975. 22.50 (*0-912338-09-1*); fiche 9.50 (*0-912338-10-5*) Lomond.

Management by Uncommon Sense. Billy B. Hair. (Illus.). 82p. 1990. 21.95 (*0-9626024-0-X*) Summit GA.

Management by Values: Towards Cultural Congruence. S. K. Chakraborty. 340p. 1993. pap. text 14.95 (*0-19-563218-4*) OUP.

Management by Vice: A Humorous Satire on R & D Life in a Fictitious Company. C. B. Don. (Illus.). 232p. 1999. 19.95 (*0-9670084-4-1*) Sterling TL.

Management Career Progress in a Japanese Organization. Mitsuru Wakabayashi. Ed. by Gunter Dufey. LC 80-23789. (Research for Business Decisions Ser.: No. 24). 395p. 1980. reprint ed. pap. 122.50 (*0-8357-1108-0*, 207006800063) Bks Demand.

Management Cases & Review Activities. Peter Goodrich. 74p. 1998. pap. text 15.80 (*1-56226-410-9*) CAT Pub.

***Management Century: A Critical Review of 20th Century Thought & Practice.** Stuart Crainer. LC 99-56006. (Strategy & Business Book Ser.: No. 5). 304p. 2000. 28.00 (*0-7879-5224-9*, Pfffr & Co) Jossey-Bass.

Management Challenge: Japanese Views. Ed. by Lester C. Thurow. 256p. 1987. pap. text 12.50 (*0-262-70033-6*) MIT Pr.

***Management Challenges for Africa in the Twenty-first Century: Theoretical & Applied Perspectives.** Felix Moses Edoho. LC 99-43112. 352p. 2000. 69.50 (*0-275-96412-4*, Praeger Pubs) Greenwood.

Management Challenges for the 21st Century. Peter F. Drucker. LC 99-17087. 224p. 1999. 27.50 (*0-88730-998-4*, HarpBusn) HarpInfo.

***Management Challenges for the 21st Century.** unabridged ed. Peter F. Drucker. 1999. audio 25.00 (*0-694-52212-0*, 698412, Pub. by HarperAudio) Lndmrk Audiobks.

Management, Challenges in the 21st Century: Insights : Readings in Small Business Management. 2nd ed. Lewis & Goodman. (SWC-Management Ser.). 1997. pap. 14.50 (*0-538-88036-8*) Sth-Wstrn College.

Management Change in East Germany. Vincent Edwards & Peter Lawrence. LC 93-45988. 192p. (C). (gr. 13). 1994. pap. 59.95 (*0-415-09187-X*, B4252) Thomson Learn.

Management Characteristics & Labour Conflict: A Study of Managerial Organisation, Attitudes & Industrial Relations. Herbert A. Turner et al. LC 77-76076. (Cambridge University, Department of Applied Economics, Paper in Industrial Relations & Labour Ser.: No. 3). 88p. reprint ed. pap. 25.10 (*0-608-12987-9*, 2024547) Bks Demand.

Management Classics. Peter Goodrich. 202p. 1997. pap. text 29.95 (*1-56226-383-8*) CAT Pub.

Management Classics: Thorstein Veblem. Peter Goodrich. 232p. 1998. pap. text 29.95 (*1-56226-396-X*) CAT Pub.

Management Clinic. White. 160p. 1993. pap. text 15.00 (*0-340-57321-X*, Pub. by E A) Routldge.

Management Communication. Arthur H. Bell & Dayle M. Smith. 560p. 1998. pap. 58.95 (*0-471-23971-2*) Wiley.

Management Communication: Principles & Practice. Michael Hattersley & Linda J. McJannet. LC 96-23243. (Illus.). 336p. (C). 1996. pap. 46.56 (*0-07-027041-4*) McGraw.

***Management Communications.** James McElroy. 66p. 2000. write for info. (*1-58692-030-8*) Copyright Mgmt.

***Management Compensation Survey for A-E-P & Environmental Consulting Firms.** 2nd ed. 176p. 1999. pap. 275.00 (*1-885002-99-8*) Zweig White.

Management Competency Development in Sport & Physical Education. Earle F. Zeigler & Gary W. Bowie. 419p. (Orig.). (C). 1995. pap. text, ring bd. 29.80 (*0-87563-563-6*) Stipes.

Management: Concepts & Applications see Management: Leadership in Action

Management Concepts & Thoughts. 2nd rev. ed. V. S. Rao & P. S. Narayana. 556p. 1990. text 45.00 (*81-220-0154-8*, Pub. by Konark Pubs Pvt Ltd) Advent Bks Div.

Management Concepts for Improving Libraries: A Guide for the Professional Librarian. Dale E. Shaffer. 1979. pap. 3.95 (*0-915060-14-0*) D E Shaffer.

Management, Concepts, Practices & Skills. 5th ed. R. Wayne Mondy et al. (Illus.). 768p. 1990. text 51.00 (*0-205-12614-6*, H26149) Allyn.

Management Consultancy: A Handbook of Best Practice. Ed. by Philip Sadler. 300p. 1998. pap. 45.00 (*0-7494-2448-6*) Kogan Page Ltd.

Management Consultancy in Schools. Ed. by H. Gray. 240p. 1988. pap. text 35.95 (*0-304-31468-4*) Continuum.

***Management Consultancy in the 21st Century.** Fiona Czerniawska. LC 99-40915. 236p. 1999. 34.95 (*1-55753-178-1*, Ichor Busn Bks) Purdue U Pr.

Management Consultancy Services in United Kingdom: A Strategic Entry Report, 1997. Compiled by Icon Group International Staff. (Illus.). 97p. 1999. ring bd. 970.00 incl. audio compact disk (*0-7418-0862-5*) Icon Grp.

***Management Consulting.** Philip A. Wickham. 256p. (Orig.). 1999. pap. 47.50 (*0-273-63811-4*, Pub. by F T P-H) Trans-Atl Phila.

Management Consulting. 2nd ed. 611p. 1982. 25.65 (*0-685-31366-2*) Taylor & Francis.

***Management Consulting: A Complete Guide to the Industry.** Sugata Biswas & Daryl Twitchell. LC 98-30144. 304p. 1998. 34.95 (*0-471-29352-0*) Wiley.

Management Consulting: A Guide to the Profession. 3rd ed. Milan Kubr. LC 96-215012. xxi, 850p. 1996. 63.00 (*92-2-109449-9*) Intl Labour Office.

Management Consulting: A Survey in the Industry & Its Large Firms. 94p. 1993. 25.00 (*92-1-104419-7*, E.93.II.A.17) UN.

Management Consulting: Theory & Tools for Small Business Interventions. Porth & Saltis. LC 97-77457. 1998. pap. 32.95 (*0-87393-737-6*) Dame Pubns.

Management Consulting Cd-Rom. Convergence Multimedia Staff. 1996. 39.95 (*0-87584-752-8*) Harvard Busn.

Management Consulting in Africa: Utilizing Local Expertise. Ed. by Frederick J. Kaijage. LC 92-34559. (Library of Management for Development). x, 213p. 1993. 36.00 (*1-56549-017-7*); pap. 18.95 (*1-56549-016-9*) Kumarian Pr.

Management Consulting, 1995. Kelly Huang. 1995. pap. text 25.00 (*0-07-103627-X*) McGraw.

Management Consulting, 1994: A Harvard Business School Career Guide. Ed. by Wai-Chan Chan. 1993. pap. text 20.00 (*0-07-103433-1*) McGraw.

Management Consulting, 1991-92, Vol. 3. Harvard Business School Press Staff. (Harvard Business Review Bk.). 1990. pap. text 20.00 (*0-07-103298-3*) McGraw.

Management Consulting, 1993: A Harvard Business School Career Guide. Ed. by Chris Wheeler. 1993. pap. text 20.00 (*0-07-103394-7*) McGraw.

Management Consulting Services in Canada: A Strategic Entry Report, 1998. Compiled by Icon Group International Staff. (Country Industry Report). (Illus.). 126p. 1999. ring bd. 1260.00 incl. audio compact disk (*0-7418-0244-9*) Icon Grp.

***Management Consulting Services in Mexico: A Strategic Entry Report, 1996.** Compiled by Icon Group International Staff. (Illus.). 145p. 1999. ring bd. 1450.00 incl. audio compact disk (*0-7418-1295-9*) Icon Grp.

Management Consulting Services in Thailand: A Strategic Entry Report, 1997. Compiled by Icon Group International Staff. (Illus.). 141p. 1999. ring bd. 1410.00 incl. audio compact disk (*0-7418-0863-3*) Icon Grp.

***Management Consulting 2000.** 1999. pap. 29.95 (*1-57851-191-7*, HBS Pr) Harvard Busn.

***Management, Containment, Risk Assessment.** Chester D. Rail. LC 00-101718. (Groundwater Contamination Ser.: Vol. 2). 192p. 2000. text 99.95 (*1-56676-897-7*) Technomic.

Management Contracting Law & Practice. Members of Freshfields' Construction & Engineering. 165p. 1994. pap. 50.00 (*1-874241-18-X*, Pub. by Cavendish Pubng) Gaunt.

Management Control. Samuel Eilon. LC 71-879031. (Studies in Management). xi, 207p. 1971. write for info. (*0-333-12938-5*) Macmillan.

Management Control. 6th ed. Anthony Young. 1998. 15.00 (*0-256-25533-4*) McGraw.

Management Control: Planning, Control, Measurement & Evaluation. Kenneth J. Euske. LC 83-12236. (A-W Paperback Series in Accounting). (Illus.). 128p. 1984. pap. text 24.75 (*0-201-10494-6*) Addison-Wesley.

Management, Control & Accountability in Nonprofit/Voluntary Organizations. Treasa Hayes. 296p. 1996. 74.95 (*1-85972-207-5*, Pub. by Avebry) Ashgate Pub Co.

Management Control & Organizational Behaviour. Phil Johnson & John Gill. LC 93-18450. 1993. 32.00 (*1-85396-163-9*, Pub. by P Chapman) Taylor & Francis.

Management Control Function. Robert N. Anthony. 260p. 1988. 27.96 (*0-07-103201-0*) McGraw.

Management Control in a Voluntary Organization: Accounting & Accountants in Organization Context. Peter Booth. LC 95-22958. (New Works in Accounting History). 304p. 1995. text 66.00 (*0-8153-2239-9*) Garland.

Management Control in Nonprofit Organizations. 2nd ed. Robert N. Anthony & Regina Herzlinger. (C). 1980. 64.95 (*0-256-02326-3*, Irwn McGrw-H) McGrw-H Hghr Educ.

Management Control in Nonprofit Organizations. 5th ed. Robert N. Anthony & David W. Young. LC 93-18016. 944p. (C). 1993. text 72.35 (*0-256-08642-7*, Irwn McGrw-H) McGrw-H Hghr Educ.

Management Control in Nonprofit Organizations. 6th ed. Robert N. Anthony & David W. Young. LC 98-7083. 888p. 1998. 89.06 (*0-256-25532-6*) McGraw.

***Management Control of Strategic Systems Beyond Y2K.** Teri Stokes. (Illus.). 32p. 2000. 39.50 (*1-930114-00-1*) Serentec Pr.

Management Control Systems. Joseph A. Maciariello. (Illus.). 720p. (C). 1984. text. write for info. (*0-318-57575-2*) P-H.

Management Control Systems. Mary T. Ziebell. (C). 1991. pap. text, teacher ed. 14.75 (*0-15-554659-7*) Harcourt Coll Pubs.

Management Control Systems. 8th ed. Robert N. Anthony & Vijay Govindarajan. LC 93-48215. (Irwin Series in Graduate Accounting). 888p. (C). 1994. text 74.85 (*0-256-13154-6*, Irwn McGrw-H) McGrw-H Hghr Educ.

Management Control Systems. 9th ed. Govinda Anthony. LC 97-21861. 1997. text 44.12 (*0-256-16878-4*, Irwn McGrw-H) McGrw-H Hghr Educ.

Management Control Systems. 10th ed. Robert N. Anthony. 2000. 69.74 (*0-07-231635-7*) McGraw.

Management Control Systems: Using Adaptive Systems to Attain Control. 2nd ed. Joseph A. Maciariello & Calvin J. Kirby. LC 93-29228. 560p. 1994. pap. text 98.00 (*0-13-098146-X*) P-H.

Management Cost Accounting: Fall 1996. 4th ed. John Drury. 1996. pap. text 24.99 (*1-86152-230-4*) Thomson Learn.

Management Crisis & Business Revolution. John Harte. LC 96-47504. 362p. 1997. text 34.95 (*1-56000-305-7*) Transaction Pubs.

Management Data Bases. R. Clay Sprowls. LC 76-6100. 398p. reprint ed. pap. 123.40 (*0-608-10843-X*, 205518500011) Bks Demand.

***Management Decision & Financial Acount Reports, Vol. 2.** Baginski. (C). 2000. pap. 11.25 (*0-324-05584-6*) Sth-Wstrn College.

Management Decision Making. Gerald L. Rose. (C). 1987. text 22.00 (*0-316-75638-5*) Little.

Management Decision Making: A Formal-Intuitive Approach. Jerome D. Braverman. LC 80-65870. 253p. reprint ed. pap. 78.50 (*0-608-12688-8*, 202350900033) Bks Demand.

***Management Decision Making: Spreadsheet Modeling, Analysis & Application.** George E. Monahan. LC 99-57330. (Illus.). 600p. 2000. write for info. (*0-521-78118-3*) Cambridge U Pr.

Management Decision Making for Nurses. 3rd ed. Bessie L. Marquis & Carol J. Huston. LC 97-24663. 464p. 1997. pap. text 29.95 (*0-397-55429-X*) Lppncott W & W.

Management Decision Making for Nurses: 101 Case Studies. Bessie L. Marquis & Carol J. Huston. (Illus.). 393p. 1987. text 26.95 (*0-397-54663-7*, Lippncott) Lppncott W & W.

Management Decision Making in Chinese Enterprises. Yuan Lu. (Studies on the Chinese Economy). 230p. 1996. text 69.95 (*0-312-15850-5*) St Martin.

Management Decisions. Sur Das. 1985. 69.00 (*0-7855-0742-6*, Pub. by Current Dist) St Mut.

Management Decisions & Actions, 6 vols., Set. 2nd ed. Richard R. Sylvester. 1983. 249.75 (*0-932010-23-7*) PhD Pub.

Management Decisions & Actions: Critical Issues & Corporate Strategy. 3rd ed. Richard R. Sylvester. (Professional Series in Quantitative Methods & Artificial Intelligence). 1988. 89.00 (*0-932010-55-5*) PhD Pub.

Management Decisions & Financial Accounting. Baginski. (AB - Accounting Principles Ser.). (C). 2000. 87.95 (*0-538-84086-2*) S-W Pub.

Management Decisions by Objectives. George S. Odiorne. 1968. 17.95 (*0-13-548529-0*) P-H.

Management Development: A Guide for the Profession. Ed. by J. Prokopenko. 1998. pap. 40.00 (*92-2-109196-1*) Intl Labour Office.

***Management Development: Strategies for Action.** Alan Mumford. 304p. 2000. pap. 56.95 (*0-8464-5108-5*) Beekman Pubs.

Management Development: Strategies for Action. Alan Mumford. 256p. (C). 1989. 110.00 (*0-85292-426-7*, Pub. by IPM Hse); 125.00 (*0-7855-4548-4*, Pub. by IPM Hse) St Mut.

Management Development: Strategies for Action. Alan Mumford. 248p. (C). 1993. pap. text 79.00 (*0-85292-518-2*, Pub. by IPM Hse) St Mut.

Management Development: Strategies for Action. Ed. by Alan Munford. 240p. (C). 1991. pap. 95.00 (*0-85292-476-3*, Pub. by IPM Hse) St Mut.

Management Development: Strategy & Practice. Jean Woodall & Diana Winstanley. LC 97-22302. 1998. 68.95 (*0-631-20840-2*) Blackwell Pubs.

Management Development: Strategy & Practice. Jean Woodall & Diana Winstanley. LC 97-22302. 288p. (C). 1998. pap. text 36.95 (*0-631-19866-0*) Blackwell Pubs.

Management Development & Training Handbook. 2nd ed. Bernard Taylor. 576p. 1985. text 84.95 (*0-07-084598-0*) McGraw.

Management Development Beyond the Fringe: A Practical Guide to Alternative Approaches. Phil Lowe & Ralph Lewis. LC 93-42469. 192p. 1994. pap. text 19.95 (*0-89397-397-1*) Nichols Pub.

Management Development in East-West Joint Ventures: A Guide for Managers in the Economies in Transition. 128p. 30.00 (*92-1-116567-9*, E.93.II.E.18) UN.

Management Development in Maternal & Child Health & Family Planning Programme: Proceedings of an Intercountry Workshop. (SEARO Technical Publications Ser.: No. 11). 124p. 1988. pap. text 6.00 (*92-9022-150-X*) World Health.

Management Development in Poland: Building Management Training Capacity with Foreign Partnerships. Senior Government & Institutions Adviser Staff et al. Ed. by Richard Thomas. LC 98-19211. 250p. 1998. text 42.95 (*1-84014-445-9*, Pub. by Ashgate Pub) Ashgate Pub Co.

Management Development in the Construction Industry: Guidelines for the Professional Engineer. 45p. 1992. pap. text 15.00 (*0-7277-1677-8*, Pub. by T Telford) RCH.

Management Development Outdoors. Bill Krouwel & Steve Goodwill. 136p. 1994. pap. 25.00 (*0-7494-1162-7*, Kogan Pg Educ) Stylus Pub VA.

Management Development Strategies. John J. Sherwood et al. 34p. 1983. pap. 35.00 (*0-685-06118-3*, Pergamon Pr) Elsevier.

Management Development Strategies. John J. Sherwood et al. (Studies in Productivity: Highlights of the Literature Ser.: Vol. 29). 29p. 1983. pap. 39.00 (*0-08-029510-X*) Work in Amer.

Management Development Through Cultural Diversity. Ronnie Lessem. LC 97-45920. 432p. (C). 1998. 100.00 (*0-415-17875-4*); pap. 34.99 (*0-415-17876-2*) Routledge.

Management Development Through Job Experiences: An Annotated Bibliography. Cynthia D. McCawley & Stephane Brutus. LC 97-23154. 116p. 1998. pap. text 20.00 (*1-882197-32-1*) Ctr Creat Leader.

Management Dictionary. Ghattas & Brech. 250p. 1984. 24.95 (*0-86685-727-3*) Intl Bk Ctr.

Management Dictionary (English-German) 5th enl. rev. ed. Werner Sommer & Hanns-Martin Schoenfeld. 621p. (C). 1979. text 52.35 (*3-11-007708-6*) De Gruyter.

Management Dilemmas: Theory of Constraints Approach to Problems. Eli Schragenheim. LC 98-41213. 240p. 1998. per. 19.95 (*1-57444-222-8*) St Lucie Pr.

Management Dimensions: New Challenges of the Mind. Owen B. Hardy & R. Clayton McWhorter. 304p. 1988. 107.00 (*0-87189-760-1*) Aspen Pub.

Management Dimensions of Development: Perspectives & Strategies. Milton J. Esman. LC 91-26410. (Library of Management for Development, New Directions in Development Management Ser.). 176p. 1991. pap. 16.95 (*0-931816-64-5*) Kumarian Pr.

Management Discipline. Burden. 400p. 1995. pap. 53.95 (*0-471-36521-1*) Wiley.

Management Discipline Professional Cop. Burden. 1995. pap. text 25.00 (*0-471-36518-1*) Wiley.

***Management Dynamics: Concepts of Management for a New Century.** 2nd ed. Jane R Flagello. 1998. pap. 34.40 (*0-536-01027-7*) Pearson Custom.

Management Dynamism. 255p. 1992. pap. 15.00 (*92-833-2114-6*) Productivity Inc.

Management Economics. 4th ed. Mansfield. Date not set. pap. text. write for info. (*0-393-97316-6*) Norton.

Management Economics: Study Guide & Casebook. 4th ed. Mansfield. 1998. pap., student ed. write for info. (*0-393-97314-X*) Norton.

Management Economics: Theory, Applications, & Cases. 4th ed. Mansfield. LC 98-18812. 1998. 91.75 (*0-393-97315-8*) Norton.

Management Economics with ABC SE 3.5 Windows. 8th ed. Hirsche. (C). 1995. 93.00 (*0-03-018757-5*) Harcourt.

Management Economics with Disk 3.5. 2nd ed. Samuels. 1995. 65.00 (*0-03-016437-0*) Harcourt.

Management Economics with Thinking Strategies. 4th ed. Mansfield et al. 1999. text. write for info. (*0-393-99030-3*) Norton.

Management Education. Robert R. Locke. LC 98-9491. (History of Management Thought Ser.). 8p. 1998. text 198.95 (*1-85521-990-5*, Pub. by Ashgate Pub) Ashgate Pub Co.

Management Education: Implications for Libraries & Library Schools; the 36th Annual Conference of the Graduate Library School, April 9-10, 1973. University of Chicago, Graduate Library School. Ed. by Herman H. Fussler et al. LC 73-92600. (Graduate Library School Papers Conference, 36th, 1973). 121p. reprint ed. pap. 37.60 (*0-608-16551-4*, 202677400052) Bks Demand.

Management Education & Development: An Annotated Resource Book. Theodore T. Herbert & Edward Yost. LC 77-91110. 211p. 1978. lib. bdg. 59.95 (*0-313-20040-8*, HME/, Greenwood Pr) Greenwood.

Management Education & Training: Understanding - Eastern European Perspectives. Ed. by George Tesar. LC 92-42910. 182p. (C). 1994. lib. bdg. 19.50 (*0-89464-741-5*) Krieger.

Management, Education & Training in Japan: Background & Practice. Lola Okasaki-Ward. LC 93-22622. 640p. (C). 1993. lib. bdg. 208.00 (*1-85333-781-1*, Pub. by Graham & Trotman) Kluwer Academic.

Management Education in Historical Perspective. Lars Engwall & Vera Negri Zamagni. LC 98-18299. xiii, 160p. 1999. 59.95 (*0-7190-5183-5*, Pub. by Manchester Univ Pr) St Martin.

Management Enzyklopaedie, 7 vols., Set. Autorentaem Staff. (GER.). 1973. 1750.00 (*0-8288-6317-2*, M7091) Fr & Eur.

Management Enzyklopaedie, 10 vols., Set, Vols. 1-10. Autorentaem Staff. (GER.). 3200p. 1975. pap. 395.00 (*0-8288-5934-5*, M7092) Fr & Eur.

Management Enzyklopaedisches Lexikon. Wolfgang J. Koschnick. (GER.). 1000p. 1993. write for info. (*0-7859-8277-9*, 3110128470) Fr & Eur.

Management Essentials for Public Works Administrators. (C). 1975. 20.00 (*0-917084-01-2*) Am Public Works.

Management Ethics: Integrity at Work. Joseph A. Petrick & John F. Quinn. LC 96-51271. (Series on Business Ethics). 384p. 1997. 58.00 (*0-8039-5796-3*); pap. 27.95 (*0-8039-5797-1*) Sage.

***Management Ethics in Sport: Excellence & Compliance.** Robert Mertzman. (C). 1999. pap. text 89.95 (*0-7872-6113-0*) Kendall-Hunt.

Management Expert Systems. Christian Ernst. (A-W Insight Ser.). (Illus.). (C). 1988. text 31.50 (*0-201-19691-3*) Addison-Wesley.

***Management Fads in Higher Education: Where They Come From, What They Do, Why They Fail.** Robert Birnbaum. 320p. 2000. 32.95 (*0-7879-4456-4*) Jossey-Bass.

Management Financial Institutions. (C). 1990. write for info. (*0-201-41711-1*) Addison-Wesley.

Management, Fitting & Grooming. Meredith Hodges. (Training Mules & Donkeys: A Logical Approach to Longears Ser.: Vol. 8). spiral bd., wbk. ed. 39.95 incl. VHS Willman Prodns.

M

An Asterisk (*) at the beginning of an entry indicates that the title is appearing for the first time.

M

Management for a Small Planet. W. Edward Stead & Jean G. Stead. (Illus.). 232p. (C). 1992. 45.00 (*0-8039-4634-1*); pap. 19.95 (*0-8039-4635-X*) Sage.
Management for a Small Planet. W. Edward Stead & Jean G. Stead. (C). 1996. pap. 22.95 (*0-7619-0294-5*) Sage.
Management for a Small Planet. 2nd ed. W. Edward Stead & Jean G. Stead. 288p. (C). 1996. 48.00 (*0-7619-0293-7*) Sage.
Management for Athletic/Sport Administration: Theory & Practice. 2nd ed. Francis J. Bridges & Libby L. Roquemore. (Illus.). 448p. (Orig.). (C). 1996. pap. text. write for info. (*0-9623126-5-7*) ESM Bks.
*__Management for Athletic/Sport Administration: Theory & Practice.__ 3rd rev. ed. Francis J. Bridges & Libby L. Roquemore. LC 00-133048. (Illus.). 410p. (Orig.). 2000. pap. 45.00 (*0-9623126-6-5*) ESM Bks.
Management for Attorneys. David Bresnick. 160p. 1987. 37.50 (*0-9610834-3-3*) Human Serv Pr.
Management for Bankers. 2nd ed. W. A. Braddick. 390p. 1991. pap. 32.00 (*0-406-00283-5*, U.K., MICHIE) LEXIS Pub.
Management for Building. Lavender. 1966. pap. text. write for info. (*0-582-26235-6*, Pub. by Addison-Wesley) Longman.
Management for Community Health Practice. Marie L. Friedmann. LC 82-20188. 288p. (C). 1983. pap. text 37.50 (*0-534-01240-X*) Jones & Bartlett.
Management for Competitiveness: Maximize Profits, Productivity & Performance. Doris Martin. LC 91-90340. 101p. (Orig.). 1991. pap. 15.95 (*0-9615541-8-5*) Martin Mgmt.
*__Management (For CPCU 7)__ rev. ed. R. Robert Rackley. (CPCU Ser.). 1999. 160.00 (*1-57195-190-3*) Insurance Achiev.
Management for Doctors. Ed. by Jenny Simpson & Richard Smith. 200p. (Orig.). (C). 1995. pap. text 27.00 (*0-7279-0858-8*, Pub. by BMJ Pub) Login Brothers Bk Co.
Management for Growth. Richard Normann. LC 77-2839. (Wiley-Interscience Publications). 216p. reprint ed. pap. 67.00 (*0-7837-1888-8*, 204208900001) Bks Demand.
*__Management for Health Professionals.__ N. Wheeler. (Illus.). 224p. 2000. pap. 30.00 (*0-7487-4038-4*, Pub. by S Thornes Pubs) Intl Spec Bk.
Management for Hospital Doctors. Maurice Burrows et al. LC 93-37792. 336p. 1994. text 85.00 (*0-7506-0880-3*) Buttrwrth-Heinemann.
Management for Librarians: Fundamentals & Issues, 33. John R. Rizzo. LC 79-8950. (Contributions in Librarianship & Information Science Ser.: No. 33). (Illus.). 339p. 1980. 55.00 (*0-313-21990-7*, RML/, Greenwood Pr) Greenwood.
Management for Nurses & Health Care Professionals. Ed. by J. E. Clark & L. Copcutt. (Illus.). 242p. 1996. pap. write for info. (*0-443-05091-0*) Church.
Management for Opticians. 2nd ed. Ray Dennis & Debra White. LC 98-27915. 295p. 1998. pap. text 45.00 (*0-7506-9756-3*) Buttrwrth-Heinemann.
Management for Privatization: Lessons from Industry & Public Service. Ed. by Joseph Prokopenko. LC 96-145880. (Management Development Ser.: Vol. 32). xiii, 300p. 1995. pap. 33.75 (*92-2-109198-8*) Intl Labour Office.
Management for Productivity. Byron N. McClenney. LC 80-134596. 128p. reprint ed. pap. 39.70 (*0-608-17104-2*, 202729400055) Bks Demand.
Management for Productivity & Business Without Bosses: How Self Managing Teams are Building High Performing Companies Businesses Without Bosses Set. 5th ed. John R. Schermerhorn et al. 880p. 1996. pap. 104.90 (*0-471-17407-6*) Wiley.
Management for Productivity & Custom Experiences for Managing Organizational Behavior, 5th Edition, Basic Organizational Behavior & Managment for Productivity, 4th Edition & Case Supplement to Accompany Management. 5th ed. John R. Schermerhorn et al. 814p. 1996. pap. 114.85 (*0-471-17406-8*) Wiley.
Management for Proprietors & Partnerships. abr. rev. ed. Intro. by Luanna C. Blagrove. (AMERCE Management Ser.). (Illus.). 250p. 1988. 24.95 (*0-939776-03-0*) Blagrove Pubns.
Management for Quality Improvement: The Seven New QC Tools. Ed. by Shigeru Mizuno. LC 88-42625. (Illus.). 323p. 1988. 65.00 (*0-915299-29-1*) Productivity Inc.
Management for Results: A "How to" Workbook for Improving the Management of Your Veterinary Practice. Michael H. Riegger. 200p. 1992. pap. 59.95 (*0-929870-06-9*) Advanstar Commns.
Management for Special Needs: Where There's a Will. Brian Walters. LC 94-195525. (Special Needs in Ordinary Schools Ser.). (Illus.). 160p. 1993. pap. 29.95 (*0-304-32799-9*) Continuum.
Management for Supervisors. Didactic Systems Staff. 1970. pap. 26.25 (*0-89401-056-5*) Didactic Syst.
Management for Supervisors. Didactic Systems Staff. (FRE.). 1970. pap. 35.00 (*0-89401-057-3*); pap. 35.00 (*0-89401-058-1*) Didactic Syst.
Management for Technologists. Arthur Mills. 272p. 1968. pap. 28.00 (*0-8464-1425-2*) Beekman Pubs.
Management for the Eyecare Practitioner. Irving Bennett. LC 92-49731. (Illus.). 220p. 1992. text 84.00 (*0-7506-9319-3*) Buttrwrth-Heinemann.
Management for the 1980s. rev. ed. William F. Christopher. LC 79-55061. 303p. reprint ed. pap. 94.00 (*0-608-13026-5*, 202352900033) Bks Demand.
Management for the Small Design Firm: Handling Your Practice, Personnel, Finances, & Projects. Jim Morgan. LC 97-7826. (Illus.). 176p. 1997. 45.00 (*0-8230-2967-0*) Watsn-Guptill.
Management for the 21st Century. Stearns. (C). 1997. text 65.00 (*0-03-006859-2*) Harcourt Coll Pubs.
Management for Your Church: How to Realize Your Church's Potential Through a Systems Approach. Norman Shawchuck & Alvin J. Lindgren. (Illus.). 160p. (C). 1985. reprint ed. pap. 12.95 (*0-938180-14-2*) Spiritual Growth.
*__Management Fundamentals.__ Lussier. LC 99-28301. (SWC-Management Ser.). 606p. 1999. pap. 59.95 (*0-324-01337-X*) Thomson Learn.
Management Fundamentals. Peter Moutsatson & Joseph T. Straub. 442p. (C). 1998. pap. text 43.95 (*1-56226-417-6*) CAT Pub.
Management Game: How to Win with People. Richard M. Greene, Jr. (Illus.). 281p. 1969. reprint ed. 24.95 (*0-934487-07-3*) R M Greene.
Management Game for the Social Services. Anthony Hall & Jimmie Algie. 1974. 25.00 (*0-7855-0834-1*, Pub. by Natl Inst Soc Work) St Mut.
*__Management, Global & Educational Issues, Vol. M.__ Ed. by M. Deistler et al. 458p. 1999. pap. 126.00 (*0-08-043224-7*) Elsevier.
Management Glossary: (English-Arabic) H. Johannsen. (ARA & ENG.). 238p. 1972. 19.95 (*0-86685-069-4*, LDL0694, Pub. by Librairie du Liban) Intl Bk Ctr.
Management Golf: What's Your Handicap? Michael J. Kami. (Illus.). 112p. (Orig.). 1997. per. 19.95 (*1-57444-105-1*) St Lucie Pr.
Management Guide for Low-Input Sustainable Apple Production. Lorraine P. Berkett. (Illus.). 54p. (Orig.). (C). 1994. pap. text 30.00 (*0-7881-0754-2*) DIANE Pub.
Management Guide to Communicating. Kate Keenan. Ed. by Anne Taute. (Management Guides Ser.). 64p. 1996. pap. 5.95 (*1-85304-789-9*, Pub. by Ravette Bks) Assoc Pubs Grp.
Management Guide to Delegating. Kate Keenan. Ed. by Anne Taute. (Management Guides Ser.). 64p. 1996. pap. 5.95 (*1-85304-797-X*, Pub. by Ravette Bks) Assoc Pubs Grp.
Management Guide to Digital Printing. 1996. 50.00 (*0-614-25535-X*, 00PO44704) Print Indus Am.
Management Guide to Health Care Information Systems. Richard M. Sneider. (Health Care Administration Ser.). 270p. 1987. 75.00 (*0-87189-855-1*) Aspen Pub.
Management Guide to Internet Resources. Byron J. Finch. LC 96-77000. 160p. (C). 1996. pap. 17.50 (*0-07-021718-1*) McGraw.
Management Guide to Leveraged Buyouts. Edward K. Crawford. LC 86-32390. (Professional Banking & Finance Ser.). 272p. 1987. 110.00 (*0-471-83232-4*) Wiley.
Management Guide to Making Time. Kate Keenan. Ed. by Anne Taute. (Management Guides Ser.). 64p. 1996. pap. 5.95 (*1-85304-787-2*, Pub. by Ravette Bks) Assoc Pubs Grp.
Management Guide to Managing. Kate Keenan. Ed. by Anne Taute. (Management Guides Ser.). 64p. 1996. pap. 5.95 (*1-85304-794-5*, Pub. by Ravette Bks) Assoc Pubs Grp.
Management Guide to Managing Yourself. Kate Keenan. Ed. by Anne Taute. (Management Guides Ser.). 64p. 1996. pap. 5.95 (*1-85304-786-4*, Pub. by Ravette Bks) Assoc Pubs Grp.
Management Guide to Meetings. Kate Keenan. 64p. 1996. pap. text 5.95 (*1-85304-793-7*) Assoc Pubs Grp.
Management Guide to Motivating. Kate Keenan. Ed. by Anne Taute. (Management Guides Ser.). 64p. 1996. pap. 5.95 (*1-85304-791-0*, Pub. by Ravette Bks) Assoc Pubs Grp.
Management Guide to Negotiating. Kate Keenan. Ed. by Anne Taute. (Management Guides Ser.). 64p. 1996. pap. 5.95 (*1-85304-796-1*, Pub. by Ravette Bks) Assoc Pubs Grp.
Management Guide to PIA Ratios see 1996 PIA Ratios
Management Guide to Planning. Kate Keenan. Ed. by Anne Taute. (Management Guides Ser.). 64p. 1996. pap. 5.95 (*1-85304-788-0*, Pub. by Ravette Bks) Assoc Pubs Grp.
Management Guide to Retrofitting Wastewater Treatment Plants. Lawrence Quick. LC 97-61845. 120p. 1997. pap. text 39.95 (*1-56676-594-3*) Technomic.
Management Guide to Selecting People. Kate Keenan. Ed. by Anne Taute. (Management Guides Ser.). 64p. 1996. pap. 5.95 (*1-85304-790-2*, Pub. by Ravette Bks) Assoc Pubs Grp.
Management Guide to Solving Problems. Kate Keenan. Ed. by Anne Taute. (Management Guides Ser.). 64p. 1996. pap. 5.95 (*1-85304-792-9*, Pub. by Ravette Bks) Assoc Pubs Grp.
Management Guide to the Protection of Information Resources. 1990. lib. bdg. 150.00 (*0-8490-4035-3*) Gordon Pr.
Management Guide to Understanding Behaviour. Kate Keenan. Ed. by Anne Taute. (Management Guides Ser.). 64p. 1996. pap. 5.95 (*1-85304-795-3*, Pub. by Ravette Bks) Assoc Pubs Grp.
Management Guidelines for Adult Nurse Practitioners. Lynne M. Hektor Dunphy. LC 98-11268. (Illus.). 568p. 1998. pap. 38.95 (*0-8036-0229-4*) Davis Co.
*__Management Guidelines for Efficient Sheep Production.__ rev. ed. G. E. Ricketts. (Illus.). 63p. 1999. pap. text 25.00 (*0-7881-8286-2*) DIANE Pub.
Management Guidelines for Gerontologic Nurse Practitioners. Laurie Kennedy-Malone et al. LC 99-15302. (Illus.). 624p. (C). 1999. pap. text 36.95 (*0-8036-0297-9*) Davis Co.
Management Guidelines for Increasing Populations of Birds That Feed on Western Spruce Budworm. Lisa A. Langelier & Edward O. Garton. (Illus.). 24p. 1997. reprint ed. pap. 3.40 (*0-89904-655-X*, Wildlife Resrch Grp) Crumb Elbow Pub.
Management Guidelines for Pediatric Nurse Practitioners. Nancy L. Hill & Linda Sullivan. LC 98-5907. (Illus.). 536p. 1999. pap. 38.95 (*0-8036-0230-8*) Davis Co.
Management Guidelines for the Treatment of Renal Anemia: Journal: American Journal of Nephrology, Vol. 10, Supplement 2, 1990. Ed. by Marsha Wolfson & W. M. Bennett. (Illus.). iv, 54p. 1990. pap. 18.50 (*3-8055-5276-9*) S Karger.
Management Guidelines for Women's Health Nurse Practitioners. Kathleen Brown. LC 99-26449. (Illus.). 464p. (C). 1999. pap. text 38.95 (*0-8036-0292-8*) Davis Co.
*__Management Gurus.__ Lv. 4. (C). 2000. 7.00 (*0-582-43046-1*) Addison-Wesley.
Management Gurus: What Makes Them & How to Become One. Adrezej A. Huczynski. (Illus.). 352p. (C). (gr. 13). 1992. pap. 36.95 (*0-415-02244-4*, A7678) Thomson Learn.
Management Gurus: What Makes Them & How to Become One. Andrzej A. Huczynski. 352p. 1996. pap. 17.50 (*1-86152-021-2*) Thomson Learn.
Management Handbook for Volunteer Programs. Margaret Price et al. Ed. by Jonathan McKallip & V. K. Lawson. 1984. pap. text 6.50 (*0-930713-37-0*) Lit Vol Am.
Management Ideas, in Brief: Preparing for the New Millennium. Sultan Kermally. LC 97-8551. 224p. 1997. pap. text 19.95 (*0-7506-3450-2*) Buttrwrth-Heinemann.
Management Ideas That Work. 1989. 25.00 (*1-878604-17-1*) Briefings Pub Grp.
Management Ideas That Work! Zweig White & Associates Staff. Ed. by Frederick D. White. 236p. 1993. pap. text 39.00 (*0-9630705-8-4*) Zweig White.
Management Impacts of Information Technology: Perspectives on Organizational Changes & Growth. Ed. by Edward J. Szewczak & Coral Snodgrass. LC 90-82960. 548p. (C). 1991. text 53.50 (*1-878289-08-X*) Idea Group Pub.
Management Impacts on Water Quality of Forests & Rangelands. Dan Binkley & Thomas C. Brown. (Illus.). 120p. 1997. reprint ed. 19.00 (*0-89904-595-2*, Bear Meadows Resrch Grp); reprint ed. pap. 13.00 (*0-89904-596-0*, Bear Meadows Resrch Grp) Crumb Elbow Pub.
Management in Action. V. S. Rao. (Dynamic Organisational Behaviour Ser.). (C). 1991. text 30.00 (*81-7141-126-6*) S Asia.
Management in Action. 2nd ed. Robert E. Stoffels. LC 73-85629. (Specialized Ser.). (Illus.). 48p. (C). 1987. spiral bd. 16.95 (*1-56016-068-3*) ABC TeleTraining.
Management in Action: Guidelines for New Managers. William D. Hitt. LC 84-18430. 304p. 1986. 24.95 (*0-935470-20-4*) Battelle.
Management in Action: Guidelines for New Managers. William D. Hitt. 304p. 1992. pap. 29.95 (*0-7803-1008-X*, PP3574) Inst Electrical.
Management in Arid & Semi-Arid Areas No. 662: WMO. I. G. Gringof & G. P. Obasi. (Technical Note Ser.). 148p. 1989. pap. write for info. (*92-63-10662-2*, Pub. by Wrld Meteorological) St Mut.
Management in Banking. Ed. by Sheffield City Poly-CIB Staff. (Bankers Workbook Ser.). (C). 1989. 125.00 (*0-85297-282-2*, Pub. by Chartered Bank) St Mut.
Management in Banking. Ed. by W. Whyte & P. Plenderleith. (C). 1989. 115.00 (*0-85297-279-2*, Pub. by Chartered Bank) St Mut.
Management in China: During & after Mao in Enterprises, Government & Party. Oiva Laaksonen. (Studies in Organization: No. 12). 379p. (C). 1988. text 57.95 (*3-11-009958-6*) De Gruyter.
Management in China: Owning in the Age of Reform. John Child. (Illus.). 352p. 1996. pap. text 22.95 (*0-521-57466-8*) Cambridge U Pr.
Management in China: The Experience of Foreign Business. Ed. by Roger Strange. LC 97-30436. (Studies in Asia Pacific Business Ser.). 288p. (C). 1997. text 37.50 (*0-7146-4842-6*, Pub. by F Cass Pubs); pap. text 19.50 (*0-7146-4398-X*, Pub. by F Cass Pubs) Intl Spec Bk.
Management in China During the Age of Reform. John Child. (Cambridge Studies in Management: No. 23). (Illus.). 352p. (C). 1994. text 64.95 (*0-521-42005-9*) Cambridge U Pr.
Management in Developing Countries. Kabinda N. Kanungo. Ed. by Alfred M. Jaeger. (Organizational Behaviour & Management Ser.). 320p. (C). (gr. 13). 1990. pap. 71.95 (*0-415-03505-8*, A4487) Thomson Learn.
*__Management in Eastern Europe.__ Vincent Edwards & Peter A. Lawrence. LC 00-42055. 2000. write for info. (*0-312-23810-X*) St Martin.
Management in Eighty Days: An Executive's Encyclopaedia of Management Practices, 10 vols. Parag Diwan. 1997. 3400.00 (*81-86830-10-3*, Pub. by Print Hse) St Mut.
Management in Engineering. 2nd ed. Gail Freeman-Bell. 496p. (C). 1996. pap. 40.00 (*0-13-233933-1*, Macmillan Coll) P-H.
Management in English Language Teaching. Ron White et al. (Illus.). 352p. (C). 1991. pap. text 26.95 (*0-521-37763-3*) Cambridge U Pr.
Management in Extension. 3rd ed. James A. Buford, Jr. et al. 380p. 1995. text 12.00 (*0-9648547-0-8*) OSU Extension.
Management in Further Education: Theory & Practice. Harriet Harper. LC 97-198255. 144p. 1997. pap. 24.95 (*1-85346-473-2*, Pub. by David Fulton) Taylor & Francis.
Management in General Practice: Practical Problems in General Practice. Ed. by Malcolm Fox. 123p. 1997. pap. 27.00 (*0-7279-1037-X*, Pub. by BMJ Pub) Login Brothers Bk Co.
Management in Geratal Practice: Health Care for Older People. Ed. by Steve Gliffe et al. 177p. 1998. pap. text 32.00 (*0-7279-1192-9*, Pub. by BMJ Pub) Login Brothers Bk Co.
Management in Government. Didactic Systems Staff. (Simulation Game Ser.). 1971. pap. 26.25 (*0-89401-059-X*) Didactic Syst.
Management in Health Care Systems. J. H. Brown. 152p. 1984. 91.00 (*0-8493-5572-9*, RA393, CRC Reprint) Franklin.
Management in International Perspective. Ed. by S. Benjamin Prasad. LC 67-10930. (Orig.). 1967. pap. text 9.95 (*0-89197-289-7*) Irvington.
Management in MGP General Practice: Procedures in General Practice. (Illus.). 177p. 1997. pap. 43.00 (*0-614-31252-3*, Pub. by BMJ Pub) Login Brothers Bk Co.
Management in Neuro-Oncology. Ed. by J. G. Hildebrand. LC 92-49588. 1993. write for info. (*3-540-56095-5*); 111.00 (*0-387-56095-5*) Spr-Verlag.
Management in Nursing. Ed. by Marjorie Cuthbert et al. (Illus.). 327p. 1992. text 45.00 (*0-7295-0380-1*) Bailliere Tindall.
Management in Nursing: An Experiential Approach That Makes Theory Work for You. Elaine L. La Monica. LC 90-9455. 464p. 1990. 51.95 (*0-8261-6580-X*) Springer Pub.
Management in Occupational Therapy. Zielfa Maslin. 1991. 45.95 (*1-56593-009-6*, 0250) Thomson Learn.
Management in Physical Therapy: An Integrated Science. Frank J. M. Walter. (Illus.). 304p. (C). (gr. 13). 1993. text 53.00 (*0-8016-6416-0*, 06416) Mosby Inc.
Management in Post-Mao China: An Insider's View. Joseph Y. Battat. LC 86-6957. (Research for Business Decisions Ser.: No. 76). (Illus.). 198p. reprint ed. pap. 61.40 (*0-8357-1663-5*, 207036200088) Bks Demand.
Management in Practice: A Framework for Managing Organizational Change. 3rd ed. Michael Jarrett & Cliff Brown. 240p. 1997. pap. text 26.95 (*0-7506-2571-6*) Buttrwrth-Heinemann.
Management in Quality A Environment. David Griffiths. LC 94-3470. 193p. 1994. 25.00 (*0-87389-222-4*, H0774) ASQ Qual Pr.
Management in Rehabilitation: A Case Study Approach. Charles P. Schuch & Darlene K. Sekerak. (Illus.). 143p. (C). 1995. pap. text 18.95 (*0-8036-7758-8*) Davis Co.
Management in Service Industries. Ed. by Peter Jones. LC 89-37324. 336p. (Orig.). reprint ed. pap. 104.20 (*0-7837-5650-X*, 205907500005) Bks Demand.
Management in Socialist Countries: U. S. S. R. & Central Europe. Witold Kiezun. (Studies in Organization: No. 27). xiv, 361p. (C). 1991. lib. bdg. 54.95 (*3-11-010670-1*) De Gruyter.
Management in the Financial Services Industry: Thriving on Organizational Change. Ian Whyte et al. 548p. 1999. pap. 100.00 (*0-85297-502-3*, Pub. by Chartered Bank) St Mut.
Management in the Fire Service. 2nd ed. 123p. 1990. pap., student ed. 14.95 (*0-945250-15-0*) Davis Pub Co.
Management in the Fire Service. 3rd ed. Harry Carter & Erwin Rausch. Ed. by Jim L. Linville. LC 89-60368. 420p. 1999. text 64.50 (*0-87765-441-7*, MFS-89) Natl Fire Prot.
Management in the Fire Service: Davis Study Guide. 2nd ed. 82p. Date not set. pap. text 14.95 (*0-614-31212-4*, S089) Davis Pub Co.
Management in the Mirror: Stress & Emotional Dysfunction in Lives at the Top. Bernadette H. Schell. LC 98-44553. 264p. 1999. 59.95 (*1-56720-197-0*, Quorum Bks) Greenwood.
Management in the Public Sector: Challenge & Change. 2nd ed. Ed. by Kester Isaac-Henry et al. (Illus.). 331p. 1997. pap. 20.99 (*0-412-73750-7*) Thomson Learn.
Management in the U. S. A. Peter Lawrence. 192p. 1996. 69.95 (*0-8039-7832-4*); pap. 24.95 (*0-8039-7833-2*) Sage.
Management in Transition. rev. ed. Sidney Sugg & Joseph Straub. 196p. (C). 1995. pap. text 33.95 (*1-56226-255-6*) CAT Pub.
Management in Transition: Transforming Managerial Practices & Organizational Strategies for a New Work Culture. Philip R. Harris. LC 85-45055. (Joint Publication in the Jossey-Bass Management Series & the Jossey-Bass Social & Behavioral Science Ser.). 487p. reprint ed. pap. 151.00 (*0-7837-2540-X*, 204269900006) Bks Demand.
Management in Two Cultures: Bridging the Gap Between U. S. & Mexican Managers. rev. ed. Eva S. Kras. LC 94-34342. 126p. 1995. pap. text 16.95 (*1-877864-32-3*) Intercult Pr.
*__Management in Western Europe.__ Peter A. Lawrence & Vincent Edwards. LC 99-45121. 2000. text 65.00 (*0-312-22944-5*) St Martin.
Management in Western Europe: Society, Culture, & Organization in Twelve Nations. Ed. by David J Hickson. (Studies in Organization: No. 47). xiv, 288p. (C). 1993. pap. text 24.95 (*3-11-012710-5*); lib. bdg. 56.95 (*3-11-014174-4*) De Gruyter.
Management Incidents. 2nd ed. Kenneth Keleman. 156p. (C). 1995. spiral bd. 27.95 (*0-8403-9131-5*) Kendall-Hunt.
Management, Industry & Trade in Cotton Textiles. Rockwood Chin. 1965. 18.95 (*0-8084-0207-2*) NCUP.
Management Information: Where to Find It. Marilyn T. Thompson. LC 81-2027. 280p. 1981. 24.00 (*0-8108-1424-2*) Scarecrow.
Management Information & Decision Support Systems in Libraries. Peter Brophy. 200p. 1986. text 54.95 (*0-566-03551-0*) Ashgate Pub Co.

An Asterisk (*) at the beginning of an entry indicates that the title is appearing for the first time.

Management, Information & Systems: An Introduction to Business Information Systems Student Note-Taking Guide. Bill Davis. Date not set. student ed. 15.00 (*0-314-22005-4*) West Pub.

*__Management Information for Marketing & Sales.__ Parkinson. 200p. 1998. pap. text 36.95 (*0-7506-4033-2*) Buttrwrth-Heinemann.

Management Information Reports: Content & Design. Ed. by Sarah A. Burke. LC 90-27329. (Illus.). 56p. (Orig.). 1991. pap. text 34.00 (*0-936742-80-1*, 32491) Robt Morris Assocs.

Management Information System: Project Cases. Lasalle. (C). 1996. pap. text. write for info. (*0-03-055752-6*) Harcourt Coll Pubs.

Management Information System Note Guide. 10th ed. Gupta. (C). 1996. mass mkt. 15.00 (*0-314-08926-8*) West Pub.

Management Information Systems. Cherian. 446p. 1998. pap. text 32.00 (*0-536-01457-4*) Pearson Custom.

Management Information Systems. Ali F. Farhoomand. Date not set. pap. text 30.00 (*0-314-71121-X*) West Pub.

Management Information Systems. Lasalle. (C). 1997. text 49.00 (*0-03-055749-6*) Harcourt Coll Pubs.

Management Information Systems. T. Lucey. 336p. 1995. pap. 59.95 (*1-85805-106-1*, Pub. by DP Publns) St Mut.

Management Information Systems. Mcgarry. 296p. 1998. pap. text 26.30 (*0-536-01633-X*) Pearson Custom.

Management Information Systems. Oz. (C). 1997. pap. 48.00 (*0-7600-4946-7*) Course Tech.

Management Information Systems. Ed. by P. Pascolo & Carlos A. Brebbia. (Management Information Systems Ser.). 516p. 2000. 248.00 (*1-85312-815-5*, 8155, Pub. by WIT Pr) Computational Mech MA.

Management Information Systems. Gerald V. Post & David Anderson. 640p. (C). 1996. text 67.95 (*0-256-17956-5*, Irwn McGrw-H) McGrw-H Hghr Educ.

Management Information Systems. Jack Rudman. (Dantes Subject Standardized Tests (DANTES) Ser.: Vol. 77). 43.95 (*0-8373-6577-5*) Nat Learn.

Management Information Systems. Stewart. 262p. (C). 1998. pap. text 26.75 (*0-536-01486-8*) Pearson Custom.

Management Information Systems. Vladimir Zwass & J. K. Pierson. 144p. (C). 1992. text 25.25 (*0-697-16845-X*, Irwn McGrw-H) McGrw-H Hghr Educ.

Management Information Systems. 2nd ed. Richard J. Lorette et al. (C). 1994. text 74.90 (*0-256-18450-X*, Irwn McGrw-H) McGrw-H Hghr Educ.

Management Information Systems. 2nd ed. Effy Oz. 700p. boxed set 72.95 (*0-7600-1091-9*, Pub. by Course Tech) Thomson Learn.

Management Information Systems. 2nd ed. Parker. 1993. teacher ed. 50.00 (*0-07-048574-7*) McGraw.

Management Information Systems. 2nd ed. Charles S. Parker. 888p. (C). 1993. text 81.75 (*0-07-048573-9*) McGraw.

Management Information Systems. 2nd ed. Post. LC 99-16364. 2000. 66.25 (*0-07-229756-5*) McGraw.

Management Information Systems. 2nd ed. Ed. by M. J. Riley. 425p. 1981. pap. text 23.95 (*0-8162-7190-9*) Holden-Day.

Management Information Systems. 3rd ed. Jerome Kanter. (Illus.). 432p. (C). 1984. text 54.20 (*0-13-549543-1*) P-H.

Management Information Systems. 3rd ed. Kroenke. 1993. 26.25 (*0-07-074752-0*) McGraw.

Management Information Systems. 3rd ed. David M. Kroenke & Richard Hatch. 800p. (C). 1993. 81.88 (*0-07-035938-5*) McGraw.

Management Information Systems. 3rd ed. David M. Kroenke & Richard Hatch. (C). 1993. text 19.74 (*0-07-035948-2*) McGraw.

*__Management Information Systems.__ 6th ed. 174p. (C). 1999. text 18.00 (*0-536-60604-8*) Pearson Custom.

Management Information Systems. 6th ed. Ed. by Prentice-Hall Staff. (C). 1999. text. write for info. (*0-13-040207-9*); text. write for info. (*0-13-040208-7*) P-H.

Management Information Systems. 6th ed. Ed. by Prentice-Hall Staff. (C). 1999. text. write for info. (*0-13-040202-8*) P-H.

Management Information Systems. 6th ed. Ed. by Prentice-Hall Staff. (C). 1999. text. write for info. (*0-13-040206-0*) P-H.

Management Information Systems. 6th ed. Ed. by Prentice-Hall Staff. (C). 2000. text. write for info. (*0-13-040204-4*); text. write for info. (*0-13-040201-X*); text. write for info. (*0-13-040209-5*) P-H.

*__Management Information Systems.__ 7th ed. 1998. write for info. (*0-13-878232-6*) P-H.

Management Information Systems. 8th ed. T. Lucey. LC 98-130408. v, 282 p. 1997. write for info. (*1-85805-303-X*) Letts Educ.

*__Management Information Systems.__ 8th ed. Raymond McLeod & George Schell. 688p. 2000. 89.33 (*0-13-019237-6*) P-H.

Management Information Systems: A Contemporary Perspective. 3rd ed. Kenneth C. Laudon & Jane P. Laudon. (Illus.). 818p. (C). 1993. write for info. (*0-318-69911-7*) Macmillan.

*__Management Information Systems: A Global Perspective.__ (C). 2001. pap. text 0.00 (*0-201-61203-8*) HEPC Inc.

Management Information Systems: A Managerial End-User Perspective. James A. O'Brien. (C). 1990. text 57.95 (*0-256-07862-9*, Irwn McGrw-H) McGrw-H Hghr Educ.

Management Information Systems: A Managerial End-User Perspective. 2nd ed. James A. O'Brien. LC 92-17554. 704p. (C). 1992. text 69.95 (*0-256-10346-1*, Irwn McGrw-H) McGrw-H Hghr Educ.

Management Information Systems: A Strategic Leadership Approach. Paul S. Licker. 188p. (C). Date not set. pap. text 28.00 (*0-03-020314-7*) Dryden Pr.

Management Information Systems: A Strategic Leadership Approach. Paul S. Licker. LC 95-71897. 562p. (C). 1997. text 77.00 (*0-15-500244-9*) Dryden Pr.

Management Information Systems: A Strategic Leadership Approach. Paul S. Licker. (C). 1996. pap. text 33.50 (*0-03-020322-8*) Harcourt Coll Pubs.

Management Information Systems: A Study of Computer-Based Information Systems. Raymond McLeod, Jr. (Illus.). 848p. (C). 1992. write for info. (*0-318-69918-4*) Macmillan.

Management Information Systems: A User Perspective. 3rd ed. Hicks. 1994. teacher ed. write for info. (*0-314-01398-9*) West Pub.

Management Information Systems: An Information Sourcebook. Patricia Loehlein. LC 87-38194. (Sourcebook Series in Business & Management). 232p. 1988. 57.50 (*0-89774-375-X*) Oryx Pr.

Management Information Systems: Apics Special Edition, the Manager's View. 2nd ed. Mary Sumner & Robert A. Schultheis. 896p. 1991. text. write for info. (*1-55623-726-X*, Irwn Prfssnl) McGraw-Hill Prof.

Management Information Systems: Learning Exercises & Applications. Sassan Rahmatian. LC 94-32648. (William R. King Series in Information Management). 304p. 1994. pap. text 38.60 (*0-13-172702-8*) P-H.

Management Information Systems: Managing Information. 3rd ed. Fritz J. Erickson & James A. O'Brien. (C). 1996. text 72.25 (*0-256-25058-8*, Irwn McGrw-H) McGrw-H Hghr Educ.

Management Information Systems: Managing Information. 3rd ed. James A. O'Brien. 752p. (C). 1995. text 35.50 (*0-256-20688-0*, Irwn McGrw-H) McGrw-H Hghr Educ.

Management Information Systems: Managing Information Technology in the Internetworked Enterprise. 4th ed. James A. O'Brien. LC 98-24795. 832p. 1998. 85.00 (*0-07-290611-1*) McGraw.

*__Management Information Systems: Organization & Technology in the Networked Enterprise.__ 6th ed. Kenneth C. Laudon & Jane P. Laudon. LC 99-16968. 662p. 1999. 90.67 (*0-13-011732-3*) P-H.

Management Information Systems: Perspectives on Management, Organization & Change. Wendy L. Currie. (Illus.). 528p. 1999. text 105.00 (*0-19-877533-4*); pap. text 45.00 (*0-19-877532-6*) OUP.

Management Information Systems: Solving Business Problems with Information Technology. Post-Anderson. 1996. text, teacher ed. write for info. (*0-256-22564-8*) McGraw.

Management Information Systems: Solving Business Problems with information Technology. Post-Anderson. 1996. pap. text 31.50 (*0-256-22566-4*) McGraw.

*__Management Information Systems: Solving Business Problems with Information Technology.__ 2nd ed. Gerald V. Post. 1999. pap., student ed. 86.25 (*0-07-238217-1*) McGraw.

Management Information Systems: The Manager's View. 3rd ed. Robert A. Schultheis. LC 94-3520. 960p. (C). 1994. text 69.65 (*0-256-13640-8*, Irwn McGrw-H) McGrw-H Hghr Educ.

Management Information Systems: The Manager's View. 4th ed. Robert A. Schultheis & Mary Summer. LC 97-25011. 1997. write for info. (*0-07-115548-1*) McGraw.

Management Information Systems: The Managers View. 4th ed. Mary Sumner & Robert A. Schultheis. LC 97-25011. 864p. (C). 1997. text 62.00 (*0-256-25195-9*, Irwn McGrw-H) McGrw-H Hghr Educ.

Management Information Systems: With Application Cases & Internet Primer. 3rd ed. James Morgan et al. (C). 1996. text, pap. text 85.00 incl. 3.5 hd (*0-256-24678-5*, Irwn McGrw-H) McGrw-H Hghr Educ.

Management, Information Systems & Computers: An Introduction. Roy Anderson. 285p. (C). 1987. 40.00 (*0-333-39852-1*); pap. text 30.00 (*0-333-39853-X*) Scholium Intl.

Management Information Systems & Organizational Behavior. 2nd ed. Pat A. Federico. LC 85-6497. 240p. 1985. 62.95 (*0-275-90097-5*, C0097, Praeger Pubs) Greenwood.

Management Information Systems & Statistics. Roland Bee & Frances Bee. 250p. (C). 1990. 75.00 (*0-85292-435-6*, Pub. by IPM Hse) St Mut.

*__Management Information Systems & Surfing Management 98-99.__ 7th ed. 1998. write for info. (*0-13-012158-4*) P-H.

Management Information Systems & Technology. Ivan Hollingsworth et al. 448p. 1996. pap. 29.95 (*0-412-71760-3*) Chapman & Hall.

*__Management Information Systems for Microfinance Institutions: A Handbook.__ Charles W. Waterfield & Nick Ramsing. (Technical Tool Ser.: No. 1). 203p. 1998. ring bd. 27.00 (*1-888753-11-0*) PACT Pubns.

Management Information Systems for the Information Age. Stephen Haag et al. LC 97-27678. (C). 1997. pap. text 63.50 (*0-07-025465-6*) McGraw.

Management Information Systems for the Information Age. 2nd ed. Stephen Haag et al. LC 98-53861. 576p. 1999. 62.50 (*0-07-231535-0*) McGraw.

Information Systems Foundation. 1997. teacher ed. 39.99 (*1-57576-547-0*) Que Educ & Trng.

Management Information Systems in Higher Education: The State of the Art. Management Information Systems Staff. Ed. by Charles B. Johnson & William G. Katzenmeyer. LC 74-109171. 215p. reprint ed. pap. 66.70 (*0-608-15072-X*, 202620600048) Bks Demand.

Management Information Systems in Human Services: Implications for the Distribution of Authority & Decision Making. Richard K. Caputo. 166p. 1987. 49.95 (*0-86656-663-5*) Haworth Pr.

Management Information Systems in Human Services: Implications for the Distribution of Authority & Decision Making. Richard K. Caputo. 166p. 1988. pap. 14.95 (*0-86656-822-0*) Haworth Pr.

Management Information Systems, International: Managerial End User Perspective. 2nd ed. James A. O'Brien. 728p. (C). 1992. text 35.50 (*0-256-10830-7*, Irwn McGrw-H) McGrw-H Hghr Educ.

Management Information Systems Lotus 2.3. 3rd ed. Mary Sumner & Robert A. Schultheis. (C). 1995. text 82.05 (*0-256-19413-0*, Irwn McGrw-H) McGrw-H Hghr Educ.

Management Information Systems, Managing with Computers. Patrick G. McKeown & Robert A. Leitch. 384p. (C). 1993. pap. text, teacher ed. 22.75 incl. trans. (*0-15-500813-7*) Dryden Pr.

Management Information Systems Specialist. Jack Rudman. (Career Examination Ser.: C-3579). 1994. pap. 39.95 (*0-8373-3579-5*) Nat Learn.

Management Informations Systems: Managing Information Technology in the Networked Enterprise. 3rd ed. James A. O'Brien. LC 95-38515. (Illus.). 752p. (C). 1998. text 69.95 (*0-256-17354-0*, Irwn McGrw-H) McGrw-H Hghr Educ.

Management Insight, 1989: Annual Planner & Sourcebook. John Nirenberg. 200p. (Orig.). 1988. pap. 19.95 (*0-945693-00-1*) Mgmt Insight.

Management Insight, 1990: Annual Planner. John Nirenberg. 176p. 1989. pap. 14.95 (*0-945693-02-8*) Mgmt Insight.

Management Intern. Jack Rudman. (Career Examination Ser.: C-1927). 1994. reprint ed. pap. 27.95 (*0-8373-1927-7*) Nat Learn.

Management International. Dorothy Marcic. Date not set. pap. text, teacher ed. write for info. (*0-314-03386-6*) West Pub.

Management Introduction to Word Processing. 1986. lib. bdg. 150.00 (*0-8490-3753-0*) Gordon Pr.

Management Involvement for High Commitment. Jerome M. Rosow & Robert Zager. Ed. by Jill Casner-Lotto. (New Roles for Managers Ser.: Pt. II). 97p. 1989. pap. 95.00 (*0-89361-046-1*) Work in Amer.

Management Issues & Operational Planning for India's Borders. Ed. by D. K. Arya & R. C. Sharma. write for info. (*0-318-71687-9*, Pub. by Promilla) Nataraj Bks.

Management Issues in Application Program Maintenance. H. Keith Cox. 68p. 1993. ring bd. 160.00 (*1-56909-002-5*) Info Systs Mgmt.

Management Issues in China: Domestic Enterprises. Ed. by David H. Brown & Robin Porter. LC 95-12696. 240p. (C). 1995. pap. 22.50 (*0-415-13002-6*) Thomson Learn.

Management Issues in China: Domestic Enterprises. Ed. by David H. Brown & Robin Porter. LC 95-12696. 288p. (C). (gr. 13). 1995. pap. 69.95 (*0-415-13001-8*) Thomson Learn.

Management Issues in China: International Enterprises. Ed. by John Child & Yuan Lu. LC 95-15788. 240p. (C). 1995. pap. 18.99 (*0-415-13004-2*) Thomson Learn.

Management Issues in China: International Enterprises. Ed. by John Child & Yuan Lu. LC 95-15788. 240p. (C). (gr. 13). 1995. pap. 69.95 (*0-415-13003-4*) Thomson Learn.

Management Issues in the Networking Environment. Ed. by Edward R. Johnson. LC 87-32940. (Journal of Library Administration: Vol. 8, Nos. 3-4). (Illus.). 141p. 1989. text 32.95 (*0-86656-692-9*) Haworth Pr.

Management Kurien-Style: The Story of the White Revolution. M. V. Kamath. 431p. 1989. text 35.00 (*81-220-0100-9*, Pub. by Konark Pubs Pvt Ltd) Advent Bks Div.

Management, Labour & Industrial Politics in Modern Europe: The Quest for Productivity Growth during the Twentieth Century. Ed. by Joseph Melling & Alan McKinlay. LC 95-49464. (Illus.). 208p. 1996. 80.00 (*1-85898-016-X*) E Elgar.

Management Laureates: A Collection of Autobiographical Essays, Vol. 1. H. Igor Ansoff. Ed. by Arthur G. Bedeian. LC 92-34213. 416p. 1992. 86.25 (*1-55938-469-7*) Jai Pr.

Management Laureates: A Collection of Autobiographical Essays, Vol. 2. Ed. by Arthur G. Bedeian. 439p. 1993. 86.25 (*1-55938-470-0*) Jai Pr.

Management Laureates: A Collection of Autobiographical Essays, Vol. 3. Ed. by ARthur G. Bedeian. 414p. 1993. 86.25 (*1-55938-471-9*) Jai Pr.

Management Laureates: A Collection of Autobiographical Essays, Vol. 4. Ed. by ARthur G. Bedeian. 1996. 86.25 (*1-55938-730-0*) Jai Pr.

Management Lauretes: A Collection of Autobiographical Essays, Vol. 5. Arthur Bedeian. 1998. 86.25 (*0-7623-0178-3*) Jai Pr.

Management Learning: Integrating Perspectives in Theory & Practice. Ed. by John Burgoyne & Michael Reynolds. 368p. 1997. 85.00 (*0-8039-7643-7*); pap. 35.00 (*0-8039-7644-5*) Sage.

Management Lessons from Engineering Failures. Ed. by Kenneth L. Gibble. LC 86-25949. 52p. 1986. pap. 13.00 (*0-87262-572-9*) Am Soc Civil Eng.

Management Live! The Video Workbook. Robert Marx et al. 400p. (C). 1991. pap. text 46.00 (*0-13-946781-5*) P-H.

Management Magic in Not-for-Profit Organizations: Internal Cost Accounting - A Basis for Change. Joe Egge. Ed. by Apple Tree Graphics Staff. 58p. 1993. pap. 16.95 (*0-9636200-3-7*) J Egge Cnslt.

Management-Manufacture-Marketing of California Black Oak, Pacific Madroue & Tanoak: A Practical Handbook on Successful Hardwood Utilization in California & Southern Oregon. Guy Hall. (Illus.). 220p. 1998. 50.00 (*0-9662264-0-2*) Wstrn Hardwd Assn.

Management, Marketing & Sales Information. Hines. pap. text. write for info. (*0-7506-4365-X*) Buttrwrth-Heinemann.

Management, Marketing & the Competitive Process. Ed. by Peter E. Earl. LC 96-23169. 416p. 1996. 100.00 (*1-85898-496-3*) E Elgar.

*__Management-Marketing-Motivation: The Keys to Running a Successful Football Program at Any Level.__ Thomas Taylor. LC 98-94020. 1999. 17.95 (*0-533-12942-7*) Vantage.

Management Masterclass: A Practical Guide to the New Realities of Business. Neil Glass. (Illus.). 354p. 1998. pap. 17.95 (*1-85788-109-5*) Nicholas Brealey.

Management Matters in 1993 LC 98-234449. 52p. 1993. write for info. (*0-7049-0591-4*) Univ of Reading.

Management Maturity: Prerequisite to Total Quality. A. Keith Barnes. LC 94-22125. 182p. (C). 1994. pap. text 26.50 (*0-8191-9646-0*); lib. bdg. 52.50 (*0-8191-9645-2*) U Pr of Amer.

Management Mess-Ups: 57 Pitfalls You Can Avoid (& Stories of Those Who Didn't) Mark Eppler. LC 96-52845. 256p. (Orig.). 1997. pap. 12.99 (*1-56414-276-0*) Career Pr Inc.

Management Metaphysics: Applying Principles of Metaphysics to Corporate Management. Ursula Hall. 1998. pap. 11.95 (*1-892896-34-6*) Buy Books.

Management Methods. Derek Torrington et al. 216p. (C). 1985. 110.00 (*0-85292-355-4*) St Mut.

Management Methods of Jesus: Ancient Wisdom for Modern Business. Bob Briner. 128p. 1996. 14.99 (*0-7852-7681-5*) Nelson.

Management Methods of Jesus: Ancient Wisdom for Modern Business. abr. ed. Bob Briner. 1998. 15.99 incl. audio (*0-8054-1265-4*) Broadman.

Management Mistakes. 6th ed. Hartley. 342p. (C). 1999. pap. 46.95 (*0-471-33311-5*) Wiley.

Management Mistakes: An Introduction. 6th ed. Hartley. pap. write for info. (*0-471-38124-1*) Wiley.

Management Model. Ivan G. Somali. 1992. pap. 25.00 (*0-7855-0240-8*, Pub. by Ratna Pustak Bhandar) St Mut.

Management Models & Industrial Applications of Linear Programming, Vol. 2. Abraham Charnes & W. W. Cooper. LC 61-14807. (Illus.). 414p. reprint ed. 128.40 (*0-8357-9928-X*, 201195000080) Bks Demand.

Management Modes for Iodine-129, Vol. 7. Ed. by W. Hebel & G. Cottone. vi, 310p. 1983. text 237.00 (*3-7186-0147-8*) Gordon & Breach.

*__Management Myth: Exploring the Essence of Future Organizations.__ Richard David Hames. (Illus.). 296p. 1999. 29.95 (*1-875680-08-X*) Business Prof of Amer.

Management Needs Assessment for the Copper River Delta, Alaska. Linda E. Kruger & Catherine B. Tyler. (Illus.). 50p. (C). 1997. reprint ed. pap. text 30.00 (*0-7881-4157-0*) DIANE Pub.

Management, 98-99. 6th ed. Fred H. Maidment. (Annual Ser.). (Illus.). 240p. 1998. pap. text 12.25 (*0-697-39181-7*, Dshkn McG-Hill) McGrw-H Hghr Educ.

Management Observation & Communication Theory. Heikki Heiskanen & G. A. Swanson. LC 91-48120. 208p. 1992. 59.95 (*0-89930-637-3*, HKC, Quorum Bks) Greenwood.

Management Odyssey: The Royal Dockyards, 1714-1914. J. M. Haas. 256p. 1994. lib. bdg. 39.00 (*0-8191-9461-1*) U Pr of Amer.

Management of a Multicultural Workforce. Monir H. Tayeb. LC 96-933. 238p. 1998. pap. 67.95 (*0-471-96276-7*) Wiley.

Management of a Public Library. Harold R. Jenkins. Ed. by Robert D. Stueart. LC 76-13957. (Foundations in Library & Information Science Ser.: Vol. 8). 258p. 1981. 78.50 (*0-89232-038-9*) Jai Pr.

Management of a Sales Force. 9th ed. William J. Stanton et al. LC 94-24843. (Marketing Ser.). 704p. (C). 1994. text 70.65 (*0-256-13818-4*, Irwn McGrw-H) McGrw-H Hghr Educ.

Management of a Sales Force. 10th ed. William J. Stanton et al. LC 98-40414. 656p. 1998. 85.00 (*0-256-21896-X*) McGraw.

Management of a Sales Force International. 9th ed. Richard Buskirk, Jr. et al. (C). 1994. pap. text, student ed. 34.50 (*0-256-18460-7*, Irwn McGrw-H) McGrw-H Hghr Educ.

Management of a Small Business. Cecile Nieuwenhuizen. 184p. 1996. pap. 28.00 (*0-7021-3785-5*, Pub. by Juta & Co) Gaunt.

Management of a Student Research Project. 2nd ed. Keith Howard & John A. Sharp. 150p. (Orig.). 1996. pap. 22.95 (*0-566-07706-X*, Pub. by Gower) Ashgate Pub Co.

Management of a Trust Department. Walter Kennedy & Philip F. Searle. LC 66-28193. 280p. reprint ed. pap. 86.80 (*0-608-16779-7*, 205218300053) Bks Demand.

Management of Abdominal Hernias. 2nd ed. Devlin. 344p. 1999. text 135.00 (*0-412-73820-1*, Pub. by E A) OUP.

Management of Acid Soils in the Humid Tropics of Asia. Ed. by E. T. Craswell & E. Pushparajah. 118p. 1989. pap. 75.00 (*1-86320-001-0*) St Mut.

Management of Acute & Chronic Pain. Ed. by Narinder Rawal et al. 231p. 1998. pap. text 43.00 (*0-7279-1193-7*) Login Brothers Bk Co.

Management of Acute & Chronic Wounds: Nursing Management. Ed. by Ruth Bryant. (Illus.). 368p. (C). (gr. 13). 1992. text 45.00 (*0-8016-0896-1*, 00896) Mosby Inc.

Management of Acute Coronary Syndromes. Christopher P. Cannon. (Contemporary Cardiology Ser.: Vol. 1). 680p. 1998. 125.00 (*0-89603-552-2*) Humana.

*Management of Acute Coronary Syndromes. Peter M. Schofield. (Illus.). 232p. 2000. pap. 49.95 (1-85317-719-9, Pub. by Martin Dunitz) Blackwell Sci.

Management of Acute Myocardial Infarction. Ed. by Desmond Julian & Eugene Braunwald. (Frontiers in Cardiology Ser.). (Illus.). 433p. 1994. text 61.00 (0-7020-1884-8, W B Saunders Co) Harcrt Hlth Sci Grp.

Management of Acute Pain. Barbara Fulton. (Illus.). 176p. 1991. pap. 32.50 (0-19-263003-2) OUP.

*Management of Acute Pain. 2nd ed. Gilbert Park et al. (Illus.). 208p. 2000. pap. text 44.95 (0-19-262467-9) OUP.

Management of Acute Respiratory Infections in Children: Practical Guidelines for Outpatient Care. (FRE.). 77p. (C). 1995. pap. 15.00 (92-4-154477-5, 1150430) World Health.

*Management of Acute Stroke. Ashfaq Shuaib & Larry B. Goldstein. LC 99-35713. (Neurological Disease & Therapy Ser.). (Illus.). 552p. 1999. text 175.00 (0-8247-7092-7) Dekker.

Management of Acute Stroke. C. M. Allen et al. LC 88-23163. (Johns Hopkins Series in Contemporary Medicine & Public Health). (Illus.). 227p. 1988. reprint ed. pap. 70.40 (0-608-05920-X, 206625600008) Bks Demand.

Management of Adnexal Cysts: Proceedings of the First European Congress of the Raoul Palmer Club of Gynecologic Endoscopy, Clermont-Ferrand, 10-11 September, 1992. Ed. by Maurice A. Bruhat. LC 93-26992. (Illus.). 264p. 1994. 125.00 (0-632-03794-6) Blackwell Sci.

Management of Adult Neurogenic Dysphagia. Maggie L. Huckabee et al. LC 98-27474. (Dysphagia Ser.). (Illus.). 350p. 1998. pap. 59.95 (1-56593-731-7, 1422) Thomson Learn.

Management of Advanced Manufacturing Technology: Strategy, Organization, & Innovation. Donald Gerwin & Harvey F. Kolodny. LC 91-16040. (Engineering & Technology Management Ser.). 416p. 1992. 130.00 (0-471-63574-X) Wiley.

Management of Advanced Melanoma. Ed. by Larry Nathanson. (Contemporary Issues in Clinical Oncology Ser.: Vol. 6). (Illus.). 272p. 1986. text 41.50 (0-685-17326-7) Church.

Management of Advanced Melanoma. fac. ed. Ed. by Larry Nathanson. LC 86-17154. (Contemporary Issues in Clinical Oncology Ser.: No. 6). (Illus.). 286p. 1986. reprint ed. pap. 88.70 (0-7837-7901-1, 204765700008) Bks Demand.

Management of Advanced Prostate Cancer. Malcolm J. Coptcoat. 64p. 1996. pap. 54.95 (0-86542-929-4) Blackwell Sci.

Management of Aerospace Programs Conference, Nov. 16-18, 1966, Columbia, MO. Ed. by Walter K. Johnson. (Science & Technology Ser.: Vol. 12). 392p. 1967. 30.00 (0-87703-040-5, Am Astronaut Soc) Univelt Inc.

Management of Aggressive Behavior: A Comprehensive Guide to Learning How to Recognize, Reduce, Manage, & Control Aggressive Behavior. Roland Ouellette. LC 92-44600. 1993. 14.95 (1-879411-22-9) Perf Dimensions Pub.

Management of Aggressive Behavior in the Elderly. Marilyn Cleland. 76p. (Orig.). 1990. text 20.00 (1-877592-13-7) GSH&MC.

*Management of Aging: The University of Geneva Experience. Ed. by J. P. Michel & P. R. Hof. LC 99-32982. (Interdisciplinary Topics in Gerontology Ser.: Vol. 30). (Illus.). 268p. 1999. 172.25 (3-8055-6860-6) S Karger.

Management of Agricultural Research: A Training Manual. V. N. Asopa et al. LC 98-210567. 10 p. 1997. (92-5-104098-2) Bernan Associates.

Management of Agropastoral Systems in Semi-Arid Regions. E. D. Ungar. 231p. 1992. pap. 200.00 (81-7089-184-1, Pub. by Intl Bk Distr) St Mut.

Management of Air Pollution. Ed. by Henry Power et al. (Advances in Air Pollution Ser.: Vol. 7). 300p. 2000. 145.00 (1-85312-528-8, 5288, Pub. by WIT Pr) Computational Mech MA.

Management of Alcohol & Drug-Related Issues in the Workplace. 61p. (Orig.). (C). 1997. pap. text 25.00 (0-7881-3887-1) DIANE Pub.

Management of Alcohol & Drug-Related Issues in the Workplace: An ILO Code of Practice. LC 97-166254. 61p. 1996. pap. 13.50 (92-2-109455-3) Intl Labour Office.

Management of Allergy in the 1990s. Ed. by M. A. Kaliner. LC 88-35245. (Illus.). 90p. (C). 1989. text 16.00 (0-920887-53-8) Hogrefe & Huber Pubs.

Management of Alzheimer's Disease. Ed. by Gordon K. Wilcock. LC 93-3404. 256p. 1993. 85.00 (1-871816-20-3, Pub. by Wrightson Biomed) Taylor & Francis.

Management of an Accounting Practice Handbook. annuals ring bd. 137.00 (0-685-48849-7) Am Inst CPA.

*Management of Aneurysmal: Subarachnoid Haemorrhage. Ed. by Iver A. Langmoen et al. LC 99-19266. (Acta Neurochirurgica Ser.). (Illus.). 100p. 1999. 89.00 (3-211-83256-4) Spr-Verlag.

Management of Aneurysmal Subarachnoid Hemorrhage. Damirez Fossett. (Illus.). 276p. (Orig.). (C). 1993. pap. 12.95 (0-929240-59-6) EMIS.

Management of Animal Waste: Environmental Health Problems & Technological Solutions. Amer V. El-Ahraf & William V. Willis. LC 95-654. 208p. 1996. 65.00 (0-275-93529-9, Praeger Pubs) Greenwood.

*Management of Antimicrobials in Infectious Diseases: Impact of Antibiotic Resistance. Ed. by Arch G. Mainous, III & Claire Pomeroy. (Infectious Disease Ser.). 353p. 2000. 99.50 (0-89603-821-1) Humana.

Management of Anxiety. 2nd ed. Diana Keable. LC 97-9852. 228p. 1997. 35.00 (0-443-05527-0) Church.

Management of Anxiety. 2nd ed. Diana Keable. LC 97-9852. 1997. pap. text. write for info. (0-443-06001-0) Church.

Management of Anxiety in Medical Disorders. David I. Mostofsky & David H. Barlow. LC 99-32656. 418p. (C). 2000. 62.50 (0-205-28704-2, Macmillan Coll) P-H.

Management of Aphasia. Ed. by Y. Lebrun & R. Hoops. (Neurolinguistics Ser.: Vol. 8). 124p. 1978. 31.00 (90-265-0280-X) Swets.

Management of Archives. T. R. Schellenberg. LC 88-600028. 420p. (C). 1988. pap. text 17.95 (0-911333-72-X, 200054) National Archives & Recs.

Management of Arterial Hypertension: A Practical Guide for the Physician & Allied Health Workers. Alberto Zanchetti et al. v, 72p. 1985. pap. text 9.90 (92-4-154197-0, 1150235) World Health.

Management of Asthma During Pregnancy. Ed. by Allan T. Luskin. (Illus.). 74p. (C). 1999. reprint ed. pap. text 20.00 (0-7881-7683-8) DIANE Pub.

Management of Autistic Behavior. Richard L. Simpson & Madelyn Regan. LC 88-30480. 450p. 1986. spiral bd. 41.00 (0-89079-196-1, 1481) PRO-ED.

Management of Back Pain. 2nd ed. Richard W. Porter. (Illus.). 368p. 1993. text 115.00 (0-443-04630-1) Church.

Management of Behaviour in Schools. Ed. by Ved P. Varma. LC 92-5637. 1993. pap. text. write for info. (0-582-07572-6) Longman.

Management of Biological Nitrogen Fixation for the Development of More Productive & Sustainable Agricultural Systems: Extended Versions of Papers Presented at the Symposium on Biological Nitrogen Fixation for Sustainable Agriculture at the 15th Congress of Soil Science, Acapulco, Mexico, 1994. Ed. by J. K. Ladha et al. (Developments in Plant & Soil Sciences Ser.: Vol. 65). 308p. (C). 1995. text 161.50 (0-7923-3413-2) Kluwer Academic.

*Management of Biotechnology. Gary Palmer. 130p. 2000. write for info. (1-58692-019-7) Copyright Mgmt.

Management of Bleeding after Open Heart Surgery. Rephael Mohr & Daniel A. Goor. LC 97-13740. (Medical Intelligence Unit Ser.). 219p. 1997. text 99.00 (1-57059-056-7) Landes Bioscience.

Management of Bleeding Disorders in Surgical Practice. C. D. Forbes & A. Cuschieri. (Illus.). 400p. 1992. 99.95 (0-632-03368-1) Blackwell Sci.

*Management of Bleeding in Cardiovascular Surgery. Roque Pifarre. LC 99-35033. 1999. 55.00 (1-56053-321-8) Hanley & Belfus.

Management of Blistering Diseases. Ed. by Fenella Wojnarowska & Robert A. Briggaman. LC 92-120868. (Illus.). 320p. reprint ed. pap. 99.20 (0-608-09741-1, 206990900007) Bks Demand.

Management of Blood Transfusion Services. Ed. by S. F. Hollan et al. (CHI, ENG, FRE & SPA.). xii, 229p. 1990. pap. text 41.00 (92-4-154406-6, 1150345) World Health.

Management of Bloodborne Infections in Sport: A\Practical Guide for Sports Health Care Providers & Coaches. Terry A. Zeigler. LC 96-44257. (Illus.). 96p. (Orig.). 1996. pap. text 18.00 (0-88011-682-X, BZEI0682) Human Kinetics.

Management of Brain-injured Children. Ed. by Richard E. Appleton & Tony Baldwin. (Illus.). 270p. 1998. pap. text 39.95 (0-19-262793-7) OUP.

Management of Breastfeeding, Module 4. Rebecca F. Black et al. LC 97-25569. (Nursing Ser.). 280p. 1998. spiral bd. 39.95 (0-7637-0193-9) Jones & Bartlett.

Management of Business. 2nd ed. J. E. Chua et al. 1983. text 10.00 (0-07-099205-3) McGraw.

Management of Business Enterprises. Ed. by Niranjan Dey. 352p. 1990. 140.00 (81-7041-251-X, Pub. by Scientific Pubs) St Mut.

Management of Business Logistics. C. Coyle et al. 631p. (C). 1988. 180.00 (0-7855-5731-8, Pub. by Inst Pur & Supply) St Mut.

Management of Business Logistics. 6th ed. John J. Coyle et al. LC 95-39258. 650p. (C). 1996. mass mkt. 95.95 (0-314-06507-5) West Pub.

Management of Business Logistics. 7th ed. John J. Coyle & Bardi. (SWC-Management Ser.). 2001. pap. 52.00 (0-324-00751-5) Thomson Learn.

Management of Business Telecommunications. Houston Carr & Charles Snyder. 560p. (C). 1996. text 55.35 (0-256-21961-3, Irwn McGrw-H) McGrw-H Hghr Educ.

Management of Business-to-Business Advertising: A Working Guide for Small to Mid-Size Companies. Stewart H. Ross. LC 85-31726. 175p. 1986. 52.95 (0-89930-163-0, RHD/, Quorum Bks) Greenwood.

Management of CAD for Construction. Stanley Port. (Illus.). 240p. (gr. 13). 1989. mass mkt. 58.95 (0-442-23698-0) Chapman & Hall.

Management of Cancer Pain. 1995. lib. bdg. 251.95 (0-8490-6780-4) Gordon Pr.

Management of Cancer Pain: Clinical Practice Guidelines. (Illus.). 257p. (Orig.). (C). 1995. pap. text 50.00 (0-7881-2061-1) DIANE Pub.

Management of Cancer Pain: Clinical Practice Guidelines. (Orig.). 1997. lib. bdg. 253.99 (0-8490-8140-8) Gordon Pr.

Management of Cancer Pain 9: Adults, Reference for Clinicians. Ada Jacox. 29p. 1994. pap. 28.00 (0-16-061533-X) USGPO.

Management of Cancer Pain, Clinical Practice 9. Ada Jacox. 276p. 1994. per. 16.00 (0-16-061531-3) USGPO.

Management of Carbon Sequestration in Soil. R. Lal. LC 97-18398. (Advances in Soil Science Ser.). 480p. 1997. boxed set 119.95 (0-8493-7442-1) CRC Pr.

Management of Cardiac Arrhythmias - Update, 1990: Journal: Cardiology, Vol. 77, No. 3, 1990. Ed. by L. S. Dreifus. (Illus.). 124p. 1990. pap. 77.50 (3-8055-5308-0) S Karger.

Management of Cataract in Adults Quick Referene Guide for Clinicians. 4th ed. Denis M. O'Day. 15p. 1994. pap. 16.00 (0-16-045245-7) USGPO.

Management of Cataract in Primary Health Care Services. (ENG, FRE & SPA.). vi, 43p. 1990. pap. text 13.50 (92-4-154408-2, 1150344) World Health.

*Management of Challenging Behaviors in Dementia. Ellen K. Mahoney et al. 288p. 2000. pap. 34.00 (1-878812-46-7, 2467) Hlth Prof Pr.

Management of Change. Harvard Business Review Staff. (Leadership Skills Ser.). 121p. 1991. pap. 19.95 (0-87584-261-5) Harvard Busn.

Management Of Change. Harvard Business School Press Staff. 150p. 1991. pap. 1995.00 (0-07-103321-1) McGraw.

Management of Change. Morrison. (GC - Principles of Management Ser.). 1997. pap. 35.00 (0-7895-0708-0) Course Tech.

Management of Change. Ian Sutton. LC 99-193963. 192p. 1998. pap. write for info. (1-57502-985-5, PO2689) Morris Pubng.

Management of Change: Administrative Logistics & Actions. Joseph W. Weiss. LC 86-9390. 228p. 1986. 59.95 (0-275-92195-6, C2195, Praeger Pubs) Greenwood.

Management of Change: Increasing School Effectiveness & Facilitating Staff Development Through Action Research. Ed. by Pamela Lomax. (BERA Dialogues Ser.: No. 1). 200p. 1989. 69.00 (1-85359-061-4, Pub. by Multilingual Matters); pap. 24.95 (1-85359-060-6, Pub. by Multilingual Matters) Taylor & Francis.

Management of Change & Innovation. Ed. by Bengt-Arne Vedin. (International Library of Management). 704p. 1994. 269.95 (1-85521-364-8, Pub. by Dartmth Pub) Ashgate Pub Co.

Management of Change in Chemical Plants: Problems & Case Histories. R. E. Sanders. LC 92-30167. 224p. 1993. text 73.95 (0-7506-1135-9) Buttrwrth-Heinemann.

Management of Change in Government. Leemans. (Development of Societies Ser.: No. 1). 1976. pap. text 152.50 (90-247-1817-1) Kluwer Academic.

Management of Change in Universities: Universities, State & Economy in Australia, Canada & the United Kingdom. Henry D. Miller. LC 94-44549. 208p. 1994. 123.00 (0-335-19089-8) OpUniv Pr.

Management of Child Development Centers. 4th ed. Verna Hildebrand & Patricia F. Hearron. LC 96-11462. 436p. 1996. pap. 53.00 (0-13-238635-6, Merrill Pub Co) Macmillan.

Management of Child Health Services. Ed. by Michael Rigby et al. LC 97-68391. (Illus.). 208p. 1997. pap. text 45.00 (0-412-59660-1, Pub. by E A) OUP.

Management of Child Protection Services: Context & Change. Robert Sanders. LC 98-40537. 416p. 1999. text 78.95 (1-85742-392-5, HV751.A6S36, Pub. by Arena) Ashgate Pub Co.

Management of Childhood Brain Tumors. Ed. by Melvin Deutsch. (Foundations of Neurological Surgery Ser.). (C). 1990. text 303.50 (0-7923-0669-4) Kluwer Academic.

Management of Children & Adolescents with Attention Deficit-Hyperactivity Disorder. 3rd ed. Ronald J. Friedman & Guy T. Doyal. LC 92-9642. 198p. (C). 1992. pap. text 26.00 (0-89079-532-0, 4038) PRO-ED.

Management of Children with Emotional & Behavioural Difficulties. Ed. by Ved P. Varma. 176p. 1989. 49.95 (0-415-02245-2, A3876); pap. 16.95 (0-415-02246-0, A3880) Routledge.

Management of Children with Emotional & Behavioural Difficulties. Ed. by Ved P. Varma. LC 89-10089. 186p. reprint ed. pap. 57.70 (0-608-20395-5, 207164800002) Bks Demand.

Management of Chronic Headaches. Edward Blanchard & F. Andraisk. 216p. (C). 1992. pap. text 60.95 (0-205-14285-0, H4285) Allyn.

*Management of Chronic Lower Limb Ischemia. Ed. by Joseph Mills. (An Arnold Publication). 224p. 2000. text 89.50 (0-340-75956-9, Pub. by E A) OUP.

Management of Chronic Pain. 2nd ed. Andrew Diamond & Stephen Coniam. LC 96-30136. (Illus.). 190p. (C). 1997. text 59.50 (0-19-262695-7) OUP.

Management of Church Music Programs. Theodore E. Minor. 83p. 1991. spiral bd. 14.95 (0-9630146-0-9) T Minor Keybd.

Management of Clinical Allergy. rev. ed. Russell I. Williams. LC 83-90909. (Illus.). 198p. 1984. pap. text 22.00 (0-9613013-0-9) R I Williams.

Management of Clubs, Recreation & Sport: Concepts & Applications. Tom Sawyer & Owen Smith. LC 98-85173. 445p. 1997. 44.95 (1-57167-027-0) Sagamore Pub.

Management of Coastal Lagoons & Enclosed Bays. Ed. by Jens Sorensen et al. LC 93-2249. (Coastlines of the World Ser.). 304p. 1993. 30.00 (0-87262-959-7) Am Soc Civil Eng.

Management of College & University Archives. William J. Maher. LC 92-11667. (Society of American Archivists Ser.). (Illus.). 430p. 1992. 52.00 (0-8108-2568-6) Scarecrow.

Management of Colorectal Cancer. Harry Blieberg et al. 408p. 1998. write for info. (1-85317-377-0, Pub. by Martin Dunitz) Mosby Inc.

Management of Common Metabolic Bone Disorders. G. A. Campbell et al. (Illus.). 180p. (C). 1994. text 80.00 (0-521-43037-2); pap. text 29.95 (0-521-43623-0) Cambridge U Pr.

Management of Common Musculoskeletal Disorders: Physical Therapy Principles & Methods. 3rd ed. Darlene Hertling & Randolph M. Kessler. LC 95-4483. (Illus.). 816p. 1995. spiral bd. 54.00 (0-397-55150-9) Lppncott W & W.

Management of Common Problems in Obstetrics & Gynecology. 3rd ed. Ed. by Daniel R. Mishell, Jr. & Paul F. Brenner. LC 93-28312. (Illus.). 912p. 1994. 99.95 (0-86542-269-9) Blackwell Sci.

Management of Common Property Natural Resources: Some Conceptual & Operational Fallacies, No. 57. Daniel W. Bromley & Michael M. Cernea. (Discussion Paper Ser.). 76p. 1989. pap. 22.00 (0-8213-1249-9, 11249) World Bank.

Management of Communication & Language Deficits. Ed. by William H. Burke. (Professional Series on Traumatic Brain Injury: Vol. 20). 56p. (Orig.). 1996. pap. 9.50 (1-882855-27-2) HDI Pubs.

Management of Communication Disorders in Multicultural. Cheng et al. 448p. 1994. pap. 39.95 (0-8016-6818-2) Mosby Inc.

Management of Company Finance. 4th ed. J. M. Samuels & F. M. Wilkes. (C). 1986. 180.00 (0-7855-4097-0, Pub. by Witherby & Co) St Mut.

Management of Company Finance. 5th ed. J. M. Samuels et al. 832p. 1990. mass mkt. 51.95 (0-412-37470-6, A5039) Chapman & Hall.

Management of Company Finance. 6th ed. (Chapman & Hall Series in Accounting & Finance). (Illus.). 1056p. 1995. text. write for info. (0-412-71850-2, Chap & Hall NY) Chapman & Hall.

Management of Company Finance. 6th ed. Samuels. 1995. pap. 26.99 (1-86152-229-0, Pub. by ITBP) Thomson Learn.

Management of Company Finance. 6th ed. J. M. Samuels et al. (Illus.). 1056p. 1995. mass mkt. 39.95 (0-412-60810-3) Chapman & Hall.

Management of Company Finance. 6th ed. J. M. Samuels et al. LC 96-44670. 1997. mass mkt. 17.99 (0-412-71860-X) Chapman & Hall.

Management of Compensation & Pension Benefits Claim Processes for Veterans. 235p. 1997. pap. 20.00 (1-57744-060-9) Nat Acad Public Admin.

*Management of Complex Cardiovascular Problems: The Consultant's Approach. Ed. by Thach N. Nguyen et al. LC 99-36190. (Illus.). 272p. 1999. pap. 45.00 (0-87993-441-7) Futura Pub.

Management of Computer Operations. Israel Borovits. (Illus.). 288p. (C). 1984. text 49.00 (0-13-549493-1) P-H.

Management of Concrete Structures for Long-Term Serviceability. Ed. by E. A. Byars & T. McNulty. LC 99-231241. 133p. 1997. 74.00 (0-7277-2654-4, 2654, Pub. by T Telford) RCH.

Management of Conflict: Interpretations & Interests in Comparative Perspective. Marc H. Ross. LC 92-47397. 232p. 1993. 32.50 (0-300-05398-3) Yale U Pr.

Management of Conflict: Interpretations & Interests in Comparative Perspective. Marc Howard Ross. 1995. pap. 15.00 (0-300-06517-5) Yale U Pr.

Management of Contaminated Site Problems. D. Kofi Asante-Duah. LC 95-11258. 432p. 1995. lib. bdg. 85.00 (1-56670-079-5, L1079) Lewis Pubs.

Management of Control Systems: Justification & Technical Auditing. N. E. Battikha. 256p. 1992. 55.00 (1-55617-199-4) ISA.

Management of Cooperative Banks in India. S. K. Sahoo. (C). 1991. 25.00 (0-8364-2664-9, Pub. by Anmol) S Asia.

Management of Coral Reef Resource Systems. Ed. by J. L. Munro & P. E. Munro. LC 96-946704. (ICLARM Conference Proceedings Ser.: No. 44). 124p. 1994. per. write for info. (971-8709-55-X, Pub. by ICLARM) Intl Spec Bk.

Management of Corporate Business Units: Portfolio Strategies for Turbulent Times. Louis E. Nevaer & Steven A. Deck. LC 87-32586. 248p. 1988. 62.95 (0-89930-284-X, NVP/, Quorum Bks) Greenwood.

Management of Corporate Communications: From Interpersonal Contacts to External Affairs. Robert L. Heath. (LEA's Communication Ser.). 320p. 1994. pap. 34.50 (0-8058-1552-X); text 59.95 (0-8058-1551-1) L Erlbaum Assocs.

Management of Correctional Institutions. Marilyn D. McShane & Frank P. Williams, III. LC 92-27791. (Current Issues in Criminal Justice Ser.: Vol. 5). 352p. 1993. text 64.00 (0-8153-1082-X, SS869) Garland.

*Management of Countertransference with Borderline Patients. Glen O. Gabbard. 2000. pap. text 25.00 (0-7657-0263-0) Aronson.

Management of Countertransference with Borderline Patients. Glen O. Gabbard & Sallye M. Wilkinson. LC 93-47462. 254p. 1994. text 35.50 (0-88048-563-9, 8563) Am Psychiatric.

Management of Criminal Justice (Recommendation & Report), No. R(95)12. 1996. 12.00 (92-871-3068-X, Pub. by Council of Europe) Manhattan Pub Co.

Management of Crop Diseases. A. Agnihotri. (C). 1992. 145.00 (81-7136-039-4, Pub. by Periodical Expert) St Mut.

Management of Culture & Knowledge. Richard Bates. 122p. (C). 1986. 60.00 (0-7300-0376-0, Pub. by Deakin Univ) St Mut.

Management of Cumulative Trauma Disorders. Ed. by Martha J. Sanders. LC 96-50459. 378p. 1997. text 52.50 (0-7506-9561-7) Buttrwrth-Heinemann.

Management of Curriculum Development. J. G. Owen. LC 72-97876. 186p. reprint ed. pap. 53.10 (0-608-13035-4, 2024506) Bks Demand.

Management of Data in Clinical Trials. Eleanor McFadden. LC 97-1251. (Probability & Statistics Ser.). 232p. 1997. 74.95 (0-471-30316-X) Wiley.

Management of Defence: Organization & Control of the United States Armed Services. John C. Ries. LC 64-18122. 247p. reprint ed. pap. 76.60 (0-608-30729-7, 200466100045) Bks Demand.

An Asterisk (*) at the beginning of an entry indicates that the title is appearing for the first time.

Management of Demonstration Programs in the Department of Health & Human Services. Thomas K. Glennan. LC 85-9398. 1985. pap. 10.00 (*0-8330-0649-5*, R-3172-HHS) Rand Corp.

Management of Depression. Stuart Checkley. LC 97-6410. (Illus.). 1998. 165.00 (*0-86542-987-1*) Blackwell Sci.

Management of Depressions with Monoamine Precursors. Ed. by Julien Mendlewicz & Herman M. Van Praag. (Advances in Biological Psychiatry Ser.: Vol. 10). (Illus.). vi, 202p. 1983. pap. 108.75 (*3-8055-3645-3*) S Karger.

Management of Design: Engineering & Management Perspectives. Ed. by Sriram Dasu. LC 94-34778. 304p. (C). 1994. lib. bdg. 124.50 (*0-7923-9509-3*) Kluwer Academic.

Management of Design Alliances. Margaret Bruce & Birgit Jevnaker. LC 97-12957. 310p. 1998. 82.95 (*0-471-97476-5*) Wiley.

Management of Design Offices. Ed. by P. A. Rutter & A. S. Martin. 99p. 1990. pap. text 28.00 (*0-7277-1383-3*, Pub. by T Telford) RCH.

Management of Developing Economics in Transition: Choice of Methods & Techniques in Economic Reform. Wuu-Long Lin & Thomas P. Chen. LC 94-42842. 200p. 1996. 55.00 (*0-275-94819-6*, Praeger Pubs) Greenwood.

Management of Diabetes Mellitus. Ed. by Rubin Bressler & David G. Johnson. LC 80-10866. 322p. reprint ed. pap. 99.90 (*0-8357-7862-2*, 203627900002) Bks Demand.

Management of Diabetes Mellitus. 3rd ed. Joia Schwartz & Sherwyn L. Schwartz. 318p. 1993. pap. 12.95 (*0-929240-60-X*) EMIS.

Management of Diabetes Mellitus: Perspectives of Care Across the Life Span. 2nd ed. Debra Haire-Joshu. LC 95-26440. (Illus.). 912p. (C). (gr. 13). 1996. text 54.95 (*0-8151-4223-4*, 26652) Mosby Inc.

Management of Diabetic Foot Problems. 2nd ed. George P. Kozak et al. LC 93-37401. (Illus.). 336p. 1994. text 79.00 (*0-7216-3284-X*, W B Saunders Co) Harcrt Hlth Sci Grp.

Management of Diabetic Retinopathy. A. M. Hamilton et al. 220p. 1996. pap. text 144.00 (*0-7279-0919-3*, Pub. by BMJ Pub) Login Brothers Bk Co.

Management of Diarrhoea & Use of Oral Rehydration Therapy: A Joint WHO-UNICEF Statement. 2nd ed. 25p. 1985. pap. text 2.70 (*92-4-156086-X*, 1150237) World Health.

Management of Difficult Glaucoma. Ed. by Eve J. Higginbotham et al. LC 93-6951. 472p. 1993. 165.00 (*0-86542-257-5*) Blackwell Sci.

Management of Digestive & Liver Disorders in Infants & Children. Ed. by Jean-Paul Buts & Etienne M. Sokal. LC 92-48383. 688p. 1993. 329.50 (*0-444-81456-6*) Elsevier.

Management of Distance Education in India. H. C. Rathore. (Illus.). x, 225p. 1993. 26.00 (*81-7024-532-X*, Pub. by Ashish Pub Hse) Nataraj Bks.

Management of Drought-Relief Maize: Technical Problems Encountered in Southern Africa During the 1992-93 Food Aid Operation. P. S. Tyler et al. 1994. pap. 25.00 (*0-85954-374-9*, Pub. by Nat Res Inst) St Mut.

Management of Drug Users in the Community. J. Roy Robertson. LC 98-232704. (Arnold Publications). (Illus.). 432p. (Orig.). 1998. pap. text 32.50 (*0-340-70013-0*) OUP.

Management of Ear, Nose & Throat Disorders in Primary Care Practice. Clarence T. Sasaki et al. (Current Clinical Practice Ser.). 300p. 1999. 74.50 (*0-89603-705-3*) Humana.

Management of Eating Disorders & Obesity. Ed. by David J. Goldstein. LC 98-53443. (Nutrition & Health Ser.). (Illus.). 384p. 1999. 99.50 (*0-89603-407-0*) Humana.

***Management of Ectopic Pregnancy.** Richard E. Leach & Steven J. Ory. LC 99-16453. (Illus.). 1999. 65.00 (*0-632-04469-1*) Blackwell Sci.

Management of Education in Muslim Institutions. Mohd A. Siddiqui. LC 95-900339. (Illus.). xii, 189p. 1995. 25.00 (*81-7024-668-7*, Pub. by Ashish Pub Hse) Nataraj Bks.

Management of Educational Change: A Case Study Approach. Ed. by Paul Oliver. (Monitoring Change in Education Ser.). 250p. 1996. text 64.95 (*1-85742-379-8*, Pub. by Arena) Ashgate Pub Co.

Management of Electronic Media. Alan B. Albarran. LC 96-19353. (Radio/TV/Film Ser.). (C). 1996. 87.95 (*0-534-26274-0*) Wadsworth Pub.

Management of Electronic Records: Curriculum Materials (ACCIS) 160p. 25.00 (*92-1-100376-8*, E.GV.92.0.15) UN.

Management of Electronic Records: Issues & Guidelines. 189p. 1989. 25.00 (*92-1-100348-2*, E.GV.89.0.15) UN.

Management of End-Stage Heart Disease. Eric Rose. LC 98-15838. 304p. 1998. text 125.00 (*0-316-75697-0*) Lppncott W & W.

Management of End Use of Computing. Houston Carr. (Illus.). 160p. 1999. pap. text 16.00 (*1-886855-28-5*) Tavenner Pub.

Management of Endocrine Disorders. Ed. by Jerome M. Hershman. LC 80-10850. 270p. reprint ed. pap. 83.70 (*0-7837-1475-0*, 205717000022) Bks Demand.

Management of Engineering: Human, Quality, Organizational, Legal & Ethical Aspects of Professional Practice. F. Lawrence Bennett. LC 95-34032. 496p. 1995. text 95.95 (*0-471-59329-X*) Wiley.

Management of Engineering of Control Systems for Water Pipelines. Compiled by American Society of Civil Engineers Staff. 141p. 1978. pap. 5.00 (*0-87262-132-4*) Am Soc Civil Eng.

Management of Engineering Projects. Intro. by Richard Stone. (Illus.). 266p. (C). 1989. text 60.00 (*0-333-40958-2*); pap. text 35.00 (*0-333-40959-0*) Scholium Intl.

Management of Environmental Protection & Safety. Institute of Chemical Engineering Staff. 174p. 1993. pap. 40.00 (*0-85295-309-7*, 9CH102, Pub. by IChemE) Gulf Pub.

Management of Epilepsy. Sudhansu Chokroverty. LC 96-16864. 414p. 1996. pap. text 49.95 (*0-7506-9754-7*) Buttrwrth-Heinemann.

Management of Epilepsy. Rosalind Troupin. write for info. (*0-444-00851-9*) Elsevier.

***Management of Epistaxis.** 3rd rev. ed. Jennifer Rubin et al. LC 99-34051. (Self-Instructional Ser.). (Illus.). 64p. 1999. pap. text 25.00 (*1-56772-073-0*) AAO-HNS.

Management of Esophageal Disease. David B. Skinner & Ronald H. Belsey. (Illus.). 864p. 1988. text 225.00 (*0-7216-8337-1*, W B Saunders Co) Harcrt Hlth Sci Grp.

Management of Esophageal Varices: Digestive Diseases, Vol. 10, Suppl. 1, 1992. Ed. by C. Scarpignato & Irvin M. Modlin. (Illus.). iv, 104p. 1992. pap. 33.25 (*3-8055-5686-1*) S Karger.

Management of Ethnic Conflict in India & Canada: A Comparative Analysis. G. Palanithurai. (C). 1993. 16.00 (*81-85475-74-1*, Pub. by Kanishka) S Asia.

Management of Ethnic Seccessionist Conflict: The Big Neighbor Syndrome. Abeysinghe M. Navaratna-Bandara. (Illus.). 208p. 1995. text 79.95 (*1-85521-698-1*, Pub. by Dartmth Pub) Ashgate Pub Co.

Management of Expatriates. IPM Committee on International Affairs Staff. Ed. by Brian Lewis. 384p. (C). 1982. 260.00 (*0-85292-304-X*) St Mut.

Management of Expertise. Harry Scarbrough. LC 95-42141. 240p. 1996. text 65.00 (*0-312-15793-2*) St Martin.

Management of Exports Marketing in India. A. K. Malviya. (C). 1990. 94.00 (*0-8364-2641-X*, Pub. by Chugh Pubns) S Asia.

Management of Extracranial Cerebrovascular Disease. Keith Calligaro. LC 96-33256. 190p. 1996. text 100.00 (*0-397-51655-X*) Lppncott W & W.

Management of Facial, Head, & Neck Pain. Cooper. 352p. 1989. text 115.00 (*0-7216-2841-9*, W B Saunders Co) Harcrt Hlth Sci Grp.

Management of Facial Lines & Wrinkles. Andrew Blitzer et al. 368p. 1999. text 99.00 (*0-7817-1551-2*) Lppncott W & W.

***Management of Failing DipSW Students: Activities & Exercises to Prepare Practice Teachers for Work with Failing Students.** Mavis Sharp & Hazel Danbury. LC 98-51475. 220p. 1999. pap. 34.95 (*1-85742-437-9*, Pub. by Ashgate Pub) Ashgate Pub Co.

Management of Farm Irrigation Systems. Glenn J. Hoffman et al. LC 90-85464. 1040p. 1990. 109.75 (*0-929355-11-3*, M0190) Am Soc Ag Eng.

Management of Federally Sponsored Libraries: Case Studies & Analysis. Ed. by Charles D. Missar. LC 94-48730. (Illus.). 112p. 1995. lib. bdg. 39.95 (*1-56024-395-3*) Haworth Pr.

Management of Financial Institutions. Alton L. Thygerson. (C). Date not set. write for info. (*0-673-55884-3*) Addson-Wesley Educ.

Management of Financial Institutions. Alton L. Thygerson. 832p. (C). 1995. text 81.50 (*0-673-99471-6*) Addson-Wesley Educ.

Management of Financial Institutions. Alton L. Thygerson. (C). 1997. teacher ed. 12.00 incl. trans., disk (*0-673-55883-5*) Addson-Wesley Educ.

Management of Food & Beverage Operations. 2nd ed. Jack D. Ninemeier. LC 90-36083. (Illus.). 370p. 1995. pap. write for info. (*0-86612-100-5*) Educ Inst Am Hotel.

***Management of Food & Beverage Operations** 3rd ed. Jack D. Ninemeier. LC 99-37315. 1999. write for info. (*0-86612-181-1*) Educ Inst Am Hotel.

Management of Food Policy. Ed. by Giulio Pontecorvo. LC 75-33468. (Individual Publications). (Illus.). 1980. lib. bdg. 17.95 (*0-405-06680-5*) Ayer.

Management of Foodservice Operations. Ed. by Peter Jones & Paul Merricks. 224p. 1995. 100.00 (*0-304-33181-3*); pap. 37.95 (*0-304-32907-X*) Continuum.

Management of Foreign Exchange: Optimal Policies for a Multinational Company. rev. ed. Raj K. Aggarwal. Ed. by Stuart Bruchey. LC 80-563. (Multinational Corporations Ser.). 1981. lib. bdg. 24.95 (*0-405-13359-6*) Ayer.

Management of Forestry Research in India. V. K. Bahuguna. 150p. (C). 1991. text 160.00 (*0-89771-542-X*, Pub. by Intl Bk Distr) St Mut.

Management of Forestry Research in India. V. K. Bahuguna. 96p. 1992. pap. 125.00 (*81-7089-178-7*, Pub. by Intl Bk Distr) St Mut.

Management of Forests. V. C. Osmanston. 384p. (C). 1985. reprint ed. pap. 175.00 (*81-7089-031-4*, Pub. by Intl Bk Distr) St Mut.

***Management of Freshwater Fisheries.** Jacques Arrignon. 600p. 1999. 95.00 (*90-5410-721-9*, Pub. by A A Balkema) Ashgate Pub Co.

Management of Freshwater Fisheries. Jacques Arrignon. LC 98-56137. 600p. 1999. text 95.00 (*1-57808-051-7*) Science Pubs.

Management of Gastric Cancer. Ed. by Paul H. Sugarbaker. (Cancer Treatment & Research Ser.). (C). 1991. text 260.50 (*0-7923-1102-7*) Kluwer Academic.

Management of Gastrointestinal Cancer. Ed. by Peter McCulloch & Andrew Kingsnorth. 416p. 1996. 128.00 (*0-7279-1071-X*, Pub. by BMJ Pub) Login Brothers Bk Co.

Management of Geological Databases. Joseph Frizado. LC 92-579. (Computer Methods in the Geosciences Ser.). 264p. 1992. 129.50 (*0-08-037951-6*, Pergamon Pr) Elsevier.

Management of Government Information Systems. 192p. 23.00 (*92-1-123113-2*, E.89.II.H.4) UN.

Management of Groundwater Observation Programmes. Yehuda Bachmat. (WMO, No. 705 & Operational Hydrology Reports: No. 31). 96p. 1989. pap. 22.00 (*92-63-10705-X*, Pub. by Wrld Meteorological) St Mut.

Management of Gunshot Wounds. Ed. by Gary Ordog. 477p. (C). 1992. pap. text 120.00 (*0-8385-5713-9*, A5713-1, Apple Lange Med) McGraw.

Management of Gypsiferous Soils. 89p. 1990. 12.00 (*92-5-102948-2*, F9482, Pub. by FAO) Bernan Associates.

Management of Hazardous Agents Vol. 1: Industrial & Regulatory Approaches, Vol. 1. Ed. by Duane G. LeVine & Arthur C. Upton. LC 92-167. (Only One Earth Ser.). 208p. 1992. 59.95 (*0-275-94322-4*, C4322, Praeger Pubs) Greenwood.

Management of Hazardous Agents Vol. 2: Social, Political, & Policy Aspects, Vol. 2. Ed. by Duane G. LeVine & Arthur C. Upton. LC 92-167. (Only One Earth Ser.). 200p. 1992. 59.95 (*0-275-94323-2*, C4323, Praeger Pubs) Greenwood.

Management of Hazardous Materials & Toxic Chemicals. Ehrlich. 600p. 1996. lib. bdg. 89.95 (*1-884015-99-9*) St Lucie Pr.

Management of Hazardous Materials & Wastes: Treatment, Minimization & Environmental Impacts. Ed. by Shyamal K. Majumdar et al. LC 89-60201. (Illus.). xviii, 474p. (C). 1989. text 45.00 (*0-9606670-9-1*) Penn Science.

Management of Hazardous Waste Policy Guidelines & Code of Practice. M. Suess & J. Huismans. (WHO Regional Publications, European Ser.: No. 14). 100p. 1983. pap. text 16.00 (*92-890-1105-X*) World Health.

Management of Head & Neck Cancer: A Multidisciplinary Approach. 2nd ed. Ed. by Rodney R. Million et al. LC 93-18326. 913p. (C). 1993. text 178.00 (*0-397-51208-2*) Lppncott W & W.

Management of Head Injuries. David G. Currie. LC 93-3454. (Oxford Handbooks in Emergency Medicine Ser.). (Illus.). 200p. (C). 1993. text 65.00 (*0-19-262385-0*, 7565) OUP.

***Management of Head Injuries: A Practical Guide for the Emergency Room.** 2nd ed. David G. Currie et al. LC 99-36446. (Illus.). 176p. 2000. pap. text 57.50 (*0-19-263078-4*) OUP.

Management of Headache. Ed. by F. Clifford Rose. LC 86-42503. 192p. 1988. reprint ed. pap. 59.60 (*0-608-03442-8*, 206414300008) Bks Demand.

Management of Headache & Headache Medications. Lawrence D. Robbins. LC 93-19226. 217p. 1994. 75.00 (*0-387-94040-5*) Spr-Verlag.

***Management of Headache & Headache Medications.** 2nd ed. Lawrence D. Robbins. LC 99-46474. 224p. 2000. pap. 49.00 (*0-387-98944-7*) Spr-Verlag.

Management of Health & Safety in Civil Engineering. Engineering Management Committee Safety Panel of t. 24p. 1995. 3.00 (*0-7277-2035-X*) Am Soc Civil Eng.

Management of Health Care. Ed. by Rosemary Stewart. LC 98-12104. (The International Library of Management). 368p. 1998. text 144.95 (*1-85521-934-4*, Pub. by Dartmth Pub) Ashgate Pub Co.

Management of Health Information: Functions & Applications. John Mattingly. 64p. (C). 1996. pap. text, teacher ed. 15.95 (*0-8273-7892-0*) Delmar.

Management of Health Information: Functions & Applications. Rozella Mattingly. (Allied Health Ser.). (Illus.). 400p. (C). 1996. mass mkt. 55.95 (*0-8273-6057-6*) Delmar.

Management of Healthcare Organizations. Carson & Carson. (Swc-Management). Date not set. write for info. (*0-534-24036-4*) Brooks-Cole.

Management of Hearing Handicap: Infants to Elderly. 3rd ed. Derek A. Sanders. LC 92-30171. Orig. Title: Aural Rehabilitation. 564p. (C). 1992. 90.00 (*0-13-051194-3*) P-H.

Management of Heart Failure. Jay Cohn & Spencer Kubo. 1990. pap. 12.95 (*0-929240-17-0*) EMIS.

Management of Hepatitis C, January 1989 Through January 1997. Ronald L. Gordner. 132p. 1997. pap. 15.00 (*0-16-061583-6*) USGPO.

Management of Heterogeneous & Autonomous Database Systems. Ahmed K. Elmagarmid et al. LC 99-214316. 432p. (C). 1998. 69.95 (*1-55860-216-X*) Morgan Kaufmann.

Management of High Quadriplegia. Ed. by Gale Whiteneck et al. LC 88-71753. (Illus.). 384p. 1988. 99.95 (*0-939957-19-1*) Demos Medical.

Management of High-Risk Pregnancy. 3rd ed. John T. Queenan. (Illus.). 632p. 1993. 89.95 (*0-86542-187-0*) Blackwell Sci.

Management of High-Risk Pregnancy. 4th ed. John T. Queenan. LC 99-24041. 14p. 1999. 99.00 (*0-632-04332-6*) Blackwell Sci.

***Management of Historic Centres.** Robert Pickard. LC 00-44058. (Conservation of the European Built Heritage Ser.). (Illus.). 2000. pap. write for info. (*0-419-23290-7*, E & FN Spon) Routledge.

Management of Historic Gardens. P. Swindells. (Illus.). 240p. 1997. text. write for info. (*0-419-21020-2*, E & FN Spon) Routledge.

Management of HIV Infection in Infants & Children. Yogev & Connor. 639p. 1991. 59.00 (*0-8016-5653-2*) Mosby Inc.

Management of HIV Infection in the Hospital. 3rd rev. ed. American Hospital Association Staff. LC 89-34355. Orig. Title: A Hospitalwide Approach to AIDS. 58p. 1988. pap. 15.00 (*0-87258-501-8*, 094642) Am Hospital.

Management of Home Care Services. Stephen Crystal et al. 192p. 1987. 24.95 (*0-8261-5660-6*) Springer Pub.

Management of Hospitality. Ed. by E. Cassee & R. Reuland. LC 82-18610. (International Series in Hospitality Management). (Illus.). 236p. 1983. 109.00 (*0-08-028107-9*, Pub. by Pergamon Repr) Franklin.

Management of Hotel & Motel Condominiums. Peter M. Gunnar & Judith A. Burkhart. (Illus.). 1978. text 17.50 (*0-937056-01-4*, A&F16) Cornell U Sch Hotel.

Management of Hotel & Motel Security. Burstein. (Occupational Safety & Health Ser.: Vol. 5). (Illus.). 216p. 1980. text 110.00 (*0-8247-1002-9*) Dekker.

Management of Human Resources for Health: Report of a WHO Expert Committee, 1987. (Technical Report Ser.: No. 783). 61p. 1989. pap. text 8.00 (*92-4-120783-3*, 1100783) World Health.

Management of Human Resources I. Jack Rudman. (Regents External Degree (REDP) Ser.: Vol. 7). 43.95 (*0-8373-5657-1*) Nat Learn.

Management of Human Resources I. Jack Rudman. (Regents External Degree Ser.: REDP-7). 1994. pap. 23.95 (*0-8373-5607-5*) Nat Learn.

Management of Human Resources II. Jack Rudman. (Regents External Degree (REDP) Ser.: Vol. 8). 43.95 (*0-8373-5658-X*) Nat Learn.

Management of Human Resources II. Jack Rudman. (Regents External Degree Ser.: REDP-8). 1994. pap. 23.95 (*0-8373-5608-3*) Nat Learn.

Management of Human Resources III. Jack Rudman. (Regents External Degree (REDP) Ser.: Vol. 9). 43.95 (*0-8373-5659-8*) Nat Learn.

Management of Human Resources III. Jack Rudman. (Regents External Degree Ser.: REDP-9). 1994. pap. 23.95 (*0-8373-5609-1*) Nat Learn.

Management of Human Resources in Hospitals: Examples of Compliance. Joint Commission on Accreditation of Healthcare Organizations. LC 96-77204. (Illus.). 199p. 1996. pap. 40.00 (*0-86688-496-3*, ED-200) Joint Comm Hlthcare.

***Management of Human Service Organizations.** (C). 2001. 46.67 (*0-205-31878-9*) Allyn.

Management of Human Service Programs. Judith A. Lewis & Michael D. Lewis. LC 82-14684. (Counseling Ser.). 228p. (C). 1983. pap. 31.00 (*0-534-01335-X*) Brooks-Cole.

Management of Human Services. Ed. by Rosemary C. Sarri & Yeheskel Hasenfeld. LC 78-9083. 376p. reprint ed. pap. 116.60 (*0-608-12654-3*, 202510800042) Bks Demand.

Management of Human Services Programs. 2nd ed. Lewis et al. LC 90-46530. 321p. (C). 1990. mass mkt. 41.00 (*0-534-13074-7*) Brooks-Cole.

Management of Human Services Programs. 3rd ed. Lewis et al. 2000. pap. text 48.00 (*0-534-36886-7*) Thomson Learn.

Management of Human Settlements: Applications of the Use of Microcomputers. Timothy J. Cartwright. 304p. (C). 1990. text 74.95 (*0-415-03124-9*) Routledge.

Management of Ideas in the Creating Organization. John E. Tropman. LC 98-4947. 280p. 1998. 69.50 (*1-56720-168-7*, Quorum Bks) Greenwood.

Management of Impotence & Infertility. Ed. by E. Douglas Whitehead & Harris M. Nagler. (Illus.). 460p. 1994. text 113.00 (*0-397-51153-1*, Lippnctt) Lppncott W & W.

Management of Independent Learning. Jo Tait & Peter Knight. 192p. 1996. pap. 29.95 (*0-7494-1949-0*, Kogan Pg Educ) Stylus Pub VA.

Management of Industrial Construction Projects. John J. O'Neill. 285p. 1990. 49.95 (*0-89397-357-2*) Nichols Pub.

Management of Industrial Pollutants by Anaerobic Processes. Alan W. Obayashi & Joseph M. Gorgan. Ed. by James M. Patterson. LC 84-23378. (Industrial Waste Management Ser.). (Illus.). 220p. 1984. 119.00 (*0-87371-001-0*, CRC Reprint) Franklin.

Management of Industrial Wastewater in Developing Countries: Proceedings of the International Symposium Held in Alexandria, Egypt, March 28-31, 1981. Ed. by D. C. Stuckey. LC 82-7671. (Illus.). 510p. 1982. 219.00 (*0-08-026286-4*, Pub. by Pergamon Repr) Franklin.

Management of Infected Arterial Grafts. Ed. by Keith D. Calligaro & Frank J. Veith. LC 94-7228. (Illus.). 243p. 1994. 75.00 (*0-942219-57-0*) Quality Med Pub.

Management of Infectious Complications in Cancer Patients. Ed. by Gary A. Noskin. LC 98-16254. (Cancer Treatment & Research Ser.). 312p. 1998. 295.00 (*0-7923-8150-5*) Kluwer Academic.

Management of Infertility: A Clinician's Manual. 2nd ed. Brian M. Cohen. 172p. 1991. pap. 12.95 (*0-929240-33-2*) EMIS.

Management of Information. Amer. Date not set. text. write for info. (*0-03-006379-5*) Harcourt Coll Pubs.

Management of Information from Archives. Michael Cook. LC 98-32250. 1999. 96.95 (*0-566-07993-3*) Ashgate Pub Co.

Management of Information Systems. 7th ed. Raymond McLeod. LC 97-13159. 655p. 1997. 93.00 (*0-13-856584-8*) P-H.

Management of Information Technology. Phil Fawcett & Graham Flower. 328p. 1996. pap. 120.00 (*0-85297-389-6*, Pub. by Chartered Bank) St Mut.

Management of Information Technology. Carroll W. Frenzel. 556p. (C). 1991. pap. 57.95 (*0-87835-508-1*) Course Tech.

Management of Information Technology. 2nd ed. Carroll Frenzel. (DC - Introduction to Computing Ser.). 544p. 1995. pap. 42.00 (*0-7895-0413-8*) Course Tech.

Management of Information Technology. 3rd ed. Frenzel. (C). 1998. pap. 60.95 (*0-7600-4990-4*) Course Tech.

M

Management of Information Technology for Construction. S. Mathur Krishan et al. 616p. 1993. text 113.00 (*981-02-1566-5*) World Scientific Pub.

Management of Innovation. Tom Burns & George M. Stalker. 304p. (Orig.). 1994. reprint ed. pap. text 22.00 (*0-19-828878-6*) OUP.

Management of Innovation. R. Charles Parker. LC 82-2737. (Illus.). 239p. reprint ed. pap. 74.10 (*0-8357-4321-7*, 203712000007) Bks Demand.

Management of Innovation in High Technology Small Firms: Innovation & Regional Development in Britain & the United States. Raymond P. Oakey et al. LC 88-11448. 224p. 1988. 55.00 (*0-89930-399-4*, OMI/, Quorum Bks) Greenwood.

Management of Insect Pests: Nuclear & Related Molecular & Genetic Techniques. IAEA Staff. 669p. 1994. pap. 190.00 (*92-0-000293-5*, STI/PUB/909, Pub. by IAEA) Bernan Associates.

Management of Intensive Care. Ed. by D. Reis Miranda et al. (Developments in Critical Care, Medicine, & Anesthesiology Ser.). (C). 1990. text 171.00 (*0-7923-0754-2*) Kluwer Academic.

Management of Intercurrent Illness & Complicated Advanced Disease: Advanced Cancer & Stroke As a Model. Ed. by James E. Cimino & Austin H. Kutscher. LC 98-71723. 120p. 1999. pap. 18.95 (*0-930194-34-9*) Ctr Thanatology.

M

Management of Intermediate & High Grade Lymphomas. 1994. lib. bdg. 250.95 (*0-8490-8528-4*) Gordon Pr.

Management of Intermediate & High Grade Lymphomas. 1995. lib. bdg. 251.99 (*0-8490-7584-X*) Gordon Pr.

Management of Internal Business Investigations: A Survival Guide. Richard B. Cole. LC 96-9152. (Illus.). 178p. 1996. text 49.95 (*0-398-06702-3*); pap. text 33.95 (*0-398-06703-1*) C C Thomas.

Management of Internal Security: Freedom from Fear. Ranjit S. Gupta. (C). 1995. 28.00 (*1-897829-65-5*, Pub. by Lancer India) S Asia.

Management of International Advertising: A Handbook & Guide for Professionals. Erdener Kaynak. LC 88-32430. 300p. 1989. 67.95 (*0-89930-142-8*, KKM/, Quorum Bks) Greenwood.

Management of International Construction Projects: Proceedings of a Conference Organized by the Institution of Civil Engineers. 188p. 1985. 39.00 (*0-7277-0220-3*, Pub. by T Telford) RCH.

*__Management of International Enterprises: A Socio-Political View.__ Monir H. Tayeb. LC 99-54952. 2000. text 69.95 (*0-312-23121-0*) St Martin.

Management of International Joint Ventures: An Organizational Learning Perspective. Andrew Inkpen. LC 95-11974. (International Business Ser.). 176p. (C). (gr. 13). 1995. pap. 74.95 (*0-415-11706-2*) Routledge.

*__Management of International Networks: Cost-Effective Strategies for the New Telecom Regulations & Services.__ Floris V. Broek. LC 99-32369. 208p. 1999. boxed set 69.95 (*0-8493-0739-2*) CRC Pr.

Management of International Oil Operations. Richard Barry, Sr. LC 93-14287. 600p. 1993. 74.95 (*0-87814-400-5*) PennWell Bks.

Management of International Tourism. Stephen F. Witt & Michael Z. Brooke. (Illus.). 224p. (C). 1991. pap. 22.95 (*0-415-08463-6*) Thomson Learn.

Management of International Tourism. Stephen F. Witt et al. 256p. 1991. 55.00 (*0-04-445124-5*, A8266); pap. 21.95 (*0-04-445993-9*) Routledge.

Management of International Tourism. 2nd ed. Stephen F. Witt et al. LC 95-13892. 240p. (C). 1995. pap. 24.95 (*0-415-12504-9*) Thomson Learn.

Management of Investment Decisions. Donald Trone et al. 500p. 1995. text 65.00 (*0-7863-0392-1*, Irwn Prfssnl) McGraw-Hill Prof.

Management of Investments. 3rd ed. Jack C. Francis. LC 92-23156. (Series in Finance). (C). 1993. text 83.75 (*0-07-021818-8*) McGraw.

Management of Irrigation & Drainage Systems. Richard G. Allen. LC 93-5107. 1216p. 1993. 99.00 (*0-87262-919-8*) Am Soc Civil Eng.

*__Management of Irrigation & Drainage Systems: A Service Approach.__ Hector M. Malano & Paul J. M. Hofwegen. (Illus.). 160p. (C). 1999. text 65.00 (*90-5410-482-1*, Pub. by A A Balkema); pap. text 38.00 (*90-5410-483-X*, Pub. by A A Balkema) Ashgate Pub Co.

*__Management of Islamic Activism: Salafis, the Muslim Brotherhood, & State Power in Jordan.__ Quintan Wiktorowicz. (C). 2001. pap. text 17.95 (*0-7914-4836-3*) State U NY Pr.

*__Management of Islamic Activism: Salafis, the Muslim Brotherhood, & State Power in Jordan.__ Quintan Wiktorowicz. (C). 2001. text 54.50 (*0-7914-4835-5*) State U NY Pr.

Management of Knowledge-Intensive Companies. Mats Alvesson. (De Gruyter Studies in Organization: Vol. 61). x, 367p. (C). 1995. lib. bdg. 79.95 (*3-11-012865-9*) De Gruyter.

Management of Labor: The British & French Iron Industries, 1860-1918. Judith E. Vichniac. LC 90-42936. (Industrial Development & the Social Fabric Ser.: Vol. 10). 244p. 1990. 73.25 (*1-55938-030-6*) Jai Pr.

Management of Labor & Delivery. Robert K. Creasey & Peter Boylan. LC 96-39912. (Illus.). 593p. 1997. 99.95 (*0-86542-416-0*) Blackwell Sci.

Management of Labour: A History of Australian Employers. Christopher Wright. (Australian Studies in Labour Relations Ser.). (Illus.). 328p. 1996. pap. text 55.00 (*0-19-553549-9*) OUP.

Management of Lakes & Ponds. 2nd ed. Intro. by George W. Bennett. LC 83-6091. 398p. (C). 1983. reprint ed. text 48.50 (*0-89874-626-4*) Krieger.

Management of Lakes & Reservoirs During Global Climate Change: NATO Advanced Research Workshop Held in Prague, 11-15 November 1995. Glen D. George. LC 98-16260. (NATO Science Ser.). 1998. 143.00 (*0-7923-5055-3*) Kluwer Academic.

Management of Lands with Religious & Charitable Institutions: A Case Study of Madhya Pradesh Bhupinder Singh et al. LC 95-906100. 132 p. 1995. write for info. (*81-241-0318-6*) S Asia.

Management of Large Capital Projects. Ed. by Institution of Civil Engineers Staff. 246p. 1978. 46.00 (*0-7277-0066-9*, Pub. by T Telford) RCH.

*__Management of Latin American River Basins: Amazon, Plata & San Francisco.__ Asit K. Biswas. LC 98-58084. 1999. pap. 29.95 (*92-808-1012-X*) UN Univ Pr.

*__Management of Leg Ulcers.__ Ed. by J. Hafner et al. LC 99-40695. (Current Problems in Dermatology Ser.: Vol. 27). (Illus.). viii, 294p. 1999. write for info. (*3-8055-6654-9*) S Karger.

Management of Leg Ulcers. 2nd ed. Terence J. Ryan. (Illus.). 110p. 1987. pap. 19.95 (*0-19-261663-3*) OUP.

Management of Library & Archival Security: From the Outside Looking In. Ed. by Robert K. O'Neill. LC 98-4912. (Journal of Library Science). 120p. 1998. 29.95 (*0-7890-0519-0*) Haworth Pr.

Management of Library & Information Studies Education. Ed. by Herman L. Totten. LC 92-10817. (Journal of Library Administration: Vol. 16, Nos. 1-2). (Illus.). 220p. 1992. 49.95 (*1-56024-252-3*) Haworth Pr.

Management of Library & Information Studies Education. Ed. by Herman L. Totten. LC 92-10817. (Journal of Library Administration: Vol. 16, Nos. 1-2). 220p. 1996. reprint ed. pap. 24.95 (*0-7890-0050-4*) Haworth Pr.

Management of Limb Inequality. Ed. by Malcolm B. Menelaus. (Current Problems in Orthopaedics Ser.). (Illus.). 236p. 1991. text 145.00 (*0-443-04298-5*) Church.

Management of Lipid Disorders: A Basis & Guide for Therapeutic Intervention. Sander J. Robins. LC 97-181155. 136p. 1997. pap. 18.95 (*0-683-30350-3*) Lppncott W & W.

Management of Lipid Disorders: A Basis & Guide for Therapy. Sander J. Robins. (Illus.). 112p. (Orig.). 1997. pap. text. write for info. (*0-89640-337-8*) Igaku-Shoin.

Management of Lipids in Clinical Practice. 2nd rev. ed. Neil J. Stone et al. 316p. 1998. pap. text 19.95 (*1-884735-37-1*) Prof Comms.

Management of Lithiasis: The Rational Deploy of Technology. Ed. by J. Talati. LC 96-32629. (Developments in Nephrology Ser.). 368p. (C). 1997. text 180.50 (*0-7923-4198-8*) Kluwer Academic.

Management of Local Government Records: A Guide for Local Officials. Bruce W. Dearstyne. LC 88-4004. 156p. 1988. reprint ed. pap. 48.40 (*0-608-04563-2*, 206530200001) Bks Demand.

Management of Local Planning. David C. Slater. LC 84-6577. (Municipal Management Ser.). (Illus.). 288p. (C). 1984. text 34.95 (*0-87326-031-7*); pap. text 28.95 (*0-87326-032-5*) Intl City-Cnty Mgt.

Management of Local Public Works. Ed. by Sam M. Cristofano & William S. Foster. (Municipal Management Ser.). 448p. 1986. text 41.95 (*0-87326-048-1*) Intl City-Cnty Mgt.

*__Management of Low Back Pain in Primary Care.__ Richard Bartley & Paul Coffey. (Illus.). 176p. 2000. pap. text 32.00 (*0-7506-4787-6*) Buttrwrth-Heinemann.

Management of Lower Extremity Fractures. Verdell Williamson et al. LC 99-188174. (Illus.). iv, 126p. 1998. pap. 65.00 (*1-892665-00-X*) Natl Assn Ortho Nurse.

Management of Maintenance & Engineering Systems in the Hospitality Industry. 4th ed. Frank D. Borsenik & Alan T. Stutts. LC 96-39997. 680p. 1997. 69.95 (*0-471-14105-4*) Wiley.

Management of Maintenance & Engineering Systems in the Hospitality Industry. 4th ed. Frank D. Borsenik & Alan T. Stutts. 228p. 1997. pap., teacher ed. write for info. (*0-471-17217-0*) Wiley.

Management of Major Trauma. 2nd ed. Colin E. Robertson & Anthony D. Redmond. (Hardbooks in Emergency Medicine Ser.: Vol. 9). (Illus.). 208p. 1994. 59.95 (*0-19-262448-2*); pap. text 27.50 (*0-19-262447-4*) OUP.

Management of Manufactured Gas Plant Sites: The Gas Research Institute's Practical Reference Guide, 2 vols., Vols. 1 & 2. Ed. by Thomas D. Hayes et al. Incl. Vol. 1: The Gas Research Institute's Practical Reference Guide, Site Investigation. LC 96-35099. (Illus.). 630p. 1996. text 119.95 (*1-884940-08-0*); Vol. 2: The Gas Research Institute's Practical Reference Guide, Risk Assessment & Site Restoration., **2 vols.** Ed. by David V. Nakles. LC 96-35099. (Illus.). 630p. 1996. text 119.95 (*1-884940-09-9*); 1600p. 1996. Set text 195.00 (*1-884940-18-8*) Amherst Sci Pubs.

Management of Marine Design. Stian Erichsen. (Illus.). 239p. 1989. 135.00 (*0-408-03237-5*) Buttrwrth-Heinemann.

Management of Marine Fisheries. John A. Gulland. LC 74-2473. (Illus.). 206p. 1974. 25.00 (*0-295-95335-7*) U of Wash Pr.

Management of Marine Fisheries in Canada. L. S. Parsons. 784p. 1993. 87.50 (*0-660-15002-6*) NRC Res Pr.

Management of Marketing. 2nd ed. M. Wilson. 150p. 1989. pap. text 25.95 (*0-7045-0609-2*, Pub. by Gower) Ashgate Pub Co.

Management of Marketing. 2nd ed. M. Wilson. 150p. 1990. text 63.95 (*0-566-02884-0*, Pub. by Gower) Ashgate Pub Co.

Management of Mass Burn Casualties & Fire Disasters. Ed. by M. Masellis. 352p. (C). 1993. text 178.50 (*0-7923-8804-6*) Kluwer Academic.

Management of Materials Research. Ed. by Dan H. Fenn & Linda M. Fernberger. LC 62-12207. (Metallurgical Society Conference Ser.: Vol. 14). 182p. reprint ed. pap. 56.50 (*0-608-11464-2*, 200067700038) Bks Demand.

Management of Medical Foodservice. 3rd ed. Catherine F. Sullivan. LC 97-26951. 400p. 1997. 59.00 (*0-8342-0921-7*, 20921) Aspen Pub.

Management of Medical Technology: A Primer for Clinical Engineers. Joseph D. Bronzino & Vernon Roosa. Ed. by Robert J. Austin-LaFrance. LC 92-21070. (Biomedical Engineering Ser.). 451p. 1992. 64.95 (*0-7506-9252-9*) Buttrwrth-Heinemann.

Management of Medical Technology: Theory, Practice & Cases. Eliezer Geisler & Ori Heller. LC 97-41934. (Management of Medical Technology Ser.). 518p. 1998. lib. bdg. 154.00 (*0-7923-8054-1*) Kluwer Academic.

Management of Memory Disorders. 2nd ed. Ed. by William H. Burke. (Professional Series on Traumatic Brain Injury: Vol. 8). 44p. (Orig.). 1995. pap. 9.50 (*1-882855-39-6*) HDI Pubs.

Management of Mentoring: Policy Issues. Derek Glover & Sue Law. 160p. 1995. pap. 29.95 (*0-7494-1598-3*, Kogan Pg Educ) Stylus Pub VA.

Management of Migraine. Egilius L. Spierings. 150p. 1995. text 49.95 (*0-7506-9623-0*) Buttrwrth-Heinemann.

Management of Migratory Shore & Upland Game Birds in North America. Ed. by Glen C. Sanderson. LC 79-23802. (Illus.). 372p. reprint ed. pap. 115.40 (*0-7837-4649-0*, 204437300002) Bks Demand.

Management of Ministry: Building Leadership in a Changing World. James D. Anderson & Ezra E. Jones. LC 93-73930. 224p. (Orig.). 1993. pap. 12.95 (*0-88177-131-7*, DR131) Discipleship Res.

Management of Motivation & Remuneration. D. A. Whitmore. 1977. 38.00 (*0-8464-0597-0*) Beekman Pubs.

Management of Motor Disorders of Children with Cerebral Palsy. Ed. by David Scrutton. (Clinics in Developmental Medicine Ser.: No. 90). (Illus.). 101p. (C). 1991. text 33.95 (*0-521-41210-2*, Pub. by Mc Keith Pr) Cambridge U Pr.

Management of Motor Speech Disorders in Children & Adults. 2nd ed. Kathryn M. Yorkston. LC 98-16735. 1999. 43.00 (*0-89079-784-6*) PRO-ED.

Management of Multiliberal Organizations, Vol. 26, NLSP. Dijkzeut. LC 96-52607. 1997. 94.00 (*90-411-0356-2*) Kluwer Law Intl.

Management of Multiple Sclerosis: An Interdisiplinary Approach. William Stuart et al. 448p. Date not set. 59.00 (*0-8342-0758-3*) Aspen Pub.

Management of Multispecies Resources & Multi-Gear Fisheries: Experience in Coastal Waters Around Japan. FAO Staff. 77p. 1989. 12.00 (*92-5-102848-6*, F8486, Pub. by FAO) Bernan Associates.

Management of Municipal Solid Waste in Europe. Alberto Quadrio Curzio et al. LC 95-119991. (Developments in Environmental Economics Ser.: Vol. 5). 262p. 1994. 155.75 (*0-444-81948-7*) Elsevier.

Management of Musculoskeletal Problems in the Haemophilias. 2nd ed. Robert B. Duthie et al. (Illus.). 298p. 1994. text 110.00 (*0-19-262317-6*) OUP.

Management of Mycorrhizas in Agriculture, Horticulture & Forestry: Proceedings of an International Symposium, Held in Perth, Western Australia, September 28-October 2, 1992. Ed. by A. D. Robson & L. K. Abbott. LC 94-685. (Developments in Plant & Soil Sciences Ser.). 248p. (C). 1994. text 136.00 (*0-7923-2700-4*) Kluwer Academic.

Management of Neurological Disorders. Ed. by C. M. Wiles. 180p. 1995. pap. text 43.00 (*0-7279-0903-7*, Pub. by BMJ Pub) Login Brothers Bk Co.

Management of New Technologies for Global Competitiveness. Ed. by Christian N. Madu. LC 92-31712. 400p. 1993. 65.00 (*0-89930-713-2*, MNH, Quorum Bks) Greenwood.

Management of Nitrogen & Phosphorus Fertilizers in Sub-Saharan Africa. Ed. by Uzo M. Mokwunye & Paul L. Vlek. (Developments in Plant & Soil Sciences Ser.). 1986. text 248.00 (*90-247-3312-X*) Kluwer Academic.

Management of Non-Hodgkin's Lymphomas in Europe. Ed. by S. Monfardini & U. Veronesi. (ESO Intercity Reports). viii, 92p. 1990. 68.95 (*0-387-52297-2*) Spr-Verlag.

Management of Non-Profit Organizations. Ed. by Sharon M. Oster. (International Library of Management). 544p. 1994. 235.95 (*1-85521-465-2*, Pub. by Dartmth Pub) Ashgate Pub Co.

Management of Nongame Wildlife in the Midwest: A Developing Art. Ed. by James B. Hale et al. 171p. 1986. pap. text 5.00 (*0-317-54821-2*) N Central Sect Wildlife.

Management of Normality: Critical Essays in Health & Welfare. Abram De Swaan. LC 89-10352. 228p. (C). 1990. pap. text 16.95 (*0-415-03200-8*, A4157) Routledge.

Management of Nutrition in Forests under Stress. Ed. by H. W. Zottl & Reinhard F. Huttl. (C). 1991. text 316.50 (*0-7923-1246-5*) Kluwer Academic.

Management of Occupational Therapy. Zielfa Maslin. Ed. by Jo Campling. (Therapy in Practice Ser.). 144p. 1990. pap. 23.00 (*0-412-33380-5*, A4414) Chapman & Hall.

Management of Ocular, Orbital, & Adnexal Trauma. Ed. by Thomas C. Spoor & Frank A. Nesi. LC 87-45469. 460p. 1988. reprint ed. pap. 142.60 (*0-608-04724-4*, 206544500004) Bks Demand.

Management of Ocular Traumas & Other Emergencies. 4th ed. Mathew MacCumber. LC 97-26482. 380p. 1997. pap. text 57.95 (*0-397-51496-4*) Lppncott W & W.

Management of Office Emergencies. Chris Barton. LC 98-35485. (Illus.). 398p. 1999. pap. text 32.00 (*0-07-006303-6*) McGraw-Hill HPD.

Management of Operations. 3rd ed. Jack R. Meredith. 148p. 1987. pap. 34.95 (*0-471-85582-0*) Wiley.

Management of Operations. 4th ed. Jack R. Meredith. LC 91-33361. 800p. (C). 1992. text 86.95 (*0-471-50909-4*) Wiley.

Management of Operations. 4th ed. Jack R. Meredith. 1992. pap. text 25.00 (*0-471-54352-7*) Wiley.

Management of Oral Cancer. Nicholas Stafford & John Waldron. (Illus.). 224p. 1990. text 65.00 (*0-19-261609-9*) OUP.

Management of Oral History Sound Archives. Frederick J. Stielow. LC 85-14716. (Illus.). 180p. 1986. lib. bdg. 52.95 (*0-313-24442-1*, SOH/, Greenwood Pr) Greenwood.

Management of Orbital & Ocular Tumors. Joseph Mauriello. 1990. 145.00 (*0-938607-19-7*) Field & Wood Inc Medical.

*__Management of Organizational Behavior: Leading Human Resources.__ 8th ed. Paul Hersey et al. LC 00-32701. 2000. write for info. (*0-13-017598-6*) Prntice Hall Bks.

Management of Organizational Behavior: Utilizing Human Resources. 7th ed. Paul Hersey & Kenneth Blanchard. LC 96-1155. 627p. (C). 1996. pap. text 66.00 (*0-13-244112-8*) P-H.

Management of Organizational Behavior: Utilizing Human Resources. 7th ed. Paul Hersey et al. LC 96-1155. 1996. text 72.00 (*0-13-261769-2*) P-H.

Management of Organizations. Patrick M. Wright. 352p. (C). 1996. text, student ed. 24.37 (*0-256-22068-9*, Irwn McGrw-H) McGrw-H Hghr Educ.

Management of Organizations: Strategies, Tactics, Analyses. Ed. by David A. Nadler et al. 600p. 1989. 54.95 (*0-88730-380-3*, HarpBusn) HarpInfo.

Management of Organizations in Africa: A Handbook & Reference. Muroki Mwaura. Ed. by J. Muruku Waiguchu & Edward Tiagha. LC 98-4975. 432p. 1999. 79.50 (*1-56720-188-1*, Quorum Bks) Greenwood.

Management of Pain. Michael A. Ashburn & Linda J. Rice. LC 97-36319. (Illus.). 729p. 1997. text 95.00 (*0-443-07679-0*) Church.

Management of Pain, 2 vols. 2nd ed. Ed. by John J. Bonica. LC 88-8983. (Illus.). 2195p. 1990. 295.00 (*0-8121-1122-2*) Lppncott W & W.

Management of Pain & Anxiety in Dental Practice. Raymond A. Dionne & J. C. Phero. 420p. 1991. pap. 89.50 (*0-444-81749-2*) Elsevier.

Management of Pain in the Hand & Wrist. Ed. by Parry C. Wynn. (Hand & Upper Limb Ser.). (Illus.). 173p. 1991. text 114.00 (*0-443-04109-1*) Church.

Management of Pakistan's Economy, 1947-1982. Viqar Ahmed & Rashid Amjad. (UGC Series in Economics). (Illus.). 328p. 1985. pap. text 24.00 (*0-19-577316-0*) OUP.

Management of Patient Care: Putting Leadership Skills to Work. 6th ed. Thora Kron & Anne Gray. (Illus.). 1987. teacher ed. write for info. (*0-7216-2842-7*, W B Saunders Co) Harcrt Hlth Sci Grp.

Management of Patient Care: Putting Leadership Skills to Work. 6th ed. Thora Kron & Anne Gray. (Illus.). 320p. 1987. pap. text 34.00 (*0-7216-2064-7*, W B Saunders Co) Harcrt Hlth Sci Grp.

*__Management of Patients at High Risk for Breast Cancer.__ Victor G. Vogel. (Illus.). 368p. 2000. 95.00 (*0-632-04323-7*) Blackwell Sci.

Management of Patients with Sexually Transmitted Diseases: Report of a WHO Study Group. (Technical Reports: No. 810). (CHI, ENG, FRE & SPA.). vii, 103p. 1991. pap. text 14.00 (*92-4-120810-4*, 1100810) World Health.

*__Management of Peace Processes.__ John Darby & Roger MacGinty. LC 99-59427. 2000. 69.95 (*0-312-23198-9*) St Martin.

Management of Pediatric Fractures. Ed. by Robert M. Letts. (Illus.). 1296p. 1993. text 294.00 (*0-443-08860-8*) Church.

Management of Pediatric Trauma. Ed. by William L. Buntain. LC 93-47168. (Illus.). 788p. 1995. text 185.00 (*0-7216-4547-X*, W B Saunders Co) Harcrt Hlth Sci Grp.

Management of People in Hotels & Restaurants. 5th ed. Donald E. Lundberg & James P. Armatas. 288p. (C). 1992. text 36.50 (*0-697-08416-7*) Brown & Benchmark.

Management of Perioperative Complications in Gynecology. Vicki V. Baker & Gunter Deppe. Ed. by Bill Schmitt. LC 96-15894. (Illus.). 288p. 1996. text 78.95 (*0-7216-5881-4*, W B Saunders Co) Harcrt Hlth Sci Grp.

Management of Personnel in Health Sciences: Index of New Information with Authors & Subjects. Denise J. Randall. 180p. 1993. 47.50 (*1-55914-858-6*); pap. 44.50 (*1-55914-859-4*) ABBE Pubs Assn.

Management of Personnel in Long Term Care. Ed. by Mildred O. Hogstel. LC 82-20579. (Illus.). 336p. 1982. text 29.95 (*0-89303-231-X*) P-H.

Management of Persons Accidentally Contaminated with Radionuclides. LC 79-91648. (Report Ser.: No. 65). 213p. 1980. 50.00 (*0-913392-49-9*) NCRP Pubns.

*__Management of Persons with Chronic Neurologic Illness.__ Mark N. Ozer. LC 99-53895. 315p. 2000. pap. text 60.00 (*0-7506-7005-3*) Buttrwrth-Heinemann.

Management of Persons with Spinal Cord Injury. Mark N. Ozer. LC 88-70004. 128p. (Orig.). 1988. pap. 29.95 (*0-939957-10-8*) Demos Medical.

Management of Philanthropic Funding for Institutional Stabilization: A History of Ford Foundation & New York City Ballet Activities. Anne B. Bennett. LC 92-26063. (Non-profit Institutions in America Ser.). 288p. 1992. text 10.00 (*0-8153-0903-1*) Garland.

Management of Physical Education & Sport. Charles Augustus Bucher & March L. Krotee. 466p. 1992. 39.95 (*0-8016-7442-5*) Mosby Inc.

An Asterisk (*) at the beginning of an entry indicates that the title is appearing for the first time.

Management of Pituitary Tumors. Powell. 1997. pap. text 49.00 (*0-443-06023-1*, W B Saunders Co) Harcrt Hlth Sci Grp.
Management of Plastic Wastes in the ECE Region. 180p. 42.00 (*92-1-116557-1*) UN.
Management of Plutonium Contaminated Waste. J. R. Grover. (Radioactive Waste Management Ser.: Vol. 3). x, 186p. 1981. text 129.00 (*3-7186-0110-9*) Gordon & Breach.
Management of Poisonous Snakebite. Thomas G. Glass, Jr. (Illus.). 210p. 1989. pap. text 39.95 (*0-9614759-1-9*) Glass Pub Co.
***Management of Police Specialized Tactical Units.** Tomas C. Mijares et al. LC 00-27308. 2000. pap. write for info. (*0-398-07070-9*) C C Thomas.
Management of Prader-Willi Syndrome. Ed. by Louise R. Greenswag & Randell C. Alexander. (Illus.). 310p. 1991. 53.00 (*0-387-96687-0*) Spr-Verlag.
Management of Prader-Willi Syndrome. 2nd ed. Louise R. Greenswag & Randall C. Alexander. LC 94-29757. 1995. write for info. (*3-540-94373-0*) Spr-Verlag.
Management of Prader-Willi Syndrome. 2nd ed. Ed. by Louise R. Greenswag & Randall C. Alexander. LC 94-29757. 1995. 75.00 (*0-387-94373-0*) Spr-Verlag.
Management of Price Fluctuations. R. Matto Aijaz. 285p. 1990. 120.00 (*81-7041-297-8*, Pub. by Scientific Pubs) St Mut.
Management of Primary Bone Tumors. 1995. lib. bdg. 259.95 (*0-8490-7583-1*) Gordon Pr.
Management of Problem Soils in Arid Ecosystems. A. Monem Balba. 272p. 1995. lib. bdg. 110.00 (*0-87371-811-9*, L811) Lewis Pubs.
Management of Process Industry Waste. Ed. by Richard Bahu & Barry Crittenden. LC 94-229322. 1997. pap. 70.00 (*0-85295-324-0*, 53240) Gulf Pub.
Management of Productivity & Technology in Manufacturing. Ed. by Paul R. Kleindorfer. LC 85-17022. 346p. 1985. 85.00 (*0-306-42032-5*, Plenum Trade) Perseus Pubng.
Management of Professionals: Insights for Maximizing Cooperation. Desmond D. Martin & Richard L. Shell. (Illus.). 348p. 1988. text 65.00 (*0-8247-7847-2*) Dekker.
Management of Program Evaluation. Frank K. Gibson & James E. Prather. LC 84-7521. 184p. pap. 7.95 (*0-89854-101-8*) U of GA Inst Govt.
Management of Programme Risk. 104p. 1995. pap. 75.00 (*0-11-330672-5*, HM06725, Pub. by Statnry Office) Balogh.
Management of Prostate Cancer. Ed. by Eric A. Klein. LC 99-34212. (Current Clinical Urology Ser.). 384p. 1999. 125.00 (*0-89603-797-5*) Humana.
Management of Prostate Cancer: A European-American Encounter, International Symposium, Munich, November 1996. Ed. by Claude C. Schulman & E. David Crawford. (European Urology Ser.: Vol. 32, Suppl. 3, 1997). (Illus.). iv, 90p. 1997. pap. 41.00 (*3-8055-6559-3*) S Karger.
Management of Prostate Diseases see Atencion de las Enfermedades Prostaticas
Management of Prostate Diseases. 2nd rev. ed. Robert E. Weiss & William R. Fair. 141p. 1997. pap. text 19.95 (*1-884735-24-X*) Prof Comms.
Management of Protection Against Ionising & Non-Ionising Radiations. H & H Scientific Consultants, Ltd. Staff. 74p. 1996. pap. 150.00 (*0-948237-27-9*, Pub. by H&H Sci Cnslts) St Mut.
Management of Protracted Social Conflict: Theory & Cases. Edward E. Azar. 168p. 1990. text 72.95 (*1-85521-063-0*, Pub. by Dartmth Pub) Ashgate Pub Co.
Management of Public Access to the Heritage Landscape. Council of Europe Staff. (Cultural Heritage Ser.: No. 24). 1992. 15.00 (*92-871-2145-1*, Pub. by Council of Europe) Manhattan Pub Co.
Management of Public Enterprises. S. A. Bhat. 132p. 1991. 60.00 (*81-7041-520-9*, Pub. by Scientific Pubs) St Mut.
Management of Public Lands in the U. S. Series, 43 bks., Set. Ed. by Stuart Bruchey. 1979. lib. bdg. 1123.50 (*0-405-11315-3*) Ayer.
Management of Quality Assurance. Madhav. N. Sinha & Walter O. Willborn. LC 85-5398. 688p. 1985. text 99.95 (*0-471-80310-3*) Wiley.
Management of Quality in Construction. John L. Ashford. 250p. 1989. 59.50 (*0-412-28840-0*) Chapman & Hall.
Management of Quality in Construction. John L. Ashford. (Illus.). 256p. (C). 1989. 95.00 (*0-419-14910-4*, E & FN Spon) Routledge.
Management of R & D & Engineering. Ed. by Dundar F. Kocaoglu. LC 92-24399. (Studies in Management Science & Systems: Vol. 20). 296p. 1992. 189.50 (*0-444-88104-2*, North Holland) Elsevier.
Management of Radioactive Materials & Wastes: Issues & Progress. Ed. by Shyamal K. Majumdar & E. Willard Miller. LC 85-61443. (Illus.). 405p. 1985. 35.00 (*0-9606670-4-0*) Penn Science.
Management of Radioactive Waste: The Issues for Local Authorities. Ed. by Stewart Kemp. 177p. 1991. pap. text 65.00 (*0-7277-1644-1*, Pub. by T Telford) RCH.
Management of Radioactive Waste in Laboratories. H & H Scientific Consultants, Ltd. Staff. 108p. 1996. pap. 150.00 (*0-948237-30-9*, Pub. by H&H Sci Cnslts) St Mut.
Management of Radioactive Wastes from the Nuclear Fuel Cycle, Vol. 1. IAEA Staff. 1976. 90.00 (*92-0-020276-4*, ISP433-1, Pub. by IAEA) Bernan Associates.
Management of Radioactive Wastes from the Nuclear Fuel Cycle, Vol. 2. IAEA Staff. 1976. pap. 85.00 (*92-0-020376-0*, ISP433-2, Pub. by IAEA) Bernan Associates.
Management of Remuneration: Paying for Effectiveness. Ian Smith. 265p. (C). 1983. 90.00 (*0-85292-305-8*) St Mut.
Management of Research & Development. George F. Thomason. 312p. 1970. pap. 25.00 (*0-8464-1171-7*) Beekman Pubs.
Management of Research & Development Organizations: Managing the Unmanageable. 2nd ed. Ravi K. Jain & Henry C. Triandis. LC 96-26912. (Wiley Series in Engineering & Technology Management). 336p. 1996. 80.00 (*0-471-14613-7*) Wiley.
Management of Resources: Conservation & Cooperation in Fishing. University of Hawaii, Honolulu Staff & Pacific Circle Consortium Staff. LC 98-199956. (Fishing in the Pacific Ser.). 55 p. 1991. write for info. (*0-937049-15-8*) Univ of Hawaii.
Management of Respiratory Tract Infections. John C. Bartlett. LC 97-13539. 120p. 1997. pap. 15.00 (*0-683-30236-1*) Lppncott W & W.
Management of Respiratory Tract Infections. 2nd ed. Bartlett. LC 99-13107. 1999. 15.00 (*0-683-30633-2*) Lppncott W & W.
Management of Retail Buying. 3rd ed. R. Patrick Cash et al. 424p. 1995. 110.00 (*0-471-07640-6*) Wiley.
Management of Rheumatoid Arthritis & Its Complications. James W. Hollingsworth. LC 77-83303. 265p. reprint ed. pap. 82.20 (*0-608-15908-5*, 203084500071) Bks Demand.
Management of Risk to Society from Potential Accidents: The Main Report of the UKAEA Working Group on the Risks to Society from Potential Major Accidents: With an Executive Summary. Ed. by F. R. Allen et al. LC 92-26262. 176p. 1992. ring bd. 183.95 (*1-85166-892-6*, Chap & Hall CRC) CRC Pr.
Management of Sales. Ed. by R. A. Hartley & Michael W. Starkey. 288p. 1996. 59.00 (*0-415-12973-7*) Routledge.
Management of Sales. R. A. Hartley & Michael W. Starky. 288p. 1996. pap. 29.95 (*0-415-12974-5*) Thomson Learn.
Management of Sales: Readings & Cases. Hartley & Starkey. 1996. pap. 20.99 (*1-86152-386-6*, Pub. by ITBP) Thomson Learn.
Management of Saline Soils & Waters. S. K. Gupta & I. C. Gupta. 1997. pap. 135.00 (*81-7233-160-6*, Pub. by Scientific Pubs) St Mut.
Management of Scale. David Collingridge. 224p. (C). 1992. mass mkt. 26.95 (*0-415-07857-1*, A9705) Routledge.
Management of Schistosomiasis. Patricia L. Rosenfield. (Resources for the Future Ser.). 148p. 1979. pap. text 11.00 (*0-8018-2328-5*) Johns Hopkins.
Management of Sci-Tech Libraries. Ed. by Ellis Mount. LC 84-6615. (Science & Technology Libraries: Vol. 4, Nos. 3-4). 169p. 1984. text 39.95 (*0-86656-280-X*); pap. text 19.95 (*0-86656-284-2*) Haworth Pr.
Management of Science: Proceedings of Section F (Economics) of the British Association for the Advancement of Science, Sheffield, 1989. British Association for the Advancement of Science. Ed. by Douglas C. Hague. LC 90-8895. 190p. 1991. text 65.00 (*0-312-05323-1*) St Martin.
Management of Sediment - Philosophy, Aims & Techniques: International Symposium on River Sedimentation, 6th, New Delhi, India, Held 1995. Ed. by C. V. Varma & A. R. Rao. (Illus.). 1204p. (C). 1996. text 160.00 (*90-5410-288-8*, Pub. by A A Balkema) Ashgate Pub Co.
Management of Self-Health & Fitness. J. G. Zilkha. (C). 1989. text 65.00 (*1-85821-029-1*, Pub. by Pentland Pr) St Mut.
Management of Separated Plutonium: The Technical Options. NEA Staff. 164p. 1997. pap. 47.00 (*92-64-15410-8*, 66-97-01-1, Pub. by Org for Econ) OECD.
Management of Serials Automation: Current Technology & Strategies for Future Planning. Ed. by Peter Gellatly. LC 82-6166. (Serials Librarian Supplement Ser.: No. 2). 287p. 1982. 69.95 (*0-917724-37-2*) Haworth Pr.
Management of Serials Automation: Current Technology & Strategies for Future Planning. Ed. by Peter Gellatly. LC 82-6166. (Serials Librarian Supplement Ser.: No. 2). 287p. 1984. pap. 29.95 (*0-86656-310-5*) Haworth Pr.
Management of Serials in Libraries. Thomas E. Nisonger. LC 98-28879. (Illus.). 440p. 1998. 70.00 (*1-56308-213-6*) Libs Unl.
Management of Service for the Restaurant Manager. Raymond J. Goodman. 320p. (C). 1979. 41.25 (*0-697-08409-4*) Brown & Benchmark.
Management of Service for the Restaurant Manager. 2nd ed. Raymond J. Goodman, Jr. LC 95-36931. 304p. (C). 1995. text 41.25 (*0-256-18737-1*, Irwn McGrw-H) McGrw-H Hghr Educ.
Management of Setting Out in Construction: ICE Design & Practice Guide. Ed. by Jim Smith. 83p. 1997. 28.00 (*0-7277-2614-5*, 2614, Pub. by T Telford) RCH.
Management of Severe & Complicated Malaria: A Practical Handbook. H. M. Gilles. (ENG, FRE & SPA.). vi, 56p. 1991. pap. text 11.00 (*92-4-154436-8*, 1150368) World Health.
Management of Severe & Complicated Malaria: An Interactive Computer Program. 1995. pap. text 78.00 incl. disk (*92-4-156174-2*, 1990004) World Health.
Management of Sexuality in Residential Treatment. Intro. by Gordon Northrup. LC 93-41273. (Residential Treatment for Children & Youth Ser.). (Illus.). 150p. 1994. lib. bdg. 39.95 (*1-56024-483-6*) Haworth Pr.
Management of Sexually Transmitted Diseases. J. Schachter et al. (Illus.). 544p. 1998. text. write for info. (*0-443-07596-4*, W B Saunders Co) Harcrt Hlth Sci Grp.
Management of Soft Tissue & Bone Sarcomas. J. A. Van Unnik. Ed. by A. T. Van Oosterom. LC 85-31703. (Monograph Series of the European Organization for Research on Treatment of Cancer: Vol. 16). 331p. 1986. reprint ed. pap. 102.70 (*0-608-00440-5*, 206115500007) Bks Demand.
Management of Software Change: Controlling Software. Nicholas Zvegintzov. 16p. 1994. pap. 35.00 (*1-884521-07-X*) Software Maint.
Management of Software Change: Managing Software. Nicholas Zvegintzov. 16p. 1994. pap. 35.00 (*1-884521-06-1*) Software Maint.
Management of Software Change: Modifying Software. Nicholas Zvegintzov. 16p. 1994. pap. 35.00 (*1-884521-08-8*) Software Maint.
Management of Solid Waste in Nigerian Cities. Richard Olowomeye. LC 90-27893. (Environment: Problems & Solutions Ser.). 224p. 1991. text 20.00 (*0-8240-9274-0*) Garland.
Management of Southwestern Desert Soils. Wallace H. Fuller. LC 74-15601. 207p. 1975. reprint ed. pap. 64.20 (*0-608-02348-5*, 206298900004) Bks Demand.
***Management of Spaticity Associated with Cerebral Palsies in Children & Adolescents.** Ed. by B. Neville & A. L. Albright. (Illus.). 160p. 2000. text. write for info. (*0-9701610-0-X*) Churchill.
Management of Speech & Swallowing. Yorkston. (C). 1998. pap. text 47.50 (*0-12-784574-7*) Acad Pr.
Management of Speech & Swallowing in Degenerative Diseases. Yorkston. LC 95-205453. 1995. 45.00 (*0-7616-7736-4*) Commun Skill.
Management of Spent Radiation Sources in the European Union: Quantities Storage, EUR 16960. C. Crumpton. 130p. 1996. pap. 25.00 (*92-827-8289-1*, CRNA-16960-ENC, Pub. by Comm Europ Commun) Bernan Associates.
Management of Spinal Cord Injury. 2nd ed. Cynthia M. Zejdlik. LC 82-23904. (Nursing-Health Science Ser.). 700p. 1991. 125.00 (*0-86720-438-9*) Jones & Bartlett.
Management of Spinal Disorders. Ed. by Dishan Singh & Aresh Hashemi-Nejad. (Stanmore Orthopedic Updates Ser.). 224p. 1998. text 68.00 (*90-5702-214-1*, Harwood Acad Pubs) Gordon & Breach.
Management of Sport. 3rd ed. Parkhouse. 2000. 46.34 (*0-07-230032-9*) McGraw.
Management of State Government Enterprises. G. Yenkatswamy. 1986. 100.00 (*81-7051-020-1*, Pub. by Archives Pubs) St Mut.
Management of Strabismus & Amblyopia. John A. Pratt-Johnson & Geraldine Tillson. LC 93-28854. 1993. 57.00 (*0-86577-499-4*) Thieme Med Pubs.
Management of Strategic Systems. 2nd ed. 490p. (C). 1997. 38.40 (*0-536-00611-3*) Pearson Custom.
Management of Stress. Ronald Dingwall. 64p. (C). 1986. 75.00 (*0-86236-026-9*, Pub. by Granary) St Mut.
***Management of Stress & Eating Disorders for Women & Children.** Jacalyn J. Robert-McComb. LC 00-39759. (Series in Modern Nutrition). 2000. write for info. (*0-8493-2027-5*) CRC Pr.
Management of Stroke: A Practical Guide for the Prevention, Evaluation & Treatment of Acute Stroke. Harold P. Adams, Jr. et al. 224p. 1998. pap. text 19.95 (*1-884735-35-5*) Prof Comms.
Management of Structure & Productivity of Boreal & Subalpine Forests. Ed. by Sune Linder & Seppo Kellomaki. (Studia Forestalia Suecica: No. 191). (Illus.). 94p. (Orig.). 1994. pap. 38.50 (*91-576-4822-0*) Coronet Bks.
Management of Struggle: Elements of Dispute Resolution Through Negotiation, Mediation & Arbitration. John W. Keltner. Ed. by Gary L. Kreps. LC 92-39491. (Speech Communication Association Applied Communication Ser.). 272p. (C). 1994. pap. text 26.50 (*1-881303-43-8*) Hampton Pr NJ.
Management of Student Teachers' Learning. Donald McIntyre et al. 120p. 1994. pap. 19.95 (*0-7494-1034-5*, Kogan Pg Educ) Stylus Pub VA.
Management of Stuttering in Adolescence: A Communication Skills Approach. Lena Rustin et al. 212p. 1995. pap. text 45.00 (*1-56593-277-3*, 0598) Thomson Learn.
Management of Superior Pulmonary Sulcus Syndrome (Pancoast Syndrome) Ed. by John J. Bonica et al. LC 82-5337. 254p. 1982. reprint ed. pap. 78.80 (*0-608-04679-5*, 206540000004) Bks Demand.
Management of Surface Transportation Systems. T. Urbanik et al. LC 98-65021. (Synthesis of Highway Practice Ser.). 26 p. 1998. write for info. (*0-309-06117-2*) Natl Acad Pr.
Management of Surgical Emergencies. Shaw Somers & William E. Thomas. (Illus.). 415p. (C). 1998. pap. text. write for info. (*0-7020-1976-3*, W B Saunders Co) Harcrt Hlth Sci Grp.
Management of System Engineering. Wilton P. Chase. LC 83-18746. 256p. 1985. reprint ed. text 30.50 (*0-89874-682-5*) Krieger.
Management of Technological Change: The Great Challenge of Management for the Future. Ernst G. Frankel. 1990. lib. bdg. 201.00 (*0-7923-0674-0*) Kluwer Academic.
***Management of Technological Innovation: An International & Strategic Approach.** Mark Dodgson. (Illus.). 300p. 2000. pap. 29.95 (*0-19-877535-0*); text 74.00 (*0-19-877536-9*) OUP.
Management of Technological Learning: Lessons from a Biotechnology Company. Mark Dodgson. (Studies in Organization: No. 29). (Illus.). xiv, 147p. (C). 1991. lib. bdg. 52.95 (*3-11-012706-7*) De Gruyter.
***Management of Technology.** Tarek Khalil. 512p. (C). 1999. 58.75 (*0-07-366149-X*) McGrw-H Hghr Educ.
Management of Technology: Change in a Society of Organized Advocacies. rev. ed. Joseph A. Raffaele. LC 79-63752. 1979. pap. text 27.00 (*0-8191-0739-5*) U Pr of Amer.
Management of Technology: The Hidden Competitive Advantage. National Research Council Staff. LC HD0045.T36. 51p. reprint ed. pap. 30.00 (*0-8357-6917-8*, 203797600009) Bks Demand.
Management of Technology & Innovation: Competing Through Technological Excellence. P. N. Rastogi. 195p. 1995. 32.00 (*0-8039-9263-7*) Sage.
Management of Technology & Operations. R. Ray Gehani. LC 97-53199. 464p. 1998. 90.00 (*0-471-17906-X*) Wiley.
Management of Technology & Regional Development in a Global Environment: An International Perspective. Ed. by Louis Lefebvre & Elizabeth Lefebvre. 192p. 1995. text 69.95 (*1-85396-297-X*, Pub. by P Chapman) Taylor & Francis.
Management of Technology in Health & Medical Care. Ed. by Cesar A. Caceres & Jacqueline L. Williams. LC 80-1117. (Artech Medical Library). (Illus.). 542p. reprint ed. pap. 168.10 (*0-8357-4189-3*, 203696700006) Bks Demand.
Management of Technology Perception & Opportunities. Chapman & Hall Staff. text 95.50 (*0-412-64370-7*) Chapman & Hall.
Management of Technology, Sustainable Development & Eco-Efficiency. L. A. Lefebvre et al. LC 97-44026. 1998. 176.75 (*0-08-043363-4*) Elsevier.
Management of Telecommunication Systems & Services: Modelling & Implementing TMN-Based Multi-Domain Management. Jane Hall. LC 96-2749. (Lecture Notes in Computer Science Ser.: Vol. 1116). 229p. 1996. 43.00 (*3-540-61578-4*) Spr-Verlag.
Management of Telecommunications. (C). Date not set. text. write for info. (*0-13-011577-0*) P-H.
Management of Temporomandibular Disorders. 1997. lib. bdg. 251.99 (*0-8490-8117-3*) Gordon Pr.
Management of Temporomandibular Disorders. 1997. lib. bdg. 252.99 (*0-8490-8151-3*) Gordon Pr.
Management of Temporomandibular Disorders: Current Bibliographies in Medicine: January 1990 Through December 1995. Martha H. Glock & James A. Lipton. 42p. 1996. pap. text 25.00 (*0-7881-3344-6*) DIANE Pub.
Management of Temporomandibular Disorders & Occlusion. 4th ed. Jeffrey P. Okeson. LC 97-35663. (Illus.). 656p. (C). (gr. 13). 1997. text 71.00 (*0-8151-6939-6*, 27162) Mosby Inc.
***Management of Temporomandibular Disorders in the General Dental Practice.** Gunnar E. Carlsson & Tomas Magnusson. LC 99-16117. 1999. write for info. (*0-86715-367-9*) Quint Pub Co.
Management of Temporomandibular Joint Degenerative Diseases: Biologic Basis & Treatment Outcome. B. Stegenga & L. G. De Bont. LC 96-10280. 1996. 119.00 (*0-8176-5286-8*) Birkhauser.
Management of Temporomandibular Joint Degenerative Diseases: Biologic Basis & Treatment Outcome. B. Stegenga & L. G. De Bont. LC 96-10280. (Illus.). 248p. 1996. 119.00 (*3-7643-5286-8*) Birkhauser.
Management of Terminal Malignant Disease. 3rd ed. Ed. by Cicely M. Saunders & Nigel Sykes. 320p. 1993. pap. text 45.00 (*0-340-56354-0*, Pub. by E A) OUP.
Management of the Absurd. Faison. 1996. text 6.95 (*0-13-259987-2*) P-H.
Management of the Absurd. Richard E. Farson. 1997. per. 11.00 (*0-684-83044-2*, Touchstone) S&S Trade Pap.
Management of the Absurd: Paradoxes in Leadership. Richard E. Farson. LC 95-25346. 176p. 1996. 20.50 (*0-684-80080-2*) S&S Trade.
Management of the Acute Coronary Attack: The J. Frank Pantridge Festschrift. Ed. by John S. Geddes. 124p. 1986. text 66.00 (*0-12-278755-2*) Acad Pr.
Management of the Acutely Ill: A Symposium Held in July, 1976. Ed. by James P. Payne & D. W. Hill. LC 77-370280. (Chartridge Symposium Ser.). (Illus.). 187p. reprint ed. pap. 58.00 (*0-8357-8943-8*, 203345800086) Bks Demand.
Management of the Acutely Ill Neurological Patient. Ed. by James Grotta. (Illus.). 208p. 1993. text 83.00 (*0-443-08870-5*) Church.
Management of the Beaver (Castor Fiber) Towards Restoration of Its Former Distribution & Ecological Function in Europe. (Nature & Environment Ser.: No. 86). 1997. 12.00 (*92-871-3211-9*, Pub. by Council of Europe) Manhattan Pub Co.
Management of the Computer in K to Twelve Environments: A Selected Bibliography. Sarah H. Huyvaert & Thomas R. Huyvaert. Ed. by William D. Milheim. LC 93-12415. (Selected Bibliography Ser.: Vol. 9). 70p. 1993. pap. 24.95 (*0-87778-261-X*) Educ Tech Pubns.
Management of the Contingency Workforce: Shaping Strategies for the 21st Century. Donald Shandler. 250p. 1996. lib. bdg. 39.95 (*1-57444-095-0*, SL0950) St Lucie Pr.
Management of the Firm. David Coleman. LC 77-86276. 1979. 13.95 (*0-930726-03-0*); pap. 9.95 (*0-930726-02-2*) Concept Pub.
Management of the Frail Elderly by the Health Care Team. John R. Walsh. 216p. 1989. pap. 32.50 (*0-87527-349-1*) Green.
Management of the Hanford Engineer Works in World War II: How the Corps, DuPont, & Metallurgical Laboratory First Tracked the Original Plutonium Works. Harry Thayer. LC 96-5570. 224p. 1996. pap. 36.00 (*0-7844-0160-8*) Am Soc Civil Eng.
***Management of the HIV Patient-LCM.** Wofsy. 1999. text 22.95 (*0-8385-6119-5*) Appleton & Lange.

M

An Asterisk (*) at the beginning of an entry indicates that the title is appearing for the first time.

Management of the Hypertensive Patient. Lawrence R. Krakoff. (Illus.). 325p. 1994. text 95.00 (*0-443-08769-5*) Church.
Management of the Infertile Woman. Helen A. Carcio. LC 97-42828. 320p. 1998. pap. text 39.95 (*0-7817-1044-8*) Lppncott W & W.
Management of the Mediterranean Wetlands. Council of Europe Staff. (Environmental Encounters Ser.: No. 12). 1992. 15.00 (*92-871-2033-1*, Pub. by Council of Europe) Manhattan Pub Co.
Management of the Menopause: Annual Review, 1998. Ed. by J. W. Studd. (Illus.). 320p. 1998. 55.00 (*1-85070-022-2*) Prthnon Pub.
***Management of the Menopause: The Millennium Review, 2000.** Ed. by J. Studd. (Illus.). 344p. 1999. 55.00 (*1-85070-079-6*) Prthnon Pub.
Management of the Mentally Disordered Offender in Prisons. Geoffrey N. Conacher. LC 97-156212. 144p. 1996. 49.95 (*0-7735-1419-8*, Pub. by McG-Queens Univ Pr) CUP Services.
***Management of the National Debt in the United Kingdom, 1900-1932.** Jeremy J. Wormell. LC 99-31072. (Explorations in Economic History Ser.). 1999. 160.00 (*0-415-21724-5*) Routledge.
Management of the Packaging Function. Harold J. Raphael & David L. Olsson. LC 76-55109. (American Management Associations. Management Briefing Ser.). 38p. reprint ed. pap. 30.00 (*0-608-11682-3*, 205130500094) Bks Demand.
Management of the Patient with Cancer. 3rd ed. Thomas F. Nealon. (Illus.). 784p. 1986. text 170.00 (*0-7216-1075-7*, W B Saunders Co) Harcrt Hlth Sci Grp.
Management of the Perimenopausal & Postmenopausal Woman: A Total Wellness Program. Barbara Kass-Annese. LC 98-26136. 416p. 1998. pap. text 38.95 (*0-7817-1654-3*) Lppncott W & W.
Management of the Severely Disturbed Adolescent. William M. Easson. LC 96-23716. xiii, 353p. 1996. 55.00 (*0-8236-3091-9*) Intl Univs Pr.
Management of the United States Navy Research & Development Centers During the Cold War Era: Survey Guide to Reports. Rodney P. Carlisle. 137p. 1997. per. 10.00 (*0-16-061335-3*) USGPO.
Management of the Veterans Administration: Improved Human Resource Planning Needed to Achieve Strategic Goals. (Illus.). 56p. (Orig.). (C). 1993. pap. text 25.00 (*1-56806-561-2*) DIANE Pub.
***Management of the Voice & Its Disorders.** 2nd ed. Morrison. 2000. pap. 54.95 (*0-7693-0054-5*) Thomson Learn.
Management of Third World Crisis in Adverse Partnership: Theory & Practice. Imtiaz H. Bokhari. LC 98-119438. 356p. 1997. 45.00 (*0-19-577757-3*) OUP.
Management of Time. James T. McCay. 1986. 14.95 (*0-13-548909-1*, Reward) P-H.
Management of Time. Ed. by A. Dale Timpe. (Art & Science of Business Management Ser.). (Illus.). 400p. 1986. 29.95 (*0-8160-1461-2*) Facts on File.
Management of Time. Ed. by A. Dale Timpe. LC 86-11511. (Art & Science of Business Management Ser.: Vol. 2). 391p. 1987. reprint ed. pap. 121.30 (*0-608-02805-3*, 206387200007) Bks Demand.
Management of Tomorrow. Ed. by Alfred D. Chandler, Jr. LC 79-7558. (History of Management Thought & Practice Ser.). 1980. reprint ed. lib. bdg. 33.95 (*0-405-12344-2*) Ayer.
Management of Toxic & Hazardous Wastes: Development from the Third Ohio Environmental Conference. Ed. by Harasiddhiprasad G. Bhatt et al. 418p. 1985. 50.00 (*0-685-18631-8*, 1023) Am Soc Civil Eng.
Management of Toxic Materials in an International Setting: A Case Study of Cadmium in the North Sea. L. Dekker et al. 130p. (C). 1987. text 91.00 (*90-6191-795-6*, Pub. by A A Balkema) Ashgate Pub Co.
Management of Trade Credit. 3rd ed. Thomas G. Hutson & John Butterworth. 224p. 1984. text 65.95 (*0-566-02419-5*) Ashgate Pub Co.
Management of Trade Marketing. Arthur Lawrence. 200p. 1983. text 78.95 (*0-566-02395-4*) Ashgate Pub Co.
Management of Transmission & Distribution Systems. O. C. Seevers. 1995. 79.00 (*0-87814-644-X*) PennWell Bks.
Management of Trauma. Bessey. Date not set. text. write for info. (*0-7216-5140-2*, W B Saunders Co) Harcrt Hlth Sci Grp.
Management of Trauma: Pitfalls & Practices. 2nd ed. Ed. by Robert F. Wilson & Alexander J. Walt. LC 96-28033. 1103p. 1996. 149.00 (*0-683-08722-3*) Lppncott W & W.
Management of Tropical Agroecosystems & the Beneficial Soil Biota. M. Vikram Reddy. (Illus.). 350p. 1999. 90.00 (*1-57808-045-2*) Science Pubs.
Management of Tropical Moist Forest Lands: Ecological Guidelines. 2nd ed. Duncan Poore & Jeffrey A. Sayer. (Illus.). 69p. 1991. pap. 17.00 (*2-8317-0071-X*, Pub. by IUCN) Island Pr.
Management of Tropical Soils. K. T. Kang. (Westview Tropical Agriculture Ser.). (C). 1996. text 25.00 (*0-8133-0124-6*) Westview.
Management of Turfgrass Diseases. 2nd ed. M. J. Vargas, Jr. LC 93-28186. 320p. 1993. lib. bdg. 85.00 (*1-56670-046-9*, L1046) Lewis Pubs.
Management of Uncertainty: Approaches, Methods & Applications. Ed. by Luc Wilkin & Alan Sutton. 1986. lib. bdg. 193.50 (*90-247-3387-1*) Kluwer Academic.
***Management of Uncertainty Learning from Chernobyl.** Angela Liberatore. 324p. 1999. text 55.00 (*90-5700-552-2*) Gordon & Breach.
Management of Upper Gastrointestinal Cancer. John M. Daly et al. (Illus.). 304p. text. write for info. (*0-7020-2147-4*) W B Saunders.
***Management of Upper Limb Hypertonicity.** Jodie Copley & Kathy Kuipers. LC 98-54875. 308p. 1999. 45.00 (*0-7616-1529-6*) Commun Skill.
Management of Upper Limb Hypertonicity. Jodie Coply & Kathy Kuipers. (Illus.). 308p. 1999. pap. 45.00 (*0-12-784596-8*) Acad Pr.
Management of Uranium Mill Tailings, Low-Level Waste & Hazardous Waste: Proceedings of the 6th Symposium, 1984. 670p. 1984. 35.00 (*0-910069-07-7*) Geotech Engineer Prog.
Management of Uranium Mill Tailings, Low-Level Waste & Hazardous Waste: Proceedings of the 7th Symposium, 2 vols. Pref. by John Nelson et al. (Orig.). 1985. pap. text 38.00 (*0-910069-08-5*) Geotech Engineer Prog.
Management of Used Treated Wood Products. 14p. 1994. pap. 1.00 (*0-931032-24-5*) Edison Electric.
Management of Values: The Ethical Difference in Corporate Policy & Performance. Charles S. McCoy. LC 84-16487. (Business & Public Policy Ser.). 394p. 1989. text 29.95 (*0-88730-431-1*, HarpBusn) HarpInfo.
Management of Visual Impairment in Childhood. Ed. by Alistair Fielder et al. (Clinics in Developmental Medicine Ser.: No. 128). (Illus.). 213p. (C). 1994. text 64.95 (*0-521-45150-7*) Cambridge U Pr.
Management of Vitreo-Retinal Disease: A Surgical Approach. D. Wong & A. H. Chignell. LC 98-20113. (Illus.). vii, 200p. 1999. pap. 99.00 (*3-540-76082-2*) Spr-Verlag.
Management of Voice Disorders. Members of the Department of Otolaryngology Staff et al. (Illus.). 256p. (C). 1994. pap. 55.00 (*1-56593-311-7*, 0464) Thomson Learn.
***Management of Voice Disorders.** Morrison. 1998. pap. 57.95 (*0-7693-0003-0*) Course Tech.
Management of Voice Disorders. Murray D. Morrison et al. LC 93-32952. (Illus.). 288p. 1993. text 59.50 (*0-412-35090-4*, Pub. by E A) OUP.
Management of Waste from Hospitals & Other Health Care Establishments. (EURO Reports & Studies: No. 97). 61p. 1985. pap. text 6.30 (*92-890-1263-3*, 1330097) World Health.
Management of Water Demand in Africa & the Middle East: Current Practices & Future Needs. Ed. by David B. Brooks et al. LC 98-700393. xi, 78p. 1997. pap. 17.50 (*0-88936-844-9*, Pub. by IDRC Bks) Stylus Pub VA.
Management of Water Resources in North America: Anticipating the 21st Century: Proceedings of the Engineering Foundation Conference Tucson, Arizona, September 4-8, 1995, Vol. III. Ed. by Nathan Buras. LC 95-35421. 160p. 1995. 22.00 (*0-7844-0113-6*) Am Soc Civil Eng.
Management of Water Treatment Plant Residuals. American Society of Civil Engineers Staff & American Water Works Association Staff. LC 96-19472. (Asce Manuals & Reports of Engineering Practice). 320p. 1996. 70.00 (*0-7844-0181-0*) Am Soc Civil Eng.
Management of Water Use in Agriculture. Ed. by K. K. Tanji & Bruno Yaron. LC 93-43691. (Advanced Series in Agricultural Sciences: No. 22). 1994. 202.95 (*0-387-57309-7*) Spr-Verlag.
Management of Wild Mammals in Captivity. Lee S. Crandall. LC 64-10498. (Illus.). 1993. lib. bdg. 40.00 (*0-226-11758-8*) U Ch Pr.
Management of Wild Mammals in Captivity. Lee S. Crandall. LC 64-10498. (Illus.). 785p. reprint ed. pap. 200.00 (*0-608-09290-8*, 205416400004) Bks Demand.
Management of Workers: Selected Arguments, 1917-1956. Ed. by Leon Stein & Philip Taft. LC 72-156430. (American Labor, Ser. 2). 1974. 25.95 (*0-405-02955-1*) Ayer.
Management of World Fisheries: Implications of Extended Coastal State Jurisdiction. Ed. by Edward L. Miles. 344p. 1990. 30.00 (*0-295-96854-0*) U of Wash Pr.
Management of Wounds & Burns. 2nd ed. Jim Wardrope & June Edhouse. LC 99-461795. (Oxford Handbooks in Emergency Medicine Ser.). (Illus.). 256p. 1999. pap. text 54.50 (*0-19-262999-9*) OUP.
Management on & off the Ward. Michael Walton. LC 95-1076. 1995. pap. 29.95 (*0-632-03447-5*) Blackwell Sci.
Management on Worldwide Web. Cynthia B. Leshin. LC 96-47385. (Illus.). 266p. (C). 1996. pap. text 13.20 (*0-13-268871-9*) P-H.
Management 136 - 1370. Gemmy Allen. (Orig.). (C). 1995. pap. 24.19 (*1-56870-179-9*) RonJon Pub.
Management, Operation & Maintenance of Irrigation & Drainage Systems. 2nd ed. Ed. by William R. Johnston & James B. Robertson. LC 91-3854. 432p. 1991. text 87.00 (*0-87262-785-3*) Am Soc Civil Eng.
Management, Operational Research & the Micro. Ed. by Alan Clementson & A. J. Clewett. 96p. 1981. pap. 17.00 (*0-08-025842-5*, Pergamon Pr) Elsevier.
Management Operations. Griffin. (C). 1992. pap., suppl. ed. 6.70 (*0-395-66818-2*) HM.
Management Organization. Wright. 1996. 51.56 (*0-256-22070-0*) McGraw.
Management Peripheral Nerve Problems. 2nd ed. Morton Spinner et al. LC 96-28473. (Illus.). 720p. 1997. text 185.00 (*0-7216-4276-4*, W B Saunders Co) Harcrt Hlth Sci Grp.
Management Personnel in Libraries. Kenneth H. Plate. 1970. 7.95 (*0-685-03095-4*) Am Faculty Pr.
Management Philosophers: The People & Ideas That Have Shaped Modern Business. Daniel A. Wren & Ronald G. Greenwood. LC 97-30036. 272p. (C). 1998. 25.00 (*0-19-511705-0*) OUP.
***Management Philosophy: A Radical-Normative Perspective.** O. Kirkeby. xvi, 274p. 2000. (*3-540-66892-6*) Spr-Verlag.
Management Planning & Control: The Printer's Path to Profitability. write for info. (*0-685-08994-0*, 1134) Print Indus Am.
Management, Planning & Ideology Vol. 2: Key Concepts for Understanding Curriculum. Colin J. Marsh. LC 97-162456. 344p. 1997. pap. 34.95 (*0-7507-0663-5*, Falmer Pr) Taylor & Francis.
Management Planning for Survival & Growth: Proceedings of a Symposium by the Engineering Management Division. Ed. by David C. Johnston. 88p. 1984. 5.00 (*0-87262-426-9*) Am Soc Civil Eng.
Management Plus: Leadership, Motivation & Power in the Changing Workplace. Lloyd M. Smigel. 288p. 1995. pap. 22.95 (*1-56565-337-8*) Lowell Hse.
Management Plus: Managing Productivity Through Motivation, Performance, & Commitment. Robert A. Fazzi. LC 93-37972. 240p. 1994. text 27.50 (*1-55623-756-1*, Irwn Prfssnl) McGraw-Hill Prof.
Management Policies in Local Government Finance. 3rd ed. Ed. by J. Richard Aronson & Eli Schwartz. LC 87-2658. (Municipal Management Ser.). 449p. 1987. 39.95 (*0-87326-075-9*) Intl City-Cnty Mgt.
Management Policies in Local Government Finance. 4th ed. Ed. by J. Richard Aronson & Eli Schwartz. LC 96-13387. (Municipal Management Ser.). 455p. 1996. 41.95 (*0-87326-108-9*) Intl City-Cnty Mgt.
Management Power the Specific Action Way: A Short Course in Management Logic. Owen Allen. LC 84-52618. (Illus.). 112p. (C). 1988. reprint ed. text 25.00 (*0-932569-00-5*) Specific Action.
Management Practices & Business Development in Pakistan, 1947-1988. Naveed Hasan. LC 96-80377. 360p. 1997. text 83.95 (*1-85972-556-2*, Pub. by Avebry) Ashgate Pub Co.
***Management Practices in Dietetics.** Hudson. LC 99-35916. (Health Sciences Ser.). 510p. 1999. pap. 60.95 (*0-534-54504-1*) Wadsworth Pub.
Management Primer. rev. ed. Karl E. Ettinger. Ed. by Ralph C. Hook, Jr. & John R. Overton. 353p. 1973. pap. text 16.25 (*92-833-1024-1*, 310241) Productivity Inc.
Management Principles & Practice: A Cybernetic Approach. R. H. Strank. (Studies in Cybernetics: Vol. 3). xiv, 144p. (C). 1983. text 156.00 (*0-677-05850-0*) Gordon & Breach.
Management Principles for Christian Schools. 3rd rev. ed. James Deuink. 448p. 1996. pap. 21.95 (*0-89084-874-2*, 094441) Bob Jones Univ.
Management Principles for Health Professionals. 2nd ed. Joan G. Liebler et al. 448p. (C). 1992. 55.00 (*0-8342-0287-5*) Aspen Pub.
Management Principles for Health Professionals. 3rd ed. Joan G. Liebler. 448p. 1999. 55.00 (*0-8342-0798-2*) Aspen Pub.
***Management Principles for Health Professionals.** 3rd ed. Joan G. Liebler & Charles R. McConnell. LC 99-34437. 524p. 1999. write for info. (*0-8342-1245-5*) Aspen Pub.
Management Principles for Physical Therapists. Larry Nosse & Deborah Friberg. (Illus.). 336p. 1991. 47.00 (*0-683-06576-9*) Lppncott W & W.
Management Principles for the Advancement Professional. Day. LC 97-39246. 289p. 1998. 59.00 (*0-8342-1040-1*) Aspen Pub.
Management Problems in Health Care. Ed. by Gunter U. Fandel. (Illus.). 310p. 1988. 100.95 (*0-387-19243-3*) Spr-Verlag.
Management Problems in Serials Work: Proceedings. Florida Atlantic University Conference. Ed. by Peter Spyers-Duran & Daniel Gore. LC 73-10775. 145p. 1973. 27.50 (*0-8371-7050-8*, SSW/, Greenwood Pr) Greenwood.
Management Procedures. Leslie Lee & Robert Comte. LC 74-18677. (Allied Health Ser.). 1975. pap. 6.35 (*0-672-61397-2*, Bobbs) Macmillan.
Management Process: A Selection of Readings for Librarians. Ed. by Ruth J. Person. LC 83-3788. 431p. reprint ed. pap. 133.70 (*0-7837-5923-1*, 204572200007) Bks Demand.
Management Processes & Functions. Michael Armstrong. 250p. (C). 1990. 95.00 (*0-85292-438-0*, Pub. by IPM Hse) St Mut.
Management Product Families. Susan Sanderson. 288p. (C). 1996. text 44.80 (*0-256-22897-3*, Irwn McGrw-H) McGrw-H Hghr Educ.
Management Program for Grease Wastes: Final Report. 95p. 1992. 20.00 (*0-317-05650-6*, P92001WAT) Assn Bay Area.
Management Project Procurement. Houston. 1996. 52.25 (*0-07-030552-8*) McGraw.
***Management Projects.** Chris Churchouse. LC 98-47108. 1999. pap. 33.95 (*0-566-08098-2*) Ashgate Pub Co.
Management Projects: Design, Research, & Presentation. Paul Raimond. LC 93-14820. 208p. 1993. mass mkt. 29.95 (*0-412-46810-7*) Chapman & Hall.
Management Pyramid: Principles & Applications. Geoffrey O. Wuzor. Ed. by Ephraim Okoro. (Illus.). 231p. (Orig.). 1995. pap. text 20.00 (*0-9647631-0-9*) G O Wuzor.
Management Quizzer. 1994. 6.95 (*0-930137-25-6*) Looseleaf Law.
Management Ratios for Colleges & Universities. Ed. & Intro. by John Minter. (Financial Management Ratios Ser.: No. 2). 500p. 1986. lib. bdg. write for info. (*0-937767-03-4*) Nat Data Service.
Management Ratios for Colleges & Universities. Ed. & Intro. by John Minter. (Financial Management Ratios Ser.: No. 3). 550p. (C). 1987. lib. bdg. 125.00 (*0-937767-30-1*) Nat Data Service.
Management Ready Notes. \ Coleman. 1998. 14.74 (*0-07-428372-3*) McGraw.
Management Redeemed: Debunking the Fads That Undermine Corporate Performance. Frederick G. Hilmer & Lex Donaldson. LC 96-20659. 223p. 1996. 23.50 (*0-684-83162-7*) S&S Trade.
Management Reform: Agencies[0012] Initial Efforts to Restructure Personnel Operations. 62p. pap. text 20.00 (*0-7881-7958-6*) DIANE Pub.
Management Reform: Completion Status of Agency Actions under the National Performance Review. (Illus.). 83p. (Orig.). (C). 1996. pap. text 25.00 (*0-7881-3479-5*) DIANE Pub.
Management Reform: GAO's Comments on the National Performance Review's Recommendations. 279p. (Orig.). (C). 1995. pap. text 50.00 (*0-7881-2159-6*) DIANE Pub.
Management Reform: Implementation of the National Performance Review's Recommendations. 539p. (Orig.). (C). 1995. pap. text 65.00 (*0-7881-1688-6*) DIANE Pub.
Management Reform: Status of Agency Reinvention Lab Efforts. 157p. (Orig.). (C). 1996. pap. text 30.00 (*0-7881-2878-7*) DIANE Pub.
Management Reform--cost, Savings, Net: Hearing Before the Subcommittee on the District of Columbia of the Committee on Government Reform & Oversight, House of Representatives, One Hundred Fifth Congress, Second Session, January 30, 1998. United States. LC 98-207649. iii, 152p. 1998. write for info. (*0-16-057072-7*) USGPO.
***Management Reform for the 21st Century: Challenges for Governance.** Donald F. Kettl. 2000. pap. write for info. (*0-8157-4917-1*) Brookings.
Management Reform in Eastern & Central Europe: Use of Pre-Communist Cultures. Magoroh Maruyama. 192p. 1993. 41.95 (*1-85521-343-5*, Pub. by Dartmth Pub) Ashgate Pub Co.
Management Reforms: Examples of Public & Private Innovations to Improve Service Delivery. 53p. pap. text 30.00 (*0-7881-4077-9*) DIANE Pub.
Management Refresher. A. Nag. 1993. 30.00 (*0-7069-6818-2*, Pub. by Vikas) S Asia.
Management Reporting, Analysis, & Behavioral Issues. 4th rev. ed. Andrew Bailey et al. Ed. by Grant Newton. (Certified Management Accountant Review Ser.: Vol. 3). (Illus.). 292p. (C). 1995. pap. text 30.00 (*0-918937-23-X*) Malibu Pub.
Management Reports on Internal Control. LC 94-235941. 64p. 1994. pap. 19.95 (*1-57073-002-4*, 507-0271) Amer Bar Assn.
Management Research: An Introduction. Mark Easterby-Smith et al. 208p. 1991. 49.95 (*0-8039-8392-1*); pap. 21.50 (*0-8039-8393-X*) Sage.
Management Research: Guide for the Institutions & Professionals. Roger Bennet. (Management Development Ser.: No. 20). viii, 245p. 1987. pap. 22.50 (*92-2-103303-1*) Intl Labour Office.
Management Research Handbook. Ed. by N. Craig Smith & Paul Dainty. 272p. (C). (gr. 13). 1991. pap. 64.95 (*0-415-04341-7*, A5684) Thomson Learn.
***Management Resource Guide - East, 4 vols.** 800p. 2000. pap. 60.00 (*1-880874-67-9*) Dorland Hlthcare.
***Management Resource Guide - Midwest, 4 vols.** 11th ed. 800p. 2000. pap. 60.00 (*1-880874-69-5*) Dorland Hlthcare.
***Management Resource Guide - South.** 800p. 2000. pap. 60.00 (*1-880874-68-7*) Dorland Hlthcare.
***Management Resource Guide (East, South, Midwest & West), 4 vols.** 800p. 2000. pap. 225.00 (*1-880874-66-0*) Dorland Hlthcare.
Management Responses to Public Issues. 3rd ed. Rogene A. Buchholz. LC 93-19558. 370p. (C). 1993. pap. text 51.00 (*0-13-554072-0*, Pub. by P-H) S&S Trade.
Management Restructuring in an FE College. Ernest Theodossin. 1986. 50.00 (*0-907659-26-8*) St Mut.
Management Review Guide: A Do-It-Yourself Practice Analysis. Mark F. Murray. 1995. 33.00 (*0-87051-168-8*) Am Inst CPA.
Management Review of the Texas State Preservation Board & the Office of the Architect. Terrell Blodgett. (Special Project Reports). 24p. 1988. pap. 5.00 (*0-89940-860-5*) LBJ Sch Pub Aff.
Management Revolution: Management Consultancy & Computer-aided Decision Making. Richard Armand et al. LC 72-190063. xvi, 319p. 1972. write for info. (*0-356-03928-5*) Janes Info Group.
Management Rights & Collective Bargaining see Human Relations & Industrial Relations Books & Management Tools
Management Rights & the Arbitration Process: Proceedings of the Ninth Annual Meeting. National Academy of Arbitrators Staff. Ed. by Jean T. McKelvey. LC HD548LN32. (National Academy of Arbitrators: Proceedings of the Annual Meeting Ser.: Vol. 9). 245p. reprint ed. pap. 76.00 (*0-608-16811-4*, 205617600054) Bks Demand.
Management Rights & Union Interests. Margaret K. Chandler. LC 78-6226. (Illus.). 329p. 1978. reprint ed. lib. bdg. 89.50 (*0-313-20495-0*, CHMA, Greenwood Pr) Greenwood.
***Management Roadmap to Information Security: Premium Edition.** John Graves. 332p. 2000. pap. 45.00 (*1-892855-06-2*) Kent Info Srvcs.
Management Science (C). 1993. pap. write for info. (*0-205-15596-0*) Allyn.
Management Science. Jeffrey D. Camm. (MB - Business/Vocational Math Ser.). (C). 1995. mass mkt., student ed. 24.95 (*0-538-82739-4*) S-W Pub.
Management Science. Evans. (Business/Vocational Math Ser.). 1996. pap. 59.95 (*0-538-86305-6*) S-W Pub.
Management Science. Hillier. LC 99-27654. 1999. 66.00 (*0-07-037816-9*) McGraw.
Management Science. Thomas Knowles. 1035p. (C). 1988. text 71.95 (*0-256-05682-X*, Irwn McGrw-H) McGrw-H Hghr Educ.
Management Science. 3rd ed. Sang M. Lee et al. 900p. 1989. text 59.00 (*0-205-12145-4*, H21454) Allyn.

M

An Asterisk (*) at the beginning of an entry indicates that the title is appearing for the first time.

Management Science. 3rd ed. Sang M. Lee et al. 900p. 1989. write for info. (*0-318-66337-6*, H21462); write for info. (*0-318-66338-4*, H21470) P-H.

Management Science. 4th ed. SangLee & Laurence J. Moore. 1993. text 105.00 (*0-205-15030-6*) Allyn.

Management Science. 7th ed. Anderson. Date not set. text, teacher ed. write for info. (*0-314-02504-9*); pap. text. write for info. (*0-314-03052-2*); pap. text, student ed. 23.25 (*0-314-03306-8*) West Pub.

Management Science. 8th ed. David R. Anderson. LC 96-25601. 900p. 1996. pap. 96.95 (*0-314-09687-6*) West Pub.

Management Science: A Decision-Support Approach. William R. King et al. (Illus.). 800p. (C). 1990. text. write for info. (*0-201-10338-9*) Addison-Wesley.

Management Science: An Introduction to Modern Quantitative Analysis & Decision Making. Gerald E. Thompson. LC 82-13071. 466p. 1982. reprint ed. lib. bdg. 42.50 (*0-89874-547-0*) Krieger.

Management Science: An Introduction to Quantitative Analysis for Management. 2nd ed. William E. Pinney & Donald B. McWilliams. (Illus.). xvii, 620p. 1987. 29.95 (*0-06-350589-4*) Valian Assocs.

Management Science: An Introduction to the Use of Decision Models. Kenneth R. Baker & Dean H. Kropp. LC 84-21959. (Illus.). 662p. reprint ed. pap. 200.00 (*0-8357-7523-2*, 203603000097) Bks Demand.

Management Science: Cases & Applications. Raj Aggarwal & Inder Khera. LC 79-65492. 1979. pap. text 21.00 (*0-8162-0096-3*); 8.00 (*0-685-02320-6*) Holden-Day.

Management Science & Decision Technology. Camm & Evans. (SWC-Management). 1999. pap. text 45.00 (*0-324-02015-5*) Sth-Wstrn College.

***Management Science & Statistics.** (C). 1999. text 63.63 (*0-536-60680-3*) Pearson Custom.

Management Science Anthology, 3 Vols., Set. Ed. by Samuel Eilon. (History of Management Thought Ser.). (Illus.). 1740p. 1996. 399.95 (*1-85521-516-0*, Pub. by Dartmth Pub) Ashgate Pub Co.

Management Science for Decision Support. Vazsonyi. (C). 1996. pap. text 6.00 (*0-03-098098-4*) Harcourt Coll Pubs.

Management Science for Energy Policy. J. E. Samouilidis. 136p. 1982. pap. 34.00 (*0-08-028172-9*, Pergamon Pr) Elsevier.

Management Science for Organization Development: A Synergistic Process Through Management Science. Richard H. Van Ness. 1996. 30.00 (*1-888753-01-3*) PACT Pubns.

Management Science in Defence. Ed. by K. C. Bowen. 105p. 1985. pap. 39.00 (*0-08-032658-7*, Pergamon Pr) Elsevier.

Management Science Information Systems: Text & Software. Mohsen Attaran. LC 92-6614. 288p. (C). 1992. pap. text 62.95 incl. disk (*0-471-52998-2*) Wiley.

Management Science Knowledge: Its Creation, Generalization, & Consolidation. Arnold Reisman. LC 91-44705. 324p. 1992. 62.95 (*0-89930-739-6*, RMK/, Quorum Bks) Greenwood.

Management Science Operations Research: A Strategic Perspective. Peter C. Bell. LC 98-8106. 1998. write for info. (*0-324-00158-4*) Sth-Wstrn College.

Management Science Operations Research: A Strategic Perspective. Peter C. Bell. 1998. 81.95 (*0-324-00466-4*) Sth-Wstrn College.

Management Science-Operations Research: Cases & Readings. James S. Dyer & Roy D. Shapiro. LC 81-19703. 274p. (C). 1982. pap. text 20.00 (*0-471-86554-0*) Wiley.

Management Science-Operations Research: Cases & Readings. Ed. by James S. Dyer & Roy D. Shapiro. LC 81-19703. 400p. reprint ed. pap. 124.00 (*0-7837-3509-X*, 205784200008) Bks Demand.

Management Science Quantitative Methods Tools for Lotus Spreadsheets. Sam L. Savage. (C). 1993. text 35.74 incl. disk (*0-07-839543-7*) McGraw.

Management Science Using Spreadsheets: Preliminary Edition. Rick Hesse. (C). 1995. pap. text. write for info. (*0-201-60736-0*) Addison-Wesley.

Management Sciences - Models & Techniques: Proceedings of the 6th International Management Institute on Management Sciences, Paris, September, 1959, 2 vols., Set. C. W. Churchman & M. Verhulst. LC 60-14193. 1960. 486.00 (*0-08-009429-5*, Pub. by Pergamon Repr) Franklin.

Management Scientist Version 3.0: Software Pkg. 3rd ed. Anderson. (SWC-Management). 1993. 3.5 hd 38.25 (*0-314-03458-7*) West Pub.

Management Scientist Version 4.0 for Windows. 8th ed. Anderson et al. 1996. 34.75 (*0-314-21646-4*) West Pub.

Management Series Vol. 1: Data, Personnel, Organizing. 518p. 1991. 175.00 (*0-88404-672-9*) Bridge Pubns Inc.

Management Series Vol. 2: Establishment Officer, Executive, Finance, Target, Computer. 510p. 1991. 175.00 (*0-88404-673-7*) Bridge Pubns Inc.

Management Series Vol. 3: Public Relations, Marketing, Admin-Know-How. 520p. 1991. 175.00 (*0-88404-674-5*) Bridge Pubns Inc.

Management Services. Institute of Personnel Management Staff. 96p. (C). 1985. 45.00 (*0-85292-345-7*, Pub. by IPM Hse) St Mut.

Management Services Organization. Sarah E. Hutchinson & Glen Coulthard. 1994. text 75.00 (*0-07-413110-9*, Irwn McGrw-H) McGrw-H Hghr Educ.

Management Services Organizations. Keith M. Korenchuk. 164p. 1994. 45.00 (*1-56829-034-9*, 4580) Med Group Mgmt.

Management Services Organizations: Cases & Analysis. Thomas M. Gorey & American Medical Association. LC 97-5171. 1997. 18.20 (*1-56793-057-3*) Health Admin Pr.

Management 7371 - 7372. Gemmy Allen. (Orig.). (C). 1995. pap. text 30.43 (*1-56870-222-1*) RonJon Pub.

Management Similarities & Differences under Different Culture. K. S. Basu. 56p. 1970. pap. text 68.00 (*0-677-61505-1*) Gordon & Breach.

Management Simulation. Hunt. (C). Date not set. pap. write for info. (*0-395-41258-7*) HM.

Management Simulations for Mental Health & Human Services Administration. Michael J. Austin. LC 78-12172. 436p. 1995. pap., student ed. 24.95 (*0-917724-07-0*) Haworth Pr.

Management Skills. Patricia M. Fandt. Date not set. pap. text, teacher ed. write for info. (*0-314-03300-9*) West Pub.

Management Skills: Practice & Experience. Patricia M. Fandt. Ed. by Leyh. LC 93-6047. 500p. (C). 1993. mass mkt. 43.75 (*0-314-02810-2*) West Pub.

Management Skills Book. Conor Hannaway & Gabriel Hunt. 246p. 1992. 55.95 (*0-566-07283-1*, Pub. by Gower) Ashgate Pub Co.

Management Skills Book. Conor Hannaway & Gabriel Hunt. 256p. 1995. pap. 26.95 (*0-566-07682-9*, Pub. by Gower) Ashgate Pub Co.

Management Skills Builder: Self-Directed Learning Strategies for Career Development. Ralph S. Hambrick. LC 91-7457. 216p. 1991. 35.00 (*0-275-94051-9*, C4051, Praeger Pubs) Greenwood.

Management Skills Correspondence Course. Mortgage Bankers Association of America Staff. 450p. (C). 1997. pap. 410.00 (*1-57599-028-8*) Mortgage Bankers.

Management Skills for a New Millenium: Inspiration, Reflection & Experience. Gareth S. Gardiner & D. K. Mathis. 256p. (C). 2000. pap. 48.00 (*0-13-863911-6*, Macmillan Coll) P-H.

Management Skills for Clinical Supervisor. Connelly. (Allied Health Ser.). 1998. pap. 31.50 (*0-8273-6154-8*) Delmar.

Management Skills for Senior Coordinators in the Primary School. Sylvia Philips. LC 99-183112. (Subject Leaders Handbks.). 238p. 1998. pap. 23.95 (*0-7507-0697-X*, Falmer Pr) Taylor & Francis.

Management Skills for the Information Manager. Lawes. 1993. 65.95 (*1-85742-019-5*) Ashgate Pub Co.

Management Skills for the New Health Care Supervisor. 3rd ed. William Umiker. LC 98-175781. xxiii, 423p. 1998. 49.00 (*0-8342-1091-6*, 10916) Aspen Pub.

Management Skills in Primary Schools. Les Bell. LC 88-31018. (Educational Management Ser.). 304p. reprint ed. pap. 94.30 (*0-608-20316-5*, 207156900002) Bks Demand.

Management Skills in Social Work: A Handbook for Social Care Managers. John Harris & Des Kelly. 116p. 1992. pap. 22.95 (*1-85742-081-0*, Pub. by Arena) Ashgate Pub Co.

Management Skills Inventory: Developing Management Skills: A Self-Directed Approach, Bk. 1. Gerald De Jaager. LC 84-51543. 78p. (Orig.). (C). 1985. pap. 20.00 (*0-916001-00-8*) Seiler-Doar.

Management Skills Series. 1994. pap. 101.95 (*1-883553-74-1*) R Chang Assocs.

Management Skills Workshop, 4 bks., Set. Date not set. per. 59.46 (*0-614-08785-6*, 557) Busn Legal Reports.

***Management Skills/Engineers & Technical Professionals.** Termini. (Electrical Trades Ser.). (C). 2000. pap. 32.25 (*0-7668-1643-5*) Delmar.

Management Small Works Minor Maintenance. Jeremy Headley et al. (C). 1997. 92.95 (*0-582-28873-8*) Addison-Wesley.

***Management, Social Work & Change.** Harlow. 208p. 2000. 64.95 (*1-84014-963-9*) Ashgate Pub Co.

Management Specialist Trainee. Jack Rudman. (Career Examination Ser.: C-3608). 1994. pap. 27.95 (*0-8373-3608-2*) Nat Learn.

Management Standards for Computer & Numerical Controls. Donald N. Smith & Lary Evans. LC 76-49742. (Illus.). 417p. reprint ed. pap. 129.30 (*0-608-17711-3*, 203010500067) Bks Demand.

Management Standards for Developing Information Systems. Norman L. Enger. LC 76-41827. 239p. reprint ed. pap. 74.10 (*0-608-12148-7*, 202390600034) Bks Demand.

***Management Strategies: A Critique of Theories & Practices.** Samuel Eilon. LC 99-44534. 1999. write for info. (*0-7923-8557-8*) Kluwer Academic.

Management Strategies: A Special Collection from the Journal of Lending & Credit Risk Management. Ed Furash. Ed. by Beverly Foster. LC 97-30371. 150p. (C). 1997. pap. 45.00 (*1-57070-018-4*) Robt Morris Assocs.

Management Strategies: Obtaining Positive Productivity from Problem Personnel. Joan E. Franklin & D. Kim Freeland. LC 96-95099. 80p. (Orig.). 1996. pap. 20.00 (*0-9655058-0-4*) Magnolia Pr TN.

Management Strategies for Culturally Diverse Classrooms. Kenneth M. Johns & Connie Espinoza. LC 96-67184. (Fastback Ser.: No. 396). 45p. (Orig.). 1996. pap. 3.00 (*0-87367-596-7*) Phi Delta Kappa.

Management Strategies for Family Planning Programs. John A. Ross et al. LC 89-6029. (Illus.). 71p. (Orig.). 1989. pap. 10.00 (*0-9620952-1-4*) CUCFP&FH.

Management Strategies for Improving Family Planning Services: The Family Planning Manager Compendium. Ed. by Janice Miller & James A. Wolff. (Illus.). 431p. 1996. spiral bd. 25.00 (*0-913723-37-1*) Mgmt Sci Health.

Management Strategies for Libraries: A Basic Reader. Ed. by Beverly P. Lynch. LC 85-5668. 682p. 1985. pap. text 55.00 (*0-918212-86-3*) Neal-Schuman.

Management Strategies for Today's Project Shop Economy. Glenn A. Bassett. LC 90-20712. 264p. 1991. 65.00 (*0-89930-574-1*, BMQ/, Quorum Bks) Greenwood.

Management Strategies in Athletic Training. Richard R. Ray, Jr. LC 93-5167. (Illus.). 280p. 1993. text 33.00 (*0-87322-582-1*, BRAY0582) Human Kinetics.

***Management Strategies in Athletic Training.** 2nd ed. Richard Ray. LC 99-27701. (Athletic Training Education Ser.). (Illus.). 328p. 2000. 45.00 (*0-88011-810-5*) Human Kinetics.

Management Strategies That Make U. S. Firms Competitive in the Global Economy. rev. ed. Ted Reingold. LC 98-9415. (Studies on Industrial Productivity). (Illus.). 250p. 1998. text 50.00 (*0-8153-3091-X*) Garland.

Management Strategy: The Effect of Management Techniques on Commercial Diversification Project Success. 2nd ed. Richard R. Sylvester. (Professional Series in Quantitative Methods & Artificial Intelligence). 1988. 65.00 (*0-932010-54-7*) PhD Pub.

Management Strategy & Information Technology: Text & Readings. Christopher Barnatt. 240p. 1996. mass mkt. 34.95 (*0-412-74950-5*) Chapman & Hall.

Management Strategy & Information Technology: Text & Readings. Christopher Barnatt. 240p. 1996. pap. 34.95 (*1-86152-025-5*, Pub. by ITBP) Thomson Learn.

Management Strategy for Information Technology. Wendy Currie. 352p. 1995. pap. 64.50 (*0-273-60700-6*, Pub. by Pitman Pub) Trans-Atl Phila.

Management Strategy in the Oil & Gas Industries: Cases & Readings. fac. ed. M. Edgar Barrett & Mary P. Cormick. LC 82-15524. 605p. pap. 187.60 (*0-7837-7417-6*, 204721200006) Bks Demand.

Management Studies in an Academic Context. Ed. by Lars Engwall & Elving Gunnarsson. LC 96-209080. (Studia Oeconomiae Negotiorum: No. 35). 218p. (Orig.). 1994. pap. 52.50 (*91-554-3238-7*) Coronet Bks.

Management Study Guide. 3rd ed. Bartol. 1997. pap. 25.31 (*0-07-006984-0*) McGraw.

Management Study of the American Educational Complex College District, Killeen, Texas. Terrell Blodgett. (Special Project Reports). 350p. 1989. pap. 10.00 (*0-89940-863-X*) LBJ Sch Pub Aff.

Management Study of the Texas State Auditor's Office. Terrell Blodgett. 167p. 1984. pap. 3.00 (*0-89940-807-9*) LBJ Sch Pub Aff.

Management Styles for the '90s. H. Gordon Baird. 140p. (Orig.). 1982. 15.00 (*0-943000-00-9*) Telstar Inc.

Management Succession: From Owner-Founder to Professional President. Maryam Tashakori. LC 80-13722. 126p. 1980. 49.95 (*0-275-90559-4*, C0559, Praeger Pubs) Greenwood.

Management Succession in Small & Growing Enterprises. Roland C. Christensen. Ed. by Stuart Bruchey & Vincent P. Carosso. LC 78-18957. (Small Business Enterprise in America Ser.). 1979. reprint ed. lib. bdg. 19.95 (*0-405-11516-4*) Ayer.

Management Supervision for Working Professionals, 2 vols. Herman Koren. 528p. 1996. text 109.90 (*1-56670-205-4*) CRC Pr.

***Management Supplement.** 6th ed. Robbins. 2000. pap., student ed. 18.67 (*0-13-019854-4*) P-H.

***Management Survival Manual for Engineers.** Ronald H. Hermone. LC 98-3479. 143p. 1998. lib. bdg. 39.95 (*0-8493-2683-4*) CRC Pr.

Management System Dynamics. R. G. Coyle. LC 76-40144. (Illus.). 475p. reprint ed. pap. 147.30 (*0-8357-5597-5*, 203523600093) Bks Demand.

Management System for Teachers. National School Services Staff. 290p. (C). 1988. 95.00 (*0-932957-88-9*); teacher ed. 110.00 (*0-932957-87-0*) Natl School.

Management System for Teachers: Guidebook. National School Services Staff. (C). 1996. 25.00 (*0-932957-78-1*) Natl School.

***Management Systems: A Viable Systems Approach.** Maurice Yolles. 352p. (Orig.). 1999. pap. 59.50 (*0-273-62018-5*, Pub. by F T P-H) Trans-Atl Phila.

Management Systems for Safety. Jeremy Stranks. (Health & Safety in Practice Ser.). 192p. (Orig.). 1994. pap. 42.50 (*0-273-60441-4*, Pub. by Pitman Pub) Trans-Atl Phila.

Management Systems to Reduce Impact of Nitrates: Proceedings of a Meeting Held in Brussels, 24-25 September 1987. Ed. by J. C. Germon. 278p. 1989. 65.00 (*1-85166-402-5*) Elsevier.

Management Tactics of Pancho Villa: The Twenty-First Century Bible. Glenn Van Warrebey. 200p. (Orig.). 1995. pap. 16.95 (*0-9642771-1-5*) G Van Warrebey.

Management-Taschenlexikon. Haas & Huelck. (GER.). 200p. 1974. 24.95 (*0-8288-6069-6*, M-7547) Fr & Eur.

Management Task. 2nd ed. Rob Dixon. LC 97-199379. (Institute of Management Ser.). 176p. 1997. pap. text 34.95 (*0-7506-3390-5*, HF) Buttrwrth-Heinemann.

Management Team Handbook: Five Key Strategies for Maximizing Group Performance. Marie G. McIntyre. LC 98-8923. 1998. 34.95 (*0-7879-3973-0*) Jossey-Bass.

Management Technician. Jack Rudman. (Career Examination Ser.: C-2751). 1994. pap. 27.95 (*0-8373-2751-2*) Nat Learn.

Management Techniques Applied to the Construction Industry. 5th ed. R. Oxley & R. Poskitt. LC 96-13801. 400p. 1996. pap. text 39.95 (*0-632-03862-4*) Blackwell Sci.

Management Techniques for Civil Engineering Construction. K. Rowe. (Illus.). x, 268p. 1975. 63.00 (*0-85334-613-5*) Elsevier.

Management Techniques for Librarians. 2nd ed. G. Edward Evans. (Library & Information Science Ser.). 1983. text 60.00 (*0-12-243856-6*) Acad Pr.

Management-Technologie als Strategischer Erfolgsfaktor. Heinz Hubner & Stefan Jahnes. 320p. 1998. pap. 42.00 (*3-11-016132-X*) De Gruyter.

Management, Technology, & Human Resources Policy in the Artic (the North) Ed. by L. Lyck & V. I. Boyko. (NATO ASI Ser.: Vol. 4). 1996. text 276.00 (*0-7923-4023-X*) Kluwer Academic.

Management Theory: From Taylorism to Japanization. John Sheldrake. 240p. 1996. pap. 34.95 (*1-86152-199-5*) Thomson Learn.

Management Theory & Library Education, 14. Sajjad U. Rehman. LC 86-22736. (New Directions in Information Management Ser.: No. 14). 158p. 1987. 49.95 (*0-313-25288-2*, RMN/, Greenwood Pr) Greenwood.

***Management Theory & Practice.** J. S. Chandan. 1999. pap. 14.00 (*0-7069-9030-7*, Pub. by Vikas) S Asia.

Management Theory & Practice: Moving to a New Era. Ed. by Gerard Griffin. 392p. 1998. pap. 39.95 (*0-7329-5045-7*, Pub. by Macmill Educ) Paul & Co Pubs.

Management Thought in Great Britain: An Original Anthology. Ed. by Alfred D. Chandler, Jr. LC 79-7523. (History of Management Thought & Practice Ser.). 1980. lib. bdg. 28.95 (*0-405-12308-6*) Ayer.

Management Thoughts on Police Administration. James Vadackumchery. xxxvi, 255p. 1998. 27.00 (*81-7024-914-7*, Pub. by APH Pubng) Nataraj Bks.

Management 302 Fall 96: Management & Organizational Behavior 2nd ed. 218p. (C). 1996. text 25.60 (*0-536-59645-X*) Pearson Custom.

Management Tools. Nadia Preyma et al. Ed. by William Schulz. (Options: Guidance for Grades 1). 140p. (Orig.). (gr. 1-8). 1989. pap., teacher ed. 8.00 (*0-920541-59-3*) Peguis Pubs Ltd.

***Management Tools & Techniques: An Executive's Guide.** Darrell K. Rigby. 69p. 2000. pap. 14.95 (*0-9656059-3-0*) Bain & Co.

Management Tools & Techniques: An Executive's Guide. rev. ed. Darrell K. Rigby. 69p. 1999. pap. 14.95 (*0-9656059-2-2*) Bain & Co.

Management Tools & Techniques: An Executive's Guide, 1998. rev. ed. Darrell K. Rigby. 69p. 1998. pap. 14.95 (*0-9656059-1-4*) Bain & Co.

Management Tools for Cosmetology Education: Worksheets to Organize Your Program. Michelle Johnson. 600p. 1992. text 49.95 (*0-87350-396-1*) Milady Pub.

Management Trainee (U. S. P. S.) Jack Rudman. (Career Examination Ser.: C-1690). 1994. pap. 29.95 (*0-8373-1690-1*) Nat Learn.

Management Training: Starting up Training & Development Programs in Medium-Sized Corporations. Colin Park. (Illus.). 180p. pap. 15.00 (*0-318-13279-6*, PAMPB) Am Soc Train & Devel.

Management Training & Corporate Strategy: How to Improve Competitive Performance. David E. Hussey. (Illus.). 210p. 1988. pap. 24.95 (*0-318-32491-1*, Pergamon Pr) Elsevier.

Management Training for Psychiatrists. Dinesh K. L. Bhugra & Alastair Burns. 264p. 1992. pap. 25.00 (*0-88048-610-4*, 8610, Pub. by Royal Coll Psych) Parkwest Pubns.

Management Training in High-Tech & R&D: Concept for Engerprises under Transition, Proceedings of the NATO Workshop on Concept of Management Training for Enterprises in High-Tech R&D, St. Petersburg, Russia, July 1-5, 1996. Ed. by C. M. Verkoeyen & Albina I. Nikkonen. LC 96-54606. (NATO Advanced Science Institutes - Partnership Sub Series 3). 182p. (C). 1997. text 104.00 (*0-7923-4431-6*) Kluwer Academic.

Management Training Today. Bob Oconnor. 1989. pap. 19.25 (*0-314-68951-6*) West Pub.

***Management 21C: New Visions for a New Millennium.** Subir Chowdhury. (Illus.). 289p. 2000. 28.00 (*0-273-63963-3*, Pub. by F T P-H) Natl Bk Netwk.

Management under Differing Labour Market & Employment Systems. Ed. by Gunther Dlugos et al. 486p. (C). 1988. lib. bdg. 161.55 (*3-11-010947-6*) De Gruyter.

Management under Differing Value Systems Vol. XIV: Political, Social & Economical Perspectives in a Changing World. Ed. by Gunter Dlugos & Klaus Weiermair. 868p. 1981. 124.00 (*3-11-008553-4*) De Gruyter.

Management Uses of Accounting Information. Jackson. (C). 2001. text. write for info. (*0-03-021092-5*); pap. text, student ed. write for info. (*0-03-021093-3*) Harcourt Coll Pubs.

Management von Umweltfonds, Vol. XIX. Henrik Wolff. (Europaische Hochschulschriften: Reihe 5: Bd. 1800). (GER.). 312p. 1995. pap. 57.95 (*3-631-48990-0*) P Lang Pubng.

Management, Welfare & Conservation of Park Deer. Ed. by D. J. Bullock & C. R. Goldspink. 107p. 1992. pap. 30.00 (*0-900767-79-0*, Pub. by Univs Fed Animal Welfare) St Mut.

Management Without Precedent: Readings to Strengthen Community-Based Organizations. 2nd rev. ed. Fran Barrett et al. Ed. by Community Resource Exchange Staff. (Illus.). 286p. 1995. pap. 29.95 (*0-9655305-0-7*) Commun Res Exchange.

Management, Work & Welfare in Modern Europe. Steve Jefferys & Michael Carpenter. 256p. 1999. 80.00 (*1-85898-281-2*) E Elgar.

Management Working Papers: Chapters 14-23. 7th ed. Skousen & Albrecht. (SWC-Accounting). 1998. pap. 19.75 (*0-538-87629-8*) S-W Pub.

Management Would Be Easy . . . If It Weren't for the People. Patricia J. Addesso. LC 96-19541. 192p. 1996. pap. 17.95 (*0-8144-7915-4*) AMACOM.

Management 100: Introduction to Management. 308p. (C). 1997. pap. text 33.00 (*0-536-00490-0*) Pearson Custom.

***Management 2000-2001.** 8th ed. Fred H. Maidment. (Annual Editions Ser.). 240p. (C). 1999. pap. 16.56 (*0-07-236402-5*) McGrw-H Hghr Educ.

Management 2001: Lecture Notes. (C). 1997. ring bd. 16.95 (*0-536-00962-7*) Pearson Custom.

Management 396. 2nd ed. Gales. 314p. 1998. pap. text 37.00 (*0-536-01814-6*) Pearson Custom.

Management 490. 2nd ed. Bickford. 1998. 29.00 (*0-07-228699-7*) McGraw.

*Managementprinzipien: Und Ihre Zusammenhange Mit Arbeitsorientierungen und Arbeitsverhalten. Markus Wendt. (GER.). 290p. 1999. 51.95 (3-631-34769-3) P Lang Pubng.
*Management's Discussion & Analysis. 16p. 1999. pap. 3.00 (0-16-050216-0) USGPO.
*Management's Discussion & Analysis. 39p. 1999. pap. 5.00 (0-16-050219-5) USGPO.
*Management's Discussion & Analysis. 39p. 2000. pap. 4.00 (0-16-050269-1) USGPO.
*Management's Discusssion & Analysis. 16p. 2000. pap. 2.00 (0-16-050270-5) USGPO.
Management's Evaluation of EDP, Vol. 2. William J. Yourwith. LC 76-46263. 1977. 30.00 (0-917818-00-8) Exec Stand.
Management's Guide to Computer Integrated Manufacturing. 93.00 (0-686-31443-3) C I M Systems.
MANAGEMNT ADMIN OFFICE SYS 2/E. 2nd ed. Burton S. Kaliski & Peter F. Meggison. 525p. (C). 1988. text 74.00 (0-15-554684-8) Dryden Pr.
*Managemt Information Systems: New Approaches to Organization & Technology. 5th ed. 1998. write for info. (0-13-922717-2) P-H.
Manager. Date not set. pap. 5.95 (0-87162-416-8) Warner Pr.
Manager & the Internal Auditor: Partners for Profit. rev. ed. Lawrence B. Sawyer & Gerald Vinten. LC 95-31232. 412p. 1996. 140.00 (0-471-96117-5) Wiley.
Manager as a Leader. Sonnenfeld. 149.95 (1-85521-551-9) Ashgate Pub Co.
*Manager as Coach & Mentor. Eric Parsloe. 96p. 2000. pap. 17.95 (0-8464-5109-3) Beekman Pubs.
Manager As Communicator. Sandra E. O'Connell. (Illus.). 206p. (C). 1986. reprint ed. pap. text 21.50 (0-8191-5402-4) U Pr of Amer.
Manager As Negotiator: Bargaining for Cooperation & Competitive Gain. David A. Lax & James K. Sebenius. 304p. 1987. 35.00 (0-02-918770-2) Free Pr.
Manager As Trainer, Coach & Leader. Jerome M. Rosow & Robert Zager. (New Roles for Managers Ser.: Pt. III). 94p. 1990. pap. 95.00 (0-89361-045-3) Work in Amer.
Manager Bookshelf Custom Edition. (C). 1997. 22.00 (0-673-67578-5) Addison-Wesley.
Manager Business Process Flows. Anupindi et al. LC 98-30746. 267p. 1999. pap. text 37.60 (0-13-907775-8) P-H.
Manager Computer Operations. Jack Rudman. (Career Examination Ser.: C-2241). 1994. pap. 34.95 (0-8373-2241-3) Nat Learn.
Manager Data Processing. (Career Examination Ser.: Vol. C-3728). 1997. pap. 34.95 (0-8373-3728-3, C3728) Nat Learn.
Manager in the International Economy. 7th ed. Raymond Vernon et al. LC 95-4955. 498p. (C). 1995. 60.80 (0-13-232539-X) P-H.
*Manager Managed Care: Secrets from a Former Case Manager. Susan Frager. LC 99-37680. 288p. 2000. pap. 39.95 (0-471-35177-6) Wiley.
Manager, Mistletoe, & the Master. Orley R. Herron. 80p. 1996. write for info. (1-889555-09-6) Stephen Aubry.
Manager Search & Selection. Ron Surz. Ed. & Illus. by Investment Management Consultants Association Staff. 79p. 1996. 100.00 (1-928974-03-1) Invest Mgmt Cons.
Manager Who Became a Superstar: The Story of Scottie Pippen. Delois B. Pippen. 78p. 1994. 10.95 (0-533-10730-X) Vantage.
Managerial Accounting, 001. Anderson. (C). 1989. mass mkt., teacher ed. 7.56 (0-395-32469-6) HM.
Managerial Accounting, 001. Anderson. (C). 1989. pap., student ed. 25.16 (0-395-32466-1); pap., wbk. ed. 31.96 (0-395-32467-X); mass mkt., teacher ed. 7.56 (0-395-32468-8) HM.
Managerial Accounting. Henry R. Anderson et al. LC 88-8138. 1989. teacher ed. 7.56 (0-318-36876-5); teacher ed., student ed. 7.56 incl. trans. (0-318-36875-7) HM.
Managerial Accounting, 001. Henry R. Anderson et al. LC 88-8138. (C). 1989. text 93.16 (0-395-32458-0) HM.
Managerial Accounting. Barfield & Cecily A. Raiborn. (AQ - Managerial Accounting Ser.). 1993. pap., teacher ed. write for info. (0-314-02319-4) West Pub.
Managerial Accounting. Chow. (AB - Accounting Principles Ser.). Date not set. write for info. (0-538-82742-4); student ed. write for info. (0-538-82743-2) S-W Pub.
Managerial Accounting. James DeLisa. 49p. (YA). (gr. 11 up). 1994. 6.95 (1-878383-27-2) C Lee Pubns.
Managerial Accounting. Calvin Engler. (C). 1989. text 61.95 (0-256-07203-5, Irwn McGrw-H) McGrw-H Hghr Educ.
Managerial Accounting. John G. Helmkamp. 752p. 1987. text 48.95 (0-471-88910-5) Wiley.
Managerial Accounting. Jiambalvo. pap. text, student ed. write for info. (0-471-28349-5) Wiley.
Managerial Accounting. Jiambalvo. 448p. 2000. text 102.95 (0-471-23823-6) Wiley.
Managerial Accounting. John Y. Lee. LC 99-234141. (Illus.). 760p. (C). 1998. text 89.95 (1-891666-00-2) Hampton Hse.
Managerial Accounting. Dale Morse & Jerold Zimmerman. 104p. (C). 1997. text 22.50 (0-256-26479-1, Irwn McGrw-H) McGrw-H Hghr Educ.
Managerial Accounting. Dale Morse & Jerold L. Zimmerman. LC 96-46238. 864p. (C). 1996. text 70.95 (0-256-18955-2, Irwn McGrw-H) McGrw-H Hghr Educ.
Managerial Accounting. Cecily A. Raiborn. Date not set. pap. text. write for info. (0-314-01757-7); pap. text, student ed. 21.00 (0-314-01613-9) West Pub.
*Managerial Accounting. Sollenberger Schneider. (SWC-Accounting Ser.). 1999. 39.95 (0-324-03310-9) Sth-Wstrn College.
Managerial Accounting. Jae K. Shim. (Illus.). 530p. 1999. ring bd. 65.00 (1-882312-04-X) Delta Pub CA.
Managerial Accounting. Sollenberger & Schneider. 1999. 74.95 (0-87393-798-8) Dame Pubns.
Managerial Accounting. Charlene W. Spoede et al. 1999. student ed. 20.00 (0-256-13117-1) McGraw.
Managerial Accounting. Flumo Stevens. 670p. (C). 1994. pap. text 48.15 (1-56226-196-7) CAT Pub.
Managerial Accounting. Jerry J. Weygandt. pap. text. write for info. (0-471-35336-1) Wiley.
Managerial Accounting. Jerry J. Weygandt. 608p. pap. text. write for info. (0-471-35318-3) Wiley.
*Managerial Accounting. Jerry J. Weygandt. 336p. 1999. pap. write for info. (0-471-35307-8) Wiley.
*Managerial Accounting. Jerry J. Weygandt. 304p. 1999. pap., student ed. 34.95 (0-471-35328-0) Wiley.
Managerial Accounting. James O. McKinsey, Jr. Ed. by Alfred D. Chandler. LC 79-7551. (History of Management Thought & Practice Ser.). 1980. reprint ed. lib. bdg. 61.95 (0-405-12335-3) Ayer.
Managerial Accounting. 2nd ed. John G. Helmkamp. 864p. 1990. text. write for info. (0-471-51422-5) Wiley.
Managerial Accounting. 2nd ed. Cecily A. Raiborn. Date not set. pap. text, teacher ed. write for info. (0-314-06403-6) West Pub.
Managerial Accounting. 2nd ed. Cecily A. Raiborn et al. LC 95-33105. 800p. (C). 1995. mass mkt. 72.50 (0-314-05826-5) West Pub.
Managerial Accounting, 2 vols. 2nd ed. Donald Ricketts. (C). 1990. pap. text, teacher ed. 6.76 (0-395-57193-6) HM.
Managerial Accounting, 2 vols. 2nd ed. Donald Ricketts. (C). 1991. pap. text, teacher ed., suppl. ed. 3.96 (0-395-57194-4) HM.
Managerial Accounting. 2nd ed. Wilson & Wai-Fong A. Siu. 1992. pap. write for info. (1-86152-357-2) Thomson Learn.
Managerial Accounting. 2nd annot. ed. Cecily A. Raiborn. Date not set. text, teacher ed. write for info. (0-314-07014-1) West Pub.
Managerial Accounting. 3rd ed. Calvin Engler. LC 92-14407. 1024p. (C). 1992. text 72.50 (0-256-10246-5, Irwn McGrw-H); text, student ed. 28.75 (0-256-11350-5, Irwn McGrw-H) McGrw-H Hghr Educ.
Managerial Accounting. 3rd ed. Philip E. Fess et al. (SWC-Accounting). (C). 1994. mass mkt. 51.75 (0-538-82185-X, AQ65CA) S-W Pub.
Managerial Accounting. 3rd ed. Ronald W. Hilton. (C). 1996. text 68.74 (0-07-029001-6); pap. text, student ed. 26.88 (0-07-028959-X) McGraw.
Managerial Accounting. 3rd ed. Raiborn & Jesse T. Barfield. LC 98-28158. (Aq - Managerial Accounting Ser.). (C). 1998. pap. 93.95 (0-538-88512-2) S-W Pub.
Managerial Accounting. 3rd ed. Raiborn & Jesse T. Barfield. (AQ - Managerial Accounting Ser.). (C). 1998. pap., student ed. 21.95 (0-538-88513-0); pap., student ed. 23.95 (0-538-88515-7) S-W Pub.
Managerial Accounting. 3rd ed. James M. Reeve. (AB - Accounting Principles Ser.). (C). 1994. mass mkt., student ed. 17.00 (0-538-82186-8) S-W Pub.
*Managerial Accounting. 4th ed. Ronald Hilton. 512p. (C). 1998. pap., student ed. 26.88 (0-07-232032-X) McGrw-H Hghr Educ.
Managerial Accounting. 4th ed. Ronald W. Hilton. LC 98-23851. 1998. 87.31 (0-07-059339-6) McGraw.
Managerial Accounting, 4 vols. 4th ed. Belverd E. Needles. LC 95-76964. (C). 1995. pap. text 60.36 (0-395-74567-5) HM.
Managerial Accounting. 5th ed. Philip E. Fess & Carl S. Warren. (AQ - Managerial Accounting Ser.). 1996. pap. 53.95 (0-538-85342-5) S-W Pub.
Managerial Accounting. 5th ed. Philip E. Fess & Carl S. Warren. (AQ - Managerial Accounting Ser.). 1996. pap., student ed. 18.95 (0-538-85343-3); pap., suppl. ed. 17.95 (0-538-85344-1) S-W Pub.
*Managerial Accounting. 5th ed. Lawrence A. Gordon. LC 99-56917. 2000. write for info. (0-07-240196-6) McGraw.
Managerial Accounting. 5th ed. Titard. LC 98-71487. (SWC-Accounting). 1999. 78.95 (0-87393-768-6); pap., student ed. 24.95 (0-87393-769-4) Dame Pubns.
Managerial Accounting. 6th ed. Maher. 1997. teacher ed. 246.00 (0-03-018197-6, Pub. by Harcourt Coll Pubs) Harcourt.
Managerial Accounting. 6th ed. Michael W. Maher. LC 96-85709. (C). 1996. text 94.50 (0-03-018193-3, Pub. by Harcourt Coll Pubs) Harcourt.
Managerial Accounting. 6th ed. Michael W. Maher. (C). 1997. pap. text, teacher ed. 42.00 (0-03-018194-1) Harcourt Coll Pubs.
Managerial Accounting. 6th ed. James M. Reeve & Carl S. Warren. (AB - Accounting Principles Ser.). 1998. pap. 75.95 (0-538-87357-4) S-W Pub.
Managerial Accounting. 7th ed. Dominiak. (AB - Accounting Principles Ser.). (C). 1994. mass mkt., student ed. 26.50 (0-538-82784-X) S-W Pub.
Managerial Accounting. 7th ed. Geraldine F. Dominiak & Joseph G. Louderback, III. LC 93-8305. (C). 1994. mass mkt. 59.00 (0-538-82534-0, AQ63CA) S-W Pub.
Managerial Accounting. 7th ed. Ray H. Garrison. 1993. pap. text 27.60 (0-256-15591-7) McGraw.
Managerial Accounting. 8th ed. Anderson. (SWC-Accounting Ser.). 1992. 41.00 (0-538-81328-8) S-W Pub.
Managerial Accounting. 8th ed. Anderson. (Swc-Accounting Ser.). 1992. teacher ed. 31.25 (0-538-81331-8) S-W Pub.
Managerial Accounting. 8th ed. Lane K. Anderson & Harold M. Sollenberger. (C). 1992. mass mkt. 55.75 (0-538-81326-1, AQ96HA) S-W Pub.
Managerial Accounting. 8th ed. Rob Anderson. (AB - Accounting Principles Ser.). (C). 1992. mass mkt., student ed. 22.50 (0-538-81327-X) S-W Pub.
Managerial Accounting. 8th ed. Copeland et al. LC 98-70890. 1998. 63.95 (0-87393-764-3) Dame Pubns.
Managerial Accounting. 8th ed. Dominiak. LC 96-19924. (AQ - Managerial Accounting Ser.). 1996. mass mkt. 66.95 (0-538-85612-2); mass mkt., student ed. 19.95 (0-538-85613-0) S-W Pub.
Managerial Accounting. 8th ed. Ray H. Garrison. 1996. text 77.50 (0-256-23752-2) Dorsey.
Managerial Accounting. 8th ed. Ray H. Garrison. 248p. (C). 1997. text, student ed., wbk. ed. 28.75 (0-256-23569-4, Irwn McGrw-H) McGrw-H Hghr Educ.
Managerial Accounting. 8th ed. Ray H. Garrison & Eric Noreen. 960p. (C). 1996. text 69.95 (0-256-16917-9, Irwn McGrw-H) McGrw-H Hghr Educ.
Managerial Accounting. 8th ed. Ray H. Garrison & Eric Noreen. (C). 1996. text, student ed. 70.95 incl. disk (0-256-23959-2, Irwn McGrw-H); text, student ed. 86.20 incl. disk (0-256-23960-6, Irwn McGrw-H); pap., text 13.95 incl. disk (0-256-24209-7, Irwn McGrw-H) McGrw-H Hghr Educ.
Managerial Accounting. 8th ed. Ray H. Garrison et al. (C). 1996. text, student ed. 85.95 incl. disk (0-256-24134-1, Irwn McGrw-H); text 19.95 (0-256-23761-1, Irwn McGrw-H) McGrw-H Hghr Educ.
Managerial Accounting. 8th ed. Ray H. Garrison et al. 896p. (C). 1996. text 82.45 incl. cd-rom (0-256-23963-0, Irwn McGrw-H) McGrw-H Hghr Educ.
Managerial Accounting. 9th ed. Geraldine J. Dominiak & Joseph G. Louderback. (SWC-Accounting). 1999. pap., student ed. 17.50 (0-324-01209-8) Thomson Learn.
Managerial Accounting. 9th ed. Dominiak & Louderback. LC 99-27838. (SWC-Accounting Ser.). 1999. pap. 91.95 (0-324-01208-X) Thomson Learn.
Managerial Accounting. 9th ed. Ray H. Garrison & Eric W. Noreen. LC 99-12837. 1999. write for info. (0-07-109249-8) McGraw.
Managerial Accounting. 9th ed. Harold M. Sollenberger & Arnold Schneider. LC 95-18421. (SWC-Accounting). (C). 1996. text 80.95 (0-538-84282-2) S-W Pub.
Managerial Accounting, Chapters 1-7. 8th ed. Dominiak & Louderback. 1996. 39.00 (0-538-87226-8) Thomson Learn.
Managerial Accounting: Chapters 14-23. 7th ed. Skousen & Albrecht. LC 99-176810. (SWC-Accounting Ser.). 1998. pap. 86.95 (0-538-88996-9) S-W Pub.
Managerial Accounting: Chapters 14-24. 6th ed. James M. Reeve & Carl S. Warren. (AB - Accounting Principles Ser.). 1998. pap. 20.25 (0-538-87363-9) S-W Pub.
Managerial Accounting: Computer Assisted Practice Set 1, 5 Disk, Ibm. 2nd ed. Louis F. Biagioni. (C). 1994. pap. text 22.00 (0-07-839911-4) McGraw.
Managerial Accounting: Concepts for Planning, Control, Decision Making. 7th ed. Ray H. Garrison. LC 93-21847. (C). 1993. pap. write for info. (0-256-13369-7, Irwn McGrw-H) McGrw-H Hghr Educ.
Managerial Accounting: Exam Questions & Explanations. 6th ed. Irvin N. Gleim & Terry Campbell. 1998. pap. text 19.95 (1-58194-031-9) Gleim Pubns.
Managerial Accounting: Information for Decisions. Robert W. Ingram et al. LC 96-39474. 1996. mass mkt. 98.95 (0-538-86717-5) S-W Pub.
Managerial Accounting: Information for Decisions. Ingram et al. 1997. 13.50 (0-538-86720-5) Thomson Learn.
Managerial Accounting: Information for Decisions. 2nd ed. Robert W. Ingram et al. (Accounting Ser.). 2000. pap. 96.95 (0-324-02441-X) Sth-Wstrn College.
*Managerial Accounting: Lecture Aid. 9th ed. Ray H. Garrison & Eric Noreen. 328p. (C). 1999. pap., student ed. 10.63 (0-07-232413-9) McGrw-H Hghr Educ.
Managerial Accounting: Method & Meaning. 2nd ed. Richard M. S. Wilson & Wai F. Chua. (Chapman & Hall Series in Accounting & Finance). (Illus.). 704p. (Orig.). 1993. mass mkt. 39.95 (0-412-43610-8, Chap & Hall NY) Chapman & Hall.
*Managerial Accounting: Ready Notes. 4th ed. Ronald Hilton. 288p. (C). 1998. pap. 11.88 (0-07-365651-8) McGrw-H Hghr Educ.
Managerial Accounting: Student Solutions Manual. 8th ed. Copeland et al. LC 98-70890. 1998. pap., student ed. 24.95 (0-87393-767-8) Dame Pubns.
Managerial Accounting: Study Guide. 8th ed. Copeland et al. LC 98-70890. 1998. pap., student ed. 21.95 (0-87393-765-1) Dame Pubns.
*Managerial Accounting: Tools for Business Decision Making. Jerry J. Weygandt et al. LC 99-11249. 648p. 1999. text 100.95 (0-471-34588-1) Wiley.
*Managerial Accounting: Tools for Business Decision Making, Working Papers. Jerry J. Weygandt et al. 458p. 1999. pap. 36.95 (0-471-35329-9) Wiley.
Managerial Accounting: Working Papers. 8th ed. Copeland et al. LC 98-70890. 1998. pap. 20.95 (0-87393-766-X) Dame Pubns.
Managerial Accounting - Working Papers. 3rd ed. James M. Reeve. (AB - Accounting Principles Ser.). (C). 1994. mass mkt., wbk. ed. 21.25 (0-538-82187-6) S-W Pub.
Managerial Accounting Activities Book. Hannon. 1999. pap. 15.95 (0-324-02012-0) Thomson Learn.
Managerial Accounting & Analysis in Multinational Enterprises. Ed. by H. Peter Holzer & Hanns-Martin W. Schoenfeld. (Illus.). xii, 270p. 1986. lib. bdg. 79.95 (3-11-010081-9) De Gruyter.
Managerial Accounting & Control: Cases & Readings. Kudar & R. Mimick. 513p. 1984. pap. 40.00 (0-13-550021-4) Prntice Hall Bks.
*Managerial Accounting Communications, Vol. II. Gee. (Accounting Ser.). 2000. pap. 10.00 (0-324-02824-5) Sth-Wstrn College.
Managerial Accounting Custom Ready Notes. 7th ed. Ray H. Garrison & Eric Noreen. (C). 1994. 7.95 (0-256-18895-5, Irwn McGrw-H) McGrw-H Hghr Educ.
Managerial Accounting for Librarians & Other Not-for-Profit Managers. G. Stevenson Smith. LC 91-11138. 256p. (C). 1991. text 75.00 (0-8389-0568-4) ALA.
Managerial Accounting for Managers. Cooper. (SWC-Accounting). 2002. pap. 62.00 (0-324-02809-1) Thomson Learn.
Managerial Accounting for the Hospitality Industry. 3rd ed. Raymond S. Schmidgall. LC 94-37385. 508p. 1994. pap. write for info. (0-86612-087-4) Educ Inst Am Hotel.
Managerial Accounting for the Hospitality Industry 4th ed. Raymond S. Schmidgall. LC 99-195671. xx, 446p. 1997. write for info. (0-86612-150-1) Educ Inst Am Hotel.
Managerial Accounting for the Hospitality Service Industries. 2nd ed. Clifford T. Fay, Jr. et al. 616p. (C). 1976. text, ring bd., boxed set 42.95 (0-697-08406-X) Brown & Benchmark.
Managerial Accounting in the Hospitality Industry. 5th ed. Peter Harris & Peter Hazzard. 352p. 1999. 44.50 (0-7487-1567-3, Pub. by S Thornes Pubs) Trans-Atl Phila.
Managerial Accounting Library. Cecily A. Raiborn. Date not set. pap. text. write for info. (0-314-01756-9) West Pub.
Managerial Accounting Notes. 8th ed. Ray H. Garrison et al. 296p. (C). 1996. text 11.25 (0-256-16943-8, Irwn McGrw-H) McGrw-H Hghr Educ.
Managerial Accounting Objective Questions & Explanations. 5th ed. Irvin N. Gleim & Terry L. Campbell. LC 96-94321. (Illus.). 696p. (C). 1996. pap. text 16.95 (0-917537-88-2) Gleim Pubns.
Managerial Accounting Package: With Workbook & Study Guide. 8th ed. Ray H. Garrison & Eric Noreen. (C). 1996. text 80.95 (0-256-24041-8, Irwn McGrw-H) McGrw-H Hghr Educ.
Managerial Accounting Primer: Corporate Approach. 2nd ed. Clo Hampton. 164p. 1996. spiral bd. 28.95 (0-7872-1935-5, 41193501) Kendall-Hunt.
Managerial Accounting Score Builders. 2nd ed. Bruce Baldwin & Diane Pattison. (C). 1994. pap. text, student ed. 13.25 (0-256-17604-3, Irwn McGrw-H) McGrw-H Hghr Educ.
Managerial Accounting Score Builders. 3rd ed. Bruce Baldwin & Diana Pattison. 224p. (C). 1994. pap. text 18.65 (1-56226-194-0) CAT Pub.
Managerial Accounting Student Lecture Aid. 8th ed. Ray H. Garrison. 296p. (C). 1996. text 9.37 (0-256-23884-7, Irwn McGrw-H) McGrw-H Hghr Educ.
*Managerial Accounting Working Papers. Weygandt. 1999. text 84.00 (0-471-37064-9) Wiley.
Managerial Accounting Working Papers. 3rd ed. Calvin Engler. 632p. (C). 1993. text 27.50 (0-256-11351-3, Irwn McGrw-H) McGrw-H Hghr Educ.
Managerial Accounting Working Papers. 8th ed. Ray H. Garrison & Eric Noreen. 528p. (C). 1996. text 27.50 (0-256-16920-9, Irwn McGrw-H) McGrw-H Hghr Educ.
Managerial Acctg. Philip E. Fess & Carl S. Warren. (Thomson Executive Press). (C). 1985. mass mkt. 41.25 (0-538-01600-0, A60) S-W Pub.
Managerial & Organisational Integration. T. G. Whiston. (Illus.). xviii, 237p. 1991. 140.95 (0-387-19663-3) Spr-Verlag.
Managerial & Organizational Cognition: Theory, Methods & Research. Colin Eden & J. C. Spender. LC 97-62468. xxi, 257 p. 1998. pap. write for info. (0-7619-5194-6) Sage.
Managerial & Supervisory Principles for Physical Therapists. Larry J. Nosse et al. LC 98-29592. 370p. 1998. 49.95 (0-683-30254-X) Lppncott W & W.
Managerial & Technical Motivation: Assessing Needs for Achievement, Power & Affiliation. Michael J. Stahl. LC 86-3221. 177p. 1986. 47.95 (0-275-92068-2, C2068, Praeger Pubs) Greenwood.
Managerial Applications of Information Technology. 778p. (C). 1995. text 81.00 (0-536-59264-0) Pearson Custom.
Managerial Applications of Operations Research. No K. Kwak & Marc J. Schniederjans. LC 81-40623. (Illus.). 452p. (Orig.). 1982. pap. text 37.00 (0-8191-2228-9) U Pr of Amer.
Managerial Applications of System Dynamics. Ed. by Edward B. Roberts. LC 77-26952. (Illus.). 669p. 1978. pap. text 25.00 (1-883823-42-0, XMNGAP) Pegasus Comm.
Managerial Applications of System Dynamics. Ed. by Edward B. Roberts. 562p. (C). reprint ed. pap. text 25.00 (0-915299-59-3) Productivity Inc.
Managerial Assessment of Water Quality & System Reliability. John Cromwell et al. LC 97-198266. (Illus.). 134p. 1997. pap. 125.00 (0-89867-905-2, 90725) Am Water Wks Assn.
Managerial Capitalism Retrospective. Marris. LC 98-16540. 300p. 1998. text 69.95 (0-312-21578-9) St Martin.
Managerial Career Plateaus. James A. Stoner et al. 1980. text 20.00 (0-317-11509-X) CU Ctr Career Res.
Managerial Challenge in the Third World. Syed M. Saeed. LC 85-28163. 400p. 1985. 65.00 (0-275-92042-9, C2042, Praeger Pubs) Greenwood.
Managerial Cognition & Organizational Information, Vol. 1. Ed. by Lee S. Sproull et al. 171p. 1984. 73.25 (0-89232-403-1) Jai Pr.
Managerial Cognition & Organizational Information Vol. 2: Research on Public Organizations. Ed. by Robert F. Coulam & Richard A. Smith. 311p. 1985. 73.25 (0-89232-425-2) Jai Pr.
Managerial Cognition & Organizational Information Vol. 3: The Cross-Functional Link of Basic & Application Research. Ed. by Sheila M. Puffer et al. 286p. 1985. 73.25 (0-89232-689-1) Jai Pr.

An Asterisk (*) at the beginning of an entry indicates that the title is appearing for the first time.

Managerial Commmunication: The Lifeline. Beck. (C). 1996. text. write for info. (*0-03-015368-9*) Harcourt Coll Pubs.

Managerial Communication. 4th ed. Mary Munter. LC 97-9000. 1996. pap. text, student ed. 25.00 (*0-13-256447-5*) P-H.

Managerial Communication: A Finger on the Pulse. 3rd ed. Paul R. Timm & Kristen B. De Tienne. LC 94-35669. 448p. 1995. pap. text 56.00 (*0-13-116196-2*) P-H.

Managerial Communication: A Strategic Approach. 2nd ed. John Waltman et al. 552p. 1991. pap. text 98.00 (*0-536-57970-9*) Pearson Custom.

Managerial Communication: Bridging Theory & Practice. Charles E. Beck. LC 98-8141. 500p. 1998. 70.00 (*0-13-849886-5*) P-H.

Managerial Communication: Strategies & Applications. Larry R. Smeltzer & Donald J. Leonard. LC 93-18311. 528p. (C). 1993. text 64.50 (*0-256-12072-2*, Irwn McGrw-H) McGrw-H Hghr Educ.

Managerial Communication: Strategies & Applications. Larry R. Smeltzer et al. (C). 1994. text 61.95 (*0-256-18177-2*, Irwn McGrw-H) McGrw-H Hghr Educ.

Managerial Communication: Strategies & Applications. 2nd ed. Leonar Smeltzer. 1997. text 51.60 (*0-256-17081-9*) McGraw.

Managerial Communication & Problem Solving. Talbott. (C). 1996. pap. text 41.25 (*0-07-063346-0*) McGraw.

Managerial Compensation. Allan Nash. (Studies in Productivity: Highlights of the Literature Ser.: Vol. 15). 56p. 1980. pap. 55.00 (*0-89361-022-4*) Work in Amer.

Managerial Compensation, Vol. 15. Allan Nash. LC 80-21044. (Work in America Institute Studies in Productivity). 1982. pap. 35.00 (*0-685-05448-9*, Pergamon Pr) Elsevier.

Managerial Competencies of Twelve Corporate Librarians: A Validation Study of New Directions in Library & Information Science Education. Marcy Murphy. LC 88-138233. (SLA Research Ser.: No. 2). 43p. reprint ed. pap. 30.00 (*0-7837-6300-X*, 204601500010) Bks Demand.

Managerial Consulting Skills. Charles J. Margerison. 224p. 1996. pap. 33.95 (*0-566-07703-5*) Ashgate Pub Co.

Managerial Consulting Skills: A Practical Guide. Charles Margerison. 256p. 1988. text 65.95 (*0-566-02793-3*, Pub. by Gower) Ashgate Pub Co.

***Managerial Consulting Skills: A Practical Guide.** 2nd ed. Charles J. Margerison. LC 00-42964. 2000. write for info. (*0-566-08292-6*, Pub. by Gower) Ashgate Pub Co.

Managerial Control of the Police: Internal Affairs & Audits. Ed. by Harry W. More & Peter C. Unsinger. 208p. 1991. pap. 29.95 (*0-398-06298-6*) C C Thomas.

Managerial Control of the Police: Internal Affairs & Audits. Ed. by Harry W. More & Peter C. Unsinger. 208p. (C). 1991. text 44.95 (*0-398-05751-6*) C C Thomas.

Managerial Cost Accounting: Planning & Control. 3rd ed. Ferrara et al. 1996. 74.95 (*0-87393-244-7*) Dame Pubns.

Managerial Cost Accounting: Planning & Control (Study Guide) 3rd ed. Pinano et al. 1996. pap., student ed. 28.95 (*0-87393-246-3*) Dame Pubns.

Managerial Cost Accounting Concepts & Standards for the Federal Government. Government Printing Office Staff. 109p. 1995. pap. 8.00 (*0-16-048130-9*) USGPO.

Managerial Cost Accounting Concepts & Standards for the Federal Government: Statement of Federal Accounting Standards, No. 4, 109p. 1996. reprint ed. pap. text 30.00 (*0-7881-3284-9*) DIANE Pub.

Managerial Craftsmanship: Getting Agencies to Work Together. Eugene Bardach. LC 98-25467. 1998. 44.95 (*0-8157-0798-3*); pap. 19.95 (*0-8157-0797-5*) Brookings.

Managerial Decision Analysis. Danny Samson. 700p. (C). 1988. pap. text. write for info. (*0-256-06683-3*, Irwn McGrw-H) McGrw-H Hghr Educ.

Managerial Decision Cases. Finnegan. 2000. pap. 31.95 (*0-324-02011-2*) Sth-Wstrn College.

Managerial Decision Making. David J. Hickson. (History of Management Thought Ser.). 1995. 163.95 (*1-85521-415-6*, Pub. by Dartmth Pub) Ashgate Pub Co.

Managerial Decision-Making Process, 4 vols. 4th ed. E. Frank Harrison. LC 94-76505. 544p. (C). 1994. text 69.16 (*0-395-70837-0*) HM.

Managerial Decision-Making Process, 4 vols. 4th ed. E. Frank Harrison. (C). 1995. text, teacher ed. 11.96 (*0-395-71188-6*) HM.

Managerial Decision Making Process. 5th ed. E. Frank Harrison. LC 98-72037. 1998. text 58.77 (*0-395-90821-3*) HM.

Managerial Decision Making with Technology. Rod F. Monger. (Studies in Productivity: No. 45). 69p. 1986. pap. text 55.00 (*0-08-029517-7*) Work in Amer.

Managerial Decisions under Uncertainty: An Introduction to the Analysis of Decision Making. 2nd ed. Bruce F. Baird. LC 88-33842. (Engineering Management Ser.). 544p. 1989. 130.00 (*0-471-85891-9*) Wiley.

Managerial Dilemmas: Cases in Social, Legal & Technological Change. Alan F. Westin & John D. Aram. LC 87-22476. 192p. 1988. pap. text 24.95 (*0-88730-181-9*, HarpBusn) HarpInfo.

Managerial Dilemmas: Cases in Social, Legal & Technological Change. Alan F. Westin & John D. Aram. LC 87-22476. 192p. 1988. write for info. (*0-88730-255-6*, HarpBusn) HarpInfo.

Managerial Dilemmas: The Political Economy of Hierarchy. Gary J. Miller. (Political Economy of Institutions & Decisions Ser.). 272p. (C). 1992. text 59.95 (*0-521-37281-X*) Cambridge U Pr.

Managerial Dilemmas: The Political Economy of Hierarchy. Gary J. Miller. (Political Economy of Institutions & Decisions Ser.). (Illus.). 272p. (C). 1993. pap. text 18.95 (*0-521-45769-6*) Cambridge U Pr.

Managerial Economics. (C). 1984. write for info. (*0-8087-5529-3*) Pearson Custom.

Managerial Economics. Boyes. 2001. text 50.97 (*0-395-82835-X*) HM.

***Managerial Economics.** Ian M. Dobbs. LC 99-24058. 1999. write for info. (*0-19-877571-7*); write for info. (*0-19-877570-9*) OUP.

Managerial Economics. Pearson Graham & Diran Bodenhorn. LC 78-67945. (Economics Ser.). (Illus.). 1980. text 19.25 (*0-201-02470-5*) Addison-Wesley.

Managerial Economics. W. Haynes. (C). 1989. 80.00 (*0-89771-427-X*, Pub. by Current Dist) St Mut.

***Managerial Economics.** Keating. 1999. pap. text 39.00 (*0-471-37819-4*) Wiley.

Managerial Economics. Barry Keating & J. Holton Wilson. 640p. (C). 1986. teacher ed. 4.55 (*0-15-554696-1*); disk. write for info. (*0-318-65141-6*) Harcourt Coll Pubs.

Managerial Economics. Robert E. McCormick. 714p. 1992. 95.00 (*0-13-544750-X*) P-H.

Managerial Economics. Ivan Png. LC 97-12043. 700p. 1997. 78.95 (*1-55786-927-8*) Blackwell Pubs.

Managerial Economics. Rabinovitch. (C). 1997. 54.95 (*1-55786-814-X*) Blackwell Pubs.

Managerial Economics. William F. Samuelson & Stephen G. Marks. 790p. (C). 1994. text 41.00 (*0-614-07780-X*) Dryden Pr.

Managerial Economics. Jae K. Shim & Joel G. Siegel. LC 98-11942. (Business Review Ser.). 356p. 1998. pap. 14.95 (*0-7641-0170-6*) Barron.

Managerial Economics. Tomic. (C). 1992. pap. text 29.50 (*0-07-065072-1*) McGraw.

Managerial Economics. Ed. by Wilbrate. (C). 1999. text. write for info. (*0-321-01077-9*) Addson-Wesley Educ.

Managerial Economics. deluxe ed. Holley H. Ulbrich. (Barron's Business Library). 320p. 1990. pap. 14.95 (*0-8120-4182-8*) Barron.

Managerial Economics. 2nd ed. Paul G. Keat & Young. 1996. pap. text, student ed. 25.00 (*0-13-230103-2*) P-H.

Managerial Economics. 2nd ed. Samuelson. LC 94-72427. (C). 1994. text 91.50 (*0-03-007559-9*) Harcourt Coll Pubs.

Managerial Economics. 2nd ed. William F. Samuelson. 240p. (C). 1994. pap. text, teacher ed., student ed. 31.00 (*0-03-007563-7*) Harcourt Coll Pubs.

Managerial Economics. 2nd ed. William F. Samuelson & Stephen Marks. 304p. (C). 1995. pap. text, teacher ed., suppl. ed. 40.00 (*0-03-007564-5*) Harcourt Coll Pubs.

Managerial Economics. 2nd ed. William F. Samuelson & Stephen G. Marks. 240p. (C). 1995. pap. text, teacher ed. 33.75 (*0-03-007562-9*) Harcourt Coll Pubs.

Managerial Economics. 3rd ed. (C). 2000. text. write for info. (*0-13-016994-3*); text. write for info. (*0-13-016995-1*); text. write for info. (*0-13-016996-X*); text. write for info. (*0-13-016997-8*) S&S Trade.

Managerial Economics. 3rd ed. Baye. LC 99-26274. 1999. 64.74 (*0-07-228917-1*) McGraw.

Managerial Economics. 3rd ed. H. Craig Peterson & W. Cris Lewis. (Illus.). 688p. (C). 1993. write for info. (*0-318-69915-X*) Macmillan.

Managerial Economics. 3rd ed. Samuelson. (C). 1998. text 56.00 (*0-03-022612-0*, Pub. by Harcourt Coll Pubs) Harcourt.

Managerial Economics. 3rd ed. William F. Samuelson. 1998. 100.50 (*0-03-022648-1*, Pub. by Harcourt Coll Pubs) Harcourt.

Managerial Economics. 4th ed. Evan J. Douglas. (C). 1992. text 53.20 (*0-13-554346-0*) P-H.

Managerial Economics. 4th ed. Peterson. (C). 1998. pap. text, student ed. 21.33 (*0-13-010296-2*) P-H.

Managerial Economics. 4th ed. Peterson & Lewis. LC 98-19387. 672p. (C). 1998. 91.93 (*0-13-976283-3*) P-H.

Managerial Economics. 4th ed. Duncan W. Reekie. 576p. (C). 1995. pap. 88.00 (*0-13-100520-0*, Macmillan Coll) P-H.

Managerial Economics. 4th ed. Truett. 1992. teacher ed. 35.25 (*0-538-81288-5*) Sth-Wstrn College.

Managerial Economics. 5th ed. Christopher R. Thomas. 320p. (C). 1994. text, wbk. ed. 23.12 (*0-256-16057-0*, Irwn McGrw-H) McGrw-H Hghr Educ.

Managerial Economics. 5th ed. Truett. (HB - Economics Ser.). (C). 1994. mass mkt., student ed. 25.95 (*0-538-84292-X*) S-W Pub.

Managerial Economics. 6th ed. Date not set. pap. text, teacher ed. write for info. (*0-314-01925-1*) West Pub.

Managerial Economics. 6th ed. S. Charles Maurice & Christopher R. Thomas. LC 98-24973. 1998. 85.93 (*0-256-17345-1*, Irwn Prfssnl) McGraw-Hill Prof.

Managerial Economics. 6th ed. James R. McGuigan. Date not set. pap. text, student ed. 20.50 (*0-314-01814-X*) West Pub.

Managerial Economics. 6th ed. James R. McGuigan. (HT - Managerial Economics Ser.). 1993. pap. 16.00 (*0-314-02278-3*) West Pub.

Managerial Economics. 6th ed. James R. McGuigan & R. Charles Moyer. Ed. by Schiller. LC 92-18132. 650p. (C). 1993. text 61.50 (*0-314-01220-6*) West Pub.

Managerial Economics. 6th ed. Truett. LC 97-17187. (Miscellaneous/Catalogs Ser.). (C). 1997. mass mkt. 90.95 (*0-538-86871-6*); mass mkt., student ed. 20.95 (*0-538-86872-4*) S-W Pub.

Managerial Economics. 7th ed. Mark Hirschey & James L. Pappas. LC 92-22542. 800p. (C). 1993. pap. text, teacher ed. 14.75 (*0-03-074806-2*) Dryden Pr.

***Managerial Economics.** 7th ed. Maurice. 2001. text 65.74 (*0-07-239291-6*); pap. text, student ed. 20.25 (*0-07-239293-2*) McGraw.

Managerial Economics. 7th ed. James R. McGuigan. Date not set. pap. text, teacher ed. write for info. (*0-314-07788-6*) West Pub.

Managerial Economics. 7th ed. James R. McGuigan. 1996. pap., student ed. 21.00 (*0-314-06516-4*) West Pub.

Managerial Economics. 7th ed. James R. McGuigan et al. LC 95-36052. 700p. (C). 1995. pap. 67.00 (*0-314-06433-8*) West Pub.

Managerial Economics. 8th ed. Mark Hirschey. (C). 1995. pap. text, teacher ed. 31.25 (*0-03-016214-9*); pap. text, student ed. 29.50 (*0-03-016217-3*, Pub. by Harcourt Coll Pubs) Harcourt.

Managerial Economics. 8th ed. Mark Hirschey. LC 95-68736. (C). 1995. text 91.50 incl. disk (*0-03-011303-2*, Pub. by Harcourt Coll Pubs) Harcourt.

Managerial Economics. 8th ed. McGuigan. LC 98-21497. (HT - Managerial Economics Ser.). (C). 1998. pap. 90.95 (*0-538-88106-2*) S-W Pub.

Managerial Economics. 8th ed. McGuigan. (HT - Managerial Economics Ser.). (C). 1998. pap., student ed. 22.95 (*0-538-88107-0*) S-W Pub.

Managerial Economics: Analysis & Strategy. 690p. (C). 1995. text 57.75 (*0-536-59095-8*) Pearson Custom.

Managerial Economics: Analysis & Strategy. 4th ed. Evan J. Douglas. 704p. (C). 1992. text. write for info. (*0-318-68774-7*) P-H.

Managerial Economics: Analysis for Business Decisions. Douglas C. Hague. LC 74-452050. (Longmans' Business Studies Ser.). 364p. reprint ed. pap. 112.90 (*0-608-13072-9*, 202520800043) Bks Demand.

Managerial Economics: Analysis, Problems, Cases. 5th ed. Truett. 1995. 75.25 (*0-538-84195-8*) Sth-Wstrn College.

***Managerial Economics: Applications, Strategy & Tactics.** 9th ed. McGuigan et al. (SWC-Business Statistics Ser.). (C). 2001. text, student ed. 19.75 (*0-324-05882-9*) Sth-Wstrn College.

Managerial Economics: Applied Microeconomics for Decision Making. 5th ed. Charles S. Maurice & Christopher R. Thomas. LC 94-26272. 752p. (C). 1994. text 69.75 (*0-256-16055-4*, Irwn McGrw-H) McGrw-H Hghr Educ.

Managerial Economics: Economic Tools for Today's Decision Makers. Paul G. Keat & Philip H. Young. LC 95-16823. 1995. write for info. (*0-614-07805-9*) Prntice Hall Bks.

Managerial Economics: Economic Tools for Today's Decision Makers. 2nd ed. Paul G. Keat & Philip K. Y. Young. 738p. 1995. 93.00 (*0-02-362183-4*, Pub. by P-H) S&S Trade.

***Managerial Economics: Economic Tools for Today's Decision Makers.** 3rd ed. Paul G. Keat & Philip K. Y. Young. LC 99-45707. 752p. 1999. 91.00 (*0-13-013538-0*) P-H.

Managerial Economics: For the Practically Minded. Hermalin. (HT - Managerial Economics Ser.). 2002. mass mkt. 64.95 (*0-538-86308-0*) S-W Pub.

Managerial Economics: Readings, Cases & Exercises. R. Charles Moyer et al. 261p. 1979. pap. text 37.00 (*0-8299-0157-4*); pap. text. write for info. (*0-314-43376-7*) West Pub.

Managerial Economics: Strategy for Profit. James G. Mulligan. 592p. 1989. teacher ed. write for info. (*0-318-63858-4*, H1973-0) P-H.

Managerial Economics: Test Bank. 8th ed. Mark Hirschey. (C). 1995. pap. text, suppl. ed. 37.00 (*0-03-016218-1*, Pub. by Harcourt Coll Pubs) Harcourt.

Managerial Economics: Text, Problems & Short Cases K. K. Seo. 664p. (C). 1994. text 60.00 (*0-536-58583-0*) Pearson Custom.

Managerial Economics: Text, Problems & Short Cases 8th ed. K. K. Seo. 208p. (C). 1994. text, student ed. 20.80 (*0-536-58572-5*) Pearson Custom.

Managerial Economics & Business Strategy. Michael Baye. 232p. (C). 1994. text 24.37 (*0-256-13730-7*, Irwn McGrw-H) McGrw-H Hghr Educ.

Managerial Economics & Business Strategy. 2nd ed. 240p. (C). 1996. text, student ed., wbk. ed. 24.37 (*0-256-17816-X*, Irwn McGrw-H) McGrw-H Hghr Educ.

Managerial Economics & Business Strategy. 2nd ed. Michael Baye. LC 96-17337. 576p. (C). 1996. text 69.75 (*0-256-17955-7*, Irwn McGrw-H) McGrw-H Hghr Educ.

***Managerial Economics & Business Strategy.** 3rd ed. Michael R. Baye. LC 99-26274. (Illus.). 2000. write for info. (*0-07-116933-4*, Irwn Prfssnl) McGraw-Hill Prof.

Managerial Economics & Business Strategy: Student Workbook Package. 2nd ed. Michael Baye. (C). 1996. text 74.75 (*0-256-21623-1*, Irwn McGrw-H) McGrw-H Hghr Educ.

Managerial Economics & Operations Research: Techniques, Applications, Cases. 5th ed. Ed. by Edwin Mansfield. 500p. (C). 1987. pap. text 21.00 (*0-393-95590-7*) Norton.

Managerial Economics & Organization. Zoltan J. Acs & Daniel A. Gerlowski. LC 95-31256. 464p. 1995. 98.00 (*0-02-300292-1*, Macmillan Coll) P-H.

Managerial Economics & Organizational Architecture. Brickley. (C). 1996. pap., student ed. 23.75 (*0-256-17232-3*) McGraw.

***Managerial Economics & Organizational Architecture.** James A. Brickley et al. LC 00-36959. 2001. write for info. (*0-07-231447-8*) McGraw.

Managerial Economics & Organizational Architecture. James Brickley et al. 576p. (C). 1996. text 66.50 (*0-256-15825-8*, Irwn McGrw-H) McGrw-H Hghr Educ.

Managerial Economics for the Service Industries. P. Bowers. 336p. 1994. mass mkt. 34.95 (*0-412-57790-9*) Chapman & Hall.

Managerial Economics in a Global Economy. 2nd ed. Dominick Salvatore. 1993. student ed. write for info. incl. disk (*0-07-054602-9*) McGraw.

Managerial Economics in a Global Economy. 3rd ed. Dominick Salvatore. (C). 1995. pap., student ed. 27.50 (*0-07-057223-2*) McGraw.

Managerial Economics in Practice. N. Branton & J. M. Livingstone. (C). 1989. 75.00 (*0-7855-4096-2*, Pub. by Witherby & Co) St Mut.

Managerial Economics Workbook. 3rd ed. Baye. 256p. 1999. pap., wbk. ed. 26.88 (*0-07-228918-X*) McGraw.

Managerial Engineering: Techniques for Improving Quality & Productivity in the Workplace. Ryuji Fukuda. 1997. pap. text 30.00 (*1-56327-174-5*) Productivity Inc.

Managerial Ethics: Morally Managing People & Processes. Ed. by Marshall Schminke. LC 98-26312. 300p. 1998. pap. 29.95 (*0-8058-2492-8*) L Erlbaum Assocs.

Managerial Excellence: McKinsey Award Winners from the Harvard Business Review, 1980-1994. Frwd. by Rajat Gupta. LC 95-36267. (Business Review Bk.). 368p. (C). 1996. 29.95 (*0-87584-670-X*) Harvard Busn.

Managerial Excellence: McKinsey Award Winners from the Harvard Business Review, 1980-1994. Harvard Business Review Staff. 335p. 1996. 29.95 (*0-07-103669-5*) McGraw.

Managerial Excellence Through Diversity: Text & Cases. Ed. by Mary C. Gentile. (Illus.). 499p. (C). 1998. reprint ed. pap. text 39.95 (*1-57766-016-1*) Waveland Pr.

Managerial Finance: Essentials. Charles O. Kroncke et al. LC 76-2048. 518p. reprint ed. pap. 160.60 (*0-608-12020-0*, 202284200030) Bks Demand.

Managerial Finance: Theory & Techniques. Dennis J. Conner & Alberto T. Bueso. (Illus.). 320p. 1981. text 54.70 (*0-13-550269-1*) P-H.

Managerial Finance: Using Frameworks for Effective Financial. Alan Parkinson. LC 97-200142. 288p. 1997. pap. text 37.95 (*0-7506-1826-4*, HG4026) Buttrwrth-Heinemann.

Managerial Finance for Business Planning. 2nd ed. David N. Reps. (Illus.). 220p. (Orig.). (C). 1996. pap. text 23.95 (*0-943025-68-0*) Cummngs & Hath.

Managerial Finance for Business Planning. 3rd rev. ed. David N. Reps. (Illus.). 248p. (Orig.). (C). 1996. pap. text 24.95 (*0-943025-88-5*) Cummngs & Hath.

Managerial Finance in the Corporate Economy. Ed. by Shahriar Khaksari & Dilip K. Ghosh. LC 94-13590. 416p. (C). (gr. 13). 1995. 125.00 (*0-415-11111-0*, B4264) Routledge.

Managerial Financial Reporting. Hans H. Jenny. Ed. by T. Jefferson Reeder. 249p. 1993. 59.95 (*0-614-17593-3*) NACUBO.

Managerial Flexibility & Accountability, Reforming the IRS: Hearing Before the Committee on Governmental Affairs, United States Senate, 105th Congress, Second Session, March 12, 1998. LC 98-193168. (S. Hrg. Ser.). iii, 76 p. 1998. write for info. (*0-16-057122-7*) USGPO.

Managerial Guide to Business Forecasting. Dennis Ellis & Jay Nathan. LC 84-81422. 165p. (Orig.). (C). 1990. pap. text 29.50 (*0-932126-11-1*) Graceway.

Managerial Guide to Judgmental Forecasting. Jain L. Chaman. 107p. (C). 1987. 24.95 (*0-932126-13-8*) Graceway.

Managerial Hierarchies: Comparative Perspectives on the Rise of the Modern Industrial Enterprise. Ed. by Alfred D. Chandler, Jr. & Herman Daems. (Studies in Business History: No. 32). (Illus.). 246p. 1980. 24.95 (*0-674-54740-3*) HUP.

Managerial Hierarchies: Comparative Perspectives on the Rise of the Modern Industrial Enterprise. Ed. by Alfred D. Chandler, Jr. & Herman Daems. (Studies in Business History: No. 32). (Illus.). 246p. 1983. pap. 9.95 (*0-674-54741-1*) HUP.

Managerial Ideology & the Social Control of Deviance in Organizations. Richard M. Weiss. LC 85-19385. 284p. 1986. 55.00 (*0-275-92105-0*, C2105, Praeger Pubs) Greenwood.

Managerial Imperative & the Practice of Leadership in Schools. Larry Cuban. LC 87-6512. (SUNY Series, Educational Leadership). 293p. (C). 1988. text 24.50 (*0-88706-593-7*) State U NY Pr.

Managerial Innovation at General Motors: An Original Anthology. Ed. by Alfred D. Chandler, Jr. LC 79-7524. (History of Management Thought & Practice Ser.). 1980. lib. bdg. 18.95 (*0-405-12309-4*) Ayer.

Managerial Innovation Change in the Metropolitan Hospital. Dalton E. McFarland. LC 79-14551. (Praeger Special Studies). 322p. 1979. 69.50 (*0-275-90390-7*, C0390, Praeger Pubs) Greenwood.

Managerial Insights from Literature. Sheila M. Puffer. 334p. (C). 1991. 37.95 (*0-534-92481-6*) S-W Pub.

Managerial Issues in Productivity Analysis. Ed. by Ali Dogramaci & Nabil R. Adam. 1985. lib. bdg. 98.00 (*0-89838-162-2*) Kluwer Academic.

Managerial Issues in the Reformed NHS. J. Rasquinha. Ed. by M. Malek et al. 280p. 1993. 175.95 (*0-471-94033-X*) Wiley.

Managerial Job Change: Men & Women in Transition. Nigel Nicholson & Michael West. (Management & Industrial Relations Ser.: No. 12). (Illus.). 288p. 1988. pap. text 22.95 (*0-521-35744-6*) Cambridge U Pr.

Managerial Kant: The Kant Critiques & the Managerial Order. Nathan D. Grundstein. (Knowledge of Strategy Ser.). 208p. 1982. 18.50 (*0-930305-02-7*) Enter Achieve.

Managerial Labour Markets in Small & Medium Sized Enterprises. Pooran Wynarczyk et al. LC 93-6921. (Small Business Ser.). 352p. (C). (gr. 13). 1993. pap. 82.95 (*0-415-10022-4*) Thomson Learn.

Managerial Leadership. Peter Wright. LC 95-12506. (Elements of Business Ser.). 224p. (C). 1996. pap. 17.99 (*0-415-11069-6*) Thomson Learn.

Managerial Leadership. Peter Wright. LC 95-12506. (Bus Press-Previous Routledge). 272p. (C). (gr. 13). 1996. pap. 64.95 (*0-415-11068-8*) Thomson Learn.

Managerial Leadership in the Post-Industrial Society. Philip Sadler. 256p. 1988. text 69.95 (*0-566-02611-2*, Pub. by Gower) Ashgate Pub Co.

M

An Asterisk (*) at the beginning of an entry indicates that the title is appearing for the first time.

Managerial Macroeconomics: Canadian Edition. Donald Daly. 480p. (C). 1987. text 49.95 (*0-256-06000-2*, Irwn McGrw-H) McGrw-H Hghr Educ.

Managerial Macroeconomics: Canadian Edition. Donald Daly. 104p. (C). 1987. teacher ed., per. write for info. (*0-256-06653-1*, Irwn McGrw-H) McGrw-H Hghr Educ.

Managerial Marketing. H. J. Kuhlmeijer. 1975. pap. text 82.50 (*90-207-0460-5*) Kluwer Academic.

Managerial Marketing Industrial. B. Charles Ames & James D. Hlavacek. 1983. 28.95 (*0-685-07561-3*) Random.

Managerial Moxie. Secretan. LC 91-31176. (Illus.). 496p. 1992. 21.95 (*1-55958-159-X*) Prima Pub.

Managerial Moxie: The 8 Proven Steps to Empowering Employees & Supercharging Your Company. Lance H. Secretan. (Illus.). 496p. 1994. pap. 14.95 (*1-55958-487-4*) Prima Pub.

Managerial Notes for Accounting. rev. ed. Allen. 1997. pap. 9.95 (*0-87393-689-2*) Dame Pubns.

Managerial Odyssey. Robert L. Focazio & Andrew Ladd. (Illus.). 192p. 1997. 14.95 (*0-9656329-0-3*) Odyssey GA.

Managerial Odyssey: Problems in Business & Its Environment. 3rd ed. Arthur Elkins & Dennis W. Callaghan. 600p. (C). 1981. text 26.25 (*0-201-03962-1*) Addison-Wesley.

Managerial Perspective. Gupta. (Management Information Systems Ser.). 1996. mass mkt. 49.95 (*0-314-08927-6*) Course Tech.

Managerial Planning: An Optimum & Stochastic Approach, 2 vols., Set. C. S. Tapiero. xxiv, 642p. 1978. text 222.00 (*0-677-05400-9*) Gordon & Breach.

Managerial Planning with Linear Programming: In Process Industry Operations. Julius S. Aronofsky et al. LC 78-2848. (Illus.). 395p. reprint ed. pap. 122.50 (*0-608-11455-3*, 205539900017) Bks Demand.

Managerial Power & Soviet Politics. Jeremy R. Azrael. LC 66-21330. (Russian Research Center Studies: No. 52). 272p. reprint ed. pap. 84.40 (*0-7837-2220-6*, 205731000004) Bks Demand.

Managerial Presidency. James P. Pfiffner. 384p. (C). 1991. pap. text 33.25 (*0-534-13194-8*) Harcourt.

Managerial Presidency. 2nd ed. Ed. by James P. Pfiffner. LC 98-30490. (Joseph V. Hughes, Jr., & Holly O. Hughes Series in the Presidency & Leadership Studies: Vol. 4). 384p. 1999. pap. 16.95 (*0-89096-860-8*) Tex A&M Univ Pr.

Managerial Presidency. 2nd rev. ed. Ed. by James P. Pfiffner. LC 98-30490. (Joseph V. Hughes, Jr., & Holly O. Hughes Series in the Presidency & Leadership Studies: Vol. 4). 384p. 1999. 29.95 (*0-89096-858-6*) Tex A&M Univ Pr.

Managerial Process for National Health Development: Guiding Principles. 1981. text. write for info. (*92-4-180005-4*) World Health.

Managerial Process in Human Service Agencies. David W. Young. LC 78-19767. (Praeger Special Studies). 331p. 1979. 69.50 (*0-275-90440-7*, C0440, Praeger Pubs) Greenwood.

Managerial Productivity. John Sweetland. (Studies in Productivity: Highlights of the Literature Ser.: Vol. 4). 40p. 1978. pap. 55.00 (*0-685-29191-X*) Work in Amer.

Managerial Promotion: The Dynamics for Men & Women. Marian N. Ruderman et al. LC 95-52022. 28p. 1996. pap. text 15.00 (*1-882197-13-5*) Ctr Creat Leader.

Managerial Psychology. 4th ed. Harold J. Leavitt. LC 77-13852. 1997. lib. bdg. 19.00 (*0-226-46974-3*) U Ch Pr.

Managerial Psychology: Managing Behavior in Organizations. 5th ed. Harold J. Leavitt & Homa Bahrami. (Illus.). 364p. 1988. 29.95 (*0-226-46973-5*) U Ch Pr.

Managerial Reality: Balancing Technique, Practice & Values. 2nd ed. Ed. by Frost Peter J. et al. LC 94-27813. 425p. (C). 1997. pap. text 51.00 (*0-673-99183-0*) Addison-Wesley Educ.

Managerial Reform & Professional Empowerment in the Public Service. Walter L. Balk. LC 95-19463. 216p. 1996. 55.00 (*1-56720-011-7*, Quorum Bks) Greenwood.

Managerial Revolution: What Is Happening in the World. James Burnham. LC 71-138102. 285p. 1972. reprint ed. lib. bdg. 38.50 (*0-8371-5678-5*, BUMR, Greenwood Pr) Greenwood.

Managerial Selected Chapters. Weygandt. pap. text 16.00 (*0-471-37386-9*) Wiley.

Managerial Skills: Explorations in Applied Knowledge. John D. Bigelow. (Illus.). 320p. 1991. text 55.00 (*0-8039-4095-5*); pap. text 25.00 (*0-8039-4096-3*) Sage.

Managerial Skills in Organizations. Chad T. Lewis et al. 350p. 1990. teacher ed. write for info. incl. disk (*0-318-66374-0*, H23377) P-H.

Managerial Spreadsheet Modeling & Analysis. Rick Hesse. 704p. (C). 1996. text 61.00 (*0-256-21530-8*, Irwn McGrw-H) McGrw-H Hghr Educ.

Managerial Spreadsheets: Modelling & Analysis. Rick Hesse. (C). 1996. pap. text. write for info. (*0-201-54215-3*) Addison-Wesley.

Managerial State: Power, Politics, & Ideology in the Remaking of Social Welfare. John Clarke & Janet Newman. 208p. 1997. 69.95 (*0-8039-7611-9*); pap. 21.95 (*0-8039-7612-7*) Sage.

Managerial Statistics. Albright. LC 99-55993. (Business Statistics). 937p. 1999. pap. 86.95 (*0-534-34981-1*) Brooks-Cole.

Managerial Statistics. Winston Albright. (Business Statistics Ser.). 2000. pap. text, student ed. 15.00 (*0-534-37139-6*) Brooks-Cole.

Managerial Transformation by Values: A Corporate Pilgrimage. S. K. Chakraborty. LC 92-42609. (Illus.). 250p. (C). 1993. text 33.50 (*0-8039-9464-8*) Sage.

Managerial Use of Accounting Data: A How-To Guide for Understanding Accounting Data & Making It Work for You. Ed. by Emerson O. Henke et al. LC 77-88600. (Illus.). 296p. reprint ed. pap. 91.80 (*0-608-18156-0*, 203284800081) Bks Demand.

Managerial Uses of Accounting Information. Joel Demski. 672p. (C). 1996. pap. text 69.95 (*0-7923-9847-5*) Kluwer Academic.

Managerial Uses of Accounting Information. Joel S. Demski. LC 93-34340. 672p. (C). 1993. lib. bdg. 105.50 (*0-7923-9406-2*) Kluwer Academic.

Managerial Woman. Margaret Henning. 1988. mass mkt. 5.99 (*0-671-67431-5*) PB.

Managerial Work. Ed. by Rosemary Stewart. LC 97-45888. 440p. 1998. text 135.95 (*1-85521-971-9*, Pub. by Ashgate Pub) Ashgate Pub Co.

Managerialism: The Emergence of a New Ideology. Willard F. Enteman. LC 93-7444. 272p. (C). 1993. pap. 17.95 (*0-299-13924-7*) U of Wis Pr.

Managerialism: The Great Debate. Mark Considine & Martin Painter. 256p. 1998. pap. 24.95 (*0-522-84759-5*, Pub. by Melbourne Univ Pr) Paul & Co Pubs.

***Managerialism & Nursing: Beyond Oppression & Profession.** Michael Traynor. LC 98-42097. 1999. pap. 29.99 (*0-415-17896-7*) Routledge.

Managers: Career Alternatives for the College Educated. Richard J. Thain. LC 78-61296. (Orig.). 1978. pap. 4.95 (*0-913936-11-1*) Coll Placement.

Managers & Innovation: The Social Construction of a Biotechnology. John Howells. LC 93-30261. 240p. (C). 1994. pap. 74.95 (*0-415-08590-X*) Thomson Learn.

Managers & Legal Environment 3. 3rd ed. Constance E. Bagley. LC 98-18789. (Business Law Ser.). 1998. pap. 98.95 (*0-538-88485-1*) S-W Pub.

***Managers & Mantras: One Company's Struggle for Simplicity.** Charlotte Butler & John Keary. LC 99-43202. 250p. 2000. 29.95 (*0-471-83558-7*) Wiley.

Managers & Missionaries: Library Service to Children & Young Adults in the Information Age. Ed. by Leslie Edmonds. (Allerton Park Institute Ser.: No. 28). (C). 1989. text 10.00 (*0-87845-075-0*) U of Ill Grad Sch.

Managers & National Culture: A Global Perspective. Ed. by Richard B. Peterson. LC 92-1747. 474p. 1993. 75.00 (*0-89930-602-0*, PMI, Quorum Bks) Greenwood.

Managers & Objects: Why Bother? Peter Coad. (C). 1999. pap. 20.25 (*0-13-555103-X*) P-H.

***Managers & the Law.** Lynden Griggs. LC 99-204625. 640p. 1999. pap. write for info. (*0-455-21642-8*) LawBk Co.

Managers & the Legal Environment of Business: Strategies for the 21st Century. Constance E. Bagley. Ed. by Clyde Perlee. 667p. (C). 1991. text 64.25 (*0-314-79790-4*) West Pub.

Managers & the Market. O'Brien. 1996. 26.95 (*0-8057-9834-X*, Twyne) Mac Lib Ref.

Managers & the Market. O'Brien. 1998. per. 15.95 (*0-8057-4502-5*) Macmillan.

Managers & Workers: Origins of the Twentieth-Century Factory System in the United States, 1880-1920. rev. ed. Daniel Nelson. LC 95-6356. 262p. 1995. 40.00 (*0-299-14880-7*); pap. 17.95 (*0-299-14884-X*) U of Wis Pr.

Managers As Employees: An International Comparison of the Changing Character of Managerial Employment. Ed. by Myron J. Roomkin. 304p. 1989. text 65.00 (*0-19-504322-7*) OUP.

Managers As Facilitators: A Practical Guide to Getting Work Done in a Changing Workplace. Richard G. Weaver & John D. Farrell. LC 97-2306. 260p. 1999. reprint ed. pap. 19.95 (*1-57675-054-X*) Berrett-Koehler.

Managers As Leaders. Harvard Business Review Staff. (Leadership Skills Ser.). 127p. 1991. pap. 19.95 (*0-87584-260-7*) Harvard Busn.

Managers As Leaders. Harvard Business School Press Staff. 150p. 1991. pap. 1995.00 (*0-07-103320-3*) McGraw.

Managers As Mentors: Building Partnerships for Learning. Chip R. Bell. LC 96-7029. 208p. 1998. reprint ed. pap. 16.95 (*1-57675-034-5*) Berrett-Koehler.

Manager's Balancing Act. Florence M. Stone. LC 97-2332. 224p. 1997. 24.95 (*0-8144-0374-3*) AMACOM.

Manager's Book of Questions: 751 Interview Questions for Hiring the Best Person. John Kador. LC 97-9029. 224p. 1997. pap. 14.95 (*0-07-034311-X*) McGraw.

Manager's Book of Quotations. Lewis D. Eigen & Jonathan P. Siegel. 528p. 1991. reprint ed. pap. 21.95 (*0-8144-7776-3*) AMACOM.

Manager's Bookshelf. 3rd ed. Jon L. Pierce & John W. Newstrom. 416p. (C). 1997. pap. 36.00 (*0-06-500707-7*) Addison-Wesley Educ.

***Manager's Bookshelf.** 5th ed. Jon L. Pierce. 2000. teacher ed. write for info. (*0-321-03061-3*) S&S Trade.

Manager's Bookshelf: A Mosaic of Contemporary Views. 5th ed. Jon L. Pierce. LC 99-43083. 374p. (C). 1999. pap. 46.67 (*0-321-01714-5*) Addison-Wesley.

Manager's Casebook of IT Systems. David Targett. 318p. 1998. pap. text 44.95 (*0-7506-3951-2*) Buttrwrth-Heinemann.

Manager's Complete Guide to Speech Writing. Burton Kaplan. 250p. 1988. 32.95 (*0-02-916951-8*) Free Pr.

Manager's Desk Book on Employment Law. Deborah Batterman. 1984. pap. 29.95 (*0-88057-196-9*) Exec Ent Pubns.

Manager's Desk Reference. Cynthia Berryman-Fink. LC 88-48035. 370p. 1991. pap. 19.95 (*0-8144-7759-3*) AMACOM.

Manager's Desk Reference. 2nd ed. Cynthia Berryman-Fink & Charles B. Fink. LC 96-12325. 384p. 1996. 24.95 (*0-8144-0342-5*) AMACOM.

Managers Divided: Organisation Politics & Information Technology Management. David Knights & Fergus Murray. 290p. 1995. 95.00 (*0-471-93586-7*) Wiley.

Managers-Entertainers-Agents Book, No. 6. 2nd ed. Walter E. Hurst. 1979. 15.00 (*0-911370-41-2*); pap. 10.00 (*0-911370-42-0*) Seven Arts.

Manager's Environment: An Economic Approach. G. H. Webster & J. M. Oliver. LC 78-563522. (Management Ser.). x, 275p. 1970. write for info. (*0-330-02638-0*) Pan.

Manager's Factomatic. Jack Horn. 536p. 1991. ring bd. 49.95 (*0-13-543984-1*, 140302) P-H.

Manager's Factomatic. 2nd enl. rev. ed. Jack Horn. LC 92-13095. 612p. (C). 1992. 49.95 (*0-13-562927-6*) P-H.

Manager's Guide: Basic Guidelines for the New Store Manager. Museum Store Association Inc. Staff. (Illus.). 144p. 1992. spiral bd. 55.00 (*0-9616104-2-5*) Museum Store.

Manager's Guide: Client-Server. Laurence Shafe. LC 94-25275. 144p. (C). 1995. pap. text 24.95 (*0-201-42790-7*) Addison-Wesley.

***Manager's Guide - Model Memos: The Classic Compedium of over 800 Indispensible Memos.** Cynthia A. Barnes. 464p. 1998. 8.98 (*1-56731-280-2*, MJF Bks) Fine Comms.

Manager's Guide for Monitoring Data Integrity in Financial Systems. 1997. lib. bdg. 250.95 (*0-8490-7694-3*) Gordon Pr.

Manager's Guide for Monitoring Data Integrity in Financial Systems. Roger F. Sies. (Illus.). 65p. (Orig.). (C). 1996. pap. text 30.00 (*0-7881-3733-6*) DIANE Pub.

Manager's Guide for Navigating Employee Resistance to Change. Edward E. Hubbard. 20p. 1995. pap. 9.95 (*1-883733-18-9*) Global Insghts.

Manager's Guide to Alternative Work Schedules. Waldon L. Booth. 267p. (C). 1982. pap. text 23.95 (*1-884566-00-6*) Inst Police Tech.

Manager's Guide to Audiovisuals. S. Allen. 1979. text 13.95 (*0-07-001093-5*) McGraw.

Manager's Guide to Behavioural Sciences. M. Brown. (C). 1986. 50.00 (*0-7855-4095-4*, Pub. by Witherby & Co) St Mut.

Manager's Guide to Benchmarking: Essential Skills for the New Competitive-Cooperative Economy. Jerome P. Finnigan. LC 96-15891. (Business & Management Ser.). 1996. 30.95 (*0-7879-0279-9*) Jossey-Bass.

Manager's Guide to Business Writing. Suzanne Sparks. LC 98-41552. (Briefcase Books Ser.). (Illus.). 187p. 1998. pap. 14.95 (*0-07-071867-9*) McGraw.

Manager's Guide to CAD-CAM Standards for Integration. CAD-CAM Alert Editors. Ed. by Jonathan Linden. (Illus.). 88p. (Orig.). 1986. 99.00 (*0-932007-07-4*, B48) Mgmt Roundtable.

Manager's Guide to CE Marking, ISO & Quality. David Kildahl. 500p. 1996. ring bd. 395.00 (*0-929321-33-2*) WEKA Pub.

Manager's Guide to Centrex. John R. Abrahams. LC 88-24218. 116p. reprint ed. pap. 36.00 (*0-7837-0412-7*, 204073400018) Bks Demand.

Manager's Guide to Change. Elmer H. Burack & Florence Torda. 226p. 1989. spiral bd. 19.95 (*0-942560-14-0*) Brace-Park.

Manager's Guide to Competitive Marketing Strategies 2nd ed. Norton Paley. LC 98-51466. 1999. 49.95 (*1-57444-234-1*) St Lucie Pr.

Manager's Guide to Computer-Aided Engineering. John K. Krouse. 232p. (C). 1993. pap. 51.95 (*1-56690-038-7*) Thomson Learn.

Manager's Guide to Computer Timesharing. Timothy P. Haidinger & Dana R. Richardson. LC 74-18413. (Illus.). 195p. reprint ed. pap. 60.50 (*0-7837-3447-6*, 205777100008) Bks Demand.

***Manager's Guide to Contingency Planning for Disasters: Protecting Vital Facilities & Critical Operations.** 2nd ed. Kenneth N. Myers. LC 99-38841. 234p. 1999. 39.95 (*0-471-35838-X*) Wiley.

Manager's Guide to Dealing with Difficult People. Brandon Toropov. LC 96-42916. 352p. 1997. text 39.95 (*0-13-520644-8*) P-H.

Manager's Guide to Distributed Environments. Richard Ptak et al. LC 98-8275. 368p. 1998. 39.99 (*0-471-19712-2*) Wiley.

Manager's Guide to Elder Care & Work. John P. Marosy. LC 98-6022. 224p. 1998. 55.00 (*1-56720-229-2*, Quorum Bks) Greenwood.

Manager's Guide to Employee Benefits: How to Select & Administer the Best Program for Your Company. Ronald M. Foster. LC 85-25419. 256p. reprint ed. pap. 79.40 (*0-7837-5338-1*, 204507800005) Bks Demand.

Manager's Guide to Employee Privacy: Laws, Policies, & Procedures. Kurt H. Decker. 288p. 1989. 74.95 (*0-471-50903-5*) Wiley.

Manager's Guide to Environmental Compliance. Joseph C. Berger & Edward P. Castorina. 164p. 1994. pap. 75.00 (*0-923606-07-6*) Amer CC Pubs.

Manager's Guide to Ergonomics in the Electronic Office. Marvin J. Dainoff & Marilyn H. Dainoff. LC 86-32493. (Illus.). 242p. reprint ed. pap. 75.10 (*0-7837-6728-5*, 204635600011) Bks Demand.

Manager's Guide to Excellence in Public Relations & Communication Management. David M. Dozier et al. (LEA's Communication Ser.). 272p. 1995. pap. 34.50 (*0-8058-1810-3*); text 59.95 (*0-8058-1809-X*) L Erlbaum Assocs.

Manager's Guide to Exporting. Nelson. (Management Ser.). 256p. 1999. pap. 19.99 (*1-86152-316-5*) Thomson Learn.

Manager's Guide to Financial Statement Analysis. Stephen F. Jablonsky & Noah P. Barsky. LC 97-32010. 304p. 1998. 67.95 (*0-471-24727-8*) Wiley.

Manager's Guide to Freight Loss & Damage Claims. Colin Barrett. Ed. by Ann A. Hunter. (Illus.). 232p. (C). 1989. text 37.50 (*0-87408-048-7*) Loft Pr.

***Manager's Guide to Freight Loss & Damage Claims.** 2nd ed. Colin Barrett. (Illus.). 300p. 2000. write for info. (*1-893846-52-0*) Loft Pr.

Manager's Guide to Getting the Answers. 2nd ed. Gillian A. Dare & K. G. Bakewell. LC 85-110400. (Illus.). 99p. reprint ed. pap. 30.70 (*0-7837-7012-X*, 204682600004) Bks Demand.

Manager's Guide to Globalization: Six Keys to Success in a Changing World. Stephen H. Rhinesmith. LC 92-19470. (Illus.). 240p. 1992. 30.00 (*1-55623-904-1*, Irwn Prfssnl) McGraw-Hill Prof.

Manager's Guide to Globalization: Six Skills for Success in a Changing World. 2nd rev. ed. Stephen H. Rhinesmith. LC 95-45171. (Illus.). 256p. 1996. text 29.95 (*0-7863-0545-2*, Irwn Prfssnl) McGraw-Hill Prof.

Manager's Guide to Health & Safety at Work. 3rd ed. Jeremy Stranks. 206p. 1994. pap. 67.95 (*0-8464-1370-1*) Beekman Pubs.

***Manager's Guide to Hiring the Best Person for Every Job.** DeAnne Rosenberg. LC 99-51372. 300p. 2000. pap. 18.95 (*0-471-38074-1*) Wiley.

Manager's Guide to International Business. Nelson. 256p. 1998. 20.00 (*1-86152-315-7*) Thomson Learn.

Managers' Guide to International Labour Standards. Alan Gladstone. (Management Development Ser.: No. 23). vi, 89p. 1990. pap. 15.75 (*92-2-105412-8*) Intl Labour Office.

Manager's Guide to Interpersonal Relations. Donald Sanzotta. LC 79-701. 176p. reprint ed. pap. 54.60 (*0-608-12861-9*, 202357800033) Bks Demand.

Manager's Guide to ISO 9000. Kenneth L. Arnold. LC 94-4413. 384p. 1994. 35.00 (*0-02-901035-7*) Free Pr.

Manager's Guide to Lawful Terminations. 2nd ed. Thomas L. Quick. 1990. pap. 29.95 (*1-55840-516-X*) Exec Ent Pubns.

Manager's Guide to Making Changes. Arnold S. Judson. LC 65-28641. 200p. reprint ed. pap. 62.00 (*0-608-10734-4*, 201398000088) Bks Demand.

Manager's Guide to Network Computing: Building, Competitive Advantage, Access to Information, Protecting Data, Measuring ROI, Training & Productivity. Billy Ward. 224p. 1998. 29.95 (*0-8144-7988-X*) AMACOM.

***Manager's Guide to Newsletters: Communicating for Results.** Robert F. Abbott. LC 98-910997. (Illus.). 200p. 1999. 49.95 (*0-9683287-1-7*) Wrd Eng Pr.

Manager's Guide to Occupational Health Services. Robert J. McCunney. LC 98-179273. viii, 47 p. 1996. 27.00 (*1-883595-06-1*) OEM Health.

Manager's Guide to Operational Research. Patrick Rivett & Russell L. Ackoff. LC 63-14115. (Illus.). 117p. reprint ed. pap. 36.30 (*0-7837-6394-8*, 204610700010) Bks Demand.

Manager's Guide to OSHA: What Every Manager Should Know. Neville C. Tompkins. Ed. by Brenda Machosky. LC 92-54632. (Fifty-Minute Ser.). 89p. (Orig.). 1993. pap. 10.95 (*1-56052-180-5*) Crisp Pubns.

***Managers' Guide to Preventing Sexual Harassment.** 4th ed. Susan Mathias Smith. Orig. Title: Federal Manager's Guide to Preventing Sexual Harassment. (Illus.). 65p. 1999. pap. 14.95 (*0-936295-93-7*) FPMI Comns.

Manager's Guide to Purchasing an Information System. Roscoe Sandlin. LC 97-204881. (Special Reports). 124p. 1996. pap. 42.00 (*0-87326-119-4*) Intl City-Cnty Mgt.

Manager's Guide to Quantitative Methods. Michael Cuming. 481p. (C). 1984. 69.00 (*0-946139-01-6*, Pub. by Elm Pubns) St Mut.

Manager's Guide to Real Estate Marketing. Harold L. Kahn. Ed. by Christopher Bettin. (Illus.). 176p. (Orig.). 1989. pap. 22.00 (*0-913652-66-0*, 131) Realtors Natl.

Manager's Guide to Safety Representatives. A. Dalton. 1996. pap. 145.00 (*1-85953-080-X*, Pub. by Tech Comm) St Mut.

Manager's Guide to Sexual Orientation in the Workplace. Bob Powers & Alan Ellis. LC 95-23654. 209p. (C). 1995. 31.99 (*0-415-91277-6*) Routledge.

Manager's Guide to Software Engineering. Roger S. Pressman. (Illus.). 528p. 1996. pap. 34.95 (*0-07-052229-4*) McGraw.

Manager's Guide to Solving Personnel Problems. Isobel Emmanuel. (Institute of Management Ser.). 192p. (Orig.). 1994. pap. 47.50 (*0-273-60695-6*, Pub. by Pitman Pub) Trans-Atl Phila.

Manager's Guide to Symphony: An Illustrated Short Course. Dennis P. Curtin. 160p. 1985. pap. 18.95 (*0-13-550047-8*) P-H.

Manager's Guide to Technology Forecasting & Strategy Analysis Methods. Stephen M. Millett & Edward J. Honton. LC 91-13690. 112p. 1991. pap. 19.95 (*0-935470-63-8*) Battelle.

Manager's Guide to the Antitrust Laws. Edward A. Matto. LC 79-54843. 207p. reprint ed. pap. 64.20 (*0-608-12149-5*, 202390700034) Bks Demand.

***Manager's Guide to the Law & Economics of Data Networks.** Jeffrey H. Matsuura. LC 99-89514. (Intellectual Property & Communications Law Library). 2000. 83.00 (*1-58053-020-6*) Artech Hse.

Manager's Guide to the New OSHA: Blueprints for Effective Training & Written Programs. Duane A. Daugherty. LC 95-46554. (AMA Management Briefing Ser.). 1995. write for info. (*0-8144-2360-4*) AMACOM.

Manager's Guide to the New Telecommunications Network. Lawrence Gasman. (Telecommunications Applications Library). 300p. 1988. text. write for info. (*0-89006-296-X*) Artech Hse.

Manager's Guide to the New Telecommunications Network. Lawrence Gasman. LC 88-19344. 249p. reprint ed. pap. 77.20 (*0-7837-1804-7*, 204200400001) Bks Demand.

An Asterisk (*) at the beginning of an entry indicates that the title is appearing for the first time.

Manager's Guide to Total Quality: Action Plans for Achieving the Ultimate Competitive Advantage. Tom Terez. (Illus.). 192p. (Orig.). 1992. pap. 17.95 (*0-9626463-4-2*) Arrow Assocs.

Manager's Guide to Wireless Telecommunications. Ron Schneiderman. LC 98-31108. 288p. 1998. 42.95 (*0-8144-0449-9*) AMACOM.

Manager's Guide to Workplace Ergonomics. rev. ed. 1991. ring bd. 129.95 (*1-55645-597-6*, 597) Busn Legal Reports.

Manager's Guidebook: Essays on Management Practice. Raymond C. Kutzer. (Illus.). v, 60p. 1998. pap., mass mkt. 8.95 (*0-9665081-0-6*) T-Love Ent.

Manager's Handbook. E. P. Nemec. LC 87-71781. (Illus.). 158p. (Orig.). 1987. pap. 4.45 (*0-9618998-0-8*) Nemec Pub.

Manager's Handbook, Vol. 2. Florists' Review Staff. (Illus.). 32p. (Orig.). 1996. pap. 5.95 (*0-9654149-1-4*) Florists Rev.

Managers in Distress: The St. Louis Stage, 1840-1844. William G. Carson. (Illus.). 1972. 23.95 (*0-405-08341-6*, Pub. by Blom Pubns) Ayer.

Managers in the Making: Careers, Development & Control in Corporate Britain & Japan. John Storey et al. 256p. 1997. 75.00 (*0-7619-5541-0*) Sage.

Managers in the Making: Careers, Development & Control in Corporate Britain & Japan. John Storey et al. (Illus.). 256p. 1997. pap. 32.00 (*0-7619-5542-9*) Sage.

Managers in the Middle. Harvard Business Review Staff. (People Management Ser.). 99p. 1991. pap. 19.95 (*0-87584-270-4*) Harvard Busn.

Managers in the Middle. Harvard Business Review Staff. 150p. 1991. pap. 19.95 (*0-07-103330-0*) McGraw.

Manager's Introduction to Tendering. Bob Lampitt. (C). 1991. pap. 60.00 (*0-85171-097-2*, Pub. by IPM Hse) St Mut.

Manager's Lifetime Guide to the Language of Power. Ed. by James Holtje. 544p. (C). 1997. text 34.95 (*0-13-894882-8*) P-H.

Managers Managing: The Workings of an Administrative System. Jane Hannaway. (Illus.). 192p. 1989. text 49.95 (*0-19-505207-2*) OUP.

Managers, Micros & Mainframes: Integrating Systems for End Users. fac. ed. Ed. by Matthias Jarke. LC 85-31490. (John Wiley Information Systems Ser.). (Illus.). 312p. pap. 96.80 (*0-7837-7367-6*, 204717600005) Bks Demand.

Manager's Negotiating Answer Book. George Fuller. LC 95-1458. 337p. 1995. 39.95 (*0-13-155921-4*) P-H.

***Manager's Negotiating Answer Book.** George T. Fuller. 337p. 1999. text 40.00 (*0-7881-5988-7*) DIANE Pub.

Managers of Discontent: Trade Union Officers & Industrial Relations Managers. Diane H. Watson. LC 88-4266. 224p. reprint ed. pap. 69.50 (*0-608-20401-3*, 207165400002) Bks Demand.

Managers of the Arts: Careers & Opinions of Administrators of U. S. Resident Theaters, Art Museums, Symphony Orchestras, & Community Arts Agencies. Paul DiMaggio. LC 87-9719. (Research Division Report, National Endowment for the Arts Ser.: No. 20). (Illus.). 104p. (Orig.). 1987. pap. 9.95 (*0-932020-50-X*) Seven Locks Pr.

Managers of Virtue: Public School Leadership in America, 1820-1980. David B. Tyack & Elisabeth Hansot. LC 81-22923. 312p. 1986. reprint ed. pap. 18.00 (*0-465-04374-7*, Pub. by Basic) HarpC.

Manager's Official Guide to Team Working. Jerry Spiegel & Cresencio Torres. LC 93-87074. (Illus.). 176p. 1994. pap. text 29.95 (*0-88390-408-X*) Jossey-Bass.

Manager's Overview of CATV. (Fiber Optics for the CATV Industry Reprint Ser.: Vol. 1). 1996. 29.95 (*0-614-18459-2*, 133ZAA) Info Gatekeepers.

Managers, Part of the Problem? Changing How the Public Sector Works. Camaron J. Thomas. LC 98-30538. 192p. 1999. 59.95 (*1-56720-268-3*, Quorum Bks) Greenwood.

***Manager's Pocket Guide to Creativity.** Alexander Hiam. 1998. pap. text 7.95 (*0-87425-436-1*) HRD Press.

***Manager's Pocket Guide to Documenting Employee Performance.** Terry Fitzwater. 1999. pap. 8.95 (*0-87425-447-7*) HRD Press.

Manager's Pocket Guide to Effective Meetings. Steve Kaye. 1998. pap. text 7.95 (*0-87425-445-9*) HRD Press.

Manager's Pocket Guide to Generation X. Bruce Tulgan. LC 97-226626. 1997. pap. text 7.95 (*0-87425-418-3*) HRD Press.

Manager's Pocket Guide to Performance Management. Sharon G. Fisher. LC 97-226606. 1997. pap. text 7.95 (*0-87425-419-1*) HRD Press.

Manager's Pocket Guide to Preventing Sexual Harassment. Terry Fitzwater. 1998. pap. text 7.95 (*0-87425-450-7*) HRD Press.

Manager's Pocket Guide to Systems Thinking. Stephen G. Haines. 1998. pap. text 7.95 (*0-87425-453-1*, HRD Pr) HRD Press.

Manager's Pocket Guide to Team Sponsorship. Sara Pope. 1997. pap. text 7.95 (*0-87425-421-3*) HRD Press.

Manager's Pocketbook. 3rd ed. John Townsend & Julie Perkins. 112p. 1999. pap. 8.95 (*1-57922-022-3*) Stylus Pub VA.

Manager's Portable Answer Book. George Fuller. 368p. (C). 1996. 39.95 (*0-13-226499-4*) P-H.

Manager's Portfolio of Hard to Write Business Letters. Bernard Heller. LC 97-2592. 366p. (C). 1997. 29.95 (*0-13-532441-6*) P-H.

Manager's Portfolio of Model Memos for Every Occasion. 2nd ed. Cynthia A. Barnes. LC 96-34632. 352p. (C). 1997. pap. text 16.95 (*0-13-242512-2*) P-H.

Manager's Portfolio of Model Memos for Every Occasion. 2nd rev. expanded ed. Cynthia A. Barnes. LC 96-34632. 352p. (C). 1997. text 39.95 (*0-13-242520-3*) P-H.

Manager's Portfolio of Model Performance Appraisals. Brandon Toropov. LC 99-19737. (C). 1998. 39.95 (*0-13-856451-5*) P-H.

Manager's Portfolio of Model Performances. Toropov. (C). 1998. pap. text. write for info. (*0-7352-0009-2*) PH Pr.

Manager's Responsibility for Communication. J. Garnett. (C). 1989. 35.00 (*0-7855-4094-6*, Pub. by Witherby & Co) St Mut.

Manager's Script Book. W. H. Weiss. 350p. (C). 1989. text 39.95 (*0-13-551839-3*) P-H.

Manager's Short Course to a Long Career: 101 Proven Techniques to Accelerate Your Managerial Worth. 2nd ed. Illus. by Ted Williams. 260p. 1998. reprint ed. pap. 21.95 (*1-893095-00-2*) Liberty Pubg Grp.

***Manager's Survival Guide to Organizational Change.** Kenneth A. Burger & Alvin E. Ray. 1999. pap. 14.95 (*0-936295-92-9*) FPMI Comns.

Managers Talk Ethics: Making Tough Choices in a Competitive Business World. B. L. Toffler. LC 86-13195. 372p. 1986. 40.00 (*0-471-83022-4*) Wiley.

Manager's Tool Kit: Practical Tips for Tackling 100 On-the-Job Problems. Cy Charney. LC 94-41742. 224p. 1995. pap. 17.95 (*0-8144-7881-6*) AMACOM.

Manager's Toolbox: Management Tools You Need to Succeed. Mark Kelly. 137p. (Orig.). 1997. pap. 11.95 (*0-9655417-0-3*) Thresher Pr.

Manager's Tough Question & Answer Book. Shirley Fulton & Al Guyant. 352p. (C). 1996. text 39.95 (*0-13-226515-X*) P-H.

Manager's Tough Questions & Answer Book. Al Guyant. 352p. (C). 1996. pap. text 16.95 (*0-13-226507-9*) P-H.

***Manager's Training Pocketbook.** Ian Fleming. 112p. 1999. pap. 8.95 (*1-870471-23-7*, Pub. by Mngmnt Pocketbks) Stylus Pub VA.

Manager's Troubleshooter: Pinpointing the Causes & Cures of 125 Tough Day-to-Day Problems. 2nd ed. Clay Carr & Mary Albright. 448p. (C). 1996. text 39.95 (*0-13-240318-8*) P-H.

Manager's Troubleshooter: Pinpointing the Causes & Cures of 125 Tough Supervisory Problems. Clay Carr & Mary A. Fletcher. 496p. (C). 1990. text 39.95 (*0-13-552647-7*) P-H.

Managers View Information. Arley R. MacDonald. LC 82-19570. (Illus.). 96p. reprint ed. pap. 30.00 (*0-7837-6302-6*, 204601700010) Bks Demand.

Manager's Violence Survival Guide. Francis J. D'Addario. (Illus.). 74p. (Orig.). 1995. pap. 15.00 (*0-9648103-1-X*); pap., wbk. ed. 15.00 (*0-9648103-0-1*) Crime Prevent Assocs.

Managers vs. Owners: The Struggle for Corporate Control in American Democracy. Allen Kaufman et al. (Ruffin Series in Business Ethics). 288p. 1995. pap. text 35.00 (*0-19-509860-9*) OUP.

Managers with God: A Way to Church Renewal. Daniel Kauffman. LC 89-77249. 176p. (Orig.). 1990. pap. 10.99 (*0-8361-3518-0*) Herald Pr.

Managing. Dunham & Pierce. (C). 1990. pap. text, student ed. 25.00 (*0-673-46168-8*) Addison-Wesley Educ.

Managing. Harold Geneen & Alvin Moscow. 1985. mass mkt. 4.95 (*0-380-69986-9*, Avon Bks) Morrow Avon.

Managing. Harold Geneen & Alvin Moscow. 320p. 1993. pap. 10.00 (*0-380-71943-6*, Avon Bks) Morrow Avon.

Managing. Salaman Graeme. LC 94-26581. 144p. 1995. 108.95 (*0-335-19364-1*); pap. 33.95 (*0-335-19363-3*) OpUniv Pr.

Managing: Pests in Your Collections. Michael Trinkley. (Illus.). 12p. 1994. pap. 2.00 (*1-58317-013-8*) Chicora Found.

Managing: The Museum Environment. Michael Trinkley. (Illus.). 12p. 1994. pap. 2.00 (*1-58317-014-6*) Chicora Found.

Managing: Yourself & Others. Dorrine Turecamo. 221p. (Orig.). 1986. pap. 12.95 (*0-937293-00-8*) Barrie Rd Bks.

***Managing Risks from Medical Product Use: Creating a Risk Management Framework, Report to the FDA Commissioner from the Task Force on Risk Management.** 168p. 1999. per. 16.00 (*0-16-050307-8*) USGPO.

Managing a Changing Workforce: Achieving Outstanding Service with Today's Employees. Bob Losyk. 210p. 1996. 24.95 (*0-9647393-4-8*) Workplace Trends Pub.

***Managing a Community Association: The Survival Manual for Volunteers.** Ellen De Haan & Debra H. Lewin. LC 00-29486. 2000. pap. write for info. (*0-944715-57-5*) CAI.

Managing a Cooperative Classroom. rev. ed. Carol Cummings. (Illus.). 108p. (C). 1997. reprint ed. pap. 5.00 (*1-881660-04-4*) Teaching WA.

Managing a Corporate Internet Strategy. Amit Maitra. 1996. 29.95 (*0-614-14507-4*, VNR) Wiley.

Managing a Crisis - Are You Prepared? Proceedings from a PATA Seminar Held January 20-21, 1997. Ed. by Bill Hastings. 72p. 1997. pap. write for info. (*1-882866-08-8*) Pac Asia Trvl.

Managing a Diverse Classroom. Carol Cummings. (Illus.). 132p. 1995. pap. 14.95 (*1-881660-03-6*) Teaching WA.

Managing a Diverse Workplace: Regaining the Competitive Edge. John P. Fernandez. 834p. 1991. 25.95 (*0-669-26903-4*) Jossey-Bass.

***Managing a Family Fixed Income.** Aaron S. Gurwitz. 2000. 58.00 (*1-883249-71-6*) F J Fabozzi.

Managing a Federal Agency: The Hidden Stimulus. Louis K. Bragaw. LC 79-27702. (Illus.). 320p. 1980. reprint ed. pap. 99.20 (*0-608-05929-3*, 206626500008) Bks Demand.

***Managing a Flexible Workforce.** Bureau of Business Practice Staff. LC 99-182040. 112 p. 1998. write for info. (*0-87622-774-4*) Aspen Pub.

Managing a Food Safety System. Educational Foundation of the National Restaurant. (Applied Foodservice Sanitation Ser.). 176p. (Orig.). 1993. pap. 35.00 (*0-915452-19-7*) Educ Found.

Managing a Foreign Exchange Department: A Manual of Effective Practice. 2nd ed. Ed. by Rudi Weisweiller. LC 91-36671. 240p. 1992. 79.50 (*0-89930-738-8*, WMF, Quorum Bks) Greenwood.

Managing a Global Enterprise: A Concise Guide to International Operations. William R. Feist et al. LC 98-27834. 232p. 1999. 59.95 (*1-56720-162-8*, Quorum Bks) Greenwood.

Managing a Law Firm for Survival. Jack A. Gottschalk & Robert J. Small. LC 91-78274. 143p. 1992. text 24.00 (*0-8318-0658-3*, B658) Am Law Inst.

Managing a Law Practice: The Human Side. Richard C. Reed. LC 88-70279. 95p. 1988. pap. 34.95 (*0-89707-351-7*, 511-0248) Amer Bar Assn.

Managing a Legend - Sterling Moss, Ken Gregory & the British Racing Partnership. Robert Edwards. LC 97-72863. 320p. 1997. 39.95 (*0-85429-988-2*) Haynes Manuals.

Managing a Local Area Network. Pinnacle Communications Staff. Ed. by Jacqueline Jonas & Patricia A. Menges. (Illus.). 160p. (C). pap. text 245.00 incl. audio (*0-917792-80-7*, 152) OneOnOne Comp Trng.

Managing a Management Development Institution. Ed. by Milan Kuhr. (Management Development Ser.: No. 18). viii, 277p. (Orig.). 1987. pap. 36.00 (*92-2-102955-7*) Intl Labour Office.

Managing a Material World: Perspectives in Industrial Ecology. P. Vellinga et al. LC 98-26527. (Environment & Policy Ser.). 348p. 1998. write for info. (*0-7923-5153-3*) Kluwer Academic.

Managing a Microsoft Windows NT Network: Notes from the Field. Microsoft Corporation Staff. LC 98-52142. 400p. 1999. pap. 39.99 (*0-7356-0647-1*) Microsoft.

***Managing a Modern Hospital.** A. V. Srinivasan. LC 99-54709. 2000. pap. write for info. (*0-7619-9412-2*) Sage.

Managing a Non-Profit Organization. Thomas A. Wolf. 320p. 1990. pap. 13.00 (*0-671-76415-2*) S&S Trade.

Managing a Nonprofit Organization in the Twenty-First Century. 3rd ed. Thomas Wolf. LC 99-21876. 368p. 1999. per. 13.00 (*0-684-84990-9*) S&S Trade.

Managing a Paint Shop. Robert D. Grear. LC 94-67171. (Illus.). 210p. 1994. 41.00 (*0-87263-453-1*) SME.

Managing a Programming Project: Process & People. 3rd ed. Philip W. Metzger & John Boddie. LC 95-44040. 400p. (C). 1995. 58.00 (*0-13-554239-1*) P-H.

Managing a Public Relations Firm for Growth & Profit. Ed. by A. C. Croft. LC 95-6818. (Illus.). 242p. 1995. 39.95 (*1-56024-955-2*) Haworth Pr.

Managing a Public Relations Firm for Growth & Profit. Ed. by A. C. Croft. LC 95-6818. 242p. 1997. pap. 19.95 (*0-7890-0130-6*) Haworth Pr.

Managing a Sales Force. 2nd rev. ed. Mike Wilson. 240p. 1983. text 86.95 (*0-566-02377-6*) Ashgate Pub Co.

Managing a Shoot. M. I. Roberts. (Illus.). 112p. 1990. 29.95 (*0-948253-43-6*, Pub. by Sportsmans Pr) Trafalgar.

Managing a Small HRD Department: You Can Do More Than You Think. Carol P. McCoy. LC 92-43607. (Management Ser.). 302p. 1993. 39.95 (*1-55542-529-1*) Jossey-Bass.

Managing a Successful Global Alliance. Margaret L. Cauley. 220p. (C). 1994. 31.88 (*0-201-42771-0*) Addison-Wesley.

Managing a Veterinary Practice. Jevring. 1995. pap. text 39.00 (*0-7020-1987-9*, W B Saunders Co) Harcrt Hlth Sci Grp.

Managing a Veterinary Practice in Canada. Jack Douglas. 265p. 1994. pap. text 39.00 (*0-920513-11-5*, Pub. by Sau1nders) Saunders.

Managing a Video Production Facility. Neil Heller. LC 96-21534. 128p. 1996. pap. 47.95 (*0-240-80274-8*, Focal) Buttrwrth-Heinemann.

Managing a Wildland Fire: A Practical Perspective. Donald G. Perry. Ed. by Carol C. Brooks. LC 89-84092. (Illus.). 145p. (Orig.). (C). 1989. pap. text 14.95 (*0-941943-01-1*) Fire Pubns.

Managing Academic Change: Interactive Forces & Leadership in Higher Education. S. V. Martorana & Eileen Kuhns. LC 74-27909. (Jossey-Bass Higher Education Ser.). 236p. reprint ed. pap. 73.20 (*0-608-15163-7*, 205216100045) Bks Demand.

Managing Academic Staff in Changing University Systems: International Trends & Comparisons. David Farnham & Society for Research into Higher Education Staff. LC 98-28628. 1998. 130.00 (*0-335-19961-5*) Taylor & Francis.

Managing Access & Entitlement in Primary Education. Barbara MacGilchrist. 32p. 1992. pap. 6.00 (*0-948080-76-0*, Trentham Bks) Stylus Pub VA.

***Managing Accounting Systems & Technology 2000 Yearbook.** annuals Andrew Dzamba. (Illus.). 200p. 2000. pap. 199.00 (*1-58673-025-8*) IOMA.

***Managing Accounts Payable, 2000 Yearbook.** annuals Ed. by Mary S. Schaeffer & David Solomon. (Illus.). 200p. 2000. pap. 199.00 (*1-58673-044-4*) IOMA.

Managing Acquisitions: Creating Value Through Corporate Renewal. Philippe C. Haspeslagh & David B. Jemison. 288p. 1991. text 35.00 (*0-02-914165-6*) Free Pr.

Managing Acquisitions & Vendor Relations: A How-to-Do-It Manual. Heather S. Miller. (How-to-Do-It Ser.). 196p. 1992. 49.95 (*1-55570-111-6*) Neal-Schuman.

Managing Across Borders: The Transnational Solution. Christopher A. Bartlett & Sumantra Ghoshal. 288p. 1991. pap. 16.95 (*0-87584-303-4*) Harvard Busn.

Managing Across Borders: The Transnational Solution. Christopher A. Bartlett & Sumantra Ghoshal. 1989. text 35.00 (*0-07-103208-8*) McGraw.

Managing Across Borders: The Transnational Solution. Harvard Business School Press Staff. 306p. 1992. pap. 1895.00 (*0-07-103314-9*) McGraw.

Managing Across Borders: The Transnational Solution. 2nd ed. Christopher A. Bartlett & Sumantra Ghoshal. LC 98-26004. 416p. 1998. 29.95 (*0-87584-849-4*) Harvard Busn.

Managing Across Cultures. Richard Punzo. (Management Booklets Ser.). Date not set. write for info. (*1-882390-94-6*) Princeton Trng.

Managing Across Cultures. Susan Schneider & Jean-Louis Barsoux. 320p. 1997. pap. text 46.67 (*0-13-272220-8*) P-H.

Managing Across Cultures: A Learning Framework. Meena S. Wilson et al. LC 96-36687. 37p. 1996. pap. text 15.00 (*1-882197-25-9*) Ctr Creat Leader.

Managing Across Cultures: Insights from Fiction & Practice. Sheila M. Puffer. 390p. (C). 1996. pap. text 36.95 (*1-55786-673-2*) Blackwell Pubs.

***Managing Across Cultures: Issues & Perspectives.** Pat Joynt & A. Warner. 1998. pap. 19.99 (*1-86152-350-5*) Thomson Learn.

Managing Across Cultures: Issues & Perspectives. Ed. by Pat Joynt & Malcolm Warner. 304p. 1996. pap. 77.95 (*0-415-13557-5*) Thomson Learn.

Managing Acting-Out Behavior. Geoffrey Colvin. 26p. 1992. pap. 169.00 incl. VHS (*1-57035-261-5*, 51KIT) Sopris.

Managing Acting-Out Behavior: A Staff Development Program to Prevent & Manage Acting-Out Behavior. Geoffrey Colvin. (C). 1992. ring bd. write for info. incl. VHS (*0-9631777-0-2*) Behav Assocs.

***Managing Active Directory for Windows 2000 Server.** Syngress Media Staff.Tr. of '. (Illus.). 608p. 2000. pap. 49.95 (*1-928994-07-5*) Syngress.

***Managing Activities.** Michael Armstrong. 320p. 2000. pap. 47.95 (*0-8464-5110-7*) Beekman Pubs.

Managing Acute & Chronic Urinary Incontinence. 1997. lib. bdg. 250.95 (*0-8490-7765-6*) Gordon Pr.

Managing Acute & Chronic Urinary Incontinence, Reference for Clinicians, 1996 2. J. Andrew Fantl. 30p. 1996. pap. 31.00 (*0-16-061544-5*) USGPO.

Managing Acute Symptoms. Town. (Nursing Education Ser.). 1995. pap. 20.95 (*0-8273-5683-8*) Delmar.

Managing ADA Projects Using Software Engineering. Jag Sodhi. 300p. 1989. 34.95 (*0-8306-0290-9*) McGraw-Hill Prof.

Managing Adjustment in Developing Countries: Economic & Political Perspectives. Marc M. Lindenberg & Noel Ramirez. LC 89-20119. 328p. 1990. 34.95 (*1-55815-053-6*); pap. 19.95 (*1-55815-054-4*) ICS Pr.

Managing Administration. Morgan et al. (Public Administration & Public Policy Ser.: Vol. 26). (Illus.). 280p. 1984. text 95.00 (*0-8247-7096-X*) Dekker.

***Managing Admissions, Records & the Law.** Kent M. Weeks. ix, 169p. (C). 1999. 60.00 (*1-881434-04-4*) Coll Legal Info.

Managing Advanced Manufacturing Systems. Brian Trought. LC 94-15636. 192p. 1994. 66.95 (*1-85628-898-6*, Pub. by Avebry) Ashgate Pub Co.

Managing Advanced Manufacturing Technology: Proceedings of the U. K. Operations Management Association Conference, 2-3 January, 1986. Ed. by Q. A. Voss. (Illus.). 460p. 1986. 206.95 (*0-387-16865-6*) Spr-Verlag.

Managing Affordable Housing: A Practical Guide to Creating Stable Communities. Bennett L. Hecht & James Stockard. LC 95-45579. (Nonprofit Law, Finance, & Management Ser.). (Illus.). 328p. 1996. 130.00 (*0-471-14064-3*) Wiley.

Managing Affordable Housing: A Practical Guide to Creating Stable Communities. Bennett L. Hecht & James Stockard. 192p. 1997. pap., suppl. ed. 55.00 (*0-471-16767-3*) Wiley.

Managing Africa's Economic Recovery. Ed. & Intro. by Phillip LeBel. 72p. 1987. pap. 7.00 (*0-944572-00-6*) MSU Ctr Econ Res Africa.

Managing Aggressive Behavior: Participant Manual. 2nd ed. Gay Phillips et al. (Illus.). 110p. 1997. student ed., wbk. ed. 10.95 (*1-878848-19-4*) Natl Res Ctr.

Managing Aggressive Behavior: Trainer's Guide. 2nd ed. Gay Phillips et al. 262p. 1997. teacher ed., ring bd. 100.00 (*1-878848-18-6*, 200C) Natl Res Ctr.

Managing Aggressive Behavior: Trainer's Guide & Participant Manual. 2nd ed. Gay Phillips et al. (Illus.). 372p. 1997. teacher ed., student ed., ring bd. 110.95 (*1-878848-17-8*, 200) Natl Res Ctr.

Managing Aging & Human Service Agencies. Edward E. Morgan, Jr. & John Hiltner. LC 91-5227. 168p. 1992. 27.95 (*0-8261-7810-3*) Springer Pub.

***Managing Agricultural Biotechnology: Addressing Research Program Needs & Policy Implications.** Joel I. Cohen. LC 99-57155. (Biotechnology in Agriculture Ser.). 350p. 2000. 85.00 (*0-85199-400-8*) OUP.

Managing Agricultural Chemicals in the Environment: The Case for a Multimedia Approach. Thomas E. Waddell & Blair T. Bower. LC 88-30246. (Illus.). 88p. (Orig.). 1988. reprint ed. pap. 30.00 (*0-608-04184-X*, 206491900011) Bks Demand.

Managing Agricultural Residues. Paul W. Unger. 764p. 1994. lib. bdg. 110.00 (*0-87371-730-9*, L730) Lewis Pubs.

Managing Agriculture Contamination of Ground Water: State Strategies. Sandra S. Batie et al. Ed. by Gerry R. Feinstein. 50p. (Orig.). 1989. pap. text 10.00 (*1-55877-057-7*) Natl Governor.

M

An Asterisk (*) at the beginning of an entry indicates that the title is appearing for the first time.

Managing Agriculture for a Better Tomorrow: The Indian Experience. Ed. by D. C. Pande. LC 98-901504. 468p. 1998. pap. 250.00 (*81-7533-067-8*, Pub. by Print Hse) St Mut.

Managing AIDS: Organizational Responses in Seven European Countries. Ed. by Patrick Kenis & Bernd Marin. LC 98-149925. (Public Policy & Social Welfare Ser.: Vol. 18). (Illus.). 400p. 1997. pap. text 46.95 (*1-85972-126-5*, Pub. by Ashgate Pub) Ashgate Pub Co.

Managing AIDS & HIV: A Practical Guide to Achieving Best Practice. A. Christie. 1996. pap. 129.00 (*1-85953-075-3*, Pub. by Tech Comm) St Mut.

Managing Air Pollution Along The US-Mexico Border. Ghosh & Molina. 59.95 (*1-84014-549-8*) Ashgate Pub Co.

Managing Alcoholism: Matching Clients to Treatment. Lars Lindstrom. (Illus.). 390p. 1992. text 69.50 (*0-19-261902-0*) OUP.

Managing American Wildlife: A History of the International Association of Fish & Wildlife Agencies. Dian O. Belanger. LC 87-30065. 264p. 1988. pap. 18.95 (*0-87023-609-1*) U of Mass Pr.

Managing America's Aging Bridge Systems: Issues & Directions. Ed. by Bernard J. Haber & Neal H. Bettigole. LC 90-86075. 1991. pap. text 30.00 (*0-939204-45-2*) Eng Found.

Managing America's Cities: A Handbook for Local Government Productivity. Roger L. Kemp. LC 97-24235. 470p. 1998. lib. bdg. 55.00 (*0-7864-0408-6*) McFarland & Co.

Managing an Alliance: The Politics of U. S. - Japanese Relations. I. M. Destler et al. LC 75-44501. 224p. 1976. 32.95 (*0-8157-1820-9*); pap. 12.95 (*0-8157-1819-5*) Brookings.

Managing an Alliance: The Politics of U. S. - Japanese Relations. I. M. Destler et al. LC 75-44501. 219p. reprint ed. pap. 67.90 (*0-608-17499-8*, 203000600067) Bks Demand.

Managing an Effective Inservice Program. large type ed. Susan M. Swap. 78p. 1984. pap. text 15.95 (*0-8077-2855-1*) Tchrs Coll.

Managing an Effective Operation. Paul Graves & Eddie Fowler. 224p. 1995. pap. text 37.95 (*0-7506-2031-5*) Buttrwrth-Heinemann.

Managing an Estate Planning Practice. rev. ed. Irving Kellogg. Ed. by Carine Archer. LC 92-70923. 478p. 1992. ring bd. 110.00 (*0-88124-483-X*, ES-31940) Cont Ed Bar-CA.

Managing an Estate Planning Practice: September 1994 Update. rev. ed. Irving Kellogg. Ed. by Mary Gerber. LC 92-70923. 120p. 1994. 25.00 (*0-88124-798-7*, ES-31941) Cont Ed Bar-CA.

Managing an Integrated Language Arts Classroom: Practical Strategies for Record Keeping... Linda P. Picciotto. 1996. pap. text 9.95 (*0-590-24543-0*) Scholastic Inc.

Managing & Allocating Time: Industrial. Harvey Lieberman & Erwin Rausch. 1976. pap. 26.25 (*0-89401-060-3*) Didactic Syst.

Managing & Allocating Time (Non-Industrial) Harvey Lieberman & Erwin Rausch. (Simulation Game Ser.). 1976. pap. 26.25 (*0-89401-061-1*) Didactic Syst.

Managing & Being Managed: Preparation for Reintegrated Professional Nursing Practice. rev. ed. Teddy L. Langford. (Illus.). 352p. (C). 1990. pap. text 26.95 (*0-9626604-1-8*) Landover Pub.

Managing & Communicating: Your Questions & Answers. Lyn Longridge. LC 98-15830. (Practice Manager Library). 1998. write for info. (*1-85775-233-3*, Radcliffe Med Pr) Scovill Paterson.

Managing & Coordinating Nursing Care. 3rd ed. Janice Rider Ellis & Celia Love Hartley. LC 99-41445. 400p. 1999. pap. text 29.95 (*0-7817-1757-4*) Lppncott W & W.

Managing & Coping with Anger. Leonard Ingram. 52p. 1998. pap. 11.95 (*1-893745-04-X*) Royal House.

Managing & Developing New Forms of Work Organisation. Ed. by George Kanawaty et al. (Management Development Ser.: No. 16). viii, 206p. 1991. pap. 22.50 (*92-2-102707-4*) Intl Labour Office.

Managing & Developing People in the Virtual Organization. Michael Colky et al. Date not set. write for info. (*1-57524-080-7*) Krieger.

*__Managing & Developing Websites & New Media Projects.__ 2nd ed. Roy Strauss & Patrick Hogan. (Illus.). 256p. 2001. pap. 26.95 (*0-240-80443-0*, Focal) Buttrwrth-Heinemann.

Managing & Maintaining Microsoft Exchange Server 5.5. Microsoft Consulting Services Staff. LC 98-22195. 300p. 39.99 incl. cd-rom (*0-7356-0529-7*) Microsoft.

Managing & Maintaining PCs. 2nd ed. Course Technology Staff. (C). 1998. pap. 35.00 (*0-7600-5073-2*) Course Tech.

Managing & Maintaining Your PC. Jean Andrews. (DC - Introduction to Computing Ser.). 320p. 1996. mass mkt. 27.95 (*0-7895-0654-8*) Course Tech.

Managing & Maintaining Your PC. Jean Andrews. (Networking Ser.). (C). 1998. pap. 37.00 (*0-7600-1116-8*) Course Tech.

Managing & Maintaining Your PC. Jean Andrews. (Networking Ser.). (C). 1998. pap., teacher ed. 18.50 (*0-7600-1117-6*) Course Tech.

*__Managing & Maintaining Your PC Marketing Piece.__ Course Technology Incorporated Staff. (Programming Ser.). (C). 1999. pap. write for info. (*0-619-01560-8*) Course Tech.

*__Managing & Marketing Technology.__ David Ford & Mike Saren. (ITBP Textbooks Ser.). 2000. write for info. (*1-86152-594-X*, Pub. by ITBP) Thomson Learn.

Managing & Marketing the Private Client Department. Brendan Hall. 100p. 1999. pap. 63.00 (*1-85811-154-4*, Pub. by CLT Prof) Gaunt.

Managing & Minimizing Construction Waste: A Practical Guide. J. Ferguson et al. 64p. 1995. 24.00 (*0-7277-2023-6*) Am Soc Civil Eng.

Managing & Modelling Complex Projects: Proceedings of the NATO Advanced Research Workshop, Kiev, Ukraine, 13-15 November 1996. Ed. by Terry M. Williams. LC 97-41583. (NATO ASI Ser.). 257p. 1997. 157.50 (*0-7923-4844-3*) Kluwer Academic.

Managing & Operating a Closely-Held Corporation. Michael Diamond. LC 90-24802. 243p. 1991. 135.00 (*0-471-52107-8*) Wiley.

Managing & Optimizing Your PC. Steven J. Vaughan-Nichols. (Illus.). 450p. 1999. pap. text 34.95 (*0-12-715170-2*) Morgan Kaufmann.

Managing & Preventing Arthritis: The Natural Alternatives. unabridged ed. George L. Redmon. LC 98-45831. 192p. 1999. pap. 12.95 (*0-934252-90-4*, Pub. by Hohm Pr) SCB Distributors.

*__Managing & Preventing Prostate Disorders: The Natural Alternatives.__ George L. Redmon. 185p. 2000. pap. 12.95 (*0-934252-97-1*, Pub. by Hohm Pr) SCB Distributors.

Managing & Training People. Edward M. Harwell. LC 74-80815. (Illus.). 1991. pap. 29.95 (*0-86730-308-5*) Lebhar Friedman.

Managing & Training Personnel in the Golf Facility. unabridged ed. (NGF Info Pacs Ser.). (Illus.). 134p. (Orig.). 1998. pap. 45.00 (*1-57701-012-4*, 99LB013) Natl Golf.

Managing & Understanding Parental Anger. rev. ed. Harriet H. Barrish & I. J. Barrish. LC 89-22503. (Coping Parent Ser.). 64p. 1989. pap. 6.95 (*0-933701-41-1*) Westport Pubs.

Managing Anger. Helen O'Neill. 1999. pap. 36.95 (*1-86156-107-5*) Whurr Pub.

Managing Anger: A Handbook of Proven Techniques. Anger Clinic Staff & Mithcell Messer. 320p. 1994. pap. text, per. 18.95 (*0-8403-9372-5*) Kendall-Hunt.

Managing Anger: A Handbook of Proven Techniques. Mitchell H. Messer et al. (Illus.). 303p. 1992. pap. 14.95 (*0-9636776-0-8*) Anger Inst.

Managing Anger: An Adults-in-Recovery Workbook. Dennis Daley. 32p. pap. 11.95 (*1-55691-173-4*) Learning Pubns.

Managing Anger: Methods for a Happier & Healthier Life. Rebecca Luhn. Ed. by Elaine Brett. LC 91-76242. (Fifty-Minute Ser.). (Illus.). 111p. (Orig.). 1992. pap. 10.95 (*1-56052-114-7*) Crisp Pubns.

Managing Anxiety: A Training Manual. 2nd ed. Helen Kennerley. (Illus.). 226p. 1995. pap. text 38.50 (*0-19-262442-3*) OUP.

Managing Aquatic Ecosystems. Ed. by H. A. Nix & M. A. Elliott. 174p. (C). 1975. text 100.00 (*0-909436-01-0*, Pub. by Surrey Beatty & Sons) St Mut.

Managing Aquatic Vegetation with Grass Carp. Ed. by J. R. Cassani. LC 96-78895. 194p. 1996. pap. 25.00 (*1-888569-02-6*, 530.26) Am Fisheries Soc.

Managing Archaeology. Ed. by John Carmen et al. LC 94-47092. (TAG Ser.). (Illus.). 280p. (C). (gr. 13). 1995. 75.00 (*0-415-10674-5*, C0033) Routledge.

Managing Architectural Projects: The Effective Project Manager. 1996. pap. 14.00 (*0-913962-37-6*, M730) AIA Press.

Managing Architectural Projects: The Process. 1996. pap. 25.00 (*0-913962-31-7*, M727) AIA Press.

Managing Architectural Projects: The Project Management Manual. 1996. pap. 25.00 (*0-913962-69-4*, M733) AIA Press.

Managing Architectural Projects: Three Case Studies. 1996. pap. 25.00 (*1-55835-102-7*, M732) AIA Press.

Managing Archival & Manuscript Repositories. Thomas Wilsted & William Nolte. (Archival Fundamentals Ser.). 120p. 1991. pap. 27.00 (*0-931828-78-3*) Soc Am Archivists.

Managing Archives & Archival Institutions. Ed. by James G. Bradsher. 320p. 1991. pap. text 23.00 (*0-226-07055-7*) U Ch Pr.

Managing Archives & Archival Institutions: A Handbook of Theories & Practices. Ed. by James G. Bradsher. LC 88-15893. xvi, 304p. 1993. 45.00 (*0-226-07054-9*) U Ch Pr.

Managing Arms in Peace Process: Cambodia. Jianwei Wang & United Nations Institute for Disarmament Research. LC 96-198802. (Disarmament & Conflict Resolution Project Ser.). 280p. 40.00 (*92-9045-111-4*) UN.

Managing Arms in Peace Process: Croatia & Bosnia-Herzegovina. LC 97-103825. (Disarmament & Conflict Resolution Project Ser.). 448p. 46.00 (*92-9045-110-6*) UN.

Managing Arms in Peace Process: Haiti. LC 97-192449. (Disarmament & Conflict Resolution Project Ser.). 136p. 28.00 (*92-9045-120-3*) UN.

Managing Arms in Peace Process: Liberia. LC 97-119591. (Disarmament & Conflict Resolution Project Ser.). 142p. 25.00 (*92-9045-117-3*) UN.

Managing Arms in Peace Process: Mozambique. LC 97-108005. (Disarmament & Conflict Resolution Project Ser.). 134p. 25.00 (*92-9045-113-0*) UN.

Managing Arms in Peace Process: Rhodesia/Zimbabwe. LC 96-167530. (Disarmament & Conflict Resolution Project Ser.). 147p. 22.00 (*92-9045-109-2*) UN.

Managing Arms in Peace Process: Somalia. United Nations Institute for Disarmament Research. LC 96-154398. (Disarmament & Conflict Resolution Project Ser.). 259p. 42.00 (*92-9045-106-8*) UN.

Managing Arms in Peace Processes: Aspects of Psychological Operations & Intelligence. LC 97-103826. (Disarmament & Conflict Resolution Project Ser.). 64p. pap. 15.00 (*92-9045-116-5*) UN.

Managing Arms in Peace Processes: Nicaragua & El Salvador. United Nations Institute for Disarmament Research. (Disarmament & Conflict Resolution Project Ser.). 244p. 1997. pap. 35.00 (*92-9045-121-1*, 85688) UN.

Managing Arms in Peace Processes: The Issues. LC 98-102516. (Disarmament & Conflict Resolution Project Ser.). 256p. 28.00 (*92-9045-119-X*) UN.

Managing As a Performing Art: New Ideas for a World of Chaotic Change. Peter B. Vaill. LC 88-32842. (Management Ser.). 260p. 1991. reprint ed. pap. 22.50 (*1-55542-369-8*) Jossey-Bass.

Managing Asbestos: OSHA & More. Daniel Swartzman & Neil Silins. pap. 39.95 (*1-57203-009-7*) Inst Real Estate.

Managing Asbestos in Place: A Building Owner's Guide to Maintenance & Operations Programs for Asbestos-Containing Materials. 1991. lib. bdg. 69.95 (*0-8490-4226-7*) Gordon Pr.

Managing Asbestos in Place: A Building Owner's Guide to Operations & Maintenance Programs for Asbestos-Containing Materials. Robert Jordan. (Illus.). 40p. (Orig.). (C). 1994. pap. text 25.00 (*0-7881-1481-6*) DIANE Pub.

Managing Assertively: How to Improve Your People Skills. 2nd ed. Madelyn Burley-Allen. LC 94-32607. (Self-Teaching Guides Ser.). 240p. 1995. pap. 17.95 (*0-471-03971-3*) Wiley.

Managing Assessment Processes: Prediction, Interaction & Control. D. Iles. LC 97-30466. (Managing Work & Organizations Ser.). 144p. 1998. 85.00 (*0-335-19037-5*); pap. 27.95 (*0-335-19036-7*) OpUniv Pr.

Managing Asset-Liability Portfolios. v, 69p. 1992. pap. text 30.00 (*1-879087-16-2*) Assn I M&R.

Managing Assets for Individual Investors. Ed. by Sanjiv Bhatia. 94p. (Orig.). 1995. pap. text 30.00 (*1-879087-53-7*) RFICFA.

Managing Associate Staff: Innovation in Primary & Secondary Schools. Peter Mortimore et al. 192p. 1993. pap. 37.50 (*1-85396-231-7*, Pub. by P Chapman) Taylor & Francis.

Managing Association Turnarounds. Charles E. Bartling. LC 98-232659. xvi, 139 p. 1997. pap. 41.95 (*0-88034-131-9*) Am Soc Assn Execs.

*__Managing Asthma.__ 2nd ed. M. Weinberger. (Illus.). 350p. 2001. pap. 42.95 (*1-85070-972-6*) Prthnon Pub.

Managing at the Speed of Change: Guidelines for Resilience in Turbulent Times. Daryl R. Conner. LC 92-20753. 1993. 24.95 (*0-679-40684-0*) Villard Books.

Managing Attention & Learning Disorders: Survival Skills for Adults with Learning or Attention Difficulties. Elaine K. McEwan. LC 97-2831. 186p. 1997. pap. 11.99 (*0-87788-181-2*, H Shaw Pubs) Waterbrook Pr.

Managing Attention & Learning Disorders in Late Adolescence & Adulthood: A Guide for Practitioners. Sam Goldstein. LC 96-6743. 512p. 1996. 75.00 (*0-471-07662-7*) Wiley.

*__Managing Attention Deficit Hyperactivity Disorder in Children: A Guide for Practitioners.__ 2nd ed. Sam Goldstein & Michael Goldstein. LC 97-36626. 896p. 1998. 85.00 (*0-471-12158-4*) Wiley.

Managing Attention Deficits. 2nd rev. ed. Ed. by William H. Burke. (Professional Series on Traumatic Brain Injury: Vol. 7). 52p. 1996. pap. 9.50 (*1-882855-49-3*) HDI Pubs.

Managing Attention Disorders in Children: A Guide for Practitioners. Sam Goldstein & Michael Goldstein. (Personality Processes Ser.). 464p. 1993. text 195.00 incl. VHS (*0-471-30317-8*) Wiley.

Managing Attitudes, Affirmation & Assertion see Leisure Wellness Series

Managing Audiovisual Records. William T. Murphy. (Illus.). 51p. (C). 1998. pap. text 25.00 (*0-7881-4766-8*) DIANE Pub.

Managing AutoCAD in the Design Firm: A Manual for Architects & Interior Designers. Karen A. Vagts. LC 95-41307. 512p. (C). 1996. pap. text 29.95 (*0-201-48960-0*) Addison-Wesley.

Managing Autonomous Schools: The Grant-Maintained Experience. Tony Bush et al. 241p. 1993. pap. 33.00 (*1-85396-202-3*, Pub. by P Chapman) Taylor & Francis.

Managing Back, Mugged by Reality. Dan Angel & Mike DeVault. 272p. 25.00 (*1-878096-37-0*, Epigram Pr) Best E TX Pubs.

Managing Back Pain. Michael S. Melnick et al. (Orig.). 1989. pap. text 4.00 (*0-9616461-6-0*) Saunders Grp.

Managing Bandwidth: Deploying QOS Across Enterprise Networks. Alistair Croll & Eric Packman. LC 99-35921. 450p. (C). 1999. 49.99 (*0-13-011391-3*, Pub. by P-H) S&S Trade.

Managing Bank Capital: Capital Allocation & Performance Measurement. Chris Matten. LC 95-53023. 224p. 1996. 155.00 (*0-471-96116-7*) Wiley.

*__Managing Bank Capital: Capital Allocation & Performance Measurement.__ 2nd ed. Matten. LC 99-59514. 350p. 2000. text 95.00 (*0-471-85196-5*) Wiley.

Managing Bank Conversions. Kent S. Belasco. LC 96-3563. 1996. text 60.00 (*0-7863-0735-8*, Irwn Prfssnl) McGraw-Hill Prof.

Managing Banking Relationships. Ed. by Gerald Leahy. 160p. 1997. 135.00 (*1-85573-326-9*, Pub. by Woodhead Pubng) Am Educ Systs.

*__Managing Banking Risks.__ Eddie Cade. 237p. 1999. 65.00 (*1-888998-63-6*) Glenlake Pub.

Managing Banking Risks. Eddie Cade. (Gresham Bks.). 256p. 1997. boxed set 155.00 (*1-85573-206-8*, Pub. by Woodhead Pubng) Am Educ Systs.

Managing Banking Risks: Reducing Uncertainty to Improve Bank Performance. Eddie Cade. LC 00-551058. (Illus.). 237p. 1999. 65.00 (*0-8144-0506-1*) AMACOM.

*__Managing Banking Risks: Reducing Uncertainty to Improve Bank Performance.__ Eddie Cade. 250p. 1999. 65.00 (*1-57958-098-X*) Fitzroy Dearborn.

Managing Bar & Beverage Operations. Lendal H. Kotschevar & Mary L. Tanke. LC 91-13954. (Illus.). 560p. 1996. pap. write for info. (*0-86612-113-7*) Educ Inst Am Hotel.

Managing Basic Skills Program. Ed. by Contemporary Book Editors. 1977. pap. 0.40 (*0-8092-7398-5*) NTC Contemp Pub Co.

*__Managing Behavior in Organizations.__ 2nd ed. 1998. write for info. (*0-13-010071-4*) P-H.

Managing Behavior in Organizations. 2nd ed. Jerald Greenberg. LC 98-38988. 380p. (C). 1998. pap. text 49.33 (*0-13-922790-3*) P-H.

Managing Behavior in the Primary School. 2nd ed. Jim Docking. 160p. 1996. pap. 24.95 (*1-85346-397-3*, Pub. by David Fulton) Taylor & Francis.

Managing Behavior on the Job: Performance Improvement. Paul L. Brown. LC 81-23063. 208p. 1982. pap. 18.95 (*0-471-86516-8*) Wiley.

Managing Behavior Problems in Children: A Guide for Parents. Reeta Peshawaria. 1991. pap. text 4.95 (*0-7069-5322-3*, Pub. by Vikas) S Asia.

Managing Behavioral Processes: Applications of Theory & Research. Richard E. Simmons. Ed. by Kenneth D. Mackenzie. LC 77-86007. (Organizational Behavior Ser.). (Illus.). (C). 1978. pap. text 15.95 (*0-88295-454-7*) Harlan Davidson.

Managing Behaviors. Warger. 1998. pap. text 43.00 (*0-12-784566-6*) Acad Pr.

Managing Behaviors: A Therapist's Guide. Cynthia Warger & Juane Heflin. 153p. 1994. pap. text 45.00 (*0-7616-7182-X*) Commun Skill.

Managing Behavioural Treatment: Policy & Practice with Delinquent Adolescents. Clive R. Hollin et al. LC 94-16008. (International Library of Psychology). 256p. (C). 1994. text 62.95 (*0-415-05005-7*, A7774) Routledge.

Managing Behavioural Treatment: Policy & Practice with Delinquent Adolescents. Clive R. Hollin et al. LC 94-16008. (International Library of Psychology). 256p. (C). 1995. pap. 27.99 (*0-415-05006-5*, A7778) Routledge.

Managing Better Schools & Colleges: The Action Research Way. Ed. by Pamela Lomax. (BERA Dialogues Ser.: No. 5). 134p. 1991. 69.00 (*1-85359-145-9*, Pub. by Multilingual Matters); pap. 24.95 (*1-85359-144-0*, Pub. by Multilingual Matters) Taylor & Francis.

Managing Beyond the Ordinary: Using Collaboration to Solve Problems, Make Decisions, & Achieve Extraordinary Results. Charles H. Kepner & Hirotsugu Ikubo. 232p. 1998. text 23.00 (*0-7881-5868-6*) DIANE Pub.

Managing Beyond the Quick Fix: A Completely Integrated Program for Creating & Maintaining Organizational Success. Ralph H. Kilmann. LC 88-46084. (Management Ser.). 256p. 1991. pap. 21.95 (*1-55542-376-0*) Jossey-Bass.

Managing Big Business: Essays from the Business History Review. Richard S. Tedlow & Richard R. John, Jr. 1986. text 30.00 (*0-07-103271-1*) McGraw.

Managing Biotechnology in Drug Development. Chi-Jen Lee. 192p. 1996. boxed set 119.95 (*0-8493-9466-X*) CRC Pr.

Managing Bloodborne Pathogens: Guidelines for Transit Managers. 7th ed. Erskine S. Walther. LC 94-77291. (Illus.). 102p. 1997. spiral bd. 50.00 (*1-885327-11-0*) Walther Cnslt.

Managing Brainpower: How to Increase Productivity & Success in the Professional Design Firm, 3 vols. Charles B. Thomsen. 400p. 1988. pap. 12.95 (*1-55835-001-2*) AIA Press.

Managing Brand Equity: Capitalizing on the Value of a Brand Name. David A. Aaker. 224p. 1991. 32.95 (*0-02-900101-3*) Free Pr.

*__Managing Brand Equity: Capitalizing on the Value of a Brand Name.__ David A. Aaker. (Illus.). 299p. 2000. reprint ed. 35.00 (*0-7881-9336-8*) DIANE Pub.

*__Managing Budgets.__ Stephen Brookson. (Illus.). 72p. 2000. pap. 6.95 (*0-7894-5969-8*) DK Pub Inc.

Managing Buildings & Building Services in Great Britain. Ed. by Gower Publications Staff. 1973. pap. 34.95 (*0-8464-0595-4*) Beekman Pubs.

Managing Business & Engineering Projects: Concepts & Implementation. John M. Nicholas. LC 89-37577. 496p. 1989. 93.33 (*0-13-551854-7*) P-H.

Managing Business Archives. Ed. by Alison Turton. LC 91-20212. 478p. reprint ed. pap. 148.20 (*0-608-20238-X*, 207149700012) Bks Demand.

Managing Business Bankruptcy. Ernest B. Williams, 4th. 1996. 84.00 (*0-89982-444-7*) Am Bankers.

Managing Business Collections in Libraries. Carolyn A. Sheehy. LC 96-2760. (Greenwood Library Management Collection). 296p. 1996. lib. bdg. 75.00 (*0-313-29650-2*) Greenwood.

Managing Business Communications. Judith B. Bogert & Karla Worley. (C). 1987. pap. text 36.80 (*0-13-548629-7*) P-H.

Managing Business Communications: An Applied Process Approach. Judith B. Bogert & Rebecca B. Worley. (Illus.). 480p. (C). 1988. pap. text. write for info. (*0-318-62138-X*) P-H.

Managing Business Ethics. John Drummond. Ed. by Bill Bain. 1994. pap. text 46.95 (*0-7506-0663-0*) Buttrwrth-Heinemann.

Managing Business Ethics: A Reader on Business Ethics for Managers & Students. Ed. by John Drummond & Bill Bain. LC 94-150795. (Management Readers Ser.). (Illus.). 223p. reprint ed. pap. 69.20 (*0-608-07420-9*, 206764700009) Bks Demand.

An Asterisk (*) at the beginning of an entry indicates that the title is appearing for the first time.

Managing Business Ethics in Global Economy: Basic Business 207. 362p. (C). 1997. text 125.00 (*0-536-59917-3*) Pearson Custom.

Managing Business Ethics 2/e. 2nd ed. Linda K. Trevino & Katherine A. Nelson. LC 98-37440. 352p. 1999. pap. 49.95 (*0-471-24652-2*) Wiley.

***Managing Business Finance.** David R. Myddelton. LC 99-89251. 2000. pap. write for info. (*0-273-64645-1*) F T P-H.

Managing Business Improvement & Quality: Implementing Key Tools & Techniques. Barrie Dale & Ruth McQuater. 200p. (C). 1998. text 68.95 (*0-631-20787-2*) Blackwell Pubs.

Managing Business Improvement & Quality: Implementing Key Tools & Techniques. Barrie Dale & Ruth McQuater. 200p. (C). 1998. pap. text 34.95 (*0-631-20788-0*) Blackwell Pubs.

Managing Business in a Changing Europe: Papers from a PATA Tourism Forum Held March 1-2, 1993. 129p. 1993. pap. 50.00 (*1-882866-34-7*) Pac Asia Trvl.

***Managing Business in Hungary: An International Perspective: Transition, Competitiveness & Economic Growth.** Ed. by Jozsef Beracs & Attila Chikan. LC 99-227257. 506p. 1999. 78.00 (*963-05-7598-1*, Pub. by Akade Kiado) Intl Spec Bk.

Managing Business Networks: An Inquiry into Managerial Knowledge in the Multimedia Industry. Christine Prange. LC 99-34927. (Illus.). XVI, 332p. 1999. pap. text 56.95 (*0-8204-3512-0*) P Lang Pubng.

Managing Business Process Flow. Anupindi. 1998. 19.25 (*0-07-232496-1*) McGraw.

Managing Business Process Flows. (C). 1999. write for info. (*0-13-015998-0*) P-H.

Managing Business Process Flows. 232p. (C). 1998. pap. text 22.00 (*0-536-00973-2*) Pearson Custom.

Managing Business Process Flows. 2nd ed. Anupindi. 328p. 1998. pap. text 31.20 (*0-536-01357-8*) S&S Trade.

***Managing Business Relationships.** I. D. Ford. LC 97-45553. 304p. 1998. pap. 54.95 (*0-471-97075-1*) Wiley.

***Managing Business Risk: An Organization-Wide Approach to Risk Management.** Peter C. Young & Steven C. Tippins. LC 00-42014. 2000. 69.95 (*0-8144-0461-8*) AMACOM.

Managing Business Risks: An Integrated Approach. (Research Reports: No. F850). 1995. 295.00 (*0-85058-850-2*) Economist Intell.

Managing Business Risks in the Information Age. Arthur Andersen. LC 99-194068. 1998. 595.00 (*0-85058-943-6*) Economist Intell.

Managing Business Transactions: Controlling the Cost of Coordinating, Communicating, & Decision Making. Paul H. Rubin. 225p. 1990. 32.95 (*0-02-927595-4*) Free Pr.

Managing Business Transactions: Controlling the Cost of Coordinating, Communicating, & Decision Making. Paul H. Rubin. 225p. 1993. pap. 19.95 (*0-02-927596-2*) Free Pr.

Managing Business Travel & Savvy Business Travel Package. Darryl Jenkins. 1992. 89.95 (*1-55623-962-9*, Irwn Prfssnl) McGraw-Hill Prof.

Managing by Consultation: Global & Asian Experience. Rama M. Kuppachi. LC 92-18619. (Illus.). 300p. (C). 1992. 32.00 (*0-8039-9433-8*) Sage.

Managing by Influence. Kenneth Schatz & Linda Schatz. 252p. 1986. 21.95 (*0-13-550591-7*, Busn) P-H.

Managing by Influence. Kenneth Schatz & Linda Schatz. LC 94-60457. 202p. 1994. reprint ed. pap. 19.00 (*0-9641364-0-6*) Windy Ent.

Managing by Listening Around: 21 Keys to Smarter Listening. Kittie W. Watson & Larry L. Barker. 1995. 6.95 (*1-877936-07-3*) SPECTRA Inc.

Managing by Measuring: How to Improve Your Organization's Performance Through Effective Benchmarking. Mark T. Czarnecki. LC 98-35080. xi, 271 p. 1999. 50.95 (*0-8144-0390-5*) AMACOM.

Managing by Priority: Thinking Strategically, Acting Effectively. Giorgio Merli. LC 96-28873. 252p. 1996. 74.50 (*0-471-96656-8*) Wiley.

***Managing by Remote Control.** Peter R. Garber. LC 99-173815. 264p. 1998. boxed set 34.95 (*1-57444-238-4*) St Lucie Pr.

Managing by Standards Skills see Productive Supervisor: A Program of Practical Managerial Skills

Managing by Storying Around. David M. Armstrong. 249p. 1995. pap. 14.00 (*0-9648027-1-6*) D M Armstrong.

Managing by the Law of the Sphere: How to Organize a Business for Maximum Profitability. David Y. Blum. (Illus.). 134p. 1999. 17.95 (*1-58244-014-X*) Rutledge Bks.

***Managing by the Numbers: A Common Sense Guide to Using Your Company's Financials.** Chuck Kremer et al. 180p. 2000. pap. 15.95 (*1-58230-019-4*, 60206) Inc Pub MA.

***Managing by the Numbers: A Complete Guide to Understanding & Using Your Company's Financials.** Chuck Kremer et al. 224p. 2000. pap. text 16.00 (*0-7382-0256-8*, Pub. by Perseus Pubng) HarpC.

Managing by the Numbers: Monitoring Your Firm's Profitability. David W. Cottle. LC 92-38936. 1992. 30.00 (*0-87051-127-0*) Am Inst CPA.

Managing by Values. Kenneth Blanchard et al. LC 96-45613. (Illus.). 154p. 1997. 20.00 (*1-57675-007-8*) Berrett-Koehler.

Managing Caddie Programs. unabridged ed. (NGF Info Pacs Ser.). (Illus.). 123p. (Orig.). 1998. pap. 45.00 (*1-57701-003-5*, 99LB011) Natl Golf.

***Managing Campus Conflict Through Alternative Dispute Resolution.** Kent M. Weeks. 181p. (C). 1999. 60.00 (*1-881434-18-4*) Coll Legal Info.

***Managing Canada Geese in Urban Environments: A Technical Guide.** Arthur E. Smith et al. (Illus.). 42p. 1998. pap. 10.50 (*1-57753-255-4*, 147IB243) Corn Coop Ext.

Managing Cancer Pain. F. De Conno. LC 96-32806. 1996. pap. text 29.00 (*0-7923-4202-X*) Kluwer Academic.

Managing Cancer Pain, Consumer Version, Clinical Practice 9. 21p. 1994. pap. 16.00 (*0-16-061532-1*) USGPO.

Managing Capital Flows & Exchange Rates: Perspectives from the Pacific Basin. Ed. by Reuven Glick. LC 97-30367. (Illus.). 375p. (C). 1998. 69.95 (*0-521-62323-5*) Cambridge U Pr.

Managing Capital Flows in East Asia. LC 95-51265. (Development in Practice Ser.). 160p. 1996. pap. 22.00 (*0-8213-3529-4*) World Bank.

Managing Capital Flows in Turbulent Times: The Experience of Europe's Emerging Market. Ed. by Zdenek Drabek & Stephany Griffith-Jones. LC 99-11328. (Illus.). 264p. 1999. text 90.00 (*0-7656-0369-1*) M E Sharpe.

Managing Capital Inflows in Latin America. (Discussion Papers: No. 8). 46p. pap. 7.50 (*92-1-126056-6*) UN.

Managing Capital Resources for Central City Revitalization. Ed. by Fritz W. Wagner et al. LC 99-26782. (Contemporary Urban Affairs Ser.: Vol. 7). 170p. 1999. 75.00 (*0-8153-3213-0*, SS1205) Garland.

Managing Capitation & Outcomes in Mental Health. Chris E. Stout. 150p. 1997. 65.00 (*1-890056-02-2*, 1995-56022) Grayson Pub.

Managing Care & Risk in Behavioral Health Care. Chris E. Stout. 240p. 1997. 39.95 (*1-890056-03-0*, 1996-56030) Grayson Pub.

Managing Care, Not Dollars: The Continuum of Mental Health Services. Ed. by Robert K. Schreter et al. 396p. 1997. text 57.00 (*0-88048-855-7*, 8855) Am Psychiatric.

***Managing Career Dilemmas.** D. Pemberton et al. (Financial Times Management Briefings Ser.). 1998. pap. 94.50 (*0-273-63731-2*, Pub. by F T P-H) Trans-Atl Phila.

***Managing Career Transitions.** 2nd ed. Kit Harrington Hayes. LC 99-18145. (Illus.). 257p. 1999. pap. text 34.40 (*0-13-924051-9*) P-H.

***Managing Career Transitions: Your Career As a Work in Progress.** 2nd ed. 1999. teacher ed. write for info. (*0-13-013136-9*) P-H.

Managing Careers. Manuel London & Stephen A. Stempf. (Management Ser.). (Illus.). 324p. 1982. pap. text 17.56 (*0-201-04559-1*) Addison-Wesley.

Managing Careers. Andrew Mayo. 320p. (C). 1991. pap. 100.00 (*0-85292-481-X*, Pub. by IPM Hse) St Mut.

Managing Careers into the 21st Century. John Arnold. LC 97-198284. 272p. 1997. pap. 29.95 (*1-85396-317-8*, Pub. by P Chapman) Taylor & Francis.

Managing Casinos: A Guide for Entrepreneurs, Management Personnel & Aspiring Managers. Ruben Martinez. LC 95-31449. (Illus.). 432p. (Orig.). 1995. 75.00 (*1-56980-045-6*) Barricade Bks.

Managing Challenging Behaviors. Lewis Polsgrove. (C). 1999. pap. text. write for info. (*0-321-03771-5*) Addison-Wesley.

Managing Challenging Behaviors. Lewis Polsgrove. (C). 2000. pap. text. write for info. (*0-321-03772-3*) Addson-Wesley Educ.

Managing Change. Colin Carnall. (Self-Development for Managers Ser.). 128p. (C). 1990. pap. 17.95 (*0-415-04463-4*, A6268) Thomson Learn.

***Managing Change.** CCTA Staff. (IS Management Guides Ser.). (Illus.). 81p. 2000. 50.00 (*1-903091-01-2*, Pub. by Format Pubg Ltd) Balogh.

Managing Change. Robert Heller. LC 99-204526. (Essential Managers Handbks.). (Illus.). 72p. 1999. pap. 6.95 (*0-7894-2897-0*) DK Pub Inc.

Managing Change. Philip Sadler. 1997. pap. text 19.95 (*0-7494-2022-7*) Kogan Page Ltd.

Managing Change: A Core Value Approach: Theory & Cases. Alma Whitely. 280p. 1994. 59.95 (*0-7329-2802-8*, Pub. by Macmill Educ); pap. 29.95 (*0-7329-2801-X*, Pub. by Macmill Educ) Paul & Co Pubs.

Managing Change: A European Perspective. 2nd ed. Bernard Burnes. (Illus.). 384p. (Orig.). 1996. pap. 62.50 (*0-273-61118-6*, Pub. by Pitman Pub) Trans-Atl Phila.

Managing Change: A Guide to British Economic Policy. Graham Ingham. pap. write for info. (*0-7190-5765-5*, Pub. by Manchester Univ Pr); text. write for info. (*0-7190-5764-7*, Pub. by Manchester Univ Pr) St Martin.

Managing Change: A Guide to Producing Innovation from Within. Ed. by Sandra J. Hale & Mary M. Williams. LC 89-22423. 194p. (Orig.). (C). 1989. pap. text 20.00 (*0-87766-431-5*) Urban Inst.

Managing Change: A How to Do It Manual for Planning, Implementing & Evaluating Change in Libraries. Susan C. Curzon. Ed. by Bill Katz. (How-to-Do-It Ser.). 128p. (Orig.). 1989. pap. text 45.00 (*1-55570-032-2*) Neal-Schuman.

***Managing Change: A Human Resource Approach.** Adrian Thornhill et al. 272p. (Orig.). 1999. pap. 49.50 (*0-273-63065-2*, Pub. by F T P-H) Trans-Atl Phila.

Managing Change: A Learning Environment Architecture. Ford et al. LC 96-28690. 144p. 1996. 112.95 (*0-335-19792-2*); pap. 38.95 (*0-335-19791-4*) OpUniv Pr.

Managing Change: A Model for Community College Leaders, 4 bks. George A. Baker, III. LC 99-163031. 32p. 1998. pap. 20.00 (*0-87117-312-3*, 1417) Comm Coll Pr Am Assn Comm Coll.

***Managing Change: A Strategic Approach to Organisational Dynamics.** 3rd ed. Bernard Burns. LC 00-36725. 2000. write for info. (*0-273-64166-2*, Pub. by Pitman Pbg) Trans-Atl Phila.

Managing Change: A Strategy for Our Time. Hugh Marlow. 174p. (C). 1975. 70.00 (*0-85292-122-5*) St Mut.

Managing Change: A Strategy for Our Time - Key Questions. Hugh Marlow. 68p. (C). 1975. 70.00 (*0-85292-123-3*) St Mut.

Managing Change: Cases & Concepts. Todd D. Jick. LC 92-24166. 432p. (C). 1992. text 67.95 (*0-256-11231-2*, Irwn McGrw-H) McGrw-H Hghr Educ.

***Managing Change: Final Report of the High-Level Group on Economic & Social Implications of Industrial Change** European Commission. LC 99-196599. (Employment & Social Affairs Ser.). 26p. 1998. write for info. (*92-828-5101-X*, Pub. by Comm Europ Commun) Bernan Associates.

Managing Change: How to Grow a Modern Enterprise. John W. Fisher & E. Bruce Geelhoed. (Business History Ser.: No. 4). (Illus.). 184p. (Orig.). 1986. pap. 7.95 (*0-913195-03-0*) BSU Bur Busn Res.

***Managing Change: Negotiating Conflict.** 2nd ed. Mark Anstey. 399p. 1999. pap. 37.95 (*0-7021-5066-5*, Pub. by Juta & Co) Intl Spec Bk.

Managing Change: Perspectives & Practice. Audley Genus. 288p. 1998. pap. 15.99 (*1-86152-047-6*) Thomson Learn.

***Managing Change: Practical Strategies for Competitive Advantage.** Kari Tuominen. LC 99-56446. 2000. write for info. (*0-87389-470-7*) ASQ Qual Pr.

Managing Change: The Challenge of Continuous Improvement. F. Michael Horton. 68p. 1993. reprint ed. pap. 31.45 (*0-913507-85-7*) New Forums.

Managing Change: Today's Challenge to Management. John E. Flaherty. 188p. 1984. reprint ed. pap. 12.95 (*0-8290-1575-2*) Irvington.

***Managing Change Vol. 7: Changing the Role of Top Public Servants.** Ed. by Peter E. Larson & Amanda Coe. (Managing the Public Service). 72p. 2000. pap. 16.95 (*0-85092-584-3*, Pub. by Comm Sec) Stylus Pub VA.

Managing Change at Work. Sheila Costello. 128p. 1994. text 10.95 (*0-7863-0162-7*, Irwn Prfssnl) McGraw-Hill Prof.

Managing Change at Work. Sheila J. Costello. LC 93-40306. 1994. write for info. (*0-7863-0104-X*, Irwn Prfssnl) McGraw-Hill Prof.

Managing Change at Work: Leading People Through Organizational Transitions. rev. ed. Cynthia D. Scott & Dennis T. Jaffe. Ed. by Michael Crisp. LC 94-71943. (Fifty-Minute Ser.). (Illus.). 82p. 1994. pap. 10.95 (*1-56052-299-2*) Crisp Pubns.

Managing Change, Changing Medicine: Park Nicollet, Seventy-Five Years. James R. Hare, Jr. LC 96-37059. 300p. (Orig.). 1996. pap. 16.00 (*0-9655104-0-9*) Park Nicollet.

Managing Change for Competitive Success. Andrew Pettigrew & Richard Whipp. 304p. 1993. pap. 31.95 (*0-631-19142-9*) Blackwell Pubs.

Managing Change for Library Support Staff. Anne Goulding. (Librarianship Ser.). 176p. 1996. 78.95 (*1-85972-249-0*, Pub. by Avebry) Ashgate Pub Co.

Managing Change for Safety & Health Professionals: A Six Step Process. F. David Pierce. LC 96-37927. 208p. 1997. 59.00 (*0-86587-563-4*) Gov Insts.

***Managing Change in a Unionized Workplace: Countervailing Collaboration.** Kirk Blackard. LC 99-40352. 272p. 2000. write for info. (*1-56720-348-5*) Greenwood.

Managing Change in Academic Libraries. Ed. by Joseph J. Branin. LC 96-10289. (Journal of Library Administration Ser.: Vol. 22, Nos. 2 & 3). 152p. (C). 1996. 29.95 (*1-56024-810-6*) Haworth Pr.

***Managing Change in Health Care: Innovative Solutions for People-Based Organizations.** M.K. Key. 1998. 35.00 (*0-07-134301-6*) McGraw.

Managing Change in Higher Education: Preparing for the 21st Century. Ed. by K. Scott Hughes & Daryl Conner. 87p. 1989. 35.00 (*0-910402-92-2*) Coll & U Personnel.

Managing Change in Old Age: The Control of Meaning in an Institutional Setting. Haim Hazan. LC 91-26575. (SUNY Series in Anthropology & Judaic Studies). 182p. (C). 1992. pap. text 21.95 (*0-7914-1064-1*) State U NY Pr.

Managing Change in Rural Schools: An Action Guide. Donald L. Horsley et al. 100p. (Orig.). 1991. pap. 10.95 (*1-878234-01-3*, 9084) Reg Lab Educ IOT NE Isls.

Managing Change in Schools. Patrick Whitaker. LC 92-23836. 1993. 110.00 (*0-335-09382-5*); pap. 42.95 (*0-335-09381-7*) OpUniv Pr.

Managing Change in the British Industry. G. Shepherd & M. Sharp. (Employment, Adjustment & Industrialisation Ser.: No. 5). xv, 159p. (Orig.). 1987. pap. 24.75 (*92-2-106154-X*) Intl Labour Office.

Managing Change in the Craft, Design & Technology Department. Peter Toft. 120p. 1989. pap. 10.00 (*0-948080-23-X*, Trentham Bks) Stylus Pub VA.

Managing Change in the 1990s: Strategies for the Operations Manager. Tom Terez. LC 90-81583. 160p. (Orig.). 1990. pap. 14.95 (*0-9626463-0-X*) Arrow Assocs.

Managing Change in the Non-Profit Sector: Lessons from the Evolution of Five Independent Research Libraries. Jed I. Bergman et al. LC 95-4705. (Nonprofit Sector Ser.). 285p. 1996. text 32.95 (*0-7879-0138-5*) Jossey-Bass.

Managing Change in the Postal & Delivery Industries. Paul R. Kleindorfer. Ed. by Michael A. Crew. LC 96-47883. (Topics in Regulatory Economics & Policy Ser.). 440p. (C). 1997. lib. bdg. 104.50 (*0-7923-9849-1*) Kluwer Academic.

Managing Change in the Printing & Publishing Industry. Pira Staff. LC 95-232937. 1998. 135.00 (*1-85802-083-2*, Pub. by Pira Pub) Bks Intl VA.

Managing Change in the U. S. S. R. The Politico-Legal Role of the Soviet Jurist. John N. Hazard. LC 83-1792. 187p. 1983. text 59.95 (*0-521-25316-0*) Cambridge U Pr.

Managing Change in the Workplace: A 12-Step Program for Success. Ralph L. Kliem & Irwin S. Ludin. LC 98-75585. (Illus.). 140p. 1998. pap. 14.95 (*0-9664286-1-7*) HNB Pubg.

Managing Change in Voluntary Organizations: A Guide to Practice. Nigel Gann. LC 96-8788. 160p. 1996. 88.00 (*0-335-19622-5*) OpUniv Pr.

***Managing Change Pocketbook.** Neil Russell-Jones. 112p. 1999. pap. 8.95 (*1-870471-31-8*, Pub. by Mngmnt Pocketbks) Stylus Pub VA.

Managing Change Reader. Paul S. Kirkbride & Jim Durcan. 304p. 1996. 69.00 (*0-415-11464-0*); pap. 23.95 (*0-415-11465-9*) Routledge.

Managing Change Through Innovation: Towards a Model for Developing & Reforming Social Work Practice & Social Service Delivery. Gerald G. Smale & Graham Tusom. 131p. 1995. lib. bdg. 7.50 (*1-899942-00-9*) U of Iowa Sch Soc Wk.

Managing Change Through Training & Development. 2nd ed. Jim Stewart. 224p. 1996. pap. 29.95 (*0-7494-1846-X*, Kogan Pg Educ) Stylus Pub VA.

Managing Change Voluntary Org: A Guide to Practice. N. Gann. LC 96-8788. 160p. 1996. pap. 27.95 (*0-335-19621-7*) OpUniv Pr.

Managing Change with Business Process Simulation. David M. Profozich. LC 97-30380. 224p. (C). 1997. 34.95 (*0-13-905837-0*) P-H.

Managing Changes: Exploring State of the Art. E. A. More. LC 98-15098. (Monographs in Organizational Behavior & Industrial Relations: Vol. 22). 1998. 78.50 (*0-7623-0415-4*) Jai Pr.

Managing Channels of Distribution: The Marketing Executive's Complete Guide. Kenneth Rolnicki. LC 97-31322. 288p. 1996. 59.95 (*0-8144-0335-2*) AMACOM.

Managing Chaos & Complexity in Government: A New Paradigm for Managing Change, Innovation & Organizational Renewal. L. Douglas Kiel. LC 94-21303. (Public Administration Ser.). 272p. 1994. 26.95 (*0-7879-0023-0*) Jossey-Bass.

Managing Chemical Risks: Corporate Response to Sara Title III. 2nd ed. Micheal S. Baram. 288p. 1992. lib. bdg. 99.95 (*0-87371-725-2*) CRC Pr.

Managing Chemicals Safely: Putting It All Together. (Illus.). 24p. (Orig.). (C). 1993. pap. text 20.00 (*1-56806-733-X*) DIANE Pub.

Managing Child Nutrition Programs: Leadership for Excellence. Josephine M. Martin et al. LC 99-13065. 768p. 1999. boxed set 65.00 (*0-8342-0917-9*, 09179) Aspen Pub.

Managing Childhood Medical Emergencies: An Action Guide for Parents & Childcare Providers. Lori Thompson. 1994. pap. text 25.00 (*0-201-49050-1*) Addison-Wesley.

Managing Children with Problems. Ved P. Varma. (Education Ser.). (Illus.). 160p. 1996. pap. 29.95 (*0-304-33331-X*); text 80.00 (*0-304-33330-1*) Continuum.

Managing Children with Psychiatric Problems. Ed. by M. Elena Garralda. 228p. 1993. pap. text 27.00 (*0-7279-0788-3*, Pub. by BMJ Pub) Login Brothers Bk Co.

Managing Children's Behaviour in the Classroom: A Practical Guide for Teachers & Students. Sonia Burnard & Heather Yaxley. LC 98-111018. 160p. 1997. pap. 27.95 (*0-7507-0722-4*, Falmer Pr) Taylor & Francis.

***Managing Children's Psychosocial Needs.** Rollins. 2000. 49.00 (*0-8342-1677-9*) Aspen Pub.

Managing Children's Services in the Public Library. 2nd ed. Adele M. Fasick. LC 97-41688. 218p. 1998. pap. 37.00 (*1-56308-526-7*) Libs Unl.

Managing Chronic Behavioral Disorders: A Desktop Reference for Mental Health & Addiction Professionals. Ed. by Karienne Stovell. 350p. 1997. 149.00 (*1-884937-48-9*) Manisses Communs.

Managing Chronic Illness: A Biopsychosocial Perspective. Ed. by Perry M. Nicassio & Timothy W. Smith. LC 95-17909. (Application & Practice in Health Psychology Ser.). 425p. 1995. text 29.95 (*1-55798-300-3*) Am Psychol.

Managing Chronic Illness in the Classroom. Dorothy B. Wishnietsky & Dan H. Wishnietsky. LC 96-67187. 108p. 1996. pap. 9.50 (*0-87367-487-1*, MCIC) Phi Delta Kappa.

Managing Chronic Orofacial Pain with Transcutaneous Electroneural Stimulation. Errol Lader. LC 85-50702. (Illus.). 300p. 1986. pap. text 85.00 (*0-9610782-5-1*) Vadare.

Managing Chronic Pain. Siang-Yang Tan. LC 96-22370. 120p. 1996. pap. 9.99 (*0-8308-1989-4*, 1989) InterVarsity.

Managing Church Conflict. Hugh F. Halverstadt. 208p. (Orig.). 1991. pap. 19.95 (*0-664-25185-4*) Westminster John Knox.

Managing Church Conflict. James A. Jones. 1973. pap. 8.00 (*0-89137-558-9*) Quality Pubns.

Managing Cisco Network Security. 704p. 2000. pap. text 60.00 (*1-57870-103-1*) Macmillan Tech.

***Managing Cisco Network Security: Building Rock-Solid Networks.** Syngress Media, Inc. Staff. 608p. 2000. pap. 59.95 (*1-928994-17-2*) Syngress.

Managing Cities: The New Urban Context. Ed. by Patsy Healey et al. LC 94-40240. 332p. 1995. pap. 59.95 (*0-471-95533-7*) Wiley.

Managing Cities in Austerity: Urban Fiscal Stress in Ten Western Countries. Ed. by Poul E. Mouritzen. (Urban Innovation Ser.: Vol. 2). 256p. 1992. 59.95 (*0-8039-8632-7*) Sage.

Managing Classroom Behavior: A Reflective Case-Based Approach. 2nd ed. James M. Kauffman et al. LC 97-36027. 224p. 1997. pap. text 37.00 (*0-205-27460-9*) P-H.

Managing Classroom Collaboration. Chris Lloyd & Jeff Beard. (Cassell Practical Handbooks Ser.). (Illus.). 128p. 1995. pap. 39.95 (*0-304-32988-6*) Continuum.

***Managing Classroom Crises.** Carlette Jackson Hardin & E. Ann Harris. (Fastback Ser.: No. 465). 48p. 2000. pap. 3.00 (*0-87367-665-3*) Phi Delta Kappa.

Managing Client Anger: What to Do When a Client Is Angry with You. Aphrodite Matasakis. LC 98-66703. 224p. 1998. 49.95 (*1-57224-123-3*) New Harbinger.

Managing Client Care. 2nd ed. Elizabeth F. Wywialowski. teacher ed. write for info. (*0-8151-4495-4*) Mosby Inc.

Managing Client Care. 2nd ed. Elizabeth F. Wywialowski. (Illus.). 384p. (C). (gr. 13). 1996. pap. text 31.00 (*0-8151-9499-4*, 28208) Mosby Inc.

Managing Coastal Erosion. Committee on Coastal Erosion Zone Management, Natl. 204p. 1990. text 24.50 (*0-309-04143-0*) Natl Acad Pr.

M

Managing Cocaine Craving. Hazelden Staff. 1996. pap. 3.00 (*0-89486-674-5*) Hazelden.

***Managing Colleges & Universities: Issues for Leadership.** Allan M. Hoffman & Randal W. Summers. LC 99-37688. 232p. 2000. 65.00 (*0-89789-645-9*) Greenwood.

Managing Collegiate Sport Clubs. Ed. by David O. Matthews. LC 86-27633. (Illus.). 255p. 1987. reprint ed. pap. 79.10 (*0-608-07093-9*, 206732000009) Bks Demand.

Managing "Command & Control" in the Persian Gulf War. Mark D. Mandeles & Thomas C. Hone. LC 95-46157. 192p. 1996. 57.95 (*0-275-95261-4*, Praeger Pubs) Greenwood.

Managing Commercial Banks. Emmanuel N. Roussakis. LC 77-4380. (Special Studies). 202p. 1977. 35.00 (*0-275-90274-9*, C0274, Praeger Pubs) Greenwood.

Managing Commodity Booms - & Busts. Panos Varangis et al. LC 95-42336. (Directions in Development Ser.). 32p. 1996. pap. 22.00 (*0-8213-3489-1*) World Bank.

Managing Commodity Price Risk in Developing Countries. Ed. by Stijn Claessens & Ronald C. Duncan. (World Bank Research Publications). 480p. 1994. text 39.95 (*0-8018-4662-5*, 44662) Johns Hopkins.

Managing Commodity Risk. Stephens. text. write for info. (*0-471-86625-3*) Wiley.

Managing Common Pool Resources: Principles & Case Studies. Katar Singh. (Illus.). 388p. 1994. 29.95 (*0-19-563398-9*) OUP.

Managing Common Property: Irrigation in India & the Philippines. Nirmal Sengupta. (Indo-Dutch Studies on Development Alternatives: No. 6). 272p. (C). 1991. 32.00 (*0-8039-9670-5*) Sage.

***Managing Communication in Changing Organizations.** R. E. Donnelly. (Management Briefings Ser.). (Illus.). 1998. pap. 89.50 (*0-273-63807-6*, Pub. by F T P-H) Trans-Atl Phila.

Managing Communication Processes: From Planning to Crisis Response. E. W. Brody. LC 90-23751. 248p. 1991. 57.95 (*0-275-93467-5*, C3467, Praeger Pubs); pap. 22.95 (*0-275-93468-3*, B3468, Praeger Pubs) Greenwood.

Managing Communications. Stowers. (SWC-Business Communication Ser.). 2000. pap. 37.50 (*0-324-01427-9*) Thomson Learn.

***Managing Communications: Lessons from Intervention in Africa.** Ed. by Ervin Rokke & Richard H. Solomon. 63p. 2000. reprint ed. pap. text 20.00 (*0-7881-8672-8*) DIANE Pub.

Managing Community & Junior Colleges: Perspectives for the Next Century. Ed. by Allan M. Hoffman & Daniel J. Julius. 266p. 1994. 40.00 (*1-878240-30-7*) Coll & U Personnel.

Managing Community Colleges: A Handbook for Effective Practice. Arthur M. Cohen et al. LC 93-43162. (Higher & Adult Education Ser.). 522p. 1994. 48.00 (*1-55542-620-4*) Jossey-Bass.

Managing Community Development in the New Federalism. Donald F. Kettl. LC 79-23504. 156p. 1980. 45.00 (*0-275-90503-9*, C0503, Praeger Pubs) Greenwood.

Managing Community Growth: Policies, Techniques, & Impacts. Eric D. Kelly. LC 92-36549. 264p. 1993. 59.95 (*0-275-94495-6*, C4495, Praeger Pubs) Greenwood.

Managing Community Growth: Policies, Techniques, & Impacts. Eric D. Kelly. LC 92-36549. 264p. 1994. pap. 22.95 (*0-275-94957-5*, Praeger Pubs) Greenwood.

Managing Community Health Services. Ed. by Allan McNaught. 200p. 1990. pap. 27.50 (*0-412-31900-4*, A5043) Chapman & Hall.

Managing Company-Wide Communication. Werner David. LC 94-74698. (Illus.). 244p. 1995. mass mkt. 32.50 (*0-412-56420-3*) Chapman & Hall.

Managing Compensation. J. Gary Berg. LC 76-9809. 256p. reprint ed. pap. 79.40 (*0-608-12153-3*, 202391000034) Bks Demand.

Managing Competition: A Blueprint for Economic Policy. Douglas N. Thompson. LC 89-62668. 341p. 1989. 19.95 (*0-9624038-0-6*) Crossroads Rsch.

Managing Competition: Meso-Corporatism, Pluralism, & the Negotiated Order in Scotland. Chris Moore & Simon A. Booth. (Illus.). 184p. 1989. text 49.95 (*0-19-827578-1*) OUP.

Managing Competitive Crisis: Strategic Choice & the Reform of Workrules. Martyn Wright. LC 98-20174. (Cambridge Studies in Management: No. 27). (Illus.). 192p. (C). 1999. text 59.95 (*0-521-64005-9*) Cambridge U Pr.

Managing Competitive Intelligence Knowledge in a Global Economy. Emily Arro et al. Ed. by Susan K. Elliott. (Illus.). 93p. 1998. spiral bd. 495.00 (*1-928593-08-9*) Am Prodtv Qual.

Managing Competitive Sport Programs in Schools. Karen E. Danylchuk. Ed. by Earle F. Zeigler. (Monograph Series on Sport & Physical Education Management). 56p. (C). 1993. pap. text 4.40 (*0-87563-450-8*) Stipes.

Managing Complex Litigation: A Practical Guide to the Use of Special Masters. Wayne D. Brazil et al. LC 83-71543. xi, 394p. 1983. 35.00 (*0-910059-03-9*, 304970) W S Hein.

Managing Complex Litigation: Procedures & Strategies for Lawyers & Courts. LC 91-58618. 680p. 1992. pap. 79.95 (*0-89707-703-2*, 519-0211, ABA Tort) Amer Bar Assn.

Managing Complex Networks: Strategies for the Public Sector. Ed. by Walter Kickert et al. 224p. 1997. pap. 26.95 (*0-7619-5548-8*); text 75.00 (*0-7619-5547-X*) Sage.

Managing Complexity: Work, Technology, Resources, & Human Relations. rev. ed. James C. Stephens. LC 77-124381. 331p. 1977. 26.50 (*0-912338-13-X*); fiche 9.50 (*0-912338-14-8*) Lomond.

Managing Complexity in High Technology Organizations. Ed. by Mary A. Von Glinow & Susan A. Mohrman. (Illus.). 344p. 1990. text 75.00 (*0-19-505720-1*) OUP.

Managing Complexity in Organizations: A View in Many Directions. Ed. by Michael R. Lissack & Hugh P. Gunz. LC 99-13621. 424p. 1999. 75.00 (*1-56720-285-3*, Quorum Bks) Greenwood.

Managing Complexity in Software Engineering. Ed. by R. J. Mitchell. (Computing Ser.: No. 17). 262p. 1990. 82.00 (*0-86341-171-1*, CM017) INSPEC Inc.

Managing Computer Based Information Systems in Developing Countries: A Cultural Perspective. Abdullah A. Gader. LC 98-42508. (Illus.). 188p. 1999. pap. 49.95 (*1-878289-49-7*) Idea Group Pub.

Managing Computer Network Operating Systems. Peter Varhol. LC 95-35592. (Illus.). 217p. 1995. pap. 285.00 (*1-56607-955-1*) Comput Tech Res.

Managing Computer Networks: A Case-Based Reasoning Approach. Lewis Lundy. LC 95-33933. 250p. 1995. 69.00 (*0-89006-799-6*) Artech Hse.

Managing Computer Numerical Control Operations: How to Get the Most Out of Your CNC Machine Tools. Mike Lynch. LC 95-70370. 372p. 1995. 83.00 (*0-87263-466-3*) SME.

Managing Computer Projects. Francois Lustman. 400p. (C). 1987. text 33.33 (*0-317-60112-1*) P-H.

Managing Computer Resources. 2nd ed. Donna Hussain & K. M. Hussain. (Information Systems Ser.). 704p. (C). 1987. text 53.95 (*0-256-03627-6*, Irwn McGrw-H) McGrw-H Hghr Educ.

Managing Computer Viruses. Eric Louw & Neil Duffy. (Illus.). 184p. 1992. pap. text 24.95 (*0-19-853974-6*) OUP.

Managing Computers: Proceedings of a Symposium Sponsored by the Engineering Management Division. Ed. by David C. Johnston. 45p. 1985. 3.00 (*0-87262-499-4*) Am Soc Civil Eng.

Managing Computers in the Hospitality Industry. 3rd ed. Michael L. Kasavana & John J. Cahill. LC 97-19743. 1997. pap. write for info. (*0-86612-147-1*) Educ Inst Am Hotel.

Managing Conduct & Data Quality of Toxicology Studies. Ed. by B. K. Hoover et al. LC 85-63837. (Illus.). 352p. 1986. 50.00 (*0-911131-93-0*) Specialist Journals.

Managing Conflict. Herb Bisno. (Human Services Guides Ser.: Vol. 52). 160p. (C). 1988. pap. text 18.95 (*0-8039-2585-9*) Sage.

Managing Conflict. Bloomfield. LC 95-73316. 229p. 1996. pap. text 35.95 (*0-312-13675-7*) St Martin.

Managing Conflict. Susanna Palomares & Terri Akins. Ed. by Dianne Schilling. (Orig.). (J). (gr. k-6). 1995. spiral bd. 19.95 (*1-56499-028-1*, IP9028) Innerchoice Pub.

Managing Conflict. 2nd ed. David A. Whetten & Kim S. Cameron. (Developing Management Skills Modules Ser.). 112p. (C). 1997. pap. 14.00 (*0-06-501591-6*) Addson-Wesley Educ.

Managing Conflict, Set. pap., wbk. ed. 139.00 incl. audio (*0-7612-0812-7*, 80186); pap., wbk. ed. 30.00 incl. audio (*0-7612-0813-5*, 80187) AMACOM.

Managing Conflict: An Interdisciplinary Approach. Ed. by M. Afzalur Rahim. LC 88-14104. 348p. 1989. 65.00 (*0-275-92683-4*, C2683, Praeger Pubs) Greenwood.

Managing Conflict: Interpersonal Dialogue & Third-Party Roles. 2nd ed. Richard E. Walton. LC 86-20679. (Organization Development Ser.). (Illus.). 160p. (C). 1987. pap. text 40.00 (*0-201-08859-2*) Addison-Wesley.

Managing Conflict: The Key to Making Your Organization Work. Dean R. Tjosvold. 1988. pap. 14.95 (*0-9621542-0-2*) Team Media.

Managing Conflict at Organizational Interfaces. L. Dave Brown. LC 82-6762. (Managing Human Resources Ser.). 250p. (C). 1983. pap. text 25.75 (*0-201-00884-X*) Addison-Wesley.

Managing Conflict at Work. Jim Murphy. LC 93-11509. (Business Skills Express Ser.). 112p. (Orig.). 1993. pap. 10.95 (*1-55623-890-8*, Irwn Prfssnl) McGraw-Hill Prof.

Managing Conflict Creatively: A Guide for Missionaries & Christian Workers. Donald C. Palmer. (Illus.). 116p. (Orig.). (C). 1991. 6.95 (*0-87808-231-X*, WCL231-X) William Carey Lib.

Managing Conflict in Organizations. 2nd ed. M. Afzalur Rahim. LC 92-7479. 248p. 1992. 57.95 (*0-275-93680-5*, C3680, Praeger Pubs) Greenwood.

***Managing Conflict in Organizations.** 3rd ed. M. Afzalur Rahim. LC 00-37271. 225p. 2000. 67.00 (*1-56720-262-4*, Q262, Quorum Bks) Greenwood.

Managing Conflict in Teams. Mescon Group Staff. (Performance Through Participation Ser.). 90p. 1996. text 14.95 (*0-538-84942-8*); text, teacher ed. 23.95 (*0-538-84943-6*) S-W Pub.

Managing Conflict in the Former Soviet Union: Russian & American Perspectives. Ed. by Alexei Arbatov et al. LC 97-11343. (CSIA Studies in International Security). (Illus.). 550p. 1997. pap. text 27.50 (*0-262-51093-6*) MIT Pr.

Managing Conflict in the Post-Cold War World: The Role of Intervention: Report of the Aspen Institute Conference. Nancy B. Dyke. (Aspen Institute Conferences on International Peace & Security Ser.). 123p. 1996. pap. 10.00 (*0-89843-192-1*) The Aspen Inst.

Managing Conservation in Museums. Suzanne Keene. LC 95-37486. (Illus.). 192p. 1996. pap. 51.95 (*0-7506-2384-5*) Buttrwrth-Heinemann.

Managing Conservation in Museums. Suzanne Keene. LC 95-37486. (Illus.). 277p. reprint ed. pap. 85.90 (*0-608-20285-1*, 207154300001) Bks Demand.

***Managing Constraints to Water Source Development** Andrew G. Graham. LC 99-39214. 1999. write for info. (*1-58321-010-5*) Am Water Wks Assn.

Managing Construction: The Contractual Viewpoint. Keith Collier. LC 93-3778. 432p. 1993. pap. 54.50 (*0-8273-5700-1*) Delmar.

Managing Construction - The Contractual Viewpoint: Instructor's Guide. Keith Collier. 75p. 1994. 16.95 (*0-8273-5702-8*) Delmar.

Managing Construction Contracts: Operational Controls for Commercial Risks. 2nd ed. Robert D. Gilbreath. LC 91-32241. 312p. 1992. 99.00 (*0-471-56932-1*) Wiley.

***Managing Construction Equipment.** 2nd ed. S. W. Nunnally. LC 99-27056. (Illus.). 399p. 1999. 75.00 (*0-13-901216-8*) P-H.

Managing Construction Industry Development: Lessons from Singapore's Experience. George Ofori. 354p. (Orig.). 1993. pap. 47.50 (*9971-69-181-7*, Pub. by Sngapore Univ Pr) Coronet Bks.

Managing Construction Purchasing. John G. McConville. 300p. 1993. 62.95 (*0-87629-316-X*, 67302) R S Means.

Managing Construction Worldwide, 3 vols., Set. Ed. by P. Lansley & P. Harlow. 1300p. 1988. lib. bdg. 235.00 (*0-419-14030-1*, E & FN Spon) Routledge.

Managing Consultants: Consultancy as the Management of Impressions. Timothy Clark. LC 95-15675. (Managing Work & Organizations Ser.). 160p. 1995. 114.95 (*0-335-19220-3*); pap. 31.95 (*0-335-19219-X*) OpUniv Pr.

Managing Contaminated Sites: Problem Diagnosis & Development of Site Restoration. D. Kofi Asante-Duah. LC 96-25954. 254p. 1997. 145.00 (*0-471-96633-9*) Wiley.

Managing Contingent Workers: How to Reap the Benefits & Reduce the Risks. Helen Axel & Stanley D. Nollen. 256p. 1995. 55.00 (*0-8144-0242-9*) AMACOM.

Managing Continual Innovation. Michel Syrett & Jean Lammiman. LC 99-182009. 200p. 1998. pap. text 29.95 (*0-7506-3700-5*) Buttrwrth-Heinemann.

Managing Continuing Professional Development in Schools. Ed. by Harry Tomlinson. LC 97-197796. (One-Off Ser.). (Illus.). 208p. 1997. pap. (*1-85396-345-3*) Corwin Pr.

Managing Contraceptive Pill Patients. 9th ed. Richard P. Dickey. LC 98-194210. 351p. 1998. pap. write for info. (*0-929240-84-7*) EMIS.

***Managing Contraceptive Pill Patients.** 9th ed. Richard P. Dickey. LC 76-29294. 1999. 17.95 (*0-917634-00-4*) EMIS.

***Managing Contraceptive Pill Patients.** 10th rev. ed. Richard P. Dickey. (Illus.). 245p. 2000. pap. 17.95 (*0-917634-05-5*) EMIS.

Managing Contracted Services: Administrating Ethical & Political Issues in Nonprofit Agencies. Susan R. Bernstein. 230p. 1991. 59.95 (*0-87722-808-6*); pap. 22.95 (*0-87722-809-4*) Temple U Pr.

Managing Contracts for IS/IT Services. 50p. 1994. pap. 40.00 (*0-11-330660-1*, HM06601, Pub. by Statnry Office) Bernan Associates.

Managing Contradiction & Avoidance: Discussion Paper & Self-Audit. Giles Darvill. 1997. pap. 23.00 (*1-899942-13-0*) Natl Inst Soc Work.

Managing Contributed Funds & Assets: The Tax-Exempt Financial Planning Manual. Paul J. Lyons. LC 85-24991. 350p. 1985. 135.00 (*0-914756-27-3*, 600009) Taft Group.

Managing Controls: The Complete Book of Motor Control Application & Maintenance. Richard L. Nailen. (Illus.). 130p. 1993. text 49.95 (*0-943876-06-0*) Barks Pubns.

***Managing Conversations with Hostile Adults: Strategies for Teachers by Georgia J. Kosmoski & Dennis R. Pollack.** Georgia J. Kosmoski & Dennis R. Pollack. LC 00-9202. 2000. pap. write for info. (*0-8039-6810-8*) Corwin Pr.

Managing Core Public Services. David McKevitt & Len Wrigley. LC 98-20901. 288p. (C). 1999. 69.95 (*0-631-19311-1*); pap. 39.95 (*0-631-19312-X*) Blackwell Pubs.

Managing Corporate Aviation Safety: Proceedings, 27th Annual Meeting, April 4-6, 1982, Houston Texas. Corporate Aviation Safety Seminar Staff. LC TL0541.6.C68. 164p. reprint ed. pap. 50.90 (*0-608-13922-X*, 201782800010) Bks Demand.

Managing Corporate Communication. Harry Irwin & Elizabeth A. More. 206p. 1994. pap. 24.95 (*1-86373-502-X*, Pub. by Allen & Unwin Pty) Paul & Co Pubs.

Managing Corporate Communications in a Competitive Climate Kathryn L. Troy & Conference Board Staff. LC 94-183583. (Conference Board Report Ser.). 38 p. 1993. write for info. (*0-8237-0471-8*) Conference Bd.

Managing Corporate Culture. Stanley M. Davis. 1990. pap. 14.95 (*0-88730-401-X*, HarpBusn) HarpInfo.

Managing Corporate Culture. Ronnie Lessem. (Illus.). 240p. 1990. text 78.95 (*0-566-02774-7*, Pub. by Gower) Ashgate Pub Co.

Managing Corporate Culture, Innovation, & Entrepreneurship. Howard W. Oden. LC 96-54283. 296p. 1997. 65.00 (*1-56720-047-8*, Quorum Bks) Greenwood.

Managing Corporate Ethics: Learning from America's Ethical Companies How to Supercharge Business. Francis J. Aguilar. LC 93-5803. (Illus.). 192p. 1994. 30.00 (*0-19-508534-5*) OUP.

***Managing Corporate Growth.** Jordi Canals. LC 99-42803. 200p. 2000. pap. 24.95 (*0-19-829668-1*); text 60.00 (*0-19-829667-3*) OUP.

Managing Corporate Health Care Programs: A Primer for Executives. Paul R. Torrens & Gary S. Whitted. LC 85-6564. 426p. 1985. 59.95 (*0-275-90236-6*, C0236, Praeger Pubs) Greenwood.

Managing Corporate Lifestyles. 2nd ed. Ichak Adizes. LC 98-52210. 384p. (C). 1998. text 26.00 (*0-7352-0057-2*) PH Pr.

***Managing Corporate Liquidity.** Ed. by Lance Moir. 250p. 1999. 65.00 (*1-57958-185-4*) Fitzroy Dearborn.

***Managing Corporate Liquidity.** Lance Moir. 196p. 1999. 65.00 (*1-888998-64-4*) Glenlake Pub.

Managing Corporate Liquidity. 2nd ed. Lance Moir. LC 00-551136. 250p. 1999. 60.00 (*0-8144-0508-8*) AMACOM.

Managing Corporate Media. 2nd ed. Eugene Marlow. (Illus.). 208p. (C). 1989. 47.95 (*0-86729-265-2*, Focal) Buttrwrth-Heinemann.

Managing Corporate Pension Plans. Dennis E. Logue. 289p. 1991. text 39.95 (*0-88730-341-2*, HarpBusn) HarpInfo.

Managing Corporation Pension Plans: The Impacts of Inflation. Dennis E. Logue & Richard J. Rogalski. LC 83-25786. (AEI Studies: No. 355). 78p. reprint ed. pap. 30.00 (*0-7837-1083-6*, 204161400021) Bks Demand.

Managing Corrosion with Plastics, Vol. 5. (Illus.). 184p. 1983. pap. 10.00 (*0-915567-63-6*) NACE Intl.

Managing Corrosion with Plastics, Vol. 8. LC 87-63179. (Illus.). 200p. 1987. pap. 10.00 (*0-915567-32-6*) NACE Intl.

Managing Corrosion with Plastics, Vol. 9. LC 77-88142. (Illus.). 364p. 1990. pap. 10.00 (*1-877914-15-0*) NACE Intl.

Managing Cost in Today's Manufacturing Environment. Peter Chalos. 1992. write for info. (*0-318-69292-9*) P-H.

Managing Costs for Profitability. Jennifer D. Belcher. (Orig.). 1996. pap. 9.95 (*0-942477-00-6*) Emprise Intl.

Managing Costs in Clinical Laboratories: A Manager's Fiscal Guide to Laboratory Cost Effectiveness. Eleanor M. Travers. LC 88-32591. (Illus.). 300p. (Orig.). 1989. pap. text 39.95 (*0-07-065121-3*, ME106) Practice Mgmt Info.

Managing County Money: A Cash Flow Problem. Dan Crippen. 1975. 1.00 (*1-55614-061-4*) U of SD Gov Res Bur.

Managing Cover Crops Profitably. (Illus.). 54p. (Orig.). (C). 1994. pap. text 20.00 (*0-7881-0755-0*) DIANE Pub.

Managing Cover Crops Profitably. 2nd ed. Sustainable Agriculture Network Staff. LC 98-9887. 1998. pap. write for info. (*1-888626-04-6*) Sustainability.

Managing Creative Assets. Henry L. Hanson. LC 85-73282. (Illus.). 130p. (Orig.). 1985. 14.95 (*0-9615945-0-0*); pap. 11.95 (*0-9615945-1-9*) Chiefton Pub.

Managing Creativity in Science & Hi-Tech. R. Kay. 240p. 1990. 39.95 (*0-387-51375-2*) Spr-Verlag.

***Managing Credit: What You Need to Know to Boost Your Buying Power.** Marc Robinson. 72p. 2000. pap. 6.95 (*0-7894-6316-4*) DK Pub Inc.

Managing Credit Department Functions: A Manager's Guide to Improving Loan Analysis, Documentation & Reporting. Kenneth R. Pirok. 225p. (C). 1995. text 50.00 (*1-55738-755-9*, Irwn Prfssnl) McGraw-Hill Prof.

***Managing Credit, Receivables & Collections, 2000 Yearbook.** annuals Ed. by Mary S. Schaeffer & Jan Bernabe. (Illus.). 200p. 2000. pap. 199.00 (*1-58673-045-2*) IOMA.

Managing Credit Risk: The Next Great Financial Challenge. Jack B. Caouette. LC 98-17660. (Frontiers in Finance Ser.). 464p. 1998. 79.95 (*0-471-11189-9*) Wiley.

***Managing Credit Risk Vol. I: Analysing Rating & Pricing the Probability of Default.** Dimitris N. Chorafas. 2000. pap. 170.00 (*1-85564-761-3*, Pub. by Euromoney) Am Educ Systs.

***Managing Credit Risk Vol. II: The Lessons of Variable Failures & Imprudent Exposure.** Dimitris N. Chorafas. 2000. pap. 170.00 (*1-85564-762-1*, Pub. by Euromoney) Am Educ Systs.

***Managing Crises Before They Happen: What Every Executive & Manager Needs to Know about Crisis Management.** Ian I. Mitroff & Gus Anagos. LC 00-30632. 2000. 24.95 (*0-8144-0563-0*) AMACOM.

***Managing Crisis: Presidential Disability & the Twenty-Fifth Amendment.** Ed. by Robert E. Gilbert. 388p. 2000. 34.95 (*0-8232-2086-9*, Pub. by Fordham); pap. 19.95 (*0-8232-2087-7*, Pub. by Fordham) BookMasters.

Managing Crisis & Change in Health Care: The Organizational Response to HIV-AIDS. Chris Bennett & Ewan Ferlie. LC 93-50137. 160p. 1994. 133.00 (*0-335-15788-2*); pap. 37.95 (*0-335-15787-4*) OpUniv Pr.

An Asterisk (*) at the beginning of an entry indicates that the title is appearing for the first time.

Managing Crisis & Risk in Mental Health Nursing. Ed. by Tony Ryan. (Illus.). 224p. 1999. pap. 28.95 (*0-7487-3336-1*) Standard Pub.

Managing Crisis Cities: The New Black Leadership & the Politics of Resource Allocation, 82. Bette Woody. LC 82-941. (Contributions in Political Science Ser.: No. 82). 228p. 1982. 59.95 (*0-313-23095-1*, WGM/, Greenwood Pr) Greenwood.

Managing Cross-Cultural Transition: A Handbook for Corporations, Employees & Their Families. Steven Shepard. LC 97-72339. 250p. 1997. pap., per. 19.95 (*0-9639260-5-5*) Aletheia.

Managing Cultural Differences. 3rd ed. Philip R. Harris & Robert T. Moran. LC 90-35354. (Managing Cultural Differences Ser.). (Illus.). 655p. 1991. reprint ed. pap. 200.00 (*0-608-07944-8*, 206791700012) Bks Demand.

Managing Cultural Differences. 4th ed. Philip R. Harris & Robert T. Moran. LC 95-45063. 402p. 1996. 39.95 (*0-88415-465-3*, 5465) Gulf Pub.

Managing Cultural Differences. 4th ed. Robert T. Moran & Philip R. Harris. 300p. 1996. pap., teacher ed. 20.00 (*0-88415-466-1*, 5466) Gulf Pub.

*__Managing Cultural Differences.__ 5th ed. 300p. 2000. pap., teacher ed. 20.00 (*0-88415-463-7*) Gulf Pub.

Managing Cultural Differences: Asian Supplement. Philip R. Harris & Robert T. Moran. 300p. 1996. pap., teacher ed. 20.00 (*0-88415-471-8*, 5471) Gulf Pub.

Managing Cultural Differences: Effective Strategy & Execution Across Cultures in Global Corporate Alliances. Morosini. LC 97-30782. (International Business & Management Ser.). 300p. 1998. 67.00 (*0-08-042762-6*, Pergamon Pr) Elsevier.

Managing Cultural Differences: European Supplement - Instructor's Manual. Moran. 300p. 1996. pap., teacher ed. 20.00 (*0-88415-472-6*, 5472) Gulf Pub.

Managing Cultural Differences: Latin American Supplement - Instructor's Manual. Moran. 300p. 1996. pap., teacher ed. 20.00 (*0-88415-470-X*, 5470) Gulf Pub.

Managing Cultural Differences: Strategies for Competitive Advantage. Lisa Hoecklin. Ed. by Michael Payne. LC 94-37013. (EIU Ser.). (C). 1994. text 41.00 (*0-201-42770-2*) Addison-Wesley.

Managing Culture. Peter Anthony. LC 93-25316. (Managing Work & Organizations Ser.). 112p. 1994. pap. 34.95 (*0-335-09788-X*) OpUniv Pr.

Managing Cultures: Making Strategic Relationships Work. Wendy Hall. LC 95-530. 336p. 1996. 69.95 (*0-471-95571-X*) Wiley.

*__Managing Currency Risk Using Foreign Exchange Options.__ Alan Hicks. 352p. 2000. text 170.00 (*1-85573-491-5*, Pub. by Woodhead Pubng) Am Educ Systs.

Managing Curricular Innovation. Numa Markee. (Cambridge Language Teaching Library). 238p. 1996. text 54.95 (*0-521-55512-4*); pap. text 20.95 (*0-521-55524-8*) Cambridge U Pr.

Managing Curriculum Materials in the Academic Library. Alice S. Clark. LC 81-16574. 227p. 1982. 30.00 (*0-8108-1482-X*) Scarecrow.

Managing Customer Credit & Collections Module, PACE: A Program for Acquiring Competence in Entrepreneurship, Level 1. rev. ed. National Center for Research in Vocational Educati. 1983. 2.50 (*0-317-06061-9*, RD240AB17) Ctr Educ Trng Employ.

Managing Customer Credit & Collections Module, PACE: A Program for Acquiring Competence in Entrepreneurship, Level 2. rev. ed. National Center for Research in Vocational Educati. 1983. 2.50 (*0-317-06062-7*, RD240BB17) Ctr Educ Trng Employ.

Managing Customer Credit & Collections Module, PACE: A Program for Acquiring Competence in Entrepreneurship, Level 3. rev. ed. National Center for Research in Vocational Educati. 1983. 2.50 (*0-318-67177-8*, RD240CB17) Ctr Educ Trng Employ.

Managing Customer Relationships: Lessons from Leaders. (Research Reports: No. N281). 1997. 395.00 (*0-85058-927-4*) Economist Intell.

Managing Customer Relationships: Lessons from Leaders. Contrib. by EIU & Anderson Consulting ED Staff. LC 99-182969. (Research Reports). 1998. 495.00 (*0-85058-471-X*) Economist Intell.

*__Managing Customer Service.__ Jenny Hayes & Frances Dredge. LC 97-77606. 168p. 1998. pap. 26.95 (*0-566-08005-2*, Pub. by Gower) Ashgate Pub Co.

Managing Customer Service on the Frontline: The ServiceWorks Method: Building Profits & Organizational Success. Edward E. Hubbard. 111p. 1990. pap. 14.95 (*1-883733-08-1*) Global Insghts.

Managing Customer Service Skillbook. Educational Foundation of the National Restaurant. (Management Skills Program Ser.). 44p. (Orig.). 1993. pap. 10.95 (*0-915452-30-8*) Educ Found.

*__Managing Customer Service 2000 Yearbook.__ annuals Ann Podolske. (Illus.). 2000p. 2000. pap. 199.00 (*1-58673-024-X*) IOMA.

Managing Customer Value: Creating Quality & Service that Customers Can See. Bradley T. Gale. LC 93-41905. 424p. 1994. 32.95 (*0-02-911045-9*) Free Pr.

Managing Danazol Patients. 2nd ed. Richard P. Dickey. 137p. 1992. pap. 12.95 (*0-929240-35-9*) EMIS.

Managing Data: From Vision to Reality. Ed. by Judith J. Newton et al. (Proceedings of the Annual DAMA Symposium Ser.: No. 4). (Illus.). 158p. (Orig.). (C). 1992. pap. text 35.00 (*1-56806-070-X*) DIANE Pub.

Managing Data with DBase. (Prisma Be an Expert! Ser.). (Illus.). 192p. (Orig.). (J). 1995. pap. 12.95 (*1-85365-386-1*, Pub. by Spectrum) Seven Hills Bk.

Managing Death. James M. Hoefler. 224p. 1999. pap. text 22.00 (*0-8133-2817-9*, Pub. by Westview) HarpC.

*__Managing Death in the ICU: The Transition from Cure to Comfort.__ Ed. by J. Randall Curtis & Gordon D. Rubenfeld. (Illus.). 384p. 2000. text 59.95 (*0-19-512881-8*) OUP.

*__Managing Death-Sentenced Inmates: A Survey of Practices.__ 2nd ed. Daniel Hudson. LC 99-48232. 1999. write for info. (*1-56991-119-3*) Am Correctional.

Managing Decline: Japan's Coal Industry Restructuring & Community Response. Suzanne Culter. LC 98-48397. (Illus.). 256p. (C). 1999. pap. 29.95 (*0-8248-2145-9*) UH Pr.

Managing Decline: Japan's Coal Industry Restructuring & Community Response. Suzanne Culter. LC 98-48397. (Illus.). 256p. (C). 1999. text 53.00 (*0-8248-2060-6*) UH Pr.

Managing Delinquency Programs That Work. Ed. by Barry Glick & Arnold P. Goldstein. 374p. 1995. pap. 49.95 (*1-56991-011-1*) Am Correctional.

Managing Democracy in Central America, a Case Study: United States Election Supervision in Nicaragua, 1927-1933. Thomas J. Dodd. LC 92-26327. 176p. (C). 1992. pap. 18.95 (*1-56000-631-5*, Pub. by U Miami N-S Ctr) L Rienner.

*__Managing Democratic Organizations, Vols. I & II.__ Ed. by Frank Heller. LC 99-41125. (Classic Research in Management Ser.). 880p. 1999. text 175.95 (*1-84014-480-7*, Pub. by Ashgate Pub) Ashgate Pub Co.

*__Managing Departments: Chairpersons & the Law.__ Kent M. Weeks. x, 191p. (C). 1999. 60.00 (*1-881434-13-3*) Coll Legal Info.

Managing Derivative Risk. Lilian Chew. (Frontiers in Finance Ser.). 332p. 1996. 99.00 (*0-471-95622-8*) Wiley.

Managing Derivatives Risk: Establishing Internal Systems & Controls. Dimitris N. Chorafas. 300p. 1995. text 65.00 (*1-55738-778-8*, Irwn Prfssnl) McGraw-Hill Prof.

Managing Development: Decentralization, Geographical Socialism & Urban Replication. P. V. Indiresan. (Illus.). 280p. (C). 1990. 27.50 (*0-8039-9638-1*) Sage.

Managing Development: State, Society, & Culture. Kathleen Staudt. (Illus.). 275p. 1991. 46.00 (*0-8039-4005-X*); pap. 21.50 (*0-8039-4006-8*) Sage.

Managing Development: The Political Dimension. Marc M. Lindenberg & Benjamin Crosby. LC 80-83345. (Library of Management for Development). 217p. (Orig.). 1981. 39.95 (*0-931816-49-1*) Transaction Pubs.

Managing Development: The Political Dimension. fac. ed. Marc M. Lindenberg & Benjamin Crosby. LC 80-83345. (Illus.). 231p. (Orig.). 1994. pap. 71.70 (*0-7837-7579-2*, 204733200007) Bks Demand.

Managing Diabetes on a Budget. Leslie Y. Dawson. LC 95-16705. 96p. 1996. pap. 7.95 (*0-945448-53-8*, 5002-01, Pub. by Am Diabetes) NTC Contemp Pub Co.

Managing Differences. Geri McArdle. Ed. by Beverly Manber. LC 93-74234. 110p. (Orig.). 1995. pap. 12.95 (*1-56052-320-4*) Crisp Pubns.

Managing Differences: How to Build Better Relationships at Work & Home. 2nd rev. ed. Daniel Dana. 240p. (Orig.). 1998. pap. 19.95 (*0-9621534-3-5*) MTI Pubns.

*__Managing Difficult, Frustrating & Hostile Conversations: Strategies for Savvy Administrators.__ Georgia J. Kosmoski & Dennis R. Pollack. LC 99-6665. 120p. 2000. pap. 19.95 (*0-8039-6809-4*); lib. bdg. 45.95 (*0-8039-6808-6*) Corwin Pr.

*__Managing Difficult People: Proven Strategies to Deal with Awkwardness in Business Situations.__ Karen Mannering. (Business Management Ser.). (Illus.). 144p. 2000. pap. 19.95 (*1-85703-573-9*, Pub. by How To Bks) Midpt Trade.

Managing Digital Workflow. Poyssick. (C). 2002. pap. 49.99 (*0-13-010911-8*) P-H.

Managing Disagreement Constructively: Conflict Management in Organizations. rev. ed. Herbert S. Kindler. Ed. by Kay Keppler. LC 95-83683. (Fifty-Minute Ser.). 88p. 1996. pap. 10.95 (*1-56052-383-2*) Crisp Pubns.

Managing Disaster: Strategies & Policy Perspectives. Ed. by Louise K. Comfort. LC 87-20049. (Illus.). xii, 420p. (C). 1988. text 69.95 (*0-8223-0800-2*) Duke.

Managing Disaster: Strategies & Policy Perspectives. Ed. by Louise K. Comfort. LC 87-20049. (Illus.). xii, 420p. (C). 1988. pap. text 29.95 (*0-8223-0816-9*) Duke.

*__Managing Disaster Risk in Mexico: Market Incentives for Mitigation Investment.__ Alcira Kreimer et al. LC 99-16468. (Disaster Risk Management Ser.). 64p. 1999. pap. 22.00 (*0-8213-4491-9*, 14491) World Bank.

Managing Discipline in Schools. Sonia Blandford. LC 97-43206. 208p. (C). 1998. pap. 24.99 (*0-415-17491-0*) Routledge.

Managing Discovery in Commercial & Business Litigation: Tools, Techniques, & Strategies. LC 92-756030. 129p. 1993. pap. 49.95 (*0-89707-815-2*, 515-0230, ABA Genl Prac) Amer Bar Assn.

Managing Diseases in Greenhouse Crops. William R. Jarvis. LC 92-71055. (Illus.). 288p. 1992. 89.00 (*0-89054-122-1*) Am Phytopathol Soc.

Managing Diseases of Greenhouse Crops see Control de Enfermedades en Cultivos de Invernadero

*__Managing Displacement: Refugees & the Politics of Humanitarianism.__ Jennifer Hyndman. LC 99-56469. (Borderlines Ser.). (C). 2000. 19.95 (*0-8166-3354-1*) U of Minn Pr.

Managing Distributed Databases: Building Bridges Between Database Islands. Donald K. Burleson. LC 95-48350. 384p. 1995. pap. 59.99 (*0-471-08623-1*) Wiley.

Managing Diversity. Ed. by Ellen Kossek & Sharon A. Lobel. 1996. pap. 38.95 (*1-55786-597-3*) Blackwell Pubs.

Managing Diversity. Nagi Condo. (C). Date not set. pap. 11.96 (*0-395-76931-0*) HM.

Managing Diversity: A Complete Desk Reference & Planning Guide. 2nd rev. ed. Lee Gardenswartz & Anita Rowe. LC 97-52603. 428p. 1998. ring bd. 99.95 (*0-07-022004-2*) McGraw-Hill Prof.

Managing Diversity: A Manager's Guide. Matthew B. Stuart. (Illus.). 144p. (Orig.). (C). 1991. pap. text 9.95 (*1-880409-02-X*) Pacific Servs.

Managing Diversity: A Practical Guide. abr. ed. Kenneth Burger & Alvin Ray. (Illus.). 70p. 1997. pap. text 14.95 (*0-936295-74-0*) FPMI Comns.

Managing Diversity: People Skills For Multiculture. 2nd ed. Norma Carr-Ruffino. LC 99-166750. 464p. 1998. pap. 40.00 (*0-536-00758-6*) Pearson Custom.

*__Managing Diversity: People Skills for Multiculture.__ 3rd ed. 456p. (C). 2000. 48.00 (*0-536-60308-1*) Pearson Custom.

*__Managing Diversity--the Courage to Lead.__ Elsie Y. Cross. LC 99-40353. 264p. 2000. write for info. (*1-56720-269-1*, Quorum Bks) Greenwood.

Managing Diversity & Change, Module 12. Deborah Ancona et al. (GI - Organizational Behavior Ser.). 1995. text 7.95 (*0-538-85892-3*) S-W Pub.

*__Managing Diversity & Multicultural Workforces E1.__ Nelarine Cornelius. 2001. pap. write for info. (*1-86152-585-0*) Thomson Learn.

Managing Diversity-Based Conflicts among Children. Charles C. Scott et al. Ed. by Donovan R. Walling. LC 97-65152. (Fastback Ser.: Vol. 414). 33p. 1997. pap. 3.00 (*0-87367-614-9*) Phi Delta Kappa.

Managing Diversity in an Equal Opportunity Workplace: A Primer for Today's Manager. Lorence L. Kessler. 130p. 1990. pap. 25.00 (*0-916559-27-0*) EPF.

Managing Diversity in Health Care. Lee Gardenswartz. LC 98-14745. xxv, 271 p. 1998. 39.95 (*0-7879-4041-0*) Jossey-Bass.

Managing Diversity in Health Care Manual: Proven Tools & Activities for Leaders & Trainers. Lee Gardenswartz. LC 99-6145. 208p. 1999. wbk. ed. 99.95 (*0-7879-4393-2*) Jossey-Bass.

Managing Diversity in Organizations. Robert T. Golembiewski. LC 94-36315. 240p. (C). 1995. pap. text 29.95 (*0-8173-0786-9*) U of Ala Pr.

Managing Diversity in the Global Workplace. Drake B. Morin. 1995. pap. 10.95 (*1-880030-37-3*) DBM Pub.

Managing Diversity in the New Reality: A Handbook for Diversity Managers. Fred Soto. 94p. 1997. pap. text 14.95 (*0-936295-77-5*) FPMI Comns.

*__Managing Diversity in the Workplace.__ (C). 2000. 35.00 (*0-536-61281-1*) Pearson Custom.

Managing Diversity Survival Guide: A Complete Collection of Checklists, Activities & Tips. Lee Gardenswartz. 192p. 1994. text 39.95 incl. disk (*0-7863-0265-8*, Irwn Prfssnl) McGraw-Hill Prof.

Managing Doctors. Alan Bruce & Sandra Hill. LC 96-187337. 64p. 1996. pap. 17.00 (*0-7486-0728-5*, Pub. by Edinburgh U Pr) Col U Pr.

Managing Doctors. Alan Sheldon. (Health Care Administration Ser.). 274p. 1986. 69.00 (*0-87094-646-3*) Aspen Pub.

Managing Documentation Projects in an Imperfect World. Gabriel Lanyi. LC 94-9111. 186p. 1994. pap. text 29.95 (*0-935470-74-3*) Battelle.

Managing Documents Across the Enterprise Fact Or Fiction? Karen V. Strong. 45p. 1997. 100.00 (*0-89258-316-9*, C136) Assn Inform & Image Mgmt.

*__Managing Domestic Dissent in First World War Britain, 1914-1918.__ Brock Millman. LC 00-25434. (British Politics & Society Ser.). 2000. write for info. (*0-7146-5054-4*) F Cass Pubs.

Managing Downsizing & Redundancy. A. Thornhill et al. 1996. pap. 129.00 (*1-85953-007-9*, Pub. by Tech Comm) St Mut.

Managing Downsizing & Redundancy. Adrian Thornhill et al. (Financial Times Management Briefings Ser.). 1997. pap. 94.50 (*0-273-63181-0*, Pub. by F T P-H) Trans-Atl Phila.

Managing Drug Supply: The Selection, Procurement, Distribution, & Use of Pharmaceuticals. 2nd expanded rev. ed. Management Sciences for Health Staff. LC 96-42268. (Books on International Development). (Illus.). 832p. 1997. pap. 84.95 (*1-56549-047-9*) Kumarian Pr.

Managing Economic Development: A Guide to State & Local Leadership Strategies. 300p. 1988. 27.95 (*0-317-05057-5*) Natl Coun Econ Dev.

*__Managing Economic Growth amid Ethnic Diversity: Malaysia, 1970-1990.__ Donald R. Snodgrass et al. 300p. 2000. 46.95 (*0-674-00362-4*); pap. 22.95 (*0-674-00363-2*) HUP.

Managing Economic Reforms in Post-Mao China. Kuotsai T. Liou. LC 97-34754. 184p. 1998. 59.95 (*0-275-95792-6*, Praeger Pubs) Greenwood.

*__Managing Economics.__ 6th ed. Maurice. 1998. pap., student ed. 25.94 (*0-256-17346-X*) McGrw-H Hghr Educ.

Managing Economics, Time & Cultural Forces see Leisure Wellness Series

Managing Education. Josylyn Owen. 1992. pap. text. write for info. (*0-582-08504-7*, Pub. by Addison-Wesley) Longman.

Managing Education: Theory & Practice. Ed. by Tony Bush. (Management in Education Ser.). 176p. 1989. pap. 34.95 (*0-335-09242-X*) OpUniv Pr.

Managing Education for Effective Schooling. John Raven. 184p. 1994. pap. 9.99 (*0-89824-531-1*, 5311) Trillium Pr.

Managing Education for Results. 3rd rev. ed. Richard W. Hostrop. LC 74-32074. (Illus.). xii, 248p. (C). 1983. 24.95 (*0-88280-022-1*) ETC Pubns.

Managing Education in Small Primary Schools. Maurice Galton. 32p. 1993. pap. 6.00 (*0-948080-77-9*, Trentham Bks) Stylus Pub VA.

Managing Effective Teaching of Mathematics: Grades 3 to 8. Suzanne Edwards. 1998. pap. text 26.95 (*1-85396-358-5*, Pub. by P Chapman) P H Brookes.

Managing Effectively in a Reinvented Government: The Federal Manager's Roadmap to Success. 2nd rev. ed. Rus Ritter. (Illus.). 133p. 1997. pap. text 14.95 (*0-936295-82-1*) FPMI Comns.

Managing Electronic Documents As Assets. Rob Allen. 41p. 1997. 100.00 (*0-89258-344-4*, C142) Assn Inform & Image Mgmt.

*__Managing Electronic Records.__ 2nd ed. William Saffady. 204p. 1998. pap. 51.00 (*0-933887-77-9*) ARMA Intl.

Managing Elephants: An Introduction to Their Training & Management. Alan Roocroft & Donald A. Zoll. 198p. (Orig.). 1994. pap. text 20.00 (*0-9640073-0-4*) Fever Tree.

Managing Emergency Medical Services: Principles & Practices. William Newkirk & Richard Linden. 272p. 1984. 27.95 (*0-317-58947-4*) P-H.

Managing Emergency Services. Tye. (Career Education Ser.). 1997. teacher ed. 14.00 (*0-8273-7373-2*) Delmar.

Managing Emergency Services. Tye. (Career Education Ser.). (C). 1998. 42.95 (*0-8273-7372-4*); pap. text, wbk. ed. 15.95 (*0-8273-7374-0*) Delmar.

Managing Emerging Market Portfolios. 1994. 30.00 (*1-879087-37-5*) Assn I M&R.

Managing Employee Internet Access: A Guide for Creating & Administering Corporate Access Policy with Monitoring & Filtering Software. Daniel Dern et al. (Illus.). 54p. (C). 1998. pap. text 25.00 (*0-7881-7070-8*) DIANE Pub.

Managing Employee Involvement & Participation. Jeff Hyman & Bob Mason. 224p. 1995. 69.95 (*0-8039-8726-9*); pap. 26.95 (*0-8039-8727-7*) Sage.

Managing Employee Performance Problems. Neville C. Thompkins. Ed. by Follin Armfield. (Professional Ser.). 200p. (Orig.). 1997. pap. 14.95 (*1-56052-428-6*) Crisp Pubns.

Managing Employee Relations in the Hotel & Catering Industry. Rosemary Lucas. LC 95-2056. (Illus.). 256p. 1995. 110.00 (*0-304-32910-X*); pap. 29.95 (*0-304-32897-9*) Continuum.

Managing Employee Rights & Responsibilities. Ed. by Chimezie A. Osigweh. LC 88-38310. 321p. 1989. 69.50 (*0-89930-336-6*, OME/, Quorum Bks) Greenwood.

Managing Employee Turnover: A Positive Approach. Edward Roseman. LC 80-69690. 277p. reprint ed. pap. 84.40 (*0-608-15007-X*, 205608800047) Bks Demand.

Managing Employees Made E-Z. E-Z Legal Staff. (Made E-Z Ser.). 1999. pap. 29.95 (*1-56382-308-X*) E-Z Legal.

*__Managing Employees' Time: A Federal Supervisor's Guide to Work Schedules, Leave, Attendance & Overtime Administration.__ 2nd rev. ed. Michael Corum. 106p. 1999. pap. 25.00 (*1-878810-54-5*) Dewey Pubns.

*__Managing Employer Liability for Employee Stress.__ D. Ashton. (Management Briefings Ser.). (Illus.). 1999. pap. 87.50 (*0-273-63253-1*, Pub. by F T P-H) Trans-Atl Phila.

Managing Employment & Training Programs. David Bresnick. (Managing the Human Services Ser.). 245p. 1986. 27.50 (*0-9610834-1-7*) Human Serv Pr.

Managing Empowerment: How to Make Business Re-Engineering Work. David Jenkins. 160p. 1997. 35.00 (*0-7126-7650-3*, Pub. by CEN3) Trafalgar.

Managing Energy Efficiency. Nebs Management. 72p. pap. text 34.95 (*0-7506-4092-8*) Buttrwrth-Heinemann.

Managing Energy Resources in Times of Dynamic Change. William H. Mashburn. LC 86-46135. 300p. 1988. text 65.00 (*0-88173-035-1*) Fairmont Pr.

Managing Energy Resources in Times of Dynamic Change. 2nd ed. Fairmont Press Staff & William H. Mashburn. 302p. 1992. 89.33 (*0-13-553496-8*) P-H.

Managing Energy Resources in Times of Dynamic Change. 2nd ed. William H. Mashburn. LC 91-3451. 290p. 1993. 74.00 (*0-88173-136-6*) Fairmont Pr.

Managing Engineering & Technology: An Introduction to Management for Engineers. 2nd ed. Daniel L. Babcock. LC 95-12378. (International Series in Industrial & Systems Engineering). 422p. 1995. 95.00 (*0-13-141392-9*) P-H.

Managing Engineering Dsgn. C. Hales. (C). 1993. 59.95 (*0-582-03933-9*, Pub. by Addison-Wesley) Longman.

Managing Engineers. Ed Repic. (Illus.). (Orig.). 1981. pap. 25.00 (*0-939740-00-1*) Effect Mgmt.

Managing Engineers & Technical Employees: How to Attract, Motivate, & Retain Excellent People. Douglas M. Soat. 184p. 1996. 59.00 (*0-89006-786-4*) Artech Hse.

Managing Environmental Disputes: Network Management As an Alternative. Ed. by Pieter Glasbergen. LC 94-27398. (Environment & Management Ser.: 5). 216p. (C). 1995. lib. bdg. 106.00 (*0-7923-3034-X*) Kluwer Academic.

Managing Environmental Disputes: Network Management As an Alternative. Ed. by Pieter Glasbergen. (Environment & Management Ser.). 200p. 1995. pap. text 55.50 (*0-7923-3625-9*) Kluwer Academic.

Managing Environmental Issues: A Casebook. Rogene A. Buchholz et al. 304p. (C). 1991. pap. text 24.60 (*0-13-563891-7*) P-H.

Managing Environmental Mandates for Multifamily Housing, 1997: A Compendium of Federal Laws & Regulations. William G. Miller. LC 96-61395. 148p. 1996. pap. text 299.95 (*0-87420-799-1*, M02) Urban Land.

Managing Environmental Mandates for Multifamily Housing, 1998: A Compendium of Federal Regulations. Urban Land Institute Staff & National Multi Housing Council/National Apartment. 150p. 1998. pap. 79.95 (*0-87420-821-1*, M25) Urban Land.

M

An Asterisk (*) at the beginning of an entry indicates that the title is appearing for the first time.

Managing Environmental Pollution. Andrew Farmer. (Routledge Environmental Management Ser.). (Illus.). 264p. (C). 1997. pap. 25.99 (*0-415-14515-5*) Routledge.

Managing Environmental Pollution. Andrew Farmer. (Routledge Environmental Management Ser.). (Illus.). 264p. (C). 1998. 80.00 (*0-415-14514-7*) Routledge.

Managing Environmental Risk: Real Estate & Business Transactions. Jennifer L. Machlin & Tomme R. Young. LC 88-17497. (Environmental Law Ser.). 1988. ring bd. 145.00 (*0-87632-603-3*) West Group.

Managing Environmental Risk Through Insurance. Paul K. Freeman & Howard Kunreuther. LC 97-8898. 50p. (Orig.). 1997. pap. 9.95 (*0-8447-4019-5*) Am Enterprise.

Managing Environmental Risk Through Insurance. Paul K. Freeman & Howard Kunreuther. LC 97-8898. (Studies in Risk & Uncertainty). (Orig.). 1997. lib. bdg. 66.00 (*0-7923-9901-3*) Kluwer Academic.

Managing Environmental Risks in Texas. Susan G. Hadden & Jurgen Schmandt. (Policy Research Project Report: No. 108). 88p. 1994. pap. 10.50 (*0-89940-716-1*) LBJ Sch Pub Aff.

Managing Environmental Risks in Texas: Background Papers, Vol. 1. Errol Brown et al. (Working Paper Ser.: Vol. 78). 166p. 1994. pap. 10.50 (*0-89940-565-7*) LBJ Sch Pub Aff.

Managing Environmental Risks in Texas: Background Papers, Vol. 2. Sylvia Amaya et al. (Working Paper Ser.: Vol. 79). 196p. 1994. pap. 10.50 (*0-89940-566-5*) LBJ Sch Pub Aff.

Managing Epilepsy in Primary Care. Malcolm P. Taylor. (Illus.). 192p. 1996. pap. 27.95 (*0-86542-972-3*) Blackwell Sci.

***Managing Equal Opportunities in Higher Education.** D. Woodward. 192p. 2000. pap. 39.95 (*0-335-19560-1*) OpUniv Pr.

Managing Ethnic Conflict in Africa: Pressures & Incentives for Cooperation. Donald S. Rothchild. LC 97-4763. 343p. 1997. 49.95 (*0-8157-7594-6*) Brookings.

Managing Ethnic Tensions in Multi-Ethnic Societies: Sri Lanka 1880-1985. Kingsley M. De Silva. 450p. (Orig.). (C). 1986. pap. text 42.00 (*0-8191-5398-2*); lib. bdg. 68.50 (*0-8191-5397-4*) U Pr of Amer.

Managing Evaluation & Innovation in Language Teaching: Building Bridges. Pauline Rea-Dickins & Kevin P. Germaine. LC 98-24975. (Applied Linguistics & Language Study Ser.). 1999. pap. text 35.63 (*0-582-30373-7*) Longman.

Managing Everyday Problems. Thomas A. Brigham. LC 88-19031. (Treatment Manuals for Practitioners Ser.). 172p. 1988. pap. text 18.95 (*0-89862-508-4*) Guilford Pubns.

Managing Existence in Naples: Morality, Action & Structure. Italo Pardo. (Cambridge Studies in Social & Cultural Anthropology: No. 104). 248p. (C). 1996. text 64.95 (*0-521-56227-9*); pap. text 25.95 (*0-521-56665-7*) Cambridge U Pr.

Managing Expectations: Working with People Who Want More, Better, Faster, Sooner, NOW! Naomi Karten. LC 93-48270. (Illus.). 240p. (Orig.). 1994. pap. 27.95 (*0-932633-27-7*) Dorset Hse Pub Co.

Managing Expert Systems. Ed. by Efraim Turban & Jay Liebowitz. LC 90-82963. 504p. (C). 1992. text 53.50 (*1-878289-11-X*) Idea Group Pub.

***Managing Explosive Corporate Growth.** Steven M. Bragg & Paul G. Lego. LC 98-27427. 336p. 1998. 34.95 (*0-471-29689-9*) Wiley.

Managing Export Entry & Expansion: Concepts & Practice. Ed. by Philip J. Rosson & Stanley D. Reid. LC 86-30330. 464p. 1987. 85.00 (*0-275-92361-4*, C2361, Praeger Pubs) Greenwood.

***Managing Exports, 2000 Yearbook.** annuals Ed. by Chris Horner & Jan C. Bernabe. (Illus.). 200p. 2000. pap. 199.00 (*1-58673-018-5*) IOMA.

Managing External Issues: Theory & Practice. Guy Stanley. LC 85-24051. (Contemporary Studies in Economic & Financial Analysis: Vol. 52). 257p. 1986. 78.50 (*0-89232-600-X*) Jai Pr.

Managing External Relations in Schools. Ed. by Nicholas Foskett. LC 92-12219. (Educational Management Ser.). 240p. 1992. pap. write for info. (*0-415-06834-7*) Routledge.

Managing Face to Face Communication: Survival Tactics for People & Products in the 21st Century. 2nd rev. ed. Allen E. Ivey. 90p. 1995. pap. text 18.95 (*0-917276-10-8*) Microtraining Assocs.

Managing Facilities Management. CCTA Staff. (IT Infrastructure Library Ser.). viii, 67p. 1990. pap. 80.00 (*0-11-330526-5*, Pub. by Statnry Office) Sftware Mgmt Network.

Managing Factory Maintenance. Joel Levitt. (Illus.). 290p. 1996. 39.95 (*0-8311-3063-6*) Indus Pr.

Managing Faculty Disputes. Jane E. McCarthy et al. LC 84-47991. (Jossey-Bass Higher Education Ser.). 292p. reprint ed. pap. 90.60 (*0-8357-4909-6*, 203783900009) Bks Demand.

Managing Fairness in Organizations. Constant D. Beugre. LC 98-6017. 168p. 1998. 49.95 (*1-56720-211-X*, Quorum Bks) Greenwood.

Managing Family Planning in General Practice. Sam Rowlands et al. LC 97-10270. 1997. write for info. (*1-85775-205-8*, Radcliffe Med Pr) Scovill Paterson.

Managing Family Trusts: Taking Control of Inherited Wealth. Robert A. Rikoon. Ed. by Larry Waschka. LC 99-18865. (Financial Advisor Ser.). (Illus.). 365p. 1999. 49.95 (*0-471-32115-X*) Wiley.

Managing Fast Growing Cities: New Approaches to Urban Planning. Nick Devas. 1993. pap. 41.95 (*0-582-09304-X*, Pub. by Addison-Wesley) Longman.

Managing Fatigue in Transportation. Ed. by American Trucking Assn. Staff. 176p. 1997. pap. text 75.00 (*0-86587-589-8*, 589) Gov Insts.

Managing Fatigue in Transportation: Selected Papers from the 3rd Fatigue in Transportation Conference, Freemantle, Western Australia, 1998. Laurence R. Hartley. LC 98-36059. 458p. 1998. 130.50 (*0-08-043357-X*, Pergamon Pr) Elsevier.

Managing Federal Assistance in the 1980s, 3 vols., Set. Office of Management & Budget Staff. 1982. reprint ed. 150.00 (*0-89941-223-8*, 201560) W S Hein.

Managing Fibromyalgia: A Six-Week Course on Self Care. Barbara Penner. 80p. 1997. 55.00 (*0-9644848-3-8*) Meerkat Graph.

Managing Field Operations: An Introduction to Incident Management. Stoffel et al. (Illus.). 80p. 1989. ring bd. 15.00 (*0-913724-42-4*) Emerg Response Inst.

Managing Finance & Financial Information. M. Collins et al. (In-Charge Ser.). 240p. (Orig.). (C). 1993. pap. text 36.95 (*0-631-19009-0*) Blackwell Pubs.

Managing Finance & Information. Ron Simpson. (Illus.). 1997. pap. 44.50 (*0-273-62637-X*, Pub. by Pitman Pub) Trans-Atl Phila.

Managing Finance for Quality: Bottom Line Results from Top Level Commitment. James A. Stoner & Frank M. Werner. 250p. 1994. text 35.00 (*0-87389-267-4*, H0823) ASQ Qual Pr.

Managing Finance in Schools. Tim Blanchard et al. Ed. by C. E. Wragg. (Education Matters Ser.). 144p. 1989. text 50.00 (*0-304-31707-1*) Continuum.

Managing Finances. David P. Anderson. (Family Life Issues Ser.). 1995. pap. 4.50 (*0-570-09491-7*, 20-2703) Concordia.

Managing Finances: Proceedings of a Symposium Sponsored by the Engineering Management Division. Ed. by David C. Johnston. 84p. 1984. 5.00 (*0-87262-397-1*) Am Soc Civil Eng.

***Managing Financial Information.** David Davies. 192p. 2000. pap. 41.95 (*0-8464-5111-5*) Beekman Pubs.

Managing Financial Institutions. 3rd ed. Mona J. Gardner. (C). 1994. teacher ed. 96.50 (*0-03-010294-4*, Pub. by Harcourt Coll Pubs) Harcourt.

***Managing Financial Institutions: A Financial Services Approach.** Scott. 2001. pap. 65.00 (*0-324-01739-1*) Thomson Learn.

Managing Financial Institutions: An Asset - Liability Approach. 3rd ed. Mona J. Gardner & Dixie L. Mills. LC 93-71151. 980p. (C). 1994. text 93.00 (*0-03-098079-8*) Dryden Pr.

***Managing Financial Institutions: An Asset/Liability Approach.** 4th ed. Mona J. Gardner. 1999. text 93.00 (*0-03-022054-8*, Pub. by Harcourt Coll Pubs) Harcourt.

Managing Financial Investments. 3rd ed. Gardner. (C). 1994. pap. text, teacher ed. 36.75 (*0-03-098080-1*) Harcourt Coll Pubs.

Managing Financial Resources. 2nd ed. Michael Broadbent & John Cullen. LC 97-199477. (Institute of Management Ser.). 480p. 1997. pap. text 35.95 (*0-7506-3392-1*, HG) Buttrwrth-Heinemann.

Managing Financial Risk. Clifford W. Smith et al. (Institutional Investor Series in Finance). 384p. 1989. 49.50 (*0-88730-371-4*, HarpBusn) HarpInfo.

Managing Financial Risk: A Guide to Derivative Products, Financial Engineering, & Value Maximization. 3rd ed. Charles W. Smithson & Clifford W. Smith, Jr. LC 98-17711. (Illus.). 620p. 1998. 70.00 (*0-07-059354-X*) McGraw.

Managing Financial Risks in Indebted Developing Countries. Donald J. Mathieson et al. (Occasional Papers: No. 65). 47p. 1989. pap. 10.00 (*1-55775-116-1*) Intl Monetary.

Managing Fire Services. 2nd ed. 257p. 1989. pap., student ed. 14.95 (*0-945250-16-9*) Davis Pub Co.

Managing Fire Services. 2nd ed. Ed. by Ronny J. Coleman & John A. Granito. (Municipal Management Ser.). 506p. 1988. text 39.95 (*0-87326-078-3*) Intl City-Cnty Mgt.

Managing Fire Services: Davis Study Guide. 2nd ed. 105p. Date not set. pap. text 14.95 (*0-614-31211-6*, S086) Davis Pub Co.

Managing Fiscal Strain in Major American Cities: Understanding Retrenchment in the Public Sector, 247. William J. Pammer, Jr. LC 89-17073. (Contributions in Political Science Ser.: No. 247). 151p. 1990. 49.95 (*0-313-26656-5*, PMF/, Greenwood Pr) Greenwood.

Managing Fiscal Stress: The Crisis in the Public Sector. Ed. by Charles H. Levine. LC 79-27266. (Chatham House Series on Change in American Politics). (Illus.). 352p. reprint ed. pap. 109.20 (*0-8357-4830-8*, 203776700009) Bks Demand.

Managing Fixed Income Portfolios. Ed. by Frank J. Fabozzi. (Illus.). 537p. 1997. 75.00 (*1-883249-27-9*) F J Fabozzi.

Managing Food Protection. DMA Staff. LC 98-183743. 202p. 1998. per. 35.00 (*0-7872-4736-7*, 41473601) Kendall-Hunt.

***Managing Food Protection.** 3rd ed. DMA Staff. 218p. 2000. per. 35.00 (*0-7872-7273-6*) Kendall-Hunt.

Managing Foodservice Facilities & Equipment: Student Manual. National Restaurant Assn. Educational Foundation S. 80p. (Orig.). 1990. pap. text. write for info. (*0-915452-50-2*) Educ Found.

Managing Foodservice Operations: A Systems Approach for Healthcare. 3rd ed. Knight. LC 97-201312. 544p. 1997. per. 60.00 (*0-7872-3374-9*, 41337401) Kendall-Hunt.

Managing for a Change: How to Run Community Development Projects. Anthony Davies & Voluntary Service Overseas Staff. LC 98-184810. xi, 164p. 1997. pap. 18.95 (*1-85339-399-1*, Pub. by Intermed Tech) Stylus Pub VA.

Managing for Accountability: Preserving the Public Trust in Public & Nonprofit Organizations. Kevin P. Kearns. (Nonprofit Sector Ser.). 250p. 1996. 28.95 (*0-7879-0228-4*) Jossey-Bass.

Managing for Commitment: Building Loyalty Within Organizations. C. Gorman. Ed. by Tony Hicks. LC 90-84926. (Fifty-Minute Ser.). (Illus.). 72p. (Orig.). 1991. pap. 10.95 (*1-56052-099-X*) Crisp Pubns.

Managing for Development. Barrie Hopson & Lifeskills International Staff. LC 99-24995. 1999. write for info. (*0-566-08140-7*) Ashgate Pub Co.

Managing for Dummies. Bob Nelson & Peter Economy. (For Dummies Ser.). (Illus.). 384p. 1996. pap. 19.99 (*1-56884-858-7*) IDG Bks.

Managing for Excellence: The Guide to Developing High Performance in Contemporary Organizations. David L. Bradford & Allan R. Cohen. (Management Series on Problem Solving, Decision Making & Strategic Thinking: 1-578). Ep. 1986. cd-rom 32.95 (*0-471-84702-X*) Wiley.

Managing for Excellence: The Guide to Developing High Performance in Contemporary Organizations. David L. Bradford & Allan R. Cohen. LC 95-50901. 320p. 1997. pap. 16.95 (*0-471-12724-8*) Wiley.

Managing for Excellence in the Public Sector. Gerrit Van Der Waldt et al. LC 98-137672. xxx, 471 p. 1997. write for info. (*0-7021-3816-9*) Juta & Co.

Managing for Greater Returns. Richard Phillips. 1962. 11.95 (*0-686-00369-1*) AG Pr.

***Managing for Growth: The Essential Business Guide to Pension Fund Management.** Asia Law & Practice Staff. 35p. 1999. pap. text 95.00 (*962-936-058-6*, Pub. by Asia Law & Practice) Am Educ Systs.

Managing for Impact in Nonprofit Organizations. rev. ed. James M. Hardy. LC 84-81456. 238p. 1995. 36.45 (*0-930381-01-7*) Essex Pr.

Managing for Joint Venture Success. Kathryn R. Harrigan. LC 85-45417. 240p. 1986. 35.00 (*0-669-11617-3*) Free Pr.

Managing for Organizational Quality: An Annotated Bibliography. 1996. lib. bdg. 251.95 (*0-8490-5962-3*) Gordon Pr.

Managing for Organizational Quality, Theory & Implementation: An Annotated Bibliography. 1995. lib. bdg. 250.99 (*0-8490-6854-1*) Gordon Pr.

Managing for Peak Performance. Alan Weiss. 1995. 18.00 (*1-886158-00-2*) Macalester.

Managing for Peak Performance: A Guide to the Power (& Pitfalls) of Personal Style. Alan Weiss. 176p. 1989. 21.95 (*0-88730-337-4*, HarpBusn) HarpInfo.

Managing for Peak Performance: A Guide to the Power (& Pitfalls) of Personal Style. Alan Weiss. 192p. 1990. pap. 12.95 (*0-88730-463-X*, HarpBusn) HarpInfo.

Managing for Performance Perfection: The Changing Emphasis, Vol. 1. William C. Pope. (Illus.). 344p. (Orig.). (C). 1990. pap. text 39.95 (*0-944453-00-7*) B Brae.

Managing for Productivity. Albert A. Vicere. 14.95 (*0-914951-11-4*) LERN.

Managing for Productivity in Data Processing. James R. Johnson. LC 80-65015. (Illus.). 188p. reprint ed. pap. 58.30 (*0-8357-7515-1*, 203601000097) Bks Demand.

Managing for Products Liability Avoidance. 2nd ed. LC 95-102154. 264p. 1996. pap. 35.00 (*0-8080-0028-4*, 04823001) CCH INC.

Managing for Profit: Improving or Maintaining the Bottom Line. LC 91-70294. 97p. 1991. pap. 49.95 (*0-89707-648-6*, 511-0288) Amer Bar Assn.

Managing for Profit in the Nonprofit World. Paul B. Firstenberg. LC 86-80827. 253p. 1986. pap. text 19.95 (*0-87954-159-8*) Foundation Ctr.

Managing for Profitability: How Winning Professionals Earn What They're Worth. David W. Cottle. 210p. 1993. 99.00 (*1-883711-00-2*) Hightower Pub.

Managing for Profits: Lumber Yard Management in the Decades Ahead. H. Jack Nunn. 87p. 1995. pap. 150.00 (*0-9645680-0-4*) CTBMA.

Managing for Quality: An Introductory Text. 450p. 1996. pap. 44.00 (*0-13-207119-3*) P-H.

Managing for Quality: How to Implement & Manage a Business Strategy of Continuous Improvement. 3rd rev. ed. Leslie L. Kossoff. LC 98-65723. Orig. Title: Closing the Gap: The Handbook for Total Quality Implementation. xii, 160p. 1998. pap. 15.95 (*0-9630724-3-9*) Kossoff Mgmt.

Managing for Quality: Integrating Quality & Business Strategy. V. Daniel Hunt. (APICS Ser.). 270p. 1992. 47.50 (*1-55623-544-5*, Irwn Prfssnl) McGraw-Hill Prof.

Managing for Quality in the Financial Services Industry. Anthony E. Ansell. LC 92-39843. (Strategic Management of Financial Institutions Ser.). 360p. 1993. mass mkt. 84.95 (*0-412-47300-3*) Chapman & Hall.

Managing for Quality in the Hospitality Industry. Robert H. Woods & Judy Z. King. LC 96-164739. (Illus.). (Orig.). 1995. pap. write for info. (*0-86612-094-7*) Educ Inst Am Hotel.

***Managing for Results.** Peter F. Drucker. 1999. pap. 13.00 (*0-06-662024-4*, HarpBusn) HarpInfo.

***Managing for Results: Agencies' Annual Performance Plans Can Help Address Strategic Planning Challenges.** Ed. by Benjamin F. Nelson. 143p. (C). 1999. pap. text 30.00 (*0-7881-8350-8*) DIANE Pub.

Managing for Results: An Agenda to Improve the Usefulness of Agencies' Annual Performance Plans. J. Christopher Mihm. 48p. (C). 1999. pap. text 20.00 (*0-7881-7631-5*) DIANE Pub.

Managing for Results: Economic Tasks & Risk-Taking Decisions. Peter F. Drucker. LC 85-45683. 240p. 1993. reprint ed. pap. 12.50 (*0-88730-614-4*, HarpBusn) HarpInfo.

Managing for Results: Effective Resource Allocation for Libraries. Sandra S. Nelson et al. LC 99-33130. (Illus.). 320p. 1999. pap. 45.00 (*0-8389-3498-6*) ALA.

Managing for Results: Experiences Abroad Suggest Insights for Federal Management Reforms. 76p. (Orig.). (C). 1995. pap. text 20.00 (*0-7881-2078-6*) DIANE Pub.

Managing for Results: Experiences of Selected Credit Programs. 56p. pap. text 20.00 (*0-7881-7947-0*) DIANE Pub.

Managing for Results: The Department of Justice's Initial Efforts to Implement GPRA. (Illus.). 76p. 1996. reprint ed. pap. text 20.00 (*0-7881-3270-9*) DIANE Pub.

Managing for Results: The Statutory Framework for Performance Based Management & Accountability. Debra R. Johnson. 51p. (C). 1998. pap. text 20.00 (*0-7881-7339-1*) DIANE Pub.

Managing for Results: Using the Results Act to Address Mission Fragmentation & Program Overlap. Michael J. Curro & Linda F. Baker. (Illus.). 44p. 1998. pap. text 20.00 (*0-7881-7076-7*) DIANE Pub.

Managing for Results in State Government. Maria P. Aristigueta. LC 98-23643. 192p. 1999. 55.00 (*1-56720-246-2*, Quorum Bks) Greenwood.

Managing for Service Effectiveness in Social Welfare Organizations. Ed. by Rino Patti et al. LC 87-22930. (Administration in Social Work Ser.: Vol. 11, Nos. 3 & 4). 295p. 1989. text 49.95 (*0-86656-687-2*) Haworth Pr.

Managing for Solvency & Profitability in Life & Health Insurance Companies. Susan Conant et al. LC 96-76706. (FLMI Insurance Education Program Ser.). (Illus.). 732p. text 71.95 (*0-939921-80-4*, Pub. by Life Office) PBD Inc.

Managing for Success. Alfred York. LC 94-43420. (Management Skills-ISM Ser.). 160p. 1995. pap. 29.95 (*0-304-33316-6*) Continuum.

Managing for Success: A Police Chief's Survival Guide. Michael Scott. LC 86-63094. 74p. (Orig.). (C). 1986. pap. 11.00 (*1-878734-11-3*) Police Exec Res.

***Managing for Success: The Latest in Management Thought & Practice from Canada's Premier Businesses.** Richard Ivey. 256p. 2000. 35.00 (*0-00-200023-7*) HarpC.

Managing for the Environment: What Every Public Manager Needs to Know. Rosemary O'Leary et al. LC 98-36772. (Business & Management Ser.). 436p. 1998. 32.95 (*0-7879-1004-X*) Jossey-Bass.

***Managing for the First Time.** Cherry Mill. 96p. 2000. pap. 17.95 (*0-8464-5179-4*) Beekman Pubs.

Managing for the Future. Deborah Ancona et al. (GI - Organizational Behavior Ser.). 1996. ring bd. 57.95 (*0-538-86158-4*) S-W Pub.

Managing for the Future. Ancona et al. 1995. 6.50 (*0-538-85895-8*); 6.50 (*0-538-85896-6*) Thomson Learn.

***Managing for the Future.** 3rd ed. Deborah Anconca. (SWC-General Business Ser.). 2001. pap. 50.00 (*0-324-05575-7*) Sth-Wstrn College.

Managing for the Future, Module 4. Deborah Ancona et al. (GI - Organizational Behavior Ser.). 1995. mass mkt. 6.25 (*0-538-85876-1*) S-W Pub.

Managing for the Future: An Ecology of Tomorrow's Organization. Alf Chattell. LC 94-43720. 1995. text 55.00 (*0-312-12431-7*) St Martin.

Managing for the Future: Organizational. 2nd ed. Deborah Ancona & Kochan. (GC - Principles of Management Ser.). 1998. 74.95 (*0-538-87546-1*) S-W Pub.

Managing for the Future: Organizational Behavior. Deborah Ancona et al. (GI - Organizational Behavior Ser.). (C). 1996. mass mkt. 69.95 (*0-538-84890-1*) S-W Pub.

Managing for the Future: The 1990s & Beyond. Peter F. Drucker. LC 93-10126. 384p. 1993. pap. 14.95 (*0-452-26984-9*, Truman Talley) St Martin.

Managing for the '90s: The Book of Solutions. Drake Beil. Ed. by Lenore Magisa. (Illus.). 212p. 1992. pap. 7.95 (*0-89610-266-1*) Island Heritage.

Managing for Tomorrow: Global Change & Local Futures. Ed. by Amy C. Paul. (Practical Management Ser.). (Illus.). 188p. 1990. 23.95 (*0-87326-061-9*) Intl City-Cnty Mgt.

Managing for Value: A Guide to Value-Based Strategic Management. Bernard C. Reimann. 256p. 1987. 33.00 (*0-912841-26-5*) Planning Forum.

Managing for World-Class Quality: A Primer for Executives & Managers. Edwin S. Shecter. (Quality & Reliability Ser.: Vol. 30). (Illus.). 288p. 1991. text 75.00 (*0-8247-7712-3*) Dekker.

Managing Foreign Exchange Reserves in Small Developing Countries. Courtney Blackman. (Occasional Paper Ser.: No. 11). 19p. 1982. pap. 7.00 (*1-56708-010-3*) Grp of Thirty.

Managing Foreign-Exchange Risk. Ed. by Richard J. Herring. LC 82-21999. (Illus.). 262p. 1986. pap. text 25.95 (*0-521-31120-9*) Cambridge U Pr.

Managing Foreign Exchange Risk: Advanced Strategies for Global Investors, Corporations. rev. ed. David F. Derosa. 304p. 1996. per. 65.00 (*1-55738-566-1*, Irwn Prfssnl) McGraw-Hill Prof.

Managing Foreign Exchange Risk: Advanced Strategies for Global Investors, Corporations, & Financial Institutions. 2nd rev. ed. David F. Derosa. Ed. by Frank J. Fabozzi. LC 96-3753. 304p. 1996. 65.00 (*0-7863-1022-7*, Irwn Prfssnl) McGraw-Hill Prof.

Managing Foreign Exchange Risk: The Tools & Techniques for Managing Currency Exposure. Dominic Bennet. (Illus.). 280p. (Orig.). 1996. 65.00 (*0-273-61976-4*) F T P H.

Managing Foreign Exchange Risks. Nick Douch. 80p. 1996. pap. 34.95 (*92-842-1202-2*, 549) ICC Pub.

Managing Foreign Investment: Lessons from Laos. Russell B. Sunshine. LC 95-42158. 1995. write for info. (*0-86638-177-5*) EW Ctr HI.

An Asterisk (*) at the beginning of an entry indicates that the title is appearing for the first time.

Managing Forest Ecosystems to Conserve Fungus Diversity & Sustain Wild Mushroom Harvests. Ed. by David Pilz & Randy Molina. 104p. (C). 1998. pap. text 35.00 (*0-7881-4343-3*) DIANE Pub.

Managing Forests as Common Property: Forestry Paper. FAO Staff. LC 98-213381. (Forestry Papers: No. 136). 1998. pap. 11.00 (*92-5-104122-9*, F41229, Pub. by FAO) Bernan Associates.

Managing Fragmented Public Mental Health Services. Richard G. Frank & Laura L. Morlock. 52p. (Orig.). 1997. pap. write for info. (*1-887748-03-2*) Milbank Memorial.

Managing Free Trade for Agriculture. Vernon O. Roningen. LC 93-87573. 200p. 1993. pap. 25.00 (*0-9640007-0-9*) Natl Ctr Food.

Managing from the Heart. Hyler Bracey et al. 242p. 1990. 16.95 (*0-9626198-0-9*, Dell Trade Pbks) Dell.

Managing from the Heart. Hyler Bracey et al. 208p. 1993. pap. 12.95 (*0-440-50472-4*, Dell Trade Pbks) Dell.

Managing from the Heart: Unfolding Spirit in People & Organizations. Arun Wakhlu. LC 98-33288. 1999. write for info. (*0-7619-9304-5*) Sage.

***Managing from the Heart: Unfolding Spirit in People & Organizations.** Arun Wakhlu. LC 98-33288. 1999. write for info. (*0-7619-9303-7*) Sage.

Managing Front Office Operations see Front Office Procedures

Managing Front Office Operations. 5th rev. ed. Michael L. Kasavana & Richard M. Brooks. LC 98-29129. (Illus.). 485p. (C). 1998. pap. 66.95 (*0-86612-179-X*) Educ Inst Am Hotel.

***Managing Frontiers in Competitive Intelligence.** Ed. by Craig S. Fleisher & David L. Blenkhorn. LC 00-37264. 300p. 2000. 69.00 (*1-56720-384-1*, Q384, Quorum Bks) Greenwood.

***Managing Frozen Foods.** Chris Kennedy. LC 00-37817. (Illus.). 2000. pap. write for info. (*0-8493-0844-5*) CRC Pr.

***Managing Frozen Foods.** Chris Kennedy. 320p. 2000. text 170.00 (*1-85573-412-5*, Pub. by Woodhead Pubng) Am Educ Systs.

Managing Gender: Affirmative Action & Organizational Power in Australian, Canadian, & New Zealand Sport. Jim McKay. LC 96-53415. (SUNY Series on Sport, Culture, & Social Relations). 217p. (C). 1997. text 56.50 (*0-7914-3421-4*); pap. text 18.95 (*0-7914-3422-2*) State U NY Pr.

Managing Gender: The State, the New Middle Class & Women Workers, 1830-1930. Desley Deacon. (Illus.). 320p. 1990. text 24.95 (*0-19-554817-5*) OUP.

***Managing Generation X: How to Bring Out the Best in Young Talen.** rev. ed. Bruce Tulgan. 2000. pap. 13.95 (*0-393-32075-8*) Norton.

Managing Generation X: How to Bring Out the Best in Young Talent. Bruce Tulgan. 275p. 1995. pap. 19.95 (*1-56343-111-4*) Silver Lake.

Managing Genetic Information: Implications for Nursing Practice. American Nurses Association Staff. 60p. 1995. pap. text 14.95 (*1-55810-111-X*, NP-102) Am Nurses Pub.

Managing Geographic Information System Projects. William E. Huxhold & Allan G. Levinsohn. LC 93-43905. (Spatial Information Systems Ser.). (Illus.). 272p. (C). 1995. text 61.00 (*0-19-507869-1*) OUP.

Managing Geographic Information Systems. Nancy J. Obermeyer & Jeffrey K. Pinto. LC 93-47119. 226p. 1994. lib. bdg. 36.00 (*0-89862-005-8*, 2005) Guilford Pubns.

Managing Gigabytes: Compressing & Indexing Documents & Images. 2nd ed. Ian H. Witten et al. Ed. by Ed Fox. LC 99-26345. (Multimedia Information & Systems Ser.). 600p. (C). 1999. text 59.95 (*1-55860-570-3*, Pub. by Morgan Kaufmann) Harcourt.

Managing Global Chaos: Sources of & Responses to International Conflict. Chester A. Crocker et al. LC 96-31858. 1996. 55.00 (*1-878379-59-3*); pap. text 29.95 (*1-878379-58-5*) US Inst Peace.

Managing Global Communication in Science & Technology, 1. Peter Hager. LC 99-14001. 365p. 1999. 74.95 (*0-471-24922-X*) Wiley.

Managing Global Corporation. 2nd ed. De La Torre. 672p. 2000. pap. 63.75 (*0-07-234798-8*) McGraw.

Managing Global Debt. Richard S. Dale & Richard P. Mattione. LC 83-72567. 50p. 1983. pap. 8.95 (*0-8157-1717-2*) Brookings.

Managing Global Information Network. Raj Ananthanpillai. LC 97-22889. (Illus.). 213p. 1997. pap. 55.00 (*0-07-001601-1*) McGraw.

Managing Global Innovation: Uncovering the Secrets of Future Competitiveness. Roman Boutellier et al. LC 98-55583. (Illus.). viii, 627p. 1999. 109.00 (*3-540-65256-6*) Spr-Verlag.

***Managing Global Innovation: Uncovering the Secrets of Future Competitiveness.** 2nd rev. ed. Roman Boutellier et al. viii, 627p. 2000. 109.00 (*3-540-66832-2*) Spr-Verlag.

Managing Global Operations: Cultural & Technical Success Factors. Scott T. Young & Winter Nie. LC 95-26267. 224p. 1996. 62.95 (*0-89930-870-8*, Quorum Bks) Greenwood.

Managing Global Projects. Richard Punzo. (Management Booklets Ser.). Date not set. write for info. (*1-882390-92-X*) Princeton Trng.

Managing Global Telecommunications: North American Perspectives. Ed. by William F. Averyt & Anne C. Averyt. 212p. (Orig.). 1988. pap. text 25.00 (*0-944799-01-9*) U VT Schl Busn Admin.

Managing Globalization in the Age of Interdependence. George C. Lodge. LC 95-17969. (Warren Bennis Executive Briefing Ser.). (Illus.). 128p. 1995. 22.50 (*0-89384-271-0*, Pfffr & Co) Jossey-Bass.

Managing Globally: A Complete Guide to Competing Worldwide. Carl A. Nelson. 320p. 1993. text 65.00 (*0-7863-0121-X*, Irwn Prfssnl) McGraw-Hill Prof.

Managing God's Mutual Funds: Yours & His - Understanding True Prosperity. Kenneth Copeland. LC 97-148010. 192p. 1997. 14.95 (*0-88114-970-5*) K Copeland Pubns.

Managing God's Organization: The Catholic Church in Society. Scott R. Safranski. Ed. by Richard Farmer. LC 85-16540. (Research for Business Decisions Ser.: No. 79). 211p. reprint ed. 65.50 (*0-8357-1669-4*, 207041500088) Bks Demand.

Managing God's Resources. James J. Newton. 100p. (Orig.). 1997. pap. 16.95 (*1-888555-08-4*) MGR Pr.

***Managing Government Records & Information.** Bruce Dearstyne. 264p. 1999. pap. 114.00 (*0-933887-83-3*) ARMA Intl.

Managing Great Britain Limited. Alfred Robens. LC 77-370608. (Lecture Ser.). 20p. 1977. write for info. (*0-903542-14-5*) Ashridge Manag College.

***Managing Green Issues.** Tom Curtin. LC 00-42078. 2000. write for info. (*0-312-23716-2*) St Martin.

Managing Green Technologies for Global Competitiveness. Christian N. Madu. LC 95-19468. 280p. 1996. 67.95 (*0-89930-827-9*, Quorum Bks) Greenwood.

Managing Grounds Maintenance. David E. Lofgren. Ed. by Gary O. Robinette. 181p. (Orig.). 1994. pap. text 29.95 (*1-882240-02-2*) Agora Comms.

Managing Group Tours: Your Complete Reference Guide to Successful Tour Management. Anita L. Fielder. Ed. by Amber Christman-Clark. (Illus.). 205p. (C). 1995. pap. 19.95 (*1-887067-51-5*) Shoreline Creat.

Managing Growing Organizations: A New Approach. Theodore D. Weinshall & Yael-Anna Raveh. LC 82-21967. 431p. reprint ed. pap. 133.70 (*0-8357-3478-1*, 203973700013) Bks Demand.

Managing Growth in America's Communities. Douglas R. Porter. LC 97-14941. (Illus.). 319p. 1997. pap. text 29.95 (*1-55963-442-1*, Shearwater Bks) Island Pr.

Managing Growth in Western Rural Communities. (State Legislative Reports: Vol. 19, No. 17). 6p. 1994. 15.00 (*1-55516-385-8*, 7302-1917) Natl Conf State Legis.

Managing Growth Through Acquisition. David F. Linowes. LC 68-31542. 192p. reprint ed. pap. 59.60 (*0-608-10731-X*, 205039400078) Bks Demand.

Managing Habitats for Conservation. Ed. by William J. Sutherland & David A. Hill. (Illus.). 411p. (C). 1995. pap. text 32.95 (*0-521-44776-3*) Cambridge U Pr.

Managing Hazardous Air Pollutants: State of the Art. Winston Chow. 608p. 1993. lib. bdg. 110.00 (*0-87371-866-6*, L866) Lewis Pubs.

Managing Hazardous Drugs: A Quick Reference for Safe Administration. Anne M. Zolaer. (Illus.). 1997. spiral bd. write for info. (*1-891814-01-X*) Found Care Mgmt.

Managing Hazardous Materials Incidents: Medical Management Guidelines for Acute Chemical Exposures, 2 vols. 1996. lib. bdg. 600.99 (*0-8490-6050-8*) Gordon Pr.

Managing Hazardous Materials Incidents Vol. I: Emergency Medical Services: A Planning Guide for the Management of Contaminated Patients. (Illus.). 77p. (Orig.). (C). 1996. pap. text 40.00 (*0-7881-3710-7*) DIANE Pub.

Managing Hazardous Materials Incidents Vol. II: Hospital Emergency Departments: A Planning Guide for the Management of Contaminated Patients. Scott V. Wright. (Illus.). 72p. (Orig.). (C). 1996. pap. text 40.00 (*0-7881-3714-X*) DIANE Pub.

Managing Hazardous Materials Incidents Vol. III: Medical Management Guidelines for Acute Chemical Exposures. Jonathan Borak et al. 495p. 1996. reprint ed. pap. text 50.00 (*0-7881-3256-3*) DIANE Pub.

Managing Hazardous Wastes: A Programmatic Approach. Ward Wright. 96p. (Orig.). 1986. pap. 15.00 (*0-87292-061-5*, C-45) Coun State Govts.

Managing Hazardous Wastes Containing Heavy Metals. Douglas Grosse. (Illus.). 170p. 1990. 29.95 (*0-925760-14-5*) SciTech Pubs.

Managing Hazards in the Transfusion Service. Harold B. Anstall et al. 212p. 1993. 47.00 (*0-89189-324-5*) Am Soc Clinical.

Managing Head Teacher Appraisal. Victor Game & Alun Morgan. 144p. 1992. pap. 35.00 (*1-85396-191-4*, Pub. by P Chapman) Taylor & Francis.

Managing Headache in Primary Care. rev. ed. Peter J. Goadsby & Stephen D. Silberstein. 464p. 1997. pap. text 39.95 (*0-86542-672-4*) Blackwell Sci.

***Managing Health & Safety in Building & Construction.** Tony Clarke. LC 99-36658. 345p. 1999. write for info. (*0-7506-4015-4*) Buttrwrth-Heinemann.

Managing Health & Safety of Contractors. R. Slade. 1996. pap. 145.00 (*1-85953-011-7*, Pub. by Tech Comm) St Mut.

Managing Health at Work. 2nd ed. C. Wilkinson. (Illus.). 256p. 1997. text write for info. (*0-412-71590-2*, Chap & Hall NY) Chapman & Hall.

Managing Health at Work: Guide for Managers & Workplace Health Specialists. Carol Wilkinson. LC 98-158700. (Illus.). 192p. (C). 1998. 60.00 (*0-419-22980-9*, E & FN Spon) Routledge.

Managing Health at Work: Guide for Managers & Workplace Health Specialists. Carol Wilkinson. (Illus.). 192p. (C). 1998. reprint ed. pap. 39.99 (*0-419-22660-5*, E & FN Spon) Routledge.

Managing Health Benefits in Small & Mid-Sized Organizations. Patricia Halo. LC 99-10715. (Illus.). 350p. 1999. 35.00 (*0-8144-0457-X*) AMACOM.

Managing Health Care. Glynn. 1995. pap. text 30.00 (*0-7020-1831-7*, W B Saunders Co) Harcrt Hlth Sci Grp.

Managing Health Care Costs: Private Sector Innovations. Sean Sullivan & Polly M. Ehrenhaft. LC 84-6390. (AEI Studies: No. 406). 112p. reprint ed. pap. 34.80 (*0-7837-1084-4*, 204161500021) Bks Demand.

Managing Health Care Demand. Robin E. MacStravic et al. LC 97-47204. 576p. 1998. 65.00 (*0-8342-0927-6*, 09276) Aspen Pub.

Managing Health Care Resources. Price. LC 98-4643. (Illus.). 336p. (C). (gr. 13). 1998. pap. text 34.95 (*0-8151-2298-5*, 27516) Mosby Inc.

Managing Health Professionals. Michael J. Nelson. 216p. 1990. pap. 25.50 (*0-412-33350-3*, A4446) Chapman & Hall.

Managing Health Promotion: Health Development in Organizations & Communities. Ina Simnett. 248p. 1996. pap. 49.95 (*0-471-95814-X*) Wiley.

Managing Health Promotion Programs. Bradley R. Wilson & Timothy E. Glaros. LC 93-38014. (Illus.). 264p. 1994. text 38.00 (*0-87322-611-9*, BWIL0000) Human Kinetics.

Managing Health Promotion Programs: Leadership Skills for the 21st Century. Donald J. Breckon. LC 96-39676. 300p. 50.00 (*0-8342-0739-7*, 20739) Aspen Pub.

Managing Health Promotion Programs: Student Workbook & Case Studies. Timothy E. Glaros & Bradley R. A. Wilson. 120p. (Orig.). 1995. pap. text, student ed. 12.00 (*0-87322-872-3*, BGLA0872) Human Kinetics.

Managing Health Service Contracts. K. Hodgson. (C). 1996. pap. text 45.00 (*0-7020-1998-4*) Harcourt.

Managing Health Service Information. R. Sheaff. 217p. 1994. pap. 34.95 (*0-335-15702-5*) OpUniv Pr.

***Managing Health Services: Cases in Organization Design & Decision Making.** Deborah Bender et al. LC 99-89904. 2000. write for info. (*1-56793-125-1*) Health Admin Pr.

Managing Health Services Organizations. 2nd ed. Beaufort B. Longest, Jr. et al. (Illus.). 550p. 1985. 42.50 (*0-7216-2045-0*, W B Saunders Co) Harcrt Hlth Sci Grp.

Managing Health Services Organizations. 3rd ed. Jonathon S. Rakich et al. LC 92-1466. 768p. 1992. 58.00 (*1-878812-09-2*) Hlth Prof Pr.

***Managing Health Services Organizations & Systems.** 4th ed. Beaufort B. Longest et al. 2000. text 78.00 (*1-878812-57-2*, 2572) Hlth Prof Pr.

Managing Health Systems Research. I. Parthamanathan. (Health System Research Training Ser.: Vol. 4). 1992. pap. 17.50 (*0-88936-588-1*, Pub. by IDRC Bks) Stylus Pub VA.

Managing Healthcare Compliance. Scott C. Withrow. LC 98-47637. 34p. 1999. 49.00 (*1-56793-096-4*) Health Admin Pr.

***Managing Healthcare Compliance: Self-Study Course.** J. Stuart Showalter. LC 00-23821. (ACHE Self-Study Program Ser.). 2000. write for info. (*1-56793-127-8*) Health Admin Pr.

***Managing Healthcare Information Systems with Web-Enabled Technologies.** Ed. by Lauren Eder. LC 99-88700. (Illus.). 300p. (C). 2000. pap. 69.95 (*1-878289-65-9*) Idea Group Pub.

Managing Heart Failure in Primary Care. Henry J. Dargie et al. (Illus.). 256p. 1996. pap. 49.95 (*0-86542-966-9*) Blackwell Sci.

Managing Hebrew Through Prayer: The Educational Director's Guide. Terry Kaye. LC 97-46473. 1998. vinyl bd. 29.95 (*0-87441-657-4*) Behrman.

Managing Herpes: How to Live & Love with a Chronic STD. rev. ed. Charles Ebel. LC 97-78101. (Illus.). 238p. 1998. pap. 27.75 (*1-885833-03-2*) Am Social Health.

Managing High Risk Flood Areas - 1985 & Beyond: Proceedings of the 8th Annual Conference of the Association of State Floodplain Managers, Portland, Maine, June 11-14, 1984. (Special Publications: No. 11). 326p. (Orig.). (C). 1985. pap. 20.00 (*0-685-28093-4*) Natural Hazards.

Managing High Tech Programs & Projects. Russell D. Archibald. LC 91-25865. 400p. 1992. 107.50 (*0-471-51327-X*) Wiley.

***Managing High Technology & Innovation.** 320p. (C). 1999. 31.50 (*0-536-60116-X*) Pearson Custom.

Managing High Technology & Innovation. Nino S. Levy. LC 97-37465. 274p. 1998. pap. text 36.20 (*0-02-370462-4*) Macmillan.

Managing Higher Education. David E. Bland. 112p. 1990. pap. text 38.00 (*0-304-32275-X*) Continuum.

Managing Higher Education As a Business. Robert L. Lenington. LC 96-7617. (American Council on Education). 184p. 1996. boxed set 29.95 (*1-57356-023-5*) Oryx Pr.

Managing Highly Usable Graphical User Interface Developmental Environments. Luke Hohmann. (C). Date not set. 35.95 (*0-13-896614-1*, Macmillan Coll) P-H.

***Managing Historic Sites & Buildings: Balancing Presentation & Preservation.** Gill Chitty & David Baker. LC 98-54678. 1999. write for info. (*0-415-20814-9*) Routledge.

Managing Historic Sites & Buildings: Balancing Presentation & Preservation. Gill Chitty & David Baker. LC 98-54678. (Issues in Heritage Management Ser.). 1999. pap. write for info. (*0-415-20815-7*) Routledge.

***Managing Historical Records Programs: A Guide for Historical Agencies.** Bruce W. Dearstyne. (American Association for State & Local History Book Ser.). 240p. 2000. 62.00 (*0-7425-0282-1*); pap. 24.95 (*0-7425-0283-X*) AltaMira Pr.

Managing Hospital-Based Patient Education. Ed. by Barbara E. Giloth. LC 92-48394. 458p. 1993. pap. 68.95 (*1-55648-097-0*, 070194) AHPI.

Managing Hospitality Engineering Systems. Michael H. Redlin & David M. Stipanuk. LC 87-15712. (Illus.). 275p. (C). 1987. pap. text. write for info. (*0-86612-037-8*) Educ Inst Am Hotel.

Managing Hospitality Human Resources. 2nd ed. Robert H. Woods. LC 97-31177. 1997. write for info. (*0-86612-151-X*) Educ Inst Am Hotel.

Managing Hospitality Marketing: Student Manual. Educational Foundation of the National Restaurant. 86p. (Orig.). 1993. pap. write for info. (*0-915452-05-7*) Educ Found.

Managing Hotels Effectively. Ed Nebel. (Illus.). 436p. 1991. text 55.95 (*0-442-23814-2*, VNR) Wiley.

Managing Hotels Effectively. Ed Nebel. 1993. pap. 22.95 (*0-442-01501-1*, VNR) Wiley.

Managing Hotels Effectively: Lessons from Outstanding General Managers. Eddystone C. Nebel. 464p. 1991. 59.95 (*0-471-28909-4*, VNR) Wiley.

***Managing Housekeeping & Custodial Operations.** Edwin B. Feldman. 492p. 2000. pap. write for info. (*0-9701478-0-5*) Natl Trade.

Managing Housekeeping Operations. 2nd ed. Margaret M. Kappa et al. LC 97-20380. 488p. 1997. write for info. (*0-86612-155-2*) Educ Inst Am Hotel.

Managing Housing Credit Apartments: A Question & Answer Handbook for Property Owners & Managers. Anker Heegaard & Charles S. Wilkins. 195p. 1998. pap. 49.95 (*0-9669944-0-X*, CG1) Comp Grp.

Managing HR in the Information Age. Ed. by Randall S. Schuler & James Walker. LC 91-21249. (SHRM/BNA Ser.: Vol. 6). 261p. 1991. reprint ed. pap. 81.00 (*0-608-00754-4*, 206154500010) Bks Demand.

Managing Human Assets: The Groundbreaking Harvard Business School Program. Bert A. Spector et al. 288p. 1984. 27.95 (*0-02-902390-4*) Free Pr.

Managing Human Development. 294p. 1988. 30.00 (*92-1-126008-6*, E.88.III.B.1) UN.

Managing Human Productivity: People Are Your Best Investment. Stephen J. Holoviak & Susan S. Sipkoff. LC 86-25247. 230p. 1987. 62.95 (*0-275-92481-5*, C2481, Praeger Pubs) Greenwood.

Managing Human Resource Development: A Practical Guide. Leonard Nadler & Garland D. Wiggs. LC 86-7339. (Management Ser.). 213p. 1986. text 30.95 (*1-55542-006-0*) Jossey-Bass.

Managing Human Resources. V. W. Eimicke. 1987. text 49.95 (*0-08-034990-0*, Pergamon Pr) Elsevier.

Managing Human Resources. V. W. Eimicke & L. E. Klimley. 230p. 1988. text 134.00 (*0-08-034767-3*, Pergamon Pr) Elsevier.

Managing Human Resources, 3 vols. French. (C). 1993. text, teacher ed., suppl. ed. 72.36 (*0-395-69089-7*) HM.

Managing Human Resources, 3 vols. French. (C). 1993. pap., teacher ed. 5.96 (*0-395-67536-7*) HM.

***Managing Human Resources.** Tom Redman. (C). 2000. pap. text. write for info. (*0-201-59613-X*) Addison-Wesley.

Managing Human Resources. Reeves. LC 94-164528. 1994. pap. text 12.75 (*0-314-03682-2*) West Pub.

Managing Human Resources. Jane Weightman. 200p. (C). 1990. 75.00 (*0-85292-437-2*, Pub. by IPM Hse) St Mut.

Managing Human Resources. Jane Weightman. 176p. 1993. pap. 39.00 (*0-85292-520-4*, Pub. by IPM Hse) St Mut.

Managing Human Resources. Ed. by Jonathan Winterton & Christopher Molander. LC 94-15560. (Elements of Business Ser.). 208p. (C). (gr. 13). 1994. mass mkt. 69.95 (*0-415-06853-3*, B4619) Routledge.

Managing Human Resources. Ed. by Jonathan Winterton & Christopher Molander. LC 94-15560. (Elements of Business Ser.). 208p. (C). 1994. pap. 17.99 (*0-415-06854-1*, B0190) Thomson Learn.

***Managing Human Resources.** 2nd ed. 1999. write for info. (*0-13-012676-4*) P-H.

Managing Human Resources. 2nd ed. Gomez & Mejia. 1997. pap. text, student ed. 16.80 (*0-13-888736-5*) P-H.

Managing Human Resources. 2nd ed. Luis R. Gomez-Mejia et al. LC 97-2384. 586p. 1997. 96.00 (*0-13-270943-0*) P-H.

***Managing Human Resources.** 3rd ed. 2000. write for info. (*0-13-018413-6*) P-H.

Managing Human Resources, 3 vols. 3rd ed. French. (C). 1993. pap. text, teacher ed. 20.76 (*0-395-69090-0*) HM.

Managing Human Resources, 3 vols. 3rd ed. Wendell French. LC 93-78694. (C). 1993. text 71.56 (*0-395-47278-4*) HM.

***Managing Human Resources.** 3rd ed. Luis R. Gomez-Mejia et al. LC 00-27878. 656p. 2000. 86.67 (*0-13-011333-6*) P-H.

Managing Human Resources. 4th ed. Mcevay. 1995. student ed. 26.56 (*0-07-011237-1*) McGraw.

Managing Human Resources. 6th ed. Cascio. 2001. 64.00 (*0-07-231716-7*) McGraw.

Managing Human Resources. 6th ed. Schuler. LC 97-26630. (GJ - Human Resources Management Ser.). 1997. mass mkt. 64.95 (*0-538-87745-6*) S-W Pub.

Managing Human Resources. 9th ed. Arthur W. Sherman, Jr. & George W. Bohlander. (C). 1991. mass mkt. 51.00 (*0-538-81075-0*, GJ83IA) S-W Pub.

Managing Human Resources. 10th ed. George W. Bohlander et al. LC 95-8634. (C). 1995. pap. 70.95 (*0-538-83925-2*) S-W Pub.

Managing Human Resources. 10th ed. Arthur W. Sherman & George W. Bohlander. (GC - Principles of Management Ser.). (C). 1995. mass mkt., student ed. 21.95 (*0-538-83926-0*) S-W Pub.

Managing Human Resources. 11th ed. George W. Bohlander. (Miscellaneous/Catalogs Ser.). 1997. mass mkt., student ed. 18.95 (*0-538-87078-8*) S-W Pub.

Managing Human Resources. 11th ed. George W. Bohlander et al. LC 97-16115. (Miscellaneous/Catalogs Ser.). 1997. mass mkt. 87.95 (*0-538-87075-3*) S-W Pub.

M

An Asterisk (*) at the beginning of an entry indicates that the title is appearing for the first time.

Managing Human Resources. 12th ed. Sherman & Bohlander. (SWC-Management Ser.). 2000. pap. 50.50 (*0-324-00724-8*) Thomson Learn.

Managing Human Resources: A Challenge to Urban Governments. Ed. by Charles H. Levine. LC 77-79869. (Urban Affairs Annual Reviews Ser.: No. 13). 319p. reprint ed. pap. 98.90 (*0-8357-8491-6*, 203476500091) Bks Demand.

Managing Human Resources: A Partnership Perspective. 7th ed. Jackson. LC 99-22218. (SWC-Management Ser.). 776p. 1999. pap. 91.95 (*0-324-00415-X*) Thomson Learn.

Managing Human Resources: A Practical Guide. Robert Chasnoff & Peter Muniz. 63p. (C). 1981. pap. text 9.25 (*0-943300-00-2*) LABS.

Managing Human Resources: Documenting the Personnel Function. V. W. Eimicke & L. E. Klimley. (Illus.). 224p. 1987. text 45.45 (*0-08-034991-9*, Pergamon Pr) Elsevier.

Managing Human Resources: Exercises, Experiments, & Applications, Set, incl. tchr's. manual. Alan B. Clardy. 136p. (C). 1995. pap., student ed. write for info. (*0-8058-1749-2*) L Erlbaum Assocs.

Managing Human Resources: Exercises, Experiments, & Applications, Set, incl. tchr's. manual. Alan B. Clardy. 176p. (C). 1995. student ed. 19.95 (*0-8058-1748-4*) L Erlbaum Assocs.

Managing Human Resources: HSM 385 Course. Mary A. Blind. 356p. (C). 1993. student ed., ring bd. write for info. (*0-933195-49-4*) CA College Health Sci.

Managing Human Resources Local Government Cases. James M. Banovetz. LC 98-40339. 1998. write for info. (*0-87326-162-3*) Intl City-Cnty Mgt.

Managing Human Resources: Productivity, Quality of Work Life, Profits. 3rd ed. Wayne F. Cascio. 1992. pap. text, student ed. write for info. (*0-318-72596-7*) McGraw.

Managing Human Resources: Productivity, Quality of Work Life, Profits. 4th ed. Wayne F. Cascio. LC 94-3480. (Management Ser.). 660p. 1994. text 79.75 (*0-07-011154-5*) McGraw.

Managing Human Resources: Productivity, Quality of Work Life, Profits. 4th ed. Wayne F. Cascio. 1995. pap. text. write for info. incl. VHS (*0-07-911791-0*) McGraw.

Managing Human Resources: Productivity, Quality of Work Life, Profits. 5th ed. Wayne F. Cascio. LC 97-30865. 752p. 1997. 81.88 (*0-07-011944-9*) McGraw.

Managing Human Resources: The Art of Full Employment. David Stern. LC 81-20517. 158p. 1982. 47.95 (*0-86569-097-9*, Auburn Hse) Greenwood.

Managing Human Resources (Canadian Version) Documenting the Personnel Function. V. W. Eimicke & L. E. Klimley. (Illus.). 224p. 1987. text 142.00 (*0-08-034768-1*, Pergamon Pr) Elsevier.

Managing Human Resources & Industrial Relations. John Storey & Keith Sisson. LC 93-10116. (Managing Work & Organizations Ser.). 224p. 1993. pap. 33.95 (*0-335-15655-X*) OpUniv Pr.

Managing Human Resources in Small & Mid-Sized Companies. 2nd ed. Diane Arthur. LC 95-412. 352p. 1995. 59.95 (*0-8144-0277-1*) AMACOM.

Managing Human Resources in Special Education. Michael J. Fimian. LC 84-17685. 336p. 1984. 65.00 (*0-275-91154-3*, C1154, Praeger Pubs) Greenwood.

Managing Human Resources in the European Tourism & Hospitality Industry: A Strategic Approach. T. Baum. (Illus.). 296p. 1995. mass mkt. 19.99 (*0-412-55630-8*) Chapman & Hall.

***Managing Human Resources in the Human Services: Supervisory Challenges.** Felice Davidson Perlmutter et al. LC 99-39955. (Illus.). 256p. 2000. text. write for info. (*0-19-512027-2*); pap. text. write for info. (*0-19-513707-8*) OUP.

Managing Human Resources in the Information Age. Ed. by Randall S. Schuler & James Walker. LC 91-21249. (SHRM-BNA Series on Human Resource Management: Vol. 6). 300p. 1991. trans. 15.00 (*0-87179-606-6*, 0606) BNA Books.

Managing Human Resources Module, PACE Level 1: A Program for Acquiring Competence in Entrepreneurship, 3 levels. rev. ed. National Center for Research in Vocational Educati. 1983. 2.50 (*0-317-06067-8*, RD240AB12) Ctr Educ Trng Employ.

Managing Human Resources Module, PACE Level 2: A Program for Acquiring Competence in Entrepreneurship, 3 levels. rev. ed. National Center for Research in Vocational Educati. 1983. 2.50 (*0-317-06068-6*, RD240BB12) Ctr Educ Trng Employ.

Managing Human Resources Module, PACE Level 3: A Program for Acquiring Competence in Entrepreneurship, 3 levels. rev. ed. National Center for Research in Vocational Educati. 1983. 2.50 (*0-317-06069-4*, RD240CB12) Ctr Educ Trng Employ.

Managing Human Resources (U. S. Version) (US Version) Documenting the Personnel Function. V. W. Eimicke & L. E. Klimley. LC 86-25273. 226p. 1987. text 158.00 (*0-08-033072-X*, Pergamon Pr) Elsevier.

Managing Human Resources. 5/e. 5th ed. Randall S. Schuler. LC 94-5533. (SWC-Management). 856p. (C). 1994. pap. 65.75 (*0-314-03908-2*) West Pub.

Managing Human Service Organizations. Lynn E. Miller. LC 88-35682. 256p. 1989. 62.95 (*0-89930-305-6*, MMN/, Quorum Bks) Greenwood.

Managing Human Services. Ed. by Wayne F. Anderson et al. LC 77-2464. (Municipal Management Ser.). (Illus.). 591p. 1977. text 30.00 (*0-87326-017-1*) Intl City-Cnty Mgt.

Managing Human Services. David A. Bresnick. 300p. 1989. text 27.50 (*0-9610834-4-1*) Human Serv Pr.

Managing Human Services Personnel. Peter J. Pecora & Michael J. Austin. (Human Services Guides Ser.: Vol. 48). 160p. (Orig.). 1987. pap. text 18.95 (*0-8039-2685-5*) Sage.

M

Managing Ignatius: The Lunacy of Lucky Dogs & Life in the Quarter. Jerry E. Strahan. LC 97-31643. (Illus.). 264p. 1998. 24.95 (*0-8071-2241-6*) La State U Pr.

Managing Ignatius: The Lunacy of Lucky Dogs & Life in the Quarter. Jerry E. Strahan. LC 98-40500. (Illus.). 256p. 1999. reprint ed. pap. 13.00 (*0-7679-0324-2*) Broadway BDD.

Managing Imitation Strategies: How Later Entrants Seize Markets from Pioneers. Steven P. Schnaars. LC 94-15203. 1994. 27.95 (*0-02-928105-9*) Free Pr.

Managing Immunization in General Practice. Michael Ingram. LC 95-15758. 1995. write for info. (*1-85775-155-8*, Radcliffe Med Pr) Scovill Paterson.

***Managing in a Business Context.** David Farnham. 368p. 2000. pap. 47.95 (*0-8464-5112-3*) Beekman Pubs.

Managing in a Changing Environment see Mastering Change Management: A Practical Guide for Turning Obstacles into Opportunities

Managing in a Competitive Environment. Mescon Group Staff. (GC - Principles of Management Ser.). 1995. text, teacher ed. 25.95 (*0-538-85042-6*) S-W Pub.

Managing in a Five Dimension Economy: Ven Matrix Architectures for New Organizations. G. D. Venerable, II. LC 98-30537. 304p. 1999. 65.00 (*1-56720-132-6*, Quorum Bks) Greenwood.

Managing in a Foreign Culture. Didactic Systems Staff. (Simulation Game Ser.). 1974. pap. 26.25 (*0-89401-062-X*) Didactic Syst.

Managing in a Global Organization: Keys to Success in a Changing World. Carol K. Goman. Ed. by Nancy Shotwell. LC 93-73183. (Illus.). 194p. (Orig.). 1994. pap. 12.95 (*1-56052-268-2*) Crisp Pubns.

Managing in a Service Economy. Heskett. 211p. 1986. 22.36 (*0-07-103240-1*) McGraw.

Managing in a Team Environment. John Robert Dew. LC 98-6018. 176p. 1998. 55.00 (*1-56720-228-4*, Quorum Bks) Greenwood.

Managing in a Time of Great Change. Peter F. Drucker. LC 95-13316. 371p. 1995. pap. 24.95 (*0-525-94053-7*, Truman Talley) St Martin.

Managing in Academics: A Health Center Model. Jill Ridky & George F. Sheldon. LC 93-23854. (Illus.). 359p. 1993. pap. 30.00 (*0-942219-11-2*) Quality Med Pub.

Managing in an Academic Health Care Environment. Ed. by William F. Minogue. LC 92-74401. 213p. (C). 1993. text 50.00 (*0-924674-18-0*) Am Coll Phys Execs.

Managing in Black & White. Ellen G. Bishop. 48p. 1989. 11.95 (*0-87920-105-3*) WNY Wares.

Managing in Britain & Germany. Rosemary Stewart et al. LC 94-20536. 224p. 1994. text 65.00 (*0-312-12237-3*) St Martin.

Managing in China: An Executive Survival Guide. Stephanie Jones. LC 97-214699. 260p. 1997. pap. 21.95 (*981-00-8086-7*, Pub. by Select Bks) Weatherhill.

Managing in Developing Countries: Strategic Analysis & Operating Techniques. James E. Austin. 1990. 40.00 (*0-02-901102-7*) Free Pr.

Managing in Government. (Illus.). 256p. 1996. text. write for info. (*0-412-73580-6*, Chap & Hall NY) Chapman & Hall.

Managing in Mexico: A Cultural Perspective. Kelley Lane et al. (SPA.). 14p. (C). 1985. pap. text 10.00 (*0-937795-05-4*) Waste-Mgmt Educ.

Managing in Organizations That Learn. Ed. by Steven Cavaleri & David Fearon. (Developmental Management Ser.). (Illus.). 650p. 1996. pap. 44.95 (*1-55786-660-0*) Blackwell Pubs.

Managing in the Age of Change: Essential Skills to Manage Today's Diverse Workplace. Ed. by Roger A. Ritvo et al. LC 94-9331. 324p. 1994. text 25.00 (*0-7863-0303-4*, Irwn Prfssnl) McGraw-Hill Prof.

Managing in the Age of Persuasion. Jay A. Conger. LC 98-9632. 224p. 1998. 24.50 (*0-684-80772-6*) S&S Trade.

Managing in the Corporate Interest: Control & Resistance in an American Bank. Vicki A. Smith. LC 90-10780. 200p. 1990. 30.00 (*0-520-06779-7*, Pub. by U CA Pr); pap. 16.95 (*0-520-07891-8*, Pub. by U CA Pr) Cal Prin Full Svc.

Managing in the Global Business Environment: Issues, Organization, & Limitations. Mark R. Eaker & Faith J. Rubenstein. LC 96-37536. 1997. mass mkt. 67.95 (*0-538-86814-7*) S-W Pub.

Managing in the Global Economy: The European Union. Harry Costin. 384p. (C). 1995. text 55.00 (*0-03-015347-6*) Dryden Pr.

Managing in the Legal Environment. 3rd ed. Meiners. (SWC-Business Law). (C). 1995. mass mkt., student ed. 20.95 (*0-314-06326-9*) S-W Pub.

Managing In The Legal Environmment. 2/e. 2nd ed. Al H. Ringleb et al. Ed. by Fenton. LC 92-30982. (SWC-Business Law). 700p. (C). 1992. text 65.75 (*0-314-01165-X*) West Pub.

***Managing in the Media.** Peter Block. (Illus.). 300p. 2000. pap. 47.95 (*0-240-51599-4*, Focal) Buttrwrth-Heinemann.

***Managing in the New Economy.** Ed. & Intro. by Joan Magretta. LC 99-24214. 304p. 1999. 29.95 (*1-57851-186-0*, HBS Pr) Harvard Busn.

Managing in the Next Millennium. Mike Johnson. LC 95-15699. 155p. 1995. pap. text 21.95 (*0-7506-1954-6*) Buttrwrth-Heinemann.

Managing in the Next Millennium. Mike Johnson. LC 95-15699. (Illus.). 176p. reprint ed. pap. 54.60 (*0-608-07414-4*, 206764100009) Bks Demand.

Managing in the NHS. Sandra Dawson & Imperial College of Science Technology Staff. LC 96-164689. xii, 265 p. 1995. write for info. (*0-11-321878-8*) Sterling.

***Managing in the Public Sector.** Connolly. 2000. pap. write for info. (*0-412-61380-8*) Thomson Learn.

Managing in the Service Economy. James L. Heskett. 211p. 1986. teacher ed. 24.95 (*0-87584-143-0*) Harvard Busn.

Managing in the Single European Market. Richard Brown. LC 94-166168. (Illus.). 198p. 1993. reprint ed. pap. 61.40 (*0-608-07425-X*, 206765200009) Bks Demand.

Managing in the Voluntary Sector: A Handbook for Managers in Voluntary & Non-Profit Organisations. Ed. by Stephen P. Osborne. (Management & Finance in the Public Services Ser.). 300p. 1997. mass mkt. 29.99 (*0-412-71840-5*) Chapman & Hall.

Managing in Time. Peter Drucker. 1998. pap. 14.95 (*0-452-27837-6*, Plume) Dutton Plume.

Managing in Times of Disorder: Hypercompetitive Organizational Responses. Anne Y. Ilinitch et al. LC 97-45402. (Organization Science Ser.). 548p. 1998. 69.95 (*0-7619-1018-2*); pap. 32.95 (*0-7619-1019-0*) Sage.

Managing in Tough Times: One Hundred One New Directions from Big Business. Doris Martin. LC 92-90898. 101p. 1992. pap. 15.95 (*1-878500-01-5*) Martin Mgmt.

***Managing in Uncertainty: Theory & Practice.** Constantin Zopounidis et al. LC 98-21505. (Applied Optimization Ser.). 29p. 1998. write for info. (*0-7923-5110-X*) Kluwer Academic.

Managing Inappropriate Sexual Behavior: Supporting Individuals with Developmental Disabilities in the Community. Karen M. Ward et al. 69p. (C). 1992. pap. text 19.00 (*0-9636593-0-8*) Ctr Human Dev.

***Managing Inclusive Education: From Policy to Experience.** Ed. by Peter Clough. 224p. 1999. pap. 27.95 (*1-85396-393-3*, Pub. by P Chapman); lib. bdg. 73.95 (*1-85396-411-5*, Pub. by P Chapman) Sage.

Managing Indian Banks: The Challenges Ahead. Vasant C. Joshi & Vinay V. Joshi. LC 98-28022. 1998. write for info. (*0-7619-9281-2*); pap. write for info. (*0-7619-9282-0*) Sage.

Managing India's Food Economy: Problems & Alternatives. D. S. Tyagi. (Illus.). 272p. 1991. text 27.50 (*0-8039-9657-8*) Sage.

***Managing Individual Performance: A Systematic, Seven Step Approach to Enhancing Employee Performance & Results.** Kieran Baldwin. (Illus.). 144p. (Orig.). 1999. pap. 19.95 (*1-85703-438-4*, Pub. by How To Bks) Trans-Atl Phila.

Managing Individual Performance: An Approach to Designing an Effective Performance Management System. Curtis H. Engelmann & Robert C. Roesch. (Building Blocks Ser.: Vol. 27). (Illus.). 24p. (Orig.). 1997. pap. 24.95 (*1-57963-037-5*, A0227) Am Compensation.

Managing Indonesia: The Modern Political Economy. John Bresnan. LC 92-23598. (East Asian Institute Ser.). 375p. (C). 1993. pap. text 23.00 (*0-231-07991-5*) Col U Pr.

Managing Indoor Air Quality. Shirley Hansen. 315p. 1991. 74.00 (*0-88173-107-2*) Fairmont Pr.

Managing Indoor Air Quality. 2nd ed. Hansen & Burroughs. 344p. 1998. 84.00 (*0-13-011665-3*) P-H.

Managing Indoor Air Quality. 2nd ed. Shirley J. Hansen & H. E. Burroughs. LC 98-34235. 334p. 1998. 89.00 (*0-88173-225-7*) Fairmont Pr.

Managing Industrial Development Projects: A Project Management Approach. Adedeji B. Badiru. LC 93-68. 386p. 1993. text 69.95 (*0-442-01087-7*, VNR) Wiley.

Managing Industrial Development Projects: A Project Management Approach. Adedeji B. Badiru. (VNR Project Management Ser.). 386p. 1993. 99.00 (*0-471-28475-0*, VNR) Wiley.

Managing Industrial Energy Conservation. American Management Association, Research Developm. LC 77-22251. (American Management Associations' Management Briefing Ser.). (Illus.). 61p. reprint ed. pap. 30.00 (*0-608-11715-3*, 205020000078) Bks Demand.

Managing Industrial Enterprise: Cases from Japan's Pre-War Experience. Ed. by William D. Wray. (East Asian Monographs: No. 142). (Illus.). 450p. 1989. 30.00 (*0-674-54770-5*) Coun East Asian Stud.

Managing Industrial Hazardous Waste: A Practical Handbook. Gary F. Lindgren. (Illus.). 404p. 1989. lib. bdg. 99.95 (*0-87371-147-5*, L147) Lewis Pubs.

Managing Industrial Risk: Getting Value for Money in Your Business. John Woodhouse. 320p. 1993. mass mkt. 99.95 (*0-412-47590-1*) Chapman & Hall.

Managing Industrial Solid Wastes from Manufacturing, Mining, Oil & Gas Production & Utility Coal Combustion. (Illus.). 130p. (Orig.). (C). 1995. pap. text 30.00 (*0-7881-2090-5*) DIANE Pub.

Managing Infectious Waste. Michael Garvin. 192p. 1995. lib. bdg. 65.00 (*0-87371-637-X*, L637) Lewis Pubs.

Managing Infiltration Sewer Systems: Inflow Analyses of Local Sewer Systems. 64p. 1977. 8.00 (*0-318-16228-8*, DG77-029) Pub Tech Inc.

***Managing Information** Judith Elkin & Derek G. Law. LC 99-16164. (Managing Universities & Colleges Ser.). 2000. 28.95 (*0-335-20339-6*) OpUniv Pr.

Managing Information. Hugh Garai & Peter Cochrane. (Gower Management Workbooks Ser.). 224p. 1997. pap. 33.95 (*0-566-07740-X*, Pub. by Gower) Ashgate Pub Co.

Managing Information: Avoiding Overload. Trevor Bentley. (CIMA Business Skills Ser.). 164p. 1998. pap. 30.00 (*0-7494-2682-9*) Kogan Page Ltd.

Managing Information: How Information Systems Impact Organizational Strategy. Gordon B. Davis & Scott Hamilton. (APICS Ser.). 300p. 1993. 47.50 (*1-55623-768-5*, Irwn Prfssnl) McGraw-Hill Prof.

Managing Information: Understanding the Impact of IT on the Financial Services. Phil Fawcett. 266p. pap. 80.00 (*0-85297-513-9*, Pub. by Chartered Bank) St Mut.

Managing Information Across the Enterprise. Robert K. Wysocki & Robert L. DeMichiell. LC 96-30257. 372p. 1996. text 87.95 (*0-471-12719-1*) Wiley.

Managing Information & Communications in a Changing Global Environment: Proceedings of the 6th IRMA International Conference. Ed. by M. Khosrowpour. 550p. 1995. 79.95 (*1-878289-31-4*) Idea Group Pub.

Managing Information & Entrepreneurship in Technology-Based Firms. Michael J. Martin. 416p. 1994. 99.00 (*0-471-57219-5*) Wiley.

***Managing Information & Knowledge in the Public Sector.** Eileen M. Milner. LC 00-20795. 2000. pap. write for info. (*0-415-20423-2*) Routledge.

***Managing Information & Statistics.** Bee & Bee. 336p. 2000. pap. 44.95 (*0-8464-5113-1*) Beekman Pubs.

Managing Information & Systems. Pearlson. 512p. 2000. pap. 73.95 (*0-471-32001-3*) Wiley.

Managing Information for Research. Elizabeth Orna & Graham Stevens. LC 95-13767. 160p. 1995. pap. 27.95 (*0-335-19397-8*) OpUniv Pr.

Managing Information for the Competitive Edge. Ed. by Ethel Auster & Chun Wei Choo. 554p. 1996. pap. 82.50 (*1-55570-215-5*) Neal-Schuman.

Managing Information Highways: The Prism Book: Principles, Methods, & Case Studies for Designing Telecommunications Management Systems. Kim Berquist & Andrew Berquist. LC 96-48513. (Lecture Notes in Computer Science Ser.: Vol. 1164). 417p. 1996. 68.00 (*3-540-62008-7*) Spr-Verlag.

***Managing Information in Healthcare: Concepts & Cases.** John Abbott Worthley. LC 00-32299. 2000. write for info. (*1-56793-131-6*) Health Admin Pr.

Managing Information in Higher Education. Ed. by E. Michael Staman. LC 85-645339. (New Directions for Institutional Research Ser.: No. IR 55). 1987. pap. 22.00 (*1-55542-947-5*) Jossey-Bass.

Managing Information Resources for Insurance. Leonard J. Watson. LC 98-71637. (C). 1998. 16.00 (*0-89463-083-0*) Am Inst FCPCU.

Managing Information Resources in the 1990's: Proceedings of the 1st IRMA International Conference. Ed. by M. Khosrowpour. 150p. 1990. 29.95 (*1-878289-06-3*) Idea Group Pub.

Managing Information Security. K. Wong & S. Watt. iv, 332p. 1990. 195.00 (*0-946395-63-2*, Pub. by Elsvr Adv Tech) Elsevier.

Managing Information Security - Achieving BS7799. B. Dodwell. (Financial Times Management Briefings Ser.). 1997. pap. 94.50 (*0-273-63305-8*, Pub. by F T P-H) Trans-Atl Phila.

Managing Information Services: An Integrated Approach. 2nd ed. Jo Bryson. LC 96-52110. 448p. 1997. text 78.95 (*0-566-07690-X*, Pub. by Gower) Ashgate Pub Co.

Managing Information Strategically: Increase Your Company's Competitiveness & Efficiency by Using Information As a Strategic Tool. James McGee & Laurence Prusak. LC 92-37939. (Ernst & Young Information Management Ser.). 272p. 1993. 39.95 (*0-471-57544-5*) Wiley.

Managing Information System Security. Gurpreet Dhillon. (Illus.). 210p. (C). 1997. pap. text 35.00 (*0-333-69260-8*, Pub. by Macmillan Ed) Scholium Intl.

Managing Information Systems: An Integrated Approach. E. Wittry. 280p. 1987. 10.50 (*0-87263-296-2*) SME.

Managing Information Systems: Strategies for Action. J. D. Mckeen & H. R. Smith. 374p. 1996. 70.00 (*0-471-96516-2*) Wiley.

Managing Information Systems & Technologies: A Basic Guide for Design, Selection, Evaluation & Use. Edwin M. Cortez & Edward J. Kazlauskas. LC 85-32013. 179p. 1986. pap. text 45.00 (*0-918212-92-8*) Neal-Schuman.

Managing Information Systems Applications. 3rd ed. O'Brien. 1996. text 75.25 (*0-256-23618-6*) McGraw.

***Managing Information Technology.** (C). 2001. text. write for info. (*0-13-017855-1*) P-H.

Managing Information Technology. 3rd ed. Martin & Dehayes & Dehayes. LC 98-21991. 716p. 1998. 90.67 (*0-13-860925-X*) P-H.

Managing Information Technology in Secondary Schools. Roger Crawford. LC 96-40270. 240p. (C). 1997. 75.00 (*0-415-10734-2*); pap. 25.99 (*0-415-10735-0*) Routledge.

Managing Information Technology in Turbulent Times. Louis Fried. 368p. 1994. pap. 39.99 (*0-471-04742-2*) Wiley.

Managing Information Technology Projects. Graham McLeod. 456p. 1995. pap. 40.00 (*0-7895-0176-7*) Course Tech.

***Managing Information Technology Resources in Organizations in the Next Millennium.** Ed. by Mehdi Khosroapour. LC 99-20249. 1156p. 1999. pap. text 149.95 (*1-878289-51-9*) Idea Group Pub.

Managing Information with Microcomputers: Database Management Systems. Donald E. Nilson & David M. Kroenke. Ed. by Dorothy P. Craig. LC 84-6651. (R BASE Ser.). (Illus.). (Orig.). 1984. 19.95 (*0-916937-00-3*) Microrim.

Managing Infotech in School Library Media Centers. L. Anne Clyde. LC 99-33116. 275p. 1999. pap. 35.00 (*1-56308-724-3*) Libs Unl.

Managing Innovation. Ed. by Jane Henry. 312p. (C). 1991. 60.00 (*0-8039-8505-3*); pap. 24.00 (*0-8039-8506-1*) Sage.

***Managing Innovation.** 8th ed. Savage. LC 99-462441. 258p. (C). 1998. pap. 1400.00 (*0-471-33169-4*) Wiley.

Managing Innovation: A Study of British & Japanese Factories. D. H. Whittaker. (Studies in Management: No. 14). (Illus.). 221p. (C). 1990. text 64.95 (*0-521-38055-3*) Cambridge U Pr.

Managing Innovation: Cases from the Services Industries. National Academy of Engineering Staff. 224p. (C). 1988. text 32.50 (*0-309-03926-6*) Natl Acad Pr.

Managing Innovation: Cases from the Services Industries. National Academy of Engineering Staff. 224p. (C). 1988. pap. text 22.50 (*0-309-03891-X*) Natl Acad Pr.

An Asterisk (*) at the beginning of an entry indicates that the title is appearing for the first time.

Managing Innovation: Integrating Technological, Market & Organizational Change. Joseph Tidd et al. LC 97-468. 390p. 1997. pap. 67.95 (*0-471-97076-X*) Wiley.

Managing Innovation & Change. Ed. by Sven B. Lunstedt & Thomas H. Moss. (C). 1989. lib. bdg. 154.50 (*0-7923-0079-3*) Kluwer Academic.

Managing Innovation & Change: People, Technology, & Strategy. John Clark. LC 95-74574. 304p. 1995. 75.00 (*0-8039-8944-X*); pap. 28.50 (*0-8039-8945-8*) Sage.

Managing Innovation for Profit. 8th ed. 366p. 1998. spiral bd. 1400.00 (*1-56217-024-4*) Tech Insights.

Managing Innovation in Policing: The Untapped Potential of the Middle Manager. William A. Geller & Guy Swanger. LC 95-71870. 216p. (Orig.). 1995. pap. text 27.50 (*1-878734-41-5*) Police Exec Res.

Managing Innovation in the Minerals Industry. Ed. by Martin C. Kuhn. LC 98-184114. (Illus.). 100p. 1998. pap. 29.00 (*0-87335-164-9*, 164-9) SMM&E Inc.

Managing Innovative Projects. A. Webb. 392p. 1996. pap. 29.99 (*1-86152-038-7*) Thomson Learn.

Managing Innovative Projects. Alan Webb. LC 93-30437. 379p. 1993. mass mkt. 79.95 (*0-412-55490-9*) Chapman & Hall.

Managing Insect Pests in the Home Vegetable Garden. Bruce A. Barrett. (Illus.). 59p. 1998. pap. text 20.00 (*0-7881-4845-1*) DIANE Pub.

Managing Insects & Mites with Spray Oils. Nita A. Davidson et al. (Illus.). 48p. 1991. pap. 6.50 (*1-879906-07-4*, 3347) ANR Pubns CA.

Managing Institutional Archives: Foundational Principles & Practices. Richard J. Cox. LC 91-34470. (Library Management Collection). 324p. 1992. lib. bdg. 65.00 (*0-313-27251-4*, CIG/, Greenwood Pr) Greenwood.

Managing Institutional Assets. Ed. by Frank J. Fabozzi. 758p. 1990. 69.95 (*0-88730-387-0*, HarpBusn) HarpInfo.

Managing Institutional Long-Term Care for the Elderly. Maurice I. May et al. 336p. 1991. 79.00 (*0-8342-0275-1*) Aspen Pub.

Managing Institutions of Higher Education into the 21st Century: Issues & Implications, 48. Ed. by Ronald R. Sims & Serbrenia J. Sims. LC 91-22990. (Contributions to the Study of Education Ser.: No. 48). 224p. 1991. 57.95 (*0-313-27470-3*, SGL, Greenwood Pr) Greenwood.

Managing Integrated Delivery Systems: A Framework for Action. David W. Young & Sheila M. McCarthy. LC 98-42820. 222p. 1999. 45.00 (*1-56793-093-X*) Health Admin Pr.

Managing Integration in CAD/CAM & Simultaneous Engineering. Chris Voss & David Twigg. (Illus.). 108p. 1992. mass mkt., wbk. ed. 84.95 (*0-412-45410-6*, Chap & Hall NY) Chapman & Hall.

***Managing Intellectual Capital: Organizational, Strategic, & Policy Dimensions.** David J. Teece. (Clarendon Lectures In Management Studies). (Illus.). 300p. 2000. 35.00 (*0-19-829541-3*) OUP.

***Managing Interactions in Smart Environments: 1st International Workshop on Managing Interactions in Smart Environments (MANSE'99), Dublin, December 1999.** Ed. by Paddy Nixon et al. LC 99-58033. (Illus.). 265p. 2000. 84.95 (*1-85233-228-X*) Spr-Verlag.

Managing Interactive Video-Multimedia Projects. Robert E. Bergman & Thomas V. Moore. LC 89-77528. (Illus.). 240p. (Orig.). (C). 1990. pap. 44.95 (*0-87778-209-1*) Educ Tech Pubns.

Managing Interest. Calomiris. 1994. pap. text 1.80 (*0-201-76503-9*) Addison-Wesley.

***Managing Interest Rate Risk.** Christopher Cuny & Catherine Lubochinsky. 256p. 2000. text 95.00 (*1-85573-513-X*, Pub. by Woodhead Pubng) Am Educ Systs.

Managing Interest Rate Risk. Clive R. Grumball. LC 86-21257. 160p. 1987. 55.00 (*0-89930-235-1*, GMG/, Quorum Bks) Greenwood.

Managing Interest Rate Risks. Nick Douch. 68p. (C). 1997. pap. 34.95 (*92-842-1228-6*, 572) ICC Pub.

Managing Intergroup Conflict in Industry. Robert R. Blake et al. LC 64-8696. 224p. reprint ed. pap. 69.50 (*0-608-18158-7*, 203285400081) Bks Demand.

Managing Intermountain Rangelands - Salt Desert Shrub Ranges. James P. Blaisdell & Ralph C. Holmgren. (Illus.). 56p. 1997. reprint ed. 13.40 (*0-89904-653-3*, Bear Meadows Resrch Grp); reprint ed. pap. 7.40 (*0-89904-654-1*, Bear Meadows Resrch Grp) Crumb Elbow Pub.

Managing International Alliances: How Cultural Compatibility Supports Success. LC 96-15944. (Management Briefing Ser.). 1996. write for info. (*0-8144-2361-2*) AMACOM.

Managing International Business. Neil Coade. LC 97-5330. (Self-Development for Managers Ser.). 104p. 1997. pap. 14.99 (*0-415-13919-8*) Thomson Learn.

Managing International Business. Griffin. (C). 1996. pap. text, student ed. write for info. (*0-201-80939-7*) Addison-Wesley.

Managing International Business. Ricky Griffin. (C). 1994. pap. text, student ed. write for info. (*0-201-57595-7*) Addison-Wesley.

Managing International Business. Rajib N. Sanyal. 632p. (C). 2001. text. write for info. (*0-201-47153-1*) Addison-Wesley.

Managing International Construction Projects: An Overview. Ed. by Richard H. Neale. LC 97-130475. (International Construction Management Ser.: Vol. 7). xv, 150p. 1996. pap. 13.50 (*92-2-108751-4*) Intl Labour Office.

***Managing International Credit & Collections 2000 Yearbook.** Mary L. Schaeffer. Ed. by Jan C. Bernabe. (Illus.). 200p. 1999. pap. 199.00 (*1-58673-017-7*) IOMA.

Managing International Distribution. Felix Wentworth & Martin Christopher. 296p. 1979. text 67.95 (*0-566-02108-0*, Pub. by Gower) Ashgate Pub Co.

Managing International Operations: A Guide for Engineers, Architects & Construction Managers. Roozbeh Kangari & Chester L. Lucas. LC 96-53243. 160p. 1997. 24.00 (*0-7844-0222-1*) Am Soc Civil Eng.

Managing International Political Risk. Theodore H. Moran. LC 98-7600. 300p. 1998. 59.95 (*0-631-20880-1*); pap. 29.95 (*0-631-20881-X*) Blackwell Pubs.

Managing International Risk. Ed. by Richard J. Herring. LC 82-19930. 286p. 1986. pap. text 25.95 (*0-521-31121-7*) Cambridge U Pr.

***Managing International Students: Recruitment to Graduation.** Christine Humfrey. LC 99-17597. (Managing Colleges & Universities Ser.). 164p. 1999. pap. 32.95 (*0-335-20307-8*) Taylor & Francis.

Managing International Technology Transfer. Min Chen. LC 95-31021. (Thunderbird/Routledge Series in International Management). 256p. 1996. pap. 60.00 (*0-415-13323-8*) Thomson Learn.

Managing Internet Information Services: World Wide Web, Gopher, FTP, & More. Cricket Liu et al. (Illus.). 400p. (Orig.). 1995. pap. 29.95 (*1-56592-062-7*) Thomson Learn.

Managing Internetworks with SNMP. 2nd ed. Mark A. Miller. LC 97-20495. (Out of Ser.). 736p. 1997. pap. text 49.95 incl. cd-rom (*1-55851-561-5*, M&T Bks) IDG Bks.

***Managing Internetworks with SNMP.** 3rd ed. Mark A. Miller. LC 99-31813. 720p. 1999. pap. 49.99 (*0-7645-7518-X*) IDG Bks.

Managing Interpersonal Conflict. William A. Donohue. (Interpersonal CommTexts Ser.: Vol. 4). 168p. (C). 1992. text 44.00 (*0-8039-3311-8*); pap. text 19.95 (*0-8039-3312-6*) Sage.

Managing Investment Portfolios: A Dynamic Process. 2nd ed. Ed. by John L. Maginn & Donald L. Tuttle. LC 89-50465. 775p. (C). 1991. text 165.00 (*0-7913-0322-5*) Warren Gorham & Lamont.

Managing Investments. Berry. (C). 1990. pap. text, teacher ed. 27.50 (*0-03-022039-4*) Harcourt Coll Pubs.

Managing Investments. Michael Berry & S. David Young. LC 88-25630. (Illus.). 608p. (C). 1990. text 61.50 (*0-03-022038-6*) Dryden Pr.

Managing Investments. 2nd ed. Berry. (C). 1996. pap. text. write for info. (*0-03-075486-0*) Harcourt Coll Pubs.

Managing IP Addresses: How to Number your Network for Growth & Change. Bill Dutcher. LC 99-49094. 310p. 1999. pap. 49.99 (*0-471-25484-3*) Wiley.

Managing IP Networks with Cisco Routers. Scott Ballew. Ed. by Michael Loukides. LC 97-223524. 352p. (Orig.). 1997. reprint ed. pap. 34.95 (*1-56592-320-0*) OReilly & Assocs.

Managing IP Traffic. 425p. 1999. 55.00 (*1-57870-106-6*) Macmillan Tech.

Managing Irrigation: Analysing & Improving the Performance of Bureaucracies. Norman Uphoff et al. (Illus.). 263p. 1991. 27.50 (*0-8039-9666-7*) Sage.

Managing Irrigation Together: Practice & Policy in India. Clarence Maloney & K. V. Raju. LC 94-7771. 340p. 1994. 36.00 (*0-8039-9175-4*) Sage.

Managing It at Board Level. 2nd ed. Kit Grindley. LC 95-199021. 224p. 1995. 40.00 (*0-273-61305-7*) F T P-H.

Managing IT for Success: The Empowering Business Partnership. Robert W. Zmud & V. Sambamurthy. LC 92-70837. 97p. (Orig.). 1992. pap. 35.00 (*0-910586-89-6*, 0100-92) Finan Exec.

Managing IT in a Global Society: Proceedings of the 2nd IRMA International Conference. 336p. 1991. 43.95 (*1-878289-13-6*) Idea Group Pub.

***Managing IT in an E-Commerce Environment.** Janet G. Butler. (Illus.). 180p. 2000. pap. 280.00 (*1-56607-086-4*) Comput Tech Res.

Managing IT Resources & Applications in the World Economy: Proceedings of the 8th IRMA International Conference. Ed. by M. Khosrowpour. 553p. 1997. 79.95 (*1-878289-45-4*) Idea Group Pub.

***Managing Key Clients.** Paul Denvir. 2000. pap. text 31.95 (*0-8264-4710-4*) Continuum.

Managing Knock Your Socks off Service. Chip R. Bell & Ron Zemke. LC 91-48064. (Illus.). 210p. 1999. pap. 17.95 (*0-8144-7784-4*) AMACOM.

***Managing Know-Who Based Companies: A Multinetworked Approach to Knowledge & Innovation Management.** Sigvald Harryson. LC 00-20483. 304p. 2000. 95.00 (*1-84064-314-5*) E Elgar.

***Managing Knowledge.** Craig Prichard. 2000. text 69.95 (*0-312-23363-9*) St Martin.

Managing Knowledge. David Wilson. 200p. 1996. pap. text 37.95 (*0-7506-2054-4*) Buttrwrth-Heinemann.

Managing Knowledge: A Practical Web Based Approach. Wayne Applehans et al. LC 98-43437. (Addison-Wesley Information Technology Ser.). 128p. (C). 1998. pap. text 29.95 (*0-201-43315-X*) Addison-Wesley.

Managing Knowledge: Experts, Agencies & Organisations. Steven Albert & Keith Bradley. 227p. (C). 1997. text 64.95 (*0-521-56150-7*); pap. text 20.95 (*0-521-59887-7*) Cambridge U Pr.

Managing Knowledge: In Cooperation & Competition. Georgh F. Von Krogh. 240p. 1996. 75.00 (*0-7619-5180-6*); pap. 29.95 (*0-7619-5181-4*) Sage.

Managing Knowledge for Design, Planning & Decision Making. Ed. by W. F. Schut & C. W. Van Lohuizen. 162p. (Orig.). 1990. pap. text 33.50 (*90-6275-645-X*, Pub. by Delft U Pr) Coronet Bks.

***Managing Knowledge in a Paper World: How Document Technologies Enable Knowledge Management.** Robert Smallwood. 256p. 2000. pap. 29.95 (*1-55558-246-X*, Digital DEC) Buttrwrth-Heinemann.

***Managing Knowledge Workers: New Skills & Attitudes to Unlock the Intellectual Capital in Your Organization.** Horibe. LC 99-201691. 320p. 1999. 29.95 (*0-471-64318-1*) Wiley.

Managing Land As Ecosystem & Economy. Ed. by Alice E. Ingerson. (Illus.). 36p. 1995. pap. 14.00 (*1-55844-125-5*) Lincoln Inst Land.

Managing Land-Use Conflicts: Case Studies in Special Area Management. Ed. by David J. Brower & Daniel S. Carol. LC 86-19881. (Duke Press Policy Studies). ix, 323p. 1987. text 59.95 (*0-8223-0560-7*) Duke.

Managing Language: The Discourse of Corporate Meetings. Francesca Bargiela-Chiappini & Sandra J. Harris. LC 97-6894. (Pragmatics & Beyond, New Ser.: Vol. 44). ix, 295p. 1997. lib. bdg. 86.00 (*1-55619-806-X*) J Benjamins Pubng Co.

Managing Language Diversity. Sue Wright et al. LC 97-47652. 81p. 1998. write for info. (*1-85359-415-6*) Multilingual.

Managing Language in "Piers Plowman" Gillian Rudd. (Piers Plowman Studies: Vol. 9). 260p. (C). 1994. 75.00 (*0-85991-392-9*, DS Brewer) Boydell & Brewer.

Managing Language Problems: A Court Interpreting Education Program Foe Judges, Lawyers, & Court Managers. William E. Hewitt et al. LC 97-228340. 1997. write for info. (*0-89656-177-1*) Natl Ctr St Courts.

Managing Large Indexing Projects: Papers from the 24th Annual Meeting of the American Society of Indexers, San Antonio, May 23, 1992. LC 93-41925. 1994. 20.00 (*0-936547-21-9*) Am Soc Index.

Managing Large Systems: Organizations for the Future. Leonard R. Sayles & Margaret K. Chandler. LC 92-19557. (Classics in Organization & Management Ser.). 370p. (C). 1992. pap. 24.95 (*1-56000-642-0*) Transaction Pubs.

Managing Large Systems: Organizations for the Future. Leonard R. Sayles & Margaret K. Chandler. LC 77-158542. 350p. reprint ed. pap. 108.50 (*0-7837-0002-4*, AU0041400017) Bks Demand.

Managing Lawfully. 88p. pap. text. write for info. (*0-7506-3320-4*) Buttrwrth-Heinemann.

Managing Learning. Ed. by Christopher Mabey & Paul Iles. LC 94-17871. 208p. (C). 1994. mass mkt. 31.95 (*0-415-11984-7*, C0461) Routledge.

Managing Learning. Ed. by Christopher Mabey & Paul Iles. LC 94-17871. 320p. (C). (gr. 13). 1994. mass mkt. 77.95 (*0-415-11983-9*, C0111) Routledge.

Managing Learning. Christopher Mabey & Paul Iles. (Bus Press-New). 320p. 1994. pap. 20.99 (*1-86152-198-7*) Thomson Learn.

***Managing Learning for Added Value.** 64p. 2000. pap. 35.95 (*0-8464-5114-X*) Beekman Pubs.

Managing Learning in Organizations. David Casey. LC 92-21156. (Managing Work & Organizations Ser.). 1993. pap. 34.95 (*0-335-15657-6*) OpUniv Pr.

Managing Learning in the Primary Classroom. Neville Bennett. 32p. 1992. pap. 6.00 (*0-948080-74-4*, Trentham Bks) Stylus Pub VA.

Managing Learning Time: A Professional Development Guide. Ida M. Halasz & Susan R. Raftery. 94p. 1985. 17.50 (*0-318-22147-0*, LT69); VHS 75.00 (*0-317-01417-X*, LT69VC) Ctr Educ Trng Employ.

Managing Learning Time: A Vocational Educator's Handbook. Ida M. Halasz & Jeanne Desy. 47p. 1984. 5.50 (*0-318-22148-9*, SN45) Ctr Educ Trng Employ.

***Managing Leave & Attendance Problems: A Guide for the Federal Supervisor.** 4th rev. ed. Robert J. Gilson et al. 62p. 1998. pap. 14.95 (*0-936295-90-2*) FPMI Comns.

Managing Legal & Security Risks in Computing & Communications. Paul Shaw. LC 97-35913. 256p. 1998. pap. 24.95 (*0-7506-9938-8*) Buttrwrth-Heinemann.

Managing Legal Uncertainty: Elite Lawyers in the New Deal. Ronen Shamir. LC 95-6279. 304p. 1995. text 49.95 (*0-8223-1650-1*); pap. text 18.95 (*0-8223-1662-5*) Duke.

Managing Leisure. Byron Grainger-Jones. LC 99-206088. viii, 231p. 1998. pap. 37.95 (*0-7506-3717-X*) Buttrwrth-Heinemann.

Managing Leviathan: Environmental Politics & the Administrative State. Ed. by Robert Paehlke & Douglas Torgerson. 310p. 1990. pap. 22.95 (*0-921149-54-9*) Broadview Pr.

Managing Liability. Ed. by J. R. King, Jr. LC 82-70764. 95p. 1982. pap. 17.00 (*0-87262-304-1*) Am Soc Civil Eng.

***Managing Liability & Overseas Programs.** Kent M. Weeks. ix, 195p. (C). 1999. 60.00 (*1-881434-17-6*) Coll Legal Info.

Managing Library Automation. 2nd ed. Marlene Clayton & Chris Batt. LC 92-14373. 1992. 63.95 (*1-85742-003-9*, Pub. by Gower) Ashgate Pub Co.

Managing Library Outreach Programs: A How-to-Do-It Manual for Librarians. Marcia Trotta. (How-to-Do-It Ser.). 150p. 1993. pap. 45.00 (*1-55570-121-3*) Neal-Schuman.

Managing Like a Man: Women & Men in Corporate Management. Judy Wajcman. LC 98-22627. 200p. 1998. 55.00 (*0-271-01840-2*); pap. 18.95 (*0-271-01848-8*) Pa St U Pr.

Managing Liquidity. 2nd ed. Lance Moir. (Association of Corporate Treasurers Ser.). 192p. 1997. pap. 45.00 (*1-85573-335-8*, Pub. by Woodhead Pubng) Am Educ Systs.

Managing Little League Baseball. Ned McIntosh. (Illus.). 192p. (Orig.). 1985. pap. 11.95 (*0-8092-5322-4*) NTC Contemp Pub Co.

***Managing Little League Baseball.** rev. ed. Ned McIntosh. LC 00-23575. (Illus.). 208p. (Orig.). 2000. pap. 12.95 (*0-8092-2525-5*, 252550, Contemporary Bks) NTC Contemp Pub Co.

Managing Livestock Production. Deere & Company Staff. 237p. 1994. teacher ed. 40.95 (*0-86691-215-0*, FBM12501T); student ed. 18.95 (*0-86691-216-9*, FBM12601W) Deere & Co.

Managing Livestock Production. Deere & Company Staff. (Farm Business Management Ser.). (Illus.). 396p. (C). 1994. pap. text 35.95 (*0-86691-235-5*, FBM12101NC) Deere & Co.

***Managing Livestock Wastes to Preserve Environmental Quality.** J. Ronald Miner et al. LC 00-33440. 2001. write for info. (*0-8138-2635-7*) Iowa St U Pr.

Managing Local Area Networks. Thomas Case & Larry Smith. 600p. (C). 1995. pap. 56.25 (*0-07-059225-X*) McGraw.

Managing Local Government. J. Fenwick. (Illus.). 216p. 1995. mass mkt. 18.99 (*0-412-49720-4*) Chapman & Hall.

Managing Local Government: Cases in Decision Making. Ed. by James M. Banovetz. LC 82-26829. (Municipal Management Ser.). 244p. 1990. pap. 28.95 (*0-87326-060-0*) Intl City-Cnty Mgt.

Managing Local Government: Cases in Decision Making. 2nd ed. Ed. by James M. Banovetz. LC 98-22838. (Municipal Management Ser.). 242p. 1998. pap. text 29.95 (*0-87326-157-7*) Intl City-Cnty Mgt.

Managing Local Government: Public Administration in Practice. Richard D. Bingham. (Illus.). 368p. 1991. text 65.00 (*0-8039-3938-8*); pap. text 27.95 (*0-8039-3939-6*) Sage.

Managing Local Government Finance: Cases in Decision Making. Ed. by James M. Banovetz. (Municipal Management Ser.). 75p. 1996. pap. 15.95 (*0-87326-111-9*) Intl City-Cnty Mgt.

Managing Local Government under Union Pressure. David T. Stanley & Carole L. Cooper. LC 73-183218. (Brookings Institution Studies of Unionism in Government). 191p. reprint ed. pap. 59.30 (*0-608-12488-5*, 202541000043) Bks Demand.

***Managing Local Services: From CCT to Best Value.** Ed. by George A. Boyne. LC 99-21019. 152p. 1999. 39.50 (*0-7146-5020-X*, Pub. by F Cass Pubs); pap. 19.50 (*0-7146-8075-3*, Pub. by F Cass Pubs) Intl Spec Bk.

Managing Logistics Change Through Innovative Information Technology. Ed. by Joseph McKeon. 220p. 1987. pap. write for info. (*0-318-61853-2*) Leaseway Trans Corp.

***Managing Logistics, 2000 Yearbook.** annuals Ed. by Cindy Dubin & Jan Bernabe. (Illus.). 200p. 2000. pap. 199.00 (*1-58673-019-3*) IOMA.

Managing Low & Moderate Income Housing. Edwin D Abrams & Edward B Blackman. LC 72-14209. (Special Studies in U. S. Economic, Social & Political Issues). 1973. 42.50 (*0-275-28816-1*) Irvington.

Managing Low Back Pain. 2nd ed. Ed. by William H. Kirkaldy-Willis. LC 87-29967. (Illus.). 419p. reprint ed. pap. 129.90 (*0-7837-2593-0*, 204275600006) Bks Demand.

Managing Low Back Pain. 3rd ed. Ed. by William H. Kirkaldy-Willis & Charles V. Burton. (Illus.). 420p. 1992. text 95.00 (*0-443-08789-X*) Church.

Managing Low Back Pain. 4th ed. William H. Kirkaldy-Willis & Thomas N. Bernard. Ed. by Marc Staruss. LC 99-19473. (Illus.). 475p. (C). 1999. text. write for info. (*0-443-07948-X*) Church.

Managing Lyric Structure. Pat Pattison. 112p. 1991. pap. 11.95 (*0-7935-1180-1*, 50481582, Berklee Pr) H Leonard.

Managing Machines? Bill Green. 154p. 1995. pap. 50.00 (*0-949823-52-X*, Pub. by Deakin Univ) St Mut.

Managing Macroeconomic Policy: The Johnson Presidency. James E. Anderson & Jared E. Hazleton. LC 85-15064. (Administrative History of the Johnson Presidency Ser.). 301p. 1986. text 30.00 (*0-292-75084-6*) U of Tex Pr.

Managing Macroeconomic Policy: The Johnson Presidency. James E. Anderson & Jared E. Hazleton. LC 85-15064. (Administrative History of the Johnson Presidency Ser.). 301p. reprint ed. pap. 93.40 (*0-608-20095-6*, 207136700011) Bks Demand.

Managing Madness. Joan Busfield. 406p. 1989. text 49.95 (*0-318-42465-7*) Routledge.

Managing Mailing Lists. Alan Schwartz. Ed. by Paula Ferguson. LC 98-208032. (Illus.). 282p. (Orig.). 1998. pap. 29.95 (*1-56592-259-X*) OReilly & Assocs.

Managing Major Accounts: Shaping & Exploring Your Firm's Tangible Assets. Chris Steward. 1996. pap. write for info. (*0-07-709069-1*) McGraw.

***Managing Major Diseases: Pulmonary Disorders.** 4th ed. Mosby. LC 99-10468. 1999. text 29.95 (*0-323-00855-0*) Harcourt.

Managing Major Sales: Practical Strategies for Improving Sales Effectiveness. Neil Rackham & Richard Ruff. 224p. 1991. 28.00 (*0-88730-508-3*, HarpBusn) HarpInfo.

Managing Managed Care. Michael C. Roberts & Linda K. Hurley. LC 97-33280. (Clinical Child Psychology Library). (Illus.). 206p. (C). 1997. 45.00 (*0-306-45670-2*, Kluwer Plenum) Kluwer Academic.

Managing Managed Care. Michael C. Roberts & Linda K. Hurley. LC 97-33280. (Clinical Child Psychology Library). 188p. 1997. pap. 21.50 (*0-306-45671-0*, Kluwer Plenum) Kluwer Academic.

Managing Managed Care: A Handbook for Mental Health Professionals. 2nd ed. Michael Goodman et al. 272p. 1996. 37.00 (*0-88048-772-0*, 8772) Am Psychiatric.

Managing Managed Care: A Practical Guide for Audiologists & Speech-Language Pathologists. Dennis Arnst et al. 150p. 1994. pap. text 40.00 (*0-910329-82-6*, 0111906) Am Speech Lang Hearing.

Managing Managed Care: Quality Improvements in Behavioral Health. Institute of Medicine Staff. Ed. by Margaret Edmonds et al. LC 97-2004. 396p. 1997. text 49.95 (*0-309-05642-X*, Joseph Henry Pr) Natl Acad Pr.

M

An Asterisk (*) at the beginning of an entry indicates that the title is appearing for the first time.

Managing Managed Care in the Medical Practice: The Physician's Handbook for Success & Survival. American Medical Association. (Practice Success Ser.). 1996. pap. 44.95 (*0-89970-757-2*, OP701095WE) AMA.

***Managing Management Development.** Graham Mole. LC 99-88205. (Managing Work & Organizations Ser.). 2000. pap. write for info. (*0-335-20134-2*) Taylor & Francis.

Managing Managers: Strategies & Techniques for Human Resource Management. Ed Snape et al. (Human Resource Management in Action Ser.). (Illus.). 240p. 1994. pap. 50.95 (*0-631-18675-1*) Blackwell Pubs.

Managing Manic Depressive Disorders. Ed. by Ved Varma. LC 97-198770. 200p. 1997. pap. write for info. (*1-85302-347-7*, Pub. by Jessica Kingsley) Taylor & Francis.

Managing Marine Environments. Richard A. Kenchington. 175p. 1990. 65.00 (*0-8448-1635-3*, Crane Russak) Taylor & Francis.

Managing Marital Disputes in Malaysia: Islamic Mediators & Conflict Resolution in the Syariah Courts. Sharifah Z. Syed Hassan & Sven Cederroth. (NIAS Monographs in Asian Studies: No. 75). 260p. (C). 1997. text 45.00 (*0-7007-0432-9*, Pub. by Curzon Pr Ltd); pap. text 23.95 (*0-7007-0454-X*, Pub. by Curzon Pr Ltd) UH Pr.

Managing Marketing: Text Cases & Reading. Thomas V. Bonoma. 512p. (C). 1984. 45.00 (*0-02-903720-4*) Free Pr.

Managing Marketing Linkages: Text, Cases & Readings. Frank V. Cespedes. 403p. 1995. pap. text 38.20 (*0-13-234923-X*) P-H.

Managing Martians. Donna Shirley & Danelle Morton. LC 98-6431. (Illus.). 288p. 1998. 25.00 (*0-7679-0240-8*) Broadway BDD.

Managing Martians. Donna Shirley & Danelle Morton. 304p. 1999. reprint ed. pap. 13.00 (*0-7679-0241-6*) Broadway BDD.

Managing Materials & Distribution. N. B. Harris et al. 87p. (C). 1988. 50.00 (*0-7855-6039-4*, Pub. by Inst Pur & Supply) St Mut.

Managing Maternal & Child Health Programmes: A Practical Guide. WHO Staff. (Western Pacific Education in Action Ser.: No. 10). 65p. 1997. 7.00 (*92-9061-140-5*) World Health.

Managing Maturing Businesses: Restructuring Declining Industries & Revitalizing Troubled Businesses. Kathryn R. Harrigan. LC 87-45966. 192p. 1988. 36.95 (*0-669-17082-8*) Free Pr.

Managing MBS Portfolios. Frank J. Fabozzi & David Yuen. LC 99-219510. (Illus.). 1998. 60.00 (*1-883249-38-4*) F J Fabozzi.

Managing Media Services: Theory & Practice. 2nd ed. William D. Schmidt & Donald A. Rieck. LC 99-23361. (Illus.). 418p. 1999. 49.00 (*1-56308-530-5*) Libs Unl.

Managing Medical Office Personnel: A Comprehensive Guide to Personnel Management in the Medical Office. rev. ed. Lynne R. Costain & Karen Moawad. Ed. by Gregg Rogers. 250p. 1994. reprint ed. student ed. 49.95 (*1-57066-006-9*, 5839M) Practice Mgmt Info.

Managing Medical Staff Change Through Bylaws & Other Strategies. Daniel A. Lang et al. 160p. 1995. pap. 56.50 (*1-55648-138-1*, 145104) AHPI.

Managing Medicine. 3rd ed. Lawrence L. Weed. Ed. by Jay S. Wakefield. (Illus.). 260p. 1983. pap. 20.00 (*0-917054-18-0*) Med Communications.

Managing Medicines: Public Policy & Therapeutic Drugs. P. Davis. LC 96-37264. 192p. 1997. pap. 30.95 (*0-335-19292-0*) OpUniv Pr.

Managing Medicines: Public Policy & Therapeutic Drugs. Peter Davis. LC 96-37264. (State of Health Ser.). 192p. 1997. 116.95 (*0-335-19293-9*) OpUniv Pr.

Managing Meetings. Tim Hindle. LC 97-38910. (Essential Managers Handbks.). (Illus.). 72p. 1999. pap. 6.95 (*0-7894-2447-9*) DK Pub Inc.

Managing Meetings: How to Prepare, How to Take Part & How to Follow up Effectively. Ann Dobson. (Business Basics Ser.). 128p. 1996. pap. 19.95 (*1-85703-222-5*, Pub. by How To Bks) Trans-Atl Phila.

***Managing Menopause Naturally with Chinese Medicine.** Honora L. Wolfe. LC 99-230464. 214p. 1999. pap. 14.95 (*0-936185-98-8*) Blue Poppy Pr.

***Managing Menopause with Diet, Vitamins & Herbs: An Essential Guide for the Pre & Post-Menopausal Years.** Leslie Beck. 288p. 2000. pap. 29.95 (*0-13-017966-3*) P-H.

Managing Mental Health Care in the Community: Chaos & Containment. Angela Foster & Vega Z. Roberts. LC 98-15339. (Illus.). 240p. (C). 1998. 80.00 (*0-415-16796-5*); pap. 25.99 (*0-415-16797-3*) Routledge.

Managing Mental Health Problems: A Practical Guide for Primary Care. rev. ed. Nick Kates & Marilyn Craven. LC 94-17533. (Illus.). 390p. (C). 1998. 49.00 (*0-88937-124-5*) Hogrefe & Huber Pubs.

Managing Mental Health Service. A. Reynolds. LC 98-30735. (Health Services Management Ser.). 1999. pap. 29.95 (*0-335-19833-3*); pap. 95.00 (*0-335-19834-1*) OpUniv Pr.

Managing Mergers & Acquisitions: A European Perspective. Ann M. Bengtsson. 192p. 1992. 63.95 (*0-566-07304-8*, Pub. by Gower) Ashgate Pub Co.

Managing Messaging Networks. Raj Ananthanpillai. LC 94-17551. 1994. 10.00 (*0-89006-703-1*) Artech Hse.

Managing Metadata with XML & RDF: Improving Workflow for Web Applications. Jeffrey Ricker. 400p. 1998. pap. 39.99 (*0-471-31519-2*) Wiley.

Managing Metrication in Business & Industry. American National Metric Council Staff. LC 75-45846. (Illus.). 215p. reprint ed. pap. 66.70 (*0-7837-0966-8*, 204127100019) Bks Demand.

Managing Mexico's Environmental Challenge. (Industrial Development Review Ser.: No. L809). 1994. 345.00 (*0-85058-809-X*) Economist Intell.

Managing Microcomputer Technology As an Organizational Resource. Ed. by Mehdi Khosrowpour & Donald Amoroso. LC 90-82961. (Illus.). 407p. (C). 1991. text 52.50 (*1-878289-07-1*) Idea Group Pub.

Managing Micrographic Records. Bonnie R. Curtin. (Illus.). 75p. 1998. pap. text 25.00 (*0-7881-4787-0*) DIANE Pub.

Managing Microsoft Exchange Server. Paul Robichaux. Ed. by Robert Denn. 450p. 1999. pap. text 34.95 (*1-56592-545-9*) OReilly & Assocs.

Managing MIDI Basics. David R. Trubitt. (Alfred Handy Guide Ser.). 48p. 1992. pap. text 4.95 (*0-88284-496-2*, 4424) Alfred Pub.

Managing Migraine in Primary Care. Anne MacGregor. LC 98-46293. (Illus.). 239p. 1998. pap. 39.95 (*0-632-05083-7*) Blackwell Sci.

***Managing Migration: Time for a New International Regime?** Ed. by Bimal Ghosh. 320p. 2000. text 72.00 (*0-19-829764-5*) OUP.

Managing Mill Maintenance: The Emerging Realities. Richard F. Baldwin. LC 89-85008. (Illus.). 302p. 1990. 45.00 (*0-87930-220-8*, 471) Miller Freeman.

Managing Misbehaviour in Schools. 2nd ed. Ed. by Tony Charlton & Kenneth David. LC 93-458. 240p. (C). 1993. pap. 25.99 (*0-415-09287-6*, B2424) Routledge.

Managing Mistakes. Ted Kowalski. (C). 1994. pap. text. write for info. (*0-8013-1344-9*) Longman.

***Managing Mistakes with Management.** 6th ed. Hartley. 1999. pap. text 87.00 (*0-471-38090-3*) Wiley.

Managing Mobile Home Parks. Steven Pappas. (IREM Monographs). (Illus.). 194p. (Orig.). (C). 1991. pap. text 44.95 (*0-944298-57-5*) Inst Real Estate.

Managing Mobility. P. S. Bawa. 1991. text 17.95 (*0-7069-5452-1*, Pub. by Vikas) S Asia.

***Managing Mobility in African Rangelands: The Legitimization of Transhumance.** Maryam Niamir-Fuller. 240p. 1999. pap. 29.95 (*1-85339-473-4*, Pub. by Intermed Tech) Stylus Pub VA.

Managing Modern Capitalism: Industrial Renewal & Workplace Democracy in the United States & Western Europe. M. Hancock et al. LC 91-37554. 384p. 1991. pap. 24.95 (*0-275-94287-2*, B4287, Greenwood Pr) Greenwood.

Managing Modern Capitalism: Industrial Renewal & Workplace Democracy in the United States & Western Europe, 125. M. Hancock et al. LC 91-9269. 400p. 1991. 69.50 (*0-313-26886-X*, Greenwood Pr) Greenwood.

Managing Money: A Center Director's Guidebook. Ed. by Roger Neugebauer & Bonnie Neugebauer. (Illus.). 160p. 1997. pap. 20.00 (*0-942702-21-2*) Child Care.

Managing Money in Higher Education: A Guide to the Financial Process & Effective Participation Within It. William E. Vandament. LC 89-45577. (Higher Education Ser.). 248p. 1989. text 32.95 (*1-55542-192-X*) Jossey-Bass.

Managing Money in Later Life. H. Finch & G. Elam. (DSS Research Report Ser.). 1995. write for info. (*0-11-762340-7*, Pub. by Statnry Office) Bernan Associates.

Managing Money with Your IBM PC. Amihai Glazer. (Illus.). 208p. 1986. 26.95 (*0-13-550658-1*) P-H.

Managing More Effectively: A Professional Approach to Get the Best Out of People. Madhurendra K. Varma. LC 97-11576. 1997. pap. write for info. (*0-8039-9374-9*) Sage.

Managing More Effectively: A Professional Approach to Get the Best Out of People. Madhurendra K. Varma. LC 97-11576. 272p. 1997. text 28.00 (*0-8039-9373-0*) Sage.

***Managing More Effectively: A Professional Approach to Get the Best Out of People.** 2nd ed. Madhurendra K. Varma. LC 00-28596. 2000. pap. write for info. (*0-7619-9452-1*) Sage.

Managing More with Less: Handling Multiple Priorities. Joanna Howard. LC 99-176075. (New Skills Portfolio Ser.). 160p. 1998. pap. text 29.95 (*0-7506-3698-X*) Buttrwrth-Heinemann.

Managing Motors: The Complete Book of Electric Motor Application & Maintenance. 2nd rev. ed. Richard L. Nailen. (Illus.). 464p. 1996. text 74.95 (*0-943876-09-5*) Barks Pubns.

Managing Multicampus Systems: Effective Administration in an Unsteady State: A Report for the Carnegie Council on Policy Studies in Higher Education. Eugene C. Lee. LC 75-24012. (Carnegie Council Ser.). 192p. reprint ed. pap. 59.60 (*0-608-14788-5*, 202566100045) Bks Demand.

Managing Multiculturalism & Diversity in the Library: Principles & Issues for Administrators. Ed. by Mark Winston. LC 99-28085. (Journal of Library Administration: Vol. 27, Nos. 1 & 2). 209p. (C). 1999. 49.95 (*0-7890-0692-8*) Haworth Pr.

Managing Multiculturalism in Substance Abuse Services. Ed. by Jacob U. Gordon. LC 94-11730. 320p. 1994. 55.00 (*0-8039-5735-1*); pap. 25.50 (*0-8039-5736-X*) Sage.

Managing Multimedia. 2nd ed. Elaine England. LC 98-222901. 440p. (C). 1999. pap. text 44.95 (*0-201-36058-6*) Addison-Wesley.

Managing Multimedia Projects. Roy Strauss. LC 96-48504. 208p. 1997. pap. 24.95 (*0-240-80244-6*, Focal) Buttrwrth-Heinemann.

***Managing Multinationals in the Middle East: Accounting & Tax Issues.** Wagdy M. Abdallah. LC 00-23932. 250p. 2000. 67.00 (*1-56720-267-5*, Q267, Quorum Bks) Greenwood.

Managing Multiple Bosses: How to Juggle Priorities, Personalities & Projects - And Make It Look Easy. Pat Nickerson. LC 98-29095. 144p. 1998. pap. 22.95 (*0-8144-7025-4*) AMACOM.

Managing Municipal Leisure Services. Ed. by Sidney G. Lutzin. LC 80-17378. (Municipal Management Ser.). 271p. 1980. pap. text 21.00 (*0-87326-023-6*) Intl City-Cnty Mgt.

Managing Muskies. Ed. by G. E. Hall. LC 86-83239. (Special Publication Ser.: No. 15). 372p. 1986. text 34.00 (*0-913235-33-4*, 510.11P) Am Fisheries Soc.

***Managing National Innovation Systems.** OECD Staff. 120p. 1999. pap. 32.00 (*92-64-17038-3*, 92 1999 03 1 P, Pub. by Org for Econ) OECD.

Managing National Park System Resources: A Handbook on Legal Duties, Opportunities & Tools. Ed. by Michael A. Mantell. LC 89-20993. 286p. 1990. reprint ed. pap. 88.70 (*0-608-04186-6*, 206492100011) Bks Demand.

Managing Nationalism: United States National Security Council Documents on the Philipines, 1953-1960. Ed. by Nick Cullather. 198p. (Orig.). 1993. pap. 12.50 (*971-10-0471-2*, Pub. by New Day Pub) Cellar.

Managing Natural Resources with GIS. Laura Lang. 117p. 1998. pap. text 19.95 (*1-879102-53-6*) ESR Inst.

Managing Negative People: Strategies for Success. S. Michael Kravitz. Ed. by Janis Paris. LC 94-68198. (Fifty-Minute Ser.). (Illus.). 71p. (Orig.). 1994. pap. 10.95 (*1-56052-306-9*) Crisp Pubns.

Managing Netware & Windows 95. 2nd ed. Farshad Nowshadi. LC 98-29668. 504p. (C). 1999. pap. text 46.88 (*0-201-17784-6*) Addison-Wesley.

***Managing Network Nodes With: Intel LANDesk Management Suite, Version 6.3.** Barbara S. Josephson & Brian K. Mason. viii, 238p. 2000. 99.95 (*1-893854-02-7*) TriTech Ed.

Managing Networks in International Business, Vol. 2. Mats Forsgren. (International Studies in Global Change). 272p. 1992. text 72.00 (*2-88124-505-6*) Gordon & Breach.

Managing New Office Technology: An Organizational Strategy. Calvin H. Pava. LC 83-47519. 224p. (C). 1984. 32.95 (*0-02-924970-8*) Free Pr.

Managing New Product & Process Development: Text & Cases. Kim B. Clark & Steven C. Wheelwright. LC 92-29067. 1992. 60.00 (*0-02-905517-2*) Free Pr.

***Managing New Product Development Process.** 2nd ed. Dolan. (C). 2000. pap. text. write for info. (*0-201-55569-7*) Addison-Wesley.

Managing New Product Innovation. Bob Jerrard. 249p. 1999. 89.00 (*0-7484-0859-2*) Taylor & Francis.

Managing New Product Innovations. William E. Souder. LC 85-40104. 272p. 1986. 37.00 (*0-669-10809-X*) Lxngtn Bks.

***Managing New Products: Using the Map System to Accelerate Growth.** 3rd ed. Thomas D. Kuczmarski. (Illus.). 288p. 2000. 34.95 (*0-9677817-0-1*, Innovation) Book Ends.

Managing New Technological Change: Case Studies in the Re-Organisation of Work. Peter Wilkins. (Avebury Business Library). 235p. 1992. 82.95 (*1-85628-336-4*, Pub. by Avebry) Ashgate Pub Co.

Managing New Technologies: The Information Revolution in Local Government. Ed. & Pref. by Costis Toregas. (Practical Management Ser.). 168p. (Orig.). 1985. pap. text 23.95 (*0-87326-047-3*) Intl City-Cnty Mgt.

Managing New Technology Development. William E. Souder. LC 93-20840. (Illus.). 348p. 1994. 50.00 (*0-07-059748-0*) McGraw.

***Managing Newsroom Employees: A Guide to Solving Common Personnel Problems.** Sharon L. Peters. 52p. 1999. pap. 12.50 (*1-930341-00-8*) NMC.

Managing NFS & NIS. Hal Stern. Ed. by Mike Larkides. LC 92-245650. (Computer Science Ser.). (Illus.). 436p. (Orig.). 1991. reprint ed. pap. 34.95 (*0-937175-75-7*) OReilly & Assocs.

Managing Nitrogren for Groundwater Quality & Farm Profitability. Ed. by R. F. Follett et al. 378p. 1991. 36.00 (*0-89118-796-0*) Soil Sci Soc Am.

Managing Non-Profit Organizations in the 20th Cenury. James P. Gelatt. LC 91-37315. 256p. 1992. pap. 29.95 (*0-89774-654-6*) Oryx Pr.

Managing Non-Proliferation Regimes in the 1990s: Power, Politics & Policies. Peter Van Ham. LC 93-38875. 1993. 14.95 (*0-87609-161-3*) Coun Foreign.

Managing Notorious Trials. 2nd ed. Timothy R. Murphy. LC 98-67361. 225p. 1998. write for info. (*0-89656-188-7*) Natl Ctr St Courts.

Managing Nuclear Operations. Ed. by Ashton B. Carter et al. LC 86-32655. 751p. 1987. 52.95 (*0-8157-1314-2*); pap. 24.95 (*0-8157-1313-4*) Brookings.

***Managing Nuisance Beavers along Roadsides: A Guide for Highway Department.** Paul G. Jensen & Paul D. Curtis. (Illus.). 14p. 1999. pap. 6.00 (*1-57753-266-X*, 47BEAV) Corn Coop Ext.

***Managing Nutrients & Pathogens from Animal Agriculture: Proceedings from "Managing Nutrients & Pathogens from Animal Agriculture, a Conference for Nutrient Management Consultants, Extension Educators & Producer Advisors," Camp Hill, Pennsylvania, March 28-30, 2000.** Ed. by Natural Resource, Agriculture & Engineering Service Conference Staff. LC 00-20869. (Illus.). 508p. 2000. pap. text 30.00 (*0-935817-54-9*, NRAES-130) NRAES.

Managing Nutrition Care of the Coronary Patient in Different Health Care Settings. Penny M. Kris-Etherton et al. 250p. 2000. 55.00 (*0-8342-1093-2*, 10932) Aspen Pub.

Managing Obesity & Eating Disorders. Nancy Gustafson. Ed. by Becky Colgan. 210p. 1997. pap. 64.95 (*1-57801-007-1*) Western Schls.

Managing Object-Oriented Software Projects. Andrew Rood. 1996. pap. text 41.91 (*0-201-63404-X*) Addison-Wesley.

Managing Object Technology. Timothy D. Korson. (C). 1998. text. write for info. (*0-201-82657-7*) Addison-Wesley.

***Managing Occupational Health & Safety a Multidisciplinary Approach.** Philip Bohle & Michael Quinlan. 512p. 2000. pap. 54.95 (*0-7329-4078-8*, Pub. by Macmill Educ) Paul & Co Pubs.

Managing Occupational Hygiene: A Challenge. B. H. Witham. 1998. pap. 150.00 (*0-948237-31-7*, Pub. by H&H Sci Cnslts) St Mut.

Managing of Police Organizations. 4th ed. R. Fred Ferguson & Paul M. Whisenand. LC 95-24336. 472p. 1995. 84.00 (*0-13-098476-0*) P-H.

Managing OFCCP Compliance Reviews. 4th ed. William F. Holmes & Jeffrey A. Norris. 1993. 125.00 (*0-916559-47-5*, 2024-TM-4045) EPF.

Managing OFCCP Compliance Reviews. 4th ed. William F. Holmes & Jeffrey A. Norris. 600p. 1993. pap. 125.00 (*0-916559-42-4*) EPF.

Managing Older Workers: Overcoming Myths & Stereotypes. Gordon F. Shea. Ed. by Kay Keppler. LC 92-54364. (Fifty-Minute Ser.). 68p. (Orig.). 1993. pap. 10.95 (*1-56052-182-1*) Crisp Pubns.

Managing on Her Own: Dr. Lillian Gilbreth & Women's Work in the Interwar Era. Laurel Graham. LC 98-13593. (Illus.). 288p. 1998. 34.95 (*0-89806-185-7*, Graham) Eng Mgmt Pr.

Managing on the Edge: How the Smartest Companies Use Conflict to Stay Ahead. Richard T. Pascale. (Illus.). 352p. 1991. pap. 12.00 (*0-671-73285-4*, Touchstone) S&S Trade Pap.

Managing One-Bank Holding Companies. Hassell H. McClellan. LC 81-4351. 314p. 1981. 42.95 (*0-275-90680-9*, C0680, Praeger Pubs) Greenwood.

Managing Online Reference Services. Ed. by Ethel Auster. LC 85-21542. 408p. 1986. pap. text 45.00 (*0-918212-93-6*) Neal-Schuman.

Managing Open Learning. Derek W. Birch & Jack Latcham. 1985. 70.00 (*0-907659-39-X*) St Mut.

Managing Open Systems. Richard Freeman. 192p. 1997. pap. 29.95 (*0-7494-2056-1*, Kogan Pg Educ) Stylus Pub VA.

***Managing Operation Inform Technology.** Hunt. 1999. 50.00 (*0-07-433559-6*, McGrw-H College) McGrw-H Hghr Educ.

***Managing Operational Risk in Financial Markets.** (Illus.). 256p. 2000. pap. 74.95 (*0-7506-4732-9*) Buttrwrth-Heinemann.

Managing Operations. Roger Cartwright et al. (In-Charge Ser.). 240p. (Orig.). (C). 1993. pap. text 40.95 (*0-631-19011-2*) Blackwell Pubs.

Managing Operations. Clark. (Illus.). 352p. 1997. text. write for info. (*0-412-74990-4*, Chap & Hall NY) Chapman & Hall.

Managing Operations. Peter Grainger. (Manager's Toolkit Ser.). 96p. 1994. pap. 12.95 (*0-7494-1251-8*, Kogan Pg Educ) Stylus Pub VA.

Managing Operations. Hart. LC 98-229119. 256p. 1998. pap. text 29.95 (*0-7506-3809-5*) Buttrwrth-Heinemann.

Managing Operations Emerging Companies. Morton. 1984. 21.95 (*0-201-15860-4*) Addison-Wesley.

Managing Operations in the Chemical Industry by Aggregate Quality. Jan M. Charvat. (European University Studies: Economics & Management: Ser. 5, Vol. 1086). (Illus.). 123p. 1990. pap. 22.00 (*3-261-04213-3*) P Lang Pubng.

Managing Oral Healthcare Delivery: A Resource for Dental Professionals. Catherine L. Ganssle. LC 94-16965. 288p. (C). 1994. mass mkt. 52.95 (*0-8273-5532-7*) Delmar.

Managing Organisations in Africa. Peter Blunt & Merrick L. Jones. (Studies in Organization: No. 40). xiv, 356p. (C). 1992. lib. bdg. 113.85 (*3-11-012646-X*) De Gruyter.

Managing Organization Behavior. 3rd ed. Stephen J. Carroll et al. LC 93-38203. 700p. 1994. pap. 50.95 (*1-55786-551-5*) Blackwell Pubs.

Managing Organizational Behavior. Philip L. Hunsaker & C. W. Cook. (C). 1986. text 53.75 (*0-201-11465-8*) Addison-Wesley.

***Managing Organizational Behavior.** 4th ed. Henry L. Tosi. LC 99-33803. 668p. 1999. 69.95 (*0-631-21257-4*) Blackwell Pubs.

Managing Organizational Behaviour. Schermerhorn. 1992. pap. text. write for info. (*0-471-64014-X*); pap. text. write for info. (*0-471-64015-8*); pap. text. write for info. incl. VHS (*0-471-64041-7*) Wiley.

Managing Organizational Behaviour. Schermerhorn. 670p. (C). 2000. text. write for info. (*0-471-64013-1*) Wiley.

Managing Organizational Change. Ed. by W. Warner Burke. LC 95-14148. 1995. 29.95 (*0-8144-6713-X*) AMACOM.

Managing Organizational Change. Wendy Carter. LC 94-10780. 126p. 1994. teacher ed. 110.00 (*0-07-011198-7*) McGraw.

Managing Organizational Change. 2nd ed. Patrick E. Connor & Linda K. Lake. LC 94-16461. 248p. 1994. 75.00 (*0-275-94652-5*, Praeger Pubs); pap. 22.95 (*0-275-94653-3*, Praeger Pubs) Greenwood.

Managing Organizational Change, Module 11. Ancona et al. (GI - Organizational Behavior Ser.). 1995. text 7.95 (*0-538-85891-5*) S-W Pub.

Managing Organizational Change: Practical Lessons for Building Commitment. Edward E. Hubbard. 45p. 1988. pap. 12.95 (*1-883733-15-4*) Global Insghts.

Managing Organizational Performance. Michael Nash. LC 82-49040. (Management Ser.). 380p. 1983. text 45.95 (*0-87589-561-1*) Jossey-Bass.

Managing Organizational Performance. Michael M. Nash. LC 82-49049. (Joint Publication in the Jossey-Bass Management Series & the Jossey-Bass Social & Behavioral Science Ser.). 382p. 1983. reprint ed. pap. 118.50 (*0-7837-2545-0*, 204270400006) Bks Demand.

An Asterisk (*) at the beginning of an entry indicates that the title is appearing for the first time.

Managing Organizational Quality. H. William Vroman & Vincent P. Luchsinger. LC 94-341. 368p. (C). 1994. text 37.50 (*0-256-14993-3*, Irwn McGrw-H) McGrw-H Hghr Educ.

Managing Organizational Transitions. Craig C. Lundberg. (C). 1989. pap. text. write for info. (*0-201-18253-X*) Addison-Wesley.

Managing Organizational Transitions in a Global Economy. Ed. by Rosalind M. Schwartz. (Monograph & Research Ser.: No. 57). 198p. 1992. 15.00 (*0-89215-175-7*) U Cal LA Indus Rel.

Managing Organizations. Dessler. LC 94-69149. (C). 1994. text 87.50 (*0-03-096612-4*) Harcourt Coll Pubs.

***Managing Organizations: Current Issues.** Ed. by Stewart R. Clegg et al. 288p. 1998. pap. 31.95 (*0-7619-6046-5*) Sage.

***Managing Organizations & People: Cases in Management, Organizational Behavior & Human Resource Management.** 6th ed. Paul F. Buller & Randall S. Schuler. LC 99-15313. 377p. 1999. pap. 46.95 (*0-324-00713-2*) Thomson Learn.

Managing Organizations by Projects: Winning Through Enterprise Project Management. Paul C. Dinsmore. LC 98-41020. 271p. 1999. 57.95 (*0-8144-0420-0*) AMACOM.

Managing Organizations in Africa: Readings, Cases & Exercises. Peter Blunt et al. LC 93-6796. (Studies in Organization: No. 49). xii, 219p. (Orig.). (C). 1993. pap. text 32.00 (*3-11-013671-6*) De Gruyter.

Managing Organizations in Developing Countries: An Operational & Strategic Approach. Moses N. Kiggundu. LC 88-13422. (Library of Management for Development, New Directions in Development Management Ser.). xx, 317p. (C). 1989. pap. text 27.95 (*0-931816-42-4*) Kumarian Pr.

Managing Orthopaedic Malpractice Risk. Ed. by Committee on Professional Liability. LC 97-102054. 80p. 1996. 25.00 (*0-89203-153-0*) Amer Acad Ortho Surg.

***Managing Osteoarthritis in Primary Care.** Gillian Hosie & John Dickson. (Illus.). 144p. 2000. pap. 29.95 (*0-632-05353-4*) Blackwell Sci.

Managing Osteogenesis Imperfecta: A Medical Manual. Ed. by Pricisalla Wacaster. (Illus.). 250p. (Orig.). 1996. pap. text 24.95 (*0-9642189-3-3*) Osteogenesis Imper.

Managing Other People's Money. Penny Letts. (C). 1989. 35.00 (*0-86242-090-3*, Pub. by Age Concern Eng) St Mut.

Managing Otitis Media with Effusion in Young Children: Reference for Clinicians. Sylvan E. Stool. 13p. 1994. pap. 43.00 (*0-16-061526-7*) USGPO.

Managing Our National Resources. 2nd ed. William Camp. 1991. pap., teacher ed. 12.00 (*0-8273-4067-2*) Delmar.

Managing Our Natural Resources. 2nd ed. William Camp. 1991. pap. 33.95 (*0-8273-4066-4*) Delmar.

Managing Our Natural Resources. 3rd ed. Camp. (Agriculture Ser.). 48p. (C). 1996. text, teacher ed. 12.75 (*0-8273-6717-1*) Delmar.

Managing Our Natural Resources. 3rd ed. Camp & Darold Hehn. (Agriculture Ser.). 144p. (C). 1995. mass mkt., wbk. ed. 17.00 (*0-8273-6926-3*) Delmar.

Managing Our Natural Resources. 3rd ed. Camp & Darold Hehn. (Agriculture Ser.). 32p. 1996. pap. text, teacher ed. 12.75 (*0-8273-6927-1*) Delmar.

Managing Our Natural Resources. 3rd ed. William G. Camp & Thomas B. Daugherty. LC 95-15154. 368p. (J). 1995. mass mkt. 55.95 (*0-8273-6716-3*) Delmar.

***Managing Our Natural Resources.** 4th ed. Camp & Daugherty. (C). 2000. text 36.00 (*0-7668-1554-4*); text, wbk. ed. 18.00 (*0-7668-1556-0*) Delmar.

Managing Our Natural Resources Activity Manual. Darold Hehn. 25p. 1994. teacher ed. 12.75 (*0-8273-6642-6*) Delmar.

Managing Our Natural Resources Activity Manual. 2nd ed. Darold Hehn. 132p. 1994. 17.00 (*0-8273-6641-8*) Delmar.

Managing Our Natural Resources CTB. 3rd ed. Camp. (Agriculture Ser.). 1996. 100.00 (*0-8273-7492-5*) Delmar.

Managing Our Selves: Building a Community of Caring. Elizabeth Power. 115p. 1992. student ed. 17.95 (*1-883307-01-5*) EPower & Assocs.

Managing Our Selves: God in Our Midst. Elizabeth Power. 63p. 1993. reprint ed. student ed. 12.95 (*1-883307-02-3*) EPower & Assocs.

Managing Our Wildlife Resources. 3rd ed. Anderson. LC 98-5859. 560p. (C). 1998. 105.00 (*0-13-901232-X*) P-H.

Managing Outcomes, Process & Cost in a Managed Care Environment. Roey Kirk. LC 96-48673. 1997. 60.00 (*0-8342-0912-8*) Aspen Pub.

Managing Outcomes Through Collaborative Care: The Application of Caremapping & Case Management. Ed. by Karen Zander. LC 94-47919. 207p. 1995. pap. text 59.95 (*1-55648-132-2*, 027103) AHPI.

Managing Outside Pressure: Strategies for Preventing Corporate Disasters. Matthias Winter & Ulrich Steger. LC 98-3084. 264p. 1998. pap. 49.95 (*0-471-97933-3*) Wiley.

Managing Overdues: A How-to-Do-It Manual for Librarians. Patsy Hansel. LC 98-16348. (How-to-Do-It Manuals Ser.). 131p. 1998. pap. 45.00 (*1-55570-291-0*) Neal-Schuman.

Managing Overseas Construction Contracting. D. A. Langford & V. R. Rowland. LC 95-209398. 192p. 1995. 67.00 (*0-7277-2029-5*) Am Soc Civil Eng.

Managing Packaged Tourism. Eric Laws. (Topics in Tourism Ser.). 248p. 1997. pap. 15.99 (*0-415-11347-4*) Thomson Learn.

Managing Paddy Rice Business of Small Farmers. V. R. Gaikwad & V. K. Gupta. xxiv, 239p. 1986. 17.00 (*0-86132-129-4*, Pub. by Popular Prakashan) S Asia.

***Managing Pain.** Reader's Digest Editors. LC 98-43587. (Health & Healing the Natural Way Ser.). 1999. write for info. (*0-7621-0144-X*) RD Assn.

Managing Pain Before It Manages You. Margaret A. Caudill. LC 94-17730. 224p. 1994. pap. text 19.95 (*0-89862-224-7*, 2224) Guilford Pubns.

Managing Participation. Marshall Sashkin. 1999. write for info. (*0-201-56346-0*) Addison-Wesley.

Managing Partner One Hundred One: A Primer on Firm Leadership. LC 90-80481. 70p. 1990. pap. 29.95 (*0-89707-543-9*, 511-0272) Amer Bar Assn.

Managing Pastoral Care. Mike Calvert & Jenny Henderson. LC 98-218268. 1998. 69.95 (*0-304-70067-3*); pap. 24.95 (*0-304-70068-1*) Continuum.

Managing Pastures & Cattle under Coconuts. Donald A. Plucknett. LC 79-5357. (Tropical Agriculture Ser.). 1980. text 63.50 (*0-89158-299-1*) Westview.

Managing Patient Expectations: The Art of Finding & Keeping Loyal Patients. Susan K. Baker. LC 98-15900. (Business & Management Ser.). 256p. 1998. 34.95 (*0-7879-4158-1*) Jossey-Bass.

Managing Payroll Systems: Payroll Accounting. 6th ed. Bernard J. Bieg. (AH - Payroll Accounting Ser.). 1996. 4.95 (*0-538-86457-5*) S-W Pub.

Managing Pediatric Emergencies. Patricia A. Moloney-Harmon. (Cardiopulmonary Arrest Ser.). (Illus.). 104p. (Orig.). 1984. pap. text 9.50 (*0-932491-03-0*) Res Appl Inc.

Managing Pension Plans: A Comprehensive Guide to Improving Plan Performance. Dennis E. Logue & Jack S. Rader. LC 97-25803. (Financial Management Association Survey & Synthesis Ser.). 432p. 1997. 45.00 (*0-87584-791-9*, HBS Pr) Harvard Busn.

Managing Pension Schemes. Norman Toulson. (C). 1986. 255.00 (*0-7855-4093-8*, Pub. by Witherby & Co) St Mut.

***Managing People.** (C). 2000. 48.00 (*0-536-61083-5*) Pearson Custom.

Managing People. Jane Churchouse & Chris Churchouse. LC 98-3178. (Management Workbook Ser.). 207p. 1998. pap. 33.95 (*0-566-08015-X*, Pub. by Gower) Ashgate Pub Co.

Managing People. M. Collins et al. (In-Charge Ser.). 272p. (Orig.). (C). 1993. pap. text 36.95 (*0-631-19012-0*) Blackwell Pubs.

Managing People. Peter Grainger. (Manager's Toolkit Ser.). 96p. 1994. pap. 12.95 (*0-7494-1249-6*, Kogan Pg Educ) Stylus Pub VA.

Managing People. Ed. by A. S. Martin & F. Grover. 142p. 1988. 30.00 (*0-7277-1354-X*, Pub. by T Telford) RCH.

Managing People. Ed. by A. Dale Timpe. (Art & Science of Business Management Ser.). 400p. 1988. 29.95 (*0-8160-1901-0*) Facts on File.

***Managing People.** Jane Weightman. 240p. 2000. pap. 47.95 (*0-8464-5115-8*) Beekman Pubs.

Managing People. Williams. LC 99-36237. (GC - Principles of Management Ser.). 1999. pap. 51.75 (*0-538-86163-0*) S-W Pub.

Managing People. Ed. by A. Dale Timpe. LC 88-3187. (Art & Science of Business Management Ser.: Vol. 6). 392p. 1988. reprint ed. pap. 121.60 (*0-608-02814-2*, 206388100007) Bks Demand.

Managing People. 2nd ed. Charles Dwyer. 200p. (C). 1996. pap. text, per. 36.95 (*0-7872-2828-1*, 41282801) Kendall-Hunt.

***Managing People.** 2nd ed. Michael Riley. 224p. 2000. pap. 29.95 (*0-7506-4536-9*) Buttrwrth-Heinemann.

Managing People. 2nd ed. Rosemary Thomson. LC 97-199406. (Institute of Management Ser.). 208p. 1997. pap. text 29.95 (*0-7506-3388-3*, HF5549) Buttrwrth-Heinemann.

Managing People: A Competence Approach to Supervisory Management. Roger Cartwright et al. LC 97-45216. 200p. 1998. pap. 38.95 (*0-631-20923-9*) Blackwell Pubs.

Managing People: A Practical Guide. 3rd ed. Byron D. Lane. LC 96-33212. (Successful Business Library). 217p. 1996. pap. 21.95 (*1-55571-380-7*, Oasis Pr) PSI Resch.

Managing People: A Practical Guide For Line Managers. Michael Armstrong. 1999. pap. text 24.95 (*0-7494-2612-8*) Kogan Page Ltd.

Managing People: One Hundred One Proven Ideas for Making You & Your People More Productive. Ed. by Sara P. Noble. 191p. (Orig.). 1992. text 24.95 (*1-880394-04-9*) Inc Pub MA.

Managing People: One Hundred One Proven Ideas for Making You & Your People More Productive. Ed. by Sara P. Noble. 191p. (Orig.). 1997. pap. 11.50 (*1-880394-02-2*) Thomson Learn.

Managing People: The Art of Leadership. 4th ed. H. C. Howlett, 2nd. (Illus.). 131p. 1992. pap., student ed. 40.00 (*1-57614-002-4*) TECHSTAR.

Managing People Across Europe. Ed. by Terry Garrison & David Rees. LC 94-185748. 190p. 1994. reprint ed. pap. 58.90 (*0-608-04550-0*, 206529200001) Bks Demand.

Managing People & Activities. Susan Curtis & Barry Curtis. (Illus.). 325p. (Orig.). 1997. pap. 49.50 (*0-273-62066-5*, Pub. by Pitman Pub) Trans-Atl Phila.

Managing People & Organizations. Gabarro. 400p. 1992. pap. 23.96 (*0-07-103362-9*) McGraw.

Managing People & Organizations. John Gabarro. 1992. pap. 30.94 (*0-07-022668-7*) McGraw.

Managing People & Organizations. Selected by John J. Gabarro. (Practice of Management Ser.). 480p. 1992. pap. 29.95 (*0-87584-311-5*) Harvard Busn.

Managing People & Problems. Quentin De la Bedoyere. 160p. 1988. text 39.95 (*0-566-02697-X*, Pub. by Gower) Ashgate Pub Co.

Managing People & Problems. Quentin De la Bedoyere. (Gower Audio Manual Ser.). 64p. 1989. pap. text 61.95 (*0-566-02763-1*, Pub. by Gower) Ashgate Pub Co.

***Managing People & Self-Part of Team Leader Development.** Palmer. 256p. 1998. pap. text 28.95 (*0-7506-3861-3*) Buttrwrth-Heinemann.

Managing People & Technological Change. John Bailey. 256p. (Orig.). 1993. pap. 53.50 (*0-273-60027-3*, Pub. by Pitman Pub) Trans-Atl Phila.

Managing People at Work. Peter J. Makin et al. LC 89-8475. 221p. 1989. 57.95 (*0-89930-505-9*, MKW/, Quorum Bks) Greenwood.

Managing People at Work: A Manager's Guide to Behavior in Organizations. John W. Hunt. 292p. (C). 1986. 60.00 (*0-85292-389-9*) St Mut.

Managing People at Work: A Manager's Guide to Behavior in Organizations. 3rd ed. John W. Hunt. LC 92-10589. 1992. write for info. (*0-07-707677-X*) McGraw.

Managing People at Work: Leadership Styles & Influence Strategies. Mahfooz A. Ansari. (Illus.). 218p. (C). 1990. 26.00 (*0-8039-9650-0*) Sage.

Managing People During Stressful Times: The Psychologically Defensive Workplace. Seth Allcorn & Michael A. Diamond. LC 96-17925. 184p. 1997. 59.95 (*1-56720-082-6*, Quorum Bks) Greenwood.

Managing People in Changing Times: Coping with the Human Impact of Organizational Change. Robert Burns. 192p. 1993. pap. text 24.95 (*1-86373-356-6*, Pub. by Allen & Unwin Pty) Paul & Co Pubs.

***Managing People in Construction.** Drucker & White. 272p. 2000. pap. 47.95 (*0-8464-5116-6*) Beekman Pubs.

Managing People in Construction. Jan Druker & Geoff White. 272p. 1996. pap. 64.00 (*0-85292-642-1*, Pub. by IPM Hse) St Mut.

Managing People in Education. Ed. by Tony Bush & David Middlewood. (Educational Management Ser.). (Illus.). 240p. 1997. pap. (*1-85396-336-4*) Corwin Pr.

***Managing People in Organizations: Applying Modern Management Theory to the Financial Services.** Ed. by David James. 244p. 1999. pap. 80.00 (*0-85297-512-0*, Pub. by Chartered Bank) St Mut.

Managing People in Professional Practices. Anne Radford. 160p. 1995. pap. 90.00 (*0-85292-571-9*, Pub. by IPM Hse) St Mut.

Managing People in Public Agencies: Personnel & Labor Relations. Jonathan Brock. LC 88-36475. (Illus.). 440p. (C). 1989. reprint ed. pap. text 32.00 (*0-8191-7277-4*) U Pr of Amer.

***Managing People in the Health Service.** Jane Weightman. 176p. 2000. pap. 47.95 (*0-8464-5117-4*) Beekman Pubs.

Managing People in the Health Service. Jane Weightman. 176p. 1996. pap. 64.00 (*0-85292-641-3*, Pub. by IPM Hse) St Mut.

Managing People in the Hotel & Catering Industry. Michael Riley. (Illus.). 240p. 1995. 29.95 (*0-7506-2289-X*) Buttrwrth-Heinemann.

Managing People in the HVAC-R Industry. Howard J. McKew. Ed. by Joanna Turpin. LC 94-33085. 120p. (Orig.). 1995. pap. 14.95 (*0-912524-97-9*) Busn News.

Managing People in Today's Law Firm: The Human Resources Approach to Surviving Change. Ellen Weisbord et al. LC 95-3780. 224p. 1995. 62.95 (*0-89930-834-1*, Quorum Bks) Greenwood.

Managing People, (Including Yourself) for Project Success. Gordon L. Culp & R. Anne Smith. (Project Management Ser.). (Illus.). 307p. 1992. text 58.95 (*0-442-00952-6*, VNR) Wiley.

Managing People (Including Yourself) for Project Success. Gordon Culp & Anne Smith. 320p. 1992. 69.95 (*0-471-29018-1*, VNR) Wiley.

Managing People Is Like Herding Cats: Warren Bennis on Leadership. Warren Bennis. LC 96-61955. 239p. 1997. 24.95 (*0-9634917-5-X*) Exec Excell.

Managing People Is Like Herding Cats: Warren Bennis on Leadership. Warren Bennis. 240p. 1999. pap. 12.00 (*1-890009-61-X*) Exec Excell.

***Managing PeopleSoft with Tivoli: Planning, Design, Management, & Optimization!** Catherine Cook. 634p. 2000. pap. text 59.00 incl. cd-rom (*0-13-016889-0*) P-H.

***Managing Performance.** CCTA Staff. (IS Management Guides Ser.). (Illus.). 99p. 2000. 50.00 (*1-903091-05-5*, Pub. by Format Pubg Ltd) Balogh.

Managing Performance: A Comprehensive Guide to Effective Supervision. Marion E. Haynes. Ed. by Rich Osborne. LC 83-17527. (Professional Ser.). 394p. 1984. pap. 22.95 (*1-56052-353-0*) Crisp Pubns.

Managing Performance: Goals, Feedback, Coaching, Recognition. Jenny Hill. (Gower Management Workbooks Ser.). 160p. 1997. pap. 33.95 (*0-566-07739-6*, Pub. by Gower) Ashgate Pub Co.

Managing Performance Improvement Projects: Preparing, Planning, & Implementing. Jim Fuller. LC 97-755. 240p. 1997. 44.95 (*0-7879-0959-9*, Pfffr & Co) Jossey-Bass.

Managing Performance... in Brief. Sultan Kermally. 160p. 1997. pap. text 28.95 (*0-7506-3607-6*, HF5001) Buttrwrth-Heinemann.

***Managing Performance Reviews: How to Ensure Your Appraisals Improve Individual Performance & Organisational Results.** 4th ed. Nigel Hunt. (Business & Management Ser.). 168p. 1999. pap. 19.95 (*1-85703-488-0*, Pub. by How To Bks) Trans-Atl Phila.

Managing Performing Arts Collections in Academic & Public Libraries. Ed. by Carolyn A. Sheehy. LC 93-35837. (Library Management Collection). 240p. 1994. lib. bdg. 65.00 (*0-313-27976-4*, Greenwood Pr) Greenwood.

Managing Personal Change: A Primer for Today's World. Dennis Jaffee & Cynthia D. Scott. Ed. by Michael G. Crisp. LC 88-72259. (Fifty-Minute Ser.). (Illus.). 71p. (Orig.). 1989. pap. 10.95 (*0-931961-74-2*) Crisp Pubns.

***Managing Personal Resources.** (Overcoming Obstacles). 32p. (YA). (gr. 6-9). 1999. pap. text 11.50 (*1-929393-06-7*) Community for Ed.

Managing Physical Education, Fitness, & Sports Programs. 2nd ed. Jim H. Railey & Peggy Railey Tschauner. x, 340p. (C). 1993. text 52.95 (*1-55934-173-4*, 1173) Mayfield Pub.

Managing Physical Education, Fitness, & Sports Programs: Instructor's Manual. 2nd ed. Jim H. Railey & Peggy Railey Tschauner. (C). 1993. pap. text, teacher ed. write for info. (*1-55934-174-2*, 1174) Mayfield Pub.

Managing Physical Plant Operations. Fairmont Press Staff & Kenneth L. Petrocelly. 332p. (C). 1993. 74.00 (*0-13-147455-3*) P-H.

Managing Physical Plant Operations. Kenneth L. Petrocelly. LC 93-35434. 312p. 1993. 74.00 (*0-88173-160-9*) Fairmont Pr.

***Managing Pig Health & the Treatment of Disease.** 608p. 1999. 460.00 (*0-9530150-0-9*, Pub. by FiveM Enterprises) St Mut.

Managing Planet Earth: Perspectives on Population, Ecology & the Law. Miguel A. Santos. LC 89-49264. 184p. 1990. 57.95 (*0-89789-216-X*, H216, Greenwood Pr) Greenwood.

Managing Planned Change. Paul C. Nutt. (Illus.). 576p. (C). 1991. teacher ed. write for info. (*0-318-69331-3*) Macmillan.

Managing Police Corruption: International Perspectives. Richard H. Ward & Robert McCormack. 363p. (C). 1987. 9.95 (*0-942511-04-2*) OICJ.

***Managing Police Operations: Nypd Crime Control Model Compstat.** MacDonald. 2000. pap. 32.00 (*0-534-53991-2*) Thomson Learn.

Managing Police Organizations. Gary W. Cordner & Dennis J. Kenney. LC 95-75512. 188p. (C). 1995. pap. 19.95 (*0-87084-142-4*) Anderson Pub Co.

Managing Police Personnel. Ed. by Dennis J. Kenny & Gary W. Cordner. LC 95-80144. 217p. (C). 1996. pap. text 18.95 (*0-87084-119-X*) Anderson Pub Co.

Managing Police Stress. Wayne D. Ford. 105p. 1998. ring bd. 39.95 (*1-879876-02-7*, 30205) Mgmt Advantage.

Managing Police Work: Issues & Analysis. Ed. by Jack R. Greene. LC 81-21263. (Perspectives in Criminal Justice Ser.: No. 4). (Illus.). 160p. reprint ed. pap. 49.60 (*0-8357-4800-6*, 203773700009) Bks Demand.

Managing Policy Change in Britain: The Politics of Water. W. A. Maloney & J. J. Richardson. LC 96-162489. 176p. 1996. 69.50 (*0-7486-0669-6*, Pub. by Edinburgh U Pr) Col U Pr.

Managing Political Change in Singapore: The Elected Presidency. Kevin Tan & Peng E. Lam. LC 96-23824. 240p. (C). 1997. 75.00 (*0-415-15632-7*) Routledge.

***Managing Post-Acute Care & Other Extented Care Services.** Margaret D. Bischel. 405p. 1998. ring bd. 225.00 (*1-893826-09-0*) Apollo Managed.

Managing Post-Polio: A Guide to Living Well with Post-Polio Syndrome. Linda S. Halstead. (Illus.). 256p. 1998. 25.00 (*1-886236-17-8*) ABI Prof Pubns.

Managing Potential Conflicts in the South China Sea. Yann H. Song. (EAI Occasional Paper Ser.). 60p. 1999. 8.00 (*981-02-3902-5*) World Scientific Pub.

Managing Poverty: The Limits of Social Assistance. Carol Walker. LC 92-28820. (State of Welfare Ser.). 1993. pap. write for info. (*0-415-08455-5*) Routledge.

Managing Power Relationships in the New Lateral Organization. Margaret A. Brindle & Lisa A. Mainiero. LC 99-27822. 192p. 2000. 59.95 (*1-56720-334-5*, Quorum Bks) Greenwood.

Managing Pressure at Work: A Practical Guide to Managing Time & Coping with Stress. Helen Froggart. (Illus.). 1996. pap. 9.95 (*0-563-36159-X*, BBC-Parkwest) Parkwest Pubns.

Managing Pressure for Peak Performance. 2nd ed. Stephen Williams. 1997. pap. text 15.95 (*0-7494-2202-5*) Kogan Page Ltd.

Managing Pressure for Real People. Stephen Williams. 1997. pap. text 19.95 (*0-7494-1239-9*, Pub. by Kogan Pg) Nichols Pub.

Managing Price Risk in Ag Commodity Markets: The Definitive Guide to Risk Management in Today's Volatile Ag Markets. (Farm Business Management Ser.). (Illus.). 176p. 1997. pap. text 28.95 (*0-86691-248-7*, FBM1510INC) Deere & Co.

Managing Price Risk in the Pakistan Wheat Market, Vol. 334. Rashid Faruqee & Jonathan R. Coleman. LC 96-22253. (World Bank Discussion Papers: No. 334). 78p. 1996. pap. 22.00 (*0-8213-3685-1*, 13685) World Bank.

***Managing Price Risks in India's Liberalized Agriculture: Can Future's Markets Help?** World Bank Staff. LC 98-51009. 1998. pap. write for info. (*0-8213-4276-2*) World Bank.

Managing Pricing Decisions: Study of Managerial Practices. A. Diamantopoulos. 168p. 1994. mass mkt. 47.00 (*0-412-49240-7*, Chap & Hall NY) Chapman & Hall.

Managing Primary Classrooms. Ed. by Ian Craig. 1997. pap. 54.50 (*0-273-62712-0*, Pub. by F T P-H) Trans-Atl Phila.

Managing Primary Health Care: Implications of the Health Transition. Richard A. Heaver. LC 95-3247. (World Bank Discussion Papers: No. 276). 58p. 1995. pap. 22.00 (*0-8213-3175-2*, 13175) World Bank.

Managing Primary Schools: A Professional Development Approach. Christopher Day et al. 224p. (C). 1986. pap. 36.00 (*0-06-318306-4*, Pub. by P Chapman) St Mut.

Managing Privacy: Information Technology & Corporate America. H. Jeff Smith. LC 93-33334. (Illus.). xvi, 298p. (C). 1994. 59.95 (*0-8078-2147-0*) U of NC Pr.

Managing Problem Behavior: Basic Skills for Paraprofessionals & Beginning Teachers. Geoffrey Colvin. (C). 1993. ring bd. write for info. incl. VHS (*0-9631777-2-9*) Behav Assocs.

M

Managing Problem Behavior: Creating Harmony in the Workplace. rev. ed. James C. Campbell. (Skill Centered Leadership Ser.). 10p. 1997. wbk. ed. 12.95 incl. audio (1-891161-69-5) ClamShell Pub.

Managing Problem Behaviors. Robert Algozzine & Festus E. Obiakor. 356p. (C). 1995. per. 50.95 (0-7872-1250-4, 41125001) Kendall-Hunt.

Managing Problem Loans. Michael J. Groves. 189p. 1989. text 42.50 (1-55520-119-9, Irwn Prfssnl) McGraw-Hill Prof.

Managing Product Development. Ed. by Toshihiro Nishiguchi. (Illus.). 320p. 1996. text 60.00 (0-19-507438-6) OUP.

Managing Product Innovation. Trueman. 1997. pap. write for info. (0-415-12701-7) Thomson Learn.

*Managing Product Liability to Achieve Highway Innovations G. L. Gittings et al. LC 98-67632. (Synthesis of Highway Practice Ser.). 63 p. 1998. 25.00 (0-309-06818-5) Natl Acad Pr.

Managing Product Life Cycles: From Start to Finish. Harvard Business Review Staff. (Marketing & Advertising Essentials Ser.). 128p. 1991. pap. 19.95 (0-87584-277-1) Harvard Busn.

Managing Product Life Cycles: From Start to Finish. Harvard Business Review Staff. 150p. 1991. pap. 19.95 (0-07-103337-8) McGraw.

Managing Production: Engineering Change & Stability. Graham Winch. (Illus.). 254p. 1995. text 52.00 (0-19-828841-7) OUP.

Managing Productive Schools. Karolyn J. Snyder. LC 85-70463. 1986. 38.75 (0-12-654030-6) Acad Pr.

Managing Productivity in Construction: JIT Operations & Measurements. Low Sui Pheng & Yue Meng Chan. LC 97-70343. 256p. 1997. text 69.95 (1-85972-607-0, Pub. by Ashgate Pub) Ashgate Pub Co.

Managing Professional & Family Life: A Comparative Study of British & French Women. Linda Hantrais. 214p. 1990. text 72.95 (1-85521-167-X, Pub. by Dartmth Pub) Ashgate Pub Co.

*Managing Professional Development in Schools. Sonia Blandford. LC 99-41939. (Educational Management Ser.). 192p. 2000. pap. write for info. (0-415-19759-7) Routledge.

Managing Professional Teachers. Nigel Bennett. 208p. 1996. text 29.95 (1-85396-269-4, Pub. by P Chapman) Taylor & Francis.

*Managing Professionals: Budgets, Controls & Ethics. Jerome J. Suran. 244p. 2000. write for info. (1-58692-028-6) Copyright Mgmt.

Managing Profits under Inflation. Curtis W. Symonds. LC 74-23167. (AMA Management Briefing Ser.). 30p. reprint ed. pap. 30.00 (0-608-30679-7, 205152100085) Bks Demand.

Managing Programming People: A Personal View. Philip W. Metzger. (Illus.). 160p. write for info. (0-318-61856-7) P-H.

Managing Projects. Willson-Murray. write for info. (0-471-33644-0) Wiley.

*Managing Projects. 2nd ed. John Nicholas. 608p. 2000. 85.33 (0-13-018328-8) P-H.

Managing Projects & Programs. Augustine, Saint. 299p. 1989. 34.95 (0-07-103204-5) McGraw.

Managing Projects for Personal Success. Charles Watson. LC 96-39625. 332p. 1997. pap. 40.00 (0-412-71740-9) Thomson Learn.

Managing Projects in Hospitality Organisations. Ed. by Richard Teare et al. 256p. 1992. pap. text 45.00 (0-304-32505-8) Continuum.

Managing Projects in Organizations: How to Make the Best Use of Time, Techniques, & People. 2nd ed. J. Davidson Frame. (Management Ser.). 270p. 1995. 34.95 (0-7879-0160-1) Jossey-Bass.

Managing Projects Made Simple. Nickson & Siodons. 96p. Date not set. pap. text. write for info. (0-7506-3471-5) Buttrwrth-Heinemann.

*Managing Projects Well. Stephen A. Bender. 220p. 1998. pap. 32.95 (0-7506-4631-4) Butterworth-Heinemann Ltd.

Managing Projects with Make. 2nd ed. Steve Talbott & Andrew Oram. (Computer Science). 152p. 1991. pap. 19.95 (0-937175-90-0) Thomson Learn.

Managing Projects with Microsoft Project: Version 4.0 for Windows & the Macintosh. 3rd ed. Gwen Lowery. 416p. 1994. pap. 34.95 (0-442-01768-5, VNR) Wiley.

Managing Projects with Microsoft Project 4.0: For Windows & Macintosh. 2nd ed. Gwen Lowery. 432p. 1994. pap. 34.95 (0-471-28611-7, VNR) Wiley.

Managing Projects with Microsoft Project '97. Gwen Lowery. 1997. pap. 34.95 (0-614-28537-2, VNR) Wiley.

Managing Projects with Microsoft Project '97. 3rd ed. Gail Lowery. LC 97-217904. (Business Technology Ser.). 400p. (Orig.). 1997. pap. 34.95 (0-442-02552-1, VNR) Wiley.

Managing Projects with Microsoft Project 98 for Windows: For Windows & Macintosh. 2nd ed. Gwen Lowery & Rob Ferrara. 400p. 1997. pap. 34.95 (0-471-29253-2, VNR) Wiley.

Managing Protected Areas in the Tropics. Ed. by Kathy MacKinnon et al. (International Union for the Conservation of Nature & Natural Resources: A Belhaven Press Book Ser.). (Illus.). 320p. 1986. pap. 51.00 (2-88032-808-X, Pub. by IUCN) Island Pr.

*Managing Public Access Computers: A How-to-Do-It Manual for Librarians. Donald Barclay. 225p. 1999. pap. 59.95 (1-55570-361-5) Neal-Schuman.

Managing Public Access Microcomputers in Health Sciences Libraries. Gale G. Hannigan & Janis F. Brown. 172p. 1990. 38.00 (0-8108-2436-1) Scarecrow.

Managing Public & Nonprofit Organizations: A Results Oriented Approach. Patrick J. Montana. 340p. (C). 1994. pap. text 29.50 (0-07-042833-6) McGraw.

Managing Public Debt: Index-Linked Bonds in Theory & Practice. Ed. by Marcello De Cecco et al. LC 96-32705. (Illus.). 240p. (C). 1997. 95.00 (1-85898-491-2) E Elgar.

Managing Public Disputes: A Practical Guide to Handling Conflict & Reaching Agreements. Susan L. Carpenter & W. J. Kennedy. LC 87-46342. (Management Ser.). 311p. 1988. text 37.45 (1-55542-080-X) Jossey-Bass.

Managing Public Enterprises. W. Stanbury. LC 82-9038. 301p. 1982. 65.00 (0-275-90909-3, C0909, Praeger Pubs) Greenwood.

Managing Public Equipment. Hilary Green & Rita E. Knorr. (Special Reports: No. 55). 153p. (Orig.). 1989. pap. text 45.00 (0-917084-05-5) Am Public Works.

*Managing Public Finances in a Small Developing Economy: The Case of Barbados. Marion V. Williams. 2001. write for info. (0-275-97031-0) Greenwood.

Managing Public Involvement. Lupton et al. LC 97-44933. (Health Services Management Ser.). 192p. 1997. 95.00 (0-335-19633-0) OpUniv Pr.

Managing Public Involvement. Lupton et al. LC 97-44933. (Health Services Management Ser.). 192p. 1998. pap. 29.95 (0-335-19632-2) OpUniv Pr.

Managing Public Lands in the Public Interest. Ed. by Benjamin C. Dysart, III & Marion Clawson. LC 87-38117. 157p. 1988. 55.00 (0-275-92990-6, C2990, Praeger Pubs) Greenwood.

Managing Public Libraries in the 21st Century. Ed. by Pat Woodrum & Sul H. Lee. LC 89-20016. (Journal of Library Administration: Vol. 11, Nos. 1-2). (Illus.). 232p. 1989. text 39.95 (0-86656-945-6) Haworth Pr.

Managing Public Organizations. Jamil E. Jreisat. (Illus.). 212p. 1994. 49.95 (1-56924-950-4) Marlowe & Co.

Managing Public Organizations. 2nd ed. Ed. by Kjell A. Eliassen & Jan Kooiman. (C). 1993. pap. text 21.95 (0-8039-7715-8) Sage.

Managing Public Organizations. 2nd ed. Ed. by Kjell A. Eliassen & Jan Kooiman. (C). 1993. text 65.00 (0-8039-7714-X) Sage.

Managing Public Organizations: Lessons from Contemporary European Experience. Ed. by Jan Kooiman & Kjell A. Eliassen. 384p. (C). 1987. text 60.00 (0-8039-8061-2) Sage.

Managing Public Programs: Balancing Politics, Administration, & Public Needs. Robert E. Cleary et al. LC 88-46089. (Public Administration Ser.). 312p. 1989. 39.95 (1-55542-143-1) Jossey-Bass.

Managing Public Relations. James E. Grunig & Todd T. Hunt. 576p. (C). 1984. text 71.00 (0-03-058337-3, Pub. by Harcourt Coll Pubs) Harcourt.

Managing Public Relations. 2nd ed. James E. Grunig. (C). pap. text, teacher ed. 4.00 (0-03-046432-3) Harcourt Coll Pubs.

Managing Public Services: Competition & Decentralization. Richard Common et al. 280p. 1993. pap. 47.95 (0-7506-0977-X) Buttrwrth-Heinemann.

Managing Public Use of Parks, Open Spaces, & Countryside. David Welch. (Leisure Management Ser.). 146p. (Orig.). 1995. pap. 64.50 (0-273-61610-2, Pub. by Pitman Pbg) Trans-Atl Phila.

Managing Publications. Robert Button. 52p. 1982. 5.00 (0-318-16332-2) Quill & Scroll.

Managing Purchasing: Making the Supply Team Work. John W. Kamauff & Kenneth Killen. (NAPM Professional Development Ser.: Vol. 2). 280p. 1995. 45.00 (0-7863-0127-9, Irwn Prfssnl) McGraw-Hill Prof.

Managing Purchasing: Organizing, Planning, & Control. Brian Farrington & Derek W. Waters. LC 93-35415. (Bus Press-Previous C&H). 264p. 1994. mass mkt. 59.95 (0-412-56760-1, Chap & Hall NY) Chapman & Hall.

Managing Purchasing: Sourcing & Contracting. Andrew Erridge. LC 96-113270. (Illus.). 224p. 1995. reprint ed. pap. 69.50 (0-608-08869-2, 206950800004) Bks Demand.

Managing Quality. Desmond Bell et al. 236p. 1994. pap. 44.95 (0-7506-1823-X) Buttrwrth-Heinemann.

*Managing Quality. Desmond Bell et al. 288p. 2001. pap. 35.95 (0-7506-4837-6) Buttrwrth-Heinemann.

Managing Quality. D. Dale & P. Plunkett. 357p. (C). 1990. 215.00 (0-7855-5716-4, Pub. by Inst Pur & Supply) St Mut.

Managing Quality. 3rd ed. Ed. by Barrie G. Dale. LC 99-16395. 480p. 1999. text 69.95 (0-631-21409-7); pap. text 39.95 (0-631-21410-0) Blackwell Pubs.

Managing Quality: A Guide to System-Wide Performance Management in Health Care. 2nd ed. Jacqueline M. Katz & Eleanor Green. LC 96-15639. (Illus.). 326p. (C). (gr. 13). 1996. text 44.95 (0-8151-4973-5, 26254) Mosby Inc.

Managing Quality: A National Perspective. LC 92-22591. 60p. 1992. 18.00 (0-309-05204-1, R1340) Transport Res Bd.

Managing Quality: A Practical Guide to Customer Satisfaction. D. B. Murthy. LC 99-11084. 1999. write for info. (0-7619-9306-1) Sage.

Managing Quality: Strategic Issues in Health Care Management. Ed. by Huw T. \Davies et al. LC 99-72982. 248p. 1999. text 69.95 (0-7546-1004-7, Pub. by Ashgate Pub) Ashgate Pub Co.

Managing Quality: Techniques for Measuring, Controlling & Monitoring Paper Quality Seminar, Elizabeth, NJ, October 11-14, 1987. Technical Association of the Pulp & Paper Industry. LC TS1080.. (TAPPI Notes Ser.). 99p. reprint ed. pap. 30.70 (0-608-17794-6, 203225900079) Bks Demand.

Managing Quality: The Strategic & Competitive Edge. David A. Garvin. 320p. 1988. 35.00 (0-02-911380-6) Free Pr.

Managing Quality & Human Resources: A Guide to Continuous Improvement. 2nd ed. Barrie Dale et al. LC 97-39508. 256p. 1997. pap. text 43.95 (0-631-20024-X) Blackwell Pubs.

Managing Quality & Productivity in Aerospace & Defense. 1991. lib. bdg. 79.95 (0-8490-4361-1) Gordon Pr.

Managing Quality & Standards. Colleen Liston. LC 98-29065. (Managing Colleges & Universities Ser.). 1998. 95.00 (0-335-20209-8); pap. 29.95 (0-335-20208-X) OpUniv Pr.

Managing Quality Child Care Centers: A Comprehensive Manual for Administrators. Pamela Schiller & Patricia M. Dyke. (Early Childhood Education Ser.). 144p. (C). 1989. text 29.00 (0-8077-2976-0); pap. text 16.95 (0-8077-2975-2) Tchrs Coll.

Managing Quality Cultural Tourism. Priscilla Boniface. LC 95-7782. 144p. (C). (gr. 13). 1995. 60.00 (0-415-09985-4) Routledge.

Managing Quality Customer Service. William B. Martin. (Better Management Skills Ser.). 1991. pap. 12.95 (0-7494-0352-7) Kogan Page Ltd.

Managing Quality Customer Service: A Practical Guide for Establishing a Service Operation. William Martin. Ed. by Elaine Fritz. LC 88-92732. (Fifty-Minute Ser.). (Illus.). 96p. (Orig.). 1989. pap. 10.95 (0-931961-83-1) Crisp Pubns.

Managing Quality Fads: How American Business Learned to Play the Quality Game. Robert E. Cole. (Illus.). 304p. 1999. 30.00 (0-19-512260-7) OUP.

Managing Quality in America's Most Admired Companies. Ed. by Jay W. Spechler. LC 92-44147. (Illus.). 434p. 1993. 49.95 (0-89806-118-0, MQAMC) Eng Mgmt Pr.

Managing Quality in Customer Care: Caterer & Hotelkeeper Hospitality Pocket Books. Julia Watson. 192p. 1998. text 24.95 (0-7506-3134-1) Buttrwrth-Heinemann.

*Managing Quality of Care in a Cost-Focused Environment. Ed. by Norbert Goldfield & David B. Nash. 227p. 2000. pap. 55.00 (0-924674-73-3) Am Coll Phys Execs.

Managing Radical Organizational Change. Karen L. Newman & Stanley D. Nollen. LC 98-9004. 1998. 47.50 (0-7619-0933-8); pap. 23.50 (0-7619-0934-6) Sage.

Managing Rape: The Feminist Anti-Rape Movement & the State. Nancy A. Matthews. LC 93-49037. (International Library of Sociology Ser.). 224p. (C). (gr. 13). 1994. 75.00 (0-415-06491-0, B3816) Routledge.

Managing Real Estate Taxes. Jerry T. Ferguson & Edward C. Spede. LC 85-6360. (Illus.). 196p. 1986. 49.95 (0-89930-106-1, FMR/, Quorum Bks) Greenwood.

*Managing Records as Evidence & Information. Richard J. Cox. 2000. write for info. (1-56720-231-4, Quorum Bks) Greenwood.

Managing Records for ISO 9000 Compliance. Eugenia K. Brumm. LC 94-46885. 437p. 1995. 50.00 (0-87389-312-3, H0870) ASQ Qual Pr.

Managing Recruitment. 4th ed. Sidney. 1988. 86.95 (0-566-02661-9) Ashgate Pub Co.

*Managing Redundancy. Alan Fowler. 160p. 2000. pap. 56.95 (0-8464-5118-2) Beekman Pubs.

Managing Redundancy in Overexploited Fisheries. Joshua John. LC 94-15942. (Discussion Paper Ser.: Vol. 240). 40p. 1994. pap. 22.00 (0-8213-2839-5, 12839) World Bank.

Managing Reforms in the East European Countries: Lessons from the Post-War Experience of Western Europe, Vol. I. (UN/ECE Discussion Papers: No. 3). 41p. 25.00 (92-1-100369-5, E.GV.92.01.) UN.

Managing Regulatory Reform: The Reagan Strategy & Its Impact. Marshall B. Goodman & Margaret T. Wrightson. LC 87-2436. 252p. 1987. 55.00 (0-275-92472-6, C2472, Praeger Pubs) Greenwood.

Managing Relations Between Government & Public Enterprises: A Handbook for Administrators & Managers. Praxy Fernandes. (Management Development Ser.: No. 25). x, 250p. (Orig.). 1986. pap. 27.00 (92-2-105594-9) Intl Labour Office.

Managing Relationship Selling. Smith. 144p. 1996. ring bd. 113.95 (0-566-07730-2) Ashgate Pub Co.

Managing Relationship Selling. David W. Smith. 144p. 1996. text 78.95 (0-566-07842-2, Pub. by Gower) Ashgate Pub Co.

Managing Relationships: How to Make a Life While Making a Living. Jagdish Parikh. 106p. 1999. 14.95 (1-900961-18-0) Capstone Pub NH.

Managing Rental Properties for Maximum Profit. Greg M. Perry. 288p. 1995. pap. 15.95 (1-55958-572-2) Prima Pub.

Managing Rental Properties for Maximum Profit. 2nd rev. ed. Greg M. Perry. LC 96-52171. 336p. 1997. pap., per. 18.00 (0-7615-0841-4) Prima Pub.

*Managing Rental Properties for Maximum Profit: Prima's Official Strategy Guide. 3rd rev. ed. Greg M. Perry. LC 99-59675. 2000. pap. 24.95 (0-7615-2531-9) Prima Pub.

Managing Rental Properties Like a Pro: How to Keep Your Buildings & Your Pockets Full. Susan J. Underhill & Ken Upshaw. 200p. 1992. pap. 16.95 (1-55738-250-6, Irwn Prfssnl) McGraw-Hill Prof.

Managing Residential Care. John Burton. LC 97-18305. (Illus.). 280p. (C). 1998. 75.00 (0-415-16487-7); pap. 24.99 (0-415-16488-5) Routledge.

Managing Resistance to Agrochemicals: From Fundamental Research to Practical Strategies. Ed. by Maurice B. Green et al. LC 89-77580. (ACS Symposium Ser.: No. 421). (Illus.). 497p. 1990. text 105.00 (0-8412-1741-6, Pub. by Am Chemical) OUP.

Managing Resource Sharing in the Electronic Age. Ed. by Amy Chang & Mary E. Jackson. LC 96-135. (Studies in Library & Information Science: Vol. 4). 125p. 1996. 39.50 (0-404-64004-4) AMS Pr.

Managing Resourceful People: Human Resource Policy & Practice. Frank Horwitz. 277p. text 45.20 (0-7021-2705-1, Pub. by Juta & Co) Intl Spec Bk.

*Managing Resources: Part of Team Leader Development. Weaver. 1998. pap. text 29.95 (0-7506-3863-X) Buttrwrth-Heinemann.

Managing Resources & Information. Roger Cartwright et al. LC 97-45214. (Illus.). 256p. 1998. pap. 41.95 (0-631-20924-7) Blackwell Pubs.

Managing Resources in a Nepalese Village Changing Dynamics of Gender Caste & Ethnicity. I. I. D. S. Staff. 1997. pap. 22.00 (0-7855-7433-6, Pub. by Ratna Pustak Bhandar) St Mut.

Managing Resources Project Planning & Financial Control: Activity Pack. John Cullen & Mick Broadbent. 300p. 1999. pap. text 175.00 (0-7506-3504-5) Buttrwrth-Heinemann.

Managing Restructuring in the Textile & Garment Subsector: Examples from Asia. Ed. by Saha D. Meyanathan. LC 93-50881. (EDI Seminar Ser.). 210p. 1994. pap. 22.00 (0-8213-2768-2, 12768) World Bank.

Managing Retail Shops in Hospitals & Other Nonprofit Institutions. Binnie Bailey. LC 93-36041. (Illus.). 224p. (Orig.). 1993. pap. 32.00 (0-87258-649-9, 019200) Am Hospital.

Managing Retirement Assets: An Approach to Administering Investments for Qualified Plans. Angela Parrish & R. Riggs Griffith. (Building Blocks Ser.: Vol. 23). (Illus.). 24p. (Orig.). 1995. pap. 24.95 (1-57963-026-X, A043) Am Compensation.

Managing Reuse. HMSO Staff. 116p. 1994. pap. 80.00 (0-11-330616-4, HM06164, Pub. by Statnry Office) Bernan Associates.

Managing Reward Systems. Michael Armstrong. LC 92-29885. (Managing Work & Organizations Ser.). 176p. 1993. 122.00 (0-335-15767-X) OpUniv Pr.

Managing Risk. Crouhy. LC 99-48928. 500p. 2000. 70.00 (0-07-135731-9) McGraw.

Managing Risk. Alan Waring & A. Glendon. 304p. 1998. pap. 49.95 (1-86152-167-7) Thomson Learn.

Managing Risk: A Leader's Guide to Creating a Successful Managed Care Provider Organization. Bruce Pyenson. LC 98-5830. 1998. 35.95 (1-55648-213-2) AHPI.

Managing Risk: How to Work Successfully with Risk. Ian Johnstone-Bryden. 240p. 1995. 74.95 (1-85972-255-5, Pub. by Avebry) Ashgate Pub Co.

*Managing Risk: Preventing Liability in Clinical Practice. Dan J. Tennenhouse. viii, 174p. 1999. pap. 64.00 (1-930548-16-8) Tennenhouse Prof Pubns.

Managing Risk Exposure in Derivatives. (Corporate Law & Practice Course Handbook, 1985-86 Ser.). 320p. 1994. pap. 99.00 (0-614-17180-6, B4-7089) PLI.

Managing Risk Exposure in Derivatives, 1995: Recent Developments. (Corporate Law & Practice Course Handbook, 1985-86 Ser.). Date not set. pap. 99.00 (0-614-17199-7, B4-7116) PLI.

*Managing Risk in Construction Projects. Nigel J. Smith. LC 98-25053. 232p. 1999. 59.95 (0-632-04243-5) Blackwell Sci.

Managing Risk in Developing Countries: National Demands & Multinational Response. Barbara C. Samuels, II. (Illus.). 280p. 1990. text 47.50 (0-691-07826-2, Pub. by Princeton U Pr) Cal Prin Full Svc.

Managing Risk in International Business: Techniques & Applications. Ephraim Clark. LC 96-38876. 304p. (gr. 13). 1996. mass mkt. 50.00 (0-412-59720-9) Chapman & Hall.

Managing Risk in Mortgage Portfolios. Alex O. Williams. LC 87-2497. 176p. 1987. 59.95 (0-89930-058-8, WMD/, Quorum Bks) Greenwood.

Managing Risk in the Foreign Exchange, Money, & Derivative Markets. Heinz Riehl. LC 98-6532. 300p. 1998. 60.00 (0-07-052673-7) McGraw.

Managing Risk in Transactional Products. Roland K. Bullard, III & Cynthia P. Yasinski. LC 85-14753. 32p. 1984. pap. text 13.00 (0-936742-18-6) Robt Morris Assocs.

Managing Risk of Construction. Shaughnessy. pap. text. write for info. (0-471-49163-2) Wiley.

Managing Risk with Financial Futures: Pricing, Hedging & Arbitrage. Robert T. Daigler. 375p. 1993. text 65.00 (1-55738-455-X, 455, Irwn Prfssnl) McGraw-Hill Prof.

Managing Risks & Decisions in Major Projects. John C. Chicken. 224p. 1994. mass mkt. 68.95 (0-412-58730-0) Chapman & Hall.

Managing Risks in Projects. Ed. by Kalle Kahkonen & Karlos A. Artto. LC 98-117583. (Illus.). 376p. (C). 1997. pap. 125.00 (0-419-22990-6, D5609) Thomson Learn.

*Managing Risks of Nitrates to Humans & the Environment. Ed. by W. S. Wilson et al. 400p. 1999. 139.00 (0-85404-768-9, Pub. by Royal Soc Chem) Spr-Verlag.

Managing Risks of Organizational Accidents. James Reason. LC 97-24648. 200p. 1997. pap. 37.95 (1-84014-105-0, Pub. by Ashgate Pub) Ashgate Pub Co.

Managing Risks of Organizational Accidents. James T. Reason. LC 97-24648. (Illus.). 252p. 1997. text 78.95 (1-84014-104-2, Pub. by Ashgate Pub) Ashgate Pub Co.

Managing Rural Development. Robert E. Meyer. (Bibliographies in Technology & Social Change Ser.: No. 2). (Illus.). 40p. (C). 1988. pap. 6.00 (0-945271-05-0) ISU-CIKARD.

Managing Rural Development: Health & Energy Programmes in India. Ed. by Hein Streefkerek & T. K. Moulik. (Indo-Dutch Studies on Development Alternatives: No. 7). 192p. (C). 1991. 32.50 (0-8039-9678-0) Sage.

Managing Rural Development: Ideas & Experience from East Africa. Robert Chambers. LC 85-23717. 216p. 1985. pap. 67.00 (0-7837-2365-2, 204004800006) Bks Demand.

Managing Rural Development: Ideas & Experience from East Africa. Robert Chambers. 216p. 1974. write for info. (*91-7106-075-8*, Pub. by Nordic Africa) Transaction Pubs.

Managing Safety & Health Programs. Raymond P. Boylston. 272p. 1990. 89.95 (*0-471-28977-9*, VNR); text 60.95 (*0-442-31900-2*, VNR) Wiley.

Managing Safety in & Around Airports. Ed. by John Van Oudenaren & Erik Frinking. LC 96-131218. (Illus.). 189p. 1995. pap. text 9.00 (*0-8330-1669-5*, CF-120-EAC) Rand Corp.

Managing Salary & Wage Systems. 2nd ed. Angela M. Bowey. (Illus.). 448p. 1989. text 96.95 (*0-566-02732-1*, Pub. by Gower) Ashgate Pub Co.

Managing Sales & Marketing Training. Ed. by Patrick Forsyth. LC 83-25381. 352p. 1984. text 78.95 (*0-566-02410-1*) Ashgate Pub Co.

Managing Sales Efforts Module, PACE Level 1: A Program for Acquiring Competence in Entrepreneurship, 3 levels. rev. ed. National Center for Research in Vocational Educati. 1983. 2.50 (*0-318-67178-6*, RD240AB14) Ctr Educ Trng Employ.

Managing Sales Efforts Module, PACE Level 2: A Program for Acquiring Competence in Entrepreneurship, 3 levels. rev. ed. National Center for Research in Vocational Educati. 1983. 2.50 (*0-317-06071-6*, RD240BB14) Ctr Educ Trng Employ.

Managing Sales Efforts Module, PACE Level 3: A Program for Acquiring Competence in Entrepreneurship, 3 levels. rev. ed. National Center for Research in Vocational Educati. 1983. 2.50 (*0-317-06072-4*, RD240CB14) Ctr Educ Trng Employ.

Managing Sales Leads. Bob Donath et al. Ed. by Anne Knudsen. LC 94-16180. (Illus.). 240p. 1995. 37.95 (*0-8442-3599-7*, NTC Business Bks) NTC Contemp Pub Co.

Managing Sales Professionals. 2nd ed. Ed. by Glenn Boseman & Kay Powell. LC 92-71834. 400p. 1993. text 40.00 (*0-943590-38-8*) Amer College.

Managing Sales Professionals: The Reality of Profitability. Joseph P. Vaccaro. LC 94-48364. 1995. 49.95 (*1-56024-946-3*) Haworth Pr.

Managing Sales Teams Effectively: A Performance Comparison of Salesmen & Saleswomen. Vincent W. Kafka. 27p. 1996. pap. 14.95 (*0-913261-34-3*) Effect Learn Sys.

Managing Salespeople. (C). 1993. 56.67 (*0-205-13715-6*, Macmillan Coll) P-H.

Managing Salespeople. Hite. Date not set. teacher ed. write for info. (*0-314-07536-4*) West Pub.

Managing Salespeople: A Relationship Approach. Robert E. Hite & Wesley J. Johnston. LC 95-31328. 600p. 1997. mass mkt. 92.95 (*0-314-06432-X*) West Pub.

Managing Salinization: Institutional Analysis of Public Irrigation Systems. Waltina Scheumann. LC 97-31664. (Illus.). 264p. 1997. 109.00 (*3-540-63328-6*) Spr-Verlag.

Managing SAP R/3 with Tivoli. Stefan Uelpenich et al. LC 00-551422. (Illus.). 320p. (C). 1999. pap. 63.00 (*0-13-015037-1*) P-H.

Managing Scarcity: Priority Setting & Rationing in the National Health Service. P. Klein et al. (State of Health Ser.). 192p. 1996. pap. 31.95 (*0-335-19446-X*) OpUniv Pr.

Managing Scarcity: Priority Setting & Rationing in the National Health Service. Rudolf Klein et al. LC 96-18743. (State of Health Ser.). 161p. 1996. 102.95 (*0-335-19447-8*) OpUniv Pr.

Managing Schizophrenia. 84p. pap. text 29.95 (*0-86471-059-3*, Pub. by Adis Intl) Lppncott W & W.

Managing School Conflict: Procedures, Conflict Lessons, Skills Lessons, Problem-Solving Lessons, Signed Agreements, & Mediating Conflicts. Richard L. Biren. LC 95-78485. 64p. 1995. 11.95 (*1-884063-69-1*) Mar Co Prods.

Managing School Development: A Practical Guide. Mel West & Mel Ainscow. 144p. (Orig.). 1991. pap. 32.95 (*0-8464-4333-3*) Beekman Pubs.

Managing School Indebtedness: The Complete Guide to School Bonding. Michael Richardson et al. LC 94-60934. 245p. 1994. text 39.95 (*1-56676-180-8*) Scarecrow.

Managing School Libraries in Elementary & Secondary Schools. Jerry L. Evans et al. 129p. 1998. pap. text 25.00 (*0-7881-4901-6*) DIANE Pub.

Managing School Library Programs. Blanche M. Woolls. xii, 182p. 1988. lib. bdg. 24.50 (*0-87287-590-3*) Libs Unl.

Managing Schools: The European Experience. Bryan T. Peck. LC 98-23871. 1998. 65.00 (*1-56072-572-9*) Nova Sci Pubs.

Managing Schools in the Community. Phil Street. 200p. 1997. text 64.95 (*1-85742-352-6*, Pub. by Gower) Ashgate Pub Co.

Managing Schools Towards High Performance & Linking School Management Theory to the School Effectiveness Knowledge Base: Linking School Management Theory to the School Effectiveness Knowledge Base. Adrie J. Visscher. LC 99-13939. (Contexts of Learning Ser.: Vol. 5). 372p. 1999. 69.00 (*90-265-1546-4*) Swets.

Managing Science. Claude Geles. LC 99-21919. 359p. 1999. 79.95 (*0-471-18508-6*) Wiley.

Managing Science Policy & Technology Acquisitions: Strategies for China. R. Lalkaka & Wu Mingyu. 544p. 1984. 40.00 (*0-86346-050-X*, Tycooly Pub) Weidner & Sons.

Managing Scientists: Leadership Strategies in Research & Development. Alice M. Sapienza. LC 94-46618. 208p. 1995. pap. 39.50 (*0-471-04367-2*) Wiley.

Managing Seagrass Systems in Western North America: Research Gaps & Needs. S. Wyllie-Echeverria & R. Thom. (Report Ser.: No. 94-01). 24p. (Orig.). 1994. pap. 3.00 (*1-56612-022-5*) AK Sea Grant CP.

Managing Secondary Classrooms: Principles & Strategies for Effective Management & Instruction. abr. ed. Williams et al. LC 98-33966. 246p. 1999. pap. text 35.00 (*0-205-26725-4*) Allyn.

Managing Section 89: The Complete Compliance Guide. Ari Cowan & Lee T. Paterson. 1989. ring bd. 195.00 (*0-932823-00-9*) Am Somerset.

Managing Selection in Changing Organizations: Human Resource Strategies. Jerard F. Kehoe. LC 99-52731. (Jossey-Bass Business & Management Ser.). 512p. 1999. 46.95 (*0-7879-4474-2*) Jossey-Bass.

Managing Self-Renewal in Secondary Education. William J. Bailey. LC 74-13352. 208p. 1975. 37.95 (*0-87778-074-9*) Educ Tech Pubns.

Managing Seniors Housing. S. Kelley Moseley. LC 88-61093. (Illus.). 214p. 1988. pap. 7.50 (*0-86718-323-3*) Home Builder.

Managing Sensitive Projects: Lateral Approach. Olivier D'Herbemont & Bruno Cesar. LC 98-20625. 232p. (C). (gr. 13). 1998. 29.95 (*0-415-92166-X*) Routledge.

Managing Serials. Ed. by Marcia Tuttle. LC 96-24349. (Foundations in Library & Information Science: Vol. 35). 1996. 78.50 (*0-7623-0100-7*) Jai Pr.

Managing Service: Student Manual. Educational Foundation of the National Restaurant. 95p. (Orig.). 1992. pap. write for info. (*0-915452-04-9*) Educ Found.

Managing Service As a Strategic Profit Center. Donald F. Blumberg. 232p. 1991. 22.95 (*0-07-006189-0*) McGraw.

Managing Service for Results. Dick Berry. LC 83-12821. (Illus.). 287p. 1983. reprint ed. pap. 89.00 (*0-7837-9044-9*, 204979500003) Bks Demand.

Managing Service for Success. John R. Beck. Ed. by Elizabeth J. Beck. 128p. (Orig.). (C). 1987. pap. 25.00 (*0-9619359-0-1*) Intl Pest Mgmt.

Managing Service in Food & Beverage Operations. Anthony M. Rey & Ferdinand Wieland. LC 85-12962. (Illus.). 395p. 1985. text. write for info. (*0-86612-023-8*) Educ Inst Am Hotel.

Managing Service in Food & Beverage Operations. 2nd ed. Ronald F. Cichy & Paul E. Wise. LC 98-28430. (Illus.). 597p. (C). 1998. pap. write for info. (*0-86612-077-7*) Educ Inst Am Hotel.

Managing Service Operations: Book & CD-ROM Pack. Nevan Wright. LC 81-70117. 256p. 1998. pap. 31.50 incl. cd-rom (*0-304-70528-1*) Continuum.

Managing Service Quality. Ed. by Paul Kunst & Jos Lemmink. 128p. 1996. pap. 47.95 (*1-85396-330-5*, Pub. by P Chapman) Taylor & Francis.

Managing Service Quality. Ed. by Paul Kunst & Jos Lemmink. LC 96-127652. 190p. 1995. pap. 65.00 (*1-85396-293-7*) St Mut.

Managing Service Quality, Vol. III. Ed. by Paul Kunst & Jos Lemmink. 208p. 1997. 69.95 (*1-85396-362-3*, Pub. by P Chapman) Taylor & Francis.

*__Managing Services.__ CCTA Staff. (IS Management Guides Ser.). (Illus.). 82p. 2000. 50.00 (*1-903091-04-7*, Pub. by Format Pubg Ltd) Balogh.

Managing Services Marketing. 3rd ed. John E. Bateson. 704p. (C). 1995. text 81.00 (*0-03-098666-4*) Dryden Pr.

Managing Services Marketing: Text & Readings. 4th ed. John E.G. Bateson et al. LC 98-73895. (Dryden Press Marketing Ser.). 471p. (C). 1998. text 81.00 (*0-03-022519-1*, Pub. by Harcourt Coll Pubs) Harcourt.

Managing Set-Aside Land for Wildlife. 146p. 1994. pap. 19.00 (*0-11-701568-7*, HM15687, Pub. by Statnry Office) Bernan Associates.

Managing Sickle Cell Disease in Low-Income Families. Shirley A. Hill. LC 93-37361. (Health, Society, & Policy Ser.). 1994. text 69.95 (*1-56639-188-1*) Temple U Pr.

Managing Single-Family Homes. Barbara K. Holland. (Series on Specific Property Types). 176p. (Orig.). 1987. 44.95 (*0-912104-92-9*, 923) Inst Real Estate.

Managing Sinusitus. Edward A. Ullmann & Steve Miller. (Illus.). 1998. pap. 10.95 (*1-892039-02-8*) Bienestar.

*__Managing Six Sigma: A Practical Guide to Understanding, Assessing & Implementing the Strategy That Yields Bottom Line Success.__ Forrest W. Breyfogle et al. LC 00-43301. 2000. write for info. (*0-471-39673-7*) Wiley.

Managing Skin Diseases. Philip C. Anderson & Kristin S. Malaker. LC 98-25827. 368p. 1998. pap. 39.95 (*0-683-30598-0*) Lppncott W & W.

Managing Small Businesses with Biz Plan B. Jian & Rob Anderson. (GG - Small Business Management Ser.). 1993. pap. 92.95 (*0-314-01784-4*); pap. 92.95 (*0-314-01815-8*) S-W Pub.

Managing Small Cities & Counties: A Practical Guide. rev. ed. Ed. by James M. Banovetz. (Municipal Management Ser.). (Illus.). 350p. (C). 1994. pap. text 34.00 (*0-87326-093-7*) Intl City-Cnty Mgt.

Managing Small Library Collections in Businesses & Community Organizations: Advice for Non-Librarians. John A. Moorman. LC 88-36877. (Illus.). 36p. 1989. reprint ed. pap. 30.00 (*0-7837-9683-8*, 206041200005) Bks Demand.

Managing Small NetWare 4.11 Networks. Douglas W. Jones. LC 96-70746. 496p. 1996. pap. text 29.99 (*0-7821-1963-8*) Sybex.

Managing Small Netware Networks. 2nd ed. Kelley J. Lindberg. 1996. pap. text 29.99 (*0-7821-1906-9*) Sybex.

Managing Small Special Libraries, 1992. 106p. 1992. 27.00 (*0-87111-404-6*) SLA.

Managing Small Tourism & Leisure Firms. Ed. by Rhodri Thomas. LC 99-217582. 224p. 1998. 69.95 (*0-304-70196-3*); pap. 27.95 (*0-304-70197-1*) Continuum.

Managing Smart: 325 High-Performance Tips Every Manager Must Know. Lynne Milgram. LC 99-13625. 400p. 1998. 26.95 (*0-88415-752-0*, 5752) Gulf Pub.

Managing Snow Removal & Ice Control Programs. (Special Reports: No. 42). 168p. 1974. 15.00 (*0-917084-09-8*) Am Public Works.

Managing Snow Removal & Ice Control Programs: A Practical Guide to the How, When, Where & Why of Effective Public Works Practices. American Public Works Association Staff. (Special Reports: No. 42). (Illus.). 168p. (Orig.). 1974. pap. text 25.00 (*0-917084-25-X*) Am Public Works.

Managing Social & Economic Change with Information Technology: Proceedings of the 5th IRMA International Conference. Ed. by M. Khosrowpour. LC 94-236142. 550p. 1994. 69.95 (*1-878289-26-8*) Idea Group Pub.

*__Managing Social Anxiety: A Cognitive-Behavioral Therapy Approach.__ Debra A. Hope et al. (Illus.). 188p. 2000. pap. text, wbk. ed. 27.50 (*0-12-784465-1*) Acad Pr.

Managing Social Policy. Ed. by Clark John et al. 256p. 1994. 69.95 (*0-8039-7768-9*); pap. 22.95 (*0-8039-7769-7*) Sage.

Managing Social Work. Terry Bamford. 200p. 1983. 25.00 (*0-422-77960-1*, NO. 3802, Pub. by Tavistock) Routldge.

Managing Socialism: From Old Cadres to New Professionals in Revolutionary Cuba. Frank T. Fitzgerald. LC 89-77246. (Illus.). 176p. 1990. 52.95 (*0-275-93414-4*, C3414, Praeger Pubs) Greenwood.

Managing Software Assets: Software Configuration & the Year 2000. Mordechai Ben-Menachem. (Slaying the Software Dragon Ser.). 1997. pap. text 39.99 (*1-85032-924-9*) ITCP.

Managing Software Development. Whitten. 1989. 19.95 (*0-07-158647-4*) McGraw.

Managing Software Development Projects: Formula for Success. Neal Whitten. 276p. 1990. 48.95 (*0-471-51255-9*) Wiley.

Managing Software Development Projects: Formula for Success. 2nd ed. Neal Whitten. LC 94-45409. 400p. 1995. 54.99 (*0-471-07683-X*) Wiley.

Managing Software Engineering: CASE Studies & Solutions. Alan C. Gillies & P. Smith. 256p. 1994. mass mkt. 49.95 (*0-412-56550-1*, Chap & Hall NY) Chapman & Hall.

Managing Software Maniacs: Finding, Managing, & Rewarding a Winning Development Team. Ken Whitaker. 232p. 1994. pap. 39.99 (*0-471-00997-0*) Wiley.

Managing Software Quality. Brian Hambling. 1995. write for info. (*0-07-709039-X*) McGraw.

Managing Software Quality & Business Risk. Martyn A. Ould. LC 99-32078. 392p. 1999. pap. 64.99 (*0-471-99782-X*) Wiley.

*__Managing Software Requirements: A Unified Approach.__ Dean Leffingwell & Don Widrig. LC 99-46571. (Object Technology Ser.). 544p. 1999. 49.95 (*0-201-61593-2*) Addison-Wesley.

Managing Software Reuse. Wayne C. Lim. LC 97-36429. 480p. (C). 1998. 57.00 (*0-13-552373-7*) P-H.

Managing Software Reuse. Donald J. Reifer. LC 97-1743. 374p. 1997. 59.99 (*0-471-57853-3*) Wiley.

Managing Software Systems Risk. Elaine M. Hall. LC 97-24703. 384p. (C). 1998. 54.95 (*0-201-25592-8*) Addison-Wesley.

Managing Solid Wastes in Developing Countries. fac. ed. Ed. by John R. Holmes. LC 83-10570. (Illus.). 316p. 1984. pap. 98.00 (*0-7837-7376-5*, 204718600005) Bks Demand.

Managing Space in Colleges. rev. ed. Grace Kenny & Ken Foster. 1986. 50.00 (*0-907659-48-9*) St Mut.

Managing Spatial Conflict: The Planning System in Switzerland. P. Gresch. (Illus.). 94p. 1985. pap. 22.00 (*0-08-032731-1*, Pub. by PPL) Elsevier.

Managing Special Collections. A. M. Scham. LC 86-16431. 201p. 1987. pap. 45.00 (*0-918212-98-7*) Neal-Schuman.

Managing Special Education: Codes, Charters, & Competition. John Fish & Jennifer Evans. LC 95-8621. 144p. 1995. pap. 31.95 (*0-335-19438-9*) OpUniv Pr.

Managing Special Event Risks: 10 Steps to Safety. 54p. 1997. pap., wbk. ed. 12.00 (*0-9637120-4-7*) Nonprof Risk Mgmt Ctr.

Managing Special Needs. Tony Bowers. 192p. 1990. 113.00 (*0-335-09257-8*) OpUniv Pr.

Managing Special Needs in Mainstream Schools: The Role of the Senco. John Dwyfor Davies. 1998. 28.95 (*1-85346-526-7*) Taylor & Francis.

Managing Special Programs in Higher Education. Ronald Simmons. 260p. 1980. 18.95 (*0-87073-064-9*); pap. text 14.95 (*0-87073-142-4*) Schenkman Bks Inc.

Managing Speed: Methods for Setting & Enforcing Speed Limits, Vol. 254. National Research Council U. S. Staff. LC 98-40323. (Special Report National Research Council, Transportation Research Board). 1998. write for info. (*0-309-06502-X*) Natl Acad Pr.

Managing Sport & Leisure Facilities: A Guide to Competitive Tendering. P. Sayers. 280p. 1991. write for info. (*0-419-17350-1*, E & FN Spon) Routledge.

Managing Sport, Fitness, & Recreation Programs: Concepts & Practices. Stier. LC 98-27304. 384p. 1998. 48.00 (*0-205-15944-3*) Allyn.

Managing Sports & Risk Management Strategies. Herb Appenzeller. LC 92-72046. (Illus.). 220p. (C). 1993. 39.95 (*0-89089-504-X*) Carolina Acad Pr.

Managing Staff: A Guide for First Time Managers. Iain Maitland. 160p. 1998. pap. 24.95 (*0-304-33470-7*) Continuum.

Managing Staff Appraisal in Schools: The Training Manual. K. J. Pratt & R. Stenning. (Illus.). 160p. (Orig.). 1989. pap. 84.95 (*0-412-43710-4*, Chap & Hall NY) Chapman & Hall.

Managing Staff Development: A Handbook for Secondary Schools. Danuta Eisner & Valerie Hall. 144p. (C). 1991. pap. text 34.00 (*1-85396-112-4*, Pub. by P Chapman) Taylor & Francis.

Managing Staff Development in Schools: An Action Research Approach. Pamela Lomax. 110p. 1990. 59.00 (*1-85359-108-4*, Pub. by Multilingual Matters); pap. 19.95 (*1-85359-107-6*, Pub. by Multilingual Matters) Taylor & Francis.

Managing Staff in Early Years Settings. Adrian Smith & Ann Langston. LC 98-40346. 1999. pap. write for info. (*0-415-17153-9*) Routledge.

*__Managing Staff on International Assignments: A Strategic Guide.__ Nick Forster. (Management Briefings Ser.). (Illus.). 1999. pap. 87.50 (*0-273-64506-4*, Pub. by F T P-H) Trans-Atl Phila.

Managing Staff Reductions in Corporations. Clifford E. Harrison. LC 86-11223. (Research for Business Decisions Ser.: No. 91). 144p. reprint ed. pap. 44.70 (*0-8357-1758-5*, 207038800088) Bks Demand.

Managing State Social Work: Front-Line Management & the Labour Process Perspective. John Harris. LC 97-78317. (Illus.). 162p. 1998. text 55.95 (*1-85972-586-4*, Pub. by Ashgate Pub) Ashgate Pub Co.

Managing Steam: An Engineering Guide to Industrial, Commercial, & Utility Systems. Ed. by Jason Makansi. 224p. 1986. 60.95 (*0-89116-462-6*) Hemisp Pub.

Managing Strategic Action: Mobilizing Change Concepts, Readings & Cases. Ed. by Cynthia Hardy. 448p. 1994. 85.00 (*0-8039-8914-8*); pap. 32.00 (*0-8039-8915-6*) Sage.

Managing Strategic Alliances. Pierre Dussuage & Bernard Garrette. LC 98-53082. 254p. 1999. 43.95 (*0-471-97492-7*) Wiley.

Managing Strategic Change: Technical, Political & Cultural Dynamics. Noel M. Tichy. LC 82-15941. (Organizational Assessment & Change Ser.). 464p. 1983. 117.95 (*0-471-86559-1*) Wiley.

*__Managing Strategic Implementation: An Organizational Perspective.__ Ed. by Patrick C. Flood et al. LC 99-87796. 1999. 64.95 (*0-631-21766-5*) Blackwell Pubs.

*__Managing Strategic Implementation: An Organizational Perspective.__ Ed. by Patrick C. Flood et al. LC 99-87796. 2000. pap. text 34.95 (*0-631-21767-3*) Blackwell Pubs.

Managing Strategic Innovation & Change: A Collection of Readings. Michael L. Tushman & Philip C. Anderson. (Illus.). 672p. (C). 1996. text 74.95 (*0-19-510010-7*); pap. text 44.95 (*0-19-510011-5*) OUP.

Managing Strategically: 101 Creative Tips. Jerry Tobin. LC 93-94000. (Illus.). 128p. 1993. pap. 11.95 (*0-9636424-0-5*) J Tobin.

Managing Strategically: 101 Creative Tips. Jerry Tobin. (Illus.). 128p. 1994. pap. 12.95 (*0-9636424-1-3*) J Tobin.

Managing Strategically in an Interconnected World. Michael A. Hitt et al. LC 98-20619. (Strategic Management Ser.). 468p. 1998. 76.95 (*0-471-98497-3*) Wiley.

*__Managing Strategy.__ David Watson. LC 99-44707. (Managing Universities & Colleges Ser.). 2000. write for info. (*0-335-20346-9*) OpUniv Pr.

Managing Strategy in Academic Institutions: Learning from Brazil. Cynthia Hardy. (Studies in Organization: No. 25). viii, 293p. (C). 1990. lib. bdg. 113.85 (*3-11-012156-5*) De Gruyter.

Managing Stress. American Institute for Preventive Medicine Staff. LC 93-40575. (For Your Information Ser.). 1993. 8.95 (*1-56420-025-6*); audio 16.00 (*1-56420-026-4*) New Readers.

Managing Stress. Kristine C. Brewer. LC 95-75173. (AMI How-to Ser.). 80p. (Orig.). 1996. pap. text 12.95 (*1-884926-30-4*, STRESS) Amer Media.

*__Managing Stress.__ Ann Edworthy. LC 00-22496. (Managing Universities & Colleges Ser.). 2000. pap. write for info. (*0-335-20405-8*, Pub. by OpUniv Pr) Taylor & Francis.

Managing Stress. David Fontana. (Problems in Practice Ser.). 128p. 1989. 25.00 (*0-901715-98-0*, Pub. by Brit Psychol Soc); pap. 10.95 (*0-901715-97-2*, Pub. by Brit Psychol Soc) Routledge.

Managing Stress. Sanford G. Kulkin. 1992. ring bd. 295.00 incl. audio (*1-58034-006-7*) IML Pubns.

Managing Stress. Ursula Markham. LC 99-193526. 1995. pap. 11.95 (*1-85230-631-9*, Pub. by Element MA) Penguin Putnam.

Managing Stress. Brian L. Seaward. (Health Science Ser.). 152p. 1994. pap. 10.00 (*0-86720-987-9*) Jones & Bartlett.

Managing Stress. Steve Shores. 1999. pap. text 6.50 (*1-57683-083-7*) NavPress.

Managing Stress. Jenny Steinmetz et al. LC 80-66389. 220p. 1980. pap. 12.95 (*0-915950-44-8*) Bull Pub.

Managing Stress. Donald H. Weiss. LC 86-47825. (Successful Office Skills Ser.). 64p. 1987. pap. 4.00 (*0-8144-7673-2*) AMACOM.

Managing Stress. 2nd ed. Brian L. Seaward. (Health Science Ser.). 160p. 1997. pap., teacher ed. 10.00 (*0-7637-0474-1*) Jones & Bartlett.

Managing Stress: A Businessperson's Guide. Jere E. Yates. LC 79-15564. 175p. reprint ed. pap. 54.30 (*0-608-17994-9*, 202904400058) Bks Demand.

Managing Stress: A Creative Journal. 2nd ed. Brian L. Seaward. LC 96-39265. (Health Science Ser.). 192p. 1996. pap. 15.00 (*0-7637-0281-1*) Jones & Bartlett.

Managing Stress: A Mindset for Health. Melody Madlem et al. LC 96-8732. 1996. write for info. (*1-56796-151-7*) WRS Group.

M

An Asterisk (*) at the beginning of an entry indicates that the title is appearing for the first time.

Managing Stress: A Practical Survival Guide. S. Mathews & A. Knight. 1996. pap. 129.00 (1-85953-081-8, Pub. by Tech Comm) St Mut.

Managing Stress: International Division. Barbara Braham. LC 93-8155. (Briefcase Bks.). 204p. 1993. per. 13.95 (0-7863-0204-6, Irwn Prfssnl) McGraw-Hill Prof.

Managing Stress: Journal Workbook. Brian L. Seaward. LC 93-40223. 96p. 1994. pap. text 13.75 (0-86720-841-4) Jones & Bartlett.

Managing Stress: Keeping Calm under Fire. Barbara J. Braham. LC 93-8155. (Briefcase Bks.). 204p. 1993. 17.00 (1-55623-855-X, Irwn Prfssnl) McGraw-Hill Prof.

Managing Stress: Learning to Pace Your Chase Through Life. Dale R. Olen. 212p. (Orig.). 1992. pap. 5.95 (1-56583-003-2) JODA.

Managing Stress: Performing under Pressure Correspondence Course, 2 bks., Set. Jeanne Stinchcomb. 444p. (Orig.). 1995. pap. 70.00 (1-56991-013-8, 163) Am Correctional.

Managing Stress: Principles & Strategies. 2nd ed. Brian L. Seaward. LC 96-26129. (Health Science Ser.). 512p. 1996. pap. 48.75 (0-7637-0233-1) Jones & Bartlett.

Managing Stress: Subjectivity & Power in the Workplace. Tim Newton. 176p. 1995. text 69.95 (0-8039-8643-2); pap. text 21.95 (0-8039-8644-0) Sage.

Managing Stress & Controlling Self-Defeating Behavior. Charles P. Giles. 150p. (Orig.). 1988. pap. text 7.95 (0-935920-62-5, Ntl Pubs Blck) P-H.

Managing Stress & Promoting Wellness. Sandy Schuster. Ed. & Illus. by Dianne Schilling. Orig. Title: Classroom Connections. 157p. (J). (gr. k-12). 1992. pap. 19.95 (1-56499-006-0, IP9006) Innerchoice Pub.

Managing Stress at Work. Williams. 2000. pap. text 39.95 (0-471-97876-0) Wiley.

Managing Stress by the Power of God's Love. Walter C. Thompson. Ed. by Creation Enterprises International Staff & Nancy Pardeiro. (Illus.). 175p. 1991. student ed. 12.95 (0-9628512-0-5, Pub. by His Image Med Mission Soc) Creation Enter Intl.

Managing Stress for Mental Fitness. 2nd rev. ed. Merill F. Raber & George Dyck. Ed. by Michael Crisp. LC 92-74205. (Fifty-Minute Ser.). 85p. 1993. pap. 10.95 (1-56052-200-3) Crisp Pubns.

Managing Stress in a Changing World. Susan Balfour. (Illus.). 144p. (Orig.). 1997. pap. 19.95 incl. audio (1-85410-448-9, Pub. by Aurum Pr) London Brdge.

Managing Stress in Families: Cognitive & Behavioural Strategies for Enhancing Coping Skills. Ian R. Falloon et al. LC 92-12221. (Strategies for Mental Health Ser.). (Illus.). 304p. (C). 1993. text 69.95 (0-415-07192-5, A7016) Routledge.

Managing Stress in Turbulent Times. Drake Beam Morin, Inc. 120p. (Orig.). 1993. pap. 22.95 incl. audio (1-880030-14-4) DBM Pub.

Managing Stress Through Positive Christian Living. Paul A. Lee & Mark Ryan. 112p. 1998. pap. 9.95 (0-88243-225-7); pap., student ed. 4.95 (0-88243-125-0) Gospel Pub.

*****Managing Stress Through the Magic of Adaptogens.** 2nd ed. Pete Billac. Ed. by Ken Kroll et al. LC 99-65296. 93p. 1999. pap. 9.95 (0-943629-42-X) Swan Pub.

Managing Stroke. Stanley N. Cohen. (Illus.). 624p. 1999. 89.00 (0-07-012045-5) McGraw-Hill HPD.

*****Managing Stroke: A Guide to Living Well After Stroke.** Ed. by Paul R. Rao et al. 320p. 2000. 27.00 (1-886236-24-0) ABI Prof Pubns.

Managing Structural Deficit Reduction. OECD Staff. LC 97-121224. (PUMA Occasional Papers: No. 11). 204p. (Orig.). 1996. pap. 30.00 (92-64-15294-6, 42-96-61-1, Pub. by Org for Econ) OECD.

Managing Student Affairs Effectively, No. 41. M. Lee Upcraft & Margaret J. Barr. LC 85-644751. (New Directions for Student Services Ser.: No. SS 41). 1988. pap. 22.00 (1-55542-926-2) Jossey-Bass.

Managing Student Affairs Programs: Methods, Models, Muddles. William L. Deegan. (Illus.). 240p. 1981. 24.95 (0-88280-083-3) ETC Pubns.

Managing Student Behavior. William E. Amos & Reginald C. Orem. LC 67-26008. 167p. reprint ed. pap. 51.80 (0-608-13998-X, 205553800028) Bks Demand.

Managing Student Behavior Problems. Daniel L. Duke & Adrienne M. Meckel. LC 80-10443. 206p. reprint ed. pap. 63.90 (0-7837-1197-2, 204172700023) Bks Demand.

Managing Student Employees in College Libraries. Compiled by Michael D. Kathman & Jane M. Kathman. (CLIP Notes: Vol. 20). 140p. (Orig.). (C). 1994. pap. 30.00 (0-8389-7752-9) Assn Coll & Res Libs.

Managing Student Library Employees: A Workshop for Supervisors. Michael D. Kathman & Jane M. Kathman. (Library Skills Ser.: No. 1). (Illus.). 124p. 1995. pap. text 30.00 (1-882208-16-1) Library Solns.

Managing Student Library Employees PLUS: A Workshop for Supervisors. Michael D. Kathman & Jane M. Kathman. LC 95-135906. (Library Skills Ser.: No. 1). (Illus.). 124p. 1995. disk 45.00 (1-882208-17-X) Library Solns.

Managing Students. John M. Gledhill. LC 98-29066. (Managing Colleges & Universities Ser.). 1999. 95.00 (0-335-20257-8); pap. 29.95 (0-335-20256-X) OpUniv Pr.

*****Managing Successful Projects with PRINCE 2.** CCTA Staff. 336p. 1998. ring bd. 110.00 (0-11-330855-8, Pub. by Statnry Office) Balogh.

*****Managing Successful Projects with PRINCE 2: Manual.** CCTA Staff. 336p. 1998. pap. 110.00 (0-11-330018-2, Pub. by Statnry Office) Balogh.

Managing Successful Teams: How to Achieve Your Objective by Working Effectively with Others. John Humphries. 144p. 1998. pap. 19.95 (1-85703-282-9, Pub. by How To Bks) Trans-Atl Phila.

Managing Succession & Developing Leadership: Growing the Next Generation of Public Service Leadership. 148p. 1997. pap. 20.00 (1-57744-059-5) Nat Acad Public Admin.

Managing Sustainable Development. Michael Carley & Ian Christie. LC 92-35224. 1993. pap. 19.95 (0-8166-2339-2) U of Minn Pr.

Managing Switched Local Area Networks: A Practical Guide. Darryl Black. LC 97-36656. (Illus.). 384p. (C). 1997. pap. text 44.95 (0-201-18554-7) Addison-Wesley.

Managing Systematic & Ethical Public Relations. 2nd ed. Mark P. McElreath. LC 96-86355. 464p. (C). 1996. text. write for info. (0-697-28882-X) Brown & Benchmark.

Managing Systems Development. 2nd ed. Jeffrey S. Keen. LC 86-15948. (Wiley Series in Information Processing). (Illus.). 398p. 1987. reprint ed. pap. 123.40 (0-7837-9503-3, 206025300005) Bks Demand.

Managing Systems for Better Health: A Facilitator's Guide. A. Rotem. (Western Pacific Education in Action Ser.: No. 2). 204p. 1988. 15.00 (92-9061-132-4) World Health.

Managing Systems in Transition: A Pragmatic View of Reengineering Methods. David Sharon. (Illus.). 300p. 1997. text 44.99 (1-85032-194-9) ITCP.

Managing Systems Maintenance. Mark Taylor. (Financial Times Management Briefings Ser.). 1997. pap. 89.50 (0-273-63215-9) F T P-H.

Managing Systems Maintenance. William E. Perry. LC 81-51630. (Illus.). 382p. reprint ed. pap. 118.50 (0-8357-8573-4, 203493900091) Bks Demand.

Managing Talent: Making the Best of the Best. Phillip Sadler. 240p. 1992. 75.00 (0-7855-2663-3) St Mut.

Managing Talent in Broadcast Advertising: Planning, Production & Use. (Orig.). 1992. pap. 19.50 (1-56318-009-X) Assn Natl Advertisers.

*****Managing TCP/IP Networks: Techniques, Tools & Security Considerations.** Gilbert Held. LC 99-44748. (Illus.). 352p. 2000. 89.95 (0-471-80003-1) Wiley.

Managing Teacher Stress. William A. Rogers. (Illus.). 129p. (Orig.). 1996. pap. 57.50 (0-273-62215-3, Pub. by Pitman Pub) Trans-Atl Phila.

Managing Teaching & Learning in Further & Higher Education. Kate Ashcroft & Lorraine Foreman P. LC 94-36524. 212p. 1994. 85.00 (0-7507-0336-9, Falmer Pr); pap. 29.95 (0-7507-0337-7, Falmer Pr) Taylor & Francis.

Managing Team Dynamics see Success Through Teamwork: A Practical Guide to Interpersonal Team Dynamics

Managing Teams. Robert Heller & Tim Hindle. LC 98-15312. (Essential Managers Handbks.). (Illus.). 72p. 1999. pap. 6.95 (0-7894-2895-4) DK Pub Inc.

Managing Teams. Lawrence Holpp. LC 98-41553. (Briefcase Books Ser.). (Illus.). 204p. 1998. pap. 14.95 (0-07-071865-2) McGraw.

*****Managing Teams.** (Illus.). 150p. 2000. reprint ed. spiral bd. 32.00 (1-57431-172-7, MT) Tech Trng Systs.

Managing Technical Assistance: A Practitioner's Handbook. Russell B. Sunshine. LC 95-42159. 1995. write for info. (0-86638-178-3) EW Ctr HI.

Managing Technical People: Innovation, Teamwork, & the Software Process. Watts S. Humphrey. LC 96-41109. (SEI Series in Software Engineering). 352p. (C). 1996. pap. text 26.95 (0-201-54597-7) Addison-Wesley.

Managing Technical Services Contracts. Bill Webb. (Career Learning Ser.). 130p. 1997. pap. 29.95 (0-940343-81-9, MTSM) Natl Contract Mgmt.

Managing Technical Services in the 90's. Ed. by Drew Racine. LC 91-24386. (Journal of Library Administration: Vol. 15, Nos. 1-2). (Illus.). 150p. 1991. lib. bdg. 39.95 (1-56024-166-7) Haworth Pr.

Managing Technological Change: Strategies for College & University Leaders. Anthony W. Bates. LC 99-44483. 320p. 1999. 34.95 (0-7879-4681-8) Jossey-Bass.

*****Managing Technological Change for Schools of the New Millennium: Problem-Based Learning Project.** Ed. by Philip Hallinger et al. x, 46p. 1999. teacher ed. 7.50 (0-86552-145-X); student ed. 7.00 (0-86552-146-8) U of Oreg ERIC.

Managing Technological Development: Strategic & Human Resources Issues. Ed. by Urs E. Gattiker & Laurie Larwood. (Technological Innovation & Human Resources Ser.: No. 1). 232p. (C). 1988. lib. bdg. 52.95 (3-11-011084-9) De Gruyter.

Managing Technological Discontinuities: The Case of the Finnish Paper Industry. Juha Laurila. LC 98-3179. 208p. (C). 1998. 90.00 (0-415-17853-3) Routledge.

Managing Technological Hazards: Research Needs & Opportunities. Ed. by Robert W. Kates. (Program on Environment & Behavior Monograph Ser.: No. 25). 175p. (Orig.). (C). 1978. pap. 20.00 (0-685-28102-7) Natural Hazards.

*****Managing Technological Innovation.** John E. Ettlie. 400p. 2000. pap. 58.95 (0-471-31546-X) Wiley.

Managing Technological Innovation. 4th ed. Brian C. Twiss. 288p. 1992. pap. 62.50 (0-273-03795-1, Pub. by Pitman Pub) Trans-Atl Phila.

Managing Technological Innovation: Competitive Advantage from Change. Frederick Betz. LC 97-20307. (Series in Engineering & Technology Management). 384p. 1997. 90.00 (0-471-17380-0) Wiley.

Managing Technology: The Strategic View. Lowell W. Steele. (Illus.). 352p. 1989. text 56.00 (0-07-060936-5) McGraw.

*****Managing Technology & Innovation for Competitive Advantage.** V. K. Narayanan. 528p. 2000. 80.00 (0-13-030506-5) P-H.

Managing Technology for Corporate Success. Chris Floyd. LC 97-28405. 261p. 1997. 86.95 (0-566-07991-7, Pub. by Gower) Ashgate Pub Co.

Managing Technology for Strategic Advantage. Geistauts-Esche. 1995. text. write for info. (0-256-08440-8) McGraw.

Managing Technology in Healthcare. Ori Heller. Ed. by Eliezer Geisler. LC 96-24589. (Management of Medical Technology Ser.: Vol. 1). 256p. (C). 1996. lib. bdg. 145.00 (0-7923-9750-9) Kluwer Academic.

Managing Technology in Society. Ed. by Arie Rip et al. LC 95-3879. 1995. write for info. (1-85567-339-8); pap. write for info. (1-85567-340-1) St Martin.

Managing Technology in Society: The Approach of the CTA. Johan Schot et al. 300p. 1995. 64.95 (1-85567-307-X); pap. 29.95 (1-85567-318-5) St Martin.

Managing Technology in the Classroom. Deborah Hayes et al. 1995. pap. 24.95 (1-55734-517-1) Tchr Create Mat.

Managing Technology in the Computer Classroom. Teacher Created Materials Staff & Susan L. Gimotty. (Illus.). 176p. (J). (gr. k-8). 1999. pap., teacher ed. 15.95 (1-57690-457-1, TCM2357) Tchr Create Mat.

Managing Technology in the Early Childhood Classroom. Hope Campbell. LC 99-180853. 256p. 1998. pap. 24.95 (1-57690-434-2) Tchr Create Mat.

Managing Technology in the Middle School Classroom. Paul Gardner. LC 97-141635. 288p. (J). (gr. 5-8). 1998. pap. 24.95 (1-55734-667-4) Tchr Create Mat.

Managing Technology Products, Vol. 1. Joseph R. Mancuso. LC 74-82598. (Modern Frontiers in Applied Science Ser.). 184p. reprint ed. pap. 57.10 (0-608-16257-4, 202716100001) Bks Demand.

Managing Teenage Pregnancy: Access to Abortion, Contraception & Sex Education. James E. Allen & Deborah Bender. LC 79-89009. 300p. 1980. 69.50 (0-275-90444-X, C0444, Praeger Pubs) Greenwood.

*****Managing Telework.** Daniels et al. 2000. pap. 34.95 (1-86152-572-9) Thomson Learn.

*****Managing Telework: Strategies for Managing the Virtual Workforce.** Jack Nilles. LC 98-13509. (Upside Bks.). 352p. 1998. 29.95 (0-471-29316-4) Wiley.

Managing Terrorism: Strategies for the Corporate Executive. Ed. by Patrick J. Montana & George S. Roukis. LC 82-11224. 182p. 1983. 52.95 (0-89930-013-8, MTE/, Quorum Bks) Greenwood.

Managing Tertiary & Sixth Form Colleges. Ed. by Simon Lambert. LC 88-2687. 134p. reprint ed. pap. 41.60 (0-7837-5179-6, 204490900004) Bks Demand.

Managing the Academic Enterprise: Case Studies for Deans & Provosts. Elwood B. Ehrle. LC 87-7877. (American Council on Education/Macmillan Series on Higher Education). 221p. reprint ed. pap. 68.60 (0-608-20856-6, 207195500003) Bks Demand.

*****Managing the Academic Unit** Allan Bolton. LC 99-16160. (Managing Universities & Colleges Ser.). 2000. 29.95 (0-335-20403-1) Taylor & Francis.

Managing the Adoption of New Technology. David A. Preece. LC 88-18309. (Management & New Information Technology Ser.). 304p. reprint ed. pap. 94.30 (0-608-20375-0, 207162800002) Bks Demand.

Managing the Aftermath of Radical Corporate Change: Reengineering, Restructuring & Reinvention. Eliezer Geisler. LC 97-8852. 240p. 1997. 59.95 (1-56720-150-4, Quorum Bks) Greenwood.

Managing the Analytical Laboratory: Plain & Simple. Clifford L. Nilsen. 337p. 1996. ring bd. 179.00 (1-57491-015-9) Interpharm.

Managing the Andrew File System. Andrew Campbell. LC 97-43581. 496p. (C). 1998. pap. text 44.99 (0-13-802729-3) P-H.

Managing the Apprehensive Dental Patient: A Management Guide for the Dentist & Staff for Effective Practice Building & Internal Marketing. Robert F. Kroeger. LC 87-80789. (Illus.). 191p. (Orig.). (C). 1987. pap. 45.00 (0-9618291-0-9) Heritage Cinn.

Managing the Audit Function: A Corporate Audit Department Procedures Guide. Michael P. Cangemi. LC 95-42391. 272p. 1995. 145.00 (0-471-01255-6) Wiley.

Managing the Big Sale. John V. Crosby. (Illus.). 256p. 1996. 37.95 (0-8442-3427-3, NTC Business Bks) NTC Contemp Pub Co.

*****Managing the Brief for Better Design.** Alastair Blyth & John Worthington. LC 00-33908. 2000. pap. write for info. (0-419-24470-0, E & FN Spon) Routledge.

*****Managing the Business: How Successful Managers Align Management Systems with Business Strategy.** Garry L. McDaniel. LC 99-44758. (Studies on Industrial Productivity). 1999. write for info. (0-8153-3691-8) Garland.

Managing the Business Environment. L. Bennett. (Illus.). 400p. 1997. mass mkt. 29.95 (0-412-62920-8) Chapman & Hall.

Managing the Business Environment. Linda Bennett. 380p. 1997. pap. 18.99 (1-86152-176-6) Thomson Learn.

Managing the Business Module, PACE Level 1: A Program for Acquiring Competence in Entrepreneurship, 3 levels. rev. ed. National Center for Research in Vocational Educati. 1983. 2.50 (0-317-06058-9, RD240AB11) Ctr Educ Trng Employ.

Managing the Business Module, PACE Level 2: A Program for Acquiring Competence in Entrepreneurship, 3 levels. rev. ed. National Center for Research in Vocational Educati. 1983. 2.50 (0-317-06059-7, RD240BB11) Ctr Educ Trng Employ.

Managing the Business Module, PACE Level 3: A Program for Acquiring Competence in Entrepreneurship, 3 levels. rev. ed. National Center for Research in Vocational Educati. 1983. 2.50 (0-317-06060-0, RD240CB11) Ctr Educ Trng Employ.

Managing the Business of Empire: Essays in Honour of David Fieldhouse. Ed. by Peter Burroughs et al. LC 98-7267. 272p. 1998. 45.00 (0-7146-4826-4, Pub. by F Cass Pubs) Intl Spec Bk.

Managing the Catalog Department. 3rd ed. Donald L. Foster. LC 86-33884. 272p. 1987. 25.50 (0-8108-1973-2) Scarecrow.

Managing the Change Process: A Field Book for Change Agents, Team Leaders & Reengineering Managers. David K. Carr & Kelvin J. Hard. LC 95-36992. (Illus.). 272p. 1995. 34.95 (0-07-012944-4) McGraw.

Managing the Chaos: Outcome-Based Case Management in Behavioral Health Care. Walter Shepperd. LC 97-92485. 64p. 1997. pap. 15.00 (0-9660256-0-1) W Shepperd.

Managing the Chemically Dependent Nurse: A Guide to Identification, Intervention & Retention. Anne M. Catanzarite. 203p. 1992. pap. 25.00 (1-886624-09-7) Creative Nursing.

Managing the Chinese Environment. Ed. by Richard Louis Edmonds. 336p. 2000. pap. text 29.95 (0-19-829635-5) OUP.

*****Managing the Church? Order & Organization in a Secular Age.** Ed. by G. R. Evans & Martyn Percy. (Lincoln Studies in Religion & Society : No. 1). 264p. 2000. 45.00 (1-84127-062-8, Pub. by Sheffield Acad) CUP Services.

Managing the City: The Aims & Impacts of Urban Policy. Ed. by Brian T. Robson. LC 87-1827. 240p. 1987. 57.00 (0-389-20731-4, N8289) B&N Imports.

Managing the Civil Service: The Lessons of Reform in Industrial Countries. Barbara Nunberg. LC 93-23872. (Discussion Paper Ser.: Vol. 204). 62p. 1995. pap. 22.00 (0-8213-2498-5, 12498) World Bank.

Managing the Civilian Workforce: A Guide for the Military Manager. 3rd rev. ed. Rus Ritter. (Illus.). 119p. 1998. pap. text 14.95 (0-936295-83-X) FPMI Comns.

Managing the Classroom: The Teacher's Part in School Administration. 2nd ed. Edwin J. Brown et al. LC 87-5983. (Douglass Series in Education). 262p. reprint ed. pap. 81.30 (0-608-08658-4, 206918100003) Bks Demand.

Managing the Clinical Drug Development Process. David M. Cocchetto & R. V. Nardi. (Drugs & the Pharmaceutical Sciences Ser.: Vol. 51). (Illus.). 232p. 1991. text 145.00 (0-8247-8595-9) Dekker.

Managing the Clinical Resource. Jones Staff. (C). 1993. pap. text 29.00 (0-7020-1681-0) Harcourt.

Managing the Code of Practice: A Whole-School Approach. Carol Goddard & Gill Tester. LC 97-195629. 88p. 1996. pap. 17.95 (1-85346-477-5, Pub. by David Fulton) Taylor & Francis.

Managing the Commons. Ed. by Garrett Hardin & John Baden. LC 76-40055. (Illus.). 294p. 1977. pap. text 12.00 (0-7167-0476-5) W H Freeman.

Managing the Commons. 2nd ed. Ed. by John A. Baden & Douglas S. Noonan. LC 97-20390. (Illus.). 264p. 1998. 39.95 (0-253-33361-X); pap. 16.95 (0-253-21153-0) Ind U Pr.

Managing the Commons. 2nd ed. John Baden & Douglas S. Noonan. LC 97-20390. 1998. pap. write for info. (0-02-532115-3) Macmillan.

Managing the Computer Power Environment: A Guide to Clean Power for Electronic Systems. rev. ed. Mark Waller. (Illus.). 192p. (C). 1992. reprint ed. pap. 24.95 (0-7906-1020-5) Prompt Publns.

Managing the Congregation: Building Effective Systems to Serve People. 1996. pap. 25.00 (0-687-08898-4) Abingdon.

Managing the Congregation: Building Effective Systems to Serve People. Norman Shawchuck & Roger Heuser. 400p. 1996. 24.95 (0-687-23072-1) Abingdon.

Managing the Construction Process. Frederick E. Gould. LC 96-21797. 338p. 1996. 75.00 (0-13-352337-3) P-H.

Managing the Construction Project: A Practical Guide for the Project Manager. Theodore J. Trauner, Jr. LC 92-17788. (Construction Business & Management Library). 208p. 1992. 99.00 (0-471-55762-5) Wiley.

Managing the Continuum of Care. Connie J. Evashwick & Lawrence J. Weiss. 440p. 1987. 92.00 (0-87189-640-0) Aspen Pub.

Managing the Cooperative Enterprise. K. K. Taimni. 1978. 12.50 (0-8364-0295-2) S Asia.

Managing the Corporate Image: The Key to Public Trust. James G. Gray, Jr. LC 85-9598. (Illus.). 174p. 1986. 49.95 (0-89930-140-1, GMC/, Greenwood Pr) Greenwood.

Managing the Corporate Intranet. Mitra Miller et al. LC 97-41086. 427p. 1998. pap. 39.99 (0-471-19978-8) Wiley.

Managing the Corporate Legal Function. D. Craig & Antonia Chaves. Vol. C1. text 82.00 (0-8205-2398-4) Bender.

Managing the Cost of Transfer Programmes. Ed. by Francois Lacasse. LC 98-133448. (Public Management Occasional Papers: No. 16). 180p. 1997. pap. 33.00 (92-64-15500-7, 42-97-66-1, Pub. by Org for Econ) OECD.

*****Managing the Costs of Instructional Technology on U. S. Campuses.** Ed. by Bernhard W. Scholz et al. 256p. 2000. boxed set 39.95 (1-57356-395-1) Oryx Pr.

*****Managing the Counterrevolution: The United States & Guatemala, 1954-1961.** Stephen M. Streeter. (Research in International Studies : Vol. 34). 368p. (C). 2000. pap. text 30.00 (0-89680-215-9, Ohio U Ctr Intl) Ohio U Pr.

Managing the Credit Function. Credit Research Foundation Staff. 40p. 1984. 40.00 (0-939050-33-1) Credit Res NYS.

Managing the Curriculum. Brighouse. 1989. pap. text. write for info. (0-582-05309-9, Pub. by Addison-Wesley) Longman.

Managing the Curriculum Effectively. Russ Russell. (Managing Colleges Effectively Ser.: No. 3). 224p. 1996. pap. write for info. (0-7507-0549-3, Falmer Pr) Taylor & Francis.

An Asterisk (*) at the beginning of an entry indicates that the title is appearing for the first time.

Managing the Curriculum for Children with Severe Motor Difficulties: A Practical Approach. Pilla A.C. Pickles. 1998. 29.95 (*1-85346-511-9*) Taylor & Francis.

Managing the Data Warehouse. W. H. Inmon et al. LC 96-31995. 386p. 1996. pap. 54.99 (*0-471-16310-4*) Wiley.

Managing the Day Care Dollars: A Financial Handbook. rev. ed. Gwen G. Morgan. LC 82-50691. 112p. 1992. pap. 7.95 (*0-942820-02-9*) Steam Pr MA.

***Managing the Demand Chain: Value Innovations for Supplier Excellence.** (Operations Management Series for Professionals). 288p. 2000. 45.00 (*0-471-38499-2*) Wiley.

Managing the Demand for Fashion Items. Rajendra R. Bhat. Ed. by Richard Farmer. LC 85-1039. (Research for Business Decisions Ser.: No. 73). 137p. reprint ed. 42.50 (*0-8357-1618-X*, 207036000088) Bks Demand.

Managing the Demands of Work & Home. Carol R. Galginaitis. LC 93-46067. (Business Skills Express Ser.). 112p. 1994. text 10.95 (*0-7863-0221-6*, Irwn Prfssnl) McGraw-Hill Prof.

Managing the Design Factory: A Toolkit for Product Developers. Donald Reinertsen. LC 97-20343. (Illus.). 256p. 1997. 29.50 (*0-684-83991-1*) Free Pr.

Managing the Development of New Products: Achieving Speed & Quality Simultaneously Through Multifunctional Teamwork. Milton D. Rosenau & John J. Moran. 272p. 1993. 69.95 (*0-471-29183-8*, VNR) Wiley.

Managing the Development Project: A Training Curriculum. 404p. 25.00 (*92-1-123118-3*, E.95.II.D2) UN.

Managing the Difficult Patient. Robert E. Hooberman & Barbara M. Hooberman. LC 97-19686. 382p. 1998. 59.95 (*1-887841-08-3*, Psychosocial) Intl Univs Pr.

Managing the Disruptive Classroom: Strategies for Educators Guide. Agency for Instructional Technology Staff. (Orig.). 1993. pap. text 7.75 (*0-7842-0721-6*) Agency Instr Tech.

Managing the Dollar. Sherman J. Maisel. (Illus.). 1973. 10.95 (*0-393-05494-2*) Norton.

Managing the Dollar: From the Plaza to the Louvre. 2nd ed. Yoichi Funabashi. LC 88-9239. 324p. (Orig.). reprint ed. pap. 100.50 (*0-608-05396-1*, 206586300006) Bks Demand.

***Managing the Dream: Reflections on Leadership & Change.** Warren G. Bennis. 256p. 2000. pap. text 15.00 (*0-7382-0332-7*) Perseus Pubng.

Managing the Dually Diagnosed. David F. O'Connell. 1990. pap. 14.95 (*0-86656-978-2*) Haworth Pr.

Managing the Dually Diagnosed Patient: Current Issues & Clinical Approaches. Ed. by David F. O'Connell. 265p. 1990. 39.95 (*0-86656-918-9*) Haworth Pr.

Managing the Dynamics of New Technology: Issues in Manufacturing Management. Hamid Noori. 352p. (C). 1989. text 57.00 (*0-13-551763-X*) P-H.

Managing the Economic Transition in South Africa. Center for Economic Research on Africa Staff. (CERAF Conference Proceedings Ser.). 108p. 1994. pap. 9.50 (*0-944572-07-3*) MSU Ctr Econ Res Africa.

Managing the Economics of Owning, Leasing & Contracting Out of Information Services. Anne Woodsworth & James Williams. 203p. 1993. 74.95 (*1-85742-018-7*, Pub. by Gower) Ashgate Pub Co.

Managing the Effective Primary School. Brent Davies & Linda Ellison. 160p. 1994. pap. 47.50 (*0-582-22868-9*, Pub. by Addison-Wesley) Trans-Atl Phila.

***Managing the Electronic Library.** Contrib. by Joan Day & Terry Hanson. LC 98-36368. xxiii, 191p. 1999. 75.00 (*1-85739-184-5*) Bowker-Saur.

Managing the Electronic Library: Papers of the 1982 Conference of the Library Management Division of Special Libraries Association. Ed. by Michael E. Koenig. LC 84-102664. (Library Management Ser.: No. 3). (Illus.). 119p. reprint ed. pap. 36.90 (*0-8357-7539-9*, 203626200001) Bks Demand.

Managing the Emergency Department: A Team Approach. American College of Emergency Physicians Staff. 1992. 120.00 (*0-07-000209-6*) McGraw.

Managing the Engineering & Construction of Small Projects: Practical Techniques for Planning, Estimating, Project Control & Computer Applications. Richard E. Westney. (Cost Engineering Ser.: Vol. 9). (Illus.). 296p. 1985. text 69.75 (*0-8247-7417-5*) Dekker.

Managing the Engineering Function. Didactic Systems Staff. (Simulation Game Ser.). 1970. pap. 26.25 (*0-89401-063-8*); pap. 35.00 (*0-89401-099-9*) Didactic Syst.

Managing the Enterprise in Transition While Coping with Inflation. Roy L. Crum et al. LC 93-40299. (EDI Seminar Ser.: No. 47). 44p. 1994. pap. 22.00 (*0-8213-2725-9*, 12725) World Bank.

Managing the Enterprise Network: In the Netware 4.X Environment. C. Alan Greene. (Illus.). 304p. 1995. pap. 29.95 (*0-9640897-2-6*) Gldn West Prods.

Managing the Enterprise with Microsoft Backoffice. Nick Gandhi & Kenneth L. Spencer. (C). 2000. pap. 44.95 (*0-13-228933-4*) P-H.

Managing the Environment. John Beaumont et al. 283p. 1993. pap. text 44.95 (*0-7506-1574-5*) Buttrwrth-Heinemann.

Managing the Environment: Business Opportunity & Responsibility. John R. Beaumont et al. LC 94-150146. (Illus.). 295p. reprint ed. pap. 91.50 (*0-608-07418-7*, 206764500009) Bks Demand.

Managing the Environment in China. Qu Geping & Wo-Yen Lee. 224p. 1984. pap. 10.00 (*0-86346-045-3*, Tycooly Pub) Weidner & Sons.

Managing the Environment, Managing Ourselves: A History of American Environmental Policy. Richard N. Andrews. LC 98-34987. 1999. 65.00 (*0-300-07358-5*) Yale U Pr.

***Managing the Environment, Managing Ourselves: A History of American Environmental Policy.** Richard N. Andrews. LC 98-34987. (Illus.). 416p. 1999. pap. 30.00 (*0-300-07795-5*) Yale U Pr.

Managing the Environment of Care: Long Term Care, Subacute Care & Dementia Units. Joint Commission on Accreditation of Healthcare Organizations. (Illus.). 156p. 1995. pap. 40.00 (*0-86688-449-1*, EC-502) Joint Comm Hlthcare.

Managing the Environment with Rapid Industrialisation: Lessons from the East Asian Experience. OECD Staff. 218p. (Orig.). 1994. pap. 27.00 (*92-64-14181-2*) OECD.

Managing the Environmental Crisis: Incorporating Competing Values in Natural Resource Administration. Daniel H. Henning & William R. Mangun. LC 89-11886. 378p. (C). 1989. pap. text 24.95 (*0-8223-0967-X*) Duke.

Managing the Environmental Crisis: Incorporating Competing Values in Natural Resource Administration 2nd ed. William R. Mangun & Daniel H. Henning. LC 99-26267. 1999. 21.95 (*0-8223-2413-X*) Duke.

***Managing the Environmental Crisis: Incorporating Competing Values in Natural Resource Administration.** 2nd ed. William R. Mangun & Daniel H. Henning. LC 99-26267. 416p. 1999. 64.95 (*0-8223-2379-6*) Duke.

***Managing the Environmental Union: Intergovernmental Relations & Environment Policy in Canada.** Ed. by Patrick C. Fafard & Kathryn Harrison. 240p. 2000. pap. 24.95 (*0-88911-837-X*, Pub. by Queens U Inst Intergov) CUP Services.

Managing the Euro in Information Systems: Strategies for Successful Changeover. Patrick O'Beirne. LC 99-28921. (Addison-Wesley Information Technology Ser.). (Illus.). 368p. (C). 1999. pap. 39.95 incl. cd-rom (*0-201-60482-5*) Addison-Wesley.

Managing the Evolving Corporation. Langdon Morris. (Industrial Engineering Ser.). 238p. 1994. text 26.95 (*0-442-01906-8*, VNR) Wiley.

Managing the Evolving Corporation. Langdon Morris. (Industrial Engineering Ser.). 238p. 1994. 26.95 (*0-471-28651-6*, VNR) Wiley.

Managing the External Environment: A Strategic Perspective. David Mercer. 312p. (C). 1992. text 60.00 (*0-8039-8628-9*); pap. text 24.00 (*0-8039-8629-7*) Sage.

Managing the Facilities Portfolio. Applied Management Engineering Staff & Sean C. Rush. 100p. 1991. 37.00 (*0-915164-59-0*) NACUBO.

Managing the Family Business: Mixing Family & Business Productively. Marshall Northington. Ed. by Janis Paris. LC 92-54372. (Small Business & Entrepreneurship Ser.). 162p. (Orig.). 1993. pap. 15.95 (*1-56052-174-0*) Crisp Pubns.

Managing the Federal Government: A Decade of Decline. 1994. lib. bdg. 256.95 (*0-8490-9055-5*) Gordon Pr.

Managing the Finance Module, PACE Level 1: A Program for Acquiring Competence in Entrepreneurship, 3 levels. rev. ed. National Center for Research in Vocational Educati. 1983. 2.50 (*0-317-06064-3*, RD240AB16) Ctr Educ Trng Employ.

Managing the Finance Module, PACE Level 2: A Program for Acquiring Competence in Entrepreneurship, 3 levels. rev. ed. National Center for Research in Vocational Educati. 1983. 2.50 (*0-317-06065-1*, RD240BB16) Ctr Educ Trng Employ.

Managing the Finance Module, PACE Level 3: A Program for Acquiring Competence in Entrepreneurship, 3 levels. rev. ed. National Center for Research in Vocational Educati. 1983. 2.50 (*0-317-06066-X*, RD240CB16) Ctr Educ Trng Employ.

Managing the Flexible Workforce. R. Pettinger. 1996. pap. 129.00 (*1-85953-071-0*, Pub. by Tech Comm) St Mut.

Managing the Flexible Workforce. Richard Pettinger. LC 98-189591. 144p. 1998. 69.95 (*0-304-70108-4*) Continuum.

Managing the Flexible Workforce. Richard Pettinger. LC 98-189591. 134p. 1998. pap. 21.95 (*0-304-70109-2*) Continuum.

Managing the Flexible Workforce. Richard Pettinger. (Financial Times Management Briefings Ser.). 1997. pap. 89.50 (*0-273-63183-7*) F T P-H.

Managing the Florida Condominium. William D. Clark. (FRE.). 116p. 1994. ring bd., suppl. ed. 42.00 (*0-614-03740-9*, MICHIE) LEXIS Pub.

Managing the Florida Condominium, 3 vols., Set. William D. Clark. 252p. 1996. ring bd. 105.00 (*0-409-26863-1*, 80886-10, MICHIE) LEXIS Pub.

Managing the Florida Condominium 99-1. Clark. 394p. 1999. ring bd. write for info. (*0-327-01167-X*, 8089018) LEXIS Pub.

Managing the Florida Condominium, 98-2. William D. Clark. 236p. 1998. ring bd. write for info. (*0-327-00613-7*, 8089017) LEXIS Pub.

Managing the Flow of Technology: Technology Transfer & the Dissemination of Technological Information Within the R & D Organization. Thomas J. Allen. 336p. 1984. pap. text 23.00 (*0-262-51027-8*) MIT Pr.

Managing the Franc Poincare, 1928-1936: Economic Understanding & Political Constraint in French Monetary Policy, 1928-1936. Kenneth Moure. (Studies in Monetary & Financial History). 318p. (C). 1991. text 89.95 (*0-521-39458-9*) Cambridge U Pr.

Managing the Future. Robert B. Tucker. 1991. reprint ed. pap. 12.00 (*0-425-13083-5*) Berkley Pub.

Managing the Future: Benchmarking Compensation Trends in Commercial Real Estate, 1994 Edition. A. Andersen. (Illus.). (Orig.). 1994. pap. text 595.00 (*0-943130-09-3*) Build Own & Man.

Managing the Future in Financial Institutions: Meeting the Challenge with Better Information. Julie Mabberley. (Illus.). 336p. 1996. 50.00 (*0-273-61975-6*) F T P-H.

Managing the Gap Between Needs & Options. Ed. by Joske F. Bunders. 96p. (Orig.). 1993. pap. 20.00 (*90-5383-173-8*, Pub. by VU Univ Pr) Paul & Co Pubs.

***Managing the General Ledger, 2000 Yearbook.** annuals Ed. by Stephen Collins & David Solomon. (Illus.). 200p. 2000. pap. 199.00 (*1-58673-020-7*) IOMA.

***Managing the Gift: Alternative Approaches for A. D. D.** Kevin Ross Emery. 176p. 2000. pap. 14.95 (*1-890405-21-3*) LightLines.

Managing the Global Commons: The Economics of Climate Change. William D. Nordhaus. LC 94-3992. (Illus.). 223p. 1994. 35.00 (*0-262-14055-1*) MIT Pr.

***Managing the Global Corporation: Case Studies in Strategy & Management.** 2nd ed. Josbe de la Torre et al. LC 00-27781. 2000. pap. write for info. (*0-07-234553-5*, McGrw-H College) McGrw-H Hghr Educ.

Managing the Global Economy. Ed. by Jonathan Michie & James G. Smith. (Illus.). 370p. 1995. text 75.00 (*0-19-828969-3*); pap. text 26.00 (*0-19-828968-5*) OUP.

Managing the Global Firm. Ed. by Christopher A. Bartlett et al. 368p. 1996. pap. 22.95 (*0-415-13518-4*) Routledge.

Managing the Global Firm. Ed. by Christopher A. Bartlett et al. 336p. (C). (gr. 13). 1989. pap. 35.95 (*0-415-03711-5*, A4199) Thomson Learn.

***Managing the Global Supply Chain.** Philip B. Schary. LC 98-106630. 1999. 51.00 (*87-16-13278-5*) Mksgaard.

Managing the Growing Plant: A Dynamic Systems Approach. William T. Walker. LC 84-19234. 384p. 1984. 59.50 (*0-87624-361-8*, Inst Busn Plan) P-H.

Managing the Heavy Metals on the Land. Geoffrey W. Leeper. LC 77-20934. (Pollution Engineering & Technology Ser.: Vol. 6). (Illus.). 143p. reprint ed. pap. 44.40 (*0-608-08949-4*, 206958400005) Bks Demand.

Managing the Hidden Organization: Strategies for Empowering Your Behind-the-Scenes Employees. Terrence E. Deal & William A. Jenkins. 384p. (Orig.). 1994. mass mkt. 10.99 (*0-446-39456-4*, Pub. by Warner Bks) Little.

Managing the High School Foreign Language Department: A Handbook for Teachers & Administrators. Ed. by Richard B. Klein & Sam L. Slick. LC 95-71538. 332p. 1998. pap. 23.35 (*0-8442-9309-1*, VS9309-1) NTC Contemp Pub Co.

Managing the Himalayan Environment. S. S. Negi. (C). 1986. 75.00 (*81-7136-006-8*, Pub. by Periodical Expert) St Mut.

***Managing the Historic Rural Landscape** Jane Grenville. LC 98-52377. (Issues in Heritage Management Ser.). 1998. pap. write for info. (*0-415-20791-6*) Routledge.

***Managing the Historic Rural Landscape.** Jane Grenville. LC 98-52377. 1998. write for info. (*0-415-20790-8*) Routledge.

Managing the "How-to" Collection & Learner's Advisory Services: A How-to-Do-It Manual for Librarians. Sy Sargent. (How-to-Do-It Ser.). 150p. 1993. 32.95 (*1-55570-143-4*) Neal-Schuman.

Managing the Human Impact on the Natural Environment Patterns & Processes. N. Newson. 282p. 1993. pap. 325.00 (*81-7089-152-3*, Pub. by Intl Bk Distr) St Mut.

Managing the Human Services in Hard Times. David A. Bresnick. LC 83-80211. (Managing the Human Services Ser.). 222p. (C). 1983. text 20.00 (*0-9610834-0-9*) Human Serv Pr.

Managing the Impact of the Euro. Simon Sear. LC 98-228625. 112p. 1998. 78.95 (*0-566-08146-6*, Pub. by Ashgate Pub) Ashgate Pub Co.

Managing the Incompetent Teacher. 2nd ed. Edwin M. Bridges. LC 90-80371. x, 98p. 1990. pap. 7.95 (*0-86552-102-6*) U of Oreg ERIC.

Managing the Industrial Labor Relation Process in Higher Education. Ed. by Daniel J. Julius. 373p. 1993. 49.00 (*1-878240-28-5*) Coll & U Personnel.

Managing the Industry - University Cooperative Research Center: A Handbook for Center Directors. Ed. by Denis O. Gray & S. George Walters. (Illus.). 332p. 1997. write for info. (*0-9658444-0-4*) Hazardous Subs Mgmt.

Managing the Industry University Cooperative Research Center: A Guide for Directors & Other Stakeholders. Denis O. Gray & S. George Walters. LC 98-23189. 1998. pap. 29.95 (*1-57477-053-5*) Battelle.

Managing the Information Ecology: A Collaborative Approach to Information Technology Management. Bruce W. Hasenyager. LC 94-39344. 248p. 1996. 59.95 (*0-89930-947-X*, Quorum Bks) Greenwood.

Managing the Initial Public Offering of Securities. Alan S. Gutterman. (Corporate Practice Ser.: No. 59). 1991. ring bd. 95.00 (*1-55871-242-9*) BNA.

Managing the Insolvency Risk of Insurance Companies. Ed. by J. David Cummins & Richard A. Derrig. (S. S. Huebner International Ser.). 1991. lib. bdg. 110.00 (*0-7923-9152-7*) Huebner Foun Insur.

Managing the Interactive Classroom: A Collection of Articles. Ed. by Kay Burke. LC 95-78185. (Illus.). 144p. (Orig.). 1995. pap. 14.95 (*1-57517-002-7*, 1343) SkyLght.

Managing the Internal Market. Ed. by Ian Tilley. 328p. 1993. pap. 37.50 (*1-85396-195-7*, Pub. by P Chapman) Taylor & Francis.

Managing the International System over the Next Ten Years: Three Essays. Bill Emmott et al. LC 97-20422. (Report to the Trilateral Commission Ser.). 60p. 1997. pap. 9.00 (*0-930503-76-7*) Trilateral Comm.

Managing the Internationalization Process: The Swedish Case. Mats Forsgren. 200p. 1989. pap. 71.95 (*0-415-03868-5*, A3773) Thomson Learn.

***Managing the Internet Controversy.** Ed. by Mark L. Smith. (Net Guides Ser.). 200p. 2000. pap. 45.00 (*1-55570-395-X*) Neal-Schuman.

Managing the Interview: A-How-to-Do-It Manual. Susan C. Curzon. LC 94-47336. (How-to-Do-It-Ser.: Vol. 47). (Illus.). 160p. (Orig.). 1995. pap. 45.00 (*1-55570-160-4*) Neal-Schuman.

Managing the Intramural-Recreational Sports Program. David O. Matthews. Ed. by Earle F. Zeigler. (Monograph Series on Sport & Physical Education Management). 62p. (Orig.). 1984. pap. text 4.00 (*0-87563-255-6*) Stipes.

Managing the Investment Firm. Ed. by James R. Vertin. (Orig.). 1991. pap. text 30.00 (*1-879087-10-3*) Assn I M&R.

Managing the Investment Professional. Ed. by James R. Vertin. 25.00 (*0-318-02105-6*) Inst Charter Finan Analysts.

***Managing the IT Value Quest: How to Capture the Business Value of IT-Based Infrastructure.** Theo J. W. Renkema. LC 99-50119. (Series in Information Systems). (Illus.). 278p. 2000. 55.00 (*0-471-98817-0*) Wiley.

Managing the Japanese Beetle: A Homeowner's Handbook. 16p. 1998. pap. 2.00 (*0-16-049529-6*, Agriculture Dept) USGPO.

***Managing the Jewish Classroom: How to Transform Yourself into a Master Jewish Teacher.** Seymour Rossel. 256p. (C). 1998. pap. 12.95 (*0-933873-96-4*) Torah Aura.

Managing the Labour Process. David Knights & Hugh Willmott. 200p. 1986. text 78.95 (*0-566-05000-5*) Ashgate Pub Co.

Managing the Large Organization: Issues, Ideas, Precepts, Innovations. David S. Brown. 300p. 1982. 27.50 (*0-912338-31-8*); fiche 19.50 (*0-912338-34-2*) Lomond.

Managing the Law Firm: Legal Practice Handbook. 2nd ed. Alan Pannett. 194p. 1995. pap. 26.00 (*1-85431-457-2*, Pub. by Blackstone Pr) Gaunt.

Managing the Learning of History. Richard Brown. (Quality in Secondary Schools & Colleges Ser.). 144p. 1995. pap. 24.95 (*1-85346-345-0*, Pub. by David Fulton) Taylor & Francis.

Managing the Learning Process in Business Education. Calfrey C. Calhoun & Bettye W. Robinson. 756p. (C). 1995. pap. text 40.00 (*1-56883-058-0*) Colonial Pr AL.

Managing the Legal Aspects of Technology. 2nd ed. Lee B. Burgunder. 2000. pap. 67.95 (*0-324-02720-6*) Thomson Learn.

Managing the Library Fire Risk. 2nd rev. ed. John Morris. LC 78-22603. (Illus.). 1979. 15.50 (*0-9602278-1-4*) J Morris.

Managing the Literacy Curriculum: How Schools Can Become Communities of Readers & Writers. Alec Webster et al. LC 95-37351. 208p. (C). 1996. 75.00 (*0-415-11294-X*); pap. 22.99 (*0-415-11295-8*) Routledge.

Managing the Living Forest. Ed. by Charles S. Roper & Andy Park. (Illus.). 450p. 1999. pap. 160.00 (*0-11-710343-8*, Pub. by Statnry Office) Balogh.

Managing the Lower Rio Grande: An Experience in International River Development. John C. Day. LC 70-129457. (University of Chicago, Department of Geography, Research Paper Ser.: No. 125). (Illus.). 289p. reprint ed. pap. 89.60 (*0-8357-3720-9*, 203644200003) Bks Demand.

Managing the Manufacturing & Industrial Engineering Functions. Didactic Systems Staff. (Simulation Game Ser.). 1970. pap. 26.25 (*0-89401-064-6*) Didactic Syst.

Managing the Manufacturing Process: A Pattern for Excellence. Ralph C. Woodgate. LC 90-42385. 240p. 1991. 99.95 (*0-471-50655-9*) Wiley.

Managing the Marginal & Unsatisfactory Performer. Lawrence L. Steinmetz. LC 78-83467. (Business Ser.). (Illus.). 1969. pap. write for info. (*0-201-07276-9*) Addison-Wesley.

Managing the Media: Proactive Strategy for Better Business-Press Relations. Fred J. Evans. LC 86-25736. 189p. 1987. 57.95 (*0-89930-156-8*, EVM/, Quorum Bks) Greenwood.

Managing the Medical Arms Race: Innovation & Public Policy in the Medical Device Industry. Susan B. Foote. (C). 1992. 45.00 (*0-520-07591-9*, Pub. by U CA Pr) Cal Prin Full Svc.

Managing the Medical Enterprise: A Study of Physician Managers. Carol L. Betson. Ed. by Richard Farmer. LC 85-31834. (Research for Business Decisions Ser.: No. 89). 205p. reprint ed. 63.60 (*0-8357-1735-6*, 207036300088) Bks Demand.

Managing the Medical Practice: The Physician's Handbook for Successful Practice Administration. Lauretta Mink. Ed. by Kay Stanley. (Practice Success Ser.). pap. 44.95 (*0-89970-755-6*, OP701295AFR) AMA.

Managing the Merger: Making It Work. Philip H. Mirvis. 400p. (C). 1991. text 26.00 (*0-13-544636-8*, Busn) P-H.

***Managing the Message.** Peter Hobday. 2000. 25.95 (*1-902809-18-1*) Allison & Busby.

Managing the Metrology System. 2nd ed. C. Robert Pennella. LC 97-10667. 176p. 1997. 28.00 (*0-87389-421-9*, H0964) ASQ Qual Pr.

Managing the Metropolis: New Life for Old City Regions. Ed. by Peter Roberts et al. 368p. 1993. 88.95 (*1-85628-383-6*, Pub. by Avebry) Ashgate Pub Co.

M

Managing the Metropolis in Japan & Texas: Sister City Relationships, Municipal Finance, & Urban Economic Development Projects. Robert C. Rickards. (Policy Research Project Report: No. 94). 92p. 1991. pap. 9.50 (*0-89940-702-1*) LBJ Sch Pub Aff.

Managing the Millennium Bug: And Its Implications for Your Organization Mike Levy & Gill Thomas. LC 99-18668. 1999. 78.95 (*0-566-08177-6*, Pub. by Gower) Ashgate Pub Co.

Managing the Modern Languages Classroom. Amanda Flint. 1994. pap. 24.00 (*1-85234-509-8*, Pub. by S Thornes Pubs) Trans-Atl Phila.

Managing the Modern Michigan Township. Kenneth Verburg. Ed. by Nancy Gendell. LC 90-620772. 432p. 1990. pap. text 22.50 (*0-941872-58-0*) MSU Dept Res Dev.

Managing the Money Side: Financial Management for Community-Based Housing Organizations. Kirby White. 140p. 1994. pap. text. write for info. (*1-886808-02-3*) Inst Comm Econ.

Managing the Morning Rush. Lee Canter. (Lee Canter Effective Parenting Bks.). (Illus.). 48p. (Orig.). 1995. pap. 5.95 (*0-939007-73-8*) Canter & Assocs.

Managing the Mortgage Maze: A Professional's Guide. Jeannine Doyle. 196p. 1997. pap. 65.90 (*0-9672223-0-3*) D&S Pubns WI.

Managing the Mosaic: Diversity in Action. Rajvinder Kandola & Johanna Fullerton. 160p. (C). 1994. pap. 50.00 (*0-85292-556-5*, Pub. by IPM Hse) St Mut.

Managing the Multicultural Workforce: Strategies for Human Resource Professionals. Ed. by Rosalind M. Schwartz. (Policy & Practice Publication: No. HR 2000). 93p. (Orig.). 1992. pap. 11.00 (*0-89215-173-0*) U Cal LA Indus Rel.

Managing the Multinational Subsidiary. James M. Hulbert & William K. Brandt. LC 80-23924. 196p. 1980. 62.95 (*0-275-91688-X*, C1688, Praeger Pubs) Greenwood.

Managing the Multinationals: An International Study of Control Mechanisms. Anne-Wil K. Harzing. LC 98-31842. (New Horizons in International Business Ser.). 448p. 1999. 100.00 (*1-84064-052-9*) E Elgar.

Managing the Museum. Michael Fopp. LC 96-34796. (Heritage Ser.). (Illus.). 256p. (C). 1997. 85.00 (*0-415-09496-8*); pap. 32.99 (*0-415-09497-6*) Routledge.

Managing the New Bank Technology. Marilyn R. Seymann. (Glenlake Business Monographs). 300p. 1998. 55.00 (*1-884964-65-6*) Fitzroy Dearborn.

Managing the New Bank Technology: An Executive Blueprint for the Future. Marilyn R. Seymann. 225p. 1997. 55.00 (*1-888998-12-1*) Glenlake Pub.

Managing the New Careerists: The Diverse Career Success Orientations of Today's Workers. Clyde B. Derr. LC 85-45901. (Joint Publication in the Jossey-Bass Management Series & the Jossey-Bass Social & Behavioral Science Ser.). 312p. reprint ed. pap. 96.80 (*0-7837-2515-9*, 204267400006) Bks Demand.

Managing the New Enterprise: The Proof, Not the Hype. Harris Kern. LC 96-164778. 240p. (C). 1995. 49.00 (*0-13-231184-4*) P-H.

Managing the New Hong Kong Economy. Ed. by David Mole. (Illus.). 162p. 1997. pap. text 32.00 (*0-19-590042-1*) OUP.

Managing the New Organization: A Blueprint for Networks & Strategic Alliances. David Limerick & Bert Cunnington. (Management Ser.). 302p. 1993. text 32.95 (*1-55542-581-X*) Jossey-Bass.

***Managing the Non-Profit Organization: Practices & Principles.** Peter F. Drucker. 1999. pap. 13.50 (*0-06-662023-6*) HarpC.

Managing the Non-Profit Organization: Principles & Practices. Peter F. Drucker. LC 89-46525. 235p. 1992. pap. 13.50 (*0-88730-601-2*, HarpBusn) HarpInfo.

Managing the Nonprofit Organization: Drucker,&Peter F., Set. abr. ed. Peter F. Drucker. 1992. audio 17.00 (*1-55994-552-4*, CPN 2283) HarperAudio.

***Managing the Nuclear Materials Threat: A Report of the CSIS Nuclear Materials Management Project.** Sam Nunn et al. LC 99-88665. (Panel Report Ser.). 118p. 1999. 24.95 (*0-89206-359-9*) CSIS.

Managing the Nursing Shortage: A Guide to Recruitment & Retention. Ed. by Terence F. Moore & Earl A. Simendinger. (Health Care Administration Ser.). 284p. 1989. 79.00 (*0-8342-0046-5*) Aspen Pub.

Managing the Obvious. Charles Coonradt. 215p. 1993. 22.00 (*1-883004-01-2*, Pub. by Game of Work) Origin Bk Sales.

Managing the Obvious: How to Get What You Want Using What You Know. 2nd rev. ed. Charles A. Coonradt. LC 93-80954. 215p. 1997. reprint ed. pap. 14.95 (*1-883004-04-7*) Game of Work.

Managing the Occupational Education Laboratory. 2nd rev. ed. George Storm. (Illus.). 216p. (C). 1993. pap. text 16.00 (*0-911168-84-2*) Prakken.

Managing the Ocean: Resources, Research, Law. Ed. by Jacques G. Richardson. LC 88-50823. 407p. 1985. 28.95 (*0-912338-49-0*); fiche 19.50 (*0-912338-50-4*) Lomond.

Managing the Ocean Resources of the United States: The Role of the Federal Marine Sanctuary Program. Daniel P. Finn. (Lecture Notes on Coastal & Estuarine Studies: Vol. 2). (Illus.). 193p. 1982. pap. 29.00 (*0-387-11583-8*) Spr-Verlag.

Managing the Office Building. rev. ed. Ed. by Mark Ingerbretsen. (Illus.). 431p. 1985. 62.95 (*0-912104-80-5*, NO. 809) Inst Real Estate.

Managing the Offshore Installation Workforce. Rhona H. Flin & Georgina Slaven. LC 96-20367. 1996. 74.95 (*0-87814-396-3*) PennWell Bks.

Managing the Oil Wealth: OPEC's Windfalls & Pitfalls. Amuzegar. 256p. 2000. text 65.00 (*1-86064-292-6*, Pub. by I B T) St Martin.

***Managing the Oracle Data Warehouse.** David Reed. 450p. 2000. pap. text 49.99 (*0-13-014923-3*) P-H.

Managing the Organizational Melting Pot: Dilemmas of Workplace Diversity. Ed. by Pushkala Prasad et al. LC 96-35610. 383p. 1997. 62.00 (*0-8039-7410-8*) Sage.

Managing the Outpatient Medical Practice: Strategies for a Changing Environment. Thomas Landholt & Coker Group Staff. LC 98-20745. 127p. 1998. 35.00 (*1-55648-242-6*) AHPI.

Managing the Patient with Type II Diabetes. Andrew L. Wilson & Ila V. Mehra. LC 97-23911. 1997. write for info. (*0-8342-1004-5*); 29.00 (*0-8342-1018-5*) Aspen Pub.

***Managing the People Side of Innovation: 8 Rules for Engaging Minds & Hearts.** A. J. Chopra. LC 99-22634. (Illus.). 211p. 1999. 24.95 (*1-56549-098-3*) Kumarian Pr.

Managing the People's Money. Chan. (Public Administration Ser.). 1997. text 49.95 (*0-534-25356-3*) Wadsworth Pub.

Managing the Performing Arts Organization: Founding Principles in the Management of the Arts. Ichak Adizes. Ed. by Patrick H. Griffin. xii, 135p. (Orig.). 1997. pap. 19.95 (*0-937120-06-5*) Adizes Inst Inc.

Managing the Pharmacy Benefit Robert Navarro & Albert I. Wertheimer. LC 96-164710. xxii, 376 p. 1996. write for info. (*0-9651745-0-6*) Emron.

Managing the Physician's Office Laboratory: Responsive Management under Regulatory & Economic Restraints. Eleanor M. Travers. 250p. (Orig.). 1994. pap. text 59.95 (*0-07-600653-0*, ME107) Practice Mgmt Info.

Managing the Policy Agendy: Organizational Options for Governors. Ed. by Mark R. Miller. 56p. (Orig.). 1992. pap. text 17.95 (*1-55877-164-6*) Natl Governor.

Managing the Poor Performer. Valerie Stewart & Andrew Stewart. 192p. 1982. text 56.95 (*0-566-02248-6*) Ashgate Pub Co.

Managing the Poor Performer. Valerie Stewart & Andrew Stewart. 192p. 1988. pap. text 26.95 (*0-7045-0594-0*) Ashgate Pub Co.

Managing the Potato Production System. Bill Dean. LC 92-1676. (Illus.). 203p. 1994. lib. bdg. 49.95 (*1-56022-025-2*) Haworth Pr.

Managing the Practice: Whose Business? June Huntington. LC 95-21406. (Primary Care Development Ser.). 140p. 1995. pap. 29.00 (*1-85775-053-5*, Radcliffe Med Pr) Scovill Paterson.

Managing the Preservation of Serial Literature. (IFLA Publications: No. 57). 291p. 1992. lib. bdg. 60.00 (*3-598-21783-8*) K G Saur Verlag.

Managing the Presidency: Carter, Reagan & the Search for Executive Harmony. Colin Campbell. LC 86-4069. (Policy & Institutional Studies). (Illus.). 352p. (Orig.). (C). 1986. pap. 15.95 (*0-8229-5412-5*) U of Pittsburgh Pr.

***Managing the Press: Origins of the Media Presidency, 1897-1933.** Stephen Ponder. LC 98-33865. 288p. 1999. text 45.00 (*0-312-21384-0*) St Martin.

Managing the Pressure in Teaching: Practical Ideas for Tutors & Their Students. Stephen Cox. LC 99-167510. 1998. 79.00 (*0-7507-0836-0*); pap. text 22.95 (*0-7507-0835-2*, Falmer Pr) Taylor & Francis.

Managing the Private Law Library: Management Challenges, New Technology & Planning for the 1990's. Lucy Curci-Gonzalez & Sharon K. French. 531p. 1991. pap. text 17.50 (*0-685-49932-4*, G4-3862) PLI.

Managing the Private Law Library, 1995: Affecting the Bottom Line. (Patents, Copyrights, Trademarks, & Literary Property Ser.). 1995. pap. 99.00 (*0-685-69465-8*, G4-3944) PLI.

Managing the Probation Service. Statham Whitehead. 1992. pap. 28.95 (*0-582-09144-6*) Ashgate Pub Co.

Managing the Product Development Process, Vol. 1. Ed. by Timothy L. Wilson. (Journal of Product Innovation Management Ser.). 108p. (Orig.). 1989. pap. 20.00 (*0-9622586-0-1*) Prod Dev Mgt Assn.

Managing the Professional Service Firm. David H. Maister. 448p. 1993. 45.00 (*0-02-919782-1*) Free Pr.

Managing the Professional Service Firm. David H. Maister. 1997. per. 25.00 (*0-684-83431-6*) Free Pr.

Managing the Project Team. Vijay K. Verma. (Human Aspects of Project Management Ser.: Vol. 3). 240p. 1997. pap. 32.95 (*1-880410-42-7*) Proj Mgmt Inst.

Managing the Prosecutor's Office: With Appendix of Sample Forms. Ed. by Patricia A. McGarry. 324p. (Orig.). 1987. pap. 25.00 (*0-910397-12-0*) NCDA.

Managing the Public Library. 2nd ed. Donald J. Sager. (Professional Librarian Ser.). 254p. 1989. 40.00 (*0-8161-1898-1*, Hall Reference); 30.00 (*0-8161-1899-X*, Hall Reference) Macmillan.

Managing the Public Sector. 5th ed. Starling. (C). 1997. pap. text, teacher ed. 31.00 (*0-15-505431-7*) Harcourt Coll Pubs.

Managing the Public Sector. 5th ed. Grover Starling. LC 96-72226. 672p. (C). 1997. text 68.00 (*0-03-019379-6*, Pub. by Harcourt Coll Pubs) Harcourt.

Managing the Public Sector: A Comparative Analysis of the United Kingdom & the United States. Andrew Massey. 240p. 1993. 90.00 (*1-85278-333-8*) E Elgar.

Managing the Publishing Process: An Annotated Bibliography, 9. Bruce W. Speck. LC 95-6289. (Bibliographies & Indexes in Mass Media & Communications Ser.: No. 9). 360p. 1995. lib. bdg. 75.00 (*0-313-27956-X*, Greenwood Pr) Greenwood.

Managing the Quality Control Function. Didactic Systems Staff. 1970. pap. 26.25 (*0-89401-065-4*) Didactic Syst.

Managing the Quality of Health Care in Developing Countries. Willy L. De Geyndt. LC 94-36278. (Technical Papers: No. 258). 92p. 1995. pap. 22.00 (*0-8213-3092-6*, 13092) World Bank.

Managing the Rapids: Stories from the Forefront of the Learning Organization. Ed. by Kellie W. O'Reilly. LC 95-69858. (Illus.). 124p. 1995. pap. 17.95 (*1-883823-08-0*, OL004) Pegasus Comm.

Managing the Recruitment Process. Christine White & Abbie W. Thorner. xv, 345p. 1982. 45.00 (*0-15-004279-5*) Harcourt.

***Managing the Reference Collection.** Christopher W. Nolan. LC 98-37178. 200p. 1998. 32.00 (*0-8389-0748-2*) ALA.

***Managing the Regulatory Process: Design, Concepts, Issues & the Latin America & Caribbean Story.** J. Luis Guasch & Pablo T. Spiller. LC 99-38444. (Latin American & Caribbean Studies). 336p. 1999. pap. 45.00 (*0-8213-4497-8*, 14497) World Bank.

Managing the Residential Treatment Center in Troubled Times. Intro. by Gordon Northrup. LC 94-17286. (Residential Treatment for Children & Youth Ser.). 111p. 1994. 39.95 (*1-56024-676-6*) Haworth Pr.

Managing the Retirement Maze - Virginia Edition Vol. 1: Retirement Living (Senior Issues, Senior Services, & Senior Living Options) Kandi Sterling & Michael R. Zervas. LC 98-71437. (Illus.). 128p. (Orig.). 1999. pap. 14.95 (*0-932045-25-1*) Dace Pub.

Managing the Revenue & Cash Flow Effects of Conservation. Vista Consulting Group Staff. LC 96-164749. (Illus.). 127p. 1996. pap. 195.00 (*0-89867-845-5*, 90686) Am Water Wks Assn.

Managing the Risks of Dam Project Development, Safety & Operation: Eighteenth Annual Uscold Lecture Series, Buffalo, New York, August 10-14, 1998. United States Committee on Large Dams. LC 98-72694. 589p. 1998. write for info. (*1-884575-13-7*) US Cttee Dams.

Managing the Risks of International Agreement. Richard B. Bilder. LC 80-52288. 315p. 1981. reprint ed. pap. 97.70 (*0-7837-9777-X*, 206050600005) Bks Demand.

Managing the School Age Child with a Chronic Health Condition: A Practical Guide for Schools, Families & Organizations. Ed. by Georgianna Larson. (Illus.). 335p. 1988. pap. text 29.95 (*0-9624814-3-2*) Sunrise River Pr.

Managing the School Library Resource Center: A Selection of Case Studies. James Henri et al. LC 91-6586. 166p. 1991. 26.00 (*0-8108-2407-8*) Scarecrow.

Managing the Secondary School. 2nd ed. Joan Dean. LC 93-13075. 1994. write for info. (*0-415-08770-8*) Routledge.

Managing the Serials Explosion: The Issues for Publishers & Librarians. David C. Taylor. LC 82-14062. (Professional Librarian Ser.). 156p. 1982. pap. 30.50 (*0-914236-54-7*) Macmillan.

Managing the Service Economy. Ed. by Robert P. Inman. (Illus.). 352p. (C). 1989. pap. text 24.95 (*0-521-37858-3*) Cambridge U Pr.

Managing the Shop-Floor: Subjectivity, Masculinity & Workplace Culture. David L. Collinson. (Studies in Organization: No. 36). (Illus.). xii, 255p. (C). 1992. lib. bdg. 54.95 (*3-11-012257-X*, 41-92) De Gruyter.

Managing the Side Effects of Chemotherapy & Radiation Therapy: A Guide for Patients & Their Families. Marylin J. Dodd. 198p. (Orig.). 1996. pap. 20.00 (*0-943671-12-4*) UCSF Schl Nursing.

Managing the Small Construction Business: A Hands-On Guide. Journal of Light Construction Staff. Ed. by Steven Bliss. LC 92-73306. (Illus.). 244p. (Orig.). 1992. pap. 27.95 (*0-9632268-1-9*) Builderburg Grp.

***Managing the Small Construction Business: A Hands-on-Guide.** 2nd rev. ed. Ed. by Steven Bliss & Josie Masterson-Glen. LC 99-75375. 336p. 1999. pap. 34.95 (*1-928580-00-9*, Jrnl Lght) Builderburg Grp.

Managing the Small to Mid-Sized Company: Concepts & Cases. James C. Collins & William C. Lazier. LC 94-30044. 688p. (C). 1994. text 68.95 (*0-256-14280-7*, Irwn McGrw-H) McGrw-H Hghr Educ.

Managing the Small Training Staff: Twelve Case Studies from the Real World of Training. American Society for Training and Development Staff. Ed. by Carol Prescott McCoy & Jack J. Phillips. LC 98-70301. (In Action Ser.). 227 p. 1998. pap. 50.00 (*1-56286-082-8*) Am Soc Train & Devel.

Managing the Social & Emotional Needs of the Gifted: A Teacher's Survival Guide. Connie C. Schmitz & Judy Galbraith. LC 85-80633. 160p. (Orig.). 1985. pap., teacher ed. 13.95 (*0-915793-05-9*) Free Spirit Pub.

Managing the Social Studies Curriculum. Kent Freeland. LC 90-71263. 380p. 1994. pap. 29.95 (*0-87762-709-6*) Scarecrow.

Managing the Software Process. Watts S. Humphrey. (Software Engineering Institute Ser.). (Illus.). 512p. (C). 1989. 59.95 (*0-201-18095-2*) Addison-Wesley.

Managing the South African War, 1899-1902: Politicians vs. Generals. Keith T. Surridge. (Studies in History, New Ser.). 224p. 1998. 55.00 (*0-86193-238-2*, Royal Historical Soc) Boydell & Brewer.

Managing the Special Library: Strategies for Success Within the Larger Organization. Herbert S. White. LC 83-24390. (Professional Librarian Ser.). 152p. 1984. 40.00 (*0-86729-088-9*, Pub. by Macmillan); 35.00 (*0-86729-087-0*, Hall Reference) Macmillan.

Managing the Spectrum: Win, Lose, or Share. Derrick C. Huang. (Illus.). 66p. (Orig.). 1993. pap. text. write for info. (*1-879716-00-3*, P-93-2) Ctr Info Policy.

Managing the Sport Club Program: From Theory to Practice. Shirley Cleave. Ed. by Earle F. Zeigler. (Monograph Series on Sport & Physical Education Management). 49p. 1984. pap. text 4.80 (*0-87563-244-0*) Stipes.

Managing the State Workforce As If Taxpayers Mattered: Data Show Colorado Is Personnel-Heavy & Pay-Heavy. Rob Fairbank. 6p. 1992. pap. text 8.00 (*1-57655-092-3*) Independ Inst.

Managing the Structured Techniques. 2nd ed. Edward Yourdon. 1979. 42.67 (*0-13-550855-X*) P-H.

Managing the Structured Techniques: Strategies for Software Development in the 1990's. 3rd ed. Edward Yourdon. (Illus.). 296p. 1985. pap. text 27.95 (*0-917072-56-1*, Yourdon) P-H.

Managing the System Life Cycle: A Software Development Methodology Overview. Edward Yourdon. LC 81-72107. (Illus.). 160p. (Orig.). 1982. pap. 29.95 (*0-917072-26-X*, Yourdon) P-H.

Managing the Team: A Guide to Successful Employee Involvement. Mick Marchington. LC 92-15428. (Human Resource Management in Action Ser.). 1992. pap. 47.95 (*0-631-18677-8*) Blackwell Pubs.

Managing the Technical Professional. Herbert S. Kindler. Ed. by Kay Keppler. LC 92-54367. (Fifty-Minute Ser.). 88p. (Orig.). 1993. pap. 10.95 (*1-56052-177-5*) Crisp Pubns.

Managing the Technical Workforce: A Study of Computer Professionals. Laurie M. Roth. 1984. pap. 17.50 (*0-317-11514-6*) CU Ctr Career Res.

Managing the Testing Process. Rex E. Black. LC 99-27358. 350p. 1999. pap. 39.99 (*0-7356-0584-X*) Microsoft.

Managing the Total Quality Transformation. Thomas H. Berry. 223p. 1991. 26.95 (*0-07-005071-6*) McGraw.

Managing the Training & Development Function. Allan Pepper. 350p. 1994. 83.95 (*0-566-02977-4*, Pub. by Gower) Ashgate Pub Co.

***Managing the Training Function.** rev. ed. (Illus.). 185p. 2000. spiral bd. 39.95 (*1-57431-158-1*) Tech Trng Systs.

Managing the Training Process: Putting the Principles into Practice. 2nd ed. Mike Wills. LC 98-9618. 321p. 1998. 69.95 (*0-566-08017-6*, Pub. by Gower) Ashgate Pub Co.

Managing the Transport Services Function. 2nd ed. F. Woodward. 334p. 1978. text 68.95 (*0-566-02032-7*) Ashgate Pub Co.

Managing the Troubled Employee. M. Douglas Clark. LC 79-91188. (Illus.). 77p. ring bd. 69.50 (*0-88061-009-3*) Intl Loss Cntrl.

Managing the Unions: The Impact of Legislation on Trade Unions' Behaviour. Ed. by Roger Undy. (Illus.). 336p. 1996. text 69.00 (*0-19-828919-7*) OUP.

Managing the United Kingdom: An Introduction to Its Political Economy & Public Policy. Richard A. Maidment & Grahame Thompson. (Illus.). 288p. (C). 1993. text 59.95 (*0-8039-8850-8*); pap. text 21.95 (*0-8039-8851-6*) Sage.

Managing the University: A Systems Approach. Ed. by Paul W. Hamelman. LC 75-186195. (Special Studies in U. S. Economic, Social & Political Issues). 1972. 32.00 (*0-275-04760-1*) Irvington.

Managing the University Curriculum: Making Common Cause. Ed. by Jean Bocock & David Watson. LC 94-28082. 160p. (Orig.). 1994. 132.00 (*0-335-19340-4*); pap. 34.95 (*0-335-19339-0*) OpUniv Pr.

Managing the Unknowable: Boundaries Between Order & Chaos in Organizations. Ralph D. Stacey. LC 92-17306. (Management Ser.). 28.95p. 1992. text 30.95 (*1-55542-463-5*) Jossey-Bass.

Managing the Unknown: By Creating New Futures. Ed. by Richard Boot et al. LC 94-15999. 1994. 27.95 (*0-07-707626-5*) McGraw.

Managing the Use of Fluoroscopy in Medical Institutions: Report of the Radiation Protection Committee Task Group #6. (Report Ser.: No. 58). 56p. 1998. pap. text 10.00 (*1-888340-13-4*) AAPM.

***Managing the Value Chain.** LC 99-28452. (Review Paperback Ser.). 2000. pap. 19.95 (*1-57851-234-4*) Harvard Busn.

Managing the Veterinary Cancer Patient: A Practice Manual. Gregory K. Ogilvie & Antony S. Moore. LC 94-61975. 540p. 1995. pap. text 68.00 (*1-884254-20-9*) Vet Lrn Syst.

Managing the Violent Patient: A Clinician's Guide. Ed. by Patricia E. Blumenreich & Susan Lewis. LC 93-12563. 176p. 1993. text 24.95 (*0-87630-707-1*) Brunner-Mazel.

***Managing the Web-Based Enterprise.** Jesse Feiler. 1999. 44.95 (*0-12-251339-8*) Morgan Kaufmann.

Managing the Welfare State: Text & Sourcebook. Tony Cutler & Barbara Waine. LC 98-215871. 1998. pap. text 19.50 (*1-85973-932-6*) NYU Pr.

Managing the Welfare State: The Politics of Public Sector Management. Tony Cutler & Barbara Waine. LC 93-23931. 192p. 1994. 47.00 (*0-85496-843-1*) Berg Pubs.

Managing the Windows NT Registry. Paul Robichaux. LC 98-178655. (Illus.). 384p. 1998. pap. 39.95 (*1-56592-378-2*) OReilly & Assocs.

***Managing the Windows 2000 Registry.** Paul Robichaux. Ed. by Robert Denn. (Illus.). 500p. 2000. pap. 39.95 (*1-56592-943-8*) OReilly & Assocs.

***Managing the Workforce: Challenges in the Manufacturing Industry.** Bikash Bhadury. LC 00-33274. 2000. pap. write for info. (*0-7619-9414-9*) Pine Forge.

Managing the Workplace Survivors: Organizational Downsizing & the Commitment Gap. Marvin R. Gottlieb & Lori Conkling. LC 95-4247. 248p. 1995. 59.95 (*0-89930-922-4*, Quorum Bks) Greenwood.

***Managing the World Economy.** John Mills. LC 00-42239. 2000. write for info. (*0-312-23579-8*) St Martin.

Managing the World Economy: Fifty Years after Bretton Woods. Ed. by Peter B. Kenen. LC 94-22350. 430p. (Orig.). (C). 1994. pap. text 25.00 (*0-88132-212-1*) Inst Intl Eco.

Managing the World Economy: The Consequences of Corporate Alliances. Peter F. Cowhey & Jonathan Aronson. LC 92-42450. 363p. 1993. reprint ed. pap. 112.60 (*0-608-02009-5*, 206266500003) Bks Demand.

M

An Asterisk (*) at the beginning of an entry indicates that the title is appearing for the first time.

Managing the World Economy: Will We Ever Learn? Stephen Marris. LC 84-19344. (Essays in International Finance Ser.: No. 155). 30p. 1984. pap. text 10.00 (*0-88165-062-5*) Princeton U Int Finan Econ.

Managing the World's Forests: Looking for Balance Between Conservation & Development. Ed. by Narendra P. Sharma. 624p. 1993. pap. text, per. 35.95 (*0-8403-7885-8*) Kendall-Hunt.

Managing the Year 2000 Crisis: Strategies & Solutions. Janet G. Butler. LC 98-6661. (Illus.). 225p. 1999. pap. 280.00 (*1-56607-056-2*) Comput Tech Res.

Managing the 4th Level of Change Pb. Price Pritchett. Date not set. pap. 14.00 (*0-88730-975-5*, HarpBusn) HarpInfo.

Managing Through Face-to-Face Communication. Didactic Systems Staff. (Simulation Game Ser.). (POR.). 1969. pap. 35.00 (*0-89401-067-0*) Didactic Syst.

Managing Through Face-to-Face Communication. Didactic Systems Staff. (Simulation Game Ser.). 1969. reprint ed. pap. 26.25 (*0-89401-066-2*) Didactic Syst.

Managing Through Incentives: How to Develop a More Collaborative, Productive & Profitable Organization. Richard B. McKenzie & Dwight R. Lee. LC 98-14526. (Illus.). 352p. 1998. 30.00 (*0-19-511901-0*) OUP.

***Managing Through Organisationss.** 2nd ed. Colin Hales. 2000. pap. write for info. (*1-86152-570-2*) Thomson Learn.

Managing Through Organization: The Management Process, Form of Organization, & the Work of Managers. Colin Hales. LC 92-33981. (Organizational Behaviour & Management Ser.). 240p. (C). (gr. 13). 1993. pap. 71.95 (*0-415-01002-0*, B0187); pap. 29.95 (*0-415-01003-9*, B0191) Thomson Learn.

Managing Through Storms of Change: A New Corporate Agenda for the 90s (Conference Proceedings) 337p. 1988. pap. 75.00 (*0-912841-29-X*) Planning Forum.

Managing Time. 80p. pap. text. write for info. (*0-7506-3324-7*) Buttrwrth-Heinemann.

Managing Time. (Open Learning for Supervisory Management Ser.). 1986. pap. text 19.50 (*0-08-070058-6*, Pergamon Pr) Elsevier.

Managing Time. NEBSM Staff. (Open Learning for Supervisory Management Ser.). 1986. pap. text 19.50 (*0-08-034055-5*, Pergamon Pr) Elsevier.

Managing Time. 2nd ed. (Open Learning Super Ser.). 1991. pap. text 26.00 (*0-08-041543-1*, Pergamon Pr) Elsevier.

Managing Time: A How-to-Do-It Manual for School & Public Librarians. Dian Walster. (How-to-Do-It Ser.). 168p. 1993. 38.50 (*1-55570-127-2*) Neal-Schuman.

Managing Time & Space in the Modern Warehouse: Practices & Procedures in Warehousing - with Ready to Use Forms, Checklists. Ernst Bolten. LC 97-3843. 240p. 1997. spiral bd. 40.00 (*0-8144-7956-1*) AMACOM.

Managing Time & Stress. Gilbert L. Whiteman. Ed. by Stephen D. Bruce. (Management Skills Workshop Ser.). 85p. 1987. reprint ed. pap. text 24.95 (*1-55645-554-2*) Busn Legal Reports.

Managing Time Effectively. Didactic Systems Staff. (Study Units Ser.). 1977. pap. 9.00 (*0-89401-112-X*) Didactic Syst.

Managing Time Effectively. Ronald Dingwall. 54p. (C). 1986. pap. 50.00 (*0-7855-2251-4*, Pub. by Granary) St Mut.

Managing Time for Sales. rev. ed. James C. Campbell. (Skill Centered Leadership Ser.). 4p. 1997. pap., wbk. ed. 12.95 incl. audio (*1-891161-72-5*) ClamShell Pub.

Managing to Achieve Multiple Goals: Financial System Reform in Japan. Christopher Weare & Eugene Smolensky. LC 98-52705. 61p. 1999. pap. 10.00 (*0-87772-386-9*) UCB IGS.

Managing to Be a Non-Smoker. Mike Dowd. 96p. 1991. pap. 9.95 (*0-9630260-9-7*) Dowd Hlthgrp.

Managing to Be Free. 1987. 5.95 (*0-918403-08-1*) Agape Ministries.

***Managing to Be Wealthy: Putting Your Financial Plan & Planner to Work for You.** John E. Sestina. LC 00-24631. (Illus.). 319p. 2000. pap. 19.95 (*0-7931-3716-0*) Dearborn.

***Managing to Care: Case Management & Service System Reform.** Ann E. P. Dill. (Social Institutions & Social Change Ser.). 176p. 2000. pap. text 18.95 (*0-202-30612-7*); lib. bdg. 37.95 (*0-202-30611-9*) Aldine de Gruyter.

Managing to Care: Public Service & the Market. Ann James. LC 94-15824. 1994. pap. text. write for info. (*0-582-23965-6*, Pub. by Addison-Wesley) Longman.

Managing to Communicate: Using Telecommunications for Increased Business Efficiency. M. P. Clark. LC 93-30453. 182p. 1994. pap. 79.95 (*0-471-94188-3*) Wiley.

Managing to Get the Job Done: How to Make Sure Your Employees Are Ready, Willing, & Able to Succeed. Peter A. Land. (Illus.). 110p. 1998. 24.95 (*0-939975-14-9*) Exec Pr NC.

Managing to Get the Job Done: How to Make Sure Your Employees Are Ready, Willing, & Able to Succeed. Peter A. Land. 128p. 1994. 24.95 (*0-471-11279-8*) Wiley.

Managing to Have Fun. Matt Weinstein. 224p. 1997. per. 11.00 (*0-684-82708-5*) S&S Trade.

Managing to Have Profits: The Secrets Japan Learned but the U. S. Forgot. Arnold J. Olenick. (Illus.). xii, 210p. 1992. reprint ed. 14.95 (*1-880561-00-X*) CashFlow Bks.

Managing to Keep the Customer: How to Achieve & Maintain Superior Customer Service Throughout the Organization. rev. ed. Robert L. Desatnick & Denis H. Detzel. LC 93-6842. 235p. 1993. 28.50 (*1-55542-415-5*) Jossey-Bass.

Managing to Learn. Patrick Whitaker. Ed. by Ron Best & Peter J. Lang. (Studies in Pastoral Care, Personal & Social Education). 176p. 1996. pap. text 37.95 (*0-304-32782-4*) Continuum.

Managing to Learn. Patrick Whitaker. Ed. by Ron Best & Peter J. Lang. (Studies in Pastoral Care, Personal & Social Education). 176p. 1996. text 100.00 (*0-304-32783-2*) Continuum.

***Managing to Make a Difference.** Bowden. 398p. 2000. 84.95 (*1-84014-859-4*) Ashgate Pub Co.

Managing to Make It. Furstenberg. LC 98-27071. 1999. 32.50 (*0-226-27391-1*) U Ch Pr.

Managing to Relate. Stephen Schoonover. (C). 1988. 22.95 (*0-201-15781-0*) Addison-Wesley.

Managing to Relate: Special Edition for General Electric. S. C. Schoonover. (C). 1988. pap. text 23.95 (*0-201-11059-8*) Addison-Wesley.

Managing to Stay Non-Union. Charles L. Hughes & Alfred DeMaria. 1979. pap. 13.95 (*0-917386-26-4*) Exec Ent Pubns.

Managing to Stay Non-Union. Charles L. Hughes & Alfred DeMaria. 196p. 1994. pap. 59.95 (*0-471-11281-X*) Wiley.

Managing to Succeed: Strategies & Systems for Manufacturing Business. Graham Smith. LC 95-22657. 512p. 1995. pap. 66.00 (*0-13-230376-0*) P-H.

Managing to Survive: Managerial Practice in Not-For-Profit Organisations. Alun C. Jackson & Frances H. Donovan. 247p. 1999. pap. 26.95 (*0-335-20353-1*) OpUniv Pr.

Managing to Survive: Working Lives in Small Firms. Monder Ram. (Warwick Studies in Industrial Relations). 256p. (C). 1994. 64.95 (*0-631-19109-7*) Blackwell Pubs.

Managing to Survive ; Five Lectures on the Industrial Future. Harold A. Watkinson. LC 75-327955. 35 p. 1975. write for info. (*0-563-10960-2*) BBC.

Managing to Teach. 2nd ed. Carol Cummings. (Illus.). 168p. (Orig.). (C). 1996. pap. text 14.95 (*0-9614574-0-6*) Teaching WA.

Managing Today! Stephen P. Robbins. LC 96-19873. 584p. (C). 1996. text 84.00 (*0-13-233313-9*) P-H.

Managing Today. 2nd ed. (C). 2000. pap. write for info. (*0-13-016496-8*); pap. write for info. (*0-13-016495-X*) P-H.

Managing Today. 2nd ed. Robbins. LC 98-50314. (Illus.). 651p. 1999. text 96.00 incl. audio compact disk (*0-13-011672-6*) P-H.

***Managing Today: Pwrpt Tran&tchnote.** 2nd ed. 1999. write for info. (*0-13-012435-4*) P-H.

Managing Today & Tomorrow. Thomas W. Johnson & John E. Stinson. LC 77-76123. (Illus.). 1978. text. write for info. (*0-201-03487-5*) Addison-Wesley.

Managing Today's Public Library: Blueprint for Change. Darlene E. Weingand. (Illus.). x, 185p. 1994. lib. bdg. 30.00 (*0-87287-807-4*) Libs Unl.

Managing Today's University. Frederick E. Balderston. LC 74-9111. (Jossey-Bass Higher Education Ser.). 325p. 1974. reprint ed. pap. 100.80 (*0-608-14785-0*, 202564900045) Bks Demand.

Managing Today's University: Strategies for Viability, Change, & Excellence. 2nd ed. Frederick E. Balderston. LC 94-25143. 421p. 1995. text 36.95 (*0-7879-0072-9*) Jossey-Bass.

Managing Tomorrow's High-Performance Unions. Thomas A. Hannigan. LC 97-15988. 320p. 1998. 59.95 (*1-56720-102-4*, Quorum Bks) Greenwood.

Managing Tools for Developing Information Systems. Ronald B. Smith. (Illus.). 200p. 1986. pap. text 19.95 (*0-89433-289-9*) Petrocelli.

Managing Tough Times. 96p. pap. text. write for info. (*0-7506-3323-9*) Buttrwrth-Heinemann.

Managing Tourism. S. Medlik. LC 91-140078. (Illus.). 358p. 1991. reprint ed. pap. 111.00 (*0-608-07965-0*, 206793700012) Bks Demand.

Managing Tourism. Ed. by S. Medlik. LC 95-195718. (Illus.). 358p. 1991. reprint ed. pap. 111.00 (*0-608-08866-8*, 206950500004) Bks Demand.

Managing Tourism Growth: Issues & Applications. Fred P. Bosselman et al. LC 99-10999. (Illus.). 420p. 1999. pap. 40.00 (*1-55963-605-X*) Island Pr.

***Managing Tourism In Cities.** Duncan Tyler et al. LC 98-5756. 264p. 1998. 74.95 (*0-471-98315-2*) Wiley.

Managing Tourism Services J. A. Bennett. LC 97-118978. 444p. 1995. write for info. (*0-627-01939-0*) J L Van Schaik.

Managing Toward the Millennium. Ed. by James E. Hennessy & Suki Robins. LC 90-55921. xiv, 303p. 1990. 25.00 (*0-8232-1298-X*); pap. 15.00 (*0-8232-1299-8*) Fordham.

Managing Towards Self-Reliance: Effectiveness of Organizations in Africa. Piet Human & Andre Zaaiman. LC 96-208836. 226p. 1997. pap. 22.95 (*0-620-18881-2*, Pub. by Juta & Co) Intl Spec Bk.

Managing Trade Relations in the New World Economy. Thomas Andersson. LC 93-9831. 192p. (C). (gr. 13). 1993. 85.00 (*0-415-09568-9*) Routledge.

Managing Training & Development in Museums: A Guide. Elaine J. Kilgour. LC 99-234515. 200p. 1997. pap. 65.00 (*0-11-495853-X*, Pub. by Statnry Office) Balogh.

Managing Training & Development Systems. William R. Tracey. LC 73-82721. 492p. 1974. reprint ed. pap. 152.60 (*0-608-14413-4*, 205169600002) Bks Demand.

Managing Training Resources & Learner Support 4. IPM Staff. (Training Design & Management Ser.: No. 4). (C). 1994. pap. 93.00 (*0-08-042167-9*, Pub. by IPM Hse) St Mut.

Managing Transboundary Stocks of Small Pelagic Fish: Problems & Options. Max Aguero & Exequiel Gonzalez. LC 96-21473. (World Bank Discussion Papers: No. 329). 56p. 1996. pap. 22.00 (*0-8213-3659-2*) World Bank.

Managing Transfer Training: Action-Packed Strategies to Ensure High Payoff from Training Investments. John W. Newstrom & Mary Broad. (Illus.). 194p. 1992. pap. 30.00 (*0-201-19274-8*) Addison-Wesley.

***Managing Transfers of Undertakings.** A. Wright. (Financial Times Management Briefings Ser.). 1998. pap. 94.50 (*0-273-63889-0*, Pub. by F T P-H) Trans-Atl Phila.

Managing Transition. N. K. Gupta & A. Ahmad. 1994. write for info. (*81-224-0668-8*, Pub. by Wiley Estrn) Franklin.

***Managing Transition & Change.** Michele Masterfano. 124p. 2000. write for info. (*1-58692-033-2*) Copyright Mgmt.

Managing Transitions: Making the Most of Change. William Bridges. (Illus.). 276p. 1991. pap. 19.00 (*0-201-55073-3*) Addison-Wesley.

Managing Traumatic Stress Through Art: Drawing from the Center. Barry M. Cohen et al. LC 95-68155. xviii, 174p. (Orig.). 1995. pap. 19.95 (*0-9629164-7-1*) Sidran Pr.

Managing Truancy in Schools. David Collins. LC 99-167631. 224p. 1999. 75.00 (*0-304-70300-1*); pap. 26.50 (*0-304-70301-X*) Continuum.

Managing Truck Fleet Operations. American Feed Manufacturers Association Staff & American Feed Manufacturers Association. 196p. 1983. 35.00 (*0-318-12576-5*, 024) Am Feed Industry.

Managing Turbulent Hearts: A Balinese Formula for Living. Unni Wikan. (Illus.). 392p. 1990. pap. text 22.00 (*0-226-89680-3*); lib. bdg. 66.00 (*0-226-89678-1*) U Ch Pr.

Managing Turfgrass Pests. Thomas L. Watschke et al. (Advances in Turfgrass Science Ser.). 384p. 1994. lib. bdg. 85.00 (*0-87371-999-9*, L999) Lewis Pubs.

Managing 12 Volts: How to Upgrade, Operate & Troubleshoot 12 Volt Systems. Harold Barre. LC 95-92383. (Illus.). 213p. (Orig.). 1996. pap. 19.95 (*0-9647386-1-9*) Summer Breeze Pub.

Managing Type Two Diabetes: Your Invitation to a Healthier Lifestyle. 2nd rev. ed. Arlene Monk et al. LC 87-20218. 192p. 1996. 11.95 (*1-885115-26-1*) Wiley.

Managing Uncertainty: A Pragmatic Approach. Harry Katzan, Jr. LC 92-16554. 320p. (C). (gr. 13). 1992. per. 52.95 (*0-442-01114-8*, Chap & Hall CRC) CRC Pr.

Managing Uncertainty: Regulating Immigration Flows in Advanced Industrial Countries. Demetrios G. Papademetriou & Kimberly Hamilton. (International Migration Policy Issues Ser.). 42p. 1995. pap. 8.95 (*0-87003-069-8*) Carnegie Endow.

Managing Uncertainty in Expert Systems. Jerzy W. Grzymala-Busse. (C). 1991. text 102.00 (*0-7923-9169-1*) Kluwer Academic.

Managing Uncertainty in the House of Representatives: Adaptation & Innovation in Special Rules. Stanley J. Bach & Steven S. Smith. 154p. 1988. 28.95 (*0-8157-0742-8*); pap. 10.95 (*0-8157-0741-X*) Brookings.

***Managing Unique Assignments: A Team Approach to Projects & Programmes.** Kor R. Twynstra & Mijnen G. Twynstra. LC 99-73719. 360p. 2000. 87.95 (*0-566-08279-9*, Pub. by Gower) Ashgate Pub Co.

Managing University Libraries. R. G. Prasher. (Illus.). 350p. 1991. 45.00 (*1-55528-250-4*, Pub. by Today Tomorrow) Scholarly Pubns.

***Managing Unmanageable Students: Practical Solutions for Administrators.** Elaine K. McEwan & Mary Damer. LC 99-50495. (Illus.). 192p. (C). 1999. pap. 32.95 (*0-8039-6787-X*); lib. bdg. 69.95 (*0-8039-6786-1*) Corwin Pr.

Managing Unstable Angina. (Clinical Practice Guidelines: No. 10). 20p. 1994. pap. 15.00 (*0-16-045276-7*) USGPO.

***Managing Up! 59 Ways to Build a Career-Advancing Relationship with Your Boss.** Michael S. Dobson & Deborah S. Dobson. LC 99-43413. 176p. 1999. pap. 16.95 (*0-8144-7042-4*) AMACOM.

Managing Upside Down: The Seven Intentions of Values-Centered Leadership. Tom Chappell. LC 99-38734. (Illus.). 240p. 1999. 25.00 (*0-688-17069-2*, Wm Morrow) Morrow Avon.

Managing Upward: Strategies for Succeeding with Your Boss. Patti Hathaway & Susan D. Schubert. Ed. by Kay Keppler. LC 91-76249. (Fifty-Minute Ser.). 118p. (Orig.). 1992. pap. 10.95 (*1-56052-131-7*) Crisp Pubns.

Managing Upwards. Jonathan Coates. LC 94-173. 112p. 1994. 51.95 (*0-566-07485-0*) Ashgate Pub Co.

Managing Urban America. 5th ed. David R. Morgan & Robert E. England. LC 98-53700. (Illus.). 416p. (C). 1998. pap. text 32.95 (*1-56643-065-8*, Chatham House Pub) Seven Bridges.

Managing Urban Government Services: Strategies, Tools, & Techniques for the Eighties. James L. Mercer et al. LC 81-66228. 256p. reprint ed. pap. 79.40 (*0-608-12155-X*, 202391200034) Bks Demand.

Managing Urban Growth in the Developing World. C. M. Rogerson. text 59.95 (*0-470-22111-9*); pap. text 24.95 (*0-470-22112-7*) Wiley.

Managing Urban Transportation As a Business. Ed. by Eric Bers & Chris Hendrickson. 382p. 1987. 32.00 (*0-87262-627-X*) Am Soc Civil Eng.

Managing Urban Transportation with Limited Resources. Ed. by Tom K. Ryden. 108p. 1983. pap. 5.00 (*0-87262-363-7*) Am Soc Civil Eng.

Managing Urinary Incontinence in the Elderly. John Schnelle. LC 90-10430. 144p. 1991. 48.00 (*0-8261-7360-8*) Springer Pub.

Managing Usenet. David Lawrence & Henry Spencer. 508p. 1998. pap. 32.95 (*1-56592-198-4*) OReilly & Assocs.

Managing User-Centred Libraries & Information Services. 2nd rev. ed. K. G. Bakewell et al. (Illus.). 290p. (C). 1996. text 110.00 (*0-7201-2270-8*) Continuum.

Managing UUCP & USENET. 10th ed. Tim O'Reilly & Grace Todino. (Computer Science). 368p. 1992. pap. 27.95 (*0-937175-93-5*) Thomson Learn.

Managing Value for Money in the Public Sector. Jonathan G. Bates. LC 92-38464. 264p. 1993. mass mkt. 79.95 (*0-412-46360-1*) Chapman & Hall.

Managing Violence in the Workplace. Thomas K. Capozzoli & R. Steve McVey. 152p. 1996. boxed set 49.95 (*1-57444-033-0*) St Lucie Pr.

Managing Virtual Private Networks. David Leon Clark. LC 99-35354. 1999. pap. text 55.00 (*0-07-135202-3*) McGraw.

Managing Virtual Teams: Practical Techniques for High-Techology Project Managers. Martha Haywood. LC 98-33847. 1998. 65.00 (*0-89006-913-1*) Artech Hse.

Managing Vocal Health. Cristine M. Sapienza et al. (Excellence in Singing Ser.: Vol. 5). Date not set. pap. 39.95 (*1-877761-20-6*) Pst.

Managing Voluntary & Non-Profit Organizations: Strategy & Structure. Richard Butler & David C. Wilson. LC 89-20437. 204p. reprint ed. pap. 63.30 (*0-608-20406-4*, 207165900002) Bks Demand.

Managing Volunteers. International Festivals & Events Assoc. Staff. Ed. by Steve Kennedy. 104p. 1996. pap. 44.95 (*1-891202-05-7*) Intl Festivals.

Managing Volunteers Effectively. Phil McSweeney & Don Alexander. LC 96-84014. 176p. 1996. 55.95 (*1-85742-294-5*, Pub. by Arena); pap. 33.95 (*1-85742-293-7*, Pub. by Arena) Ashgate Pub Co.

Managing Warehouse & Distribution Operations. Theodore H. Allegri, Sr. LC 93-17608. 336p. (C). 1993. text 79.95 (*0-13-564618-9*) P-H.

Managing Wastewater in Coastal Urban Areas. National Research Council Staff. LC 93-1845. 496p. (Orig.). (C). 1993. text 49.95 (*0-309-04826-5*) Natl Acad Pr.

Managing Water: Coping with Scarcity & Abundance. Ed. by Marchall English & Andras Szollosi-Nagy. LC 97-17973. (Water for a Changing Global Community Ser.). 960p. 1997. 64.00 (*0-7844-0271-X*) Am Soc Civil Eng.

Managing Water As an Economic Resource. James T. Winpenny. LC 93-10560. 176p. (C). 1994. pap. 18.95 (*0-415-10378-9*) Routledge.

Managing Water-Drive Gas Reservoirs. Gas Research Institute Staff. 1994. 55.00 (*0-88415-104-2*, 5104) Gulf Pub.

Managing Water for Drought: National Study of Water Management During Drought. William J. Werick & William Whipple, Jr. (Illus.). 180p. (C). 1997. reprint ed. pap. text 40.00 (*0-7881-4171-6*) DIANE Pub.

Managing Water for Peace in the Middle East: Alternative Strategies. Masahiro Murakami. LC 96-149708. 309p. 1997. pap. write for info. (*92-808-0858-3*, Pub. by UN Univ Pr) Brookings.

Managing Water Quality: Economics, Technology, Institutions. Allen V. Kneese & Blair T. Bower. LC 84-17998. 328p. 1984. pap. 18.95 (*0-915707-13-6*) Resources Future.

Managing Water-Related Conflicts: The Engineer's Role. Warren Viessman, Jr. & Ernest T. Smerdon. 293p. 1990. pap. text 5.00 (*0-87262-744-6*) Am Soc Civil Eng.

Managing Water Resources. Ed. by John Cairns, Jr. & Ruth Patrick. LC 86-18215. (Environmental Regeneration Ser.). 144p. 1986. 49.95 (*0-275-92200-6*, C2200, Praeger Pubs) Greenwood.

Managing Water Resources During Global Change: AWRA 28 Annual Conference & Symposium, an International Conference, Reno, NV, November 1-5, 1992. American Water Resources Association Staff. Ed. by Raymond Herrmann. LC 92-74227. (American Water Resources Association Technical Publication Ser.: Vol. TPS-92-4). (Illus.). 874p. 1992. reprint ed. pap. 200.00 (*0-7837-9224-7*, 204997500004) Bks Demand.

Managing Water Resources in the West under Conditions of Climate Uncertainty: A Proceedings. National Research Council Staff. 358p. (C). 1991. pap. text 39.00 (*0-309-04677-7*) Natl Acad Pr.

***Managing Water Supply & Sanitation in Emergencies.** John Adams. (Skills & Practice Ser.). 1999. pap. text 15.00 (*0-85598-378-7*) Oxfam Pubns.

Managing Watersheds: Combining Water Quality Protection & Community Planning. Graham Trelstad et al. (Illus.). 112p. (Orig.). Date not set. pap. text. write for info. (*0-938085-07-7*) Regional Plan Assn.

***Managing Web-Based Training: How to Keep Your Program on Track & Make It Successful.** Alan L. Ellis et al. LC 99-72434. 180p. 1999. pap. 27.95 (*1-56286-115-8*) Am Soc Train & Devel.

***Managing Web-Enabled Technologies in Organizations: A Global Perspective.** Ed. by Mehdi Khosrowpour. LC 99-48157. 300p. (C). 2000. pap. 69.95 (*1-878289-72-1*) Idea Group Pub.

***Managing Welfare Reform in Five States: The Challenge of Devolution.** Sarah F. Liebschutz. LC 00-42211. 2000. pap. write for info. (*0-914341-77-4*, Rockefeller Inst Pr) Nelson Rockefeller Inst Govt.

Managing White & Lutz Spruce Stands in South-Central Alaska for Increased Resistance to Spruce Beetle. John S. Hard & Edward H. Holsten. (Illus.). 30p. 1997. reprint ed. pap. 4.00 (*0-89904-927-3*, Ecosytems Resrch) Crumb Elbow Pub.

Managing Wild Turkeys in Florida. Lovett E. Williams, Jr. (Illus.). 104p. (Orig.). 1992. pap. 3.00 (*0-9624809-1-6*) Real Turkeys Pubs.

Managing Wildlife: On Private Lands in Alabama & the Southeast. Greg K. Yarrow et al. LC 98-35971. 1998. write for info. (*1-58173-157-4*) Sweetwater Pr.

Managing Wildlife As an Agricultural Enterprise. 245p. 1997. pap. text, teacher ed. 65.95 (0-86691-257-6, FBM1650IT); pap. text, student ed. 35.95 (0-86691-258-4, FBM1660IW) Deere & Co.

Managing Wildlife As an Agricultural Enterprise: A Practical Guide Book to Increasing Agricultural Revenue. 150p. 1997. pap. text 25.95 (0-86691-251-7, FBM1610INC) Deere & Co.

*__Managing Wildlife Habitat on Golf Courses.__ Ronald G. Dodson. LC 99-53028. (Illus.). 177p. 2000. 45.00 (1-57504-028-X, Ann Arbor Press) Sleepng Bear.

*__Managing Windows NT Logons.__ Kathy Ivens. Ed. by Sue Miller. LC 99-89457. (Illus.). 224p. 2000. pap. 29.95 (1-56592-637-4) OReilly & Assocs.

Managing Windows NT Server. 1997. 49.99 (1-56205-795-2) New Riders Pub.

*__Managing Windows 2000 Network Services.__ Syngress Media Staff. (Illus.). 608p. 2000. pap. 49.95 (1-928994-06-7) Syngress.

Managing Wine & Wine Sales. Joseph Fattorini. 200p. 1997. mass mkt. 18.99 (0-412-72190-2) Chapman & Hall.

Managing with a Conscience: How to Improve. Frank K. Sonnenberg. (Illus.). 261p. 1996. pap. 14.95 (0-07-059660-3) McGraw.

Managing with a Global Mindset. Jean-Pierre Jeannet. 272p. 2000. 28.00 (0-273-63276-0, Pub. by F T P-H) Trans-Atl Phila.

Managing with a Heart: 100 Plus Ways to Make Your Employees Feel Appreciated. Sharon Good. LC 94-21636. (Illus.). 64p. (Orig.). 1994. pap. 8.95 (1-885064-00-4) Excalibur Pub.

Managing with Appraisal: Achieving Quality Schools Through Management. David Trethowan. 1991. pap. 34.00 (1-85396-135-3, Pub. by P Chapman) Taylor & Francis.

Managing with Authority. Nebsm Staff. 96p. pap. text. write for info. (0-7506-3310-7) Buttrwrth-Heinemann.

Managing with Dual Strategies: Mastering the Present, Preempting the Future. Derek F. Abell. 294p. 1993. 32.95 (0-02-900145-5) Free Pr.

Managing With Infomation Technology. Bullen. 1995. text, teacher ed. 23.00 (0-07-008913-2) McGraw.

Managing with Information Technology. Ed. by Richard Ennals & Phil Molyneux. LC 93-6018. (Illus.). 297p. 1993. 46.95 (0-387-19795-8) Spr-Verlag.

Managing with Integrity: Insights from America's CEOs. Charles E. Watson. LC 90-48582. 392p. 1991. 49.95 (0-275-93865-4, C3865, Praeger Pubs) Greenwood.

Managing with Integrity for Long Term Care. K. J. Langlais. LC 97-10673. 250p. 1997. 35.00 (0-7863-1097-9, Irwn Prfssnl) McGraw-Hill Prof.

Managing with Less: A Book of Readings. Ed. by Elizabeth K. Kellar. LC 79-26163. 160p. 1979. pap. 12.00 (0-87326-995-0) Intl City-Cnty Mgt.

Managing with Microsoft Project. Lisa Bucki. (Essentials Ser.). 528p. 1996. per. 35.00 (0-7615-0688-8) Prima Pub.

*__Managing with Microsoft Project.__ Prima. 2000. pap. 39.95 (0-7615-1986-6) Prima Pub.

*__Managing with Microsoft Project 98.__ Lisa Bucki. LC 97-75645. 528p. 1998. per. 29.99 (0-7615-1420-1) Prima Pub.

Managing with Passion: Making the Most of Your Job & Your Life. Sigmund G. Ginsburg. LC 96-222172. 254p. 1996. pap. 14.95 (0-471-14558-0) Wiley.

Managing with People. Raymond J. Burby. 1968. pap. text 9.00 (0-201-00723-1) Addison-Wesley.

Managing with People: A Manager's Handbook of Organization Development. 2nd ed. Jack K. Fordyce & Raymond Weil. 1979. 19.95 (0-201-02031-9) Addison-Wesley.

Managing With People In Mind. Harvard Business School Press Staff. 250p. 1991. pap. 3500.00 (0-07-103325-4) McGraw.

Managing with Power. Pfeffer. 400p. 1992. 34.95 (0-07-103360-2) McGraw.

Managing with Power: Politics & Influence in Organizations. Jeffrey Pfeffer. LC 91-26237. 400p. 1992. 24.95 (0-87584-314-X) Harvard Busn.

Managing with Power: Politics & Influence in Organizations. Jeffrey Pfeffer. 400p. 1994. pap. 16.95 (0-87584-440-5) Harvard Busn.

Managing with Power: Politics & Influence in Organizations. Jeffrey Pfeffer. 1993. pap. text 16.95 (0-07-103452-8) McGraw.

Managing with Scarce Resources. Ed. by William B. Simpson. LC 85-645339. (New Directions for Institutional Research Ser.: No. IR 79). 99p. (Orig.). 1993. pap. 22.00 (1-55542-724-3) Jossey-Bass.

Managing with Success. Orley R. Herron. 80p. 1996. write for info. (1-889555-06-1) Stephen Aubry.

Managing with Systems Thinking: Making Dynamics Work for You in Business Decision Making. Michael Balle. LC 94-7631. 1994. 21.95 (0-07-707951-5) McGraw.

Managing with the Power of NLP: Neuro-Linguistic Programming for Competitive Advantage. David Molden. (Illus.). 225p. (Orig.). 1996. pap. 17.95 (0-273-62063-0) F T P-H.

Managing with the Wisdom of Love: Uncovering Virtue in People & Organizations. Dorothy Marcic. LC 97-1668. (Jossey-Bass Business & Management Ser.). 1997. 25.95 (0-7879-0173-3) Jossey-Bass.

Managing with Wisdom. Jack H. Grossman. LC 95-31933. 160p. 1996. 17.95 (1-56554-112-X) Pelican.

Managing Without Management: A Post-Management Manifesto for Business Simplicity. Richard Koch & Ian Godden. LC 96-20244. (Illus.). 256p. 1998. pap. 16.00 (1-85788-166-4) Nicholas Brealey.

*__Managing without Profit: The Art of Managing Third Sector Organizations.__ Mike Hudson. 336p. 1999. pap. 22.95 (0-14-026953-3, Pub. by Pnguin Bks Ltd) Trafalgar.

Managing Women: Feminism & Power in Educational Management. Sue Adler et al. LC 92-34666. (Gender & Education Ser.). 144p. 1993. pap. 30.95 (0-335-15780-7) OpUniv Pr.

Managing Work & Family. (Illus.). 96p. 1997. write for info. (0-945100-66-3) Parlay Intl.

Managing Work & Family Life: The U. S. Response. Viola M. Lechner & Michael Creedon. (Social Work Ser.). (Illus.). 200p. 1994. 34.95 (0-8261-8470-7) Springer Pub.

Managing Work-in-Process Inventory. Kenneth Kivenko. (Industrial Engineering Ser.: Vol. 5). (Illus.). 240p. 1981. text 135.00 (0-8247-1268-4) Dekker.

Managing Worker Safety & Health for Excellence. Margaret Richardson. LC 97-9095. (Illus.). 416p. 1997. 59.95 (0-442-02393-6, VNR) Wiley.

Managing Worker Safety Health. Margaret R. Richardson. (Occupational Health & Safety Ser.). 382p. 1997. 69.95 (0-471-28801-2, VNR) Wiley.

Managing Worker's Compensation: A Guide to Injury Reduction & Effective Claim Management. Keith Wertz & C. Bradley Layton. (Occupational Safety & Health Guide Ser.). Date not set. 59.95 (1-56670-348-4, L1348) Lewis Pubs.

*__Managing Workforce Diversity in Organizations.__ Mak Khojasteh. 244p. (C). 1998. pap. text 39.95 (0-87563-742-6) Stipes.

Managing Workforce Reduction: An International Survey. Ed. by Michael Cross. LC 84-18088. 224p. 1985. 57.95 (0-275-90080-0, C0080, Praeger Pubs) Greenwood.

Managing Workforce 2000: Gaining the Diversity Advantage. David Jamieson & Julie O'Mara. LC 90-22120. (Management Ser.). 272p. 1991. text 30.95 (1-55542-264-0) Jossey-Bass.

Managing Workplace Conflict. Jean Lebedun. Ed. by Karen M. Miller. LC 98-72097. (How-to Book Ser.). 104p. 1998. pap. 12.95 (1-884926-93-2, SOLV2) Amer Media.

*__Managing Workplace Negativity.__ Gary S. Topchik. 2000. 21.95 (0-8144-0582-7) AMACOM.

Managing Workplace Stress. Cary L. Cooper & Susan Cartwright. LC 96-25274. 185p. 1996. 34.00 (0-7619-0192-2); pap. 15.95 (0-7619-0193-0) Sage.

*__Managing World Economic Change: International Political Economy.__ 3rd ed. Robert A. Isaak. LC 99-39016. 354p. (C). 1999. pap. text 47.00 (0-13-011775-7) P-H.

Managing World Economic Change: International Political Economy. 3rd ed. Ed. by Prentice-Hall Staff. (C). 2000. text. write for info. (0-13-040211-7) P-H.

*__Managing Your Academic Career: Strategies for Success.__ Royce Sadler. 224p. 2000. pap. 24.95 (1-86448-984-7, Pub. by Allen & Unwin Pty) Paul & Co Pubs.

Managing Your Anxiety: Regaining Control When You Feel Stressed, Helpless & Alone. Christopher J. McCullough. Ed. by Robert W. Mann. 320p. 1994. reprint ed. mass mkt. 6.50 (0-425-14295-7) Berkley Pub.

Managing Your Band: Artist Management: The Ultimate Responsibility. 2nd rev. ed. Stephen Marcone. LC 99-176419. 250p. (Orig.). 1998. pap. text 27.95 (0-9651250-2-5) HiMarks Pubng.

*__Managing Your Bluewater Cruise.__ Rory Burke. 2000. pap. 29.95 (0-473-03822-6) PROMATEC Intl.

*__Managing Your Boss & Colleagues.__ Steve Gravett. (Business & Management Ser.). (Illus.). 144p. 1999. pap. 19.95 (1-85703-498-8, Pub. by How To Bks) Trans-Atl Phila.

Managing Your Business: Milady's Guide to the Salon. Edgerton. LC 93-8191. (SalonOvations Ser.). 212p. 1992. pap. 24.95 incl. audio (1-56253-084-4) Milady Pub.

*__Managing Your Business Accounts: How to Keep the Books & Maintain Financial Control Over Your Business.__ 5th ed. Peter Taylor. (Small Business Ser.). (Illus.). 229p. 1999. pap. 19.95 (1-85703-536-4, Pub. by How To Bks) Trans-Atl Phila.

Managing Your Business for Profitable Results! Edward E. Hubbard. 180p. 1990. pap. 19.95 (1-883733-09-X) Global Insghts.

Managing Your Business with QuickBooks 6. 2nd ed. Charles Rubin & Diane Parssinen. LC 98-228290. 312p. (C). 1998. pap. text 19.95 (0-201-35356-3, Pub. by Peachpit Pr) Addison-Wesley.

Managing Your Career. D. Unwin. 1996. pap. 129.00 (1-85953-030-3, Pub. by Tech Comm) St Mut.

Managing Your Career. Don Urwin. (Financial Times Management Briefings Ser.). 1997. pap. 94.50 (0-273-63184-5, Pub. by F T P-H) Trans-Atl Phila.

*__Managing Your Career for Dummies.__ Max Messmer. (For Dummies (Lifestyles) Ser.). 384p. 2000. pap. 19.99 (0-7645-5253-8) IDG Bks.

Managing Your Career in a Changing Workplace: Taking Control of Your Career. Jane Ballback & Jan Slater. LC 96-85724. (Personal Growth & Development Collection). (Illus.). 123p. 1996. pap. 14.95 (1-883553-76-8) R Chang Assocs.

Managing Your Career in Nursing. Frances C. Henderson & Barbara O. McGettigan. 276p. (C). 1986. pap. text 17.25 (0-201-12958-2) Addison-Wesley.

Managing Your Career in Nursing. 2nd ed. Barbara McGettigan & Frances Henderson. LC 95-102019. 1994. 24.95 (0-88737-629-0) Natl League Nurse.

Managing Your Career with Power. Gerald M. Sturman. 1990. write for info. (0-9626887-1-1) Bierman Hse.

Managing Your Child's Crohn's Disease & Ulcerative Colitis. Keith J. Benkov & Harland S. Winter. 200p. 1995. 21.95 (1-57101-023-8) MasterMedia Pub.

Managing Your Child's Eating Problems During Cancer Treatments. (Illus.). 32p. (Orig.). (C). 1995. pap. text 15.00 (0-7881-1964-8) DIANE Pub.

Managing Your City or Town: A Reference Guide for the New Public Official. Kenton G. Griffin. LC 93-44355. 292p. (Orig.). (C). 1994. pap. text 37.50 (0-8191-9404-2); lib. bdg. 62.50 (0-8191-9403-4) U Pr of Amer.

Managing Your Classroom. Barbara Gruber. (Instant Idea Bks.). (Illus.). 64p. 1983. 7.95 (0-86734-048-7, FS-8302) Schaffer Pubns.

Managing Your College Experince. 2nd ed. Lee. 226p. (C). 1998. pap. text 16.90 (0-536-01288-1) Pearson Custom.

Managing Your Computer Physique: How to Manage the Human Body in a Computer Environment. Maribeth C. Yarnell. (Illus.). 69p. (Orig.). 1994. pap. 12.95 (1-885879-00-8) Eaglecliff.

Managing Your Documentation Projects. JoAnn T. Hackos. 656p. 1994. pap. 49.99 (0-471-59099-1) Wiley.

Managing Your Drug or Alcohol Problem Client Workbook. Dennis C. Daley. 1999. pap. text 26.00 (0-12-785039-2) Acad Pr.

Managing Your Drug or Alcohol Problem Therapist Guide. Dennis C. Daley. 1999. pap. text 37.50 (0-12-785038-4) Acad Pr.

Managing Your Emotions Instead of Your Emotions Managing You. Joyce Meyer. 288p. 1997. 17.99 (1-57794-026-1, HH2-026) Harrison Hse.

Managing Your Employees. 1996. pap. text 16.95 (0-89384-302-4) P-H.

Managing Your Employees. George Devine. LC 96-39736. 224p. (C). 1997. pap. text 13.95 (0-13-603341-5) P-H.

*__Managing Your Epilepsy.__ Ilo E. Leppik. (Illus.). 130p. 2000. pap. 29.95 (1-884065-81-3, Hndbks Hlth Care) Assocs in Med.

Managing Your Ewe: And Her Newborn Lambs. rev. ed. Laura Lawson. LC 93-79480. (Illus.). 352p. (Orig.). 1997. pap. 34.95 (0-9633923-1-X) LDF Pubns.

Managing Your Finances. T. W. McRae. LC 97-12805. 1997. 17.99 (1-86152-049-2, Pub. by ITBP) Thomson Learn.

*__Managing Your First Computer: How to Perform Core Tasks & Gain Knowledge & Confidence.__ 2nd ed. Carol Dolman & Marcus Saunders. (Computer Basics Ser.). (Illus.). 144p. 1999. pap. 19.95 (1-85703-502-X, Pub. by How To Bks) Trans-Atl Phila.

Managing Your First Years in Industry: The Essential Guide to Career Transition & Success. David J. Wells. LC 94-29513. 200p. 1994. 29.95 (0-7803-1021-7, PP3707) Inst Electrical.

Managing Your 401(k) It's Just What You Need to Know. Marc Robinson. LC 96-40388. (Your Money Matters Ser.). (Illus.). 40p. (gr. 11). 1997. 4.95 (0-7835-4812-5) Time-Life.

Managing Your Future As an Association: Thinking about Trends & Working with Their Consequences, 1993-2020. Joseph F. Coates & Jennifer Jarret. LC 94-20958. 156p. 1994. 60.00 (0-88034-084-3) Am Soc Assn Execs.

Managing Your Goals. Alec Mackenzie. 1993. 16.00 incl. audio (0-671-87993-6) S&S Trade.

Managing Your Hazardous Waste: A Step-by-Step Guide. Mary Baver & Elizabeth J. Kellar. 214p. 1992. pap. text 79.00 (0-86587-311-9) Gov Insts.

Managing Your Health: Assessment & Action. David A. Birch & Michael J. Cleary. LC 96-1779. (Health Science Ser.). 304p. 1996. pap. 29.50 (0-7637-0139-4) Jones & Bartlett.

Managing Your Health Care: Making the Most of Your Medical Resources. Martin Gipson et al. LC 95-46188. 96p. 1996. pap. 9.95 (0-934793-59-X) Pathfinder CA.

Managing Your Healthcare: A Consumer Guide to Navigating Today's Health Care Systems. William F. McNally. 216p. 1997. pap. 19.95 (1-886346-20-8) Warde Pubs.

*__Managing Your Independent Contract Fleet Survey: A Nationwide Survey of Trucking Companies Utilizing Owner-Operators.__ American Trucking Association National Accounting. 37p. 1999. pap. text 95.00 (0-88711-375-3) Am Trucking Assns.

Managing Your Inheritance: Getting It, Keeping It, Growing It; Making the Most of an Inheritance. Emily Card & Adam Miller. LC 95-13765. 288p. 1997. pap. 15.00 (0-8129-2600-5, Times Bks) Crown Pub Group.

Managing Your Institution's Effectiveness: A User Guide. Midlands Technical College Staff. (AACC Strategies & Solutions Ser.). (Illus.). 102p. 1997. pap. 35.00 (0-87117-299-2, 1392) Comm Coll Pr Am Assn Comm Coll.

Managing Your Investment Manager. 3rd ed. Ed. by Arthur Williams, III. 400p. 1992. text 55.00 (1-55623-515-1, Irwn Prfssnl) McGraw-Hill Prof.

Managing Your Investment Manager: The Complete Guide to Selection, Measurement & Control. 2nd ed. Arthur Williams, III. 250p. 1985. text 45.00 (0-87094-723-0, Irwn Prfssnl) McGraw-Hill Prof.

Managing Your Investments, Savings & Credit: The Basics & Beyond. Esme E. Faerber. (Investor's Quick Reference Ser.). 150p. 1991. per. 14.95 (1-55738-245-X, Irwn Prfssnl) McGraw-Hill Prof.

Managing Your Kitchen & Bathroom Firm's Finances for Profit. Don Quigley. (Illus.). 207p. (Orig.). 1997. pap. text 30.00 (1-887127-10-0, 5302) Natl Kit Bath.

Managing Your Law Practice: The Big Picture Perspective, Developing a Long-Term Strategy for the Legal Industry. John W. Michener, Jr. Ed. by C. Joseph Miles. LC 96-78021. 250p. 1996. pap. text. write for info. (0-7620-0081-3) West Group.

Managing Your Marketing Career. Andrew Crofts. 1991. text 49.95 (0-7506-0152-3) Buttrwrth-Heinemann.

Managing Your Medical Practice. Charles Wold. 1278p. 1988. text 135.00 (1-887515-00-3) AHAB Press.

Managing Your Migraine: A Migraine-Sufferer's Practical Guide. Susan L. Burks. LC 94-4712. 264p. 1994. pap. 14.50 (0-89603-324-4) Humana.

Managing Your Mind: The Mental Fitness Guide. Gillian Butler & Tony Hope. (Illus.). 384p. 1995. pap. 2.00 (0-19-262383-4) OUP.

Managing Your Mind: The Mental Fitness Guide. Gillian Butler & Tony Hope. (Illus.). 448p. 1997. reprint ed. pap. 12.95 (0-19-511125-7) OUP.

Managing Your Mind & Mood Through Food. Judith J. Wurtman. LC 87-45676. (Illus.). 288p. 1988. reprint ed. pap. 13.00 (0-06-097138-X, PL-7138, Perennial) HarperTrade.

*__Managing Your Money.__ Bailey. (Cliffs Consumer Extension Ser.). 128p. 1999. 8.99 (0-7645-8516-9) IDG Bks.

Managing Your Money. Richard Fish. (Christian Living Ser.). 28p. 1991. pap. 3.50 (0-8341-1402-X) Beacon Hill.

Managing Your Money. 2nd ed. Robert K. Heady. LC 98-87594. (Complete Idiot's Guide Ser.). (Illus.). 329p. 1998. pap. text 18.95 (0-02-862722-9) Macmillan Gen Ref.

Managing Your Mouth: An Owner's Manual for Your Most Important Business Asset. Robert L. Genua. LC 92-1406. 192p. 1992. pap. 17.95 (0-8144-7803-4) AMACOM.

Managing Your Move to Object Technology: Guidelines & Strategies for a Smooth Transition. Barry McGibbon. (Managing Object Technology Ser.: No. 2). 290p. 1995. pap. 34.95 (0-13-242009-0) Cambridge U Pr.

*__Managing Your Organization's Records.__ Elizabeth Parker. (Successful LIS Professional Ser.). 181p. 1999. 30.00 (1-85604-335-5, Pub. by Library Association) Bernan Associates.

*__Managing Your Own Learning.__ James R. Davis & Adelaide B. Davis. 200p. 2000. pap. 15.95 (1-57675-067-1) Berrett-Koehler.

Managing Your Own Learning at the University. Aidan Moran. 128p. 1997. pap. 10.95 (1-900621-04-5) Dufour.

Managing Your Own Money: A Financial Guide for the Average Wage Earner. James F. Tucker. LC 87-30594. 1988. 17.95 (0-942637-00-3, Dembner NY) Barricade Bks.

Managing Your Personal Finances. 1991. lib. bdg. 79.95 (0-8490-5050-2) Gordon Pr.

Managing Your Personal Finances. 1997. lib. bdg. 251.99 (0-8490-6125-3) Gordon Pr.

Managing Your Personal Finances. Ryan. (OX - Home Economics Ser.). 1984. mass mkt. 46.95 (0-538-08030-2) S-W Pub.

Managing Your Personal Finances. 2nd ed. Ryan. (HM - Consumer Education Ser.). 1989. mass mkt. 49.95 (0-538-60084-5); mass mkt., wbk. ed. 16.95 (0-538-60085-3) S-W Pub.

Managing Your Personal Finances. 3rd ed. Ryan. (OX - Home Economics Ser.). 1996. mass mkt., wbk. ed. 16.95 (0-538-62897-9) S-W Pub.

Managing Your Personal Finances. 3rd ed. Ryan. (HM - Consumer Education Ser.). 1996. mass mkt. 56.95 (0-538-62896-0) S-W Pub.

Managing Your Personal Finances. 3rd ed. Ryan. (HM - Consumer Education Ser.). 1997. text, teacher ed. 16.95 (0-538-63399-9) S-W Pub.

Managing Your Personal Finances. 3rd ed. Ryan. 1997. pap. 45.25 (0-538-68336-8) Thomson Learn.

*__Managing Your Personal Finances: How to Achieve Your Own Financial Security, Wealth & Independence.__ 3rd ed. John Claxton. (Illus.). 160p. (Orig.). 1999. pap. 19.95 (1-85703-471-6, Pub. by How To Bks) Trans-Atl Phila.

Managing Your Personal Finances: How to Use Savings, Investments, Insurance, & Credit to Best Achieve Your Financial Goals in Times of Inflation, Unemployment & Retirement. 1991. lib. bdg. 79.95 (0-8490-5169-X) Gordon Pr.

Managing Your Personal Finances: Tests. 2nd ed. Ryan. (HM - Consumer Education Ser.). 1989. 3.95 (0-538-60086-1) S-W Pub.

Managing Your Priorities from Start to Success. William J. Bond. (Briefcase Bks.). 156p. 1996. text 16.95 (0-7863-0387-5, Irwn Prfssnl) McGraw-Hill Prof.

Managing Your Renovation or Move to New Offices. Robert E. Weber. LC 86-30583. 254p. 1987. 67.95 (0-89930-245-9, WHT/, Quorum Bks) Greenwood.

Managing Your Rental Properties for Maximum Profit: Save Time & Money with Greg Perry's Fool-Proof System. Greg M. Perry. 288p. 1993. 22.95 (1-55958-314-2) Prima Pub.

Managing Your Reputation: How to Plan & Run Communications Programmes That Win Friends & Build Success. Roger Haywood. LC 94-19178. 1994. 18.95 (0-07-707740-7) McGraw.

Managing Your Safety Manager. Charles V. Culbertson. 46p. 1981. 4.95 (0-937802-01-8) RMSP.

*__Managing Your Sales Team: A Practical Guide to Sales Leadership.__ 2nd ed. John Humphries. 160p. (Orig.). 1999. pap. 19.95 (1-85703-494-5, Pub. by How To Bks) Trans-Atl Phila.

*__Managing Your School Counseling Program: K-12 Developmental Strategies.__ 2nd rev. ed. Joe Wittmer. LC 99-68919. 372p. (Orig.). (C). 2000. pap. 32.95 (0-932796-98-2) Ed Media Corp.

Managing Your Self: Management by Detached Involvement. Jagdish Parikh. (Developmental Management Ser.). 1994. pap. 30.95 (0-631-19307-3) Blackwell Pubs.

Managing Your Software Project: A Student's Guide. Ian W. Ricketts. LC 97-34671. xiii, 103p. (C). 1997. pap. 19.95 (3-540-76046-6) Spr-Verlag.

An Asterisk (*) at the beginning of an entry indicates that the title is appearing for the first time.

Managing Your Stress: How to Relax & Enjoy. rev. ed. Jerry V. Teplitz & Shelly Kellman. LC 81-80175. (Illus.). 128p. 1985. pap. 15.00 (*0-87040-402-4*) Happiness Unltd.

Managing Your Time. Ted W. Engstrom & Alec R. Mackenzie. LC 67-17239. (Orig.). 1968. pap. 4.25 (*0-310-24262-2*, 9572P) Zondervan.

***Managing Your Time.** Iain Maitland. 96p. 2000. pap. 17.95 (*0-8464-5119-0*) Beekman Pubs.

Managing Your Time. Lisa Rogak. LC 99-12221. (Smart Guides Ser.). 192p. 1999. pap. 10.95 (*0-471-31886-8*) Wiley.

Managing Your Time: Practical Guidelines on the Effective Use of Time. rev. ed. Ted W. Engstrom & Alec R. Mackenzie. 240p. 1988. pap. 9.95 (*0-310-24261-4*, 9571P) Zondervan.

Managing Your Time to Achieve Your Goals, Set. pap., wbk. ed. 139.00 incl. audio (*0-7612-0823-2*, 80196); pap., wbk. ed. 30.00 incl. audio (*0-7612-0824-0*, 80197) AMACOM.

***Managing Yourself.** Lisa Davis. LC 99-204259. 96p. 1998. pap. text 44.95 (*0-7506-3661-0*) Buttrwrth-Heinemann.

Managing Yourself: Practical Help for Christians in Personal Planning, Time Scheduling & Self-Control. Stephen B. Douglass & Al Janssen. LC 78-70647. 223p. Date not set. pap. 8.99 (*0-918956-49-8*) Integrtd Res.

Managing Yourself; A Competence Approach to Supervisory Management, Revised ed. Roger Cartwright. LC 98-14602. 1998. pap. text 41.95 (*0-631-20925-5*) Blackwell Pubs.

***Managing Youth Ministry Chaos.** Mike Woodruff. LC 99-44725. 2000. 14.99 (*0-7644-2143-3*) Group Pub.

Managing Youth Violence Prevention: A Guide for Local Governments. William P. Fischer & International City-County Management Association S. LC 96-41292. 1996. write for info. (*0-87326-120-8*) Intl City-Cnty Mgt.

Managment Accounting for Business. David Crowther. 320p. 1999. pap. 52.50 (*0-7487-2246-7*, Pub. by S Thornes Pubs) Trans-Atl Phila.

Managment & Financial Road: Agenda Reference. 208p. 1997. pap. 22.00 (*0-8213-3476-X*, 13476) World Bank.

Managment & Marketing Dictionary, German-English. W. Schafer. (ENG & GER.). 1995. 25.00 (*0-7859-9732-6*) Fr & Eur.

Managment in Museums. Ed. by Kevin Moore. LC 98-30552. 285p. 1999. pap. 33.95 (*0-485-90008-4*, Pub. by Athlone Pr) Transaction Pubs.

Managment of Information Technology. 2nd ed. Frenzel. (C). 1998. pap. 42.00 (*0-7600-5894-6*) Course Tech.

Managua, Nicaragua Earthquake of December 23, 1972. J. F. Meehan et al. 214p. 1973. pap. 12.00 (*0-318-16321-7*, EP-12) Earthquake Eng.

Manalapan & Englishtown. Richard Dalik. (Images of America Ser.). (Illus.). 128p. 1998. pap. 16.99 (*0-7524-0910-7*) Arcadia Publng.

***Manalive.** G. K. Chesterton. LC 00-31388. 2000. pap. write for info. (*0-486-41405-1*) Dover.

Manana: Christian Theology from a Hispanic Perspective. Justo L. Gonzalez. LC 90-36110. 1990. pap. 14.95 (*0-687-23067-5*) Abingdon.

Manana del Armagedon. Nicky Cruz.Tr. of Armageddon by Morning. (SPA.). 275p. 1994. 7.99 (*1-56063-415-4*, 550131) Editorial Unilit.

Manana "Detras del Generalisimo" (Biografia de Bernarda Gomez de Toro) Ena Curnow. LC 93-74825. (Coleccion Cuba y sus Jueces). (SPA., Illus.). 445p. (Orig.). 1995. pap. 29.00 (*0-89729-719-9*) Ediciones.

Mananitas: Black & White Nellie Edge I Can Read & Sing Big Books. Tr. by Hector Pichardo. (Illus.). (J). (ps-2). 1996. 20.00 (*0-922053-40-5*) N Edge Res.

Manantiales de Avivamiento. C PETER WAGNER. 1998. pap. text 9.99 (*0-88113-525-9*) Caribe Betania.

Manantiales en el Desierto. rev. ed. L. B. Cowman. (SPA.). 480p. 1998. pap. 12.50 (*0-311-40056-6*) Baptist Spanish.

Manantiales en el Desierto, No. 2. Charles E. Cowman. Vol. 2.Tr. of Streams in the Dessert. (SPA.). 304p. 1989. pap. 6.99 (*0-945792-51-4*, 498521) Editorial Unilit.

Manantiales en el Desierto: Streams in the Desert. Charles E. Cowman & Antonio Serrano. 1973. reprint ed. pap. 10.50 (*0-311-40028-0*, Edit Mundo) Casa Bautista.

Manantiales en el Desierto: Streams in the Desert. rev. ed. Charles E. Cowman. Ed. by Jose Luis & Violeta Martinez. Tr. by Antonio Serrano from ENG. (SPA.). 368p. 1992. pap. 12.50 (*0-311-40055-8*) Casa Bautista.

Manantiales en el Desierto (Streams in the Desert) Cowman. (SPA.). 1998. 10.99 (*0-88113-022-2*, B000-0222) Caribe Betania.

Manara's Kama Sutra. Milo Manara. Tr. by Joe Johnson from FRE. LC 98-193978. (Illus.). 67p. 1998. pap. 12.95 (*1-56163-206-6*, Eurotica) NBM.

Mana's Story. Peter Dickinson. (Kin Ser.). (Illus.). 160p. (J). (gr. 5-9). 1998. 14.99 (*0-399-23350-4*, G & D) Peng Put Young Read.

Mana's Story: The Kin. Peter Dickinson. (Kin Ser.). (Illus.). 211p. (YA). (gr. 5-9). 1998. pap. 3.99 (*0-448-41712-X*, G & D) Peng Put Young Read.

Manasquan. Mary Birkhead Ware. (Images of America Ser.). (Illus.). 128p. 1998. pap. 16.99 (*0-7524-0925-5*) Arcadia Publng.

***Manasquan Revisited: New Jersey.** Mary A. Birckhead Ware. LC 00-100091. (Images of America Ser.). (Illus.). 128p. 2000. pap. 18.99 (*0-7385-0092-5*) Arcadia Publng.

***Manassas.** James Reasoner. LC 98-52494. (Civil War Battles Ser.: Vol. 1). 352p. 1999. 22.95 (*1-58182-008-9*) Cumberland Hse.

***Manassas: A Novel of the Civil War.** Upton Sinclair. 414p. 2000. pap. 19.95 (*0-8173-1044-4*) U of Ala Pr.

Manassas: A Novel of the War. Upton Sinclair. LC 04-23761. 1969. reprint ed. 39.00 (*0-403-00060-2*) Scholarly.

Manassas: (Revised as Theirs Be the Guilt) Upton Sinclair. (Collected Works of Upton Sinclair). 412p. 1999. reprint ed. lib. bdg. 118.00 (*1-58201-825-1*) Classic Bks.

Manassas to Appomattox: The Civil War Memoirs of Pvt. Edgar Warfield - 17th Virginia Infantry. Edgar Warfield. Ed. by Friends of Fort Ward Staff. LC 96-48089. Orig. Title: A Confederate Soldier's Memoirs. (Illus.). 216p. 1996. pap. 12.95 (*1-889324-04-3*, EPM) Howell Pr VA.

***Manassas, Virginia: A Place of Passages.** Kathleen Mulvaney & Manassas Museum Systems Staff. (Images of America Ser.). (Illus.). 128p. 1999. pap. 18.99 (*0-7385-0147-6*) Arcadia Publng.

Manasseh Through the Eyes of the Deuteronomists: The Manasseh Account (2 Kings 21:1-18) & the Final Chapters of the Deuteronomistic History. Percy S. Van Keulen. 250p. 1996. 91.50 (*90-04-10666-9*) Brill Academic Pubs.

Manatee. Photos by Rei Ohara. LC 98-12678. (Illus.). 96p. 1998. 14.95 (*0-8118-1920-5*) Chronicle Bks.

Manatee. Claire Price-Goff. LC 98-53230. (Overview Ser.). (Illus.). 128p. (YA). (gr. 4-12). 1999. lib. bdg. 23.70 (*1-56006-445-5*) Lucent Bks.

Manatee. Jean H. Sibbald. LC 89-26048. (Remarkable Animals Ser.). (Illus.). 60p. (J). (gr. 3 up). 1990. lib. bdg. 13.95 (*0-87518-429-4*, Dillon Silver Burdett) Silver Burdett Pr.

Manatee. Jean H. Sibbald. (Remarkable Animals Ser.). (Illus.). 60p. (J). (gr. 4). 1995. pap. 5.95 (*0-382-39233-7*) Silver Burdett Pr.

Manatee. Alvin Silverstein et al. LC 95-1961. (Endangered in America Ser.). (Illus.). 64p. (J). (gr. 4-6). 1995. lib. bdg. 23.90 (*1-56294-551-3*) Millbrook Pr.

Manatee. Alvin Silverstein et al. LC 95-1961. (Endangered in America Ser.). (Illus.). 64p. (J). (gr. 4-6). 1996. pap. 6.95 (*0-7613-0163-1*) Millbrook Pr.

Manatee: A First BIG Book. large type ed. Donna Corey. (Illus.). 32p. (Orig.). (J). 1997. pap. 7.00 (*1-879488-07-8*) Sundiver.

Manatee: A First Book. 3rd rev. ed. Donna Corey. LC 96-70668. (Illus.). 48p. (J). 1997. 7.00 (*1-879488-08-6*) Sundiver.

Manatee: Gentle Giants in Peril. rev. ed. Mary Unterbrink. (Illus.). 48p. 1995. pap. 3.95 (*0-8200-9914-7*) Great Outdoors.

Manatee: On Location. Kathy Darling. (Illus.). (J). (gr. 4-7). 1991. 17.00 (*0-688-09030-3*) Lothrop.

Manatee: The Screenplay. Mark Mulligan. (Illus.). 121p. (Orig.). (YA). (gr. 9-12). 1993. pap. 9.95 (*1-882444-00-0*) Blvd Bks FL.

Manatee Book & Toy. Donna S. Corey. 1997. 12.00 (*1-879488-16-7*) Sundiver.

Manatee Christmas. Tim Thomas. Ed. by Barbara Mulligan. (Illus.). 32p. (J). 1995. pap. 9.95 (*1-882444-02-7*); pap., student ed. 6.95 (*1-882444-04-3*) Blvd Bks FL.

Manatee Magic for Kids see Animal Magic for Kids

Manatee Mania! A Teaching Guide. Donna Corey. (Illus.). 48p. 1997. pap., teacher ed. 12.00 (*1-879488-12-4*) Sundiver.

Manatee Morning. Jim Arnosky. LC 99-39430. (J). 2000. per. 14.00 (*0-689-81604-9*) S&S Childrens.

***Manatee Morning.** Jim Arnosky. (J). 2001. per. 5.99 (*0-689-81605-7*) S&S Childrens.

Manatee Winter. Kathleen W. Zoehfeld. LC 94-158. (Smithsonian Oceanic Collection). (Illus.). 32p. (J). (ps-2). 1994. 15.95 (*1-56899-075-8*) Soundprints.

Manatee Winter. unabridged ed. Kathleen W. Zoehfeld. LC 94-158. (Smithsonian Oceanic Collection). (Illus.). 32p. (J). (ps-2). 1994. 19.95 incl. audio (*1-56899-079-0*) Soundprints.

Manatee Winter, Incl. large toy. Kathleen W. Zoehfeld. LC 94-158. (Smithsonian Oceanic Collection). (Illus.). 32p. (J). (ps-2). 1994. 29.95 (*1-56899-077-4*) Soundprints.

Manatee Winter, Incl. micro bk. & small toy. Kathleen W. Zoehfeld. LC 94-158. (Smithsonian Oceanic Collection). (Illus.). 32p. (J). (ps-2). 1994. 9.95 (*1-56899-078-2*) Soundprints.

Manatees see Manaties

Manatees. Marianne Johnston. LC 96-46607. (Giant Animals Ser.). (J). (gr. k-4). 1997. lib. bdg. 17.27 (*0-8239-5146-4*, PowerKids) Rosen Group.

Manatees. Emilie U. Lepthien. LC 90-21138. (New True Books Ser.). (Illus.). 48p. (J). (gr. k-4). 1991. lib. bdg. 21.00 (*0-516-01114-6*) Childrens.

Manatees. Emilie U. Lepthien. LC 90-21138. (New True Books Ser.). (Illus.). 48p. (J). (ps-3). 1991. pap. 5.50 (*0-516-41114-4*) Childrens.

Manatees. Mary A. McDonald. LC 97-38097. (Nature Books Ser.). (Illus.). 32p. (J). (gr. 2-6). 1998. lib. bdg. 22.79 (*1-56766-475-X*) Childs World.

Manatees. Sarah Palmer. (Sea Mammal Discovery Library). (Illus.). 24p. (J). (gr. k-5). 1989. 8.95 (*0-685-58620-0*) Rourke Corp.

Manatees. Sarah Palmer. (Sea Mammal Discovery Library). (Illus.). 24p. (J). (gr. k-4). 1989. lib. bdg. 14.60 (*0-86592-359-0*) Rourke Enter.

Manatees. Homer Seward. LC 98-24062. (Sea Monsters Ser.). 1998. (*1-57103-237-1*) Rourke Pr.

Manatees. Frank J. Staub. LC 97-33005. (Early Bird Nature Books Ser.). (Illus.). 48p. (J). (gr. 2-4). 1998. 22.60 (*0-8225-3023-6*) Lerner Pub.

Manatees. Sally M. Walker. LC 98-31325. (Nature Watch Ser.). 48p. (J). (gr. 3-6). 1999. 22.60 (*1-57505-299-7*, Carolrhoda) Lerner Pub.

Manatees - Our Vanishing Mermaids. M. Timothy O'Keefe. LC 93-79803. (Illus.). 128p. (Orig.). 1993. pap. text 8.95 (*0-936513-43-8*) Larsens Outdoor.

Manatees & Dugongs see Endangered! - Group 3

Manatees & Dugongs. John E. Reynolds, III & Daniel K. Odell. (Illus.). 192p. 1991. 24.95 (*0-8160-2436-7*) Facts on File.

Manatees & Dugongs of the World. Jeff Ripple. LC 99-22721. (Illus.). 144p. 1999. 29.95 (*0-89658-393-7*) Voyageur Pr.

Manatees for Kids. Patricia Corrigan. LC 95-32806. (Wildlife for Kids Ser.). (Illus.). 48p. (Orig.). (J). (gr. 3-7). 1996. pap. 6.95 (*1-55971-539-1*, NorthWord Pr) Creat Pub Intl.

Manatees of Florida. Bill Lund. (Animals of the World Ser.). (Illus.). 24p. (J). (gr. k-3). 1997. lib. bdg. 14.00 (*0-531-11463-5*, Hlltop Bks) Capstone Pr.

Manatees of Florida. Bill Lund. LC 97-12673. (Animals of the World Ser.). (J). 1998. lib. bdg. write for info. (*1-56065-579-8*) Capstone Pr.

***Manatees 2000.** (Illus.). 1999. pap. 10.95 (*1-55971-694-0*, NorthWord Pr) Creat Pub Intl.

Manati: Un Libro Inicial. Donna Corey. LC 92-64397. (Illus.). 48p. (J). (ps-6). 1992. pap. 5.00 (*1-879488-01-9*) Sundiver.

Manaties. Sarah Palmer. (Mamifero Marino Ser.).Tr. of Manatees. 24p. (J). (gr. k-4). 1991. lib. bdg. 14.60 (*0-86592-672-7*) Rourke Enter.

Manaus: Social Life & Work in Brazil's Free Trade Zone. Leo A. Despres. LC 90-35150. (SUNY Series in Anthropological Studies of Contemporary Issues). 322p. (C). 1991. pap. text 24.95 (*0-7914-0537-0*) State U NY Pr.

Manav Mootra (Auto-Urine Therapy) 6th ed. Raojibhai M. Patel. 252p. 1994. reprint ed. pap. 12.95 (*0-8464-4820-3*) Beekman Pubs.

Manava Dharma Sastra. G. C. Haughton. 406p. 1986. reprint ed. 25.00 (*0-8364-1758-5*, Pub. by Manohar) S Asia.

***Manawydan Uab Llyr: Text from the Diplomatic Edition of the White Book of Rhydderch, by J. Gwenogvryn Evans.** Patrick K. Ford & J. Gwenogvryn Evans. LC 00-29378. (ENG & WEL.). 2000. write for info. (*0-926689-07-X*) Ford & Bailie Pubs.

Manayunk & Other Places: Paintings & Drawings by Francis Speight. William Hull. (Illus.). 48p. 1974. pap. 5.00 (*0-911209-04-2*) Palmer Mus Art.

Mance Lipscomb Texas Blues Guitar Solos. Mance Lipscomb. Tr. by Dan Bowden. 80p. 1994. pap. 10.95 (*0-7866-0087-X*, 95239) Mel Bay.

Mance Lipscomb/Texas Blues Guitar Solos. Transcribed by Dan Bowden. 80p. 1994. pap. 25.95 incl. audio compact disk (*0-7866-1237-1*, 95239CDP) Mel Bay.

Manch. Mary E. Bryan. (Works of Mary (Edwards) Bryan). 1989. reprint ed. lib. bdg. 79.00 (*0-7812-2121-8*) Rprt Serv.

Manchac Swamp: Louisiana's Undiscovered Wilderness. Photos by Julia Sims. LC 96-13365. (Illus.). 144p. (C). 1996. 39.95 (*0-8071-2021-9*) La State U Pr.

Manchas Aprenda a Ladrar. (SPA.). 1995. pap. 2.98 (*1-85854-314-2*) Brimax Bks.

Manchas del Sapo (How the Toad Got Its Spots) Marjorie E. Herrman. (Fabulas Bilingues Ser.). (ENG & SPA.). (J). 1978. 10.15 (*0-606-01314-8*, Pub. by Turtleback) Demco.

Manche & Peten: The Hazards of Itza Deceit & Barbarity. Fray A. Cano. Tr. by Charles P. Bowditch & Guillermo Rivera from SPA. LC 83-83344. 32p. 1984. pap. 10.00 (*0-911437-02-9*) Labyrinthos.

Manchester. Dawn Dearborn. LC 99-70092. 256p. 1999. 22.95 (*1-57197-168-8*) Pentland Pr.

***Manchester.** David Hands. (Illus.). 320p. 2000. pap. 15.00 (*1-899858-77-6*, Pub. by Ellipsis) Norton.

Manchester. C. Makepeace. LC 97-130405. (Best of Britain in Old Photographs Ser.). (Illus.). 128p. 1998. pap. 15.95 (*0-7509-1204-9*, Pub. by Sutton Pub Ltd) Intl Pubs Mktg.

Manchester. Gary Samson. LC 96-227596. (Images of America Ser.). 128p. 1996. pap. 25.00 (*0-7524-0103-3*) Arcadia Publng.

Manchester: A Celebration. Brian Redhead. (Illus.). 170p. 1994. 45.00 (*0-233-98816-5*, Pub. by Andre Deutsch) Trafalgar.

Manchester: A Neighborhood Sketchbook. Dennis McFadden & Paul Rosenblatt. (Illus.). 48p. 1998. pap. 5.00 (*0-88039-035-2*) Mus Art Carnegie.

***Manchester: An Architectural History.** John J. Parkinson-Bailey. LC 99-55329. (Illus.). 352p. 2000. 39.95 (*0-7190-5606-3*) Manchester Univ Pr.

Manchester: Brief Record of Its Past, Also a Picture of Its Present, Including an Account of Its Settlement & of Its Growth...& Sketches of Its Representative Citizens. John B. Clarke. 463p. 1997. reprint ed. lib. bdg. 49.50 (*0-8328-6010-7*) Higginson Bk Co.

Manchester - 50 Years of Change. LC 96-187782. 113p. 1995. pap. 30.00 (*0-11-702006-0*, HM20060, Pub. by Statnry Office) Bernan Associates.

Manchester Affair. large type ed. Elizabeth Elgin. 1998. 26.95 (*0-7531-5861-2*) T T Beeler.

***Manchester Affair.** large type unabridged ed. Elizabeth Elgin. 1999. pap. 19.95 (*0-7531-5876-0*, 158760, Pub. by ISIS Lrg Prnt) ISIS Pub.

Manchester & Milford Railway. J. S. Holden. 152p. (C). 1985. 45.00 (*0-85361-244-7*) St Mut.

***Manchester Benchmarks for Rail Vechile Simulation.** Ed. by S. Iwnicki. LC 99-16967. (Supplement to Vehicle System Dynamics Ser.: Vol. 31). (Illus.). 242p. 1999. 100.00 (*90-265-1551-0*) Swets.

Manchester-by-the-Sea, (MA) Frank L. Floyd. (Illus.). 209p. 1993. reprint ed. lib. bdg. 29.00 (*0-8328-3199-9*) Higginson Bk Co.

Manchester City Greats. Ian Whittell. 180p. (C). 1996. pap. 24.00 (*0-85976-352-8*, Pub. by J Donald) St Mut.

Manchester Concerto Partbooks, 2 vols., Set. Ed. by John Caldwell, pseud. LC 89-7887. (Outstanding Dissertations in Music from British Universities Ser.). 664p. 1990. text 10.00 (*0-8240-0194-X*) Garland.

Manchester Experiment: A History of Manchester Business School, 1965-1990. J. F. Wilson. 176p. 1992. 49.50 (*1-85396-158-2*, Pub. by P Chapman) Taylor & Francis.

Manchester Fourteen Miles. Margaret Penn. LC 80-40707. 247p. reprint ed. pap. 70.40 (*0-608-15763-5*, 2031706) Bks Demand.

Manchester in the Age of the Factory: The Business Structure of Cottonoplis in the Industrial Revolution. Roger Lloyd-Jones & M. J. Lewis. 272p. 1988. lib. bdg. 75.00 (*0-7099-4158-7*, Pub. by C Helm) Routldge.

Manchester Memories. George Mould. 132p. (C). 1988. 85.00 (*0-900963-41-7*, Pub. by T Dalton) St Mut.

Manchester Men, Soldiers & Sailors in the Civil War, 1861-66. George C. Gilmore. (Illus.). 167p. 1997. reprint ed. pap. 21.00 (*0-8328-6009-3*) Higginson Bk Co.

Manchester Merchants & Foreign Trade, 1794-1858. Arthur Redford. LC 73-1675. 251p. 1973. reprint ed. 37.50 (*0-678-00750-0*) Kelley.

***Manchester Mills: A World Within a World.** Gary Sampson. (Images of America Ser.). (Illus.). 128p. 2000. pap. 18.99 (*0-7385-0477-7*) Arcadia Publng.

Manchester (NH) A Brief Record of Its Past & a Picture of Its Present. (Illus.). 463p. 1994. reprint ed. lib. bdg. 47.50 (*0-8328-3977-9*) Higginson Bk Co.

Manchester of Yesterday: A Human Interest Story of Its Past, with One Hundred Illustrations, Including Rate Wood Engravings of Old Pioneers & Places. L. Ashton Thorp. (Illus.). 561p. 1996. reprint ed. lib. bdg. 59.00 (*0-8328-5058-6*) Higginson Bk Co.

***Manchester Pride.** large type ed. Freda Lightfoot. 448p. 2000. write for info. (*0-7505-1478-7*, Pub. by Mgna Lrg Print) Ulverscroft.

Manchester Road & Rail. Edward Gray. (Britain in Old Photographs Ser.). (Illus.). 1996. pap. 17.95 (*0-7509-1172-7*, Pub. by Sutton Pub Ltd) Intl Pubs Mktg.

Manchester Rosh Yeshiva. 22.99 (*0-89906-287-3*, RSEH); pap. 18.99 (*0-89906-288-1*, RSEP) Mesorah Pubns.

Manchester Ship Canal. Edward Gray. LC 98-139365. (Illus.). 160p. 1998. pap. 19.95 (*0-7509-1459-9*, Pub. by Sutton Pub Ltd) Intl Pubs Mktg.

Manchester Ship Canal & the Rise of the Port of Manchester. D. A. Farni. 128p. (C). 1980. 30.00 (*0-7190-0795-X*, Pub. by Manchester Univ Pr) St Martin.

***Manchester Streetcars.** O. R. Cummings. LC 00-100094. (Images of America Ser.). (Illus.). 128p. 2000. pap. 18.99 (*0-7385-0412-2*) Arcadia Publng.

Manchester Terrier: A Complete & Reliable Handbook. Pat Dresser. (Illus.). 96p. 1998. 19.95 (*0-7938-0755-7*, RX-105) TFH Pubns.

Manchester Union Leader in New Hampshire Elections. Eric P. Veblen. LC 74-15446. 217p. reprint ed. pap. 67.30 (*0-608-11920-2*, 202323400032) Bks Demand.

***Manchester Unlimited: The Money, Egos & Infighting Behind the World's Richest Soccer Club.** Mihir Bose. (Illus.). 2000. 27.95 (*1-58799-008-3*) Texere.

Manchild in the Promised Land. Claude Brown. 416p. 1990. 55.00 (*0-02-517325-1*, Hudson Rvr Edtn) S&S Trade.

Manchild in the Promised Land. Claude Brown. LC 90-34905. 416p. 1999. per. 12.00 (*0-684-86418-5*, Touchstone) S&S Trade Pap.

Manchos del Sapo. Dorothy S. Bishop et al.Tr. of How the Toad Got Its Spots. (ENG & SPA., Illus.). 64p. (J). 1994. pap. 4.95 (*0-8442-7171-3*, Natl Textbk Co) NTC Contemp Pub Co.

Manchoukuo: Child of Conflict. K. K. Kawakami. LC 79-94317. reprint ed. 20.00 (*0-404-03639-2*) AMS Pr.

***Manchu: A Textbook for Reading Documents.** Gertraude Roth Li. LC 99-58186. 416p. 2000. pap. text 29.00 (*0-8248-2206-4*) UH Pr.

Manchu Blood. Hugh Wiley. (Short Story Index Reprint Ser.). 1977. reprint ed. 20.95 (*0-8369-3932-8*) Ayer.

Manchu Monarch: An Interpretation of Chia Ch'ing. Alexandra E. Grantham. LC 75-32313. (Studies in Chinese History & Civilization). 223p. 1976. reprint ed. lib. bdg. 62.50 (*0-313-26973-4*, U6973, Greenwood Pr) Greenwood.

***Manchu-Mongol Relations on the Eve of the Qing Conquest: A Documentary History.** Nicola Di Cosmo & Dalizhabu Bao. (Illus.). 170p. 2000. 62.00 (*90-04-11777-6*) Brill Academic Pubs.

Manchu Palaces. Jeanne Larsen. (Illus.). 88p. 1995. 19.95 (*0-8050-1111-0*) H Holt & Co.

***Manchuria.** LC 99-47570. 2000. write for info. (*1-57588-596-4*) W S Hein.

Manchuria: Cradle of Conflict. rev. ed. Owen Lattimore. LC 72-4435. reprint ed. 37.50 (*0-404-10632-3*) AMS Pr.

Manchurian Candidate. Richard Condon. (Read-Along Ser.). (YA). pap., student ed. 34.95 incl. audio (*0-88432-966-6*, S23910) Audio-Forum.

Manchurian Candidate. Richard Condon. 320p. 1988. mass mkt. 6.99 (*0-515-09441-2*, Jove) Berkley Pub.

Manchurian Candidate. Richard Condon. 1993. pap. 5.25 (*0-8222-1339-7*) Dramatists Play.

Manchurian Crisis, 1931-1932: A Tragedy in International Relations. Sara R. Smith. LC 73-104235. 281p. 1970. reprint ed. lib. bdg. 35.00 (*0-8371-3344-0*, SMMC, Greenwood Pr) Greenwood.

***Manchurian Legacy: Memoirs of a Japanese Colonist.** Kazuko Kuramoto. LC 99-6503. (Illus.). 210p. 1999. 28.95 (*0-87013-510-4*) Mich St U Pr.

***Manchurian Myth: Nationalism, Resistance & Collaboration During the Manchurian Crisis, 1931-33.** Rana Mitter. LC 99-46738. 326p. 2000. 45.00 (*0-520-22111-7*, Pub. by U CA Pr) Cal Prin Full Svc.

Manchus. Pamela K. Crossley. LC 96-17702. (Peoples of Asia Ser.). 1997. 31.95 (*1-55786-560-4*) Blackwell Pubs.

***Manchus & Han: Ethnic Relations & Political Power in Late Qing & Early Republican China, 1861-1928.** Edward J. M. Rhoads. LC 00-8470. (Illus.). 384p. 2000. 55.00 (*0-295-97938-0*) U of Wash Pr.

Manchus: or The Reigning Dynasty of China: Their Rise & Progress. John Ross. LC 70-38080. (China Ser.). (Illus.). reprint ed. 89.00 (*0-404-56944-7*) AMS Pr.

Mancini - Brimhall EP. 64p. 1996. pap. 10.95 (*0-7692-1154-2*, AF9617) Wrner Bros.

Manciple's Tale. Geoffrey Chaucer. Ed. by Donald C. Baker. LC 83-14734. (Variorum Edition of the Works of Geoffrey Chaucer, The Canterbury Tales Ser.: Vol. II, Pt. 10). (Illus.). 176p. 1984. 49.95 (*0-8061-1872-5*) U of Okla Pr.

Mancroft Essays. Arthur M. Samuel. LC 76-99723. (Essay Index Reprint Ser.). 1977. 21.95 (*0-8369-1378-7*) Ayer.

Mancrow's Feather: A Story from Jamaica. Janet Palazzo-Craig. (First-Start Legends Ser.). (Illus.). 32p. (Orig.). (J). (gr. k-2). 1996. pap. 4.95 (*0-8167-3998-6*) Troll Communs.

Mancrow's Feather: A Story from Jamaica. enl. ed. Janet Palazzo-Craig. (Orig.). 1999. pap. text 18.95 (*0-8167-3999-4*) Troll Communs.

Mancuso's Small Business Basics: Start, Buy or Franchise Your Way to a Successful Business. 2nd rev. ed. Joseph R. Mancuso. LC 97-50090. 224p. 1997. pap. 12.95 (*1-57071-212-3*) Sourcebks.

Mancuso's Small Business Resource Guide. rev. ed. Joseph R. Mancuso. LC 95-36910. (Small Business Sourcebooks Ser.). 208p. 1995. pap. 9.95 (*1-57071-066-X*) Sourcebks.

Manda: Excavation at an Island Port on the Kenya Coast. Neville Chittick. (Illus.). 258p. 1984. 45.00 (*1-872566-05-7*, Pub. by Brit Inst Estrn Africa) David Brown.

M&A Dictionary: Mergers & Acquisitions Definitions, Phrases & Examples. Ed. by Roland DeSilva et al. 360p. 1999. pap. 19.95 (*0-9670699-0-4*) Fulcurm Info Serv.

Mandaean Book of Black Magic. E. S. Drower. 1990. pap. 5.95 (*1-55818-139-3*) Holmes Pub.

Mandak Realities: Person & Power in Central New Ireland. Brenda J. Clay. LC 85-22054. 327p. 1986. reprint ed. pap. 101.40 (*0-7837-5661-5*, 205908700005) Bks Demand.

Mandal Commision & Mandalisation: A Critique. S. R. Maheshwari. (C). 1990. text 21.00 (*81-7022-338-5*, Pub. by Concept) S Asia.

Mandal Commission Controversy. Ed. by Asghar E. Engineer. (C). 1991. text 30.00 (*81-202-0312-7*, Pub. by Ajanta) S Asia.

Mandala. Ed. by Robert Adkinson. LC 95-60472. (Sacred Symbols Ser.). (Illus.). 80p. 1995. 10.00 (*0-500-06020-7*, Pub. by Thames Hudson) Norton.

Mandala: A Novel of India. Pearl Synderstricker Buck. 384p. 1995. pap. 9.95 (*1-55921-037-0*) Moyer Bell.

Mandala: Luminous Symbols for Healing. Judith Cornell. (Illus.). 154p. 1994. pap. 25.95 (*0-8356-0710-0*, Quest) Theos Pub Hse.

Mandala: Path of Beauty. Joan Kellogg. 112p. 1992. pap. text 10.00 (*0-9631949-1-7*) Graphic Pub Williamsbrg.

Mandala: Poems - Monotypes by Galen Garwood. Sam Hamill. LC 91-3370. (Illus.). 80p. 1991. pap. 12.95 (*0-915943-52-2*) Milkweed Ed.

Mandala: Sacred Circle in Tibetan Buddhism. Martin Brauen. (Illus.). 152p. 1998. pap. 25.00 (*1-57062-380-5*, Pub. by Shambhala Pubns) Random.

Mandala & Landscape. A. W. MacDonald. (Illus.). xiv, 460p. (C). 1997. 99.00 (*81-246-0060-0*, Pub. by D K Printwrld) Nataraj Bks.

Mandala Coloring Book. Jonathan Quintin. (Illus.). 140p. 1998. pap. 10.00 (*1-56170-542-X*, 569) Hay House.

***Mandala Designs.** Martha Bartfeld. 2000. pap. 2.95 (*0-486-41034-X*) Dover.

Mandala Gardens. Tarthang Tulku. (Illus.). 115p. 1992. 35.00 (*0-945798-65-2*) Kabouter Prods.

Mandala Journey. Sheri L. Bortz. (Illus.). 28p. (Orig.). 1997. pap. 16.95 (*0-9658154-0-4*) Wise Snail.

Mandala Quilt Designs. Katie Pasquini. LC 94-40103. (Needlework Ser.). (Illus.). 112p. 1995. pap. text 8.95 (*0-486-28491-3*) Dover.

Mandala Two to the Fifth Power. limited ed. Vasanti. LC 75-176131. (Living Poets' Library). pap. 2.50 (*0-686-01283-6*) Dragons Teeth.

Mandalas of the Celts. Klaus Holitzka. LC 99-176933. (Illus.). 64p. 1998. pap. 9.95 (*0-8069-5729-8*) Sterling.

Mandalas of the World. Rudiger Dahlke & Katharina Von Martius. LC 91-42009. (Illus.). 286p. 1992. pap. 21.95 (*0-8069-8526-7*) Sterling.

Mandalay: Travels from the Golden City. Paul Strachan. (Illus.). 240p. 1995. 40.00 (*1-870838-96-3*, Pub. by Kiscadale) Weatherhill.

Mandalay's Child: A Novel. Prem Sharma. LC 98-50088. 392p. 1999. pap. 12.00 (*1-880404-20-6*) Bkwrights.

Mandalorian Armor. K. W. Jeter. (Star Wars: Bk. 1). 416p. (YA). (gr. 5 up). 1998. mass mkt. 5.99 (*0-553-57885-5*, Spectra) Bantam.

Mandamiento Olvidado: Sed Santos. William Macdonald. 176p. 1997. pap. 8.99 (*0-8254-1460-1*) Kregel.

Mandan. David O. Roberts. (Cops of Discovery Ser.: Vol. 1). (Illus.). 400p. 1998. pap. 15.00 (*0-9668531-0-5*) Hoka Hey Pr.

Mandan & Hidatsa Music. Frances Densmore. (Bureau of American Ethnology Bulletins Ser.). 192p. 1995. lib. bdg. 79.00 (*0-7812-4080-8*) Rprt Serv.

Mandan & Hidatsa Music. Frances Densmore. LC 72-1886. (Music Ser.). (Illus.). 236p. 1972. reprint ed. lib. bdg. 27.50 (*0-306-70514-1*) Da Capo.

Mandan Mesa. large type ed. Buck Thompson. (Linford Western Library Ser.). 272p. 1997. pap. 16.99 (*0-7089-5135-X*, Linford) Ulverscroft.

Mandana Misra's Distinction of the Activity Bhavanaviveka: With Introduction, English Translation with Notes, & Sanskrit Text. Ed. by V. P. Bhatta. LC 93-910452. 6, 307p. (C). 1994. 30.00 (*81-85133-81-6*, Pub. by Eastern Bk Linkers) Nataraj Bks.

Mandans. rev. ed. Emilie U. Lepthien. LC 89-22235. (New True Books Ser.). (Illus.). 48p. (J). (ps-3). 1992. lib. bdg. 21.00 (*0-516-01180-4*) Childrens.

Mandans, a Study of Their Culture, Archaeology & Language. George F. Will & Herbert J. Spinden. (HU PMP Ser.: Vol. 3, No. 4). (Illus.). 1906. 18.00 (*0-527-01195-9*) Periodicals Srv.

Mandarin: Phrasebook. 4th ed. Justin Ben-Adam Rudelson. LC 97-109758. (CHI., Illus.). 250p. 1996. pap. 5.95 (*0-86442-344-6*) Lonely Planet.

Mandarin - English Mini-Books Set with Audio, 11 bks. Claudia Schwalm. (ENG & MAN., Illus.). (Orig.). (J). (gr. k-6). 1997. pap. 21.95 incl. audio (*0-614-24739-X*) Cultural Cnnect.

Mandarin--Chinese. DK Publishing Staff. LC 98-53896. (Eyewitness Travel Guide Phrase Bks.). 1999. pap. text 6.95 (*0-7894-4188-8*) DK Pub Inc.

Mandarin (And Other Stories) And Other Stories. 2nd ed. Jose Maria Eca de Queiroz. Ed. by Robert Webb. Tr. by Margaret J. Cozta from POR. (European Classics). 128p. 1999. reprint ed. pap. 10.99 (*0-946626-98-7*, Pub. by Dedalus) Hippocrene Bks.

Mandarin & the Cadre: China's Political Cultures. Lucian W. Pye. LC 88-27727. (Michigan Monographs in Chinese Studies: No. 59). 224p. 1989. pap. text 20.00 (*0-89264-083-9*) Ctr Chinese Studies.

***Mandarin Chinese.** Kindersley Dorling. 144p. 2000. pap. 9.95 (*0-7894-6546-9*) DK Pub Inc.

Mandarin Chinese. rev. ed. Frank Hill. (LanguageCard Pac Ser.). 1993. 4.00 (*0-88699-007-6*) Travel Sci.

Mandarin Chinese. unabridged ed. Henry C. Fenn et al. Ed. by M. Gardner Tewksbury. (CHI.). 238p. pap. text 185.00 incl. audio (*0-88432-027-8*, AFM201) Audio-Forum.

***Mandarin Chinese.** 2nd ed. Rough Guides Staff. (Phrasebooks Ser.). (Illus.). 288p. 2000. pap. 6.50 (*1-85828-607-7*, Pub. by Rough Guides) Penguin Putnam.

Mandarin Chinese, Vol. 1. John H. Lu. LC 89-183898. 119p. (C). 1989. pap. 29.95 incl. audio (*0-9626654-0-1*) East Oak Hse.

Mandarin Chinese, Vol. II. John H. Lu. LC 89-183898. 129p. 1994. pap. 35.95 incl. audio (*0-9626654-1-X*) East Oak Hse.

Mandarin Chinese: A Functional Reference Grammar. Charles N. Li & Sandra A. Thompson. LC 80-6054. 1981. pap. 27.50 (*0-520-06610-3*, Pub. by U CA Pr) Cal Prin Full Svc.

***Mandarin Chinese: An Introduction.** Mobo C. F. Gao. 224p. 2000. pap. 24.95 (*0-19-554002-6*) OUP.

Mandarin Duck. Christopher Lever. (Natural History Ser.: No. 24). (Illus.). 24p. 1989. pap. 5.25 (*0-7478-0055-3*, Pub. by Shire Pubns) Parkwest Pubns.

Mandarin Everyday. Singapore Broadcasting Corporation Staff. 1984. pap. 375.00 incl. audio, VHS (*0-88432-151-7*, SV0022) Audio-Forum.

Mandarin of Mayfair. large type ed. Patricia Veryan. LC 96-10455. 1996. 23.95 (*0-7862-0702-7*) Thorndike Pr.

Mandarin Plaid. S. J. Rozan. LC 96-8499. Vol. 3. 288p. 1996. text 22.95 (*0-312-14674-4*) St Martin.

Mandarin Plaid. S. J. Rozan. 1997. mass mkt. 5.99 (*0-614-27790-6*) St Martin.

Mandarin Plaid, Vol. 1. S. J. Rozan. 288p. 1997. mass mkt. 5.99 (*0-312-96283-5*) St Martin.

Mandarin Primer: An Intensive Course in Spoken Chinese. Yuen R. Chao. LC 48-8224. 344p. 1948. reprint ed. pap. 106.70 (*0-7837-2234-6*, 205732400004) Bks Demand.

Mandarin Squares: Mandarins & Their Insignia. Valery M. Garrett. (Images of Asia Ser.). (Illus.). 74p. 1991. text 22.00 (*0-19-585239-7*) OUP.

Mandarin y Los Pajaros (The Mandarin's Birds) Fernando Alonso. (Superbks./Superlibros). (SPA.). (J). (gr. k-1). 1989. pap. 6.95 (*0-88272-503-3*); pap. 6.95 (*0-88272-505-X*) Santillana.

Mandarin y Los Pajaros (The Mandarin's Birds), Big Book. Fernando Alonso. (Superbks./Superlibros). (SPA.). (J). (gr. k-1). 1989. 21.95 (*0-88272-502-5*); 21.95 (*0-88272-504-1*) Santillana.

Mandarins. Simone de Beauvoir. 1999. pap. 16.00 (*0-393-31883-4*) Norton.

Mandarins. Simone de Beauvoir. LC 79-65852. 610p. 1979. reprint ed. pap. 9.95 (*0-89526-898-1*) Regnery Pub.

Mandarins, 2 vols., Set. Simone de Beauvoir. (Folio Ser.: Nos. 769 & 770). (FRE.). 1972. 10.95 (*0-685-57720-1*) Schoenhof.

Mandarins, Vol. 1. Simone de Beauvoir. (FRE.). 512p. 1978. pap. 10.95 (*0-8288-3652-3*, F85765) Fr & Eur.

Mandarins, Vol. 1. Simone de Beauvoir. (Folio Ser.: Nos. 769 & 770). (FRE.). 1972. pap. 11.95 (*2-07-036769-X*) Schoenhof.

Mandarins, Vol. 2. Simone de Beauvoir. (FRE.). 512p. 1978. pap. 10.95 (*0-8288-3653-1*, F85764) Fr & Eur.

Mandarins, Vol. II. Simone de Beauvoir. (Folio Ser.: Nos. 769 & 770). (FRE.). 1972. pap. write for info. (*2-07-036770-3*) Schoenhof.

Mandarins: The Circulation of Elites in China, 1600 to 1900. Robert M. Marsh. Ed. by Harriet Zuckerman & Robert K. Merton. LC 79-9013. (Dissertations on Sociology Ser.). 1980. lib. bdg. 31.95 (*0-405-12981-5*) Ayer.

Mandarins & Marigolds: A Child's Journey Through Color. Diz Wallis. LC 95-16598. (Illus.). 32p. (J). (gr. 2 up). 1995. lib. bdg. 21.27 (*0-8368-1391-X*) Gareth Stevens Inc.

Mandarins, Jews & Missionaries: The Jewish Experience in the Chinese Empire. Michael Pollak. LC 98-171038. 436p. 1998. reprint ed. pap. text 22.50 (*0-8348-0419-0*) Weatherhill.

Mandate Days: British Lives in Palestine, 1918-1948. A. J. Sherman. LC 97-60234. (Illus.). 264p. 1998. 27.50 (*0-500-25116-9*, Pub. by Thames Hudson) Norton.

Mandate for Leadership Vol. 4: Turning Ideas into Action. Ed. by Stuart M. Butler & Kim R. Holmes. (Illus.). 759p. (Orig.). (C). 1997. 29.95 (*0-89195-064-8*); pap. 24.95 (*0-89195-065-6*) Heritage Found.

Mandate for Mercy: A Call to Compassionate Action for a Hurting World. Don Stephens. 157p. 1995. pap. 8.99 (*0-927545-81-0*) YWAM Pub.

Mandate in Moreland: The American Government of Muslim Filipinos, 1899-1920. Peter Gordon Gowing. (Illus.). ixx, 411p. 1983. pap. 22.50 (*971-10-0101-2*, Pub. by New Day Pub) Cellar.

Mandate of Heaven: A New Generation of Entrepreneurs, Dissidents, Bohemians, & Technocrats Lay Claim to China's Future. Orville Schell. 464p. 1994. 25.00 (*0-671-70132-0*) S&S Trade.

Mandate of Heaven: A Record of Civil War, China, 1945-49. John F. Melby. LC 68-9736. (Illus.). 327p. reprint ed. pap. 101.40 (*0-608-11792-7*, 201436300090) Bks Demand.

Mandate of Heaven: In China, A New Generation of Entreprenurs, Dissidents, Bohemians & Technocra. Orville Schell. 464p. 1995. per. 14.00 (*0-684-80447-6*, Touchstone) S&S Trade Pap.

Mandate of Heaven: Marx & Mao in Modern China. Nigel Harris. 12.50 (*0-7043-2191-2*, Pub. by Quartet); pap. 4.95 (*0-686-85786-0*, Pub. by Quartet) Charles River Bks.

Mandate of Heaven: The Divine Command & the Natural Order. Michael Keeling. 1995. pap. 27.95 (*0-567-29281-9*) Bks Intl VA.

Mandate to Educate: The Law & Handicapped Children. Maggie Hume. LC 87-70906. 117p. (Orig.). 1987. 14.95 (*0-937925-27-6*, MEHC) Capitol VA.

Mandated Benefits: A Practical Guide to Cost-Effective Compliance. McGladre & Pullen. LC 96-216135. 688p. 1995. pap. 106.00 (*1-56706-085-4*) Panel Pubs.

Mandated Benefits: 1997 Compliance Guide. McGladrey. LC 97-118902. 688p. 1996. 125.00 (*1-56706-403-5*) Panel Pubs.

***Mandated Benefits: 2000 Compliance Guide, 1.** Ed. by RSM McGladrey Inc. Staff. 1104p. 1999. pap. text 165.00 (*0-7355-0491-1*) Panel Pubs.

Mandated Health Care: Issues & Strategies. Donald L. Westerfield. LC 90-14331. 224p. 1991. 57.95 (*0-275-93813-1*, C3813, Praeger Pubs) Greenwood.

Mandated Reporting of Suspected Child Abuse: Ethics, Law & Policy. 2nd rev. ed. Seth C. Kalichman. LC 99-28737. 1999. text 39.95 (*1-55798-602-9*, 431-733A) Am Psychol.

Mandated Reporting of Suspected Child Abuse: Ethics' Laws' & Policy. Seth C. Kalichman. 235p. 2000. 39.95 (*1-55798-197-3*) Am Psychol.

Mandated Science. L. Salter. (C). 1988. pap. text 50.50 (*1-55608-077-8*) Kluwer Academic.

Mandated Science. Liora Salter & William Leiss. 226p. (C). 1988. text 130.50 (*1-55608-057-3*) Kluwer Academic.

***Mandates & Empire: The League of Nations & Africa, 1914-1931.** Michael D. Callahan. LC 99-20795. 304p. 1999. 75.00 (*1-902210-23-9*, Pub. by Sussex Acad Pr) Intl Spec Bk.

Mandates, Dependencies, & Trusteeship. H. D. Hall. (Studies in the Administration of International Law & Organization: No. 9). 1948. reprint ed. pap. 45.00 (*0-527-00887-7*) Periodicals Srv.

Mandates Under the League of Nations. Quincy Wright. LC 68-57649. (Illus.). 726p. 1969. reprint ed. lib. bdg. 95.00 (*0-8371-0765-2*, WRLN, Greenwood Pr) Greenwood.

Mandating Academic Excellence: High School Responses to State Curriculum Reform. Bruce L. Wilson & Gretchen B. Rossman. LC 92-45749. (Sociology of Education Ser.). 272p. (C). 1993. text 44.00 (*0-8077-3264-8*); pap. text 21.95 (*0-8077-3263-X*) Tchrs Coll.

Mandating Health Insurance. John C. Goodman et al. 1989. pap. 10.00 (*0-943802-40-7*, 136) Natl Ctr Pol.

Mandative Subjunctive in American & British English in the 20th Century. Gerd Overgaard. LC 96-226108. (Studia Anglistica Upsaliensia Ser.: No. 94). 139p. (Orig.). 1995. pap. 37.50 (*91-554-3676-5*) Coronet Bks.

Mandatory Celibacy in the Catholic Church: A Handbook for the Laity. Michele Prince. LC 92-16145. 114p. (C). 1992. pap. 9.95 (*0-932727-60-3*, N Paradigm Bks); lib. bdg. 16.95 (*0-932727-61-1*, N Paradigm Bks) Hope Pub Hse.

***Mandatory Community Service in High School: The Legal Dimension.** Ronald T. Hyman. 160p. 1999. text 24.00 (*1-56534-074-4*) Ed Law Assn.

Mandatory Continuing Education for Texas Real Estate Professionals. Ralph Tamper. LC 98-48417. 1999. pap. 25.95 (*0-7931-2925-7*) Dearborn.

Mandatory Financial Information & Capital Market Equilibrium in Belgium. Pierre A. Michel. (Accounting Thought & Practice Ser.). 225p. 1987. text 10.00 (*0-8240-7852-7*) Garland.

Mandatory HIV Testing of Pregnant Women: A Threat to the Reproductive Rights of All Women. Leslie R. Wolfe & Karen Schneider. 20p. (Orig.). 1997. pap. 5.00 (*1-877966-35-5*) Ctr Women Policy.

Mandatory Minimum Drug Sentences: Throwing Away the Key or the Taxpayer's Money? Jonathan P. Caulkins et al. LC 97-8234. (Illus.). 220p. 1997. pap. 15.00 (*0-8330-2453-1*, MR-827-DPRC) Rand Corp.

Mandatory Minimum Penalties in the Federal Criminal Justice System. pap. text. write for info. (*0-314-03583-4*) West Pub.

Mandatory Minimum Penalties in the Federal Criminal Justice System. Barbara Meierhoefer. (Illus.). 244p. 1997. reprint ed. pap. text 45.00 (*0-7881-4677-7*) DIANE Pub.

Mandatory Motorcycle Helmets? Harvey Bjornstad. 112p. (Orig.). 1996. pap. 7.95 (*1-888824-03-4*) Bridgeport Bks.

***Mandatory Package Digital Signal Processing.** Sanjit K. Mitra. (C). 1999. pap., lab manual ed. 33.13 (*0-07-232876-2*) McGrw-H Hghr Educ.

Mandatory Parties. Dylotta Dye. 32p. (Orig.). (J). 1994. pap. 3.90 (*1-885148-01-1*) Lavots Press.

***Mandatory Purchase of Flood Insurance Guidelines.** Ed. by Barry Leonard. (Illus.). 150p. (C). 1999. reprint ed. pap. text 25.00 (*0-7881-7866-0*) DIANE Pub.

Mandatory Workplace Posters in California. 4th ed. Lee T. Paterson. 1992. pap. 30.00 (*1-55943-094-X*, MICHIE) LEXIS Pub.

Mandatory Workplace Posters in California. 5th ed. Lee T. Paterson. 140p. pap. 35.00 (*0-250-47262-7*) LEXIS Pub.

Mandatory Workplace Posters in California. 5th ed. Lee T. Paterson. 140p. 1994. pap. 35.00 (*0-250-47242-2*) Parker Pubns.

Mandatum Novum - "A New Commandment" An Exhortation to Keep the Commandments of Christ. Peter Toon. (Catechetical Ser.). 52p. 3.95 (*1-886412-11-1*) Preserv Press.

Mande Blacksmiths: Knowledge, Power, & Art in West Africa. Patrick R. McNaughton. LC 86-46347. (Traditional Arts of Africa Ser.). (Illus.). 270p. 1993. pap. 15.95 (*0-253-20798-3*) Ind U Pr.

***Mande Music.** Eric S. Charry. 1999. pap. text 39.00 (*0-226-10162-2*); lib. bdg. 89.00 (*0-226-10161-4*) U Ch Pr.

Mande Potters & Leatherworkers: Art & Heritage in West Africa. Barbara E. Frank. LC 97-27477. (Illus.). 192p. 1998. 45.00 (*1-56098-794-4*) Smithsonian.

Mandela. Ronald Harwood. 176p. 1988. 40.00 (*1-85283-204-5*, Pub. by Boxtree) St Mut.

Mandela: An Illustrated Autobiography. Nelson Mandela. LC 96-77497. (Illus.). 208p. (gr. 8). 1996. 29.95 (*0-316-55038-8*) Little.

Mandela: From the Life of the South African Statesman. Floyd Cooper. LC 95-19639. (Illus.). 40p. (J). (gr. 1-5). 1996. 15.95 (*0-399-22942-6*, Philomel) Peng Put Young Read.

***Mandela: From the Life of the South African Statesman.** Floyd Cooper. LC 95-19639. (Illus.). 40p. (J). (gr. k-5). 1999. pap. 6.99 (*0-698-11816-2*) Putnam Pub Group.

Mandela: The Authorized Biography. Anthony Sampson. LC 99-18498. 688p. 1999. 30.00 (*0-375-40019-2*) Knopf.

***Mandela: The Authorized Biography.** Anthony Sampson. (Illus.). 736p. 2000. pap. 17.00 (*0-679-78178-1*) Knopf.

Mandela: The Man, the Struggle, the Triumph. Dorothy Hoobler & Thomas Hoobler. (Illus.). 160p. (YA). (gr. 9-12). 1992. lib. bdg. 24.00 (*0-531-11141-5*) Watts.

Mandela for Young Beginners. Sue Adler. (Illus.). 64p. (J). (gr. 3). 1997. pap. 8.00 (*0-86316-174-X*) Writers & Readers.

Mandela, Tambo, & the African National Congress: The Struggle Against Apartheid, 1948-1990 - A Documentary Study. Ed. by Sheridan Johns & R. Hunt Davis, Jr. (Illus.). 376p. (C). 1991. pap. text 23.95 (*0-19-505784-8*) OUP.

***Mandela's Children: Growing-Up in a Post-Apartheid South Africa.** Oscar A. Barbarin & Linda M. Richter. LC 00-31134. 2000. pap. write for info. (*0-415-92469-3*) Routledge.

Mandelbaum Gate. Muriel Spark. 272p. 1992. pap. 9.00 (*0-380-71569-4*, Avon Bks) Morrow Avon.

Mandelbaum's Donut. Bradd Hopkins. 1999. write for info. (*1-891954-40-7*) Russell Dean.

***Mandelbrot Set, Theme & Variations.** Ed. by Tan Lei. LC 99-54508. (London Mathematical Society Lecture Note Ser.: No. 274). (Illus.). 286p. 2000. pap. 44.95 (*0-521-77476-4*) Cambridge U Pr.

***Mandell, Douglas & Bennett's Principles & Practice of Infectious Diseases, 2 vols.** 5th ed. Gerald L. Mandell et al. LC 99-16736. 1999. text. write for info. (*0-443-07593-X*, W B Saunders Co) Harcrt Hlth Sci Grp.

Mandelso's Travels in Western India, AD 1638-1639. M. S. Commissariat. (C). 1995. reprint ed. 18.00 (*81-206-0714-7*, Pub. by Asian Educ Servs) S Asia.

Mandelstam & 'Der Nister' Files: An Introduction to Stalin-Era Prison & Labor Camp Records. Peter B. Maggs. LC 95-41480. (Illus.). 184p. (C). (gr. 13). 1995. text 69.95 (*1-56324-175-7*) M E Sharpe.

Mandelstam Centenary Conference - Stoletie Mandelshtama. Joseph Brodsky et al. Ed. by Robin Aizlewood & Diana Myers. LC 93-50155. (ENG & RUS.). 352p. (Orig.). 1994. pap. 25.00 (*1-55779-058-2*) Hermitage Pubs.

Mandelstam the Reader. Nancy Pollak. (Parallax). 240p. 1995. text 42.00 (*0-8018-5006-1*) Johns Hopkins.

Mandeville: A Guide for the Marketing of Professional Services. Stuart W. Rose. 379p. 1995. lthr. 89.00 (*1-887133-00-3*) Prof Dev Res.

Mandeville: A Tale of the Seventeenth Century in England, 3 vols., 2 bks., Set. William Godwin. LC 79-8272. reprint ed. 84.50 (*0-404-61871-5*) AMS Pr.

Mandeville Studies. Primer. (International Archives of the History of Ideas Ser.: No. 81). 1975. lib. bdg. 126.50 (*90-247-1686-1*) Kluwer Academic.

Mandeville's Travels: From MS. Cotton Titus C. xvi, Vol. II. Ed. by P. Hamelius. (EETS Original Ser.: Vol. 154). 1963. reprint ed. 30.00 (*0-19-722154-8*, Pub. by EETS) Boydell & Brewer.

An Asterisk (*) at the beginning of an entry indicates that the title is appearing for the first time.

Mandeville's Travels Pt. II: Notes & Introduction. Ed. by P. Hamelias. (EETS, OS Ser.: Vol. 154). 1969. reprint ed. pap. 30.00 (*0-8115-4845-7*) Periodicals Srv.

Mandeville's Travels from the French, Pt. 1. John Mandeville. Ed. by P. Hamelius. (EETS, OS Ser.: No. 153). 1916. 45.00 (*0-527-00150-3*) Periodicals Srv.

Mandevilles Used Book Price Guide. Richard L. E.D.T. Collins. 1998. 93.00 (*0-911182-12-8*) Price Guide.

Mandeville's Used Book Price Guide: Five Year, 1989 Edition. Ed. by Richard Collins. 604p. 1988. 89.00 (*0-911182-88-8*) Price Guide.

Mandeville's Used Book Price Guide: Five Year, 1994 Edition. Ed. by Richard L. Collins. 604p. 1993. text 90.00 (*0-911182-94-2*) Price Guide.

Mandi & the Fairies. Elizabeth Newman. 1992. pap. 9.95 (*0-938645-78-1*) In His Steps.

Mandiani Drum & Dance: Djimbe Performance & Black Aesthetics. Mark Sunkett. LC 93-37626. (Performance in World Music Ser.: No. 11). 192p. 1995. pap. 19.95 (*0-941677-76-1*, Pub. by White Cliffs Media) Words Distrib.

Mandibles of "Sinanthropus Pekinensis" A Comparative Study. Franz Weidenreich. LC 77-86448. (China. Geological Survey. Palaeontologia Sinica. New Ser. D.: Vol. 7, Fasc. 3). (Illus.). reprint ed. 25.50 (*0-404-16691-1*) AMS Pr.

Mandibular Reconstruction. Arnold Komisar. LC 96-36513. (Illus.). 160p. 1997. text 85.00 (*0-86577-614-8*) Thieme Med Pubs.

Mandie: My Diary. Lois G. Leppard. 256p. (J). 1997. text 9.99 (*0-7642-2022-5*, 232022) Bethany Hse.

Mandie & Her Missing Kin. Lois G. Leppard. (Mandie Bks.: No. 25). 16p. (J). (gr. 4-7). 1995. mass mkt. 4.99 (*1-55661-511-6*) Bethany Hse.

Mandie & Her Missing Kin. Lois G. Leppard. (Mandie Bks.: No. 25). (J). (gr. 4-7). 1995. 10.09 (*0-606-10868-8*, Pub. by Turtleback) Demco.

Mandie & Joe's Christmas Suprise. Lois G. Leppard. 128p. (J). (gr. 3-8). 1995. text 9.99 (*1-55661-552-3*) Bethany Hse.

*__Mandie & Joe's Christmas Surprise.__ Lois G. Leppard. 128p. (J). (gr. 3-9). 2000. mass mkt. 4.99 (*0-7642-2414-X*) Bethany Hse.

Mandie & Jonathan's Predicament. Lois G. Leppard. LC 97-21027. (Mandie Bks.: No. 28). 176p. (J). (gr. 4-7). 1997. mass mkt. 4.99 (*1-55661-555-8*) Bethany Hse.

Mandie & Mollie: The Angel's Visit. Lois G. Leppard. LC 97-45479. 128p. (J). 1998. text 9.99 (*0-7642-2063-2*) Bethany Hse.

Mandie & the Abandoned Mine. Lois G. Leppard. LC 87-70883. (Mandie Bks.: No. 8). 16p. (J). (gr. 4-9). 1987. mass mkt. 4.99 (*0-87123-932-9*) Bethany Hse.

Mandie & the Abandoned Mine. Lois G. Leppard. (Mandie Bks.: No. 8). (J). (gr. 4-9). 1987. 10.09 (*0-606-06123-1*, Pub. by Turtleback) Demco.

Mandie & the Angel's Secret. Lois G. Leppard. (Mandie Bks.: No. 22). 16p. (J). (gr. 4-7). 1993. mass mkt. 4.99 (*1-55661-370-9*) Bethany Hse.

Mandie & the Angel's Secret. Lois G. Leppard. (Mandie Bks.: No. 22). (J). (gr. 4-7). 1993. 10.09 (*0-606-06124-X*, Pub. by Turtleback) Demco.

*__Mandie & the Buried Stranger.__ Lois G. Leppard. LC 99-6446. (Mandie Bks.: No. 31). 176p. (J). (gr. 4-7). 1999. pap. text 4.99 (*1-55661-384-9*) Bethany Hse.

Mandie & the Charleston Phantom. Lois G. Leppard. LC 86-7098. (Mandie Bks.: No. 7). 144p. (J). (gr. 4-7). 1986. mass mkt. 4.99 (*0-87123-650-8*) Bethany Hse.

Mandie & the Charleston Phantom. Lois G. Leppard. (Mandie Bks.: No. 7). (J). (gr. 4-7). 1986. 10.09 (*0-606-06125-8*, Pub. by Turtleback) Demco.

Mandie & the Cherokee Legend. Lois G. Leppard. LC 83-70894. (Mandie Bks.: No. 2). 144p. (J). (gr. 4-8). 1983. mass mkt. 4.99 (*0-87123-321-5*) Bethany Hse.

Mandie & the Cherokee Legend. Lois G. Leppard. (Mandie Bks.: No. 2). (J). (gr. 4-7). 1983. 10.09 (*0-606-06126-6*, Pub. by Turtleback) Demco.

Mandie & the Courtroom Battle. Lois G. Leppard. LC 96-51197. (Mandy Ser.: No. 27). 176p. (J). (gr. 4-7). 1996. mass mkt. 4.99 (*1-55661-554-X*) Bethany Hse.

Mandie & the Courtroom Battle. Lois G. Leppard. (Mandie Bks.: No. 27). (J). (gr. 4-7). 1996. 10.09 (*0-606-10869-6*, Pub. by Turtleback) Demco.

Mandie & the Dangerous Imposter. Lois G. Leppard. LC 93-74539. (Mandie Bks.: No. 23). 176p. (J). (gr. 4-7). 1994. mass mkt. 4.99 (*1-55661-459-4*) Bethany Hse.

Mandie & the Dark Alley. Lois G. Leppard. (Mandie Bks.: No. 33). (J). (gr. 4-7). mass mkt. 4.99 (*0-7642-1674-0*) Bethany Hse.

*__Mandie & the Dark Alley.__ Lois G. Leppard. (Mandie Bks.: No. 33). (Illus.). 176p. (J). (gr. 4-7). 2000. mass mkt. 4.99 (*1-55661-674-0*) Bethany Hse.

Mandie & the Fiery Rescue. Lois G. Leppard. (Mandie Bks.: No. 21). 16p. (J). (gr. 4-7). 1993. mass mkt. 4.99 (*1-55661-289-3*) Bethany Hse.

Mandie & the Fiery Rescue. Lois G. Leppard. (Mandie Bks.: No. 21). (J). (gr. 4-7). 1993. 10.09 (*0-606-06127-4*, Pub. by Turtleback) Demco.

Mandie & the Forbidden Attic. Lois G. Leppard. LC 84-72710. (Mandie Bks.: No. 4). 128p. (J). (gr. 4-7). 1985. mass mkt. 4.99 (*0-87123-822-5*) Bethany Hse.

Mandie & the Forbidden Attic. Lois G. Leppard. (Mandie Bks.: No. 4). (J). (gr. 4-7). 1985. 10.09 (*0-606-06128-2*, Pub. by Turtleback) Demco.

Mandie & the Foreign Spies. Lois G. Leppard. (Mandie Bks.: No. 15). 16p. (J). (gr. 4-7). 1990. mass mkt. 4.99 (*1-55661-147-1*) Bethany Hse.

Mandie & the Foreign Spies. Lois G. Leppard. (Mandie Bks.: No. 15). (J). (gr. 4-7). 1990. 10.09 (*0-606-06129-0*, Pub. by Turtleback) Demco.

Mandie & the Ghost Bandits. Lois G. Leppard. LC 84-71151. (Mandie Bks.: No. 3). 128p. (J). (gr. 4-7). 1984. mass mkt. 4.99 (*0-87123-442-4*) Bethany Hse.

Mandie & the Ghost Bandits. Lois G. Leppard. (Mandie Bks.: No. 3). (J). (gr. 4-7). 1984. 10.09 (*0-606-06130-4*, Pub. by Turtleback) Demco.

Mandie & the Hidden Treasure. Lois G. Leppard. LC 87-71606. (Mandie Bks.: No. 9). 16p. (J). (gr. 4-7). 1987. mass mkt. 4.99 (*0-87123-977-9*) Bethany Hse.

Mandie & the Hidden Treasure. Lois G. Leppard. (Mandie Bks.: No. 9). (J). (gr. 4-7). 1987. 10.09 (*0-606-06131-2*, Pub. by Turtleback) Demco.

Mandie & the Holiday Surprise. Lois G. Leppard. LC 88-71502. (Mandie Bks.: No. 11). 16p. (J). (gr. 4-7). 1988. mass mkt. 4.99 (*1-55661-036-X*) Bethany Hse.

Mandie & the Holiday Surprise. Lois G. Leppard. (Mandie Bks.: No. 11). (J). (gr. 4-7). 1988. 10.09 (*0-606-06132-0*, Pub. by Turtleback) Demco.

Mandie & the Invisible Troublemaker. Lois G. Leppard. LC 94-25134. (Mandie Bks.: No. 24). 176p. (J). (gr. 4-7). 1994. mass mkt. 4.99 (*1-55661-510-8*) Bethany Hse.

Mandie & the Jumping Juniper. Lois G. Leppard. (Mandie Bks.: No. 18). 16p. (J). (gr. 4-7). 1991. mass mkt. 4.99 (*1-55661-200-1*) Bethany Hse.

Mandie & the Jumping Juniper. Lois G. Leppard. (Mandie Bks.: No. 18). (J). (gr. 4-7). 1991. 10.09 (*0-606-06133-9*, Pub. by Turtleback) Demco.

Mandie & the Long Goodbye. Lois G. Leppard. (Mandie Bks.: No. 30). 16p. (J). (gr. 4-7). 1998. mass mkt. 4.99 (*1-55661-557-4*) Bethany Hse.

Mandie & the Medicine Man. Lois G. Leppard. LC 85-73426. (Mandie Bks.: No. 6). 128p. (J). (gr. 4-7). 1986. mass mkt. 4.99 (*0-87123-891-8*) Bethany Hse.

Mandie & the Medicine Man. Lois G. Leppard. (Mandie Bks.: No. 6). (J). (gr. 4-7). 1986. 10.09 (*0-606-06134-7*, Pub. by Turtleback) Demco.

Mandie & the Midnight Journey. Lois G. Leppard. (Mandie Bks.: No. 13). 16p. (J). (gr. 4-7). 1989. mass mkt. 4.99 (*1-55661-084-X*) Bethany Hse.

Mandie & the Midnight Journey. Lois G. Leppard. (Mandie Bks.: No. 13). (J). (gr. 4-7). 1989. 10.09 (*0-606-06135-5*, Pub. by Turtleback) Demco.

Mandie & the Mysterious Bells. Lois G. Leppard. LC 87-72792. (Mandie Bks.: No. 10). 16p. (J). (gr. 4-7). 1988. mass mkt. 4.99 (*1-55661-000-9*) Bethany Hse.

Mandie & the Mysterious Bells. Lois G. Leppard. (Mandie Bks.: No. 10). (J). (gr. 4-7). 1988. 10.09 (*0-606-06136-3*, Pub. by Turtleback) Demco.

Mandie & the Mysterious Fisherman. Lois G. Leppard. (Mandie Bks.: No. 19). 176p. (J). (gr. 4-7). 1992. mass mkt. 4.99 (*1-55661-235-4*) Bethany Hse.

Mandie & the Mysterious Fisherman. Lois G. Leppard. (Mandie Bks.: No. 19). (J). (gr. 4-7). 1992. 10.09 (*0-606-06137-1*, Pub. by Turtleback) Demco.

Mandie & the Schoolhouse's Secret. Lois G. Leppard. (Mandie Bks.: No. 26). 176p. (J). (gr. 4-7). 1996. mass mkt. 4.99 (*1-55661-553-1*) Bethany Hse.

Mandie & the Schoolhouse's Secret. Lois G. Leppard. (Mandie Bks.: No. 26). (J). (gr. 4-7). 1996. 10.09 (*0-606-10870-X*, Pub. by Turtleback) Demco.

Mandie & the Seaside Rendezvous. Lois G. Leppard. (Mandie Bks.: No. 32). 176p. (J). (gr. 4-7). 1999. pap. text 4.99 (*1-55661-673-2*) Bethany Hse.

Mandie & the Secret Tunnel. Lois G. Leppard. LC 82-74053. (Mandie Bks.: No. 1). 144p. (J). (gr. 4-7). 1983. mass mkt. 4.99 (*0-87123-320-7*) Bethany Hse.

Mandie & the Secret Tunnel. Lois G. Leppard. (Mandie Bks.: No. 1). (J). (gr. 4-7). 1983. 10.09 (*0-606-06138-X*, Pub. by Turtleback) Demco.

Mandie & the Shipboard Mystery. Lois G. Leppard. (Mandie Bks.: No. 14). 16p. (J). (gr. 4-7). 1990. mass mkt. 4.99 (*1-55661-120-X*) Bethany Hse.

Mandie & the Shipboard Mystery. Lois G. Leppard. (Mandie Bks.: No. 14). (J). (gr. 4-7). 1990. 10.09 (*0-606-06139-8*, Pub. by Turtleback) Demco.

Mandie & the Silent Catacombs. Lois G. Leppard. (Mandie Bks.: No. 16). 16p. (J). (gr. 4-7). 1990. mass mkt. 4.99 (*1-55661-148-X*) Bethany Hse.

Mandie & the Silent Catacombs. Lois G. Leppard. (Mandie Bks.: No. 16). (J). (gr. 4-7). 1990. 10.09 (*0-606-06140-1*, Pub. by Turtleback) Demco.

Mandie & the Singing Chalet. Lois G. Leppard. (Mandie Bks.: No. 17). 176p. (J). (gr. 4-7). 1991. mass mkt. 4.99 (*1-55661-198-6*) Bethany Hse.

Mandie & the Singing Chalet. Lois G. Leppard. (Mandie Bks.: No. 17). (J). (gr. 4-7). 1991. 10.09 (*0-606-06141-X*, Pub. by Turtleback) Demco.

Mandie & the Trunk's Secret. Lois G. Leppard. (Mandie Bks.: No. 5). (J). (gr. 4-7). 1985. 10.09 (*0-606-06142-8*, Pub. by Turtleback) Demco.

Mandie & the Trunk's Secret, Bk. 5. Lois G. Leppard. LC 85-71474. (Mandie Bks.: No. 5). 128p. (J). (gr. 4-7). 1985. mass mkt. 4.99 (*0-87123-839-X*) Bethany Hse.

Mandie & the Unwanted Gift, 29. Lois G. Leppard. LC 97-33827. (Mandie Bks.: No. 29). 176p. (J). (gr. 4-7). 1997. mass mkt. 4.99 (*1-55661-556-6*) Bethany Hse.

Mandie & the Washington Nightmare. Lois G. Leppard. (Mandie Bks.: No. 12). (J). (gr. 4-7). 1989. 10.09 (*0-606-06143-6*, Pub. by Turtleback) Demco.

Mandie & the Washington Nightmare, Bk. 12. Lois G. Leppard. LC 88-63464. (Mandie Bks.: No. 12). 176p. (J). (gr. 4-7). 1989. mass mkt. 4.99 (*1-55661-065-3*) Bethany Hse.

Mandie & the Windmill's Message. Lois G. Leppard. LC 92-73061. (Mandie Bks.: No. 20). 16p. (J). (gr. 4-7). 1992. mass mkt. 4.99 (*1-55661-288-5*) Bethany Hse.

Mandie & the Windmill's Message. Lois G. Leppard. (Mandie Bks.: No. 20). (J). (gr. 4-7). 1992. 10.09 (*0-606-06144-4*, Pub. by Turtleback) Demco.

Mandie Books. Lois G. Leppard. 1998. pap., boxed set 24.99 (*0-7642-8390-1*) Bethany Hse.

Mandie Books Boxed Set: Mandie & the Holiday Surprise; Mandie & the Washington Nightmare; Mandie & the Midnight Journey; Mandie & the Shipboard Mystery; Mandie & the Foreign Spies. Lois G. Leppard. (Mandie Bks.: Nos. 11-15). (J). (gr. 4-7). 1990. boxed set 24.99 (*1-55661-758-5*) Bethany Hse.

Mandie Books Boxed Set: Mandie & the Medicine Man; Mandie & the Charleston Phantom; Mandie & the Abandoned Mine; Mandie & the Hidden Treasure; Mandie & the Mysterious Bells. Lois G. Leppard. (Mandie Bks.: Nos. 6-10). (J). (gr. 4-7). 1988. pap., boxed set 24.99 (*1-55661-752-6*, 252752) Bethany Hse.

Mandie Books Boxed Set: Mandie & the Secret Tunnel; Mandie & the Cherokee Legend; Mandie & the Ghost Bandits; Mandie & the Forbidden Attic; Mandie & the Trunk's Secret. Lois G. Leppard. (Mandie Bks.: Nos. 1-5). (J). (gr. 4-7). 1987. boxed set 24.99 (*1-55661-750-X*) Bethany Hse.

Mandie Books Boxed Set: Mandie & the Silent Catacombs; Mandie & the Singing Chalet; Mandie & the Jumping Juniper; Mandie & the Mysterious Fisherman; Mandie & the Windmill's Message. Lois G. Leppard. (Mandie Bks.: Nos. 16-20). (J). (gr. 4-7). 1992. boxed set 24.99 (*1-55661-769-0*) Bethany Hse.

Mandie's Cookbook. Lois G. Leppard. 112p. (Orig.). (J). (gr. 3-8). 1991. pap. 9.99 (*1-55661-224-9*) Bethany Hse.

Mandingo Kingdoms of the Senegambia: Traditionalism, Islam & European Expansion. Charlotte A. Quinn. LC 77-154831. 235p. reprint ed. 72.90 (*0-8357-9463-6*, 201530700093) Bks Demand.

Mandinko: The Ethnography of a West African Holy Land. Matt Schaffer & Christine Cooper. (Illus.). 116p. 1987. pap. text 10.50 (*0-88133-294-1*) Waveland Pr.

Mandolin Chord Book. James Major. 1984. pap. 5.95 (*0-8256-2296-4*, AM34729) Music Sales.

Mandolin Chords: In Picture & Diagram Form. Bay, Mel, Publications, Inc. Staff. (Illus.). 32p. 1963. pap. 4.95 (*0-87166-863-7*, 93257) Mel Bay.

Mandolin Chords, Plus. Ron Middlebrook. 8p. 1995. pap. text 3.95 (*1-57424-007-2*) Centerstream Pub.

Mandolin Classics. Ross Cherednik & Ken Eidson. 68p. 1986. pap. 9.95 (*0-87166-943-9*, 94043) Mel Bay.

Mandolin Classics in Tablature. Arranged by Robert Bancalari. 56p. 1995. pap. 8.95 (*0-7866-0197-3*, 95353) Mel Bay.

Mandolin Crosspicking Techniques. Mickey Cochran. 128p. 1997. pap. 14.95 (*0-7866-2891-X*, 96613) Mel Bay.

Mandolin Method. 64p. 1996. pap. 14.95 (*0-7935-6878-1*) H Leonard.

Mandolin Music in America: Thirty-Eight Hundred Pieces for Mandolin & Where to Find Them. Ed. by Joshua Bell. 68p. (Orig.). 1993. pap. 10.00 (*0-9614120-3-8*) Plucked.

Mandolin Picker's Fake Book. David Brody. 1984. pap. 24.95 (*0-8256-0239-4*, OK64352, Oak) Music Sales.

Mandolin Player's Pastime: A Collection of Reels, Hornpipes, Jigs, & Other Dance Tunes for Mandolin. Philip L. Williams. LC 91-68107. 62p. (Orig.). 1992. pap. 10.00 (*0-9631484-4-3*) Voyager Rec.

Mandolin Pocket Book. 32p. 1980. pap. 0.95 (*0-87166-548-4*, 93703) Mel Bay.

Mandolin Primer. 5th ed. Bert Casey. Ed. by Geoff Hohwald. (Illus.). 56p. 1988. reprint ed. pap. text 14.95 (*1-893907-33-3*, MP) Cassett & Video.

Mandolin Scales & Studies. Ray Bell. 152p. 1995. spiral bd. 16.95 (*0-7866-0839-0*, 95542) Mel Bay.

Mandolin Songbook. Ken Eidson. 72p. 1980. pap. 8.95 (*1-56222-240-6*, 93680) Mel Bay.

*__Mandolin Tablature Pad.__ William Bay. 48p. 1999. pap. 4.95 (*0-7866-3397-2*) Mel Bay.

Mandolina y Otros Cuentos: Coleccion de Cuentos y Cantos Sefarditas. Berta Savariego. LC 88-81442. (Coleccion Caniqui). (SPA.). 88p. (Orig.). 1989. pap. 9.00 (*0-89729-493-9*) Ediciones.

Mandragola. Niccolo Machiavelli. Tr. by Henry Paolucci & Anne A. Paolucci. LC 57-14629. 64p. 1957. pap. 10.00 (*0-672-60231-8*, LLA58, Bobbs) Macmillan.

Mandragola. Niccolo Machiavelli. Tr. by Mera J. Flaumenhaft from ITA. LC 80-54106. 64p. (C). 1981. pap. text 5.25 (*0-917974-57-3*) Waveland Pr.

Mandragola. Niccolo Machiavelli. Ed. by Vincent Luciani. (ITA & ENG.). (C). 1997. pap. 10.95 (*0-913298-19-0*) S F Vanni.

Mandragola: Machiavelli. Henry Paolucci. 80p. (C). 1957. pap. text 8.20 (*0-02-391350-9*, Macmillan Coll) P-H.

Mandrake. Niccolo Machiavelli. Tr. by Wallace Shawn. 1978. pap. 5.25 (*0-8222-0728-1*) Dramatists Play.

Mandrell Family Cookbook. Matt Dudney et al. LC 99-28592. (Illus.). 175p. 1999. 19.95 (*1-55853-752-X*) Rutledge Hill Pr.

Mandschu-Sprachkunde in Korea. Hiu Lie. LC 70-635028. (Uralic & Altaic Ser.: Vol. 114). (Illus.). 304p. (Orig.). 1971. 19.00 (*0-87750-162-9*) Res Inst Inner Asian Studies.

Manductio ad Ministerium. Cotton Mather. (Notable American Authors Ser.). 1999. reprint ed. lib. bdg. 125.00 (*0-7812-3971-0*) Rprt Serv.

Mandukopanisad. Tr. by Swami Nikhilananda. 5.95 (*81-7505-022-5*, Pub. by Advaita Ashrama) Vedanta Pr.

Mandukya Upanishad. Tr. by Swami Gambhirananda from SAN. (Upanishads with Shankara's Commentary Ser.). 240p. 1980. pap. 3.95 (*0-87481-202-X*) Vedanta Pr.

Mandy. Barbara D. Booth. LC 90-19989. (Illus.). 32p. (J). (gr. 1 up). 1991. 16.00 (*0-688-10338-3*) Lothrop.

Mandy. Mary C. Borntrager. LC 96-2461. (Ellie's People Ser.: Vol. 9). 144p. (Orig.). (J). (gr. 4 up). 1996. pap. 7.99 (*0-8361-9046-7*) Herald Pr.

Mandy. Julie Edwards. LC 76-157901. (Illus.). 192p. (J). (gr. 4-7). 1971. 13.95 (*0-06-021802-9*) HarpC Child Bks.

Mandy. Julie Edwards. LC 76-157901. (Trophy Bk.). (Illus.). 144p. (J). (gr. 3-6). 1989. pap. 4.95 (*0-06-440296-7*, HarpTrophy) HarpC Child Bks.

Mandy. Julie Edwards. LC 76-157901. (Illus.). 192p. (J). (gr. 4-7). 1990. lib. bdg. 14.89 (*0-06-021803-7*) HarpC Child Bks.

Mandy. Julie Edwards. 1989. 9.60 (*0-606-12413-6*, Pub. by Turtleback) Demco.

Mandy. Margaret Phelan. LC 97-65965. 200p. (Orig.). 1997. pap. 9.95 (*1-57197-060-6*) Pentland Pr.

Mandy. large type ed. Barbara D. Booth. (Illus.). 1993. 9.50 (*0-614-09841-6*, L-34096-00) Am Printing Hse.

Mandy. large type ed. Mary C. Borntrager. (Ellie's People Ser.: Vol. 9). 144p. (Orig.). (J). 1996. pap. 8.99 (*0-8361-9048-3*) Herald Pr.

Mandy, Amanda. C. P. Shields. LC 96-90181. 1996. 14.95 (*0-533-11938-3*) Vantage.

Mandy & the Kookalocka. Margaret H. Matens. LC 93-77130. (Illus.). 32p. (J). (gr. k-5). 1993. 14.95 (*1-882959-53-1*) Foxglove TN.

Mandy Meets a Millionaire. Tracy Sinclair. 1996. per. 3.99 (*0-373-24072-4*, 1-24072-0) Silhouette.

Mandy Miami & the Miracle Motel No. 2. Juanita Phillips. (Newspaper Kids Ser.). 1998. pap. text 5.95 (*0-207-19152-2*) HarpC.

Mandy Miller Fights Back. Created by Francine Pascal. (Sweet Valley Twins Ser.: No. 48). 144p. (J). (gr. 3-7). 1991. pap. 3.50 (*0-553-15880-5*) Bantam.

Mandy Miller Fights Back. Jamie Suzanne. (Sweet Valley Twins Ser.: No. 48). (J). (gr. 3-7). 1991. 8.60 (*0-606-04971-1*, Pub. by Turtleback) Demco.

*__Mandy Moore: The Unofficial Book.__ Molly MacDermot. (Illus.). (J). 2000. pap. 12.95 (*0-8230-8374-8*, Billboard Bks) Watsn-Guptill.

Mandy Oxendine: A Novel. Charles Waddell Chesnutt. Ed. by Charles Hackenberry. LC 93-553. 112p. 1994. 11.95 (*0-252-06347-3*); text 27.50 (*0-252-02051-0*) U of Ill Pr.

Mandy's Backyard. J. David Loeb. LC 97-162667. (Illus.). 32p. (Orig.). (J). (gr. k-4). 1997. pap. 5.95 (*1-885744-04-8*) Otter Creek.

Mandy's Wash Tub & Other Stories. Irving L. Stevens. Ed. by Brenda Hall & Joshua Hall. (Illus.). 140p. (Orig.). 1992. pap. 9.95 (*0-9609208-1-1*) Moosehead Prods.

*__Mane Thing.__ Kevin Mancuso. LC 98-49591. (Illus.). 144p. (gr. 8). 1999. 25.00 (*0-316-16614-6*) Little.

Maneater. Sophie G. Bird. (Orig.). 1993. mass mkt. 6.95 (*1-56333-103-9*, Rhinoceros) Masquerade.

Maneaters. Peter H. Capstick. (Illus.). 200p. 1981. 17.95 (*0-8227-3023-5*) Petersen Pub.

Maneaters. Peter H. Capstick. (Illus.). 178p. 1993. 24.95 (*1-57157-117-5*) Safari Pr.

Maneaters of Tsavo. J. H. Patterson. 240p. 1996. per. 6.99 (*0-671-00306-2*) PB.

*__Manege: Poems from Hollywood.__ Mark Dunster. 11p. 1999. pap. 5.00 (*0-89642-808-7*) Linden Pubs.

Maneige Royal. Antoine De Pluvinel. Tr. by Hilda Nelson. 170p. 1990. 110.00 (*0-85131-452-X*, Pub. by J A Allen) Trafalgar.

*__MaNejar el Comportamiento Deticil: En la Sala de Clase: Una Guia de Bolsillo Para.__ Grad L. Plick. Tr. by Mary Weeks. (Illus.). 130p. 1999. pap. write for info. (*1-928633-51-X*) Seacoast MS.

Manejo de Conflictos y Reconciliacion (Conflict Management & Reconciliation) J. Wendell Lowe. (Equipped to Serve Ser.: No. 4). (SPA.). Date not set. pap. text. write for info. (*1-889505-32-3*) White Wing Pub.

Manejo de Riego por Goteo. (SPA.). 560p. 1990. pap. 10.00 (*0-9621805-2-1*) UPR Agr Exper Sta.

Manejo Del Comportamiento . . . No Puedes Obligarme! Judith Schneider. (SPA.). 60p. 1997. pap. 10.95 (*0-944454-29-1*) CAPE Center.

Manejo Integrado de los Insectos, Acaros, y Enfermedades en los Cultivos Ornamentales. Charles C. Powell & Richard K. Lindquist. Ed. by Veronica Hoyos De Martens. LC 94-28537. (SPA., Illus.). 118p. 1994. pap. text 28.95 (*1-883052-06-8*, B022) Ball Pub.

Manejo Popular de los Desastres Naturales. Andrew Maskrey. (SPA.). 208p. 1989. pap. 19.00 (*1-85339-368-1*, Pub. by Intermed Tech) Stylus Pub VA.

Manel Anoro: Los Colores del Mediterraneo. Claudia Gioseffi. LC 95-695359. (Illus.). 144p. 1995. 100.00 (*1-884495-04-4*) Caldwell Snyder.

Manel Anoro: Los Colores del Mediterraneo. deluxe ed. Claudia Gioseffi. LC 95-695359. (Illus.). 144p. 1995. 1200.00 (*1-884495-02-2*) Caldwell Snyder.

Manel Anoro: The Explorers Civilization Found. Susan Jacoby. LC 99-188316. (Illus.). 40p. 1998. 25.00 (*1-884495-09-5*) Caldwell Snyder.

Manent European Liberty. 1983. lib. bdg. 71.50 (*90-247-2869-X*) Kluwer Academic.

Manera Biblica de Reunirse y de Servir para la Edificacion del Cuerpo De Cristo. Witness Lee.Tr. of SCRIPTURAL WAY TO MEET AND TO SERVE FOR THE BUILDING UP OF THE BODY OF CHRIST. (SPA.). 315p. 1988. per. 10.25 (*0-87083-423-1*, 12-018-002) Living Stream Ministry.

Manera de Ensayo. Susan C. Schaffer & Rebeca Acevedo. (SPA.). 306p. (C). 1997. pap. text 36.76 (*0-669-21999-1*) HM Trade Div.

Manera de Practicar el Recobro Actual Del Senor. Witness Lee.Tr. of Way to Practice the Lord's Present Recovery. (SPA.). 54p. 1989. pap. 3.75 (*0-87083-472-X*, 12-026-002) Living Stream Ministry.

Manera Ordenada Por Dios de Practicar la Economia Neotestamentaria. Witness Lee.Tr. of God-Ordained Way to Practice the New Testament Economy. (SPA.). 183p. 1987. per. 8.00 (*0-87083-329-4*, 12-006-002) Living Stream Ministry.

Manera Practica de Llevar una Vida Conforme a la Cumbre de la Revelacion Divinae Contenida En Las Santas Escrituras. Witness Lee.Tr. of PRACTICAL WAY TO LIVE A LIFE ACCORDING TO THE HIGH

M

PEAK OF THE DIVINE REVELATION IN THE HOLY SCRIPTURES. (SPA.). 50p. 1994. pap. 4.50 (*0-87083-825-3*, 04-033-002) Living Stream Ministry.

Manera Viva y Practica de Disfrutar a Cristo. Witness Lee.Tr. of Living & Practical Way to Enjoy Christ. (SPA.). 72p. 1994. pap. 3.75 (*0-87083-790-7*, 07-040-002) Living Stream Ministry.

Maneras de Narrar: Contraste de Lino Novas Calvo y Alfonso Hernandez Cata. A. Gutierrez De La Solana. 1972. 10.95 (*0-88303-017-9*); pap. 8.95 (*0-685-73219-3*) E Torres & Sons.

Maneras Maravillosas De Amar A Un Adolescente. Judy Ford. (SPA.). 227p. 1997. pap. text 10.98 (*968-13-3112-5*) Edit Diana.

Maneras Maravillosas Para Amar A Su Hijo. Judy Ford. (SPA.). 203p. 1997. pap. text 10.98 (*968-13-3014-5*) Edit Diana.

Maneras Maravillosas Para Amar a un Adolescente. Judy Ford. 208p. 1999. pap. text 9.95 (*1-57324-182-2*) Conari Press.

***Maneras Maravillosas Para Amar a un Hijo.** Judy Ford. 208p. 1999. pap. text 9.95 (*1-57324-181-4*) Conari Press.

Manes & Tails. Valerie Watson. (Illus.). 24p. (Orig.). 1987. pap. 12.00 (*0-901366-32-3*) Half Halt Pr.

Manes Sperber: Un Combat Contre la Tyrannie (1934-1960) Anne-Marie Corbin-Schuffels. (Contacts Ser.: Series III, Vol. 34). (FRE.). 568p. 1996. 63.95 (*3-906754-39-1*, Pub. by P Lang) P Lang Pubng.

Manet. Chelsea House Publishing Staff. (World's Greatest Artists Ser.). 1997. 17.95 (*1-85813-908-2*) Chelsea Hse.

Manet. Pierre Courthion. (Masters of Art Ser.). (Illus.). 1984. 24.95 (*0-8109-1318-6*, Pub. by Abrams) Time Warner.

Manet. DK Publishing Staff. (Eyewitness Books). 64p. (J). (gr. 4-7). 1999. 15.95 (*0-7894-4879-3*, D K Ink) DK Pub Inc.

Manet. Nathaniel Harris. 80p. (YA). (gr. 7 up). 1997. 17.95 (*1-85813-585-0*) Chelsea Hse.

Manet. John Richardson. (Color Library). (Illus.). (C). 1994. reprint ed. pap. 14.95 (*0-7148-2755-X*, Pub. by Phaidon Press) Phaidon Pr.

Manet: A New Realism. Barron's Educational Editors. (Great Artists Ser.). (Illus.). 32p. 1997. pap. text 5.95 (*0-7641-0295-8*) Barron.

***Manet: A Visionary Impressionist.** Henri Lallemand. 1998. 16.98 (*1-880908-14-X*) Todtri Prods.

Manet: And the Painters of Contemporary Life. Alan Krell. LC 95-60470. (World of Art Ser.). (Illus.). 216p. (Orig.). 1996. pap. 14.95 (*0-500-20289-3*, Pub. by Thames Hudson) Norton.

***Manet: Le Dejeuner sur l'Herbe.** Federico Zeri. (One Hundred Paintings Ser.). (Illus.). 48p. 2000. 14.95 (*1-55321-005-0*, Pub. by NDE Pub) IPG Chicago.

Manet: The Influence of the Modern. Francoise Cachin. Tr. by Rachel Kaplan. (Discoveries Ser.). (Illus.). 176p. 1995. pap. 12.95 (*0-8109-2892-2*, Pub. by Abrams) Time Warner.

***Manet: The Still-Life Paintings.** George L. Mauner et al. LC 00-42009. 2000. write for info. (*0-8109-4391-3*) Abrams.

Manet & Modern Paris: One Hundred Paintings, Drawings, Prints, & Photographs by Manet & His Contemporaries. Theodore Reff. LC 82-18965. (Illus.). 280p. 1992. 39.95 (*0-226-70720-2*) U Ch Pr.

Manet & the French Impressionists. Theodore Duret. Tr. by J. E. Crawford Flitch. (Select Bibliographies Reprint Ser.). 1977. reprint ed. 26.95 (*0-8369-6687-2*) Ayer.

Manet by Himself. Juliet W. Bareall. 1995. 32.98 (*0-7858-0429-3*) Bk Sales Inc.

Manet, Monet, & the Gare Saint-Lazare. Juliet W. Bareau. LC 97-44389. 224p. 1998. 40.00 (*0-300-07510-3*); pap. write for info. (*0-89468-230-X*) Yale U Pr.

Manet's Contemplation at the Gare Saint-Lazare. Harry Rand. LC 86-25077. (Illus.). 168p. 1987. 48.00 (*0-520-05967-0*, Pub. by U CA Pr) Cal Prin Full Svc.

Manet's Graphic Work: A Catalogue Raisonne. rev. ed. Jean C. Harris. (Illus.). 256p. 1990. 125.00 (*1-55660-042-9*) A Wofsy Fine Arts.

Manet's "Le Dejeuner sur l'Herbe" Paul H. Tucker. LC 97-27062. (Masterpieces in Western Painting Ser.). (Illus.). 192p. (C). 1998. text 49.95 (*0-521-47466-3*) Cambridge U Pr.

Manet's "Le Dejeuner sur l'Herve" Paul H. Tucker. LC 97-27062. (Masterpieces in Western Painting Ser.). (Illus.). 192p. (C). 1998. pap. text 15.95 (*0-521-47984-3*) Cambridge U Pr.

Manets Modernism. Fried. 1998. pap. text 35.00 (*0-226-26217-0*) U Ch Pr.

Manet's Modernism: or The Face of Painting in the 1860s. Michael Fried. LC 95-14461. (Illus.). 664p. 1996. 50.00 (*0-226-26216-2*) U Ch Pr.

Manet's Silence & the Poetics of Bouquets. James H. Rubin. LC 93-38505. (Illus.). 192p. 1994. 44.50 (*0-674-54802-7*) HUP.

Manet's Silence & the Poetics of Bouquets. James H. Rubin. LC 93-38505. (Essays in Art & Culture Ser.). (Illus.). 256p. (C). 1995. text 25.95 (*0-674-54803-5*) HUP.

***Maneuver & Firepower (Cloth Editon) The Evolution of Divisions & Separate Brigades.** John B. Wilson. 489p. 1999. boxed set 36.00 (*0-16-049571-7*) USGPO.

Maneuver Warfare: An Anthology. Ed. by Richard D. Hooker, Jr. LC 93-8900. 416p. 1994. pap. 17.95 (*0-89141-518-1*) Presidio Pr.

Maneuver Warfare Handbook. William S. Lind. (Replica Edition Ser.). 152p. (C). 1985. pap. 32.00 (*0-86531-862-X*, Pub. by Westview) HarpC.

Maneuvering the Maze of Managed Care. Corooran. 1996. 28.00 (*0-02-874126-9*) Free Pr.

Maneuvering the Maze of Managed Care: A Survival Guide for Clinicians in Public & Private Settings. Corcoran. 1995. 18.00 (*0-02-874062-9*) Free Pr.

Maneuvering the Maze of Managed Care: A Survival Guide for Clinicians in Public & Private Settings. Kevin Corcoran. 1996. 35.00 (*0-684-82310-1*) Free Pr.

Maneuvering the Maze of Managed Care: A Survival Guide for Clinicians in Public & Private Settings. Kevin Corcoran & Vicki Vandiver. 224p. 1996. 20.00 (*0-684-82309-8*) Free Pr.

Maneuvers: Poems from Hollywood. Mark Dunster. 11p. 1998. pap. 5.00 (*0-89642-516-9*) Linden Pubs.

Maneuvers: The International Politics of Militarizing Women's Lives. Cynthia Enloe. LC 99-28136. 428p. 1999. 45.00 (*0-520-22070-6*, Pub. by U CA Pr); pap. 17.95 (*0-520-22071-4*, Pub. by U CA Pr) Cal Prin Full Svc.

***Maneuvers in Terror.** Joe E. Law. 173p. 1999. pap. 13.95 (*0-7414-0142-8*) Buy Books.

Maneuvers with Number Patterns. David A. Page & Kathryn Chval. (Maneuvers with Math Ser.). (Illus.). 118p. (Orig.). 1994. teacher ed. 15.95 (*0-86651-935-1*) Seymour Pubns.

Maneuvers with Number Patterns. David A. Page & Kathryn Chval. (Maneuvers with Math Ser.). (Illus.). 116p. (Orig.). (J). (gr. 5-8). 1994. student ed. 5.50 (*0-86651-934-3*) Seymour Pubns.

Manfred Bergmeister: Schmiedearbeiten = Smithery. Klaus Pracht & Manfred Bergmeister. LC 98-197177. (ENG & GER.). 183p. 1997. write for info. (*3-8030-5066-9*) E J Wasmuth.

Manfred Schwartz: The Last Ten Years. Jean-Patrice Marandel. LC 73-93335. (Illus.). 1974. pap. 3.00 (*0-911517-27-8*) Mus of Art RI.

Manfrone: or The One-Handed Monk, 2 vols., Set. Mary-Anne Radcliffe. LC 79-131339. (Gothic Novels Ser.). 1979. reprint ed. 53.95 (*0-405-00818-X*) Ayer.

Manga! Manga! The World of Japanese Comics. Frederick L. Schodt. LC 82-48785. (Illus.). 260p. 1986. pap. 22.00 (*0-87011-752-1*) Kodansha.

***Manga! Manga! The World of Japanese Comics.** Frederik L. Schodt. 1998. pap. text 25.00 (*4-7700-1252-7*, Pub. by Kodansha Intl) Kodansha.

Manga! Manga! The World Of Japanese Comics. Frederik L. Schodt. 1998. pap. text 45.00 (*4-7700-2305-7*, Pub. by Kodansha Intl) Kodansha.

Manga Reva. Robert L. Eskridge. 296p. 1988. reprint ed. mass mkt. 5.95 (*0-935180-35-4*) Mutual Pub HI.

Mangaboom. Charlotte Pomerantz. LC 96-10416. (Illus.). 40p. (J). (gr. k up). 1997. 16.00 (*0-688-12956-0*, Grenwillow Bks) HarpC Child Bks.

Mangajin's Japanese Grammar Through Comics. Wayne P. Lammers. (JPN., Illus.). 256p. (Orig.). (C). 1997. pap. write for info. (*0-9634335-5-5*) Mangajin.

Manganese. (Metals & Minerals Ser.). 1993. lib. bdg. 250.75 (*0-8490-8989-1*) Gordon Pr.

Manganese. (Environmental Health Criteria Ser.: No. 17). 110p. 1981. pap. text 13.00 (*92-4-154077-X*, 1160017) World Health.

Manganese. Arthur H. Sully. LC TN0490.M3S85. (Metallurgy of the Rarer Metals Ser.: No. 3). 319p. reprint ed. pap. 98.90 (*0-608-15054-1*, 202575800046) Bks Demand.

Manganese Pt. C: The Compounds: Section 2, Manganate Compounds with Metals, from Li to U. Planck, Max, Society for the Advancement of Scienc. (Gmelin Handbuch der Anorganischen Chemie Ser.). (Illus.). 302p. 1975. 445.00 (*0-387-93287-9*) Spr-Verlag.

Manganese Dioxide Electrode Theory & Practice for Electrochemical Applications: Proceedings of the Symposium. Symposium on Manganese Dioxide Electrode Theory &. Ed. by B. Schumm, Jr. et al. LC 85-70834. (Electrochemical Society Ser.: No. 85-4). (Illus.). 695p. 1985. reprint ed. pap. 200.00 (*0-608-04435-0*, 205257100012) Bks Demand.

Manganese Dioxide-Zinc Batteries. 2nd ed. K. Kordesch & Manfred Weissenbacher. Date not set. write for info. (*0-8247-9880-5*) Dekker.

Manganese in Health & Disease. Dorothy Klimas-Tavantzis. 224p. 1993. boxed set 169.00 (*0-8493-7841-9*) CRC Pr.

Manganese in Soils & Plants. Ed. by R. D. Graham et al. (Developments in Plant & Soil Sciences Ser.). (C). 1988. text 173.50 (*90-247-3758-3*) Kluwer Academic.

Manganese Mineralization. Ed. by K. Nicholson et al. (Geological Society Special Publication Ser.: No. 119). vi, 346p. 1996. 115.00 (*1-897799-74-8*, 360, Pub. by Geol Soc Pub Hse) AAPG.

Manganese Modules: Dimensions & Perspectives. United Nations Ocean Economics & Technology Office. (Natural Resources Forum Library). 1979. pap. text 70.50 (*90-277-0902-5*); lib. bdg. 88.00 (*90-277-0500-3*) Kluwer Academic.

Manganese Modules & Sediments in the Equatorial North Pacific Ocean: "Sonne" Cruise SO 25, 1982. U. Von Stackelberg & H. Beiersdorf. (Geologisches Jahrbuch Reihe D Ser.: Heft 87). (Illus.). 403p. 1987. pap. text 135.80 (*0-945345-19-4*) Lubrecht & Cramer.

Manganese Ores of Supergene Zone: Geochemistry of Formation. Igor M. Varentsov. (Solid Earth Science Library). 356p. (C). 1996. text 195.00 (*0-7923-3906-1*) Kluwer Academic.

Manganese Redox Enzymes. Ed. by Vincent L. Pecoraro. (Illus.). 290p. 1992. 110.00 (*0-89573-729-9*, Wiley-VCH) Wiley.

Manganese Sulfate from the People's Republic of China: An International Trade Investigation. Jonathan Seiger. (Illus.). 74p. (Orig.). (C). 1995. pap. text 50.00 (*0-7881-1610-X*) DIANE Pub.

Mangarayi. Francesca C. Merlan. (Descriptive Grammars Ser.). 264p. 1986. pap. 72.50 (*0-7099-3567-6*, Pub. by C Helm) Routldge.

Mangas Coloradas: Chief of the Chiricahua Apaches. Edwin R. Sweeney. LC 98-9616. (Civilization of American Indian Ser.: No. 231). (Illus.). 608p. 1998. 34.95 (*0-8061-3063-6*) U of Okla Pr.

Mangeclous. Albert Cohen. (Solal Et les Solal Ser.: Vol. II). (FRE.). 448p. 1983. pap. 13.95 (*0-7859-1909-0*, 2070371700) Fr & Eur.

Mangeclous. Albert Cohen. (Folio Ser.: No. 1170). (FRE.). pap. 13.95 (*2-07-037170-0*) Schoenhof.

Manger see Pesebre

Manger & Mystery: An Advent Adventure. Marilyn Brown-Oden. Ed. by Rita Collett. LC 98-55298. 128p. 1999. pap. 10.00 (*0-8358-0861-0*) Upper Room Bks.

Mangerial Accounting: Ready Notes. Morse. 1997. pap., student ed. 24.69 (*0-256-19594-3*) McGraw.

***Mangerialism & Nursing: Beyond Oppression & Profession.** Michael Traynor. LC 98-42097. 1999. 90.00 (*0-415-17895-9*) Routledge.

Mangeront-Ils? Victor Hugo. 272p. 27.50 (*0-686-54080-8*) Fr & Eur.

Manger's Guide Globalization 3/e. Stephen H. Rhinesmith. 2000. 29.95 (*0-07-135480-8*) McGraw.

Mangeurs D'Etoiles. Romain Gary. (Comedie American Ser.: No. I). (FRE.). 448p. 1981. pap. 11.95 (*0-7859-2642-9*, 207037257X) Fr & Eur.

Mangeurs D'Etoiles. Romain Gary. (Folio Ser.: No. 1257). (FRE.). 1966. 10.95 (*2-07-037257-X*) Schoenhof.

Mangeux D'Terre. Gaston Coute. (FRE.). 1995. pap. 49.95 (*2-86808-041-3*) Intl Scholars.

Mangia Cookbook. Ricardo Diaz & Sasha Muniak. 1999. write for info. (*0-316-18464-0*) Little.

Mangia, Little Italy! Secrets from a Sicilian Family Kitchen. Francesca Romina. LC 97-34027. 320p. 1997. pap. text 18.95 (*0-8118-1533-1*) Chronicle Bks.

Mangia Pasta! TK. Mary A. Esposito. Ed. by Pam Hoenig. LC 98-22866. (Illus.). 192p. 1998. 23.00 (*0-688-16189-8*, Wm Morrow) Morrow Avon.

Mangiare E'Squisito - Food Is Love: Antonia's Italian & American Cuisine. 2nd ed. Antonia F. Martin. LC 95-95335. (Illus.). 120p. (Orig.). 1996. reprint ed. spiral bd. 15.00 (*0-9653902-0-9*) Food Is Love.

Mangione/Love Notes: Piano. 19p. 1982. pap. 8.95 (*0-7692-1155-0*, PF0167) Wrner Bros.

Manglares del Gran Caribe: Hacia un Manejo Sostenible. Richard Bossi & Gilberto Cintron. Tr. by Jose Gonzalez from ENG. (SPA., Illus.). 48p. (Orig.). 1991. pap. write for info. (*1-879358-02-6*) Panos Inst.

Mangle of Practice: Time, Agency & Science. Andrew Pickering. LC 94-44546. 296p. 1995. pap. text 17.95 (*0-226-66803-7*); lib. bdg. 45.00 (*0-226-66802-9*) U Ch Pr.

Mangled Hands. Johnny Stanton. (New American Fiction Ser.: No. 2). 320p. 1985. 30.00 (*0-940650-41-X*) Sun & Moon CA.

Mangnificent One: Selected Verses from Rumi. Tr. by Nevit O. Ergin. 112p. 1996. pap. 10.95 (*0-614-21307-X*, 747) Kazi Pubns.

Mango: Botany, Production & Uses. Ed. by Richard E. Litz. LC 96-48881. (A CAB International Publication). 601p. 1997. text 140.00 (*0-85199-127-0*) OUP.

***Mango-coloured Fish.** Kavery Nambisan. LC 98-917645. 1998. write for info. (*0-14-027814-1*) Penguin Books.

Mango Days: A Teenager Facing Eternity Reflects on the Beauty of Life. Patty Smith. LC 92-10039. (Illus.). 135p. (Orig.). (YA). (gr. 9-12). 1992. pap. 11.95 (*0-932727-77-8*); lib. bdg. 19.95 (*0-932727-59-X*) Hope Pub Hse.

Mango Diseases & Their Management: A World Review. Om Prakash & K. C. Srivastava. 180p. 1987. 59.00 (*1-55528-101-X*, Pub. by Today Tomorrow) Scholarly Pubns.

Mango Elephants in the Sun: How Life in an African Village Let Me Be in My Skin. Susana Herrera. 270p. (J). 1999. text 22.50 (*1-57062-376-7*, Pub. by Shambhala Pubns) Random.

***Mango Elephants in the Sun: How Life in an African Village Let Me Be in My Skin.** Susana Herrera. (Illus.). 280p. (J). 2000. pap. 14.95 (*1-57062-572-7*, Pub. by Shambhala Pubns) Random.

Mango Grove. Lorenzo Mans. 41p. 1993. pap. text 3.95 (*1-885901-11-9*) Presbyters Peartree.

Mango Hill. Diana Hansen-Young. (Illus.). 32p. (J). (gr. 2-3). 1989. write for info. (*0-318-64670-6*) Kahaluu Pr.

Mango Lady & Other Stories from Hawaii. Ted Gugelyk. (Illus.). 160p. (Orig.). 1997. pap. 12.95 (*0-9653971-1-4*) Anoai Pr.

***Mango Opera.** Tom Corcoran. 1999. mass mkt. 5.99 (*0-312-96988-0*, Minotaur) St Martin.

Mango Opera, Vol. 1. Tom Corcoran. LC 98-4804. 304p. 1998. text 22.95 (*0-312-18628-2*) St Martin.

Mango Shoes: And Other Stories. Paul Drexel. Ed. by Cordelia McIntyre. (Illus.). (Orig.). 1995. pap. 8.95 (*0-9640300-8-X*) Galhattan Pr.

Mango Spice. Gloria Cameron. (J). pap. write for info. (*0-7136-2107-9*, 93118, Pub. by A & C Blk) Midpt Trade.

Mango Tree Church. D. G. McKenzie. 84p. (C). 1990. pap. text 30.00 (*0-86439-039-4*, Pub. by Boolarong Pubns) St Mut.

Mango Walk. large type ed. Rhona Martin. (Ulverscroft Large Print Ser.). 736p. 1997. 27.99 (*0-7089-3762-4*) Ulverscroft.

Mangod, No. 1. Bernard J. Gill. 300p. 1986. 15.00 (*0-9616510-0-8*); pap. 12.95 (*0-685-13309-5*) B J Gill.

Mangoes & Bullets. John Agard. 80p. (Orig.). 1991. pap. 12.95 (*1-85242-124-X*) Serpents Tail.

Mangoes & Chappaties. Margaret R. Drucker. LC 98-90664. (Orig.). 1999. pap. 14.95 (*0-533-12870-6*) Vantage.

***Mangoes & Quince.** Carol Field. 2001. 23.95 (*1-58234-114-1*) Bloomsbury Pubg.

Mangoes or Bananas? The Quest for an Authentic Asian Christian Theology. Hwa Yung. 273p. 1997. reprint ed. pap. 30.00 (*1-870345-25-8*, Pub. by Regnum Bks) OM Literature.

***Mangoes Restaurant Key West, Cool Recipes for Turned-On Cooks: Anthology of a Restaurant.** Paul Orchard. Ed. by Amy Culver-Aversa. (Illus.). 46p. 1998. pap. 20.00 (*0-9673660-0-3*) P A G Key West.

Mangos, Bananas & Coconuts: A Cuban Love Story. Himilce Novas. LC 95-37661. 168p. 1996. 9.95 (*1-55885-092-9*) Arte Publico.

Mangos, Mangos, Mangos: Recipes & Art from Hawaii. Charles K. Smoyer. LC 89-180569. (Illus.). 232p. (Orig.). 1989. pap. write for info. (*0-9623332-0-4*) Hawaiian Island.

***Mangrove Coast.** Randy Wayne White. LC 98-22243. 256p. 1998. 22.95 (*0-399-14372-6*, G P Putnam) Peng Put Young Read.

***Mangrove Coast.** Randy Wayne White. 1999. reprint ed. mass mkt. 6.50 (*0-425-17194-9*, Prime Crime) Berkley Pub.

***Mangrove Ecosystem of Deep Bay & the Mai Po Marshes, Hong Kong.** Ed. by Shing Yip Lee. 196p. 1999. pap. (*962-209-485-6*) HK Univ Pr.

Mangrove Mama. Janwillem Van de Wetering. (Illus.). 296p. 1995. 30.00 (*0-939767-23-6*) D McMillan.

Mangrove Man: Dialogics of Culture in the Sepik Estuary. David Lipset. LC 96-50213. (Studies in Social & Cultural Anthropology: Vol. 106). (Illus.). 358p. (C). 1997. text 59.95 (*0-521-56434-4*); pap. text 23.95 (*0-521-56435-2*) Cambridge U Pr.

Mangrove Squeeze. Laurence Shames. 1999. mass mkt. 6.99 (*0-345-43306-8*) Ballantine Pub Grp.

Mangrove Squeeze. Laurence Shames. LC 97-35880. 320p. 1998. 22.45 (*0-7868-6301-3*, Pub. by Hyperion); mass mkt. 5.99 (*0-7868-8945-4*) Hyperion.

Mangrove Swamps of the Sundarbans: An Ecological Perspective. Naskar Guha. (C). 1987. 57.50 (*81-85109-49-4*, Pub. by Naya Prokash) S Asia.

Mangrove Vegetation. P. Lin. 150p. 1988. 29.50 (*0-387-15718-2*) Spr-Verlag.

Mangroves. Jeremy Stafford-Deitsch. 288p. (C). 1995. pap. 51.00 (*0-907151-93-0*, Pub. by IMMEL Pubng) St Mut.

Mangroves de la Caraibe: Pour une Gestion Durable. Richard Bossi & Gilberto Cintron. Tr. by Fota Kamara from ENG. (FRE., Illus.). 48p. (Orig.). 1991. pap. write for info. (*1-879358-03-4*) Panos Inst.

Mangroves of Orissa Coast & Their Ecology. L. K. Banerjee & T. A. Rao. (Illus.). 118p. 1990. text 17.50 (*81-211-0028-3*, Pub. by Mahendra Pal Singh) Lubrecht & Cramer.

Mangroves of the Wider Caribbean: Toward Sustainable Management. Richard Bossi & Gilberto Cintron. (Illus.). 52p. (Orig.). 1990. pap. write for info. (*1-879358-00-X*) Panos Inst.

***Mangroves to Major League: A Timeline of St. Petersburg, Florida (Pre-History to 2000 A.D.)** Rick Baker. (Illus.). 400p. 2000. 34.95 (*0-941072-38-X*) Southern Herit.

Manhaj al Bahth al Ijtima'i Bayna al Wad'iyah wa al Mi'yariyah: The Method of Social Research Between Subjectivity & Standardization. Muhammad M. Imiziyan. LC 91-14262. (Silsilat al Rasa'il al Jami'iyah Ser.: No. 4). (ARA.). 516p. (Orig.). 1991. 15.00 (*0-912463-87-2*); pap. 10.00 (*0-912463-88-0*) IIIT VA.

Manhattan. (Frommer's Irreverent Guides Ser.). 1996. pap. 12.95 (*0-614-12828-5*) Macmillan.

Manhattan. Carol M. Highsmith & Ted Landphair. LC 97-18034. (Pictorial Souvenir). 64p. 1998. 7.99 (*0-517-18762-0*) Crown Pub Group.

Manhattan. Ted Landphai & Carol M. Highsmith. LC 96-44146. (Photographic Tour Ser.). (Illus.). 128p. 1997. 14.99 (*0-517-18332-3*) Random Hse Value.

Manhattan. Jean Zimmerman & Gil Reavill. LC 94-17972. (Compass American Guides Ser.). (Illus.). 304p. 1994. pap. 17.95 (*1-878867-37-7*) Fodors Travel.

Manhattan. 3rd ed. Eugene Fodor. LC 98-3441. (Compass American Guides Ser.). 1999. pap. 19.95 (*0-679-00228-6*) Fodors Travel.

Manhattan: A Tour about Town. (Little Bks.). (Illus.). 80p. 1996. 4.95 (*0-8362-1055-7*) Andrews & McMeel.

Manhattan: An Island in Focus. Photos by Jake Rajs. LC 85-43056. (Illus.). 256p. 1991. 55.00 (*0-8478-0670-7*, Pub. by Rizzoli Intl) St Martin.

Manhattan: Between the Rivers. Jeff Hirsch. LC 98-87139. (Images of America Ser.). 1998. write for info. (*0-7524-0812-7*) Arcadia Publng.

Manhattan: Postcard Book. Jon Ortner. 30p. 1996. pap. text 10.95 (*1-55670-455-0*) Stewart Tabori & Chang.

Manhattan Apartment Finder. Stephen T. Leven & David M. Elwell. 97p. (Orig.). 1996. pap. 19.95 (*0-9651014-0-1*, 1001) Greener Pastures.

***Manhattan City Diary Deluxe with Clasp & Pen.** 1999. 35.50 (*1-57499-119-1*) Per Annum.

Manhattan Class Company - Class 1 Acts: A Collection of One-Acts. 1992. pap. 5.25 (*0-8222-1311-7*) Dramatists Play.

Manhattan College - Then & Now. Photos by Sepp Seitz. (First Edition Ser.). (Illus.). 112p. 1991. 39.95 (*0-916509-85-0*) Harmony Hse Pub.

Manhattan Company: Managing a Multi-Unit Corporation in New York, 1799-1842. Gregory S. Hunter. LC 89-48491. (Studies in Entrepreneurship). 350p. 1990. reprint ed. text 20.00 (*0-8240-4670-6*) Garland.

***Manhattan Daily-Plan It 2000.** (Illus.). 214p. 1999. write for info. (*1-57499-109-4*) Per Annum.

***Manhattan Daily-Plan It 2000, Leather.** (Illus.). 214p. 1999. write for info. (*1-57499-111-6*) Per Annum.

***Manhattan Daily Plan-It 2001: Black.** (Illus.). 214p. 2000. lthr. 60.00 (*1-57499-087-X*) Per Annum.

An Asterisk (*) at the beginning of an entry indicates that the title is appearing for the first time.

***Manhattan Daily Plan-It 2001: Burgundy.** (Illus.). 214p. 2000. lthr. 35.00 (*1-57499-088-8*) Per Annum.

***Manhattan Daily Plan-It 2001: Refill.** (Illus.). 214p. 2000. 18.00 (*1-57499-086-1*) Per Annum.

Manhattan Dance School Directory. Ed. by Barbi L. O'Reilly. LC 78-10411. (Dance Program Ser.: Vol. 13). 191p. reprint ed. pap. 59.30 (*0-608-16660-X*, 202781500054) Bks Demand.

Manhattan Dawn & Dusk. Photos by Jon Ortner. LC 95-22256. (Illus.). 208p. 1995. 60.00 (*1-55670-426-7*) Stewart Tabori & Chang.

Manhattan Diary 2000. (Illus.). 214p. 1999. 17.00 (*1-57499-108-6*) Per Annum.

***Manhattan Diary 2000, Black Leather.** (Illus.). 214p. 1999. 32.50 (*1-57499-106-X*) Per Annum.

***Manhattan Diary 2000, Burgundy Leather.** (Illus.). 214p. 1999. 32.50 (*1-57499-107-8*) Per Annum.

***Manhattan Diary 2001.** (Illus.). 214p. 2000. im. lthr. 18.00 (*1-57499-085-3*) Per Annum.

***Manhattan Diary 2001: Black.** (Illus.). 214p. 2000. lthr. 32.50 (*1-57499-084-5*) Per Annum.

***Manhattan Diary 2001: Burgundy.** (Illus.). 214p. 2000. lthr. 32.50 (*1-57499-089-6*) Per Annum.

Manhattan Directory of Private Nursery Schools. 4th rev. ed. Linda Faulhaber. 360p. 1998. pap. 24.00 (*1-56947-128-2*) Soho Press.

Manhattan District History: Nonscientific Aspects of Los Alamos Project Y, 1942 Through 1946. Edith C. Truslow. Ed. by Kasha V. Thayer. LC 91-8207. (Illus.). viii, 111p. (Orig.). 1991. reprint ed. pap. 12.95 (*0-941232-11-5*) Los Alamos Hist Soc.

Manhattan Doctor Guide: New York's Most Talked about Doctors. Richard D. Topp. LC 98-202009. 164p. 1998. pap. 14.95 (*0-9663834-0-0*) Radcomm Inc.

Manhattan Family Guide to Private Schools. 3rd rev. ed. Victoria Goldman & Catherine Hausman. 448p. 1999. pap. 25.00 (*1-56947-148-7*) Soho Press.

Manhattan for Rent, 1785-1850. Elizabeth Blackmar. LC 88-47926. (Illus.). 336p. 1991. pap. text 17.95 (*0-8014-9973-9*) Cornell U Pr.

Manhattan for Sale or Rent: Upper East Side. (Illus.). 160p. 1997. pap. 19.95 (*0-9660096-0-6*) Aaron Publ.

***Manhattan for Sale or Rent No. 1: Upper East Side.** (Illus.). 215p. 1999. pap. 19.95 (*0-9660096-4-9*, Pub. by Aaron Publ) Midpt Trade.

Manhattan for Sale or Rent - Upper West Side, Vol. 2. Jenny Henry. (Illus.). 114p. 1997. pap. 19.95 (*0-9660096-1-4*) Aaron Publ.

***Manhattan for Sale or Rent - Upper West Side: Everything You Need to Know to Successfully Find Your Own Apartment on Manhattan's West Side.** Jenny Henry. 180p. 2000. pap. 19.95 (*0-9660096-5-7*, Pub. by Aaron Publ) Midpt Trade.

Manhattan for Sale or Rent-Downtown. Jenny Henry. (Illus.). 233p. 1998. pap. 19.95 (*0-9660096-3-0*) Aaron Publ.

Manhattan for Sale or Rent-Midtown: Everything You Need to Know to Successfully Find Your Own Apartment. Jenny Henry. 1998. pap. 19.95 (*0-9660096-2-2*) Aaron Publ.

Manhattan 'Forty-Five. Jan Morris. 288p. 1990. reprint ed. pap. 9.95 (*0-19-506664-2*) OUP.

Manhattan, 1945. Jan Morris. LC 98-12937. 286p. 1998. reprint ed. pap. 15.95 (*0-8018-5957-3*) Johns Hopkins.

Manhattan Ghost Story. T. M. Wright. 384p. 1994. mass mkt. 4.99 (*0-8125-1950-7*, Pub. by Tor Bks) St Martin.

Manhattan Goodbye. Seymour Hakim. 1970. pap. 3.50 (*0-913054-01-1*) Poet Gal Pr.

Manhattan Gothic. Mel Arrighi. LC 99-60521. 250p. 1999. reprint ed. pap. 16.00 (*1-892323-80-X*) Vivisphere.

Manhattan Health Pages: A Directory of Resources for Living Healthy in New York City. Lyn Skreczko & Virginia Bell. LC 98-66462. 300p. 1998. pap. 16.95 (*0-9641262-8-1*) Little Bkrm.

Manhattan Heat. Alice H. Orr. (Intrigue Ser.). 1996. per. 3.75 (*0-373-22369-2*, 1-22369-2) Harlequin Bks.

Manhattan Hotels, 1880-1920. Jeff Hirsch. (Images of America Ser.). 1999. pap. 16.99 (*0-7524-0843-7*) Arcadia Publng.

Manhattan in Maps, 1556-1990. Paul E. Cohen & Robert T. Augustyn. LC 97-19200. (Illus.). 176p. 1997. 50.00 (*0-8478-2052-1*, Pub. by Rizzoli Intl) St Martin.

Manhattan in 1638, As Desribed in the . . . Autographed Letter of Jonas Michaelius...with a Review of the Letter & an Historical Sketch of New Netherland to 1628. Dingman Versteeg. (Illus.). 203p. 1997. reprint ed. lib. bdg. 32.00 (*0-8328-6171-5*) Higginson Bk Co.

***Manhattan Is My Beat.** Jeffery Deaver. 304p. 2000. mass mkt. 6.99 (*0-553-58176-7*) Bantam.

Manhattan Lightscape. Photos by Nathaniel Lieberman. (Illus.). 124p. 2000. 45.00 (*1-55859-121-4*) Abbeville Pr.

Manhattan Lightscape Postcard Book. 1993. pap. 7.95 (*1-55859-646-1*) Abbeville Pr.

Manhattan Living. Bruce Levine. Ed. by Michael Weisberg. (Illus.). 304p. (Orig.). 1985. pap. 14.95 (*0-9614421-0-7*) M K L Ltd.

Manhattan Living. Ed. by Noah Sarlat. (Illus.). 275p. (Orig.). 1986. pap. 7.95 (*0-9614421-1-5*) M K L Ltd.

***Manhattan Loverboy.** Arthur Nersesian. LC 99-96428. 203p. 2000. pap. 13.95 (*1-888451-09-2*, AKB06, Pub. by Akashic Bks) SPD-Small Pr Dist.

Manhattan Lullaby. Olivia De Grove. 206p. 1990. pap. 5.95 (*0-7736-7258-3*) Genl Dist Srvs.

Manhattan Magic. large type ed. Jean Davidson. 1990. pap. 16.99 (*0-7089-6928-3*, Linford) Ulverscroft.

Manhattan Maneater. James T. Sledge, Jr. (Illus.). vii, 209p. 1997. pap. 9.95 (*0-9660010-0-1*) Up-To-Minute.

***Manhattan Memoir.** Mary Cantwell. LC 99-52553. 440p. 2000. pap. 17.95 (*0-14-029190-3*) Viking Penguin.

Manhattan Messiah. Michael Guerra. Ed. by Cynthia Burris. LC 98-93915. 530p. 1998. pap. text 14.95 (*0-9668116-0-7*) Destiny Grp Inc.

Manhattan Music. rev. ed. Meena Alexander. LC 96-53344. (Illus.). 256p. (Orig.). 1997. reprint ed. pap. 14.95 (*1-56279-092-7*) Mercury Hse Inc.

Manhattan North Homicide. Thomas Mckenna. 1997. mass mkt. 5.99 (*0-312-96009-3*) St Martin.

Manhattan Ocean Club Seafood Cookbook. Jonathan Parker. LC 99-23463. 1999. 30.00 (*1-56799-798-8*, Friedman-Fairfax) M Friedman Pub Grp Inc.

Manhattan Odyssey: A Memoir. Herman G. Weinberg. (Illus.). 206p. 1982. 20.00 (*0-911689-10-9*); pap. 10.00 (*0-911689-09-5*) Anthology Film.

Manhattan on Film: Walking Tours of Hollywood's Fabled Front Lot. Chuck Katz. LC 99-41345. (Illus.). 176p. 1999. pap. 14.95 (*0-87910-283-7*) Limelight Edns.

Manhattan On-Street Parking: A Street by Street Guide to Parking Regulations from 72nd Street to the Battery. Jeffrey M. Keller. (Illus.). 96p. (Orig.). 1987. pap. 6.95 (*0-942313-00-3*) Sandhill Pubns.

Manhattan Pastures. Sandra Hochman. LC 75-21577. (Yale Series of Younger Poets: No. 59). reprint ed. 18.00 (*0-404-53859-2*) AMS Pr.

Manhattan Project. Daniel Cohen. 144p. (YA). (gr. 7 up). 1999. 21.90 (*0-7613-1309-5*, Copper Beech Bks) Millbrook Pr.

Manhattan Project. Daniel Cohen. LC 98-44499. (Illus.). 128p. 1999. lib. bdg. 22.95 (*0-7613-0359-6*) TFC Bks NY.

Manhattan Project. Ed. by Kenneth M. Deitch. LC 94-71896. (Perspectives on History Ser.). (Illus.). 64p. (C). 1995. pap. 6.95 (*1-878668-41-2*) Disc Enter Ltd.

Manhattan Project. Richard C. Stein. LC 93-12686. (Cornerstones to Freedom Ser.). (Illus.). 32p. (J). (gr. 3-6). 1993. pap. 5.95 (*0-516-46670-4*) Childrens.

Manhattan Project. Richard C. Stein. LC 93-12686. (Cornerstones to Freedom Ser.). (Illus.). 32p. (J). (gr. 4-7). 1993. lib. bdg. 19.50 (*0-516-06670-6*) Childrens.

Manhattan Project: A Documentary Introduction to the Atomic Age. Michael B. Stoff. 320p. (C). 1991. pap. 19.69 (*0-07-557209-5*) McGraw.

Manhattan Project: Making the Atomic Bomb. F. G. Gosling. (Illus.). 66p. 1999. pap. text 20.00 (*0-7881-7880-6*) DIANE Pub.

***Manhattan Project & the Atomic Bomb.** Doreen Gonzales. LC 99-16690. (In American History Ser.). (Illus.). 128p. (gr. 5 up). 2000. lib. bdg. 20.95 (*0-89490-879-0*) Enslow Pubs.

Manhattan Rhapsody. Carl Shapiro. 100p. 1985. pap. 8.50 (*0-914937-01-4*) Ind Pubns.

Manhattan Shores: An Expedition Around Manhattan Island. Laura Rosen. LC 98-60187. (Illus.). 160p. 1998. 35.00 (*0-500-54221-X*, Pub. by Thames Hudson) Norton.

Manhattan Skyscrapers. Eric Nash. LC 98-50603. (Illus.). 1999. 45.00 (*1-56898-181-3*) Princeton Arch.

Manhattan Tales 1920-1945. Isabel Butterfield. (Illus.). 182p. 1999. 29.50 (*1-85776-367-X*, Pub. by Book Guild Ltd) Trans-Atl Phila.

Manhattan Transcripts. Bernard Tschumi. 1995. 35.00 (*1-85490-381-0*) Academy Ed UK.

Manhattan Transcripts. Bernard Tschumi. (Illus.). 1982. pap. 9.95 (*0-312-51286-4*) St Martin.

Manhattan Transfer. John Dos Passos. Date not set. lib. bdg. 27.95 (*0-8488-0986-6*) Amereon Ltd.

Manhattan Transfer. John Dos Passos. (FRE.). 499p. 1976. pap. 11.95 (*0-7859-1831-0*, 2070368254) Fr & Eur.

Manhattan Transfer. John Dos Passos. 410p. 1991. pap. 14.95 (*0-395-57423-4*) HM.

Manhattan Transfer. John E. Stith. 384p. 1994. mass mkt. 4.99 (*0-8125-1952-3*, Pub. by Tor Bks) St Martin.

Manhattan Transfer. John Dos Passos. 1980. reprint ed. lib. bdg. 22.00 (*0-8376-0433-8*) Bentley Pubs.

Manhattan Transfer Meets Tubby the Tuba. Paul Tripp et al. (Illus.). 32p. (J). 1994. pap. Price not set. incl. audio (*0-9642066-0-9*) MK Prods.

Manhattan Transfer Songbook. 72p. 1982. per. 14.95 (*0-7935-2081-9*, 00357470) H Leonard.

Manhattan up Close: District to District, Street by Street. Fiona Duncan & Leonie Glass. (Illus.). 160p. 1994. pap. 12.95 (*0-8442-9450-0*, 94500, Passprt Bks) NTC Contemp Pub Co.

Manhattan User's Guide: The Guide to New York for New Yorkers. Charles Suisman. LC 96-21582. (Illus.). 512p. (J). 1996. pap. 17.45 (*0-7868-8152-6*, Pub. by Hyperion) Time Warner.

***Manhattan Water-Bound: Manhattan's Waterfront from the Seventeenth Century to the Present.** 2nd ed. Ann L. Buttenwieser. LC 98-55154. (New York City History & Culture Ser.). 296p. 1999. pap. 19.95 (*0-8156-2801-3*) Syracuse U Pr.

Manhattan, When I Was Young. Mary Cantwell. 224p. 1996. pap. 12.95 (*0-14-023223-0*, Penguin Bks) Viking Penguin.

***Manhattan with a Twist.** unabridged ed. Jan Arrigo. (Illus.). 126p. 2000. 36.95 (*1-891643-71-1*, Winter Bks LA) Pontalba Pr.

Manhattan Woman. unabridged ed. Sam Oakland. LC 98-75117. 116p. 1999. pap. 15.00 (*0-9658601-2-4*) Sweetbriar Co.

Manhattaner in New Orleans: or Phases of Crescent City Life. A. Oakey Hall. Ed. by Henry A. Kmen. LC 75-21960. xxviii, 195p. 1976. reprint ed. 35.00 (*0-8071-0167-2*, HMANHA) Claitors.

Manhattans & Murder. Jessica Fletcher & Donald Bain. (Murder She Wrote Ser.: Vol. 1). 304p. (Orig.). 1994. mass mkt. 5.99 (*0-451-18142-5*, Sig) NAL.

Manhattans & Murder. large type ed. Donald Bain. LC 98-14731. 267p. 1998. 19.95 (*0-7838-0133-5*, G K Hall & Co) Mac Lib Ref.

Manhattan's First Retail Discount Directory. Nexus Network Inc. Staff. (Nexusguide Ser.). 1998. pap. 20.00 (*1-892983-00-1*) Nexus Network Inc.

Manhattanville College - Then & Now. Photos by Tom Sobolik. (First Edition Ser.). (Illus.). 112p. 1992. 39.95 (*0-916509-92-3*) Harmony Hse Pub.

Manheimer's Cataloging & Classification. 4th expanded rev. ed. J. D. Saye. LC 99-38007. (Books in Library & Information Sciences). (Illus.). 395p. 1999. text 45.00 (*0-8247-9476-1*, 9476-1) Dekker.

Manheimer's Cataloging & Classification: A Workbook. 3rd ed. Jerry D. Saye. (Books in Library & Information Science: Vol. 53). (Illus.). 296p. 1991. text 39.75 (*0-8247-8493-6*) Dekker.

Manhole Covers. Mimi Melnick. (Illus.). 272p. 1994. 45.00 (*0-262-13302-4*) MIT Pr.

Manhole Covers. Mimi Melnick. (Illus.). 274p. 1996. pap. text 22.50 (*0-262-63174-1*) MIT Pr.

Manhole Covers of Ft. Wayne, Indiana. Kathryn Moore. (Illus.). 128p. (Orig.). Date not set. pap. 10.95 (*0-89708-191-9*) And Bks.

Manhole Inspection & Rehabilitation. American Society of Civil Engineers Staff. LC 97-26967. (ASCE Manuals & Reports on Engineering Practice: Vol. 92). (Illus.). 96p. 1997. 39.00 (*0-7844-0285-X*, 40285-X) Am Soc Civil Eng.

Manhood: A Journey from Childhood into the Fierce Order of Virility. Michel Leiris. Tr. by Richard Howard. LC 91-48195. 184p. (Orig.). 1992. pap. 13.95 (*0-226-47141-1*) U Ch Pr.

Manhood: An Action Plan for Changing Men's Lives. Steve Biddulph. LC 98-42354. 272p. 1999. pap. 12.95 (*0-89087-852-8*) Celestial Arts.

Manhood & Morality: Sex, Violence, & Ritual in GISU Society. Suzette Heald. LC 98-38229. 1999. 75.00 (*0-415-18577-7*) Routledge.

Manhood & Morality: Sex, Violence & Ritual in GISU Society. Suzette Heald. LC 98-38229. ix, 192 p. 1999. pap. 24.99 (*0-415-18578-5*) Routledge.

Manhood & Politics: A Feminist Reading in Political Thought. Wendy L. Brown. LC 87-12850. (New Feminist Perspectives Ser.). 248p. 1988. 66.00 (*0-8476-7576-9*); pap. 23.00 (*0-8476-7577-7*) Rowman.

Manhood & the American Renaissance. David Leverenz. LC 88-47914. 384p. 1989. text 47.50 (*0-8014-2281-7*) Cornell U Pr.

Manhood & the American Renaissance. David Leverenz. LC 88-47914. 384p. 1990. reprint ed. pap. text 18.95 (*0-8014-9743-4*) Cornell U Pr.

Manhood at Harvard: William James & Others. Kim Townsend. (Illus.). 336p. 1998. pap. text 16.95 (*0-674-54804-3*) HUP.

Manhood Development in Urban African-American Communities. Ed. by Roderick J. Watts & Robert J. Jagers. LC 97-45551. 167p. 1998. 29.95 (*0-7890-0377-5*); pap. 19.95 (*0-7890-0505-0*) Haworth Pr.

***Manhood God's Style.** Wilbur Conway. 112p. 1999. pap. 8.99 (*1-56043-318-3*) Destiny Image.

Manhood in America. Michael Kimmel. 1997. pap. 17.95 (*0-684-83712-9*) S&S Trade.

Manhood in America: A Cultural History. Michael Kimmel. LC 95-32619. (Illus.). 506p. 1995. 29.50 (*0-02-874067-X*) Free Pr.

***Manhood in Early Modern England: Honor, Sex & Marriage.** Elisabeth Foyster. LC 98-42933. 264p. (C). 1999. pap. 32.46 (*0-582-30735-X*) Longman.

Manhood in Early Modern England: Honor, Sex & Marriage. Elizabeth Foyster. LC 98-42933. 1999. text 68.95 (*0-582-30734-1*) Addison-Wesley.

Manhood in the Making: Cultural Concepts of Masculinity. David D. Gilmore. 1991. pap. 16.00 (*0-300-05076-3*) Yale U Pr.

Manhood of Humanity. 2nd ed. Alfred Korzybski. 326p. 1950. 15.00 (*0-937298-00-X*) Inst Gen Seman.

Manhood 101. Ed Cole. LC 96-122342. 1996. pap. 6.99 (*1-56292-051-0*, HB-051) Honor Bks OK.

Manhood Redux: Standing up to Feminism. Carleton H. Freedman. Ed. by J. Leiman. 294p. (Orig.). 1985. pap. 7.95 (*0-935985-00-X*) Samson Pubs.

Manhood 501 see Taking the Lead: Following the Example of Paul, Timothy & Silvans

***Manhunt.** Wayne Barton. (Orig.). 2000. mass mkt. 5.99 (*0-425-17339-9*) Berkley Pub.

Manhunt. Wayne Barton & Stan Williams. Ed. by Doug Grad. 224p. (Orig.). 1992. pap. 3.50 (*0-671-74576-X*) PB.

Manhunt. large type ed. Wayne Stan & Baron Williams. LC 97-30531. 293p. 1997. 20.95 (*0-7838-8305-6*, G K Hall Lrg Type) Mac Lib Ref.

Manhunt: The Book. Harvey C. Altes et al. LC 98-66795. (Illus.). 452p. 1998. pap. write for info. (*0-9664959-1-8*) TFA Publishing.

Manhunt: The Pursuit of Harry Tracy. Bill Gullick. Ed. by Wayne Cornell. LC 99-10642. (Illus.). 240p. 1999. pap. 18.95 (*0-87004-392-7*) Caxton.

Manhunt: USA Vs. Militia. Ian Slater. 1999. mass mkt. 6.99 (*0-449-15046-1*) Fawcett.

Manhunt in the Desert. Akhter Ahsen. 1979. pap. 9.95 (*0-913412-26-0*) Brandon Hse.

Manhunter. large type ed. Lauran Paine. LC 94-45644. 214p. 1995. 18.95 (*0-7862-0397-8*) Thorndike Pr.

Manhunter. large type ed. Gordon D. Shirreffs. (Linford Western Library). 304p. 1988. pap. 16.99 (*0-7089-6495-8*, Linford) Ulverscroft.

Manhunter: The Astounding True Story of the U. S. Marshal Who Tracked down the World's Most Evil Criminals. John Pascucci & Cameron Stauth. 384p. 1996. 23.00 (*0-671-88518-9*) PB.

Manhunter: The Astounding True Story of the U. S. Marshal Who Tracked down the World's Most Evil Criminals. John Pascucci & Cameron Stauth. 367p. 1997. per. 6.50 (*0-671-88517-0*, Pocket Star Bks) PB.

Manhunter: The Life & Times of Frank Hamer. Gene Shelton. 304p. 1997. mass mkt. 5.99 (*0-425-15973-6*) Berkley Pub.

Manhunter: The Special Edition. Archie Goodwin. (Illus.). 104p. 1999. pap. text 9.95 (*1-56389-374-6*, Pub. by DC Comics) Time Warner.

Manhunters. Elmer Kelton. LC 94-6499. (Texas Tradition Ser.: Vol. 22). 208p. (C). 1994. 19.95 (*0-87565-132-1*); pap. 12.95 (*0-87565-134-8*) Tex Christian.

Manhunters: Hounds of the Big T. William D. Tolhurst. Ed. by Lena F. Reed. (Illus.). 284p. 1985. 16.00 (*0-9617723-0-1*) Hound Dog Pr.

Manhunting. Jennifer Crusie. (Temptation Ser.). 1993. per. 2.99 (*0-373-25563-2*, 1-25563-7) Harlequin Bks.

***Manhunting.** Jennifer Crusie. 2000. mass mkt. 4.50 (*0-373-82215-4*, 1-82215-4) Harlequin Bks.

***Manhunting.** Jennifer Crusie. 2000. mass mkt. 5.99 (*1-55166-618-9*, 1-66618-9, Mira Bks) Harlequin Bks.

Manhunting in Manhattan. Carolyn Andrews. (Temptation Ser.). 1998. per. 3.75 (*0-373-25773-2*, 1-25773-2) Harlequin Bks.

Manhunting in Memphis. Heather MacAllister. (Temptation Ser.: No. 669). 1998. per. 3.75 (*0-373-25769-4*, 1-25769-0) Harlequin Bks.

Manhunting in Miami. Alyssa Dean. (Temptation Ser.). 1998. per. 3.75 (*0-373-25781-3*, 0-25781-6) Harlequin Bks.

Manhunting in Mississippi. Stephanie Bond. (Temptation Ser.). 1998. per. 3.75 (*0-373-25785-6*, 1-25785-6) Harlequin Bks.

Manhunting in Montana. Vicki L. Thompson. (Temptation Ser.: Vol. 677). 1998. per. 3.75 (*0-373-25777-5*, 1-25777-3) Harlequin Bks.

Manhunts & Massacres. Leo W. Banks. (Wild West). 144p. 1999. pap. 7.95 (*0-916179-63-X*) Ariz Hwy.

***Mani: His Life & Work Transforming Evil.** Richard Seddon. 96p. 1998. pap. 16.95 (*0-904693-95-3*, Pub. by Temple Lodge) Anthroposophic.

Mani & Manichaeism. rev. ed. George Widengren. Tr. by George Kessler from GER. LC 82-45825. (Orthodoxies & Heresies in the Early Church Ser.). (Illus.). reprint ed. 37.50 (*0-404-62396-4*) AMS Pr.

Mania: Clinical & Research Perspectives. Ed. by Paul J. Goodnick. 478p. 1998. text 62.00 (*0-88048-728-3*, 8728) Am Psychiatric.

Mania: New Research & Treatment. Ed. by Alan C. Swann. LC 86-10911. (Clinical Insights Ser.). 212p. reprint ed. pap. 65.80 (*0-8357-7840-1*, 203621500002) Bks Demand.

Mania & Depression: A Classificiation of Syndrome & Disease. George Winokur. LC 91-6345. (Series in Contemporary Medicine & Public Health). 256p. 1991. text 50.00 (*0-8018-4187-9*) Johns Hopkins.

Mania & Literary Style: The Rhetoric of Enthusiasm from the Ranters to Christopher Smart. Clement Hawes. (Studies in Eighteenth-Century English Literature & Thought: No. 29). 255p. (C). 1996. text 59.95 (*0-521-55022-X*) Cambridge U Pr.

Maniac. John Peel. (YA). (gr. 7 up). 1995. mass mkt. 3.50 (*0-671-88735-1*, Archway) PB.

Maniac in the Bushes: And More Tales of Cleveland Woe. John S. Bellamy, II. LC 97-33939. (Illus.). 304p. 1997. pap. 13.95 (*1-886228-19-1*) Gray & Co Pubs.

Maniac in the Cellar: Sensation Novels of the 1860s. Winifred Hughes. LC 80-7530. 222p. reprint ed. pap. 68.90 (*0-8357-8944-6*, 205228400085) Bks Demand.

***Maniac Magee.** 1999. 9.95 (*1-56137-348-6*) Novel Units.

***Maniac Magee.** Phyllis A. Green. 44p. (J). 1999. student ed., wbk. ed. 11.95 (*1-56137-604-3*) Novel Units.

Maniac Magee. Michael Levin. (Literature Unit Ser.). (Illus.). 48p. 1995. pap., teacher ed. 7.95 (*1-55734-537-6*) Tchr Create Mat.

Maniac Magee. Jerry Spinelli. LC 89-27144. 184p. (J). (gr. 4-7). 1990. 15.95 (*0-316-80722-2*, Joy St Bks) Little.

***Maniac Magee.** Jerry Spinelli. LC 89-27144. (Illus.). 192p. (J). (gr. 4-7). 1999. pap. 5.95 (*0-316-80906-3*) Little.

Maniac Magee. Jerry Spinelli. (Pathways to Critical Thinking Ser.). 32p. (YA). 1997. pap. text 19.95 (*1-58303-026-3*) Pthways Pubng.

Maniac Magee. Jerry Spinelli. (Assessment Packs Ser.). 15p. (J). 1998. pap. text 15.95 (*1-58303-050-6*) Pthways Pubng.

Maniac Magee. Jerry Spinelli. (J). 1992. 10.05 (*0-606-00864-0*, Pub. by Turtleback) Demco.

Maniac Magee. Jerry Spinelli & Scholastic, Inc. Staff. (Literature Guide Ser.). 16p. (J). 1997. pap. text 3.95 (*0-590-36644-0*) Scholastic Inc.

Maniac Magee. large type ed. Jerry Spinelli. (J). 1995. 50.00 (*0-614-09600-6*, L-81911-00) Am Printing Hse.

Maniac Magee. large type ed. Jerry Spinelli. 221p. (J). 1993. reprint ed. lib. bdg. 15.95 (*1-56054-621-2*) Thorndike Pr.

Maniac Magee: A Study Guide. Kathleen Fischer. Ed. by J. Friedland & R. Kessler. (Novel-Ties Ser.). (J). (gr. 5-7). 1992. pap. text, student ed. 15.95 (*0-88122-731-5*) Lrn Links.

Maniac Magee: A Unit Plan. Barbara M. Linde. 208p. 1997. teacher ed., ring bd. 26.95 (*1-58337-162-1*) Teachers Pet Pubns.

Maniac Magee: L-I-T Guide. Charlotte Jaffe & Barbara Roberts. (J). (gr. 4-10). Date not set. pap. 8.95 (*1-56644-980-4*, 980-4AP) Educ Impress.

***Maniac Magee Study Guide.** Andrew Clausen. 68p. (YA). (gr. 6-8). 1999. student ed., ring bd. 12.99 (*1-58609-153-0*) Progeny Pr WI.

***Maniac Monkeys on Magnolia Street.** Angela Johnson. (J). 2000. pap. 4.99 (*0-375-80208-8*, Pub. by Knopf Bks Yng Read) Random.

M

Maniac Monkeys on Magnolia Street. Angela Johnson. LC 98-33503. 97p. (J). 1998. 16.00 (0-679-89053-X, Pub. by Random Bks Yng Read) Random.

Manias & Delusions. (Library of Curious & Unusual Facts). 1992. write for info. (0-8094-7731-9) Time-Life.

*__Manias, Panics & Crashes: A History of Financial Crashes.__ 4th ed. Charles P. Kindleberger. (Investment Classics Ser.). 264p. 2000. 39.95 (0-471-38946-3) Wiley.

Manias, Panics, & Crashes: A History of Financial Crises. rev. ed. Charles P. Kindleberger. LC 89-42516. 320p. 1989. pap. 20.00 (0-465-04404-2, Pub. by Basic) HarpC.

Manias, Panics, & Crashes: A History of Financial Crises. 3rd ed. Charles P. Kindleberger. LC 96-23919. (Wiley Investment Classics Ser.). 320p. 1996. 39.95 (0-471-16192-6) Wiley.

*__Manias, Panics, & Crashes: A History of Financial Crises.__ 4th ed. Charles P. Kindleberger. (Investment Classics Ser.). 2000. pap. 19.95 (0-471-38945-5) Wiley.

Manias, Panics & Crashes: A History of Financial Crisis. Charles P. Kindleberger. LC 96-23919. 288p. 1996. pap. 19.95 (0-471-16171-3) Wiley.

*__Manic Depression: How to Live While Loving a Manic Depressive.__ Lynn Bradley. 240p. 1999. pap. 16.95 (1-885373-28-7, Pub. by Emerald Ink) ACCESS Pubs Network.

Manic-Depression: Illness or Awakening. Robert E. Kelly. Ed. by Jennifer Carey & Marjorie Pannell. (Illus.). 266p. 1995. 19.95 (0-9639451-4-9) Knowldge Unltd.

Manic Depression & Creativity. D. Jablow Hershman & Julian Lieb. LC 98-27043. 310p. 1998. reprint ed. pap. 18.95 (1-57392-241-2) Prometheus Bks.

Manic-Depressive Illness. Frederick K. Goodwin & Kay R. Jamison. (Illus.). 962p. 1990. text 78.50 (0-19-503934-3) OUP.

Manic-Depressive Illness: History of a Syndrome. Edward A. Wolpert. LC 76-46817. 604p. 1977. 90.00 (0-8236-3095-1) Intl Univs Pr.

Manic-Depressive Insanity & Paranoia. Emil Kraepelin. Tr. by R. Mary Barclay from GER. LC 75-16712. (Classics in Psychiatry Ser.). (Illus.). 1977. reprint ed. 28.95 (0-405-07441-7) Ayer.

Manic Monkeys on Magnolia Street. Angela Johnson. LC 98-33503. 97p. (J). 1998. lib. bdg. 17.99 (0-679-99053-4, Pub. by Random Bks Yng Read) Random.

*__Manic Moon: Romance... Suspense Mystery.__ Joanna Wolfe. 295p. 2000. pap. 18.95 (1-928867-04-9) Warren Intl.

Manic Society. Peter Whybrow. 1999. write for info. (0-375-50174-6) Random.

Manic Street Preachers. Mick St. Michael. (Illus.). 94p. (Orig.). pap. 12.95 (0-7119-6011-9, OP 47852) Omnibus NY.

Manic Street Preachers: In Their Own Words. Martin Power. 95p. 1998. pap. text 15.95 (0-7119-6906-X, OP48068) Music Sales.

*__Manic Street Preachers: Prole Art Threat.__ Ben Roberts. (Illus.). 2000. pap. 18.95 (0-946719-25-X, Pub. by SAF Pub) Interlink Pub.

*__Manic Street Preachers Biography.__ Mike Middlesworth. 2000. pap. 19.95 (0-7119-7738-0) Omnibus NY.

*__Manichaean Body: In Discipline & Ritual.__ Jason BeDuhn. LC 99-45879. 2000. 42.50 (0-8018-6270-1) Johns Hopkins.

Manichaean Literature: Representative Texts Chiefly from Middle Persian & Parthian Writings. Ed. & Tr. by Jes P. Asmussen from PER. LC 74-22063. (Persian Heritage Ser.: Vol. 22). 148p. 1975. text 25.00 (0-8201-1141-4) Bibliotheca Persica.

Manichaeische Religionssystem, Nach den Quellen Neu Untersucht. Ferdinand C. Baur. (GER.). xi, 500p. 1973. reprint ed. write for info. (3-487-04736-5) G Olms Pubs.

Manichaeism in Central Asia & China. Samuel N. Lieu. LC 97-47631. (Nag Hammadi & Manichaean Studies). 1998. 97.00 (90-04-10405-4) Brill Academic Pubs.

Manichaeism in Mesopotamia & the Roman East. Samuel N. Lieu. LC BT1410.L46 1994. (Religions in the Graeco-Roman World Ser.: Vol. 118). 325p. 1994. 113.50 (90-04-09742-2) Brill Academic Pubs.

Manichaeism in the Later Roman Empire & Medieval China. Samuel N. Lieu. (WissUNT Neuen Testament Ser.: No. 63). 400p. 1992. 117.50 (3-16-145820-6, Pub. by JCB Mohr) Coronet Bks.

Manicheisme: Son Fondateur, Sa Doctrine (Musee Guimet. Bibliotheque de diffusion, t. 56) Henri-Charles Puech. LC 82-45821. (Orthodoxies & Heresies in the Early Church Ser.). reprint ed. 27.50 (0-404-62391-3) AMS Pr.

Manicuring. Ahern. Date not set. pap. text, teacher ed., wbk. ed. write for info. (0-314-78617-1); pap. text, wbk. ed. 15.00 (0-314-78618-X) West Pub.

Manicuring: The Knowledge of Maintaining Beautiful Nails & Hands. Betty A. Alfonso. Ed. by Laborde Printers Staff. (Illus.). 85p. (Orig.). 1992. pap. write for info. (0-9634492-0-6) Betty Bks.

*__Manicuring for the Salon & Spa.__ McCormick. LC 99-46252. 1999. 29.95 (1-56253-460-2) Thomson Learn.

Manicurist (Nail Specialty License) (Career Examination Ser.: Vol. C-3792). 1997. pap. 29.95 (0-8373-3792-5) Nat Learn.

Maniere Universelle de Monsieur Desargues. Abraham Bosse. (FRE., Illus.). 520p. (C). 1998. reprint ed. pap. 240.00 (1-85297-027-8, Pub. by Archival Facs) St Mut.

Manierismo e Condizione Della Scrittura in Anton Francesco Doni. Giuseppe Candela. LC 93-25226. (Studies in Italian Culture: Vol. 15). 190p. (C). 1994. text 41.95 (0-8204-2271-1) P Lang Pubng.

Manifest; & Furthermore. William Bronk. 86p. 1995. reprint ed. 16.00 (1-883689-27-9); reprint ed. pap. 7.95 (1-883689-26-0) Talisman Hse.

Manifest Design: Anxious Aggrandizement in Late Jacksonian America. Thomas R. Hietala. LC 84-45808. 304p. 1990. reprint ed. pap. text 16.95 (0-8014-9776-0) Cornell U Pr.

*__Manifest Destinies: Americanizing Immigrants & Internationalizing Americans.__ Ed. by David W. Haines & Carol A. Mortland. LC 00-29843. 192p. 2000. 61.00 (0-275-96703-4, C6703, Praeger Pubs) Greenwood.

Manifest Destiny. Brian Garfield. 416p. 1989. 19.95 (0-89296-382-4, Pub. by Mysterious Pr) Little.

Manifest Destiny. Ed. by Norman A. Greabner. LC 67-21402. 1968. pap. 6.90 (0-672-60072-2, AHS48, Bobbs) Macmillan.

*__Manifest Destiny.__ Richard Worth. LC 00-9280. (In American History Ser.). 2001. write for info. (0-7660-1457-6) Enslow Pubs.

Manifest Destiny: A Study of Nationalist Expansionism in American History. Albert K. Weinberg. LC 75-41293. reprint ed. 41.50 (0-404-14706-2) AMS Pr.

Manifest Destiny: A Study of Nationalist Expansionism in American History. Albert K. Weinberg. (History - United States Ser.). 559p. 1993. reprint ed. lib. bdg. 99.00 (0-7812-4856-6) Rprt Serv.

Manifest Destiny: American Expansion & the Empire of Right. Anders Stephanson. 144p. 1996. 7.95 (0-8090-1584-6) Hill & Wang.

Manifest Destiny & Empire: American Antebellum Expansion. Ed. by Sam W. Haynes & Christopher Morris. LC 97-25072. (Walter Prescott Webb Memorial Lectures: No. 31). 192p. 1997. 24.95 (0-89096-756-3) Tex A&M Univ Pr.

Manifest Destiny & Mission in American History. Frederick Merk. 304p. (Orig.). (C). 1995. pap. text 16.50 (0-674-54805-1) HUP.

Manifest Destiny & Mission in American History. Frederick Merk. (Orig.). 1966. pap. text 8.95 (0-07-553693-5) McGraw.

Manifest Destiny & Mission in American History: A Reinterpretation. Frederick Merk & Lois B. Merk. LC 82-25146. 265p. (C). 1983. reprint ed. lib. bdg. 41.50 (0-313-23844-8, MERM, Greenwood Pr) Greenwood.

Manifest Destiny & the Coming of the Civil War, 1840-1860. Don E. Fehrenbacher. LC 72-118950. (Goldentree Bibliographies Series in American History). (C). 1970. pap. text 6.95 (0-88295-512-8) Harlan Davidson.

Manifest Dream & Its Use in Therapy. Roy M. Mendelsohn. LC 93-30140. 300p. 1990. 50.00 (0-87668-766-4) Aronson.

Manifest in Flesh: The Epiphany Christology of the Pastoral Epistles. Andrew Y. Lau. LC 96-221067. (WissUnt Zum Neuen Testament Ser.: No. 2-86). 336p. (Orig.). 1996. pap. 82.50 (3-16-146302-1) Coronet Bks.

Manifest Manners: Narratives on Postindian Survivance. Gerald R. Vizenor. LC 99-38527. 197p. 1999. pap. 15.00 (0-8032-9621-5, Bison Books) U of Nebr Pr.

Manifest Rationality: A Pragmatic Theory of Argument. Ralph H. Johnson. LC 99-58491. 350p. 1999. write for info. (0-8058-2173-2); pap. write for info. (0-8058-2174-0) L Erlbaum Assocs.

Manifest Victory. Rufus Moseley. 1985. pap. 9.95 (0-910924-92-9) Macalester.

Manifest Your Destiny: Life Planning with Punch. rev. ed. Larry Boldt. Ed. by Kim Grant. LC 87-80391. (Illus.). 346p. 1987. pap. 24.95 (0-9617762-0-X); ring bd. 149.95 (0-9617762-9-3) Lightning Pr.

Manifest Your Destiny: The Nine Spiritual Principles for Getting Everything You Want. Wayne W. Dyer. LC 96-48248. 192p. 1997. 23.00 (0-06-017528-1) HarpC.

Manifest Your Destiny: The Nine Spiritual Principles for Getting Everything You Want. Wayne W. Dyer. LC 96-48248. 192p. 1998. pap. 13.00 (0-06-092892-1) HarpC.

Manifest Your Destiny: The Nine Spiritual Principles for Getting Everything You Want. Wayne W. Dyer. 240p. 1999. mass mkt. 6.99 (0-06-109494-3, Harp PBks) HarpC.

Manifest Your Destiny: The Nine Spiritual Principles for Getting Everything You Want. abr. ed. Wayne W. Dyer. 1997. audio 18.00 (0-694-51778-X, CPN 2620) HarperAudio.

*__Manifesta: Young Women, Feminism & the Future.__ Jennifer Baumgardner & Amy Richards. 240p. 2000. pap. 13.00 (0-374-52622-2) FS&G.

Manifestation of Analogous Being in the Dialectic of the Space-Time Continuum: A Philosophical Study in Freedom. David A. Harris. LC 92-20134. (American University Studies: Philosophy: Ser. V, Vol. 140). XXXIV, 130p. (C). 1993. text 39.95 (0-8204-1928-1) P Lang Pubng.

*__Manifestation of Aphasic Symptoms in Different Languages.__ Paradis. 2000. 65.00 (0-08-043662-5, Pergamon Pr) Elsevier.

*__Manifestation of His Presence.__ Sophia Grant. 2000. pap. 8.99 (0-88270-805-8) Bridge-Logos.

Manifestation of the Spirit. Robert E. Tourville. 13p. (Orig.). (C). 1985. pap. 2.00 (0-912981-15-6) Hse BonGiovanni.

Manifestation of the Tathagata: Buddhahood According to the Avatamsaka Sutra. Cheng C. Bhikshu. LC 93-24080. 192p. 1993. pap. 12.50 (0-86171-054-1) Wisdom MA.

Manifestations. William T. Hall. Ed. by Dorothy P. Koger. 1999. pap. write for info. (1-882821-12-2) DPK Pubns.

Manifestations: Poems & Aphorisms by Ralph Aquila. Ralph Aquila. 1997. pap. write for info. (1-57553-507-6) Watermrk Pr.

Manifestations of Cancer & Treatment. Susan L. Groenwald. 1991. pap. 44.95 (0-86720-304-8) Jones & Bartlett.

Manifestations of Discontent in Germany on the Eve of the Reformation. Gerald Strauss. LC 75-135014. 270p. 1971. pap. 83.70 (0-608-05045-8, 205970600004) Bks Demand.

Manifestations of Grace. Elizabeth Dreyer. (Theology & Life Ser.: Vol. 29). 246p. 1990. pap. 19.95 (0-8146-5759-1, M Glazier) Liturgical Pr.

Manifestations of Karma. Rudolf Steiner. 2000. reprint ed. pap. text. write for info. (1-85584-058-8, Pub. by R Steiner Pr) Anthroposophic.

Manifestations of Reason: Life, Historicity, Culture: Phenomenology at the Adriatic. Ed. by Anna-Teresa Tymieniecka. LC 93-557. (Analecta Husserliana Ser.: Vol. 40). 464p. 1993. lib. bdg. 223.00 (0-7923-2215-0, Pub. by Kluwer Academic) Kluwer Academic.

Manifestations of the Electron-Phonon Interaction - 2nd Cinvestav Superconductivity Sym. R. Baquero. 224p. 1994. text 109.00 (981-02-1545-2) World Scientific Pub.

Manifestations of Thought. Molana S. Angha. LC 88-20599. 126p. (Orig.). 1988. lib. bdg. 41.50 (0-8191-7135-2) U Pr of Amer.

Manifestations of Thought. Molana S. Angha. LC 88-20599. 126p. (Orig.). 1996. pap. 22.50 (0-8191-7136-0) U Pr of Amer.

Manifestations of Thought. Shah Maghsoud & Sadegh Angha. LC 97-69690. 87p. (Orig.). 1997. pap. 9.95 (0-910735-70-0) MTO Printing & Pubn Ctr.

*__Manifestations Throughout Church History.__ Lee A. Howard. 68p. 1998. pap. 5.95 (0-9647573-2-X) Beautiful Ft Pubng.

Manifested Sons of God. Joseph C. Hedgecock. Ed. by Patricia T. Ross. 300p. 1988. pap. 6.95 (0-945255-14-4) J C Hedgecock Pubns.

Manifestes du Surrealisme. Andre Breton. (FRE.). 1985. pap. 12.95 (0-7859-2792-1) Fr & Eur.

Manifestes du Surrealisme. Andre Breton. (Folio Essais Ser.: No. 5). (FRE.). 9.95 (2-07-032279-3) Schoenhof.

Manifesting: A Master's Manual. Khit Harding. (Becoming Ser.). (Illus.). 95p. (Orig.). (C). 1988. pap. 7.95 (0-9615868-2-6) Adams Pub Co.

*__Manifesting Medicine: Bodies & Machines.__ Ed. by Robert Bud et al. 174p. 1999. text 46.00 (90-5702-408-X, Harwood Acad Pubs); pap. text 24.00 (90-5702-430-6, Harwood Acad Pubs) Gordon & Breach.

Manifesting Power: Gender & the Interpretation of Power in Archaeology. Tracy Sweely. LC 98-39602. 2p. 1999. write for info. (0-415-17179-2); pap. 24.99 (0-415-19744-9) Routledge.

Manifesting the Holy Ghost. Rodney M. Howard-Browne. 32p. 1991. pap. 1.50 (0-9583066-7-2, RHB667) Revival Minst Intl.

Manifesting the Life of Your Dreams. abr. ed. Robert A. Robinson. (Magic Magnifying Mind Ser.). 1991. pap. text 8.95 incl. audio (1-884780-02-4) Phoenix Pubng.

Manifesting Your Desires: How to Apply Timeless Spiritual Truths to Achieve Fulfillment. 2nd expanded rev. ed. Victoria Loveland-Coen. (Illus.). 200p. (Orig.). 1998. pap. 19.95 (0-9644765-0-9) Self-Mastery Pr.

Manifesting Your Heart's Desire. Fred Fengler & Todd Varnum. 215p. 1994. pap. 13.95 (0-9641305-0-5) Heart Light.

*__Manifesto: A Century of Isms.__ Ed. by Mary Ann Caws. 768p. 2000. pap. 35.00 (0-8032-6407-0, Bison Books) U of Nebr Pr.

Manifesto: A Radical Strategy for Britain's Future Francis Cripps. LC 82-101165. (Politics Ser.). 224 p. 1981. write for info. (0-330-26402-8) Pan.

Manifesto: Cosa Nostra di Poesia. Ronald F. Sauer. 8p. (Orig.). 1988. pap. text 1.50 (1-879594-14-5) Androgyne Bks.

Manifesto: The Mad Farmer Liberation Front & Other Articles. Voices from a Multi-Racial Movement for Nonviolenc. (Common Ground Ser.: Vol. III). (Illus.). 48p. (Orig.). 1987. pap. 5.00 (1-884478-02-6) Common Grnd.

Manifesto Destiny: Radical Manifestos in American History. Ed. by Tom Darling. 224p. (Orig.). 1996. pap. 12.00 (1-889543-01-2) Beachchair Pr.

Manifesto for a New Medicine. James S. Gordon. 1997. pap. 13.00 (0-201-89828-4) Addison-Wesley.

Manifesto for a New Medicine: Your Guide to Healing Partnerships & the Wise Use of Alternative Therapies. James S. Gordon. 358p. 1999. text 25.00 (0-7881-6182-2) DIANE Pub.

Manifesto for Christians. 1992. lib. bdg. 74.95 (0-8490-5404-4) Gordon Pr.

Manifesto for Philosophy. Alian Badiou. Tr. by Norman Madarasz from FRE. LC 98-43903. (SUNY Series, Intersections). 128p. (C). 1999. text 44.50 (0-7914-4219-5, Suny Pr) State U NY Pr.

Manifesto for Philosophy: Followed by Two Essays: "The (Re)Turn of Philosophy Itself" & "Definition of Philosophy" Alian Badiou. Ed. & Intro. by Norman Madarasz. LC 98-43903. (Suny Series, Intersections: Philosophy & Critical Theory). 181p. (C). 1999. pap. text 14.95 (0-7914-4220-9, Suny Pr) State U NY Pr.

Manifesto for the Dead. Domenic Stansberry. LC 99-30775. 182p. 2000. 22.00 (1-57962-059-0) Permanent Pr.

Manifesto for the Millennium. Paul Johnson. 2000. pap. 14.00 (0-06-093123-X) HarpC.

Manifesto for the Nation. R. K. Allday. (C). 1989. text 30.00 (0-902662-00-7, Pub. by R K Pubns) St Mut.

*__Manifesto of a Passionate Moderate.__ Susan Haack. 2000. pap. 13.00 (0-226-31137-6) U Ch Pr.

Manifesto of a Passionate Moderate: Unfashionable Essays. Susan Haack. LC 98-22658. 1998. 22.50 (0-226-31136-8) U Ch Pr.

Manifesto of a Tenured Radical. Cary Nelson. LC 96-51305. 1997. text 50.00 (0-8147-5794-4); pap. text 18.00 (0-8147-5797-9) NYU Pr.

Manifesto of Capitalism: An Analysis & Summary of Adam Smith's "Wealth of Nations" 7th ed. Frank H. Solomon. LC 93-144287. 131p. (C). 1996. pap. text 10.00 (0-9625163-2-5) Light Brigade Pub Hse.

*__Manifesto of Capitalism: An Analysis & Summary of Adam Smith's "Wealth of Nations"__ 8th rev. unabridged ed. Frank H. Solomon. LC 93-144287. 175p. 2000. per. 10.00 (0-9625163-3-3) Light Brigade Pub Hse.

Manifesto of Destruction. 3rd ed. Christian C. Abraham. 104p. 1996. reprint ed. pap. 5.00 (0-9654986-2-X) IMXMI Pub.

Manifesto of Freedom. Leslie Citron. 160p. (C). 1993. text 25.50 (0-88033-254-9, 357, Pub. by East Eur Monographs) Col U Pr.

Manifesto of Men's Liberation. 4th rev. ed. Richard F. Doyle. 1995. pap. 4.00 (0-917212-03-7) Poor Richards.

Manifesto of the Communist Party. Karl Marx & Friedrich Engels. (Reprint Series in Social Sciences). (C). 1993. reprint ed. pap. text 3.90 (0-8290-2655-X, S-455) Irvington.

Manifesto: or A Declaration of the Doctrines & Practice of the Church of Christ. John Dunlavy. LC 74-134416. reprint ed. 49.50 (0-404-08460-5) AMS Pr.

Manifesto Photography. Photos by Armando Rumayor. (Illus.). 1994. write for info. (0-614-04252-6) Focal Point Pr.

Manifestoes & the Trouble with the Modern. Janet Lyon. LC 98-36507. 1999. write for info. (0-8014-3635-4); pap. write for info. (0-8014-8591-6) Cornell U Pr.

Manifestoes of Surrealism. Andre Breton. Tr. by Richard Seaver & Helen R. Lane from FRE. 316p. 1969. pap. text 17.95 (0-472-06182-8, 06182, Ann Arbor Bks) U of Mich Pr.

Manifestos Manifest. Vicente Huidobro. Tr. by Gilbert Alter-Gilbert. (Green Integer Bks.: No. 20). 128p. 1999. pap. 12.95 (1-892295-08-3, Pub. by Green Integer) SPD-Small Pr Dist.

Manifiesto Comunista. Karl Marx & Friedrich Engels. Ed. by Luis Madrid. (SPA.). 63p. (Orig.). (C). 1992. pap. 5.00 (0-87348-751-6) Pathfinder NY.

Manifiesto Democrata. Carlos M. Mendez. LC 82-71115. (Coleccion Cuba y sus Jueces). (SPA.). 40p. (Orig.). 1982. pap. 2.00 (0-89729-313-4) Ediciones.

Manifiesto Educativo. Natalio Dominguez. (SPA.). 156p. 1992. pap. write for info. (0-929441-34-6) Pubns Puertorriquenas.

Manifiestos Humanistas I y II. Tr. by Francisco Samaranch. 40p. (C). 1975. pap. 1.50 (0-8477-2808-0) U of PR Pr.

*__Manifold: Time.__ Stephen Baxter. LC 99-42045. 528p. 2000. 24.00 (0-345-43075-1, Del Rey) Ballantine Pub Grp.

*__Manifold: Time.__ Stephen Baxter. 2000. mass mkt. 6.99 (0-345-43076-X) Ballantine Pub Grp.

Manifold Annihilation: A Novel. Aimable Twagilimana. LC 96-22465. 260p. 1996. 15.95 (0-944957-87-0) Rivercross Pub.

Manifold Destiny: The One & Only Guide to Cooking on Your Car Engine. Bill Scheller. LC 99-215318. 144p. 1998. pap. 9.95 (0-375-75140-8) Villard Books.

Manifold Grace: Revealed in Blood, Water & Spirit. Ken Gurley. LC 92-21228. 200p. (Orig.). 1993. pap. 8.99 (1-56722-007-X) Word Aflame.

Manifolds All of Whose Geodesics Are Closed. A. L. Besse. (Ergebnisse der Mathematik und Ihrer Grenzgebiete Ser.: Vol. 93). (Illus.). 1978. 93.95 (0-387-08158-5) Spr-Verlag.

Manifolds & Geometry. Ed. by P. De Bartolomeis et al. (Symposia Mathematica Ser.: No. 36). (Illus.). 329p. (C). 1996. text 69.95 (0-521-56216-3) Cambridge U Pr.

Manifolds & Lie Groups: Papers in Honor of Yozo Matsushima. Ed. by Jun-Ichi Hano. (Progress in Mathematics Ser.: 14). 608p. (C). 1981. 73.00 (0-8176-3053-8) Birkhauser.

Manifolds of Differentiable Mappings. P. W. Michor. (Shiva Mathematics Ser.: 3). 160p. (Orig.). 1980. 16.95 (0-906812-03-8) Birkhauser.

Manifolds, Tensor Analysis, & Applications. R. Abraham et al. (Applied Mathematical Sciences Ser.: Vol. 75). (Illus.). 650p. 1996. 69.95 (0-387-96790-7) Spr-Verlag.

Manifolds Tokyo, 1973: Proceedings of the International Conference on Manifolds & Related Topics in Topology, Tokyo, 1973. International Conference on Manifolds & Related To. Ed. by Akio Hattori. LC 74-81990. 443p. 1975. reprint ed. pap. 137.40 (0-608-01210-6, 206189900001) Bks Demand.

Manifolds with Cusps of Rank One. W. Mueller. (Lecture Notes in Mathematics Ser.: Vol. 1244). xi, 158p. 1987. 34.95 (0-387-17696-9) Spr-Verlag.

Manifolds with Group Actions & Elliptic Operators. Vladimir Lin & Yehuda Pinchover. LC 94-26456. (Memoirs of the American Mathematical Society Ser.: No. 540). 78p. 1994. pap. 31.00 (0-8218-2604-2, MEMO/112/540) Am Math.

Manifolds with Singularities & the Adams-Novikov Spectral Sequence. Boris I. Botvinnik. (London Mathematical Society Lecture Note Ser.: No. 170). (Illus.). 197p. (C). 1992. pap. text 44.95 (0-521-42608-1) Cambridge U Pr.

Manigances. Boileau-Narcejac. (FRE.). 373p. 1986. pap. 11.95 (0-7859-2037-4, 2070377431) Fr & Eur.

Manigances. Pierre Boileau & Thomas Narcejac. (Folio Ser.: No. 1743). (FRE.). 373p. 1971. pap. 10.95 (2-07-037743-1) Schoenhof.

Manigua en Paris: Correspondencia Diplomatica De Betances. Ed. by Felix O. Reyes. (SPA.). 156p. (Orig.). 1984. pap. 6.00 (1-878483-09-9) Hunter Coll CEP.

Manikin: A Novel. Joanna Scott. LC 95-21734. 276p. 1995. 22.50 (0-8050-3974-0) H Holt & Co.

Manikin: A Novel. Joanna Scott. 288p. 1998. pap. text 12.00 (0-8050-5591-6) H Holt & Co.

An Asterisk (*) at the beginning of an entry indicates that the title is appearing for the first time.

Manila Declaration on the Agenda for Action on Social Development in the ESCAP Region. 45p. pap. 7.50 (92-1-127038-3) UN.

Manila Envelopes: Oregon Volunteer Lt. George F. Telfer's Spanish American War Letters. George F. Telfer. Ed. by Sara Bunnett. (Illus.). (Orig.). 1987. pap. 15.95 (0-87595-129-5) Oregon Hist.

Manila Fugue. Luisita Lopez. Date not set. write for info. (0-393-03374-0) Norton.

Manila Ransomed: The British Assault on Manila in the Seven Years War. Nicholas Tracy. LC 96-157268. (Illus.). 128p. 1995. pap. text 29.95 (0-85989-426-6, Pub. by Univ Exeter Pr) Northwestern U Pr.

Manila Time: A Novel. Jack Trolley. 304p. 1995. 21.00 (0-7867-0255-9) Carroll & Graf.

Manila Workers' Unions, 1900-1950. Melinda T. Kerkvliet. 206p. (Orig.). 1992. pap. 16.50 (971-10-0475-5, Pub. by New Day Pub) Cellar.

Manilii. rev. ed. Ed. by Goold. (LAT.). 1998. 53.50 (3-8154-1528-4, T1528, Pub. by B G Teubner) U of Mich Pr.

Manilius - Concordantia in Manilii Astronomica. Ed. by Manfred Wacht. (Alpha-Omega, Reihe A Ser.: Bd. CVI). (GER.). vii, 502p. 1990. write for info. (3-487-09230-1) G Olms Pubs.

Manimekhalai (The Dancer with the Magic Bowl) Merchant-Prince Shattan. Tr. by Alain Danielou from TAM. LC 88-39885. 256p. 1989. 21.95 (0-8112-1097-9, Pub. by New Directions); pap. 11.95 (0-8112-1098-7, NDP674, Pub. by New Directions) Norton.

Manin & the Venetian Revolution of 1848. George M. Trevelyan. LC 75-80597. xvi, 284p. 1974. reprint ed. 40.00 (0-86527-122-4) Fertig.

Manioc in Africa. William O. Jones. (Stanford University Food Research Institute Studies in Tropical Development). ix, 315p. 1959. 42.50 (0-8047-0002-8) Stanford U Pr.

Manioc in Africa. fac. ed. William O. Jones. LC 59-12468. (Stanford University Food Research Institute Studies in Tropical Development). (Illus.). 331p. 1959. reprint ed. pap. 30.00 (0-7837-7908-9, 204766400008) Bks Demand.

Manip. Math - Multiplication & Division. Jo E. Moore. (Mathematics Ser.). (Illus.). 32p. (J). (gr. 2-3). 1997. pap., teacher ed. 2.95 (1-55799-459-5, 4061) Evan-Moor Edu Pubs.

Manipulated City. D. Gale & Eric Moone. 366p. 1975. 11.95 (0-416-60111-1, NO. 2863) Routledge.

***Manipulated Mind: Brainwashing, Conditioning & Indoctrination.** Denise Winn. LC 99-53289. 217p. 2000. reprint ed. pap. 19.00 (1-883536-22-7, Malor Bks) ISHK.

Manipulated Path to the White House - 1996: Maximizing Advantage in the Presidential Selection Process. Robert D. Loevy. LC 97-49697. 400p. (C). 1998. 64.00 (0-7618-1023-4); pap. 37.50 (0-7618-1024-2) U Pr of Amer.

***Manipulating Hegemony: State Power, Labour & the Marshall Plan in Britain.** Rhiannon Vickers. LC 99-49749. 2000. text 69.95 (0-312-23045-1) St Martin.

Manipulating Language: How to Move Students Successfully from Composition to Literary Analysis. Lillian D. Roland. 284p. (C). 1997. per. 47.95 (0-7872-3477-X) Kendall-Hunt.

Manipulating Life: Debating the Genetic Revolution. Ed. by Gary E. McCuen. (Ideas in Conflict Ser.). (Illus.). 136p. (YA). (gr. 7-12). 1985. lib. bdg. 15.95 (0-86596-054-2) G E M.

Manipulating Meetings: How to Get What You Want, When You Want It. rev. ed. David Martin. (Institute of Management Foundation Ser.). 186p. (Orig.). 1996. pap. 47.50 (0-273-62193-9, Pub. by Pitman Pub) Trans-Atl Phila.

Manipulating Needs. Conrad Lodziak. (C). 49.95 (0-7453-0853-8, Pub. by Pluto GBR); pap. 15.95 (0-7453-0854-6, Pub. by Pluto GBR) Stylus Pub VA.

Manipulating Secondary Metabolism in Culture. Ed. by R. J. Robins & M. J. Rhodes. (Illus.). 324p. (C). 1989. text 69.95 (0-521-36254-7) Cambridge U Pr.

Manipulating Soviet Population Resources. Jeff Chinn. LC 77-11683. 163p. 1978. 34.50 (0-8419-0345-X) Holmes & Meier.

Manipulating the Ether: The Power of Broadcast Radio in Thirties America. Robert J. Brown. LC 97-43336. 324p. 1998. lib. bdg. 48.50 (0-7864-0397-7) McFarland & Co.

Manipulating the Market: Understanding Economic Sanctions, Institutional Change, & the Political Unity of White Rhodesia. David M. Rowe. (Illus.). 284p. (C). text 52.50 (0-472-11187-6, 11187) U of Mich Pr.

Manipulating the Mouse Embryo: A Laboratory Manual. 2nd ed. Brigid Hogan et al. (Illus.). 500p. (C). 1994. text 190.00 (0-87969-392-4); pap. text 105.00 (0-87969-384-3) Cold Spring Harbor.

Manipulation. Bernard Haring. (C). 1988. 85.00 (0-85439-121-5, Pub. by St Paul Pubns); pap. 39.00 (0-85439-115-0, Pub. by St Paul Pubns) St Mut.

Manipulation. Beverley J. Townsend. 397p. mass mkt. 4.99 (1-55197-360-X) Picasso Publ.

Manipulation & Expression of Recombinant DNA: A Laboratory Manual. Dominique Robertson et al. LC 97-195982. (Illus.). 224p. 1997. spiral bd. 45.00 (0-12-589765-0) Morgan Kaufmann.

Manipulation & Mobilization: Extremity & Spinal Techniques. Susan L. Edmond. LC 92-49998. 304p. (gr. 13). 1992. text 45.00 (0-8016-6305-9, 06305) Mosby Inc.

Manipulation of Air-Sensitive Compounds. 2nd ed. D. F. Shriver & M. A. Drezdon. LC 86-11012. 336p. 1986. 110.00 (0-471-86773-X) Wiley.

Manipulation of Consent: The State & Working-Class Consciousness in Brazil. Youssef Cohen. LC 89-5403. (Latin American Ser.). 194p. 1989. pap. 15.95 (0-8229-5806-6) U of Pittsburgh Pr.

Manipulation of Growth in Farm Animals. Ed. by J. F. Roche & D. O'Callaghan. (Current Topics in Veterinary Medicine & Animal Science Ser.). 316p. 1984. text 115.00 (0-685-08511-2) Kluwer Academic.

Manipulation of Mammalian Development, Vol. 4. R. B. Gwatkin. LC 85-3406. (Developmental Biology Ser.). (Illus.). 402p. (C). 1986. text 95.00 (0-306-42166-6, Kluwer Plenum) Kluwer Academic.

Manipulation of the American Voter: Political Campaign Commercials. Karen S. Johnson-Cartee & Gary A. Copeland. LC 96-20688. (Political Communication Ser.). 232p. 1997. 55.00 (0-275-95588-5, Praeger Pubs) Greenwood.

Manipulation of the Avian Genome. Robert J. Etches. 352p. 1992. lib. bdg. 119.00 (0-8493-4216-3, SF492) CRC Pr.

Manipulation of the Young Mind: Human Biography. Brenda Lee. Ed. by Hired Pen. (Illus.). 400p. 1997. 21.00 (0-9649571-9-1) Princess Lee.

Manipulation on Trial: Economic Analaysis & the Hunt Silver Case. Jeffrey Williams. (Illus.). 266p. (C). 1995. text 47.95 (0-521-44028-9) Cambridge U Pr.

Manipulation Robots. Felix L. Chernousko. 288p. 1993. boxed set 157.95 (0-8493-4457-3, TJ211) CRC Pr.

Manipulation Therapy for the Naturopathic Physician. David J. Shipley. (Illus.). 172p. 1997. pap. text 42.00 (0-9662564-0-9) Ascelapias Pub.

Manipulations Viscerales see Visceral Manipulation

Manipulative Child: How to Regain Control & Raise Resilient, Resourceful, & Independent Kids. Ernest W. Swihart & Patrick Cotter. 272p. 1998. pap. 11.95 (0-553-37949-6) Bantam.

Manipulative Child: How to Regain Control & Raise Resilient, Resourceful, & Independent Kids. Ernest W. Swihart & Patrick Cotter. LC 96-15974. 240p. 1996. 22.95 (0-02-861254-X) Macmillan.

***Manipulative Child: How to Regain Control & Raise Resilient, Resourceful, & Independent Kids.** Ernest W. Swihart & Patrick Cotter. 209p. 2000. reprint ed. text 23.00 (0-7881-6972-6) DIANE Pub.

Manipulative Interludes for Algebra I. Margaret A. Smart & Mary Laycock. (Illus.). 80p. (Orig.). (YA). (gr. 7-12). 1990. pap. 9.95 (0-918932-95-5, A-1670) Activity Resources.

Manipulative Math - Addition & Subtraction. Jo E. Moore. (Mathematics Ser.). (Illus.). 32p. (J). (gr. 1-2). 1996. pap., teacher ed. 2.95 (1-55799-444-7, 4046) Evan-Moor Edu Pubs.

Manipulative Math - Addition & Subtraction. Jo Ellen Moore. (Illus.). 29p. (J). (gr. 1-2). 1995. pap., wbk. ed. 2.50 (1-58610-066-1, Learn on the Go) Learn Horizon.

Manipulative Memos: The Art of Control Through the Medium of the Memo. Arthur D. Rosenberg. 148p. 1994. 18.95 (0-89815-614-9) Ten Speed Pr.

Manipulative Participation in the Study of Elementary Industrial Arts. Theresa C. Gunther. LC 70-176825. (Columbia University. Teachers College. Contributions to Education Ser.: No. 490). reprint ed. 37.50 (0-404-55490-3) AMS Pr.

Manipulative Resource I. Ed. by Barbara Nophlin. 1988. student ed. 99.50 (0-88076-128-8, 15645) Kaplan Pr.

Manipulative Resource II. Ed. by Barbara Nophlin. 1988. student ed. 175.50 (0-88076-129-6, 15646) Kaplan Pr.

Manipulative Surgery. A. S. Bankart. 150p. 1997. reprint ed. spiral bd. 12.50 (0-7873-0070-5) Hlth Research.

Manipulative Therapy in Rehabilitation Locomotor System. 3rd ed. Lewit. LC 98-54113. 320p. 1999. pap. text 70.00 (0-7506-2964-9) Buttrwrth-Heinemann.

Manipulative Therapy in the Rehabilitation of the Motor System. 2nd ed. Karel Lewit. (Illus.). 320p. 1991. 70.00 (0-7506-1123-5) Buttrwrth-Heinemann.

Manipulatives for Keyboard Capers. Anne C. May. 40p. 1993. 37.95 (1-884098-03-7); 20.00 (1-884098-02-9) Elijah Co.

Manipulator: A Novel of Deceit. Mary W. Syreen. LC 96-94724. 257p. (Orig.). 1997. per. 11.95 (0-9645798-5-5) Lakesde Pr.

Manipulator: A Psychoanalytic View. Ben Bursten. LC 72-92553. 287p. reprint ed. pap. 89.00 (0-608-30593-6, 201741700007) Bks Demand.

Manipulators: Personality & Politics in Multiple Perspectives. A. W. Lerner. 168p. (C). 1989. text 39.95 (0-8058-0335-1) L Erlbaum Assocs.

Manipulus Vocabulorum. Peter Levens. (Camden Society, London. Publications, First Ser.: No. 95). reprint ed. 90.00 (0-404-50195-8) AMS Pr.

Manipulus Vocabulorum: Rhyming Dictionary of the English Language. Peter Levens. (EETS, OS Ser.: No. 27). 1969. reprint ed. 63.00 (0-527-00027-2) Periodicals Srv.

Manipur: The Glorious Past. A. K. Sharma. LC 94-905528. (C). 1994. 60.00 (81-7305-050-3, Pub. by Aryan Bks Intl) S Asia.

***Manisa Nach Evliya Celebi: Aus Dem Neunten Band des Seyahat-Name Edition, Ubersetzung Und Kommentar.** Nuran Tezcan. (Evliya Celebi's Book of Travels, 4 Ser.). (Illus.). 355p. 1999. 106.00 (90-04-11485-8) Brill Academic Pubs.

Manish. Alfred L. Woods. (Illus.). 55p. 1989. pap. 8.00 (0-88378-122-0) Third World.

Manito Masks: Dramatizations, with Music, of American Indian Spirit Legends. Hartley Alexander. LC 77-94335. (One-Act Plays in Reprint Ser.). (Illus.). 1978. reprint ed. 25.00 (0-8486-2031-3) Roth Pub Inc.

Manito Park: A Reflection of Spokane's Past. Tony Bamonte & Suzanne S. Bamonte. LC 98-90257. (Illus.). 128p. 1998. 21.95 (0-9652219-2-X) Tornado Creek.

***Manitoba.** (Canada in the Tweny First Century Ser.). (Illus.). (J). 2000. 18.95 (0-7910-6063-2) Chelsea Hse.

Manitoba. Harry Beckett. LC 97-7672. (Journey Across Canada Ser.). 24p. (J). (gr. 3-5). 1997. lib. bdg. 18.60 (1-55916-203-1) Rourke Bk Co.

***Manitoba.** Sarah Yates. (Hello Canada Ser.). (Illus.). 1999. pap. 7.95 (1-55041-259-0) Fitzhenry & W Ltd.

Manitoba. Sarah Yates. LC 95-4223. (Hello Canada Ser.). (Illus.). 76p. (J). 1996. lib. bdg. 19.93 (0-8225-2756-1, Lerner Publctns) Lerner Pub.

Manitoba: A Color Guidebook. Ed. by Marilyn Morton. (Illus.). 200p. 1995. pap. 19.95 (0-88780-322-9, Pub. by Formac Publ Co) Seven Hills Bk.

Manitoba: A History. William Lewis Morton. LC 67-4598. 561p. reprint ed. pap. 174.00 (0-608-12876-7, 202365400033) Bks Demand.

Manitoba: The Keystone Province: An Illustrated History. Kenneth S. Coates. 192p. (YA). (gr. 7 up). 1988. 32.95 (0-89781-257-3) Am Historical Pr.

***Manitoba & Saskatchewan Birds.** James Kavanagh. (Pocket Naturalist Ser.). (Illus.). 1999. 5.95 (1-58355-038-0, Pub. by Waterford WA) Falcon Pub Inc.

***Manitoba Business Directory, 1999-2000.** rev. ed. American Business Directories Staff. 544p. 1999. boxed set 395.00 incl. cd-rom (0-7687-0186-4) Am Busn Direct.

***Manitoba Highway Map.** Rob McLennan. 84p. 1999. pap. 10.50 (0-921411-89-8) Genl Dist Srvs.

Manitoba Reports, 1883-1962, Vols. 1-67, Set. 1970. 1850.00 (1-57588-328-7, 302540) W S Hein.

Manitoba Scrip. rev. ed. Gail Morin. 352p. 1996. pap. 40.00 (1-886560-02-1, 096547) Quintin Pub RI.

Manitou: The Sacred Landscape of New England's Native Civilization. James W. Mavor & Byron E. Dix. LC 89-17106. (Illus.). 392p. 1992. pap. 18.95 (0-89281-078-5) Inner Tradit.

***Manitou, a Mythological Journey in Time.** unabridged ed. Ramona Du Houx et al. (Illus.). 196p. 1999. pap. 7.99 (1-882190-77-7, Pub. by Polar Bear ME) Maine Writers.

Manitou & Providence: Indians, Europeans & the Making of New England, 1500-1643. Neal Salisbury. (Illus.). 330p. 1984. pap. text 23.95 (0-19-503454-6) OUP.

Manitou, Fountains of the Deep: The Crash of Flight 585, March 3, 1991, Widefield, Colorado. Daniel A. Lauing. 320p. 1999. per. 13.50 (0-9641269-0-7) Benchmark Invest.

Manitou, Fountains of the Deep: The Crash of Flight 585, March 3, 1991, Widefield, Colorado. Daniel A. Lauing. 2000. boxed set 23.50 (0-9641269-1-5) Benchmark Invest.

***Manitou Man.** Graham Masterton. 237p. 1998. pap. 18.95 (0-9524153-4-8, Pub. by BFS) Firebird Dist.

Manitou, Saratoga of the West. 2nd ed. Sharon A. Cunningham. LC 99-173079. 75 p. 1998. write for info. (0-9663939-0-2) S A Cunningham.

Manitous: The Spiritual World of the Ojibway. Basil Johnston. 272p. 1996. pap. 13.00 (0-06-092735-6) HarpC.

Maniyadanabon of Shin Sandalinka. Tr. by L. E. Bagshawe. 132p. 1981. pap. 7.00 (0-87727-115-1, DP 115) Cornell SE Asia.

Maniyadanabon of Shin Sandalinka. Shin Sandalinka. LC 82-132590. (Cornell University, Southeast Asia Program, Data Paper Ser.: No. 115). 161p. reprint ed. pap. 50.00 (0-8357-3683-0, 203640700003) Bks Demand.

Manjinn Moon. Denise Vitola. 272p. 1998. mass mkt. 5.99 (0-441-00521-7) Ace Bks.

Mankato: Its First Fifty Years . . . with Brief Biographies of Early Settlers & Active Upbuilders of the City, 1852-1902. (Illus.). 347p. 1997. reprint ed. lib. bdg. 39.50 (0-8328-6805-1) Higginson Bk Co.

Mankiller. large type ed. Elliot Long. (Linford Western Library). 256p. 1996. pap. 16.99 (0-7089-7949-1, Linford) Ulverscroft.

Mankiller: A Chief & Her People. Michael Wallis. 2000. pap. 14.95 (0-312-20662-3) St Martin.

Mankiller: A Chief & Her People. Michael Wallis & Wilma P. Mankiller. 320p. 1994. pap. 13.95 (0-312-11393-5) St Martin.

Mankind: A Journey Through Human Emotions. Ed. by Bert Hower. (Illus.). 99p. 1995. pap. write for info. (0-936945-54-0) Creat with Wds.

***Mankind: Child of the Stars.** Max H. Flind & Otto O. Binder. 275p. 1999. pap. 15.00 (1-886940-06-1) Ozark Mountn.

Mankind: The Macro Plays, No. 1. LC 76-133702. (Tudor Facsimile Texts. Old English Plays Ser.: No. 3). reprint ed. 49.50 (0-404-53303-5) AMS Pr.

Mankind at the Crossroads. Edward M. East. LC 76-46074. (Anti-Movements in America Ser.). 1977. reprint ed. lib. bdg. 27.95 (0-405-09947-9) Ayer.

Mankind in Barbary: The Individual & Society in the Novels of Norman Mailer. Stanley T. Gutman. LC 75-18290. 238p. reprint ed. pap. 73.80 (0-8357-6514-8, 203588500097) Bks Demand.

Mankind in Transition: A View of the Distant Past, the Present & the Far Future. Masse Bloomfield. LC 91-90359. vi, 187p. (C). 1993. 29.95 (1-879981-01-7) Jarren Pr.

Mankind's Oedipal Destiny: Libidinal & Aggressive Aspects of Sexuality. Ed. by Peter Hartocollis. 263p. 2000. 32.50 (0-8236-3097-8, 03097) Intl Univs Pr.

Mankind's Quest for Identity. Herbert B. Gerstner. LC 80-84797. 312p. 1981. 37.00 (0-930376-23-4) Chem-Orbital.

Mankind's Road to the Stars. Vitali Sevstyanov & Vladimir Pryakhin. (C). 1989. 9.50 (0-8364-2435-2, Pub. by Allied Pubs) S Asia.

Manley Art of Librarianship. Will Manley. LC 92-56664. (Illus.). 248p. 1993. lib. bdg. 32.50 (0-89950-866-9) McFarland & Co.

Manlike Monsters on Trial: Early Records & Modern Evidence. Ed. by Marjorie M. Halpin & Michael M. Ames. (Illus.). 370p. 1980. pap. 19.95 (0-7748-0288-X) U of Wash Pr.

Manliness & Civilization: A Cultural History of Gender & Race in the United States, 1880-1917. Gail Bederman. xiv, 308p. 1996. pap. text 19.00 (0-226-04139-5) U Ch Pr.

Manliness & Civilization: A Cultural History of Gender & Race in the United States, 1880-1917. Gail Bederman. LC 94-26936. (Women in Culture & Society Ser.). 322p. 1998. 27.50 (0-226-04138-7) U Ch Pr.

Manly Adventures & Other Delusions. Tom Wilson. LC 95-70803. (Illus.). 93p. (Orig.). (C). 1995. pap. 9.95 (1-880222-23-X) Red Apple Pub.

Manly Adventures II & Other Delusions: Sudden Impact. Tom Wilson. LC 98-68706. (Illus.). 96p. 1999. per. 9.95 (1-880222-31-0) Red Apple Pub.

Manly Anniversary Studies in Language & Literature. John M. Manly. LC 68-22110. (Essay Index Reprint Ser.). 1977. reprint ed. 24.95 (0-8369-0673-X) Ayer.

Manly Art: Bare-Knuckle Prize Fighting in America. Elliott J. Gorn. LC 86-6410. (Illus.). 320p. 1986. 42.50 (0-8014-1920-4); pap. text 16.95 (0-8014-9582-2) Cornell U Pr.

Manly Family: Account of the Descendants of Captain Basil Manly of the Revolution, & Related Families. Louise Manly. (Illus.). 351p. 1994. reprint ed. pap. 54.50 (0-8328-4030-0); reprint ed. lib. bdg. 64.50 (0-8328-4029-7) Higginson Bk Co.

M

Manly Movie Guide. Harold Schechter & David Everitt. LC 97-226342. 304p. 1997. pap. 11.00 (1-57297-308-0) Blvd Books.

***Manly Pursuits.** Ann Harries. 352p. 1999. 24.95 (1-58234-019-6) Bloomsbury Pubg.

***Manly Pursuits.** Ann Harries. 2000. pap. 13.95 (1-58234-073-0) Bloomsbury Pubg.

Manly-Rickert Text of the Canterbury Tales. Roy V. Ramsey. LC 93-50809. 716p. 1994. 139.95 (0-7734-9128-7) E Mellen.

***Manly States: Masculinities, International Relations, & Gender Politics.** Charlotte Hooper. 224p. 2000. text 45.00 (0-231-12074-5); pap. text 18.50 (0-231-12075-3) Col U Pr.

Manly Weight Loss: For Men Who Hate Aerobics & Carrot-Stick Diets. Charles Poliquin et al. (Illus.). 80p. 1998. pap. 19.95 (0-9662752-1-7) Dayton Pubns.

Manly Writing: Gender, Rhetoric, & the Rise of Composition. Miriam Brody. LC 92-32129. 272p. (C). 1993. 29.95 (0-8093-1691-9) S Ill U Pr.

***Manmade for Murder.** David Burton. 2000. per. 4.99 (0-373-26342-2) Harlequin Bks.

Manmade for Murder. David Burton. 296p. 1997. 20.95 (1-885173-33-4) Write Way.

Manmade Heartbreak. Patty Rice. 48p. 1998. 5.00 (1-889289-33-7) Ye Olde Font Shoppe.

Manmade Monsters see Monsters

Manmade Wonders. LC 97-48425. (Explore America Ser.). 1998. write for info. (0-7621-0052-4) RD Assn.

Manmohan's India & Other Current Writings. V. S. Mahajan. (C). 1994. text 29.00 (81-7100-640-X, Pub. by Deep & Deep Pubns) S Asia.

Mann: Der Tod in Venedig. Ed. by D. Jackson. (German Texts Ser.). (GER.). 104p. 1996. pap. 19.95 (1-85399-468-5, Pub. by Brist Class Pr) Focus Pub-R Pullins.

Mann: Doctor Faustus. Michael Beddow. LC 93-49364. (Landmarks of World Literature Ser.). 132p. (C). 1994. text 34.95 (0-521-37575-4); pap. text 12.95 (0-521-37592-4) Cambridge U Pr.

Mann: The Short Story Cycle. LC 88-18685. 243p. 1988. lib. bdg. 55.00 (0-313-25081-2, MSS, Greenwood Pr) Greenwood.

Mann: Tonio Kroger. Ed. by J. White. (Bristol German Texts Ser.). (GER.). 228p. 1996. pap. 18.95 (1-85399-345-X, Pub. by Brist Class Pr) Focus Pub-R Pullins.

Mann: Two Stories: Unordnung und Fruhes Leid. 2nd ed. Ed. by W. Witte. (German Texts Ser.). (GER.). 128p. 1995. pap. 18.95 (1-85399-366-2, Pub. by Brist Class Pr) Focus Pub-R Pullins.

***Mann in der Kinst, Band 5.** Ed Cervone. 1998. pap. 24.95 (3-925443-55-X) Janssen.

***Mann in der Kinst, Band 6.** Willibrord Haas. 1998. pap. text 24.95 (3-925443-66-5) Janssen.

Mann-Mallin Fantasy Baseball Guide - 1992. Steve Mann & Ken Mallin. (Illus.). 184p. 1998. reprint ed. pap. text 5.00 (0-7881-5152-5) DIANE Pub.

Mann of Amman: The Life of Dai Davies. Phil Melling. 135p. 1994. pap. 23.95 (0-8464-4667-7) Beekman Pubs.

Mann Zu Viel. (Easy Reader Ser.: Level 1). 32p. 1991. 5.25 (3-468-49682-6) Langenscheidt.

Manna: An Historical Geography. R. A. Donkin. (Biogeographica Ser.: No. 17). (Illus.). vii, 160p. 1980. text 148.50 (90-6193-218-1) Kluwer Academic.

Manna: For the Mandelstams for the Mandelas. Helene Cixous. Tr. & Intro. by Catherine A. MacGillivray. LC 93-34674. (Emergent Literatures Ser.). 1994. 24.95 (0-8166-2114-4) U of Minn Pr.

Manna: Poems from Hollywood. Mark Dunster. 12p. 1998. pap. 5.00 (0-89642-429-4) Linden Pubs.

Manna & Mystery: A Jungian Approach to Hebrew Myth & Legend. Bettina L. Knapp. LC 94-3553. 184p. (Orig.). 1995. pap. 16.95 (0-933029-80-2) Chiron Pubns.

Manna for a Desert of Busyness: Praying Advent Sunday Scripture. Joseph A. Tetlow. LC 88-90351. 112p. (Orig.). 1988. pap. 7.95 (1-55612-181-4) Sheed & Ward WI.

Manna for a Desert of Busyness: Praying Lenten Sunday Scripture. Joseph A. Tetlow. LC 87-63376. 112p. (Orig.). 1988. pap. 6.95 (1-55612-119-9) Sheed & Ward WI.

An Asterisk (*) at the beginning of an entry indicates that the title is appearing for the first time.

Manna for a Modern Age: Essential Nourishment for Total Well-Being & Life-Long Personal Success. Larry J. Aufiero. 250p. Date not set. pap. 14.95 (0-9679839-2-4) Horizon NY.

Manna for the Hungry-Hearted. Robert B. Burnette. 56p. 1989. pap. 3.95 (1-881202-01-1) Anointed Pubns.

Manna for Winter. Michael Cole. 30p. 1994. pap. 7.00 (0-937669-52-0) Owl Creek Pr.

Manna from Heaven: Spiritual Food from the Word of God. Ivor C. Powell. 224p. 1996. pap. 9.99 (0-8254-3546-3) Kregel.

Manna in the Morning. 6th ed. Stephen F. Olford. 13p. 1962. 0.50 (1-879028-01-8) Encounter Minist.

Manna in the Wilderness: A Harvest of Hope. Bill Williams. LC 98-55924. (Illus.). 96p. 1999. pap. 9.95 (0-8192-1782-4) Morehouse Pub.

Manna Machine. George Sassoon & Rodney Dale. LC 78-320824. 300p. reprint ed. pap. 93.00 (0-8357-7682-4, AU0039200002) Bks Demand.

Manna of Heaven. Dennis W. Van De Mark. LC 93-80638. (Orig.). 1994. pap. text 19.95 (0-9639721-0-3) Midlands Pubng.

Manna Project: Business Opportunities in Outer Space. G. Harry Stine. (Illus.). 240p. 1998. 21.95 (0-87131-867-9) M Evans.

Manned Laboratories in Space: Proceedings of the International Astronautical Congress, New York, October 18, 1968. International Astronautical Congress Staff. Ed. by S. Fred Singer. (Astrophysics & Space Science Library: No.16). 133p. 1969. text 85.50 (90-277-0140-7) Kluwer Academic.

Manned Lunar Flight (AAS/AAAS Symposium) Dec. 19, 1961, Denver, CO: Proceedings of the AAA/AAAS Symposium, Denver, CO, Dec. 19, 1961. Ed. by George W. Morgenthaler & Horace Jacobs. LC 57-43769. (Advances in the Astronautical Sciences Ser.: Vol. 10). 310p. 1963. 35.00 (0-87703-011-1, Am Astronaut Soc) Univelt Inc.

Manned Space Flight: A Source Guide. 1991. lib. bdg. 76.00 (0-8490-4912-1) Gordon Pr.

Manned Space Reliability Symposium, Jun. 9, 1964, Anaheim, CA. Ed. by Paul Horowitz. (Science & Technology Ser.: Vol. 1). 112p. 1964. 20.00 (0-87703-029-4, Am Astronaut Soc) Univelt Inc.

Manned Spacecraft: Engineering Design & Operation. Ed. by Paul E. Purser et al. LC 64-24708. (Illus.). 523p. reprint ed. pap. 162.20 (0-608-11525-8, 201174500079) Bks Demand.

Mannequin. J. Robert Janes. LC 98-18970. (Soho Crime Ser.). 266p. 1998. 22.00 (1-56947-129-0) Soho Press.

Mannequin. J. Robert Janes. (Soho Crime Ser.). 272p. 1999. pap. 12.00 (1-56947-176-2) Soho Press.

Mannequin d'Osier. Anatole France, pseud. (FRE.). 1965. pap. 10.95 (0-8288-9760-3, F101281) Fr & Eur.

Mannequin d'Osier see Romans et Contes

***Mannequins' Ball.** Bruno Jasienski. Ed. by Daniel Gerould. (Illus.). 84p. 1998. pap. text 22.00 (90-5755-053-9, Harwood Acad Pubs) Gordon & Breach.

***Mannequins' Ball.** Bruno Jasienski. Ed. by Daniel Gerould. (Illus.). 100p. 2000. text 28.00 (90-5755-052-0, Harwood Acad Pubs) Gordon & Breach.

Manner of Correspondence: A Study of the Scriblerus Club. Patricia C. Bruckmann. LC 98-103948. 200p. 1997. 55.00 (0-7735-1546-1, Pub. by McG-Queens Univ Pr) CUP Services.

Manner of Death. Stephen White. LC 98-26697. 368p. 1999. 23.95 (0-525-94440-0) NAL.

***Manner of Death.** large type ed. Stephen White. LC 99-11200. 1999. 26.95 (1-57490-177-X) T T Beeler.

***Manner of Death.** Stephen White. 2000. reprint ed. mass mkt. 7.50 (0-451-19703-8, Sig) NAL.

Manner of Man That Kills. L. Vernon Briggs. (Historical Foundations of Forensic Psychiatry & Psychology Ser.). (Illus.). 444p. 1983. reprint ed. lib. bdg. 45.00 (0-306-76182-3) Da Capo.

Manner Ohne Fraune - Parsifal. Markus Lupertz. 1994. pap. 20.00 (1-881616-31-2) Dist Art Pubs.

***Mannerakt 2.** Herausgegeben Von Volk Janssen. 1998. 44.95 (3-925443-43-6) Janssen.

Mannerism. John Shearman. (J). (gr. 4-7). 1991. pap. 11.95 (0-14-013759-9) Viking Penguin.

Mannerism: The Crisis of the Renaissance & the Origin of Modern Art. Arnold Hauser. (Illus.). 688p. (Orig.). 1986. pap. 26.50 (0-674-54815-9) HUP.

Mannerism & Anti-Mannerism in Italian Painting. Walter Friedlaender. 1990. text 57.50 (0-231-02024-4) Col U Pr.

Mannerism & Anti-Mannerism in Italian Painting. Walter Friedlander. 1990. pap. text 17.00 (0-231-08388-2) Col U Pr.

Mannerism in Arabic Poetry: A Structural Analysis of Selected Texts (3rd Century AH-9th Century AD-5th Century AH-11th Century AD) Stefan Sperl. (Cambridge Studies in Islamic Civilization). 240p. (C). 1989. text 69.95 (0-521-35485-4) Cambridge U Pr.

Mannerism in Art, Literature, & Music: A Bibliography. Richard Studing & Elizabeth Kruz. LC 79-63612. (Checklists in the Humanities & Education Ser.). 81p. reprint ed. pap. 30.00 (0-8357-6352-8, 203562700096) Bks Demand.

Mannerisms: The Five Phases of Manfred Mann. Greg Russo. (Illus.). 275p. (Orig.). 1995. pap. 22.95 (0-9648157-1-0) Crossfire NY.

Mannerisms of Speech & Gestures in Everyday Life. Sandor S. Feldman. LC 59-6713. 167p. (Orig.). 1969. reprint ed. pap. 24.95 (0-8236-8144-0, 023100) Intl Univs Pr.

Mannerist Prints: International Style in the Sixteenth Century. Bruce Davis. LC 88-12674. (Illus.). 336p. 1988. text 29.95 (0-87587-147-X) LA Co Art Mus.

Mannerphantasien, Vol. 2 see Male Fantasies, Vol. 2, The Male Body: Psychoanalyzing the White Terror

Manners. Gail Aemmer & Lynette Pyne. (Home Workbooks Ser.). (Illus.). 64p. (Orig.). (J). (ps-1). 1996. pap., wbk. ed. 2.49 (0-88724-368-1, CD-6865) Carson-Dellos.

Manners. Aliki. LC 89-34622. 32p. (J). (ps-3). 1990. 16.00 (0-688-09198-9, Grenwillow Bks) HarpC Child Bks.

Manners. Aliki. LC 89-34622. 32p. (J). (ps-3). 1990. 15.89 (0-688-09199-7, Grenwillow Bks) HarpC Child Bks.

Manners. Aliki. LC 92-43788. (Illus.). 40p. (J). (ps-3). 1997. mass mkt. 4.95 (0-688-04579-0, Wm Morrow) Morrow Avon.

Manners. Aliki. 1997. 10.15 (0-606-11596-X, Pub. by Turtleback) Demco.

Manners. Marcia Crots. LC 97-69233. (Illus.). 24p. (J). (gr. k-3). 1998. pap. 6.95 (1-57197-086-X) Pentland Pr.

Manners. Judy Klare. (Looking Good Ser.). (Illus.). 32p. (J). (gr. 5 up). 1990. lib. bdg. 11.95 (0-685-36384-8) Rourke Corp.

Manners. Judy Klare. (Looking Good Ser.: Set II). (Illus.). 32p. (YA). (gr. 5 up). 1990. lib. bdg. 19.93 (0-86625-419-6) Rourke Pubns.

Manners. Shelly Nielsen. Ed. by Rosemary Wallner. LC 91-73042. (Values Matter Ser.). (J). 1992. lib. bdg. 14.98 (1-56239-066-X) ABDO Pub Co.

Manners. Eric Suben. LC 98-48388. 32p. 1999. lib. bdg. write for info. (1-55916-234-1) Rourke Bk Co.

Manners, Reading Level 2. Elaine Goley. (Learn the Value Ser.: Set II). (Illus.). 32p. (J). (gr. 1-4). 1989. 11.95 (0-685-58787-8) Rourke Corp.

Manners: Happy Homes & Good Society All the Year Round. Sarah Josephbuell Hale. LC 72-2606. (American Women Ser.: Images & Realities). 384p. 1974. reprint ed. 26.95 (0-405-04461-5) Ayer.

Manners & Customs. James Barmier. (Life in America 100 Years Ago Ser.). (Illus.). 104p. (YA). (gr. 5 up). 1995. lib. bdg. 19.95 (0-7910-2844-5) Chelsea Hse.

Manners & Customs in the Bible. rev. ed. Victor H. Matthews. (Illus.). 284p. 1991. 17.95 (0-943575-77-X); pap. 9.95 (0-943575-81-8) Hendrickson MA.

Manners & Customs of Bible Lands see Usos y Costumbres de las Tierras Biblicas

***Manners & Customs of Bible Times.** Broadman & Holman Publishing Staff. LC 99-54865. (Shepherd's Notes Bible Summary Ser.). 1999. pap. 5.95 (0-8054-9376-X) Broadman.

Manners & Customs of Mankind, 2 vols., Set. Ed. by J. A. Hammerton. 1977. lib. bdg. 250.00 (0-8490-2202-9) Gordon Pr.

Manners & Customs of the Bible. James M. Freeman. LC 97-208500. (Illus.). 528p. 1996. pap. 17.99 (0-88368-290-7) Whitaker Hse.

Manners & Customs of the Modern Egyptians. E. W. Lane. 616p. 1986. 360.00 (1-85077-115-4, Pub. by Darf Pubs Ltd) St Mut.

Manners & Customs of the New Zealanders, 2 vols. Joel S. Polack. LC 75-35263. reprint ed. 64.50 (0-404-14435-7) AMS Pr.

Manners & Customs of the Rwala Bedouins. Alois Musil. LC 77-87091. (American Geographical Society Oriental Explorations & Studies: No. 6). reprint ed. 74.50 (0-404-60236-3) AMS Pr.

Manners & Meaning in West Sumatra: The Social Context of Consciousness. Frederick K. Errington. LC 83-21893. (Illus.). 189p. reprint ed. pap. 58.60 (0-7837-6217-8, 208020400003) Bks Demand.

Manners & Morals. Mary P. Thaman. LC 77-8129. 1977. reprint ed. lib. bdg. 65.00 (0-8371-9679-5, THMM, Greenwood Pr) Greenwood.

Manners & Morals of Yesterday. Sam Tuttle, pseud. (Illus.). 109p. 1994. pap. 14.95 (0-914166-19-0) Americana Rev.

Manners & Rules of Good Society or Solecisms to be Avoided (1924) "A Member of the Aristocracy" Staff. 280p. 1999. reprint ed. pap. 18.95 (0-7661-0824-4) Kessinger Pub.

Manners & Social Usages. Mary E. Sherwood. LC 75-1869. (Leisure Class in America Ser.). (Illus.). 1975. reprint ed. 36.95 (0-405-06935-9) Ayer.

***Manners & Violence.** Ignacio L. Gotz. LC 00-25466. 168p. 2000. 52.00 (0-275-97007-8, C7007) Greenwood.

"Manners Are Fun!" with Katherine the Great. Paula G. Edwards. (Illus.). 135p. (J). (gr. k-6). 1996. spiral bd. 11.99 (0-9656566-0-8) River Side.

Manners at Work: A Guide to What Every Office Worker Should Know. Christine Ekkebus. 64p. (Orig.). 1994. pap. text 2.57 (0-9639073-1-X) C Ekkebus.

Manners Can Be Fun. 2nd rev. ed. Munro Leaf. LC 84-48459. (Trophy Picture Bk.). (Illus.). 48p. (J). (gr. k-3). 1985. pap. 4.95 (0-06-443053-7, HarpTrophy) HarpC Child Bks.

Manners Can Be Fun. 3rd ed. Munro Leaf. LC 84-48459. (Illus.). 48p. (J). (gr. k-3). 1985. lib. bdg. 12.89 (0-397-32118-X) HarpC Child Bks.

***Manners, Customs, & Antiquities of the Indians of North & South America.** Samuel G. Goodrich. (LC History-America-E). 336p. 1999. reprint ed. lib. bdg. 89.00 (0-7812-4256-8) Rprt Serv.

Manners for the Metropolis: An Entrance Key to the Fantastic Life of the 400. Francis W. Crowninshield. LC 75-1838. (Leisure Class in America Ser.). (Illus.). 1975. reprint ed. 17.95 (0-405-06907-3) Ayer.

Manners for the Modern Dog. Gwen Bohnenkamp. 34p. 1990. pap. text 9.95 (0-9644601-0-6) Perfect Paws.

Manners Matter. Debbie Pincus. (Illus.). 112p. (J). (gr. 3-7). 1992. student ed. 12.99 (0-86653-688-4, 1422) Good Apple.

Manners of Interpretation: The Ends of Argument in Literary Studies. Miguel Tamen. LC 92-2412. (SUNY Series, The Margins of Literature). 211p. (C). 1993. text 64.50 (0-7914-1503-1); pap. text 21.95 (0-7914-1504-X) State U NY Pr.

Manners, Please! Poems & Activities That Teach Responsible Behavior. Greta B. Lipson. Ed. by Judy Mitchell. (Illus.). 96p. (Orig.). (J). (gr. k-3). 1995. pap., teacher ed. 9.95 (1-57310-014-5) Teachng & Lrning Co.

Manners That Matter: For People under Twenty-One. Ideal Instructional Fair Staff. 1999. pap. text 9.95 (1-56822-851-1) Instruct Fair.

***Manners That Sell: Adding the Polish That Builds Profits.** Lydia Ramsey. (Illus.). 2000. pap. 19.95 (0-9670012-0-X) L Ramsey.

Mannheim Christmas in the Aire Fingerstyle Guitar. 48p. 1996. pap. 12.95 (0-7935-6715-7) H Leonard.

Mannheim Steamroller: Christmas in the Aire. 80p. 1996. otabind 12.95 (0-7935-6668-1) H Leonard.

Mannheim Steamroller: Fresh Aire 1 - Solo Piano. 40p. 1986. otabind 12.95 (0-7935-3742-8, 00357475) H Leonard.

Mannheim Steamroller: Fresh Aire 2 - One Piano, Four Hands. 80p. 1988. otabind 12.95 (0-7935-3741-X, 00357474) H Leonard.

Mannheim Steamroller: Fresh Aire 3. C. Davis. 64p. 1988. otabind 12.95 (0-7935-2749-X, 00357476) H Leonard.

Mannheim Steamroller: Fresh Aire 4. 72p. 1988. otabind 12.95 (0-7935-3739-8, 00357477) H Leonard.

***Mannheim Steamroller: Live.** 72p. 1998. otabind 15.95 (0-7935-9925-3) H Leonard.

Mannheim Steamroller Christmas for Fingerstyle Guitar. 48p. 1995. pap. 12.95 (0-7935-5627-9, 00650042) H Leonard.

Mannich Bases: Chemistry & Uses. Tramotini & Angi. 304p. 1994. boxed set 178.95 (0-8493-4430-1) CRC Pr.

Manning. Peyton Manning. 2000. mass mkt. 6.99 (0-06-102024-9) HarpC.

***Manning: A Father, His Sons & a Football Legacy.** Peyton Manning et al. (Illus.). 256p. 2000. 24.00 (0-06-105136-5, HarpEntertain) Morrow Avon.

Manning Clark: Essays on His Place in History. Ed. by Carl Bridge. LC 95-105052. 184p. 1994. pap. 29.95 (0-522-84640-8, Pub. by Melbourne Univ Pr) Paul & Co Pubs.

Manning Clark's History of Australia: An Abridgement. Abr. by Michael Cathcart. 588p. 1993. 45.00 (0-522-84523-1, Pub. by Melbourne Univ Pr) Paul & Co Pubs.

Manning Clarks's History of Australia: Special Anniversary Edition. abr. ed. Michael Cathart. LC 98-222510. 592p. 1997. 85.00 (0-522-84779-X, Pub. by Melbourne Univ Pr) Paul & Co Pubs.

Manning on Decoupage. Hiram Manning. (Illus.). 254p. 1980. reprint ed. pap. 9.95 (0-486-24028-2) Dover.

Manning on Estate Planning. 5th ed. Jerome A. Manning et al. 720p. 1995. ring bd. 145.00 (0-614-17124-5, D1-0165) PLI.

Manning the New Navy: The Development of a Modern Naval Enlisted Force, 1899-1940, 68. Frederick S. Harrod. LC 77-82697. (Contributions in American History Ser.: No. 68). 276p. 1978. 55.00 (0-8371-9759-7, HEM/, Greenwood Pr) Greenwood.

Manny. unabridged ed. Isaac Rosen. LC 96-42294. 1996. 20.00 (1-880909-52-9) Baskerville.

Manny: A Criminal-Addict's Story. Richard P. Rettig. 202p. (C). 1999. pap. 11.95 (1-57766-058-7) Waveland Pr.

Manny: Memoirs of a Night Beat Cabbie. LaVonne Sullivan. (One-Act Plays Ser.). 30p. 1994. pap. 5.00 (1-885800-08-8) PineTree Pr.

Manny Almeida's Ringside Lounge: The Cape Verdeans' Struggle for Their Neighborhood. Sam Beck. LC 92-72593. (Illus.). 118p. (Orig.). 1992. pap. text 12.50 (0-943722-18-7) Gavea-Brown.

Manny Farber. Amy Goldin. LC 78-58402. 103p. (Orig.). 1978. pap. 9.00 (0-934418-01-2) Mus Contemp Art.

Manny Farber: Paintings of the '80s. Sally Yard. Ed. by Julie Dunn. LC 90-63842. (Illus.). 48p. (Orig.). 1991. per. 20.00 (0-9628536-0-7) Quint Contempo.

Manny Ramirez. Charlie Vascellaro. LC 99-54106. (Latinos in Baseball Ser.). (Illus.). 64p. (YA). (gr. 6-12). 2000. lib. bdg. 18.95 (1-58415-020-3) M Lane Pubs.

Manny Shinwell. Slowe. LC 93-29494. 352p. (C). 59.95 (0-7453-0736-1, Pub. by Pluto GBR); pap. 22.95 (0-7453-0737-X, Pub. by Pluto GBR) Stylus Pub VA.

***Manny the Happy Hanukkah Menorah.** Dorothy Fish & Betty Cohen. (Illus.). 24p. (J). (ps-3). 2000. pap. 5.50 (0-914080-42-3) Shulsinger Sales.

Manny's a Thief. Getzel. 1992. 9.99 (0-89906-414-0) Mesorah Pubns.

Mano del Amo. Tomas Eloy Martinez. 1999. pap. text 18.95 (968-406-753-4) F Planeta.

Mano en la Arena, Level 1. Fernanco Uria. (Leer en Espanol Ser.). (SPA.). (C). 1998. pap. 5.95 (84-294-3479-8) Santillana.

Mano Majra see Train to Pakistan

Mano Manca. Ivonne Acosta. 156p. 1995. pap. text. write for info. (1-56758-040-8) Edit Cultl.

***Mano Sobre Mano.** Karen M. Rogers. Tr. by Ana M. Alvarado. (Think-Kids Book Collection).Tr. of Hand over Hand. (SPA., Illus.). 16p. (J). 2000. pap. 2.95 (1-58237-053-2) Creat Think.

Manoa: The Story of a Valley. Ed. by Glen Grant. (Illus.). 320p. 1994. 35.00 (1-56647-067-6) Mutual Pub HI.

Manoah Bodman Series, 7 bks. Ed. by Edward Foster. 1998. 20.00 (1-893032-10-8) Jensen Daniels.

Manobos of Mindanao. John M. Garvan. LC 77-86951. (National Academy of Sciences, Washington, D.C. Memoirs Ser.: Vol. 23). reprint ed. 82.50 (0-404-16715-2) AMS Pr.

Manoeuvring & Control of Marine Craft. Ed. by P. A. Wilson. LC 92-70439. 650p. 1992. 199.00 (1-56252-109-8) Computational Mech MA.

Manoeuvring & Control of Marine Craft: Proceedings of the 4th IFAC Conference, Brijuni, Croatia, 10-12 September 1997. Ed. by Z. Vukic & G. N. Roberts. 216p. 1998. pap. 67.00 (0-08-042934-3, Pergamon Pr) Elsevier.

Manoir Enchante et Quatre Autres Oeuvres Inedites. Alfred Jarry. (FRE.). 256p. 1974. 12.95 (0-7859-0103-5, M3597) Fr & Eur.

Manolithography - A Borderland Between STM, EB & X-Ray Lithographies: Proceedings of the NATO Advanced Research Workshop, Frascati, Roma, Italy, April 6-8, 1993. M. Gentili. (NATO Advanced Science Institutes Series C: Mathematical & Physical Sciences). 228p. (C). 1994. text 156.00 (0-7923-2794-2) Kluwer Academic.

Manolo: Escultura, Pintura y Dibujo. Montserrat Blanch. (Grandes Monografias). (SPA., Illus.). 338p. 1993. 200.00 (84-343-0087-7) Elliots Bks.

***Manolo Blahnik.** Colin McDowell. 208p. 2000. 50.00 (0-06-019684-X, HarpCollins) HarperTrade.

***Manolo Valdes.** Thomas Llorens. (SPA.). 2000. text 75.00 (958-9393-79-9, Pub. by Villegas Ed) St Martin.

Manometer Tables: ISA Standard RP2.1. 1978. pap. 40.00 (0-87664-325-X, RP2.1) ISA.

***Manon.** Melanie N. Jackson. 320p. 2000. mass mkt. 4.99 (0-8439-4737-3, Leisure Bks) Dorchester Pub Co.

Manon. Jules Massenet. Ed. by Nicholas John. Tr. by Tracey Edmund from FRE. LC 84-755667. (English National Opera Guide Series: Bilingual Libretto, Articles: No. 25). (Illus.). 112p. 1984. pap. 9.95 (0-7145-4041-2) Riverrun NY.

Manon. Abbe Prevost. Tr. by Helen Waddell from FRE. LC 88-60594. 262p. 1988. reprint ed. pap. 14.95 (0-948166-15-0, Pub. by Soho Bk Co) Dufour.

Manon: Alone in Front of the Net. Manon Rheaume. 1993. pap. write for info. (0-00-638029-8) HarpC.

Manon: Alone in Front of the Net. Manon Rheaume & Chantal Gilbert. Tr. by Mark Daley. LC 95-5213. (Illus.). ix, 179p. 1998. mass mkt. 5.50 (0-00-638031-X) HarpC.

Manon: Vocal Score: Five Acts. Jules Massenet. (ENG & FRE.). 396p. 1986. pap. 35.00 (0-7935-2547-0, 50338380) H Leonard.

Manon des Sources. Marcel Pagnol. (FRE.). 320p. 1976. 13.95 (0-8288-9894-4, F117461) Fr & Eur.

Manon des Sources. Marcel Pagnol. (FRE.). 318p. 1988. pap. 13.95 (0-7859-1657-1, 2877060551) Fr & Eur.

Manon des Sources see Eau des Collines

Manon in Full Score. Jules Massenet. 1997. 21.95 (0-486-29871-X, 741688Q) Dover.

Manon Lescaut. Abbe Prevost. (FRE.). 1976. pap. 8.95 (0-7859-3078-7) Fr & Eur.

Manon Lescaut. Abbe Prevost. (FRE.). (C). pap. 7.95 (0-8442-1832-4, VF1832-4) NTC Contemp Pub Co.

Manon Lescaut. Abbe Prevost. (Folio Ser.: No. 757). (FRE.). 249p. 1988. pap. 8.95 (2-07-036757-6) Schoenhof.

Manon Lescaut. Abbe Prevost. Tr. by Leonard W. Tancock. 192p. 1992. pap. 10.95 (0-14-044559-5, Penguin Classics) Viking Penguin.

Manon Lescaut. unabridged ed. Abbe Prevost. (FRE.). pap. 5.95 (2-87714-196-9, Pub. by Bookking Intl) Distribks Inc.

Manon Lescaut in Full Score. Giacomo Puccini. 496p. pap. text 22.95 (0-486-28590-1) Dover.

Manopause: Boomer Hits the Big Fifty. Mark P. Poncy. LC 97-90295. x, 64p. (Orig.). 1997. pap. 9.95 (0-533-12345-3) Vantage.

Manor & Cottages: Albemarle Park, Asheville, North Carolina, a Historic Planned Residential Community. Jane G. Mathews & Richard A. Mathews. (Illus.). 112p. (Orig.). 1991. pap. 19.95 (0-9630437-0-6) Albemarle Pk.

Manor Houses & Castles of Sweden: A Voyage Through Five Centuries. Maita Di Niscemi. LC 87-60276. (Illus.). 216p. 1994. 55.00 (0-935748-73-3) Antique Collect.

Manor Houses & Historic Homes of the Hudson Valley. Harold D. Eberlein. 327p. 1993. reprint ed. lib. bdg. 89.00 (0-7812-5294-6) Rprt Serv.

Manor Houses in Normandy. Regis Faucaon & Yves Lescroart. (Illus.). 400p. 1998. 39.95 (3-89508-703-3, 520364) Konemann.

Manor Life in Old France: From the Journal of the Sire de Gouberville for the Years 1549-1562. Katharine Fedden. LC 70-168013. reprint ed. 29.50 (0-404-02374-6) AMS Pr.

Manor of Eden. Sheryl J. Stevens. (Orig.). 1993. pap. 9.95 (0-9637084-0-6) Osborn Pub.

Manor of Fordham & Its Founder. Harry C. Melick. LC 50-11879. (Illus.). 234p. reprint ed. pap. 72.60 (0-7837-5584-8, 204537600005) Bks Demand.

Manor of Springettsbury: Its History & Early Settlers. Neal O. Hively. (York County, PA Land Records Ser.: Vol. 6). 272p. 1993. pap. 18.00 (0-9638435-0-8) N O Hively.

Manor on Cranton-Barry Hill. Petey. 136p. 1998. pap. 9.95 (0-9662636-0-X) Starr-Vision.

Manor Spirits. Tony Foster. 154p. (YA). (gr. 4-9). 1998. pap. 4.95 (1-85594-184-8, Pub. by Attic Press) Intl Spec Bk.

Manor, the Plowman, & the Shepherd: Agrarian Themes & Imagery in Late Medieval & Early Renaissance English Literature. Ordelle G. Hill. LC 91-51054. 1993. 42.50 (0-945636-42-3) Susquehanna U Pr.

Manorial Domestic Buildings in England & Northern France. Ed. by Gwyn Merion-Jones & Michael Jones. (Society of Antiquaries Occasional Papers: No. 15). (Illus.). 223p. 1994. pap. 35.00 (0-85431-263-3, Pub. by Soc Antiquaries) David Brown.

Manorma. Leoda A. Buckwalter. LC 91-71664. 176p. 1991. pap. 7.95 (0-916035-46-8) Evangel Indiana.

Manos. Robert James. (SPA.). (J). 1995. lib. bdg. 14.60 (1-57103-133-2) Rourke Pr.

An Asterisk (*) at the beginning of an entry indicates that the title is appearing for the first time.

***Manos.** Dana Meachen Rau. (Rookie Espanol Ser.). (SPA., Illus.). (J). 2000. 15.00 (*0-516-22021-7*) Childrens.

***Manos: Oraciones Antes de Comer.**Tr. of Hands! Mealtime Prayers. (SPA., Illus.). (J). 2000. 2.99 (*0-7899-0396-2*, 494041) Editorial Unilit.

***Manos: Oraciones Antes de Dormir.**Tr. of Hands! Bedtime Prayers. (SPA., Illus.). (J). 2000. 2.99 (*0-7899-0398-9*, 494043) Editorial Unilit.

***Manos: Oraciones de Alabanza.**Tr. of Hands! Prayers of Praise. (SPA., Illus.). (J). 2000. 2.99 (*0-7899-0397-0*, 494042) Editorial Unilit.

***Manos: Oraciones Infantiles Clasicas.**Tr. of Hands! Classic Childrens Prayers. (SPA., Illus.). (J). 2000. 2.99 (*0-7899-0399-7*, 494044) Editorial Unilit.

Manos a la Obra: The Story Behind Operation Bootstrap. Pedro A. Rivera. 25p. 1986. pap. 7.00 (*1-878483-18-8*) Hunter Coll CEP.

Manos en el Agua. Carlos Murciano. (J). (gr. 3-5). 1997. pap. text 7.50 (*84-279-3337-1*) Lectorum Pubns.

Manplay Vol. 3: True Gay Encounters. Ed. by Winston Leyland. 192p. (Orig.). 1986. pap. 10.00 (*0-943595-06-1*) Leyland Pubns.

Manpower & Employment in Arab Countries: Some Critical Issues. 1979. 14.00 (*92-2-103504-2*, ILO68) Intl Labour Office.

Manpower & Merger: The Impact of Merger upon Personnel Policies in the Carpet & Furniture Industries. Steven S. Plice. LC 76-21151. (Manpower & Human Resources Studies: No. 5). 168p. reprint ed. pap. 52.10 (*0-608-14850-4*, 202590900047) Bks Demand.

Manpower & Vocational Education Planning Processes: Four Regional Case Studies. Kenneth W. Tolo. (Policy Research Project Report Ser.: No. 9). 76p. 1975. pap. 3.00 (*0-89940-605-X*) LBJ Sch Pub Aff.

Manpower Connection: Education & Work. Eli Ginzberg. 288p. 1976. 34.95 (*0-674-54810-8*) HUP.

Manpower Counselor. Jack Rudman. (Career Examination Ser.: C-2435). 1994. pap. 34.95 (*0-8373-2435-1*) Nat Learn.

Manpower Development Planning: Theory & an African Case Study. Berhanu Abegaz. (Making of Modern Africa Ser.). 240p. 1994. 72.95 (*1-85628-521-9*, Pub. by Avebry) Ashgate Pub Co.

Manpower Development Specialist. Jack Rudman. (Career Examination Ser.: C-2688). 1994. pap. 34.95 (*0-8373-2688-5*) Nat Learn.

Manpower for Energy Production: An International Guide to Sources with Annotations, 5. Compiled by Djehane A. Hosni. LC 86-19377. (Bibliographies & Indexes in Economics & Economic History Ser.: No. 5). 171p. 1986. lib. bdg. 55.00 (*0-313-25089-8*, HMP/) Greenwood.

Manpower Grants Technician. Jack Rudman. (Career Examination Ser.: C-2822). 1994. pap. 29.95 (*0-8373-2822-5*) Nat Learn.

Manpower in Homebuilding: A Preliminary Analysis. Howard G. Foster. LC 74-12751. (Manpower & Human Resources Studies: No. 3). 200p. reprint ed. pap. 62.00 (*0-8357-3158-8*, 203942100012) Bks Demand.

Manpower Information & Liaison Specialist. Jack Rudman. (Career Examination Ser.: C-2807). 1994. pap. 39.95 (*0-8373-2807-1*) Nat Learn.

Manpower Needs in the Omaha SMSA. David W. Hinton. 60p. (Orig.). 1975. pap. 4.50 (*1-55719-066-6*) U NE CPAR.

Manpower Placement: Service Delivery for the Hard-to-Employ. Yeheskel Hasenfeld. LC 73-620092. (Policy Papers in Human Resources & Industrial Relations Ser.: No. 21). 95p. 1973. 10.00 (*0-87736-124-X*); pap. 5.00 (*0-87736-125-8*) U of Mich Inst Labor.

Manpower Planning: Strategy & Techniques in an Organizational Context. Ed. by John Edwards et al. LC 82-23813. 216p. reprint ed. pap. 67.00 (*0-7837-6729-3*, 204635700011) Bks Demand.

Manpower Planning & the Development of Human Resources. Thomas H. Patten. LC 76-137109. 747p. reprint ed. pap. 200.00 (*0-608-13285-3*, 205576000037) Bks Demand.

Manpower Planning in a Free Society. Richard A. Lester. LC 66-14890. 241p. reprint ed. pap. 74.80 (*0-8357-8945-4*, 203339800085) Bks Demand.

Manpower Planning Workbook. 2nd ed. Barrie O. Pettman. LC 83-18488. 127p. 1984. text 76.95 (*0-566-02468-3*) Ashgate Pub Co.

Manpower Policies & Development in the Persian Gulf Region. Robert E. Looney. LC 93-14137. 216p. 1994. 62.95 (*0-275-94217-1*, C4217, Praeger Pubs) Greenwood.

Manpower Problem in Mental Hospitals: A Consultant Team Approach. Philip F. Seitz et al. LC 76-18935. xiii, 253p. (C). 1977. 37.50 (*0-8236-3110-9*) Intl Univs Pr.

Manpower Program Administrator. Jack Rudman. (Career Examination Ser.: C-2671). 1994. pap. 39.95 (*0-8373-2671-0*) Nat Learn.

Manpower Program Coordinator. Jack Rudman. (Career Examination Ser.: C-2316). 1994. pap. 39.95 (*0-8373-2316-9*) Nat Learn.

Manpower Programs in the Policy Mix. Ed. by Lloyd Ulman. LC 72-11850. 176p. reprint ed. pap. 54.60 (*0-608-11905-9*, 202311600032) Bks Demand.

Manpower Resources & Population under Socialism: Socialism Today. V. Aperyan. 198p. 1979. 40.00 (*0-317-53795-4*, Pub. by Collets) St Mut.

Manpower Services Commission in Scotland. Ed. by Alice Brown & John Fairley. (Edinburgh Education & Society Ser.). 324p. 1990. 55.00 (*0-7486-0126-0*, Pub. by Edinburgh U Pr) Col U Pr.

Manpower Services Commission in Scotland. Ed. by Alice Brown & John Fairley. 324p. 1991. pap. 20.00 (*0-7486-0141-4*, Pub. by Edinburgh U Pr) Col U Pr.

Manpower Substitution in the Hospital Industry: A Study of New York City Voluntary & Municipal Hospital Systems. Myron D. Fottler. LC 73-173280. (Special Studies in U. S. Economic, Social & Political Issues). 1972. 52.50 (*0-275-06150-7*) Irvington.

Manpower Tomorrow: Prospects & Priorities - Conference Report of the W. E. Upjohn Institute for Employment Research, 1966. Ed. by Irving H. Siegel. LC 67-29747. viii, 219p. 1968. 35.00 (*0-678-00343-2*) Kelley.

Manpower Training Coordinator. Jack Rudman. (Career Examination Ser.: C-1554). 1994. pap. 39.95 (*0-8373-1554-9*) Nat Learn.

Manpower Training in Saudi Arabia: A Strategic Entry Report, 1997. Compiled by Icon Group International Staff. (Illus.). 135p. 1999. ring bd. 1350.00 incl. audio compact disk (*0-7418-0815-3*) Icon Grp.

Manprint: Approach to Systems Integration. Harold R. Booher. 1990. text 59.95 (*0-442-00383-8*, VNR) Wiley.

Manresa: The Spiritual Exercises of St. Ignatius. 364p. 1996. reprint ed. spiral bd. 23.00 (*0-7873-0002-0*) Hlth Research.

Manresa: or The Spiritual Exercises of St. Ignatius. Catholic Publication Society Staff. 394p. 1996. reprint ed. pap. 21.95 (*1-56459-923-X*) Kessinger Pub.

Manresa: The Spiritual Exercises of St. Ignatius - For General Use see Spiritual Exercises of St. Ignatius Loyola or Manresa: Explained Step-by-Step for Independent Use

Manroot. A. Steinberg. mass mkt. 11.95 (*0-7472-4501-0*, Pub. by Headline Bk Pub) Trafalgar.

Man's Accidents & God's Purposes: Multiplicity in Hawthorne's Fiction. James K. Folsom. 1963. pap. 13.95 (*0-8084-0208-0*) NCUP.

Man's Anger & God's Silence: The Book of Job. Dermot Cox & Board of St. Paul Editorial Staff. 144p. (C). 1996. pap. 39.95 (*0-85439-316-1*, Pub. by St Paul Pubns) St Mut.

Man's Ascent to God. I. Parker Maxey. 1993. pap. 12.99 (*0-88019-306-9*) Schmul Pub Co.

Man's Being, His Destiny & World Evolution. 3rd ed. Rudolf Steiner. Tr. by Erna McArthur & William Riggins from GER. 123p. (Orig.). 1984. pap. 8.95 (*0-88010-090-7*) Anthroposophic.

Man's Best Friend. Nina Coombs. 368p. (Orig.). 1997. mass mkt. 5.50 (*0-505-52205-5*, Love Spell) Dorchester Pub Co.

Man's Best Friend. Photos by William Wegman. (Illus.). 64p. 1999. 12.98 (*0-8109-8174-2*, Pub. by Abrams) Time Warner.

Man's Best Friend. Laurence Wieder. (Illus.). 64p. 1982. pap. 16.95 (*0-8109-2266-5*, Pub. by Abrams) Time Warner.

Man's Best Friend Is His Doggerel. Vince Danca. 44p. 1992. pap. write for info. (*0-9602390-0-6*) V Danca.

***Man's Body: An Owner's Manual, 1.** rev. ed. Diagram Group Staff. LC 99-11777. 480p. 1999. pap. 16.95 (*0-8092-2619-7*, 261970, Contemporary Bks) NTC Contemp Pub Co.

Man's Book. Randy Smith. LC 97-75507. 120p. 1998. pap. 15.00 (*1-57197-089-4*) Pentland Pr.

Man's Book of the Spirit: Daily Meditations for a Mindful Life. Bill Alexander. 384p. (Orig.). 1994. pap. 10.00 (*0-380-77175-6*, Avon Bks) Morrow Avon.

Man's Changing Mask: Modes & Methods of Characterization in Fiction. Charles C. Walcutt. LC 66-24088. 378p. reprint ed. pap. 117.20 (*0-608-15960-3*, 203324200084) Bks Demand.

Man's Check-Up. Dave Ray. 56p. 1994. 9.95 (*1-57326-015-0*) Core Ministries.

Mans City Plan. (Grafocarte Maps Ser.). 1995. 8.95 (*2-7416-0021-X*, 80021) Michelin.

Man's Confidence. Jack W. Hayford. (Power-to-Become Book-Pak Ser.: Bk. 2). 94p. 1992. pap. text 3.95 (*0-916847-11-X*) Living Way.

Man's Confidence. Jack W. Hayford. LC 96-103794. (Power to Become Ser.: No. 02). 1995. pap. 4.99 (*0-7852-7791-9*) Nelson.

Man's Courage. Joseph Vogel. LC 88-39973. (New York Classics Ser.). 336p. 1989. reprint ed. pap. text 16.95 (*0-8156-0233-2*) Syracuse U Pr.

Man's Dependence on the Earth: The Role of Geosciences in the Environment. Ed. by A. A. Archer et al. (Illus.). xiii, 216p. 1987. text 41.00 (*3-510-65128-6*, Pub. by E Schweizerbartsche) Balogh.

Man's Destiny in Eternity. Arthur H. Compton. LC 75-117821. (Essay Index Reprint Ser.). 1977. 21.95 (*0-8369-1762-6*) Ayer.

Man's Divine Parentage & Destiny: The Great Rounds & Races. Gertrude W. Van Pelt. Ed. by W. Emmett Small & Helen Todd. (Theosophical Manual Ser.: No. 7). 64p. 1975. pap. 5.00 (*0-913004-24-3*, 913004-24) Point Loma Pub.

Man's Earth-Lease Is about to Expire. C. C. Cribb. LC 77-70210. pap. 2.95 (*0-932046-01-0*) Manhattan Ltd NC.

Man's Estate. large type ed. Nigel Tranter. 1977. 27.99 (*0-7089-0037-2*) Ulverscroft.

Man's Eternal Quest. Paramahansa Yogananda. LC 75-17183. (Illus.). 503p. 1982. 16.50 (*0-87612-233-0*); pap. 12.50 (*0-87612-232-2*) Self Realization.

Man's Fate. Andre Malraux. 360p. (C). 1965. 8.44 (*0-07-553654-4*) McGraw.

Man's Fate. Andre Malraux. Tr. by Haakon M. Chevalier. 1965. pap. 4.50 (*0-685-06615-0*) Modern Lib NY.

Man's Fate. Andre Malraux. 1990. pap. 13.00 (*0-679-72574-1*) Vin Bks.

Man's Field Guide to Dating: The Guide. Robert A. Wray. 235p. 1999. pap. 17.95 (*0-9669723-0-9*) net Image.

Mans Forgeries: A Chapter from the History of Church Property in the Ninth Century. Walter A. Goffart. LC 66-18246. (Historical Studies: No. 76). 397p. 1966. 25.00 (*0-674-51875-6*) HUP.

Man's Future Birthright: Essays on Science & Humanity. Ed. by Hermann Joseph Muller & Elof A. Carlson. LC 79-171215. 164p. (C). 1973. text 24.50 (*0-87395-097-6*) State U NY Pr.

Man's Game. Newton Thornburg. 304p. 1996. 22.95 (*0-312-85923-6*) Forge NYC.

Man's Game. Newton Thornburg. 1997. mass mkt. 6.99 (*0-8125-5374-8*, Pub. by Forge NYC) St Martin.

***Man's Garden.** Warren Schultz. (Illus.). 160p. 2001. 40.00 (*0-618-00392-4*) HM.

Man's Great Future. Christian Science Monitor Editors. Ed. by Erwin D. Canham. LC 71-37866. (Essay Index Reprint Ser.). 1977. reprint ed. 20.95 (*0-8369-2585-8*) Ayer.

Man's Greatest Fear: The Final Phase of Human Evolution. Tim Marshall. LC 96-104113. (Illus.). 180p. (Orig.). 1995. pap. 11.00 (*0-9645750-0-0*) Athena Bks.

Man's Greatest Questions. Ronnie W. Lowe. 1992. pap. 7.15 (*0-89137-132-X*) Quality Pubns.

Man's Guide to (And from) Infidelity. Elissa Gough. 130p. 1998. pap. 19.95 (*1-891863-02-9*) Face Reality.

Man's Guide to Being a Woman's Best Friend. Michael Levin. 96p. (Orig.). 1996. pap. 4.95 (*0-8362-2581-3*) Andrews & McMeel.

Man's Guide to Coping with Disability. 2nd ed. Resources for Rehabilitation Staff. LC 98-55559. 1999. pap. 44.95 (*0-929718-23-2*) Resc Rehab.

Man's Guide to Mexico & Central America, 1996-97. annuals Senor Cordova. Ed. by Joe Torres, 3rd. LC 95-70191. (Illus.). 204p. (Orig.). 1996. pap. 18.95 (*0-9639054-2-2*) Centurion CA.

Man's Guide to Mexico & Central America, 1998-99. Senor Cordova. (Illus.). 225p. (Orig.). 1997. pap. text 18.95 (*0-9639054-3-0*) Centurion CA.

Man's Guide to Mexico, 1995-96. Senor Cordova. Ed. by Joe Torres, 3rd. (Illus.). 192p. 1995. pap. 16.95 (*0-9639054-1-4*) Centurion CA.

Man's Guide to Prayer: New Ideas, Prayers & Meditations from Many Traditions . . . Linus Mundy. LC 98-7754. 192p. 1998. pap. 13.95 (*0-8245-1762-8*, Crsrd) Crossroad NY.

Man's Guide to the Caribbean, 1998-99. Senor Cordova. (Illus.). 225p. (Orig.). 1997. pap. text 18.95 (*0-9639054-4-9*) Centurion CA.

Man's Guide to the Justification of Golf. Bob Peck & Sandy Silver. LC 96-86679. 128p. (Orig.). 1997. pap. 6.95 (*0-8362-2755-7*) Andrews & McMeel.

Man's Guide to Understanding What She Really Means. Susan H. Grant & Michael Levin. LC 96-86636. 96p. (Orig.). 1997. pap. 4.95 (*0-8362-2709-3*) Andrews & McMeel.

Man's Health Book. Mike Oppenheim. LC 94-4872. 370p. (C). 1994. pap. text 16.95 (*0-13-880550-4*) P-H.

Man's Health Sourcebook. 2nd ed. Alfred M. Dashe. LC 99-43149. (Illus.). 288p. 1999. pap. 17.95 (*0-7373-0109-0*, 01090W) NTC Contemp Pub Co.

Man's Health Sourcebook. 2nd ed. Alfred M. Dashe. (Illus.). 288p. 1997. reprint ed. pap. 15.00 (*1-56565-813-2*, Anodyne) Lowell Hse.

Man's Higher Consciousness. rev. ed. Hilton Hotema. 300p. (Orig.). 1997. reprint ed. pap. 23.00 (*0-7873-0440-9*) Hlth Research.

Man's Highest Purpose: The Lost Word Regained. Karel Weinfurter. 254p. 1992. reprint ed. pap. 17.95 (*0-922802-11-4*) Kessinger Pub.

***Man's Illegal Life.** K. Heller. 1998. mass mkt. 9.95 (*0-7472-5685-3*, Pub. by Headline Bk Pub) Trafalgar.

Man's Image & Identity. Jack W. Hayford. (Power-to-Become Book-Pak Ser.: Bk. 4). 96p. 1993. pap. text 3.95 (*0-916847-13-6*) Living Way.

Man's Image & Identity. Jack W. Hayford. LC 96-103815. (Power to Become Ser.: No. 04). 1995. pap. 4.99 (*0-7852-7794-3*) Nelson.

Man's Image in Medicine & Anthropology. Ed. by Iago Galdston. LC 63-19871. (Institute of Social & Historical Medicine Monographs: No. 4). 525p. 1963. 67.50 (*0-8236-3120-6*) Intl Univs Pr.

Man's Impact on Forests & Rivers see Change in the Amazon Basin

Man's Impact on the Global Environment: Assessment & Recommendations for Action. Ed. by William H. Matthews, III. (Study of Critical Environmental Problems Ser.). 1970. pap. text 10.95 (*0-262-69027-6*) MIT Pr.

Man's Impact on Vegetation. W. Holzner et al. (Geobotany Ser.). 1983. text 318.00 (*90-6193-685-3*) Kluwer Academic.

Man's Impossibilities-God's Possibilities see Imposibilidades del Hombre-Posibilidades para Dios

Man's Impossibility, God's Possibility. Kenneth E. Hagin, Jr. 1978. pap. 4.95 (*0-89276-700-6*) Faith Lib Pubns.

Man's Integrity. Jack W. Hayford. (Power-to-Become Book-Pak Ser.: Bk. 5). 96p. 1993. pap. text 3.95 (*0-916847-14-4*) Living Way.

Man's Integrity. Jack W. Hayford. (Power to Become Ser.: No. 05). 1995. pap. 4.99 (*0-7852-7795-1*) Nelson.

***Man's Journey to Simple Abundance.** Sarah Ban Breathnach et al. 2000. 22.00 (*0-7432-0061-6*) Scribner.

Man's Judgement Call - The Irrevocable Master Contract. Kenna. write for info. (*0-318-59097-2*) Port Love Intl.

Man's Kitchen: North Georgia's Favorite Recipes. Bruce Mitchell. (Illus.). 392p. (Orig.). 1987. pap. 9.95 (*0-9619975-0-8*) Cooking Angles.

Man's Knife among the Eskimo: A Study in the Collections of the U. S. National Museum. fac. ed. Otis T. Mason. (Shorey Indian Ser.). (Illus.). 20p. 1999. reprint ed. pap. 10.00 (*0-8466-4051-1*, I-51) Shoreys Bkstore.

Man's Knife among the North American Indians: A Study in the Collections of the U. S. National Museum, 1897. Otis T. Mason. 16.95 (*0-8488-0035-4*, J M C & Co) Amereon Ltd.

Man's Life. James Martin. LC 94-27683. 150p. 1995. pap. 5.95 (*0-9642188-9-5*) Four Seasns.

Man's Life: An Autobiography. Roger Wilkins. LC 90-25715. (Illus.). 392p. 1991. reprint ed. pap. 18.95 (*0-918024-83-8*) Ox Bow.

Man's Life: The Complete Instructions. Denis Boyles. LC 96-15766. 480p. 1996. pap. 20.00 (*0-06-095141-9*, Perennial) HarperTrade.

Man's Life on Earth & in the Spiritual Worlds. Rudolf Steiner. 86p. (Orig.). 1960. reprint ed. spiral bd. 9.00 (*0-7873-0822-6*) Hlth Research.

Man's Loving Family. Keith Heller. 224p. mass mkt. 11.95 (*0-7472-5686-1*, Pub. by Headline Bk Pub) Trafalgar.

Man's Made Hell. Bennie Beard. 104p. 1999. pap. 11.00 (*0-8059-4700-0*) Dorrance.

Man's Mathematical Mind: From Thales to Weiner. John Kreitner. 26p. (gr. 7-12). 1976. reprint ed. pap. 1.50 (*0-913098-14-0*) Orion Society.

Man's Measure: A Study of the Greek Image of Man from Homer to Sophocles. Laszlo Versenyi. LC 73-17420. 274p. (C). 1974. text 29.50 (*0-87395-254-5*) State U NY Pr.

Man's Most Dangerous Myth: The Fallacy of Race. 6th ed. Ashley Montagu. LC 97-21132. 704p. 1997. 45.00 (*0-8039-4647-3*) AltaMira Pr.

Man's Most Dangerous Myth: The Fallacy of Race. 6th abr. ed. Ashley Montagu. LC 97-21132. 304p. 1997. pap., student ed. 19.95 (*0-8039-4648-1*) AltaMira Pr.

***Man's New Cycle.** Melford Okilo. 45p. 1999. pap. 5.00 (*1-879605-65-1*) U Sci & Philos.

Man's Onotological Predicament: A Detailed Analysis of Soren Kierkegaard's Concept of Sin with Special Reference to the Concept of Dread. Edward Harris. (Studia Doctrinae Christianae Upsaliensia: No. 24). 138p. (Orig.). 1984. pap. 31.00 (*91-554-1532-6*, Pub. by Uppsala Univ Acta Univ Uppsaliensis) Coronet Bks.

Man's Origin, Man's Destiny. A. E. Wilder-Smith. 284p. 1993. pap. 7.99 (*0-936728-44-2*) Word for Today.

Man's Pilgrimage Towards the "New Earth" Jose Barriuso & Raffaele Angelisanti. 42p. 1979. 2.00 (*0-9607590-4-2*) Action Life Pubns.

Man's Place. Annie Ernaux. Tr. by Tanya Leslie. LC 91-43106. 99p. 1992. 15.95 (*1-888363-19-3*) Seven Stories.

Man's Place: Masculinity & the Middle-Class Home in Victorian England. John Tosh. LC 98-31422. (Illus.). 288p. 1999. 30.00 (*0-300-07779-3*) Yale U Pr.

Man's Place in Evolution. 2nd ed. British Museum, Geological Department Staff. (Illus.). 103p. (YA). (gr. 7 up). 1991. pap. 14.95 (*0-521-40864-4*) Cambridge U Pr.

Man's Place in Nature. Huxley. (Illus.). (C). pap. text. write for info. (*0-472-08514-X*) U of Mich Pr.

Man's Place in the Natural Order: A Study of Ernest Hemingway's Major Works. Sarah P. Unfried. 99 p. 1976. lib. bdg. 250.00 (*0-87968-458-5*) Gordon Pr.

Man's Plague? Insects & Agriculture. Vincent G. Dethier. LC 75-15216. 245p. 1976. reprint ed. pap. 76.00 (*0-608-01041-3*, 205254700001) Bks Demand.

Man's Problem - God's Solution, Lessons from Genesis 1 to 3: Discover Course. Wilberta L. Chinn. (Illus.). 24p. 1998. pap., student ed. 1.95 (*0-937673-21-8*) Peacock Ent LA.

Man's Problem - God's Solution, Lessons from Genesis 1 to 3: Discovery Course. Wilberta L. Chinn. (Discovery Course Ser.: Vol. 1). (Illus.). 24p. 1998. pap., teacher ed. 1.95 (*0-937673-18-8*) Peacock Ent LA.

Man's Proper Study. Richard J. Moore-Colyer. 182p. (C). 1982. 30.00 (*0-85088-944-8*, Pub. by Gomer Pr) St Mut.

Man's Psychic Life: Elements & Structures. Omraam M. Aivanhov. (Izvor Collection: Vol. 222). (Illus.). 205p. 1987. pap. 7.95 (*2-85566-389-X*, Pub. by Prosveta) Prosveta USA.

Man's Quest for God: Studies in Prayer & Symbolism. Abraham Joshua Heschel. LC 54-10371. (Hudson River Editions Ser.). 176p. 1981. 30.00 (*0-684-16829-4*, Scribners Ref) Mac Lib Ref.

Man's Quest for God: Studies in Prayer & Symbolism. Abraham Joshua Heschel. 192p. 1998. reprint ed. pap. 16.95 (*0-943358-48-5*) Aurora Press.

Man's Quest for Security. Ed. by Edwin J. Faulkner. LC 74-117790. (Essay Index Reprint Ser.). 1977. 20.95 (*0-8369-1921-1*) Ayer.

Man's Questions - God's Answers. Sotirios J. Noussias. LC 96-85003. 240p. (Orig.). 1997. pr. 12.95 (*0-9652284-0-1*) Flower Pub.

Man's Rage for Chaos: Biology, Behavior & the Arts. Morse Peckham. 360p. 1997. pap. 19.95 (*0-944624-36-7*) Maisonneuve Pr.

***Man's Reach.** Elmer L. Andersen. LC 00-8891. 2000. pap. write for info. (*0-8166-3739-3*) U of Minn Pr.

Man's Reach. Glenn Clark. 1977. reprint ed. pap. 11.00 (*0-910924-82-1*) Macalester.

Man's Reach: American Autobiography. Glenn Clark. 314p. 1995. lib. bdg. 89.00 (*0-7812-8480-5*) Rprt Serv.

Man's Relation to the Universe. Alred C. Lovell. LC 84-1443. 266p. reprint ed. pap. 82.50 (*0-608-08666-5*, 206918900003) Bks Demand.

Man's Relationship with God: The Theory of Indwelling in Human Behavior. David Wagstaff. LC 96-48800. (Toronto Studies in Theology: Vol. 72). 356p. 1997. text 99.95 (*0-7734-8964-9*) E Mellen.

M

M

Man's Role in Changing the Face of the Earth, 2 vols. in 1. Ed. by William L. Thomas, Jr. LC 56-5865. (Illus.). 1213p. 1956. lib. bdg. 54.00 (*0-226-79603-5*) U Ch Pr.

Man's Role in Changing the Face of the Earth, 2 vols., Vol. 1. Ed. by William L. Thomas, Jr. LC 56-5865. (Illus.). 476p. 1996. reprint ed. pap. text 15.00 (*0-226-79604-3*, P390) U Ch Pr.

Man's Role in Changing the Face of the Earth, 2 vols., Vol. 2. Ed. by William L. Thomas, Jr. LC 56-5865. (Illus.). 1996. reprint ed. pap. text 20.00 (*0-226-79605-1*, P391) U Ch Pr.

Man's Role in the Shaping of the Eastern Mediterranean Landscape: Proceedings of the Symposium on the Impact of Ancient Man on the Landscape of the Eastern Mediterranean Region & the Near East, Groningen, 6-9 March 1989. Ed. by S. Bottema et al. (Illus.). 352p. (C). 1990. text 123.00 (*90-6191-138-9*, Pub. by A A Balkema) Ashgate Pub Co.

Man's Ruin: Poster Art of Frank Kozik. Frank Kozik. 96p. 1995. pap. 24.95 (*0-86719-397-2*) Last Gasp.

***Man's Search for Meaning.** Viktor E. Frankl. 2000. 20.00 (*0-8070-1426-5*) Beacon Pr.

Man's Search for Meaning. Viktor E. Frankl. 226p. 1993. reprint ed. lib. bdg. 31.95 (*1-56849-011-9*) Buccaneer Bks.

Man's Search for Meaning. rev. ed. Viktor E. Frankl. 221p. 1988. mass mkt. 5.99 (*0-671-66736-X*) PB.

Man's Search for Meaning: An Introduction to Logotherapy. Viktor E. Frankl. 1997. per. 5.99 (*0-671-02337-3*, Pocket Books) PB.

Man's Search for Meaning: An Introduction to Logotherapy. 3rd ed. Viktor E. Frankl. 192p. 1984. pap. 11.00 (*0-671-24422-1*) S&S Trade Pap.

Man's Search for Meaning: An Introduction to Logotherapy. 4th ed. Viktor E. Frankl. 192p. 1992. 20.00 (*0-8070-2918-1*) Beacon Pr.

Man's Search for the Good Life. Scott Nearing. 143p. 1974. pap. 9.95 (*0-911394-12-5*) Good Life Ctr.

Man's Search for Ultimate Meaning. Viktor E. Frankl. LC 97-23940. (Illus.). 194p. (C). 1997. 24.95 (*0-306-45620-6*, Plen Insight) Perseus Pubng.

***Man's Search for Ultimate Meaning.** Viktor E. Frankl. 208p. 2000. reprint ed. pap. text 13.00 (*0-7382-0354-8*, Pub. by Perseus Pubng) HarpC.

***Man's Secret Power.** Melford Okilo. 19p. 1999. pap. 5.00 (*1-879605-64-3*) U Sci & Philos.

Man's Self-Interpretation-in-Existence. Anna-Teresa Tymieniecka. 504p. (C). 1990. lib. bdg. 248.50 (*0-7923-0324-5*, Pub. by Kluwer Academic) Kluwer Academic.

Man's Soul: An Introductory Essay in Philosophical Psychology. S. L. Frank. Tr. by Boris Jakim. 312p. (C). 1993. text 39.95 (*0-8214-1061-X*) Ohio U Pr.

Man's Starting Place. Jack W. Hayford. (Power-to-Become Book-Pak Ser.: Bk. 1). 96p. 1992. pap. text 3.95 (*0-916847-10-1*) Living Way.

Man's Starting Place. Jack W. Hayford. LC 96-103799. (Power to Become Ser.: No. 01). 1995. pap. 4.99 (*0-7852-7792-7*) Nelson.

***Man's Storm: A Novel of Crime Set in London, 1703.** Keith Heller. 1998. pap. (*0-7472-5684-5*) Headline Bk Pub.

Man's Subtle Bodies & Centers: The Aura, the Solar Plexus, the Chakras. 4th ed. Omraam M. Aivanhov. (Izvor Collection: Vol. 219). (Illus.). 154p. 1986. pap. 7.95 (*2-85566-383-0*, Pub. by Prosveta) Prosveta USA.

Man's Supersensory Powers. Hodson. 1999. 7.95 (*0-8356-7162-3*, Quest) Theos Pub Hse.

***Man's Threefold Nature: His Body, Soul & Spirit, Vol. 1.** B. R. Hicks. Orig. Title: The Threefold Nature of Man. (Illus.). 398p. 2000. 19.95 (*1-58363-136-4*) Christ Gospel.

Man's Touch. Charles Stanley. LC 92-13029. 112p. 1992. 8.99 (*0-89693-062-9*, 6-1062, Victor Bks) Chariot Victor.

Man's Touch. Rosalyn West. 352p. (Orig.). 1996. mass mkt. 5.50 (*0-380-78511-0*, Avon Bks) Morrow Avon.

Man's Town: Inequality Between Women & Men in Rural Australia. Ken Dempsey. 336p. (C). 1993. pap. text 29.95 (*0-19-554997-X*) OUP.

Man's Turf: The Perfect Lawn. Warren Schultz. LC 98-19139. (Illus.). 180p. 1999. 35.00 (*0-609-60068-0*) C Potter.

***Man's Turf: The Perfect Lawn.** Warren Schultz. (Illus.). 2000. pap. 24.95 (*0-609-80569-X*, Crown) Crown Pub Group.

Man's Twin. Kaukab Siddique. 150p. (C). 1995. pap. 5.00 (*0-942978-16-1*) Am Soc Ed & Rel.

Man's Two Natures, Human & Divine. 3rd rev. ed. Omraam M. Aivanhov. (Izvor Collection: Vol. 213). (Illus.). 152p. 1984. pap. 7.95 (*2-85566-326-1*, Pub. by Prosveta) Prosveta USA.

Man's Ultimate Commitment. Henry N. Wieman. 330p. (C). 1990. pap. 26.50 (*0-8191-7947-7*); lib. bdg. 51.50 (*0-8191-7946-9*) Foun Phil Creat.

Man's Unconquerable Mind. Gilbert Highet. LC 54-6133. 138p. 1954. text 46.00 (*0-231-02016-3*) Col U Pr.

Man's Unconquerable Mind. Gilbert Highet. LC 54-6133. 138p. 1960. pap. text 16.50 (*0-231-08501-X*) Col U Pr.

Man's Unconquerable Mind. Raymond W. Chambers. LC 67-30811. (Studies in Poetry: No. 38). (Illus.). 1969. reprint ed. lib. bdg. 75.00 (*0-8383-0711-6*) M S G Haskell Hse.

Man's Unconscious Passion (1920) Wilfrid Lay. 254p. 1999. reprint ed. pap. 19.95 (*0-7661-0774-4*) Kessinger Pub.

Man's Unconscious Spirit: The Psychoanalysis of Spiritism (1921) Wilfrid Lay. 338p. 1998. reprint ed. pap. 27.95 (*0-7661-0559-8*) Kessinger Pub.

Man's Universes. Denys Wilkinson. 213p. 1991. text 55.00 (*0-231-07184-1*) Col U Pr.

Man's Value to Society: Studies in Self-Culture & Character (1896) Newell D. Hillis. 330p. 1998. reprint ed. pap. 24.95 (*0-7661-0519-9*) Kessinger Pub.

Man's Venture in Culture. Thorne Deuel. (Story of Illinois Ser.: No. 6). (Illus.). 40p. (J). (ps-12). 1955. pap. 1.00 (*0-89792-008-2*) Ill St Museum.

Man's Victorious Spirit: How to Release the Victory Within You. Jack H. Holland. LC 76-179668. 127p. 1971. pap. 5.00 (*0-87852-001-5*) Inst Human Growth.

Man's View of Life & Love. Michael Lane. Ed. by Betty Allums. 57p. (Orig.). 1988. pap. 8.00 (*0-932211-02-X*) BA Cross Ctrl.

Man's Viewpoint: Viewing Gender Issues Through Men's Eyes. Rob Mazzeo. LC 97-91253. (Illus.). 276p. 1998. pap. 17.95 (*0-9660666-0-X*) Viewpt Publ.

Man's Walk with God. Jack W. Hayford. (Power-to-Become Book-Pak Ser.: Bk. 3). 96p. 1993. pap. text 3.95 (*0-916847-12-8*) Living Way.

Man's Walk with God. Jack W. Hayford. LC 96-103806. (Power to Become Ser.: No. 03). 1995. pap. 4.99 (*0-7852-7793-5*) Nelson.

Man's Woman. Frank Norris. LC 71-108125. 1970. reprint ed. 35.00 (*0-404-04789-0*) AMS Pr.

Man's Woman. Frank Norris. (BCL1-PS American Literature Ser.). 286p. 1992. reprint ed. lib. bdg. 79.00 (*0-7812-6810-9*) Rprt Serv.

Man's Work. Frank Endersby. 12p. (J). (gr. 4 up). 1981. 2.99 (*0-85953-270-4*) Childs Play.

***Man's Work.** Annie Kubler. LC 99-57967. 1999. 2.99 (*0-85953-587-8*) Childs Play.

Man's Work. Teresa O'Brien. (GRE.). (J). 1981. 3.99 (*0-85953-868-0*); 3.99 (*0-85953-631-9*) Childs Play.

Man's Worldly Goods. Leo Huberman. 352p. (YA). (gr. 9-12). 1968. pap. 15.00 (*0-85345-070-6*, Pub. by Monthly Rev) NYU Pr.

Man's Worship & Witness. Jack W. Hayford. (Power-to-Become Book-Pak Ser.: Bk. 6). 96p. 1993. pap. text 3.95 (*0-916847-15-2*) Living Way.

Man's Worship & Witness. Jack W. Hayford. LC 96-103804. (Power to Become Ser.: No. 06). 1995. pap. 4.99 (*0-7852-7797-8*) Nelson.

Mansa Musa: The Goldne King of Ancience Mali. Akbarall Thobhani. LC 99-178971. 190p. (C). 1998. per. 28.95 (*0-7872-4559-3*, 41455901) Kendall-Hunt.

Mansa Musa: The Lion of Mali. Khephra Burns. LC 97-50559. (Illus.). (J). 2000. 20.01 (*0-15-200375-4*) Harcourt.

Mansara on Architecture & Sculpture: Sanskrit Text with Critical Notes. Prasana K. Acharya. 1979. reprint ed. 64.00 (*0-8364-2609-6*, Pub. by M Manoharial) S Asia.

Manscapes: An American Journey. Colin Henfrey. LC 73-163601. 285 p. 1973. write for info. (*0-233-96054-6*) Andre Deutsch.

Manse. Lisa W. Cantrell. 352p. 1987. pap. 3.95 (*0-8125-1673-7*) Tor Bks.

Manse: One Man's War. Wilton Earle. LC 96-83128. (Illus.). 416p. 1996. 24.00 (*0-9632422-2-9*) Adept.

Mansex. Max Exander. (Orig.). 1994. mass mkt. 4.95 (*1-56333-160-8*, Badboy) Masquerade.

Mansex Fine: Religion, Manliness & Imperialism in Nineteenth-Century Britain. Alderson. 25p. 1998. text 79.95 (*0-7190-5275-0*, Pub. by Manchester Univ Pr) St Martin.

Mansfield. Andrew J. Todesco & Kevin B. McNatt. LC 98-88252. (Images of America Ser.). 1998. write for info. (*0-7385-0010-0*) Arcadia Publng.

Mansfield & Vietnam: A Study in Rhetorical Adaptation. Gregory A. Olson. 1995. 39.95 (*0-87013-386-1*) Mich St U Pr.

Mansfield College, Oxford: It's Origin, History, & Significance. Elaine Kaye. (Illus.). 357p. (C). 1996. text 70.00 (*0-19-920180-3*) OUP.

Mansfield Letters: A Sequel to Mansfield Park. Paula Atchia. 170p. 1996. 36.50 (*1-85776-118-9*, Pub. by Book Guild Ltd) Trans-Atl Phila.

Mansfield Manuscripts & the Growth of English Law in the Eighteenth Century, 2 vols., Set. James Oldham. LC 91-46199. (Studies in Legal History). (C). 1992. 250.00 (*0-8078-2052-0*) U of NC Pr.

Mansfield Park. Jane Austen. 227p. Date not set. 21.95 (*0-8488-2533-0*) Amereon Ltd.

Mansfield Park. Jane Austen. 400p. 1983. mass mkt. 4.95 (*0-553-21276-1*, Bantam Classics) Bantam.

Mansfield Park. Jane Austen. 1987. lib. bdg. 20.95 (*0-89966-244-7*) Buccaneer Bks.

***Mansfield Park.** Jane Austen. 419p. 1999. pap. 10.95 (*0-7868-8524-6*, Pub. by Disney Pr) Time Warner.

Mansfield Park. Jane Austen. LC 97-24777. 496p. 1997. 18.50 (*0-385-48726-6*) Doubleday.

Mansfield Park. Jane Austen. 1992. 20.00 (*0-679-41269-7*) Everymns Lib.

Mansfield Park. Jane Austen. (Cloth Bound Pocket Ser.). 240p. 1998. 7.95 (*3-89508-459-X*) Konemann.

Mansfield Park. Jane Austen. 1995. 15.50 (*0-679-60194-5*) Modern Lib NY.

Mansfield Park. Jane Austen. 1996. mass mkt. 4.95 (*0-451-52629-5*, Sig Classics) NAL.

Mansfield Park. Jane Austen. Ed. by Claudia L. Johnson. LC 96-49462. (Critical Editions Ser.). (C). 1998. pap. text 11.25 (*0-393-96791-3*, Norton Paperbks) Norton.

Mansfield Park. Jane Austen. Ed. by James Kinsley. (Oxford World's Classics Ser.). 474p. 1998. pap. 5.95 (*0-19-283363-4*) OUP.

Mansfield Park. Jane Austen. (Signet Classics). 1996. 10.05 (*0-606-03852-3*, Pub. by Turtleback) Demco.

Mansfield Park. Jane Austen. Ed. by Pamela Norris. 512p. 1993. pap. 3.95 (*0-460-87294-X*, Everyman's Classic Lib) Tuttle Pubng.

Mansfield Park. Jane Austen. Ed. by Kathryn Sutherland. LC 95-72351. 464p. 1996. pap. 6.95 (*0-14-043414-3*, Viking) Viking Penguin.

Mansfield Park. Jane Austen. (Classics Library). 345p. 1998. pap. 3.95 (*1-85326-032-0*, 0320WW, Pub. by Wrdsworth Edits) NTC Contemp Pub Co.

Mansfield Park. Mary Evans et al. Ed. by Nigel Wood. LC 92-32423. (Theory in Practice Ser.). 208p. 1993. pap. 29.95 (*0-335-09628-X*) OpUniv Pr.

Mansfield Park. large type ed. Jane Austen. 547p. 1988. 27.99 (*0-7089-8504-1*, Charnwood) Ulverscroft.

Mansfield Park see Oxford Illustrated Jane Austen

***Mansfield Park: A Screenplay.** Patricia Rozema. LC 00-37026. 2000. 10.95 (*0-7868-8603-X*, Pub. by Hyperion) Time Warner.

Manship School Guide to Political Communication. Ed. by David D. Perlmutter. LC 99-23661. (Illus.). 400p. 1999. text 49.95 (*0-8071-2480-X*); pap. text 24.95 (*0-8071-2481-8*) La State U Pr.

Mansion. William Faulkner. 448p. 1965. pap. 12.00 (*0-394-70282-4*) Random.

Mansion & Its Murder. Bernard Bastable. LC 98-16788. 192p. 1998. 22.00 (*0-7867-0515-9*) Carroll & Graf.

Mansion in the Mist. John Bellairs. 176p. (YA). (gr. 5 up). 1993. pap. 4.99 (*0-14-034933-2*, PuffinBks) Peng Put Young Read.

Mansion in the Mist. John Bellairs. (J). 1993. 9.09 (*0-606-05450-2*, Pub. by Turtleback) Demco.

Mansion in the Mountains: The Story of Moses & Bertha Cone & Their Blowing Rock Mansion. Philip T. Noblitt. LC 96-6277. (Illus.). 225p. 1996. pap. 14.95 (*1-887905-02-2*) Pkway Pubs.

Mansion Is Built for You in Paradise. Theodore Fitch. 63p. 1986. reprint ed. spiral bd. 10.50 (*0-7873-1238-X*) Hlth Research.

Mansion (1959) Typescript Draft. William Faulkner. Ed. by Michael Millgate. LC 86-9853. (William Faulkner Manuscripts). 1088p. 1986. text 135.00 (*0-8240-6832-7*) Garland.

Mansion of Magnanimitie: Wherein Is Shewed the Acts of Sundrie English Kings, No. 722. Richard Crompton. LC 74-28841. 1975. reprint ed. 20.00 (*90-221-0722-1*) Walter J Johnson.

Mansion of Smiling Masks. large type ed. Daoma Winston. LC 94-9230. 277p. 1994. lib. bdg. 20.95 (*0-7862-0216-5*) Thorndike Pr.

Mansion of the Gods. Rene de Goscinny. (Asterix Ser.: No. 11). (Illus.). (J). 1976. pap. text 9.95 (*0-340-19269-0*) Intl Lang.

Mansion on the Hill: Dylan, Young, Geffen, Springstein & the Head-On Collision of Rock & Commerce. Fred Goodman. 1998. pap. 14.00 (*0-679-74377-4*) Vin Bks.

Mansion on Turtle Creek Cookbook. Dean Fearing. LC 87-21535. (Illus.). 320p. 1987. 32.50 (*0-8021-1397-4*, Grove) Grove-Atltic.

Mansions & the Shanties (Sobrados E Mucambos) The Making of Modern Brazil. Gilberto Freyre. Tr. by Harriet De Onis from POR. LC 80-10887. (Illus.). 431p. 1980. reprint ed. lib. bdg. 89.50 (*0-313-22148-0*, FRMA, Greenwood Pr) Greenwood.

Mansions in the Clouds: The Skyscraper Palazzi of Emery Roth. Steven R. Ruttenbaum. (Illus.). 224p. 1986. 48.00 (*0-917439-09-0*) Balsam Pr.

Mansions of Darkness. Chelsea Quinn Yarbro. 432p. 1997. pap. 15.95 (*0-312-86382-9*) St Martin.

Mansions of Darkness. Chelsea Quinn Yarbro. 432p. 1996. 24.95 (*0-312-85759-4*) Tor Bks.

Mansions of Limbo. Dominick Dunne. 1999. 14.95 (*0-449-00437-6*) Fawcett.

Mansions of Limbo. large type ed. Dominick Dunne. (General Ser.). 440p. 1992. pap. 16.95 (*0-8161-5371-X*, G K Hall Lrg Type) Mac Lib Ref.

Mansions of Long Island's Gold Coast. Monica Randall. LC 86-31558. (Illus.). 256p. 1988. reprint ed. pap. 35.00 (*0-8478-0821-1*, Pub. by Rizzoli Intl) St Martin.

***Mansions of Morris County.** John W. Rae. (Images of America Ser.). 1999. pap. 18.99 (*0-7385-0064-X*) Arcadia Publng.

Mansions of Paris. Oliver Blanc. (Illus.). 208p. 1998. pap. text 27.50 (*2-87939-180-6*, Pub. by Pierre Terrail) Rizzoli Intl.

Mansions of the Gods. Rene de Goscinny & M. Uderzo. (Illus.). (J). 1990. 24.95 (*0-8288-4979-X*) Fr & Eur.

Mansions of the Gods. Rene Goscinny. (Adventures of Asterix Ser.). (Illus.). 44p. (J). 1995. reprint ed. pap. 9.95 (*0-917201-60-4*, Pub. by Dargaud) Distribks Inc.

Mansions of the Soul. Lewis H. Spencer. LC 30-34218. 229p. 1930. pap. 14.95 (*0-912057-43-2*, 501960) GLELJ AMORC.

***Manslaughter, Markets & Moral Economy: Violent Disputes over Property Rights in 18th-Century China.** Thomas M. Buoye. (Cambridge Studies in Chinese History, Literature & Institutions). (Illus.). 288p. (C). 2000. 59.95 (*0-521-64045-8*) Cambridge U Pr.

***Manson: The Unholy Trail of Charlie & The Family.** Ron Kenner. 1999. pap. text 15.95 (*1-878923-13-7*) Amok Bks.

Manson Behind the Scenes. Bill Nelson. LC 97-65212. 400p. (Orig.). 1997. pap. 19.95 (*0-9629084-1-X*) Pen Power.

Manson Family Picnic. large type rev. ed. R. Downey & Garth Powell. (Illus.). 44p. 1998. pap. 6.50 (*0-9660958-0-4*) Playroom Pr.

Manson Impact Structure, Iowa: Anatomy of an Impact Crater. Ed. by Christian Koeberl & Raymond R. Anderson. (Special Papers: No. 302). (Illus.). 476p. 1996. pap. 99.50 (*0-8137-2302-7*) Geol Soc.

Manson in His Own Words. Nuel Emmons. LC 86-45257. (Illus.). 256p. 1988. pap. 11.95 (*0-8021-3024-0*, Grove) Grove-Atltic.

Manson Murders: A Philosophical Inquiry. Ed. by David Cooper & Peter French. LC 73-78119. 141p. 1974. pap. text 15.95 (*0-87073-533-0*) Schenkman Bks Inc.

Manson's Tropical Disease. 20th ed. Cook. 1995. text 125.00 (*0-7020-1764-7*, W B Saunders Co) Harcrt Hlth Sci Grp.

Mansoul or the Riddle of the World. Charles M. Doughty. 1971. reprint ed. 29.00 (*0-403-00574-4*) Scholarly.

Manspeak: What He Says - What He Really Means. Marnie Winston-Macauley. LC 96-84527. 128p. (Orig.). 1996. pap. 5.95 (*0-8362-2225-3*) Andrews & McMeel.

Manspell-Godspell. Sam Bradley. 80p. 1975. pap. 13.95 (*0-900977-93-0*, Pub. by Anvil Press) Dufour.

Manston's Flea Markets, Antique Fairs & Auctions of France. Peter B. Manston. LC 86-30909. (Manston's Travel Key Guide Ser.). (Illus.). 196p. 1987. 9.95 (*0-931367-06-9*) Travel Keys.

Manston's Flea Markets, Antique Fairs & Auctions of Germany. Peter B. Manston. LC 86-30908. (Illus.). 224p. 1987. pap. 9.95 (*0-931367-08-5*) Travel Keys.

Manston's Italy. Peter B. Manston. (Illus.). 352p. 1990. pap. 10.95 (*0-931367-12-3*) Travel Keys.

Manston's Travel Key Britain. Peter B. Manston. LC 89-4488. (Illus.). 384p. (Orig.). 1996. pap. 9.95 (*0-931367-11-5*) Travel Keys.

Mansul. Chen Li. (Asian Folk Tales Ser.). (Illus.). 24p. (J). 1995. 9.95 (*983-9808-68-0*, Pub. by Delta Edits) Weatherhill.

Mansurs Find a Home. Saima Shofi. 30p. (J). 1996. pap. write for info. (*0-9642101-5-0*) Al-Huda Prnting.

Mantalk. Jerry Douglas. (Illus.). 222p. (Orig.). 1991. pap. 12.95 (*0-943383-02-1*) FirstHand Ltd.

***MANTECH Project Book (1995)** Ed. by Barry Leonard. (Illus.). 120p. (C). 1999. reprint ed. pap. text 50.00 (*0-7881-2667-9*) DIANE Pub.

MANTECH Project Book, 1992. (Illus.). 229p. (Orig.). (C). 1993. pap. text 50.00 (*1-56806-605-8*) DIANE Pub.

Mantegna. Nike Batzner. (Masters of Italian Art Ser.). (Illus.). 140p. 1998. 19.95 (*3-8290-0252-1*, 520532) Konemann.

Mantegna. Ettore Camesasca. (Grandes Maestros del Arte Ser.). (SPA., Illus.). 80p. (Orig.). 1992. pap. 12.99 (*1-878351-25-7*) Riverside NY.

Mantegna. Ettore Camesasca. Tr. by Susan M. Lister from ITA. LC 98-158629. (Library of Great Masters). (Illus.). 80p. (Orig.). 1992. pap. 12.99 (*1-878351-16-8*) Riverside NY.

Mantegna & Painting As Historical Narrative. Jack M. Greenstein. (Illus.). 316p. 1992. 38.50 (*0-226-30707-7*) U Ch Pr.

Mantegna to Rubens: The Weld-Blundell Drawings Collection. Xanthe Brooke. LC 98-205350. (Illus.). 208p. 1998. 65.00 (*1-85894-052-4*, Pub. by Merrell Holberton) U of Wash Pr.

Mantegna to Rubens: The Weld-Blundell Drawings Collection. Xanthe Brooke et al. LC 98-205350. 208p. 1998. pap. write for info. (*1-85894-053-2*) Merrell Holberton.

Mantel-Piece Minstrels, & Other Stories. John K. Bangs. LC 78-85689. (Short Story Index Reprint Ser.). 1977. 16.95 (*0-8369-3030-4*) Ayer.

Mantel's Folks Redner: Mantel's Sermons & Address in Yiddish Language for All Jewish Holidays & Many Other Occasions. Herman Mantel & Hugo Mantel. (ENG & YID.). 320p. 27.50 (*0-87559-148-5*) Shalom.

***Manteniendo Pentecostes Pentecostal: Hacia un Avivamiento Permanente.** Nino Gonzalez. 1998. 5.99 (*0-8297-2200-9*) Vida Pubs.

***Manteniendo un Balance: Impactos Economicos, Ambientales y Sociales del Cultivo de Camaron en Latinoamerica.** James A. Tobey et al. (Coastal Management Report Ser.: Vol. 2202). (SPA., Illus.). 62p. 1998. pap. write for info. (*1-885454-22-8*) Coastal Res.

Mantenimiento de Calidad: Caro Defectos a Traves de la Gestion del Equipo. Seiji Tsuchiya. (ENG & SPA.). 202p. 1995. pap. 55.00 (*84-87022-16-2*) Productivity Inc.

Mantenimiento Delacuario: Healthy Aquarium. Neville Carrington. (SPA.). 1995. 11.95 (*1-56465-180-0*) Tetra Pr.

***Manteo: A Roanoke Island Town.** Angel Ellis Khoury. LC 00-25747. (Illus.). 2000. write for info. (*1-57864-099-7*) Donning Co.

Manter & Gatz's Essentials of Clinical Neuroanatomy & Neurophysiology. 9th ed. Sid Gilman & Sarah W. Newman. LC 95-49487. (Illus.). 309p. (C). 1996. pap. text 28.95 (*0-8036-0144-1*) Davis Co.

Manticore. Robertson Davies. 312p. 1977. pap. 12.95 (*0-14-016793-5*, Penguin Bks) Viking Penguin.

Mantik in Ugarit: Keilalphabetische Texte der Opferschau - Omensammlungen Nekromantie. Manfried Dietrich & Oswald Loretz. (Abhandlungen Zur Literatur Alt-Syrien-Palastinas Ser.: Vol. 3). x, 307p. 1990. text 71.00 (*3-927120-05-7*, Pub. by UGARIT) Eisenbrauns.

Mantinades: Selected Love Distichs of Crete. Tr. by Stylianos V. Spyridakis. (Hellenism: Ancient, Mediaeval, Modern Ser.: Vol. 23). 1996. text 25.00 (*0-89241-577-0*) Caratzas.

Mantique Apollinienne a Delphes: Essai sur le Fonctionnement de L'Oracle. Pierre Amandry. LC 75-10627. (Ancient Religion & Mythology Ser.). (FRE., Illus.). 1976. reprint ed. 25.95 (*0-405-07003-9*) Ayer.

Mantis. Richard La Plante. 352p. 1995. 5.99 (*0-8125-3019-5*) Tor Bks.

Mantis Carol. Laurens Van Der Post. 166p. (C). 1983. reprint ed. pap. 16.95 (*0-933280-21-1*) Island Pr.

Mantissa. John Fowles. LC 82-145758. 192 p. 1982. 6.95 (*0-224-02938-X*) Jonathan Cape.

Mantissa. John Fowles. 208p. 1997. pap. 11.95 (*0-316-29027-0*) Little.

Mantissa Plantarum, 1767-71, 2 Vols. in 1. Carl Linnaeus. 1960. 97.50 (*3-7682-0037-X*) Lubrecht & Cramer.

Mantle & Lower Crust Exposed in Oceanic Ridges & in Ophiolites: Proceedings: Specialized Symposium on Mantle Denudation in Slow Spreading Ridges & in Ophiolites (1993: Strasbourg) Ed. by R. L. Vissers et al. LC 95-17077. (Petrology & Structural Geology Ser.: Vol. 6). 214p. (C). 1995. text 115.00 (0-7923-3491-4) Kluwer Academic.

Mantle & Other Stories. Nikolai Vasilevich Gogol. Tr. by Claude Field from RUS. LC 77-152940. (Short Story Index Reprint Ser.). 1977. reprint ed. 18.95 (0-8369-3799-6) Ayer.

Mantle Convection: Plate Tectonics & Global Dynamics. Ed. by W. Richard Peltier. 882p. 1988. 198.00 (0-677-22102-9) Gordon & Breach.

Mantle Convection: Plate Tectonics & Global Dynamics, Vol. 4. W. Richard Peltier. viii, 882p. 1989. text 383.00 (0-677-22120-7) Gordon & Breach.

Mantle Dynamics & Plate Interactions in East Asia. Martin F. Flower. LC 98-3504. (Geodynamics Ser.: Vol. 27). 419p. 1998. 62.00 (0-87590-529-3) Am Geophysical.

Mantle Flow & Melt Generation at Mid-Ocean Ridges. Ed. by Jason P. Morgan et al. LC 93-812. (Geophysical Monograph Ser.: No. 71). 1993. 46.00 (0-87590-035-6) Am Geophysical.

Mantle Metasomatism & Alkaline Magmatism. Ed. by Ellen M. Morris & Jill D. Pasteris. LC 87-17390. (Geological Society of America Ser.: Vol. 215). (Illus.). 393p. 1987. reprint ed. pap. 121.90 (0-608-07741-0, 206782900010) Bks Demand.

Mantle of Abbadon. G. T. Hesse. LC 99-475825. 1998. 22.95 (0-9666642-0-5) Azel Pub.

Mantle of Elijah: The Redaction Criticism of the Prophetical Books. Terence Collins. (Biblical Seminar Ser.: Vol. 20). 197p. 1993. pap. 23.00 (1-85075-425-X, Pub. by Sheffield Acad) CUP Services.

Mantle of Heroism: Tarawa & the Struggle for the Gilberts, November 1943. Michael B. Graham. (Illus.). 384p. 1998. pap. 17.95 (0-89141-652-8) Presidio Pr.

Mantle of Kendis-Dai: A Starshield Novel. Margaret Weis & Tracy Hickman. 1997. mass mkt. 6.99 (0-345-39761-4, Del Rey) Ballantine Pub Grp.

***Mantle of the Mountain Man.** Rod Bell, Sr. LC 99-28466. 1999. 15.95 (1-57924-272-3) Bob Jones Univ.

***Mantle of the Prophet.** Roy Mottahedeh. 2000. pap. 25.95 (1-85168-234-1, Pub. by Onewrld Pubns) Penguin Putnam.

***Mantle Plumes.** Yu. P. Orovetskii. (Illus.). 250p. 1999. text 95.00 (90-5410-792-8, Pub. by A A Balkema) Ashgate Pub Co.

Mantle Sample: Inclusions in Kimberlites & Other Volcanics: Proceedings of the Second International Kimberline Conference, Vol. 2. Ed. by F. R. Boyd & H. O. Meyer. (Illus.). 424p. 1979. 25.00 (0-87590-213-8) Am Geophysical.

Mantle Xenoliths. fac. ed. Ed. by Peter H. Nixon. LC 86-15705. (Illus.). 895p. 1994. pap. 200.00 (0-7837-7663-2, 204741600007) Bks Demand.

Mantlemann's Imaging Guide. Lee Mantlemann. 34.95 (0-936648-67-8) Telecom Bks.

Mantles of Glory. Bill Panko & Margaret Panko. 250p. (Orig.). Date not set. pap. 19.95 (1-885342-20-9) Creative Ways.

Mantodea (Insecta) with a Review of Aspects of Functional Morphology & Biology see Fauna of New Zealand Series

Mantor Book of American Poetry. Oscar Williams. 1962. mass mkt. 7.99 (0-451-62791-1) NAL.

Mantra. Ed. by Harvey P. Alper. LC 87-6489. (SUNY Series in Religious Studies). 343p. (C). 1988. pap. text 21.95 (0-88706-599-6) State U NY Pr.

Mantra: Hearing the Divine in India. Harold G. Coward & David J. Goa. LC 96-28527. 1996. 15.50 (0-231-10783-8) Col U Pr.

Mantra & Meditation. Pandit Usharbudh Arya & D. Lih. LC 81-84076. 237p. 1981. pap. 14.95 (0-89389-074-X) Himalayan Inst.

***Mantra Is a Prayer to God.** Cecilia Miller. (Illus.). 24p. (J). 2000. reprint ed. 12.95 (0-911307-92-3, 205426, Pub. by SYDA Found) Words Distrib.

Mantra, Kirtana, Yantra & Tantra. Swami Jyotirmayananda. (Illus.). 1974. pap. 5.99 (0-934664-06-4) Yoga Res Foun.

Mantra Voyage: Le Son Comme Moyen de Realisation de Soi. Partrick Bernhardt. (FRE.). 1998. 21.95 (2-89466-020-0) Edns Roseau.

Mantracking: Introduction to the Step-by-Step Method. Roland Robbins. Ed. by Elizabeth Anderson et al. LC 77-77680. (Illus.). 1977. pap. 39.00 (0-9603392-0-5) Search & Rescue.

Mantram Handbook. 5th rev. ed. Elenath Easwaran. 224p. 1998. pap. 12.95 (0-915132-98-2) Nilgiri Pr.

Mantramotion: The Next Step in Mind-Body Fitness. Hal F. Atkinson, III. 13p. 1997. pap. 14.95 incl. audio (0-9667003-0-9) Mantramotion Inc.

Mantrap. large type ed. Alan Evans. (Linford Mystery Library). 272p. 1989. pap. 16.99 (0-7089-6730-2, Linford) Ulverscroft.

Mantrapping. Ragnar Benson. (Illus.). 88p. 1981. pap. 15.00 (0-87364-215-5) Paladin Pr.

Mantras: A Musical Path to Peace. Henry Marshall. LC 98-43115. (Illus.). 144p. 1999. pap. 18.95 incl. audio compact disk (1-885394-34-9) Bluestar Communs.

Mantras: Helpful or Harmful? Ralph Rath. (Get the Facts Ser.: Series I). 30p. (Orig.). 1993. pap. 2.95 (0-9640167-2-9) Peter Pubns.

Mantras: Words of Power. Sivananda Radha. 1998. pap. write for info. (81-207-1677-9) Sterling Pubs.

Mantras: Words of Power. rev. ed. Sivananda Radha. Ed. by Karin Lenman. LC 93-46477. (Illus.). 208p. 1994. pap. 14.95 (0-931454-66-2) Timeless Bks.

Mantras for the Season. Paul Page. 1998. pap. 16.95 (0-937690-44-9, 7194) Wrld Lib Pubns.

Mantras from a Poet: Jessica Powers. Robert F. Morneau. LC 90-64032. 134p. (Orig.). 1991. pap. 8.95 (1-55612-420-1, LL1420) Sheed & Ward WI.

Mantras, Menorahs, & Minarets: Encountering Other Faiths. Gary Wilde. (Generation Why: Vol. 2:7). 44p. (YA). (gr. 9-12). 1997. pap. 12.95 (0-87303-272-1) Faith & Life.

Mantras of the Agnuyupasthana & the Sautramani. J. Gonda. (Verhandelingen der Koninklijke Nederlandse Akademie van Wetenschappen, Afd. Letterkunde, Nieuwe Reeks Ser.: No. 104). 202p. 1980. pap. 53.25 (0-7204-8493-6) Elsevier.

Mantras of the Mother. Mother. 1983. 5.00 (0-89071-319-7, Pub. by SAA) Acrpls Bks CO.

Mantras of the Mother. 2nd ed. Mother. 276p. 1994. 4.95 (81-7058-179-6, Pub. by SAA) E-W Cultural Ctr.

Mantras Sacred Word of Power. John E. Blofeld. 106p. 1977. 11.95 (0-04-294097-4) Asia Bk Corp.

Mantras, Yantras, & Fabulous Gems... Healing Secrets of the Ancient Vedas. deluxe ed. Howard Beckman. (Illus.). 1995. write for info. (0-9525172-5-6) Balaji Pub.

Manu: The Biodiversity of Southeastern Peru. Ed. by Don E. Wilson & Abelardo Sandoval. LC 97-138020. (Illus.). 672p. (Orig.). 1997. pap. text 35.00 (1-56098-710-3) Smithsonian.

***Manu & the Talking Fish.** Illus. by Roberta Arenson. 32p. (J). (ps-3). 2000. 15.95 (1-84148-032-0) Barefoot Bks NY.

Manu Forti: A History of the Herefordshire Regiment 1860-1967. T. J. Hill. (Illus.). 192p. 1996. 30.95 (0-7509-1182-4, Pub. by Sutton Pub Ltd) Intl Pubs Mktg.

Manu Smriti: A Sociological Analysis. Deepali Bhargva. (C). 1989. 21.50 (81-7033-078-5, Pub. by Rawat Pubns) S Asia.

Manual. Hoobler. 160p. (C). 1998. pap. text 20.80 (0-536-00730-6) S&S Trade.

Manual. Mangina. 1994. write for info. (0-8058-1760-3) L Erlbaum Assocs.

***Manual: An Easy Key to Self Publishing.** rev. ed. Mikael Hakansson. 45p. 2000. pap. 6.95 (0-9676112-2-9) Notherway.

Manual: Art in General, 1993 & 1994. Ed. by Catherine Ruello. (Illus.). 96p. (Orig.). 1994. pap. 15.00 (1-883967-02-3) Art in General.

***Manual: Church of the Nazarene, 1997-01.** 352p. 1998. 11.99 (0-8341-1689-8) Nazarene.

Manual: Distance Writing & Computer Assisted Training in Mental Health. Luciano L'Abate & Margaret S. Baggett. 101p. 1997. pap. 19.95 (0-9662839-0-2) Inst Life Empower.

MANUAL AMER ENGL PRONNC PB 4/E. 4th ed. Clifford H. Prator, Jr. & Betty W. Robinett. LC 84-25222. 244p. (C). 1985. pap. text 20.00 (0-03-000703-8, Pub. by Harcourt Coll Pubs) Harcourt.

Manual & Atlas of Fine Needle Aspiration Cytology. 2nd ed. Svente R. Orell et al. (Illus.). 341p. 1992. text 240.00 (0-443-04239-X) Church.

Manual & Correction Key. Mangina. 1994. 19.75 (0-8058-1758-1) L Erlbaum Assocs.

Manual & Digital Gymnastics. Adrian Bezdechi. (Illus.). (Orig.). 1957. pap. 7.95 (0-9604092-1-1) Interstate Piano.

Manual & Industrial Education at Girard College, 1831-1965: An Era in American Educational Experimentation. Louis A. Romano. Ed. by Francesco Cordasco. LC 80-1075. (American Ethnic Groups Ser.). 1981. lib. bdg. 47.95 (0-405-13450-9) Ayer.

Manual Asymmetries in Motor Performance. Ed. by Digby Elliott & Eric A. Roy. 272p. 1996. boxed set 104.95 (0-8493-8999-2) CRC Pr.

Manual Biblico de Bolsillo. Ed. by Walter A. Elwell.Tr. of Pocket Bible Handbook. (SPA., Illus.). 352p. 15.99 (0-89922-501-2, C072-5012) Caribe Betania.

Manual Biblico de Unger. Merrill F. Unger. Orig. Title: Unger's Bible Handbook. (SPA.). 976p. 1976. 20.99 (0-8254-1777-5, Edit Portavoz); pap. 15.99 (0-8254-1778-3, Edit Portavoz) Kregel.

Manual Bibliografico de Estudos Brasileiros. Borba De Moraes & William Berrien. 1976. lib. bdg. 59.95 (0-8490-2203-7) Gordon Pr.

Manual Bibliographique des Science Physiques ou Occultes, 3 vols. Albert Caillet. (Illus.). 1907p. 1997. reprint ed. 195.00 (1-57898-004-6) Martino Pubng.

Manual Car Asia, No. 3. Hillis. 1987. 10.95 (0-316-36404-5) Little.

Manual Car ISE, No. 3. Hillis. 1987. 15.95 (0-316-36403-7) Little.

Manual Catolico Esencial: Con Referencias al Catecismo de la Iglesia Catolica. rev. ed. Una Publicacion Pastoral Redentorista Staff. LC 94-75248. (SPA.). 192p. 1994. 14.95 (0-89243-694-8) Liguori Pubns.

Manual Communication: A Basic Text & Workbook with Practical Exercises. Dean A. Christopher. LC 75-38884. (Illus.). 544p. 1976. pap. 39.00 (0-936104-63-5, 1107) PRO-ED.

Manual Communication: Implications for Education. Ed. by Harry Bornstein. LC 90-40934. (Illus.). 208p. 1990. text 34.95 (0-930323-57-2) Gallaudet Univ Pr.

Manual Communication Vol. 1: Fingerspelling & the Langauge of Signs. fac. ed. Barbara E. Babbini. LC 72-94999. (Illus.). 391p. 1974. pap. 121.30 (0-7837-7607-1, 204736000001) Bks Demand.

Manual Communication Vol. 2: Fingerspelling & the Langauge of Signs, Vol. 2. fac. ed. Barbara E. Babbini. LC 72-94999. (Illus.). 203p. 1974. pap. 63.00 (0-7837-7608-X, 204736000002) Bks Demand.

Manual Compartiendo la Fe: Faith-Sharing Manual. Samuel de la Rosa et al. (SPA.). 96p. 1996. pap. 8.95 (0-88177-185-6, DR185) Discipleship Res.

Manual Complete Urology Asia. Martin I. Resnick. 1989. 10.95 (0-316-74052-7, Little Brwn Med Div) Lppncott W & W.

Manual Complete Urology ISE. Martin I. Resnick. 1989. 15.95 (0-316-74053-5, Little Brwn Med Div) Lppncott W & W.

Manual Completo de los Verbos en Ingles: Complete Handbook of English Verbs. Jaime G. Bores. (ENG & SPA., Illus.). 208p. 1994. pap. 8.95 (0-8442-7102-0, Natl Textbk Co) NTC Contemp Pub Co.

Manual Completo De Verbos Auziliares E Irregulares En Ingles. Garza & Jamie Borez. (SPA.). 206p. 1997. pap. text 13.98 (968-13-2504-4) Libros Fronteras.

Manual CRDV Asia, No. 3. Joseph S. Alpert. 1988. 10.95 (0-316-03521-1) Little.

Manual de Accordes Para Guitarra. Peter Pickow. (SPA.). 48p. 1997. pap. 5.95 (0-8256-1540-2, AM 91802) Music Sales.

Manual de Adoracion: Worship Manual. Magda Ramirez. (SPA.). 56p. 1996. pap. 7.95 (0-88177-184-8, DR184) Discipleship Res.

Manual de Aire Acondicionado. Carrier Air Conditioning Co. Staff. (SPA.). 848p. 1977. 150.00 (0-8288-5499-8, S30875) Fr & Eur.

Manual de Asesoramiento Permarital. Norman Wright.Tr. of Premarital Counseling Handbook. (SPA.). 100. pap. 10.99 (1-56063-828-1, 497264) Editorial Unilit.

Manual de Astrologia - The Astrologer's Handbook. Frances Sokoian & Louis S. Acker. 480p. 1994. 12.00 (0-06-633702-X) Addson-Wesley Educ.

Manual de Bailes Folkloricos. Paquita Pescador de Umpierre. 290p. (C). 1981. pap. 5.00 (0-8477-2501-4) U of PR Pr.

Manual de Bibliografia de la Literatura Espanola. Homero Seris. 1948. pap. 4.00 (0-87535-061-5) Hispanic Soc.

Manual de Billy Graham: Obreros Cristianos. Billy Graham.Tr. of Billy Graham's Handbook for Christian Workers. (SPA.). 297p. 1995. 8.99 (0-7899-0040-8, 497658) Editorial Unilit.

Manual de Biografia y de Bibliografia de los Escritores Espanoles del Siglo, No. XIX. Manuel Ovilo y Otero. vii, 540p. 1976. reprint ed. write for info. (3-487-05861-8) G Olms Pubs.

Manual de Circuitos Electronicos. John Markus. 984p. 1974. 125.00 (0-7859-0873-0, S-30723) Fr & Eur.

Manual de Como Sobrevivir el Jardin de Ninos: La Lista Pre-Escolar y una Guia para los Padres. rev. ed. Allana Elovson. Tr. by Lita C. Arellanos. (SPA., Illus.). 96p. 1993. per. 12.95 (1-879888-07-6) Parent Ed.

Manual de Concentracion (Concentration Workbook) Carlos Gonzalez. (SPA.). 1991. write for info. (1-56491-039-3) Imagine Pubs.

Manual de Control de Gestion. Yves Dupuy & Gerard Rolland. (SPA.). 329p. 1992. pap. 31.00 (84-7978-044-4, Pub. by Ediciones Diaz) IBD Ltd.

Manual de Controle de Incendio de Buques. (SPA.). (C). 1989. 175.00 (0-89771-705-8, Pub. by Lorne & MacLean Marine) St Mut.

Manual de Controle de Incendio de Buques. Lorne & MacLean Marine & Offshore Publications Sta. (SPA.). (C). 1987. 165.00 (0-7855-4383-X, Pub. by Lorne & MacLean Marine) St Mut.

Manual de Controle de Incendio de Buques. OCS Marine Staff. (SPA.). (C). 1989. text 195.00 (0-7855-6968-5, Pub. by Lorne & MacLean Marine) St Mut.

***Manual de Creacion de Paginas Web en Espanol con CD-ROM: Crea, Publica y Promociona Tu Sitio Web en Internet.** Fernando Casale & Gustavo Katcheroff. (Manuales PC Users Ser.). (SPA., Illus.). 223p. 1999. pap. 17.90 incl. cd-rom (987-9131-54-1, Pub. by MP Ediciones) Am Wholesale.

Manual de Cultivos Hidroponicos. 1994. write for info. (92-806-3118-7) U N I C E.

Manual de Defensa Personal. Editorial America, S. A. Staff. Ed. by Maria E. Del Real. (SPA., Illus.). 224p. (Orig.). 1990. pap. 3.95 (0-944499-53-8) Editorial Amer.

Manual de Derecho Procesal Civil. 2nd rev. ed. Rafael H. Colon. 450p. 1981. pap. 25.00 (0-88063-499-5, MICHIE) LEXIS Pub.

Manual de Desembolsos - Disbursement Handbook. (SPA.). 148p. 1994. pap. 22.00 (0-8213-2520-5, 12520) World Bank.

Manual de Diagnostico y Terapeutica Medica en Atencion Primaria. 2nd ed. R. Ruiz de Adana. (SPA.). 1221p. 1996. pap. 52.00 (84-7978-255-2, Pub. by Ediciones Diaz) IBD Ltd.

Manual de Doctrina Cristiana. 4th ed. Louis Berkhof. (SPA.). 296p. 1991. pap. 12.00 (0-939125-03-X) CRC Wrld Lit.

Manual de Doctrinas Basicas: Una Compilacion de Referencias Biblicas. David K. Bernard. Tr. by Grover J. Medina. (SPA.). 112p. (Orig.). 1996. mass mkt. 5.99 (1-56722-141-6) Word Aflame.

Manual de Eclesiologia: A Manual of Ecclesiology. H. E. Dana. Tr. by Adolfo Robleto. 1987. 10.99 (0-311-17018-8) Casa Bautista.

Manual de Ejercicios Para Pacientes en el Post-Operatorio de Cabeza y Cuello. (SPA.). 1984. 5.00 (0-940876-09-4) City Hope.

Manual de Ejercicios Para Pacientes Mastecjomizada y con Remocion de Nodulas Axilares. (SPA.). 1984. 5.00 (0-940876-08-6) City Hope.

Manual De Ejercicios Y De Laboratorio to Accompany Contigo: Essentials. 3rd ed. Oscar Ozete. (SPA.). (C). 1994. wbk. ed., lab manual ed. 40.50 (0-15-501077-8) Harcourt Coll Pubs.

Manual de Ensenanza de Medicamentos En Espanol: A Guide to Patient Drug Information in Spanish. Tr. of Medication Teaching Manual. (SPA.). 760p. (Orig.). 1995. pap. text 70.00 (1-879907-60-7) Am Soc Hlth-Syst.

Manual De Espanol, 2. rev. ed. Maria Arsuaga De Vila. LC 80-36752. 253p. (C). 1980. 5.00 (0-8477-3165-0) U of PR Pr.

Manual De Espanol, Set. rev. ed. Maria Arsuaga De Vila. LC 80-36752. 253p. (C). 1980. 15.00 (0-8477-3177-4) U of PR Pr.

Manual De Espanol, Vol. 1, Pt. 1. rev. ed. Maria Arsuaga De Vila. LC 80-36752. 253p. (C). 1980. 5.00 (0-8477-3195-2) U of PR Pr.

Manual De Espanol, Vol. 1, Pt. 2. rev. ed. Maria Arsuaga De Vila. LC 80-36752. 253p. (C). 1980. 5.00 (0-8477-3196-0) U of PR Pr.

Manual de Espanol Correcto, 2 vols. L. Gomex Torrego. (SPA.). 818p. 1996. pap. 68.00 (84-7635-057-0, Pub. by Acro Libros) IBD Ltd.

Manual de Estilo. Jose L. Albertos & Luisa S. Suarez. Ed. by Centro Tecnico de la Sociedad Staff & Interamericana de Prensa Staff. (SPA.). 224p. (Orig.). (C). 1993. pap. text 21.00 (0-89730-225-7, Inter Am Pr) R J Berg.

***Manual de Estilo de Publicaciones de la American Psychological Association.** American Psychological Association Staff. 480p. 1998. pap. 21.95 (968-426-793-2) Am Psychol.

Manual de Estudios Profeticos. K. Nigh.Tr. of Manual of Prophetic Studies. (SPA.). 272p. 1995. pap. 11.99 (0-8297-1988-1) Vida Pubs.

Manual de Evangelismo: Envagelism Manual. Roberto Gomez et al. (SPA.). 56p. 1996. pap. 7.95 (0-88177-186-4, DR186) Discipleship Res.

***Manual de Excel para Secretarias en Espanol: Aproveche al Maximo el Poder del Programa Excel.** Claudio Sanchez. (Computacion para Secretarias Ser.). (SPA., Illus.). 232p. 1999. pap. 13.90 (987-9131-90-8, Pub. by MP Ediciones) Am Wholesale.

***Manual de Exploracion.** Portavoz Editorial Staff. (Sabio & Prudente Ser.: Vol. 4). 96p. 1999. pap. 3.75 (0-8254-0939-X, Edit Portavoz) Kregel.

***Manual de Exporacion.** Portavoz Editorial Staff. (Sabio & Prudente Ser.: Vol. 4). 96p. 1999. pap., teacher ed. 4.99 (0-8254-0938-1, Edit Portavoz) Kregel.

Manual de Extension de la Escuela Dominical: Church School Extension Manual. Mary Lou Santillan-Baert et al. (SPA.). 56p. 1996. pap. 7.95 (0-88177-187-2, DR187) Discipleship Res.

Manual de Formacion de Personal. L. Rae. Orig. Title: Skills of Training. (SPA.). 263p. 1994. pap. 25.00 (84-7978-121-1, Pub. by Ediciones Diaz) IBD Ltd.

Manual De Fundamentos de Higiene Industrial. 1284p. 120.00 (0-318-17998-9) Inter-Am Safety.

Manual de Genetica Cuantitativa. rev. ed. Walter Alvin Becker. Tr. by Oliver Deaton & Rafael Vera from ENG. LC 86-71091.Tr. of Manual of Quantitative Genetics. (SPA.). 176p. (C). 1986. pap. 19.95 (0-931399-01-7) Academic Enter.

***Manual de Gerencia para una Escuela de Calidad.** C. Crespo et al. 102p. 1999. write for info. (92-806-3515-8) U N I C E.

***Manual De Gramatica.** 2nd ed. Dozier. 1998. pap., student ed. 34.00 (0-8384-1025-1) Heinle & Heinle.

Manual de Gramatica. 2nd ed. Eleanor Dozier. (SPA.). 1998. pap. text 51.95 (0-8384-9832-9) Heinle & Heinle.

Manual de Gramatica: A Reference Tool for Intermediate-Level Spanish Students. Eleanor Dozier & Zulma Iguina. LC 94-26367. (SPA.). (C). 1995. pap. 31.25 (0-8384-5888-2) Heinle & Heinle.

***Manual de Gramatica Espanola.** (SPA.). 1998. pap. 12.95 (84-03-27081-X) Santillana.

Manual de Guerra Espiritual. Ed Murphy.Tr. of Handbook for Spiritual Warfare. (SPA.). 688p. 1995. 19.99 (0-88113-212-8) Caribe Betania.

Manual de Herramientas de Calidad: El Enfoque Japones. Kazuo Ozeki & Tetsuichi Asaka. LC 89-43211. (SPA., Illus.). 281p. 1992. pap. 60.00 (84-87022-92-8) Productivity Inc.

Manual de Historia de Espana Vol. 1: Prehistoria, y Edad Antigua. T. M. Blazquez. 562p. 1989. 125.00 (84-239-5091-3) Elliots Bks.

Manual de Historia de Espana Vol. 2: Edad Media (711-1500) M. Riu y Riu. 644p. 1989. 125.00 (84-239-5092-1) Elliots Bks.

Manual de Historia de Espana Vol. 3: Edad Moderna (1474-1808) Pere Molas Ribalta. 582p. 1989. 125.00 (84-239-5093-X) Elliots Bks.

Manual de Historia de Espana Vol. 4: Edad Contemporanea, I (1808-1898) Vincente P. Atard. (SPA.). 644p. 1991. 125.00 (84-239-5094-8) Elliots Bks.

Manual de Homiletica Para Laicos. Justo C. Anderson.Tr. of Homiletic for Laymen. (SPA., Illus.). 128p. (C). 1987. reprint ed. 6.50 (0-311-42073-7) Casa Bautista.

Manual de Identificacao e Controle de Plantas Daninhas (Manual for the Identification & Control of Weeds. 4th ed. Harri Lorenzi. (POR., Illus.). 300p. 1994. 65.00 (85-86714-04-6, Pub. by Inst Plantarum) Balogh.

Manual de Instrucciones - Sistema de Gas Inerte. (SPA.). (C). 1989. 600.00 (0-7855-6720-8, Pub. by Lorne & MacLean Marine) St Mut.

Manual de Instrucciones - Sistema de Gas Inerte. Lorne & MacLean Marine & Offshore Publications Sta. (SPA.). (C). 1987. 600.00 (0-7855-4370-8, Pub. by Lorne & MacLean Marine) St Mut.

Manual de Intercesion Misionera. Comibam.Tr. of Manual for Missionary Intercession. (SPA.). 101p. 1986. pap. 3.99 (1-56063-398-0, 498548) Editorial Unilit.

M

Manual de Interpretacion - LSM Dictionary: Mexican Sign Language Dictionary. Leonel M. Matute. (ENG & SPA., Illus.). 254p. 1997. pap. 19.95 (*0-915035-70-7*) Dawn Sign.

Manual de Investigacion Intelectual. Adela Rodriguez Forteza. (UPREX, Manuales Ser.: No. 7). 114p. (C). 1972. pap. 1.50 (*0-8477-0007-0*) U of PR Pr.

Manual de la Mama Perfecta. deluxe ed. Ed. by Adrianne Lange. (SPA., Illus.). 192p. 1999. pap. 5.95 (*0-939193-37-X*) Edit Concepts.

***Manual de la Sociedad Internacional de Transferencia de Embriones: Guia de Procedimientos e Informacion General para el Uso de la Technologia de la Transferencia de Embriones con Especial Enfasis.** 3rd ed. Ed. by David A. Stringfellow & Sarah Seidel. LC 00-91206. Orig. Title: Manual of the International Embryo Transfer Society. (SPA., Illus.). 185p. 2000. pap. text 35.00 (*0-9662386-2-1*) Intl Embryo Trans.

***Manual de la Societe Internationale de Transfert Embryonnaire: Guide Methodologique et Informations Generales sur l'Utilisation du Transfert Embryonnaire Avec Attention Particuliere sur les Precautions d'Ordre Sanitaire.** 3rd ed. Ed. by David A. Stringfellow & Sarah Seidel. LC 00-131492. Orig. Title: Manual of the International Embyo Transfer Society. (FRE., Illus.). 185p. 2000. pap. text 35.00 (*0-9662386-1-3*) Intl Embryo Trans.

M

Manual de la Super Mama. Adrianne Lange. (SPA.). 224p. (Orig.). 1987. pap. 4.95 (*0-939193-11-6*) Edit Concepts.

Manual de la Teneper: Tarea Energetica Personal. Waldo Vieira. Tr. by Paloma Cabadas from POR. (SPA., Illus.). 145p. 1996. pap. 11.95 (*85-86019-17-8*) Intl Inst Proj.

Manual de la Vida Cristiana. Paul A. Kienel.Tr. of Handbook for Christian Living. (SPA.). 336p. 1996. 11.99 (*0-88113-147-4*, B001-1474) Caribe Betania.

Manual de la Vida (Manual of the Life) Samuel Alpizar. (SPA., Illus.). 16p. (Orig.). 1993. pap. 5.00 (*0-9655165-0-4*) S Alpizar.

Manual de Liberacion para Obreros Cristianos. Marzullo & Snyder.Tr. of Manual for the Deliverance Worker. (SPA.). 90p. 1994. 3.99 (*958-95462-0-X*, 550061) Editorial Unilit.

Manual de Lideres de Lideres. Mike Phillipps & Marilyn Phillipps. (SPA.). 100p. 1995. pap. text. write for info. (*1-884794-17-3*) Eden Pubng.

Manual de Literatura Espanola, 12 vols. Felipe B. Pedraza Jimenez & Milagros Rodriguez Caceres. Ed. by Cenlit Ediciones Staff. (SPA., Illus.). 628.00 (*0-8485-1104-2*) Cenlit Ediciones.

Manual de Literatura Hispanoamericana, Vols. 1-3. Felipe B. Pedraza Jimenez & Milagros Rodriguez Caceres. Ed. by Cenlit Ediciones Staff. (SPA.). 180.00 (*84-85511-26-3*) Cenlit Ediciones.

Manual de los Postreros Dias. Robert P. Lightner.Tr. of Last Days Handbook. (SPA.). 159p. 1995. 8.99 (*0-88113-193-8*, B001-1938) Caribe Betania.

Manual de Metodos de Campo para el Monitoreo de Aves Terrestres. C. John Ralph et al. (SPA., Illus.). 52p. 1997. reprint ed. 11.50 (*0-89904-677-0*, Wildlife Resrch Grp); reprint ed. pap. 6.20 (*0-89904-675-4*, Wildlife Resrch Grp) Crumb Elbow Pub.

Manual de Ministerios con Familias: Family Ministries Manual. Hideliza Amores. (SPA.). 52p. 1996. pap. 7.95 (*0-88177-188-0*, DR188) Discipleship Res.

Manual de Ministerios con Jovenes: Youth Ministries Manual. Ada Chong & Elena de la Pena. (SPA.). 52p. 1996. pap. 6.95 (*0-88177-190-2*, DR190) Discipleship Res.

***Manual de MS FrontPage 2000 en Espanol - Spanish con CD-ROM: Diseno, Publicacion y Mantenimiento de Sitios Web.** Jorge A. Rolando. (Manuales para PC Users Ser.). (SPA., Illus.). 255p. 1999. pap. 19.90 incl. cd-rom (*987-526-017-7*, Pub. by MP Ediciones) Am Wholesale.

Manual de Neurofisiologia. D. P. Cardinali. (SPA.). 339p. 1992. pap. 28.50 (*84-7978-005-3*, Pub. by Ediciones Diaz) IBD Ltd.

Manual de Nociones y Ejercicios Gramaticales: Unidad de Composicion y Otras Destrezas Linguisticas. enl. rev. ed. Departamento De Espanol, Facultad De Estudios Gene. LC 76-4501. (SPA.). 148p. (C). 1989. pap. text 5.95 (*0-8477-3164-2*) U of PR Pr.

Manual de Odontologia Infantil. Ed. by Luis A. Marini. (SPA.). 463p. (Orig.). (C). 1982. 12.00 (*0-8477-2330-5*) U of PR Pr.

Manual de Oleohidraulica Industrial: 935100-E. 5th rev. ed. (Illus.). 600p. (C). 1995. pap. text 39.00 (*0-9634162-3-5*) Vickers Inc Trng Ctr.

Manual de Orientacion al Maestro. Dalila Rodriguez Irlanda. (SPA.). 262p. 1990. pap. write for info. (*0-929441-03-6*) Pubns Puertorriquenas.

Manual de Pediatria Practica. 4th ed. M. Pombo Arias. (SPA.). 693p. 1992. 37.50 (*84-7978-055-X*, Pub. by Ediciones Diaz) IBD Ltd.

***Manual de Pintura y Caligrafia.** Jose Saramago. (SPA.). 2000. pap. 31.95 (*968-19-0561-X*) Aguilar.

Manual de Planeacion Empresarial. Courtney H. Price & R. Mack Davis. Orig. Title: Entrepreneur's Fast Trac Planning Handbook. (SPA.). 150p. 1998. spiral bd. write for info. (*0-944303-23-4*) Entre Ed Fndtn.

Manual de Prevencion de Accidentes en la Construccion. 280p. 40.00 (*0-318-17997-0*) Inter-Am Safety.

Manual de Primeros Auxilios. Editorial America, S. A. Staff. Ed. by Maria E. Alvarez del Real. (SPA., Illus.). 224p. (Orig.). 1989. pap. 3.50 (*0-944499-06-6*) Editorial Amer.

Manual de Primeros Auxilios. 7th ed. Norman G. Kirby. 1985. text 14.95 (*0-07-104013-7*) McGraw.

Manual de Procedimiento Parlamentario. 7th rev. ed. Reece B. Bothwell. 225p. (C). 1990. 7.00 (*0-8477-3028-X*) U of PR Pr.

Manual de Procedimientos. E. Reyes.Tr. of Operations Manual. (SPA.). 224p. 1994. pap. 9.99 (*0-8297-2040-5*) Vida Pubs.

Manual de Productos Cuimicos, 3 vols., Vols. 1, 2 & 3. IASC Staff. 225.00 (*0-317-04173-8*) Inter-Am Safety.

Manual de Redaccion. Jose R. Feliciano. (SPA.). 209p. (C). 1995. pap. text 14.95 (*1-56328-037-X*) Edit Plaza Mayor.

Manual De Reparacion y Mantenimiento Del Autoestima. B. David Brooks & Rex K. Dalby. Ed. by Paula J. Hunter. Tr. by Adolfo Martinez.Tr. of Self-Esteem Repair & Maintenance Manual. (ENG & SPA., Illus.). 143p. 1991. reprint ed. pap. 14.95 (*968-38-0251-6*, Pub. by Panorama Edit) Routldge.

Manual de Sistemas de Labranza para America Latina. (SPA.). 208p. 1992. 25.00 (*92-5-303253-7*, FSP2537, Pub. by FAO) Bernan Associates.

Manual de Sociologia de la Salud. P. Donati. (SPA.). 419p. 1994. pap. 29.75 (*84-7978-143-2*, Pub. by Ediciones Diaz) IBD Ltd.

Manual de Teatro Escolar. William Padin Zamot. (SPA.). 168p. 1995. 17.95 (*0-8477-0227-8*) U of PR Pr.

Manual de Tecnicas de Investigacion Social. Ronald J. Duncan et al. LC 80-23411. (Illus.). 73p. 1980. 5.00 (*0-913480-46-0*) Inter Am U Pr.

Manual de Tecnicas de Redaccion Periodistica. Jorge Covarrubias. Ed. by Jose Abreu. LC 96-84354. (SPA.). 233p. (Orig.). 1996. pap. text 13.95 (*0-917360-13-3*) Assoc Pr.

Manual de Tecnicas Microquimicas de Campo para la Arqueologia. Luis Barba et al. 36p. 1991. pap. 2.50 (*968-36-2184-8*, UN002) UPLAAP.

Manual de Tecnicas Quirurgicas. J. Sanchez Fernandez. (SPA.). 291p. 1992. pap. 27.00 (*84-7978-058-4*, Pub. by Ediciones Diaz) IBD Ltd.

***Manual de Windows 98 en Espanol: Domine Su PC con la Ultima Tecnologia de Win'98.** Ricardo Goldberger. (Manuales PC Users Ser.). (SPA., Illus.). 301p. 1999. pap. 16.90 (*987-9131-77-0*, Pub. by MP Ediciones) Am Wholesale.

Manual Del Administrador de Planificacion Familiar: Tecnicas para Mejorar la Gestion de Programas. Ed. by James A. Wolff et al. (SPA., Illus.). 345p. (Orig.). 1994. pap. write for info. (*0-913723-32-0*) Mgmt Sci Health.

***Manual del Ama de Casa Desordenada.** S. Felton.Tr. of Messies Manual. (SPA.). 2000. 8.99 (*0-7899-0589-2*, 498670) Editorial Unilit.

Manual Del Automovil en 5 Idiomas: Diccionario Idiomatico del Automovil. Equipo Reactor de Ceac Staff. (ENG, FRE, GER, ITA & SPA.). 240p. 1974. 24.95 (*0-8288-6071-8*, S-50224) Fr & Eur.

Manual Del Buen Modal y Otras Ocurrencias "Light" Juan A. Ramos. 1993. 7.95 (*0-8477-0185-9*) U of PR Pr.

***Manual del Codigo Penal y las Leyes de Vehiculos y Transito de Puerto Rico: Codigo Penal y Ley de Vehiculos y Transito.** (SPA.). 1100p. 2000. write for info. (*0-327-13680-4*, 3182410) LEXIS Pub.

Manual del Cristiano Lleno del Espiritu. Derek Prince.Tr. of Spirit Filled Believer's Handbook. (SPA.). 500p. 1996. 14.99 (*1-56063-745-5*, 550071) Editorial Unilit.

Manual Del Discipulado: Hagamos Discipulos. Rodrigo Zapata.Tr. of Let's Make Disciples. (SPA.). 220p. 1990. pap. 6.99 (*1-56063-018-3*, 498451) Editorial Unilit.

Manual Del Maestro - A Handbook for Christian Maturity. Bright. (Diez Grados Basicos - Ten Basic Steps Ser.). (SPA.). teacher ed. write for info. (*1-56063-470-7*) Editorial Unilit.

Manual del Maestro - Progresa con las Matematicas. Cicely Banks & Noemi Alvarado. (SPA.). 80p. 1998. pap. text 12.00 (*0-9624192-3-0*) N Bacchus.

Manual del Perfecto Ateo. Rius. 1997. pap. text 12.98 (*968-419-161-8*) Grijalbo Edit.

Manual Del Perfecto Idiota Latinamericano. Plinio Apuleyo Mendoza. (SPA.). 336p. 1997. mass mkt. 9.99 (*0-553-06060-0*) Bantam.

***Manual Del Perfecto Sinverguenza.** Jose M. Muzaurrieta. Ed. by Jose A. Madrigal & Carlos A. Montaner. LC 99-65162. (Coleccion Cuba y Sus Jueces). (SPA., Illus.). 94p. 1999. pap. 9.95 (*0-89729-907-8*) Ediciones.

Manual del Profesor. (SPA.). 80p. (C). 1995. write for info. (*0-201-65399-0*) P-H Intl.

Manual del Temperamento: Descubra Su Potencial. Tim F. LaHaye.Tr. of Your Temperament: Discover Its Potential. (SPA.). 1987. 16.99 (*0-8423-6322-X*, 490214); write for info. (*0-614-27078-2*) Editorial Unilit.

Manual Del Ujier. Les Parrott.Tr. of Usher's Manual. (SPA.). 68p. 1992. pap. 4.99 (*0-8297-0329-2*) Vida Pubs.

Manual Derm Asia, No. 4. Andreas Arndt. 1988. 10.95 (*0-316-05179-9*, Little Brwn Med Div) Lppncott W & W.

Manual Derm ISE, No. 4. Andreas Arndt. 1988. 15.95 (*0-316-05178-0*) Little.

***Manual d'exercises-pour Accompagner: A la Francaise-Correct French for English Speakers.** Marie Gontier Geno & Denis M. Provencher. 168p. 2000. pap. 24.50 (*0-7618-1606-2*) U Pr of Amer.

Manual Dictionary for Wine & Spirits Merchants see Dictionnaire-Manuel du Negociant en Vins et Spiriteaux et du Maitre de Chai

Manual Didactico para Investigadores de Delitos Financieros. Ed. by Magnum School, Inc. Staff & Tobias Zylberglait. (SPA.). 134p. (Orig.). 1995. lab manual ed. 29.95 (*0-945406-03-7*) Magnum Schl.

Manual Drive Train & Axles. Knowles. (Automotive Technology Ser.). 1997. student ed. 14.95 (*0-8273-7657-X*) Delmar.

Manual Drive Trains & Axles. 2nd ed. Thomas W. Birch. LC 98-6983. 422p. (C). 1998. pap. text 65.00 (*0-13-924069-1*) P-H.

Manual Drive Trains & Axles: For ASE Test A3. Chek-Chart Staff. (Chek-Chart's ASE Study Guides Ser.). 112p. 1998. pap. 19.95 (*0-02-862661-3*) Macmillan.

Manual DX Imaging ISE, No. 2. William H. Straub. 1989. 15.95 (*0-316-81888-7*, Little Brwn Med Div) Lppncott W & W.

Manual Electr ISE, No. 2. Gilbert H. Mudge, Jr. 1986. 15.95 (*0-316-58919-5*) Little.

Manual Evaluating Stormwater Effects in Receiving Waters. G. Allen Burton, Jr. 250p. 1999. 59.95 (*0-87371-924-7*, L924) Lewis Pubs.

Manual Fetal Echocardiology. Lindsey D. Allan. 1986. text 89.00 (*0-85200-988-7*) Kluwer Academic.

Manual First Congregational Church Marblehead, Massachusetts. large type ed. Ed. by Charles D. Townsend. LC 98-220645. (Illus.). 107p. 1997. reprint ed. pap. 15.00 (*1-878545-32-9*) ACETO Bookmen.

Manual Flora of Egypt, 2 vols. in one. R. Muschler. (Illus.). 1971. reprint ed. 250.00 (*3-7682-0678-5*) Lubrecht & Cramer.

Manual for a Perfect Government: How to Harness the Laws of Nature to Bring Maximum Success to Government Administration. John S. Hagelin. (Illus.). 171p. 1998. pap. 15.00 (*0-923569-22-7*) Maharishi U Mgmt Pr.

Manual for a Province Congregation see Guide for Delegates to a Province Congregation

Manual for a Technological Approach to Ground Stone Analysis. Jenny L. Adams. (Illus.). 81p. (Orig.). 1996. pap. 15.00 (*1-886398-30-5*) Desert Archaeol.

Manual for Acolytes: The Duties of the Server at Liturgical Celebrations. Dennis G. Michno. LC 80-81096. (Illus.). 96p. 1991. pap. 8.95 (*0-8192-1272-5*) Morehouse Pub.

Manual for Acute Postoperative Pain Management. Ferne B. Sevarino & Linda M. Preble. 256p. 1992. text 63.00 (*0-88167-866-X*) Lppncott W & W.

***Manual for Administration in Occupational Theraphy.** Hunt Prabst. 2001. pap. 44.00 (*0-7693-0096-0*) Thomson Learn.

Manual for Administrative Law Judges. 1997. lib. bdg. 251.95 (*0-8490-8228-5*) Gordon Pr.

Manual for Agency Accreditation. rev. ed. Council on Accreditation of Services for Families. LC 91-77835. 1080p. 1991. disk 90.00 (*0-685-59101-8*) Coun Accred Srvs Fam & Child.

Manual for Agency Accreditation, Set. rev. ed. Council on Accreditation of Services for Families. LC 91-77835. 1080p. 1991. per. 75.00 (*1-880853-01-9*) Coun Accred Srvs Fam & Child.

Manual for Animal Health Auxiliary Personnel. 392p. 1984. 40.00 (*92-5-101475-2*, F2582, Pub. by FAO) Bernan Associates.

Manual for Annual Conference Commission on Archives & History, 1993-1996. 41p. 1996. pap. text 5.00 (*1-880927-15-2*) Gen Comm Arch.

Manual for Arabic Translators with Emphasis on the Useage in the United Nations System, 2 Vols., Set. 793p. 150.00 (*0-685-35072-X*, AE.89.III.E.2) UN.

Manual for Assertiveness Trainers: 1990 Edition with 1995 Supplement. 3rd ed. Robert E. Alberti & Michael L. Emmons. LC 90-5326. 160p. 1995. pap. 10.95 (*0-915166-14-3*) Impact Pubs CA.

Manual for Assessing Health Practices & Designing Practice Policies: The Explicit Approach. Council of Medical Specialty Societies Task Force & David M. Eddy. 144p. 1992. pap. 34.00 (*0-943126-18-5*, MAH91) Amer Coll Phys.

***Manual for Assessing Progress in Coastal Management.** Stephen B. Olsen et al. (Coastal Management Report Ser.: Vol. 2211). (Illus.). 1999. pap. write for info. (*1-885454-11-2*) Coastal Res.

Manual for Basic Laboratory Exercises. Mohamed Elhelu. 1984. per. 16.65 (*0-88252-157-8*) Paladin Hse.

Manual for Becoming a Jester. Stephanie West Allen & Edd Nichols. (Illus.). (Orig.). 1999. pap. 19.95 (*0-9644207-1-6*) KiteShade Pubng.

Manual for Better Training Statistics: Conceptual, Measurement & Survey Issues. Terry Murphy & Murray Klee. LC 99-162671. 280p. 1997. pap. 35.00 (*92-64-15566-X*, 91-97-01-1, Pub. by Org for Econ) OECD.

Manual for Bird Watching in the Americas. Donald S. Heintzelman. (Illus.). 255p. 1998. pap. text 15.00 (*0-7881-5318-8*) DIANE Pub.

Manual for Bishops. rev. ed. Thomas J. Green. 96p. (C). 1992. pap. 7.95 (*1-55586-496-1*) US Catholic.

Manual for Building Sound Self-Esteem. Lilburn S. Barksdale. 86p. 1978. pap. 39.95 (*0-918588-03-0*, 203) Barksdale Foun.

Manual for Cancer Registry Personnel. D. Esteban & S. Whelan. (IARC Technical Report Ser.: No. 10). 322p. 1995. text 45.00 (*92-832-1424-2*) World Health.

Manual for Change. Terry Wilson. 191p. 1994. 86.95 (*0-566-07460-5*, Pub. by Gower) Ashgate Pub Co.

Manual for Child Health Workers in Major Disasters. 1986. lib. bdg. 79.95 (*0-8490-3796-4*) Gordon Pr.

Manual for Children's Deliverance. Hammond. LC 98-162042. 1996. pap. 7.95 (*0-89228-078-6*) Impact Christian.

Manual for Christian School Secretaries. Association of Christian Schools International Staff. Ed. by Bonnie Damon. 1992. reprint ed. 17.95 (*1-58331-026-6*) Assn Christ Sch.

Manual for Christian Workers see Manual para Obreros Cristianos

Manual for Clinical Psychology Trainees, No. 10. 3rd ed. James P. Choca & Eric J. Van Denburg. LC 96-8894. (Basic Principles into Practice Ser.: Vol. 10). 256p. 1996. pap. text 27.95 (*0-87630-814-0*) Brunner-Mazel.

***Manual for Clinical Trials Nursing.** Ed. by Angela Klimaszewski et al. (Illus.). 400p. 2000. pap. text 50.00 (*1-890504-12-2*) Oncology Nursing.

Manual for Complex Insurance Coverage Litigation. John D. Shugrue & Committee on Insurance Coverage Litigation Task Fo. LC 93-37855. 286p. 1993. ring bd. 136.00 (*0-13-109323-1*) Aspen Law.

Manual for Complex Litigation, 2 vols. 1997. lib. bdg. 600.95 (*0-8490-8227-7*) Gordon Pr.

Manual for Complex Litigation. 2nd ed. Federal Judicial Center Staff. LC 85-31435. (Federal Court Rules Ser.). 1986. ring bd. 145.00 (*0-87632-492-8*) West Group.

Manual for Complex Litigation. 3rd ed. Ed. by Federal Judicial Center Staff. 568p. (C). 1995. pap. text. write for info. (*0-314-07009-5*) West Pub.

Manual for Computer-Assisted Legal Research. James A. Sprowl. LC 76-45588. 126p. 1976. reprint ed. pap. 39.10 (*0-608-12376-5*, 205213000038) Bks Demand.

Manual for Computer Literacy. Hugh L. McHenry. 200p. (C). 1995. spiral bd. 14.95 (*0-7872-1048-X*) Kendall-Hunt.

Manual for Condition Evaluation of Bridges. (Bridges Ser.). 148p. (C). 1994. pap. text 28.00 (*1-56051-067-6*, MCEB) AASHTO.

Manual for Cooperation Between State & Federal Courts. James G. Apple et al. 251p. (C). 1998. pap. text 35.00 (*0-7881-7472-X*) DIANE Pub.

Manual for Corporations Officers: The Law, Procedures & Forms. William J. Grange. LC 67-14483. 852p. reprint ed. pap. 200.00 (*0-608-30531-6*, 201584600002) Bks Demand.

Manual for Country Economists. Marcello Caiola. 1995. write for info. (*1-55775-460-8*) Intl Monetary.

Manual for Courts-Martial, U. S. (Illus.). 800p. 1997. reprint ed. pap. text 95.00 (*0-7881-3298-9*) DIANE Pub.

Manual for Courts-Martial United States. Ed. by Barry Leonard. 800p. (C). 1999. pap. text 95.00 (*0-7881-7756-7*) DIANE Pub.

***Manual for Courts Martial, United States: 1998.** 864p. 1998. per. 57.00 (*0-16-061141-5*) USGPO.

Manual for Data Administration. (Illus.). 110p. (Orig.). (C). 1994. pap. text 30.00 (*1-56806-362-8*) DIANE Pub.

Manual for Determining Physical Properties of Fertilizer. 2nd ed. David W. Rutland. LC 93-3133. (Reference Manual Ser.: No. R-10). (Illus.). 115p. (Orig.). 1993. pap. text 30.00 (*0-88090-101-2*) Intl Fertilizer.

Manual for Discussion Moderators. Walter Gray, Jr. 1964. pap. 4.00 (*0-910092-00-1*) Am Inst Disc.

Manual for Emigrants to America. Calvin Colton. LC 69-18767. (American Immigration Collection. Series 1). 1969. reprint ed. 12.95 (*0-405-00515-6*) Ayer.

Manual for Evaluation of Industrial Projects. 216p. pap. 16.00 (*92-1-106111-3*, E.80-II.B.2) UN.

Manual for Eye Examination & Diagnosis. 4th ed. Mark W. Leitman. 1993. pap. 36.95 (*0-86542-339-3*) Blackwell Sci.

***Manual for Eye Examination & Diagnosis.** 5th ed. Mark W. Leitman. (Illus.). 98p. (C). 2000. pap. 39.95 (*0-632-04542-6*) Blackwell Sci.

Manual for Flash Point Standards & Their Use: Methods & Regulations. Ed. by Harry Wray. LC 91-45892. (Manual Ser.: No. 9). (Illus.). 180p. 1991. text 54.00 (*0-8031-1410-9*, MNL9) ASTM.

Manual for Florida Legal Secretaries, 3 vols. Florida Association of Legal Secretaries Staff. 1984. ring bd. 180.00 (*0-327-00958-6*, 80876, MICHIE) LEXIS Pub.

Manual for Florida Legal Secretaries, Issue 99-1. Florida Association of Legal Secretaries Staff. 264p. 1999. ring bd. write for info. (*0-327-00965-9*, 8088220) LEXIS Pub.

Manual for Florida Legal Secretaries, 1984-1994, 3 vols. Florida Association of Legal Secretaries Staff. 1987. ring bd., suppl. ed. 39.00 (*0-685-11450-3*, MICHIE) LEXIS Pub.

Manual for Florida Legal Secretaries, 1984-1994, 3 vols., Set. Lloyd Davidson & Florida Association of Legal Secretaries Staff. 108p. 1997. ring bd. 180.00 (*0-409-26252-8*, 80876-10, MICHIE) LEXIS Pub.

***Manual for Florida Legal Secretaries 99-2, 3 vols., Set.** Florida Ass'n of Legal Secretaries Staff. 110p. 1999. ring bd. write for info. (*0-327-01529-2*, 8088221) LEXIS Pub.

Manual for Florida Legal Secretaries 98-4, Vols. 1-3. Florida Association of Legal Secretaries Staff. 248p. 1998. ring bd. write for info. (*0-327-00887-3*, 8088219) LEXIS Pub.

Manual for Functional Training. 3rd ed. Lynn M. Palmer & Janice E. Toms. LC 91-34541. (Illus.). 351p. 1992. pap. text 29.95 (*0-8036-6759-0*) Davis Co.

Manual for General Chemistry Laboratory I. 4th ed. James C. Horvath. (Illus.). 280p. 1996. pap. text, lab manual ed. 21.95 (*0-89892-143-0*, 2045L) Contemp Pub Co of Raleigh.

Manual for General Chemistry Laboratory II (2046L) 2nd ed. James C. Horvath. (Illus.). 250p. (C). 1993. lab manual ed. 21.95 (*0-89892-147-3*) Contemp Pub Co of Raleigh.

Manual for Graphological Researchers. Ed. by Willa Smith. 50p. (C). 1989. pap. text 6.95 (*1-877772-01-1*) AHAF.

Manual for Group Facilitators. Brian Auvine et al. (Illus.). 89p. 1999. pap. 16.00 (*0-9602714-7-3*) Fllwshp Intent.

Manual for Group Facilitators. Center for Conflict Resolution Staff. 89p. 1978. 12.95 (*0-318-17938-5*; E03A) NASCO.

Manual for Group Leaders & Participants Vol. 4: Parenthood in a Free Nation. Ethel Kawin. 213p. 1970. pap. 1.75 (*0-931682-08-8*) Purdue U Pubns.

Manual for Hazardous Waste Management: Reference Text, 2 vols., Vols. I & II. 562p. wbk. ed. 75.00 (*92-1-119687-6*) UN.

An Asterisk (*) at the beginning of an entry indicates that the title is appearing for the first time.

Manual for Health Officers. J. Scott MacNutt. Ed. by Barbara G. Rosenkrantz. LC 76-40634. (Public Health in America Ser.). (Illus.). 1977. reprint ed. lib. bdg. 54.95 (*0-405-09825-1*) Ayer.

Manual for History Museums. Arthur C. Parker. LC 36-985. reprint ed. 20.00 (*0-404-04887-0*) AMS Pr.

Manual for Horticultural Export Quality Assurance. 1994. pap. 150.00 (*0-85954-382-X*, Pub. by Nat Res Inst) St Mut.

Manual for Human Dissection: Photographs with Clinical Applications. Gerald Callas. (Illus.). 203p. (C). 1994. pap. text 34.95 (*0-8385-6133-0*, A6133-1, Apple Lange Med) McGraw.

Manual for Indexing see INIS: Manual for Subject Analysis

Manual for Intensive Brief & Emergency Psychotherapy Manual. Leopold Bellak. LC 87-23865. 50p. (Orig.). 1987. pap. text 9.50 (*0-918863-01-5*) CPS Inc.

Manual for Introduction to Spe Ech Disorders. Ronald W. Isele & Donald Fucci. 128p. (C). 1994. spiral bd. (*0-7872-0184-7*) Kendall-Hunt.

Manual for Introductory Experiments in Parapsychology. 2nd ed. Louisa E. Rhine. LC 68-70901. 24p. 1977. 2.00 (*0-911106-01-4*) Parapsych Pr.

Manual for IV Therapy Procedures. 3rd ed. Shila Hayden. Ed. by Jill C. Brittenham. LC 92-49992. (Illus.). 361p. (C). 1992. 25.00 (*1-878487-50-7*, ME221) Practice Mgmt Info.

Manual for Judiciary Interpreters. M. Eta Trabing. (ENG & SPA.). 256p. (Orig.). 1998. pap. 34.95 (*1-884570-87-9*) Research Triangle.

Manual for Kinship Analysis. Ernest L. Schusky. Ed. by Louise S. Spindler & George D. Spindler. (Studies in Anthropological Method). 99p. 1982. reprint ed. pap. text 6.95 (*0-8290-0924-8*) Irvington.

Manual for Kinship Analysis. 2nd ed. Ernest L. Schusky. LC 83-14669. 104p. (C). 1983. reprint ed. pap. text 14.50 (*0-8191-3493-7*) U Pr of Amer.

Manual for Laboratory Work in Mammalian Physiology. 3rd ed. Illus. by Fred E. D'Amour et al. LC 65-17285. 1996. pap. text 23.00 (*0-226-13563-2*) U Ch Pr.

Manual for Land Application of Treated Municipal Wastewater & Sludge. Scientific Publishers Staff. (C). 1988. 250.00 (*81-85312-01-X*, Pub. by Scientific) St Mut.

Manual for Land Application of Treated Municipal Wastewater & Sludge Environment, Canada. Scientific Publishers Staff. (C). 1989. text 160.00 (*0-7855-0105-3*, Pub. by Scientific Pubs) St Mut.

Manual for Lawyers & Legal Assistants: Real Estate. 2nd ed. Peter G. Seward & M. Catherine Cantor. LC 79-57456. 450p. 1980. pap., ring bd. 65.00 (*0-685-47730-4*, 79-116) U MI Law CLE.

Manual for Lay Eucharistic Ministers. Beth W. Ely. LC 91-12433. 80p. (Orig.). 1991. pap. 8.95 (*0-8192-1573-2*) Morehouse Pub.

Manual for Legal Assistants. National Association of Legal Assistants, Inc. Sta. 529p. 1979. 18.95 (*0-318-15095-6*) Natl Assn Legal Secys.

Manual for Legal Assistants 2E. 2nd ed. National Association of Legal Assistants, Inc. Sta. Ed. by Hannan. (Paralegal). 397p. (C). 1991. mass mkt. 53.50 (*0-314-80780-2*) West Pub.

Manual for Legal Investigators. rev. ed. John R. Rose. LC 96-158224. 319p. (C). 1995. 50.00 (*1-881170-05-5*) Rose Pub OR.

Manual for Library Binding. 1991. lib. bdg. 95.00 (*0-8490-5401-X*) Gordon Pr.

Manual for Light Artillery, 1863. Ed. by Jacques N. Jacobsen. 1989. 10.00 (*0-913150-90-8*) Pioneer Pr.

Manual for Living. Epictetus. Ed. by Sharon Lebell. LC 94-2721. (Little Book of Wisdom Ser.). 96p. 1994. pap. 9.00 (*0-06-251111-4*, Pub. by Harper SF) HarpC.

Manual for Management of Diabetes Mellitus. Juliana C. Chan et al. Date not set. pap. 23.95 (*962-201-757-6*, Pub. by Chinese Univ) U of Mich Pr.

Manual for Managing the Law Office. ring bd. write for info. (*0-318-57375-X*) P-H.

Manual for Midwives see Home Birth: Step-by-Step Instructions for Natural & Emergency Childbirth

Manual for Missionary Intercession see Manual de Intercesion Misionera

Manual for Mosquito Rearing & Experimental Techniques No. 5: Bulletin. American Mosquito Control Association Staff. 105p. 1970. 3.50 (*0-318-12862-4*) Am Mosquito.

Manual for North Carolina Jury Commissioners. 2nd ed. James C. Drennan & John L. Saxon. 46p. (C). 1993. pap. text 9.00 (*1-56011-215-8*, 92.08) Institute Government.

Manual for Northern Herb Growers. Seija Halva & Lyle E. Craker. LC 96-78191. (Illus.). 101p. (Orig.). 1996. spiral bd. 25.00 (*0-9629868-1-X*) HSMP Pr.

Manual for Notaries Public of Michigan. 2nd ed. Ed. by Eugene E. Hines & Lisa K. Fisher. 38p. 1997. 9.45 (*0-685-68061-4*) Am Soc Notaries.

Manual for Notaries Public of Virginia. American Society of Notaries Staff et al. LC 82-72541. (Illus.). viii, 83p. 1982. 9.95 (*0-317-00824-2*) Am Soc Notaries.

Manual for Nursing Care of Children. Frances R. Martin. 352p. 1993. spiral bd. 31.95 (*0-8403-8616-8*) Kendall-Hunt.

Manual for Nurture for Baptist Churches: The Church Training Guide for the National Baptist Convention, U. S. A., Inc. Amos Jones, Jr. LC 95-16126. 1995. write for info. (*0-910683-32-8*) Townsnd-Pr.

Manual for One Hundred Percent Export Units, Free Trade & Export Processing Zones, 1991. N. Nabhi. (C). 1990. 110.00 (*0-89771-311-7*) St Mut.

Manual for Overhaul, Repair & Handling of Hamilton 35-Size Chronometer Watch with Parts Catalog. Navy Department Staff. (Illus.). 63p. 1988. pap. 9.95 (*0-930163-35-4*) Arlington Bk.

Manual for Overhaul, Repair & Handling of U. S. Navy Mechanical, Boat & Deck Clocks: Chelsea Type with Parts Catalog. Navy Department Staff. (Illus.). 101p. 1988. pap. 14.95 (*0-930163-20-6*) Arlington Bk.

Manual for Owners of Historic Buildings. (Illus.). 104p. 1995. pap. 20.00 (*1-880067-33-1*) SC Dept of Arch & Hist.

Manual for Pharmacy Technician. Keresztes. 1997. pap. text. write for info. (*0-7216-5007-4*, W B Saunders Co) Harcrt Hlth Sci Grp.

Manual for Pharmacy Technicians. 2nd rev. ed. LC 98-228601. 416p. 1998. 69.00 (*1-879907-79-8*) Am Soc Hlth-Syst.

Manual for Pharmacy Technicians, Pts. 1 & 2. 349p. 1993. ring bd. 50.00 (*1-879907-34-8*) Am Soc Hlth-Syst.

Manual for Physical Agents. 4th ed. Karen W. Hayes. (Illus.). 240p. (C). 1993. pap. text 29.95 (*0-8385-6143-8*, A6143-0) Appleton & Lange.

Manual for Physical Agents. 5th rev. ed. Karen Hayes. LC 99-22306. (Illus.). 169p. (C). 1999. 29.95 (*0-8385-6128-4*, A-6128-1) Appleton & Lange.

Manual for Planetary Leadership. Joshua D. Stone. (Easy-to-Read Encyclopedia of the Spiritual Path Ser.: Vol. 9). 283p. 1998. pap. 14.95 (*1-891824-05-8*) Light Tech Pubng.

Manual for Planning & Implementing the Living Standards Measurement Study Survey. Margaret E. Grosh & Juan Munoz. (Living Standards Measurement Study Ser.: No. 126R). (RUS.). 312p. 1998. pap. 22.00 (*0-8213-4155-3*, 14155) World Bank.

Manual for Planning & Implementing the Living Standards Measurement Study Survey. Margaret E. Grosh & Juan Munoz. (Living Standards Measurement Study Ser.: No. 126S). (SPA.). 304p. 1999. pap. 22.00 (*0-8213-4316-5*, 14316) World Bank.

Manual for Practice Before Boards of Contract Appeals, Recent Developments. 58p. 1983. pap. text 2.50 (*1-56986-092-0*) Federal Bar.

Manual for Practice Before Boards of Government Contract Appeals. 130p. 1981. pap. text 5.00 (*1-56986-091-2*) Federal Bar.

Manual for Practice of International Trade Law. 455p. 1984. pap. text 15.00 (*1-56986-208-7*) Federal Bar.

Manual for Preventing Spills of Hazardous Substances at Fixed Facilities. L. Unterberg et al. 208p. 1988. 48.95 (*0-89116-068-X*) Hemisp Pub.

Manual for Priests. Ed. by Earle H. Maddux. 301p. 1996. reprint ed. 29.95 (*1-886412-19-7*) Preserv Press.

Manual for Professionals Who Work with the Substance Abusing Mentally Ill. Robert D. Thompson. (Illus.). 103p. (Orig.). 1989. pap. 15.00 (*0-9624700-0-7*) Arapahoe Mental Hlth Ctr.

Manual for Profile Measurement: Operation Field Guidelines. 130p. (C). 1994. pap. text 20.00 (*0-309-05759-0*, SHRP-P-378) SHRP.

Manual for Quality Control for Plants & Production of Architectural Precast Concrete. 226p. 30.00 (*0-937040-06-1*, MNL-117-77) P-PCI.

Manual for Quality Control for Plants & Production of Precast Prestressed Concrete Products. 3rd ed. 1985. 60.00 (*0-937040-05-3*, MNL-116-85) P-PCI.

Manual for Radiation Oncology Nursing Practice & Education. rev. ed. Ed. by Deborah Watkins-Broner et al. (Illus.). 80p. 1998. pap. text 25.00 (*1-890504-07-6*) Oncology Nursing.

Manual for Rapid Laboratory Viral Diagnosis. J. Almeida & P. Atanasiu. (WHO Offset Publications: No. 47). 48p. 1979. 4.00 (*92-4-170047-5*) World Health.

Manual for Regulating Air Conditioning Installations (Including Set of Forms) BSRIA Staff. (C). 1975. 60.00 (*0-86022-009-5*, Pub. by Build Servs Info Assn) St Mut.

Manual for Regulating Water Systems. BSRIA Staff. (C). 1979. 75.00 (*0-86022-069-9*, Pub. by Build Servs Info Assn) St Mut.

Manual for Retirement Counselors. Harold Geist. LC 87-90980. 1988. 15.00 (*0-87212-206-9*) Libra.

Manual for Rural Water Supply. Ed. by University of Saint-Gall Switzerland, Swiss Centre. (C). 1988. 250.00 (*0-7855-6703-8*, Pub. by Scientific) St Mut.

Manual for Selection of Consultants. rev. ed. Christopher K. Ahoy & Frederick W. King. Ed. by Ken Meraw et al. LC 88-70743. (Illus.). 248p. (C). 1991. student ed. 85.00 (*0-317-90976-2*) Compr Facilities Mgmt.

Manual for Setting up Prepared Childbirth Classes for Cesarean Parents. 2nd ed. Beth Shearer. 56p. 1983. pap. text 7.00 (*0-318-41356-6*) C Sec.

Manual for SIS Micro-Computer Software System. Arthur R. Rasch. Ed. by Robert Ussery. (Illus.). 101p. (C). 1987. student ed. 45.00 (*0-317-91111-2*, SIS030-M) Summa Info Systs.

Manual for Small & Medium-Sized Law Libraries. Devra L. Altman. LC 76-372536. (Research Contributions of the American Bar Foundation Ser.: 1976, No. 2). 35p. reprint ed. pap. 30.00 (*0-608-12377-3*, 205212900038) Bks Demand.

Manual for Small Industrial Business: Project Design & Appraisal. LC 95-210766. (UNIDO General Stuides). 275p. 25.00 (*92-1-106295-0*, E.UNIDO.94.11.E) UN.

Manual for Social Skills Training in Young People with Parent & Teacher Programmes. Lindy Petersen & Anne F. Gannoni. (C). 1992. 100.00 (*0-86431-116-8*, Pub. by Aust Council Educ Res) St Mut.

Manual for Social Surveys on Food Habits & Consumption in Developing Countries. A. P. Den Hartog et al. 153p. 1995. pap. 16.00 (*3-8236-1237-9*, Pub. by Backhuys Pubs) Balogh.

Manual for Staging of Cancer. 2nd ed. American Joint Committee on Cancer. Ed. by Oliver H. Beahrs & Max H. Myers. (Illus.). 220p. 1983. text 19.50 (*0-397-50594-9*, 65-07594, Lppncott) Lppncott W & W.

Manual for Staging of Cancer. 5th ed. Irvin D. Fleming et al. (Illus.). 300p. 1997. pap. text 49.00 (*0-397-58414-8*) Lppncott W & W.

Manual for State Legislative Programs - Prepared by the State Legislation Committee, American Institute of Certified Public Accountants. 2nd ed. American Institute of Certified Public Accountants. LC 82-199346. 59p. reprint ed. pap. 30.00 (*0-7837-0080-6*, 204033800016) Bks Demand.

Manual for Stewardship Development Programs in the Congregation. Thomas R. Gossen et al. LC 98-8757. 48p. 1996. pap. 11.95 (*0-8192-1679-8*) Morehouse Pub.

Manual for Structured Group Treatment with Adolescent Sexual Offenders. Ineke F. Way & Thomas J. Balthazor. LC 90-91853. 132p. (Orig.). 1990. pap. 18.95 (*0-9627375-0-X*) Jalice Pubs.

Manual for Successful Hunters: Why 10of the Hunters Harvest 90of the Game. Tony Russ. (Illus.). 400p. (Orig.). 1999. pap. 24.95 (*0-9639869-1-0*) Northern Pubng.

Manual for Survival for Women in Nontraditional Employment. Assn. for Union Democracy Women's Project Staff & NOW Legal Defense & Education Fund Staff. 154p. 1993. pap. 6.00 (*0-614-29600-5*) Assn Union Demo.

Manual for Targeted Intervention Research on Sexually Transmitted Illnesses with Community Members. Deborah L. Helitzer-Allen & Hubert A. Allen, Jr. (Illus.). vii, 122p. 1994. pap. text 25.00 (*0-9641694-0-1*) H Allen & Assocs.

Manual for Teacher Training in the African American Church. Oneal C. Sandidge. (Illus.). 64p. 1996. pap. text, teacher ed. 16.95 (*1-886094-31-4*) Chicago Spectrum.

Manual for Teacher Training in the African American Church. Oneal C. Sandidge. (Illus.). 48p. 1995. pap. 9.00 (*0-8059-3773-0*) Dorrance.

Manual for Teachers to Accompany Cases & Materials on Contracts. Edward Allan Farnsworth & William F. Young. (University Casebook Ser.). 282p. 1995. pap. text. write for info. (*1-56662-326-X*) Foundation Pr.

Manual for Teachers to Accompany Payment Systems & Credit Instruments. Clayton P. Gillette et al. (University Casebook Ser.). 636p. 1996. pap. text, teacher ed. write for info. (*1-56662-436-3*) Foundation Pr.

Manual for the Adjudication of Grievances. rev. ed. 29p. 1989. 7.00 (*0-87101-163-8*) Natl Assn Soc Wkrs.

Manual for the American Negro: His History & Literature. Daniel C. Smith. (Series I). 1969. pap. 2.00 (*0-405-01802-9*, 115) Ayer.

Manual for the Basic Course in English: Structure. Ester Torrado de Marcano & Rhenna L. Adams. xi, 287p. (C). 1985. reprint ed. student ed. 8.75 (*0-8477-3314-9*) U of PR Pr.

Manual for the Calligraphic Arts. Ed. by M. Jane Van Milligen. (Illus.). 124p. (Orig.). 1986. pap. 14.95 (*0-9617137-0-4*) Ctr Callig KS.

Manual for the Certification on Labs Analyzing Drinking Water. 4th rev. ed. U. S. Environmental Protection Agency Staff. (Illus.). 260p. 1997. 34.00 (*1-892209-05-5*, 1832) Env Compli Rep.

Manual for the Chemical Analysis of Metals, No. 25. Ed. by Thomas R. Dulski. LC 96-1836. (Manual Ser.: Vol. 25). (Illus.). 260p. 1996. text 89.00 (*0-8031-2066-4*, MNL25) ASTM.

Manual for the Child Behavior Checklist - 2-3 & 1992 Profile. Thomas M. Achenbach. LC 92-60136. 210p. (Orig.). 1992. pap. 25.00 (*0-938565-20-6*) U of VT Psych.

Manual for the Child Behavior Checklist 4-18 & 1991 Profile. Thomas M. Achenbach. LC 90-72107. (Illus.). 288p. (Orig.). 1991. pap. 25.00 (*0-938565-08-7*) U of VT Psych.

Manual for the Deliverance Worker see Manual de Liberacion para Obreros Cristianos

Manual for the Deliverance Worker. Frank Marzullo & Tom Snyder. 112p. 1990. pap. write for info. (*1-892363-07-0*) Christian Covenant.

Manual for the Determination of Supercompressibility Factors of Natural Gas. American Gas Association Pipeline Research Committ. 407p. 1963. pap. 12.00 (*0-318-12650-8*, L00340) Am Gas Assn.

Manual for the Determination of the Clinical Role of Anaerobic Microbiology. Ed. by Lorraine S. Gall & Phyllis E. Riely. 96p. 1981. 58.00 (*0-8493-5935-X*, QR67, CRC Reprint) Franklin.

Manual for the Development of Criminal Justice Statistics. (Studies in Methods, Series F: No. 43). 68p. pap. 8.50 (*92-1-161269-1*, E.86.XVII.16) UN.

Manual for the Development of Statistical Information for Disability: Programmes & Policies. LC 96-173818. 132p. pap. 12.50 (*92-1-161380-9*) UN.

Manual for the Examination of Bone. Colin Anderson. 128p. 1982. 78.00 (*0-8493-0725-2*, RC930, CRC Reprint) Franklin.

Manual for the Homemaker/Home Health Aide. Elizabeth Hazen Willborn. LC 65-5443. (Illus.). 342p. 1988. pap. text 25.95 (*0-397-54635-1*, Lippncott) Lppncott W & W.

***Manual for the Identification of Plants Cultivated in Europe, Both Out-of-Doors & Under Glass: Dicotyledons Part IV - Longaniaceae to Compositae, Vol. 6.** Ed. by The European Garden Flora Editorial Committee & James Cullen. (The European Garden Flora). (Illus.). 750p. (C). 2000. text Price not set. (*0-521-42097-0*) Cambridge U Pr.

Manual for the Identification of the Birds of Minnesota & Neighboring States. rev. ed. Thomas S. Roberts. LC QL0684.M6R47. (Illus.). 295p. 1955. reprint ed. pap. 91.50 (*0-608-00840-0*, 206163100010) Bks Demand.

Manual for the Laboratory Assistant. Seth A. Morgan. pap. 4.95 (*0-89741-007-6*) Gila River.

Manual for the Lawyer's Assistant. 2nd ed. National Association of Legal Secretaries (NALS) S. 1118p. 1991. reprint ed. text 32.95 (*0-314-41162-3*) West Pub.

Manual for the Lawyer's Assistant. 3rd ed. LC 98-193434. 1060p. 1998. 44.95 (*0-314-21467-4*) West Pub.

Manual for the Lawyer's Assistant (NALS) 3rd ed. Kaye Aoki. 1200p. (C). 1994. pap. text. write for info. (*0-314-04069-2*) West Pub.

Manual for the Legal Assistant. 2nd ed. Nala. Date not set. pap. text, teacher ed. 21.50 (*0-314-92995-9*) West Pub.

Manual for the Medical Officers of the United States Army. Charles Greenleaf. (American Civil War Medical Ser.: No. 9). 199p. 1992. reprint ed. 45.00 (*0-930405-39-0*) Norman SF.

Manual for the Organization of Scientific Congresses. Helena B. Lemp. 1978. pap. 28.75 (*3-8055-2962-7*) S Karger.

Manual for the Peacemaker: An Iroquois Legend to Heal Self & Society. Jean Houston. (Illus.). 214p. 1995. 18.00 (*0-8356-0709-7*, Quest) Theos Pub Hse.

Manual for the Peacemaker: An Iroquois Legend to Heal Self & Society. Jean Houston. (Illus.). 177p. 1997. pap. 12.00 (*0-8356-0735-6*, Quest) Theos Pub Hse.

Manual for the Penitent. 48p. 1992. pap. 1.95 (*0-8146-6014-2*, Pueblo Bks) Liturgical Pr.

Manual for the Pikunas Graphoscopic Scale. 3rd ed. Justin Pikunas. LC 81-43841. (Illus.). 70p. (Orig.). 1982. 16.50 (*0-8191-2351-X*) U Pr of Amer.

Manual for the Practice of U. S. Import Law (1990) Federal Bar Association Staff. 250p. 1995. ring bd. 200.00 (*90-6544-962-0*) Kluwer Law Intl.

Manual for the Preparation of Assignments on Audio Cassette. Deakin University Press Staff. 71p. (C). 1987. 24.00 (*0-7300-0261-6*, Pub. by Deakin Univ) St Mut.

Manual for the Preparation of Industrial Feasibility Studies. 386p. 45.00 (*92-1-106270-5*, E.91.III.E.18) UN.

Manual for the Preparation of Industrial Feasibility Studies. 386p. 1991. 45.00 (*92-1-062705-9*); 25.00 (*92-1-106269-1*, 91.III.E.18) UN.

Manual for the Preparation of Industrial Feasibility Studies. 1979. reprint ed. pap. 22.00 (*92-1-106109-1*, E.78.II.B.5) UN.

Manual for the Primary Animal Health Care Worker. LC 96-127666. 326p. 1994. 45.00 (*92-5-103258-0*, F32580, Pub. by FAO) Bernan Associates.

Manual for the Proper Use of Inoculants & Pelleting for Legumes. V. Iswaran. (Illus.). 195p. 1983. 15.00 (*0-88065-239-X*) Scholarly Pubns.

Manual for the Provision of Intrauterine Devices IUDS. R. Gray. (Nonserial Publication). 51p. 1980. pap. text 10.00 (*92-4-154143-1*, 1150121) World Health.

Manual for the Safe Handling of Flammable & Combustible Liquids & Other Hazardous Products. U. S. Coast Guard Staff. (Illus.). 154p. 1976. reprint ed. pap. 16.00 (*0-934114-92-7*, BK-454) Marine Educ.

Manual for the Selection of Optimal Maintenance Levels of Service. (National Cooperative Highway Research Program Report Ser.: No. 273). 80p. 1984. 9.20 (*0-309-03853-7*, NR273) Transport Res Bd.

Manual for the Semistructured Clinical Interview for Children & Adolescents. Stephanie H. McConaughy & Thomas M. Achenbach. 228p. (Orig.). 1994. pap. 25.00 (*0-938565-32-X*) U of VT Psych.

Manual for the Shapiro Control Inventory. Deane H. Shapiro, Jr. 200p. (Orig.). 1994. pap. 39.50 (*1-879858-01-0*) Behaviordyne.

Manual for the Solution of Military Ciphers. Parker Hitt. 119p. 1976. reprint ed. pap. 20.80 (*0-89412-001-8*) Aegean Park Pr.

Manual for the SVIB-SII (Strong Interest Inventory, Form T325 of the Strong Vocational Interest Blanks) 3rd ed. Jo-Ida C. Hansen. 1981. write for info. (*0-8047-1104-6*) Stanford U Pr.

Manual for the Teacher's Report Form & 1991 Profile. Thomas M. Achenbach. LC 90-72108. (Illus.). viii, 214p. (Orig.). 1991. pap. 25.00 (*0-938565-10-9*) U of VT Psych.

Manual for the Use of Law Books. George B. Weisiger. LC 94-76711. Vol. 13. ix, 107p. 1994. reprint ed. 45.00 (*0-89941-891-0*, 308350) W S Hein.

Manual for the Use of Prospectors on the Mineral Lands of the U. S. 5th ed. Henry N. Copp. Ed. by Stuart Bruchey. LC 78-53538. (Development of Public Land Law in the U. S. Ser.). 1979. reprint ed. lib. bdg. 16.95 (*0-405-11371-4*) Ayer.

Manual for the Uses of General Aptitude Test Battery, Section 1: Administration & Scoring (forms C & D) (controlled Item) Government Printing Office Staff. 149p. 1986. ring bd. 13.00 (*0-16-003950-9*) USGPO.

Manual for the Videofluorographic Study of Swallowing. 2nd rev. ed. Jerilyn A. Logemann. LC 92-41623. (C). 1993. spiral bd. 44.00 (*0-89079-584-3*, 6599) PRO-ED.

Manual for the Young Adult Self-Report & Young Adult Behavior Checklist. Thomas M. Achenbach. LC 96-61686. (Illus.). 212p. (Orig.). 1997. pap. 25.00 (*0-938565-45-1*) U of VT Psych.

Manual for the Youth Self-Report & 1991 Profile. Thomas M. Achenbach. LC 90-72109. (Illus.). 221p. (Orig.). 1991. pap. 25.00 (*0-938565-09-5*) U of VT Psych.

Manual for Theory & Practice of Counseling & Psychotherapy. 5th ed. Gerald Corey. LC 95-15144. 230p. 1995. pap., student ed. 16.50 (*0-534-33857-7*) Brooks-Cole.

Manual for Theory & Practice of Group Counseling. 2nd ed. Gerald Corey. (Psychology-Counseling Ser.). 160p. (C). 1984. pap. 12.00 (*0-534-03428-4*) Brooks-Cole.

M

An Asterisk (*) at the beginning of an entry indicates that the title is appearing for the first time.

Manual for Traditional American Rug Hooking. rev. ed. Jeanne H. Fallier. (Illus.). 60p. 1987. pap. 8.95 (*0-9611554-4-2*) Rugging Rm.
Manual for Training in Research & Innovation Management. A. Forti. 144p. 1994. text 53.00 (*981-02-1653-X*) World Scientific Pub.
Manual for Training Leaders in Exploring Parenting. (Exploring Parenting Curriculum Ser.). 49p. 1988. write for info. (*1-55672-034-3*) US HHS.
Manual for Training Reclamation Inspectors in the Fundamentals of Soils & Revegetation. Willis G. Vogel. (Illus.). 178p. (C). 1998. pap. text 35.00 (*0-7881-7306-5*) DIANE Pub.
Manual for Training the Program Assistant in Adult Day Care. 163p. 1993. ring bd. write for info. (*0-910883-68-8*, 2052) Natl Coun Aging.
Manual for Translators of Mathematical Russian. rev. ed. S. H. Gould. LC 91-20605. 42p. 1991. pap. 21.00 (*0-8218-0172-4*, MTR) Am Math.
Manual for Travel Counsellors. 15th rev. ed. Kenneth N. Carlson. LC 89-114573. (Illus.). 304p. 1996. pap. text 27.50 (*0-938428-08-X*) Rain Belt.
Manual for Ultasonography in Medicine. Jeffrey I. Schwartz. Ed. by Laura Becker. 209p. (Orig.). 1996. text 55.00 (*0-9655671-0-9*) EMI Medical.
Manual for Use of the New Dale-Chall Readability Formula. Jeanne S. Chall & Edgar Dale. 40p. (Orig.). 1994. pap. text 14.95 (*1-57129-012-5*) Brookline Bks.
Manual for Using the MMPI-2 As a Therapeutic Intervention. Stephen E. Finn. LC 96-33867. (C). 1996. 16.95 (*0-8166-2885-8*) U of Minn Pr.
Manual for Writers of Term Papers, Theses, & Dissertations. Kate L. Turabian. LC 95-43267. (Chicago Guides to Writing, Editing & Publishing Ser.). (C). 1996. 27.50 (*0-226-81626-5*) U Ch Pr.
Manual for Writers of Term Papers, Theses & Dissertations. 4th ed. Kate L. Turabian. LC 73-77792. 1997. pap. 6.95 (*0-226-81621-4*); lib. bdg. 16.00 (*0-226-81620-6*, P46) U Ch Pr.
Manual for Writers of Term Papers, Theses, & Dissertations. 5th ed. Kate L. Turabian. LC 86-19128. x, 310p. (C). 1997. 26.50 (*0-226-81624-9*); pap. 9.95 (*0-226-81625-7*) U Ch Pr.
Manual for Writers of Term Papers, Theses & Dissertations. 6th ed. Kate L. Turabian. LC 95-43267. (Illus.). 318p. 1996. pap. 13.00 (*0-226-81627-3*) U Ch Pr.
***Manual Fraga Iribarne & the Rebirth of Spanish Conservatism, 1939-1990.** John Gilmour. LC 99-21895. (Spanish Studies: Vol. 3). 360p. 1999. text 99.95 (*0-7734-8029-3*) E Mellen.
Manual Gastro ISE. Gregory Eastwood. 1988. 15.95 (*0-316-20399-8*, Little Brwn Med Div) Lppncott W & W.
***Manual Greek Lexicon of the New Testament.** G. Abbott-Smith. 528p. 1999. pap. 24.95 (*0-567-08684-4*) T&T Clark Pubs.
Manual Greek Lexicon of the New Testament. 3rd ed. G. Abbott-Smith. 528p. 1937. 34.95 (*0-567-01001-5*, Pub. by T & T Clark) Bks Intl VA.
Manual Gyn Asia. 2nd ed. Carol S. Havens. 1991. 10.95 (*0-316-35099-0*, Little Brwn Med Div) Lppncott W & W.
Manual Gyn-Onc ISE. M. Steven Piver. 1989. 15.95 (*0-316-70937-9*, Little Brwn Med Div) Lppncott W & W.
Manual Handling. Neville Williams. (Safety Instruction Booklet Ser.). (Illus.). 24p. 1994. pap. 45.00 (*1-85573-168-1*, Pub. by Woodhead Pubng) Am Educ Systs.
***Manual Handling Law & Litigation.** Jeffry Zindani. 256p. 1998. 54.50 (*1-85811-181-1*, Pub. by CLT Prof) Gaunt.
Manual ICU Asia, No. 2. James M. Rippe. 1989. 10.95 (*0-316-74714-9*) Little.
Manual ICU ISE. 2nd ed. James M. Rippe. 1989. 15.95 (*0-316-74713-0*, Little Brwn Med Div) Lppncott W & W.
Manual ICU Medicine. 2nd ed. James M. Rippe. 614p. 1989. spiral bd. 38.00 (*0-316-74712-2*) Lppncott W & W.
Manual Ilustrado de Laboratorio Para Botanica. 2nd ed. Sarah Lugo de Kaplan. 145p. (C). 1990. pap. text, student ed. 24.95 (*1-881375-10-2*) Libreria Univ.
Manual Ilustrado de Laboratorio Para Curso Basico de Biologia. Sarah Lugo de Kaplan. 124p. (C). 1980. pap. text, student ed. 24.95 (*1-881375-09-9*) Libreria Univ.
Manual Ilustrado de Laboratorio Para Zoologia. Virgilio Biaggi. 129p. (C). 1975. pap. text, student ed. 24.95 (*1-881375-11-0*) Libreria Univ.
Manual Intentional Logic. Johan Van Bentham. 1986. pap. text 8.95 (*0-226-12210-7*) U Ch Pr.
Manual Internacional de Seguranca Maritima. Lorne & MacLean Marine & Offshore Publications Sta. (POR.). (C). 1987. 250.00 (*0-7855-4375-9*, Pub. by Lorne & MacLean Marine) St Mut.
Manual Joslin para la Diabetes: The Joslin Guide to Diabetes. Richard S. Beaser & Joan V. Hill. 352p. 1996. per. 15.00 (*0-684-82387-X*, Libros) S&S Trade Pap.
Manual Kinesiology. (C). 1993. 11.00 (*0-8087-9369-1*) Pearson Custom.
Manual Labor: Building Computer Manuals That Really Work. Susan B. Smith & Lisa M. Ruddolo. (Technical Writing Ser.). 200p. 1993. pap. 27.95 (*1-883140-00-5*) Sftware Res.
Manual Material Handling: Understanding & Preventing Back Trauma. Ed. by AIHA Ergonomics Committee. (Illus.). (C). 1993. reprint ed. pap. 40.00 (*0-932627-54-4*, 149-ER-89) Am Indus Hygiene.
Manual Materials Handling: Design & Injury Control Through Ergonomics. M. M. Ayoub & Anil Mital. 350p. 1989. 126.00 (*0-85066-383-0*) Taylor & Francis.
***Manual Medicine: Therapy.** W. Schneider et al. (Illus.). 2001. 49.00 (*0-86577-926-0*) Thieme Med Pubs.
Manual Medicine - Diagnostics. 2nd ed. Jiri Dvorak et al. (Illus.). 1990. text 85.00 (*0-86577-306-8*) Thieme Med Pubs.
Manual Medicine - Therapy. Schneider. (Illus.). 160p. 1988. 65.00 (*0-86577-266-5*) Thieme Med Pubs.
Manual Merck de Diagnostico y Terapeutica. 9th ed. Merck & Co., Inc. Staff. Ed. by Robert Berkow. (SPA.). 3122p. 1994. 150.00 (*0-7859-9597-8*) Fr & Eur.
Manual Metal-Arc Welding. 1987. 60.00 (*0-85083-026-5*) St Mut.
Manual Nutritional: International Edition. 2nd ed. David H. Alpers. 1988. 15.95 (*0-316-03514-9*) Little.
Manual Nutritional Therapeutics: Asia. 2nd ed. David H. Alpers. 1988. 10.95 (*0-316-03517-3*) Little.
Manual Ocular, No. 3. Deborah Pavan-Langston. 1991. 10.95 (*0-316-69548-3*, Little Brwn Med Div) Lppncott W & W.
Manual of a Mystic. Tr. by F. L. Woodward from PLI. (C). 1916. 26.50 (*0-86013-003-7*, Pub. by Pali Text) Elsevier.
Manual of a Perfect Atheist. Eduardo Del Rio Garcia. Tr. by Samuel Miller from SPA. (Illus.). 156p. (Orig.). 1984. reprint ed. pap. 13.00 (*0-910309-71-X*, 5441) Am Atheist.
Manual of Accident & Emergency Resuscitation. Ed. by Colin E. Robertson & Keith Little. LC 83-1290. (Wiley-Medical Publication). (Illus.). 191p. reprint ed. pap. 59.30 (*0-8357-3927-9*, 203666200004) Bks Demand.
Manual of Accident Prevention in Construction. rev. ed. 296p. 1977. 10.00 (*0-318-13522-1*); 15.00 (*0-318-13523-X*) Assn Gen Con.
Manual of Accreditation Standards for Adventure Programs, 1995. 1995. 65.00 (*0-929361-12-1*) Assn Exper Ed.
Manual of Activities to Improve Perceptual Motor Skills. Michael A. Horvat. (Illus.). 190p. (Orig.). 1989. teacher ed. 35.00 (*1-878276-03-4*) Educ Systs Assocs Inc.
Manual of Acute Coronary Care: A Guide to Patient Management. M. J. Walsh. (Illus.). 118p. 1999. pap. text 19.95 (*1-86036-011-4*, Pub. by E A) OUP.
Manual of Acute Hand Injuries. Ed. by David S. Martin & E. Dale Collins. LC 97-17955. (Illus.). 696p. (C). (gr. 13). 1997. pap. text 49.95 (*0-8151-5861-0*, 25196) Mosby Inc.
Manual of Acute Orthopaedic Therapeutics. 4th ed. Larry D. Iversen & Marc F. Swiontkowski. LC 94-22476. 368p. 1995. spiral bd. 34.95 (*0-316-43439-6*) Lppncott W & W.
Manual of Acute Orthopaedic Therapeutics. 5th ed. Marc F. Swiontkowski. 400p. spiral bd. 39.95 (*0-7817-1909-7*) Lppncott W & W.
Manual of Acute Orthopaedic Therapeutics: International. 3rd ed. Larry D. Iversen. 1986. 15.95 (*0-316-43433-7*, Little Brwn Med Div) Lppncott W & W.
Manual of Acute Pain Management in Children. Ian M. McKenzie. LC 97-3034. 1997. pap. text 35.00 (*0-443-05321-9*) Church.
Manual of Admitting Orders & Therapeutics. 3rd ed. Eric B. Larson & W. Conrad Lilies, Jr. LC 93-26134. 1994. pap. text 31.95 (*0-7216-5268-9*, W B Saunders Co) Harcrt Hlth Sci Grp.
Manual of Adult & Paediatric Medical Oncology. Ed. by S. Monfardini et al. (Illus.). 420p. 1987. 58.95 (*0-387-15347-0*) Spr-Verlag.
Manual of Advanced Prehospital Care. Gail Walraven. (Illus.). 430p. 1978. pap. text 15.95 (*0-87618-995-8*) P-H.
Manual of Advanced Prehospital Care. 2nd ed. Gail Walraven. (Illus.). 416p. 1984. pap. text 28.00 (*0-89303-252-2*) P-H.
***Manual of Advanced Veterinary Nursing.** Alasdair Moore. (Illus.). 250p. 2000. pap. text 99.95 (*0-905214-51-X*, Pub. by BSAVA) Iowa St U Pr.
Manual of Adverse Drug Interactions. 5th ed. J. P. Griffin & P. F. D'Arcy. LC 97-8345. 664p. 1997. write for info. (*0-444-82406-5*) Elsevier.
Manual of Aesthetic Surgery. Ed. by J. C. Fisher et al. (Comprehensive Manuals of Surgical Specialties Ser.). (Illus.). 115p. 1985. 220.00 (*0-387-96045-7*) Spr-Verlag.
Manual of Agricultural Nematology. Ed. by William R. Nickle. (Illus.). 1064p. 1991. text 275.00 (*0-8247-8397-2*) Dekker.
Manual of Akkadian. David Marcus. LC 78-63068. 1978. pap. text 19.50 (*0-8191-0608-9*) U Pr of Amer.
Manual of Allergy & Immunology. 3rd ed. Ed. by Glenn J. Lawlor, Jr. et al. LC 94-26782. 608p. 1995. spiral bd. 38.00 (*0-316-51681-3*, Little Brwn Med Div) Lppncott W & W.
Manual of Ambulatory Care. Ed. by K. R. Epstein. (Illus.). 416p. 1995. pap. 44.95 (*0-86542-340-7*) Blackwell Sci.
***Manual of Ambulatory General Surgery.** Shukri K. Shami & Delilah A. Hassanally. LC 99-17030. (Illus.). xiii, 140p. 1999. 88.00 (*1-85233-131-3*, Pub. by Spr-Verlag) Spr-Verlag.
Manual of Ambulatory Pediatrics. 4th ed. Rose W. Boynton. LC 97-35923. 528p. 1998. spiral bd. 38.95 (*0-397-55472-9*) Lppncott W & W.
Manual of Ambulatory Surgery. Ed. by K. J. Kassity. (Comprehensive Manuals of Surgical Specialties Ser.). (Illus.). 266p. 1982. 155.00 (*0-387-90700-9*) Spr-Verlag.
Manual of Analytical Methods for Measuring Chemical Exposures in the Workplace. 1995. lib. bdg. 9995.95 (*0-8490-7523-8*) Gordon Pr.
Manual of Anatomy & Physiology: Brief Version. Anne B. Donnersberger et al. (Life Science Ser.). 344p. (C). 1989. pap., teacher ed. 10.00 (*0-669-18012-2*) Jones & Bartlett.
Manual of Ancient Sculpture. Pierre Paris. Ed. by Jane E. Harrison. (Illus.). xvi, 369p. 1984. lib. bdg. 55.00 (*0-89241-373-5*) Caratzas.
Manual of Anesthesia. 3rd ed. John C. Snow. (Spiral Manual Ser.). 1988. spiral bd. 19.50 (*0-316-80223-9*, Little Brwn Med Div) Lppncott W & W.
Manual of Anesthesia in Cancer Care. Ed. by William S. Howland et al. LC 86-16797. 333p. (Orig.). reprint ed. pap. 103.30 (*0-7837-6263-1*, 204597500010) Bks Demand.
Manual of Anesthesiology. 2nd ed. John C. Snow. 1982. 32.95 (*0-316-80222-0*, Little Brwn Med Div) Lppncott W & W.
Manual of Ankle & Foot Arthroscopy. Richard O. Lundeen. (Manuals in Podiatric Surgery Ser.). (Illus.). 121p. (Orig.). 1991. pap. text 49.00 (*0-443-08694-X*) Church.
Manual of Antenatal Pathology & Hygiene: The Embryo. John W. Ballantyne. (Classics in Human Development Ser.: Issue 1). 697p. 1991. reprint ed. text 75.00 (*1-879554-00-3*) Greenwood-Gene.
Manual of Antibiotics & Infectious Diseases. 8th ed. John E. Conte, Jr. LC 94-23078. (Illus.). 384p. 1995. pap. 32.00 (*0-683-02068-4*) Lppncott W & W.
Manual of Antibiotics & Infectious Diseases. 9th ed. John E. Conte, Jr. 512p. pap. text 39.95 (*0-7817-2316-7*) Lppncott W & W.
***Manual of Antisense Methodology.** Gunther H. Hartmann & Stefan Endres. LC 99-24715. (Perspectives in Antisense Science Ser.). 205p. 1999. write for info. (*0-7923-8539-X*) Kluwer Academic.
Manual of Aphasia Therapy. Nancy Helm-Estabrooks. pap. 22.50 (*0-316-35523-2*) Little.
Manual of Aphasia Therapy. Nancy Helm-Estabrooks & Martin L. Albert. LC 90-5630. (Illus.). 284p. 1991. pap. text 31.00 (*0-89079-404-9*, 1588) PRO-ED.
***Manual of Applied Field Hydrogeology.** Willis D. Weight. (Illus.). 640p. 2000. 79.95 (*0-07-069639-X*) McGraw.
Manual of Applied Geology for Engineers. Ed. by Institution of Civil Engineers Staff. 414p. 1976. pap. 37.00 (*0-7277-0038-3*, Pub. by T Telford) RCH.
Manual of Applied Techniques for Biological Electron Microscopy. Michael J. Dykstra. LC 93-23118. (Illus.). 272p. (C). 1993. text 39.50 (*0-306-44449-6*, Kluwer Plenum) Kluwer Academic.
Manual of Aquatic Plants. rev. ed. Norman C. Fassett. (Illus.). 416p. 1957. 29.95 (*0-299-01450-9*) U of Wis Pr.
Manual of Aquatic Sediment Sampling. Alena Mudroch & Jose Azcue. 240p. 1995. lib. bdg. 65.00 (*1-56670-029-9*, L1029) Lewis Pubs.
***Manual of Archival Description.** 3rd ed. Margaret Procter & Michael Cook. LC 00-21004. 352p. 2000. 104.95 (*0-566-08258-6*, Pub. by Ashgate Pub) Ashgate Pub Co.
Manual of Archival Description 2nd Edition. Cook. 1990. 78.95 (*0-566-03634-7*) Ashgate Pub Co.
Manual of Archival Reprography. Ed. & Compiled by Lajos Kormendy. (ICA Handbook Ser.: Vol. 5). 233p. 1989. lib. bdg. 40.00 (*3-598-20277-6*) K G Saur Verlag.
Manual of Archival Techniques. rev. ed. Ed. by Roland Baumann. LC 82-623264. 150p. 1982. pap. 5.95 (*0-89271-020-9*) Pa Hist & Mus.
Manual of Arms for the Sharps Rifle. 1961. reprint ed. 3.50 (*0-913150-33-9*) Pioneer Pr.
Manual of Arryth Asia. Stephen E. Vlay. 1988. 10.95 (*0-316-90478-3*, Little Brwn Med Div) Lppncott W & W.
Manual of Arryth ISE. Stephen E. Vlay. 1988. 15.95 (*0-316-90477-5*, Little Brwn Med Div) Lppncott W & W.
Manual of Articulation & Phonological Disorders: Infancy Through Adulthood. Ken M. Bleile. (Clinical Competence Ser.). (Illus.). 404p. (C). 1995. pap. 51.95 (*1-56593-343-5*, 0641) Thomson Learn.
Manual of Articulatory Phonetics. rev. ed. William A. Smalley. (Illus.). 528p. (C). 1989. reprint ed. pap. text 42.00 (*0-8191-7398-3*) U Pr of Amer.
Manual of Artistic Colouring, As Applied to Photographs. Alfred H. Wall. LC 72-9244. (Literature of Photography Ser.). 1973. reprint ed. 20.95 (*0-405-04948-X*) Ayer.
Manual of Assessment Keys for Plant Disease. W. C. James. 90p. 1971. 24.00 (*0-89054-081-0*) Am Phytopathol Soc.
Manual of Asthma Management. O'Byrne. 1995. pap. text 52.50 (*0-7020-1781-7*, W B Saunders Co) Harcrt Hlth Sci Grp.
Manual of Astrology. Sepharial. 279p. 1981. pap. 25.00 (*0-89540-066-9*, SB-066, Sun Bks) Sun Pub.
Manual of Athletic Taping: U. S. Version. Sports Medicine Council of British Columbia Staff. (Illus.). 117p. (C). 1995. pap. text 24.95 (*0-8036-0115-8*) Davis Co.
Manual of Australian Constitutional Law. 4th ed. P. H. Lane. xxii, 565p. 1987. pap. 74.50 (*0-455-20771-2*, Pub. by LawBk Co) Gaunt.
Manual of Automotive Radiator Construction & Repair see Automotive Radiator Construction & Restoration for Antique & Classic
Manual of Avian Practice. Agnes E. Rupley. Ed. by Stephanie Donley. LC 96-34618. (Illus.). 576p. 1997. pap. text 49.00 (*0-7216-4083-4*, W B Saunders Co) Harcrt Hlth Sci Grp.
Manual of Aviation Fuel Quality Control Procedures. Ed. by Rick Waite. LC 89-17651. (Manual Ser.: No. 5). (Illus.). 83p. 1989. pap. text 28.00 (*0-8031-1192-4*, MNL5) ASTM.
Manual of Avionics. 3rd ed. Brian Kendal. (Illus.). 300p. 1993. pap. 55.00 (*0-632-03472-6*) Blackwell Sci.
Manual of Babylonian Jewish Aramaic. David Marcus. LC 80-6073. 104p. (Orig.). (C). 1981. pap. text 16.00 (*0-8191-1363-8*) U Pr of Amer.
Manual of Basic Neuropathology. 3rd ed. Jacques Poirier et al. 292p. 1990. pap. text 40.00 (*0-7216-3464-8*, W B Saunders Co) Harcrt Hlth Sci Grp.
Manual of Bed Oncology. Dennis A. Casciato. 1988. 10.95 (*0-316-13069-9*, Little Brwn Med Div) Lppncott W & W.
Manual of Bedfordshire Lace. Pam Robinson. 74p. 1987. pap. 24.50 (*0-903585-20-0*) Robin & Russ.
Manual of Behavior Management Techniques for Physical Educators & Recreators. Ed. by Ron French & Barry Lavay. 435p. (Orig.). 1990. teacher ed. 45.00 (*1-878276-04-2*) Educ Systs Assocs Inc.
Manual of Below-Grade Waterproofing Systems. Justin Henshell. Ed. by C. W. Griffin. (Illus.). 1999. write for info. (*0-9670476-1-7*) Davon Pr.
***Manual of Below-Grade Waterproofing Systems.** Justin Henshell. LC 99-42180. 304p. 1999. 69.95 (*0-471-37730-9*) Wiley.
Manual of Bibliography. Walter T. Rogers. 1977. lib. bdg. 75.00 (*0-8490-2204-5*) Gordon Pr.
Manual of Bioassessment of Aquatic Sediment Quality. Alena Mudroch & Jose M. Azcue. LC 98-229734. 1998. lib. bdg. 79.95 (*1-56670-343-3*) Lewis Pubs.
Manual of Biological Corrosion. Wilkes. LC 96-41145. 304p. 1996. lib. bdg. 75.00 (*0-87371-726-0*, L726) Lewis Pubs.
Manual of Biological Markers of Disease. R. N. Maini. Ed. by W. J. Van Venrooij. LC 96-31174. 744p. (C). 1997. lib. bdg. 330.00 (*0-7923-4242-9*) Kluwer Academic.
Manual of Biological Markers of Disease. Ed. by W. J. Van Venrooij. 744p. (C). 1997. pap. text 102.50 (*0-7923-4243-7*) Kluwer Academic.
Manual of Biological Markers of Disease: Basic Work. Ed. by W. J. Van Venrooij. LC 93-3227. 744p. (C). 1996. ring bd. 337.00 (*0-7923-2219-3*) Kluwer Academic.
Manual of Bone & Soft Tissue Tumors. David Present. 350p. 1996. text 79.50 (*0-397-51414-X*) Lppncott W & W.
***Manual of Bone Densitometry Measurements: An Aid to the Interpretation of Bone Densitometry Measurements in a Clinical Setting.** John Fordham. LC 00-26565. (Illus.). 2000. write for info. (*1-85233-278-6*) Spr-Verlag.
Manual of Bone Marrow Examination. Ed. by Anwarul Islam. 124p. 1997. text 42.00 (*90-5702-009-2*) Gordon & Breach.
Manual of Bone Marrow Examination. Ed. by Anwarul Islam. (Illus.). 160p. 1998. pap. 65.00 (*90-5702-010-6*, Harwood Acad Pubs) Gordon & Breach.
Manual of British Standards in Building Construction & Engineering. Ed. by Edward Smith. (C). 1987. 275.00 (*0-09-170760-9*, Pub. by S Thornes Pubs) St Mut.
Manual of British Standards in Engineering Drawing & Design. Maurice Parker. 226p. (C). 1999. pap. 75.00 (*0-7487-1031-0*, Pub. by S Thornes Pubs) Trans-Atl Phila.
Manual of Buddhism for Advanced Students. Carolina A. Davids. LC 78-72410. reprint ed. 32.50 (*0-404-17274-1*) AMS Pr.
Manual of Buddhism in Its Modern Development. R. Spence Hardy. 550p. (C). 1995. reprint ed. 43.50 (*81-215-0677-8*, Pub. by M Manoharial) Coronet Bks.
Manual of Buddhism in Its Modern Development. Robert S. Hardy. LC 78-72439. reprint ed. 46.50 (*0-404-17305-5*) AMS Pr.
Manual of Buddhist Historical Traditions - Saddhamma - Sangaha. Dhamma-Kitti. Tr. by Bimala Churn Law. LC 78-72418. reprint ed. 21.50 (*0-404-17279-2*) AMS Pr.
Manual of Buddhist Historical Traditions (Saddhammma-sangaha) Dhammakitti et al. LC 99-932500. vi, 140 p. 1999. write for info. (*81-206-1386-4*, Pub. by Asian Educ Servs) S Asia.
Manual of Buddhist Philosophy. William M. McGovern. LC 78-70097. reprint ed. 27.50 (*0-404-17346-2*) AMS Pr.
Manual of Bulbs. Ed. by John Bryan & Mark Griffiths. (Illus.). 446p. 1995. 49.95 (*0-88192-339-7*) Timber.
Manual of Burn Care. fac. ed. Joan E. Nicosia & Jane A. Petro. LC 82-25499. (Illus.). 166p. pap. 51.50 (*0-7837-7288-2*, 204701800005) Bks Demand.
Manual of Burns. W. S. McDougal et al. LC 78-18210. (Comprehensive Manuals of Surgical Specialties Ser.). (Illus.). 1978. 107.00 (*0-387-90319-4*) Spr-Verlag.
Manual of Business French: A Comprehensive Language Guide. Stuart Williams & Nathalie McAndrew-Cazorla. LC 95-37168. (Language Manuals for Business Ser.). 432p. (C). 1996. 85.00 (*0-415-09267-1*); pap. 24.99 (*0-415-12901-X*) Routledge.
Manual of Business German: A Comprehensive Language Guide. Paul Hartley & Gertrud Robins. LC 95-37167. (Language Manuals for Business Ser.). 400p. (C). 1996. 85.00 (*0-415-09266-3*); pap. 24.99 (*0-415-12902-8*) Routledge.
Manual of Business Italian: A Comprehensive Language Guide. Vincent Edwards & Gianfranca G. Shepheard. LC 95-37166. (Language Manuals for Business Ser.). 416p. (C). 1995. 85.00 (*0-415-09265-5*) Routledge.
Manual of Business Italian: A Comprehensive Language Guide. Vincent Edwards & Gianfranca G. Shepheard. LC 95-37166. (Language Manuals for Business Ser.). (ITA.). 416p. (C). 1996. pap. 24.99 (*0-415-12904-4*) Routledge.
Manual of Business Library Practice. 2nd ed. Ed. by Malcolm J. Campbell. LC 84-43215. 248p. 1985. reprint ed. pap. 76.90 (*0-608-02477-5*, 206312100004) Bks Demand.
Manual of Business Spanish: A Comprehensive Language Guide. Michael Gorman & Maria-Luisa Henson. LC 95-36056. (Language Manuals for Business Ser.). 448p. (C). 1996. pap. 24.99 (*0-415-12903-6*) Routledge.
Manual of Business Spanish: A Comprehensive Language Guide. Maria-Luisa Henson & Michael Gorman. LC 95-36056. (Language Manuals for Business Ser.). (SPA.). 448p. (C). 1996. 85.00 (*0-415-09264-7*) Routledge.

M

An Asterisk (*) at the beginning of an entry indicates that the title is appearing for the first time.

*Manual of Cable Osteosyntheses. R. Labitzke. 200p. 2000. (3-540-66508-0) Spr-Verlag.

Manual of Cancer Pain Management. Richard B. Patt. (Illus.). 450p. 1992. write for info. (0-318-69535-9) Lppncott W & W.

Manual of Canine & Feline Cardiology. 2nd ed. Michael S. Miller & Larry P. Tiley. (Illus.). 528p. 1994. pap. text 65.00 (0-7216-5940-3, W B Saunders Co) Harcrt Hlth Sci Grp.

Manual of Canine & Feline Cardiology. 3rd ed. Larry Patrick Tilley & John-Karl Goodwin. (Illus.). 575p. (C). 1999. text. write for info. (0-7216-7721-5, W B Saunders Co) Harcrt Hlth Sci Grp.

*Manual of Canine & Feline Emergency & Critical Care. Ed. by Richard Hammond & Lesley King. (Illus.). 374p. 1999. pap. 92.95 (0-905214-40-4, Pub. by BSAVA) Iowa St U Pr.

Manual of Canine & Feline Gastroenterology. Ed. by D. A. Thomas et al. (Illus.). 268p. 1996. pap. 82.95 (0-8138-1597-5) Iowa St U Pr.

Manual of Canine & Feline Nephrology & Urology. Ed. by John Bainbridge & Jonathan Elliott. (BSAVA Ser.). (Illus.). 232p. 1996. pap. 82.95 (0-8138-1879-6) Iowa St U Pr.

Manual of Canine & Feline Wound Management & Reconstruction. Ed. by John Williams & David A. Fowler. (Illus.). 200p. 1999. pap. 89.95 (0-905214-38-2, Pub. by BSAVA) Iowa St U Pr.

Manual of Canine Behaviour. 2nd ed. Valerie O'Farrell. (Illus.). 132p. 1994. pap. text 51.95 (0-905214-17-X, Pub. by BSAVA) Iowa St U Pr.

Manual of Cardiac Anesthesia. Ed. by Stephen J. Thomas. LC 84-4227. (Illus.). 481p. (Orig.). reprint ed. pap. 149.20 (0-7837-1608-7, 204190000024) Bks Demand.

Manual of Cardiac Anesthesia. 2nd ed. Ed. by Stephen J. Thomas. (Illus.). 608p. (Orig.). 1993. pap. text 72.00 (0-443-08580-3) Church.

Manual of Cardiac Anesthesia. 3rd ed. Thomas. 2000. text 69.00 (0-443-07922-6, W B Saunders Co) Harcrt Hlth Sci Grp.

Manual of Cardiac Surgery. 2nd ed. Bradley J. Harland et al. LC 93-47190. (Illus.). 378p. 1994. 210.00 (0-387-94220-3) Spr-Verlag.

Manual of Cardiac Surgery, Vol. I. B. J. Harlan et al. (Comprehensive Manuals of Surgical Specialties Ser.). (Illus.). 204p. 1980. 120.00 (0-387-90393-3) Spr-Verlag.

Manual of Cardiac Surgery, Vol. II. B. J. Harlan. (Comprehensive Manuals of Surgical Specialties Ser.). (Illus.). 347p. 1981. 161.00 (0-387-90563-4) Spr-Verlag.

Manual of Cardiac Surgical Intensive Care. pap. text. write for info. (0-340-52855-9, Pub. by E A) Routldge.

Manual of Cardiopulmonary Transplantation. A. Kirk et al. 80p. 1993. pap. text 22.50 (0-340-56756-2, Pub. by E A) OUP.

Manual of Cardiovascular Anesthesiology. Charles Kingsley & Kane High. (Illus.). 656p. 1999. pap. text 39.95 (0-07-034773-5) McGraw-Hill HPD.

Manual of Cardiovascular Diagnosis & Therapy. 2nd ed. Joseph S. Alpert & James M. Rippe. (Spiral Manual Ser.). 426p. 1985. spiral bd. 21.00 (0-316-03510-6, Little Brwn Med Div) Lppncott W & W.

Manual of Cardiovascular Diagnosis & Therapy. 4th ed. Joseph S. Alpert & James M. Rippe. LC 95-24885. 416p. 1996. spiral bd. 39.00 (0-316-03531-9) Lppncott W & W.

Manual of Cardiovascular Medicine. Steven Marso et al. LC 99-42919. 600p. 1999. 34.95 (0-683-30685-5) Lppncott W & W.

Manual of Cartomancy & Occult Divination. Arthur E. Waite. 260p. 1994. reprint ed. pap. 16.95 (1-56459-434-3) Kessinger Pub.

Manual of Cartomancy, Fortune-Telling & Occult Divination. Grand Orient. 278p. 1996. reprint ed. spiral bd. 18.00 (0-7873-0646-0) Hlth Research.

Manual of Cataract & Intraocular Lens Surgery. Richard B. Packard & Fiona C. Kinear. (Illus.). 144p. 1991. 90.00 (0-443-04091-5) Church.

Manual of Cataract Surgery. Robert M. Sinskey & Jay V. Patel. 99p. 1987. pap. text 50.00 (0-7506-9958-2) Buttrwrth-Heinemann.

*Manual of Cataract Surgery. 2nd ed. Gavin G. Bahadur & Robert M. Sinskey. LC 99-29627. 128p. 1999. pap. text 45.00 (0-7506-7082-7) Buttrwrth-Heinemann.

Manual of Celestial Photography. 2nd ed. E. S. King. (Illus.). 192p. 1988. reprint ed. pap. 12.95 (0-933346-46-8) Sky Pub.

Manual of Cementing Technique. 2nd ed. K. Draenert et al. LC 99-17758. 140p. 1999. 129.00 (3-540-65437-2) Spr-Verlag.

Manual of Chemical & Biological Methods for Seawater Analysis. Y. Parsons et al. (Illus.). 144p. 1984. text 51.00 (0-08-030288-2, Pergamon Pr); pap. text 35.25 (0-08-030287-4, Pergamon Pr) Elsevier.

Manual of Chemical Peels: Superficial & Medium Depth. Mark G. Rubin. 200p. 1995. text 104.00 (0-397-51506-5) Lppncott W & W.

Manual of Child Development. Sundara Lingham & David R. Harvey. LC 87-15861. (Manual Ser.). (Illus.). 120p. 1988. pap. text 24.95 (0-443-03784-1) Church.

Manual of Child Language Disorders. Stephen M. Camarata. 300p. 2000. 60.95 (1-56593-842-9, 1644) Thomson Learn.

Manual of Child Neurology. Owen B. Evans. (Illus.). 435p. (Orig.). 1986. text 44.95 (0-443-08435-1) Church.

Manual of Childhood Infections. Meredith Davies. (C). 1996. pap. text 41.00 (0-7020-1832-5) Harcourt.

Manual of Chinese-Manchurian Place Names. Times Shuppansha. 1943. 20.00 (0-911586-32-6) Wahr.

Manual of Chinese Metaphor. Charles A. Williams. LC 71-38094. reprint ed. 41.50 (0-404-56969-2) AMS Pr.

Manual of Chiropractic Diagnosis & Therapeutics. National College of Chiropractic Staff. 500p. 1993. pap. 39.95 (0-8016-6468-3) Mosby Inc.

Manual of Christian Doctrine. Louis Berkhof. 1939. pap. 18.00 (0-8028-1647-9) Eerdmans.

Manual of Christian Reformed Church Government. rev. ed. Leonard J. Hofman & Richard R. De Ridder. LC 94-28868. 1994. pap. 14.95 (1-56212-067-0) CRC Pubns.

Manual of Church History, 2 vols. Franz X. Von Funk. Tr. by Luigi Cappadelta. LC 78-168077. 1910. 110.00 (0-404-02646-X) AMS Pr.

Manual of Church History, 2 vols., Set. Albert H. Newman. 1977. lib. bdg. 250.00 (0-8490-2205-3) Gordon Pr.

Manual of Church Order. John L. Dagg. 1992. 21.99 (0-87377-976-2) GAM Pubns.

Manual of Civil Engineering Plant & Equipment. 2nd ed. Ed. by J. M. Paxton. (Illus.). 592p. 1977. 158.50 (0-85334-500-7) Elsevier.

Manual of Class Action Notice Forms. American Bar Association Staff. LC 79-50160. 320p. 1979. pap. 10.00 (0-685-07097-2, 5030023) Amer Bar Assn.

Manual of Classical Bibliography, 2 vols., Set. 2nd ed. Joseph Moss. LC 76-101049. reprint ed. lib. bdg. 193.00 (0-8046-0714-1) Irvington.

Manual of Classification, 1996. Government Printing Office Staff. 1983. ring bd. 126.00 (0-16-016455-9) USGPO.

Manual of Clay Tennis Court Maintenance. Michael R. Humphrey. (Illus.). 74p. 1982. 7.50 (0-9610438-0-6) Bacon St Pr.

Manual of Climbers & Wall Plants. Ed. by J. K. Burras & Mark Griffiths. (New Royal Horticultural Society Dictionary Ser.). (Illus.). 282p. 1994. 72.50 (0-333-61537-9, Pub. by Pan) Trans-Atl Phila.

Manual of Climbers & Wall Plants. J. K. Burras & Mark Griffiths. (Illus.). 304p. 1995. 39.95 (0-88192-299-4) Timber.

Manual of Clinical Child & Adolescent Psychiatry. 2nd rev. ed. Ed. by Kenneth S. Robson. Orig. Title: Manual of Clinical Child Psychiatry. 497p. 1994. spiral bd. 44.50 (0-88048-528-0, 8528) Am Psychiatric.

Manual of Clinical Child Psychiatry see Manual of Clinical Child & Adolescent Psychiatry

Manual of Clinical Child Psychiatry. Kenneth S. Robson. LC 85-26869. 334p. 1986. reprint ed. pap. 103.60 (0-608-02023-0, 206267900003) Bks Demand.

Manual of Clinical Colposcopy. Thomas Julian et al. (Illus.). 212p. 1998. 115.00 (1-85070-639-5) Prthnon Pub.

Manual of Clinical Dietetics. 4th ed. Chicago Dietetic Association Staff & South Surburban Dietetic Association Staff. LC 92-49557. 1992. ring bd. 62.00 (0-88091-108-5, 0127A) Am Dietetic Assn.

Manual of Clinical Dietetics. 5th ed. Chicago Dietetic Association Staff. LC 96-36492. 868p. 1996. 70.00 (0-88091-153-0) Am Dietetic Assn.

Manual of Clinical Evaluation. Mark D. Aronson & Thomas L. Delbanco. (Brown Spiral Manual Ser.). (Illus.). 350p. 1988. 31.95 (0-316-05210-8, Little Brwn Med Div) Lppncott W & W.

Manual of Clinical Exercise Testing, Prescription & Rehabilitation. Ziya Altug & Janet L. Hoffman. Ed. by Jerome L. Martin. (Illus.). 384p. (C). 1993. pap. text 37.95 (0-8385-0241-5, A0241-8) Appleton & Lange.

Manual of Clinical Hematology. 2nd ed. Ed. by Joseph J. Mazza. LC 94-26649. 382p. 1995. spiral bd. 35.95 (0-316-55220-8, Little Brwn Med Div) Lppncott W & W.

Manual of Clinical Hospital Psychiatry. 2nd ed. Ed. by Ole J. Thienhaus. 432p. 1995. spiral bd. 48.50 (0-88048-550-7, 8550) Am Psychiatric.

Manual of Clinical Hysteroscopy: Diagnostic & Therapeutic. R. F. Valle et al. LC 97-18022. (Illus.). 160p. 1998. 89.00 (1-85070-641-7) Prthnon Pub.

Manual of Clinical Laboratory Immunology. 3rd ed. American Society for Microbiology Staff et al. Ed. by Noel R. Rose. LC 85-26675. 1026p. reprint ed. pap. 200.00 (0-7837-4037-9, 204386700011) Bks Demand.

Manual of Clinical Laboratory Immunology. 5th rev. ed. Ed. by Noel R. Rose et al. LC 96-49032. (Illus.). 1282p. 1997. 125.00 (1-55581-118-3) ASM Pr.

Manual of Clinical Laparoscopy. Michael P. Diamond et al. LC 97-18021. (Illus.). 120p. 1998. 72.00 (1-85070-640-9) Prthnon Pub.

Manual of Clinical Magnetic Resonance Imaging: A Practical Guide to Conducting Magnetic Resonance Imaging Examinations of the Head & Body. 2nd ed. Ed. by Jay P. Heiken & Jeffrey J. Brown. 192p. 1990. spiral bd. 39.00 (0-88167-744-2) Lppncott W & W.

Manual of Clinical Magnetic Resonance Imaging: A Practical Guide to Conducting Magnetic Resonance Imaging Examinations of the Head & Body. 2nd ed. Ed. by Jay P. Heiken & Jeffrey J. Brown. LC 90-9036. (Illus.). 192p. reprint ed. pap. 59.60 (0-608-09750-0, 206992300007) Bks Demand.

Manual of Clinical Microbiology. American Society for Microbiology Staff et al. Ed. by Edwin H. Lennette. LC 84-28304. 1165p. reprint ed. pap. 200.00 (0-7837-4036-0, 204386600011) Bks Demand.

Manual of Clinical Microbiology. 7th rev. ed. Ed. by Patrick R. Murray. LC 98-46075. (Illus.). 1800p. 1999. 129.95 (1-55581-126-4) ASM Pr.

Manual of Clinical Nephrology. Jhoong S. Cheich et al. Ed. by Kurt H. Stenzel & Albert L. Rubin. 470p. 1981. text 180.50 (90-247-2397-3) Kluwer Academic.

Manual of Clinical Nutrition. Wiley Staff. 584p. 1994. pap. text 54.95 (0-471-34916-X) Wiley.

Manual of Clinical Nutrition. Robert Goodhart & Michael G. Wohl. LC 64-14481. 279p. reprint ed. pap. 86.50 (0-608-13669-7, 205542800022) Bks Demand.

Manual of Clinical Oncology. 3rd ed. Ed. by Dennis A. Casciato & Barry B. Lowitz. LC 95-9993. 720p. 1995. spiral bd. 37.95 (0-316-13279-9) Lppncott W & W.

Manual of Clinical Oncology. 4th ed. Dennis A. Casciato & Barry B. Lowitz. 704p. spiral bd. 39.95 (0-7817-2159-8) Lppncott W & W.

Manual of Clinical Oncology. 4th rev. ed. Ed. by UICC Staff & International Union Against Cancer Staff. (Illus.). 380p. 1987. pap. 28.00 (0-387-17367-6) Spr-Verlag.

Manual of Clinical Oncology. 5th ed. Ed. by D. K. Hossfeld et al. (UICC International Union Against Cancer Ser.). (Illus.). 384p. 1992. pap. 45.00 (0-387-52769-9) Spr-Verlag.

Manual of Clinical Oncology. 7th ed. Ed. by Raphael E. Pollock et al. (UICC - International Union Against Cancer Ser.). 840p. 1999. pap. 69.95 (0-471-23828-7, Wiley-Liss) Wiley.

Manual of Clinical Oncology: UICC International Union Against Cancer. 6th ed. Ed. by R. R. Love et al. LC 94-37384. 802p. 1994. 49.00 (0-387-58193-6) Spr-Verlag.

Manual of Clinical Problems in Adult Ambulatory Care: With Annotated Key References. 3rd ed. Ed. by Laurie Dornbrand et al. LC 97-1675. (Illus.). 784p. 1997. spiral bd. 34.95 (0-316-19038-1) Lppncott W & W.

Manual of Clinical Problems in Cardiology: With Annotated Key References. 5th ed. David Hillis et al. LC 94-34559. 579p. 1995. spiral bd. 38.00 (0-316-36493-2) Lppncott W & W.

Manual of Clinical Problems in Gastroenterology: With Annotated Key References. 2nd ed. Ed. by Michael M. Van Ness & Sarkis J. Chobanian. LC 93-19183. 352p. 1993. spiral bd. 39.00 (0-316-89726-4) Lppncott W & W.

Manual of Clinical Problems in Infectious Disease. 2nd ed. Nelson M. Gantz et al. 420p. 1986. 28.50 (0-316-30352-6, Little Brwn Med Div) Lppncott W & W.

Manual of Clinical Problems in Infectious Disease. 3rd ed. Nelson M. Gantz et al. LC 94-11938. 528p. 1994. spiral bd. 38.00 (0-316-30349-6) Lppncott W & W.

*Manual of Clinical Problems in Infectious Disease 4th ed. Nelson M. Gantz. LC 98-46884. 13p. 1999. write for info. (0-7817-1910-0) Lppncott W & W.

Manual of Clinical Problems in Nephrology. Burton D. Rose & Robert Black. 375p. 1988. 31.95 (0-316-75637-7, Little Brwn Med Div) Lppncott W & W.

Manual of Clinical Problems in Neurology: With Annotated Key References. J. P. Mohr. (Spiral Manual Ser.). 1984. spiral bd. 21.00 (0-316-57747-2, Little Brwn Med Div) Lppncott W & W.

Manual of Clinical Problems in Obstetrics & Gynecology. 4th ed. Ed. by Michel E. Rivlin & Rick W. Martin. LC 93-35803. 544p. 1994. spiral bd. 34.95 (0-316-74777-7) Lppncott W & W.

Manual of Clinical Problems in Obstetrics & Gynecology. 5th ed. Michel E. Rivlin et al. LC 99-25744. 512p. 1999. spiral bd. 34.95 (0-7817-1723-X) Lppncott W & W.

Manual of Clinical Problems in Obstetrics & Gynecology: With Annotated Key References. 2nd ed. Michael E. Rivlin et al. 448p. 1986. 22.50 (0-316-74769-6, Little Brwn Med Div) Lppncott W & W.

Manual of Clinical Problems in Oncology. 2nd ed. Carol S. Portlock & Donald R. Goffinet. 1986. 27.00 (0-316-71425-9, Little Brwn Med Div) Lppncott W & W.

Manual of Clinical Problems in Ophthalmology. John W. Gittinger. 1987. 10.95 (0-316-31473-0, Little Brwn Med Div) Lppncott W & W.

Manual of Clinical Problems in Pediatrics. 2nd ed. Kenneth B. Roberts. 1985. spiral bd. 22.50 (0-316-74990-7, Little Brwn Med Div) Lppncott W & W.

Manual of Clinical Problems in Pediatrics: With Annotated Key References. 4th ed. Ed. by Kenneth B. Roberts. LC 94-22643. (Illus.). 600p. 1995. spiral bd. 35.95 (0-316-75006-9, Little Brwn Med Div) Lppncott W & W.

Manual of Clinical Problems in Psychiatry. Steven E. Hyman. 1990. 15.95 (0-316-38725-8) Little.

Manual of Clinical Problems in Psychiatry. Steven E. Hyman. 1990. 10.95 (0-316-38723-1, Little Brwn Med Div) Lppncott W & W.

Manual of Clinical Problems in Psychiatry: With Annotated Key References. Steven E. Hyman. 1990. 34.95 (0-316-38722-3, Little Brwn Med Div) Lppncott W & W.

Manual of Clinical Problems in Pulmonary Medicine. Richard A. Bordow. 1991. 10.95 (0-316-10271-7, Little Brwn Med Div) Lppncott W & W.

Manual of Clinical Problems in Pulmonary Medicine. 2nd ed. Ed. by Richard A. Bordow et al. (Spiral Manual Ser.). 1985. 24.50 (0-316-10265-2, Little Brwn Med Div) Lppncott W & W.

Manual of Clinical Problems in Pulmonary Medicine: With Annotated Key References. 4th ed. Ed. by Richard A. Bordow & Kenneth M. Moser. 576p. 1995. spiral bd. 37.95 (0-316-10270-9) Lppncott W & W.

Manual of Clinical Problems in Urology. Martin I. Resnick. 298p. 1989. spiral bd. 36.00 (0-316-74054-3, Little Brwn Med Div) Lppncott W & W.

Manual of Clinical Procedures in the Dog & Cat. 2nd ed. Stephen Crow. 271p. 1997. pap. text 34.95 (0-397-51588-X) Lppncott W & W.

Manual of Clinical Psychiatric Nursing. 2nd ed. Sue Ritter & Kevin Gournay. (Illus.). 352p. 1999. pap. 42.50 (0-7487-3299-3) Standard Pub.

Manual of Clinical Psychopharmacology. 2nd ed. Alan F. Schatzberg & Jonathan O. Cole. LC 91-162254. (Illus.). 388p. 1991. reprint ed. pap. 120.30 (0-608-06650-8, 206684700009) Bks Demand.

Manual of Clinical Psychopharmacology. 3rd ed. Alan F. Schatzberg et al. LC 96-24026. 499p. 1997. spiral bd. 52.95 (0-88048-921-9, 8921) Am Psychiatric.

Manual of Clinical Trauma Care: The First Hour. 3rd ed. Susan B. Sheehy. LC 98-26666. 464p. 1998. pap. text 37.95 (0-323-00305-2) Mosby Inc.

Manual of Clinical Virology. Danny L. Wiedbrauk & Sheryl L. Johnston. LC 92-49313. 288p. 1992. pap. text 75.00 (0-88167-984-4) Lppncott W & W.

Manual of Coating Work for Light-Water Nuclear Power Primary Containment & Other Safety-Related Facilities, 201p. 1979. 63.00 (0-8031-0394-8, 03-401079-14) ASTM.

Manual of Colloquial Tibetan. Ed. by Charles Bell. (Illus.). (C). 1979. reprint ed. 180.00 (0-89771-117-3, Pub. by Ratna Pustak Bhandar) St Mut.

Manual of Combined Movements: Their Use in the Examination & Treatment of Mechanical VCDs. Brian C. Edwards. (Illus.). 131p. 1992. text 50.00 (0-443-04666-2) Church.

Manual of Combined Movements: Their Use in the Examination & Treatment of Musculoskeletalvertebral Column Disorders. 2nd ed. B. C. Edwards. LC 99-12515. 149p. 1999. pap. text 43.00 (0-7506-4290-4) Buttrwrth-Heinemann.

Manual of Common Bedside Surgical Procedures. Herbert Chen et al. LC 95-4786. (Illus.). 400p. 1996. spiral bd. 25.95 (0-683-01549-4) Lppncott W & W.

*Manual of Common Bedside Surgical Procedures. 2nd ed. Herbert Chen et al. LC 99-40830. 2000. write for info. (0-683-30792-4) Lppncott W & W.

Manual of Common Ophthalmic Surgical Procedures. Ed. by Charles D. Phelps & E. J. Hansjoerg. LC 86-17157. (Illus.). 203p. (Orig.). reprint ed. pap. 63.00 (0-7837-2557-4, 204271600006) Bks Demand.

Manual of Complete Internal Medicine Asia, No. 4. Jerry L. Spivak. 1990. 10.95 (0-316-80741-9, Little Brwn Med Div) Lppncott W & W.

Manual of Complete Internal Medicine ISE, No. 4. Jerry L. Spivak. 1990. 15.95 (0-316-80742-7, Little Brwn Med Div) Lppncott W & W.

Manual of Complete Neph ISE. Burton D. Rose. 1988. 15.95 (0-316-75635-0, Little Brwn Med Div) Lppncott W & W.

Manual of Complete Pediatrics ISE, No. 3. Roberts. 1989. 15.95 (0-316-74992-3, Little Brwn Med Div) Lppncott W & W.

Manual of Complications During Anesthesia. Ed. by Nikolaus Gravenstein. LC 90-6357. (Illus.). 736p. 1991. reprint ed. pap. 200.00 (0-608-07309-1, 206753700009) Bks Demand.

Manual of Congregational Church of Simisbury Connecticut. Ed. by Charles D. Townsend. LC 98-222177. 1998. reprint ed. pap. 15.00 (1-878545-27-2) ACETO Bookmen.

Manual of Congregational Church Waterbury, Vermont. Intro. by Charles D. Townsend. 45p. 1995. reprint ed. pap. 5.00 (1-878545-15-9) ACETO Bookmen.

Manual of Coniferae, Containing a General Review of the Order. James Veitch. (Illus.). 350p. 1980. reprint ed. text 60.00 (0-934454-96-5) Lubrecht & Cramer.

Manual of Construction Documentation. Glenn E. Wiggins. (Illus.). 224p. 1989. pap. 29.95 (0-8230-3002-4, Whitney Lib) Watsn-Guptill.

Manual of Contact Lens Prescribing & Fitting. Milton M. Hom. LC 96-50456. 418p. 1997. pap. text 47.50 (0-7506-9741-5) Buttrwrth-Heinemann.

*Manual of Contact Lens Prescribing & Fitting with CD-ROM. Milton H. Hom. (Illus.). 528p. 2000. pap. 55.00 incl. cd-rom (0-7506-7215-3) Buttrwrth-Heinemann.

Manual of Contract Documents for Highway Works: A User's Guide & Commentary, 1993-1994 Amendments. Bill Money & Geoff Hodgson. 284p. 1996. 48.00 (0-7277-2088-0) Am Soc Civil Eng.

Manual of Cooperative Group Therapy for Aphasia. Jan R. Avent. LC 97-21508. 174p. 1997. pap. text 32.50 (0-7506-9921-3) Buttrwrth-Heinemann.

Manual of Corneal Surgery. Ed. by William E. Bruner et al. LC 86-23280. (Illus.). 149p. reprint ed. pap. 46.20 (0-7837-6251-8, 204596300010) Bks Demand.

Manual of Corporate Forms for Securities Practice, 3 vols., Set. Arnold S. Jacobs. LC 81-3857. (Securities Law Ser.). 1981. ring bd. 395.00 (0-87632-302-6) West Group.

Manual of Cotton Spinning: Opening & Cleaning, Vol. 2, Pt. 2. C. Shrigley. 229p. 1973. 45.00 (0-7855-7205-8) St Mut.

Manual of Cotton Spinning: The Characteristics of Raw Cotton, Vol. 2, Pt. 1. E. Lord. 333p. 1971. 60.00 (0-7855-7204-X) St Mut.

Manual of Cranial Computerized Tomography. K. Y. Chynn & N. Finby. (Illus.). vi, 106p. 1982. 172.25 (3-8055-3432-9) S Karger.

*Manual of Credit & Commercial Laws. 91st ed. 1264p. 1999. 125.00 (0-471-29949-9) Wiley.

*Manual of Credit & Commercial Laws: January 2000 Supplement. 91st ed. Ed. by Charles M. Tatelbaum & John K. Pearson. 96p. 2000. pap. 25.00 (0-471-36145-3) Wiley.

Manual of Critical Care: Applying Nursing Diagnosis to Adult Critical Illness. 3rd ed. Pamela L. Swearingen. (Illus.). 864p. (C). (gr. 13). 1995. text 41.95 (0-8151-7500-0, 24500) Mosby Inc.

Manual of Critical Care Medicine. Ed. by M. H. Weil & P. L. DaLuz. LC 77-24959. (Illus.). 1978. 118.00 (0-387-90270-8) Spr-Verlag.

M

M

Manual of Critical Care Nursing. Jennifer Hebra & Merrily Kuhn. 500p. 1996. spiral bd. 29.95 (0-316-35596-8, Little Brwn Med Div) Lppncott W & W.

*Manual of Critical Care Nursing. 4th ed. Swearingen. 2000. text. write for info. (0-323-00998-0) Mosby Inc.

Manual of Crop Experimentation. write for info. (0-85264-289-X) Lubrecht & Cramer.

Manual of Cross-Connection Control. 9th rev. ed. Foundation for Cross-Connection Control & Hydrauli & Manual Review Committee. (Illus.). 310p. 1993. pap. text 48.00 (0-9638912-0-0) USC Fnd Cross-Connect.

Manual of Cryptography. Luigi Sacco. 203p. 1977. reprint ed. pap. 26.80 (0-89412-016-6) Aegean Park Pr.

Manual of Cultivated Broad-Leaved Trees & Shrubs Vol. III: Pru-Z. Gerd Krussmann. Ed. by Gilbert S. Daniels. Tr. by Michael E. Epp from GER.Tr. of Handbuch der Laubgeholze. (Illus.). 678p. 1986. 65.00 (0-88192-006-1) Timber.

Manual of Cultivated Conifers. Gerd Krussmann. Ed. by Gilbert S. Daniels. Tr. by Michael E. Epp from GER. Orig. Title: Handbuch der Nadelgeholze. (Illus.). 521p. 1985. 69.95 (0-88192-007-X) Timber.

Manual of Cultivated Orchard Species. 3rd ed. Helmut Bechtel et al. (Illus.). 500p. 1992. 85.00 (0-262-02339-3) MIT Pr.

Manual of Curatorship: A Guide to Museum Practice. 2nd ed. Ed. by John M. Thompson. 720p. 1992. 139.95 (0-7506-0351-8) Buttrwrth-Heinemann.

Manual of Cutaneous Laser Techniques. Tina S. Alster. LC 96-37985. 200p. 1997. text 116.00 (0-397-58429-6) Lppncott W & W.

*Manual of Cutaneous Laser Techniques. 2nd ed. Tina S. Alster. LC 99-43217. 259p. 1999. write for info. (0-7817-1960-7, Lippnctt) Lppncott W & W.

Manual of Cytotechnology. 7th ed. Ed. by Catherine M. Keebler & Theresa M. Somrak. LC 82-22818. 1993. 145.00 (0-89189-352-0) Am Soc Clinical.

Manual of Darkroom Technique: WHO Basic Radiological System. P. E. Palmer. (CHI, FRE & SPA.). 25p. 1985. pap. text 8.00 (92-4-154178-4, 1150238) World Health.

Manual of Dermatologic Surgery Techniques. Susana Leal-Khouri et al. 320p. 1998. spiral bd. write for info. (0-397-51497-2) Lppncott W & W.

Manual of Dermatologic Therapeutics. 5th ed. Kenneth A. Arndt et al. LC 94-24451. 382p. 1995. spiral bd. 38.00 (0-316-05175-6) Lppncott W & W.

Manual of Dermatologic Therapeutics: With Essentials of Diagnosis. 6th ed. Kenneth A. Arndt. 400p. spiral bd. 39.95 (0-7817-2170-9) Lppncott W & W.

Manual of Dermatological Therapeutics. 3rd ed. Kenneth A. Arndt. 1983. 19.50 (0-316-05181-0, Little Brwn Med Div) Lppncott W & W.

Manual of Dermatology: An Introduction to Diagnosis & Treatment. Jeffrey P. Callen et al. LC 79-19865. (Illus.). 306p. reprint ed. pap. 94.90 (0-8357-8577-7, 203494300091) Bks Demand.

Manual of Dermatology for Developing Countries. 2nd ed. Orlando Canizares. LC 92-49991. (Illus.). 392p. 1993. 85.00 (0-19-262293-5); pap. 29.50 (0-19-262294-3) OUP.

Manual of Dermatology in Chinese Medicine. Nissi Wang et al. LC 94-61962. (Illus.). 381p. (C). 1996. text 45.00 (0-939616-20-3) Eastland.

Manual of Design for Slow Sand Filtration. 284p. 1991. 82.00 (0-89867-551-0, 90578) Am Water Wks Assn.

Manual of Developmental & Behavioral Problems in Children. Vidya Bhushan Gupta. LC 98-46421. (Pediatric Habilitation Ser.: Vol. 9). (Illus.). 336p. 1998. text 69.75 (0-8247-1938-7) Dekker.

Manual of Diagnosis & Professional Practice in Mental Retardation. Ed. by John W. Jacobson & James A. Mulick. 540p. 1996. 39.95 (1-55798-341-0) Am Psychol.

Manual of Diagnostic Imaging: A Clinician's Guide to Clinical Problem Solving. William H. Straub. (Spiral Manual Ser.). 320p. 1984. spiral bd. 21.00 (0-316-81887-9, Little Brwn Med Div) Lppncott W & W.

Manual of Diagnostic Ultrasound. Ed. by P. E. Palmer. (FRE & SPA., Illus.). 334p. (C). 1995. pap. 65.00 (92-4-154461-9, 1150393) World Health.

Manual of Dietetic Practice: Edited for the British Dietetic Association by Briony Thomas. 2nd ed. Ed. by Briony Thomas. LC 93-20867. (Illus.). 752p. 1994. pap. 89.95 (0-632-03003-8) Blackwell Sci.

Manual of Dipterocarps for Foresters: Borneo Island Light Hardwoods. M. F. Newman et al. (Manual Ser.). (Illus.). x, 278p. 1996. pap. 40.00 (1-872291-76-7, Pub. by Royal Botanic Edinburgh) Balogh.

Manual of Dipterocarps for Foresters: Philippines. M. F. Newman et al. (Manual Ser.). (Illus.). x, 126p. 1996. pap. 23.00 (1-872291-61-9, Pub. by Royal Botanic Edinburgh) Balogh.

Manual of Dipterocarps for Foresters: Sumatra Light Hardwoods. M. F. Newman et al. (Manuals Ser.). (Illus.). x, 158p. 1996. pap. 31.00 (1-872291-91-0, Pub. by Royal Botanic Edinburgh) Balogh.

Manual of Diseases of the Nervous System, 2 vols. William R. Gowers. Ed. by James Taylor. Incl. Vol. 1. Diseases of the Nerves & Spinal Cord. (Illus.). 1970. Vol. 2. Diseases of the Brain & Cranal Nerves: General & Functional Diseases of the Nerves System. (Illus.). 1970. 1970. reprint ed. 76.00 (0-02-845390-5) Hafner.

Manual of District Health Management for Uganda. Gilbert Bukenya et al. LC 97-37032. 128p. 1997. pap. 20.00 (1-56474-251-2) Fithian Pr.

Manual of Dosimetry in Radiotherapy. John B. Massey. (Technical Reports: No. 110). (Illus.). (Orig.). 1970. pap. 25.00 (92-0-115370-8, IDC110, Pub. by IAEA) Bernan Associates.

Manual of Drilling Technology. Ed. by C. P. Chugh. 596p. (C). 1985. text 47.00 (90-6191-553-8, Pub. by A A Balkema) Ashgate Pub Co.

Manual of Drug & Alcohol Abuse: Guidelines for Teaching in Medical & Health Institutions. A. Arif & J. Westmeyer. LC 88-22414. (Illus.). 350p. (C). 1988. text 65.00 (0-306-42890-3, Kluwer Plenum) Kluwer Academic.

Manual of Drug Interactions for Anesthesiology. Robert A. Mueller & Dag B. Lundberg. LC 88-20410. 384p. reprint ed. pap. 119.10 (0-7837-2564-7, 204272300006) Bks Demand.

Manual of Drug Interactions for Anesthesiology. 3rd ed. Robery A. Mueller & Dag B. Lundberg. LC 96-29164. 1996. pap. text 42.00 (0-443-07764-9) Church.

Manual of Drug Therapy. Ed. by David A. Scheinberg & Labe Scheinberg. LC 85-2378. (Illus.). 399p. 1985. reprint ed. pap. 123.70 (0-608-05780-0, 205974500007) Bks Demand.

Manual of Dwarf Conifers. rev. ed. Humphrey J. Welch. (Illus.). 1976. 20.00 (0-913728-07-1) Theophrastus.

Manual of Dysphagia Assessment in Adults. Joseph Murray. LC 98-41268. (Illus.). 248p. 1998. pap. 49.95 (1-56593-871-2, 1702) Thomson Learn.

Manual of Eastern Orthodox Prayers. 2nd ed. Intro. by Alexander Schmemann. 113p. 1983. reprint ed. pap. text 5.95 (0-88141-012-8) St Vladimirs.

Manual of Ecclesiastical Architecture. W. W. Martin. 1977. lib. bdg. 75.00 (0-8490-2206-1) Gordon Pr.

Manual of Educational Risk Management. Frank Cody & John H. Dise. 937p. 1991. 225.00 (0-9630262-0-8) Educ Risk.

Manual of Electrical Contracting Forms & Procedures. Ralph E. Johnson & Gene Whitson. LC 95-10809. 323p. 1995. 49.50 (0-07-032699-1) McGraw.

Manual of Electrocardiography. Gilbert H. Mudge, Jr. 1986. spiral bd. 32.95 (0-316-58918-7, Little Brwn Med Div) Lppncott W & W.

Manual of Elementary Law: Being a Summary of the Fundamental Principles of American Law. William P. Fishback & Arnold B. Hall. LC 97-49244. xxxi, 515p. 1998. reprint ed. 65.00 (0-8377-2141-5, Rothman) W S Hein.

Manual of Emergency Airway Management. Ron M. Walls et al. 272p. pap. text 39.95 (0-7817-2616-6) Lppncott W & W.

Manual of Emergency Care. 5th ed. Susan B. Sheehy & Gail P. Lenehan. LC 98-8531. 672p. 1998. pap. text 42.95 (0-323-00304-4) Mosby Inc.

Manual of Emergency Medical Therapeutics. 2nd ed. Gideon Bosker. 5760p. (C). (gr. 13). 1995. 36.95 (0-8151-0992-X, 28453) Mosby Inc.

Manual of Emergency Medical Treatment for the Dental Team. 2nd ed. Robert J. Braun & Bruce J. Cutilli. LC 98-19198. 139p. 1998. pap. 29.95 (0-683-30270-1) Lppncott W & W.

Manual of Emergency Medicine. 3rd ed. Jon L. Jenkins et al. LC 94-45589. 592p. 1995. spiral bd. 34.95 (0-316-46061-3) Lppncott W & W.

Manual of Emergency Medicine. 6th ed. George L. Sternbach & Michael Jay Bresler. LC 97-27604. (Illus.). 640p. (C). (gr. 13). 1997. pap. text 35.95 (0-8151-1142-8, 27233) Mosby Inc.

Manual of Emergency Medicine: Diagnosis & Treatment. Jon L. Jenkins & Joseph Loscalzo. 493p. 1986. 24.50 (0-316-46052-4, Little Brwn Med Div) Lppncott W & W.

Manual of Emergency Medicine: Diagnosis & Treatment. 4th ed. Jon L. Jenkins & G. Richard Braen. LC 99-27742. 592p. 2000. spiral bd. 40.00 (0-7817-1726-4) Lppncott W & W.

Manual of Emergency Nursing. Judy Selfridge-Thomas. LC 95-2409. (Illus.). 476p. 1995. pap. text 41.00 (0-7216-5452-5, W B Saunders Co) Harcrt Hlth Sci Grp.

Manual of Emergency Orthopaedics. Phillip M. Segelov. (Illus.). 234p. (Orig.). 1986. pap. text 53.00 (0-443-03341-2) Church.

Manual of Emergency Orthopedics. William M. Green et al. 480p. write for info. (0-683-03760-9) Lppncott W & W.

Manual of Emergency Outpatient Technique, Vol. 1. 2nd ed. Klippel. (Illus.). 1996. 22.95 (0-316-49869-6, Little Brwn Med Div) Lppncott W & W.

Manual of Emergency Pediatrics. 4th ed. Ed. by Robert M. Reece. (Illus.). 586p. 1992. pap. text 69.00 (0-7216-3289-0, W B Saunders Co) Harcrt Hlth Sci Grp.

Manual of Endocrine Surgery. 2nd ed. A. J. Edis et al. (Comprehensive Manuals of Surgical Specialties Ser.). (Illus.). 280p. 1984. 160.00 (0-387-90921-4) Spr-Verlag.

Manual of Endocrinology & Metabolism. Norman Lavin. 770p. 1986. pap. text 21.00 (0-316-51651-1, Little Brwn Med Div) Lppncott W & W.

Manual of Endocrinology & Metabolism. 2nd ed. Ed. by Norman Lavin. LC 93-874. (Illus.). 688p. 1993. spiral bd. 35.95 (0-316-51657-0, Little Brwn Med Div) Lppncott W & W.

Manual of Endocrinology & Metabolism. 3rd ed. Norman Lavin. 720p. spiral bd. 39.95 (0-7817-2014-1) Lppncott W & W.

Manual of Endoscopic Aesthetic Surgery. Oscar M. Ramirez & Rollin K. Daniel. LC 94-30008. 1994. 245.00 (0-387-92623-2) Spr-Verlag.

Manual of English for the Overseas Doctor. 4th ed. Joy E. Parkinson. (Illus.). 286p. 1991. pap. text 32.00 (0-443-04188-1) Church.

Manual of English for the Overseas Doctor. 5th ed. Joy E. Parkinson. LC 98-31755. 1998. write for info. (0-443-06136-X) Church.

Manual of English Grammar. Doris Torregrosa et al. 142p. 1986. pap. 5.00 (0-8477-3336-X) U of PR Pr.

Manual of English Grammar. Doris Torregrosa et al. 100p. 1987. pap. 5.00 (0-8477-3335-1) U of PR Pr.

Manual of English Grammar for Spanish Speakers: Workbooks, 4 units, Set. rev. ed. Doris Torregrosa de Torres. (C). pap. 20.00 (0-8477-3334-3) U of PR Pr.

Manual of English Grammar for Spanish Speakers Vol. III: Word Order (Workbook) 3rd rev. ed. La Verne Walker et al. xviii, 169p. (C). 1982. 5.00 (0-8477-3337-8) U of PR Pr.

Manual of English Grammar for Spanish Speakers Vol. IV: Verb Tenses: Active & Passive Voice. 3rd rev. ed. La Verne Walker et al. xv, 189p. (C). 1982. 5.00 (0-8477-3338-6) U of PR Pr.

Manual of English-Gujarati Dictionary. Rustam N. Rahina. 1981. write for info. (0-8288-1769-3) Fr & Eur.

Manual of English Gujarati Dictionary. N. Ranina Rustam. (ENG & GUJ.). 640p. 1910. 59.95 (0-7859-9830-6) Fr & Eur.

Manual of English Meters. Joseph Malof. LC 77-823. 236p. 1978. reprint ed. lib. bdg. 59.50 (0-313-20293-1, MAMEM, Greenwood Pr) Greenwood.

Manual of Environmental Microbiology. Ed. by Christon J. Hurst et al. LC 96-18805. (Illus.). 850p. 1996. 109.95 (1-55581-087-X) ASM Pr.

Manual of Environmental Protection Law: The Pollution Control Functions of the Environment Agency & SEPA. Michael Fry. 886p. 1997. pap. text 72.00 (0-19-826233-7) OUP.

Manual of Environmental Protection Law: The Pollution Control Functions of the Environmental Agency & S. E. P. A. Ed. by Michael Fry. LC 97-181233. 886p. 1997. text 140.00 (0-19-826230-2) OUP.

Manual of Environmental Safety & Health Abbreviations. Jonathan Klane. 1997. pap. 19.00 (1-882417-18-6, 9672) Am Conf Govt Indus Hygienist.

Manual of Epidemiology & Epidemiological Services in Malaria Programmes. R. H. Black. (Illus.). 223p. 1968. pap. text 8.00 (92-4-154015-X, 1150098) World Health.

Manual of Epidemiology for District Health Management. Ed. by J. P. Vaughan & R. H. Morrow. (ENG & FRE.). vii, 198p. 1989. pap. text 35.00 (92-4-154404-X, 1150335) World Health.

Manual of Equine Anaesthesia. 2nd ed. Clarke. 1998. pap. text 37.00 (0-7020-1806-6, W B Saunders Co) Harcrt Hlth Sci Grp.

Manual of Equine Emergencies: Treatment & Procedures. 6th ed. James A. Orsini & Thomas J. Divers. Ed. by Stephanie Donley. LC 97-35784. (Illus.). 592p. (C). 1998. text 55.00 (0-7216-2425-1, W B Saunders Co) Harcrt Hlth Sci Grp.

Manual of Equine Neonatal Medicine. 2nd rev. ed. John E. Madigan. (Illus.). 363p. 1994. pap. text 29.95 (0-9629517-0-6) Live Oak CA.

Manual of Equine Neonatal Medicine. 3rd ed. John E. Madigan. (Illus.). 415p. 1997. pap. 42.00 (0-9629517-1-4) Live Oak CA.

Manual of Equine Practice. Reuben J. Rose & David R. Hodgson. LC 92-21745. (Illus.). 544p. 1992. pap. text 72.00 (0-7216-3739-6, W B Saunders Co) Harcrt Hlth Sci Grp.

Manual of Equine Practice. 2nd ed. Reuben J. Rose & David R. Hodgson. Ed. by Stephanie Donley. LC 98-28631. 750p. 1999. text. write for info. (0-7216-8665-6, W B Saunders Co) Harcrt Hlth Sci Grp.

Manual of Equine Reproduction. Blanchard. (Illus.). 224p. (gr. 13). 1997. pap. text 39.95 (0-8151-4378-8, 31124) Mosby Inc.

*Manual of Equipment & Design for the Foodservice Industry. 2nd ed. James W. Stevens. (Illus.). 350p. (C). 1999. 65.00 (0-9669712-2-1) Chips Bks.

Manual of ERCP. Martin. (C). 1998. text 169.00 (0-443-05117-8, W B Saunders Co) Harcrt Hlth Sci Grp.

Manual of Ethics. J. N. Sinha. (C). 1989. 40.00 (0-89771-450-4, Pub. by Current Dist) St Mut.

Manual of Ethnobotany. S. K. Jain. 225p. (C). 1987. 55.00 (0-7855-2274-3, Pub. by Scientific) St Mut.

Manual of European Environmental Law. 2nd ed. Alexandre C. Kiss & Dinah Shelton. 666p. (C). 1997. text 125.00 (0-521-59122-8); pap. text 59.95 (0-521-59888-5) Cambridge U Pr.

Manual of European Languages for Librarians. 2nd ed. C. G. Allen. LC 99-13806. 994p. 1999. 215.00 (1-85739-241-8) Bowker-Saur.

Manual of Examination & Treatment of the Spine & Extremities. Carolyn Wadsworth et al. (Illus.). 229p. 1988. pap. 37.00 (0-683-08600-6) Lppncott W & W.

Manual of Examination of the Eyes. E. Landolt. LC 78-20773. (Classics in Ophthalmology Ser.). 328p. 1979. reprint ed. lib. bdg. 31.50 (0-88275-843-8) Krieger.

Manual of Exercise Testing. 2nd ed. Victor F. Froelicher. LC 93-38016. (Illus.). 304p. (C). (gr. 13). 1994. pap. text 59.00 (0-8151-3346-4, 23774) Mosby Inc.

Manual of Exorcism. J. D. Brady & Eunice Beyersdorf. 1974. 5.00 (0-87535-138-7) Hispanic Soc.

Manual of Exotic Pets. Ed. by Peter H. Beynon & John E. Cooper. (Illus.). 312p. 1994. pap. text 72.95 (0-8138-2294-7) Iowa St U Pr.

Manual of Experimental Embryology. rev. ed. Viktor Hamburger. LC 60-14069. (Illus.). 1994. lib. bdg. 15.00 (0-226-31471-5) U Ch Pr.

Manual of Facial Growth: A Computer Analysis of Longitudinal Cephalometric Growth Data. S. N. Bhatia & B. C. Leighton. LC 93-2900. (Illus.). 560p. 1993. text 230.00 (0-19-261770-2) OUP.

Manual of Family Practice. Robert B. Taylor. LC 96-271. 592p. 1996. spiral bd. 36.95 (0-316-83390-8, Little Brwn Med Div) Lppncott W & W.

Manual of Federal Evidence, 3 vols. 4th ed. Richard A. Givens. Date not set. 210.00 (0-07-172346-3, 67041-10, MICHIE) LEXIS Pub.

Manual of Federal Practice, 3 vols. 4th ed. Richard A. Givens. 2344p. 1991. text 210.00 (0-07-172028-6) Shepards.

Manual of Federal Practice, Vol. 1. 5th ed. Richard A. Givens. LC 98-85324. 1998. text. write for info. (0-327-00222-0, 67041-11) LEXIS Pub.

Manual of Federal Practice, Vol. 2. 5th ed. Richard A. Givens. LC 98-85324. 1998. text. write for info. (0-327-00223-9, 67041-11) LEXIS Pub.

Manual of Federal Practice, Vol. 3. 5th ed. Richard A. Givens. LC 98-85324. 1998. text. write for info. (0-327-00224-7, 67041-11) LEXIS Pub.

Manual of Federal Practice, 3 vols., Vols. 1-3. 5th ed. Richard A. Givens. LC 98-85324. 1998. text 235.00 (0-327-00139-9, 67041-11) LEXIS Pub.

Manual of Federal Practice: Forms, 2 vols. Richard A. Givens. LC 94-6819. Date not set. ring bd. 195.00 (0-07-172496-6, 67065-10, MICHIE) LEXIS Pub.

*Manual of Federal Practice: Forms, 1999. 2nd rev. ed. Richard Givens. 1200p. 1999. ring bd. write for info. (0-327-01379-6, 6706511) LEXIS Pub.

Manual of Federal Practice: 1996 Cumulative Supplement. 4th ed. Richard A. Givens. Ed. by Russ Davis. 814p. 1996. pap. text, suppl. ed. write for info. (0-7620-0047-3) West Group.

Manual of Federal Practice: 1999 First Cumulative Supplement. 5th ed. Richard A. Givens. 216p. 1999. pap. write for info. (0-327-01323-0, 6705115) LEXIS Pub.

Manual of Federal Practice Forms: June 1998 Supplement. Richard A. Givens. LC 94-6819. 150p. 1998. ring bd. write for info. (0-327-00240-9, 67076-11) LEXIS Pub.

Manual of Federal Practice, 1998 Supplement. 5th ed. Richard A. Givens. 222p. 1998. pap. write for info. (0-327-00605-6, 6705114) LEXIS Pub.

Manual of Federal Trade Commission Practice. 2nd ed. J. Thomas Rosch. (Corporate Practice Series Portfolio: No. 21). 1989. ring bd. 92.00 (1-55871-144-9) BNA.

Manual of Federal Wildlife Regulations, 2 vols. American Association of Zoological Parks & Aquariu et al. 1985. 200.00 (0-317-01290-8) Am Assoc Z Pk.

Manual of Feline Behaviour. Peter Neville & Valerie O'Farrell. Ed. by Christopher S. Ross. (Illus.). 84p. 1994. pap. text 42.95 (0-905214-24-2, Pub. by BSAVA) Iowa St U Pr.

Manual of Fertilizer Processing. Francis T. Nielsson. (Fertilizer Science & Technology Ser.: Vol. 5). (Illus.). 544p. 1986. text 250.00 (0-8247-7522-8) Dekker.

Manual of Field Excavation: Handbook for Field Archaeologists. Ed. by William G. Dever & H. Darrell Lance. iv, 240p. 1978. pap. text 20.00 (0-87820-303-6) Hebrew Union Coll Pr.

Manual of Field Hydrogeology. Laura L. Sanders. LC 97-45597. 381p. (C). 1998. pap. text 60.00 (0-13-227927-4) P-H.

*Manual of Fingerweaving. Robert J. Austin. Ed. by Earl C. Fenner. (Illus.). 56p. 2000. pap. text 17.95 (1-929572-00-X) C C T P Reddick.

Manual of First-Aid Practices for School Bus Drivers. William R. Nesbitt. (Illus.). 80p. 1998. pap. text 20.00 (0-7881-7122-4) DIANE Pub.

Manual of First Congregational Church of Brimfield, MA & Town History. Ed. by Charles D. Townsend. LC 98-222238. 95p. 1998. reprint ed. pap. 20.00 (1-878545-36-1) ACETO Bookmen.

Manual of Fish Eggs & Larvae from Asian Mangrove Waters. M. J. Prince Jeyaseelan. Ed. by M. Vannucci. LC 98-197916. (Titles Published Solely by UNESCO Ser.: Vol. 02000001). 1998. 40.00 (92-3-103449-9, U3449, Pub. by UNESCO) Bernan Associates.

Manual of Fish Health. Chris Andrews & Neville Carrington. (Illus.). 210p. 1995. 26.95 (1-56465-160-6, 16068) Tetra Pr.

Manual of Flight: Private & Commercial Pilot. Aero Products Research, Inc., Department of Aviati. 332p. 1973. pap. 14.95 (0-685-62814-0) Aero Products.

Manual of Flood Control Methods & Practices. 1983. 20.00 (81-85068-07-0) US Comm Irrigation.

Manual of Fluorometric & Spectrophotometric Experiments. Allesia M. Gillespie. x, 150p. 1985. text 85.00 (2-88124-005-4) Gordon & Breach.

Manual of Food Quality Control 15: Imported Food Inspection. FAO Staff. (Food & Nutrition Papers: 14-15). 94p. 1994. 14.00 (92-5-103415-X, F3415x, Pub. by FAO) Bernan Associates.

Manual of Foraminifera. J. J. Galloway. 1961. reprint ed. 25.00 (0-934454-60-4) Lubrecht & Cramer.

Manual of Forest Zoology for India. E. P. Stebbing. 229p. 1987. pap. 225.00 (81-7089-089-6, Pub. by Intl Bk Distr) St Mut.

Manual of Forest Zoology for India. E. O. Stebbing. 229p. (C). 1977. reprint ed. 250.00 (0-7855-3090-8, Pub. by Intl Bk Distr) St Mut.

Manual of Forestry. W. R. Fischer. (C). 1990. 2500.00 (81-7136-015-7, Pub. by Periodical Expert) St Mut.

Manual of Formulas: Recipes, Methods & Secret Processes. LC 79-66410. 1979. pap. text 6.95 (0-934188-00-9) Evans Pubns.

Manual of Formulas: Recipes, Methods & Secret Processes. 1995. lib. bdg. 300.00 (0-8490-5637-3) Gordon Pr.

Manual of Four-Handed Dentistry. J. Ellis Paul. (Illus.). 155p. 1980. text 60.00 (0-931386-09-8) Quint Pub Co.

Manual of Free Flaps. Russell & Zamboni. (Illus.). 320p. (C). (gr. 13). 1999. text 195.00 (0-8151-9013-1, 29110) Mosby Inc.

Manual of Freemasonry: The First Three Degrees; the Royal Arch & Knights Templar Druids. Richard Carlile. 311p. 1992. reprint ed. pap. 30.00 (1-56459-197-2) Kessinger Pub.

Manual of French Literature. F. Brunetiere. LC 71-127998. (Studies in French Literature: No. 45). 1970. reprint ed. lib. bdg. 75.00 (0-8383-1149-0) M S G Haskell Hse.

An Asterisk (*) at the beginning of an entry indicates that the title is appearing for the first time.

Manual of Freshwater Algae. L. A. Whitford & George Schumacher. 35.00 (*0-916822-01-X*) Sparks Pr.
Manual of Furniture Restoration. V. J. Taylor. (Illus.). 224p. 1994. pap. 19.95 (*0-7153-0250-7*, Pub. by D & C Pub) Sterling.
Manual of Gastoenterologic Procedures. 2nd ed. Ed. by Douglas A. Drossman. LC 86-42509. 283p. reprint ed. pap. 87.80 (*0-7837-7119-3*, 204694800004) Bks Demand.
Manual of Gastroenterologic Procedures. 3rd ed. Ed. by Douglas A. Drossman. LC 92-17142. (Illus.). 304p. 1992. spiral bd. 40.00 (*0-88167-944-5*, 2424) Lppncott W & W.
Manual of Gastroenterology: Diagnosis & Therapy. 2nd ed. Gregory L. Eastwood & Canan Avunduk. LC 93-47188. 512p. 1994. spiral bd. 41.00 (*0-316-19992-3*, Little Brwn Med Div) Lppncott W & W.
Manual of Gastrointestinal Fluoroscopy: Performance of Procedures. David J. Ott et al. (Illus.). 212p. (C). 1996. text 52.95 (*0-398-06555-1*) C C Thomas.
***Manual of Gastrointestinal Procedures.** 4th rev. ed. Society of Gastroenterology Staff. (Illus.). x, 236p. 2000. 85.00 (*0-9702133-0-1*) Scty Gastro.
Manual of Gastrointestinal Procedures Pediatric Supplement: A Publication of the Society of Gastroenterology Nurses & Associates. 2nd ed. Nancy Rayhorn. 35p. 1995. pap. write for info. (*0-683-07182-3*) Lppncott W & W.
Manual of Gear Design, Vols. 1-3. rev. ed. Eliot K & Earle Buckingham. 1980. text 49.95 (*0-8311-3116-0*) Indus Pr.
Manual of Gear Design Sect. 1: Gear Ratio & Mathematical Tables. rev. ed. Eliot K & Earle Buckingham. 161p. 1981. text 19.95 (*0-8311-3113-6*) Indus Pr.
Manual of Gear Design Sect. 2: Spur & Internal Gears, Vol. 2. rev. ed. Eliot K & Earle Buckingham. 153p. 1980. text 19.95 (*0-8311-3114-4*) Indus Pr.
Manual of Gear Design Sect. 3: Helical & Internal Gears, Vol. 3. rev. ed. Eliot K & Earle Buckingham. 158p. 1980. text 19.95 (*0-8311-3115-2*) Indus Pr.
Manual of Geology for Civil Engineers. John Pitts. 228p. 1985. text 48.00 (*9971-978-05-9*); pap. text 23.00 (*9971-978-12-1*) World Scientific Pub.
Manual of Gerontologic Nursing. 2nd ed. Charlotte Eliopoulos. LC 98-17792. 416p. 1998. 34.95 (*0-323-00177-7*) Mosby Inc.
Manual of GI Fluoroscopy. Bruce R. Javors. (Illus.). 232p. 1995. pap. 31.00 (*0-86577-607-5*) Thieme Med Pubs.
Manual of Glaucoma: Diagnosis & Management. fac. ed. Theodore Krupin. LC 88-20321. (Illus.). 265p. pap. 82.20 (*0-7837-7232-7*, 204706600005) Bks Demand.
Manual of Grammar of Greek in the New Testament. H. E. Dana. 1957. 53.00 (*0-02-327070-5*, Macmillan Coll) P-H.
Manual of Graphic Techniques, Vol. 1. Tom Porter & Bob Greenstreet. (Illus.). 128p. 1980. pap. write for info. (*0-408-50012-3*, VNR) Wiley.
Manual of Graphic Techniques, Vol. 1. Tom Porter & Robert Greenstreet. (Illus.). 112p. 1980. pap. 15.95 (*0-684-16504-X*, Scribners Ref) Mac Lib Ref.
Manual of Graphic Techniques, Vol. 2. Tom Porter & Sue Goodman. (Illus.). 128p. 1982. pap. write for info. (*0-408-50007-7*, VNR) Wiley.
Manual of Graphic Techniques, Vol. 3. Tom Porter & Sue Goodman. (Illus.). 128p. 1983. pap. write for info. (*0-408-50008-5*, VNR) Wiley.
Manual of Graphic Techniques, Vol. 4. Tom Porter & Sue Goodman. (Illus.). 128p. 1985. pap. write for info. (*0-7506-1627-X*, VNR) Wiley.
Manual of Graphic Techniques Vol. 3: For Architects, Graphic Designers & Artists, Vol. 3. Tom Porter & Sue Goodman. (Illus.). 128p. 1983. pap. 12.95 (*0-684-18018-9*, Scribners Ref) Mac Lib Ref.
Manual of Grasses. Frederick Darke & Mark Griffiths. (Illus.). 218p. 1995. 39.95 (*0-88192-300-1*) Timber.
Manual of Grasses. Ed. by Rick Darke & Mark Griffiths. (Illus.). 169p. 1994. 72.50 (*0-333-61535-2*, Pub. by Pan) Trans-Atl Phila.
Manual of Grasses of the United States, 2 vols. 2nd ed. A. S. Hitchcock. (Illus.). 1990. 51.50 (*0-8446-0309-0*) Peter Smith.
Manual of Greek Forms. James L. Boyer. pap. 4.99 (*0-88469-007-5*) BMH Bks.
Manual of Ground Water Sampling Procedures. William Dunlap et al. 96p. 1981. 15.00 (*1-56034-026-6*, T029) Natl Grnd Water.
Manual of Ground Water Sampling Procedures. William Dunlap et al. 96p. (C). 1987. 160.00 (*0-7855-6704-6*, Pub. by Scientific) St Mut.
Manual of Ground-Water Sampling Procedures. Ed. by Marion R. Scalf et al. (C). 1988. text 250.00 (*0-7855-3139-4*, Pub. by Scientific) St Mut.
Manual of Guitar Technology: History & Technology of Plucked String Instruments. Franz Jahnel & J. C. Harvey. (Illus.). 1999. pap. 64.95 incl. 5.25 hd (*0-933224-27-3*, T034) Bold Strummer Ltd.
Manual of Gymnosperms of India & Adjacent Countries. K. C. Sahni. (Illus.). 275p. 1990. text 30.00 (*81-211-0047-X*, Pub. by Mahendra Pal Singh) Lubrecht & Cramer.
Manual of Gynecologic Surgery. 2nd ed. B. J. Masterson. (Comprehensive Manuals of Surgical Specialties Ser.). (Illus.). 379p. 1986. 290.00 (*0-387-96193-3*) Spr-Verlag.
Manual of Gynecology & Obstetrics. Johns Hopkins Staff. 1997. spiral bd. write for info. (*0-316-46703-0*) Lppncott W & W.
Manual of Gynecology Asia. 3rd ed. Carol S. Havens. 1995. 32.95 (*0-316-35014-1*) Little.
Manual of Gynecology ISE, No. 3. Michael E. Rivlin. 1990. 15.95 (*0-316-74773-4*, Little Brwn Med Div) Lppncott W & W.
Manual of Hadith. Maulana Myhammad. 1987. 10.95 (*0-913321-15-X*) Ahmadiyya Anjuman.
Manual of Hadith: The Traditions of the Prophet Muhammad. Maulana Ali. (ARA & ENG.). 424p. 1988. 45.00 (*0-7007-0110-9*, Pub. by Curzon Pr Ltd) Paul & Co Pubs.
Manual of Haematology. Annabelle S. Baughan et al. LC 85-11286. (Illus.). 274p. 1986. pap. text 19.95 (*0-443-02564-9*) Church.
Manual of Hand-Made Bobbin Lace Work. Margaret Maidment. (Illus.). 1983. 22.50 (*0-7134-3855-X*) Robin & Russ.
Manual of Harmonics. Nicomachus the Pythagorean. Tr. by Flora Levin from GRE. (Illus.). 200p. (Orig.). 1993. pap. 18.00 (*0-933999-43-7*) Phanes Pr.
Manual of Hawaiian Mosses. E. B. Bartram. (BMB Ser.: No. 101). 1969. reprint ed. 45.00 (*0-527-02207-1*) Periodicals Srv.
Manual of Health & Safety References. EEMUA Staff. (C). 1988. 125.00 (*0-85931-038-8*, Pub. by EEMUA) St Mut.
Manual of Herbaceous Ornamental Plants. 4th ed. Steven Still. (Illus.). (C). 1993. text 52.80 (*0-87563-434-6*); pap. text 38.80 (*0-87563-433-8*) Stipes.
Manual of Heritage Management. Richard Harrison. LC 94-3941. (Illus.). 464p. 1994. 155.00 (*0-7506-0822-6*) Buttrwrth-Heinemann.
Manual of Hermeneutics. Luis Alonso Schokel. (Biblical Seminar Ser.: Vol. 54). 181p. 1998. pap. 28.50 (*1-85075-850-6*, Pub. by Sheffield Acad) CUP Services.
Manual of High-Risk Pregnancy & Delivery. 2nd ed. Elizabeth Stepp Gilbert & Judith S. Harmon. LC 97-46588. (Illus.). 848p. (C). (gr. 13). 1998. pap. text 36.95 (*0-8151-4462-8*, 30688) Mosby Inc.
Manual of Hindu Astrology: Correct Casting of Horoscopes. Bangalore V. Raman. (BVR Astrology Ser.). (C). 1992. pap. 4.50 (*81-85674-29-9*, Pub. by UBS Pubs Dist) S Asia.
Manual of Histological Techniques. John D. Bancroft & Harry C. Cook. (Illus.). 274p. (Orig.). 1984. pap. text 32.00 (*0-443-02870-2*) Church.
Manual of Histological Techniques & Their Diagnostic Applications. 2nd ed. John D. Bancroft & Harry C. Cook. LC 93-35533. 1994. text 59.95 (*0-443-04534-8*) Church.
Manual of HIV - AIDS Therapy, 1997 Edition: Current Clinical Strategies. 2nd ed. Douglas C. Princeton. 102p. 1997. pap. 12.75 (*1-881528-05-7*) Current Clin Strat.
***Manual of HIV-AIDS Therapy: 2001 Edition.** rev. ed. Douglas C. Princeton. (Current Clinical Strategies Ser.). 83p. 2000. pap. 28.95 incl. cd-rom (*1-881528-88-X*) Current Clin Strat.
Manual of HIV-AIDS Therapy, 2001 Edition: Current Clinical Strategies. rev. ed. Douglas C. Princeton. 1999. pap. 12.95 (*1-881528-87-1*) Current Clin Strat.
Manual of HIV Therapeutics. Ed. by William Powderly. LC 97-8075. (Illus.). 400p. 1997. spiral bd. 42.00 (*0-316-71510-7*) Lppncott W & W.
Manual of Home Care for Arthritis. Judith K. Sands. 1989. pap. text 35.95 (*0-8273-4353-1*) Delmar.
Manual of Home Care Nursing Orientation. Carolyn J. Humphrey & Paula Milone-Nuzzo. LC 95-21179. 392p. Date not set. ring bd. 145.00 (*0-8342-0512-2*, S147) Aspen Pub.
Manual of Home Health Nursing Procedures. Robyn Rice. (Illus.). 400p. (C). (gr. 13). 1994. text 115.00 (*0-8016-6945-6*, 06945) Mosby Inc.
***Manual of Home Health Nursing Procedures.** 2nd ed. Robyn Rice. LC 99-26972. 1999. text 55.00 (*0-323-00912-3*) Harcourt.
***Manual of Home Health Nursing Procedures: Update.** Robyn Rice. (Illus.). 400p. 1998. write for info. (*1-55664-414-0*) Mosby Inc.
Manual of Hospital Administration. Howard S. Rowland & Beatrice L. Rowland. LC 92-10857. ring bd. 249.00 (*0-8342-0324-3*) Aspen Pub.
Manual of Hospital Paediatrics. Garry Hambleton. (Illus.). 360p. (Orig.). 1988. pap. text 34.00 (*0-443-03512-1*) Church.
Manual of House Monsters. Stanislav Marijanovic. LC 99-20138. 32p. (J). (ps-3). 1999. 15.95 (*1-57255-718-4*) Mondo Pubng.
Manual of Hydraulic Fracturing for Well Stimulation & Geologic Studies. S. Smith. LC 88-34024. 120p. 1988. 22.50 (*1-56034-072-X*, T431) Natl Grnd Water.
Manual of Hydrotherapy & Massage. Fred B. Moor et al. LC 64-23214. 169p. 1964. 12.99 (*0-8163-0023-2*, 13160-7) Pacific Pr Pub Assn.
Manual of Hypertension. J. D. Swales. LC 94-30757. (Illus.). 200p. 1995. pap. 44.95 (*0-86542-861-1*) Blackwell Sci.
Manual of I. V. Therapeutics. 2nd ed. Lynn D. Phillips. LC 96-40183. (Illus.). 644p. (C). 1997. pap. text 29.95 (*0-8036-0131-X*) Davis Co.
Manual of Immunocytochemical Techniques. K. J. Morrell et al. (Illus.). 208p. 1997. text. write for info. (*0-443-04861-4*) Church.
Manual of Immunological Methods. Canadian Networking Toxicology Center Staff. LC 98-3373. (Pharmacology & Toxicology Ser.). 160p. 1998. per. 64.95 (*0-8493-8558-X*) CRC Pr.
Manual of Immunology Asia, No. 2. Glenn J. Lawlor, Jr. 1987. 10.95 (*0-316-51669-4*, Little Brwn Med Div) Lppncott W & W.
Manual of Immunology ISE, No. 2. Glenn J. Lawlor, Jr. 1987. 15.95 (*0-316-51667-8*, Little Brwn Med Div) Lppncott W & W.
Manual of Income Tax. Julie Cassidy. 332p. 1997. pap. 49.00 (*1-86287-261-9*, Pub. by Federation Pr) Gaunt.
Manual of Indian Buddhism. H. Kern. (C). 1989. reprint ed. 14.50 (*81-208-0457-0*, Pub. by Motilal Bnarsidass) S Asia.
Manual of Indian Edible Mushrooms. R. P. Purkayastha & Aindrila Chandra. (International Bioscience Monographs: No. 16). 267p. 1985. 37.00 (*1-55528-070-6*) Scholarly Pubns.
Manual of Indian Edible Mushrooms. R. P. Purkayastha & Anidrila Chendra. Ed. by R. K. Jain. (International Bioscience Monographs: Vol. 16). (Illus.). xvi, 267p. (C). 1985. lib. bdg. 37.00 (*1-55528-001-3*) Scholarly Pubns.
Manual of Indian Forestry Botany. N. L. Bor. 441p. 1953. 200.00 (*0-7855-6634-1*, Pub. by Intl Bk Distr) St Mut.
Manual of Indian Gaming Law. Ralph Reeser. 1300p. 1995. ring bd. 329.00 (*1-882800-00-1*) Falmouth Inst.
Manual of Indian Timbers. H. H. Gamble. 868p. (C). 1972. text 350.00 (*0-89771-623-X*, Pub. by Intl Bk Distr) St Mut.
Manual of Indian Timbers. H. H. Gamble. 868p. 1972. reprint ed. 200.00 (*0-7855-3057-6*, Pub. by Intl Bk Distr) St Mut.
Manual of Indian Wood Technology. H. P. Brown. 121p. 1985. pap. 175.00 (*0-7855-0379-X*, Pub. by Intl Bks & Periodicals) St Mut.
Manual of Individual Water Supply System. USEPA Staff. (C). 1987. text 90.00 (*81-85046-62-X*, Pub. by Scientific Pubs) St Mut.
Manual of Individual Water Supply Systems. Ed. by Scientific Publishers Staff. (C). 1988. text 125.00 (*0-7855-5996-5*, Pub. by Scientific) St Mut.
Manual of Industrial Corrosion Standards & Control. American Society for Testing & Materials Staff. Ed. by F. H. Cocks. LC 73-75375. (ASTM Special Technical Publication: No. 534). 308p. reprint ed. pap. 95.50 (*0-608-15315-X*, 205633100060) Bks Demand.
Manual of Industrial Marketing Research: Prepared under the Auspices of the Industrial Marketing Research Association. Ed. by Allan Rawnsley. LC 77-7272. (Illus.). 206p. reprint ed. pap. 63.90 (*0-8357-3082-4*, 203933900012) Bks Demand.
Manual of Industrial Microbiology & Biotechnology. 2nd rev. ed. Ed. by Arnold L. Demain & Julian E. Davies. LC 98-44884. (Illus.). 600p. 1999. 93.95 (*1-55581-128-0*) ASM Pr.
Manual of Infection Control in Respiratory Care. Arthur J. McLaughlin. 179p. 1983. spiral bd. 27.50 (*0-316-56096-0*, Little Brwn Med Div) Lppncott W & W.
Manual of Instructions for Enlisting & Discharging Soldiers. Roberts S. Bartholow. (American Civil War Medical Ser.: No. 6). 276p. 1991. reprint ed. 45.00 (*0-930405-37-4*) Norman SF.
Manual of Instructions for Etant Donnes: Il la Chuted'eau, Z'Legaz D'Eclairage. Marcel Duchamp. (Illus.). 56p. 1987. 40.00 (*0-87633-072-3*) Phila Mus Art.
Manual of Intensional Logic: Center for the Study of Language & Information. rev. ed. Johan Van Benthem. LC 87-34935. (CSLI Lecture Notes Ser.: No. 1). 142p. (Orig.). 1988. pap. 17.95 (*0-937073-29-6*) CSLI.
Manual of Intensional Logic: Center for the Study of Language & Information. 2nd rev. ed. Johan Van Benthem. LC 87-34935. (CSLI Lecture Notes Ser.: No. 1). 142p. (Orig.). 1988. 54.95 (*0-937073-30-X*) CSLI.
Manual of Intensive Care Medicine. James M. Rippe & Marie Csete. (Spiral Manual Ser.). 465p. 1983. spiral bd. 22.50 (*0-316-74708-4*, Little Brwn Med Div) Lppncott W & W.
***Manual of Intensive Care Medicine: With Annotated Key References.** 3rd ed. Richard S. Irwin & James M. Rippe. LC 99-87836. 2000. write for info. (*0-7817-1986-0*) Lppncott W & W.
Manual of Intergroup Relations. John P. Dean et al. LC 79-14226. 190p. reprint ed. pap. 58.90 (*0-608-08674-6*, 206919700003) Bks Demand.
Manual of Interior Photography. Michael G. Harris. LC 92-41310. (Illus.). 128p. 1993. pap. text 39.95 (*0-240-51296-0*, Focal) Buttrwrth-Heinemann.
Manual of Internal Fixation. 2nd rev. ed. M. E. Mueller et al. LC 78-20743. (Illus.). 1979. 230.00 (*3-540-92113-3*) Spr-Verlag.
Manual of Internal Fixation. 3rd rev. ed. Ed. by M. E. Muller et al. (Illus.). 750p. 1995. 249.00 (*0-387-52523-8*) Spr-Verlag.
Manual of Internal Fixation in Small Animals. Ed. by Wade O. Brinker et al. (Illus.). 304p. 1983. 266.00 (*0-387-10629-4*) Spr-Verlag.
Manual of Internal Fixation in Small Animals. Ed. by Wade O. Brinker et al. (Illus.). 304p. 1984. 316.00 (*0-387-92118-4*) Spr-Verlag.
Manual of Internal Fixation in Small Animals. 2nd enl. rev. ed. Ed. by H. P. Berlien & P. P. Schmittenbecher. LC 97-20200. (Illus.). 450p. 1997. write for info. (*3-540-63000-7*) Spr-Verlag.
Manual of Internal Fixation in the Cranio-Facial Skeleton: Techniques As Recommended by the AO/ASIF-Maxillofacial Group. Ed. by J. Prein. LC 97-35559. (Illus.). 235p. 1997. 185.00 (*3-540-61810-4*) Spr-Verlag.
Manual of Internal Fixation of the Spine. Ed. by John S. Thalgott & Max Aebi. (Principles & Techniques in Spine Surgery Ser.). 305p. 1995. text 160.00 (*0-397-51621-5*) Lppncott W & W.
Manual of Internal Medicine. 4th ed. Jerry L. Spivak. 1990. 32.95 (*0-316-80738-9*, Little Brwn Med Div) Lppncott W & W.
Manual of Invertebrate Paleontology. Judith Dyer & Frederick R. Schram. (Illus.). 165p. (Orig.). (C). 1983. pap. text 8.25 (*0-87563-237-8*) Stipes.
Manual of IV Medications. Lynn D. Phillips & Marrily K. Kuhn. LC 95-21517. 700p. 1996. spiral bd. 29.95 (*0-316-70601-9*, Little Brwn Med Div) Lppncott W & W.
Manual of IV Medications. 2nd ed. Lynn D. Phillips & Merrily A. Kuhn. LC 98-2987. 816p. 1998. spiral bd. 29.95 (*0-7817-1546-6*) Lppncott W & W.
Manual of Karate. Ernest J. Harrison. 21.95 (*0-685-22028-1*) Wehman.
Manual of Lab & Diagnostic Tests for Nursing. Wilson. (Illus.). 1997. spiral bd. write for info. (*0-316-94410-6*) Lppncott W & W.
Manual of Laboratory & Diagnostic Tests. 5th ed. Frances T. Fischbach. LC 95-9601. 1,120p. 1995. pap. text 31.95 (*0-397-55186-X*) Lppncott W & W.
***Manual of Laboratory & Diagnostic Tests.** 6th ed. Frances T. Fischbach. LC 99-27740. 1152p. 1999. pap. text 31.95 (*0-7817-1969-0*) Lppncott W & W.
Manual of Laboratory Immunology. 2nd ed. Linda Miller et al. LC 89-13712. (Illus.). 427p. 1991. pap. text 45.50 (*0-8121-1319-5*) Lppncott W & W.
Manual of Laparoscopic Surgery. Christian Klaiber & Joseph B. Petelin. LC 92-48741. (Illus.). 264p. 1993. 146.00 (*0-88937-091-5*) Hogrefe & Huber Pubs.
Manual of Law French. 2nd ed. J. H. Baker. (Illus.). 160p. 1990. text 86.95 (*0-85967-745-1*, Pub. by Scolar Pr) Ashgate Pub Co.
Manual of Law Librarians. MOYS. (C). 1976. text 55.00 (*0-89158-637-7*) Westview.
Manual of Law Librarianship: The Use & Organization of Legal Literature. 2nd ed. Ed. by Elizabeth M. Moys. (Professional Librarian Ser.). 952p. 1987. 70.00 (*0-8161-1854-X*, Hall Reference) Macmillan.
Manual of Life. Samuel Alpizar. 18p. 1998. pap. 5.00 (*0-9655165-1-2*) S Alpizar.
Manual of Liver Surgery. W. P. Longmire, Jr. & R. K. Tompkins. (Comprehensive Manuals of Surgical Specialties Ser.). (Illus.). 267p. 1981. 185.00 (*0-387-90212-0*) Spr-Verlag.
Manual of Lizards & Snakes. Marc Staniszewski. (Illus.). 158p. 24.95 (*3-89356-040-8*, 16048) Tetra Pr.
Manual of Low-Slope Roof Systems. 3rd ed. C. W. Griffin & R. L. Fricklas. 480p. 1996. 74.95 (*0-07-024784-6*) McGraw.
Manual of Lower Gastrointestinal Surgery. C. E. Welch et al. LC 79-9534. (Comprehensive Manuals of Surgical Specialties Ser.). (Illus.). 1980. 160.00 (*0-387-90205-8*) Spr-Verlag.
***Manual of Lung Transplant Medical Care.** University of Minnesota Staff & Fairview Health Services Staff. Ed. by Marshall I. Hertz. LC 99-43215. 96p. 1999. spiral bd. 20.00 (*1-57749-092-4*) Fairview Press.
Manual of Mammalogy. 2nd ed. Anthony F. DeBlase & Robert E. Martin. 448p. (C). 1980. text. write for info. (*0-697-04591-9*, WCB McGr Hill) McGrw-H Hghr Educ.
Manual of Management Training Exercises. John Payne. (Illus.). 236p. 1989. ring bd. 245.95 (*1-85904-046-2*, Pub. by Gower) Ashgate Pub Co.
Manual of Manuscript Transcription for the Dictionary of the Old Spanish Language. 5th rev. ed. Ed. by Ray Harris-Northall. vii, 53p. 1997. 40.00 (*1-56954-067-5*) Hispanic Seminary.
Manual of Maple Street Church, Danvers Massachusetts. Ed. by Charles D. Townsend. 55p. 1997. reprint ed. pap. 10.00 (*1-878545-31-0*) ACETO Bookmen.
Manual of Marine Invertebrates. Martyn Haywood & Sue Well. (Illus.). 230p. 1995. 26.95 (*1-56465-139-8*, 16038) Tetra Pr.
Manual of Materia Medica & Pharmacology. 7th ed. David M. Culbreth. 667p. 1996. reprint ed. pap. 35.00 (*0-7873-0229-5*) Hlth Research.
Manual of Maternal-Newborn Nursing. Patricia A. Dunn. LC 96-3206. 450p. 1996. spiral bd. 29.95 (*0-316-19659-2*) Lppncott W & W.
Manual of Medical Care. 4th ed. R. Timothy Coussons. 1990. 34.95 (*0-316-77493-6*, Little Brwn Med Div) Lppncott W & W.
Manual of Medical Care Asia, No. 4. R. Timothy Coussons. 1990. 10.95 (*0-316-77490-1*, Little Brwn Med Div) Lppncott W & W.
Manual of Medical Care of the Surgical Patient. 3rd ed. Solomon Papper et al. 304p. 1985. 24.50 (*0-316-69058-9*, Little Brwn Med Div) Lppncott W & W.
Manual of Medical Mycology. John T. Crissey et al. LC 94-3339. (Illus.). 300p. 1995. 79.95 (*0-86542-363-6*) Blackwell Sci.
Manual of Medical Nutrition Therapy. 4th ed. Crozer-Chester Medical Center Clinical Nutrition S. 376p. 1998. ring bd. 100.00 (*0-9662274-0-9*) Crozer-Keystone.
Manual of Medical Procedures. Ed. by Michael J. Ford. (Illus.). 204p. 1987. pap. 22.00 (*0-443-03598-9*) Church.
Manual of Medical Procedures. Paul M. Suratt & Robert S. Gibson. LC 82-3457. (Illus.). 400p. (C). (gr. 13). 1982. spiral bd. 27.95 (*0-8016-4850-5*, 04850) Mosby Inc.
Manual of Medical-Surgical Nursing. Debra Daly-Gawenda. LC 96-9848. (Nursing Fact Finder Ser.). 700p. 1996. spiral bd. 29.95 (*0-316-21792-1*) Lppncott W & W.
Manual of Medical Surgical Nursing Care: Interventions & Collaborative Management, No. 4. 4th ed. Pamela L. Swearingen. LC 98-22562. (Illus.). 896p. (C). (gr. 13). 1998. pap. text 36.95 (*0-8151-2744-8*, 31305) Mosby Inc.
Manual of Medical Therapeutics. 25th ed. Washington University Department of Medicine et al. 500p. 1986. 22.50 (*0-316-92393-1*, Little Brwn Med Div) Lppncott W & W.
Manual of Medical Therapeutics. 28th ed. 1996. 99.95 (*1-56712-266-3*, F0300) Franklin Elect.
Manual of Medical Therapeutics. 28th ed. Washington University Department of Medicine. 640p. 1995. spiral bd. 34.95 (*0-316-92433-4*) Little.

M

Manual of Medical Therapy, No. 26. Washington University Department of Medicine. 1989. 24.50 (*0-316-92400-8*, Little Brwn Med Div) Lppncott W & W.

Manual of Medical Therapy Asia. 26th ed. Washington University Department of Medicine. 1989. 10.95 (*0-316-92390-7*, Little Brwn Med Div) Lppncott W & W.

Manual of Medicinal Poisoning. V. Anantharaman & P. P. Tan. 280p. 1995. text 61.00 (*981-02-1093-0*) World Scientific Pub.

Manual of Medicine. Rodes. (SPA.). 1995. 73.00 (*84-458-0093-0*, Little Brwn Med Div) Lppncott W & W.

Manual of Mental & Physical Tests, 2 vols., 1 bk. Guy M. Whipple. LC 73-2997. (Classics in Psychology Ser.). 1974. reprint ed. 47.95 (*0-405-05169-7*) Ayer.

Manual of Mental Subnormality. Roberto Moran. (SPA.). 482p. 1968. 7.00 (*0-8477-2900-1*) U of PR Pr.

Manual of Methods & Identification of Toxins in Seafood & Seafood Products. Mark L. Tamplin. 1999. 90.00 (*0-8493-8975-5*, 8975) CRC Pr.

Manual of Methods for General Bacteriology. American Society for Microbiology Staff. Ed. by Philipp Gerhardt. LC 80-22275. (Illus.). 536p. reprint ed. pap. 166.20 (*0-8357-7509-7*, 203600100097) Bks Demand.

Manual of Microbiologic Monitoring of Laboratory Animals. Kim Waggie. 339p. 1994. per. 28.00 (*0-16-044918-9*) USGPO.

Manual of Microbiologic Monitoring of Laboratory Animals. 2nd ed. Ed. by Kim Waggie et al. 226p. (C). 1994. pap. text 50.00 (*0-7881-1071-3*) DIANE Pub.

Manual of Microcomputers Speech Language Pathology & Audiology. Katz. 1998. 27.00 (*1-56593-230-7*) Singular Publishing.

Manual of Microsurgery. Ed. by Sun Lee. (Illus.). 160p. 1985. 92.00 (*0-8493-0726-0*, RD33, CRC Reprint) Franklin.

Manual of Microsurgery on the Laboratory Rat, Pt. 1. Ed. by J. J. Van Dongen et al. (Techniques in the Behavioral & Neural Sciences Ser.: No. 4). (Illus.). 294p. 1990. 210.00 (*0-444-81138-9*); pap. 75.75 (*0-685-40077-8*) Elsevier.

Manual of Microsurgery on the Laboratory Rat, Pt. 1. J. J. Van Dongen & R. Remie. (Techniques in the Behavioral & Neural Sciences Ser.: Vol. 4). 294p. 1990. pap. 82.25 (*0-444-81139-7*, TBN 4) Elsevier.

*__Manual of Middle Ear Surgery, 3 vols.__ Mirkos Tos. 1480p. 2000. 427.00 (*0-86577-820-5*) Thieme Med Pubs.

Manual of Middle Ear Surgery Vol. 1: Approaches, Myringoplasty, Ossiculoplasty & Tympanoplasty, Vol. 1. M. Tos. (Illus.). 413p. 1993. 159.00 (*0-86577-498-6*) Thieme Med Pubs.

Manual of Middle Ear Surgery Vol. 2: Mastoid Surgery & Reconstructive Procedures, Vol. 2. M. Tos. (Illus.). 448p. 1995. 159.00 (*0-86577-589-3*) Thieme Med Pubs.

Manual of Middle Ear Surgery Vol. 3: External Auditory Canal, Vol. 3. Mirkos Tos. (Illus.). 384p. 1997. 149.00 (*0-86577-608-3*) Thieme Med Pubs.

Manual of Military Surgery. Samuel D. Gross. LC 88-60872. (American Civil War Surgery Ser.: No. 1). 186p. 1988. reprint ed. 45.00 (*0-930405-04-8*) Norman SF.

Manual of Military Surgery: Prepared for the Use of the Confederate States Army. Intro. by Samuel P. Moore & Ira M. Rutkow. LC 88-60874. (American Civil War Surgery Ser.: No. 2). (Illus.). 297p. 1989. reprint ed. 75.00 (*0-930405-14-5*) Norman SF.

Manual of Military Surgery: Suregeons in the Confederate States Army. J. Julian Chisolm. (Illus.). 581p. 1997. reprint ed. 45.00 (*0-89029-068-7*) Morningside Bkshop.

Manual of Military Surgery, for the Use of Surgeons in the Confederate States Army: With an Appendix of the Rules & Regulations of the Medical Department in the Confederate Army. John J. Chisolm. LC 88-60871. (American Civil War Surgery Ser.: No. 4). 447p. 1989. reprint ed. 60.00 (*0-930405-03-X*) Norman SF.

Manual of Mineralogy. Cornelis Klein & Cornelius Hurlbut. LC 84-19556. 704p. 1993. text 87.95 (*0-471-57452-X*) Wiley.

Manual of Mineralogy. rev. ed. Cornelis Klein & Cornelius S. Hurlbut. LC 98-23230. 704p. 1998. text 102.95 (*0-471-31266-5*) Wiley.

Manual of Mineralogy: With Minerals & Rocks Exercises in Crystallography Mineralogy & Home Specimen Petrology. 21st rev. ed. Cornelis Klein & Cornelius S. Hurlbut. 1120p. 1994. text 69.50 (*0-471-11549-5*) Wiley.

Manual of Mineralogy (After James D. Dana) Cornelius Klein & Cornelius S. Hurlbut. 1995. pap. 25.00 (*0-471-14679-X*) Wiley.

Manual of Minor Surgery. John H. Packard. LC 88-60670. (American Civil War Surgery Ser.: No. 10). 288p. 1989. reprint ed. 45.00 (*0-930405-08-0*) Norman SF.

Manual of Model Civil Jury Instructions for the District Courts of the Eighth Circuit. William A. Knox. 150p. 1993. pap. text. write for info. (*0-314-01861-1*) West Pub.

Manual of Model Civil Jury Instructions for the District Courts of the Eighth Circuit: 1995 Edition. William A. Knox. 231p. (C). 1995. pap. text. write for info. (*0-314-06218-1*) West Pub.

Manual of Model Civil Jury Instructions for the Ninth Circuit. Model Jury Instructions Committee. 303p. (C). 1993. pap. text. write for info. (*0-314-02583-9*) West Pub.

Manual of Model Criminal Jury Instructions for the District Courts of the Uniteds States Eighth Circuit, 1994 Edition. William A. Knox. 425p. 1994. pap. text. write for info. (*0-314-04194-X*) West Pub.

Manual of Model Jury Criminal Jury Instructions, for the District Courts of the U. S. Eighth Circuit. William A. Knox. 375p. (C). 1992. pap. text. write for info. (*0-314-01039-4*) West Pub.

Manual of Modern Greek, Vol. I. Anne Farmakides. LC 82-48915. (Yale Linguistic Ser.: Vol. 18). 304p. 1983. pap. 25.00 (*0-300-03019-3*) Yale U Pr.

Manual of Mongolian Astrology & Divination. Francis W. Cleaves. 1990. pap. 7.00 (*0-674-54825-6*) HUP.

Manual of Monocular Subjective Refraction. Harry Freeman. (C). 1989. 100.00 (*0-9507635-0-0*, Pub. by Assn Brit Dispen Opticians) St Mut.

Manual of Morphometry in Diagnostic Pathology. J. P. Baak & J. Oort. (Illus.). 230p. 1983. 78.95 (*0-387-11431-9*) Spr-Verlag.

Manual of Motivational Strategies: Text & Transparencies in Composition & Grammar. 4th ed. Joel Littauer. Ed. & Intro. by Joan Ashkenas. 60p. 1999. ring bd. 45.00 (*0-943327-05-9*) JAG Pubns.

Manual of Museum Management. Barry Lord & Gail D. Lord. 261p. 1997. pap. 49.00 (*0-11-290518-8*, HM05188, Pub. by Statnry Office) Balogh.

*__Manual of Museum Planning.__ 2nd ed. Ed. by Gail D. Lord & Barry Lord. 480p. 2000. pap. 49.95 (*0-7425-0406-9*) AltaMira Pr.

Manual of Musical Copyright Law for the Use of Music-Publishers & Artists & of the Legal Profession. Edward Cutler. xx, 132, lxiiip. 1996. reprint ed. 35.00 (*0-8377-2058-3*, Rothman) W S Hein.

Manual of Mythology: Greek & Roman, Norse & Old German, Hindoo & Egyptian Mythology. Alexander V. Murray. Ed. by Gina R. Gross. (Illus.). 368p. 1993. reprint ed. pap. 12.95 (*0-87877-182-4*) Newcastle Pub.

Manual of Mythology in Relation to Greek Art. M. Collignon. Tr. by J. Ellen Harrison. xvi, 335p. (C). 1982. reprint ed. lib. bdg. 55.00 (*0-89241-141-4*) Caratzas.

Manual of Nail Disease & Surgery. 2nd ed. Robert Baran et al. LC 97-5904. (Illus.). 112p. 1997. pap. text 69.95 (*0-86542-638-4*) Blackwell Sci.

*__Manual of Nail Disorders.__ P. Rich. 2001. write for info. (*1-84214-035-3*) Prthnon Pub.

Manual of Natural History Curatorship. Museum & Galleries Commission Staff. Ed. by Geoff Stansfield et al. 306p. 1994. pap. 79.95 (*0-11-290513-7*, HM05137, Pub. by Statnry Office) Balogh.

Manual of Natural Therapy. Moshe Olshevsky et al. 384p. 1990. pap. 14.95 (*0-8065-1202-4*, Citadel Pr) Carol Pub Group.

Manual of Natural Therapy: A Practical Guide to Alternative Medicine. Moshe Olshevsky et al. (Illus.). 386p. 1999. reprint ed. 39.95 (*0-7351-0088-8*) Replica Bks.

Manual of Natural Therapy: A Succint Catalog of Complementary Treatments. Moshe Olshevsky et al. LC 88-24410. (Illus.). 384p. reprint ed. pap. 119.10 (*0-7837-6694-7*, 204631100011) Bks Demand.

Manual of Nature Conservation Law. Michael Fry. 536p. 1995. pap. text 54.00 (*0-19-826048-2*) OUP.

Manual of Nature Conservation Law. Ed. by Michael Fry. 536p. 1995. text 89.00 (*0-19-825958-1*) OUP.

Manual of Navaho Grammar. Berard Haile. LC 73-15402. reprint ed. 47.50 (*0-404-11240-4*) AMS Pr.

Manual of Neonatal Care. 2nd ed. John P. Cloherty & Ann R. Stark. 688p. 1985. 25.50 (*0-316-14756-7*, Little Brwn Med Div) Lppncott W & W.

Manual of Neonatal Care. 4th ed. Ed. by John P. Cloherty & Ann R. Stark. LC 97-22777. (Illus.). 688p. 1997. spiral bd. 34.95 (*0-316-14765-6*) Lppncott W & W.

Manual of Neonatal Emergency X-Ray Interpretation. P. W. Meerstadt & Catherine Gyll. (Illus.). 301p. 1995. pap. text 33.95 (*0-7020-1567-9*, Pub. by W B Saunders) Saunders.

Manual of Neonatal Intensive Care. 3rd ed. N. R. Robertson. 416p. 1993. pap. text 24.95 (*0-340-55572-6*, Pub. by E A) OUP.

*__Manual of Neonatal Respiratory Care.__ Ed. by Sunil K. Sinha & Steven M. Donn. LC 99-39510. (Illus.). 600p. 2000. write for info. (*0-87993-444-1*) Futura Pub.

Manual of Neotropical Birds: Spheniscidae (Penguins) to Laridae (Gulls & Allies), Vol. 1. Emmet R. Blake. LC 75-43229. (Illus.). 714p. 1977. lib. bdg. 120.00 (*0-226-05641-4*) U Ch Pr.

Manual of Nephrology. 2nd ed. Robert W. Schrier. (Diagnosis & Therapy Ser.). 291p. 1985. 22.50 (*0-316-77478-2*, Little Brwn Med Div) Lppncott W & W.

Manual of Nephrology. 4th ed. Ed. by Robert W. Schrier. LC 94-22850. 320p. 1995. spiral bd. 38.00 (*0-316-77464-2*, Little Brwn Med Div) Lppncott W & W.

*__Manual of Nephrology.__ 5th ed. Ed. by Robert W. Schrier. LC 99-33657. 310p. 1999. pap. 37.95 (*0-7817-2172-5*) Lppncott W & W.

*__Manual of Nerve Conduction Studies.__ Ralph M. Buschbacher. (Illus.). 304p. 1999. pap. text 49.95 (*1-888799-36-6*, Pub. by Demos Medical) SCB Distributors.

Manual of Nerve Conduction Velocity & Clinical Neurophysiology. 3rd ed. Joel A. DeLisa et al. LC 93-21370. 512p. 1994. spiral bd. 49.95 (*0-7817-0138-4*) Lppncott W & W.

Manual of Nerve Conduction Velocity & Somatosensory Evoked Potentials. 2nd fac. ed. Joel A. DeLisa et al. LC 85-43145. 288p. pap. 89.30 (*0-7837-7272-6*, 204703300005) Bks Demand.

Manual of Neural Therapy According to Huneke: Therapy with Local Anesthetics. Peter Dosch. (Illus.). 498p. 1985. 98.00 (*3-7760-0702-8*, Pub. by K F Haug Pubs) Medicina Bio.

Manual of Neurologic Therapeutics. 6th ed. Martin A. Samuels. LC 98-41269. 512p. 1998. spiral bd. 34.95 (*0-7817-1645-4*) Lppncott W & W.

Manual of Neurologic Therapeutics: With Essentials of Diagnosis. 3rd ed. Martin A. Samuels. (Spiral Manual Ser.). 1986. spiral bd. 22.50 (*0-316-76992-4*, Little Brwn Med Div) Lppncott W & W.

Manual of Neurologic Therapeutics: With Essentials of Diagnosis. 5th ed. Samuels. 472p. 1994. spiral bd. 33.95 (*0-316-77004-3*, Little Brwn Med Div) Lppncott W & W.

Manual of Neurology. 2nd ed. J. P. Mohr. 1989. 32.95 (*0-316-57748-0*, Little Brwn Med Div) Lppncott W & W.

Manual of Neurology Asia, No. 4. Martin A. Samuels. 1990. 10.95 (*0-316-76999-1*, Little Brwn Med Div) Lppncott W & W.

Manual of Neurology ISE. 2nd ed. J. P. Mohr. 1989. 15.95 (*0-316-57749-9*, Little Brwn Med Div) Lppncott W & W.

Manual of Neurology ISE, No. 4. Martin A. Samuels. 1990. 15.95 (*0-316-77001-9*, Little Brwn Med Div) Lppncott W & W.

Manual of Neurology NSG. 2nd ed. Nancy Swift-Bandin & Ban. 1982. 16.00 (*0-316-82541-7*) Little.

Manual of Neurosurgery. Palmer. 1995. pap. text 58.00 (*0-443-05391-X*, W B Saunders Co) Harcrt Hlth Sci Grp.

Manual of Newborn Care Plans. Mary L. Rang. (Spiral Manual Ser.). 1981. 14.00 (*0-316-73380-6*, Little Brwn Med Div) Lppncott W & W.

Manual of Normal Neonatal Care. 2nd ed. N. R. Robertson. (Arnold Publication). 368p. 1996. pap. 27.95 (*0-340-61375-0*) OUP.

Manual of Nuclear Medicine Imaging. Christopher C. Kuni & Rene P. Du Cret. LC 96-48078. (Illus.). 336p. 1996. pap. text 35.00 (*0-86577-568-0*) Thieme Med Pubs.

Manual of Nuclear Medicine Procedures. 4th ed. Ed. by James E. Carey et al. 248p. 1983. 139.00 (*0-8493-0708-2*, R78, CRC Reprint) Franklin.

Manual of Nuer Law: Being an Account of Customary Law, Its Evolution & Development in the Courts Established by the Sudan Government. Paul P. Howell. LC 55-14160. (Illus.). 278p. reprint ed. pap. 86.20 (*0-8357-3008-5*, 205709400010) Bks Demand.

Manual of Nurse Recruitment & Retention. Kate M. Fenner & Peter Fenner. 250p. ring bd. 159.00 (*0-8342-0037-6*, S14) Aspen Pub.

Manual of Nursing Diagnosis, 1997-1998. Marjory Gordon. 512p. (C). (gr. 13). 1996. text 24.00 (*0-8151-3494-0*, 27933) Mosby Inc.

*__Manual of Nursing Home Practice for Psychiatrists.__ American Psychiatric Association Staff. LC 99-48771. 2000. write for info. (*0-89042-283-4*) Amer Psych Assn.

Manual of Nursing Quality Assurance. Ed. by Howard S. Rowland & Beatrice L. Rowland. ring bd. 289.00 (*0-87189-875-6*, S08) Aspen Pub.

Manual of Nursing Staff Development. Brown & Stewart. (Illus.). 432p. (C). (gr. 13). 1995. text 98.00 (*0-8016-6609-0*, 06609) Mosby Inc.

Manual of Nursing Therapeutics: Applying Nursing Diagnoses to Medical Disorders. Pamela L. Swearingen. 556p. (C). 1986. pap. text 22.95 (*0-201-12940-X*, Health Sci) Addison-Wesley.

Manual of Nutritional Therapeutics. 3rd ed. David H. Alpers. (Spiral Manual Ser.). 624p. 1995. spiral bd. 38.00 (*0-316-03524-6*) Lppncott W & W.

Manual of Obstetric & Gynecologic Ultrasound. Richard Jaffe & Jacques S. Abramowicz. LC 96-53903. 400p. 1997. pap. text 47.95 (*0-397-51595-2*) Lppncott W & W.

*__Manual of Obstetrics.__ 6th ed. Arthur T. Evans & Kenneth R. Niswander. LC 99-48129. 2000. write for info. (*0-7817-2404-X*) Lppncott W & W.

Manual of Obstetrics: Diagnosis & Therapy. 3rd ed. Kenneth R. Niswander. 1987. spiral bd. 22.50 (*0-316-61139-5*, Little Brwn Med Div) Lppncott W & W.

Manual of Obstetrics: Diagnosis & Therapy. 5th ed. Ed. by Kenneth R. Niswander & Authur T. Evans. 538p. 1995. spiral bd. 32.95 (*0-316-61172-7*, Little Brwn Med Div) Lppncott W & W.

Manual of Obstetrics Asia, No. 3. Kenneth R. Niswander. 1987. 10.95 (*0-316-61135-2*, Little Brwn Med Div) Lppncott W & W.

Manual of Obstetrics Asia, No. 4. Kenneth R. Niswander. 1991. 10.95 (*0-316-61171-9*, Little Brwn Med Div) Lppncott W & W.

Manual of Obstetrics ISE, No. 3. Kenneth R. Niswander. 1987. 15.95 (*0-316-61136-0*, Little Brwn Med Div) Lppncott W & W.

Manual of Occultism. A. Sepharial. 356p. 1996. reprint ed. pap. 30.00 (*0-7873-0764-5*) Hlth Research.

Manual of Occultism. A. Sepharial. 360p. 1996. reprint ed. pap. 24.95 (*1-56459-815-2*) Kessinger Pub.

Manual of Ocular Diagnosis & Therapy. 2nd ed. Deborah Pavan-Langston. 494p. 1985. 24.50 (*0-316-69544-0*, Little Brwn Med Div) Lppncott W & W.

Manual of Ocular Diagnosis & Therapy. 4th ed. Ed. by Deborah Paven-Langston. LC 95-31695. 506p. 1995. spiral bd. 35.95 (*0-316-69534-3*, Little Brwn Med Div) Lppncott W & W.

Manual of Ocular Diagnosis for Asia. Deborah Pavan-Langston. 1995. 32.95 (*0-316-69560-2*) Little.

Manual of Ocular Fundus Examination. Theo Dorion. LC 98-2711. 576p. 1998. pap. text 65.00 (*0-7506-9987-6*) Buttrwrth-Heinemann.

Manual of Oculoplastic Surgery. Ed. by Mark R. Levine. LC 88-18903. (Illus.). 284p. reprint ed. pap. 88.10 (*0-7837-6254-2*, 204596600010) Bks Demand.

Manual of Oculoplastic Surgery. 2nd ed. Mark Levine. (Illus.). 336p. 1996. text 70.00 (*0-7506-9634-6*, Focal) Buttrwrth-Heinemann.

Manual of Oil & Gas Terms: Annotated. 10th ed. Kramer & Martin. LC 98-163473. 1983. reprint ed. pap. write for info. (*0-8205-1821-2*) Bender.

Manual of Oncologic Therapeutics. 3rd ed. John D. MacDonald et al. 576p. 1995. spiral bd. 49.00 (*0-397-51394-1*) Lppncott W & W.

Manual of Oncology Nursing Practice: Nursing Diagnoses. Reidun Daeffler & Barbara A. Petrosino. 314p. 1990. 100.00 (*0-8342-0114-3*, 20114) Aspen Pub.

Manual of Online Search Strategies. 2nd ed. Chris Armstrong & Andy Large. (Professional Librarian Ser.). 200p. 1992. 65.00 (*0-8161-1992-9*, Hall Reference) Macmillan.

*__Manual of Online Search Strategies, 3 vols.__ 3rd ed. Ed. by C. J. Armstrong & Andrew Large. LC 00-25154. 1088p. 2000. 400.00 (*0-566-07990-9*, Pub. by Ashgate Pub) Ashgate Pub Co.

*__Manual of Online Search Strategies, 3 vols.__ 3rd ed. C. J. Armstrong & J. A. Large. LC 00-25154. 2000. write for info. (*0-566-08305-1*, Pub. by Gower) Ashgate Pub Co.

Manual of Operation for the Automatic Sequence Controlled Calculator. Harvard Computation Laboratory Staff. 585p. 1985. reprint ed. 75.00 (*0-262-01084-4*) MIT Pr.

Manual of Ophthalmology. John W. Gittinger. 1987. 15.95 (*0-316-31472-2*, Little Brwn Med Div) Lppncott W & W.

Manual of Oral & Maxillofacial Surgery. 3rd ed. Massachusetts General Hospital Staff. Ed. by R. Bruce Donoff. (Illus.). 448p. (C). (gr. 13). 1996. text 46.95 (*0-8151-2755-3*, 26586) Mosby Inc.

Manual of Orbital Lacrimal Surgery. 4th ed. McNab. 160p. 1998. pap. text 65.00 (*0-7506-3997-0*) Buttrwrth-Heinemann.

Manual of Orchestral Bowings. Charles Gigante. 133p. 1986. 27.50 (*0-89917-469-8*) Am String Tchrs.

Manual of Orchidaceous Plants. V. Veitch. 1070p. (C). 1981. 260.00 (*0-7855-3281-1*, Pub. by Scientific) St Mut.

Manual of Orchids. Ed. by Joyce Stewart & Mark Griffiths. (Illus.). 448p. 1995. 49.95 (*0-88192-334-6*) Timber.

Manual of Organic Materia Medica: Drugs from Natural Sources. J. M. Maisch. (Alternative Medicine Ser.). 1992. lib. bdg. 275.95 (*0-8490-5441-9*) Gordon Pr.

Manual of Organizational Development: The Psychology of Change. Claire Huffington et al. 112p. 1997. pap. 27.00 (*1-85575-128-3*, Pub. by H Karnac Bks Ltd) Other Pr LLC.

Manual of Organizational Development: The Psychology of Change. Claire Huffington et al. LC 97-1576. xiv, 98p. 1997. 26.50 (*1-887841-06-7*, 63143, Psychosocial) Intl Univs Pr.

Manual of Ornament. (Reference Library). (Illus.). 208p. 1998. pap. 6.95 (*1-85326-347-8*, 3478WW, Pub. by Wrdsworth Edits) NTC Contemp Pub Co.

Manual of Ornamental Fish. Ed. by Ray L. Butcher. (Illus.). 200p. 1994. pap. text 64.95 (*0-905214-18-8*, Pub. by BSAVA) Iowa St U Pr.

Manual of Ornithology: Avian Structure & Function. Noble S. Proctor. (Illus.). 352p. 1993. pap. 25.00 (*0-300-07619-3*) Yale U Pr.

Manual of Ornithology: Avian Structure & Function. Noble S. Proctor. LC 92-17066. (Illus.). 352p. (C). 1993. 50.00 (*0-300-05746-6*) Yale U Pr.

Manual of Orthopaedic Surgery for Spasticity. Mary A. Keenan et al. LC 92-48983. 176p. 1993. text 79.00 (*0-7817-0000-0*) Lppncott W & W.

Manual of Orthopaedic Terminology, No. 6. 6th ed. Carolyn T. Blauvelt & Fred Nelson. LC 98-10711. (Illus.). 475p. (C). (gr. 13). 1998. pap. text 36.95 (*0-8151-2787-1*, 31249) Mosby Inc.

Manual of Orthopedic Anesthesia & Related Pain Syndromes. Ralph L. Bernstein & Andrew D. Rosenberg. (Illus.). 496p. (Orig.). 1993. pap. text 72.00 (*0-443-08843-8*) Church.

Manual of Otolaryngology: A Symptom-Oriented Text. Raymond P. Wood. Ed. by Jerry L. Northern. LC 78-31442. 252p. reprint ed. pap. 78.20 (*0-608-14654-4*, 202315000032) Bks Demand.

Manual of Otolaryngology: Diagnosis & Therapy. Strome Marshall. 212p. 1985. 25.50 (*0-316-81967-0*, Little Brwn Med Div) Lppncott W & W.

Manual of Otolaryngology: Head & Neck Therapeutics. Ed. by Arnold E. Katz. LC 85-238. 547p. reprint ed. pap. 169.60 (*0-7837-2719-4*, 204309900006) Bks Demand.

Manual of Outpatient Gynecology. Carol S. Havens et al. 280p. 1986. 25.50 (*0-316-35097-4*, Little Brwn Med Div) Lppncott W & W.

Manual of Outpatient Gynecology. 3rd ed. Patti Tilton et al. LC 95-16986. 320p. 1995. spiral bd. 35.95 (*0-316-35000-1*) Lppncott W & W.

Manual of Paediatric Dentistry. 4th ed. R. J. Andlaw & W. P. Rock. LC 96-39210. (C). 1998. pap. text 49.50 (*0-443-05372-3*) Church.

Manual of Paediatric Intensive Care Nursing. Ed. by Bernadette Carter. LC 92-49068. 1993. 63.75 (*1-56593-042-8*, 0290) Thomson Learn.

Manual of Pain Management. Ed. by Carol A. Warfield. LC 65-10440. (Illus.). 416p. 1991. pap. text 54.00 (*0-397-50879-4*, Lippnctt) Lppncott W & W.

Manual of Pain Management. 2nd ed. Carol A. Warfield & Hilary Fausett. 420p. pap. text 59.95 (*0-7817-2313-2*) Lppncott W & W.

Manual of Panic-Focused Psychodynamic Psychotherapy. Barbara Milrod et al. 128p. 1997. text 29.00 (*0-88048-871-9*, 8871) Am Psychiatric.

Manual of Parliamentary Practice: For the Use of the Senate of the United States. Thomas Jefferson. LC 92-43244. 144p. 1993. pap. 10.95 (*1-55709-202-8*) Applewood.

Manual of Partnership Relations. Thomas Conyngton. LC 06-693. (Business Enterprises Reprint Ser.). 221p. 1982. reprint ed. lib. bdg. 40.00 (*0-89941-178-9*, 302130) W S Hein.

An Asterisk (*) at the beginning of an entry indicates that the title is appearing for the first time.

Manual of Patent Examining Procedure. 16th ed. Patent & Trademark Office Staff. (IP Ser.). 1993. pap. 60.00 (*0-614-07304-9*) West Group.

Manual of Patent Examining Procedure, 1998. Government Printing Office Staff. 1984. ring bd. 216.00 (*0-16-016459-1*) USGPO.

Manual of Patient Care in Neurosurgery. 2nd ed. James R. Howe. 1983. 22.50 (*0-316-37575-6*, Little Brwn Med Div) Lppncott W & W.

Manual of Patient Care Standards. Anne MacGuire. ring bd. 249.00 (*0-87189-765-2*, S15) Aspen Pub.

Manual of Patient Classification: Systems & Techniques for Practical Application. Elizabeth N. Lewis. 432p. 1988. 167.00 (*0-87189-898-5*, 510) Aspen Pub.

Manual of Peace: Embracing I, Evils & Remedies of War, II, Suggestions on the Law of Nations, III, Consideration of a Congress of Nations. Thomas C. Upham. LC 79-143433. (Peace Movement in America Ser.). 408p. 1972. reprint ed. lib. bdg. 48.95 (*0-89198-086-5*) Ozer.

Manual of Pediatric Anesthesia. 3rd ed. David J. Steward. (Illus.). 446p. 1990. pap. text 37.95 (*0-443-08573-0*) Church.

Manual of Pediatric Anesthesia. 4th ed. David J. Steward. LC 94-34674. 1994. pap. text 50.00 (*0-443-08942-6*) Church.

Manual of Pediatric Critical Care. Mary F. Hazinski. (Illus.). 700p. (C). (gr. 13). 1998. pap. text 39.95 (*0-8151-4230-7*, 24849) Mosby Inc.

Manual of Pediatric Critical Care. Narendra C. Singh. Ed. by Judy Fletcher. LC 96-7417. (Illus.). 448p. 1997. pap. text 42.00 (*0-7216-5949-7*, W B Saunders Co) Harcrt Hlth Sci Grp.

Manual of Pediatric Emergencies. Ed. by Joseph R. Zanga. LC 86-21586. (Illus.). 527p. reprint ed. pap. 163.40 (*0-7837-6249-6*, 204596100010) Bks Demand.

Manual of Pediatric Gastroenterology. Joseph F. Fitzgerald & Joseph H. Clark. (Illus.). 216p. 1988. pap. text 38.95 (*0-443-08538-2*) Church.

Manual of Pediatric Hematology & Oncology. Philip Lanzkowsky et al. LC 89-470. 468p. reprint ed. pap. 145.10 (*0-7837-1613-3*, 204190500024) Bks Demand.

Manual of Pediatric Hematology & Oncology. 2nd ed. Philip Lanzkowsky. LC 94-32744. 1994. text 115.00 (*0-443-08969-8*) Church.

***Manual of Pediatric Hematology & Oncology.** 3rd ed. Philip Lanzkowsky. (Illus.). 816p. 2000. 99.95 (*0-12-436635-X*) Acad Pr.

***Manual of Pediatric Intensive Care.** Haresh M. Kirpalani et al. 300p. 1999. pap. 24.95 (*1-55009-089-5*) DEKR.

Manual of Pediatric Nursing. Ed. by Janet M. Brucker & Kelly D. Wallin. LC 95-52479. (Peds Fact Finder Ser.). 450p. 1996. spiral bd. 29.95 (*0-316-11451-0*) Lppncott W & W.

Manual of Pediatric Nursing Practice. Massachusetts General Hospital Department of Nursi. Ed. by Barbara H. Pikl. 1981. pap. 16.00 (*0-316-54959-2*, Little Brwn Med Div) Lppncott W & W.

Manual of Pediatric Nursing Procedures. Nedra Skale. (Illus.). 608p. 1992. pap. text 28.95 (*0-397-54782-X*) Lppncott W & W.

***Manual of Pediatric Nutrition.** Kristy M. P. Hendricks et al. 560p. 1999. pap. 34.95 (*1-55009-091-7*) DEKR.

Manual of Pediatric Nutrition. Wiley Staff. 560p. 1997. pap. text 54.95 (*0-471-34917-8*) Wiley.

Manual of Pediatric Nutrition. 3rd ed. 555p. 1997. ring bd. 59.95 (*1-56561-118-7*) Wiley.

Manual of Pediatric Therapeutics. 6th ed. Ed. by John W. Graef. LC 97-1436. (Illus.). 688p. 1997. spiral bd. 35.95 (*0-316-14171-2*) Lppncott W & W.

Manual of Pediatrics Emergency Nursing. Treesa E. Soud & Janice Steiner Rogers. LC 97-14312. (Illus.). 792p. (C). (gr. 13). 1997. pap. text 39.95 (*0-8016-7891-9*, 07891) Mosby Inc.

Manual of Pelvic Surgery. Ed. by M. J. Webb. (Illus.). 350p. 1994. 145.00 (*0-387-56865-4*) Spr-Verlag.

Manual of Penny Stocks. Ed. by Harry K. Eisenberg. 608p. 1998. pap. 45.00 (*0-9652088-3-4*, 98P) Walkers Manual.

Manual of Perinatal Anesthesia & Critical Care. Diaz. (Illus.). 416p. 1991. pap. text 64.00 (*0-7216-1874-X*, W B Saunders Co) Harcrt Hlth Sci Grp.

Manual of Perioperative Care in Cardiac & Thoracic Surgery. 2nd ed. Robert M. Bojar. LC 93-31153. (Illus.). 512p. 1994. pap. 44.95 (*0-86542-347-4*) Blackwell Sci.

Manual of Perioperative Care in Cardiac Surgery. 3rd ed. Robert M. Bojar & Kenneth G. Warner. LC 98-33471. (Illus.). 1998. pap. 51.95 (*0-632-04365-2*) Blackwell Sci.

Manual of Peritoneal Dialysis. G. A. Coles. (C). 1988. pap. text 72.50 (*0-7462-0081-1*) Kluwer Academic.

Manual of Permanent Plot Procedures for Tropical Rain Forests. T. J. Synnott. 1979. 42.00 (*0-85074-031-2*) St Mut.

Manual of Personnel Policies, Procedures & Operations. 2nd ed. Joseph D. Leveque. LC 93-9305. 512p. (C). 1993. ring bd. 79.95 (*0-13-020231-2*) P-H.

Manual of Pesticide Residue Analysis, Vol. 2. Ed. by H. P. Thier & J. Kirchhoff. (Illus.). 482p. 1992. 175.00 (*3-527-27017-5*, Wiley-VCH) Wiley.

Manual of Petrographic Methods, 2 vols., Set. 1991. lib. bdg. 188.96 (*0-8490-4506-1*) Gordon Pr.

Manual of Petroleum Measurement Standards. American Petroleum Institute Staff. LC 80-67080. (Chapter 11.1 -- Volume Correction Factors Ser.: Vol. II). (Illus.). 592p. 1980. 90.00 (*0-89364-023-9*, 852-27015) Am Petroleum.

Manual of Petroleum Measurement Standards. American Petroleum Institute Staff. LC 80-67080. (Chapter 11.1 -- Volume Correction Factors Ser.: Vol. III). (Illus.). 563p. 1980. 90.00 (*0-89364-024-7*, 852-27032) Am Petroleum.

Manual of Petroleum Measurement Standards. American Petroleum Institute Staff. LC 80-67080. (Chapter 11.1 -- Volume Correction Factors Ser.: Vol. IV). (Illus.). 878p. 1980. 90.00 (*0-89364-025-5*, 852-27045) Am Petroleum.

Manual of Petroleum Measurement Standards. American Petroleum Institute Staff. LC 80-67080. (Chapter 11.1 -- Volume Correction Factors Ser.: Vol. IX). (Illus.). 587p. 1980. 90.00 (*0-89364-032-8*, 852-27130) Am Petroleum.

Manual of Petroleum Measurement Standards. American Petroleum Institute Staff. LC 80-67080. (Chapter 11.1 -- Volume Correction Factors Ser.: Vol. V). (Illus.). 812p. 1980. 90.00 (*0-89364-026-3*, 852-27060) Am Petroleum.

Manual of Petroleum Measurement Standards. American Petroleum Institute Staff. LC 80-67080. (Chapter 11.1 -- Volume Correction Factors Ser.: Vol. VI). (Illus.). 563p. 1980. 90.00 (*0-89364-027-1*, 852-27085) Am Petroleum.

Manual of Petroleum Measurement Standards. American Petroleum Institute Staff. LC 80-67080. (Chapter 11.1 -- Volume Correction Factors Ser.: Vol. VII). (Illus.). 958p. 1980. 90.00 (*0-89364-029-8*, 852-27100) Am Petroleum.

Manual of Petroleum Measurement Standards. American Petroleum Institute Staff. (Chapter 11.1 -- Volume Correction Factors Ser.: Vol. VIII). (Illus.). 881p. 1980. 90.00 (*0-89364-030-1*, 852-27115) Am Petroleum.

Manual of Petroleum Measurement Standards. American Petroleum Institute Staff. LC 80-67080. (Chapter 11.1 -- Volume Correction Factors Ser.: Vol. X). (Illus.). 420p. 1980. 90.00 (*0-89364-033-6*, 852-27145) Am Petroleum.

Manual of Philatelic Judging. 3rd rev. ed. Ed. by APS Judges Accreditation Committee Staff & William H. Bauer. 120p. 1990. pap. 8.50 (*0-318-41175-X*) Am Philatelic Society.

Manual of Philatelic Judging: How Exhibits Are Judged. 4th rev. ed. Ed. by William H. Bauer. (Illus.). 88p. 1999. pap. text 12.00 (*0-933580-21-5*) Am Philatelic Society.

Manual of Phonology. Charles F. Hockett. (International Journal of America Linguistic: No. 21-4, Pt. 1). 252p. 1988. pap. text 19.50 (*0-226-34574-2*) U Ch Pr.

Manual of Photographic Interpretation. 2nd ed. Warren R. Philipson. (Illus.). 700p. 1997. 124.00 (*1-57083-039-8*, 4725) ASP & RS.

Manual of Photographic Manipulation Treating of the Practice of the Art & Its Various Applications to Nature. 2nd ed. William L. Price. LC 72-9223. (Literature of Photography Ser.). 1973. reprint ed. 24.95 (*0-405-04930-7*) Ayer.

Manual of Photography. 3rd ed. Robert Hunt. LC 72-9212. (Literature of Photography Ser.). 1973. reprint ed. 28.95 (*0-405-04920-X*) Ayer.

Manual of Photography. 8th ed. Ralph E. Jacobson et al. (Illus.). 384p. 1988. pap. text 54.95 (*0-240-51268-5*, Focal) Buttrwrth-Heinemann.

Manual of Phycology: An Introduction to the Algae & Their Biology. Ed. by Gilbert M. Smith. 375p. 1994. pap. 300.00 (*81-7233-091-X*, Pub. by Scientific Pubs) St Mut.

Manual of Physical Medicine & Rehabilitation. Tan. LC 97-22255. (Illus.). 848p. (C). (gr. 13). 1997. text 36.95 (*0-8151-8708-4*, 25352) Mosby Inc.

Manual of Physical Status & Performance in Childhood Vol. 1: Physical Status, Set with Vol. 2. Ed. by Alex F. Roche & Robert M. Malina. LC 82-16515. 1456p. 1983. 195.00 (*0-306-41136-9*, Plenum Trade) Perseus Pubng.

Manual of Physical Status & Performance in Childhood Vol. 2: Physical Performance. Ed. by Alex F. Roche & Robert M. Malina. LC 82-16515. 814p. 1983. 145.00 (*0-306-41137-7*, Plenum Trade) Perseus Pubng.

Manual of Physical Therapy. Ed. by Otto D. Payton et al. (Illus.). 761p. 1989. text 69.95 (*0-443-08499-8*) Church.

Manual of Piety: Die Hauspostille. Bertolt Brecht. Tr. by Eric Bentley from GER. LC 91-20789. 336p. 1970. pap. 11.95 (*0-8021-3245-6*, Grove) Grove-Atltic.

Manual of Pig Production in the Tropics. H. Serres. Tr. by J. Wiseman. (CAB International Publication Ser.). (Illus.). 288p. (Orig.). 1992. pap. text 45.00 (*0-85198-784-2*) OUP.

Manual of Pistol & Revolver Cartridges, 2 vols. 1987. lib. bdg. 300.00 (*0-8490-3934-7*) Gordon Pr.

Manual of Plastics Analysis. T. R. Crompton. LC 98-20244. (Illus.). 524p. (C). 1998. text 135.00 (*0-306-45912-4*, Kluwer Plenum) Kluwer Academic.

Manual of Pleural Procedures. Henri Colt & Praveen N. Mathur. 22p. 1998. pap. text 34.95 (*0-7817-1476-1*) Lppncott W & W.

Manual of Poisonous Plants: Chiefly of Eastern North America, with Brief Notes on Economic & Medicinal Plants. L. H. Pammel. (Illus.). 977p. 1992. reprint ed. lib. bdg. 75.00 (*0-945345-43-7*) Lubrecht & Cramer.

Manual of Policy & Procedure for Your Internal Security Force. Michael Maxwell. 1992. pap. 149.50 (*0-614-05762-0*) Abbott Langer Assocs.

Manual of Political Economy. E. Peshine Smith. LC 66-17864. (Reprints of Economic Classics Ser.). x, 269p. 1966. reprint ed. 39.50 (*0-678-00127-8*) Kelley.

Manual of Political Economy: With Particular Reference to the Institutions, Resources & Condition of the U. S. Willard Phillips. LC 65-26373. (Reprints of Economic Classics Ser.). 278p. 1968. reprint ed. 45.00 (*0-678-00278-9*) Kelley.

Manual of Political Economy: 1863 Edition. (Works of Henry & Millicent Garrett Fawcett). 626p. 1996. reprint ed. 96.00 (*1-85506-368-9*) Bks Intl VA.

Manual of Pollution Control Laws in India. G. Goyal. (C). 1988. 85.00 (*0-7855-3707-4*) St Mut.

Manual of Positive Attitude Training Techniques for Children & Young Adults. Nicola M. Tauraso & L. Richard Batzler. LC 82-82068. 1982. 25.00 (*0-935710-03-5*) Hid Valley MD.

Manual of Postoperative Management in Adult Cardiac Surgery. Carlos Moreno-Cabral et al. (Illus.). 112p. 1988. pap. 29.00 (*0-683-06146-1*) Lppncott W & W.

Manual of Pottery & Porcelain Restoration. 2nd ed. David Everett. (Illus.). 142p. 1991. pap. 13.95 (*0-7090-4705-3*, Pub. by R Hale Ltd) Antique Collect.

Manual of Poultry Production in the Tropics. R. R. Say. 119p. (Orig.). 1996. pap. text 29.95 (*0-85198-590-4*) C A B Intl.

Manual of Practical Devotion to St. Joseph. Patrignani. LC 82-50594. 328p. (J). 1988. reprint ed. pap. 15.00 (*0-89555-175-6*) TAN Bks Pubs.

***Manual of Practical Neuropathology Techniques.** Tim P. Dawson & J. S. Neal. (Illus.). 256p. 2000. pap. 75.00 (*0-7506-9086-0*) Buttrwrth-Heinemann.

Manual of Practical Pain Management. Beth Minzter. (Illus.). 600p. (C). 1999. pap. 54.95 (*0-8385-8116-1*) McGraw.

Manual of Practical Pediatrics. fac. ed. Stephen H. Sheldon. LC 80-5675. 301p. pap. 93.40 (*0-7837-7183-5*, 204711600005) Bks Demand.

Manual of Practical Pipeline Construction. Brian Schurr. LC 82-11810. 168p. reprint ed. pap. 52.10 (*0-8357-2562-6*, 204025300015) Bks Demand.

Manual of Prayers. James D. Watkins. 446p. 29.95 (*0-87973-640-2*) Our Sunday Visitor.

Manual of Prayers. 2nd ed. Ed. by James D. Watkins. (Illus.). xx, 425p. 1997. reprint ed. 30.00 (*1-890177-03-2*) Midwest Theol.

Manual of Primary Eye Care. Narciss Okhravi. LC 97-144804. (Illus.). 192p. 1997. text 45.00 (*0-7506-2221-0*) Buttrwrth-Heinemann.

***Manual of Primary Eye Care.** Narciss Okhravi. 176p. 1999. reprint ed. 35.00 (*0-7506-4467-2*) Buttrwrth-Heinemann.

Manual of Primary Health Care: Its Nature & Organization. 2nd ed. Peter M. Pritchard. (Illus.). (C). 1981. pap. text 18.95 (*0-19-261355-3*) OUP.

***Manual of Procedures.** rev. ed. Diane Levitan & Jeanne Wildman. Ed. by Lori Burfield. (Illus.). 164p. 2000. 33.00 (*1-930866-02-X*) IES.

Manual of Procedures & Form Book for the Construction Industry. 9th ed. Robert O. Wilhelm. 260p. 1995. ring bd. 69.95 (*1-55701-120-6*) BNI Pubns.

Manual of Procedures for Private Law Libraries. rev. ed. Elizabeth Finley. LC 66-15518. (AALL Publications Ser.: No. 8). xi, 176p. 1966. 35.00 (*0-8377-0106-6*, Rothman) W S Hein.

Manual of Procedures for Private Law Libraries: 1984 Supplement. American Association of Law Librarians Staff & Susan K. Dyer. LC 84-11589. (AALL Publications: No. 21). ix, 130p. 1984. 18.50 (*0-317-00875-7*) Am Assn Law Libs.

Manual of Procedures for Private Law Libraries: 1984 Supplement. Susan K. Dyer. LC 84-11589. (AALL Publications Ser.: No. 21). ix, 130p. 1984. suppl. ed. 22.50 (*0-8377-0119-8*, Rothman) W S Hein.

Manual of Prophetic Studies see Manual de Estudios Profeticos

Manual of Protective Actions for Nuclear Incidents. (Illus.). 220p. (Orig.). (C). 1996. pap. text 50.00 (*0-7881-2653-9*) DIANE Pub.

Manual of Protective Linings for Flue Gas Desulfurization Systems, Vol. STP 837. 35p. 1984. pap. 22.00 (*0-8031-0216-X*, STP837) ASTM.

Manual of Psittacine Birds. Ed. by Peter H. Beynon et al. LC 96-159979. (Illus.). 240p. 1996. pap. text 72.95 (*0-8138-2349-8*, Pub. by BSAVA) Iowa St U Pr.

Manual of Psychiatric Consultation & Emergency Care. Ed. by Frederick G. Guggenheim & Myron F. Weiner. LC 84-477. 400p. 1984. 60.00 (*0-87668-666-8*) Aronson.

Manual of Psychiatric Disorders. Ed. by George M. Simpson. (Illus.). 200p. (Orig.). 1995. pap. text. write for info. (*0-9645991-0-4*) Impact Commun.

Manual of Psychiatric Emergencies. 3rd ed. Ed. by Steven E. Hyman & George E. Tesar. LC 93-1834. (Spiral Manual Ser.). (Illus.). 400p. 1993. spiral bd. 34.95 (*0-316-38728-2*) Lppncott W & W.

Manual of Psychiatric Quality Assurance: A Report of the APA Committee on Quality Assurance. Ed. by Marlon R. Mattson. LC 91-25954. 254p. 1992. pap. text 27.50 (*0-89042-232-X*, 2232) Am Psychiatric.

Manual of Psychiatric Therapeutics. 2nd ed. Ed. by Richard I. Shader. LC 93-25998. (Spiral Manual Ser.). (Illus.). 368p. 1994. spiral bd. 32.95 (*0-316-78223-8*, Little Brwn Med Div) Lppncott W & W.

Manual of Psychology. J. N. Sinha. (C). 1989. 45.00 (*0-89771-453-9*, Pub. by Current Dist) St Mut.

Manual of Psychology, 9. George F. Stout. LC 77-72191. (Contributions to the History of Psychology Ser.: Pt. A, Vol. IX, Orientations). 642p. 1977. reprint ed. lib. bdg. 95.00 (*0-313-26933-5*, U6933, Greenwood Pr) Greenwood.

Manual of Psychosocial Nursing Interventions: Promoting Mental Health in Medical-Surgical Settings. Lewis et al. 288p. 1989. text 44.00 (*0-7216-5763-X*, W B Saunders Co) Harcrt Hlth Sci Grp.

Manual of Pteridology. Ed. by Frans Verdoorn. (Illus.). 1967. reprint ed. 79.00 (*90-6123-093-4*) Lubrecht & Cramer.

Manual of Public International Law. UNESCO Staff. (Unesco Ser.). 1296p. (C). 1992. lib. bdg. 252.50 (*92-3-102716-6*) Kluwer Academic.

Manual of Public International Law. Thomas A. Walker. xxviii, 244p. 1984. reprint ed. 43.00 (*0-8377-1330-7*, Rothman) W S Hein.

Manual of Pulmonary Function Testing. 7th ed. Gregg Ruppel. LC 97-26485. (Illus.). 384p. (C). (gr. 13). 1997. pap. text 36.00 (*0-8151-2299-3*, 27686) Mosby Inc.

Manual of Pulmonary Surgery. E. W. Humphrey. (Comprehensive Manuals of Surgical Specialties Ser.). (Illus.). 259p. 1982. 171.00 (*0-387-90732-7*) Spr-Verlag.

Manual of Quantitative Genetics see Manual de Genetica Cuantitativa

Manual of Quantitative Genetics. 5th ed. Walter Alvin Becker. LC 91-71883. 192p. (C). 1992. pap. text 29.95 (*0-931399-11-4*) Academic Enter.

Manual of Quantitative Pathology in Cancer Diagnosis & Prognosis. 2nd ed. J. P. Baak. (Illus.). 696p. 1991. 250.00 (*0-387-51275-6*) Spr-Verlag.

Manual of Queensland Succession Law. 3rd ed. W. A. Lee. xlviii, 295p. 1991. pap. 49.00 (*0-455-21034-9*, Pub. by LawBk Co) Gaunt.

***Manual of Rabbit Medicine & Surgery.** Paul Flecknell. (Illus.). 160p. 2000. pap. text 84.95 (*0-905214-46-3*, Pub. by BSAVA) Iowa St U Pr.

Manual of Radiographic Interpretation for General Practitioners: WHO Basic Radiological System. W. P. Cockshott et al. (CHI, FRE & SPA., Illus.). 216p. 1985. pap. text 34.00 (*92-4-154177-6*, 1150231) World Health.

Manual of Radiographic Technique: WHO Basic Radiological System. T. Holm et al. (CHI, FRE & SPA., Illus.). 256p. 1986. pap. text 30.00 (*92-4-154179-2*, 1150240) World Health.

Manual of Radiology. John Eng. LC 96-42148. 300p. 1996. pap. text 38.00 (*0-397-51768-8*) Lppncott W & W.

Manual of Radiology. Charles E. Kahn. 1992. pap. text 25.00 (*0-07-033647-4*) McGraw.

Manual of Railway Laws. B. Bhatnagar. (C). 1990. 110.00 (*0-89771-247-1*) St Mut.

Manual of Ready-Mixed Concrete. 2nd ed. J. D. Dewar & R. Anderson. (Illus.). 256p. 1992. text 70.50 (*0-7514-0079-3*, Pub. by B Acad & Prof) Routldge.

Manual of Real Estate Law & Procedures. William J. Grange & Thomas C. Woodbury. LC 67-26183. 472p. reprint ed. pap. 146.40 (*0-608-30530-8*, 201584100097) Bks Demand.

Manual of Recommended Practice for Combustible Gas Indicators & Portable Direct-Reading Hydrocarbon Detectors. 2nd ed. Ed. by C. F. Chelton. 61p. (C). 1993. pap. 28.00 (*0-932627-48-X*, 158SI93) Am Indus Hygiene.

Manual of Recommended Practice for Portable Direct-Reading Carbon Monoxide Indicators. AIHA Gas & Vapor Detection Systems Committee. Ed. by Patrick R. Frazee. 46p. 1985. 25.00 (*0-932627-22-6*) Am Indus Hygiene.

Manual of Recommended Practices for the Installation of Thermoplastic Water Well Casing. 64p. 1980. 15.00 (*1-56034-027-4*, T030) Natl Grnd Water.

Manual of Refraction. 3rd ed. Albert E. Sloane & George E. Garcia. 1979. 23.00 (*0-316-79844-4*, Little Brwn Med Div) Lppncott W & W.

Manual of Regulations & Procedures for Federal Radio Frequency Management. Government Printing Office Staff. 1989. ring bd. 133.00 (*0-16-016464-8*) USGPO.

Manual of Remote Sensing: Principles of Remote Sensing, Vol. 4. Wang. 800p. 198.00 (*0-471-31792-6*) Wiley.

Manual of Remote Working. Kevin Curran & Geoff Williams. LC 96-32170. 352p. 1997. 113.95 (*0-566-07839-2*, Pub. by Gower) Ashgate Pub Co.

Manual of Renal Transplantation. Richard D. Allen & Jeremy Chapman. (Illus.). 320p. 1994. pap. text 49.95 (*0-340-55154-2*, Pub. by E A) OUP.

Manual of Reptiles. Ed. by Peter H. Beynon et al. (Illus.). 228p. 1994. pap. text 72.95 (*0-8138-2296-3*) Iowa St U Pr.

Manual of Respiratory Care Procedures. 2nd ed. Blodgett. LC 65-8782. 1987. text 19.50 (*0-397-50714-3*, Lippncott) Lppncott W & W.

***Manual of Retinal Surgery.** 2nd ed. Andrew J. Packer. (Illus.). 144p. 2000. pap. 45.00 (*0-7506-7106-8*) Buttrwrth-Heinemann.

***Manual of Rheumatology & Outpatient Orthopaedic Disorders: Diagnosis & Therapy.** 4th ed. Stephen A. Paget. LC 99-45307. 568p. 2000. 36.95 (*0-7817-2442-2*) Lppncott W & W.

Manual of Rheumatology & Outpatient Orthopaedic Disorders: Diagnosis & Therapy. 4th ed. Stephen A. Paget et al. 512p. spiral bd. 34.95 (*0-7817-1576-8*) Lppncott W & W.

Manual of Rheumatology & Outpatient Orthopedic Disorders: Diagnosis & Therapy. 3rd ed. Cornell University Medical College Staff. Ed. by Paul M. Pellicci et al. LC 92-49265. (Illus.). 400p. 1993. spiral bd. 35.95 (*0-316-68846-0*) Lppncott W & W.

Manual of Rifling & Rifle Sights. fac. ed. Viscount Bury. (Illus.). 48p. 1995. reprint ed. pap. 11.95 (*1-880677-07-5*) Excalibur AZ.

This is a facsimile edition of an 1864 manual produced for the British National Rifle Association. The book gives details on contemporary rifling, fore sights, middle sights & back sights. In addition, the manual features woodcuts of sights & other inventions by Medford, Bury, the British government, Kerr, Blanch, Turner, Elcho, Vernon & London Armoury Co. Includes four pages of fold out diagrams at the back of the book. 165 illustrations & woodcuts are featured in the manual. Contact Excalibur Publications, PO Box 35369, Tucson, AZ 85740-5369. Voice: (520) 575-9057. Fax: (520) 575-9068. *Publisher Paid Annotation.*

Manual of Roman Law. Peter Spiller. 262p. 1986. pap. write for info. (*0-409-05755-X*, MICHIE) LEXIS Pub.

Manual of Roman Law. Peter Spiller. (Illus.). 262p. 1986. pap. 43.00 (*0-614-05465-6*, SA, MICHIE) LEXIS Pub.

Manual of Roman Private Law. 2nd ed. William W. Buckland. LC 94-75667. xxx, 434p. 1994. reprint ed. 105.00 (*1-56169-092-9*) Gaunt.

M

An Asterisk (*) at the beginning of an entry indicates that the title is appearing for the first time.

Manual of Rules, Classifications & Interpretations for Workers Compensation Insurance. 1991. 209.00 (*1-886813-15-9*) Intl Risk Mgt.

Manual of Sail Trim. Stuart H. Walker. (Illus.). 1985. pap. 21.95 (*0-393-03296-5*) Norton.

Manual of Scandinavian Mythology: Containing a Popular Account of the Two Eddas & of the Religion of Odin. Grenville Pigott. Ed. by Kees W. Bolle. LC 77-79152. (Mythology Ser.). 1978. reprint ed. lib. bdg. 30.95 (*0-405-10561-4*) Ayer.

Manual of School Health. Helen Thomson & Keeta D. Lewis. (Illus.). 288p. (C). 1986. pap. text 45.94 (*0-201-15292-4*, Health Sci) Addison-Wesley.

Manual of Sclerotherapy. Neil S. Sadick. LC 99-16112. (Illus.). 272p. 1998. text 126.50 (*0-397-51742-4*) Lppncott W & W.

*__Manual of 2nd Congregational Church of Chicopee, MA.__ Ed. by Charles D. Townsend. 78p. 1998. reprint ed. pap. 15.00 (*1-878545-44-2*) ACETO Bookmen.

Manual of Sedimentary Petrography: Sampling, Preparation for Analysis, Mechanical Analysis & Statistical Analysis, by W. C. Krumbein. II Shape Analysis, Mineralogical Analysis, Chemical Analysis & Mass Properties, by F. J. Pettijohn. William C. Krumbein. LC QE0471.K786. (SEPM Reprint Ser.: No. 13). (Illus.). 571p. 1988. reprint ed. pap. 177.10 (*0-608-02977-7*, 206344500006) Bks Demand.

Manual of Sequential Art Activities for Classified Children & Adolescents. Rocco A. Fugaro. (Illus.). 246p. (C). 1985. pap., spiral bd. 41.95 (*0-398-05085-6*) C C Thomas.

Manual of Sexually Transmitted Diseases. H. Hunter Handsfield & Walter E. Stamm. 324p. 1983. write for info. (*0-07-060694-3*) McGraw.

Manual of Sheep Production in the Humid Tropics of Africa. Tr. by Alan Leeson. 250p. (Orig.). 1992. pap. 35.00 (*0-85198-795-8*) OUP.

Manual of Sixteenth-Century Contrapuntal Style. Charlotte Smith. LC 87-40064. (Illus.). 144p. 1989. 45.00 (*0-87413-327-0*) U Delaware Pr.

Manual of Skin Surgery: A Practical Guide to Dermatologic Procedures. David J. Leffell & Marc D. Brown. LC 96-30884. 250p. 1997. pap. 69.95 (*0-471-13411-2*) Wiley.

Manual of Skull Base Dissection, Vol. 1. Ed. by Takanori Fukushima. LC 96-84288. (Illus.). 136p. (Orig.). 1996. ring bd. 180.00 (*0-9651986-0-X*) AF NeuroVid.

Manual of Small Animal Anesthesia. 2nd ed. Robert R. Paddleford. Ed. by Ray Kersey. LC 98-15368. (Illus.). 320p. (C). 1998. pap. text 39.95 (*0-7216-4060-5*, W B Saunders Co) Harcrt Hlth Sci Grp.

Manual of Small Animal Anesthesia & Analgesia. Ed. by Chris Seymour & Robin Gleed. (Illus.). 320p. 1999. pap. 84.95 (*0-905214-48-X*, Pub. by BSAVA) Iowa St U Pr.

Manual of Small Animal Arthrology. Ed. by John E. Houlton & Robert W. Collinson. (Illus.). 344p. 1994. pap. text 74.95 (*0-8138-2869-4*) Iowa St U Pr.

Manual of Small Animal Cardiorespiratory Medicine & Surgery. Ed. by Virginia Fuentes & Simon Swift. (Illus.). 320p. 1998. pap. text 116.95 (*0-905214-33-1*, Pub. by BSAVA) Iowa St U Pr.

Manual of Small Animal Dentistry. 2nd ed. Ed. by D. A. Crossley & Sue Penman. (Illus.). 245p. 1995. pap. text 82.95 (*0-905214-28-5*) Iowa St U Pr.

Manual of Small Animal Dermatology. Ed. by P. Harvey Locke et al. (Illus.). 280p. 1994. pap. text 72.95 (*0-905214-20-X*, Pub. by BSAVA) Iowa St U Pr.

Manual of Small Animal Diagnostic Imaging. Ed. by Robin Lee. 200p. 1995. pap. 69.95 (*0-905214-26-9*, Pub. by BSAVA) Iowa St U Pr.

Manual of Small Animal Endocrinology. 2nd ed. Ed. by Andrew Torrance & Carmel Mooney. (Illus.). 250p. (C). 1998. pap. text 82.95 (*0-905214-42-0*, Pub. by BSAVA) Iowa St U Pr.

*__Manual of Small Animal Internal Medicine.__ Richard W. Nelson & C. Guillermo Couto. (Illus.). 944p. (C). (gr. 13). 1998. pap. text 39.95 (*0-8151-7297-4*, 27769) Mosby Inc.

Manual of Small Animal Nephrology & Urology. Dennis J. Chew & Stephen P. DiBartola. LC 86-17134. 350p. (Orig.). reprint ed. pap. 108.50 (*0-7837-1373-8*, 204152200021) Bks Demand.

Manual of Small Animal Ophthalmology. Ed. by Simon M. Petersen-Jones & Sheila M. Crispin. (Illus.). 304p. 1994. pap. text 82.95 (*0-905214-21-8*, Pub. by BSAVA) Iowa St U Pr.

Manual of Small Animal Postoperative Care. Robert A. Taylor & Robin A. McGehee. LC 94-4929. 1994. write for info. (*0-8121-1765-4*) Lppncott W & W.

Manual of Small Animal Postoperative Care. Robert Taylor & Robin McGehee. (Illus.). 220p. 1995. write for info. (*0-683-08125-X*) Lppncott W & W.

Manual of Small Animal Reproduction & Neonatology. Ed. by Gillian M. Simpson et al. (Illus.). 235p. 1998. pap. 83.95 (*0-905214-36-6*, Pub. by BSAVA) Iowa St U Pr.

Manual of Small Animal Surgical Therapeutics. Ed. by C. W. Betts & Stephen W. Crane. (Illus.). 440p. 1986. text 49.00 (*0-7216-5924-1*, W B Saunders Co) Harcrt Hlth Sci Grp.

Manual of Small Public Water Supply Systems. U. S. EPA Office of Drinking Water Staff. 224p. 1992. boxed set 83.95 (*0-87371-864-X*, TK) Smoley.

Manual of Soccer Coaching. Roy Rees. 1988. pap. text 14.95 (*0-937347-19-1*) C & D Intl.

Manual of Soft-Tissue Tumor Surgery. J. P. Neifeld et al. (Comprehensive Manuals of Surgical Specialties Ser.). (Illus.). 214p. 1983. 189.00 (*0-387-90843-9*) Spr-Verlag.

Manual of Soil & Water Analysis. P. Buurman et al. 314p. 1996. pap. 53.00 (*90-73348-58-7*, Pub. by Backhuys Pubs) Balogh.

*__Manual of Soil Laboratory Testing: Effective Stress Tests.__ 2nd ed. K. H. Head. 442p. 1998. 165.00 (*0-471-97795-0*) Wiley.

Manual of Soil Laboratory Testing, Vol. 3, Effective Stress Tests, Vol. 3, Effective Stress Tests. 2nd ed. K. H. Head. (Manual of Soil Laboratory Testing Ser.). 495p. 1996. 165.00 (*0-471-96411-5*) Wiley.

Manual of Soil Laboratory Testing, 2E, Vol. 2, Permeability, Shear Strength & Compressibility Tests, Vol. 2, Permeability, Shear Strength and Compressi. 2nd ed. K. H. Head. 454p. 1996. 130.00 (*0-471-96410-7*) Wiley.

Manual of Sound Archive Administration. Alan Ward. 272p. 1990. text 78.95 (*0-566-05571-6*, Pub. by Gower) Ashgate Pub Co.

*__Manual of Special Education Law for Educators & Parents.__ M. Jean Rawson & Annette Kocal. 150p. 2000. pap. 17.95 (*0-9676206-0-0*) Morgen Pubg Inc.

Manual of Specialised Lexicography: The Preparation of Specialised Dictionaries. Ed. by Henning Bergenholtz & Sven Tarp. LC 95-19988. (Benjamins Translation Library: No. 12). 256p. 1995. 50.00 (*1-55619-693-8*) J Benjamins Pubng Co.

Manual of Spectrofluorometric & Spectropotometric Derivative Experiments. Allesia M. Gillespie, Jr. LC 93-26029. 224p. 1993. lib. bdg. 69.95 (*0-8493-6390-X*) CRC Pr.

Manual of Sports Medicine. Safran. (Illus.). 1997. spiral bd. 32.95 (*0-316-77111-2*) Lppncott W & W.

Manual of Sports Surgery. Ed. by C. L. Shields. (Comprehensive Manuals of Surgical Specialties Ser.). (Illus.). xvii, 206p. 1986. 292.00 (*0-387-96415-0*) Spr-Verlag.

Manual of Standardized Methods for Veterinary Microbiology. National Research Council, Subcommittee on Metabolism Staff. Ed. by George E. Cottral. LC 77-90900. 733p. reprint ed. pap. 200.00 (*0-608-08087-X*, 206904600002) Bks Demand.

Manual of Standards for Erosion & Sediment Control Measures. 275p. 1981. 20.00 (*0-318-22703-7*); 20.00 (*0-317-05667-0*, P81003WAT) Assn Bay Area.

Manual of Steel Construction Allowable Stress Design. 9th rev. ed. AISC Manual Committee. (Illus.). 1144p. (C). 1991. text 72.00 (*1-56424-000-2*, M016) Am Inst Steel Construct.

Manual of Steel Construction Load & Resistance Factor Design Vol. I: Structural Members, Specifications & Codes. 2nd rev. ed. William A. Thornton et al. (Illus.). 1280p. 1998. 72.00 (*1-56424-046-0*, M018L) Am Inst Steel Construct.

Manual of Steel Construction, Load & Resistance Factor Design Vol. II: Connections. 2nd rev. ed. William A. Thornton et al. 783p. 1998. 72.00 (*1-56424-047-9*, M019L) Am Inst Steel Construct.

Manual of Stroke Rehabilitation. Karl J. Sandin & Kristin D. Mason. LC 95-44678. (Physical Medicine & Rehabilitation Clinical Practice Manuals Ser.). 194p. 1996. pap. text 45.00 (*0-7506-9489-0*) Buttrwrth-Heinemann.

*__Manual Of Structural Kinesiology.__ 14th ed. Clem W. Thompson & Ed D. Floyd. (Illus.). 288p. 2000. Price not set. (*0-07-232917-3*) McGraw.

Manual of Style: A Guide for Authors & Editors. 9th ed. American Medical Association & Cheryl Iverson. LC 97-19246. 660p. 1997. 34.95 (*0-683-40206-4*) Lppncott W & W.

Manual of Style for Business Letters, Memos, & Reports. 4th ed. Erwin M. Keithley & Marie E. Flatley. 144p. (C). 1988. mass mkt. 18.00 (*0-538-05230-9*, E23) S-W Pub.

Manual of Suggested Practice for Administration of Local Sales & Use Taxes. Lennox L. Moak & Frank Cowan, Jr. LC 61-18038. (Illus.). 311p. 1961. 8.00 (*0-317-34948-1*) Municipal.

Manual of Surgery Asia, No. 7. Condon. 1988. 10.95 (*0-316-15260-9*, Little Brwn Med Div) Lppncott W & W.

Manual of Surgery ISE, No. 7. Condon. 1988. 15.95 (*0-316-15259-5*, Little Brwn Med Div) Lppncott W & W.

Manual of Surgery of the Gallbladder, Bile Ducts, & Exocrine Pancreas. R. E. Hermann. (Comprehensive Manuals of Surgical Specialties Ser.). (Illus.). 1979. 174.00 (*0-387-90351-8*) Spr-Verlag.

Manual of Surgical Pathology Gross Room Procedures. Juan Rosai. (Illus.). 132p. (C). 1981. pap. 29.95 (*0-8166-1027-4*) U of Minn Pr.

Manual of Surgical Therapeutics. 7th ed. Robert E. Condon & Lloyd M. Nyhus. 480p. 1988. 23.50 (*0-316-15261-7*, Little Brwn Med Div) Lppncott W & W.

Manual of Surgical Therapeutics. 9th ed. Robert E. Condon & Lloyd M. Nyhus. LC 95-333. (Illus.). 439p. 1995. spiral bd. 34.95 (*0-316-15402-4*) Lppncott W & W.

Manual of Surgical Therapeutics. 9th ed. Ed. by Robert E. Condon & Lloyd M. Nyhus. LC 95-333. 1996. 34.95 (*0-316-15396-6*, Little Brwn Med Div) Lppncott W & W.

Manual of Systematic Corneal Surgery. Arthur D. Steele & Colin M. Kirkness. (Illus.). 104p. 1992. text 85.00 (*0-443-04284-5*) Church.

Manual of Systematic Corneal Surgery. 2nd ed. Arthur D. Steele & Colin M. Kirkness. (Illus.). 164p. 1999. text 90.00 (*0-7506-3720-X*) Buttrwrth-Heinemann.

Manual of Systematic Corneal Surgery 2Ed. 2nd ed. Steele & Kirkness. 104p. Date not set. pap. text. write for info. (*0-7506-3722-6*) Buttrwrth-Heinemann.

*__Manual of Systematic Eyelid Surgery.__ 2nd ed. J. R. O. Collin. 166p. 1999. 80.00 (*0-7506-4572-5*) Buttrwrth-Heinemann.

*__Manual of Systematic Eyelid Surgery.__ 3rd ed. J. R. O. Collin. (Illus.). 192p. 2000. pap. 65.00 (*0-7506-4550-4*) Buttrwrth-Heinemann.

Manual of Sytematic Eyelid Surgery. 2nd ed. J. R. Collin. (Illus.). 166p. 1989. text 54.95 (*0-443-04009-5*) Church.

Manual of Tabular Presentation. 1991. lib. bdg. 79.95 (*0-8490-4505-3*) Gordon Pr.

Manual of Tank Busters. Gina Sandford & Richard Crow. (Illus.). 160p. 1991. 21.95 (*3-89356-041-6*, 16011) Tetra Pr.

Manual of Techniques in Insect Pathology. Ed. by Lawrence A. Lacey. (Biological Techniques Ser.). (Illus.). 432p. 1997. boxed set 110.00 (*0-12-432555-6*) Morgan Kaufmann.

Manual of Tests for Syphilis. 8th ed. Ed. by Sandra A. Larsen et al. 208p. 1990. 30.00 (*0-87553-174-1*) Am Pub Health.

*__Manual of Tests for Syphilis.__ 9th ed. Ed. by Sandra A. Larsen et al. LC 98-72440. 361p. 1998. pap. 48.00 (*0-87553-234-9*) Am Pub Health.

Manual of Textual Analysis. Vinton A. Dearing. LC 82-20947. 108p. 1983. reprint ed. lib. bdg. 49.50 (*0-313-23734-4*, DEMA, Greenwood Pr) Greenwood.

Manual of the Administration of the Madras Presidency, 3 vols., Set, Vols. I-III. C. D. Maclean. (C). 1987. reprint ed. 168.50 (*0-8364-2415-8*, Pub. by Asian Educ Servs) S Asia.

Manual of the Andamanese Languages. M. V. Portman. 1987. 19.95 (*0-7859-9826-8*) Fr & Eur.

Manual of the Botany of the Northern United States. Asa Gray. (Notable American Authors Ser.). 1992. reprint ed. lib. bdg. 75.00 (*0-7812-2945-6*) Rprt Serv.

Manual of the Central Baptist Church of Providence, Rhode Island. Ed. by Charles D. Townsend. 65p. 1998. reprint ed. pap. 15.00 (*1-878545-40-X*) ACETO Bookmen.

Manual of the Church of Illumination. R. Swinburne Clymer. 100p. 1952. 5.95 (*0-932785-28-X*) Philos Pub.

Manual of the Church of Illumination. deluxe ed. R. Swinburne Clymer. 100p. 1952. 20.00 (*0-932785-89-1*) Philos Pub.

Manual of the Common North American Species of the Aquatic Leafmining Genus Hydrellia (Diptera: Ephydridae) D. L. Deonier. Ed. by Virendra K. Gupta. LC 98-19928. (Memoirs on Entomology, International Ser.: Vol. 12). (Illus.). 368p. 1998. 65.00 (*1-56665-069-0*) Assoc Pubs FL.

Manual of the Congregational Church of Dorset & East Rupert, Vermont. Intro. by Charles D. Townsend. 58p. 1996. reprint ed. pap. 10.00 (*1-878545-16-7*) ACETO Bookmen.

Manual of the Congregational Church Thompson Connecticut, 1730-1901. Ed. by Charles D. Townsend. LC 98-221864. 78p. 1998. pap. 15.00 (*1-878545-33-7*) ACETO Bookmen.

*__Manual of the Congregational Church Westbook, CT.__ Ed. by Charles D. Townsend. 63p. 1999. reprint ed. pap. 20.00 (*1-878545-47-7*) ACETO Bookmen.

Manual of the Coniferae. J. Veitch. 350p. (C). 1980. text 375.00 (*0-89771-672-8*, Pub. by Intl Bk Distr) St Mut.

Manual of the Constitution of the United States of America. Timothy Farrar. xii, 532p. 1993. reprint ed. 55.00 (*0-8377-2137-7*, Rothman) W S Hein.

*__Manual of the First Congregational Church of Suffield, Connecticut.__ Charles D. Townsend. 42p. 1999. reprint ed. pap. 15.00 (*1-878545-45-0*) ACETO Bookmen.

Manual of the Flowering Plants of California. Willis L. Jepson. 1992. reprint ed. lib. bdg. 75.00 (*0-7812-5056-0*) Rprt Serv.

Manual of the Flowering Plants of Hawaii, 2 vols. rev. ed. Warren L. Wagner et al. LC 98-51798. (Bernice B. Bishop Museum Special Publications: Vol. 97). (Illus.). 1900p. 1999. 95.00 (*0-8248-2166-1*) UH Pr.

Manual of the Grasses of the United States, 2 vols., Vol. 1. 2nd ed. A. S. Hitchcock. (Illus.). 1971. reprint ed. pap. 13.95 (*0-486-22717-0*) Dover.

Manual of the Grasses of the United States, 2 vols., Vol. 2. 2nd ed. A. S. Hitchcock. (Illus.). 1971. reprint ed. pap. 12.95 (*0-486-22718-9*) Dover.

Manual of the Grasses of the West Indies. A. S. Hitchcock. (Illus.). 439p. 1986. text 40.00 (*81-211-0000-3*) Lubrecht & Cramer.

Manual of the History of the Political System of Europe & Its Colonies. Arnold H. Heeren. LC 71-154153. (Select Bibliographies Reprint Ser.). 1977. reprint ed. 31.95 (*0-8369-5769-5*) Ayer.

Manual of the International Embryo Transfer Society see Manual de la Sociedad Internacional de Transferencia de Embriones: Guia de Procedimientos e Informacion General para el Uso de la Technologia de la Transferencia de Embriones con Especial Enfasis

Manual of the International Embryo Transfer Society: A Procedural Guide & General Information for the Use of Embryo Transfer Technology, Emphasizing Sanitary Precautions. 3rd ed. D. A. Stringfellow et al. LC 98-70383. 170 p. 1998. write for info. (*0-9662386-0-5*) Intl Embryo Trans.

Manual of the International Embyo Transfer Society see Manual de la Societe Internationale de Transfert Embryonnaire: Guide Methodologique et Informations Generales sur l'Utilisation du Transfert Embryonnaire Avec Attention Particuliere sur les Precautions d'Ordre Sanitaire

Manual of the Legislature of New Jersey, Two Hundred & Sixth Legislature, First Session, 1995. rev. ed. Skinder-Strauss Staff. 1040p. 1995. 35.00 (*1-57741-000-9*) Skinder-Strauss.

Manual of the Lodge (1898): or Monitorial Instructions in the Degrees of Entered Apprentice, Fellow Craft, & Master Mason Arranged in Accordance with the American System of Lectures: To Which Are Added the Ceremonies of the Order Past Master, Relating to Installations, Dedications, Consecrations, Laying of Corner-Stones, Etc. Albert G. Mackey. 275p. 1995. reprint ed. pap. 24.95 (*1-56459-518-8*) Kessinger Pub.

Manual of the Mercenary Soldier: A Guide to Mercenary War, Money & Adventure. Paul Balor. 320p. 1988. text 29.95 (*0-87364-474-3*) Paladin Pr.

Manual of the Mother Church. Mary M. Eddy. (Notable American Authors Ser.). 1992. reprint ed. lib. bdg. 75.00 (*0-7812-2757-7*) Rprt Serv.

Manual of the Mother Church: The First Church of Christ, Scientist, in Boston, Massachusetts. Mary Baker Eddy. reprint ed. 18.00 (*0-87952-084-1*) Writings of Mary Baker.

Manual of the Mother Church: The First Church of Christ, Scientist, in Boston, Massachusetts. 88th ed. Mary Baker Eddy. 138p. (C). 1994. reprint ed. 15.95 (*0-930227-23-9*) Bookmark CA.

Manual of the Northwood Meadows State Park. M. Edward Burtt. (Illus.). 25p. (Orig.). 1991. pap. write for info. (*1-888913-00-2*) M E Burtt.

Manual of the Ornithology of the United States & Canada, 2 vols., Set. Thomas Nuttall. LC 73-17833. (Natural Sciences in America Ser.). 1332p. 1974. reprint ed. 96.95 (*0-405-05751-2*) Ayer.

Manual of the Ornithology of the United States & Canada, 2 vols., Vol. 1. Thomas Nuttall. LC 73-17833. (Natural Sciences in America Ser.). 1332p. 1974. reprint ed. 48.95 (*0-405-05752-0*) Ayer.

Manual of the Ornithology of the United States & Canada, 2 vols., Vol. 2. Thomas Nuttall. LC 73-17833. (Natural Sciences in America Ser.). 1332p. 1974. reprint ed. 48.95 (*0-405-05753-9*) Ayer.

Manual of the Penicillia. K. B. Raper & Charlesthom. 172p. 1984. pap. 175.00 (*0-7855-0380-3*, Pub. by Intl Bks & Periodicals) St Mut.

Manual of the Recent & Fossil, Marine Pelecypod Mollusks of the Hawaiian Islands. W. H. Dall et al. (BMB Ser.: No. 153). 1969. reprint ed. 40.00 (*0-527-02261-6*) Periodicals Srv.

Manual of the System of Teaching: 1816 Edition. Joseph Lancaster. Ed. & Intro. by Jeffrey Stern. (Classics in Education Ser.). 96p. 1996. reprint ed. 65.00 (*1-85506-274-7*) Bks Intl VA.

Manual of the Terminology of Public International Law & International Organizations. Isaac Paenson. 1983. text 301.00 (*90-6544-052-6*) Kluwer Law Intl.

Manual of the Terminology of Public International Law & Organizations. Isaac Paenson. (ENG, FRE, RUS & SPA.). 846p. 1983. 295.00 (*0-8288-0413-3*, M6435) Fr & Eur.

Manual of the Terminology of Public International Law (Law of Peace) & of International Organizations. Isaac Paenson. (ENG, FRE & SPA.). xlviii, 846p. 1983. write for info. (*3-598-07558-8*) K G Saur Verlag.

Manual of the Terminology of the Law of Armed Conflicts & of International Humanitarian Organizations. Isaac Paenson. (ENG, FRE & SPA.). xxxviii, 844p. 1989. write for info. (*3-598-07559-6*) K G Saur Verlag.

Manual of the Terminology of the Law of Armed Conflicts & of International Humanitarian Organizations. Isaac Paenson. (ENG, FRE, RUS & SPA.). 864p. 1989. lib. bdg. 359.00 (*90-247-3466-5*) Kluwer Academic.

Manual of the Trees of North America, Vol. 2. Charles S. Sargent. (Illus.). 1962. 14.50 (*0-8446-2864-6*) Peter Smith.

Manual of the Trees of North America, 2 vols., Vol. 1. 2nd ed. Charles S. Sargent. (Illus.). 1961. pap. text 13.95 (*0-486-20277-1*) Dover.

Manual of the Trees of North America, 2 vols., Vol. 2. 2nd ed. Charles S. Sargent. (Illus.). 1961. pap. text 13.95 (*0-486-20278-X*) Dover.

Manual of the Union Congregational Church Marlboro, Massachusetts: Catalogue of Its Officers & Members. Ed. by Charles D. Townsend. LC 98-222127. 57p. 1997. reprint ed. pap. 10.00 (*1-878545-30-2*) ACETO Bookmen.

Manual of the Vanni Districts, Ceylon. J. P. Lewis. (C). 1993. text 32.50 (*81-7013-113-8*, Pub. by Navarang) S Asia.

Manual of the Vascular Flora of the Carolinas. Albert E. Radford et al. LC 68-28264. (Illus.). lxii, 1183p. 1968. 45.00 (*0-8078-1087-8*) U of NC Pr.

*__Manual of the Vascular Plants of Mongolia, 2 vols.__ Ed. by V. I. Grubov. (Illus.). 850p. 2000. text 180.00 (*1-57808-073-8*) Science Pubs.

Manual of the Writings in Middle English, 1050-1400. John E. Wells. (BCL1-PR English Literature Ser.). 941p. 1992. reprint ed. lib. bdg. 119.00 (*0-7812-7032-4*) Rprt Serv.

Manual of the Writings in Middle English, 1050-1400, Supp. 1. John E. Wells. (Connecticut Academy of Arts & Sciences Ser., Trans.). 1919. 49.50 (*0-685-30605-4*) Elliots Bks.

Manual of the Writings in Middle English, 1050-1400, Supp. 2. John E. Wells. (Connecticut Academy of Arts & Sciences Ser., Trans.). 1923. 49.50 (*0-685-30604-6*) Elliots Bks.

Manual of the Writings in Middle English, 1050-1400, Supp. 3. John E. Wells. (Connecticut Academy of Arts & Sciences Ser., Trans.). 1926. 49.50 (*0-685-30603-8*) Elliots Bks.

Manual of the Writings in Middle English, 1050-1500, Vol. 1. 2nd ed. Ed. by J. Burke Severs. 338p. 1967. reprint ed. 49.50 (*0-208-01831-X*) CT Acad Arts & Sciences.

Manual of the Writings in Middle English, 1050-1500, Vol. 3. Ed. by Albert E. Hartung. LC 67-7687. 291p. 1972. 49.50 (*0-208-01220-6*) CT Acad Arts & Sciences.

Manual of the Writings in Middle English, 1050-1500, Vol. 4. Ed. by Albert E. Hartung. LC 67-7687. 351p. 1973. 49.50 (*0-208-01342-3*) CT Acad Arts & Sciences.

Manual of the Writings in Middle English 1050-1500, Vol. 5. Ed. by Albert E. Hartung. LC 67-7687. 412p. (C). 1975. 49.50 (*0-208-01459-4*) CT Acad Arts & Sciences.

Manual of the Writings in Middle English 1050-1500, Vol. 6. Ed. by Albert E. Hartung. LC 67-7687. 468p. (C). 1980. 49.50 (*0-208-01715-1*) CT Acad Arts & Sciences.

Manual of the Writings in Middle English 1050-1500, Vol. 7. Ed. by Albert E. Hartung. LC 67-7687. 400p. (C). 1986. 49.50 (*0-208-02107-8*) CT Acad Arts & Sciences.

Manual of the Writings in Middle English 1050-1500, Vol. 8. Ed. by Albert E. Hartung. LC 67-7687. 359p. (C). 1989. 49.50 (*0-208-02158-2*) CT Acad Arts & Sciences.

Manual of the Writings in Middle English 1050-1500, Vol. 9. Ed. by Albert E. Hartung. LC 67-7687. 635p. 1993. 59.50 (*1-878508-05-9*) CT Acad Arts & Sciences.

Manual of Theology, 3 vols. in 1. John L. Dagg. 1992. 23.99 (*0-87377-977-0*) GAM Pubns.

Manual of Theology . . . Christian Doctrine . . . Church Order, 2 Vols. John L. Dagg. Ed. by Edwin S. Gaustad. LC 79-52592. (Baptist Tradition Ser.). 1980. reprint ed. lib. bdg. 63.95 (*0-405-12459-7*) Ayer.

Manual of Therapeutic Medications & Pesticides for Worm Growers. Charlie Morgan. (Illus.). 1979. pap. 8.00 (*0-914116-16-9*) Shields.

Manual of Therapeutics for Addictions. Ed. by Norman S. Miller et al. LC 96-30946. 364p. 1997. pap. 67.50 (*0-471-56176-2*) Wiley.

Manual of Therapy for Skin Diseases. Timothy Berger et al. 349p. 1990. pap. text 35.00 (*0-443-08477-7*) Church.

Manual of Thoracic Surgery. 2nd ed. Arndt Von Hippel. 1986. pap. 40.00 (*0-9615808-1-X*) Stone Age Pr.

Manual of Tibetan Being: A Guide to the Colloquial Speech of Tibet in a Series of Progressive Exercises. Thomas H. Lewin. (C). 1985. reprint ed. 18.50 (*0-8364-2411-5*, Pub. by Asian Educ Servs) S Asia.

Manual of Toxicologic Emergencies. Eric K. Noji. 1989. 99.95 (*0-685-25523-9*) Mosby Inc.

Manual of Traditional Wood Carving. Paul N. Hasluck. (Illus.). 576p. 1977. pap. 12.95 (*0-486-23489-4*) Dover.

Manual of Traffic Signal Design. 2nd ed. James H. Kell & Iris J. Fullerton. (Illus.). 256p. 1998. reprint ed. text 80.00 (*0-935403-19-1*, TB-005A) Inst Trans Eng.

Manual of Trauma Resuscitation, Anaesthesia & Intensive Care. Oakley. (Illus.). 320p. (C). 1997. text. write for info. (*0-412-61850-8*, Chap & Hall NY) Chapman & Hall.

Manual of Travel Agency Practice. 2nd ed. Gwenda Syratt. LC 94-39184. 260p. 1995. pap. 37.95 (*0-7506-2163-X*) Buttrwrth-Heinemann.

Manual of Travel Medicine: A Guide to Disease Prevention & Treatment. Seymour I. Schlager. 352p. spiral bd. write for info. (*0-7817-2032-X*) Lppncott W & W.

***Manual of Travel Medicine & Health.** Robert Steffen & Herbert L. DuPont. 300p. 1999. pap. 28.95 (*1-55009-078-X*) DEKR.

Manual of Tropical Dermatology. J. H. Pettit et al. (Illus.). 270p. 1984. 146.00 (*0-387-90987-7*) Spr-Verlag.

***Manual of Tropical Pediatrics.** Ed. by M. D. Seear. (Illus.). 504p. (C). 2000. 80.00 (*0-521-65835-7*) Cambridge U Pr.

Manual of Tropical Veterinary Parasitology. M. Shah-Fischer & R. R. Say. 473p. (Orig.). 1996. pap. text 85.00 (*0-85198-584-X*) OUP.

Manual of Tumbling & Apparatus Stunts. 8th ed. Otto E. Ryser & James R. Brown. 272p. (C). 1989. text. write for info. (*0-697-10418-4*) Brown & Benchmark.

Manual of Tumescent Liposculpture & Laser Cosmetic Surgery: Including the Weekend Alternative to the Facelift. William R. Cook. LC 98-50220. 217p. 1999. write for info. (*0-7817-1987-9*) Lppncott W & W.

Manual of Ultrasound. H. Lutz & R. Meudt. (Illus.). 160p. 1983. 73.95 (*0-387-12377-6*) Spr-Verlag.

***Manual of Unarmed Self-Defense.** Michael Vassolo. LC 00-41342. (Illus.). 2000. write for info. (*1-56980-167-3*) Barricade Bks.

Manual of Upper Gastrointestinal Surgery. William H. ReMine et al. (Comprehensive Manuals of Surgical Specialties Ser.). (Illus.). xiv, 124p. 1985. 162.00 (*0-387-96148-8*) Spr-Verlag.

Manual of Urologic Surgery. A. T. Cockett & Ken Koshiba. (Comprehensive Manuals of Surgical Specialties Ser.). (Illus.). 284p. 1979. 161.00 (*0-387-90423-9*) Spr-Verlag.

Manual of Urology. Michael B. Siroky. 1990. 32.95 (*0-316-79296-9*, Little Brwn Med Div) Lppncott W & W.

Manual of Urology Asia. Michael B. Siroky. 1990. 10.95 (*0-316-79298-5*, Little Brwn Med Div) Lppncott W & W.

Manual of Urology ISE. Michael B. Siroky. 1990. 15.95 (*0-316-79297-7*, Little Brwn Med Div) Lppncott W & W.

Manual of Usage. John A. Myers, Jr. 1986. teacher ed. 6.96 (*0-88334-076-3*, 75752); student ed. 7.50 (*0-8013-0088-6*, 75752) Longman.

Manual of Vascular Access, Organ Donation, & Transplantation. John S. Najarian et al. (Comprehensive Manuals of Surgical Specialties Ser.). (Illus.). 355p. 1984. 207.00 (*0-387-90965-6*) Spr-Verlag.

Manual of Vascular Plants of Northeastern United States & Adjacent Canada. 2nd ed. Henry Allan Gleason & Arthur Cronquist. (C). 1991. text 69.00 (*0-89327-365-1*) NY Botanical.

Manual of Vascular Surgery, Pt. 1. E. J. Wylie et al. Ed. by R. H. Egdahl. LC 79-18226. (Comprehensive Manuals of Surgical Specialties Ser.). (Illus.). 320p. 1980. 99.00 (*3-540-90408-5*) Spr-Verlag.

Manual of Vascular Surgery, Vol. 2. E. J. Wylie et al. (Comprehensive Manuals of Surgical Specialties Ser.). (Illus.). 360p. 1986. 377.00 (*0-387-90409-3*) Spr-Verlag.

Manual of Veneering. Paul Villiard. (Illus.). 174p. 1975. reprint ed. pap. 6.95 (*0-486-23217-4*) Dover.

***Manual of Veterinary Care.** Sue Dallas. (Illus.). 256p. 2000. pap. text 56.95 (*0-905214-49-8*, Pub. by BSAVA) Iowa St U Pr.

Manual of Veterinary Echocardiography. June A. Boon. LC 97-43333. 478p. 1998. 79.00 (*0-683-00938-9*) Lppncott W & W.

***Manual of Veterinary Nursing.** Margaret Moore. (Illus.). 208p. 2000. pap. text 69.95 (*0-905214-50-1*, Pub. by BSAVA) Iowa St U Pr.

Manual of Voice Therapy. Rex J. Prater & Roger W. Swift. LC 90-50380. 288p. (C). 1984. spiral bd. 31.00 (*0-89079-279-8*, 1773) PRO-ED.

***Manual of Voice Therapy.** 2nd ed. Rex J. Prater et al. LC 99-31323. 1999. write for info. (*0-89079-825-7*) PRO-ED.

Manual of Voice Treatment. 2nd rev. ed. Moya L. Andrews. LC 98-37605. (Illus.). 700p. 1999. pap. 59.95 (*1-56593-998-0*, 1976) Thomson Learn.

Manual of Voice Treatment: Pediatrics to Geriatrics. Moya L. Andrews. LC 94-40347. (Illus.). 632p. (C). 1994. pap. 59.95 (*1-56593-162-9*, 0472) Thomson Learn.

Manual of Wastewater Collection. Ed. by Clayton H. Billings. (Illus.). 232p. 1981. text 16.19 (*0-933317-03-4*) Texas Water.

Manual of Wastewater Treatment. 5th ed. Ed. by Clayton H. Billings. (Illus.). 572p. 1983. text 19.19 (*0-933317-02-6*) Texas Water.

Manual of Water Utility Operations. Ed. by Charles K. Foster. (Illus.). 800p. 1989. reprint ed. text 18.19 (*0-933317-01-8*) Texas Water.

Manual of Water Well Maintenance & Rehabilitation Technology. Tyler E. Gass & T. Bennett. Ed. by J. Miller & R. Miller. 244p. 1980. 18.75 (*1-56034-030-4*, T033) Natl Grnd Water.

Manual of Weight Training. 4th ed. Ed. by George W. Kirkley & John Goodbody. (Illus.). 272p. 1994. pap. 24.95 (*0-09-177540-X*, Pub. by S Paul) Trafalgar.

Manual of Wildlife in India. S. S. Negi. 1993. pap. 175.00 (*81-7089-166-3*, Pub. by Intl Bk Distr) St Mut.

Manual of Woody Landscape Plants. 3rd ed. Michael A. Dirr. (Illus.). 1983. pap. text 26.80 (*0-87563-226-2*) Stipes.

***Manual of Woody Landscape Plants: Their Identification, Ornamental Characteristics, Culture, Propagation & Uses.** 5th ed. Michael A. Dirr. LC 98-61065. (Illus.). 1250p. 1998. 59.80 (*0-87563-800-7*); pap. text 50.80 (*0-87563-795-7*) Stipes.

Manual of Worship. John E. Skoglund & Nancy E. Hall. LC 92-46117. 304p. 1993. pap. 18.00 (*0-8170-1184-6*) Judson.

Manual of Writer's Tricks. David L. Carroll. 127p. 1995. pap. 9.95 (*1-56924-877-X*) Marlowe & Co.

***Manual of Writer's Tricks: Essential Advice for Fiction & Nonfiction Writers.** David L. Carroll. 144p. 2000. reprint ed. pap. 12.95 (*1-56924-607-6*) Marlowe & Co.

***Manual of Writings in Middle English 1050-1500: Works of Science & Information.** George R. Keiser. Ed. by Albert E. Hartung. (Manual of Writings in Middle English Ser.: No. 10). 1998. 59.95 (*1-878508-18-0*) CT Acad Arts & Sciences.

Manual of Yearbook Studies. William C. Bolland. LC 85-81801. (Cambridge Studies in English Legal History). 184p. 1986. reprint ed. 48.00 (*0-912004-40-1*) Gaunt.

Manual of Zen Buddhism. Ed. by D. T. Suzuki. LC 60-7637. 208p. (Orig.). 1969. pap. 12.00 (*0-8021-3065-8*, Grove) Grove-Atltic.

Manual on Acquisition Review. LC 94-73554. 153p. 1995. pap. 59.95 incl. disk (*1-57073-104-7*, 507-0283) Amer Bar Assn.

Manual on Aircraft Loads. J. Taylor. LC 64-24959. 1965. 157.00 (*0-08-010949-7*, Pub. by Pergamon Repr) Franklin.

Manual on Aquatic Ecotoxicology. Ed. by H. A. Kruijf et al. (C). 1989. text 160.00 (*0-7923-0177-3*) Kluwer Academic.

Manual on Aquatic Ecotoxicology. Ed. by H. A. M. De Kruijf et al. (C). 1990. reprint ed. 58.00 (*0-8364-2736-X*, Pub. by Allied Pubs) S Asia.

Manual on Asbestos Control: Removal, Management, & the Visual Inspection Process. Ed. by Andrew F. Oberta. LC 95-25365. (MNL, Manual Ser.: No. 23). (Illus.). 86p. 1995. text 43.00 (*0-8031-2067-2*, MNL23) ASTM.

Manual on Assisted Reproduction. T. Rabe et al. LC 96-30572. (Illus.). 300p. 1996. 159.00 (*3-540-61134-7*) Spr-Verlag.

***Manual on Assisted Reproduction.** 2nd ed. T. Rabe et al. LC 00-38608. 2000. pap. write for info. (*3-540-67299-0*) Spr-Verlag.

Manual on Bookselling: Practical Advice for the Bookstore Professional. 5th ed. Ed. by Kate Whouley et al. 824p. 1996. pap. 24.95 (*1-879556-18-9*) ABA.

Manual on Chemical Pollution Section 1: Problem Assessment & Response Arrangements. International Maritime Organization Staff. 1987. text 70.00 (*0-89771-972-7*, Pub. by Intl Maritime Org) St Mut.

Manual on Chemical Pollution Section 2: Search & Recovery of Packaged Goods Lost at Sea. International Maritime Organization Staff. 1991. text 100.00 (*0-89771-973-5*, Pub. by Intl Maritime Org) St Mut.

Manual on Chlorosilane Emergency Response Guidelines. Ed. by John T. Higgins et al. LC 98-9980. (Manual (MNL) Ser.: Vol. 33). 39p. 1998. pap. 60.00 (*0-8031-2076-1*, MNL33) ASTM.

Manual on Civil Rights in Vocational Education. Michael Brustein et al. 1984. write for info. (*0-318-57735-6*) NYS Ed Dept.

***Manual on Coaching.** 5th ed. Fairman Rogers. 5p. 2000. reprint ed. 60.00 (*1-880499-09-6*) Carriage Museum.

Manual on Community Pediatrics. 2nd ed. Polnay. 1996. pap. text 24.95 (*0-443-05352-9*, W B Saunders Co) Harcrt Hlth Sci Grp.

Manual on Compost & Other Organic Manures. R. Krishnamurthy. (Illus.). 150p. 1977. 4.00 (*0-88065-148-2*) Scholarly Pubns.

Manual on Construction Layout. NSPS Construction Standards Survey Committee Staff. 40p. 1993. pap. 20.00 (*0-614-06108-3*, S309) Am Congrs Survey.

Manual on Consumer Sensory Evaluation - STP 682. Ed. by E. E. Schaefer. 61p. 1986. 15.00 (*0-8031-0396-4*, STP682) ASTM.

Manual on Cutting of Metals, with Single-Point Tools. 2nd ed. American Society of Mechanical Engineers Staff. LC 53-1487. 560p. reprint ed. pap. 173.60 (*0-608-11620-3*, 200472300046) Bks Demand.

Manual on Demonology: Diary of an Exorcist. Roy Bryant. 1997. 19.95 (*0-89228-123-5*) Impact Christian.

Manual on Descriptive Analysis Testing for Sensory Evaluation. Ed. by Robert C. Hootman. LC 92-13840. (ASTM Manual Ser.: Vol. 13). 1992. 29.00 (*0-8031-1756-6*, MNL13) ASTM.

Manual on Determination of Volatile Organic Compound (VOC) Content in Paints, Inks, & Related Coating Products, MNL 4. 2nd ed. Ed. by John Brezinski. LC 93-20769. (ASTM Manual Ser.: No. MNL 4). 175p. 1993. text 39.00 (*0-8031-2054-0*, MNL4) ASTM.

Manual on Documentation & Information Systems for Furniture & Joinery Plants in Developing Countries. 244p. 1990. 39.00 (*92-1-106245-4*, 90.III.E.7) UN.

Manual on Drilling, Sampling, & Analysis of Coal. Ed. by ASTM Subcommittees DO5.18 & DO5.23 Joint Task Grou & Ronald W. Stanton. LC 92-5556. (Manual Ser.: Vol. MNL 11). (Illus.). 60p. 1992. text 35.00 (*0-8031-1464-8*, MNL11) ASTM.

Manual on Drug Dependence. Ed. by J. F. Kramer & D. C. Cameron. 1975. pap. text 24.00 (*92-4-154045-1*, 1150113) World Health.

Manual on Drug Dependence. Gabriel G. Nahas. (Illus.). 268p. (Orig.). 1992. pap. 12.95 (*0-929240-46-4*) EMIS.

Manual on Economic Accounts for Agriculture & Forestry. European Communities Staff. (E. C. Comprehensive Standing Order English Editions Ser.: Vol. 81450000). 123p. 1997. pap. 18.00 (*92-828-2225-7*, CA-07-97-490ENC, Pub. by Comm Europ Commun) Bernan Associates.

Manual on Economic Development Projects. 279p. 15.50 (*92-1-121053-4*) UN.

Manual On Elastic-Plastic Fracture: Laboratory Test Procedures. Ed. by James A. Joyce. LC 96-17228. (ASTM Manual Ser.). (Illus.). 80p. 1996. 59.00 (*0-8031-2069-9*, MNL27) ASTM.

Manual on Electron Metallography Techniques - STP 547. 78p. 1973. pap. 5.25 (*0-8031-0397-2*, STP547) ASTM.

Manual on Electronic Surveillance. 1991. lib. bdg. 75.00 (*0-8490-4770-6*) Gordon Pr.

Manual on Employment Discrimination & Civil Rights Actions in the Federal Courts: Attorneys' Edition. rev. ed. Charles R. Richey. (Commercial Law Library). 610p. 1988. 85.00 (*1-55834-010-6*, MICHIE) LEXIS Pub.

Manual on Employment Discrimination Law & Civil Rights Actions in the Federal Courts. Charles R. Richey. LC 85-9640. 1985. ring bd. 100.00 (*0-87632-465-0*) West Group.

Manual on Employment Discrimination Law & Civil Rights Actions in the Federal Courts. 2nd ed. Charles R. Richey. 1994. 140.00 (*0-318-72689-0*) West Group.

Manual on Employment Discrimination Law & Civil Rights Actions in the Federal Courts, 1988 Replacement Edition. Charles R. Richey. 630p. 1988. 80.00 (*0-685-28794-7*, MICHIE) LEXIS Pub.

Manual on Emu Farming. Phillip Minnaar. (Illus.). 44p. (Orig.). 1989. pap. 18.00 (*0-9643741-0-2*) Nyoni Pubng.

Manual on Evaporation & Its Restriction from Free Water Surfaces. Ed. by C. V. Varma. LC 99-227623. (Illus.). 98p. (C). 1996. text 67.00 (*90-5410-714-6*, Pub. by A A Balkema) Ashgate Pub Co.

Manual on Exorcism. H. A. Whyte. 128p. 1974. mass mkt. 5.99 (*0-88368-029-7*) Whitaker Hse.

Manual on Experimental Methods for Mechanical Testing of Composites. 2nd ed. C H Jenkins. LC 97-26505. 281p. 1998. pap. text 109.00 (*0-13-907684-0*) P-H.

Manual on Experimental Methods for Mechanical Testing of Composites. 2nd ed. C. H. Jenkins & Society for Experimental Mechanics (U. S.) Staff. LC 97-26505. 264p. 1997. 105.00 (*0-88173-284-2*) Fairmont Pr.

Manual on Fire Assaying & Determination of the Noble Metals in Geological Materials. 2nd ed. Joseph Haffty et al. LC 77-608100. (Illus.). 64p. 1977. reprint ed. pap. 7.95 (*0-9653923-1-7*) Western Tales.

Manual on Gas Dispatching. 175p. 1976. 4.00 (*0-318-12651-6*, XJ0576) Am Gas Assn.

Manual on Government Finance Statistics. International Monetary Fund Staff. LC 85-2373. 375p. reprint ed. pap. 116.30 (*0-608-17995-7*, 202908600058) Bks Demand.

Manual on How to Establish a Trust & Reduce Taxation. rev. ed. 1982. 295.00 (*0-935036-04-0*) Liberty Lobby.

Manual on How to Play the 5-String Banjo for the Complete Ignoramus! Wayne Erbsen. 52p. 1977. pap. 7.95 (*0-8258-0000-5*, PCB 103) Fischer Inc NY.

Manual on Human Rights Reporting. 203p. 1991. 42.00 (*92-1-154082-8*, E.91.XIV.1) UN.

Manual on Human Rights Reporting: Under Six Major International Human Rights Instruments. United Nations Institute for Training & Research. 550p. 1997. pap. 29.00 (*92-1-100752-6*, K3240) UN.

Manual on Hydrocarbon Analysis. American Society for Testing & Materials Staff. Ed. by A. W. Drews. LC 88-37542. (ASTM Data Ser.: MNL 3). (Illus.). 854p. reprint ed. pap. 200.00 (*0-7837-4794-2*, 204483500003) Bks Demand.

Manual on Hydrocarbon Analysis. 5th ed. Ed. by A. W. Drews. LC 92-38461. 840p. 1992. pap. 68.00 (*0-8031-1497-4*) ASTM.

Manual on Hydrocarbon Analysis. 5th ed. Ed. by A. W. Drews. LC 92-38461. (ASTM Manual Ser.: MNL 3). (Illus.). 840p. 1992. text 68.00 (*0-8031-1767-1*, MNL3) ASTM.

Manual on Hydrocarbon Analysis. 6th ed. Ed. by A. W. Drews. LC 98-25886. (Manual Ser.: Vol. 3). (Illus.). 1000p. 1998. reprint ed. pap. 129.00 (*0-8031-2080-X*, MNL3) ASTM.

Manual on Hymn Playing: A Handbook for Organists. David Heller. 160p. 1992. spiral bd. 19.95 (*0-941050-31-9*, G-3642) GIA Pubns.

Manual on Industrial Water & Industrial Waste Water. 2nd ed. American Society for Testing & Materials Staff. LC 67-4371. 148-I. 1007p. reprint ed. pap. 180.00 (*0-317-10882-4*, 2000636) Bks Demand.

Manual on Information Technology Applications in Correctional Administration. Council of Europe Staff. LC 98-220024. 27p. 1998. write for info. (*92-871-3617-3*) Council of Europe.

Manual on Investigating Child Custody Reports. Mary E. Lindley. 194p. 1988. pap. 29.95 (*0-398-06241-2*) C C Thomas.

Manual on Investigating Child Custody Reports. Mary E. Lindley. 194p. (C). 1988. text 45.95 (*0-398-05487-8*) C C Thomas.

Manual on Irrigation Agronomy. R. D. Misra. 422p. (C). 1987. 18.00 (*81-204-0184-0*, Pub. by Oxford IBH) S Asia.

Manual on KF: The Library of Congress Classification Schedule for Law of the United States. Patricia L. Piper et al. LC 72-86471. (AALL Publications Ser.: No. 11). viii, 135p. 1972. 25.00 (*0-8377-0109-0*, Rothman) W S Hein.

Manual on Legal Problems Facing the Released Psychiatric Patient. 178p. 1984. 13.00 (*0-685-30187-7*, 37,516) NCLS Inc.

Manual on Low Cycle Fatigue Testing. American Society for Testing & Materials Staff. LC 70-97730. (ASTM Special Technical Publication: No. 465). 210p. reprint ed. pap. 65.10 (*0-608-12575-X*, 202398700035) Bks Demand.

Manual on Maintenance Coatings for Nuclear Power Plants. Ed. by Timothy Shugart. LC 90-15589. (MNL Ser.: MNL 8). (Illus.). 41p. 1990. text 35.00 (*0-8031-1404-4*, MNL8) ASTM.

Manual on Membrand Lipids. Ed. by R. Prasad. (Springer Lab Manuals Ser.). 224p. 1996. ring bd. 79.00 (*3-540-59448-5*) Spr-Verlag.

Manual on Methodology for Food Consumption Studies. Ed. by Margaret E. Cameron & Wija A. Van Staveren. (Illus.). 284p. 1988. 70.00 (*0-19-261577-7*) OUP.

Manual on Moisture Control in Buildings. Ed. by Heinz R. Trechsel. LC 93-43304. (ASTM Manual Ser.: MNL18). (Illus.). 480p. 1994. text 89.00 (*0-8031-2051-6*, MNL18) ASTM.

Manual on Motion Economy Techniques. 1986. 5.00 (*0-940876-11-6*) City Hope.

Manual on National Accounts at Constant Price. 8.00 (*92-1-161168-7*, E.79.XVII.5) UN.

Manual on Oil Pollution Section I: Prevention. International Maritime Organization Staff. 1983. text 85.00 (*0-89771-958-1*, Pub. by Intl Maritime Org) St Mut.

Manual on Oil Pollution Section II: Contingency Planning. International Maritime Organization Staff. 1988. text 75.00 (*0-7855-6894-8*, Pub. by Intl Maritime Org) St Mut.

Manual on Oil Pollution Section III: Salvage. International Maritime Organization Staff. 1983. text 95.00 (*0-89771-959-X*, Pub. by Intl Maritime Org) St Mut.

Manual on Oil Pollution Section IV: Combating Oil Spills. International Maritime Organization Staff. 1988. text 150.00 (*0-89771-960-3*, Pub. by Intl Maritime Org) St Mut.

Manual on Operational Methods for the Measurement of Sediment Transport. Long Yuqian. (WMO, No. 686 & Operational Hydrology Reports: No. 29). 169p. 1989. pap. 22.00 (*92-63-10686-X*, Pub. by Wrld Meteorological) St Mut.

Manual on Plant Layout & Materials Handling. Economic Development Foundation Staff. (Illus.). 80p. 1972. pap. text 11.75 (*92-833-1012-8*, 310128) Productivity Inc.

Manual on Population Census Data Processing Using Microcomputers. 136p. 25.00 (*92-1-161326-4*, 90.XVII.19) UN.

Manual on Presentation of Data & Control Chart Analysis, MNL 7. LC 89-18047. (Manual Ser.). (Illus.). 125p. 1990. pap. text 22.00 (*0-8031-1289-0*, MNL7) ASTM.

Manual on Radiation Dosimetry. Ed. by Niels W. Holm & Roger J. Berry. LC 73-84775. 466p. reprint ed. 144.50 (*0-8357-9086-X*, 205500300007) Bks Demand.

Manual on Radiation Protection in Hospitals & General Practice. Incl. Vol. 1. Basic Protection Requirements. C. B. Braestrup & K. J. Vikterlof. 1974. 12.00 (*92-4-154038-9*); Vol. 2. Unsealed Sources. D. Frost & H. Jammet. 1975. 24.00 (*92-4-154039-7*); Vol. 3. X-Ray Diagnosis. B. E. Keane & K. B. Tikhonov. 1975. 18.00 (*92-4-154040-0*); write for info. (*0-318-56480-7*) World Health.

Manual on Radiation Protection in Hospitals & General Practice: Personnel Monitoring Services, Vol. 5. W. Minder & S. Osborn. (Nonserial Publication). 56p. 1980. pap. text 9.00 (*92-4-154042-7*, 1150112) World Health.

Manual on Radiation Protection in Hospitals & General Practice: Radiation Protection in Dentistry, Vol. 4. K. Koren & A. Wuehrmann. (Nonserial Publication). 52p. 1977. pap. text 10.00 (*92-4-154041-9*, 1150111) World Health.

M

Manual on Radiation Sterilization of Medical & Biological Materials. (Technical Reports: No. 149). (Illus.). 327p. (Orig.). 1973. pap. 60.00 (*92-0-115073-3*, IDC149, Pub. by IAEA) Bernan Associates.

Manual on Recurring Problems in Criminal Trials. 4th ed. Donald S. Voorhees. 162p. (C). 1997. pap. text 40.00 (*0-7881-4531-2*) DIANE Pub.

Manual on Requirements, Handling & Quality Control of Gas Turbine Fuel-STP 531. 200p. 1973. 20.00 (*0-8031-0764-1*, STP531) ASTM.

Manual on Sawmill Operational Maintenance. 69p. 1990. 12.00 (*92-5-102913-X*, F913X, Pub. by FAO) Bernan Associates.

Manual on Selection & Use of Engine Coolants & Cooling System Chemicals. 4th ed. Ed. by Joseph A. Lima & George R. Otterman. LC 89-342. (Manual Ser.: No. MNL 6). (Illus.). 16p. 1989. pap. text 12.00 (*0-8031-1265-3*, MNL6) ASTM.

Manual on Sensory Testing Methods. American Society for Testing & Materials Staff. LC 68-15545. (ASTM Special Technical Publication: No. 434). 84p. reprint ed. pap. 30.00 (*0-7837-4702-0*, 204484900003) Bks Demand.

Manual on Sensory Testing Methods - STP 434. 82p. 1993. pap. 13.00 (*0-8031-0018-3*, STP434) ASTM.

Manual on Significance of Tests for Petroleum Products. 6th ed. Ed. by George V. Dryoff. LC 93-39717. (Manual Ser.: No. 1). 127p. 1993. 33.00 (*0-8031-2050-8*, MNL1) ASTM.

M

***Manual on Small Animal Surgery.** Fossum. LC 99-26587. 1999. pap. text 49.95 (*0-323-00562-4*) Harcourt.

Manual on Species & Provenance Research with Particular Reference to the Tropics. J. Burley & P. J. Wood. 1976. 62.50 (*0-85074-016-9*) St Mut.

Manual on Species & Provenance Research with Particular Reference to the Tropics. J. Burley & P. J. Wood. 1977. 30.00 (*0-85074-024-X*) St Mut.

Manual on Statistical Planning & Analysis for Fatigue Experiments-STP 588. 157p. 1975. 15.00 (*0-8031-0501-0*, STP588) ASTM.

Manual on Technology Transfer Negotiations. LC 97-105610. (General Studies). 344p. 50.00 (*92-1-106302-7*) UN.

Manual on Test Sieving Methods: Guidelines for Establishing Sieve Analysis Procedures. American Society for Testing & Materials Staff. LC 69-17122. (ASTM Special Technical Publication: No. 447A). 49p. reprint ed. pap. 30.00 (*0-608-16278-7*, 202666500051) Bks Demand.

Manual on Test Sieving Methods: Guidelines for Establishing Sieve Analysis Procedures. 4th ed. Ed. by Lawrence C. Pope. LC 98-22472. (Manual Ser.: Vol. 32). (Illus.). 50p. 1998. pap. 26.00 (*0-8031-2495-3*, MNL32) ASTM.

Manual on Test Sieving Methods - STP 447B. LC 85-22816. 50p. 1985. pap. text 16.00 (*0-8031-0476-6*, STP447B) ASTM.

Manual on the Building of Materials Databases. Ed. by Crystal H. Newton. LC 93-36460. (ASTM Manual Ser.: No. MNL 19). (Illus.). 105p. 1993. text 45.00 (*0-8031-2052-4*, MNL19) ASTM.

Manual on the Causes & Control of Activated Sludge Bulking & Foaming. 2nd ed. David Jenkins et al. 224p. 1993. lib. bdg. 75.00 (*0-87371-873-9*, L873) Lewis Pubs.

Manual on the Culture of Small Fruits. Edward P. Roe. (Notable American Authors Ser.). 1999. reprint ed. lib. bdg. 125.00 (*0-7812-8828-2*) Rprt Serv.

***Manual on the Development & Use of FAO Specifications for Plant Protection Products.** 5th ed. FAO Staff. (Illus.). 188p. 1999. pap. 22.00 (*92-5-104271-3*, Pub. by FAO) Bernan Associates.

Manual on the Diagnosis of Rinderpest: Animal Health Manual. 2nd ed. J. Anderson et al. (Animal Health Ser.: No. 1). (Illus.). 143p. 1997. pap. 28.00 (*92-5-103814-7*, F38147, Pub. by FAO) Bernan Associates.

Manual on the Effective Prevention & Investigation of Extra-Legal Arbitrary Summary Executions. 72p. pap. 15.00 (*92-1-130142-4*) UN.

Manual on the Global Data-Processing System, 2 vols. in 1, Set. World Meteorological Organization Staff. (WMO Ser.: No. 485). ring bd. 66.00 (*92-63-10485-9*, Pub. by Wrld Meteorological) St Mut.

Manual on the Global Telecommunication System, 2 vols. in 1. World Meteorological Organization Staff. No. 386. (Illus.). suppl. ed. write for info. (*0-318-68022-X*, Pub. by Wrld Meteorological); write for info. (*0-318-68021-1*, Pub. by Wrld Meteorological); write for info. (*0-318-68020-3*, Pub. by Wrld Meteorological) St Mut.

Manual on the Global Telecommunication System, 2 vols. in 1, Set. World Meteorological Organization Staff. (WMO Ser.: No. 386). (Illus.). 1992. ring bd. 157.00 (*92-63-12386-1*, Pub. by Wrld Meteorological) St Mut.

Manual on the Liturgy: Lutheran Book of Worship. Philip H. Pfatteicher & Carlos R. Messerli. LC 78-68179. 1979. 31.50 (*0-8066-1676-8*, 3-2015, Augsburg) Augsburg Fortress.

Manual on the Production & Use of Live Food for Aquaculture. (Fisheries Technical Papers: No. 361). 295p. 1997. pap. 41.00 (*92-5-103934-8*, F39348, Pub. by FAO) Bernan Associates.

Manual on the Use of Consultants in Developing Countries. 176p. reprint ed. pap. 12.00 (*92-1-106056-7*, E.72.II.B.10) UN.

Manual on the Use of Rock in Hydraulic Engineering. Netherlands Centre for Civil Engineering Research. 800p. 1995. 368.00 (*90-5410-605-0*, Pub. by A A Balkema) Ashgate Pub Co.

***Manual on the Use of the LP-System in Milk Handling & Preservation.** Food & Agriculture Organization Staff. 36p. 1999. pap. 8.00 (*92-5-104254-3*, Pub. by FAO) Bernan Associates.

Manual on the Use of Thermocouples in Temperature Measurement. Ed. by Richard M. Parks. LC 92-47237. (Manual Ser.: No. MNL 12). (Illus.). 311p. 1993. text 49.00 (*0-8031-1466-4*, MNL12) ASTM.

Manual on the Use of Thermocouples in Temperature Measurement. 3rd ed. (Special Technical Publication Ser.: No. 470A). 275p. 1981. 17.50 (*0-8031-0502-9*, STP470A) ASTM.

Manual on the Use of Thermocouples in Temperature Measurement. 3rd ed. American Society for Testing & Materials Staff. LC 80-69066. (ASTM Special Technical Publication: Vol. 470B). (Illus.). 276p. 1981. reprint ed. pap. 85.60 (*0-7837-8943-2*, 204965400002) Bks Demand.

Manual on Trading with the Socialist Countries of Eastern Europe. 130p. 1991. 26.00 (*92-1-112288-0*, 90.II.D.3) UN.

Manual on Uniform Traffic Control Devices: Standards & Guides for Traffic Controls for Street & Highway Construction, Maintenance, Utility, & Incident Management Operations. 6th rev. ed. Transportation Department, Federal Highway Adminis. (FHWA-SA-89-006. ANSI D6.1e-1989 Ser.). (Illus.). 203p. 1994. per. 19.00 (*0-16-043015-1*, 050-001-00316-3) USGPO.

Manual on Uniform Traffic Control Devices for Streets & Highways, 2 vols. (Transportation Ser.). Orig. Title: Work Zone Traffic Control: Standards & Guidelines. 1990. lib. bdg. 600.00 (*0-8490-4014-0*) Gordon Pr.

Manual on Uniform Traffic Control Devices for Streets & Highways & Guides for Traffic Construction, Maintenance, Utility, & Incident Management Operations, 2 vols. 1997. lib. bdg. 600.95 (*0-8490-6118-0*) Gordon Pr.

Manual on Urban Air Quality Management. Ed. by S. R. Craxford & Michael J. Suess. (WHO Regional Publications). 1976. pap. text 36.00 (*92-9020-101-0*, 1310001) World Health.

Manual on Usage & Style. 8th ed. Texas Law Review Association Staff. 90p. 1995. pap. 4.00 (*1-878674-51-X*) U TX Law Pubns.

Manual on User Benefit Analysis & Bus Transit Improvements. 1978. pap. 35.00 (*0-686-24170-3*, UBA) AASHTO.

Manual on Using the Light. John-Roger. 1976. pap. 5.00 (*0-88238-960-2*) Mandeville LA.

Manual on Using the Light. John-Roger. 73p. 1995. pap. 5.00 (*0-914829-13-0*) Mandeville LA.

Manual on Vapor Degreasing, MNL2. 3rd rev. ed. Ed. by ASTM Subcommittee D26.02 on Vapor Degreasing Staff. LC 88-35141. 48p. 1989. pap. text 21.00 (*0-8031-1217-3*, MNL2) ASTM.

Manual on Water. 4th ed. American Society for Testing & Materials Staff. Ed. by C. E. Hamilton. LC 78-51579. (ASTM Special Technical Publication: No. 442A). 480p. reprint ed. pap. 148.80 (*0-7837-6484-7*, 204651100001) Bks Demand.

Manual on Water-Quality Monitoring: Planning & Implementation of Sampling & Field Testing. World Meteorological Organization Staff. (WMO, No. 680 & Operational Hydrology Reports: No. 27). (Illus.). 197p. 1988. pap. 27.00 (*92-63-10680-0*, Pub. by Wrld Meteorological) St Mut.

Manual on Zirconium & Hafnium - STP 639. Ed. by J. H. Schemel. 108p. 1977. 9.50 (*0-8031-0505-3*, STP639) ASTM.

Manual Oncology, No. 2. Carol S. Portlock. 1986. 15.95 (*0-316-71426-7*, Little Brwn Med Div) Lppncott W & W.

Manual Para Comites de Supervision. Felix J. Martinez & Benjamin Rosario. Ed. by Carmen M. Bauza. (Cooperatives Ser.). (SPA.). 84p. (Orig.). 1990. 5.95 (*0-934885-03-6*) Edit Nosotros.

Manual para Comunidades Eclesiales de Base. M.A.C.C. Team Staff. (SPA.). 36p. 1991. write for info. (*0-614-04890-7*) Mex Am Cult.

Manual para Controlar los Accidentes Ocupacionales. 470p. 40.00 (*0-318-17994-6*) Inter-Am Safety.

Manual Para el Catolico de Hoy: Con Referencias Al Catecismo de la Iglesia Catolica. rev. ed. Una Publicacion Pastoral Redentorista Staff. LC 94-75246. (SPA.). 112p. 1994. pap. 2.95 (*0-89243-673-5*) Liguori Pubns.

Manual para la Crianza Del Emu. rev. ed. Phillip Minnaar. Ed. by Maria Minnaar. Tr. by Kathryn Nava. (SPA., Illus.). 58p. (C). 1997. 20.00 (*0-9643741-6-1*) Nyoni Pubng.

Manual para la Familia Catolica Hispana de Hoy: Practicas y Oraciones de la Iglesia Catolica. Una Publicacion Pastoral Redentorista Staff. Ed. by John McPhee. Tr. by Olimpia Diaz. (SPA.). 64p. 1979. pap. 3.95 (*0-89243-123-7*) Liguori Pubns.

Manual Para la Implementacion Del Just-in-Time: Una Guia Completa Para la Reconversion a la Fabricacion JIT, 2 Vol. Set, Vol. 1 & 2. Hirano. 1991. teacher ed., boxed set 995.00 (*84-87022-83-9*) Productivity Inc.

Manual Para la Practica Docente: Programa a Base de Competencias. Objectivos Operacionales-Instrumentos de Evaluacion. Christina W. Needham & Carmen A. Morales. (SPA.). 82p. 1980. pap. 5.00 (*0-8477-2744-0*) U of PR Pr.

Manual para la Preparacion de Informes y Tesis. Irma G. Deserrano. LC 76-11003. (C). 1992. pap. 8.25 (*0-8477-2312-7*) U of PR Pr.

Manual para la Secretaria Legal. 3rd rev. ed. Ignacio R. Garcia. 420p. 1990. 45.00 (*0-88063-698-X*, 82932-10, MICHIE) LEXIS Pub.

***Manual para las Exportaciones y Ventas Internacionales: Como Preparar y Hacer Ventas Internacionales.** Ed. by Marie Vacca. Tr. by Professional Translation Services, Inc. Staff from ENG. Orig. Title: Export Sales & Marketing Manuel. (SPA., Illus.). xvi, 555p. 1999. pap. 295.00 (*0-9674938-0-3*) DowWarner Enter.

Manual para los Discipulos de Hoy. rev. ed. D. Duane Cummins. Tr. by Conchita Delgado from ENG. LC 83-15489.Tr. of Handbook for Today's Disciples. (SPA.). 80p. (Orig.). 1999. pap. 3.75 (*0-8272-2326-9*) Chalice Pr.

Manual para Monografias Musicales. Donald Thompson & Annie Figueroa de Thompson. LC 80-21247. (SPA.). 59p. (Orig.). (C). 1980. pap. text 4.00 (*0-8477-2113-2*) U of PR Pr.

Manual para Obreros Cristianos. C. L. Neal.Tr. of Manual for Christian Workers. (SPA.). 184p. 1961. pap. 6.99 (*0-311-05017-4*) Casa Bautista.

Manual para Plantar Iglesias. Larry L. Lewis.Tr. of Church Planter's Handbook. (SPA.). 176p. 1997. pap. text 6.99 (*0-311-13863-2*) Casa Bautista.

Manual para Predicadores Laicos: Manual for the Lay Preachers Student. J. D. Crane. 122p. 1967. reprint ed. pap. 9.99 (*0-311-42039-7*) Casa Bautista.

Manual para Proclamadores de la Palabra, 1999. Juan Alfaro. (SPA.). 216p. 1998. pap. 12.00 (*1-56854-219-4*, SWL99) Liturgy Tr Pubns.

Manual Para Tecnicos de Pulpa y Papel. Gary A. Smook. Tr. by Jose C. Pastor from ENG.Tr. of Handbook for Pulp & Paper Technologists. (SPA.). 1991. 103.00 (*0-89852-055-X*, 0102B055) TAPPI.

Manual Para Tubos Drager. 9th ed. Tr. by Language Center Staff from GER.Tr. of Drager-Tube Handbook. 367p. (Orig.). 1995. pap. 25.00 (*0-9650423-0-8*) National Draeger.

Manual Paralegal. Ignacio R. Garcia. 400p. 1984. 45.00 (*0-88063-518-5*, 82928-10, MICHIE) LEXIS Pub.

***Manual Pediatra Practico.** 3rd ed. Beryl J. Rosenstein. (C). 1998. text 24.49 (*84-8174-344-5*) Mosby Inc.

***Manual Pediatrico para los Duenos del Nueva Bebe: Guia para el Cuidado y Mantenimiento de su Nuevo Bebe.** Horst D. Weinburg.Tr. of Pediatrician's New Baby Owner's Manual. (SPA., Illus.). 208p. 1999. pap. 12.95 (*1-884956-06-8*) Quill Driver.

***Manual Personal del Obrero Cristiano.** Leadership Ministries Worldwide Staff. (SPA.). 272p. 1999. pap. 9.99 (*0-8254-1019-3*, Edit Portavoz) Kregel.

Manual Portavoz del Templo Judio. Robert Backhouse.Tr. of Kregel Pictorial Guide to the Temple. (SPA.). 32p. 1996. pap. 8.99 (*0-8254-1047-9*, Edit Portavoz) Kregel.

Manual Practico de Homiletica. K. Silva.Tr. of Practical Homiletics Manual. (SPA.). 155p. 1995. 6.99 (*1-56063-502-9*, 498448) Editorial Unilit.

Manual Practico de las Ventas. Benito Avanti. (SPA., Illus.). 98p. (Orig.). 1997. pap. 8.99 (*1-890701-01-7*) La Mancha.

***Manual Relating to Special Verdicts & Special Findings by Juriers.** George B. Clementson. lxi,350p. 1999. reprint ed. 124.50 (*1-56169-450-9*) Gaunt.

Manual Screw Press for Small-Scale Oil Extraction. Kathryn H. Potts & Keith Machell. 72p. (Orig.). 1995. pap. 17.50 (*1-85339-198-0*, Pub. by Intermed Tech) Stylus Pub VA.

Manual SLRs. Joseph Meehan. LC 95-151239. (Magic Lantern Guides Ser.). (Illus.). 176p. (Orig.). (C). 1998. pap. 19.95 (*1-883403-10-3*, H 153, Silver Pixel Pr) Saunders Photo.

Manual Sobre Investigaciones de Especies y Procedencias con Referencia Especial a Los Tropicos. J. Burley & P. J. Wood. 1979. 50.00 (*0-85074-058-4*) St Mut.

Manual Terapeutico para el Adulto Con Dificultades Del Habla y Lenguaje Tomo 1: Una Seleccion de Materiales de Estimulo. Kathryn Kilpatrick & Cynthia L. Jones. Tr. by Ingrid Bahler & Katherine G. Gatto. (SPA., Illus.). 433p. 1985. student ed. 37.00 (*1-880504-01-4*) Visit Nurse.

Manual Therapy. Ed. by Jensen & Farrell. 104p. 1993. pap. 21.00 (*0-912452-83-8*, P-87) Am Phys Therapy Assn.

Manual Therapy: Improve Muscle & Joint Functioning. L. A. Warmerdam. Ed. by Barbara Field. LC 97-91614. (Illus.). 329p. 1998. text. write for info. (*0-9657910-0-9*) Pine NY.

Manual Therapy Case Studies. Spencer. 1998. pap. text 39.95 (*0-443-05696-X*, W B Saunders Co) Harcrt Hlth Sci Grp.

Manual Therapy for Functional Mobility: A Neuromuscular Approach. Darlene Hertling. 400p. text. write for info. (*0-7817-1459-1*) Lppncott W & W.

***Manual Therapy of Peripheral Joints.** Ed. by J. D. Boyling. (Illus.). 592p. 1998. text. write for info. (*0-443-04349-3*) Church.

Manual Thermal Diagnosis. Jean-Pierre Barral. (Illus.). 130p. (C). 1996. text 35.00 (*0-939616-24-6*) Eastland.

Manual to Determine Benefits of Separating Pedestrians & Vehicles. (National Cooperative Highway Research Program Report Ser.: No. 240). 56p. 1981. 7.20 (*0-309-03300-4*, NR240) Transport Res Bd.

Manual to Physics. 5th ed. Arthur Beiser. (C). 1991. pap. text, student ed. 28.00 (*0-201-16868-5*) Addison-Wesley.

***Manual to the Palms of Ecuador.** Finn Borchsenius et al. (AAU Reports: Vol. 37). (Illus.). 217p. 1998. pap. 12.95 (*87-87600-53-6*, Pub. by Aarhus Univ Pr) David Brown.

Manual Training School. Calvin M. Woodward. LC 79-89254. (American Education; Its Men, Institutions, & Ideas. Series 1). 1978. reprint ed. 19.95 (*0-405-01492-9*) Ayer.

Manual Transmission Clutch Systems. Ray Shaver & SAE Clutch Standards Committee. LC 96-51095. 1997. 79.00 (*1-56091-923-X*, AE-17) Soc Auto Engineers.

Manual Transmissions. Jana. (EZ Auto Ser.). (C). 1996. pap. text, wbk. ed. 13.50 (*0-8273-8060-7*) Delmar.

Manual Transmissions. Jana. (EZ Auto Ser.). (C). 2001. text 39.00 (*0-8273-8059-3*) Delmar.

Manual Transmissions. John White. 320p. 1987. pap. 36.50 (*0-8273-2609-2*) Delmar.

Manual Transmissions. John White. 320p. 1987. teacher ed. 13.50 (*0-8273-2610-6*) Delmar.

Manual Transmissions & Transaxles, 2 vols., Set. Jack Erjavec. LC 93-33478. (Today's Technician Ser.). 1993. write for info. (*0-8273-6181-5*) Delmar.

Manual Treatment of Back Pain. Vincent C. Nwuga. LC 84-3965. 224p. (C). 1986. lib. bdg. 23.50 (*0-89874-753-8*) Krieger.

Manual Urologic Surgery. H. Ramsey Fowler. 1990. 115.00 (*0-316-28951-5*, Little Brwn Med Div) Lppncott W & W.

Manual Vacuum Aspiration: A Summary of Clinical & Programmatic Experience Worldwide. Forrest C. Greenslade et al. LC 93-8963. 1993. pap. write for info. (*1-882220-03-X*) IPAS.

Manual Vacuum Aspiration Guide for Clinicians see Guia de Aspiracao Manual Intrauterina para Medicos

Manual Vacuum Aspiration Guide for Clinicians see Guia Practica para la Aspiracion Manual Endouterina

Manual Vacuum Aspiration Guide for Clinicians. Laura Yordy et al. LC 93-39549. 1993. pap. write for info. (*1-882220-04-8*) IPAS.

Manual with IBM 3.5 Disk. pap. 26.00 (*0-393-96262-8*) Norton.

Manual with IBM 3.5 Disk/Pged with Shorter Edition Text. pap. 40.50 (*0-393-96267-9*) Norton.

Manual with IBM 3.5 Disk/Pkged with Text. pap. 43.00 (*0-393-96264-4*) Norton.

Manual with IBM 5.25 Disk. pap. 26.00 (*0-393-96263-6*) Norton.

Manual with IBM 5.25 Disk/Pkged with Shorter Edition Text. pap. 40.50 (*0-393-96268-7*) Norton.

Manual with IBM 5.25 Disk/Pkged with Text. Constance Gefvert. pap. 36.50 (*0-393-96259-8*) Norton.

Manual with IBN 5.25 Disk. Constance Gefvert. pap. 26.00 (*0-393-96257-1*) Norton.

Manual with IBM 3.5 Disk/Pkged with Text. Edwin Mansfield. 1994. pap. 67.00 (*0-393-96538-4*) Norton.

Manual with 5.25 Disk/Pkged with Text. pap. 43.00 (*0-393-96265-2*) Norton.

***Manualde Diseno y Construacion de Templos.** Ladson Saylor. (SPA.). 1999. pap. 12.99 (*0-7899-0522-1*) Spanish Hse Distributors.

Manuale Congregationis Provinciae see Guide for Delegates to a Province Congregation

Manuale Di Grammatica Italiana. Annamaria Napolitano & Maria T. Devine. (C). 1979. pap. text 29.50 (*0-915838-98-2*) Anma Libri.

Manuale Di Pronuncia Italiana. Luciano Canepari. (ITA.). 416p. 1993. 150.00 incl. audio (*0-8288-9429-9*) Fr & Eur.

Manually Actuated Signaling Boxes for Use with Fire-Protective Signaling Systems, UL 38. 7th ed. (C). 1999. pap. text 95.00 (*1-55989-515-2*) Underwrtrs Labs.

***Manuals of Dhamma.** 280p. 1999. pap. 14.95 (*81-7414-202-9*) Vipassana Res Pubns.

Manuals of Dipterocarps for Foresters: Singapore. M. F. Newman et al. (Illus.). 104p. 1995. pap. 23.00 (*1-872291-31-7*, Pub. by Royal Botanic Edinburgh) Balogh.

Manuals of Food Quality Control: Food for Export. rev. ed. 149p. 1990. 20.00 (*92-5-103014-6*, F0146, Pub. by FAO) Bernan Associates.

Manuals of Food Quality Control: Training in Mycotoxins Analysis. 116p. 1990. 25.00 (*92-5-102947-4*, F9474, Pub. by FAO) Bernan Associates.

Manuals of Food Quality Control No. 1: The Food Control Laboratory. rev. ed. P. G. Martin & J. Weatherwax. (Food & Nutrition Papers: No. 14-1). (Illus.). 67p. (Orig.). 1987. pap. text 12.00 (*92-5-102489-8*, F3038, Pub. by FAO) Bernan Associates.

Manuals of Food Quality Control No. 4: Microbiological Analysis. rev. ed. (Food & Nutrition Papers: No. 14). 348p. 1992. 41.00 (*92-5-103189-4*, F31894, Pub. by FAO) Bernan Associates.

Manuals of Food Quality Control No. 7: Food Analysis, General Techniques, Additives, Contaminants & Composition. (Food & Nutrition Papers: No. 14). (Illus.). 238p. 1986. text 35.00 (*92-5-102399-9*, F2998, Pub. by FAO) Bernan Associates.

Manuals of Food Quality Control No. 8: Food Analysis, Quality, Adulteration, & Tests of Identity. (Food & Nutrition Papers: No. 14-8). (Illus.). 326p. 1987. lib. bdg. 45.00 (*92-5-102412-X*, F2997, Pub. by FAO) Bernan Associates.

Manuals of Food Quality Control No. 11: Management of Food Control Programmes. (Food & Nutrition Papers: No. 14). 50p. 1991. 20.00 (*92-5-103050-2*, F0502, Pub. by FAO) Bernan Associates.

Manuals of Food Quality Control No. 12: Quality Assurance in the Food Control Microbiological Laboratory. Food & Agriculture Organization Staff. (Food & Nutrition Papers: No. 14). 164p. 1992. 25.00 (*92-5-103053-7*, F0537, Pub. by FAO) Bernan Associates.

Manuals of Food Quality Control No. 13: Pesticide Residue Analysis in the Food Control Laboratory. FAO Staff. (Food & Nutrition Papers). 348p. 1993. 25.00 (*92-5-103269-6*, F32396, Pub. by FAO) Bernan Associates.

Manuals of Food Quality Control No. 14: Quality Assurance in Food Control Chemical Laboratory. FAO Staff. (Food & Nutrition Papers: 14-14). 136p. 1994. 19.00 (*92-5-103403-6*, F34036, Pub. by FAO) Bernan Associates.

Manuals of Plants. Ed. by F. E. Fritsch. 1991. 200.00 (*81-7158-247-8*, Pub. by Scientific Pubs) St Mut.

Manuals Set (DCM & MCC) 2nd rev. ed. Ann Morrison. 1994. 485.00 (*0-614-05008-1*, MSET) Capitol Publns.

An Asterisk (*) at the beginning of an entry indicates that the title is appearing for the first time.

Manuals That Work. IA Associates Staff. (Illus.). 192p. 1986. student ed. 79.50 (*0-87683-829-8*); ring bd. 149.50 incl. VHS (*0-87683-837-9*) GP Courseware.

Manuals that Work: A Guide for Writers. rev. ed. Michael Davis et al. 128p. 1990. pap. 27.50 (*0-89397-353-X*) Nichols Pub.

Manuductio Administerium, Directions for a Candidate of the Ministry. Cotton Mather. LC 75-41190. reprint ed. 36.50 (*0-404-14685-6*) AMS Pr.

Manuel Alphabetique de Psychiatrie Clinique et Therapeutique. 6th ed. Ed. by Antoine Porot. (FRE.). 768p. 1984. 135.00 (*0-7859-4832-5*, M6391) Fr & Eur.

Manuel Altolaguirre: Vida y Literatura. Carmen D. Hernandez de Trelles. (Coleccion Mente y Palabra). 190p. (C). 1974. 5.00 (*0-8477-0510-2*); pap. 4.00 (*0-8477-0511-0*) U of PR Pr.

Manuel Alvarez Bravo. Susan Kismaric. (Illus.). 240p. 1997. 60.00 (*0-87070-133-9*, 0-8109-6171-7, Pub. by Mus of Modern Art); pap. 27.50 (*0-87070-114-2*) Mus of Modern Art.

Manuel Alvarez Bravo. 2nd ed. A. D. Coleman. (Masters of Photography Ser.). (Illus.). 96p. 1997. reprint ed. 18.95 (*0-89381-742-2*) Aperture.

***Manuel & the Madman.** Gerald W. Haslam & Janice E. Haslam. 206p. 2000. pap. 9.95 (*0-915685-11-6*, Pub. by Devil Mountain Bks) SPD-Small Pr Dist.

Manuel Bibliographique des Sciences Psychiques Ou Occultes, 3 vols., Set. Albert Caillet. (FRE.). 1831p. 1964. text 325.00 (*90-6004-024-4*, Pub. by B De Graaf) Coronet Bks.

Manuel de Bacteriologie Clinique, 2 vols. J. Freney et al. 1760p. pap. 211.00 (*2-906077-57-7*) Elsevier.

Manuel de Bibliographie Litteraire pour les XVIe, XVIIe, XVIIIe Siecles Francais (1921-1935), 2 tomes. (FRE.). write for info. (*0-8288-7766-1*) Fr & Eur.

Manuel de Bibliographie Litteraire pour les XVIe, XVIIe, XVIIIe Siecles Francais (1921-1935), 2 tomes, Set. Victor Giraud. 35.75 (*0-685-35966-2*) Fr & Eur.

Manuel de Composition Francais. Pierre Limouzy. (FRE.). 1970. 14.00 (*0-394-30363-6*) Random.

Manuel de Composition Francaise. 2nd ed. Pierre Limouzy & Jacques A. Bourgeacq. 288p. (C). 1990. 44.69 (*0-07-037903-3*) McGraw.

Manuel de Composition Francaise. 2nd ed. Pierre Limouzy & Jacques A. Bourgeacq. (C). 1990. pap. text, teacher ed. 12.18 (*0-07-037904-1*) McGraw.

Manuel de Defectos de la Fundicion. (SPA., Illus.). 197p. 1991. pap. 44.00 (*0-685-67384-7*, GM9100) Am Foundrymen.

Manuel De Diplomatique. Arthur Giry. xvi, 944p. 1972. reprint ed. write for info. (*3-487-04513-3*) G Olms Pubs.

Manuel de Ensenanza Autodidactica 1. (GER.). 80p. 1997. pap. write for info. (*3-468-49772-5*) Langenscheidt.

Manuel de Falla. Suzanne Demarquez. LC 82-23640. (Music Reprint Ser.). viii, 253p. 1983. reprint ed. lib. bdg. 32.50 (*0-306-76204-8*) Da Capo.

Manuel de Falla: A Bio-Bibliography, 68. Nancy Lee Harper. LC 98-28638. (Bio-Bibliographies in Music: Vol. 68). 288p. 1998. lib. bdg. 65.00 (*0-313-30292-8*, Greenwood Pr) Greenwood.

***Manuel de Falla: His Life & Works.** Ed. by Manzani Diaz Agen & Juan Perez de Ayala. Tr. by Chi Qui Abril. (Illus.). 303p. 1999. pap. text 34.95 (*0-7119-6909-4*, OP48U71) Omnibus NY.

Manuel de Falla & Spanish Music. John B. Trend. 1988. reprint ed. lib. bdg. 49.00 (*0-7812-0796-7*) Rprt Serv.

Manuel de Falla & Spanish Music. John B. Trend. LC 74-181283. 184p. 1934. reprint ed. 49.00 (*0-403-01706-8*) Scholarly.

Manuel de Falla & the Spanish Musical Renaissance Burnett James. LC 79-315764. 172 p. 1979. write for info. (*0-575-02645-6*) Trafalgar.

Manuel de Falla, 1876-1946. Javier Suarez-Pajares. 1999. 45.00 (*84-8048-224-9*) Vanderbilt U Pr.

Manuel de Fixation des Dunes. (FRE.). 68p. 1988. 9.00 (*92-5-202658-4*, FF6584, Pub. by FAO) Bernan Associates.

Manuel de Formation Pratique pour la Transplantation Embryonnaire Chez la Brebis & la Chevre. (FRE.). 198p. 1993. 15.00 (*92-5-203388-2*, FF3882, Pub. by FAO) Bernan Associates.

***Manuel de Gestion Financiere.** (FRE.). 127p. 1998. pap. 15.00 (*0-9700770-2-5*) Ctr Intl Private Enter.

Manuel de Gramatica Comercial. A. Lugo-Guernelli et al. (ENG & SPA.). 204p. 1976. pap. 14.95 (*0-8288-5741-5*, S50369) Fr & Eur.

Manuel de l'Amateur de Livres du XIXe Siecle, 1801-1893. Georges Vicaire. LC 73-87062. 510p. 1973. reprint ed. lib. bdg. write for info. (*0-85964-028-0*) Chadwyck-Healey.

Manuel de Lideres - Una Guia Estructarada e Introduccion a la No Violencia Segun los Principios de King: Filosofia y Metodologia. David C. Jehnsen & Bernard LaFayette. (Illus.). 155p. 1999. pap. text 40.00 (*1-888615-07-9*) Inst Human Rghts.

Manuel de Lideres de la Comunidad: El Programs del Dr. King de Reconciliacion Contro lo Violencia Estrategis Para Responder Conflicto y Violencia. David C. Jehnsen & Bernard LaFayette. 1998. pap. text 25.00 (*1-888615-05-2*) Inst Human Rghts.

Manuel de l'Inquisiteur, 2 vols. in 1. Bernardus Guidonis. Ed. by G. Mollat. LC 78-63183. (Heresies of the Early Christian & Medieval Era Ser.: Second Ser.). reprint ed. 79.50 (*0-404-16199-5*) AMS Pr.

Manuel de Numismatique Orientale de l'Antiquite et du Moyen Age. J. DeMorgan. (FRE., Illus.). 1979. reprint ed. 30.00 (*0-916710-44-0*) Obol Intl.

Manuel de Recherche Operationnelle en Matiere de Planification Familiale. Andrew Fisher et al.Tr. of Handbook for Family Planning Operations Research Design. (FRE.). 1991. write for info. (*0-87834-055-6*) Population Coun.

Manuel d'Economie Politique. Vilfredo Pareto. Tr. by Alfred Bonnet. LC 79-108770. reprint ed. 55.00 (*0-404-04879-X*) AMS Pr.

Manuel Del Ministro. rev. ed.Tr. of Minister's Manual. (SPA.). 112p. 1995. 5.99 (*0-8297-2004-9*) Vida Pubs.

Manuel des Etudes de la Litterature Francaise - 17th. Pierre-Georges Castex et al. 261p. 1966. 19.95 (*0-8288-7441-7*) Fr & Eur.

Manuel Des Etudes Litteraires Francaises, 6 tomes, Tome 1: Moyen Age. Pierre-Georges Castex & P. Surer. (Illus.). 5.95 (*0-685-11344-2*) Fr & Eur.

Manuel Des Etudes Litteraires Francaises, 6 tomes, Tome 2: 16e Siecle. Pierre-Georges Castex & P. Surer. (Illus.). 14.95 (*0-685-11345-0*) Fr & Eur.

Manuel Des Etudes Litteraires Francaises, 6 tomes, Tome 3: 17e Siecle. Pierre-Georges Castex & P. Surer. (Illus.). 14.95 (*0-685-11346-9*) Fr & Eur.

Manuel Des Etudes Litteraires Francaises, 6 tomes, Tome 4: 18e Siecle. Pierre-Georges Castex & P. Surer. (Illus.). 14.95 (*0-685-11347-7*) Fr & Eur.

Manuel Des Etudes Litteraires Francaises, 6 tomes, Tome 5: 19e Siecle. Pierre-Georges Castex & P. Surer. (Illus.). 15.95 (*0-685-11348-5*) Fr & Eur.

Manuel Des Etudes Litteraires Francaises, 6 tomes, Tome 6: 20e Siecle. Pierre-Georges Castex & P. Surer. (Illus.). 16.95 (*0-685-11349-3*) Fr & Eur.

Manuel des Etudes Litteraires Francaises, 6 tomes, Vol. 1. Pierre-Georges Castex & P. Surer. 13.95 (*0-8288-7640-1*, F13980) Fr & Eur.

Manuel Diaz Rodriguez: Evolution & Dynamics of the Stylist, Vol. 107. Marianna M. Matteson. LC 93-18340. (Scripta Humanistica Ser.). 101 p. 1993. 48.50 (*1-882528-02-6*) Scripta.

Manuel du Libraire et de l'Amateur des Livres. J. P. Brunet. 7449p. 1990. 1200.00 (*0-7859-5218-7*) Fr & Eur.

Manuel du Libraire et de l'Amateur des Livres, 7 tomes, Set. J. P. Brunet. 995.00 (*0-685-11350-7*) Fr & Eur.

Manuel du Traducteur Pour le Livre du Levitique see Handbook on Leviticus

Manuel Elementaire Pour Coconseillers see Fundamentals of Co-Counseling Manual

Manuel Gallego. Erica Witschey & Manuel Gallego. LC 98-6995. 1998. write for info. (*0-8176-5916-1*) Birkhauser.

Manuel Gallego. Erica Witschey & Manuel Gallego. LC 98-6995. (Illus.). 176p. 1998. 49.95 (*3-7643-5916-1*) Birkhauser.

Manuel Galvez. Myron I. Lichtblau. LC 71-169627. (Twayne's World Authors Ser.). 152p. (C). 1972. lib. bdg. 20.95 (*0-8290-1737-2*) Irvington.

***Manuel Garcia, 1775-1832: Chronicle of the Life of a Bel Canto Tenor at the Dawn of Romanticism.** James Radomski. LC 99-48687. 384p. 2000. write for info. (*0-19-816373-8*) OUP.

Manuel Gonzalez Prada: A Chronology. V. Munoz. Tr. by W. Scott Johnson. (Libertarian & Anarchist Chronology Ser.). 1979. lib. bdg. 59.95 (*0-8490-3046-3*) Gordon Pr.

Manuel Gutierrez Najera y Sus Cuentos: De la Cronica Periodistica al Relato de Ficcion. Jose I. Gutierrez. (Currents in Comparative Romance Languages & Literatures Ser.: Vol. 68). VII, 459p. (C). 1999. text 66.95 (*0-8204-3919-3*) P Lang Pubng.

Manuel Lisa. Walter B. Douglas. Ed. by Abraham P. Nasatir. (Illus.). 1964. reprint ed. 25.00 (*0-87266-006-0*) Argosy.

Manuel M. Ponce & the Guitar. Corazon Otera. Tr. by J. D. Roberts. (Illus.). 96p. 1995. reprint ed. 24.95 (*0-933224-84-2*, T320) Bold Strummer Ltd.

Manuel Mantero: New Songs for the Ruins of Spain. Manuel Mantero & Betty J. Craige. LC 84-46101. 120p. 1986. 29.50 (*0-8387-5094-X*) Bucknell U Pr.

Manuel Merck de Diagnostic et Therapeutic. Robert Berkow. (FRE.). 1988. lib. bdg. 195.00 (*0-8288-3829-1*, F120190) Fr & Eur.

Manuel Neri: Early Work, 1953-1978. Jack Cowart et al. LC 96-11220. (Illus.). 424p. 1997. 65.00 (*0-88675-046-6*, Pub. by Hudson Hills) Natl Bk Netwk.

Manuel Ocampo: Heridas de la Lengua. Kevin Power & Chon Noriega. (Illus.). 96p. 1997. pap. 30.00 (*1-889195-10-3*) Smart Art Pr.

Manuel Ponce: Some of My Poems. Manuel Ponce. Ed. by Yvette E. Miller. Tr. & Intro. by Maria-L. Rodriguez-Lee. LC 87-3407. (Discoveries Ser.). (ENG & SPA.). 126p. (C). 1987. pap. 11.50 (*0-935480-28-5*) Lat Am Lit Rev Pr.

Manuel Ponce & the Guitar. Corazon Otero. Tr. by J. D. Roberts from SPA. (Guitar Study Ser.). (Illus.). 90p. 1995. pap. 19.95 (*0-933224-85-0*, T321) Bold Strummer Ltd.

Manuel Pratique de Composition Francaise. Beaugrand. 16.50 (*0-685-36705-3*, F140310); 7.95 (*0-8288-7608-8*, F140310) Fr & Eur.

Manuel Pratique de Curietherapie see Practical Manual of Brachytherapy

Manuel Puig. Jonathan Tittler. (Twayne's World Authors Ser.). 160p. 1993. 23.95 (*0-8057-8289-3*, Twyne) Mac Lib Ref.

***Manuel Puig & the Spider Woman.** Suzanne J. Levine. LC 99-39130. (Illus.). 426p. 2000. text 27.50 (*0-374-28190-4*) FS&G.

Manuel Sanguily: Historia de un Ciudadano. 2nd ed. Octavio R. Costa. LC 89-83536. (Coleccion Cuba y sus Jueces). (SPA.). 156p. 1989. pap. 9.95 (*0-89729-532-3*) Ediciones.

Manuel sur l'Amenagement des Peches dans les Lagunes Cotieres: La Bordigue Mediterraneenne. (FRE.). 83p. 1988. 12.00 (*92-5-202716-5*, FF7165, Pub. by FAO) Bernan Associates.

Manuel Tamayo y Baus. Gerald Flynn. LC 72-7978. (Twayne's World Authors Ser.). 158p. (C). 1973. lib. bdg. 20.95 (*0-8290-1752-6*) Irvington.

Manuel Zeno Gandia: Estetica & Sociedad. Ernesto Alvarez. LC 86-16082. 253p. 1987. pap. 12.00 (*0-8477-3520-6*) U of PR Pr.

Manuela Color Canela (Manuela, Color of Cinnamon) Elena Dreser. (SPA.). 32p. (J). (gr. 1-3). 1994. 12.99 (*968-16-4572-3*, Pub. by Fondo) Continental Bk.

***Manuela's Gift.** Kristyn Estes. LC 98-39605. (Illus.). 32p. (J). (gr. k-3). 1999. 15.95 (*0-8118-2085-8*) Chronicle Bks.

Manufactura: Calidad Y Productividad. (C). 1994. pap. 14.33 (*0-201-62187-8*) HEPC Inc.

Manufacture & Processing of PVC. Ed. by R. H. Burgess. (Illus.). 276p. (C). (gr. 13). 1981. 140.00 (*0-85334-972-X*, E & FN Spon) Routledge.

Manufacture & Refining of Raw Cane Sugar. 2nd ed. V. E. Baikow. (Sugar Ser.: Vol. 2). xx,588p. 1982. 362.00 (*0-444-41896-2*) Elsevier.

Manufacture & Use of the Functional Foot Orthosis. R. J. Anthony. (Illus.). xiv, 220p. 1991. 172.25 (*3-8055-5298-X*) S Karger.

Manufacture of Beauty. Ruth Kanin. 190p. (Orig.). (C). 1990. pap. 12.95 (*0-8283-1934-0*) Branden Bks.

Manufacture of Bone Fish Hooks in the Little Miami Valley. F. W. Putnam. (Ohio History, Prehistoric Indians, Archaeology Ser.). (Illus.). 8p. (C). 1994. reprint ed. pap. 1.30 (*1-56651-105-4*) A W McGraw.

Manufacture of Ceramic Components: Proceedings: Design for Manufacturability & Manufacture of Ceramic Components Symposium (96th: 1994: Indianapolis, Indiana) Ed. by Basavaraj V. Hiremath et al. LC 95-10175. (Ceramic Transactions Ser.: Vol. 49). (Illus.). 222p. 1995. 88.00 (*0-944904-87-4*, CT049) Am Ceramic.

Manufacture of Evil: Ethics, Evolution & the Industrial State. Lionel Tiger. 1991. pap. 14.95 (*0-7145-2929-X*) M Boyars Pubs.

Manufacture of Madness: A Comparative Study of the Inquisition & the Mental Health Movement. Thomas Szasz. LC 96-48784. 426p. 1997. reprint ed. pap. 19.95 (*0-8156-0461-0*) Syracuse U Pr.

Manufacture of News: Deviance, Social Problems & the Mass Media. rev. ed. Ed. by Stanley Cohen & Jock Young. LC 81-50585. (Communication & Society Ser.). 506p. 1981. reprint ed. pap. 156.90 (*0-608-02796-0*, 206386300007) Bks Demand.

Manufacture of Paper. Charles T. Davis. LC 72-5042. (Technology & Society Ser.). (Illus.). 625p. 1972. reprint ed. 37.95 (*0-405-04694-4*) Ayer.

Manufacture of Precision Parallel Axis Gears. J. Cadish & E. J. Bartholet. (1984 Fall Technical Meeting Ser.: Vol. 84FTM5). 10p. 1984. pap. text 30.00 (*1-55589-087-3*) AGMA.

Manufacture of Pulp & Paper: Science & Engineering Concepts. (Illus.). 113p. (J). 1988. pap. 6.00 (*0-89852-448-2*, 0101R148) TAPPI.

Manufacture of Rubber Goods, 1909-1990. A. Heil & Wesch. Tr. by Edward Lewis. (Illus.). 237p. 1991. pap. 35.00 (*0-87556-801-7*) Saifer.

Manufacture of Scottish History. Whatley Donnachie. 1992. 20.00 (*0-7486-6120-4*, Pub. by Polygon) Subterranean Co.

Manufacture of Soap, Other Detergents & Glycerine. E. Woollatt. (Applied Science & Industrial Technology Ser.). 1985. text 181.00 (*0-470-20234-3*) P-H.

Manufacture of Soda with Special Reference to the Ammonia Process: A Practical Treatise. Te-pang Hou. LC 33-34998. (American Technical Society Monograph Ser.: No. 65). (Illus.). 618p. reprint ed. pap. 191.60 (*0-608-11550-9*, 201523600095) Bks Demand.

Manufacture of Sulfuric Acid. Ed. by Werner W. Duecker & James R. West. LC 59-15498. (ACS Monograph Ser.: Vol. 144). (Illus.). 525p. 1959. reprint ed. pap. 162.80 (*0-608-06932-9*, 206714000009) Bks Demand.

Manufacture of Superconducting Materials: An International Conference, 8-10 November, 1976, Port Chester, New York, Proceedings. Ed. by Robert W. Meyerhoff. LC 77-11148. (Materials-Metalworking Technology Ser.). (Illus.). 239p. reprint ed. pap. 74.10 (*0-608-10721-2*, 201947800013) Bks Demand.

Manufacture of Whiskey, Brandy & Cordials. 1996. lib. bdg. 253.99 (*0-8490-8328-1*) Gordon Pr.

Manufactured Abrasives in Gear Lapping. H. J. Willis. (Technical Papers: Vol. P64). (Illus.). 4p. 1928. pap. text 30.00 (*1-55589-220-5*) AGMA.

Manufactured & Patented Spokeshaves & Similar Tools: Identification of the Artifacts & Profiles of the Makers & Patentees. Thomas C. Lamond. LC 97-93162. (Illus.). 450p. 1997. 95.00 (*0-9655401-0-3*) T C Lamond.

Manufactured Carbon. H. W. Davidson et al. 1968. 61.00 (*0-08-012667-7*, Pub. by Pergamon Repr) Franklin.

Manufactured Carbon - Self Lubricating/Mechanical Division. Paxton. 192p. 1979. lib. bdg. 75.00 (*0-8493-5655-5*) CRC Pr.

Manufactured Crisis. David Berliner. (C). 1995. pap. text. write for info. (*0-8013-1671-5*) Addison-Wesley.

Manufactured Crisis: Myths, Fraud & the Attack on America's Public Schools. David C. Berliner & Bruce J. Biddle. LC 95-3271. 432p. 1995. 25.00 (*0-201-40957-7*) Addison-Wesley.

Manufactured Crisis: Myths, Fraud & the Attack on America's Public Schools. David C. Berliner et al. 432p. 1996. pap. 16.00 (*0-201-44196-9*) Addison-Wesley.

Manufactured Exports of East Asian Industrializing Economies & Possible Regional Cooperation. Ed. by Chu-Chin Yang. LC 93-27326. 304p. (gr. 13). 1994. pap. text 38.95 (*1-56324-462-4*) M E Sharpe.

Manufactured Exports of East Asian Industrializing Economies & Possible Regional Cooperation. Ed. by Shu-Chin Yang. LC 93-27326. 304p. (gr. 13). 1994. text 85.95 (*1-56324-245-1*) M E Sharpe.

***Manufactured Home Community Management.** 3rd rev. ed. George Allen. 242p. 1998. pap. 60.00 (*1-878350-07-2*) PMN Pub.

Manufactured Home Installation in Flood Hazard Areas. (Illus.). 110p. (Orig.). (C). 1995. pap. text 25.00 (*0-7881-1014-4*) DIANE Pub.

Manufactured Homes: Making Sense of a Housing Opportunity. Thomas E. Nutt-Powell. LC 81-14846. 219p. 1982. 62.95 (*0-86569-086-3*, Auburn Hse) Greenwood.

Manufactured Houses. A. M. Watkins. 200p. 1994. pap. 14.95 (*0-7931-1149-8*, 19130302, Real Estate Ed) Dearborn.

Manufactured Housing: Regulation, Design Innovations, & Development Options. Welford Sanders & Manufactured Housing Institute Staff. LC 98-234398. (American Planning Association, Planning Advisory Service Report Ser.). 115p. 1998. 32.00 (*1-884829-20-1*) Am Plan Assn.

Manufactured Housing: What It Is, Where It Is, How It Operates. Ed. by Shepard D. Robinson. 1988. pap. 60.00 (*0-9603502-1-7*) Ingleside.

Manufactured Housing in Nonmetropolitan Areas: A Data Review. Housing Assistance Council Staff. (Illus.). 60p. 1996. 4.00 (*1-58064-015-X*) Housing Assist.

Manufactured Wiring Systems, UL 183. 2nd ed. (C). 1993. pap. text 95.00 (*1-55989-448-2*) Underwrtrs Labs.

M

Manufacturer: The British Merchant; The Weaver. Daniel Defoe. Ed. by Robert Gosselink. LC 78-11810. 1979. reprint ed. 75.00 (*0-8201-1324-7*) Schol Facsimiles.

***Manufacturer to Manufacturer Part Number Cross Reference.** Howard W. Sams & Company Engineering Staff. LC 99-69259. 287p. 2000. 29.95 (*0-7906-1207-0*, 61207) H W Sams.

Manufacturers A-Z: Anglo American Microelectronics Data 1968-69, 2 vols., Set. Geoffrey W. Dummer & J. M. Robertson. LC 68-20388. 1968. 1330.00 (*0-08-012880-7*, Pub. by Pergamon Repr) Franklin.

Manufacturers & Distributors of Premises Cabling & Wiring Apparatus, 1993: Strategic Assessment & Competitive Analysis. Amadee Bender et al. 100p. 1993. pap. text 2400.00 (*1-878218-41-7*) World Info Tech.

***Manufacturers Directory 2001.** American Business Directory Staff. 2000. 595.00 (*0-7687-0327-1*) Am Busn Direct.

Manufacturers' Experience with New Plant Machinery, Equipment & Systems. 32p. 1976. 20.00 (*0-318-19684-0*) Clothing Mfrs.

Manufacturer's Guide to Business Marketing: How Small & Mid-Size Companies Can Increase Profits with Limited Resources. Michael P. Collins. LC 94-11216. 240p. 1994. text 45.00 (*1-55623-837-1*, Irwn Prfssnl) McGraw-Hill Prof.

***Manufacturer's Guide to Implementing the Theory of Constraints.** Mark Woeppel. 1999. ring bd. 42.95 (*1-57444-268-6*) St Lucie Pr.

Manufacturer's Reengineering Guide: How to Use Time As Your Competitive Weapon. Mary Wish & James Wish. LC 94-73221. 304p. 1995. pap. 24.95 (*1-886507-14-7*) Loose Threads.

***Manufacturers Reference Guide: Plumbing - Heating - Cooling.** Ed. by Mert Kennedy. 400p. 2000. pap. 39.95 (*0-915955-21-0*) Trade Srv Corp.

Manufacturer's Specifications & Reference Synopsis Catalog: Antibodies. 3rd ed. Robert V. Weimer. 1801p. 1995. 89.00 (*0-9643268-3-3*) Aerie Corp.

Manufacturers-Systems see Machine Vision for Robotics & Automated Inspection: Technical Report for Engineers & Managers

Manufactures: General Report & Analysis see Census of the United States: 13th Decennial Census, 1910

Manufactures, Pt. II, Reports by States see Census of the United States: 13th Decennial Census, 1910

Manufactures, Pt. III, Reports for Principal Industries see Census of the United States: 13th Decennial Census, 1910

Manufactures of Poverty see Fabricantes de Miseria

Manufactures: United States by Industries see Decennial Census Reports of the United States, 12th Census, 1900

Manufacturing. (Best Practices Ser.: No. 1771). 1994. 175.00 (*0-85058-771-9*) Economist Intell.

Manufacturing. Minton. (Techknowledge Reference Ser.). (J). (gr. k-12). 1998. pap. 18.95 (*0-538-66140-2*) S-W Pub.

Manufacturing: A Basic Text for Industrial Arts. 2nd ed. James Fales et al. (Illus.). 1986. 34.47 (*0-02-675730-3*, B82088) Glencoe.

Manufacturing: A Basic Text for Industrial Arts. 2nd ed. James Fales et al. (Illus.). 1986. teacher ed. 16.73 (*0-02-675750-8*); student ed. 8.48 (*0-02-675740-0*) Glencoe.

Manufacturing: A Historiographical & Bibliographical Guide, 1. Ed. by David O. Whitten & Bessie E. Whitten. LC 89-25921. (Handbook of American Business History Ser.: No. 1). 520p. 1990. lib. bdg. 105.00 (*0-313-25198-3*, WBU/, Greenwood Pr) Greenwood.

***Manufacturing: Beyond Lean & World Class.** Steve Brown. (Illus.). 288p. 2000. 39.00 (*0-273-64322-3*, Pub. by F T P H) Trans-Atl Phila.

Manufacturing Across Borders & Oceans: Japan, the United States, & Mexico. Ed. by Gabriel Szekely et al. (Monographs: No. 36). 123p. (C). 1991. pap. 12.95 (*1-878367-00-5*, MN-36) UCSD Ctr US-Mex.

***Manufacturing Advantage: Why High Performance Work Systems Pay Off.** Eileen Appelbaum et al. LC 99-48690. 2000. pap. 19.95 (*0-8014-8655-6*) Cornell U Pr.

Manufacturing Africa: Performance & Prospects of Seven Countries in Sub-Saharan Africa. Roger C. Riddel et al. 419p. (C). 1990. pap. 30.00 (*0-435-08050-4*, 08050) Heinemann.

Manufacturing & Operation's Management: Basic Business 204. 206p. (C). 1997. text 91.00 (*0-536-59914-9*) Pearson Custom.

Manufacturing & Services Vol. 15. Ed. by Claes G. Alvstam. (National Atlas of Sweden Ser.). (Illus.). 176p. 1998. text 99.50 (*91-87760-34-7*) Coronet Bks.

Manufacturing & the Environment. Glasgow Caledonian University. pap., student ed. 50.00 (*1-86125-042-8*) Institute of Management Consultants.

Manufacturing & the Internet. Sarah E. Hutchinson & Stacey Sawyer. 1996. text 34.95 (*0-07-413144-3*, Irwn McGrw-H) McGrw-H Hghr Educ.

Manufacturing & the Internet: An Information Guide for Professionals in Manufacturing... Richard G. Mathieu. LC 96-17830. 480p. 1996. pap. text 34.95 (*0-89806-164-4*, MFGNET) Eng Mgmt Pr.

Manufacturing Apartheid: State Corporations in South Africa. Nancy L. Clark. LC 93-48316. (Yale Historical Publications). 264p. 1994. 40.00 (*0-300-05638-9*) Yale U Pr.

Manufacturing Aspects in Electronic Packaging. Ed. by Y. C. Lee & T. J. Bennett. (EEP Series, Vol. 2: PED: Vol. 60). 220p. 1992. 57.50 (*0-7918-1112-3*, G00756) ASME.

Manufacturing Aspects in Electronic Packaging, 1993. Ed. by Y. C. Lee et al. LC 93-73267. 125p. pap. 40.00 (*0-7918-1032-1*) ASME.

Manufacturing Automation. Cohen-Apte. LC 96-29709. 352p. 1997. 75.00 (*0-256-14606-3*) McGraw.

***Manufacturing Automation: Metal Cutting Mechanics, Machine Tool Vibrations & CNC Design.** Yusuf Altintas. (Illus.). 304p. (C). 2000. 90.00 (*0-521-65029-1*); pap. 39.95 (*0-521-65973-6*) Cambridge U Pr.

Manufacturing Automation at the Crossroads: Standardization in CIM Software. Ed. by Louis Pau & Jan-Olaf Willums. LC 93-78479. 181p. (gr. 12). 1993. pap. 70.00 (*90-5199-137-1*, Pub. by IOS Pr) IOS Press.

Manufacturing Babies & Public Consent: Debating the New Reproductive Technologies. Jose Van Dyck. 224p. (C). 1994. pap. text 19.50 (*0-8147-8786-X*) NYU Pr.

Manufacturing Babies & Public Consent: Debating the New Reproductive Technologies. Jose Van Dyck et al. LC 94-30373. 224p. (C). 1995. text 45.00 (*0-8147-8785-1*) NYU Pr.

Manufacturing 'Bad Mothers' A Critical Perspective on Child Neglect. Karen Swift. 256p. 1995. pap. text 18.95 (*0-8020-7435-9*) U of Toronto Pr.

Manufacturing 'Bad Mothers' A Critical Perspective on Child Neglect. Karen J. Swift. 218p. 1995. text 45.00 (*0-8020-2978-7*) U of Toronto Pr.

Manufacturing Beyond Joe's Garage: Value Based Manufacturing. William B. Miller & Vicki L. Schenk. 128p. (Orig.). 2000. pap. 9.95 (*0-9630439-9-4*) Bayrock.

Manufacturing Business. Andrews. 328p. 1994. 65.95 (*0-7512-0292-4*) Ashgate Pub Co.

Manufacturing Cells: A Systems Engineering View. Ed. by Colin Moodie et al. LC 96-133476. 398p. 1995. 59.95 (*0-7484-0327-2*, Pub. by Tay Francis Ltd) Taylor & Francis.

Manufacturing CEO's Secret Tips for Improving Profit. Richard Ludwig. LC 95-22725. 237p. 1996. 34.95 (*0-471-12555-5*) Wiley.

Manufacturing Confucianism: Chinese Traditions & Universal Civilization. Lionel M. Jensen. LC 97-29986. (Illus.). 444p. 1997. pap. 19.95 (*0-8223-2047-9*) Duke.

Manufacturing Confucianism: Chinese Traditions & Universal Civilizations. Lionel M. Jensen. LC 97-29986. (Illus.). 408p. 1997. lib. bdg. 59.95 (*0-8223-2034-7*) Duke.

Manufacturing Consent: Changes in the Labor Process under Monopoly Capitalism. Michael Burawoy. LC 79-10188. xviii, 286p. (C). 1982. pap. text 16.00 (*0-226-08038-2*) U Ch Pr.

Manufacturing Consent: The Political Economy of the Mass Media. Edward S. Herman & Noam Chomsky. LC 88-42614. 1988. pap. 18.95 (*0-679-72034-0*) Pantheon.

Manufacturing Consent - Noam Chomsky & the Media: A Primer in Intellectual Self-Defence. Ed. by Mark Achbar. LC 94-154599. (Illus.). 265p. 1998. 52.99 (*1-55164-003-1*, Pub. by Black Rose); pap. 23.99 (*1-55164-002-3*, Pub. by Black Rose) Consort Bk Sales.

Manufacturing Consumption of Energy, 2 vols., Set. 1996. lib. bdg. 608.99 (*0-8490-5955-0*) Gordon Pr.

***Manufacturing Consumption of Energy, 1994.** 544p. 1998. per. 47.00 (*0-16-063505-5*) USGPO.

Manufacturing Cost Engineering Handbook. Malstrom. (Cost Engineering Ser.: Vol. 5). (Illus.). 472p. 1984. text 175.00 (*0-8247-7126-5*) Dekker.

Manufacturing Cost Estimating. Ed. by Phillip F. Ostwald. LC 79-67648. 266p. reprint ed. pap. 82.50 (*0-608-13390-6*, 205573800034) Bks Demand.

Manufacturing Data Structures: Building Foundations for Excellence with Bills of Materials & Process Information. Jerrt Clement et al. LC 92-60537. 276p. 1992. 129.00 (*0-939246-27-9*) Wiley.

Manufacturing Data Structures A: Building Foundations for Excellence with Bills of Materials & Process Information, 0000. Jerry Clement et al. 288p. 1995. 50.00 (*0-471-13269-1*) Wiley.

Manufacturing Databases & Computer Integrated Systems. Dimitris N. Chorafas. 320p. 1993. boxed set 89.95 (*0-8493-8689-6*) CRC Pr.

Manufacturing Desire: Media, Popular Culture, & Everyday Life. Arthur A. Berger. 287p. (C). 1996. text 34.95 (*1-56000-226-3*) Transaction Pubs.

Manufacturing Development Applications: Guidelines for Attaining Quality & Productivity. Andre McHose. 1993. 29.95 (*0-89806-122-9*, DEVAPP) Eng Mgmt Pr.

Manufacturing Development Applications: Guidelines for Attaining Quality & Productivity. Andre McHose. 275p. 1992. 45.00 (*1-55623-572-0*, Irwn Prfssnl) McGraw-Hill Prof.

***Manufacturing Engineering.** (C). 1999. text. write for info. (*0-201-61085-X*) Addison-Wesley.

Manufacturing Engineering: An Introduction to the Basic Functions. 2nd ed. Ed. by John P. Tanner. (Manufacturing Engineering & Materials Processing Ser.: Vol. 36). (Illus.). 424p. 1990. text 79.75 (*0-8247-8402-2*) Dekker.

Manufacturing Engineering: Principles for Optimization. 2nd ed. Daniel T. Koenig. LC 94-18098. 1994. 69.95 (*1-56032-301-9*) Hemisp Pub.

Manufacturing Engineering & System Handbook. Jay Lee & Robert Schafrik. (Mechanical Engineering Ser.). 1999. 125.00 (*0-8493-9582-8*) CRC Pr.

Manufacturing Engineering & Technology. Serope Kalpakjian. (Illus.). 944p. (C). 1989. text 44.76 (*0-201-12849-7*) Addison-Wesley.

Manufacturing, Engineering & Technology. 4th ed. Serope Kalpakjian. LC 00-26331. 1168p. (C). 2000. 105.00 (*0-201-36131-0*) Peachpit Pr.

Manufacturing Engineering & Technology: Solutions Manual. 3rd ed. Serope Kalpakjian. 336p. 1995. write for info. (*0-201-53847-4*) Addison-Wesley.

Manufacturing Engineering Processes. 2nd expanded rev. ed. Leo Alting. (Manufacturing Engineering & Materials Processing Ser.: Vol. 40). (Illus.). 512p. 1993. text 69.75 (*0-8247-9129-0*) Dekker.

Manufacturing Engineering Techniques. 3rd ed. Serope Kalpakjian. (C). 1995. pap. text. write for info. (*0-201-84552-0*) Addison-Wesley.

Manufacturing Engineering Transactions, Vol. 3. Society of Manufacturing Engineers Staff. LC 76-646280. 224p. reprint ed. pap. 69.50 (*0-608-13112-1*, 202417200003) Bks Demand.

Manufacturing Engineering Transactions, Vol. 4. Society of Manufacturing Engineers Staff. LC 76-646280. 445p. reprint ed. pap. 138.00 (*0-608-13125-3*, 202417400004) Bks Demand.

Manufacturing Enterprise Reference Model: Continuous Business Process Improvement Is Model Driven. Dennis E. Wisnosky. (Illus.). 154p. 1998. pap. 495.00 (*1-893990-02-8*) Wizdom Systems.

Manufacturing Excellence in Global Markets. Chapman & Hall Staff. LC 97-131163. 1997. text 180.50 (*0-412-80520-0*) Chapman & Hall.

Manufacturing Extension Programs: Manufacturers' View about Delivery & Impact of Services. 54p. (Orig.). (C). 1996. pap. text 20.00 (*0-7881-2881-7*) DIANE Pub.

Manufacturing Facilities: Location, Planning & Design. Dileep R. Sule. 672p. (C). 1988. text 69.95 (*0-534-91971-5*) PWS Pubs.

Manufacturing Facilities: Location, Planning & Design. 2nd ed. Dileep R. Sule. LC 93-34245. (C). 1994. mass mkt. 82.95 (*0-534-93435-8*) PWS Pubs.

***Manufacturing Facilities Design & Material Handling.** 2nd ed. Fred E. Meyers & Matthew P. Stephens. LC 99-19587. (Illus.). 415p. 1999. 98.00 (*0-13-674821-X*) P-H.

Manufacturing for Competitive Advantage: Becoming a World-Class Manufacturer. Thomas G. Gunn. LC 87-1093. 240p. 1987. text 34.95 (*0-88730-154-1*, HarpBusn) HarpInfo.

Manufacturing for Export in the Developing World: Problems & Possibilities. Ed. by G. K. Helleiner. LC 94-47338. 232p. (C). (gr. 13). 1995. 85.00 (*0-415-12387-9*) Routledge.

Manufacturing for Survival: The How-to Guide for Practitioners & Managers. Blair Williams. 480p. (C). 1996. pap. 45.00 (*0-201-63373-6*) Addison-Wesley.

Manufacturing for the Security of the United States: Reviving Competitiveness & Reducing Deficits. Robert E. McGarrah. LC 89-28942. 200p. 1990. 59.95 (*0-89930-427-3*, MDG/, Quorum Bks) Greenwood.

Manufacturing from Recyclables: 24 Case Studies of Successful Recycling Enterprises. Ed. by Michael Lewis. (Illus.). 115p. (C). 1999. pap. text 25.00 (*0-7881-7605-6*) DIANE Pub.

Manufacturing Frontier: Pioneer Industry in Antebellum Wisconsin 1830-1860. Margaret Walsh. LC 72-619513. 263p. 1972. 12.50 (*0-87020-119-0*) State Hist Soc Wis.

Manufacturing Guidelines for Processed Beef Products. National Live Stock & Meat Board Staff & B. C. Breidenstein. (Illus.). 60p. 1983. 10.00 (*0-88700-001-0*) Natl Live Stock.

Manufacturing Guidelines for Processed Pork Products. National Live Stock & Meat Board Staff. (Illus.). 60p. (Orig.). (C). 1985. pap. text 10.00 (*0-88700-005-3*) Natl Live Stock.

Manufacturing Guitars for the American Parlor: James Ashborn's Wolcottville, Connecticut, Factory, 1851-56. Philip F. Gura. (Illus.). 38p. 1994. pap. 11.50 (*0-944026-58-3*) Am Antiquarian.

Manufacturing High Technology Handbook. Tijunelis & McKee. (Manufacturing Engineering & Materials Processing Ser.: Vol. 22). (Illus.). 816p. 1987. text 250.00 (*0-8247-7720-4*) Dekker.

Manufacturing Ideology: Scientific Management in Twentieth-Century Japan. William M. Tsutsui. LC 97-48505. 288p. 1998. text 29.95 (*0-691-05808-3*, Pub. by Princeton U Pr) Cal Prin Full Svc.

Manufacturing in America: A Legacy of Excellence. Robert Muccigrosso & Ceila D. Robbins. LC 95-38734. (Illus.). 160p. 1995. write for info. (*0-944641-15-6*) Greenwich Pub Group.

Manufacturing in Europe: Research in Robotics, Design Methodologies, & Concurrent Engineering. D. E. Whitney. 30p. (Orig.). (C). 1993. pap. text 30.00 (*1-56806-298-2*) DIANE Pub.

Manufacturing in Technology Education: 42nd Yearbook. Council on Technology Teacher Education Staff. Ed. by R. B. Seymour & Shackelford. 1999. 18.96 (*0-02-677140-3*) Glencoe.

Manufacturing in Texas. Ed. by Lois G. Shrout. LC 92-76048. 100p. (Orig.). 1993. pap. 16.50 (*0-87755-331-9*) Bureau Busn TX.

Manufacturing in the Nineties: How to Become a Mean, Lean, World Class Competetor. Harold J. Steudel & Paul Desruelle. (VNR Competitive Manufacturing Ser.). 374p. 1991. 69.95 (*0-471-28391-6*, VNR) Wiley.

Manufacturing in the '90s: How to Become a Mean, Lean World-Class Competitor. Harold J. Steudel. (Illus.). 320p. 1992. text 55.95 (*0-442-00182-7*, VNR) Wiley.

Manufacturing in the Ottoman Empire & Turkey, 1500-1950. Ed. by Donald Quataert. LC 93-36571. (SUNY Series in the Social & Economic History of the Middle East). 175p. (C). 1994. pap. text 19.95 (*0-7914-2016-7*) State U NY Pr.

Manufacturing in the Ottoman Empire & Turkey, 1500-1950. Ed. by Donald Quataert. LC 93-36571. (SUNY Series in the Social & Economic History of the Middle East). 175p. (C). 1994. text 59.50 (*0-7914-2015-9*) State U NY Pr.

Manufacturing in Transition. Rick Delbridge & James Lowe. LC 97-51636. 288p. (C). 1998. 95.00 (*0-415-18271-9*); pap. 29.99 (*0-415-18272-7*) Routledge.

Manufacturing Industries & Economic Development in the SADCC Countries. Richard H. Peet. (Energy, Environment & Development in Africa Ser.: No. 5). 119p. 1984. write for info. (*91-7106-233-5*, Pub. by Nordic Africa) Transaction Pubs.

***Manufacturing Industry.** 254p. 1998. pap. 21.00 (*0-16-062323-5*) USGPO.

Manufacturing Inequality: Gender Division in the French & British Metalworking Industries, 1914-1939. Laura L. Downs. (Wilder House Ser.). (Illus.). 344p. 1995. text 42.50 (*0-8014-3015-1*) Cornell U Pr.

***Manufacturing Innovations & Technological Operations: Theory & Application.** John J. Liu. 2000. 74.00 (*981-02-4179-8*) World Scientific Pub.

Manufacturing Insecurity: The Rise & Fall of Brazil's Military-Industrial Complex. Ken Conca. 290p. 1996. lib. bdg. 58.00 (*1-55587-695-1*, 876951) L Rienner.

Manufacturing Intelligence. Paul K. Wright & David A. Bourne. (Mechanical Engineering Ser.). (Illus.). 312p. (C). 1988. text 38.36 (*0-201-13576-0*) Addison-Wesley.

***Manufacturing Job Shops.** Mildred S. Ponzer & Catherine M. Frank. (Industry-at-a-Glance Ser.). 90p. 1999. pap. write for info. (*0-9679123-0-X*) Univ of MO-Rolla.

Manufacturing Knowledge: A History of the Hawthorne Experiments. Richard Gillespie. (Studies in Economic History & Policy: The United States in the Twentieth Century). (Illus.). 292p. (C). 1991. text 64.95 (*0-521-40358-8*) Cambridge U Pr.

Manufacturing Knowledge: A History of the Hawthorne Experiments. Richard Gillespie. (Studies in Economic History & Policy: The United States in the Twentieth Century). (Illus.). 294p. (C). 1993. pap. text 18.95 (*0-521-45643-6*) Cambridge U Pr.

Manufacturing Management. John Hughes. (C). 2000. pap. text. write for info. (*0-201-40393-5*) Addison-Wesley.

Manufacturing Management: Learning Through Case Studies. David G. Coward. (Illus.). 204p. (C). 1998. pap. text 30.00 (*0-333-64777-7*, Pub. by Macmillan Ed) Scholium Intl.

Manufacturing Management: Principles & Systems. Richard Burman. LC 94-44158. 1995. 19.95 (*0-07-709044-6*) McGraw.

Manufacturing Message Specification: Companion Standard for Process Control S72.02. ANSI/ISA Staff. 1993. pap. 95.00 (*1-55617-519-1*, S72.02) ISA.

Manufacturing Militance: Workers' Movements in Brazil & South Africa, 1970-1985. Gay W. Seidman. LC 92-35866. 1993. 50.00 (*0-520-07519-6*, Pub. by U CA Pr); pap. 16.95 (*0-520-08303-2*, Pub. by U CA Pr) Cal Prin Full Svc.

Manufacturing Mining & Labour. Michael G. Morony. 114.95 (*0-86078-707-9*) Ashgate Pub Co.

Manufacturing Numbers: How Inaccurate Statistics Conceal U. S. Industrial Decline. Lawrence R. Mishel. LC 88-81375. 103p. (Orig.). 1988. pap., per. 12.00 (*0-944826-03-2*) Economic Policy Inst.

Manufacturing of Electronic Materials & Components. Ed. by Asish Ghosh et al. (Ceramic Transactions Ser.: Vol. 90). (Illus.). 188p. 1998. 95.00 (*1-57498-044-0*, CT090) Am Ceramic.

Manufacturing of Polymer Composites. B. T. Astrhom. LC 98-120935. xxi, 469 p. 1997. 57.50 (*0-412-81960-0*) Chapman & Hall.

Manufacturing of Porcelain & Glass. D. Lardner. 320p. 1994. pap. 25.00 (*0-87556-795-9*) Saifer.

Manufacturing on the Internet: Use 21st Century Techniques to Speed Your Product Cycles. LC 98-225527. 84p. 1997. pap. 995.00 (*0-471-29012-2*) Wiley.

Manufacturing on the Move. Robert W. Crandall. 111p. (C). 1993. 32.95 (*0-8157-1598-6*) Brookings.

Manufacturing on the Move. Robert W. Crandall. LC 92-43320. 111p. (C). 1993. pap. 12.95 (*0-8157-1597-8*) Brookings.

Manufacturing Operations Audit: Key to Organizational Improvement. D. Wynn. (Quality & Reliability Ser.). Date not set. write for info. (*0-8247-9964-X*) Dekker.

Manufacturing Organization & Management. 6th ed. Harold T. Amrine et al. LC 92-12867. (International Industrial & Systems Engineering Ser.). 608p. 1992. 91.00 (*0-13-554858-6*) P-H.

Manufacturing Output, 1929-1937. Solomon Fabricant. (Occasional Papers: No. 1). 31p. 1940. reprint ed. 20.00 (*0-87014-316-6*) Natl Bur Econ Res.

Manufacturing Overhead Allocations. Ansari. 1997. 4.00 (*0-256-26392-2*) McGrw-H Hghr Educ.

Manufacturing Phone Book U. S. A., 1997. Ed. by Darren L. Smith. 1997. pap. 125.00 (*0-7808-0299-3*) Omnigraphics Inc.

Manufacturing Planning: Key to Improving Industrial Productivity. Kelvin F. Cross. (Industrial Engineering Ser.: Vol. 12). (Illus.). 304p. 1986. text 135.00 (*0-8247-7324-1*) Dekker.

Manufacturing Planning & Control in Process Industries. Ed. by Steven F. Bolander et al. LC 81-68512. 162p. 1981. pap. 20.00 (*0-935406-04-2*) Am Prod & Inventory.

Manufacturing Planning & Control Systems. 3rd ed. William L. Berry et al. (APICS Series in Production Management). 900p. 1991. 65.00 (*1-55623-608-5*, Irwn Prfssnl) McGraw-Hill Prof.

Manufacturing Planning & Control Systems. 3rd ed. William L. Berry et al. 912p. (C). 1991. text 58.00 (*0-256-08808-X*, Irwn McGrw-H) McGrw-H Hghr Educ.

Manufacturing Planning & Control Systems. 4th ed. William L. Berry et al. 864p. 1997. text 65.00 (*0-7863-1209-2*, Irwn McGrw-H) McGrw-H Hghr Educ.

Manufacturing Planning & Control Systems. 4th ed. Thomas E. Vollmann et al. LC 96-52736. 896p. (C). 1997. text 74.95 (*0-256-13899-0*, Irwn McGrw-H) McGrw-H Hghr Educ.

Manufacturing Planning Scheduling & Control. Tomas Sam. (C). 1993. pap. 69.95 (*0-13-554304-5*) P-H.

Manufacturing Planning Systems. Bill Scott. LC 94-9515. 367p. 1994. 39.95 (*0-07-707743-1*) McGraw.

Manufacturing Plant Layout: Fundamentals & Fine Points of Optimum Facility Design. Edward J. Phillips. LC 97-65261. (Illus.). 259p. 1997. 59.00 (*0-87263-484-1*, 2570) SME.

Manufacturing Population of England. Peter Gaskell. LC 73-38266. (Evolution of Capitalism Ser.). viii, 361 p. 1980. reprint ed. 28.95 (*0-405-04120-9*) Ayer.

***Manufacturing Powerlessness in the Black Diaspora: Inner City Youth & the New Global Frontier, 1 vol.** Charles Green. 240p. 2000. 65.00 (*0-7425-0268-6*); pap. 24.95 (*0-7425-0269-4*) AltaMira Pr.

Manufacturing Practices & Technologies for Electronic Ceramic Products. Ed. by Basavaraj V. Hiremath et al. (Ceramic Transactions Ser.: Vol. 70). 1997. 95.00 (*1-57498-024-6*) Am Ceramic.

Manufacturing Principles & Practices Seminar. LC 89-80583. (Illus.). 235p. (Orig.). 1989. 20.00 (*1-55822-017-8*) Am Prod & Inventory.

Manufacturing Principles & Practices Seminar Proceedings. 258p. 1990. 20.00 (*1-55822-050-X*) Am Prod & Inventory.

Manufacturing Principles & Practices Seminar Proceedings: Spring Training for the Manufacturing Professional. 217p. 1991. 20.00 (*1-55822-036-4*) Am Prod & Inventory.

Manufacturing Problems in India: The Cummins Diesel Experience. Jack Baranson. LC 67-26917. 168p. reprint ed. pap. 52.10 (*0-608-15216-1*, 202741000055) Bks Demand.

Manufacturing Process. Harold V. Johnson. 1979. text 29.20 (*0-02-664940-3*); student ed. 9.00 (*0-02-664950-0*) Glencoe.

Manufacturing Process. 2nd ed. Johnson. 1984. 29.20 (*0-02-664990-X*) Macmillan Info.

Manufacturing Process Controls for the Industries of the Future. National Research Council Staff. LC 99-177575. (Compass Ser.). 72p. 1998. pap. text 15.00 (*0-309-06184-9*) Natl Acad Pr.

Manufacturing Process Design & Optimization. Robert F. Rhyder. LC 97-5719. (Manufacturing Engineering & Materials Processing Ser.: Vol. 50). (Illus.). 351p. 1997. text 137.50 (*0-8247-9909-7*) Dekker.

Manufacturing Processes. Serope Kalpakjian. (Metallurgy & Metals Ser.). (Illus.). 800p. 1984. pap. text, teacher ed. 1.50 (*0-201-11691-X*) Addison-Wesley.

Manufacturing Processes. Linton. (Mechanical Technology Ser.). 1996. pap. text 41.95 (*0-8273-7710-X*) Delmar.

Manufacturing Processes. Loper. (C). 1987. pap. text 47.50 (*0-03-071643-8*) Harcourt Coll Pubs.

Manufacturing Processes. 2nd ed. Serope Kalpakjian. (C). 1991. pap. text. write for info. (*0-201-60702-6*) Addison-Wesley.

Manufacturing Processes. 8th ed. B. H. Amstead et al. LC 86-19094. 736p. 1987. text 92.95 (*0-471-84236-2*) Wiley.

Manufacturing Processes: Ceramics. T. Gregor. 1976. pap. text 10.16 (*0-13-555664-3*) P-H.

Manufacturing Processes: Course Outline Lab Activity Manual. Lynn Mosher. 62p. (C). 1998. per. 18.95 (*0-7872-5159-3*, 41515901) Kendall-Hunt.

Manufacturing Processes: Metals. Hercules C. Kazanas. 1976. pap. text 10.16 (*0-13-555680-5*) P-H.

Manufacturing Processes: Plastics. D. Jambro. 1976. pap. text 10.16 (*0-13-555623-6*) P-H.

Manufacturing Processes: Woods. G. Cheek. 1975. 7.20 (*0-13-555656-2*); pap. text 10.16 (*0-13-555649-X*) P-H.

Manufacturing Processes & Equipment. Jiri Tlusty. LC 99-32425. 928p. (C). 1999. 105.00 (*0-201-49865-0*, Prentice Hall) P-H.

Manufacturing Processes & Systems. 9th ed. Phillip F. Ostwald & Jairo Munoz. LC 96-47300. 800p. 1997. text 106.95 (*0-471-04741-4*) Wiley.

Manufacturing Processes Experimentation. Eyada. LC 94-219289. 154p. (C). 1994. pap. text 26.20 (*0-536-58563-6*) Pearson Custom.

Manufacturing Processes For Engineering Materials. Serope Kalpakjian. (Metallurgy & Metals Ser.). (Illus.). 800p. 1984. text 41.56 (*0-201-11690-1*) Addison-Wesley.

Manufacturing Processes for Engineering Materials. 3rd ed. Serope Kalpakjian. LC 96-31465. 960p. (C). 1996. 105.00 (*0-201-82370-5*) Addison-Wesley.

Manufacturing Processes for Technology. William O. Fellers & William W. Hunt. LC 94-7909. 544p. (C). 1994. 80.00 (*0-02-336881-0*, Macmillan Coll) P-H.

***Manufacturing Processes for Technology.** 2nd ed. William O. Fellers & William W. Hunt. 496p. 2000. 70.67 (*0-13-017791-1*) P-H.

Manufacturing Processes in Canada. Ed. by K. C. Livingston & T. C. Graham. LC 60-4680. (Illus.). 308p. reprint ed. pap. 95.50 (*0-608-11643-2*, 201430100095) Bks Demand.

Manufacturing Processes Reference Guide. Robert H. Todd et al. (Illus.). 512p. 1994. 44.95 (*0-8311-3049-0*) Indus Pr.

Manufacturing Processes Reprints. American Production & Inventory Control Society St. 199p. 1993. 23.00 (*1-55822-080-1*) Am Prod & Inventory.

Manufacturing Processing. Wysk. 2000. 37.74 (*0-07-303324-3*) McGraw.

Manufacturing-Processing Machine Setting. 1982. 50.00 (*0-7855-2891-1*) St Mut.

Manufacturing Profits: Industry Week's Guide to Driving Business Growth. Ted Kinni. 256p. 1997. 29.95 (*0-471-16001-6*) Wiley.

Manufacturing Prosperity: Ideas for Industry, Technology & Employment. Ed. by Rodin Genoff & Roy Green. 262p. 1998. pap. 44.00 (*1-86287-285-6*, Pub. by Federation Pr) Gaunt.

***Manufacturing Rationality: The Engineering Foundations of the Managerial Revolution.** Yehouda A. Shenhav. LC 99-37909. 256p. 2000. write for info. (*0-19-829630-4*) OUP.

Manufacturing Religion: The Discourse of Sui Generis Religion & the Politics of Nostalgia. Russell T. McCutcheon. LC 96-22755. (Illus.). 272p. 1997. text 35.00 (*0-19-510503-6*) OUP.

Manufacturing Renaissance. Pisano. 1995. 29.95 (*0-07-103620-2*) McGraw.

Manufacturing Renaissance: A Harvard Business Review Book. Ed. by Gary P. Pisano & Robert H. Hayes. LC 94-43320. (Business Review Bk.). 384p. 1995. 29.95 (*0-87584-610-6*) Harvard Busn.

Manufacturing Resource Planning. Oliver W. Wight. 488p. 1995. 45.00 (*0-471-13274-8*) Wiley.

Manufacturing Revolution. Skinner. Date not set. write for info. (*0-02-929130-5*) P-H.

Manufacturing Science. A. Ghosh & A. K. Mallik. (Engineering Science Ser.). 1986. text 69.95 (*0-470-20312-9*) P-H.

Manufacturing Science & Engineering. Ed. by Jay Lee. LC 99-191723. 965p. 1998. pap. text 240.00 (*0-7918-1606-0*) ASME.

Manufacturing Science & Engineering: Proceedings, ASME International Mechanical Engineering Congress & Exposition, 1996, Atlanta, Georgia. Ed. by K. Subramanian et al. LC 96-78687. (MED Ser.: Vol. 4). 824p. 1996. pap. text 280.00 (*0-7918-1545-5*) ASME Pr.

Manufacturing Science & Engineering, 1997: Proceedings, ASME International Mechanical Engineering Congress & Exposition, Dallas, TX, 1997, 2 vols. Ed. by Gloria J. Wiens et al. LC 98-190287. (MED Ser.: Vol. 6-1). 954p. 1997. pap. 300.00 (*0-7918-1849-7*, TS167) ASME Pr.

Manufacturing Science & Engineering, 1994 Vol. 1: International Mechanical Engineering Congress & Exposition, Chicago, Illinois - November 6-11, 1994. LC 94-79144. (PED Ser.: Vol. 68-1). 480p. 1994. 110.00 (*0-7918-1435-1*, G0930A) ASME.

Manufacturing Science & Engineering, 1995 Vol. 2-3: Manufacturing Science & Engineering, 2 vols., Set, Vols. 1 & 2. Ed. by J. Mills et al. LC 95-81272. (1995 ASME International Mechanical Engineering Congress & Exposition Ser.: MED-Vol. 2/MH-Vol. 3). 1352p. 1995. 360.00 (*0-7918-1738-5*, H01020) ASME.

Manufacturing Science & Engineering, 1994: International Mechanical Engineering Congress & Exposition, Chicago, Illinois - November 6-11, 1994, 2 vols., Set. (PED Ser.: Vols. 68-1 & 68-2). 1000p. 1994. 190.00 (*0-614-05618-7*, GX0930) ASME.

Manufacturing Science & Engineering, 1994 Vol. 2: International Mechanical Engineering Congress & Exposition, Chicago, Illinois - November 6-11, 1994. (PED Ser.: Vol. 68-2). 520p. 1994. 114.00 (*0-614-05617-9*, G0930B) ASME.

***Manufacturing Science & Engineering, 1999: International Mechanical Engineering Congress & Exposition, Nashville, TN, 1999.** Ed. by John W. Sutherland. (MED Ser.: Vol. 10). 961p. 1999. 240.00 (*0-7918-1646-X*) ASME Pr.

Manufacturing Science & Technology Area Plan, FY 94: Air Force Material Command. (Illus.). 56p. (Orig.). (C). 1994. pap. text 30.00 (*0-7881-0641-4*) DIANE Pub.

Manufacturing Science & Technology of the Future. Ed. by Nam P. Suh. 230p. 1986. pap. 55.00 (*0-08-033451-2*, Pub. by PPL) Elsevier.

Manufacturing Simulation. 148p. 415.00 (*0-317-65597-3*) TBC Inc.

Manufacturing Simulation. Richard K. Miller. LC 89-17111. 178p. 1989. pap. text 95.00 (*0-88173-104-8*) Fairmont Pr.

Manufacturing Simulation. Richard K. Miller & Fairmont Press Staff. 186p. (C). 1989. pap. 95.00 (*0-13-555517-5*) P-H.

Manufacturing Simulation. Richard K. Miller & Terri C. Walker. LC 88-72190. (Survey on Technology & Markets Ser.: No. 35). 50p. 1989. pap. text 200.00 (*1-55865-096-2*) Future Tech Surveys.

Manufacturing Social Distress: Psychopathy in Everyday Life. Robert W. Rieber. LC 96-52872. (PATH in Psychology Ser.). (Illus.). 238p. (C). 1928. 39.50 (*0-306-45346-0*, Plenum Trade) Perseus Pubng.

***Manufacturing, Social Effects, Scheduling.** Ed. by T. Y. Chai et al. Vol. A. 506p. 1999. pap. 126.00 (*0-08-043212-3*) Elsevier.

Manufacturing Software. Richard K. Miller & Terri C. Walker. LC 88-81640. (Survey on Technology & Markets Ser.: No. 49). 50p. 1989. pap. text 200.00 (*1-55865-048-2*) Future Tech Surveys.

Manufacturing Solutions Based on Engineering Sciences: Presented at the Winter Annual Meeting of the American Society of Mechanical Engineers, Washington, D.C., November 15-20, 1981. American Society of Mechanical Engineers Staff. Ed. by L. Kops. LC 81-69018. (PED Ser.: Vol. 3). (Illus.). 213p. reprint ed. pap. 66.10 (*0-8357-2827-7*, 203906300010) Bks Demand.

Manufacturing Standards & Specifications for Textbooks. National Association of State Textbook Administrat et al. 1976. write for info. (*0-318-55921-8*) Textbk Specif.

Manufacturing Strategy: Formulation & Implementation. Garry R. Greenhalgh. (C). 1991. text 24.33 (*0-201-50983-0*) Addison-Wesley.

Manufacturing Strategy: How to Formulate & Implement a Winning Plan. John Miltenburg. (Illus.). 392p. 1995. 45.00 (*1-56327-071-4*) Productivity Inc.

Manufacturing Strategy: Process & Content. Ed. by C. A. Voss. 416p. 1995. pap. 35.00 (*0-412-63480-5*) Chapman & Hall.

Manufacturing Strategy: Text & Cases. 2nd ed. Terry Hill. LC 93-17064. 592p. (C). 1993. text 74.95 (*0-256-10666-5*, Irwn McGrw-H) McGrw-H Hghr Educ.

Manufacturing Strategy: The Research Agenda for the Next Decade. Ed. by John E. Ettlie. (C). 1990. lib. bdg. 150.00 (*0-7923-9065-2*) Kluwer Academic.

Manufacturing Success: How to Manage Your Competitive Edge. Roland Toone. LC 94-11047. 300p. (C). 1995. pap. text 62.00 (*0-13-102773-5*) P-H.

Manufacturing Systems. R. Thomas Wright. LC 98-53010. 413p. 2000. 38.60 (*1-56637-584-3*) Goodheart.

Manufacturing Systems: Foundations of World-Class Practice. Committee on Foundations of Manufacturing, Nationa. Ed. by W. Dale Compton & Joseph A. Heim. 280p. 1991. 34.95 (*0-309-04588-6*) Natl Acad Pr.

Manufacturing Systems: Foundations of World-Class Practice. Committee on Foundations of Manufacturing, Nationa. Ed. by W. Dale Compton & Joseph A. Heim. 288p. 1992. pap. 19.95 (*0-309-04678-5*) Natl Acad Pr.

Manufacturing Systems: Modelling Management & Control: A Postprint Volume from the IFAC Workshop, Vienna, Austria, 3-5 February 1997. Ed. by Peter Kopacek. LC 97-23732. (IFAC Postprint Ser.). 1997. pap. text. write for info. (*0-08-042616-6*, Pergamon Pr) Elsevier.

Manufacturing Systems: Theory & Practice. G. Chryssolouris. (Texts in Mechanical Engineering Ser.). (Illus.). xvi, 419p. 1993. 79.95 (*0-387-97754-6*) Spr-Verlag.

Manufacturing Systems: Theory & Practice. 2nd ed. G. Chryssolouris. (Texts in Mechanical Engineering Ser.). (Illus.). xvi, 419p. 1993. text. write for info. (*3-540-97754-6*) Spr-Verlag.

Manufacturing Systems Engineering. Ed. by Katsundo Hitomi. LC 97-104007. 320p. 1996. text 99.00 (*0-7484-0323-X*, Pub. by Tay Francis Ltd); pap. text 44.95 (*0-7484-0324-8*, Pub. by Tay Francis Ltd) Taylor & Francis.

Manufacturing Systems Engineering. Katsundo Hitomi. 508p. 1996. 99.00 (*0-7484-0522-4*, Pub. by Tay Francis Ltd); pap. 49.95 (*0-7484-0523-2*, Pub. by Tay Francis Ltd) Taylor & Francis.

Manufacturing Systems Explained. Ed. by Dennis Kroon. 18p. 1990. pap., wbk. ed. 7.00 (*0-943008-11-5*, T11) Bergwall.

Manufacturing Systems Explained. Dennis K. Kroon. (Technology Education Ser.). 18p. (YA). (gr. 10 up). 1990. student ed. 7.00 (*0-8064-0396-9*) Bergwall.

Manufacturing Tales: Sex & Money in Contemporary Legends. Gary A. Fine. LC 91-46237. 224p. 1992. pap. 17.95 (*0-87049-755-3*); text 38.95 (*0-87049-754-5*) U of Tenn Pr.

Manufacturing, Teams & Improvement: The Human Art of Manufacturing. Michael Quirk. LC 98-28547. 322p. 1998. 71.00 (*0-13-924226-0*) P-H.

Manufacturing Techniques for Surface Mounted Assemblies. R. J. Wassink & M. M. Verguld. 510p. 1997. pap. 380.00 (*0-901150-30-4*) St Mut.

Manufacturing Technology. 1990. lib. bdg. 75.00 (*0-8490-4004-3*) Gordon Pr.

Manufacturing Technology. Horton. (Tech & Industrial Education Ser.). 1990. pap., teacher ed. 12.00 (*0-8273-3464-8*) Delmar.

Manufacturing Technology. Andrew C. Horton. (Tech & Industrial Education Ser.). 1990. text 36.95 (*0-8273-3462-1*) Delmar.

Manufacturing Technology. Stanley A. Komacek et al. 1991. pap., teacher ed. 65.95 (*0-8273-4626-3*) Delmar.

Manufacturing Technology. John R. Lindbeck. 640p. 1995. pap. text 100.00 (*0-13-211690-1*) P-H.

Manufacturing Technology: Engineering Materials, Vol. 1. J. M. Alexander et al. (Mechanical Engineering Ser.). 238p. 1987. text 57.95 (*0-470-20815-5*) P-H.

Manufacturing Technology: Factors Affecting Adoption. (Illus.). 182p. (Orig.). (C). 1994. pap. text 35.00 (*0-7881-0243-5*) DIANE Pub.

Manufacturing Technology: Prevalence & Plans for Use, 1993. (Illus.). 134p. (Orig.). (C). 1995. pap. text 30.00 (*0-7881-2275-4*) DIANE Pub.

Manufacturing Technology: Today & Tomorrow. Robert A. Daiber & Erekson. 152p. 1999. teacher ed. 10.13 (*0-02-675752-4*) Glencoe.

Manufacturing Technology: Today & Tomorrow. Robert A. Daiber & Erekson. (Illus.). 192p. (YA). (gr. 6-12). 1999. student ed., wbk. ed. 8.87 (*0-02-675753-2*) Glencoe.

Manufacturing Technology: Today & Tomorrow. annot. ed. Robert A. Daiber & Erekson. 510p. 1999. teacher ed. 44.40 (*0-02-675757-5*) Glencoe.

***Manufacturing Technology: Volume I, Vol. I.** 3rd ed. Timings. 440p. (C). 1998. pap. text 59.95 (*0-582-35693-8*, Prentice Hall) P-H.

Manufacturing Technology Activities. Henry Harms. (Tech & Industrial Education Ser.). 1988. pap. 37.95 (*0-8273-3239-4*) Delmar.

Manufacturing, Technology & Economic Growth. Carlos Sabillon. LC 99-27549. 448p. 2000. text 81.95 (*0-7656-0513-9*) M E Sharpe.

Manufacturing Technology Centers Program, 1992: Proposal Evaluation. (Illus.). 67p. (Orig.). (C). 1993. pap. text 25.00 (*1-56806-632-5*) DIANE Pub.

Manufacturing Technology Directorate: Project Book Update, 1996-97. (Illus.). 93p. (C). 1998. pap. text 25.00 (*0-7881-4041-8*) DIANE Pub.

Manufacturing Technology for Technician. Timings. 1990. pap. text. write for info. (*0-582-03039-0*, Pub. by Addison-Wesley) Longman.

Manufacturing Technology in the Electronics Industry: An Introduction. P. R. Edwards. (Illus.). 224p. (gr. 13). 1991. pap. text 39.95 (*0-412-37130-8*) Chapman & Hall.

Manufacturing Technology of Continuous Glass Fibres. 3rd rev. ed. K. L. Lowenstein. LC 92-39909. (Glass Science & Technology Ser.: Vol.6). 368p. 1993. 269.25 (*0-444-89346-6*) Elsevier.

Manufacturing Technology Program: U. S. Air Force. (Illus.). 98p. (Orig.). (C). 1993. pap. text 35.00 (*1-56806-639-2*) DIANE Pub.

Manufacturing Technology Today & Tomorrow. Robert A. Daiber. 1990. 38.47 (*0-02-675751-6*) Glencoe.

Manufacturing the Employee: Management Knowledge from the 19th to 21st Centuries. Roy Jacques. 256p. 1996. 75.00 (*0-8039-7915-0*); pap. 26.95 (*0-8039-7916-9*) Sage.

Manufacturing the Future: A History of Western Electric. Stephen B. Adams & Orville R. Butler. LC 98-34294. 288p. (C). 1999. text 34.95 (*0-521-65118-2*) Cambridge U Pr.

Manufacturing the Self: Orshi Drozdik. John C. Welchman. (Illus.). 32p. (C). 1994. 7.95 (*0-935519-18-1*) Anderson Gal.

***Manufacturing Time: Global Competition in the Watch Industry, 1795-2000.** Amy K. Glasmeier. (Perspectives on Economic Change Ser.). 340p. 2000. lib. bdg. 40.00 (*1-57230-589-4*, C0589) Guilford Pubns.

***Manufacturing U. S. A., 2 Vols. Set.** 7th ed. 2300p. 2000. 230.00 (*0-7876-3737-8*, UXL) Gale.

Manufacturing U. S. A: Industry Statistics, 2 vols. 6th ed. 1998. 210.00 (*0-7876-2782-8*, 00148845) Gale.

Manufacturing Victims: How the Psychology Business Wants to Keep Your Dependent for Life. Tana Dineen. 320p. 1996. pap. text 16.99 (*1-895854-58-X*, Pub. by R Davies Pub) Genl Dist Srvs.

Manufacturing Virtue. James R. Kincaid. 1999. pap. 23.95 (*0-670-85843-9*) Viking Penguin.

Manufacturing with Materials. Lyndon Edwards & Mark Endean. 430p. 2000. pap. text 49.95 (*0-7506-2754-9*) Buttrwrth-Heinemann.

Manufacturing Worldwide: Industry Analysis Statistics. 3rd ed. 885p. 1999. 210.00 (*0-7876-2447-0*) Gale.

Manufacturing Yield Evaluation of VLSI - WSI Systems. Ed. by Bruno Ciciani. LC 94-20185. 448p. 1995. pap. 58.00 (*0-8186-6292-1*, BP06292) IEEE Comp Soc.

Manuleae: A Tribe of Scrophulariaceae. O. M. Hilliard. (Illus.). 600p. 1994. 140.00 (*0-7486-0489-8*, Pub. by Edinburgh U Pr) Col U Pr.

Manumission of Slaves in Early Christianity. 2nd ed. J. Albert Harrill. (Hermeneutische Untersuchungen zur Theologie Ser.: No. 32). 273p. 1998. pap. 75.00 (*3-16-146935-6*, Pub. by JCB Mohr) Coronet Bks.

Manure, Meadows & Milkshakes. Eric Jorgensen et al. Ed. by Elizabeth Hone. (Illus.). 132p. (Orig.). (J). (ps-8). 1986. reprint ed. pap. text, teacher ed. 9.95 (*0-318-20228-X*) Trust Hidden Villa.

Manus O'Donnell's Life of Colum Cille. Brian Lacey. LC 98-233154. 256p. 1998. pap. 19.95 (*1-85182-395-6*, Pub. by Four Cts Pr) Intl Spec Bk.

Manus O'Donnell's Life of Colum Cille. limited ed. Brian Lacey. LC 98-233154. 256p. 1998. 120.00 (*1-85182-394-8*, Pub. by Four Cts Pr) Intl Spec Bk.

Manuscript. 7th rev. ed. Ed. by Karger, S., AG Staff. (Illus.). iv, 52p. 1981. pap. 13.25 (*3-8055-2563-X*) S Karger.

***Manuscript Book.** William Bay. (QwikGuide Ser.). 64p. 2000. pap. 5.95 (*0-7866-5718-9*, 99162) Mel Bay.

Manuscript Book Ten-Stave. 32p. 1980. pap. 3.95 (*0-87166-563-8*, 93679) Mel Bay.

Manuscript Book Twelve Stave. 32p. 1980. pap. 3.95 (*0-87166-672-3*, 93303) Mel Bay.

Manuscript Books of Emily Dickinson: A Facsimile Edition, 2 vols. Emily Dickinson. Ed. by Ralph W. Franklin. LC 80-17861. 1480p. 1981. 173.00 (*0-674-54828-0*) Belknap Pr.

Manuscript by Aonghus MacArtain. Aonghus MacArtain. 105p. 1992. pap. 19.00 (*0-685-67869-5*) A MacRaonuill.

Manuscript by Domhnull MacDhomhnuill. Domhnull MacDhomhnuill. 282p. 1992. pap. 51.00 (*0-685-67870-9*) A MacRaonuill.

Manuscript Catalog of American Jewish Archives. 1991. suppl. ed. 400.00 (*0-8161-0518-9*, G K Hall & Co) Mac Lib Ref.

Manuscript Catalog of the American Jewish Archives. American Jewish Archives Staff. 1971. 505.00 (*0-8161-1430-7*, G K Hall & Co) Mac Lib Ref.

Manuscript Catalog of the American Jewish Archives, Supplement 1. American Jewish Archives Staff. 1978. suppl. ed. 175.00 (*0-8161-1436-6*, G K Hall & Co) Mac Lib Ref.

Manuscript Chapters of Persuasion: Jane Austen Library. Jane Austen. Ed. by R. W. Chapman. LC 85-6174. (C). 1985. text 37.50 (*0-485-10502-0*, Pub. by Athlone Pr) Humanities.

Manuscript Collections of the Maryland Historical Society. A. J. Pedley. LC 68-23074. 1968. 20.00 (*0-938420-08-9*) MD Hist.

Manuscript Documents from Spain Dating from the 12th through the 18th Centuries Housed in the Special Collection of the Margaret I King Library, Univer. of Ky. John Lihani. LC 84-50663. (University of Kentucky Libraries Occasional Papers). 117p. (Orig.). 1984. lib. bdg. 7.00 (*0-917519-01-9*) U of KY Libs.

Manuscript Emblem Books of Henry Peacham. Alan R. Young. (Index Emblematicus Ser.). (Illus.). 400p. 1998. text 120.00 (*0-8020-0987-5*) U of Toronto Pr.

Manuscript Essays & Notes. William James. Ed. by Frederick Burkhardt & Fredson Bowers. LC 86-18412. (Works of William James). (Illus.). 599p. 1988. 79.50 (*0-674-54829-9*) HUP.

M

Manuscript Facsimiles of Various Lafcadio Hearn Writings in the Tenri Central Library Collection, Tokyo, Japan, 5 vols. Lafcadio Hearn. reprint ed. 387.00 (*0-404-13211-1*) AMS Pr.

Manuscript Found: The Complete Original "Spaulding Manuscript" Ed. by Kent Jackson. 1997. 18.95 (*1-57008-297-9*) Bookcraft Inc.

Manuscript Found in Saragossa. Jan Potocki. lib. bdg. 35.95 (*0-8488-2012-6*) Amereon Ltd.

Manuscript Found in Saragossa. Jan Potocki. 656p. 1996. pap. 14.95 (*0-14-044580-3*, Viking) Viking Penguin.

Manuscript Glosses to the Canterbury Tales. Stephen Partridge. (Chaucer Studies). 352p. 2000. 110.00 (*0-85991-533-6*) Boydell & Brewer.

Manuscript Handwriting. Frank Schaffer Publications Staff. 1997. pap. text 3.95 (*0-7647-0232-7*) Schaffer Pubns.

Manuscript Handwriting. Jo E. Moore. (Reading & Writing Ser.). (Illus.). 32p. (J). (gr. k-2). 1996. pap., teacher ed. 2.95 (*1-55799-420-X*, 4022) Evan-Moor Edu Pubs.

Manuscript Handwriting Practice. Frank Schaffer Publications, Inc. Staff. (Skill Builders Ser.). (Illus.). 128p. 1996. wbk. ed. 10.95 (*0-86734-919-0*, 32063) Schaffer Pubns.

Manuscript in the British American World of Print. David S. Shields. 1993. pap. 7.00 (*0-944026-43-5*) Am Antiquarian.

Manuscript Index to the Index of Middle English Verse. Richard Hamer. 64p. 1994. pap. 36.00 (*0-7123-0387-1*) U of Toronto Pr.

Manuscript Ivrea, Biblioteca Capitolare 115. Karl Kugle. LC 97-138142. (Musicological Studies Ser.: Vol. 69). (ENG & LAT., Illus.). 362p. 1997. 76.00 (*1-896926-04-5*) Inst Mediaeval Mus.

Manuscript Lectures. William James. LC 87-8804. (Works of William James). (Illus.). 736p. 1988. 98.95 (*0-674-54826-4*) HUP.

Manuscript Material, Correspondence, & Graphic Material in the Fiske Islandic Collection: A Descriptive Catalogue. Compiled by Thorunn Sigurdardottir. LC 93-29520. (Islandica Ser.: Vol. XLVIII). 312p. 1994. text 47.50 (*0-8014-2993-5*) Cornell U Pr.

Manuscript Mechanics. Shirley Warren. (Illus.). 20p. 1990. pap. 5.00 (*1-877801-08-9*) Still Waters.

Manuscript Murders. large type ed. Roy H. Lewis. (Linford Mystery Library). 304p. 1987. pap. 16.99 (*0-7089-6389-7*) Ulverscroft.

***Manuscript, Narrative, Lexicon: Essays on Literary & Cultural Transmission in Honor of Whitney F. Bolton.** Robert Boenig & Kathleen Davis. LC 99-55721. (Illus.). 264p. 2000. 44.50 (*0-8387-5440-6*) Bucknell U Pr.

Manuscript Notes on Weaving, 2 bks. James Holmes. LC 85-51975. (Illus.). 320p. 1985. 15.00 (*0-9616526-1-6*) Tunstede.

Manuscript of a Black Caucasian. Dorothy E. Miller. 149p. 1994. pap. 14.99 (*0-9638844-0-9*) Miller & Seymour.

Manuscript of Al-Malik Al-Afdal: A Medieval Arabic Anthology from the Yemen. Ed. by Daniel M. Varisco & G. Rex Smith. (ARA.). 542p. 1998. reprint ed. 160.00 (*0-906094-32-1*) David Brown.

Manuscript of Dove, Vol. 1. Aonghus MacAoidh. 186p. 1992. pap. 34.00 (*0-685-62622-9*) A MacRaonuill.

Manuscript of Dove, Vol. 2. Aonghus MacAoidh. 200p. 1992. pap. 36.00 (*0-685-62623-7*) A MacRaonuill.

Manuscript of Dove, Vol. 3. Aonghus MacAoidh. 162p. 1992. pap. 30.00 (*0-685-66249-7*) A MacRaonuill.

Manuscript of Jow Smithwitz. Monty Robins. 323p. (C). 1989. text 50.00 (*1-872795-58-7*, Pub. by Pentland Pr) St Mut.

Manuscript Pad for Children. 96p. 1996. pap. 4.95 (*1-56222-124-8*, 94521) Mel Bay.

Manuscript Painting at the Court of France: The Fourteenth Century (1310-1380) Francois Avril. LC 77-78721. (Illus.). 120p. 1978. pap. 11.95 (*0-8076-0879-3*, Pub. by Braziller) Norton.

Manuscript Paper. (Illus.). 96p. 1963. pap. 7.95 (*0-8256-2117-8*, AM40486) Music Sales.

Manuscript Paper, 10 Stave. 64p. 1987. 5.95 (*0-7390-0597-9*, 177) Alfred Pub.

Manuscript Poems in the British Library: Facsimiles of the Hyperion Holograph & of George Keats' Notebook of Holographs & Transcripts. John Keats. Ed. & Intro. by Jack Stillinger. LC 88-33406.

(Manuscripts of the Younger Romantics & the Bodleian Shelley Manuscripts: Vol. 5). xvi, 184p. 1989. reprint ed. text 42.00 (*0-8240-7020-8*) Garland.

Manuscript Poems of A. E. Housman: Eight Hundred Lines of Hitherto Uncollected Verse from the Author's Notebooks. Alfred E. Housman. Ed. by Tom B. Haber. LC PR4809.H15. (Illus.). 160p. reprint ed. pap. 49.60 (*0-8357-8946-2*, 203322600085) Bks Demand.

*__Manuscript Practice: Modern Handwriting.__ Ed. by Maria McKinney & Amy Gamble. (Illus.). 32p. (J). (gr. 1-3). 1999. pap. 4.95 (*0-88724-504-8*, CD-0878) Carson-Dellos.

*__Manuscript Practice: Traditional Handwriting.__ Ed. by Maria McKinney & Amy Gamble. (Illus.). 32p. (J). (gr. 1-3). 1999. pap. 4.95 (*0-88724-505-6*, CD-0879) Carson-Dellos.

Manuscript, Print, & the English Renaissance Lyric. Arthur F. Marotti. 336p. 1995. text 49.95 (*0-8014-2291-4*); pap. text 21.95 (*0-8014-8238-0*) Cornell U Pr.

Manuscript Records of the French & Indian War in the Library of the American Antiquarian Society. Charles H. Lincoln. 267p. 1993. reprint ed. pap. text 20.00 (*1-55613-739-7*) Heritage Bk.

Manuscript Remains: Critical Debates (1809-1818), Vol. II. Arthur Schopenhauer. Tr. by E. F. Payne. 524p. 1989. 53.00 (*0-85496-539-4*) Berg Pubs.

Manuscript Remains: Early Manuscripts (1809-1819), Vol. 1. Arthur Schopenhauer. Tr. by E. F. Payne. 560p. 1988. 53.00 (*0-85496-538-6*) Berg Pubs.

Manuscript Remains: The Manuscript Books of (1830-1852), Vol. IV, Bk. 1. Arthur Schopenhauer. Tr. by E. F. Payne. LC 87-27815. 530p. 1990. 53.00 (*0-85496-541-6*) Berg Pubs.

Manuscript Remains Vol. III: Berlin Manuscripts (1818-1830) Arthur Schopenhauer. Ed. by Arthur Hubscher. Tr. by E. F. Payne. LC 87-27815. 784p. 1989. 53.00 (*0-85496-540-8*) Berg Pubs.

Manuscript Remains of Buddhist Literature Found in Eastern Turkestan: Facsimiles with Transcripts Translations & Notes Edited in Conjunction with Other Scholars. A. F. Hoernle. (Bibliotheca Indo-Buddhica Ser.: No. 48). (C). 1988. reprint ed. 60.00 (*81-7030-158-0*) S Asia.

*__Manuscript Review & Introduction to Cursive, Bk. M/C.__ Thomas Wasylyk. (Illus.). 64p. (J). (gr. 2). 1999. pap. 2.75 (*1-56762-111-2*) Modern Learn Pr.

Manuscript Sources in the Rosenberg Library: A Selective Guide. Ed. by Jane A. Kenamore & Michael E. Wilson. LC 82-45896. (Illus.). 184p. 1983. 24.95 (*0-89096-146-8*) Tex A&M Univ Pr.

Manuscript Sources of American History. Justin Winsor. (Notable American Authors Ser.). 1999. reprint ed. lib. bdg. 125.00 (*0-7812-9994-2*) Rprt Serv.

Manuscript Sources of Medieval Medicine: A Book of Essays. Ed. by Margaret R. Schleissner. LC 94-15149. (Medieval Casebooks Ser.: Vol. 8). 224p. 1995. text 42.00 (*0-8153-0815-9*, H1576) Garland.

Manuscript Sources of Seventeenth-Century Italian Lute Music. rev. ed. Victor Coelho. LC 94-36302. 736p. 1995. text 127.00 (*0-8153-1382-9*) Garland.

Manuscript Sources of the History of Irish Civilization. 1989. 1375.00 (*0-8161-1751-9*, G K Hall & Co) Mac Lib Ref.

Manuscript Sources of the History of Irish Civilization, Supplement 1. 1989. suppl. ed. 495.00 (*0-8161-1752-7*, G K Hall & Co) Mac Lib Ref.

Manuscript Submission. Scott Edelstein. (Elements of Fiction Writing Ser.). 176p. 1990. 14.99 (*0-89879-398-X*, Wrtrs Digest Bks) F & W Pubns Inc.

Manuscript Tradition of Propertius. James L. Butrica. LC 84-225780. (Phoenix Supplementary Ser.: No. 17). (Illus.). 383p. reprint ed. pap. 118.80 (*0-8357-3658-X*, 203638500003) Bks Demand.

Manuscript Tradition of the Tragedies of Aeschylus. Aleksander Turyn. 147p. 1943. reprint ed. lib. bdg. 32.37 (*0-685-13784-8*, 05101572) G Olms Pubs.

Manuscript Tradition of the Tragedies of Aeschylus. Aleksander Turyn. vi, 141p. 1967. reprint ed. write for info. (*0-318-71055-2*) G Olms Pubs.

Manuscript Writing. Joan Hoffman. (I Know It! Book Ser.). (Illus.). 32p. (J). (ps-3). 1981. student ed. 2.49 (*0-938256-01-7*, 02001) Sch Zone Pub Co.

*__Manuscript Writing, Bk. M.__ Thomas Wasylyk. (Illus.). 64p. (J). (gr. 2). 1999. pap. 2.75 (*1-56762-110-4*) Modern Learn Pr.

Manuscript Writing: Reading & Writing Skills. Jo Ellen Moore. (Illus.). 32p. (J). (gr. k-2). 1995. pap., wbk. ed. 2.50 (*1-58610-041-6*, Learn on the Go) Learn Horizon.

Manuscript Writing: Words Book 1 & 2, Bk. 1. Ann Arbor Publishers Editorial Staff. (Manuscript Writing Words Ser.). (J). (gr. 3-6). 1994. 10.00 (*0-87879-787-4*, Ann Arbor Div) Acad Therapy.

Manuscript Writing: Words Book 1 & 2, Bk. 2. Ann Arbor Publishers Editorial Staff. (Manuscript Writing Words Ser.). (J). (gr. 3-6). 1994. 10.00 (*0-87879-788-2*, Ann Arbor Div) Acad Therapy.

Manuscripts: The First Twenty Years. Ed. by Priscilla S. Taylor & Herbert E. Klingelhofer. LC 84-3846. (Illus.). 429p. 1984. 65.00 (*0-313-24281-X*, MNU/, Greenwood Pr) Greenwood.

Manuscripts & Documents: Their Deterioration & Restoration. 2nd ed. William J. Barrow. LC 72-89855. (Illus.). 112p. reprint ed. pap. 34.80 (*0-8357-3144-8*, 203940700012) Bks Demand.

Manuscripts & Government Records in the United Kingdom & Ireland Relating to Canada. Ed. by Bruce G. Wilson. 705p. 1993. 123.50 (*0-660-57424-1*, Pub. by Canadian Govt Pub) Accents Pubns.

Manuscripts & Libraries in the Age of Charlemagne. Bernhard Bischoff. Tr. & Compiled by Michael M. Gorman. LC 92-44509. (Studies in Palaeography & Codicology: No. 1). (ENG & GER.). 211p. (C). 1994. text 69.95 (*0-521-38346-3*) Cambridge U Pr.

Manuscripts & Memories: Chapters in Our Literary Tradition. Michael Earls. LC 67-26735. (Essay Index Reprint Ser.). 1977. 20.95 (*0-8369-0397-8*) Ayer.

Manuscripts & the Text of the New Testament: An Introduction for English Readers. Keith Elliott & Ian Moir. (Illus.). 144p. 1996. pap. 14.95 (*0-567-29298-3*, Pub. by T & T Clark) Bks Intl VA.

Manuscripts at Oxford. (Illus.). 155p. 1987. pap. 16.95 (*0-900177-64-0*, 76-4, Pub. by Ashmolean Mus) A Schwartz & Co.

Manuscripts Collections of the Minnesota Historical Society No. 2: Guide. Minnesota Historical Society Staff et al. LC 35-27911. (Publications of the Minnesota Historical Society). 228p. reprint ed. pap. 70.70 (*0-8357-3315-7*, 203953900013) Bks Demand.

Manuscripts Collections of the Minnesota Regional Research Centers No. 2: Guide. Compiled by James E. Fogerty. LC 80-25374. 92p. 1979. pap. 4.50 (*0-87351-150-6*) Minn Hist.

Manuscripts in the Department of Middle American Research see Studies in Middle America

Manuscripts of a Passage to India. Ed. by E. M. Forster & Oliver Stallybrass. LC 78-26698. (Abinger Edition of E. M. Forster Ser.). 589p. 1979. 125.00 (*0-8419-0470-7*) Holmes & Meier.

Manuscripts of Allan George Finch, 1692 & Addenda, 1690-1691. Francis L. Bickley. (Reports & Calendars, Series 58: Vol. 4). 626p. 1965. 16.00 (*0-11-440140-3*, HM01403, Pub. by Statnry Office) Bernan Associates.

Manuscripts of D. H. Lawrence. L. C. Powell. 1972. 200.00 (*0-87968-020-2*) Gordon Pr.

Manuscripts of D. H. Lawrence. Lawrence C. Powell. (Studies in D. H. Lawrence: No. 20). 1970. reprint ed. pap. 27.95 (*0-8383-0099-5*) M S G Haskell Hse.

Manuscripts of Early Norman England (c.1066-1130) Richard Gameson. (British Academy Postdoctoral Fellowship Monographs). (Illus.). 200p. 2000. text 60.00 (*0-19-726190-6*) OUP.

Manuscripts of "Piers Plowman" The B-Version. C. David Benson & Lynne S. Blanchfield. LC 97-28792. (Illus.). 352p. 1997. 110.00 (*0-85991-501-8*, DS Brewer) Boydell & Brewer.

Manuscripts of Sedulius: A Provisional Handlist. Carl P. Springer. LC 94-78523. (Transactions Ser.: Vol. 85, Pt. 5). (Illus.). 244p. 1995. pap. 15.00 (*0-87169-855-2*, T855-spc) Am Philos.

Manuscripts of the Bible: Greek Bibles in the British Library. rev. ed. T. S. Pattie. (Illus.). 48p. (C). 1995. pap. 9.95 (*0-7123-0403-7*, Pub. by B23tish Library) U of Toronto Pr.

Manuscripts of the Dibner Collection: Manuscripts in the History of Science & Technology in the Smithsonian Institution Libraries. Sil. LC 85-11576. (Illus.). 176p. 1985. 35.00 (*0-88135-025-7*) Watson Pub Intl.

Manuscripts of the Earl of Dartmouth, 3 vols., Set. Great Britain Historical Manuscripts Commission. Ed. by George A. Billias. LC 72-8795. (American Revolutionary Ser.). 1592p. reprint ed. lib. bdg. 201.00 (*0-8398-0802-X*) Irvington.

Manuscripts of the Greek Bible: An Introduction to Paleography. Bruce M. Metzger. (Illus.). 160p. (C). 1981. text 60.00 (*0-19-502924-0*) OUP.

Manuscripts of the Marquess of Downshire, Papers of William Trumbull the Elder, September 1616 - December 1618. Ed. by Sonia P. Anderson & G. Dynfallt Owen. (Reports & Calendars, Series 75: Vol. 6). 1995. 245.00 (*0-11-440230-2*, HM402302, Pub. by Statnry Office) Bernan Associates.

Manuscripts of the Marquess of Downshire, Papers of William Trumbull the Elder, 1613-1614. Ed. by A. B. Hinds. (Reports & Calendars, Series 75: Vol. 4). 604p. 1940. 6.00 (*0-11-440134-9*, HM01349, Pub. by Statnry Office) Bernan Associates.

Manuscripts of the Marquess of Salisbury, Addenda 1562-1605. Ed. by G. Dyfnallt Owen. (Reports & Calendars, Series 9: Vol. 23). 294p. 1973. 7.00 (*0-11-440042-3*, HM00423, Pub. by Statnry Office) Bernan Associates.

Manuscripts of the Marquess of Salisbury, Addenda 1605-1668. Ed. by G. Dynfallt Owen. (Reports & Calendars, Series 9: Vol. 24). 417p. 1976. 19.00 (*0-11-440062-8*, HM00628, Pub. by Statnry Office) Bernan Associates.

Manuscripts on Microform of the Hilandar Research Library (The Ohio State University) Resources in Medieval Slavic Studies, 2 vols., Set. Predrag Matejic & Hannah Thomas. xxix, 1196p. 1992. 79.95 (*0-89357-225-X*) Slavica.

Manuscripts on Slavery: Guide to the Xavier University Library-Heartman Manuscript Collection. Xavier University Library, New Orleans Staff. 238p. 1982. 160.00 (*0-8161-0375-5*, G K Hall & Co) Mac Lib Ref.

Manuscripts Speculum Humanae. E. Peters. 1998. 118.95 (*90-6831-773-3*, Pub. by Peeters Pub) Bks Intl VA.

Manuscript/6 Stave PB. 32p. 1996. pap. 0.95 (*0-7866-1751-9*, 95751) Mel Bay.

Manuscrit de Ma Mere. Alphonse D. Lamartine. 200p. 65.00 (*0-686-54278-9*) Fr & Eur.

Manuscrit du Roi, 2 vols. Ed. by Jean Beck & Louise Beck. (Chansonniers des troubadours et des trouveres Ser.: Vol. 2). (Illus.). 1970. reprint ed. lib. bdg. 200.00 (*0-8450-0003-9*) Broude.

*__Manuscrito de Miramar.__ Olga Nolla. (SPA.). 211p. 2000. pap. 14.95 (*968-19-0455-9*) Aguilar.

Manuscrits Arabes de l'Escurial Decrits, Vol. 1. Hartwig Derenbourg. (Publications De 'Ecole Des Langues Orientales Vivantes Ser. No. 2: Vol. X). xliii, 525p. 1976. reprint ed. write for info. (*3-487-06091-4*) G Olms Pubs.

Manuscrits Francais de la Bibliotheque Parker: Actes Due Colloque 24-27 Mars, 1993 Parker Library, Corpus Christi College, Cambridge. Ed. by Nigel Wilkins. 184p. (C). 1995. pap. 45.00 (*1-897852-01-0*) Boydell & Brewer.

Manuscrits Latins du Ve au XIIIe Siecle Conserves a la Bibliotheque Imperiale de Saint-Petersbourg, 2 vols., Set. Antonio Staerk. 664p. 1976. reprint ed. write for info. (*3-487-05957-6*) G Olms Pubs.

Manuskript. 5th ed. Ed. by Karger, S., AG Staff. (Illus.). 1980. pap. 13.25 (*3-8055-0182-X*) S Karger.

Manusmrti with Sanskrit Commentary Manvarthamuktavali of Kulluka Bhatta. Ed. by S. C. Banerjee. (C). 1990. reprint ed. 26.00 (*81-208-0765-0*, Pub. by Motilal Bnarsidass) S Asia.

Manwatching. Morris. pap. 18.95 (*0-586-04887-1*) HarpC.

Manx: Everything about Purchase, Care, Nutrition, Behavior & Training. Karen Commings. LC 98-46012. 1999. 7.95 (*0-7641-0754-2*) Barron.

*__Manx: The Cat with No Tail.__ Jennifer Quasha. LC 98-53562. 1999. write for info. (*0-8239-5512-5*, PowerKids) Rosen Group.

Manx, a Course in the Spoken Language. Manx Gaelic Society. 1974. pap. 12.50 (*0-89979-025-9*) British Am Bks.

Manx Ballads & Music. Ed. by Arthur W. Moore. LC 78-72642. (Celtic Language & Literature Ser.: Goidelic & Brythonic). reprint ed. 32.50 (*0-404-17575-9*) AMS Pr.

Manx Cat. Stuart A. Kallen. LC 95-12655. (Illus.). 24p. (J). (ps-4). 1995. lib. bdg. 13.98 (*1-56239-449-5*) ABDO Pub Co.

*__Manx Cats.__ Karen Commings. (Complete Pet Owner's Manual Ser.). (Illus.). 104p. 1999. pap. 6.95 (*0-7641-0753-4*) Barron.

Manx-English Dictionary. 1979. 35.00 (*0-89979-026-7*) British Am Bks.

Manx Idioms & Phrases. J. J. Kneen. 1978. pap. 12.50 (*0-89979-027-5*) British Am Bks.

Manx Murders: A Niccolo Benedetti Mystery. William L. DeAndrea. 256p. 1994. 20.00 (*1-883402-66-2*) S&S Trade.

Manx Railways & Tramways. Edward Gray. (Sutton's Photographic History of Railways Ser.). (Illus.). 160p. 1998. pap. 21.95 (*0-7509-1827-6*, Pub. by Sutton Pub Ltd) Intl Pubs Mktg.

Manxman. Hall Caine. LC 79-8243. reprint ed. 44.50 (*0-404-61801-4*) AMS Pr.

Many a Fine Harvest: Sauk County, 1840-1990. Michael J. Goc. (Illus.). 192p. 1991. 25.95 (*0-938627-11-2*) New Past Pr.

Many a Good Crusade. Virginia C. Gildersleeve. LC 79-8795. (Signal Lives Ser.). (Illus.). 1980. reprint ed. lib. bdg. 50.95 (*0-405-12841-X*) Ayer.

*__Many Adventures of Johnny Mutton.__ James Proimos. LC 00-9219. (Illus.). (J). 2001. write for info. (*0-15-202413-1*) Harcourt.

Many Adventures of Minnie. Jan S. Hart. (Illus.). 111p. (J). (gr. 3-6). 1997. reprint ed. 12.95 (*0-9644559-2-7*) Hart Publ.

Many Adventures of Winnie the Pooh. Mousework Staff. LC 99-159377. (Illus.). 96p. (J). 1998. 7.98 (*1-57082-804-0*, Pub. by Mouse Works) Time Warner.

Many Adventures of Winnie the Pooh: A Classic Disney Treasury. Disney Staff. LC 97-80021. (Illus.). 192p. (J). (ps-2). 1997. 19.95 (*0-7868-3138-3*, Pub. by Disney Pr) Time Warner.

Many-Agent Simulation & Artificial Life. J. Stender & E. Hillebrand. LC 94-78819. (Frontiers in Artificial Intelligence Applications Ser.: Vol. 25). 252p. (YA). (gr. 12). 1994. pap. 75.00 (*90-5199-191-6*) IOS Press.

Many Americas: Critical Perspectives on Race, Racism, & Ethn. Gregory R. Campbell. LC 98-73129. 432p. (C). 1998. per. 69.95 (*0-7872-4987-4*) Kendall-Hunt.

Many & More: A Celebration of Love in Later Life. Ed. by Jane Mead. LC 94-5303. 246p. 1994. 20.00 (*0-943221-21-8*) Timken Pubs.

Many & the Few: A Chronicle of the Dynamic Auto Workers. 2nd ed. Henry Kraus. 328p. 1985. reprint ed. pap. text 15.95 (*0-252-01199-6*) U of Ill Pr.

Many Are Called. Pat Arrowsmith. 1998. pap. text 10.99 (*0-906500-59-1*) Onlywomen Pr.

Many Are Called but Few Are Chosen. H. Verlan Andersen. Ed. by Hans V. Andersen, Jr. 110p. 1997. pap. 8.95 (*1-57636-043-1*) SunRise Pbl.

Many Are Called but Few Are Chosen. Verlan Andersen. 96p. 1967. pap. 3.95 (*0-89036-002-2*) Liahona Pub Trust.

Many Are Called, but Most Leave Their Phone off the Hook. Doug Peterson. 256p. 1992. pap. 9.99 (*0-310-57431-5*) Zondervan.

Many Are Chosen: Divine Election & Western Nationalism. Ed. by William R. Hutchison & Hartmut Lehmann. LC 94-16621. (Harvard Theological Studies: Vol. 38). 176p. (Orig.). (C). 1996. pap. 16.00 (*1-56338-244-X*) TPI PA.

Many Are the Crimes: McCarthyism in America. Ellen Schrecker. 1999. pap. 17.95 (*0-691-04870-3*, Pub. by Princeton U Pr) Cal Prin Full Svc.

Many Aspects of Mobile Home Living: A Novel. Martin Clark. 352p. 2000. 24.00 (*0-375-40725-1*) Knopf.

Many Aspire/Few Attain. Elbert Willis. 20p. 1996. pap. 2.00 (*0-614-31153-5*) Fill the Gap.

Many-Atom Interactions in Solids: Proceedings of the International Workshop, Pajulahti, Finland, June 5-9, 1989. Ed. by R. M. Nieminen et al. (Proceedings in Physics Ser.: Vol. 48). (Illus.). viii, 319p. 1990. 68.00 (*0-387-52657-9*) Spr-Verlag.

Many Avenues of Healing. Judith D. Parr. Ed. by Dorothy Rome. (Illus.). 169p. 1989. pap. 11.00 (*0-941971-06-6*) Peacock CO.

Many Blessings Cookbook: A Celebration of Harvest Home, Family, & Country Cooking. Jane W. Hopping. LC 92-46055. 1993. 21.00 (*0-679-14754-3*) Villard Books.

Many-Body Atomic Physics. Ed. by James J. Boyle & M. S. Pindzola. LC 96-14068. (Illus.). 440p. (C). 1998. text 69.95 (*0-521-47006-4*) Cambridge U Pr.

Many-Body Methods in Quantum Chemistry. Ed. by U. Kaldor. (Lecture Notes in Chemistry Ser.: Vol. 52). (Illus.). v, 349p. 1989. 53.95 (*0-387-51027-3*) Spr-Verlag.

Many-Body Physics: Proceedings of the International Conference. C. F. Fiolhais et al. 484p. 1994. text 116.00 (*981-02-1828-1*) World Scientific Pub.

Many-Body Problem: An Encyclopedia of Exactly Solved Models. D. C. Mattis. 984p. 1994. pap. text 74.00 (*981-02-1476-6*) World Scientific Pub.

Many-Body Problem: An Encyclopedia of Exactly Solved Models 1D. 2nd ed. Ed. by Elliott H. Lieb & D. C. Mattis. 800p. 1994. text 109.00 (*981-02-0975-4*) World Scientific Pub.

Many-Body Problem in Quantum Mechanics. unabridged ed. Norman H. March et al. 471p. 1995. reprint ed. pap. text 14.95 (*0-486-68754-6*) Dover.

Many-Body Problems. David Pines. LC 97-43363. 1997. 39.00 (*0-201-32834-8*) Addison-Wesley.

Many-Body Theory of Atomic Structure & Photoionization. 420p. 1993. 46.00 (*981-02-0877-4*) World Scientific Pub.

Many-Body Theory of Atomic Structure & Photoionization. T. N. Chang. 500p. 1993. text 143.00 (*981-02-0876-6*) World Scientific Pub.

Many-Body Theory of Correlated Fermion Systems: Proceedings of the VI Hispalensis International School Oromana, Seville, Spain 9-21 June, 1997. Ed. by Jose M. Arias et al. LC 99-170956. 330p. 1998. 78.00 (*981-02-3383-3*) World Scientific Pub.

Many-Body Tree Methods in Physics. Susanne Pfalzner & Paul Gibbon. (Illus.). 177p. (C). 1996. text 54.95 (*0-521-49564-4*) Cambridge U Pr.

Many Californias: Literature from the Golden State. 2nd rev. ed. Ed. by Gerald Haslam. LC 98-48029. (Western Literature Ser.). (Illus.). 424p. 1998. pap. 18.95 (*0-87417-325-6*) U of Nev Pr.

*__Many Candles: Millennium Graduates - Timeless Wisdom.__ Anastasia K. Hurlin. LC 99-68541. (Illus.). 195p. 2000. pap. 12.95 (*1-887472-74-6*, Pub. by Sunstar Pubng) Midpt Trade.

Many Cargoes. William W. Jacobs. LC 71-103520. (Short Story Index Reprint Ser.). 1977. 20.95 (*0-8369-3262-5*) Ayer.

Many Children: Religions Around the World. M. Angele Thomas & Mary L. Ramey. LC 87-91771. (Illus.). 70p. (Orig.). (J). (gr. 2-6). 1987. pap. text 6.95 (*0-9619293-0-8*) M A Thomas.

Many Children Coloring Book. M. Angele Thomas & Mary L. Ramey. (Illus.). 24p. (J). 1988. pap. 1.50 (*0-9619293-1-6*) M A Thomas.

Many Circles, Many Paths: A Native American Larning Story. Paula Underwood. LC 94-78237. (Illus.). 49p. 1994. pap. 9.00 (*1-879678-10-1*) Tribe Two Pr.

Many Circles Many Paths: A Native American Learning Story. Paula Underwood. Ed. by Jeanne Slobod. (Illus.). 51p. 1994. pap. 9.00 (*1-879678-11-X*) Tribe Two Pr.

Many Colored Buffalo: Transformation Through the Council of Many Voices. William S. Taegel. Ed. by Edward Tick. LC 90-46541. (Frontiers in Psychotherapy Ser.). 192p. (C). 1990. text 73.25 (*0-89391-739-7*) Ablx Pub.

Many Colored Coat: Countee Cullen. Houston A. Baker, Jr. (Broadside Critics Ser.: No. 4). (YA). (gr. 12 up). 1974. pap. 3.00 (*0-910296-36-7*) Broadside Pr.

Many-Colored Land. Julian May. 480p. 1985. mass mkt. 5.99 (*0-345-32444-7*, Del Rey) Ballantine Pub Grp.

Many-Colored Toga: Diary. Henry F. Ashurst. Ed. by George F. Sparks. LC 62-10625. (Illus.). 435p. reprint ed. pap. 124.30 (*0-608-02354-X*, 2062995) Bks Demand.

Many Colors of Mother Goose. Ceryl W. Hudson. LC 97-73797. (Illus.). 32p. (J). 1997. 10.95 (*0-940975-77-7*) Just Us Bks.

*__Many Colors of Mother Goose.__ Cheryl Willis Hudson. (Illus.). (J). 2000. pap. 7.95 (*0-940975-91-2*) Just Us Bks.

Many Crimes: McCarthyism in America. Ellen Schrecker. LC 97-42269. (Illus.). 592p. (gr. 8). 1998. 29.95 (*0-316-77470-7*) Little.

Many Cultures. Doris Roettger. (It's a Student's World Ser.). 64p. (J). (gr. 4-6). 1996. 8.99 (*0-86653-867-4*, FE3867) Fearon Teacher Aids.

Many Cultures: One in Christ. Ed. by Julie Garber. LC 92-43594. (Covenant Bible Studies). 80p. 1992. pap. 5.95 (*0-87178-547-1*, 8471) Brethren.

Many Cultures, One People: A Multicultural Handbook for Vermont Teachers. Compiled by Gregory Sharrow. LC 92-28437. 1992. write for info. (*0-916718-12-3*) VT Folklife Ctr.

Many Danes, Some Norwegians: Karen Miller's Diary, 1894. Karen Miller. (Illus.). xviii, 173p. 1997. pap. 14.95 (*0-930697-02-2*) Lur Pubns.

Many Deadly Returns: An Inspector Henry Tibbett Mystery. Patricia Moyes. LC 87-15015. 256p. 1995. pap. 5.95 (*0-8050-0598-6*, Owl) H Holt & Co.

An Asterisk (*) at the beginning of an entry indicates that the title is appearing for the first time.

Many Deaths of Danny Rosales: And Other Plays. Carlos Morton. LC 82-72277. 160p. (Orig.). (C). 1983. pap. 10.00 (0-934770-16-6) Arte Publico.

Many Deaths of Danny Rosales: Playscript. Carlos Morton. LC 90-53684. 50p. (Orig.). 1991. pap. 6.00 (0-88734-232-9) Players Pr.

Many Deaths of George Robertson. George Little. 137p. 1990. pap. 10.95 (0-86492-124-1, Pub. by Goose Ln Edits) Genl Dist Srvs.

Many Different Roads: A Common Path. Jock W. Rolfe & Gladys Knight. (YA). (gr. 8-12). 1998. pap. write for info. (1-890984-51-5) Rolfe Lrdrship.

Many Dimensions see Novels

***Many Dimensions of Aging.** Ed. by Robert L. Rubinstein et al. LC 99-31415. 256p. 1999. 42.95 (0-8261-1247-1) Springer Pub.

Many Dimensions of Family Practice. North American Symposium on Family Practice Staff. LC 80-14847. 340p. 1983. 45.00 (0-87668-427-4) Aronson.

Many Dimensions of the Human Person. E. Ecker Steger. LC 90-36346. (American University Studies, V, Philosophy: Vol. 96). 204p. (C). 1994. pap. text 35.95 (0-8204-2568-0) P Lang Pubng.

Many Disappointments of Flexible Exchange Rates. Robert M. Dunn, Jr. LC 83-26543. (Essays in International Finance Ser.: No. 154). 36p. 1983. pap. text 10.00 (0-88165-061-7) Princeton U Int Finan Econ.

Many Dogs There Be. Walter A. Dyer. LC 71-122695. (Short Story Index Reprint Ser.). 1977. 18.95 (0-8369-3528-4) Ayer.

***Many-Electron Densities & Reduced Density Matrices.** Jerzy Ciolowski. LC 00-42336. (Mathematical & Computational Chemistry Ser.). 2000. write for info. (0-306-46454-3) Plenum.

Many Excellent People: Power & Privilege in North Carolina, 1850-1900. Paul D. Escott. LC 84-28107. (Fred W. Morrison Series in Southern Studies). xxii, 344p. 1988. reprint ed. pap. 18.95 (0-8078-4228-1) U of NC Pr.

Many-Eyed Landscapes. Ed. by Peggy Z. Lynch & Edmund C. Lynch. (Illus.). 88p. 1991. lib. bdg. 10.95 (1-878149-05-9) Counterpoint Pub.

Many Faces: An Anthology of Oregon Autobiography. Ed. by Stephen D. Beckham. (Oregon Literature Ser.: Vol. 2). (Illus.). 352p. (Orig.). 1993. pap. 21.95 (0-87071-372-8); text 35.95 (0-87071-371-X) Oreg St U Pr.

Many Faces - Many Spaces: Artists of Ontario. Olga Dey-Bergmoser & Khaletum Majumder. (Illus.). 128p. 1993. 29.95 (0-88962-350-3) Mosaic.

***Many Faces, Many Microbes: Personal Reflections in Microbiology.** Ed. by Ronald Atlas. (Illus.). 340p. 2000. pap. 39.95 (1-55581-190-6) ASM Pr.

Many Faces, Many Visions: The Story of Montrose, Colorado. Elaine H. Jones. 80p. 1995. pap. write for info. (0-9647490-0-9) E H Jones.

Many Faces, Many Voices: Multicultural Literary Experience for Youth. Virginia Hamilton Conference Staff. Ed. by Anthony L. Manna & Carolyn S. Brodie. LC 92-31119. (Illus.). 183p. 1993. pap. text 19.00 (0-917846-12-5, 95516) Highsmith Pr.

***Many Faces Mata Ortiz: The Postcard Book.** Susan Lowell et al. (Illus.). 32p. 2000. pap. 9.95 (1-887896-19-8, Rio Nuevo) Treas Chest Bks.

Many Faces of Abuse: Treating the Emotional Abuse of High-Functioning Women. Joan Lachkar. 240p. 1998. 50.00 (0-7657-0065-4) Aronson.

Many Faces of Angels. Harvey Humann. LC 86-72703. (Illus.). 107p. (Orig.). 1987. pap. 9.95 (0-87516-586-9) DeVorss.

Many Faces of Anti-Semitism. George Salomon & Rose Feitelson. 44p. 1978. 1.50 (0-87495-045-7) Am Jewish Comm.

Many Faces of Babylon: The Babylonian Influences upon Our Churches. 2nd rev. ed. Paul Hunter. (Illus.). 208p. 1994. reprint ed. pap. 10.00 (0-9642820-1-1) Revelation NY.

Many Faces of Bereavement: The Nature & Treatment of Natural, Traumatic & Stigmatized Grief. Ginny Sprang & John McNeill. 216p. 1995. text 28.95 (0-87630-756-X) Brunner-Mazel.

Many Faces of Cuilapan: A Historical Digest of a Sixteenth-Century Dominican Monastery & Church Complex & Village, Oaxaca, Mexico. Eleanor F. Sleight. LC 88-60066. (Illus.). 200p. 1988. 25.00 (0-9619949-0-8) E F Sleight.

Many Faces of Deceit: Omissions, Lies & Disguise in Psychotherapy. Helen K. Gediman & Janice S. Lieberman. LC 95-18353. 272p. 1996. 45.00 (1-56821-592-4) Aronson.

Many Faces of Dependency in Old Age. Margret M. Baltes. (Illus.). 203p. (C). 1996. text 54.95 (0-521-49684-5); pap. text 16.95 (0-521-49804-X) Cambridge U Pr.

Many Faces of Dyslexia. Margaret B. Rawson. 270p. 1992. pap. 18.50 (0-89214-003-8) Intl Dyslexia.

Many Faces of Eros: A Psychoanalytic Exploration of Human Sexuality. Joyce McDougall. 256p. 1995. 30.00 (0-393-70215-4) Norton.

Many Faces of Evil: Reflections on the Sinful, the Tragic, the Demonic & the Ambiguous. Kenneth Cauthen. LC 96-38674. (Orig.). 1997. pap. 14.95 (0-7880-1004-2) CSS OH.

Many Faces of Evil: The Study Guide. Kenneth Cauthen. 1997. 8.95 (0-7880-1070-0) CSS OH.

Many Faces of Faith. John H. Hampsch. 16p. 1997. pap. 1.25 (1-57918-026-4, 7126) Queenship Pub.

Many Faces of Gay: Activists Who Are Changing the Nation. Arthur D. Kahn. LC 96-26283. 352p. 1997. 45.00 (0-275-95366-1, Praeger Pubs) Greenwood.

Many Faces of Giftedness: Lifting the Mask. Alexinia Y. Baldwin & Wilma Vialle. LC 98-10691. (C). 1998. pap. 46.95 (0-7668-0006-7) Delmar.

Many Faces of Homosexuality: Anthropological Approaches to Homosexual Behavior. Ed. by Evelyn Blackwood. LC 85-17757. (Journal of Homosexuality Ser.: Vol. 11, Nos. 3 & 4). 217p. 1986. pap. 19.95 (0-918393-20-5, Harrington Park) Haworth Pr.

Many Faces of Imitation in Language Learning. Ed. by G. Speidel & K. E. Nelson. (Language & Communication Ser.: Vol. 24). (Illus.). 390p. 1989. 137.00 (0-387-96885-7) Spr-Verlag.

Many Faces of India, Nepal & the Philippines. Pepper Worthington. (Illus.). 310p. (Orig.). 1995. pap. 25.00 (1-880994-32-1) Mt Olive Coll Pr.

***Many Faces of Islam.** Nissim Rejwan. LC 00-32587. 2000. write for info. (0-8130-1807-2) U Press Fla.

Many Faces of Jack the Ripper. M. J. Trow. 192p. 1998. 25.95 (1-84024-016-4, Pub. by Summers) Howell Pr VA.

Many Faces of Judaism: Orthodox, Conservative, Reconstructionist, & Reform. Moshe Ben-Aharon et al. Ed. by Seymour Rossel. LC 78-25898. 1979. pap., teacher ed. 14.95 (0-87441-339-7) Behrman.

Many Faces of Judaism: Orthodox, Conservative, Reconstructionist, & Reform. Gilbert S. Rosenthal. Ed. by Seymour Rossel. LC 78-25898. (YA). (gr. 9-10). 1979. pap. 7.95 (0-87441-311-7) Behrman.

Many Faces of Judaism: Orthodox, Conservative, Reconstructionist, & Reform. Ellen Singer et al. Ed. by Seymour Rossel. LC 78-25898. (YA). (gr. 9-10). 1979. pap., wbk. ed. 4.95 (0-87441-332-X) Behrman.

***Many Faces of Leadership.** Taking the Lead Staff. (Leadership Ser.). (Illus.). 42p. 2000. pap. text 14.95 (1-930390-00-9, Taking The Lead) Ctr for Career Dev in Educ.

Many Faces of Lincoln: Selected Articles from the Lincoln Herald. Ed. by Charles M. Hubbard et al. LC 97-70467. (Illus.). 390p. 1997. pap. 19.95 (1-878044-53-2) Mayhaven Pub.

Many Faces of Long-Term Care: Today's Bitter Pill or Tommorrow's Cure : Hearing Before the Special Committee on Aging, United States Senate, One Hundred Fifth Congress, First Session, Las Vegas, NV, January 12, 1998, Reno, NV, January 13, 1998. United States Staff. LC 98-175718. (Real Lives Ser.). iv, 426 p. 1998. write for info. (0-16-056532-4) USGPO.

Many Faces of Mary: A Love Story. Bob Lord & Penny Lord. (Illus.). 242p. (Orig.). 1987. 13.95 (0-926143-06-9); pap. 9.95 (0-926143-07-7) Journeys Faith.

Many Faces of Mary: A Love Story see Muchos Rostros de Maria: Una Storia di Amor

Many Faces of Mata Ortiz. Susan Lowell et al. (Illus.). 224p. 1999. 50.00 (1-887896-18-X, Rio Nuevo); pap. 29.95 (1-887896-08-2, Rio Nuevo) Treas Chest Bks.

Many Faces of Mexico. Charlene Wear Simmons et al. 66p. 1997. pap. write for info. (1-58703-058-6) CA St Libry.

Many Faces of Mexico. 2nd rev. ed. Meredith Sommers et al. (Illus.). 352p. (YA). (gr. 7-12). 1998. pap. text 39.95 (0-9617743-9-8) Res Ctr Amer.

Many Faces of Michael Jackson. Lee Pinkerton. LC 98-178581. (Illus.). 62p. 1997. pap. text 16.95 (0-7119-6783-0, 02100023, Pub. by Ozone Bks) Omnibus NY.

Many Faces of Modern Architecture: Building in Germany Between the World Wars. Ed. by John Zukowsky. (Illus.). 256p. 1994. 75.00 (3-7913-1366-5, Pub. by Prestel) te Neues.

Many Faces of Murukan: The History & Meaning of a South Indian God. Fred W. Clothey. (Religion & Society Ser.: No. 6). 1978. text 83.85 (90-279-7632-5) Mouton.

Many Faces of National Security in the Arab World. Ed. by Bahgat Korany et al. LC 92-19906. 1993. text 49.95 (0-312-08368-8) St Martin.

Many Faces of National Security in the Arab World. Ed. by Bahgat Korany et al. (International Political Economy Ser.). 344p. (C). 1993. pap. 19.95 (0-312-08378-5) St Martin.

Many Faces of Neutron Stars. R. Buccheri et al. LC 98-28190. (NATO ASI Ser.). 608p. 1998. 80.00 (0-7923-5194-0) Kluwer Academic.

Many Faces of Pamela. Jane V. Bertolino. (Literary Criticism Ser.). 138p. (Orig.). (C). 1990. pap. 12.00 (0-921252-12-9) LEGAS.

Many Faces of Passion. Carmen M. Pursifull. LC 95-82261. (Illus.). 112p. 1996. pap. 10.00 (1-881900-04-5) Hawk Prods.

Many Faces of Play. Association for the Anthropological Study of Play, Meeting (9th: 1983: Baton Rouge, LA) Staff. Ed. by Kendall Blanchard et al. LC 85-30602. (Association for the Anthropological Study of Play Ser.: No. 9). (Illus.). 288p. reprint ed. pap. 89.30 (0-608-06454-8, 206729200009) Bks Demand.

Many Faces of Play. Association for the Anthropological Study of Play, Meeting (9th: 1983: Baton Rouge, LA) Staff. Ed. by Kendall Blanchard et al. LC 85-30602. 288p. reprint ed. pap. 89.30 (0-608-20820-5, 207191900003) Bks Demand.

***Many Faces of Prejudice.** BRANSCOMBE SPEARS. 2001. pap. 46.00 (0-534-57133-6) Thomson Learn.

Many Faces of RNA. Ed. by Drake Eggleston et al. LC 97-45534. (Illus.). 240p. 1998. text 99.95 (0-12-233210-5) Morgan Kaufmann.

Many Faces of Sandinista Democracy. Katherine C. Hoyt. LC 96-43208. (Monographs in International Studies, Latin America Ser.: Vol. 27). 204p. (Orig.). (C). 1997. pap. text 23.00 (0-89680-197-7) Ohio U Pr.

***Many Faces of Science.** Byerly. 2000. 65.00 (0-8133-6550-3, Pub. by Westview) HarpC.

***Many Faces of Science.** 2nd ed. Byerly. 304p. 2000. pap. 25.00 (0-8133-6551-1, Pub. by Westview) HarpC.

Many Faces of Science: Scientists, Values & Society. Leslie Stevenson & Henry Byerly. LC 94-46510. 257p. (C). 1995. pap. 25.00 (0-8133-2017-8, Pub. by Westview) HarpC.

Many Faces of Shame. Ed. by Donald L. Nathanson. LC 86-31937. 370p. 1987. lib. bdg. 47.00 (0-89862-705-2) Guilford Pubns.

Many Faces of Slavery. Alexia J. Helsley. LC 99-458892. 1999. pap. text 14.25 (1-880067-52-8) SC Dept of Arch & Hist.

Many Faces of Socialism: Essays in Comparative Sociology & Politics. Paul Hollander. LC 82-19458. 362p. 1983. 44.95 (0-87855-480-7); pap. 24.95 (0-88738-740-3) Transaction Pubs.

Many Faces of Teaching. Ed. by Thomas H. Buxton et al. LC 86-26648. 504p. (Orig.). 1987. pap. text 34.00 (0-8191-5764-3); lib. bdg. 62.00 (0-8191-5763-5) U Pr of Amer.

Many Faces of the Christ: The Christologies of the New Testament & Beyond. Ben Witherington, III. LC 97-37547. (Companion to the New Testament Ser.). 1998. pap. 19.95 (0-8245-1705-9) Crossroad NY.

Many Faces of the Divine. Ed. by Hermann Haring et al. 150p. (Orig.). 1995. pap. 15.00 (0-88344-883-1) Orbis Bks.

***Many Faces of the Face.** Brigitte Baumbusch. LC 99-15470. (Art for Children Ser.). (Illus.). 29p. (J). (ps-3). 1999. pap. 9.95 (1-55670-968-4) Stewart Tabori & Chang.

Many Faces of the Hero: Odysseus, Theseus & Jason. Robert Wilhelm. (Ancient Greek & Roman Resource Ser.). (Illus.). 100p. 24.95 (1-56696-137-8) Jackdaw.

Many Faces of the Sun: A Summary of Results from NASA's Solar Maximum Mission. Ed. by K. Strong et al. LC 98-11970. (Illus.). 624p. 1998. 79.00 (0-387-98481-X) Spr-Verlag.

***Many Faces of the Superworld: Yuri Golf & Memorial Volume.** M. A. Shifman. 1999. 103.00 (981-02-4206-9) World Scientific Pub.

Many Faces of William Shakespeare. Jeffrey W. Ryback. Ed. by William-Alan Landes. LC 97-20145. 51p. (Orig.). 1997. pap. 6.00 (0-88734-245-0) Players Pr.

Many Faces of Zane Grey. G. M. Garley. 1976. 23.95 (0-8488-0267-5) Amereon Ltd.

Many-Facet Rasch Measurement. 2nd ed. John M. Linacre. LC 94-76939. (Illus.). 157p. 1994. pap. text 30.00 (0-941938-02-6) Mesa Pr.

Many-Faceted Jacksonian Era: New Interpretations, 67. Edward Pessen. LC 77-24621. (Contributions in American History Ser.: No. 67). (Illus.). 331p. 1977. 59.95 (0-8371-9720-1, PJE/, Greenwood Pr) Greenwood.

Many Facets of Chemistry: Reflections & Changes. Olah. 300p. 24.95 (0-471-15743-0) Wiley.

Many Facets of Nuclear Physics. Ed. by A. Molinari et al. 288p. (C). 1989. text 86.00 (9971-5-0630-0) World Scientific Pub.

Many Facets of Stephen King. Michael R. Collings. LC 85-12598. (Starmont Studies in Literary Criticism: No. 11). (Illus.). vi, 190p. 1985. pap. 21.00 (0-930261-14-3) Millefleurs.

Many Facets of Touch. Catherine C. Brown et al. (Pediatric Round Table Ser.: No. 10). 207p. 1984. 10.00 (0-931562-12-0) J & J Consumer Prods.

Many Families, Many Literacies. Denny Taylor. 1997. pap. 19.95 (0-614-28104-0) Heinemann.

Many Families, Many Literacies: An International Declaration of Principles. Ed. by Denny Taylor. LC 97-7124. 1997. pap. 25.95 (0-435-08130-6) Heinemann.

Many Fires. Kathleen Sage. 352p. (Orig.). 1995. mass mkt. 5.99 (0-515-11781-1, Jove) Berkley Pub.

Many Friends Many Colors. Charles L. Cleek. (Illus.). 44p. (gr. 3-8). 1997. pap. write for info. (0-9660543-0-X) GIFTGO.

Many Furrows. Alfred G. Gardiner. LC 77-121469. (Essay Index Reprint Ser.). 1977. 20.95 (0-8369-1807-X) Ayer.

Many Futures, Many Worlds: Theme & Form in Science Fiction. Ed. by Thomas D. Clareson. LC 76-42448. 313p. reprint ed. pap. 97.10 (0-7837-1357-6, 204150500020) Bks Demand.

Many Generations of Davis Dimock Cheever, 1851-1920, Lest We Forget. Robert D. Lawrence. (Illus.). 64p. 1983. pap. text 5.00 (0-9617907-0-9) Lawrence KS.

Many Gifts for the Multi-Talented Man see Ild'anach Ild'irech: A Festschrift for Proinsias Mac Cana

Many Glancing Colours: An Essay in Reading Tennyson, 1809-1850. Kenneth M. McKay. 301p. 1988. text 40.00 (0-8020-2658-3) U of Toronto Pr.

Many Gods & Many Voices: The Role of the Prophet in English & American Modernism. Louis L. Martz. LC 97-40320. (Illus.). 248p. 1998. 34.95 (0-8262-1148-8) U of Mo Pr.

Many Gods, Many Lords: Christianity Encounters World Religions. Daniel B. Clendenin. LC 95-39849. 192p. 1996. pap. 11.99 (0-8010-2059-X) Baker Bks.

Many Hands: Making a Communal Quilt. Elaine Miles. (Illus.). 75p. (Orig.). 1982. 6.95 (0-936810-02-5) M & M.

Many Hands Counting Book: Level One, Red. Illus. by Brita Granstrom. LC 98-88073. (Reading Together Ser.). 32p. (J). 1999. pap. write for info. (0-7636-0853-X) Candlewick Pr.

Many Hands, Many Miracles. Dan Madigan & Ann Bancroft. LC 97-1801. 1997. pap. 16.00 (0-268-01426-4) U of Notre Dame Pr.

Many Hands of My Relations: French & Indians on the Lower Missouri. Tanis C. Thorne. (Illus.). 320p. (C). 1996. 39.95 (0-8262-1083-X) U of Mo Pr.

Many Happy Returns. Mary B. Craft. LC 96-86072. 38p. (Orig.). 1996. pap. 4.95 (1-56883-065-3) Colonial Pr AL.

Many Happy Returns: How to Return Unwanted, Used or Old Items for Cash Refunds. Tiina Harris. LC 88-70877. 1988. 14.95 (0-929419-00-6); pap. 9.95 (0-929419-01-4) Bountiful Pr.

Many Happy Returns: Recollections of a Great Grandmother, Grandmother, Mothers & a Daughter. Vivian B. Kline et al. (Illus.). 161p. 1998. pap. 19.95 (0-9635046-1-4) Vidan Pr.

Many Happy Returns & Fast Women: Two One Act Plays. Willie Reale. 1983. pap. 3.25 (0-8222-0729-X) Dramatists Play.

Many Hats Many Faces. (Illus.). 83p. 1995. write for info. (0-9653945-1-4) N Shepard Arts.

Many Hats of Mr. Minches. unabridged ed. Paulette Bourgeois. (Illus.). 32p. (J). (ps up). 1994. 12.95 (0-7737-2839-2) STDK.

Many Hats of Mr. Minches. unabridged ed. Paulette Bourgeois. (Illus.). 32p. (J). (ps up). 1996. pap. 7.95 (0-7737-5703-1) STDK.

***Many-Headed Hydra: The Hidden History of the Revolutionary Atlantic.** Peter Linebaugh & Marcus Rediker. LC 00-8881. (Illus.). 352p. 2000. pap. 30.00 (0-8070-5006-7) Beacon Pr.

Many Heads, Arms & Eyes: Origin, Meaning & Form of Multiplicity in Indian Art. Doris M. Srinivasan. LC 97-11187. (Studies in Asian Art & Archaeology, Continuation of Studies in South Asian Culture: Vol. 20). xii, 436p. 1997. 159.50 (90-04-10758-4) Brill Academic Pubs.

Many Hearts & Many Hands: The History of Ferry Hall & Lake Forest Academy. Jay Pridmore. Ed. by Anne Gendler. 264p. 1994. 50.00 (0-9643350-0-X) Lke Forest Acad.

Many Hills Yet to Climb. John Minassian. 300p. (Orig.). 1986. pap. write for info. (0-936941-00-6) Jim Cook.

"Many Histories Deep" The Personal Landscape Poets in Egypt, 1940-45. rev. ed. Roger Bowen. LC 94-34717. (Illus.). 248p. 1995. 39.50 (0-8386-3567-9) Fairleigh Dickinson.

Many Horses (Sequel to Quest for Courage) Stormy Rudolph. (Indian Culture Ser.). (Illus.). 79p. (J). (gr. 4-10). 1987. pap. 8.95 (0-89992-112-4) Coun India Ed.

Many Houses. Charles Gullans. 40p. 1981. 30.00 (0-936576-04-9) Symposium Pr.

***Many Indias, Many Literatures: New Critical Essays.** Panja. 1999. 20.00 (81-86423-34-6, Pub. by Gyan Publishing Hse) S Asia.

Many Infallible Proofs: Evidences for the Christian Faith. Henry M. Morris. LC 74-81484. 400p. 1997. pap. 11.95 (0-89051-005-9) Master Bks.

Many Landfalls of John Cabot. Peter E. Pope. LC 98-112689. (Illus.). 208p. 1997. pap. 17.95 (0-8020-7150-3); text 50.00 (0-8020-0786-4) U of Toronto Pr.

Many Latitudes. Fryniwyd T. Jesse. LC 76-116957. (Short Story Index Reprint Ser.). 1977. reprint ed. 20.95 (0-8369-3461-X) Ayer.

Many Laughs for Many Days. Irvin S. Cobb. (Collected Works of Irvin S. Cobb). 243p. 1998. reprint ed. lib. bdg. 88.00 (1-58201-600-3) Classic Bks.

Many Lifetimes. Joan Grant & Denys Kelsey. 240p. 1997. pap. 12.95 (0-89804-161-9) Ariel GA.

Many Lifetimes. Denys Kelsey & Joan M. Grant. 1980. 25.95 (0-405-11786-8) Ayer.

Many Lights in Many Windows: Twenty Years of Great Fictions & Poetry from the Writers Community. Ed. by Laurel Blossom. LC 97-11722. 324p. (Orig.). 1997. pap. 16.95 (1-57131-218-8) Milkweed Ed.

Many Literacies: Modules for Training Adult Beginning Readers & Tutors. Marilyn Gillespie. (Illus.). 140p. (Orig.). 1990. spiral bd. 12.50 (0-932288-83-9) Ctr Intl Ed U of MA.

***Many Lives.** M. R. Kukrit Pramoj. Tr. by Meredith Borthwick. 240p. 2000. pap. 14.50 (974-7100-67-3, Pub. by Silk Worm Bks) U of Wash Pr.

Many Lives & Secret Sorrows of Josephine B. A Novel. Sandra Gulland. LC 98-51453. 448p. 1999. per. 14.00 (0-684-85606-9, Scribner Pap Fic) S&S Trade Pap.

Many Lives, Many Masters. Brian L. Weiss. 224p. 1988. per. 11.00 (0-671-65786-0) S&S Trade.

Many Lives of Academic Presidents: Association of Governing Boards & Universities & Colleges. Clark Kerr & Marian L. Gade. 260p. 1986. 26.00 (0-318-21457-1) Assn Gov Bds.

Many Lives of Andrew Carnegie. Milton Meltzer. LC 96-40144. (Meltzer Biographies Ser.). 160p. (YA). (gr. 7 up). 1997. lib. bdg. 28.00 (0-531-11427-9) Watts.

Many Lives of Andrew Carnegie. Milton Meltzer. LC 96-40144. (Milton Meltzer Biographies Ser.). (J). 1997. write for info. (0-531-11388-4) Watts.

Many Lives of Benjamin Franklin. Mary Pope Osborne. (Illus.). (J). (gr. 5 up). 1990. 13.95 (0-685-31008-6, Dial Yng Read) Peng Put Young Read.

Many Lives of Elton John. Susan Crimp & Patricia Burstein. (Illus.). 288p. 1992. 19.95 (1-55972-111-1, Birch Ln Pr) Carol Pub Group.

Many Lives of Ministry Wives. Sharon Hoffman. Ed. by Cindy G. Spear. 8p. 1997. 19.95 incl. audio (1-57052-086-0) Chrch Grwth VA.

Many Lives of Yokasta Sneed. Judy L. Vernon. 130p. (Orig.). 1987. pap. 7.95 (0-9617776-3-X) J Vernon.

Many Loves & Other Plays. William C. Williams. LC 61-9334. 1965. pap. 9.95 (0-8112-0232-1, NDP191, Pub. by New Directions) Norton.

Many Loves of Dobie Gillis. Max Shulman. 107p. (YA). (gr. 7 up). 1961. pap. 5.50 (0-87129-925-9, M16) Dramatic Pub.

Many Loves of Dobie Gillis. Max Shulman. 220p. reprint ed. lib. bdg. 21.95 (0-89190-982-6, Rivercity Pr) Amereon Ltd.

Many Loves of Dobie Gillis. Max Shulman. 1993. reprint ed. lib. bdg. 19.95 (1-56849-221-9) Buccaneer Bks.

M

An Asterisk (*) at the beginning of an entry indicates that the title is appearing for the first time.

Many Luscious Lollipops: A Book about Adjectives. Ruth Heller. (Illus.). 48p. (J). (ps-3). 1989. 17.99 (0-448-03151-5, G & D) Peng Put Young Read.

Many Luscious Lollipops: A Book about Adjectives. Ruth Heller. (World of Language Ser.). (Illus.). 48p. (J). (gr. k-3). 1998. pap. 6.99 (0-698-11641-0, PapStar) Peng Put Young Read.

Many Luscious Lollipops: A Book about Adjectives. Ruth Heller. (J). 1992. 13.15 (0-606-05451-0, Pub. by Turtleback) Demco.

Many Mansions: A Christian's Encounter with Other Faiths. 2nd ed. Harvey Cox. LC 91-28603. 240p. 1992. pap. 13.00 (0-8070-1213-0) Beacon Pr.

Many Mansions: An Introduction to the Development & Diversity of Medieval Theology. David N. Bell. 1996. 34.95 (0-614-19804-6) Cistercian Pubns.

Many Mansions: An Introduction to the Development & Diversity of Medieval Theology. David N. Bell. LC 96-213134. (Illus.). 1996. pap. 15.95 (0-87907-546-5) Cistercian Pubns.

Many Mansions: The Edgar Cayce Story. Gina Cerminara. 291p. 1988. mass mkt. 6.99 (0-451-16817-8) NAL.

Many, Many Times. James Riddell. LC 98-76192. 250p. 1999. write for info. (1-893766-03-9) Aeon Pub Co.

Many Marriages. Sherwood Anderson. (Collected Works of Sherwood Anderson). 290p. 1998. reprint ed. lib. bdg. 88.00 (1-58201-502-3) Classic Bks.

Many Marriages by Sherwood Anderson. Ed. by Douglas G. Rogers. LC 78-2353. 316p. 1978. 31.00 (0-8108-1122-7) Scarecrow.

Many Masks: A Life of Frank Lloyd Wright. Brendan Gill. LC 98-17356. (Illus.). 544p. 1998. reprint ed. pap. 17.95 (0-306-80872-2) Da Capo.

Many Meanings of Play: A Psychoanalytic Perspective. Ed. by Albert J. Solnit et al. LC 92-48988. 358p. (C). 1993. 42.50 (0-300-05438-6) Yale U Pr.

Many Mexicos. 4th rev. ed. Lesley B. Simpson. LC 66-19101. (Illus.). 405p. reprint ed. pap. 125.60 (0-7837-4675-X, 204442100003) Bks Demand.

Many Mexicos: Silver Anniversary Edition. rev. ed. Lesley B. Simpson. (YA). (gr. 9 up). 1966. pap. 17.95 (0-520-01180-5, Pub. by U CA Pr) Cal Prin Full Svc.

Many Miles to Bethlehem: Stories for Advent & Christmas. Dina Strong. (Storyteller Ser.). (Illus.). 32p. (J). 1996. pap. 4.95 (1-889108-10-3) Liv Good News.

Many Miles to Bethlehem Storyteller's Kit: Stories for Advent & Christmas. Dina Strong & Liz Riggleman. (Storyteller Ser.). 16p. (J). 1996. pap., suppl. ed. 4.95 (1-889108-13-8) Liv Good News.

Many Minds. Maurice Hutton. LC 71-99703. (Essay Index Reprint Ser.). 1977. 23.95 (0-8369-1415-5) Ayer.

Many Minds. Carl Van Doren. LC 73-17657. 242p. 1975. reprint ed. lib. bdg. 59.50 (0-8371-7261-6, VAMM, Greenwood Pr) Greenwood.

Many Minds. Carl Van Doren. (BCL1-PS American Literature Ser.). 242p. 1992. reprint ed. lib. bdg. 79.00 (0-7812-6625-4) Rprt Serv.

Many Minds: Information for People Who Have Multiple Personalities. Lauren Lund & David Lund. (Illus.). 34p. (Orig.). 1993. pap. text 4.95 (0-9637149-0-2) Soft Words.

Many Mirrors: Body Image & Social Relations. Ed. by Nicole Sault. LC 93-37997. 360p. (C). 1994. text 45.00 (0-8135-2079-7); pap. text 16.95 (0-8135-2080-0) Rutgers U Pr.

Many Moods: A Volume of Verse. John A. Symonds. 1988. reprint ed. lib. bdg. 49.00 (0-7812-0129-2) Rprt Serv.

Many Moods: A Volume of Verse. John A. Symonds. LC 74-115280. (Illus.). 1970. reprint ed. 29.00 (0-403-00275-3) Scholarly.

Many Moons. Diana Brueton. 1992. per. 16.00 (0-13-553355-4) P-H.

Many Moons. Diana Brueton. (Illus.). 256p. 1992. pap. 14.00 (0-671-76801-8, Fireside) S&S Trade Pap.

Many Moons. James Thurber. LC 43-51250. (Illus.). 45p. (J). (gr. 1-5). 1943. 16.00 (0-15-251873-8, Harcourt Child Bks) Harcourt.

Many Moons. James Thurber. LC 89-36465. (Illus.). 48p. (J). (ps-3). 1998. pap. 7.00 (0-15-201895-6) Harcourt.

Many Moons. James Thurber. 1943. 12.20 (0-606-03914-7, Pub. by Turtleback) Demco.

Many Moons. James Thurber. 1946. 5.50 (0-87129-414-1, M17) Dramatic Pub.

Many Moons. James Thurber. LC 43-51250. (Voyager Picture Bks.). (Illus.). 45p. (J). (gr. 1-5). 1973. reprint ed. pap. 7.00 (0-15-656980-9, Voyager Bks) Harcourt.

Many Moons: Featuring New Artwork. James Thurber. LC 89-36465. (Illus.). 48p. (J). (ps-3). 1990. 14.95 (0-15-251872-X) Harcourt.

Many More Mountains, Vol. 2. Allen Nossaman. (Illus.). 352p. 1993. 39.00 (0-913582-57-3) Sundance.

Many More Mountains Vol. 3: Rails into Silverton. Allen Nossaman. (Illus.). 352p. 1998. 39.00 (0-913582-64-6, 0258) Sundance.

Many Mountains Moving, Vol. 1 No. 2. Ed. by Naomi Horii & Marilyn Krysl. (Illus.). 144p. 1995. pap. 6.50 (1-886976-00-7) Many Mntns.

Many Mountains Moving, Vol. 2 No. 3. Michael Ramos. (Illus.). 170p. 1996. pap. 6.50 (1-886976-05-8) Many Mntns.

Many Mountains Moving, Vol. 3, No. 1. Homero Aridjis et al. (Illus.). 1996. pap. 6.50 (1-886976-06-6) Many Mntns.

***Many Mountains Moving, Vol. 3, No. 2.** 215p. 1999. pap. 6.50 (1-886976-07-4, Pub. by Many Mntns) SPD-Small Pr Dist.

***Many Mountains Moving, Vol. 3, No. 3.** 191p. 1999. pap. 6.50 (1-886976-08-2, Pub. by Many Mntns) SPD-Small Pr Dist.

Many Mountains Moving Vol. 1 No. 3: Feature: Poets from India. Tr. by Peter Michelson. (Illus.). 176p. 1995. pap. 6.50 (1-886976-02-3) Many Mntns.

Many Mountains Moving Vol. 2 No. 1: Burning Issues. Ed. by Luis A. Urrea. (Illus.). 190p. 1995. pap. 6.50 (1-886976-03-1) Many Mntns.

Many Mountains to Climb: Lessons on the True Meaning of Success from the First American Woman to Top Mt. Everest. Stacy Allison. LC 99-38520. 270p. 1999. pap. 15.95 (1-58151-011-X) BookPartners.

Many Mouthed Birds: Contemporary Writings by Chinese Canadians. Ed. by Bennett Lee & Jim Wong-Chu. LC 91-19664. 250p. 1991. 26.95 (0-295-97149-5) U of Wash Pr.

Many Names of Country People: An Historical Dictionary from the Twelfth Century Onward. John T. Schlebecker. LC 88-16549. 337p. 1989. lib. bdg. 65.00 (0-313-26417-1, SYN/, Greenwood Pr) Greenwood.

Many Nations: A Library of Congress Resource Guide for the Study of Indian & Alaska Native Peoples of the United States. Ed. by Patrick Frazier. (Illus.). 334p. (Orig.). 1997. pap. text 50.00 (0-7881-3988-6) DIANE Pub.

Many Nations: A Library of Congress Resource Guide for the Study of Indian & Alaska Native Peoples of the United States. Library of Congress Staff. Ed. by Patrick Frazier. LC 96-42503. (Library of Congress Resource Guide Ser.). (Illus.). 334p. 1996. pap. 33.00 (0-8444-0904-9) Lib Congress.

Many Nations: An Alphabet of Native America. Joseph Bruchac. LC 97-12271. (Illus.). 32p. (J). (ps-2). 1997. 15.95 (0-8167-4389-4) BrdgeWater.

Many Nations: An Alphabet of Native America. Joseph Bruchac. (Illus.). 32p. (J). (ps-2). 1998. pap. 5.95 (0-8167-4460-2) Troll Communs.

Many Nations: Library of Congress Resource Guide for Study of Indian & Alaska Native Peoples of the United States. Patrick Frazier. 354p. 1996. per. 38.00 (0-16-061804-5, Library of Cong) USGPO.

Many Nations Under God. Silhouette Romances Staff. LC 97-199907. (Illus.). 144p. 1997. pap. text 7.99 (1-56309-194-1, N973108, New Hope) Womans Mission Union.

Many-Particle Dynamics & Kinetic Equations. Carlo Cercignani et al. Tr. by K. Petrina & V. Gredzhuk from RUS. LC 97-23958. (Mathematics & Its Applications Ser.: Vol. 420). 244p. 1997. text 164.00 (0-7923-4696-3) Kluwer Academic.

Many-Particle Hamiltonians: Spectra & Scattering. R. Minlos. (Advances in Soviet Matheamtics Ser.: Vol. 5). 194p. 1991. text 75.00 (0-8218-4104-1, ADVSOV/5) Am Math.

Many-Particle Physics. 2nd ed. G. D. Mahan. (Physics of Solids & Liquids Ser.). (Illus.). 1046p. (C). 1990. text 145.00 (0-306-43423-7, Kluwer Plenum) Kluwer Academic.

***Many-Particle Physics.** 3rd ed. Gerald D. Mahan. LC 00-39101. (Physics of Solids & Liquids Ser.). (Illus.). 2000. write for info. (0-306-46338-5, Kluwer Plenum) Kluwer Academic.

Many-Particle Theory. E. K. Gross et al. (Illus.). 448p. 1991. 223.00 (0-7503-0072-8); pap. 61.00 (0-7503-0155-4) IOP Pub.

Many Paths: A Catholic Approach to Religious Pluralism. Eugene Hillman. LC 88-37470. (Faith Meets Faith Ser.). 112p. (Orig.). reprint ed. pap. 34.80 (0-608-20194-4, 207145300012) Bks Demand.

***Many Paths, One Spirit.** Utne Reader Staff. 2000. pap. write for info. (0-688-17453-1, Quil) HarperTrade.

Many Paths, One Truth. Carole Addelstone. LC 96-33087. (Illus.). 142p. (Orig.). 1997. lib. bdg. 26.95 (0-89334-264-5) Humanics Ltd.

Many Paths to God? Can You Choose Any Spiritual Path & Find God? Rose Zerra. (Orig.). 1992. pap. 0.50 (1-882187-00-8) Earth-Salt Bks.

Many Patrols. large type ed. R. D. Symons. 320p. 1995. pap. 17.95 (1-55050-083-X, Pub. by Coteau) Genl Dist Srvs.

Many Patrols: Reminiscences of a Conservation Officer. R. D. Symons. (Illus.). 320p. 1995. 12.95 (1-55050-073-2, Pub. by Coteau) Genl Dist Srvs.

Many People Many Faiths. 6th ed. Ellwood et al. LC 98-33937. 510p. (C). 1999. pap. 43.00 (0-13-010735-2) P-H.

Many People, One Nation. rev. ed. Bernard A. Weisberger. (American Heritage Library). 1987. pap. 10.64 (0-8281-1200-2) HM.

Many Peoples, Many Faiths: An Introduction to the Religious Life of Humankind. 5th ed. Robert S. Ellwood. LC 95-1201. 464p. 1995. 50.00 (0-13-183039-2) P-H.

***Many Peoples, One Land: A Guide to New Multicultural Literature for Children & Young Adults.** Alethea K. Helbig. LC 00-25111. 425p. 2000. 55.00 (0-313-30967-1) Greenwood.

Many Petals of the Lotus: Five Asian Buddhist Communities in Toronto. Janet McLellan. 352p. 1999. text 60.00 (0-8020-4421-2); pap. text 24.95 (0-8020-8225-4) U of Toronto Pr.

Many Pleasures of Ironwood. 2nd ed. Don Winslow. (Orig.). 1998. reprint ed. mass mkt. 6.95 (1-56333-661-8) Masquerade.

Many Presences of Christ. Ed. by David A. Lysik. LC 99-25798. 214p. 1999. pap. 16.00 (1-56854-313-1) Liturgy Tr Pubns.

Many Pretty Toys. Hazard Adams. LC 98-21577. (SUNY Series in Postmodern Culture). 256p. (C). 1999. text 31.50 (0-7914-4085-0) State U NY Pr.

Many Pretty Toys. Hazard Adams. LC 98-21577. (SUNY Series in Postmodern Culture). (C). 2000. pap. text 19.95 (0-7914-4086-9) State U NY Pr.

Many Rains Ago: A Historical & Theological Reflection on the Role of the Episcopate in the Evangelization of African Americans. Secretariat for Black Catholics Staff & National Conference of Catholic Bishops. 56p. (Orig.). (C). 1990. pap. 4.95 (1-55586-319-1) US Catholic.

Many Ramayanas: The Diversity of a Narrative Tradition in South Asia. Ed. by Paula Richman. LC 91-7273. 280p. 1991. 50.00 (0-520-07281-2, Pub. by U CA Pr); pap. 18.95 (0-520-07589-7, Pub. by U CA Pr) Cal Prin Full Svc.

Many Reasons Why: The American Involvement in Vietnam. Michael Charlton & Anthony Moncrieff. 250p. 1997. reprint ed. pap. text 10.00 (0-7881-5173-8) DIANE Pub.

Many Religions: One God. Carol R. Murphy. LC 66-30689. (Orig.). 1966. pap. 4.00 (0-87574-150-9) Pendle Hill.

***Many Religions, One Covenant.** Ratzinger Cardinal. 1999. pap. 11.95 (0-89870-753-6) Ignatius Pr.

Many Rivers to Cross. large type ed. Steve Frazee. LC 98-18670. 248p. 1998. pap. 21.95 (0-7838-0204-8, G K Hall & Co) Mac Lib Ref.

Many Rivers to Cross: Good Running Water, Trout & Remains of Wilderness. M. R. Montgomery. (Illus.). 256p. 1996. per. 12.00 (0-684-81829-9, Touchstone) S&S Trade Pap.

Many Rivers to Cross: Of Good Running Water, Native Trout & the Remains of Wilderness. M. R. Montgomery. 254p. 1999. reprint ed. text 22.00 (0-7881-6428-7) DIANE Pub.

Many Roads One Journ. Charlotte D. Kasl. LC 90-56435. 448p. 1992. pap. 17.00 (0-06-096518-5, Perennial) HarperTrade.

***Many Roads to Justice: The Law Related Work of Ford Foundation Grantees Around the World.** Mary McClymont & Stephen Golub. LC 99-89905. 2000. write for info. (0-916584-54-2) Ford Found.

***Many Rooms: Classic Religious Themes in Literature.** John C. Benzinger. 235p. 2000. pap. 19.95 (0-940121-54-9, Pub. by Cross Cultural Pubns) BookWorld.
This is an anthology of religious works by Anthony Burgess, Albert Camus, Stephen Crane, Jean Giano, Herman Hesse, C.S. Lewis, Joyce Carol Oates, N. Scott Peck, Chaim Potok, William Saroyan, Alexander Solzhenitsyn, John Steinbeck, John Updike & Alice Walker. Selected & introduced by Reverend John Bensinger, a theologian, chaplain & teacher for over thirty years. ***Publisher Paid Annotation.***

Many Rooms in a Winter Night. Ruth L. Schechter. 52p. (Orig.). 1989. pap. 8.95 (0-317-93455-4) Croton Review.

Many Roomsoms. Steve Jaech. (Orig.). 1982. pap. 3.00 (0-942648-00-5) Vardaman Pr.

Many Seasons of Love. Theodore K. Candan. 100p. 1999. pap. 9.95 (0-7392-0056-9, 2869) Morris Pubng.

Many Servants: An Introduction to Deacons. Ormonde Plater. LC 91-622. 218p. (Orig.). 1991. pap. 13.95 (1-56101-043-X) Cowley Pubns.

***Many Shades of Light: Reflections in Poetry.** Diana Hunter. 168p. 1999. pap. 24.95 (0-9673895-0-X) Great Spirit Enterp.

Many Shades of Red: State Policy & Collective Agriculture. Ed. by Mieke Meurs. LC 98-41936. 320p. 1998. 62.00 (0-8476-9038-5); pap. 21.95 (0-8476-9039-3) Rowman.

Many-Sided Franklin. Paul L. Ford. LC 73-38353. (Select Bibliographies Reprint Ser.). 1977. reprint ed. 37.95 (0-8369-6770-4) Ayer.

Many-Sided Franklin. Paul L. Ford. (Notable American Authors Ser.). 1992. reprint ed. lib. bdg. 75.00 (0-7812-2882-4) Rprt Serv.

Many Sides of a Woman's Heart, 2 vols. in 1. Brenda Hunter. 448p. 1997. 11.99 (0-88365-989-1) Galahad Bks.

Many Sides of America. Frazier. (C). 1996. pap. text 31.50 (0-15-502077-3, Pub. by Harcourt Coll Pubs) Harcourt.

Many Simple Things. Michael Hettich & Robert Bixby. 20p. 1997. pap. 6.00 (1-882983-37-8) March Street Pr.

Many Sleepless Nights: The World of Organ Transplantation. Lee Gutkind. LC 89-40585. 368p. 1990. reprint ed. pap. 15.95 (0-8229-5905-4) U of Pittsburgh Pr.

Many-Sorted Calculus Based on Resolution & Paramodulation. Christoph Walther. (Research Notes in Artificial Intelligence Ser.). 160p. (Orig.). (C). 1987. pap. text 36.95 (0-934613-49-4) Morgan Kaufmann.

Many-Sorted Logic & Its Applications. Ed. by Karl Meinke. LC 93-138982. (Wiley Professional Computing Ser.). (Illus.). 415p. 1993. reprint ed. pap. 128.70 (0-608-05263-9, 206580100001) Bks Demand.

Many Specialties, One Corps: A Pictorial History of the Medical Services [sic] Corps. David P. Gray. LC 97-3179. (Illus.). 1997. write for info. (0-89865-994-9) Donning Co.

Many Species Populations, Ecosystems, & Systems Analysis see Statistical Ecology

Many-Splendored Fishes of Hawaii. Gar Goodson. LC 84-40783. (Illus.). 96p. 1985. reprint ed. pap. 7.95 (0-8047-1270-0) Stanford U Pr.

Many Stars & More String Games. Camilla Gryski. LC 85-4875. (Illus.). 80p. (J). (gr. 3 up). 1985. pap. 7.95 (0-688-05792-6, Wm Morrow) Morrow Avon.

Many Steps. David Blot. 96p. (Orig.). (C). 1984. pap. text 4.50 (0-317-93601-8) D Blot Pubns.

***Many Stones.** Carolyn Coman. 2000. 15.95 (1-886910-55-3, Front Street) Front Str.

***Many Streams Make a River: Proceedings of National Conference on Community Systems Building & Services Integration, September 14-15, 1997.** Contrib. by National Conference on Community Systems-Building and Services Integration et al. LC 98-68316. (Illus.). 96p. 1998. pap. write for info. (1-57285-055-8) Nat Ctr Educ.

Many Strong & Beautiful Voices. Quinn Eli. LC 97-66638. (Illus.). 370p. 1997. 12.95 (0-7624-0168-0) Running Pr.

Many Tables: The Eucharist in the New Testament & Liturgy Today. Dennis E. Smith & Hal E. Taussig. LC 90-31941. 128p. (Orig.). (C). 1990. pap. text 10.00 (0-334-02443-9) TPI PA.

Many Tender Ties: Women in Fur-Trade Society, 1670-1870. Sylvia Van Kirk. LC 82-40457. (Illus.). 301p. 1983. pap. 17.95 (0-8061-1847-4) U of Okla Pr.

Many Thanks: A Book of Gratitude. Andrews & McMeel Staff. (Tiny Tomes Ser.). 1998. 3.95 (0-8362-5248-9) Andrews & McMeel.

***Many Thanks for the Blessings in My Life: A Gratitude Journal.** Illus. by Wendy Wegner. (Guided Journals). 128p. 1999. 11.99 (0-88088-246-8, Inspire Bks) Peter Pauper.

Many Thanks for the Things in My Life: A Guided Gratitude Journal. Illus. by Wendy Wegner & Lesley Ehlers. (Guided Journals). 128p. 1999. 11.99 (0-88088-214-X) Peter Pauper.

Many Thanks to You. Julie Otlewis. Ed. by Patrick Caton. 80p. (Orig.). 1996. pap. 7.95 (1-56245-249-5) Great Quotations.

Many Theories of the Business. Demetri Kantarelis. 59.95 (1-85972-650-X) Ashgate Pub Co.

Many Things in Parables: Expository Studies. Ronald S. Wallace. 226p. 1997. pap. 19.00 (1-57910-060-0) Wipf & Stock.

Many Things in Parables: Reflections for Life. Joseph Fictner. LC 88-17. 80p. 1988. pap. 7.95 (0-8189-0536-0) Alba.

Many Things to Tell You: Natural Poetry. Thomas E. Heinzen. 196p. (Orig.). 1996. pap. 10.00 (1-885778-14-7) Seaburn.

Many Thousand Gone: African Americans from Slavery to Freedom. Virginia Hamilton. (J). (gr. 4-9). 1995. pap. 12.00 (0-679-97936-0) Random.

Many Thousand Gone: African Americans from Slavery to Freedom. Virginia Hamilton. (J). 1997. 17.10 (0-606-12414-4, Pub. by Turtleback) Demco.

***Many Thousands Gone: The First Two Centuries of Slavery in North America.** Ira Berlin. LC 98-19336. (Illus.). 497p. 1998. 29.95 (0-674-81092-9) Belknap Pr.

***Many Thousands Gone: The First Two Centuries of Slavery in North America.** Ira Berlin. 2000. pap. 16.95 (0-674-00211-3) HUP.

Many Tongues of Literacy. Ray B. Browne. LC 92-71958. 201p. (C). 1992. 40.95 (0-87972-559-1); pap. 20.95 (0-87972-560-5) Bowling Green Univ Popular Press.

Many Troubles of Andy Russell. David A. Adler. LC 98-10788. (Illus.). 133p. (J). (gr. 3-5). 1998. 14.00 (0-15-201295-8) Harcourt.

Many Troubles of Andy Russell. David A. Adler. LC 98-10788. (Illus.). 144p. (J). 1999. pap. 4.95 (0-15-201900-6, Voyager Bks) Harcourt.

Many-Valued Approach to Deduction & Reasoning for Artificial Intelligence. Cary G. DeBessonet. (International Series in Engineering & Computer Science, VLSI, Computer Architecture, & Digital Screen Processing). 272p. 1991. text 102.00 (0-7923-9138-1) Kluwer Academic.

Many-Valued Logic. Nicholas Rescher. (Modern Revivals in Philosophy Ser.). 376p. 1993. 67.95 (0-7512-0274-6, Pub. by Gregg Revivals) Ashgate Pub Co.

Many-Valued Logics. Grzegorz Malinowski. LC 93-36413. (Oxford Logic Guides Ser.: No. 25). 138p. (C). 1994. text 45.00 (0-19-853787-5, Clarendon Pr) OUP.

Many-Valued Logics, Vol. 1. Leonard Bolc & P. Borowik. LC 92-34076. 1992. write for info. (3-540-55926-4); 69.95 (0-387-55926-4) Spr-Verlag.

Many-Valued Logics 2: Automated Reasoning & Practical Applications. L. Bolc & P. Borowik. xvi, 282p. 1998. 59.95 (3-540-64507-1) Spr-Verlag.

Many Verses! The Importance of Reading the Scriptures in Reformed Worship. Ernest Springer, III. 75p. (Orig.). pap. text 7.95 (0-9632557-2-X) Old Paths Pubns.

Many Visions Many Aims: A Cross-National Investigation of Curricular Intentions in School Mathematics. Ed. by William H. Schmidt et al. 1997. pap. text 55.00 (0-7923-4437-5) Kluwer Academic.

Many Visions Many Aims: A Cross-National Investigation of Curricular Intentions in School Mathematics, Vol. 2. Ed. by William H. Schmidt et al. LC 97-3667. 308p. 1997. 99.00 (0-7923-4438-3) Kluwer Academic.

Many Visions, Many Aims: A Cross-National Investigation of CUrricular Intentions in School Science, Vol. 2. Ed. by William H. Schmidt et al. 308p. 1997. pap. 49.00 (0-7923-4439-1) Kluwer Academic.

Many Visions Many Aims Vol. 1: A Cross-National Investigation of Curricular Intentions in School Mathematics. Ed. by William H. Schmidt et al. LC 97-3667. 1997. lib. bdg. 120.00 (0-7923-4436-7) Kluwer Academic.

Many Voices. Ed. by Mona Swann. LC 72-149166. (Granger Index Reprint Ser.). 1977. 23.95 (0-8369-6248-6) Ayer.

***Many Voices: A Multicultural Reader.** Watkins-Goffman, Linda & Richard W. Goffman. LC 99-56714. 2001. write for info. (0-13-975624-8) P-H.

Many Voices: Multicultural Reader. (C). 2001. pap. text 0.00 (0-13-016987-0) HEPC Inc.

Many Voices: Multicultural Responses to the Minor Prophets. Ed. by Alice O. Bellis. 116p. (Orig.). (C). 1995. pap. text 23.50 (0-8191-9837-4) U Pr of Amer.

An Asterisk (*) at the beginning of an entry indicates that the title is appearing for the first time.

Many Voices: Multicultural Responses to the Minor Prophets. Ed. by Alice O. Bellis. (Illus.). 116p. (Orig.). (C). 1995. lib. bdg. 42.00 (*0-8191-9836-6*) U Pr of Amer.

Many Voices: The Autobiography of a Medium. Eileen J. Garrett. (Collector's Library of the Unknown). 254p. 1991. reprint ed. write for info. (*0-8094-8079-4*); reprint ed. lib. bdg. write for info. (*0-8094-8080-8*) Time-Life.

Many Voices: True Tales from America's Past. National Storytelling Association Staff. Ed. by Mary C. Weaver. LC 95-21310. 224p. (J). 1995. pap. 14.95 (*1-879991-17-9*, Natl Storytell) Natl Storytlng Network.

Many Voices - Many Lands, Vol. I, No. 2. Ed. by Will Stratford. (Illus.). 160p. 1988. 45.00 (*0-940861-01-1*) Poetry Ctr Pr.

Many Voices - Many Lands, Vol. II, No. 2. Ed. by Will Stratford. (Illus.). 1989. 50.00 (*0-940861-03-8*) Poetry Ctr Pr.

Many Voices-Many Lands Vol. I, No. 1: Poetry Anthology. Ed. by Will Stratford. (Illus.). 160p. 1987. 45.00 (*0-940861-00-3*) Poetry Ctr Pr.

Many Voices, Many Opportunities: Cultural Pluralism & American Arts Policy. Clement A. Price. LC 93-34290. (Illus.). 96p. (Orig.). 1993. pap. 10.00 (*1-879903-16-4*, ACA Bks) Am for the Arts.

Many Voices, Many Rooms: A New Anthology of Alabama Writers. Ed. by Philip D. Beidler. LC 97-13084. 384p. 1997. pap. 22.95 (*0-8173-0904-7*); text 39.95 (*0-8173-0867-9*) U of Ala Pr.

Many Voices of Paws: A Workbook for Young Stutterers. Julie D. Reville. (Illus.). 64p. (J). (ps-3). 1989. 18.95 (*0-937857-11-4*, 1568) Speech Bin.

Many Voices, One God: Being Faithful in a Pluralistic World; In Honor of Shirley Guthrie. Shirley C. Guthrie. Ed. by Walter Brueggemann & George W. Stroup. LC 97-30707. 232p. 1998. pap. 28.95 (*0-664-25757-7*) Westminster John Knox.

Many Voices Teacher's Guide. Ed. by Mary C. Weaver. 96p. 1995. pap. 7.95 (*1-879991-20-9*) Natl Storytlng Network.

Many Waters. Madeleine L'Engle. 310p. (YA). (gr. 5-9). 1987. pap. 5.50 (*0-440-40548-3*) Dell.

Many Waters. Madeleine L'Engle. (J). 1991. mass mkt. 4.99 (*0-440-80265-2*) Dell.

Many Waters. Madeleine L'Engle. LC 86-14911. 310p. (J). (gr. 4 up). 1986. 17.00 (*0-374-34796-4*) FS&G.

Many Waters. Madeleine L'Engle. 1986. 9.60 (*0-606-05091-4*, Pub. by Turtleback) Demco.

***Many Waters.** Madeleine L'Engle. 1998. 10.60 (*0-606-13596-0*, Pub. by Turtleback) Demco.

Many Waters. anniversary rev. ed. Madeleine L'Engle. (Illus.). 336p. (J). (gr. 8-12). 1998. mass mkt. 5.99 (*0-440-22770-4*) BDD Bks Young Read.

Many Waters: Poems from West Virginia. Llewellyn McKernan. LC 93-27131. (Poetry Ser.: Vol. 7). 1993. pap. 14.95 (*0-88946-568-1*, Mellen Poetry Pr) E Mellen.

Many Were Called, Few Were Chosen: The Story of the Earth-Based Volunteers. Heather A. Harder. LC 93-80637. (Illus.). 156p. 1994. pap. 13.95 (*1-884410-00-6*) Light Pubng.

Many Wests: Place, Culture, & Regional Identity. Ed. by David M. Wrobel & Michael C. Steiner. LC 97-23019. (Illus.). 320p. 1997. 45.00 (*0-7006-0861-3*); pap. 19.95 (*0-7006-0862-1*) U Pr of KS.

Many Wives, Many Powers: Authority & Power in Polygynous Families. Remi Clignet. LC 75-89821. 400p. (C). reprint ed. pap. 124.00 (*0-8357-9464-4*, 201025800068) Bks Demand.

Many Wonders of Heaven. Donald F. Ginkel. 1993. pap., text 4.50 (*0-9642122-0-X*) Church Press.

Many Wonders of Heaven Leader's Guide. Donald F. Ginkel. 1993. pap., text 2.95 (*0-9642122-1-8*) Church Press.

Many Worlds. Herrick. (C). 1993. pap. text, student ed. 24.00 (*0-15-501723-3*, Pub. by Harcourt Coll Pubs) Harcourt.

Many Worlds: A Russian Life. Sophie Koulomzin. LC 80-19332. 368p. 1980. pap. 10.95 (*0-913836-72-9*) St Vladimirs.

***Many Worlds: The New Universe & Its Theological Implications.** Steven J. Dick. LC 00-20804. 256p. 2000. 22.95 (*1-890151-37-8*) Templeton Fnd.

***Many Worlds: The New Universe & Its Theological Implications.** Steven J. Dick. LC 00-20804. 256p. 2000. pap. 14.95 (*1-890151-42-4*) Templeton Fnd.

Many-Worlds Interpretation of Quantum Mechanics. Ed. by Bryce S. DeWitt & Neill Graham. LC 72-12116. (Princeton Series in Physics). (Illus.). 255p. reprint ed. pap. 79.10 (*0-7837-1942-6*, 204215700001) Bks Demand.

Many Worlds of Gershon Shofman. Norman Tarnor. (C). 1989. pap. text 15.95 (*0-87441-482-2*) Behrman.

Many Worlds of Larry Niven: A Checklist of Works by Larry Niven. Paul Cruptill. (Booklet Ser.: No. 33). 63p. (Orig.). 1989. pap. text 4.50 (*0-936055-44-8*) C Drumm Bks.

***Many Worlds of Literature.** (C). 2000. 43.00 (*0-536-60939-X*) Pearson Custom.

Many Worlds of Logic. Herrick. (C). 1994. pap. text, teacher ed. 5.75 (*0-15-501455-2*) Harcourt Coll Pubs.

Many Worlds of Logic. 2nd ed. Herrick. (C). 1999. text 69.50 (*0-15-507165-3*, Pub. by Harcourt Coll Pubs) Harcourt.

Many Worlds of Manoj Das. P. Raja. (Orig.). (C). 1993. 8.50 (*81-7018-761-3*, Pub. by BR Pub) S Asia.

Many Worlds of Peter Mohyla. Ihor Sevcenko. 44p. 1994. write for info. (*0-9609822-7-2*) Ukrainian Studies Fund.

Many Yankee Faces: Essays on Ernest Hemingway, Henry James, Paul Laurence Dunbar, Erskine Caldwell, John Hawkes & White Women in Black Literature. Roger Whitlow. 1979. lib. bdg. 250.00 (*0-8490-2860-4*) Gordon Pr.

Many Young Men of Twenty. John B. Keane. 56p. 1997. pap. 9.95 (*1-898175-04-7*, Pub. by Mercier Pr) Irish Amer Bk.

Manya's Story: Faith & Survival in Revolutionary Russia. Bettyanne Gray. LC 94-32393. 109p. (YA). (gr. 6 up). 1995. lib. bdg. 19.95 (*0-8225-3156-9*, Runestone Pr) Lerner Pub.

Manyfaced Glass: Tennyson's Dramatic Monologues. Linda K. Hughes. LC 86-23599. 320p. 1987. text 34.95 (*0-8214-0853-4*) Ohio U Pr.

Manzanar Martyr: An Interview with Harry Y. Ueno. limited ed. Ed. by Arthur A. Hansen et al. 13.95 (*0-317-46863-4*) CA St U Religious.

***Manzanas.** Ann Burckhardt. LC 98-18749. (Primeros Lectores Ciencias: Alimentos Ser.). 1999. 14.00 (*1-56065-785-5*) Capstone Pr.

Manzanas. Capstone Press Staff. (J). 1998. 14.00 (*0-516-21381-4*) Childrens.

Manzanas Por Vida (Apples for Life) Adan Zepeda. Tr. by Olga Larimer. (SPA., Illus.). 32p. 1999. text 13.00 (*0-9651440-1-1*) Apples For Life.

***Manzanitas of California: Also of Mexico & the World.** Philip V. Wells. LC 00-130148. (Illus.). xvi, 151p. (C). 2000. lib. bdg. 50.00 (*0-933994-22-2*, Pub. by Comstock Bon) Wells.

Manzano: A Study of Community Disorganization. Wesley R. Hurt. LC 88-35132. (Immigrant Communities & Ethnic Minorities in the U. S. & Canada Ser.: No. 34). 1989. 54.00 (*0-404-19444-3*) AMS Pr.

Manzano, Manzano! (Big Book) Alma F. Ada. (Cuento Mas Ser.). (SPA., Illus.). 24p. (Orig.). (J). (gr. k-3). 1989. pap. text 29.95 (*0-917837-09-6*) Hampton-Brown.

Manzoni & the Aesthetics of the Lombard Seicento: Art Assimilated into the Narrative of I Promessi Sposi. Glenn P. Pierce. LC 97-40777. (Illus.). 256p. 1998. 42.50 (*0-8387-5367-1*) Bucknell U Pr.

Manzoni Family. Natalia Ginzburg. Tr. by Marie Evans from ITA. 1987. 19.95 (*0-8050-0613-3*) Seaver Bks.

Manzoni Family. Natalia Ginzburg. Ed. & Tr. by Marie Evans from ITA. (Illus.). 384p. 1989. reprint ed. pap. 9.70 (*1-55970-030-0*, Pub. by Arcade Pub Inc) Time Warner.

Mao. Shaun Breslin. LC 98-19456. (Profiles in Power Ser.). 240p. (C). 1998. pap. 24.60 (*0-582-21525-0*) Longman.

Mao: A Biography. expanded rev. ed. Ross Terrill. LC 99-17082. (Illus.). 526p. 1997. pap. 18.95 (*0-8047-2921-2*) Stanford U Pr.

Mao: A Life. Philip Short. LC 99-41839. (Illus.). 782p. 2000. 35.00 (*0-8050-3115-4*) H Holt & Co.

Mao: A Young Man from the Yangtze Valley. Bernadette P. Shih. Ed. by Billie Young. LC 74-76433. 1974. 22.95 (*0-87949-026-8*) Ashley Bks.

Mao - The Mother of All Amine Oxidases. Ed. by J. P. Finberg et al. (Journal of Neural Transmission: Suppl. 52, 1997). (Illus.). 400p. 1998. 165.00 (*3-211-83038-3*) Spr-Verlag.

Mao & Matisse. Ed Friedman. LC 95-9870. 96p. 1995. 20.00 (*1-882413-21-0*); pap. 12.00 (*1-882413-20-2*) Hanging Loose.

Mao & the Workers: The Hunan Labor Movement, 1920-1923. Lynda N. Shaffer. LC 82-5923. 272p. 1982. reprint ed. pap. 84.40 (*0-8357-2618-5*, 204010100014) Bks Demand.

Mao-B-Inhibitor Selegiline (R-(-)-Deprenyl) Ed. by P. Riederer & H. Przuntek. (Journal of Neural Transmission: Suppl. 25). (Illus.). 220p. 1987. 69.95 (*0-387-82009-4*) Spr-Verlag.

Mao for Beginners. Rius. 176p. 1993. pap. 9.95 (*0-906386-07-1*) Writers & Readers.

Mao Game. Joshua Miller. LC 97-5847. 224p. 1998. pap. 12.00 (*0-380-73182-7*, Avon Bks) Morrow Avon.

Mao Game. Joshua Miller. LC 97-5847. 224p. 1997. 21.00 (*0-06-039185-5*, ReganBks) HarperTrade.

Mao Kung Ting. John Way. (Illus.). 200p. (C). 1983. 28.80 (*0-88691-001-3*) Yen Wen Pub.

***Mao Memorabilia: The Man & the Myth.** Lynn Pan. (Illus.). 130p. 1999. pap. 38.00 (*962-7283-20-7*, Pub. by FormAsia) Weatherhill.

Mao Myth & the Legacy of Stalinism in China. Tom Kerry. LC 77-81290. 190p. 1977. pap. 14.95 (*0-87348-522-X*); lib. bdg. 45.00 (*0-87348-521-1*) Pathfinder NY.

Mao Tiang Pelos Tiesos. Del Amo Montserrat. pap. text 8.50 (*84-216-3153-5*) Bruno Edit.

Mao Tse-Tung & I Were Beggars. Siao-Yu. LC 59-15411. (Illus.). 1959. 39.95 (*0-8156-0015-1*) Syracuse U Pr.

Mao Tse-Tung & I Were Beggars. Yu Hsiao. LC 59-15411. (Illus.). 266p. 1959. reprint ed. pap. 82.50 (*0-608-07627-9*, 205994200010) Bks Demand.

Mao Tse Tung on Guerrilla Warfare. 2nd ed. Tr. by Samuel B. Griffith. 160p. 1992. reprint ed. 22.95 (*1-877853-10-0*) Nautical & Aviation.

***Mao Tse-Tung's Ch'I & the Chinese Political Economy: With Special Reference to the Post-Mao Modernization Revolution.** Lam Lai Sing. LC 00-21171. (Chinese Studies: Vol. 13). 356p. 2000. text 99.95 (*0-7734-7813-2*) E Mellen.

Mao Tse-Tung's Immortal Contributions. Bob Avakian. 1978. 12.95 (*0-89851-020-1*); pap. 4.95 (*0-89851-021-X*) RCP Pubns.

Mao Tse-Tung's Purposive Contention with the Superpowers: The Theory of Ch'i. Lai S. Lam. LC 94-13504. 216p. 1994. text 89.95 (*0-7734-2289-7*) E Mellen.

Mao Tse-Tung's Theory of Dialectic. Francis Y. Soo. 205p. 1981. text 135.00 (*90-277-1206-9*, D Reidel) Kluwer Academic.

Mao II. Don DeLillo. 256p. 1992. pap. 12.95 (*0-14-015274-1*, Penguin Bks) Viking Penguin.

Mao-Wu see Biographical Dictionary of Republican China

Mao Zedong. Delia Davin. LC 98-111033. (New Pocket Biographies Ser.). (Illus.). 128p. 1998. pap. 9.95 (*0-7509-1531-5*, Pub. by Sutton Pub Ltd) Intl Pubs Mktg.

Mao Zedong. Jonathan D. Spence. LC 99-26970. (Penguin Lives Ser.). 160p. 1999. 19.95 (*0-670-88669-6*) Viking Penguin.

Mao Zedong: A Bibliography, 3. Alan Lawrance. LC 91-8424. (Bibliographies of World Leaders Ser.: No. 3). 232p. 1991. lib. bdg. 65.00 (*0-313-28222-6*, LMZ/, Greenwood Pr) Greenwood.

Mao Zedong: Founder of the People's Republic of China. Rebecca Stefoff. LC 95-24662. (Illus.). 128p. (YA). (gr. 7 up). 1996. lib. bdg. 22.40 (*1-56294-531-9*) Millbrook Pr.

***Mao Zedong: His Thoughts & Works.** Ed. by Subrata Mukherjee & Sushila Ramaswamy. 1998. 36.00 (*81-7100-774-0*) Deep & Deep Pubns.

***Mao Zedong & China's Revolutions.** Cheek. 2001. pap. text. write for info. (*0-312-25626-4*) St Martin.

Mao Zedong & the Communist Policies, 1927-1978. B. E. Shinde. (C). 1991. 16.00 (*81-7154-530-0*, Pub. by Popular Prakashan) S Asia.

Mao Zedong on Dialectical Materialism: Writings on Philosophy, 1937. Ed. by Nick Knight. LC 89-49016. (Chinese Studies on China). 304p. (gr. 13). 1990. text 79.95 (*0-87332-682-2*) M E Sharpe.

***Mao Zedong, Zhou Enlai & the Evoultion of the Chinese Communist Leadership.** Thomas Kampen. 2000. 45.00 (*87-87062-80-1*, Pub. by NIAS); pap. 19.95 (*87-87062-76-3*, Pub. by NIAS) Paul & Co Pubs.

Mao Zedong's Posters. Cheung Yau. 55.00 (*962-217-625-9*); pap. 35.00 (*962-217-640-2*) Norton.

Mao Zedong's "Talks at the Yan'an Conference on Literature & Art" A Translation of the 1943 Text with Commentary. Bonnie S. McDougall. LC 80-18443. (Michigan Monographs in Chinese Studies: No. 39). 112p. 1980. pap. text 15.00 (*0-89264-039-1*) Ctr Chinese Studies.

Mao Zedong's World View: From Youth to Yanan. Jianfei Xin. LC 98-169318. 248p. (C). 1998. 39.00 (*0-7618-1034-X*) U Pr of Amer.

Maoism & Chinese Culture. Zongli Tang & Bing Zuo. LC 96-8857. (Illus.). 279p. (C). 1996. lib. bdg. 85.00 (*1-56072-353-X*) Nova Sci Pubs.

***Maoism vs. Bolshevism: The 1965 Catastrophe in Indonesia, China's "Cultural Revolution" & the Disintegration of World Stalinism** Joseph Hansen. LC 99-185310. 75 p. 1998. write for info. (*0-87348-886-5*) Pathfinder NY.

Maoist Economics & the Revolutionary Road to Communism: The Shanghai Textbook. Afterword & Intro. by Raymond Lotta. LC 94-94131. 346p. (Orig.). (C). 1994. pap. text 15.00 (*0-916650-41-3*) Banner Pr Intl.

Maoist Insurgency since Vietnam. Thomas A. Marks. LC 95-5364. 320p. (C). 1996. pap. 26.50 (*0-7146-4123-5*, Pub. by F Cass Pubs); text 57.50 (*0-7146-4606-7*, Pub. by F Cass Pubs) Intl Spec Bk.

Maoists in Andhra Pradesh. Shantha Sinha. 320p. (C). 1989. 52.00 (*81-212-0252-3*, Pub. by Gian Publng Hse) S Asia.

Maomao & Mimi. Florence C. Chang. LC 81-80784. (Chinese Can Be Fun Bks.: Level 3). (Illus.). 80p. (Orig.). (J). (gr. 5-6). 1981. pap. 5.00 (*0-936620-05-6*) Ginkgo Hut.

Maori. Robert Macdonald. LC 93-35530. (Threatened Cultures Ser.). (Illus.). 48p. (J). (gr. 4-6). 1994. lib. bdg. 24.26 (*1-56847-151-3*) Raintree Steck-V.

Maori, 2 vols., Set. Elsdon Best. LC 75-35231. reprint ed. 165.00 (*0-404-14310-5*) AMS Pr.

Maori: A Photographic & Social History. rev. ed. Michael King. LC 97-198408. (Illus.). 289 p. 1996. write for info. (*0-7900-0500-X*) Reed Pubng.

Maori: A Study in Acculturation. H. D. Hawthorn. LC 44-47267. (American Anthropological Association Memoirs Ser.: No. 64). 1969. reprint ed. 25.00 (*0-527-00563-0*) Periodicals Srv.

Maori: Art & Culture. Ed. by D. C. Starzecka. (Illus.). 168p. 1996. pap. 29.50 (*1-878529-18-8*) Art Media Resources.

Maori & Polynesian, Their Origin, History & Culture. John M. Brown. LC 75-35240. reprint ed. 41.50 (*0-404-14415-2*) AMS Pr.

Maori & the Crown: An Indigenous People's Struggle for Self-Determination, 68. Ed. by Dora Alves. LC 98-50236. (Contributions to the Study of World History Ser.: Vol. 68). 216p. 1999. 55.00 (*0-313-31058-0*) Greenwood.

Maori Canoe. Elsdon Best. LC 75-35234. 1923. reprint ed. 74.50 (*0-404-14411-X*) AMS Pr.

Maori King Movement in New Zealand. Thomas Buddle. LC 75-35241. reprint ed. 32.50 (*0-404-14416-0*) AMS Pr.

Maori Land Tenure: Studies of a Changing Institution. Ian H. Kawharu. 1977. 39.50 (*0-19-823177-6*) OUP.

Maori Life in Ao-tea. Johannes C. Andersen. LC 75-35221. reprint ed. 74.50 (*0-404-14400-4*) AMS Pr.

Maori Music. Mervyn McLean. (Illus.). 430p. 1997. 45.00 (*1-86940-144-1*, Pub. by Auckland Univ) Paul & Co Pubs.

Maori Music, with Its Polynesian Background. Johannes C. Andersen. LC 75-35222. reprint ed. 87.50 (*0-404-14401-2*) AMS Pr.

Maori Oral Literature - As Seen by a Classicist. Agatha Thornton. 1987. pap. 21.95 (*0-908569-43-2*, Pub. by Univ Otago Pr) Intl Spec Bk.

Maori Origins & Migrations: The Genesis of Some Pakeha Myths & Legends. M. P. Sorrenson. (Illus.). 104p. 1991. pap. 19.95 (*1-86940-053-4*) OUP.

Maori People Today: A General Survey. Ivan L. Sutherland. LC 75-30085. (Institute of Pacific Relations Ser.). reprint ed. 42.50 (*0-404-59563-4*) AMS Pr.

Maori Race. Edward Tregear. LC 73-12314. (Illus.). reprint ed. 30.00 (*0-404-11222-6*) AMS Pr.

Maori Religion & Mythology. Elsdon Best. LC 75-35236. reprint ed. 62.50 (*0-404-14412-8*) AMS Pr.

Maori Religion & Mythology. Edward Shortland. LC 75-35268. reprint ed. 31.50 (*0-404-14437-3*) AMS Pr.

Maori String Figures. Johannes C. Andersen. LC 75-35223. reprint ed. 41.50 (*0-404-14402-0*) AMS Pr.

Maori Tales & Legends. Kate M. Clark. LC 78-67696. (Folktale Ser.). (Illus.). reprint ed. 32.50 (*0-404-16067-0*) AMS Pr.

Maori Tohunga & His Spirit World. Johannes C. Andersen. LC 75-35224. reprint ed. 37.50 (*0-404-14403-9*) AMS Pr.

Maori Tribe Choreographies, Vol. II, Bk. 21. Vicki Corona. (Celebrate the Cultures Ser.). (Illus.). 28p. 1989. pap. 14.95 (*1-58513-011-7*) Dance Fantasy.

Maori Tribe of New Zealand Costume-Making, Vol. II, Bk. 22. Vicki Corona. (Celebrate the Cultures Ser.). (Illus.). 28p. 1989. pap. 15.95 (*1-58513-012-5*) Dance Fantasy.

Maori Warrior. Alan Taylor. (Pamphlets Polynesia Ser.: No. 6). (Illus.). 32p. (C). 1987. pap. 3.50 (*0-939154-43-9*) Inst Polynesian.

Maori Wars of the Nineteenth Century. 2nd enl. ed. Stephenson P. Smith. LC 75-35271. reprint ed. 41.50 (*0-404-14440-3*) AMS Pr.

***Mao's Children in New China: Voices From the Red Guard Generation.** Ed. by Yarong Jiang & David Ashley. LC 99-49313. (Asia's Transformations Ser.). 240p. (C). 2000. text 85.00 (*0-415-22330-X*) Routledge.

***Mao's Children in New China: VoicesFrom the Red Guard Generation.** Ed. by Yarong Jiang & David Ashley. LC 99-49313. (Asia's Transformations Ser.). 240p. (C). 2000. pap. 24.99 (*0-415-22331-8*) Routledge.

Mao's China: Party Reform Documents, 1942-44. Mao Tse-Tung. Tr. by Boyd Compton from CHI. LC 82-6102. 278p. 1982. reprint ed. lib. bdg. 59.75 (*0-313-23593-7*, MAMAC, Greenwood Pr) Greenwood.

Mao's China & After. enl. rev. ed. Maurice Meisner. 1986. pap. 18.95 (*0-02-920880-7*) Free Pr.

Mao's China & After. 3rd rev. ed. Maurice Meisner. 1998. 16.00 (*0-02-920882-3*) Free Pr.

Mao's China & After: A Histroy of the People's Republic. 3rd ed. Maurice Meisner. LC 98-31734. 608p. 1999. 19.95 (*0-684-85635-2*) S&S Trade.

Mao's Generals: Chen Yi & the New Fourth Army. Lanzin Xiang. LC 98-6658. 256p. 1998. 37.00 (*0-7618-1129-X*) U Pr of Amer.

Mao's Graphic Voice: Pictorial Posters from the Cultural Revolution. Patricia Powell & Shitao Huo. LC 97-153281. (Illus.). 16p. 1996. pap. 3.00 (*0-932900-41-0*) Elvejhem Mus.

Mao's Military Romanticism: China & the Korean War, 1950-1953. Shu G. Zhang. LC 95-18532. (Modern War Studies). 352p. (C). 1995. 45.00 (*0-7006-0723-4*) U Pr of KS.

Mao's People: Sixteen Portraits of Life in Revolutionary China. B. Michael Frolic. (Illus.). 278p. 1980. 34.95 (*0-674-54846-9*) HUP.

Mao's People: Sixteen Portraits of Life in Revolutionary China. B. Michael Frolic. (Illus.). 278p. 1980. pap. 19.95 (*0-674-54845-0*) HUP.

Mao's Revolution & the Chinese Political Culture. Richard H. Solomon. LC 98-12268. (Michigan Monographs in Chinese Studies: Vol. 82). 630p. 1999. reprint ed. 75.00 (*0-89264-132-0*) Ctr Chinese Studies.

Mao's Road to Power Vol. V: Revolutionary Writings, 1912-1949, Vol. V. Stuart R. Schram. LC 92-26783. 846p. 1999. text 165.00 (*0-7656-0349-7*, East Gate Bk) M E Sharpe.

Mao's Road to Power: Revolutionary Writings, 1912-1949: From the Jinggangshan to the Establishment of the Jiangxi, Vol. III. Ed. by Stuart R. Schram. LC 92-26783. 848p. (C). (gr. 13). 1995. text 169.95 (*1-56324-439-X*, East Gate Bk) M E Sharpe.

Mao's Road to Power: Revolutionary Writings, 1912-1949: National Revolution & Social Revolution, Vol. II. Ed. by Stuart R. Schram. LC 92-26783. 608p. (C). (gr. 13). 1995. text 169.95 (*1-56324-430-6*, East Gate Bk) M E Sharpe.

Mao's Road to Power: Revolutionary Writings, 1912-1949: The Rise & Fall of the Chinese Soviet Republic, 1931-1934, Vol. IV. Ed. by Stuart R. Schram. LC 92-26783. (Illus.). 1110p. (C). (gr. 13). 1997. text 165.95 (*1-56324-891-3*, East Gate Bk) M E Sharpe.

Mao's Road to Power: Revolutionary Writings, 1912-1949 Vol. I: The Pre-Marxist Period, 1912-1920. Ed. by Stuart R. Schram. LC 92-26783. 688p. (C). (gr. 13). 1992. pap. text 65.95 (*1-56324-457-8*, East Gate Bk) M E Sharpe.

Mao's Road to Power: Revolutionary Writings, 1912-1949 Vol. I: The Pre-Marxist Period, 1912-1920, Vol. I. Ed. by Stuart R. Schram. LC 92-26783. 688p. (C). (gr. 13). 1992. text 169.95 (*1-56324-049-1*, East Gate Bk) M E Sharpe.

Maot Chittim see Mitzvah of the Month

Map: Programa Co-Creativo de Asistencia Medica de la Hermandad Blanca. Machaelle S. Wright. Tr. by Maria Siccardi. LC 95-92820.Tr. of The Co-Creative White Brotherhood Medical Assistance Program. (SPA., Illus.). 374p. 1996. pap. 16.95 (*0-927978-23-7*) Perelandra Ltd.

Map: Rediscovering Rock & Roll a Journey. Paul Williams. LC 87-7300. 272p. (Orig.). 1988. pap. 9.95 (*0-89708-166-8*) And Bks.

Map: The Co-Creative White Brotherhood Medical Assistance Program. 2nd ed. Machaelle S. Wright. LC 94-65465. (Illus.). 317p. 1994. pap. 14.95 (*0-927978-19-9*) Perelandra Ltd.

M

An Asterisk (*) at the beginning of an entry indicates that the title is appearing for the first time.

Map Aid to Laos, 1959-1972. Peter A. Liebchen. 200p. 1993. reprint ed. pap. 22.00 (*0-8373135-51-0*) Dalley Bk Service.

Map & Coordinate Supervisor. Jack Rudman. (Career Examination Ser.: C-3330). 1994. pap. 34.95 (*0-8373-3330-X*) Nat Learn.

Map & Entertainment Directory of Palm Beach: With Indexed Streets, Brief History, Wining & Dining & Shopping Guides, & Special Sight-Seeing Comments. James J. Sheeran. (Illus.). 24p. 1995. 2.50 (*0-9622977-1-2*) Palm Beach Soc.

Map & Globe Skills. Dianne K. Salerni. 1997. 4.95 (*1-55708-553-6*, MCR650) McDonald Pub Co.

Map & Guide to Tuolumne Meadows. Steven P. Medley. (Illus.). 1994. pap. 2.50 (*0-939666-72-3*) Yosemite Assn.

Map & Guide to Wawona & Mariposa Grove. Steven P. Medley. Tr. by Reineck & Reineck Staff. (Illus.). 1991. pap. 2.95 (*0-939666-29-4*) Yosemite Assn.

Map & Guide to Yosemite Valley see Karte & Fuhrer Zum Yosemite Valley

Map & Guide to Yosemite Valley. Dean Shenk. Tr. by Reineck & Reineck Staff. (Illus.). 1991. pap. 2.50 (*0-939666-17-0*) Yosemite Assn.

Map & Industrial LANS. Richard K. Miller & Terri C. Walker. LC 88-81647. (Survey on Technology & Markets Ser.: No. 56). 50p. 1989. pap. text 200.00 (*1-55865-055-5*) Future Tech Surveys.

Map & Maze Puzzles. Sarah Dixon. (Superpuzzles Ser.). (Illus.). 48p. (J). (gr. 7-12). 1993. pap. 7.95 (*0-7460-1579-8*, Usborne) EDC.

Map & Maze Puzzles. Sarah Dixon. (Superpuzzles Ser.). (Illus.). 48p. (J). (gr. 7 up). 1993. lib. bdg. 15.95 (*0-88110-525-2*, Usborne) EDC.

Map & Track: State Initiatives to Encourage Responsible Fatherhood. Stanley Bernard et al. LC 97-24729. 80p. 1997. pap. 19.95 (*0-926582-22-4*) NCCP.

Map & Track: State Initiatives to Encourage Responsible Fatherhood, 1999 Edition. Stanley Bernard et al. LC 99-32963. 200p. 1999. pap. 19.95 (*0-926582-24-0*) NCCP.

Map & Track: State Initivatives for Young Children & Families, 1998 Edition. Jane Knitzer & Stephen Page. LC 98-4430. 1998. pap. 19.95 (*0-926582-23-2*) NCCP.

Map Attack: Understanding Globes & Maps. Jack Warner. (Illus.). 176p. (J). (gr. 5-8). 1991. pap. text 7.00 (*0-13-962903-3*, 640122) P-H.

Map-Building & Exploration Strategies of a Simple Sonar-Equipped Mobile Robot: An Experimental, Quantitative Evaluation. D. C. Lee. LC 96-15187. (Distinguished Dissertations in Computer Science Ser.: No. 13). (Illus.). 239p. 1996. text 64.95 (*0-521-57331-9*) Cambridge U Pr.

***Map-by-Map Directory.** Richard J. A. Talbert. (Illus.). 2000. 150.00 (*0-691-04945-9*) Princeton U Pr.

Map Collections in the United States & Canada: A Directory. 3rd ed. David K. Carrington & Richard W. Stephenson. LC 77-26685. 240p. 1978. reprint ed. pap. 74.40 (*0-608-14562-9*, 202496000040) Bks Demand.

Map Color Theorem. G. Ringel. LC 73-17986. (Grundlehren der Mathematischen Wissenschaften Ser.: Vol. 209). (Illus.). 220p. 1974. 86.95 (*0-387-06548-2*) Spr-Verlag.

Map Coloring, Polyhedra & the Four-Color Problem. David W. Barnette. (Dolciani Mathematical Expositions Ser.: Vol. 8). 1984. text 8.00 (*0-88385-309-4*, DOL-08) Math Assn.

Map, Compass, & Campfire: A Handbook for the Outdoorsman. Donald E. Ratliff. LC 64-8453. (Illus.). 64p. 1993. reprint ed. pap. 7.95 (*0-8323-0129-9*) Binford Mort.

***Map, Compass, GPS: An Introduction.** Robert J. Rutten. (Illus.). 110p. (YA). (gr. 7 up). 2000. pap. write for info. (*0-9678156-0-6*) Outdoor Comm Co.

Map Corner. Arnold B. Cheyney & Donald Capone. (Illus.). 128p. (Orig.). 1983. pap. 12.95 (*0-673-16615-5*, GoodYrBooks) Addson-Wesley Educ.

Map Crosswords. S. Finch. 64p. (gr. 4-8). 1997. pap. 9.95 (*0-590-89646-6*) Scholastic Inc.

Map Dowsing. Verne L. Cameron. (Dowser's Hdbk. Ser.: No. 1). 40p. 1970. pap. 5.75 (*0-88234-003-4*) Life Understanding.

Map Drafter. Jack Rudman. (Career Examination Ser.: C-3729). 1994. pap. 27.95 (*0-8373-3729-1*) Nat Learn.

Map Generalization. Robert Weibel. 80p. 1995. pap. 125.00 (*0-7855-2837-7*, Pub. by R-I-C-S Bks) St Mut.

Map Generalization: Making Rules for Knowledge Representation. B. P. Buttenfield. 1991. 115.32 (*0-582-08062-2*, Pub. by Addison-Wesley) Longman.

***Map Guide Sydney Portier.** 56p. 2000. pap., student ed. 8.95 (*0-312-24639-0*) St Martin.

Map Guide to American Migration Routes: 1735-1815. William Dollarhide. LC 98-145522. 1997. pap. text 9.95 (*1-877677-74-4*) Herit Quest.

Map Guide to the U. S. Federal Censuses, 1790-1920. William Thorndale & William Dollarhide. (Illus.). 445p. 2000. reprint ed. pap. 39.95 (*0-8063-1188-6*, 5785) Genealog Pub.

Map History of the Ancient World. Don Barrett et al. 1988. pap. text 19.44 (*0-582-66350-4*, 74671) Longman.

Map History of the United States. Brian Catchpole. (YA). (gr. 7). 1972. pap. text 15.00 (*0-435-31158-1*, 31158) Heinemann.

***Map in the Mystery Machine.** Gail Herman. Vol. 1. (Illus.). 32p. (ps-3). 2000. pap. text 3.99 (*0-439-16167-3*) Scholastic Inc.

Map Index to Topographic Quadrangles of the United States, 1882-1940. Riley M. Moffat. LC 84-21984. (Occasional Papers: No. 10). (Illus.). 238p. (Orig.). 1986. 32.50 (*0-939112-12-4*) Western Assn Map.

Map Is a Picture. Barbara Rinkoff. LC 65-11648. (Let's-Read-&-Find-Out Science Bks.). (Illus.). (J). (gr. k-3). 1965. lib. bdg. 10.89 (*0-690-51793-9*) HarpC Child Bks.

Map Is Not Territory: Studies in the History of Religions. Jonathan Z. Smith. LC 92-36231. xx, 352p. (C). 1992. pap. text 17.95 (*0-226-76357-9*) U Ch Pr.

Map It! Tools for Charting the Vast Territories of Your Mind, 5 bks., Set. Contrib. by Nancy Margulies. (Interactive Comics Ser.). (Illus.). 36p. (Orig.). 1995. pap., teacher ed. 16.00 (*1-56976-008-X*) Zephyr Pr AZ.

***Map Kinases in Plant Signal Transduction.** Ed. by H. Hirt. LC 99-30056. (Results & Problems in Cell Differentiation Ser.: Vol. 27). (Illus.). 150p. 1999. 125.00 (*3-540-65625-1*) Spr-Verlag.

Map Librarianship. 2nd ed. Harold Nichols. LC 82-126289. 272p. 1982. reprint ed. pap. 84.40 (*0-608-07776-3*, 206786400010) Bks Demand.

Map Librarianship: An Introduction. 3rd ed. Mary L. Larsgaard. LC 98-15451. (Illus.). 475p. 1998. 68.50 (*1-56308-474-0*) Libs Unl.

Map Link Academic Section, 1995: Maps for the Entire World. Paul Watson. (Illus.). 289p. 1995. pap. 10.00 (*0-929591-25-9*) Map Link.

Map Madness & Compass Caper. Dispezio. 1998. spiral bd. write for info. (*0-201-33998-6*) Addison-Wesley.

Map Mysteries. Mark Falstein. Ed. by Clark Editorial & Design Staff. (Illus.). 96p. (Orig.). (J). (gr. 4-6). 1997. pap. 10.95 (*0-88160-297-3*, LW367) Learning Wks.

Map of a Small Place. Linda Johnson. 15p. (Orig.). 1993. pap. 2.00 (*1-884047-56-4*) Mass Extinct.

Map of Addy's World. Pleasant Company Staff. (American Girls Collection). (YA). (gr. 2 up). 1996. 5.95 (*1-56247-493-6*) Pleasant Co.

Map of All My Youth: Early Works, Friends, & Influences. W. H. Auden. Ed. by Katherine Bucknell & Nicholas Jenkins. (Auden Studies Ser.). 256p. (C). 1990. text 65.00 (*0-19-812964-5*) OUP.

Map of American Indian Nations. 3rd ed. George L. Russell. (J). (gr. 6 up). 1993. pap. 15.00 (*1-881933-02-4*) Russell Pub AZ.

Map of Cheshire County, New Hampshire, 1858. 1981st ed. L. Fagan. (Illus.). 36p. 1981. reprint ed. boxed set 27.95 (*0-911653-00-7*) Old Maps.

Map of Days. Shuntaro Tanikawa. Ed. by Thomas Fitzsimmons. Tr. by Harold Wright from JPN. LC 96-43436. (Asian Poetry in Translation: Japan Ser.: No. 19).Tr. of Hibi No Chizu. (Illus.). 112p. 1997. 25.00 (*0-942668-49-9*); pap. text 15.00 (*0-942668-50-2*) Katydid Bks.

Map of Desire: Sensuality & Self-Discovery. David Kantor & Tom Monte. 304p. 1997. 22.95 (*1-57322-054-X*, Riverhead Books) Putnam Pub Group.

Map of Europe Has to Be Re-Made see Five Views on European Peace

Map of Europe Redrawn. Ed. by Eva Klimas. (Oxford in North America Ser.: No. 9). 45p. (Orig.). 1993. pap. write for info. (*1-883718-04-X*) Oxford U Dev.

Map of Felicity's World. Pleasant Company Staff. (American Girls Collection). (YA). (gr. 2 up). 1996. 5.95 (*1-56247-491-X*) Pleasant Co.

Map of Goodhue County, Minnesota, 1877, with Index & Introduction. Kathryn Ericson. LC 91-70207. (Illus.). 100p. (Orig.). 1991. pap. 14.50 (*0-9617197-2-9*) Goodhue County Hist Soc.

Map of Historical Scotland. Collins1. 1997. pap. 11.95 (*0-00-448687-0*, 0-8437-6646-8) Hammond World.

Map of Hope: Women's Writing on Human Rights. Ed. by Marjorie Agosin. LC 98-44985. 395p. (C). 1999. pap. 18.00 (*0-8135-2626-4*); text 49.00 (*0-8135-2625-6*) Rutgers U Pr.

Map of Italy. Passport Books Staff. 1991. pap. 9.95 (*0-8442-9594-9*) NTC Contemp Pub Co.

Map of Kirsten's World. Pleasant Company Staff. (American Girls Collection). (YA). (gr. 2 up). 1996. 5.95 (*1-56247-492-8*) Pleasant Co.

***Map of Knowledge Humanities.** Alan Hausman. 234p. (C). 1999. per. 62.95 (*0-7872-6367-2*, 41636701) Kendall-Hunt.

Map of Leaving. Jack Heflin. 52p. (Orig.). 1985. pap. 5.95 (*0-939872-04-8*) MRP.

Map of Life. F. J. Sheed. 1994. pap. text 8.95 (*0-89870-474-X*) Ignatius Pr.

Map of Life: A Simple Study of the Catholic Faith. Francis J. Sheed. LC 93-80278. 147p. pap. 8.95 (*0-89870-473-1*) Ignatius Pr.

***Map of Love.** Ahdaf Soueif. LC 99-490981. 529p. 1999. write for info. (*0-7475-4367-4*) Blmsbury Pub.

***Map of Love.** Ahdaf Soueif. 2000. pap. write for info. (*0-7475-4563-4*) Blmsbury Pub.

***Map of Love.** Ahdaf Soueif. LC 00-35531. 544p. 2000. 14.00 (*0-385-72011-4*, Anchor NY) Doubleday.

Map of Making Dances. Stuart Hodes. (Illus.). 293p. (C). 1998. pap. text 29.95 (*1-880157-61-6*) Ardsley.

Map of Mexico City Blues: Jack Kerouac As Poet. James T. Jones. LC 91-40769. 216p. (C). 1992. 26.95 (*0-8093-1828-8*) S Ill U Pr.

Map of Minnesota Territory, 1850. Minnesota Historical Society Staff. (Borealis Bks.). 16p. 1999. pap. 9.95 (*0-87351-374-6*, Borealis Book) Minn Hist.

Map of Misreading. Harold Bloom. 218p. 1980. pap. 13.95 (*0-19-502809-0*) OUP.

Map of Molly's World. Pleasant Company Staff. (American Girls Collection). (YA). (gr. 2 up). 1996. 5.95 (*1-56247-495-2*) Pleasant Co.

Map of Oregon Trail: The Highway of the Pioneers to the Pacific Northwest. W. McIlwraith. (J). (gr. 3-6). 1986. pap. 5.95 (*0-8323-0052-7*) Binford Mort.

Map of Philadelphia. Tim Kerner. (Illus.). 1.50 (*0-9619081-0-6*) Kerner Graphics.

Map of Samantha's World. Pleasant Company Staff. (American Girls Collection). (YA). (gr. 2 up). 1996. 5.95 (*1-56247-494-4*) Pleasant Co.

Map of Shakespeare's London. Chester Garrison. (Illus.). 8p. 1970. pap. 3.95 (*0-87071-083-4*) Oreg St U Pr.

Map of the Counties Cass, Van Buren & Berrien, Michigan, 1860. Ed. by Harley Geil Siverd et al. (Illus.). 66p. 1983. reprint ed. pap. 15.00 (*0-9615358-1-4*) Cass County His.

Map of the East. Photos by Leo Rubinfien. (Illus.). 132p. 1992. pap. 25.00 (*0-87923-943-3*) Godine.

Map of the Inland Waterways of England & Wales. Imray Laurie Norie & Wilson, Ltd. Staff. (Illus.). (C). 1990. 125.00 (*0-85288-031-6*, Pub. by Laurie Norie & Wilson Ltd) St Mut.

Map of the Inland Waterways of France. Wilson Limited Staff & Imray L. Norie. (Illus.). (C). 1998. 125.00 (*0-85288-033-2*, Pub. by Laurie Norie & Wilson Ltd) St Mut.

Map of the Mind: Toward a Science of Psychotherapy. Richard Brockman. LC 98-11890. 375p. 1998. 37.95 (*1-887841-14-8*, Psychosocial) Intl Univs Pr.

Map of the New Country: Women & Christianity. Sara Maitland. LC 82-13142. 280p. 1984. pap. 13.95 (*0-7100-9301-2*, Routledge Thoemms) Routledge.

Map of the Province of Nova Scotia. Seven Hills Staff. 1996. pap. text 14.95 (*0-88780-288-5*) Formac Dist Ltd.

Map of the Province of Nova Scotia. 4th rev. ed. (Illus.). 92p. 1995. 29.95 (*0-88780-230-3*, Pub. by Formac Publ Co); pap. 14.95 (*0-88780-228-1*, Pub. by Formac Publ Co) Seven Hills Bk.

Map of the Rivers Cam & Lower Great Ouse: Cambridge to Denver. Derek Bowskill. (Illus.). 1996. spiral bd. 125.00 (*0-85288-374-9*, Pub. by Laurie Norie & Wilson Ltd) St Mut.

Map of the Ruins of Dzibilchaltun, Yucatan, Mexico. George E. Stuart et al. (Publications: No. 47). (Illus.). 1979. 20.00 (*0-939238-52-7*) Tulane MARI.

Map of the Upper Ouse Bedford to Pope's Corner. Derek Bowskill. (Illus.). 1996. spiral bd. 125.00 (*0-85288-364-1*, Pub. by Laurie Norie & Wilson Ltd) St Mut.

Map of the World. Jane Hamilton. 400p. 1992. pap. 12.95 Doubleday.

***Map of the World.** Jane Hamilton. 352p. 1999. 24.95 (*0-385-50076-9*); pap. 12.95 (*0-385-72010-6*, Anchor NY) Doubleday.

Map of Twentieth Century Theology: Readings from Karl Barth to Radical Pluralism. Ed. by Carl Braaten & Robert W. Jenson. 400p. 1995. pap. 29.00 (*0-8006-2686-9*, 1-2686) Augsburg Fortress.

Map of Where I Live. S. Shankar. LC 97-530. 167p. 1997. pap. 14.95 (*0-435-08143-8*, 08143) Heinemann.

Map of Who We Are: A Novel. Lawrence R. Smith. LC 97-11212. (American Indian Literature & Critical Studies Ser.: Vol. 24). (Illus.). 320p. 1997. 24.95 (*0-8061-2956-5*) U of Okla Pr.

Map of You, Map of Me. Eliot Greenspan. (Illus.). 80p. (Orig.). 1994. pap. 8.00 (*1-882775-05-8*) Selva Edit.

Map Projection: Theory & Applications. Ed. by Plaison. 384p. 1990. lib. bdg. 139.00 (*0-8493-6888-X*, GA110) CRC Pr.

Map Projection Methods. Frederick Pearson, II. Ed. by John L. Junkins. (Applied Mathematics for Science & Engineering Ser.). (Illus.). 304p. 1984. 31.00 (*0-915313-00-6*) Sigma Sci Inc.

Map Projection Software. Frederick Pearson, II. Ed. by John L. Junkins. (Applied Mathematics for Science & Engineering Ser.). (Illus.). 50p. 1984. 110.00 incl. disk (*0-317-06090-2*) Sigma Sci Inc.

***Map Projection Transformation Principles & Applications.** Oihe Yang. 1999. pap. text 45.00 (*0-7484-0668-9*) Tay Francis Ltd.

Map Projections: A Reference Manual. Lev M. Bugayevskiy & John P. Snyder. LC 94-45668. 1995. 95.00 (*0-7484-0303-5*, Pub. by Tay Francis Ltd); pap. 45.00 (*0-7484-0304-3*, Pub. by Tay Francis Ltd) Taylor & Francis.

Map Projections: A Working Manual, 2 vols., Set. 1995. lib. bdg. 602.95 (*0-8490-6711-1*) Gordon Pr.

MAP-R for Windows: Multitrait/Multi-Item Analysis Program - Revised User's Guide. rev. ed. John E. Ware, Jr. et al. (Illus.). vi, 191p. 1996. pap. 170.00 (*1-891941-00-3*) Health Assess.

Map Rap: A Fun Way to Learn Geography Through Rap. Earl Jones, Sr. LC 90-84037. (Illus.). 60p. (Orig.). (J). (gr. 2-12). 1990. pap. 12.75 (*0-935132-18-X*) C H Fairfax.

Map Reader. Graham Duncan. 28p. 1987. pap. 3.00 (*0-9613465-6-6*) Great Elm.

Map Reading. Jack Rudman. (General Aptitude & Abilities Ser.: Vol. 59). pap. 19.95 (*0-8373-6759-X*) Nat Learn.

***Map Reading: Grades K-2.** Lynn Backer & Debbie Cline. (Illus.). 64p. 1998. pap., teacher ed. 6.95 (*1-889369-25-X*, TI0100) Teaching Ink.

***Map Reading: Grades 3-4.** Lynn Smith & Ruth Emmel. (Illus.). 64p. 1998. pap., teacher ed. 6.95 (*1-889369-26-8*, TI0101) Teaching Ink.

***Map Reading: Grades 5-6.** Lynn Smith & Ruth Emmel. (Illus.). 64p. 1998. pap., teacher ed. 6.95 (*1-889369-27-6*, TI0102) Teaching Ink.

Map Reading & Land Navigation. (Illus.). 1990. lib. bdg. 250.00 (*0-8490-3987-8*) Gordon Pr.

***Map Reading for GCSE.** John Wilson. (Illus.). (YA). (gr. 9-11). 1999. pap. 33.00 (*0-7217-1072-7*, Pub. by Schofield) St Mut.

Map Reading for the Caribbean. MacPherson. Date not set. pap. text. write for info. (*0-582-76609-5*, Pub. by Addison-Wesley) Longman.

***Map Reading, Laitude, Longitude, & Time.** Myrl Shireman. (Illus.). 80p. (YA). (gr. 5). 1998. pap. text 9.95 (*1-58037-079-9*, Pub. by M Twain Media) Carson-Dellos.

Map Report. Jack Hollingum. (Illus.). 180p. 1987. 205.95 (*0-387-16354-9*) Spr-Verlag.

Map Room Clerk. Jack Rudman. (Career Examination Ser.: C-3730). 1994. pap. 23.95 (*0-8373-3730-5*) Nat Learn.

Map Room Files of President Roosevelt, 1941-1945: Map Room Ground Operations Files, 1941-1945. LC 94-42746. (World War II Research Collections). 1994. 3860.00 (*1-55655-513-X*) U Pubns Amer.

Map Room Messages of President Truman (1945-1946) Harry S. Truman et al. LC 86-893389. (The Presidential Documents Ser.). 5 p. 1980. write for info. (*0-89093-352-9*) U Pubns Amer.

Map Selected Reading, 1999. PCPS MAP Committee Staff. 1999. pap. 38.75 (*0-87051-254-4*, 090451) Am Inst CPA.

Map Selected Readings, 1996. American Institute of Certified Public Accountants Staff. LC 86-655896. 575p. Date not set. reprint ed. pap. 178.30 (*0-608-20764-0*, 207186300003) Bks Demand.

***Map Skills: Inventive Exercises to Sharpen Skills & Raise Achievement.** Imogene Forte & Marjorie Frank. Ed. by Jennifer Streams. (Basic Not Boring Ser.). (Illus.). 64p. (YA). (gr. 6-8). 2000. pap. text 6.95 (*0-86530-440-8*, IP 402-4) Incentive Pubns.

Map Skills Bilingual English, Haitian Creole: Ladres nan Jeyografi. Fequiere Vilsaint. 54p. (J). (gr. 4-8). Date not set. pap. 4.00 (*1-881839-71-0*) Educa Vision.

Map Skills for Texas History & Geography Students. William B. Conroy. 48p. 1995. pap. 8.95 (*0-937460-36-2*) Hendrick-Long.

Map Stamps of the World. American Topical Association Carto-Philatelists-Ma. (Illus.). 39p. (Orig.). 1982. pap. 7.00 (*0-614-25041-2*) Am Topical Assn.

Map Supplies: Charthead Only. 16.00 (*0-687-23306-2*) Abingdon.

Map Supplies: Charthead 502. 16.00 (*0-687-23503-0*) Abingdon.

Map Supplies: Tripod Only. 40.00 (*0-687-23502-2*) Abingdon.

***Map That Lies Between Us: New & Collected Poems, 1980-2000.** Anne George. LC 00-9748. 2000. write for info. (*1-880216-88-4*) Black Belt Communs.

MAP-34, Client - Server Control, Security & Audit. Javier F. Kuong. (Illus.). 200p. 1996. text 175.00 (*0-940706-31-8*) Management Advisory Pubns.

Map 3.0 Specification, 1993 Release. Ed. by C. J. Gardner. 1750p. pap. text 95.00 (*0-9639941-1-5*) Open I T.

Map Through the Maze: A Guide to Surviving the Criminal Justice System with Advice for Families of Offenders. Ned Rollo & Louis W. Adams. (Illus.). 119p. (Orig.). 1993. pap. 8.95 (*1-878436-14-7*) OPEN TX.

***Map to Clear Messages: Conversations with a Wizard & a Warrior.** Nadine Udall Fischer et al. LC 99-56838. 1999. write for info. (*0-9643824-3-1*) WREXpress.

Map to the End of Time: Wayfarings with Friends & Philosophers. Ronald J. Manheimer. LC 98-33336. 332p. 1999. 24.95 (*0-393-04725-3*) Norton.

Map to the Next World. Joy Harjo. pap. 13.00 (*0-393-32096-0*) Norton.

Map to the Next World. Joy Harjo. LC 99-41099. 128p. 2000. text 22.95 (*0-393-04790-3*) Norton.

Map Turtles & Diamond Back Terrapins. W. P. Mara. (Illus.). 64p. 1997. 9.95 (*0-7938-2068-5*, RE-156) TFH Pubns.

Map 25: How to Audit EDP Contingency Planning & Recovery Provisions. Javier F. Kuong. 208p. 1989. pap. text 60.00 (*0-940706-21-0*) Management Advisory Pubns.

Map Use: Reading, Analysis & Interpretation. 2nd ed. Phillip C. Muehrcke. LC 78-70573. (Illus.). 525p. (C). 1986. pap. text 25.00 (*0-9602978-2-0*) JP Pubns WI.

Map Use: Reading, Analysis & Interpretation. 3rd rev. ed. Phillip C. Muehrcke & Juliana O. Muehrcke. LC 92-71696. (Illus.). 600p. 1992. pap. text 40.00 (*0-9602978-3-9*) JP Pubns WI.

Map Use: Reading, Analysis & Interpretation. 4th rev. ed. Phillip Muehrcke & Juliana Muehrcke. LC 97-73803. (Illus.). 648p. 1998. pap. text 40.00 (*0-9602978-4-7*) JP Pubns WI.

Map Use & Analysis. 2nd ed. John Campbell. 448p. (C). 1993. text. write for info. (*0-697-13579-9*, WCB McGr Hill) McGrw-H Hghr Educ.

Map Use & Analysis. 3rd ed. John Campbell. LC 96-78490. 464p. (C). 1997. text. write for info. (*0-697-22969-6*, WCB McGr Hill) McGrw-H Hghr Educ.

Map Use & Analysis. 4th ed. John Campbell. 384p. 2000. pap. 59.38 (*0-07-303748-6*) McGraw.

Map Uses, Scales & Accuracies for Engineering & Associated Purposes. 172p. 1983. pap. 17.00 (*0-87262-379-3*) Am Soc Civil Eng.

Map with Utopia: Oscar Wilde's Theory for Social Transformation. Jody Price. LC 94-22374. (American University Studies IV: Vol. 162). 249p. (C). 1996. text 44.95 (*0-8204-2069-7*) P Lang Pubng.

Map Work. 5th ed. 48p. (C). 1999. pap. Price not set. (*0-13-012465-6*) P-H.

Map Workshop: Proceedings of the Meeting at the State University of New York at Stony Brook, March 15, 1984. Ed. by Barbara Shupe. x, 76p. (Orig.). 1986. pap. 15.00 (*0-938435-00-0*) LI Lib Resources.

Mapa de Cuauhtlantzinco. Frederick Starr. LC 74-9026. (University of Chicago, Dept. of Anthropology. Bulletin Ser.: No. 3). reprint ed. 27.50 (*0-404-11904-2*) AMS Pr.

Mapa de la Poesia Negra Americana. Ed. by Emilio Ballagas. (B. E. Ser.: No. 8). (SPA.). 1946. 35.00 (*0-8115-2959-2*) Periodicals Srv.

An Asterisk (*) at the beginning of an entry indicates that the title is appearing for the first time.

Mapa de Ninguna Parte (A Map of Nowhere) Gillian Cross. (SPA.). (YA). 1997. pap. 6.99 (*968-16-5096-4*, Pub. by Fondo) Continental Bk.

Mapaches. Lynn M. Stone. (Animales Norteamericanos Ser.).Tr. of Raccoons. 24p. (J). (gr. k-4). 1991. lib. bdg. 14.60 (*0-86592-798-7*) Rourke Enter.

Mapai in Israel: Political Organisation & Government in a New Society. Peter Y. Medding. LC 75-184900. 338p. reprint ed. pap. 96.40 (*0-608-16859-9*, 2027240) Bks Demand.

Mapas. Chris Jaeggi. (I Know about Ser.). (Illus.). 1995. pap. 2.50 (*0-528-83740-0*) Rand McNally.

Mapas de Monte Alban: Proyecto Especial Monte Alban, 1992-1994. Damon E. Peeler. (SPA., Illus.). 162p. 1994. pap. 70.00 (*1-877812-75-7*, UC006) UPLAAP.

***Mapas para la Fiesta.** Otto Maduro. (SPA.). 214p. 1999. pap. 14.95 (*0-9657839-6-0*) AETH Bks.

Mapas Y Globos Terraqueos. Jack Knowlton. (SPA.). 1996. 12.15 (*0-606-09591-8*, Pub. by Turtleback) Demco.

MapBasic Developer's Guide. Angela Whitener & Breck Ryker. 608p. (C). 1996. pap. 54.95 (*1-56690-113-8*) Thomson Learn.

Mapbook of Michigan Counties. LC 83-63020. 128p. 1984. pap. 9.95 (*0-941912-08-6*) Mich Nat Res.

Mapfre Dictionary of Insurance: Trilingual Glossary in Spanish, English, & French. 3rd ed. M. J. Castelo. (ENG, FRE & SPA.). 1992. 150.00 (*0-7859-8956-0*) Fr & Eur.

MapHead. Lesley Howarth. LC 94-48604. 160p. (YA). (gr. 8-10). 1994. 14.95 (*1-56402-416-4*) Candlewick Pr.

MapHead. Lesley Howarth. LC 93-48604. (J). (gr. 6-10). 1996. pap. 4.99 (*1-56402-858-5*) Candlewick Pr.

MapHead. Lesley Howarth. 1996. 10.09 (*0-606-09592-6*, Pub. by Turtleback) Demco.

MapHead: The Return. Lesley Howarth. LC 97-519. 240p. (YA). (gr. 8-10). 1997. 15.99 (*0-7636-0344-9*) Candlewick Pr.

MAPI Survey on Potential Impact of U. S.-Mexico Free Trade Agreement on U. S. Manufacturers. 15.00 (*0-317-05110-5*, ER-228); 10.00 (*0-317-05111-3*, ER-228) Manu All Prod & Innov.

Maple. William C. Bauldry et al. LC 95-127133. 296p. 1994. pap. 31.95 (*0-471-06368-1*) Wiley.

Maple: A Comprehensive Introduction. Roy A. Nicolaides & Noel J. Walkington. (Illus.). 485p. 1996. text 42.95 (*0-521-56230-9*) Cambridge U Pr.

Maple: An Introduction & Reference. Michael Kofler. LC 97-202358. 544p. (C). 1997. pap. text 49.69 (*0-201-17899-0*) Addison-Wesley.

Maple: Introduction Reference&cd. (C). 1997. text. write for info. (*0-201-33135-7*) S&S Trade.

***Maple Approach to Calculus.** Gresser. LC QA303.5.C65G74 1999. 284p. (C). 1998. pap. text 20.00 (*0-13-010583-X*) P-H.

Maple Companion: Calculus. 5th ed. Grossman. (C). 1993. pap. text 24.50 (*0-03-096778-3*) Harcourt Coll Pubs.

Maple Computer Manual for Advanced Engineering Mathematics. Erwin Kreyszig & E. J. Norminton. 528p. 1993. pap. text 19.50 (*0-471-31126-X*) Wiley.

***Maple Dale, 1.** MaryAnn Myers. LC 98-94135. 1999. pap. text 12.95 (*0-9668780-1-9*) Lighthouse Lit.

Maple V: Mathematics & Its Application. Ed. by R. J. Lopez. LC 94-29119. 234p. 1994. 42.50 (*0-8176-3791-5*) Birkhauser.

Maple V by Example. 2nd ed. Martha L. Abell & James P. Braselton. LC 98-38819. (Illus.). 644p. (C). 1998. boxed set 44.95 incl. cd-rom (*0-12-041558-5*) Acad Pr.

Maple V Calculus Labs. Abi Fattahi. 95p. (C). 1992. pap., wbk. ed. 12.60 (*0-534-19272-6*) Brooks-Cole.

Maple V Flight Manual. Wade Ellis, Jr. et al. (Mathematics Ser.). 1993. mass mkt. 26.50 (*0-534-21235-2*) Brooks-Cole.

Maple V Flight Manual. Wade Ellis et al. 224p. (C). 1992. pap. 22.95 (*0-534-17338-1*) Brooks-Cole.

Maple V Flight Manual Release 4. 2nd ed. Wade Ellis, Jr. et al. (Mathematics Ser.). 1995. mass mkt., lab manual ed. 24.95 (*0-534-26208-2*) Brooks-Cole.

***Maple V for Engineers.** Douglas Meade & Etan Bourkoff. 1999. teacher ed. write for info. (*0-8053-6446-3*) Benjamin-Cummings.

Maple V for Engineers: Toolkit. Douglas Meade & Etan Bourkoff. 128p. 1997. pap. 23.33 (*0-8053-6445-5*) Benjamin-Cummings.

Maple Five Language Reference Manual. B. W. Char et al. xv, 267p. 1995. 26.00 (*0-387-97622-1*) Spr-Verlag.

Maple V Learning Guide. Waterloo Maple Software Staff. 269p. 1996. 26.95 (*0-387-94536-9*) Spr-Verlag.

Maple V Learning Guide: Release 5. 2nd ed. Waterloo Maple Incorporated Staff. LC 97-43751. (Illus.). 296p. 1997. pap. text 26.95 (*0-387-98397-X*) Spr-Verlag.

Maple V.3: Getting Started. 3rd ed. Waterloo Maple Software Staff. (Mathematics Ser.). 1995. 13.95 (*0-534-25573-6*); 13.95 (*0-534-25574-4*) Brooks-Cole.

Maple V.3: Release Notes. 3rd ed. Waterloo Maple Software Staff. (Mathematics Ser.). 1995. 13.95 (*0-534-25568-X*) Brooks-Cole.

Maple V Primer: Release 4. Frank Garvan. LC 96-34579. 160p. 1996. per. 15.95 (*0-8493-2681-8*) CRC Pr.

Maple V Programming Guide. Waterloo Maple Software Staff. 379p. 1996. 37.95 (*0-387-94537-7*) Spr-Verlag.

Maple V Programming Guide: Release 5. 2nd ed. Waterloo Maple Incorporated Staff. LC 97-43752. 391p. 1997. pap. text 37.95 (*0-387-98398-8*) Spr-Verlag.

Maple V Quick Reference. Nancy R. Blachman & Michael J. Mossinghoff. LC 94-10459. 1994. mass mkt. 26.50 (*0-534-20478-3*) Brooks-Cole.

Maple V Release 5: Student Version. 2nd ed. Waterloo Maple Inc. Staff. 288p. 1998. pap. 99.00 incl. cd-rom (*0-387-14240-1*) Spr-Verlag.

Maple V Student Version. Waterloo Maple Software Staff. 50p. 1993. 82.50 incl. 3.5 hd (*0-387-14211-8*) Spr-Verlag.

Maple V Student Version. Waterloo Maple Software Staff. 50p. 1994. 90.95 incl. 3.5 hd (*0-387-14209-6*) Spr-Verlag.

Maple V Student Version: Release 3., DOS/Windows. Waterloo Maple Software Staff. 70p. 1994. 90.95 (*0-387-14216-9*) Spr-Verlag.

Maple V Student Version: Release 4. Waterloo Maple, Inc. Staff. 288p. 1997. 69.00 incl. cd-rom (*0-387-14232-0*) Spr-Verlag.

Maple for Algebra. Richard Parker. LC 96-44278. (Trade/Tech Math Ser.). 320p. (C). 1996. text, mass mkt. 20.95 incl. disk (*0-8273-7407-0*) Delmar.

Maple for Basic Calculus. Richard Parker. LC 97-4462. (Trade/Tech Math Ser.). 352p. (C). 1997. 19.95 incl. disk (*0-8273-7408-9*) Delmar.

Maple for Trigonometry. Richard Parker. LC 97-159703. (Trade/Tech Math Ser.). (C). 1997. pap. 20.95 (*0-8273-7409-7*) Thomson Learn.

Maple Handbook. Darren Redfern. 400p. 1993. write for info. (*3-540-94054-5*) Spr-Verlag.

Maple Handbook. 2nd ed. Darren Redfern. LC 94-25796. 1995. 29.00 (*0-387-94331-5*) Spr-Verlag.

Maple Handbook. 4th ed. Darren Redfern. 495p. 1998. 31.95 (*0-387-98418-6*) Spr-Verlag.

Maple Handbook: Maple V Release 4. 3rd ed. Darren Redfern. 495p. 1996. 31.95 (*0-387-94538-5*) Spr-Verlag.

***Maple Kids Go to the Zoo.** large type ed. Derrick M. Dandridge. (Maple Kids Ser.). (Illus.). 32p. (ps-2). 1999. pap. 5.00 (*1-928694-01-2*, Pub. by Modern Star Bks) Allnce Hse.

Maple Leaf: A Civil War Shipwreck. 2nd ed. Sandra Dunnavant et al. Ed. by Vicki Cole. (Series of Lesson Plans: Ser. 2, No. 18). (Illus.). 12p. (J). (gr. k-12). 1997. write for info. (*1-889030-11-2*) FL Div Hist Res.

Maple Leaf Adventures. James Houston. 1990. mass mkt. 6.95 (*0-7710-4242-6*) McCland & Stewart.

Maple Leaf Against the Axis: Canada's Second World War. David Bercuson. 336p. 1998. pap. 21.95 (*0-7737-5952-2*) Stoddart Publ.

Maple Leaf & the White Eagle: Canadian-Polish Relations, 1918-1978. Aloysius Balawyder. (East European Monographs: No. 66). 300p. 1980. text 68.50 (*0-914710-59-1*, Pub. by East Eur Monographs) Col U Pr.

Maple Leaf Rag. Ellen Banks. 1989. 50.00 (*0-932526-63-2*) Nexus Pr.

Maple Leaf Rag. Sott Joplin. 12p. 1997. per. 4.95 (*0-7935-8321-7*) H Leonard.

Maple Leaf Rag. large type ed. Stephen Brook. 1989. 27.99 (*0-7089-2100-0*) Ulverscroft.

Maple Leaf Rag: An Anthology of New Orleans Poetry. Ed. by Maxine Cassin et al. (Illus.). 116p. (Orig.). 1980. pap. 25.00 (*0-938498-01-0*) New Orleans Poetry.

Maple Leaf Rag: Poetry Anthology from New Orleans. anniversary ed. 192p. 1994. pap. 15.00 (*0-916620-99-9*) Portals Pr.

Maple Leaves. Marilyn S. Doheny. 1996. 10.95 (*0-945169-13-2*) Doheny Pubns.

Maple Library Reference Manual. B. W. Char et al. xxv, 698p. 1993. 43.95 (*0-387-97592-6*) Spr-Verlag.

Maple Magic. Sherri Eldridge. (Illus.). 32p. 1998. pap. 2.95 (*1-886862-28-1*, MN MAP, Coastal New England Pubns) Harv Hill ME.

***Maple Moon.** Connie B. Crook. (Illus.). 32p. (ps-3). 2000. pap. 6.95 (*0-7737-6098-9*) Stoddart Publ.

Maple Moon. unabridged ed. Connie B. Crook. LC 98-108655. (Illus.). 32p. (YA). (ps-2). 1998. 15.95 (*0-7737-3017-6*) STDK.

Maple Ode Lab Book. Darren Redfern & E. Chandler. LC 97-1341. 160p. 1996. pap. 29.95 (*0-387-94733-7*) Spr-Verlag.

Maple Sampler. Jan Siegrist. (Illus.). 48p. (Orig.). 1985. pap. 3.95 (*0-933050-33-X*) New Eng Pr VT.

Maple Sugar. Roberta Hall. (Illus.). 64p. 1998. pap. 10.50 (*1-56770-444-1*) S Scheewe Pubns.

Maple Sugar. Robert L. Merriam. (Illus.). 32p. (Orig.). 1982. 35.00 (*0-685-05823-9*); pap. 2.50 (*0-686-35762-0*) R L Merriam.

***Maple Sugar, Vol. 3.** Roberta Hall. (Illus.). 72p. 1999. pap. 10.50 (*1-56770-471-9*) S Scheewe Pubns.

***Maple Sugar, Vol. 4.** Roberta Hall. (Illus.). 82p. 2000. pap. 10.50 (*1-56770-481-6*) S Scheewe Pubns.

Maple Sugar Book. Helen Nearing & Scott Nearing. (Illus.). 271p. 1950. 14.95 (*0-911394-02-8*) Good Life Ctr.

Maple Sugar Book. Helen Nearing & Scott Nearing. LC 73-148417. (Illus.). 271p. 1970. pap. 11.95 (*0-911394-03-6*) Good Life Ctr.

***Maple Sugar Book: 50th Anniversary Edition - A Good Life Center Book.** anniversary ed. Helen Nearing & Scott Nearing. (Illus.). 328p. 2000. pap. 17.95 (*1-890132-63-2*) Chelsea Green Pub.

***Maple Sugar Festivals: Tapping for Sap.** Lisa Gabbert. (Illus.). 24p. (J). (gr. k-4). 1999. 17.26 (*0-8239-5340-8*, PowerKids) Rosen Group.

Maple Sugar Language in Vermont; Comments on PADS 5 & 6; Supplementing Word-Lists. Margaret M. Bryant et al. (Publications of the American Dialect Society: No. 8). 41p. 1947. pap. 4.50 (*0-8173-0608-0*) U of Ala Pr.

Maple Sugar Murders. Steve Sherman. LC 98-76206. 224p. 1999. mass mkt. 5.99 (*0-9627162-5-1*) Appledore Bks.

***Maple Sugar II.** Roberta Hall. (Illus.). 82p. 1999. pap. 10.50 (*1-56770-461-1*) S Scheewe Pubns.

Maple Sugaring Story: A Guide for Teaching & Learning the Maple Industry. Betty A. Lockhart. Ed. by Donald G. Lockhart. (Illus.). 84p. 1990. teacher ed. 4.50 (*1-880327-04-X*) Perceptions.

***Maple Supplement for Statics.** 144p. (C). 1999. pap. 21.00 (*0-13-011427-8*) P-H.

Maple Syrup. Elaine Elliot. (Flavours Ser.). (Illus.). 64p. 1998. pap. 9.95 (*0-88780-420-9*, Pub. by Formac Publ Co) Seven Hills Bk.

Maple Syrup Baking & Dessert Cookbook. large type ed. Ken Haedrich. (Illus.). 48p. (Orig.). 1985. pap. 4.50 (*0-942550-00-5*) Am Impress Bk Co.

Maple Syrup Book. Julie Aldis. 96p. 2000. 19.95 (*1-55046-207-5*, Pub. by Boston Mills) Genl Dist Srvs.

Maple Syrup Book. unabridged ed. Marilyn Linton & Lesley Fairfield. (Illus.). 48p. (J). (gr. 3-7). 1983. pap. 9.95 (*0-919964-52-4*, Pub. by Kids Can Pr) Genl Dist Srvs.

Maple Syrup Cookbook. Ken Haedrich. Ed. by Andrea Chesman. LC 88-45485. (Illus.). 144p. 1989. pap. 12.95 (*0-88266-523-5*, Garden Way Pub) Storey Bks.

Maple Tree, No. 3066. David M. Schwartz. Ed. by Sue Lewis & Elaine Pascoe. (Life Cycles Ser.). 16p. 1999. pap. 2.99 (*1-57471-556-9*) Creat Teach Pr.

Maple Trees. Marcia S. Freeman. LC 98-18294. (Trees Ser.). (Illus.). 24p. (J). 1998. 13.25 (*0-7368-0092-1*, Cpstone High Low) Capstone Pr.

Maple Trees, 1 vol. Marcia S. Freeman. (Trees (Captstone) Ser.). (J). 1998. 13.25 (*0-516-21504-3*) Childrens.

Maple via Calculus: Tutorial Approach. Robert J. Lopez. LC 94-28246. xiii, 166p. 1994. 18.50 (*0-8176-3771-0*) Birkhauser.

Maple 4.2.1: Profess Single User Version. Symbolic Computation Group Staff. (Math). (C). 1990. 384.00 (*0-534-10224-7*) Brooks-Cole.

***Maples & the Stream.** Lien Chao. 136p. 1999. 14.95 (*0-920661-83-1*) TSAR Pubns.

***Maples & the Stream: A Narrative Poem.** Lien Chao. 125p. 1999. pap. 14.95 (*0-920661-81-5*, Pub. by TSAR Pubns) SPD-Small Pr Dist.

Maples Fine Furnishers. Hugh Barty-King. 1992. 29.95 (*1-870948-67-X*, Pub. by Quiller Pr) St Mut.

Maples for Gardens: A Color Encyclopedia. C. J. Van Gelderen & D. M. Van Gelderen. LC 98-44064. 294p. 1999. 49.95 (*0-88192-472-5*) Timber.

Maples in the Mist. Minfong Ho. LC 95-17357. (Illus.). 32p. 1996. 16.00 (*0-688-12044-X*) Lothrop.

Maples in the Mist. Minfong Ho. LC 95-17357. (Illus.). 32p. (J). 1996. lib. bdg. 14.93 (*0-688-14723-2*) Lothrop.

Maples of the World. D. M. Van Gelderen et al. Ed. by Theodore R. Dudley. LC 92-46361. (Illus.). 478p. 1994. 65.00 (*0-88192-000-2*) Timber.

Maplewood. John C. Bausmith. LC 98-86896. (Images of America Ser.). (Illus.). 128p. 1998. pap. 16.99 (*0-7524-1279-5*) Arcadia Publng.

Maplin Electronic Circuit Handbook. 2nd ed. Michael H. Tooley. (Illus.). 320p. 1995. pap. text 34.95 (*0-7506-2331-4*) Buttrwrth-Heinemann.

Maplin Home Security Projects: A Collection of Useful Design Ideas for Security Devices around the Home. Maplin Staff. (Illus.). 208p. 1999. pap. text 26.95 (*0-7506-2603-8*) Buttrwrth-Heinemann.

Maplin Power Supply Projects. Maplin Staff. (Maplin Project Ser.). (Illus.). 208p. 1996. pap. text 26.95 (*0-7506-2602-X*) Buttrwrth-Heinemann.

Mapmaker: Poems. Beatriz Badikian. 84p. (Orig.). 1994. pap. 8.95 (*0-9641825-0-5*) Gladsome Bks.

***Mapmakers.** John N. Wilford. LC 99-49957. 2000. 30.00 (*0-375-40929-7*) Knopf.

Mapmaker's Art: An Illustrated History of Cartography. John Goss. LC 93-4963. (Illus.). 1993. 100.00 (*0-528-83620-X*) Rand McNally.

Mapmaker's Art: Three-Hundred Years of British Cartography. Elisabeth R. Fairman. (Illus.). 16p. (Orig.). (C). 1989. pap. 3.00 (*0-685-62658-X*) Yale Ctr Brit Art.

Mapmaker's Dream: The Meditations of Fra Mauro, Cartographer to the Court of Venice. James Cowan. LC 96-7439. 208p. 1996. 18.00 (*1-57062-196-9*, Pub. by Shambhala Pubns) Random.

Mapmaker's Dream: The Meditations of Fra Mauro, Cartographer to the Court of Venice. James Cowan. LC 97-26164. 176p. 1997. mass mkt. 10.99 (*0-446-67338-2*, Pub. by Warner Bks) Little.

***Mapmakers of Spitalfields.** Syed M. Islam. LC 98-130969. 144p. 1999. pap. 12.95 (*1-900715-08-2*, Pub. by Peepal Tree Pr) Paul & Co Pubs.

Mapmakers of the Western Trails: The Story of John Charles Fremont. Natalie Nelson-Hernandez. LC 97-181478. (Illus.). 128p. (J). (gr. 3-8). 1997. pap. 9.95 (*0-9644386-2-3*) Santa Ines Pub.

Mapmaking with Children: Sense-Of Place Education for the Elementary Years. David Sobel. LC 98-14641. 164p. 1998. pap. 24.50 (*0-325-00042-5*) Heinemann.

Mapondera: Soldier of Zimbabwe. Solomon M. Mutswairo. 133p. 1978. pap. 10.00 (*1-57889-046-2*) Passeggiata.

Mapoteca Geologica Americana: A Catalogue of Geological Maps of America (North & South), 1752-1881. Jules Marcou & John B. Marcou. 184p. 1997. reprint ed. 65.00 (*1-891396-02-1*) Pober Pub.

Mapoteca Geologica Americana: A Catalogue of Geological Maps of America, 1752-1881. Jules Marcou & John B. Marcou. 189p. 1997. reprint ed. 60.00 (*1-57898-060-7*) Martino Pubng.

Mapp & Lucia. E. F. Benson. LC 98-52500. 234p. 2000. pap. 12.95 (*1-55921-232-2*) Moyer Bell.

***Mapp & Lucia.** E. F. Benson. (Humour Classics). 2000. 14.95 (*1-85375-390-4*, Pub. by Prion) Trafalgar.

MAPP to Aquarius: Mark Age Period & Program. Nada-Yolanda. LC 85-62167. (Illus.). 351p. 1985. 20.00 (*0-912322-05-5*); pap. 15.00 (*0-912322-53-5*) Mark-Age.

Mapp vs. Ohio: Evidence & Search Warrants. Deborah A. Persico. LC 96-21295. (Landmark Supreme Court Cases Ser.). (Illus.). 128p. (YA). (gr. 6 up). 1997. lib. bdg. 20.95 (*0-89490-857-X*) Enslow Pubs.

Mappa Mundi: The Hereford World Map. P. D. Harvey. (Illus.). 64p. 1996. 40.00 (*0-8020-0985-9*); pap. 20.00 (*0-8020-7945-8*) U of Toronto Pr.

Mappamundi: New & Selected Poems. Mac Hammond. 149p. 1989. 24.95 (*0-933466-05-6*); pap. 19.95 (*0-933466-04-8*) Bellevue Pr.

Mapped Out! The Search for Snookums. Carol Baicker-McKee. LC 96-27680. (Illus.). 32p. (YA). (gr. 3 up). 1997. 19.95 (*0-87905-788-2*) Gibbs Smith Pub.

Mappila Muslims of Kerala: A Study of Islamic Trends. 2nd enl. rev. ed. Roland E. Miller. 389p. 1992. 22.00 (*0-86311-270-6*, Pub. by Sangam Bks Ltd) S Asia.

Mapping. Frances Colpitt. 40p. 1994. pap. 18.00 (*0-9640911-0-0*) U TX San Antonio.

Mapping. Daniel Dorling. 208p. (C). 1997. pap. text 24.60 (*0-582-28972-6*) Addison-Wesley.

Mapping. rev. ed. David Greenhood. LC 63-20905. 302p. 1964. pap. 23.00 (*0-226-30697-6*, P521) U Ch Pr.

Mapping. rev. ed. David Greenhood. LC 63-20905. 1992. lib. bdg. 25.00 (*0-226-30696-8*) U Ch Pr.

Mapping: Earth Science Translated. Alfred DeVito. (Illus.). 130p. 1986. pap. 14.95 (*0-942034-05-8*) Creat Ventures IN.

Mapping a Changing World. Yvette La Pierre. (Illus.). 64p. 1996. 17.95 (*0-9650308-4-9*) Lickle Pubng.

Mapping a Winning Training Approach: A Practical Guide to Choosing the Best Training Approach. Joe B. Wilson. (High-Impact Training Ser.). (Illus.). 120p. 1995. pap. 14.95 (*0-7879-5099-8*) R Chang Assocs.

M

***Mapping African America.** Ed. by Maria Diedrich et al. (Forecast Forum for European Contributions to African American Studies). 252p. 1999. pap. 32.95 (*3-8258-3328-3*, Pub. by CE24) Transaction Pubs.

Mapping American Culture. Ed. by Wayne Franklin & Michael Steiner. LC 92-10421. (American Land & Life Ser.). (Illus.). 318p. 1992. text 32.95 (*0-87745-379-9*); pap. text 15.95 (*0-87745-518-X*) U of Iowa Pr.

Mapping American History: Student Activities. (C). 1991. pap. text 12.19 (*0-673-53768-4*) Addison-Wesley.

Mapping America's Past: A Historical Atlas. Mark C. Carnes. (Illus.). 288p. 1996. 50.00 (*0-8050-4927-4*) H Holt & Co.

Mapping an Empire. Andrew T. Edney. LC 96-39703. 1997. 35.00 (*0-226-18487-0*) U Ch Pr.

Mapping an Empire: The Geographical Construction of British India, 1765-1843. Matthew H. Edney. LC 96-39703. (Illus.). 458p. 1999. pap. text 25.00 (*0-226-18488-9*) U Ch Pr.

Mapping & Naming the Moon: A History of Lunar Cartography & Nomenclature. Ewen A. Whitaker. (Illus.). 242p. (C). 1999. 59.95 (*0-521-62248-4*) Cambridge U Pr.

Mapping & Remote Sensing Tools for the 21st Century, 1994. 248p. 1994. 25.00 (*1-57083-012-6*) ASP & RS.

Mapping & Spatial Modelling for Navigation. Ed. by Louis F. Pau. (NATO ASI Series F: Computer & Systems Sciences, Special Programme AET: Vol. 65). (Illus.). viii, 357p. 1990. 91.95 (*0-387-52711-7*) Spr-Verlag.

Mapping & Topographic Drafting. John D. Bies. (Drafting Ser.). 1983. teacher ed. 17.50 (*0-538-33331-6*); text 42.95 (*0-538-33330-8*) S-W Pub.

***Mapping Animal Movements.** rev. ed. Katherine Barrett. Ed. by Lincoln Bergman & Kay Fairwell. (Great Explorations in Math & Science (GEMS) Ser.). (Illus.). 56p. (J). 1999. pap. 10.50 (*0-924886-24-2*, GEMS) Lawrence Science.

Mapping Between X.400 (1988) - ISO 100 21 & RFC 822. Steve Hardcastle-Kille. 96p. (Orig.). (C). 1993. pap. text 40.00 (*1-56806-321-0*) DIANE Pub.

***Mapping Boston.** Ed. by Alex Krieger et al. LC 99-20991. (Illus.). 277p. 1999. 50.00 (*0-262-11244-2*) MIT Pr.

***Mapping Careers with LD & ADD Clients: Guidebook & Case Studies.** Raizi Abby Janus. LC 98-51485. 384p. 1999. 42.00 (*0-231-10978-4*) Col U Pr.

***Mapping Chengde: The Qing Landscape Enterprise.** Philippe Foret. LC 99-88190. (Illus.). 204p. 2000. text 60.00 (*0-8248-1980-2*) UH Pr.

***Mapping Chengde: The Qing Landscape Enterprise.** Philippe Foret. LC 99-88190. (Illus.). 204p. 2000. pap. text 32.95 (*0-8248-2293-5*) UH Pr.

Mapping Christian Education: Approaches to Congregational Learning. Ed. by Jack L. Seymour. LC 96-51888. 144p. 1997. pap. 15.95 (*0-687-00812-3*) Abingdon.

***Mapping Cities.** Naomi Miller. (Illus.). 92p. 2000. pap. 20.00 (*1-881450-13-9*) U of Wash Pr.

Mapping Class Groups & Moduli Spaces of Reimann Surfaces: Proceedings of Workshops Held June 24-28, 1991 & August 6-10, 1991 in Gottingen, Germany & Seattle, Washington. Ed. by Carl-Freidrich Bodigheimer & Richard M. Hain. LC 93-14150. (Contemporary Mathematics Ser.: Vol. 150). 372p. 1993. pap. 51.00 (*0-8218-5167-5*, CONM/150) Am Math.

Mapping Class Groups of Low Genus & Their Cohomology. D. Benson & F. Cohen. LC 90-26421. (Memoirs Ser.: Vol. 90/443). 104p. 1991. pap. 21.00 (*0-8218-2506-2*, MEMO/90/443) Am Math.

Mapping Codes: A Collection of New Writing from Moscow to San Francisco. Ed. by Aleka Chase et al. (Review Ser.: No. 8/9). 286p. (Orig.). 1990. pap. 9.00 (*0-9618409-8-6*) Five Fingers.

Mapping Crime in Its Community Setting: Event Geography Analysis. M. D. Maltz et al. (Illus.). 152p. 1990. 82.95 (*0-387-97381-8*) Spr-Verlag.

Mapping Cultural Spaces: Postcolonial Indian Literature in English : Essays in Honour of Nissim Ezekiel. Nissim Ezekiel et al. LC 98-917124. 376p. 1998. write for info. (*81-7094-311-6*) Vision.

M

Mapping Curricular Reform in Library & Information Studies: The American Mosaic. Ed. by Virgil L. Blake. LC 95-37925. (Public & Access Services Quarterly Ser.: Vol. 1, No. 3). 130p. 1995. 39.95 (*1-56024-740-1*) Haworth Pr.

***Mapping Cyberspace.** Martin Dodge & Rob Kitchin. LC 00-38247. 2000. pap. write for info. (*0-415-19884-4*) Routledge.

Mapping Cyberspace: Social Research on the Electronic Frontier. Joseph E. Behar. (Dowling Studies in the Humanities & the Social Sciences). 256p. 1997. pap. 17.00 (*1-883058-43-0*, Dowling College) Global Pubns.

Mapping Desire: Geographies of Sexualities. Ed. by David Bell & Gill Valentine. LC 94-34825. (Illus.). 500p. (C). (gr. 13). 1995. pap. 25.99 (*0-415-11164-1*, C0058) Routledge.

Mapping Educational Success: Strategic Thinking & Planning for School Administrators. rev. ed. Roger Kaufman. Ed. by Fenwick W. English. (Successful Schools Ser.). (Illus.). 208p. 1994. pap. 24.95 (*0-8039-6203-7*) Corwin Pr.

***Mapping Epidemics: A Historical Atlas of Disease.** Charles H. Calisher. (Reference Ser.). (Illus.). (YA). 2000. pap. 19.95 (*0-531-16487-X*) Watts.

***Mapping Epidemics: A Historical Atlas of Disease** Brent H. Hoff et al. LC 99-16502. 2000. 38.00 (*0-531-11713-8*) Watts.

Mapping Fate: A Memoir of Family, Risk, & Genetic Research. Alice Wexler. LC 96-16801. (Illus.). 319p. (C). 1996. pap. 15.95 (*0-520-20741-6*, Pub. by U CA Pr) Cal Prin Full Svc.

***Mapping Fish Habitats.** rev. ed. Katherine Barrett & Cary I. Sneider. Ed. by Lincoln Bergman & Kay Fairwell. (Great Explorations in Math & Science (GEMS) Ser.). (Illus.). 60p. 1999. pap. 10.50 (*0-924886-25-0*, GEMS) Lawrence Science.

Mapping Florida Outdoors. Joan L. Scalpone. (Illus.). 64p. 1992. pap. 9.98 (*0-929198-11-5*) Mini DayTrip Bks.

Mapping for Stonewall: The Civil War Service of Jed Hotchkiss. William J. Miller. LC 93-18611. (Illus.). 176p. 1993. 29.95 (*1-880216-11-6*, Elliott Clark) Black Belt Communs.

Mapping Genomes: A Laboratory Manual. Ed. by Bruce Birren et al. (Genome Analysis Ser.: No. 4). (Illus.). 650p. (C). 1998. text 230.00 (*0-87969-514-5*); pap. text 140.00 (*0-87969-515-3*) Cold Spring Harbor.

Mapping Great Debates: Can Computers Think?: 7 Maps & a Handbook, 8 vols. Robert E. Horn et al. LC 98-96437. (Illus.). 450p. (C). 1998. 125.00 (*1-892637-08-1*) MacroVU Inc.

Mapping Hegemony: Television News & Industrial Conflict. Robert Goldman & Arvind Rajagopal. 272p. 1991. pap. 39.50 (*0-89391-819-9*); text 73.25 (*0-89391-697-8*) Ablx Pub.

Mapping Hidden Dimensions of the Urban Scene. Janos Szego. (Urban Studies). (Illus.). 266p. 1994. pap. 82.50 (*91-540-5651-9*) Coronet Bks.

Mapping Hypertext. Robert E. Horn. (Illus.). 300p. (Orig.). (C). 1990. pap. 39.50 (*0-9625565-0-5*) Lexington Inst.

Mapping Ideology. Ed. by Slavo Zizek. (Mappings Ser.). 288p. (C). 1995. pap. 22.00 (*1-85984-055-8*, B4579, Pub. by Verso) Norton.

Mapping Inner Space: Learning & Teaching Mind Mapping. Nancy Margulies. (Illus.). 128p. (J). (gr. k-12). 1991. 32.00 (*0-913705-56-X*) Zephyr Pr AZ.

Mapping Islamic Studies: Genealogy, Continuity & Change. Ed. by Azim Nanji. LC 97-15820. (Religion & Reason Ser.). 270p. 1997. text 132.00 (*3-11-014187-6*) Mouton.

Mapping It Out: Expository Cartography for the Humanities & Social Sciences. Mark Monmonier. LC 92-39894. (Chicago Guides to Writing, Editing & Publishing Ser.). (Illus.). 316p. (C). 1993. pap. 15.95 (*0-226-53417-0*); lib. bdg. 41.00 (*0-226-53416-2*) U Ch Pr.

Mapping Jewish Identities. Silberstein. text 60.00 (*0-8147-9768-7*); pap. text 20.00 (*0-8147-9769-5*) NYU Pr.

Mapping Literary Modernism: Time & Development. Ricardo J. Quinones. LC 84-42899. 314p. 1985. reprint ed. pap. 97.40 (*0-608-02905-X*, 206396900008) Bks Demand.

***Mapping Male Sexuality: Nineteenth-Century England.** Jay Losey & William D. Brewer. LC 99-53165. 2000. write for info. (*0-8386-3828-7*) Fairleigh Dickinson.

Mapping Maryland. Willard Hackerman Collection Staff. LC 99-168129. 1999. 20.00 (*0-938420-64-X*) MD Hist.

Mapping, Measuring & Modelling the Universe. Ed. by Peter Coles et al. (ASP Conference Series Proceedings: Vol. 94). 383p. 1996. 34.00 (*1-886733-15-5*) Astron Soc Pacific.

Mapping Men & Empire: A Geography of Adventure. Richard Phillips. LC 96-10899. (Illus.). 224p. (C). 1996. 85.00 (*0-415-13771-3*); pap. 25.99 (*0-415-13772-1*) Routledge.

Mapping Mortality: The Persistence of Memory & Melancholy in Early Modern England. William E. Engel. LC 95-12794. (Massachusetts Studies in Early Modern Culture). (Illus.). 304p. (C). 1996. 50.00 (*0-87023-998-8*) U of Mass Pr.

Mapping Multiculturalism. Ed. by Avery Gordon & Christopher Newfield. (Illus.). 504p. 1996. pap. 24.95 (*0-8166-2547-6*); text 62.95 (*0-8166-2546-8*) U of Minn Pr.

Mapping New Schools, Vol. 1. Beverly L. Taylor. LC 79-108535. 153p. 1980. reprint ed. pap. 47.50 (*0-608-02751-0*, 205255900001) Bks Demand.

Mapping New Schools, Vol. 2. Beverly L. Taylor. LC 79-108535. 167p. 1980. reprint ed. pap. 51.80 (*0-608-02752-9*, 205255900002) Bks Demand.

Mapping New Schools, Vol. 3. Beverly L. Taylor. LC 79-108535. 159p. 1980. reprint ed. pap. 49.30 (*0-608-02753-7*, 205255900003) Bks Demand.

Mapping New Schools, Vol. 4. Beverly L. Taylor. LC 79-108535. 183p. 1980. reprint ed. pap. 56.80 (*0-608-02754-5*, 205255900004) Bks Demand.

Mapping of America. Ronald V. Tooley. 522p. (C). 1988. 270.00 (*0-7855-4040-7*) St Mut.

Mapping of Australia. Ed. by Ronald V. Tooley. (Holland Press Cartographica Ser.: Vol. 1). (Illus.). 1979. 75.00 (*0-900470-87-9*, Pub. by Holland Press) Book East.

Mapping of Australia. deluxe limited ed. Ed. by Ronald V. Tooley. (Holland Press Cartographica Ser.: Vol. 1). (Illus.). 1979. 180.00 (*0-900470-88-7*) W G Arader.

Mapping of Geological Structures. Kenneth R. McClay. (Geological Society of London Professional Handbook Ser.: No. 1572). 168p. 1991. pap. 59.95 (*0-471-93243-4*) Wiley.

Mapping of Geological Structures. 2nd ed. Kenneth McClay. (Geological Society of London Professional Handbook Ser.). 2000. pap. text 20.00 (*0-471-96635-5*) Wiley.

Mapping of New Spain: Indigenous Cartography & the Maps of the Relaciones Geograficas. Barbara E. Mundy. LC 96-15824. (Illus.). 256p. 1996. 40.00 (*0-226-55096-6*) U Ch Pr.

Mapping of North America. John Goss. 1990. 29.98 (*1-55521-672-2*) Bk Sales Inc.

Mapping of Ohio: The Delineation of the State of Ohio Through the Use of Manuscript Maps, Printed Maps, & Plats, Sketches & Plans from Original Map Makers with a Narrative Which Describes Each Map from Contemporary Sources. Thomas H. Smith. LC 75-99081. 268p. reprint ed. pap. 83.10 (*0-7837-2026-2*, 205245400002) Bks Demand.

Mapping of the American Southwest. Ed. by Dennis Reinhartz & Charles C. Colley. LC 86-22992. (Special Collections Publication of the University of Texas at Arlington Ser.: No. 1). (Illus.). 112p. 1987. reprint ed. 29.95 (*0-89096-237-5*) Tex A&M Univ Pr.

***Mapping of the Entradas into the Greater Southwest.** annot. ed. Ed. by Dennis Reinhartz & Gerald D. Saxon. (Illus.). 256p. 1998. 37.50 (*0-8061-3047-4*) U of Okla Pr.

Mapping of the Great Lakes in the Seventeenth Century: 22 Maps from the George S. & Nancy B. Parker Collection: A Portfolio with an Introduction & Commentary. fac. ed. Kevin Kaufman. (Illus.). 108p. 1989. 165.00 (*0-916617-34-3*) J C Brown.

Mapping of the Heavens. Peter Whitfield. (Illus.). 144p. 1995. 35.00 (*0-87654-475-8*) Pomegranate Calif.

Mapping of the World. Rodney Shirley. (Illus.). 720p. 1998. 295.00 (*1-85368-271-3*, Pub. by New5 Holland) Sterling.

Mapping of the World. Rodney W. Shirley. 718p. (C). 1988. 750.00 (*0-946323-03-8*, Pub. by New5 Holland) St Mut.

Mapping Our Genes: Genome Projects - How Big, How Fast? Congress of the United States Office of Technology. LC 88-45401. 224p. 1988. text 37.50 (*0-8018-3755-3*) Johns Hopkins.

Mapping Our Genes: Genome Projects: How Big, How Fast? United States Congress, Office of Technology Asses. LC 88-17572. (Illus.). 232p. reprint ed. pap. 72.00 (*0-608-08801-3*, 206944000004) Bks Demand.

Mapping Our Genes: The Genome Projects. 1990. lib. bdg. 250.00 (*0-87700-911-2*) Revisionist Pr.

Mapping Our Selves: Canadian Women's Autobiography. Helen M. Buss. 248p. 1993. 65.00 (*0-7735-0975-5*, Pub. by McG-Queens Univ Pr) CUP Services.

Mapping Our Selves: Canadian Women's Autobiography. Helen M. Buss. (Illus.). 252p. 1994. pap. 24.95 (*0-7735-1244-6*, Pub. by McG-Queens Univ Pr) CUP Services.

Mapping Our World. Martyn Bramwell. LC 97-50150. (Maps & Mapmakers Ser.). (YA). (gr. 4-12). 1998. 16.95 (*0-8225-2924-6*) Lerner Pub.

Mapping Our World: Group 1. (Illus.). 64p. (YA). (gr. 4 up). lib. bdg. 108.29 (*0-7614-0366-3*) Marshall Cavendish.

Mapping Our World Boxed Set, 4 vols. Fran Sammis. (J). 2000. 108.29 (*0-7614-0375-2*, Benchmark NY) Marshall Cavendish.

Mapping Out a Strategy to Witness in Your Jerusalem, Judea, Samaria & to the Ends of His Earth. Mark Schaufler. 14p. 1995. spiral bd. 2.00 (*1-886904-25-1*) MST Minist.

***Mapping Penny's World.** Loreen Leedy. LC 99-48327. (Illus.). 32p. (gr. k-3). 2000. text 17.00 (*0-8050-6178-9*) St Martin.

Mapping Project: Liberty & Equality. Murrin. 1996. pap. text 14.00 (*0-15-503676-9*, Pub. by Harcourt Coll Pubs) Harcourt.

Mapping Project: Liberty & Equality. Murrin. (C). 1996. wbk. ed. 14.00 (*0-15-503581-9*, Pub. by Harcourt Coll Pubs) Harcourt.

Mapping Public Policy for Genetic Technologies: A Legislator's Resource Guide. Brenda Trolin & National Conference of State Legislatures Education. LC 98-217945. 214p. 1998. 30.00 (*1-55516-790-X*) Natl Conf State Legis.

Mapping Reality. King. LC 96-140400. 1996. text 49.95 (*0-312-12704-9*) St Martin.

Mapping Reality: An Evolutionary Realist Methodology for the Natural & Social Sciences. Jane Azevedo. LC 96-2367. (SUNY Series in the Philosophy of the Social Sciences). (Illus.). 322p. (C). 1997. pap. text 22.95 (*0-7914-3208-4*) State U NY Pr.

Mapping Reality: An Evolutionary Realist Methodology for the Natural & Social Sciences. Jane Azevedo. LC 96-2367. (SUNY Series in the Philosophy of the Social Sciences). (Illus.). 322p. (C). 1997. text 68.50 (*0-7914-3207-6*) State U NY Pr.

Mapping Reality: An Exploration of Cultural Cartographies. Geoff King. 224p. 1996. pap. 19.95 (*0-312-12706-5*) St Martin.

Mapping Regional Freeze - Thaw Patterns with Satellite Microwave Radiometry. Anthony W. England et al. LC QC0902.. (University of Michigan Reports: No. 027396-1-F). 25p. reprint ed. pap. 30.00 (*0-7837-6290-9*, 204600500010) Bks Demand.

Mapping Russia & Its Neighbors: The New Atlas of the Changed Geographical Face of the Former Soviet Union. Godfrey Harris & Sergei Diakonov. (Illus.). 1993. 29.95 (*0-935047-14-X*) Americas Group.

Mapping Skills. Meryl Meisser & Evelyn Popper. Ed. by Stephanie Pliakas. (Thinking Skills Library). (Illus.). 110p. (Orig.). (J). (gr. 2-5). 1997. pap., teacher ed. 9.95 (*1-56784-711-0*) Newbridge Educ.

***Mapping Social Networks, Spatial Data & Hidden Populations.** Jean J. Schensul et al. LC 98-40072. (Ethnographer's Toolkit Ser.: Vol. 4). (Illus.). 224p. 1998. pap. 19.95 (*0-7619-9112-3*) AltaMira Pr.

Mapping Social Theory. Ed. by Sebastian Budgen. 320p. 1999. 60.00 (*1-85984-700-5*, Pub. by Verso); pap. 20.00 (*1-85984-227-5*, Pub. by Verso) Norton.

Mapping Strategies in Chemical Oceanography. Ed. by Alberto Zirino. LC 85-20265. (Advances in Chemistry Ser.: No. 209). 465p. 1985. lib. bdg. 98.95 (*0-8412-0862-X*) Am Chemical.

Mapping Strategies in Chemical Oceanography. Ed. by Alberto Zirino. LC 84-20265. (Advances in Chemistry Ser.: Vol. 209). 480p. 1985. reprint ed. pap. 148.80 (*0-608-03511-4*, 206423000008) Bks Demand.

Mapping Subaltern Studies & the Postcolonial. Vinayak Chaturvedi. 1999. pap. text 20.00 (*1-85984-214-3*, Pub. by Verso) Norton.

***Mapping Subaltern Studies & the Postcolonial.** Vinayak Chaturvedi. 1999. 60.00 (*1-85984-723-4*, Pub. by Verso) Norton.

Mapping Technician. Jack Rudman. (Career Examination Ser.: C-3462). 1994. pap. 27.95 (*0-8373-3462-4*) Nat Learn.

Mapping Technologist. Jack Rudman. (Career Examination Ser.: C-3463). 1994. pap. 29.95 (*0-8373-3463-2*) Nat Learn.

Mapping Texas & the Gulf Coast: The Contributions of Saint-Denis, Olivan, & Le Maire. Jack Jackson et al. LC 90-36494. (Illus.). 104p. 1990. 29.50 (*0-89096-439-4*) Tex A&M Univ Pr.

Mapping "The American Promise" Historical Geography Workbook, Vol. II. Mark Newman. 1997. pap. text, wbk. ed. 1.33 (*0-312-18026-8*) St Martin.

Mapping the American Revolutionary War. Lawrence W. Towner et al. LC 77-8023. (Kenneth Nebenzahl, Jr., Lectures in the History of Cartography). (Illus.). 1994. 39.95 (*0-226-21631-9*) U Ch Pr.

***Mapping the American West.** Judy Alter. LC 00-23533. (Illus.). (J). 2001. write for info. (*0-516-21599-X*) Childrens.

Mapping the Beat: Popular Music & Contemporary Theory. Ed. by Thomas Swiss et al. LC 96-39868. 224p. (C). 1997. text 62.95 (*1-57718-077-1*); pap. text 24.95 (*1-57718-078-X*) Blackwell Pubs.

Mapping the Big Picture: Integrating Curriculum & Assessment K-12. Heidi H. Jacobs. LC 97-16708. 110p. (Orig.). 1997. pap. 16.95 (*0-87120-286-7*, 197135) ASCD.

Mapping the Boundary Between Continuous & Discontinuous Permafrost in Alaska. Anthony W. England. LC G 0070.4. (University of Michigan Reports: No. 028676-1-F). 50p. 1995. reprint ed. pap. 30.00 (*0-608-02393-0*, 206303400004) Bks Demand.

Mapping the Boundary Between Continuous & Discontinuous Permafrost in Alaska: Water Resources Research Grant Program. Tony England et al. LC QC0973.. (University of Michigan Reports: No. 028676-1-T). 24p. reprint ed. pap. 30.00 (*0-7837-6284-4*, 204599900010) Bks Demand.

Mapping the Brain & Its Functions: Integrating Enabling Technologies into Neuroscience Research. Institute of Medicine, Committee on a National Neu. Ed. by Constance M. Pecura & Joseph B. Martin. 180p. 1991. text 24.95 (*0-309-04497-9*) Natl Acad Pr.

Mapping the Chaos. Rhea Tregebov. Ed. by Michael Harris. (Signal Editions Ser.). 64p. (Orig.). 1995. pap. 9.95 (*1-55065-070-X*, Pub. by Vehicule Pr) Genl Dist Srvs.

Mapping the Civil War: Featuring Rare Maps from the Library of Congress. Christopher Nelson. LC 92-17799. (Illus.). 176p. 1992. 39.95 (*1-56373-001-4*) Fulcrum Pub.

Mapping the Code: The Human Genome Project & the Choices of Modern Science. Joel L. Davis. LC 90-12572. 294p. 1991. 19.95 (*0-471-50383-5*) Wiley.

***Mapping the Course of the Chinese Language Field.** Ed. by Madeline Chu. (Monograph Ser.: Vol. III). (Illus.). xii, 350p. 1999. pap. text 20.00 (*1-891637-01-0*) Chinese Lang Teach.

Mapping the Cultural Space of Journalism: How Journalists Distinguish News from Entertainment. Samuel P. Winch. LC 96-33190. 208p. 1998. pap. 19.95 (*0-275-96467-1*, Praeger Pubs) Greenwood.

Mapping the Cultural Space of Journalism: How Journalists Distinquish News from Entertainment. Samuel P. Winch. LC 96-33190. 208p. 1997. 55.00 (*0-275-95763-2*, Praeger Pubs) Greenwood.

***Mapping the Deep: The Extraordinary Story of Ocean Science.** Robert Kunzig. (Illus.). 432p. 2000. reprint ed. pap. 15.95 (*0-393-32063-4*, Norton Paperbks) Norton.

Mapping the Distance. Alicia Hokanson. LC 88-8175. 80p. 1989. 14.95 (*0-932576-69-9*); pap. 8.95 (*0-932576-70-2*) Breitenbush Bks.

***Mapping the Edge.** Sarah Dunant. 2001. 25.00 (*0-375-50323-4*) Random.

Mapping the Empty: Eight Artists & Nevada. William L. Fox. LC 98-39801. 1999. 34.95 (*0-87417-314-0*) U of Nev Pr.

Mapping the Energy Future: Energy Modelling & Climate Change. IEA Staff. 88p. 1998. pap. 50.00 (*92-64-16184-8*, 6198211P) OECD.

Mapping the Faerie Queene: Quest Structures & the World of the Poem. Wayne Erickson. LC 95-50636. (Studies in the Renaissance: Vol. 3). 160p. 1996. text 40.00 (*0-8153-1658-5*, H1835) Garland.

Mapping the Farm: The Chronicle of a Family. John Hildebrand. 1996. pap. 13.00 (*0-679-75033-9*) Random.

Mapping the Future: Young People & Career Guidance. Caroline St. John-Brooks & A. G. Watts. 160p. (Orig.). 1996. pap. 23.00 (*92-64-15319-5*, 96-96-08-1) OECD.

Mapping the Futures: Local Cultures, Global Change. Ed. by Jon Bird et al. LC 92-8718. (Futures Ser.). (Illus.). 256p. (C). 1993. pap. 23.99 (*0-415-07018-X*, A7914) Routledge.

Mapping the Godzone: A Primer on New Zealand Literature & Culture. William J. Schafer. LC 98-10181. 272p. 1998. pap. text 23.00 (*0-8248-2016-9*) UH Pr.

Mapping the Great Irish Famine: An Atlas of the Famine Years. Ed. by L. A. Clarkson et al. 240p. 1999. pap. 30.00 (*1-85182-357-3*, Pub. by Four Cts Pr); boxed set 60.00 (*1-85182-353-0*, Pub. by Four Cts Pr) Intl Spec Bk.

***Mapping the Heart: Reflections on Place & Poetry.** Wesley McNair. 2000. 30.00 (*1-56792-160-4*) Godine.

Mapping the Human Genome: Reality, Morality, & Deity. Theodore C. Kent. 154p. (C). 1995. pap. text 22.50 (*0-8191-9779-3*); lib. bdg. 43.00 (*0-8191-9784-X*) U Pr of Amer.

Mapping the Internet Information Space. Patrik Faltstrom & Leslie L. Daigle. (C). 1999. text 48.00 (*0-13-856550-3*) P-H.

Mapping the Invisible Landscape: Folklore, Writing, & the Sense of Place. Kent C. Ryden. LC 92-46529. (American Land & Life Ser.). (Illus.). 362p. 1993. text 39.95 (*0-87745-406-X*); pap. text 17.95 (*0-87745-414-0*) U of Iowa Pr.

***Mapping the Journey: Case Studies in Developing & Implementing Sustainable Development Strategies.** Russell Baron. 224p. 2000. pap. 30.00 (*1-874719-26-8*) Chelsea Green Pub.

Mapping the Land: Aerial Imagery for Land Use Information. J. B. Campbell. (C). 1987. text 49.00 (*81-85046-51-4*, Pub. by Scientific Pubs) St Mut.

Mapping the Land: Aerial Imagery for Land Use Information. James B. Campell. Ed. by C. Gregory Knight. 85p. (Orig.). 1983. pap. 15.00 (*0-89291-167-0*) Assn Am Geographers.

Mapping the Land: Aerial Imagery for Land Use Information. James B Campell. (Orig.). 1987. 75.00 (*0-7855-1973-4*, Pub. by Scientific) St Mut.

Mapping the Language of Racism: Discourse & the Legitimation of Exploitation. Margaret Wetherell & Jonathan Potter. LC 92-30481. (C). 1993. pap. 19.00 (*0-231-08261-4*); text 57.50 (*0-231-08260-6*) Col U Pr.

Mapping the Local. Rothfield. (C). 1999. write for info. (*0-415-06057-5*); pap. write for info. (*0-415-06058-3*) Routledge.

Mapping the Map Projection to the Need. American Cartographic Association Staff. 28p. 1991. pap. 20.00 (*0-614-06089-3*, C170) Am Congrs Survey.

Mapping the Maze of SIIS. Lynn B. Grandlund. 15p. 1993. 10.00 (*1-886306-06-0*) Nevada Policy.

Mapping the Media: A Media Literacy Guidebook. Paul O. Johnston. (Illus.). 48p. 1997. pap. 9.50 (*0-9637643-3-0*) M & T Communs.

***Mapping the Millennium: Behind the Plans of the New World Order.** Terry M. Boardman. (Illus.). 192p. 1998. pap. 10.95 (*0-904693-97-X*, Pub. by Temple Lodge) Anthroposophic.

***Mapping the Mind.** Rita Carter. LC 98-70490. (Illus.). 221p. 1999. 29.95 (*0-520-21937-6*, Pub. by U CA Pr) Cal Prin Full Svc.

***Mapping the Mind.** Rita Carter. 224p. 2000. pap. 22.95 (*0-520-22461-2*) U CA Pr.

Mapping the Mind. Hunter B. Shirley. LC 82-24664. (Illus.). 376p. 1983. text 49.95 (*0-911012-19-2*) Burnham Inc.

Mapping the Mind: Domain Specificity in Cognition & Culture. Ed. by Lawrence A. Hirschfeld & Susan A. Gelman. (Illus.). 530p. (C). 1994. pap. text 27.95 (*0-521-42993-5*) Cambridge U Pr.

***Mapping the Mind: The Intersection of Psychoanalysis & Neuroscience.** Fred Levin. 1999. pap. 39.95 (*0-88163-320-8*) Analytic Pr.

Mapping the Mind: The Secrets of the Human Brain & How It Works. Joel Davis. (Illus.). 384p. 1996. 24.95 (*1-55972-344-0*, Birch Ln Pr) Carol Pub Group.

Mapping the Mind: The Secrets of the Human Brain & How It Works. Joel Davis. (Illus.). 304p. 1999. reprint ed. 33.95 (*0-7351-0091-8*) Replica Bks.

Mapping the Moral Domain. Ed. by Carol Gilligan et al. 384p. 1990. pap. 14.95 (*0-674-54831-0*) HUP.

Mapping the Moral Domain: A Contribution of Women's Thinking to Psychological Theory & Education. Ed. by Carol Gilligan et al. LC 87-72418. (Illus.). 432p. 1989. 30.00 (*0-674-54832-9*) HUP.

Mapping the Nation. Ed. by Gopal Balakrishnan. (Mappings Ser.). 288p. (C). 1996. pap. 22.00 (*1-85984-060-4*, B4636, Pub. by Verso) Norton.

Mapping the North Carolina Coast: Sixteenth-Century Cartography & the Roanoke Voyages. William P. Cumming. (America's 400th Anniversary Ser.). (Illus.). xii, 144p. (Orig.). 1988. pap. 12.00 (*0-86526-232-2*) NC Archives.

An Asterisk (*) at the beginning of an entry indicates that the title is appearing for the first time.

Mapping the Planets & Space. Martyn Bramwell. LC 97-12188. (Maps & Mapmakers Ser.). (J). 1998. lib. bdg. 22.60 (*0-8225-2922-X*, Lerner Publctns) Lerner Pub.

Mapping the Renaissance World: The Geographical Imagination in the Age of Discovery. Frank Lestringant. LC 93-40812. (New Historicism: Studies in Cultural Poetics). 1994. 45.00 (*0-520-08871-9*, Pub. by U CA Pr) Cal Prin Full Svc.

Mapping the Seas & Airways. Martyn Bramwell. LC 97-12190. (Maps & Mapmakers Ser.). (J). 1998. lib. bdg. 22.60 (*0-8225-2921-1*, Lerner Publctns) Lerner Pub.

Mapping the Sky: Past Heritage & Future Directions. S. Debardat. Ed. by J. A. Eddy et al. (C). 1988. pap. text 76.50 (*90-277-2810-0*); lib. bdg. 188.00 (*90-277-2809-7*) Kluwer Academic.

Mapping the Social Landscape: Readings in Sociology. 2nd rev. ed. Susan J. Ferguson. LC 98-36974. xxxii, 652p. (C). 1998. pap. text 26.95 (*0-7674-0616-8*, 0616-8) Mayfield Pub.

Mapping the Subject: Geographies of Cultural Transformation. Ed. by Steve Pile & Nigel Thrift. LC 94-23747. (Illus.). 512p. (C). 1995. pap. 27.99 (*0-415-10226-X*) Routledge.

Mapping the Subject: Geographies of Cultural Transformation. Ed. by Steve Pile & Nigel Thrift. LC 94-23747. (Illus.). 512p. (C). (gr. 13). 1995. 90.00 (*0-415-10225-1*) Routledge.

Mapping the Terrain: New Genre Public Art. Ed. by Suzanne Lacy. LC 94-35417. (Illus.). 296p. (Orig.). 1995. pap. 18.95 (*0-941920-30-5*) Bay Pr.

Mapping the Terrain of the Heart: Passion, Tenderness & the Capacity to Love. Ed. by Stephen Goldbart & David Wallin. 312p. 1996. pap. 30.00 (*1-56821-790-0*) Aronson.

Mapping the Third Sector: Voluntarism in a Changing Social Economy. Jo Van Til. LC 88-3610. 270p. (Orig.). (C). 1988. pap. 24.95 (*0-87954-240-3*) Foundation Ctr.

Mapping the Transmississippi West, 6 vols. Carl I. Wheat. (Illus.). 2000p. 1995. reprint ed. 1000.00 (*1-57898-002-X*) Martino Pubng.

Mapping the U. K. R. B. Parry & C. R. Perkins. 448p. 1996. 210.00 (*1-85739-030-X*) Bowker-Saur.

Mapping the Unknown. Peter Chrisp. LC 96-8344. (Remarkable World Ser.). (Illus.). 48p. (J). (gr. 3-8). 1996. lib. bdg. 24.26 (*0-8172-4535-9*) Raintree Steck-V.

Mapping the West: Nineteenth-Century American Landscape Photography from the Boston Public Library. Kim Sichel. (Illus.). 28p. 1992. pap. 3.00 (*1-881450-00-7*) Boston U Art.

Mapping the West European Left. Ed. by Perry Anderson & Patrick Camiller. (Mapping Ser.). 288p. (C). 1994. pap. 19.00 (*0-86091-927-7*, A2706, Pub. by Verso) Norton.

Mapping the Women's Movement. Ed. by Monica Threlfall. 288p. (C). 1996. 60.00 (*1-85984-984-9*, Pub. by Verso); pap. 22.00 (*1-85984-120-1*, Pub. by Verso) Norton.

Mapping the World. Sylvia A. Johnson. LC 98-7858. (Illus.). 32p. (J). 1999. 16.00 (*0-689-81813-0*) Atheneum Yung Read.

Mapping the World in the Mind: An Investigation of the Unwritten Knowledge of Micronesian Navigators. Ed. by David Turnbull. 75p. (C). 1995. pap. 40.00 (*0-7300-1221-2*, HUS101, Pub. by Deakin Univ) St Mut.

Mapping the World of Education: Comparative Database System, Overview, Description, & Coding Structure. 1997. lib. bdg. 250.75 (*0-8490-7731-1*) Gordon Pr.

Mapping the World's Vegetation: Regionalization of Formations & Flora. David J. De Laubenfels. LC 75-25934. (Syracuse Geographical Ser.: No. 4). (Illus.). 266p. reprint ed. pap. 82.50 (*0-8357-3123-5*, 203938400012) Bks Demand.

Mapping Time: The Calendar & Its History. E. G. Richards. LC 98-24957. (Illus.). 464p. 1999. 35.00 (*0-19-850413-6*) OUP.

***Mapping Time: The Calendar & Its History.** E. G. Richards. (Illus.). 460p. 2000. pap. 16.95 (*0-19-286205-7*) OUP.

Mapping Time & Space: How Medieval Mapmakers Viewed Their World. Evelyn Edson. (British Library Studies in Map History: Vol. 1). (Illus.). 256p. 1999. text 60.00 (*0-7123-4535-3*) U of Toronto Pr.

Mapping Upper Canada, 1780-1867: An Annotated Bibliography of Manuscript & Printed Maps. Joan Winearls. 976p. 1991. text 175.00 (*0-8020-2794-6*) U of Toronto Pr.

Mapping Was Our Mission: The Military History of the 650th Engineer Topographic Battalion. Otto A. Ewaldsen. LC 96-86352. (Illus.). xv, 702p. 1996. 49.95 (*0-9654542-0-7*) Alden Pub.

Mapping We Will Go. 1996. pap., teacher ed. write for info. (*0-89359-112-2*) Afton Pub.

Mapping We Will Go. (J). (gr. 4). 1996. pap., student ed. write for info. (*0-89359-111-4*) Afton Pub.

***Mapping Websites: Digital Media Design.** Paul Kahn. (Illus.). 2000. pap. 39.50 (*2-88046-464-1*, Rotovision) Watsn-Guptill.

***Mapping Wildfire Hazards & Risks.** R. Neil Sampson et al. LC 00-39406. 2000. pap. write for info. (*1-56022-073-2*, Food Products) Haworth Pr.

***Mapping Wisconsin History: Teacher's Guide & Student Materials.** Bobbie Malone & Wisconsin Cartographers Guild Staff. LC 00-30122. (Illus.). 2000. pap. write for info. (*0-87020-318-5*) State Hist Soc Wis.

Mapping with Microsoft Office. Angela Whitener & Wilgus Creath. 304p. (C). 1996. pap. 29.95 (*1-56690-112-X*) Thomson Learn.

Mapping Work Processes. Dianne Galloway. LC 94-13349. 89p. 1994. 22.00 (*0-87389-266-6*, H0822) ASQ Qual Pr.

Mapping World Communication: War, Progress, Culture. Armand Mattelart. Tr. by Susan Emanuel & James A. Cohen from FRE. LC 93-32250. 1994. pap. 19.95 (*0-8166-2262-0*); text 49.95 (*0-8166-2261-2*) U of Minn Pr.

Mapping Your Business. Barbara Shupe & Colette O'Connell. LC 83-14729. (Illus.). 96p. reprint ed. pap. 30.00 (*0-7837-3403-4*, 204336300008) Bks Demand.

***Mapping Your Community: Using Geographic Information to Strengthen Community Initiatives.** Frwd. by Andrew Cuomo. (Illus.). 145p. (C). 2000. reprint ed. pap. text 25.00 (*0-7881-8589-6*) DIANE Pub.

Mapping Your Future: A Lifework Planning Guide for Health Professionals. Leland R. Kaiser. Ed. by Alys Novak. 120p. 1990. 76.00 (*0-933948-26-3*) Med Group Mgmt.

Mapping Your Legacy: A Hook It Up Journey. Charles R. Eitel. (Illus.). 160p. 1998. text 19.95 (*0-9645953-3-8*); pap. text 11.95 (*0-9645953-4-6*) Peregrinzilla.

Mapping Your Risk Management Course in Ambulatory Care. American Hospital Association Staff. (Illus.). 52p. (Orig.). 1995. pap. 20.00 (*0-87258-694-4*) Am Hospital.

Mapping Your Risk Management Course in Home Health Care. American Hospital Association Staff. (Illus.). 32p. (Orig.). 1995. pap. 20.00 (*0-87258-701-0*) Am Hospital.

Mapping Your Risk Management Course in Integrated Delivery Networks. American Hospital Association Staff. (Illus.). 40p. (Orig.). 1995. pap. 20.00 (*0-87258-697-9*) Am Hospital.

Mapping Your Risk Management Course in Stand-Alone Hospitals. American Hospital Association Staff. (Illus.). 50p. (Orig.). 1996. pap. 20.00 (*0-87258-702-9*) Am Hospital.

Mappings. Ed. by Denis Cosgrove. (Critical Views Ser.). (Illus.). 320p. 1999. pap. 27.00 (*1-86189-021-4*, Pub. by Reaktion Bks) Consort Bk Sales.

Mappings: Feminism & the Geographies of Encounter. Susan S. Friedman. LC 98-11525. 360p. 1998. pap. text 19.95 (*0-691-05804-0*, Pub. by Princeton U Pr) Cal Prin Full Svc.

***Mappings: Feminism & the Geographies of Encounter.** Susan S. Friedman. LC 98-11525. 360p. 1998. text 65.00 (*0-691-05803-2*, Pub. by Princeton U Pr) Cal Prin Full Svc.

Mappings in Thought & Language. Gilles Fauconnier. LC 96-23820. 217p. 1997. pap. text 17.95 (*0-521-59953-9*) Cambridge U Pr.

Mappings in Thought & Language. Gilles Fauconnier. (Illus.). 217p. (C). 1997. text 54.95 (*0-521-46062-X*) Cambridge U Pr.

Mappings of Operator Algebras. Huzihiro Araki & Richard V. Kadison. (Progress in Mathematics Ser.: Vol. 84). 300p. 1990. 64.00 (*0-8176-3476-2*) Birkhauser.

Mappings of the Biblical Terrain: The Bible As Text. Ed. by Vincent L. Tollers & John Maier. (Review Ser.: Vol. 33, No. 2). 1990. 22.00 (*0-8387-5172-5*) Bucknell U Pr.

Mapplethorpe. Robert Mapplethorpe. LC 92-50154. 1992. 125.00 (*0-679-40804-5*) Random.

Mapplethorpe: A Biography. Patricia Morrisroe. LC 96-43819. (Illus.). 512p. 1997. reprint ed. pap. 16.95 (*0-306-80766-1*) Da Capo.

Mapplethorpe - Assault with a Deadly Camera: A Pop Culture Memoir - An Outlaw Reminiscence. Jack Fritscher & John Fritscher. (Illus.). 306p. 1998. 24.95 (*1-890834-29-7*) Palm Drive.

Mapplethorpe Portraits. Robin Gibson & Terence Pepper. (Illus.). 96p. 1988. pap. 35.00 (*0-904017-91-5*, Pub. by Natl Port Gall) Antique Collect.

Maps see Discovering Geography

Maps. Nuruddin Farah. LC 99-25060. 288p. 1999. 23.95 (*1-55970-485-3*, Pub. by Arcade Pub Inc) Time Warner.

***Maps.** Nuruddin Farah. (Illus.). 2000. pap. 13.00 (*0-14-029643-3*) Penguin Putnam.

***Maps.** Barbara Taylor. (Make It Work! Geography Ser.). (Illus.). (J). (gr. 4-7). 2000. pap. 6.95 (*1-58728-250-X*) Two Can Pub.

Maps, Vol. 3929. Joellyn T. Cicciarelli. Ed. by Rozanne L. Williams. (Social Studies Learn to Read Ser.). (Illus.). 16p. (J). (ps-2). 1996. pap. 2.75 (*1-57471-134-2*, 3929) Creat Teach Pr.

Maps, Vol. 3973. Joellyn T. Cicciarelli. Ed. by Rozanne L. Williams. (Social Studies Big Bks.). (Illus.). 16p. (J). (ps-2). 1997. pap. 12.98 (*1-57471-180-6*, 3972) Creat Teach Pr.

Maps: Craft Essays, Fiction, Poetry. Ed. by Alan R. Davis. (Illus.). (Orig.). 1986. pap. 6.00 (*0-9617312-0-6*) MoonsQuilt Pr.

Maps: Getting from Here to There. Harvey Weiss. LC 90-25069. (Illus.). 64p. (J). (gr. 3-6). 1995. pap. 7.95 (*0-395-72028-1*, Sandpiper) HM.

Maps: Getting from Here to There. Harvey Weiss. (J). 1991. 11.40 (*0-606-07839-8*) Turtleback.

Maps: Plotting Places on the Globe. Paula B. Pratt. (Encyclopedia of Discovery & Invention Ser.). (Illus.). 96p. (J). (gr. 5-9). 1995. lib. bdg. 23.70 (*1-56006-255-X*, 255X) Lucent Bks.

Maps - the World & United States. Karen Sevaly. (Illus.). 104p. (Orig.). (J). (gr. k-8). 1991. pap. text 9.95 (*0-943263-20-4*, TF1702) Teachers Friend Pubns.

Maps & Atlases of the World War I Period: A List of Atlases & Maps Applicable to the World War. Philip L. Phillips. 207p. 1995. reprint ed. lib. bdg. 45.00 (*0-9649000-0-9*, T Nova Pr) G B Manasek.

***Maps & Charts of North America & the West Indies.** John R. Sellers & Al Sellers. 495p. 2000. reprint ed. 75.00 (*1-57898-217-0*) Martino Pubng.

Maps & Charts Published in America Before 1800: A Bibliography, Vol. 3. rev. ed. James C. Wheat & Christian F. Brun. (Illus.). 1979. 125.00 (*0-900470-89-5*, Pub. by Holland Press) Book East.

Maps & Civilization: Cartography in Culture & Society. 2nd ed. Norman J. Thrower. Orig. Title: Maps & Man. (Illus.). 352p. 1997. lib. bdg. 55.00 (*0-226-79971-9*) U Ch Pr.

Maps & Civilization: Cartography in Culture & Society. 2nd ed. Norman J. Thrower. Orig. Title: Maps & Man. (Illus.). 352p. 2000. pap. text 17.95 (*0-226-79972-7*) U Ch Pr.

***Maps & Civilization: Cartography in Culture & Society.** 2nd ed. Norman J. W. Thrower. Orig. Title: Maps & Man. 1999. pap. text 18.00 (*0-226-79973-5*) U Ch Pr.

Maps & Compasses. 2nd ed. Percy W. Blandford. 256p. 1991. 22.95 (*0-8306-2141-5*, 5007); pap. 14.95 (*0-8306-2140-7*) McGraw-Hill Prof.

Maps & Compasses: A User's Handbook. Percy W. Blandford. (Illus.). 252p. (Orig.). 1984. pap. 12.95 (*0-8306-1644-6*) McGraw-Hill Prof.

Maps & Dreams: Indians & the British Columbia Frontier. Hugh Brody. (Illus.). 294p. (C). 1997. reprint ed. pap. text 14.95 (*0-88133-965-2*) Waveland Pr.

Maps & Globes see Step-by-Step Geography

Maps & Globes. Jack Knowlton. LC 85-47537. (Illus.). 48p. (J). (gr. 2-5). 1985. 15.95 (*0-690-04457-7*) HarpC Child Bks.

Maps & Globes. Jack Knowlton. LC 85-47537. (Trophy Nonfiction Bk.). (Illus.). 48p. (J). (gr. 4-7). 1986. pap. 6.95 (*0-06-446049-5*, HarpTrophy) HarpC Child Bks.

Maps & Globes. Jack Knowlton. 1985. 11.15 (*0-606-01902-2*, Pub. by Turtleback) Demco.

***Maps & Globes.** David Petersen & Christine E. Petersen. LC 00-30716. (True Bks.). (Illus.). (J). 2001. write for info. (*0-516-22044-6*) Childrens.

Maps & Globes: An Integrated Unit. Kathy Rogers. (Primary Thematic Units Ser.). (Illus.). 96p. (Orig.). 1993. pap. 12.95 (*0-944459-76-5*) ECS Lrn Systs.

Maps & Guide to Microdissection of the Rat Brain. Miklos Palkovits & Brownstein. (Illus.). 262p. (C). 1987. pap. text 70.00 (*0-8385-6159-4*, A6159-6, Apple Lange Med) McGraw.

Maps & History: Constructing Images of the Past. Jeremy Black. LC 96-41293. (Illus.). 278p. 1997. 40.00 (*0-300-06976-6*) Yale U Pr.

***Maps & History: Constructing Images of the Past.** Jeremy Black. (Illus.). 278p. 2000. pap. 18.95 (*0-300-08693-8*) Yale U Pr.

Maps & History in South West England. Ed. by Barker & Kain. 159p. 1991. pap. text 24.95 (*0-85989-373-1*) Northwestern U Pr.

Maps & Journeys. Kate Petty. (Around & About Ser.). (Illus.). 32p. (J). (gr. 2-4). 1993. pap. 5.95 (*0-8120-1235-6*) Barron.

Maps & Man see Maps & Civilization: Cartography in Culture & Society

***Maps & Map-Making in Local History.** Jacinta Prunty. (Maynooth Research Guides for Irish Local History Ser.). 64p. 2000. pap. 14.50 (*0-7165-2727-8*, Pub. by Irish Acad Pr) Intl Spec Bk.

***Maps & Mapmakers of the Civil War.** Earl B. McElfresh. LC 99-28098. (Illus.). 272p. 1999. 55.00 (*0-8109-3430-2*, Pub. by Abrams) Time Warner.

***Maps & Mapmaking.** Fran Sammis. LC 98-49883. (Mapping Our World Ser.). (J). (gr. 4-7). 1999. 27.07 (*0-7614-0367-1*) Marshall Cavendish.

Maps & Mapping. Barbara Taylor. (Young Discoverers Ser.). (J). 1993. 12.15 (*0-606-05305-0*, Pub. by Turtleback) Demco.

Maps & Mapping: Geography Facts & Experiments. Barbar Taylor. LC 92-23373. (Young Discoverers Ser.). (Illus.). 32p. (J). (ps-3). pap. 7.95 (*1-85697-936-9*) LKC.

Maps & Mapping of Africa. John McIlwaine. LC 97-13251. 1997. 100.00 (*1-873836-76-7*) Bowker-Saur.

Maps & Mazes: A First Guide to Mapmaking. Gillian Chapman & Pam Robson. LC 93-1234. (Illus.). 32p. (J). (gr. 2-4). 1993. pap. 6.95 (*1-56294-715-X*) Millbrook Pr.

Maps & Models for Ministry. Ed. by David Whitelaw et al. (Illus.). 160p. (Orig.). 1996. pap. write for info. (*0-9652698-1-7*) Pt Loma Pr.

Maps & Mythology. Edward F. Henderson. (Illus.). 1982. pap. 1.00 (*0-318-01025-9*) Am Educ Trust.

Maps & Politics. Jeremy Black. LC 97-28355. 192p. 1998. 35.00 (*0-226-05493-4*) U Ch Pr.

Maps & Prints: Aspects of the English Booktrade. Ed. by Robin Myers & Michael Harris. (Publishing History Occasional Ser.). (Illus.). 130p. 1984. pap. write for info. (*0-902692-33-X*) Chadwyck-Healey.

***Maps & Related Cartographic Materials: Cataloging, Classification & Bibliographic Control.** Ed. by Paige G. Andrew & Mary Lynette Lasrgaard. LC 99-51487. (Monograph Published Simultaneously as Cataloging & Classification Quarterly Ser.: Vol. 27, Nos. 1-4). 487p. 1999. pap. text 39.95 (*0-7890-0813-0*) Haworth Pr.

***Maps & Related Cartographic Materials: Cataloging, Classification & Bibliographic Control.** Ed. by Paige G. Andrew & Mary Lynette Lasrgaard. LC 99-51487. (Monograph Published Simultaneously as Cataloging & Classification Quarterly Ser.: Vol. 27, Nos. 1-4). 487p. (C). 1999. 69.95 (*0-7890-0778-9*) Haworth Pr.

Maps & Scale Drawing see Let's Investigate - Group 3

Maps & Statistics. Peter A. Lewis. 336p. 1977. pap. 22.50 (*0-416-65380-4*, NO. 6180) Routledge.

Maps & Statistics for California's New Congressional Districts. Douglas Johnson & Tatia Van Note. 35p. 1992. pap. text 150.00 (*1-883638-14-3*) Rose Inst.

Maps & Surveys of Malawi. C. G. Martin. 280p. (C). 1980. text 162.00 (*90-6191-092-7*, Pub. by A A Balkema) Ashgate Pub Co.

Maps & Surveys of the Pueblo Lands of San Diego: 1602-1874. Neal Harlow. 1988. 100.00 (*0-87093-189-X*) Dawsons.

Maps & Symbols. Angela Royston. LC 97-46959. (Geography Starts Here Ser.). (J). 1998. write for info. (*0-8172-5113-8*) Raintree Steck-V.

Maps & Symbols. Angela Royston. LC 97-46959. (Geography Starts Here Ser.). 1998. write for info. (*0-7502-1987-4*) Raintree Steck-V.

Maps & the Columbian Encounter: An Interpretive Guide. J. B. Harley. (Illus.). 160p. (Orig.). 1990. pap. 12.95 (*1-879281-00-7*) G Meir Lib.

***Maps & the Writing of Space in Early Modern England & Ireland.** Bernhard Klein. LC 00-33348. 2000. write for info. (*0-312-23573-9*) St Martin.

Maps & Views of Washington & District of Columbia. 2nd ed. P. Lee Phillips. LC 97-119747. (Illus.). 87p. 1996. reprint ed. text, lib. bdg. 45.00 (*0-9649000-2-5*, T Nova Pr) G B Manasek.

Maps Are Territories: Science in an Atlas. David Turnbull et al. 66p. (C). 1995. pap. 50.00 (*0-7300-0688-3*, HUS204, Pub. by Deakin Univ) St Mut.

Maps Are Territories: Science is an Atlas: A Portfolio of Exhibits. David Turnbull. LC 93-11239. 72p. 1994. reprint ed. pap. text 17.95 (*0-226-81705-9*) U Ch Pr.

Maps As Prints in the Italian Renaissance: Makers, Distributors & Consumers. David Woodward. (Illus.). 128p. 1996. pap. 30.00 (*0-7123-4502-7*, Pub. by B23tish Library) U of Toronto Pr.

Maps, Charts, Globes: Five Centuries of Exploration. Sandra Sider et al. 1992. 40.00 (*0-87535-145-X*) Hispanic Soc.

Maps, Charts, Graphs, & Diagrams. John Carratello & Patty Carratello. (Illus.). 80p. (gr. 3-6). 1990. student ed. 9.95 (*1-55734-169-9*) Tchr Create Mat.

Maps Contained in the Publications of the American Bibliography, 1639-1819: An Index & Checklist. Jim Walsh. LC 88-31916. 383p. 1989. 41.50 (*0-8108-2193-1*) Scarecrow.

***Maps for Family History.** William Foot. (Readers' Guides Ser.: No. 9). (Illus.). 93p. 1999. pap. 14.95 (*1-873162-17-0*, Pub. by PRO Pubns) Midpt Trade.

Maps, Genealogies, & Lists: A Companion to Irish History, Pt. II. T. W. Moody et al. (New History of Ireland Ser.: No. 9). (Illus.). 688p. 1984. text 198.00 (*0-19-821745-5*) OUP.

Maps, Globes, Atlases & Geographies Through the Year 1800: The Eleanor Houston & Lawrence M. C. Smith Cartographic Collection. Compiled by James E. Mooney. (Illus.). 168p. (C). 1988. 75.00 (*0-939561-03-4*) Univ South ME.

Maps in a Mirror: The short fiction of Orson Scott Card. Orson Scott Card. 544p. 1990. 24.95 (*0-312-85047-6*, Pub. by Tor Bks) St Martin.

Maps in Everyday Life. Martyn Bramwell. LC 97-27282. (Maps & Mapmakers Ser.). (J). 1997. lib. bdg. 22.60 (*0-8225-2923-8*) Lerner Pub.

Maps in the Geoscience Community: Proceedings of the Nineteenth Meeting of the Geoscience Information Society, November 5-8, 1984. Geoscience Information Society Staff. Ed. by Claren M. Kidd. LC QE0048.85.G4. (Geoscience Information Society Proceedings Ser.: Vol. 15). 219p. reprint ed. pap. 67.90 (*0-7837-5635-6*, 204554400005) Bks Demand.

Maps in Tudor England. P. D. Harvey. LC 93-11710. 128p. 1993. 29.95 (*0-226-31878-8*) U Ch Pr.

Maps, Maps, Maps: A Collection of Alaskan Maps. Ed. by Jane Niebergall. (Illus.). 113p. 1996. pap. 11.95 (*1-878051-48-2*) Circumpolar Pr.

Maps of Africa. 2nd rev. ed. Ed. by Jeffrey Stone. LC 97-120230. (Illus.). 450p. 1997. lib. bdg. 100.00 (*0-9649000-4-1*) G B Manasek.

Maps of Connecticut, 2 vols., Set. Edmund Thompson. (Illus.). 177p. 1995. reprint ed. lib. bdg. 115.00 (*0-9649000-1-7*) G B Manasek.

Maps of Englishness: Writing Identity in the Culture of Colonialism. Simon Gikandi. LC 96-26173. 268p. 1996. 52.00 (*0-231-10598-3*); pap. 18.50 (*0-231-10599-1*) Col U Pr.

Maps of Fiji: A Selective & Annotated Cartobibliography. Mason S. Green. LC 78-24066. (Occasional Papers: No. 5). (Illus.). 90p. (Orig.). 1978. pap. 4.00 (*0-939112-06-X*) Western Assn Map.

Maps of Flesh & Light: The Religious Experience of Medieval Women Mystics. Ed. by Ulrike Wiethaus. 272p. (Orig.). 1992. pap. text 19.95 (*0-8156-2611-8*) Syracuse U Pr.

Maps of Flesh & Light: The Religious Experience of Medieval Women Mystics. Ed. by Ulrike Wiethaus. LC 91-33315. 272p. (Orig.). 1992. 45.00 (*0-8156-2560-X*) Syracuse U Pr.

Maps of Heaven, Maps of Hell: Religious Terror as Memory from the Puritans to Stephen King. Edward J. Ingebretsen. 256p. 1995. 29.95 (*1-55778-638-0*); pap. 16.95 (*1-55778-728-X*) M E Sharpe.

Maps of Heaven, Maps of Hell: Religious Terror as Memory from the Puritans to Stephen King. Edward J. Ingebretsen. LC 94-39041. 280p. (gr. 13). 1996. pap. 27.95 (*1-56324-872-7*) M E Sharpe.

Maps of Heaven, Maps of Hell: Religious Terror as Memory from the Puritans to Stephen King. Edward J. Ingebretsen. LC 94-39041. 280p. (C). (gr. 13). 1996. 41.95 (*1-56324-871-9*) M E Sharpe.

Maps of Indiana Counties in 1876: Reprinted from Illustrated Historical Atlas of the State of Indiana. (Illus.). 95p. 1979. reprint ed. pap. 16.00 (*0-87195-059-6*) Ind Hist Soc.

Maps of Meaning: An Introduction to Cultural Geography. Peter Jackson. Ed. by Derek Gregory. (Contours Ser.). 192p. 1989. pap. text 17.95 (*0-04-445366-3*) Routledge.

Maps of Meaning: An Introduction to Cultural Geography. Peter Jackson. LC 92-18073. (Illus.). 192p. (C). 1989. pap. 24.99 (*0-415-09088-1*) Routledge.

***Maps of Meaning The Architecture of Belief.** Jordan B. Peterson. LC 98-37486. 1999. 80.00 (*0-415-92221-6*) Routledge.

M

M

Maps of Meanings: The Architecture of Belief. Jordan B. Peterson. LC 98-37486. 1999. pap. 35.00 (*0-415-92222-4*) Routledge.

Maps of Mughal India: Drawn by Jean-Baptiste-Joseph Gentil, Agent for the French Government to the Court of Shuja-ud-daula at Faizabad, in 1770. Ed. by Susan Gole. (Illus.). 1990. 85.00 (*0-7103-0347-5*) Routledge.

Maps of San Francisco Bay: From the Spanish Discovery in 1769 to the American Occupation. Neal Harlow. (Illus.). 160p. 1996. reprint ed. 110.00 (*1-888262-95-8*) Martino Pubng.

Maps of Texas & the Southwest, 1513-1900. James C. Martin & Robert S. Martin. (Illus.). 190p. 1998. 39.95 (*0-87611-169-X*) Tex St Hist Assn.

Maps of Texas, 1527-1900. James M. Day. 597p. 1997. reprint ed. 65.00 (*1-57898-054-2*) Martino Pubng.

Maps of the Ancient Sea Kings: Evidence of Advanced Civilization in the Ice Age. Charles H. Hapgood. 1997. pap. text 19.95 (*0-932813-42-9*) Adventures Unltd.

Maps of the California Gold Region, 1848-1857: A Biblio-Cartography of an Important Decade. Carl I. Wheat. (Illus.). xlii, 148p. 1995. reprint ed. 125.00 (*1-888262-01-X*) Martino Pubng.

***Maps of the California Trail.** Gregory M. Franzwa. (Illus.). 287p. 1999. pap. 29.95 (*1-880397-32-3*); spiral bd. 34.95 (*1-880397-33-1*) Patrice Pr.

Maps of the Civil War: The Roads They Took. David Phillips. (Illus.). 160p. 1998. 24.98 (*1-56799-586-1*, MetroBooks) M Friedman Pub Grp Inc.

Maps of the Isle of Man, 1280-1760. Ed. by Shearwater Press Staff. 1986. 120.00 (*0-904980-00-6*) St Mut.

Maps of the Oregon Trail. 3rd ed. Gregory M. Franzwa. Ed. by Arielle North. LC 82-675039. (Illus.). 299p. 1990. pap. 18.95 (*0-935284-83-4*); spiral bd. 24.95 (*0-935284-82-6*) Patrice Pr.

Maps of the Shaker West: A Journey of Discovery. Martha H. Boice. LC 97-197398. (Illus.). 140p. 1997. pap. write for info. (*0-9655018-1-7*, Pub. by Knot Grdn Pr) Partners Bk Dist.

Maps of the U. S. A. Joy Evans & Leslie Tryon. (Illus.). 64p. (J). (gr. 1-6). 1989. pap. text 6.95 (*1-55799-148-0*, EMC 191) Evan-Moor Edu Pubs.

Maps of the U. S. A. Jo Ellen Moore & Leslie Tryon. Ed. by Marilyn Evans. (Partners in Learning). (Illus.). 63p. (J). (gr. 3-6). Date not set. pap., wbk. ed. 6.95 (*1-58610-141-2*) Learn Horizon.

Maps of the World, 10 vols. (Illus.). 800p. (YA). (gr. 5 up). 1997. lib. bdg. 335.00 (*0-7172-7662-7*) Grolier Educ.

Maps on File: 1997 Editon. Facts on File Staff. 592p. 1997. 195.00 (*0-8160-3668-3*) Facts on File.

Maps on File: 1997 Update. Facts on File Staff. 1997. ring bd. 45.00 (*0-8160-3669-1*) Facts on File.

Maps on File: 1998 Edition, 2 vols. Diagram Group Staff. (Illus.). 592p. 1998. ring bd. 195.00 (*0-8160-3816-3*) Facts on File.

Maps on File: 1999 Edition, 2 vols. (Illus.). 590p. 1999. ring bd. 195.00 (*0-8160-4003-6*, Checkmark) Facts on File.

Maps on File Annual Update, 1995. (Illus.). 1995. ring bd. 45.00 (*0-8160-3188-6*) Facts on File.

Maps on File Annual Update, 1996. 1996. ring bd. 45.00 (*0-8160-3452-4*) Facts on File.

Maps on File Updates: 1998 Update. Diagram Group Staff. (Illus.). 1998. ring bd. 45.00 (*0-8160-3817-1*) Facts on File.

Maps on File Updates: 1999 Updates. 1999. ring bd. 45.00 (*0-8160-4004-4*, Checkmark) Facts on File.

***Maps on File 2000.** Facts on File Publishing Staff. 2000. 45.00 (*0-8160-4166-0*) Facts on File.

***Maps on File 2000, 2 vols.** Facts on File Publishing Staff. (Illus.). 590p. 2000. 195.00 (*0-8160-4165-2*) Facts on File.

Maps on the Ceiling: Libyan Poems. Philip Ward. (Modern Poets Ser.: Vol.9). 1968. 5.95 (*0-902675-02-8*) Oleander Pr.

Maps to Anywhere. Bernard Cooper. LC 89-11864. 160p. 1997. pap. 12.95 (*0-8203-1946-5*) U of Ga Pr.

Maps to Ecstacy: A Healing Journey for the Untamed Spirit. 2nd rev. ed. Gabrielle Roth & John Loudon. LC 98-35180. (Illus.). 240p. 1998. pap. 12.95 (*1-57731-045-4*) New Wrld Lib.

Maps with Moving Parts. Walid Bitar. 60p. 1988. pap. 9.95 (*0-919626-37-8*, Pub. by Brick Bks) Genl Dist Srvs.

Maps with the News: The Development of American Journalistic Cartography. Mark Monmonier. LC 88-23829. (Illus.). 346p. 1989. 29.95 (*0-226-53411-1*) U Ch Pr.

Maps with the News: The Development of American Journalistic Cartography. Mark Monmonier. 1999. pap. 16.00 (*0-226-53413-8*) U Ch Pr.

Mapsco Ellis & Johnson: A Routing & Delivery System for Ellis & Johnson Counties: with Additional Coverage for Corsicana, Hillsboro & Selected Areas. Mapsco Inc Staff. LC 96-675589. 1995. write for info. (*1-56966-047-6*) Mapsco Inc.

Mapsco Street Guide & Directory. Mapsco Inc. 25.95 (*1-56966-541-9*) Mapsco Inc.

Mapskill Atlas. Kemp. 1992. pap. text. write for info. (*0-582-09246-9*, Pub. by Addison-Wesley) Longman.

Mapskills Copymasters. Richard Kemp & David Lean. 1989. pap. text 38.88 (*0-582-04087-6*, 78445) Longman.

Mapstart 2. S. Catling. Date not set. pap. text. write for info. (*0-582-00187-0*, Pub. by Addison-Wesley) Longman.

Maptime . . . U. S. A. Jerry Aten. 64p. (J). (gr. 4 up). 1982. 8.99 (*0-86653-093-2*, GA 422) Good Apple.

Mapuche Indians of Chile. Louis C. Faron. (Illus.). 120p. (C). 1986. reprint ed. pap. text 10.50 (*0-88133-247-X*) Waveland Pr.

MapView User's Guide. Larry McDonough et al. LC 93-10349. 1993. pap. 9.00 (*0-8330-1363-7*, MR-160-AF/A) Rand Corp.

Mapworks. Pamela A. Klawitter. LC 92-81914. (World Geography Ser.). 48p. (J). (gr. 4-8). 1994. 6.95 (*0-88160-206-X*, LW254) Learning Wks.

Maqaddimat Al-Istitba: Al-Sharq Mawjud Bi-Ghayrih la Bi-Dhatih. Ghrighwar M. Marshu. LC 96-33950. 1996. write for info. (*1-56564-241-4*) IIIT VA.

Maqasid al 'Ammah lil Shari'ah al Islamiyah: The General Objectives of Islamic Law. Yusuf H. Alim. LC 91-3222. (Silsilat al Rasa'il al Jami'iyah Ser.: No. 5). (ARA.). 614p. (Orig.). 1991. 20.00 (*0-912463-83-X*); pap. 15.00 (*0-912463-84-8*) IIIT VA.

Maqasid al-Ri'ayah li-Huquq Allah 'Azza wa-Jall, aw Mukhtasar Ri'ayat al-Muhasabi. Al-Izz Bin Abd al-Salam. 192p. 1995. pap. 5.95 (*1-57547-210-4*) Dar Al-Fikr.

Maqasid al-Salah. Al-Izz B. Abd-al-Salam. (Writings of Al-'Izz bin 'Abd-al-Salam Ser.). (ARA.). 48p. (Orig.). 1995. pap. 2.95 (*1-57547-226-0*) Dar Al-Fikr.

Maqasid al-Sawm. Al-Izz B. Abd-al-Salam. (Writings of al-'Izz bin Abd-al-Salam Ser.). (ARA.). 64p. (Orig.). 1995. pap. 2.95 (*1-57547-224-4*) Dar Al-Fikr.

Maquette for Murder. Gretchen Sprague. LC 99-56342. 240p. 2000. text 22.95 (*0-312-19920-1*, Minotaur) St Martin.

Maquiavelo. Gautier. (Breviarios Ser.). (SPA.). pap. 5.99 (*968-16-0019-3*, Pub. by Fondo) Continental Bk.

Maquila Directory. 71p. (Orig.). (C). 1996. pap. text 39.95 (*0-937795-15-1*) Waste-Mgmt Educ.

Maquiladora Industry: Economic Solution or Problem? Ed. by Khosrow Fatemi. LC 89-26537. 280p. 1990. 65.00 (*0-275-93357-1*, C3357, Greenwood Pr) Greenwood.

Maquiladora Reader: Cross Border Organizing since NAFTA. Ed. by Rachael Kamel & Anya Hoffman. 131p. 1999. pap. 14.95 (*0-910082-35-9*) Am Fr Serv Comm.

Maquiladora Revolution in Guatemala. Kurt Petersen. LC 92-23067. (Occasional Paper Ser.: Vol. 2). xvi, 244p. (Orig.). (C). 1992. pap. text 7.95 (*1-881862-00-3*) O H Schell Yale Law Schl.

Maquiladora Supplier Guidebook. 16p. (Orig.). (C). 1993. pap. text 10.00 (*0-937795-16-X*) Waste-Mgmt Educ.

Maquiladoras: Annotated Bibliography & Research Guide to Mexico's In-Bond Industry, 1980-1988. Leslie Sklair. (Monographs: No. 24). 1988. pap. 12.95 (*0-935391-96-7*, MN-24) UCSD Ctr US-Mex.

Maquiladoras: Assembly & Manufacturing Plants on the United States Border: An International Guide. Ed. by Martin H. Sable. (Behavioral & Social Sciences Librarian: Vol. 7, Nos. 3-4). 150p. 1989. 49.95 (*0-86656-904-9*) Haworth Pr.

***Maquillajo Basico.** Cindy Crawford. 1998. 34.95 (*84-08-01907-4*) Planeta.

Maquinarias. Karen Bryant-Mole. (Images Ser.). (SPA., Illus.). 24p. 1996. pap. text 4.95 (*0-382-39576-X*) Silver Burdett Pr.

Maquinarias. Karen Bryant-Mole. (Imagenes Ser.). 1997. 10.15 (*0-606-10473-9*, Pub. by Turtleback) Demco.

Maquinas e Inventos (Machines & Inventions) see Enciclopedia Ilustrada de Ciencia Naturaleza (Understanding Science & Nature)

Maquinas Simples, 2 vols. Capstone Press Staff. 1998. 28.00 (*0-516-29817-8*) Childrens.

Maquinas Vivientes. Isaura Meza. (Ciencia para Todos Ser.). (SPA.). pap. 6.99 (*968-16-4988-5*, Pub. by Fondo) Continental Bk.

Maquis: A History of the French Resistance Movement. Claude Chambard. Tr. by Elaine P. Halperin from FRE. LC 75-6400. (Illus.). 372p. 1976. 15.00 (*0-672-52156-3*, Bobbs) Macmillan.

Mar. Isidro Sanchez & Carme Peris. (World of Sports Ser.). (SPA., Illus.). 32p. (J). (ps-1). 1992. pap. 6.95 (*0-8120-4869-5*) Barron.

Mar de Espuma: Marti y la Literatura Infantil. Eduardo Lolo. (SPA.). 1995. pap. 18.00 (*0-89729-771-7*) Ediciones.

Mar de Mi Infancia see Sea of My Infancy

Mar de Puerto Rico: Una Introduccion a las Pesquerias De la Isla. Jose A. Suarez-Caabro. (SPA., Illus.). 257p. 1979. 15.00 (*0-8477-2323-2*) U of PR Pr.

Mar Es Mala Mujer. Raul Guerra Garrido & Juan Cruz Mendizabal. (Nueva Austral Ser.: Vol. 210). (SPA.). 1991. pap. text 24.95 (*84-239-7210-0*) Elliots Bks.

Mar, Gran Enciclopedia Salvat, 10 vols., Set. Salvat Staff. (SPA.). 3000p. 1975. 495.00 (*0-8288-5936-1*, S50560) Fr & Eur.

Mar Inclinida see Sea on Its Side

Mar morto see Sea of Death

Mar Ratacit (Stray Apple) Poems. Alex A. Calin. Ed. by H & H Promotions Staff. (ENG & RUM., Illus.). x, 158p. 1998. pap. 10.00 (*0-9664844-1-X*) H & H Promotions.

Mar (Seaside) Maria Rius & Josep M. Parramon. (Let's Discover Ser.). (SPA., Illus.). 32p. (J). (ps). 1986. pap. 7.95 (*0-8120-3751-0*) Barron.

Mar y Tu. Julia de Burgos. LC 81-68710. (Illus.). 1981. pap. 6.75 (*0-940238-46-2*) Ediciones Huracan.

***Mara: A Novel.** Tova Reich. LC 00-35396. (Library of Modern Jewish Literature). 2000. write for info. (*0-8156-0659-1*) Syracuse U Pr.

Mara: Celtic Shamaness, Vol. 2. Dennis Cramer. 36. pap. 19.95 (*1-56097-294-7*, Pub. by Fantagraph Bks) Seven Hills Bk.

Mara & Dann: An Adventure. Doris Lessing. LC 98-30782. 416p. 1999. 25.00 (*0-06-018294-6*, HarperFlamingo) HarpC.

Mara & Dann: An Adventure. Doris Lessing. 416p. 2000. pap. 14.00 (*0-06-093056-X*) HarpC.

Mara, Daughter of the Nile. Eloise J. McGraw. LC 85-567. 280p. (J). (gr. 5-9). 1985. pap. 4.99 (*0-14-031929-8*, PuffinBks) Peng Put Young Read.

Mara of the Celts. Dennis Cramer. (Eros Graphic Novel Ser.: No. 17). 136p. 1995. pap. 16.95 (*1-56097-215-7*) Fantagraph Bks.

***Mara Strikes Back.** Kosuke Fujishima. (Oh My Goddess! Ser.: Vol. 6). (Illus.). 176p. (YA). 2000. pap. 14.95 (*1-56971-449-5*) Dark Horse Comics.

Maraazan. Nevil Shute. 1977. mass mkt. 1.95 (*0-345-25078-8*, Ballantine) Ballantine Pub Grp.

Maraazan. Nevil Shute. 1970. mass mkt. 0.95 (*0-345-22088-9*) Fawcett.

Marabi Dance. Modikwe Dikobe. (African Writers Ser.). 118p. (C). 1973. pap. 8.95 (*0-435-90124-9*, 90124) Heinemann.

Marabi Nights: Early South African Jazz & Vaudeville. Christopher Ballantine. (Illus.). 116p. (Orig.). (C). 1994. pap. text 24.95 (*0-86975-439-4*, Pub. by Ravan Pr) Ohio U Pr.

Marabou Stork Nightmares: A Novel. Irvine Welsh. 264p. 1996. 21.00 (*0-393-03845-9*) Norton.

Marabou Stork Nightmares: A Novel. Irvine Welsh. 284p. 1997. pap. 13.00 (*0-393-31563-0*) Norton.

Marabout. K. Petit. (FRE.). 480p. 1960. pap. 17.95 (*0-7859-5541-0*, M-6445) Fr & Eur.

Marabout & the Muse: New Aspects of Islam in Africa. Ed. by Kenneth W. Harrow. LC 96-25668. 300p. 1996. pap. 22.00 (*0-435-08983-8*) Heinemann.

Marabout Dictionary of Micro-Computers: Dictionnaire Marabout de la Micro-Informatique. Ilya Virgatchik. (FRE.). 250p. 1984. pap. 12.95 (*0-8288-1356-6*, M14877) Fr & Eur.

Marabout Synonyms Dictionary: Dictionnaire Marabout des Synonymes. Georges Younes. (FRE.). 452p. 1981. pap. 16.95 (*0-8288-1955-6*, M14203) Fr & Eur.

***Marac A: The Biodiversity & Environment of an Amazonian Rainforest.** William Milliken & J. A. Ratter. LC 97-41832. 528p. 1998. 185.00 (*0-471-97917-1*) Wiley.

Marac, Franz. R. Marz. 72p. (C). 1987. 80.00 (*0-7855-4521-2*, Pub. by Collets) St Mut.

***Maraca.** Sonia Canals. (J). 1999. pap. 6.95 (*1-899607-72-2*) Levinson Bks.

MarAd Systematic Series of Full-Form Ship Models. Ed. by Donald P. Roseman. 421p. 1987. 50.00 (*0-614-06722-7*) Soc Naval Arch.

Maradona: The Man with the Magic Feet. Lian Goodall. (Champion Sports Biography Ser.). (Illus.). 86p. (YA). (gr. 7-12). 1999. pap. 8.95 (*1-894020-53-7*) Warwick Publ.

Maraging Steels: Recent Developments & Applications: Proceedings of a Symposium Sponsored by the Ferrous Metallurgy Committee of the Minerals, Metals & Materials Society, & Held at the TMS Annual Meeting in Phoenix, Arizona, January 25-26, 1988. Ed. by Richard K. Wilson. LC 88-42858. 323p. reprint ed. pap. 100.20 (*0-7837-1458-0*, 205243400023) Bks Demand.

Marah. William A. Christian. LC 76-39079. (Black Heritage Library Collection). 1977. reprint ed. 28.95 (*0-8369-9017-X*) Ayer.

***Maraini: Acts of Photography, Acts of Love.** Fosco Maraini. (Illus.). 160p. 1999. 60.00 (*1-55670-973-0*) Stewart Tabori & Chang.

Maralinga: British A-Bomb Australian Legacy. Adrian Tame & F. P. Robotham. LC 82-174416. (Fontana Original Ser.). 272 p. 1982. 5.95 (*0-00-636391-1*) Collins SF.

Maram Nagas: A Socio-Cultural Study. Joseph Athickal. (C). 1992. 28.00 (*81-7099-354-7*, Pub. by Mittal Pubs Dist) S Asia.

Maramar (Novel in Arabic) Naguib Nahfouz. (ARA.). 141p. 1980. pap. 8.95 (*0-86685-159-3*, LDL538) Intl Bk Ctr.

Maramures County, Vol. 5. Bela Bartok. (Rumanian Folk Music Ser.). 1975. lib. bdg. 185.00 (*90-247-1738-8*) Kluwer Academic.

Marana Community in the Hohokam World. Ed. by Suzanne K. Fish et al. LC 92-8510. (Anthropological Papers: No. 56). (Illus.). 120p. (Orig.). 1992. 18.95 (*0-8165-1314-7*) U of Ariz Pr.

Maranao Dictionary. Howard P. McKaughan & Batua A. Macaraya. LC 67-13668. 878p. reprint ed. pap. 200.00 (*0-8357-9825-9*, 201611300098) Bks Demand.

Maranatha: Our Lord, Come! Renald E. Showers. LC 94-78233. 1995. 16.95 (*0-915540-22-3*) Frnds Israel.

Maranatha Vol. 2: My Many Phases. Belva Carey. (Illus.). 117p. (Orig.). 1997. pap. 8.00 (*0-614-28589-5*) Careys Pub Co.

***Marangoni & Interfacial Phenomena in Materials Processing.** Ed. by E. D. Hondros et al. 268p. 1999. 90.00 (*1-86125-056-8*, Pub. by Inst Materials) Ashgate Pub Co.

***Marangraphic Skids.** 1999. write for info. (*0-13-002319-1*) P-H.

MaranGraphics' Development Group Learn at First Sight Windows 3.1. Marangraphics' Development Group Staff. 1994. write for info. (*0-318-72421-9*) P-H.

Maraniello. Mainolfi Maraniello. (Illus.). 64p. 1999. pap. 24.95 (*88-8158-188-4*, Pub. by Charta) Dist Art Pubs.

Mararoko: A Study in Melanesian Religion. Mary N. MacDonald. LC 90-35291. (American University Studies: Anthropology & Science: Ser. XI, Vol. 45). (Illus.). XVII, 592p. (C). 1991. text 85.95 (*0-8204-1194-9*) P Lang Pubng.

Marasmieae (Basidiomycetes-Tricholomataceae) Rolf Singer. LC 76-21378. (Flora Neotropica Monographs: No. 17). (Illus.). 347p. 1976. pap. 25.00 (*0-89327-009-1*) NY Botanical.

***Marassa Concept.** Florence H. Robertson. 182p. (C). 1999. per. 33.95 (*0-7872-6373-7*, 41637301) Kendall-Hunt.

Marat - Sade, the Investigaiton, & the Shadow of the Coachman's Body. Peter Weiss. Ed. by Robert Cohen. LC 81-71132. (The German Library). 324p. 1998. 39.95 (*0-8264-0962-8*); pap. 19.95 (*0-8264-0963-6*) Continuum.

Marat-Sade. Peter Weiss & Geoffrey Skelton. 1964. 5.95 (*0-87129-507-5*, M18) Dramatic Pub.

Maratha Confederacy: A Study of Its Origin & Development. V. S. Kadam. (C). 1993. 14.00 (*0-685-68100-9*, Pub. by M Manoharial) S Asia.

Maratha Confederacy: A Study of Its Origin & Development. V. S. Kadam. 172p. 1993. 33.50 (*81-215-0570-4*, Pub. by M Manoharial) Coronet Bks.

Maratha Rajas of Tanjore. K. R. Subramanian. (C). 1988. reprint ed. 14.50 (*81-206-0399-0*, Pub. by Asian Educ Servs) S Asia.

Maratha War Papers of Arthur Wellesley: April to December 1803. Anthony S. Bennell. 1999. 74.00 (*0-7509-2069-6*) A Sutton.

Marathas & Dekhani Musalmans: Handbooks for the Indian Army. R. M. Betham. (C). 1996. 24.00 (*81-206-1204-3*, Pub. by Asian Educ Servs) S Asia.

Marathas, Marauders & State Formation in Eighteenth-Century India. Stewart Gordon. (Illus.). 240p. 1999. pap. 11.95 (*0-19-564748-3*) OUP.

Marathas, 1600-1818. Stewart Gordon. LC 92-16525. (New Cambridge History of India Ser.: II: 4). 219p. (C). 1993. text 54.95 (*0-521-26883-4*) Cambridge U Pr.

Mãrathi. Rajeshwari Pandharipande. LC 96-38089. (Descriptive Grammars Ser.). 680p. (C). 1997. 190.00 (*0-415-00319-9*) Routledge.

Marathi English Dictionary. J. T. Molesworth. 952p. 1989. 95.00 (*0-8288-8470-6*, F27270) Fr & Eur.

Marathi English Dictionary. J. T. Molesworth & Candy T. Molesworth. 1986. reprint ed. 50.00 (*0-8364-1702-X*, Pub. by Popular Prakashan) S Asia.

Marathi-Oriya-Panjabi-Sanskrit see National Bibliography of Indian Literature, 1901-1953

Marathi Proverbs. Ed. by A. Manwaring. (C). 1991. reprint ed. 15.00 (*81-206-0704-X*, Pub. by Asian Educ Servs) S Asia.

Marathon! Jeff Galloway. 197p. 1996. pap. 13.95 (*0-9647187-1-5*) Phidippides.

Marathon. Clarence DeMar. LC 81-83460. (Illus.). 156p. 1981. reprint ed. 9.95 (*0-933050-09-7*) New Eng Pr VT.

Marathon: The Anatomy of a Race Mile by Mile. Robert De Castella & Ardy Friedberg. 1989. text 17.95 (*0-07-016199-2*) McGraw.

Marathon: The Clarence DeMar Story. Clarence DeMar. 92p. 1991. reprint ed. pap. 12.95 (*0-915297-09-4*, CDM) Cedarwinds.

Marathon: The Official Strategy Guide. Tuncer Deniz. 1995. pap. 19.95 (*0-7615-0084-7*) Prima Pub.

Marathon: The Ultimate Training & Racing Guide. Hal Higdon. (Illus.). 224p. (Orig.). 1993. pap. 15.95 (*0-87596-159-2*) Rodale Pr Inc.

***Marathon: The Ultimate Training Guide.** Hal Higdon. LC 99-35214. 224p. 1999. pap. 15.95 (*1-57954-171-2*) Rodale Pr Inc.

Marathon, Cross Country & Road Running. Cliff Temple. (Illus.). 256p. 1990. pap. 22.95 (*0-09-174331-1*, Pub. by S Paul) Trafalgar.

Marathon Dad: Setting a Pace That Works for Working Fathers. John Evans. LC 98-4033. 256p. 1998. mass mkt. 23.00 (*0-380-97520-3*, Avon Bks) Morrow Avon.

***Marathon Dad: Setting a Pace That Works for Working Fathers.** John Evans. 256p. 1999. pap. 14.00 (*0-380-79321-0*, Avon Bks) Morrow Avon.

Marathon Flyers & the Flights to Nowhere. Russell Plehinger. (Illus.). 192p. 1989. 27.00 (*0-8187-0112-9*) Harlo Press.

***Marathon Love.** Ameritonia Staff. Ed. by Sarah Holmes. 215p. 2000. pap. write for info. (*0-9701345-0-9*) Ameritonia Inspir.

Marathon Man. William Goldman. 22.95 (*0-88411-653-0*) Amereon Ltd.

Marathon Man. William Goldman. 1993. reprint ed. lib. bdg. 27.95 (*1-56849-201-4*) Buccaneer Bks.

Marathon, My Marathon: A Novel. Jon Foyt & Lois Foyt. 128p. (Orig.). 1996. 16.95 (*1-56474-161-3*); pap. 9.95 (*1-56474-160-5*) Fithian Pr.

Marathon of Faith. Rex E. Lee et al. LC 96-10450. xiii, 194p. 1996. 15.95 (*1-57345-163-0*) Deseret Bk.

Marathon 33. June Havoc. 1969. pap. 5.25 (*0-8222-0730-3*) Dramatists Play.

Marathon Training: The Proven 100-Day Program for Success. Joe Henderson. LC 96-43355. (Illus.). 264p. (Orig.). 1997. pap. 14.95 (*0-88011-591-2*, PHEN0591) Human Kinetics.

Marathoning. Manfred Steffny. Tr. by George Beinhorn. LC 78-64388. (Illus.). 176p. 1979. reprint ed. pap. 5.95 (*0-89037-156-3*) Anderson World.

Marathoning 101: How to Finish Your First Marathon! Scott Demaree & Eric Steele. (Illus.). 112p. 1999. pap. 14.95 (*0-9665512-1-4*) Stone Mason Inc.

Marathoning Start to Finish. Patti Finke & Warren Finke. (Illus.). 186p. (Orig.). 1986. pap. 10.00 (*0-9616865-0-2*) wYeast Consult.

Marati' al-Mu'minin fi Riyad al-Salihin. Muhammad A. Salim. 192p. 1994. pap. 2.95 (*1-57547-199-X*) Dar Al-Fikr.

Marauder Squadron Albums - A Trilogy from the 455th Bombardment Squadron: Includes Marauder Memoirs - History of the 455th Bombardment Squadron in WW II - World War II Combat Drawings & Memoirs of Benedict I. Goldsmith - Prisoners of War . . . Missing in Action & the Squadron Beyond, 3 vols. Members of the 455th Bomb Squadron Association. Ed. by Paul E. Mulrenin. LC 97-70441. (Illus.). 1230p. (C). 1997. pap. 75.00 (*0-9619535-2-7*) Four Fifty Fifth.

***Marauders - Day of the Halfbreeds, 2 vols. in 1.** Peter McCurtin. (Sundance Ser.: Vols. 3 & 5). 368p. 1999. mass mkt. 5.50 (*0-8439-4521-4*, Leisure Bks) Dorchester Pub Co.

Marauders' Moon. large type ed. Luke Short. 315p. 1991. reprint ed. lib. bdg. 17.95 (*1-56054-231-4*) Thorndike Pr.

An Asterisk (*) at the beginning of an entry indicates that the title is appearing for the first time.

Marauders of Gor. John Norman. 1998. reprint ed. mass mkt. 6.95 (*1-56333-662-6*, Masquerade SF) Masquerade.
Marauders of the Indian Nations: The Bill Cook Gang & Cherokee Bill. Glenn Shirley. LC 94-27935. (Illus.). 190p. 1994. 21.95 (*0-935269-15-0*) Western Pubns.
Maravich: Pistol Pete. 1969. pap. 4.95 (*1-57980-028-9*) Claitors.
Maravilla. Laura Del Fuego. (Mujer Latina Ser.). 233p. (Orig.). 1990. pap. 19.95 (*0-915745-15-1*) Floricanto Pr.
Maravilla. Alfredo Vea, Jr. LC 93-31582. 1994. pap. 13.95 (*0-452-27160-6*, Plume) Dutton Plume.
Maravillas Con Variaciones Acrosticas en el Jardin de Miro. deluxe limited aut. ed. Rafael Alberti. (Ediciones Especiales y de Bibliofilo Ser.). (CAT., Illus.). 118p. 1975. 17500.00 (*84-343-0226-8*) Elliots Bks.
Maravillas de la Ciencia. Dale McCreedy & Jean N. Kuhn. (National Science Partnership para Girl Scouts y Museos de Ciencia Ser.). Orig. Title: Science Wonders. (ENG & SPA., Illus.). 37p. 1997. pap. 8.00 (*1-889939-04-8*) Franklin PA.
Maravillas de la Humanidad (Man-Made Wonders) Series, 6 bks., Set VI. Jason Cooper. (SPA.). (J). 1991. 87.60 (*0-86592-899-1*) Rourke Enter.
Maravillas de la Naturaleza (Wonders in Nature) Scandinavia Staff. (SPA.). 4.99 (*0-685-74951-7*, 491398) Editorial Unilit.
Maravillas de la Selva. Janet Craig. (SPA.). (J). 1997. pap. 3.50 (*0-8167-3258-2*) Troll Communs.
Maravillas de Mexico. Laura Conlon. (Al Sur de Nuestra Frontera Ser.).Tr. of Wonders of Mexico. 24p. (J). (gr. k-4). 1994. lib. bdg. 17.27 (*1-55916-075-6*) Rourke Bk Co.
Maravillas del Agua. Dale McCreedy & Julia Andrews. Orig. Title: Water Wonders. (ENG & SPA., Illus.). 69p. 1997. pap. 8.00 (*1-889939-06-4*) Franklin PA.
Maravillas del Pantano. Francene Sabin. (J). 1997. pap. 3.50 (*0-8167-3340-6*) Troll Communs.
Maravillas District. Rosa Chacel. Tr. by D. A. Demers from SPA. LC 92-8098. (European Women Writers Ser.). 286p. 1992. pap. 14.95 (*0-8032-6353-8*, Bison Books) U of Nebr Pr.
Maravillosa Medician de Jorge: George's Marvelous Medicine. Roald Dahl. (J). 1995. pap. text 8.95 (*84-204-3609-7*) Santillana.
Maravillosa Medicina de Jorge. Roald Dahl. 1996. 14.05 (*0-606-10442-9*, Pub. by Turtleback) Demco.
Maravillosa Vida Llena del Espiritu. Charles Stanley.Tr. of Wonderful Spirit-Filled Life. (SPA.). 304p. 1994. 10.99 (*0-89922-526-8*, C001-5268) Caribe Betania.
Maravilloso Jesus! L. Parry & A. Parry.Tr. of Wonderful Jesus!. (SPA.). 5p. (J). 1995. 9.99 (*1-56063-719-6*, 498749) Editorial Unilit.
Maravilloso Mago de Oz (Wizard of Oz) L. Frank Baum. (SPA., Illus.). 160p. (Orig.). (J). 1996. pap. 2.95 (*0-486-28968-0*) Dover.
Maravilloso Mundo de los Aracnidos. Anita Hoffmann. (Ciencia para Todos Ser.). (SPA.). pap. 6.99 (*968-16-4214-7*, Pub. by Fondo) Continental Bk.
Marbin Besimho. P. S. Pollak. 15.00 (*0-87559-083-7*); pap. 10.00 (*0-87559-084-5*) Shalom.
***Marble.** Beth Maye. Ed. by Noreen Wise. (Lemonade Collection). 96p. (YA). (gr. 4 up). 2000. pap. 6.95 (*1-58584-264-8*) Huckleberry CT.
Marble: Art Historical & Scientific Perspectives on Ancient Sculpture. Ed. by Marion True. LC 90-42216. (Illus.). 299p. 1990. pap. 49.95 (*0-89236-174-3*, Pub. by J P Getty Trust) OUP.
Marble: The History of a Culture. Luciana Mannoni & Tiziano Mannoni. LC 86-160034. (Illus.). 284p. reprint ed. pap. 88.10 (*0-8357-4254-7*, 203704300007) Bks Demand.
Marble Vol. 1: A Town Built on Dreams. Oscar McCollum, Jr. (Illus.). 352p. 1992. 42.00 (*0-913582-55-7*, 0248) Sundance.
Marble Vol. 2: A Town Built on Dreams. Oscar McCollum, Jr. (Illus.). 352p. 1993. 42.00 (*0-913582-56-5*, 0249) Sundance.
Marble & Stone Slab Veneer. James E. Amrhein & Michael W. Merrigan. (Illus.). 138p. (Orig.). 1989. pap. text 20.00 (*0-940116-08-1*) Masonry Inst Am.
Marble & Tile: The Selection & Care of Stone & Tile Surfaces. Frederick M. Hueston. LC 96-68655. (Illus.). 234p. 1996. pap. 29.95 (*0-9652577-0-3*) NTC Enter.
Marble Book & the Marbles. Richie Chevat. LC 96-604. (Illus.). 192p. (J). (ps-7). 1996. pap. 9.95 (*0-7611-0449-6*, 10449) Workman Pub.
Marble City: A Photographic Tour of Knoxville's Graveyards. Jack Neely. LC 98-40116. (Illus.). 88p. 1999. 34.00 (*1-57233-043-0*); pap. 16.00 (*1-57233-036-8*, 9840116) U of Tenn Pr.
***Marble Clocks.** Peter Wotton & Brian Oliver. 1999. pap. 24.00 (*0-7478-0431-1*, Pub. by Shire Pubns) St Mut.
Marble Faun. Nathaniel Hawthorne. Ed. by William Charvat et al. (Centenary Edition of the Works of Nathaniel Hawthorne: Vol. 4). (Illus.). 610p. 1969. text 80.00 (*0-8142-0062-1*) Ohio St U Pr.
Marble Faun. Nathaniel Hawthorne. Ed. by Malcolm Bradbury. 424p. 1995. pap. 6.95 (*0-460-87532-9*, Everyman's Classic Lib) Tuttle Pubng.
Marble Faun. Nathaniel Hawthorne. 480p. 1990. pap. 9.95 (*0-14-039077-4*, Penguin Classics) Viking Penguin.
Marble Faun. Nathaniel Hawthorne. (Notable American Authors Ser.). 1992. reprint ed. lib. bdg. 75.00 (*0-7812-3041-1*) Rprt Serv.
Marble Faun: Hawthorne's Transformations. Evan Carton. 170p. (C). 1992. 23.95 (*0-8057-9448-4*, Twyne) Mac Lib Ref.
Marble Faun: or The Romance of Monte Beni. Ed. by Richard H. Rupp. LC 73-134464. 1971. pap. 7.60 (*0-672-61026-4*, Bobbs) Macmillan.
Marble Fly. Jamie McKendrick. 64p. 1997. pap. 11.95 (*0-19-283256-5*) OUP.
Marble Game, Vols. 1-4. Geoffrey W. Brown. 936p. (Orig.). 1986. pap. 19.95 (*0-936061-00-6*) Foothills.
***Marble Goddesses with Technicolor Skins.** Corinne Robins. 108p. 2000. pap. 11.95 (*0-937804-84-3*, Pub. by Segue NYC) SPD-Small Pr Dist.
Marble Head & Other Poems. Ludwig Zeller. (Illus.). 96p. 1995. pap. 12.95 (*0-88962-335-X*) Mosaic.
***Marble Hill Annealing Demonstration Evaluation.** C. B. Oland. 164p. 1998. per. 38.00 (*0-16-062902-0*) USGPO.
***Marble Hill Annealing Demonstration Evaluation.** C. B. Oland et al. LC 98-174523. xvii, 117p. 1998. write for info. (*0-16-049502-4*) USGPO.
Marble in Antiquity: Collected Papers of J. B. Ward-Perkins. Hazel Dodge & Bryan Ward-Perkins. (Archaeological Monographs). (Illus.). 182p. 1992. pap. 45.00 (*0-904152-20-0*, Pub. by British Schl Rome) David Brown.
Marble in the Water: Essays on Contemporary Writers of Fiction for Children & Young Adults. David Rees. LC 80-16623. 224p. 1980. pap. 9.95 (*0-87675-281-4*) Horn Bk.
Marble Jungle. Clay Richards. 1961. 12.95 (*0-8392-1064-7*) Astor-Honor.
Marble Man: Robert E. Lee & His Image in American Society. Thomas L. Connelly. LC 76-41778. 272p. 1978. pap. 14.95 (*0-8071-0474-4*) La State U Pr.
Marble Mania. Stanley Block. LC 98-18146. 192p. 1998. 34.95 (*0-7643-0014-8*) Schiffer.
Marble Manifesto: Poems. Byron Vazakas. (Orig.). 1964. 4.50 (*0-8079-0079-6*); pap. 1.95 (*0-8079-0080-X*) October.
***Marble Mask.** Archer Mayor. 320p. 2000. 23.95 (*0-89296-723-4*) Mysterious Pr.
Marble Mountain Wilderness. 2nd ed. David Green & Greg Ingold. LC 96-13123. 180p. (Orig.). 1996. pap. 15.95 (*0-89997-183-0*) Wilderness Pr.
Marble Orchard. William F. Nolan. 224p. 1995. 20.95 (*0-312-14011-8*) St Martin.
Marble Orchard. large type ed. Basil Copper. (Linford Mystery Large Print Ser.). 256p. 1998. pap. 17.99 (*0-7089-5265-8*, Linford) Ulverscroft.
Marble Palaces, Temples of Art: Art Museums, Architecture, & American Culture, 1890-1930. Ingrid A. Steffensen-Bruce. LC 98-4527. (Illus.). 272p. 1998. 60.00 (*0-8387-5351-5*) Bucknell U Pr.
Marble Princess. 2nd rev. ed. Menelaos Stefanidis. (Folk Tales from Greece Ser.: Vol. 3). (Illus.). 64p. (J). (gr. 1-6). 1996. lib. bdg. 27.50 (*960-425-055-8*, Pub. by Sigma Publns) Cosmos.
Marble Prophecy, & Other Poems. Josiah G. Holland. LC 72-4964. (Romantic Tradition in American Literature Ser.). 122p. 1972. reprint ed. 20.95 (*0-405-04635-9*) Ayer.
Marble Quarry: The James H. Ricau Collection of Sculpture at the Chrysler Museum of Art. H. Nichols Clark & William H. Gerdts. LC 97-15397. (Illus.). 280p. 1997. 75.00 (*1-55595-131-7*, Pub. by Hudson Hills) Natl Bk Netwk.
Marble Queens & Captives: Women in Nineteenth-Century American Sculpture. Joy S. Kasson. 320p. (C). 1990. 42.00 (*0-300-04596-4*) Yale U Pr.
Marble Shoot. Dave Johnson. 65p. 1995. pap. 12.00 (*0-9649765-1-X*) Hmmingbrd NC.
Marble, Stone & Ceramic Tile. Frederick M. Hueston. 38p. (Orig.). 1996. pap. 2.99 (*0-9652577-1-1*) NTC Enter.
Marble Threshing Floor. Philip Sherrard. LC 73-117893. (Select Bibliographies Reprint Ser.). 1977. 31.95 (*0-8369-5346-0*) Ayer.
Marble Woman: Unknown Thrillers of Louisa May Alcott. Louisa May Alcott. Ed. by Madeleine B. Stern. Orig. Title: Plots & Counterplots. 320p. 1995. reprint ed. pap. 11.00 (*0-380-72677-7*, Avon Bks) Morrow Avon.
Marble Words from Hays, Kansas. S. J. Sackett. (Publications of the American Dialect Society: No. 37). 29p. 1962. pap. 4.20 (*0-8173-0637-4*) U of Ala Pr.
Marble Workers' Manual. Tr. by M. L. Booth. (Illus.). 295p. 1985. reprint ed. pap. text 25.00 (*0-87556-352-X*) Saifer.
Marbled Paper: Its History, Techniques, & Patterns. Richard J. Wolfe. LC 89-14614. (Illus.). 260p. 1990. text 130.00 (*0-8122-8188-8*) U of Pa Pr.
Marbled Vignettes: Including Muir Dawson & Norma Rubovits in Conversation. Norma Rubovits. 8p. 1992. 125.00 (*0-87093-278-0*); 600.00 (*0-87093-279-9*) Dawsons.
Marblehead, Vol. I. John Hardy Wright. LC 97-149487. (Images of America Ser.). 1999. pap. 16.99 (*0-7524-0450-4*) Arcadia Publng.
Marblehead, Vol. II. John Hardy Wright. (Images of America Ser.). 1997. pap. 16.99 (*0-7524-0482-2*) Arcadia Publng.
Marblehead Boat Names: From Achiever to Zephyr . . . How These Boats Really Got Their Names. Susan C. Fischer. LC 94-227992. (Illus.). 120p. (Orig.). 1994. pap. text 10.95 (*0-9641013-0-0*) Marblehead Lghthse.
Marblehead Lighthouse: Lake Erie's Eternal Flame. Betty Neidecker. Ed. by Rose Kernan. (Illus.). 112p. (Orig.). 1996. pap. 16.95 (*0-9649679-0-1*) Hawks Cry.
Marbleheart. Don Callander. 1998. mass mkt. 5.99 (*0-441-00538-1*) Ace Bks.
Marbles. Shar Levine. LC 98-26083. (Illus.). 96p. 1998. 17.95 (*0-8069-4262-2*) Sterling.
Marbles. Oxford Stroud. 1991. 19.95 (*0-15-157055-8*) Harcourt.
Marbles. Oxford Stroud. 312p. 1992. pap. 8.95 (*0-15-657200-1*, Harvest Bks) Harcourt.
Marbles. 2nd expanded rev. ed. Robert Block. LC 98-143835. (Illus.). 160p. 1998. pap. 19.95 (*0-7643-0454-2*) Schiffer.
Marbles: A Forgotten Part of Salem History. Dale E. Shaffer. 49p. (Orig.). 1983. pap. 2.50 (*0-915060-18-3*) D E Shaffer.
Marbles: A Guide to Machine-Made Marbles. Larry Castle & Marlow Peterson. (Illus.). 75p. (Orig.). 1991. pap. 15.00 (*0-9624185-1-X*) UT Marble Connection.
Marbles: A Play in Three Acts. Joseph Brodsky. Tr. by Alan Myers. (Noonday Ser.). 80p. 1990. pap. 11.00 (*0-374-52116-6*) FS&G.
***Marbles: A Player's Guide.** Shar Levine. (J). 1999. pap. text 9.95 (*0-8069-6257-7*) Sterling.
Marbles: Identification & Price Guide. 3rd rev. ed. Robert Block. LC 99-31912. (Illus.). 160p. 1999. pap. 19.95 (*0-7643-0888-2*) Schiffer.
Marbles: The Guide to Cat's-Eyes Marbles. Larry Castle & Marlow Peterson. (Illus.). 32p. 1998. pap. 8.95 (*0-9624185-3-6*) UT Marble Connection.
Marbles: The Guide to Machine-Made Marbles. 2nd ed. Larry Castle & Marlow Peterson. LC 95-60961. (Illus.). 118p. 1995. pap. 19.95 (*0-9624185-2-8*) UT Marble Connection.
Marbles: 101 Ways to Play. Joanna Cole. (Illus.). 128p. (J). (gr. k-3). 1998. mass mkt. 8.95 (*0-688-12207-8*, Wm Morrow) Morrow Avon.
Marbles: 101 Ways to Play. Joanna Cole. LC 97-36251. (Illus.). 127p. (J). 1998. 16.00 (*0-688-12205-1*, Wm Morrow) Morrow Avon.
Marbles Illustrated: Prices at Auction. Robert Block. (Illus.). 160p. 1999. pap. 16.95 (*0-7643-0970-6*) Schiffer.
Marbles, Roller Skates, Doorknobs: Simple Machines That Are Really Wheels. Christopher Lampton. LC 92-34332. (Gateway Simple Machines Ser.). (Illus.). 32p. (J). (gr. 2-4). 1991. pap. 4.80 (*1-878841-45-9*) Millbrook Pr.
Marblesized Paper Patterns in Full Color. Lauren Clark. LC 92-12032. (Pictorial Archive Ser.). 64p. 1992. pap. 9.95 (*0-486-27220-6*) Dover.
Marbling: A Complete Guide to Creating Beautiful Patterned Papers & Fabrics. Diane V. Maurer. (Illus.). 120p. 1994. pap. 11.95 (*1-56799-113-0*, Friedman-Fairfax) M Friedman Pub Grp Inc.
Marbling Methods & Receipts from Four Centuries. Barry McKay. 105p. 1990. 125.00 (*0-938768-21-2*, 30757) Oak Knoll.
Marbling on Fabric. Anne Chambers. (Illus.). 48p. 1995. pap. 12.95 (*0-85532-788-X*, 2788X, Pub. by Srch Pr) A Schwartz & Co.
Marbling on Fabric. Daniel Cohen et al. LC 89-78121. (Illus.). 94p. (Orig.). 1990. pap. 12.95 (*0-934026-54-8*) Interweave.
Marbling on Fabric. Polly Fox. (Illus.). 1989. 14.95 (*0-9623586-1-4*) Fresh Ink Pr.
Marbling on Paper Using Oil Paints. Anne Chambers. 64p. (Orig.). 1993. pap. 15.95 (*0-85532-709-X*, 709-X, Pub. by Srch Pr) A Schwartz & Co.
Marbling Techniques: How to Create Traditional & Contemporary Designs on Paper & Fabric. Wendy A. Medieros. LC 94-19095. (Illus.). 144p. 1994. pap. 24.95 (*0-8230-3005-9*) Watsn-Guptill.
Marblous Story. John McGahee. LC 96-86374. 1996. mass mkt., spiral bd. 9.95 (*1-889131-05-9*) CasAnanda.
Marburg & Ebola Virus Infections: A Guide for Their Diagnosis, Management & Control. D. Simpson. (WHO Offset Publications: No. 36). 28p. 1977. 4.00 (*92-4-170036-X*) World Health.
Marburg & Ebola Viruses. Ed. by H. D. Klenk et al. (Current Topics in Microbiology & Immunology Ser.: Vol. 235). (Illus.). 220p. 1999. 149.00 (*3-540-64729-5*) Spr-Verlag.
Marburg, Universitat: Personen- und Ortsregister zu der Matrikel und den Annalen der Universitat Marburg, 1527-1652. Compiled by W. Falckenheiner. (Alumni of German Universities Ser.). 1990. reprint ed. 50.00 (*0-8115-3774-9*) Periodicals Srv.
Marburg, Universitat. Catalogi Studiosorum Marpurgensium cum Annalibus Coniuncti Series Recentior: Fasciculi I-XII. Annos, 1653-1830. (Alumni of German Universities Ser.). 1990. reprint ed. 80.00 (*0-8115-3772-2*) Periodicals Srv.
Marburg Virus. large type ed. Stanley Johnson. 496p. 1984. 27.99 (*0-7089-1142-0*) Ulverscroft.
Marburger Informations, Dokumentations und Administrations-System (MIDAS) Handbuch: Lutz Heusinger. Ed. by Bildarchiv Foto Marburg Staff & Deutches Dokumentationszentrum fur Kuntsgeschichte. (Literatur und Archiv Ser.). (GER.). xxvi, 577p. 1992. lib. bdg. 54.00 (*3-598-22086-3*) K G Saur Verlag.
Marbury vs. Madison: Powers of the Supreme Court. David DeVillers. LC 97-24865. (Landmark Supreme Court Cases Ser.). (Illus.). 112p. (YA). (gr. 6 up). 1998. lib. bdg. 20.95 (*0-89490-967-3*) Enslow Pubs.
***Marbury vs. Madison: The Origins & Legacy of Judicial Review.** William E. Nelson. (Landmark Law Cases & American Society Ser.). 2000. 29.95 (*0-7006-1061-8*) U Pr of KS.
***Marbury vs. Madison: The Origins & Legacy of Judicial Review.** William E. Nelson. 2000. pap. 12.95 (*0-7006-1062-6*) U Pr of KS.
Marbury vs. Madison & Judicial Review. Robert L. Clinton. LC 89-34651. xii, 332p. 1989. pap. 19.95 (*0-7006-0517-7*) U Pr of KS.
Marc. S. Partsch. 1994. pap. 9.99 (*3-8228-0544-0*) Taschen Amer.
Marc. Susanna Partsch. 1996. pap. 12.99 (*3-8228-0673-0*) Benedikt Taschen.
Marc. Taschen Staff. (Illus.). 1996. pap. 8.99 (*3-8228-8678-5*) Taschen Amer.
MARC - AACR2 - Author Control Tagging: Blitz Cataloging Workbooks. Bobby Ferguson. Ed. by Sheila Intner. LC 98-2811. 176p. 1998. pap., wbk. ed. 25.00 (*1-56308-644-1*) Libs Unl.
***Marc Anthony.** Michael-Anne Johns. (Illus.). (J). 2000. 4.95 (*0-7407-0790-6*) Andrews & McMeel.
Marc-Antoine Charpentier: Music for Moliere's Comedies. Moliere & Marc-Antoine Charpentier. Ed. by John S. Powell. (Recent Researches in the Music of the Baroque Era Ser.: No. RRB63). (Illus.). 93, xliiip. 1990. pap. 45.00 (*0-89579-239-7*) A-R Eds.
Marc-Antoine Charpentier: Nine Settings of the "Litanies de la Vierge" Marc-Antoine Charpentier. Ed. by David C. Rayl. (Recent Researches in Music of the Baroque Era Ser.: Vol. RRB72). (Illus.). xx, 242p. 1994. pap. 80.00 (*0-89579-302-4*) A-R Eds.
Marc-Antoine Charpentier: Vocal Chamber Music. Marc-Antoine Charpentier. Ed. by Robert Preston. (Recent Researches in Music of the Baroque Era Ser.: Vol. RRB48). (Illus.). xxi, 98p. 1986. pap. 40.00 (*0-89579-202-8*) A-R Eds.
Marc Aurele. Jules Romains, pseud. (FRE.). 252p. 1968. pap. 16.95 (*0-7859-1411-0*, 2080603620) Fr & Eur.
Marc Bessange. Marc Bessange. (Illus.). 1998. pap. text 7.95 (*3-86187-125-4*) B Gmunder.
Marc Bloch: A Life in History. Carole Fink. (Illus.). 400p. (C). 1989. text 52.95 (*0-521-37300-X*) Cambridge U Pr.
Marc Bloch: A Life in History. Carole Fink. (Canto Book Ser.). (Illus.). 391p. (C). 1991. pap. 12.95 (*0-521-40671-4*) Cambridge U Pr.
Marc Bloch, Sociology & Geography: Encountering Changing Disciplines. Susan W. Friedman. (Cambridge Studies in Historical Geography: No. 24). (Illus.). 270p. (C). 1996. text 54.95 (*0-521-56157-4*) Cambridge U Pr.
Marc Bolan. Virgin Publishing Staff. (Illus.). 1999. pap. 9.95 (*1-85227-683-5*, Pub. by Virgin Bks) London Brdge.
Marc Bolan: A Tribute. (Illus.). 128p. 1992. pap. 19.95 (*0-7119-2995-5*, AM89180) Music Sales.
***Marc Brown.** Mae Woods. LC 99-88856. (Children's Authors Ser.). 2000. write for info. (*1-57765-111-1*) ABDO Pub Co.
***Marc Brown Arthur Chapter, Bks. 1-3.** Marc Brown. 208p. (J). 2000. 9.95 (*0-316-12096-0*, Pub. by Little) Time Warner.
Marc Brown Connection. Will C. Howell. 1991. 10.99 (*0-8224-4378-3*) Fearon Teacher Aids.
Marc Chagall. (Prestel Postcard Bks.). (Illus.). 18p. 1995. pap. 8.95 (*3-7913-1457-2*, Pub. by Prestel) te Neues.
***Marc Chagall.** Howard Greenfeld. (Essential Ser.). (Illus.). 112p. 2000. 12.95 (*0-7407-0727-2*, Abrams Essential) Andrews & McMeel.
***Marc Chagall.** Howard Greenfield. (Essential Ser.). 2000. pap. 12.95 (*0-8109-5815-5*, Pub. by Abrams) Time Warner.
Marc Chagall. Andrew Kagan. (Modern Masters Ser.). (Illus.). 128p. 1989. 35.00 (*0-89659-932-9*); pap. 14.95 (*0-89659-935-3*) Abbeville Pr.
***Marc Chagall.** Mike Venezia. LC 99-41807. (Getting to Know the World's Greatest Artists Ser.). (J). 2000. 22.00 (*0-516-21055-6*) Childrens.
***Marc Chagall.** Mike Venezia. (Getting to Know the World's Greatest Artists Ser.). (Illus.). 32p. (J). (gr. 3-4). 2000. pap. 6.95 (*0-516-27041-9*) Childrens.
Marc Chagall. James J. Sweeney. LC 74-86433. (Museum of Modern Art Publications in Reprint). (Illus.). 1969. reprint ed. 18.95 (*0-405-01552-6*) Ayer.
Marc Chagall: A First Impressions Book. Howard Greenfeld. (First Impressions Ser.). (Illus.). 80p. (YA). (gr. 7 up). 1990. 19.95 (*0-8109-3152-4*, Pub. by Abrams) Time Warner.
Marc Chagall: An Intimate Biography. Sidney Alexander. (Illus.). 526p. 1994. pap. 16.95 (*1-56924-980-6*) Marlowe & Co.
Marc Chagall: An Introduction. Howard Greenfeld. LC 80-14277. (Illus.). 176p. 1981. reprint ed. 16.95 (*0-87951-115-X*, Pub. by Overlook Pr) Penguin Putnam.
Marc Chagall: Arabian Nights. Tr. by Richard F. Burton from ARA. LC 98-54867. (Pegasus Library). (Illus.). 164p. 1999. 25.00 (*3-7913-2081-5*) te Neues.
Marc Chagall: Daphnis & Chloe. Marc Chagall. (Pegasus Library). (Illus.). 152p. 1994. 25.00 (*3-7913-1373-8*, Pub. by Prestel) te Neues.
***Marc Chagall: Daphnis & Chloe.** Longus. (Illus.). 2000. pap. 9.95 (*3-7913-2336-9*) Prestel Pub NY.
Marc Chagall: Life Is a Dream. Brigitta Hopler. LC 99-179476. (Adventures in Art Ser.). (Illus.). 30p. (J). (gr. 1-6). 1998. 14.95 (*3-7913-1986-8*) Prestel.
Marc Chagall: My Life - My Dream: Berlin & Paris, 1922-1940. Susan Compton et al. (Illus.). 268p. 1990. 70.00 (*3-7913-1064-X*, Pub. by Prestel) te Neues.
Marc Chagall: Origins & Paths. Roland Doschka. (Illus.). 232p. 1998. 65.00 (*3-7913-1989-2*) te Neues.
Marc Chagall: Painter of Dreams. Natalie S. Bober. LC 91-25463. (Illus.). 124p. (J). (gr. 4-8). 1991. 14.95 (*0-8276-0379-7*) JPS Phila.
Marc Chagall: Paintings. Exhibition Catalogue. Marc Chagall. (Illus.). 24p. 1980. pap. 15.00 (*0-8150-0004-9*) Wittenborn Art.
Marc Chagall: The Land of My Heart: Russia. Sylvie Forestier & Mikhail Guerman. (Great Painters Ser.). (Illus.). 192p. 1996. 40.00 (*1-85995-110-4*) Parkstone Pr.
Marc Chagall: The Lithographs; La Collection Sorlier. Mark Chagall. Ed. by Ulrike Gauss. (Illus.). 415p. 1999. 125.00 (*1-891024-07-8*) Dist Art Pubs.
***Marc Chagall: What Colour Is Paradise?** Elisabeth Lemke & Thomas David. (Illus.). 30p. 2000. 14.95 (*3-7913-2393-8*) Prestel.
Marc Chagall - Arabian Nights: Four Tales from 1001 Arabian Nights. Frwd. by Norbert Nobis et al. (Illus.). 176p. 1995. 60.00 (*3-7913-0842-4*, Pub. by Prestel) te Neues.
Marc Chagall, 1887-1985. Jacob Baal-Teshuva. (Illus.). 280p. 1998. 39.99 (*3-8228-8271-2*) Taschen Amer.
Marc Chagall Postcard Book. Marc Chagall. 1998. pap. 5.99 (*3-8228-7968-1*) Taschen Amer.
Marc Edmund Jones Five Hundred, Vol. 1. Marc E. Jones. LC 77-2634. 1978. pap. 14.95 (*0-88231-040-2*) ASI Pubs Inc.

M

An Asterisk (*) at the beginning of an entry indicates that the title is appearing for the first time.

MARC for Library Use: Understanding Integrated USMARC. 2nd ed. Walt Crawford. (Professional Librarian Ser.). 376p. 1989. 45.00 (0-8161-1887-6, Hall Reference) Macmillan.
Marc-Francois Beche's Collection of Eleven Grands Motets by Esprit-Joseph-Antoine Blanchard (1696-1770) Tai W. Li. (American University Studies XX: Vol. 27). XV, 206p. (C). 1996. text 42.95 (0-8204-2745-4) P Lang Pubng.
Marc Friedland Invitations. Marc Friedland. LC 98-9182. (Illus.). 96p. 1998. 25.00 (0-609-60303-5) C Potter.
*__Marc Leuthold.__ Thomas E. Piche, Jr. et al. (Illus.). 36p. 1999. pap. 9.95 (0-914407-21-X) Everson Mus.
Marc-Making It Manageable: Version 3. Ed. by Winnebago Software Staff. (Illus.). 1997. pap. 7.95 (0-927875-74-8, 7220) Winnebago.
MARC Manual: Understanding & Using MARC Records. 2nd ed. Deborah J. Byrne. LC 97-35961. (Illus.). 263p. 1998. pap. 45.00 (1-56308-176-8) Libs Unl.
Marc Miller's Traveller. rev. ed. Marc Miller & Lester Smith. Ed. by Tony Lee. (Traveller Ser.). (Illus.). (YA). (gr. 9 up). pap. 25.00 (0-614-18941-1) Imperium Games.
*__Marc Mimram, Minimal Design: Solferino Bridge in Paris (english/french)__ Francoise Fromonot. (Illus.). 112p. 2000. 42.00 (3-7643-6335-5) Birkhauser.
*__Marc Newsom.__ Marc Newsom. 1999. pap. 59.95 (1-86154-062-0) Booth-Clibborn.

M

Marc Riboud: Photographs at Home & Abroad. Intro. by Claude Roy. (Illus.). 120p. 1988. 45.00 (0-8109-1566-9, Pub. by Abrams) Time Warner.
Marc Riboud in China: Forty Years of Photography. Tr. by Ruth Sharman from FRE. LC 96-85654. (Illus.). 176p. 1997. 49.50 (0-8109-4430-8, Pub. by Abrams) Time Warner.
Marc Simont at the Library of Congress: A Lecture for International Children's Book Day, Presented on May 8, 1992 by Marc Simont. Marc Simont. Ed. by Sybille A. Jagusch. LC 94-44463. 1995. write for info. (0-8444-0870-0) Lib Congress.
*__MARC 21 Concise Formats, 2000.__ Library of Congress Staff & National Library of Canada Staff. LC 99-87123. 2000. write for info. (0-8444-1002-0) Lib Congress.
*__MARC 21 Format for Bibliographic Data 2 vols. Including Guidelines for Content Designation (1999), 2 vols.__ Contrib. by Library of Congress Network Development and MARC Standards Office Staff. LC 99-31117. 1999. 70.00 (0-8444-0989-8) Lib Congress.
*__MARC 21 Specifications for Record Structure, Character Sets & Exchange Media, 1999.__ Library of Congress Staff & National Library of Canada Staff. LC 99-87122. 2000. write for info. (0-8444-1006-3) Lib Congress.
*__Marca de La Bestia.__ Peter LaLonde & Paul LaLonde.Tr. of Mark of the Beast. (SPA.). 184p. 1998. pap. 8.99 (0-88113-500-3) Caribe Betania.
*__Marcabru: A Critical Edition.__ Marcabrun. Ed. by Simon Gaunt et al. LC 99-56191. 2000. 162.00 (0-85991-574-3, DS Brewer) Boydell & Brewer.
Marcal Paper Mills: A Report on the Company's Environmental Policies & Practices. (Illus.). 31p. (C). 1994. reprint ed. pap. text 40.00 (0-7881-0962-6, Coun on Econ) DIANE Pub.
Marc'Antonio Ingegneri: Il Secondo Libro de Madrigali a Quattro Voci (Venice, 1579) Ed. by Jessie A. Owens. LC 93-18257. (Sixteenth-Century Madrigal Ser.: Vol. 16). 104p. 1993. text 61.00 (0-8240-5516-0) Garland.
Marc'Antonio Pasqualini (1614-1691), Vol. 3. Ed. by Margaret Murata. (Italian Cantata in the Seventeenth Century Ser.). 300p. 1986. text 25.00 (0-8240-8877-8) Garland.
Marcas del Discipulo. P. Doyle.Tr. of Mark of a Disciple. write for info. (1-56063-945-8, 497463) Editorial Unilit.
Marcel: Premier Dialogue de la Cite Harmonieuse. Charles Peguy. (FRE.). 208p. 1973. pap. 11.95 (0-686-54858-2, 2070284658) Fr & Eur.
Marcel & Mona Lisa. Rabley. Date not set. pap. text. write for info. (0-582-06075-3, Pub. by Addison-Wesley) Longman.
Marcel & the Shakespeare Letters. Rabley. 1996. pap. text. write for info. (0-582-08136-X, Pub. by Addison-Wesley) Longman.
Marcel & White Star. Stephen Rabley. 1990. pap. text. write for info. (0-582-04610-6, Pub. by Addison-Wesley) Longman.
Marcel Breuer: A Memoir. Bob Gatje. (Illus.). 368p. 2000. pap. 40.00 (1-58093-029-8, Pub. by Monacelli Pr) Penguin Putnam.
Marcel Carne. Jean Queval. (Film Ser.). 1979. lib. bdg. 59.95 (0-8490-2970-8) Gordon Pr.
Marcel Dadi: Fingers Crossing. Marcel Dadi. (Illus.). 80p. 1996. pap. 22.95 incl. audio compact disk (0-7866-1461-7, 95677BCD) Mel Bay.
Marcel Dadi/Fingerpicking Guitar Legend, Vol. 1. Marcel Dadi. 128p. 1997. spiral bd. 22.95 incl. audio compact disk (0-7866-3142-2, 94851BCD) Mel Bay.
Marcel Dadi/Fingerpicking Guitar Legend, Vol. 2. Marcel Dadi. 84p. 1997. spiral bd. 22.95 incl. audio compact disk (0-7866-3143-0, 95115BCD) Mel Bay.
Marcel Duchamp. Dawn Ades et al. LC 98-61434. (World of Art Ser.). (Illus.). 224p. 1999. pap. 14.95 (0-500-20322-9, Pub. by Thames Hudson) Norton.
Marcel Duchamp. Ed. by Anne D'Harnoncourt & Kynaston McShine. (Illus.). 360p. 1989. 65.00 (3-7913-1018-6, Pub. by Prestel) te Neues.
Marcel Duchamp. Gloria Moure. LC 88-42716. (Twentieth Century Artists Ser.). (Illus.). 128p. 1988. 27.50 (0-8478-0978-1, Pub. by Rizzoli Intl) St Martin.
Marcel Duchamp: A Life in Pictures. Jennifer Gough-Cooper & Jacques Caumont. (Illus.). 27p. 1999. 8.95 (1-900565-15-3, Pub. by Atlas Pr) SPD-Small Pr Dist.
Marcel Duchamp: Appearance Stripped Bare. Octavio Paz. Tr. by Rachel Phillips & Donald Gardner. 1991. pap. 9.70 (1-55970-138-2, Pub. by Arcade Pub Inc) Time Warner.
Marcel Duchamp: Artist of the Century. Ed. by Rudolf E. Kuenzli & Francis M. Naumann. (Illus.). 272p. 1989. reprint ed. pap. text 18.00 (0-262-61072-8) MIT Pr.
*__Marcel Duchamp: Respirateur.__ Marcel Duchamp. 2000. 39.95 (3-7757-0895-2) Gerd Hatje.
Marcel Duchamp: The Art of Making Art in the Age of Mechanical Reproduction. Francis M. Naumann & Marcel Duchamp. LC 99-29063. (Illus.). 336p. 2000. 70.00 (0-8109-6334-5, Pub. by Abrams) Time Warner.
*__Marcel Duchamp: The Art of Making Art in the Age of Mechanical Reproduction - An Exhibition Catalogue.__ Achim Moeller & Francis M. Naumann. (Illus.). 48p. 1999. pap. 35.00 (0-9646052-4-4) A Moeller Fine Art.
Marcel Duchamp: Work & Life. Ed. by Pontus Hulten. LC 93-77531. (Illus.). 616p. 1993. 75.00 (0-262-08225-X) MIT Pr.
Marcel Duchamp: Works from the John & Mable Ringling Museum of Art Collection. Michael Auping. LC 83-81504. (Illus.). 50p. (Orig.). 1983. pap. 4.95 (0-916758-13-3) Ringling Mus Art.
Marcel Duchamp & Max Ernst: The Bride Shared. David Hopkins. LC 97-43396. (Clarendon Studies in the History of Art). (Illus.). 230p. 1998. text 115.00 (0-19-817513-2) OUP.
*__Marcel Dzama.__ (Illus.). 130p. 1999. pap. write for info. (0-921381-21-2, Pub. by Plug In Editions) RAM Publications.
Marcel Goes Hollywood. Rabley. 1992. pap. text. write for info. (0-582-06252-7, Pub. by Addison-Wesley) Longman.
Marcel Grossmann Meeting: Fifth (in 2 Vols.) D. G. Blair & M. J. Buckingham. (Proceedings of the Fifth Meeting Ser.). 1989. pap. 94.00 (9971-5-0785-4); text 282.00 (9971-5-0784-6) World Scientific Pub.
Marcel Grossmann Meeting on General Relativity, 2 vols. 1792p. 1993. 88.00 (981-02-0951-7) World Scientific Pub.
Marcel Mauss Vol. 1: A Centenary Tribute. Ed. by Wendy James & N. J. Allen. LC 98-28121. 256p. 1998. pap. 22.50 (1-57181-705-0) Berghahn Bks.
Marcel Mauss Vol. 1: A Centenary Tribute. Ed. by Wendy James & N. J. Allen. LC 98-28121. 260p. 1998. 59.95 (1-57181-703-4) Berghahn Bks.
Marcel Moyse: Voice of the Flute. Ann McCutchan. LC 93-33357. (Illus.). 344p. 1994. 29.95 (0-931340-68-3, Amadeus Pr) Timber.
Marcel Odenbach. Dan Cameron et al. LC 98-66517. (Illus.). 56p. 1998. pap. 22.00 (0-915557-82-7) New Mus Contemp Art.
Marcel Pagnol M'a Raconte. Raymond Castans. (FRE.). 1976. pap. 10.95 (0-7859-1826-4, 2070367932) Fr & Eur.
Marcel Proust. Ed. by Barbara J. Bucknall. LC 87-19. (Critical Essays Ser.). 224p. 1987. 49.00 (0-8161-8833-5, Hall Reference) Macmillan.
Marcel Proust. Georges Cattaui. Tr. by Ruth Hall from FRE. 125p. 1967. 17.95 (0-8464-1159-8) Beekman Pubs.
Marcel Proust. Diane De Margerie. (Maison D'Ecrivain Collection). (FRE., Illus.). 1995. pap. 49.95 (0-614-14006-4) Intl Scholars.
Marcel Proust. Ed. by Legeton Hodson. (Critical Heritage Ser.). 440p. (C). 1997. 140.00 (0-415-15913-X) Routledge.
Marcel Proust. Ed. by Leighton Hodson. (Critical Heritage Ser.). 400p. 1989. 95.00 (0-415-02821-3) Routledge.
Marcel Proust. Edmund White. LC 98-22119. 153p. 1999. 19.95 (0-670-88057-4) Viking Penguin.
Marcel Proust: A Biography, 2 vols. George D. Painter. 1978. pap. 4.95 (0-685-04271-5) Vin Bks.
Marcel Proust: A Critical Panorama. Ed. by Larkin B. Price. LC 72-83033. 302p. reprint ed. pap. 93.70 (0-608-13934-3, 202022600016) Bks Demand.
*__Marcel Proust: A Life.__ William C. Carter. LC 99-53701. (Illus.). 921p. 2000. 35.00 (0-300-08145-6) Yale U Pr.
*__Marcel Proust: A Life.__ Jean-Yves Tadie. LC 00-20565. (Illus.). 960p. 2000. 45.00 (0-670-87655-0, Viking) Viking Penguin.
Marcel Proust: A Reference Guide, 1950-1970. Janet C. Stock. (Reference Guides to Literature Ser.). 363p. (C). 1991. 50.00 (0-8161-8987-0, Hall Reference) Macmillan.
Marcel Proust: An English Tribute. Ed. by C. K. Scott-Moncrieff. LC 73-18100. (Studies in French Literature: No. 45). 1974. lib. bdg. 65.00 (0-8383-1741-3) M S G Haskell Hse.
Marcel Proust: Remembrance of Publishers Past. Franck Lhomeau & Alain Coelho. Tr. by Sabine Destree from FRE. 320p. 2000. 24.45 (1-55970-058-0, Pub. by Arcade Pub Inc) Time Warner.
Marcel Proust: Romancier, 2 tomes, Set. Bardeche. 31.95 (0-685-37073-9, F119810) Fr & Eur.
Marcel Proust & the Creative Encounter. George Stambolian. LC 72-77645. 264p. reprint ed. pap. 81.90 (0-608-15108-4, 202578900046) Bks Demand.
Marcel Proust & the Strategy of Reading. Walter Kasell. (Purdue University Monographs in Romance Languages: No 4). x, 125p. 1980. 35.00 (90-272-1714-9) J Benjamins Pubng Co.
Marcel Proust & the Text as Macrometaphor. Lois M. Jaeck. 272p. 1990. text 55.00 (0-8020-2715-6) U of Toronto Pr.
Marcel Proust As a Social Critic. Richard L. Kopp. LC 73-149406. 230p. 1975. 32.50 (0-8386-7898-X) Fairleigh Dickinson.
Marcel Proust at UAB: A Checklist of Proust Holdings at the Mervyn H. Sterne Library. Richard Bleiler & Dieu Van Tong. 59p. (C). 1988. pap. text 7.95 (0-9620942-0-X) M H Sterne Lib.
Marcel Proust Lexikon. Philippe Michel-Thiriet. (GER.). 514p. 1992. 125.00 (0-7859-8407-0, 3518403907) Fr & Eur.
Marcel Proust on Art & Literature, 1896-1919. Marcel Proust. Tr. by Sylvia T. Warner. LC 97-17483. 416p. 1997. pap. 13.95 (0-7867-0454-3) Carroll & Graf.
Marcel Proust Revisited. Barbara J. Bucknall. LC 92-12879. (Twayne's World Authors Ser.: No. 830). 160p. 1992. 32.00 (0-8057-8274-5, Twyne) Mac Lib Ref.
Marcel Proust's a la Recherche du Temps Perdu: A Search for Certainty. Jack L. Jordan. LC 93-83302. (Marcel Proust Studies: Vol. 3). 143p. 1993. lib. bdg. 30.95 (0-917786-97-1) Summa Pubns.
Marcel Proust's Combray. Gabriel N. Seymour & Marcel Proust. Tr. by C. K. Scott-Moncrieff. LC 79-17314. (Illus.). 160p. 1979. 32.50 (0-915998-04-1) Lime Rock Pr.
Marcel Pursued by the Hounds. Michel Tremblay. LC 97-113818. 80p. 1996. pap. 10.95 (0-88922-326-2, Pub. by Talonbks) Genl Dist Srvs.
Marcel Riesz Collected Papers. Ed. by L. Hormander & L. Garding. 1000p. 1988. 160.00 (0-387-18115-6) Spr-Verlag.
Marcel Super Dice GM, No. 2. TSR Staff. 1998. 8.95 (0-7869-0739-8) TSR Inc.
Marcelino Pan y Vino. Jose M. Sanchez-Silva. Ed. by Edward R. Mulvihill & Roberto G. Sanchez. (Illus.). 128p. 1961. pap. text 15.95 (0-19-501043-4) OUP.
Marcella: A Raggedy Ann Story. Johnny Gruelle. LC 98-47801. (Illus.). 96p. (J). (gr. k-3). 1999. 16.00 (0-689-82878-0) S&S Bks Yung.
Marcella - Discipula et Magistra: Auf den Spuren einer romischen Christin des 4. Jahrhunderts. Silvia Letsch-Brunner. 304p. 1998. 105.00 (3-11-015808-6) De Gruyter.
Marcella Cucina. Marcella Hazan. LC 97-1253. 480p. 1997. 35.00 (0-06-017103-0) HarpC.
Marcella's Italian Kitchen. Marcella Hazan. 368p. 1995. pap. 22.00 (0-679-76437-2) Random.
*__Marcella's Once upon a Time Stories for Grandma's & Other Kids, Too.__ S. Jaye Woodington. vii, 175p. 1999. pap. 10.00 (0-9676223-0-1) S J Woodington.
Marcellin Caillou. Jean-Jacques Sempe. (Folio - Junior Ser.: No. 561). (FRE.). 162p. (J). (gr. 5-10). 1990. pap. 8.95 (2-07-033561-5) Schoenhof.
Marcellinus Comes: Index Marcellinianus. Compiled by Massimo Grusso. (Alpha-Omega, Reihe A Ser.: Bd. CLXXXIII). (GER.). xiv, 172p. 1996. write for info. (3-487-10100-9) G Olms Pubs.
Marcello Cervini & Ecclesiastical Government in Tridentine Italy. William V. Hudon. LC 92-1301. 271p. 1992. lib. bdg. 35.00 (0-87580-169-2) N Ill U Pr.
Marcello Giovanetti (1598-1631) A Poet of the Early Roman Baroque. William R. Crelly. LC 89-9418. (Illus.). 456p. 1989. lib. bdg. 109.95 (0-88946-146-5) E Mellen.
Marcello Malpighi & the Evolution of Embryology, 5 vols. Howard B. Adelmann. (Publications in the History of Science). (Illus.). 2548p. 1966. boxed set 250.00 (0-8014-0004-X) Cornell U Pr.
Marcello Mastorianni: An Intimate Biography. Donald Dewey. (Illus.). 288p. 1993. 21.95 (1-55972-158-8) Carol Pub Group.
Marcello Mastroianni. Matilde Hochkofler. 1994. 29.95 (88-7301-011-3, Pub. by Gremese Intl) Natl Bk Netwk.
*__Marcello Mastroianni: His Life & Art.__ Donald Dewey. (Illus.). 312p. 2000. reprint ed. 22.00 (0-7881-9393-7) DIANE Pub.
Marcellus. Lorraine Simeon. (Illus.). 24p. (J). (ps-3). 1995. 10.95 (0-86316-223-1) Writers & Readers.
Marcellus' Birthday Cake. Lorraine Simeon. (Illus.). 16p. (J). (ps-3). Date not set. 7.95 (0-86316-221-5) Writers & Readers.
Marcellus Empiricus: Concordantiae in Marcellum Empiricum, 3 vols. Sergio Sconocchia. write for info. (0-318-71959-2) G Olms Pubs.
Marcellus Empiricus: Marcelli de Medicamentis Librorum Concordantiae. Sergio Sconocchia. (GER.). 1500p. 1995. write for info. (3-487-09960-8) G Olms Pubs.
Marcellus Empiricus - Concordantiae in Marcellum Empiricum. Ed. by Sergio Sconocchia. write for info. (0-318-70675-X) G Olms Pubs.
Marcelo el Murcielago (Marcelo the Bat) Laura Navarro. LC 97-202990. (ENG & SPA., Illus.). 40p. (J). (gr. k-3). 1997. 8.95 (0-292-75567-8) Bat Conserv.
*__March.__ (Monthly Patterns & Projects Ser.). (Illus.). 80p. (J). (ps-2). 2000. pap. 7.95 (1-58273-131-4) Newbridge Educ.
March. Ed. by Paul Burns. (Butler's Lives of the Saints Ser.). 293p. 1999. 24.95 (0-8146-2379-4) Liturgical Pr.
March. John Francois. LC 98-74231. 184p. 1999. 17.95 (0-9667806-0-4) Attakapas Pr.
March. Walter R. Holland. (Orig.). 1996. mass mkt. 6.95 (1-56333-429-1, Hard Candy) Masquerade.
March. Richard Kostelanetz. (Chapbook Ser.). 24p. 1990. pap. 5.00 (0-945112-12-2) Generator Pr.
March. Larcom. (Illus.). 32p. (ps-3). 14.95 (0-06-024307-4); lib. bdg. 14.89 (0-06-024308-2) HarpC.
March. Daniel Parker. LC 98-46984. (Countdown Ser.: No. 3). 128p. (YA). (gr. 7-12). 1999. per. 3.99 (0-689-81821-1) Aladdin.
March, Before Spring. Stephanie Mendel. 32p. 1999. reprint ed. pap. 13.00 (0-9668431-1-8, Pub. by O & W Pub) SPD-Small Pr Dist.
March-December, 1781 see Papers of James Madison
March 1831 - December 1832 see Diary of Charles Francis Adams
March 18: What Your Birth Date Reveals about You. (Birth Date Book Ser.). (Illus.). 80p. 1998. 4.95 (0-8362-5992-0) Andrews & McMeel.
March 8: What Your Birth Date Reveals about You. (Birth Date Book Ser.). (Illus.). 80p. 1998. 4.95 (0-8362-5981-5) Andrews & McMeel.
March 11: What Your Birth Date Reveals about You. (Birth Date Book Ser.). (Illus.). 80p. 1998. 4.95 (0-8362-5985-8) Andrews & McMeel.
March Essentials: Idea Booklet & Pocket Folder Organizer. Karen Sevaly. (Illus.). 16p. 1997. pap., teacher ed., wbk. ed. 3.99 (1-57882-003-0, TF-1253) Teachers Friend Pubns.
March 15: What Your Birth Date Reveals about You. (Birth Date Book Ser.). (Illus.). 80p. 1998. 4.95 (0-8362-5989-0) Andrews & McMeel.
March 5: What Your Birth Date Reveals about You. (Birth Date Book Ser.). (Illus.). 80p. 1998. 4.95 (0-8362-5978-5) Andrews & McMeel.
March 5, 1987 Ecuador Earthquake: Mass Wasting & Socioeconomic Effects. National Research Council Staff. (Natural Disaster Studies: Vol. 5). 184p. 1991. pap. text 19.00 (0-309-04444-8) Natl Acad Pr.
March 1: What Your Birth Date Reveals about You. (Birth Date Book Ser.). (Illus.). 80p. 1998. 4.95 (0-8362-5974-2) Andrews & McMeel.
March 1 to August 31, 1781 see Letters of Delegates to Congress, 1774-1789, Vol. 25, March 1, 1788-July 25, 1789, with Supplement, 1774-87
March for Justice: Martin Luther King's Rise to Fame. rev. ed. Dorothy Swygert. 111p. (YA). (gr. 6 up). 1997. 25.00 (0-9648737-0-2, RST01) Rekindlng Heart.
March 14: What Your Birth Date Reveals about You. (Birth Date Book Ser.). (Illus.). 80p. 1998. 4.95 (0-8362-5988-2) Andrews & McMeel.
March 4: What Your Birth Date Reveals about You. (Birth Date Book Ser.). (Illus.). 80p. 1998. 4.95 (0-8362-5977-7) Andrews & McMeel.
March from "Symphonic Suite" for Orchestra: Score. Williams Clifton. LC M 1247. 159p. reprint ed. pap. 49.30 (0-608-10799-9, 200289300015) Bks Demand.
March Hare. Padraic Breathnach. Tr. by Gabriel Rosenstock from IRI. LC 95-115821. 154p. pap. 14.95 (1-874700-03-6, Pub. by Clo Iar-Chonnachta) Dufour.
*__March Hare.__ Illus. by Barry Moser. (Barry Moser Ser.). 160p. 1998. 9.95 (1-55156-081-X, Pub. by Paperblank) Andrews & McMeel.
March Hare Network. Jack L. Chalker. (Wonderland Gambit Ser.: Bk. 2). 1996. pap. 11.00 (0-614-97803-3, Del Rey) Ballantine Pub Grp.
March Hare Network. Jack L. Chalker. (Wonderland Gambit Ser.: Bk. 2). 1996. mass mkt. 5.99 (0-345-38848-8, Del Rey) Ballantine Pub Grp.
March Hares see Collected Works of Harold Frederic
March Hares. Harold Frederic. (Collected Works of Harold Frederic). 1988. reprint ed. lib. bdg. 59.00 (0-7812-1193-X) Rprt Serv.
March Idea Book: A Creative Idea Book for the Elementary Teacher, Ps-6. rev. ed. Karen Sevaly. (Illus.). 144p. (Orig.). 1997. pap. 10.95 (0-943263-06-9, TF-0300) Teachers Friend Pubns.
March Madness. Stanley Wagner. LC 98-85365. 192p. 1999. pap. 11.95 (1-56315-186-3, Pub. by SterlingHse) Natl Bk Netwk.
*__March Mania.__ Tess Eileen Kindig. LC 00-8210. (Slam Dunk Ser.). (J). 2000. write for info. (0-570-07092-9) Concordia.
March Militaire Francaise. Composed by Saint-Seans. 1996. pap. text 29.95 (0-7935-6598-7) H Leonard.
March Monthly Activities. Janet Hale. (Monthly Activities Ser.). (Illus.). 80p. (J). (gr. 1-5). 1989. pap., wbk. ed. 9.95 (1-55734-157-5, No. TCM157) Tchr Create Mat.
March Monthly Activities. Dona H. Rice. (Illus.). 80p. 1996. pap., teacher ed. 9.95 (1-55734-876-6, TCM876) Tchr Create Mat.
March Monthly Activities. Dona H. Rice. (Monthly Activities Ser.). 80p. (J). (ps-k). 1997. pap. 9.95 (1-55734-866-9) Tchr Create Mat.
March Music Melodies. Norman E. Smith. LC 93-92697. 544p. 1997. reprint ed. pap. 35.00 (0-9617346-2-0) Program Note Pr.
March Music Notes. N. E. Smith. LC 87-404894. 559p. 1996. reprint ed. pap. 30.00 (0-9617346-1-2) Program Note Pr.
March 1991 Direct Mail Catalog. 1991. text. write for info. (1-55623-557-7, Irwn Prfssnl) McGraw-Hill Prof.
March 1934 - August 1935 see Franklin D. Roosevelt & Foreign Affairs
March, 1939: A Study in the Continuity of British Foreign Policy. Simon K. Newman. 264p. 1976. text 55.00 (0-19-822532-6) OUP.
March 19: What Your Birth Date Reveals about You. (Birth Date Book Ser.). (Illus.). 80p. 1998. 4.95 (0-8362-5993-9) Andrews & McMeel.
March 9: What Your Birth Date Reveals about You. (Birth Date Book Ser.). (Illus.). 80p. 1998. 4.95 (0-8362-5982-3) Andrews & McMeel.
March of Centuries: Lawyers & the Law in Jacksonville 1564 to 1997. Gary Moore. LC 97-73764. (Illus.). 113p. 1997. 30.00 (0-9659460-0-2) Jacksnvl Bar Assn.
*__March of Das Reich.__ Philip Vickers. 2000. pap. 16.95 (1-58097-047-8, 970478) Combined Pub.
March of Dimes Statbook: Statistics for Monitorins Maternal & Infant Health. March of Dimes Birth Defects Foundation Staff. LC 97-20539. 1997. write for info. (0-86525-078-2) March of Dimes.
March of Dimes Substance Abuse Curriculum for Obstetricians & Gynecologists. Cynthia Chazotte et al. Ed. by Rochelle K. Rosen et al. LC 95-36651. 1995. write for info. (0-86525-066-9) March of Dimes.
March of Faith: The Story of Religion in America since 1865. Winfred E. Garrison. LC 79-138112. 332p. 1971. reprint ed. lib. bdg. 65.00 (0-8371-5688-2, GAMF, Greenwood Pr) Greenwood.

An Asterisk (*) at the beginning of an entry indicates that the title is appearing for the first time.

March of Fascism. Stephen Raushenbush. 1939. 69.50 (*0-686-83616-2*) Elliots Bks.
March of Folly: From Troy to Vietnam. Barbara W. Tuchman. 1985. pap. 16.00 (*0-345-30823-9*) Ballantine Pub Grp.
March of Freedom: Modern Classics in Conservative Thought. Ed. by Edwin J. Feulner, Jr. LC 98-10678. (Illus.). 400p. 1998. 29.95 (*0-9653208-8-X*) Spence Pub.
***March of Freedom: Modern Classics in Conservative Thought.** Edwin J. Feulner, Jr. LC 98-10678. (Illus.). 375p. 1999. pap. 18.95 (*1-890626-14-7*) Spence Pub.
March of Glory. Carla Joinson. 125p. (YA). (gr. 9-12). 1994. pap. 9.99 (*0-88092-083-1*) Royal Fireworks.
March of Industry. Robert G. Cleland. 1992. reprint ed. lib. bdg. 75.00 (*0-7812-5014-5*) Rprt Serv.
March of Islam: Time Frame Six Hundred - Eight Hundred AD. Time-Life Books Editors. (Time Frame Ser.). (Illus.). 176p. (Orig.). 1988. pap. write for info. (*0-8094-6423-3*); text. write for info. (*0-8094-6422-5*); lib. bdg. 25.93 (*0-8094-6421-7*) Time-Life.
March of Liberty: A Constitutional History of the United States, Vol. 2. Melvin I. Urofsky. (C). 1987. pap. text 29.00 (*0-07-553698-6*) McGraw.
March of Literature: From Confucius' Day to Our Own. Ford Madox Ford. LC 93-21208. 898p. 1994. reprint ed. pap. 16.95 (*1-56478-051-1*) Dalkey Arch.
March of Medicine Laity Lectures, No. 4. New York Academy of Medicine Staff. LC 78-142677. (Essay Index Reprint Ser.). 1977. reprint ed. 19.95 (*0-8369-2212-3*) Ayer.
March of Medicine Laity Lectures, No. 5. New York Academy of Medicine Staff. LC 78-142677. (Essay Index Reprint Ser.). 1977. 19.95 (*0-8369-2115-1*) Ayer.
March of Medicine Laity Lectures, No. 6. New York Academy of Medicine Staff. LC 78-142677. (Essay Index Reprint Ser.). 1977. 19.95 (*0-8369-2116-X*) Ayer.
March of Medicine Laity Lectures, No. 7. New York Academy of Medicine Staff. LC 78-142677. (Essay Index Reprint Ser.). 1977. 20.95 (*0-8369-2117-8*) Ayer.
March of Medicine Laity Lectures, 1943. New York Academy of Medicine Staff. LC 78-142677. (Essay Index Reprint Ser.). 1977. reprint ed. 19.95 (*0-8369-2466-5*) Ayer.
March of Medicine Laity Lectures, 1944. New York Academy of Medicine Staff. LC 78-142677. (Essay Index Reprint Ser.). 1977. reprint ed. 17.95 (*0-8369-2467-3*) Ayer.
March of Portola: And the Log of the San Carlos. Zoeth S. Eldridge & E. J. Molera. (Illus.). 71p. (C). 1909. reprint ed. pap. text 8.44 (*1-55567-617-0*) Coyote Press.
March of Science: A First Quinquennial Review, 1931-1935. British Association For The Advancement Of Science. LC 68-55841. (Essay Index Reprint Ser.). 1977. 19.95 (*0-8369-0254-8*) Ayer.
March of the Columns: Chronicle of the 1876 Indian War, June 27-September 16, 1876. James Willert. LC 94-60906. (Custer Trails Ser.: Vol. 4). (Illus.). 643p. 1994. 85.00 (*0-912783-23-0*) Upton & Sons.
***March of the Goblins.** George Peter Tingley. 4p. 1999. pap. 2.50 (*0-7390-0294-5*, 18525) Alfred Pub.
March of the Iron Men: A Social History of Union Through Invention. Roger Burlingame. LC 75-22805. (America in Two Centuries Ser.). (Illus.). 1976. reprint ed. 46.95 (*0-405-07677-0*) Ayer.
March of the Lemmings. James R. Newton. LC 75-42491. (Let's-Read-&-Find-Out Science Bks.). (Illus.). 40p. (J). (gr. k-3). 1976. lib. bdg. 11.89 (*0-690-01085-0*) HarpC Child Bks.
March of the Lonely see Marsh Odinokikh
March of the Millennia: A Key to Looking at History. Isaac Asimov & Frank White. 224p. 1990. 18.95 (*0-8027-1122-7*) Walker & Co.
March of the Montana Column: A Prelude to the Custer Disaster. James H. Bradley. Ed. by Edgar I. Stewart. LC 61-6494. (American Exploration & Travel Ser.: Vol. 32). (Illus.). 216p. 1991. pap. 11.95 (*0-8061-2316-8*) U of Okla Pr.
March of the Mounted Riflemen: From Fort Leavenworth to Fort Vancouver, May to October 1849. Ed. by Raymond W. Settle. LC 89-4936. (Illus.). 378p. 1989. reprint ed. pap. 12.95 (*0-8032-9196-5*, Bison Books) U of Nebr Pr.
March of the Seventy Thousand. Henry Baerlein. LC 72-115506. (Russia Observed Ser.). (Illus.). 1971. reprint ed. 23.95 (*0-405-03076-2*) Ayer.
***March of the Women: A Revisionist Analysis of the Campaign for Women's Suffrage, 1866-1914.** Martin Pugh. 320p. 2000. text 35.00 (*0-19-820775-1*) OUP.
March on London: Covert Operations in the Battle of the Bulge December 1944. Charles Whiting. (Illus.). 181p. (Orig.). 1996. pap. 16.95 (*0-85052-502-0*, Pub. by Leo Cooper) Trans-Atl Phila.
March on Washington, 1963: Gathering to Be Heard. Tricia Andryszewski. LC 96-1217. (Spotlight on American History Ser.). (Illus.). 64p. (J). (gr. 4-6). 1996. lib. bdg. 21.90 (*0-7613-0009-0*) Millbrook Pr.
March Patterns, Projects & Plans: To Perk up Early Learning Programs. Imogene Forte. Ed. by Sally D. Sharpe. (Illus.). 80p. (Orig.). (J). (gr. 1-6). 1990. pap. text 9.95 (*0-86530-138-7*, IP 167-3) Incentive Pubns.
March 2: What Your Birth Date Reveals about You. (Birth Date Book Ser.). (Illus.). 80p. 1998. 4.95 (*0-8362-5975-0*) Andrews & McMeel.
March 17: What Your Birth Date Reveals about You. (Birth Date Book Ser.). (Illus.). 80p. 1998. 4.95 (*0-8362-5991-2*) Andrews & McMeel.
March 7: What Your Birth Date Reveals about You. (Birth Date Book Ser.). (Illus.). 80p. 1998. 4.95 (*0-8362-5980-7*) Andrews & McMeel.
March 16: What Your Birth Date Reveals about You. (Birth Date Book Ser.). (Illus.). 80p. 1998. 4.95 (*0-8362-5990-4*) Andrews & McMeel.
March 6: What Your Birth Date Reveals about You. (Birth Date Book Ser.). (Illus.). 80p. 1998. 4.95 (*0-8362-5979-3*) Andrews & McMeel.
March 10: What Your Birth Date Reveals about You. (Birth Date Book Ser.). (Illus.). 80p. 1998. 4.95 (*0-8362-5983-1*) Andrews & McMeel.
March 10, 1784 - March 28, 1786 see Papers of James Madison
March 3: What Your Birth Date Reveals about You. (Birth Date Book Ser.). (Illus.). 80p. 1998. 4.95 (*0-8362-5976-9*) Andrews & McMeel.
March 13: What Your Birth Date Reveals about You. (Birth Date Book Ser.). (Illus.). 80p. 1998. 4.95 (*0-8362-5987-4*) Andrews & McMeel.
March 30: What Your Birth Date Reveals about You. (Birth Date Book Ser.). (Illus.). 80p. 1998. 4.95 (*0-8362-6006-6*) Andrews & McMeel.
March 31: What Your Birth Date Reveals about You. (Birth Date Book Ser.). (Illus.). 80p. 1998. 4.95 (*0-8362-6007-4*) Andrews & McMeel.
March Time. (In Classical Mood Ser.: Vol. 40). (Illus.). 1998. write for info. incl. cd-rom (*1-886614-66-0*) Intl Masters Pub.
March to Armageddon: The United States & the Nuclear Arms Race, 1939 to the Present. Ronald E. Powaski. 318p. 1989. reprint ed. pap. 9.95 (*0-19-504411-8*) OUP.
March to Calumny. Albert D. Biderman. Ed. by Richard H. Kohn. LC 78-22376. (American Military Experience Ser.). 1980. reprint ed. lib. bdg. 23.95 (*0-405-11853-8*) Ayer.
***March to Capitalism in the Transition Countries.** Irving Michelman. LC 98-71401. (Avebury Series in Philosophy). 130p. 1998. text 59.95 (*1-84014-101-8*) Ashgate Pub Co.
March to Madness: A View from the Floor in the Atlantic Coast Conference. John Feinstein. 1998. pap. 14.00 (*0-316-19103-5*) Little.
March to Madness: A View from the Floor in the Atlantic Coast Conference. John Feinstein. (Illus.). 512p. 1999. pap. 14.00 (*0-316-27712-6*) Little.
***March to Madness: The View from the Floor in the Atlantic Coast Conference.** John Feinstein. (Illus.). 464p. 2000. text 25.00 (*0-7881-9014-8*) DIANE Pub.
March to Madness: The View from the Floor in the Atlantic Coast Conference. John Feinstein. LC 97-31060. (Illus.). 448p. (gr. 8). 1998. 24.95 (*0-316-27740-1*) Little.
March to the Finals: The History of College Basketball's Illustrious Finale. Alan Minsky. LC 96-39799. 96p. 1997. 12.98 (*1-56799-387-7*, MetroBooks) M Friedman Pub Grp Inc.
March to the Finals: The History of College Basketball's Illustrious Finales. rev. ed. Alan Minsky. LC 99-228231. 1999. 15.98 (*1-56799-705-8*, MetroBooks) M Friedman Pub Grp Inc.
March to the Monteria. B. Traven. 21.95 (*0-89190-458-1*) Amereon Ltd.
March to the Monteria. B. Traven. LC 93-40750. 240p. 1994. reprint ed. pap. 10.95 (*1-56663-046-0*, Pub. by I R Dee) Natl Bk Netwk.
March to the Sea. 2nd ed. William R. Scaife. (Illus.). 129p. (Orig.). 1993. pap. 18.50 (*0-9619508-4-6*) W R Scaife.
March to the Sea & Beyond: Sherman's Troops in the Savannah & Carolinas Campaigns. Joseph T. Glatthaar. LC 84-29496. 336p. (C). 1995. pap. 16.95 (*0-8071-2028-6*) La State U Pr.
March to the Sea: Franklin & Nashville see Sherman's March to the Sea: Hood's Tennessee Campaign & the Carolina Campaigns of 1865
March to War. Ed. & Intro. by James Ridgeway. LC 91-11607. 244p. 1991. pap. 9.95 (*0-941423-61-1*) FWEW.
March 12: What Your Birth Date Reveals about You. (Birth Date Book Ser.). (Illus.). 80p. 1998. 4.95 (*0-8362-5986-6*) Andrews & McMeel.
March 12-September 30, 1783 see Letters of Delegates to Congress, 1774-1789, Vol. 25, March 1, 1788-July 25, 1789, with Supplement, 1774-87
March 20: What Your Birth Date Reveals about You. (Birth Date Book Ser.). (Illus.). 80p. 1998. 4.95 (*0-8362-5994-7*) Andrews & McMeel.
March 28: What Your Birth Date Reveals about You. (Birth Date Book Ser.). (Illus.). 80p. 1998. 4.95 (*0-8362-6003-1*) Andrews & McMeel.
March 28, 1882-May 18, 1882 see Germans to America: Lists of Passengers Arriving at U. S. Ports, 1850-1893
March 28, 1749 - March 19, 1750 see Journal of the Commons House of Assembly: Series One
March 25: What Your Birth Date Reveals about You. (Birth Date Book Ser.). (Illus.). 80p. 1998. 4.95 (*0-8362-6000-7*) Andrews & McMeel.
March 21: What Your Birth Date Reveals about You. (Birth Date Book Ser.). (Illus.). 80p. 1998. 4.95 (*0-8362-5995-5*) Andrews & McMeel.
March 24: What Your Birth Date Reveals about You. (Birth Date Book Ser.). (Illus.). 80p. 1998. 4.95 (*0-8362-5999-8*) Andrews & McMeel.
March 29: What Your Birth Date Reveals about You. (Birth Date Book Ser.). (Illus.). 80p. 1998. 4.95 (*0-8362-6005-8*) Andrews & McMeel.
March 22: What Your Birth Date Reveals about You. (Birth Date Book Ser.). (Illus.). 80p. 1998. 4.95 (*0-8362-5996-3*) Andrews & McMeel.
March 27: What Your Birth Date Reveals about You. (Birth Date Book Ser.). (Illus.). 80p. 1998. 4.95 (*0-8362-6002-3*) Andrews & McMeel.
March 26: What Your Birth Date Reveals about You. (Birth Date Book Ser.). (Illus.). 80p. 1998. 4.95 (*0-8362-6001-5*) Andrews & McMeel.
March 23: What Your Birth Date Reveals about You. (Birth Date Book Ser.). (Illus.). 80p. 1998. 4.95 (*0-8362-5997-1*) Andrews & McMeel.
March up Country: A Modern Translation of the Anabasis. Xenophon. Tr. by W. H. Rouse. 224p. 1958. pap. text 15.95 (*0-472-06095-3*, 06095, Ann Arbor Bks) U of Mich Pr.
March We Onward: A Centennial History of the First Baptist Church of Walnut Ridge, Arkansas, 1889-1989. Kenneth M. Startup. 75p. (Orig.). 1989. pap. 6.00 (*0-685-28029-2*) FBC AR.
Marcha del Imperialismo Hacia el Fascismo y la Guerra (Imperialism's March Toward Fascism & War) Jack Barnes. Ed. by Martin Koppel. (SPA.). 365p. 1995. pap. 15.00 (*0-87348-795-8*) Pathfinder NY.
Marchando Hacia la Madurez Espiritual. J. Dwight Pentecost. (SPA.). 384p. 1979. mass mkt. 8.99 (*0-8254-1554-3*, Edit Portavoz) Kregel.
Marchantia I: The New World Species. H. Bischler. (Bryophytorum Bibliotheca Ser.: Vol. 26). (Illus.). 228p. 1984. text 48.00 (*3-7682-1401-X*) Lubrecht & Cramer.
Marchantia L. The Asiatic & Oceanic Taxa. Helene Bischler-Causse. Ed. by S. R. Gradstein. (Bryophytorum Bibliotheca: Vol. 38). (GER., Illus.). 317p. 1989. pap. text 77.00 (*3-443-62010-8*, Pub. by Gebruder Borntraeger) Balogh.
Marchantia L. The European & African Taxa. Helene Bischler-Causse. Ed. by S. R. Gradstein. (Bryophytorum Bibliotheca: Vol. 45). (GER., Illus.). 129p. 1993. pap. 42.00 (*3-443-62017-5*, Pub. by Gebruder Borntraeger) Balogh.
Marchants Aviso, 1589. John Browne. Ed. by Patrick McGrath. (Kress Library of Business & Economics Publication: No. 11). xxxvi, 64p. 1957. pap. 9.95 (*0-678-09906-5*) Kelley.
Marchants Mapp of Commerce. Lewes Roberts. LC 74-80203. (English Experience Ser.: No. 689). 468p. 1974. reprint ed. 126.00 (*90-221-0689-6*) Walter J Johnson.
Marche de l'Imperialisme Vers le Fascisme et la Guerre (Imperialism's March Toward Fascism & War) Jack Barnes. Ed. by Michel Prairie. (FRE.). 376p. 1995. pap. 15.00 (*0-87348-803-2*) Pathfinder NY.
Marche du Fou. Henriette Jelinek. (FRE.). 320p. 1974. pap. 10.95 (*0-7859-2347-0*, 2070366154) Fr & Eur.
Marche Mondial de la Propriete Intellectuelle: Droits Traditionnels et Indigenes. Darrell A. Posey & Graham Dutfield. LC 97-900048.Tr. of Beyond Intellectual Property. (ENG & FRE.). 1997. pap. 24.00 (*0-88936-823-6*, Pub. by IDRC Bks) Stylus Pub VA.
Marchen see Fairy Tales of Hermann Hesse
Marchen. Hermann Hesse.Tr. of Fairy Tales. (GER., Illus.). (C). 1975. 13.95 (*0-8442-2763-3*, X2763-3) NTC Contemp Pub Co.
Marchen. unabridged ed. Hauff. (World Classic Literature Ser.). (GER.). pap. 5.95 (*3-89507-029-7*, Pub. by Bookking Intl) Distribks Inc.
Marchen Cycle. Bruce McClelland. LC 80-10183. (Illus.). 50p. 1980. pap. 6.00 (*0-930794-25-7*) Station Hill Pr.
Marchen Der 692. Nacht-reitergeschichte-erlebnis De Marchalls Von Bassompierre. Hugo von Hofmannsthal. 1999. pap. text 16.95 (*3-596-13136-7*) Fischer Taschen.
Marchen, Schwanke und Gebrauche Aus Stadt und Stift Hildesheim. Karl Seifart. (GER.). 124p. 1996. write for info. (*3-487-09668-4*) G Olms Pubs.
Marchen und Sagen Aus Walschtirol. Christian Schneller. (GER.). vii, 256p. 1976. reprint ed. write for info. (*3-487-05971-1*) G Olms Pubs.
Marchen von Rosenblattchen see Legend of Rosepetal
***Marches.** (Illus.). 240p. 2000. pap. 16.95 (*88-365-1467-7*, Pub. by Tour Club Ital) Abbeville Pr.
Marches. Prod. by Zobeida Perez. 16p. (Orig.). (J). 1994. pap. 17.00 (*0-89898-753-9*, BMR05067) Wrner Bros.
Marches: Marches for Alto Sax. (That's Easy! Ser.). Date not set. 9.95 (*0-7119-4026-6*, AM 91910) Music Sales.
Marches: Marches for Clarinet. (That's Easy! Ser.). Date not set. 9.95 (*0-7119-4024-X*, AM 91908) Music Sales.
Marches: Marches for Flute. (That's Easy! Ser.). Date not set. 9.95 (*0-7119-4025-8*, AM 91909) Music Sales.
Marches: Marches for Tenor Sax. (That's Easy! Ser.). Date not set. 9.95 (*0-7119-4237-4*, AM 92111) Music Sales.
Marches: Marches for Trumpet. (That's Easy! Ser.). Date not set. 9.95 (*0-7119-4027-4*, AM 91911) Music Sales.
Marches de Sable. Andree Chedid. (FRE.). 1990. pap. 10.95 (*0-7859-3281-X*, 2277228869) Fr & Eur.
Marches of the Dragoons in the Mississippi Valley, 1833-1850. Louis Pelzer. LC 75-116. (Mid-American Frontier Ser.). 1975. reprint ed. 26.95 (*0-405-06882-4*) Ayer.
Marchesa D'. Summer on the Lakes in 1843. Sarah M. Ossoli. (BCL1 - United States Local History Ser.). 256p. 1991. reprint ed. lib. bdg. 79.00 (*0-7812-6320-4*) Rprt Serv.
Marchesi & Music: Passages from the Life of a Famous Singing-Teacher. Mathilde Marchesi. LC 77-27354. (Music Reprint Ser.: 1978). 1978. reprint ed. lib. bdg. 39.50 (*0-306-77577-8*) Da Capo.
Marchin' the Pilgrims Home: Leadership & Decision-Making in an Afro-Caribbean Faith, 10. Stephen D. Glazier. LC 82-24179. (Contributions to the Study of Religion Ser.: No. 10). (Illus.). 165p. 1983. 52.95 (*0-313-23464-7*, GPI/) Greenwood.
Marching Along: Recollections of Men, Women & Music. John P. Sousa. 384p. 1990. reprint ed. lib. bdg. 79.00 (*0-7812-9091-0*) Rprt Serv.
Marching Along: Recollections of Men, Women & Music. rev. ed. John P. Sousa. Ed. by Paul E. Bierley. LC 94-77091. (Illus.). 486p. 1994. 24.95 (*0-918048-11-7*) Integrity.
Marching & More. Elte Shuppan Editors. (Pose File Ser.: Vol. 3). (Illus.). 160p. 1993. pap. 49.95 (*4-87199-030-3*, Pub. by Erute-Shuppan) Bks Nippan.
Marching As to War. Rose L. Goldemberg. 1972. pap. 3.25 (*0-8222-0731-1*) Dramatists Play.
Marching Band see Set 1
Marching Band. LC 97-32449. (P. B. Bear Ser.). (Illus.). 24p. (J). (ps). 1998. 6.95 (*0-7894-3108-4*) DK Pub Inc.
Marching Band. Desmond Graham. 66p. 1996. pap. 14.95 (*1-85411-158-2*, Pub. by Seren Bks) Dufour.
Marching Band Director. 206p. 1985. spiral bd. 40.00 (*0-7935-1089-9*) H Leonard.
Marching Band Fundamentals. Al Wright. (Illus.). 263p. (Orig.). 1963. pap. 15.00 (*0-8258-0008-0*, 04283) Fischer Inc NY.
Marching Band Handbook: Competitions, Instruments, Clinics, Fundraising, Publicity, Uniforms, Accessories, Trophies, Drum Corps, Twirling, Color Guard, Indoor Guard, Music, Travel, Directories, Bibliographies, Index. 2nd ed. Compiled by Kim R. Holston. LC 93-42227. (Illus.). 188p. 1994. pap. 34.50 (*0-89950-922-3*) McFarland & Co.
Marching Drummer's Companion. 2nd ed. George Kusel. 52p. 1981. pap. 4.95 (*0-9604476-0-1*) Kusel.
Marching Forward Vol. 3: Women's First in the Northwest, 1444 Role Models. James A. Long. (Illus.). 202p. 1999. pap. 29.95 (*1-882635-01-9*) Pumpkin Ridge.
Marching Ghosts of the Civil War. Brad Steiger. 2000. 16.95 (*1-880090-52-X*) Galde Pr.
***Marching into a New Millennium: Challenges to Educational Leadership.** Patrick M. Jenlink & National Council of Professors of Educational Administration Staff. LC 00-44050. 2000. write for info. (*0-8108-3839-7*) Scarecrow.
Marching into Tyranny. David W. Ridley. LC 97-215875. x, 268p. (Orig.). 1997. pap. 12.95 (*0-9658784-2-2*) Ridley Assocs.
Marching! Marching! Clara Strang. LC 74-22824. (Labor Movement in Fiction & Non-Fiction Ser.). reprint ed. 45.00 (*0-404-58483-7*) AMS Pr.
Marching! Marching! Clara Weatherwax. (Proletarian Literature Ser.). 1990. reprint ed. lib. bdg. 38.00 (*1-55888-295-2*) Omnigraphics Inc.
Marching Men. Sherwood Anderson. (Collected Works of Sherwood Anderson). 314p. 1998. reprint ed. lib. bdg. 98.00 (*1-58201-503-1*) Classic Bks.
Marching Men. Sherwood Anderson. 1993. reprint ed. lib. bdg. 89.00 (*0-7812-5421-3*) Rprt Serv.
Marching Orders. Ed. by William Barclay. (C). 1990. pap. 30.00 (*0-85305-251-4*, Pub. by Arthur James) St Mut.
Marching Orders: A Novel. Olov Hartman. LC 73-103447. 192p. reprint ed. pap. 59.60 (*0-608-30607-X*, 201299400083) Bks Demand.
***Marching Orders: The Civil War Diary of Alex Crawford Gwin.** Ed. by Joseph Campbell. 87p. 1999. 8.75 (*0-9670553-1-8*) Daisy Pubg.
Marching Orders: The Role of the Military in South Korea's "Economic Miracle," 1961-1971, 92. John H. Huer. LC 88-38381. (Contributions in Economics & Economic History Ser.: No. 92). 235p. 1989. 57.95 (*0-313-26648-4*, HFC/, Greenwood Pr) Greenwood.
Marching Orders for the End of Battle. Corrie Ten Boom. 1980. mass mkt. 5.99 (*0-87508-024-3*) Chr Lit.
Marching Out. Yngwie Malmsteen. 104p. 1987. per. 19.95 (*0-88188-765-X*) H Leonard.
***Marching Season.** Daniel Silva. LC 99-91482. 366p. 2000. mass mkt. 7.50 (*0-449-00211-X*) Ballantine Pub Grp.
Marching Season. Daniel Silva. LC 98-53464. 418p. 1999. 25.95 (*0-375-50089-8*) Random.
Marching Season. Daniel Silva. LC 98-51567. 1999. pap. 25.95 (*0-375-70638-0*) Random Hse Lrg Prnt.
Marching Through Chaos: The Descent of Armies in Theory & Practice. John A. English. LC 96-29354. 232p. 1996. 65.00 (*0-275-94657-6*, Praeger Pubs) Greenwood.
Marching Through Chaos: The Descent of Armies in Theory & Practice. John A. English. LC 96-29354. 232p. 1998. pap. 24.95 (*0-275-96392-6*, Praeger Pubs) Greenwood.
***Marching Through Culpepper: A Novel of Culpepper, Virginia - Crossroads of the Civil War.** Virginia B. Morton. LC 00-103914. (Illus.). xiv, 520p. (C). 2000. 27.99 (*0-615-11642-6*) Edgehill Bks.
Marching Through Georgia: The Story of Soldiers & Civilians During Sherman's Campaign. Lee B. Kennett. 448p. 1996. pap. 15.00 (*0-06-092745-3*) HarpC.
Marching Through Nostalgia. Allen R. Harris. (Illus.). 71p. (Orig.). 1987. pap. 6.95 (*0-9618807-0-8*) Allen R Harris.
Marching Through Time: A Play about Turns-of-Centuries. Susan B. Pickford. (J). (gr. 5-9). 1996. pap., wbk. ed. 10.00 (*1-878668-57-9*) Disc Enter Ltd.
Marching to a Different Drummer. Martin Goldfarb & S. Thomas Axworthy. 176p. 1988. 19.95 (*0-7737-2230-0*) Genl Dist Srvs.
Marching to a Different Drummer. Jim Raymo. (Orig.). 1996. pap. 8.95 (*0-87508-719-1*, 719) Chr Lit.
Marching to a Different Drummer: Unrecognized Heroes of American History. Robing K. Berson. LC 93-49533. 368p. 1994. 49.95 (*0-313-28802-X*, Greenwood Pr) Greenwood.
Marching to a Different Tune: Diary about an Adhd Boy. Jacky Fletcher. LC 99-41649. 1999. pap. 16.95 (*1-85302-810-X*) Jessica Kingsley.
Marching to Captivity: The War Diaries of a French Peasant, 1939-1945. Gustave Folcher. Ed. & Tr. by Christopher J. Hill from FRE. Ed. by Remy Cazals. (Illus.). 300p. (Orig.). 1996. 27.95 (*1-85753-166-3*, Pub. by Brasseys) Brasseys.
Marching to Different Drummers. 2nd ed. Pat Burke Guild & Stephen Garger. 193p. 1998. pap. 17.95 (*0-87120-306-5*, 198186) ASCD.
Marching to Different Drummers: Evolution of the Army's Environmental Program. David Rubenson et al. LC 94-28610. 1994. pap. 15.00 (*0-8330-1564-8*, MR-453-A) Rand Corp.

M

Marching to Freedom: The Story of Martin Luther King Jr. Joyce Milton. 96p. (Orig.). (J). (gr. k-6). 1987. pap. 3.99 (*0-440-45433-6*, YB BDD) BDD Bks Young Read.

Marching to Freedom: The Story of Martin Luther King, Jr. Joyce Milton. (Dell Yearling Biography Ser.). (J). 1987. 8.45 (*0-606-03023-9*, Pub. by Turtleback) Demco.

Marching to Glory. Edward H. McKinley. 290p. reprint ed. pap. 8.95 (*0-86544-039-5*) Salv Army Suppl South.

Marching to Slavery: South Africa's Descent into Communism. Sipo E. Mzimela. Ed. by Dennis Wheeler. 258p. (Orig.). (C). 1993. pap. 12.50 (*0-9626646-8-5*) Soundview Pubns.

***Marching to the Drums: Eyewitness Accounts of War from the Charge of the Light Brigade to the Siege of Ladysmith.** Ed. by Ian Knight. LC 99-35088. (Illus.). 288p. 1999. 34.95 (*1-85367-372-2*, Pub. by Greenhill Bks) Stackpole.

Marching to the Sound of Gunfire: North-West Europe, 1944-1945. Patrick Delaforce. LC 96-20728. (Illus.). 224p. 1996. 30.95 (*0-7509-0780-0*, Pub. by Sutton Pub Ltd) Intl Pubs Mktg.

Marching to Valhalla: A Novel of Custer's Last Days. Michael Blake. 304p. 1997. pap. 12.95 (*0-449-00044-3*) Fawcett.

Marching to Valhalla: A Novel of Custer's Last Days. large type ed. Michael Blake. LC 97-4448. 412p. 1997. 23.95 (*0-7838-8091-X*, G K Hall Lrg Type) Mac Lib Ref.

***Marching to Victory, 6 vols., Vol. 6.** Charles Coffin. 496p. 2000. write for info. (*1-889128-71-6*) Mantle Ministries.

Marching to War. London News Staff. 192p. 1989. 24.95 (*0-385-25217-X*) Doubleday.

Marching to Zaragoza: A Novel of Mexico. Barding Dahl. LC 97-44158. 228p. 1998. pap. 14.95 (*1-56474-256-3*) Fithian Pr.

Marching to Zion. Perry A. Klopfenstein. LC 83-71702. 660p. 1984. 15.00 (*0-9611836-0-8*) Apostolic Christ Ch.

Marching to Zion: A Collection of Ira North's Sermons. Ira North. 1995. pap. 10.99 (*0-89225-454-8*) Gospel Advocate.

Marching to Zog. Gyeorgos C. Hatonn. (Phoenix Journals). 209p. 1993. pap. 6.00 (*1-56935-024-8*) Phoenix Source.

Marching Together: Women of the Brotherhood of Sleeping Car Porters. Melinda M. Chateauvert. LC 97-4579. (Working Class in American History Ser.). 320p. 1997. text 46.95 (*0-252-02340-4*); pap. text 17.95 (*0-252-06636-7*) U of Ill Pr.

Marching Toward Freedom: Blacks in the Civil War, 1861-1865. James M. McPherson. (Library of American History). (Illus.). 160p. (YA). (gr. 7-12). 1991. 19.95 (*0-8160-2337-9*) Facts on File.

Marching Toward Freedom: Blacks in the Civil War, 1861-1865. James M. McPherson. (Library of American History). (Illus.). 160p. 1994. reprint ed. pap. 8.95 (*0-8160-3092-8*) Facts on File.

Marching Toward Freedom: From the Founding of the Southern Christian Leadership Conference to the Assassination of Malcolm X (1957-1965) Robert Weisbrot. (Milestones in Black American History Ser.). (Illus.). 128p. (YA). (gr. 5 up). 1994. pap. 8.95 (*0-7910-2682-5*) Chelsea Hse.

Marching Towards the 21st Century: Military Manpower & Recruiting, 154. Ed. by Mark J. Eitelberg & Stephen L. Mehay. LC 93-33517. (Contributions in Military Studies Ser.: No. 154). 272p. 1994. 62.95 (*0-313-28566-7*, Greenwood Pr) Greenwood.

Marching under Darkening Skies: The American Military & the Impending Urban Operations Threat. Russell W. Glenn. LC 98-41329. 30p. 1999. pap. 7.50 (*0-8330-2658-5*, MR-1007-A) Rand Corp.

Marching with Sherman: Passages from the Letters & Campaign Diaries of Henry Hitchcock, Major & Assistant Adjutant General of Volunteers, November 1864-May 1865. Henry Hitchcock. Ed. & Intro. by M. A. Howe. Intro. by Brooks D. Simpson. LC 95-2996. (Illus.). xix, 344p. 1995. pap. 12.95 (*0-8032-7276-6*, Bison Books) U of Nebr Pr.

***Marching with Sousa.** 33rd ed. Norma Jean Lutz. (American Adventure Ser.: No. 33). (Illus.). (J). (gr. 3-7). 1998. pap. 3.97 (*1-57748-406-1*) Barbour Pub.

Marchlands: A Novel. Karla Kuban. LC 97-37254. 272p. 1998. 22.50 (*0-684-83165-1*) S&S Trade.

Marchlands: A Novel. Karla Kuban. 272p. 1999. pap. 12.00 (*0-684-85444-9*) S&S Trade.

Marchman. Nigel Tranter. 320p. 1997. 27.00 (*0-340-65994-7*, Pub. by Hodder & Stought Ltd); pap. 11.95 (*0-340-65995-5*, Pub. by Hodder & Stought Ltd) Trafalgar.

Marchmont. Charlotte Smith. LC 88-38440. 340p. 1989. 50.00 (*0-8201-1436-7*) Schol Facsimiles.

Marchmont in Edinburgh. Malcolm Cant. 176p. (C). 1989. pap. 23.00 (*0-85976-099-5*, Pub. by J Donald) St Mut.

March's Thesaurus & Dictionary of the English Language. Francis March et al. 1324p. 1980. pap. 10.95 (*0-89659-161-1*) Abbeville Pr.

Marci Aurelii, Antonini, Libri XII. Ed. by Dalfen. (GRE.). 1987. 39.50 (*3-322-00355-8*, T1046, Pub. by B G Teubner) U of Mich Pr.

Marci Books: Dragon Who Chewed Purple Bubble Gum, Papsee's Pup, Calling All Detectives, Woody & Wendy Woodpecker, 4 bks. 2nd ed. Marcia Rodenbaugh. (Illus.). 56p. 1983. pap. text 1.00 (*1-57543-047-9*) Mar Co Prods.

Marcia Adams' Christmas in the Heartland: Recipes, Decorations & Traditions for Joyous Celebrations. Marcia Adams. (Illus.). 176p. 1992. 25.00 (*0-517-58572-3*) C Potter.

Marcia Adam's Heirloom Recipes: Hidden Treasures from America's Kitchens. Marcia Adams. LC 94-7662. (Illus.). 320p. 1994. 22.50 (*0-517-59347-5*) Crown Pub Group.

Marcia Clark. Clifford L. Linedecker. 1995. pap. 5.99 (*0-7860-0218-2*) Kensgtn Pub Corp.

Marcia Clark, Voice for the Victims. Katherine E. Krohn. LC 96-16428. (J). 1996. lib. bdg. 19.93 (*0-8225-2892-4*, Lerner Publctns) Lerner Pub.

Marcia Gygli King. Christina M. Strassfield. (Illus.). 12p. 1995. pap. 5.00 (*0-933793-34-0*) Guild Hall.

***Marcia Lippman: Sacred Encounters, East & West.** Photos by Marcia Lippman. (Illus.). 2000. 70.00 (*3-908163-26-9*, Pub. by Edit Stemmle) Abbeville Pr.

Marcia Lippman's Angels. Marcia Lippman. 1995. pap. 8.95 (*0-8118-1191-3*) Chronicle Bks.

Marcia of the Doorstep: A Romance. Edgar Rice Burroughs & Ned Dameron. 1999. 60.00 (*1-880418-41-X*); 30.00 (*1-880418-42-8*) D M Grant.

Marcia Schuyler. Grace Livingston Hill. reprint ed. lib. bdg. 25.95 (*0-89190-028-4*, Rivercity Pr) Amereon Ltd.

Marcia Schuyler, No. 89. Grace Livingston Hill. (Grace Livingston Hill Ser.: Vol. 83). 1995. pap. 4.99 (*0-8423-4036-X*) Tyndale Hse.

Marcie. Beverly B. Kelly. LC 90-92018. 104p. (Orig.). 1990. pap. 3.95 (*0-9627838-1-1*) B B Kelly.

Marcie & the Monster of the Bayou. Betty Hager. LC 93-44490. (Tales from the Bayou Ser.: Bk. 4). 128p. (J). (gr. 3-7). 1994. pap. 5.99 (*0-310-38431-1*) Zondervan.

Marciea's Melody. Carol L. Williams. Ed. by Jennifer Utley. LC 96-7770. (Latter-Day Daughters Ser.). (Illus.). 80p. (J). (gr. 3-9). 1996. pap. 4.95 (*1-56236-509-6*, Pub. by Aspen Bks) Origin Bk Sales.

Marcion. Robert S. Wilson. LC 78-63176. (Heresies of the Early Christian & Medieval Era Ser.: Second Ser.). reprint ed. 39.50 (*0-404-16194-4*) AMS Pr.

Marcion: Das Evangelium Vom Fremden Gott, eine Monographie zur Gerschichte der Grundlegung der katholischen Kirche. 2., verb. und verm. Aufl. Adolf Von Harnack. LC 82-45820. (Orthodoxies & Heresies in the Early Church Ser.). reprint ed. 62.50 (*0-404-62388-3*) AMS Pr.

Marcion & His Influence. Edwin C. Blackman. LC 77-84695. reprint ed. 39.50 (*0-404-16103-0*) AMS Pr.

Marcion & Sein Apostolos: Rekonstruktion & Historische Einordnung der Marcionitischen Paulusbriefausgabe. Ulrich Schmid. (Arbeiten zur Neutestamentlichen Textforschung Ser.: Bd. 25). (GER.). xviii, 381p. (C). 1995. lib. bdg. 164.40 (*3-11-014695-9*) De Gruyter.

Marcion & the New Testament. John Knox. LC 78-63168. (Heresies of the Early Christian & Medieval Era Ser.: Second Ser.). reprint ed. 31.00 (*0-404-16183-9*) AMS Pr.

Marcion, Muhammad & the Mahatma: Exegetical Perspectives on the Encounter of Cultures & Faith. Heikki Raisanen. (Illus.). 1997. pap. 27.00 (*0-334-02693-8*) TPI PA.

Marciusi Front (The March Front) Imre Kovacs. LC 80-83193. (Tanuk Korukrol Ser.). 96p. 1980. pap. 7.00 (*0-910539-01-4*) Hungarian Alumni.

***Marco: The Making of Marco Pierre White, Sharpest Chef in History.** Charles A. Hennessy. (Illus.). 224p. 2000. 29.95 (*0-09-186819-X*, Pub. by Ebury Pr) Trafalgar.

Marco & Michela. Satu Repo et al. (Where We Live Ser.). (Illus.). 79p. (J). 1985. pap. 5.95 (*0-88862-172-8*, Pub. by J Lorimer); bds. 12.95 (*0-88862-181-7*, Pub. by J Lorimer) Formac Dist Ltd.

Marco Del Lenguaje (The Framework of Language) Roman Jakobson. (SPA.). 127p. 1988. pap. 8.99 (*968-16-2873-X*, Pub. by Fondo) Continental Bk.

Marco Juridico Para el Combate Al Narcotrafico. Mario R. Massieu. (SPA.). pap. 5.99 (*968-16-4340-2*, Pub. by Fondo) Continental Bk.

Marco Markets: Creating Institutions for Managing Society's Largest Economic Risks. Robert J. Shiller. (Clarendon Lectures in Economics). 268p. 1998. reprint ed. pap. text 19.95 (*0-19-829418-2*) OUP.

Marco Paul's Travels on the Erie Canal. (Illus.). 203p. 1987. reprint ed. pap. 6.95 (*0-932334-99-7*, NY70056, Empire State Bks) Hrt of the Lakes.

Marco Polo see What Would You Ask?

***Marco Polo.** Alexandra Bandon & Patrick O'Brien. LC 99-48893. (Explorers & Exploration Ser.). 48p. (J). 2000. lib. bdg. write for info. (*0-7398-1485-0*) Raintree Steck-V.

Marco Polo. Anita Ganeri. LC 99-19320. (What Would You Ask? Ser.). (J). 1999. write for info. (*0-382-42125-6*) Silver Burdett Pr.

Marco Polo. Bob Italia. Ed. by Rosemary Walner. LC 90-82626. (Explorers of the Past & Present Ser.). (Illus.). 32p. (J). (gr. 4). 1990. lib. bdg. 11.96 (*0-939179-92-X*) ABDO Pub Co.

***Marco Polo.** Ed. by Jackie Jones. 350p. (C). 2002. pap. 7.95 (*0-9676706-7-5*) Robbie Jones.

Marco Polo. Jonathan Levy. 1977. pap. 5.25 (*0-8222-0732-X*) Dramatists Play.

***Marco Polo.** Fiona MacDonald. (World in the Time of... Ser.). (Illus.). (J). 2000. 17.95 (*0-7910-6033-0*) Chelsea Hse.

Marco Polo. Susan Roth. 1990. 15.00 (*0-385-44522-9*) Doubleday.

Marco Polo see Discovery Biographies

Marco Polo: A Journey Through China. Fiona MacDonald & Mark Bergin. (Expedition Ser.). (Illus.). 32p. (J). (gr. 2-9). 1998. pap. 7.95 (*0-531-15340-1*) Watts.

Marco Polo: A Journey Through China. Fiona MacDonald & David Salariya. LC 97-7533. (Expedition Ser.). (Illus.). 32p. (J). (gr. 5 up). 1998. 21.00 (*0-531-14453-4*) Watts.

Marco Polo: Overland to Medieval China. Clint Twist. LC 93-30744. (Beyond the Horizon Ser.). 48p. (J). 1994. lib. bdg. 24.26 (*0-8114-7251-5*) Raintree Steck-V.

Marco Polo: Voyager. Houghton Mifflin Company Staff. (Literature Experience 1993 Ser.). (J). (gr. 7). 1992. pap. 11.04 (*0-395-61844-4*) HM.

***Marco Polo & the Discovery of the World.** John Larner. LC 99-24887. (Illus.). 288p. 1999. 29.95 (*0-300-07971-0*) Yale U Pr.

Marco Polo & the Medieval Explorers. Rebecca Stefoff. Ed. by William H. Goetzmann. (World Explorers Ser.). (Illus.). 120p. (YA). (gr. 5 up). 1992. lib. bdg. 19.95 (*0-7910-1294-8*) Chelsea Hse.

Marco Polo & the Wonders of the East. Hal Marcovitz. LC 99-22255. (Explorers of the New World Ser.). (Illus.). 64p. 1999. 16.95 (*0-7910-5511-6*) Chelsea Hse.

Marco Polo at the Millennium. Laurie O'Brien. 31p. (Orig.). pap. 8.95 (*0-916092-24-0*) Tex Ctr Writers.

Marco Polo Croatian Adventurer. Adam S. Eterovich. 50p. 1987. pap. 5.00 (*0-918660-53-X*) Ragusan Pr.

Marco Polo, If You Can. William F. Buckley, Jr. 1983. pap. 3.95 (*0-380-61424-3*, Avon Bks) Morrow Avon.

Marco Polo, If You Can. William F. Buckley, Jr. LC 96-21123. 288p. 1996. reprint ed. pap. 10.95 (*1-888952-11-3*) Cumberland Hse.

Marco Polo Official Secrets & Solutions. Michael Rymaszewski. 1995. pap. text 14.95 (*0-7615-0262-9*) Prima Pub.

Marco Polo Sings a Solo. John Guare. 1977. pap. 5.25 (*0-8222-0733-8*) Dramatists Play.

Marco Polo's Book. John S. Critchley. 224p. 1993. 83.95 (*0-86078-361-8*, Pub. by Variorum) Ashgate Pub Co.

Marco Raconte: Thirteen Histoires Vraies. Marc Guiguin. (Serie Rouge). (Illus.). 72p. (C). 1994. pap. 7.50 (*0-521-44983-9*) Cambridge U Pr.

Marconi: The Man & His Wireless. rev. ed. Orrin E. Dunlap, Jr. LC 72-161142. (History of Broadcasting: Radio to Television Ser.). 1976. reprint ed. 35.95 (*0-405-03563-2*) Ayer.

Marconi Wireless on Cape Cod: South Wellfleet, Massachusetts, 1901-1917. Michael E. Whatley. (Illus.). 32p. (Orig.). 1987. pap. 2.95 (*0-9618300-0-X*) Nauset Marsh.

Marconi's Battle for Radio. Beverley Birch. (Science Stories Ser.). (Illus.). 48p. (J). (gr. 4-7). 1996. 10.95 (*0-8120-6620-0*); pap. text 5.95 (*0-8120-9792-0*) Barron.

Marconi's Battle for Radio. Beverley Birch. (Science Stories Ser.). (Illus.). 48p. (J). (gr. 2-4). 1996. lib. bdg. 14.95 (*1-56674-191-2*) Forest Hse.

Marconi's Battle for Radio. Beverly Birch. (Science Stories). 1996. 11.15 (*0-606-11597-8*, Pub. by Turtleback) Demco.

Marconi's Cottage. Medbh McGuckian. LC 91-67446. 112p. 1992. pap. 8.95 (*0-916390-51-9*) Wake Forest.

Marconi's International Register. annuals 99th ed. 1998. 150.00 (*0-916446-20-4*) Tele Cable.

Marconi's International Register: 98th Annual. annuals 99th rev. ed. Ed. by Joanne Clark. LC 31-15824. 1300p. 1998. pap. 150.00 (*0-916446-23-9*) Tele Cable.

Marcos. Guillermo Cook & Ricardo Foulkes. (Comentario Biblico Hispanoamericano Ser.). 372p. 1990. 19.99 (*0-89922-377-X*) Caribe Betania.

Marcos Against the Church: Economic Development & Political Repression in the Philippines. Robert L. Youngblood. LC 90-55135. 236p. reprint ed. pap. 73.20 (*0-608-20959-7*, 207206000003) Bks Demand.

Marcos Against the Church: Economic Development & Political Repression in the Phillipines. Robert L. Youngblood. LC 90-55135. 240p. 1990. 37.50 (*0-8014-2305-8*) Cornell U Pr.

Marcos (Comentario Biblico Portavoz) Ralph Earle. (SPA.). 128p. 1996. pap. 6.99 (*0-8254-1197-1*, Edit Portavoz) Kregel.

Marcos File. Charles C. McDougald. 356p. 1987. 22.95 (*0-940777-05-3*) SF Pubs.

Marcos, la Genial Impostura. Bertrand de La Grange. 1998. pap. 12.95 (*968-19-0434-6*) Santillana.

Marco's Monster. Meredith S. Willis. LC 96-14606. 128p. (J). (gr. 3-7). pap. 4.50 (*0-06-440662-8*) HarpC Child Bks.

***Marco's Run.** Wesley Cartier & Reynold Ruffins. LC 00-9727. (Green Light Readers Series). (Illus.). (J). 2001. write for info. (*0-15-216249-6*) Harcourt.

Marcovaldo: Level B. Italo Calvino. text 8.95 (*0-88436-993-5*) EMC-Paradigm.

Marcovaldo: The Seasons in the City. Italo Calvino. Tr. by William Weaver from ITA. LC 83-4372. (Helen & Kurt Wolff Bk.). 128p. 1983. pap. 9.00 (*0-15-657204-4*, Harvest Bks) Harcourt.

***Marcus.** Marcus Allen & Carleton Stowers. LC 99-41905. 430p. 1999. 29.95 (*1-56000-457-6*) Transaction Pubs.

Marcus, Vol. 1. Allen. 1998. 6.99 (*0-312-96623-7*, Pub. by Tor Bks) St Martin.

Marcus Allen. Marcus Allen & Carl Stowers. LC 97-16522. (Illus.). 352p. 1997. text 24.95 (*0-312-16924-8*) St Martin.

Marcus Alonzo Hanna. Herbert D. Croly. 1993. reprint ed. lib. bdg. 89.00 (*0-7812-5352-7*) Rprt Serv.

Marcus Alonzo Hanna: His Life & Work. Herbert D. Croly. (History - United States Ser.). 495p. 1992. reprint ed. lib. bdg. 99.00 (*0-7812-6197-X*) Rprt Serv.

Marcus & Lionel. Ronne P. Randall. (Teddy Bear Tales Ser.: No. S897-5). (J). 1989. pap. 3.95 (*0-7214-5228-0*, Ladybrd) Penguin Putnam.

Marcus & Narcissa Whitman & the Opening of Old Oregon. Clifford M. Drury. (Illus.). 911p. 1986. reprint ed. pap. 19.95 (*0-914019-08-2*) NW Interpretive.

Marcus Aurelius: A Biography. Henry D. Sedgwick. LC 77-137290. reprint ed. 31.50 (*0-404-05691-1*) AMS Pr.

Marcus Aurelius: A Biography. rev. ed. Anthony R. Birley. LC 86-51355. 334p. reprint ed. pap. 103.60 (*0-7837-2349-0*, 208024400004) Bks Demand.

Marcus Aurelius: Aspects of Civic & Cultural Policy in the East. James H. Oliver. LC 72-22588. (Hesperia Supplement Ser.: No. 13). (Illus.). xv, 160p. 1970. pap. 15.00 (*0-87661-513-2*) Am Sch Athens.

Marcus Aurelius & the Later Stoics. Frederick W. Bussell. 1976. lib. bdg. 59.95 (*0-8490-2207-X*) Gordon Pr.

Marcus Aurelius Antoninus. Paul B. Watson. LC 76-148904. (Select Bibliographies Reprint Ser.). 1977. reprint ed. 27.95 (*0-8369-5667-2*) Ayer.

Marcus Aurelius, His Life & His World. Arthur Farguharson. Ed. & Pref. by D. A. Rees. LC 74-11854. (Illus.). 154p. 1975. reprint ed. lib. bdg. 35.00 (*0-8371-8139-9*, FAMAU, Greenwood Pr) Greenwood.

Marcus Cardiac Imaging: A Companion to Braunwald's Heart Disease, 2 vols. 2nd rev. ed. Eugene Braunwald et al. LC 95-19482. (Illus.). 1318p. 1996. text 215.00 (*0-7216-4687-5*, W B Saunders Co) Harcrt Hlth Sci Grp.

Marcus Clarke. Ed. by Michael Wilding. (Portable Austrailian Authors Ser.). 690p. 1977. pap. 16.95 (*0-7022-1181-8*) Intl Spec Bk.

Marcus Contectual Grammars. Gheorghe Pun. LC 97-34636. (Studies in Linguistic & Philosophy 7). 392p. 1997. text 140.50 (*0-7923-4783-8*) Kluwer Academic.

Marcus-Evangelium see Itala: Das Neue Testament in Altlateinischer Ueberlieferung

Marcus Garvey: An Annotated Bibliography. Compiled by Lenwood G. Davis & Janet L. Sims. LC 80-653. 192p. 1980. lib. bdg. 49.95 (*0-313-22131-6*, DMG/, Greenwood Pr) Greenwood.

Marcus Garvey: Anti-Colonial Champion. Rupert Lewis. LC 87-72598. 280p. 1988. 29.95 (*0-86543-061-6*); pap. 18.95 (*0-86543-062-4*) Africa World.

Marcus Garvey: Black Nationalist Leader. Mary Lawler. Ed. by Nathan I. Huggins. (Black Americans of Achievement Ser.). (Illus.). 124p. (YA). (gr. 5 up). 1987. lib. bdg. 19.95 (*1-55546-587-0*) Chelsea Hse.

Marcus Garvey: Black Nationalist Leader. Mary Lawler. Ed. by Nathan I. Huggins. (Black Americans of Achievement Ser.). (Illus.). 124p. (YA). (gr. 5 up). 1989. pap. 8.95 (*0-7910-0203-9*) Chelsea Hse.

Marcus Garvey: Black Nationalist Leader. Mary Lawler. (Black American Ser.). 192p. (YA). 1990. mass mkt. 3.95 (*0-87067-568-0*, Melrose Sq) Holloway.

Marcus Garvey: Life & Lessons. Marcus M. Garvey. Ed. by Robert A. Hill & Barbara Bair. 350p. (C). 1987. 45.00 (*0-520-06214-0*, Pub. by U CA Pr); pap. 17.95 (*0-520-06265-5*, Pub. by U CA Pr) Cal Prin Full Svc.

Marcus Garvey: The F. B. I. Investigation Files. Sitamon M. Youssef. LC 97-36559. 500p. 1997. pap. text 21.95 (*0-86543-571-5*) Africa World.

Marcus Garvey: The F. B. I. Investigation Files. Sitamon M. Youssef. 1997. 24.95 (*0-614-27372-2*); pap. 21.95 (*0-614-27373-0*) Africa World.

Marcus Garvey: The F. B. I. Investigation Files. Ed. & Intro. by Sitamon M. Youssef. LC 97-36559. 500p. 1998. 79.95 (*0-86543-570-7*) Africa World.

Marcus Garvey - Makis Gave. Florie N. Chevry-Saintil. (Illus.). 21p. (J). (gr. 1-6). 1996. pap. text 9.95 (*0-912469-32-3*) Majority Pr.

Marcus Garvey & Universal Negro Improvement Association Papers: June 1921-December 1922. Robert Hill. 1996. 70.00 (*0-520-20211-2*, Pub. by U CA Pr) Cal Prin Full Svc.

Marcus Garvey & Universal Negro Improvement Association Papers Vol. I: 1826-1919, Vol. I: 1826 to Augu. Marcus M. Garvey. Ed. by Robert A. Hill. (C). 1986. 85.00 (*0-520-04456-8*, Pub. by U CA Pr) Cal Prin Full Svc.

Marcus Garvey & Universal Negro Improvement Association Papers Vol. II: Aug. 1919 - Aug. 1920, Vol. II: August 1919. Marcus M. Garvey. Ed. by Robert A. Hill. (C). 1986. 85.00 (*0-520-05091-6*, Pub. by U CA Pr) Cal Prin Full Svc.

Marcus Garvey & Universal Negro Improvement Association Papers Vol. III: Sept. 1920 - Aug. 1921, Vol. III: September. Marcus M. Garvey. Ed. by Robert A. Hill. (C). 1986. 85.00 (*0-520-05257-9*, Pub. by U CA Pr) Cal Prin Full Svc.

Marcus Garvey & Universal Negro Improvement Association Papers Vol. IV: Sept. 1921 - Sept. 1922, Vol. IV: September 1. Marcus M. Garvey. Ed. by Robert A. Hill. (C). 1986. 85.00 (*0-520-05446-6*, Pub. by U CA Pr) Cal Prin Full Svc.

Marcus Garvey & Universal Negro Improvement Association Papers Vol. V: Sept. 1922 - Aug. 1924, Vol. V: September 19. Marcus M. Garvey. Ed. by Robert A. Hill. (C). 1987. 85.00 (*0-520-05817-8*, Pub. by U CA Pr) Cal Prin Full Svc.

Marcus Garvey & Universal Negro Improvement Association Papers Vol. VI: Sept. 1924 - Dec. 1927. Marcus M. Garvey. Ed. by Robert A. Hill. 1989. 85.00 (*0-520-06568-9*, Pub. by U CA Pr) Cal Prin Full Svc.

Marcus Garvey & Universal Negro Improvement Association Papers Vol. VII: Nov. 1927 - Aug. 1940. Ed. by Robert A. Hill & Barbara Bair. LC 82-13379. (Illus.). 1146p. 1990. 85.00 (*0-520-07208-1*, Pub. by U CA Pr) Cal Prin Full Svc.

Marcus Garvey & Universal Negro Improvement Association Papers Vol. VIII: March 1917 - June 1921. Ed. by Robert A. Hill. 784p. 1995. 65.00 (*0-520-20210-4*, Pub. by U CA Pr) Cal Prin Full Svc.

Marcus Garvey, Hero: A First Biography. Tony Martin. LC 83-61113. (New Marcus Garvey Library: No. 3). (Illus.). x, 179p. 1983. pap. text 9.95 (*0-912469-05-6*) Majority Pr.

Marcus Garvey's Footsoldiers of the Universal Negro Improvement Association (Their Own Words) Jeannette Smith-Irvin. LC 88-83118. 110p. (C). 1989. 19.95 (*0-86543-110-8*); pap. 7.95 (*0-86543-111-6*) Africa World.

Marcus Is Walking: Scenes from the Road. Joan Ackermann. 1999. pap. 5.25 (*0-8222-1655-8*) Dramatists Play.

Marcus Iunius Nypsus: Introduction, Text, Translation, & Commentary. Jelle Bouma. LC 93-309. (Studien zur Klassischen Philologie).Tr. of Fluminis varatio, Limitis Repositio. (ENG & LAT., Illus.). 196p. 1993. 37.00 (*3-631-45588-7*) P Lang Pubng.

Marcus Jones: Western Geologist, Mining Engineer & Botanist. Lee W. Lenz. LC 85-61956. (Illus.). xv, 486p. 1986. 28.00 (*0-9605808-2-4*) Rancho Santa Ana.

Marcus la Puce A l'Ecole. Gilles Gauthier. (Novels in the Premier Roman Ser.). (FRE.). 64p. (J). (gr. 2-5). 1991. pap. 8.95 (*2-89021-145-2*, Pub. by La Courte Ech) Firefly Bks Ltd.

Marcus Mosiah Garvey, Jr. Great Nubian Quiz. Al I. Obaba. (Great Nubian Quiz Bks.). (Illus.). 43p. (YA). 1989. pap. 5.95 (*0-916157-15-6*) African Islam Miss Pubns.

***Marcus Pfister Favorites Board Book Package: The Rainbow Fish/hopper/penguin Pete.** Marcus Pfister. 1999. 14.95 (*0-7358-1228-4*) North-South Bks NYC.

Marcus Roberts: Gershwin for Lovers. Ed. by Tony Esposito. 96p. (Orig.). 1997. pap. 19.95 (*0-7692-0083-4*, 00843) Wrner Bros.

Marcus Schenkenberg. Marcus Shcenkenberg. LC 97-60135. (Illus.). 144p. 1997. pap. 27.50 (*0-7893-0097-4*, Pub. by Universe) St Martin.

Marcus Thrane: A Norwegian Radical in America. Terje I. Leiren & Odd Sverre Lovoll. (Biographical Series: Special Publications). (Illus.). 167p. 1987. 15.00 (*0-87732-073-X*) Norwegian-Am Hist Assn.

Marcus Tullius Ciceroes Thre Bokes of Duties. Marcus Tullius Cicero. Ed. by Gerald O'Gorman. Tr. by Nicolas Grimalde. LC 86-46408. (Renaissance English Text Society Ser.: No. 12). (Illus.). 272p. 1990. 37.50 (*0-918016-93-2*) Folger Bks.

Marcus Whitman: The Great Command. Nard Jones. LC 59-11883. (Illus.). 414p. 1987. 16.95 (*0-8323-0063-2*) Binford Mort.

Marcuse: Critical Theory & the Promise of Utopia. Robert Pippin et al. LC 87-20002. 288p. 1987. 59.95 (*0-89789-106-6*, Bergin & Garvey); pap. 24.95 (*0-89789-107-4*, Bergin & Garvey) Greenwood.

Marcuse: From the New Left to the Next Left. Ed. by John Bokina & Timothy J. Lukes. LC 93-40249. 256p. 1994. 35.00 (*0-7006-0658-0*); pap. 16.95 (*0-7006-0659-9*) U Pr of KS.

Marcy Wigglewasher & the Bad News Bully. Cristine S. Burke. Ed. by Ann B. Faccenda. (Marcy Wigglewasher Ser.). (Illus.). 24p. (Orig.). (J). (gr. k-5). 1995. pap. 3.95 (*0-9638237-2-8*) Playgrnd Bks.

Marcy Wigglewasher's Not So Boring Summer. Cristine S. Burke. Ed. by Ann B. Faccenda. (Marcy Wigglewasher Ser.). (Illus.). 24p. (Orig.). (J). (gr. k-5). 1995. pap. 3.95 (*0-9638237-1-X*) Playgrnd Bks.

Marcy Wigglewasher's Small Adventure. Cristine S. Burke. Ed. by Ann B. Faccenda. (Marcy Wigglewasher Ser.). (Illus.). 24p. (Orig.). (J). (gr. k-5). 1995. pap. 3.95 (*0-9638237-3-6*) Playgrnd Bks.

Marcy's Granny. Peaches Smith. LC 96-33900. (Illus.). 62p. (J). 1996. 12.95 (*1-56763-184-3*); pap. 2.95 (*1-56763-185-1*) Ozark Pub.

Mardarin Chinese in Three Months. H. D. R. Baker. LC 98-31747. (Hugo's Simplified Language Course Ser.). 304p. 1999. pap. text 14.95 (*0-7894-4214-0*) DK Pub Inc.

Marder III. Horst Scheibert. LC 98-134342.Tr. of Waffen Arsenal-der Panzerjager Marder III - in Den Vers. (Illus.). 48p. 1998. pap. 9.95 (*0-7643-0394-5*) Schiffer.

Mardi. Herman Melville. (FRE.). 1983. pap. 20.95 (*0-7859-4190-8*) Fr & Eur.

Mardi. Herman Melville. Ed. by Tyrus Hillway. (Masterworks of Literature Ser.). 1973. 25.95 (*0-8084-0016-9*); pap. 18.95 (*0-8084-0017-7*) NCUP.

Mardi. Herman Melville. Ed. by Harrison Hayford et al. LC 67-21602. (Northwestern-Newberry Edition of the Writings of Herman Melville: Vol. 3). 1970. 79.95 (*0-8101-0015-0*); pap. text 29.95 (*0-8101-0014-2*) Northwestern U Pr.

Mardi. annot. ed. Herman Melville. Ed. by Nathalia Wright. (Complete Works of Herman Melville Ser.). 1990. 29.95 (*0-87532-015-5*) Hendricks House.

Mardi: And a Voyage Thither. Herman Melville. LC 98-29409. (Northwestern-Newberry Edition of the Writings of Herman Melville). 704p. 1998. pap. 17.95 (*0-8101-1690-1*) Northwestern U Pr.

Mardi: And a Voyage Thither, 2 vols., Set. Herman Melville. (BCL1-PS American Literature Ser.). 1992. reprint ed. lib. bdg. 150.00 (*0-7812-6795-1*) Rprt Serv.

***Mardi Gras.** (Body Glitter Art Kits Ser.). (Illus.). (J). (gr. 4-7). 1999. 8.95 (*1-57054-439-5*) Klutz.

Mardi Gras. Dianne M. MacMillan. LC 96-43563. (Best Holiday Bks.). (Illus.). 48p. (J). (gr. 1-4). 1997. lib. bdg. 18.95 (*0-89490-819-7*) Enslow Pubs.

Mardi Gras: A Cajun Country Celebration. Diane Hoyt-Goldsmith. LC 94-42707. (Illus.). 32p. (J). (gr. 4-6). 1995. lib. bdg. 15.95 (*0-8234-1184-2*) Holiday.

Mardi Gras! A Celebration. Errol Laborde. Ed. by Mary A. Rogers. (Illus.). 200p. 1981. 29.95 (*0-937430-03-X*); pap. 15.95 (*0-937430-02-1*) Picayune Pr.

***Mardi Gras: A City's Masked Parade.** Lisa Gabbert. LC 98-3526. (Festivals! U. S. A. Ser.). (Illus.). 24p. (J). (gr. k-4). 1999. 17.26 (*0-8239-5337-8*, PowerKids) Rosen Group.

Mardi Gras: A Pictorial History of Carnival in New Orleans. 2nd ed. Leonard V. Huber. (Illus.). 96p. 1989. reprint ed. pap. 9.95 (*0-88289-160-X*) Pelican.

Mardi Gras: New Orleans. Henri Schindler. LC 97-26362. (Illus.). 192p. 1997. 50.00 (*2-08-013615-1*, Pub. by Flammarion) Abbeville Pr.

Mardi Gras . . . As It Was. Robert Tallant. 276p. 1989. pap. 8.95 (*0-88289-722-5*) Pelican.

Mardi Gras Dictionary. Beverly B. Vidrine. LC 97-33568. (Illus.). 32p. (gr. 4-7). 1997. 14.95 (*1-56554-332-7*) Pelican.

Mardi Gras Guide, 1986. 10th ed. Arthur Hardy. (Illus.). 128p. 1986. pap. 2.50 (*0-930892-10-0*) A Hardy & Assocs.

Mardi Gras in Calcasieu Parrish: A Pictorial History. Nola M. Ross. (Illus.). 111p. 1991. 30.00 (*1-887144-01-3*) N M Ross.

Mardi Gras Indians. Michael P. Smith. LC 92-9972. (Illus.). 160p. 1994. 39.95 (*0-88289-896-5*) Pelican.

***Mardi Gras Madness: Stories of Murder & Mayhem in New Orleans.** Ed. by Martin H. Greenburg & Russell Davis. LC 99-58601. 240p. 2000. pap. 12.95 (*1-58182-077-1*, Cumberland Hearthside) Cumberland Hse.

Mardi Gras Mix-Up. Linda Lowery Keep. LC 99-20703. (Hannah & the Angels Ser.: No. 6). (J). (gr. 3-6). 1999. pap. 3.99 (*0-375-80096-4*) Random.

***Mardi Gras Swamp Parade.** Susan McKnight & Suzi Thornton. (Illus.). 38p. (J). (gr. k-6). 2000. pap. 14.00 (*1-882913-12-4*) Thornton LA.

***Mardi Gras Treasures: Invitations of the Golden Age.** Henri Schindler. LC 00-39150. (Illus.). 2000. 34.95 (*1-56554-722-5*) Pelican.

***Mardi Gras Treasures: Postcard Book.** Henri Schindler. (Illus.). 30p. 2000. pap. text 9.95 (*1-56554-746-2*) Pelican.

Mardi Gras 2000. Vladimir Swirynsky. Ed. by Susan L. Hassenzahl. (Illus.). 52p. pap. 5.00 (*1-881786-44-7*) New Kiev Pub.

Mardu Aborigines: Living the Dream in Australia's Desert. 2nd ed. Robert Tonkinson. Ed. by Louise S. Spindler & George D. Spindler. (Case Studies in Cultural Anthropology). (Illus.). 150p. (C). 1991. pap. text 23.50 (*0-03-032282-0*) Harcourt Coll Pubs.

Marduk the Mighty & Other Stories of Creation. Andrew Matthews. LC 96-41710. (Illus.). 96p. (J). (gr. 2 up). 1997. lib. bdg. 22.40 (*0-7613-0204-2*) Millbrook Pr.

***Mare.** Emanuele Martino. 2000. pap. 29.95 (*88-8158-260-0*) Charta.

Mare among the Geldings: Biography of Georgie Connell Sicking. Glorianne Weigand. (Illus.). 200p. 1998. pap. 14.95 (*0-9644141-4-7*) One-Hund-One Ranch.

Mare & Beast. C. W. Hume. Ed. by Universities Federation for Animal Welfare Staff. 1982. reprint ed. 25.00 (*0-7855-1111-3*) St Mut.

Mare au Diable. George Sand. 256p. 1973. write for info. (*0-318-63489-9*) Fr & Eur.

Mare au Diable. George Sand. (Folio Ser.: No. 892). (FRE.). 256p. 1973. 8.95 (*2-07-036892-0*) Schoenhof.

Mare au Diable. George Sand. Ed. by Salomon & Mallion. (FRE.). 1992. pap. 4.95 (*0-7859-3286-0*, 2277231940) Fr & Eur.

Mare au Diable. unabridged ed. George Sand. (FRE.). pap. 5.95 (*2-87714-192-6*, Pub. by Bookking Intl) Distribks Inc.

Mare au Diable, Francois le Champi. George Sand. Ed. by Salomon & Mallion. (Coll. Prestige). 27.95 (*0-685-34995-0*) Fr & Eur.

Mare Clasum see Of the Dominion: or Ownership of the Sea

Mare for Young Wolf. Janice J. Shefelman. LC 91-42749. (Step into Reading Ser.: A Step 3 Book). (Illus.). 48p. (J). (gr. 1-3). 1993. pap. 3.99 (*0-679-83445-1*, Pub. by Random Bks Yng Read) Random.

Mare for Young Wolf. Janice J. Shefelman. (Step into Reading Ser.: A Step 3 Book). (J). (gr. 2-3). 1993. 9.19 (*0-606-12415-2*, Pub. by Turtleback) Demco.

***Mare Kin: The Language We Speak Instead of English.** Dana Wall. 190p. 1999. pap. 12.95 (*0-7392-0447-5*, PO3733) Morris Pubng.

Mare on the Hill. Thomas Locker. (J). 1995. 11.19 (*0-606-07840-1*) Turtleback.

Maree du Soir: Carnets, 1968-1971. Henry De Montherlant. 17.50 (*0-685-36983-8*); pap. 9.95 (*0-686-55525-2*) Fr & Eur.

Marei Mekomot, Hagaot V'Haorot Ketzarot l'Sefer Shel, Vol. 1. Menachem M. Schneerson. (HEB., Illus.). 54p. 1995. pap. 5.00 (*0-8266-5154-2*) Kehot Pubn Soc.

Marek's Disease. Ed. by L. N. Payne. (Developments in Veterinary Virology Ser.). 1985. text 146.50 (*0-89838-730-2*) Kluwer Academic.

Marek's Disease I: Genetics & Virology. Gad Zeitlin et al. (Herpesvirus-Related Diseases Ser.). 1974. 27.50 (*0-8422-7166-X*) Irvington.

Marek's Disease II: Pathogenicity & Immunology. Ed. by H. Graham et al. (Herpesvirus-Related Diseases Ser.). 320p. 1974. text 31.50 (*0-8422-7167-8*) Irvington.

***Maremaid: A Pony's Tale.** Stacy Erin Myers. (Illus.). 32p. (J). (ps-3). 2000. 15.95 (*1-929845-11-1*) DeFranco Ent.

Maremma Senese Nella Crisi Del Seicento. Giuseppe Pallanti. Ed. by Stuart Bruchey. LC 80-2820. (Dissertations in European Economic History Ser.).Tr. of Sienese Maremma in the Crisis of the Seventeenth Century. (Illus.). 1981. lib. bdg. 23.95 (*0-405-14004-5*) Ayer.

***Marengo & Hohenlinden: Napoleon's Rise to Power.** James R. Arnold. (Illus.). x, 301p. 1999. 34.00 (*0-9670985-0-5*) Napoleon Bks.

***Marengo 1800: Napoleon's Greatest Gamble.** David Hollins. (Campaign Ser.: Vol. 70). (Illus.). 96p. 2000. pap. 17.95 (*1-85532-965-4*) Osprey.

Marenos: Tradition & Transition in Huave Community Organization. Charles C. Cheney. (Vanderbilt University Publications in Anthropology: No. 15). (Illus.). 1976. pap. 3.10 (*0-935462-04-X*) VUPA.

Maren's Hope. Launi K. Anderson. LC 95-33437. (Latter-Day Daughters Ser.). (Illus.). 80p. (J). 1995. pap. 4.95 (*1-56236-503-7*, Pub. by Aspen Bks) Origin Bk Sales.

Maren's Nest. Bowen. 48p. (J). Date not set. pap. 6.95 (*0-06-440790-X*) HarpC Child Bks.

Mare's Egg. Carole Spray. (Illus.). 56p. (J). (gr. 1-6). 1981. pap. 4.99 (*0-920656-07-2*) Firefly Bks Ltd.

***Mares Foals & Foaling.** Andrist. 2000. pap. 5.95 (*0-85131-447-3*, Pub. by J A Allen) Trafalgar.

Mares, Foals & Foaling. Friedrich Andrist. 1990. pap. 25.00 (*0-85131-053-2*, Pub. by J A Allen) St Mut.

Mares, Mud & Manure: Poems for Horse Lovers. unabridged ed. Nancy Callery. (Illus.). 80p. 1996. 14.95 (*0-9656068-0-5*) N Callery.

***Mare's Nest.** Gary Bowen. (Illus.). 48p. (J). (gr. 1-5). 2000. 17.95 (*0-06-028408-0*); lib. bdg. 17.89 (*0-06-028407-2*) HarpC Child Bks.

Mareva Injunction & Related Orders. 2nd ed. Mark Hoyle. 240p. 1989. 85.00 (*1-85044-161-8*) LLP.

Mareva Injunctions. Ed. by Marion Hetherington. xv, 122p. 1983. 47.50 (*0-455-20493-4*, Pub. by LawBk Co) Gaunt.

***Marfan.** Peter Reading. 2000. pap. 16.95 (*1-85224-516-6*, Pub. by Bloodaxe Bks) Dufour.

Marfan Syndrome. 4th ed. Reed E. Pyeritz & Cheryll Gasner. (Illus.). 48p. 1994. pap. 4.00 (*0-918335-09-4*) Natl Marfan Foun.

Marfan Syndrome. 5th ed. Reed E. Pyeritz & Cheryll Gasner. (Illus.). 44p. Date not set. pap. text 5.00 (*0-918335-10-8*) Natl Marfan Foun.

Marfan Syndrome: A Booklet for Teachers. Barbara A. Bernhardt. 1992. pap. text 3.00 (*0-918335-07-8*) Natl Marfan Foun.

Marfan Syndrome: A Booklet for Teenagers. Barbara A. Bernhardt et al. (Illus.). 20p. (YA). 1988. pap. 3.00 (*0-918335-03-5*) Natl Marfan Foun.

Marfan Syndrome: Physical Activity Guidelines for Physical Educators, Coaches & Physicians. Thomas J. Romeo. 77p. pap. 15.00 (*0-918335-08-6*) Natl Marfan Foun.

Marfan Syndrome: Physical Activity Guidelines for Physical Educators, Coaches & Physicians. Thomas J. Romeo. 78p. 1992. pap. 15.00 (*0-918335-06-X*) Natl Marfan Foun.

Marga. Mark Dunster. (Rin Ser.: Pt. 4). 61p. (Orig.). 1982. pap. 4.00 (*0-89642-086-8*) Linden Pubs.

Margaret. H. Rider Haggard. reprint ed. lib. bdg. 26.95 (*0-89190-709-2*) Amereon Ltd.

Margaret. Sylvester Judd. LC 68-57536. (Muckrakers Ser.). reprint ed. lib. bdg. 22.00 (*0-8398-0959-X*) Irvington.

Margaret: A Woman of Conflict. large type ed. Paul James. 300p. 1992. 22.95 (*1-85089-561-9*, Pub. by ISIS Lrg Prnt) Transaction Pubs.

Margaret: Remembering a Life That Was Poetry. Ed. by Marta Knobloch et al. (Illus.). 96p. 1998. pap. 11.95 (*0-944806-12-0*) Icarus Press.

Margaret & Dusty. Alice Notley. LC 84-27472. (Illus.). 80p. (Orig.). 1985. pap. 8.95 (*0-918273-08-0*) Coffee Hse.

Margaret & Her Friends: or Ten Conversations with Margaret Fuller upon the Mythology of the Greeks & Its Expression in Art. Caroline H. Dall. LC 72-4961. (Romantic Tradition in American Literature Ser.). 166p. 1978. reprint ed. 20.95 (*0-405-04633-2*) Ayer.

Margaret & Margarita, Margarita y Margaret. Lynn Reiser. LC 92-29012. 1996. 10.15 (*0-606-10482-8*, Pub. by Turtleback) Demco.

Margaret & Margarita, Margarita y Margaret. Lynn W. Reiser. LC 92-29012. (SPA., Illus.). 32p. (J). (ps-3). 1993. 15.95 (*0-688-12239-6*, Grenwillow Bks) HarpC Child Bks.

Margaret & Margarita, Margarita y Margaret. Lynn W. Reiser. LC 92-29012. (SPA & ENG., Illus.). 32p. (J). (ps up). 1993. lib. bdg. 15.93 (*0-688-12240-X*, Grenwillow Bks) HarpC Child Bks.

Margaret & Margarita, Margarita y Margaret. Lynn Reisser. LC 92-29012. (Illus.). 32p. (J). 1996. mass mkt. 5.95 (*0-688-14734-8*, Wm Morrow) Morrow Avon.

***Margaret & Me.** William J. Thomas. 208p. 2000. pap. 9.95 (*0-7737-6106-3*) Stoddart Publ.

Margaret & Me: All Humor Needs a Victim - And My Mother Should Come First. William Thomas. LC 99-206594. 208p. 2000. 17.95 (*0-7737-3051-6*) Stoddart Publ.

***Margaret Atwood.** Harold Bloom. LC 99-52023. (Modern Critical Views Ser.). 300p. 2000. 34.95 (*0-7910-5659-7*) Chelsea Hse.

Margaret Atwood. Howells. 1997. text 15.95 (*0-333-51916-7*, Pub. by Macmillan) St Martin.

Margaret Atwood: A Biography. Nathalie Cooke. LC 98-225308. (Illus.). 336p. 1998. text 24.95 (*1-55022-308-9*, Pub. by ECW) Genl Dist Srvs.

Margaret Atwood: A Critical Inquiry. Philip H. Rees. LC 84-433. (Women Writers Ser.). 352p. (C). 1984. 50.00 (*0-389-20742-X*, 08034) B&N Imports.

Margaret Atwood: A Critical Inquiry. Barbara H. Rigney. LC 87-1370. (Women Writers Ser.). (C). 1987. pap. 19.50 (*0-389-20743-8*, N8301) B&N Imports.

Margaret Atwood: A Feminist Poetics. Frank Davey. LC 85-103362. 178p. 1984. pap. 13.95 (*0-88922-217-7*, Pub. by Talonbks) Genl Dist Srvs.

Margaret Atwood: A Reference Guide. Judith McCombs & Carole L. Palmer. (Reference Guides to Literature Ser.). 300p. 1991. 65.00 (*0-8161-8940-4*, Hall Reference) Macmillan.

Margaret Atwood: An Annotated Bibliography (Poetry) Alan J. Horne. 53p. (C). 1980. pap. text 9.00 (*1-920763-49-X*, Pub. by ECW) Genl Dist Srvs.

Margaret Atwood: An Annotated Bibliography (Prose) Alan J. Horne. 46p. (C). 1979. pap. text 9.00 (*0-920763-48-0*, Pub. by ECW) Genl Dist Srvs.

Margaret Atwood: Conversations. Ed. & Intro. by Earl G. Ingersoll. LC 89-29944. (Critical Ser.). 251p. 1990. 19.95 (*0-86538-070-8*) Ontario Rev NJ.

Margaret Atwood: Conversations. Ed. & Intro. by Earl G. Ingersoll. LC 89-29944. (Critical Ser.). 251p. 1991. pap. 14.95 (*0-86538-074-0*) Ontario Rev NJ.

Margaret Atwood: Vision & Forms. Ed. by Kathryn Van Spanckeren & Jan G. Castro. LC 88-6452. (Ad Feminam: Women & Literature Ser.). (Illus.). 302p. 1988. text 31.95 (*0-8093-1408-8*) S Ill U Pr.

Margaret Atwood: Works & Impact. Ed. by Reingard Nischik. (Illus.). 272p. 2000. 55.00 (*1-57113-139-6*, Pub. by Camden Hse) Boydell & Brewer.

Margaret Atwood Reads: Atwood,&Margaret. abr. ed. Margaret Atwood. 1993. audio 12.00 (*1-55994-838-8*, DCN 1537) HarperAudio.

Margaret Atwood Revisited. Karen F. Stein. LC 99-33696. 1998. 28.95 (*0-8057-1614-9*, Twyne) Mac Lib Ref.

Margaret Atwood's Fairy-Tale Sexual Politics. Sharon R. Wilson. LC 93-30903. (Illus.). 350p. 1993. text 37.50 (*0-87805-639-4*) U Pr of Miss.

Margaret Atwood's Power: Mirrors, Reflections, Images in Select Fiction & Poetry. Shannon Hengen. 175p. 1993. pap. 12.95 (*0-929005-49-X*, Pub. by Sec Story Pr) LPC InBook.

Margaret Avison & Her Works. David A. Kent. (Canadian Author Studies). 58p. (C). 1989. pap. text 9.95 (*1-55022-008-X*, Pub. by ECW) Genl Dist Srvs.

Margaret Ayer Barnes. Lloyd C. Taylor. Ed. by Sylvia E. Bowman. LC 73-15837. (Twayne's United States Authors Ser.). 149p. (C). 1974. lib. bdg. 20.95 (*0-8057-0037-4*) Irvington.

Margaret Aylward, 1810-1889: Lady of Charity, Sister of Faith. Jacinta Prunty. LC 99-198046. 192p. 1999. pap. 19.95 (*1-85182-438-3*, Pub. by Four Cts Pr) Intl Spec Bk.

Margaret Bourke-White. Catherine A. Welch. LC 95-11695. (On My Own Bks.). (Illus.). (J). (gr. k-3). 1996. lib. bdg. 18.60 (*0-87614-890-9*, Carolrhoda) Lerner Pub.

Margaret Bourke-White. Catherine A. Welch. (Illus.). 56p. (J). (gr. k-3). 1996. pap. 5.95 (*0-87614-956-5*) Lerner Pub.

***Margaret Bourke-White: Her Pictures Were Her Life.** Susan Goldman Rubin. LC 98-53967. (Illus.). 96p. (YA). (gr. 5-8). 1999. 19.95 (*0-8109-4381-6*, Pub. by Abrams) Time Warner.

Margaret Bourke-White: Photographer see Women of Achievement

Margaret Bourke-White: Photographing the World. Eleanor H. Ayer. LC 91-39800. (People in Focus Ser.). (Illus.). 112p. (YA). (gr. 5 up). 1992. lib. bdg. 13.95 (*0-87518-513-4*, Dillon Silver Burdett) Silver Burdett Pr.

Margaret Bourke-White: Racing with a Dream. Catherine A. Welch. LC 97-37939. (gr. 5 up). 1997. 16.95 (*1-57505-049-8*) Lerner Pub.

Margaret Bourke-White, Photographer. Photos by Margaret Bourke-White. LC 98-71654. (Illus.). 160p. (gr. 8). 1998. 65.00 (*0-8212-2490-5*) Little.

Margaret Cape: A Novel. Wylene Dunbar. LC 96-48108. 352p. (C). 1997. 23.00 (*0-15-100248-7*) Harcourt.

Margaret Cavendish: Sociable Letters. James Fitzmaurice. LC 96-20565. (Literature-Reference Ser.). 264p. 1997. text 50.00 (*0-8153-2451-0*) Garland.

Margaret Cavendish & the Exiles of the Mind. Anna Battigelli. LC 97-47261. (Studies in the English Renaissance). 192p. 1998. 32.00 (*0-8131-2068-3*) U Pr of Ky.

Margaret Chase Smith: Beyond Convention. Patricia L. Schmidt. LC 96-31038. 1996. pap. write for info. (*0-89101-089-0*) U Maine Pr.

Margaret Chase Smith: Beyond Convention. Patricia L. Schmidt. LC 96-31038. 1996. 26.95 (*0-89101-088-2*) U Maine Pr.

Margaret Chase Smith: Model Public Servant, 27. Marlene B. Vallin. LC 97-53290. (Great American Orators Ser.: Vol. 27). 264p. 1998. lib. bdg. 69.50 (*0-313-29163-2*, Greenwood Pr) Greenwood.

Margaret Chase Smith's Skowhegan. Frank H. Sleeper. LC 96-209947. (Images of America Ser.). 128p. 1996. pap. 16.99 (*0-7524-0436-9*) Arcadia Publng.

Margaret Clitherow, 1556-1586. Mary Claridge. LC 66-19228. 208p. reprint ed. pap. 64.50 (*0-7837-5595-3*, 204550100005) Bks Demand.

Margaret Drabble: A Reader's Guide. Valerie G. Myer. LC 91-10737. (Critical Studies of Key Texts). 224p. 1991. text 29.95 (*0-312-06104-8*) St Martin.

Margaret Drabble: Existing Within Structures. Mary H. Moran. LC 83-332. 144p. 1983. 21.95 (*0-8093-1080-5*) S Ill U Pr.

Margaret Drabble's Female Bildungstromane: Theory, Genre, & Gender. Ian Wojcik-Andrews. LC 92-12163. (Writing about Women: Vol. 6). XIII, 224p. (C). 1995. text 49.95 (*0-8204-1901-X*) P Lang Pubng.

Margaret Ebner: Major Works. Margaret Ebner. Ed. & Tr. by Leonard P. Hindsley. LC 92-46650. (Classics of Western Spirituality Ser.). 240p. 1993. 24.95 (*0-8091-0462-8*); pap. 17.95 (*0-8091-3397-0*) Paulist Pr.

***Margaret Fell.** Ed. by Isabel Ross. 1999. pap. 30.00 (*1-85072-185-8*, Pub. by W Sessions) St Mut.

Margaret Fell: Mother of Quakerism. Isabel Ross. (C). 1989. pap. 36.00 (*0-900657-83-9*, Pub. by W Sessions) St Mut.

Margaret Fell & the Rise of Quakerism. Bonnelyn Y. Kunze. LC 92-85445. 280p. (C). 1993. 42.50 (*0-8047-2154-8*) Stanford U Pr.

Margaret Fell Speaking. Hugh Barbour. LC 76-4224. (Orig.). 1976. pap. 4.00 (*0-87574-206-8*) Pendle Hill.

Margaret Fleming. James A. Herne. Ed. & Intro. by Walter J. Meserve. (On Stage, America! Ser.). 45p. 1996. spiral bd. 4.95 (*0-937657-32-8*) Feedbk Theabks & Prospero.

Margaret, Frank, & Andy: Three Writers' Stories. Cynthia Rylant. LC 95-45526. (Illus.). 56p. (J). 1996. 15.00 (*0-15-201083-1*) Harcourt.

Margaret Fuller. Arthur W. Brown. Ed. by Sylvia E. Bowman. LC 63-20612. (Twayne's United States Authors Ser.). 155p. (C). 1964. text 17.95 (*0-8290-1712-7*) Irvington.

Margaret Fuller. Eve Kornfeld. LC 96-86774. 272p. 1997. text 35.00 (*0-312-16387-8*) St Martin.

Margaret Fuller. David Watson. LC 88-4311. (Women's Ser.). 128p. 1989. 19.50 (*0-85496-181-X*) Berg Pubs.

M

An Asterisk (*) at the beginning of an entry indicates that the title is appearing for the first time.

Margaret Fuller. Julia W. Howe. (Notable American Authors Ser.). 1992. reprint ed. lib. bdg. 75.00 (*0-7812-3221-X*) Rprt Serv.

Margaret Fuller: A Biography. Margaret Bell, Jr. LC 72-164587. (Select Bibliographies Reprint Ser.). 1977. reprint ed. 23.95 (*0-8369-5871-3*) Ayer.

Margaret Fuller: A Descriptive Bibliography. Joel Myerson. LC 78-4203. (Series in Bibliography). (Illus.). 178p. 1978. 100.00 (*0-8229-3381-0*) U of Pittsburgh Pr.

Margaret Fuller: A Psychological Biography. Katharine S. Anthony. (BCL1-PS American Literature Ser.). 223p. 1992. reprint ed. lib. bdg. 79.00 (*0-7812-6818-4*) Rprt Serv.

Margaret Fuller: An American Romantic Life: The Private Years. Charles Capper. (Illus.). 456p. 1992. text 65.00 (*0-19-504579-3*) OUP.

**Margaret Fuller: An Annotated Bibliography of Criticism, 1983-1995, 27.* Compiled by Joel Myerson. LC 97-49188. (Bibliographies & Indexes in Women's Studies: Vol. 27). 160p. 1998. lib. bdg. 69.50 (*0-313-29577-8*, Greenwood Pr) Greenwood.

Margaret Fuller: Brief Biography. Kornfeld. LC 96-86774. 272p. 1996. pap. text 12.95 (*0-312-12009-5*) St Martin.

Margaret Fuller: The Public Years. Charles Capper. (Illus.). 320p. Date not set. 29.95 (*0-19-506313-9*) OUP.

Margaret Fuller: Visionary of the New Age. Ed. by Marie Urbawski. LC 93-87696. 1994. 37.00 (*1-880811-14-6*) North Lights.

Margaret Fuller: Whetstone of Genius. Mason Wade. LC 75-122077. xvi, 304p. 1973. reprint ed. 45.00 (*0-678-03178-9*) Kelley.

Margaret Fuller an American Romantic Life: The Private Years, Vol. 1. Charles Capper. (Illus.). 456p. 1994. reprint ed. pap. 18.95 (*0-19-509267-8*) OUP.

***Margaret Fuller, Critic: Writings from the New York Tribune, 1844-1846.** Margaret Fuller et al. LC 99-87879. 2000. 75.00 (*0-231-11132-0*) Col U Pr.

Margaret Fuller (Marchesa Ossoli) Julia Howe. LC 68-24938. (American Biography Ser.: No. 32). 1969. reprint ed. lib. bdg. 75.00 (*0-8383-0201-7*) M S G Haskell Hse.

Margaret Fuller (Marchesa Ossoli) Julia W. Howe. LC 69-13936. 298p. 1970. reprint ed. lib. bdg. 59.75 (*0-8371-4089-7*, HOMF, Greenwood Pr) Greenwood.

Margaret Fuller (Marchesa Ossoli) Julia W. Howe. (BCL1-PS American Literature Ser.). 298p. 1992. reprint ed. lib. bdg. 79.00 (*0-7812-6820-6*) Rprt Serv.

Margaret Fuller Ossoli. Thomas Higginson. LC 68-24937. (American Literature Ser.: No. 49). 1968. reprint ed. lib. bdg. 75.00 (*0-8383-0955-0*) M S G Haskell Hse.

Margaret Fuller Ossoli. Thomas W. Higginson. (BCL1-PS American Literature Ser.). 323p. 1992. reprint ed. lib. bdg. 89.00 (*0-7812-6819-2*) Rprt Serv.

Margaret Fuller Ossoli. Thomas W. Higginson. (Notable American Authors Ser.). 1992. reprint ed. lib. bdg. 75.00 (*0-7812-3105-1*) Rprt Serv.

***Margaret Fuller's Cultural Critique: Her Age & Legacy.** Ed. by Fritz Fleischmann. LC 99-30008. (Early American Literature & Culture Through the American Renaissance Ser.: Vol. 3). 296p. 2000. text 55.95 (*0-8204-3952-5*) P Lang Pubng.

Margaret Fuller's New York Journalism: A Biographical Essay & Key Writings. Ed. by Catherine C. Mitchell. LC 94-18710. (Illus.). 240p. (C). 1995. text 32.50 (*0-87049-870-3*) U of Tenn Pr.

Margaret Fuller's Woman in the Nineteenth Century: A Literary Study of Form & Content, of Sources & Influences, 13. Marie M. Urbanski. LC 79-7475. (Contributions in Women's Studies: No. 13). 189p. 1980. 49.95 (*0-313-21475-1*, UMF/) Greenwood.

Margaret George Assortment. Margaret George. 1999. pap. 150.50 (*0-312-24517-3*) St Martin.

Margaret Gillies RWS, Unitarian Painter of Mind & Emotion (1803-1887) Charlotte Yeldham. LC 97-24676. (Studies in Art & Religious Interpretation: Vol. 19). (Illus.). 228p. 1997. text 89.95 (*0-7734-8637-2*) E Mellen.

Margaret Helfand Architects: Evolution of an Elemental Style Work in Progress. Margaret Helfand & Marti Cowan. (Work in Progress Ser.). (Illus.). 192p. 1999. pap. text 35.00 (*1-885254-93-8*, Pub. by Monacelli Pr) Penguin Putnam.

Margaret Howth. Rebecca H. Davis. LC 77-104437. 266p. reprint ed. lib. bdg. 32.50 (*0-8398-0353-2*) Irvington.

Margaret Howth. Rebecca H. Davis. 266p. (C). 1986. reprint ed. pap. text 9.95 (*0-8290-1949-9*) Irvington.

Margaret Hurley: An Oral History. Contrib. by Laurie Mercier. (Illus.). xii, 211p. (Orig.). 1995. pap. write for info. (*1-889320-01-3*) WA St Oral Hist.

Margaret Jourdain's Regency Furniture, 1795-1830. Ralph Fastnedge. 1997. 49.50 (*1-85149-181-3*) Antique Collect.

***Margaret Knight.** Illus. by Marlene Targ Brill & Joanne H. Friar. LC 99-45145. (J). 2000. lib. bdg. write for info. (*0-7613-1756-2*) Millbrook Pr.

Margaret Laurence: An Appreciation. Ed. by Christl Verduyn. 268p. 1988. 12.95 (*0-921149-20-4*) Broadview Pr.

Margaret Laurence: The Long Journey Home. rev. ed. Patricia Morley. 200p. (C). 1991. reprint ed. pap. text 24.95 (*0-7735-0856-2*, Pub. by McG-Queens Univ Pr) CUP Services.

Margaret Laurence's The Fire-Dwellers. Nora F. Stovel. (Canadian Fiction Studies: No. 24). 120p. (C). 1993. pap. text 14.95 (*1-55022-127-2*, Pub. by ECW) Genl Dist Srvs.

Margaret Maron Presents: Malice Domestic #8. Margaret Maron et al. 256p. 1999. mass mkt. 5.99 (*0-380-79407-1*, Avon Bks) Morrow Avon.

Margaret McCurry: Constructing Twenty-Five Short Stories. Margaret McCurry. LC 99-53960. (Illus.). 192p. 2000. pap. 40.00 (*1-58093-046-8*, Pub. by Monacelli Pr) Penguin Putnam.

Margaret McMillan: Portrait of a Pioneer. Elizabeth Bradburn. 272p. 1989. 69.50 (*0-415-01254-6*) Routledge.

Margaret McWilliams: An Interwar Feminist. Mary Kinnear. (Illus.). 232p. 1991. 60.00 (*0-7735-0857-0*, Pub. by McG-Queens Univ Pr) CUP Services.

Margaret Mead. Liza N. Burby. LC 96-41733. (Making Their Mark Ser.). (J). 1997. lib. bdg. 15.93 (*0-8239-5026-3*, PowerKids) Rosen Group.

Margaret Mead. Julie Castiglia. (Pioneers in Change Ser.). (Illus.). 144p. (J). (gr. 5-9). 1989. lib. bdg. 13.95 (*0-382-09525-1*) Silver Burdett Pr.

Margaret Mead. Rafael Tilton. LC 93-21840. (Importance of Ser.). 112p. (J). (gr. 5-8). 1994. lib. bdg. 22.45 (*1-56006-039-5*) Lucent Bks.

Margaret Mead: Anthropologist see Women of Achievement

***Margaret Mead: Bringing World Cultures Together.** Michael Pollard. LC 98-47864. (Giants of Science Ser.). (Illus.). 64p. (J). (gr. 5-8). 1999. lib. bdg. 18.95 (*1-56711-327-3*) Blackbirch.

Margaret Mead: Coming of Age in America. Joan Mark. Ed. by Owen Gingerich. LC 98-18604. (Oxford Portraits in Science Ser.). (Illus.). 112p. (YA). (gr. 6-12). 1999. 22.00 (*0-19-511679-8*) OUP.

Margaret Mead: The Complete Bibliography, 1925-1975. Ed. by Joan Gordan. 1976. text 43.85 (*90-279-3026-0*) Mouton.

Margaret Mead & Ruth Benedict: The Kinship of Women. Hilary Lapsley. LC 98-54185. (Illus.). 376p. 1999. 34.95 (*1-55849-181-3*) U of Mass Pr.

Margaret Mead & Samoa. Freeman. (Australian National University Press Ser.). 1996. text. write for info. (*0-08-032990-X*, Pergamon Pr) Elsevier.

Margaret Mead & Samoa: The Making & Unmaking of an Anthropological Myth. Derek Freeman. LC 82-15620. 403p. reprint ed. pap. 125.00 (*0-7837-2261-3*, 205734900004) Bks Demand.

Margaret Mead, Gregory Bateson, & Highland Bali: Fieldwork Photographs of Bayung Gede, 1936-1939. Gerald Sullivan. LC 98-55903. (Illus.). 220p. 1999. 45.00 (*0-226-38434-9*) U Ch Pr.

***Margaret Mead Made Me Gay: Personal Essays, Public Ideas.** Esther Newton. LC 00-29400. (Series Q). (Illus.). 360p. 2000. pap. 18.95 (*0-8223-2612-4*); lib. bdg. 54.95 (*0-8223-2604-3*) Duke.

Margaret Mee: Return to the Amazon. Ruth Stiff & Royal Botanic Gardens Kew Staff. (Illus.). viii, 199p. 1998. reprint ed. pap. 50.00 (*0-11-250113-3*, Pub. by Statnry Office) Balogh.

Margaret Mitchell. Elizabeth I. Hanson. (Twayne's United States Authors Ser.: No. 566). 136p. (C). 1990. 21.95 (*0-8057-7608-7*, Twayne) Mac Lib Ref.

Margaret Mitchell & John Marsh: The Love Story Behind Gone with the Wind. Marianne Walker. 1995. pap. text 16.95 (*1-56145-104-5*) Peachtree Pubs.

***Margaret Mitchell & John Marsh: The Love Story Behind Gone with the Wind.** 2nd ed. Marianne Walker. (Illus.). 608p. 2000. 29.95 (*1-56145-231-9*) Peachtree Pubs.

***Margaret Mitchell, Reporter.** Margaret Mitchell. 2000. 23.95 (*1-892514-86-9*) Hill St Pr.

Margaret Murie. Bryant. (J). 1995. 14.95 (*0-8050-2125-6*) H Holt & Co.

Margaret Murie's Wilderness Life. Jennifer Bryant. (J). 1993. 19.93 (*0-516-07398-2*) Childrens.

Margaret Newman: Health As Expanding Consciousness. Joanne Marchione. (Notes on Nursing Theories Ser.: Vol. 6). (Illus.). 60p. 1992. 22.95 (*0-8039-4796-8*); pap. 9.95 (*0-8039-4797-6*) Sage.

***Margaret of Anjou.** Betty King. 336p. 2000. 31.99 (*0-7089-4231-8*) Ulverscroft.

Margaret of Anjou: Queen of England. Phillipe Erlanger. Tr. by Edward Hyams. LC 79-161438. (Illus.). 251p. 1970. 19.95 (*0-87024-214-8*) U of Miami Pr.

Margaret of Castello: Unwanted One. LC 90-84543. 64p. 1991. pap. 5.95 (*0-916927-14-8*) Growth Unltd.

Margaret of the Imperfections: Stories. Lynda Sexson. LC 88-4150. 224p. 1989. pap. 9.95 (*0-89255-147-X*) Persea Bks.

Margaret of York, Simon Marmion, & "The Visions of Tondal" Ed. by Thomas Kren. LC 91-33413. (Illus.). 272p. 1992. pap. 49.95 (*0-89236-204-9*, Pub. by J P Getty Trust) OUP.

Margaret Ogilvy. J. M. Barrie. 1980. 29.00 (*0-403-00243-5*) Scholarly.

Margaret Ogilvy & Others see Works of J. M. Barrie: Peter Pan Edition

Margaret Oliphant: Critical Essays on a Gentle Subversive. Ed. by D. J. Trela. LC 94-19751. 1995. 33.50 (*0-945636-72-5*) Susquehanna U Pr.

Margaret Olley. France Christine. (Illus.). 180p. 1990. text 37.00 (*0-947131-36-1*) Gordon & Breach.

Margaret Rinkovsky: The "Odyssey Landscapes" Reconsidered. Janina Darling. 1995. pap. 10.00 (*0-945952-01-5*) Mus Art Hist.

***Margaret River Style.** Shelley Cullen et al. (Illus.). 200p. 1999. pap. 24.95 (*1-86368-285-6*, Pub. by Fremantle Arts) Intl Spec Bk.

Margaret Sanger. Deborah Bachrach. LC 92-46878. (Importance of Ser.). (Illus.). 112p. (J). (gr. 5-8). 1993. lib. bdg. 22.45 (*1-56006-032-8*) Lucent Bks.

***Margaret Sanger: An Autobiography.** Intro. by Kathryn Cullen-DuPont. (Illus.). 516p. 1999. pap. 17.95 (*0-8154-1015-8*) Cooper Sq.

Margaret Sanger: An Autobiography. Margaret H. Sanger. (American Biography Ser.). 504p. 1991. reprint ed. lib. bdg. 99.00 (*0-7812-8338-8*) Rprt Serv.

Margaret Sanger: Every Child a Wanted Child. Nancy Whitelaw. LC 93-13635. (People in Focus Ser.). (Illus.). 160p. (J). (gr. 4 up). 1994. lib. bdg. 13.95 (*0-87518-581-9*, Dillon Silver Burdett) Silver Burdett Pr.

Margaret Sanger: Father of Modern Society. 3rd rev. ed. Elasah Drogin. (Illus.). 128p. 1985. pap. 4.00 (*1-892875-00-4*, 0101, Remnant Israel) New Hope Publicatns.

Margaret Sanger: Mini-Play. (Women's Studies). (YA). (gr. 6 up). 1978. 6.50 (*0-89550-310-7*) Stevens & Shea.

Margaret Sanger, an Autobiography see Works

Margaret Sanger & the Birth Control Movement: A Bibliography, 1911-1984. Ronald Moore & Gloria Moore. LC 86-10119. 230p. 1986. 30.00 (*0-8108-1903-1*) Scarecrow.

Margaret Sanger Papers: Collected Documents Series. Margaret Sanger et al. LC 97-25564. (Collected Documents Ser.). 1997. 2485.00 (*1-55655-635-7*) U Pubns Amer.

Margaret Sanger Papers: Documents from the Sophia Smith Collection & College Archives, Smith College. Ed. by Esther Katz et al. LC 95-52040. (Research Collections in Women's Studies). 1995. 12020.00 (*1-55655-529-6*) U Pubns Amer.

Margaret Sanger Story & the Fight for Birth Control. Lawrence Lader. LC 73-11855. (Illus.). 348p. 1975. reprint ed. lib. bdg. 69.50 (*0-8371-7076-1*, LAMS, Greenwood Pr) Greenwood.

Margaret Shepherd's Calligraphy Projects for Pleasure & Profit. Ed. by Margaret Shepherd. (Illus.). 96p. (Orig.). 1983. pap. 8.95 (*0-399-50908-9*, Perigee Bks) Berkley Pub.

Margaret Tafoya: A Tewa Potter's Heritage & Legacy. Laurence R. Blair & Mary E. Blair. Ed. by Susan McDonald. LC 86-62249. 200p. 1986. 45.00 (*0-88740-080-9*) Schiffer.

***Margaret Thatcher.** Sean Connolly. LC 99-89880. (Profiles Ser.). (Illus.). 2000. lib. bdg. write for info. (*1-57572-224-0*) Heinemann Lib.

Margaret Thatcher. Kenneth Harris. (Illus.). 288p. 1988. 19.95 (*0-316-34837-6*) Little.

Margaret Thatcher. Marietta D. Moskin. (In Focus Biographies Ser.). (Illus.). 128p. (J). 1990. lib. bdg. 13.98 (*0-671-69632-7*, Julian Messner) Silver Burdett Pr.

Margaret Thatcher. Marietta D. Moskin. (In Focus Biographies Ser.). (Illus.). 128p. (YA). (gr. 9). 1990. pap. 7.95 (*0-671-69633-5*, Julian Messner) Silver Burdett Pr.

Margaret Thatcher: A Bibliography, 18. Faysal Mikdadi. LC 92-38071. (Bibliographies of British Statesmen Ser.: No. 18). 288p. 1993. lib. bdg. 89.50 (*0-313-28288-9*, MKE/) Greenwood.

Margaret Thatcher: In Victory & Downfall, 1987 & 1990. E. Bruce Geelhoed. LC 91-35146. 248p. 1992. 59.95 (*0-275-94148-5*, C4148, Praeger Pubs) Greenwood.

Margaret Thatcher: Madam Prime Minister: A Biography of Margaret Thatcher. Libby Hughes. LC 89-11974. (People in Focus Ser.). (Illus.). 128p. (YA). (gr. 5 up). 1989. lib. bdg. 13.95 (*0-87518-410-3*, Dillon Silver Burdett) Silver Burdett Pr.

Margaret Thatcher's Doctrine on Recognition of Croatia. Margaret S. Omrcanin. 82p. (Orig.). 1992. pap. 5.00 (*1-878716-07-7*) Ivor Pr.

Margaret the Queen. Nigel Tranter. 1998. mass mkt. 11.95 (*0-340-26545-0*) Trafalgar.

Margaret, Tom, & Mary's Authentic Hungarian Cookbook. Barbara Jean Prince. (Illus.). 56p. 1998. pap. 9.95 (*0-8059-4160-6*) Dorrance.

Margaret Tomkins. (Illus.). 1977. pap. 10.00 (*0-87422-044-0*) Wash St U Pr.

Margaret Tomkins, 1975-1981. Sue A. Kendall. LC 82-971409. (Illus.). 24p. (Orig.). 1982. pap. 5.00 (*0-942342-01-1*) Bellevue Art.

Margaret Truman: Three Complete Novels. Margaret Truman. 1993. 11.99 (*0-517-08480-5*) Random Hse Value.

Margaret Watson Parker: A Collector's Legacy. Museum Practice Program Graduate Students. (Illus.). 30p. 1982. pap. 3.00 (*0-912303-26-3*) Michigan Mus.

Margaret Webster: A Bio-Bibliography, 47. Milly S. Barranger. LC 93-37191. (Bio-Bibliographies in the Performing Arts Ser.: No. 47). 256p. 1994. lib. bdg. 75.00 (*0-313-28439-3*, Greenwood Pr) Greenwood.

Margaret Winthrop. Alice M. Earle. 341p. 1975. reprint ed. 26.95 (*0-87928-065-4*) Corner Hse.

Margaret Winthrop. Alice M. Earle. LC 67-30156. 1968. reprint ed. 20.00 (*0-87152-041-9*) Reprint.

***Margaret Winthrop: Biography of a Puritan Woman, the Wife of John Winthrop, First Governor of the Massachusetts Bay Colony.** Alice M. Earle. 341p. 1999. reprint ed. text 25.00 (*0-7881-6369-8*) DIANE Pub.

Margaret Wise Brown: Author of Goodnight Moon. Carol Greene. LC 92-34471. (Rookie Biographies Ser.). (Illus.). 48p. (J). (gr. k-3). 1993. pap. 4.95 (*0-516-44254-6*) Childrens.

Margaret Wise Brown: Awakened by the Moon. Leonard S. Marcus. LC 99-37202. (Illus.). 352p. 1999. pap. 14.00 (*0-688-17188-5*, Quil) HarperTrade.

Margaret Wise Brown's Pussy Willow. Margaret W. Brown. (Little Golden Storybks.). (J). 1997. 3.99 (*0-307-16069-6*, 16069, Goldn Books) Gldn Bks Pub Co.

Margaret Yorke. Kathleen Norris. reprint ed. lib. bdg. 17.95 (*0-89190-307-0*, Rivercity Pr) Amereon Ltd.

Margarete Steiff: Toy Maker. Carol Greene. LC 93-16855. (Rookie Biographies Ser.). (Illus.). 48p. (J). (gr. k-3). 1993. pap. 4.95 (*0-516-44257-0*) Childrens.

Margarethe. Caroline A. Fischer. (Fruhe Frauenliteratur in Deutschland Ser.: Vol. 3). (GER.). 354p. 1988. reprint ed. write for info. (*3-487-09067-8*) G Olms Pubs.

Margarethe von Trotta. Renate Hehr. (GER & ENG., Illus.). 128p. 58.00 (*3-930698-92-7*) Edition A Menges.

Margaret's Magnificent Colorado Adventure. Julie Danneberg. LC 98-31232. (Illus.). 48p. (J). (gr. 4-7). 1999. pap. 14.95 (*1-56579-329-3*) Westcliffe Pubs.

Margaret's Peace. Linda Hall. LC 97-40805. 300p. 1998. pap. 9.99 (*1-57673-216-9*, Multnomah Fiction) Multnomah Pubs.

Margaret's Peace. Linda Hall. LC 98-39760. 1998. 22.95 (*0-7862-1652-2*) Thorndike Pr.

Margaret's Story. large type ed. Eugenia Price. LC 92-18864. 723p. 1993. 22.95 (*1-56054-468-6*) Thorndike Pr.

Margarita. Ruben Dario. (Illus.). 48p. (J). 5.95 (*980-257-053-2*, Pub. by Ediciones Ekare) Kane-Miller Bk.

***Margarita: A Guatemalan Peace Corps Experience.** Marjorie DeMoss Casebolt. 224p. (C). 2000. pap. 14.95 (*1-880222-38-8*) Red Apple Pub.

***Margarita: The Case of the Numbers Kidnapper.** Michele W. Campanelli. 1999. pap. write for info. (*1-928781-19-5*) Hollis Bks.

***Margaritas: Recipes for Margaritas & South-of-the-Border Snacks.** Barbara Albright. (Illus.). 2000. 4.95 (*0-7407-1033-8*) Andrews & McMeel.

***Margaritaville Cookbook.** Olaf Nordstrom. (Illus.). 288p. 2000. pap. 18.00 (*1-883684-22-6*, Margaritaville Bks) Peninsula MA.

Marge. Andre P. De Mandiargues. (FRE.). 1981. pap. 10.95 (*0-7859-4152-5*) Fr & Eur.

Marge! Margaret H. McDonnell. (Illus.). 192p. (Orig.). 1997. pap. write for info. (*1-885527-10-1*) Feather Fables.

Marge Piercy. Sparks. 1996. 22.95 (*0-8057-4032-5*, Twyne) Mac Lib Ref.

Marge Piercy: An Annotated Bibliography, 25. Patricia Doherty. LC 96-53091. (Bibliographies & Indexes in American Literature Ser.: 25). 240p. 1997. lib. bdg. 67.95 (*0-313-30194-8*, Greenwood Pr) Greenwood.

Marge Site: Late Archaic & Emergent Mississippian Occupations in the Palmer Creek Locality (11-Mo-99) Andrew C. Fortier. LC 96-10030. (American Bottom Archaeology Ser.: Vol. 27). 416p. 1996. pap. text 29.95 (*0-252-06607-3*) U of Ill Pr.

Margenes Literarios Del Juego: Una Poetica del Naipe (Siglos XVI-XVIII) Jean-Pierre Etienvre. (Monagrafias A Ser.: No. 142). (SPA., Illus.). 352p. 1991. 72.00 (*1-85566-004-0*, Pub. by Tamesis Bks Ltd) Boydell & Brewer.

Margery Allingham: A Biography. Julia Thorogood. LC 92-171169. xxii, 423 p. 1991. write for info. (*0-434-77906-7*) Buttrwrth-Heinemann.

Margery Allingham Omnibus. Margery Allingham. Incl. Crime at Black Dudley. 1983. Look to the Lady. 1983. Mystery Mile. 1983. 592p. 1983. Set pap. 7.95 (*0-14-006058-8*, Penguin Bks) Viking Penguin.

Margery Fish's Country Gardening. Timothy Clark. 1999. 39.50 (*1-870673-31-X*) Garden Art Pr.

Margery Fry. Enid Huws Jones. 1999. pap. 21.00 (*1-85072-066-5*, Pub. by W Sessions) St Mut.

Margery Kempe. Robert Gluck. 204p. (Orig.). 1994. pap. 11.99 (*1-85242-334-X*, High Risk Bks) Serpents Tail.

Margery Kempe: A Book of Essays. Ed. by Sandra J. McEntire. LC 92-6437. 280p. 1992. text 20.00 (*0-8153-0378-5*) Garland.

Margery Kempe & Translations of the Flesh. Karma Lochrie. 1994. pap. text 16.95 (*0-8122-1557-5*) U of Pa Pr.

Margery Kempe of Lynn & Medieval England. Margaret Gallyon. (Illus.). 221p. (Orig.). 1996. pap. 16.95 (*1-85311-111-2*, 848, Pub. by Canterbury Press Norwich) Morehouse Pub.

***Margery Kemper.** 2000. write for info. (*0-582-36809-X*) Pearson Educ.

Margery Kempe's Dissenting Fictions. Lynn S. Johnson. LC 93-23046. 1993. 40.00 (*0-271-01030-4*); pap. 18.95 (*0-271-01031-2*) Pa St U Pr.

Margery Nahl: California Impressionist. Anna MacDonnel. (Illus.). 140p. 1994. 37.50 (*0-9640481-0-8*) M W Morse.

Margery Perham & British Rule in Africa. Ed. by Alison Smith & Mary Bull. 1992. text 37.50 (*0-7146-3451-4*, Pub. by F Cass Pubs) Intl Spec Bk.

Margery Williams "The Velveteen Rabbit" Margery Williams. Ed. by David Eastman. LC 87-11269. (Illus.). 32p. (J). (gr. k-4). 1988. lib. bdg. 15.85 (*0-8167-1061-9*) Troll Communs.

Margery Williams "The Velveteen Rabbit" Margery Williams. Ed. by David Eastman. LC 87-11269. (Illus.). 32p. (J). (gr. k-4). 1997. pap. 3.95 (*0-8167-1062-7*) Troll Communs.

Marge's Diner. Gail Gibbons. LC 88-26789. (Illus.). 32p. (J). (gr. 1-4). 1989. lib. bdg. 13.89 (*0-690-04606-5*) HarpC Child Bks.

Margherita of Cortona & the Lorenzetti: Sienese Art & the Cult of a Holy Woman in Medieval Tuscany. Joanna Cannon & Andre Vauchez. LC 97-48436. 1998. 80.00 (*0-271-01756-2*) Pa St U Pr.

Margiad Evans. Ceridwen Lloyd-Evans. LC 98-212231. (Border Lines Ser.). (Illus.). 156p. 1998. 39.95 (*1-85411-219-8*, Pub. by Seren Bks); pap. 19.95 (*1-85411-220-1*, Pub. by Seren Bks) Dufour.

Margie Hughto: A Ten Year Survey, 1980-1990. Peter Doroshenko. Ed. by Thomas E. Piche. LC 91-70277. (Illus.). 64p. 1991. pap. 10.00 (*0-914407-15-5*) Everson Mus.

Margie the Cat. Edna M. Blunt. pap. 6.95 (*0-681-02740-1*) Booklines Hawaii.

Margin. large type ed. Ian Stuart. (Linford Mystery Library). 480p. 1997. pap. 16.99 (*0-7089-7993-9*, Linford) Ulverscroft.

An Asterisk (*) at the beginning of an entry indicates that the title is appearing for the first time.

Margin: Restoring Emotional, Physical, Financial, & Time Reserves to Overloaded Lives. Richard A. Swenson. (Illus.). 275p. 1994. pap. 12.00 (*0-89109-888-7*) NavPress.

Margin-Alias: Language & Colonization in Canadian & Quebecois Fiction. Sylvia Soderlind. (Theory - Culture Ser.). 232p. 1991. text 45.00 (*0-8020-5903-1*); pap. text 17.95 (*0-8020-6845-6*) U of Toronto Pr.

Margin Book. Martin Torosian. 1985. 36.00 (*0-9603592-0-6*) MTA Financial Servs.

Margin for Error. Bruce Spicer. 260p. (Orig.). 1990. pap. 9.95 (*0-9624569-9-3*) ATA Pub Co.

Margin for Error: Manuscript Edition. Clare Boothe Luce. 1940. pap. 13.00 (*0-8222-1456-3*) Dramatists Play.

Margin in Time. Laura Hayden. 352p. 1995. mass mkt. 4.99 (*0-8217-0109-6*, Zebra Kensgtn) Kensgtn Pub Corp.

Margin of Appreciation Doctrine in the Dynamics of European Human Rights Jurisprudence. Howard C. Yourow. LC 94-46497. (International Studies in Human Rights: Vol. 28). 1996. lib. bdg. 86.00 (*0-7923-3338-1*, Pub. by M Nijhoff) Kluwer Academic.

*__Margin of Error.__ large type ed. Edna R. Buchanan. 488p. 2000. write for info. (*0-7089-4189-3*) Ulverscroft.

Margin of Error. large type ed. Edna R. Buchanan. LC 98-6707. 1998. pap. 23.95 (*1-56895-563-4*, Wheeler) Wheeler Pub.

Margin of Error. Edna R. Buchanan. 384p. 1998. reprint ed. mass mkt. 5.99 (*0-7868-8931-4*, Pub. by Hyperion) Time Warner.

*__Margin of Error: The Ethics of Mistakes in Clinical Medicine.__ Ed. by Susan B. Rubin & Laurie Zoloth. 384p. 2000. pap. 29.95 (*1-55572-053-6*) Univ Pub Group.

*__Margin of Error: The Ethics of Mistakes in Clinical Medicine.__ Ed. by Susan B. Rubin & Laurie Zoloth. 384p. (C). 2000. lib. bdg. 65.00 (*1-55572-077-1*) Univ Pub Group.

Margin of Life see Al Margen de la Vida: Poblacion y Pobreza en America Central

*__Margin of Safety: Risk-Averse Value Investing Strategies for the Thoughtful Investor.__ Seth A. Klarman. LC 00-23626. 2000. pap. write for info. (*1-893122-81-6*) Beard Bks.

Margin Power: A Stock Market Strategy. Sheldon Zerden. LC 81-10749. 231p. 1981. 49.95 (*0-275-91706-1*, C1706, Praeger Pubs) Greenwood.

Margin That Remains: A Study of Aging in Literature. Janice Sokoloff. (American University Studies: English Language & Literature: Ser. IV, Vol. 37). VIII, 135p. (C). 1987. text 26.00 (*0-8204-0287-7*) P Lang Pubng.

Marginal Account Profile. Credit Research Foundation Staff. 8p. 1983. 40.00 (*0-939050-34-X*) Credit Res NYS.

Marginal & Footnote Poetry. Kathy Metcalfe & Myrle Olson. 1977. pap. 3.95 (*0-910286-56-6*) Boxwood.

Marginal Approach to Joint Cost Allocation: Theory & Application. Rene P. Manes & C. S. Agnes Cheng. (Studies in Accounting Research: No. 29). 219p. 1988. 20.00 (*0-86539-068-1*) Am Accounting.

*__Marginal Catholic: Challenge, Don't Crush.__ rev. ed. Joseph M. Champlin. LC 00-33153. (Orig.). 2000. write for info. (*0-8189-0882-3*) Alba.

Marginal Catholics. Ivan Clutterbuck. 304p. 1993. pap. 14.95 (*0-85244-234-3*, 947, Pub. by Gracewing) Morehouse Pub.

*__Marginal Communities & Social Development__ Snehlata Chandra. LC 98-901715. vi, 329 p. 1998. write for info. (*81-7391-245-9*) S Asia.

Marginal Consciousness. Aron Gurwitsch. Ed. by Lester Embree. LC 84-11877. (Series in Continental Thought : Vol. 7). 172p. (C). 1985. text 26.95 (*0-8214-0789-9*) Ohio U Pr.

Marginal Conventions: Popular Culture, Mass Media & Social Deviance. Ed. by Clinton R. Sanders. LC 90-81336. 183p. (C). 1990. 35.95 (*0-87972-489-7*); pap. 17.95 (*0-87972-490-0*) Bowling Green Univ Popular Press.

Marginal Cost Analysis & Pricing of Water & Electrical Power: Methodology Notes. Yves Albouy. 230p. 1983. 18.50 (*0-940602-10-5*) IADB.

Marginal Europe: The Contribution of Marginal Lands Since the Middle Ages. Sidney Pollard. LC 97-1021. 334p. 1997. text 75.00 (*0-19-820608-0*) OUP.

Marginal Forces - Cultural Centers: Tolson, Pynchon, & the Politics of the Canon. Michael Berube. LC 91-55555. 368p. 1992. pap. text 17.95 (*0-8014-9921-6*) Cornell U Pr.

*__Marginal Groups & Mainstream American Culture.__ Yolanda Estes. (Feminist Ethics Ser.). 2000. 40.00 (*0-7006-1047-2*); pap. 17.95 (*0-7006-1048-0*) U Pr of KS.

Marginal Jew - Rethinking the Historical Jesus Vol. 1: Roots of the Problem & the Person, Vol. 1. John P. Meier. 496p. 1991. 39.95 (*0-385-26425-9*) Doubleday.

Marginal Jew - Rethinking the Historical Jesus Vol. 2: Mentor, Message & Miracles, Vol. 2. John P. Meier. 1136p. 1994. 37.50 (*0-385-46992-6*) Doubleday.

Marginal Man in a Colonial Society: Abdoel Moeis' Salah Asuhan. David H. De Queljoe. LC 74-620028. (Papers in International Studies: Southeast Asia Ser.: No. 32). 52p. reprint ed. pap. 30.00 (*0-608-10994-0*, 200745100062) Bks Demand.

Marginal Nation: Transborder Migration from Bangladesh to West Bengal. LC 98-28021. 1998. 32.00 (*0-7619-9283-9*) Sage.

Marginal Notes for the New Testament. Ed. by R. G. Bratcher. vi, 125p. 1980. pap. 12.99 (*0-8267-0026-8*, 102701) Untd Bible Soc.

Marginal Notes for the Old Testament. Ed. by R. G. Bratcher. vi, 186p. 1980. pap. 21.99 (*0-8267-0025-X*, 102700) Untd Bible Soc.

Marginal Oilfield & Tanker Conversion '85. Ed. by Lorne & MacLean Marine & Offshore Publications Sta. 1985. 500.00 (*0-7855-1048-6*, Pub. by Lorne & MacLean Marine) St Mut.

Marginal Oilfield Development Manual. (C). 1989. 395.00 (*0-89771-715-5*, Pub. by Lorne & MacLean Marine) St Mut.

Marginal Oilfield Development Manual. OCS Marine Staff. (C). 1989. text 350.00 (*0-906314-35-6*, Pub. by Lorne & MacLean Marine) St Mut.

Marginal Regeneration. V. A. Nierstrasz. (Illus.). 108p. (Orig.). 1996. pap. 62.50 (*90-407-1237-9*, Pub. by Delft U Pr) Coronet Bks.

Marginal Scotland, Set. John N. Buchanan. (American University Studies: History: Ser. IX, Vols. 64 & 65). (Illus.). 361 + 348p. 1990. text 103.50 (*0-8204-0900-6*) P Lang Pubng.

Marginal Sculpture in Medieval France: Towards the Deciphering of an Enigmatic Pictoral Language. Nurith Kenaan-Kedar. LC 94-20428. (Illus.). 228p. 1995. 104.95 (*1-85928-109-5*, Pub. by Scolar Pr) Ashgate Pub Co.

Marginal Sights: Staging the Chinese in America. James S. Moy. LC 93-17415. (Studies in Theatre History & Culture). (Illus.). 172p. 1993. text 29.95 (*0-87745-427-2*) U of Iowa Pr.

Marginal Sights: Staging the Chinese in America. James S. Moy. LC 93-17415. (Studies in Theatre History & Culture). (Illus.). 172p. 1993. reprint ed. pap. text 14.95 (*0-87745-448-5*) U of Iowa Pr.

Marginal Spaces. Ed. by Michael P. Smith. LC 95-9319. (Comparative Urban & Community Research Ser.: Vol. 5). 146p. 1995. pap. 21.95 (*1-56000-812-1*) Transaction Pubs.

Marginal Teacher: A Step-by-Step Guide to Fair Procedures for Identification & Dismissal. C. Edward Lawrence et al. 192p. 1993. pap., student ed. 32.95 (*0-8039-6048-4*) Corwin Pr.

Marginal Teacher: A Step-by-Step Guide to Fair Procedures for Identification & Dismissal. C. Edward Lawrence et al. 192p. 1993. pap., wbk. ed. 29.95 (*2-8106-6048-4*) NEA.

Marginal Voices: Selected Stories. Julio R. Ribeyro. Tr. by Dianne Douglas from SPA. LC 92-30359. (Texas Pan American Ser.). 153p. (Orig.). (C). 1993. pap. 11.95 (*0-292-77058-8*); text 27.50 (*0-292-77057-X*) U of Tex Pr.

Marginal Workers, Marginal Jobs: The Underutilization of American Workers. Teresa A. Sullivan. LC 77-26727. 245p. reprint ed. pap. 76.00 (*0-7837-1014-3*, 204132500020) Bks Demand.

Marginal World of Oe Kenzaburo: A Study of Themes & Techniques. Michiko N. Wilson. LC 85-22150. 168p. (gr. 13). 1986. 65.95 (*0-87332-343-2*, East Gate Bk); pap. 35.95 (*1-56324-580-9*, East Gate Bk) M E Sharpe.

Marginal Worth: Teaching & the Academic Labor Market. Lionel S. Lewis. 163p. 1996. text 34.95 (*1-56000-263-8*) Transaction Pubs.

Marginal Zones. Peter Sirr. 46p. 1984. pap. 11.95 (*0-904011-70-4*) Dufour.

Marginalia. Doran Larson. 176p. 1997. 22.00 (*1-877946-90-7*) Permanent Pr.

Marginalia. Gail Sher. 94p. 1997. 10.00 (*1-887289-29-1*) Rodent Pr.

Marginalia. Edgar Allan Poe. LC 80-22585. (Illus.). 255p. reprint ed. pap. 79.10 (*0-8357-3133-2*, 203939600012) Bks Demand.

*__Marginalia: Sherlock to Unidentified, 12.__ H. J. Jackson. (Collected Works of Samuel Taylor Colerid Ser.). 2000. 150.00 (*0-691-09958-8*, Pub. by Princeton U Pr) Cal Prin Full Svc.

Marginalism & Discontinuity: Tools for the Crafts of Knowledge & Decision. Martin Krieger. LC 89-10047. 224p. 1989. 32.50 (*0-87154-488-1*) Russell Sage.

Marginalist. Don Welch. (Plains Poetry Ser.: Vol. 8). 28p. 1992. pap. 4.00 (*0-911015-18-3*) Sandhills Pr.

Marginality. Gino Germani. LC 78-62978. 148p. 1980. 32.95 (*0-87855-235-9*) Transaction Pubs.

Marginality: Speech Writing & the African Woman Writer. Obioma Nnaemeka. (Opening Out: Feminism for Today Ser.). 256p. (C). 1999. write for info. (*0-415-06811-8*); pap. write for info. (*0-415-06812-6*) Routledge.

Marginality: The Key to Multicultural Theology. Jung-Young Lee. LC 94-31475. 224p. 1995. pap. 22.00 (*0-8006-2810-1*, 1-2810, Fortress Pr) Augsburg Fortress.

Marginality & Dissent in Twentieth-Century American Sociology: The Case of Elizabeth Briant Lee & Alfred McClung Lee. John F. Galliher & James M. Galliher. LC 94-29612. (SUNY Series in Deviance & Social Control). 249p. (C). 1995. text 54.50 (*0-7914-2483-9*); pap. text 17.95 (*0-7914-2484-7*) State U NY Pr.

Marginality & Modernity: Ethnicity & Change in Post-Colonial Balochistan. Ed. by Paul Titus. LC 97-180625. (Illus.). 360p. 1997. text 32.00 (*0-19-577633-X*) OUP.

Marginality in Space - Past, Present & Future: Theoretical & Methodological Aspects of Cultural, Social & Economic Parameters of Marginal & Critical Regions. Ed. by Heikki Jussila et al. LC 98-74504. (IGU - Dynamics of Marginal & Critical Regions (in Association with) Ser.). 360p. 1999. text 78.95 (*1-84014-934-5*) Ashgate Pub Co.

Marginalization & Social Welfare in China. Linda J. Wong. LC 97-25913. 256p. (C). 1998. 85.00 (*0-415-13312-2*) Routledge.

Marginalization of Poetry: Language, Writing & Literary History. Bob Perelman. 224p. 1996. text 39.50 (*0-691-02139-2*, Pub. by Princeton U Pr); pap. text 15.95 (*0-691-02138-4*, Pub. by Princeton U Pr) Cal Prin Full Svc.

Marginalized in the Middle. Alan Wolfe. 291p. 1996. 27.50 (*0-226-90516-0*) U Ch Pr.

Marginalized in the Middle. Alan Wolfe. 292p. 1998. pap. 15.00 (*0-226-90517-9*) U Ch Pr.

Marginalized Places & Populations: A Structurationist Agenda. David Wilson & James O. Huff. LC 93-32900. 280p. 1994. 69.50 (*0-275-94614-2*, Praeger Pubs) Greenwood.

Marginellas. Robert E. Lipe. 40p. (Orig.). 1991. pap. 15.95 (*0-9637681-0-7*) Shell Store.

Margins: A Naturalist Meets Long Island Sound. Mary P. Buckles. LC 96-47946. 288p. 1997. 23.00 (*0-86547-516-4*) N Point Pr.

Margins: A Naturalist Meets Long Island Sound. Mary P. Buckles. (Illus.). 286p. 1998. pap. text 13.00 (*0-86547-532-6*) N Point Pr.

*__Margins: A Novel.__ Terri De la Pena. (Djuna Bks.). 336p. 2000. pap. 12.95 (*1-58005-039-5*) Seal Pr WA.

Margins: A Research Initiative for Interdisciplinary Studies of the Processes Attending Lithospheric Extension & Convergence. National Research Council, Commission on Physical. 296p. 1990. pap. text 30.00 (*0-309-04188-0*) Natl Acad Pr.

Margins & Mainstreams: Asians in American History & Culture. Gary Y. Okihiro. LC 93-44382. 222p. (C). 1994. 25.00 (*0-295-97338-2*); pap. 13.95 (*0-295-97339-0*) U of Wash Pr.

Margins & Marginality: The Printed Page in Early Modern England. Evelyn B. Tribble. (Illus.). 224p. 1993. text 35.00 (*0-8139-1472-8*) U Pr of Va.

Margins & Minorities: The Peripheral Areas & Peoples of Malaysia. Ed. by Victor J. King & Michael J. Parnwell. (Illus.). (Orig.). 1991. pap. text 19.95 (*0-85958-490-9*, Pub. by Univ of Hull Pr) Paul & Co Pubs.

*__Margins in European Integration.__ Noel Parker & Bill Armstrong. LC 99-59898. 2000. 65.00 (*0-312-22958-5*) St Martin.

Margins in the Classroom: Teaching Literature. Ed. by Kostas Myrsiades & Linda S. Myrsiades. LC 93-8692. (Pedagogy & Cultural Practices Ser.: Vol. 2). 1994. pap. 17.95 (*0-8166-2320-1*); text 44.95 (*0-8166-2319-8*) U of Minn Pr.

Margins of Erasure: Purdah in the Subcontinental Novel in English. Ed. by Jasbir Jain & Amina Amin. LC 95-901722. (C). 1995. write for info. (*81-207-1744-9*) Sterling Pubs.

Margins of European Law. Ward. LC 96-15989. 230p. 1996. text 65.00 (*0-312-16150-6*) St Martin.

Margins of Insecurity: Minorities & International Security. Ed. by Sam C. Nolutshungu. 328p. 1996. pap. 24.95 (*1-878822-75-6*) Univ Rochester Pr.

Margins of Insecurity: Minorities & International Security. Ed. by Sam C. Nolutshungu. LC 95-51461. 328p. (C). 1996. 60.00 (*1-878822-63-2*) Univ Rochester Pr.

Margins of Orthodoxy: Heterodox Writing & Cultural Response, 1660-1750. Ed. by Roger D. Lund. 312p. (C). 1996. text 64.95 (*0-521-47177-X*) Cambridge U Pr.

Margins of Philosophy. Jacques Derrida. Tr. by Alan Bass from FRE. LC 82-11137. 360p. (C). 1984. pap. text 16.95 (*0-226-14326-0*) U Ch Pr.

Margins of Political Discourse. Fred Dallmayr. LC 88-30582. (SUNY Series in Contemporary Continental Philosophy). 271p. 1989. text 21.50 (*0-7914-0034-4*) State U NY Pr.

Margins of Reality. Robert G. Jahn & Brenda J. Dunne. (Illus.). 430p. 1989. pap. 24.00 (*0-15-657246-X*) Harcourt.

Margins of Reality: The Role of Consciousness in the Physical World. Robert F. Jahn & Brenda J. Dunne. (Illus.). 1987. 27.95 (*0-15-157148-1*) Harcourt.

Margins of the City: Gay Men's Urban Lives. Ed. by Stephen Whittle. (Popular Cultural Studies). 184p. 1994. 59.95 (*1-85742-201-5*, Pub. by Arena); pap. 24.95 (*1-85742-202-3*, Pub. by Arena) Ashgate Pub Co.

Margins of the Text. Ed. by D. C. Greetham. 392p. (C). 1997. text 49.50 (*0-472-10667-8*, 10667) U of Mich Pr.

Margins of Utopia: Shui-Hu Hou-Chuan & the Literature of Ming Loyalism. Ellen Widmer. LC 86-24382. (East Asian Monographs: No. 128). 300p. 1986. 28.00 (*0-674-54847-7*) HUP.

Margit Kovacs. Ilona Pataky-Brestyanszky. 196p. 1989. 65.00 (*963-13-2628-4*, Pub. by Corvina Bks) St Mut.

Margo: Aviation Insurance. 3rd ed. Rod D. Margo. 1997. write for info. (*0-406-89101-X*, MAIL3, MICHIE) LEXIS Pub.

Margo: The Life & Theatre of Margo Jones. Helen Sheehy. LC 89-42892. (Illus.). 328p. 1989. 24.95 (*0-87074-296-5*) SMU Press.

*__Margo & the Secret Pond.__ John M. Ferrone. (Illus.). 36p. (J). (ps-5). 1999. pap. 16.95 (*1-928811-03-5*) Story Stuff.

*__Margo & the Trail Ride.__ John M. Ferrone. (Illus.). 36p. (J). (ps-5). 2000. pap. 16.95 (*1-928811-05-1*) Story Stuff.

*__Margo Goes on Safari.__ John M. Ferrone. (Illus.). 36p. (J). (ps-5). 2000. pap. 16.95 (*1-928811-04-3*) Story Stuff.

Margo Leavin Gallery - 25 Years: A Catalogue Documenting 25 Years of the Margo Leavin Gallery. Ed. by Margo L. Gallery. (Illus.). 128p. 1995. 45.00 (*1-880641-02-X*) M Leavin Gal.

Margo Oliver's Cookbook for Seniors: Nutritious Recipes for One- Two- or More. Margo Oliver. (Retirement Ser.). (Illus.). 272p. 1989. pap. 9.95 (*0-88908-695-8*) Self-Counsel Pr.

Margo's House. Peni R. Griffen. LC 95-51796. 128p. (J). (gr. 7 up). 1996. 16.00 (*0-689-80944-1*) S&S Bks Yung.

Margot. Julian Grenfell. 586p. 1984. 16.95 (*0-88191-002-3*) Freundlich.

Margot: Queen of the Night. Jerome Chabyn. 1996. 14.95 (*1-882931-15-7*) Heavy Metal Magazine.

Margot Fonteyn. Alistair Macaulay. (Illus.). 128p. 1998. pap. 9.95 (*0-7509-1579-X*, Pub. by Sutton Pub Ltd) Intl Pubs Mktg.

Margot in Badtown. Jerome Charyn. Ed. by Fershid Bharucha. Tr. by Mary Irwin from FRE. (Illus.). 48p. 1991. reprint ed. 14.95 (*1-879450-61-5*) Kitchen Sink.

Margrave House. large type ed. Elizabeth York. 1996. pap. 18.99 (*1-85389-583-0*, Dales) Ulverscroft.

*__Margret & H. A. Rey's Curious George Goes to a Costume Party.__ Margret Rey et al. LC 00-21804. (J). 2000. pap. write for info. (*0-618-06569-5*) HM.

*__Margret & H. A. Rey's Curious George Goes to an Ice Cream Shop.__ Margret Rey & H. A. Rey. Ed. by Vipah Interactive Staff. LC 00-21117. (Illus.). (J). 2000. bds. write for info. (*0-618-06575-X*) HM.

Margret Howth. Rebecca H. Davis. LC 90-3684. 312p. 1990. reprint ed. 35.00 (*1-55861-030-8*); reprint ed. pap. 11.95 (*1-55861-036-7*) Feminist Pr.

Margueret, le 3rd Reich. 1977. lib. bdg. 40.50 (*90-286-0307-7*) Kluwer Academic.

Marguerita & Sarabella's Glad Day. large type ed. Patricia L. Cromwell. (Illus.). 16p. (J). (ps-6). 1997. pap. 4.50 (*0-9664794-0-8*, 041998) Patty Cake.

Marguerite: A Journey of a Sephardic Woman. Gloria S. Stein. (Illus.). 198p. 1997. pap. 12.95 (*1-883294-52-5*) Masthof Pr.

Marguerite Bourgeoys & Montreal, 1640-1665. Patricia Simpson. (McGill-Queen's Studies in the History of Religion Ser.). (Illus.). 264p. 1997. 49.95 (*0-7735-1607-7*, Pub. by McG-Queens Univ Pr); pap. 19.95 (*0-7735-1641-7*, Pub. by McG-Queens Univ Pr) CUP Services.

*__Marguerite Bourgeoys et Montreal, 1640-1665.__ Patricia Simpson. (FRE., Illus.). 296p. 1999. pap. 19.95 (*0-7735-2008-2*) McG-Queens Univ Pr.

Marguerite Clark: America's Darling of Broadway & the Silent Screen. Curtis Nunn. LC 81-4178. (Illus.). 188p. 1981. pap. 15.00 (*0-912646-69-1*) Tex Christian.

Marguerite De la Roque: A Story of Survival. Elizabeth Boyer. LC 75-20805. 1975. 20.00 (*0-915964-01-5*) Veritie Pr.

Marguerite de Navarre: Les Prisons XX: A French & English Edition: Les Prisons XX: A French & English Edition. Claire L. Wade. (American University Studies: Romance Languages & Literature: Ser. II, Vol. 99). XXI, 143p. 1989. text 34.95 (*0-8204-0802-6*) P Lang Pubng.

Marguerite de Navarre's Heptameron: Themes, Language & Structure. Marcal Tetel. LC 72-88735. 223p. reprint ed. pap. 69.20 (*0-608-12822-8*, 202346000033) Bks Demand.

*__Marguerite De Valois.__ Alexandre Dumas. 252p. 2000. pap. 9.95 (*0-594-02836-1*) Eightn Hundrd.

*__Marguerite Duras.__ Laure Adler. 1999. 35.00 (*0-226-00758-8*) U Ch Pr.

Marguerite Duras. Aliette Armel. (FRE.). 152p. 1998. pap. 49.95 (*2-86808-117-7*) Intl Scholars.

Marguerite Duras: A Bio-Bibliography, 5. Robert Harvey & Helene Volat. LC 96-53093. (Bio-Bibliographies in World Literature Ser.: 5). 296p. 1997. lib. bdg. 75.00 (*0-313-28898-4*, Greenwood Pr) Greenwood.

Marguerite Duras: Apocalyptic Desires. Leslie Hill. LC 92-34599. 288p. (C). (gr. 13). 1993. pap. 23.99 (*0-415-05048-0*, B2388) Routledge.

Marguerite Duras: Etude sur l'Oeuvre Litteraire, Theatrale et Cinematographique de Marguerite Duras. Marguerite Duras et al. (Illus.). 200p. 1976. 14.95 (*0-8288-9601-1*) Fr & Eur.

Marguerite Duras: Fascinating Vision & Narrative Cure. Deborah Glassman. LC 88-46147. (Illus.). 152p. 1991. 34.50 (*0-8386-3337-4*) Fairleigh Dickinson.

Marguerite Duras: Une Experience Interieure: "Le Gommage de l'Etre en Faveur du Tout, Vol. 6. Noelle Carruggi. (Francophone Cultures & Literatures Ser.). (FRE.). 170p. (C). 1995. 40.95 (*0-8204-2643-1*) P Lang Pubng.

Marguerite Duras: Writing on the Body. Sharon Willis. LC 86-4289. 204p. 1987. text 24.95 (*0-252-01335-2*) U of Ill Pr.

Marguerite Duras Lives On. Janine Ricouart. LC 98-24668. 256p. 1998. 39.50 (*0-7618-1206-7*) U Pr of Amer.

Marguerite Duras, Revisited. Marilyn R. Schuster. LC 93-9411. (World Authors Ser.: No. 840). 185p. 1993. 32.00 (*0-8057-8298-2*, Twyne) Mac Lib Ref.

Marguerite, Go Wash Your Feet!, 001. Illus. & Compiled by Wallace Tripp. LC 85-7616. 48p. 1985. pap. 8.95 (*0-395-39894-0*) HM.

Marguerite Henry Biography. Henry & Flood. 1996. pap. 5.95 (*0-02-043097-3*) S&S Childrens.

Marguerite Henry's Album of Horses: A Pop-Up Book. Illus. by Marguerite Henry & Ezra Tucker. 12p. (J). (gr. k-3). 1993. bds. 14.95 (*0-689-71685-0*) Aladdin.

Marguerite Henry's Horseshoe Library: Stormy, Misty's Foal, Sea Star, Orphan of Chincoteague; Misty of Chincoteague, 3 bks., Set. Marguerite Henry. (Illus.). (J). (gr. 3-7). 1992. pap. 11.85 (*0-689-71624-9*) Aladdin.

Marguerite Long: A Life in French Music, 1874-1966. Cecilia Dunoyer. LC 93-9354. (Illus.). 1993. 29.95 (*0-253-31839-4*) Ind U Pr.

*__Marguerite Makes a Book.__ Bruce Robertson. LC 98-31222. (Getty Trust Publications). (Illus.). 48p. (YA). (gr. 2-5). 1999. 18.95 (*0-89236-372-X*, Pub. by J P Getty Trust) OUP.

Marguerite Maury's Guide to Aromatherapy. Daniele Ryman. 108p. 1989. pap. 17.95 (*0-85207-163-9*, Pub. by C W Daniel) Natl Bk Netwk.

Marguerite Maury's Guide to Aromatherapy. 3rd ed. Ed. by Daniele Ryman. 240p. pap. 26.95 (*0-8464-4249-3*) Beekman Pubs.

Marguerite Neilson's Cats. M. Neilson. Ed. by Grace McHattie. (Illus.). 1999. pap. 23.00 (*0-900767-69-3*, Pub. by Univs Fed Animal Welfare) St Mut.

*__Marguerite Patten's Complete Book of Teas.__ Marguerite Patten. (Illus.). 144p. 1999. reprint ed. pap. text 17.00 (*0-7881-6686-7*) DIANE Pub.

Marguerite Porete: The Mirror of Simple Souls. Marguerite Porete. LC 93-14479. (Classics of Western Spirituality Ser.).Tr. of Miroir des Simples Ames. 288p. 1993. 24.95 (*0-8091-0464-4*); pap. 17.95 (*0-8091-3427-6*) Paulist Pr.

Marguerite Porete et Marguerite d'Oingt de l'Autre Cote du Miroir. Catherine M. Muller. (Currents in Comparative Romance Languages & Literatures Ser.: Vol. 72). (FRE.). XVI, 213p. (C). 1999. text 47.95 (*0-8204-4010-8*, 40108) P Lang Pubng.

Marguerite Potter's Complete Book of Teas. Marguerite Patten. (Illus.). 144p. (Orig.). 1997. pap. text 14.95 (*0-7499-1691-5*, Pub. by Piatkus Bks) London Brdge.

Marguerite Wolff: Adventures of a Concert Pianist. Robert Clarson-Leach. 137p. 1985. 110.00 (*0-946444-01-3*, Pub. by Artmusique Pub Co) St Mut.

Marguerite Young, Our Darling: Tributes & Essays. Ed. by Miriam Fuchs. LC 94-7330. (Illus.). 160p. 1994. 24.95 (*1-56478-055-4*) Dalkey Arch.

Marguerite Yourcenar: Inventing a Life. Josyane Savigneau. (Illus.). 584p. (C). 1993. 25.00 (*0-226-73544-3*) U Ch Pr.

***Marguerite Yourcenar: Reading the Visual.** Nigel Saint. (Legenda Ser.: Vol. 5). 200p. (C). 2000. pap. 49.50 (*1-900755-39-4*, Pub. by E H R C) David Brown.

Marguerite Yourcenar: Vers la Rive d'Une Ithaque Interieure. Nadia Harris. (Stanford French & Italian Studies: No. 78). (FRE.). 152p. 1994. pap. 56.50 (*0-915838-94-X*) Anma Libri.

Marguerite Yourcenar in Counterpoint. C. Frederick Farrell, Jr. & Edith R. Farrell. 126p. (Orig.). 1984. pap. text 17.00 (*0-8191-3608-5*) U Pr of Amer.

Marguerites de la Marguerite des Princesses, 4 vols. in 1. Marguerite D'Angouleme. 1970. reprint ed. 90.00 (*0-8288-9919-3*, F30280) Fr & Eur.

Mari. Donna Anders. (Historical Ser.: No. 73). 1991. per. 3.95 (*0-373-28673-2*) Harlequin Bks.

Mari: A Novel. Jane V. Barker. LC 97-15919. (Women's West Ser.: No. 2). 200p. 1997. 19.95 (*0-87081-452-4*) Univ Pr Colo.

Mari & the Bible. Abraham Malamat. LC 97-18282. (Studies in the History & Culture of the Ancient Near East). viii, 270p. 1998. 84.50 (*90-04-10863-7*) Brill Academic Pubs.

Mari & the Early Israelite Experience: The Schweich Lectures, 1984. Abraham Malamat. (Schweich Lectures on Biblical Archaeology, British Academy Ser.). (Illus.). 174p. 1992. reprint ed. pap. text 28.00 (*0-19-726117-5*) OUP.

Mari in Retrospect: Fifty Years of Mari & Mari Studies. Ed. by Gordon D. Young. LC 91-37606. xvi, 345p. 1991. text 39.50 (*0-931464-28-5*) Eisenbrauns.

Mari Inoubliable. Jeanne Allan. (Azur Ser.: No. 732). (FRE.). 1998. mass mkt. 3.50 (*0-373-34732-4*, 1-34732-7) Harlequin Bks.

***Mari pour Melody.** Sandra Steffen. 1999. mass mkt. 3.99 (*0-373-39536-1*) Silhouette.

Mari Sandoz: A Study in Post-Colonial Discourse. Laura R. Villiger. LC 93-23327. (Swiss American Historical Society Publications: Vol. 3). X, 215p. (C). 1995. text 39.95 (*0-8204-2365-3*) P Lang Pubng.

Mari Sandoz: Story Catcher of the Plains. Helen W. Stauffer. LC 81-22014. (Illus.). xiv, 322p. 1982. pap. text 12.95 (*0-8032-9134-5*, Bison Books) U of Nebr Pr.

Mari Sandoz a Wildflower. Evelyn B. Hisel. LC 93-94161. (Illus.). 129p. 1993. pap. 9.95 (*0-9638163-0-6*) Hisel Bk Ends.

Maria see Mary: Yesterday, Today, Tomorrow

Maria. Margaret Haswell. LC 95-68517. 145p. 1995. pap. 15.95 (*1-57197-004-5*) Pentland Pr.

***Maria.** Jorge Isaacs. 2000. pap. 4.98 (*968-15-0036-9*) Ed Mex.

Maria. Jorge Isaacs. (SPA.). pap. 9.50 (*968-432-141-4*, Pub. by Porrua) Continental Bk.

Maria. Jorge Isaccs. (SPA.). 1997. pap. 4.98 (*968-15-0817-3*) Edit Diana.

Maria. Eugenia Price. 432p. 1984. mass mkt. 6.99 (*0-553-26362-5*) Bantam.

Maria. Arleta Richardson. 157p. 1998. pap. 5.95 (*0-89367-227-0*) Light & Life Comm.

Maria. Todd Tarbox. (J). 1993. pap. 6.60 (*0-8442-7218-3*) NTC Contemp Pub Co.

Maria. Todd Tarbox. (NTC Bilingual Ser.). (ENG & SPA.). (J). 1979. 11.80 (*0-606-01347-4*, Pub. by Turtleback) Demco.

Maria. Theodore Taylor. 80p. (J). (gr. 4-7). 1993. mass mkt. 3.99 (*0-380-72120-1*, Avon Bks) Morrow Avon.

Maria. large type ed. Eugenia Price. LC 92-20070. 701p. 1993. 22.95 (*1-56054-467-8*) Thorndike Pr.

Maria: A Christmas Story. Theodore Taylor. (J). 1993. 9.19 (*0-606-05452-9*, Pub. by Turtleback) Demco.

Maria: A Christmas Story. abr. ed. Theodore Taylor. LC 92-809. (Illus.). 96p. (J). (gr. 3-7). 1992. 15.00 (*0-15-217763-9*, Harcourt Child Bks) Harcourt.

Maria: A South American Romance. Jorge Isaacs. Tr. by Rollo Ogden. 1977. lib. bdg. 59.95 (*0-685-01968-3*) Gordon Pr.

***Maria: Eugenia Price Commemorative Edition.** Ed. by Eugenia Price. LC 99-23553. (Florida Trilogy Ser.: Vol. 1). 408p. 1999. pap. 14.95 (*1-57736-152-0*) Providence Hse.

Maria: Goddess of the Teche. Morris Raphael. (Illus.). 48p. (J). (gr. 4-9). 1991. 19.95 (*0-9608866-8-0*) M Raphael.

Maria: The Legend, the Legacy. Susan B. McGreevy & R. C. Gorman. LC 81-14512. (Illus.). 32p. (Orig.). 1982. 4.50 (*0-86534-005-6*) Sunstone Pr.

Maria: The Potter of San Ildefonso. Alice Marriott. LC 48-2101. (Civilization of the American Indian Ser.: Vol. 27). (Illus.). 320p. 1987. pap. 16.95 (*0-8061-2048-7*) U of Okla Pr.

Maria - A Woman of Valor. Beverly J. Ballard. 206p. 1999. 18.95 (*0-9667364-2-7*) Novelle Publ.

Maria & Mr. Feathers. (Illus.). (J). (ps-2). 1991. pap. 5.10 (*0-8136-5624-9*); lib. bdg. 7.95 (*0-8136-5124-7*) Modern Curr.

Maria Bella. Austin Goodrich. LC 98-60793. 165p. 1998. pap. 10.00 (*0-9664172-0-8*) Thistlefld Studio.

***Maria Callas.** Giandonato Crico. 2000. pap. 12.95 (*88-7301-394-5*) Gremese Intl.

Maria Callas. Andre Tubeuf. 80p. 1999. 18.95 (*0-7893-0381-7*) Universe.

Maria Callas: Sacred Monster. Stelios Galatopoulos. (Illus.). 544p. 1999. 35.00 (*0-684-85985-8*) S&S Trade.

***Maria Callas: The Tigress & the Lamb.** David Bret. 380p. 1999. pap. 14.95 (*1-86105-257-X*) Robson.

Maria Callas: The Tigress & the Lamb. David Bret. LC 98-70052. (Illus.). 380p. 1998. 32.95 (*1-86105-110-7*, Pub. by Robson Bks) Parkwest Pubns.

***Maria Callas Remembered.** Nadia Stancioff. 320p. 2000. pap. text 17.00 (*0-306-80967-2*) Da Capo.

Maria Calleja's Gozo: A Life History. Intro. by Micheline Galley. (UNESCO Collection of Representative Works, Series of Translations from the Literature of the Union of Soviet Socialist Republics). (Illus.). 245p. (C). 1994. 20.00 (*0-87421-169-7*) Utah St U Pr.

Maria Cebotari see Maria Cebotari, das Leben Einer Sangerin

Maria Cebotari, das Leben Einer Sangerin. Antonio Mingotti. Ed. by Andrew Farkas. LC 76-29955. (Opera Biographies Ser.).Tr. of Maria Cebotari. (GER., Illus.). 1977. reprint ed. lib. bdg. 19.95 (*0-405-09696-8*) Ayer.

Maria Celeste. Carmen Posadas. (SPA., Illus.). 44p. (J). (gr. 3-4). 1993. pap. 5.99 (*968-16-4039-X*, Pub. by Fondo) Continental Bk.

Maria Ceniczienta. George Crespo. 1999. 15.99 (*0-525-45346-6*) NAL.

Maria Chapdelaine. Louis Hemon. (FRE.). 1989. pap. 8.95 (*0-7859-3068-X*, 2253005665) Fr & Eur.

Maria Chapdelaine. Louis Hemon. (Illus.). 161p. 1992. pap. 5.95 (*0-7736-7388-1*) Genl Dist Srvs.

Maria Chapdelaine. Louis Hemon. (FRE., Illus.). 96p. (YA). (gr. 5 up). 1989. 19.99 (*0-88776-239-5*) Tundra Bks.

Maria Chapdelaine. Louis Hemon. LC 89-50775. (Illus.). 192p. (YA). 1991. pap. 9.95 (*0-88776-242-5*) Tundra Bks.

Maria Chapdelaine. Louis Hemon. Tr. by Alan Brown from FRE. LC 89-50775. (Illus.). 96p. (YA). (gr. 6 up). 1989. reprint ed. 19.99 (*0-88776-236-0*) Tundra Bks.

Maria Contra Viento y Marea. Magolo Cardenas. (SPA., Illus.). 191p. 1994. pap. 6.99 (*968-16-4229-5*, Pub. by Fondo) Continental Bk.

Maria Dabrowska. Zbigniew Folejewski. LC 67-12267. (Twayne's World Authors Ser.). 1967. lib. bdg. 20.95 (*0-8057-2260-2*) Irvington.

***Maria de Estrada: Gypsy Conquistadora.** Gloria Duran. LC 99-16679. 227p. (YA). 1999. pap. 14.95 (*1-891270-01-X*, Pub. by Lat Am Lit Rev Pr) Consort Bk Sales.

Maria de Sautuola: Discoverer of the Bulls in the Cave. Dennis Fradin. LC 96-5027. (Remarkable Children Ser.: No. 2). (Illus.). (J). 1996. pap. 5.95 (*0-382-39471-2*); lib. bdg. 15.95 (*0-382-39470-4*) Silver Burdett Pr.

Maria de Sautuola: Los Toros de la Cueva. Dennis Fradin. LC 96-47637. (Remarkable Children Ser.). (J). 1997. pap. text 5.95 (*0-382-39844-0*) Silver Burdett Pr.

Maria de Sautuola: Los Toros de la Cueva. Ed Martinez. (Remarkable Children Ser.).Tr. of Bulls in the Cave. (SPA.). (J). (gr. k-5). 1997. pap. 5.95 (*0-614-29055-4*, Silver Pr NJ) Silver Burdett Pr.

Maria de Sautuola: The Bulls in the Cave. Ed Martinez. (Remarkable Children Ser.). (J). (gr. k-5). 1997. 15.95 (*0-614-29056-2*, Silver Pr NJ); pap. 6.95 (*0-614-29057-0*, Silver Pr NJ) Silver Burdett Pr.

Maria de Zayas: The Dynamics of Discourse. Ed. by Amy R. Williamsen & Judith A. Whitenack. LC 94-19476. (Illus.). 264p. (C). 1995. 41.50 (*0-8386-3572-5*) Fairleigh Dickinson.

Maria Edgeworth. James Newcomer. LC 77-125886. (Irish Writers Ser.). 94p. 1975. pap. 1.95 (*0-8387-7732-5*) Bucknell U Pr.

Maria Edgeworth: Chosen Letters. Maria Edgeworth. LC 75-41083. reprint ed. 45.00 (*0-404-14536-1*) AMS Pr.

Maria Edgeworth in France & Switzerland: Selections from the Edgeworth Family Letters. Maria Edgeworth. Ed. by Christina Colvin. (Illus.). 1979. 67.00 (*0-19-812518-6*) OUP.

Maria Edgeworth's Art of Prose Fiction. McWhorter & O. Elizabeth Harden. 258p. 1971. text 35.40 (*3-10-800307-0*) Mouton.

Maria Edgeworth's Irish Writing. Hollingsworth. LC 97-23090. 220p. 1997. text 55.00 (*0-312-17746-1*) St Martin.

Maria Escapes. Gillian Avery. LC 91-36730. (Illus.). 272p. (J). (gr. 4-8). 1992. pap. 15.00 (*0-671-77074-8*) S&S Bks Yung.

Maria Fernanda Cardoso. Ron Platt. (Illus.). 32p. (Orig.). 1994. pap. 5.00 (*0-938437-46-1*) MIT List Visual Arts.

Maria Gonds of Bastar. Wilfred Grigson. (Illus.). 528p. 1992. 28.00 (*0-19-562855-1*) OUP.

Maria Grever: Poeta y Compositora. Maria L. Rodriguez-Lee. 175p. 54.50 (*1-882528-05-0*) Scripta.

Maria Irene Fornes: Plays. Maria I. Fornes. 1986. pap. 13.95 (*0-933826-83-4*) PAJ Pubns.

Maria Irene Fornes & Her Critics, 70. Assunta B. Kent. LC 95-25604. (Contributions in Drama & Theatre Studies: Vol. 70). 256p. 1996. 59.95 (*0-313-29735-5*, Greenwood Pr) Greenwood.

Maria Izquierdo, 1902-1955. Teresa Del Conde & Louis-Martin Lozano. Tr. by Colin White & Alejandro Velasco from SPA. LC 97-217454. (ENG & SPA., Illus.). 126p. 1997. pap. 29.95 (*1-889410-00-4*) Mexican Fine Arts.

Maria la Voz y Otras Historias (Maria the Voice) 2nd ed. Juan De La Cabada. (SPA.). 184p. 1984. pap. 7.99 (*968-16-1631-6*, Pub. by Fondo) Continental Bk.

Maria Lacerda de Moura: A Chronology. V. Munoz. Tr. by W. Scott Johnson. (Libertarian & Anarchist Chronology Ser.). 1979. lib. bdg. 59.95 (*0-8490-3053-6*) Gordon Pr.

Maria Luisa Bombal: Apreciaciones Criticas. Marjorie Agosin et al. LC 87-70082. 280p. 1987. pap. 22.00 (*0-916950-73-5*) Biling Rev-Pr.

Maria Luisa Bombal: Realidad y Fantasia. Gloria G. Lira. 28.50 (*0-916379-25-6*) Scripta.

***Maria Maddalena de' Pazzi: Selected Revelations.** Tr. & Intro. by Armando Maggi. LC 99-88285. (CWS Ser.: Vol. 98). 365p. 2000. pap. 39.95 (*0-8091-0509-8*); pap. 29.95 (*0-8091-3923-5*) Paulist Pr.

Maria Magdalena: De Mythe Voorbij; Op Zoek Naar Wie Zij Werkelijkis see Mary Magdalene: Beyond the Myth

Maria Making Pottery: The Story of the Famous New Mexico Potter. rev. ed. Hazel Hyde. LC 83-5093. (Illus.). 32p. 1991. pap. 4.95 (*0-86534-156-7*) Sunstone Pr.

Maria Malibran: A Biography of the Singer. Howard Bushnell. LC 79-14880. (Illus.). 1979. 35.00 (*0-271-00222-0*) Pa St U Pr.

Maria Malibran: Diva of the Romantic Age. April FitzLyon. (Illus.). 330p. 1988. 12.95 (*0-253-32408-4*) Ind U Pr.

Maria Martinez. Mary C. Nelson. LC 78-172871. (Story of an American Indian Ser.). 77 p. 1972. write for info. (*0-87518-038-8*, Dillon Silver Burdett) Silver Burdett Pr.

Maria Martinez. Mary C. Nelson. LC 74-12323. (Story of an American Indian Ser.). 74 p. 1974. write for info. (*0-87518-098-1*, Dillon Silver Burdett) Silver Burdett Pr.

Maria Mazzarello see St. Mary Mazzarello

Maria Meneghini Callas. Michael Scott. LC 92-17103. 320p. 1992. text 29.95 (*1-55553-146-6*) NE U Pr.

Maria, Mi Madre. Lawrence G. Lovasik. (San Jose de Libros en Laminas Ser.). (SPA., Illus.). (J). 1990. pap. 1.50 (*0-89942-463-5*, 463/S) Catholic Bk Pub.

Maria Mitchell: The Soul of an Astronomer. Beatrice Gormley. LC 95-21980. 128p. (J). (gr. 5-9). 1995. pap. 8.00 (*0-8028-5099-5*, Eerdmans Bks) Eerdmans.

Maria Mitchell, Life, Letters & Journals. Maria Mitchell. (American Biography Ser.). 293p. 1991. reprint ed. lib. bdg. 69.00 (*0-7812-8285-3*) Rprt Serv.

Maria Molina & the Days of the Dead. Kathleen Krull. LC 94-14535. (Illus.). 32p. (J). (gr. k-3). 1994. mass mkt. 15.95 (*0-02-750999-0*, Mac Bks Young Read) S&S Childrens.

Maria Montessori: A Biography. Rita Kramer. (Radcliffe Biography Ser.). (Illus.). 416p. 1988. pap. 21.50 (*0-201-09227-1*) Addison-Wesley.

Maria Montessori: Her Life & Work. E. M. Standing. LC 98-11403. 1998. pap. 13.95 (*0-452-27989-5*, Plume) Dutton Plume.

Maria Montessori: Teacher of Teachers. Marie T. Shephard. LC 96-350. (YA). 1996. lib. bdg. 23.93 (*0-8225-4952-2*, Lerner Publctns) Lerner Pub.

Maria Montoya Martinez: Master Potter. Elsie K. Kreischer. LC 95-8198. (Illus.). 96p. (J). (gr. 4-7). 1995. 13.95 (*1-56554-098-0*) Pelican.

Maria, Mota, & the Grandmother: A Novel. Stella H. Alico. Ed. by Laura Ware. LC 92-31237. (Illus.). 128p. (C). 1993. pap. 12.95 (*0-86534-190-7*) Sunstone Pr.

Maria Nordman: Trabajos en la Ciudad de Ondas. Ronald J. Onorato. LC 85-80104. (Illus.). 20p. 1985. 5.00 (*0-934418-23-3*) Mus Contemp Art.

Maria of Olonets. Bishop Nikodim. (Illus.). 111p. 1996. pap. 8.95 (*0-938635-74-3*) St Herman Pr.

Maria: or The Wrongs of Woman. Mary Wollstonecraft Shelley. 1994. pap. 9.95 (*0-393-31169-4*) Norton.

Maria Paradox: How Latinas Can Merge Old World Traditions with New World Self-Esteem. Rosa M. Gill & Carmen I. Vazquez. 288p. 1997. pap. 14.00 (*0-399-52309-X*, Perigee Bks) Berkley Pub.

Maria Paradox: How Latinas Can Merge Old World Traditions with New World Self-Esteem see Paradoja de Maria: Como Pueden las Latinas Fortalecer Su Autoestima, Sin Abandonar Sus Tradiciones

Maria Rodale's Organic Gardening: Your Seasonal Companion to Creating a Beautiful & Delicious Garden. Maria Rodale. LC 98-8913. (Illus.). 352p. 1998. text 35.00 (*0-87596-799-X*) Rodale Pr Inc.

***Maria Rodale's Organic Gardening Companion.** Maria Rodale. (Illus.). 96p. 2000. pap. 19.95 (*0-87596-835-X*) Rodale Pr Inc.

Maria-Rosa Mystica. A. M. Weigl. 200p. 1993. pap. 6.00 (*1-890137-21-9*) One Hund-One Fnd.

Maria Sabina: Saint Mother of the Mushrooms. John W. Allen. 28p. 1997. pap. 7.00 (*0-9631518-9-4*) Mltilingl Bks.

Maria Sibylla Merian: Artist & Naturalist. Maria S. Merian. Ed. by Kurt Wettengl. (Illus.). 256p. 1998. text 65.00 (*3-7757-0723-9*, 810812, Pub. by Gerd Hatje) Dist Art Pubs.

Maria Sibylla Merian: Artist & Naturalist, 1647-1717. Maria Sibylla Merian. 1998. 65.00 (*3-7757-0751-4*, Pub. by Gerd Hatje) Dist Art Pubs.

***Maria Sibylla Merian: The New Book of Flowers.** Ed. by Thomas Burger. LC 99-62668. (Illus.). 96p. 1999. 25.00 (*3-7913-2080-7*, Pub. by Prestel) te Neues.

***Maria Sibylla Merian - Neues Blumenbuck: (New Book of Flowers)** Pref. by Maria S. Merian. (Illus.). 80p. 1999. 125.00 (*3-7913-2060-2*) te Neues.

Maria Sklodowska-Curie: Centenary Lectures. (Proceedings Ser.). (Illus.). 198p. 1968. pap. 25.00 (*92-0-030168-1*, ISP179, Pub. by IAEA) Bernan Associates.

Maria Stuart. Schiller. (GER.). (C). 1986. 6.95 (*0-8442-2942-3*, X2942-3) NTC Contemp Pub Co.

Maria Stuart. Friedrich Schiller. Ed. by Wolfgang Wittkowski. (GER.). 237p. (C). 1992. reprint ed. pap. text 10.50 (*0-88133-706-4*) Waveland Pr.

Maria Tallchief: America's Prima Ballerina. Maria Tallchief. (Illus.). 351p. 1995. 27.50 (*0-8050-3302-5*) H Holt & Co.

Maria Tallchief: Native American Ballerina. Paul Lang. LC 96-52555. (Native American Biographies Ser.). (Illus.). 128p. (YA). (gr. 6 up). 1997. lib. bdg. 20.95 (*0-89490-866-9*) Enslow Pubs.

Maria Tallchief, Prima Ballerina. Vee Browne. (Illus.). (J). (gr. 1-4). 1995. pap. 4.99 (*0-8136-5767-9*); lib. bdg. 10.60 (*0-8136-6081-5*) Modern Curr.

Maria Teresa. 2nd ed. Mary Atkinson. LC 79-90393. (ENG & SPA., Illus.). 39p. (J). 1979. 5.95 (*0-914996-21-5*) Lollipop Power.

Maria Theresa. Petra Mathers. LC 84-48346. (Illus.). 32p. (J). (ps-3). 1985. 13.95 (*0-06-024109-8*) HarpC Child Bks.

Maria Theresa. Petra Mathers. LC 84-48346. (Trophy Picture Bk.). (Illus.). 32p. (J). (gr. k-3). 1992. pap. 4.95 (*0-06-443282-3*, HarpTrophy) HarpC Child Bks.

Maria Theresa. William J. McGill, Jr. LC 85-17856. (Twayne's Rulers & Statesmen of the World Ser.). 169p. (C). 1972. lib. bdg. 17.95 (*0-8290-1738-0*) Irvington.

Maria Theresa. James F. Bright. LC 71-154145. (Select Bibliographies Reprint Ser.). 1977. reprint ed. 20.95 (*0-8369-5761-X*) Ayer.

***Maria-Theresien-Thaler.** Carl Peez et al. (Social Research on Africa Ser.: Vol. 5). 128p. 1999. pap. 22.95 (*3-8258-3765-3*, Pub. by CE24) Transaction Pubs.

Maria Tiefenthaller. Muriel Cerf. (FRE.). 1984. pap. 15.95 (*0-7859-2003-X*, 2070376168) Fr & Eur.

Maria Tolete. Houghton Mifflin Company Staff. (Literature Experience 1993 Ser.). (J). (gr. 3). 1992. pap. 9.48 (*0-395-61795-2*) HM.

Maria Treben's Cures: Letters & Accounts of Cures Through the Herbal, "Health Through God's Pharmacy" 4th ed. Maria Treben. (Illus.). 96p. 1995. pap. text 23.95 (*3-85068-224-2*, Pub. by Ennsthaler) Am Educ Systs.

Maria von Oignies: Eine Hochmittelalterliche Mystikerin Zwischen Ketzerei und Rechtglaubigkeit. Iris Geyer. (Europaische Hochschulschriften Ser.: Reihe 23, Bd. 454). (GER.). 252p. 1992. 45.80 (*3-631-44704-3*) P Lang Pubng.

Maria W. Stewart, America's First Black Woman Political Writer: Essays & Speeches. Ed. by Marilyn Richardson. LC 86-43048. (Blacks in the Diaspora Ser.). (Illus.). 160p. 1987. 26.95 (*0-253-36342-X*); pap. 9.95 (*0-253-20446-1*, MB-446) Ind U Pr.

Maria Who? Created by Francine Pascal. (Sweet Valley High Senior Year Ser.: No. 8). 175p. (YA). (gr. 7-12). 1999. mass mkt. 3.99 (*0-553-49280-2*) Bantam.

Maria Woodworth-Etter: Her Life & Ministry. Maria Woodworth-Etter. 1960. per. 3.95 (*0-89985-022-7*) Christ for the Nations.

***Maria Woodworth-Etter: The Complete Collection of Her Life Teachings.** Roberts Liardon. 1032p. 2000. 34.99 (*1-57778-122-8*) Albury Pub.

Maria X. Joan V. Herndon. LC 96-70830. 304p. 1996. 25.95 (*1-56167-338-2*) Noble Hse MD.

Maria y la Tumba Vacia. Alice J. Davidson. (SPA.). 1998. 3.99 (*0-8297-2488-5*) Vida Pubs.

Maria Zef. Paola Drigo. Tr. & Intro. by Blossom S. Kirschenbaum. LC 88-37837. (European Women Writers Ser.). xiv, 182p. 1989. pap. 15.00 (*0-8032-6577-8*, Bison Books) U of Nebr Pr.

Mariachi Bishop: The Life of Patrick Flores, First Mexican-American Bishop in the U. S. Martin McMurtrey. LC 87-70378. (Illus.). 181p. (Orig.). 1987. pap. 6.95 (*0-931722-56-X*) Corona Pub.

Mariachi... Y Mas. Lonnie Dai Zovi. (SPA.). 71p. 1994. pap. 28.50 incl. audio (*0-935301-67-4*); pap. 31.50 incl. audio compact disk (*0-935301-77-1*) Vibrante Pr.

***Mariage.** Diane Johnson. 320p. 2000. 23.95 (*0-525-94518-0*, Dutt) Dutton Plume.

Mariage a Hollywood. Sandra Marton. (Azur Ser.). (FRE.). 1997. pap. 3.50 (*0-373-34655-7*, 1-34655-0) Harlequin Bks.

Mariage a l'Improviste. Elizabeth Duke. (Azur Ser.: Vol. 753). (FRE.). 1999. mass mkt. 3.50 (*0-373-34753-7*, 1-34753-3) Harlequin Bks.

Mariage au Montana. Anne Eames. (FRE.). 1998. mass mkt. 3.50 (*0-373-37480-1*, 1-37480-0) Harlequin Bks.

Mariage Blanc & the Hunger Artist Departs: Two Plays. Tadeusz Rozewicz. Tr. by Adam Czerniawski from POL. LC 82-12859. 112p. 1983. 13.50 (*0-7145-2775-0*); pap. 7.95 (*0-7145-2776-9*) M Boyars Pubs.

Mariage de Conte de Fees. Day Leclaire. (Horizon Ser.: No. 518). (FRE.). 1999. mass mkt. 3.99 (*0-373-39518-3*, 1-39518-5) Harlequin Bks.

Mariage de Figaro. Beaumarchais. (FRE.). (C). 1985. pap. 9.95 (*0-8442-1830-8*, VF1830-8) NTC Contemp Pub Co.

Mariage de Figaro. Pierre De Beaumarchais. 192p. 1970. 5.95 (*0-686-54084-0*) Fr & Eur.

Mariage de Figaro. Jean-Pierre De Beaumarchais. (FRE.). 1965. pap. 9.95 (*0-8288-9336-5*, F46096) Fr & Eur.

***Mariage de Figaro: Advanced Placement French Literature.** Lison Baselis-Bitoun. (FRE.). 95p. (YA). (gr. 9-12). 1999. student ed., wbk. ed. 7.33 (*1-877653-68-3*) Wayside Pub.

Mariage de Figaro - La Mere Coupable. Pierre De Beaumarchais. (FRE.). 1984. pap. 18.95 (*0-7859-1986-4*, 2070375277) Fr & Eur.

Mariage de Figaro - La Mere Coupable. Pierre-Augustin C. De Beaumarchais. (Folio Ser.: No. 1527). (FRE.). 1984. pap. 14.95 (*2-07-037527-7*) Schoenhof.

Mariage de Figaro - Le Barbier de Seville. unabridged ed. Pierre De Beaumarchais. (FRE.). pap. 5.95 (*2-87714-212-4*, Pub. by Bookking Intl) Distribks Inc.

An Asterisk (*) at the beginning of an entry indicates that the title is appearing for the first time.

Mariage de M. le Trouhadec. Jules Romains, pseud. (FRE.). 160p. 1959. pap. 10.95 (*0-7859-1313-0*, 2070255271) Fr & Eur.

Mariage Eclair. Vanessa Grant. (Azur Ser.: No. 713). (FRE.). 1998. pap. 3.50 (*0-373-34713-8*, 1-34713-7) Harlequin Bks.

Mariage en Dix Recettes. Stephanie Bond. (Rouge Passion Ser.: No. 519). (FRE.). 1999. mass mkt. 3.99 (*0-373-37519-0*, 1-37519-5) Harlequin Bks.

Mariage en Droit Canonique Oriental. Jean Dauvillier. LC 80-2357. reprint ed. 35.00 (*0-404-18905-9*) AMS Pr.

***Mariage Force: A Comedie-Ballet by Molier.** Julia Preston. (FRE.). 1999. pap. 24.95 (*0-85989-643-9*) Univ Exeter Pr.

Mariage Imprevisible. Lucy Gordon. (Azur Ser.: No. 729). (FRE.). 1998. mass mkt. 3.50 (*0-373-34729-4*, 1-34729-3) Harlequin Bks.

Mariage Piege. Sandy Steen. (Rouge Passion Ser.: No. 474). (FRE.). 1998. pap. 3.50 (*0-373-37474-7*, 1-37474-3) Harlequin Bks.

Mariage Princier. Kathryn Jensen. (Rouge Passion Ser.: No. 481). (FRE.). 1998. mass mkt. 3.50 (*0-373-37481-X*, 1-37481-8) Harlequin Bks.

Mariage, Separation, Divorce: L'Etat du Droit au Quebec. 2nd rev. ed. Jean Pineau. LC 77-565419. (FRE.). 314p. 1978. reprint ed. pap. 97.40 (*0-7837-6947-4*, 204677600003) Bks Demand.

Mariages des Iles-de-la-Madeleine, PQ, 1794-1900. Dennis Boudreau. xliv, 325p. 1984. per. 21.00 (*1-929920-25-3*) American French.

Mariah. Sandra Canfield. (Calloway Corners Ser.). 1993. per. 3.50 (*0-373-83278-8*, 1-83278-1) Harlequin Bks.

Mariah Carey. 80p. 1991. per. 14.95 (*0-7935-0491-0*, 00308098) H Leonard.

***Mariah Carey, Vol. 1.** 104p. 1999. otabind 16.95 (*0-634-00202-3*) H Leonard.

Mariah Carey. Sam Wellman. (Illus.). 64p. 1999. 17.95 (*0-7910-5233-8*) Chelsea Hse.

Mariah Carey. Sam Wellman. LC 99-31804. (Galaxy of Superstars Ser.). (Illus.). 64p. (YA). (gr. 4-7). 1999. pap. 9.95 (*0-7910-5333-4*) Chelsea Hse.

Mariah Carey. large type ed. Melanie Cole. LC 97-21843. (Real Life Reader Biographies Ser.). (Illus.). 32p. (J). (gr. 3-8). 1997. lib. bdg. 15.95 (*1-883845-51-3*) M Lane Pubs.

Mariah Carey: Emotions. (Piano-Vocal-Guitar Ser.). 80p. (Orig.). 1992. otabind 14.95 (*0-7935-1222-0*, 00308127) H Leonard.

Mariah Carey: Her Story. Chris Nickson. LC 95-9883. 1995. pap. 9.95 (*0-312-13121-6*) St Martin.

Mariah Carey: Merry Christmas. 56p. 1994. per. 14.95 (*0-7935-3965-X*, 00306007) H Leonard.

Mariah Carey: Music Box. 56p. 1994. otabind 14.95 (*0-7935-2986-7*, 00308214) H Leonard.

Mariah Carey: Music Box. 56p. 1995. pap. 9.95 (*0-7935-4720-2*, 00316001) H Leonard.

Mariah Carey: Music Box, No. 381. 48p. 1995. pap. 7.95 (*0-7935-3186-1*, 00102305) H Leonard.

***Mariah Carey: Rainbow.** 96p. 2000. otabind 16.95 (*0-634-01492-7*) H Leonard.

Mariah Carey: Unplugged. 48p. 1992. pap. 9.95 (*0-7935-1777-X*, 00308159) H Leonard.

***Mariah Carey Butterfly.** 80p. 1998. per. 16.95 (*0-7935-8986-X*) H Leonard.

Mariah Carey Revisited. Chris Nickson. LC 98-23938. 192p. 1998. pap. 11.95 (*0-312-19512-5*, St Martin Griffin) St Martin.

***Mariah Delany Lending Library Disaster.** Sheila Greenwald. (Illus.). 128p. (J). 2000. pap. 4.95 (*0-618-04929-0*) HM.

***Mariah Delany's Author-of-the-Month Club.** Sheila Greenwald. (Illus.). 128p. (J). 2000. pap. 4.95 (*0-618-04928-2*) HM.

Mariah Delany's Author-of-the-Month Club. Sheila Greenwald. (J). 1997. pap. 2.95 (*0-8167-3000-8*) Troll Communs.

Mariah Keeps Cool. Mildred P. Walter. LC 89-23981. 144p. (J). (gr. 3-7). 1990. lib. bdg. 15.00 (*0-02-792295-2*, Bradbury S&S) S&S Childrens.

Mariah Loves Rock. large type ed. Mildred P. Walter. 1993. 34.00 (*0-614-09842-4*, L-34112-00) Am Printing Hse.

Mariah's Diary. Valerie F. Harris & Eula V. Jones. 26p. (J). (gr. k-6). Date not set. pap. write for info. (*1-889654-01-9*) Enricharamics.

Mariah's Prize. Miranda Jarrett. (Historical Ser.). 1994. per. 3.99 (*0-373-28827-1*, 1-28827-3) Harlequin Bks.

Mariamne. Hardy. Ed. by Howe. (Exeter French Texts Ser.: Vol. 73). (FRE.). 134p. Date not set. pap. text 19.95 (*0-85989-303-0*, Pub. by Univ Exeter Pr) Northwestern U Pr.

Marian. large type ed. Catherine J. Todd. (General Fiction Ser.). 688p. 1993. 27.99 (*0-7089-2978-8*) Ulverscroft.

Marian: The Life of George Eliot. Simon Dewes. LC 74-28384. (English Literature Ser.: No. 33). 1974. lib. bdg. 75.00 (*0-8383-1745-6*) M S G Haskell Hse.

Marian Anderson: A Great Singer. Patricia McKissack & Fredrick McKissack. LC 90-19163. (Great African Americans Ser.). (Illus.). 32p. (J). (gr. 1-4). 1991. lib. bdg. 14.95 (*0-89490-303-9*) Enslow Pubs.

***Marian Anderson: A Singer's Journey.** Allan Keiler. LC 99-43319. (Illus.). 448p. 2000. 29.50 (*0-684-80711-4*) Scribner.

Marian Anderson: An Annotated Bibliography & Discography. Compiled by Janet L. Sims. LC 80-1787. (Illus.). 243p. 1981. lib. bdg. 42.95 (*0-313-22559-1*, SIM/, Greenwood Pr) Greenwood.

Marian Anderson: Singer see Women of Achievement

***Marian Anderson: Singer & Humanitarian.** Andrea Broadwater. LC 99-36258. (African-American Biographies Ser.). (Illus.). 128p. (gr. 6 up). 2000. lib. bdg. 20.95 (*0-7660-1211-5*) Enslow Pubs.

Marian Anderson, a Portrait. Kosti Vehanen. LC 74-100184. 270p. 1970. reprint ed. lib. bdg. 35.00 (*0-8371-4051-X*, VEMA, Greenwood Pr) Greenwood.

Marian Apparitions Today - Why So Many? Edward D. O'Connor. LC 96-67811. (Illus.). 148p. (Orig.). 1996. pap. 7.95 (*1-882972-71-6*, 3391) Queenship Pub.

Marian Catechism. Robert J. Fox. 128p. 1985. 1.75 (*0-911988-66-1*, 36122) AMI Pr.

Marian Child Mass Book, Black/Red. 1981. 7.95 (*0-88271-077-X*) Regina Pr.

Marian Dogma Whose Time Has Come. Robert J. Payesko. 100p. 1998. pap. 5.95 (*1-57918-074-4*, 3576) Queenship Pub.

Marian Engel & Her Works. Elizabeth Brady. (Canadian Author Studies). 69p. (C). 1987. pap. text 9.95 (*0-920763-27-8*, Pub. by ECW) Genl Dist Srvs.

***Marian Engel's Notebooks: "Ah, Mon Cahier, Ecoute..."** Marian Engel. Ed. by Christl Verduyn. (Life Writing Ser.). 576p. (C). 1999. pap. 28.95 (*0-88920-349-0*) Wilfrid Laurier.

***Marian Engel's Notebooks: "Ah, Mon Cahier, Ecoute..."** Ed. by Christl Verduyn. (Life Writing Ser.: Vol. 8). (Illus.). 576p. 1999. 54.95 (*0-88920-333-4*) Wilfrid Laurier.

Marian Mass Book. 1982. pap. 5.95 (*0-88271-075-3*) Regina Pr.

Marian Mass Book. 1984. 15.95 (*0-88271-084-2*) Regina Pr.

Marian Mass Book, Black/Gold. 1980. pap. 9.95 (*0-88271-079-6*) Regina Pr.

Marian Mass Book, Boys Picture. (J). (gr. 4-7). 1981. pap. 11.95 (*0-88271-082-6*) Regina Pr.

Marian Mass Book, White. 1982. pap. 5.95 (*0-88271-076-1*) Regina Pr.

Marian Mass Book, White. 1985. 4.95 (*0-88271-101-6*) Regina Pr.

Marian Mass Book, White/Gold. (J). (gr. 4-7). 1980. pap. 9.95 (*0-88271-080-X*) Regina Pr.

Marian Mass Book, White/Orange. 1981. 7.95 (*0-88271-078-8*) Regina Pr.

Marian Mass Book, White/Pearl. (J). (gr. 4-7). 1984. pap. 16.95 (*0-88271-083-4*) Regina Pr.

Marian Mass Book for Boys, Black. 1985. 4.95 (*0-88271-100-8*) Regina Pr.

Marian Mass Book for Boys, Black/Gold. 1992. 8.95 (*0-88271-240-3*) Regina Pr.

Marian Mass Book for Girls, White. 1992. 8.95 (*0-88271-239-X*) Regina Pr.

Marian Mass Book for Girls, White/Gold. 1992. 8.95 (*0-88271-241-1*) Regina Pr.

Marian McPartland - Piano Jazz. Ed. by Tony Esposito. 72p. (Orig.). (C). 1993. pap. text 14.95 (*0-7692-0695-6*, TPF0160) Wrner Bros.

Marian McPartland - Piano Jazz 2. 63p. 1992. pap. 14.95 (*0-7692-1156-9*, AF9575) Wrner Bros.

Marian McPartland - Willow Creek. 41p. 1985. pap. 14.95 (*0-7692-1157-7*, TPF0156) Wrner Bros.

***Marian Profile: In the Ecclesiology of Hans Urs von Balthasar.** Brendan Leahy. (Illus.). 2000. pap. 14.95 (*1-56548-139-9*) New City.

Marian Protestantism: Six Studies. Andrew Pettegree. (St. Andrews Studies in Reformation History). 224p. 1996. 86.95 (*1-85928-176-1*, Pub. by Scolar Pr) Ashgate Pub Co.

Marian Reflections: The Angelus Messages of Pope John Paul II. John Paul, II, pseud. Ed. & Anno. by David O. Brown. LC 90-82367. 140p. 1990. 5.95 (*0-911988-96-3*, 38344) AMI Pr.

***Marian Representations in the Miracle Tale of Thirteenth-Century Spain & France.** David A. Flory. LC 99-35484. 2000. 49.95 (*0-8132-0956-0*) Cath U Pr.

***Marian Shrines of the United States Series 1: A Pilgrim's Travel Guide.** Theresa S. Czarnopys & Thomas M. Santa. LC 98-20164. (Illus.). 240p. 1998. pap. 13.95 (*0-7648-0227-5*) Liguori Pubns.

Marian Spirituality of Pope John Paul II. Frederick L. Miller. (Queen of Apostles Ser.: Vol. XII). 19p. 1992. pap. 0.65 (*1-56036-050-X*, 49743) AMI Pr.

Marian Studies: Proceedings, Vol. 31. Mariological Society of America. New York City Con. 238p. 12.00 (*0-318-14800-5*) Mariological Soc.

Marian Studies: Proceedings, Mariological Society of America. Baltimore Convention, 1978, Vol. 29. 206p. 12.00 (*0-318-14794-7*) Mariological Soc.

Marian Studies: Proceedings, Mariological Society of America. New York City Convention, 1970, Vol. 21. 249p. 12.00 (*0-318-14799-8*) Mariological Soc.

Marian Studies: Proceedings, Mariological Society of America. Tampa Convention, 1979, Vol. 30. 198p. 12.00 (*0-318-14803-X*) Mariological Soc.

Marian Studies: Proceedings, Mariological Society of America. Tampa Convention, 1981, Vol. 32. 160p. 12.00 (*0-318-17247-X*) Mariological Soc.

Marian Studies: Proceedings, Mariological Society of America. Washington, D. C. Convention, 1984, Vol. 35. 190p. 12.00 (*0-318-17634-3*) Mariological Soc.

Marian Studies: Proceedings, Mariological Society of America. Washington, D. C. 1987, Vol. 38. 207p. 12.00 (*0-318-23202-2*) Mariological Soc.

Marian Studies Vol. 39: Proceedings. Mariological Society of America, East Aurora Conve. 224p. 12.00 (*0-318-50038-8*) Mariological Soc.

Marian Studies Vol. 40: Proceedings. Mariological Society of America, Burlingame, Calif. 279p. 12.00 (*0-318-50039-6*) Mariological Soc.

Marian Studies Vol. 41: Proceedings. Mariological Society of America, Providence, R. I. 203p. 12.00 (*0-317-04171-1*) Mariological Soc.

Marian Studies - Proceedings Vol. 42: Chicago Convention, 1991. Mariological Society of America Staff. 1991. 12.00 (*0-317-04172-X*) Mariological Soc.

Marian Withers, 3 vols., 1 bk. Geraldine E. Jewsbury. LC 79-8144. reprint ed. 44.50 (*0-404-61948-7*) AMS Pr.

Marian Wright Edelman: Defender of Children's Rights. Steven Otfinoski. LC 91-598. (Famous Women Ser.). (Illus.). 64p. (J). (gr. 4-6). 1992. lib. bdg. 14.95 (*0-8239-1206-X*) Rosen Group.

Marian Wright Edelman: Fighting for Children's Rights. Wendie C. Old. LC 95-7508. (People to Know Ser.). (Illus.). 128p. (YA). (gr. 6 up). 1995. lib. bdg. 20.95 (*0-89490-623-2*) Enslow Pubs.

Marian Wright Edelman: The Making of a Crusader. Beatrice Siegel. LC 94-41245. (Illus.). 160p. (J). (gr. 5-8). 1995. mass mkt. 15.00 (*0-02-782629-5*) S&S Bks Yung.

Marian Wright Edelman, Children's Champion. Joann J. Burch. LC 94-2260. (Gateway Biographies Ser.). (Illus.). 48p. (J). (gr. 2-4). 1994. pap. 6.95 (*1-56294-742-7*); lib. bdg. 20.90 (*1-56294-457-6*) Millbrook Pr.

Mariana. Kearsley. 1995. 6.99 (*0-552-14262-X*) Transworld Publishers Ltd.

Mariana. Susanna Kearsley. 352p. 1995. mass mkt. 5.50 (*0-553-57376-4*, Fanfare) Bantam.

***Mariana & the Merchild: A Folk Tale from Chile.** Caroline Pitcher. LC 99-39926. (Illus.). 32p. (J). (ps-7). 2000. 17.00 (*0-8028-5204-1*, Eerdmans Bks) Eerdmans.

Mariana Mesa: Seven Prehistoric Settlements in West-Central New Mexico. Charles R. McGimsey, III. LC 79-57109. (Peabody Museum Papers: Vol. 72). (Illus.). 298p. 1980. pap. 25.00 (*0-87365-198-7*) Peabody Harvard.

Mariana O el Alba. Rene Marques. (SPA.). 243p. 1968. 7.50 (*0-8288-7059-4*, S5041) Fr & Eur.

Mariana Pineda. Federico Garcia Lorca. (SPA.). 109p. 1969. 15.95 (*0-8288-7147-7*) Fr & Eur.

Mariana Pineda. Federico Garcia Lorca. (SPA.). 230p. 1984. 15.95 (*0-8288-7013-6*, S8991) Fr & Eur.

Mariana Pineda. Federico Garcia Lorca. (SPA.). 368p. 1991. pap. 15.95 (*0-7859-4975-5*) Fr & Eur.

Mariana Pineda. Federico Garcia Lorca & Andres Soria Olmedo. (Nueva Austral Ser.: Vol. 145). (SPA.). pap. 12.95 (*84-239-1945-5*) Elliots Bks.

Mariana Pineda: A Popular Ballad in Three Engravings. Federico Garcia Lorca. Ed. by Robert G. Havard. (Hispanic Classics Ser.). 1987. 59.95 (*0-85668-333-7*, Pub. by Aris & Phillips); pap. 22.00 (*0-85668-334-5*, Pub. by Aris & Phillips) David Brown.

Mariana Pineda - La Savetiere Prodigieuse - Les Amours. Federico Garcia Lorca. (FRE.). 288p. 1984. pap. 15.95 (*0-7859-2493-0*, 2070375897) Fr & Eur.

Mariana Pineda, la Zapatera Prodigiosa, Asi Que Pasen Cinco Anos, Dona Rosita la Soltera, la Casa De Bernarda Alba, Primeras Canciones, Canciones. Federico Garcia Lorca. (SPA.). 1992. pap. 9.95 (*968-432-111-2*) Colton Bk.

Marianela. Benito P. Galdos. (SPA.). pap. 15.95 (*84-206-9985-3*, Pub. by Alianza Editorial) Continental Bk.

Marianela. Benito P. Galdos. (SPA.). pap. 18.50 (*84-376-0380-3*, Pub. by Ediciones Catedra) Continental Bk.

Marianela. Perez Galdos. 1995. pap. text 6.95 (*968-416-731-8*) Fernandez USA.

Marianela, Level 3. Adapted by Benito Perez Galdos. (Leer en Espanol Ser.). (SPA.). (C). 1998. pap. 5.95 (*84-294-3433-X*) Santillana.

Marianela: Classic Spanish Literature. Alberto Romo. (C). 1987. pap. text 14.80 (*0-13-556069-1*) P-H.

Marianela, Miau. Benito P. Galdos. (SPA.). pap. 11.95 (*968-432-292-5*, Pub. by Porrua) Continental Bk.

Marianna Von Martines: Dixit Dominus. Marianna Von Martines. Ed. by Irving Godt. (Recent Researches in Music of the Classic Era Ser.: Vol. RRC48). (Illus.). xiii, 93p. 1997. pap. 35.00 (*0-89579-384-9*) A-R Eds.

Mariannas Prehistory: Archaeological Survey & Excavations on Saipan, Tinian & Rota. Alexander Spoehr. LC 57-12368. (Field Museum of Natural History, Publication 184, Anthropological Ser.: No. 48). 187p. 1957. reprint ed. pap. 58.00 (*0-608-02107-5*, 206275600004) Bks Demand.

Marianne. George Sand. 176p. 1998. pap. 10.95 (*0-7867-0538-8*) Carroll & Graf.

Marianne & the Lords of the East Juliette Benzoni. LC 76-365189. 242 p. 1975. write for info. (*0-434-06609-5*) Buttrwrth-Heinemann.

Marianne Burkhalter & Chrstian Sumi. (Illus.). 176p. 1999. 55.00 (*1-56898-186-4*) Princeton Arch.

Marianne Burkhalter, Christian Sumi: Burkhalter + Sumi. Katja Steiner et al. LC 99-12305. 1999. write for info. (*3-7643-5929-3*) Birkhauser.

Marianne Ehrmann: Reason & Emotion in Her Life & Works. Helga S. Madland. (Women in German Literature Ser.: Vol. 1). X, 340p. (C). 1998. text 57.95 (*0-8204-3929-0*) P Lang Pubng.

Marianne Faithfull's Cigarette. Gerry G. Pearlberg. LC 97-47575. 144p. 1998. pap. 12.95 (*1-57344-034-5*) Cleis Pr.

Marianne Moore see Modern Critical Views Series

Marianne Moore. rev. ed. Bernard F. Engel. 176p. 1988. 32.00 (*0-8057-7525-0*, TUSAS 54, Twyne) Mac Lib Ref.

Marianne Moore: A Descriptive Bibliography. Craig S. Abbott. LC 76-5922. (Series in Bibliography). 280p. 1977. 100.00 (*0-8229-3319-5*) U of Pittsburgh Pr.

Marianne Moore: A Literary Life. Charles Molesworth. 472p. 1991. reprint ed. pap. text 20.00 (*1-55553-115-6*) NE U Pr.

Marianne Moore: An Introduction to the Poetry. George W. Nitchie. LC 79-96998. (Introduction to Twentieth Century American Poetry Ser.). 205p. 1972. pap. text 23.00 (*0-231-08312-2*) Col U Pr.

Marianne Moore: Imaginary Possessions. Bonnie Costello. LC 81-1133. 281p. 1981. 28.00 (*0-674-54848-5*) HUP.

Marianne Moore: Questions of Authority. Cristanne Miller. LC 95-7167. 320p. (C). 1995. 43.00 (*0-674-54862-0*) HUP.

Marianne Moore: The Art of a Modernist. Ed. by Joseph Parisi. LC 89-20476. (Studies in Modern Literature: No. 109). 202p. (C). reprint ed. 62.70 (*0-8357-2031-4*, 207066500016) Bks Demand.

Marianne Moore: The Poetry of Engagement. Grace Schulman. LC 85-21006. 152p. 1987. 24.95 (*0-252-01270-4*) U of Ill Pr.

Marianne Moore: The Poet's Advance. Laurence Stapleton. LC 78-51193. 301p. 1979. reprint ed. pap. 93.40 (*0-608-02903-3*, 206396700008) Bks Demand.

Marianne Moore: Vision into Verse. Patricia C. Willis. (Illus.). 103p. 1987. pap. 18.50 (*0-939084-21-X*) R Mus & Lib.

Marianne Moore: Woman & Poet. Ed. by Patricia C. Willis. LC 90-63357. 636p. 1991. pap. 35.00 (*0-915032-71-6*) Natl Poet Foun.

Marianne Moore: Woman & Poet. Ed. by Patricia C. Willis. LC 90-63357. (Man & Poet Ser.). 636p. 1991. 55.00 (*0-915022-85-0*) Natl Poet Foun.

***Marianne Moore & China: Orientalism & a Writing of America.** Cynthia Stamy. 240p. 2000. text 70.00 (*0-19-818460-3*) OUP.

Marianne Moore & the Visual Arts: Prismatic Color. Linda Leavell. (Illus.). 232p. 1995. text 32.50 (*0-8071-1986-5*) La State U Pr.

Marianne Straub. May Schoeser. 124p. 1987. 80.00 (*0-85072-153-9*) St Mut.

Marianne Williamson on Abundance: Williamson,&Marianne. unabridged ed. Marianne Williamson. 1997. audio 11.00 (*0-694-51659-7*, DCN 10076) HarpC.

Marianne Williamson on Body Vs Spirit: Williamson,&Marianne. unabridged ed. Marianne Williamson. 1997. audio 11.00 (*0-694-51626-0*, DCN 10075) HarperAudio.

Marianne Williamson On Commitment: Williamson,&Marianne. unabridged ed. 1995. audio 11.00 (*0-694-51504-3*, DCN 10044) HarperAudio.

Marianne Williamson on Communication: Williamson,&Marianne. unabridged ed. 1994. audio 11.00 (*1-55994-886-8*, DCN 10011) HarperAudio.

Marianne Williamson on Dealing With Anger: Williamson,&Marianne. abr. ed. Marianne Williamson. (Marianne Williamson Lecture Ser.). 1992. audio 11.00 (*1-55994-713-6*) HarperAudio.

Marianne Williamson on Death & Dying: Williamson,&Marianne. abr. ed. Marianne Williamson. (Marianne Williamson Lecture Ser.). 1992. audio 11.00 (*1-55994-591-5*) HarperAudio.

Marianne Williamson on Emotional Healing: Williamson,&Marianne. unabridged ed. Marianne Williamson. 1996. audio 11.00 (*0-694-51624-4*) HarperAudio.

Marianne Williamson on Forgiving Your Parents: Williamson,&Marianne. unabridged ed. 1994. audio 11.00 (*1-55994-983-X*, DCN 10029) HarperAudio.

Marianne Williamson on Hope & Happiness: Williamson,&Marianne. unabridged ed. 1994. audio 11.00 (*1-55994-720-9*, DCN 10049) HarperAudio.

Marianne Williamson on Intimacy: Williamson,&Marianne. unabridged ed. 1993. audio 11.00 (*1-55994-839-6*, DCN 10001) HarperAudio.

Marianne Williamson on Love: Williamson,&Marianne. abr. ed. Marianne Williamson. (Marianne Williamson Lecture Ser.). 1992. audio 11.00 (*1-55994-714-4*) HarperAudio.

Marianne Williamson On Miracles: Williamson,&Marianne. unabridged ed. 1995. audio 11.00 (*0-694-51506-X*, DCN 10046) HarperAudio.

Marianne Williamson on Money: Williamson,&Marianne. abr. ed. Marianne Williamson. (Marianne Williamson Lecture Ser.). 1993. audio 11.00 (*1-55994-756-X*) HarperAudio.

Marianne Williamson on Relationships: Williamson,&Marianne. abr. ed. Marianne Williamson. (Marianne Williamson Lecture Ser.). 1992. audio 11.00 (*1-55994-589-3*) HarperAudio.

Marianne Williamson on Self-Esteem: Williamson,&Marianne. abr. ed. Marianne Williamson. (Marianne Williamson Lecture Ser.). 1992. audio 11.00 (*1-55994-592-3*) HarperAudio.

Marianne Williamson on Simplicity: Williamson,&Marianne. abr. ed. Marianne Williamson. 1997. audio 11.00 (*0-694-51658-9*, DCN10077) HarperAudio.

Marianne Williamson On Spirituality: Williamson,&Marianne. unabridged ed. 1995. audio 11.00 (*0-694-51505-1*, DCN 10045) HarperAudio.

Marianne Williamson on Success: Williamson,&Marianne. abr. ed. Marianne Williamson. (Marianne Williamson Lecture Ser.). 1993. audio 11.00 (*1-55994-710-1*) HarperAudio.

Marianne Williamson On Transforming Your Life: Williamson,&Marianne. unabridged ed. Marianne Williamson. 1996. audio 11.00 (*0-694-51625-2*, CPN 10074, Caedmon) HarperAudio.

Marianne Williamson on Work/Career: Williamson,&Marianne. abr. ed. Marianne Williamson. (Marianne Williamson Lecture Ser.). 1992. audio 11.00 (*1-55994-590-7*) HarperAudio.

Marianne's Magical Journey. Kathleen G. Rand. (Illus.). 15p. (J). (ps-8). 1998. pap. 6.95 (*1-880710-18-8*) Monterey Pacific.

***Marianne's Smile.** Chris Gutierrez. 2000. pap. write for info. (*1-58235-341-7*) Watermrk Pr.

Mariano Brull y la Poesia Pura en Cuba. Ricardo Larraga. (SPA.). 1994. pap. 19.00 (*0-89729-735-0*) Ediciones.

M

Mariano Cosimo Italian-Latin Dictionary. Mariano Cosimo. (ITA & LAT.). 1644p. 1988. 95.00 (*0-8288-7341-0*) Fr & Eur.
Mariano de Larra & Spanish Political Rhetoric. Pierre L. Ullman. LC 72-133239. 440p. reprint ed. pap. 136.40 (*0-8357-6781-7*, 203545800095) Bks Demand.
Mariano Jose de Larra: A Directory of Historical Personages. Alvin F. Sherman, Jr. (American University Studies: Romance Languages & Literature: Ser. II, Vol. 196). XI, 552p. (C). 1993. text 79.95 (*0-8204-1931-1*) P Lang Pubng.
Marianthe's Story: Painted Words & Spoken Memories (Double Book), 2 bks. in 1. Aliki. LC 97-36312. (Illus.). 64p. (J). (gr. k-3). 1998. 16.00 (*0-688-15661-4*, Grenwillow Bks) HarpC Child Bks.
***Marianthe's Story: Painted Words & Spoken Memories (Double Book), 2 bks. in 1.** Aliki. LC 97-36312. (Illus.). 64p. (J). (gr. k-3). 1998. 15.89 (*0-688-15662-2*, Grenwillow Bks) HarpC Child Bks.
Maria's Bubble Stick. Maria-Natalie Kent. (Illus.). 30p. (Orig.). (J). (gr. 1-6). 1996. pap. 10.95 (*1-879418-91-6*) Audenreed Pr.
Maria's Comet. Deborah Hopkinson. LC 97-46676. (Illus.). 32p. (J). 1999. 16.00 (*0-689-81501-8*) Atheneum Yung Read.
Maria's Girls. Jerome Charyn. 288p. 1993. mass mkt. 5.50 (*0-446-40046-7*, Pub. by Warner Bks) Little.
Maria's Revenge: A Novel. Makeda Silvera. 168p. 1999. pap. 12.95 (*0-88974-084-4*, Pub. by Press Gang Pubs) LPC InBook.
Maria's Secret. June Toretta-Fuentes. LC 92-9866. (Illus.). 32p. (J). 1992. pap. 3.95 (*0-8091-6606-2*) Paulist Pr.
Mariategui & Latin American Marxist Theory. Marc Becker. LC 93-3211. (Monographs in International Studies, Latin America Ser.: No. 20). 239p. (C). 1993. pap. text 20.00 (*0-89680-177-2*) Ohio U Pr.
Mariategui y la Argentina: Un Caso de Lentes Ajenos. Elizabeth Garrels. LC 82-71934. (SPA.). 144p. (Orig.). 1982. pap. 7.25 (*0-935318-08-9*) Edins Hispamerica.
Maribel y la Extrana Familia. Miguel Nijura. (Nueva Austral Ser.: Vol. 123). (SPA.). 1991. pap. text 24.95 (*84-239-1923-4*) Elliots Bks.
Maribor Papers in Naturalized Semantics. Ed. by Dunja Jutronic. LC 98-158522. 428p. (C). 1997. pap. 22.00 (*86-80693-32-4*) Ridgeview.
Maricela de la Luz Lights the World. Jose Rivera. 52p. (J). (gr. 1 up). 1998. pap. 5.50 (*0-87129-894-5*, MB3) Dramatic Pub.
Maricopa Morphology & Syntax. Lynn Gordon. (Publications in Linguistics: Vol. 108). 1986. pap. 30.00 (*0-520-09965-6*, Pub. by U CA Pr) Cal Prin Full Svc.
Mariculture: A Source Guide. 1991. lib. bdg. 76.00 (*0-8490-4885-0*) Gordon Pr.
***Marido de Conveniencia.** Jacqueline Baird.Tr. of Husband of Convenience. (ENG & SPA.). 2000. per. 3.50 (*0-373-33539-3*) Harlequin Bks.
Marido Perfecto (The Perfect Husband) Patty Salier. (SPA.). 1999. mass mkt. 3.50 (*0-373-35274-3*, 1-35274-9) Harlequin Bks.
Marie. Kirsten Thorup. Tr. by Alexander Taylor from DAN. 20p. (Orig.). 1982. pap. 3.00 (*0-917061-11-X*) Top Stories.
Marie: An Invitation to Dance. Kathleen V. Kudlinski. LC 96-15062. (Girlhood Journeys Ser.: No. 3). (J). 1996. pap. 5.99 (*0-689-80985-9*) S&S Childrens.
Marie: An Invitation to Dance. unabridged ed. Kathleen V. Kudlinski. (Girlhood Journeys Ser.). (Illus.). (J). (gr. 6-8). 1996. pap. write for info. (*0-614-22042-4*) Aladdin.
Marie: An Invitation to Dance, France, 1775. Kathleen V. Kudlinski. (Girlhood Journeys Ser.). 1996. 11.19 (*0-606-10823-8*, Pub. by Turtleback) Demco.
Marie: Classic Friendly Tale. Mouse Works Staff. 10p. 1999. bds. 6.99 (*0-7364-1013-9*, Pub. by Mouse Works) Time Warner.
Marie: Summer in the Country, Paris, 1775. Girlhood Journeys, Inc., Staff. LC 97-11101. (Girlhood Journeys Ser.: 3). (Illus.). 69p. (J). (gr. 4-6). 1997. per. 5.99 (*0-689-81562-X*) S&S Childrens.
Marie No. 2: Mystery at the Paris Ballet. Lyn Durham. LC 96-39353. (Girlhood Journeys Ser.: Bk. 2). (J). 1997. 12.95 (*0-689-81205-1*) S&S Childrens.
Marie No. 2: Mystery at the Paris Ballet. Jacqueline D. Greene. (Girlhood Journeys Ser.). (Illus.). (J). (gr. 2-6). 1997. pap. 5.99 (*0-614-29079-1*) Aladdin.
Marie No. 3: An Invitation to Dance. Kathleen V. Kudlinski. (Illus.). 72p. (J). (gr. 2-6). 1996. per. 13.00 (*0-689-81139-X*) S&S Childrens.
***Marie Adrien Persac: Louisiana Artist.** Ed. by H. Parrott Bacot et al. (Illus.). 144p. 2000. 39.95 (*0-8071-2641-1*); pap. 24.95 (*0-8071-2642-X*) La State U Pr.
Marie & Bruce. Wallace Shawn. 1980. pap. 5.25 (*0-8222-0734-6*) Dramatists Play.
Marie & Bruce. Wallace Shawn. LC 80-991. 80p. 1987. pap. 10.00 (*0-8021-3018-6*, Grove) Grove-Atltic.
Marie & Pierre Curie. John Senior. LC 99-185101. (Pocket Biographies Ser.). 1998. pap. 9.95 (*0-7509-1527-7*, Pub. by Sutton Pub Ltd) Intl Pubs Mktg.
Marie Antoinette. Conrad Bishop & Elizabeth Fuller. 62p. (C). 1994. pap. 5.00 (*0-9624511-2-6*) WordWorkers.
***Marie Antoinette.** Fiona MacDonald. (World in the Time of... Ser.). (Illus.). (J). 2000. 17.95 (*0-7910-6034-9*) Chelsea Hse.
Marie Antoinette. Hilaire Belloc. LC 70-37871. (Select Bibliographies Reprint Ser.). 1977. reprint ed. 37.95 (*0-8369-6708-9*) Ayer.
***Marie Antoinette: A Biography.** Evelyne Lever. Tr. by Catherine Temerson from FRE. (Illus.). 352p. 2000. 30.00 (*0-374-19938-8*) FS&G.
***Marie Antoinette: Princess of Versailles, Austria-France 1544.** Kathryn Lasky. LC 99-16804. (Royal Diaries Ser.). (Illus.). 240p. (J). (gr. 4-8). 2000. 10.95 (*0-439-07666-8*) Scholastic Inc.
Marie-Antoinette & Count Fersen: The Untold Love Story. Evelyn Farr. LC 96-145913. (Illus.). 256p. 1996. 39.95 (*0-7206-0960-7*, Pub. by P Owen Ltd) Dufour.
***Marie Barber's 515 Inspirational Cross Stitch Designs.** Marie Barber. LC 98-46796. 1999. 24.95 (*0-8069-6255-0*) Sterling.
Marie Blythe: A Novel. Howard Frank Mosher. (Contemporay American Fiction Ser.). 464p. 1989. pap. 12.95 (*0-14-007659-X*, Penguin Bks) Viking Penguin.
Marie Bonaparte. Celia Bertin. LC 86-51356. 304p. 1987. pap. 17.00 (*0-300-03901-8*, Y-654) Yale U Pr.
Marie Cardinal. Barbara J. Bucknall. 1999. 22.95 (*0-8057-4559-9*, Twyne) Mac Lib Ref.
Marie Cardinal: Les Mots pour le Dire. Ed. by P. Powrie. (FRE.). 1993. pap. 20.95 (*1-85399-336-0*, Pub. by Brist Class Pr) Focus Pub-R Pullins.
Marie Cardinal: Motherhood & Creativity. Lucille Cairns. 296p. 1993. 60.00 (*0-85261-339-3*, Pub. by Univ of Glasgow) St Mut.
Marie-Claire Blais. Mary J. Green. LC 94-44449. (World Authors Ser.: Vol.856). 1995. 32.00 (*0-8057-4547-5*, Twyne) Mac Lib Ref.
Marie Corelli: The Writer & the Woman. F. G. Coates & R. S. Bell. 1977. lib. bdg. 59.95 (*0-8490-2208-8*) Gordon Pr.
Marie Corelli: The Writer & the Woman. T. F. Coates & R. S. Bell. 352p. 1996. reprint ed. pap. 17.25 (*1-56459-693-1*) Kessinger Pub.
Marie Corelli: The Writer & the Woman. T. F. Coates & Warren Bell. 352p. 1996. reprint ed. spiral bd. 18.50 (*0-7873-0186-8*) Hlth Research.
Marie Curie see What Would You Ask?
***Marie Curie.** Beverley Birch. LC 00-8806. (Illus.). 64p. (gr. 4-7). 2000. write for info. (*1-56711-333-8*) Blackbirch.
Marie Curie. Liza N. Burby. LC 96-41734. (Making Their Mark Ser.). (J). 1997. lib. bdg. 15.93 (*0-8239-5024-7*, PowerKids) Rosen Group.
Marie Curie. Leonard Everett Fisher. LC 93-40211. (Illus.). 32p. (J). 1994. mass mkt. write for info. (*0-02-735375-3*, Mac Bks Young Read) S&S Childrens.
Marie Curie. Ibi Lepscky. (Famous People Ser.). (Illus.). 28p. (J). (gr. k-3). 1993. pap. 5.95 (*0-8120-1558-4*) Barron.
Marie Curie. Ibi Lepscky. LC 92-38955. (Famous People Ser.). (Illus.). 28p. (J). (ps-3). 1993. 9.95 (*0-8120-6340-6*) Barron.
Marie Curie. Greg Linder. LC 98-46104. (Photo-Illustrated Biographies Ser.). (Illus.). 1999. write for info. (*0-7368-0206-1*, Bridgestone Bks) Capstone Pr.
Marie Curie. Greg Linder. 1999. 14.00 (*0-516-21764-X*) Capstone Pr.
Marie Curie. Mary Montgomery & Severino Baraldi. (What Made Them Great Ser.). (Illus.). 104p. (J). (gr. 5-8). 1990. lib. bdg. 12.95 (*0-382-09981-8*) Silver Burdett Pr.
Marie Curie. Susan Quinn. 512p. 1996. pap. 17.50 (*0-201-88794-0*) Addison-Wesley.
***Marie Curie.** Dana Meachen Rau. (Early Biographies Ser.). (Illus.). (J). (gr. 1-2). 2000. write for info. (*0-7565-0017-6*) Compass Point.
Marie Curie: A Life. Francoise Giroud. Tr. by Lydia Davis from FRE. LC 85-27241.Tr. of Une Femme Honorable. 350p. 1986. 39.95 (*0-8419-0977-6*) Holmes & Meier.
Marie Curie: And the Science of Radioactivity. Naomi Pasachoff. (Oxford Portraits in Science Ser.). (Illus.). 112p. (YA). (gr. 7 up). 1997. reprint ed. pap. 11.95 (*0-19-512011-6*) OUP.
Marie Curie: Brave Scientist. Keith Brandt. LC 82-16092. (Illus.). 48p. (J). (gr. 4-6). 1996. pap. 3.95 (*0-89375-856-6*) Troll Communs.
Marie Curie: Brave Scientist. Keith Brandt. LC 82-16092. (Illus.). 48p. (J). (gr. 4-6). 1997. lib. bdg. 17.25 (*0-89375-855-8*) Troll Communs.
Marie Curie: Discoverer of Radium. Margaret Poynter. LC 93-21224. (Great Minds of Science Ser.). (Illus.). 128p. (J). (gr. 4-10). 1994. lib. bdg. 20.95 (*0-89490-477-9*) Enslow Pubs.
***Marie Curie & Ann Fullick.** Ann Fullick. LC 00-24352. (J). 2000. lib. bdg. write for info. (*1-57572-374-3*) Heinemann Lib.
Marie Curie & Her Daughter Irene. Rosalynd Pflaum. LC 92-2453. (YA). (gr. 6-9). 1993. lib. bdg. 23.93 (*0-8225-4915-8*, Lerner Publctns) Lerner Pub.
Marie Curie & Radium see Science Discoveries
Marie Curie & Radium. Steve Parker. LC 92-3616. (Science Discoveries Ser.). (Illus.). 32p. (J). (gr. 3-7). 1992. pap. 5.95 (*0-06-446143-2*, HarpTrophy) HarpC Child Bks.
Marie Curie & the Discovery of Radium. Anne Steinke. (Solutions Ser.). (Illus.). 144p. (J). (gr. 3-6). 1987. pap. 6.95 (*0-8120-3924-6*) Barron.
Marie Curie & the Science of Radioactivity: And the Science of Radioactivity. Naomi Pasachoff. (Oxford Scientists Ser.). (Illus.). 112p. (YA). (gr. 7 up). 1996. 22.00 (*0-19-509214-7*) OUP.
Marie Curie, Brave Scientist. Keith Brandt. (J). 1983. 8.70 (*0-606-03118-9*, Pub. by Turtleback) Demco.
Marie Curie's Search for Radium. Beverley Birch. (Science Stories Ser.). (Illus.). 48p. (J). (gr. 4-7). 1996. 10.95 (*0-8120-6621-9*); pap. text 5.95 (*0-8120-9791-2*) Barron.
Marie Curie's Search for Radium. Beverley Birch. (Science Stories Ser.). (Illus.). 48p. (J). (gr. 2-4). 1996. lib. bdg. 14.95 (*1-56674-192-0*) Forest Hse.
Marie Curie's Search for Radium. Beverly Birch. (Science Stories). 1996. 11.15 (*0-606-11598-6*, Pub. by Turtleback) Demco.
***Marie D'Agoult: The Rebel Countess.** Richard Bolster. LC 99-55838. (Illus.). 256p. 2000. 25.00 (*0-300-08246-0*) Yale U Pr.
Marie de France: Lais. Ed. by A. Ewert & T. Hemming Ewert. (French Texts Ser.). (FRE.). 295p. 1995. pap. 19.95 (*1-85399-416-2*, Pub. by Brist Class Pr) Focus Pub-R Pullins.
Marie de France: Thirty-Two Fables. Harriet Spiegel. 1995. reprint ed. pap. text 17.95 (*0-8020-7636-X*) U of Toronto Pr.
Marie de Medicis & the French Court in the Seventeenth Century. Louis Batiffol. Ed. by H. W. Davis. Tr. by Mary King from FRE. LC 72-137368. (Select Bibliographies Reprint Ser.). 1977. reprint ed. 19.95 (*0-8369-5569-2*) Ayer.
Marie Dressler: The Unlikeliest Star. Betty Lee. LC 97-15244. (Illus.). 336p. 1997. 27.50 (*0-8131-2036-5*) U Pr of Ky.
Marie Dubois. Jacques Audiberti. (FRE.). 288p. 1952. pap. 22.95 (*0-7859-0363-1*, F83800) Fr & Eur.
Marie en Cavale. Leandra Logan. (Rouge Passion Ser.: No. 487). (FRE.). 1998. mass mkt. 3.50 (*0-373-37487-9*, 1-37487-5) Harlequin Bks.
Marie-Eve et le Piege a Genies (Leanna Builds a Genie Trap) Hazel J. Hutchins. (Picture Bks.). (FRE., Illus.). 32p. (J). (ps-3). 1996. pap. 5.95 (*1-55037-088-X*, Pub. by Les Editions) Firefly Bks Ltd.
Marie-Gabrielle. Georges Pichard. 136p. 1995. pap. 15.95 (*1-56163-138-8*, Eurotica) NBM.
Marie in Fourth Position: The Story of Degas's "The Little Dancer" Amy Littlesugar. LC 95-40827. (Illus.). 32p. (J). (ps-3). 1996. 15.99 (*0-399-22794-6*, Philomel) Peng Put Young Read.
Marie in Fourth Position: The Story of Degas's "The Little Dancer" Amy Littlesugar. (gr. k up). 1999. pap. 6.99 (*0-698-11769-7*, PapStar) Peng Put Young Read.
Marie-Jo Lafontaine. (Illus.). 52p. 1992. 30.00 (*3-89322-384-3*, Pub. by Edition Cantz) Dist Art Pubs.
Marie-Jo LaFontaine. Marie-Jo Lafontaine. 1999. 42.95 (*3-89322-947-7*) Dist Art Pubs.
Marie Karpovna. Henri Troyat. (FRE.). 1986. pap. 7.95 (*0-7859-3276-3*, 2277219258) Fr & Eur.
Marie Laurencin: Catalogue Raisonne of the Graphic Work. Daniel Marchesseau. (FRE., Illus.). 184p. 1981. pap. 135.00 (*1-55660-064-X*) A Wofsy Fine Arts.
Marie Laurencin: Catalogue Raisonne of the Paintings. Daniel Marchesseau. (FRE., Illus.). 554p. 1986. 575.00 (*1-55660-065-8*) A Wofsy Fine Arts.
Marie Laurencin: Paintings 1903-1946. Daniel Marchesseau. (FRE & JPN., Illus.). 176p. 1980. pap. 95.00 (*0-8150-0028-6*) Wittenborn Art.
Marie Laveau: Voodoo Queen & Folk Tales along the Mississippi. Raymond J. Martinez. 96p. 1983. pap. 7.95 (*0-911116-83-4*) Pelican.
Marie Lloyd: Queen of the Music-Halls. large type ed. Richard A. Baker. (Lythway Ser.). 240p. 1992. 21.50 (*0-7451-1410-5*, G K Hall Lrg Type) Mac Lib Ref.
Marie Magdalens Funeral Teares. Robert Southwell. LC 74-22099. 180p. 1975. 50.00 (*0-8201-1144-9*) Schol Facsimiles.
Marie of Bayou Teche. Billie T. Signer, pseud. (Wind Star Ser.). (Illus.). 128p. (Orig.). (J). (gr. 6-8). 1995. pap. 4.95 (*0-8198-4780-1*) Pauline Bks.
Marie of the Incarnation: Selected Writings. Ed. by Irene Mahoney. (Sources of American Spirituality Ser.). 1989. 24.95 (*0-8091-0428-8*) Paulist Pr.
Marie, or Slavery in the United States. Gustave De Beaumont. LC 98-31234. 282p. 1998. pap. 15.95 (*0-8018-6064-4*) Johns Hopkins.
Marie, or Slavery in the United States: A Novel of Jacksonian America. Gustave A. De Beaumont. Tr. by Barbara Chapman from FRE. xx, 252p. 1958. 35.00 (*0-8047-0545-3*) Stanford U Pr.
Marie: or Slavery in the United States: A Novel of Jacksonian America. Gustave De Beaumont. Tr. by Barbara Chapman from FRE. LC 58-11693. 252p. 1958. reprint ed. pap. 30.00 (*0-608-01658-6*, 2062310) Bks Demand.
Marie Steiner: Her Place in World Karma. Hans P. Van Manen. Tr. by J. Collis. 48p. 1995. pap. 9.95 (*0-904693-76-7*, Pub. by Temple Lodge) Anthroposophic.
Marie Steiner-Von Sivers: Fellow Worker with Rudolf Steiner. Marie Savitch. Tr. by Juliet Compton-Burnett from GER. (Illus.). 239p. 1967. 14.50 (*0-85440-057-5*, Pub. by R Steiner Pr) Anthroposophic.
Marie-Toi, et Huit Autres Scenarios. Boris Vian. (FRE.). 1992. pap. 16.95 (*0-7859-3204-6*, 2264017376) Fr & Eur.
Marie von Ebner-Eschenbach: The Victory of a Tenacious Will. Doris M. Klostermaier. LC 96-34901. (Studies in Austrian Literature, Culture & Thought). 376p. 1997. 39.95 (*1-57241-038-8*) Ariadne CA.
***Marie von Ebner-Eschenbach: 100 Jahre Spater: Eine Analyse Aus der Sicht des Ausgehenden 20, Jahrhunderts Mit Berucksichtigung der Mutterfigur, der Ideologie des Matriarchats und Formaler Aspekte.** Gudrun Gorla. 222p. 1999. 37.95 (*3-906762-22-X*, Pub. by P Lang) P Lang Pubng.
Marie von Egner-Eschenbach: Leben & Werk. Edith Toegel. LC 95-49573. (Austrian Culture Ser.: Vol. 25). (ENG & GER.). VII, 150p. (C). 1997. text 41.95 (*0-8204-3080-3*) P Lang Pubng.
Mariee en Fuite. Sally Carr. (Azur Ser.: Vol. 705). 1998. mass mkt. 3.50 (*0-373-34705-7*, 1-34705-3) Harlequin Bks.
Mariel & the Cookie. Claire J. Saintil. (J). (gr. k-3). 1999. pap. 6.95 (*0-533-12743-2*) Vantage.
***Mariel of Redwall.** Brian Jacques. (Redwall Ser.). (Illus.). 370p. (J). (gr. 8-12). 2000. mass mkt. 6.99 (*0-441-00694-9*) Ace Bks.
Mariel of Redwall. Brian Jacques. LC 91-17157. (Redwall Ser.: Vol. 4). (Illus.). 400p. (J). (gr. 4-7). 1999. mass mkt. 5.99 (*0-380-71922-3*, Avon Bks) Morrow Avon.
Mariel of Redwall. Brian Jacques. LC 91-17157. (Redwall Ser.: Vol. 4). (Illus.). 400p. (J). (gr. 3-7). 1992. 21.99 (*0-399-22144-1*, Philomel) Peng Put Young Read.
***Marieluise Fleisser (1901-1974) et le Theatre Populaire Critique en Allemagne, Vol. 19.** Gerard Thieriot. xii, 387p. 1999. 54.95 (*3-906762-02-5*) P Lang Pubng.
***Marienberg.** Janice Huber Stangl. 2000. write for info. (*1-891193-10-4*) ND State Univ.
Marienkafer. (Meyers Kleine Kinderbibliothek Ser.). 24p. 1991. 13.25 (*3-411-08431-6*, Pub. by Bibliogr Inst Brockhaus) Langenscheidt.
Marienkafer die Wunderbare Verwandlung aus dem Ei see Life of the Ladybug
Marie's Journey. Yvonne Rimmer. LC 98-36364. 128p. 1998. pap. 6.99 (*1-56722-224-2*) Word Aflame.
Marie's Melting Pot: Italian, Sicilian, French, Creole, Spanish & American Recipes. Marie L. Tusa. Ed. by Spielman Company Editors. (Illus.). 288p. 1980. spiral bd. 10.95 (*0-9607062-9-1*) T & M.
Marietta. Francis M. Crawford. (Works of Francis Marion Crawford). 1990. reprint ed. lib. bdg. 79.00 (*0-7812-2552-3*) Rprt Serv.
***Marietta, GA, 1833-2000.** James Bolan Glover, V & Joe McTyre. (Illus.). 128p. 1999. pap. 18.99 (*0-7385-0322-3*) Arcadia Publng.
Marietta Holley. Jane Curry. (Twayne's United States Authors Ser.: vol. 658). 114p. 1995. 32.00 (*0-8057-4020-1*) Macmillan.
Marietta Holley: Life with "Josiah Allen's Wife" Kate H. Winter. (Illus.). 224p. 1984. text 34.95 (*0-8156-2324-0*) Syracuse U Pr.
Marietta, Ohio: The Continuing Erosion of a Speech Island. Thomas L. Clark. (Publications of the American Dialect Society: Vol. 57). 55p. 1974. pap. text 5.85 (*0-8173-0657-9*) U of Ala Pr.
Marietta Wetherill: Life with the Navajos in Chaco Canyon. Ed. by Kathryn Gabriel. LC 97-116. (Illus.). 242p. 1997. pap. 16.95 (*0-8263-1820-7*) U of NM Pr.
Mariette in Ecstasy: A Novel. Ron Hansen. LC 90-56362. 192p. 1994. pap. 12.00 (*0-06-098118-0*, E Burlingame Bks) HarpC.
Mariette Lydis. Henry De Montherlant. (Illus.). 65.75 (*0-685-36997-8*) Fr & Eur.
Marigold. Joan Sisson. (Illus.). 24p. (Orig.). (J). (ps-5). 1988. pap. 4.00 (*0-317-93622-0*) J Sisson.
Marigold. large type ed. Nancy Cato. (Charnwood Ser.). 240p. 1994. 27.99 (*0-7089-8753-2*, Charnwood) Ulverscroft.
Marigold. Grace Livingston Hill. 299p. reprint ed. lib. bdg. 23.95 (*0-89190-056-X*, Rivercity Pr) Amereon Ltd.
Marigold, No. 15. Grace Livingston Hill. (Grace Livingston Hill Ser.: Vol. 15). 256p. 1990. pap. 3.95 (*0-8423-4037-8*) Tyndale Hse.
Marigold: Calendula Officinalis: A Step-by-Step Guide. Jill R. Davies. (In a Nutshell Ser.). 2000. 7.95 (*1-86204-558-5*, Pub. by Element MA) Penguin Putnam.
Marigold: The Music of Billy Mayerl. Peter Dickinson. (Illus.). 328p. 2000. 45.00 (*0-19-816213-8*) OUP.
Marigold & Grandma on the Town. Stephanie Calmenson. (I Can Read Bks.). (Illus.). 64p. (J). (gr. 1-3). 1994. lib. bdg. 15.89 (*0-06-020813-9*) HarpC Child Bks.
Marigold & Grandma on the Town. Stephanie Calmenson. (I Can Read Bks.). (J). (gr. 1-3). 1997. 8.95 (*0-606-10871-8*, Pub. by Turtleback) Demco.
***Marigold Field.** Pearson. 2000. pap. 5.95 (*0-552-10271-7*, Pub. by Transworld Publishers Ltd) Trafalgar.
Marigold Gold: Verses of the Ozarks. Mary E. Mahnkey. Ed. by Ellen Gray Massey. LC 99-73189. 158p. 1999. pap. 9.95 (*0-934426-90-2*) NAPSAC Reprods.
Marigold Poems. Margaret Renkl. 28p. (Orig.). 1992. pap. 5.00 (*1-877801-25-9*) Still Waters.
Marigold Summers. Emma Stirling. 572p. 1995. mass mkt. 11.95 (*0-7472-4604-1*, Pub. by Headline Bk Pub) Trafalgar.
Marigolds for Mourning. Audrey Stallsmith. (Thyme Will Tell Mystery Ser.: Bk. 2). 304p. 1998. pap. 6.95 (*1-57856-054-3*) Waterbrook Pr.
Marigolds for Mourning. large type ed. Audrey Stallsmith. LC 99-32536. 391p. 1999. pap. 22.95 (*0-7862-2062-7*) Mac Lib Ref.
Marigolds in August & the Guest: Two Screenplays. Athol Fugard & Ross Devenish. LC 92-17448. 136p. 1992. reprint ed. pap. 10.95 (*1-55936-059-3*) Theatre Comm.
Marigold's Marriages. Sandra Heath. (Signet Book Ser.). 224p. 1999. mass mkt. 4.99 (*0-451-19682-1*) NAL.
Marihuana: The First Twelve Thousand Years. E. L. Abel. LC 80-15606. (Illus.). 302p. (C). 1980. 44.50 (*0-306-40496-6*, Plenum Trade) Perseus Pubng.
Marihuana - Cannaboids: Neurobiology & Neurophysiology. Ed. by Andrei Bartke. 608p. 1992. boxed set 198.95 (*0-8493-7931-8*, QP801) CRC Pr.
Marihuana, America's New Drug Problem: A Sociologic Question with Its Basic Explanation Dependent on Biologic & Medical Principles. Robert P. Walton & E. M. Geiling. LC 75-17248. (Social Problems & Social Policy Ser.). 1976. 19.95 (*0-405-07523-5*) Ayer.
Marihuana & Medicine. Ed. by Gabriel G. Nahas et al. LC 99-13481. 848p. 1999. 135.00 (*0-89603-593-X*) Humana.
Marihuana-Biological Effects, Analysis, Metabolism, Cellular Responses, Reproduction & Brain: Proceedings of the Satellite Symposium to the International Congress of Pharmacology, 7th, Reims, 1978. International Congress of Pharmacology Staff. Ed. by Gabriel G. Nahas & William D. Paton. (Illus.). 777p. 1979. 100.00 (*0-08-023759-2*, Pergamon Pr) Elsevier.
Marihuana Conviction: A History of Marihuana Prohibition in the United States. Richard J. Bonnie & Charles H. Whitebread. LC 73-89907. 384p. reprint ed. pap. 119.10 (*0-608-13912-2*, 202032200017) Bks Demand.

M

An Asterisk (*) at the beginning of an entry indicates that the title is appearing for the first time.

Marihuana Dictionary: Words, Terms, Events & Persons Relating to Cannabis. Ernest L. Abel. LC 81-13427. 136p. 1982. lib. bdg. 55.00 (*0-313-23252-0*, ABM/, Greenwood Pr) Greenwood.

Marihuana in Science & Medicine. Gabriel G. Nahas. LC 84-11697. 326p. 1984. reprint ed. pap. 101.10 (*0-608-03433-9*, 206413400008) Bks Demand.

Marihuana, Motherhood & Madness: Three Screenplays from the Exploitation Cinema of Dwain Esper. Ed. by Bret Wood & Anthony Slide. LC 97-31262. (Illus.). 272p. 1998. 38.00 (*0-8108-3375-1*) Scarecrow.

Marihuana Reconsidered. 2nd ed. Lester Grinspoon. 474p. 1994. pap. 19.95 (*0-932551-13-0*) Quick Am Pub.

Marihuana the Burning Bush of Moses: Mysticism & Cannabis Experience. Robert Thorne. LC 99-94818. xvi, 400p. 1999. pap. 22.95 (*0-9671056-0-9*) Clarus Bks.

Marihuana, the Forbidden Medicine. James B. Bakalar & Lester Grinspoon. 1995. pap. 13.00 (*0-300-05994-9*) Yale U Pr.

Marihuana, the Forbidden Medicine. rev. ed. Lester Grinspoon & James B. Bakalar. LC 97-981. 312p. 1997. pap. 16.00 (*0-300-07086-1*) Yale U Pr.

Marihuana, the Forbidden Medicine. rev. ed. Lester Grinspoon & James B. Bakalar. LC 97-981. 312p. 1997. 35.00 (*0-300-07085-3*) Yale U Pr.

Marihuana, Tobacco, Alcohol, & Reproduction. Ernest L. Abel. 256p. 1983. 146.00 (*0-8493-6480-9*, RG580, CRC Reprint) Franklin.

Marii Victorini: Opera Theologica. Ed. by Locher. (LAT.). 1976. 39.50 (*3-322-00185-7*, T1929, Pub. by B G Teubner) U of Mich Pr.

Marii VictoriniCommentarii in Epistulas Pauli: Ad Galatas, Ad Philippenses, Ad Ephesios. Ed. by Locher. (LAT.). 1972. 36.50 (*3-322-00186-5*, T1928, Pub. by B G Teubner) U of Mich Pr.

Marijke Van Warmerdam: Single, Double, Crosswise. Text by Lynn Cooke & Kees van Gelder. LC 99-213630. (Illus.). 96p. 1999. 44.00 (*90-70149-70-2*, 915028, Pub. by S V Abbemuseum) Dist Art Pubs.

Marijuana. Ed. by William Dudley. LC 98-35006. (At Issue Ser.). 96p. (YA). (gr. 9-12). 1998. lib. bdg. 19.95 (*0-7377-0007-6*) Greenhaven.

***Marijuana.** Ed. by William Dudley. LC 98-35006. (At Issue Ser.). 95p. (YA). (gr. 9-12). 1998. pap. 12.45 (*0-7377-0006-8*) Greenhaven.

Marijuana. M. S. Gold. LC 88-32427. (Drugs of Abuse: Vol. 1). (Illus.). 276p. (C). 1989. text 42.50 (*0-306-43062-2*, Kluwer Plenum) Kluwer Academic.

Marijuana. Ed. by Steven L. Jaffe. LC 98-51362. (Illus.). 80p. (J). (gr. 4-8). 1999. lib. bdg. 19.95 (*0-7910-5176-5*) Chelsea Hse.

***Marijuana.** Angela Royston. LC 99-88168. (Learn to Say No! Ser.). (Illus.). (J). 2000. lib. bdg. write for info. (*1-57572-238-0*) Heinemann Lib.

Marijuana. Elizabeth Schleichert. (Drug Library Ser.). (Illus.). 104p. (YA). (gr. 6 up). 1996. lib. bdg. 20.95 (*0-89490-740-9*) Enslow Pubs.

Marijuana. Sandra L. Smith. (Drug Abuse Prevention Library). 64p. (gr. 7-12). 1997. pap. 6.95 (*1-56838-167-0*, 1759 A) Hazelden.

Marijuana. rev. ed. David L. Ohlms. Ed. & Intro. by GWC, Inc. Staff. 17p. 1993. 2.50 (*1-56168-030-3*, B106) GWC Inc.

***Marijuana.** rev. ed. Sandra Lee Smith. (Drug Abuse Prevention Library). (Illus.). 64p. (YA). (gr. 7-12). 1999. 17.95 (*0-8239-3007-6*) Rosen Group.

Marijuana: A Dangerous "High" Way. rev. ed. Barbara H. Leahy. Ed. by Lee Farrell et al. LC 82-62440. (Illus.). 173p. (Orig.). (J). (gr. 4-9). 1983. pap. 6.95 (*0-9610312-1-2*) B Leahy.

Marijuana: A Short Course Updated for the Eighties. Paul R. Robbins. LC 75-22753. 80p. 1983. pap. 11.95 (*0-8283-1856-5*) Branden Bks.

Marijuana: Costs of Abuse, Costs of Control, 22. Mark A. Kleiman. LC 88-7712. (Contributions in Criminology & Penology Ser.). 217p. 1989. 49.95 (*0-313-25853-8*, KCM, Greenwood Pr) Greenwood.

Marijuana: Facts for Teens. 16p. 1996. pap. 33.00 (*0-16-061511-9*) USGPO.

Marijuana: Facts Parents Need to Know. 28p. 1996. pap. 48.00 (*0-16-061510-0*) USGPO.

Marijuana: Facts Parents Need to Know. Government Printing Office Staff. 28p. 1996. pap. 2.00 (*0-16-048873-7*) USGPO.

Marijuana: Health Effects. rev. ed. Sara Macintosh. 2000. pap. 0.50 (*0-89230-161-9*) Do It Now.

Marijuana: Its Effects on Mind & Body. William J. Hermes & Anne Galperin. (Encyclopedia of Psychoactive Drugs Ser.: No. 1). (Illus.). 124p. (YA). (gr. 7 up). 1992. lib. bdg. 19.95 (*0-87754-754-8*) Chelsea Hse.

Marijuana: Medical Uses. Jim Parker. 1999. pap. 0.50 (*0-89230-159-7*) Do It Now.

Marijuana: Not Guilty As Charged. David R. Ford. 260p. 1997. 24.95 (*0-9655932-5-8*, Pub. by Good Press) ACCESS Pubs Network.

Marijuana: Personality & Behavior. rev. ed. Sara Macintosh. 2000. pap. 0.50 (*0-89230-160-0*) Do It Now.

Marijuana: Your Legal Rights. Richard Moller. LC 81-621. 1981. pap. 9.95 (*0-201-04777-2*) Addison-Wesley.

Marijuana & AIDS: Pot, Politics & PWAs in America. Robert C. Randall. LC 91-77140. 183p. (Orig.). 1991. pap. 12.95 (*0-936485-07-8*, Galen Pr DC) Lkng Glass Pubns.

Marijuana & Medicine: Assessment of the Science Base. Institute of Medicine Staff. Ed. by John A. Benson et al. LC 99-6484. 288p. 1999. 39.95 (*0-309-07155-0*) Natl Acad Pr.

Marijuana & the Workplace: Interpreting Research on Complex Social Issues. Ed. by Charles R. Schwenk & Susan L. Rhodes. LC 99-27819. 208p. 1999. 59.95 (*1-56720-291-8*, Quorum Bks) Greenwood.

***Marijuana as Medicine: The Science Beyond the Controversy.** Alison Mack. 240p. 1999. pap. 16.95 (*0-309-06531-3*, Joseph Henry Pr) Natl Acad Pr.

Marijuana Beer. Ed Rosenthal. (Illus.). 53p. 1996. pap. 14.95 (*0-932551-22-X*) Quick Am Pub.

Marijuana Botany. 3rd ed. Robert C. Clarke. (Illus.). 197p. 1995. pap. 24.95 (*0-914171-78-X*) Ronin Pub.

Marijuana Chemistry. 2nd ed. Michael Starks. 199p. 1990. pap. 22.95 (*0-914171-39-9*) Ronin Pub.

Marijuana Conspiracy: The Truth about Marijuana, a Natural Resource. 1991. lib. bdg. 250.00 (*0-8490-4659-9*) Gordon Pr.

Marijuana Conviction: History of Marijuana Prohibition. Richard J. Bonnie & Charles H. Whitebread, II. LC 99-15034. 368p. 1999. pap. text 14.95 (*1-891385-06-2*, Pub. by Open Soc Inst) BookWorld.

Marijuana Drug Dangers. Gary L. Somdahl. LC 98-51536. (Drug Dangers Ser.). (Illus.). 64p. (YA). (gr. 4-10). 1999. lib. bdg. 19.95 (*0-7660-1214-X*) Enslow Pubs.

***Marijuana Drug Dangers.** Gary L. Somdahl. LC 98-51536. (Drug Dangers Ser.). (Illus.). 64p. (YA). (gr. 4-10). 1999. pap. 10.95 (*0-7660-1740-0*) Enslow Pubs.

Marijuana Effects on the Endocrine & Reproductive Systems. 1986. lib. bdg. 250.00 (*0-8490-3518-X*) Gordon Pr.

Marijuana Flower Forcing: Secrets of Designer Growing. Tom Flowers. (Illus.). 144p. (Orig.). 1997. pap. text 16.95 (*0-9647946-1-6*) Flowers Pubng.

Marijuana Grower's Guide Deluxe. 4th rev. ed. Mel Frank. LC 96-231573. (Illus.). 352p. 1997. reprint ed. pap. 19.95 (*0-929349-03-2*); reprint ed. spiral bd. 23.95 (*0-929349-04-0*) Red Eye Pr.

Marijuana Grower's Handbook: The Indoor High Yield Guide. 3rd ed. Ed Rosenthal. (Illus.). 282p. 1998. pap. text 19.95 (*0-932551-25-4*) Quick Am Pub.

Marijuana Grower's Handbook: The Indoor High Yield Guide. 3rd rev. ed. Ed Rosenthal. (Illus.). 282p. 1998. spiral bd. 23.95 (*0-932551-26-2*) Quick Am Pub.

Marijuana Grower's Insider's Guide. Mel Frank. Ed. by Aidan Kelly. (Illus.). 369p. (Orig.). (C). 1988. pap. 19.95 (*0-929349-00-8*) Red Eye Pr.

Marijuana Growing Tips. Ed Rosenthal. (Illus.). 128p. 1986. reprint ed. pap. 12.95 (*0-932551-05-X*) Quick Am Pub.

Marijuana Growing Tips. 2nd ed. Ed Rosenthal. (Illus.). 111p. 1999. pap. 12.95 (*0-932551-31-9*) Quick Am Pub.

Marijuana Herbal Cookbook: Recipes for Recreation & Health. Tom Flowers. (Illus.). 96p. (Orig.). 1995. pap. 14.95 (*0-9647946-0-8*) Flowers Pubng.

Marijuana Horticulture Indoors. (Drug Abuse Ser.). 1991. lib. bdg. 78.95 (*0-8490-4716-1*) Gordon Pr.

Marijuana Hydroponics: High Tech Water Culture. Daniel Storm. (Illus.). 120p. 1987. pap. 16.95 (*0-914171-07-0*) Ronin Pub.

***Marijuana in the Movies: The Complete Guide to the Hollywood High.** Kip Kay. 136p. (C). 1999. write for info. (*0-9674705-0-1*) MediaGreen.

Marijuana Jail Terms: Costly & Hasty. David B. Kopel. (Issue Papers: No. 5-91). 1991. pap. text 8.00 (*1-57655-040-0*) Independ Inst.

Marijuana Law: A Comprehensive Legal Manual. 2nd rev. ed. Richard G. Boire. (Illus.). 288p. (Orig.). 1996. pap. 15.95 (*0-914171-86-0*) Ronin Pub.

Marijuana Medical Handbook: A Guide to Therapeutic Use. Ed Rosenthal et al. 270p. 1996. pap. 16.95 (*0-932551-16-5*) Quick Am Pub.

***Marijuana Medicine: A World Tour of the Healing & Visionary Powers of Cannabis.** Christian Ratsch. (Illus.). 224p. 2001. pap. 24.95 (*0-89281-933-2*) Inner Tradit.

Marijuana, Medicine & the Law: Direct Testimony of Witnesses on Marijuana's Medical Use. Ed. by Richard C. Randall. LC 88-80330. 502p. (Orig.). 1988. pap. 29.95 (*0-936485-02-7*, Galen Pr DC) Lkng Glass Pubns.

Marijuana, Medicine & the Law Vol. II: The Legal Argument. Ed. by Richard C. Randall. LC 88-80330. 484p. (Orig.). pap. 25.95 (*0-936485-04-3*, Galen Pr DC) Lkng Glass Pubns.

Marijuana Mystery: A Novel. Guy Mount. 168p. 1993. per. 9.95 (*0-9604462-8-1*) Sweetlight.

Marijuana Myths Marijuana Facts: A Review of the Scientific Evidence. Lynn Zimmer. pap. 12.95 (*0-9641568-4-9*, 578-003) Open Soc Inst.

Marijuana Question? Ask Ed: The Encyclopedia of Marijuana. Ed Rosenthal. (Illus.). 284p. 1987. reprint ed. pap. 19.95 (*0-932551-01-7*) Quick Am Pub.

Marijuana Reappraised: Two Personal Accounts. Martin Croes & Andre McNicoll. LC 77-15695. 20p. 1977. pap. 1.00 (*0-913098-08-6*) Orion Society.

Marijuana Research Findings. 1992. lib. bdg. 88.95 (*0-8490-8823-2*) Gordon Pr.

Marijuana Research Findings: Marijuana Chemistry, Metabolism & Its Effect on Human Health. 1992. lib. bdg. 79.00 (*0-8490-5463-X*) Gordon Pr.

***Marijuana Run.** Joseph Hawkins. 264p. 2000. pap. 13.95 (*0-9637583-2-2*) Sunrise Pr GA.

Marijuana Rx: The Patients' Fight for Medicinal Pot. Robert C. Randall & Alice M. O'Leary. LC 98-27499. 528p. 1999. pap. 14.95 (*1-56025-166-2*, Thunders Mouth) Avalon NY.

Marijuana Softdrink. Buck Downs. 1999. pap. 11.00 (*1-890311-02-2*, Pub. by Edge Bks) SPD-Small Pr Dist.

Marijuana Use in America: Hearing Before the Committee on the Judiciary, U. S. House of Representatives. Composed by Diane Publishing Staff. (Illus.). 191p. (C). 1998. pap. text 35.00 (*0-7881-4921-0*) DIANE Pub.

***Marika - A Bulgarian Odyssey: Adventures of Bulgarian Dreamers.** Joanne Temcov. LC 99-61927. (Illus.). 216p. 1999. pap. 28.00 (*0-9651935-1-9*, Prmetheus Pr) Fisher Ent.

***Marika - a Bulgarian Odyssey: Adventures of Bulgarian Dreamers.** Joanne L. Temcov. LC 99-61927. (Illus.). 216p. 1999. 28.00 (*0-9651935-2-7*, Prmetheus Pr) Fisher Ent.

Mariken van Nieumeghen. Ed. by Therese Decker & Martin Walsh. (Medvl Ser.). viii, 144p. 1994. 55.00 (*1-879751-20-8*) Camden Hse.

***Marikes World.** Catherine M. Rae. 2000. text 21.95 (*0-312-26199-3*) St Martin.

Mariko Mori. Dominic Molon et al. LC 98-8268. (Illus.). 80p. 1998. pap. 20.00 (*0-933856-57-1*) Mus Art Chicago.

Mariko Wears Her Thinking Cap. Carol Apacki et al. (Illus.). 24p. (J). (gr. k-2). 1993. pap. text 12.95 (*1-56095-083-8*) Quest Intl.

Marilu Henner's Total Health Makeover. Marilu Henner. 480p. 1999. mass mkt. 6.99 (*0-06-109828-0*) HarpC.

Marilu Henner's Total Health Makeover: Ten Steps to Your B. E. S. T. Body. Marilu Henner & Laura Morton. LC 98-158673. 352p. 1998. 24.00 (*0-06-039216-9*, ReganBks) HarperTrade.

***Marilu Henner's Total Health Makeover: Ten Steps to Your B. E. S. T. Body.** unabridged ed. Marilu Henner & Laura Morton. 1998. audio 12.00 (*0-694-51927-8*) HarperAudio.

Marilyn. Marie Cahill. (Illus.). 64p. 1994. write for info. (*1-57215-031-9*) World Pubns.

***Marilyn.** Diana Karanikas Harvey. LC 98-47387. (Life in Pictures Ser.). (Illus.). 11p. 1999. 13.98 (*1-56799-774-0*) M Friedman Pub Grp Inc.

Marilyn. Marilyn Monroe. 176p. 1995. pap. 14.95 (*0-85965-145-2*, Pub. by Plexus) Publishers Group.

Marilyn. Gloria Steinem. (Illus.). 182p. 1996. reprint ed. 14.98 (*1-56731-125-3*, MJF Bks) Fine Comms.

Marilyn: A Hollywood Farewell: The Death & Funeral of Marilyn Monroe. Leigh A. Wiener. Ed. by Phil Syracopoulos & Joyce W. Wiener. (Illus.). 94p. 1990. 100.00 (*0-9619146-3-7*) Seventy Four Ten.

Marilyn: Her Life & Legend. 256p. 1991. 29.99 (*0-88176-825-1*) Pubns Intl Ltd.

Marilyn: Shades of Blonde. Carole Nelson Douglas. 1998. pap. 15.95 (*0-312-86688-7*) St Martin.

Marilyn: Story of a Woman. Kathryn Hyatt. (Illus.). 144p. 1996. pap. 14.95 (*1-888363-06-1*) Seven Stories.

Marilyn: The Encyclopedia. Adam Victor. LC 99-37838. 352p. 1999. 55.00 (*0-87951-718-2*, Pub. by Overlook Pr) Penguin Putnam.

Marilyn: The Last Take. Peter H. Brown & Patte B. Barham. 23.00 (*0-685-61645-2*, Dutt) Dutton Plume.

***Marilyn: The Last 24 Hours.** Allan Silverman. (Illus.). 2000. pap. 9.95 (*1-902588-07-X*) Glitter Bks.

Marilyn: Ultimate Look at the Legend. James Haspiel. (Illus.). 208p. 1995. pap. 19.95 (*0-8050-2965-6*) H Holt & Co.

Marilyn - Her Life in Her Own Words: Marilyn Monroe's Revealing Last Words & Photographs. Photos & Compiled by George Barris. LC 95-19254. (Illus.). 192p. 1995. 24.95 (*1-55972-306-8*, Birch Ln Pr) Carol Pub Group.

Marilyn & Me: Sisters, Rivals, Friends. Susan Strasberg. 288p. 1993. mass mkt. 5.99 (*0-446-36425-8*, Pub. by Warner Bks) Little.

Marilyn Bridges: The Sacred & the Secular: A Decade of Aerial Photography. Ed. by Anne H. Hoy & Tom Bridges. (Illus.). 94p. (Orig.). 1991. pap. 19.95 (*0-933642-13-X*) Intl Ctr Photo.

Marilyn by Moonlight. Jack Allen. (Illus.). 1996. 50.00 (*0-614-20389-9*, Barclay House) Zinn Pub Grp.

Marilyn by Moonlight: A Remembrance in Rare Photos. Jack Allen. LC 96-19148. 1996. 50.00 (*0-935016-45-7*) Zinn Pub Grp.

Marilyn Conspiracy. Milo A. Speriglio. 1986. pap. 3.50 (*0-671-62612-4*) PB.

Marilyn Had Hands Full of Eyes. Al Miltal. (Orig.). 1989. pap. 5.00 (*0-941720-66-7*) Slough Pr TX.

Marilyn la Dingue. Jerome Charyn.Tr. of Marilyn the Wild. (FRE.). 246p. 1988. pap. 10.95 (*0-7859-2106-0*, 2070380920) Fr & Eur.

Marilyn Manson: God of Fuck. Kurt Reighley. LC 97-46172. 192p. 1998. pap. 10.95 (*0-312-18133-7*) St Martin.

***Marilyn Manson: In His Own Words.** Chuck Weiner. (Illus.). 96p. 2000. pap. 15.95 (*0-7119-7916-2*, OP48168) Omnibus NY.

Marilyn Manson: The Unauthorized Biography. Kalen Rogers. 78p. 1997. pap. 19.95 (*0-8256-1643-3*, OP48034) Omnibus NY.

Marilyn Miglin. Marilyn Miglin. 192p. 2000. write for info. (*1-886094-68-3*) Chicago Spectrum.

Marilyn Monroe see Pop Culture Legends

Marilyn Monroe. Ariel Books Staff. (Illus.). 80p. 1995. 4.95 (*0-8362-3115-5*, Arie Bks) Andrews & McMeel.

Marilyn Monroe. Barbara Leaming. LC 98-18738. (Illus.). 448p. 1998. 27.50 (*0-517-70260-6*) Crown Pub Group.

***Marilyn Monroe.** Barbara Leaming. 464p. 2000. pap. 15.00 (*0-609-80553-3*, Three Riv Pr) Crown Pub Group.

Marilyn Monroe. Sheridan Morley & Ruth Leon. (Get a Life...Pocket Biographies Ser.). (Illus.). 1997. pap. 9.95 (*0-7509-1510-2*, Pub. by Sutton Pub Ltd) Intl Pubs Mktg.

Marilyn Monroe. Adam Woog. LC 96-22300. (Mysterious Deaths Ser.). (Illus.). (YA). 1997. lib. bdg. 22.45 (*1-56006-265-7*) Lucent Bks.

Marilyn Monroe: A Biography. Dan Spoto. (Illus.). 864p. 1994. mass mkt. 6.99 (*0-06-109166-9*, Harp PBks) HarpC.

Marilyn Monroe: A Life of the Actress. Carl E. Rollyson. LC 86-11322. (Studies in Cinema: No. 39). (Illus.). 269p. reprint ed. pap. 83.40 (*0-8357-1771-2*, 207052000097) Bks Demand.

Marilyn Monroe: A Life of the Actress. Carl E. Rollyson, Jr. (Illus.). 269p. 1993. reprint ed. pap. 14.95 (*0-306-80542-1*) Da Capo.

Marilyn Monroe: A Postcard Book. Ed. by Running Press Staff. (Postcard Bks.). (Illus.). 64p. (Orig.). 1989. pap. text 8.95 (*0-89471-766-9*) Running Pr.

Marilyn Monroe: Cover-To-Cover. Clark Kidder. LC 99-60080. 160p. 1999. pap. 24.95 (*0-87341-740-2*) Krause Pubns.

Marilyn Monroe: From Beginning to End. Michael Ventura. (Illus.). 144p. pap. 14.95 (*0-7137-2738-1*, Pub. by Blandford Pr) Sterling.

Marilyn Monroe: From Beginning to End. Michael Ventura. (Illus.). 144p. 1997. 24.95 (*0-7137-2686-5*, Pub. by Blandford Pr) Sterling.

Marilyn Monroe: Murder Cover-Up. Milo A. Speriglio. LC 82-51319. (Illus.). 276p. (Orig.). 1983. pap. 7.95 (*0-930990-77-3*) Seville Pub.

Marilyn Monroe: Norma Jean's Dream. Katherine E. Krohn. LC 96-26526. (J). 1996. lib. bdg. 23.93 (*0-8225-4930-1*) Lerner Pub.

Marilyn Monroe: Photographs, 1945-1962. Schirmer's Visual Library Staff. (Schirmer's Visual Library). (Illus.). 1998. pap. 13.95 (*0-393-30938-X*, Norton Paperbks) Norton.

Marilyn Monroe: Poems by Lyn Lifshin. Lyn Lifshin. Ed. by Brian C. Hamilton & Lynn D. DelMargo. 143p. (Orig.). 1994. pap. 8.95 (*1-882550-02-1*) Quiet Lion Pr.

Marilyn Monroe: Price & Identification Guide. 4th rev. ed. Denis C. Jackson. 56p. 2000. pap. 8.95 (*1-888687-07-X*) Illust Collectors.

Marilyn Monroe: The Body in the Library. Graham McCann. LC 87-26522. (Illus.). 220p. (C). 1988. pap. 14.95 (*0-8135-1303-0*) Rutgers U Pr.

Marilyn Monroe: The Collector's & Dealer's Price & Identification Guide. 3rd rev. ed. Denis C. Jackson. 52p. (Orig.). 1996. pap. 8.95 (*1-888687-01-0*) Illust Collectors.

***Marilyn Monroe: The Complete Last Sitting.** Bert Stern. (Illus.). 464p. 2000. 125.00 (*3-8238-5483-6*) te Neues.

Marilyn Monroe - Paper Dolls. Tom Tierney. (J). 1998. pap. 4.95 (*0-486-23769-9*) Dover.

Marilyn Monroe & Other Poems. Ernesto Cardenal. 136p. 1994. pap. 21.00 (*0-85532-358-2*, Pub. by Srch Pr) St Mut.

***Marilyn Monroe & the Camera.** Jane Russell. (Illus.). 245p. 2000. pap. 35.00 (*3-8238-5467-4*) te Neues.

***Marilyn Monroe Collectibles: A Comprehensive Guide to the Memorabilia of an American Legend.** Clark Kidder. (Confident Collector Ser.). 336p. 1999. pap. 15.00 (*0-380-79909-X*, Avon Bks) Morrow Avon.

Marilyn Monroe in Hollywood: A Guide. Marsha Bellavance-Johnson. (Famous Footsteps Ser.). (Illus.). (Orig.). 1992. pap. 4.95 (*0-929709-10-1*) Computer Lab.

***Marilyn Monroe Story.** Jesse Monroe Walker. 20p. 1999. pap. write for info. (*1-882194-58-6*) TN Valley Pub.

Marilyn, Norma Jean & Me. large type ed. Joseph Ajlouny. 54p. 1999. pap. 7.95 (*0-929957-14-8*, Push-Pull Pr) JSA Pubns.

***Marilyn Price & Friends Present the Alphabet from Alef to Bet.** Joel Lurie Grishaver et al. (HEB., Illus.). 96p. (J). (gr. k-3). 1998. pap. 9.95 (*0-933873-99-9*) Torah Aura.

Marilyn Tapes. E. J. Gorman. 416p. 1995. mass mkt. 5.99 (*0-8125-2236-2*, Pub. by Forge NYC) St Martin.

Marilyn the Wild see Marilyn la Dingue

Marilyn Wood's Wonderful Weekends. 3rd ed. Marilyn Wood. 688p. 1996. 17.95 (*0-02-860929-8*, Pub. by Macmillan) S&S Trade.

Marilyn's Machine-Stitched Sew Simple Quilts! Marilyn Greene. (Spiraling Log Cabin Design Ser.). (Illus.). 62p. (C). 1986. 12.95 (*0-9614798-1-7*) Dav-A-Lynn Ent.

Marilyn's Machine-Stitched Sew Simple Quilts! Fly'n Geese 'n Rainbows. Marilyn Greene. (Illus.). 56p. 1988. 12.95 (*0-9614798-3-3*) Dav-A-Lynn Ent.

Marilyn's Machine-Stitched Sew Simple Quilts! Squares n' Strips. Marilyn Greene. (Illus.). 58p. 1987. 12.95 (*0-9614798-2-5*) Dav-A-Lynn Ent.

Marimba. 1994. write for info. (*92-806-3038-5*) U N I C E.

Marimba. Richard Hoyt. 352p. 1993. mass mkt. 4.99 (*0-8125-1563-3*) Tor Bks.

Marimba de Guatemala: Te' son, Chinab' o K'ojom. 2nd ed. Jose B. Camposeco. (SPA., Illus.). 95p. 1995. pap. 4.75 (*1-886502-02-1*, Ediciones Yax Te) Yax Te Found.

Marin. Photos by Hal Lauritzen. (Illus.). 120p. 1996. pap. 18.95 (*0-8118-1424-6*) Chronicle Bks.

Marin. Photos by Hal Lauritzen. (Illus.). 120p. 1993. 35.00 (*0-8118-0022-9*) Chronicle Bks.

Marin Bike Paths: A Guide to Easy Rides & Interesting Sights. rev. ed. Tacy Dunham. (Marin Trail Guide Ser.). (Illus.). 56p. (Orig.). 1989. reprint ed. pap. 6.95 (*0-685-27208-7*) Cttnwd Pr.

Marin Coast: The Enchanted Coast. 1992. 4.95 (*0-916310-04-3*) North of San Francisco.

Marin County Bike Trails: Easy to Challenging Bicycle Rides for Touring & Mountain Bikes. Phyllis L. Neumann. (Bay Area Bike Trails Ser.). (Illus.). 128p. (Orig.). 1996. pap. 12.95 (*0-9621694-0-4*) Penngrove Pubns.

Marin County Breeding Bird Atlas: A Distributional & Natural History of Coastal California Birds. W. David Shuford. (California Avifauna Ser.: No. 1). (Illus.). 479p. (Orig.). 1993. pap. 24.95 (*0-9633050-0-X*) Bushtit Bks.

Marin County Jail Alternatives. 7.00 (*0-318-20311-1*) Natl Coun Crime.

Marin County Street Guide & Directory: 1999 Edition. Thomas Bros. Maps Staff. (Illus.). 64p. 1998. pap. 16.95 (*1-58174-024-7*) Thomas Bros Maps.

***Marin County Street Guide & Directory: 2000 Edition.** (Illus.). 64p. 1999. pap. 16.95 (*1-58174-129-4*) Thomas Bros Maps.

Marin de Gibraltar. Marguerite Duras. (FRE.). 1977. pap. 13.95 (*0-8288-3638-8*, F99870) Fr & Eur.
Marin de Gibraltar. Marguerite Duras. (Folio Ser.: No. 943). (FRE.). 429p. 1977. 10.95 (*2-07-036943-9*) Schoenhof.
Marin Flora: Manual of the Flowering Plants & Ferns of Marin County, California. 2nd ed. John T. Howell. LC 71-100608. 1970. pap. 19.95 (*0-520-05621-3*, Pub. by U CA Pr) Cal Prin Full Svc.
Marin Headlands: Portals of Time. Harold Gilliam & Ann Gilliam. (Illus.). 56p. 1993. pap. 7.95 (*1-883869-13-7*) Gldn Gate Natl Parks Assoc.
Marin Headlands Trail Guide: Golden Gate National Recreation Area. rev. ed. Tacy Dunham. (Marin Trail Guide Ser.). (Illus.). 56p. 1989. reprint ed. pap. 6.95 (*0-685-27204-4*) Cttnwd Pr.
Marin Kasimir: Fragments of Longing. (Illus.). 120p. 1990. pap. 30.00 (*90-72191-13-7*, Pub. by Imschoot) Dist Art Pubs.
Marin Marais: Six Suites for Violin Thorough Bass. Marin Marais. Ed. by Gordon J. Kinney. (Recent Researches in Music of the Baroque Era Ser.: Vol. RRB21-22). (Illus.). xxi, 126p. 1976. pap. 55.00 (*0-89579-069-6*, RRB21-22) A-R Eds.
Marin Mountain Bike Guide. A. Todd. (Illus.). 135p. 1998. 12.95 (*0-9623537-6-0*) A Todd.
Marin Mountain Bike Guide. Armor Todd. (Illus.). 110p. 1995. pap. 10.95 (*0-9623537-5-2*) A Todd.
***Marin, Napa & Sonoma 2000.** Don McCormack. (Illus.). 1999. pap. 13.95 (*1-929365-03-9*, Pub. by McCormacks Guides) Bookpeople.
Marin Rejete par la Mer. Yukio Mishima, pseud. (FRE.). 1979. pap. 10.95 (*0-7859-4122-3*) Fr & Eur.
Marina: A Dramatic Romance. William Shakespeare. LC 71-177860. reprint ed. 31.50 (*0-404-06904-5*) AMS Pr.
Marina: The Story of a Princess. Sophia Watson. (Illus.). 288p. 1997. pap. (*1-85799-970-3*) Phoenix Hse.
Marina & Boatyard Industry Financial Performance. Robert A. Comerford. (Illus.). 66p. (Orig.). 1988. pap. 20.00 (*0-929803-01-9*) Intl Marina Inst.
***Marina Carr: Plays 1: Low in the Dark; The Mai; Portia Coughlan; By the Bog of Cats...** Marina Carr. 368p. 2000. pap. 17.00 (*0-571-20011-7*) Faber & Faber.
Marina Design & Engineering Conference Technical Papers. Intro. by Neil W. Ross. (Illus.). 305p. (Orig.). (C). 1987. pap. 65.00 (*0-929803-00-0*) Intl Marina Inst.
Marina Developments. Ed. by R. Blain. 301p. 1993. 81.00 (*0-614-16833-3*, CM149) Am Soc Civil Eng.
Marina Environment, 1990. Ed. by Neil W. Ross. (Illus.). 322p. (Orig.). (C). 1990. pap. 65.00 (*0-929803-10-8*) Intl Marina Inst.
Marina Investment & Appraisal Notebook. Ed. by Neil W. Ross. (Illus.). 327p. 1995. 75.00 (*0-929803-12-4*) Intl Marina Inst.
***Marina, Marine Goods, Marina Services in Japan: A Strategic Entry Report, 1996.** Compiled by Icon Group International Staff. (Illus.). 162p. 1999. ring bd. 1620.00 incl. audio compact disk (*0-7418-1362-9*) Icon Grp.
Marina Research, 1989. Ed. by Neil W. Ross. (Illus.). 344p. (Orig.). (C). 1989. pap. 75.00 (*0-929803-04-3*) Intl Marina Inst.
Marina Research, 1990. Ed. by Neil W. Ross. (Illus.). 255p. (Orig.). (C). 1990. pap. 75.00 (*0-929803-05-1*) Intl Marina Inst.
Marina Research, 1991. Ed. by Neil W. Ross. (Illus.). 178p. (C). 1991. 75.00 (*0-929803-11-6*) Intl Marina Inst.
Marina Technology. Ed. by W. R. Blain. 644p. 1992. 198.00 (*1-85312-161-4*) Computational Mech MA.
Marina Technology. Ed. by W. R. Blain. 632p. 1992. text 156.00 (*0-7277-1689-1*, Pub. by T Telford) RCH.
Marina Technology II. Ed. by W. R. Blain. LC 91-77630. (Marinas Ser.: Vol. 2). 644p. 1992. 198.00 (*1-56252-089-X*, 1614) Computational Mech MA.
Marina III: Planning, Design & Operation. Ed. by W. R. Blain. 338p. 1995. 147.00 (*1-85312-312-9*) Computational Mech MA.
Marina Tsvetaeva: A Pictorial Biography. Ed. by Ellendea C. Proffer. (Illus.). 1980. pap. 15.95 (*0-88233-359-3*) Ardis Pubs.
Marina Tsvetaeva: Stikhotvoreniia I Poemy V 5-I Tomakh, 5 vols., 3. Marina I. Tsvetaeva. Ed. by Alexander Sumerkin. LC 80-51177. (RUS.). (Orig.). 1980. pap. 36.50 (*0-89830-019-3*) Russica Pubs.
Marina Tsvetaeva: Stikhotvoreniia I Poemy V 5-I Tomakh, 5 vols., 4. Marina I. Tsvetaeva. Ed. by Alexander Sumerkin. LC 80-51177. (RUS.). (Orig.). 1980. pap. 32.00 (*0-89830-020-7*) Russica Pubs.
Marina Tsvetaeva: Stikhotvoreniia I Poemy V 5-I Tomakh, 5 vols., Set. Marina I. Tsvetaeva. Ed. by Alexander Sumerkin. LC 80-51177. (RUS.). (Orig.). 1980. pap. 148.50 (*0-89830-016-9*) Russica Pubs.
Marina Tsvetaeva: Stikhotvoreniia I Poemy V 5-I Tomakh, 5 vols., Vol. 1. Marina I. Tsvetaeva. Ed. by Alexander Sumerkin. LC 80-51177. (RUS.). (Orig.). 1980. pap. 32.00 (*0-89830-017-7*) Russica Pubs.
Marina Tsvetaeva: Stikhotvoreniia I Poemy V 5-I Tomakh, 5 vols., Vol. 2. Marina I. Tsvetaeva. Ed. by Alexander Sumerkin. LC 80-51177. (RUS.). (Orig.). 1982. pap. 34.50 (*0-89830-018-5*) Russica Pubs.
Marina Tsvetaeva: Stikhotvoreniia I Poemy V 5-I Tomakh, 5 vols., Vol. 5. Marina I. Tsvetaeva. Ed. by Alexander Sumerkin. LC 80-51177. (RUS.). (Orig.). 1993. pap. 38.50 (*0-89830-021-5*) Russica Pubs.
Marina Tsvetaeva: The Double Beat of Heaven & Hell. Lily Feiler. LC 94-9243. (Illus.). 336p. 1994. text 37.95 (*0-8223-1482-7*) Duke.
Marina Tsvetaeva, One Hundred Years: Papers from the Tsvetaeva Centenary Symposium. Ed. by Viktoria Schweitzer et al. (Modern Russian Literature & Culture, Studies & Texts: Vol. 32). (ENG & RUS., Illus.). 286p. (Orig.). (C). 1994. pap. 20.00 (*1-57201-006-1*) Berkeley Slavic.
Marina Tsvetaeva V Zhizni: Neizdannye Vospominaniia Sovremennikov. Veronique Losskaia. LC 88-32032. (Russian Ser.). (Illus.). 332p. 1989. pap. 15.00 (*1-55779-011-6*) Hermitage Pubs.
Marina Tsvetaeva's Orphic Journeys in the Worlds of the Word. Olga P. Hasty. (Studies in Russian Literature & Theory). 290p. 1996. text 49.95 (*0-8101-1315-5*) Northwestern U Pr.
Marina Tsvetayeva: A Critical Biography. Maria Razumovsky. Tr. by Aleksey Gibson. LC 88-70234. (Illus.). 400p. 1995. reprint ed. 65.00 (*1-85224-045-8*, Pub. by Bloodaxe Bks) Dufour.
***Marinade for Murder.** Claudia Bishop. 2000. mass mkt. 5.99 (*0-425-17611-8*, Prime Crime) Berkley Pub.
Marinade Recipes. S. J. Fretz. 36p. (Orig.). 1996. pap. 3.25 (*1-886367-32-9*) Wellspring.
Marinades: Dry Rubs, Pastes & Marinades for Poultry, Meat, Seafood, Cheese & Vegetables. Jim Tarantino. (Illus.). 240p. (Orig.). 1992. pap. 16.95 (*0-89594-531-2*) Crossing Pr.
Marinades: Make Ordinary Foods Extraordinary. Dona Z. Meilach. (Illus.). 176p. 1995. pap. 8.95 (*1-55867-119-6*, Nitty Gritty Ckbks) Bristol Pub Ent CA.
Marinades: The Secret of Great Grilling. Melanie Barnard. LC 96-26200. 176p. (Orig.). 1997. pap. 11.00 (*0-06-095162-1*, Perennial) HarperTrade.
Marinas: Recommendations for Design, Construction & Management, Vol. 1. Clint Chamberlain. 169p. 35.00 (*0-318-17794-3*) Natl Marine Mfrs.
Marinas along the Intracoastal Waterway. 3rd ed. Robert D. Reib. LC 97-91147. 98p. 1999. pap. 14.00 (*0-9662208-0-3*, Marinas97) Skip Bob.
Marinas, Parks & Recreation Developments: Proceedings of the International Conference. Ed. by Marshall Flug & Fred A. Klanchik. LC 94-18093. 620p. 1994. 60.00 (*0-7844-0028-8*) Am Soc Civil Eng.
***Marinating the Soul: Writing Poetry with Aspiring Writers.** Sigmund A. Boloz. Ed. by Patricia Moriarty. (Illus.). 64p. 1999. pap. 10.00 (*1-886635-16-1*) Wooded Hill AZ.
Marind-Anim Von Hollandischsud-Neu-Guinea, 2 vols. Paul Wirz. Ed. by Kees W. Bolle. (Mythology Ser.). (GER.). 1978. reprint ed. lib. bdg. 59.95 (*0-405-10569-X*) Ayer.
Marine: A Guided Tour of a Marine Expeditionary Unit. Tom Clancy. LC 96-224067. 352p. 1996. pap. 16.00 (*0-425-15454-8*) Berkley Pub.
Marine: The French Colonial Soldier in Canada, 1745-1761. Andrew Gallup & Donald F. Shaffer. (Illus.). x, 274p. (Orig.). 1992. pap. text 22.00 (*1-55613-711-7*) Heritage Bk.
Marine! The Life of Chesty Puller. Burke Davis. 400p. (YA). 1991. mass mkt. 6.99 (*0-553-27182-2*) Bantam.
Marine Accident Investigation Branch Annual Report 1996. Marine Accident Investigation Branch, Department of Transport Staff. (Marine Accident Investigation Branch Reports Ser.). 52p. 1997. 35.00 (*0-11-551934-3*, Pub. by Statnry Office) Balogh.
Marine Affairs Bibliography: A Comprehensive Index to Marine Law & Policy Literature Cumulation, 1980-1985. Christian L. Wiktor & Leslie A. Foster. 702p. 1987. lib. bdg. 296.00 (*90-247-3570-X*) Kluwer Academic.
Marine Air Power Vol. III: Real Heroes. Randy Jolly. Ed. by J. A. Papay. (Real Heroes Ser.). (Illus.). 224p. 1996. 29.95 (*1-885347-02-2*) Aero Graphics.
Marine Algae & Coastal Environment of Tropical West Africa. 2nd ed. G. W. Lawson & David M. John. (Nova Hedwigia Beihefte Ser.: Vol. 93). (Illus.). vi, 415p. 1987. pap. 130.00 (*3-443-51015-9*, Pub. by Gebruder Borntraeger) Balogh.
***Marine Algae Control Secrets: Remedies for the Marine & Reef Aquarium.** Bob Goemans. 40p. 2000. pap. 8.99 (*0-9664549-4-4*) M Weiss Cos.
Marine Algae in Pharmaceutical Science. Ed. by Hoppe. (C). 1979. 180.80 (*3-11-007375-7*) De Gruyter.
Marine Algae (Morphology, Reproduction & Biology) V. S. Sundaralingam. (Illus.). 258p. 1990. text 27.50 (*81-211-0041-0*, Pub. by Mahendra Pal Singh) Lubrecht & Cramer.
Marine Algae of California. Isabella A. Abbott. xvi, 828p. (C). 1992. pap. 34.50 (*0-8047-2152-1*) Stanford U Pr.
Marine Algae of California. Isabella A. Abbott & George J. Hollenberg. LC 74-82774. (Illus.). xvi, 828p. 1976. 39.50 (*0-8047-0867-3*) Stanford U Pr.
Marine Algae of Florida: With Special Reference to Dry Tortugas. W. R. Taylor. (Bibliotheca Phycologica Ser.: Vol.2). 1967. reprint ed. 96.00 (*3-7682-0504-5*) Lubrecht & Cramer.
Marine Algae of New England & Adjacent Coast. W. C. Farlow. (Illus.). 1969. reprint ed. pap. 80.00 (*3-7682-0582-7*) Lubrecht & Cramer.
Marine Algae of New Zealand, Vol. 3. Valentine J. Chapman. Incl. Pt. 1. Bangiophycidate & Florideophycidate. 1970. 24.00 (*3-7682-0591-6*); Pt. 2. Florideophycidae: Rhodymeniales. F. I. Dromgoole. 1970. 20.00 (*3-7682-0592-4*); (Illus.). 1970. write for info. (*0-318-54143-2*) Lubrecht & Cramer.
Marine Algae of New Zealand: Section 3 Rhodophyceae. Valentine J. Chapman & P. G. Parkinson. (Florideophycidae: Cryptonemiales Ser.: Pt. 3). (Illus.). 278p. 1974. pap. text 32.00 (*3-7682-0593-2*) Lubrecht & Cramer.
Marine Algae of New Zealand Pt. 4: Section 3 Rhodophyceae: Florideophycidae: Gigartinales. Ed. by Valentine J. Chapman. (Illus.). 510p. 1979. pap. text 64.00 (*3-7682-0594-0*) Lubrecht & Cramer.
Marine Algae of the Danish West Indies, 3 pts. in 1. Frederik Boergesen. (Dansk Botanisk Arkiv Ser.: Bind 1-3). (Illus.). 726p. 1985. reprint ed. 200.00 (*3-87429-253-3*, 001419, Pub. by Koeltz Sci Bks) Lubrecht & Cramer.
Marine Algae of the Pacific Coast of North America, 1919-1929, 3 pts. in 1. N. L. Gardener & William A. Setchell. (Bibliotheca Phycologica Ser.). 1967. 117.00 (*3-7682-0454-5*) Lubrecht & Cramer.
Marine Algae of the West Coast of Florida. Clinton J. Dawes. LC 73-22107. (Illus.). 272p. 1990. pap. 20.00 (*0-87024-258-X*) U of Miami Pr.
Marine Algae of Virginia. Harold J. Humm. LC 78-16319. (Special Papers in Marine Science: No. 3). 272p. reprint ed. pap. 84.40 (*0-8357-2710-6*, 203982300013) Bks Demand.
Marine Algen der Karibischen Kuest E. von Kolumbien: Chlorophyceae, Vol. II. R. Schnetter. (Bibliotheca Phycologica Ser.: No. 42). (Illus.). 1978. lib. bdg. 42.00 (*3-7682-1204-1*) Lubrecht & Cramer.
Marine Algen der Pazifikkueste von Kolumbien (Algas Marinas del litoral pacifico de Colombia) Chlorophyceae, Phaeophyceae, Rodophyceae: Synoptic Edition-German & Spanish. R. Schnetter & G. Bula. (Bibliotheca Phycologica Ser.: No. 60). (Illus.). 288p. 1983. text 80.00 (*3-7682-1347-1*) Lubrecht & Cramer.
Marine & Coastal Biodiversity in the Tropical Island Pacific Region. Ed. by James E. Maragos et al. LC 95-34642. 1996. pap. write for info. (*0-86638-175-9*) EW Ctr HI.
Marine & Coastal Biodiversity National Reports. (Black Sea Environmental Ser.). 131p. 20.00 (*92-1-126041-8*) UN.
Marine & Coastal Biodiversity Regional Overview. (Black Sea Environmental Ser.). 150p. 20.00 (*92-1-126042-6*) UN.
***Marine & Coastal Geographical Information Systems.** Dawn J. Wright & Darius J. Bartlett. LC 99-32009. (Research Monographs in GIS). 2000. 0.00 (*0-7484-0870-3*, Pub. by Tay Francis Ltd) Taylor & Francis.
Marine & Coastal Law: Cases & Materials. Dennis W. Nixon. LC 93-30986. 392p. 1994. text 69.50 (*0-275-93763-1*, Praeger Pubs) Greenwood.
***Marine & Freshwater Products Handbook.** Ed. by Roy C. Martin et al. LC 00-101386. 984p. 2000. text 149.95 (*1-56676-889-6*) Technomic.
Marine & Intermodal Transportation: Freight Movement & Environmental Issues. LC 92-17371. (Transportation Research Record Ser.: No. 1333). 64p. 1992. 17.00 (*0-309-05172-X*) Transport Res Bd.
Marine & Maritime Careers. Wm. Ray Heitzmann. LC 98-40925. (Opportunities in...Ser.). 160p. 1999. 14.95 (*0-8442-1833-2*, 18332, VGM Career) NTC Contemp Pub Co.
Marine & Oceanography: Experiments & Activities. 7th enl. rev. ed. Carol L. Matthews. Ed. & Illus. by Douglas L. Matthews. (Expert Systems for Teachers Ser.). 636p. 1999. teacher ed. 238.00 incl. cd-rom (*0-9629357-3-5*) Water Pr.
Marine & Offshore Computer Applications. Ed. by T. K. Murthy et al. LC 88-71664. (CADMO Ser.: Vol. 2). 812p. 1988. 149.00 (*0-945824-05-X*) Computational Mech MA.
Marine & Offshore Computer Applications. Ed. by T. K. Murthy & J. C. Dern. 810p. 1988. 206.95 (*0-387-50172-X*) Spr-Verlag.
Marine & Pocket Chronometers. Hans Von Bertele. LC 90-64231. (Illus.). 216p. 1991. 135.00 (*0-88740-303-4*) Schiffer.
Marine & Recreational Vehicles Law of New York State. 310p. 2000. ring bd. 16.95 (*0-930137-71-X*) Looseleaf Law.
Marine & Terminal Operations Survey Guidelines. OCIMF Staff. (C). 1983. 90.00 (*0-900886-86-2*, Pub. by Witherby & Co) St Mut.
Marine Angelfishes. Joachim Frische. (Illus.). 64p. 1998. 12.95 (*0-7938-0231-8*, WW-065) TFH Pubns.
Marine Angelfishes. J. Smartt et al. (Illus.). 144p. 1996. 35.95 (*0-7938-0090-0*, TS217) TFH Pubns.
Marine Animals of Baja California: A Guide to the Common Fishes & Invertebrates. 2nd ed. Daniel W. Gotshall. Ed. by Ken Hashagen. LC 87-62975. (Illus.). 113p. 1987. pap. 18.95 (*0-930118-15-4*, 43G) ProStar Pubns.
Marine Animals of Southern New England & New York: Identification Keys to Common Nearshore & Shallow Water Macrofauna. Howard M. Weiss et al. (State Geological & Natural History Survey Bulletin Ser.: Vol. 115). (Illus.). 344p. 1995. 45.00 (*0-942081-06-4*) CT DEP CGNHS.
Marine Animals Stained Glass Pattern Book. Carolyn Relei. (Illus.). 64p. 1992. pap. 6.95 (*0-486-27016-5*) Dover.
Marine Anti-Fouling Paint Compounding. John A. Wills. (Illus.). 100p. 1986. pap., lab manual ed. 14.50 (*0-9667133-4-6*) John A Wills.
Marine Aquaculture: Opportunities for Growth. Committee on Assessment of Technology & Opportunit. 304p. 1992. text 34.95 (*0-309-04675-0*) Natl Acad Pr.
Marine Aquaculture in the Black Sea Region: Current Status & Development Options. (Black Sea Environmental Ser.: No. 2). 255p. 30.00 (*92-1-126039-6*) UN.
Marine Aquaria. Warren E. Burgess. (Illus.). 96p. text 9.95 (*0-87666-533-4*, KW-088) TFH Pubns.
Marine Aquaria & Miniature Reefs. Cliff W. Emmens. (Illus.). 320p. 1990. 47.95 (*0-86622-087-9*, TS-133) TFH Pubns.
Marine Aquarist Manual: Comprehensive Edition. Hans Baensch & Paul V. Loiselle. (Illus.). 286p. 26.95 (*3-89356-130-7*, 16031) Tetra Pr.
Marine Aquarist's Manual. Hans A. Baensch. (Illus.). 1991. 10.95 (*3-923880-15-4*, 16030) Tetra Pr.
***Marine Aquarists' Quiz Book.** Martin Moe & Barbara Moe. 224p. 2000. pap. 15.95 (*0-939960-10-9*) Green Turtle Pubns.
Marine Aquarium. Chelsea House Publishing Staff. (Fish Ser.). (Illus.). 64p. (YA). (gr. 3 up). 1999. lib. bdg. 17.95 (*0-7910-5092-0*) Chelsea Hse.
Marine Aquarium Companion Vol. 1: Southeast Asia. Pabloo Tepoot. Ed. by Ian Tepoot & Diane Grindol. (Illus.). 367p. 1996. 65.00 (*0-9645058-2-7*, New Life Press) New Life Exotic Fish.
Marine Aquarium Companion Vol. 1: Southeast Asia. Pabloo Tepoot. Ed. by Ian Tepoot & Diane Grindol. (Illus.). 358p. 1996. 65.00 (*0-9645058-3-5*, New Life Press) New Life Exotic Fish.
Marine Aquarium Fish. Book Sales Staff. 1998. pap. text 4.99 (*0-7858-0967-8*) Bk Sales Inc.
Marine Aquarium Handbook: Beginner to Breeder. 2nd ed. Martin A. Moe, Jr. LC 92-4908. (Illus.). 320p. (Orig.). 1992. pap. 16.95 (*0-939960-07-9*) Green Turtle Pubns.
Marine Aquarium in Theory & Practice. rev. ed. Cliff W. Emmens. (Illus.). 208p. 1989. 23.95 (*0-86622-742-3*, PS-735) TFH Pubns.
Marine Aquarium Keeping. 2nd ed. Stephen H. Spotte. (Illus.). 192p. 1993. pap. 24.95 (*0-471-59489-X*) Wiley.
Marine Aquarium Problem Solver: Over 500 Questions Answered. Nick Dakin. (Illus.). 208p. 1996. 28.95 (*1-56465-187-8*) Tetra Pr.
Marine Aquariums. Richard F. Stratton. (Illus.). 64p. 1996. 19.95 (*0-7938-0108-7*, WW010) TFH Pubns.
Marine Architecture: Directions for Carrying on a Ship (1739) Intro. by Brian Lavery. LC 93-13766. (Scholars' Facsimiles & Reprints, Maritime History Ser.: Vol. 481). 102p. 1993. 75.00 (*0-8201-1481-2*) Schol Facsimiles.
Marine Arsenal Wunderwaffe Elektro-UBoot Type XXI see German U-Boat Type XXI
***Marine Art & Antiques: Jack Tar - A Sailor's Life 1750-1910.** J Welles Henderson. 287p. 1999. 65.00 (*1-85149-326-3*) Antique Collect.
Marine Atlas: The Joint Aquarium Care of Invertebrates & Tropical Marine Fishes. rev. ed. Hans A. Baensch et al. Tr. & Rev. by Gero W. Fischer. LC 93-46617. 1994. 59.95 (*1-56465-113-4*, 16820) Tetra Pr.
Marine Atlas Vol. I: Olympia to Malcolm Island. 12th rev. ed. George A. Bayless. (Illus.). 50p. 1997. write for info. (*0-9674750-0-7*, Pub. by Bayless Enter Inc) Fish Supply.
Marine Atlas Vol. II: Port Hardy to Skagway. 12th rev. ed. George A. Bayless. (Illus.). 50p. 1997. write for info. (*0-9674750-1-5*, Pub. by Bayless Enter Inc) Fish Supply.
Marine Atlas of the Hawaiian Islands. A. P. Balder. LC 91-45699. (Illus.). 120p. 1992. pap. text 39.00 (*0-8248-1444-4*) UH Pr.
Marine Auxiliary Machinery. 7th ed. H. David McGeorge. LC 95-3360. (Illus.). 572p. 1995. 84.95 (*0-7506-1843-4*, Focal) Buttrwrth-Heinemann.
Marine Aviation in the Persian Gulf. Tom Hayden. LC 99-89630. (Illus.). 350p. 1997. 34.95 (*1-877853-44-5*) Nautical & Aviation.
Marine Aviation in the Philippines. Charles W. Boggs, Jr. (Elite Unit Ser.: No. 30). (Illus.). 184p. reprint ed. 34.95 (*0-89839-168-7*) Battery Pr.
Marine Benthic Flora of Southern Australia, Pt. 1. H. B. Womersley. (Flora & Fauna of South Australia Handbooks Ser.). (Illus.). 329p. 1984. pap. 26.50 (*0-7243-4552-3*) Lubrecht & Cramer.
Marine Benthic Vegetation: Recent Changes & the Effects of Eutrophication. Ed. by W. Schramm & P. N. Nienhuis. (Ecological Studies: Vol. 123). 448p. 1996. 149.00 (*0-387-58106-5*) Spr-Verlag.
Marine Benthic Vegetation: Recent Changes & the Effects of Eutrophication. Ed. by Winfried Schramm & Pieter H. Nienhuis. LC 96-3923. (Ecological Studies: Vol. 123). 1996. write for info. (*3-540-58106-5*) Spr-Verlag.
Marine Bio. 2nd ed. H. H. Webber & Harold V. Thurman. 388p. (C). 1997. pap. text 86.00 (*0-673-39913-3*) Addson-Wesley Educ.
Marine Bio Acoustics: Proceedings of Symposium on Lener Marine, Bimini, Bahamas, April 1963. William N. Tavolga. LC 63-23207. 1964. 189.00 (*0-08-010557-2*, Pub. by Pergamon Repr) Franklin.
Marine Bio Acoustics: Proceedings of the 2nd Symposium on Marine Bio Acoustics, New York, Apr. 1966. William N. Tavolga. LC 63-23207. 1967. 164.00 (*0-08-012293-0*, Pub. by Pergamon Repr) Franklin.
Marine Biodeterioration: Advanced Techniques Applicable to the Indian Ocean. Ed. by Mary-Frances Thompson et al. (Illus.). 858p. (C). 1988. text 233.00 (*90-6191-488-4*, Pub. by A A Balkema) Ashgate Pub Co.
Marine Biodiversity. United States Government Printing Office Staff. LC 91-602044. v, 98 p. 1991. write for info. (*0-16-036833-2*) USGPO.
Marine Biodiversity: Patterns & Processes. Ed. by Rupert F. Ormond et al. LC 96-9334. (Illus.). 472p. (C). 1998. text 80.00 (*0-521-55222-2*) Cambridge U Pr.
Marine Biogenic Lipids, Fats, & Oils, 2 vols., Vol. I. R. G. Ackman. 368p. 1989. lib. bdg. 215.95 (*0-8493-4889-7*, QH91) CRC Pr.
Marine Biogenic Lipids, Fats, & Oils, 2 vols., Vol. II. R. G. Ackman. 416p. 1989. lib. bdg. 249.00 (*0-8493-4890-0*, QH91) CRC Pr.
Marine Biological Association of the United Kingdom, Library. Catalogues of the Library of the Marine Biological. 1978. 1890.00 (*0-8161-0076-4*, G K Hall & Co) Mac Lib Ref.
***Marine Biologist.** Jim Dawson. 1999. 19.93 (*0-516-21889-1*) Capstone Pr.

An Asterisk (*) at the beginning of an entry indicates that the title is appearing for the first time.

*Marine Biologist. Jennifer Wendt. LC 99-35396. (Career Exploration Ser.). (Illus.). 48p. (YA). (gr. 4-7). 1999. 19.93 (0-7368-0330-0) Capstone Pr.
Marine Biologist: Swimming with the Sharks. Keith Greenberg. Ed. by Bruce Glassman. LC 95-20196. (Risky Business Ser.). (Illus.). 32p. (J). (gr. 2-5). 1995. lib. bdg. 16.95 (1-56711-156-4) Blackbirch.
Marine Biology. Lorraine Conway. 64p. (J). (gr. 5 up). 1982. 7.99 (0-86653-056-8, GA 400) Good Apple.
Marine Biology. Matthew Lerman. (Illus.). 510p. (C). 1986. pap. text 57.00 (0-8053-6402-1) Benjamin-Cummings.
Marine Biology. Pechenik & Sumich. 1998. 16.00 (0-697-16520-5, WCB McGr Hill) McGrw-H Hghr Educ.
Marine Biology. 2nd ed. Peter Castro & Michael Huber. LC 95-78746. 480p. (C). 1996. text. write for info. (0-697-24360-5, WCB McGr Hill) McGrw-H Hghr Educ.
Marine Biology. 2nd ed. Peter Castro & Miichael Huber. 480p. (C). 1996. write for info. (0-697-31312-3, WCB McGr Hill) McGrw-H Hghr Educ.
Marine Biology. 3rd ed. Peter Castro & Michael E. Huber. LC 98-53832. 464p. 1999. 62.50 (0-07-012197-4) McGraw.
Marine Biology. 4th ed. Castro. 2002. 49.00 (0-07-029421-6) McGraw.
Marine Biology: A Port Erin Perspective. Ed. by Steven Hawkins & Richard Hartnoll. 238p. (C). 1990. 135.00 (0-907151-95-7, Pub. by IMMEL Pubng) St Mut.
Marine Biology: An Ecological Approach. James W. Nybakken. 446p. (C). 1982. write for info. (0-06-364800-8) Addson-Wesley Educ.
Marine Biology: An Ecological Approach. 4th ed. James W. Nybakken. LC 96-645. 446p. (C). 1997. 73.00 (0-673-99451-1) Addison-Wesley Educ.
Marine Biology: Ecology of the Sea. rev. ed. Joey Tanner. (Learning Packets - Science Ser.). (Illus.). 66p. (J). (gr. k-8). 1992. ring bd. 18.00 (0-913705-05-5) Zephyr Pr AZ.
Marine Biology: Function, Biodiversity, Ecology. Jeffrey S. Levinton. (Illus.), 448p. (C). 1995. text 62.95 (0-19-508573-6) OUP.
Marine Biology: Index of New Information with Authors & Subjects. Pauline T. Wetterby. LC 92-54247. 180p. 1990. 47.50 (1-55914-642-7); pap. 44.50 (1-55914-643-5) ABBE Pubs Assn.
Marine Biology: True Homosexual Military Stories. Ed. by Winston Leyland. (Military Sex Stories Ser.: Vol. 4). 160p. (Orig.). 1994. pap. 14.95 (0-943595-49-5) Leyland Pubns.
Marine Biology & Oceanography: Experiments & Activities. 7th ed. Carol L. Matthews. Ed. & Illus. by Douglas L. Matthews. (Expert Systems for Teachers Ser.). 636p. 1991. pap., teacher ed. 258.00 (0-9629357-2-7); pap., student ed. 16.00 (0-9629357-1-9) Water Pr.
Marine Biology Coloring Book. Thomas M. Niesen. (Illus.). 224p. 1982. pap. 18.00 (0-06-460303-2, CO 303, Harper Ref) HarpC.
*Marine Biology Coloring Book. 2nd ed. Concepts Coloring Staff. 272p. 2000. pap. 17.95 (0-06-273718-X) HarpC.
Marine Biology, Environment, Diversity, & Ecology. Clare Clark. 560p. (C). 1987. pap. text 57.00 (0-201-23221-9) Addison-Wesley.
Marine Biology, Oceanography, Environmental & Freshwater Science Professional Sample Copy: Experiments & Activities. 7th ed. Carol L. Matthews. Ed. & Illus. by Douglas L. Matthews. (Expert Systems for Teachers Ser.). 302p. 1991. pap., teacher ed. 18.00 (0-9629357-0-0) Water Pr.
Marine Biology of Polar Regions & Effects of Stress on Marine Organisms: Proceedings of the 18th European Marine Biology Symposium, University of Oslo, Norway, 14-20 August 1983. European Marine Biology Symposium Staff. Ed. by J. S. Gray & M. E. Christiansen. LC 84-3257. (Illus.). 659p. reprint ed. pap. 200.00 (0-7837-6377-8, 204609000010) Bks Demand.
Marine Biology of the South China Sea, 2 vols. Brian Morton. 772p. 1994. pap. 125.00 (962-209-356-6, Pub. by HK Univ Pr) Coronet Bks.
Marine Biology of the South China Sea III, 2 vols. Ed. by Brian Morton. (Illus.). 704p. 1998. pap. 99.50 (962-209-461-9, Pub. by HK Univ Pr) Coronet Bks.
*Marine Bioprocess Engineering: Proceedings of an International Symposium Organized under Auspices of the Working Party on Applied Biocatalysis of the European Federation of Biotechnology & the European Society for Marine Biotechnology, Noordwijkerhour, the Netherlands, Nobember 8-11, 1998. R. Osinga et al. LC 99-89648. (Progress in Industrial Microbiology Ser.). 414p. 2000. write for info. (0-444-50387-0) Elsevier.
Marine Biotechnology Vol. 1: Pharmaceutical & Bioactive Natural Products. D. H. Attaway & O. R. Zaborsky. (Illus.). 520p. (C). 1993. text 110.00 (0-306-44174-8, Kluwer Plenum) Kluwer Academic.
Marine Biotechnology & Developing Countries. Raymond A. Zilinskas & Carl G. Lundin. LC 93-26137. (Discussion Paper Ser.: No. 210). 132p. 1993. pap. 22.00 (0-8213-2590-6, 12590) World Bank.
Marine Birds see Birds up Close Series
Marine Birds see Birds up Close Series
Marine Blowers UL 1128. 3rd ed. (C). 1997. pap. text 250.00 (0-7629-0218-3) Underwrtrs Labs.
Marine Boilers. 3rd ed. Flanagan. 128p. 1990. pap. 39.95 (0-7506-1821-3) Buttrwrth-Heinemann.
Marine Book: A Portrait of America's Military Elite. rev. ed. Chuck Lawliss. LC 91-67311. (Illus.). 192p. 1992. pap. 19.95 (0-500-27665-X, Pub. by Thames Hudson) Norton.
Marine Botany. 2nd ed. Clinton J. Dawes. LC 97-10372. 328p. 1998. 90.00 (0-471-19208-2) Wiley.
Marine Buoyant Devices, UL 1123. 6th ed. (C). 1996. pap. text 330.00 (0-7629-0029-6) Underwrtrs Labs.
Marine Cargo Claims. 4th ed. W. Tetley. 1498p. (C). 1990. 199.00 (0-685-32733-7, MICHIE) LEXIS Pub.
Marine Cargo Clauses: A Collection of Non-Institute Clauses. Joe Felice-Pace. 150p. 1997. pap. 100.00 (1-85609-145-7, Pub. by Witherby & Co) St Mut.
Marine Cargo Delays. Max Ganado & Hugh M. Kindred. 175p. 1990. 110.00 (1-85044-235-5) LLP.
Marine Cargo Operations. 2nd ed. Charles L. Sauerbier & Robert J. Meurn. LC 84-20920. 704p. 1985. 105.00 (0-471-88616-5) Wiley.
Marine Casuality Response: Salvage Engineering. ASNE (Cronin) Staff. 800p. text (0-7872-3465-6) Kendall-Hunt.
Marine Chaplain, 1943-1946. George W. Wickersham. (World War II Monograph Ser.: No. 227). (Illus.). 162p. 1998. 42.95 (1-57638-134-X, M227-H); pap. 34.95 (1-57638-133-1, M227-S) Merriam Pr.
*Marine Chemistry. Ed. by P. J. Wangersky. (Handbook of Environmental Chemistry Ser.: Vol. 5). xiv, 228p. 2000. 109.00 (3-540-66020-8) Spr-Verlag.
Marine Chemistry, Vol. 1. 2nd ed. Dean F. Martin. LC 72-169633. (Illus.). 401p. 1972. reprint ed. pap. 124.40 (0-608-08271-6, 205506900001) Bks Demand.
Marine Chemistry: An Environmental Analytical Chemistry Approach. Antonio Gianguzza et al. LC 97-19834. (Water, Science & Technology Library). 1997. text 194.00 (0-7923-4622-X) Kluwer Academic.
Marine Chemistry: Theory & Applications, Vol. 2. Dean F. Martin. LC 68-27532. (Illus.), 463p. 1970. reprint ed. pap. 143.60 (0-608-08270-8, 203301100082) Bks Demand.
Marine Chemistry in the Coastal Environment. Ed. by Thomas M. Church. LC 75-28151. (ACS Symposium Ser.: Vol. 18). 720p. 1975. reprint ed. pap. 200.00 (0-608-03552-1, 206427100008) Bks Demand.
Marine Chronometer. Rupert T. Gould. (Illus.). 402p. 1990. 59.50 (0-907462-05-7) Antique Collect.
Marine Chronometer. Rupert T. Gould. (Illus.). 1960. pap. 25.00 (0-87556-106-3) Saifer.
Marine Claims. Christof Cuddeke. 295p. 1993. 105.00 (1-85044-540-0) LLP.
Marine Claims: Collected Papers. J. K. Goodacre. (C). 1980. 100.00 (0-7855-4092-X, Pub. by Witherby & Co) St Mut.
Marine Claims Handbook. 4th ed. N. G. Hudson & J. C. Allen. 1984. 40.00 (0-907432-91-3) LLP.
Marine Claims Handbook. 4th ed. N. G. Hudson & J. C. Allen. (C). 1984. 160.00 (0-7855-4091-1, Pub. by Witherby & Co) St Mut.
Marine Clastic Reservoirs: Examples & Analogues. E. G. Rhodes & T. F. Moslow. Ed. by A. H. Bouma. (Frontiers in Sedimentary Geology Ser.). (Illus.). 360p. 1992. 161.00 (0-387-97788-0) Spr-Verlag.
Marine Clastic Sediment. J. K. Leggett. 1987. text 265.00 (0-86010-864-3) Kluwer Academic.
Marine Clastic Sedimentology. Ed. by J. K. Leggett. (C). 1987. lib. bdg. 105.00 (0-86010-897-X, Pub. by Graham & Trotman) Kluwer Academic.
Marine Climate, Weather & Climate Changes in Fisheries & Ocean Resources. Taivo Laevastu. 204p. 1993. text 69.95 (0-470-22049-X) Halsted Pr.
Marine Coastal Europhication. R. A. Vollenweider et al. 1310p. 1992. 323.50 (0-444-89990-1) Elsevier.
*Marine, Coastal, Interwaterway Pollution Equipment & Services in Thailand: A Strategic Entry Report, 1996. Compiled by Icon Group International Staff. (Illus.). 143p. 1999. ring bd. 1430.00 incl. audio compact disk (0-7418-1396-3) Icon Grp.
Marine Coatings. Henry R. Bleile & Stephen Rodgers. (Illus.). 28p. 1989. pap. 30.00 (0-934010-29-3) Fed Soc Coat Tech.
Marine Coatings. 2nd ed. (Illus.). Date not set. pap. 30.00 (0-934010-30-7) Fed Soc Coat Tech.
*Marine Combat Correspondent: World War 2 in the Pacific. Sammuel E. Stavisky. 1999. mass mkt. 6.99 (0-8041-1865-5) Ivy Books.
Marine Combustible Gas Indicators, UL 1110. 3rd ed. 1997. write for info. (0-7629-0216-7) Underwrtrs Labs.
Marine Communications in Desert Shield & Desert Storm. John T. Quinn. 136p. 1996. per. 14.00 (0-16-048749-8) USGPO.
Marine Community Aquarium. (Illus.). 1988. 23.95 (0-86622-892-6, H-1101) TFH Pubns.
*Marine Composites. 2nd ed. Eric Greene. 1999. pap. 50.00 (0-9673692-0-7) E Greene Assoc.
Marine Computing Directory. 2nd ed. Ed. by H. W. Bonnett & M. B. Bonnett. 1996. text 35.00 (0-07-006653-1) McGraw.
Marine Concrete. A. Marshall. (gr. 13). 1990. text 155.95 (0-442-30297-5) Chapman & Hall.
Marine Conservation for the 21st Century. Hillary Viders. LC 95-78019. (Illus.). 350p. 1995. 19.95 (0-941332-47-0, D705H); pap. 17.50 (0-941332-46-2, D705S) Best Pub Co.
Marine Control Practice. D. A. Taylor & Billis. (Illus.). 424p. 1987. 82.95 (0-408-01313-3) Buttrwrth-Heinemann.
Marine Corps: A Handbook. 1991. lib. bdg. 79.95 (0-8490-4240-2) Gordon Pr.
Marine Corps: Improving Amphibians Capability Would Require Larger Share of Budget Than Previously Provided. (Illus.). 53p. (Orig.). (C). 1996. pap. text 20.00 (0-7881-3019-6) DIANE Pub.
*Marine Corps Air Station El Toro. Thomas O'Hara. (Images of America Ser.). (Illus.). 128p. 1999. pap. 18.99 (0-7385-0186-7) Arcadia Publng.
Marine Corps Aviation Association: Chronolog 1912-1954, Vol. I. Turner Publishing Company Staff. LC 89-50043. (Illus.). 152p. 1989. 44.95 (0-938021-39-7) Turner Pub KY.
Marine Corps Aviation Association: Chronolog 1955-1996, Vol. II. Turner Publishing Company Staff. LC 89-50043. (Illus.). 136p. 1996. 49.95 (1-56311-207-8) Turner Pub KY.
Marine Corps Book of Lists: A Definitive Compendium of Marine Corps Facts, Feats & Traditions. Albert A. Nofi. LC 97-16681. (Illus.). 240p. 1998. pap. 14.95 (0-938289-89-6, 289896) Combined Pub.
*Marine Corps Gallantry: Or Psychosis Sgt. Macdonald. A. S. Macdonald. 244p. 2000. per. 15.00 (0-9676941-0-8) ASM Pubng.
Marine Corps Reserve. U. S. Marine Corps Staff. LC 75-8635. 311p. 1966. reprint ed. 25.00 (0-403-01776-9) Scholarly.
Marine Corps' Search for a Mission, 1880-1898. Jack Shulimson. LC 93-7181. (Modern War Studies). 256p. (C). 1993. 35.00 (0-7006-0608-4) U Pr of KS.
Marine Corps Sourcing Competitions: Historical Performance & Direction for Improvement. Nancy Y. Moore et al. (Illus.). 71p. 1999. pap. 6.00 (0-8330-2692-5, DB-250-USMC) Rand Corp.
Marine Corrosion of Stainless Steel: Chlorination & Microbial Effects. (European Federation of Corrosion Publications Ser.). 224p. 1993. pap. 116.00 (0-901716-33-2, Pub. by Inst Materials) Ashgate Pub Co.
Marine Damage Survey Guide. Richard A. Cady. (Illus.). 157p. (Orig.). 1977. pap. text 26.00 (0-934114-68-4, BK-121) Marine Educ.
Marine Data Systems Symposium, 1989: Proceedings. Ed. by Lester Gray. 260p. 1989. pap. text 49.00 (0-933957-05-X) Marine Tech Soc.
Marine Debris: Sources, Impacts & Solutions. James M. Coe & Donald B. Rogers. LC 96-18351. (Environmental Management Ser.). 416p. 1996. 86.95 (0-387-94759-0) Spr-Verlag.
Marine Diatoms see Diatomeenschalen im Elektronenmikroskopischen Bild
Marine Diatoms Associated with Mangrove Prop Roots in the Indian River, Florida, U. S. A. J. Nelson Navarro. (Bibliotheca Phycologica Ser.: Vol. 61). (Illus.). 151p. (Orig.). 1982. pap. text 35.00 (3-7682-1337-4) Lubrecht & Cramer.
Marine Dictionary, French & English see Dictionnaire de Marine, Francais et Anglais
Marine Diesel Engines: Maintenance, Troubleshooting, & Repair. 2nd ed. Nigel Calder. 1991. 24.95 (0-07-009612-0) McGraw.
Marine Diesel Engines: Maintenance, Troubleshooting & Repair. 2nd ed. Nigel Calder. 224p. 1991. 24.95 (0-87742-313-X) Intl Marine.
Marine Disposal System. Garber. (Water Science & Technology Ser.). 294p. 1992. pap. 105.75 (0-08-042186-5, Pergamon Pr) Elsevier.
Marine Disposal Systems, 1994. Ed. by I. Ozturk et al. 310p. 1995. 115.00 (0-08-042671-9, Pergamon Pr) Elsevier.
Marine Dive-Bomber Pilot at Guadalcanal. John H. McEniry. LC 86-16053. (Illus.). 195p. 1987. reprint ed. pap. 60.50 (0-608-01674-8, 206233000002) Bks Demand.
Marine-Dredged Materials Management in Massachusetts: Issues, Options & the Future. Eric J. Dolin & Judith Pederson. 46p. (Orig.). 1992. write for info. (1-56172-006-2) MIT Sea Grant.
Marine Ecological Processes. I. Valiela. (Advanced Texts in Life Sciences Ser.). (Illus.). 536p. 1993. 54.00 (0-387-90929-X) Spr-Verlag.
Marine Ecological Processes. 2nd ed. Ivan Valiera. LC 94-41484. (Illus.). 686p. 1995. 54.95 (0-387-94321-8) Spr-Verlag.
*Marine Ecologonomics. A. V. Souvorov. (Developments in Environmental Economics Ser.). 313p. 1999. write for info. (0-444-82659-9) Elsevier.
Marine Ecology: A Comprehensive, Integrated Treatise on Life in Ocean & Coastal Waters: Ocean Management - Ecosystems & Organic Resources: Environmental Factors. Ed. by Otto Kinne. LC 79-121779. 577p. 1972. reprint ed. pap. 178.90 (0-608-03960-8, 205205200001) Bks Demand.
Marine Ecology: A Comprehensive, Integrated Treatise on Life in Oceans & Coastal Waters. Ed. by Otto Kinne. LC 79-121779. (Ocean Management Ser.: Vol. 5, Pt. 1). (Illus.). 666p. 1982. reprint ed. pap. 200.00 (0-608-07548-5, 201505800006) Bks Demand.
Marine Ecology: A Comprehensive, Integrated Treatise on Life in Oceans & Coastal Waters. Otto Kinne. LC 79-121779. (Ocean Management Ser.: Vol. 5, Pt. 2). (Illus.). 466p. 1983. reprint ed. pap. 144.50 (0-608-07549-3, 201505800007) Bks Demand.
Marine Ecology: A Comprehensive, Integrated Treatise on Life in Oceans & Coastal Waters. Ed. by Otto Kinne. LC 79-121779. (Ocean Management Ser.: Vol. 5, Pt. 4). (Illus.). 396p. 1984. reprint ed. pap. 122.80 (0-608-07550-7, 201505800008) Bks Demand.
Marine Ecology: A Comprehensive, Integrated Treatise on Life in Oceans & Coastal Waters, Vol. 1, Pt. 3: Environmental Factors. Ed. by Otto Kinne. LC 79-221779. 547p. 1970. pap. 155.90 (0-608-16253-1, 2015058) Bks Demand.
Marine Ecology: A Comprehensive, Integrated Treatise on Life in Oceans & Coastal Waters, Vol. 2, Pt. 2: Physiological Mechanisms. Ed. by Otto Kinne. LC 79-121779. 557p. 1975. pap. 172.70 (0-608-03963-2, 201505800093) Bks Demand.
Marine Ecology: A Comprehensive, Integrated Treatise on Life in Oceans & Coastal Waters, Vol. 3, Pt. 1: Cultivation. Ed. by Otto Kinne. LC 79-221779. 593p. 1976. pap. 183.90 (0-608-03964-0, 201505800094) Bks Demand.
Marine Ecology: A Comprehensive, Integrated Treatise on Life in Oceans & Coastal Waters: Ocean Management - Ecosystems & Organic Resources, 5 vols., Vol. 1, Pt. 1: Environmental Factors. Ed. by Otto Kinne. LC 79-121779. (Illus.). 697p. 1970. reprint ed. pap. 200.00 (0-608-03959-4, 201505800001) Bks Demand.
Marine Ecology: A Comprehensive, Integrated Treatise on Life in Oceans & Coastal Waters: Ocean Management - Ecosystems & Organic Resources, 5 vols., Vol. 2, Pt. 1: Physiological Mechanisms. Ed. by Otto Kinne. LC 79-121779. (Illus.). 465p. 1970. reprint ed. pap. 144.20 (0-608-03962-4, 201505800002) Bks Demand.
Marine Ecology: A Comprehensive, Integrated Treatise on Life in Oceans & Coastal Waters: Ocean Management - Ecosystems & Organic Resources, 5 vols., Vol. 3, Pt. 2: Cultivation. Ed. by Otto Kinne. LC 79-121779. (Illus.). 736p. 1970. reprint ed. pap. 200.00 (0-608-03965-9, 201505800095) Bks Demand.
Marine Ecology: A Comprehensive, Integrated Treatise on Life in Oceans & Coastal Waters: Ocean Management - Ecosystems & Organic Resources, 5 vols., Vol. 3, Pt. 3: Cultivation. Ed. by Otto Kinne. LC 79-121779. (Illus.). 242p. 1970. reprint ed. pap. 75.10 (0-608-03966-7, 201505800096) Bks Demand.
Marine Ecology: A Comprehensive, Integrated Treatise on Life in Oceans & Coastal Waters: Ocean Management - Ecosystems & Organic Resources, 5 vols., Vol. 4: Dynamics. Ed. by Otto Kinne. LC 79-121779. (Illus.). 762p. 1970. reprint ed. pap. 200.00 (0-608-03967-5, 201505800097) Bks Demand.
Marine Ecology Vol. 5, Pt. 3: A Comprehensive, Integrated Treatise on Life in Oceans & Coastal Waters. fac. ed. Ed. by Otto Kinne. LC 79-121779. 545p. reprint ed. pap. 169.00 (0-7837-8633-6, 201505800005) Bks Demand.
Marine Ecology of Birds in the Ross Sea, Antarctica. David G. Ainley et al. 97p. 1984. 15.00 (0-943610-39-7) Am Ornithologists.
Marine Ecology of the Arabian Region: Patterns & Processes in Extreme Tropical Environments. Charles Sheppard et al. (Illus.). 368p. 1992. text 83.00 (0-12-639490-3) Acad Pr.
*Marine Education: A Bibliography of Educational Materials Available from the Nation[0012]s Sea Grant College Programs (5th ed.) 5th ed. (Illus.). 67p. 2000. reprint ed. pap. text 20.00 (0-7881-8668-X) DIANE Pub.
Marine Electric Motors & Generators (Cranking, Outdrive Tilt, Trim Tab, Generators, Alternators) UL 1112. 3rd ed. 1997. write for info. (0-7629-0214-0, UL 1112) Underwrtrs Labs.
Marine Electrical & Electronics Bible. 2nd rev. ed. John C. Payne. LC 98-27298. (Illus.). 432p. 1998. 39.95 (1-57409-060-7) Sheridan.
*Marine Electrical Basics Workbook. 4th rev. ed. William A. Young. 196p. 2000. pap. text 49.00 (0-86587-681-9, 681) Gov Insts.
Marine Electrical Equipment & Practice. 2nd ed. H. David McGeorge. 160p. 1993. pap. 39.95 (0-7506-1647-4) Buttrwrth-Heinemann.
Marine Electrical Practice. 6th rev. ed. G. O. Watson. 308p. 1991. 145.00 (0-7506-1013-1) Buttrwrth-Heinemann.
Marine Electrochemistry. Ed. by Joan B. Berkowitz et al. LC 73-75170. (Illus.). 414p. reprint ed. pap. 128.40 (0-608-10962-2, 205044500081) Bks Demand.
Marine Electrochemistry: A Practical Introduction. Ed. by M. Whitfield & D. Jagner. LC 80-42023. (Illus.). 543p. reprint ed. pap. 168.40 (0-608-18415-2, 203044400069) Bks Demand.
Marine Electronic Navigation. 2nd ed. S. F. Appleyard. 600p. (C). 1988. 110.00 (0-415-06600-X) Routledge.
Marine Electronics Handbook. Colin Jones. (Illus.). 176p. 1997. 29.95 (1-85310-882-0, Pub. by Airlife) Motorbooks Intl.
Marine Encyclopaedic Dictionary 5th ed. Eric Sullivan. LC 99-160700. 452p. 1996. write for info. (1-85978-043-1) LLP.
Marine Encyclopaedic Dictionary. 5th rev. ed. Eric Sullivan. 550p. 1995. 94.00 (1-85044-970-8) LLP.
Marine Engine Ignition Systems & Components, UL 1120. 3rd ed. 1997. write for info. (0-7629-0217-5) Underwrtrs Labs.
Marine Engine Lay-Up: A Step-by-Step Guide to Decommissioning Inboards, Stern Drives, & Outboard Motors. Tom Banse. LC 95-30192. 1995. write for info. (0-934523-39-8) Middle Coast Pub.
Marine Engine Room Blue Book. 4th ed. William D. Eglinton. LC 83-46035. (Illus.). 428p. 1993. pap. text 25.00 (0-87033-447-6) Cornell Maritime.
Marine Engineer. Jack Rudman. (Career Examination Ser.: C-1363). 1994. pap. 29.95 (0-8373-1363-5) Nat Learn.

Marine Engineering. rev. ed. Ed. by Roy L. Harrington. (Illus.). 968p. (C). 1992. 175.00 (0-939773-10-4) Soc Naval Arch.
More than twenty years have passed since the previous edition of MARINE ENGINEERING was published. During that period, many changes have occurred in the body of technology that is collectively known as "marine engineering." Most of the changes have been of an evolutionary nature; as examples, diesels have continued to supplant steam turbines for most ship propulsion applications in the commercial

M

arena, & gas turbines have become more firmly established as propulsion engines, particularly for warships of the frigate class. Because of some of the evolutionary nature of the technology changes, the coverage of some subjects has been reduced in comparison with that in the previous edition, e.g., Boilers & Combustion. Noise Control has been given a more thorough treatment. In addition, the introductory chapter has been broadened to include several topics, such as Design for Production, which has been given increased emphasis since publication of the previous edition. This book offers a complete review of marine engineering including power plants, transmissions, auxiliary components, shipboard systems & supporting technology, & provides a basic understanding of marine engineering principles to persons who are nominally second-year engineering students. Price: $95.00 members; $190 non-members. The Society of Naval Architects & Marine Engineers, 601 Pavonia Ave., Jersey City, NJ 07306. phone: 201-798-4800. FAX: 201-798-4975. website: http://www.sname.org. ***Publisher Paid Annotation.***

M

Marine Engineering: Design & Operation of Ships & Offshore Structures. Ed. by T. K. S. Murthy & C. A. Brebbia. 276p. 1994. 152.00 (*1-85312-248-3*) Computational Mech MA.

Marine Engineering Economics & Cost Analysis. Everett C. Hunt & Boris S. Butman. LC 94-35353. 496p. 1995. text 50.00 (*0-87033-458-1*) Cornell Maritime.

Marine Engineering with Copper-Nickel: Proceedings of the Conference Held at the City Conference Centre, London, on 19-20 April, 1988. 104p. 1989. pap. text 37.80 (*0-901462-52-7*, Pub. by Inst Materials) Ashgate Pub Co.

Marine Engineer's Guide to Fluid Flow. Peter G. Robinson. LC 75-25933. (Illus.). 88p. 1975. reprint ed. pap. 30.00 (*0-7837-9066-X*, 204981500003) Bks Demand.

Marine Engines for Recreational Boats: Characteristics, Comparisons, Maintenance & Troubleshooting. Hugh G. Stocker. LC 90-10139. (Illus.). 100p. 1990. text 75.00 (*0-937041-82-3*); pap. text 45.00 (*0-937041-83-1*) Systems Co.

Marine Environment. Ed. by John D. Milliman & W. Redwood Wright. 1986. 81.25 (*0-86720-066-9*) Jones & Bartlett.

Marine Environment & Oil Facilities. Ed. by Institution of Civil Engineers Staff. 168p. 1979. 39.00 (*0-7277-0075-8*, Pub. by T Telford) RCH.

Marine Environment & Sustainable Development: Law, Policy, & Science, 25th Annual Conference Proceedings. Ed. by Alastair Couper et al. 688p. 1993. 58.00 (*0-911189-25-4*) Law Sea Inst.

Marine Environment Law. John H. Bates & Charles J. Benson. (Lloyd's Shipping Law Library). ring bd. 395.00 (*1-85044-452-8*) LLP.

Marine Environment Law in the United Nations Environment Programme: An Emergent Ecoregime. P. H. Sand. 292p. 1988. text 90.00 (*1-85148-024-2*, Tycooly Pub) Weidner & Sons.

Marine Environmental Studies in Boca de Quadra & Smeaton Bay: Chemical & Geochemical. D. C. Burrell. (IMS Reports: No. R82-2). 307p. 1980. pap. 19.25 (*0-914500-16-3*) U of AK Inst Marine.

Marine Environmental Studies in Boca de Quadra & Smeaton Bay: Physical & Chemical, 1979. D. C. Burrell et al. (Science Technical Reports: No. R80-1). (Illus.). 144p. pap. 10.50 (*0-914500-10-4*) U of AK Inst Marine.

Marine Environmental Studies in Boca de Quadra & Smeaton Bay: Physical Oceanography, 1980. Burrell & D. Nebert. (IMS Report: No. R81-5). 59p. 5.25 (*0-914500-12-0*) U of AK Inst Marine.

Marine Environments of the Virgin Islands. D. Grigg et al. (Illus.). 191p. 1976. 25.00 (*0-318-14616-9*) Isl Resources.

Marine Equipment Buyers' Guide, 1995. Lloyd's of London Press Staff. 1995. pap. 185.00 (*1-85044-553-2*) LLP.

Marine Eutrophication. Robert J. Livingston. (Marine Science Ser.). 2000. 89.95 (*0-8493-9062-1*) CRC Pr.

Marine Fauna of the British Isles & Northwest Europe Vol. 1: Introduction & Protozoans to Arthropods. Ed. by Peter J. Hayward & John S. Ryland. (Illus.). 688p. 1991. text 195.00 (*0-19-857356-1*) OUP.

Marine Fauna of the British Isles & Northwest Europe Vol. 2: Mollusks to Chordates. Ed. by Peter J. Hayward & John S. Ryland. (Illus.). 386p. 1991. text 195.00 (*0-19-857515-7*) OUP.

Marine Field Course Guide 1: Rocky Shores. Stephen Hawkins & Hugh D. Jones. 112p. (C). 1995. pap. 45.00 (*0-907151-58-2*, Pub. by IMMEL Pubng) St Mut.

Marine Fighting Squadron 121: (VMF-121) Thomas Doll. (Illus.). 72p. (Orig.). 1996. pap. 12.95 (*0-89747-369-8*, 6177) Squad Sig Pubns.

***Marine Fire Fighting.** Ed. by John F. Lewis & David Merk. (Illus.). 400p. 2000. pap. 30.00 (*0-87939-177-4*) IFSTA.

Marine Fire Prevention, Firefighting & Fire Safety. 1995. lib. bdg. 251.95 (*0-8490-7517-3*) Gordon Pr.

Marine Fire Prevention, Firefighting & Fire Safety. 388p. 1979. per. 32.00 (*0-16-000321-0*) USGPO.

Marine Fire Prevention, Firefighting & Fire Safety. Joseph Connor. (Illus.). 404p. 1979. pap. text 21.95 (*0-87618-994-X*) P-H.

Marine Fire Prevention, Firefighting & Fire Safety: A Comprehensive Training & Reference Manual. (Illus.). 388p. (Orig.). (C). 1994. pap. text 65.00 (*0-7881-0478-0*) DIANE Pub.

Marine Fish Behaviour in Capture & Abundance Estimation. Ferno & Steiner Olson. 1994. 85.00 (*0-85238-211-1*) Blackwell Sci.

Marine Fish Culture. John W. Tucker. LC 98-42062. 1998. write for info. (*0-7923-8349-4*) Kluwer Academic.

Marine Fish Farming for India. J. Hornell. 86p. 1984. pap. 175.00 (*0-7855-0381-1*, Pub. by Intl Bks & Periodicals) St Mut.

***Marine Fisheries Ecology.** Simon Jennings. (Illus.). 384p. 2000. pap. 49.95 (*0-632-05098-5*) Blackwell Sci.

Marine Fisheries Economics & Development in India. Ed. by S. M. Ali. LC 96-904824. 208p. 1996. pap. 163.00 (*81-7533-009-0*, Pub. by Print Hse) St Mut.

***Marine Fisheries Products (Seafood) in Portugal: A Strategic Entry Report, 1996.** Compiled by Icon Group International Staff. (Illus.). 103p. 1999. ring bd. 1030.00 incl. audio compact disk (*0-7418-1322-X*) Icon Grp.

Marine Fisheries Review. Government Printing Office Staff. pap. 10.00 (*0-16-009593-X*) USGPO.

Marine Fishery Resources of Sri Lanka. G. Bruin et al. LC 96-146477. (FAO Species Identification Guide for Fishery Purpose Ser.). 425p. 1994. pap. 75.00 (*92-5-103293-9*) Food & Agri Org UN.

Marine Fishes. Herbert R. Axelrod & Warren E. Burgess. (Illus.). 96p. 1979. 9.95 (*0-87666-513-X*, KW-031) TFH Pubns.

Marine Fishes. rev. ed. Dick Mills. (Fishkeeper's Guide Ser.). (Illus.). 120p. 1991. 11.95 (*1-56465-129-0*, 16064) Tetra Pr.

***Marine Fishes: 500 Essential-to-Know Aquarium Species.** Scott W. Michael. LC 99-35858. (PocketExpert Guide Ser.: Vol. 1). (Illus.). 448p. 1999. pap. 24.95 (*1-890087-38-6*) Microcosm Ltd.

Marine Fishes & Invertebrates in Your Own Home. Cliff W. Emmens. (Illus.). 192p. 1988. 35.95 (*0-86622-790-3*, H-1103) TFH Pubns.

Marine Flora & Fauna of Hong Kong & Southern China 11, 3 vols., Set. Ed. by Brian Morton. 1322p. (C). 1990. pap. text 257.50 (*962-209-241-1*, Pub. by HK Univ Pr) Coronet Bks.

Marine Flora & Fauna of Hong Kong & Southern China: Proceedings of the First International Marine Biological Workshop, Hong Kong, 18 April-10 May 1980, 2 vols., 1. International Marine Biological Workshop Staff. Ed. by Brian Morton & C. K. Tseng. LC 82-223457. 562p. reprint ed. pap. 174.30 (*0-7837-1975-2*, 204224800001) Bks Demand.

Marine Flora & Fauna of Hong Kong & Southern China: Proceedings of the First International Marine Biological Workshop, Hong Kong, 18 April-10 May 1980, 2 vols., 2. International Marine Biological Workshop Staff. Ed. by Brian Morton & C. K. Tseng. LC 82-223457. 387p. reprint ed. pap. 120.00 (*0-7837-1976-0*, 204224800002) Bks Demand.

Marine Flora & Fauna of Hong Kong & Southern China III: Proceedings of the 4th International Workshop on the Marine Flora & Fauna of Hong Kong, Hong Kong, April 11-29, 1989, 2 vols. Ed. by B. Morton. 928p. 1992. pap. 197.00 (*90-73348-17-X*, Pub. by Backhuys Pubs) Balogh.

Marine Flora & Fauna of Hong Kong & Southern China III: Proceedings of the 4th International Workshop on the Marine Flora & Fauna of Hong Kong, Hong Kong, April 11-29, 1989, 2 vols. Ed. by Brian Morton. (Illus.). 928p. 1993. pap. 225.00 (*962-209-293-4*, Pub. by HK Univ Pr) Coronet Bks.

Marine Flora & Fauna of Hong Kong & Southern China IV, Vol. IV. Ed. by Brian Morton. 540p. (Orig.). 1997. pap. 99.50 (*962-209-437-6*, Pub. by HK Univ Pr) Coronet Bks.

Marine Foods: Lebensmittel Aus Dem Meer. Ed. by J. C. Somogyi & D. Hoetzel. (Bibliotheca Nutritio et Dieta Ser.: No. 46). (Illus.). xii, 130p. 1990. 117.50 (*3-8055-5219-X*) S Karger.

***Marine from Boston: A First Person Story of a U. S. Marine in World War II: Boot Camp, New River, Samoa, Guadalcanal, Bougainville.** John J. Carey. LC 00-34109. 2000. write for info. (*1-880774-26-7*) Ferguson.

Marine Fuels - STP 878. Ed. by Cletus H. Jones. LC 85-15642. 293p. 1985. text 43.00 (*0-8031-0425-1*, STP878) ASTM.

Marine Gear Drives. A. A. Ross. (Technical Papers: Vol. P65). (Illus.). 8p. 1921. pap. text 30.00 (*1-55589-403-8*) AGMA.

Marine Gearing. I. Short. (Technical Papers: Vol. P137). (Illus.). 17p. 1936. pap. text 30.00 (*1-55589-406-2*) AGMA.

Marine Geochemistry. R. Chester. 416p. 1989. pap. text 59.95 (*0-04-551109-8*) Routledge.

***Marine Geochemistry.** Ed. by H. D. Schulz & M. Zabel. LC 99-50190. (Illus.). 487p. 2000. 89.95 (*3-540-66453-X*) Spr-Verlag.

Marine Geochemistry. 2nd ed. Roy Chester. LC 99-17623. (Illus.). 1999. 175.00 (*0-632-05432-8*) Blackwell Sci.

Marine Geological & Geophysical Atlas of the Circum-Antarctic to 30 Degrees S. Ed. by D. E. Hayes. (Antarctic Research Ser.: Vol. 54). (Illus.). 60p. 1991. 54.00 (*0-87590-811-X*) Am Geophysical.

Marine Geological Surveying & Sampling. Ed. by Ernest A. Hailwood & Robert B. Kidd. (C). 1990. text 195.50 (*0-7923-0788-7*) Kluwer Academic.

Marine Geology. James P. Kennett. (Illus.). 813p. (C). 1981. 93.33 (*0-13-556936-2*) P-H.

Marine Geology: A Planet Earth Perspective. rev. ed. Roger N. Anderson. 336p. 1989. pap. 87.95 (*0-471-50407-6*) Wiley.

Marine Geology: Undersea Landforms & Life Forms. Jon Erickson. LC 95-22109. (Changing Earth Ser.). 256p. 1996. 26.95 (*0-8160-3354-4*) Facts on File.

Marine Geology & Oceanography of the Pacific Manganese Nodule Province. Ed. by J. L. Bischoff & D. Z. Piper. LC 79-12475. (Marine Science Ser.: Vol. 9). 856p. 1979. 145.00 (*0-306-40187-8*, Plenum Trade) Perseus Pubng.

Marine Geology & Palaeoceanography see Proceedings of the 30th International Geological Congress

Marine Geology, Geophysics, & Geochemistry of the Woodlark Basin: Solomon Islands. Ed. by Brian Taylor & Neville F. Exon. (Earth Science Ser.: Vol. 7). (Illus.). 365p. 1987. pap. 10.00 (*0-933687-07-9*, 832-28) Circum-Pacific.

***Marine Geology of Korean Seas.** 2nd ed. Sung Kwun Chough et al. LC 00-26493. 2000. write for info. (*0-444-50438-9*) Elsevier.

Marine Geophysics Jones Staff. LC 98-47324. 474p. 1999. pap. 54.95 (*0-471-98694-1*) Wiley.

***Marine Geophysics** Jones Staff. LC 98-47324. 474p. 1999. 125.00 (*0-471-98693-3*) Wiley.

Marine Geophysics, Plate Tectonics, & the Earth's Core. Ed. by G. A. Harrison. 192p. 1981. reprint ed. 15.00 (*0-87590-226-X*) Am Geophysical.

Marine Geotechnics. H. G. Poulos. (Illus.). 448p. 1988. mass mkt. 200.50 (*0-04-620024-X*) Routledge.

Marine Geotechnique: Proceedings. International Research Conference on Marine Geotechnique (1966: Allerton House) Ed. by Adrian F. Richards. LC 67-27773. (Illus.). 335p. reprint ed. 103.90 (*0-8357-9688-4*, 201493600097) Bks Demand.

Marine Geotechnology & Nearshore-Offshore Structures. Ed. by R. C. Chaney & Hsai-Yang Fang. LC 86-22200. (Special Technical Publication Ser.: No. 923). (Illus.). 380p. 1986. text 48.00 (*0-8031-0490-1*, STP923) ASTM.

Marine Gyro Compasses for Ship's Officers. A. Frost. (C). 1987. 80.00 (*0-85174-426-5*) St Mut.

Marine Hawser Towing Guide. Richard A. Cady. (Illus.). 123p. (Orig.). 1985. reprint ed. pap. text 26.00 (*0-934114-65-X*, BK-120) Marine Educ.

Marine Helo: Helicopter War in Vietnam with the U. S. Marine Corps. David Petteys. (Illus.). 240p. 1995. pap. 20.00 (*0-9671793-0-0*) D M Petteys.

Marine Hydrodynamics. John N. Newman. 1977. 63.00 (*0-262-14026-8*) MIT Pr.

Marine Hydrotherman Systems & the Origin of Life: Report of SCOR Working Group 91. N. G. Holm. 248p. (C). 1992. text 185.00 (*0-7923-2018-2*) Kluwer Academic.

Marine Inboard Engines: Petrol & Diesel. Loris Goring. (Illus.). 196p. 1990. pap. 35.00 (*0-229-11842-9*, Pub. by Adlard Coles) Sheridan.

Marine Insurance: Cargo Practice, Vol. 2. 4th ed. Robert H. Brown. (C). 1985. 225.00 (*0-7855-6043-2*, Pub. by Witherby & Co) St Mut.

Marine Insurance: Hull Practice, Vol. 3. Robert H. Brown. 425p. 1975. 81.00 (*0-900886-13-7*, Pub. by Witherby & Co) St Mut.

Marine Insurance: Hull Practice, Vol. 3. Ed. by Robert H. Brown. 1200p. (C). 1995. 395.00 (*0-948691-45-X*, Pub. by Witherby & Co) St Mut.

Marine Insurance: Principles & Basic Practice, Vol. 1. 5th ed. Robert H. Brown. (C). 1986. write for info. (*0-7855-2604-8*, Pub. by Witherby & Co) St Mut.

Marine Insurance: Templeman on Principles & Practice. 6th ed. R. J. Lambeth. (C). 1986. 600.00 (*0-7855-4086-5*, Pub. by Witherby & Co) St Mut.

Marine Insurance Vol. 1: Principles & Basic Practice. Robert H. Brown. 343p. (C). 1986. 155.00 (*0-948691-19-0*, Pub. by Witherby & Co) St Mut.

***Marine Insurance Vol. 1: Principles & Basic Practice.** Robert H. Brown. 408p. 1998. 140.00 (*1-85609-150-3*, Pub. by Witherby & Co) St Mut.

Marine Insurance Vol. 2: Cargo Practice. Robert H. Brown & J. J. Novitt. 450p. (C). 1985. 200.00 (*0-900886-83-8*, Pub. by Witherby & Co) St Mut.

Marine Insurance Vol. 2: Cargo Practice. 5th ed. Robert H. Brown. 630p. 1998. 180.00 (*1-85609-132-5*, Pub. by Witherby & Co) St Mut.

Marine Insurance Abbreviations. Robert H. Brown. 91p. 1974. 60.00 (*0-900886-00-5*, Pub. by Witherby & Co) St Mut.

Marine Insurance Abbreviations. Robert H. Brown. (C). 1984. 100.00 (*0-7855-4090-3*, Pub. by Witherby & Co) St Mut.

Marine Insurance & Average: The Law & Practice, 2 vols. A. Parks. (C). 1988. 1145.00 (*0-7855-6044-0*, Pub. by Witherby & Co) St Mut.

Marine Insurance & Reinsurance Abbreviations. Robert H. Brown. 130p. (C). 1994. pap., per. 50.00 (*0-948691-63-8*, Pub. by Witherby & Co) St Mut.

Marine Insurance-Arnould On: British Shipping Laws, 2 vols. 16th ed. Witherby & Co. Ltd. Staff. (C). 1981. 1170.00 (*0-7855-6045-9*, Pub. by Witherby & Co) St Mut.

Marine Insurance Claims. J. K. Goodacre. (C). 1981. 350.00 (*0-7855-4088-1*, Pub. by Witherby & Co) St Mut.

Marine Insurance Claims. J. Kenneth Goodacre. 1016p. 1981. 350.00 (*0-900886-53-6*, Pub. by Witherby & Co) St Mut.

Marine Insurance Claims 3rd ed. J. Kenneth Goodacre. LC 98-231402. lxvii,1439p. 1996. write for info. (*1-85609-104-X*) Witherby & Co.

Marine Insurance Digest. Hugh A. Mullins. LC 59-15426. 308p. reprint ed. 95.50 (*0-8357-9073-8*, 201910500010) Bks Demand.

Marine Insurance Fraud in International Trade. Michael Ford. 312p. (C). 1993. 395.00 (*1-85609-047-7*, Pub. by Witherby & Co) St Mut.

Marine Insurance Law of Canada. Rui M. Fernandes. (C). 1987. 520.00 (*0-7855-4087-3*, Pub. by Witherby & Co) St Mut.

Marine Insurance, Non-Marine Insurance, General Average, Salvage, 1919-1991. (Lloyd's Law Reports Consolidated Index, 1919-1994 Ser.: Vol. 3). 1992. 125.00 (*1-85044-427-7*) LLP.

Marine Invertebrate Fisheries: Their Assessment & Management. Ed. by John F. Caddy. LC 87-32436. 768p. 1989. 190.00 (*0-471-83237-5*) Wiley.

Marine Invertebrates. Chris Andrews. (Illus.). 1988. pap. 3.15 (*3-923880-49-9*, 16853) Tetra Pr.

Marine Invertebrates: Comparative Physiology. Carl S. Hammen. LC 80-51505. 142p. reprint ed. pap. 44.10 (*0-8357-6515-6*, 203588600097) Bks Demand.

Marine Invertebrates & Plants of the Living Reef. Patrick L. Colin. (Illus.). 512p. (YA). (gr. 7 up). 1988. 35.95 (*0-86622-875-6*, H-971) TFH Pubns.

Marine Invertebrates in the Aquarium. Richard F. Stratton. (Illus.). 64p. 1998. 12.95 (*0-7938-0333-0*, WW092) TFH Pubns.

Marine Invertebrates in the Home Aquarium. U. Erich Friese. (Illus.). 119p. 1973. 23.95 (*0-86622-708-3*, PS-658) TFH Pubns.

Marine Invertebrates Pacific Northwest. Kozloff. (Illus.). 511p. 1996. pap. 40.00 (*0-295-97562-8*) U of Wash Pr.

Marine Jet Drive, 1961-1996. Clarence W. Coles. (Marine Tune-Up & Repair Manuals). (C). 1998. pap. text 34.95 (*0-89330-029-2*, Pub. by Seloc) Natl Bk Netwk.

Marine Laws: Navigation & Safety, 2 vols. 4th ed. 1700p. 1993. boxed set 195.00 (*0-88063-468-5*, MICHIE) LEXIS Pub.

Marine Laws: Navigation & Safety, 2 vols. 4th ed. Warren Freedman. Ed. by Butterworths Staff. 1700p. 1993. ring bd. 195.00 (*0-250-40701-9*, 83165-10, MICHIE) LEXIS Pub.

Marine Liabilities Guidelines to Exposures & Insurance of Port Authorities & Other Port Related Industries or Activities. A. S. Bashford. 41p. 1989. 75.00 (*0-948691-82-4*, Pub. by Witherby & Co) St Mut.

Marine Liabilities Guidelines to Exposures & Insurance of Port Authorities & Other Port Related Industries or Activities. A. S. Bashford. (C). 1989. 90.00 (*0-948691-29-8*, Pub. by Witherby & Co) St Mut.

Marine Life. Ed. by Christine J. Dillon. (My First Report Ser.). (Illus.). 48p. (J). (gr. 1-3). 1995. ring bd. 5.95 (*1-57896-042-8*, 2224) Hewitt Res Fnd.

Marine Life & the Sea. David H. Milne. LC 94-20337. 459p. 1994. 80.95 (*0-534-16314-9*) Wadsworth Pub.

Marine Life of Southern California. Donald J. Reish. 240p. (C). 1995. pap. text 21.00 (*0-7872-1045-5*) Kendall-Hunt.

Marine Life of the North Atlantic: Canada to New England. Andrew J. Martinez. (Illus.). 265p. (Orig.). pap. 30.00 (*0-9640131-0-X*) Martinez & Katz.

Marine Life of the North Atlantic: Canada to New England. 2nd ed. Andrew J. Martinez. LC 98-48695. (Illus.). 272p. (Orig.). 1999. pap. 30.00 (*0-89272-455-2*) Down East.

Marine Life of the Pacific & Indian Oceans. Gerald R. Allen. (Illus.). 96p. 1997. pap. 19.95 (*962-593-016-7*, Periplus Eds) Tuttle Pubng.

Marine Life of the Pacific & Indian Oceans: A Periplus Nature Guide. Gerald Allen. 1997. pap. 19.95 (*0-614-27433-8*) Periplus.

Marine Light Field Statistics. Ronald E. Walker. (Pure & Applied Optics Ser.). 675p. 1994. 129.95 (*0-471-31046-8*) Wiley.

Marine Lighting: RP-12-97. rev. ed. Marine Committee. (Recommended Practices Ser.). (Illus.). 25p. 1996. pap. 25.00 (*0-87995-127-3*, RP-12-96) Illum Eng.

Marine Lipids. Rita Elkins. (The Woodland Health Ser.). 1997. pap. text 3.95 (*1-885670-50-8*) Woodland UT.

Marine Lover of Friedrich Nietzsche. Luce Irigaray. Tr. by Gillian C. Gill from FRE. 1991. text 43.00 (*0-231-07082-9*) Col U Pr.

Marine Lover of Friedrich Nietzsche. Luce Irigaray. 1993. pap. 18.00 (*0-231-07083-7*) Col U Pr.

Marine Maintenance & Repair Industry: Guides to Pollution Prevention. (Illus.). 64p. (Orig.). (C). 1995. pap. text 25.00 (*0-7881-2142-1*) DIANE Pub.

Marine Maintenance Foreman. Jack Rudman. (Career Examination Ser.: C-3070). 1994. pap. 29.95 (*0-8373-3070-X*) Nat Learn.

Marine Mammal Commission Compendium of Selected Treaties, International Agreements, & Other Relevant Documents on Marine Resources, Wildlife & the Environment (First Update) Ed. by Richard L. Wallace. 1017p. (C). 1999. reprint ed. pap. text 95.00 (*0-7881-7591-2*) DIANE Pub.

***Marine Mammal Commission Compendium of Selected Treaties, International Agreements Other Relevant Documents on Marine Resources, Wildlife & the Environment: First Update.** Richard L. Wallace. 1037p. 1998. per. 63.00 (*0-16-049316-1*) USGPO.

***Marine Mammal Research in the Southern Hemisphere.** Ed. by Surrey Beatty Staff. 220p. 1999. pap. 180.00 (*0-949324-76-0*, Pub. by Surrey Beatty & Sons) St Mut.

Marine Mammal Sensory Systems. J. A. Thomas et al. LC 92-35373. (Illus.). 788p. (C). 1993. text 165.00 (*0-306-44351-1*, Kluwer Plenum) Kluwer Academic.

***Marine Mammal Survey & Assessment Methods: Proceedings of the Symposium on Marine Mammal Survey & Assessment Methods, Seattle, WA, 21-25.02.1998.** Ed. by G. W. Garner et al. (Illus.). 13p. 1999. 95.00 (*90-5809-043-4*, Pub. by A A Balkema) Ashgate Pub Co.

Marine Mammals: Evolutionary Biology. Annalisa Berta & Sumich. 460p. 1999. 59.95 (*0-12-093225-3*) Acad Pr.

An Asterisk (*) at the beginning of an entry indicates that the title is appearing for the first time.

Marine Mammals & Fisheries. Ed. by R. J. Beverton et al. (Illus.). 350p. (C). 1985. text 100.00 (*0-04-639003-0*) Routledge.

***Marine Mammals & Low-Frequency Sound: Progress since 1994.** Ocean Studies Board Staff et al. 160p. 2000. pap. 35.00 (*0-309-06886-X*) Natl Acad Pr.

Marine Mammals & Noise. W. John Richardson. 1998. pap. text 39.95 (*0-12-588441-9*) Acad Pr.

Marine Mammals & the "Exxon Valdez" Ed. by Thomas R. Loughlin. (Illus.). 395p. 1994. text 53.00 (*0-12-456160-8*) Acad Pr.

Marine Mammals, Coastal & River Issues. Belle Mickelson. (Alaska Sea Week Curriculum Ser.). (Illus.). 186p. 1994. reprint ed. teacher ed., ring bd. 12.50 (*1-56612-023-3*) AK Sea Grant CP.

Marine Mammals of Australasia: Field Biology & Captive Management. Ed. by M. L. Augee. 140p. (C). 1988. text 55.00 (*0-7855-0032-4*, Pub. by Surrey Beatty & Sons) St Mut.

Marine Mammals of California. Robert T. Orr et al. LC 78-165233. (California Natural History Guides Ser.: No. 29). 92p. 1972. pap. 12.95 (*0-520-06515-8*, Pub. by U CA Pr) Cal Prin Full Svc.

***Marine Mammals of the Gulf of Mexico.** Bernd G. Wursig et al. LC 99-36385. (Natural History Ser.). (Illus.). 304p. 2000. 34.95 (*0-89096-909-4*) Tex A&M Univ Pr.

Marine Mammals of the Wadden Sea: Final Report of the Section "Marine Mammals" of the Wadden Sea WorkinG Group. Ed. by W. J. Wolff & Peter J. Reijinders. 64p. (C). 1982. text 51.00 (*90-6191-057-9*, Pub. by A A Balkema) Ashgate Pub Co.

Marine Mammals of the World Species Identification Guide. T. Jefferson & Stephen Leatherwood. (Illus.). 328p. 1994. pap. 56.00 (*92-5-103292-0*, F32920, Pub. by FAO) Bernan Associates.

Marine Management in Disputed Areas: The Case of the Barents Sea. Robin Churchill & Geir Ulfstein. LC 91-37180. (Ocean Management & Policy Ser.). 208p. (C). 1992. 100.00 (*0-415-03811-1*, A7209) Routledge.

Marine Manufacturer's Identification Code Book, Vol. 2. Intertec Publishing Staff. LC 96-78271. 193p. (Orig.). 1996. pap. 26.95 (*0-87288-630-1*, MM1C-3) Intertec Pub.

Marine Mesocosms: Biological & Chemical Research in Experimental Ecosystems. Ed. by G. D. Grice & M. R. Reeve. (Illus.). 450p. 1981. 157.00 (*0-387-90579-0*) Spr-Verlag.

Marine Microbiology: A Monograph on Hydrobacteriology. C. E. Zobell. (Illus.). 240p. 1990. reprint ed. text 49.00 (*81-211-0044-5*, Pub. by Mahendra Pal Singh) Lubrecht & Cramer.

Marine Micropaleontology of China. P. Wang. LC 85-1468. (Illus.). 380p. 1985. 175.95 (*0-387-13147-7*) Spr-Verlag.

Marine Mineral Exploration. Ed. by H. Kunzendorf. (Elsevier Oceanography Ser.: Vol. 41). 300p. 1986. 162.50 (*0-444-42627-2*) Elsevier.

Marine Mineral Resources. Fillmore C. Earney. LC 89-38875. (Illus.). 400p. (C). 1990. 150.00 (*0-415-02255-X*, A3912) Routledge.

Marine Minerals: Advances in Research & Resource Assessment. Ed. by P. G. Teleki et al. 1987. text 256.00 (*90-277-2436-9*) Kluwer Academic.

Marine Mollusca of the Maltese Islands Pt. 2: Neotaenioglossa. C. Cachia et al. (Illus.). 228p. 1996. pap. 48.00 (*90-73348-48-X*, Pub. by Backhuys Pubs) Balogh.

Marine Molluscan Genera of Western North America: An Illustrated Key. 2nd ed. A. Myra Keen & Eugene Coan. LC 73-80625. (Illus.). 224p. 1974. 35.00 (*0-8047-0839-8*) Stanford U Pr.

Marine Molluscan Genera of Western North America: An Illustrated Key. 2nd ed. Angeline M. Keen & Eugene Coan. LC 73-80625. (Illus.). 216p. 1974. reprint ed. pap. 30.00 (*0-7837-6817-6*, 204664900003) Bks Demand.

Marine Molluscan Remains from Franchthi Cave: Fascicle 4. Judith C. Shackleton. LC 87-45115. (Excavations at Franchthi Cave, Greece Ser.: No. 4). (Illus.). 208p. 1989. pap. 35.00 (*0-253-31976-5*) Ind U Pr.

Marine Mollusks of Cape Cod. Donald J. Zinn. (Natural History Ser.: No. 2). (Illus.). 80p. 1984. pap. 6.95 (*0-916275-00-0*) Cape Cod Mus Nat His.

Marine Motifs on Ancient Coins. J. Ringel. (Illus.). 96p. 1984. lib. bdg. 25.00 (*965-222-008-6*) Maureen Mack.

Marine, Municipal & Industrial Waste Water Disposal: Proceedings, Sorrento, Italy see Progress in Water Technology

Marine Musings: Illustrated Poetry. Yon Swanson. (Illus.). 111p. 1973. 12.95 (*0-913042-01-3*) Holland Hse Pr.

***Marine Mystique.** Frank Hernandez. LC 00-190724. 2000. 25.00 (*0-7388-1950-6*); pap. 18.00 (*0-7388-1951-4*) Xlibris Corp.

Marine Natural Products Diversity & Biosynthesis. Ed. by Paul J. Scheuer. (Topics in Current Chemistry Ser.: Vol. 167). (Illus.). 197p. 1993. 118.95 (*0-387-56513-2*) Spr-Verlag.

Marine Navigation: Piloting & Celestial & Electronic Navigation. 3rd ed. Richard R. Hobbs. LC 90-30116. (Illus.). 672p. (C). 1990. 39.95 (*0-87021-294-X*) Naval Inst Pr.

Marine Navigation: Piloting & Celestial & Electronic Navigation. 4th ed. Richard R. Hobbs. LC 97-34676. (Illus.). 640p. 1997. 49.95 (*1-55750-381-8*) Naval Inst Pr.

Marine Navigation Workbook: Piloting & Celestial & Electronic Navigation. 3rd ed. Richard R. Hobbs. 1990. wbk. ed. 18.95 (*1-55750-551-9*) Naval Inst Pr.

Marine Navigation Workbook: Piloting & Celestial & Electronic Navigation. 4th ed. Richard R. Hobbs. (Illus.). 200p. 1997. pap. 24.95 (*1-55750-385-0*) Naval Inst Pr.

Marine Observation Satellite, Vol. 1. K. Tsuchiya et al. (Remote Sensing Reviews Ser.: Vol. 3, No. 1). 56p. 1987. pap. text 63.00 (*3-7186-0420-5*) Gordon & Breach.

Marine Officers Guide. 1987. lib. bdg. 69.00 (*0-8490-3955-X*) Gordon Pr.

Marine Officer's Guide. 6th rev. ed. Kenneth W. Estes. LC 95-3307. (Illus.). 520p. 1995. 26.95 (*1-55750-567-5*) Naval Inst Pr.

Marine, Offshore & Ice Technology. Ed. by T. K. S. Murthy et al. 416p. 1994. 213.00 (*1-85312-344-7*) Computational Mech MA.

Marine, Offshore & Ice Technology: Proceedings of CADMO 94 & ITC 94. Ed. by T. K. Murthy et al. LC 94-72458. (CADMO Ser.: Vol. 4). 416p. 1994. 213.00 (*1-56252-268-X*, 3447) Computational Mech MA.

Marine Oiler. Jack Rudman. (Career Examination Ser.: C-471). 1994. pap. 27.95 (*0-8373-0471-7*) Nat Learn.

Marine Olaf. Gordon Hoban. LC 89-92327. 155p. (Orig.). 1990. pap. 12.95 (*0-944204-09-0*) Omniun.

Marine Organism As Indicators. Ed. by D. F. Soule & G. S. Kleppel. (Illus.). 425p. 1988. 208.00 (*0-387-96565-3*) Spr-Verlag.

Marine Outfall Systems: Planning, Design, & Construction. Robert A. Grace. 1978. 89.00 (*0-13-556951-6*) Ocean Sci-Tech.

Marine Paintings & Drawings in Mystic Seaport Museum. Dorothy E. Brewington. (Illus.). ix, 219p. 1982. 40.00 (*0-913372-25-0*) Mystic Seaport.

Marine Paintings & Drawings in the Peabody Museum of Salem. rev. ed. Marion V. Brewington & Dorothy Brewington. (Illus.). xvii, 530p. 1981. 125.00 (*0-87577-066-5*, PEMP140, Peabody Museum) Peabody Essex Mus.

Marine Palaeoenvironmental Analysis from Fossils. Ed. by D. W. Bosence & P. A. Allison. (Special Publication Ser.: No. 83). (Illus.). 272p. 1995. pap. 64.00 (*1-897799-31-4*, 221, Pub. by Geol Soc Pub Hse) AAPG.

Marine Particles: Analysis & Characterization. Ed. by D. C. Hurd & D. W. Spencer. (Geophysical Monograph Ser.: Vol. 63). 482p. 1991. 56.00 (*0-87590-029-1*, GM0630291) Am Geophysical.

Marine Pelagic Cyanobacteria: Trichodesmium & Other Diazotrophs. Ed. by E. J. Carpenter et al. (C). 1992. text 185.00 (*0-7923-1614-2*) Kluwer Academic.

Marine Personnel Safety Manual. (C). 1989. 130.00 (*0-89771-719-8*, Pub. by Lorne & MacLean Marine) St Mut.

Marine Phosphorites. Ed. by Y. K. Bentor. (Special Publications: NO. 29). 247p. 1980. 33.50 (*0-918985-09-9*) SEPM.

Marine Physics. J. Dera. (Oceanography Ser.: Vol. 53). 516p. 1991. 245.00 (*0-444-98716-9*) Elsevier.

Marine Phytoplankton & Productivity: Proceedings of the Invited Lectures to a Symposium Organized within the 5th Conference of the European Society for Cooperative Physiology & Biochemistry, Taurmina, Sicily, Sept. 5-8, 1983. Ed. by O. Holm-Hansen et al. (Lecture Notes on Coastal & Estaurine Studies: Vol. 8). vii, 175p. 1984. pap. 29.00 (*0-387-13333-X*) Spr-Verlag.

Marine Pioneers: The Unsung Heroes of World War II. Kerry Lane. LC 96-70487. (Illus.). 272p. 1997. 29.95 (*0-7643-0227-2*) Schiffer.

Marine Planarians of the World. R. Sluys. 1994. 99.00 (*3-540-14191-X*) Spr-Verlag.

Marine Planarians of the World. R. Sluys. 1996. cd-rom 99.00 (*3-540-14192-8*) Spr-Verlag.

Marine Plankton Diatoms of the West Coast of North America. Easter E. Cupp. (Bulletin of the Scripps Institute of Oceanography, Techn. Ser.: Vol. 5, Pt. 1). (Illus.). 237p. 1977. reprint ed. 95.00 (*3-87429-125-1*, 002145, Pub. by Koeltz Sci Bks) Lubrecht & Cramer.

Marine Plankton Life Cycle Strategies. Karen A. Steidinger & Linda M. Walker. 168p. 1984. 100.00 (*0-8493-5222-3*, QH91, CRC Reprint) Franklin.

Marine Planktonic Ostracode. M. Angel. Ed. by Expert-Center for Taxonomic Identification (ETI) S. (World Biodiversity Database Ser.). 1998. pap. 109.00 incl. cd-rom (*3-540-14680-6*) Spr-Verlag.

Marine Plant Biomass of the Pacific Northwest Coast: A Potential Economic Resource. Ed. by Robert W. Krauss. (Illus.). 416p. 1978. text 29.95 (*0-87071-447-3*) Oreg St U Pr.

Marine Plants of the Caribbean: A Field Guide from Florida to Brazil. Diane S. Littler et al. LC 88-43157. (Illus.). 272p. (C). 1989. pap. 24.95 (*0-87474-607-8*) Smithsonian.

Marine Policy & Management in Southeast Asian Seas: A Selected Bibliography. Mark J. Valencia & Diana C. Shepherd. vii, 58p. (Orig.). 1981. pap. text 3.00 (*0-86638-035-3*) EW Ctr HI.

Marine Pollution. 1981. 75.95 (*0-387-10940-4*) Spr-Verlag.

Marine Pollution. Ed. by J. Albaiges. (Proceedings of the Arab School of Science & Technology Ser.). (Illus.). 225p. 1989. 115.00 (*0-89116-862-1*) Hemisp Pub.

Marine Pollution. 4th ed. Robert Clark. (Illus.). 172p. 1997. pap. text 37.00 (*0-19-850069-6*) OUP.

Marine Pollution. 4th ed. Robert Clark. (Illus.). 172p. (C). 1997. text 75.00 (*0-19-850070-X*) OUP.

Marine Pollution: ACOPS Yearbook, 1990. Ed. by Advisory Committee on Pollution of the Sea, London. (Advisory Committee on the Pollution of the Sea Ser.: Vol. 1). (Illus.). 188p. 1990. pap. 77.50 (*0-08-040809-5*, Pergamon Pr) Elsevier.

Marine Pollution & International Law: Principles & Practices. Douglas Brubaker. 420p. 1993. 79.95 (*0-85293-273-1*, BH3273) CRC Pr.

Marine Pollution & International Law: Principles & Practices. Douglas Brubaker. 485p. 1994. 79.95 (*1-85293-273-2*) Halsted Pr.

Marine Pollution & Sea Life. Ed. by Mario Ruivo. 1978. 100.00 (*0-7855-6936-7*) St Mut.

Marine Pollution & the Law of the Sea, 4 vols. in 6. John W. Kindt. LC 84-81482. 1986. lib. bdg. 595.00 (*0-89941-327-7*, 303250) W S Hein.

Marine Pollution by Oil. Institute of Petroleum Staff. (Illus.). 198p. 1974. 43.00 (*0-85334-452-3*) Elsevier.

Marine Pollution in International & Middle Eastern Law. S. H. Amin. 1986. 60.00 (*0-946706-26-3*, Pub. by Royston Ltd) St Mut.

Marine Pollution Laws of the Australasian Region. Michael James Denham White. LC 94-238133. 334p. 1994. 79.00 (*1-86287-139-6*, Pub. by LawBk Co) Gaunt.

Marine Polymetallic Sulfides: A National Overview & Future Needs. Ed. by Mary B. Hatem. 1983. pap. 1.50 (*0-943676-21-5*) MD Sea Grant Col.

Marine Populations: An Essay on Population Regulation & Speciation. Michael Sinclair. (Illus.). 260p. 1988. pap. 15.00 (*0-295-96634-3*) U of Wash Pr.

Marine Products Directory, 1997. (C). 1997. pap. text 10.00 (*0-7629-0106-3*) Underwrtrs Labs.

Marine Propellers & Propulsion. J.S. Carlton. LC 94-222746. 432p. 1994. 215.00 (*0-7506-1143-X*) Buttrwrth-Heinemann.

Marine Propulsion: Presented at the Winter Annual Meeting of the ASME, New York, NY, December 5-10, 1976. American Society of Mechanical Engineers Staff. Ed. by J. Sladky. LC 76-28850. (American Society of Mechanical Engineers, Applied Mechanics Division Ser.: Vol. 2). (Illus.). 235p. reprint ed. pap. 72.90 (*0-608-10776-X*, 201681500005) Bks Demand.

Marine Propulsion: Principles & Evolution. Robert Taggart. LC 79-75731. (Illus.). 380p. reprint ed. pap. 117.80 (*0-608-18168-4*, 203287400081) Bks Demand.

Marine Propulsion: The Most Comprehensive Source on Marine Propulsion Worldwide. (Illus.). 1999. 890.00 (*0-7106-1515-9*) Janes Info Group.

Marine Prosobranch Gastropods from Oceanic Islands off Brazil. J. H. Leal. (Illus.). 419p. 1991. pap. 99.00 (*90-73348-11-0*, Pub. by Backhuys Pubs) Balogh.

Marine Protected Areas & Ocean Conservation. Tundi Agardy. 1997. text 69.95 (*0-12-044455-0*) Acad Pr.

Marine Protected Areas Needs in the South Asian Seas Region Vol. 4: Pakistan. Ed. by John C. Pernetta. 42p. (C). 1993. pap. text 13.50 (*2-8317-0177-5*, Pub. by IUCN) Island Pr.

Marine Protected Areas Needs in the South Asian Seas Region Vol. 5: Sri Lanka. Ed. by John C. Pernetta. 67p. (C). 1993. pap. text 13.50 (*2-8317-0178-3*, Pub. by IUCN) Island Pr.

Marine Radionavigation & Communications. Jeffrey W. Monroe & Thomas L. Bushy. LC 98-38876. (Illus.). 336p. 1998. text 40.00 (*0-87033-510-3*) Cornell Maritime.

Marine Radiotelephone Logbook. 66p. 1998. pap. 12.00 (*1-879778-69-6*) Marine Educ.

***Marine Recreation Equipment in Indonesia: A Strategic Entry Report, 1996.** Compiled by Icon Group International Staff. (Illus.). 165p. 1999. ring bd. 1650.00 incl. audio compact disk (*0-7418-1444-7*) Icon Grp.

Marine Recreational Fisheries. Ed. by Henry Clepper & Richard H. Stroud. (Illus.). 174p. (C). 1976. text 15.00 (*0-935217-04-5*) Intl Game Fish.

Marine Recreational Fisheries. Richard H. Stroud. Ed. by Henry Clepper. 1976. 15.00 (*0-686-21852-3*); pap. 12.00 (*0-686-21853-1*) Sport Fishing.

Marine Recreational Fisheries, No. 2. Ed. by Henry Clepper & Richard H. Stroud. (Illus.). 220p. (C). 1977. text 15.00 (*0-935217-05-3*) Intl Game Fish.

Marine Recreational Fisheries, No. 3. Ed. by Henry Clepper. 176p. (C). 1978. text 15.00 (*0-935217-06-1*) Intl Game Fish.

Marine Recreational Fisheries, No. 4. Ed. by Henry Clepper. (Illus.). 169p. (C). 1979. text 15.00 (*0-935217-07-X*) Intl Game Fish.

Marine Recreational Fisheries, No. 5. Ed. by Henry Clepper. 226p. (C). 1980. text 15.00 (*0-935217-08-8*) Intl Game Fish.

Marine Recreational Fisheries, No. 6. Frank E. Carlton. Ed. by Henry Clepper. 1981. 15.00 (*0-685-10270-X*) Sport Fishing.

Marine Recreational Fisheries, No. 6. Ed. by Henry Clepper. 212p. (C). 1981. text 15.00 (*0-935217-09-6*) Intl Game Fish.

Marine Recreational Fisheries, No. 7. Frank E. Carlton. Ed. by Henry Clepper. 1982. 15.00 (*0-685-10271-8*) Sport Fishing.

Marine Recreational Fisheries, No. 7. Ed. by Richard H. Stroud. 180p. 1982. 15.00 (*0-935217-10-X*) Intl Game Fish.

Marine Recreational Fisheries, Vol. 3. Frank E. Carlton. Ed. by Henry Clepper. LC 76-22389. 1978. 15.00 (*0-686-65030-1*) Sport Fishing.

Marine Recreational Fisheries, Vol. 4. Frank E. Carlton. Ed. by Henry Clepper. LC 76-22389. 1979. 15.00 (*0-686-65031-X*) Sport Fishing.

Marine Recreational Fisheries, Vol. 5. Frank E. Carlton. Ed. by Henry Clepper. LC 76-22389. 1980. 15.00 (*0-686-70340-5*) Sport Fishing.

Marine Recreational Fisheries, Vol. 8. Frank E. Carlton. Ed. by Henry Clepper. 1983. 15.00 (*0-317-45803-5*) Sport Fishing.

Marine Recreational Fisheries, Vol. 9. Frank E. Carlton. Ed. by Henry Clepper. 1984. 15.00 (*0-317-30084-9*) Sport Fishing.

Marine Recreational Fisheries, Vol. 10. Frank E. Carlton. Ed. by Henry Clepper. 1986. write for info. (*0-318-60770-0*) Sport Fishing.

Marine Recreational Fisheries, Vol. 11. Ed. by Richard H. Stroud. 1987. 15.00 (*0-685-38065-3*) Sport Fishing.

Marine Recreational Fisheries, Vol. 12. Ed. by Richard H. Stroud. 1988. 15.00 (*0-685-38066-1*) Sport Fishing.

Marine Recreational Fisheries, 2 pts., Vol. 13. Richard H. Stroud. 1989. 15.00 (*0-685-38067-X*) Sport Fishing.

Marine Recreational Fisheries, Vol. 14. Frank E. Carlton. Ed. by Henry Clepper. 199p. write for info. (*0-318-69747-5*) Sport Fishing.

Marine Recreational Fisheries: A Symposium, Vol. 2. Ed. by Richard H. Stroud & Henry Clepper. LC 76-22389. 1977. 15.00 (*0-686-22998-3*) Sport Fishing.

Marine Recreational Fisheries No. 8: Marine Recreational Fisheries at the Crossroads. Ed. by Richard H. Stroud. 236p. 1983. text 15.00 (*0-935217-11-8*) Intl Game Fish.

Marine Recreational Fisheries No. 9: Marine Recreational Fisheries Development. Ed. by Richard H. Stroud. (Illus.). 218p. (C). 1984. text 15.00 (*0-935217-12-6*) Intl Game Fish.

Marine Recreational Fisheries No. 10: Recreational Uses, Production & Management of Anadromous Pacific Salmonids. Ed. by Richard H. Stroud. 217p. 1985. text 15.00 (*0-935217-13-4*) Intl Game Fish.

Marine Recreational Fisheries No. 11: Multi-Jurisdictional Management of Marine Fisheries, No. 11. Ed. by Richard H Stroud. (Illus.). 237p. 1986. text 15.00 (*0-935217-14-2*) Intl Game Fish.

Marine Red Algae of Pacific Mexico: Ceramiales, Dasyaceae, Rhodomelaceae, Part 8. E. Y. Dawson. (Illus.). 1963. pap. 15.00 (*3-7682-0209-7*) Lubrecht & Cramer.

Marine Red Algae of the Hawaiian Islands. Isabella A. Abbott. LC 99-22307. 465p. 1999. 60.00 (*1-58178-003-6*) Bishop Mus.

Marine Reef Aquarium Handbook. Robert J. Goldstein. LC 96-38130. (Illus.). 180p. 1997. pap. 12.95 (*0-8120-9598-7*) Barron.

Marine Reinforced Plastics Construction: Manufacture & Repair. John A. Wills. (Illus.). 256p. 1998. pap. 29.95 (*1-888671-15-7*) Tiller.

Marine Reinsurance. Robert H. Brown & P. B. Reed. (C). 1981. 210.00 (*0-7855-4085-7*, Pub. by Witherby & Co) St Mut.

Marine Reinsurance. Robert Brown & Peter Reed. 343p. 1987. 230.00 (*0-900886-61-7*, Pub. by Witherby & Co) St Mut.

Marine Reinsurance Terms & Abbreviations. Robert H. Brown. 32p. 1982. 85.00 (*0-900886-58-7*, Pub. by Witherby & Co) St Mut.

Marine Reserves & Conservation of Mediterranean Coastal Habitats. Council of Europe Staff. (Nature & Environment Ser.: No. 50). 1990. 18.00 (*92-871-1889-2*, Pub. by Council of Europe) Manhattan Pub Co.

Marine Resources Technician. Jack Rudman. (Career Examination Ser.: C-1369). 1994. pap. 29.95 (*0-8373-1369-4*) Nat Learn.

Marine Safety Manual: Administration & Management, Vol. 1. Government Printing Office Staff. ring bd. 76.00 (*0-16-036201-6*) USGPO.

Marine Safety Manual: Investigations, Vol. 5. Government Printing Office Staff. 1989. ring bd. 50.00 (*0-16-017442-2*) USGPO.

***Marine Safety Manual: Marine Industry Personnel, Vol. 3.** Government Printing Office Staff. 1998. ring bd. 41.00 (*0-16-017439-2*) USGPO.

Marine Safety Manual: Materiel Inspection. Government Printing Office Staff. ring bd. 84.00 (*0-16-017435-X*) USGPO.

Marine Safety Manual: Merchant Marine Technical Manual, Vol. 4. Government Printing Office Staff. ring bd. 73.00 (*0-16-017441-4*) USGPO.

Marine Safety Manual: Port Security, Vol. 7. Government Printing Office Staff. 1991. ring bd. 74.00 (*0-16-029072-4*) USGPO.

Marine Safety Manual: Ports & Waterways Activities. Government Printing Office Staff. 1986. ring bd. 76.00 (*0-16-017444-9*) USGPO.

Marine Salvage: A Guide for Boaters & Divers. George H. Reid. LC 96-16995. (Illus.). 176p. 1996. 23.50 (*0-924486-99-6*) Sheridan.

Marine Salvage: Proceedings of the Third International Symposium. Ed. by Charles A. Bookman. 188p. 1985. pap. text 21.00 (*0-933957-01-7*) Marine Tech Soc.

Marine Salvage in the United States. National Research Council (U. S.), Marine Board St. LC VK1491.M36. 159p. reprint ed. pap. 49.30 (*0-8357-7706-5*, 203606100002) Bks Demand.

Marine Science Careers: A Sea Grant Guide to Ocean Opportunities. Steve Adams & Tracey Crago. (Illus.). 40p. 1996. pap. text 5.00 (*0-9649529-0-4*) Maine-NHamp SGCP.

***Marine Science Careers: A Sea Grant Guide to Ocean Opportunities.** rev. ed. Ed. by Steve Adams & Tracey Crago. (Illus.). 32p. 2000. pap. text 5.00 (*0-9649529-2-0*) Maine-NHamp SGCP.

Marine Science Journals & Serials: An Analytical Guide, 7. Judith B. Barnett. LC 86-7594. (Annotated Bibliographies of Serials: A Subject Approach Ser.: No. 7). 191p. 1986. lib. bdg. 59.95 (*0-313-24717-X*, BMS/, Greenwood Pr) Greenwood.

Marine Science of the Arabian Sea. Ed. by Mary F. Thompson & Nasima M. Tirmizi. (Illus.). 700p. 1988. 25.00 (*0-936829-01-X*) Am Inst Bio Sci.

***Marine Science on File.** Diagram Group Staff. (On File Ser.). (Illus.). 288p. 2000. 165.00 (*0-8160-4251-9*) Facts on File.

Marine Scientific Research. LC 94-198305. (The Law of the Sea Ser.). 185p. 25.00 (*92-1-133469-1*) UN.

Marine Seismic Source. Gregg Parkes & Les Hatton. 1986. text 113.00 (*90-277-2228-5*) Kluwer Academic.

Marine Shells of the West Coast of North America, 4 vols., Set. Ida S. Oldroyd. (Illus.). 1530p. 1927. 149.50 (*0-8047-0987-4*) Stanford U Pr.

Marine Shipboard Cable, UL 1309. (C). 1995. pap. text 95.00 (*1-55989-874-7*) Underwrtrs Labs.

Marine Shop Service Set, 10 vols., Set. 1991. 179.95 (*0-87288-260-8*, MARSS) Intertec Pub.

Marine Shrimp Culture: Principles & Practices. A. W. Fast & L. J. Lester. (Developments in Aquaculture & Fisheries Science Ser.: Vol. 23). xvi,862p. 1992. 195.50 (*0-444-88606-0*) Elsevier.

Marine Simulation & Ship Manoeuvrability: Proceedings of an International Conference, Copenhagen, 8-13 September 1996. Ed. by Erich Kasper & M. S. Chislett. (Illus.). 600p. (C). 1996. 181.00 (*90-5410-831-2*, Pub. by A A Balkema) Ashgate Pub Co.

Marine Sniper: 93 Confirmed Kills. Charles Henderson. 291p. 1988. mass mkt. 6.50 (*0-425-10355-2*) Berkley Pub.

Marine Sniper: 93 Confirmed Kills. Charles W. Henderson. 274p. 1995. 22.95 (*1-886681-01-5*) Claymore Pub.

Marine Snow. Karen Mac Cormack. LC 96-118782. 64p. 1995. pap. 12.00 (*1-55022-258-9*, Pub. by ECW) Genl Dist Srvs.

Marine Special Warfare & Elite Unit Tactics. Bob Newman. (Illus.). 184p. 1995. pap. 25.00 (*0-87364-845-5*) Paladin Pr.

Marine Specially Protected Area: The General Aspects & the Mediterranean Regional System. Tullio Scovazzi. LC 98-49925. (International Environmental Law & Policy Ser.). 1999. 141.00 (*90-411-1129-8*) Kluwer Law Intl.

Marine Species & Their Distributions in China's Seas. Huang Zongguo. 1999. write for info. (*1-57524-103-X*) Krieger.

Marine SSB Operation: A Small Boat Guide to Single Sideband Radio. J. Michael Gale. 96p. (C). 1990. text 70.00 (*0-906754-74-7*, Pub. by Fernhurst Bks) St Mut.

Marine SSB Operation: A Small Boat Guide to Single Sideband Radio. J. Michael Gale. 1998. pap. text 18.95 (*1-898660-40-9*) Fernhurst Bks.

Marine Stingers. John Williamson. (Illus.). 1996. 69.95 (*0-86840-229-X*, Pub. by New South Wales Univ Pr) Intl Spec Bk.

Marine Stoker. Jack Rudman. (Career Examination Ser.: C-472). 1994. pap. 23.95 (*0-8373-0472-5*) Nat Learn.

Marine Structures Research Recommendations: Recommendations for the Interagency Ship Structure Committee's 1998-1999 Research Program. National Research Council Staff. 108p. (C). 1997. pap. text 21.75 (*0-309-05786-8*) Natl Acad Pr.

Marine Survey Practice Compendium. Richard A. Cady. (Illus.). 362p. (Orig.). 1980. pap. text 54.00 (*0-934114-69-2*, BK-134) Marine Educ.

Marine Surveyor's Notebook. N. A. Vlassopulos. (C). 1987. 60.00 (*0-85174-354-4*) St Mut.

Marine Survival & Rescue Systems. David J. House. 317p. 1997. 120.00 (*1-986091-27-9*, Pub. by Witherby & Co) St Mut.

Marine Survival Equipment & Maintenance. Hank Pennington. (Education Publication: No. 6). (Illus.). 30p. 1990. pap. text 4.00 (*1-56612-030-6*) AK Sea Grant CP.

***Marine Tank Battles in the Pacific.** Oscar E. Gilbert. 2000. 34.95 (*1-58097-050-8*) Combined Pub.

Marine Technical Consultancy: A Guide to the Principles & Practice of Consulting Marine Engineering & Ship Surveying. Society of Consulting Marine Engineers & Ship Surv. 190p. 1992. 90.00 (*1-85609-043-4*, Pub. by Witherby & Co) St Mut.

Marine Technology, No. III. Ed. by T. Graczyk et al. (Marine & Maritime Ser.). 720p. 1999. 338.00 (*1-85312-699-3*, 6993, Pub. by WIT Pr) Computational Mech MA.

Marine Technology & Transportation. Ed. by T. Graczyk et al. 848p. 1995. 364.00 (*1-85312-330-7*) Computational Mech MA.

Marine Technology Programs: Where We Are & Where We're Going. Angelo C. Gillie & Arden L. Pratt. LC 78-28301. 57p. reprint ed. pap. 30.00 (*0-608-11524-X*, 202057000018) Bks Demand.

Marine Technology Reference Book. Nina Morgan. (Illus.). 500p. 1990. 280.00 (*0-408-02784-3*) Buttrwrth-Heinemann.

Marine Technology II. Ed. by Carlos A. Brebbia et al. LC 97-66367. (Marine Technology Ser.: Vol. 2). 568p. 1997. 268.00 (*1-85312-467-2*, 4672) Computational Mech MA.

Marine Tells It to You. Frederic M. Wise & Meigs O. Frost. 366p. 1981. reprint ed. 8.95 (*0-940328-02-X*) Marine Corps.

Marine Terminal Survey Guidelines. Ed. by Chemical Gas & Oil Terminals Staff. 1995. 125.00 (*1-85609-062-0*, Pub. by Witherby & Co) St Mut.

Marine Thraustochytrids & Chytridiomycetes in the North Sea Area & in Selected Other Regions. Annemarie Ulken. (Bibliotheca Mycologica: Vol. 137). (GER., Illus.). 93p. 1990. 53.00 (*3-443-59038-1*, Pub. by Gebruder Borntraeger) Balogh.

Marine Tourism: Development, Impacts & Management. Mark Orams. LC 98-18191. 1998. write for info. (*0-415-19572-1*); pap. 14.95 (*0-415-13938-4*) Routledge.

Marine Toxins: Origin, Structure, & Molecular Pharmacology. Ed. by Sherwood Hall & Gary R. Strichartz. LC 89-18505. (ACS Symposium Ser.: No. 418). (Illus.). 300p. 1990. 74.95 (*0-8412-1733-5*) Am Chemical.

Marine Transport: A Guide to Libraries. Marine Libraries Association Staff. 76p. 1983. pap. 65.00 (*0-946347-00-X*, Pub. by Witherby & Co) St Mut.

Marine Transportation. Questech Staff. (Illus.). 120p. 1997. text 99.95 (*1-58100-026-X*) Beckley Cardy.

Marine Transportation in War: The U. S. Army Experience, 1775-1860. Charles D. Gibson & E. Kay Gibson. LC 92-73583. (Army's Navy Ser.: Vol. 1). (Illus.). 192p. (C). 1992. lib. bdg. 27.00 (*0-9608996-2-6*) Ensign Pr.

Marine Transportation Management. Henry S. Marcus. LC 86-22188. 323p. 1986. 65.00 (*0-86569-158-4*, Auburn Hse) Greenwood.

Marine Transportation of LNG (Liquefied Natural Gas) & Related Products. Richard G. Wooler. LC 75-23457. 360p. 1975. reprint ed. pap. 111.60 (*0-608-02464-3*, 206310800004) Bks Demand.

Marine Tropical Aquarium Guide. Frank De Graaf. (Illus.). 282p. 1982. 17.95 (*0-87666-805-8*, PL-2017) TFH Pubns.

Marine Tropical Fish. John Green. (Little Activity Bks.). (J). 1994. pap. 1.00 (*0-486-28095-0*) Dover.

Marine Turtles in the Comoro Archipelago. J. Frazier. (Verhandelingen der Koninklijke Nederlandse Akademie van Wetenschappen, Afd. Natuurkunde Ser.: No. 84). 196p. pap. 59.50 (*0-444-85629-3*) Elsevier.

Marine Turtles in the Mediterranean: Distribution, Population Status, Conservation. Council of Europe Staff. (Nature & Environment Ser.: No. 48). 1990. 18.00 (*92-871-1864-7*, Pub. by Council of Europe) Manhattan Pub Co.

Marine Turtles in the Republic of the Seychelles: Status & Management : Report on Project 1809 (1981-1984) Jeanne A. Mortimer. LC 86-123064. vii, 80 p. 1984. write for info. (*2-88032-901-9*, Pub. by IUCN) Island Pr.

***Marine under the Mistletoe: Bachelor Battalion.** Maureen Child. (Desire Ser.). 1999. mass mkt. 3.75 (*0-373-76258-5*) Silhouette.

Marine VHF Operation. rev. ed. J. Michael Gale. (C). 1990. text 59.00 (*0-906754-27-5*, Pub. by Fernhurst Bks) St Mut.

Marine War Risks. 2nd ed. Michael D. Miller. 621p. 1994. 185.00 (*1-85044-516-8*) LLP.

Marine Way. Sam E. Clagg. Ed. by McClain Printing Co., Staff. (Illus.). 588p. 1989. 24.95 (*0-9623827-0-1*) McClain.

This is a factual story of Marine training & military activities in the Pacific during World War II. The detailed relating was made possible by over 900 pages of material personally logged at the time of the actual events. A portion of the content has been embellished in an effort to generate reader interest & to maintain continuity. Time may have eroded the specifics from the minds of most, but all warriors past & present should be able to identify with THE MARINE WAY. The work, accurate & in place & chronology, is approached in the manner of oral history. *Publisher Paid Annotation.*

***Marine Weather Forecasting.** Frank Brumbaugh. Ed. by John P. O'Connor, Jr. (Illus.). 96p. 2000. spiral bd. 15.95 (*1-892216-22-1*) Bristol Fash.

***Marine Weather Hazards Manual: West Coast Edition.** 3rd ed. Canada Environment Staff. 1999. pap. 22.50 (*0-660-17774-9*) Can Mus Nature.

Marine Wildlife: From Puget Sound Through the Inside Passage. Steve Yates. LC 98-26966. (Illus.). 264p. 1998. reprint ed. pap. 14.95 (*1-57061-158-0*) Sasquatch Bks.

Marine Wildlife of Atlantic Europe. Amanda Young & Paul G. Kay. (Illus.). 192p. (C). 1995. pap. 45.00 (*0-907151-81-7*, Pub. by IMMEL Pubng) St Mut.

Marine Zoology of Tropical Central Pacific. C. H. Edmondson et al. (BMB Ser.: No. 27). 1969. reprint ed. 25.00 (*0-527-02130-X*) Periodicals Srv.

Marine Zoology of West Coast. H. James. 148p. 1909. pap. 175.00 (*0-7855-0382-X*, Pub. by Intl Bks & Periodicals) St Mut.

Marinello Haircutting Manual. Milady Publishing Company Staff. (Cosmetology Ser.). 1969. pap. 23.50 (*0-87350-486-0*, VNR) Wiley.

Mariner Cheney: My Dad. Harriet C. Nealand-Staley. (Illus.). 136p. 1992. 19.95 (*1-882266-00-5*) Newburyport.

Mariner Missions to Mars. John Hamilton. LC 97-34678. (Mission to Mars Ser.). (J). 1998. lib. bdg. 14.95 (*1-56239-828-8*) ABDO Pub Co.

Mariner Outboard Vol. 2: Tune-Up & Repair Manual, 3, 4 & 6 Cylinder In-Line, V-6 with EFI. Joan Coles & Clarence W. Coles. (Marine Tune-Up & Repair Manuals: Vol. 2). (Illus.). 616p. (C). 1998. pap. 34.95 (*0-89330-016-0*, Pub. by Seloc) Natl Bk Netwk.

Mariner Outboard 1977-1989 Vol. 1: Tune-Up & Repair Manual, 1 & 2 Cylinder. Joan Coles & Clarence W. Coles. LC 95-118717. (Marine Tune-Up & Repair Manuals: Vol. 1). (Illus.). 456p. (C). 1998. pap. 34.95 (*0-89330-015-2*, Pub. by Seloc) Natl Bk Netwk.

Mariner Outboard Shop Manual 2-220 HP, 1976-1989. 2nd rev. ed. LC 90-55692. (Illus.). 720p. 1991. pap. 36.95 (*0-89287-542-9*, B714) Intertec Pub.

Mariner 2.5-275 Horse-Power Outboards, 1990-1993. LC 93-78505. (Illus.). 640p. Date not set. pap. 36.95 (*0-89287-606-9*, B715) Intertec Pub.

Mariner/Marlin: "anywhere, anytime" Turner Publishing Company Staff. LC 91-67163. (Illus.). 168p. 1992. 49.95 (*1-56311-074-1*) Turner Pub KY.

***Mariners.** Matt Silverman. (Total Baseball Companions Ser.). 96p. 2000. mass mkt. 2.50 (*1-892129-63-9*) Total Sprts.

Mariners & Markets. Charles P. Kindleberger. LC 92-26909. 106p. (C). 1992. text 45.00 (*0-8147-4644-6*) NYU Pr.

Mariner's & More! Virginia People, Places & Things Everyone Should Know. Carole Marsh. (Carole Marsh Virginia Bks.). (Illus.). (YA). (gr. 9-12). 1994. pap. 19.95 (*0-7933-0001-0*); lib. bdg. 29.95 (*0-7933-0000-2*); disk 29.95 (*0-7933-0002-9*) Gallopade Intl.

***Mariner's Atlas: South Florida, the Keys & the Bahama Islands the Dry Tortugas, Shark River & Okeechobee Waterway.** A. P. Balder. 132p. 2000. pap. 59.95 (*0-930151-23-2*, Pub. by Chartcrafters Pubs) Firefly Bks Ltd.

***Mariner's Atlas: Southern New England, Long Island Sound & the South Shore.** A. P. Balder. 132p. 2000. pap. 59.95 (*0-930151-22-4*, Pub. by Chartcrafters Pubs) Firefly Bks Ltd.

Mariner's Book of Days. Desk. 1999. 12.95 (*0-937822-52-3*) WoodenBoat Pubns.

Mariner's Book of Days. Peter H. Spectre. 1996. pap. text 14.50 (*0-07-060035-X*) McGraw.

Mariner's Bride. Bronwyn Williams. (Family Continuity Program Ser.: No. 25). 1999. per. 4.50 (*0-373-82173-5*, 1-82173-5) Harlequin Bks.

Mariner's Celestial Navigation. William P. Crawford. (Illus.). 1979. 19.95 (*0-393-60003-3*) Norton.

***Mariner's Compass.** Earlene Fowler. LC 98-47182. (Benni Harper Mystery Ser.). 336p. 1999. pap. 21.95 (*0-425-16891-3*, Prime Crime) Berkley Pub.

***Mariner's Compass.** Earlene Fowler. (Benni Harper Mystery Ser.: Vol. 6). 322p. 2000. mass mkt. 6.50 (*0-425-17408-5*) Berkley Pub.

Mariner's Compass Quilts: New Directions. Judy Mathieson. LC 95-18374. (Illus.). 80p. 1995. pap. 21.95 (*0-914881-97-3*, 10119) C & T Pub.

Mariner's Compass Quilts: New Quilts from an Old Favorite. Victoria Faoro. LC 97-12180. 1997. 16.95 (*0-89145-797-6*, 4911, Am Quilters Soc) Collector Bks.

Mariner's Directory & Guide, 1998-1999 - Worldwide Maritime Source Book (Directory & Guide) 2nd expanded rev. ed. James L. Pelletier. Ed. by Aaron Levine. LC 97-94345. (Periodic Chapter/Serial Updates Ser.: No. 1). Orig. Title: Mariner's Employment Guide. (Illus.). 1212p. 1999. pap. 350.00 (*0-9644915-1-6*) Marine Techn.

Mariner's Employment Guide see Mariner's Directory & Guide, 1998-1999 - Worldwide Maritime Source Book (Directory & Guide)

Mariner's Employment Guide - 1997/1998 Edition. 5th expanded rev. ed. James L. Pelletier. LC 94-96822. (Illus.). 357p. 1999. 85.00 (*0-9644915-0-8*) Marine Techn.

Mariner's Fancy: The Whaleman's Art of Scrimshaw. Nina Hellman & Norman J. Brouwer. (Illus.). 96p. (J). 1992. pap. 22.50 (*0-917439-14-7*) Balsam Pr.

Mariners Guide to G. M. D. S. S. A Practical Solution. Kurt J. Breitfeller. (Illus.). 80p. 1999. pap. 34.95 (*0-7392-0237-5*, PO3279) Morris Pubng.

Mariner's Guide to Radiofacsimile Weather Charts. Joseph M. Bishop. (Illus.). 115p. (Orig.). 1981. pap. 14.95 (*0-9607004-1-2*) Alden Electronics.

Mariner's Guide to Single Sideband. 5th ed. Frederick Graves. Ed. by Jill S. Berry et al. (Illus.). 136p. 1987. 11.95 (*0-911677-01-1*) SEA Inc.

Mariner's Guide to the Rules of the Road. 2nd ed. William H. Tate. LC 81-85441. (Illus.). 159p. 1982. 18.95 (*0-87021-355-5*) Naval Inst Pr.

Mariner's Gyro-Navigation Manual for Masters, Mates, Marine Engineers. Walter J. O'Hara. LC 51-7444. (Illus.). 192p. reprint ed. pap. 59.60 (*0-608-30806-4*, 201130500076) Bks Demand.

Mariner's Medallion Using Foundation Paper Piecing. M'Liss R. Hawley. LC 98-30689. (Illus.). 56p. 1999. pap. 16.95 (*1-56477-246-2*, B358, That Patchwrk Pl) Martingale & Co.

Mariners, Merchants & Oceans: Studies Maritime History. K. S. Mathew. LC 95-905821. (C). 1995. 38.00 (*81-7304-075-3*, Pub. by Manohar) S Asia.

Mariners of the American Revolution. Marion J. Kaminkow & Jack Kaminkow. 274p. 1993. reprint ed. 25.00 (*0-8063-4872-0*, Pub. by Clearfield Co) ACCESS Pubs Network.

Mariner's Periodical Directory, 1989 Edition. La Vaughn Fuhriman. 160p. (Orig.). 1989. text 29.95 (*0-685-28849-8*); pap. text 19.95 (*0-685-28850-1*) Quad A Ventures.

Mariner's Photo Log. Weems & Plath Staff. (Illus.). 98p. (Orig.). 1994. pap. 15.95 (*1-878797-12-3*) Weems & Plath.

Mariner's Pocket Companion, 1998. Wallace E. Tobin, III. (Illus.). 224p. 1997. pap. 13.95 (*1-55750-569-1*) Naval Inst Pr.

Mariner's Pocket Companion, 1999. Wallace E. Tobin, 3rd. (Illus.). 224p. 1998. pap. 13.95 (*1-55750-570-5*) Naval Inst Pr.

***Mariner's Pocket Companion 2000.** 2000th ed. Wallace E. Tobin. 224p. 1999. pap. text 14.95 (*1-55750-558-6*) Naval Inst Pr.

Mariner's Trip Log. W. D. Kline. 127p. 1997. text 9.95 (*0-9647051-1-7*) One River Pr.

Mariner's Trivia Book. Rustie Brown. LC 85-73570. 280p. (Orig.). 1986. pap. 9.95 (*0-9605278-1-8*) Blue Harbor.

Mariner's Weather. William P. Crawford. (Illus.). 312p. 1992. pap. 22.00 (*0-393-30884-7*) Norton.

Mariner's Weather Handbook: A Guide to Forecasting & Tactics. Steve Dashew & Linda Dashew. LC 98-93808. 594p. 1998. 69.95 (*0-9658028-2-5*) Beowulf.

Mariners Weather Log. Government Printing Office Staff. pap. 10.00 (*0-16-009596-4*) USGPO.

***Marines.** Octavio Diez. (Illus.). 96p. 2000. pap. 16.95 (*84-95323-40-0*) Lema Pubns.

Marines. Ed. by Edwin H. Simmons & J. Robert Moskin. (Illus.). 360p. 1998. 75.00 (*0-88363-198-9*, Pub. by H L Levin) Publishers Group.

Marines: Official Magazine of the United States Marine Corps. Government Printing Office Staff. 1984. pap. 22.00 (*0-16-010238-3*) USGPO.

Marines & Helicopters, 1962-1973. William R. Fails. (Illus.). 253p. (Orig.). (C). 1995. pap. text 45.00 (*0-7881-1818-8*) DIANE Pub.

Marines & Military Law in Vietnam: Trial by Fire. 1995. lib. bdg. 251.95 (*0-8490-6732-4*) Gordon Pr.

Marines & Others: A Few Good Men from the Old Corps. Charles Waterhouse & Edward H. Simmons. Ed. by Jane Waterhouse. (Illus.). 280p. 1994. 75.00 (*0-9640264-0-6*) C Waterhouse.

Marines & You. Dorothy Hole. LC 92-9771. (Armed Forces Ser.). (Illus.). 48p. (J). (gr. 5-6). 1993. lib. bdg. 12.95 (*0-89686-768-4*, Crstwood Hse) Silver Burdett Pr.

Mariner's Guide to the Inland Rules. Mark Tilford & William D. Kline. (Illus.). 192p. 1999. text 29.95 (*1-893184-00-5*) River School.

Marines in Santo Domingo! Victor Perlo. 1965. pap. 0.20 (*0-87898-004-0*) New Outlook.

Marines in the Central Solomons. John N. Rentz. (Elite Unit Ser.: No. 24). (Illus.). 216p. 1989. reprint ed. 39.95 (*0-89839-143-1*) Battery Pr.

Marine's Letters: World War II & the Korean War. Fred T. Klemm. 187p. 1993. pap. write for info. (*0-9635729-1-1*) Colohi Prods.

***Marines of Autumn: A Novel of the Korean War.** James Brady. LC 00-25472. 288p. 2000. 24.95 (*0-312-26200-0*, Thomas Dunne) St Martin.

***Marines II World War II: From Pearl Harbor to Tokyo Bay.** Christopher J. Anderson. LC 00-30809. (G. I. Ser.). (Illus.). 2000. write for info. (*1-85367-426-5*, Pub. by Greenhill Bks) Stackpole.

Maring Hunters & Traders: Production & Exchange in the Papua New Guinea Highlands. Christopher Healey. LC 89-20649. (Studies in Melanesian Anthropology: No. 8). (Illus.). 350p. 1990. 55.00 (*0-520-06840-8*, Pub. by U CA Pr) Cal Prin Full Svc.

Maring Subject(s) Literature & the Emergence of the National Identity. Allen Carey-Webb. Ed. by Jonathan Hart. LC 97-32709. (Comparative Literature & Cultural Studies Ser.: Vol. 4). (Illus.). 256p. 1998. text 55.00 (*0-8153-2896-6*, H2072) Garland.

***Marin/North Bay Entertainment, 2000.** (Illus.). 550p. 1999. pap. 25.00 (*1-880248-39-5*, 0009) Enter Pubns.

Marino: On the Record. Dan Marino. (Illus.). 1996. pap. 25.00 (*0-614-20473-9*) HarpC.

Marino, Giovan Battista la Lira a Cura di Ottavio Besomi Janina Hauser, Giovanni Sporanzi. Marino et al. (Archivio Tematico della Lirica Ser.: Vol. 1). (ITA.). 488p. 1991. pap. 102.50 (*0-614-97982-X*) G Olms Pubs.

Marino Marini. (Illus.). 21p. (Orig.). 1989. pap. 10.00 (*0-9624615-4-7*) Nahan Editions.

***Marino Marini.** Ed. by Pierre Case. 332p. 2000. 45.00 (*88-8118-631-4*, Pub. by Skira IT) Abbeville Pr.

Marino Marini: Catalogue Raisonne, Sculpture. Contrib. by Giovanni Carandente. (Illus.). 384p. 1999. boxed set 90.00 (*88-8118-390-0*, Pub. by Skira IT) Abbeville Pr.

Marino Marini, Catalogue Raisonne of the Graphic Work, 1919-1980. Giorgio Guastalla & Guido Guastalla. (Illus.). 280p. 1993. 225.00 (*1-55660-146-8*) A Wofsy Fine Arts.

Marinship at War: Shipbuilding & Social Change in Wartime Sausalito. Charles Wollenberg. (Western Heritage of California Ser.). (Illus.). 188p. (Orig.). 1990. pap. 8.95 (*0-9621956-1-8*) Wstrn Heritage.

***Marinus Willett: Defender of the Northern Frontier.** Larry Lowenthal. LC 00-32352. (New Yorkers & the Revolution Ser.). 2000. pap. write for info. (*1-930098-07-3*) Purple Mnt Pr.

Mario & Luigi's Recital: Duets Elementary Piano. 24p. (J). 1992. pap. 5.95 (*0-7935-1497-5*, 00290372) H Leonard.

Mario & the Murgatrons. Illus. by Bryan Hayes. 169p. (Orig.). (YA). (gr. 9-12). 1996. pap. 9.95 (*0-9653682-0-3*) Blue Steel Publng.

***Mario & the Tarantula.** E. G. Walker. (Illus.). 46p. (ps-5). 1999. pap. 6.95 (*0-7392-0268-5*, PO3351) Morris Pubng.

Mario Andretti. G. S. Prentzas. LC 95-8238. (Race Car Legends Ser.). 64p. (YA). (gr. 3 up). 1996. lib. bdg. 15.95 (*0-7910-3176-4*) Chelsea Hse.

Mario Andretti Photo Album. Peter Nygaard. (World Champion Driver Ser.). (Illus.). 112p. 1999. pap. 19.95 (*1-58388-009-7*, Pub. by Iconografix) Motorbooks Intl.

Mario Bellini, Architecture, 1982-1995. Ed. by Ermanno Ranzani. (Illus.). 300p. 1996. 62.00 (*3-7643-5375-9*) Birkhauser.

Mario Bellini, Designer. Cara McCarty. (Illus.). 80p. (Orig.). 1987. pap. 9.95 (*0-87070-224-6*, 0-8109-6014-1) Mus of Modern Art.

***Mario Botta.** Philip Jodidio. 1999. 29.99 (*3-8228-6612-1*) Taschen Amer.

Mario Botta. 3rd expanded ed. Emilio Pizzi. (Illus.). 256p. 1998. pap. 29.95 (*3-7643-5438-0*) Birkhauser.

Mario Botta: Public Buildings, 1990-1998. Contrib. by Werner Oechslin et al. LC 99-492916. (Illus.). 228p. 1999. 35.00 (*88-8118-321-8*, Pub. by Skira IT) Abbeville Pr.

Mario Botta: Seen by Pino Musi. Pino Musi & Mario Botta. (Illus.). 342p. 1997. 195.00 (*3-87135-032-X*, Pub. by Daco-Verlag) U of Wash Pr.

Mario Botta: The Complete Works, 3 vols. Emilio Pizzi. (Illus.). 800p. 1997. 250.00 (*3-7643-5767-3*, Pub. by Birkhauser) Princeton Arch.

Mario Botta Vol. 1: The Complete Works, 1960-1985. Emilio Pizzi. (Mario Botta Ser.). (Illus.). 256p. 1993. 98.00 (*3-7643-5530-1*, Pub. by Birkhauser) Princeton Arch.

Mario Botta Vol. 2: The Complete Works, 1985-1990. Emilio Pizzi. 280p. 1994. 98.00 (*3-7643-5538-7*, Pub. by Birkhauser) Princeton Arch.

Mario Botta Vol. 3: The Complete Works, 1990-1997. Emilio Pizzi. LC 94-200100. (Illus.). 256p. 1997. 98.00 (*3-7643-5541-7*, Pub. by Birkhauser) Princeton Arch.

Mario Botta/Enzo Cucchi: The Chapel of Monte Tamaro. Created by Enzo Cucchi. (ENG & ITA., Illus.). 132p. 1998. pap. 59.95 (*88-422-0531-1*) Gingko Press.

An Asterisk (*) at the beginning of an entry indicates that the title is appearing for the first time.

Mario Bottinelli Montandon. Mario Bottinelli Montandon. (Illus.). 128p. 1999. pap. 35.00 (*88-8158-218-X*, Pub. by Charta) Dist Art Pubs.

Mario Cravo Neto: Photographs. Peter Weiermair. (Illus.). 92p. 1994. 45.00 (*3-905514-33-8*, Pub. by Edit Stemmle) Dist Art Pubs.

Mario Cucinella: Space & Light/lo Spazio E La Luce. Maurizio Vitta. 1999. pap. text 25.00 (*88-7838-057-1*) L'Arca IT.

***Mario de Andrade: The Crative Works.** Jose I. Suarez & Jack E. Tomlins. LC 99-41817. 200p. 2000. 37.50 (*0-8387-5426-0*) Bucknell U Pr.

Mario des Bellini. Cara McCarty. (Illus.). 80p. 1990. pap. 12.95 (*0-8109-6014-1*, Pub. by Abrams) Time Warner.

Mario Giacomelli. Mario Giacomelli. Ed. by James Alinder. LC 83-81265. (Untitled Ser.: No. 32). (Illus.). 1983. pap. 7.98 (*0-933286-34-1*) Frnds Photography.

Mario Lanza: A Biography. Derek Mannering. (Illus.). 176p. pap. 14.95 (*0-7090-5052-6*, Pub. by R Hale Ltd) Seven Hills Bk.

Mario Lanza: Tenor in Exile. Roland L. Bessette. LC 98-24135. (Illus.). 306p. 1999. 24.95 (*1-57467-044-1*, Amadeus Pr) Timber.

Mario Lemieux. Bob Italia. Ed. by Rosemary Wallner. LC 92-19751. 32p. (J). 1992. lib. bdg. 13.98 (*1-56239-124-0*) ABDO Pub Co.

***Mario Lemieux.** Suzanne J. Murdico. (Overcoming the Odds Ser.). (Illus.). 48p. (J). (gr. 4-7). 1998. pap. 7.95 (*0-8172-8004-9*) Raintree Steck-V.

Mario Lemieux. Suzanne J. Murdico. LC 97-36691. (Overcoming the Odds Ser.). (J). (gr. 4-6). 1998. 24.26 (*0-8172-4126-4*) Raintree Steck-V.

Mario Lemieux. Brian Tracy. LC 97-27365. (Ice Hockey Legends Ser.). (Illus.). 64p. (YA). (gr. 3 up). 1999. lib. bdg. 15.95 (*0-7910-4558-7*) Chelsea Hse.

Mario Lemieux: Beating the Odds. Jim Haskins & Kathleen Benson. (Illus.). 64p. (J). (gr. 1-4). 1996. pap. 5.95 (*0-8225-9717-9*) Lerner Pub.

Mario Lemieux: Beating the Odds. Morgan Hughes. LC 95-38964. (Achievers Ser.). 1996. lib. bdg. 19.93 (*0-8225-2884-3*, Lerner Publctns) Lerner Pub.

Mario Lemieux: Best There Ever Was. Pittsburgh Post-Gazette Staff. (Illus.). 160p. 1997. 24.95 (*1-57028-161-0*, Mstrs Pr) NTC Contemp Pub Co.

Mario Lemieux: Star Center. Ken Rappoport. LC 97-49431. (Sports Reports Ser.). 104p. (YA). (gr. 4-10). 1998. lib. bdg. 20.95 (*0-89490-932-0*) Enslow Pubs.

Mario Lemieux: The Final Period. Mario Lemieux & Tom McMillan. (Illus.). 128p. 1997. 50.00 (*1-57243-253-5*) Triumph Bks.

Mario Lemieux: The Ice Hockey Great Who Has Hodgkin's Disease. Jeff Z. Klein. LC 94-31522. (Great Achievers Ser.). (Illus.). 120p. (YA). (gr. 5 up). 1995. lib. bdg. 19.95 (*0-7910-2400-8*) Chelsea Hse.

Mario Lemieux: Wizard with a Puck. Bill Gutman. LC 92-5003. (Millbrook Sports World Ser.). (Illus.). 48p. (J). (gr. 3-6). 1992. pap. 5.95 (*1-56294-826-1*) Millbrook Pr.

Mario Lemieux: Wizard with a Puck. Bill Gutman. (Millbrook Sports World Ser.). (J). 1992. 11.15 (*0-606-07842-8*) Turtleback.

Mario Merz. (Parkett Art Magazine Ser.: No. 15). (Illus.). 200p. 1988. 19.50 (*3-907509-65-X*, Pub. by Parkett Verlag AG) Dist Art Pubs.

Mario Merz. VICENTE TODOLT. 1999. 35.00 (*88-7757-091-1*) Hopefulmonster Editore.

***Mario Party 2 Official Strategy Guide.** Ed. by BradyGames Staff. (Bradygames Strategy Guides Ser.). (Illus.). 112p. (J). 2000. pap. 12.99 (*1-56686-973-0*, BradyGAMES) Brady Pub.

***Mario Party 2.** Don Tica et al. (Official Strategy Guides Ser.). (Illus.). 96p. (YA). 2000. pap. 14.99 (*0-7615-2767-2*) Prima Pub.

Mario Sanchez: Before & After. Nance Frank. Ed. by John Sundin. (Illus.). 50p. Date not set. 19.95 (*0-9661053-0-3*) Key West Pr.

***Mario Sironi & Italian Modernism: Art & Politics under Fascism.** Emily Braun. (Illus.). 336p. (C). 2000. 60.00 (*0-521-48015-9*) Cambridge U Pr.

Mario 64 Survival Guide. J. Douglas Arnold & Zach Meston. (Gaming Mastery Ser.). (Illus.). 160p. (Orig.). 1996. pap. 12.95 (*1-884364-19-5*) Sandwich Islands.

Mario the Magician. Thomas Mann. 1991. reprint ed. lib. bdg. 19.95 (*1-56849-035-6*) Buccaneer Bks.

Mario Vargas Llosa. Dick Gerdes. (Twayne World Authors Ser.: No. 762). 232p. 1985. 26.95 (*0-8057-6612-X*, Twayne) Mac Lib Ref.

Mario Vargas Llosa: Critical Essays on Characterization. Roy A. Kerr. 1990. 43.50 (*0-916379-78-7*) Scripta.

***Marion.** Judith Rosbe. (Images of America Ser.). (Illus.). 128p. 2000. pap. 18.99 (*0-7385-0419-X*) Arcadia Publng.

Marion: A History of the United States Watch Company. William Muir & Bernard Kraus. Ed. by Eugene T. Fuller. LC 85-61588. (Illus.). 218p. 1985. 24.15 (*0-9614984-0-4*) Natl Assn Watch & Clock.

***Marion - Lake & Sumter Counties, Florida.** C. J. Janis. 257p. 1999. spiral bd. 34.95 (*1-882829-07-7*, 59478-82907) Map & Globe.

Marion, American Pocket Watch Encyclopedia & Price Guide Vol. 3: Identification & Price Guide. Roy Ehrhardt et al. 130p. 1987. spiral bd. 35.00 (*0-913902-54-3*) Heart Am Pr.

Marion Bridge. Daniel MacIvor. 128p. 1999. pap. 11.95 (*0-88922-407-2*) Talonbks.

Marion Brown's Southern Cook Book. rev. ed. Marion Brown. LC 68-14365. ix, 489p. 1968. 34.95 (*0-8078-1065-7*); pap. 19.95 (*0-8078-4078-5*) U of NC Pr.

Marion County Arkansas Census, 1850. Courtney York & Gerlene York. 58p. (Orig.). 1969. pap. 12.00 (*0-916660-02-8*) Hse of York.

Marion County, Arkansas, Tax Records, 1841-1866. Ed. by Desmond W. Allen. 179p. 1988. pap. 19.50 (*0-941765-35-0*) Arkansas Res.

Marion County History, No. 15. (Illus.). 200p. 1998. pap. 30.95 (*0-943297-02-8*) Marion Coun Hist Soc.

Marion County History, Vol. 1. Ed. by Chester C. Kaiser & Mirpah Blair. (Illus.). 36p. 1955. pap. 5.00 (*0-943297-16-8*) Marion Coun Hist Soc.

Marion County History, Vol. 2. Ed. by Mirpah Blair & Sylvia Kraps. (Illus.). 62p. 1956. pap. 5.00 (*0-943297-15-X*) Marion Coun Hist Soc.

Marion County History, Vol. 3. Ed. by Orcutt W. Frost & Chester C. Kaiser. (Illus.). 1957. pap. 5.00 (*0-943297-14-1*) Marion Coun Hist Soc.

Marion County History, Vol. 4. Ed. by Chester C. Kaiser et al. (Illus.). 64p. 1958. pap. 5.00 (*0-943297-13-3*) Marion Coun Hist Soc.

Marion County History, Vol. 5. Ed. by Chester C. Kaiser et al. (Illus.). 72p. 1959. pap. 5.00 (*0-943297-12-5*) Marion Coun Hist Soc.

Marion County History, Vol. 6. Ed. by Chester C. Kaiser et al. (Illus.). 48p. 1960. pap. 5.00 (*0-943297-11-7*) Marion Coun Hist Soc.

Marion County History, Vol. 7. Ed. by Chester C. Kaiser et al. (Illus.). 40p. 1961. pap. 5.00 (*0-943297-10-9*) Marion Coun Hist Soc.

Marion County History, Vol. 8. Ed. by Chester C. Kaiser et al. (Illus.). 48p. 1964. pap. 5.00 (*0-943297-09-5*) Marion Coun Hist Soc.

Marion County History, Vol. 9. Ed. by Chester C. Kaiser & Helen Pearce. (Illus.). 52p. 1968. pap. 5.00 (*0-943297-08-7*) Marion Coun Hist Soc.

Marion County History, Vol. 10. (Illus.). 64p. 1971. pap. 5.00 (*0-943297-07-9*) Marion Coun Hist Soc.

Marion County History, Vol. 11. Ed. by Mary E. Eyre & George G. Strozut. (Illus.). 56p. 1976. pap. 5.00 (*0-943297-06-0*) Marion Coun Hist Soc.

Marion County History, Vol. 12. Ed. by Mary E. Eyre et al. (Illus.). 72p. 1978. pap. 5.00 (*0-943297-05-2*) Marion Coun Hist Soc.

Marion County History, Vol. 13. (Illus.). 92p. 1982. pap. 10.00 (*0-943297-04-4*) Marion Coun Hist Soc.

Marion County History, Vol. 14. Ed. by Alfred C. Jones. (Illus.). 120p. 1984. pap. 11.00 (*0-943297-03-6*) Marion Coun Hist Soc.

Marion County History: Index. Ed. by Lucile Fidler. 31p. 1981. pap. 5.00 (*0-943297-17-6*) Marion Coun Hist Soc.

Marion County, Miss., Miscellaneous Records: (Orphans Ct. Records, Wills & Estates, 1812-1859; Deeds 1812-1840; Territorial & Federal Census Recs. & Mortality Schedules; Old Road Books; 1813 Lawrence County Tax Lists) E. Russ Williams. 376p. 1985. reprint ed. pap. 32.50 (*0-89308-341-0*, MS 2) Southern Hist Pr.

Marion County, Ohio. Sylvia D. Wilson & Ruth E. Wilson. 370p. 1993. reprint ed. lib. bdg. 42.00 (*0-8328-2832-7*) Higginson Bk Co.

Marion County South Carolina Abstracts of Deeds, 1800-1811, Vol. 1, Bks. A-E. Alita W. Sutcliffe. LC 96-85713. xii, 218p. 1996. 31.75 (*0-9649207-0-0*, 001) Forebears Pr.

Marion County South Carolina Abstracts of Deeds, 1811-1823, Vol. 2, Bks. F-I & K. Alita W. Sutcliffe. LC 96-85713. xii, 238p. 1997. 34.95 (*0-9649207-1-9*, 002) Forebears Pr.

Marion County, West Virginia: A Pictorial History. Thomas J. Koon. LC 95-617. 1995. write for info. (*0-89865-948-5*) Donning Co.

Marion Cunningham's Good Eating: The Breakfast Book & the Supper Book. Marion Cunningham. LC 98-28799. (Illus.). 576p. 1999. 9.99 (*0-517-20402-9*) Random Hse Value.

Marion Fay. Anthony Trollope. Ed. by R. H. Super. LC 82-7036. (Illus.). 465p. 1982. pap. 15.95 (*0-932282-18-0*) Caledonia Pr.

Marion Fay, 3 vols. Anthony Trollope. LC 80-1902. (Selected Works of Anthony Trollope). 1981. reprint ed. lib. bdg. 99.95 (*0-405-14191-2*) Ayer.

Marion Harland's Autobiography. Mary V. Terhune. Ed. by Annette K. Baxter. LC 79-8816. (Signal Lives Ser.). 1980. reprint ed. lib. bdg. 56.95 (*0-405-12860-6*) Ayer.

Marion Huse: An Artist's Evolution. Brockton Art Museum Publications Staff & Peter J. Baldaia. Ed. by Elizabeth C. Haff. LC 85-47809. (Illus.). 94p. (Orig.). 1985. pap. 10.00 (*0-934358-15-X*) Fuller Mus Art.

***Marion Jones.** (Illus.). 56p. 2001. pap. 12.95 (*1-892920-40-9*) G H B Pubs.

***Marion Jones: Fast & Fearless.** Rachel Rutledge. LC 00-30514. (Track & Field's New Wave Ser.). (Illus.). (YA). 2000. lib. bdg. write for info. (*0-7613-1870-4*) Millbrook Pr.

Marion Jones: Sprinting Sensation. Mark Stewart. LC 99-23008. (Sports Stars Ser.). 48p. (J). (gr. 3-4). 1999. 19.00 (*0-516-21661-9*) Childrens.

***Marion Jones: Sprinting Sensation.** Mark Stewart. (Sports Stars Ser.). (J). 2000. pap. text 5.95 (*0-516-27004-4*) Childrens.

***Marion Jones: World Class Runner.** Heather Feldman. LC 00-36710. (Reading Power Ser.). (Illus.). (J). 2001. write for info. (*0-8239-5718-7*, PowerKids) Rosen Group.

***Marion May: (trollope 1997)** Skilton. 1999. 48.00 (*1-870587-53-7*) Ashgate Pub Co.

Marion Pike: The Art & the Artist. Illus. by Michel F. Sarda. LC 86-60950. 176p. 1990. pap. 24.95 (*0-9270015-01-3*) Bridgewood Pr.

Marion Post Wolcott: A Photographic Journey. Forrest J. Hurley. LC 88-20690. (Illus.). 240p. 1989. reprint ed. pap. 74.40 (*0-608-04127-0*, 206486000011) Bks Demand.

Marion Press: A Survey & a Checklist. Thomas A. Larremore & Amy Hopkins. LC 85-51272. 293p. 1981. reprint ed. 35.00 (*0-938768-04-2*) Oak Knoll.

Marion Quebec Studies in Philosophy of Science Pt. II: Biology, Psychology, Cognitive Science & Economics, Vol. 178. Ed. by Mathieu Marion. (Boston Studies in the Philosophy of Science). 326p. (C). 1995. lib. bdg. 154.00 (*0-7923-3560-0*, Pub. by Kluwer Academic) Kluwer Academic.

***Marion, South Carolina.** Historic Marion Association Staff. (Images of America Ser.). (Illus.). 128p. 1999. pap. 18.99 (*0-7385-0231-6*) Arcadia Publng.

Marion Weinstein's Handy Guide to Tarot Cards. Marion Weinstein. LC 98-72161. 104p. 2000. pap. 8.95 (*1-890733-05-9*) Earth Magic.

Marion Weinstein's Handy Guide to the I Ching. Marion Weinstein. LC 98-72162. 96p. 2000. pap. 8.95 (*1-890733-06-7*) Earth Magic.

Marion Zimmer Bradley. Rosemarie Arbur. Ed. by Roger C. Schlobin. LC 85-2721. (Starmont Reader's Guide Ser.: Vol. 27). ii, 138p. 1985. lib. bdg. 29.00 (*0-916732-96-7*) Millefleurs.

Marion Zimmer Bradley's Darkover. Marion Zimmer Bradley. 352p. (Orig.). 1993. mass mkt. 4.99 (*0-88677-593-0*, Pub. by DAW Bks) Penguin Putnam.

***Marionetoj.** Carmel Mallia. (ESP.). 62p. 1999. pap. 5.50 (*1-882251-28-8*) Eldonejo Bero.

Marionette Actor. Ralph Chesse. 114p. (Orig.). (C). 1987. text 43.00 (*0-8026-0011-5*); pap. text 22.50 (*0-8026-0012-3*) Univ Pub Assocs.

Marionette Magic: From Concept to Curtain Call. Bruce Taylor. (Illus.). 176p. 1988. 19.95 (*0-8306-9091-3*, 3091) McGraw-Hill Prof.

Marionettes. Susan Hestenes. 1975. 3.50 (*0-686-17212-4*) Sandollar Pr.

Marionettes. limited ed. William Faulkner. LC 75-27485. (Illus.). 1979. boxed set 125.00 (*0-916242-01-3*) Yoknapatawpha.

Marionettes: Easy to Make Fun to Use. Edith F. Ackley. (Illus.). (J). (gr. 5-9). 1939. lib. bdg. 12.89 (*0-397-31409-4*) HarpC Child Bks.

Marionettes: How to Make & Work Them. Helen Fling. (Illus.). 185p. 1973. reprint ed. pap. 6.95 (*0-486-22909-2*) Dover.

Marionettes: With an Introduction & Textual Apparatus by Noel Polk. William Faulkner. LC 77-8994. (Linton R. Massey Memorial Publication Bk.). 140p. reprint ed. pap. 43.40 (*0-7837-2429-2*, 204257700005) Bks Demand.

Marionettes & String Puppets: Collector's Reference Guide. Daniel E. Hodges. LC 98-71058. (Illus.). 168p. 1998. pap. 24.95 (*0-930625-94-3*, Antique Trader) Krause Pubns.

***Marion's Magic Shoes.** Wanda L. Groves. LC 99-69144. (Illus.). 74p. (J). (gr. 3-7). 2000. 13.95 (*1-58244-060-3*) Rutledge Bks.

Mario's Big Question: A Child's Guide to Adoption. Carolyn Nystrom. 48p. (J). (gr. 4-7). 1994. pap. 4.99 (*0-7459-2923-0*) Lion USA.

Mario's Mayan Journey. Michelle McCunney. LC 95-39407. (Illus.). (J). (gr. 2-6). 1996. pap. 4.95 (*1-57255-203-4*) Mondo Pubng.

Mario's Vineyard. large type ed. Michael Legat. 752p. 1983. 27.99 (*0-7089-8099-6*, Charnwood) Ulverscroft.

Mariotti. Franz Schulze & Taro Yomasaki. (Illus.). 208p. 1987. 35.00 (*0-917001-07-9*) Herring Pr.

Mariposa. Francisco Jimenez. (SPA.). 40p. (J). (gr. 1-5). 1998. 16.00 (*0-395-91738-7*) HM.

Mariposa. Francisco Jimenez. LC 96-27664. (Illus.). 40p. (J). (gr. 1-5). 1998. 16.00 (*0-395-81663-7*) HM.

***Mariposa.** Francisco Jimenez. (SPA.). 2000. pap. 5.95 (*0-618-07317-5*) HM.

Mariposa Bailarina. Carlos Ruvalcaba. (SPA.). 1995. pap. text 8.95 (*1-56014-617-6*) Santillana.

Mariposa Blues. Ronald Koertge. 176p. (J). 1993. mass mkt. 3.50 (*0-380-71761-1*, Avon Bks) Morrow Avon.

Mariposa Blues. Ronald Koertge. 1991. 8.60 (*0-606-02737-8*, Pub. by Turtleback) Demco.

Mariposa Courthouse: "A Shrine to Justice" Scott Pinkerton. (Illus.). 112p. 1989. pap. 5.95 (*0-685-29449-8*) Mariposa Heritage Pr.

Mariposa de Obsidiana (with 33 RPM Recording in Spanish) Octavio Paz. (Ediciones Especiales y de Bibliofilo Ser.). (ENG & SPA., Illus.). 1993. 200.00 (*84-343-0343-4*) Elliots Bks.

Mariposa Indian War, 1850-1851: Diaries of Robert Eccleston: The California Gold Rush, Yosemite, & the High Sierra. Robert Eccleston. Ed. by C. Gregory Crampton. LC 58-62761. 177p. reprint ed. pap. 54.90 (*0-608-14812-1*, 202590100047) Bks Demand.

Mariposa y el Monstruo del Pantano (Butterfly & the Swamp Monster) Nancy Krulik & Joanna Cole. (Autobus Magico Ser.). (ENG & SPA., Illus.). (J). (gr. 1-4). 1996. pap. text 2.99 (*0-590-85965-X*) Scholastic Inc.

Mariposas Entre los Antiguos Mexicanos (Butterflies among the Ancient Mexicans) Carlos Beutelspacher. (SPA.). 104p. 1989. 23.99 (*968-16-3042-4*, Pub. by Fondo) Continental Bk.

Mariposas Tropicales. Hugo Achugar. (SPA.). 80p. 1986. pap. 8.50 (*0-910061-30-0*, 1404) Ediciones Norte.

Mariquita. Sylvaine Perios. (SPA.). 13.00 (*84-348-3467-7*, Pub. by SM Ediciones) IBD Ltd.

Mariquitas Son Verdaderos Escarabajos. Arthur Morton. Tr. by Angelita L. Aguilar. (SPA., Illus.). (J). (gr. k-3). 1996. 12.50 (*1-57842-051-2*) Delmas Creat.

Maris. Grace Livingston Hill. 313p. reprint ed. lib. bdg. 20.95 (*0-89190-052-7*, Rivercity Pr) Amereon Ltd.

Maris, No. 17. Grace Livingston Hill. (Grace Livingston Hill Ser.: Vol. 17). 292p. 1995. mass mkt. 4.99 (*0-8423-4042-4*) Tyndale Hse.

Marisa. Linda L. Bartell. 384p. (Orig.). 1988. pap. 3.95 (*0-380-75380-4*, Avon Bks) Morrow Avon.

Marisa: Italian Stories. Ben B. Cumella. 80p. 1988. pap. 7.50 (*0-89304-654-X*) Cross-Cultrl NY.

Mariska. Lance Martin. (Illus.). 64p. (Orig.). 1995. pap. 19.95 (*0-930400-13-5*) Pleasure Trove.

Marisol: Y el Mensajero Amarillo. Emilie Smith-Ayala.Tr. of Marisol & the Yellow Messenger. (SPA., Illus.). 32p. (YA). (gr. k-3). 1995. pap. 5.95 (*1-55037-985-2*, Pub. by Annick) Firefly Bks Ltd.

Marisol & Magdalena: The Sound of Our Sisterhood. Veronica Chambers. 141p. (YA). (gr. 5-8). 1998. 14.95 (*0-7868-0437-8*, Pub. by Hyperion); lib. bdg. 15.49 (*0-7868-2385-2*, Pub. by Hyperion) Little.

Marisol & Other Plays. Jose Rivera. LC 97-5736. 240p. (Orig.). 1997. pap. 14.95 (*1-55936-136-0*) Theatre Comm.

Marisol & the Yellow Messenger see Marisol: Y el Mensajero Amarillo

Marisol & the Yellow Messenger. Emilie Smith-Ayala. (Illus.). 32p. (J). (gr. 1-4). 1994. pap. 4.95 (*1-55037-972-0*, Pub. by Annick); lib. bdg. 14.95 (*1-55037-973-9*, Pub. by Annick) Firefly Bks Ltd.

Marisol from Puerto Rico. Yuko Green. 1998. pap. 1.00 (*0-486-40319-X*) Dover.

Marisol y Magdalena: The Sound of Our Sisterhood. Veronica Chambers. 128p. (J). 1998. pap. 5.95 (*0-7868-1304-0*, Pub. by Hyperion) Time Warner.

Marisol y Magdelena, Bk. 2. Chambers. (J). 1998. 15.00 (*0-689-81025-3*) S&S Childrens.

Marisol y Magdelena Book, No. 1. John W. Chambers. LC 97-34365. (J). 1998. 15.00 (*0-689-81024-5*) S&S Trade.

Marissa the Tooth Fairy. Karla Andersdatter. 100p. (J). 1979. per. 5.95 (*0-935430-03-2*) In Between.

Marissa's Dance. Francess L. Lantz. LC 93-43225. (Boys' School Girls Ser.). (Illus.). 128p. (J). (gr. 3-7). 1994. pap. text 2.95 (*0-8167-3475-5*) Troll Communs.

Marita. Evelyn Hege. (Illus.). 293p. (YA). (gr. 7-10). 1991. 10.10 (*0-7399-0115-X*, 2329) Rod & Staff.

Marita: Missing in Mexico. Mari Vawn Bailey. 278p. 1996. 14.95 (*1-56236-227-5*, Pub. by Aspen Bks) Origin Bk Sales.

Marita - Perdida en Mexico. Mari V. Bailey. Tr. by Blanca Keogan & Mireya C. Raygoza. (ENG & SPA., Illus.). 342p. 1998. pap. 11.95 (*1-888031-06-9*, Edit Rosa d Desierto) Liahona Dev.

Marita No Sabe Dibujar (Marita Doesn't Know How to Draw) Monique Zepeda. (SPA., Illus.). 32p. (J). (gr. 1-3). 1997. 12.99 (*968-16-5186-3*, Pub. by Fondo) Continental Bk.

Maritain-Mounier: Correspondance, 1929-1939. Jacques Maritain. Ed. by Emmanuel Mounier. (FRE.). 272p. 1973. 34.95 (*0-7859-0107-8*, M3734) Fr & Eur.

Maritain's Ontology of the Work of Art. J. W. Hanke. 138p. 1973. pap. text 57.00 (*90-247-5149-7*, Pub. by M Nijhoff) Kluwer Academic.

Marital Adjustment in Tribal & Non-Tribal Working Women. Dhruv Tanwani. LC 99-931769. 126p. 1997. pap. 100.00 (*81-7533-054-6*, Pub. by Print Hse) St Mut.

***Marital & Family Processes in Depression: A Scientific Foundation for Clinical Practice.** Steven R. H. Beach. LC 00-29321. 2000. write for info. (*1-55798-695-9*) Am Psychol.

Marital & Family Therapy. 3rd ed. Ira D. Glick et al. Ed. by John F. Clarkin & David R. Kessler. LC 87-81507. 623p. 1987. text 19.95 (*0-88048-525-6*, 8525) Am Psychiatric.

***Marital & Family Therapy.** 4th ed. Ira D. Glick et al. LC 99-47724. 2000. write for info. (*0-88048-548-5*) Am Psychiatric.

Marital & Parental Torts: A Guide to Causes of Action, Arguments, & Damages. LC 90-55359. 140p. 1990. pap. 44.95 (*0-89707-555-2*, 513-0031) Amer Bar Assn.

Marital Assets. Bruce Ducker. LC 92-31161. 252p. 1993. 22.00 (*1-877946-26-5*) Permanent Pr.

Marital Bliss & Other Oxymorons. Joel Kohl. Ed. by Cliff Carle. 1994. pap. 4.99 (*0-918259-75-4*) CCC Pubns.

Marital Check-up. Steven G. Pittman. 26p. 1994. wbk. ed. 149.95 incl. audio (*0-9670678-0-4*) S G Pittman.

Marital Communication & Decision Making: Analysis, Assessment, & Change. Edwin J. Thomas. LC 75-41551. 1977. pap. 19.95 (*0-02-932570-6*) Free Pr.

Marital Compatibility Test: Hundreds of Questions for Couples to Answer Together. Susan Adams. LC 97-626. 160p. 1997. pap. 9.95 (*0-8065-1880-4*, Citadel Pr) Carol Pub Group.

***Marital Compatibility Test: 100's of Questions for Couples to Answer Together.** Susan Adams. LC 99-53973. 2000. 11.95 (*1-886039-46-1*) Addicus Bks.

Marital Conflicts: Role Play Peacegames. David W. Felder. LC 95-90517. 98p. 1996. 24.95 (*0-910959-21-8*, B&G 21H); teacher ed. 44.95 (*0-910959-41-2*, B&G 21T) Wellington Pr.

Marital Counseling: A Biblical Behavioral Cognitive Approach. Norman Wright. iii, 421p. 1981. 16.95 (*0-938786-00-8*) Chr Marriage.

***Marital Discord & Family Pathology: Impact on Children.** Archana Dogra. 119p. 1999. 15.00 (*81-241-0645-2*, Pub. by Har-Anand Pubns) Nataraj Bks.

Marital Distress: Cognitive Behavioral Interventions for Dysfunctional Couples (A1) Jill H. Rathus & William Sanderson. LC 98-21980. 1998. 50.00 (*0-7657-0000-X*) Aronson.

Marital Equality: Its Relationship to the Well-Being of Husbands & Wives. Janice M. Steil. LC 97-4797. (Series on Close Relationships: Vol. 16). 170p. 1997. 30.00 (*0-8039-5250-3*); pap. 12.99 (*0-8039-5251-1*) Sage.

Marital Instability: A Social & Behavioral Study of the Early Years. Joseph Veroff et al. LC 94-42825. 208p. 1995. 55.00 (*0-275-95031-X*, Praeger Pubs) Greenwood.

Marital Instability & Divorce Outcomes: Issues for Therapists & Educators. Craig A. Everett. (Journal of Divorce & Remarriage: Vol. 15, Nos. 1-2). (Illus.). 209p. 1991. text 6.95 (*1-56024-115-2*) Haworth Pr.

M

An Asterisk (*) at the beginning of an entry indicates that the title is appearing for the first time.

Marital Intimacy: A Traditional Jewish Approach. Cary A. Friedman. LC 95-19974. 160p. 1996. 22.50 (*1-56821-461-8*) Aronson.

Marital Intimacy: A Traditional Jewish Approach. Avraham P. Friedman. LC 95-19974. 160p. 1997. reprint ed. pap. 25.00 (*0-7657-9999-5*) Aronson.

Marital Power in Dickens' Fiction, Vol. 3. Rita Lubitz. (Dickens' Universe Ser.). XI, 146p. (C). 1996. text 39.95 (*0-8204-2729-2*) P Lang Pubng.

***Marital Property Classification Handbook.** Linda Roberson et al. 80p. 1999. pap. 29.00 (*1-57862-025-2*) State Bar WI.

Marital Property Law. 2nd ed. John Tingley & Nicholas B. Svalina. 1994. 115.00 (*0-8366-0029-0*) West Group.

Marital Property Law in Wisconsin, 3 vols. 2nd ed. Keith A. Christiansen et al. 1400p. 1984. ring bd. 195.00 (*0-945574-34-7*) State Bar WI.

Marital Relationship of Parents & the Emotionally Disturbed Child. Ezra F. Vogel. LC 90-13948. (Harvard Studies in Sociology: Vol. 18). 525p. 1990. text 35.00 (*0-8240-2565-2*) Garland.

Marital-Relationship Therapy Casebook: Theory & Application of the Intersystem Model. Ed. by Gerald R. Weeks & Larry Hof. LC 94-4079. 272p. 1994. text 32.95 (*0-87630-733-0*) Brunner-Mazel.

Marital Relationships Seminar. Douglas E. Brinley. 24p. 1988. pap. 2.95 (*1-55503-064-5*, 0111812) Covenant Comms.

Marital Spirituality: The Search for the Hidden Ground of Love. Patrick J. McDonald & Claudette M. McDonald. LC 99-39713. 208p. 1999. pap. 14.95 (*0-8091-3891-3*) Paulist Pr.

Marital Status & Living Arrangements. 1994. lib. bdg. 256.95 (*0-8490-9047-4*) Gordon Pr.

Marital Status & Living Arrangements in the U. S. Population. (Illus.). 99p. (Orig.). (C). 1993. pap. text 20.00 (*1-56806-456-X*) DIANE Pub.

Marital Tensions: Clinical Studies Towards a Psychological Theory of Interaction. Henry V. Dicks. 368p. 1993. pap. text 33.00 (*1-85575-064-3*, Pub. by H Karnac Bks Ltd) Other Pr LLC.

Marital Tensions: Clinical Studies Towards a Psychological Theory of Interaction. Henry V. Dicks. 189p. 1984. reprint ed. pap. 13.95 (*0-7102-0037-4*, Routledge Thoemms) Routledge.

Marital Therapy. Brown. 2001. 40.00 (*0-534-52732-9*) Wadsworth Pub.

Marital Therapy: A Combined Psychodynamic-Behavioral Approach. R. Taylor Segraves. LC 82-16653. (Critical Issues in Psychiatry Ser.). 314p. 1982. 45.00 (*0-306-40936-4*, Plenum Trade) Perseus Pubng.

Marital Therapy: A Hypnoanalytic Approach. John Scott, Sr. 250p. 1989. text 29.95 (*0-8290-2411-5*) Irvington.

Marital Therapy: An Integrative Approach. William C. Nichols. LC 88-11179. (Family Therapy Ser.). 282p. 1988. lib. bdg. 35.00 (*0-89862-102-X*) Guilford Pubns.

Marital Therapy: Integrating Theory & Technique. Len Sperry & Jon Carlson. LC 90-60833. 1991. pap. 29.95 (*0-89108-215-8*) Love Pub Co.

Marital Therapy: Research, Practice & Organisation. J. D. Haldane. (Malcolm Millar Lectures). 36p. 1988. pap. text 3.90 (*0-08-036578-7*, Pub. by Aberdeen U Pr) Macmillan.

Marital Therapy: Strategies Based on Social Learning & Behavior Exchange Principles. Neil S. Jacobson & Gayla Margolin. LC 79-728. 432p. 1986. text 47.95 (*0-87630-199-5*) Brunner-Mazel.

Marital Therapy in Britain Vol. 1: Context & Therapeutic Approaches. Wendy Dryden. 368p. 1985. pap. 28.00 (*0-335-09812-6*) OpUniv Pr.

Marital Therapy in Britain Vol. 2: Special Areas. Wendy Dryden. 368p. 1985. pap. 28.00 (*0-335-09813-4*) OpUniv Pr.

Maritime Accidents: What Went Wrong? Edward T. Gates. LC 89-11745. 144p. 1989. reprint ed. pap. 44.70 (*0-608-01574-1*, 206199400001) Bks Demand.

Maritime Adaptations of the Pacific. Ed. by Richard W. Casteel & George I. Quimby. (World Anthropology Ser.). x, 320p. 1975. 60.00 (*90-279-7619-8*) Mouton.

Maritime Air Operations. Ben Laite. (Air Power: Aircraft, Weapons Systems & Technology Ser.: Vol. 11). (Illus.). 200p. 1992. 40.00 (*0-08-040705-6*, Pub. by Brasseys); 25.00 (*0-08-040706-4*, Pub. by Brasseys) Brasseys.

Maritime Album: 100 Photographs & Their Stories. Richard Benson & Mariners' Museum (Newport News, Va.) Staff. LC 97-22154. (Illus.). 245p. 1997. pap. 24.95 (*0-917376-48-X*) Mariners Mus.

Maritime Album: 100 Photographs & Their Stories. John Szarkowski & Richard Benson. LC 97-22154. (Illus.). 320p. 1997. 40.00 (*0-300-07342-9*) Yale U Pr.

Maritime Album: 100 Photographs & Their Stories. John Szarkowski et al. LC 97-22154. (Illus.). 320p. 1997. pap. 24.50 (*0-300-07399-2*) Yale U Pr.

Maritime America: Art & Artifacts from America's Great Nautical Collections. Peter Neill. (Illus.). 256p. 1988. 45.00 (*0-917439-11-2*) Balsam Pr.

Maritime America: Art & Artifacts from America's Great Nautical Collections. Ed. by Peter Neill. (Illus.). 250p. 1988. 45.00 (*0-8109-1527-8*, PEMP141) Peabody Essex Mus.

Maritime & Coastal Forts of India. M. S. Naravane. LC 97-906960. (Illus.). xvi, 196p. (C). 1998. 39.00 (*81-7024-910-4*, Pub. by APH Pubng) Nataraj Bks.

Maritime & Fishing Technical Dictionary. (CHI, ENG & FRE.). 617p. 1994. 95.00 (*0-7859-8890-4*) Fr & Eur.

Maritime & Offshore Structure Maintenance. Illus. by Institution of Civil Engineers Staff. 368p. 1986. 63.00 (*0-7277-0273-4*, Pub. by T Telford) RCH.

Maritime & Pipeline Transportation of Oil & Gas: Problems & Outlook - Proceedings of the Conference HEC-Montreal, April 23 & 24, 1990. 2nd ed. Ed. by A. Poirier & G. Zaccour. (Illus.). 320p. (C). 1991. pap. 95.00 (*2-7108-0606-1*, 9ET10) Gulf Pub.

Maritime & Pipeline Transportation of Oil & Gas, Problems & Outlook: Proceedings of the Conference HEC-Montreal, April 23 & 24, 1990. Ed. by A. Poirier & G. Zaccour. 320p. 1991. 505.00 (*0-7855-2697-8*, Pub. by Edits Technip) Enfield Pubs NH.

Maritime Arbitration, Charter-Parties (Time & Voyage) Contracts of Affreightment: Sale of Ship, 1919-1991. (Lloyd's Law Reports Consolidated Index, 1919-1994 Ser.: Vol. 1). 1991. 125.00 (*1-85044-425-0*) LLP.

***Maritime Archaeology: A Reader of Substantive & Theoretical Contributions.** L. E. Babits & H. Van Tilburg. LC 97-49977. (Series in Underwater Archaeology). (Illus.). 425p. (C). 1998. 95.00 (*0-306-45330-4*, Plenum Trade); pap. 49.50 (*0-306-45331-2*, Plenum Trade) Perseus Pubng.

Maritime Archaeology in Australia. Graeme Henderson. 201p. 1986. 29.95 (*0-85564-241-6*, Pub. by Univ of West Aust Pr) Intl Spec Bk.

Maritime Arts & Artisans: The Collection of the San Francisco Maritime National Historical Park. Robert Schwendinger. Ed. by Carole Austin. LC 89-61259. (Illus.). 50p. (Orig.). 1989. pap. 7.50 (*1-877742-00-7*) SF Craft & Folk.

Maritime Baselines. (Law of the Sea Ser.). 79p. pap. 8.50 (*92-1-133308-3*, E.88.V.5) UN.

Maritime Boundaries. Ed. by Gerald H. Blake. LC 93-35761. (World Boundaries Ser.: Vol. 5). (Illus.). 192p. (C). 1994. 85.00 (*0-415-08835-6*) Routledge.

Maritime Boundaries & Ocean Resources. Ed. by Gerald H. Blake. LC 87-907. 304p. 1987. 65.50 (*0-389-20726-8*, N8284) B&N Imports.

Maritime Boundaries of the Indian Ocean Region. Vivian L. Forbes. LC 95-948109. (Illus.). 264p. 1995. 67.50 (*9971-69-192-2*, Pub. by Sngapore Univ Pr); pap. 49.50 (*9971-69-189-2*, Pub. by Sngapore Univ Pr) Coronet Bks.

Maritime Boundary. Pood & S. P. Jagota. 1985. lib. bdg. 153.00 (*90-247-3133-X*, Pub. by M Nijhoff) Kluwer Academic.

Maritime Boundary Agreements, 1985-1996. (Law of the Sea Ser.). 97p. pap. 15.00 (*92-1-133422-5*) UN.

Maritime Boundary Agreements, 1942-1969. (The Law of the Sea Ser.). 105p. 25.00 (*92-1-133416-0*, E.91.V.11) UN.

Maritime Boundary Agreements, 1970-1984, Vol. 12. (The Law of the Sea Ser.). 315p. 38.00 (*92-1-133302-4*, E.87.V.12) UN.

Maritime Capital: The Shipping Industry in Atlantic Canada, 1820-1914. Eric W. Sager & Gerald E. Panting. (Illus.). 320p. (C). 1990. text 65.00 (*0-7735-0764-7*, Pub. by McG-Queens Univ Pr) CUP Services.

Maritime Capital: The Shipping Industry in Atlantic Canada, 1820-1914. Eric W. Sager & Gerald E. Panting. (Illus.). 320p. 1996. pap. 24.95 (*0-7735-1520-8*, Pub. by McG-Queens Univ Pr) CUP Services.

Maritime Claims in the Arctic: Canadian & Russian Perspectives. Erik Franckx. LC 93-19520. 360p. (C). 1993. lib. bdg. 149.00 (*0-7923-2218-5*) Kluwer Academic.

Maritime Commerce & English Power: Southeast India, 1750-1800. Sinnappah Arasaratnam. 1996. write for info. (*81-207-1814-3*) Sterling Pubs.

Maritime Commerce & English Power: Southeast India, 1750-1800. Sinnappah Arasaratnam. LC 96-33879. 336p. 1996. 83.95 (*0-86078-610-2*, Pub. by Variorum) Ashgate Pub Co.

Maritime Communications - Electronic Warfare Systems. Charles LeMesurier & Marc Arnold. (Special Reports). 1996. 695.00 (*0-7106-1394-6*) Janes Info Group.

Maritime Dictionary English-Estonian-Russian. Kulno Olev. (ENG, EST & RUS.). 560p. 1981. 35.00 (*0-8288-0430-3*, M 15461) Fr & Eur.

Maritime Dictionary English-Spanish - Spanish-English. 2nd ed. Rodriguez Barrientos. (ENG & SPA.). 248p. 1995. 49.95 (*0-7859-9767-9*) Fr & Eur.

Maritime Dictionary Swedish-English. H. E. Eklund. (ENG & SWE.). 184p. 1980. 49.95 (*0-8288-0426-5*, F26550) Fr & Eur.

Maritime Disasters. Elaine Landau. LC 98-46910. (Watts Library). 63p. (J). (gr. 4-7). 1999. 24.00 (*0-531-20344-1*) Watts.

***Maritime Disasters.** Elaine Landau. (Illus.). (J). 2000. pap. 8.95 (*0-531-16427-6*) Watts.

Maritime Economics. Martin Stopford. (Illus.). 400p. (C). 1988. text 55.00 (*0-04-623016-5*); pap. text 27.95 (*0-04-623017-3*) Routledge.

Maritime Economics: Management & Marketing. 3rd ed. A. Branch. 496p. 1998. pap. 83.00 (*0-7487-3986-6*) St Mut.

Maritime Economics II. 2nd ed. Martin Stopford. LC 97-14490. 512p. (C). 1997. 99.95 (*0-415-15309-3*); pap. 29.95 (*0-415-15310-7*) Routledge.

Maritime Economy of Malaysia. Abdul Aziz Abdul Rahman et al. LC 98-944384. 119p. 1997. write for info. (*967-978-572-6*) Pelanduk.

Maritime Engineering & Ports II. Ed. by J. Olivella & Carlos A. Brebbia. (Water Studies). 350p. 2000. 173.00 (*1-85312-829-5*, 8295, Pub. by WIT Pr) Computational Mech MA.

Maritime Flavors Guidebook & Cookbook. Elaine Elliot & Virginia Lee. (Illus.). 176p. 1995. pap. 19.95 (*0-88780-252-4*, Pub. by Formac Publ Co) Seven Hills Bk.

***Maritime Flavours: Guidebook & Cookbook.** 4th ed. Elaine Elliot et al. (Maritime Flavours Ser.). (Illus.). 176p. 2000. pap. write for info. (*0-88780-506-X*, Pub. by Formac Publ Co) Formac Dist Ltd.

Maritime Flavours Guidebook & Cookbook: 1997 Edition. rev. ed. Elaine Elliot et al. LC 97-950006. (Maritime Flavours Ser.). (Illus.). 170p. 1997. pap. 19.95 (*0-88780-406-3*, Pub. by Formac Publ Co) Formac Dist Ltd.

Maritime Fraud. Barbara Conway. 170p. 1990. 75.00 (*1-85044-257-6*) LLP.

Maritime Heritage: The Ships & Seamen of Southern Ceredigion. J. Geraint Jenkins. 265p. (C). 1982. text 75.00 (*0-85088-985-5*, Pub. by Gomer Pr) St Mut.

***Maritime Heritage of the Cayman Islands.** Roger C. Smith. (Illus.). 200p. 2000. 49.95 (*0-8130-1773-4*) U Press Fla.

Maritime History, Set, Vols. 1 & 2. Ed. by John B. Hattendorf. LC 94-24805. (Open Forum Ser.). (Illus.). (Orig.). (C). 1997. text 62.50 (*1-57524-013-0*) Krieger.

Maritime History: A Hand-List of the Maritime Books (1474-1860) in the John Carter Brown Library with a Special Section on Sir Francis Drake. Danial C. Elliott. 339p. 1979. pap. 20.00 (*0-916617-00-9*) J C Brown.

Maritime History Vol. 1: The Age of Discovery. Ed. by John B. Hattendorf. LC 94-24805. 348p. (C). 1995. pap. 29.50 (*0-89464-834-9*) Krieger.

Maritime History Vol. 1: The Eighteenth Century & the Classic Age of Sail. Ed. by John B. Hattendorf. LC 94-24805. (Open Forum Ser.). (Illus.). (Orig.). (C). 1997. 39.00 (*1-57524-010-6*) Krieger.

Maritime History Vol. 2: The Eighteenth Century & the Classic Age of Sail. Ed. by John B. Hattendorf. LC 94-24805. (Open Forum Ser.). (Illus.). 320p. (Orig.). (C). 1997. 36.50 (*1-57524-007-6*); pap. 26.50 (*0-89464-944-2*) Krieger.

Maritime History of Alaska. William S. Hanable. (Illus.). 350p. 1997. 34.95 (*1-877853-43-7*) Nautical & Aviation.

Maritime History of Bath, Maine & the Kennebec River Regions, 2 vols., 1. William A. Baker. LC 73-85867. (Illus.). 564p. 1973. write for info. (*0-937410-08-X*) ME Maritime Mus.

Maritime History of Bath, Maine & the Kennebec River Regions, 2 vols., 2. William A. Baker. LC 73-85867. (Illus.). 596p. 1973. write for info. (*0-937410-09-8*) ME Maritime Mus.

Maritime History of Bath, Maine & the Kennebec River Regions, 2 vols., Set. William A. Baker. LC 73-85867. (Illus.). 1160p. 1973. 60.00 (*0-937410-10-1*) ME Maritime Mus.

Maritime History of Devon. Oppenheim. 202p. 1968. text 35.00 (*0-900771-00-3*, Pub. by Univ Exeter Pr) Northwestern U Pr.

Maritime History of Massachusetts, 1783-1860. Samuel Eliot Morison. LC 79-5422. 433p. 1979. reprint ed. pap. text 20.00 (*0-930350-04-9*) NE U Pr.

Maritime History of New York. Federal Writers' Project Staff. LC 76-44939. (American Guidebook Ser.). 1980. reprint ed. lib. bdg. 69.00 (*0-403-03823-5*) Somerset Pub.

Maritime History of New York. New York Writer's Program Staff. LC 72-2083. (American History & Americana Ser.: No. 47). 1972. reprint ed. lib. bdg. 75.00 (*0-8383-1460-0*) M S G Haskell Hse.

Maritime History of Russia, 848-1948. Mairin Mitchell. LC 75-94278. (Select Bibliographies Reprint Ser.). 1977. 46.95 (*0-8369-5052-6*) Ayer.

Maritime History of Southampton in Picture Postcards. Rodney Baker & Alan Leonard. (C). 1989. 39.00 (*1-85455-032-2*, Pub. by Ensign Pubns & Print) St Mut.

Maritime History of the Pacific Coast, 1540-1980. James H. Hitchman. 226p. (Orig.). (C). 1990. pap. text 23.50 (*0-8191-7817-9*); lib. bdg. 40.00 (*0-8191-7816-0*) U Pr of Amer.

Maritime History of the World, 2 vols., Set. (Teredo Books Ltd.). 960p. 1985. 450.00 (*0-903662-10-8*) St Mut.

Maritime India: Ports & Shipping. Animesh Ray. (Illus.). 746p. (C). 1995. reprint ed. 67.50 (*81-215-0691-3*, Pub. by M Manoharial) Coronet Bks.

Maritime India in the Seventeenth Century. Sinnappah Arasaratnam. (Illus.). 304p. 1994. text 27.00 (*0-19-563424-1*) OUP.

Maritime Indonesia Moving into the Next Century. S. Hengst. (Illus.). 108p. 1997. 36.50 (*90-407-1473-8*, Pub. by Delft U Pr) Coronet Bks.

Maritime Industry: Cargo Preference Laws - Estimated Costs & Effects. (Illus.). 58p. (Orig.). 1994. pap. text 40.00 (*1-57979-080-1*) DIANE Pub.

Maritime Industry: Cargo Preference Laws - Estimated Costs & Effects. (Illus.). 58p. (Orig.). (C). 1995. pap. text 30.00 (*0-7881-1242-2*) DIANE Pub.

Maritime Industry: Federal Assessments Levied on Commercial Vessels. 196p. (Orig.). (C). 1993. pap. text 45.00 (*0-7881-0005-X*) DIANE Pub.

Maritime Interception & U. N. Sanctions: Resolving Issues in the Persian Gulf War, the Conclict in the Former Yugoslavia, & the Haiti Crisis. Lois E. Fielding. LC 96-31267. 368p. 1997. 69.95 (*1-57292-007-6*) Austin & Winfield.

Maritime Interception & U. N. Sanctions: Resolving Issues in the Persian Gulf War, the Conclict in the Former Yugoslavia, & the Haiti Crisis. Lois E. Fielding. LC 96-31267. 368p. 1997. pap. 49.95 (*1-57292-006-8*) Austin & Winfield.

Maritime Issues in the Caribbean: Proceedings of a Conference Held at Florida International University, 13 April 1981. Ed. by Farrokh Jhabvala. LC 82-20115. 142p. 1983. reprint ed. pap. 44.10 (*0-608-04488-1*, 206523300001) Bks Demand.

Maritime Labour Conventions & Recomendations. 4th rev. ed. LC 98-213628. 276p. 1998. pap. 27.00 (*92-2-110332-3*) Intl Labour Office.

Maritime Labour Conventions & Recommendations. 3rd ed. LC 94-233158. vi, 194p. 1994. pap. 20.25 (*92-2-107111-1*) Intl Labour Office.

Maritime Law. 3rd ed. Christopher Julius Starforth Hill. 500p. 1995. 65.00 (*1-85044-888-4*) LLP.

Maritime Law & Practice. 2nd ed. Florida Bar Members. LC 87-81291. 594p. 1991. ring bd. 75.00 (*0-910373-85-X*, 228) FL Bar Legal Ed.

Maritime Law Handbook. Ed. by Roger Heward & Hans-Christian Albrecht. 1984. ring bd. 226.00 (*90-6544-332-0*) Kluwer Law Intl.

Maritime Law (1993) 348p. 1993. pap. text 45.00 (*1-56986-238-9*) Federal Bar.

Maritime Law Reporter. Ed. by Paul S. Edelman. 1987. pap. 195.00 (*0-88063-173-2*, 81539-10, MICHIE) LEXIS Pub.

Maritime Litigation. John T. Maher et al. LC 94-34469. 1994. ring bd. 100.00 (*0-250-40734-5*, MICHIE) LEXIS Pub.

Maritime Memories of Puget Sound. Joe Williamson & Jim Gibbs. LC 76-18150. (Illus.). 184p. 1987. reprint ed. pap. 19.95 (*0-88740-044-2*) Schiffer.

Maritime Museums of North America, Including Canada: With Selected Lighthouse & Canal Museums. rev. ed. Robert H. Smith. (Illus.). 512p. 1998. pap. 19.95 (*1-887678-14-X*) Finley-Greene Pubns.

Maritime Nantucket. Paul C. Morris. LC 96-77311. (Illus.). 272p. 1996. 40.00 (*0-936972-16-5*) Lower Cape.

***Maritime Neutrality to 1780: A History of the Main Principles Governing Neutrality & Belligerency to 1780-1936.** Carl J. Kulsrud. LC 99-38825. 2000. 65.00 (*1-58477-027-9*) Lawbk Exchange.

Maritime New York in Nineteenth Century Photographs. Harry Johnson & Frederick S. Lightfoot. (Illus.). 160p. (Orig.). 1980. pap. 14.95 (*0-486-23963-2*) Dover.

Maritime Northwest Garden Guide: Planning Calendar for Year-Round Organic Gardening. Carl W. Elliott & Rob Peterson. LC 98-60058. (Illus.). 82p. 1998. pap. 10.00 (*0-931380-17-0*) Seattle Tilth Assn.

Maritime Operations in the Russo-Japanese War, 1904-1905, 2 vols., Set. Julian S. Corbett. LC 94-34316. 1072p. 1994. 79.95 (*1-55750-129-7*) Naval Inst Pr.

***Maritime Paintings of Early Australia, 1788-1900.** Martin Terry. (Illus.). 128p. 1999. 59.95 (*0-522-84688-2*, Pub. by Melbourne Univ Pr) Paul & Co Pubs.

Maritime Paintings of Robert Taylor. Charles Walker & Robert Taylor. (Illus.). 80p. 1999. 65.00 (*0-7153-0935-8*, Pub. by D & C Pub) Sterling.

Maritime Personal Injury Defense: An Outline. James R. Walsh et al. LC 99-62680. (Illus.). viii, 184p. 1999. pap. 23.50 (*0-9669612-0-X*) Walsh Dono.

Maritime Personal Injury Litigation: Jurisdiction & Damages. LC 92-54476. 152p. 1992. pap. 34.95 (*0-89707-825-X*, 519-0213, ABA Tort) Amer Bar Assn.

Maritime Power & the Twenty-First Century. Harold Kearsley. 150p. 1992. 66.95 (*1-85521-288-9*, Pub. by Dartmth Pub) Ashgate Pub Co.

***Maritime Power in the 20th Century: The Australian Experience.** Ed. by David Stevens. (Illus.). 352p. 1999. 39.95 (*1-86448-736-4*, Pub. by Allen & Unwin Pty) Paul & Co Pubs.

Maritime Province Reports, 1929-1967, Vols. 1-53. 1980. 1595.00 (*1-57588-329-5*, 302550) W S Hein.

Maritime Provinces: Off the Beaten Path: A Guide to Unique Places. 2nd ed. Trudy Fong. LC 98-51075. (Off the Beaten Path Ser.). (Illus.). 225p. 1999. pap. 12.95 (*0-7627-0402-0*) Globe Pequot.

Maritime Provinces Atlas. 2nd ed. Robert J. McCalla. (Illus.). 96p. 1991. 29.95 (*0-921921-05-5*, Pub. by Formac Publ Co) Formac Dist Ltd.

Maritime Provinces Prehistory. James A. Tuck. (Canadian Prehistory Ser.). (Illus.). 112p. 1984. pap. 16.95 (*0-660-10759-7*, Pub. by CN Mus Civilization) U of Wash Pr.

Maritime Radio & Satellite Communications Manual. Ian Waugh. 1996. pap. text 34.95 (*0-07-068609-2*) McGraw.

Maritime Regime for North-East Asia. Mark J. Valencia. (Illus.). 340p. 1996. text 75.00 (*0-19-587595-8*) OUP.

Maritime Regulations in the Kingdom of Saudi Arabia. Hussein El-Sayed. 400p. 1987. lib. bdg. 349.50 (*0-86010-736-1*) G & T Inc.

Maritime Rights Movement, 1919-1927: A Study in Canadian Regionalism. Ernest R. Forbes. 260p. 1979. pap. 27.95 (*0-7735-0330-7*, Pub. by McG-Queens Univ Pr) CUP Services.

Maritime Rights Movement, 1919-1927: A Study in Canadian Regionalism. Ernest R. Forbes. LC 79-308545. 258p. reprint ed. pap. 80.00 (*0-7837-1021-6*, 204133200020) Bks Demand.

***Maritime Scotland.** Brian Lavery. (Historic Scotland Ser.). 1999. pap. 23.95 (*0-7134-8583-3*) B T B.

Maritime Sector, Institutions & Sea Power of Premodern China, 212. Gang Deng. LC 99-11267. (Contributions in Economics & Economic History Ser.: Vol. 212). 312p. 1999. 69.50 (*0-313-30712-1*) Greenwood.

Maritime Security. Kenneth G. Hawkes. LC 88-43525. (Illus.). 367p. 1989. text 45.00 (*0-87033-395-X*) Cornell Maritime.

Maritime Security: The Building of Confidence. 163p. 40.00 (*92-9045-074-6*, E.GV.92.0.31) UN.

Maritime Security & Peacekeeping. Ed. by Michael Pugh. LC 94-28597. (Illus.). 240p. 1995. text 29.95 (*0-7190-4563-0*, Pub. by Manchester Univ Pr) St Martin.

Maritime Services Directory, 1995. Ed. by John A. Meanley. 960p. 1995. pap. 89.00 (*0-9623031-2-7*) Aegis Pubns.

Maritime Services Directory, 1999. Ed. by John A. Meanley. 1999. pap. 95.00 (*0-9623031-7-8*) Aegis Pubns.

An Asterisk (*) at the beginning of an entry indicates that the title is appearing for the first time.

Maritime Simulation. Ed. by M. R. Heller. (Illus.). xii, 290p. 1985. 72.95 (0-387-15620-8) Spr-Verlag.
Maritime Sketches. Paul C. Morris. LC 85-50662. (Illus.). 88p. 1985. pap. 10.00 (0-936972-07-6) Lower Cape.
Maritime Solidarity: Pacific Coast Unionism, 1929-1938. Ottilie Markholt. LC 98-68428. (Illus.). 461p. 1999. pap. 19.95 (0-9664397-0-8) Pac Coast Maritime.
Maritime Southeast Asia to 1500. Lynda N. Shaffer. LC 95-36663. (Sources & Studies in World History). (Illus.). 144p. (C). (gr. 13). 1996. text 56.95 (1-56324-143-9) M E Sharpe.
Maritime Southeast Asia to 1500. Lynda N. Shaffer & Kevin Reilly. LC 95-36663. (Sources & Studies in World History). (Illus.). 144p. (YA). (gr. 13). 1996. pap. text 23.95 (1-56324-144-7) M E Sharpe.
Maritime Strategy & Continental Wars. K. R. Menon. LC 97-28051. (Naval Policy & History Ser.: No. 3). 232p. (C). 1998. 47.50 (0-7146-4793-4, Pub. by F Cass Pubs); pap. 22.50 (0-7146-4348-3, Pub. by F Cass Pubs) Intl Spec Bk.
Maritime Strategy & the Nuclear Age. 2nd ed. Geoffrey Till. Date not set. pap. text 13.00 (0-333-35968-2, Pub. by Macmillan) Humanities.
Maritime Strategy, Geopolitics, & the Defense of the West. Colin S. Gray. LC 86-62424. 96p. (Orig.). 1986. pap. text 8.95 (0-915071-02-9) Ramapo Pr.
Maritime Strategy or Coalition Defense? Robert W. Komer. 234p. 1984. reprint ed. pap. text 22.00 (0-8191-4118-6) U Pr of Amer.
***Maritime Supremacy & the Opening of the Western Mind: Naval Campaign That Shaped the Modern World, 1588-1782.** Peter Padfield. LC 99-58999. (Illus.). 340p. 2000. 35.00 (1-58567-002-2, Pub. by Overlook Pr) Penguin Putnam.
Maritime Terror: Protecting Yourself, Your Vessel & Your Crew Against Piracy. Jim Gray et al. (Illus.). 72p. 1999. pap. 14.00 (1-58160-015-1) Paladin Pr.
Maritime Terrorism & International Law. Ed. by Natalino Ronzitti. (C). 1990. lib. bdg. 92.00 (0-7923-0734-8) Kluwer Academic.
Maritime Texas Prior to 1836. Jean L. Epperson & Bill J. Doree. 250p. 25.00 (0-9614104-1-8) Texana Herit Serv.
Maritime Thematic Dictionary English & French. 2nd ed. A. Bruno & Claude Mouilleron-Becar. (ENG & FRE.). 472p. 1994. pap. 225.00 (0-7859-8895-5) Fr & Eur.
***Maritime Trade & Transportation.** Ed. by Chip Moore. (Illus.). 128p. (C). 2000. pap. text 30.00 (0-7567-0030-2) DIANE Pub.
Maritime Trade of the East Anglian Ports, 1550-1590. N. J. Williams. (Oxford Historical Monographs). (Illus.). 344p. 1988. 69.00 (0-19-822943-7) OUP.
Maritime Trade, Society & European Influence in South Asia, 1600-1800. Sinnappah Arasaratnam. (Collected Studies: No. CS471). 320p. 1995. 106.95 (0-86078-452-5, Pub. by Variorum) Ashgate Pub Co.
Maritime Transport Crisis. Hans J. Peters. LC 93-41296. (Discussion Paper Ser.). 60p. 1993. pap. 22.00 (0-8213-2714-3, 12714) World Bank.
Maritime Transport, 1995: (1997 Edition) OECD Staff. 180p. (Orig.). 1997. pap. 35.00 (92-64-15411-6, 76-97-01-1, Pub. by Org for Econ) OECD.
Maritime Zones of Islands in International Law. C. R. Symmons. (Developments in International Law Ser.: No. 1). 1979. lib. bdg. 86.50 (90-247-2171-7) Kluwer Academic.
Maritne Franck: One Day to the Next. Frwd. by John Berger. LC 98-86913. (Illus.). 168p. 1999. 45.00 (0-89381-845-3) Aperture.
Marius. Marcel Pagnol. (FRE., Illus.). 297p. 1973. 13.95 (0-8288-9895-2, F117470) Fr & Eur.
Marius Barbeau's Photographic Collection: The Nass River. Ed. by Linda Riley. (Mercury Ser.: CES No. 109). (Illus.). 204p. 1988. pap. 16.95 (0-660-10766-X, Pub. by CN Mus Civilization) U of Wash Pr.
Marius the Epicurean: His Sensations & Ideas. Walter Pater. 224p. 1985. reprint ed. pap. 18.95 (0-948166-02-9, Pub. by Soho Bk Co) Dufour.
Marivaux & Moliere: A Comparison. Alfred Cismaru. 139p. 1977. 12.95 (0-89672-055-1) Tex Tech Univ Pr.
Marivaux & Reason: A Study in Early Enlightenment Thought. D. J. Culpin. LC 92-34832. (American University Studies: Romance Languages & Literature: Ser. II, Vol. 200). IX, 152p. (C). 1993. text 37.95 (0-8204-2024-7) P Lang Pubng.
Marivaux et l'Angleterre: Essai sur une Creation Dramatique Originale. Desvignes-Parent. 52.50 (0-685-34043-0) Fr & Eur.
Marivaux Plays. Pierre Carlet de Chamblain de Marivaux. (Methuen World Dramatists Ser.). (Illus.). 559p. (Orig.). (C). 1988. pap. write for info. (0-413-18560-5, A0343, Methuen Drama) Methn.
Mariy-El Republic: Economy, Industry, Government, Business. 2nd rev. ed. Russian Information & Business Center, Inc. Staff. (Russian Regional Business Directories Ser.). (Illus.). 200p. 1997. pap. 99.00 (1-57751-364-9) Intl Business Pubns.
***Mariy el Republic Regional Investment & Business Guide.** Global Investment & Business Center, Inc. Staff. (Russian Regional Investment & Business Guides Ser.: Vol. 45). (Illus.). 350p. 1999. pap. 99.00 (0-7397-0816-3) Intl Business Pubns.
***Mariy el Republic Regional Investment & Business Guide.** Contrib. by Global Investment & Business Center, Inc. Staff. (Russian Regional Investment & Business Guides Ser.: Vol. 45). (Illus.). 350p. 2000. pap. 99.95 (0-7397-2993-4) Intl Business Pubns.
Marje: The Guilt & the Gingerbread. large type ed. Angela Palmore. 24.95 (1-85695-121-9, Pub. by ISIS Lrg Prnt) Transaction Pubs.
Marjorie Daw & Other People. Thomas Bailey Aldrich. (Short Story Index Reprint Ser.). 1977. 20.95 (0-8369-3230-7) Ayer.
Marjorie Daw & Other People. Thomas Bailey Aldrich. (Works of Thomas Bailey Aldrich). 243p. reprint ed. 44.00 (0-7812-0819-X) Rprt Serv.
Marjorie Daw & Other People. Thomas Bailey Aldrich. (Works of Thomas Bailey Aldrich). 1989. reprint ed. lib. bdg. 79.00 (0-7812-1665-6) Rprt Serv.
Marjorie Daw & Other Stories. Thomas Bailey Aldrich. (Short Story Index Reprint Ser.). 1977. 20.95 (0-8369-3231-5) Ayer.
Marjorie Daw & Other Stories. Thomas Bailey Aldrich. 1972. reprint ed. lib. bdg. 18.00 (0-8422-8001-4) Irvington.
Marjorie Daw & Other Stories. Thomas Bailey Aldrich. (C). 1986. reprint ed. pap. text 6.95 (0-8290-1943-X) Irvington.
Marjorie Holmes: The Inspirational Writings: A Collection Consisting of Love & Laughter;..., 3 vols. in 1. Marjorie Holmes. 480p. 1995. 14.98 (0-88486-120-1) Galahad Bks.
Marjorie Holmes' Secrets of Health, Energy, & Staying Young. rev. ed. Marjorie Holmes. 384p. 1989. mass mkt. 4.50 (0-380-70707-1, Avon Bks) Morrow Avon.
Marjorie Kinnan Rawlings: A Descriptive Bibliography. Rodger L. Tarr. LC 95-24171. (Pittsburgh Series in Bibliography). 320p. (C). 1996. text 100.00 (0-8229-3920-7) U of Pittsburgh Pr.
Marjorie Kinnan Rawlings: Sojourner at Cross Creek. Elizabeth Silverthorne. 375p. 1988. 24.95 (0-87951-308-X, Pub. by Overlook Pr) Penguin Putnam.
Marjorie Kinnan Rawlings: Sojourner at Cross Creek. Elizabeth Silverthorne. 374p. 1990. pap. 16.95 (0-87951-320-9, Pub. by Overlook Pr) Penguin Putnam.
Marjorie Kinnan Rawlings & the Florida Crackers. Sandra W. Sammons & Nina McGuire. (Southern Pioneer Ser.). (Illus.). 72p. (Orig.). (J). (gr. 4 up). 1995. pap. 14.95 (0-9631241-5-3) Tail Tours.
***Marjorie Main: Rural Documentary Poetry.** John Sherman. Tr. by John F. Sherman. LC 99-91362. 82p. 1999. pap. 8.95 (0-9607220-1-7) Mesa Verde.
Marjorie Morningstar. Herman Wouk. LC 55-6485. 565p. 1992. pap. 13.95 (0-316-95513-2) Little.
***Marjorie Morningstar.** Herman Wouk. 1998. pap. 13.95 (0-316-19076-4, Back Bay) Little.
Marjorie Morningstar. large type ed. Herman Wouk. LC 96-43538. (Core Ser.). 896p. 1996. 26.95 (0-7838-1993-5) Thorndike Pr.
Marjorie Morningstar. Herman Wouk. LC 55-6485. 1994. reprint ed. lib. bdg. 27.95 (1-56849-559-5) Buccaneer Bks.
Marjorie Phillips & Her Paintings. Marjorie Phillips. Ed. by Sylvia Partridge. (Illus.). 1985. 35.00 (0-393-02290-0) Norton.
Marjorie Sykes - Quaker Grandhian. Martha Dart. LC 99-936354. (Illus.). 1999. pap. 24.00 (1-85072-125-4, Pub. by W Sessions) St Mut.
Marjorie's Magical Tail. Marc P. Mannino & Angelica L. Mannino. LC 93-86041. (Illus.). 32p. (Orig.). (J). (ps-5). 1993. pap. 7.95 (0-9638340-0-2) Sugar Sand.
Marjorie's Vacation. Carolyn Wells. 315p. (J). 1980. reprint ed. lib. bdg. 12.95 (0-89967-012-1, Harmony Rain) Buccaneer Bks.
Marjorie's Vacation. Carolyn Wells. 232p. (J). 1981. reprint ed. lib. bdg. 16.95 (0-89966-337-0) Buccaneer Bks.
Marjory Stoneman Douglas: Guardian of the Everglades. Kem K. Sawyer. (Illus.). 72p. (YA). (gr. 5-12). 1994. pap. 7.95 (1-878668-28-5); lib. bdg. 14.95 (1-878668-20-X) Disc Enter Ltd.
Marjory Stoneman Douglas: Voice of the River. Marjory S. Douglas. LC 87-2242. (Illus.). 268p. 1990. pap. 9.95 (0-910923-94-9) Pineapple Pr.
Marjory Stoneman Douglas: Voice of the River. 5th ed. Marjory S. Douglas & John Rothchild. LC 87-2242. (Illus.). 268p. 1990. 17.95 (0-910923-33-7) Pineapple Pr.
Marjory Stoneman Douglas & the Florida Everglades. Sandra W. Sammons. (Southern Pioneer Ser.). (Illus.). 72p. (gr. 4 up). 1998. pap. 14.95 (1-892629-00-3) Tail Tours.
Marjory Stoneman Douglas, Friend of the Everglades. Tricia Andryszewski. LC 93-26731. (Gateway Green Biography Ser.). (Illus.). 48p. (J). (gr. 2-4). 1994. lib. bdg. 21.90 (1-56294-384-7) Millbrook Pr.
Mark see Commentaries on the New Testament
Mark see Rey Siervo: Marcos
Mark. (LifeChange Ser.). 1995. pap. 7.00 (0-89109-910-7) NavPress.
Mark. (Life Application Bible Study Guide Ser.). 128p. 1992. pap. 5.99 (0-8423-2878-5, 02-2878-5) Tyndale Hse.
***Mark.** Anonimo. (Sermon Outline Ser.). 308p. 1998. pap. 19.99 (0-8254-1008-8) Kregel.
Mark. Louis Barbieri. LC 96-207803. (Gospel Commentaries Ser.). pap. 21.99 (0-8024-5450-X, 516) Moody.
Mark. William Barclay. 384p. 1993. pap. 25.00 (0-7152-0272-3, Pub. by St Andrew) St Mut.
Mark. Bruce B. Barton et al. LC 94-3689. (Life Application Bible Commentary Ser.). 507p. 1994. pap. 14.99 (0-8423-3028-3, 75-3028-3) Tyndale Hse.
Mark. C. Clifton Black. (Abingdon New Testament Commentaries Ser.). pap. 23.95 (0-687-05841-4) Abingdon.
Mark. Broadman & Holman Staff. LC 99-11542. (Shepherd's Notes Ser.). 100p. 1999. pap. 5.95 (0-8054-9071-X) Broadman.
Mark. James A. Brooks. (New American Commentary Ser.: Vol.23). 288p. 1991. 27.99 (0-8054-0123-7) Broadman.
Mark. Keith L. Brooks. (Teach Yourself the Bible Ser.). pap. 5.99 (0-8024-5200-0, 520) Moody.
***Mark.** Rodney L. Cooper. (Holman New Testament Commentary Ser.: Vol. 2). 2000. 16.99 (0-8054-0202-0) Broadman.
Mark. Richard L Deibert. (Interpretation Bible Studies). (Illus.). 144p. 1999. pap. 7.00 (0-664-50078-1) Geneva Press.
Mark. Geoffrey Grogan. (Focus on the Bible Commentary Ser.). 9.99 (1-85792-114-3, Pub. by Christian Focus) Spring Arbor Dist.
Mark. Douglas R. Hare. (Westminster Bible Companion Ser.). 224p. 1996. pap. 17.00 (0-664-25551-5) Westminster John Knox.
Mark. H. Harrington. 1989. pap. 22.00 (0-86217-003-6, Pub. by Veritas Pubns) St Mut.
Mark. William Hendriksen. LC 54-924. (New Testament Commentary Ser.). 712p. 1975. 34.99 (0-8010-4114-7) Baker Bks.
Mark. James Hoover. (LifeGuide Bible Studies). 96p. (Orig.). 1985. pap., wbk. ed. 4.99 (0-8308-1004-8, 1004) InterVarsity.
Mark. Henry A. Ironside. LC 94-5184. (Ironside Commentaries). 165p. 1993. pap. 9.99 (0-87213-426-1) Loizeaux.
***Mark.** Jerry B. Jenkins & Tim LaHaye. (Left Behind Ser.: No. 8). 2000. 22.99 (0-8423-3225-1) Tyndale Hse.
Mark. Gary Lacy. 48p. 2000. pap. 8.00 (0-8059-4832-5) Dorrance.
Mark. Matthew Lipman. LC 80-80849. (Philosophy for Children Ser.). 86p. (gr. 11-12). 1980. pap. 10.50 (0-916834-13-1, TX 752-903) Inst Advncmnt Philos Child.
***Mark.** John MacArthur. (MacArthur Bible Study Guides Ser.). 2000. pap. 7.99 (0-8499-5539-4) Word Pub.
Mark. J. Vernon McGee. (Thru the Bible Commentary Ser.: Vol. 36). 1997. pap. 6.97 (0-7852-0654-X) Nelson.
Mark. David L. McKenna. (Communicator's Commentary Ser.: Vol. 2). 332p. 1982. 22.99 (0-8499-0155-3) Word Pub.
Mark. David L. McKenna. (Mastering the Old & New Testament Ser.: Vol. 2). 1991. pap. 14.99 (0-8499-3318-8) Word Pub.
Mark. Dennis M. Sweetland. (Spiritual Commentaries on the New Testament Ser.). 2000. pap. 10.95 (1-56548-117-8) New City.
Mark. William R. Telford. (New Testament Guides Ser.: No. 2). 162p. 1995. pap. 12.50 (1-85075-728-3, Pub. by Sheffield Acad) CUP Services.
Mark. Tyndale House Publishers Staff. (Life Application Bible Studies). 114p. 1999. pap. 5.99 (0-8423-3417-3) Tyndale Hse.
Mark. Harold E. Wicke. (People's Bible Commentary Ser.). 241p. (Orig.). 1992. pap. 10.99 (0-570-04593-2, 12-8011) Concordia.
Mark. Harold E. Wicke. LC 87-61757. (People's Bible Ser.). 241p. (Orig.). 1988. pap. 10.99 (0-8100-0271-X, 15N0426) Northwest Pub.
Mark. Lamar Williamson, Jr. LC 82-17161. (Interpretation: A Bible Commentary for Teaching & Preaching Ser.). 289p. (C). 1983. 27.00 (0-8042-3121-4) Westminster John Knox.
Mark. abr. ed. J. C. Ryle. LC 92-45785. (Classic Commentaries Ser.). 288p. 1993. pap. 15.90 (0-89107-727-8) Crossway Bks.
Mark. J. C. Ryle. 370p. 1984. reprint ed. pap. 9.99 (0-85151-441-3) Banner of Truth.
Mark. rev. ed. R. Alan Cole. Ed. by Leon Morris. (Tyndale New Testament Commentaries Ser.). 340p. 1989. pap. 14.00 (0-8028-0481-0) Eerdmans.
***Mark.** rev. ed. James Hoover. (Orig.). 1999. pap. 4.99 (0-8308-3004-9) InterVarsity.
Mark see Preacher's Outline & Sermon Bible - New Testament Set
Mark. 2nd enl. rev. ed. Paul J. Achtemeier. Ed. by Gerhard A. Krodel. LC 85-46020. (Proclamation Commentaries Ser.: the New Testament Witnesses for Preaching). 138p. 1986. pap. 14.00 (0-8006-1916-1, 1-1916, Fortress Pr) Augsburg Fortress.
Mark, 2. Willard H. Taylor. Ed. by A. Elwood Sanner & William M. Greathouse. (Beacon Bible Exposition Ser.: Vol. 2). 255p. 1978. 14.99 (0-8341-0313-3) Beacon Hill.
Mark, Vol. 2. Larry W. Hurtado. LC 96-6228. (New International Biblical Commentary Ser.). 306p. 1989. pap. 11.95 (0-943575-16-8) Hendrickson MA.
Mark: A Bible Commentary for Every Day. R. T. France. LC 98-2542. (Doubleday Bible Commentaries Ser.). 224p. 1998. pap. 12.95 (0-385-49017-8) Doubleday.
Mark: A Gospel for Today. Danes. 1989. pap. 16.95 (0-7459-1504-3, Pub. by Lion Pubng) Trafalgar.
Mark: A New Translation with Introduction & Commentary. C. S. Mann. LC 85-4433. (Anchor Bible Ser.: Vol. 27). (Illus.). 752p. 1986. 44.95 (0-385-03253-6, Anchor NY) Doubleday.
Mark: A Reader-Response Commentary. Bas M. Van Iersel. (JSNT Supplement Ser.: Vol. 164). 560p. 1998. 85.00 (1-85075-829-8, Pub. by Sheffield Acad) CUP Services.
Mark: A Very Human Jesus. Robert Knopp. (Gospel Images for Prayer Ser.). 216p. 1998. pap. 7.95 (0-8198-3085-2) Pauline Bks.
Mark: A War Correspondent's Memoir of Vietnam & Cambodia. Jacques Leslie. LC 94-38062. (Illus.). 305p. 1995. 22.00 (1-56858-024-X) FWEW.
Mark: Evangelist & Theologian. Ralph P. Martin. (Contemporary Evangelical Perspective Ser.). 249p. (C). 1986. pap. 12.95 (0-310-28801-0, 18118P) Zondervan.
Mark: God in Action. Chuck Christensen & Winnie Christensen. LC 72-88935. (Fisherman Bible Studyguide Ser.). 94p. 1972. pap. 4.99 (0-87788-309-2, H Shaw Pubs) Waterbrook Pr.
Mark: Good News for Hard Times - A Popular Commentary on the Earliest Gospel. George T. Montague. 197p. 1992. 9.95 (0-940535-53-X, UP 153) Franciscan U Pr.
Mark: Gospel of Action. Ralph Earle. (Everyman's Bible Commentaries Ser.). pap. 9.99 (0-8024-2041-9, 483) Moody.
Mark: Hope for Hurting People. rev. ed. Marilyn Kunz & Catherine Schell. 112p. 1993. pap. 5.99 (1-880266-06-7) Neighborhood Bible.
Mark: Images of an Apostolic Interpreter. C. Clifton Black. LC 93-37578. (Studies on Personalities of the New Testament). 347p. (C). 1994. text 34.95 (0-87249-973-1) U of SC Pr.
Mark: Jesus, Servant & Savior, Vol. I. R. Kent Hughes. LC 89-50322. (Preaching the Word Ser.). 240p. 1999. 19.99 (0-89107-522-4) Crossway Bks.
Mark: Jesus, Servant & Savior, Vol. II. R. Kent Hughes. LC 89-50322. (Preaching the Word Ser.). 240p. 1999. 19.99 (0-89107-537-2) Crossway Bks.
Mark: New Testament II see Ancient Christian Commentary on Scripture
Mark: Realistic Theologian: The Jesus of Mark. Wilfrid J. Harrington. 152p. (Orig.). 1996. pap. 14.95 (1-85607-169-3, Pub. by Columba Press) Whitecap Bks.
***Mark: The Beginning of the Gospel.** Peter Bolt & Tony Payne. (Faith Walk Bible Studies). 80p. 2000. 4.99 (1-58134-147-4) Crossway Bks.
Mark: The Good News Preached to the Romans. Philip J. Cunningham. LC 94-41670. 192p. (Orig.). 1995. pap. 10.95 (0-8091-3554-X) Paulist Pr.
Mark: The Gospel As Story. Ernest E. Best. Ed. by John E. Riches. 164p. 1989. pap. 24.95 (0-567-29153-7, Pub. by T & T Clark) Bks Intl VA.
Mark: The Serving Christ. (God's Word for Today Ser.). 102p. 1996. pap. 5.50 (0-570-09542-5, 20-2650) Concordia.
***Mark: The Way for All Nations.** Willard M. Swartley. 248p. 1999. pap. 23.00 (1-57910-235-2) Wipf & Stock.
Mark: Visionary of Early Christianity. Leonard Doohan. LC 86-72485. (Scripture for Worship Ser.). 192p. (Orig.). (C). 1993. pap. text 10.95 (0-89390-261-6) Resource Pubns.
Mark: What Is He Saying? Robert G. Davidson. 88p. 1998. pap. 7.95 (1-57438-025-7, 6621) Ed Ministries.
Mark, a Devotional Commentary: Meditations on the Gospel According to St. Mark. Ed. by Leo Zanchettin. LC 99-182822. 200p. 1998. pap. 19.95 (0-932085-13-X) Word Among Us.
***Mark A. Smith's Guide to Safe, Common Sense off Road Driving.** 2nd rev. ed. Mark A. Smith. (Illus.). 81p. 2000. pap. 6.95 (0-9658763-3-0) Cedar Ridge.
***Mark Akenside: A Reassessment.** Robin Dix. LC 00-33571. 2000. write for info. (0-8386-3882-1) Fairleigh Dickinson.
Mark Allen's Total Triathlete. Mark Allen & Bob Babbitt. (Illus.). 176p. (Orig.). 1988. pap. 12.95 (0-8092-4589-2, 458920, Contemporary Bks) NTC Contemp Pub Co.
Mark & His Friend. Michael J. Belloise. LC 94-77012. 269p. 1994. 18.95 (0-9641541-0-2) Lieto Pubng.
Mark & Livy: The Love Story of Mark Twain & the Woman Who Almost Tamed Him. Resa Willis. 352p. 1992. text 25.00 (0-689-12154-7) Atheneum Yung Read.
***Mark & Livy: The Love Story of Mark Twain & the Woman Who Almost Tamed Him.** Resa Willis. LC 99-55505. (Illus.). 368p. 2000. pap. 16.00 (1-57500-096-2, Pub. by TV Bks) HarpC.
Mark & Luke in Poststructuralist Perspectives: Jesus Begins to Write. Stephen D. Moore. LC 91-30523. 192p. (C). 1992. 30.00 (0-300-05197-2) Yale U Pr.
Mark & Method: New Approaches in Biblical Studies. Ed. by Janice C. Anderson & Stephen D. Moore. LC 92-17158. 192p. 1992. pap. 18.00 (0-8006-2655-9, 1-2655) Augsburg Fortress.
Mark & Q. E. Peters. 1998. 56.95 (90-6831-712-1, Pub. by Peeters Pub) Bks Intl VA.
Mark & the Knowledge: Social Stigma in Classic American Fiction. Marjorie Pryse. LC 78-23229. 189p. reprint ed. pap. 58.60 (0-608-09868-X, 206983300006) Bks Demand.
Mark Antony. Pat Southern. (Illus.). 160p. 1998. 27.50 (0-7524-1406-2, Pub. by Tempus Pubng) Arcadia Publng.
Mark Antony: A Biography. Eleanor G. Huzar. (Classical Lives Ser.). (Illus.). 347p. (Orig.). (C). 1986. reprint ed. pap. 16.95 (0-7099-4719-4, Pub. by C Helm) Routldge.
Mark As Recovery Story: Alcoholism & the Rhetoric of Gospel Mystery. John C. Mellon. LC 94-24082. 296p. 1995. 26.95 (0-252-02165-7) U of Ill Pr.
Mark as Story: An Introduction to the Narrative of a Gospel. 2nd ed. David Rhoads et al. LC 99-12061. 192p. 1999. pap. 18.00 (0-8006-3160-9, 1-3160, Fortress Pr) Augsburg Fortress.
Mark at the Farm see Early Phonetic Readers - Set C
***Mark Borthwick: 2000-1 Maison Martin Margiela Autumn/winter 1998-99.** Mark Borthwick. 1999. pap. text 30.00 (2-9512460-0-5) MIAS.
Mark Brewster of Hull England & Allied Families in America Including: Atkey, Carpenter, Dare, Fowler, Hiscock, Hewitt, Potter & Yelf. Marcus V. Brewster. Ed. by Janet B. Brewster. (Biographical & Genealogical Ser.). (Illus.). 340p. 1990. 30.00 (0-89308-449-2) J B Brewster.
***Mark Brunnell: Super Southpaw.** Pete Prisco. (SuperStar Series: Vol. 5). 96p. (J). 1999. pap. 4.95 (1-58261-166-1, Pub. by Sprts Pubng) Partners-West.
Mark Catesby's Natural History of America: Watercolours from the Royal Library, Windsor Castle. Henrietta McBurney. LC 97-181018. 1997. 40.00 (1-85894-039-7, Pub. by Merrell Holberton) U of Wash Pr.
Mark Catesby's Natural History of America: Watercolours from the Royal Library, Windsor Castle. Henrietta McBurney. (Illus.). 144p. 1997. 40.00 (1-85894-038-9, Pub. by Merrell Holberton) U of Wash Pr.

M

Mark Catesby's Natural History of America: Watercolours from the Royal Library, Windsor Castle. Henrietta McBurney et al. LC 97-3931. 1997. pap. write for info. (*0-89090-081-7*) Mus Fine TX.

Mark Curtis Hoax: How the Socialist Workers Party Tried to Dupe the Labor Movement. Martin McLaughlin. (Illus.). 253p. (Orig.). (C). 1990. pap. 11.95 (*0-929087-46-1*) Mehring Bks.

Mark Di Suvero: At Storm King Art Center. Irving Sandler. LC 94-35360. (Illus.). 128p. 1996. pap. write for info. (*0-8109-2614-8*) Abrams.

Mark Di Suvero: At Storm King Art Center. Irving Sandler. LC 94-35360. (Illus.). 128p. 1996. 45.00 (*0-8109-3218-0*, Pub. by Abrams) Time Warner.

Mark Di Suvero: Valence. 1994. pap. 40.00 (*1-881616-43-6*) Dist Art Pubs.

Mark Di Suvero in Venice. Giouanni Carandente. (Illus.). 52p. 1996. pap. text 29.95 (*88-8158-035-7*, Pub. by Charta) Dist Art Pubs.

Mark di Suvero/Orange County. Bruce Guenther et al. (Illus.). 40p. 1998. pap. 12.95 (*0-917493-26-5*) Orange Cnty Mus.

Mark Dion. Lisa G. Corrin. (Illus.). 160p. 1997. pap. 29.95 (*0-7148-3659-1*, Pub. by Phaidon Press) Phaidon Pr.

Mark 8:27-16:20. Craig A. Evans. (Biblical Commentary Ser.: Vol. 34b). 320p. 2000. 32.99 (*0-8499-0253-3*) Word Pub.

Mark 8:22-16:20 Vol. 2: Introducing the Gospel According to Mark. Eugene LaVerdiere. (Beginning of the Gospel Ser.). 1999. pap. text 29.95 (*0-8146-2574-6*) Liturgical Pr.

Mark Eugenicus & the Council of Florence: A Historical Re-Evaluation of His Personality. 2nd ed. Constantine N. Tsirpanlis. 125p. 1986. pap. 26.95 (*0-317-36318-2*) EO Pr.

Mark Freedom Paid: A Combat Anthology. Ed. by Lee Steedle. LC 97-60560. (Illus.). 190p. 1998. reprint ed. pap. 12.95 (*0-9657649-0-7*) Eighty-Third Chem.

Mark Goodson Collection. (Illus.). 64p. (Orig.). 1995. pap. 20.00 (*1-878283-56-1*) PaceWildenstein.

Mark Grace: Winning with Grace. Barry Rozner. Ed. by Rob Rains. (Super Star Ser.). 96p. (J). 1999. pap. 4.95 (*1-58261-056-8*) Sprts Pubng.

Mark Hopkins & the Log: Williams College, 1836-1872. 2nd rev. ed. Ed. by Frederick Rudolph. (Illus.). 288p. 1996. pap. 19.95 (*0-915081-03-2*) Williams Coll.

Mark Hughes. Mark Hughes. (Illus.). 224p. 1994. 29.95 (*1-85158-680-6*, Pub. by Mainstream Pubng) Trafalgar.

Mark in the Closet. G. Van Denend. Ed. by J. Vreeman. (Illus.). 16p. (Orig.). (J). 1985. pap. 3.95 (*0-918789-01-X*) FreeMan Prods.

Mark Innerst: Landscape & Beyond. Contrib. by Barry Blinderman. (Illus.). 48p. 1988. 20.00 (*0-945558-02-3*) ISU Univ Galls.

Mark Is Ready: 666. David F. Webber. LC 97-181927. 94p. (Orig.). 1997. pap. 10.00 (*0-937422-37-1*, 2037) Midnight Call.

Mark It Like It Is. Frederick Binkley. LC 87-90901. 1988. 15.00 (*0-87212-205-0*) Libra.

Mark It with a Stone: A Moving Account of a Young Boy's Struggle to Survive the Nazi Death Camps. Joseph Horn. LC 95-51075. 224p. 1996. 20.00 (*1-56980-068-5*) Barricade Bks.

Mark J. Millard Architectural Collection. National Gallery of Art (U. S.) Staff et al. LC 93-4308. 1993. write for info. (*0-89468-265-2*) Natl Gallery Art.

Mark Kistler's Draw Squad. Mark Kistler. (Illus.). 224p. 1988. per. 16.00 (*0-671-65694-5*, Fireside) S&S Trade Pap.

Mark Kistler's Drawing in 3-D Wacky Workbook. Mark Kistler. LC 99-225814. (Illus.). 192p. 1998. pap., wbk. ed. 8.00 (*0-684-85337-X*, Fireside) S&S Trade Pap.

Mark Kistler's Imagination Station: Learn How to Draw in 3-D with Public Television's Favorite Drawing Teacher. Mark Kistler. 288p. 1994. per. 16.00 (*0-671-50013-9*, Fireside) S&S Trade Pap.

***Mark Kistler's Web Wizards: Build Your Own Homepage with Public TV's Favorite Cybercartoonist & His Pal Web Master Dennis.** Mark Kistler. LC 00-20838. (Illus.). 96p. (gr. 5-9). 2000. pap. 10.00 (*0-684-86322-7*, Fireside) S&S Trade Pap.

Mark Knopfler - Guitar Styles, Vol. II. Ed. by Jeannette DeLisa. 104p. (Orig.). (YA). 1994. reprint ed. pap. text 19.95 (*0-89898-767-9*, P1065GTX) Wrner Bros.

Mark Knopfler Golden Heart. 72p. 1997. otabind 16.95 (*0-7935-7369-6*); otabind 19.95 (*0-7935-7370-X*) H Leonard.

Mark Lere. Suzanne Muchnic & Julie Courtney. (Illus.). 36p. (Orig.). 1986. pap. 4.00 (*0-939351-00-5*) Temple U Tyler Gal.

Mark Lindquist: Revolutions in Wood. Hobbs. (Illus.). 88p. 1996. pap. 22.95 (*0-295-97506-7*) U of Wash Pr.

Mark Luyten: On a Balcony: A Novel. Mark Luyten et al. LC 96-52684. (Illus.). 112p. (Orig.). 1997. pap. 16.95 (*0-935640-54-1*) Walker Art Ctr.

Mark Manning's Mission: or The Story of a Shoe Factory Boy. Horatio Alger. 268p. 1974. reprint ed. lib. bdg. 23.95 (*0-88411-804-5*) Amereon Ltd.

Mark Martin. Tara Baukus Mello. LC 99-15640. (Illus.). 64p. 1999. 16.95 (*0-7910-5411-X*) Chelsea Hse.

Mark Martin. Tara Baukus Mello. (Race Car Legends Ser.). (Illus.). 64p. (gr. 4-7). 1999. pap. 7.95 (*0-7910-5677-5*) Chelsea Hse.

Mark Martin: Driven to Race. Bob Zeller. (Illus.). 159p. (Orig.). 1997. pap. 24.95 (*0-9649722-3-9*, SMMB) D Bull.

Mark Mason's Victory. Horatio Alger, Jr. (Works of Horatio Alger Jr.). 1989. reprint ed. lib. bdg. 79.00 (*0-685-27577-9*) Rprt Serv.

***Mark McGuire: Home Run King.** C. A. Piparo. (All-Star Bks.). (Illus.). 32p. (J). (ps-3). 1999. pap. 3.95 (*1-58260-017-1*, Pub. by Infnty Plus One) Assoc Pubs Grp.

***Mark McGwire.** Richard Brenner. (Illus.). 32p. (J). (gr. 1-4). 1999. pap. 4.50 (*0-688-17085-4*, Wm Morrow) Morrow Avon.

Mark McGwire. Terri Dougherty. LC 98-43248. 1999. 6.95 (*1-57765-347-5*) ABDO Pub Co.

***Mark McGwire.** Terri Dougherty. LC 98-43248. (Jam Session Ser.). (Illus.). 32p. 1999. lib. bdg. 19.93 (*1-57765-349-1*, ABDO & Dghtrs) ABDO Pub Co.

Mark McGwire. David Fisher. LC 98-89166. 1999. 4.95 (*0-8362-1462-5*) Andrews & McMeel.

Mark McGwire. Jim Gallagher. LC 99-25370. (Real-Life Reader Biography Ser.). (Illus.). 32p. (J). (gr. 3-8). 1999. lib. bdg. 15.95 (*1-58415-017-3*) M Lane Pubs.

***Mark McGwire.** GHB Publishers Staff & Mike Eisenbath. 2000. pap. text 12.95 (*1-892920-33-6*) G H B Pubs.

***Mark McGwire.** Rob Kirkpatrick. LC 99-42490. (Great Record Breakers in Sports Ser.). (Illus.). (J). 2000. lib. bdg. 18.60 (*0-8239-5630-X*, PowerKids) Rosen Group.

***Mark McGwire.** Intro. by Jim Murray. LC 98-51065. (Baseball Legends Ser.). (Illus.). 64p. (YA). (gr. 3-7). 1999. 16.95 (*0-7910-5155-2*) Chelsea Hse.

Mark McGwire. Carrie Muskat. (Baseball Legends Ser.). 1999. pap. 7.95 (*0-7910-5491-8*) Chelsea Hse.

***Mark McGwire.** Phelan Powell. (Sports Heroes Ser.). 48p. (YA). (gr. 5 up). 2000. lib. bdg. 21.26 (*0-7368-0578-8*, Capstone Bks) Capstone Pr.

Mark McGwire. Rob Rains. 1999. mass mkt. 5.99 (*0-312-97109-5*) St Martin.

Mark McGwire. Mark Stewart. LC 98-48386. (Sports Stars Ser.). 48p. (J). (gr. 3-4). 1999. 18.00 (*0-516-21612-0*) Childrens.

Mark Mcgwire. Bob Temple. LC 99-18541. (Illus.). 24P32p. 1999. lib. bdg. 21.36 (*1-56766-662-0*) Childs World.

***Mark McGwire.** Bob Temple. LC 00-40493. (Illus.). (J). 2000. lib. bdg. write for info. (*1-56766-830-5*) Childs World.

Mark McGwire: A Biography. Jonathan Hall. LC 99-199277. 1998. per. 4.99 (*0-671-03273-9*, Archway) PB.

Mark McGwire: Home Run Hero. Rob Rains. LC 98-38326. (Illus.). 227p. 1998. 22.95 (*0-312-20162-1*) St Martin.

***Mark McGwire: Home Run King.** Jeff Savage. LC 98-43684. (Sports Achievers Biographies Ser.). 64p. (YA). (gr. 4-9). 1999. pap. 5.95 (*0-8225-9845-0*, LernerSports) Lerner Pub.

***Mark McGwire: Home Run King.** Jeff Savage. LC 98-43684. (Sports Achievers Biographies Ser.). 80p. (YA). (gr. 4-9). 1999. 21.27 (*0-8225-3675-7*, LernerSports) Lerner Pub.

Mark McGwire: Home Run King. Mark Stewart. (Sports Stars Ser.). 1999. lib. bdg. 5.95 (*0-516-26512-1*) Childrens.

Mark McGwire: "Mac Attack!" Rob Rains. (SuperStar Ser.). 96p. (YA). (gr. 7-10). 1998. pap. 5.95 (*1-58261-004-5*) Sprts Pubng.

***Mark McGwire: On the Record, 1.** Beckett Publications Editors. LC 98-232598. 1998. 19.95 (*1-887432-63-9*) Beckett Pubns.

Mark McGwire: Record Breaker see Reading Power Set 1: Power Player

Mark McGwire: Slugger! Rob Rains. Ed. by Sporting News Staff. (Illus.). 50p. (J). (gr. k-5). 1998. 15.95 (*1-58261-005-3*) Sprts Pubng.

Mark McGwire: Star Home Run Hitter. Stew Thornley. LC 98-33313. (Sports Reports Ser.). (Illus.). 104p. (J). (gr. 4-10). 1999. lib. bdg. 20.95 (*0-7660-1329-4*) Enslow Pubs.

Mark McGwire & Chipper Jones. J. Gelberg. (J). 1997. pap. 4.99 (*0-943403-43-X*) East End.

Mark Medoff. Rudolf Erben. LC 95-75724. (Western Writers Ser.: No. 117). (Illus.). 55p. (C). 1995. pap. 4.95 (*0-88430-116-8*) Boise St U W Writ Ser.

***Mark Messier.** (Illus.). 56p. 2000. pap. 12.95 (*1-892920-37-9*) G H B Pubs.

Mark Messier. Barry Wilner. LC 97-27364. (Ice Hockey Legends Ser.). (Illus.). 64p. (YA). (gr. 3 up). 1999. lib. bdg. 15.95 (*0-7910-4559-5*) Chelsea Hse.

Mark Messier: Star Center. Michael J. Sullivan. LC 96-52295. (Sports Reports Ser.). 104p. (YA). (gr. 4-10). 1997. lib. bdg. 20.95 (*0-89490-801-4*) Enslow Pubs.

Mark Miller's Indian Market: Recipes from Santa Fe's Famous Coyote Cafe. Mark Miller et al. LC 95-4212. (Illus.). 217p. 1995. text 39.95 (*0-89815-620-3*) Ten Speed Pr.

Mark Miller's Networking Libra. Miller. 1997. 145.00 (*1-55851-575-5*, M&T Bks) IDG Bks.

***Mark Minasi's Windows 2000 Resource Kit.** Mark Minasi. 2448p. 2000. pap. 124.96 (*0-7821-2614-6*) Sybex.

Mark Morris. Joan Acocella. LC 93-13697. 1993. 27.50 (*0-374-20295-8*) FS&G.

Mark Morris. Joan Acocella. 306p. 1995. pap. 17.00 (*0-374-52418-1*, Noonday) FS&G.

Mark Morrisroe. Klaus Ottmann. (Illus.). 220p. 1999. 60.00 (*0-944092-62-4*) Twin Palms Pub.

Mark My Words: A Commentary on the Gospel of Mark. Joseph O'Hanlon. 316p. 1996. pap. 19.95 (*0-85439-472-9*, Pub. by St Paul Pubns) St Mut.

Mark My Words: Instruction & Practice in Proofreading. rev. ed. Penny Smith. 342p. 36.50 (*0-614-25534-1*, 00PO44693) Print Indus Am.

Mark My Words: Instruction & Practice in Proofreading. 3rd ed. Peggy Smith. LC 97-47038. 1997. pap. 35.00 (*0-935012-23-0*) E E I Pr.

Mark O'Connor - The Championship Years. Mark O'Connor & Stacy Phillips. 500p. 1991. spiral bd. 17.95 (*1-56222-201-5*; 94585) Mel Bay.

Mark of a Champion. Ron Brown. 32p. 1996. pap. 2.95 (*1-887002-33-2*) Cross Trng.

Mark of a Christian: Studies from Second Corinthians. James Thompson. 127p. 1993. pap. 6.95 (*0-945441-15-0*) Res Pubns AR.

Mark of a Disciple see Marcas del Discipulo

Mark of a Man. Elisabeth Elliot. LC 80-25108. 178p. 1984. pap. 9.99 (*0-8007-5121-3*) Revell.

Mark of a Murderer. Mike McAlary. 2000. pap. write for info. (*0-7868-8424-X*, Pub. by Disney Pr) Little.

Mark of a Shadow. Darrick Moore. (Illus.). 72p. 1998. pap. 10.00 (*0-9667048-0-0*) SilkWorks.

Mark of Blasphemy: An Exposition of Revelation 13:16-18. Marjorie B. Matheny & James F. Matheny. 108p. 1995. pap. text 6.95 (*0-939422-08-5*) Jay & Assocs.

Mark of Cain. Ruth Mellinkoff. LC 80-18589. (Quantum Bks.: No. 20). 128p. 1981. 45.00 (*0-520-03969-6*, Pub. by U CA Pr) Cal Prin Full Svc.

Mark of Cain. Andrew Lang. LC 68-54278. reprint ed. 37.50 (*0-404-03828-X*) AMS Pr.

Mark of Circumcision: A History of the World's Most Controversial Surgery. David L. Gollaher. LC 99-40015. 224p. 2000. 15.00 (*0-465-04397-6*, Pub. by Basic) HarpC.

Mark of Flesh. Sylvester. 1999. pap. 11.00 (*0-393-31910-5*) Norton.

Mark of Flesh. Janet Sylvester. LC 96-45127. 64p. (C). 1997. 19.00 (*0-393-04094-1*) Norton.

Mark of God Vol. 1: How to Get the Mark of God on Your Forehead. Cheryl A. Alexander. ix, 54p. 1997. pap. 6.99 (*0-9660632-9-5*) C A Alexander.

Mark of God or Mark of the Beast. Betty Miller. (End Times Ser.). 112p. 1991. pap. 5.00 (*1-57149-019-1*) Christ Unltd.

Mark of Mandragora: A Doctor Who Graphic Novel. Andrew Donkin. (Illus.). 90p. 1999. reprint ed. pap. text 20.00 (*0-7881-6062-1*) DIANE Pub.

Mark of Murder: A Lieutenant Luis Mendoza Mystery. Dell Shannon. 240p. 1986. mass mkt. 3.95 (*0-445-40262-8*, Pub. by Warner Bks) Little.

Mark of Our Moccasins. Colleen L. Reece. (Indian Culture Ser.). 45p. (J). (gr. 5-12). 1982. 5.95 (*0-89992-081-0*) Coun India Ed.

***Mark of the Angel.** Nancy Huston. (International Ser.).Tr. of L'Empreinte de l'ange. (Illus.). 240p. 2000. pap. text 12.00 (*0-375-70921-5*) Vin Bks.

***Mark of the Angel.** large type ed. Nancy Huston. LC 99-50156.Tr. of L'Empreinte de l'ange. 1999. 24.95 (*1-57490-244-X*, Beeler LP Bks) T T Beeler.

Mark of the Angel: A Novel. Nancy Huston. LC 99-16682.Tr. of L'Empreinte de l'ange. 215p. 1999. 21.00 (*1-883642-64-7*) Steerforth Pr.

Mark of the Assassin. Daniel Silva. 1999. mass mkt. 6.99 (*0-449-22531-3*, Crest) Fawcett.

***Mark of the Assassin.** Daniel Silva. 2000. mass mkt. 6.99 (*0-449-45939-X*, Crest) Fawcett.

Mark of the Bear: Legend & Lore of an American Icon. Ed. by Paul D. Schullery. LC 96-17650. (Illus.). 120p. 1996. 30.00 (*0-87156-903-5*, Pub. by Sierra) Random.

Mark of the Beast see Marca de La Bestia

Mark of the Beast. Ed. & Intro. by Pat Bryant. (Southern Exposure Ser.). (Illus.). 112p. (Orig.). 1980. pap. 3.00 (*0-943810-09-4*) Inst Southern Studies.

Mark of the Beast, 2 vols. Yisrayl Hawkins. Incl. Vol. 1. (Illus.). 240p. 1985. 20.00 (*1-890967-01-7*); Vol. 2. (Illus.). 439p. 1986. 25.00 (*1-890967-02-5*); 39.00 (*1-890967-03-3*) Hse of Yahweh.

Mark of the Beast. Trevor Ravenscroft & Tim Wallace-Murphy. 256p. 1992. pap. 12.95 (*0-8065-1322-5*, Citadel Pr) Carol Pub Group.

Mark of the Beast, Vol. 1. rev. ed. Yisrayl Hawkins. 1997. pap. 20.00 (*1-890967-20-3*) Hse of Yahweh.

Mark of the Beast: Death & Degradation in the Literature of the Great War. Alfredo Bonadeo. LC 88-27645. 184p. 1989. 24.95 (*0-8131-1680-5*) U Pr of Ky.

Mark of the Beast: The Continuing Story of the Spear of Destiny. 2nd ed. Trevor Ravenscroft & T. Wallace Murphy. LC 96-14629. (Illus.). 256p. 1997. reprint ed. pap. 12.95 (*0-87728-870-4*) Weiser.

Mark of the Beast: The Medieval Bestiary in Art, Life, & Literature. Ed. by Debra Hassig. LC 98-36629. (Medieval Casebks.: No. 22). (Illus.). 252p. 1998. 65.00 (*0-8153-2952-0*, H2076) Garland.

Mark of the Beast: Your Money, Computers, & the End of the World. Peter Lalonde & Paul Lalonde. LC 93-43734. 1994. pap. 9.99 incl. VHS (*1-56507-218-9*) Harvest Hse.

Mark of the Beast: 666. Martin Stone. Ed. by Flo Wishmeyer. LC 98-87914. 280p. 1999. pap. 17.95 (*0-9666848-0-X*) La Casa Pr.

Mark of the Beast & the Jerusalem Temple. Michael Penny. (Illus.). 24p. (Orig.). 1993. pap. text 2.50 (*1-880573-08-3*) Bible Search Pubns.

Mark of the Beast, Six Six Six. Robert B. Benson. 132p. (Orig.). 1993. pap. 7.50 (*0-9616327-0-4*) Brandt Bks.

Mark of the Blue Tattoo. Franklin W. Dixon. (Hardy Boys Mystery Stories Ser.: No. 146). (J). (gr. 3-6). 1997. per. 3.99 (*0-671-00058-6*) PB.

Mark of the Blue Tattoo. Franklin W. Dixon. (Hardy Boys Mystery Stories Ser.: No. 146). (J). (gr. 3-6). 1997. 9.09 (*0-606-13460-3*, Pub. by Turtleback) Demco.

***Mark of the Bundesbank: Germany's Role in EMC.** Dorothee Heisenberg. LC 98-29705. 214p. 1998. lib. bdg. 49.95 (*1-55587-689-7*) L Rienner.

Mark of the Cat. Andre Norton. 1993. mass mkt. 4.99 (*0-441-51971-7*) Ace Bks.

Mark of the Chadwicks. Jo-Ann Power. 288p. 1993. mass mkt. 3.99 (*0-8217-4072-5*, Zebra Kensgtn) Kensgtn Pub Corp.

Mark of the Christian. Francis A. Schaeffer. 38p. (Orig.). 1970. pap. 5.99 (*0-87784-434-8*, 434) InterVarsity.

***Mark of the Crown.** Jude Watson. 131p. (gr. 3-7). 1999. mass mkt. 4.99 (*0-590-51934-4*) Scholastic Inc.

***Mark of the Galilean.** E. Noah Sarath. LC 00-190106. 276p. 2000. 25.00 (*0-7388-1548-9*); pap. 18.00 (*0-7388-1549-7*) Xlibris Corp.

Mark of the Grizzly: True Stories of Recent Bear Attacks & the Hard Lessons Learned. Scott McMillion. LC 98-16427. 249p. 1998. pap. 14.95 (*1-56044-636-6*) Falcon Pub Inc.

Mark of the Lion Trilogy. Francine Rivers. 1998. pap. text 29.99 (*0-8423-3952-3*) Tyndale Hse.

Mark of the Maker. Tom Hegg. (Illus.). 48p. (YA). (gr. 10 up). 1991. 10.95 (*0-931674-18-2*) Waldman Hse Pr.

Mark of the Maker: A Portrait of Helen Waddell. Monica Blackett. LC 73-161815. 258p. reprint ed. pap. 80.00 (*0-608-15681-7*, 203199700077) Bks Demand.

Mark of the Man-Wolf. Marvel Comics Staff. (Spiderman Ser.: No. 3). 1996. mass mkt. 3.99 (*0-8125-4408-0*, Pub. by Tor Bks) St Martin.

Mark of the New World Order. Terry Cook. 280p. 1995. pap. 29.95 (*0-9647860-0-1*) Virtue Intl Pubng.

Mark of the New World Order. Terry Cook. LC 97-108. 385p. 1996. pap. 12.99 (*0-88368-466-7*) Whitaker Hse.

Mark of the Scots: Their Astonishing Contributions to History, Science, Democracy, Literature, Duncan A. Bruce. LC 98-29039. (Illus.). 368p. 1998. pap. 18.95 (*0-8065-2060-4*, Citadel Pr) Carol Pub Group.

Mark of the Scots: Their Astonishing Contributions to History, Science, Democracy, Literature & the Arts. Duncan A. Bruce. LC 95-50374. (Illus.). 320p. 1996. 21.95 (*1-55972-356-4*, Birch Ln Pr) Carol Pub Group.

Mark of the Scots: Their Astonishing Contributions to History, Science, Democracy, Literature & the Arts. Duncan A. Bruce. 1998. pap. 24.95 (*0-8065-1754-9*, Citadel Pr) Carol Pub Group.

Mark of the Social: Discovery or Invention? Ed. by John D. Greenwood. 248p. 1996. pap. text 24.95 (*0-8476-8308-7*); lib. bdg. 60.50 (*0-8476-8307-9*) Rowman.

***Mark of the Spirit? A Charismatic Critique of the Toronto Blessing.** Ed. by Lloyd Pietersen. x, 121p. 1998. reprint ed. pap. 12.99 (*0-85364-861-1*, Pub. by Paternoster Pub) OM Literature.

Mark of the Wolf. Derek Adams. (Orig.). 1996. mass mkt. 5.95 (*1-56333-361-9*, Badboy) Masquerade.

Mark of Z: The Original Zorro. Johnston McCulley. 1976. reprint ed. lib. bdg. 24.95 (*0-89190-999-0*, Rivercity Pr) Amereon Ltd.

Mark of Zorro. Johnston McCulley. 288p. 1997. mass mkt. 4.99 (*0-8125-4007-7*, Pub. by Forge NYC) St Martin.

***Mark of Zorro.** Johnston McCulley. 1998. 10.09 (*0-606-13597-9*, Pub. by Turtleback) Demco.

Mark of Zorro. Johnston McCulley. 1990. reprint ed. lib. bdg. 25.95 (*0-89968-541-2*) Buccaneer Bks.

Mark on the Door. rev. ed. Franklin W. Dixon. LC 67-20847. (Hardy Boys Mystery Stories Ser.: No. 13). (Illus.). 180p. (J). (gr. 4-7). 1934. 5.99 (*0-448-08913-0*, G & D) Peng Put Young Read.

Mark 1-8: A New Translation with Introduction & Commentary. Joel Marcus. LC 98-8741. (Anchor Bible Ser.). 592p. 2000. 42.50 (*0-385-42349-7*) Doubleday.

***Mark 1-8:21.** Eugene A. LaVerdiere. LC 98-44957. 227p. 1999. pap. 24.95 (*0-8146-2478-2*, Liturg Pr Bks) Liturgical Pr.

Mark 1-8:26. Robert A. Guelich. (Biblical Commentary Ser.: Vol. 34A). 1989. 29.99 (*0-8499-0233-9*) Word Pub.

Mark Only. Theodore F. Powys. (Literature Ser.). 270p. 1972. reprint ed. 25.00 (*0-403-00692-9*) Scholarly.

***Mark R. Smith: Tent City, Mosh Pit, Trampled Clover.** Mark R. Smith. Ed. by Terri M. Hopkins. 2000. pap. 2.00 (*0-914435-35-3*) Marylhurst Art.

Mark Romanek: Music Video Stills. Photos by Mark Romanek. (Illus.). 200p. 2000. 50.00 (*1-892041-08-1*, Tondo Bks) Arena Editions.

Mark Rothco. James E. Breslin. 700p. 1998. pap. 27.50 (*0-226-07406-4*) U Ch Pr.

Mark Rothko. Peter H. Selz. LC 76-169316. (Museum of Modern Art Publications in Reprint). 1980. 10.95 (*0-405-01574-7*) Ayer.

Mark Rothko. Diane Waldman. (Illus.). 304p. 1978. 65.00 (*0-8109-1587-1*, Pub. by Abrams) Time Warner.

Mark Rothko. Jeffrey Weiss. LC 97-51532. (Illus.). 352p. 1998. 65.00 (*0-300-07505-7*) Yale U Pr.

***Mark Rothko.** Jeffrey Weiss. (Illus.). 376p. 2000. pap. 35.00 (*0-300-08098-0*) Yale U Pr.

Mark Rothko. Jeffrey Weiss et al. LC 97-51532. 1998. pap. write for info. (*0-89468-229-6*) Natl Gallery Art.

Mark Rothko: A Biography. James E. Breslin. (Illus.). 712p. (C). 1993. 39.95 (*0-226-07405-6*) U Ch Pr.

Mark Rothko: Subjects in Abstraction. Anna C. Chave. (Illus.). 224p. (C). 1991. reprint ed. pap. 30.00 (*0-300-04961-7*) Yale U Pr.

Mark Rothko: The Chapel Commission. David Anfam & Carol Mancusi-Ungaro. (Illus.). 32p. 1996. pap. 12.95 (*0-939594-38-2*, Menil Collection) Menil Found.

Mark Rothko: The Works on Canvas: A Catalogue Raisonne. David Anfam. LC 98-25970. (Illus.). 708p. 1998. 125.00 (*0-300-07489-1*) Yale U Pr.

Mark Rothko: Works on Paper. Bonnie Clearwater. LC 83-22843. (Illus.). 144p. 1984. 25.00 (*0-933920-54-7*, Pub. by Hudson Hills) Natl Bk Netwk.

Mark Rothko Multiforms. Contrib. by Mark Stevens. (Illus.). 48p. 1990. pap. write for info. (*1-878283-03-0*) PaceWildenstein.

Mark Rothko, 1903-1970. Mark Rothko. (Illus.). 205p. 1997. pap. 45.00 (*1-55670-550-6*) Stewart Tabori & Chang.

An Asterisk (*) at the beginning of an entry indicates that the title is appearing for the first time.

Mark Rothko, 1903-1970: A Retrospective. Diane Waldman. LC 78-58411. (Illus.). 38.00 (*0-89207-014-5*); pap. 19.95 (*0-686-96878-6*) S R Guggenheim.
Mark Rothko's Harvard Murals. Marjorie B. Cohn et al. (Illus.). 62p. 1988. pap. 12.95 (*0-916724-69-7*) Harvard Art Mus.
Mark Rutherford: The Mind & Art of William Hale White. Catherine R. Harland. LC 87-11286. 330p. reprint ed. pap. 102.30 (*0-608-09683-0*, 2069798) Bks Demand.
Mark Rutherford: (William Hale White) Stephen Merton. 189p. 1967. 49.50 (*0-685-63213-X*) Elliots Bks.
Mark Satern's Illustrated Guide to Video's Best: Master Edition. 2nd ed. Mark A. Satern. (Illus.). 704p. 1995. 19.95 (*0-9643171-1-7*) Satern Pr.
Mark Satern's Illustrated Guide to Video's Best: Winter, 1995. Mark A. Satern. (Illus.). 1994. pap. 16.95 (*0-9643171-0-9*) Satern Pr.
Mark Skousen's Thirty-Day Plan to Financial Independence. Mark Skousen. 1995. 19.95 (*0-89526-478-1*) Regnery Pub.
Mark Stark's Amazing Jewish Cookbook: For the Entire Family. Mark Stark. LC 97-12164. (Illus.). 320p. (Orig.). 1997. pap. 19.95 (*1-881283-19-4*) Alef Design.
Mark Strand & the Poet's Place in Contemporary Culture. David Kirby. LC 90-32578. 112p. 1990. pap. 12.95 (*0-8262-0743-X*) U of Mo Pr.
Mark Strong's Napa Valley, 1886-1924. deluxe ed. David Kernberger & Kathleen Kernberger. (Illus.). 1978. spiral bd. 12.00 (*0-933206-00-3*) Historic Photos.
Mark T-W-A-I-N! A Story about Samuel Clemens. David R. Collins. LC 93-15164. (Creative Minds Ser.). (Illus.). (J). (gr. 3-6). 1993. lib. bdg. 19.95 (*0-87614-801-1*, Carolrhoda) Lerner Pub.
Mark T-W-A-I-N! A Story about Samuel Clemens. David R. Collins. (Illus.). 56p. (J). (gr. 3-6). 1994. pap. 5.95 (*0-87614-640-X*, Carolrhoda) Lerner Pub.
Mark Tansey: Art & Source. Patterson Sims. LC 90-52862. (Illus.). 40p. (Orig.). 1990. pap. 14.95 (*0-932216-36-6*) Seattle Art.
Mark the Music: The Life & Work of Marc Blitzstein. Eric A. Gordon. LC 88-29891. (Illus.). 605p. 1989. 29.95 (*0-910278-61-X*) Boulevard.
Mark the Wind's Power. George Cerveny. 299p. 1982. 10.95 (*0-87770-272-1*); pap. 5.95 (*0-87770-273-X*) Ye Galleon.
Mark the World. Tor Norretranders. 400p. 1999. pap. 14.95 (*0-14-023012-2*, PuffinBks) Peng Put Young Read.
Mark These Men. J. Sidlow Baxter. LC 91-41881. 168p. 1992. pap. 9.99 (*0-8254-2197-7*) Kregel.
Mark Time. Robert Hinson. vi, 58p. (Orig.). (YA). (gr. 6-9). 1997. pap. 5.95 (*1-890424-03-X*) Dyn-Novel.
Mark-to-Market: Managing the Bank Portfolio under FASB No. 115. John E. Bowen. 125p. (C). 1993. text 60.00 (*1-55738-701-X*, Irwn Prfssnl) McGraw-Hill Prof.
Mark to Turn: A Reading of William Stafford's Poetry. Jonathan Holden. LC 76-2024. xii, 92p. (C). 1976. 12.95 (*0-7006-0145-7*); pap. 7.95 (*0-7006-0146-5*) U Pr of KS.
Mark Tobey. William C. Seitz. 1981. 18.95 (*0-405-12893-2*) Ayer.
Mark Tobey: A New Look. 1988. pap. 8.50 (*0-910524-16-5*) Eastern Wash.
Mark Tobey: Art & Belief. Arthur L. Dahl et al. (Illus.). 128p. (Orig.). 1984. 24.95 (*0-85398-179-5*); pap. 13.95 (*0-85398-180-9*) G Ronald Pub.
Mark Tobey: Paintings (1920-1960) Paul Cummings & Paul Jenkins. Ed. by Ivy S. Iglesia. (Illus.). 80p. (Orig.). 1994. pap. 25.00 (*0-9626731-9-6*) Yoshii Gallery.
Mark Trail in the Smokies: A Naturalists Look at GSMNP & the Southern Appalachians. Ed Dodd & Jack Elrod. Ed. by Stan Canter et al. (Illus.). 48p. (Orig.). 1989. pap. text 1.95 (*0-937207-11-X*) GSMNH.
Mark Twain. Ed. by Frederick Anderson. (Critical Heritage Ser.). 364p. (C). 1997. 140.00 (*0-415-15932-6*) Routledge.
Mark Twain. Intro. by Harold Bloom. (Modern Critical Views Ser.). 222p. 1986. 29.95 (*0-87754-698-3*) Chelsea Hse.
Mark Twain. Harold Bloom. LC 98-54082. (Bloom's Short Story Writers Ser.). 112p. (YA). (gr. 8 up). 1999. lib. bdg. 18.95 (*0-7910-5124-2*) Chelsea Hse.
Mark Twain. Harold Bloom. LC 99-33402. 120p. 1999. 19.95 (*0-7910-5256-7*) Chelsea Hse.
Mark Twain. Ken Chowder. 1998. write for info. (*0-679-45061-0*) Knopf.
Mark Twain. Ed. by Katie De Koster. (Literary Companion Ser.). 1996. lib. bdg. 26.20 (*1-56510-471-4*) Greenhaven.
Mark Twain. Ed. by Katie De Koster. LC 95-51236. (Literary Companion Ser.). 1996. pap. 16.20 (*1-56510-470-6*) Greenhaven.
Mark Twain. Cassandra Eason. (Little Brown Notebook Ser.). (Illus.). 256p. 1995. 6.95 (*0-8069-3972-9*) Sterling.
Mark Twain. John C. Gerber. (United States Authors Ser.: No. 535). 184p. 1988. 32.00 (*0-8057-7518-8*, Twyne) Mac Lib Ref.
Mark Twain. A. Henderson. LC 74-10996. (American Literature Ser.: No. 49). 1974. lib. bdg. 75.00 (*0-8383-1742-1*) M S G Haskell Hse.
Mark Twain. Stephen Leacock. LC 73-21633. (Mark Twain Ser.: No. 76). 1974. lib. bdg. 75.00 (*0-8383-1789-8*) M S G Haskell Hse.
Mark Twain. Peter B. Messent. LC 96-9831. (Modern Novelists Ser.). 248p. 1997. text 29.95 (*0-312-16479-3*) St Martin.
Mark Twain. Museum Quilts Publications Staff. (Little Brown Notebooks Ser.). 1998. 9.99 (*1-897954-74-3*, Pub. by Mus Quilts Pub) Sterling.
Mark Twain. Skip Press. LC 93-1827. (Importance of Ser.). 112p. (J). (gr. 5-8). 1994. lib. bdg. 22.45 (*1-56006-043-3*) Lucent Bks.
Mark Twain. Jill C. Wheeler. (Illus.). 32p. 1995. lib. bdg. 14.98 (*1-56239-519-X*) ABDO Pub Co.
Mark Twain: A Bibliography of the Collections of the Mark Twain Memorial & the Stowe-Day Foundation. William M. McBride. (Illus.). 512p. 1984. 60.00 (*0-930313-00-3*) McBride Pub.
Mark Twain: A Biography, 3 vols. Albert B. Paine. Ed. by Daniel Aaron. LC 96-51552. (American Men & Women of Letters Ser.). 600p. 1997. 134.95 (*0-7910-4539-0*) Chelsea Hse.
Mark Twain: A Collection of Critical Essays. Ed. by Henry N. Smith. 1963. 12.95 (*0-13-933317-7*, Spectrum IN) Macmillan Gen Ref.
Mark Twain: A Descriptive Guide to Biographical Sources. Jason G. Horn. LC 98-54311. (Illus.). 144p. 1999. 32.50 (*0-8108-3630-0*) Scarecrow.
***Mark Twain: A Literary Life.** Everett H. Emerson. LC 99-34173. 392p. 1999. 34.95 (*0-8122-3516-9*) U of Pa Pr.
Mark Twain: A Portrait. Edgar Lee Masters. LC 66-15216. 1938. 30.00 (*0-8196-0171-3*) Biblo.
Mark Twain: A Study of the Short Fiction. Ed. by Tom Quirk. LC 97-3445. Vol. 66. 1997. 29.00 (*0-8057-0867-7*, Twyne) Mac Lib Ref.
Mark Twain: A Writer's Life. Milton Meltzer. LC 85-5108. (Illus.). 128p. (YA). (gr. 9-12). 1985. lib. bdg. 28.00 (*0-531-10072-3*) Watts.
Mark Twain: American Skeptic. Ed. by Victor Doyno. LC 82-60382. (Illus.). 450p. 1995. pap. 19.95 (*0-87975-972-0*) Prometheus Bks.
Mark Twain: An Anthology of Recent Criticism. Ed. by Prafulla C. Kar. 1993. 27.95 (*81-85753-00-8*, Pub. by Pencraft International) Advent Bks Div.
Mark Twain: Critical Assessments, 4 vols., Set. Ed. by Stuart Hutchinson. (Critical Assessments of Writers in English Ser.). (Illus.). 1816p. (C). (gr. 13 up). 1993. text, boxed set 535.00 (*1-873403-09-7*) Routledge.
Mark Twain: Four Complete Novels. Mark Twain, pseud. (Illus.). 704p. 1993. 12.99 (*0-517-09289-1*) Random Hse Value.
Mark Twain: Great American Series. Compiled by Nancy Skarmeas. LC 98-7980. (Illus.). 96p. (J). 1998. 17.95 (*0-8249-4085-7*) Ideals.
Mark Twain: Great American Short Stories I. Illus. by Tracy Hall. LC 94-75014. (Classic Short Stories Ser.). 80p. 1994. pap. 5.95 (*0-7854-0578-X*, 40003) Am Guidance.
Mark Twain: His Adventures at Aurora & Mono Lake. George J. Williams, III. LC 86-16021. (Mark Twain in the West Ser.). (Illus.). 100p. (YA). (gr. 5 up). 1986. pap. 8.95 (*0-935174-17-6*); lib. bdg. 18.95 (*0-935174-18-4*) Tree by River.
Mark Twain: His Life in Virginia City, Nevada. George J. Williams, III. Ed. by Bill Dalton. LC 85-16483. (Mark Twain in the West Ser.). (Illus.). 200p. (YA). (gr. 5 up). 1986. 24.95 (*0-935174-16-8*); pap. 10.95 (*0-935174-15-X*) Tree by River.
Mark Twain: Legendary Writer & Humorist. Lynda Pflueger. LC 98-31293. (Historical American Biographies Ser.). (Illus.). 128p. (YA). (gr. 6 up). 1999. lib. bdg. 20.95 (*0-7660-1093-7*) Enslow Pubs.
Mark Twain: Legendary Writer & Humorist. Lynda Pflueger. LC 98-31293. (Historical American Biographies Ser.). 1999. write for info. (*0-07-601093-7*) McGraw.
Mark Twain: Mysterious Stranger & Other Curious Tales. Mark Twain, pseud. 448p. 1997. 9.99 (*0-517-15073-5*) Random Hse Value.
Mark Twain: Protagonist for the Popular Culture, 18. Marlene B. Vallin. LC 92-17861. (Great American Orators Ser.: No. 18). 208p. 1992. lib. bdg. 59.95 (*0-313-27353-7*, VMB, Greenwood Pr) Greenwood.
Mark Twain: Ritual Clown: A Collection of Critical Essays. Ed. by Mary Fitzgerald-Hoyt. 174p. 1990. 5.95 (*1-882520-00-9*) Siena Coll Res.
Mark Twain: Selections from the Collection of Nick Karanovich. Nick Karanovich et al. (Illus.). 72p. 1991. pap. 15.00 (*1-879598-01-9*) IN Univ Lilly Library.
***Mark Twain: Short Stories & Tall Tales.** Mark Twain, pseud. (Literary Classics Ser.). 320p. (YA). (gr. 4 up). 1999. 5.98 (*0-7624-0549-X*) Running Pr.
***Mark Twain: The Contemporary Reviews.** Ed. by Louis J. Budd. LC 98-38097. (American Critical Archives Ser.: No. 11). 850p. (C). 1999. 125.00 (*0-521-39024-9*) Cambridge U Pr.
Mark Twain: The Development of a Writer. Henry N. Smith. LC 62-19224. 224p. reprint ed. pap. 69.50 (*0-7837-2497-7*, 205746100005) Bks Demand.
Mark Twain: The Ecstasy of Humor. Louis J. Budd. (Quarry Farm Papers: Vol. 6). 28p. 1995. pap. 5.00 (*1-880817-08-X*) EC Ctr Mark T Stu.
Mark Twain: The Fate of Humor. James M. Cox. LC 66-11966. 331p. reprint ed. pap. 102.70 (*0-7837-1938-8*, 204215300001) Bks Demand.
Mark Twain: The Man & His Adventures. Richard B. Lyttle. LC 93-11247. (Illus.). 192p. (YA). (gr. 5 up). 1994. write for info. (*0-689-31712-3*) Atheneum Yung Read.
Mark Twain: The Youth Who Lived on in the Sage. John S. Tuckey. (Quarry Farm Papers: No. 2). 17p. 1990. pap. 5.00 (*1-880817-02-0*) EC Ctr Mark T Stu.
Mark Twain: Tom Sawyer - Huckleberry Finn. Stuart Hutchinson. LC 98-39505. (Critical Guides Ser.). 192p. 1999. pap. 14.50 (*0-231-11541-5*) Col U Pr.
***Mark Twain: Tom Sawyer - Huckleberry Finn.** Stuart Hutchinson. LC 98-39505. (Critical Guides Ser.). 192p. 1999. 39.50 (*0-231-11540-7*) Col U Pr.
Mark Twain: Young Writer. Miriam E. Mason. LC 90-23768. (Childhood of Famous Americans Ser.). (Illus.). 192p. (J). (gr. 3-7). 1991. reprint ed. mass mkt. 4.95 (*0-689-71480-7*) Aladdin.
Mark Twain - America's Humorist, Dreamer, Prophet: A Biography. Clinton Cox. LC 94-18624. 240p. (J). (gr. 3-9). 1995. 14.95 (*0-590-45642-3*, Scholastic Hardcover) Scholastic Inc.
***Mark Twain - America's Humorist, Dreamer, Prophet: A Biography.** Clinton Cox. 1999. pap. text 4.50 (*0-590-45641-5*) Scholastic Inc.
Mark Twain, a Biography, 3 vols. Albert B. Paine. 1992. reprint ed. lib. bdg. 225.00 (*0-7812-5072-2*) Rprt Serv.
Mark Twain A to Z: The Essential Reference to His Life & Writings. R. Kent Rasmussen. LC 94-39156. (Illus.). 512p. 1995. 45.00 (*0-8160-2845-1*) Facts on File.
Mark Twain A to Z: The Essential Reference to His Life & Writings. R. Kent Rasmussen. LC 96-26826. (Illus.). 576p. 1996. reprint ed. pap. 21.50 (*0-19-511028-5*) OUP.
Mark Twain Abroad: The Cruise of the Quaker City. Dewey Ganzel. LC 68-16691. 344p. reprint ed. pap. 106.70 (*0-608-16401-1*, 202721200054) Bks Demand.
Mark Twain & Bret Harte. Margaret Duckett. LC 64-21709. (Illus.). 390p. reprint ed. 120.90 (*0-8357-9734-1*, 201009100068) Bks Demand.
Mark Twain & His Illustrators, 1869-1875, Vol. I. Beverly R. David. LC 85-51269. (Illus.). xii, 268p. 1986. 45.00 (*0-87875-307-9*) Whitston Pub.
Mark Twain & Huckleberry Finn. Stewart Ross. LC 98-29892. (Illus.). (gr. 5 up). 1999. 16.99 (*0-670-88181-3*) Viking Penguin.
Mark Twain & "Life on the Mississippi" Horst H. Kruse. LC 81-7570.Tr. of Eine Entstehungs-und Quellengeschichtliche Untersuchung Zu Mark Twain's "Standard Work". (Illus.). 208p. 1982. lib. bdg. 30.00 (*0-87023-330-0*) U of Mass Pr.
Mark Twain & Little Satan: The Writing of "the Mysterious Stranger" John S. Tuckey. LC 72-7511. 101p. 1973. reprint ed. lib. bdg. 38.50 (*0-8371-6521-0*, TUMT, Greenwood Pr) Greenwood.
Mark Twain & Me, Mikey T., Vol. 1. Thomas Gilding. LC 97-159432. 160p. (Orig.). (J). (gr. 4-8). 1996. pap. 6.95 (*1-889817-35-X*) M Twain Ent.
Mark Twain & Religion: A Mirror of American Eclecticism. John Q. Hays. Ed. by Fred A. Rodewald. (American University Studies: American Literature: Ser. XXIV, Vol. 9). XVI, 226p. (C). 1989. text 36.60 (*0-8204-0854-9*) P Lang Pubng.
Mark Twain & Shakespeare: A Cultural Legacy. Anthony J. Berret. 218p. (C). 1993. lib. bdg. 48.00 (*0-8191-9220-1*) U Pr of Amer.
Mark Twain & Southwestern Humor. Kenneth S. Lynn. LC 70-176135. (Illus.). 300p. 1972. reprint ed. lib. bdg. 59.75 (*0-8371-6270-X*, LMTPB, Greenwood Pr) Greenwood.
Mark Twain & the Backwoods Angel: The Matter of Innocence in the Works of Samuel L. Clemens. William C. Spengemann. LC 66-28208. (Kent Studies in English: No. 4). 160p. reprint ed. pap. 49.60 (*0-8357-9369-9*, 201015300068) Bks Demand.
Mark Twain & the Bible. Allison Ensor. LC 76-80092. 140p. reprint ed. pap. 43.40 (*0-608-13083-4*, 201951700013) Bks Demand.
Mark Twain & the Feminine Aesthetic. Peter Stoneley. (Cambridge Studies in American Literature & Culture: No. 54). (Illus.). 221p. (C). 1992. text 64.95 (*0-521-40549-1*) Cambridge U Pr.
Mark Twain & the Gilded Age: The Book That Named an Era. Bryant M. French. LC 65-24438. 391p. reprint ed. pap. 121.30 (*0-608-17199-9*, 202700400053) Bks Demand.
Mark Twain & the Happy Island. E. Wallace. LC 73-20383. (Mark Twain Ser.: No. 76). 1974. lib. bdg. 75.00 (*0-8383-1756-1*) M S G Haskell Hse.
Mark Twain & the Jumping Frog of Calaveras County. George J. Williams, III. (Illus.). 110p. 1998. 16.95 (*0-935174-46-X*, Mus Bus Bks); pap. 8.95 (*0-935174-45-1*, Mus Bus Bks) Tree by River.
Mark Twain & the Limits of Power: Emerson's God in Ruins. James L. Johnson. LC 81-16052. 216p. reprint ed. pap. 67.00 (*0-7837-1319-3*, 204146700020) Bks Demand.
Mark Twain & the Novel: The Double-Cross of Authority. Lawrence Howe. LC 97-41131. (Studies in American Literature & Culture: No. 116). 288p. (C). 1998. 54.95 (*0-521-56168-X*) Cambridge U Pr.
Mark Twain & the Queens of the Mississippi. Cheryl Harness. LC 97-40799. (Illus.). 40p. (J). (gr. 1-5). 1998. per. 16.00 (*0-689-81542-5*) S&S Childrens.
Mark Twain & the South. Arthur G. Pettit. LC 73-86405. 240p. 1974. 27.50 (*0-8131-1310-5*) U Pr of Ky.
Mark Twain & the Starchy Boys. Edgar M. Branch. 97p. (Orig.). 1992. pap. 10.00 (*1-880817-04-7*) EC Ctr Mark T Stu.
Mark Twain & the Three R's: Race, Religion, Revolution & Related Matters. Ed. by Maxwell Geismar. LC 72-9882. 1973. 8.95 (*0-672-51705-1*, Bobbs); pap. 4.95 (*0-672-51820-1*, Bobbs) Macmillan.
Mark Twain & West Point: America's Favorite Storyteller at the U. S. Military Academy. Philip W. Leon. LC 97-200367. (Illus.). 276p. 1996. pap. 15.95 (*1-55022-277-5*, Pub. by ECW) LPC InBook.
Mark Twain & William James: Crafting a Free Self. Jason G. Horn. 200p. (C). 1996. 34.95 (*0-8262-1072-4*) U of Mo Pr.
Mark Twain As Critic. Sydney Krause. LC 67-14925. 320p. reprint ed. pap. 99.20 (*0-8357-8214-X*, 203412600088) Bks Demand.
Mark Twain at the "Buffalo Express" Articles & Sketches by America's Favorite Humorist. Mark Twain, pseud. Ed. by Joseph B. McCullough & Janice McIntire-Strasburg. LC 99-20031. 320p. 1999. 30.00 (*0-87580-249-4*) N Ill U Pr.
***Mark Twain at the Buffalo Express: Articles & Sketches by America's Favorite Humorist.** Mark Twain, pseud. (Illus.). 2000. pap. 18.00 (*0-87580-585-X*) N Ill U Pr.
Mark Twain Book. Oliver Howard & Goldena Howard. LC 84-61875. (Illus.). 147p. 1985. 14.95 (*0-685-73843-4*) Ralls Cnty Bk.
Mark Twain, Boy of Old Missouri. Miriam Evangeline Mason. (Childhood of Famous Americans Ser.). (J). 1991. 10.34 (*0-606-07843-6*) Turtleback.
Mark Twain, Business Man: American Autobiography. Mark Twain, pseud. 409p. 1995. lib. bdg. 99.00 (*0-7812-8482-1*) Rprt Serv.
Mark Twain, Culture & Gender: Envisioning America Through Europe. John D. Stahl. LC 93-12347. 216p. (C). 1994. 35.00 (*0-8203-1559-1*) U of Ga Pr.
Mark Twain Dreaming. James Walker & Carl Farinelli. 1998. pap. 4.00 (*1-57514-329-1*) Encore Perform Pub.
Mark Twain Encyclopedia. Ed. by J. R. LeMaster & James D. Wilson. LC 92-45662. 888p. 1993. text 100.00 (*0-8240-7212-X*, H1249) Garland.
Mark Twain in Hawaii. Mark Twain, pseud. Ed. by William R. Jones. LC 97-34478. (Illus.). 96p. 1997. reprint ed. pap. 4.95 (*0-89646-070-3*) Vistabooks.
Mark Twain in Hawaii: Roughing It in the Sandwich Islands. A. Grove Day. 144p. 1990. reprint ed. mass mkt. 4.95 (*0-935180-93-1*) Mutual Pub HI.
Mark Twain in the Company of Women. Laura E. Skandera-Trombley. (Illus.). 256p. (C). 1994. text 31.50 (*0-8122-3218-6*) U of Pa Pr.
Mark Twain in the Company of Women. Laura E. Skandera-Trombley. (Illus.). 248p. 1997. pap. text 16.50 (*0-8122-1619-9*) U of Pa Pr.
***Mark Twain in the Margins: The Quarry Farm Marginalia & "A Connecticut Yankee in King Arthur's Court"** Joe B. Fulton. LC 99-50647. 224p. 2000. text 34.95 (*0-8173-1033-9*) U of Ala Pr.
Mark Twain in the "St. Louis Post-Dispatch", 1874-1891. abr. ed. James McWilliams. LC 95-61176. viii, 291p. 1997. 39.00 (*0-87875-469-5*) Whitston Pub.
Mark Twain in the U. S. A. A Guide. Marsha Bellavance-Johnson. (Famous Footsteps Ser.). (Illus.). (Orig.). 1990. pap. 4.95 (*0-929709-07-1*) Computer Lab.
Mark Twain in Virginia City Nevada. Mark Twain, pseud. (Illus.). 1986. 14.95 (*0-913814-84-9*); pap. 7.95 (*0-913814-78-4*) Nevada Pubns.
Mark Twain International: A Bibliography & Interpretation of His Worldwide Popularity. Ed. by Robert M. Rodney. LC 81-13441. 275p. 1982. lib. bdg. 65.00 (*0-313-23135-4*, RMT/, Greenwood Pr) Greenwood.
Mark Twain Library Cookbook: A Treasury of Redding Recipes, Vol. III. (Illus.). 256p. (Orig.). 1988. pap. 10.95 (*0-9620120-0-9*) Mark Twain Lib Assn.
Mark Twain Made Me Do It & Other Plains Adventures. Bryan L. Jones. LC 96-8534. (Illus.). xi, 210p. 1997. pap. 15.00 (*0-8032-7592-7*, Bison Books) U of Nebr Pr.
Mark Twain Murders: A Beth Austin Mystery. Edith Skom. 304p. 1990. mass mkt. 5.99 (*0-440-20608-1*) Dell.
Mark Twain Notebook for 1892. Daniel M. McKeithan. (Essays & Studies on American Language & Literature: Vol. 17). (Orig.). 1965. pap. 25.00 (*0-8115-0197-3*) Periodicals Srv.
Mark Twain on the Loose: A Comic Writer & the American Self. Bruce Michelson. LC 94-37579. 280p. 1995. pap. 18.95 (*0-87023-967-8*) U of Mass Pr.
Mark Twain Overseas. Robert M. Rodney. (Time - Place Ser.: No. 5). 350p. 1993. pap. 20.00 (*1-57889-055-1*) Passeggiata.
Mark Twain Postcard Book. Starhill Press Staff. (Illus.). 6.95 (*0-913515-77-9*, Starhill Press) Black Belt Communs.
Mark Twain Remembers. Thomas Hauser. LC 99-31446. 208p. 1999. 20.00 (*1-56980-154-1*) Barricade Bks.
Mark Twain Returns. Robert R. Leichtman & Carl Japikse. LC 81-69185. (From Heaven to Earth Ser.). 80p. (Orig.). 1982. pap. 3.50 (*0-89804-067-1*) Ariel GA.
Mark Twain Sampler, Miniature bk. Mark Twain, pseud. (Illus.). 64p. 1980. 17.50 (*0-915998-17-3*) Lime Rock Pr.
Mark Twain Selected Works. deluxe ed. Mark Twain, pseud. 704p. 1990. 19.99 (*0-517-05357-8*) Random Hse Value.
Mark Twain Speaks for Himself. Mark Twain, pseud. Ed. by Paul Fatout. LC 77-81462. 1997. pap. 16.95 (*1-55753-101-3*, NotaBell) Purdue U Pr.
Mark Twain Tales: For Children, 5 vols. Thomas Gilding & Mary Gilding. Incl. Vol. 1. Jim Smiley & His Jumping Frog. Illus. by Robert Marr. 24p. (J). (gr. k-4). 1996. pap. 2.00 (*1-889817-01-5*); Vol. 2. Buffalo Climbed a Tree? Illus. by Robert Marr. 24p. (Orig.). (J). (gr. k-4). 1996. pap. 2.00 (*1-889817-02-3*); Vol. 3. Blue Jay Yarn. Illus. by Robert Marr. 24p. (Orig.). (J). (gr. k-4). 1996. pap. 2.00 (*1-889817-03-1*); Vol. 4. Ant Is a Fraud. Illus. by Robert Marr. 24p. (Orig.). (J). (gr. k-4). 1996. pap. 2.00 (*1-889817-04-X*); Vol. 5. Fable Vol. 5: A Cat, a Mirror & a Picture. Illus. by Matt Bowers. 24p. (Orig.). (J). (gr. k-4). 1996. pap. 2.00 (*1-889817-05-8*); 1997. Set pap. 10.00 (*1-889817-00-7*) M Twain Ent.
Mark Twain to Mrs. Fairbanks: American Autobiography. Mark Twain, pseud. 286p. 1995. lib. bdg. 79.00 (*0-7812-8483-X*) Rprt Serv.
Mark Twain Wit & Wisecracks. Mark Twain, pseud. LC 98-219867. (Pocket Gift Editions Ser.). (Illus.). 1998. 4.95 (*0-88088-080-5*) Peter Pauper.
Mark Twain, Young Reporter in Virginia City. Katherine Hillyer. (Illus.). 92p. 1967. pap. 6.95 (*0-913814-69-5*) Nevada Pubns.
Mark Twain's Adventures of Huckleberry Finn see Modern Critical Interpretations
Mark Twain's America. Bernard DeVoto. LC 96-37754. (Illus.). xxiii, 351p. 1997. pap. 15.00 (*0-8032-6607-3*, Bison Books) U of Nebr Pr.

M

An Asterisk (*) at the beginning of an entry indicates that the title is appearing for the first time.

Mark Twain's America. Bernard A. De Voto. LC 78-4109. (Illus.). 351p. 1978. reprint ed. lib. bdg. 69.50 (0-313-20368-7, DEVMT, Greenwood Pr) Greenwood.

Mark Twain's Autobiography, 2 vols. Mark Twain, pseud. (American Biography Ser.). 1991. reprint ed. lib. bdg. 148.00 (0-7812-8075-3) Rprt Serv.

Mark Twain's Autobiography & First Romance. Mark Twain, pseud. LC 74-128410. (American Biography Ser.: No. 32). 1970. reprint ed. lib. bdg. 75.00 (0-8383-1152-0) M S G Haskell Hse.

Mark Twain's Book for Bad Boys & Girls. Ed. by R. Kent Rasmussen. LC 95-32766. (Illus.). 192p. 1995. 12.95 (0-8092-3398-3, 339830, Contemporary Bks) NTC Contemp Pub Co.

Mark Twain's Correspondence with Henry Huttleston Rogers, 1893-1909. Mark Twain, pseud. Ed. by Lewis Leary. LC 68-23900. (Mark Twain Papers: No. 4). 1969. 60.00 (0-520-01467-7, Pub. by U CA Pr) Cal Prin Full Svc.

Mark Twain's Damned Human Race. Jules Tasca. Ed. by Neil Johnson. pap. 7.95 (1-56861-021-1) Swift Lrn Res.

Mark Twain's Escape from Time: A Study of Patterns & Images. Susan K. Harris. LC 82-1981. 181p. reprint ed. pap. 56.20 (0-7837-2357-1, AU0042200006) Bks Demand.

Mark Twain's Ethical Realism: The Aesthetics of Race, Class, & Gender. Joe B. Fulton. LC 97-33411. 192p. 1998. 27.50 (0-8262-1144-5) U of Mo Pr.

Mark Twain's Fables of Man. Ed. by John S. Tuckey. (Mark Twain Papers). 1972. 60.00 (0-520-02039-1, Pub. by U CA Pr) Cal Prin Full Svc.

Mark Twain's German Critical Reception, 1875-1986: An Annotated Bibliography, 22. Compiled by J. C. Kinch. LC 89-11880. (Bibliographies & Indexes in World Literature Ser.: No. 22). 288p. 1989. lib. bdg. 72.95 (0-313-26229-2, KHA/, Greenwood Pr) Greenwood.

Mark Twain's Hannibal, Huck & Tom. Mark Twain, pseud. Ed. by Walter Blair. LC 69-10575. (Mark Twain Papers: No. 5). 512p. 1969. 60.00 (0-520-01501-0, Pub. by U CA Pr) Cal Prin Full Svc.

Mark Twain's Huckleberry Finn. Rita Grauer. (J). 1999. pap. 7.00 (0-87602-371-5) Anchorage.

Mark Twain's Humor: Critical Essays. David E. Sloane et al. (Garland Studies in Humor: No. 3). (Illus.). xxvi, 635p. 1996. reprint ed. 95.00 (0-9652668-0-X) D Sloane.

Mark Twain's Last Years As a Writer. William R. MacNaughton. LC 78-19846. 264p. reprint ed. pap. 81.90 (0-7837-3201-5, AU0042900007) Bks Demand.

Mark Twain's Letter to William Bowen. Mark Twain, pseud. LC 75-22382. (Studies in Mark Twain: No. 76). (Illus.). 11p. 1975. lib. bdg. 49.00 (0-8383-2089-9) M S G Haskell Hse.

Mark Twain's Letter to William Bowen: Buffalo, February 6, 1870. Mark Twain, pseud. (American Biography Ser.). 11p. 1991. reprint ed. lib. bdg. 59.00 (0-7812-8076-1) Rprt Serv.

Mark Twain's Letters. Mark Twain, pseud. (Works of Samuel Clemens). 1989. reprint ed. lib. bdg. 79.00 (0-685-28381-X) Rprt Serv.

Mark Twain's Letters, 2 vols., Set. Mark Twain, pseud. LC 74-6025. (BCL Ser.: No. II). (Illus.). 855p. reprint ed. 124.50 (0-404-11545-4) AMS Pr.

Mark Twain's Letters, 2 vols., Set. Mark Twain, pseud. (BCL1-PS American Literature Ser.). 1992. reprint ed. lib. bdg. 150.00 (0-7812-6689-0) Rprt Serv.

Mark Twain's Letters, 1853-1886, Vol. 1. Mark Twain, pseud. Ed. by Edgar M. Branch et al. LC 87-5963. (Mark Twain Papers: No. 9). 1987. 50.00 (0-520-03668-9, Pub. by U CA Pr) Cal Prin Full Svc.

Mark Twain's Letters, 1870-1871, Vol. 4. Mark Twain, pseud. Ed. by Victor Fischer et al. LC 87-5963. (Mark Twain Papers). (Illus.). 850p. 1995. 55.00 (0-520-20360-7, Pub. by U CA Pr) Cal Prin Full Svc.

Mark Twain's Letters, 1872-1873, Vol. 5. Mark Twain, pseud. Ed. by Lin Salamo & Harriet E. Smith. LC 87-5963. (Illus.). 974p. 1997. 60.00 (0-520-20822-6, Pub. by U CA Pr) Cal Prin Full Svc.

Mark Twain's Letters, 1869, Vol. 3. Ed. by Victor Fischer et al. LC 78-51761. (Illus.). 775p. 1992. 55.00 (0-520-03670-0, Pub. by U CA Pr) Cal Prin Full Svc.

Mark Twain's Letters, 1867-1868, Vol. 2. Ed. by Harriet E. Smith et al. (Illus.). 1990. 55.00 (0-520-03669-7, Pub. by U CA Pr) Cal Prin Full Svc.

Mark Twain's Letters from Hawaii. Mark Twain, pseud. Ed. by A. Grove Day. LC 74-31359. (Pacific Classics Ser.: No. 5). 316p. 1975. reprint ed. pap. 11.95 (0-8248-0288-8) UH Pr.

Mark Twain's Letters in the Muscatine Journal: American Autobiography. Mark Twain, pseud. 28p. 1995. lib. bdg. 69.00 (0-7812-8484-8) Rprt Serv.

***Mark Twain's Library of Humor.** Mark Twain, pseud. Ed. by Martin. LC 00-25971. (Illus.). 624p. 2000. pap. 15.95 (0-679-64036-3) Modern Lib NY.

Mark Twain's Margins on Thackeray's "Swift" Coley B. Taylor. LC 75-22075. (Mark Twain Ser.: No. 76). 1975. lib. bdg. 49.00 (0-8383-2087-2) M S G Haskell Hse.

Mark Twain's Mysterious Stranger Manuscripts. Mark Twain, pseud. Ed. by William M. Gibson. LC 69-10576. (Mark Twain Papers: No. 6). 1969. 60.00. (0-520-01473-1, Pub. by U CA Pr) Cal Prin Full Svc.

Mark Twain's Notebook. Mark Twain, pseud. (American Biography Ser.). 413p. 1991. reprint ed. lib. bdg. 89.00 (0-7812-8077-X) Rprt Serv.

Mark Twain's Notebooks & Journals, 1855-1873, Vol. 1. Mark Twain, pseud. Ed. by Frederick Anderson et al. (Mark Twain Papers: No. 8). 700p. 1976. 60.00 (0-520-02326-9, Pub. by U CA Pr) Cal Prin Full Svc.

Mark Twain's Notebooks & Journals, 1877-1883, Vol. 2. Mark Twain, pseud. Ed. by Frederick Anderson et al. (Mark Twain Papers: No. 8). 700p. 1976. 60.00 (0-520-02542-3, Pub. by U CA Pr) Cal Prin Full Svc.

Mark Twain's Notebooks & Journals, 1883-1891, Vol. 3. Mark Twain, pseud. Ed. by Frederick Anderson et al. (Mark Twain Papers: No. 8). 1980. 60.00 (0-520-03383-3, Pub. by U CA Pr) Cal Prin Full Svc.

Mark Twain's Own Autobiography: The Chapters from the North American Review. Mark Twain, pseud. Ed. by Michael J. Kiskis. LC 90-50091. (Studies in American Autobiography). 340p. (Orig.). (C). 1990. pap. 15.95 (0-299-12544-0) U of Wis Pr.

Mark Twain's Personal Recollections of Joan of Arc: Modern English from the Original Unpublished Manuscript in the National Archives of France. Mark Twain, pseud. Tr. by Jean F. Alden. LC 97-40780. (Studies in American Literature: Vol. 28). (Illus.). 500p. 1997. reprint ed. 109.95 (0-7734-8456-6) E Mellen.

Mark Twain's Pudd'n Head Wilson: Race, Conflict, & Culture. Ed. by Susan Gillman & Forrest Robinson. LC 89-49753. 279p. (C). 1990. pap. text 20.95 (0-8223-1046-5) Duke.

Mark Twain's Quarrel with Heaven. Mark Twain, pseud. Ed. by Ray B. Browne. (Masterworks of Literature Ser.). 126p. 1970. 16.95 (0-8084-0018-5); pap. 12.95 (0-8084-0019-3) NCUP.

Mark Twain's Relatives. Paul O. Selby. 25p. Date not set. 16.95 (0-8488-2661-2) Amereon Ltd.

Mark Twain's Rubaiyat. Mark Twain, pseud. Ed. by Alan Gribben. (Illus.). 67p. 1983. 25.00 (0-8363-0170-6, PA2-111-3385) Jenkins.

Mark Twain's San Francisco. Mark Twain, pseud. Ed. by Bernard Taper. LC 77-19241. (Illus.). 263p. 1978. reprint ed. lib. bdg. 59.75 (0-313-20254-0, CLMT, Greenwood Pr) Greenwood.

Mark Twain's Satires & Burlesques. Mark Twain, pseud. Ed. by Franklin R. Rogers. (Mark Twain Papers: No. 3). 1967. 50.00 (0-520-01081-7, Pub. by U CA Pr) Cal Prin Full Svc.

Mark Twain's Sketches New & Old. Mark Twain, pseud. (Works of Samuel Clemens). 1989. reprint ed. lib. bdg. 79.00 (0-7812-1124-7) Rprt Serv.

Mark Twain's Speeches. Mark Twain, pseud. (Works of Samuel Clemens). 1989. reprint ed. lib. bdg. 79.00 (0-7812-1374-6) Rprt Serv.

Mark Twain's The Adventures of Huckleberry Finn see Bloom's Notes

Mark Twain's the Adventures of Tom Sawyer. Mark Twain, pseud. (C). 3.95 (0-671-00696-7, Arco) Macmillan Gen Ref.

Mark Twain's Travels with Mr. Brown. Mark Twain, pseud. (American Biography Ser.). 296p. 1991. reprint ed. lib. bdg. 69.00 (0-7812-8078-8) Rprt Serv.

Mark Twain's Virginia City: Nevada Territory. Mark Twain, pseud. Ed. by William R. Jones. (Illus.). 64p. 1982. reprint ed. pap. 4.95 (0-89646-074-6) Vistabooks.

***Mark Twain's Visit to Heaven & Other Short Stories.** George Hammond. LC 99-91285. 1999. 25.00 (0-7388-0734-6); pap. 18.00 (0-7388-0735-4) Xlibris Corp.

Mark Twain's "Which Was the Dream?" & Other Symbolic Writings of the Later Years. Mark Twain, pseud. Ed. by John S. Tuckey. (Mark Twain Papers: No. 1). 1966. 50.00 (0-520-01285-2, Pub. by U CA Pr) Cal Prin Full Svc.

Mark-Up Clerk (U. S. P. S.) Jack Rudman. (Career Examination Ser.: C-2459). 1994. pap. 19.95 (0-8373-2459-9) Nat Learn.

Mark Van Doren. J. T. Ledbetter. LC 96-7124. (American University Studies XXIV: Vol. 67). XII, 175p. (C). 1997. 35.95 (0-8204-3334-9) P Lang Pubng.

Mark Whitfield: The Guitar Collection. 88p. 1996. otabind 19.95 (0-7935-4467-X, 00672320) H Leonard.

Mark Wilson's Cyclopedia of Magic: A Complete Course. Mark Wilson. (Illus.). 640p. 1995. pap. 9.95 (1-56138-613-8) Running Pr.

***Mark Wilson's Little Book of Card Tricks.** Mark Wilson. (Illus.). 2000. 4.95 (0-7624-0834-0) Running Pr.

Mark Wilson's Tips to Better Musicianship: A Self-Help Manual for the Creative Guitarist & Bassist. Mark A. Wilson. LC 90-90364. (Illus.). (Orig.). 1990. pap. 12.95 (1-878134-00-0) Five Star Mus.

Mark World. Tor Norretranders. Tr. by Jonathan Sydenham. LC 97-39580. 400p. 1999. text 27.95 (0-7139-9182-8) Viking Penguin.

Markagunt Megabreccia: Large Miocene Gravity Slides Mantling the Northern Markagunt Plateau, Southwestern Utah. John J. Anderson. (Miscellaneous Publication Ser.: Vol. 93-2). (Illus.). 37p. 1993. pap. 5.00 (1-55791-321-8, MP-93-2) Utah Geological Survey.

Markan Public Debate: Literary Technique, Concentric Structure, & Theology in Mark 2: 1-3: 6. Joanna Dewey. LC 79-17443. (Society of Biblical Literature. Dissertation Ser.: No. 48). 289p. reprint ed. pap. 89.60 (0-7837-5441-8, 204520600005) Bks Demand.

Markan Sandwich Stories: Narration, Definition, & Function. Tom Shepherd. (Andrews University Seminary Doctoral Dissertation Ser.: Vol. 18). 436p. 1993. pap. 19.99 (1-883925-00-2) Andrews Univ Pr.

Markarian Album: The Richard R. Markarian Collection of Oriental Rugs. Walter B. Denny & Daniel Walker. Ed. by Jon M. Anderson & Russell S. Fling. (Illus.). 432p. 1989. 195.00 (0-9621115-0-3) Markarian Found.

Markborough Decision. Garth Clark. 25.00 (0-614-05188-6, PECO191.5M) ASFE.

***Marked Bible.** Charles L. Taylor. 128p. 2000. pap. 2.49 (0-8163-0803-9) Pacific Pr Pub Assn.

Marked by Fire. Joyce C. Thomas. 160p. (YA). (gr. 7 up). 1982. mass mkt. 4.50 (0-380-79327-X, Avon Bks) Morrow Avon.

***Marked by Fire, 1.** Joyce Carol Thomas. LC 99-95318. 176p. (gr. 7-12). 1999. mass mkt. 6.99 (0-380-81434-X, Avon Bks) Morrow Avon.

Marked Cards. George R. R. Martin. (Wild Cards Ser.: Vol. 2). 448p. (Orig.). 1994. mass mkt. 5.99 (0-671-72212-3) Baen Bks.

Marked for Death. large type ed. Ben Bridges. (Linford Western Library). 272p. 1994. pap. 16.99 (0-7089-7581-X, Linford) Ulverscroft.

Marked for Life: Prayer in the Easter Christ. Maria Boulding. 128p. 1995. pap. 11.95 (0-687-06628-X) Abingdon.

Marked for Life: The Crime & Redemption of Todd Ice. Walter Butler. 1998. mass mkt. write for info. (0-345-41252-4) Ballantine Pub Grp.

Marked Individuals in the Study of Bird Population. Ed. by J. D. Lebreton & Ph. M. North. LC 93-3400. (Advances in Life Sciences Ser.). xviii, 397p. 1993. 109.00 (0-8176-2780-4, Pub. by Birkhauser) Princeton Arch.

Marked Men. Aris Fakinos. LC 73-137868. 288p. 1971. 6.95 (0-87140-516-4, Pub. by Liveright) Norton.

Marked Men. Aris Fakinos. LC 73-137868. 288p. 1972. pap. 2.45 (0-87140-263-7, Pub. by Liveright) Norton.

***Marked Men: Stories.** Michael C. White. 208p. 2000. pap. 17.95 (0-8262-1294-8) U of Mo Pr.

***Marked Men: White Masculinity in Crisis.** Sally Robinson. LC 00-25916. 2000. pap. 17.50 (0-231-11293-9); text 49.50 (0-231-11292-0) Col U Pr.

Marked Paper. David Lockwood. 62p. 1995. pap. 13.95 (0-8464-4786-X) Beekman Pubs.

Marked Point Proceddes on the Real Line: The Dynamical Approach. A. Brandt & G. Last. Ed. by J. Gani et al. (Probability & Its Applications Ser.). 494p. 1995. 60.95 (0-387-94547-4) Spr-Verlag.

Marked Ref Prophecy. Ed. by R. Jeffrey, Jr. LC 98-61544. 2000. 34.99 (0-310-92064-7) Zondervan.

Marked Reference Prophecy Study Bible. Prophecy Study Staff. 1999. bond lthr. 59.99 (0-310-92065-5) Zondervan.

Marked Reference Prophecy Study Bible: Indexed. Prophecy Study Staff. 1999. bond lthr. 69.99 (0-310-92067-1) Zondervan.

Marked Reference Prophecy Study Bible: King James Version. Prophecy Study Staff. 1700p. 1999. bond lthr. 59.99 (0-310-92068-X) Zondervan.

Marked Reference Prophecy Study Bible: New International Version. Propecy Study Staff. 1999. bond lthr. 59.99 (0-310-90864-7) Zondervan.

Marked Reference Prophecy Study Bible: New International Version. Prophecy Study Staff. 1999. bond lthr. 59.99 (0-310-90863-9) Zondervan.

Marked Reference Prophecy Study Bible: New International Version, Indexed. Propecy Study Staff. 1999. bond lthr. 69.99 (0-310-90865-5) Zondervan.

Marked Reference Prophecy Study Bible: New International Version, Indexed. Prophecy Study Staff. 1999. bond lthr. 69.99 (0-310-90866-3) Zondervan.

Marked Reference Prophecy Study Bible, King James Version. 1999. bond lthr. 69.99 (0-310-92069-8, 162023) Zondervan.

Markedness. Ed. by Fred R. Eckman et al. LC 86-15096. 352p. 1986. 75.00 (0-306-42372-3, Plenum Trade) Perseus Pubng.

Markedness: The Evaluative Superstructure of Language. Edwin L. Battistella. LC 89-29453. (SUNY Series in Linguistics). 265p. (C). 1990. text 89.50 (0-7914-0369-6); pap. text 29.95 (0-7914-0370-X) State U NY Pr.

Markedness Theory: The Union of Asymmetry & Semiosis in Language. Edna Andrews. Ed. by C. H. Van Schooneveld. LC 89-7906. (Sound & Meaning: The Roman Jakobson Series in Linguistics & Poetics). 200p. 1989. text 49.95 (0-8223-0959-9) Duke.

Markell von Ankyra: Die Fragmente & der Brief an Julius von Rom. Markus Vinzent. (Vigiliae Christianae, Supplements Ser.: Vol. 39). (GER & GRE.). 304p. 1997. 115.75 (90-04-10907-2) Brill Academic Pubs.

***Markennamen Sprachliche Strukturen, Ahnlichkeit und Verwechselarkeit: Ein Beitrag Zur Forensischen Linguistik des Markenrechts.** Kai U. Stoll. (GER., Illus.). XII, 246p. 1999. 45.95 (3-631-33808-2) P Lang Pubng.

Marker. Lowell Cauffiel. LC 97-9111. 1997. text 23.95 (0-312-15583-2) St Martin.

Marker. Lowell Cauffiel. 1998. mass mkt. 6.50 (0-312-96497-8) St Martin.

Marker Magic. Richard M. McGarry. LC 92-6773. (Illus.). 192p. 1993. text 39.95 (0-442-00769-8, VNR) Wiley.

Marker Magic: The Rendering Problem Solver for Beginners. Richard McGarry. 146p. 1992. 44.95 (0-471-28434-3, VNR) Wiley.

Marker Mania. Illus. by Diana Fisher. (Art Start Kits Ser.). 32p. (J). (gr. 3-7). 1999. pap. 6.95 (1-56010-349-3, AS01) W Foster Pub.

Marker Proteins in Inflammation: Proceedings of the Symposium; Lyon, France, April 22-25, 1981, Vol. 1. Robert M. Suskind. Ed. by Robert C. Allen et al. (Illus.). 608p. 1982. 180.80 (3-11-008625-5) De Gruyter.

Marker Proteins in Inflammation: Proceedings of the 2nd Symposium, Lyon, France, June 27-30, 1983, Vol. 2. Ed. by Jacques Bienvenu et al. LC 84-9462. (Illus.). xix, 687p. 1984. 165.40 (3-11-009872-5) De Gruyter.

Marker Proteins in Inflammation Vol. 3: Proceedings of the 3rd Symposium, Lyon, France, June 26-28, 1985. Ed. by Jacques Bienvenu et al. (Illus.). xv, 693p. 1986. lib. bdg. 296.15 (3-11-010639-6) De Gruyter.

Marker Rendering. Todd Murrison. (Artist's Library). (Illus.). 64p. (Orig.). 1995. pap. 7.95 (1-56010-127-X, AL24) W Foster Pub.

Markers. Isidro Sanchez. (I Draw, I Paint Ser.). (Illus.). 48p. (J). (gr. 3 up). 1992. pap. 7.95 (0-8120-1375-1) Barron.

Markers: The Journal of the Association for Gravestone Studies, No. 7. Ed. by Theodore Chase. LC 81-642903. (Illus.). 281p. (Orig.). (C). 1990. pap. text 13.00 (1-878381-00-8) Assn Gravestone Studies.

Markers: The Journal of the Association for Gravestone Studies, No. 9. Ed. by Theodore Chase. LC 81-642903. (Markers Ser.). (Illus.). 288p. (Orig.). 1992. pap. 16.00 (1-878381-02-4) Assn Gravestone Studies.

Markers: The Journal of the Association for Gravestone Studies, No. 10. Ed. by Richard E. Meyer. LC 81-642903. (Illus.). 256p. 1992. pap. 25.00 (1-878381-03-2) Assn Gravestone Studies.

Markers: The Journal of the Association for Gravestone Studies, No. 11. Ed. by Richard E. Meyer. LC 81-642903. (Illus.). 233p. 1993. pap. 25.00 (1-878381-04-0) Assn Gravestone Studies.

Markers: The Journal of the Association for Gravestone Studies, No. 13. Ed. by Richard E. Meyer. LC 81-642903. (Illus.). 243p. 1996. pap. 25.00 (1-878381-06-7) Assn Gravestone Studies.

Markers: The Journal of the Association for Gravestone Studies, Vol. 8. Ed. by Richard E. Meyer et al. LC 81-642903. (Illus.). 352p. (C). 1991. 25.00 (1-878381-01-6) Assn Gravestone Studies.

Markers: The Journal of the Association for Gravestone Studies, Vol. 15. Ed. by Richard E. Meyer. LC 81-642903. (Illus.). 356p. 1998. 42.00 (1-878381-08-3) Assn Gravestone Studies.

Markers: The Materials, Techniques, & Exercises to Teach Yourself to Draw & Paint with Markers. Sanchez I. Sanchez. (I Draw, I Paint Ser.). (J). 1992. 13.15 (0-606-01632-5, Pub. by Turtleback) Demco.

Markers No. 2: The Journal of the Association for Gravestone Studies. Ed. by David Watters. LC 81-642903. (Illus.). 226p. (Orig.). (C). 1983. pap. text 28.50 (0-8191-3464-3) U Pr of Amer.

Markers No. 4: The Journal of the Association for Gravestone Studies. Ed. by David Watters. LC 81-642903. (Illus.). 182p. (Orig.). (C). 1987. text 48.00 (0-8191-5956-5); pap. text 24.00 (0-8191-5957-3) U Pr of Amer.

Markers No. 6: The Journal of the Association for Gravestone Studies. Ed. by Theodore Chase. LC 81-642903. (Illus.). 245p. (Orig.). (C). 1989. 25.00 (0-8191-7316-9); pap. 13.00 (0-8191-7317-7) U Pr of Amer.

Markers & Meaning in Paul: An Analysis of 1 Thessalonians, Philippians & Galatians. Jonas Holmstrand. (Coniectanea Biblica - New Testament Ser.: No. 28). 244p. 1997. pap. 57.50 (91-22-01761-5, Pub. by Almqvist Wiksell) Coronet Bks.

Markers in English-Influenced Swahili Conversation: Influenced Swahili Conversation. Carol M. Eastman. LC PL8702.E3. (Papers in International Studies: Africa Ser.: No. 13). 32p. reprint ed. pap. 30.00 (0-608-10981-9, 200741700063) Bks Demand.

Markers in Urology: Journal: European Urology, Vol. 21, Suppl. 1, 1992. Ed. by F. Di Silverio. (Illus.). iv, 116p. 1992. pap. 36.75 (3-8055-5612-8) S Karger.

Markers in Urology, Abstracts Vol. 19, Suppl. 2: Journal: European Urology, Vol. 19, Suppl. 1. Ed. by F. Di Silverio. xvi, 44p. 1991. pap. 18.50 (3-8055-5453-2) S Karger.

Markers of Colonic Cell Differentiation. Ed. by Sandra R. Wolman & Anthony J. Mastromarino. LC 82-42747. (Progress in Cancer Research & Therapy Ser.: Vol. 29). 455p. 1984. reprint ed. pap. 141.10 (0-608-00401-4, 206111500007) Bks Demand.

Markers of Human Neuroectodermal Tumors. Ed. by Gerard E. Staal & Cees W. van Veelen. 288p. 1986. 146.00 (0-8493-6414-0, RC280, CRC Reprint) Franklin.

Markers of Neuronal Injury & Degeneration. Ed. by Jan N. Johannessen. LC 93-13753. (Annals Ser.: Vol. 679). 432p. 1993. write for info. (0-89766-795-6); pap. 120.00 (0-89766-796-4) NY Acad Sci.

Markers Wet & Wild. Charles Hayden. (Illus.). 144p. 1993. pap. 24.95 (0-8230-0277-2) Watsn-Guptill.

Market! Ted Lewin. LC 95-7439. (Illus.). 48p. (J). (gr. k up). 1996. lib. bdg. 15.93 (0-688-12162-4) Lothrop.

Market! Ted Lewin. LC 95-7439. (Illus.). 32p. (J). (ps up). 1996. 16.00 (0-688-12161-6) Lothrop.

***Market!** Ted Lewin. LC 95-7439. (Illus.). 48p. (YA). (gr. k-3). 2000. mass mkt. 5.95 (0-688-17520-1, Wm Morrow) Morrow Avon.

Market: Ethics Knowledge & Politics. LC 97-44673. (Economics as Social Theory Ser.). 256p. (C). 1998. 85.00 (0-415-09827-0) Routledge.

Market: Ethics Knowledge & Politics. LC 97-44673. (Economics as Social Theory Ser.). 240p. (C). 1998. pap. 25.99 (0-415-15422-7) Routledge.

Market a la Mode: Fashion, Commodity, & Gender in the Tatler & the Spectator. Erin S. Mackie. LC 97-4442. 328p. 1997. text 39.95 (0-8018-5588-8) Johns Hopkins.

Market Access after the Uruguay Round: Investment, Competition & Technology Perspectives. OECD Staff. 225p. (Orig.). 1996. pap. 48.00 (92-64-14823-X, Pub. by Org for Econ) OECD.

Market Access Guides: The Baltic States. Ed. by Thomas M. Timberman. LC 92-73199. (Illus.). 1992. pap. 20.50 (0-9633925-0-6) LOI.

Market Access Issues for U. S. Agricultural Exports: Hearing Before the Subcommittee on International Trade of the Committee on Finance, United States Senate, 105th Congress, First Session, May 15, 1997. LC 98-193103. (S. Hrg. Ser.). iv, 102p. 1997. write for info. (0-16-056595-2) USGPO.

Market Access Issues in the Automobile Sector. Ed. by Denis Audet. LC 98-136145. 264p. 1997. pap. 32.00 (92-64-15680-1, 22-97-01-1, Pub. by Org for Econ) OECD.

Market Action. 2nd ed. Bonnarens. 1995. 32.50 (0-256-19867-5) McGraw.

Market Analysis: Assessing Your Business Opportunities. Robert E. Stevens et al. 240p. (Orig.). 1993. pap. 19.95 (*1-56024-269-8*) Haworth Pr.

Market Analysis: Assessing Your Business Opportunities. Robert E. Stevens et al. LC 92-220. (Illus.). 240p. (Orig.). 1993. lib. bdg. 49.95 (*1-56024-268-X*) Haworth Pr.

Market Analysis for Nebraska City. David R. DiMartino & Murray Frost. 95p. (Orig.). 1985. pap. 7.50 (*1-55719-001-1*) U NE CPAR.

Market Analysis for Valuation Appraisals. Stephen Fanning et al. 400p. 1994. 41.25 (*0-922154-18-X*) Appraisal Inst.

Market Analysis of ISDN CPE Vendors: Profiles & Strategies. IGIC, Inc. Staff. 250p. 1994. pap. 1195.00 (*0-918435-80-3*, IGIC-28) Info Gatekeepers.

Market & Beyond: Co-Operation & Competition in Information Technology in the Japanese System. Martin Fransman. (Illus.). 349p. (C). 1993. pap. text 22.95 (*0-521-43525-0*) Cambridge U Pr.

***Market & Community: The Bases of Social Order, Revolution & Relegitimation.** Mark Irving Lichbach & A. Seligman. LC 00-35620. 2000. write for info. (*0-271-02081-4*) Pa St U Pr.

Market & Health. David Reisman. LC 93-17299. 254p. 1993. text 45.00 (*0-312-09981-9*) St Martin.

Market & Institutional Regulation in Chinese Industrialization, 1978-94. Dic Lo. LC 96-27846. (Illus.). 280p. 1997. text 69.95 (*0-312-16422-X*) St Martin.

Market & Its Critics. Noel W. Thompson. 224p. 1988. lib. bdg. 57.50 (*0-415-00380-6*) Routledge.

Market & Non-Market Hierarchies: Theory of Institutional Failure. Christos N. Pitelis. LC 93-16051. 258p. 1993. reprint ed. pap. 29.95 (*0-631-19061-9*) Blackwell Pubs.

Market & Plan under Socialism: The Bird in the Cage. Jan S. Prybyla. (Publication Ser.: No. 422). 348p. (C). 1987. text 15.98 (*0-8179-8351-1*); pap. text 7.58 (*0-8179-8352-X*) Hoover Inst Pr.

***Market & Political Reforms in Algeria.** Mohammed Akacem. 2000. 55.00 (*0-8133-3658-9*, Pub. by Westview) HarpC.

Market & Sales Forecasting. 3rd ed. Gordon Bolt. (Marketing & Sales Ser.). 1994. pap. 29.95 (*0-7494-0913-4*) Kogan Page Ltd.

Market & Technology Trends in Diagnostics. (Market Research Reports: No. 300). 136p. 1993. 795.00 (*0-317-05463-5*) Theta Corp.

***Market & the Environment: The Effectiveness of Market-Based Policy Instruments for Environmental Reform.** Ed. by Thomas Sterner. LC 99-19520. (International Studies in Environmental Policy Making Ser.). 520p. 2000. 120.00 (*1-85898-906-X*) E Elgar.

Market & the State. David B. Audretsch. (C). 1991. text 57.50 (*0-8147-1432-3*) NYU Pr.

Market & the State: Essays in Honour of Adam Smith. Ed. by Thomas W. Wilson & Andrew S. Skinner. (Illus.). 372p. 1977. text 45.00 (*0-19-828406-3*) OUP.

Market & the State in Economic Development in the 1990s. Ed. by Alvaro A. Zini, Jr. LC 92-36911. (Contributions to Economic Analysis Ser.: Vol. 212). 292p. 1992. 98.50 (*0-444-89460-8*, North Holland) Elsevier.

***Market Approach to Education: An Analysis of America's First Voucher Program.** John F. Witte. LC 99-28151. (Illus.). 232p. 2000. 29.95 (*0-691-00944-9*, Pub. by Princeton U Pr) Cal Prin Full Svc.

***Market Approach to Valuing Companies.** Shannon P. Pratt. 250p. 2000. 85.00 (*0-471-35928-9*) Wiley.

Market Approaches to Education: Vouchers & School Choice. Elchanan Cohn. LC 96-41664. 600p. 1996. 96.00 (*0-08-042567-4*, Pergamon Pr) Elsevier.

Market-Based Approaches to Environmental: Regulatory Innovations to the Fore. Richard F. Kosobud & Jennifer M. Zimmerman. LC 96-45349. (General Science & Technology Ser.). 450p. 1997. 69.95 (*0-442-02483-5*, VNR) Wiley.

Market-Based Approaches to Environmental Policy: Regulatory Innovations to the Fore. Ed. by Richard F. Kosobud & Jennifer M. Zimmerman. (General Science Ser.). 354p. 1997. 99.00 (*0-471-28826-8*, VNR) Wiley.

Market-Based Control: A Paradigm for Distributed Resource Allocation. Ed. by Scott H. Clearwater. LC 95-35276. 300p. 1996. 62.00 (*981-02-2254-8*) World Scientific Pub.

Market-Based Debt Reduction for Developing Countries: Principles & Prospects. Stijn Claessens et al. (Policy & Research Ser.: No. 16). 72p. 1991. pap. 22.00 (*0-8213-1732-6*, 11732) World Bank.

***Market Based Instruments for Environmental Management.** Mikael Skou Andersen & Rolf-Ulrich Sprenger. LC 99-49220. (International Studies in Environmental Policy Making Ser.). 288p. 2000. text 100.00 (*1-84064-039-1*) E Elgar.

Market-Based Instruments for Environmental Policymaking in Latin America & the Caribbean: Lessons from Eleven Countries. Richard M. Huber et al. LC 97-39131. (Discussion Paper Ser.: No. 381). 89p. 1998. pap. 22.00 (*0-8213-4149-9*, 14149) World Bank.

***Market-Based Management: Strategies for Growing Customer Value & Profitability.** 2nd ed. Roger J. Best. LC 99-37126. (Illus.). 385p. 1999. pap. 51.00 (*0-13-014546-7*) P-H.

Market Based Public Policy. Ed. by Richard Hula. 192p. (Orig.). 1986. pap. 15.00 (*0-918592-80-1*) Pol Studies.

Market-Based Solutions for Air Service Problems at Medium-Sized Communities: Hearing Before the Subcommittee on Aviation of the Committee on Transportation & Infrastructure, House of Representatives, 105th Congress, 1st Session, June 25, 1997. USGPO Staff. LC 98-143865. v, 259 p. 1997. pap. write for info. (*0-16-056163-9*) USGPO.

Market Behaviour & Macroeconomic Modelling Steven Brakman et al. LC 98-13604. xvi, 416p. 1998. write for info. (*0-333-71836-4*, Pub. by Macmillan) St Martin.

Market Bell. Ed. by Ian Robinson & Elaine Mencher. 322p. (C). 1989. 95.00 (*0-907839-42-8*, Pub. by Brynmill Pr Ltd) St Mut.

Market Book Containing a Historical Account of the Public Markets in the Cities of New York, Boston, Philadelphia & Brooklyn Vol. 1: A History of the Public Markets in the City of New York. Thomas F. De Voe. LC 72-121319. (Library of Early American Business & Industry: No. 40). xiv, 621p. 1970. reprint ed. lib. bdg. 65.00 (*0-678-00685-7*) Kelley.

Market, Bureaucracy & Com: A Student's Guide to Organisation. Colebatch. LC 93-33091. 144p. (C). 44.95 (*0-7453-0762-0*, Pub. by Pluto GBR); pap. 15.95 (*0-7453-0763-9*, Pub. by Pluto GBR) Stylus Pub VA.

Market Capitalism & Moral Values: Proceedings of Section F (Economics) of the British Association for the Advancement of Science, 1993. Ed. by Samuel Brittan & Alan Hamlin. 168p. 1995. 85.00 (*1-85898-080-1*) E Elgar.

Market Centers & Hinterlands in Baden-Wurttemberg: Marktzentren und Hinterlander in Baden-Wurttemberg. H. Gardiner Barnum. LC 65-28149. (University of Chicago, Department of Geography, Research Paper Ser.: No. 103). 195p. reprint ed. pap. 60.50 (*0-7837-0389-9*, 204071000018) Bks Demand.

Market Centers & Rural Development: A Study in Chitwan District Nepal. U. C. Pradhan & Routray. 1994. pap. 80.00 (*0-7855-0460-5*, Pub. by Ratna Pustak Bhandar) St Mut.

***Market Communication: A Holistic Approach for Increased Profitability.** Otto Ottesen. 2000. Price not set. (*87-16-13335-8*, Pub. by Copenhagen Busn Schl) Bks Intl VA.

Market, Competition & Democracy: A Critique of Neo-Austrian Economics. Stavros Ioannides. 208p. 1992. 95.00 (*1-85278-531-4*) E Elgar.

Market Conduct Examiners Handbook. 7th ed. Ed. by Paula Kitt. (C). 1996. ring bd. 100.00 (*0-89382-402-X*, EXC-ZM) Nat Assn Insurance.

***Market Conduct for Life Insurance Agents.** Dearborn Financial Publishing Staff. LC 99-42796. 100p. 1999. pap. 29.00 (*0-7931-3299-1*) Dearborn.

Market Control & Planning in Communist China. Dwight H. Perkins. LC 66-10808. (Economic Studies: No. 128). (Illus.). 299p. 1966. 17.50 (*0-674-54950-3*) HUP.

Market Control in the Alumininum Industry. Donald H. Wallace. Ed. by Mira Wilkins. LC 76-29774. (European Business Ser.). (Illus.). 1977. reprint ed. lib. bdg. 53.95 (*0-405-09786-7*) Ayer.

Market Cultures: Society & Morality in the New Asian Capitalisms. Ed. by Robert W. Hefner. LC 97-36705. 336p. (C). 1997. pap. 26.00 (*0-8133-3360-1*, Pub. by Westview); text 79.00 (*0-8133-3359-8*, Pub. by Westview) HarpC.

Market Day. Eve Bunting. LC 95-5604. (Illus.). 32p. (J). (ps-3). 1996. 15.95 (*0-06-025364-9*); lib. bdg. 15.89 (*0-06-025368-1*) HarpC Child Bks.

Market Day. Eve Bunting. LC 95-5604. (Illus.). 32p. (J). (ps-3). 1999. pap. 5.95 (*0-06-443517-2*, HarpTrophy) HarpC Child Bks.

***Market Day: A Story Told with Folk Art.** Lois Ehlert. LC 99-6252. (Illus.). 36p. (J). (ps-2). 2000. 16.00 (*0-15-202158-2*, Harcourt Child Bks) Harcourt.

Market Day Sticker Book. Ed. by Heather Amery. (Farmyard Tales Sticker Bks.). (Illus.). 18p. (J). (ps-3). 1999. text 6.95 (*0-7460-3516-0*, Usborne) EDC.

Market Demand. W. Trockel. (Lecture Notes in Economics & Mathematical Systems Ser.: Vol. 223). viii, 205p. 1984. 34.00 (*0-387-12881-6*) Spr-Verlag.

Market Demand: Theory & Empirical Evidence. Werner Hildenbrand. LC 93-5910. 220p. 1994. text 62.50 (*0-691-03428-1*, Pub. by Princeton U Pr) Cal Prin Full Svc.

Market Demand Assessment, 1995. (VDT-2000 Ser.: Vol. 3). 1995. 2995.00 (*0-614-18340-5*, IGIC-94) Info Gatekeepers.

Market Demand for Dairy Products. Ed. by S. R. Johnson et al. LC 91-26898. (Illus.). 322p. 1992. text 64.95 (*0-8138-0289-X*) Iowa St U Pr.

Market Democracy: The Decline of American Ideals & Rise of a Two Class Society. Rory Blake. LC 96-85861. 288p. 1997. pap. text 15.00 (*0-9653521-0-2*) BC Bks.

Market Design: Client Relations & Organizational Power in the Management Consulting Firm. Richard Schneider. 324p. 1988. text 32.50 (*0-8290-1808-5*) Irvington.

Market Developments in Mercosur Countries Affecting Leading U. S. Exporters. William Greene. (Illus.). 66p. (C). 1998. pap. text 20.00 (*0-7881-7455-X*) DIANE Pub.

Market Dominance: How Firms Gain, Hold, or Lose It & the Impact on Economic Performance. Ed. by David I. Rosenbaum. LC 97-27004. 280p. 1998. 69.50 (*0-275-95604-0*, Praeger Pubs) Greenwood.

Market Dominance & Antitrust Policy. Michael A. Utton. 352p. 1995. 95.00 (*1-85278-358-3*) E Elgar.

Market-Driven Health Care: Who Wins, Who Loses in the Transformation of America's Largest Service Industry. Regina Herzlinger. LC 96-30199. 416p. 1996. 25.00 (*0-201-48994-5*) Perseus Pubng.

Market-Driven Healthcare: Who Wins, Who Loses in the Transformation of America's Largest Service Industry. Regina Herzlinger. LC 99-61216. 416p. 1999. pap. text 16.00 (*0-7382-0136-7*, Pub. by Perseus Pubng) HarpC.

Market Driven Journalism: Let the Citizen Beware? John H. McManus. LC 93-49517. 302p. (C). 1994. text 52.00 (*0-8039-5252-X*); pap. text 24.00 (*0-8039-5253-8*) Sage.

***Market-Driven Management: An Introduction to Marketing.** Jean-Jacques Lambin. LC 00-21421. 608p. 2000. text 85.00 (*0-312-23185-7*) St Martin.

Market-Driven Management: Lessons Learned from 20 Successful Associations. Donald M. Norris. 154p. (Orig.). 1990. pap. 45.00 (*0-88034-044-4*) Am Soc Assn Execs.

Market Driven Management: Prescriptions for Success in a Turbulent World. 2nd ed. B. Charles Ames. LC 96-9326. 208p. 1996. text 29.95 (*0-7863-0540-1*, Irwn Prfssnl) McGraw-Hill Prof.

Market-Driven Management: Using the New Marketing Concept to Create a Customer-Oriented Company. Frederick W. Webster. LC 93-39184. 336p. 1994. 29.95 (*0-471-59576-4*) Wiley.

Market Driven Management (Charles Ames Company Special Edition) 2nd ed. Charles Ames & James D. Hlavacek. 1996. text 29.95 (*0-7863-1227-0*, Irwn McGrw-H) McGrw-H Hghr Educ.

Market-Driven Nursing: Developing & Marketing Patient Care Services. American Organization of Nurse Executives Staff. LC 98-45912. (AONE Leadership Ser.). 172p. 1999. 36.00 (*1-55648-247-7*) AHPI.

Market Driven Organization: Understanding, Attracting & Keeping Valuable Customers. George S. Day. LC 99-16155. (Illus.). 304p. 1999. 28.00 (*0-684-86467-3*) Free Pr.

Market-Driven Strategy: An Executive Guide to Health Care's Integrated Environment. Linda MacCracken. LC 97-28826. 210p. 1997. 55.00 (*1-55648-211-6*) AHPI.

Market Driven Strategy: Processes for Creating Value. George S. Day. 420p. 1990. 35.00 (*0-02-907211-5*) Free Pr.

***Market Driven Strategy: Processes for Creating Value.** George S. Day. LC 99-30544. (Illus.). 432p. 1999. 35.00 (*0-684-86536-X*) Free Pr.

Market-Driving Strategies. Ed. by Carpenter. (C). 1998. text. write for info. (*0-321-01414-6*) Addson-Wesley Educ.

Market Driving Strategies. Ed. by Carpenter. (C). 1996. text. write for info. (*0-321-40453-X*) Addson-Wesley Educ.

Market-Driving Strategies: A Reader. Ed. by Carpenter. LC 97-195665. 540p. (C). 1997. pap. text 49.00 (*0-321-01413-8*) Addson-Wesley Educ.

Market Dynamics & Entry. Paul A. Geroski. 320p. (C). 1991. text 70.95 (*0-631-15554-6*) Blackwell Pubs.

Market Economics & Political Change: Comparing China & Mexico. Ed. by Juan D. Lindau & Timothy Cheek. LC 98-10415. 360p. 1998. 65.00 (*0-8476-8732-5*); pap. 24.95 (*0-8476-8733-3*) Rowman.

Market Economy: A Reader. Ed. by James L. Doti & Dwight R. Lee. LC 90-19524. 360p. (C). 1991. pap. text. write for info. (*0-935732-26-8*) Roxbury Pub Co.

***Market Economy & Christian Ethics.** Peter H. Sedgwick. LC 98-53577. (New Studies in Christian Ethics: No. 14). 346p. (C). 1999. 59.95 (*0-521-47048-X*) Cambridge U Pr.

Market Economy & Civil Society in Hungary. Ed. by C. M. Hann. 230p. 1990. text 37.50 (*0-7146-3396-8*, Pub. by F Cass Pubs) Intl Spec Bk.

Market Economy & Planned Economy: An Encyclopedic Dictionary, 2 vols., Set. Saur, K. G., Staff. (ENG, GER & RUS.). 1045p. 1992. 250.00 (*0-8288-7379-8*, 3598110707) Fr & Eur.

Market Education: The Unknown History. Andrew J. Coulson. LC 98-44583. 430p. 1999. 54.95 (*1-56000-408-8*); pap. 24.95 (*0-7658-0496-4*) Transaction Pubs.

Market Efficiency: Stock Market Behavior in Theory & Practice, 2 vols. Ed. by Andrew W. Lo. LC 97-3805. (International Library of Critical Writings in Economics Ser.: No. 3). 1224p. 1997. 430.00 (*1-85898-161-1*) E Elgar.

Market Efficiency & Inflation: Two Documents from the Cabinet Committee on Price Stability of the Johnson Administration, 1969. United States Cabinet Committee on Price Stability. LC 70-83785. 1969. 13.95 (*0-405-00055-3*) Ayer.

***Market Elections: How Democracy Serves the Rich.** Vincent Copeland. LC 99-53590. 2000. write for info. (*0-89567-134-4*) World View Forum.

Market Evolution: Competition & Cooperation. Ed. by Arjen Van Witteloostuijn. LC 94-48185. (Studies in Industrial Organization: Vol. 20). 1995. lib. bdg. 132.50 (*0-7923-3350-0*) Kluwer Academic.

Market Evolution in Developing Countries: The Unfolding of the Indian Market. Subhash C. Jain. LC 92-22619. (Original Book Ser.). (Illus.). 329p. 1993. lib. bdg. 79.95 (*1-56024-360-0*) Haworth Pr.

Market Experience. Robert E. Lane. 640p. (C). 1991. pap. text 29.95 (*0-521-40737-0*) Cambridge U Pr.

Market Failure in Training? New Economic Analysis & Evidence on Training of Adult Employees. Ed. by D. Stern et al. (Studies in Contemporary Economics). vii, 233p. 1992. 47.95 (*0-387-54622-7*) Spr-Verlag.

Market Focused Production Systems: Design & Implementation. David J. Bennett & Paul L. Forrester. 250p. (C). 1993. pap. 24.95 (*0-13-322157-1*) P-H.

Market for Antifungals. Market Intelligence Staff. 310p. 1992. 3700.00 (*1-56753-674-3*, A2500) Frost & Sullivan.

Market for Antihypertensive Agents (U. S.) 1992. 3800.00 (*0-685-61791-2*, A2498) Frost & Sullivan.

Market for Bakery Products. T. Chirco. 1999. 1295.00 (*0-685-08040-4*) Busn Trend.

Market for Bakery Snacks. LC 99-208366. 227p. 1997. write for info. (*1-56241-464-X*) FIND-SVP.

Market for Bathroom Products & Deodorants (Europe) Market Intelligence Staff. 305p. 1992. 1250.00 (*1-56753-736-7*, E1580) Frost & Sullivan.

Market for Breakfast Foods: Past Performance, Current Trends & Opportunities for Growth. V. Seeno. 395p. 1999. 1495.00 (*0-317-55214-7*) Busn Trend.

Market for Canned, Frozen & Cured Seafood: A Product-by-Product Marketing Analysis & Competitor Profile. 500p. 1996. 1095.00 (*0-317-55188-4*) Busn Trend.

Market for Cellular Communications (Europe) Market Intelligence Staff. 272p. 1992. 3850.00 (*1-56753-746-4*, E1586) Frost & Sullivan.

Market for Children & Family Dining. 140p. 1991. pap. 45.00 (*0-614-31118-7*, CS680) Natl Restaurant Assn.

Market for Children's Toys & Games. Ed. by Peter Allen. 222p. 1985. pap. 295.00 (*0-931634-49-0*) FIND-SVP.

Market for Coffee & Tea. Find/SVP (Firm) Staff. LC 99-163381. (A Market Intelligence Report). xi, 221 p. 1996. write for info. (*1-56241-434-8*) FIND-SVP.

Market for Collectible Dolls. Ed. by Peter Allen. 248p. 1985. pap. text 295.00 (*0-931634-53-9*) FIND-SVP.

Market for College-Trained Manpower: A Study in the Economics of Career Choice. Richard B. Freeman. LC 70-139726. 292p. reprint ed. pap. 90.60 (*0-608-14208-5*, 202159300022) Bks Demand.

Market for Craft & Specialty Beer. LC 99-171346. (Market Intelligence Report Ser.). 215 p. 1997. write for info. (*1-56241-459-3*) FIND-SVP.

Market for Dairy Products (Europe) Butter Cheese & Fermented Products. Market Intelligence Staff. 400p. 1992. 1200.00 (*1-56753-726-X*, E1616) Frost & Sullivan.

Market for Dairy Products (Europe) Milk, Cream & Dairy Drinks. Market Intelligence Staff. 290p. 1992. 1200.00 (*1-56753-725-1*, E1617) Frost & Sullivan.

Market for Dairy Products (Europe) Yogurt, Dairy Desserts & Ice Cream. Market Intelligence Staff. 325p. 1992. 1200.00 (*1-56753-724-3*, E1618) Frost & Sullivan.

Market for Decubitus Ulcer Treatment: Products, Drugs & Devices. 238p. 1986. 1950.00 (*0-931634-50-4*) FIND-SVP.

Market for Dried Fruit in the United Kingdom, the Federal Republic of Germany & France. G. Harman & N. Anaand. 69p. 1990. pap. 30.00 (*0-85954-268-8*, Pub. by Nat Res Inst) St Mut.

Market for Electrical Generating Equipment. Bruce T. Allen & Arie Melnik. LC 73-620027. (MSU Public Utilities Papers: Vol. 1973). 91p. reprint ed. pap. 30.00 (*0-608-20488-9*, 207174000002) Bks Demand.

Market for Emerging Ethnic Foods. LC 99-171142. 135 p. 1996. write for info. (*1-56241-377-5*) FIND-SVP.

Market for Energy. Ed. by Dieter R. Helm et al. (Illus.). 464p. 1989. text 85.00 (*0-19-828608-2*) OUP.

Market for Environmental Equipment Services in Russia: A Strategic Entry Report, 1996. Compiled by Icon Group International Staff. (Illus.). 247p. 1999. ring bd. 2470.00 incl. audio compact disk (*0-7418-1410-2*) Icon Grp.

Market for Ethnic Personal Care Products: A Strategic Marketing Analysis & Biennial Review of Products Designed for the Black Consumer. K. Soscia. 205p. 1999. 1995.00 (*0-317-55207-4*) Lead Edge Reports.

Market for Facsimile Equipment (Europe) Market Intelligence Staff. 259p. 1992. 3800.00 (*1-56753-711-1*, E1562) Frost & Sullivan.

Market for Fats & Oils. V. Seeno. 540p. 1998. 1295.00 (*0-318-04395-5*) Busn Trend.

Market for Ferrous & Nonferrous Metal Stampings. M. Gallagher. 183p. 1997. 1995.00 (*0-945235-37-2*) Lead Edge Reports.

Market for Fortified Foods & Beverages. Packaged Facts (Firm) Staff. LC 98-186522. xi, 144 p. 1996. write for info. (*1-56241-373-2*) FIND-SVP.

Market for Fragrances (Europe) Market Intelligence Staff. 383p. 1992. 1250.00 (*1-56753-710-3*, E1576) Frost & Sullivan.

Market for Fresh Produce. Ed. by Peter Allen. 200p. 1989. pap. 1295.00 (*0-318-41824-X*) FIND-SVP.

Market for Frozen Dinners & Entrees. 193p. 1998. 1995.00 (*0-685-43150-9*, H138) Lead Edge Reports.

Market for Fruit & Vegetable Juices. Ed. by Peter Allen. 340p. 1986. pap. text 1250.00 (*0-318-18886-4*) FIND-SVP.

Market for Funeral & Cremation Services. K. Soscia. 230p. 1998. 995.00 (*0-318-04400-5*) Busn Trend.

Market for Genitourinary Pharmaceuticals. Find/SVP (Firm) Staff. LC 99-182695. (Market Intelligence Report Ser.). xii, 247 p. 1996. write for info. (*1-56241-407-0*) FIND-SVP.

Market for Golf Equipment in Netherlands: A Strategic Entry Report, 1998. Compiled by Icon Group International. (Country Industry Report). (Illus.). 124p. 1999. ring bd. 1240.00 incl. audio compact disk (*0-7418-0349-6*) Icon Grp.

Market for Gourmet Coffees & Teas. Ed. by Peter Allen. 157p. 1988. pap. 495.00 (*0-941285-33-2*) FIND-SVP.

Market for Hair Care (Europe) Market Intelligence Staff. 397p. 1992. 1250.00 (*1-56753-708-1*, E1579) Frost & Sullivan.

Market for Hazardous Waste Management (Europe) Market Intelligence Staff. 412p. 1992. 3900.00 (*1-56753-707-3*, E1590) Frost & Sullivan.

Market for Heat Exchangers (U. S.) Market Intelligence Staff. 253p. 1992. 2450.00 (*1-56753-706-5*, A2547) Frost & Sullivan.

Market for Heating, Air Conditioning & Refrigeration Equipment. 750p. 1997. 1195.00 (0-318-03908-7) Busn Trend.

Market for High Power Semiconductors (Europe) 1992. 2300.00 (0-685-61918-4, E1615) Frost & Sullivan.

Market for High Power Semiconductors (Europe) Market Intelligence Staff. 386p. 1992. 2300.00 (0-685-70257-X) Frost & Sullivan.

Market for Home Textiles. Ed. by Peter Allen. 100p. 1989. pap. 695.00 (0-317-01800-0) FIND-SVP.

Market for Ice Cream & Frozen Desserts. (Illus.). 340p. 1997. spiral bd. 1150.00 (0-685-21992-5) Busn Trend.

Market for Ice Cream & Other Frozen Desserts. Find/SVP (Firm) Staff. LC 97-229128. (A Market Intelligence Reports). xiii, 381 p. 1996. write for info. (1-56241-241-8) FIND-SVP.

Market for Industrial Adhesives. Ed. by Peter Allen. 193p. 1988. 1795.00 (0-941285-35-9) FIND-SVP.

Market for Industrial & Institutional Cleaners. C. Broyles. 450p. 1999. pap. 1995.00 (0-685-43869-4) Lead Edge Reports.

Market for Industrial Chemicals in Vietnam: A Strategic Entry Report, 1997. Compiled by Icon Group International Staff. (Illus.). 145p. 1999. ring bd. 1450.00 incl. audio compact disk (0-7418-0854-4) Icon Grp.

Market for Information Technology (IT) Security Products & Services (Europe) Market Intelligence Staff. 415p. 1992. 3400.00 (1-56753-787-1, E1513) Frost & Sullivan.

Market for Intimate Apparel & Women's Hosiery. T. Chirco. 930p. 1999. 1495.00 (0-685-17773-4) Busn Trend.

Market for Intravenous Therapy & Interal Nutrition (Europe) Market Intelligence Staff. 405p. 1992. 3800.00 (1-56753-786-3, E1584) Frost & Sullivan.

Market for Juices, Ades & Noncarbonated Drinks. K. Soscia. 280p. 1998. 1195.00 (0-318-04394-7) Busn Trend.

Market for LAN Value Added Resellers (U. S.) Market Intelligence Staff. 300p. 1992. 2400.00 (1-56753-781-2, A2456) Frost & Sullivan.

Market for Lasers in Medicine. Ed. by Peter Allen. 239p. 1989. pap. 1495.00 (0-941285-49-9) FIND-SVP.

Market for Lawn, Garden, & Snow Equipment. T. Dowd. (Illus.). 400p. 1999. spiral bd. 1295.00 (0-317-65738-0) Busn Trend.

Market for Leather Accessories & Travelware: A Product-by-Product Marketing Analysis & Competitor Profile. L. Levine. 300p. 1999. 1295.00 (0-317-55201-5) Busn Trend.

Market for Liberty. Morris Tannehill & Linda Tannehill. 169p. 1993. reprint ed. pap. 12.95 (0-930073-08-8) Fox & Wilkes.

Market for Lifestyle & Ready-to-Assemble Furniture. Ed. by Peter Allen. 125p. 1989. pap. 695.00 (0-941285-47-2) FIND-SVP.

Market for Liquid - Solid Separation Equipment (U. S.) Market Intelligence Staff. 301p. 1992. 2800.00 (1-56753-780-4, A2568) Frost & Sullivan.

Market for Local Area Network (LAN) Maintenance (Europe) Market Intelligence Staff. 272p. 1992. 3200.00 (1-56753-779-0, E1556) Frost & Sullivan.

Market for Low-Fat, Nonfat & Reduced-Fat Foods. LC 99-171320. (Market Intelligence Report Ser.). 253 p. 1997. write for info. (1-56241-413-5) FIND-SVP.

Market for Low Power Semiconductors - Smart Power ICs (Europe) Market Intelligence Staff. 387p. 1992. 2300.00 (1-56753-778-2, E1614) Frost & Sullivan.

Market for Make-Up (Europe) Market Intelligence Staff. 394p. 1992. 1250.00 (1-56753-777-4, E1577) Frost & Sullivan.

Market for Manufacturing Systems Integration (U. S.) Market Intelligence Staff. 250p. 1992. 2400.00 (1-56753-775-8, A2551) Frost & Sullivan.

Market for Material Handling Equipment. 390p. 1998. 1095.00 (0-318-00498-4) Busn Trend.

Market for Meat & Meat Products (Europe) Carcass Meats. Market Intelligence Staff. 382p. 1994. 1200.00 (1-56753-774-X, E1619) Frost & Sullivan.

Market for Meat & Meat Products (Europe) Comminuted Meat Products. Market Intelligence Staff. 389p. 1992. 1200.00 (1-56753-773-1, E1621) Frost & Sullivan.

Market for Meat & Meat Products (Europe) Prepared Meat & Associated Products. Market Intelligence Staff. 411p. 1992. 1200.00 (1-56753-772-3, E1620) Frost & Sullivan.

Market for Metal Doors, Windows, Sash & Trim: Nonwood Doors, Windows, Sash & Trim. J. Terra. 430p. 1999. 1195.00 (0-317-55197-3) Busn Trend.

Market for Metropolitan Area Networks (U. S.) Market Intelligence Staff. 233p. 1992. 3300.00 (1-56753-770-7, A2540) Frost & Sullivan.

Market for Military Automated Mission Planning (U. S.) Market Intelligence Staff. 300p. 1992. 2700.00 (1-56753-769-3, A2516) Frost & Sullivan.

Market for Military C3I (Europe) Market Intelligence Staff. 302p. 1992. 2900.00 (1-56753-768-5, E1632) Frost & Sullivan.

Market for Military Passive Night Vision (U. S.) Market Intelligence Staff. 250p. 1992. 2450.00 (1-56753-755-3, A2495) Frost & Sullivan.

Market for Military Power Supplies (U. S.) Market Intelligence Staff. 250p. 1992. 2700.00 (1-56753-756-1, A2541) Frost & Sullivan.

Market for Mobile Satellite Communications David Williams & Ronald J. Lepkowski. LC 89-175107. iv, 325p. 1989. write for info. (0-934960-63-1) Phillips Business.

Market for Money & the Market for Credit. Ed. by Pieter Korteweg & P. D. Van Loo. 1977. pap. text 66.50 (90-207-0685-3) Kluwer Academic.

Market for Multichip Modules (MCMs) (U. S.) Market Intelligence Staff. 215p. 1992. 2200.00 (1-56753-760-X, A2530) Frost & Sullivan.

Market for Multimedia (Europe) Market Intelligence Staff. 340p. 1992. 3700.00 (1-56753-762-6, E1646) Frost & Sullivan.

Market for Murder. large type ed. Frank Gruber. (Linford Mystery Library). 304p. 1992. pap. 16.99 (0-7089-7231-4, Linford) Ulverscroft.

Market for Musical Instruments. T. Chirco. 560p. 1999. 1295.00 (0-685-08045-5) Busn Trend.

Market for North American Video & Audio Post-Production Equipment (U. S.) Market Intelligence Staff. 200p. 1992. 1450.00 (1-56753-765-0) Frost & Sullivan.

Market for Office Furniture & Equipment. Ed. by Peter Allen. 200p. 1989. pap. 1495.00 (0-318-41825-8) FIND-SVP.

***Market for Oil Refinery Equipment in Poland: A Strategic Entry Report, 1996.** Compiled by Icon Group International Staff. (Illus.). 184p. 1999. ring bd. 1840.00 incl. audio compact disk (0-7418-1342-4) Icon Grp.

Market for Ophthalmic Goods. J. Wichert. 410p. 1998. 1095.00 (0-318-00519-0) Busn Trend.

Market for Oral Hygiene Products (Europe) Market Intelligence Staff. 384p. 1992. 1250.00 (1-56753-800-2, E1581) Frost & Sullivan.

Market for Osteoporosis Diagnostics, Therapeutics & Disease Management. Find/SVP (Firm) Staff. LC 99-182961. (A Market Intelligence Report). xiii, 194p. 1997. write for info. (1-56241-447-X) FIND-SVP.

Market for Outsourcing Services (U. S.) Market Intelligence Staff. 246p. 1992. 2450.00 (1-56753-802-9, A2497) Frost & Sullivan.

Market for PC Cad Hardware, Software & Systems in Europe. J. J. & J. Consultants. (Illus.). 116p. 1987. 1495.00 (0-914849-08-5) TBC Inc.

Market for PC-LAN Hardware, Software, File Servers & Value Added Services in the Office Environment (Europe) 250p. 1992. 3300.00 (0-685-62155-3, E1647) Frost & Sullivan.

Market for Pet Healthcare Products (Europe) Market Intelligence Staff. 405p. 1992. 3800.00 (1-56753-823-1, E1608) Frost & Sullivan.

Market for Physical Fitness & Exercise Equipment. Ed. by Peter Allen. 250p. 1987. pap. 1250.00 (0-931634-74-1) FIND-SVP.

Market for Pleasure Boats & Related Products. Business Trend Analysts, Inc. Staff. (Illus.). 270p. 1998. spiral bd. 1195.00 (0-685-24423-7) Busn Trend.

Market for Poultry & Small Game. L. Levine. (Illus.). 270p. 1999. pap. 1995.00 (0-318-04171-5) Lead Edge Reports.

Market for Power-Driven Hand Tools. J. Terra. 420p. 1999. 1195.00 (0-318-02835-2) Busn Trend.

Market for Process Control: Flow & Level Instrumentation. Market Intelligence Staff. 176p. 1993. 1900.00 (1-56753-490-2) Frost & Sullivan.

Market for Process Control: Temperature Instrumentation. Market Intelligence Staff. 180p. 1993. 1900.00 (1-56753-489-9) Frost & Sullivan.

Market for Process Control Pressure - Differentiation Pressure Instrumentation. Market Intelligence Staff. 180p. 1993. 1900.00 (1-56753-491-0) Frost & Sullivan.

Market for Professional Studio & Portable Video Equipment in North America (U. S.) Market Intelligence Staff. 200p. 1992. 1450.00 (1-56753-805-3, A2462) Frost & Sullivan.

Market for Rapid in Vitro Diagnostic Tests. Find/SVP (Firm) Staff. LC 99-182735. (A Market Intelligence Report). xvii, 313p. 1997. write for info. (1-56241-454-2) FIND-SVP.

Market for Recycling Goods, Services in Mexico: A Strategic Entry Report, 1996. Compiled by Icon Group International Staff. (Illus.). 177p. 1999. ring bd. 1770.00 incl. audio compact disk (0-7418-1411-0) Icon Grp.

Market for Rugs & Carpeting. Ed. by Peter Allen. 120p. 1989. pap. 695.00 (0-941285-58-8) FIND-SVP.

Market for Salted Snacks. Ed. by Peter Allen. 200p. 1987. pap. 1250.00 (0-941285-04-9) FIND-SVP.

Market for Scientific Equipment in Vietnam: A Strategic Entry Report, 1997. Compiled by Icon Group International Staff. (Illus.). 145p. 1999. ring bd. 1450.00 incl. audio compact disk (0-7418-1044-1) Icon Grp.

***Market for Security Systems in Indonesia: A Strategic Entry Report, 1996.** Compiled by Icon Group International Staff. (Illus.). 165p. 1999. ring bd. 1650.00 incl. audio compact disk (0-7418-1439-0) Icon Grp.

Market for Self-Improvement Products & Services. 36p. 1999. 59.00 (0-9632529-8-4) Mktdata Ent.

Market for Shelter in Indonesian Cities. Raymond J. Struyk et al. LC 90-30366. (Illus.). 500p. 1990. lib. bdg. 80.00 (0-87766-444-7) Urban Inst.

Market for Skin Care (Europe) Market Intelligence Staff. 394p. 1992. 1250.00 (1-56753-809-6, E1578) Frost & Sullivan.

Market for Small Engines. 400p. 1996. 1995.00 (0-614-10252-9) Lead Edge Reports.

Market for Small Engines: A Product-by-Product Analysis of the Market for Small Nonautomotive Engines & Outboard Motors. 185p. 1996. 1995.00 (0-685-74758-1) Lead Edge Reports.

Market for Stress Management Products & Services. 22p. 1996. 59.00 (0-9632529-1-7) Mktdata Ent.

Market for Teletext in the United States, 2 vols. Richard Adler et al. 203p. 1983. 20.00 (0-318-19202-0, R-57) Inst Future.

Market for Tissues Transplantation. (Report Ser.: No. B-103). 351p. 1996. 2950.00 (1-56965-359-3) BCC.

Market for Toiletries & Cosmetics: A Product-by-Product Marketing Analysis & Competitor Profile. J. Terra. 765p. 1999. 1495.00 (0-317-55199-X) Busn Trend.

Market for Tourism to the Usa in Italy: A Strategic Entry Report, 1998. Compiled by Icon Group International. (Country Industry Report). (Illus.). 148p. 1999. ring bd. 1480.00 incl. audio compact disk (0-7418-0384-4) Icon Grp.

Market for Toys & Games: An Analysis of Current Markets & Prospects for Future Growth. V. Seeno. 520p. 1999. 1295.00 (0-318-03739-4) Busn Trend.

Market for Training: International Perspectives on Theory, Methodology & Policy. Ed. by Robert McNabb & Keith Whitfield. 416p. 1994. 96.95 (1-85628-599-5, Pub. by Avebry) Ashgate Pub Co.

Market for Trunked Radio Equipment for SMRs & Users (U. S.) Market Intelligence Staff. 225p. 1992. 2900.00 (1-56753-819-3, A2510) Frost & Sullivan.

***Market for Turbines & Generators in Indonesia: A Strategic Entry Report, 1998.** Compiled by Icon Group International Staff. (Country Industry Report). (Illus.). 175p. 1999. ring bd. 1750.00 incl. audio compact disk (0-7418-0182-5) Icon Grp.

Market for TV Transmission Systems Technology in North America (U. S.) Market Intelligence Staff. 397p. 1992. 1850.00 (1-56753-820-7, A2461) Frost & Sullivan.

Market for UNIX (Europe) Market Intelligence Staff. 350p. 1992. 3900.00 (1-56753-821-5, E1593) Frost & Sullivan.

Market for VANs (Europe) Market Intelligence Staff. 291p. 1992. 3900.00 (1-56753-855-X, E1601) Frost & Sullivan.

Market for Visual Simulation/Virtual Reality Systems: A Study Conducted by CyberEdge Information Services. Ben Delaney. (Illus.). 33p. (C). 1997. pap. 775.00 (1-929696-00-0) CyberEdge Info.

***Market for Visual Simulation/Virtual Reality Systems: A Study Conducted by CyberEdge Information Services.** 2nd ed. Ben Delaney. (Illus.). 118p. (C). 1999. pap. 1820.00 (1-929696-02-7) CyberEdge Info.

Market for Watches & Clocks. T. Chirco. 430p. 1999. 1295.00 (0-318-00526-3) Busn Trend.

Market for Water Rights in Chile: Major Issues. Monica R. Brehm & Jorge Q. Castro. (World Bank Technical Papers: No. 285). 40p. 1995. pap. 22.00 (0-8213-3307-0, 13307) World Bank.

Market for Window Coverings. V. Seeno. 490p. 1999. pap. 1195.00 (0-318-03740-8) Busn Trend.

Market Forces & World Development. Ed. by Renee Prendergast & Frances Stewart. LC 93-25823. 1994. text 85.00 (0-312-10175-9) St Martin.

Market Forces in China: Competition & Small Business: The Wenzhou Debate. Ed. by Peter Nolan & D. Fureng. LC 89-70608. (Illus.). 208p. (C). 1997. pap. 19.95 (0-86232-833-0, Pub. by St Martin); text 49.95 (0-86232-832-2, Pub. by St Martin) St Martin.

Market Guide for Young Writers: Where & How to Sell What You Write. 5th ed. Kathy Henderson. LC 95-44903. (Illus.). 320p. (YA). 1996. pap. 16.99 (0-89879-721-7, Wrtrs Digest Bks) F & W Pubns Inc.

Market Hunter. Dave Kimball & Jim Kimball. pap. write for info. (0-87518-011-6, Dillon Silver Burdett) Silver Burdett Pr.

Market Integration in the European Community. Jacques Pelkmans. LC 84-8138. (Studies in Industrial Organization: Vol. 5). 1984. lib. bdg. 122.50 (90-247-2978-5) Kluwer Academic.

***Market Integration, Regionalism & the Global Economy.** Ed. by Richard E. Baldwin et al. LC 99-11548. (Illus.). 352p. (C). 1999. 69.95 (0-521-64181-0); pap. 25.95 (0-521-64589-1) Cambridge U Pr.

Market Intelligence: Indonesia. 17p. 1994. pap. 35.00 (1-882866-79-7) Pac Asia Trvl.

Market Intelligence: Singapore. 21p. 1993. pap. 35.00 (1-882866-20-7) Pac Asia Trvl.

Market Intelligence: South Africa. 26p. 1993. pap. 35.00 (1-882866-78-9) Pac Asia Trvl.

Market Intelligence: Thailand. 27p. 1993. pap. 35.00 (1-882866-75-4) Pac Asia Trvl.

Market Intelligence Report: Hong Kong. 19p. 1993. pap. 35.00 (1-882866-80-0) Pac Asia Trvl.

Market It Write: Entrepreneur's Guide to Publicity in the Chicago Area Press. Jim Peters. LC 95-90279. 149p. (Orig.). 1995. pap. 15.95 (0-9646583-0-5) Eastview Pub.

***Market Killing.** 2000. write for info. (0-582-38236-X) Pearson Educ.

Market Lady & the Mango Tree. Pete Watson. LC 93-7725. (Illus.). 32p. (J). 1994. 14.00 (0-688-12970-6, Wm Morrow) Morrow Avon.

***Market Leadership: Managing the Customer Focused Team.** Joe Calloway. 80p. 1999. pap. write for info. (0-9675911-1-2) Busn Resources.

Market Leadership Strategies for Service Companies: Creating Growth, Profits & Customer Loyalty. Arthur Middlebrooks & Craig Terrill. LC 99-10338. 288p. 1999. 39.95 (0-8442-2441-3, 24413, Natl Textbk Co) NTC Contemp Pub Co.

***Market-Led Strategic Change.** Nigel Piercy. 2000. pap. 37.95 (0-7506-4382-X) Buttrwrth-Heinemann.

Market-Led Strategic Change: Making Marketing Happen in Your Organization. Nigel Piercy. LC 92-250048. (Marketing Ser.). (Illus.). 416p. 1992. reprint ed. pap. 129.00 (0-608-07432-2, 206765900009) Bks Demand.

Market-Led Strategic Change: Transforming the Process of Going to Market. 2nd ed. Nigel Piercy. LC 98-135256. (Marketing Ser.). 480p. 1998. pap. text 42.95 (0-7506-3285-2) Buttrwrth-Heinemann.

Market Liberalisation, Equity & Development. Ed. by Geoffrey T. Renshaw. xiv, 181p. 1989. pap. 22.50 (92-2-106397-6) Intl Labour Office.

Market Liberalism: A Paradigm for the 21st Century. Ed. by David Boaz & Edward H. Crane. LC 92-42550. 352p. 1993. 25.95 (0-932790-98-4) Cato Inst.

Market Liberalism: American Foreign Policy Toward China. Gordon Cheung. LC 98-18320. 328p. 1998. text 34.95 (1-56000-378-2) Transaction Pubs.

Market Magic: Riding the Greatest Bull Market of the Century. Louise Yamada. LC 97-45104. (Investments Ser.). (Illus.). 272p. 1998. 34.95 (0-471-19759-9) Wiley.

***Market Magic: Riding the Greatest Bull Market of the Century.** Louise Yamada. LC 97-45104. (Illus.). 224p. 2000. pap. 18.95 (0-471-38368-6) Wiley.

Market Maker. Michael Ridpath. 384p. 1999. mass mkt. 6.99 (0-451-19752-6) NAL.

***Market Makers.** Spulber. 1999. write for info. (0-07-134895-6) McGraw.

Market Makers: How Leading Companies Are Creating & Winning Markets. Daniel F. Spulber. LC 98-6168. (Illus.). 320p. 1998. 24.95 (0-07-060584-X) McGraw.

***Market Maker's Edge: Day Trading Tactics from a Wall Street Insider.** Josh Lukeman. LC 00-21162. (Illus.). 288p. 2000. 34.95 (0-07-135975-3) McGraw.

Market Management. 5th ed. Guiltinan. 1993. teacher ed. 42.81 (0-07-048972-6) McGraw.

Market Mechanism & Economic Reforms in China. William A. Byrd. LC 90-8105. (Studies on Contemporary China). 264p. (C). (gr. 13). 1991. text 72.95 (0-87332-719-5, East Gate Bk) M E Sharpe.

Market Mechanisms & the Health Sector in Central & Eastern Europe. Alexander S. Preker & Richard G. Feachem. (Technical Papers: Vol. 293). 64p. 1996. pap. 22.00 (0-8213-3331-3, 13331) World Bank.

Market Meets Its Match: Restructuring the Economies of Eastern Europe. Alice H. Amsden et al. LC 94-18600. 232p. 1994. text 43.50 (0-674-54983-X, AMSMAR) HUP.

Market Meets Its Match: Restructuring the Economies of Eastern Europe. Alice H. Amsden et al. (Illus.). 264p. 1998. pap. 18.95 (0-674-54984-8) HUP.

Market Meets the Environment: Economic Analysis of Environmental Policy. Ed. by Bruce Yandle. LC 99-27982. 336p. 1999. pap. text 24.95 (0-8476-9625-1) Rowman.

***Market Meets the Environment: Economic Analysis of Environmental Policy.** Ed. by Bruce Yandle. LC 99-27982. (The Political Economy Forum Ser.). 336p. 1999. text 65.00 (0-8476-9624-3) Rowman.

Market Microstructure: Intermediaries & the Theory of The Fire. Daniel F. Spulber. LC 98-34680. (Illus.). 450p. (C). 1998. 69.95 (0-521-65025-9) Cambridge U Pr.

Market Microstructure: Intermediaries & the Theory of the Fire. Daniel F. Spulber. LC 98-34680. (Illus.). 450p. (C). 1999. pap. text 24.95 (0-521-65978-7) Cambridge U Pr.

Market Microstructure & Capital Market Information Content Research. Philip Brown et al. (Studies in Accounting Research: No. 32). 183p. 1992. 15.00 (0-86539-078-9) Am Accounting.

Market Microstructure Theory. Maureen O'Hara. LC 94-28078. (Illus.). 300p. (C). 1994. text 55.95 (1-55786-443-8) Blackwell Pubs.

Market Microstructure Theory. Maureen O'Hara. LC 94-28078. (Illus.). 300p. (C). 1997. pap. text 36.95 (0-631-20761-9) Blackwell Pubs.

Market Morality & Company Size. Ed. by Brian Harvey. 240p. (C). 1991. lib. bdg. 107.00 (0-7923-1342-9, Pub. by Kluwer Academic) Kluwer Academic.

Market Morals & Public Policy. Lionel Orchard & Robert Dare. 240p. 1989. pap. 41.00 (1-86287-624-X, Pub. by Federation Pr) Gaunt.

Market Movers. Nancy Dunnan & Jay J. Pack. 352p. (Orig.). 1993. mass mkt. 14.99 (0-446-39340-1, Pub. by Warner Bks) Little.

Market Movers: Understanding & Using Economic Indicators from the Big Five Economies. Mark Jones & Ken Ferris. LC 92-16103. 320p. 1993. 34.95 (0-07-707556-0) McGraw.

Market Neutral: Long & Short Strategies for Every Market Environment. Jess Lederman. 288p. 1996. 65.00 (0-7863-0733-1, Irwn McGrw-H) McGrw-H Hghr Educ.

Market Neutral Investing: The Essential Strategies. Joseph G. Nicholas. 65.00 (1-57660-037-8, Pub. by Bloomberg NJ) Norton.

Market of Plastic Optical Fiber in Data Communications. 1997. 2995.00 (0-614-26450-2) Info Gatekeepers.

Market Opportunities for Innovative Site Clean-Up Technologies: Mid-Atlantic States. Environmental Protection Agency Staff. (Illus.). 175p. 1995. ring bd. 24.00 (1-892209-08-X) Env Compli Rep.

Market Opportunity Analysis for Short-Range Public Transportation Planning: Economic, Energy, & Environmental Impacts. (National Cooperative Highway Research Program Report Ser.: No. 210). 45p. 1979. 6.00 (0-309-03002-1, NR210) Transport Res Bd.

Market Opportunity Analysis for Short-Range Public Transportation Planning: Goals & Policy Development, Institutional Constraints, & Alternative Organizational Arrangements. (National Cooperative Highway Research Program Report Ser.: No. 211). 161p. 1979. 9.20 (0-309-03003-X, NR211) Transport Res Bd.

Market Opportunity Analysis for Short-Range Public Transportation Planning: Procedures for Evaluating Alternative Service Concepts. (National Cooperative Highway Research Program Report Ser.: No. 208). 80p. 1979. 6.80 (0-309-03000-5, NR208) Transport Res Bd.

Market Opportunity Analysis for Short-Range Public Transportation Planning: Transportation Services for the Transportation Disadvantaged. (National Cooperative Highway Research Program Report Ser.: No. 209). 52p. 1979. 6.00 (0-309-03001-3, NR209) Transport Res Bd.

Market or Mafia: Russian Managers on the Difficult Road Towards an Open Society. Wilhelm Eberwein & Jochen Tholen. 272p. 1997. text 73.95 (*1-85972-395-0*, Pub. by Avebry) Ashgate Pub Co.

Market Orientation in Food & Agriculture. Klaus G. Grunert et al. 304p. (C). 1995. lib. bdg. 127.00 (*0-7923-9649-9*) Kluwer Academic.

Market-Oriented Pricing: Strategies for Management. Michael H. Morris & Gene Morris. LC 89-10712. 218p. 1990. 62.95 (*0-89930-402-8*, MBY/, Greenwood Pr) Greenwood.

Market-Oriented Systemic Transformations in Eastern Europe: Problems, Theoretical Issues, & Policy Options. Paul J. Welfens. LC 92-25886. (Illus.). xii, 261p. 1992. 100.95 (*0-387-55793-8*) Spr-Verlag.

Market Outlook for Major Energy Products, Metals, & Minerals. World Bank Staff. LC 94-207874. 200p. 1994. pap. 60.00 (*0-8213-2765-8*, 12765) World Bank.

Market Outlook for Web Offset Printers, 1995-1996. Web Offset Association Staff. 166p. 100.00 (*0-614-25555-4*, 00BT60015) Print Indus Am.

Market Overview, 1995. (Telecom Power-2000 Ser.: Vol. 1). 1994. 2495.00 (*0-614-18332-4*, IGIC-87) Info Gatekeepers.

Market Overview, 1994. (VDT-2000 Ser.: Vol. 1). 1994. 2995.00 (*0-614-18338-3*, IGIC-92) Info Gatekeepers.

Market Panacea: Agrarian Transformation in LDCs & Former Socialist Economies. Max Spoor. 160p. 1997. pap. 26.95 (*1-85339-414-9*, Pub. by Intermed Tech) Stylus Pub VA.

Market Place. Intro. by Edward Cashin. (Illus.). 1986. 8.95 (*0-9615980-0-X*) Augusta Jr Womans.

Market Place see Collected Works of Harold Frederic

Market Place. Harold Frederic. (Collected Works of Harold Frederic). 1988. reprint ed. lib. bdg. 59.00 (*0-7812-1196-4*) Rprt Serv.

Market-Place: Text Established by Charlyne Dodge, History of the Text by Stanton Garner. Harold Frederic. LC 81-8853. (Harold Frederic Edition Ser.: Vol. 2). 497p. 1981. reprint ed. pap. 154.10 (*0-608-04619-1*, 206248800002) Bks Demand.

Market, Plan & State: The Strengths & Weaknesses of the Two World Economic Systems. Adam Zwass. LC 86-15581. 208p. (gr. 13). 1987. text 93.95 (*0-87332-396-3*) M E Sharpe.

Market-Planned Economy of Yugoslavia. Svetozar Pejovich. LC 66-18868. (Illus.). 172p. reprint ed. pap. 53.40 (*0-608-15974-3*, 203328100084) Bks Demand.

Market Planning. Didactic Systems Staff. (Simulation Game Ser.). 1972. pap. 26.25 (*0-89401-068-9*) Didactic Syst.

Market Planning. Paisley College Staff. (Marketing for Manufacturing Managers Ser.). 1989. 105.00 (*0-08-037127-2*) Elsevier.

Market Planning see Marketing for Manufacturing Managers

Market Planning Guide. 4th ed. David H. Bangs, Jr. LC 94-46609. 240p. 1994. pap. 19.95 (*0-936894-72-5*, 610003-04) Dearborn.

Market Planning Guide: Creating a Plan to Successfully Market Your Business, Products or Service. 5th ed. David H. Bangs. LC 97-44730. 224p. 1998. write for info. (*1-57410-098-X*) Dearborn.

Market Planning Guide: Gaining & Maintaining the Competitive Edge. David H. Bangs, Jr. 164p. 1989. pap. 19.95 (*0-936894-03-2*, 6100-0303) Dearborn.

Market Plays. Stephen Gray. LC 87-100501. 190 p. 1986. write for info. (*0-86852-070-5*) Ad Donker.

Market Pledge & Gender Bargain: Commercial Relations in French Farce, 1450-1550. Sharon L. Collingwood. LC 95-33323. (Studies in the Humanities: Vol. 23). XII, 209p. (C). 1997. text 44.95 (*0-8204-2869-8*) P Lang Pubng.

Market Power & Business Strategy: In Search of the Unified Organization. David J. Morris, Jr. LC 95-50742. 224p. 1996. 57.95 (*1-56720-045-1*, Quorum Bks) Greenwood.

Market Power & Price Levels in the Ethical Drug Industry. Hugh D. Walker. LC 68-64122. (Indiana University Social Science Ser.: No. 28). 271p. reprint ed. 84.10 (*0-8357-9224-2*, 201583800097) Bks Demand.

Market Power & the Economy: Industrial, Corporate, Government & Political Aspects. Ed. by Wallace C. Peterson. (C). 1988. lib. bdg. 91.00 (*0-89838-267-X*) Kluwer Academic.

Market Power, Vertical Linkages, & Government Policy: The Fish Industry in Peninsular Malaysia. Ishak H. Omar. (South-East Asian Social Science Monographs). (Illus.). 204p. 1995. text 49.95 (*967-65-3056-5*) OUP.

Market Process: Essays in Contemporary Austrian Economics. Ed. by Peter J. Boettke & David L. Prychitko. 328p. 1994. 95.00 (*1-85278-854-2*) E Elgar.

Market Process Theories, 2 vols. Ed. by Peter J. Boettke & David L. Prychitko. LC 98-10076. (International Library of Critical Writings in Economics Ser.: Vol. 91). 976p. 1998. 350.00 (*1-85898-556-0*) E Elgar.

Market Profile. Specialists in Business Information Inc. Staff. LC 99-182585. (Market Intelligence Report Ser.). 1997. write for info. (*1-56241-457-7*); write for info. (*1-56241-456-9*) FIND-SVP.

Market Profiles for Medicare Risk Contracting, 1997: North Central. 1997. pap. 310.00 (*1-57372-086-0*) HCIA.

Market Profiles for Medicare Risk Contracting, 1997: Northeastern. 1997. pap. 310.00 (*1-57372-085-2*) HCIA.

Market Profiles for Medicare Risk Contracting, 1997: Southern. 1997. pap. 310.00 (*1-57372-087-9*) HCIA.

Market Profiles for Medicare Risk Contracting, 1997: Western. 1997. pap. 310.00 (*1-57372-088-7*) HCIA.

Market Profiles, 1998. 1998. pap. 310.00 (*1-880678-79-9*) HCIA.

Market Prospects for Pulses in South Asia International & Domestic Trade. Economic Commission for Europe. (Studies in Trade & Investment: 30). 144p. 1997. pap. 15.00 (*92-1-119784-8*) UN.

Market Reform Act of 1990 Legislative History of Public Law No. 101-432: Congressional Response to the Stock Market Crash of October 1987. Ed. by Bernard D. Reams, Jr. LC 94-78778. Part 6. 1994. 125.00 (*0-89941-908-9*, 308510) W S Hein.

Market Reform in Vietnam: Building Institutions for Development. Ed. by Dennis A. Rondinelli & Jennie I. Litvak. LC 98-44555. 216p. 1999. 59.95 (*1-56720-288-8*, Quorum Bks) Greenwood.

Market Reforms in Health Care: Current Issues, New Directions, Strategic Decisions. Ed. by Jack A. Meyer. LC 82-22678. (AEI Symposia Ser.: No. 82F). 352p. reprint ed. pap. 109.20 (*0-8357-4503-1*, 203735900008) Bks Demand.

Market Reforms in Socialist Societies: Comparing China & Hungary. Ed. by Peter Van Ness. LC 88-34563. 326p. 1989. lib. bdg. 35.00 (*1-55587-096-1*) L Rienner.

Market Relations. James Butler. 224p. 1996. pap. 43.50 (*0-273-62203-X*, Pub. by F T P-H) Trans-Atl Phila.

***Market Rep: The Odyssey of a Still-Struggling Commodity Trader.** Art Collins. 230p. 2000. 24.95 (*0-934380-61-9*) Traders Pr.

Market Research. Charles Falk & Patrick Miller. 51p. 14.95 (*0-914951-15-7*) LERN.

Market Research. Sudman. 1997. 65.25 (*0-07-913670-2*) McGraw.

Market Research: A Guide to British Library Collections. 8th ed. Ed. by Michael Leydon & Leathea Lee. (Key to British Library Holdings Ser.). 320p. 1994. pap. 59.95 (*0-7123-0804-0*, Pub. by SRIS) L Erlbaum Assocs.

Market Research: A Guide to Planning, Methodology & Evaluation. Paul Hague & Peter Jackson. 224p. 1996. reprint ed. pap. 29.95 (*0-7494-1785-4*) Kogan Page Ltd.

***Market Research: A Guide To Planning, Methodology & Evaluation.** 2nd ed. Paul Hague. 1999. pap. text 25.00 (*0-7494-2917-8*) Kogan Page Ltd.

Market Research: Using Forecasting in Business. Peter Clifton et al. LC 93-118001. (Illus.). 280p. 1992. reprint ed. pap. 86.80 (*0-608-07428-4*, 206765500009) Bks Demand.

Market Research & Alternate Media. 4th ed. Jackaki. (SWC-Management Ser.). 1998. pap., wbk. ed. 11.50 (*0-324-00185-1*) Thomson Learn.

Market Research & Sales Forecast. Paisley College Staff. (Marketing for Manufacturing Managers Ser.). 1989. pap. text 84.00 (*0-08-040466-9*, Pergamon Pr) Elsevier.

Market Research & Using Microsoft Excel: A Learning Tool. 4th ed. Sounderpandian. 1998. pap. 13.50 (*0-324-00186-X*) Thomson Learn.

Market Research Council, 1958-1989. Hugh M. Beville & A. B. Blankenship. (Illus.). 144p. 1989. 60.00 (*1-877633-02-X*) Luthers.

Market Research for Shopping Centers. Intro. by Ruben A. Roca. LC 79-92292. 210p. (Orig.). 1988. pap. 28.95 (*0-685-68040-1*) Intl Coun Shop.

Market Research for Shopping Centers. Intro. by Ruben A. Roca. LC 79-92292. 210p. (Orig.). 1988. pap. 39.95 (*0-913598-11-9*, 504) Intl Coun Shop.

Market Research for the Private Investigator. Larry W. Smith. Date not set. pap. 29.95 (*1-57914-036-X*) Campbell-Smith.

Market Research in Action. Ray Kent. LC 92-47341. 224p. (C). 1993. pap. 29.95 (*0-415-06760-X*, A7683) Thomson Learn.

Market Research in Action. Ray Kent. LC 92-47341. 224p. (C). (gr. 13). 1993. pap. 75.95 (*0-415-06759-6*, A7679) Thomson Learn.

Market Research in Federal Contracting. unabridged ed. Donna S. Ireton & Ron Smith. LC 97-78421. (Illus.). ix, 198p. 1998. pap. 58.00 (*0-9662828-2-5*) Adv Systs Dev.

***Market Research in Health & Social Care.** Mike Luckovich et al. LC 99-87923. 200p. 2000. write for info. (*0-415-20754-1*); pap. write for info. (*0-415-20755-X*) Routledge.

Market Research in Travel & Tourism. Brunt. 200p. 1997. pap. 39.95 (*0-7506-3082-5*) Buttrwrth-Heinemann.

***Market Research in Travel & Tourism, Vol. 1.** Paul Brunton. 1998. pap. 34.95 (*0-7506-4347-1*) Buttrwrth-Heinemann.

***Market Research Matters: Tools & Techniques for Aligning Your Business.** Robert S. Duboff & Jim Spaeth. 224p. 2000. text 34.95 (*0-471-36005-8*) Wiley.

Market Research Problem Solve Appr. Sudman. 1997. 65.25 (*0-07-062482-8*) McGraw.

Market Research Toolbox: A Concise Guide for Beginners. Edward F. McQuarrie. (Illus.). 184p. 1996. 46.00 (*0-8039-5856-0*); pap. 19.50 (*0-8039-5857-9*) Sage.

Market Response Models: Econometric & Time-Series Analysis. Dominique M. Hanssens et al. (C). 1989. lib. bdg. 149.00 (*0-7923-9013-X*) Kluwer Academic.

Market Revolution: Jacksonian America, 1815-1846. Charles C. Sellers. 512p. (C). 1992. text 39.95 (*0-19-503889-4*) OUP.

Market Revolution: Jacksonian America, 1815-1846. Charles C. Sellers. 512p. 1994. reprint ed. pap. 19.95 (*0-19-508920-0*) OUP.

Market Revolution & Its Limits: A Price for Everything. Alan Shipman. LC 98-35365. 1999. write for info. (*0-415-15735-8*); pap. write for info. (*0-415-15736-6*) Routledge.

Market Revolution in America: Social, Political, & Religious Expressions, 1800-1880. Ed. by Melvyn Stokes & Stephen Conway. LC 95-42346. 416p. (C). 1996. text 55.00 (*0-8139-1649-6*); pap. text 22.50 (*0-8139-1650-X*) U Pr of Va.

Market Risk Amendment: Understanding the Marking-To-Model & Value-at-Risk. Dimitris N. Chorafas. LC 97-8664. 1997. 75.00 (*0-7863-1224-6*, Irwn Prfssnl) McGraw-Hill Prof.

***Market Risk Practice & Applications.** Lore & Borodovsky. 2001. 74.95 (*0-7506-5022-2*) Buttrwrth-Heinemann.

Market Rule or Public Policy? Willner. 68.95 (*1-85521-639-6*) Ashgate Pub Co.

***Market Savvy Investor: Profit from the Techniques of the Top Traders.** Howard Abell & Robert Koppel. LC 99-36071. 256p. 1999. 28.00 (*0-7931-2792-0*, 56807001) Dearborn.

***Market Scope - Category Sales Volume: The Desktop Guide to Category Sales, Vol. II.** Ed. by Lynda Gutierrez et al. 358p. 2000. 179.00 (*1-891856-13-8*) Trade Dimensns.

Market Scope, 1994. rev. ed. Ed. by Adrienne Toth et al. (Illus.). 1994. 299.00 (*0-911790-16-0*) Trade Dimensns.

***Market Scope 1999 Vol. I: Supermarket Share Volume: A Desktop Guide to Supermarket Share.** rev. ed. Ed. by Lynda Gutierrez et al. 847p. 1999. 325.00 (*1-891856-02-2*, Progress Grocer) Trade Dimensns.

***Market Scope 1999 Vol. II: Category Sales Volume: The Desktop Guide to Supermarket Share.** rev. ed. Ed. by Lynda Gutierrez et al. 353p. 1999. 179.00 (*1-891856-03-0*, Progress Grocer) Trade Dimensns.

***Market Scope 2000 - Supermarket Share Volume: The Desktop Guide to Supermarket Share, Vol. I.** Ed. by Lynda Gutierrez et al. 358p. 2000. 325.00 (*1-891856-12-X*) Trade Dimensns.

Market Segmentation: A Step-by-Step Approach to Creating Profitable Market Segments. Ian Dunbar & Malcolm B. McDonald. 271p. 1995. pap. 42.50 (*0-333-63723-2*, Pub. by Macmillan) Trans-Atl Phila.

Market Segmentation: A Step-by-Step Guide to Profitable New Business. Michael J. Croft. LC 94-9064. (Marketing for Managers Ser.). (Illus.). 176p. (C). 1994. pap. 14.99 (*0-415-09736-3*, B4747) Thomson Learn.

Market Segmentation: Conceptual & Methodological Foundations. Michel Wedel & Wagner A. Kamakura. LC 97-38555. (International Series in Quantitative Marketing: No. 7). 400p. 1997. 99.95 (*0-7923-8071-1*) Kluwer Academic.

Market Segmentation: How to Do It. How to Profit from It. 2nd ed. Malcolm McDonald & Ian Dunbar. (Illus.). 376p. 1998. pap. 64.50 (*0-333-73369-X*, Pub. by Macmillan) Trans-Atl Phila.

Market Segmentation: Using Demographics, Psychographics & Other Niche Marketing Techniques. Art Weinstein. LC 94-116089. 1993. text 32.50 (*1-55738-492-4*, Irwn Prfssnl) McGraw-Hill Prof.

Market Segmentation Workbook: Target Marketing for Marketing Managers. Sally Dibb & Lyndon Simkin. LC 95-35968. (Marketing Workbooks Ser.). 240p. (C). 1996. pap. 19.99 (*0-415-11892-1*) Thomson Learn.

***Market Share Planner.** 500p. 1999. 1000.00 (*0-86338-884-1*, Pub. by Euromonitor PLC) St Mut.

Market Share Reporter: 2000 Edition. 10th ed. 600p. 1999. 245.00 (*0-7876-2449-7*, GML00299-111973, Gale Res Intl) Gale.

Market Share Reporter, 1998. 8th ed. 1997. 235.00 (*0-7876-1460-2*, 00156651) Gale.

Market Share Reporter, 1994. 4th ed. 1993. 235.00 (*0-8103-8185-0*) Gale.

Market Share Reporter, 1995. 5th ed. Ed. by Arsen J. Darnay & Marlita A. Reddy. 720p. 1994. 235.00 (*0-8103-8954-1*) Gale.

Market Share Reporter, 1991. Ed. by Arsen J. Darnay. 624p. 1990. 235.00 (*0-8103-7872-8*, 100913-M94801) Gale.

Market Share Reporter, 1997. 7th ed. Arsen J. Darnay. 1996. 235.00 (*0-8103-0209-8*) Gale.

Market Share Reporter, 1996: An Annual Compilation of Reported Market Share Data on Companies, Products, & Services, Set. 6th ed. Ed. by Arsen J. Darnay & Robert S. Lazich. (Market Share Reporter Ser.). 725p. 1995. 235.00 (*0-8103-0208-X*, 101968) Gale.

Market Share Reporter, 1992. 2nd ed. Arsen J. Darnay. 1992. 235.00 (*0-8103-7947-3*) Gale.

Market Share Reporter, 1993. 3rd ed. 1993. 235.00 (*0-8103-8184-2*) Gale.

Market Share Reporter 1999. 9th ed. 1998. 235.00 (*0-7876-2448-9*) Gale.

Market Share Reports for Top One-Hundred Life & Fraternal Insurance Companies by State in 1993. 186p. (C). 1995. per. 125.00 (*0-89382-304-X*) Nat Assn Insurance.

Market Share Reports for Top Ten Property-Casualty Groups & Company Groups by State in 1993. 370p. (C). 1995. per. 125.00 (*0-89382-302-3*) Nat Assn Insurance.

***Market Shock.** Todd G. Buchholz. 320p. 2000. pap. 15.00 (*0-88730-950-X*, HarpBusn) HarpInfo.

Market Shock: An Agenda for the Socio-Economic Reconstruction of Central & Eastern Europe. Ed. by Jan Kregel et al. 144p. 1992. pap. text 18.95 (*0-472-08204-3*, 08204) U of Mich Pr.

Market Shock: 9 Economic & Social Upheavals That Will Shake Your Financial Future - And What to Do about Them. Todd Buchholz. LC HD30.27.B83 1999. 297p. 2000. 26.00 (*0-88730-949-6*, HarpBusn) HarpInfo.

Market Signaling: The Information Structure of Hiring & Related Processes. A. Michael Spence. LC 73-83419. (Economic Studies: No. 143). 224p. 1974. 17.95 (*0-674-54990-2*) HUP.

Market Sketchbook: 25th Anniversary Edition. anniversary ed. Victor Steinbrueck. (Illus.). 200p. 1996. pap. 17.95 (*0-295-97556-3*) U of Wash Pr.

Market Smarter, Not Harder. Pamela Truax & Monique Myron. 400p. 1996. pap. text, per. 29.95 (*0-7872-2079-5*) Kendall-Hunt.

Market Socialism: Debate among Socialists. Ed. by Bertell Ollman. LC 97-18313. 192p. (C). 1997. pap. 20.99 (*0-415-91967-3*) Routledge.

Market Socialism: Debate among Socialists. Bertell Ollman. LC 97-18313. 192p. (C). 1998. 70.00 (*0-415-91966-5*) Routledge.

Market Socialism or the Restoration of Capitalism? Ed. by Anders Aslund. (International Council for Soviet & East European Studies). (Illus.). 226p. (C). 1991. text 69.95 (*0-521-41193-9*) Cambridge U Pr.

***Market, Socialist & Mixed Economies: Comparative Policy & Performance: Chile, Costa Rica & Cuba** Carmelo Mesa-Lago. LC 99-42559. 2000. 75.00 (*0-8018-6172-1*) Johns Hopkins.

Market Solution to Economic Development in Eastern Europe. Ed. by Robert W. McGee. LC 92-16214. 332p. 1992. lib. bdg. 99.95 (*0-7734-9545-2*) E Mellen.

Market Square. Miss Read. Date not set. lib. bdg. 21.95 (*0-8488-1696-X*) Amereon Ltd.

Market Square Dog. James Herriot. (Illus.). 32p. (J). 1991. pap. 6.95 (*0-312-06567-1*) St Martin.

Market Square Dog. James Herriot. (J). 1989. 12.15 (*0-606-05453-7*, Pub. by Turtleback) Demco.

Market, State, & Community: Theoretical Foundations of Market Socialism. David Miller. 370p. 1991. pap. text 35.00 (*0-19-827864-0*) OUP.

***Market, State & Feminism: The Economics of Feminist Policy.** Graham Dawson & Linda Watson-Brown. 240p. 2000. write for info. (*1-85898-231-6*) E Elgar.

Market Strategy. Didactic Systems Staff. (Simulation Game Ser.). 1970. pap. 26.25 (*0-89401-069-7*) Didactic Syst.

Market Strategy. Didactic Systems Staff. (Simulation Game Ser.). (POR.). 1970. pap. 35.00 (*0-89401-118-9*) Didactic Syst.

Market Strategy. 3rd ed. Jean-Claude Larreche. 1998. text 52.95 incl. 3.5 hd (*0-538-86759-0*) S-W Pub.

Market Strategy & Structure. Ed. by J. M. Gee & George Norman. LC 92-10785. 1992. 80.00 (*0-7450-0940-9*) P-H.

Market Structure & Behavior. Martin Shubik & Richard Levitan. LC 79-27108. (Illus.). 267p. 1980. 37.95 (*0-674-55026-9*) HUP.

***Market Structure & Competition Policy: Game-Theoretic Approaches.** Ed. by George Norman & Jacques-Francois Thisse. (Illus.). 300p. 2001. write for info. (*0-521-78333-X*) Cambridge U Pr.

Market Structure & Foreign Trade: Increasing Returns, Imperfect Competition, & the International Economy. Elhanan Helpman & Paul R. Krugman. 288p. 1987. pap. text 18.50 (*0-262-58087-X*) MIT Pr.

Market Structure & Performance: The Empirical Research, Vol. 28. J. S. Cubbin. viii, 80p. 1988. pap. text 44.00 (*3-7186-4842-3*) Gordon & Breach.

Market Structure & Technological Change, Vol. 17. William L. Baldwin & John T. Scott. (Fundamentals of Pure & Applied Economics Ser.: Vol. 1). viii, 170p. 1987. pap. text 58.00 (*3-7186-0375-6*) Gordon & Breach.

Market Structure, Corporate Performance, & Innovative Activity. Paul A. Geroski. (Illus.). 186p. 1995. text 55.00 (*0-19-828855-7*) OUP.

Market Structure of International Oil with Special Reference to the Organization of Petroleum Exporting Countries. Hussein A. Abdel-Barr. Ed. by Stuart Bruchey. LC 78-22653. (Energy in the American Economy Ser.). (Illus.). 1979. lib. bdg. 33.95 (*0-405-11958-5*) Ayer.

Market Structure of Sports. Gerald W. Scully. 214p. 1995. pap. text 15.00 (*0-226-74395-0*) U Ch Pr.

Market Structure of Sports. Gerald W. Scully. 214p. 1997. lib. bdg. 39.95 (*0-226-74394-2*) U Ch Pr.

Market Supermarket & Hypermarket Design. Intro. by Martin M. Pegler. (Illus.). 224p. 1990. 49.95 (*0-934590-33-8*) Visual Refer.

Market Supermarket & Hypermarket Design, No. 2. Ed. by Martin M. Pegler. (Illus.). 224p. 1992. 49.95 (*0-934590-44-3*) Visual Refer.

***Market Survey of the Energy Industry 2000-2001.** Albert Thumann & Ruth Bennett Fowler. LC 99-45242. (Illus.). 85p. 2000. 68.00 (*0-88173-343-1*) Fairmont Pr.

***Market Survey of the Energy Industry 2000/20.** Albert Thumann & Ruth B. Fowler. 96p. 2000. pap. 68.00 (*0-13-019733-5*, Prentice Hall) P-H.

Market System, Structural Change & Efficient Economies: The International Trend Towards Indicative Targeting. Ed. by Bodo B. Gemper. 207p. 1989. pap. 24.95 (*0-88738-805-1*) Transaction Pubs.

Market Tells Them So: The World Bank & Economic Fundamentalism in Africa. John Mihevc. LC 95-13678. (Illus.). 320p. (C). 1996. text 25.00 (*1-85649-328-6*, Pub. by Zed Books) St Martin.

Market the Arts. Joseph V. Melillo. 1995. pap. text 26.00 (*1-884345-04-2*) ARTS Action.

Market Theory of Money. John Richard Hicks. 150p. 1989. text 48.00 (*0-19-828724-0*) OUP.

Market Timing: Market Timing. Ed. by Laurence A. Connors. (Best of the Professional Traders Journal Ser.). 56p. 1999. pap. 39.95 (*0-9650461-8-4*) M Gordon Pubng.

Market Timing for the Nineties: The Five Key Signals for When to Buy, Hold, & Sell. Stephen Leeb & Roger S. Conrad. LC 92-5433. 256p. 1993. reprint ed. 22.00 (*0-88730-641-1*, HarpBusn) HarpInfo.

Market Timing Models: Constructing, Implementing & Optimizing a Market Timing Based Investment Strategy. Richard Anderson. LC 96-20989. 240p. 1996. 50.00 (*0-7863-1099-5*, Irwn Prfssnl) McGraw-Hill Prof.

M

Market to Market. Service League of Hickory NC, Inc. Staff. 424p. (Orig.). 1983. pap. 14.50 (*0-9611356-0-3*) Serv Leag Hickory.

***Market Trading Tactics: Beating the Odds Through Technical Analysis & Money Management.** Daryl Guppy. LC 00-20411. 368p. 2000. 39.95 (*0-471-84663-5*) Wiley.

Market Transformation. Ed. by Ralph Prahl & Jeff Schlegel. 70p. 1996. pap. 20.00 (*0-8058-9933-2*) L Erlbaum Assocs.

Market Trends for Advanced Paints & Coatings. C. Broyles. 470p. 1998. 1495.00 (*0-945235-33-X*) Busn Trend.

Market Trends for Selected Chemical Products, 1965-90 & Prospects to 1995. 96p. 28.00 (*92-1-116603-9*) UN.

Market 2000: An Examination of Current Equity Market Developments, 2 vols., Set. 1996. lib. bdg. 612.99 (*0-8490-5986-0*) Gordon Pr.

Market Unbound: Unleashing Global Capitalism. Lowell L. Bryan & Diana Farrell. LC 95-50490. 268p. 1996. 27.95 (*0-471-14446-0*) Wiley.

Market Value Process: Bridging Customer & Shareholder Value. Alan S. Cleland & Albert V. Bruno. LC 96-10106. (Business & Management Ser.). 244p. 1996. 39.95 (*0-7879-0275-6*) Jossey-Bass.

***Market Values in American Higher Education: Pitfalls & Promises.** Charles W. Smith. LC 99-89685. 232p. 2000. 60.00 (*0-8476-9563-8*); pap. 22.95 (*0-8476-9564-6*) Rowman.

Market Volatility. Robert J. Shiller. (Illus.). 480p. 1990. 49.00 (*0-262-19290-X*) MIT Pr.

Market Volatility. Robert J. Shiller. 480p. 1992. reprint ed. pap. text 24.50 (*0-262-69151-5*) MIT Pr.

***Market Wedding.** Cary Fagan. (Illus.). 32p. (J). (gr. 2-5). 2000. 16.95 (*0-88776-492-4*) Tundra Bks.

Market What You Grow: A Practical Manual for Home Gardeners, Market Gardeners & Small Farmers. Ralph J. Hils, Jr. LC 89-7268. 56p. 1989. pap. 9.95 (*0-913845-02-7*) Chicot Pr.

***Market Whys & Human Wherefores: Thinking Again about Markets, Politics & People.** David Jenkins. (Illus.). 2000. pap. 28.95 (*0-304-70608-6*) Continuum.

Market Wizards. Jack D. Schwager. 458p. (C). 1989. text 24.95 (*0-13-556093-4*) P-H.

Market Wizards: Interviews with Top Traders. Jack D. Schwager. 450p. 1989. 19.95 (*0-317-02017-X*) NY Inst Finance.

Market Wizards: Interviews with Top Traders. Jack D. Schwager. LC 89-46228. 480p. 1993. reprint ed. pap. 15.00 (*0-88730-610-1*, HarpBusn) HarpInfo.

***Market Your College Degree.** Dorothy Rogers & Craig Bettinson. (Here's How Ser.). 168p. 1999. pap. 14.95 (*0-8442-2623-8*) NTC Contemp Pub Co.

Market Your Financial Plan. Kruse. Date not set. pap. text. write for info. (*0-582-19160-2*, Pub. by Addison-Wesley) Longman.

***Market Your Small Business Made E-Z.** Cohen & Reddick. 224p. 2000. pap. 17.95 (*1-56382-454-X*) E-Z Legal.

Market Yourself. Ed Cerny. 50p. (Orig.). 1987. student ed. 9.95 (*0-317-65549-3*) Cane Patch.

Market Yourself & Your Career. 2nd ed. Jeff Davidson. LC 99-20339. 1999. pap. 12.95 (*1-58062-119-8*) Adams Media.

Market Yourself for Success. Cynthia Schoeppel. 125p. 1995. pap. text 9.95 (*1-887608-00-1*) HRC Pub.

Marketable Surplus & Market Dependence: A Study of a Millet Region. M. V. Nadkarni. 176p. 1980. 24.95 (*0-940500-80-9*, Pub. by Allied Pubs) Asia Bk Corp.

Marketable Surplus & Market Dependence in a Millet Region. M. V. Nadkarnia. 176p. 1980. 24.95 (*0-318-37333-5*) Asia Bk Corp.

Marketable Treasury Securities. 1991. lib. bdg. 79.95 (*0-8490-5153-3*) Gordon Pr.

Marketer: A Simulation, 2 vols. 2nd ed. Jerald R. Smith. (C). 1987. pap. text 21.96 (*0-395-42546-8*) HM.

Marketers Collide to Media, 98-99: Media Trends, Rates & Demographics. Ed. by Rick McClintic. 304p. 1998. pap. 75.00 (*1-891204-10-6*) Adweek Direct.

Marketer's Guide to Media Vehicles, Methods & Options: A Sourcebook in Advertising & Promotion. Ann Grossman. LC 87-2473. 252p. 1987. 65.00 (*0-89930-266-1*, GMK/, Quorum Bks) Greenwood.

Marketer's Guide to Selling Products Abroad. Robert E. Weber. LC 88-11316. 276p. 1989. 65.00 (*0-89930-325-0*, WMG/, Quorum Bks) Greenwood.

Marketer's Guide to Successful Package Design. Herbert M. Meyers & Murray J. Lubliner. LC 97-50260. (Illus.). 304p. 1998. 49.95 (*0-8442-3438-9*, NTC Business Bks) NTC Contemp Pub Co.

Marketers Handbook, 1990: Pennsylvania, Vol. I. Pennsylvania State Data Center Staff. 160p. 1993. pap. text 35.00 (*0-939667-31-2*) Penn State Data Ctr.

Marketer's Handbook of Tips & Checklists. Phyllis W. Haserot. LC 96-44881. 1996. pap. write for info. (*0-9636246-7-9*) Andrews Pubns.

Marketer's Planning Guide. Eric P. Canada. (Illus.). 226p. (Orig.). 1995. wbk. ed. 30.00 (*0-9650270-0-7*) Blane Canada.

***Marketg Engrg: Comptr Asst Mktg Analy Plnng.** 2nd ed. (C). 2001. pap. text 0.00 (*0-321-03706-5*) HEPC Inc.

***Marketimg & Product Management.** Fransson. 206p. (C). 1998. pap. text 10.00 (*0-536-01269-5*) Pearson Custom.

Marketing see Branch Banking Series

Marketing. (Quick Study Academic Ser.). 4p. pap. 3.95 (*1-57222-254-9*) Barcharts.

Marketing. (Best Practices Ser.: No. 1807). 1993. 175.00 (*0-85058-807-3*) Economist Intell.

***Marketing.** 320p. 2000. write for info. (*0-273-63407-0*, Finc Times) F T P-H.

Marketing. 1992. pap. text 41.00 (*0-13-093469-0*) P-H.

Marketing. (Prentice Hall College Titles Ser.). (C). 1996. text 125.00 (*0-13-287392-3*, Macmillan Coll) P-H.

Marketing. 1992. 21.00 (*0-387-55136-0*); 23.00 (*0-387-55177-8*) Spr-Verlag.

Marketing. William O. Bearden et al. 520p. (C). 1995. text, student ed. 26.25 (*0-256-16344-8*, Irwn McGrw-H) McGrw-H Hghr Educ.

Marketing. P. D. Bennett et al. 800p. (C). 1987. text 69.25 (*0-07-004721-9*) McGraw.

Marketing. Gilbert A. Churchill & J. Paul Peter. 304p. (C). 1995. text, student ed. 26.25 (*0-256-17474-1*, Irwn McGrw-H) McGrw-H Hghr Educ.

Marketing. David W. Cravens & Robert B. Woodruff. LC 84-24357. 800p. (C). 1986. text 29.56 (*0-201-10840-2*); pap. text 80.00 (*0-201-10842-9*); student ed. 15.16 (*0-201-10843-7*) Addison-Wesley.

Marketing. Ed. by J. Eliashberg & Gary L. Lilien. LC 93-10556. (Handbook in Operations Research & Management Science Ser.: Vol. 5). 910p. 1993. 165.00 (*0-444-88957-4*, North Holland) Elsevier.

Marketing. C. B. Giles. 236p. (C). 1990. 80.00 (*0-7855-5658-3*, Pub. by Inst Pur & Supply) St Mut.

Marketing. Seth Godin. 224p. (Orig.). 1995. pap. 14.00 (*0-399-51904-1*, Perigee Bks) Berkley Pub.

Marketing. Elizabeth Hill & Terry O'Sullivan. LC 96-3877. (Modular Texts in Business & Economics Ser.). 1996. write for info. (*0-582-26255-0*, Pub. by Addison-Wesley) Longman.

Marketing, 2 vols. Ed. by Stanley Hollander & Kathleen Rassuli. (International Library of Critical Writings in Business History: Vol. 6). 1336p. 1993. 470.00 (*1-85278-601-9*) E Elgar.

Marketing. Geoff Lancaster. 258p. 1995. pap. text 37.95 (*0-7506-2055-2*) Buttrwrth-Heinemann.

Marketing. Lindgren. (C). 1995. pap. text, student ed. 54.50 (*0-03-017479-1*) Harcourt Coll Pubs.

Marketing. Carl McDaniel, Jr. & Darden. 768p. 1986. teacher ed. write for info. (*0-318-61505-3*, H0517-6); write for info. (*0-318-61506-1*, H0518-4); write for info. (*0-318-61508-8*, H1313-9); trans. write for info. (*0-318-61507-X*, H05192) P-H.

Marketing. Ed. by Jill Muehrcke. (Leadership Ser.). 90p. 1993. spiral bd. 20.00 (*0-614-07103-8*) Soc Nonprofit Org.

Marketing. J. Naylor. 1985. 60.00 (*0-85297-071-4*, Pub. by Chartered Bank) St Mut.

Marketing. Ed. by N. Naylor. (C). 1989. 40.00 (*0-85297-175-3*, Pub. by Chartered Bank) St Mut.

Marketing, 9 vols. William M. Pride. (C). Date not set. pap., teacher ed., suppl. ed. 11.96 (*0-395-72150-4*); pap., teacher ed., suppl. ed. 11.96 (*0-395-72149-0*) HM.

Marketing, 9 vols. William M. Pride. (C). 1995. text 80.76 (*0-395-73890-3*) HM.

Marketing. Carolyn Seigel. 472p. (C). 1995. text, student ed. 14.00 (*0-256-20834-4*, Irwn McGrw-H) McGrw-H Hghr Educ.

Marketing. Steven J. Skinner. (C). 1989. pap. text 3.96 (*0-395-53258-2*) HM.

Marketing. Steven J. Skinner. (C). 1990. 149.56 (*0-395-53260-4*) HM.

Marketing. Steven J. Skinner. (C). 1990. 21.96 (*0-395-53261-2*) HM.

Marketing, 2 vols. Steven J. Skinner. (C). 1993. pap., teacher ed. 5.96 (*0-395-68365-3*); pap., teacher ed., suppl. ed. 5.56 (*0-395-68366-1*) HM.

Marketing. Michael R. Solomon & Elnora W. Stuart. 736p. (C). 1996. text 86.00 (*0-205-15206-6*) Allyn.

Marketing. Solomon & Stuart. (C). 1996. pap. text, student ed. 23.80 (*0-13-619511-3*) P-H.

Marketing. Margery Steinberg. (VGM Career Planner Ser.). (Illus.). 128p. 1993. pap. 7.95 (*0-8442-8678-8*, NTC Business Bks) NTC Contemp Pub Co.

Marketing. Walter B. Wentz. (Illus.). 639p. 1979. text, teacher ed. write for info. (*0-8299-0581-2*) West Pub.

Marketing. William C. Zikmund & Michael D'Amico. LC 83-23521. 734p. (C). 1984. text 27.45 (*0-471-86493-5*) Wiley.

Marketing. William C. Zikmund & Michael D'Amico. LC 83-23521. 734p. (C). 1984. pap. text 15.00 (*0-471-80068-6*) Wiley.

Marketing. William C. Zikmund & Michael D'Amico. LC 83-23521. 734p. (C). 1984. pap. text 5.00 (*0-471-80065-1*) Wiley.

Marketing. deluxe ed. Robert D. Hisrich. (Barron's Business Library). 320p. 1990. pap. 18.95 (*0-8120-4180-1*) Barron.

Marketing. E. T. Martin. Ed. by Wilfried R. Vanhonacker. LC 83-1708. (Core Business Program Ser.). 127p. reprint ed. pap. 39.40 (*0-7837-2669-4*, 204303400006) Bks Demand.

Marketing. Ed. by A. Dale Timpe. LC 88-26838. (Art & Science of Business Management Ser.: Vol. 8). 380p. 1989. reprint ed. pap. 117.80 (*0-608-02816-9*, 206388300007) Bks Demand.

Marketing. 2nd ed. (Open Learning Super Ser.). 1991. pap. text 26.00 (*0-08-041674-8*, Pergamon Pr) Elsevier.

Marketing. 2nd ed. Courtland L. Bovee et al. LC 94-12132. (Series in Marketing). (C). 1994. text 65.25 (*0-07-006879-8*) McGraw.

Marketing. 2nd ed. Courtland L. Bovee et al. (C). 1994. pap. text, student ed. 23.75 (*0-07-006911-5*) McGraw.

Marketing. 2nd ed. Churchill. 1998. pap. 7.19 (*0-256-26617-4*) McGraw.

Marketing. 2nd ed. Griffis. 160p. 1995. pap. text, student ed. 22.80 (*0-13-125956-3*) P-H.

***Marketing.** 2nd ed. Robert D. Hisrich. LC 00-21669. (Business Library). (Illus.). 288p. 2000. pap. 14.95 (*0-7641-1404-2*) Barron.

Marketing. 2nd ed. Warren Keegan et al. LC 94-12523. 848p. 1994. text 28.80 (*0-13-016387-2*) P-H.

Marketing. 2nd ed. David Mercer. (Illus.). 576p. (C). 1996. pap. 38.95 (*0-631-19638-2*) Blackwell Pubs.

Marketing. 2nd ed. Richard L. Sandhuser. (Business Review Ser.). 480p. 1993. pap. 13.95 (*0-8120-1548-7*) Barron.

Marketing, 2 vols. 2nd ed. Steven J. Skinner. LC 93-78653. (C). 1993. text 70.76 (*0-395-62147-X*) HM.

Marketing, 2 vols. 2nd ed. Steven J. Skinner. (C). 1993. pap. text, student ed. 20.76 (*0-395-68364-5*) HM.

Marketing. 2nd ed. William C. Zikmund & Michael D'Amico. LC 85-91283. 764p. 1986. text 47.95 (*0-471-82198-5*) Wiley.

Marketing. 3rd ed. Bearden. 2000. 36.94 (*0-07-232297-7*) McGraw.

Marketing. 3rd ed. David L. Kurtz & Louis E. Boone. 800p. (C). 1986. disk. write for info. (*0-03-009978-1*) Dryden Pr.

Marketing. 3rd ed. Charles W. Lamb, Jr. et al. LC 95-2874. 1995. pap. 75.95 (*0-538-84948-7*) S-W Pub.

Marketing. 3rd ed. Matulich & Charles W. Lamb. (SB - Marketing Education Ser.). 1995. mass mkt., student ed. 22.95 (*0-538-84949-5*) S-W Pub.

***Marketing** 3rd ed. Richard Sandhusen. LC 99-16325. (Business Review Ser.). 1999. 14.95 (*0-7641-1277-5*) Barron.

Marketing. 4th ed. Armstrong. 1996. pap. text, teacher ed. write for info. (*0-13-252850-9*) Allyn.

Marketing. 4th ed. Armstrong. 1996. pap. text, teacher ed. write for info. (*0-13-252909-2*) Allyn.

Marketing. 4th ed. Beckman. (C). 1990. pap. write for info. (*0-03-998099-5*) Harcourt Coll Pubs.

Marketing. 4th ed. Ed. by G. B. Giles. (C). 1983. 55.00 (*0-7855-4083-0*, Pub. by Witherby & Co) St Mut.

***Marketing.** 4th ed. Hair & Lamb. (Swc-Marketing Ser.). (C). 1999. pap. 89.95 (*968-7529-44-X*) Sth-Wstrn College.

Marketing. 4th ed. Hair & Charles W. Lamb. LC 97-17422. (Miscellaneous/Catalogs Ser.). (C). 1997. pap. 61.50 (*0-538-87011-7*) S-W Pub.

Marketing. 4th ed. William G. Zikmund. Date not set. pap. text, teacher ed. write for info. (*0-314-01779-8*) West Pub.

Marketing. 5th ed. Berkowitz. 1996. 69.25 (*0-256-22074-3*) McGraw.

Marketing. 5th ed. Eric N. Berkowitz et al. LC 96-21378. 752p. (C). 1996. text 68.95 (*0-256-18968-4*, Irwn McGrw-H) McGrw-H Hghr Educ.

Marketing. 5th ed. William G. Zikmund. Date not set. pap. text, teacher ed. write for info. (*0-314-09215-3*) West Pub.

Marketing. 5th annot. ed. William G. Zikmund. Date not set. text. write for info. (*0-314-07170-9*) West Pub.

***Marketing.** 6th ed. Berkowitz. LC 99-30269. 1999. 65.25 (*0-07-365645-3*) McGraw.

***Marketing.** 6th ed. Eric Berkowitz et al. 350p. (C). 1999. pap., student ed. 28.75 (*0-07-365817-0*) McGrw-H Hghr Educ.

Marketing. 6th ed. Brooks. 1995. pap. text, student ed. 28.60 (*0-13-207853-8*) P-H.

Marketing. 6th ed. Richard J. Semenik & Roy T. Shaw. 480p. (C). 1988. text. write for info. (*0-538-80010-0*, SB74FA) S-W Pub.

Marketing. 6th ed. Zikmund. LC 98-18863. (Marketing Management Ser.). 1998. pap. 94.95 (*0-538-88215-8*); pap., student ed. 18.95 (*0-538-88233-6*) S-W Pub.

Marketing. 7th ed. (Prentice Hall College Titles Ser.). (C). 1996. text 125.00 (*0-13-287095-9*, Macmillan Coll) P-H.

Marketing. 7th ed. 1996. 250.00 (*0-13-242678-1*); 125.00 (*0-13-242686-2*); 125.00 (*0-13-253055-4*) P-H.

***Marketing.** 7th ed. (Prentice Hall College Titles Ser.). 1998. write for info. (*0-13-242694-3*) P-H.

Marketing. 7th ed. Evans. 1996. pap. text, teacher ed. write for info. (*0-13-242652-8*); pap. text, teacher ed. write for info. incl. trans. (*0-13-242645-5*) Allyn.

***Marketing.** 7th ed. Zikmund & D'Amico. 2000. pap., student ed. 19.75 (*0-324-02813-X*) Sth-Wstrn College.

Marketing. 7th ed. Damico Zikmund. (SWC-General Business Ser.). 2000. pap. 65.00 (*0-324-02811-3*) Thomson Learn.

Marketing, 9 vols. 9th ed. William M. Pride. LC 94-76541. (C). 1994. pap. text 43.96 (*0-395-70746-3*) HM.

Marketing. 9th ed. David P. Stone et al. 448p. (C). 1997. pap. text, student ed. 36.00 (*0-03-019029-0*) Dryden Pr.

Marketing, 10 vols. 10th ed. William M. Pride. (C). 1996. pap. text 43.96 (*0-395-78574-X*) HM.

Marketing. 11th ed. Michael J. Etzel et al. LC 96-19807. (McGraw-Hill Series in Marketing). (C). 1996. pap. text 43.00 (*0-07-018954-4*) McGraw.

Marketing. 11th ed. Michael J. Etzel et al. (C). 1996. pap., student ed. 16.25 (*0-07-061038-X*) McGraw.

Marketing. 12th ed. Etzel. 2000. teacher ed. 80.93 (*0-07-228369-6*) McGraw.

***Marketing.** 12th ed. Michael J. Etzel et al. LC 00-27784. (Series in Marketing). (Illus.). 2001. write for info. (*0-07-366031-0*) Gregg-McGraw.

Marketing. 16th ed. Richardson. 1994. 12.74 (*1-56134-282-3*) McGraw.

Marketing. 17th ed. Richardson. 1995. 12.74 (*1-56134-362-5*) McGraw.

Marketing, Vol. 3. 1991. 22.00 (*0-387-53802-X*) Spr-Verlag.

Marketing: A How-to-Do-It Manual for Librarians. Suzanne Walters. (How-to-Do-It Ser.). 112p. 1992. 45.00 (*1-55570-095-0*) Neal-Schuman.

Marketing: A Practical Guide for Fish Farmers. Susan A. Shaw. (Illus.). 96p. 1990. 34.95 (*0-85238-176-X*) Blackwell Sci.

Marketing: A Situational Approach. Walters & Bergiel. LC 97-77453. 1998. pap. 69.95 (*0-87393-430-X*) Dame Pubns.

Marketing: A Southeast Asian Perspective. Ed. by Ian McGovern. LC 95-40594. 1997. write for info. (*0-201-88910-2*) Addison-Wesley.

Marketing: A Strategic Perspective. James M. Hulbert. 186p. 1985. text 29.95 (*0-9614952-0-0*) Impact Pub NY.

Marketing: An Active Learning Approach. Elizabeth Barnes. 1997. pap. text 50.95 (*0-631-20182-3*) Blackwell Pubs.

Marketing: An Analytical Framework & Perspect. Peter Mudie. LC 96-40334. 312p. 1997. pap. 55.00 (*0-13-357757-0*) P-H.

Marketing: An Interactive Learning System. 2nd ed. Shimp. (C). 1999. pap. text. write for info. (*0-03-023651-7*) Harcourt Coll Pubs.

Marketing: An Introduction. 2nd ed. Hutt. (SB - Marketing Education Ser.). 1991. mass mkt., wbk. ed. 22.95 (*0-538-60820-X*) S-W Pub.

Marketing: An Introduction. 2nd ed. Kotler. (C). 1990. 17.67 (*0-13-556531-6*, Macmillan Coll) P-H.

***Marketing: An Introduction.** 5th ed. Told to Gary Armstrong. LC 99-35215. 596p. 1999. 64.00 (*0-13-012771-X*) S&S Trade.

***Marketing: An Introduction.** 5th ed. Simon & Schuster Staff. (C). 2000. write for info. (*0-13-013738-3*) S&S Trade.

Marketing: An Introductory Text. M. J. Baker. 503p. (C). 1985. 175.00 (*0-7855-5657-5*, Pub. by Inst Pur & Supply) St Mut.

Marketing: An Introductory Text. M. J. Baker. 503p. (C). 1988. 70.00 (*0-7855-3781-3*, Pub. by Inst Pur & Supply) St Mut.

Marketing: An Introductory Text. M. J. Baker. 503p. (C). 1989. 135.00 (*0-7855-4627-8*, Pub. by Inst Pur & Supply) St Mut.

Marketing: Basic Concepts & Decisions. William M. Pride & O. C. Ferrell. LC 83-83389. 768p. (C). 1984. disk 45.00 (*0-395-36498-1*) HM.

Marketing: Basic Concepts & Decisions. 6th ed. William M. Pride & O. C. Ferrell. 1988. write for info. (*0-318-63331-0*); trans., VHS. write for info. (*0-318-63332-9*) HM.

Marketing: Best Practices. Michael R. Czinkota. (C). 1999. text 88.50 (*0-03-021109-3*, Pub. by Harcourt Coll Pubs) Harcourt.

Marketing: Best Practices. Schaffer. (C). 1998. text 29.50 (*0-03-022927-8*, Pub. by Harcourt Coll Pubs) Harcourt.

***Marketing: Building Relationships & Loyalty with Customers.** 3rd ed. 206p. (C). 1998. 55.00 (*0-536-00561-3*) Pearson Custom.

***Marketing: Business Week Edition.** 2nd ed. (C). 1998. 57.81 (*0-07-289682-5*) McGrw-H Hghr Educ.

Marketing: Business Week Edition. 2nd ed. Churchill-Peter. 1998. 72.74 (*0-07-013748-X*) McGraw.

Marketing: Concepts & Decision Making. Charles W. Gross & Robin T. Peterson. LC 86-26676. (Illus.). 700p. (C). 1987. text 69.75 (*0-314-85242-5*); pap. text. write for info. (*0-314-34782-8*); pap. text, teacher ed. write for info. (*0-314-34781-X*); pap. text, student ed. 21.75 (*0-314-34783-6*) West Pub.

Marketing: Concepts & Strategies, 3 vols. 3rd ed. Dibb. (C). 1995. pap. text 47.16 (*0-395-79005-0*) HM.

Marketing: Concepts & Strategies, 10 vols. 10th ed. William M. Pride & O. C. Ferrell. (C). 1996. pap. text, student ed. 15.16 (*0-395-83689-1*) HM.

Marketing: Concepts & Strategies, 10 vols. 10th ed. William M. Pride & O. C. Ferrell. (C). 1997. pap. text, teacher ed. 11.96 (*0-395-83685-9*) HM.

Marketing: Connecting with Customers. Harrell et al. LC 98-27613. 640p. (C). 1998. pap. text 50.00 (*0-02-350251-7*) Macmillan.

***Marketing: Connecting with Customers Companion Website.** 1999. write for info. (*0-13-012214-9*) P-H.

Marketing: Contemporary Concepts & Practices. 4th ed. William F. Schoell & Joseph P. Guiltinan. 1989. text 53.00 (*0-205-12071-7*, H20712) Allyn.

Marketing: Contemporary Concepts & Practices. 4th ed. William F. Schoell & Joseph P. Guiltinan. 1989. student ed. 20.00 (*0-685-18771-3*, H21009) P-H.

Marketing: Contemporary Concepts & Practices. 6th ed. William F. Schoell. 762p. 1995. text 87.00 (*0-205-15602-9*) Allyn.

Marketing: Creating Customer Value. Gilbert A. Churchill & J. Paul Peter. LC 94-8479. (C). 1994. text 68.95 (*0-256-12539-2*, Irwn McGrw-H) McGrw-H Hghr Educ.

Marketing: Creating Value for Customers. 2nd ed. Gilbert A. Churchill & J. Paul Peter. LC 97-13807. 704p. (C). 1997. text 87.25 (*0-256-22877-9*, Irwn McGrw-H) McGrw-H Hghr Educ.

Marketing: Defining Dictionary. A. Dzhincharadze. 224p. (C). 1991. text 80.00 (*0-569-09911-0*, Pub. by Collets) St Mut.

***Marketing: Early Theories of Business & Management, 8 vols.** Ed. & Intro. by Morgen Witzel. (Early Theories of Business & Management Ser.). 2680p. 2000. 950.00 (*1-85506-628-9*) Thoemmes Pr.

Marketing: Everybody's Business. 2nd ed. Dransfield & Needham. 1997. 24.95 (*0-435-45025-5*) Heinemann.

Marketing: Foundations & Applications. Carolyn F. Siegel. LC 95-4179. 608p. (C). 1995. text 24.70 (*0-256-16298-0*, Irwn McGrw-H) McGrw-H Hghr Educ.

Marketing: Foundations & Applications with Irwin Multimedia Business Reference Library CD-ROM. Irwin Staff & Carolyn F. Siegel. 608p. (C). 1996. text, per. 29.70 incl. cd-rom (*0-256-24123-6*, Irwn McGrw-H) McGrw-H Hghr Educ.

Marketing: Insights & Applicatons. Frederick Crane & Stephen Grant. 512p. (C). 1997. per. 47.96 (*0-256-19520-X*, Irwn McGrw-H) McGrw-H Hghr Educ.

Marketing: Interact with CD ROM. Lindgre. (C). 1995. student ed. 88.50 (*0-03-018563-7*) Harcourt.

Marketing: Introduction. 4th ed. (Prentice Hall College Titles Ser.). 1996. 250.00 (*0-13-253188-7*) P-H.

***Marketing: Introduction.** 5th ed. (C). 2000. text. write for info. (*0-13-016530-1*) P-H.

An Asterisk (*) at the beginning of an entry indicates that the title is appearing for the first time.

Marketing: Laserdisc Guide, 2 vols. Steven J. Skinner. (C). 1993. pap. 5.96 (*0-395-69871-5*) HM.

Marketing: Lecture. 4th ed. William G. Zikmund. Date not set. pap. text, suppl. ed. write for info. (*0-314-01781-X*) West Pub.

Marketing: Marketing-Politics, Vol. 2. 1992. 31.00 (*0-387-55176-X*) Spr-Verlag.

Marketing: Mastering Your Small Business. Gloria Green & Jeff Williams. LC 95-39461. 256p. 1996. pap. 22.95 (*1-57410-020-3*, 6100-9201) Dearborn.

Marketing: Media Guide. Lindgren & Shrimp. (C). 1995. pap. text, teacher ed., student ed. 28.00 (*0-03-017572-0*) Harcourt Coll Pubs.

Marketing: Modules. 5th ed. William G. Zikmund. Date not set. pap. text. write for info. (*0-314-09008-8*) West Pub.

Marketing: New Homes. David F. Parker. LC 98-52745. 1999. write for info. (*0-86718-447-7*) Home Builder.

***Marketing: One Color Reprint.** 7th ed. Joel Evans & Bary Berman. 1999. 92.00 (*0-13-017546-3*, Prentice Hall) P-H.

Marketing: Practices & Principles. 5th ed. Ralph Mason et al. Ed. by Richard Lynch. 1995. text 38.25 (*0-02-635601-5*) Glencoe.

Marketing: Principles & Perspectives. William O. Bearden et al. LC 94-31421. (Marketing Ser.). 631p. (C). 1994. text 68.95 (*0-256-11319-X*, Irwn Prfssnl) McGraw-Hill Prof.

Marketing: Principles & Perspectives. 2nd ed. William Bearden. (C). 1997. text 12.25 (*0-256-26953-X*) McGraw.

Marketing: Principles & Practice. Tom Cannon. 512p. 1998. pap. 27.95 (*0-304-70294-3*) Continuum.

Marketing: Principles & Practice. 5th ed. Tom Cannon. 512p. 1998. 60.00 (*0-304-70293-5*) Continuum.

Marketing: Principles & Practices. Fred C. Allvine. 868p. (C). 1987. text 66.00 (*0-15-555101-9*) Dryden Pr.

***Marketing: Real People & Real Choices.** 2nd ed. Michael R. Solomon. LC 99-30606. 580p. 1999. 93.33 (*0-13-021304-7*) P-H.

Marketing: Real People, Real Choices. Michael R. Solomon & Elnora W. Stuart. 1p. (C). 1997. pap. text 83.60 (*0-13-795683-5*) P-H.

***Marketing: Real People, Real Choices.** 2nd ed. 1999. text, teacher ed. write for info. (*0-13-013610-7*) P-H.

***Marketing: Real People, Real Choices.** 2nd ed. 2000. write for info. (*0-13-031959-7*) P-H.

Marketing: Relationships, Quality, & Value. William G. Nickels & Marian B. Wood. LC 96-60599. 768p. 1996. text 58.20 (*1-57259-144-7*) Worth.

Marketing: Relationships, Quality, & Value. William G. Nickels & Marian B. Wood. 1997. pap. text, student ed. 12.80 (*1-57259-311-3*) Worth.

Marketing: Relationships, Quality, Value - Instructor's Manual, Vol. I. Gayle M. Ross & William G. Nickels. 1997. teacher ed. write for info. (*1-57259-315-6*) Worth.

Marketing: Relationships, Quality, Value - Instructor's Manual, Vol. II. Gayle M. Ross & William G. Nickels. 1997. teacher ed. write for info. (*1-57259-358-X*) Worth.

Marketing: The Encyclopedic Dictionary. David Mercer. LC 98-26085. 576p. 1998. 69.95 (*0-631-19107-0*); pap. 39.95 (*0-631-21126-8*) Blackwell Pubs.

Marketing: Trivia. 5th ed. William G. Zikmund. Date not set. pap. text. write for info. (*0-314-09483-0*) West Pub.

Marketing: Wall Street Journal Readings. 4th ed. Eric N. Berkowitz et al. (C). 1999. text, student ed. 73.95 (*0-256-18179-9*, Irwn McGrw-H) McGrw-H Hghr Educ.

Marketing 1999-2000 Edition. 21st ed. Richardson. 1998. pap., student ed. 16.56 (*0-07-041175-1*) McGraw.

Marketing a Country: Promotion As a Tool for Attracting Foreign Investment. Louis T. Wells, Jr. & Alvin G. Wint. (Foreign Investment Advisory Service Occasional Paper Ser.). 80p. 1990. pap. 22.00 (*0-8213-1539-0*, 11539) World Bank.

Marketing Across Cultures. 3rd ed. Jean-Claude Usunier. LC 99-25726. 600p. 2000. 46.00 (*0-13-010668-2*) P-H.

Marketing Across Cultures: A Cultural Approach. 2nd ed. Jean-Claude Usunier. (College Titles Ser.). 584p. (C). 1996. pap. 46.00 (*0-13-236175-2*, Macmillan Coll) P-H.

Marketing Action. Peterson. Date not set. pap. text, teacher ed. write for info. (*0-314-36530-3*) West Pub.

Marketing Advantage: How to Get & Keep the Clients You Want. Ed. by Colette P. Nassutti. LC 93-47895. 1993. 85.00 (*0-87051-146-7*) Am Inst CPA.

Marketing Advantage II: New Ideas on Getting & Keeping Clients. PCPS Staff. LC 98-20402. 200p. 1998. pap. 43.95 (*0-87051-225-0*, 090437) Am Inst CPA.

Marketing Aesthetics. Alex Simonson & Bernd H. Schmitt. LC 97-9426. 368p. 1997. 29.50 (*0-684-82655-0*) Free Pr.

Marketing Africa's High-Value Foods: Comparative Experiences of an Emergent Private Sector. World Bank Staff (Jaffee). 512p. 1994. pap. text, per. 44.95 (*0-8403-9760-7*) Kendall-Hunt.

Marketing Agricultural Commodities. Wayne Purcell. Ed. by Ralph Reynold & H. Evan Drummond. (Farm Business Management Ser.). (Illus.). (Orig.). 1995. pap. text, student ed. 25.95 (*0-86691-219-3*, FBM14601W) Deere & Co.

Marketing Agricultural Commodities. Wayne Purcell. Ed. by Ralph Reynold & H. Evan Drummond. (Farm Business Management Ser.). (Illus.). (Orig.). (C). 1995. pap. text, teacher ed. 44.95 (*0-86691-218-5*, FBM14501T) Deere & Co.

Marketing Allied Health Educational Programs: Eight Low Cost Steps You Need to Know. Patricia L. Hassel & David R. Palmer. LC 92-22068. 1992. 39.95 (*1-881566-10-2*) Eagle Pub & Comms.

Marketing Ambulatory Care Services. Ed. by William J. Winston. LC 84-27902. (Health Marketing Quarterly Ser.: Vol. 2, Nos. 2 & 3). 209p. 1985. text 6.95 (*0-86656-387-3*); pap. text 24.95 (*0-86656-448-9*) Haworth Pr.

Marketing an Orthopedic Practice. John B. Pinto. 160p. (Orig.). 1991. pap. 19.95 (*1-879952-02-5*) Inst Spine.

Marketing Analysis & Decision Making: Text & Cases with Spreadsheets. 2nd ed. Darral Clarke. 480p. (C). 1992. teacher ed. write for info. (*0-89426-231-9*) Course Tech.

Marketing & Advertising For The Salon. Henry Gambino. (Salon Business Ser.). 368p. 1996. 31.95 (*1-56253-262-6*) Thomson Learn.

Marketing & Business Planning with the IBM PCs: A Guide to the Productive Use of Personal Computers for Business & Marketing Professionals. Michael V. Laric & M. Ronald Stiff. (Illus.). 224p. 1985. pap. 16.95 (*0-13-557067-0*) P-H.

Marketing & Communications Strategies: An Action Plan for Camps. American Camping Association Staff. 124p. 1991. pap. 250.00 (*0-87603-130-0*) Am Camping.

Marketing & Consumer Behavior Research in the Public Interest. Ronald P. Hill. LC 95-36413. 340p. 1995. 56.00 (*0-8039-7190-7*); pap. 26.00 (*0-8039-7191-5*) Sage.

Marketing & Design Management. Margaret Bruce & Rachel Cooper. 256p. 1996. pap. 59.00 (*0-415-12008-X*) Thomson Learn.

Marketing & Design Management. Margaret Bruce & Rachel Cooper. 256p. 1997. pap. 19.99 (*1-86152-173-1*) Thomson Learn.

Marketing & Development for Community Colleges. Ed. by G. Jeremiah Ryan & Nanette J. Smith. 252p. 1989. 20.00 (*0-89964-270-5*, 23901) Coun Adv & Supp Ed.

Marketing & Distribution in the Third World. Ronan Paddison. (Routledge Introductions to Development Ser.). (Illus.). 128p. (C). 1998. pap. 14.99 (*0-415-05583-0*) Routledge.

Marketing & Distributive Education. Jack Rudman. (National Teacher Examination Ser.: NT-46). 1994. pap. 23.95 (*0-8373-8466-4*) Natl Learn.

Marketing & Economic Development. Erdener Kaynak. LC 86-91548. 222p. 1986. 55.00 (*0-275-90003-7*, C0003, Praeger Pubs) Greenwood.

Marketing & Entrepreneurship: Research Ideas & Opportunities. Ed. by Gerald E. Hills. LC 93-6763. 352p. 1994. 69.50 (*0-89930-765-5*, HMF/, Quorum Bks) Greenwood.

Marketing & Entrepreneurship in SME's: An Innovative Approach. David Carson. 296p. 1996. pap. text 35.00 (*0-13-150970-5*) P-H.

***Marketing & Essential Math Skills.** 4th ed. Stull. 1998. pap., teacher ed. 21.00 (*0-538-68113-6*) Sth-Wstrn College.

***Marketing & Feminism: Current Issues & Research.** Miriam Catterall et al. LC 00-20069. (Interpretive Marketing Research Ser.). 2000. pap. write for info. (*0-415-21973-6*) Routledge.

Marketing & Finance: Working the Interface. David Walters & Michael Halliday. 304p. 1998. pap. 55.00 (*1-86448-426-8*, Pub. by Allen & Unwin Pty) Paul & Co Pubs.

Marketing & Healthcare Organizations. Colin Gilligan & Robin Lowe. LC 95-24339. 1995. write for info. (*1-85775-190-6*, Radcliffe Med Pr) Scovill Paterson.

Marketing & Information Technology. John O'Connor & Eamonn Galvin. 320p. 1997. pap. 62.50 (*0-273-62644-2*, Pub. by Pitman Pub) Trans-Atl Phila.

Marketing & Maintainig a Family Law Mediation Practice. Paula James. LC 99-208375. 179p. 1994. write for info. (*1-879590-67-0*) Amer Law Media.

***Marketing & Management Maximizer for Your: Investing Practice.** Jack Murray. (Private Investigation Ser.). (Illus.). 89p. 1999. spiral bd. 38.00 (*1-891247-33-6*) Thomas Investigative.

Marketing & Managing Local Enterprise Zones. Mia Purcell. Ed. by Andrea Kailo. 32p. (Orig.). 1985. pap. 16.00 (*0-317-04905-4*) Natl Coun Econ Dev.

Marketing & Managing Services. Shugan. 1997. text. write for info. (*0-256-13190-2*, Irwn McGrw-H) McGrw-H Hghr Educ.

Marketing & Managing Your Refractive Surgery Venture. Mark S. Danzo. (Illus.). 158p. 1997. pap. write for info. (*1-929196-07-5*) Am Opthlmc Admin.

Marketing & Marketing Game. William O. Bearden et al. (C). 1994. text 87.90 (*0-256-19380-0*, Irwn McGrw-H) McGrw-H Hghr Educ.

Marketing & Modernity. Marianne Lien. LC 98-119929. 1997. pap. 19.50 (*1-85973-996-2*, Pub. by Berg Pubs) NYU Pr.

Marketing & Modernity. Miller. LC 98-119929. 1997. 55.00 (*1-85973-991-1*, Pub. by Berg Pubs) NYU Pr.

***Marketing & Multicultural Diversity.** Ed. by C. P. Rao. 2001. write for info. (*1-56720-074-5*) Greenwood.

Marketing & Preventive Health Care: Interdisciplinary & Interorganizational Perspectives. Ed. by Philip D. Cooper et al. LC 77-25849. (American Marketing Association, Proceedings Ser.). 142p. reprint ed. pap. 44.10 (*0-608-13822-3*, 201777900008) Bks Demand.

Marketing & Pricing of Milk & Dairy Products in the United States. Kenneth W. Bailey. LC 97-5474. (Illus.). 296p. 1997. 39.95 (*0-8138-2750-7*) Iowa St U Pr.

***Marketing & Product Managemt.** 2nd ed. Fransson & Chase Staff. 222p. 1999. pap. text 12.00 (*0-536-02825-7*) Pearson Custom.

Marketing & Production Decisions. Tinniswood. 1992. pap. text. write for info. (*0-582-06772-3*, Pub. by Addison-Wesley) Longman.

Marketing & Promoting Floral Products. Redbook Florist Services Educational Advisory Comm. LC 92-85370. (Encycloflora Ser.). (Illus.). 468p. (Orig.). 1993. pap. text 39.95 (*1-56963-018-6*) Redbk Florist.

Marketing & Promotion for Design Professionals. John P. Bachner & Naresh K. Khosla. LC 76-57975. (Illus.). 368p. reprint ed. pap. 114.10 (*0-608-11328-X*, 201490200094) Bks Demand.

Marketing & Promotion from A to Z: For Home Fashions Retailers & Interior Designers. Kay L. Pegram. 157p. (Orig.). 1992. pap. 22.95 (*0-9634747-0-7*) Kaymar Bks.

Marketing & Public Policy Proceedings, Vol. 6. Ed. by Ronald P. Hill & C. Ray Taylor. 212p. 1996. pap. 45.00 (*0-87757-260-7*) Am Mktg.

Marketing & Public Policy Proceedings, Vol. 7. Ed. by Easwar Iyer & George Milne. 99p. 1997. pap. 45.00 (*0-87757-265-8*) Am Mktg.

***Marketing & Public Policy Proceedings, Vol. 8.** Ed. by Alan Andreasen et al. 117p. 1998. pap. 45.00 (*0-87757-272-0*) Am Mktg.

Marketing & Public Relations for Libraries. Cosette N. Kies. LC 86-20219. (Library Administration Ser.: No. 10). 214p. 1987. 24.00 (*0-8108-1925-2*) Scarecrow.

***Marketing & Public Relations Handbook for Museums, Galleries & Heritage Attractions.** Ed. by Sue Rungard & Ylva French. 304p. 2000. pap. 44.95 (*0-7425-0407-7*) AltaMira Pr.

Marketing & Retail Pharmacy. Colin Gilligan et al. LC 97-28563. 1997. write for info. (*1-85775-202-3*, Radcliffe Med Pr) Scovill Paterson.

Marketing & Sales Across Cultures. Tim Walker & Danielle Walker. (Management Booklets Ser.). Date not set. write for info. (*1-882390-88-1*) Princeton Trng.

Marketing & Sales Career Directory. 4th ed. R. Fry. 1992. 17.95 (*0-8103-9430-8*) Visible Ink Pr.

Marketing & Sales Career Directory. 4th ed. Ed. by Bradley J. Morgan. (Career Advisor Ser.). 300p. 1992. 39.00 (*0-8103-5609-0*, 101581) Visible Ink Pr.

Marketing & Selling. Nebsm. 88p. pap. text. write for info. (*0-7506-3299-2*) Buttrwrth-Heinemann.

Marketing & Selling Architecture & Engineering Services: The Complete Guide to Creating Your Own Program. Scott C. Gladden & Arnold Olitt. 120p. 1996. pap. 30.00 (*0-7844-0100-4*) Am Soc Civil Eng.

***Marketing & Selling Black & White Portrait Photography.** Helen T. Boursier. (Illus.). 128p. 2000. pap. 29.95 (*1-58428-015-8*) Amherst Media.

Marketing & Selling Design Services: The Designer - Client Relationship. Mary V. Knackstedt. 1993. text 36.95 (*0-442-01073-7*, VNR) Wiley.

Marketing & Selling the Travel Product. James Burke & Barry Resnick. 332p. 1991. pap., teacher ed. write for info. (*0-538-70278-8*) S-W Pub.

Marketing & Selling the Travel Product. Resnick. (Hospitality, Travel & Tourism Ser.). (C). 1990. mass mkt. 36.50 (*0-538-70277-X*) S-W Pub.

Marketing & Selling the Travel Product. 2nd ed. Burke. (Hospitality, Travel & Tourism Ser.). 1998. teacher ed. 12.00 (*0-8273-7649-9*) Delmar.

Marketing & Selling the Travel Product. 2nd ed. Burke. LC 99-43258. (Hospitality, Travel & Tourism Ser.). (C). 1999. pap. 56.95 (*0-8273-7648-0*) Delmar.

Marketing & Selling to Associations & Nonprofits in the New Millennium: A Service Providers Guide to Understanding a Changing Association Marketplace. Stephen C. Carey. 75p. 1999. pap. text 38.50 (*0-9666966-0-3*) Assn Mktg Mgmt Res.

Marketing & Selling Variable & Fixed Annuities: A Guide for the Financial Professional. Bruce F. Wells. 1995. 50.00 (*1-55738-909-8*, Irwn Prfssnl) McGraw-Hill Prof.

Marketing & Selling Your Accent Reduction Programs: How to Find, & Contact Accented Speakers & Sell Your Program. Daniel P. Dato. LC 92-71984. 121p. 1992. pap. text 19.95 (*1-881336-00-X*) Bilingual Cl.

Marketing & Selling Your Film Around the World: A Guide for Independent Filmmakers. John Durie et al. (Illus.). 260p. 1998. pap. 22.95 (*1-879505-43-6*) Silman James Pr.

Marketing & Semiotics: New Directions in the Study of Signs for Sale. Ed. by Jean Umiker-Sebeok. (Approaches to Semiotics Ser.: No. 77). 556p. (C). 1988. text 161.55 (*0-89925-276-1*) Mouton.

Marketing & Semiotics: Selected Papers from the Copenhagen Symposium. Ed. by H. Hartvig Larsen et al. 240p. (Orig.). 1991. pap. 110.00 (*87-17-03591-0*) Coronet Bks.

Marketing & Social Structure in Rural China. G. William Skinner. 399p. 1993. reprint ed. pap. 10.00 (*0-614-97993-5*) Assn Asian Studies.

Marketing & the Black Consumer: An Annotated Bibliography. Ed. by Thomas E. Barry et al. LC 76-3722. (American Marketing Association Bibliography Ser.: No. 22). 52p. reprint ed. pap. 30.00 (*0-608-11537-1*, 201462200093) Bks Demand.

Marketing & the Laws. M. A. Sujan & H. Sujan. 1994. write for info. (*81-224-0634-3*, Pub. by Wiley Estrn) Franklin.

Marketing & the Library. Ed. by Gary T. Ford. LC 84-668. (Journal of Library Administration: Vol. 4, No. 4). 80p. 1984. text 39.95 (*0-86656-307-5*) Haworth Pr.

Marketing & the Poor. Linda F. Alwitt & Thomas Donley. (Illus.). 320p. 1996. 46.00 (*0-8039-7211-3*); pap. 19.95 (*0-8039-7212-1*) Sage.

Marketing & the Quality of Life. Ed. by Fred D. Reynolds & Hiram C. Barksdale. LC 78-17765. (American Marketing Association, Proceedings Ser.). 88p. reprint ed. pap. 30.00 (*0-608-11941-5*, 202336200032) Bks Demand.

Marketing & the Quality-of-Life Interface. Ed. by A. Coskun Samli. LC 86-8118. 366p. 1987. 79.50 (*0-89930-124-X*, SMQ/, Quorum Bks) Greenwood.

Marketing & Trade of Forest Produce. D. N. Tewari. LC 95-910425. 1995. pap. 99.00 (*81-7089-228-7*, Pub. by Intl Bk Distr) St Mut.

***Marketing &Selling Construction Services.** Smyth Hedley. LC 99-37765. 1999. write for info. (*0-632-04987-1*) Blackwell Sci.

Marketing Apocalypse: Eschatology, Escapology, & the Illusion of the End. Ed. by Stephen Brown & Jim Bell. 314p. (C). 1997. 90.00 (*0-415-14822-7*) Routledge.

Marketing Apocalypse: Eschatology, Escapology, & the Illusion of the End. Stephen Brown et al. LC 97-16140. 312p. (C). 1998. pap. 29.99 (*0-415-17356-6*) Routledge.

Marketing Approach to Physician Recruitment: Haworth Marketing Resources. James O. Hacker et al. LC 93-41669. (Illus.). 130p. 1995. pap. 14.95 (*1-56024-899-8*) Haworth Pr.

Marketing Approach to Physician Recruitment: Haworth Marketing Resources. James O. Hacker et al. LC 93-41669. (Illus.). 130p. 1995. lib. bdg. 39.95 (*1-56024-898-X*) Haworth Pr.

Marketing Architectural & Engineering Services. 2nd ed. Weld Coxe. LC 89-31795. (Illus.). 310p. (C). 1990. reprint ed. lib. bdg. 39.50 (*0-89464-377-0*) Krieger.

Marketing Architectural Services for Health Care. 1996. pap. 10.50 (*1-55835-003-9*, N303) AIA Press.

Marketing As Social Behavior: A General Systems Theory. M. Joseph Sirgy. LC 84-2150. 284p. 1984. 45.00 (*0-275-91270-1*, C1270, Praeger Pubs) Greenwood.

Marketing Aspects of International Business. Gerald M. Hampton & Aart Van Gent. 1983. lib. bdg. 97.50 (*0-89838-136-3*) Kluwer Academic.

Marketing Audit Checklists: A Guide to Effective Marketing Resource Realization. 2nd rev. ed. Aubrey Wilson. LC 92-20723. (Marketing for Professionals Ser.). 1992. write for info. (*0-07-707760-1*) McGraw.

Marketing Bank Services see Installment Credit Series

Marketing Basics for Designers: A Sourcebook of Strategies & Ideas. Jane D. Martin & Nancy Knoohuizen. LC 95-13176. 272p. 1995. 45.00 (*0-471-11871-0*) Wiley.

Marketing Beef in Japan. William A. Kerr et al. LC 93-23224. (Illus.). 204p. 1994. lib. bdg. 69.95 (*1-56022-044-9*) Haworth Pr.

Marketing Behavior & Executive Action. Wroe Alderson. Ed. by Henry Assael. LC 78-222. (Century of Marketing Ser.). 1979. reprint ed. lib. bdg. 44.95 (*0-405-11162-2*) Ayer.

Marketing Behaviour in Asia. Pecotich. 1999. pap. 34.95 (*0-07-470480-X*) McGraw.

Marketing Blueprint. Christine T. Ennew. LC 92-32455. 208p. 1993. pap. 37.95 (*0-631-18715-4*) Blackwell Pubs.

Marketing Boards in Tropical Africa. Kwame Arhin et al. (Monographs from the African Studies Centre, Leiden). (Illus.). 350p. 1985. 69.50 (*0-7103-0109-X*) Routledge.

***Marketing Book.** 4th ed. Ed. by Michael J. Baker. 718p. 1999. pap. text 49.95 (*0-7506-4114-2*) Buttrwrth-Heinemann.

Marketing Booze to Blacks. George A. Hacker & Ronald K. Collins. 69p. 1987. pap. 4.95 (*0-89329-015-7*) Ctr Sci Public.

Marketing Builder Express. Jian Software Staff. (SS - Marketing Management Ser.). 1997. mass mkt. 16.95 (*0-538-87574-7*) S-W Pub.

Marketing Building. Jian. (C). 1998. 30.95 (*0-13-095499-3*, Macmillan Coll) P-H.

Marketing by Association. Tracy Schneider. 40p. 1993. 7.50 (*0-9638712-1-8*) TLS Mktg.

Marketing by Design: Creating the Competitive Image: Merchandising in the 90s. D. K. Holland. (Illus.). 256p. 1996. 49.99 (*1-56496-109-5*) Rockport Pubs.

Marketing by Matrix: 100 Practical Ways to Improve Your Strategic & Tactical Marketing. Malcolm McDonald & John W. Leppard. LC 92-161964. (Illus.). 174p. 1992. reprint ed. pap. 54.00 (*0-608-07967-7*, 206793900012) Bks Demand.

***Marketing by Menu, 3E.** 3rd ed. Nancy L. Scanlon. LC 98-8155. 272p. 1999. 44.95 (*0-471-25330-8*) Wiley.

Marketing Campaigns. Ros Jay. LC 98-209338. (ITBP PROFESSIONAL). 256p. 1998. pap. 24.95 (*1-86152-245-2*) Thomson Learn.

Marketing (Canadian) Eric Berkowitz & Roger Kerin. 344p. (C). 1991. student ed., per. 19.95 (*0-256-10229-5*, Irwn McGrw-H) McGrw-H Hghr Educ.

Marketing, Canadian. 2nd ed. Eric N. Berkowitz et al. 800p. (C). 1995. text 48.95 (*0-256-12088-9*, Irwn McGrw-H) McGrw-H Hghr Educ.

Marketing Career Guide. William O. Bearden et al. 160p. (C). 1995. text 10.25 (*0-256-18369-4*, Irwn McGrw-H) McGrw-H Hghr Educ.

Marketing Case Studies: How to Tackle Them, How To. Massingham & Lancaster. 214p. 1965. pap. 34.95 (*0-7506-2011-0*) Buttrwrth-Heinemann.

Marketing Case Studies & a Training Curriculum for SME Managers in the APEC Region. Education Forum (Asia Pacific Economic Cooperation). Staff. LC 97-945713. iii, 182 p. 1996. write for info. (*981-00-8119-7*) AgBe Pub.

Marketing Casebase: Short Examples of Marketing Practice. Brian MacNamee & Ray MacDonnell. LC 94-31229. 240p. (C). 1995. pap. 14.99 (*0-415-10321-5*, C0029) Thomson Learn.

Marketing Casebook. Sally Dibb & Lyndon Simkin. 150p. (C). 1993. pap., teacher ed. 62.95 (*0-415-10513-7*) Thomson Learn.

***Marketing Casebook.** 2nd ed. 600p. 2000. write for info. (*0-273-63896-3*) F T P H.

Marketing Casebook: Cases & Concepts. Sally Dibb & Lyndon Simkin. LC 93-9645. 356p. (C). 1993. pap. 29.95 (*0-415-08950-6*) Thomson Learn.

M

***Marketing Casebook: Cases & Concepts.** 2nd ed. Dibb & Simkin. 2000. pap. write for info. (*1-86152-624-5*, Pub. by ITBP) Thomson Learn.

Marketing Casebook: Keynote Cases. Dibb & Simkin. 1993. pap. write for info. (*1-86152-471-4*, Pub. by ITBP) Thomson Learn.

Marketing Cases, 9 vols. 9th ed. William M. Pride. (C). 1988. pap. text 31.96 (*0-395-49594-6*) HM.

Marketing CD- Rom. John Shimp. LC 95-72013. (C). 1995. bds. 50.00 (*0-03-098916-7*) Harcourt Coll Pubs.

Marketing Challenge. Laura Mazur & Annik Hogg. LC 93-15369. 298p. (C). 1993. 44.00 (*0-201-63191-1*) Addison-Wesley.

Marketing Challenge of 1992. John A. Quelch et al. (Illus.). 350p. (C). 1989. pap. text 21.50 (*0-201-51562-8*) Addison-Wesley.

Marketing Challenges: Cases & Exercises. 3rd ed. Ed. by Christopher H. Lovelock & Charles B. Weinberg. LC 92-38991. (Marketing Ser.). 1993. write for info. (*0-07-911577-2*) McGraw.

***Marketing Challenges in the Transition Economies of Europe, Baltic States & the CIS.** Ed. by Gopalkrishnan R. Iyer & Lance A. Masters. LC 99-51400. (Journal of East-West Business Monograph Ser.: Vol. 5, Nos. 1/2). 221p. 1999. 59.95 (*0-7890-0961-7*, Intl Busn Pr) Haworth Pr.

***Marketing Challenges in the Transition Economies of Europe, Baltic States & the CIS.** Ed. by Gopalkrishnan R. Iyer & Lance A. Masters. LC 99-51400. (Journal of East-West Business Monograph Ser.: Vol. 5, Nos. 1/2). 221p. (C). 1999. pap. text 39.95 (*0-7890-0979-X*, Intl Busn Pr) Haworth Pr.

Marketing Channel Development & Management. Russell W. McCalley. LC 92-15768. 300p. 1992. 62.95 (*0-89930-780-9*, MKB, Quorum Bks) Greenwood.

Marketing Channel Management: An Instructor's Manual. Russell W. McCalley. 80p. 1996. pap., teacher ed. 5.95 (*0-275-95547-8*, Praeger Pubs) Greenwood.

Marketing Channel Management: People, Products, Programs & Markets. Russell W. McCalley. LC 95-26517. 288p. 1996. text 38.00 (*0-275-95439-0*, Praeger Pubs) Greenwood.

Marketing Channels. Barry Berman. LC 95-36680. 736p. 1995. text 93.95 (*0-471-57748-0*) Wiley.

Marketing Channels. 2nd ed. Pelton. 1999. 67.50 (*0-07-289512-8*) McGraw.

Marketing Channels. 5th ed. Rosenbloom. (C). 1995. pap. text, teacher ed. 49.75 (*0-03-010493-9*) Harcourt Coll Pubs.

Marketing Channels. 5th ed. Louis W. Stern & Adel I. El-Ansary. LC 95-36321. 576p. 1995. 97.00 (*0-13-205865-0*, Pub. by P-H) S&S Trade.

***Marketing Channels.** 6th ed. Anne T. Coughlan. LC 00-55058. 2000. write for info. (*0-13-012772-8*) P-H.

Marketing Channels. 6th ed. Rosenbloom. LC 97-78266. (C). 1998. text 91.50 (*0-03-024482-X*, Pub. by Harcourt Coll Pubs); text, teacher ed. 66.50 (*0-03-024786-1*) Harcourt Coll Pubs.

Marketing Channels: A Management View. 5th ed. Bert Rosenbloom. LC 94-70288. 774p. (C). 1994. text 91.00 (*0-03-097736-3*) Dryden Pr.

Marketing Channels: Domestic & International Perspectives. Ed. by Michael G. Harvey & Robert F. Lusch. 1982. 15.00 (*0-317-02578-3*) U OK Ctr Econ.

Marketing Channels Text & Software. Berman. 1997. text 65.00 (*0-471-25507-6*) Wiley.

Marketing Child Care Programs: Why & How. Ed. by Mary Frank. LC 84-27948. (Journal of Children in Contemporary Society: Vol. 17, No. 2). 107p. 1985. text 39.95 (*0-86656-330-X*) Haworth Pr.

Marketing Classics 25th Anniversary: A Selection of Influential Articles. 8th anniversary ed. Ben M. Enis et al. LC 94-11406. 578p. (C). 1994. pap. text 57.00 (*0-205-15988-5*) Allyn.

***Marketing Communication.** Duncan. 2001. 63.74 (*0-256-21476-X*) McGraw.

***Marketing Communications.** (C). 2000. write for info. (*0-13-016103-9*) Prntice Hall Bks.

Marketing Communications. Jim Blythe. LC 99-25715. 356p. 2000. 42.50 (*0-273-63960-9*) F T P H.

Marketing Communications. 2nd ed. Edgar Crane. LC 72-4505. (Marketing Ser.). 510p. (C). reprint ed. 158.10 (*0-8357-9929-8*, 201311600084) Bks Demand.

Marketing Communications: A Bridge to Better Sales for Molders & Moldmakers. Clare Goldsberry. LC 99-17340. (IMM Book Club Strategies for Molders & Moldmakers Ser.). (Illus.). 99p. 1999. pap. 29.95 (*1-893677-02-8*) Abby Communs.

Marketing Communications: An Integrated Approach. 2nd ed. Paul Smith. 450p. 1998. pap. 40.00 (*0-7494-2699-3*) Kogan Page Ltd.

***Marketing Communications: Contexts, Contents & Strategies.** 2nd ed. Chris Fill. LC 98-29818. 560p. 1999. pap. text 37.95 (*0-13-010229-6*) P-H.

***Marketing Communications: Cornerstones, Instruments, & Applications.** Patrick de Pelsmacker et al. LC 99-49461. 472p. 2000. write for info. (*0-273-63871-8*) F T P H.

Marketing Communications: From Fundamentals to Strategies. Michael Rothschild. LC 86-80486. (Illus.). 765p. (C). 1987. text 68.76 (*0-669-07210-9*) HM Trade Div.

Marketing Communications: From Fundamentals to Strategies. Michael Rothschild. LC 86-80486. (Illus.). 765p. (C). 2000. pap. text, teacher ed. 2.66 (*0-669-07209-5*) HM Trade Div.

Marketing Communications: Planning, Implementation & Control. Gilligan. 320p. 1999. pap. text 32.95 (*0-7506-1923-6*) Buttrwrth-Heinemann.

***Marketing Communications: Principles & Practice.** Philip J. Kitchen. 1998. pap. text 19.99 (*1-86152-196-0*) Thomson Learn.

***Marketing Communications Classics.** David Arnott & Maureen Fitzgerald. 256p. 1999. pap. 21.99 (*1-86152-507-9*) ITBP.

Marketing Communications for Solicitors: A Practical Guide to Promoting Your Firm. Mark Oglesby. 247p. 1995. pap. 34.00 (*1-874241-19-8*, Pub. by Cavendish Pubng) Gaunt.

Marketing Communications Strategy 1998-99. Yeshin. 200p. pap. text. write for info. (*0-7506-4029-4*) Buttrwrth-Heinemann.

Marketing Company Shares. David Fanning. 288p. 1982. text 59.95 (*0-566-02174-9*) Ashgate Pub Co.

Marketing Computer Graphics Equipment in Europe: Analyses, Strategies, Forecasts. JJ & J Consultants. (Illus.). 230p. 1983. 675.00 (*0-914849-00-X*) TBC Inc.

Marketing Concepts for Libraries & Information Services. Eileen E. De Saez. 144p. 1993. 45.00 (*0-85157-448-3*, LAP4483, Pub. by Library Association) Bernan Associates.

Marketing Cooperatives & Peasants in Kenya. Torben Bager. (Centre for Development Research Publications: No. 5). 116p. 1980. write for info. (*91-7106-174-6*, Pub. by Nordic Africa) Transaction Pubs.

Marketing Core Concepts. Assael. LC 97-74497. (C). 1997. text 37.00 (*0-03-024811-6*) Harcourt Coll Pubs.

Marketing Core Concepts. Assael. (C). 1997. pap. text, teacher ed. 26.75 (*0-03-024812-4*) Harcourt Coll Pubs.

Marketing Core Concepts. Assael. (C). 1998. pap. text 29.50 (*0-03-024813-2*, Pub. by Harcourt Coll Pubs) Harcourt.

Marketing Corporate Image: The Company As Your Number One Product. James R. Gregory. 272p. 1993. pap. 27.95 (*0-8442-3283-1*) NTC Contemp Pub Co.

Marketing Corporate Image: The Company As Your Number One Product. James R. Gregory & Jack G. Wiechmann. 272p. 1994. 39.95 (*0-8442-3282-3*, NTC Business Bks) NTC Contemp Pub Co.

Marketing Corporate Image: Your Company As Your Number One Product. James R. Gregory & Jack G. Wiechmann. LC 98-25043. 288p. 1998. 29.95 (*0-8442-3307-2*, NTC Business Bks) NTC Contemp Pub Co.

Marketing Cost Analysis for Performance Measurement & Decision Support. Michael Schiff & Jonathan B. Schiff. Ed. by Claire Barth. 80p. 1994. pap. 40.00 (*0-86641-235-2*, 94298) Inst Mgmt Account.

Marketing CPS - Textmaps: A Chapter-by-Chapter Guide for Exploring Main Ideas & Terms in Marketing. 4th rev. ed. Eric N. Berkowitz et al. (C). 1995. 14.00 (*0-256-19139-5*, Irwn McGrw-H) McGrw-H Hghr Educ.

Marketing Credit Union Services: The Role of Perceived Value. Peter Dacin & F. Wadsworth. 50p. 1995. pap. 100.00 (*1-880572-20-6*) Filene Res.

***Marketing Cultural Organisations: New Strategies for Attracting Audiences to Classical Music, Dance, Museums, Theatre & Opera.** Bonita M. Kolb. 240p. 2000. pap. 18.95 (*1-86076-141-0*, Pub. by Oak Tr) Midpt Trade.

***Marketing Customer Interface (CIM 2000)** 5th ed. Craig J. Simmons & Rosemary Phipps. 338p. 1999. pap. text 36.95 (*0-7506-4369-2*) Buttrwrth-Heinemann.

Marketing Data: A Guide to Sources of Market Statistics in the Building Service Industry. A. King. 1989. pap. 25.00 (*0-86022-199-7*, Pub. by Build Servs Info Assn) St Mut.

***Marketing de Guerrilla: Los Secretos Para Obtener Grandes Ganancias de Sus Pequenas y Medianas Empresas.** Jay Conrad Levinson. Ed. by Steve Savage. Tr. by Helena Zambrano.Tr. of Guerrilla Marketing. (SPA.). 432p. 2000. pap. 19.95 (*0-9627848-1-8*) Savage Mktg.

Marketing Decision for New & Mature Products. 2nd ed. Robert Hisrich. LC 90-49108. 516p. (C). 1991. 61.00 (*0-675-20647-2*, Merrill Coll) P-H.

Marketing Decision Maker: From MKIS to MDSS. 2nd rev. ed. Leyland F. Pitt & Derek Bromfield. (Illus.). 209p. (C). pap. text 37.00 (*0-7021-3042-7*, Pub. by Juta & Co) Intl Spec Bk.

Marketing Decision Making Using Lotus 1-2-3. John Bedient. 176p. (C). 1989. pap. text. write for info. incl. 5.25 hd (*0-538-80358-4*, SS80A81); pap. text. write for info. incl. 3.5 hd (*0-538-80480-7*, SS80A8H88) S-W Pub.

Marketing Decision Models. Ed. by Randall L. Schultz & A. A. Zoltners. 1981. 75.00 (*0-444-00426-2*) P-H.

Marketing Decisions under Uncertainty. Dung Nguyen. LC 97-24859. (International Series in Quantitative Marketing). 1997. lib. bdg. 121.00 (*0-7923-9964-1*) Kluwer Academic.

***Marketing Democracy: Changing Opinion about Inequality & Politics in East Central Europe.** David S. Mason & James R. Kluegel. LC 00-37284. 2000. write for info. (*0-7425-0153-1*) Rowman.

***Marketing Democracy: Power & Social Movements in Post-Dictatorship Chile.** Julia Paley. LC 00-37405. 2001. pap. write for info. (*0-520-22768-9*) U CA Pr.

Marketing Democracy: Public Opinion & Media Formation in Democratic Societies. Romain Laufer & Catherine Paradeise. 347p. 1989. 49.95 (*0-88738-199-5*) Transaction Pubs.

Marketing Dermatology. Cynthia Hough. (Illus.). 77p. 1997. pap. 26.00 (*1-890018-13-9*) Anadem Pubng.

Marketing des Assurances de Personnes: FLMI 320. Dennis W. Goodwin. Ed. by Joel V. Basarich. Tr. by TRIUS Staff. (FLMI Insurance Education Program Ser.). (FRE.). 564p. (C). text 100.00 (*0-939921-37-5*, Pub. by Life Office) PBD Inc.

Marketing Designs for Nonprofit Organizations. Jack Christian. 250p. 1992. 49.00 (*0-930807-38-3*, 600316) Fund Raising.

Marketing Disease to Hispanics. Bruce Maxwell & Michael F. Jacobson. (Illus.). 100p. (Orig.). 1989. pap., per. 6.95 (*0-89329-020-3*) Ctr Sci Public.

***Marketing, Distribution & Users of Annuities.** Mary C. Bickley et al. LC 00-30200. 2000. write for info. (*1-57974-077-4*) Life Office.

Marketing Doctoral Dissertation Abstracts, 1979. American Marketing Association. LC HF5415.M2977. (American Marketing Association Bibliography Ser.: No. 34). 162p. reprint ed. pap. 50.30 (*0-608-16297-3*, 202667000051) Bks Demand.

Marketing Doctoral Dissertation Abstracts, 1980. American Marketing Association. Ed. by Thomas Greer. LC Z 7164.M18A5. (American Marketing Association Bibliography Ser.: No. 39). 209p. reprint ed. pap. 64.80 (*0-608-16300-7*, 202667100051) Bks Demand.

Marketing Economics Guide, 1982-1983: Current Market Dimensions for 1500 Cities, All 3100 Counties, All Metro Area. Ed. by Alfred Hong. LC 73-647896. (Illus.). 264p. 1982. 25.00 (*0-914078-46-1*) Marketing Econs.

Marketing Economics Guide, 1980-1981: Current Market Dimensions for 1500 Cities, All 3100 Counties, All Metro Areas. Ed. by Alfred Hong. LC 73-647896. (Illus.). 264p. 1980. 20.00 (*0-914078-43-7*) Marketing Econs.

Marketing Economics Guide, 1981-1982: Current Market Dimensions for 1500 Cities, All 3100 Counties, All Metro Areas. Ed. by Alfred Hong. LC 73-647896. (Illus.). 264p. 1981. 25.00 (*0-914078-44-5*) Marketing Econs.

Marketing Economics Guide, 1983-1984: Current Market Dimensions for 1500 Cities, All 3100 Counties, All Metro Areas. Ed. by Alfred Hong. LC 73-647896. (Illus.). 264p. 1983. 25.00 (*0-914078-47-X*) Marketing Econs.

Marketing Economics Guide, 1985-1986: Current Market Dimensions for 1500 Cities, All 3100 Counties, All Metro Counties. Ed. by Alfred Hong. LC 73-647896. (Illus.). 264p. 1985. 25.00 (*0-914078-50-X*) Marketing Econs.

Marketing Economics Guide, 1984-1985: Current Market Dimensions for 1500 Cities, All 3100 Countries, All Metro Areas. Ed. by Alfred Hong. LC 73-647896. (Illus.). 264p. 1984. 25.00 (*0-914078-49-6*) Marketing Econs.

Marketing Economics Guide, 1973-1974: Current Market Dimensions for 1500 Cities, All 3100 Counties, All Metro Areas. Ed. by Alfred Hong. (Illus.). 264p. 1973. 20.00 (*0-914078-09-7*) Marketing Econs.

Marketing Economics Guide, 1974-1975: Current Market Dimensions for 1500 Cities, All 3100 Counties, All Metro Areas. Ed. by Alfred Hong. (Illus.). 280p. 1974. 20.00 (*0-914078-10-0*) Marketing Econs.

Marketing Economics Guide, 1975-1976: Current Market Dimensions for 1500 Cities, All 3100 Counties, All Metro Areas. Ed. by Alfred Hong. LC 73-647896. (Illus.). 280p. 1975. 20.00 (*0-914078-11-9*) Marketing Econs.

Marketing Economics Guide, 1976-1977: Current Market Dimensions for 1500 Cities, All 3100 Counties, All Metro Areas. Alfred Hong. LC 76-647896. (Illus.). 280p. 1976. 20.00 (*0-914078-21-6*) Marketing Econs.

Marketing Economics Guide, 1977-1978: Current Market Dimensions for 1500 Cities, All 3100 Counties, All Metro Areas. Ed. by Alfred Hong. LC 73-647896. (Illus.). 1977. 20.00 (*0-914078-22-4*) Marketing Econs.

Marketing Economics Guide, 1978-1979: Current Market Dimensions for 1500 Cities, All 3100 Counties All Metro Areas. Ed. by Alfred Hong. LC 73-647896. (Illus.). 1978. 20.00 (*0-914078-32-1*) Marketing Econs.

Marketing Economics Guide, 1979-1980: Current Market Dimensions for 1500 Cities, All 3100 Counties All Metro Areas. Ed. by Alfred Hong. LC 73-647896. (Illus.). 1979. 20.00 (*0-914078-33-X*) Marketing Econs.

Marketing Economics Key Plants, 1975-1976, Set. Alfred Hong. Incl. Guide to Industrial Purchasing Power: (East South Central) LC 73-642154. 43p. 1975. 13.00 (*0-914078-18-6*); Guide to Industrial Purchasing Power: (Middle Atlantic) LC 73-642154. 72p. 1975. 13.00 (*0-914078-14-3*); Guide to Industrial Purchasing Power: (Mountain & Pacific) LC 73-642154. 65p. 1975. 13.00 (*0-914078-20-8*); Guide to Industrial Purchasing Power: (New England) LC 73-642154. 43p. 1975. 13.00 (*0-914078-13-5*); Guide to Industrial Purchasing Power: (North Central) LC 73-642154. 79p. 1975. 13.00 (*0-914078-15-1*); Guide to Industrial Purchasing Power: (South Atlantic) LC 73-642154. 63p. 1975. 13.00 (*0-914078-17-8*); Guide to Industrial Purchasing Power: (West North Central) LC 73-642154. 37p. 1975. 13.00 (*0-914078-16-X*); Guide to Industrial Purchasing Power: (West South Central) LC 73-642154. 39p. 1975. 13.00 (*0-914078-19-4*); LC 73-642154. 1975. 70.00 (*0-914078-12-7*) Marketing Econs.

Marketing Economics Key Plants, 1979-1980: The Guide to Industrial Purchasing Power. Alfred Hong. LC 73-642154. 1979. 90.00 (*0-914078-34-8*) Marketing Econs.

Marketing Economics Key Plants, 1981-1982: The Guide to Industrial Purchasing Power. Alfred Hong. LC 73-642154. 632p. 1981. 95.00 (*0-914078-45-3*) Marketing Econs.

Marketing Economics Key Plants, 1977-1978: The Guide to Industrial Purchasing Power, National Edition. Ed. by Alfred Hong. LC 73-642154. 1977. 90.00 (*0-914078-23-2*) Marketing Econs.

Marketing Economics Key Plants, 1984-1985: The Guide to Industrial Purchasing Power, National Edition. Alfred Hong. LC 73-642154. 632p. 1984. 100.00 (*0-914078-48-8*) Marketing Econs.

Marketing Edge: Making Strategies Work. Thomas V. Bonoma. 240p. 1985. 32.95 (*0-02-904200-3*) Free Pr.

Marketing Edge: The New Leadership Role of Sales & Marketing in Manufacturing. George E. Palmatier & Joseph E. Shull. LC 88-51917. 183p. 1988. 40.00 (*0-939246-08-2*) Wiley.

Marketing Edge: The New Leadership Role of Sales & Marketing in Manufacturing. George E. Palmatier & Joseph S. Shull. 208p. 1995. 42.50 (*0-471-13270-5*) Wiley.

Marketing Education. Lynton Gray. 176p. 1991. 128.95 (*0-335-09676-X*) OpUniv Pr.

Marketing Education. Jane Kenway. 1995. pap. 100.00 (*0-949823-50-3*, Pub. by Deakin Univ) St Mut.

Marketing Education: A Future Perspective. Richard L. Lynch. 86p. 1983. 8.75 (*0-318-22150-0*, SN37) Ctr Educ Trng Employ.

Marketing Educator's Guide see Skills for the Changing Workplace

Marketing Engineering: Computer-Assisted Marketing Analysis & Planning, Revised Edition, Compatible with Office 97. Gary L. Lilien. 400p. (C). 1998. text 123.00 incl. audio compact disk (*0-321-03050-8*, Prentice Hall) P-H.

Marketing Environment & Practices in Nepal. V. Verma & D. R. Dahal. 1988. 65.00 (*0-7855-0244-0*, Pub. by Ratna Pustak Bhandar) St Mut.

Marketing Essentials. (C). 1999. write for info. (*0-13-557224-X*, Macmillan Coll) P-H.

Marketing Essentials. Lois Farese. 1990. 37.47 (*0-02-820000-4*) Glencoe.

Marketing Essentials. Lois Farese et al. 620p. 1997. text 38.50 (*0-02-640601-2*) Glencoe.

Marketing Essentials: Teacher's Wraparound Edition. Lois Farese et al. 1997. write for info. (*0-02-640602-0*) Glencoe.

Marketing Ethics. Bodo Schlegelmilch. 256p. 1997. pap. 27.95 (*0-415-12588-X*) Thomson Learn.

Marketing Ethics: A Selected, Annotated Bibliography of Articles. Ed. by Jan Willem Bol et al. 84p. pap. 26.00 (*0-87757-237-2*) Am Mktg.

Marketing Ethics: An International Perspective. Bodo Schlegelmilch. LC 98-144542. 256p. 1998. pap. 22.00 (*1-86152-191-X*) Thomson Learn.

Marketing Exchange Relationships, Transactions, & Their Media. Ed. by Franklin S. Houston. LC 93-14126. 336p. 1994. 69.50 (*0-89930-809-0*, Q809, Quorum Bks) Greenwood.

Marketing Exchange Transactions & Relationships. Franklin S. Houston et al. LC 92-9569. 192p. 1992. 49.95 (*0-89930-735-3*, HMH, Quorum Bks) Greenwood.

Marketing Financial Services. Colin McIver & Geoffrey Naylor. 292p. 1981. 75.00 (*0-85297-054-4*, Pub. by Chartered Bank); pap. 39.00 (*0-85297-055-2*, Pub. by Chartered Bank) St Mut.

Marketing Financial Services. Ed. by M. McIver & N. Naylor. (C). 1989. 110.00 (*0-85297-145-1*, Pub. by Chartered Bank) St Mut.

Marketing Financial Services. Robert C. Perez. LC 83-4230. 175p. 1983. 52.95 (*0-275-91723-1*, C1723, Praeger Pubs) Greenwood.

Marketing Financial Services. Mary Ann Pezzullo. (Illus.). 415p. (C). 1978. 18.00 (*0-89982-062-X*) Am Bankers.

Marketing Financial Services. T. Watkins & M. Wright. 152p. 1986. boxed set 54.00 (*0-406-50270-6*, U.K., MICHIE) LEXIS Pub.

Marketing Financial Services. T. Watkins & M. Wright. (C). 1986. 210.00 (*0-7855-4082-2*, Pub. by Witherby & Co) St Mut.

Marketing Financial Services. David B. Zenoff. (Institutional Investor Series in Finance). 456p. 1989. text 49.50 (*0-88730-298-X*, HarpBusn) HarpInfo.

***Marketing Financial Services Through Retail Outlets.** Ian Youngman. 2000. 270.00 (*1-85573-455-9*, Pub. by Woodhead Pubng) Am Educ Systs.

Marketing Food to Women: How to Reach the Growing New Women's Food Product & Service Market. About Women Inc. Staff. LC 98-145117. 35 p. 1997. write for info. (*1-890211-05-2*) About Women.

Marketing for a Full House. Dewitt Coffman. (Illus.). 1984. pap. 10.00 (*0-937056-03-0*, M1) Cornell U Sch Hotel.

Marketing For Artichtects & Engineers: New Approach. Brian Richardson. 152p. (C). (gr. 13). 1996. pap. 32.99 (*0-419-20290-0*) Chapman & Hall.

Marketing for Attorneys & Law Firms. Ed. by William J. Winston. LC 92-1685. (Original Book Ser.). (Illus.). 323p. (Orig.). 1993. pap. 24.95 (*1-56024-325-2*); lib. bdg. 39.95 (*1-56024-324-4*) Haworth Pr.

Marketing for Bankers. 2nd ed. Mary A. Pezzullo. (Illus.). 564p. (C). 1988. text 45.00 (*0-89982-352-8*) Am Bankers.

Marketing for Bankers. 4th ed. Mary A. Pezzullo. (Illus.). 570p. (C). 1993. pap. text 45.00 (*0-89982-317-3*) Am Bankers.

Marketing for Building Service Contractors. Barbara Darraugh. 1997. pap. 50.00 (*1-892725-11-8*, RP145) Building Serv.

Marketing for Churches & Ministries. Robert E. Stevens & David L. Loudon. LC 91-4069. (Illus.). 176p. 1992. lib. bdg. 39.95 (*1-56024-177-2*) Haworth Pr.

Marketing for Congregations: Choosing to Serve People More Efficiently. Philip Kotler et al. 384p. 1992. 24.95 (*0-687-23579-0*) Abingdon.

Marketing for CPAs, Accountants, & Tax Professionals. William J. Winston. LC 93-41763. (Illus.). 386p. 1995. pap. 19.95 (*1-56024-873-4*); lib. bdg. 49.95 (*1-56024-872-6*) Haworth Pr.

Marketing for Design Firms in the 1990s. Roger L. Pickar. 112p. (Orig.). 1991. pap. 20.00 (*1-55835-037-3*) AIA Press.

Marketing for Dummies. Alexander Hiam. LC 97-71817. (For Dummies Ser.). 400p. 1997. pap. 19.99 (*1-56884-699-1*) IDG Bks.

An Asterisk (*) at the beginning of an entry indicates that the title is appearing for the first time.

Marketing for Engineers. J. S. Bayliss. (Management of Technology Ser.: No. 4). 391p. 1984. 45.00 (*0-86341-035-9*, MTO04Z) INSPEC Inc.

Marketing for Engineers. Stan Haavik. (Guide to Business Ser.: Vol. 10). 150p. 1996. pap. 19.95 (*0-7803-2264-9*, EG110) Inst Electrical.

Marketing for Financial Services. Ed. by William J. Winston. LC 86-309. (Journal of Professional Services Marketing: Vol. 1, No. 3). 143p. 1986. text 39.95 (*0-86656-548-5*) Haworth Pr.

Marketing for Health & Wellness Programs. Donald R. Self & James W. Busbin. LC 90-34020. (Health Marketing Quarterly Ser.: Vol. 7, Nos. 3 & 4). 248p. 1990. text 49.95 (*1-56024-014-8*) Haworth Pr.

Marketing for Hospitality & Tourism. 2nd ed. Ed. by Prentice-Hall Staff. (C). 1999. write for info. (*0-13-013698-0*) P-H.

Marketing for Keeps: Building Your Business by Retaining Your Customers. Carla B. Furlong. LC 92-40872. 256p. 1993. 24.95 (*0-471-54017-X*) Wiley.

Marketing for Law Firms. Andrew Williamson et al. 182p. 1994. pap. 49.50 (*1-85811-029-7*, Pub. by CLT Prof) Gaunt.

Marketing for Libraries & Information Agencies. Darlene E. Weingand. LC 83-25793. (Libraries & Information Science). 176p. 1984. text 73.25 (*0-89391-155-0*) Ablx Pub.

Marketing for Managers: A Practical Approach. Leyland F. Pitt. LC 98-178282. 288p. 1998. pap. 32.00 (*0-7021-4222-0*, Pub. by Juta & Co) Intl Spec Bk.

Marketing for Manufacturing Managers see Marketing for Manufacturing Managers

Marketing for Manufacturing Managers. Paisley College Staff. Incl. Marketing for Manufacturing Managers., **6 vols.** 1989. pap. text 435.00 (*0-08-040476-6*, Pergamon Pr); 1. Introduction to Marketing. 1989. pap. text 84.00 (*0-08-040464-2*, Pergamon Pr); 3. Product Development. 1989. pap. text 84.00 (*0-08-040468-5*, Pergamon Pr); 4. Pricing for Profit. 1989. pap. text 84.00 (*0-08-040470-7*, Pergamon Pr); 5. Market Planning. 1989. pap. text 84.00 (*0-08-040472-3*, Pergamon Pr); 6. Strategic Marketing. 1989. pap. 84.00 (*0-08-040474-X*, Pergamon Pr); 1989. 22.00 (*0-08-040475-8*, Pergamon Pr) Elsevier.

Marketing for Mental Health Services. Ed. by William J. Winston. LC 83-27534. (Health Marketing Quarterly Ser.: Vol. 1, Nos. 2 & 3). 180p. 1984. text 39.95 (*0-86656-278-8*); pap. text 17.95 (*0-86656-313-X*) Haworth Pr.

Marketing for Mission. Rebecca K. Leet. 24p. 1998. pap. text 12.00 (*0-925299-82-0*) Natl Ctr Nonprofit.

Marketing for Multimedia Guides. William G. Zikmund. Date not set. pap. text. write for info. (*0-314-02262-7*) West Pub.

Marketing for Non-Profit Organizations. Siri N. Espy. 160p. (C). 1992. pap. text 25.95 (*0-925065-34-X*) Lyceum IL.

Marketing for Non-Profit Organizations. 2nd ed. David L. Rados. LC 95-13609. 480p. 1996. text 59.95 (*0-86569-254-8*, Auburn Hse) Greenwood.

Marketing for Nonmarketers: Principles & Tactics That Everyone in Business Must Know. 2nd ed. Houston G. Elam & Norton Paley. LC 91-41985. (Illus.). 253p. 1992. pap. 78.50 (*0-7837-8360-4*, 204915000010) Bks Demand.

Marketing for Nonprofit Cultural Organizations. Nancy J. Church. LC 86-72772. (Illus.). 136p. (Orig.). 1986. pap. 5.00 (*0-9617701-0-4*) C E F Lib Syst.

Marketing for Parks, Recreation, & Leisure. Ellen L. O'Sullivan. LC 91-65916. 275p. 1991. 28.95 (*0-910251-43-6*) Venture Pub PA.

Marketing for People Not in Marketing. Ed. by Rick Crandall. 180p. (Orig.). 1997. pap. 14.95 (*0-9644294-8-9*) Select Pr.

Marketing for Profitable Results. James Brennan. 1992. 53.00 (*0-929442-10-5*, 2220PP) Prof Prnting & Pub.

Marketing for Schools. Ian Evans. (Cassell Education Ser.). (Illus.). 144p. 1995. 100.00 (*0-304-33253-4*); pap. 33.95 (*0-304-33255-0*) Continuum.

Marketing for Small Publishers. Bill Godber. (C). 1993. text 38.50 (*0-85172-034-X*); pap. text 14.95 (*0-85172-035-8*) Westview.

Marketing for Small Publishers. Bill Godber et al. (C). 42.50 (*1-85172-034-0*, Pub. by Pluto GBR); pap. 14.95 (*1-85172-035-9*, Pub. by Pluto GBR) Stylus Pub VA.

Marketing for Success: Creative Marketing Tools for the Agriculture Industry. Robert J. Matarazzo. (Illus.). (Orig.). 1996. pap. 16.95 (*0-9653385-0-9*) Doe Hollow.

Marketing for the Developing Company. John Winkler. 1969. pap. 28.00 (*0-8464-0608-X*) Beekman Pubs.

Marketing for the Home-Based Business. 2nd ed. Jeffrey P. Davidson. LC 98-26818. 256p. 1999. pap. text 10.95 (*1-58062-078-7*) Adams Media.

***Marketing for the Legal Nurse Consultant: A Guide to Getting All the Clients You Can Handle Using Proven, Low-Cost Strategies.** Betty Joos & John Joos. LC 99-91290. (Illus.). XI, 211p. 2000. pap. 39.95 (*0-9674730-0-4*, Sky Lake) Inform Decisions.

Marketing for the Manufacturer. J. Paul Peter. (APICS Ser.). 270p. 1992. 47.50 (*1-55623-648-4*, Irwn Prfssnl) McGraw-Hill Prof.

Marketing for the New Millennium: Applying New Techniques. Jay Tolman. LC 97-52778. (Illus.). 128p. 1998. pap. 19.95 (*1-55571-432-3*, MNMLP) PSI Resch.

Marketing for Therapists: A Handbook for Success in Managed Care. Ed. by Jeri Davis & Michael A. Freeman. LC 95-44177. (Psychology Ser.). 208p. (Orig.). 1996. pap. 28.95 (*0-7879-0207-1*) Jossey-Bass.

Marketing for Tourism. 3rd ed. Holloway. 1995. pap. 35.95 (*0-582-27748-5*, Pub. by Addison-Wesley) Longman.

***Marketing for Volunteer Managers: Mastering Its Magic in a New Millennium.** 72p. 1999. pap. write for info. (*1-58534-031-6*) Points of Light.

***Marketing for Volunteer Managers: Mastering Its Magic in a New Millennium - Self Study Booklet.** 15p. 1999. pap. write for info. (*1-58534-032-4*) Points of Light.

Marketing Forest Products: Gaining the Competitive Edge. Jean Mater et al. (Illus.). 300p. 1992. 49.00 (*0-87930-193-7*, 412) Miller Freeman.

Marketing-Forschung fur Agrarfakultaten: Analyse der Berufsfelder & Evaluierung des Studiums der Studiengange Allgemeine Agrarwissenschaften & Agrarbiologie. Wolfgang Bischoff. (GER., Illus.). XVI, 304p. 1996. 57.95 (*3-631-30529-X*) P Lang Pubng.

Marketing Foundations & Functions. Burrow. (Marketing Education Ser.). 1994. pap. 5.95 (*0-538-62549-X*) S-W Pub.

Marketing Foundations & Functions. James L. Burrow. (SB - Marketing Education Ser.). 1994. mass mkt. 59.95 (*0-538-62541-4*); mass mkt. 10.95 (*0-538-62545-7*); mass mkt., wbk. ed. 13.95 (*0-538-62542-2*); mass mkt., wbk. ed. 10.95 (*0-538-62548-1*) S-W Pub.

Marketing 4 Modules. William G. Zikmund. Date not set. pap. text. write for info. (*0-314-01778-X*) West Pub.

Marketing Fundamentals. Lancaster & Withey. pap. text. write for info. (*0-7506-4366-8*) Buttrwrth-Heinemann.

Marketing Game. Eric Schulz. LC 99-28138. 304p. 1999. 24.95 (*1-58062-222-4*) Adams Media.

Marketing Geography with Special Reference to Retailing. Ross L. Davies. 320p. 1977. pap. 15.95 (*0-416-70070-9*, 6079) Routledge.

Marketing Globally. A. Coskum Samli & John S. Hill. LC 98-182654. 480p. 1998. 56.95 (*0-8442-3308-0*) NTC Contemp Pub Co.

Marketing Glossary: Glosario de Mercadeo. Rossi Fischer. (ENG & SPA.). 208p. 1982. pap. 13.50 (*0-8288-0131-2*, S35178) Fr & Eur.

Marketing Glossary: Key Terms, Concepts, & Applications. Mark N. Clemente. 470p. 1992. 34.95 (*0-8144-5030-X*) AMACOM.

Marketing Golf to Women. unabridged ed. (NGF Info Pacs Ser.). (Illus.). 161p. (Orig.). 1998. pap. 45.00 (*0-9638647-6-9*, 99LB009) Natl Golf.

Marketing Government Geographic Information: Issues & Guidelines. Ed. by William J. Bamberger & Nora Sherwood Bryan. (Illus.). vii, 108p. 1993. pap. 45.00 (*0-916848-00-0*) Urban & Regional Information Systems.

Marketing Grain & Livestock. Gary F. Stasko. LC 97-8897. (Illus.). 300p. 1997. 39.95 (*0-8138-2832-5*) Iowa St U Pr.

***Marketing Growth & Shareholder Value.** Peter Doyle. 356p. 2000. pap. 47.95 (*0-7506-4613-6*) Buttrwrth-Heinemann.

Marketing Guide for Money Market Mutual Funds. Cynthia C. Andrade et al. 82p. 1996. write for info. (*0-913755-35-4*) IBC Financial.

Marketing Guide for Small Business. David T. Maloch. 62p. (Orig.). 1989. pap. 7.95 (*0-9623457-0-9*) Perfidia Pr.

Marketing Guidebook, 1998 & Supermarket Census: The Book of Supermarket Distribution Facts. rev. ed. Ed. by Lynda Gutierrez et al. 880p. 1997. 340.00 (*0-911790-65-9*, Progress Grocer) Trade Dimensns.

Marketing Guidebook, 1994. rev. ed. Ed. by Adrienne Toth et al. (Illus.). 1993. pap. 320.00 (*0-911790-14-4*) Trade Dimensns.

Marketing Guidebook, 1999: The Book of Supermarket Distribution Facts. rev. ed. Ed. by Lynda Gutierrez et al. 968p. 1998. 340.00 (*0-911790-72-1*, Progress Grocer) Trade Dimensns.

***Marketing Guidebook, 2000: The Book of Supermarket Distribution Facts.** rev. ed. Ed. by Lynda Gutierrez et al. 1008p. 1999. 340.00 (*1-891856-05-7*) Trade Dimensns.

Marketing Handbook for Tourism. English Tourist Board Staff. 1993. pap. text. write for info. (*0-582-21321-5*, Pub. by Addison-Wesley) Longman.

Marketing-hardback. 2nd ed. Bearden Et Al. 1997. 83.44 (*0-256-26907-6*) McGraw.

Marketing Health Behavior: Principles, Techniques, & Applications. L. W. Frederiksen et al. LC 84-3271. (Illus.). 216p. (C). 1984. 47.50 (*0-306-41523-2*, Plenum Trade) Perseus Pubng.

Marketing Health Care. Carole A. Letheren & Richard Mathieu. (Illus.). 127p. (C). 1991. text 29.95 (*1-878487-32-9*, ME043) Practice Mgmt Info.

Marketing Health Care into the Twenty-First Century: The Changing Dynamic. Alan K. Vitberg. LC 94-44795. (Illus.). 210p. 1996. 39.95 (*1-56024-979-X*) Haworth Pr.

Marketing Healthcare to Women: Meeting New Demands for Products & Services. Patricia Braus. (Illus.). 200p. 1997. 42.50 (*0-936889-40-3*) American Demo.

Marketing Health/Fitness Services. Richard F. Gerson. LC 88-13078. (Illus.). 134p. 1989. reprint ed. pap. 41.60 (*0-608-06455-6*, 206729300009) Bks Demand.

Marketing High Technology: An Insider's View. William H. Davidow. 224p. 1986. 35.00 (*0-02-907990-X*) Free Pr.

***Marketing High Technology Services.** Colin V. Sowter. LC 00-24870. 264p. 2000. 99.95 (*0-566-08237-3*, Pub. by Ashgate Pub) Ashgate Pub Co.

Marketing Higher Education: A Handbook for College Administrators. George C. Dehne et al. 126p. (Orig.). 1991. 18.00 (*1-879994-02-X*) Consortium Advan.

Marketing Hospitality. (Service Management Ser.). 1990. pap. text, teacher ed. write for info. (*0-471-84502-7*) Wiley.

Marketing Hospitality. Tom Powers. 148p. 1990. pap., student ed., suppl. ed. 29.95 (*0-471-62298-2*) Wiley.

Marketing Hospitality. 2nd ed. Tom Powers. LC 96-36091. 464p. 1997. 54.95 (*0-471-12703-5*) Wiley.

Marketing Hospitality: Sales & Marketing for Hotels, Motels, & Resorts. Dennis L. Foster. 190p. 1992. text 41.07 (*0-02-808755-0*) Glencoe.

Marketing, Hospitality & Tourism. 2nd ed. Philip Kotler. LC 98-25191. (Illus.). 816p. 1998. 81.00 (*0-13-080795-8*) P-H.

Marketing Housing to an Aging Population. Andre Shashaty. LC 90-19580. xiv, 110p. (Orig.). 1991. pap. text 15.00 (*0-86718-356-X*) Home Builder.

Marketing Human Services: Selling Your Services under Managed Care. Nancy W. Veeder. LC 98-44118. (Illus.). 152p. 1998. 32.95 (*0-8261-1205-6*) Springer Pub.

Marketing Idea Generator. Frederick J. Dotzler. (Illus.). 76p. (Orig.). 1982. pap. 14.95 (*0-9609906-0-7*) Innovex.

Marketing Ideas for Small Service Business. 1992. lib. bdg. 79.95 (*0-8490-5375-7*) Gordon Pr.

Marketing Identities: The Invention of Jewish Ethnicity in Ost und West. David Brenner. LC 97-50452. (Illus.). 256p. 1998. pap. 21.95 (*0-8143-2684-6*) Wayne St U Pr.

Marketing Image CD-ROM. Dryden. (C). 1995. 246.00 (*0-03-018127-5*) Harcourt Coll Pubs.

Marketing Imagination. Associated Equipment Distributors Staff. 10.00 (*0-318-19185-7*) Assn Equip Distrs.

Marketing Imagination. Theodore Levitt. LC 83-47989. 256p. (C). 1983. 9.95 (*0-02-918840-7*) Free Pr.

Marketing Imagination. enl. ed. Theodore Levitt. 218p. 1986. pap. 16.95 (*0-02-919090-8*) Free Pr.

Marketing in a Global Economy - Post Secondary Version. Turner. (SB - Marketing Education Ser.). 1995. mass mkt. 17.00 (*0-538-71429-8*) S-W Pub.

Marketing in a Multicultural World: Ethnicity, Nationalism & Cultural Identity. Janeen A. Costa & Gary J. Bamossy. (Illus.). 352p. 1995. text 58.00 (*0-8039-5327-5*); pap. text 26.95 (*0-8039-5328-3*) Sage.

Marketing in a Regulated Environment. George S. Dominguez. LC 77-22099. (Marketing Management Ser.). 359p. reprint ed. 111.30 (*0-8357-9525-X*, 205525500011) Bks Demand.

Marketing in a Slow Growth Economy: The Impact of Stagflation on Consumer Psychology. Avraham Shama. LC 79-26312. (Praeger Special Studies). (Illus.). 166p. 1980. 45.00 (*0-275-90550-0*, C0550, Praeger Pubs) Greenwood.

Marketing in Action: An Experiential Approach. Robin T. Peterson et al. (Illus.). 259p. 1978. teacher ed. write for info. (*0-8299-0565-0*) West Pub.

Marketing in Action: Readings & Cases. A. Forman et al. (C). 1986. pap. write for info. (*0-201-10844-5*) Addison-Wesley.

Marketing in an Electronic Age. Buzzell. 1985. 39.95 (*0-07-103217-7*) McGraw.

Marketing in Australia. (Illus.). 50p. (Orig.). (C). 1994. pap. text 40.00 (*0-7881-1159-0*) DIANE Pub.

Marketing in Central & Eastern Europe. Ed. by Jan Nowak. LC 97-762. (Journal of East-West Business Monograph Ser.: Vol. 3, No. 1). 101p. (C). 1997. 29.95 (*0-7890-0039-3*, Intl Busn Pr) Haworth Pr.

Marketing in College Admissions: A Broadening of Perspectives. 170p. (Orig.). 1980. pap. 9.95 (*0-87447-133-8*) College Bd.

Marketing in Commercial Banks. W. Ogden Ross. LC 68-579749. 1968. 19.95 (*0-912164-07-7*) Masterco Pr.

Marketing in Europe. John Nicholls & Malcom Sargent. LC 95-83290. (Perspectives on Europe Ser.). 192p. 1996. 72.95 (*1-85972-141-9*, Pub. by Avebry) Ashgate Pub Co.

Marketing in Europe: Case Studies. Jordie M. Esade. (European Management Ser.). 256p. (C). 1994. text 69.95 (*0-8039-8955-5*); pap. text 29.95 (*0-8039-8956-3*) Sage.

Marketing in Hospitality & Tourism: A Consumer Focus. Richard Teare et al. (Hotel & Catering Ser.). 256p. 1995. 90.00 (*0-304-32823-5*); pap. 45.00 (*0-304-32825-1*) Continuum.

Marketing In-House Seminars. Ralph Elliot. 31p. 49.95 (*0-914951-17-3*) LERN.

Marketing In-House Training Programs. Don M. Schrello. (Illus.). 44p. (Orig.). 1984. pap. 5.95 (*0-935823-02-6*) Schrello Market.

Marketing in Ireland. 30p. (Orig.). (C). 1993. pap. text 20.00 (*1-56806-969-3*) DIANE Pub.

***Marketing in Japan.** Ian Melville. (Illus.). 256p. 2000. pap. text 39.95 (*0-7506-4145-2*) Buttrwrth-Heinemann.

Marketing in Management: Basic Principles. Mike Worsam & D. Berkeley Wright. (Illus.). 594p. (Orig.). 1995. pap. 57.50 (*0-273-60736-7*, Pub. by Pitman Pub) Trans-Atl Phila.

Marketing in Nonprofit Organizations. Ed. by Patrick J. Montana. LC 78-18322. 316p. reprint ed. pap. 98.00 (*0-608-12806-6*, 202354700033) Bks Demand.

Marketing in Practice. W. G. Leader & N. Kyritsis. Ed. by Stanley Thornes. 256p. (C). 1999. pap. 67.50 (*0-7487-0512-0*, Pub. by S Thornes Pubs) Trans-Atl Phila.

Marketing in Practice, 1999-2000. Mike Hyde & Gill Kelley. 172p. 2000. pap. text 34.95 (*0-7506-4363-3*) Buttrwrth-Heinemann.

Marketing in Publishing. Patrick Forsyth & Robin Birn. LC 96-45646. (Illus.). 208p. (C). 1997. pap. 24.99 (*0-415-15134-1*) Routledge.

Marketing in Publishing. Patrick Forsyth & Robin Birn. LC 96-45646. (Illus.). 176p. (C). 1997. 80.00 (*0-415-15133-3*) Routledge.

Marketing in Saudi Arabia. Abdel A. AbuNabaa. LC 83-17819. 228p. 1984. 59.95 (*0-275-91111-X*, C1111, Praeger Pubs) Greenwood.

Marketing in the Cyber Age: Paradigms, Perspectives & Implementation. Kurt Rohner. LC 98-3083. 240p. 1998. pap. 74.95 (*0-471-97023-9*) Wiley.

***Marketing in the Digital Age.** 2nd ed. 304p. 2000. write for info. (*0-273-64195-6*) F T P H.

Marketing in the Hospitality Industry. 3rd ed. Ronald A. Nykiel. LC 96-30823. (Illus.). 308p. 1996. pap. write for info. (*0-86612-143-9*) Educ Inst Am Hotel.

***Marketing in the Music Industry.** 2nd ed. 379p. (C). 1998. pap. 31.00 (*0-536-00819-1*) Pearson Custom.

Marketing in the New Era: Combating Competition in a Globalizing Economy. J. S. Panwar. LC 97-10585. 1997. pap. write for info. (*0-8039-9383-8*) Sage.

Marketing in the New Era: Combating Competition in a Globalizing Economy. J. S. Panwar. LC 97-10585. 272p. 1997. 36.00 (*0-8039-9382-X*) Sage.

***Marketing in the New Millennium.** 168p. (C). 1999. 18.00 (*0-536-60160-7*) Pearson Custom.

Marketing in the New Millennium: 36 Trends That Will Change Business & Marketing. M. J. Xavier. 1999. 24.00 (*81-259-0694-0*, Pub. by Vikas) S Asia.

Marketing in the NHS. W. R. Sheaff. 1990. 113.00 (*0-335-15428-X*); pap. 40.95 (*0-335-15427-1*) OpUniv Pr.

Marketing in the Not-for-Profit Sectors. Margaret Kinnell-Evans & Jennifer MacDougall. (Illus.). 256p. 1997. pap. text 34.95 (*0-7506-2234-2*) Buttrwrth-Heinemann.

Marketing in the Service Industries. Ed. by Gordon Foxall. (Illus.). 222p. 1985. 35.00 (*0-7146-3270-8*, Pub. by F Cass Pubs) Intl Spec Bk.

Marketing in the Third World. Ed. by Denise M. Johnson & Erdener Kaynak. LC 96-20073. (Journal of Global Marketing: Vol. 9, No. 4). 126p. 1996. 29.95 (*1-56024-830-0*, Intl Busn Pr) Haworth Pr.

Marketing in the Tourism Industry: The Promotion of Destination Regions. Goodall. 1987. 79.95 (*0-415-04545-2*) Thomson Learn.

Marketing in the Tourism Industry: The Promotion of Destination Regions. Ed. by Brian Goodall & Gregory J. Ashworth. 256p. 1988. lib. bdg. 62.50 (*0-7099-5811-0*, Pub. by C Helm) Routldge.

***Marketing in Travel & Tourism.** Victor T. C. Middleton. 394p. 2000. pap. 37.95 (*0-7506-4471-0*) Buttrwrth-Heinemann.

Marketing in Travel & Tourism. 2nd ed. Victor Middleton. LC 94-240552. 480p. 1994. pap. 36.95 (*0-7506-0973-7*) Buttrwrth-Heinemann.

Marketing Information. Incl. GAMIS-GATF Source-Book 1988. 50.00 Pira Handbook of Statistical Sources. 2nd ed. 95.00 write for info. (*0-318-58037-3*) Print Indus Am.

Marketing Information & Decision Support Systems. Sisodia. (C). 1996. text 61.25 (*0-03-096969-7*) Harcourt Coll Pubs.

Marketing Information Revolution. Blattberg. 1993. 39.95 (*0-07-103428-5*) McGraw.

Marketing Information Revolution. Ed. by Robert C. Blattberg et al. LC 93-15849. 384p. 1994. 35.00 (*0-87584-329-8*) Harvard Busn.

Marketing Information Systems: Selected Readings. Ed. by Charles D. Schewe. LC 76-3791. 193p. reprint ed. pap. 59.90 (*0-608-14218-2*, 202152200022) Bks Demand.

***Marketing Insights & Outrages.** Drayton Bird. 2000. pap. 17.95 (*0-7494-3215-2*) Kogan Page Ltd.

Marketing Insights for the Asia Pacific Rim. 2nd ed. Chin T. Tan. LC 98-117883. 332p. 1997. pap. text 29.95 (*9971-64-532-7*) Buttrwrth-Heinemann.

Marketing Institute Chartbook: Succeeding in an Increasingly Competitive Market: Marketing Tools for the Behavioral Health & Social Services Fields. Monica E. Oss & John H. Clary. (Illus.). 258p. 1998. spiral bd. 295.00 (*1-878586-26-2*, HB-33) Open Minds PA.

Marketing Institution. Ralph F. Breyer. Ed. by Henry Assael. LC 78-245. (Century of Marketing Ser.). 1979. reprint ed. lib. bdg. 31.95 (*0-405-11160-6*) Ayer.

Marketing Institutional Money Management Services: Meeting the Needs of Today's Plan Sponsors & Corporate Treasurers. Philip Halpern. 200p. 1995. text 50.00 (*1-55738-859-8*, Irwn Prfssnl) McGraw-Hill Prof.

Marketing Instructional Media: A Handbook for Sales Personnel. Robert G. Harding & Paul C. Oddo. LC 77-83617. (Illus.). 1978. pap. 3.95 (*0-87783-141-6*) Oddo.

Marketing Instructional Services: Applying Private Sector Techniques to Plan & Promote Bibliographic Instruction. Ed. by Carolyn A. Kirkendall. LC 86-60025. (Library Orientation Ser.: No. 15). 168p. 1986. 25.00 (*0-87650-201-X*) Pierian.

Marketing Insurance: A Practical Guide. Ed. by Nigel Dyer & Trevor Watkins. (C). 1988. 400.00 (*0-7855-4081-4*, Pub. by Witherby & Co) St Mut.

Marketing Intelligence: Discover What Your Customers Really Want & What Your Competitors Are up To. Jack Savidge. (Illus.). 224p. 1992. text 32.50 (*1-55623-579-8*) J Savidge & Co.

Marketing Internacional de Productos Insustriales. (C). 1994. pap. 14.00 (*0-201-82175-3*) HEPC Inc.

Marketing Introductory Text. Baker. 1997. text 25.95 (*0-333-55686-0*, Pub. by Macmillan) St Martin.

Marketing Investigations. William J. Reilly. Ed. by Henry Assael. LC 78-251. (Century of Marketing Ser.). 1979. reprint ed. lib. bdg. 23.95 (*0-405-11176-2*) Ayer.

Marketing Investment Real Estate. 3rd ed. Stephen D. Messner et al. Ed. by Helene Berlin. LC 81-86402. (Illus.). 546p. 1985. reprint ed. text 22.95 (*0-913652-59-8*, BK. 139) Realtors Natl.

Marketing Issues. Harrell. 176p. 1998. pap. text 50.00 (*0-536-01662-3*) Pearson Custom.

Marketing Issues in Pacific Area Tourism. Ed. by John C. Crotts & Chris A. Ryan. LC 96-52392. (Journal of Travel & Tourism Marketing Monograph Ser.: Vol. 6, No. 1). 136p. (C). 1997. 39.95 (*0-7890-0029-6*); pap. text 14.95 (*0-7890-0310-4*) Haworth Pr.

M

M

*Marketing Issues in Transitional Economies Rajeev Batra & William Davidson Institute Staff. LC 99-35795. (Series on Transitional & Emerging Economies). 1999. write for info. (0-7923-8498-9) Kluwer Academic.
Marketing Japanese Style. Paul Herbig. LC 95-19467. 312p. 1995. 65.00 (1-56720-009-5, Quorum Bks) Greenwood.
*Marketing Kit for Dummies. Alexander Hiam. 384p. 2000. pap. 24.99 incl. cd-rom (0-7645-5238-4) IDG Bks.
Marketing Kit for Family Day Care Providers. National Council of Jewish Women Staff. 1990. 10.00 (0-614-06656-5) NCJW.
*Marketing Know-How: Your Guide to the Best Marketing Tools & Sources. Peter Francese. (Illus.). 1998. 69.38 (0-936889-42-X) American Demo.
Marketing Know-How: Your Guide to the Best Tools & Sources. 4th rev. ed. Peter K. Francese. 1996. text 49.95 (0-936889-38-1) American Demo.
Marketing Leadership Hospitali. 2nd ed. Lewis. 1997. pap. text. write for info. (0-471-28647-8) Wiley.
Marketing Leadership in Hospitality. 2nd ed. Robert C. Lewis. (Hospitality, Travel & Tourism Ser.). 860p. 1994. text 55.95 (0-442-01888-6, VNR) Wiley.
Marketing Leadership in Hospitality: Foundations & Practices. 2nd ed. Robert C. Lewis et al. (Hospitality, Travel & Tourism Ser.). 880p. 1994. 59.95 (0-471-28646-X, VNR) Wiley.
*Marketing Leadership in Hospitality: Foundations & Practices. 3rd ed. Robert C. Lewis & Richard E. Chambers. LC 99-19482. 960p. (C). 2000. 64.95 (0-471-33270-4) Wiley.
Marketing Led, Sales Driven. Keith Steward. LC 93-135317. (Marketing Ser.). (Illus.). 333p. reprint ed. pap. 103.30 (0-608-06259-6, 206658800008) Bks Demand.
*Marketing Legal Services. Colin Gilligan et al. 264p. 1999. 66.00 (1-85811-194-3, Pub. by CLT Prof) Gaunt.
Marketing Legal Services: Developing & Growing Client Relationships for the 1990s. Richard K. Rodgers. 212p. 1993. student ed., spiral bd. write for info. (0-9641994-0-8) K Rodgers Grp.
Marketing Levies & Bond Issues for Public Schools. Gordon Wise et al. 1987. pap. 15.75 (0-932429-02-5, 51163) Univ Monographs.
Marketing Life Insurance in a Bank or Thrift. Ed. by Jerome R. Corsi. (Professional Handbooks on the New Banking Ser.). 233p. 1986. pap. text 51.50 (0-8133-7205-4) Westview.
Marketing Literature. Robert Bartels. Ed. by Henry Assael. LC 78-228. (Century of Marketing Ser.). 1979. lib. bdg. 47.95 (0-405-11165-7) Ayer.
Marketing Livestock & Meat. William Lesser. 471p. 1993. pap. 59.95 (1-56022-017-1) Haworth Jrnl Co-Edits.
Marketing Livestock & Meat. William Lesser. LC 91-32989. (Illus.). 484p. 1993. lib. bdg. 69.95 (1-56022-016-3) Haworth Pr.
Marketing Logistics. Martin Christopher. LC 97-179025. 192p. 1997. pap. text 37.95 (0-7506-2209-1) Buttrwrth-Heinemann.
Marketing Long-Term & Senior Care Services. William J. Winston. LC 84-6716. (Health Marketing Quarterly Ser.: Vol. 1, No. 4). 113p. 1984. 39.95 (0-86656-289-3) Haworth Pr.
Marketing Machine: How to Produce Inquiries That Turn into Sales. (Marketing Machine Business Development Ser.). 1994. pap. 10.00 (0-9642750-0-7) Mktg Machine.
Marketing Made Easier: Guide to Free Product Publicity. 2nd ed. Ed. by Barry T. Klein. 175p. 2001. pap. 50.00 (0-915344-62-9) Todd Pubns.
Marketing Made Easy. F. Lee Reid. Ed. by Dorris Tennyson. 96p. 1994. write for info. (0-86718-428-0) Home Builder.
Marketing Made Easy! Basics for Home Builders. E. Lee Reid. LC 94-46812. (Illus.). (Orig.). 1995. pap. 24.75 (0-86718-403-5) Home Builder.
Marketing Made Easy for the Small Accounting Firm. Jo A. Rosen. LC 95-31172. 244p. 1997. pap. 19.95 (0-471-17411-4) Wiley.
*Marketing Made Simple. 4th ed. Smith. 256p. 2001. write for info. (0-7506-4771-X) Buttrwrth-Heinemann.
Marketing Madness: A Survival Guide for a Consumer Society. Michael F. Jacobson. 260p. (C). 1995. pap. text 30.00 (0-8133-1981-1, Pub. by Westview) HarpC.
Marketing Madness: (Power Marketing for Portrait Wedding Photographers) 2nd ed. Helen T. Boursier. (Illus.). 205p. 1992. reprint ed. pap. 39.50 (0-934420-13-0) Studio Pr NE.
Marketing Magic: A Program for Major & Planned Gifts. Lynda Moersbacher. 1999. pap. 40.00 (1-56625-135-4) Bonus Books.
Marketing Magic: Action-Oriented Strategies That Will Help You. Don Debelak. 1997. pap. text 9.95 (1-55850-704-3) Adams Media.
Marketing Magnetico. John Graham. (SPA.). 193p. 1992. 27.75 (84-7978-000-2, Pub. by Ediciones Diaz) IBD Ltd.
Marketing, Majoring in the Rest of Your Life. 3rd ed. (C). 1993. 72.00 (0-13-178633-4) P-H.
*Marketing Management. 1p. (C). 2000. write for info. (0-321-06771-1) Addison-Wesley.
*Marketing Management. 480p. (C). 2000. (0-321-06769-X) Addson-Wesley Educ.
Marketing Management. 1999. 49.00 (0-07-023736-0) McGraw.
Marketing Management. (C). 1999. write for info. (0-13-016400-3) P-H.
*Marketing Management. (C). 2000. write for info. (0-13-016797-5) P-H.
*Marketing Management. 264p. (C). 1999. pap. text. write for info. (0-321-06770-3) Addison-Wesley.
*Marketing Management. (C). 1999. pap. text. write for info. (0-321-07601-X) Addson-Wesley Educ.
*Marketing Management. (C). 2000. pap. text 0.00 (0-321-07600-1) HEPC Inc.
Marketing Management. Weistein Annavarjula. (General Business Ser.). 2000. pap. 43.95 (0-324-02737-0) Sth-Wstrn College.
Marketing Management. Richard P. Bagozzi et al. LC 97-36484. 718p. 1998. 96.00 (0-02-305162-0) P-H.
Marketing Management. Stephen Calver et al. (Resource Based Series for Hospitality & Tourism). 60p. 1994. pap. 23.95 (0-304-32926-6) Continuum.
Marketing Management. David W. Cravens & Robert B. Woodruff. LC 84-24357. 800p. (C). 1986. pap. text 16.00 (0-201-10853-4) Addison-Wesley.
Marketing Management. Michael R. Czinkota et al. (Illus.). 700p. 1996. 74.95 (1-55786-694-5) Blackwell Pubs.
Marketing Management. Irwin. 1997. pap. 18.25 (0-07-218843-X) McGraw.
Marketing Management. Geoffrey Lancaster & Lester Massingham. LC 92-25428. 1993. 16.95 (0-07-707420-3) McGraw.
Marketing Management. Lewison. (C). 1996. pap. text, teacher ed. 28.00 (0-03-016227-0) Harcourt Coll Pubs.
Marketing Management. Marshall. 2001. write for info. (0-538-89036-3) S-W Pub.
Marketing Management. Stayman & Kotler. 178p. 1998. pap. text 16.75 (0-536-01414-0) Pearson Custom.
Marketing Management. Russell Winer. LC 99-28523. 576p. (C). 2000. text. write for info. (0-321-04656-0) Addison-Wesley Educ.
*Marketing Management. Russell Winer. LC 99-28523. (Illus.). 551p. (C). 1999. pap. 77.00 (0-321-01421-9, Prentice Hall) P-H.
*Marketing Management. abr. ed. 396p. (C). 2000. 35.00 (0-536-60195-X) Pearson Custom.
Marketing Management. 2nd ed. Dickson. (C). 1997. pap. text 33.50 (0-03-018093-7) Harcourt.
Marketing Management. 2nd ed. Dickson. (C). 1997. pap. text, teacher ed. 70.00 (0-03-018094-5) Harcourt.
Marketing Management. 2nd ed. Dickson. (C). 1998. teacher ed. 29.50 (0-03-019554-3) Harcourt.
Marketing Management. 2nd ed. Dickson. 1996. 246.00 (0-03-018084-8) Harcourt Coll Pubs.
Marketing Management. 2nd ed. Peter R. Dickson. LC 96-83162. 852p. (C). 1996. text 101.50 (0-03-017742-1) Dryden Pr.
*Marketing Management. 2nd ed. Mercer & Masaaki Kotabe. 2000. pap. text 18.75 (0-324-04171-3) Thomson Learn.
Marketing Management. 3rd ed. Harper W. Boyd & Orville C. Walker. LC 97-22528. 608p. (C). 1997. text 58.95 (0-256-22632-6, Irwn McGrw-H) McGrw-H Hghr Educ.
Marketing Management. 4th ed. Boyd. 2001. 54.00 (0-07-231523-7) McGraw.
Marketing Management. 5th ed. Guiltinan. 1994. 112.81 (0-07-074689-3) McGraw.
Marketing Management. 7th ed. Dalrymple. 720p. (C). 1999. text 99.95 (0-471-33238-0) Wiley.
Marketing Management 7th ed. Dalrymple. pap. text. write for info. (0-471-36201-8) Wiley.
*Marketing Management. 10th ed. Simon & Schuster Staff. (C). 2000. write for info. (0-13-013737-5) S&S Trade.
*Marketing Management: A Relationship to Marketing Perspective. Cranfield. LC 00-21419. 370p. 2000. text 79.95 (0-312-23186-5) St Martin.
Marketing Management: A Strategic Approach with a Global Orientation. 2nd ed. Harper W. Boyd et al. LC 94-20955. (Marketing Ser.). 576p. (C). 1994. text 58.95 (0-256-12576-7, Irwn Prfssnl) McGraw-Hill Prof.
Marketing Management: A Strategic Approach with a Global Orientation. 3rd ed. Harper W. Boyd et al. LC 97-22528. 1997. write for info. (0-07-115429-9) McGraw.
*Marketing Management: An Asian Perspective. 2nd ed. Philip Kotler & Swee Hoon Ang. 920p. 1999. pap. text 52.00 (0-13-010980-0, Prentice Hall) P-H.
Marketing Management: Analysis, Planning, Implementation, & Control. 9th ed. Phillip Kotler. LC 96-1649. (International Series in Marketing). (Illus.). 789p. (C). 1996. text 89.00 (0-13-243510-1) P-H.
Marketing Management: Casebook. 3rd ed. Robert Davis et al. (C). 1980. 45.50 (0-256-02347-6, Irwn McGrw-H) McGrw-H Hghr Educ.
*Marketing Management: Cbc Phc Library Video. 10th ed. 2000. text. write for info. (0-13-014595-5) S&S Trade.
Marketing Management: CPS-Select Cases. 4th ed. James Donnelly & Paul J. Peter. (C). 1994. 20.95 (0-256-19023-2, Irwn McGrw-H) McGrw-H Hghr Educ.
Marketing Management: Creating & Leveraging Competitive Advantage. Rajendra Srivastava. (C). 1995. text. write for info. (0-201-50578-9) Addison-Wesley.
Marketing Management: Integrating Theory & Practice. T. Proctor. (Illus.). 528p. 1995. pap. 24.99 (0-412-62350-1) Thomson Learn.
Marketing Management: Issues in Ambulatory Health Care. Robert E. Sweeney. (Journal of Ambulatory Care Marketing: Vol. 4 No. 2). (Illus.). 192p. 1991. text 49.95 (1-56024-122-5) Haworth Pr.
Marketing Management: Knowledge & Skills. 4th ed. James H. Donnelly, Jr. & J. Paul Peter. LC 94-7621. (Marketing Ser.). 864p. (C). 1994. text 70.95 (0-256-13727-7, Irwn McGrw-H) McGrw-H Hghr Educ.
Marketing Management: Knowledge & Skills. 5th ed. J. Paul Peter & James H. Donnelly. LC 97-20733. (Irwin Series in Marketing). (C). 1997. text 95.14 (0-256-22633-4, Irwn Prfssnl) McGraw-Hill Prof.
Marketing Management: Knowledge & Skills. 6th ed. J. Paul Peter. 896p. 2000. 85.63 (0-07-231557-1) McGraw.
Marketing Management: Knowledge & Skills CPS - Finance 1 Course (Pace University) 3rd ed. J. Paul Peter et al. (C). 1994. 15.95 (0-256-19142-5, Irwn McGrw-H) McGrw-H Hghr Educ.
Marketing Management: Knowledge & Skills CPS Selected. 4th ed. Paul J. Peter & James Donnelly. (C). 1994. 29.95 (0-256-19134-4, Irwn McGrw-H) McGrw-H Hghr Educ.
Marketing Management: Millenium Edition. 10th ed. (C). 1999. pap. 13.33 (0-13-016280-9) P-H.
Marketing Management: Millenium Edition. 10th ed. (C). 2000. pap. write for info. (0-13-016398-8) P-H.
*Marketing Management: Millenium Edition. 10th ed. Simon & Schuster Staff. LC 98-52099. (C). 1999. 81.33 (0-13-012217-3) S&S Trade.
*Marketing Management: Millennium Edition. 10th ed. 2000. write for info. (0-13-088090-6) P-H.
*Marketing Management: Millennium Edition. 10th ed. (C). 2000. write for info. (0-13-017287-1) P-H.
Marketing Management: Providing, Communicating & Delivering Value. Frank Bradley. 990p. 1995. pap. 84.00 (0-13-065343-8) P-H.
Marketing Management: Skillbook. Educational Foundation of the National Restaurant. (Management Skills Program Ser.). 58p. (Orig.). 1992. pap. text 10.95 (0-915452-94-4) Educ Found.
*Marketing Management: Stanford Graduate School of Business. 374p. (C). 1999. 50.00 (0-536-60262-X) Pearson Custom.
Marketing Management: Strategies & Programs. 5th ed. Joseph P. Guiltinan & Gordon W. Paul. LC 93-22754. (Series in Marketing). (C). 1993. text 75.50 (0-07-048971-8) McGraw.
Marketing Management: Strategies & Programs. 6th ed. Joseph P. Guiltinan et al. LC 96-27233. (Marketing Ser.). 496p. (C). 1996. 83.44 (0-07-049097-X) McGraw.
Marketing Management: Technology As a Social Process. Ed. by George Fisk. LC 86-8202. 323p. 1986. 69.50 (0-275-92177-8, C2177, Praeger Pubs) Greenwood.
Marketing Management: Text & Cases. John A. Quelch et al. LC 92-31499. (Series in Marketing). (Illus.). 960p. (C). 1993. text 70.95 (0-256-10955-9, Irwn McGrw-H) McGrw-H Hghr Educ.
Marketing Management: Text & Cases. 6th ed. Douglas J. Dalrymple & Leonard J. Parsons. LC 94-26245. 1008p. 1994. text 92.95 (0-471-55255-0) Wiley.
Marketing Management Vol. 1: Principles, Analysis, & Applications. Benson P. Shapiro et al. (C). 1985. text 50.95 (0-256-03153-3, Irwn McGrw-H) McGrw-H Hghr Educ.
Marketing Management & Cases in Marketing Management: Select Chapters. 3rd ed. J. Paul Peter et al. (C). 1994. text 36.95 (0-256-18210-8, Irwn McGrw-H) McGrw-H Hghr Educ.
*Marketing Management & Strategy. 2nd ed. Peter Doyle. 544p. (C). 1998. pap. 72.00 (0-13-262239-4) P-H.
Marketing Management & Strategy: A Reader. 4th ed. Philip Kotler & Keith K. Cox. (Illus.). 400p. (C). 1988. pap. text 41.20 (0-13-558453-1) P-H.
Marketing Management & Strategy: Marketing Engineering Applications. Gary Lilien. 128p. (C). 1998. pap. text 33.00 (0-321-04640-4, Prentice Hall) P-H.
Marketing Management & Wall Street Journal. 4th ed. James Donnelly et al. (C). 1994. 62.95 (0-256-19096-8, Irwn McGrw-H) McGrw-H Hghr Educ.
Marketing Management for Non-Profit Organizations. Adrian Sargeant. LC 98-36853. (Illus.). 318p. 1999. text 70.00 (0-19-877567-9); pap. text 45.00 (0-19-877566-0) OUP.
Marketing Management for the Hospitality Industry: A Strategic Approach. Allen Z. Reich. LC 94-47535. 530p. 1997. 59.95 (0-471-31012-3) Wiley.
Marketing Management for Travel & Tourism. Lesley Pender. (Illus.). 320p. 1999. pap. 45.00 (0-7487-2783-3, Pub. by S Thornes Pubs) Trans-Atl Phila.
Marketing Management in the Fee-for-Service Prepaid Medical Group. Robert G. Shouldice. (Going Prepaid Ser.). 102p. (Orig.). 1987. pap. 24.00 (0-933948-78-6, 963) Ctr Res Ambulatory.
*Marketing, Management Support Systems - Principles, Tools & Implementation. Berend Wierenga & Gerrit Van Bruggen. 360p. 2000. 120.00 (0-7923-8615-9) Kluwer Academic.
Marketing Management Workbook. Ed. by C. J. Jooste. 260p. 1998. pap., wbk. ed. 31.00 (0-7021-3597-6, Pub. by Juta & Co) Intl Spec Bk.
*Marketing Managerial Foundations. Michael Baker et al. 560p. 2000. pap. 64.95 (0-7329-5211-5, Pub. by Macmill Educ) Paul & Co Pubs.
Marketing Managers Handbook. (C). 2000. pap. write for info. (0-13-016110-1) P-H.
*Marketing Manager's Troubleshooter. Rice. (C). 2000. 59.95 (0-13-923574-4, Macmillan Coll) P-H.
Marketing Manager's Yearbook: 1998 Edition. 1999. pap. 125.00 (0-906247-78-0) Kogan Page Ltd.
Marketing Manual: A Resource Guide. 126p. (C). 1997. ring bd. 35.00 (0-910329-89-3, 0112028) Am Speech Lang Hearing.
Marketing: Mastering Your Small Business see Tecnicas Cruciales de Marketing
Marketing Masters. Ed. by American Marketing Association Staff. LC 91-32691. 278p. (Orig.). 1991. pap. 24.95 (0-87757-219-4) Am Mktg.
Marketing Masters: Secrets of America's Best Companies. Gene Walden & Edmund O. Lawler. LC 92-54750. (Illus.). 256p. 1993. 22.50 (0-88730-590-3, HarpBusn) HarpInfo.
Marketing Mastery: Your Seven Step Guide to Success. 2nd ed. Harriet Stephenson et al. Ed. by Erin Wait. LC 94-47632. (Successful Business Library). (Illus.). 240p. 1995. pap. 19.95 (1-55571-357-2, Oasis Pr) PSI Resch.
Marketing Math. 3rd ed. Stull. (SB - Marketing Education Ser.). 1990. mass mkt., wbk. ed. 19.95 (0-538-60448-4) S-W Pub.
Marketing Math. 4th ed. Stull. (SB - Marketing Education Ser.). (C). Date not set. pap., teacher ed. 40.95 (0-538-68114-4) S-W Pub.
Marketing Matters: An SLA Information Kit, 1997. 94p. 1997. pap. 27.00 (0-87111-461-5, Z731) SLA.
Marketing Megaworks: The Top 150 Books & Articles. Ed. by Larry M. Robinson & Roy D. Adler. LC 86-25248. 224p. 1987. 57.95 (0-275-92318-5, C2318, Praeger Pubs) Greenwood.
Marketing Men's Clothing under U. S. - Canada Free Trade Agreement. 55p. 1989. 10.00 (0-317-01978-3) Clothing Mfrs.
Marketing Mental Health Services in a Managed Care Environment. Norman Winegar & John L. Bistline. LC 92-1697. (Illus.). 202p. 1994. pap. 14.95 (1-56024-362-7); lib. bdg. 49.95 (1-56024-361-9) Haworth Pr.
*Marketing Metrics. Tim Ambler. 256p. 2000. pap. 29.00 (0-273-64248-0) F T P H.
Marketing Miso & Soy Sauce: Labels, Ads, Posters & Other Graphics. Ed. by Akiko Aoyagi. (Marketing Soyfoods Ser.). 148p. 1988. spiral bd. 59.20 (0-933332-35-1) Soyfoods Center.
Marketing Mistakes. 7th ed. Robert F. Hartley. LC 97-14092. 384p. 1997. pap. 40.95 (0-471-15905-0) Wiley.
*Marketing Mistakes. 8th ed. Robert F. Hartley. LC 00-38172. 384p. 2000. pap. 35.00 (0-471-37060-6) Wiley.
Marketing Mix Analysis with Lotus 1-2-3. Gary L. Lilien. 250p. 1986. 42.50 incl. 3.5 hd (0-89426-168-1) Course Tech.
Marketing Models. Gary L. Lilien. LC 91-34512. 1995. pap. text 39.00 (0-13-545641-X, Pub. by P-H) S&S Trade.
Marketing Modernism in Fin-de-Siecle Europe. Robert Jensen. 376p. 1994. pap. text 18.95 (0-691-02926-1, Pub. by Princeton U Pr) Cal Prin Full Svc.
Marketing Modernisms: Self-Promotion, Canonization, & Rereading. Ed. by Kevin J. Dettmar & Stephen Watt. 384p. (Orig.). 1996. text 44.50 (0-472-09641-9, 09641); pap. text 19.95 (0-472-06641-2, 06641) U of Mich Pr.
*Marketing, Morality & the Natural Environment. Andrew Crane. LC 00-35310. (Advances in Management & Business Studies). 2001. write for info. (0-415-21382-7) Routledge.
Marketing Myths That Are Killing Business: The Cure for Death Wish Marketing. Kevin J. Clancy & Robert S. Shulman. 308p. 1995. pap. 14.95 (0-07-011361-0) McGraw.
Marketing New Homes. Clark Parker Associates Staff. 129p. 1989. pap. 22.00 (0-86718-332-2) Home Builder.
Marketing New Mexico's Natural Gas to Mexico. Ed. by Patricia A. Sullivan. 46p. (Orig.). (C). 1993. pap. text 10.00 (0-937795-03-8) Waste-Mgmt Educ.
Marketing, 1991-92. Harvard Business School Press Staff. 1990. pap. text 50.00 (0-07-103299-1) McGraw.
Marketing, 1996-1997. annuals 18th ed. Ed. by John E. Richardson. 256p. (C). 1995. text. write for info. (0-697-31545-2) Brown & Benchmark.
Marketing, 98-99. 20th ed. John E. Richardson. (Annual Ser.). (Illus.). 240p. 1998. pap. text 12.25 (0-697-39180-9, Dshkn McG-Hill) McGrw-H Hghr Educ.
Marketing Nonprofit Programs & Services: Proven & Practical Strategies to Get More Customers, Members & Donors. Douglas B. Herron. LC 96-25356. (Nonprofit Sector Ser.). 1996. 30.95 (0-7879-0326-4) Jossey-Bass.
Marketing Nuts & Bolts. Zweig White & Associates Staff. Ed. by Susan E. Marshall. 139p. 1998. pap. 39.00 (1-885002-58-0) Zweig White.
Marketing of Agricultural Products. 8th ed. Richard L. Kohls & Joseph N. Uhl. LC 97-3807. 560p. 1997. 99.00 (0-13-231275-1) P-H.
Marketing of Agriculture Products 8th ed. (C). 1997. text, teacher ed. write for info. (0-13-270893-0, Macmillan Coll) P-H.
Marketing of Cooperative Advertising. Elaine Bastl. (Illus.). 110p. 1983. 15.95 (0-912875-00-3) Basbery Pub.
Marketing of Engineering Services. Brian Scanlon. 120p. 1988. 25.00 (0-7277-1348-5, Pub. by T Telford) RCH.
Marketing of Financial Services. Jane Cowdell & Christ Farrance. 465p. 1990. pap. 125.00 (0-85297-337-3, Pub. by Chartered Bank) St Mut.
Marketing of Hedge Funds: A Key Strategic Variable in Defining Possible Roles of an Emerging Investment Force. 2nd ed. Matthias Bekier. (European University Studies: Vol. 1902). 557p. (C). 1997. pap. text 63.95 (3-906759-43-1) P Lang Pubng.
Marketing of Hospitality Services. William Lazer & Roger Layton. LC 99-217175. (Illus.). (C). 1998. pap. 77.95 (0-86612-157-9) Educ Inst Am Hotel.
Marketing of Ideas & Social Issues. Seymour H. Fine. LC 81-850. 227p. 1981. 45.00 (0-275-90623-X, C0623, Praeger Pubs) Greenwood.
Marketing of Ideas & Social Issues. Seymour H. Fine. LC 81-850. 1981. 28.95 (0-03-059277-1) Holt R&W.
Marketing of Nations. Phillip Kotler et al. LC 97-1285. 1997. 40.00 (0-684-83488-X) S&S Trade.
Marketing of Petroleum Products. Marshall C. Howard. Ed. by Stuart Bruchey & Vincent P. Carosso. LC 78-18964. (Small Business Enterprise in America Ser.). 1979. lib. bdg. 31.95 (0-405-11468-0) Ayer.
Marketing of Polymer Modifiers & Additives: Technical Papers, Regional Technical Conference, September 23-25, 1991, Ramada Renaissance Hotel, East Brunswick, NJ. Society of Plastics Engineers Staff. LC TA0455.. (Illus.). 180p. reprint ed. pap. 55.80 (0-7837-1788-1, 204198700001) Bks Demand.

An Asterisk (*) at the beginning of an entry indicates that the title is appearing for the first time.

Marketing of Services. Hoffman. (C). 1996. pap. text, teacher ed. 70.00 (*0-03-017803-7*) Harcourt Coll Pubs.

Marketing of Services. Ken Irons. LC 96-32496. (Marketing for Professionals Ser.). 1996. pap. write for info. (*0-07-709084-5*) McGraw.

Marketing of Shellfish. W. S. Nowak. 1978. 50.00 (*0-7855-6937-5*) St Mut.

Marketing of the President: Political Marketing As Campaign Strategy. Bruce I. Newman. LC 93-32450. (C). 1993. text 48.00 (*0-8039-5137-X*); pap. text 21.00 (*0-8039-5138-8*) Sage.

Marketing of Tourism Products: Concepts, Issues & Cases. A. V. Seaton. 564p. 1996. pap. 24.99 (*1-86152-302-5*) Thomson Learn.

Marketing of Tradition: Perspectives on Folklore, Tourism & the Heritage Industry. Ed. by Teri Brewer. 1994. pap. 19.50 (*1-874312-21-4*, Pub. by Hisarlik Pr) Intl Spec Bk.

Marketing of Traffic Safety. OECD Staff. 120p. (Orig.). 1993. pap. 35.00 (*92-64-13903-6*) OECD.

Marketing on a Budget. Ros Jay. LC 98-149152. (ITBP PROFESSIONAL). 256p. 1998. pap. 24.95 (*1-86152-146-4*) Thomson Learn.

Marketing on the Internet. Ekin. 2000. pap. text 11.97 (*0-395-97220-5*) HM.

Marketing on the Internet: A Proven 7 Step Plan for Selling Your Products & Services & Image to Millions over the Information Superhighway. 3rd ed. Jan Zimmerman. LC 98-9088. 1998. pap. 34.95 (*1-885068-26-3*) Maximum Pr.

Marketing on the Internet: A 7 Step Plan for Selling Your Products, Service, & Image to Millions over the Information Superhighway. 4th rev. ed. Jan Zimmerman. (Illus.). 276p. 1999. pap. 34.95 (*1-885068-36-0*) Maximum Pr.

***Marketing on the Internet: A 7-Step Plan for Selling Your Products, Services & Image to Millions over the Information Superhighway.** 5th ed. Jan Zimmerman. 276p. 2000. pap. 34.95 (*1-885068-49-2*, Pub. by Maximum Pr) IPG Chicago.

Marketing on the Internet: Multimedia Strategies for the World Wide Web. 2nd rev. expanded ed. Jill H. Ellsworth & Matthew V. Ellsworth. LC 96-41394. 464p. 1996. pap. 29.99 (*0-471-16504-2*) Wiley.

***Marketing on the Internet: Principles of On-Line Marketing.** Judy Strauss & Raymond D. Frost. LC 98-56092. 383p. (C). 1999. pap. text 52.67 (*0-13-010585-6*) P-H.

***Marketing on the Web: Building Your Business Using the Internet.** David Schincariol. 280p. 1999. pap. text 19.95 (*1-55180-237-6*) Self-Counsel Pr.

Marketing I. Jack Rudman. (Regents External Degree (REDP) Ser.: Vol. 10). 43.95 (*0-8373-5660-1*) Nat Learn.

Marketing I. Jack Rudman. (Regents External Degree Ser.: REDP-10). 1994. pap. 23.95 (*0-8373-5610-5*) Nat Learn.

Marketing Online for Dummies. Bud E. Smith. LC 98-70125. (For Dummies Ser.). 368p. 1998. pap. 24.99 incl. cd-rom (*0-7645-0335-9*) IDG Bks.

Marketing Operations. Delaughter. 1998. 23.50 (*0-07-230286-0*) McGraw.

Marketing Operations, 1997-98. Worsam. 416p. 1997. pap., wbk. ed. 39.95 (*0-7506-3584-3*) Buttrwrth-Heinemann.

***Marketing Operations 1998-99.** Worsam. 416p. 1999. pap. text 34.95 (*0-7506-4030-8*) Buttrwrth-Heinemann.

Marketing Ophthalmology: A Comprehensive Marketing Guide for Ophthalmologists. Stanley R. Joseph. (Illus.). 231p. 1995. pap. write for info. (*1-929196-01-6*) Am Ophthlmc Admin.

Marketing Opportunities for the 1990's in Fiber Optics Long-Distance Telecommunications Network in North America. 4th ed. IGIC, Inc. Staff. 260p. 1989. pap. 1495.00 (*0-918435-86-2*, IGIC-12) Info Gatekeepers.

Marketing Opportunities in Ireland. Peter Nabney. 246p. 1985. 450.00 (*0-903706-75-X*, Pub. by Euromonitor PLC) St Mut.

Marketing Opportunities in West Germany. 1985. 550.00 (*0-903706-74-1*, Pub. by Euromonitor PLC) St Mut.

Marketing Organisation: An Analysis of Information Processing, Power & Politics. Nigel Piercy. (Illus.). 224p. 1985. text 34.95 (*0-04-658245-2*) Routledge.

Marketing Organization & Magagement: Basic Business 206 (3-4) 374p. (C). 1997. text 135.00 (*0-536-59916-5*) Pearson Custom.

Marketing Organization & Management: Basic Business 206 (1-2) 426p. (C). 1997. text 115.00 (*0-536-59915-7*) Pearson Custom.

Marketing Paper. 2nd ed. Churchill. 1999. 41.60 (*0-07-236922-1*) McGraw.

Marketing para Todos. Alan West. (SPA.). (C). 1994. pap. text 15.00 (*0-201-62579-2*) Addison-Wesley.

Marketing Paradigm: A Guide for General Managers. Paul R. Messinger. LC 94-41608. (C). 1995. 26.50 (*0-538-84494-9*) S-W Pub.

Marketing Peanut Butter: A Microcomputer Simulation. C. Lewis et al. 1984. 271.72 (*0-07-079588-6*) McGraw.

Marketing Performance Assesment. Bonoma. 218p. 1988. pap. 15.16 (*0-07-103211-8*) McGraw.

Marketing Perspectives on a Potential Pacific Spice Industry. Grant Vinning. 1990. pap. 60.00 (*1-86320-006-1*, Pub. by ACIAR) St Mut.

Marketing Pharmaceutical Services: Patron Loyalty, Satisfaction, & Preferences. Ed. by Harry A. Smith & Stephen J. Coons. LC 91-22251. (Illus.). 386p. 1992. lib. bdg. 59.95 (*1-56024-208-6*) Haworth Pr.

Marketing Pharmaceutical Services: Patron Loyalty, Satisfaction, & Preferences. Ed. by Harry A. Smith & Stephen J. Coons. 368p. 1992. pap. 24.95 (*1-56024-209-4*) Haworth Pr.

Marketing Pharmacy Services, 1990, Level 2. 182p. 1990. ring bd. 63.00 (*1-879907-12-7*, P322) Am Soc Hlth-Syst.

Marketing Piece. 4th ed. (C). 1999. Price not set. (*0-13-022291-7*) P-H.

Marketing Places: Attracting Investment, Industry, & Tourism to Cities, States, & Regions. Philip Kotler et al. 404p. 1993. 40.00 (*0-02-917596-8*) Free Pr.

Marketing Plan see Marketing Plan: Step-by-Step Workbook

Marketing Plan. David S. Hopkins. (Report: No. 801). (Illus.). vi, 138p. 1981. pap. text 80.00 (*0-8237-0237-5*) Conference Bd.

Marketing Plan. MacDonald. 96p. 1987. pap. text 34.95 (*0-7506-0678-9*) Buttrwrth-Heinemann.

Marketing Plan. 2nd ed. William A. Cohen. LC 97-12926. 352p. 1997. pap. 48.95 (*0-471-18033-5*) Wiley.

Marketing Plan: A Practitioner's Guide. 2nd ed. John Westwood. 217p. pap. 44.95 (*0-8464-4318-X*) Beekman Pubs.

Marketing Plan: A Practitioner's Guide 2nd. 2nd ed. John Westwood. 1998. pap. text 30.00 (*0-7494-2614-4*) Kogan Page Ltd.

Marketing Plan: How to Prepare & Implement It. 2nd expanded ed. William M. Luther. LC 92-17618. 208p. 1992. pap. 17.95 (*0-8144-7805-0*) AMACOM.

Marketing Plan: Step-by-Step Workbook. 3rd rev. ed. Michael O'Donnell. Ed. by Bruce Gjovig. Orig. Title: The Marketing Plan. 160p. 1998. wbk. ed. 29.95 (*0-9626855-5-0*) Ctr for Innov.

Marketing Plan - Step-by-Step. Michael O'Donnell. 150p. (Orig.). 1991. pap. 49.95 (*0-930204-30-1*) Lord Pub.

***Marketing Plan in Color: A Pictorial Guide for Managers.** 4th ed. Malcolm McDonald & Peter Morris. (Illus.). 96p. 2000. pap. 24.95 (*0-7506-4759-0*) Buttrwrth-Heinemann.

Marketing Plan in the 1990s. Howard Sutton. (Report: No. 951). (Illus.). 62p. (Orig.). 1990. pap. text 80.00 (*0-8237-0397-5*) Conference Bd.

Marketing Plan Project - Marketing. 3rd ed. Charles W. Lamb. (SB - Marketing Education Ser.). 1995. mass mkt. 15.95 (*0-538-84951-7*) S-W Pub.

Marketing Plan Workbook. James C. Makens. 240p. (C). 1988. pap. text 24.95 (*0-13-558537-6*) P-H.

Marketing Planning. Dibb & Simkin. 1996. pap., wbk. ed. 19.99 (*1-86152-349-1*, Pub. by ITBP) Thomson Learn.

Marketing Planning: A Step-by-Step Guide. James W. Taylor. 272p. (C). 1996. pap. 24.95 (*0-13-242041-4*); text 49.95 (*0-13-242058-9*) P-H.

***Marketing Planning: A Step-by-Step Guide.** James W. Taylor. (Illus.). 364p. 2000. reprint ed. pap. text 25.00 (*0-7881-9113-6*) DIANE Pub.

***Marketing Planning: Strategy, Tactics & Implementation.** Barry Davies & Claudio Vignali. 352p. (Orig.). 2000. pap. 50.00 (*0-273-62862-3*) F T P H.

Marketing, Planning & Strategy. Subhash C. Jain. LC 95-51292. 1996. write for info. (*0-614-95888-1*) S-W Pub.

Marketing Planning & Strategy. 2nd ed. Subhash C. Jain. (SWC-Marketing). (C). 1985. 40.50 (*0-538-19130-9*, S13) S-W Pub.

Marketing Planning & Strategy. 3rd ed. Subhash C. Jain. (C). 1989. 54.50 (*0-538-80251-0*, SS90CA) S-W Pub.

Marketing Planning & Strategy. 4th ed. Subhash C. Jain. LC 92-31418. (C). 1992. 65.50 (*0-538-82648-7*) S-W Pub.

Marketing Planning & Strategy. 5th ed. Jain. (SS - Marketing Management Ser.). 1996. pap. 71.95 (*0-538-85283-6*) S-W Pub.

***Marketing Planning & Strategy Case Book.** Jain. (Swc-Marketing Ser.). (C). 2000. pap. 15.00 (*0-324-06262-1*) Sth-Wstrn College.

Marketing Planning for the Pharmaceutical Industry. John Lidstone. 250p. 1987. text 109.95 (*0-566-02630-9*, Pub. by Gower) Ashgate Pub Co.

***Marketing Planning for the Pharmaceutical Industry.** 2nd ed. John Lidstone & Janice MacLennan. LC 98-41233. 200p. 1999. 160.00 (*0-566-08112-1*) Ashgate Pub Co.

Marketing Planning Guide. Robert E. Stevens et al. LC 90-27355. 308p. (C). 1991. text 49.95 (*1-56024-083-0*); pap. text 19.95 (*1-56024-084-9*) Haworth Pr.

Marketing Planning Guide. 2nd ed. Robert E. Stevens et al. LC 97-1572. (Illus.). 343p. (C). 1997. pap. 29.95 (*0-7890-0241-8*) Haworth Pr.

Marketing Planning Guide. 2nd ed. Robert E. Stevens et al. LC 97-1572. (Illus.). 343p. (C). 1997. 49.95 (*0-7890-0112-8*) Haworth Pr.

Marketing Planning in a Total Quality Environment. Robert E. Linneman & John L. Stanton. LC 94-48363. (Illus.). 461p. 1995. lib. bdg. 79.95 (*1-56024-938-2*) Haworth Pr.

Marketing Planning Strategy. 6th ed. Jain. LC 99-35181. (Swc-Marketing Ser.). 1999. pap. 96.95 (*0-324-01480-5*) Thomson Learn.

Marketing Planning Workbook: Effective Marketing for Marketing Managers. Sally Dibb et al. LC 95-30550. (Marketing Workbooks Ser.). 256p. (C). 1996. pap. 29.95 (*0-415-11891-3*) Thomson Learn.

Marketing Plans: How to Prepare Them: How to Use Them. 3rd ed. Malcolm H. Mcdonald. (Professional Development Ser.). 360p. 1999. pap. text 39.95 (*0-7506-2213-X*) Buttrwrth-Heinemann.

Marketing Plans: How to Prepare Them, How to Use Them. 4th ed. Malcolm H. B. McDonald. 578p. 2000. pap. text 44.95 (*0-7506-4116-9*) Buttrwrth-Heinemann.

Marketing Plans: With a Winning Edge. Angela Hatton. (Pitman Marketing Ser.). (Illus.). 320p. 1995. pap. text 19.95 (*0-273-61693-5*) F T P-H.

***Marketing Plans for Lemonade Stands: The Micro-Business Owner's How-To Guide to More Sales & Bigger Profits.** Michael E. Odell. 112p. 1999. pap. text 24.00 (*0-924380-03-9*) Veritas Rsch Pub.

***Marketing Plans That Work.** 2nd ed. Malcolm McDonald & Warren J. Keegan. 2001. pap. 21.95 (*0-7506-7307-9*) Buttrwrth-Heinemann.

Marketing Plans That Work: Targeting Growth & Profitability. Malcolm H. McDonald & Warren J. Keegan. LC 97-7401. 240p. 1997. pap. text 19.95 (*0-7506-9828-4*) Buttrwrth-Heinemann.

Marketing Policy Determination by a Major Firm in a Capital Goods Industry. Kenneth H. Myers. LC 75-41773. (Companies & Men: Business Enterprises in America Ser.). 1976. 47.95 (*0-405-08087-5*) Ayer.

Marketing Portfolio Planner. Malcolm McDonald. Date not set. audio compact disk 340.00 (*0-7506-4893-7*) Buttrwrth-Heinemann.

Marketing Practices & Principles. 3rd ed. Ralph E. Mason et al. (Illus.). 1980. text 24.88 (*0-07-040693-6*) McGraw.

Marketing Practices & Principles. 4th ed. Ralph E. Mason et al. 448p. 1985. text 21.24 (*0-07-040705-3*) McGraw.

Marketing Practices in Small Scale Industries. R. P. Hooda. (C). 1991. 18.00 (*81-7026-168-6*, Pub. by Heritage IA) S Asia.

Marketing Precedes the Miracle: More Cartoons. Illus. by Calvin Grondahl. LC 88-151150. 96p. 1987. pap. 7.95 (*0-941214-63-X*) Signature Bks.

Marketing Preview. 5th ed. Berkowitz. 1996. 37.50 (*0-256-22890-6*) McGraw.

Marketing Principles & Perspectives. 2nd ed. William O. Bearden et al. LC 97-24735. (Irwin-McGraw-Hill Series in Marketing). (C). 1997. text 52.50 (*0-256-21897-8*, Irwn Prfssnl) McGraw-Hill Prof.

Marketing Principles & Practice. 3rd ed. Dennis Adcock & Ray Bradfield. 464p. (Orig.). 2000. pap. write for info. (*0-273-62798-8*) F T P H.

Marketing Problems of Forestry Industry in India. Indra Kumar & Alok Kumar. 1990. 32.00 (*81-7169-037-8*, Commonwealth) S Asia.

Marketing Professional Services: Practical Apractical Approaches To Practice Development. Patrick Forsyth. 1999. pap. text 29.95 (*0-7494-2982-8*, Kogan Pg Educ) Stylus Pub VA.

Marketing Public Health: Strategies to Promote Social Change. Michael Siegel & Lynn Doner. LC 98-24163. 208p. 1998. 49.00 (*0-8342-1071-1*, 10711) Aspen Pub.

***Marketing Public Relations: The HOWS That Make It Work.** Rene A. Henry, Jr. LC 99-89008. 296p. 2000. pap. 29.95 (*0-8138-2207-6*) Iowa St U Pr.

Marketing-Public Relations for Lawyers. Jack A. Gottschalk. (Illus.). 160p. (Orig.). 1990. pap. 40.00 (*0-939457-00-8*) NJ Inst CLE.

Marketing Public Transit: A Strategic Approach. Christopher H. Lovelock et al. LC 87-11583. (Public & Nonprofit Sector Marketing Ser.). 238p. 1987. 52.95 (*0-275-92499-8*, C2499, Praeger Pubs) Greenwood.

Marketing Reader. Ed. by Dale Littler & Dominic Wilson. (Management Reader Ser.). 300p. 1995. pap. text 41.95 (*0-7506-0662-2*) Buttrwrth-Heinemann.

***Marketing Reader C55,0001.** Williams. 1999. 35.00 (*0-07-432904-9*, McGrw-H College) McGrw-H Hghr Educ.

Marketing Real Estate. 3rd ed. William M. Shenkel. LC 92-35168. 396p. (C). 1993. 51.80 (*0-13-555079-3*) P-H.

Marketing Real Estate Internationally. M. A. Hines. LC 87-24935. 240p. 1988. 62.95 (*0-89930-205-X*, HMR/, Quorum Bks) Greenwood.

Marketing Rehabilitation Facility Product & Services. Goodwill Industries of America Staff & Christopher A. Smith. (Illus.). 156p. (Orig.). (C). 1987. pap. write for info. (*0-916671-47-X*) TRR.

Marketing Representative. Jack Rudman. (Career Examination Ser.: C-2465). 1994. pap. 29.95 (*0-8373-2465-3*) Nat Learn.

***Marketing Research.** (C). 1999. 24.00 (*0-321-02013-8*) Addison-Wesley.

***Marketing Research.** (C). 1998. write for info. (*0-13-017289-8*) P-H.

Marketing Research. Bush. LC 99-27710. 1999. 65.00 (*0-256-19555-2*) McGraw.

Marketing Research. Kerr. 1136p. 1999. pap. text, teacher ed. write for info. (*0-02-362790-5*) P-H.

Marketing Research. Don Lehmann. (C). 1998. text. write for info. (*0-321-02879-1*) Addison-Wesley.

Marketing Research. Don Lehmann. LC 97-34741. (Illus.). 950p. (C). 1997. 98.00 (*0-321-01416-2*, Prentice Hall) P-H.

Marketing Research. Myers. (General Business & Business Education Ser.). 1996. pap. 13.00 (*0-8273-6252-8*) Delmar.

Marketing Research. A. Parasuraman. (C). 1986. text 39.96 (*0-201-06051-5*, 85-1354) Addison-Wesley.

Marketing Research. 2nd ed. E. Edward Harris. Ed. by Eugene L. Dorr. (Occupational Manuals & Projects in Marketing Ser.). (Illus.). (gr. 7-12). 1978. text 12.28 (*0-07-026837-1*) McGraw.

Marketing Research. 2nd ed. Sudman. 2000. 65.25 (*0-07-231477-X*) McGraw.

Marketing Research. 2nd ed. Wong Toon Quee. LC 97-219758. 512p. 1996. reprint ed. pap. 44.95 (*9971-64-312-X*) Heinemann.

***Marketing Research.** 3rd ed. Alvin C. Burns & Ronald F. Bush. LC 99-47150. 640p. 1999. 105.00 (*0-13-014411-8*) P-H.

Marketing Research. 3rd ed. Peter M. Chisnall. (Marketing Ser.). 312p. (C). 1986. text 30.75 (*0-07-084155-1*) McGraw.

***Marketing Research.** 3rd ed. Wong-Toon Quee. 360p. 2000. pap. 39.95 (*0-7506-4707-8*) Buttrwrth-Heinemann.

Marketing Research. 5th ed. Peter M. Chisnall. LC 96-38336. 1996. pap. write for info. (*0-07-709175-2*) McGraw.

Marketing Research. 6th ed. David A. Aaker et al. LC 97-21710. 792p. 1997. text 99.95 (*0-471-17069-0*) Wiley.

Marketing Research. 6th ed. Gilbert A. Churchill. 824p. (C). 1994. pap. text, teacher ed. 49.75 (*0-03-006888-6*) Harcourt Coll Pubs.

***Marketing Research.** 7th ed. D. Aaker et al. 816p. 2000. write for info. (*0-471-36340-5*) Wiley.

Marketing Research: An Aid to Decision Making. Alan T. Shao. LC 98-23818. 650p. 1998. pap. 75.95 (*0-538-88192-5*) S-W Pub.

Marketing Research: An Applied Approach. 5th ed. Thomas C. Kinnear & James R. Taylor. LC 95-22571. (Series in Marketing). 1995. 24.95 (*0-07-034799-9*) McGraw.

Marketing Research: An Applied Approach. 5th ed. Thomas C. Kinnear & James R. Taylor. (C). 1995. text 80.50 incl. disk (*0-07-912252-3*) McGraw.

Marketing Research: Applications & Problems. Ed. by Arun K. Jain et al. LC 81-14651. 569p. reprint ed. pap. 176.40 (*0-608-15938-7*, 203305100083) Bks Demand.

***Marketing Research: Applied Orientation.** 3rd ed. (C). 1999. write for info. (*0-13-031547-8*) P-H.

***Marketing Research: European Edition.** 752p. 2000. write for info. (*0-13-922964-7*) P-H.

M

Marketing Research: Marketing Engineering Applications. Gary Lilien. 152p. (C). 1998. pap. text 40.00 (*0-321-04646-3*, Prentice Hall) P-H.

Marketing Research: Methodological Foundations. 6th ed. Gilbert A. Churchill. 1117p. (C). 1994. text 91.00 (*0-03-098366-5*) Dryden Pr.

Marketing Research: Methodological Foundations. 6th ed. Gilbert A. Churchill, Jr. 444p. (C). 1995. pap. text, teacher ed. 40.00 (*0-03-006889-4*, Pub. by Harcourt Coll Pubs) Harcourt.

Marketing Research: Methodological Foundations. 7th ed. Gilbert A. Churchill. LC 98-71246. 1998. text 91.50 (*0-03-023816-1*, Pub. by Harcourt Coll Pubs) Harcourt.

Marketing Research: Methodological Foundations. 7th ed. Gilbert A. Churchill, Jr. (C). 1998. pap. text 74.00 (*0-03-023818-8*) Harcourt Coll Pubs.

Marketing Research: Private & Public Sector Decisions. David A. Aaker & George S. Day. LC 79-18532. (Wiley Series in Marketing). (Illus.). 648p. reprint ed. pap. 200.00 (*0-7837-3502-2*, 205783500008) Bks Demand.

***Marketing Research: State-of-the-Art Perspectives: Handbook of the American Marketing Association & the Professional Marketing Research Society.** Chuck Chakrapani et al. LC 00-35565. 2000. write for info. (*0-87757-283-6*) Am Mktg.

Marketing Research & Exercise. 3rd ed. McDaniel & Gates. 1995. 60.20 (*0-314-08609-9*) Sth-Wstrn College.

***Marketing Research Essentials.** Carl D. McDaniel & Roger H. Gates. LC 00-36524. 2001. write for info. incl. disk (*0-324-03713-9*) Sth-Wstrn College.

Marketing Research Essentials. Carl McDaniel, Jr. & Roger H. Gates. LC 94-20227. (SWC-Marketing). 550p. (C). 1995. pap. 50.25 (*0-314-04283-0*) West Pub.

Marketing Research Essentials. 2nd ed. Carl McDaniel & Roger Gates. LC 97-12978. (SC - Marketing Research Ser.). 512p. 1997. pap. 79.95 (*0-538-87669-7*) Thomson Learn.

Marketing Research Guide. Robert E. Stevens et al. LC 96-19070. (Illus.). 488p. 1997. 79.95 (*1-56024-339-2*) Haworth Pr.

Marketing Research in a Marketing Environment. 3rd ed. William R. Dillon et al. LC 93-24883. 784p. (C). 1993. text 67.50 (*0-256-10517-0*, Irwn McGrw-H) McGrw-H Hghr Educ.

Marketing Research in a Marketing Environment: International. 3rd ed. William R. Dillon et al. (C). 1994. text, student ed. 32.50 (*0-256-10829-3*, Irwn McGrw-H) McGrw-H Hghr Educ.

Marketing Research in a Marketing Environment: International Version. 2nd ed. William R. Dillon et al. (C). 1989. text 30.95 (*0-256-08403-3*, Irwn McGrw-H) McGrw-H Hghr Educ.

Marketing Research in Action. 2nd rev. ed. Raymond Kent. 384p. 1998. pap. 19.99 (*1-86152-155-3*) Thomson Learn.

Marketing Research in the Global Construction Industry. Low S. Pheng. (Illus.). 138p. (C). 1993. pap. 39.50 (*9971-69-173-6*, Pub. by Sngapore Univ Pr) Coronet Bks.

***Marketing Research Process.** 5th ed. Len Tiu Wright & Margaret Crimp. LC 99-51903. 400p. 2000. write for info. (*0-13-011753-6*) P-H.

Marketing Research Project Manual. 3rd ed. Glen R. Jarboe. 200p. 1996. pap. 19.00 (*0-314-07690-5*) West Pub.

Marketing Research Project Manual. 4th ed. Jarboe. LC 98-193236. (SWC-Marketing Ser.). 1998. pap. 27.95 (*0-538-89148-3*) S-W Pub.

Marketing Research Quickprint. (C). 1999. 20.95 (*0-536-02231-3*) Pearson Custom.

Marketing Research Reprint. Crask & Fox. 1997. pap. text 40.00 (*0-13-911025-9*) P-H.

Marketing Research That Pays Off: Case Histories of Marketing Research Leading to Success in the Marketplace. Ed. by Larry Percy. LC 96-25516. (Illus.). 266p. (C). 1997. pap. text 24.95 (*0-7890-0197-7*); lib. bdg. 49.95 (*1-56024-949-8*) Haworth Pr.

Marketing Research the Right Way. Harvard Business Review Staff. (Marketing & Advertising Essentials Ser.). 150p. 1991. pap. 19.95 (*0-87584-276-3*) Harvard Busn.

Marketing Research the Right Way. Harvard Business Review Staff. 150p. 1991. pap. 19.95 (*0-07-103336-X*) McGraw.

M

*__Marketing Reserch for Effective Decision Making.__ 178p. (C). 1999. pap. 35.00 (*0-536-02149-X*) Pearson Custom.

Marketing Revolution: A Radical Manifesto for Dominating the Marketplace. Kevin J. Clancy. 1992. 22.00 (*0-88730-481-8*, HarpBusn) HarpInfo.

Marketing Revolution: Understanding Major Changes in How Businesses Market. Richard L. Bencin. LC 84-7646. 220p. 1985. 32.50 (*0-915601-01-X*) Swansea Press.

*__Marketing, Sales & Customer Service.__ Charley Watkins. 244p. 1999. pap. 80.00 (*0-85297-511-2*, Pub. by Chartered Bank) St Mut.

Marketing Scales Handbook: A Compilation of Multi-Item Measures. Gordon C. Bruner & Paul J. Hensel. LC 92-18858. 1320p. 1992. 149.95 (*0-87757-226-7*) Am Mktg.

Marketing Scales Handbook: A Compilation of Multi-Item Measures. Gordon C. Bruner & Paul J. Hensel. 1320p. 1994. pap. 89.95 (*0-87757-251-8*) Am Mktg.

Marketing Scales Handbook: A Compilation of Multi-Item Measures. Gordon C. Bruner & Paul J. Hensel. 1068p. 1996. 149.95 (*0-87757-261-5*) Am Mktg.

Marketing Secrets of a Mail Order Maverick: Stories & Lessons on the Power of Direct Marketing to Start a Successful Business, Create a Famous Brand Name & Sell Any Product or Service see Sugarman Secrets

Marketing Secrets of a Mail Order Maverick: Stories & Lessons on the Power of Direct Marketing to Start a Successful Business, Create a Famous Brand Name & Sell Any Product or Service. Joseph Sugarman. (Illus.). 400p. 1998. 39.95 (*1-891686-06-2*, D00200) DelStar Bks.

Marketing Services: Competing Through Quality. Leonard L. Berry & A. Parasuraman. (Illus.). 228p. 1991. 32.95 (*0-02-903079-X*) Free Pr.

Marketing Services: Special Edition. 254p. (C). 1996. text 51.00 (*0-536-59406-6*) Pearson Custom.

Marketing, Services & Sales. John Marsh. 89p. 1990. pap. 125.00 (*0-85297-371-3*, Pub. by Chartered Bank) St Mut.

Marketing Sheets: Promoting Your Program: A Step-by-Step Guide to Preparing an Effective Marketing Sheet see Communications Series

Marketing Small Shopping Centers: How to Increase Retail Traffic & Sales. Kim A. Fraser. (Illus.). 150p. (Orig.). 1991. pap. 69.95 (*0-913598-97-6*) Intl Coun Shop.

Marketing Small Shopping Centers: How to Increase Retail Traffic & Sales. rev. ed. Kim A. Fraser. (Illus.). 150p. (Orig.). 1997. pap. 39.95 (*0-927547-74-0*) Intl Coun Shop.

Marketing Social Change: Changing Behavior to Promote Health, Social Development, & the Environment. Alan A. Andreasen. (Nonprofit Sector, Public Administration & Health Ser.). 367p. 1995. text 30.95 (*0-7879-0137-7*) Jossey-Bass.

Marketing Solar Energy Innovations. Avraham Shama. LC 81-11870. 303p. 1981. 69.50 (*0-275-90717-1*, C0717, Praeger Pubs) Greenwood.

Marketing Soymilk & Soymilk Products: Labels, Ads, Posters & Other Graphics. Ed. by Akiko Aoyagi. (Marketing Soyfoods Ser.). 174p. 1988. spiral bd. 69.60 (*0-933332-34-3*) Soyfoods Center.

Marketing Soynuts, Natto, & Modern Soy Protein Products: Company Letterheads: Labels, Ads, Posters & Other Graphics. William Shurtleff & Akiko Aoyagi. (Marketing Soyfoods Ser.). 88p. 1988. spiral bd. 35.20 (*0-933332-36-X*) Soyfoods Center.

Marketing Straight to the Heart: From New Product Development to Advertising. Barry Feig. LC 96-52678. 224p. 1997. 24.95 (*0-8144-0355-7*) AMACOM.

Marketing Strategies: A Resource for Registered Dietitians. Marcia Ward. (Illus.). (Orig.). 1984. pap. 12.95 (*0-9613444-0-7*) M Ward.

Marketing Strategies: A Road Map for Molders & Moldmakers. Clare Goldsberry. LC 98-43823. (The Imm Book Club Strategies for Molders & Moldmakers Ser.: 3). 113p. 1998. pap. 12.95 (*1-893677-01-X*) Abby Communs.

Marketing Strategies: A Road Map for Molders & Moldmakers, 4 vols., Set. Clare Goldsberry. LC 98-43823. (IMM Book Club Strategies for Molders & Moldmakers Ser.). (Illus.). 1998. lib. bdg. 275.00 (*0-9642570-3-3*) Abby Communs.

Marketing Strategies: New Approaches New Techniques. Ed. by Malcolm B. McDonald. (Best of Long Range Planning Ser.: No. 2). 250p. 1995. text 57.50 (*0-08-042572-0*, Pergamon Pr) Elsevier.

Marketing Strategies for Design-Build Contracting. W. D. Booth. (Illus.). 183p. (gr. 13). 1995. text 44.95 (*0-412-99591-3*) Chapman & Hall.

Marketing Strategies for Engineers. J. G. Snyder. LC 93-9409. 80p. 1993. 17.00 (*0-87262-859-0*) Am Soc Civil Eng.

Marketing Strategies for Growth in Uncertain Times. Allan J. Magrath. Ed. by Anne Knudsen. LC 94-20721. (Illus.). 192p. 1995. 29.95 (*0-8442-3323-4*, NTC Business Bks) NTC Contemp Pub Co.

Marketing Strategies for Growth in Uncertain Times. Allan J. Magrath. (Illus.). 192p. 1996. pap. 17.95 (*0-8442-3314-5*, NTC Business Bks) NTC Contemp Pub Co.

Marketing Strategies for Human & Social Service Agencies. Ed. by William J. Winston. LC 85-8534. (Health Marketing Quarterly Ser.: Vol. 2, No. 4). 157p. 1985. text 39.95 (*0-86656-355-5*); pap. text 17.95 (*0-86656-468-3*) Haworth Pr.

Marketing Strategies for Local Economic Development: From Design to Implementation. Kenneth Poole. Ed. by Jenny Murphy & Andrea Kailo. 44p. (Orig.). 1986. pap. 17.50 (*0-317-04902-X*) Natl Coun Econ Dev.

Marketing Strategies for Nurse Managers: A Guide for Developing & Implementing a Nursing Marketing Plan. Vi Kunkle. 276p. (C). 1990. 58.00 (*0-8342-0110-0*, 20110) Aspen Pub.

Marketing Strategies for Services: Globalization, Client-Orientation, Deregulation. Ed. by M. M. Kostecki. LC 93-39236. 264p. 1994. text 68.00 (*0-08-042389-2*, Pergamon Pr) Elsevier.

Marketing Strategies for Small Business. Richard F. Gerson. Ed. by Beverly Manber. LC 92-54355. (Small Business & Entrepreneurship Ser.). 309p. (Orig.). 1996. pap. 15.95 (*1-56052-172-4*) Crisp Pubns.

Marketing Strategies for the Mature Market. George P. Moschis. LC 94-8542. 216p. 1994. 59.95 (*0-89930-887-2*, Quorum Bks) Greenwood.

Marketing Strategies for the New Europe: A North American Perspective in 1992. John K. Ryans, Jr. & Pradaeep A. Rau. LC 89-18279. 202p. 1990. 29.95 (*0-87757-203-8*) Am Mktg.

Marketing Strategies for the Online Industry. Frederic Saunier. (Professional Librarian Ser.). 1988. 40.00 (*0-8161-1863-9*, Hall Reference); 30.00 (*0-8161-1879-5*, Hall Reference) Macmillan.

Marketing Strategies for Writers. Michael H. Sedge. LC 99-47781. 224p. 1999. pap. text 16.95 (*1-58115-040-7*) Allworth Pr.

Marketing Strategique see Marketing Strategy: A New European Approach

*__Marketing Strategy.__ Egan. 356p. 2000. 42.95 (*0-7506-4354-4*) Buttrwrth-Heinemann.

Marketing Strategy. Ferrell. LC 98-70999. (C). 1998. text 57.50 (*0-03-024801-9*) Harcourt Coll Pubs.

Marketing Strategy. 3rd ed. Orville C. Walker et al. LC 98-8631. 416p. (C). 1998. pap. 61.56 (*0-256-26118-0*) McGraw.

Marketing Strategy: A Customer-Driven Approach. Steven P. Schnaars. LC 90-43633. 384p. 1991. 40.00 (*0-02-927953-4*) Free Pr.

Marketing Strategy: A Customer-Driven Approach. 2nd rev. ed. Steven P. Schnaars. LC 97-21554. (Illus.). 256p. 1997. pap. 29.95 (*0-684-83191-0*) Free Pr.

Marketing Strategy: A Marketing Decision Game. 2nd ed. Louis E. Boone & Edwin C. Hackleman. LC 74-27870. iv, 156 p. 1975. write for info. (*0-675-08713-9*) Mrrill.

Marketing Strategy: A New European Approach. Jean-Jacques Lambin. LC 93-21714. (Marketing for Professionals Ser.).Tr. of Marketing Strategique. 1993. 22.50 (*0-07-707795-4*) McGraw.

Marketing Strategy: How to Prepare It, How to Implement It. 2nd ed. Paul Fifield. LC 99-165810. 352p. 2000. pap. text 37.95 (*0-7506-3284-4*) Buttrwrth-Heinemann.

Marketing Strategy: Planning & Implementation. 2nd ed. Orville C. Walker et al. LC 95-22508. (Series in Marketing). 416p. (C). 1995. text 51.95 (*0-256-13692-0*, Irwn McGrw-H) McGrw-H Hghr Educ.

Marketing Strategy: Relationships, Offerings, Timing & Resource Allocation. Devanathan Sudharshan. LC 94-39777. 500p. (C). 1995. 98.00 (*0-02-418264-8*, Macmillan Coll) P-H.

*__Marketing Strategy: The Challenge of the External Environment.__ David Mercer. LC 97-62267. viii, 325p. 1998. pap. write for info. (*0-7619-5876-2*) Sage.

Marketing Strategy: Training Activities for Entrepreneurs, 1. Suzanne Kindervatter & Maggie Range. LC 86-61561. (Appropriate Business Skills for Third World Women Ser.). (Illus.). 96p. (Orig.). 1986. pap. 15.50 (*0-912917-08-3*) UNIFEM.

Marketing Strategy & Competitive Positioning. 2nd ed. Graham J. Hooley et al. LC 97-45173. 1998. write for info. (*0-13-371253-2*) P-H.

Marketing Strategy & Uncertainty. Sharan Jagpal. LC 98-16307. (Illus.). 352p. (C). 1998. text 57.95 (*0-19-512573-8*) OUP.

*__Marketing Strategy for Home Health Care Agencies.__ Gwen N. Walker. 180p. 1999. pap. 19.95 (*0-9672052-1-2*) Montg Pubg Co.

Marketing Strategy in Action. Alfred Tack. 254p. 1986. text 36.50 (*0-566-02668-6*, Pub. by Gower) Ashgate Pub Co.

Marketing Strategy, International: Planning & Implementation. Harper W. Boyd, Jr. et al. (C). 1991. text, student ed. 32.50 (*0-256-11271-1*, Irwn McGrw-H) McGrw-H Hghr Educ.

Marketing Strategy Portfolio One: A Resource Guide. 1990. 580.00 (*3-9520013-3-3*, Pub. by Strategic Direction) St Mut.

Marketing Strategy Portfolio Two: A Special Study. 1990. 390.00 (*3-9520013-4-1*, Pub. by Strategic Direction) St Mut.

Marketing Study Guide. 5th ed. Eric N. Berkowitz et al. 344p. (C). 1996. text 26.25 (*0-256-21971-0*, Irwn McGrw-H) McGrw-H Hghr Educ.

Marketing Study Guide. 12th ed. Etzel. 2000. student ed. 22.74 (*0-07-228367-X*) McGraw.

Marketing Success Stories: Personal Interviews with 66 Rainmakers. Hollis Hatfield. LC 97-70253. 272p. 1997. pap. 89.95 (*1-57073-399-6*, 511-0382) Amer Bar Assn.

Marketing Tactics. Sneppenger. 2000. pap. text 11.97 (*0-395-97217-5*) HM.

Marketing Techniques for Office Staff. William Draves. 32p. 5.98 (*0-914951-14-9*) LERN.

Marketing Techniques for Physical Therapists. Kathryn Schaefer. LC 90-14570. 204p. 1991. 51.00 (*0-8342-0208-5*) Aspen Pub.

Marketing Technology Products. Ed. by Joseph R. Mancuso. LC 77-352039. (Technology Products Ser.: No. 2). (Illus.). 205p. reprint ed. pap. 63.60 (*0-8357-4182-6*, 203696000006) Bks Demand.

*__Marketing Telecommunications Services: New Approaches for a Changing Environment.__ Karen G Strouse. LC 99-30838. 6p. 1999. 69.00 (*1-58053-015-X*) Artech Hse.

Marketing Tempeh & Tempeh Products: Labels, Ads, Posters & Other Graphics. Ed. by Akiko Aoyagi. (Marketing Soyfoods Ser.). 175p. 1988. spiral bd. 70.00 (*0-933332-33-5*) Soyfoods Center.

Marketing the American Creed Abroad: Diasporas in the U. S. & Their Homelands. Yossi Shain. LC 98-11676. (Cambridge Studies in Comparative Politics). 250p. 1999. pap. text 17.95 (*0-521-64531-X*) Cambridge U Pr.

Marketing the American Creed Abroad: Diasporas in the U. S. & Their Homelands. Yossi Shain. LC 98-11676. 304p. (C). 1999. text 54.95 (*0-521-64225-6*) Cambridge U Pr.

Marketing the Arts: Praeger Series in Public & Nonprofit Sector Marketing. Michael P. Mokwa et al. Ed. by Steven E. Permut. LC 79-26603. (Praeger Special Studies). 286p. 1980. 59.95 (*0-275-90526-8*, C0526, Praeger Pubs) Greenwood.

Marketing the Church: What They Never Taught You about Church Growth. George Barna. LC 88-60625. 175p. (Orig.). 1988. pap. 9.00 (*0-89109-250-1*) NavPress.

Marketing the City: The Role of Flagship Developments in Urban Regeneration. Hedley Smyth. LC 93-34338. (Illus.). 312p. (C). 1993. 85.00 (*0-419-18610-7*, E & FN Spon) Routledge.

Marketing the College. Primary Research Group Staff. 110p. 1998. per. 85.00 (*1-57440-015-0*) Primary Research.

Marketing the Complete Awakening. Pando C. Papantoniou. (C). 1990. 85.00 (*1-872684-30-0*, Pub. by P A S S Pubns); pap. 60.00 (*1-872684-18-1*, Pub. by P A S S Pubns) St Mut.

Marketing the Continuum of Care: Hospital Marketing Strategies for Developing Community Service. Vicki Mason. LC 97-25979. 1997. 45.00 (*0-7863-1154-1*, Irwn Prfssnl) McGraw-Hill Prof.

Marketing the Group Practice: Practical Methods for the Health Care Practitioner. Ed. by William J. Winston. LC 83-13039. (Health Marketing Quarterly Ser.: Vol. 1, No. 1). 107p. 1983. text 39.95 (*0-86656-264-8*) Haworth Pr.

Marketing the Law Firm: Business Development Techniques. Sally J. Schmidt. 450p. 1991. ring bd. 90.00 (*0-317-05399-X*, 00613) NY Law Pub.

Marketing the Library. Benedict A. Leerburger. LC 81-18132. (Professional Librarian Ser.). 124p. 1982. pap. 26.50 (*0-914236-89-X*, Hall Reference) Macmillan.

Marketing the Mediterranean As a Region. 300p. 1997. pap. 20.00 (*92-844-0177-1*, WTO0177, Pub. by Wrld Tourism Org) Bernan Associates.

Marketing the Menacing Fetus in Japan. Helen Hardacre. LC 96-28732. (Twentieth-Century Japan Ser.). (Illus.). 332p. 1997. 40.00 (*0-520-20553-7*, Pub. by U CA Pr) Cal Prin Full Svc.

*__Marketing the Menacing Fetus in Japan.__ Helen Hardacre. 344p. 1999. pap. 17.95 (*0-520-21654-7*, Pub. by U CA Pr) Cal Prin Full Svc.

Marketing the Most Important Product - Yourself: Resumes & Cover Letters That Get Results. Daryl Kerr. 94p. (C). 1996. pap. text, spiral bd. 20.95 (*0-7872-2776-5*) Kendall-Hunt.

Marketing the Museum. Fiona Mclean. LC 96-22435. (Illus.). 272p. (C). 1997. 85.00 (*0-415-10392-4*); pap. 32.99 (*0-415-15293-3*) Routledge.

Marketing the One Person Business. Michael F. Rounds & Nancy Miller. LC 97-94834. (Illus.). 112p. 1998. pap. 19.95 (*0-9629944-3-X*) CPM Systems.

*__Marketing the Physician Practice.__ 1999. 40.00 (*1-57947-010-6*) AMA.

Marketing the Program. William A. Keim & Marybelle C. Keim. LC 80-84266. 127 p. 1981. 6.95 (*0-87589-814-9*) Jossey-Bass.

Marketing the Public Sector: Promoting the Causes of Public & Nonprofit Agencies. Seymour H. Fine et al. 384p. (C). 1992. pap. 29.95 (*1-56000-610-2*) Transaction Pubs.

Marketing the Value of Excellence. Terry R. Bacon et al. (Illus.). 94p. 1994. write for info. (*1-57740-005-4*, ILW003) Intl LrningWrk.

Marketing Theory. Michael Baker. (ITBP Textbooks Ser.). 1933. text. write for info. (*1-86152-593-1*, Pub. by ITBP) Thomson Learn.

Marketing Theory: Distinguished Contributions. Ed. by Stephen W. Brown & Raymond P. Fisk. LC 83-23452. (Theories in Marketing Ser.). (Illus.). 388p. reprint ed. pap. 120.30 (*0-7837-3503-0*, 205783600008) Bks Demand.

Marketing Theory: Evolution & Evaluation. Jagdish N. Sheth et al. LC 88-10162. (Theories in Marketing Ser.). 256p. 1988. text 68.95 (*0-471-63527-8*) Wiley.

Marketing Theory & Metatheory. Robert Bartels. LC 72-105536. 310p. reprint ed. 96.10 (*0-8357-9035-5*, 201778900008) Bks Demand.

Marketing Theory & Practice: 1989 AMA Winter Educators' Conference. American Marketing Association Staff. Ed. by Terry L. Childers et al. LC 89-272. (American Marketing Association Proceedings Ser.). (Illus.). 408p. 1989. reprint ed. pap. 126.50 (*0-608-04082-7*, 206481400011) Bks Demand.

Marketing III. Jack Rudman. (Regents External Degree (REDP) Ser.: Vol. 12). 43.95 (*0-8373-5662-8*) Nat Learn.

Marketing III. Jack Rudman. (Regents External Degree Ser.: REDP-12). 1994. pap. 23.95 (*0-8373-5612-1*) Nat Learn.

Marketing 3. 2nd ed. 1995. 17.00 (*3-540-58748-9*) Spr-Verlag.

*__Marketing to American Latinos Pt. 1: A Guide to the In-Culture Approach.__ Isabel Valdes. (Illus.). 190p. 2000. 54.95 (*0-9671439-3-4*, 1002) Paramount Mrkt.

Marketing to Americans with Disabilities. Packaged Facts Staff & Scenehouse Productions Staff. LC 99-182782. 1997. write for info. (*1-56241-422-4*) FIND-SVP.

Marketing to & Through Kids. Selina S. Guber & Jon Berry. 234p. 1993. 24.95 (*0-07-025111-8*) McGraw.

Marketing to Changing Consumer Markets: Environmental Scanning. Ronald D. Michman. 188p. 1983. 52.95 (*0-275-91045-8*, C1045, Praeger Pubs) Greenwood.

Marketing to China. Xu B. Yi. 160p. 1994. 24.95 (*0-8442-3395-1*, NTC Business Bks) NTC Contemp Pub Co.

Marketing to China: One Billion New Customers. Xu B. Yi. 160p. 1990. pap. 16.95 (*0-8442-3388-9*, NTC Business Bks) NTC Contemp Pub Co.

Marketing to Consumers with Disabilities: How to Identify & Meet the Growing Market Needs of 43 Million Americans. Joel Reedy. 240p. 1993. text 32.50 (*1-55738-478-9*, Irwn Prfssnl) McGraw-Hill Prof.

*__Marketing to Ethnic Consumers: An Annotated Bibliography.__ Geng Cui & Pravat K. Choudhury. LC 00-44760. (Bibliography Ser.). 2000. pap. write for info. (*0-87757-285-2*) Am Mktg.

Marketing to Generation X: Strategies for a New Era. Karen Ritchie. 1995. 25.00 (*0-02-926545-2*) Free Pr.

Marketing to Managed Care Organizations. Kathleen S. Penkert. LC 97-42357. 1998. pap. 9.95 (*0-87868-727-0*, CWLA Pr) Child Welfare.

Marketing to Older Consumers: A Handbook of Information for Strategy Development. George P. Moschis. LC 91-47642. 352p. 1992. 69.50 (*0-89930-764-7*, MOV, Quorum Bks) Greenwood.

Marketing to Pharmacists: Understanding Their Role & Influence. Benjamin F. Banahan. LC 98-33324. 165p. 1998. 69.95 (*0-7890-0686-3*, Pharmctl Prods) Haworth Pr.

*__Marketing to Pharmacists: Understanding Their Role & Influence.__ Ed. by Benjamin F. Banahan, III. 165p. 2000. pap. 29.95 (*0-7890-1009-7*, Pharmctl Prods) Haworth Pr.

Marketing to Schools: A Textbook for the Education Market. Bob Stimolo & Lynn Stimolo. 288p. 1998. 39.95 (*0-9622067-1-7*) SMRI Inc.

Marketing to the Affluent. Thomas J. Stanley. 336p. 1997. pap. 19.95 (*0-07-061047-9*) McGraw.

Marketing to the Affluent. Thomas J. Stanley. 450p. 1988. text 55.00 (*1-55623-105-9*, Irwn Prfssnl) McGraw-Hill Prof.

Marketing to the Mind: Right Brain Strategies for Advertising & Marketing. Richard C. Maddock & Richard L. Fulton. LC 95-50743. 304p. 1996. 59.95 (*1-56720-031-1*, Quorum Bks) Greenwood.

Marketing to the New America. Tharp. Date not set. 25.00 (*0-02-932466-1*) Jossey-Bass.

Marketing to the New Natural Consumer: Consumer Trends Forming the Wellness Category. Harvey Hartman. (Illus.). 100p. 1999. pap. 39.95 (*1-929027-00-1*) Hartman Grp.

Marketing to the Paper & Pulp Industry: 1984 Seminar Notes. Technical Association of the Pulp & Paper Industry. LC TS1109.. 100p. 1984. reprint ed. pap. 31.00 (*0-608-12032-4*, 202280000030) Bks Demand.

Marketing to the Pulp & Paper Industry Seminar, 1990: Scanticon Conference Center, Minneapolis, MN, June 5-8. Technical Association of the Pulp & Paper Industry. LC HD9827.M37. (TAPPI Notes Ser.). (Illus.). 296p. reprint ed. pap. 91.80 (*0-8357-4326-8*, 203712600007) Bks Demand.

Marketing to the Pulp & Paper Industry, 1986: Proceedings of Conference, Hotel Intercontinental, Hilton Head, SC, May 28-30, 1986. Technical Association of the Pulp & Paper Industry. LC HD9820.5.A1. 242p. pap. 75.10 (*0-608-15246-3*, 202917500059) Bks Demand.

Marketing to the Pulp & Paper Seminar, 1989: May 30-June 2, Hyatt Regency, Savannah, GA. Technical Association of the Pulp & Paper Industry. LC HD9827.M37. (TAPPI Notes Ser.). (Illus.). 273p. pap. 84.70 (*0-8357-6332-3*, 203560500096) Bks Demand.

Marketing to Win: How You Can Build Your Client Base in the New Highly Competitive Service Economy. Frank K. Sonnenberg. 256p. 1990. 29.95 (*0-88730-420-6*, HarpBusn) HarpInfo.

Marketing Today. G. Oliver. 425p. (C). 1988. 100.00 (*0-7855-3782-1*, Pub. by Inst Pur & Supply) St Mut.

Marketing Today. Ed. by G. Oliver. 425p. (C). 1989. 173.00 (*0-7855-4626-X*, Pub. by Inst Pur & Supply) St Mut.

Marketing Today. G. Oliver. 425p. (C). 1990. 200.00 (*0-7855-5656-7*, Pub. by Inst Pur & Supply) St Mut.

Marketing Today. 3rd ed. David Rachman. (C). 1994. text 30.25 (*0-03-000559-0*) Harcourt Coll Pubs.

Marketing Today. 4th ed. Gordon Oliver. 550p. 1995. pap. 63.00 (*0-13-203001-2*) P-H.

Marketing Today's Fashion. 3rd ed. Carol S. Mueller. LC 94-17476. 320p. 1994. pap. text 85.00 (*0-13-043001-3*) P-H.

Marketing Tofu: Labels, Ads, Posters & Other Graphics. Ed. by Akiko Aoyagi. (Marketing Soyfoods Ser.). 180p. (Orig.). 1988. spiral bd. 71.00 (*0-933332-30-0*) Soyfoods Center.

Marketing Tofu Second Generation Products: Labels, Ads, Posters & Other Graphics. Ed. by Akiko Aoyagi. (Marketing Soyfoods Ser.). 176p. 1988. spiral bd. 70.40 (*0-933332-32-7*) Soyfoods Center.

Marketing Tofutti & Other Soy Ice Creams: Labels, Articles, Ads, Posters & Other Graphics. Ed. by Akiko Aoyagi. (Marketing Soyfoods Ser.). 214p. 1985. pap., spiral bd. 75.00 (*0-933332-37-8*) Soyfoods Center.

Marketing Tourism. Lickorish & Jefferson. 1988. pap. text. write for info. (*0-582-03340-3*, Pub. by Addison-Wesley) Longman.

Marketing Tourism Destinations: A Strategic Planning Approach. Ernie Heath & Geoffrey Wall. LC 91-33980. 240p. 1992. 59.95 (*0-471-54067-6*) Wiley.

Marketing Tourism, Hospitality & Leisure in Europe. Horner. (ITBP Textbooks Ser.). 1996. pap. 23.99 (*1-86152-303-3*) Thomson Learn.

Marketing Tourism, Hospitality & Leisure in Europe. S. Horner & J. Swarbrooke. (Illus.). 352p. 1996. mass mkt. 35.95 (*0-412-62170-3*) Chapman & Hall.

Marketing Tourism Places. Gregory J. Ashworth & Brian Goodall. 304p. (C). (gr. 13). 1990. pap. 74.95 (*0-415-03810-3*, A4064) Thomson Learn.

Marketing Training Services. Ian Linton. LC 97-3420. 210p. 1997. text 74.95 (*0-566-07549-0*, Pub. by Gower) Ashgate Pub Co.

Marketing Trends: An Analysis of Marketing Activities. Etra Corporation Staff. 55p. (Orig.). 1992. pap. 29.00 (*1-889394-27-0*) Credit Union Execs.

***Marketing Trends in Australasia: Essays & Case Studies.** Michael Harker et al. 300p. 2000. pap. 39.95 (*0-7329-5498-3*, Pub. by Macmill Educ) Paul & Co Pubs.

Marketing II. Jack Rudman. (Regents External Degree (REDP) Ser.: Vol. 11). 43.95 (*0-8373-5661-X*) Nat Learn.

Marketing II. Jack Rudman. (Regents External Degree Ser.: REDP-11). 1994. pap. 23.95 (*0-8373-5611-3*) Nat Learn.

Marketing 2000: Future Perspectives on Marketing: an Annotated Bibliography of Articles. Allen E. Smith et al. LC 89-33053. (Bibliography Ser.). 299p. 1989. reprint ed. pap. 92.70 (*0-7837-9758-3*, 206048600005) Bks Demand.

Marketing 2000 & Beyond: Future Perspectives in Marketing. William Lazer. LC 89-29851. 246p. 1990. 25.00 (*0-87757-204-6*) Am Mktg.

***Marketing, 2000 Edition.** William M. Pride & O. C. Ferrell. 2000. pap. 39.57 (*0-395-97483-6*) HM.

Marketing 2370: Principles of Marketing. Gemmy Allen. (C). 1995. 21.03 (*1-56870-200-0*) RonJon Pub.

Marketing University Outreach Programs. Ed. by Ralph S. Foster, Jr. et al. LC 94-34200. (Journal of Nonprofit & Public Sector Marketing). (Illus.). 262p. 1995. lib. bdg. 49.95 (*1-56024-610-3*) Haworth Pr.

Marketing Us. 11th ed. Etzel. 1996. pap., student ed. 16.25 (*0-07-021897-8*) McGraw.

Marketing Video Guide, 2 vols. Steven J. Skinner. (C). 1993. pap. 3.96 (*0-395-69867-7*) HM.

Marketing Warfare. Al Ries & Jack Trout. (Illus.). 216p. 1986. 24.95 (*0-07-052730-X*) McGraw.

Marketing Warfare. Al Ries & Jack Trout. 216p. 1997. pap. 12.95 (*0-07-052726-1*) McGraw.

Marketing Windows Powerpoint. Nickels & Wood. 1997. 109.20 (*1-57259-319-9*) Worth.

***Marketing with E-Mail: A Spam-Free Guide to Increasing Awareness, Building Loyalty & Increasing Sales.** 2nd ed. Shannon Kinnard. (Illus.). 250p. 2000. pap. 24.95 (*1-885068-51-4*, Pub. by Maximum Pr) IPG Chicago.

Marketing with Email: A Spam-Free Guide to Increasing Awareness, Building Loyalty & Increasing Sales by Using the Internet's Most Powerful Tool. Shannon Kinnard. LC 99-6945. 284p. 1999. pap. 24.95 (*1-885068-40-9*, Pub. by Maximum Pr) IPG Chicago.

Marketing with Newsletters: How to Boost Sales, Add Members, Raise Donations, & Further Your Cause with a Printed, Faxed or Web Site Newsletter. 2nd rev. ed. Elaine Floyd. (Illus.). 250p. 1996. pap. 29.95 (*0-9630222-4-5*) EFG Inc MO.

Marketing with Seminars & Newsletters. Herman R. Holtz. LC 85-12304. (Illus.). 243p. 1986. 62.95 (*0-89930-099-5*, HZM/, Quorum Bks) Greenwood.

Marketing with Speeches & Seminars: Your Key to More Clients & Referrals. Miriam Otte. LC 98-96086. ix, 200p. 1998. pap. 16.95 (*0-9663131-0-0*) Zest Pr.

Marketing Without a Marketing Budget. Craig S. Rice. (Illus.). 320p. 1989. pap. 10.95 (*1-55850-986-0*) Adams Media.

Marketing Without Advertising. 2nd rev. ed. Michael Phillips & Salli Rasberry. LC 96-50111. (Illus.). 240p. 1997. pap. 19.00 (*0-87337-369-3*) Nolo com.

Marketing Without Frontiers: International Version. Kathryn Wilson. (Illus.). (Orig.). (C). 1995. pap. text 40.00 (*0-7881-2279-7*) DIANE Pub.

Marketing Without Frontiers: The RMI Guide to International Marketing. 3rd ed. (Illus.). vi, 283p. 1995. pap. 80.00 (*0-9656560-4-7*) DIANE Pub.

***Marketing Without Frontiers: The Royal Mail Guide to International Direct Marketing.** 4th ed. Frwd. by David Robottom. (Illus.). 330p. 2000. reprint ed. pap. text 65.00 (*0-7881-8911-5*) DIANE Pub.

Marketing Without Megabucks: How to Sell Anything on a Shoestring. Shel Horowitz. Ed. by David J. Dunton. LC 93-12633. 384p. (Orig.). 1993. pap. 12.00 (*0-671-76036-X*) Accurate Writing.

Marketing Without Money! 175, Cheap & Offbeat Ways for Small Businesses to Increase Sales! Nichola E. Bade. LC 97-50528. (Illus.). 160p. 1994. pap. 12.95 (*0-8442-3343-9*) NTC Contemp Pub Co.

Marketing Without Money! 175 Free, Cheap & Offbeat Ways for Small Businesses to Increase Sales! Nicholas E. Bade. LC 92-76216. 148p. 1993. pap. 12.95 (*1-882923-12-X*) Halle Hse Pub.

Marketing Without Money! 175 Free Cheap & Offbeat Ways for Small Businesses to Increase Sales! Nicholas E. Bade. LC 93-44562. (Illus.). 160p. 1994. 19.95 (*0-8442-3335-8*, NTC Business Bks) NTC Contemp Pub Co.

***Marketing Without Money for Small & Midsize Businesses! 300 FREE & Cheap Ways to Increase Your Sales!** Nicholas E. Bade. LC 99-73072. 164p. 1999. pap. 16.95 (*1-882923-20-0*) Halle Hse Pub.

Marketing Without Mystery for NPOs: A Practical Guide to Marketing Fund Raisers. Sally H. Daniel & Laura M. Dirks. (Illus.). 196p. 1996. student ed. 34.95 (*1-878681-03-6*) McCormick Pub.

Marketing Women around the World. Bartos. 338p. 1989. 29.95 (*0-07-103209-6*) McGraw.

Marketing Women's Health Care. Ruthie H. Dearing et al. 292p. (C). 1987. 85.00 (*0-87189-633-8*) Aspen Pub.

Marketing Words: The Writer's Guide to Marketing Income. Jessica P. Morrell. 8p. (Orig.). 1996. pap. 2.50 (*1-884241-40-9*, EWO020) Energeia Pub.

Marketing Workbook: Strategy & Management. Baker. LC 98-228280. 288p. 1998. pap. text 32.95 (*0-7506-3652-1*) Buttrwrth-Heinemann.

Marketing Workbook for Nonprofit Organizations Vol. I: Develop the Plan. Gary J. Stern. LC 90-83183. (Illus.). 132p. (Orig.). 1990. pap. 28.00 (*0-940069-01-6*) A H Wilder.

Marketing Workbook for Nonprofit Organizations Vol. II: Mobilize People for Marketing Success. Gary J. Stern. Ed. by Vincent Hyman. (Illus.). 208p. (Orig.). 1997. pap. text 28.00 (*0-940069-10-5*) A H Wilder.

Marketing Wright: A Real Estate Guide for Unique Properties. Frank Lloyd Wright Building Conservancy Staff. 12p. 1992. pap. 3.95 (*0-9629087-2-X*) F L Wright Build.

Marketing y Ventas en la Oficina de Farmacia. Antonio Merinero. (SPA.). 304p. 1997. pap. 29.00 (*84-7978-316-8*, Pub. by Ediciones Diaz) IBD Ltd.

Marketing Yearbook. Sunny Baker & Kim Baker. (C). 1992. 79.95 (*0-13-554486-6*, Macmillan Coll) P-H.

Marketing Your Arts & Crafts. Steve Long & Cindy Long. (Illus.). 192p. (Orig.). (C). 1987. pap. text 14.95 (*0-9618894-0-3*) Idahome Pubns.

Marketing Your Arts & Crafts: Creative Ways to Profit from Your Work. Janice West. Ed. by Sara Schroeder. LC 94-5493. (Illus.). 270p. 1994. 24.95 (*1-56530-127-7*, Pub. by Summit TX) BookWorld.

Marketing Your Budget: Creative Ways to Engage Citizens in the Bottom Line. Frank Benest. Ed. by William Mascenik. 125p. 1997. pap. text 38.00 (*1-882403-34-7*) The Innovation Grps.

Marketing Your Church: Concepts & Strategies. John J. Considine. 136p. (Orig.). 1995. pap. 14.95 (*1-55612-800-2*) Sheed & Ward WI.

Marketing Your City, U. S. A. A Guide to Developing a Strategic Tourism Marketing Plan. Ronald A. Nykiel & Elizabeth Jascolt. LC 98-17980. (Illus.). 112p. 1998. pap. text 19.95 (*0-7890-0592-1*); lib. bdg. 29.95 (*0-7890-0591-3*) Haworth Pr.

Marketing Your Clinical Practice: Ethically, Effectively, Economically. Neil Baum & Gretchen Henkel. 316p. 1991. 80.00 (*0-8342-0233-6*) Aspen Pub.

***Marketing Your Clinical Practice: Ethically, Effectively, Economically.** 2nd ed. Neil Baum. 2000. 75.00 (*0-8342-1745-7*) Aspen Pub.

Marketing Your Community. Jeffrey P. Davison. LC 86-62165. 125p. (Orig.). 1986. pap. 40.00 (*1-55657-000-7*) Pub Tech Inc.

Marketing Your Consultancy: How to Establish Yourself As the Expert. J. Stephen Lanning. 28p. 1998. write for info. (*1-891558-05-6*) New Ventures Pub.

Marketing Your Consulting & Professional Services. 3rd ed. Dick Connor & Jeffrey P. Davidson. LC 97-22965. 288p. 1997. 34.95 (*0-471-13392-2*) Wiley.

Marketing Your Consulting or Professional Services. David Karlson. Ed. by Michael G. Crisp. LC 87-72482. (Fifty-Minute Ser.). (Illus.). 108p. (Orig.). 1988. pap. 10.95 (*0-931961-40-8*) Crisp Pubns.

Marketing Your Expert Witness Practice. 324p. 1989. 49.95 (*0-9602962-6-3*) Natl Forensic.

Marketing Your Hospital: A Strategy for Survival Norman H. McMillan. LC 81-10892. ix, 117 p. 1981. write for info. (*0-87258-298-1*) Am Hospital.

Marketing Your Hospital: A Strategy for Survival. Norman H. McMillan. LC 84-21576. ix, 117 p. 1981. 20.00 (*0-939450-51-8*) AHPI.

Marketing Your Indexing Services. Ed. by Anne Leach. LC 94-46408. 1995. 15.00 (*0-936547-28-6*) Am Soc Index.

Marketing Your Indexing Services. 2nd ed. Ed. by Anne Leach. LC 98-21547. 70p. 1998. pap. 20.00 (*1-57387-054-4*) Info Today Inc.

Marketing Your Invention. 28p. 1989. pap. 2.00 (*0-89707-448-3*, 537-0055-01) Amer Bar Assn.

Marketing Your Invention. 2nd ed. Thomas E. Mosley. LC 97-2315. 1997. pap. 22.95 (*1-57410-072-6*, 6100-1702) Dearborn.

Marketing Your Legal Services. Ira S. Kalb. (Illus.). 200p. 1992. 42.95 (*0-924050-03-9*) K & A Pr.

Marketing Your Novel, Vol. 3. Lynn Bradley. (Your Novel Ser.: No. 3). 24p. 1998. pap., wbk. ed. 9.95 (*0-9637150-6-2*) Talent By Lb.

Marketing Your Practice: A Practical Guide to Client Development. Austin G. Anderson. LC 86-82074. (Illus.). 204p. 1986. pap. 54.95 (*0-89707-258-8*, 511-0215) Amer Bar Assn.

Marketing Your Practice: A Practical Guide to Client Development. Austin G. Anderson. LC 86-82074. (ABA Law Practice Management Section Ser.). 204p. 1986. pap. 60.00 (*0-685-22731-6*, 87-017) U MI Law CLE.

Marketing Your Practice: Creating Opportunities for Success. American Psychological Association Practice Direct. (APA Practitioner's Toolbox Ser.). 82p. 1996. pap. 29.95 (*1-55798-358-5*) Am Psychol.

Marketing Your Practice in an Era of Medical Reform. (Illus.). 245p. 1998. pap. 45.00 (*1-58383-000-6*, MARKET9) Robert D Keene.

Marketing Your Product. 3rd ed. Donald G. Cyr. 170p. 1998. pap. text 14.95 (*1-55180-145-0*) Self-Counsel Pr.

Marketing Your Product to the Federal Government: An Introduction to GSA Schedule Contracts. National Office Products Association Staff. (Illus.). 183p. write for info. (*0-318-62124-X*) Bus Prod Indust.

Marketing Your Professional Services Through Advertising. George A. Harris & Jeffrey S. Moses. LC 87-62198. 75p. (Orig.). 1987. pap. 16.70 incl. audio (*0-943158-23-0*, MYPSBP) Pro Resource.

Marketing Your Remodeling Services: Putting the Pieces Together. Carol Davitt. LC 93-31673. (Illus.). 128p. (Orig.). 1993. pap. 20.00 (*0-86718-388-8*) Home Builder.

Marketing Your Restaurant: So Easy, Effective, & Inexpensive Ideas That You Can Use Today! Rick A. Alderfer. LC 98-90424. 84p. 1998. pap. 12.95 (*0-9664822-0-4*) Strategic Pr.

Marketing Your Service. 3rd ed. Jean Withers. 150p. 1998. pap. text 14.95 (*1-55180-147-7*) Self-Counsel Pr.

Marketing Your Services: A Step-by-Step Guide for Small Businesses & Professionals. Anthony O. Putman. 256p. 1990. 39.95 (*0-471-50948-5*) Wiley.

Marketing Your Services: For People Who Hate to Sell. Rick Crandall. 320p. 1996. pap. 16.95 (*0-8092-3157-3*, 315730, Contemporary Bks) NTC Contemp Pub Co.

Marketing Your Services: For People Who Hate to Sell. Rick Crandall. LC 94-74836. 149p. 1995. pap. 15.95 (*0-9644294-0-3*) Select Pr.

Marketing Your Shopping Center. S. Albert Wenner. 194p. (Orig.). 1987. pap. 79.95 (*0-913598-55-0*, 817) Intl Coun Shop.

Marketing Your Skills: How Smart Loan Originators Sell More. Gordon Schlicke. (Learning System Ser.). (Illus.). ix, 161p. 1997. ring bd. 345.00 (*1-929246-07-2*) Schl Mortg Lend.

Marketing Your Software: Strategies for Success. William G. Nisen et al. (Illus.). 224p. 1984. pap. 16.95 (*0-201-00105-5*) Addison-Wesley.

Marketing Your Software Skills. Michael Griffin. 141p. 1992. pap. 15.95 (*0-9634441-5-8*) Micom.

Marketing Your Start-Up Business: A Step-by-Step Guide. Rebecca Amble. 152p. (Orig.). 1994. pap. text. write for info. (*0-9643203-1-2*) Future Focus.

Marketing Your Veterinary Practice. Shawn Messonnier. 168p. 1994. 29.95 (*0-939674-56-4*) Am Vet Pubns.

Marketing Your Veterinary Practice, Vol. II. Shawn Messonnier. LC 96-37947. (Illus.). 176p. (gr. 13). 1997. pap. text 28.95 (*0-8151-8583-9*, 28819) Mosby Inc.

Marketing Yourself & Your Career: Promoting Your Skills & Accomplishments. Jane Ballback & Jan Slater. LC 96-85830. (Personal Growth & Development Collection). (Illus.). 106p. 1996. pap. 14.95 (*1-883553-78-4*) R Chang Assocs.

Marketing Yourself As a Psychotherapist. John M. Curtis & Marc R. Hamer. LC 96-96841. (Illus.). 103p. (C). 1997. per. 29.95 (*0-9653956-0-X*) Discobolos.

Marketing Yourself to the Top: Communicating to Win in a Competitive Marketplace. Susan St. John. 160p. 1994. pap. text, per. 13.95 (*0-8403-9432-2*) Kendall-Hunt.

Marketing Yourself to the Top Business Schools. Phil Carpenter & Carol Carpenter. 224p. 1995. pap. 15.95 (*0-471-11817-6*) Wiley.

Marketing Yourself with Technical Writing: A Guide for Today's Professionals. William V. Vatavuk. 176p. 1992. lib. bdg. 54.95 (*0-87371-478-4*, L478) Lewis Pubs.

Marketing 1996/97. 18th annot. ed. Richardson. 1996. teacher ed. 13.12 (*0-697-31546-0*, WCB McGr Hill) McGrw-H Hghr Educ.

***Marketing 2000-2001.** 22nd ed. John Richardson. (Annual Editions Ser.). 240p. 1999. pap. 16.56 (*0-07-236400-9*) McGrw-H Hghr Educ.

Marketing 4e. 4th ed. William G. Zikmund & Michael D'Amico. Ed. by Leyh. LC 92-19091. (SWC-Marketing). 800p. (C). 1993. text 53.50 (*0-314-01132-3*) West Pub.

Marketing 5e. 5th ed. William G. Zikmund & Michael D'Amico. LC 95-23375. (SWC-Marketing). (Illus.). 800p. (C). 1996. pap. 67.50 (*0-314-06214-9*) West Pub.

Marketing/Administrative Pay: The Facts You Need to Establish Motivational Pay Plans for Software Marketing & Administrative Professionals. Culpepper & Associates Staff. (Illus.). 252p. 1997. ring bd. 695.00 (*1-58128-014-9*, DR) Culpepper.

Marketingbuilder: Academic Version, Reference Guide. Jian Software Inc. Staff. LC 97-161422. 1996. 37.75 (*0-538-86423-0*) Thomson Learn.

Marketing/Planning Library & Information Services. 2nd ed. Darlene E. Weingand. LC 99-31433. 210p. 1999. 47.50 (*1-56308-612-3*) Libs Unl.

Marketing's New Strategic Direction. Stephen J. Garone & Conference Board. LC 98-216050. (Reports). 46 p. 1995. write for info. (*0-8237-0561-7*) Conference Bd.

Marketing's Role in Economic Development. Allan C. Reddy & David P. Campbell. LC 93-27715. 160p. 1993. 49.95 (*0-89930-766-3*, Quorum Bks) Greenwood.

Market/Internet Guide. 11th ed. Etzel. 1996. 43.00 (*0-07-913261-8*) McGraw.

***Marketization & Democracy: East Asian Experiences.** Samantha F. Ravich. (RAND Studies in Policy Analysis). (Illus.). 292p. (C). 2000. 39.95 (*0-521-66165-X*) Cambridge U Pr.

***Marketization of Social Security.** Ed. by John Dixon & Mark Hydeman. 2001. write for info. (*1-56720-325-6*) Greenwood.

Marketization, Restructuring & Competition in Transition Industries of Central & Eastern Europe. Ed. by Marvin Jackson & Wouter Biesbrouck. (LICOS Studies on the Transitions in Central & Eastern Europe: Vol. 2). 384p. (C). 1995. text 91.95 (*1-85972-047-1*, Pub. by Avebry) Ashgate Pub Co.

Marketizing Education & Health in Developing Countries: Miracle or Mirage? Christopher Colclough. (IDS Development Studies). (Illus.). 388p. 1998. text 95.00 (*0-19-829255-4*) OUP.

***Marketplace.** Laura Antoniou. 2000. pap. 13.95 (*0-9645960-4-0*) Mystic Rose.

Marketplace. Claudette C. Mitchell et al. (Visions: African-American Experiences: Vol. 35). (Illus.). 8p. (Orig.). (J). (gr. k-1). 1996. pap. text 3.00 (*1-57518-077-4*) Arborlake.

Marketplace. 2nd ed. Laura Antoniou. 1998. mass mkt. 7.95 (*1-56333-602-2*, Rhinoceros) Masquerade.

Marketplace Vol. II: The Management of Strategy in the Marketplace. Ernest R. Cadotte & Harry J. Bruce. (Illus.). 398p. 1997. pap. text 25.00 (*1-891622-00-5*) Univ TN Div.

Marketplace for Telecommunications Regulation & Deregulation in Industrialized Democracies. Marcellus S. Snow. (Illus.). 304p. 1986. text 48.95 (*0-582-28600-X*, 71626) Longman.

Marketplace of Broadcasters' Ideas. Vigdor Schreibman. LC 87-6206. (Essays on the Impact of the Constitution & Legal System on American Life & Government Ser.: No. 3). (Illus.). 109p. (Orig.). 1987. pap. 24.00 (*0-942539-02-8*) Amicas Pubns.

Marketplace of Print: Pamphlets & the Public Sphere in Early Modern England. Alexandra Halasz. LC 96-44204. (Cambridge Studies in Renaissance Literature & Culture: Vol. 17). 254p. (C). 1997. text 59.95 (*0-521-58209-1*) Cambridge U Pr.

Marketplace Operating Manual Vol. III: A Guide to Marketplace Decisions. Ernest R. Cadotte. 182p. 1997. pap. 18.00 (*1-891622-01-3*) Univ TN Div.

Marketplace Preaching: How to Return the Sermon to Where It Belongs. Calvin Miller. LC 94-32754. 192p. 1995. pap. 12.99 (*0-8010-6320-5*) Baker Bks.

Markets. Ed. by Grahame Thompson. (The U. S. in the Twentieth Century Ser.). 288p. 1995. text 14.95 (*0-340-59688-0*, Pub. by E A) St Martin.

Markets: From Barter to Bar Codes. Jeanne Bendick & Robert Bendick. LC 96-41673. (First Bks.). (Illus.). (J). 1997. lib. bdg. 22.00 (*0-531-20263-1*) Watts.

Markets: From Barter to Bar Codes. Jeanne Bendick & Robert Bendick. (First Bks.). (J). 1997. pap. text 6.95 (*0-531-15850-0*) Watts.

Markets & Dealers: The Economics of the London Financial Markets. Ed. by David Cobham. LC 92-20208. 1992. pap. text. write for info. (*0-582-07851-2*) Longman.

Markets & Democracy: Participation, Accountability, & Efficiency. Ed. by Samuel Bowles et al. LC 92-30242. (Illus.). 358p. (C). 1993. text 69.95 (*0-521-43223-5*) Cambridge U Pr.

Markets & Democracy in Latin America: Conflict or Convergence? Ed. by Philip Oxhorn & Pamela K. Starr. LC 98-7421. 290p. 1998. lib. bdg. 55.00 (*1-55587-716-8*) L Rienner.

Markets & Famines. Martin Ravallion. (Illus.). 212p. 1990. reprint ed. pap. text 24.00 (*0-19-828727-5*) OUP.

Markets & Health Care: A Comparative Analysis. Wendy Ranade. LC 97-37202. 272p. (C). 1998. pap. text 25.75 (*0-582-28985-8*) Longman.

Markets & Hierarchies: Analysis & Antitrust Implications. Oliver E. Williamson. 320p. 1983. reprint ed. pap. 16.95 (*0-02-934780-7*) Free Pr.

Markets & Innovations in Wound Care. Ed. by Peter Allen. 200p. 1989. pap. 1795.00 (*0-318-41827-4*) FIND-SVP.

Markets & Institutions: A Contemporary Introduction to Financial Services. 2nd ed. William L. Scott. LC 98-7620. (FI - Financial Institutions Ser.). 1998. pap. 93.95 (*0-538-85963-6*) S-W Pub.

Markets & Justice. Ed. by John W. Chapman & J. Roland Pennock. (Nomos Ser.: Vol. 31). 384p. (C). 1989. text 45.00 (*0-8147-1421-8*) NYU Pr.

Markets & Majorities: The Political Economy of Public Policy. Steven M. Sheffrin. LC 93-21722. 1993. 35.00 (*0-02-928651-4*) Free Pr.

Markets & Marketing: Proceedings of the 1984 Meeting of the Society for Economic Development. Ed. by Stuart Plattner. (Monographs in Economic Anthropology: No. 4). (Illus.). 438p. 1985. pap. text 37.00 (*0-8191-4605-6*); lib. bdg. 55.00 (*0-8191-4604-8*) U Pr of Amer.

Markets & Merchants of the Late Seventeenth Century: The Marescoe-David Letters, 1668-1680. Henry Roseveare. (Records of Social & Economic History, New Series British Academy: No. XII). (Illus.). 700p. 1992. reprint ed. pap. text 85.00 (*0-19-726106-X*) OUP.

Markets & Mortality: Economics, Dangerous Work & the Value of Human Life. Peter Dorman. 286p. (C). 1996. text 54.95 (*0-521-55306-7*) Cambridge U Pr.

Markets & Networks: Contracting in Community Health Services. R. Flynn et al. LC 96-22704. 192p. 1996. 108.95 (*0-335-19457-5*) Taylor & Francis.

Markets & Networks: Contracting in Community Health Services. Flynn et al. LC 96-22704. 192p. 1996. pap. 33.95 (*0-335-19456-7*) OpUniv Pr.

Markets & Organization. Ed. by R. Arena & Christian Longhi. LC 97-50107. (Illus.). vi, 697p. 1998. pap. 99.00 (*3-540-63810-5*) Spr-Verlag.

Markets & People: The Czech Reform Experience in a Comparative Perspective. Jiri Vecernik. 320p. 1996. text 82.95 (*1-85972-406-X*, Pub. by Avebry) Ashgate Pub Co.

Markets & Politicians: Politicized Economic Choice. Ed. by Arye L. Hillman. (C). 1991. lib. bdg. 122.00 (*0-7923-9135-7*) Kluwer Academic.

***Markets & Power: Understanding the West's Modern Command Economy.** Eric A. Schutz. (Illus.). 208p. 2000. 58.95 (*0-7656-0500-7*) M E Sharpe.

Markets & Socialism. Ed. by Alec Nove & Ian Thatcher. (International Library of Critical Writings in Economics: Vol. 39). 584p. 1994. 240.00 (*1-85278-842-9*) E Elgar.

M

Markets & States in Tropical Africa: The Political Basis of Agricultural Policies. Robert H. Bates. LC 80-39732. (California Series on Social Choice & Political Economy: Vol. 1). 176p. 1981. pap. 19.95 (*0-520-05229-3*, Pub. by U CA Pr) Cal Prin Full Svc.

Markets & the Media: Competition, Regulation & the Interests of Consumers. M. E. Beesley et al. (IEA Readings Ser.: No. 43). 146p. 1996. pap. 37.50 (*0-255-36378-8*, Pub. by Inst Economic Affairs) Coronet Bks.

Markets at Work: Dynamics of the Residential Real Estate Market in Hong Kong. Ed. by Bertrand Renaud et al. LC 98-170590. (Illus.). 128p. 1997. pap. 32.50 (*962-209-438-4*, Pub. by HK Univ Pr) Coronet Bks.

Markets, Choice & Equity in Education. Sharon Gewirtz et al. LC 95-14758. 224p. 1995. pap. 33.95 (*0-335-19369-2*) OpUniv Pr.

Markets, Civil Society & Democracy in Kenya. Ed. by Peter Gibbon. LC 96-229036. 179p. 1995. 62.50 (*91-7106-371-4*) Coronet Bks.

Markets, Corporate Behaviour & the State. Ed. by Alexis P. Jacquemin & H. W. DeJong. (Nijenrode Studies in Economics: No. 1). 1976. lib. bdg. 85.50 (*90-247-1845-7*) Kluwer Academic.

Markets Directory, 1991: Focus Facilities, Test Kitchens, Malls, Moderators by Location in Every Major Market in the United States. James Roxton. 261p. 1990. pap. 40.00 (*0-9628135-0-8*) Dobbs Dirs.

Markets, Firms & the Management of Labour in Modern Britain. Howard Gospel. (Cambridge Studies in Management: No. 17). 270p. (C). 1992. text 59.95 (*0-521-41527-6*) Cambridge U Pr.

***Markets for Clean Air: The U. S. Acid Rain Program.** A. Denny Ellerman et al. (Illus.). 375p. 2000. 39.95 (*0-521-66083-1*) Cambridge U Pr.

Markets for Electronic Information Services in the European Economic Area: Supply, Demand & Information Infrastructure. (Illus.). 271p. (Orig.). (C). 1997. pap. text 60.00 (*0-7881-3782-4*) DIANE Pub.

Markets for Federal Water: Subsidies, Property Rights, & the Bureau of Reclamation. Richard W. Wahl. LC 89-32192. 308p. 1989. 30.00 (*0-915707-48-9*) Resources Future.

Markets for Home Security & Energy Management Systems. Ed. by Peter Allen. 158p. 1988. 1495.00 (*0-941285-34-0*) FIND-SVP.

Markets for Innovation, Ownership & Control: Proceedings of the International Conference, Saltsjobaden, Sweden, June 12-15, 1988. Ed. by Richard H. Day et al. LC 93-14648. (Studies in Economic Decision, Organization & Behavior: Vol. 2). 456p. 1993. 166.50 (*0-444-89675-9*, North Holland) Elsevier.

Markets for PC Hardware, Software & Systems in Europe. 116p. 1495.00 (*0-317-65609-0*) TBC Inc.

Markets for Recovered Glass. (Illus.). 34p. (Orig.). (C). 1994. pap. text 20.00 (*0-7881-0449-7*) DIANE Pub.

Markets for Salt-Free & Sugar-Free Foods: A Product-by-Product Marketing Analysis & Competitor Profile. L. Levine. 300p. 2000. 1995.00 (*0-317-55191-4*) Lead Edge Reports.

Markets for Spectrometric Equipment, No. YGB-168. Cort Wrotnowski. 256p. 1993. 2650.00 (*1-56965-202-3*) BCC.

***Markets for Water: Potential & Performance.** K. William Easter et al. LC 98-39005. (Natural Resource Management & Policy Ser.). 1998. 99.95 (*0-7923-8256-0*) Kluwer Academic.

Markets, Hierarchies & Networks: The Coordinator of Social Life. Ed. by Grahame Thompson et al. (Illus.). 304p. (C). 1992. 55.00 (*0-8039-8589-4*); pap. 19.95 (*0-8039-8590-8*) Sage.

Markets in Developing Countries: Parallel, Fragmented & Black. Michael Roemer & Christine Jones. 267p. 1991. pap. 12.95 (*1-55815-082-X*); 6.95 (*1-55815-142-7*) ICS Pr.

Markets in Education. Simon Marginson. LC 99-488378. 352p. 1998. pap. 35.00 (*1-86448-432-2*, Pub. by Allen & Unwin Pty) Paul & Co Pubs.

Markets in the Firm: A Market-Process Approach to Management. Tyler Cowen & David Parker. (Hobart Paper Ser.: No. 134). 95p. 1997. pap. 22.50 (*0-255-36405-9*, Pub. by Inst Economic Affairs) Coronet Bks.

Markets, Information & Uncertainty: Essays in Economic Theory in Honor of Kenneth Arrow. Ed. & Contrib. by Graciela Chichilnisky. LC 97-25548. (Illus.). 424p. (C). 1998. text 69.95 (*0-521-55355-5*) Cambridge U Pr.

Markets, Managers & Theory in Education. John Halliday. 224p. 1990. 69.95 (*1-85000-877-9*, Falmer Pr); pap. 29.95 (*1-85000-878-7*, Falmer Pr) Taylor & Francis.

***Market's Measure: An Illustrated History of America Told Through the Dow Jones Industrial Average.** Ed. by John A. Prestbo. (Illus.). 188p. 1999. 39.95 (*1-881944-25-5*) Dow Jones & Co.

Markets, Money & Empire: The Political Economy of the Australian Wool Industry. Kosmas Tsokhas. 244p. 1990. pap. 29.95 (*0-522-84417-0*, Pub. by Melbourne Univ Pr) Paul & Co Pubs.

Markets Myths. Tony Weymouth et al. LC 95-47529. 256p. (C). 1996. pap. text 33.75 (*0-582-27565-2*, Pub. by Addison-Wesley) Longman.

Markets of Asia-Pacific, 12 vols. Survey Research Group Staff. Incl. Australia. 1982. 75.00 (*0-87196-592-5*); China. 1982. 75.00 (*0-87196-595-X*); Hong Kong & Macau. 75.00 (*0-87196-588-7*); Indonesia. 75.00 (*0-87196-587-9*); Malaysia. (Orig.). 75.00 (*0-87196-585-2*); Philippines. 75.00 (*0-87196-590-9*); Singapore. 75.00 (*0-87196-584-4*); South Korea. 1982. 75.00 (*0-87196-591-7*); Taiwan. 1982. 75.00 (*0-87196-589-5*); Thailand. 75.00 (*0-87196-586-0*); write for info. (*0-318-56678-8*) Facts on File.

Markets of Governments: Choosing Between Imperfect Alternatives. 2nd ed. Charles Wolf, Jr. LC 93-18730. (Illus.). 178p. 1993. 30.00 (*0-262-23172-7*); pap. text 17.50 (*0-262-73104-5*) MIT Pr.

***Markets of One: Creating Customer-Unique Value Through Mass Customization.** James H. Gilmore & B. Joseph Pine, II. LC 99-32967. (Review Book Ser.). 2000. 29.95 (*1-57851-238-7*) Harvard Busn.

Markets of Provence. Ruthanne Long & Dixon Long. (Illus.). 1996. 19.95 (*0-614-95771-0*) Harper SF.

Markets of Provence: A Culinary Tour of Southern France. Ruthanne Long & Dixon Long. LC 95-42042. (Illus.). 144p. 1996. 22.00 (*0-00-225061-6*) Collins SF.

Markets of the Sixties. Fortune Magazine Editors. LC 74-167340. (Essay Index Reprint Ser.). 1977. reprint ed. 29.95 (*0-8369-2769-9*) Ayer.

Markets of the United States for Business Planners: Historical & Current Profiles of 183 U. S. Urban Economies by Major Section & Industry with Maps, Graphics & Commentary. 2nd ed. Ed. by Thomas F. Conroy. (Illus.). 1688p. 1995. lib. bdg. 240.00 (*0-7808-0019-2*) Omnigraphics Inc.

***Markets on Line: The Future of Financial Markets in the Digital World.** Stephen Eckett. 256p. 1998. pap. 57.50 (*0-273-63542-5*, Pub. by F T P-H) Trans-Atl Phila.

Markets, Politics, & Change in the Global Political Economy. Ed. by William P. Avery & David P. Rapkin. LC 89-3626. (International Political Economy Yearbook Ser.: No. 4). 225p. 1989. lib. bdg. 40.00 (*1-55587-148-8*) L Rienner.

Markets, Politics & Globalization. Neil Fligstein. (Acta Universitatis Upsaliensis Studia Oeconomiae Negotiorum: No. 42). 47p. 1997. pap. 33.50 (*91-554-3889-X*, Pub. by Almqvist Wiksell) Coronet Bks.

Markets, Risk & Money: Essays in Honor of Maurice Allais. Ed. by Bertrand R. Munier. LC 93-36635. (Theory & Decision Library Series B: Vol. 26). 388p. (C). 1995. lib. bdg. 213.50 (*0-7923-2578-8*) Kluwer Academic.

Markets, States & Housing Provision: Four European Growth Regions Compared. James Barlow & Simon Duncan. (Progress in Planning Ser.: Vol. 38). 88p. 1992. 64.00 (*0-08-042059-1*, Pergamon Pr) Elsevier.

Markets, States & Public Policy. Nikolaos Zahariadis. LC 94-46259. 248p. 1995. text 42.50 (*0-472-10542-6*, 10542) U of Mich Pr.

Markets, the State & the Environment. Robyn Eckersley. 316p. 1996. 64.95 (*0-7329-3095-2*, Pub. by Macmill Educ); pap. 32.95 (*0-7329-3069-3*, Pub. by Macmill Educ) Paul & Co Pubs.

Markets, Unemployment, & Economic Policy: Essays in Honour of Geoff Harcourt, Vol. 2. Ed. by Philip Arestis & Gabriel Palma. LC 97-155047. (Illus.). 576p. (C). 1997. 125.00 (*0-415-13390-4*) Routledge.

Markets Within Planning: Socialist Economic Management in the Third World. Ed. by E. V. Fitzgerald & Marc E. Wuyts. 218p. 1989. text 42.50 (*0-7146-3342-9*, Pub. by F Cass Pubs) Intl Spec Bk.

Marketwise. Victoria Ryce. (Illus.). 170p. 1988. pap. 18.95 (*0-7737-5143-2*) Genl Dist Srvs.

Markham: Canada's Community of the Future. Wendy Priesnitz. 1990. 34.95 (*0-89781-327-8*) Am Historical Pr.

Markham: Shaping a Destiny. Ed. by Jerry Amernic & Maryanne Tefft. LC 98-38584. (Illus.). 160p. 1998. 39.00 (*1-885352-78-6*) Community Comm.

Markham in Peru: The Travels of Clements R. Markham, 1852-1853. Clements R. Markham. Ed. by Peter Blanchard. (Illus.). 168p. (Orig.). 1991. pap. 10.95 (*0-292-75127-3*); text 25.00 (*0-292-71132-8*) U of Tex Pr.

Markheim. Robert Louis Stevenson. Ed. by Raymond Harris. (Classics Ser.). (Illus.). 48p. (gr. 6-12). 1982. audio 13.00 (*0-89061-252-8*, 456, Jamestwn Pub) NTC Contemp Pub Co.

Markheim. Robert Louis Stevenson. Ed. by Raymond Harris. (Classics Ser.). (Illus.). 48p. (YA). (gr. 6-12). 1982. teacher ed. 7.32 (*0-89061-251-X*, 457, Jamestwn Pub); pap. text 5.99 (*0-89061-250-1*, 455, Jamestwn Pub) NTC Contemp Pub Co.

Markhoff & Lagrange Spectra. T. Cusick & E. Flahive. LC 89-14867. (Mathematical Surveys & Monographs: Vol. 30). 97p. 1989. text 49.00 (*0-8218-1531-8*, SURV/30) Am Math.

Markie & the Hammond Cousins. unabridged ed. Wanda Yoder. (Illus.). 1994. pap. 5.95 (*0-87813-556-1*) Christian Light.

Marking for Telecommunications: A Handbook to the Telecommunications Directives. Patrick Braster & Pieter De Beer. LC 97-42751. 1997. write for info. (*1-55937-947-2*) IEEE Standards.

Marking Her Questions. Lois M. Hirshkowitz. LC 93-20913. 64p. 1993. pap. 14.95 (*0-7734-2787-2*, Mellen Poetry Pr) E Mellen.

Marking Missouri History. Ed. by James W. Goodrich & Lynn W. Gentzler. LC 98-214523. (Illus.). 302p. 1998. pap. 17.50 (*0-9622891-3-2*) SHS MO.

Marking Our Times: Aboriginal & Torees Strait Islander Art. Avrill Quail. LC 95-61182. (Illus.). 100p. (Orig.). 1996. pap. 19.95 (*0-500-97431-4*, Pub. by Thames Hudson) Norton.

Marking Residential Care Work: Structure & Culture in Children's Homes. Elizabeth Brown et al. LC 98-70907. (Dartington Social Research Ser.: Vol. 1). 176p. 1998. text 51.95 (*1-84014-499-8*, Pub. by Ashgate Pub) Ashgate Pub Co.

Marking the City Boundaries: Art & Design Profile 25. Academy Editions Staff. 1992. pap. 26.95 (*0-312-08107-3*) St Martin.

Marking the Magic Circle: An Intimate Geography. George Venn. LC 86-19185. (Illus.). 208p. 1987. 24.95 (*0-87071-352-3*); pap. 15.95 (*0-87071-353-1*) Oreg St U Pr.

***Marking the Sparrow's Fall: The Making of the American West.** Wallace Stegner. 384p. 1999. pap. text 14.00 (*0-8050-6296-3*, Owl) H Holt & Co.

Marking the Sparrow's Fall: Wallace Stegner's American West. Wallace Stegner. LC 97-49281. 384p. 1998. text 25.00 (*0-8050-4464-7*) St Martin.

***Ma(r)king the Text: The Presentation of Meaning on the Literary Page.** Joe Bray et al. LC 00-34850. 2000. write for info. (*0-7546-0168-4*, Pub. by Ashgate Pub) Ashgate Pub Co.

Marking Time. Jean Harris. 1993. mass mkt. 4.99 (*0-8217-4312-0*, Zebra Kensgtn) Kensgtn Pub Corp.

Marking Time. Elizabeth J. Howard. 416p. 1995. per. 14.00 (*0-671-52794-0*, WSP) PB.

Marking Time. Elizabeth J. Howard. Ed. by Bill Grose. 416p. 1995. 12.00 (*0-671-52794-2*) PB.

***Marking Time.** E. A. Markham. 264p. 2000. 16.95 (*1-900715-29-5*, Pub. by Peepal Tree Pr) Paul & Co Pubs.

Marking Time. Elizabeth J. Howard. Ed. by Bill Grose. xvi, 512p. 1994. reprint ed. mass mkt. 5.50 (*0-671-70910-0*) PB.

Marking Time: The Epic Quest to Invent the Perfect Calendar. Duncan Steel. LC 99-51369. 422p. 1999. 27.95 (*0-471-29827-1*) Wiley.

***Marking Time with Faulkner: A Study of the Symbolic Importance of the Mark & of Related Actions.** unabridged ed. Margaret A. Harrell. (Illus.). 191p. 1999. pap. 20.00 (*973-98216-7-7*, MTF, Pub. by Hermann Pr) Harrell Comm.

Marking Your Children for God. 2nd ed. 94p. 1996. reprint ed. pap. 5.00 (*0-9651279-0-7*) Ark Pubng.

Markings. Dag Hammarskjold. (Epiphany Bks.). 1985. mass mkt. 5.99 (*0-345-32741-1*) Ballantine Pub Grp.

Markings. Dag Hammarskjold. 1994. lib. bdg. 21.95 (*1-56849-473-4*) Buccaneer Bks.

Markings. Dag Hammarskjold. 1964. 27.50 (*0-394-43532-X*) Knopf.

Markings: Aerial Views of Sacred Landscapes. Marilyn Bridges. (Illus.). 96p. 1986. 60.00 (*0-89381-228-5*) Aperture.

***Markings: Poems & Drawings.** Cilla McQueen. (Illus.). 64p. 2000. pap. 24.95 (*1-877133-92-2*, Pub. by Univ Otago Pr) Intl Spec Bk.

Markita. Alissa Nash. LC 95-128561. 1997. pap. text 7.95 (*0-913543-39-X*) African Am Imag.

Markland. Jean P. Waterbury. LC 89-61112. (Illus.). 64p. (Orig.). 1989. pap. 10.95 (*0-917553-09-8*) St Augustine Hist.

Markland Operations Management. Date not set. student ed. write for info. (*0-314-05424-3*); pap. text, teacher ed. write for info. (*0-314-05422-7*) West Pub.

Marklin: Great Toys, 1895-1914. Charlotte P. Crooke. (Illus.). 180p. 1995. pap. text 29.95 (*1-872727-18-2*) Pincushion Pr.

Marko Songs from Hercegovina a Century after Karadzic. Laura G. Fisher. Ed. by Albert B. Lord. LC 90-2976. (Harvard Dissertations in Folklore & Oral Literature Ser.). 304p. 1990. reprint ed. text 20.00 (*0-8240-2790-6*) Garland.

Markology. Mark O'Connor. Ed. by Wayne Kiser. Tr. by John Carlini. 96p. 1997. spiral bd. 16.95 (*0-7866-1654-7*, 95695) Mel Bay.

Markology. Mark O'Connor. Tr. by John Carlini. 96p. 1997. spiral bd. 31.95 incl. audio compact disk (*0-7866-1656-3*, 95695CDP) Mel Bay.

Markops. 2nd ed. Jean-Claude Larreche. 180p. 1992. teacher ed. 32.50 incl. disk (*0-89426-204-1*); teacher ed. 32.50 incl. disk (*0-89426-205-X*); teacher ed. 32.50 incl. disk (*0-685-74392-6*); pap. 32.50 (*0-685-74391-8*) Course Tech.

Markov Cell Structures near a Hyperbolic Set. Tom Farrell & Lowell Jones. LC 93-464. (Memoirs of the American Mathematical Society Ser.: No. 491). 138p. 1993. pap. 32.00 (*0-8218-2553-4*, MEMO/103/491) Am Math.

Markov Chain Models - Rarity & Exponentiality. J. Keilson. (Applied Mathematical Sciences Ser.: Vol. 28). 1979. 58.95 (*0-387-90405-0*) Spr-Verlag.

Markov Chain Monte Carlo: Stochastic Simulation for Bayesian Inference. Dani Gamerman. (Texts in Statistical Science Ser.). 512p. 1997. ring bd. 54.95 (*0-412-81820-5*, Chap & Hall NY) Chapman & Hall.

Markov Chain Monte Carlo in Practice. W. R. Gilks. LC 98-33429. 512p. (gr. 13). 1995. boxed set 74.95 (*0-412-05551-1*, Chap & Hall CRC) CRC Pr.

Markov Chains. J. Norris. LC 96-31570. (Cambridge Series in Statistical & Probabilistic Mathematics: No. 2). 253p. 1997. text 49.95 (*0-521-48181-3*) Cambridge U Pr.

Markov Chains. J. Norris. (Series in Statistical & Probabilistic Mathematics: Vol. 2). (Illus.). 253p. (C). 1998. pap. text 24.95 (*0-521-63396-6*) Cambridge U Pr.

Markov Chains. William J. Stewart. 616p. (C). 1995. text 199.50 (*0-7923-9550-6*) Kluwer Academic.

Markov Chains. B. Freedman. (Illus.). 382p. 1983. reprint ed. 79.95 (*0-387-90808-0*) Spr-Verlag.

Markov Chains. rev. ed. Daniel Revuz. (Mathematical Library: Vol. 11). 374p. 1984. 149.50 (*0-444-86400-8*, I-548-83, North Holland) Elsevier.

Markov Chains: Gibbs Fields, Monte Carlo Simulation & Queues. P. Bremaud. Ed. by J. E. Marsden et al. LC 98-17539. (Texts in Applied Mathematics Ser.: Vol. 31). 550p. 1998. 49.95 (*0-387-98509-3*) Spr-Verlag.

Markov Chains: Theory & Applications. Dean L. Isaacson & Richard W. Madsen. LC 84-27792. 270p. 1985. reprint ed. lib. bdg. 43.50 (*0-89874-834-8*) Krieger.

Markov Chains & Monte Carlo Calculations in Polymer Science. Ed. by George G. Lowry. LC 70-84777. (Monographs in Macromolecular Chemistry). 338p. reprint ed. pap. 104.80 (*0-608-30342-9*, 205504800008) Bks Demand.

Markov Chains & Stochastic Stability. S. P. Meyn & R. L. Tweedie. (Communications & Control Engineering Ser.). (Illus.). xvi, 548p. 1996. 119.95 (*0-387-19832-6*) Spr-Verlag.

Markov Decision Processes. D. J. White. 238p. 1993. 219.95 (*0-471-93627-8*) Wiley.

Markov Decision Processes: Discrete Stochastic Dynamic Programming. Martin L. Puterman. (Series in Probability & Mathematical Statistics). 672p. 1994. 129.95 (*0-471-61977-9*) Wiley.

Markov Fields over Countable Partially Ordered Sets: Extrema & Splitting. Ed. by I. V. Evstigneev & P. E. Greenwood. LC 94-26459. (Memoirs of the American Mathematical Society Ser.: No. 537). 100p. 1994. pap. 32.00 (*0-8218-2597-6*, MEMO/112/537) Am Math.

Markov Models & Linguistic Theory: An Experimental Study of a Model for English. Frederick J. Damerau. LC 78-135666. (Janua Linguarum, Ser. Minor: No. 95). (Orig.). 1971. pap. text 53.85 (*90-279-1707-8*) Mouton.

Markov Models & Optimization. Mark H. Davis. LC 92-39557. 296p. (gr. 13). 1993. ring bd. 78.95 (*0-412-31410-X*, Chap & Hall CRC) CRC Pr.

Markov Moment Problem & Extremal Problems. M. G. Krein & A. A. Nudel'Man. LC 77-11716. (Translations of Mathematical Monographs: Vol. 50). 417p. 1977. text 108.00 (*0-8218-4500-4*, MMONO/50) Am Math.

Markov Point Processes & Their Applications. M. N. Van Lieshout. 200p. 1998. 38.00 (*1-86094-071-4*, Pub. by Imperial College) World Scientific Pub.

Markov Processes: An Introduction for Physical Scientists. Daniel T. Gillespie. (Illus.). 565p. (C). 1991. text 65.00 (*0-12-283955-2*) Acad Pr.

Markov Processes: Characterization & Convergence. S. N. Ethier & T. G. Kurtz. LC 85-12078. (Probability & Mathematical Statistics: Applied Probability & Statistics Section Ser.). 544p. 1986. 199.95 (*0-471-08186-8*) Wiley.

Markov Processes: Ray Processes & Right Processes, Vol. 440. R. K. Getoor. (Lecture Notes in Mathematics Ser.). v, 118p. 1975. 26.95 (*0-387-07140-7*) Spr-Verlag.

Markov Processes: Structure & Asymptotic Behavior. Murray Rosenblatt. LC 70-161441. (Grundlehren der Mathematischen Wissenschaften Ser.: Vol. 184). 1971. 75.00 (*0-387-05480-4*) Spr-Verlag.

Markov Processes & Differential Equations: Asymptotic Problems. Mark Freidlin. LC 96-6160. (Lectures in Mathematics ETH Zurich). 152p. 1996. 34.95 (*0-8176-5392-9*); pap. 34.95 (*3-7643-5392-9*) Birkhauser.

Markov Processes & Related Problems of Analysis. E. B. Dynkin. LC 81-38438. (London Mathematical Society Lecture Note Ser.: No. 54). 320p. reprint ed. pap. 91.20 (*0-608-17519-6*, 2030605) Bks Demand.

Markov Processes for Stochastic Modeling. M. Kijima. LC 96-86521. (Illus.). 341p. 1997. ring bd. 65.95 (*0-412-60660-7*, Chap & Hall CRC) CRC Pr.

Markov Random Field Modeling in Computer Vision. S. Z. Li. Ed. by Toshiyasu L. Kunii. LC 95-23304. (Computer Science Workbench Ser.). (Illus.). 280p. 1995. 135.00 (*0-387-70145-1*) Spr-Verlag.

Markov Random Fields. Yuri A. Rozanov. Tr. by C. M. Elson from RUS. (Illus.). 201p. 1982. 118.95 (*0-387-90708-4*) Spr-Verlag.

Markov Random Fields: Theory & Applications. Ed. by Rama Chellappa & Anil Jain. (Illus.). 581p. 1993. text 88.00 (*0-12-170608-7*) Acad Pr.

Markov Random Fields & Their Applications. Ross Kindermann & J. Laurie Snell. LC 80-22764. (Contemporary Mathematics Ser.: Vol. 1). 142p. 1981. reprint ed. pap. 19.00 (*0-8218-5001-6*, CONM/1) Am Math.

Markov Set-Chains, Vol. 169. D. J. Hartfiel. LC 98-29369. (Lecture Notes in Mathematics Ser.: Vol. 1695). (Illus.). viii, 131p. 1998. pap. 27.00 (*3-540-64775-9*) Spr-Verlag.

Markov-Switching Vector Autoregressions: Modelling, Statistical Inference & Application to Business Cycle Analysis. Hans-Martin Krolzig. LC 97-19163. (Lecture Notes in Economics & Mathematical Systems Ser.: Vol. 454). xiv, 357p. 1997. pap. write for info. (*3-540-63073-2*) Spr-Verlag.

Markovian Decision Processes. Hisashi Mine & Shunji Osaki. LC 70-116709. (Modern Analytic & Computational Methods in Science & Mathematics Ser.: No. 25). 152p. reprint ed. pap. 47.20 (*0-608-16325-2*, 202626400049) Bks Demand.

Markrich Sportsworld, Inc. An Audit Practice Case. 3rd ed. William H. Holley, Jr. (C). 1988. pap. text 36.95 (*0-256-07372-4*, Irwn McGrw-H) McGrw-H Hghr Educ.

Markrich Sportsworld, Inc. An Audit Practice Case. 4th ed. Charles L. Holley. 272p. (C). 1992. text 38.95 (*0-256-09211-7*, Irwn McGrw-H) McGrw-H Hghr Educ.

Mark's Account of Peter's Denial: A History of Its Interpretation. Robert W. Herron, Jr. 212p. (C). 1992. pap. text 28.00 (*0-8191-8353-9*); lib. bdg. 53.00 (*0-8191-8352-0*) U Pr of Amer.

Marks & Monograms on European & Oriental Pottery & Porcelain. William Chaffers. 1983. 45.00 (*0-87505-067-0*) Borden.

Marks & Remarks on a Year of Traveling. Kourtney M. Braff. (Illus.). 146p. (Orig.). 1993. 75.00 (*0-9637534-0-1*); pap. 25.00 (*0-9637534-1-X*) Thalagoya Pr.

Marks & Spencer: Anatomy of Britain's Most Efficiently Managed Company. K. K. Tse. (Illus.). 247p. 1984. text 79.25 (*0-08-030211-4*, Pergamon Pr); pap. text 38.50 (*0-08-030212-2*, Pergamon Pr) Elsevier.

An Asterisk (*) at the beginning of an entry indicates that the title is appearing for the first time.

Mark's Attachable Words: A Reader's List of Hard-to-Remember Words & Their Meanings. Mark Howell. LC 99-231701. 40p. 1998. pap. 5.95 (*0-9636577-5-5*) Trego-Hill.

Mark's Audience: The Literary & Social Setting of Mark 4.11-12. Mary Ann Beavis. (JSNT Supplement Ser.: No. 33). 262p. 1989. 75.00 (*1-85075-215-X*, Pub. by Sheffield Acad) CUP Services.

Marks' Electronic Standard Handbook for Mechanical Engineers. Ed. by McGraw-Hill Staff. 1995. 150.00 incl. cd-rom (*0-07-005368-5*) McGraw.

Mark's Endless Gospel: How You Complete the Story. James A. Harnish. LC 89-62041. 80p. 1989. pap. 6.95 (*0-917851-41-2*) Bristol Hse.

Mark's Gospel. John Painter. LC 96-9727. (New Testament Readings Ser.). 272p. (C). 1997. 65.00 (*0-415-11364-4*); pap. 24.99 (*0-415-11365-2*) Routledge.

Mark's Gospel Enrollment in the School of Discipleship. Catherine Nerney. 1987. pap. 2.50 (*0-8091-9331-0*) Paulist Pr.

Marks in the Field: Essays on the Uses of Manuscripts by Friends of the Houghton Library. Ed. by Rodney Dennis. (Illus.). 176p. 1992. pap. 25.00 (*0-914630-07-5*) Houghton Lib.

Mark's Kwanzaa Celebration. Diane Hoyt-Goldsmith. Ed. by Susan Evento. (Big America Ser.). (Illus.). 16p. (Orig.). (J). (gr. 1-3). 1996. pap. 3.95 (*1-56784-199-6*); pap. 17.95 (*1-56784-198-8*) Newbridge Educ.

Mark's Memory of the Future: A Study in the Art of Theology. Bascom Wallis. LC 95-16050. 256p. 1995. pap. 14.95 (*0-941037-34-7*, BIBAL Press) D & F Scott.

Marks of a Christian. Earl Robinson. pap. 2.99 (*0-88019-179-1*) Schmul Pub Co.

Marks of Achievement. write for info. (*0-318-66725-8*) Abrams.

Marks of American Potters. Edwin A. Barber. (Illus.). 1976. reprint ed. 37.95 (*0-89344-001-9*) Ars Ceramica.

Marks of American Potters - With Facsimilies of 1000 Marks & Illustrations of Rare Examples of American Wares. Edwin A. Barber. 1976. reprint ed. 59.00 (*0-403-06291-8*, Regency) Scholarly.

Marks of American Silversmiths in the Ineson-Bissell Collection. Louise C. Belden. LC 78-31816. 518p. reprint ed. pap. 160.60 (*0-7837-1766-0*, 204190900001) Bks Demand.

Marks of Christian Maturity: Becoming the Kind of Christian God Wants You to Be. George Duncan. 159p. 1987. pap. 4.95 (*0-310-55282-6*, 19028P) Zondervan.

Marks of Civilization: Artistic Transformations of the Human Body. Arnold Rubin & Robert S. Bianchi. LC 88-195361. (Illus.). 280p. (C). 1988. pap. 35.00 (*0-930741-12-9*); text 49.00 (*0-930741-13-7*) UCLA Fowler Mus.

Marks of Excellence: The History & Taxonomy of Trademarks. Per Mollerup. (Illus.). 240p. 1997. 75.00 (*0-7148-3448-3*, Pub. by Phaidon Press) Phaidon Pr.

Marks of Excellence: The History & Taxonomy of Trademarks. Per Mollerup. 1999. pap. text 29.95 (*0-7148-3838-1*) Phaidon Press.

Marks of Identity. Juan Goytisolo. 352p. 1992. pap. 15.95 (*1-85242-134-7*) Serpents Tail.

Marks of Our Brothers. Jane Lindskold. 256p. (Orig.). 1995. mass mkt. 4.99 (*0-380-77847-5*, Avon Bks) Morrow Avon.

Marks of Stone, Bk. 4. Terence Munsey. LC 96-94015. (Stoneman Ser.). 312p. (Orig.). (YA). (gr. 7 up). 1996. mass mkt. 5.99 (*0-9697066-3-4*, 70663) Munsey Music.

Marks of the Body of Christ. Ed. by Carl E. Braaten & Robert W. Jenson. LC 98-49966. 184p. 1999. pap. 18.00 (*0-8028-4617-3*) Eerdmans.

Marks of the Maker. Jan Bush. 256p. 1997. pap. 9.95 (*1-896836-09-7*) NStone Publ.

Marks on German, Bohemian & Austrian Porcelain. rev. ed. Robert E. Rontgen. 640p. 1998. 95.00 (*0-7643-0353-8*) Schiffer.

Marks Rackets Practice Set. Edmonds. 1995. 24.69 (*0-07-021399-2*) McGraw.

Mark's Sketch Book of Christ. Helen Tenney. 1975. spiral bd. 11.99 (*0-85151-075-2*) Banner of Truth.

Marks Standard Handbook for Mechanical Engineers. 9th ed. Ed. by E. A. Avalione & Theodore Baumeister, III. 2048p. 98.00 (*0-685-70908-6*, E00028) ASME Pr.

Mark's Standard Handbook for Mechanical Engineers. 10th ed. Ed. by E. A. Avallone & Theodore Baumeister. (Illus.). 1792p. 1996. 150.00 (*0-07-004997-1*) McGraw.

Mark's Story of Jesus. Werner H. Kelber. LC 78-14668. 96p. 1979. pap. 12.00 (*0-8006-1355-4*, 1-1355, Fortress Pr) Augsburg Fortress.

***Mark's Story of Jesus: Messiah for All Nations.** Dewey Mulholland. 224p. 1999. pap. 20.00 (*1-57910-251-4*) Wipf & Stock.

Mark's Superb Gospel. Ivor C. Powell. LC 85-25615. (Ivor Powell Commentaries Ser.). 432p. 1986. pap. 16.99 (*0-8254-3510-2*) Kregel.

Marksizm i Filosofija Jazyka: Osnovnye Problemy Sociologiceskogo Metoda V Nauke O Jazyke. V. N. Volosinov. (Janua Linguarum, Ser. Anastatica: No. 5). 1972. reprint ed. pap. 36.95 (*90-279-2007-9*) Mouton.

Marksmanship with Rifles: A Basic Guide. 2nd ed. Jay Peter Merkley. (Illus.). 67p. (C). 1984. pap. text 9.95 (*0-89641-141-9*) American Pr.

MARKSTRAT 2. 2nd ed. Jean-Claude Larreche & Hubert A. Gatignon. 240p. (C). 1990. pap. text, teacher ed. 38.50 (*0-89426-125-8*) Course Tech.

MARKSTRAT 2. 2nd ed. Jean-Claude Larreche & Hubert A. Gatignon. 240p. (C). 1990. mass mkt. 40.25 incl. disk (*0-89426-164-9*) Course Tech.

Markstrat3: The Strategic Marketing Simulation. 3rd ed. Jean-Claude Larreche et al. 1997. pap. text 65.95 (*0-538-88089-9*) Sth-Wstrn College.

Markt Drivng Strat Rdr. Carpenter et al. (C). 1995. text 25.00 (*0-673-99601-8*) Addson-Wesley Educ.

Marktchance Wirtschaftsdeutsch Level 2: Begleitheft. Juergen Bolten. (GER.). 46p. (C). 1993. pap. text 23.25 (*3-12-675142-3*, Pub. by Klett Edition) Intl Bk Import.

Marktchance Wirtschaftsdeutsch Level 2: Lehrbuch. Juergen Bolten. (GER.). 160p. (C). 1993. pap. text 25.25 (*3-12-675140-7*, Pub. by Klett Edition); audio 29.75 (*3-12-675141-5*, Pub. by Klett Edition) Intl Bk Import.

Marktonderzoek met SPSS. Groerland. (C). 1993. pap. text. write for info. (*0-201-54532-2*) Addison-Wesley.

MarktprozeB und Erwartungen: Studien zur Theorie der Marktwirtschaft. Ludwig M. Lachman. Tr. by Leonhard Walentik & W. Grinder from ENG. 336p. 1984. 105.00 (*3-88405-035-4*) Philosophia Pr.

Markup & Profit: A Contractor's Guide. Michael Stone. LC 98-42265. 192p. 1998. pap. 32.50 (*1-57218-071-4*) Craftsman.

Markup of H. R. 1432--African Growth & Opportunity Act Markup Before the Subcommittee on Africa of the Committee on International Relations, House of Representatives, 105th Congress, 1st Session, May 22, 1997. USGPO Staff. LC 97-217028. iii, 68 p. 1997. pap. write for info. (*0-16-055381-4*) USGPO.

Markups of H. R. 363, H. R. 437, H. R. 1271, H. R. 1272, H. R. 1273, H. R. 1277, H. R. 1275, H. R. 1274, H. R. 1276 & H. R. 1278: Markups Before the Committee on Science, U. S. House of Representatives, 105th Congress, 1st Session, April 16, 1997. USGPO Staff. LC 98-110355. iii, 540p. 1997. pap. write for info. (*0-16-055392-X*) USGPO.

Markus Lupertz: Drawings, 1964-1985. (Illus.). 212p. 1986. 160.00 (*3-906127-01-X*, Pub. by Gachnang & Springer) Dist Art Pubs.

Markus Raetz: In the Realm of the Possible. Marcia Tucker. Ed. by Karen Fiss. (Illus.). 64p. (Orig.). 1988. pap. 8.00 (*0-915557-62-2*) New Mus Contemp Art.

Markuspassion: Eine Redaktionsgeschicht Liche Untersuchung. Johannes Schreiber. (Beiheft zur Zeitschrift fuer die Neuetestamentliche Wissenschaft Ser.: Bd 68). (GER.). xv, 562p. (C). 1993. lib. bdg. 167.70 (*3-11-014153-1*) De Gruyter.

***Markwirtschaftliche Reformsteuerung: Die Rolle Von Iwf Und Weltbank in Mittelosteuropa Nach 1990.** C. Goricki. Vol. 4.Tr. of Free Enterprise Reform Management:The Role of IMF & World Bank in Central Europe after 1990. (GER.). 308p. 1999. text 52.00 (*90-5708-047-8*) Gordon & Breach.

***Marky & the Cat.** Deanna Luke. LC 99-91778. (Marky Ser.: No. 2). (Illus.). 40p. (J). (gr. 2). 2000. 8.95 (*1-928777-06-6*) Blessing Our Wrld.

***Marky & the Mouse.** Deanna Luke. LC 99-91777. (Marky Ser.: No. 1). (Illus.). 32p. (J). (gr. 2-7). 2000. 8.95 (*1-928777-05-8*) Blessing Our Wrld.

***Marky & the Rat.** Deanna Luke. LC 99-91779. (Marky Ser.: No. 3). (Illus.). 40p. (J). (gr. 2-7). 2000. 8.95 (*1-928777-07-4*) Blessing Our Wrld.

Marla. Ethel Van Pelt. 154p. 1982. pap. 4.25 (*0-89084-155-1*, 017905) Bob Jones Univ.

Marlboro Man & Japanese Import Policy Toward Cigarettes. Michael Ryan et al. (Pew Case Studies in International Affairs). 50p. (C). 1995. pap. text 3.50 (*1-56927-719-2*, GU Schl Foreign) Geo U Inst Dplmcy.

***Marlboro Township.** Randall Gabrielan. (Images of America Ser.). 128p. 1999. pap. 18.99 (*0-7524-1221-3*) Arcadia Publng.

Marlborough As Military Commander. David Chandler. (Illus.). 408p. 1996. 35.00 (*1-885119-30-5*) Sarpedon.

Marlborough As Military Commander. David Chandler. 408p. 1997. 100.00 (*0-946771-12-X*, Pub. by Spellmnt Pubs) St Mut.

Marlborough County, South Carolina, Minutes of the County Court, 1785-1799 & Minutes of the Court of Ordinary 1791-1821. Brent Holcomb. 152p. 1982. 20.00 (*0-89308-298-8*) Southern Hist Pr.

Marlborough Downs: A Later Bronze Age Landscape & Its Origins. Christopher Gingell. (Illus.). 166p. 1992. pap. 54.00 (*0-947723-04-8*) David Brown.

Marlborough-Godolphin Correspondence, 3 vols. Ed. by Henry I. Snyder. 1976. 169.00 (*0-19-822381-1*) OUP.

Marlborough's Army, 1702-11. Michael Barthrop. (Men-at-Arms Ser.: No. 97). (Illus.). 48p. pap. 11.95 (*0-85045-346-1*, 9007, Pub. by Ospry) Stackpole.

Marlene. Marlene Dietrich. 304p. 1990. mass mkt. 4.95 (*0-380-71088-9*, Avon Bks) Morrow Avon.

Marlene. Pam Gems. 96p. 1999. pap. 12.95 (*1-84002-064-4*) Theatre Comm.

Marlene. Mariarosa Sclauzero. 128p. (Orig.). 1988. pap. 6.95 (*0-87286-226-7*) City Lights.

Marlene Dietrich see Notable Biographies

Marlene Dietrich. Alexander Walker. (Legends Ser.). (Illus.). 156p. 2000. pap. 9.95 (*1-55783-352-4*) Applause Theatre Bk Pubs.

***Marlene Dietrich: Life & Legend.** Steven Bach. (Illus.). 672p. 2000. pap. text 18.00 (*0-306-80934-6*) Da Capo.

***Marlene Dietrich: The Songbook.** Leonard, Hal, Corporation Staff. 1999. pap. text 14.95 (*0-7119-7022-X*) H Leonard.

Marlene Dumas. Marlene Dumas. LC 99-475008. (Contemporary Artists Ser.). 1999. pap. 29.95 (*0-7148-3823-3*) Phaidon Press.

Marlene Dumas. Jolie Van Leeuwen. Ed. by Elsa Longhauser. (Illus.). 8p. 1993. pap. 10.00 (*1-58442-011-1*) Galleries at Moore.

Marlene My Friend: An Intimate Biography. David Bret. (Illus.). 280p. 1996. pap. 31.95 (*0-86051-844-2*, Robson-Parkwest) Parkwest Pubns.

Marler Family History. Sherry W. Manuel et al. (Illus.). 431p. (Orig.). 1996. pap. 35.00 (*1-887745-06-8*) Dogwood TX.

Marley & Her Scrooge. Emily Dalton. (American Romance Ser.: No. 706). 1997. per. 3.75 (*0-373-16706-7*, 1-16706-3) Harlequin Bks.

Marley & Me: The Real Bob Marley Story. Don Taylor. LC 94-45789. 256p. 1995. pap. 14.95 (*1-56980-044-8*) Barricade Bks.

Marley's Ghost. Mark H. Osmun. LC 99-64220. 336p. 2000. pap. 12.99 (*0-9673079-0-2*, 1225) Twelfth Ngt Pr.

Marlfox. Brian Jacques. LC PZ7.J15317Mare 1999. (Redwall Ser.). (Illus.). 386p. (J). (gr. 4-8). 1998. 22.99 (*0-399-23307-5*, Philomel) Peng Put Young Read.

***Marlfox.** Brian Jacques. (Redwall Ser.). (Illus.). 365p. (J). (gr. 4-7). 2000. reprint ed. mass mkt. 6.50 (*0-441-00693-0*) Ace Bks.

Marlik: The Complete Excavation Report. Ezat O. Negahban. LC 94-32410. (University Museum Monographs: Vol. 87). (Illus.). 408p. 1996. 195.00 (*0-924171-32-4*) U Museum Pubns.

Marlin! limited ed. Ernest Hemingway. Ed. by John Miller. (Illus.). 104p. 1992. reprint ed. 35.00 (*0-9632508-0-9*) Big Fish Bks.

Marlin & Ballard, Arms & History, 1861-1978: All Varieties. Bill West. LC 77-77900. (West Arms Library - Classic Bks.). (Illus.). 1977. 52.00 (*0-911614-07-9*) John Babish.

Marlin Firearms: A History of the Guns & the Company That Made Them. William S. Brophy. LC 88-38768. (Illus.). 704p. 1989. 75.00 (*0-8117-0877-2*) Stackpole.

Marlin Justice. Eugene D. Wheeler. LC 89-72152. 192p. (Orig.). 1990. 9.95 (*0-934793-25-5*); pap. 7.95 (*0-934793-26-3*) Pathfinder CA.

Marlina & McGee. Beverley B. Ashwill. LC 86-73031. (Illus.). 32p. (J). (ps-3). 1987. pap. 5.95 (*0-941381-00-5*) BJO Enterprises.

Marline Spike Seamanship: The Art of Handling, Splicing & Knotting Wire. L. Popple. (C). 1987. 50.00 (*0-85174-138-X*) St Mut.

Marlinespikes & Monkey's Fists: Traditional Arts & Knot-Tying Skills of Maritime Workers. LuAnne G. Kozma. Ed. by Ruth D. Fitzgerald. 60p. (Orig.). 1994. pap. write for info. (*0-944311-07-5*) MSU Museum.

Marling Hall. Angela M. Thirkell. 400p. 1995. pap. 11.95 (*0-7867-0273-7*) Carroll & Graf.

Marling Menu-Master for France. William E. Marling & Clare F. Marling. 112p. (Orig.). 1971. pap. 8.95 (*0-912818-03-4*) Altarinda Bks.

Marling Menu-Master for Germany. William E. Marling & Clare F. Marling. 88p. (Orig.). 1970. pap. 8.95 (*0-912818-01-8*) Altarinda Bks.

Marling Menu-Master for Italy. William E. Marling & Clare F. Marling. 108p. (Orig.). 1971. pap. 8.95 (*0-912818-02-6*) Altarinda Bks.

Marling Menu-Master for Spain. William E. Marling & Clare F. Marling. 112p. (Orig.). 1973. pap. 8.95 (*0-912818-04-2*) Altarinda Bks.

***Marlins.** Matt Silverman. (Total Baseball Companions Ser.). 96p. 2000. mass mkt. 2.50 (*1-892129-66-3*) Total Sprts.

Marlinspike Sailor. Hervey G. Smith. 1993. pap. 15.95 (*0-87742-412-8*) Intl Marine.

Marlinspike Sailor. rev. ed. Hervey G. Smith. 131p. 1993. pap. 15.95 (*0-07-059218-7*) McGraw.

Marlon Brando: Larger Than Life. Nellie Bly. 320p. 1994. mass mkt. 4.99 (*0-7860-0086-4*, Pinncle Kensgtn) Kensgtn Pub Corp.

Marlovian Tragedy: The Play of Dilation. Troni Y. Grande. LC 98-36204. 224p. 1999. 38.50 (*0-8387-5374-4*) Bucknell U Pr.

Marlovian World Picture. William Godshalk. (Studies in English Literature: No. 93). 224p. 1974. pap. text 60.00 (*90-279-3252-2*) Mouton.

Marlow see Major Literary Characters

Marlow & Shakespeare see Way of Life

Marlow Chronicles. Lawrence Sanders. 224p. 1986. mass mkt. 6.99 (*0-425-09963-6*) Berkley Pub.

Marlowe: Doctor Faustus. John D. Jump. LC 70-403540. (Casebook Ser.). 235p. 1969. write for info. (*0-333-06086-5*) Macmillan.

Marlowe: The Critical Heritage, Fifteen Eighty-Eight to Eighteen Ninety-Six. Ed. by Millar MacLure. 1979. 69.50 (*0-7100-0245-9*, Routledge Thoemms) Routledge.

Marlowe & His Circle: A Biographical Survey. Frederick S. Boas. (BCL1-PR English Literature Ser.). 159p. 1992. reprint ed. lib. bdg. 69.00 (*0-7812-7249-1*) Rprt Serv.

Marlowe & His Circle: A Biographical Survey. Frederick S. Boas. (BCL1-PR English Literature Ser.). 159p. 1992. reprint ed. lib. bdg. 69.00 (*0-7812-7260-2*) Rprt Serv.

Marlowe & His Poetry. John H. Ingram. LC 72-120965. (Poetry & Life Ser.). reprint ed. 27.50 (*0-404-52522-9*) AMS Pr.

Marlowe Canon. Tucker Brooke. 51p. (Orig.). (C). 1922. reprint ed. pap. 39.95 (*0-8383-0010-3*) M S G Haskell Hse.

***Marlowe, History & Sexuality: New Critical Essays on Christopher Marlowe.** unabridged ed. Paul Whitfield White. LC 97-24447. (Studies in the Renaissance: Vol. 35). 257p. 1998. text 59.99 (*0-404-62335-2*) AMS Pr.

Marlowe, Shakespeare, & the Economy of Theatrical Experience. Thomas Cartelli. LC 91-21173. 264p. (C). 1991. text 39.95 (*0-8122-3102-3*) U of Pa Pr.

Marlowe, Shakespeare, & the Economy of Theatrical Experience. Thomas Cartelli. LC 91-21173. reprint ed. pap. 80.30 (*0-608-07408-X*, 2067635) Bks Demand.

Marlowe's Counterfeit Profession: Ovid, Spenser, Counter-Nationhood. Patrick Cheney. LC 98-146977. 368p. 1997. text 60.00 (*0-8020-0971-9*) U of Toronto Pr.

Marlowe's Poems. Christopher Marlowe. Ed. by L. C. Martin. LC 66-23027. (Works & Life of Christopher Marlowe Ser.: Vol. 4). 304p. 1966. reprint ed. 50.00 (*0-87752-193-X*) Gordian.

Marlusk the Warrior. Micah Sapaugh. (Illus.). 48p. (Orig.). (J). (gr. k-8). 1993. text 11.95 (*1-56763-092-8*); pap. text 5.95 (*1-56763-093-6*) Ozark Pub.

Marlwych Mystery: or Parson Thring's Secret. Arthur W. Marchmont. 1976. lib. bdg. 15.80 (*0-89968-066-6*, Lghtyr Pr) Buccaneer Bks.

Marmac Guide to Atlanta. 9th ed. Ed. by Diane C. Thomas. (Marmac Guide Ser.). (Illus.). 304p. 1995. pap. 14.95 (*1-56554-088-3*) Pelican.

Marmac Guide to Dallas. Yves Gerem. (Illus.). 304p. 1999. pap. 14.95 (*1-56554-407-2*) Pelican.

Marmac Guide to Forth Worth & Arlington. Yves Gerem. (Illus.). 320p. 1999. pap. 14.95 (*1-56554-429-3*) Pelican.

Marmac Guide to Los Angeles. 3rd ed. Joe Jares. (Marmac Guide Ser.). (Illus.). 336p. 1995. pap. 14.95 (*1-56554-079-4*) Pelican.

***Marmac Guide to New Orleans.** 4th ed. Cecilia Casrill Dartez. LC 85-646121. (Illus.). 328p. 1999. pap. 14.95 (*1-56554-424-2*) Pelican.

***Marmaduke: Everlovin'** Anderson. 1999. mass mkt. 3.50 (*0-8125-1743-1*) Tor Bks.

Marmaduke: I Am Lovable. Brad Anderson. (Illus.). 128p. 1991. pap. 3.50 (*0-8125-1293-6*, Pub. by Tor Bks) St Martin.

Marmaduke: It's a Dog's Life. Brad Anderson. (Illus.). 128p. 1989. pap. 2.95 (*0-8125-7355-2*, Pub. by Tor Bks) St Martin.

Marmaduke: Laps it. Anderson. 1989. mass mkt. 2.95 (*0-8125-0309-0*) Tor Bks.

Marmaduke: Large & Loveable. Brad Anderson. (Illus.). 128p. (Orig.). 1990. pap. 2.95 (*0-8125-1281-2*, Pub. by Tor Bks) St Martin.

***Marmaduke: The Magic Cat.** C. West. (Illus.). (J). 1999. mass mkt. 7.95 (*0-340-72663-6*, Pub. by Hodder & Stought Ltd) Trafalgar.

Marmaduke: Up & at 'Em. Brad Anderson. (Illus.). 128p. 1990. pap. 2.95 (*0-8125-0597-2*, Pub. by Tor Bks) St Martin.

Marmaduke Laps it Up. Brad Anderson. (Illus.). 128p. 1989. pap. 2.95 (*0-8125-7335-8*, Pub. by Tor Bks) St Martin.

Marmaduke Multiply's Merry Method of Making Minor Mathematicians. E. F. Bleiler. 103p. 1971. pap. 4.95 (*0-486-22773-1*) Dover.

Marmalade. William Benton. LC 97-74601. (Illus.). 52p. 1997. pap. 11.95 (*0-9660170-0-5*) G Adams Gal.

Marmalade Days: Fall - Complete Units for Busy Teachers of Young Children. Carol T. Bond. 1987. pap. 27.95 (*0-933212-35-6*) Partner Pr.

Marmalade Days: Spring - Complete Units for Busy Teachers of Young Children. Carol T. Bond. 1988. pap. 27.95 (*0-933212-37-2*) Partner Pr.

Marmalade Days: Winter - Complete Units for Busy Teachers of Young Children. Carol T. Bond. 1987. pap. 27.95 (*0-318-35167-6*) Partner Pr.

Marmalade Me. expanded ed. Jill Johnston. LC 97-21727. (Illus.). 343p. 1998. pap. 22.95 (*0-8195-6314-5*, Wesleyan Univ Pr) U Pr of New Eng.

Marmee's Surprise: A Little Women Story. Louisa May Alcott. LC 95-30266. (Step into Reading Ser.: A Step 3 Book). (Illus.). (J). (gr. 2-3). 1997. pap. 3.99 (*0-679-87579-4*, Pub. by Random Bks Yng Read); lib. bdg. 11.99 (*0-679-97579-9*, Pub. by Random Bks Yng Read) Random.

Marmee's Surprise: A Little Women Story. Louisa May Alcott. (Step into Reading Ser.: A Step 3 Book). (J). (gr. 2-3). 1997. 9.19 (*0-606-12765-8*, Pub. by Turtleback) Demco.

Marmol, Bronce y Barro. Ethel Rios De Betancourt. LC 81-10286. (Illus.). 499p. 1984. 20.00 (*0-8477-0874-8*) U of PR Pr.

Marmoset Periodontium in Health & Disease. Barnet M. Levy et al. Ed. by H. M. Myers. (Monographs in Oral Science: Vol. 1). 1972. 34.00 (*3-8055-1366-6*) S Karger.

Marmosets in Captivity. Mike Moore. (C). 1989. 50.00 (*0-946873-95-X*, Pub. by Basset Pubns) St Mut.

Marmosets in Experimental Medicine: Proceedings. Conference on Marmosets in Experimental Medicine,. Ed. by J. Moor-Jankowski et al. (Primates in Medicine Ser.: Vol. 10). (Illus.). 1978. 133.25 (*3-8055-2750-0*) S Karger.

Marmots: Social Behavior & Ecology. David P. Barash. LC 89-4284. (Illus.). 384p. 1989. 55.00 (*0-8047-1534-3*) Stanford U Pr.

Marne. Edith Wharton. (Collected Works of Edith Wharton). 138p. 1998. reprint ed. lib. bdg. 88.00 (*1-58201-987-8*) Classic Bks.

Marnie. Winston Graham. 1976. 23.95 (*0-8488-0169-5*) Amereon Ltd.

Marnie Ritter's Canvas Patterns, Bk. 2. Marnie Ritter. 109p. 1992. pap. text 27.95 (*0-9635593-0-3*) Marnies Crewel.

Marnie Ritter's Canvas Patterns, Bk. 2. Marnie Ritter. (Illus.). 100p. 1994. pap. text 28.00 (*0-9635593-2-X*) Marnies Crewel.

Marnie's Kitchen Shortcuts. Marnie Swedberg. 256p. 1996. pap. 11.95 (*0-312-14119-X*) St Martin.

Marni's Mirror. Cheryl Silva. LC 98-45083. 115p. (J). (gr. 4-7). 1999. pap. 8.95 (*0-87159-230-4*) Unity Bks.

Maroc. (FRE.). 1999. 9.95 (*2-06-656401-X*) Michelin.

Maroc. Michelin Staff. (FRE.). 24.95 (*0-8288-6146-3*) Fr & Eur.

Maroc Green Guide. 6th ed. Michelin Staff. (FRE.). 1995. pap. 19.95 (*0-7859-9141-7*) Fr & Eur.

Maroc Green Guide: Afrique. 2nd ed. Michelin Staff. (FRE., Illus.). 1997. pap. 20.00 (*2-06-054402-5*, 544) Michelin.

Maroni De Chypre. Jane Johnson. (Studies in Mediterranean Archaeology: Vol. LIX). (Illus.). 130p. (Orig.). 1980. pap. 52.50 (*91-85058-94-7*) P Astroms.

Maronite Historians of Medieval Lebanon. Kamal S. Salibi. LC 78-63369. (Crusades & Military Orders Ser.: Second Series). reprint ed. 55.00 (*0-404-17035-8*) AMS Pr.

M

An Asterisk (*) at the beginning of an entry indicates that the title is appearing for the first time.

Maronites in History. Matti Moosa. LC 86-1919. 400p. 1986. reprint ed. pap. 124.00 (*0-608-06966-3*, 206717400009) Bks Demand.
Maroo of the Winter Caves. Ann Turnbull. 144p. (J). (gr. 4-7). 1990. pap. 6.95 (*0-395-54795-4*, Clarion Bks) HM.
Maroo of the Winter Caves. Ann Turnbull. (J). 1984. 12.05 (*0-606-04740-9*, Pub. by Turtleback) Demco.
Maroof the Cobbler. Librairie du Liban Staff. (J). 1986. 9.95 (*0-86685-566-1*) Intl Bk Ctr.
Maroon Arts: Cultural Vitality in the African Diaspora. Richard Price & Sally Price. LC 98-29572. (Illus.). 384p. 1999. 37.50 (*0-8070-8550-2*) Beacon Pr.
***Maroon Arts: Cultural Vitality in the African Diaspora.** Sally Price & Richard Price. 2000. pap. 25.00 (*0-8070-8551-0*) Beacon Pr.
Maroon Bells. Ansel Adams. 1995. 30.00 (*0-8212-2185-X*, Pub. by Bulfinch Pr) Little.
Maroon Bells - Redstone-Marble, CO. rev. ed. Ed. by Trails Illustrated Staff. 1995. 8.99 (*0-925873-48-9*) Trails Illustrated.
Maroon Lives: For Grenadian Freedom Fighters. Lasana M. Sekou. (Illus.). 36p. 1983. pap. text 5.00 (*0-913441-03-1*) Hse of Nehesi.
Maroon on Georgetown. 2nd abr. rev. ed. Photos & Text by Fred J. Maroon. LC 97-17174. (Illus.). 160p. 1997. 50.00 (*1-890674-01-X*) Lickle Pubng.
Maroon Societies: Rebel Slave Communities in the Americas. 3rd ed. Ed. by Richard Price. LC 96-26927. 445p. 1996. reprint ed. pap. text 16.95 (*0-8018-5496-2*) Johns Hopkins.
Maroon Within Us: Selected Essays on the African American Community Socialization 1981-1993. Asa G. Hilliard, III. LC 94-78760. 220p. 1994. pap. 16.95 (*0-933121-84-9*) Black Classic.
Marooned. Christie Golden. (Star Trek: No. 14). 1997. per. 5.99 (*0-671-01423-4*) PB.
Marooned on Eden. Robert L. Forward & Martha D. Forward. 1993. mass mkt. 4.99 (*0-671-72180-1*) Baen Bks.
***Marooned with a Marine.** Maureen Child. (Desire Ser.: Bk. 1325). 2000. mass mkt. 3.99 (*0-373-76325-5*, 1-76325-9) Silhouette.
Maroons of Jamaica. Mavis C. Campbell. LC 88-70992. 225p. 1992. reprint ed. pap. 14.95 (*0-86543-096-9*) Africa World.
Maroons of Jamaica: A History of Resistance, Collaboration & Betrayal. Mavis C. Campbell. LC 88-10413. 302p. 1988. 65.00 (*0-89789-148-1*, Bergin & Garvey) Greenwood.
Marowitz Shakespeare: Adaptations & Collages of Hamlet, Macbeth, the Taming of the Shrew, Measure for Measure & The Merchant of Venice. Charles Marowitz. 288p. 1990. pap. 15.00 (*0-7145-2651-7*) M Boyars Pubs.
Marowitz Shakespeare: Caesar, The Tempest, Timon, Vol. 2. Charles Marowitz. 1999. pap. text 16.95 (*0-7145-3052-2*) M Boyars Pubs.
Marpel is Stuck! And Other Really Good Reasons to Forgive. Sandy Silverthorne. LC 98-55699. 32p. 1999. 10.99 (*0-7814-3241-3*) Chariot Victor.
Marpingen: Apparitions of the Virgin Mary in Bismarckian Germany. David Blackbourn. LC 92-46119. (Illus.). 480p. 1993. text (*0-19-821783-8*) OUP.
Marple & Newtown Townships. Michael Mathis. LC 98-87697. (Images of America Ser.). (Illus.). 128p. 1998. pap. 16.99 (*0-7524-1246-9*) Arcadia Publng.
Marplot Marriage. Beth Andrews. 224p. 1999. 19.95 (*1-929085-02-8*); lib. bdg. 17.95 (*1-929085-03-6*); mass mkt. 4.95 (*1-929085-01-X*) Rgncy Pr.
Marplot Marriage. large type ed. Beth Andrews. 336p. 1999. lib. bdg. 23.95 (*1-929085-04-4*); per. 19.95 (*1-929085-05-2*) Rgncy Pr.
Marpol 73/78. International Maritime Organization Staff. LC 98-133344. v, 78 p. 1996. write for info. (*92-801-1417-4*, Pub. by Intl Maritime Org) St Mut.
Marpol, 72-78. International Maritime Organization Staff. 1991. text 380.00 (*0-89771-944-1*, Pub. by Intl Maritime Org) St Mut.
Marq Brown Sight Book: Compiled by an Instructor in Navigation. Brown, Son & Ferguson Ltd. Staff. (C). 1987. 60.00 (*0-85174-101-0*) St Mut.
Marquard & Seeley. Noel Hynd. LC 96-1988. 256p. 1996. 19.95 (*0-940160-64-1*) Parnassus Imprints.
Marquensan Encounters: Melville & the Meaning of Civilization. T. Walter Herbert, Jr. 247p. 1990. 34.95 (*0-674-55066-8*) HUP.
Marques de Collections de Dessins & d'Estampes. Frits Lugt. LC 75-21068. (FRE., Illus.). 608p. 1975. reprint ed. 125.00 (*0-915346-08-7*) A Wofsy Fine Arts.
Marques de Collections de Dessins et d'Estampes: Supplement. Frits Lugt. (FRE., Illus.). 476p. 1988. reprint ed. 125.00 (*1-55660-023-2*) A Wofsy Fine Arts.
Marques de Mantua. Hortensia Ruiz del Vizo. 1971. pap. 5.00 (*0-89729-138-7*) Ediciones.
Marques des Porcelaines, Faiences et Poteries. Graesse. (FRE.). 272p. 1991. reprint ed. 150.00 (*0-8288-7304-6*, 2859170650) Fr & Eur.
Marquesa. Stephen A. Bly. LC 98-33717. (Heroines of the Golden West Ser.). 1998. pap. text 10.99 (*1-58134-025-7*) Crossway Bks.
Marquesa. Stephen A. Bly. LC 99-22371. (Heroines of the Golden West Ser.). 1999. 23.95 (*0-7838-8608-X*, G K Hall & Co) Mac Lib Ref.
Marquesa: A Place & Time with Fish. Jeffrey Cardenas. (Illus.). 125p. 1995. 50.00 (*0-9620609-9-2*) Meadow Run Pr.
Marquesa Rosalinda, Farsa Sentimental y Grotesca. Ramon Del Valle-Inclan. Ed. by Cesar Oliva. (Nueva Austral Ser.: Vol. 113). (SPA.). 1991. pap. text 24.95 (*84-239-1913-7*) Elliots Bks.
Marquesan Insects: Environment. A. M. Adamson. (BMB Ser.: No. 139). 1969. reprint ed. 25.00 (*0-527-02245-4*) Periodicals Srv.
Marquesan Insects, 1932-1939, No. 1. (BMB Ser.). 1969. reprint ed. 35.00 (*0-527-02204-7*) Periodicals Srv.
Marquesan Insects, 1932-1939, No. 2. (BMB Ser.). 1969. reprint ed. 55.00 (*0-527-02220-9*) Periodicals Srv.
Marquesan Insects, 1932-1939, No. 3. (BMB Ser.). 1969. reprint ed. 40.00 (*0-527-02248-9*) Periodicals Srv.
Marquesan Legends. E. S. Handy. (BMB Ser.: No. 69). 1969. reprint ed. 25.00 (*0-527-02175-X*) Periodicals Srv.
Marquesan Notion of the Person. John Kirkpatrick. LC 83-18317. (Studies in Cultural Anthropology: No. 3). (Illus.). 292p. 1983. reprint ed. pap. 90.60 (*0-608-06866-7*, 206707200009) Bks Demand.
Marquesan Societies: Inequality & Political Transformation in Eastern Polynesia. Nicholas Thomas. (Illus.). 272p. 1990. text 65.00 (*0-19-827748-2*) OUP.
Marquesas Islands - Mave Mai. Sharon Chester et al. (Illus.). 114p. 1998. pap. 20.00 (*0-9638511-8-7*) Wander Albatross.
Marquese Von O. unabridged ed. Kleist. (World Classic Literature Ser.). (GER.). pap. 7.95 (*3-89507-003-3*, Pub. by Bookking Intl) Distribks Inc.
Marquess Lends a Hand. Monique Ellis. 320p. 1996. mass mkt. 4.50 (*0-8217-5522-6*, Zebra Kensgtn) Kensgtn Pub Corp.
Marquesta Kar-Thon. Tina Daniell. (DragonLance Warriors Ser.). 320p. (Orig.). 1995. pap. 5.99 (*0-7869-0134-9*, Pub. by TSR Inc) Random.
Marquet: Travels. (Rhythem & Color Two Ser.). 1970. 9.95 (*0-8288-9518-X*) Fr & Eur.
Marquetry. David Hume. (Illus.). 80p. 1994. pap. 16.95 (*0-85532-763-4*, 763-4, Pub. by Srch Pr) A Schwartz & Co.
***Marquetry.** Parramon Studios Staff. (Woodworking Class Ser.). (Illus.). 64p. 2000. 12.95 (*0-7641-5244-0*) Barron.
***Marquetry.** Pierre Ramond. (Illus.). 238p. 1998. 110.00 (*2-85101-005-0*) Antique Collect.
Marquetry. Pierre Ramond. Tr. by Jackqueline Derenne et al from FRE. LC 88-51885. (Illus.). 240p. 1995. 75.00 (*0-942391-19-5*, 70098) Taunton.
Marquetry: How to Make Pictures & Patterns in Wood Veneers. David Hume. (Illus.). 80p. 1998. pap. 16.95 (*0-8117-2850-1*) Stackpole.
Marquetry: The How to Do It Book. Jack Garide. LC 92-13174. (Illus.). 52p. (Orig.). 1996. pap. 14.95 (*1-879511-01-0*, Vestal Pr) Madison Bks UPA.
Marquetry & Inlay: Twenty Decorative Projects. Alan Bridgewater & Gill Bridgewater. (Illus.). 192p. 1991. 24.95 (*0-8306-8426-3*, 3426); pap. 15.95 (*0-8306-3426-6*) McGraw-Hill Prof.
Marquetry Manual. William A. Lincoln. LC 94-41869. (Illus.). 272p. (Orig.). 1990. reprint ed. pap. 21.95 (*0-941936-19-8*) Linden Pub Fresno.
Marquetry Techniques. Colin Holcombe. (Illus.). 128p. 1998. pap. 24.95 (*1-86126-057-1*, Pub. by Crolwood) Trafalgar.
***Marquette.** Gabriel N. Downs & Michael C. Downs. (Images of America Ser.). 1999. pap. 18.99 (*0-7385-0056-9*) Arcadia Publng.
Marquette: The Biography of an Iowa Railroad Town. Cecil Cook. LC 75-7184. (Illus.). 240p. 1975. 9.95 (*0-942240-03-0*) D Rehder.
Marquette: Then & Now. Sonny Longtime & Laverne Chappell. (Illus.). 280p. 1999. pap. 24.95 (*0-9670793-0-6*) North Shore Pubns.
Marquette on a Vanishing Frontier. Richard F. O'Dell. (Illus.). 16p. 1978. pap. 2.50 (*0-938746-09-X*) Marquette Cnty.
Marquette's Explorations: The Narratives Reexamined. Raphael N. Hamilton. LC 78-121768. (Illus.). 299p. reprint ed. pap. 92.70 (*0-8357-6201-7*, 203427900089) Bks Demand.
Marquis & the Chevalier: A Study in the Psychology of Sex As Illustrated by the Lives & Personalities of the Marquis De Sade, 1740-1814 & the Chevalier Von Sacher-Masoch, 1836-1905. James Cleugh. LC 70-142317. (Illus.). 295p. 1972. reprint ed. lib. bdg. 65.00 (*0-8371-5920-2*, CLMC) Greenwood.
Marquis at Bay: Novel. Albert B. Davis. LC 91-29369. 336p. 1992. 24.95 (*0-8071-1737-4*) La State U Pr.
Marquis de Custine & His Russia in 1839. George F. Kennan. LC 75-143818. (Illus.). 161p. reprint ed. pap. 50.00 (*0-7837-0560-3*, 204090400019) Bks Demand.
Marquis de La Fayette in the American Revolution, 2 Vols., Set. Charlemagne Tower. LC 70-169778. (Select Bibliographies Reprint Ser.). 1977. reprint ed. 68.95 (*0-8369-5998-1*) Ayer.
Marquis de Lafayette & a Flag That Never Comes Down, 1834-1989. limited ed. Robert L. Wells. (Illus.). 10p. 1989. 1.50 (*0-934021-30-9*) Natl Flag Foun.
Marquis de Mores at War in the Bad Lands. Usher L. Burdick. 27p. 1986. pap. 4.95 (*0-87770-379-5*) Ye Galleon.
Marquis de Sade. O. Beliard. (FRE.). 317p. 1958. pap. 25.00 (*0-87556-953-6*) Saifer.
***Marquis de Sade: A Life.** Neil Schaeffer. 592p. 2000. pap. 18.95 (*0-674-00392-6*) HUP.
Marquis de Sade: A Life. Neil Schaeffer. LC 98-12640. 592p. 1999. 35.00 (*0-679-40407-4*) Knopf.
Marquis de Sade: The Man & His Age. Iwan Bloch. Tr. by James Bruce. LC 72-9613. (Human Sexual Behavior Ser.). reprint ed. 45.00 (*0-404-57412-2*) AMS Pr.
Marquis de Sade's Elements of Style. Derek Pell. (Illus.). 64p. (Orig.). 1996. pap. 5.95 (*1-882633-20-2*) Permeable.
Marquis de Villemer. George Sand. (FRE.). 240p. 1976. pap. 10.95 (*0-7859-1443-9*, 2203220015) Fr & Eur.
Marquis Demores at War in the Bad Lands. Usher L. Burdick. (Shorey Historical Ser.). 27p. pap. 10.00 (*0-8466-0220-2*, S220) Shoreys Bkstore.
Marquis et la Marquise de Sade. A. M. Laborde. (American University Studies: Romance Languages & Literature: Ser. II, Vol. 108). 216p. (C). 1990. text 41.95 (*0-8204-0899-9*) P Lang Pubng.
***Marquis' Kiss.** Regina Scott. (Regency Romance Ser.). 256p. 2000. mass mkt. 4.99 (*0-8217-6705-4*, Zebra Kensgtn) Kensgtn Pub Corp.
Marquis of Carabas. Elizabeth Brodnax. 224p. 1991. 18.95 (*0-8027-1130-8*) Walker & Co.
Marquis of Carabas. large type ed. Elizabeth Brodnax. LC 91-16987. 270p. 1991. reprint ed. lib. bdg. 19.95 (*1-56054-188-1*) Thorndike Pr.
Marquis of Lossie. George MacDonald. 1994. 27.50 (*0-940652-54-4*) Sunrise Bks.
Marquis of Lossie. George MacDonald. (George MacDonald Original Works Ser.: Series V). 390p. 1995. reprint ed. 22.00 (*1-881084-32-9*) Johannesen.
Marquis of Montrose: Prion Lost Treasures. John Buchan. 325p. 1997. pap. 14.95 (*1-85375-224-X*) Trafalgar.
***Marquis Takes a Bride.** large type ed. Marion Chesney. LC 99-44278. (Romance Ser.). 1999. 27.95 (*0-7838-8777-9*, G K Hall & Co) Mac Lib Ref.
***Marquise & Pauline: Two Novellas.** George Sand. Tr. by Sylvie Charron & Sue Huseman from FRE. LC 98-19508. 200p. 1998. 23.00 (*0-89733-449-3*) Academy Chi Pubs.
Marquise de Sarde. 2nd ed. Rachilde. Tr. & Abr. by Liz Heron. LC 96-120965. (Decadence Ser.). 279p. 1999. reprint ed. pap. 14.95 (*1-873982-06-2*, Pub. by Dedalus) Hippocrene Bks.
Marquise des Ombres. Catherine Hermary-Vielle. (FRE.). 639p. 1985. pap. 12.95 (*0-7859-2505-8*, 2070376559) Fr & Eur.
Marquise of O & Other Stories. Heinrich Von Kleist. Tr. by David Luke & Nigel Reeves from GER. (Classics Ser.). 320p. 1978. pap. 11.95 (*0-14-044359-2*, Penguin Classics) Viking Penguin.
Marquise Sortit a Cinq Heures. Claude Mauriac. (FRE.). 1984. pap. 13.95 (*0-7859-4201-7*) Fr & Eur.
Marra Familia. William Martin et al. 64p. 1994. pap. 14.95 (*1-85224-221-3*, Pub. by Bloodaxe Bks) Dufour.
Marrano. Barry Goldensohn. LC 87-62233. 100p. 1988. pap. 12.95 (*0-943373-00-X*) Natl Poet Foun.
Marrano. Howard Rose. LC 92-60817. 256p. 1992. 20.00 (*1-878352-08-3*); pap. 10.00 (*1-878352-09-1*) R Saroff Pub.
Marrano As Metaphor: The Jewish Presence in French Writing. Elaine Marks. LC 95-9627. (Illus.). 224p. 1996. pap. text 30.50 (*0-231-10308-5*) Col U Pr.
Marrano Poets of the Seventeenth Century: An Anthology. Ed. & Tr. by Timothy Oelman from SPA. (Littman Library of Jewish Civilization). (Illus.). 296p. 1985. 29.95 (*0-19-710047-3*) OUP.
Marrano Prince. Auner Gold. (Ruach Ami Ser.). (Illus.). 286p. (YA). (gr. 9-12). 1988. 13.95 (*0-935063-39-0*); text 14.95 (*0-935063-40-4*) CIS Comm.
Marranos of Spain: From the Late 14th to the Early 16th Century (According to Contemporary Hebrew Sources) 3rd expanded rev. ed. B. Netanyahu. LC 98-55165. 304p. 1999. 42.50 (*0-8014-3586-2*) Cornell U Pr.
Marranos of Spain: From the Late 14th to the Early 16th Century According to Contemporary Hebrew Sources. 3rd expanded rev. ed. B. Netanyahu. LC 98-55165. 302p. 1999. pap. 16.95 (*0-8014-8568-1*) Cornell U Pr.
Marriage. Ariel Books Staff. (Illus.). 80p. 1992. 4.95 (*0-8362-3007-8*, Arie Bks) Andrews & McMeel.
Marriage. Witold Gombrowicz. 158p. 1986. pap. 10.95 (*0-8101-0725-2*) Northwestern U Pr.
Marriage. Concept by L. Ron Hubbard. 32p. 1994. pap. 4.00 (*0-88404-920-5*) Bridge Pubns Inc.
Marriage. Paul Johnson & Nicole Johnson. LC 98-56165. (SelectScripts Ser.: Vol. 1). 64p. 1999. pap. 14.99 (*0-8054-2023-1*) Broadman.
Marriage. Gloria Nagy. 432p. 1996. mass mkt. 5.99 (*1-57566-098-9*, Knsington) Kensgtn Pub Corp.
Marriage. Karl Rahner. 1970. pap. 4.95 (*0-87193-118-4*) Dimension Bks.
Marriage. Dallas Schulze. 384p. 1999. per. 5.99 (*1-55166-464-X*, 1-66464-8, Mira Bks) Harlequin Bks.
Marriage. J. C. Willke & Wilke. 1979. pap. 3.95 (*0-910728-13-5*) Hayes.
Marriage. adapted ed. Nikolai Vasilevich Gogol. 1987. pap. 5.25 (*0-8222-0735-4*) Dramatists Play.
Marriage see Works of Henry James Jr.: Collected Works
Marriage see Works of H. G. Wells
Marriage. Leon Blum. Tr. by Warre B. Wells from FRE. LC 72-9703. (Illus.). reprint ed. 42.50 (*0-404-57416-5*) AMS Pr.
Marriage. Edward Westermarck. LC 97-13491. 115p. 1997. reprint ed. lib. bdg. 40.00 (*0-7808-0273-X*) Omnigraphics Inc.
Marriage. 2nd ed. Susan Ferrier. LC 97-10835. (The World's Classics Ser.). 524p. 1998. pap. 10.95 (*0-19-282524-0*) OUP.
***Marriage.** 2nd ed. Susan Ferrier. (Oxford World Classics Ser.). 1999. pap. 10.95 (*0-19-283893-8*) OUP.
Marriage. 4th ed. Diane Johnson. 1995. 3.25 (*0-697-29104-9*, WCB McGr Hill) McGrw-H Hghr Educ.
Marriage: A Celebration. (Illus.). 64p. 1997. 9.95 (*1-85967-398-8*, Lorenz Bks) Anness Pub.
Marriage: A Covenant of Seasons. Mary V. Holt. LC 93-77227. (Illus.). 176p. (Orig.). 1993. pap. 7.95 (*0-89243-537-2*) Liguori Pubns.
Marriage: A Path to Sanctity. Javier Abad & E. Fenoy. 200p. 1997. pap. 9.95 (*971-11-7107-4*) Scepter Pubs.
Marriage: A Powerful Partnership. Mark McGaughey. 49p. (Orig.). 1996. teacher ed. 9.00 (*1-888220-02-3*) Reality Living.
Marriage: A Powerful Partnership. Mark McGaughey. 49p. (Orig.). 1996. student ed. 9.00 (*1-888220-03-1*) Reality Living.
Marriage: A Psychological & Moral Approach. Institute of Pastoral Psychology Staff. Ed. by William C. Bier. LC 64-25381. (Pastoral Psychology Ser.: No. 4). 288p. reprint ed. pap. 89.30 (*0-7837-0439-9*, 204076200018) Bks Demand.
Marriage: A Shared Sacrament. Center for Learning Network Staff. 65p. (YA). (gr. 9-12). 1993. teacher ed., spiral bd. 12.95 (*1-56077-286-7*) Ctr Learning.
Marriage: A Spiritual Leading for Lesbian, Gay & Straight Couples. Leslie Hill. LC 93-83951. 32p. (Orig.). 1993. pap. 4.00 (*0-87574-308-0*) Pendle Hill.
Marriage: A Treasury of Words to Live By. Robert B. Luce. (Illus.). 1992. 8.95 (*0-8378-2501-6*) Gibson.
Marriage: An Examination of the Man-Woman Relationship. 2nd ed. Herman R. Lantz & Eloise C. Snyder. LC 69-16038. (Illus.). 278p. reprint ed. pap. 86.20 (*0-608-10751-4*, 201372200087) Bks Demand.
Marriage: An Orthodox Perspective. John Meyendorff. LC 75-14241. 144p. 1975. pap. 9.95 (*0-913836-05-2*) St Vladimirs.
Marriage: Building Real Intimacy. Bill Hybels. (Interactions). 96p. 1996. pap., student ed. 5.99 (*0-310-20675-8*) Zondervan.
***Marriage: Celebrate Your Commitment - Leader's Guide.** Drew Gordon. (Discover Life Ser.). 38p. 1999. pap., teacher ed. 5.75 (*1-56212-438-2*, 1970-0325) CRC Pubns.
***Marriage: Celebrate Your Commitment - Study Guide.** Drew Gordon. 18p. 1999. pap., student ed. 3.45 (*1-56212-439-0*, 1970-0320) CRC Pubns.
Marriage: Claiming God's Promises. Zan Zoller & Jack Gilbert. LC 97-66523. 64p. 1998. pap. 15.95 (*0-88177-218-6*, DR218) Discipleship Res.
Marriage: Dead or Alive. Adolf Guggenbuhl-Craig. Tr. by Murray Stein from GER. LC 86-10054. 150p. 1997. pap. 14.50 (*0-88214-309-3*) Spring Pubns.
Marriage: Disillusion & Hope: Papers Celebrating Forty Years of the Tavistock Institute of Marital Studies. Ed. by Christopher Clulow. 128p. 1990. reprint ed. pap. text 21.95 (*0-946439-93-1*, Pub. by H Karnac Bks Ltd) Brunner-Mazel.
Marriage: First Things First. Grace H. Ketterman. (Framing Better Families Ser.: Bk. 1). 112p. 1995. pap. 8.99 (*0-8341-1562-X*) Beacon Hill.
Marriage: God's Design for Intimacy. James Reapsome & Martha Reapsome. (LifeGuide Bible Studies). 64p. 1986. pap., wbk. ed. 4.99 (*0-8308-1056-0*, 1056) InterVarsity.
***Marriage: God's Design for Intimacy.** rev. ed. James Reapsome & Martha Reapsome. (Life Guide Bible Studies Ser.). 63p. 1999. pap. 4.99 (*0-8308-3056-1*, 3056) InterVarsity.
Marriage: God's Way. Henry Brandt & Kerry L. Skinner. LC 99-23279. 1999. 18.99 (*0-8054-1971-3*) Broadman.
Marriage: In the Christian Church. Herbert O'Driscoll. 56p. (Orig.). 1998. pap. 2.95 (*0-88028-191-X*, 1439) Forward Movement.
Marriage: Its Ethic & Religion. Peter T. Forsyth. 152p. 1996. pap. 15.00 (*1-57910-010-4*) Wipf & Stock.
Marriage: Its History, Character, & Results. Thomas L. Nichols. LC 78-22161. (Free Love in America Ser.). reprint ed. 36.50 (*0-404-60955-4*) AMS Pr.
Marriage: Learning from Couples in Scripture. R. Paul Stevens & Gail Stevens. (Fisherman Bible Studyguide Ser.). 80p. 1991. pap. text 4.99 (*0-87788-533-8*, H Shaw Pubs) Waterbrook Pr.
Marriage: Past & Present. Margaret I. Cole. LC 72-9632. reprint ed. 41.50 (*0-404-57431-9*) AMS Pr.
Marriage: Past & Present: A Debate Between Robert Briffault & Bronislaw Malinowski. Robert Briffault & Bronislaw Malinowski. (Extending Horizons Ser.). 90p. (C). 1956. reprint ed. 3.95 (*0-87558-027-0*); reprint ed. pap. 2.45 (*0-87558-028-9*) Porter Sargent.
Marriage: Seasons of Growth. Serendipty House Staff. (101 Beginner Bible Study Ser.). 1998. pap. 5.99 (*1-57494-050-3*) Serendipty Hse.
Marriage: Sex, Celebration & Law. Joan Carreras. 192p. 1999. pap. 18.00 (*1-85182-280-1*, Pub. by Four Cts Pr) Intl Spec Bk.
Marriage: The Best Resources to Help Yours Thrive. Ed. by Rich Wemhoff. 237p. 1999. pap. 24.95 (*1-892148-05-6*) Res Pathways.
Marriage: The Biblical Perspective. Wilbur T. Dayton et al. 84p. 1984. pap. 5.99 (*0-89827-022-7*, BKZ65) Wesleyan Pub Hse.
Marriage: The Mystery of Faithful Love. Dietrich Von Hildebrand. LC 91-36153. 116p. 1997. reprint ed. pap. 9.95 (*0-918477-00-X*) Sophia Inst Pr.
Marriage: The Phoenix Contract. Dale D. Cornell & Frances G. Erickson. 175p. 1990. pap. 22.50 (*0-87527-264-9*) Green.
Marriage: The Rock on Which the Family Is Built. William E. May. LC 94-79300. 143p. (Orig.). 1995. pap. 9.95 (*0-89870-537-1*) Ignatius Pr.
Marriage: The Second Blood Covenant. Betty J. Jackson. (Illus.). 120p. 1998. pap. 20.00 (*1-890301-10-8*) M Bey.
Marriage: Theology & Reality. Cathy Molloy. LC 97-112581. 96p. (Orig.). 1996. pap. 12.95 (*1-85607-166-9*, Pub. by Columba Press) Whitecap Bks.
Marriage: This Time Will Be Perfect. Alan Schlossberg. 224p. (Orig.). pap. 6.99 (*1-878010-93-X*) A Schlossberg.
***Marriage: Whose Dream?** Paul David Tripp. (Resources for Changing Lives Ser.). 20p. 1999. pap. 1.75 (*0-87552-675-6*) P & R Pubng.

An Asterisk (*) at the beginning of an entry indicates that the title is appearing for the first time.

Marriage - The Early Years. Center for Learning Network Staff. (Religion Ser.). 44p. 1995. 6.00 (*1-56077-340-5*) Ctr Learning.

Marriage - The Early Years (Leader's Guide) Center for Learning Network Staff. (Religion Ser.). 20p. 1995. spiral bd. 3.00 (*1-56077-339-1*) Ctr Learning.

Marriage - The Sacrament of Divine-Human Communion: A Commentary on St. Bonaventures Breviloquium. Paula J. Miller. (Illus.). 268p. 1996. pap. 24.95 (*0-8199-0967-X*) Franciscan Pr.

Marriage, a Keepsake. Ed. by Helen Exley. (Suedel Giftbooks Ser.). (Illus.). 64p. 1994. 12.00 (*1-85015-464-3*) Exley Giftbooks.

Marriage, a Keepsake. Ed. by Helen Exley. (Sharon Bassin Covers Ser.). (Illus.). 64p. 1997. 9.00 (*1-85015-898-3*) Exley Giftbooks.

Marriage a la Mode. John Dryden. Ed. by David Crane. (New Mermaids Ser.). (C). 1991. pap. text 11.25 (*0-393-90064-9*) Norton.

Marriage a la Mode. John Dryden. Ed. by Mark S. Auburn. LC 80-51043. (Regents Restoration Drama Ser.). xxxii, 144p. 1981. pap. text 7.95 (*0-8032-6556-5*) U of Nebr Pr.

Marriage Abandoned Wife Jewish Law. Broyde. write for info. (*0-88125-678-1*); pap. write for info. (*0-88125-679-X*) Ktav.

Marriage Across Frontiers. Agustin Barbara. 104p. 1989. 59.00 (*1-85359-042-8*, Pub. by Multilingual Matters); pap. 24.95 (*1-85359-041-X*, Pub. by Multilingual Matters) Taylor & Francis.

Marriage Across the Color Line. Ed. by Clotye M. Larsson. LC 65-21549. 204p. 1965. 4.95 (*0-87485-014-2*) Johnson Chicago.

***Marriage after Modernity: Christian Marriage in Postmodern Times.** Adrian Thatcher. LC 99-29691. 320p. 1999. text 60.00 (*0-8147-8250-7*); pap. text 19.50 (*0-8147-8251-5*) NYU Pr.

***Marriage after Modernity: Christian Marriage in Postmodern Times.** Adrian Thatcher. (Studies in Theology & Sexuality: Vol. 3). 330p. 1999. 65.00 (*1-85075-944-8*, Pub. by Sheffield Acad); pap. 19.95 (*1-85075-948-0*, Pub. by Sheffield Acad) CUP Services.

Marriage after Mourning. Judy Pearson. 256p. 1994. pap. text, per. 18.95 (*0-7872-0205-3*) Kendall-Hunt.

Marriage, after Sex. Andrew Ames. Ed. by Jared A. March. LC 95-80305. 96p. (Orig.). 1995. pap. 7.95 (*0-931673-03-8*) J March Pub Grp.

Marriage Ain't Easy: Love, Honor & Negotiate Your Way to Happiness. Betty Carter & Joan K. Peters. 352p. 1997. per. 14.00 (*0-671-89625-3*) PB.

Marriage Alliance. large type ed. Mira Stables. 288p. 1995. 27.99 (*0-7089-3249-5*) Ulverscroft.

Marriage Alliance in Late Medieval Florence. Anthony Molho. LC 93-8470. (Harvard Historical Studies: No. 117). (Illus.). 472p. 1994. text 59.00 (*0-674-55070-6*) HUP.

Marriage among Indian Christians. Mariamma Joseph. (C). 1994. text 30.00 (*81-7033-215-X*) S Asia.

Marriage among Muslims. H. Donnan. 250p. 1996. 60.00 (*0-614-21515-3*, 754) Kazi Pubns.

Marriage among the Religions of the World. Ed. by Arlene A. Swidler. LC 90-19295. (Religions in Dialogue Ser.: Vol. 2). 180p. 1990. lib. bdg. 79.95 (*0-88946-310-7*) E Mellen.

Marriage-Analysis, Treatment & Results: Index of New Information with Authors & Subjects. Edith Marie Christos. (Illus.). 180p. 1992. 47.50 (*1-55914-696-6*); pap. 44.50 (*1-55914-697-4*) ABBE Pubs Assn.

Marriage & Adoption in China, 1845-1945. Arthur P. Wolf & Chieh-shan Huang. LC 78-66182. xxii, 426p. 1980. 57.50 (*0-8047-1027-9*) Stanford U Pr.

Marriage & Burials from the Frederick, Maryland, Evangelical Lutheran Church, 1743-1811. Frederick S. Weiser. 183p. 1985. lib. bdg. 19.00 (*0-915156-38-5*, SP 38) Natl Genealogical.

Marriage & Census Indexes for Family Historians. 7th ed. Jeremy Sumner Wycherley Gibson & Elizabeth Hampson. LC 98-71833. 47p. 1998. pap. 7.50 (*0-8063-1573-3*) Genealog Pub.

***Marriage & Customs of Tribes of India.** J. P. Singh Rana. LC 99-931535. 223p. 1998. pap. 200.00 (*81-7533-087-2*, Pub. by Print Hse) St Mut.

Marriage & Death Notices: From Raleigh Register & North Carolina State Gazette, 1799-1825. Carrie L. Broughton. LC 66-26935. 178p. 1995. reprint ed. pap. 18.50 (*0-8063-0052-3*) Clearfield Co.

Marriage & Death Notices Extracted from the Genius of Liberty & Fayette Advertiser of Uniontown, Pa., 1805-1854. Jean Rentmeister. 52p. 1981. per. 8.50 (*0-933227-41-8*, 244) Closson Pr.

Marriage & Death Notices from Baptist Newspapers of South Carolina, 1835-1865. Brent H. Holcomb. LC 81-17710. 150p. 1996. 25.00 (*0-87152-354-X*) Reprint.

Marriage & Death Notices from Baptist Newspapers of South Carolina, 1866-1887, Vol. 2. Brent H. Holcomb. 354p. 1996. 35.00 (*0-913363-23-5*) SCMAR.

Marriage & Death Notices from Columbia, South Carolina, Newspapers, 1792-1839. Brent H. Holcomb. 114p. 1981. 20.00 (*0-89308-270-8*) Southern Hist Pr.

Marriage & Death Notices from Extant Asheville, N. C., Newspapers 1840-1870. Ed. by Robert M. Topkins. LC 75-314671. 139p. 1983. reprint ed. 18.00 (*0-936370-02-5*) N C Genealogical.

Marriage & Death Notices from Raleigh, N. C., Newspapers, 1796-1826. Silas Lucas, Jr. & Brent Holcomb. 168p. 1978. reprint ed. 20.00 (*0-89308-046-2*) Southern Hist Pr.

Marriage & Death Notices from the Charleston Observer, 1827-1845. Brent Holcomb. 287p. 1991. reprint ed. pap. 21.50 (*1-55613-419-3*) Heritage Bk.

Marriage & Death Notices from the Griffin (Georgia) Weekly News & the Griffin Weekly News & Sun, 1882-1896. Fred R. Hartz & Emilie K. Hartz. 369p. 1987. 42.00 (*0-937503-00-2*) Gwendolyn Pr.

Marriage & Death Notices from the "South Western Baptist" Newspaper. Michael Kelsey et al. 223p. (Orig.). 1995. pap. 19.50 (*0-7884-0338-9*) Heritage Bk.

Marriage & Death Notices from the Southern Patriot, 1815-1830, Vol. 1. Theresa E. Wilson & Janice L. Grimes. 262p. 1982. 25.00 (*0-89308-279-1*) Southern Hist Pr.

Marriage & Death Notices from the Southern Patriot, 1831-1848, Vol. 2. Janice L. Grimes & Theresa E. Wilson. 248p. 1985. 25.00 (*0-89308-280-5*) Southern Hist Pr.

Marriage & Death Notices from the Up Country of South Carolina As Taken from Greenville Newspapers, 1826-1863. Brent H. Holcomb. 269p. 1983. 30.00 (*0-913363-02-2*) SCMAR.

***Marriage & Death Notices in "Raleigh Register & North Carolina State Gazette," 1826-1845.** Carrie L. Broughton. LC 68-17004. 402p. 1999. reprint ed. pap. 32.50 (*0-8063-0053-1*) Clearfield Co.

Marriage & Death Notices of Wheeling, Western Virginia & the Tri-State Area, 1818-1857, Vol. 1. Carol A. Scott. 90p. 1987. per. 9.50 (*0-933227-63-9*, 505) Closson Pr.

Marriage & Death Notices of Wheeling, Western Virginia & the Tri-State Area, 1858-1865, Vol. 2. Carol A. Scott. 104p. 1987. per. 9.50 (*0-933227-65-5*, 507) Closson Pr.

Marriage & Death Notices Transcribed from the Pages of the Lebanon Valley Standard. Robert A. Heilman. 292p. (Orig.). 1995. pap. text 23.00 (*0-7884-0181-5*) Heritage Bk.

Marriage & Disability. Ed. by Betty Garee. 88p. (Orig.). 1992. pap. 7.95 (*0-915708-34-5*) Cheever Pub.

Marriage & Divorce. Margaret C. Jasper. LC 94-207825. (Legal Almanac Ser.). 96p. 1994. text 22.50 (*0-379-11187-X*) Oceana.

***Marriage & Divorce.** J. Vernon McGee. LC 97-36461. 240p. 1998. 16.99 (*0-7852-7454-5*) Nelson.

Marriage & Divorce. Ed. by Tamara L. Roleff & Mary E. Williams. LC 97-4941. (Current Controversies Ser.). (J). (gr. 5-12). 1997. pap. 16.20 (*1-56510-567-2*); lib. bdg. 26.20 (*1-56510-568-0*) Greenhaven.

Marriage & Divorce, Vol. 1. McCaffrey. 1996. 125.00 (*0-316-55342-5*) Little.

Marriage & Divorce: A Social & Economic Study. rev. ed. Hugh Carter & Paul C. Glick. (Vital & Health Statistics Monographs, American Public Health Association). 483p. (C). 1970. 49.95 (*0-674-55076-5*) HUP.

Marriage & Divorce: A Social & Economic Study. rev. ed. Hugh Carter & Paul C. Glick. LC 79-105369. (Vital & Health Statistics Monographs, American Public Health Association). 483p. 1970. 12.00 (*0-674-55075-7*) HUP.

Marriage & Divorce, a Contemporary Perspective. Ed. by Carol C. Nadelson & Derek C. Polonsky. LC 83-1567. (Guilford Family Therapy Ser.). (Illus.). 285p. 1984. reprint ed. pap. 88.40 (*0-608-07577-9*, 205989100010) Bks Demand.

Marriage & Divorce in Islamic South-East Asia. Gavin W. Jones. LC 93-38170. (South-East Asian Social Science Monographs). (Illus.). 376p. 1994. text 49.95 (*967-65-3047-6*) OUP.

***Marriage & Divorce in the Bible & the Church.** Alex R. G. Deasley. LC 99-87528. 2000. pap. 19.99 (*0-8341-1763-0*) Beacon Hill.

Marriage & Divorce in the Thought of Martin Bucer. Herman J. Selderhuis. Tr. by John Vriend & Lyle D. Bierma. LC 98-16686. (Sixteenth Century Essays & Studies: Vol. 48). Orig. Title: Huwelijk en Echtscheiding Bij Martin Bucer. 436p. 1998. 45.00 (*0-943549-68-X*) Truman St Univ.

Marriage & Divorce in the United States, 1867-1886. Carroll D. Wright. LC 75-38146. (Demography Ser.). (Illus.). 1976. reprint ed. 84.95 (*0-405-07999-0*) Ayer.

Marriage & Divorce Laws in Europe: A Study in Comparative Legislation. Frederic R. Coudert, Jr. 1993. reprint ed. 32.50 (*0-8377-2021-4*, Rothman) W S Hein.

Marriage & Divorce Laws of the World. Ed. by Hyacinthe Ringrose. 270p. 1988. reprint ed. 45.00 (*0-8377-2540-2*, Rothman) W S Hein.

Marriage & Divorce Practices in Native California. Kyerstie Nelson. (Archaeological Research Facility, Dept. of Anthropology, Miscellaneous Papers, Berkeley CA). 51p. (C). 1975. pap. 6.25 (*1-55567-647-2*) Coyote Press.

Marriage & Divorce Records from Maine Freewill Baptist Publications, 1819-1851. David C. Young & Elizabeth K. Young. 726p. (Orig.). 1995. pap. text 46.00 (*0-7884-0136-X*) Heritage Bk.

Marriage & Divorce Statistics. (OPCS Ser.: No. 22). 102p. 1997. pap. 45.00 (*0-11-620930-5*, HM09305, Pub. by Statnry Office) Bernan Associates.

Marriage & Divorce Statistics. LC 98-178904. (OPCS Series FM2, 1995: No. 23). (Illus.). 102p. 1998. pap. 55.00 (*0-11-621028-1*, HM10281, Pub. by Statnry Office) Bernan Associates.

Marriage & Families. Kenneth C. Kammeyer & Constance L. Shehan. 1997. pap. text, student ed. 20.00 (*0-205-26193-0*) Allyn.

***Marriage & Family.** (C). 2000. write for info. (*0-13-019891-9*) P-H.

Marriage & Family. Davidson & Moore. 1996. pap. text, student ed. 20.00 (*0-205-18432-4*) Allyn.

Marriage & Family. Kenneth C. Kammeyer. 1986. text 44.00 (*0-205-08624-1*, H86242) Allyn.

Marriage & Family. Pocs. 1994. 12.74 (*1-56134-283-1*) McGraw.

Marriage & Family. Ed. by L. Stone. LC 98-33930. (Contemporary Perspectives Ser.). (YA). (gr. 9-12). 1998. pap. 22.45 (*1-56510-902-3*); lib. bdg. 39.95 (*1-56510-903-1*) Greenhaven.

Marriage & Family. Thompson. (C). Date not set. pap. text 16.36 (*0-395-90254-1*) HM.

Marriage & Family. 4th ed. Lauer. 168p. 1999. pap., student ed. 19.38 (*0-07-234189-0*) McGraw.

Marriage & Family. 4th ed. Lauer. LC 99-30977. 1999. 37.50 (*0-07-231572-5*) McGraw.

Marriage & Family. 22nd annot. ed. Gilbert. 1996. teacher ed. (*0-697-31712-9*, WCB McGr Hill) McGrw-H Hghr Educ.

Marriage & Family: A Complete Course. Robert J. Hannon & Anastasia S. Slattery. 172p. (Orig.). (YA). (gr. 11 up). 1978. teacher ed. 30.00 (*0-9606040-0-6*) Patio Pubns.

Marriage & Family: A Study Guide. Wolf. (C). 1996. student ed. 64.00 (*0-673-98419-2*) Addison-Wesley.

Marriage & Family: An Introduction Using ExplorIt. 2nd ed. Kevin Demmitt. (C). 1999. pap. text 18.00 (*0-922914-35-4*) Thomson Learn.

Marriage & Family: Change & Continuity. 2nd ed. J. Kenneth Davidson, Sr. & Nelwyn B. Moore. LC 95-39047. 704p. 1996. 79.00 (*0-205-16747-0*) Allyn.

Marriage & Family: Change & Continuity, Examination Copy. J. Kenneth Davidson & Nelwyn B. Moore. 864p. (C). 1996. write for info. (*0-205-18408-1*, H8408-0) Allyn.

Marriage & Family: Experiencing the Church's Teaching in Married Life. Ed. by Pontifical Council for the Family Staff. LC 88-81273. 175p. (Orig.). 1989. pap. 9.95 (*0-89870-218-6*) Ignatius Pr.

Marriage & Family: The Quest for Intimacy. 3rd ed. Robert H. Lauer & Jeanette C. Lauer. LC 96-83188. 544p. (C). 1996. text. write for info. (*0-697-24452-0*, WCB McGr Hill) McGrw-H Hghr Educ.

***Marriage & Family: The Quest for Intimacy.** 4th ed. Robert Lauer. 532p. (C). 1999. pap. 47.81 (*0-07-236163-8*) McGrw-H Hghr Educ.

Marriage & Family 1999-2000 Edition. 25th ed. Gilbert. 1999. pap., student ed. 16.56 (*0-07-041153-0*) McGraw.

Marriage & Family Assessment: A Sourcebook for Family. Ed. by Erik E. Filsinger. LC 83-11087. (Illus.). 342p. 1983. reprint ed. pap. 106.10 (*0-608-01169-X*, 205946900001) Bks Demand.

Marriage & Family Enrichment. Wallace Denton. LC 86-308. (Journal of Psychotherapy & the Family: Vol. 2, No. 1). 125p. 1986. text 39.95 (*0-86656-495-0*) Haworth Pr.

Marriage & Family Experience. Strong. (Adaptable Courseware-Softside Ser.). Date not set. 43.00 (*0-534-15919-2*); pap. 43.00 (*0-534-56610-3*) Wadsworth Pub.

Marriage & Family Experience. 5th ed. Bryan Strong & Christine DeVault. Ed. by Grumney. 582p. (C). 1992. text 54.25 (*0-314-88136-0*) West Pub.

Marriage & Family Experience. 6th ed. Strong. (Sociology-Upper Level Ser.). 1995. pap., student ed. 15.75 (*0-314-06032-4*) Wadsworth Pub.

Marriage & Family Experience. 6th ed. Bryan Strong & Christine DeVault. LC 94-45224. 806p. (C). 1995. mass mkt. 46.75 (*0-314-04390-X*) West Pub.

Marriage & Family Experience. 7th ed. Strong. 1998. pap., student ed. 17.25 (*0-534-53758-8*) Brooks-Cole.

***Marriage & Family Experience.** 8th ed. Bryan Strong et al. (Sociology-Upper Level Ser.). 2000. 19.50 (*0-534-55675-2*) Wadsworth Pub.

Marriage & Family Experience. 8th ed. Devault Saya Strong. 2000. 5475.00 (*0-534-55674-4*) Thomson Learn.

Marriage & Family Experience: Intimate Rel Changing Society. 7th ed. Brian Strong et al. LC 97-35925. (Sociology-Upper Level). (C). 1997. mass mkt. 50.75 (*0-534-53757-X*) Wadsworth Pub.

Marriage & Family Experience with Infotrac. 7th ed. Strong & Devault. 1997. 52.75 incl. cd-rom (*0-534-53765-0*) Wadsworth Pub.

Marriage & Family in a Changing Society. 4th ed. Ed. by James M. Henslin. 1992. pap. 16.95 (*0-02-914475-2*) Free Pr.

Marriage & Family in a Changing Society. 4th ed. Ed. by James M. Henslin. 1992. teacher ed. 4.95 (*0-02-914476-0*) S&S Trade.

Marriage & Family in Islam. Mohammad M. Hussaini. Ed. by Sumaiyah Bintulislam. 64p. (Orig.). 1996. pap. write for info. (*0-911119-73-6*) Igram Pr.

Marriage & Family in Transition. Ed. by John N. Edwards & David H. Demo. 496p. 1990. pap. text 56.00 (*0-205-12641-3*, H26412) Allyn.

Marriage & Family Law Agreements, 1. Samuel Green & John V. Long. (Family Law Library). 476p. 1998. boxed set 140.00 (*0-471-11223-2*) Wiley.

Marriage & Family Law Agreements, Set. Samuel Green & John V. Long. 476p. 1984. text 75.00 (*0-07-024275-5*) Shepards.

Marriage & Family Life Code of the Jewish Faith. Bernard Abramowitz. (HEB.). 16.00 (*0-87559-098-5*) Shalom.

Marriage & Family, 1996-1997. annuals 22nd ed. Katleen R. Gilbert. 256p. (C). 1996. text. write for info. (*0-697-31711-0*) Brown & Benchmark.

Marriage & Family, 98-99. 24th ed. Kathleen R. Gilbert. (Annual Ser.). (Illus.). 240p. 1998. pap. text 12.25 (*0-697-39179-5*, Dshkn McG-Hill) McGrw-H Hghr Educ.

Marriage & Family Presentation Sourcebook. Laurie Cope Grand. LC 99-55827. 304p. 2000. pap. text 49.95 incl. disk (*0-471-37444-X*) Wiley.

Marriage & Family Relations. Feinman. (C). 1998. text 36.25 (*0-03-076579-X*); pap. text, teacher ed. 28.00 (*0-03-076582-X*); pap. text, teacher ed., suppl. ed. 31.00 (*0-03-076583-8*, Pub. by Harcourt Coll Pubs); pap. text, student ed. 13.75 (*0-03-076581-1*) Harcourt Coll Pubs.

Marriage & Family Relationships. Strong. Date not set. 43.00 (*0-534-15860-9*) Wadsworth Pub.

Marriage & Family Review see Publishing in Journals on the Family: A Survey & Guide for Scholars, Practitioners, & Students

Marriage & Family Therapy: A Sociocognitive Approach. Nathan Hurvitz & Roger A. Straus. LC 90-25788. (Marriage & Family Review Ser.). 240p. (C). 1991. text 49.95 (*1-56024-060-1*); pap. text 19.95 (*1-56024-061-X*) Haworth Pr.

Marriage & Family Today. 3rd ed. Keith Melville. 492p. (C). 1983. text. write for info. (*0-318-57008-4*) Random.

***Marriage & Family Workbook: An Interactive Reader.** Robert Manis. 208p. 2000. wbk. ed. 20.00 (*0-205-30931-3*) Allyn.

Marriage & Fertility: Studies in Interdisciplinary History. Ed. by Robert I. Rotberg & Theodore Rabb. LC 80-7816. (Illus.). 384p. 1980. reprint ed. pap. 119.10 (*0-7837-9428-2*, 206016900004) Bks Demand.

Marriage & Friendship in Medieval Spain: Social Relations According to the Fourth Partida of Alfonso X. Marilyn Stone. (American University Studies: Romance Languages & Literature: Ser. II, Vol. 131). (Illus.). 200p. (C). 1990. text 42.00 (*0-8204-1177-9*) P Lang Pubng.

M

Marriage & Inequality in Chinese Society. Ed. by Rubie S. Watson & Patricia B. Ebrey. LC 90-10839. (Studies on China: Vol. 12). (Illus.). 400p. 1991. 58.00 (*0-520-06930-7*, Pub. by U CA Pr); pap. 17.95 (*0-520-07124-7*, Pub. by U CA Pr) Cal Prin Full Svc.

Marriage & Inequality in Classless Societies. Jane F. Collier. LC 87-19132. xx, 290p. 1988. 42.50 (*0-8047-1365-0*) Stanford U Pr.

Marriage & Inequality in Classless Societies. Jane Fishburne Collier. xx, 290p. 1993. pap. 17.95 (*0-8047-2177-7*) Stanford U Pr.

Marriage & Its Values: An Interactive Approach. Jesse J. Thomas. 126p. Date not set. pap. 11.95 (*0-930626-09-5*) Psych & Consul Assocs.

Marriage & Life Choices: Teacher's Wraparound Edition. David Thomas. 1999. pap. write for info. (*0-02-655912-9*, Benzger Pub) Glencoe.

Marriage & Mandatory Abortion among the 17th-Century Siraya. John R. Shepherd. LC 95-15069. (American Ethnological Society Monograph Ser.: No. 6). 99p. 1995. pap. 15.00 (*0-913167-71-1*) Am Anthro Assn.

Marriage & Mental Illness: A Sex-Roles Perspective. R. Julian Hafner. LC 85-17693. (Guilford Family Therapy Ser.). 269p. 1986. reprint ed. pap. 83.40 (*0-608-07875-1*, 205989200010) Bks Demand.

Marriage & Miracles. Miranda Lee. LC 96-415. 185p. 1995. per. 3.25 (*0-373-11784-1*, 1-11784-5) Harlequin Bks.

Marriage & Miscellaneous from Hudson, NY Newspapers Vol. 2: The Balance & Columbian Repository, 1802-1811. Arthur C. Kelly. 208p. 1980. lib. bdg. 30.00 (*1-56012-046-0*, 45) Kinship Rhinebeck.

Marriage & Morals. Bertrand Russell. LC 70-114377. 1970. pap. 13.95 (*0-87140-211-4*, Pub. by Liveright) Norton.

Marriage & Motherhood: What's That? Sarah W. Utterbach. 28p. (Orig.). 1995. pap. 2.00 (*1-887770-01-1*) Redeeming Love.

Marriage & Parentage. Henry C. Wright. LC 73-20651. (Sex, Marriage & Society Ser.). 330p. 1974. reprint ed. 28.95 (*0-405-05823-3*) Ayer.

***Marriage & Patterns of Partnership.** Beulah Woods. 204p. 1998. reprint ed. pap. 11.99 (*1-85078-316-0*, Pub. by O M Pubng) OM Literature.

Marriage & Personal Development. Rubin Blanck & Gertrude Blanck. LC 68-9577. 191p. 1968. text 52.50 (*0-231-03150-5*) Col U Pr.

Marriage & Property. Ed. by Elizabeth M. Craik. (SWSS Ser.). 202p. 1991. pap. text 13.90 (*0-08-041205-X*, Pub. by Aberdeen U Pr) Macmillan.

Marriage & Property. Ed. by Elizabeth M. Craik. 208p. 1984. text 31.00 (*0-08-028448-5*, Pergamon Pr) Elsevier.

Marriage & Race Death. Morrison I. Swift. 1977. lib. bdg. 59.95 (*0-8490-2211-8*) Gordon Pr.

Marriage & Rank in Bengali Culture. Ronald B. Inden. 161p. 1976. 10.95 (*0-7069-0435-4*) Asia Bk Corp.

Marriage & Rank in Bengali Culture: A History of Caste & Clan in Middle Period Bengal. Ronald B. Inden. LC 73-85789. 173p. reprint ed. pap. 53.70 (*0-608-17470-X*, 202995200066) Bks Demand.

Marriage & Relationship Encounter: A Guide to Improved Relationships. Frank H. Kim. Ed. by Hayley R. Mitchell. 208p. (Orig.). 1996. pap. 8.50 (*0-9653151-0-X*) Sheila-Na-Gig.

Marriage & Sacrament: A Theology of Christian Marriage. Michael G. Lawler. LC 93-22619. 122p. (Orig.). 1993. pap. text 9.95 (*0-8146-5051-1*, M Glazier) Liturgical Pr.

Marriage & Sexuality in Islam: A Translation of Al-Ghazali's Book on the Etiquette of Marriage from the Ihya. Madelain Farah. LC 83-27365. 197p. reprint ed. pap. 61.10 (*0-608-15654-X*, 203191300077) Bks Demand.

Marriage & Single: or Marriage & Celibacy Contrasted. Timothy S. Arthur. (Works of Timothy Shay Arthur). 1989. reprint ed. lib. bdg. 79.00 (*0-685-27488-8*) Rprt Serv.

Marriage & the Christian Home. Michael B. Henning. (Orig.). 1987. pap. 3.50 (*0-913026-66-2*) St Nectarios.

Marriage & the English Reformation. Eric J. Carlson. (Family, Sexuality & Social Relations in Past Times Ser.). 352p. (C). 1994. 66.95 (*0-631-16864-8*) Blackwell Pubs.

Marriage & the Family. Perry. (C). 2000. text 48.00 (*0-205-18544-4*) Allyn.

An Asterisk (*) at the beginning of an entry indicates that the title is appearing for the first time.

Marriage & the Family. Harold T. Christensen & Kathryn P. Johnsen. LC 71-155205. 554p. reprint ed. pap. 171.80 (*0-608-31000-X*, 201247600081) Bks Demand.

Marriage & the Family. 2nd ed. Lasswell & Gillette. (Sociology - Introductory Level Ser.). 1987. pap., student ed. 10.00 (*0-534-07585-1*) Wadsworth Pub.

Marriage & the Family. 2nd ed. Lasswell & Gillette. (Sociology - Introductory Level Ser.). 1987. pap., teacher ed. write for info. (*0-534-07586-X*) Wadsworth Pub.

Marriage & the Family. 2nd ed. Marcia Lasswell & Thomas E. Lasswell. 596p. (C). 1987. pap. write for info. (*0-534-07584-3*) Wadsworth Pub.

Marriage & the Family: A Brief Introduction. Knox. LC 98-8095. (Sociology-Upper Level Ser.). 1998. pap. 28.75 (*0-534-55287-0*) Wadsworth Pub.

Marriage & the Family: A Christian Perspective. 2nd rev. ed. Stephen A. Grunlan. LC 99-27098. 416p. 1999. write for info. (*0-310-20156-X*) Zondervan.

Marriage & the Family: Current Critical Issues. Ed. by Marvin B. Sussman. LC 79-53232. (Collected Essay Ser.). 63p. 1979. pap. 9.95 (*0-917724-08-9*) Haworth Pr.

Marriage & the Family: Diversity & Strengths. 3rd ed. David H. Olson & John D. DeFrain. LC 99-22761. xxviii, 692p. 1999. text 63.95 (*0-7674-1209-5*, 12095) Mayfield Pub.

Marriage & the Family: New Directions, New Integrations. Ed. by John T. Chirban. (Series on Medicine, Psychology & Religion). (Illus.). 94p. (Orig.). pap. 4.95 (*0-916586-63-4*) Holy Cross Orthodox.

M

Marriage & the Family: The Domestic Church. Luis Alessio & Hector Munoz. Tr. by Aloysius Owen from SPA. LC 82-6853. 121p. 1982. pap. 3.95 (*0-8189-0433-X*) Alba.

Marriage & the Family & Child-Rearing Practices. Sheila Corwin. Ed. by Therese A. Zak. (Lifeworks Ser.). (Illus.). 160p. 1981. text 13.96 (*0-07-013198-8*) McGraw.

Marriage & the Family in the Documents of the Magisterium: A Course in the Theology of Marriage. Ramon G. De Haro. Tr. by William E. May. LC 93-78531. 350p. 1993. 24.95 (*0-89870-459-6*) Ignatius Pr.

Marriage & the Family in the Middle Ages. Frances Gies & Joseph Gies. LC 87-45048. 320p. 1989. reprint ed. pap. 14.00 (*0-06-091468-8*, PL 1468, Perennial) HarperTrade.

***Marriage & the Family Study Guide: Diversity & Strength.** 3rd ed. David H. Olson et al. iv, 220p. (C). 1999. pap. text 19.95 (*0-7674-1211-7*, 1211-7) Mayfield Pub.

Marriage & the Family under Challenge: An Outline of Issues, Trends, & Alternatives. 2nd ed. Dorothy F. Beck. LC 76-26307. 107p. reprint ed. pap. 33.20 (*0-608-18322-9*, 203159600075) Bks Demand.

Marriage & the Spirituality of Intimacy. Leif Kehrwald. 112p. (Orig.). 1997. pap. 7.95 (*0-86716-253-8*, B2538) St Anthony Mess Pr.

Marriage & Virginity. Augustine Hippo. Ed. by John E. Rotelle & David Hunter. Tr. by Ray Kearney from LAT. (Works of St. Augustine). 272p. 1998. 35.00 (*1-56548-104-6*) New City.

Marriage & You. Bernard J. Oliver, Jr. 1964. 14.95 (*0-8084-0211-0*); pap. 16.95 (*0-8084-0212-9*) NCUP.

Marriage Around the Clock: Fifty-Two Ways to Stay Happily Married Even Though Your Husband's.... Phoebe Hichens. 1992. pap. text 9.95 (*1-870948-26-2*, Pub. by Quiller Pr) St Mut.

Marriage Arranged. large type ed. Mira Stables. 184p. 1992. 15.95 (*0-7451-1561-6*, G K Hall Lrg Type) Mac Lib Ref.

Marriage As a Covenant: A Study of Biblical Law & Ethics Governing Marriage Developed from the Perspective of Malachi. Gordon Hugenberger. LC 93-40730. (Supplements to Vetus Testamentum Ser.: No. 52). 350p. 1993. 134.50 (*90-04-09977-8*, NLG155) Brill Academic Pubs.

Marriage as a Covenant: Biblical Law & Ethics as Developed from Malachi. Gordon P. Hugenberger. LC 98-38841. (Biblical Studies Library). 448p. (YA). (gr. 13). 1998. pap. 34.99 (*0-8010-2192-8*) Baker Bks.

Marriage As a Path to Holiness: Lives of Married Saints. David Ford & Mary Ford. LC 94-14011. 1994. write for info. (*1-878997-52-1*) St Tikhons Pr.

Marriage As a Search for Healing. Jerry M. Lewis. LC 96-54242. 320p. 1997. 34.95 (*0-87630-831-0*) Brunner-Mazel.

Marriage As an Economic Partnership: How One State Made It Happen. Jo Staab. LC 98-24535. xx, 258 p. 1998. 24.95 (*1-891859-26-9*) Atwood Pub LLC. .

Marriage As Evangelism. Ronald J. Sider. Date not set. pap. 10.99 (*0-310-20653-7*) Zondervan.

***Marriage at a Distance.** Sara Craven. (Presents Ser.). 2000. per. 3.99 (*0-373-12093-1*) Harlequin Bks.

Marriage at Antibes. Carol Azadeh. 224p. 2000. 22.95 (*0-7867-0708-9*) Carroll & Graf.

Marriage at Its Best see Matrimonio en Toda Su Excelencia

***Marriage Badge: The Blackwell Brothers.** Sharon De Vita. 2000. per. 3.50 (*0-373-19443-9*) Silhouette.

Marriage Bait. Eva Rutland. 1997. per. 3.25 (*0-373-03439-3*, 1-03439-6) Silhouette.

Marriage Bait. large type ed. Eva Rutland. (Simply the Best Ser.). 1997. per. 3.25 (*0-373-15685-5*) Harlequin Bks.

***Marriage Bargain.** Susan Fox. (Romance Ser.: Vol. 3606). 2000. per. 3.50 (*0-373-03606-X*) Harlequin Bks.

***Marriage Bargain.** Michelle McMaster. 320p. 2000. pap. 4.99 (*0-8439-4750-0*, Leisure Bks) Dorchester Pub Co.

Marriage Bargain. Jennifer Mikels. 1998. per. 4.25 (*0-373-24168-2*, 1-24168-6) Silhouette.

***Marriage Bargain.** Victoria Pade. (Montana Mavericks Ser.: Vol. 4). 256p. 2000. mass mkt. 4.50 (*0-373-65049-3*, 1-65049-8) Harlequin Bks.

Marriage Bargain. large type ed. Rachelle Edwards. (Linford Romance Library). 256p. 1995. pap. 16.99 (*0-7089-7743-X*, Linford) Ulverscroft.

***Marriage Bargain.** large type ed. Susan Fox. Vol. 452. 2000. per. 3.50 (*0-373-15852-1*) Harlequin Bks.

Marriage Bargain: Women & Dowries in European History. Ed. by Marion A. Kaplan. LC 84-15707. (Women & History Ser.: No. 10). 182p. 1985. text 39.95 (*0-86656-311-3*) Haworth Pr.

Marriage Bargain: Women & Dowries in European History. Ed. by Marion A. Kaplan. LC 84-25272. (Women & History Ser.: No. 10). 182p. 1985. pap. text 14.95 (*0-918393-16-7*, Harrington Park) Haworth Pr.

***Marriage Basket.** Sharon De Vita. (Special Edition Ser.: Vol. 134). 2000. mass mkt. 4.50 (*0-373-24307-3*) Silhouette.

Marriage Beat: He's My Hero. Doreen Roberts. (Romance Ser.: Bk. 1380). 1999. per. 3.50 (*0-373-19380-7*, 1-19380-4) Silhouette.

Marriage Bed. Stephanie Mittman. 400p. 1996. mass mkt. 5.99 (*0-440-22182-X*) Dell.

Marriage Bed. large type ed. Catherine George. LC 94-42533. (Nightingale Ser.). 268p. 1995. pap. 17.95 (*0-7838-1191-8*, G K Hall Lrg Type) Mac Lib Ref.

***Marriage Betrayed.** Emma Darcy. (Harlequin Presents Ser.). 1999. mass mkt. 3.75 (*0-373-12069-9*, Harlequin) Harlequin Bks.

***Marriage Betrayed.** large type ed. Emma Darcy. (Harlequin Romance Ser.). 2000. 22.95 (*0-263-16406-3*) Mills & Boon.

Marriage Blessed by God see Matrimonio Bendecido por Dios

Marriage Bliss. Dick Mills. Orig. Title: How to Have a Happy Marriage. 91p. 1996. mass mkt. 5.99 (*0-88368-394-6*) Whitaker Hse.

Marriage Bond. large type ed. Denise Robins. (Dales Large Print Ser.). 352p. 1998. pap. 19.99 (*1-85389-768-X*, Dales) Ulverscroft.

Marriage Bonds & Ministers' Returns of Halifax County Marriages, Seventeen Fifty-Six to Eighteen Hundred. Catherine L. Knorr. 142p. 1982. reprint ed. 18.50 (*0-89308-259-7*, VA 22) Southern Hist Pr.

***Marriage Bonds & Other Marriage Records of Amherst County, Virginia, 1763-1800: Published with Marriage Records of Amherst County, Virginia, 1815-1821.** William Montgomery Sweeny. 130p. 1999. reprint ed. pap. 16.50 (*0-8063-4919-0*, Pub. by Clearfield Co) ACCESS Pubs Network.

Marriage Bonds & Other Marriage Records of Amherst County, Virginia, 1763-1800: Published with Marriage Records of Amherst County, Virginia 1815-1821 & Subscription for Building St. Mark's Church, Amherst. William M. Sweeny. 102p. 1997. reprint ed. 14.00 (*0-8063-0573-8*, 5685) Clearfield Co.

Marriage Bonds of Bedford County, Virginia, 1755-1800: (Reprinted with) Bedford County, Virginia: Index of Wills, from 1754 to 1830. Earle S. Dennis & Jane E. Smith. LC 75-4010. 99p. 1989. reprint ed. pap. 7.00 (*0-8063-0669-6*) Genealog Pub.

Marriage Bonds of Fleming County, Kentucky, 1798-1825. Gareth L. Mark. 184p. 1991. pap. 14.95 (*0-9617478-0-3*) Lineages Inc.

Marriage Bonds of Franklin County, Virginia, 1786-1858: With a New Index of Brides, Parents, & Sureties. Marshall Wingfield. 299p. 1997. reprint ed. pap. 27.50 (*0-8063-0575-4*, 6445) Clearfield Co.

Marriage Bonds of Ontario, 1803-1834. Thomas B. Wilson. 445p. 1985. lib. bdg. 25.00 (*0-912606-26-6*) Hunterdon Hse.

Marriage Book. Ebury Press Staff. (Illus.). 96p. 1994. 14.95 (*0-09-177877-8*, Pub. by Ebury Pr) Trafalgar.

Marriage Book: Words of Wisdom Men & Women Should Know Before Marrying. Ed. by Ron Thunder-Ten-Tronck. LC 97-74584. 112p. 1998. pap. 9.95 (*0-943213-29-0*) Axiom Info Res.

Marriage Bowl. large type ed. Mary Minton. 512p. 31.99 (*0-7505-1242-3*, Pub. by Mgna Lrg Print) Ulverscroft.

Marriage Bracelet. Rebecca Winters. (Romance Ser.: No. 192). 1992. pap. 2.89 (*0-373-03192-0*, 1-03192-1) Harlequin Bks.

Marriage Breakdown. 1999. 84.00 (*1-85431-854-3*, Pub. by Blackstone Pr) Gaunt.

Marriage Breakdown & Divorce Law Reform. S. Jaffer Hussain. 240p. 1983. 24.95 (*0-318-36836-6*) Asia Bk Corp.

Marriage Breakdown & Divorce Law Reform in Contemporary Society: A Comparative Study of U. S. A., U. K. & India. S. Jaffer Hussain. (C). 1990. 35.00 (*0-89771-162-9*) St Mut.

Marriage Builder. Crabb, Jr. & J. Lawrence. 1986. 12.99 (*0-88469-185-3*) BMH Bks.

Marriage Builder: A Blueprint for Couples & Counselors. 176p. 1992. reprint ed. pap. 10.99 (*0-310-54801-2*) Zondervan.

Marriage Business. Jessica Steele. (Romance Ser.). 1996. per. 3.25 (*0-373-03407-5*, 1-03407-3) Harlequin Bks.

Marriage by Arrangement. Sally Wentworth. 1997. per. 3.50 (*0-373-11882-1*, 1-11882-7) Harlequin Bks.

Marriage by Arrangement. large type ed. Sally Wentworth. 1997. 20.95 (*0-263-14824-6*) Mac Lib Ref.

Marriage by Contract. Sandra Steffen. (Thirty-Six Hours Ser.). 1998. per. 4.50 (*0-373-65013-2*, 1-65013-4) Harlequin Bks.

Marriage by Default: Concept Two Thousand. Michael Sammaritano. LC 92-96898. 192p. 1993. 24.95 (*0-9634366-0-0*); pap. 19.95 (*0-9634366-1-9*) Sunrise Intl.

Marriage by Design, 1. Jill Metcalf. 320p. 1999. mass mkt. 4.99 (*0-8439-4553-2*) Dorchester Pub Co.

Marriage by Design. Cathy Gillen Thacker et al. 1994. per. 4.99 (*0-373-83295-8*, 1-83295-5) Harlequin Bks.

Marriage by Mistake. Mollie Molay. LC 96-2789. (American Romance Ser.). 248p. 1996. per. 3.50 (*0-373-16616-8*, 1-16616-4) Harlequin Bks.

Marriage by Necessity. Christine Rimmer. 1998. per. 4.25 (*0-373-24161-5*, 1-24161-1) Silhouette.

Marriage by the Book: Florida, Bk. 9. Joan Johnston. (Born in the U. S. A. Ser.). 1997. per. 4.50 (*0-373-47159-9*, 1-47159-8) Harlequin Bks.

Marriage Campaign. Helen Bianchin. (Presents Ser.). 1998. per. 3.75 (*0-373-11960-7*, 1-11960-1) Harlequin Bks.

Marriage Campaign. large type ed. Helen Bianchin. 1998. 21.95 (*0-263-15747-4*, Pub. by Mills & Boon) Chivers N Amer.

Marriage Can Be Fun. Jon Kardatzke. (Illus.). 132p. 1997. 16.95 (*0-9643362-1-9*) New Wings Minist.

Marriage, Census & Other Indexes for Family Historians. (C). 1987. 40.00 (*0-7855-2051-1*, Pub. by Birmingham Midland Soc) St Mut.

Marriage Chase. Natalie Patrick. (Romance Ser.). 1996. per. 2.99 (*0-373-19130-8*, 1-19130-3) Silhouette.

Marriage Chests. large type ed. Anne Herries. 688p. 1995. 27.99 (*0-7089-3219-3*) Ulverscroft.

Marriage, Class & Colour in Nineteenth-Century Cuba. Verena Martinez-Alier. 224p. 1989. pap. text 16.95 (*0-472-06405-3*, 06405) U of Mich Pr.

Marriage, Class & Colour in Nineteenth-Century Cuba: A Study of Racial Attitudes & Sexual Values in a Slave Society. Verena M. Alier. LC 73-82463. (Cambridge Latin American Studies: No. 17). 212p. reprint ed. pap. 60.50 (*0-608-16458-5*, 2026347) Bks Demand.

Marriage Clinic: A Scientifically Based Marital Therapy. John M. Gottman. LC 99-18916. 1999. 49.00 (*0-393-70282-0*) Norton.

Marriage Clinic: Manual, a Scientifically Based Marital Therapy. John M. Gottman. 1999. pap. text 12.00 (*0-393-70292-8*) Norton.

Marriage Clues for the Clueless: God's Word in Your World. Illus. by Elwood Smith. (Clues for the Clueless Ser.). 256p. 1999. pap. 8.99 (*1-57748-564-5*) Barbour Pub.

Marriage Collection: Keys to Make Your Marriage Better. Compiled by Fritz Ridenour. 528p. 1989. pap. 14.99 (*0-310-20961-7*) Zondervan.

Marriage Conditions in a Palestinian Village, 2 vols., Set. Hilma N. Granqvist. LC 72-9644. reprint ed. 105.00 (*0-404-57450-5*) AMS Pr.

Marriage Conference Manual. Family Life Staff. 164p. 1994. 12.00 (*1-57229-022-6*) FamilyLife.

***Marriage Contract.** Anna Adams. (Superromance Ser.). 2000. mass mkt. 4.50 (*0-373-70959-5*, 1709591) Harlequin Bks.

Marriage Contract. Cathy Forsythe. (Romance Ser.: No. 1167). 1996. per. 3.25 (*0-373-19167-7*, 1-19167-5) Silhouette.

Marriage Contract. Alexandra Jones. (Scarlet Ser.). (Orig.). 1997. mass mkt. 3.99 (*1-85487-966-9*, Pub. by Scarlet Bks) London Brdge.

***Marriage Contract.** Lisa Mondello. 148p. 2000. pap. 12.95 (*1-58345-471-3*) Domhan Bks.

Marriage Contract in Islamic Law: In the Shari'ah & Personal Status Laws of Egypt & Morocco. Dawoud S. El Alami. (Arab & Islamic Laws Ser.). 224p. (C). 1992. lib. bdg. 91.50 (*1-85333-719-6*, Pub. by Graham & Trotman) Kluwer Academic.

Marriage Contracts & Couple Therapy: Hidden Forces in Intimate Relationships. Clifford J. Sager. 335p. 1998. reprint ed. text 27.00 (*0-7881-5617-9*) DIANE Pub.

Marriage Counseling. Norman Wright. Ed. by Virginia Woodward. 335p. 1995. pap. 14.99 (*0-8307-1766-8*, 5422551, Regal Bks) Gospel Lght.

Marriage Counseling: A Christian Approach to Counseling Couples. Everett L. Worthington, Jr. LC 89-1697. 382p. 1993. reprint ed. pap. 19.99 (*0-8308-1769-7*, 1769) InterVarsity.

Marriage Counseling Handbook: A Guide to Practice. George Thorman. (Illus.). 146p. (C). 1996. text 33.95 (*0-398-06557-8*); pap. text 19.95 (*0-398-06558-6*) C C Thomas.

Marriage Covenant. (ENG & IND.). 1992. pap. write for info. (*0-934920-26-5*, B-31IN) Derek Prince.

Marriage Covenant. Derek Prince. 121p. 1995. mass mkt. 5.99 (*0-88368-333-4*) Whitaker Hse.

Marriage Covenant: A Biblical Study on Marriage, Divorce & Remarriage. 4th deluxe ed. Ed. by Samuele Bacchiocchi. (Biblical Perspectives Ser.: Vol. 9). 223p. (YA). 1991. pap. 20.00 (*1-930987-08-0*) Biblical.

Marriage Curse. Carolyn Andrews. (Temptation Ser.). 1996. per. 3.50 (*0-373-25681-7*, 1-25681-7) Harlequin Bks.

Marriage Customs. Anita Compton. LC 93-16317. (Comparing Religions Ser.). (Illus.). 32p. (J). (gr. 4-8). 1993. lib. bdg. 22.83 (*1-56847-033-9*) Raintree Steck-V.

Marriage Customs of the World. H. N. Hutchinson. 348p. 1989. 29.95 (*0-318-36839-0*) Asia Bk Corp.

Marriage Dance. Jillian James. (Scarlet Ser.). 1998. mass mkt. 3.99 (*1-85487-870-0*, Pub. by Scarlet Bks) London Brdge.

Marriage Dead or Alive. Adolf Guggenbuhl-Craig. Tr. by Murray Stein. 150p. 2000. pap. 14.50 (*0-88214-378-6*) Spring Pubns.

***Marriage Decider.** Emma Darcy. 1999. per. 3.75 (*0-373-12020-6*, 1-12020-3, Harlequin) Harlequin Bks.

Marriage Decider. large type ed. Emma Darcy. (Harlequin Ser.). 1999. 21.95 (*0-263-16102-1*, Pub. by Mills & Boon) Ulverscroft.

***Marriage Devotional Bible.** 2000. 44.99 (*0-310-91120-6*); pap. text 14.99 (*0-310-90878-7*) Zondervan.

Marriage Diaries of Robert & Clara Schumann: From Their Wedding Day to the Russia Trip. Gerd Nauhaus. Tr. & Pref. by Peter F. Ostwald. (Illus.). 256p. 1993. text 35.00 (*1-55553-171-7*) NE U Pr.

Marriage Dictionary. Tom Carey. (Illus.). 128p. (Orig.). 1993. pap. 6.95 (*1-877590-99-1*) DE Pr IL.

Marriage, Divorce, & Children in Ancient Rome. Ed. by Beryl Rawson. (Illus.). 266p. (C). 1996. pap. text 32.00 (*0-19-815045-8*) OUP.

Marriage, Divorce & Children's Adjustment. Robert E. Emery. (Developmental Clinical Psychology & Psychiatry Ser.: Vol. 14). 160p. (C). 1988. text 42.00 (*0-8039-2780-0*); pap. text 18.95 (*0-8039-2781-9*) Sage.

***Marriage, Divorce & Children's Adjustment.** 2nd ed. Robert E. Emery. LC 98-40280. (Developmental Clinical Psychology & Psychiatry Ser.: Vol. 14). 164p. 1999. 55.00 (*0-7619-0251-1*) Sage.

Marriage, Divorce & Children's Adjustment. 2nd ed. Robert E. Emery. LC 98-40280. (Developmental Clinical Psychology & Psychiatry Ser.). 160p. 1999. 21.95 (*0-7619-0252-X*) Sage.

Marriage, Divorce & Nullity: A Guide to the Annulment Process in the Catholic Church. Geoffrey Robinson. 96p. 1988. pap. 8.95 (*0-8146-1570-8*) Liturgical Pr.

Marriage, Divorce & Remarriage see Matrimonio, Divorcio y Nuevo Matrimonio

Marriage, Divorce, & Remarriage in the Bible. Jay Edward Adams. (Jay Adams Library). 128p. 1986. pap. 10.99 (*0-310-51111-9*, 12123P) Zondervan.

***Marriage, Divorce & the Believer.** 53p. 1999. pap. 8.50 (*0-9673443-0-1*) Restoration.

Marriage, Divorce & the Children. Dave Roberson. 28p. 1997. pap. 1.00 (*1-929339-03-8*) D Roberson Min.

Marriage, Divorce, Remarriage. Andrew J. Cherlin. LC 81-2901. (Social Trends in the United States Ser.). (Illus.). 158p. (C). 1981. 28.50 (*0-674-55080-3*) HUP.

Marriage, Divorce, Remarriage. Theodore H. Epp. pap. 3.99 (*0-8474-1127-3*) Revival Lit.

Marriage, Divorce, Remarriage. enl. rev. ed. Andrew J. Cherlin. (Illus.). 244p. 1992. pap. 16.95 (*0-674-55082-X*) HUP.

Marriage, Divorce, Remarriage, Woman & the Bible. Arthur F. Ide. LC 94-1884. (Women in History Ser.: Vol. 23). 106p. (Orig.). 1995. pap. 10.00 (*0-934667-10-1*) Tangelwuld.

Marriage, Duty, & Desire in Victorian Poetry & Drama. Richard D. McGhee. LC 80-11962. x, 318p. (C). 1980. 35.00 (*0-7006-0203-8*) U Pr of KS.

Marriage Encounter for Just the Two of You. Ed. by Casey Peterson. 50p. 1988. pap. 2.50 (*0-936098-59-7*) Intl Marriage.

Marriage Enrichment: Preparation, Mentoring, & Outreach. Richard A. Hunt et al. LC 98-25594. 1998. pap. 24.95 (*0-87630-914-7*) Brunner-Mazel.

***Marriage Enrichment: Preparation, Mentoring & Outreach.** Richard A. Hunt et al. LC 98-25594. 275p. 1998. text 59.95 (*0-87630-913-9*) Brunner-Mazel.

Marriage Enrichment Handbook: Godly Principles for a Successful Marriage. Andrew Merritt. Ed. by Temperance Publishing House Staff. (Illus.). 197p. (Orig.). 1993. pap. 9.95 (*0-9637640-1-2*) A & V Pub.

Marriage Enrichment Workbook: A Workbook for Couples in Marital Therapy. Murray D. Callahan. (MARC Ser.). (Illus.). 200p. (Orig.). 1997. pap. 35.00 (*1-888916-05-2*) Counselsource.

Marriage Exchange: Property, Social Place & Gender in Cities of the Low Countries, 1300-1500. Martha C. Howell. LC 97-37905. (Women in Culture & Society Ser.). 256p. 1998. pap. text 19.00 (*0-226-35516-0*); lib. bdg. 52.00 (*0-226-35515-2*) U Ch Pr.

Marriage, Families & Close Relationships. Seccombe. (Sociology-Upper Level Ser.). 2001. pap. 47.00 (*0-534-55881-X*) Wadsworth Pub.

***Marriage, Family & Law in Medieval Europe: Collected Studies.** Michael M. Sheehan. Ed. by James K. Farge. 362p. 1998. reprint ed. pap. text 21.95 (*0-8020-8137-1*) U of Toronto Pr.

Marriage Family & Relationships: A Cross-Cultural Encyclopedia. Gwen J. Broude. (Human Experience Ser.). 372p. 1995. lib. bdg. 49.50 (*0-87436-736-0*) ABC-CLIO.

***Marriage, Family & Sexuality.** Ed. by Kerby Anderson. LC 99-33450. (Issues in Focus Ser.). 160p. 1999. pap. 10.99 (*0-8254-2031-8*) Kregel.

Marriage, Family, Human Capital & Fertility: Proceedings of a Conference, June 4-5, 1973, Sponsored by National Bureau of Economic Research & the Population Council. Ed. by Theodore W. Schultz. LC 74-176066. (Supplement to the Journal of Political Economy Ser.: Vol. 82, No. 2, Pt. 2, March-April, 1984). 240p. pap. 74.40 (*0-608-15345-1*, 205636100061) Bks Demand.

Marriage Fool. Richard Vetere. 71p. 1996. pap. 5.60 (*0-87129-731-0*, M97) Dramatic Pub.

Marriage for a Lifetime: Honest Talk about What Makes a Partnership Last. Harriett Thatcher & Floyd W. Thatcher. 248p. 1995. 9.99 (*0-87788-505-2*, H Shaw Pubs) Waterbrook Pr.

Marriage for a Year see Matrimonsio por un Ano: Instant Mother

Marriage for Keeps. Karen Young et al. (Promo Ser.). (Orig.). 1999. per. 5.99 (*0-373-83407-1*, 1-83407-6, Harlequin) Harlequin Bks.

***Marriage for Maggie.** Trisha David. 288p. 2000. 26.99 (*0-263-16441-1*, Pub. by Mills & Boon) Ulverscroft.

***Marriage for Sale.** Carol Devine. (Desire Ser.). 2000. per. 3.99 (*0-373-76284-4*) Silhouette.

Marriage for Three. Elizabeth Seifert. 1974. reprint ed. lib. bdg. 22.95 (*0-88411-031-1*) Amereon Ltd.

Marriage from God's Perspective: Love Your Mate! Judith A. Brumbaugh. (Illus.). 44p. (Orig.). 1993. student ed. 9.00 (*0-9624603-5-4*) Comt Restoration Fam.

An Asterisk (*) at the beginning of an entry indicates that the title is appearing for the first time.

Marriage-Go-Round. Katherine Ransom. (American Romance Ser.: No. 440). 1992. per. 3.39 (*0-373-16440-8*, 1-16440-9) Harlequin Bks.
Marriage-Go-Round: Practical Guidelines for a Successful Marriage. Judy Segraves. LC 90-30558. (Illus.). 138p. (Orig.). (YA). 1990. pap. 10.00 (*0-932581-64-1*) Word Aflame.
***Marriage: God's Wonderful Gift of Love.** Theodore Archibald. 2000. pap. text 12.95 (*0-7880-0990-7*) CSS OH.
Marriage, Good Better Best. Bobbi Thurman. 52p. 1998. pap. write for info. (*1-57502-692-9*, PO1687) Morris Pubng.
Marriage Guide: or Natural History of Generation. Frederick Hollick. LC 73-20628. (Sex, Marriage & Society Ser.). (Illus.). 438p. 1974. reprint ed. 35.95 (*0-405-05804-7*) Ayer.
Marriage Has Been Arranged. Anne Weale. 1997. per. 3.25 (*0-373-03474-1*, 1-03474-3) Harlequin Bks.
Marriage Has Been Arranged. large type ed. Anne Weale. 1997. per. 3.25 (*0-373-15720-7*) Harlequin Bks.
Marriage Has Been Arranged. large type ed. Anne Weale. (Harlequin Ser.). 1997. 20.95 (*0-263-15301-0*) Thorndike Pr.
Marriage Hearse. Larry Duberstein. 1988. mass mkt. 4.50 (*0-440-20195-0*, LE) Dell.
Marriage Hearse. Larry Duberstein. LC 86-62450. 160p. 1987. 22.00 (*0-932966-76-4*) Permanent Pr.
Marriage in a Bottle. Carolyn Zane. (Romance Ser.). 1996. per. 3.25 (*0-373-19170-7*, 1-19170-9) Silhouette.
Marriage in a Culture of Divorce. Karla B. Hackstaff. LC 99-25159. (Women in the Political Economy Ser.). (Illus.). 292p. 1999. 59.50 (*1-56639-724-3*); pap. 22.95 (*1-56639-725-1*) Temple U Pr.
Marriage in a Suitcase. Kasey Michaels. (Romance Ser.). 1993. pap. 2.75 (*0-373-08949-X*, 5-08949-5) Silhouette.
***Marriage in America: A Communitarian Perspective.** Ed. by Martin King Whyte. 400p. 2000. 68.00 (*0-7425-0770-X*); pap. 24.95 (*0-7425-0771-8*) Rowman.
Marriage in Black & White. Joseph R. Washington, Jr. 368p. (Orig.). (C). 1993. reprint ed. pap. text 34.00 (*0-8191-9068-3*) U Pr of Amer.
Marriage in Christ. 48p. 1983. pap. 1.25 (*0-8146-1293-8*) Liturgical Pr.
Marriage in Domoni: Husbands & Wives in an Indian Ocean Community. Martin Ottenheimer. 106p. (C). 1994. reprint ed. pap. text 11.50 (*1-879215-23-3*) Sheffield WI.
Marriage in Haste. large type ed. Sue Peters. (Linford Romance Library). 384p. 1985. pap. 16.99 (*0-7089-6100-2*, Linford) Ulverscroft.
Marriage in Islam: A Manual. 6th ed. Muhammad A. Rauf. LC 96-42977. 87p. 1996. reprint ed. pap. text 5.00 (*1-881963-48-9*) Al-Saadawi Pubns.
Marriage in Italy, 1300-1650. Jacqueline Musacchio & Piet Van Boxel. Ed. by Trevor Dean & K. J. Lowe. LC 97-10266. (Illus.). 318p. (C). 1998. text 59.95 (*0-521-55402-0*) Cambridge U Pr.
Marriage in Jeopardy. Daphne Clair. LC 95-4580. (Presents Ser.). 189p. 1995. per. 3.25 (*0-373-11730-2*, 1-11730-8) Harlequin Bks.
Marriage in Jeopardy. large type ed. Miranda Lee. (Harlequin Ser.). 1994. lib. bdg. 19.95 (*0-263-13714-7*) Thorndike Pr.
Marriage in Jeopardy: Presents Plus. Miranda Lee. (Presents Ser.). 1995. per. 3.25 (*0-373-11728-0*, 1-11728-2) Harlequin Bks.
Marriage in Maradi: Gender & Culture in a Hausa Society in Niger, 1900-1989. B. Cooper. LC 97-1610. (Social History of Africa Ser.). 1997. pap. 23.95 (*0-435-07413-X*, 07413) Heinemann.
Marriage in Maradi: Gender & Culture in a Hausa Society in Niger, 1900-1989. B. Cooper. LC 97-1610. (Social History of Africa Ser.). 1997. 60.00 (*0-435-07414-8*, 07414) Heinemann.
Marriage in Maradi: Gender & Culture in a Hausa Society in Niger, 1900-1989. Barbara M. Cooper. LC 97-1610. l, 228 p. 1997. pap. write for info. (*0-85255-627-6*) Heinemann.
Marriage in Men's Lives. Steven L. Nock. LC 98-21949. (Illus.). 176p. 1998. 29.95 (*0-19-512056-6*) OUP.
***Marriage in Motion: The Natural Ebb & Flow of Lasting Relationships.** Richard S. Schwartz & Jacqueline Olds. 224p. 2000. text 24.00 (*0-7382-0238-X*, Pub. by Perseus Pubng) HarpC.
Marriage in Name Only. Doreen O. Malek. (Intimate Moments Ser.). 1995. per. 3.75 (*0-373-07620-7*, 1-07620-7) Silhouette.
Marriage in New Hampshire: A Handbook for Justices of the Peace. 2nd ed. Charles G. Douglas, III. 1987. 7.00 (*0-88063-480-4*, MICHIE) LEXIS Pub.
***Marriage in Sri Lanka: A Century of Change.** Bruce Caldwell. LC 99-931663. (Studies in Sociology & Social Anthropology). xvi, 233p. 1999. write for info. (*81-7075-048-2*) S Asia.
Marriage in the Early Church. Ed. & Tr. by David G. Hunter. LC 92-3694. (Sources of Early Christian Thought Ser.). 144p. 1992. pap. 15.00 (*0-8006-2652-4*, 1-2652) Augsburg Fortress.
Marriage in the Early Republic: Elizabeth & William Wirt & the Companionate Ideal. Anya Jabour. LC 97-52180. (Gender Relations in the American Experience Ser.). (Illus.). 288p. 1998. 42.00 (*0-8018-5877-1*) Johns Hopkins.
Marriage in the Lord. William P. Steinhauser et al. LC 85-201865. (Marriage & Marriage Preparation Ser.). (Illus.). 84p. 1985. 3.75 (*0-940679-01-9*) CCOC.
Marriage in the Making. Natalie Fox. (Presents Ser.: Vol. 90). 1998. per. 3.75 (*0-373-18690-8*, 1-18690-7) Harlequin Bks.
Marriage In The Trees. Stanley Plumly. LC 96-18589. 96p. 1997. 22.00 (*0-88001-487-3*) HarpC.
***Marriage In The Trees.** Stanley Plumly. LC 96-18589. 96p. 1998. pap. 14.00 (*0-88001-546-2*) HarpC.
Marriage in the United States. Auguste Carlier. LC 70-169376. (Family in America Ser.). 200p. 1977. reprint ed. 23.95 (*0-405-03853-4*) Ayer.
Marriage in the Western Church: The Christianization of Marriage During the Patristic Medieval Periods. Philip L. Reynolds. LC 94-570. (Supplements to Vigiliae Christianae Ser.: Vol. 24). 1994. 134.50 (*90-04-10022-9*) Brill Academic Pubs.
Marriage in the Whirlwind: 7 Skills for Couples Who Can't Slow Down. Bill Farrel & Pam Farrel. LC 96-17398. 175p. 1996. pap. 9.99 (*0-8308-1953-3*, 1953, Saltshaker Bk) InterVarsity.
Marriage in Trouble: A Time of Decision. Eleanor C. Haspel. LC 76-4780. 192p. 1976. text 29.95 (*0-88229-222-6*) Burnham Inc.
Marriage in Wittenwiler's Ring. C. G. Fehrenbach. LC 70-140019. (Catholic University Studies in German: No. 15). reprint ed. 37.50 (*0-404-50235-0*) AMS Pr.
***Marriage Incorporated.** Debbi Rawlins. 2000. mass mkt. 4.50 (*0-373-82209-X*, 1-82209-7) Harlequin Bks.
Marriage Incorporated: In Name Only. Debbi Rawlins. LC 95-6864. (American Romance Ser.). 249p. 1995. per. 3.50 (*0-373-16580-3*, 1-16580-3) Harlequin Bks.
Marriage Institution. Douglas Kennedy. 1995. 27.00 (*0-8050-3090-5*) H Holt & Co.
Marriage Insurance. Betty Doty. LC 77-92285. (Illus.). 1978. pap. 8.95 (*0-930822-01-3*) Bookery.
Marriage Is a Covenant, Not a Contract. Glover Shipp. (Small Group Studies). 32p. 1997. pap. 4.99 (*0-89900-704-X*, T96-704-X) College Pr Pub.
Marriage Is a For-Better Word. Diane Pfeifer. (Illus.). 128p. 1995. pap. 6.95 (*1-887987-00-2*) Strawberry GA.
Marriage Is a Great Career. Lillian S. Knore. 156p. 1994. 18.95 (*1-57087-061-6*) Prof Pr NC.
Marriage Is a Promise of Love see Matrimonio es una Promesa de Amor
Marriage Is a Promise of Love. Ed. by Susan Polis Schutz. LC 90-80732. (Illus.). 64p. 1990. pap. 8.95 (*0-88396-282-9*) Blue Mtn Art.
Marriage Is for Keeps: Foundations for Christian Marriage. John F. Kippley. LC 93-73126. 125p. (Orig.). 1993. pap. 5.95 (*0-926412-11-6*) Couple to Couple.
Marriage Is for Keeps: Foundations for Christian Marriage, Wedding Edition. John F. Kippley. 168p. (Orig.). 1994. pap. 6.95 (*0-926412-12-4*) Couple to Couple.
***Marriage Is for Life: No Broken Promises, No Shattered Dreams.** Al Wingfield. LC 99-69844. 145p. 2000. pap. 9.99 (*1-930260-03-2*) C T S Family.
Marriage Is for Loving. Muriel James. (Illus.). 1979. pap. 9.57 (*0-201-03455-7*) Addison-Wesley.
Marriage Is for Those Who Love God & One Another. Thomas B. Warren. 1976. 9.00 (*0-934916-37-3*) Natl Christian Pr.
Marriage Is God's Plan. 3rd ed. Dyrel W. Collins. 28p. 1996. pap. 2.95 (*1-56794-152-4*, C2465) Star Bible.
Marriage Is Just the Beginning. Betty J. Sanders. 1997. per. 3.25 (*0-373-19245-2*, 1-19245-9) Silhouette.
Marriage Is Murder. Nancy Pickard. Ed. by Linda Marrow. 1988. mass mkt. 5.50 (*0-671-73428-8*) PB.
Marriage Journey: Preparations & Provisions for Life Together. Linda Grenz & Delbert Glover. LC 96-8077. 156p. (Orig.). 1996. pap. 13.95 (*1-56101-127-4*) Cowley Pubns.
Marriage, Kinship, & Power in Northern China. Jennifer Holmgren. (Collected Studies: Vol. CS516). 352p. 1995. 113.95 (*0-86078-554-8*, Pub. by Variorum) Ashgate Pub Co.
Marriage Knot. Mary McBride. (Historical Ser.: No. 465). 1999. per. 4.99 (*0-373-29065-9*, 1-29065-9, Harlequin) Harlequin Bks.
Marriage Laws in Africa. Arthur Phillips & Henry I. Morris. LC 75-28914. 239p. reprint ed. pap. 74.10 (*0-8357-3028-X*, 205711500010) Bks Demand.
Marriage Laws in the United States, 1887-1906. S. N. North. Ed. by Desmond W. Allen. 91p. 1994. pap. 14.95 (*0-941765-89-X*) Arkansas Res.
Marriage Laws of the British Empire. William P. Eversley & William F. Craies. xxxvii, 375p. 1989. reprint ed. 47.50 (*0-8377-2105-9*, Rothman) W S Hein.
Marriage License Bonds of Accomack County, Virginia from 1774 to 1806. Stratton Nottingham. 49p. 1997. reprint ed. pap. 9.00 (*0-8063-0263-1*, 4180) Clearfield Co.
Marriage License Bonds of Lancaster County, Virginia, from 1701 to 1848. Stratton Nottingham. 106p. 1996. reprint ed. pap. 13.50 (*0-8063-4638-8*, 9282) Clearfield Co.
Marriage License Bonds of Westmoreland County, Virginia from 1786 to 1850. Stratton Nottingham. 97p. 1995. reprint ed. pap. 12.00 (*0-8063-0651-3*, 4195) Clearfield Co.
Marriage Licenses of Caroline County, Maryland, 1774-1815. Henry D. Cranor. LC 75-986. 62p. 1998. reprint ed. pap. 12.50 (*0-8063-0667-X*) Clearfield Co.
Marriage Life Choices. 1993. 19.48 (*0-02-655911-0*) Glencoe.
Marriage Litigation in Medieval England. R. H. Helmholz. LC 85-81808. (Cambridge Studies in English Legal History). 256p. 1986. reprint ed. 65.00 (*0-912004-47-9*) Gaunt.
Marriage Made at Woodstock. Cathie Pelletier. Ed. by Donna Ng. 288p. 1995. reprint ed. pap. 14.00 (*0-671-51694-9*, WSP) PB.
Marriage Made in Heaven. Ann Coleman. LC 97-65640. 192p. (Orig.). 1997. pap. 13.95 (*1-57736-032-X*) Providence Hse.
Marriage Made in Heaven. Alexandra Mark. LC 89-50407. 256p. 1989. pap. 14.95 (*0-914918-90-7*, Whitford) Schiffer.
***Marriage Made in Heaven: A Love Story in Letters.** Vatsala Sperling & Ehud Sperling. LC CT275.S6238A3 2000. (Illus.). 288p. 2000. 24.95 (*1-58008-182-7*) Ten Speed Pr.
Marriage Made in Heaven: Or Too Tired for an Affair. Erma Bombeck. 304p. 1994. mass mkt. 6.99 (*0-06-109202-9*, Harp PBks) HarpC.
Marriage Made in Heaven: The Sexual Politics of Hebrew & Yiddish. Naomi Seidman. LC 96-39172. (Contraversions Ser.). (Illus.). 188p. 1997. 45.00 (*0-520-20193-0*, Pub. by U CA Pr) Cal Prin Full Svc.
Marriage Made in Heaven--Or Too Tired to Have an Affair: Bombeck,&Erma. abr. ed. Erma Bombeck. 1993. audio 18.00 (*1-55994-741-1*, CPN 2352) HarperAudio.
Marriage Made in Heaven: or Too Tired for an Affair. large type ed. Erma Bombeck. LC 93-39610. 1993. 24.95 (*1-56895-024-1*) Wheeler Pub.
Marriage Made in Joeville. Anne Eames. (Desire Ser.: No. 1078). 1997. per. 3.50 (*0-373-76078-7*, 1-76078-4) Silhouette.
***Marriage Made Me Fat!** Edward Abramson. (Illus.). 267p. 2000. mass mkt. 5.99 (*1-57566-556-5*) Kensgtn Pub Corp.
Marriage Made Simple: 50 Hints on Building Long Lasting Love. Kris Conover & Gayle M. Gardner. LC 98-30257. 128p. 1999. pap. 10.95 (*0-452-28038-9*, Plume) Dutton Plume.
Marriage Make Up. large type ed. Penny Jordan. 1999. 21.95 (*0-263-15808-X*, G K Hall & Co) Mac Lib Ref.
Marriage Make Up: (Top Author/The Big Event) Penny Jordan. (Presents Ser.: Vol. 1983). 1998. per. 3.75 (*0-373-11983-6*, 1-11983-3) Harlequin Bks.
Marriage Maker Be's: How to Make a Marriage Last a Lifetime. 2nd ed. Everett Thurman. 84p. 1994. pap. 11.95 (*0-88100-085-X*) Natl Writ Pr.
Marriage Manual. Krysta Kavenaugh. 56p. 1993. pap. 5.00 (*0-936098-71-6*) Intl Marriage.
Marriage Manual. rev. ed. Perry H. Biddle, Jr. 192p. 1994. pap. 16.00 (*0-8028-0699-6*) Eerdmans.
Marriage Manual for Newlyweds: Suggestions for Beginners. Paul H. Thibert. (Illus.). 78p. 1992. 12.95 (*0-9637299-0-X*) T-Bear Assocs.
Marriage Marathon: How to Go the Distance As Husband & Wife. Timothy J. Demy & Gary P. Stewart. LC 98-15295. 208p. 1998. pap. text 10.99 (*0-8254-2356-2*) Kregel.
Marriage Mart. Norma L. Clark. 240p. 1990. pap. 3.50 (*0-318-50081-7*, Sig) NAL.
Marriage Mart. large type ed. Patricia Burns. 1995. 27.99 (*0-7089-3306-8*) Ulverscroft.
Marriage Masque. large type ed. Catherine Fellows. 336p. 1986. 27.99 (*0-7089-1457-8*) Ulverscroft.
Marriage Material. Ruth Wind. (Special Edition Ser.: No. 1108). 1997. per. 3.99 (*0-373-24108-9*, 1-24108-2) Silhouette.
Marriage Matters! Growing Together Through the Differences & Surprises of Life Together. Stuart Briscoe & Jill Briscoe. LC 93-40582. 272p. 1994. pap. 9.99 (*0-87788-532-X*, H Shaw Pubs) Waterbrook Pr.
Marriage Maze: McLaird's Field Guide for the Journey. George L. McLaird. Ed. by Doris Donaldson & Jill Fugaro. LC 95-79114. (Illus.). 256p. (Orig.). 1995. pap. 17.95 (*1-887182-01-2*) AED.
Marriage Mediator: The Street Smart Guide to a Successful Marriage. Karl Schmidt. Ed. by Fran H. Grimes. LC 98-91612. (Illus.). 220p. 1999. 19.95 (*0-9664989-2-5*) OnTrack Pubg.
Marriage Meltdown. Emma Darcy. 1997. per. 3.50 (*0-373-11900-3*, 1-11900-7) Harlequin Bks.
Marriage Meltdown. large type ed. Emma Darcy. (Harlequin Romance Ser.). 288p. 1998. 20.95 (*0-263-15398-3*) Thorndike Pr.
Marriage Mender: A Couple's Guide for Staying Together. Thomas A. Whiteman & Thomas Bartlett. 160p. (Orig.). 1996. pap. 12.00 (*0-89109-925-5*, 99255) NavPress.
***Marriage Menders.** large type ed. Patricia Wendorf. 559p. 2000. 27.95 (*0-7838-9021-4*) Mac Lib Ref.
Marriage Mentor Manual: Couples Encouraging Couples in the First Year of Marriage. Leslie Parrott. 80p. 1995. pap. 5.99 (*0-310-50131-8*) Zondervan.
Marriage Merger: Loving the Boss. Vivian Leiber. (Romance Ser.: No. 1366). 1999. per. 3.50 (*0-373-19366-1*, 1-19366-3) Silhouette.
Marriage Mile & Marathon. Mel M. Murphy. LC 96-71985. 100p. 1996. pap. text 7.95 (*1-57636-031-8*) SunRise Pbl.
Marriage Minded. Kayla Daniels. 1996. per. 3.99 (*0-373-24068-6*, 1-24068-8) Silhouette.
Marriage-Minded Man? The Lone Star Social Club. Linda Turner. (Intimate Moments Ser.: No. 829). 1998. per. 3.99 (*0-373-07829-3*, 1-07829-4) Silhouette.
Marriage Minutes: Inspirational Readings to Share with Your Spouse. Robert Moeller & Cheryl Moeller. LC 98-204278. 284p. 1998. 16.99 (*0-8024-2146-6*) Moody.
Marriage Mishap. Judith Stacy. 1997. per. 4.99 (*0-373-28982-0*, 1-28982-6) Harlequin Bks.
Marriage Moments: Heart to Heart Times to Deepen Your Love. David Arp & Claudia Arp. LC 98-15318. 178p. 1998. 9.97 (*1-56955-091-3*, Vine Bks) Servant.
Marriage Money: The Social Shaping of Money in Marriage & Banking. Supriya Singh. 208p. 1998. pap. 29.95 (*1-86448-328-8*, Pub. by Allen & Unwin Pty) Paul & Co Pubs.
***Marriage Movement: A Statement of Principles.** CMFCE Staff & Institute for American Values Staff. 36p. (C). 2000. 7.00 (*0-9659841-6-8*) Inst for Am Val.
Marriage 911. Becky Freeman. LC 95-10921. 192p. 1996. pap. 10.99 (*0-8054-6178-7*, 4261-78) Broadman.
Marriage 911: The Truth about Marriage, Vol. 1. 1996. 19.95 incl. VHS (*1-890553-06-9*, CV 606) Double Vision.
Marriage Notices, Dutchess & Columbia County, New York, 1859-1936: From Red Hook Newspapers. Margaret E. Herrick. 206p. 1991. lib. bdg. 38.00 (*1-56012-117-3*, 111) Kinship Rhinebeck.
Marriage Notices for the Whole United States, 1785-1794. Charles Bolton. 139p. 1989. reprint ed. lib. bdg. 18.00 (*1-56012-104-1*, 96) Kinship Rhinebeck.
Marriage Notices from Dutchess County, NY, Newspapers, 1826-1851. Arthur C. Kelly. LC 83-180800. 406p. 1983. lib. bdg. 49.50 (*1-56012-060-6*, 59) Kinship Rhinebeck.
Marriage Notices from Extant Issues of the "Rockingham Register," Harrisonburg, Virginia, 1822-1870. Dorothy A. Boyd-Rush. viii, 495p. (Orig.). 1993. pap. 33.50 (*1-55613-822-9*) Heritage Bk.
Marriage Notices from Richmond, Virginia, Newspapers, 1821-1840. Pref. by Annabelle Osborne & Benjamin B. Weisiger. 238p. 1999. reprint ed. pap. 20.00 (*1-888192-01-1*) VA Geneal Soc.
Marriage Notices from Richmond, Virginia, Newspapers, 1841-1853. Ed. by Wesley E. Pippenger. 360p. 1997. pap. 25.00 (*1-888192-02-X*) VA Geneal Soc.
Marriage Notices from Steuben County, New York, Newspapers, 1797-1884. Mary S. Jackson & Edward F. Jackson. LC 99-159363. 483p. 1998. pap. 44.00 (*0-7884-0995-6*, J018) Heritage Bk.
Marriage Notices from the Ohio Observer Series, 1827-1855. James F. Caccamo. LC 95-157023. 208p. 1995. per. 19.95 (*1-55856-189-7*, 191) Closson Pr.
Marriage Notices from the Southern Christian Advocate, 1867-1878. Brent H. Holcomb. 1994. 35.00 (*0-913363-17-0*) SCMAR.
Marriage Notices from Washington Co. NY, Newspapers, 1799-1880. Mary Jackson & Edward Jackson. 449p. (Orig.). 1995. pap. 32.00 (*0-7884-0342-7*) Heritage Bk.
Marriage Notices in Charleston Courier, 1803-1808. Alexander S. Salley. 83p. 1994. reprint ed. 10.00 (*0-8063-0727-7*, 5115) Clearfield Co.
Marriage Notices in the South-Carolina & American General Gazette, 1766 to 1781 & the Royal Gazette, 1781-1782. Alexander S. Salley, Jr. 52p. 1990. reprint ed. pap. 5.00 (*0-8063-0726-9*, 5120) Clearfield Co.
Marriage Notices in the South-Carolina Gazette, & Its Successors (1732-1801) Ed. by Alexander S. Salley, Jr. (Illus.). 174p. 1995. reprint ed. pap. 19.50 (*0-8328-5119-1*) Higginson Bk Co.
***Marriage Notices of Ontario, 1813-1854.** William D. Reid. 550p. 2000. reprint ed. pap. 38.50 (*0-8063-4983-2*, Pub. by Clearfield Co) ACCESS Pubs Network.
Marriage Notices, 1785-1794, for the Whole United States from the Massachusetts Centinel & the Columbian Centinel. Charles K. Bolton. LC 65-28304. 139p. 1985. reprint ed. 15.00 (*0-8063-0045-0*) Genealog Pub.
Marriage of Agreement: Conveniently Wed. Judith Duncan. (Intimate Moments Ser.). 2000. mass mkt. 4.25 (*0-373-07975-3*, 1-07975-5) Silhouette.
Marriage of Bette & Boo. Christopher Durang. 1986. pap. 5.25 (*0-8222-0736-2*) Dramatists Play.
Marriage of Bette & Boo. Christopher Durang. LC 86-33468. 112p. 1987. pap. 13.00 (*0-8021-3365-7*, Grove) Grove-Atltic.
Marriage of Cadmus & Harmony. Roberto Calasso. 416p. 1994. pap. 14.00 (*0-679-73348-5*) Random.
Marriage of Cadmus Harmony Tent Card. Calasso Roberto. 1994. pap. 1.00 (*0-394-25870-3*) Random.
Marriage of Catherine & David. LaVonne R. Hanlon. LC 82-82540. (Illus.). 68p. (Orig.). 1982. pap. text 7.00 (*0-9609326-0-7*) Fay-West Her.
Marriage of Catherine & David: The Rowe Addendum. LaVonne R. Hanlon. 78p. (Orig.). 1985. pap. text 7.50 (*0-9609326-1-5*) Fay-West Her.
Marriage of Claudia. large type ed. Rose Franken. 352p. 1982. 27.99 (*0-7089-0860-8*) Ulverscroft.
***Marriage of Continents: Multiculturalism in Modern Literature.** Guy Amirthanayagam. LC 99-51876. 384p. 2000. 49.50 (*0-7618-1575-9*) U Pr of Amer.
Marriage of Contraries: Bernard Shaw's Middle Plays. J. L. Wisenthal. LC 73-85183. 288p. 1974. 37.95 (*0-674-55085-4*) HUP.
Marriage of Convenience. Lois Stewart. 224p. 1996. mass mkt. 4.50 (*0-8217-5427-0*, Zebra Kensgtn) Kensgtn Pub Corp.
Marriage of Convenience: Business & Social Work in Toronto, 1918-1957. Gale Wills. 256p. 1995. pap. text 17.95 (*0-8020-7369-7*) U of Toronto Pr.
Marriage of Convenience: Ideal & Ideology in the 'Novelas Ejemplares' Theresa A. Sears. LC 92-8804. (Cervantes & His Times Ser.: Vol. 3). 225p. (C). 1994. text 51.95 (*0-8204-1906-0*) P Lang Pubng.
***Marriage of Convenience: Loving, Injured Innocent, Six-Month Marriage.** Penny Jordan. 2001. mass mkt. 6.99 (*0-373-20181-8*, 1-20181-3) Harlequin Bks.
Marriage of Convenience: The New Zionist Organization & the Polish Government, 1936-1939. Laurence Weinbaum. 295p. 1993. 43.50 (*0-88033-266-2*, 369, Pub. by East Eur Monographs) Col U Pr.
Marriage of East & West. Bede Griffiths. 180p. 1982. pap. 12.95 (*0-87243-105-3*) Templegate.
Marriage of Figaro see Nozze di Figaro: Libretto
Marriage of Figaro. Pierre De Beaumarchais. 1991. pap. 6.95 (*0-88145-099-5*) Broadway Play.
Marriage of Figaro. Pierre A. De Beaumarchais. Ed. & Tr. by Bernard Sahlins. LC 94-26337. (Plays for Performance Ser.). (FRE.). 112p. 1994. pap. 7.95 (*1-56663-065-7*, Pub. by I R Dee); lib. bdg. 15.95 (*1-56663-066-5*, Pub. by I R Dee) Natl Bk Netwk.
Marriage of Figaro. Wolfgang Amadeus Mozart. 144p. 1999. 19.98 (*1-57912-065-2*) Blck Dog & Leventhal.

M

Marriage of Figaro. Wolfgang Amadeus Mozart. Ed. by Nicholas John. Tr. by Edward Dent from ITA. (English National Opera Guide Series: Bilingual Libretto, Articles: No. 17). (Illus.). 1982. pap. 9.95 (*0-7145-3771-3*) Riverrun NY.

Marriage of Figaro: Complete Orchestral Score. Wolfgang Amadeus Mozart. LC 78-67726. 448p. 1979. reprint ed. pap. 18.95 (*0-486-23751-6*) Dover.

Marriage of Figaro; Beaumarchais: One-Act Adaptation. Beaumarchais. (Illus.). 38p. 1968. pap. 3.25 (*0-88680-127-3*) I E Clark.

Marriage of Figaro; Beaumarchais: One-Act Adaptation - Director's Script. Beaumarchais. (Illus.). 38p. 1968. pap. 10.00 (*0-88680-128-1*) I E Clark.

***Marriage of Heaven & Earth: Alchemical Regeneration in the Works of Taylor, Poe, Hawthorne & Fuller, 6.** Randall A. Clack. LC 99-58878. (Contributions to the Study of American Literature: Vol. 5). 176p. 2000. 59.95 (*0-313-31269-9*, Greenwood Pr) Greenwood.

Marriage of Heaven & Hell. William Blake. LC 94-13248. (Illus.). 82p. 1975. pap. text 13.95 (*0-19-281167-3*) OUP.

Marriage of Heaven & Hell. Peter Dally. LC 99-52175. 352p. 1999. text 24.95 (*0-312-20559-7*) St Martin.

Marriage of Heaven & Hell. limited ed. William Blake. (Illus.). 50p. 1993. 3000.00 (*1-887123-03-2*) Granary Bks.

Marriage of Heaven & Hell: A Facsimile in Full Color. William Blake. LC 94-471. (Illus.). 48p. 1994. reprint ed. pap. 4.95 (*0-486-28122-1*) Dover.

Marriage of Hindu Widows. I. Vidyasagar. 144p. 1976. 12.95 (*0-318-37059-X*) Asia Bk Corp.

Marriage of Inconvenience. Marion Chesney. 184p. 1996. 22.00 (*0-7278-5121-7*) Severn Hse.

Marriage of Inconvenience. large type ed. Marion Chesney. LC 98-7843. (Romance Ser.). 197 p. 1998. pap. write for info. (*0-7540-3415-1*) Chivers N Amer.

Marriage of Inconvenience: The Persecution of Ruth & Seretse Khama. Michael Dutfield. 256p. 1990. text 24.95 (*0-04-440495-6*) Routledge.

Marriage of Lit-lit. Jack London. (Jamestown Classics Ser.). 1995. pap., teacher ed. 7.32 (*0-89061-045-2*, Jamestwn Pub) NTC Contemp Pub Co.

Marriage of Lit-lit. Jack London. (Jamestown Classics Ser.). (J). 1995. pap., student ed. 5.99 (*0-89061-044-4*, Jamestwn Pub) NTC Contemp Pub Co.

Marriage of Mademoiselle Gimel, & Other Stories. Rene Bazin. Tr. by Edna K. Hoyt. LC 71-128719. (Short Story Index Reprint Ser.). 1977. 19.95 (*0-8369-3610-8*) Ayer.

Marriage of Masks. M. T. Dohaney. LC 95-173288. 176p. 1995. pap. 10.95 (*0-921556-56-X*, Pub. by Gynergy-Ragweed) U of Toronto Pr.

Marriage of Meggotta. large type ed. Edith Pargeter. 1995. 27.99 (*0-7505-0713-6*, Pub. by Mgna Lrg Print) Ulverscroft.

***Marriage of Minds: Collaborative Fiction Writing.** Nikoo McGoldrick & James McGoldrick. LC 00-26784. 160p. 2000. pap. 12.95 (*0-325-00232-0*) Heinemann.

Marriages of Phelps County Missouri, 1880-1881, Bk. 2. Contrib. by Robert M. Doerr. 4p. Date not set. pap. write for info. (*1-893474-13-5*) Phelps Cnty Gene.

Marriage of Poets. Arthur Knight & Kit Knight. 64p. 1984. pap. 3.95 (*0-933180-61-6*) Spoon Riv Poetry.

Marriage of Secrets. Emma Stirling. 160p. 22.00 (*0-7278-5128-4*) Severn Hse.

Marriage of Sense & Soul: Integrating Science & Religion. Ken Wilber. LC 98-51501. (Illus.). 240p. 1999. reprint ed. pap. 13.00 (*0-7679-0343-9*) Broadway BDD.

Marriage of Sense & Soul: Integrating Science & Religion, Set. unabridged ed. Ken Wilber. 1998. pap. 24.95 incl. audio (*1-55927-510-3*) Audio Renaissance.

Marriage of Sense & Soul: One Taste. Ken Wilber. (Collected Works of Ken Wilber: Vol. 8). (Illus.). 592p. 1999. 40.00 (*1-57062-508-5*, Pub. by Shambhala Pubns) Random.

Marriage of Sense & Thought: Imaginative Participation in Science. John Davy et al. LC 96-29674. (Renewal in Science Ser.). 160p. 1997. pap. 16.95 (*0-940262-82-7*, Lindisfarne) Anthroposophic.

***Marriage of Spirit: Principles for Balancing Your Life & Clearing Shadow.** Leslie Temple-Thurston. 2000. 22.88 (*0-9660182-0-6*) Corelight Pubns.

***Marriage of Steel: Life & Times W & P Verity.** 86p. (C). 2000. 125.00 (*0-536-60371-5*) Pearson Custom.

***Marriage of Sticks.** Jonathan Carroll. 2000. pap. 14.95 (*0-312-87243-7*) St Martin.

***Marriage of Sticks.** Jonathan Carroll. 1999. mass mkt. write for info. (*0-8125-7618-7*) Tor Bks.

***Marriage of Sticks.** Jonathan Carroll. LC 99-33233. 256p. 1999. 23.95 (*0-312-87193-7*, Pub. by Tor Bks) St Martin.

Marriage of the Lamb. J. Gordon Powell. (Illus.). 296p. 1997. pap. 17.00 (*0-8059-4144-4*) Dorrance.

Marriage of the Living Dark. David Wingrove. 480p. 1999. pap. 14.95 (*0-385-25736-8*) Bantam.

Marriage of the Mind: Processes of Insight & Integration. George F. Buletza. LC 97-66324. (Illus.). 250p. 1997. pap. 11.95 (*0-912057-94-7*, 510813) GLELJ AMORC.

Marriage of the Portuguese. Sam Pereira. LC 78-71826. 53p. (Orig.). 1978. pap. 3.75 (*0-934332-09-6*) LEpervier Pr.

***Marriage of the Rain Goddess: A South African Myth.** Margaret Wolfson. (Illus.). 32p. (J). (gr. 1-5). 2000. pap. 6.99 (*1-84148-233-1*) Barefoot Bks NY.

Marriage of the Rain Goddess: A South African Myth. Margaret Olivia Wolfson. (Illus.). 32p. (J). (gr. 1-5). 1999. 15.95 (*1-84148-100-9*) Barefoot Bks NY.

Marriage of the Sun & the Moon: A Quest for Unity in Consciousness. Andrew Weil. LC 98-28460. 1998. pap. 14.00 (*0-395-91154-0*) HM.

Marriage of True Minds - Walt Whitman to Dora. Compiled by Dilys Gold. 87p. (C). 1990. 50.00 (*0-7212-0801-0*, Pub. by Regency Pr GBR) St Mut.

Marriage of William Ashe. Humphry Ward. 562p. 1977. reprint ed. lib. bdg. 22.35 (*0-89966-196-3*) Buccaneer Bks.

Marriage of William Bull. Eager. 4.95 (*0-686-14960-2*) T E Henderson.

Marriage of Wit & Science. LC 77-133705. (Tudor Facsimile Texts. Old English Plays Ser.: No. 43). reprint ed. 49.50 (*0-404-53343-4*) AMS Pr.

Marriage on Demand. Susan Mallery. (Special Edition Ser.). 1995. per. 3.75 (*0-373-09939-8*, 1-09939-9) Silhouette.

Marriage on Demand. large type ed. Susan Mallery. (Silhouette Romance Ser.). 1996. lib. bdg. 19.95 (*0-373-59745-2*, G K Hall Lrg Type) Mac Lib Ref.

Marriage on His Mind. Susan Crosby. 1997. per. 3.50 (*0-373-76108-2*, 1-76108-9) Silhouette.

Marriage on His Terms. Val Daniels. (Romance Ser.). 1998. per. 3.50 (*0-373-03497-0*, 1-03497-4) Harlequin Bks.

Marriage on His Terms. large type ed. Val Daniels. (Bachelor Territory Ser.). 1998. per. 3.50 (*0-373-15743-6*, Harlequin) Harlequin Bks.

Marriage on Paper see Matrimonio de Papel

Marriage on the Edge: The Barons. Sandra Marton. (Presents Ser.: No. 2027). 1999. per. 3.75 (*0-373-12027-3*, 1-12027-8) Harlequin Bks.

***Marriage on the Edge: The Barons.** large type ed. Sandra Marton. 288p. 1999. 25.99 (*0-263-16174-9*, Pub. by Mills & Boon) Ulverscroft.

Marriage on the Rebound. Michelle Reid. (Presents Ser.: Vol. 1973). 1998. per. 3.75 (*0-373-11973-9*, 1-11973-4) Harlequin Bks.

Marriage on the Rebound. large type ed. Michelle Reid. (Mills & Boon Large Print Ser.). 288p. 1998. 24.99 (*0-263-15564-1*, Pub. by Mills & Boon) Ulverscroft.

Marriage on the Rock. Jimmy Evans. 1996. pap. text 13.00 (*0-00-519035-5*) Majestic Media.

Marriage on the Rock: Creating Your Dream Marriage. Jimmy Evans. Ed. by Kimberly Fritts. 1996. 19.95 (*0-9647435-1-5*) Majestic Media.

Marriage on the Rock: Creating Your Dream Marriage. Jimmy Evans. 318p. 1995. reprint ed. pap. 14.95 (*0-9647435-0-7*) Majestic Media.

Marriage on the Rocks: Learning to Live with Yourself & An Alcoholic. Janet G. Woititz. 148p. 1986. pap. 6.95 (*0-932194-17-6*) Health Comm.

Marriage on Trial. Ziba Mir-Hosseini. 256p. 1997. text 24.50 (*1-86064-182-2*, Pub. by I B T) St Martin.

***Marriage on Trial.** Lee Wilkinson. (Presents Ser.: Vol. 209). 2000. mass mkt. 3.99 (*0-373-12090-7*) Harlequin Bks.

Marriage on Trial: Islamic Family Law in Iran & Morocco. Ziba Mir-Hosseini. (Society & Culture in the Modern Middle East Ser.). 288p. 1993. text 65.00 (*1-85043-685-1*, Pub. by I B T) St Martin.

Marriage 101: Back to the Basics. Barry Rosen. (Marriage & Family Romance SelfHelp Ser.). 98p. 1993. pap. 4.25 (*0-9625593-1-8*) B R Pub Co TN.

***Marriage 101: Building a Healthy Relationship with Your Mate.** Myles Munroe. 1999. pap. 5.99 (*1-56229-139-4*) Pneuma Life Pub.

Marriage or Celibacy? The Daily Telegraph on a Victorian Dilemma. John M. Robson. 366p. 1996. pap. text 29.95 (*0-8020-7798-6*) U of Toronto Pr.

Marriage or Mistake: A Workbook for Couples Who Are Thinking about Marriage. Neal E. Desch. 110p. 1993. write for info. (*0-9635884-0-0*) Life Improve Sem.

Marriage Other Alternative. 2nd ed. Lucille Duberman. (C). 1977. pap. write for info. (*0-03-038336-6*) Harcourt Coll Pubs.

Marriage, Outlaw Style: Outlaw Hearts. Cindy Gerard. (Desire Ser.: No. 1185). 1998. per. 3.75 (*0-373-76185-6*, 1-76185-7) Silhouette.

Marriage Owner's Manual. 2nd rev. ed. Linda H. Dykstra. (Illus.). xvii, 214p. 1998. pap. 14.95 (*0-9665503-0-7*) Medit Ctr Grnd.

Marriage Pact. R. Winning. 20p. 1983. write for info. (*0-943216-03-6*) MoonsQuilt Pr.

Marriage Partnership: Handbook for a Healthy Christian Marriage. Louise A. Ferrebee. LC 98-34499. 1998. pap. write for info. (*0-8054-9054-X*) Broadman.

Marriage, Perversion, & Power: The Construction of Moral Discourse in Southern Rhodesia, 1894-1930. Diana Jeater. LC 92-26360. (Oxford Studies in African Affairs). 290p. 1993. text 79.00 (*0-19-820379-9*, Clarendon Pr) OUP.

Marriage Plan. Judy Jackson. 400p. (Orig.). 1997. mass mkt. 3.99 (*1-85487-907-3*, Pub. by Scarlet Bks) London Brdge.

Marriage Plan. Catherine R. Puglisi. LC 98-88292. 325p. 1998. pap. 15.00 (*0-7388-0146-1*) Xlibris Corp.

Marriage Plan: How to Marry Your Soul Mate in a Year - or Less. Aggie Jordan. LC 98-88292. 325p. 1998. 25.00 (*0-7388-0145-3*) Xlibris Corp.

Marriage Plan: How to Marry Your Soul Mate in a Year or Less. Aggie Jordan. 226p. 1999. pap. text 15.95 (*0-9668463-1-1*, Pub. by Butte Pubg) Seven Hills Bk.

***Marriage Plan: How to Marry Your Soul Mate in One Year--or Less.** Aggie Jordan. LC 00-24887. 2000. pap. write for info. (*0-7679-0602-0*) Broadway BDD.

***Marriage Plan: How to Marry Your Soul Mate in One Year-Or Less.** Aggie Jordan. 224p. 2000. 18.95 (*0-7679-0601-2*) Broadway BDD.

Marriage Play. Edward Albee. LC 96-208087. 1995. pap. 5.25 (*0-8222-1422-9*) Dramatists Play.

Marriage Poems. Ed. by John Hollander. 256p. 1997. 12.50 (*0-679-45515-9*) Everymns Lib.

Marriage Poems & Satires, 1670-1800. Ed. by William C. Horne. LC 86-22576. 352p. 1987. 60.00 (*0-8201-1419-7*) Schol Facsimiles.

***Marriage Population & Society: Demographic Perspectives of a Social Institution.** M. M. Krishna Reddy. LC 98-906907. 1998. 34.00 (*81-7391-255-6*, Pub. by Kaniska Pubs Dist) S Asia.

***Marriage Prey.** Annette Broadrick. (Desire Ser.: Bk. 1327). 2000. mass mkt. 3.99 (*0-373-76327-1*, 1-76327-5) Silhouette.

***Marriage Prize.** Virginia Henley. LC 99-59897. 400p. 2000. 22.95 (*0-385-31823-5*) Delacorte.

***Marriage Promise.** Sharon DeVita. (Special Edition Ser.). 2000. per. 4.50 (*0-373-24313-8*) Silhouette.

Marriage, Property, & Law in Late Imperial Russia. William G. Wagner. (Historical Monographs). (Illus.). 428p. 1994. text 65.00 (*0-19-820447-7*) OUP.

Marriage Proposal see Plays

Marriage Proposal. Paul Caywood & Anton Chekhov. (Half Hour Classics Ser.). 1997. pap. 2.50 (*1-57514-316-X*, 3106) Encore Perform Pub.

Marriage Proposal. Anton Chekhov. Ed. by William-Alan Landes. Tr. by Sergius Ponomarov from RUS. LC 90-53061. (Players Press Chekhov Collection). (Illus.). 20p. 1990. pap. 5.00 (*0-88734-318-X*) Players Pr.

Marriage Protection Program: Cameron, Utah. Margaret Watson. (Intimate Moments Ser.: No. 951). 1999. mass mkt. 4.25 (*0-373-07951-6*, 1-07951-6) Silhouette.

Marriage Puzzle. Shirley Cook. 128p. (Orig.). 1985. pap. 4.70 (*0-310-33611-2*, 11718P) Zondervan.

***Marriage Quest.** large type ed. Helen Brooks. 288p. 1999. 25.99 (*0-263-16204-4*, Pub. by Mills & Boon) Ulverscroft.

Marriage: Questions Women Ask see Matrimonio, Cosas Que las Mujeres Preguntan

Marriage Quizzes to a Street Preacher. Charles M. Carty & Leslie Rumble. (Radio Replies Quizzes to a Street Preacher Ser.). 32p. 1992. reprint ed. pap. 1.50 (*0-89555-115-2*) TAN Bks Pubs.

Marriage Record of Caughnawaga Reformed Church, Fonda NY, Now the Reformed Church of Fonda, 1772-1899. Arthur C. Kelly. (Palatine Transcripts Ser.). 140p. 1986. lib. bdg. 28.00 (*1-56012-077-0*, 76) Kinship Rhinebeck.

Marriage Record of First & Second Reformed Churches of Coxsackie NY, 1797-1899: Reformed Church, Coxsackie NY, 1797-1899; 2nd Reformed Church, Coxsackie NY, 1834-1899. Arthur C. Kelly. LC 77-153350. (Palatine Transcripts Ser.). 118p. 1977. lib. bdg. 24.00 (*1-56012-036-3*, 35) Kinship Rhinebeck.

Marriage Record of Four Lutheran Congregations of Southern Columbia County, NY, Including Manorton, Churchtown, Germantown, Barrytown (of Dutchess County), 1794-1899: St. John's Lutheran Church, Manorton, 1794-1872; St. Thomas Lutheran Church, Churchtown, 1804-1899; Christ Lutheran Church, Germantown, 1811-1899; Sylvania Lutheran Church, Barrytown, 1893. Arthur C. Kelly. LC 74-191753. (Palatine Transcripts Ser.). 124p. 1974. lib. bdg. 24.00 (*1-56012-026-6*, 25) Kinship Rhinebeck.

Marriage Record of Four Reformed Congregations in the Towns of Germantown, Gallatin, Copake, & Hillsdale, Columbia County, NY, 1736-1899: Germantown Reformed Church, 1736-1899; Gallatin Reformed Church, 1755-1899; West Copake Reformed Church, 1784-1899; Hillsdale Reformed Church, 1781-1792. Arthur C. Kelly. LC 71-29760. (Palatine Transcripts Ser.). 121p. 1971. lib. bdg. 26.00 (*1-56012-016-9*, 16) Kinship Rhinebeck.

Marriage Record of German Flats Reformed Church, 1781-1814 & Herkimer Reformed Church, 1801-1899, Herkimer, NY, 1781-1899. Arthur C. Kelly. LC 83-244837. (Palatine Transcripts Ser.). 154p. 1983. lib. bdg. 30.00 (*1-56012-063-0*, 62) Kinship Rhinebeck.

Marriage Record of Kinderhook Reformed Church, Kinderhook NY, 1717-1899. Arthur C. Kelly. LC 86-215779. (Palatine Transcripts Ser.). 103p. 1986. lib. bdg. 22.00 (*1-56012-076-2*, 75) Kinship Rhinebeck.

Marriage Record of Linlithgo Reformed Church, Livingston, NY, 1723-1899. Arthur C. Kelly. LC 73-15395. (Palatine Transcripts Ser.). 67p. 1970. lib. bdg. 16.00 (*1-56012-011-8*, 11) Kinship Rhinebeck.

Marriage Record of Reformed Church, Claverack, NY, 1727-1899. Arthur C. Kelly. LC 75-22133. (Palatine Transcripts Ser.). 200p. 1970. lib. bdg. 36.00 (*1-56012-013-4*, 13) Kinship Rhinebeck.

Marriage Record of Schenectady Reformed Church, 1694-1852, Schenectady, NY. Donald A. Keefer. Ed. by Arthur C. Kelly. LC 89-125329. (Palatine Transcripts Ser.). 154p. 1988. lib. bdg. 30.00 (*1-56012-084-3*, 83) Kinship Rhinebeck.

Marriage Record of the Four Reformed Congregations of Old Rhinebeck, Dutchess County, NY, 1731-1899: St. John's Low Dutch Reformed Church of Upper Red Hook, 1795-1899; Red Church of Tivoli (Old Red Hook Church), 1795-1899; German Reformed Zion's Church of Rhinebeck, 1756-1899; Reformed Church Rhinebeck, 1731-1899. Arthur C. Kelly. LC 73-27430. (Palatine Transcripts Ser.). 168p. 1971. lib. bdg. 33.00 (*1-56012-015-0*, 15) Kinship Rhinebeck.

Marriage Record of the Lutheran Churches of Athens & West Camp, NY, 1705-1899: Zion Lutheran Church, Athens NY, 1705-1899; St. Paul's Lutheran Church, West Camp NY, 1709-1899. Arthur C. Kelly. LC 77-354783. (Palatine Transcripts Ser.). 99p. 1976. lib. bdg. 22.00 (*1-56012-033-9*, 32) Kinship Rhinebeck.

***Marriage Record of the Tappan Reformed Church, Rockland County, N. Y., 1831-1901.** Transcribed by Arthur C. M. Kelly. 100p. 2000. pap. 16.00 (*1-56012-169-6*) Kinship Rhinebeck.

Marriage Record of Three Lutheran Congregations of Rhinebeck, NY, 1746-1899: St. Peters, Lutheran Church, 1746-1899; St. Paul's Lutheran Church, Wurtemburg, 1766-1899; Third Lutheran Church, Rhineback Village, 1843-1899. Arthur C. Kelly. LC 77-16665. (Palatine Transcripts Ser.). 152p. 1969. lib. bdg. 29.00 (*1-56012-006-1*, 6) Kinship Rhinebeck.

Marriage Record of Two Early Schoharie, NY, Churches: Reformed Church, 1732-1892; St. Paul's Lutheran Church, 1743-1899. Arthur C. Kelly. LC 78-107861. (Palatine Transcripts Ser.). 185p. 1978. lib. bdg. 34.00 (*1-56012-040-1*, 39) Kinship Rhinebeck.

Marriage Record of Two Early Stone Arabia NY Churches: Reformed Church, 1739-1895; Trinity Lutheran Church, 1763-1899. Arthur C. Kelly. LC 83-136974. (Palatine Transcripts Ser.). 134p. 1982. lib. bdg. 27.00 (*1-56012-059-2*, 58) Kinship Rhinebeck.

Marriage Records: Shawnee County, Kansas & Index to Microfilmed Marriage Licenses January 1, 1891 to June 10, 1906 with Bride's Index, Vol. 2. Topeka Genealogical Society Staff. LC 83-162208. 234p. (Orig.). 1983. pap. 18.12 (*0-943259-10-X*) Topeka Geneal Soc.

Marriage Records, Barbour County, Alabama, 1838-1859. Helen Foley. 100p. 1990. pap. 20.00 (*0-89308-657-6*, AL 20) Southern Hist Pr.

Marriage Records, 1811-1853: Mecklenburg County, Virginia. (Katherine B. Elliott Books on Southern Virginia). 236p. 1962. 28.50 (*0-89308-417-4*, VA 52); pap. 24.00 (*0-89308-375-5*, VA 51) Southern Hist Pr.

Marriage Records in the Virginia State Library: A Researcher's Guide. 2nd ed. John Vogt & T. William Kethley. LC 88-34675. 246p. (Orig.). 1988. pap. 14.00 (*0-935931-00-7*) Iberian Pub.

Marriage Records Index 1865-1895 of Yavapai County, Prescott, Arizona. Dora M. Whiteside. 47p. (Orig.). 1983. pap. 8.00 (*0-938353-01-2*) D M Whiteside.

Marriage Records Marshall County Alabama, 1849-1869. fac. ed. Mazie C. Brooks. iv, 86p. 1982. spiral bd. 15.00 (*0-944619-19-3*) Gregath Pub Co.

Marriage Records of Accomack Co., VA, 1776-1854 Recorded in Bonds, Licenses, & Ministers' Returns. Nora M. Turman. 394p. (Orig.). 1994. pap. text 28.50 (*0-7884-0135-1*) Heritage Bk.

Marriage Records of Accomack County, VA, 1854-1895. Barry W. Miles & Moody K. Miles, III. LC 97-210564. vi, 414p. 1997. 29.00 (*0-7884-0680-9*, M353) Heritage Bk.

Marriage Records of Barre & of Berlin, Washington County, Vermont. William T. Dewey & James F. Dewey. 64p. 1984. pap. 7.00 (*0-912606-24-X*) Hunterdon Hse.

***Marriage Records of Brunswick County, Virginia, 1730-1852.** Augusta B. Fothergill. LC 75-34969. 153p. 1999. reprint ed. pap. 18.50 (*0-8063-0704-8*) Clearfield Co.

Marriage Records of Cabell County, 1809-1851. Compiled by Annie W. Bell. (Illus.). 90p. 1997. reprint ed. pap. 17.50 (*0-8328-6942-2*) Higginson Bk Co.

Marriage Records of Hancock County, Maine Prior to 1892. Ed. by Alice M. Long. LC 91-67682. 576p. 1992. 45.00 (*0-929539-55-9*, 1330) Picton Pr.

Marriage Records of Hempstead County, Arkansas, 1817-1875. Bobbie J. McLane & Capitola Glazner. 182p. (Orig.). 1969. pap. 22.00 (*0-929604-15-6*) Arkansas Ancestors.

Marriage Records of Highland County, Ohio, 1805-1880. David N. McBride & Jane N. McBride. (Vital Records of Highland County, Ohio Ser.). 416p. 1982. reprint ed. lib. bdg. 37.00 (*0-941000-01-X*) S Ohio Genealog.

Marriage Records of Hunterdon County, New Jersey, 1795-1875. rev. ed. Hiram E. Deats. 378p. 1986. lib. bdg. 25.00 (*0-912606-28-2*) Hunterdon Hse.

Marriage Records of Independence County, Arkansas 1826-1877. Bobbie J. McLane & Mary S. Harris. 350p. 1970. pap. 28.00 (*0-929604-22-9*) Arkansas Ancestors.

Marriage Records of Jefferson County, Ohio, 1850-1866, Bk. 7. Leila S. Francy. 274p. 1993. per. 21.95 (*1-55856-127-7*, 090) Closson Pr.

Marriage Records of Jefferson County, Ohio, 1865-1874, Bk. 8, Pt. 1. Leila S. Francy. 159p. 1993. per. 14.95 (*1-55856-132-3*, 092) Closson Pr.

***Marriage Records of Lawrence County, Arkansas, 1820-1850.** James Logan Morgan. 50p. 2000. pap. 12.00 (*1-56546-167-3*) Arkansas Res.

Marriage Records of Notre Dame RC Church 1873-1879, Central Falls, RI. Ed. by Robert J. Quintin. 350p. 1982. pap. 25.00 (*1-886560-13-7*) Quintin Pub RI.

Marriage Records of the City of Fredericksburg & of Orange, Spotsylvania, & Stafford Counties, Virginia, 1722-1850. Therese A. Fisher. 268p. (Orig.). 1990. pap. 21.50 (*1-55613-345-6*) Heritage Bk.

Marriage Records of Townsend, Massachusetts, 1737-1830. Ithamar B. Sawtelle. 60p. 1984. reprint ed. pap. 6.50 (*0-912606-19-3*) Hunterdon Hse.

Marriage Records of Waldo County, Maine Prior to 1892. Tr. by Elizabeth M. Mosher. 634p. 1990. lib. bdg. 95.00 (*0-929539-20-6*, 1120) Picton Pr.

Marriage Records of Washington County, Tennessee, 1787-1840. Norma R. Grammer & Marion D. Mullins. LC 73-8035. 68p. 1991. reprint ed. pap. 6.00 (*0-8063-0564-9*) Genealog Pub.

Marriage Records, 1749-1840: Cumberland County, Virginia. (Katherine B. Elliott Books on Southern Virginia). 198p. 1969. 27.50 (*0-89308-425-5*, VA 68); pap. 22.50 (*0-89308-382-8*, VA 67) Southern Hist Pr.

Marriage Records, 1765-1810: Mecklenburg County, Virginia. 190p. 1963. 27.50 (*0-89308-416-6*, VA 49); pap. 22.50 (*0-89308-376-3*, VA 50) Southern Hist Pr.

Marriage Records, Shawnee County, Kansas: Index to Microfilmed Marriage Licenses, 11 Jun 1906 - 1 May 1913, Vol. 3. Topeka Genealogical Society Staff. LC 83-162208. 152p. (Orig.). 1984. pap. 15.23 (*0-943259-09-6*) Topeka Geneal Soc.

An Asterisk (*) at the beginning of an entry indicates that the title is appearing for the first time.

Marriage Records, Shawnee County, Kansas & Index to Microfilmed Marriage Licenses, February 1 1856 Thru December 31, 1980 (with Bride's Index), Vol. 1. Topeka Genealogical Society Staff. LC 83-162208. 206p. 1982. pap. 18.12 (*0-943259-11-8*) Topeka Geneal Soc.

Marriage Records, Wyoming County, West Virginia, 1854-1880. Ed. by Norma P. Evans. LC 79-56632. (Illus.). 1980. reprint ed. pap. 15.00 (*0-937418-01-3*) N P Evans.

Marriage Registers of Upper Canada/Canada West Dan Walker & Robert W. Calder. LC 96-120667. 1995. write for info. (*1-896264-17-4*) Norsim Resrch.

Marriage Repair Kit. Bob Moorehead. 115p. 1988. pap. 7.99 (*0-9639496-1-6*) Overlake Press.

***Marriage Repair Manual.** Scott Anthony. 64p. 1999. pap. 7.95 (*0-9666115-5-1*, Our Ladys Pr) Eureka Pub.

***Marriage Resolution.** large type ed. Penny Jordan. (Thorndike Harlequin Romance Ser.). 2000. 22.95 (*0-263-16353-9*) Mills & Boon.

***Marriage Resolution: (Sweet Revenge/Seduction)** Penny Jordan. (Presents Ser.: No. 2079). 2000. per. 3.99 (*0-373-12079-6*, 1-12079-9, Harlequin) Harlequin Bks.

Marriage Returns for Oakland County, 1836-1884. Ed. by Ruth S. Kennedy. 225p. (Orig.). 1989. pap. 23.00 (*1-879766-04-3*) OCG Society.

Marriage Returns of Cumberland County, Maine Prior to 1892. Ed. by Judith H. Kelley & Clayton R. Adams. LC 98-84520. (Maine Genealogical Society Special Publication Ser.: No. 29). 1056p. 1998. 69.50 (*0-89725-173-3*, 1518) Picton Pr.

Marriage Returns of Oxford County, Maine, Prior to 1892. rev. ed. Ed. by Donald McAllister & Lucille Naas. 352p. 1993. 37.50 (*0-89725-141-5*, 1455) Picton Pr.

Marriage Returns of Penobscot County, Maine Prior to 1892, 2 vols., Set. Ed. by Ruth Gray. 1408p. 1994. 95.00 (*0-89725-172-5*, 1452) Picton Pr.

Marriage Returns of Washington County, Maine, Prior to 1892. Ed. by Alice M. Long. 128p. 1993. 24.50 (*0-89725-140-7*, 1454) Picton Pr.

Marriage Returns of York County, Maine Prior to 1892. Ed. by John E. Frost & Joseph C. Anderson, II. LC 93-83380. 576p. 1993. 45.00 (*0-89725-104-0*, 1423) Picton Pr.

Marriage Ring: 'Til Death Do Us Part? Dewitt Talmage. Ed. by Robert Van Alstine. (Orig.). 1996. mass mkt. 6.25 (*0-87508-321-8*, 321) Chr Lit.

Marriage Risk. Debbie Macomber. LC 96-455. 189p. 1995. per. 2.99 (*0-373-03383-4*) Harlequin Bks.

Marriage Rites. Michael Joncas. 2000. pap. 10.00 (*1-56854-126-0*, MRITES) Liturgy Tr Pubns.

Marriage Rites. large type ed. Pauline Bentley. 350p. 1995. 23.99 (*0-263-14424-0*, Pub. by Mills & Boon) Ulverscroft.

Marriage Rituals & Songs of Bengal. Buddhaved Roy. 1985. 6.50 (*0-8364-1290-7*, Pub. by Mukhopadhyaya) S Asia.

***Marriage Sabbatical.** Jarvis. 2000. pap. 26.00 (*0-7382-0339-4*, Pub. by Perseus Pubng) HarpC.

Marriage Savers: A Study Guide. Michael J. McManus. 96p. 1994. pap. text 4.00 (*1-885481-02-0*) Quadrus Media.

Marriage Savers Revised Edition: Helping Your Friends & Family Stay Married. 2nd rev. ed. Michael J. McManus. 320p. 1995. pap. 14.99 (*0-310-38661-6*) Zondervan.

Marriage Scheme. Carla Cassidy. (Romance Ser.). 1994. per. 2.75 (*0-373-08996-1*, 5-08996-6) Silhouette.

Marriage Secrets: How to Have a Lifetime Love Affair. Roseanne Rosen. LC 93-9442. 1993. 17.95 (*1-55972-166-9*, Birch Ln Pr) Carol Pub Group.

Marriage Service. Church of Scotland Panel on Worship Staff. 1993. pap. 12.00 (*0-86153-009-8*, Pub. by St Andrew) St Mut.

Marriage Service for You. Robert J. Peterson. 1977. 5.95 (*0-89536-160-4*) CSS OH.

Marriage Settlements, 1601-1740. Lloyd Bonfield. LC 85-82331. (Cambridge Studies in English Legal History). 154p. 1986. reprint ed. 48.00 (*0-912004-55-X*) Gaunt.

Marriage, Sexuality & Celibacy: A Greek Orthodox Perspective. Demetrios J. Constantelos. 1975. pap. 8.95 (*0-937032-15-8*) Light&Life Pub Co MN.

Marriage Shock: The Transformation of Women into Wives. 206p. text 23.00 (*0-7881-6925-4*) DIANE Pub.

Marriage-Shy. large type ed. Karen Van Der Zee. (Mills & Boon Large Print Ser.). 288p. 1997. 23.99 (*0-263-15070-4*, Pub. by Mills & Boon) Ulverscroft.

Marriage Solution. Helen Brooks. (Presents Ser.: Vol. 1987). 1998. per. 3.75 (*0-373-11987-9*, 1-11987-4) Harlequin Bks.

Marriage Sourcebook. Ed. by J. Robert Baker et al. LC 94-25324. (Illus.). 236p. (Orig.). 1994. pap. 15.00 (*1-56854-039-6*, MARRSB) Liturgy Tr Pubns.

***Marriage Spirit: Finding the Passion & Joy of Soul Centered Love.** Evelyn Moschetta. LC 97-40029. (Illus.). 320p. 2000. per. 13.00 (*0-684-85198-9*) S&S Trade.

Marriage Spirit: Finding the Passion & Joy of Soul-Centered Love. Paul Moschetta & Evelyn Moschetta. LC 97-40029. 288p. 1998. 22.50 (*0-684-83450-2*) S&S Trade.

Marriage Stability, Divorce, & the Law. Max Rheinstein. LC 79-169582. 496p. 1995. lib. bdg. 42.00 (*0-226-71773-9*) U Ch Pr.

Marriage Stempede: Wrangers & Lace. Julianna Morris. (Romance Ser.: No. 1375). 1999. per. 3.50 (*0-373-19375-0*, 1-19375-4) Silhouette.

Marriage Studies, Vol. IV. Ed. by John Alesandro. 188p. 1990. pap. 7.00 (*0-943616-48-4*) Canon Law Soc.

Marriage Studies: Reflections in Canon Law & Theology, Vol. 1. Ed. by Thomas P. Doyle. 155p. 1980. pap. 3.00 (*0-943616-03-4*) Canon Law Soc.

Marriage Study. Zondervan Publishing Staff. Date not set. 32.99 (*0-310-90133-2*) Zondervan.

Marriage Surrender. Michelle Reid. (Presents Ser.: No. 2014). 1999. per. 3.75 (*0-373-12014-1*, 1-12014-6) Harlequin Bks.

***Marriage Takeover.** Lee Wilkinson. (Presents Ser.: Vol. 2107). 2000. per. 3.99 (*0-373-12107-5*) Harlequin Bks.

Marriage Takes More Than Love. Jack Mayhall & Carole Mayhall. (NavClassics Ser.). 1996. pap. 12.00 (*0-89109-946-8*) NavPress.

Marriage Test. Madeline Harper. (Temptation Ser.). 1996. per. 3.50 (*0-373-25689-2*, 1-25690-8) Harlequin Bks.

Marriage That Did Succeed for Mary, Queen of Scots. James W. Deppa. LC 89-81233. (Illus.). 325p. 1990. 14.50 (*0-9623620-1-8*) Ironwood MD.

Marriage the Covenant or the Curse. Tom Smith. 100p. 1998. pap. 8.95 (*1-57502-701-1*, PO1978) Morris Pubng.

Marriage, the Family & Women in India. VV Prakasa Rao & V Nandini Rao. 1982. 19.50 (*0-8364-0850-0*) S Asia.

Marriage: The Mystery of Christ & the Church see Marriage, the Mystery of Christ & the Church: The Covenant-Bond in Scripture & History

Marriage, the Mystery of Christ & the Church: The Covenant-Bond in Scripture & History. 2nd rev. ed. David J. Engelsma. LC 97-75395. Orig. Title: Marriage: The Mystery of Christ & the Church. 239p. 1999. 24.95 (*0-916206-59-9*) Refrd Free Pub Assn.

Marriage Therapy: Index of New Information for the Married, Divorced, Live-Ins & Professional Counselors. Lynne E. Langeston. 179p. 1997. 47.50 (*0-7883-1604-4*); pap. 44.50 (*0-7883-1605-2*) ABBE Pubs Assn.

Marriage Ticket. Sharon Brondos. (Superromance Ser.). 1993. per. 3.50 (*0-373-70557-3*, 1-70557-3) Harlequin Bks.

Marriage-to-Be? Gail Link. 1996. per. 3.99 (*0-373-24035-X*, 1-24035-7) Silhouette.

Marriage to Death: The Conflation of Wedding & Funeral Rituals in Greek Tragedy. Rush Rehm. LC 93-39939. 264p. 1994. text 37.50 (*0-691-03369-2*, Pub. by Princeton U Pr); pap. text 16.95 (*0-691-02916-4*, Pub. by Princeton U Pr) Cal Prin Full Svc.

Marriage to Fight For. Raina Lynn. 1997. per. 3.99 (*0-373-07804-8*, 1-07804-7) Silhouette.

Marriage to Remember. Cathryn Clare. (Intimate Moments Ser.: No. 795). 1997. per. 3.99 (*0-373-07795-5*, 1-07795-7) Silhouette.

Marriage to Remember: Top Author. Carole Mortimer. (Presents Ser.: No. 1929). 1998. per. 3.50 (*0-373-11929-1*, 1-11929-6) Harlequin Bks.

Marriage Trap. large type ed. Joan Mellows. 455p. 1989. 27.99 (*0-7089-1935-9*) Ulverscroft.

Marriage Triangle: Man, Woman & God. Louise S. Murphy. 66p. (Orig.). 1984. pap. text 1.95 (*0-937580-40-6*) Sumrall Pubng.

Marriage Ultimatum. Lindsay Armstrong. (Presents Ser.: Bk. 2075). 2000. per. 3.75 (*0-373-12075-3*, 1-12075-7) Harlequin Bks.

***Marriage Ultimatum.** large type ed. Lindsay Armstrong. (Thorndike Harlequin Romance Ser.). 2000. 22.95 (*0-263-16366-0*) Mills & Boon.

Marriage under Suspicion. Sara Craven. (Presents Ser.: No. 2058). 1999. per. 3.75 (*0-373-12058-3*, 1-12058-3) Harlequin Bks.

Marriage Visa Kit: Obtaining US Residency for Alien Spouse. American Immigration Center Ser. (Do-It-Yourself Immigration Ser.). 40p. 1998. pap. 69.00 (*0-9663425-3-4*) Amer Immig Ctr.

Marriage Vow: Poetry & Reflections Celebrating the Married Life. 2nd rev. ed. Adam W. Seligman & Julie A. Furger. (Illus.). 80p. (Orig.). 1996. pap. 9.95 (*0-9650733-0-0*, ECHO-001) Echolalia Pr.

Marriage Vows see Votos de Matrimonio: Marriage Vows

Marriage Vows, 2000: The New Marriage Contract for the Next Millennium. Ken G. Wolf. 130p. 1999. pap. 16.95 (*0-9665598-0-0*, 98-5-50) G T C Pr.

Marriage Wanted: From This Day Forward. Debbie Macomber. (Special Edition Ser.). 1993. per. 3.50 (*0-373-09842-1*, 5-09842-1) Silhouette.

Marriage War see Guerra Matrimonial

Marriage War. Charlotte Lamb. 1997. per. 3.50 (*0-373-11913-5*, 1-11913-0) Harlequin Bks.

Marriage War. large type ed. Charlotte Lamb. (Harlequin Romance Ser.). 288p. 1997. 20.95 (*0-263-15289-8*) Thorndike Pr.

"Marriage: What Is It? Why Do It? How Do You Do It?" Lavada Jefferson Weathers. (Illus.). 32p. (Orig.). 1998. pap. text 7.00 (*0-9669416-0-8*) Vada K.

Marriage Wish. Dee Henderson. (Love Inspired Ser.: No. 17). 1998. per. 4.50 (*0-373-87017-5*, 1-87017-9, Steeple Hill) Harlequin Bks.

***Marriage with an Attitude: How to Build an Exciting Marriage with a Fantastic Attitude.** Chuck Rife & Eileen Rife. 150p. 2000. pap. text 10.00 (*0-7392-0504-8*) Morris Pubng.

Marriage with My Kingdom: The Courtships of Elizabeth I. Alison Plowden. 2000. pap. 15.95 (*0-7509-2197-8*, Pub. by Sutton Pub Ltd) Intl Pubs Mktg.

Marriage with Papers. Mohammed Mrabet. Tr. by Paul Bowles. LC 85-52107. 88p. (Orig.). 1986. pap. 6.00 (*0-939180-32-4*) Tombouctou.

Marriage with Papers. deluxe ed. Mohammed Mrabet. Tr. by Paul Bowles. LC 85-52107. 88p. (Orig.). 1986. 35.00 (*0-939180-29-4*) Tombouctou.

***Marriage Without Regrets: International Edition.** Kay Arthur. 250p. 2000. pap. 11.99 (*0-7369-0440-9*) Harvest Hse.

Marriage Without Regrets: Your Life Together As God Intended. Kay Arthur. LC 99-14080. 250p. 2000. 18.99 (*1-56507-451-3*) Harvest Hse.

***Marriage Without Regrets Study Guide.** Kay Arthur. 144p. 2000. pap., student ed. 6.99 (*0-7369-0439-5*) Harvest Hse.

Marriage Work-out Book. Kirk. 1996. pap. 12.95 (*0-7459-3352-1*, Pub. by Lion Pubng) Trafalgar.

Marriage Worth Keeping. Kate Denton. 1997. per. 3.25 (*0-373-03482-2*, 1-03482-6) Harlequin Bks.

Marriage Worth Keeping. large type ed. Denton. 1997. per. 3.25 (*0-373-15728-2*, Harlequin) Harlequin Bks.

***Marriage You've Always Wanted: How to Grow a Stronger More Intimate Relationship.** Tim Clinton & Julie Clinton. 172p. 2000. pap. 12.99 (*0-8499-3745-0*) Word Pub.

Marriages. Arlene H. Eakle. 48p. 1993. pap. 16.50 (*0-940764-43-1*) Genealog Inst.

Marriages. Alan Ebert. 432p. 1988. mass mkt. 4.95 (*0-380-89855-1*, Avon Bks) Morrow Avon.

Marriages, Vol. 60. James Hillman et al. Ed. by Charles Boer & Jay Livernois. (Illus.). 150p. (Orig.). 1997. pap. 17.50 (*1-882670-09-4*) Spring Jrnl.

Marriages: Northampton County, VA. Jean M. Mihalyka. (1660-1854 Ser.). 177p. (Orig.). 1995. reprint ed. pap. text 16.50 (*0-7884-0166-1*) Heritage Bk.

Marriages & Baptisms of St. Michael Catholic Church, Swansea, MA (Ocean Grove) 1922-1995. American-French Genealogical Society Staff. vi, 409p. 1996. spiral bd. 30.00 (*1-929920-36-9*) American French.

Marriages & Death from Mississippi Newspapers, 1837-1863, Vol. 1. Betty C. Wiltshire. viii, 280p. (Orig.). 1987. pap. 20.00 (*1-55613-058-9*) Heritage Bk.

Marriages & Deaths from Baltimore Newspapers, 1796-1816. Robert Barnes. LC 78-61144. 383p. 2000. reprint ed. pap. 32.50 (*0-8063-0826-5*, Pub. by Clearfield Co) ACCESS Pubs Network.

Marriages & Deaths from Mississippi Newspapers, 1850-1861, Vol. 4. Betty C. Wiltshire. 365p. (Orig.). 1990. pap. 20.00 (*1-55613-284-0*) Heritage Bk.

Marriages & Deaths from Tarboro, N. C., Newspapers, 1824-1865. Hugh B. Johnston. 168p. 1985. pap. 20.00 (*0-89308-558-8*) Southern Hist Pr.

Marriages & Deaths from the American Democrat (Carlisle, Pa) Newspaper, 1851-1858. Mary Anne Wilson. LC 98-70558. iv, 137p. 1998. per. 15.00 (*1-55856-267-2*, 119) Closson Pr.

Marriages & Deaths from the American Volunteer (Carlisle, PA) Newspaper, 1839-1848. Mary Anne Capell Wilson. LC 98-70606. 1998. per. 10.00 (*1-55856-270-2*, 117) Closson Pr.

Marriages & Deaths from the Cambria Tribune, Vol. 1. Ed. by Patricia W. Collins. 32p. 1981. per. 7.00 (*0-933227-18-3*, 304) Closson Pr.

Marriages & Deaths from the Cambria Tribune, Vol. 2. Ed. by Patricia W. Collins. 61p. 1982. per. 8.00 (*0-933227-23-X*, 305) Closson Pr.

Marriages & Deaths from the Cambria Tribune, Vol. 4. Patricia W. Collins. 242p. 1985. per. 18.00 (*0-933227-42-6*, 307) Closson Pr.

Marriages & Deaths from the Carlisle Herald (PA) Newspaper, 1866, 1868-1872. Mary Anne Capell Wilson. LC 98-70559. iii, 134 p. 1998. per. 15.00 (*1-55856-266-4*, 123) Closson Pr.

Marriages & Deaths from the "Maryland Gazette," 1727-1839. Robert W. Barnes. 243p. 1997. reprint ed. pap. 24.00 (*0-8063-0580-0*, 355, Pub. by Clearfield Co) ACCESS Pubs Network.

Marriages & Deaths from the New Yorker: Double Quatro Edition 1836-1841. Kenneth Scott. LC 80-80958. 301p. 1980. 21.75 (*0-915156-46-6*, SP46) Natl Genealogical.

Marriages & Families. 2nd ed. Nijole V. Benokraitis. 1996. pap. text, student ed. 22.00 (*0-13-209529-7*) P-H.

Marriages & Families. 2nd ed. Lamanna & Riedmann. (Sociology - Introductory Level Ser.). 1985. pap. 7.25 (*0-534-04048-9*) Wadsworth Pub.

Marriages & Families. 3rd ed. Benokraitis. 1998. pap. text, student ed. 19.00 (*0-13-922197-2*) P-H.

Marriages & Families. 3rd ed. Lamanna & Riedmann. (Sociology - Introductory Level Ser.). 1988. pap., student ed. 10.00 (*0-534-08665-9*) Wadsworth Pub.

Marriages & Families. 4th ed. Lamanna. (Sociology - Intro Level Ser.). 1991. pap. 39.00 (*0-534-12723-1*) Wadsworth Pub.

Marriages & Families. 4th ed. Lamanna & Riedmann. (Sociology - Intro Level Ser.). 1991. pap., student ed. 12.00 (*0-534-12721-5*); mass mkt., teacher ed. write for info. (*0-534-12722-3*) Wadsworth Pub.

Marriages & Families. 5th ed. Lamanna & Agnes Riedmann. (Sociology Ser.). 1993. mass mkt., student ed. 15.00 (*0-534-18740-4*) Wadsworth Pub.

Marriages & Families. 6th ed. Mary A. Lamanna. (Sociology Ser.). 1996. pap., student ed. 18.00 (*0-534-50555-4*) Wadsworth Pub.

Marriages & Families. 6th ed. Mary A. Lamanna & Agnes Riedmann. LC 96-18509. (Sociology - Intro Level). (C). 1996. pap. 49.00 (*0-534-50553-8*) Wadsworth Pub.

Marriages & Families. 7th ed. Lamanna. LC 99-33896. (Sociology - Intro Level). 1999. pap. 73.95 (*0-534-52507-5*) Wadsworth Pub.

Marriages & Families. 7th ed. Mary A. Lamanna. (Sociology - Intro Level). 1999. pap., student ed. 20.25 (*0-534-52508-3*) Wadsworth Pub.

Marriages & Families: Changes, Choices, & Constraints. 3rd ed. Nijole V. Benokraitis. LC 98-5440. 603p. (C). 1998. 74.67 (*0-13-915935-5*) P-H.

***Marriages & Families: Changing Choices & Constraints.** 3rd ed. (C). 1999. pap. write for info. (*0-13-016500-X*) P-H.

***Marriages & Families: Diversity & Change.** 3rd ed. Mary Ann Schwartz & Barbara Marliene Scott. LC 99-34372. 552p. 1999. pap. 58.00 (*0-13-010431-0*) P-H.

Marriages & Families: Enrichment Through Communication. Ed. by Sherod Miller. LC 75-27012. (Sage Contemporary Social Science Issues Ser.: No. 20). 126p. reprint ed. pap. 39.10 (*0-608-10113-3*, 202193300026) Bks Demand.

Marriages & Families: Making Choices & Facing Change. 3rd ed. Mary A. Lamanna & Agnes Riedmann. 656p. (C). 1988. pap. write for info. (*0-534-08664-0*) Wadsworth Pub.

Marriages & Families: Making Choices & Facing Change. 4th ed. Mary A. Lamanna & Agnes Riedmann. 711p. (C). 1991. pap. 48.95 (*0-534-12720-7*) Wadsworth Pub.

Marriages & Families: Making Choices & Facing Change. 5th ed. Mary A. Lamanna & Agnes Riedmann. 709p. (C). 1993. mass mkt. 42.00 (*0-534-18738-2*) Wadsworth Pub.

Marriages & Families: Making Choices Throughout the Life Cycle. 2nd ed. Mary A. Lamanna & Agnes Riedmann. 704p. (C). 1985. pap. write for info. (*0-534-04047-0*) Wadsworth Pub.

Marriages & Families: New Problems & New Opportunities. 3rd ed. 382p. (C). 1994. text 45.00 (*0-536-58627-6*) Pearson Custom.

Marriages & Families: Reflections of a Gendered Society. Constance L. Shehan & Kenneth C. Kammeyer. LC 96-32261. 484p. 1996. pap. text 57.00 (*0-205-13973-6*) Allyn.

Marriages & Families: Reflections of a Gendered Society, Examination Copy. Constance L. Shehan & Kenneth C. Kammeyer. 512p. (C). 1996. write for info. (*0-205-26448-4*, T6448-9) Allyn.

Marriages & Families: Reflections of a Gendered Society: Instructor's Manual & Test Bank. Constance L. Shehan & Kenneth C. Kammeyer. (C). 1996. pap. text, teacher ed. write for info. (*0-205-26191-4*, T6191-5) Allyn.

Marriages & Families in a Diverse Society. (C). 1997. 67.00 (*0-06-502058-8*) Allyn.

Marriages & Families in a Diverse Society. Laurence A. Basirico. 368p. (C). 1997. pap., student ed. 25.00 (*0-06-502013-8*) Addson-Wesley Educ.

Marriages & Families in a Diverse Society. Robin Wolf. 576p. (C). 1997. 74.00 (*0-06-047185-9*) Addson-Wesley Educ.

Marriages & Families in a Diverse Society. 2nd ed. Wolf. (C). 1999. text. write for info. (*0-321-02281-5*) Addson-Wesley Educ.

Marriages & Much Miscellaneous from Rhinebeck New York Newspapers, 1846-1899, Vol. 2, Marriages. Arthur C. Kelly. LC 79-101054. 160p. 1978. lib. bdg. 24.00 (*1-56012-042-8*, 41) Kinship Rhinebeck.

Marriages & Obituaries from Early Georgia Newspapers. 464p. 1989. 40.00 (*0-89308-655-X*) Southern Hist Pr.

Marriages & Obituaries from the Macon Messenger, 1818-1865. Willard Rocker. 588p. 1988. 47.50 (*0-89308-340-2*, GA 65) Southern Hist Pr.

Marriages & Obituaries from the Tennessee Baptist, 1844-1862. Russell P. Baker. 137p. 1979. 18.50 (*0-89308-127-2*) Southern Hist Pr.

Marriages & Related Items Abstracted from Clayton Enterprise Newspaper of Clayton, Adams County, IL, 1879-1900. Beals. 206p. 1997. pap. 18.00 (*0-7884-0766-X*, B107) Heritage Bk.

Marriages & Related Items Abstracted from the Mendon Dispatch of Mendon, Adams County Illinois, 1877-1905. Joseph J. Beals & Sandy Kirchner. LC 98-104804. vi, 231p. 1997. pap. 16.00 (*0-7884-0749-X*, B103) Heritage Bk.

Marriages & Vital Records of Western Pennsylvania & Eastern Ohio. Compiled by Catherine L. Gowdy. LC 96-85286. 109p. 1996. per. 10.95 (*1-55856-230-3*, 277) Closson Pr.

Marriages Copied from the Private Record of Rev. Caleb Bradley of Westbrook (Maine) 21p. 1986. reprint ed. pap. 3.50 (*0-935207-46-5*) Danbury Hse Bks.

Marriages, Deaths, Divorces, 1870-1875, Medina County Gazette, Medina, Ohio. Sharon L. Kraynek. 124p. 1993. per. 9.95 (*1-55856-131-5*, 429) Closson Pr.

Marriages, 1809-1850, Cabell Co., VA/WV. rev. ed. Carrie Eldridge. (Illus.). 47p. 1988. spiral bd. 15.00i (*1-928979-05-X*) C Eldridge.

Marriages (1895-1905) & Deaths (1895-1900) & Related Items Abstracted from the Golden New Era of Golden Adams County, IL. Beals & Sandra Kirchner. LC 98-117876. 98p. 1998. pap. 17.00 (*0-7884-0792-9*, B109) Heritage Bk.

Marriages from Early Tennessee Newspapers, 1794-1851. Silas E. Lucas, Jr. 1981. reprint ed. 37.50 (*0-89308-092-6*) Southern Hist Pr.

Marriages from the Saugerties Telegraph,1846-1870 & Obituaries, Death Notices & Genealogical Gleanings from the Ulster Telegraph, 1846-1848. Audrey M. Klinkenberg. LC 99-197760. 437p. 1999. pap. 35.00 (*0-7884-1078-4*, K436) Heritage Bk.

Marriages from Venango County Sources: 1795-1885 (All) 1886-1921 (Outside the County) 2nd ed. Joan S. Hanson & Kenneth L. Hanson. 381p. 1994. per. 35.95 (*1-55856-178-1*) Closson Pr.

Marriages in Montpelier, Vermont. William T. Dewey. 1984. reprint ed. pap. 6.00 (*0-912606-17-7*) Hunterdon Hse.

Marriages in Russia: Couples During the Economic Transition. Dana Vannoy et al. LC 98-33619. 256p. 1999. 65.00 (*0-275-96147-8*, Praeger Pubs) Greenwood.

Marriages in the Roman Catholic Diocese of Tuam, Ireland, 1821-1829. Helen M. Murphy & James R. Reilly. x, 192p. (Orig.). 1993. pap. text 28.50 (*1-55613-812-1*) Heritage Bk.

Marriages in Utah Territory, 1850-1884: Deseret News, 1850-1872, Elias Smith Journal 1850-1884. Ed. by Judith W. Hansen. LC 98-60501. 140p. 1998. per. 15.00 (*1-892229-01-3*) Utah Geneolog.

Marriages in Woodford County: For the Period of Years 1788 to 1851. Annie W. Burns. 32p. 1997. reprint ed. pap. 7.00 (*0-8328-6741-1*) Higginson Bk Co.

Marriages Meant to Be: True Stories of How Couples Met & Married & the Astonishing Role Fate & Destiny Played! 176p. (Orig.). 1997. pap. 9.95 (*0-9651472-0-7*) Magic Moments.

Marriages, 1901-1919, Mason County, Illinois. 67p. 1988. pap. text 5.00 (*1-877869-16-3*) Mason Cnty Hist Proj.

***Marriages Northampton County, Virginia 1660-1854.** Jean M. Mihalyka. 168p. 2000. pap. 20.50 (*0-7884-1506-9*, 1506) Heritage Bk.

Marriages of Alleghany County, Virginia, 1822-1872. Carletta L. Nelson. 508p. (Orig.). 1994. pap. text 35.00 (*0-7884-0038-X*) Heritage Bk.

Marriages of Amelia County, Virginia, 1735-1815. Kathleen Booth Williams. 165p. 2000. reprint ed. pap. 21.50 (*0-8063-0835-4*, 6380, Pub. by Clearfield Co) ACCESS Pubs Network.

Marriages of Blessed Sacrament Catholic Church, Fall River, MA, 1892-1995. American-French Genealogical Society Staff. vii, 204p. 1996. spiral bd. 30.00 (*1-929920-18-0*) American French.

M

Marriages of Campbell County, Virginia, 1782-1810. Lucy H. Baber & Hazel L. Williamson. LC 79-56412. (Illus.). 185p. 2000. reprint ed. pap. 22.50 (*0-8063-0879-6*, Pub. by Clearfield Co) ACCESS Pubs Network.

Marriages of Caroline Co, VA, 1777-1853. Therese Fisher. LC 98-150267. xiii, 272 p. 1998. pap. 22.50 (*0-7884-0855-0*, F378) Heritage Bk.

Marriages of Goochland County, Virginia, 1733-1815. Kathleen B. Williams. 148p. 1998. pap. 17.00 (*0-8063-0836-2*, 6385) Clearfield Co.

Marriages of Granville County, North Carolina, 1753-1868. Brent H. Holcomb. LC 98-169163. 431p. 1997. reprint ed. pap. 35.00 (*0-8063-0945-8*, 2769) Clearfield Co.

Marriages of Halifax County, Virginia, 1801-1830. Marian D. Chiarito & James H. Prendergast. 183p. 1985. 25.00 (*0-945503-08-3*) Clarkton Pr.

Marriages of Henrico County, Virginia, 1680-1808. Joycey H. Lindsay. 96p. 1983. reprint ed. pap. 15.00 (*0-89308-364-X*) Southern Hist Pr.

Marriages of Isle of Wight County, Virginia, 1628-1800. Blanche Adams Chapman. 124p. 1999. reprint ed. pap. 16.50 (*0-8063-0710-2*, 950, Pub. by Clearfield Co) ACCESS Pubs Network.

Marriages of Jacob: A Poem Novella. Charlotte Mandel. LC 91-10855. 110p. (Orig.). 1991. pap. 10.00 (*0-916288-32-3*) Micah Pubns.

Marriages of Jefferson County, Tennessee, 1792-1836. Edythe R. Whitley. LC 81-84359. 110p. 1998. reprint ed. pap. 15.00 (*0-8063-0967-9*) Clearfield Co.

Marriages of Loudoun County, Virginia, 1757-1853. Mary A. Wertz. LC 84-81902. 231p. 1990. 15.00 (*0-8063-1103-7*) Clearfield Co.

Marriages of Lunenburg County, Virginia, 1746-1853. Emma R. Matheny & Helen K. Yates. (Illus.). 177p. 1997. reprint ed. pap. 18.00 (*0-8063-0833-8*, 3805) Clearfield Co.

Marriages of Mecklenburg County, Virginia, from 1765 to 1810. Stratton Nottingham. 71p. 1996. reprint ed. pap. 10.00 (*0-8063-4639-6*, 9283) Clearfield Co.

Marriages of Mobile County, Alabama, 1856-1875. Clinton P. King & Merlem A. Barlow. LC 86-71322. 181p. 20.00 (*0-943609-02-X*) AL Ancestors.

Marriages of Mobile County, Alabama, 1813-1855. Clinton P. King & Merlem A. Barlow. 181p. 20.00 (*0-8063-1135-5*, Pub. by Clearfield Co) ACCESS Pubs Network.

Marriages of Notre Dame de la Consolation RC Church (1895-1978), Pawtucket, RI. Robert J. Quintin. 200p. 1978. pap. 20.00 (*1-886560-16-1*) Quintin Pub RI.

Marriages of Patrick County, Virginia, 1791-1850. Lela C. Adams. 165p. 1984. reprint ed. pap. 20.00 (*0-89308-357-7*, VA 46) Southern Hist Pr.

Marriages of Phelps County Missouri Bk. 1: 28 Mar 1867-12 May 1881. Jerome T. Berry. 47p. 1944. pap. write for info. (*1-893474-12-7*) Phelps Cnty Gene.

Marriages of Pittsylvania County, Virginia, 1806-1830. Kathleen B. Williams. LC 80-68125. 229p. 1999. reprint ed. pap. 24.00 (*0-8063-0903-2*, Pub. by Clearfield Co) ACCESS Pubs Network.

Marriages of Precieux-Sang RC Church (1873-1977), Woonsocket, RI. Julien Hamelin. 250p. pap. 25.00 (*1-886560-17-X*) Quintin Pub RI.

***Marriages of Precious Blood Catholic Church, Woonsocket, RI, 1870-1995: Indexed by Men & Women, 2 vols.** American-French Genealogical Society Staff. 1998. spiral bd. 60.00 (*1-929920-29-6*) American French.

Marriages of Richmond County, Virginia, 1668-1853. George H. King. (Illus.). 312p. 1985. reprint ed. 28.50 (*0-89308-579-0*) Southern Hist Pr.

Marriages of Robertson County, Tennessee, 1839-1861. Edythe R. Whitley. LC 80-84319. 135p. 1999. reprint ed. pap. 18.00 (*0-8063-0920-2*, Pub. by Clearfield Co) ACCESS Pubs Network.

Marriages of Rowan County, North Carolina, 1753-1868. Brent H. Holcomb. 506p. 1998. reprint ed. pap. 37.50 (*0-8063-0942-3*, 2772) Clearfield Co.

Marriages of Rutherford County, Tennessee, 1804-1872. Edythe R. Whitley. LC 80-84318. 352p. 1999. reprint ed. pap. 29.50 (*0-8063-0921-0*, Pub. by Clearfield Co) ACCESS Pubs Network.

Marriages of Sacred Heart Catholic Church, North Attleboro, MA, 1904-1990. American-French Genealogical Society Staff. vii, 242p. 1993. spiral bd. 35.00 (*1-929920-19-9*) American French.

***Marriages of St. Ambrose Catholic Church, Albion, RI, 1905-1986.** American-French Genealogical Society Staff. viii, 59p. 1999. spiral bd. 12.50 (*1-929920-30-X*) American French.

***Marriages of Saint Anne Catholic Church, Fall River, Massachusetts, 1869-1996, 2 vols.** American-French Genealogical Society Staff. 1999. spiral bd. 70.00 (*1-929920-41-5*) American French.

Marriages of St. Anne's RC Church 1869-1930, Fall River, Massachusetts. Robert J. Quintin. 300p. 1980. pap. 25.00 (*1-886560-11-0*) Quintin Pub RI.

Marriages of St. Cecilia's Catholic Church, Pawtucket, RI (1910-1986) American-French Genealogical Society Staff. iv, 398p. 1987. per. 35.00 (*1-929920-11-3*) American French.

Marriages of St. Jean Baptist Church (1901-1979), Fall River, Massachusetts. Ed. by Robert J. Quintin. 85p. 1980. pap. 15.00 (*1-886560-12-9*) Quintin Pub RI.

***Marriages of St. Jean-Baptiste Catholic Church: Fall River, Massachusetts (1901-1996)** American-French Genealogical Society Staff. viii, 300p. 2000. spiral bd. 35.00 (*1-929920-57-1*) American French.

Marriages of St. John the Baptist Catholic Church, West Warwick, RI (ARCTIC) 1873-1980, 2 vols. American-French Genealogical Society Staff. 1987. per. 50.00 (*1-929920-10-5*) American French.

Marriages of St. John the Evangelist Catholic Church, Slatersville, RI, 1872-1986. American-French Genealogical Society Staff. x, 310p. 1988. per. 28.50 (*1-929920-13-X*) American French.

Marriages of St. Joseph Catholic Church, Pascoag, RI, 1893-1991. American-French Genealogical Society Staff. vii, 276p. 1993. spiral bd. 35.00 (*1-929920-56-3*) American French.

Marriages of St. Joseph's Catholic Church, Ashton, RI, 1872-1986. American-French Genealogical Society Staff. x, 246p. 1988. per. 24.00 (*1-929920-01-6*) American French.

Marriages of St. Joseph's Catholic Church, Attleboro, MA, 1905-1986. American-French Genealogical Society Staff. viii, 232p. 1988. per. 22.50 (*1-929920-02-4*) American French.

Marriages of St. Joseph's Catholic Church, Natick, RI, 1875-1989. American-French Genealogical Society Staff. viii, 410p. 1993. spiral bd. 40.00 (*1-929920-53-9*) American French.

Marriages of St. Mathieu, RC Church 1906-1978, Central Falls, RI. Alfred Gaboury. 125p. 1979. pap. 20.00 (*1-886560-14-5*) Quintin Pub RI.

***Marriages of St. Matthew Catholic Church, Central Falls, RI, 1906-1988.** American-French Genealogical Society Staff. vii, 466p. 1999. spiral bd. 40.00 (*1-929920-28-8*) American French.

Marriages of St. Matthew's Catholic Church, Fall River, MA, 1888-1986. American-French Genealogical Society Staff. x, 309p. 1987. per. 27.00 (*1-929920-00-8*) American French.

Marriages of St. Stephen's Catholic Church, Attleboro, MA (Dodgeville) 1880-1986. American-French Genealogical Society Staff. vi, 225p. 1988. per. 19.95 (*1-929920-12-1*) American French.

Marriages of St. Theresa Catholic Church, Blackstone, MA, Jul 1929-Jun 1987. American-French Genealogical Society Staff. viii, 132p. 1987. spiral bd. 15.00 (*1-929920-31-8*) American French.

Marriages of St. Theresa Catholic Church, Nasonville, RI, 1923-1986. American-French Genealogical Society Staff. vii, 65p. 1993. spiral bd. 15.00 (*1-929920-32-6*) American French.

Marriages of Some Virginia Residents, 1607-1800, 7 vols. in 2. Dorothy F. Wulfeck. 2259p. 1995. reprint ed. 120.00 (*0-8063-1141-X*) Genealog Pub.

Marriages of Sumner County, Tennessee, 1787-1838. Edythe R. Whitley. LC 80-84317. 150p. 1999. pap. 18.50 (*0-8063-0922-9*) Clearfield Co.

Marriages of Surry County, North Carolina 1779-1868. Brent H. Holcomb. 272p. 1998. reprint ed. pap. 25.00 (*0-8063-0975-X*, 2773) Clearfield Co.

Marriages of the Bourbons, 2 vols. Denis A. Bingham. LC 70-113557. (Illus.). reprint ed. 95.00 (*0-404-00890-9*) AMS Pr.

Marriages of Washington County, Arkansas, 1845-71. Lois N. Miller. 118p. (Orig.). 1982. 31.50 (*1-878193-00-7*); pap. 25.00 (*1-878193-01-5*) L N Miller Geog Pubns.

Marriages of Washington County, Arkansas, 1871-91. Lois N. Miller. 194p. 1985. 27.00 (*1-878193-02-3*); pap. 22.00 (*1-878193-03-1*) L N Miller Geog Pubns.

Marriages of Washington County, Arkansas, 1901-10. Lois N. Miller et al. 166p. 1990. 31.50 (*1-878193-04-X*); pap. 25.00 (*1-878193-05-8*) L N Miller Geog Pubns.

Marriages of Washington County, Arkansas, 1911-21. Lois N. Miller et al. 218p. 1990. 31.50 (*1-878193-06-6*); pap. 25.00 (*1-878193-07-4*) L N Miller Geog Pubns.

Marriages of Washington County, Arkansas, 1922-30. Lois N. Miller et al. 156p. 1990. 31.50 (*1-878193-08-2*); pap. 25.00 (*1-878193-09-0*) L N Miller Geog Pubns.

Marriages of Washington County, Arkansas, 1930-41. Lois N. Miller. 260p. 1990. 37.50 (*1-878193-10-4*); pap. 30.00 (*1-878193-11-2*) L N Miller Geog Pubns.

Marriages of Wilkes County, North Carolina 1778-1868. Brent H. Holcomb. 243p. 1998. reprint ed. pap. 24.00 (*0-8063-1008-1*, 2782) Clearfield Co.

Marriages Recorded in the Town of Blackstone, MA, 1845-1900. American-French Genealogical Society Staff. vii, 601p. 1994. spiral bd. 35.00 (*1-929920-52-0*) American French.

Marriages Recorded in the Town Reports of Peterboro, NH, 1887-1948. American-French Genealogical Society Staff. vii, 559p. 1995. spiral bd. 35.00 (*1-929920-33-4*) American French.

Married? Annette Broadrick. (Here Come the Grooms Ser.: No. 27). 1996. per. 3.99 (*0-373-30127-8*, 1-30127-4) Harlequin Bks.

Married? Annette Broadrick. (Romance Ser.: No. 742). 1990. per. 2.25 (*0-373-08742-X*) Silhouette.

Married . . . With Twins! Jennifer Mikels. (Special Edition Ser.). 1996. per. 3.99 (*0-373-24054-6*, 1-24054-8) Silhouette.

Married & Alone: The Way Back. P. M. Rosenzweig. (Illus.). 282p. (C). 1992. 24.50 (*0-306-44125-X*, Plen Insight) Perseus Pubng.

Married & How to Stay That Way: A Treasury of Practical Solutions Based Solely on Gods Word. Steve Carr. 304p. 1998. pap. 12.99 (*0-9656749-3-2*) ACW Press.

Married & Making a Living: Couples Who Own Small Franchise Businesses. Barbara Kranendonk. LC 97-36984. (Studies in Entrepreneurship). (Illus.). 173p. 1997. text 48.00 (*0-8153-2996-2*) Garland.

Married & Single Life. Audrey Riker. (gr. 9-12). 1984. text 19.40 (*0-02-665040-1*) Glencoe.

Married & Single Life: Teacher's Annotated Edition. 6th annot. ed. Riker & Brisbane. 512p. 1999. teacher ed. 43.69 (*0-02-643001-0*) Glencoe.

Married at Midnight. Kathleen E. Woodiwiss et al. 400p. 1996. mass mkt. 6.99 (*0-380-78615-X*, Avon Bks) Morrow Avon.

Married at Midnight. large type ed. Kathleen E. Woodiwiss et al. LC 96-50225. 424p. 1997. 25.95 (*1-56895-401-8*, Compass) Wheeler Pub.

Married by a Thread. Kia Cochrane. 1994. per. 3.50 (*0-373-07600-2*, 1-07600-9) Harlequin Bks.

Married by Accident: Conveniently Yours. Christine Rimmer. (Special Edition Ser.: No. 1250). 1999. per. 4.25 (*0-373-24250-6*, 1-24250-2) Silhouette.

Married by Christmas. large type ed. 1999. 21.95 (*0-263-15934-5*) Chivers N Amer.

Married by Christmas: (Top Author) Carole Mortimer. 1998. per. 3.75 (*0-373-11995-X*, 1-11995-7) Harlequin Bks.

Married by High Noon. Leigh Greenwood. Vol. 1295. 250p. 2000. mass mkt. 4.25 (*0-373-24295-6*, 1-24295-7) Silhouette.

***Married by Midnight.** Mollie Molay. (American Romance Ser.: Vol. 815). 2000. mass mkt. 4.25 (*0-373-16815-2*) Harlequin Bks.

Married by Mistake! Renee Roszel. (Harlequin Romance Ser.: No. 3488). 1998. per. 3.25 (*0-373-03488-1*, 1-03488-3) Harlequin Bks.

Married by Mistake! large type ed. Renee Roszel. 1998. per. 3.25 (*0-373-15734-7*) Harlequin Bks.

Married Cooperators. J. Don Bloom. LC 97-71454. (Illus.). 160p. 1997. text 59.95 (*1-85972-691-7*, Pub. by Ashgate Pub) Ashgate Pub Co.

Married for Good. R. Paul Stevens. 168p. (Orig.). 1997. pap. 15.95 (*1-57383-087-9*) Regent College.

Married for Life: Couple's Manual. Mike Phillipps & Marilyn Phillipps. 208p. 1983. pap. text. write for info. (*1-884794-02-5*) Eden Pubng.

Married for Life: Couple's Manual. Mike Phillipps & Marilyn Phillipps. 195p. 1995. pap. text. write for info. (*1-884794-19-X*) Eden Pubng.

Married for Life: Leader's Manual. Mike Phillipps & Marilyn Phillipps. 320p. 1983. pap. text. write for info. (*1-884794-01-7*) Eden Pubng.

Married for Life: Leader's Manual. Mike Phillipps & Marilyn Phillipps. Tr. by Valentina Bren. (RUS.). 320p. 1992. pap. text, teacher ed. write for info. (*1-884794-25-4*) Eden Pubng.

Married for Life: Leader's Manual. Mike Phillipps & Marilyn Phillipps. 320p. 1995. pap. text. write for info. (*1-884794-18-1*) Eden Pubng.

Married for Life, Couples. Mike Phillipps & Marilyn Phillipps. (TAG.). 195p. (Orig.). 1995. pap. text. write for info. (*1-884794-12-2*) Eden Pubng.

Married for Life, Couples. Mike Phillipps & Marilyn Phillipps. Tr. by Valentina Bren. (RUS.). 195p. (Orig.). 1995. pap. text. write for info. (*1-884794-24-6*) Eden Pubng.

Married for Life Leder Hanbog. Mike Phillipps & Marilyn Phillipps. Tr. by Lena Thorslund from ENG. (DAN.). 322p. (Orig.). 1994. pap. write for info. (*1-884794-07-6*) Eden Pubng.

Married for Real. Lindsay Armstrong. (Presents Ser.: No. 1925). 1997. per. 3.50 (*0-373-11925-9*, 1-11925-4) Harlequin Bks.

Married for Real. large type ed. Lindsay Armstrong. (Mills & Boon Large Print Ser.). 288p. 1997. 23.99 (*0-263-14991-9*) Ulverscroft.

Married in a Moment. Jessica Steele. (Romance Ser.). 1998. per. 3.50 (*0-373-03499-7*, 1-03499-0) Harlequin Bks.

Married in a Moment. large type ed. Jessica Steele. (Whirlwind Weddings Ser.). 1998. per. 3.50 (*0-373-15745-2*, Harlequin) Harlequin Bks.

Married in a Moment. large type ed. Jessica Steele. 1998. 21.95 (*0-263-15751-2*, Pub. by Mills & Boon) Chivers N Amer.

Married... In Business: What You Must Know & Achieve to Survive & Thrive in This All-Important Partnership. Jack Wyman & Elaine Wyman. LC 99-94625. (Illus.). 236p. 1999. pap. 16.95 (*0-9639180-0-1*) Doer Pubns.

Married in Friendship. J. Conner. 1990. pap. 30.00 (*0-7220-5264-2*) St Mut.

***Married in Haste.** Cathy Maxwell. LC 99-94774. 372p. 1999. mass mkt. 6.50 (*0-380-80831-5*, Avon Bks) Morrow Avon.

Married in Haste. Dani Sinclair. (Intrigue Ser.: Vol. 481). 1998. per. 3.99 (*0-373-22481-8*, 1-22481-5) Harlequin Bks.

***Married in the Sight of God: Theology, Ethics, & Church Debates over Homosexuality.** Christian Batalden Scharen. 2000p. 2000. 49.00 (*0-7618-1768-9*) U Pr of Amer.

Married Lady's Companion: or Poor Man's Friend. 2nd ed. Samuel K. Jennings. LC 77-180580. (Medicine & Society in America Ser.). 308p. 1978. reprint ed. 23.95 (*0-405-03957-3*) Ayer.

Married Life. Arnold Bennett. LC 74-17077. (Collected Works of Arnold Bennett: Vol. 52). 1977. reprint ed. 19.95 (*0-518-19133-8*) Ayer.

Married Life. Edith L. O'Shaughnessy. LC 71-52952. (Short Story Index Reprint Ser.). 1977. reprint ed. 20.95 (*0-8369-3867-4*) Ayer.

Married Love. Kent Thompson. 95p. 1988. pap. 7.95 (*0-86492-077-6*, Pub. by Goose Ln Edits) Genl Dist Srvs.

Married Love: Delights of Wisdom Relating to Married Love Followed by Pleasures of Insanity Relating to Licentious Love. Emanuel Swedenborg. Tr. by N. Bruce Rogers from LAT. LC 95-10807. 618p. 1995. 15.00 (*0-945003-06-4*) General Church.

Married Love: Delights of Wisdom Relating to Married Love Followed by Pleasures of Insanity Relating to Licentious Love, The Word Edition. Emanuel Swedenborg. Tr. by N. Bruce Rogers from LAT. LC 95-10807. 618p. 1995. 15.00 (*0-945003-07-2*) General Church.

***Married Lovers, Married Friends.** Steve Chapman. 160p. 1999. pap. 9.99 (*0-7642-2226-0*) Bethany Hse.

***Married Man: A Love Story.** Edmund White. LC 99-53980. 336p. 2000. 25.00 (*0-375-40005-2*) Knopf.

Married, Middle-Brow, & Militant: Sarah Grand & the New Woman Novel. Teresa Mangum. LC 98-40079. (Illus.). 304p. 1998. text 47.50 (*0-472-10977-4*, 10977) U of Mich Pr.

Married Priests & the Reforming Papacy: The 11th Century Debates. Anne L. Barstow. LC 82-7914. (Texts & Studies in Religion: Vol. 12). 288p. 1982. lib. bdg. 89.95 (*0-88946-987-3*) E Mellen.

Married Saints. Selden P. Delany. LC 69-17573. (Essay Index Reprint Ser.). 1977. 20.95 (*0-8369-0071-5*) Ayer.

Married Saints. John F. Fink. LC 98-28459. 148p. 1999. mass mkt. 9.95 (*0-8189-0822-X*) Alba.

Married to a Mistress. large type ed. Lynne Graham. 1998. 21.95 (*0-263-15750-4*, Pub. by Mills & Boon) Chivers N Amer.

Married to a Mistress: The Husband Hunters. Lynne Graham. 1998. per. 3.75 (*0-373-12001-X*, 1-12001-3, Mira Bks) Harlequin Bks.

Married to a Pastor: How to Stay Happily Married in the Ministry. H. B. London, Jr. & Neil B. Wiseman. Ed. by Wil Simon. LC 99-28718. 264p. 1999. pap. 12.99 (*0-8307-2505-9*) Gospel Lght.

Married to a Stranger. Connie Bennett. (Superromance Ser.). 1996. per. 3.99 (*0-373-70695-2*, 1-70695-1) Harlequin Bks.

***Married to a Stranger.** Allison Leigh. (Special Edition Ser.: Bk. 1336). 2000. mass mkt. 4.50 (*0-373-24336-7*, 1-24336-9) Silhouette.

Married to a Stranger. Nahid Rachlin. 232p. (Orig.). 1993. pap. 12.95 (*0-87286-276-3*) City Lights.

Married to a Traveling Spouse. Cindy L. Houfek. LC 97-90033. ix, 195p. (Orig.). 1997. pap. 12.95 (*0-9656675-0-2*) Extricare Pub.

Married to Dance: The Irina & Frank Pal Story. Lynn Hoggard. (Illus.), 350p. 1995. 25.00 (*0-915323-08-7*) Midwestern St U Pr.

***Married to Laughter.** large type ed. Jerry Stiller. 2000. 25.00 (*0-375-43092-X*) Random.

***Married to Laughter: A Love Story Featuring Anne Meara.** Jerry Stiller. (Illus.). 320p. 2000. 25.00 (*0-684-86903-9*) S&S Trade.

Married to Murder. large type ed. E. Radford & M. A. Radford. (Linford Mystery Library). 416p. 1995. pap. 16.99 (*0-7089-7734-0*, Linford) Ulverscroft.

Married to My Husband: A Personal Testimony on How to Develop a God-Centered Marriage. Helen R. Spears. 192p. (Orig.). 1996. per. 10.00 (*0-939513-43-9*) Joy Pub SJC.

Married to Sinclair. Danielle Shaw. (Scarlet Ser.). (Orig.). 1997. mass mkt. 3.99 (*1-85487-956-1*, Pub. by Scarlet Bks) London Brdge.

***Married to the Amadeus: Life with a String Quartet.** Muriel Nissel. (Illus.). 184p. 2000. pap. 22.95 (*1-900357-12-7*, Pub. by Giles Mare Pubs) Trafalgar.

***Married to the Boss.** Lori Foster. (Maitland Maternity Ser.: Bk. 3). 2000. mass mkt. 4.50 (*0-373-65064-7*, 1-65064-7) Harlequin Bks.

Married to the Church. Raymond Hedin. LC 95-5918. 272p. 1995. 29.95 (*0-253-32943-4*) Ind U Pr.

Married to the Enemy. Ann Major. (Desire Ser.: No. 716). 1992. per. 2.89 (*0-373-05716-4*, 5-05716-1) Harlequin Bks.

Married to the Foreign Service. Jewell Fenzi. (Twayne's Oral History Ser.). 250p. 1994. 28.95 (*0-8057-9123-X*, Twyne); per. 13.95 (*0-8057-9122-1*, Twyne) Mac Lib Ref.

Married to the Iceman: A True Account of Life with a Mafia Hitman & the Inside Story of His Crimes. Barbara Kuklinski & John Driver. LC 94-11194. (Illus.). 352p. 1999. pap. 22.95 (*0-525-93786-2*, Dutt) Dutton Plume.

Married to the Man. Ann Charlton. (Presents Ser.: No. 1892). 1997. per. 3.50 (*0-373-11892-9*, 1-11892-6) Harlequin Bks.

Married to the Man. large type ed. Ann Charlton. (Mills & Boon Large Print Ser.). 288p. 1997. 23.99 (*0-263-14923-4*) Ulverscroft.

An Asterisk (*) at the beginning of an entry indicates that the title is appearing for the first time.

Married to the Man (Reunited) Judith Arnold. (Superromance Ser.). 1996. per. 3.99 (*0-373-70684-7*, 1-70684-5) Harlequin Bks.

Married to the SAS. Andy McNab. (Illus.). 290p. 1997. 25.95 (*1-85782-166-1*, Pub. by Blake Publng) Seven Hills Bk.

Married to the SAS. Frances Nicholson. 1997. 25.95 (*0-614-28056-7*) Blake Pub.

Married to the Sheik: Virgin Bride. Carol Grace. (Romance Ser.: No. 1391). 1999. mass mkt. 3.50 (*0-373-19391-2*, 1-19391-1) Silhouette.

Married to Their Careers: Career & Family Dilemmas in Doctors' Lives. Lane A. Gerber. 272p. 1983. pap. 13.95 (*0-422-78250-5*, NO. 3812, Pub. by Tavistock) Routldge.

Married to Tolstoy. Cynthia Asquith. (Illus.). 283p. 1964. 9.95 (*0-251-15039-9*) Dufour.

Married White Male in Search Of . . . An Offbeat Look at Family Life, Faith Life & Mid-Life. Mark Collins. LC 97-52263. 176p. 1998. pap. 11.00 (*0-7648-0179-1*, Liguori Triumph) Liguori Pubns.

Married Widows: The Wives of Men in Long-Term Care. Maria C. Bartlett. LC 93-22707. (Studies on the Elderly in America). 136p. 1993. text 15.00 (*0-8153-1535-X*) Garland.

Married with Careers: Coping with Role Strain. Jacqueline B. Stanfield. LC 96-83249. 112p. 1996. 58.95 (*1-85972-334-9*, Pub. by Avebry) Ashgate Pub Co.

Married with Pleasure. Patricia W. Holt. (Illus.). 125p. 1994. pap. 8.95 (*0-9643719-0-1*) P W Holt.

Married Woman. Laurie John. (Sweet Valley University Ser.: No. 5). (YA). (gr. 7 up). 1994. 9.09 (*0-606-06790-6*, Pub. by Turtleback) Demco.

Married Woman. Created by Francine Pascal. (Sweet Valley University Ser.: No. 5). 240p. (YA). (gr. 7 up). 1994. mass mkt. 4.50 (*0-553-56309-2*) Bantam.

Married Woman's Private Medical Companion. A. M. Mauriceau. LC 73-20635. (Sex, Marriage & Society Ser.). 256p. 1974. reprint ed. 23.95 (*0-405-05811-X*) Ayer.

Married Women & the Law of Property in Nineteenth-Century Ontario. Lori Chambers. LC 97-210553. 272p. 1997. pap. text 18.95 (*0-8020-7839-7*) U of Toronto Pr.

Married Women vs. Husbands' Names. Una Stannard. LC 73-87334. 1973. 10.00 (*0-914142-00-3*) Germainbooks.

***Married Women Who Love Women.** Carren Strock. LC 99-87155. 228p. 2000. pap. 12.95 (*1-55583-555-4*, Pub. by Alyson Pubns) Consort Bk Sales.

Married Women's Separate Property in England, 1660-1833. Susan Staves. (Illus.). 304p. 1990. 47.00 (*0-674-55088-9*) HUP.

Married Wowen & the Law of Property in Nineteenth-Century Ontario. Lori Chambers. LC 97-210553. 272p. 1997. text 55.00 (*0-8020-0854-2*) U of Toronto Pr.

Marriott's Legacy. Margaret Callaghan. (Scarlet Ser.). 1999. mass mkt. 3.99 (*1-85487-557-4*, Pub. by Scarlet Bks) London Brdge.

Marriott's Practical Electrocardiography. 9th ed. Galen S. Wagner. LC 93-30277. (Illus.). 416p. 1994. 32.00 (*0-683-08604-9*) Lppncott W & W.

Marriott's Practical Electrocardiography. 10th ed. Galen Wagner. 450p. 36.00 (*0-683-30746-0*) Lppncott W & W.

***Marrow.** Robert Reed. 384p. 2000. 25.95 (*0-312-86801-4*, Pub. by Tor Bks) St Martin.

Marrow. William Shaw. Ed. by Brian Browning & Joe Dionne. (Illus.). 24p. 1991. pap. 10.00 (*0-945950-05-5*) Canoe Pr MI.

Marrow: And Other Stories. Nora Gold. LC 98-206668. (Illus.). 224p. 1998. pap. 16.95 (*1-894020-31-6*) Warwick Publ.

Marrow & Stem Cell Processing for Transplantation. Ed. by Larry C. Lasky & Phyllis Warkentin. (Illus.). (C). 1995. text 35.00 (*1-56395-042-1*) Am Assn Blood.

Marrow Controversy, 1718-1723: An Historical & Theological Analysis. David C. Lachman. LC 92-5154. (Rutherford Studies in Historical Theology). 516p. 1992. reprint ed. lib. bdg. 119.95 (*0-7734-1649-8*) E Mellen.

Marrow of Alchemy. George Ripley. Ed. by J. D. Holmes. 1994. reprint ed. pap. 6.95 (*1-55818-281-0*) Holmes Pub.

***Marrow of Flame: Poems of the Spiritual Journey.** Dorothy Walters. LC 99-89501. 128p. 2000. pap. 12.00 (*0-934252-96-3*, Pub. by Hohm Pr) SCB Distributors.

Marrow of Theology. William Ames. Tr. by John D. Eusden. 368p. 1997. pap. text 24.99 (*0-8010-2038-7*, Labyrinth) Baker Bks.

Marrow of Tradition. Bentley. 2001. pap. write for info. (*0-312-19406-4*) St Martin.

Marrow of Tradition. Charles Waddell Chesnutt. 1976. 25.95 (*0-8488-0962-9*) Amereon Ltd.

Marrow of Tradition. Charles Waddell Chesnutt. LC 70-83927. (Black Heritage Library Collection). 1977. 16.95 (*0-8369-8539-7*) Ayer.

Marrow of Tradition. Charles Waddell Chesnutt. Ed. & Intro. by Eric J. Sundquist. LC 92-31334. (Twentieth-Century Classics Ser.). 128p. 1993. pap. 13.95 (*0-14-018686-7*, Penguin Classics) Viking Penguin.

Marrow of Tradition. large type ed. Charles Waddell Chesnutt. LC 99-14583. 450p. 1999. 27.95 (*1-56000-493-2*) Transaction Pubs.

Marrow of Tradition. Charles Waddell Chesnutt. LC 72-1564. reprint ed. 42.50 (*0-404-00014-2*) AMS Pr.

Marrow of Tradition. 2nd ed. Charles Waddell Chesnutt. (Illus.). 352p. 1969. pap. text 14.95 (*0-472-06147-X*, 06147) U of Mich Pr.

Marrow of Tradition: American Negro. Charles Waddell Chesnutt. LC 69-18585. (His History & Literature Ser.: No. 2). 1968. reprint ed. 16.95 (*0-405-01855-X*) Ayer.

Marrow Protection: Transduction of Hematopoietic Cells with Drug Resistance Genes. Ed. by J. R. Bertino. LC 99-25603. (Progress in Experimental Tumor Research Ser.: Vol. 36). (Illus.). 180p. 1999. 174.00 (*3-8055-6828-2*) S Karger.

Marrow Stromal Cell Culture. Ed. by Jon Beresford & Maureen Owen. LC 97-30196. (Handbooks in Practical Animal Cell Biology). (Illus.). 166p. (C). 1998. text 64.95 (*0-521-58021-8*); pap. text 24.95 (*0-521-58978-9*) Cambridge U Pr.

Marry for Money. Faith Baldwin. 1976. reprint ed. lib. bdg. 22.95 (*0-88411-621-2*) Amereon Ltd.

Marry in Haste. Moyra Tarling. 1997. per. 3.25 (*0-373-19242-8*, 1-19242-6) Silhouette.

Marry in Haste. large type ed. Gail Mallin. 350p. 1996. 23.99 (*0-263-14689-8*, Pub. by Mills & Boon) Ulverscroft.

Marry in Haste: Whirlwind Weddings. Heather Allison. (Romance Ser.: No. 3487). 1998. per. 3.25 (*0-373-03487-3*, 1-03487-5) Harlequin Bks.

Marry in Haste: Whirlwind Weddings. large type ed. Heather Allison. 1998. per. 3.25 (*0-373-15733-9*) Harlequin Bks.

Marry Me. Heather Allison. (Romance Ser.). 1997. per. 3.25 (*0-373-03445-8*, 1-03445-3) Harlequin Bks.

Marry Me. Pat Booth. 384p. 1997. mass mkt. 5.99 (*1-57566-191-8*, Knsington) Kensgtn Pub Corp.

Marry Me! John Updike. 303p. 1996. pap. 12.95 (*0-449-91215-9*) Fawcett.

Marry Me. large type ed. Heather Allison. 1997. per. 3.25 (*0-373-15691-X*, Harlequin) Harlequin Bks.

Marry Me. large type ed. Pat Booth. 528p. 1996. lib. bdg. 25.95 (*0-7838-1865-3*, G K Hall Lrg Type) Mac Lib Ref.

Marry Me! A Romance. John Updike. 1976. 22.95 (*0-394-40856-X*) Knopf.

Marry Me! Courtships & Proposals of Legendary Couples. Wendy H. Goldberg & Betty Goodwin. LC 94-31939. (Illus.). 164p. 1994. 18.95 (*1-883318-21-1*) Angel City Pr.

***Marry Me! Three Professional Men Reveal How to Get Mr. Right to Pop the Question.** Christopher Pizzo. 256p. 2000. 22.95 (*0-06-019539-8*, Cliff Street) HarperTrade.

Marry Me Again. Suzanne Carey. (Silhouette Romance Ser.). 1994. per. 2.75 (*0-373-19001-8*, 5-19001-2) Harlequin Bks.

Marry Me Again. Suzanne Carey. (Romance Ser.). 1997. per. 95.76 (*0-373-91001-0*, 5-91001-3) Silhouette.

Marry Me, Baby. Debbi Rawlins. 1997. per. 3.75 (*0-373-16691-5*, 1-16691-7) Harlequin Bks.

Marry Me Christmas. JoAnn Algermissen. 1996. per. 3.50 (*0-373-52034-4*, 1-52034-5) Silhouette.

Marry Me, Cowboy! Susan Fox & Margaret Way. 1995. per. 4.99 (*0-373-83299-0*) Harlequin Bks.

Marry Me, Cowboy! Peggy Moreland. (Desire Ser.: No. 1084). 1997. per. 3.50 (*0-373-76084-1*, 1-76084-2) Silhouette.

Marry Me in Amarillo. Celeste Hamilton. (Special Edition Ser.). 1997. per. 3.99 (*0-373-24091-0*, 1-24091-0) Silhouette.

Marry Me Kate. Tracy Sinclair. (Special Edition Ser.). 1994. per. 3.50 (*0-373-09868-5*, 5-09868-6) Silhouette.

Marry Me, Kate: Lucky Charm Sisters. Judy Christenberry. (Romance Ser.). 1998. per. 3.50 (*0-373-19344-0*, 1-19344-0) Silhouette.

Marry Me, Now! Allison Hayes. 1996. per. 3.99 (*0-373-24032-5*, 1-24032-4) Silhouette.

***Marry Me Stranger.** Kay Gregory. LC 00-35358. 2000. write for info. (*0-7862-2635-8*) Five Star.

Marry Me Stranger. Kay Gregory. 400p. 1996. mass mkt. 3.99 (*1-85487-483-7*, Pub. by Scarlet Bks) London Brdge.

Marry Me Tonight: Weddings, Inc. Marisa Carroll. LC 95-7133. (Superromance Ser.). 297p. 1995. per. 3.75 (*0-373-70635-9*, 1-70635-7) Harlequin Bks.

Marry Only in the Lord. Bruce R. Curd. 72p. (Orig.). 1987. pap. 1.95 (*0-940999-12-9*, C-2062) Star Bible.

Marry-Out or Die-Out: A Cross Cultural Examination of Exogamy & Survival Value. Gay E. Kang. (Council on International Studies & Programs Special Studies: No. 148). 213p. 1982. pap. text 15.00 (*0-924197-00-5*, 148) SUNYB Coun Intl Studies.

Marry Sunshine. Anne McAllister. (Here Come the Grooms Ser.: No. 36). 1996. per. 3.99 (*0-373-30136-7*, 1-30136-5) Harlequin Bks.

***Marry Yes Marry No: Marriage for the Clueless.** Mari P. Saunders. LC 99-91446. 2000. 25.00 (*0-7388-0792-3*); pap. 18.00 (*0-7388-0793-1*) Xlibris Corp.

Marry Your Muse: Making a Lasting Commitment to Your Creativity. Jan Phillips. LC 97-19472. (Illus.). 320p. 1997. pap. 18.00 (*0-8356-0759-3*, Quest) Theos Pub Hse.

***Marrying a Delacourt.** Sherryl Woods. (Special Edition Ser.: Bk. 1352). 2000. mass mkt. 4.50 (*0-373-24352-9*, 1-24352-6) Silhouette.

Marrying an Older Man. Arlene James. (Special Edition Ser.: No. 1235). 1999. per. 4.25 (*0-373-24235-2*, 1-24235-3) Harlequin Bks.

Marrying & Burying: Rites of Passage in a Man's Life. Ronald L. Grimes. LC 94-29698. 263p. (C). 1994. pap. text 25.00 (*0-8133-2460-2*, Pub. by Westview) HarpC.

Marrying by Lot. Charlotte Mortimer. 1993. reprint ed. lib. bdg. 89.00 (*0-7812-5494-9*) Rprt Serv.

Marrying Communism to the Market: Institutional Foundation of China's Post-mao Hyper-growth. Lance L. P. Gore. LC 98-37358. (Illus.). 368p. 1999. text 49.95 (*0-19-590758-2*) OUP.

Marrying for Life: A Handbook of Marriage Skills. Raymond E. Vath & Daniel O'Neill. (Illus.). 144p. (Orig.). 1982. 6.95 (*0-86683-674-8*) Harper SF.

Marrying for Love. large type ed. Sally Blake. (Mills & Boon Large Print Ser.). 350p. 1998. 24.99 (*0-263-15528-5*, Pub. by Mills & Boon) Ulverscroft.

Marrying Game. large type ed. Lindsay Armstrong. 1990. lib. bdg. 18.95 (*0-263-12351-0*) Mac Lib Ref.

Marrying Harriet. large type ed. Marion Chesney. (School for Manners Ser.: Vol. 6). 252p. 1992. pap. 15.95 (*0-8161-5158-X*, G K Hall Lrg Type) Mac Lib Ref.

Marrying Jake. Beverly Bird. 1997. per. 3.99 (*0-373-07802-1*, 1-07802-1) Silhouette.

***Marrying Jezebel.** Hillary Fields. 368p. 2000. mass mkt. 5.99 (*0-312-97567-8*) St Martin.

Marrying Kind. Beverly Bird. (Intimate Moments Ser.). 1996. per. 3.99 (*0-373-07732-7*, 1-07732-0) Silhouette.

***Marrying Maddy.** Kasey Michaels. (Silhouette Romance Ser.: Vol. 1469). 2000. mass mkt. 3.50 (*0-373-19469-2*, 1-19469-5) Harlequin Bks.

Marrying Malcolm Murgatroyd. Mame Farrell. LC 95-5420. 128p. (J). (gr. 4-7). 1995. 14.00 (*0-374-34838-3*) FS&G.

Marrying Malcolm Murgatroyd. Mame Farrell. 128p. (YA). (gr. 4-7). 1998. pap. 4.95 (*0-374-44744-6*) FS&G.

Marrying Man? Lindsay Armstrong. 1998. per. 3.75 (*0-373-18695-9*, 1-18695-6, Mira Bks) Harlequin Bks.

***Marrying Man.** Millie Criswell. 2000. per. 4.99 (*0-373-29108-6*) Harlequin Bks.

Marrying Man? large type ed. Lindsay Armstrong. (Harlequin Romance Ser.). 1997. 20.95 (*0-263-15119-0*) Mac Lib Ref.

***Marrying Margot.** large type ed. Barbara McMahon. 288p. 2000. 22.95 (*0-263-16488-8*) Thorndike Pr.

***Marrying Margot, Vol. 458.** large type ed. Barbara McMahon. (Large Print Ser.). 2000. mass mkt. 3.50 (*0-373-15858-0*) Harlequin Bks.

***Marrying Margot: Beaufort Brides.** Barbara McMahon. 2000. mass mkt. 3.50 (*0-373-03612-4*) Harlequin Bks.

Marrying Mary. Betty A. Neels. (Romance Ser.: No. 3492). 1998. per. 3.50 (*0-373-03492-X*, 1-03492-5) Harlequin Bks.

Marrying Mary. large type ed. Betty A. Neels. 1998. per. 3.50 (*0-373-15738-X*, Harlequin) Harlequin Bks.

Marrying Mary. large type ed. Betty A. Neels. (Harlequin Romance Ser.). 1996. lib. bdg. 19.95 (*0-263-14594-8*) Mac Lib Ref.

Marrying Mattie. Victoria Dark. 320p. 1999. mass mkt. 4.99 (*0-8217-6101-3*) Kensgtn Pub Corp.

***Marrying Mike... Again: (Men In Blue)** Alicia Scott. (Intimate Moments Ser.: No. 980). 2000. per. 4.50 (*0-373-07980-X*, 1-07980-5) Harlequin Bks.

Marrying Mom. Olivia Goldsmith. 352p. 1999. mass mkt. 6.50 (*0-06-109554-0*, Harp PBks) HarpC.

Marrying Mom. large type ed. Olivia Goldsmith. LC 96-47454. (Basic Ser.). 336p. 1997. lib. bdg. 25.95 (*0-7862-0954-2*) Thorndike Pr.

Marrying Mr. Right: White Weddings. Carolyn Greene. (Romance Ser.: No. 3573). 1999. per. 3.50 (*0-373-03573-X*, 1-03573-2) Harlequin Bks.

Marrying Mr. Right: White Weddings. large type ed. Carolyn Greene. (Larger Print Ser.: No. 419). 1999. per. 3.50 (*0-373-15819-X*, 1-15819-5) Harlequin Bks.

Marrying Nicky. Vivian Leiber. (American Romance Ser.: No. 655). 1996. per. 3.75 (*0-373-16655-9*, 1-16655-2) Harlequin Bks.

***Marrying of Anne of Cleves: Royal Protocol in Tudor England.** Retha M. Warnicke. (Illus.). 342p. 2000. 24.95 (*0-521-77037-8*) Cambridge U Pr.

Marrying off Mother: And Other Stories. Gerald Durrell. 208p. 1993. reprint ed. pap. 10.45 (*1-55970-213-3*, Pub. by Arcade Pub Inc) Time Warner.

Marrying O'Malley. Elizabeth August. (Romance Ser.: No. 1386). 1999. per. 3.50 (*0-373-19386-6*, 1-19386-1) Silhouette.

***Marrying Owen, Vol. 57.** Colleen Faulkner. 2000. mass mkt. 3.99 (*0-8217-6667-8*) Kensgtn Pub Corp.

Marrying Smart. Kalyn W. Gibbens. 176p. 1996. 20.00 (*0-7615-0659-4*) Prima Pub.

Marrying Smart! A Practical Guide for Attracting Your Mate. Kalyn W. Gibbens. Ed. by Douglas Gibbens. LC 94-75125. 128p. (Orig.). 1994. pap. 10.95 (*1-884517-15-3*) Just Your Type.

Marrying Stone. Pamela Morsi. 336p. 1994. mass mkt. 5.50 (*0-515-11431-6*, Jove) Berkley Pub.

Marrying the Animals. Cornelia Hoogland. LC 96-105573. 80p. 1995. pap. 11.95 (*0-919626-84-X*, Pub. by Brick Bks) Genl Dist Srvs.

Marrying the Boss! Leigh Michaels. (Romance Ser.). 1996. per. 3.25 (*0-373-03423-7*, 1-03423-0) Harlequin Bks.

Marrying the Boss! large type ed. Leigh Michaels. (Harlequin Romance Ser.). 1997. 20.95 (*0-263-15124-7*) Mac Lib Ref.

Marrying the Enemy! Elizabeth Power. (Presents Ser.: No. 100). 1999. mass mkt. 3.75 (*0-373-18700-9*, 1-18700-4) Harlequin Bks.

***Marrying the Mistress.** Joanna Trollope. LC 99-462175. 293p. 2000. 23.95 (*0-670-89150-9*, Viking) Viking Penguin.

***Marrying the Mistress.** Joanna Trollope. LC 00-30705. 2000. write for info. (*1-56895-910-9*) Wheeler Pub.

Marrying the Natives: Love & Interracial Marriage. Peter M. Rinaldo. LC 95-92343. 120p. 1996. 14.95 (*0-9622123-9-3*) DorPete Pr.

Marrying Type. Judith Arnold. 1994. mass mkt. 3.50 (*0-373-16553-6*, 1-16553-9) Harlequin Bks.

***Marrying Walker McKay.** Lori Copeland. 384p. 2000. mass mkt. 5.99 (*0-380-80249-X*, Avon Bks) Morrow Avon.

Marrying Well. Lynda Simons. (Yours Truly Ser.). 1997. per. 3.50 (*0-373-52042-5*, 1-52042-8) Silhouette.

Marrying William. Trisha David. (Romance Ser.: No. 449). 1999. mass mkt. 3.50 (*0-373-17449-7*, 1-17449-9) Harlequin Bks.

Mars see Kuntu Drama

Mars see Images

Mars see Galaxy Series

Mars. Ben Bova. 560p. 1993. mass mkt. 6.99 (*0-553-56241-X*) Bantam.

Mars. Arthur Boyd & Peter Porter. (Illus.). 112p. 1989. 34.95 (*0-233-98006-7*, Pub. by Andre Deutsch) Trafalgar.

Mars. Larry D. Brimner. LC 97-42072. (True Bks.). (J). 1998. 21.00 (*0-516-20618-4*) Childrens.

Mars. Larry D. Brimner. LC 97-42072. (True Books: Space (Paper) Ser.). (Illus.). 48p. (J). (gr. 3-5). 1999. pap. text 6.95 (*0-516-26435-4*) Childrens.

Mars. Norma Cole. LC 93-80298. (Poetry Ser.: No. 1). 128p. 1994. pap. text 10.00 (*0-9639321-0-1*) Listening Chamber.

Mars. Michael George. LC 96-47045. (Our Universe Ser.). (Illus.). 32p. (J). (gr. 2-6). 1997. lib. bdg. 22.79 (*1-56766-389-3*) Childs World.

***Mars.** Robin Kerrod. LC 99-31617. (Planet Library Ser.). (Illus.). 32p. (J). (gr. 4-7). 2000. 22.60 (*0-8225-3906-3*, Lerner Publctns) Lerner Pub.

Mars. Ed. by Hugh H. Kieffer et al. LC 92-10951. (Space Science Ser.). (Illus.). 1498p. 1992. 95.00 (*0-8165-1257-4*) U of Ariz Pr.

Mars. Steve Kipp. (Galaxy Ser.). (Illus.). 24p. (J). (gr. k-3). 1997. lib. bdg. 14.00 (*0-516-20892-6*) Childrens.

***Mars.** Steven L. Kipp. (Galaxy Ser.). (Illus.). 24p. (J). (ps-3). 2000. lib. bdg. 15.93 (*0-7368-0520-6*, Bridgestone Bks) Capstone Pr.

Mars. Elaine Landau. LC 90-13097. (First Bks.). (Illus.). 64p. (J). (gr. 4-6). 1991. lib. bdg. 22.00 (*0-531-20012-4*) Watts.

Mars. Elaine Landau. LC 98-46327. (First Bks.). 63p. (J). (gr. 5-7). 1999. lib. bdg. 24.00 (*0-531-20388-3*) Watts.

***Mars.** Elaine Landau. (Illus.). (J). 2000. pap. 8.95 (*0-531-16428-4*) Watts.

Mars. Annalisa McMorrow. (Illus.). 48p. (J). (gr. 1-3). 1998. pap. 7.95 (*1-57612-058-9*, MM2072) Monday Morning Bks.

Mars. Judith Murray. 64p. (Orig.). 1986. write for info. (*0-9617376-0-3*) Murpubco.

Mars. Ed. by Jeff Nicholas. (Wish You Were Here Postcard Book Ser.). (Illus.). 20p. 1998. pap. 4.95 (*0-939365-87-1*) Panorama Intl.

Mars. Seymour Simon. LC 86-31106. (Illus.). 32p. (J). (ps-3). 1987. 18.00 (*0-688-06584-8*, Wm Morrow) Morrow Avon.

Mars. Seymour Simon. LC 86-31106. (Illus.). 32p. (J). (ps-3). 1990. mass mkt. 6.95 (*0-688-09928-9*, Wm Morrow) Morrow Avon.

Mars. Seymour Simon. (J). 1987. 11.15 (*0-606-04741-7*, Pub. by Turtleback) Demco.

Mars. Gregory L. Vogt. LC 93-11219. (Gateway Solar System Ser.). (Illus.). 32p. (J). (gr. 2-4). 1994. lib. bdg. 19.90 (*1-56294-392-8*) Millbrook Pr.

Mars. Gregory L. Vogt. (Gateway Solar System Ser.). (Illus.). 32p. (J). (gr. 2-4). 1996. pap. 6.95 (*0-7613-0156-9*) Millbrook Pr.

Mars. Elaine Landau. (First Bks.). (Illus.). 64p. (J). (gr. 4-6). 1996. reprint ed. pap. 6.95 (*0-531-15773-3*) Watts.

Mars: A Science Fiction Vision. Richard Grossinger. (Illus.). 230p. 1971. pap. 3.50 (*0-913028-00-2*) North Atlantic.

Mars: A Source Guide. 1991. lib. bdg. 59.95 (*0-8490-4891-5*) Gordon Pr.

Mars: Back Care. Oliver. 1996. 3.5 hd 205.00 (*0-7506-2672-0*) Buttrwrth-Heinemann.

***Mars: Exploring the Red Planet.** Wolfgang Engelhardt. (Start Me Up Ser.). (Illus.). 64p. 1999. 15.95 (*1-58185-012-3*) Quadrillion Media.

Mars: Past, Present, & Future. Ed. by E. B. Pritchard. (PAAS Ser.: Vol. 145). 324p. 1992. 69.95 (*1-56347-043-8*, V-145) AIAA.

Mars: The Law of Insolvency in South Africa. 8th ed. E. De La Rey. 824p. 1988. 107.00 (*0-7021-2176-2*, Pub. by Juta & Co) Gaunt.

Mars: The Living Planet. Barry DiGregorio. LC 96-37580. (Illus.). 300p. 1997. 25.00 (*1-883319-58-7*) Frog Ltd CA.

Mars: The Next Step. Arthur E. Smith. (Illus.). 168p. 1989. pap. 39.00 (*0-85274-026-3*) IOP Pub.

***Mars: The Red Planet.** Patricia Demuth. LC 98-13996. (All Aboard Reading Ser.). (Illus.). 48p. (J). (gr. 2-4). 1998. pap. 3.99 (*0-448-41843-6*, G & D) Peng Put Young Read.

Mars: The Red Planet, Level 3. Patricia Demuth. LC 98-13996. (All Aboard Reading Ser.). (Illus.). 32p. (J). (gr. 2-3). 1998. lib. bdg. 13.89 (*0-448-41888-6*, G & D) Peng Put Young Read.

Mars: The War Lord. Alan Leo. 99p. 1993. reprint ed. spiral bd. 9.00 (*0-7873-0550-2*) Hlth Research.

Mars: Uncovering the Secrets of the red Planet. Paul Raeburn. LC 98-13991. 232p. 1998. 40.50 (*0-7922-7373-7*) Natl Geog.

***Mars: Uncovering the Secrets of the Red Planet.** Paul Raeburn. 232p. 2000. per. 25.00 (*0-7922-7614-0*) Natl Geog.

Mars No. 2: Gods of Mars. Edgar Rice Burroughs. 190p. 1985. mass mkt. 4.99 (*0-345-32439-0*, Del Rey) Ballantine Pub Grp.

Mars No. 9: Synthetic Men of Mars. Edgar Rice Burroughs. 160p. 1986. mass mkt. 5.99 (*0-345-33930-4*, Del Rey) Ballantine Pub Grp.

Mars - Earth Catastrophes. Donald W. Patten. 1988. 19.95 (*0-685-20125-2*); pap. 14.95 (*0-685-20126-0*) Pacific Mer.

***Mars, a Growing Nation.** Lenora Lewis-Stratford. LC 00-90313. 2000. pap. 10.95 (*0-533-13532-X*) Vantage.

Mars & Her Children. Marge Piercy. 1992. pap. 15.00 (*0-679-73877-0*) Knopf.

M

Mars & Venus Book of Days: 365 Inspriations to Enrich Your Relationships. John Gray. LC 98-40600. 368p. 1998. 22.00 (*0-06-019277-1*) HarpC.

Mars & Venus in Love: Gray,&John. abr. ed. John Gray. 1996. audio 18.00 (*0-694-51713-5*, CPN 2579) HarperAudio.

Mars & Venus in Love: Inspiring & Heartfelt Stories of Relationships That Work. John Gray. LC 96-20228. 192p. 1996. 18.00 (*0-06-017471-4*) HarpC.

Mars And Venus In Love: Inspiring & Heartfelt Stories of Relationships that Work. John Gray. 256p. 1999. mass mkt. 6.50 (*0-06-109829-9*) HarpC.

Mars & Venus in the Bedroom see Mars et Venus sur l'oreiller

***Mars & Venus in the Bedroom.** John Gray. 1999. audio 20.00 (*0-694-52215-5*) HarpC.

Mars & Venus in the Bedroom, Set. abr. ed. John Gray. 1995. audio 18.00 (*1-55994-883-3*, CPN 2486, Pub. by HarperAudio) Lndmrk Audiobks.

Mars & Venus in the Bedroom: A Guide to Lasting Romance & Passion. John Gray. LC 95-1125. 224p. 1995. 24.00 (*0-06-017212-6*) HarpC.

Mars & Venus in the Bedroom: A Guide to Lasting Romance & Passion. John Gray. 224p. 1997. pap. 13.00 (*0-06-092793-3*, Perennial) HarperTrade.

Mars & Venus on a Date: A Guide for Navigating the 5 Stages of Dating to Create a Loving & Lasting Relationship. John Gray. LC 97-19991. 400p. 1997. 25.00 (*0-06-017472-2*) HarpC.

Mars & Venus on a Date: A Guide for Navigating the 5 Stages of Dating to Create a Loving & Lasting Relationship. John Gray. 496p. 1998. mass mkt. 6.99 (*0-06-104463-6*) HarpC.

Mars & Venus on a Date: A Guide for Navigating the 5 Stages of Dating to Create a Loving & Lasting Relationship. John Gray. 400p. 1999. pap. 13.00 (*0-06-093221-X*) HarpC.

Mars & Venus on a Date: Gray,&John. abr. ed. John Gray. 1997. audio 18.00 (*0-694-51845-X*, CPN 2658) HarperAudio.

Mars & Venus Starting Over: A Practical Guide for Finding Love Again after a Painful Breakup. large type ed. John Gray. 384p. 1999. pap. 25.00 (*0-06-093303-8*) HarpC.

Mars & Venus Starting Over: A Practical Guide for Finding Love Again after a Painful Breakup, Divorce, or the Loss of a Loved One. John Gray. LC 98-175566. 352p. 1998. 25.00 (*0-06-017598-2*) HarpC.

Mars & Venus Starting Over: A Practical Guide for Finding Love Again after a Painful Breakup, Divorce, or the Loss of a Loved One. John Gray. 432p. 1999. mass mkt. 6.99 (*0-06-109838-8*) HarpC.

***Mars & Venus Starting Over: A Practical Guide for Finding Love Again after a Painful Breakup, Divorce, Or the Loss of a Loved One.** John Gray. 334p. 2000. pap. 14.00 (*0-06-093027-6*) HarpC.

***Mars & Venus Starting Over: Gray,&John, Set.** abr. ed. John Gray. 1998. audio 18.00 (*0-694-51976-6*, JG19R, Pub. by HarperAudio) Lndmrk Audiobks.

Mars & Venus Together Forever: A Practical Guide to Creating Lasting Intimacy. John Gray. 368p. 1998. mass mkt. 6.99 (*0-06-104457-1*) HarpC.

Mars & Venus Together Forever: Relationship Skills for Lasting Love. rev. ed. John Gray. 288p. 1996. pap. 13.00 (*0-06-092661-9*, Harp PBks) HarpC.

Mars Arena. James Axler. 1997. per. 5.50 (*0-373-62538-3*, 1-62538-3, Wrldwide Lib) Harlequin Bks.

Mars Attacks. Troll Communications Staff. 1996. pap. 3.95 (*0-8167-4314-2*) Troll Communs.

***Mars Attacks!, Vol. No. 4.** Lianne Sentar. 1999. pap. 4.99 (*1-892213-27-3*) Mixx Enter Inc.

Mars Book: A Guide to Your Personal Energy & Motivation. Donna Van Toen. 302p. (Orig.). 1988. pap. 12.95 (*0-87728-666-3*) Weiser.

***Mars Crossing.** Geoffrey A. Landis. 1999. write for info. (*0-8125-7648-9*) Tor Bks.

***Mars Crossing.** Geoffrey A. Landis. 2000. text 24.95 (*0-312-87201-1*) Tor Bks.

Mars Effect: A French Test of over 1,000 Sports Champions. Claude Benski et al. LC 95-44463. 157p. 1996. pap. 21.00 (*0-87975-988-7*) Prometheus Bks.

Mars et Venus sur l'oreiller. Tr. of Mars & Venus in the Bedroom. (FRE., Illus.). pap., boxed set 14.95 incl. audio (*2-89517-023-1*, Pub. by Coffragants) Penton Overseas.

Mars Gun. large type ed. Fred Harrison. 304p. 1992. pap. 16.99 (*0-7089-7247-0*, Linford) Ulverscroft.

Mars in Myth: A Science. John Hamilton. LC 97-34677. (Mission To Mars Ser.). (J). 1998. lib. bdg. 14.95 (*1-56239-827-X*) ABDO Pub Co.

***Mars Internet Guide.** 50p. 2000. pap. 10.00 (*1-883573-21-1*, Lightning Rod) Pride & Imprints.

Mar's Meanderings: Things You Thought You Didn't Know - A Compilation of Educational, Humorous, & Thought-Provoking Articles. Mary R. Dees. 128p. (Orig.). 1993. pap. 7.95 (*0-9630600-1-5*) Marmor.

Mars Mystery: The Secret Connection Linking Earth's Ancient Civilization & the Red Planet. Graham Hancock. 1999. pap. 16.00 (*0-609-80223-2*, Crown) Crown Pub Group.

***Mars Mystery: The Secret Connection Linking Earth's Ancient Civilization & the Red Planet.** Graham Hancock et al. (Illus.). 320p. 1998. 16.95 (*0-385-25684-1*) Doubleday.

Mars Mystery: The Secret Connection Linking Earth's Ancient Civilization & the Red Planet. Graham Hanscock & Robert Bauval. LC 98-17933. 16p. 1998. 26.00 (*0-609-60086-9*) Crown Pub Group.

Mars Observer Mission: Return to the Red Planet. (Illus.). 59p. (Orig.). (C). 1996. pap. text 25.00 (*0-7881-2671-7*) DIANE Pub.

Mars Pathfinder Approach to "Faster-Better-Cheaper" Hand of from the NASA - JPL Pathfinder Team on How Limitations Can Guide You to Breakthroughs. Price Pritchett & Brian Muirhead. LC 98-154527. (Illus.). 85p. 1998. pap. 9.95 (*0-944002-74-9*) Pritchett Assocs.

Mars Plus. Frederik Pohl & Thomas T. Thomas. 352p. 1994. 20.00 (*0-671-87605-8*) Baen Bks.

Mars Plus. Frederik Pohl & Thomas T. Thomas. 352p. 1995. mass mkt. 5.99 (*0-671-87665-1*) Baen Bks.

***Mars Project.** 2001. write for info. (*0-06-105184-5*, HarpEntertain) Morrow Avon.

Mars Project. Wernher Von Braun. 112p. 1991. pap. text 9.95 (*0-252-06227-2*) U of Ill Pr.

Mars Reference Atmosphere, Vol. 2, Pt. 2. Ed. by A. J. Kliore. (Illus.). 107p. 1982. pap. 43.00 (*0-08-029126-0*, Pergamon Pr) Elsevier.

Mars Underground. William K. Hartmann. LC 97-1398. 352p. 1997. text 24.95 (*0-312-86342-X*) St Martin.

Mars Underground. William K. Hartmann. 1999. mass mkt. 6.99 (*0-8125-8039-7*, Pub. by Tor Bks) St Martin.

Mars Underground Cities Discovered. Ruth E. Norman. (Tesla Speaks Ser.: Vol. 12). (Illus.). 344p. 1977. 14.00 (*0-932642-35-7*) Unarius Acad Sci.

***Mars Unmasked: The Changing Face of Urban Operations.** Sean J. A. Edwards. (Illus.). xxiv, 108p. 2000. pap. 15.00 (*0-8330-2820-0*) Rand Corp.

Marsalis on Music. Wynton Marsalis. Date not set. pap. write for info. (*0-393-31530-4*) Norton.

Marsalis on Music. Wynton Marsalis. (Illus.). 175p. (YA). (gr. 5 up). 1995. 29.95 (*0-393-03881-5*) Norton.

Marschalck in Hispanien. Jeronimo. Ed. by Willi Flemming. 298p. 1973. reprint ed. write for info. (*3-487-04389-0*) G Olms Pubs.

Marsden: Calculo Vectorial. 2nd ed. (SPA.). 688p. (C). 1991. pap. text 30.00 (*0-201-62935-6*) Addison-Wesley.

Marsden Hartley. Bruce Robertson. LC 93-46820. (Illus.). 160p. 1995. 45.00 (*0-8109-3416-7*, Pub. by Abrams) Time Warner.

Marsden Hartley: An American Modern. Patricia McDonnell. LC 97-13221. (Illus.). 86p. 1997. pap. 22.95 (*1-885116-04-7*) Weisman Art.

Marsden Hartley: Paintings & Drawings. Text by Lawrence Salander. (Illus.). 52p. 1988. pap. 30.00 (*1-58821-039-1*) Salander OReilly.

Marsden Hartley: Paintings & Drawings. Text by Karen Wilken. (Illus.). 80p. 1985. pap. 35.00 (*1-58821-040-5*) Salander OReilly.

Marsden Hartley: Six Berlin Paintings. Text by Gail Levin. (Illus.). 1992. pap. 15.00 (*1-58821-038-3*) Salander OReilly.

Marsden Hartley: The Biography of an American Artist. Townsend Ludington. LC 98-29358. (Illus.). 325p. 1998. pap. text 21.00 (*0-8014-8580-0*) Cornell U Pr.

Marsden Hartley: The Late Figure Works. Frwd. by Lawrence Salander. (Illus.). 69p. 1990. pap. write for info. (*1-58821-037-5*) Salander OReilly.

Marsden Hartley in Maine. Scribner Ames. LC 73-153218. 1972. 8.95 (*0-89101-025-4*) U Maine Pr.

Marse Henry: A Biography of Henry Watterson. Isaac F. Marcosson. LC 74-156200. (Illus.). 269p. 1971. reprint ed. lib. bdg. 65.00 (*0-8371-6150-9*, MAMH) Greenwood.

Marse Henry: An Autobiography, 2 vols, Set. Henry Watterson. (American Newspapermen 1790-1933 Ser.). (Illus.). 629p. 1974. reprint ed. 45.00 (*0-8464-0002-2*) Beekman Pubs.

Mars/Earth Enigma: A Sacred Message to Mankind. DeAnna Emerson. LC 95-23023. (Illus.). 320p. 1996. pap. 19.95 (*1-880090-18-X*) Galde Pr.

Marseille Agglomeration City Plan. (Grafocarte Maps Ser.). 1995. 8.95 (*2-7416-0022-8*, 80022) Michelin.

Marseille Centre City Plan. (Grafocarte Maps Ser.). 1993. 8.95 (*2-7416-0062-7*, 80062) Michelin.

Marseilles, Genoa & Pisa: A Beatrix Potter Photograph Album Representing a Pictorial Biography. fac. ed. Ed. & Frwd. by Ivy Trent. LC 98-86673. (Illus.). 1998. write for info. (*0-9666084-0-2*) Cotsen Occas Pr.

Marseilles Tarot. Stuart R. Kaplan. 1977. pap. 16.00 (*0-913866-60-1*, 1803) US Games Syst.

Marseille/Toulon/Nice Map. 1998. 6.95 (*2-06-700084-5*, 84) Michelin.

Marsena & Other Stories of the Wartime. Harold Frederic. LC 72-110191. (Short Story Index Reprint Ser.). 1977. 19.95 (*0-8369-3342-7*) Ayer.

Marsena & Other Stories of the Wartime see Collected Works of Harold Frederic

Marsena & Other Stories of the Wartime. Harold Frederic. (Collected Works of Harold Frederic). 1988. reprint ed. lib. bdg. 59.00 (*0-7812-1190-5*) Rprt Serv.

***Marsfile.com.** Gary Tigerman. 2001. write for info. (*0-380-97670-6*, Wm Morrow) Morrow Avon.

***Marsfile.com.** Gary Tigerman. 2002. mass mkt. write for info. (*0-380-79920-0*) Morrow Avon.

Marsh Flies of California: (Diptera, Sciomyzidae) fac. ed. T. W. Fisher & Robert E. Orth. LC 82-13428. (Bulletin of the California Insect Survey Ser.: No. 24). 125p. 1983. reprint ed. pap. 38.80 (*0-7837-8126-1*, 204793300008) Bks Demand.

Marsh (Gavkhuni) Jafar Modarres-Sadeqi. Tr. by Afkham Darbandi from PER. LC 96-44379. (Bibliotheca Iranica Ser.: No. 3).Tr. of Gavkhuni. 110p. (Orig.). 1996. pap. 8.95 (*1-56859-044-X*) Mazda Pubs.

Marsh Genealogy, Giving Several Thousand Descendants of John Marsh of Hartford, Connecticut, 1636-1895. D. W. Marsh. (Illus.). 585p. 1989. reprint ed. pap. 87.60 (*0-8328-0853-9*); reprint ed. lib. bdg. 95.60 (*0-8328-0852-0*) Higginson Bk Co.

Marsh Island. Sarah Orne Jewett. (Collected Works of Sarah Orne Jewett). 1988. reprint ed. lib. bdg. 59.00 (*0-7812-1307-X*) Rprt Serv.

Marsh King. Mark Dunster. 10p. (Orig.). (J). 1990. pap. 4.00 (*0-89642-184-8*) Linden Pubs.

***Marsh King's Daughter.** Elizabeth Chadwick. 416p. 2000. 25.95 (*0-312-26491-7*) St Martin.

Marsh, Meadow, Mountain: Natural Places of the Delaware Valley. Ed. by John J. Harding. LC 85-17297. (Illus.). 256p. 1986. 29.95 (*0-87722-391-2*) Temple U Pr.

Marsh, Meadow, Mountain: Natural Places of the Delaware Valley. Ed. by John J. Harding. LC 85-17297. (Illus.). 288p. 1986. pap. 16.95 (*0-87722-401-3*) Temple U Pr.

Marsh Odinokikh. limited ed. Sergei Dovlatov. Ed. by Roman Sonynn. LC 83-61816.Tr. of March of the Lonely. (RUS.). 100p. 1983. pap. text 20.00 (*0-914265-06-7*) New Eng Pub MA.

Marsh Tales: Market Hunting, Duck Trapping, & Gunning. William N. Smith. LC 85-40531. (Illus.). 240p. 1985. 18.95 (*0-87033-338-0*, Tidewtr Pubs) Cornell Maritime.

Marsha Gets Mad. Judy Mullican. (HRL Big Bks.). (Illus.). 8p. (J). (ps-k). 1995. pap. text 10.95 (*1-57332-013-7*) HighReach Lrning.

***Marsha Is Only a Flower.** Bottner. (Illus.). 48p. (J). 2000. write for info. (*0-307-46330-3*) Gldn Bks Pub Co.

***Marsha Is Only a Flower.** Illus. by Barbara Bottner & Denise Brunkus. LC 99-24650. (Road to Reading Ser.). 48p. (J). 2000. pap. text 3.99 (*0-307-26330-4*, Whitman Coin) St Martin.

Marsha Makes Me Sick. Barbara Bottner. LC 98-5800. (Road to Reading Ser.). (Illus.). 32p. (J). 1998. pap. 3.99 (*0-307-26302-9*, 26302) Gldn Bks Pub Co.

***Marsha Makes Me Sick.** Barbara Bottner. (J). 1999. 9.44 (*0-606-16139-2*) Turtleback.

Marsha McCloskey's Block Party: A Quilter's Extravaganza of 120 Rotary-Cut Block Patterns. Marsha McCloskey. LC 98-25353. (Illus.). 256p. 1998. text 29.95 (*0-87596-756-6*) Rodale Pr Inc.

***Marsha McCloskey's Block Party: A Quilter's Extravaganza of 120 Rotary-Cut Block Patterns.** Marsha McCloskey. (Illus.). 256p. 2000. pap. 18.95 (*1-57954-266-2*) Rodale Pr Inc.

Marsha Norman: A Casebook. Ed. by Linda G. Brown. LC 95-52416. (Casebooks on Modern Dramatists Ser.: Vol. 19). 272p. 1996. text 60.00 (*0-8153-1352-7*, H1750) Garland.

Marsha Norman Vol. 1: Collected Plays. Marsha Norman. LC 97-7665. (Contemporary American Playwrights Ser.). 336p. (Orig.). 1997. pap. 19.95 (*1-57525-029-2*) Smith & Kraus.

Marshal. Lauran Paine. 154p. 1985. 14.95 (*0-8027-4053-7*) Walker & Co.

Marshal. large type ed. Frank Gruber. 1990. pap. 16.99 (*0-7089-6941-0*, Linford) Ulverscroft.

Marshal for Lawless. large type ed. Ray Hogan. LC 95-2471. 144p. 1995. reprint ed. pap. 17.95 (*0-7838-1281-7*, G K Hall Lrg Type) Mac Lib Ref.

Marshal from Deadwood. large type ed. Todhunter Ballard. LC 97-40245. (Sagebrush Large Print Westerns Ser.). 1997. lib. bdg. 18.95 (*1-57490-094-3*) T T Beeler.

Marshal Law: Blood Sweat & Fears Collection. Pat Mills & Kevin O'Neill. (Illus.). 168p. 1993. pap. 15.95 (*1-878574-95-7*) Dark Horse Comics.

Marshal Law: The Deadlands Reference Screen. Shane Hensley. (Illus.). 40p. (Orig.). 1996. pap. 15.00 (*1-889546-09-7*) Pinnacle Ent.

Marshal Matt & the Case of the Freezing Fingers. Nancy I. Sanders. LC 96-53870. (Marshal Matt, Mysteries with a Value Ser.). (Illus.). (J). (ps-2). 1997. 4.99 (*0-570-04811-7*, 56-1826) Concordia.

Marshal Matt & the Case of the Secret Code. Nancy I. Sanders. LC 96-24209. (Marshal Matt Ser.). (Illus.). 48p. (J). (ps-2). 1997. pap. 4.99 (*0-570-04798-6*, 56-1818) Concordia.

Marshal Matt & the Puzzling Prints. Nancy I. Sanders. LC 96-9627. (Marshal Matt Ser.). (Illus.). 48p. (J). (ps-2). 1997. pap. 4.99 (*0-570-04799-4*, 56-1819) Concordia.

Marshal Matt & the Slippery Snacks Mystery. Nancy I. Sanders. LC 96-10620. (Marshal Matt, Mysteries with a Value Ser.). (Illus.). 48p. (J). (ps-2). 1996. pap. 4.99 (*0-570-04796-X*, 56-1816) Concordia.

Marshal Matt & the Topsy-Turvy Trail Mystery. Nancy I. Sanders. LC 96-10621. (Marshal Matt, Mysteries with a Value Ser.: Bk. 2). (Illus.). 48p. (J). (ps-2). 1996. pap. 4.99 (*0-570-04797-8*, 56-1817) Concordia.

Marshal of Borado. large type ed. Alan Irwin. (Linford Western Large Print Ser.). 240p. 1998. pap. 17.99 (*0-7089-5203-8*, Linford) Ulverscroft.

Marshal of Borg City. large type ed. Walt Santee. (Linford Western Library). 272p. 1992. pap. 16.99 (*0-7089-7182-2*, Linford) Ulverscroft.

Marshal of Sangaree. large type ed. Louis Trimble. (Linford Romance Library). 256p. 1988. pap. 16.99 (*0-7089-6611-X*, Linford) Ulverscroft.

Marshal of Twisted Fork. large type ed. Wade A. Bronson. 221p. 1994. pap. 18.99 (*1-85389-440-0*, Dales) Ulverscroft.

Marshal Redleaf. large type ed. A. A. Andrews. (Linford Western Library). 1991. pap. 16.99 (*0-7089-7009-5*) Ulverscroft.

Marshal Royal: Jazz Survivor. Marshal Royal & Claire P. Gordon. (Bayou Jazz Ser.). 224p. 2000. 27.95 (*0-304-33836-2*) Continuum.

Marshal Tito: A Bibliography, 1. April Carter. LC 89-31984. (Bibliographies of World Leaders Ser.: No. 1). 160p. 1989. lib. bdg. 75.00 (*0-313-28087-8*, CMT/, Greenwood Pr) Greenwood.

Marshal Without a Badge. large type ed. Bret Rey. (Linford Western Library). 272p. 1993. pap. 16.99 (*0-7089-7362-0*, Linford) Ulverscroft.

Marshaling Social Support: Formats, Processes, & Effects. Ed. by Benjamin H. Gottlieb. LC 87-26305. 337p. 1988. reprint ed. pap. 104.50 (*0-608-01170-3*, 205947000001) Bks Demand.

Marshaling Technology for Development: Proceedings of a Symposium. National Research Council Staff et al. LC 95-71477. 264p. (Orig.). (C). 1995. pap. text 35.00 (*0-309-05349-8*) Natl Acad Pr.

Marshall. Lauran Paine. 176p. 1987. pap. 2.50 (*0-380-70187-1*, Avon Bks) Morrow Avon.

Marshall - Covington, Oklahoma. Seekers of Oklahoma Heritage Staff. (Illus.). 699p. 1987. 50.00 (*0-88107-082-3*) Curtis Media.

Marshall & the Heiress. large type ed. Patricia Potter. LC 96-38771. 1997. 23.95 (*0-7862-0925-9*) Thorndike Pr.

Marshall Art of Creative Writing. Jimmie B. Marshall. 1998. write for info. (*0-9625557-3-8*) Excelsior Cee.

Marshall Asphalt for Airfield Pavement Works. 92p. 1995. pap. 35.00 (*0-11-772689-3*, HM26893, Pub. by Statnry Office) Bernan Associates.

Marshall Attack Made Easy. John Elburg. 42p. (Orig.). 1994. pap. 6.50 (*0-945470-41-X*) Chess Ent.

Marshall, Barrett & Co. A Word Processing Simulation. Mark W. Lehman et al. (C). 1989. pap. text 29.95 (*0-538-80124-7*, WS60AC) S-W Pub.

Marshall Cavendish International Wildlife Encyclopedia, 25 vols. Ed. by Maurice Burton & Robert Burton. (Illus.). 3000p. 1991. reprint ed. lib. bdg. 499.95 (*0-86307-734-X*) Marshall Cavendish.

Marshall County, Kentucky. Leon L. Freeman & Edward C. Olds. (Illus.). 344p. 1993. reprint ed. lib. bdg. write for info. (*0-8328-2965-X*) Higginson Bk Co.

Marshall County, Mississippi Probate & Will Records. Betty C. Wiltshire. 306p. (Orig.). 1996. pap. 25.00 (*1-885480-10-5*) Pioneer Pubng.

Marshall County, MS: From the Collection of Chesley Thorne Smith. Mary Carol Miller. (Images of America Ser.). (Illus.). 128p. 1998. pap. 16.99 (*0-7524-1211-6*) Arcadia Publng.

Marshall Elliot, a Retrospect. Edward C. Armstrong. (Elliott Monographs: Vol. 15). 1923. pap. 25.00 (*0-527-02618-2*) Periodicals Srv.

Marshall Family: or A Genealogical Chart of the Descendants of John Marshall & Elizabeth Markham, His Wife. W. M. Paxton. (Illus.). 415p. 1989. reprint ed. pap. 62.00 (*0-8328-0855-5*); reprint ed. lib. bdg. 70.00 (*0-8328-0854-7*) Higginson Bk Co.

***Marshall Faulk.** Rob Rains. (Illus.). 1999. pap. 4.95 (*1-58261-167-X*) Sprts Pubng.

***Marshall Faulk: Rushing to Glory.** Rob Rains. (SuperStar Series: Vol. 8). 96p. (J). 1999. pap. 4.95 (*1-58261-191-2*, Pub. by Sprts Pubng) Partners-West.

Marshall Festus, Vol. 3. Gary McCarthy. (Gunsmoke Ser.). 1999. mass mkt. 5.99 (*0-425-16974-X*) Berkley Pub.

Marshall Fowler Album. A. Condie. (Illus.). 104p. 1996. pap. 29.95 (*1-85638-005-X*, MBI 123494AE, Pub. by A T Condie Pubns) Motorbooks Intl.

Marshall Gambit in the French & Sicilian Defenses. Riley Sheffield & Rick Kennedy. (Openings Ser.). (Illus.). 68p. (Orig.). 1988. 8.00 (*0-939433-06-0*) Caissa Edit.

***Marshall Islands: A Country Study Guide.** Global Investment & Business Center, Inc. Staff. (World Country Study Guides Library: Vol. 109). (Illus.). 350p. 2000. pap. 59.00 (*0-7397-2407-X*) Intl Business Pubns.

Marshall Islands - A Country Study Guide: Basic Information for Research & Pleasure. Global Investment Center, USA Staff. (World Country Study Guide Library: Vol. 109). (Illus.). 350p. 1999. pap. 59.00 (*0-7397-1506-2*) Intl Business Pubns.

***Marshall Islands Business Intelligence Report, 190 vols.** Global Investment & Business Center, Inc. Staff. (World Business Intelligence Library: Vol. 109). (Illus.). 350p. 2000. pap. 99.95 (*0-7397-2607-2*) Intl Business Pubns.

***Marshall Islands Business Law Handbook, 190 vols.** Global Investment & Business Center, Inc. Staff. (Global Business Law Handbooks Library: Vol. 109). (Illus.). 350p. 2000. pap. 99.95 (*0-7397-2007-4*) Intl Business Pubns.

Marshall Islands Business Law Handbook-98. Russian Information & Business Center, Inc. Staff. (World Business Law Library-98). (Illus.). 350p. 1998. pap. 99.00 (*1-57751-840-3*) Intl Business Pubns.

***Marshall Islands Business Opportunity Yearbook.** Global Investment & Business Center, Inc. Staff. (Global Business Opportunity Yearbooks Library: Vol. 109). (Illus.). 2000. pap. 99.95 (*0-7397-2207-7*) Intl Business Pubns.

***Marshall Islands Business Opportunity Yearbook: Export-Import, Investment & Business Opportunities.** International Business Publications, U. S. A. Staff & Global Investment Center, U. S. A. Staff. (Global Business Opportunity Yearbooks Library: Vol. 109). (Illus.). 350p. 1999. pap. 99.95 (*0-7397-1307-8*) Intl Business Pubns.

***Marshall Islands Country Review 2000.** Robert C. Kelly et al. (Illus.). 60p. 1999. pap. 39.95 (*1-58310-533-6*) CountryWatch.

***Marshall Islands Foreign Policy & Government Guide.** Contrib. by Global Investment & Business Center, Inc. Staff. (World Foreign Policy & Government Library: Vol. 105). (Illus.). 350p. 1999. pap. 99.00 (*0-7397-3603-5*) Intl Business Pubns.

***Marshall Islands Foreign Policy & Government Guide.** Global Investment & Business Center, Inc. Staff. (World Foreign Policy & Government Library: Vol. 105). (Illus.). 350p. 2000. pap. 99.95 (*0-7397-3807-0*) Intl Business Pubns.

***Marshall Islands Investment & Business Guide.** Global Investment & Business Center, Inc. Staff. (Global Investment & Business Guide Library: Vol. 109). (Illus.). 2000. pap. 99.95 (*0-7397-1807-X*) Intl Business Pubns.

M

An Asterisk (*) at the beginning of an entry indicates that the title is appearing for the first time.

Marshall Islands Investment & Business Guide: Economy, Export-Import, Business & Investment Climate, Business Contacts. Contrib. by Russian Information & Business Center, Inc. Staff. (Russia, NIS & Emerging Markets Investment & Business Library-98). (Illus.). 350p. 1998. pap. 99.00 (1-57751-897-7) Intl Business Pubns.

***Marshall Islands Investment & Business Guide: Export-Import, Investment & Business Opportunities.** International Business Publications, USA Staff & Global Investment Center, USA Staff. (World Investment & Business Guide Library-99: Vol. 109). (Illus.). 350p. 1999. pap. 99.95 (0-7397-0304-8) Intl Business Pubns.

Marshall Islands 1996 Economic Report. Asian Development Bank Staff. 161p. 1998. pap. 10.00 (971-561-121-4, Pub. by Asian Devel Bank) Paul & Co Pubs.

***Marshall Loeb's 52 Weeks to Financial Fitness.** Marshall Loeb. 2000. 25.00 (0-8129-3337-0, Times Business) Crown Pub Group.

Marshall Loeb's Lifetime Financial Strategies: The Ultimate Guide to Future Wealth & Security. Marshall Loeb. LC 95-17011. (Illus.). 880p. 1996. 27.95 (0-316-53075-1, Pub. by Bulfinch Pr) Little.

Marshall Loeb's Lifetime Financial Strategies: Your Ultimate Guide to Future Wealth & Security. Marshall Loeb. 1996. 27.95 (0-614-15440-5) Little.

Marshall Loeb's Money Guide, 1989. rev. ed. Marshall Loeb. 512p. 1988. pap. 12.95 (0-316-53067-0) Little.

Marshall Loeb's Money Guide, 1990, Vol. 1. Marshall Loeb. 1989. pap. 13.95 (0-316-53064-6) Little.

Marshall McLuhan: The Medium & the Messenger. Philip Marchand. (Illus.). 352p. 1989. 19.45 (0-89919-485-0, Pub. by Ticknor & Fields) HM.

Marshall McLuhan: The Medium & the Messenger. rev. ed. Philip Marchand. LC 98-65303. 336p. 1998. pap. text 17.50 (0-262-63186-5) MIT Pr.

Marshall Plan. Allen W. Dulles. LC 92-15793. 160p. 1993. 30.00 (0-85496-350-2) Berg Pubs.

Marshall Plan: America, Britain, & the Reconstruction of Western Europe, 1947-1952. Michael J. Hogan. 496p. 1989. reprint ed. pap. text 21.95 (0-521-37840-0) Cambridge U Pr.

Marshall Plan & Its Legacy. Peter Grose. (C). 1998. pap. 9.95 (0-87609-207-5) Coun Foreign.

Marshall Plan Days. Charles P. Kindleberger. 280p. (C). 1987. text 45.00 (0-04-332142-9) Routledge.

Marshall Plan Fifty Years after. Martin A. Schain. text 45.00 (0-312-22962-3) St Martin.

Marshall Plan for Novel Writing. Evan Marshall. LC 98-35710. 240p. 1998. 17.99 (0-89879-848-5, Wrtrs Digest Bks) F & W Pubns Inc.

Marshall Plan for the 1990s: An International Roundtable on World Economic Development. Ed. by Charles A. Cerami. LC 88-27503. 276p. 1989. 59.95 (0-275-93137-4, C3137, Praeger Pubs) Greenwood.

***Marshall Plan from Those Who Made It Succeed.** Ed. & Pref. by Constantine C. Menges. 424p. 2000. pap. 39.50 (0-7618-1658-5) U Pr of Amer.

***Marshall Plan in Austria.** Ed. by Gunter Bischoff et al. LC 99-87781. (Contemporary Austrian Studies: Vol. 8). 475p. 2000. pap. 40.00 (0-7658-0679-7) Transaction Pubs.

Marshall Plan Revisited: The European Recovery Program in Economic Perspective, 55. Imanuel Wexler. LC 83-5694. (Contributions in Economics & Economic History Ser.: No. 55). (Illus.). 327p. 1983. 42.95 (0-313-24011-6, WMR/) Greenwood.

Marshall, the Courthouse Mouse: A Tail of the U. S. Supreme Court. Peter W. Barnes & Cheryl S. Barnes. LC 98-90151. (Illus.). 32p. (J). (gr. 2-5). 1997. 15.95 (0-9637688-6-7) Vacation Spot.

Marshall Trimble's Original Arizona Trivia. Marshall Trimble. 1996. pap. 8.95 (1-885590-05-9) Golden West Pub.

Marshall Valuation Service. Marshall & Swift Staff. 1998. ring bd. 229.95 (1-56842-067-6) Marshall & Swift.

Marshall Valuation Service. Marshall & Swift Staff. 1999. ring bd. 246.95 (1-56842-073-0) Marshall & Swift.

***Marshall Valuation Service.** Marshall & Swift Staff. 2000. ring bd. 349.95 incl. cd-rom (1-56842-079-X) Marshall & Swift.

Marshall Yesterday: An Adventure Back in Time for Children & Adults. Anne T. Dennis. 36p. (J). (gr. 4 up). 1991. pap. 5.00 (1-879703-00-9) Marshall Regnl Arts.

Marshallese-English Dictionary. Takaji Abo et al. LC 76-26156. (PALI Language Texts, Micronesia Ser.). 626p. 1976. pap. text 25.00 (0-8248-0457-0) UH Pr.

***Marshalling of Securities.** Paul A. U. Ali. 260p. 1999. text 160.00 (0-19-826865-3) OUP.

Marshalls, Increasing the Tempo. Robert D. Heinl & John Crown. (Elite Unit Ser.: No. 29). (Illus.). 208p. reprint ed. 39.95 (0-89839-164-4) Battery Pr.

Marshall's Iowa Title Opinions & Standards Annotated. 2nd ed. George F. Madsen. 65.00 (0-327-12319-2) LEXIS Pub.

Marshall's Mission to China: December 1945 to January 1947, 2 vols., Vol. I: The Report. George C. Marshall. Ed. by Lyman P. Van Slyke. LC 76-43634. 465p. 1976. lib. bdg. 65.00 (0-313-26910-6, U6910) Greenwood.

Marshall's Mission to China: December 1945 to January 1947, 2 vols., Vol. 2. George C. Marshall. Ed. by Lyman P. Van Slyke. LC 76-43634. 522p. 1976. lib. bdg. 65.00 (0-313-26911-4, U6911) Greenwood.

Marshall's Physiology of Reproduction Vol. 2: Reproduction Function in the Male. 4th ed. Ed. by G. E. Lamming. (Illus.). 704p. 1990. text 125.00 (0-443-01967-3) Church.

***Marshall's Tendencies: What Can Economists Know?** John Sutton. LC 00-29196. (Eyskens Lectures). (Illus.). 112p. 2000. 22.95 (0-262-19442-2) MIT Pr.

Marshes & Swamps. Illus. by Gail Gibbons. LC 97-17995. 32p. (J). (ps-3). 1998. lib. bdg. 16.95 (0-8234-1347-0) Holiday.

***Marshes & Swamps.** Gail Gibbons. (Illus.). (J). 1999. pap. 6.95 (0-8234-1515-5) Holiday.

Marshes of Southwestern Lake Erie. Louis W. Campbell & Claire Gavin. LC 94-21052. (Illus.). 247p. 1994. pap. 24.95 (0-8214-1094-6) Ohio U Pr.

Marshes of Southwestern Lake Erie. Louis W. Campbell & Claire Gavin. LC 94-21052. (Illus.). 247p. 1995. 45.00 (0-8214-1107-1) Ohio U Pr.

Marshes of the Ocean Shore: Development of an Ecological Ethic. Joseph V. Siry. LC 82-45899. (Environmental History Ser.: No. 6). (Illus.). 264p. 1984. 29.95 (0-89096-150-6) Tex A&M Univ Pr.

Marshfield: A Town of Villages, 1640-1990. Cynthia H. Krusell et al. (Illus.). 256p. 1990. 40.00 (0-9627871-0-8) Hist Res Assocs.

Marshland Bird Walk. Lang Elliott. (Illus.). 28p. 1998. boxed set 12.95 incl. audio (1-878194-30-5); boxed set 16.95 incl. audio compact disk (1-878194-31-3) Nature Sound Studio.

Marshland Trinity. unabridged ed. Chris Segura. 497p. 1997. 29.95 (0-9655342-0-0) Win or Lose Ink.

***Marshmallow.** Clare Turlay Newberry. LC 98-75100. (Clare Newberry Classics Ser.). (Illus.). 32p. (J). (ps-3). 1999. 9.98 (0-7651-0951-4) Smithmark.

Marshmallow Autumn: Fire Safety. Debra Milligan. (Child Safety Ser.). (Illus.). 48p. 1986. 5.95 (0-513-01830-1) Denison.

Marshmallow Muscles, Banana Brainstorms. Karen T. Taha. LC 88-14785. 144p. (J). (gr. 3-7). 1988. 13.95 (0-15-200525-0, Gulliver Bks) Harcourt.

***Marshmellow Kisses.** Linda Crotta Brennan. LC 99-36271. (Illus.). 32p. (J). 2000. 15.00 (0-395-73872-5) HM.

Marsh's California Corporation Law, 3 vols. 2nd ed. Harold Marsh, Jr. 1981. write for info. (0-318-65477-6, H39921) P-H.

Marsh's California Corporation Law, 4 vols. 3rd ed. Harold Marsh, Jr. & R. Roy Finkle. 4166p. ring bd. 457.00 (0-13-559014-0, 55901) Aspen Law.

Marsh's California Corporation Law, 4 vols., Set. 3rd ed. Harold Marsh, Jr. & R. N. Roy Finkle. 3730p. 1990. ring bd. 435.00 (0-13-564626-X) Aspen Law.

***Marsh's Dinosaurs: The Collections from Como Bluff** John H. Ostrom & John S. McIntosh. LC 99-32467. (Illus.). 416p. 2000. 85.00 (0-300-08208-8) Yale U Pr.

Marsigli's Europe, 1630-1730: The Life & Times of Luigi Ferdinando Marsigli, Soldier & Virtuoso. John W. Stoye. LC 93-24053. (Illus.). 448p. 1994. 47.50 (0-300-05542-0) Yale U Pr.

Marsilio Ficino & the Phaedran Charioteer. Marsilio Ficino. Ed. & Tr. by Michael J. Allen. LC 80-20439. (Center for Medieval & Renaissance Studies, UCLA: Contribution: No. 14). 1981. 60.00 (0-520-04222-0, Pub. by U CA Pr) Cal Prin Full Svc.

Marsilio Ficino, Pietro Bembo, Baldassare Castiglione: Philosophical, Aesthetic, & Political Approaches in Renaissance Platonism. Christine Raffini. LC 95-37316. (Renaissance & Baroque Ser.: Vol. 21). (Illus.). XII, 173p. (C). 1998. text 41.95 (0-8204-3023-4) P Lang Pubng.

Marsilio Ficino, Three Books on Life: A Critical Edition & Translation. Ed. by Carol V. Kaske & John R. Clark. (Medieval & Renaissance Texts & Studies: Vol. 57). 528p. 1998. reprint ed. 40.00 (0-86698-041-5, MR57) MRTS.

Marsilius of Inghen. Egbert P. Bos. 1983. lib. bdg. 162.50 (90-277-1343-X) Kluwer Academic.

***Marsilius of Inghen.** Ed. by Manuel S. Noya et al. (Studies in the History of Christian Thought). 344p. 1999. 126.50 (90-04-11224-3) Brill Academic Pubs.

***Marsilius of Inghen.** Ed. by Manuel S. Noya. 336p. 1999. 109.00 (90-04-11312-6) Brill Academic Pubs.

Marsilius of Inghen: Divine Knowledge in Late Medieval Thought. Maarten J. Hoenen. LC 92-29893. (Studies in the History of Christian Thought: Vol. 50). 1992. 100.50 (90-04-09563-2) Brill Academic Pubs.

Marsilius of Padua, 2 vols., Set. Alan Gewirth. Ed. by J. P. Mayer. LC 78-67352. (European Political Thought Ser.). 1980. reprint ed. lib. bdg. 68.95 (0-405-11699-3) Ayer.

Marston Genealogy, 2 pts. N. W. Marston. (Illus.). 607p. 1989. reprint ed. pap. 91.00 (0-8328-0857-1); reprint ed. lib. bdg. 99.00 (0-8328-0856-3) Higginson Bk Co.

Marsupial Biology: Recent Research & New Perspectives. Norman Saunders & Lyn Hinds. LC 98-110382. 450p. 1997. 130.00 (0-86840-311-3, Pub. by New South Wales Univ Pr) Intl Spec Bk.

Marsupial Nutrition. Ian D. Hume. LC 98-24765. (Illus.). 384p. (C). 1999. text. write for info. (0-521-59406-5) Cambridge U Pr.

Marsupial Nutrition. Ian D. Hume. LC 98-24765. (Illus.). 384p. (C). 1999. pap. text 54.95 (0-521-59555-X) Cambridge U Pr.

Marsupiales, Bebes de Bolsa. Arthur Morton. Tr. by Angelita L. Aguilar. (SPA.). (J). (gr. k-3). 1995. 12.50 (1-57842-056-3) Delmas Creat.

Marsupials. Annalisa McMorrow. (Illus.). (J). (gr. 1-3). 1998. pap. 7.95 (1-57612-056-2, MM2070) Monday Morning Bks.

Marsupials: An Educational Coloring Book. pap. 1.99 (0-86545-217-2) Spizzirri.

Marsupials, Pouch Babies. Arthur Morton. (Illus.). (J). (gr. k-3). 1995. 12.50 (1-57842-055-5) Delmas Creat.

***Mars/Venus Affair: Astrology's Sexiest Planets.** Wendell Perry. LC 99-54273. (Illus.). 480p. 2000. pap. 17.95 (1-56718-517-7) Llewellyn Pubns.

Mart n'Oublie Personne. Didier Daeninckx. (FRE.). 192p. 1990. pap. 10.95 (0-7859-2142-7, 2070382567) Fr & Eur.

Mart Series, 4 Bks. Incl. Accommodating an HIV Infected Client. Ed. by Mibile Aids Resource Team Staff. 32p. 1994. pap. text 5.00 (1-885565-04-6); Recovery, Sexuality & HIV. 32p. 1991. 5.00 (1-885565-01-1); Sponsoring Someone with HIV Infection. 28p. 1992. 5.00 (1-885565-03-8); Substance Abuse Treatment: Considerations for Lesbians & Gay Men. 60p. 1991. 5.00 (1-885565-02-X); write for info. (1-885565-00-3) Mart.

Mart Stam, 1899-1986, Rassegna 47. (Illus.). 110p. 1991. pap. 35.00 (88-85322-05-0, Pub. by Birkhauser) Princeton Arch.

Marta. large type ed. Peggy O'More. 1994. 27.99 (0-7089-3205-3) Ulverscroft.

Marta, a Refugee's Story Marta Gabre-Tsadick & Sandra P. Aldrich. LC 83-202138. 128p. 1983. write for info. (0-281-04074-5) Society Prom Christ Know.

Marta Abreu, una Mujer Comprendida. Panfilo D. Camacho. (SPA.). 1995. pap. 16.00 (0-89729-743-1) Ediciones.

MARTA'S At-Grade Acoustical Barrier. (PCI Journal Reprints Ser.). 3p. 1981. pap. 9.00 (0-686-40149-2, JR245) P-PCI.

Marta's Magnets. Wendy Pfeffer. LC 94-37223. (Illus.). 32p. (J). (gr. k-2). 1995. pap. 5.95 (0-382-24932-1); lib. bdg. 15.95 (0-382-24930-5) Silver Burdett Pr.

Marta's Magnets. Wendy Pfeffer. LC 94-37223. (Illus.). (J). (gr. 1 up). 1995. 13.95 (0-382-24931-3) Silver Burdett Pr.

Marte Y Venus En El Dormitorio: Rivela,&Francisco, Set. abr. ed. John Gray. (SPA.). 1996. audio 18.00 (0-694-51676-7, 394090, Pub. by HarperAudio) Lndmrk Audiobks.

Marte y Venus en el Dormitorio: Una guia para hacer durar el romance y la pasion. John Gray. (SPA.). 208p. 1996. pap. 11.00 (0-06-095180-X) HarpC.

Marte y Venus Juntos Para Siempre. John Gray. (SPA.). 288p. 1997. pap. 11.00 (0-06-095236-9) HarpC.

Marteau Sans Maitre: Avec: Le Moulin Premier (1927-1935) Rene Char. 128p. 12.50 (0-686-54158-8) Fr & Eur.

Martello Towers. Sheila Sutcliffe. LC 72-9566. (Illus.). 181p. 1973. 29.50 (0-8386-1313-6) Fairleigh Dickinson.

Martelly (John S. De) The Prints. Vic Zink. (Illus.). 48p. 1990. pap. 25.00 (1-55660-154-9) A Wofsy Fine Arts.

Martens, Sables, & Fishers: Biology & Conservation. Ed. by Steven W. Buskirk et al. (Comstock Bk.). (Illus.). 512p. 1994. text 67.50 (0-8014-2894-7) Cornell U Pr.

Martensite: A Tribute to Morris Cohen. Morris Cohen. Ed. by G. B. Olson & W. S. Owen. LC 91-76275. (Illus.). 345p. 1992. reprint ed. pap. 107.00 (0-608-02644-1, 206330300004) Bks Demand.

Martensite: Fundamentals & Technology. Evan R. Petty. LC 70-546066. 217p. reprint ed. pap. 67.30 (0-608-11413-8, 200364800038) Bks Demand.

Martensitic Transformation in Science & Technology: Proceedings of the European Conference 1989. Ed. by E. Hornbogen & N. Jost. (Illus.). 550p. 1990. 103.00 (3-88355-153-8, Pub. by DGM Metallurgy Info) IR Pubns.

Martensitic Transformations. Ed. by B. C. Muddle. 714p. (C). 1990. text 241.00 (0-87849-610-6, Pub. by Trans T Pub) Enfield Pubs NH.

Martereau. Nathalie Sarraute. (FRE.). 1972. pap. 10.95 (0-8288-3739-2, F124441) Fr & Eur.

Martereau. Nathalie Sarraute. (Folio Ser.: No. 136). (FRE.). 256p. 1972. 8.95 (2-07-036136-5) Schoenhof.

Martereau. Nathalie Saurraute. 1994. pap. 11.95 (0-7145-0369-X) Riverrun NY.

Martes de Carnaval. Ramon Del Valle-Inclan. Ed. by Jesus Rubio Jimenez. (Nueva Austral Ser.: Vol. 256). (SPA.). 1991. pap. text 24.95 (84-239-7256-9) Elliots Bks.

Martha. F. V. Flotow. 272p. 1986. pap. 30.00 (0-7935-1213-1, 50337300) H Leonard.

Martha Alf Vol. 1: Retrospective. Photos by Martha Alf. LC 83-83032. (Illus.). 79p. (Orig.). 1984. pap. 16.00 (0-911291-09-1) Fellows Cont Art.

Martha & Elvira: A Play. Diana Braithwaite. 96p. 1993. per. 10.95 (0-920813-64-X) Sister Vis Pr.

Martha & Mary: A Woman's Relationship to Her Home. Josephine M. Benton. (C). 1947. pap. 4.00 (0-87574-036-7) Pendle Hill.

Martha & Mary: Friends of Jesus. C. MacKenzie. (BibleTime Bks.). (J). 1995. 2.99 (0-906731-67-4, Pub. by Christian Focus) Spring Arbor Dist.

Martha & Mary: Meeting Christ As Friend. Anastasio Ballestrero. 118p. 1996. pap. 22.00 (0-85439-483-4, Pub. by St Paul Pubns) St Mut.

***Martha & Skits.** Susan Meddaugh. LC 00-23988. (Illus.). (J). 2000. 15.00 (0-618-05776-5) HM.

Martha & the Nightbird. Helena C. Pittman. (J). (ps-3). 1986. 10.95 (0-89845-491-3, Caedmon) HarperAudio.

Martha Berry: A Woman of Courageous Spirit & Bold Dreams. Joyce Blackburn. (J). (gr. 7-12). 1992. pap. 8.95 (1-56145-071-5) Peachtree Pubs.

Martha Black: Her Story from the Dawson Gold Fields to the Halls of Parliament. 3rd ed. Martha L. Black & Florence Whyard. LC 98-18361. (Caribou Classics Ser.). (Illus.). ix, 190 p. 1998. pap. 8.95 (0-88240-508-X, Alaska NW Bks) Gr Arts Ctr Pub.

Martha Blah Blah. Susan Meddaugh. (Illus.). 32p. (J). 1996. 14.95 (0-395-79755-1) HM.

Martha Blah Blah. Susan Meddaugh. LC 95-53275. (Illus.). 32p. (J). (ps-3). 1998. pap. 5.95 (0-395-90118-9) HM.

Martha Calling. Illus. by Susan Meddaugh. 32p. (J). 1994. 14.95 (0-395-69825-1) HM.

Martha Calling. Illus. by Susan Meddaugh. LC 93-50611. 32p. (J). (ps-3). 1996. pap. 5.95 (0-395-82741-8) HM.

Martha Calling. Susan Meddaugh. LC 93-50611. 1994. 10.15 (0-606-10259-0, Pub. by Turtleback) Demco.

***Martha Contemplates the Universe.** Peggy Miller. 28p. 1999. pap. 6.00 (0-9648232-8-4) Frith Pr.

Martha Counts Her Kittens. Mike Walsh. (Illus.). 12p. (J). (ps). 1997. 14.95 (0-7613-0250-6) Millbrook Pr.

***Martha Dandridge Custis Washington, 1731-1802.** Charnan Simon. LC 99-16989. (Encyclopedia of First Ladies Ser.). (J). 2000. 33.00 (0-516-20480-7) Childrens.

Martha E. Rogers: Her Life & Her Work. Ed. by Violet M. Malinski & Elizabeth A. Barrett. LC 94-6137. (Illus.). 366p. 1994. 50.00 (0-8036-5807-9) Davis Co.

Martha et Edouard see Martha Et Edouard

Martha et Edouard see Brenda & Edward

Martha Et Edouard, Mini Bk. Maryann Kovalski.Tr. of Martha et Edouard. (FRE.). (J). mass mkt. 3.99 (0-590-74819-X) Scholastic Inc.

Martha Finley Collector Guide. Harmony Raine. (Orig.). (C). 1984. pap. 4.95 (0-89966-499-7) Buccaneer Bks.

Martha Gellhorn: Her Life & Times. Carl Rollyson. 1999. text. write for info. (0-312-04348-1) St Martin.

***Martha Graham.** Alice Helpern. (Illus.). 120p. 1999. pap. text 21.00 (90-5755-098-9, Harwood Acad Pubs) Gordon & Breach.

Martha Graham. Paula B. Pratt. LC 94-10883. (Importance of...Biographies Ser.). (Illus.). 112p. (J). (gr. 5-8). 1995. lib. bdg. 22.45 (1-56006-056-5) Lucent Bks.

Martha Graham. Kathilyn S. Probosz. LC 94-8992. (People in Focus Ser.). (Illus.). (YA). (gr. 5 up). 1995. pap. 7.95 (0-382-24961-5, Dillon Silver Burdett) Silver Burdett Pr.

Martha Graham: A Dancer's Life. Russell Freedman. LC 97-15832. (Illus.). 175p. (J). (gr. 4 up). 1998. 18.00 (0-395-74655-8, Clarion Bks) HM.

Martha Graham: Founder of Modern Dance. Gerald Newman & Eleanor Newman Layfield. LC 98-20410. (Book Report Biography Ser.). (J). 1998. 22.00 (0-531-11442-2) Watts.

Martha Graham: Sixteen Dances in Photographs. rev. ed. Barbara Morgan. LC 80-81766. (Illus.). 168p. 1980. reprint ed. 125.00 (0-87100-176-4, 2176) Morgan.

Martha Graham: The Early Years. Ed. by Merle Armitage. LC 78-17608. (Series in Dance). (Illus.). 1978. reprint ed. pap. 12.95 (0-306-80084-5); reprint ed. lib. bdg. 25.00 (0-306-79504-3) Da Capo.

Martha Grimes, 4 vols. Martha Grimes. 1990. pap., boxed set 13.50 (0-440-36024-2) Dell.

Martha Grimes: The Dirty Duck, Help the Poor Struggler, Jerusalem Inn, Set. Martha Grimes. 1986. boxed set 11.40 (0-440-13279-7) Dell.

Martha Habla (Martha Speaks) Illus. by Susan Meddaugh. Date not set. 14.95 (1-880507-32-3) Lectorum Pubns.

Martha Jackson Collection at the Albright-Knox Art Gallery. Linda Cathcart. LC 75-24230. (Illus.). 1976. pap. 4.95 (0-914782-04-5) Buffalo Fine-Albrght-Knox.

Martha Jane & Me. large type ed. Mavis Nicholson. 1993. 39.95 (0-7066-1014-8, Pub. by Remploy Pr) St Mut.

Martha Jane & Me: A Girlhood in Wales. Mavis Micholson. (Illus.). 288p. 1992. 34.95 (0-7011-3355-4, Pub. by Chatto & Windus) Trafalgar.

Martha Landscapes. Colleen Thibaudeau. 76p. 1984. pap. 9.95 (0-919626-24-6, Pub. by Brick Bks) Genl Dist Srvs.

Martha, Martha! Marge Green. 1964. 10.95 (0-89137-401-9); pap. 7.15 (0-89137-400-0) Quality Pubns.

***Martha, Martha: How Christians Worry.** Ed. by Elaine Leong Eng. LC 99-39460. 150p. (C). 2000. pap. text 14.95 (0-7890-0866-1, Haworth Pastrl); lib. bdg. 39.95 (0-7890-0865-3, Haworth Pastrl) Haworth Pr.

***Martha Matilda Harper & the American Dream: How One Woman Changed the Face of American Business.** Jane Plitt. LC 99-85982. (Women's Studies). (Illus.). 224p. 2000. text 26.95 (0-8156-0638-9) Syracuse U Pr.

Martha Maxwell: Pioneer Naturalist. Jane V. Barker & Sybil Downing. (Women of the West Ser.). (Illus.). 138p. (J). 1982. pap. 7.95 (1-878611-12-7) Silver Rim Pr.

Martha Maxwell, Rocky Mountain Naturalist. Maxine Benson. LC 86-6936. (Women in the West Ser.). (Illus.). 335p. 1986. text 50.00 (0-8032-1192-9, Bison Books) U of Nebr Pr.

Martha Maxwell, Rocky Mountain Naturalist. Maxine Benson. LC 86-6936. (Women in the West Ser.). (Illus.). 335p. 1999. pap. 15.95 (0-8032-6155-1, Bison Books) U of Nebr Pr.

***Martha Mitchell of Possum Walk Road: Texas Quiltmaker.** Melvin Rosser Mason. LC 99-39376. (Illus.). 80p. 1999. pap. 19.95 (1-881515-22-2) TX Review Pr.

Martha Moody: A Fantastical Western Novel. Susan Stinson. LC 95-10941. 224p. 1995. 10.95 (1-883523-07-9) Spinsters Ink.

Martha Mouse & Baby Bear: Present Preschool Voice Worksheets. Monica Gustafson. (Illus.). 64p. (J). (ps-3). 1997. spiral bd., wbk. ed. 15.95 (1-58650-063-5, BK-260) Super Duper.

***Martha Novel, Vol. 4.** Melissa Peterson. 304p. (J). (gr. 3-7). 2001. 15.95 (0-06-027986-9) HarpC Child Bks.

***Martha Novel, Vol. 4.** Melissa Peterson. (J). 2002. lib. bdg. 15.89 (0-06-028205-3) HarpC Child Bks.

Martha Odum: Watercolors. Jennifer Deprima et al. LC 96-52377. (Illus.). 80p. 1997. pap. 20.00 (0-915977-32-X) Georgia Museum of Art.

Martha Ostenso & Her Works. Stan Atherton. (Canadian Author Studies). 43p. (C). 1990. pap. 9.95 (1-55022-053-5, Pub. by ECW) Genl Dist Srvs.

Martha Paints with Her Kittens. Mike Walsh. LC 98-217144. (Illus.). 12p. (J). (ps). 1997. 14.95 (0-7613-0285-9) Millbrook Pr.

***Martha Peake: A Novel of the Revolution.** Patrick McGrath. 400p. 2000. 24.95 (0-375-50081-2) Random.

Martha Polo. Mateo Lettunich. 272p. 1998. 24.00 (1-887750-92-4) Rutledge Bks.

M

Martha Quest. Doris Lessing. LC 95-33106. (Children of Violence Ser.: Vol. 1). 336p. 1995. pap. 14.00 (0-06-097666-7, Perennial) HarperTrade.

Martha Rogers: The Science of Unitary Human Beings. Louette R. Lutjens. (Notes on Nursing Theories Ser.: Vol. 1). (Illus.). 40p. (C). 1991. 22.95 (0-8039-4578-7) Sage.

Martha Rogers: The Science of Unitary Human Beings, No. 1. Louette R. Lutjens. (Notes on Nursing Theories Ser.: Vol. 1). (Illus.). 40p. (C). 1991. pap. 9.95 (0-8039-4229-X) Sage.

Martha Root: Lioness at the Threshold. M. R. Garis. LC 83-3913. (Illus.). 578p. 1983. pap. 15.95 (0-87743-185-X) Bahai.

Martha Rosler: Positions in the Life World. Ed. by Catherine De Zegher. LC 98-89291. (Illus.). 256p. 1999. 40.00 (0-262-04174-X) MIT Pr.

Martha Schofield & the Reeducation of the South, 1839-1916. Katherine Smedley. LC 87-17370. (Studies in Women & Religion: Vol. 24). 328p. 1987. lib. bdg. 99.95 (0-88946-525-8) E Mellen.

Martha Schwartz: Transfiguration of the Commonplace. Ed. by Heidi Landecker. (Illus.). 178p. 1997. pap. 45.00 (1-888931-01-9) Spacemkr Pr.

Martha Schwartz, Incorporated. Spacemaker Press Staff. 1996. pap. 35.00 (0-688-15063-2, Wm Morrow) Morrow Avon.

Martha Speaks. Susan Meddaugh. LC 91-48455. (Illus.). 32p. (J). (ps-3). 1992. 15.00 (0-395-63313-3) HM.

Martha Speaks. Susan Meddaugh. LC 91-48455. (Illus.). 32p. (J). (ps-3). 1995. pap. 5.95 (0-395-72952-1, Sandpiper) HM.

Martha Speaks. Susan Meddaugh. (J). 1995. 10.85 (0-606-07844-4, Pub. by Turtleback) Demco.

Martha Stewart: America's Lifestyle Expert. Sarah M. Wooten. LC 98-3899. (Library of Famous Women). (Illus.). 64p. (J). (gr. 4-7). 1998. lib. bdg. 16.95 (1-56711-254-4) Blackbirch.

Martha Stewart: Successful Businesswoman. Virginia Meachum. LC 97-43578. (People to Know Ser.). 112p. (YA). (gr. 6 up). 1998. lib. bdg. 20.95 (0-89490-984-3) Enslow Pubs.

Martha Stewart - Just Desserts: The Unauthorized Biography. Jerry Oppenheimer. 496p. 1998. mass mkt. 6.99 (0-380-73164-9, Avon Bks) Morrow Avon.

Martha Stewart Cookbook. Martha Stewart. 1996. 27.50 (0-614-12881-1) Crown Pub Group.

Martha Stewart Cookbook: Collected Recipes for Every Day. Martha Stewart. (Illus.). 640p. 1995. 30.00 (0-517-70335-1) Random.

***Martha Stewart Hors D'Oeuvres.** Martha Stewart. 1999. write for info. (0-609-50162-3) Random Hse Value.

Martha Stewart Living: Arranging Flowers. 1999. pap. 19.95 (0-8487-1843-7) Oxmoor Hse.

Martha Stewart Living: Christmas with Martha Stewart. Martha Stewart. 1997. pap. 19.95 (0-8487-1639-6) Oxmoor Hse.

Martha Stewart Living: Decorating Details. Martha Stewart. LC 97-44131. 1998. pap. 19.95 (0-8487-1663-9, 109118) Oxmoor Hse.

Martha Stewart Living Cookbook. Martha Stewart Living Editors. Date not set. write for info. (0-609-50338-3) Crown Pub Group.

***Martha Stewart Living Cookbook.** Ed. by Martha Stewart Living Magazine Staff. (Illus.). 2000. 35.00 (0-609-60750-2, Crown) Crown Pub Group.

Martha Stewart Living Wreaths. 1996. pap. 19.95 (0-8487-1531-4, 102587) Oxmoor Hse.

Martha Stewart's Christmas: Entertaining, Decorating & Giving in the Holiday Season. Martha Stewart. 1989. 25.00 (0-517-57416-0) C Potter.

Martha Stewart's Christmas: Entertaining, Decorating & Giving in the Holiday Season. Martha Stewart. 1993. pap. 18.00 (0-517-88102-0) C Potter.

Martha Stewart's Collected Recipes for Every Day. 1995. 27.50 (0-614-15465-0) C Potter.

***Martha Stewart's Creating America.** Martha Stewart. 1998. write for info. (0-517-70461-7) C Potter.

Martha Stewart's Gardening: Month by Month. Martha Stewart. (Illus.). 348p. 1991. 50.00 (0-517-57413-6) C Potter.

Martha Stewart's Healthy & Light. Martha Stewart. 1995. write for info. (0-517-70157-X) C Potter.

Martha Stewart's Healthy Quick Cook. Martha Stewart. 224p. 1997. 32.50 (0-517-57702-X) Random Hse Value.

Martha Stewart's Hors d'Oeuvres: The Creation & Presentation of Fabulous Finger Food. Martha Stewart. (Illus.). 1984. 21.95 (0-517-55455-0) C Potter.

Martha Stewart's Hors D'Oeuvres: The Creation & Presentation of Fabulous Finger Food. Martha Stewart. 176p. 1992. pap. 20.00 (0-517-58950-8) C Potter.

Martha Stewart's Hors D'Oeuvres Handbook. Martha Stewart. LC 98-39161. (Illus.). 495p. 1999. 35.00 (0-609-60310-8) C Potter.

Martha Stewart's Menus for Entertaining. Martha Stewart. (Illus.). 224p. 1994. 30.00 (0-517-59099-9) C Potter.

Martha Stewart's New Old House: Restoration, Renovation, Decoration. Martha Stewart. LC 92-15900. (Illus.). 252p. 1992. 45.00 (0-517-57701-1) C Potter.

Martha Stewart's Pies & Tarts. Martha Stewart. (Martha Stewart Food & Entertaining Bk.). (Illus.). 224p. 1985. 23.95 (0-517-55751-7) C Potter.

Martha Stewart's Pies & Tarts. Martha Stewart. LC 91-38464. 224p. 1992. pap. 18.00 (0-517-58953-2) C Potter.

Martha Stewart's Quick Cook. Martha Stewart et al. (Illus.). 224p. 1983. 23.95 (0-517-55096-2) C Potter.

Martha Stewart's Quick Cook: Two Hundred Easy & Elegant Recipes. Martha Stewart. 224p. 1992. pap. 18.00 (0-517-58952-4) C Potter.

Martha Stewart's Quick Cook Menus: Fifty-Two Meals You Can Make in under an Hour. Martha Stewart. (Illus.). 1988. 22.95 (0-517-57064-5) C Potter.

Martha Stewart's Quick Cook Menus: Fifty-Two Meals You Can Make in under an Hour. Martha Stewart. (Illus.). 224p. 1992. pap. 18.00 (0-517-58951-6) C Potter.

Martha Stuart's Better Than You at Entertaining: A Parody. Tom Connor & Jim Downey. LC 96-155402. (Illus.). 64p. 1996. pap. 10.00 (0-06-095171-0, Perennial) HarperTrade.

Martha Stuart's Excruciatingly Perfect Weddings. Tom Connor. LC 98-3808. 64p. 1998. pap. 10.00 (0-06-095238-5, Perennial) HarperTrade.

***Martha to the Max! Balanced Living for Perfectionists.** Debi Stack. LC 00-41586. 2000. write for info. (0-8024-5389-9) Moody.

Martha Walks the Dog. Susan Meddaugh. LC 97-47172. 32p. (J). (gr. k-3). 1998. 15.00 (0-395-90494-3) HM.

Martha Washington: America's First First Lady. Jean B. Wagoner. LC 86-10737. (Childhood of Famous Americans Ser.). (Illus.). 192p. (J). (gr. 3-7). 1986. reprint ed. mass mkt. 4.95 (0-02-042160-5, Pub. by Macmillan) S&S Trade.

Martha Washington: First Lady. Stephanie McPherson. LC 97-23478. (Historical American Biographies Ser.). (Illus.). 128p. (YA). (gr. 6 up). 1998. lib. bdg. 20.95 (0-7660-1017-1) Enslow Pubs.

Martha Washington: First Lady of the Land see Discovery Biographies

Martha Washington, America's First First Lady. Jean B. Wagoner. (Illus.). (J). (gr. 3-7). 1959. 7.16 (0-672-52733-2, 913458) Macmillan.

Martha Washington, America's First First Lady. Jean B. Wagoner. (Childhood of Famous Americans Ser.). (J). 1986. 10.05 (0-606-03249-5, Pub. by Turtleback) Demco.

Martha Washington Goes to War. Frank Miller & Dave Gibbons. (Illus.). 144p. 1995. pap. 17.95 (1-56971-090-2) Dark Horse Comics.

***Martha Washington Saves the World.** Frank Miller. 112p. 1999. pap. 12.95 (1-56971-384-7) Dark Horse Comics.

Martha Washington's Book of Cookery & Book of Sweetmeats. Ed. by Karen Hess. LC 97-200909. 518p. 1996. pap. 20.00 (0-231-04931-5) Col U Pr.

Martha Wetherbee's Handbook of New Shaker Baskets. Martha Wetherbee. (Illus.). 28p. (Orig.). 1987. reprint ed. pap. 4.00 (0-9609384-0-0) M Wetherbee.

Martha White's Southern Sampler: From Cornbread to Cobbler, the Best Recipes from Martha White's Kitchens. Martha White. LC 89-39568. (Illus.). 192p. 1989. 19.95 (1-55853-035-5) Rutledge Hill Pr.

Martha's Ark. Charlotte Moore. 272p. 1998. pap. 10.95 (0-09-955351-1, Pub. by Arrow Bks) Trafalgar.

Martha's Attic: Program Guide for Public T. V. Series 400. Martha Pullen. Ed. by Kathy McMakin. LC 96-920960. (Illus.). 344p. 1996. text 19.95 (1-878048-06-6) M Pullen.

Martha's Got Nothin' on Me: The Pre-Fab Cookbook. Debbie Bishop & Cori Berg. (Illus.). 174p. 1998. pap. 14.95 (0-9664737-0-1, PF2001) Lft Field Prods.

Martha's Kitchen: Home Cooking. Martha E. Goodwin. 262p. 1996. spiral bd. 11.00 (1-56383-064-7, 162) G & R Pub.

***Martha's Madness.** ed. Mary Taffs. (Second Chances Ser.: Vol. II). 250p. 1999. 4.50 (1-928670-42-3) Awe Struck E Bks.

Martha's New Puppy. Danielle Steel. (Illus.). 32p. (J). 1990. 9.95 (0-385-30166-9) Delacorte.

Martha's Pet. Joe Marcotte. 24p. (J). (ps-5). 1995. pap. 5.95 (0-9648807-0-9) Spking With Insight.

Martha's Sewing Room: Program Guide for Public T. V. Series-100. Martha C. Pullen. (Illus.). 274p. 1994. 19.95 (1-878048-03-1) M Pullen.

Martha's Vineyard. Peter W. Barnes & Cheryl S. Barnes. (Illus.). 32p. (J). (gr. k-6). 1995. 15.95 (0-9637688-3-2) Vacation Spot.

Martha's Vineyard. Insight Guides Staff. (Insight Guides). 1998. pap. text 7.95 (0-88729-545-2) Langenscheidt.

Martha's Vineyard: An Affectionate Memoir. Ralph Graves. LC 94-41486. (Illus.). 144p. 1995. 29.95 (1-55859-866-9) Abbeville Pr.

Martha's Vineyard: Gardens & Houses. Elizabeth Talbot & Taylor Lewis. 288p. 1994. 30.00 (0-671-88106-X) S&S Trade.

Martha's Vineyard: Houses & Gardens. Photos by Lisl Dennis. (Illus.). 240p. 1992. 50.00 (0-316-18083-1) Little.

Martha's Vineyard ABC's. Jan Paul. Ed. by Richard Rooney. (Illus.). 32p. (Orig.). (J). 1996. pap. 12.95 (0-9654165-0-X) ABC Graphics.

Martha's Vineyard & Nantucket. Bill Harris. (Illus.). 140p. 1997. 12.95 (1-85833-699-6, Pub. by CLib Bks) Whitecap Bks.

Martha's Vineyard Cookbook. 3rd ed. Louise T. King & Jean S. Wexler. LC 99-49132. (Illus.). 356p. 1999. pap. 16.95 (0-7627-0569-8) Globe Pequot.

Martha's Vineyard Nature Guide. Sylvia S. Mader. (Illus.). 96p. (Orig.). 1985. pap. 7.99 (0-317-40346-X) Mader Enter.

Martha's Will. John Hankins. 408p. 1999. pap. 21.95 (1-889260-01-0) Writers Bk Club.

Marthe: Histoire d'Une Fille: Les Soeurs Vatard. Joris-Karl Huysmans. (FRE.). 448p. 1975. 17.95 (0-7859-0121-3, M5283) Fr & Eur.

Marthe ou les Amantes Tristes. Jean Freustie. (FRE.). 1979. pap. 12.95 (0-7859-2401-9, 2070370119) Fr & Eur.

Marthe Robin: The Cross & the Joy. Raymond Peyret. Tr. by Clare W. Faulhaber from FRE. LC 83-15591. (Illus.). 135p. 1983. pap. 6.95 (0-8189-0464-X) Alba.

***Marthellen & the Major.** Stephen Bly. 260p. 2000. pap. 10.99 (1-56955-159-6) Servant.

Marth's 1999 Florida Guide: State's Premier Media & Source Directory. 9th rev. ed. Del Marth et al. (Illus.). 220p. 1999. spiral bd. 39.50 (1-885034-12-1) Suwannee River.

Marth's 1998 Florida Guide: State's Premier Media & Source Directory. 8th rev. ed. Del Marth & Marty Marth. (Illus.). 200p. 1998. spiral bd. 39.50 (1-885034-10-5) Suwannee River.

Marth's 1997 Florida Guide: State's Premier Media & Sources Directory. 7th rev. ed. Del Marth & Marty Marth. 192p. (Orig.). 1997. pap., spiral bd. 39.50 (1-885034-06-7) Suwannee River.

Marth's 2000 Florida Guide: State's Premier Media & Source Directory. 10th rev. ed. Marty Marth et al. (Illus.). 200p. 2000. spiral bd. 39.50 (1-885034-14-8) Suwannee River.

Marti: Apostle of Freedom. Jorge Manach. (Illus.). 9.50 (0-8159-6201-0) Devin.

Marti el Apostol. Jorge Manach. (SPA.). 248p. 1998. reprint ed. pap. 12.00 (84-239-0252-8, Pub. by Espasa Calpe) IBD Ltd.

***Marti el Poeta.** Ricardo R. Sardina. LC 99-64536. (Coleccion Clasicos Cubanos: Vol. 20). (Illus.). 307p. 1999. pap. 19.00 (0-89729-906-X) Ediciones.

Marti Ideario. Carlos Ripoll. 94p. (C). 1994. pap. text 5.00 (1-884619-03-7) Endowment CAS.

Marti, Martyr of Cuban Independence. Felix Lizaso. LC 73-20502. (Illus.). 260p. 1974. reprint ed. lib. bdg. 60.00 (0-8371-7329-9, LIMA, Greenwood Pr) Greenwood.

Marti y el Krausismo. Tomas G. Oria. LC 86-63038. (SPA.). 176p. 1987. pap. 30.00 (0-89295-047-1) Society Sp & Sp-Am.

Marti y Su Concepcion de la Sociedad, 2 pts., Tomo II. Roberto D. Agramonte & Portada De Rafael Rosa. 1984. pap. 10.50 (0-8477-3517-6) U of PR Pr.

Marti y Su Concepcion de la Sociedad Tomo II, Parte 1: Teoria General de la Sociedad. Roberto D. Agramonte & Portada de Rafael Rosa. (Illus.). 232p. 1979. pap. 4.95 (0-8477-2467-0) U of PR Pr.

Marti y Su Concepcion de la Sociedad Tomo II, Parte 2: Patria y Humanidad 1. Roberto Agramonte. LC 81-10377. (Illus.). 394p. 1984. pap. 5.50 (0-8477-3500-1) U of PR Pr.

Marti y Su Concepcion Del Mundo. Roberto Agramonte. 815p. (C). 1971. 7.50 (0-8477-3102-2) U of PR Pr.

Martial. J. P. Sullivan. LC 92-26826. (Classical Heritage Ser.: Vol. 3). 272p. 1992. text 48.00 (0-8153-0335-1, H1456) Garland.

Martial Bk. V: The Epigrams. Martial. Ed. & Tr. by Peter Howell from LAT. (Classical Texts Ser.). 176p. 1995. 59.99 (0-85668-589-5, Pub. by Aris & Phillips); pap. 22.00 (0-85668-590-9, Pub. by Aris & Phillips) David Brown.

***Martial Bk. IX: A Commentary.** Christer Henriksben. LC 99-159038. 224p. 1998. 57.50 (91-554-4293-5, Pub. by Uppsala Univ Acta Univ Uppsaliensis) Coronet Bks.

***Martial & Friendship Love Poetically Highlighted.** Abraham J. Heller. 2000. write for info. (1-58235-580-0) Watermrk Pr.

Martial Art Touch of the Tiger: The Martial Art of Charles Jones Touch of the Tiger. Charles Jones. Ed. by Barbara Archie. (Illus.). 88p. (Orig.). Date not set. pap. 10.95 (0-9643501-2-2) C & C Jones.

Martial Artist As a Work of Art: A Biography. Ronald P. Mombello. LC 91-73108. 70p. 1991. pap. 14.95 (0-9631732-0-0) Document Wks.

Martial Artist's Book of Five Rings: A New Interpretation of Miyamoto Musashi's Classic Book of Strategy. Stephen F. Kaufman. LC 94-7394. 128p. (Orig.). 1994. pap. 12.95 (0-8048-3020-7) Tuttle Pubng.

Martial Artist's Book of the Five Rings. Hanshi Steve Kaufman. 1999. 6.99 (0-7858-1127-3) Bk Sales Inc.

Martial Artist's Guide to American Law. Regina A. Brice. (Illus.). 537p. 1994. ring bd. 65.00 (0-9643872-1-2) Sanshin Consulting.

Martial Artist's Guide to Ancient Chinese Weapons: An Easy Reference Guide. Jwing-Ming Yang. LC 98-61696. (Illus.). 160p. 1999. pap. 16.95 (1-886969-67-1) YMAA Pubn.

Martial Artist's Guide to Korean Terms, Translation, & Han-gul. Richard L. Mitchell et al. (ENG & KOR.). 322p. 1998. pap. 22.00 (1-884583-00-8) Lilley Gulch.

Martial Artist's Way: Achieve Your Peak Performance. Sifu G. Doyle. LC 98-46199. (Orig.). 1999. pap. 14.95 (0-8048-3195-5) Tuttle Pubng.

Martial Arts. David Armentrout. LC 97-12421. (Sports Challenge Ser.). 24p. (J). (gr. 3-7). 1997. lib. bdg. 18.60 (1-55916-217-1) Rourke Bk Co.

Martial Arts. Bernie Blackall. LC 98-19590. (Top Sport Ser.). 1998. write for info. (1-57572-705-6) Heinemann Lib.

***Martial Arts.** Ann G. Gaines. (Composite Guides Ser.). (Illus.). 2000. pap. 5.95 (0-7910-5875-1) Chelsea Hse.

***Martial Arts.** Bob Knotts. (True Bks.). (Illus.). (YA). 2000. pap. 6.95 (0-516-27028-1) Childrens.

Martial Arts. Susan Ribner & Richard Chin. LC 76-58713. (Trophy Bk.). (Illus.). 160p. (J). (gr. 5 up). 1984. pap. 4.95 (0-06-440139-1, HarpTrophy) HarpC Child Bks.

***Martial Arts.** Stuart Schwartz. 1999. 59.79 (0-516-29623-X) Capstone Pr.

Martial Arts. Stuart Schwartz & Craig Conley. (Illus.). 192p. 76.00 (0-7368-0125-1) Capstone Pr.

Martial Arts. Daniel Sidlik. 108p. 2000. pap. 17.95 (1-56072-486-2, Nova Kroshka Bks) Nova Sci Pubs.

Martial Arts: A Complete Illustrated History. Michael Finn. LC 88-42773. (Illus.). 224p. 1989. 35.00 (0-87951-335-7, Pub. by Overlook Pr) Penguin Putnam.

Martial Arts: An Introduction to Self-Defense. Sean X. Cai. (Illus.). 200p. (C). 1999. pap. text 34.00 (1-893435-07-5) Lakeshore Comm.

Martial Arts: Mastering the Self. Louise Rafkin & Leslie McGrath. LC 96-35407. 1997. write for info. (0-316-73450-0) Little.

Martial Arts: Origins, Philosophy, Practice. Peter Lewis. 192p. 1997. pap. 11.95 (1-85375-206-1) Prion.

Martial Arts: The Spiritual Dimension. Peter Payne. LC 86-51575. (Art & Imagination Ser.). (Illus.). 1987. pap. 15.95 (0-500-81025-7, Pub. by Thames Hudson) Norton.

Martial Arts - Physical Development. Bryant Lloyd. LC 98-22411. (Martial Arts Ser.). (J). 1998. (1-57103-231-2) Rourke Pr.

Martial Arts - Techniques. Bryant Lloyd. LC 98-22415. (Martial Arts Ser.). (J). 1998. (1-57103-230-4) Rourke Pr.

Martial Arts after 40. Sang H. Kim. LC 99-44144. (Illus.). 272p. 1999. pap. 16.95 (1-880336-29-4, Pub. by Turtle CT) ACCESS Pubs Network.

Martial Arts Almanac. Date not set. boxed set 55.60 (1-56565-823-X) NTC Contemp Pub Co.

Martial Arts Almanac. rev. ed. Ngo Vinh-Hoi. LC 97-74073. 88p. (J). 1997. pap. text 6.95 (1-56565-822-1, 08221W, Pub. by Lowell Hse) NTC Contemp Pub Co.

Martial Arts America: A Western Approach to Eastern Arts. Bob Orlando. LC 97-38087. (Illus.). 200p. 1998. pap. 14.95 (1-883319-67-6) Frog Ltd CA.

Martial Arts & Arts of Management see Black Belt Manager: Martial Arts Strategies for Power, Creativity, & Control

Martial Arts & Sports in Japan. (Illustrated Japan in Your Pocket Ser.: No. JTB 16). (Illus.). 192p. 1994. pap. 17.95 (4-533-01995-1, Pub. by Japan Trvl Bur) Bks Nippan.

Martial Arts Are Not Just for Kicking Butt: An Anthology of Writings on Martial Arts. Ed. by Antonio Cuevas & Jennifer Lee. LC 97-50055. (Illus.). 200p. 1998. pap. 15.95 (1-55643-266-6) North Atlantic.

Martial Arts Around the World. John S. Soet. 148p. (Orig.). 1991. pap. 12.95 (0-86568-151-1, 140) Unique Pubns.

Martial Arts Athlete: Mental & Physical Conditioning for Peak Performance. Tom Seabourne. Ed. by Andrew Murray. LC 98-60688. (Martial Arts-External Ser.). (Illus.). 160p. 1998. pap. 19.95 (1-886969-65-5, B033/655, Pub. by YMAA Pubn) Natl Bk Netwk.

Martial Arts Companion. S. Danielson & J. Curtis. (Rolemaster Standard System Ser.). (Illus.). 128p. 1997. pap. 18.00 (1-55806-313-7, 5602) Iron Crown Ent Inc.

Martial Arts Dynamic Management & Marketing Seminar Book. Byung K. Cho. 450p. 1992. 99.00 (0-9631874-0-6) Chos Black Belt.

Martial Arts Encyclopedia. Jennifer Lawler. (Illus.). 328p. (Orig.). 1996. pap. 19.95 (1-57028-068-1, 80681H, Mstrs Pr) NTC Contemp Pub Co.

Martial Arts for Beginners. Ron Sieh. (Illus.). 160p. 1995. pap. 11.00 (0-86316-171-5) Writers & Readers.

Martial Arts for Kids: The Road to Inner Strength, Self-Awareness & a Peaceful World. Richard Devens & Norman Sandler. LC 97-28591. 1997. pap. write for info. (0-8348-0401-8) Weatherhill.

Martial Arts for Women: A Practical Guide. Jennifer Lawler. LC 97-27231. (Illus.). 256p. (Orig.). 1998. pap. 19.95 (1-880336-16-2) Turtle CT.

***Martial Arts Home Training: The Complete Guide to the Construction & Use of Home Training Equipment.** Mike Young. LC 99-28144. (Illus.). 160p. 1999. pap. write for info. (0-8048-3170-X) Tuttle Pubng.

***Martial Arts in Action.** (Sports in Action Ser.). (Illus.). 32p. (J). (gr. 1-4). 2000. pap. 5.95 (0-7787-0181-6); lib. bdg. 19.96 (0-7787-0169-7) Crabtree Pub Co.

Martial Arts Index: An Annotated Bibliography. Randy F. Nelson. LC 88-11243. 456p. 1988. text 25.00 (0-8240-4435-5, SS451) Garland.

Martial Arts Information Guide. Chris Pellitte. (Illus.). 77p. 1998. spiral bd. 7.95 (0-9668079-0-1) C Pellitteri Martial Arts.

***Martial Arts Madness: A User's Guide to the Esoteric Martial Arts.** Glenn Morris. LC 98-36693. 1999. pap. text 14.95 (1-883319-77-3) Frog Ltd CA.

Martial Arts Masters: The Greatest Teachers, Fighters & Performers. Ngo Vinh-Hoi. LC 96-41912. 1996. write for info. (1-56565-559-1) Lowell Hse.

***Martial Arts Mind & Body.** Claudio Iedwab & Roxanne Standefer. LC 00-27092. (Illus.). 200p. 2000. pap. 17.95 (0-7360-0125-5) Human Kinetics.

***Martial Arts of Renaissance Europe.** Sydney Anglo. LC 99-89407. (Illus.). 400p. 2000. 45.00 (0-300-08352-1) Yale U Pr.

Martial Arts... Personal Development. Bryant Lloyd. LC 98-22413. (Martial Arts Ser.). (J). 1998. (1-57103-229-0) Rourke Pr.

***Martial Arts Talk: Conversations with Leading Authorities on the Martial Arts.** Mark V. Wiley. LC 99-27411. 184p. 2000. pap. write for info. (0-8048-3182-3) Tuttle Pubng.

Martial Arts Teachers on Teaching. Ed. by Carol A. Wiley. LC 95-19456. (Illus.). 242p. (Orig.). (C). 1995. pap. 14.95 (1-883319-09-9) Frog Ltd CA.

***Martial Arts Teaching Tales of Power & Paradox: Freeing the Mind, Focusing Chi, & Mastering the Self.** Pascal Fauliot. 160p. 2000. pap. 12.95 (0-89281-882-4, Inner Trad) Inner Tradit.

Martial Arts... The Class: The Class. Bryant Lloyd. LC 98-22420. (Martial Arts Ser.). (J). 1998. 18.60 (1-57103-226-6) Rourke Pr.

Martial Arts... The History. Bryant Lloyd. LC 98-20430. (Martial Arts Ser.). (J). 1998. (1-57103-228-2) Rourke Pr.

Martial Arts... The Student. Bryant Lloyd. LC 98-22412. (Martial Arts Ser.). (J). 1998. (1-57103-227-4) Rourke Pr.

Martial Arts Training Diary for Kids. Art Brisacher. (Illus.). 96p. (J). (gr. 2-6). 1997. pap., wbk. ed. 9.95 (*1-880336-17-0*, MATKD) Turtle CT.

Martial Dance: Total Fitness with Martial Arts Aerobics. Chaz Wilson. (Illus.). 176p. (Orig.). 1987. pap. 9.95 (*0-85030-758-9*, Pub. by Aqrn Pr) Harper SF.

Martial Face: The Military Portrait in Britain, 1760-1900. Pref. by Peter Harrington. (Illus.). 152p. (Orig.). 1991. pap. 20.00 (*0-933519-20-6*) D W Bell Gallery.

Martial Justice: The Last Mass Execution in the United States. Richard Whittingham. LC 97-26227. (Bluejacket Books Ser.). (Illus.). 304p. 1997. pap. 16.95 (*1-55750-945-X*) Naval Inst Pr.

Martial Medley. Ed. by Eric Partridge et al. LC 73-117905. (Select Bibliographies Reprint Ser.). 1977. 29.95 (*0-8369-5358-4*) Ayer.

Martial Metropolis: U. S. Cities in War & Peace, 1900-1970. Ed. by Roger W. Lotchin. LC 83-21250. 242p. 1984. 59.95 (*0-275-91219-1*, C1219, Praeger Pubs) Greenwood.

Martial Musician's Mentor: A Complete Course of Instruction for the Fife, Pt. 1. 2nd rev. ed. George Kusel. (Illus.). 52p. (YA). (gr. 6 up). 1979. pap. 4.95 (*0-9604476-1-X*) Kusel.

***Martial Musings: A Portrayal of Martial Arts in the 20th Century.** Robert W. Smith. (Illus.). 1999. 39.95 (*1-893765-00-8*) Via Media Pub.

Martial Power Exemplified in Mrs. Packard's Trial: And Self-Defense from the Charge of Insanity; or Three Years' Imprisonment for Religious Beliefs by the Arbitrary Will of a Husband, with an Appeal to the Government to So Change the Laws As to Protect the Rights of Married Women. E. P. Packard. (Women & the Law Reprint Ser.). xxiv, 137p. 1994. reprint ed. 37.50 (*0-8377-2552-6*, Rothman) W S Hein.

Martial Spirit. Walter Millis. Ed. by Richard H. Kohn. LC 78-22389. (American Military Experience Ser.). (Illus.). 1980. reprint ed. lib. bdg. 37.95 (*0-405-11866-X*) Ayer.

Martial Spirit: An Introduction to the Origin, Philosophy & Psychology of the Martial Arts. Herman Kauz. LC 77-77808. (Illus.). 1978. 21.95 (*0-87951-067-6*, Pub. by Overlook Pr) Penguin Putnam.

Martial Spirit: An Introduction to the Origin, Philosophy, & Psychology of the Martial Arts. Herman Kauz. (Illus.). 144p. 1988. pap. 12.95 (*0-87951-327-6*, Pub. by Overlook Pr) Penguin Putnam.

Martialis, M. Valerii. Ed. by Shackleton Bailey. (LAT.). 1990. 110.00 (*3-519-01531-5*, T1531, Pub. by B G Teubner) U of Mich Pr.

Martialis, M. Valerius: Martial-Konkordanz. Marcus Valerius Martialis Martialis. Ed. by Edgar Siedschlag. (Alpha-Omega, Reihe A Ser.: Bd. XXXVIII). iv, 968p. 1979. write for info. (*3-487-06821-4*) G Olms Pubs.

Martial's Catullus: The Reception of an Epigrammatic Rival. B. W. Swann. (Spudasmata Ser.: Vol. 54). viii, 180p. 1994. write for info. (*3-487-09931-4*) G Olms Pubs.

Martian. George L. Du Maurier. LC 77-144991. (Illus.). 1971. reprint ed. 69.00 (*0-403-00919-7*) Scholarly.

Martian. George DuMaurier. 1988. reprint ed. lib. bdg. 59.00 (*0-7812-0458-5*) Rprt Serv.

Martian Chronicles. Ray Bradbury. 22.95 (*0-88411-862-2*) Amereon Ltd.

Martian Chronicles. Ray Bradbury. 192p. 1984. mass mkt. 6.50 (*0-553-27822-3*, Bantam Classics) Bantam.

Martian Chronicles. Ray Bradbury. 1986. pap. 5.50 (*0-87129-211-4*, M64) Dramatic Pub.

Martian Chronicles. Ray Bradbury. LC 99-24658. 1999. 24.95 (*0-7838-8635-7*) Mac Lib Ref.

Martian Chronicles. Ray Bradbury. 288p. 1997. 16.00 (*0-380-97383-9*, Avon Bks) Morrow Avon.

Martian Chronicles. Ray Bradbury. 1950. 11.09 (*0-606-01042-4*, Pub. by Turtleback) Demco.

Martian Chronicles. Ray Bradbury. 1991. reprint ed. lib. bdg. 25.95 (*1-56849-085-2*) Buccaneer Bks.

Martian Chronicles: Curriculum Unit. Center for Learning Network Staff & Ray Bradbury. (Novel Ser.). 94p. (YA). (gr. 9-12). 1995. spiral bd. 18.95 (*1-56077-317-0*) Ctr Learning.

Martian Enigmas: The Face, Pyramids & Other Unusual Objects on Mars. Mark Carlotto. LC 91-32489. (Illus.). 123p. 1991. 29.95 (*1-55643-092-2*) North Atlantic.

Martian Enigmas - A Closer Look: The Face, Pyramids & Other Unusual Objects on Mars. 2nd ed. Mark J. Carlotto. LC 96-49796. (Illus.). 160p. 1997. pap. 18.95 (*1-55643-242-9*) North Atlantic.

Martian Fossils on Earth: The Story of Meteorite ALH 84001. Fred Bortz. LC 97-6190. (Illus.). 64p. (J). (gr. 5 up). 1997. lib. bdg. 21.40 (*0-7613-0270-0*) Millbrook Pr.

***Martian Genesis: The Extraterrestrial Origins of the Human Race.** Herbie Brennan. 272p. 2000. mass mkt. 6.50 (*0-440-23557-X*) Dell.

Martian Goo. Lynn Salem & Josie Stewart. (Illus.). 8p. (J). (gr. k-1). 1993. pap. 3.75 (*1-880612-13-5*) Seedling Pubns.

Martian Homecoming at the All-American Revival Church. Richard Grossinger. 124p. (Orig.). 1974. pap. 3.00 (*0-913028-21-5*) North Atlantic.

Martian Mask. Scholastic, Inc. Staff. LC 97-116803. (Mask Ser.). 46p. (J). (ps-3). 1996. pap. text 3.99 (*0-590-50204-2*) Scholastic Inc.

Martian Metamorphoses: The Planet Mars in Ancient Myth & Religion. Ev Cochrane. (Illus.). 200p. (Orig.). 1997. pap. 20.00 (*0-9656229-0-8*) Aeon Press.

***Martian Race.** Gregory Benford. LC 99-52492. 352p. 1999. 23.95 (*0-446-52633-9*, Pub. by Warner Bks) Little.

***Martian Race.** Gregory Benford. 2001. mass mkt. 6.99 (*0-446-60890-4*, Aspect) Warner Bks.

Martian Rock. Carol Diggory Shields. LC 98-51273. (Illus.). 40p. (J). (ps-2). 1999. text 15.99 (*0-7636-0598-0*) Candlewick Pr.

Martian Sends a Postcard Home. Craig Raine. 54p. 1980. pap. 9.95 (*0-19-211896-X*) OUP.

Martian Spring. Michael L. Williams. 288p. 1986. pap. 3.50 (*0-380-89633-8*, Avon Bks) Morrow Avon.

Martian Time-Slip. Philip K. Dick. LC 94-42802. 1995. pap. 11.00 (*0-679-76167-5*) Vin Bks.

Martian Viking. Timothy R. Sullivan. 272p. (Orig.). 1991. pap. 3.50 (*0-380-75814-8*, Avon Bks) Morrow Avon.

Martian Way & Other Stories. Isaac Asimov. LC 81-15009. 224p. 1982. reprint ed. 16.00 (*0-8376-0463-X*) Bentley Pubs.

Martiani Capellae: De Nuptiis Mercurii et Philologiae. Ed. by Willis. (LAT.). 1983. 110.00 (*3-322-00238-1*, T1540, Pub. by B G Teubner) U of Mich Pr.

Martiani Capellae: De Nuptiis Mercurii et Philologiae. rev. ed. Ed. by Dick & Preaux. (LAT.). 1978. reprint ed. 69.50 (*3-519-01532-3*, T1532, Pub. by B G Teubner) U of Mich Pr.

Martians. Kim Stanley Robinson. LC 99-13115. 352p. 1999. 24.95 (*0-553-80117-1*, Spectra) Bantam.

***Martians.** Kim Stanley Robinson. 2000. mass mkt. 6.99 (*0-553-57401-9*) Bantam.

Martians & Misplaced Clues: The Life & Work of Fredric Brown. Jack Seabrook. LC 93-71000. 312p. (C). 1993. 39.95 (*0-87972-590-7*); pap. 16.95 (*0-87972-591-5*) Bowling Green Univ Popular Press.

Martians Don't Take Temperatures. Debbie Dadey & Marcia Thornton Jones. LC 00-5333. (Adventures of the Bailey School Kids Ser.: No. 18). 67p. (J). (gr. 4-7). 1996. pap. 2.99 (*0-590-50960-8*) Scholastic Inc.

Martians Don't Take Temperatures. Debbie Dadey & Marcia Thornton Jones. (Adventures of the Bailey School Kids Ser.: No. 18). (J). (gr. 2-4). 1995. 8.70 (*0-606-08565-3*, Pub. by Turtleback) Demco.

Martians in Maggody: An Arly Hanks Mystery. large type ed. Joan Hess. LC 95-1979. 365p. 1995. lib. bdg. 20.95 (*0-7862-0422-2*) Thorndike Pr.

***Martians, Monsters, & Madonna: Fiction & Form in the World of Martin Amis.** John A. Dern. LC 98-54323. (Studies in Twentieth-Century British Literature: No. 2). 208p. (C). 2000. pap. text 25.95 (*0-8204-4457-X*) P Lang Pubng.

Martianus Capella - Concordantia in Martianum Capellam. Ed. by Matthias Korn & Stefan Reitzer. write for info. (*0-318-70666-0*); write for info. (*0-318-71170-2*); write for info. (*0-318-71983-5*) G Olms Pubs.

Martianus Capella & the Seven Liberal Arts: The Marriage of Philology & Mercury. William H. Stahl & E. L. Burge. LC 76-121876. (Records of Western Civilization Ser.: Vol. 2). 389p. 1977. pap. 22.50 (*0-231-09636-4*); text 69.50 (*0-231-03719-8*) Col U Pr.

Martianus Capella & the Seven Liberal Arts Vol. 1: The Quadrivium of Martianus Capella. William H. Stahl et al. LC 76-121876. 1991. text 76.00 (*0-231-03254-4*) Col U Pr.

Martie, the Unconquered. Kathleen Norris. (Collected Works of Kathleen Norris). 376p. 1999. reprint ed. lib. bdg. 98.00 (*1-58201-796-4*) Classic Bks.

Martin - God's Court Jester: Luther in Retrospect. Eric W. Gritsch. 289p. 1991. reprint ed. pap. 21.00 (*0-9623642-1-5*) Sigler Pr.

Martin A. Hansen. Faith Ingwersen & Niels Ingwersen. LC 76-21278. (Twayne's World Authors Ser.). 197p. (C). 1976. text 17.95 (*0-8057-6259-0*) Irvington.

Martin Adan, el Hermoso Crepusculo. Aguilar. (SPA.). pap. 16.99 (*968-16-3791-7*, Pub. by Fondo) Continental Bk.

Martin Aircraft, 1909-1960. John R. Breihan et al. LC 92-91184. (American Aircraft Manufacturers Ser.: Vol. 2). (Illus.). 208p. (Orig.). 1995. pap. 33.95 (*0-913322-03-2*) Jonathan T Pub.

Martin AM-1 - IQ Mauler. Bob Kowalski. (Naval Fighters Ser.: No. 24). 82p. 1994. pap. 14.95 (*0-942612-24-8*) Naval Fighters.

Martin Amis. Baxter. 1998. 23.95 (*0-8057-7804-7*, Twyne) Mac Lib Ref.

Martin & Guild: Free Movement of Persons in the European Union. Denis Martin & Elspeth Guild. 1996. write for info. (*0-406-06564-0*, GMMP, MICHIE) LEXIS Pub.

Martin & John. Dale Peck. LC 93-34064. 240p. 1994. reprint ed. pap. 13.00 (*0-06-097588-1*, Perennial) HarperTrade.

Martin & John: A Novel. Dale Peck. LC 92-1622. 1993. 21.00 (*0-374-20311-3*) FS&G.

Martin & Kunigunda Krotsch: Their Story, Their Ancestors, Their Descendants. Jane K. Klasen. (Illus.). 377p. 1988. 35.00 (*0-9620113-0-4*) J K Klasen.

Martin & Malcolm & America: A Dream or a Nightmare. James H. Cone. LC 90-14159. (Illus.). 358p. 1992. pap. 16.00 (*0-88344-824-6*) Orbis Bks.

Martin & Meditations on the South Valley. Jimmy S. Baca. LC 87-10983. 128p. 1987. pap. 8.95 (*0-8112-1032-4*, NDP648, Pub. by New Directions) Norton.

Martin & the Mountaintop: An Illustrated Tribute to Dr. Martin Luther King, Jr. Richard D. Gordon. LC 88-92651. (Illus.). 85p. (YA). (gr. 7 up). 1988. 14.95 (*0-9621308-0-X*) CMark Pr.

Martin & the Teacher's Pet. Bernice Chardiet & Grace Maccarone. (School Friends Ser.: No. 5). (Illus.). 48p. (J). (ps-3). 1992. pap. text 2.50 (*0-590-44931-1*) Scholastic Inc.

Martin Andersen: Editor, Publisher, Galley Boy. Ormund Powers. LC 96-41241. 1996. write for info. (*0-8092-3044-5*) NTC Contemp Pub Co.

Martin B. Hellriegel: Pastoral Liturgist. Noel J. Barrett. (Illus.). 209p. (Orig.). 1990. pap. 10.00 (*0-9626257-1-X*) CBCCU Amer.

Martin B-26 Marauder. J. K. Havener. (Illus.). 272p. 1988. pap. 16.95 (*0-8306-8287-2*, 22387) McGraw-Hill Prof.

***Martin B-26 Marauder.** Frederick A. Johnsen. (WarbirdTech Ser.: Vol. 29). (Illus.). 100p. 2000. pap. 16.95 (*1-58007-029-9*, Pub. by Specialty Pr) Voyageur Pr.

Martin B-26 Marauder. 2nd ed. J. K. Havener. (Illus.). 276p. 1988. reprint ed. pap. 18.95 (*0-941072-27-4*) Southern Herit.

Martin B-26 Marauder: A Bibliography & Guide to Research Sources. Ed. by John O. Moench. 200p. 1992. pap. text 7.95 (*1-877597-03-1*) Malia Enterprises.

Martin B-26 Marauder: A Bibliography, 1990. John O. Moench & Esther M. Oyster. 43p. (Orig.). 1990. pap. 6.50 (*1-877597-02-3*) Malia Enterprises.

Martin B-57 Canberra. Robert Mikesh. 0.00 (*0-88740-772-2*) Schiffer.

***Martin Bauman: or A Sure Thing: A Novel.** David Leavitt. LC 00-27589. 352p. 2000. 26.00 (*0-395-90243-6*) HM.

***Martin Bear & Friends: Tales of Enchantment for the Child in All of Us.** SHARON PUBLISHING STAFF. 1999. 22.95 (*0-9669973-1-X*) Sharon.

Martin Bonehouse: One Man's Look Within. Mark Stewart-Jones. 224p. 1996. 42.50 (*1-85776-039-5*, Pub. by Book Guild Ltd) Trans-Atl Phila.

Martin Book: A Complete History of Martin Guitars. Walter Carter. (Illus.). 108p. 1995. 22.95 (*0-87930-354-9*) Miller Freeman.

Martin Bormann: Nazi in Exile. Paul Manning. (Illus.). 320p. (C). 1981. 14.95 (*0-8184-0309-8*) Carol Pub Group.

Martin Boyd: A Life. Brenda Niall. 24p. 1989. reprint ed. pap. 19.95 (*0-522-84400-6*, Pub. by Melbourne Univ Pr) Paul & Co Pubs.

***Martin Brassey's Commentary on the Labour Relations Act.** Garth Abraham et al. 1999. ring bd. 96.50 (*0-7021-5118-1*, Pub. by Juta & Co) Gaunt.

Martin Brodeur. Robert Schnakenberg. (Ice Hockey Legends Ser.). (Illus.). 64p. (YA). (gr. 3 up). 1999. lib. bdg. 16.95 (*0-7910-5011-4*) Chelsea Hse.

***Martin Brodeur: Picture Perfect.** Phil Coffey. (SuperStar Ser.: Vol. 6). (Illus.). 96p. 1999. pap. 4.95 (*1-58261-157-2*, Pub. by Sprts Pubng) Partners-West.

Martin Brothers Potters. Malcolm Haslam. (Illus.). 172p. 1978. 95.00 (*0-903685-06-X*, Pub. by R Dennis) Antique Collect.

Martin Buber: A Centenary Volume. Haim Gordon. 1983. 49.50 (*0-88125-026-0*) Ktav.

Martin Buber: Prophet of Religious Secularism. 2nd rev. ed. Donald J. Moore. LC 95-46078. xxxiii, 298p. 1996. 32.50 (*0-8232-1639-X*); pap. 18.00 (*0-8232-1640-3*) Fordham.

Martin Buber: The Hidden Dialogue. Dan Avnon. LC 97-41158. (Twentieth Century Political Thinkers Ser.). 256p. 1998. pap. 21.95 (*0-8476-8688-4*) Rowman.

Martin Buber: The Hidden Dialogue. Dan Avnon. LC 97-41158. (Twentieth Century Political Thinkers Ser.). 256p. 1998. 58.00 (*0-8476-8687-6*) Rowman.

Martin Buber: The Life of Dialogue. 3rd rev. ed. Maurice Friedman. 1995. pap. text 16.00 (*0-226-26356-8*) U Ch Pr.

Martin Buber - Erich Foerster - Paul Tillich: Evangelische Theologie und Religionsphilosophie an der Universitat Frankfurt a.M. 1914 Bis 1933. Ed. by Dieter Stoodt. (GER., Illus.). 186p. 1990. 21.80 (*3-631-42500-7*) P Lang Pubng.

Martin Buber & the Eternal. Maurice Friedman. 191p. 1986. 29.95 (*0-89885-284-6*, Kluwer Acad Hman Sci) Kluwer Academic.

Martin Buber & the Human Sciences. Ed. by Maurice Friedman. LC 95-19176. 415p. (C). 1996. pap. text 18.95 (*0-7914-2876-1*) State U NY Pr.

Martin Buber & the Human Sciences. Ed. by Maurice Friedman. LC 95-19176. 415p. (C). 1996. text 54.50 (*0-7914-2875-3*) State U NY Pr.

Martin Buber-Carl Rogers Dialogue: A New Transcript with Commentary. Rob Anderson & Kenneth N. Cissna. LC 96-44106. (SUNY Series in Speech Communication). 138p. (C). 1997. text 29.50 (*0-7914-3437-0*); pap. text 9.95 (*0-7914-3438-9*) State U NY Pr.

Martin Buber on Psychology & Psychotherapy: Essays, Letters, & Dialogue. Martin Buber & Judith B. Agassi. LC 98-37835. 1998. 45.00 (*0-8156-0582-X*) Syracuse U Pr.

Martin Buber's Formative Years: From German Culture to Jewish Renewal, 1897-1909. Gilya G. Schmidt. LC 94-24877. (Judaic Studies). (Illus.). 192p. 1995. text 34.95 (*0-8173-0769-9*) U of Ala Pr.

Martin Buber's Life & Work, 3 vols. Maurice Friedman. LC 87-25415. (Illus.). 1408p. 1988. 79.00 (*0-8143-1947-5*) Wayne St U Pr.

Martin Buber's Life & Work: The Early Years, 1878-1923. Maurice Friedman. 400p. 1994. 45.00 (*0-85532-516-X*, Pub. by Srch Pr) St Mut.

Martin Buber's Life & Work: The Early Years, 1878-1923. Maurice S. Friedman. LC 87-25415. (Illus.). 463p. reprint ed. pap. 143.60 (*0-608-10588-0*, 207120900009) Bks Demand.

Martin Buber's Ontology: An Analysis of I & Thou. Robert E. Wood. LC 73-82510. (Studies in Phenomenology & Existential Philosophy). 139p. 1969. pap. 16.95 (*0-8101-0650-7*) Northwestern U Pr.

Martin Buber's Philosophy of Education. Daniel Murphy. 240p. 1988. 45.00 (*0-7165-2427-9*, Pub. by Irish Acad Pr) Intl Spec Bk.

Martin Buber's Philosophy of Interhuman Relation. Alexander S. Kohanski. LC 80-70626. 300p. 1982. 39.50 (*0-8386-3085-5*) Fairleigh Dickinson.

Martin Buber's Ten Rungs: Collected Hasidic Sayings. Martin Buber. 126p. 1995. pap. 6.95 (*0-8065-1593-7*, Citadel Pr) Carol Pub Group.

Martin Bucer: Reforming Church & Community. Ed. by D. F. Wright. LC 93-28910. 209p. (C). 1994. text 69.95 (*0-521-39144-X*) Cambridge U Pr.

Martin Bucer & Sixteenth Century Europe: Actes du Colloque de Strasbourg (28-31 Aout 1991), 2 Vols., Set. Ed. by Christian Krieger & Marc Linehard. LC 93-11160. (Studies in Medieval & Reformation Thought: Vol. 52-53). (Illus.). xvi, xiv 781p. 1993. 307.00 (*90-04-09886-0*) Brill Academic Pubs.

Martin Chambi: Photographs, 1920-1950. Intro. by Edward Ranney & Publio L. Mondejar. LC 92-62314. (Illus.). 115p. (Orig.). 1993. pap. 39.95 (*1-56098-244-6*) Smithsonian.

***Martin Chuzzelwit.** Charles Dickens. (Penguin Classics Ser.). 912p. 2000. pap. 10.95 (*0-14-043614-6*, Penguin Classics) Viking Penguin.

Martin Chuzzlewit. Charles Dickens. 1995. 20.00 (*0-679-43884-X*) Everymns Lib.

Martin Chuzzlewit. Charles Dickens. Ed. by Margaret Cardwell. (Clarendon Dickens Ser.). (Illus.). 940p. 1983. text 145.00 (*0-19-812488-0*) OUP.

Martin Chuzzlewit. Charles Dickens. Ed. by Sylvere Monod & Claude Rawson. (Unwin Critical Library). 192p. 1985. text 55.00 (*0-04-800028-0*) Routledge.

Martin Chuzzlewit. Charles Dickens. Ed. by P. N. Furbank. (English Library). 1968. pap. 10.95 (*0-14-043031-8*, Penguin Classics) Viking Penguin.

Martin Chuzzlewit. Charles Dickens. (Classics Library). 765p. 1998. pap. 3.95 (*1-85326-205-6*, 2056WW, Pub. by Wrdsworth Edits) NTC Contemp Pub Co.

Martin Chuzzlewit. Charles Dickens. Ed. & Intro. by Margaret Cardwell. (Oxford World's Classics Ser.). (Illus.). 766p. 1998. reprint ed. pap. 9.95 (*0-19-283461-4*) OUP.

Martin Chuzzlewit: An Annotated Bibliography. Robert Lougy. LC 89-23263. (Dickens Bibliographies Ser.: Vol. 10). 320p. 1990. text 20.00 (*0-8240-4608-0*, H01083) Garland.

Martin County Architectural Heritage: The Historic Structures of a Rural North Carolina County. Ed. by Thomas R. Butchko. LC 97-76490. 500p. 1999. 45.00 (*0-9626609-3-0*) MCH Soc NC.

Martin County Magazine, 1993: Covering Martin, Northern Palm Beach - St. Lucie Counties. (Illus.). 128p. 1993. 5.95 (*1-883117-03-8*) Mohr Graphics.

Martin County Magazine, 1992: For Visitors, New Residents, Businesses. (Illus.). 112p. 1992. 5.95 (*1-883117-02-X*) Mohr Graphics.

***Martin County, North Carolina.** Fred Harrison, Jr. (Images of America Ser.). (Illus.). 128p. 1999. pap. 18.99 (*0-7385-0272-3*) Arcadia Publng.

Martin County, North Carolina Abstracts of Deed Book A, 1774-1787. Library Committee Staff & Doris L. Wilson. 136p. 1993. pap. 25.00 (*0-9626609-2-2*) MCH Soc NC.

Martin County, North Carolina Abstracts of Deed Books B & C, 1787-1801. LC 97-70314. 170p. 1997. pap. 35.00 (*0-9626609-4-9*) MCH Soc NC.

Martin County, North Carolina Abstracts of Will Books 3 & 4, 1868-1910, Vol. 11. Ed. by Doris L. Wilson. 110p. 1990. pap. 20.00 (*0-9626609-1-4*) MCH Soc NC.

Martin County, North Carolina Abstracts of Will, 1774-1868, Bks. 1 & 2. Ed. by Doris L. Wilson. 240p. 1990. pap. 35.00 (*0-9626609-0-6*) MCH Soc NC.

***Martin Crimp: Plays 1: Dealing with Clair; Play with Repeats; Getting Attention; The Treatment.** Martin Crimp. 352p. 2000. pap. 17.00 (*0-571-20345-0*) Faber & Faber.

***Martin Del Rio: Investigation into Magic.** P. G. Maxwell-Stuart. 2000. text. write for info. (*0-7190-4976-8*, Pub. by Manchester Univ Pr) St Martin.

Martin Delany, Frederick Douglass, & the Politics of Representative Identity. Robert S. Levine. LC 96-9614. 352p. (C). (gr. 13). 1997. 49.95 (*0-8078-2323-6*); pap. 19.95 (*0-8078-4633-3*) U of NC Pr.

Martin, Descendants of John Martin of Brunswick & Old Bristol, Maine. Kenneth A. Clark. (Illus.). 81p. 1993. pap. 16.00 (*0-8328-3579-X*); lib. bdg. 26.00 (*0-8328-3578-1*) Higginson Bk Co.

Martin Dies. William Gellermann. LC 77-151620. (Civil Liberties in American History Ser.). 1972. reprint ed. lib. bdg. 37.50 (*0-306-70200-2*) Da Capo.

Martin Dressler: The Tale of an American Dreamer. Steven Millhauser. 1997. pap. 12.00 (*0-679-78127-7*) Vin Bks.

Martin Eden. Jack London. (Airmont Classics Ser.). (J). (gr. 9 up). 1969. mass mkt. 3.50 (*0-8049-0209-7*, CL-209) Airmont.

Martin Eden. Jack London. lib. bdg. 27.95 (*0-8488-1992-6*) Amereon Ltd.

Martin Eden. Ed. by Jack London. (Twelve-Point Ser.). 365p. 1999. lib. bdg. 24.00 (*1-58287-101-9*) North Bks.

Martin Eden. Jack London. 480p. 1994. pap. 12.95 (*0-14-018772-3*, Penguin Classics) Viking Penguin.

***Martin Eden.** Jack London. (Collected Works of Jack London). 411p. 1998. reprint ed. lib. bdg. 108.00 (*1-58201-726-3*) Classic Bks.

***Martin Eve Remembered.** Ed. by Walter Kemsley. 101p. 2000. pap. 14.95 (*0-85036-485-X*, Pub. by MRLN) Paul & Co Pubs.

Martin Faber. William Gilmore Simms. Ed. by Glenn Reed. (Masterworks of Literature Ser.). 1991. 11.95 (*0-8084-0435-0*) NCUP.

Martin Faber: The Story of a Criminal & Other Tales, 2 vols. William Gilmore Simms. LC 75-32784. (Literature of Mystery & Detection Ser.). 1976. reprint ed. 41.95 (*0-405-07899-4*) Ayer.

Martin Family, of Ireland, U. S. & Canada. G. C. Martin. 144p. 1993. reprint ed. pap. 25.00 (*0-8328-3716-4*); reprint ed. lib. bdg. 35.00 (*0-8328-3715-6*) Higginson Bk Co.

M

Martin Fierro. Jose Hernandez. (SPA.). 9.95 (968-432-424-3, Pub. by Porrua) Continental Bk.
Martin Fierro. Jose Hernandez. (Clasicos Ser.). (SPA.). 275p. 1997. pap. write for info. (1-881713-00-8) Pubns Puertorriquenas.
Martin Fierro. Jose Hernandez et al. Ed. by Frank G. Carrino & Alberto Carlos. LC 67-63759. 507p. (C). 1967. text 24.50 (0-87395-026-7) State U NY Pr.
Martin Fierro. 2nd ed. Jose Hernandez. 304p. 1989. pap. 10.95 (0-7859-5192-X) Fr & Eur.
Martin Gardner's New Mathematical Diversions from Scientific American. Martin Gardner. LC 83-12352. (Illus.). 254p. 1984. pap. 9.95 (0-226-28247-3) U Ch Pr.
Martin Gardner's Science Tricks. Martin Gardner. (Illus.). 96p. (J). 1998. 5.95 (0-8069-9544-0) Sterling.
Martin Gardner's Sixth Book of Mathematical Diversions from Scientific American. Martin Gardner. LC 83-12332. (Illus.). x, 262p. 1983. pap. 7.95 (0-226-28250-3) U Ch Pr.
Martin Gardner's Table Magic. Martin Gardner. LC 98-28297. (Illus.). 128p. 1998. pap. 5.95 (0-486-40403-X) Dover.
Martin Genealogy: Tied to the History of Germanna, Virginia. William A. Martin. 382p. (Orig.). 1995. pap. text 28.50 (0-7884-0184-X) Heritage Bk.
Martin Grove Brumbaugh: A Pennsylvanian's Odyssey from Sainted Schoolman to Bedeviled World War I Governor, 1862-1930. Earl C. Kaylor, Jr. LC 95-31882. (Illus.). 384p. 1995. 45.00 (0-8386-3689-6) Fairleigh Dickinson.
Martin Guitars. Reader's Digest Editors. (Woodworking Ser.). 264p. 1999. 40.00 (0-7621-0174-1, Pub. by RD Assn) Penguin Putnam.
*__Martin Hayes - Under the Moon.__ Martin Hayes. 48p. 1999. pap. 9.95 (0-7866-4090-1, 97291) Mel Bay.
*__Martin Hays - Under the Moon.__ Transcribed by Allan Smith. 48p. 1999. pap. 24.95 (0-7866-4092-8, 97291CDP) Mel Bay.
Martin Heidegger. George Steiner. LC 87-17647. x, 184p. (C). 1987. pap. text 12.00 (0-226-77232-2) U Ch Pr.
Martin Heidegger: A Bibliography. Ed. by Joan Nordquist. (Social Theory: A Bibliographic Ser.: No. 17). 64p. (Orig.). (C). 1990. pap. 20.00 (0-937855-33-2) Ref Rsch Serv.
Martin Heidegger: Between Good & Evil. Rudiger Safranski. Tr. by Ewald Osers from GER. LC 97-40754. 480p. 1999. text 36.50 (0-674-38709-0) HUP.
Martin Heidegger: Between Good & Evil. Rudiger Safranski. 496p. 1999. pap. 17.95 (0-674-38710-4) HUP.
Martin Heidegger: Critical Assessments, 4 vols., Set. Ed. by Christopher E. Macann. LC 91-46751. (Illus.). 1472p. (C). (gr. 13). 1992. text, boxed set 655.00 (0-415-04982-2, A7593) Routledge.
Martin Heidegger: Politics, Art, & Technology. Karsten Harries. LC 94-6413. 280p. (C). 1994. text 42.50 (0-8419-1334-X) Holmes & Meier.
Martin Heidegger No. 42: A Bibliography. Ed. by Joan Nordquist. (Social Theory: A Bibliographic Ser.: No. 42). (Orig.). 1996. pap. 20.00 (0-937855-83-9) Ref Rsch Serv.
Martin Heidegger & European Nihilism. Karl Lowith. Ed. by Richard Wolin. Tr. by Gary Steiner from GER. LC 94-48411. (European Perspectives Ser.). 256p. 1995. 47.50 (0-231-08406-4) Col U Pr.
Martin Heidegger & European Nihilism. Karl Lowith. 304p. 1998. pap. 17.50 (0-231-08407-2) Col U Pr.
Martin Heidegger & the Holocaust. Ed. by Alan Milchman & Alan Rosenberg. 288p. (C). 1996. text 60.00 (0-391-03925-3) Humanities.
Martin Heidegger & the Holocaust. Ed. by Alan Milchman & Alan Rosenberg. LC 95-21824. 288p. (C). 1997. pap. 17.50 (0-391-04015-4) Humanities.
Martin Heidegger & the Question of Literature: Toward a Postmodern Literary Hermeneutics. Ed. by William V. Spanos. LC 79-84261. (Studies in Phenomenology & Existential Philosophy). 349p. reprint ed. pap. 108.20 (0-7837-3728-9, 205790600009) Bks Demand.
Martin Hewitt, Investigator. Arthur Morrison. LC 75-32769. (Literature of Mystery & Detection Ser.). (Illus.). 1976. reprint ed. 19.95 (0-405-07888-9) Ayer.
Martin Hotine: Differential Geodesy. Ed. by J. D. Zund. (Illus.). 200p. 1991. 139.95 (0-387-53799-6) Spr-Verlag.
Martin Jessop Price: The Coinage in the Name of Alexander the Great & Philip Arrhidaeus, a British Museum Catalogue. 1991. 200.00 (3-908103-00-2) Classical Numismatic Grp.
Martin John Spalding: American Churchman. Thomas W. Spalding. LC 74-171040. 387p. reprint ed. pap. 120.00 (0-608-17282-0, 202952400061) Bks Demand.
*__Martin Johnson Heade.__ Theodore E. Stebbins, Jr. LC 99-60202. (Illus.). 208p. 1999. 50.00 (0-300-08169-3) Yale U Pr.
Martin Johnson Heade: A Survey: 1840-1900. Barbara Novak & Timothy A. Eaton. LC 96-61842. (Illus.). 80p. 1996. 39.95 (0-9655819-0-X); pap. 29.00 (0-9655819-1-8) Eaton Fine Art.
Martin Johnson's Amazing Maritime Models. Martin Johnson. (Illus.). 128p. 1995. 27.95 (0-7153-0186-1, Pub. by D & C Pub) Sterling.
Martin Kippenberger. Martin Kippenberger. 1997. pap. text 19.95 (3-89322-900-0, Pub. by Edition Cantz) Dist Art Pubs.
Martin Kippenberger: Heavy Madel. Stuart Morgan. (Illus.). 112p. 1992. pap. 35.00 (1-56466-014-1) Archer Fields.
Martin Kippenberger: Hotel-Hotel. Martin Kippenberger. (Illus.). 494p. (Orig.). 1993. pap. 49.50 (3-88375-143-X, Pub. by Walther Konig) Dist Art Pubs.
Martin Kippenberger: Hotel-Hotel. deluxe ed. Martin Kippenberger. (Illus.). 494p. (Orig.). 1993. pap. 90.00 (0-685-66695-6, Pub. by Walther Konig) Dist Art Pubs.
Martin Larson's Best. 1985. write for info. (0-935036-06-7) Liberty Lobby.
Martin Larson's Best. Martin Larson. 1982. 5.95 (0-935036-02-4) Liberty Lobby.
Martin-Leake: The First Man Ever to Be Awarded the Victoria Cross Twice. Ann Clayton. (Illus.). 256p. 1994. 31.95 (0-85052-397-4, Pub. by Leo Cooper) Trans-Atl Phila.
Martin Lebowitz: His Thought & Writings. Martin Lebowitz. Ed. by Robert E. Jones. LC 97-34876. 496p. (C). 1997. text 29.95 (0-7618-0933-3) U Pr of Amer.
Martin Luther. Compiled by E. R. Chamberlin. 39.00 (1-56696-070-3) Jackdaw.
Martin Luther. Mike Fearon. (Men of Faith Ser.). 144p. 1993. mass mkt. 4.99 (1-55661-306-7) Bethany Hse.
Martin Luther. Lindsay. 1996. pap. 11.99 (1-85792-261-1, Pub. by Christian Focus); pap. 11.99 (1-85792-262-X, Pub. by Christian Focus) Spring Arbor Dist.
Martin Luther. Sally Stepanek. (World Leaders Past & Present Ser.). (Illus.). 120p. (YA). (gr. 5 up). 1986. lib. bdg. 19.95 (0-87754-538-3) Chelsea Hse.
Martin Luther. Gustav Freytag. LC 78-144612. reprint ed. 34.50 (0-404-02577-3) AMS Pr.
Martin Luther. Estelle Ross. LC 83-45673. (Illus.). reprint ed. 37.50 (0-404-19862-7) AMS Pr.
Martin Luther: A Destiny. Lucien Febvre. Tr. by Roberts Tapley. LC 83-45640. reprint ed. 37.50 (0-404-19850-3) AMS Pr.
Martin Luther: An Introduction to His Life & Work. Bernhard Lohse. Tr. by Robert C. Schultz from GER. LC 85-45496. 304p. 1986. pap. 23.00 (0-8006-1964-1, 1-1964, Fortress Pr) Augsburg Fortress.
Martin Luther: German Monk Who Changed the Church. Ben Alex. (Heroes of Faith & Courage Ser.). (Illus.). 51p. (J). (gr. 3-12). 1998. reprint ed. pap. 7.99 (1-884543-13-8) O M Lit.
Martin Luther: His Life & Work. Hartmann Grisar. Ed. by Arthur Preuss. LC 71-137235. reprint ed. 49.50 (0-404-02935-3) AMS Pr.
Martin Luther: His Road to Reformation, 1483-1521. Martin Brecht. Tr. by James L. Schaaf. 592p. 1985. pap. 29.00 (0-8006-2813-6, 1-2813) Augsburg Fortress.
*__Martin Luther: Hitler's Spiritual Ancestor.__ 2nd rev. ed. Peter F. Weiner. LC 99-43327. (Illus.). 126p. 1999. pap. 11.00 (1-57884-954-3, 5516) Am Atheist.
Martin Luther: Knowledge & Mediation in the Renaissance. Jan Lindhardt. LC 86-17940. (Texts & Studies in Religion: Vol. 29). 270p. 1986. lib. bdg. 89.95 (0-88946-817-6) E Mellen.
Martin Luther: Learning for Life. Marilyn J. Harran. LC 97-33547. (Concordia Scholarship Today Ser.). 1997. 16.99 (0-570-05315-3, 12-3365) Concordia.
Martin Luther: Prophet to the Church Catholic. James Atkinson. LC 83-16462. 232p. reprint ed. 72.00 (0-608-16650-2, 202753500055) Bks Demand.
Martin Luther: Reformer or Heretic? Thomas E. Patten. 1991. pap. 5.50 (1-55673-407-7, 9220) CSS OH.
Martin Luther: Selections from His Writings. Martin Luther. Ed. by John Dillenberger. LC 61-9503. 560p. 1958. pap. 12.95 (0-385-09876-6, Anchor NY) Doubleday.
Martin Luther: Shaping & Defining the Reformation, 1521-1532. Martin Brecht. LC 84-47911. 560p. 1994. pap. 29.00 (0-8006-2814-4, 1-2814, Fortress Pr) Augsburg Fortress.
*__Martin Luther: Spy for the Night Riders.__ Julia Pferdehirt et al. (Trailblazer Books Curriculum Guides). (Illus.). 24p. 2000. pap. 4.99 (0-7642-2347-X) Bethany Hse.
Martin Luther: The Christian Between God & Death. Richard Marius. LC 98-36856. (Illus.). 592p. 1999. 35.00 (0-674-55090-0) HUP.
*__Martin Luther: The Christian Between God & Death.__ Richard Marius. 592p. 2000. pap. 17.95 (0-674-00387-X) HUP.
Martin Luther: The German Monk Who Changed the Church. Ben Alex. (Heroes of Faith & Courage Ser.). (Illus.). 42p. (J). (gr. 4-9). 1995. 11.99 (1-56476-475-3, 6-3475, Victor Bks) Chariot Victor.
Martin Luther: The Great Reformer. Edwin P. Booth. LC 98-24325. (Heroes of the Faith Ser.). 208p. (YA). (gr. 5 up). 1999. lib. bdg. 17.95 (0-7910-5037-8) Chelsea Hse.
Martin Luther: The Great Reformer. Dan Harmon. LC 96-132230. (Heroes of the Faith Ser.). 208p. 1998. pap. 3.97 (1-55748-727-8) Barbour Pub.
Martin Luther: The Great Reformer. J. A. Morrison. Ed. by Michael J. McHugh. (Illus.). 108p. (YA). (gr. 6-12). 1994. pap. text 3.95 (1-930092-16-4, CLP29915) Christian Liberty.
Martin Luther: The Man & the Image. Herbert D. Rix. 335p. 1983. text 37.50 (0-8290-0554-4) Irvington.
*__Martin Luther: The Preservation of the Church, 1532-1546.__ Martin Brecht. 1999. pap. text 29.00 (0-8006-2815-2) Augsburg Fortress.
Martin Luther Vol. 3: The Preservation of the Church, 1532-1546. Martin Brecht. Tr. by James L. Schaaf. 544p. 1993. 48.00 (0-8006-2704-0) Augsburg Fortress.
Martin Luther - Faith in Christ & the Gospel: Selected Spiritual Writings. Martin Luther. Ed. by Eric W. Gritsch. LC 95-34532. 192p. 1996. pap. 11.95 (1-56548-041-4) New City.
Martin Luther & George Fox, Vol. 3 of 7. Gordon Lindsay. (Men Who Changed the World Ser.: Vol. 3). 1965. 1.50 (0-89985-256-4) Christ for the Nations.
*__Martin Luther & John Wesley on the Sermon on the Mount.__ Tore Meistad. LC 98-45129. (Pietist & Wesleyan Studies: No. 10). (Illus.). 352p. 1999. 55.00 (0-8108-3567-3) Scarecrow.
*__Martin Luther & the Jews.__ Ed. by Martin Sasse. 12p. 1998. pap. 2.00 (0-944379-35-4) CPA Bk Pub.
Martin Luther & the Modern Mind: Freedom, Conscience, Toleration, Rights. Ed. by Manfred Hoffman. LC 85-3054. (Toronto Studies in Theology: Vol. 22). 296p. 1985. lib. bdg. 89.95 (0-88946-766-8) E Mellen.
Martin Luther & the Reformation: An Annotated Bibliography. Leona R. Phillips. 1985. lib. bdg. 250.00 (0-8490-3242-3) Gordon Pr.
Martin Luther & the Reformation in Germany until the Close of the Diet of Worms. Charles Austin Beard. LC 83-45638. reprint ed. 49.50 (0-404-19822-8) AMS Pr.
*__Martin Luther, German Saviour: German Evangelical Theological Factions & the Interpretation of Luther, 1917-1933.__ James M. Stayer. 192p. 2000. 55.00 (0-7735-2044-9, Pub. by McG-Queens Univ Pr) CUP Services.
Martin Luther, Hero of the Reformation. John Ritchie. (Illus.). 63p. 1996. pap. 4.99 (0-88019-357-3) Schmul Pub Co.
Martin Luther Jr. & His Family Paper Dolls in Full Color. 70th ed. Tom Tierney. (Illus.). (J). (gr. k-3). 1993. pap. 4.95 (0-486-27523-X) Dover.
Martin Luther King. (Illus.). 128p. 1999. pap. 9.95 (0-7509-1932-9) A Sutton.
Martin Luther King. Rosemary L. Bray. LC 93-41002. (Illus.). 48p. (J). (gr. 2 up). 1995. lib. bdg. 15.93 (0-688-13132-8, Grenwillow Bks) HarpC Child Bks.
Martin Luther King. Rosemary L. Bray. LC 93-41002. (Illus.). 48p. (J). (gr. 4-7). 1995. 16.00 (0-688-13131-X, Grenwillow Bks) HarpC Child Bks.
Martin Luther King. Rosemary L. Bray. LC 93-41002. (Illus.). 48p. (J). 1997. mass mkt. 5.95 (0-688-15219-8, Wm Morrow) Morrow Avon.
Martin Luther King. Rosemary L. Bray. 1997. 11.15 (0-606-11599-4, Pub. by Turtleback) Demco.
*__Martin Luther King.__ Marshall Frady. 2000. text. write for info. (0-670-88231-3, Viking) Viking Penguin.
Martin Luther King. Sande Smith. 80p. 1997. 10.98 (0-7858-0805-1) Bk Sales Inc.
Martin Luther King. abr. large type ed. (Great Illustrated Classics Ser.: Vol. 223-7). (Illus.). 240p. (YA). (gr. 3-7). 1995. 9.95 (0-86611-917-5) Playmore Inc.
Martin Luther King: A Man & His Dream. Stuart A. Kallen. LC 93-2296. (I Have a Dream Ser.). (YA). (gr. 7 up). 1993. lib. bdg. 15.98 (1-56239-256-5) ABDO Pub Co.
Martin Luther King: Peaceful Warrior. Ed Clayton. (J). (gr. 3 up). 1996. pap. 3.50 (0-614-15694-7, Archway) PB.
Martin Luther King: Striding Towards Freedom. Martin Tierney. 1989. pap. 22.00 (0-86217-217-9, Pub. by Veritas Pubns) St Mut.
Martin Luther King: The Inconvenient Hero. Vincent Harding. LC 95-26580. 150p. (Orig.). 1996. pap. 12.00 (1-57075-064-5) Orbis Bks.
Martin Luther King: The Man Behind the Myth. Des Griffin. (Illus.). 60p. (Orig.). 1987. pap. 7.00 (0-941380-04-1) Emissary Pubns.
Martin Luther King: The Peaceful Warrior. Ed Clayton. Ed. by Pat MacDonald. (Illus.). 128p. (J). (gr. 4-6). 1991. per. 3.50 (0-671-73242-0, Archway) PB.
Martin Luther King: The Peaceful Warrior. Edward Taylor Clayton. 1996. 8.35 (0-606-03932-5, Pub. by Turtleback) Demco.
Martin Luther King , Jr. - Spirit-Led Prophet: A Biography. Richard L. Deats. LC 99-51952. (Christian Living Ser.). 160p. 1999. pap. 9.95 (1-56548-097-X) New City.
Martin Luther King Biography. Walter Dean Myers. 32p. (gr. k-3). 15.89 (0-06-027704-1) HarpC.
Martin Luther King Day. Linda Lowery. (Carolrhoda On My Own Bks.). (Illus.). 56p. (J). (gr. k-3). 1987. lib. bdg. 18.60 (0-87614-299-4, Carolrhoda) Lerner Pub.
Martin Luther King Day. Linda Lowery. (Illus.). (J). (gr. 1-6). 1987. pap. 15.95 incl. audio (0-87499-070-X) Live Oak Media.
Martin Luther King Day. Linda Lowery. (Holiday on My Own Bks.). (Illus.). 56p. (J). (gr. k-3). 1988. reprint ed. pap. 5.95 (0-87614-468-7, Carolrhoda) Lerner Pub.
Martin Luther King Day. unabridged ed. Linda Lowery. (Illus.). (J). (gr. 1-6). 1987. 24.95 incl. audio (0-87499-071-8) Live Oak Media.
Martin Luther King Day, 4 bks., Set. unabridged ed. Linda Lowery. (Illus.). (J). (gr. 1-6). 1987. teacher ed. 33.95 incl. audio (0-87499-072-6) Live Oak Media.
Martin Luther King Day: Let's Meet Martin Luther King, Jr. Barbara DeRubertis. (Holidays & Heroes Ser.). (Illus.). (Orig.). (J). (gr. 1-5). 1992. pap. 4.95 (0-7915-1932-5) Kane Pr.
Martin Luther King, Jr. Jean Darby. (Lerner Biography Ser.). (Illus.). 112p. (YA). (gr. 6-9). 1990. lib. bdg. 23.96 (0-8225-4902-6, Lerner Publctns) Lerner Pub.
Martin Luther King, Jr. Jean Darby. (Illus.). 144p. (YA). (gr. 6-9). 1992. pap. 6.95 (0-8225-9611-3, Lerner Publctns) Lerner Pub.
Martin Luther King, Jr. Ebony Editors. LC 68-29476. (Ebony Picture Biography Ser.). (Illus.). 82p. 1968. pap. 5.00 (0-87485-025-8) Johnson Chicago.
Martin Luther King, Jr. V. P. Franklin. LC 98-22898. (Illus.). 192p. (J). 1998. 20.00 (0-517-20098-8) Random Hse Value.
Martin Luther King, Jr. Caroline Lazo. LC 93-9069. (Peacemakers Ser.). (Illus.). 64p. (J). (gr. 4 up). 1994. lib. bdg. 13.95 (0-87518-618-1, Dillon Silver Burdett) Silver Burdett Pr.
Martin Luther King, Jr. Carol Murphy. (Famous People Ser.). (Illus.). (J). (gr. k-6). 1991. 13.95 (0-89868-230-4); pap. 22.00 (0-89868-231-2) ARO Pub.
Martin Luther King, Jr. Diane Patrick. LC 89-24800. (First Bks.). (Illus.). 64p. (J). 1990. lib. bdg. 21.00 (0-531-10892-9) Watts.
Martin Luther King, Jr. Valerie Schloredt. (People Who Have Helped the World Ser.). 1990. 13.15 (0-606-04972-X, Pub. by Turtleback) Demco.
Martin Luther King, Jr. Nancy F. Shuker. (World Leaders Past & Present Ser.). (Illus.). 120p. (Orig.). (YA). (gr. 5 up). 1987. lib. bdg. 19.95 (0-87754-567-7) Chelsea Hse.
Martin Luther King, Jr. Nancy F. Shuker. (World Leaders Past & Present Ser.). (Illus.). 120p. (Orig.). (YA). (gr. 5 up). 1989. pap. 8.95 (0-7910-0219-5) Chelsea Hse.
*__Martin Luther King, Jr.__ Thomas Siebold. LC 99-38367. (People Who Made History Ser.). (Illus.). 144p. (gr. 9). 2000. 27.45 (0-7377-0227-3) Greenhaven.
*__Martin Luther King, Jr.__ Thomas Siebold. LC 99-38367. (People Who Made History Ser.). (Illus.). 144p. (YA). (gr. 9-12). 2000. pap. 17.45 (0-7377-0226-5) Greenhaven.
Martin Luther King, Jr. Kathie B. Smith. (Great Americans Ser.). (Illus.). 24p. (J). (gr. k-5). 1987. pap. 2.50 (0-671-63632-4) Litle Simon.
Martin Luther King, Jr. Flossie E. Thompson-Peters & Debra J. Behrens. Ed. by Lisa E. Jeffery. (African-American Heritage Ser.). (Illus.). 94p. (Orig.). (J). (gr. 3-12). 1992. pap. 8.00 (1-880784-06-8) Atlas Pr.
Martin Luther King, Jr. Jacqueline Woodson. Ed. by Bonnie Brook. (Let's Celebrate Ser.). (Illus.). 32p. (J). (gr. k-2). 1990. lib. bdg. 6.95 (0-671-69106-6) Silver Burdett Pr.
Martin Luther King, Jr. John F. Wukovits. LC 98-36197. (Importance of Ser.). (Illus.). (YA). (gr. 4-12). 1998. lib. bdg. 23.70 (1-56006-483-8) Lucent Bks.
Martin Luther King, Jr. Adam Fairclough. LC 94-4171. 168p. 1995. reprint ed. pap. 12.95 (0-8203-1653-9) U of Ga Pr.
Martin Luther King, Jr. A Big Biography. J. C. Reed. 16p. (J). (gr. 2-4). 1994. pap. 16.95 (1-56784-350-6) Newbridge Educ.
Martin Luther King, Jr. A Biography for Young Children. Carol H. Schlank & Barbara Metzger. LC 88-64160. (Illus.). 24p. (J). (ps-3). 1989. pap. 7.00 (0-9613271-2-X) RAEYC.
Martin Luther King, Jr. A Documentary . . . Montgomery to Memphis. Ed. by Flip Schulke. (Illus.). 224p. (YA). (gr. 8 up). 1999. pap. 17.95 (0-393-07492-7) Norton.
Martin Luther King, Jr. A History of His Religious Witness & of His Life. Russell Moldovan. LC 99-27995. 284p. 1999. 74.95 (1-57309-346-7); pap. 54.95 (1-57309-345-9) Intl Scholars.
Martin Luther King Jr. A Story For Children. Margurite Thompson. 24p. (J). (gr. k-3). 1983. pap. 3.50 (0-912444-25-8) DARE Bks.
Martin Luther King, Jr. An Annotated Bibliography, 12. Compiled by Sherman E. Pyatt. LC 86-7593. (Bibliographies & Indexes in Afro-American & African Studies: No. 12). 166p. 1986. lib. bdg. 55.00 (0-313-24635-1, PML/, Greenwood Pr) Greenwood.
Martin Luther King, Jr. And the March Toward Freedom. Rita Hakim. (Gateway Civil Rights Ser.). (Illus.). 32p. (J). (gr. 2-4). 1991. pap. 3.80 (1-878841-33-5); lib. bdg. 20.90 (1-878841-13-0) Millbrook Pr.
Martin Luther King, Jr. Civil Rights Leader. Robert Jakoubek. Ed. by Nathan I. Huggins. (Black Americans of Achievement Ser.). (Illus.). 124p. (YA). (gr. 5 up). 1989. lib. bdg. 19.95 (1-55546-597-8) Chelsea Hse.
Martin Luther King, Jr. Civil Rights Leader. Robert Jakoubek. (Black Americans of Achievement Ser.). (Illus.). 124p. (YA). (gr. 5 up). 1990. pap. 8.95 (0-7910-0243-8) Chelsea Hse.
Martin Luther King, Jr. Civil Rights Leader. Kathy K. Lambert. (Junior Black Americans of Achievement Ser.). (Illus.). 76p. (J). (gr. 3-6). 1992. pap. 4.95 (0-7910-1954-3) Chelsea Hse.
Martin Luther King, Jr. Civil Rights Leader. Kathy K. Lambert. LC 91-34986. (Junior Black Americans of Achievement Ser.). (Illus.). 76p. (J). (gr. 5-7). 1993. lib. bdg. 15.95 (0-7910-1759-1) Chelsea Hse.
Martin Luther King, Jr. Civil Rights Leader. Joseph Nazel. (Black American Ser.). (Illus.). 192p. (YA). 1992. mass mkt. 3.95 (0-87067-573-7, Melrose Sq) Holloway.
*__Martin Luther King Jr. Dream of Freedom.__ Ariel. (Illus.). 80p. 1999. 4.95 (0-7407-0072-3) Andrews & McMeel.
Martin Luther King, Jr. Free at Last. David A. Adler. LC 86-4670. (Illus.). 48p. (J). (gr. k-3). 1986. lib. bdg. 15.95 (0-8234-0618-0) Holiday.
Martin Luther King, Jr. Leader for Civil Rights. Michael A. Schuman. LC 95-42797. (African-American Biographies Ser.). 128p. (YA). (gr. 6 up). 1996. lib. bdg. 20.95 (0-89490-687-9) Enslow Pubs.
Martin Luther King, Jr. Let's Meet Martin Luther King, Jr. Barbara DeRubertis. (Holidays & Heroes Ser.). (Illus.). 32p. (Orig.). (J). (gr. 1-5). 1996. pap. 7.95 incl. audio (1-57565-010-X) Kane Pr.
Martin Luther King, Jr. Man of Peace. Patricia McKissack & Fredrick McKissack. LC 90-19156. (Great African Americans Ser.). (Illus.). 32p. (J). (gr. 1-4). 1991. lib. bdg. 14.95 (0-89490-302-0) Enslow Pubs.
Martin Luther King, Jr: Mini Play. (Black Americans Ser.). (J). (gr. 5 up). 1977. 6.50 (0-89550-363-8) Stevens & Shea.
*__Martin Luther King, Jr. Nonviolent Strategies & Tactics for Social Change.__ John J. Ansbro. 2000. reprint ed. pap. 18.95 (1-56833-169-X, Pub. by Madison Bks UPA) Natl Bk Netwk.
Martin Luther King, Jr. Personalism & the Sacredness of the Human Personality. AESOP Enterprises, Inc. Staff & Gwendolyn J. Crenshaw. (Heroes & Sheroes Ser.). 16p. (J). (gr. 3-12). 1991. pap. write for info. incl. audio (1-880771-01-2) AESOP Enter.
Martin Luther King, Jr. The Dream of Peaceful Revolution. Della Rowland. Ed. by Richard Gallin. (Civil Rights Ser.). (Illus.). 128p. (J). (gr. 5 up). 1990. lib. bdg. 12.95 (0-382-09924-9) Silver Burdett Pr.

An Asterisk (*) at the beginning of an entry indicates that the title is appearing for the first time.

Martin Luther King, Jr. The Dream of Peaceful Revolution. Della Rowland. Ed. by Richard Gallin. (Civil Rights Ser.). (Illus.). 128p. (YA). (gr. 5 up). 1990. pap. 7.95 (*0-382-24062-6*) Silver Burdett Pr.

Martin Luther King, Jr. The Dream of Peaceful Revolution. Della Rowland. (History of the Civil Rights Movement Ser.). (J). 1990. 13.15 (*0-606-04742-5*, Pub. by Turtleback) Demco.

Martin Luther King, Jr: The Evolution of a Revolutionary. Manu Ampim. (Illus.). 1994. pap. write for info. (*0-9636447-4-2*) Advan The Res.

Martin Luther King, Jr. Young Man with a Dream. Dharathula H. Millender. (Childhood of Famous Americans Ser.). (J). 1986. 10.05 (*0-606-03247-9*, Pub. by Turtleback) Demco.

Martin Luther King, Jr. Young Man with a Dream. Dharathula H. Millender. LC 86-10739. (Childhood of Famous Americans Ser.). (Illus.). 192p. (J). (gr. 3-7). 1986. reprint ed. mass mkt. 4.95 (*0-02-042010-2*) Macmillan.

Martin Luther King, Jr. & His Birthday. Jacqueline Woodson. 32p. (J). (ps-3). 1996. pap. text 4.95 (*0-382-39476-3*) Silver Burdett Pr.

Martin Luther King, Jr. & His Birthday. Jacqueline Woodson. LC 89-49536. (Let's Celebrate Ser.). 1990. 10.15 (*0-606-10260-4*, Pub. by Turtleback) Demco.

Martin Luther King, Jr. & Our January 15th Holiday for Children. Eunice Cauper. (Illus.). 32p. (Orig.). (J). (gr. k-3). 1991. pap. text 6.00 (*0-9617551-3-X*) E Cauper.

Martin Luther King, Jr. & the Freedom Movement. Lillie Patterson. Ed. by John A. Scott. (Makers of America Ser.). (Illus.). 192p. (YA). (gr. 7-12). 1989. 19.95 (*0-8160-1605-4*) Facts on File.

Martin Luther King, Jr. & the Freedom Movement. Lillie Patterson. Ed. by John A. Scott. (Makers of America Ser.). (Illus.). 192p. (YA). (gr. 7-12). 1993. pap. 8.95 (*0-8160-2997-0*) Facts on File.

Martin Luther King, Jr. & the March Toward Freedom. Rita Hakim. (Gateway Civil Rights Ser.). 1991. 10.15 (*0-606-01457-8*, Pub. by Turtleback) Demco.

Martin Luther King, Jr., & the Sermonic Power of Public Discourse. Ed. by Carolyn Calloway-Thomas & John L. Lucaites. LC 92-21236. (Studies in Rhetoric & Communication). 256p. (C). 1993. text 34.95 (*0-8173-0689-7*) U of Ala Pr.

Martin Luther King, Jr. Companion: Quotations from the Speeches, Essays, & Books of Martin Luther King, Jr. Martin Luther King, Jr. LC 92-40818. (Illus.). xiii, 108p. 1992. text 9.95 (*0-312-09063-3*) St Martin.

Martin Luther King, Jr. Companion: Quotations from the Speeches, Essays, & Books of Martin Luther King, Jr. Martin Luther King, Jr. LC 98-51196. 1998. text 12.95 (*0-312-19990-2*) St Martin.

Martin Luther King, Jr. Companion: Quotations from the Speeches, Essays, & Books of Martin Luther King, Jr. Martin Luther King, Jr. LC 94-24627. (Illus.). xiii, 108p. 1994. pap. 7.95 (*0-312-11851-1*) St Martin.

Martin Luther King, Jr. Day. Mir Tamim Ansary. LC 98-14378. (Holiday Histories Ser.). (Illus.). 32p. (J). (ps-3). 1999. lib. bdg. 13.95 (*1-57572-873-7*) Heinemann Lib.

***Martin Luther King, Jr. Day.** Helen Frost. LC 99-49390. (National Holidays Ser.). (Illus.). 24p. (J). (ps-2). 2000. lib. bdg. 13.25 (*0-7368-0543-5*, Pebble Bks) Capstone Pr.

Martin Luther King, Jr. Day. Dianne M. MacMillan. LC 91-43097. (Best Holiday Bks.). (Illus.). 48p. (J). (gr. 1-4). 1992. lib. bdg. 18.95 (*0-89490-382-9*) Enslow Pubs.

***Martin Luther King, Jr. Day.** David F. Marx. LC 00-22638. (Rookie Read-About Holidays Ser.). (Illus.). 2001. write for info. (*0-516-22211-2*) Childrens.

Martin Luther King, Jr. Day. Lynda Sorensen. LC 94-17840. (J). 1994. lib. bdg. 14.60 (*1-57103-068-9*) Rourke Pr.

Martin Luther King, Jr. Day Activities. Pamela Friedman. 32p. 1997. pap. 2.95 (*1-57690-067-3*) Tchr Create Mat.

Martin Luther King, Jr. on Leadership: Inspiration & Wisdom for Challenging Times. Donald T. Phillips. LC 98-3795. 272p. 1999. 22.00 (*0-446-52367-4*, Pub. by Warner Bks) Little.

Martin Luther King, Jr., on Leadership: Inspiration & Wisdom for Challenging Times. Donald T. Phillips. 384p. 2000. mass mkt. 13.95 (*0-446-67546-6*, Pub. by Warner Bks) Little.

Martin Luther King Jr. Pop Up. (J). 1996. pap. 8.95 (*0-8167-2569-1*) Troll Communs.

Martin Luther King, Jr. Lola M. Schaefer. LC 98-19960. (J). 1998. 13.25 (*0-7368-0111-1*, Pebble Bks) Capstone Pr.

Martin Luther King, Jr. Lola M. Schaefer. (Famous Americans Ser.). 1998. 13.25 (*0-516-21503-5*) Childrens.

***Martin Luther King, Jr. A Man with a Dream.** Jayne Pettit. LC 00-36646. (Book Report Biography Ser.). (Illus.). 2001. write for info. (*0-531-11670-0*) Watts.

***Martin Luther King, Jr. Minister & Civil Rights Leader.** Brendan January. LC 00-37618. (Career Biographies Ser.). (Illus.). 2000. write for info. (*0-89434-342-4*) Ferguson.

Martin Luther King Poster Book. D. J. Arneson. (Illus.). 6p. (J). 1992. pap. 2.95 (*1-56156-161-4*) Kidsbks.

Martin Luther, the Hero of the Reformation. Henry E. Jacobs. LC 72-170838. reprint ed. 47.50 (*0-404-03544-2*) AMS Pr.

Martin Luther, Theologian of the Church: Collected Essays. George W. Forell. Ed. by William R. Russell. LC 94-61151. (Word & World Supplement Ser.: 2). 280p. (Orig.). 1994. pap. text 14.95 (*0-9632389-1-4*) Luther Seminary.

Martin Luther's Basic Theological Writings. Ed. by Timothy F. Lull. LC 89-34201. 752p. (Orig.). 1989. pap. 30.00 (*0-8006-2327-4*, 1-2327, Fortress Pr) Augsburg Fortress.

Martin Luther's Christmas Book. Ed. by Roland H. Bainton. LC 97-28979. 96p. 1997. pap. 10.99 (*0-8066-3577-0*, 9-3577, Augsburg) Augsburg Fortress.

Martin Luther's Christology & Ethics. Dietmar Lage. LC 89-77128. (Texts & Studies in Religion: Vol. 45). 192p. 1990. lib. bdg. 79.95 (*0-88946-834-6*) E Mellen.

Martin Luther's Easter Book. Ed. by Roland H. Bainton. LC 97-28980. (Illus.). 96p. 1997. pap. text 10.99 (*0-8066-3578-9*, 9-3578, Augsburg) Augsburg Fortress.

Martin Luther's Friends. Noel C. Leroque. 1997. pap. text 18.95 (*1-57736-022-2*) Providence Hse.

Martin Luther's Theology: Its Historical & Systematic Development. Bernhard Lohse. Tr. by Roy Harrisville from GER. LC 99-22239. 1999. 43.00 (*0-8006-3091-2*, Fortress Pr) Augsburg Fortress.

Martin Marauder & the Franklin Allens: A Wartime Love Story. Ed. by Donald J. Mrozek et al. (Illus.). 544p. 1980. pap. 10.00 (*0-89745-007-8*) Sunflower U Pr.

Martin Margiela. Martin Margiela. LC 98-141031. (Illus.). 90p. 1997. pap. 40.00 (*90-6918-180-0*) Dist Art Pubs.

Martin Marietta Corp. A Report on the Company's Environmental Policies & Practices. (Illus.). 51p. (C). 1994. reprint ed. pap. text 40.00 (*0-7881-0905-7*, Coun on Econ) DIANE Pub.

Martin Marprelate, Gentleman: Master Job Throkmorton Laid Open in His Colors. Leland H. Carlson. LC 80-26442. (Illus.). 467p. 1981. reprint ed. pap. 144.80 (*0-608-03170-4*, 206362300007) Bks Demand.

Martin Mars XPB2M-1 & JRM Flying Boats. Steve Ginter. (Naval Fighters Ser.: Vol. 29). (Illus.). 72p. (Orig.). 1995. pap. 14.95 (*0-942612-29-9*) Naval Fighters.

Martin Merrivale. John T. Trowbridge. (Notable American Authors). 1999. reprint ed. lib. bdg. 125.00 (*0-7812-9792-3*) Rprt Serv.

Martin Munkacsi: An Aperture Monograph. Susan Morgan. (Illus.). 80p. 1992. 53.00 (*0-89381-516-0*) Aperture.

Martin of Tours: Parish Priest, Mystic & Exorcist. Christopher Donaldson. (Illus.). 196p. 1985. pap. 9.95 (*0-7102-0682-8*, Routledge Thoemms) Routledge.

Martin of Tours: The Shaping of Celtic Spirituality. Christopher Donaldson. LC 99-170726. 176p. 1997. pap. 15.95 (*1-85311-157-0*, 1982, Pub. by Canterbury Press Norwich) Morehouse Pub.

Martin P. Catherwood Library of the New York State School of Industrial & Labor Relations: Cumulation of the Library Catalog Supplements, 9 vols., Set. Cornell University, New York State School of Indus. 1977. suppl. ed. 1625.00 (*0-8161-0022-5*, G K Hall & Co) Mac Lib Ref.

Martin. Peter Martin, 1741-1807: A Revolutionary Soldier of Virginia Buried in Shelby Co., Ky.; His Washington Co., Ind., & Many Other Descendants. Marjorie A. Souder. 464p. 1995. reprint ed. pap. 69.50 (*0-8328-4798-4*); reprint ed. lib. bdg. 79.50 (*0-8328-4797-6*) Higginson Bk Co.

Martin Pring on Market Momentum. Martin J. Pring. 335p. 1997. pap. 29.95 (*0-7863-1176-2*, Irwn Prfssnl) McGraw-Hill Prof.

Martin Pring's Introduction to Technical Analysis: A CD-ROM Seminar & Workbook. Martin J. Pring. 1997. pap. text, wbk. ed. write for info. (*0-07-913621-4*) McGraw.

***Martin Pring's Introduction to Technical Analysis: A CD-ROM Seminar & Workbook.** Martin J. Pring. LC 97-9028. (Illus.). 304p. 1998. pap. 49.95 incl. cd-rom (*0-07-032933-8*) McGraw.

Martin Puryear. Neal Benezra. LC 91-2366. (Illus.). 160p. 1991. pap. 29.95 (*0-86559-092-3*) Art Inst Chi.

Martin Puryear. Neal Benezra. LC 91-65308. (Illus.). 160p. 1993. pap. 29.95 (*0-500-27702-8*, Pub. by Thames Hudson) Norton.

Martin Reef: Lightship to Lighthouse/Another Chapter in Les Cheneaux History. John J. Sellman. Ed. by Philip M. Pittman. LC 96-85265. (Illus.). 71p. 1996. pap. 7.50 (*0-9673493-0-3*) Les Cheneaux Hist.

Martin Reis, Sport bei Horaz, Band 2. (Supplement-Reihe/Supplement Ser.). (GER.). vi, 120p. 1994. 49.80 (*3-615-00136-2*, Pub. by Weidmann) Lubrecht & Cramer.

Martin Rico y Ortega in the Collection. Elizabeth D. Trapier. (Illus.). 1937. 10.00 (*0-87535-042-9*) Hispanic Soc.

Martin Rivas. Alberto Blest Gana. Tr. by Charles Whitham. 1977. lib. bdg. 59.95 (*0-8490-2212-6*) Gordon Pr.

Martin Rivas. Alberto Blest Gana. Ed. by Jaime Concho. Tr. by Tess O'Dwyer. LC 99-47790. (Library of Latin America). 448p. 2000. 30.00 (*0-19-510713-6*); pap. 18.95 (*0-19-510714-4*) OUP.

Martin Said So: About Martin Luther King Jr. Wanda Schell & Kenny Bento. (Illus.). 28p. 1991. pap. 3.50 (*0-88680-344-6*) I E Clark.

Martin Schmiel: Personalbibliographie Eines Wirtschafts- und Berufspadagogen. Gerhard Schannewitzky. 127p. 1998. 28.95 (*3-631-33348-X*) P Lang Pubng.

Martin Scorcese - Close Up: The Making of His Movies. Andy Dougan. (Illus.). 144p. 1998. pap. text 13.95 (*1-56025-161-1*, Thunders Mouth) Avalon NY.

Martin Scorsese. Lester Keyser. (Twayne's Filmmakers Ser.). 160p. 1992. 26.95 (*0-8057-9315-1*, Twyne); pap. 13.95 (*0-8057-9321-6*, Twyne) Mac Lib Ref.

Martin Scorsese: A Journey. 2nd ed. Mary P. Kelly. 320p. 1997. pap. text 13.95 (*1-56025-116-6*, Thunders Mouth) Avalon NY.

Martin Scorsese: An Analysis of His Feature Films, with a Filmography of His Entire Directorial Career. Marie K. Connelly. LC 92-56636. (Illus.). 192p. 1993. lib. bdg. 31.50 (*0-89950-845-6*) McFarland & Co.

Martin Scorsese: Interviews. Ed. by Peter Brunette. LC 98-28414. (Interviews with Filmmakers Ser.). (Illus.). 256p. 1999. pap. 18.00 (*1-57806-072-9*); text 45.00 (*1-57806-071-0*) U Pr of Miss.

Martin Secker & Warburg: The First Fifty Years: A Memoir. George M. Thomson. LC 86-205995. 86p. 1986. write for info. (*0-436-52054-0*) M Secker & Warburg.

Martin Shares His Cloak. Regine Schindler. (Illus.). (C). 1990. text 35.00 (*0-7855-6908-1*, Pub. by St Paul Pubns) St Mut.

Martin Simpson - Smoke & Mirrors. Martin Simpson. 48p. 1997. pap. 9.95 (*0-7866-1760-8*, 95717) Mel Bay.

Martin Simpson-Smoked Mirrors. Martin Simpson. 48p. 1997. pap. 24.95 incl. audio compact disk (*0-7866-3094-9*, 95717CDP) Mel Bay.

Martin Smith Ceramics, 1976-1996: Balance & Space. Dorris U. Kuyken-Schneider & Martin Smith. LC 97-168451. (Illus.). 128p. 1997. pap. 27.95 (*90-6918-172-X*, Pub. by Boymans Mus) U of Wash Pr.

Martin Taylor - Jazz Guitar Artistry. Martin Taylor. 1990. pap. 16.95 (*0-7935-8670-4*) H Leonard.

Martin the Cavebine. Sara Nickerson. LC 88-71369. (Illus.). 28p. (Orig.). (J). (gr. 2-4). 1988. pap. 9.00 (*0-935529-06-3*) Comprehen Health Educ.

Martin the Cobbler. Leo Tolstoy. (Illus.). 32p. (J). (gr. k-12). 1982. 10.45 (*0-86683-638-1*) Harper SF.

Martin "The Hero" Merriweather. Bobby L. Jackson & Michael C. Carter. LC 93-77056. (Illus.). 48p. (Orig.). (J). (gr. 4-8). 1993. 15.95 (*0-9634932-2-1*); pap. 7.95 (*0-9634932-3-X*) Multicult Pubns.

Martin the Warrior. Brian Jacques. (Redwall Ser.: Vol. 6). (Illus.). 384p. (J). (gr. 8-12). 1995. mass mkt. 5.99 (*0-441-00186-6*) Ace Bks.

Martin the Warrior. Brian Jacques. LC 93-26434. (Redwall Ser.: Vol. 6). (Illus.). 400p. (J). (gr. 3-7). 1994. 21.99 (*0-399-22670-2*, Philomel) Peng Put Young Read.

Martin the Warrior. Brian Jacques. (Redwall Ser.: 6). (J). (gr. 4-8). 1996. 12.15 (*0-606-12990-1*, Pub. by Turtleback) Demco.

Martin Van Buren. Jim Hargrove. LC 87-16023. (Encyclopedia of Presidents Ser.). (Illus.). 100p. (J). (gr. 3 up). 1987. lib. bdg. 24.00 (*0-516-01391-2*) Childrens.

Martin Van Buren. Anne Welsbacher. LC 98-4338. (United States Presidents Ser.). (J). 1998. 14.95 (*1-57765-238-X*) ABDO Pub Co.

Martin Van Buren. Edward M. Shepard. Ed. by John T. Morse, Jr. LC 76-128964. (American Statesmen Ser.: No. 18). reprint ed. 49.50 (*0-404-50868-5*) AMS Pr.

Martin Van Buren: Eighth President of the United States. Rafaela Ellis. Ed. by Richard G. Young. LC 88-24535. (Presidents of the United States Ser.). (Illus.). (J). (gr. 5-9). 1989. lib. bdg. 21.27 (*0-944483-12-7*) Garrett Ed Corp.

Martin Van Buren: Law, Politics, & the Shaping of Republican Ideology. Jerome Mushkat & Joseph G. Rayback. LC 97-8710. 272p. 1997. lib. bdg. 35.00 (*0-87580-229-X*) N Ill U Pr.

***Martin Van Buren: The Romantic Age of American Politics.** John Niven. Ed. by Katherine Speirs. (Signature Ser.). (Illus.). 715p. 2000. reprint ed. 37.50 (*0-945707-25-8*) Amer Political.

Martin Van Buren & the American Political System. Donald B. Cole. LC 84-3402. 492p. reprint ed. pap. 152.60 (*0-7837-0099-7*, 204037700016) Bks Demand.

Martin von Nathusius und die Anfange Protestantischer Wirtschafts - Und Sozialethik. Thomas Schlag. 450p. 1998. 124.00 (*3-11-015862-0*) De Gruyter.

Martin Wagner: Urban Projects in Rural Contexts 1988-1993. Lars Lerup et al.Tr. of Urbane Provekte Im Landlichen Umfeld 1988-1993. (Illus.). 120p. 1996. 50.00 (*0-9651144-0-6*) W K Stout.

Martin XB-51. Scott Libis. Ed. by Steve Ginter. (Air Force Legends Ser.: No. 201). (Illus.). 48p. 1998. pap. 10.95 (*0-942612-00-0*, NFAF201) Naval Fighters.

Martin Yan's Asia: Favorite Recipes from Hong Kong, Malaysia, Singapore, Philippines & Japan. Martin Yan. LC 97-36267. (Illus.). 256p. (Orig.). 1997. pap. 19.95 (*0-912333-32-4*) BB&T Inc.

Martin Yan's Culinary Journey Through China. Martin Yan. LC 95-18719. (Illus.). 224p. (Orig.). 1995. pap. 18.95 (*0-912333-64-2*) BB&T Inc.

Martin Yan's Feast: The Best of Yan Can Cook. Martin Yan. (Illus.). 400p. 1998. 34.95 (*0-912333-31-6*) BB&T Inc.

***Martin Yan's Invitation to Chinese Cooking.** Martin Yan. LC 99-53496. (Illus.). 240p. 2000. pap. 24.95 (*1-57959-504-9*) BB&T Inc.

Martin Yesterday. Brad Fraser. LC 99-186298. 128p. 1999. pap. 13.95 (*1-896300-26-X*) Genl Dist Srvs.

Martin Zweig's Winning on Wall Street. rev. ed. Martin E. Zweig. 304p. 1994. mass mkt. 13.99 (*0-446-67014-6*, Pub. by Warner Bks) Little.

Martin Zweig's Winning on Wall Street. rev. ed. Martin E. Zweig. LC 97-165426. 304p. 1997. mass mkt. 14.99 (*0-446-67281-5*, Pub. by Warner Bks) Little.

Martina: The Lives & Times of Martina Navratilova. Adrianne Blue. 240p. 1995. 19.95 (*1-55972-300-9*, Birch Ln Pr) Carol Pub Group.

***Martina Hingis.** Christin Ditchfield. (Women Who Win Ser.). (Illus.). 2000. pap. 7.95 (*0-7910-6157-4*) Chelsea Hse.

***Martina Hingis.** Christin Ditchfield. LC 00-22841. (Women Who Win Ser.). 2001. 17.95 (*0-7910-5797-6*) Chelsea Hse.

Martina Hingis. Richard Rambeck. LC 97-44094. (Illus.). (J). 1998. lib. bdg. 21.36 (*1-56766-519-5*) Childs World.

Martina Hingis Linda Shaughnessy. LC 98-33153. (Taking Part Ser.). 2000. write for info. (*0-382-42145-0*, Dillon Silver Burdett) Silver Burdett Pr.

Martina Kaposchi Erzaehlt Deutsche Maerchen: Es War Einmal. Martina Kaposchi. (GER., Illus.). 57p. 1992. student ed. 32.95 incl. audio (*0-9646575-0-3*) CEMSCO.

Martina Navratilova see Notable Biographies

Martina Navratilova. Ed. by Puffin Books Staff. (Women of Our Time Ser.). (J). (gr. 2-6). 1989. pap. 3.50 (*0-14-033218-9*, PuffinBks) Peng Put Young Read.

***Martindale: The Complete Drug Reference.** 32nd ed. Kathleen Parfitt. 1999. 299.00 (*0-85369-429-X*, Pub. by Pharmaceutical Pr) Rittenhouse.

Martindale & Brztwa. Joyce J. Elam & Betty Vandenbosch. 6p. (C). 1997. pap. 4.00 (*0-13-632712-5*, Macmillan Coll) P-H.

Martindale Extra Pharmacopoeia. 31st ed. Ed. by James Reynolds. 2739p. 1996. text 299.00 (*0-85369-342-0*, Pub. by Pharmaceutical Pr) Rittenhouse.

Martindale-Hubbell Bar Register of Preeminent Lawyers, 1998 In The United States, Canada & Other Countries. Martindale-Hubbell Staff. 1998. 195.00 (*1-56160-321-X*) Martindale-Hubbell.

Martindale-Hubbell Bar Register of Preeminent Lawyers, 1998: In The United States, Canada & Other Countries. Martindale-Hubbell Staff. 1998. 195.00 (*1-56160-320-1*) Martindale-Hubbell.

***Martindale Hubbell Law Directory 2000.** Ed. by Martindale-Hubbell Staff. 2000. 695.00 (*1-56160-376-7*) Martindale-Hubbell.

Martine Aballea. Martine Aballea & Jerome Sans. (Illus.). 68p. 1992. pap. 20.00 (*2-908257-02-5*, Pub. by F R A C) Dist Art Pubs.

Martines De Pasqually, 2 vols. in 1. Gerard Van Rijnberk. (Saint-Martin, Oeuvres Completes Ser.: No. 2, Vol. 1). 390p. 1982. reprint ed. write for info. (*3-487-07274-2*) G Olms Pubs.

Martine's Handbook of Etiquette. Arthur Martine. LC 95-37797. 176p. 1996. reprint ed. pap. 12.95 (*1-55709-429-2*) Applewood.

Martingale Approximations. Ed. by Yu V. Borovskikh & Vladimir S. Korolyuk. LC 99-496394. (Illus.). 334p. 1997. 187.50 (*90-6764-271-1*, Pub. by VSP) Coronet Bks.

Martingale Hardy Spaces & Their Applications in Fourier-Analysis. Ferenc Weisz. LC 93-49415. (Lecture Notes in Mathematics Ser.: Vol. 1568). viii, 217p. 1994. 43.95 (*0-387-57623-1*) Spr-Verlag.

Martingale Methods in Financial Modeling: Theory & Applications. Merek Musiela & Marek Rutkowski. Ed. by I. Karatzas & M. Yor. LC 97-11586. (Applications of Mathematics Ser.: No. 36). 504p. 1997. 79.95 (*3-540-61477-X*) Spr-Verlag.

Martingales & Stochastic Analysis. James Yeh. (Series on Multivariate Analysis: Vol. 1). 450p. 1995. 78.00 (*981-02-2477-X*) World Scientific Pub.

Martini. Andrews & McMeel Staff. (Little Bks.). 1998. 4.95 (*0-8362-5220-9*) Andrews & McMeel.

***Martini.** Guy Buffet. 2000. 10.95 (*0-7407-0597-0*) Andrews & McMeel.

Martini. Ed. by Running Press Staff. (Illus.). 60p. 1998. pap. 8.95 (*0-7624-0371-3*) Running Pr.

***Martini, Vol. 1.** Alexander B. Struminger. 1998. pap. text 6.98 (*1-57717-022-9*) Todtri Prods.

Martini: Shaken Not Stirred. Barnaby Conrad, III. LC 94-17325. (Illus.). 132p. 1995. 24.95 (*0-8118-0717-7*) Chronicle Bks.

Martini Book: Fun Facts, Fanciful Quotes & Other Really Cool Stuff. Dove Jones. 1997. pap. text 5.95 (*1-889913-05-7*) Accommodating Vices.

Martini Book: How to Fashion & Savor the Perfect Drink. Sally A Berk. 192p. 1997. 10.98 (*1-884822-98-3*) Blck Dog & Leventhal.

Martini Buceri Opera Latina: Consilium, Vol. IV. Intro. by Pierre Fraenkel. (Studies in Medieval & Reformation Thought: No. 42). (FRE & LAT.). xxxii, 194p. 1989. 84.00 (*90-04-08602-1*) Brill Academic Pubs.

Martini Companion: The Connoisseur's Guide. Gary Regan & Mardee H. Regan. (Illus.). 192p. 1997. 19.95 (*0-7624-0061-7*) Running Pr.

Martini Effect. B. J. Morison. LC 92-31610. (Little Maine Murder Ser.). 1992. 17.95 (*0-945980-38-8*) Nrth Country Pr.

M

M

Martini Madness. Robert Chirico. 32p. 1997. pap. 3.95 (*0-942320-60-3*) Am Cooking.

Martini Man: The Life of Dean Martin. William Schoell. LC 99-37616. 336p. 1999. 24.95 (*0-87833-231-6*) Taylor Pub.

***Martini Shot: A Hollywood Novel.** Peter Craig. LC 97-41898. 288p. 2000. pap. 12.00 (*0-688-17581-3*, Quil) HarperTrade.

***Martini Shot: A Hollywood Novel.** Peter Craig. LC 97-41898. 256p. 1998. 22.00 (*0-688-15658-4*, Wm Morrow) Morrow Avon.

Martini, Straight Up: The Classic American Cocktail. Lowell Edmunds. LC 98-18257. (Illus.). 184p. 1998. 24.95 (*0-8018-5971-9*) Johns Hopkins.

Martinique. Compiled by Janet Crane. LC 96-192593. (World Bibliographical Ser.: Vol. 175). 174p. 1995. lib. bdg. 55.00 (*1-85109-151-3*) ABC-CLIO.

Martinique. Wilson Ltd. Staff & Imray L. Norie. (C). 1990. 65.00 (*0-7855-5927-2*, Pub. by Laurie Norie & Wilson Ltd) St Mut.

Martinique: Ulysses Travel Guide. 3rd ed. Claude Morneau. Ed. by Ulysses Travel Guide Staff. (Illus.). 256p. 1998. 17.95 (*2-89464-136-2*) Globe Pequot.

Martinique, Charmeuse des Serpents. Andre Breton. 1972. 9.95 (*0-7859-0928-1*, M3137) Fr & Eur.

Martinique, Guateloupe, Dominica & St. Lucia. Lynne Sullivan. (Alive Guides Ser.). (Illus.). 700p. 1999. pap. 19.95 (*1-55650-857-3*) Hunter NJ.

Martinique Revisited: The Changing Plant Geographies of a West Indian Island. Clarissa T. Kimber. LC 86-30203. (Illus.). 480p. 1988. 78.50 (*0-89096-297-9*) Tex A&M Univ Pr.

Martinique to Tobago & Barbados. Wilson Ltd. Staff & Imray L. Norie. (C). 1989. 65.00 (*0-7855-5917-5*, Pub. by Laurie Norie & Wilson Ltd) St Mut.

Martinique to Trinidad, Vol. 4. rev. ed. Donald M. Street, Jr. (Street's Cruising Guide to the Eastern Caribbean Ser.). (Illus.). 224p. 1997. pap. 125.00 (*0-393-03523-9*, Pub. by Laurie Norie & Wilson Ltd) St Mut.

Martinis. (Tiny Tomes Ser.). (Illus.). 128p. 1998. 3.95 (*0-8362-6816-4*) Andrews & McMeel.

Martinliners. Gary Killion. Ed. by John Wegg. (Illus.). 200p. 1999. 37.50 (*0-9653993-2-X*, A-14) Airways Intnl.

***Martins: Dream Big.** 64p. 1999. otabind 14.95 (*0-634-01134-0*) H Leonard.

***Martin's & Miller's Greensboro.** J. Stephen Catlett. (Images of America Ser.). (Illus.). 128p. 1999. pap. 18.99 (*0-7385-0315-0*) Arcadia Publng.

***Martin's Big Words.** Doreen Rappaport. (Illus.). 40p. (J). 2001. 15.99 (*0-7868-0714-8*, Pub. by Disney Pr) Time Warner.

Martin's Concise Japanese Dictionary: Fully Romanized with Complete Kanji & Kana. Samuel E. Martin. (JPN., Illus.). 768p. 1994. pap. 16.95 (*0-8048-1912-2*) Tuttle Pubng.

Martin's Father. 2nd ed. Margrit Eichler. LC 77-81779. (Illus.). 31p. 1977. 5.00 (*0-914996-16-9*) Lollipop Power.

Martin's Hundred. rev. ed. Ivor Noel Hume. 400p. 1991. pap. text 17.50 (*0-8139-1323-3*) U Pr of Va.

Martin's Last Chance. Heidi Schmidt. 1999. pap. text 5.99 (*1-85792-425-8*) Christian Focus.

Martin's Mice. Dick King-Smith. (J). 1990. pap. 4.99 (*0-440-80214-8*) Dell.

Martin's Mice. Dick King-Smith. (Illus.). 128p. (J). 1998. pap. 4.99 (*0-679-89098-X*) Knopf.

Martin's Mice. Dick King-Smith. 1998. 10.09 (*0-606-13598-7*, Pub. by Turtleback) Demco.

Martin's Mice. large type ed. Dick King-Smith. (J). (gr. 4-7). 1989. 16.50 (*0-7451-0956-X*, G K Hall Lrg Type) Mac Lib Ref.

Martin's MINI Mysteries. Bruce Martin. LC 98-72684. 186p. 1998. 19.95 (*0-9622899-5-7*) Creative Consort Inc.

Martins Pocket Dictionary: English-Japanese - Japanese-English. Samuel E. Martin. 700p. 1989. pap. 9.95 (*0-8048-1588-7*) Tuttle Pubng.

Martin's Quest. Diane M. Moore. (Illus.). 96p. (Orig.). (J). (gr. 5-12). 1995. pap. 8.00 (*1-884725-05-8*) Blue Heron LA.

Martin's Quest. Diane M. Moore. (Illus.). (Orig.). (J). (gr. 5-12). 1995. 10.00 (*1-884725-12-0*) Blue Heron LA.

***Martin's Quick-E - Critical Care: Clinical Nursing Reference.** Martin Schiavenato. (Martin's Quick-E Clinical Reference Guide Ser.). (Illus.). 40p. 1999. spiral bd. 19.95 (*1-929693-02-8*) Bandido Bks.

***Martin's Quick-E - E. R. Clinical Nursing Reference.** Martin Schiavenato. (Martin's Quick-E Clinical Reference Guide Ser.). (Illus.). 40p. 1999. spiral bd. 19.95 (*1-929693-01-X*) Bandido Bks.

***Martin's Quick-E - Med-Surg: Clinical Nursing Reference.** Martin Schiavenato. (Martin's Quick-E Clinical Reference Guide Ser.). (Illus.). 46p. 1999. spiral bd. 19.95 (*1-929693-00-1*) Bandido Bks.

***Martin's Quick-E - Peds: Clinical Nursing Reference.** Martin Schiavenato. (Martin's Quick-E Clinical Reference Guide Ser.). (Illus.). 40p. 1999. spiral bd. 19.95 (*1-929693-03-6*) Bandido Bks.

***Martin's Quick-E - Spanish Guide: Clinical Nursing Reference.** Martin Schiavenato. (Martin's Quick-E Clinical Reference Guide Ser.). (SPA., Illus.). 36p. 1999. spiral bd. 19.95 (*1-929693-04-4*) Bandido Bks.

***Martin's Quick-E Clinical Nursing Reference IV: Intravenous Nursing.** Martin Schiavenato. (Martin's Quick-E Clinical Nursing Reference Ser.). 60p. 2000. pap. 19.95 (*1-929693-05-2*) Bandido Bks.

***Martin's Quick-E Clinical Nursing Reference OB: Obstetric Nursing.** Martin Schiavenato. (Martin's Quick-E Clinical Nursing Reference Ser.). (Illus.). 60p. 2000. pap. 19.95 (*1-929693-06-0*) Bandido Bks.

***Martin/St. Lucie Entertainment, 2000.** (Illus.). 422p. 1999. pap. 35.00 (*1-880248-40-9*, 0049) Enter Pubns.

Martinsville: A Pictorial History. Joanne R. Stuttgen. (Indiana Pictorial History Ser.). (Illus.). 160p. 1995. write for info. (*0-943963-51-6*) G Bradley.

Martinsville Seven: Race, Rape, & Capital Punishment. Eric W. Rise. 256p. (C). 1995. 27.95 (*0-8139-1567-8*) U Pr of Va.

Martinsville Seven: Race, Rape & Capital Punishment. Eric W. Rice. (Constitutionalism & Democracy Ser.). 226p. 1998. reprint ed. pap. 14.50 (*0-8139-1830-8*) U Pr of Va.

Martinsville Speedway, Half-Mile of Thunder. Andres R. Alonso & Mike Smith. (Illus.). 160p. 1999. 29.95 (*0-9670545-0-8*) Foto Vision.

Martinu. Brian Large. LC 75-45082. (Illus.). 198p. 1976. 45.00 (*0-8419-0256-9*) Holmes & Meier.

Martinus Myklevolls Sjfartsminner. Martinus Myklevoll. (NOR.). (Orig.). 1989. pap. 8.95 (*0-9621657-0-0*) Jest Pubns.

Martir de las Catacumbas. Tr. of Martyr of the Catacombs. (SPA., Illus.). 160p. 1984. mass mkt. 4.99 (*0-8254-1466-0*, Edit Portavoz) Kregel.

Martires. Ignacio Solares. (SPA.). pap. 8.99 (*968-16-5322-X*, Pub. by Fondo) Continental Bk.

Martiros Saryan. Alexander Kamensky. (Illus.). 345p. 1989. 125.00 (*0-943071-07-0*) Sphinx Pr.

Martlesham Heath: A History of the Royal Air Force Station, 1917-1973. Gordon Kinsey. 264p. 1990. 55.00 (*0-86138-023-1*, Pub. by T Dalton) St Mut.

Martorell's Tirant lo Blanch: A Program for Military & Social Reform in Fifteenth-Century Christendom. Edward T. Alward. LC 85-2916. (North Carolina Studies in the Romance Languages & Literatures: No. 225). 224p. reprint ed. pap. 69.50 (*0-608-20065-4*, 207133700011) Bks Demand.

***Marty Aardvark.** Barbara DeRubertis. LC 97-44312. (Let's Read Together Ser.). (Illus.). 32p. (J). (ps-3). 1998. pap. 4.95 (*1-57565-042-8*) Kane Pr.

Marty & the Million Man March. Joseph D. Trimble. Ed. by Jacqueline A. Trimble. (Illus.). 24p. (J). 1995. pap. 5.95 (*0-9650427-0-7*) J Trimble.

Marty Frye, Private Eye. Janet Tashjian. LC 98-13770. (Illus.). 80p. (J). (gr. 1-3). 1998. 15.95 (*0-8050-5888-5*) H Holt & Co.

***Marty Frye, Private Eye.** Janet Tashjian. (Illus.). 80p. (J). (gr. 1-3). 2000. pap. 3.99 (*0-439-09557-3*) Scholastic Inc.

Marty Makes a Difference. Joseph D. Trimble. Ed. by Jacqueline A. Trimble. (Illus.). 24p. (J). (gr. k-4). 1997. pap. 6.95 (*0-9650427-1-5*) J Trimble.

Marty Mule. Dave Sargent & Pat Sargent. LC 97-27200. (Illus.). (J). 1998. write for info. (*1-56763-378-1*); pap. write for info. (*1-56763-379-X*) Ozark Pub.

Marty Robbins: Fast Cars & Country Music. Barbara J. Pruett. LC 90-8709. (Illus.). 621p. 1990. 62.50 (*0-8108-2325-X*) Scarecrow.

Marty Robbins Songbook. 48p. 1983. pap. 9.95 (*0-7935-1908-X*, 00357480) H Leonard.

Marty Stouffer's Wild America. Marty Stouffer. (Illus.). 384p. 1988. 30.00 (*0-8129-1610-7*, Times Bks) Crown Pub Group.

Marty Stuart - Honky Tonkin's What I Do Best. Ed. by Carol Cuellar. 64p. (Orig.). (C). 1996. pap. text 16.95 (*1-57623-659-5*, PF9641) Wmer Bros.

Marty the Little Lost Martian. Fowler Companies, Inc. Staff & Daddy Rabbit. LC 97-94728. (Illus.). iii, 29p. (J). (ps-6). 1998. 14.95 (*0-9661365-0-0*) Fowler Cos.

Marty the Marathon Bear. Bill Wood. (Illus.). 136p. (Orig.). (J). (gr. 3-7). 1988. pap. text 6.95 (*0-317-93376-0*) Rallysport Commun.

Martydom of Man. Winwood Reade. 342p. 1995. reprint ed. 36.00 (*1-896032-46-X*) Battered Silicon.

Martyrdom of St. Paul: Historical & Judicial Context, Traditions & Legends. H. W. Tajra. LC 95-164650. (WissUNT Zum Neuen Testament Ser.). 240p. (Orig.). 1994. pap. text 36.50 (*3-16-146239-4*, Pub. by JCB Mohr) Coronet Bks.

Martyn Brewster. Simon Olding. LC 97-66328. (Illus.). 96p. 1997. text 39.95 (*1-85928-414-0*, Pub. by Ashgate Pub) Ashgate Pub Co.

Martyn Brewster. limited ed. Simon Olding. LC 97-66328. (Illus.). 96p. 1997. text 209.95 (*1-85928-415-9*, Pub. by Ashgate Pub) Ashgate Pub Co.

Martyn Lloyd Jones: From Wales To Westminster. Christopher Catherwood. 1999. pap. text 5.99 (*1-85792-349-9*) Christian Focus.

Martyr. Peter David. (Star Trek: Bk. 5). 282p. 1998. mass mkt. 6.50 (*0-671-02036-6*, Star Trek) PB.

Martyr. Douglas E. Love. LC 90-90401. (Illus.). (Orig.). 1990. pap. 5.00 (*0-9628240-0-3*) D E Love.

Martyr. Morteza Mutahhari. Tr. by A. Yasin from PER. 28p. pap. 2.00 (*0-941722-07-4*) Book Dist Ctr.

***Martyr: Bhagat Singh - Experiments in Revolution.** Kuldip Nayar. 2000. 19.50 (*81-241-0700-9*, Pub. by Har-Anand Pubns) S Asia.

Martyr Age of the United States. Harriet Martineau. LC 73-82206. (Anti-Slavery Crusade in America Ser.). 1978. reprint ed. 18.95 (*0-405-00644-6*) Ayer.

Martyr Bishop: The Life of St. Oliver Plunkett. John McKee. 181p. 1975. 8.95 (*0-912414-21-9*) Lumen Christi.

Martyr Bishop Confessors under Communism. Elena Lopeshinskaya. (RUS.). pap. 5.00 (*0-89981-055-1*) Eastern Orthodox.

Martyr for Sin: Rochester's Critique of Polity, Sexuality, & Society. Kirk Combe. LC 97-40382. 192p. 1998. 35.00 (*0-87413-647-4*) U Delaware Pr.

Martyr of the Catacombs see Martir de las Catacumbas

Martyr of the Catacombs. LC 90-36537. 144p. 1990. reprint ed. mass mkt. 5.99 (*0-8254-2143-8*) Kregel.

Martyr of the Catacombs. 1993. reprint ed. pap. 3.95 (*0-87813-957-5*) Christian Light.

Martyrdom According to John Chrysostom: To Live Is Christ, to Die Is Gain. Gus G. Christo. LC 96-37777. 228p. 1997. text 89.95 (*0-7734-2290-0*) E Mellen.

Martyrdom & Political Resistance: Essays from Asia & Europe. Ed. by Joyce Pettigrew. (Comparative Asian Studies: Vol. 18). 180p. 1997. pap. 19.50 (*90-5383-501-6*, Pub. by VUB Univ Pr) Paul & Co Pubs.

Martyrdom & Rome. G. W. Bowersock. 118p. (C). 1995. text 34.95 (*0-521-46539-7*) Cambridge U Pr.

Martyrdom & the Politics of Religion: Progressive Catholicism in El Salvador's Civil War. Anna L. Peterson. LC 96-367. 211p. (C). 1996. text 54.50 (*0-7914-3181-9*); pap. text 17.95 (*0-7914-3182-7*) State U NY Pr.

Martyrdom, 1990-1995. Stephen W. Sweigart. (Computer Poetry Ser.). (C). 1992. 85.00 (*0-9604252-4-1*) Parpaglion.

Martyrdom of Lovejoy: An Account of the Life, Trials, & Perils of Rev. Elijah P. Lovejoy. Henry Tanner. LC 68-18603. (Illus.). 233p. 1971. reprint ed. lib. bdg. 39.50 (*0-678-00744-6*) Kelley.

Martyrdom of Man. W. Winwood Reade. 1981. lib. bdg. 300.00 (*0-686-71630-2*) Revisionist Pr.

Martyrdom of Man. unabridged ed. Winwood Reade. (Classic Reprint Ser.). (Illus.). 455p. 1997. reprint ed. 45.00 (*0-936128-83-6*) De Young Pr.

Martyrdom of Perpetua. Ed. by Monica Furlong. (Visionary Women Ser.). 64p. (Orig.). 1999. pap. 7.95 (*0-85305-352-9*, Pub. by Arthur James) St Mut.

Martyrdom of St. Menas. 1998. pap. 1.95 (*0-89979-108-5*) British Am Bks.

Martyrdom of St. Polycarp: The Encyclical Epistle of the Church at Smyrna Concerning the Martyrdom of the Holy Polycarp. Tr. by James Donaldson & Alexander Roberts. 1986. pap. 1.50 (*0-89981-056-X*) Eastern Orthodox.

Martyrdom of Sts. Nicander & Marcian, Timothy & Maura, St. Euphemia, & St. Maximus. Tr. by J. A. Fastre. 1992. pap. 3.95 (*0-89981-132-9*) Eastern Orthodox.

Martyrdom of the Bab: A Compilation. (Illus.). 110p. 1992. 14.95 (*0-933770-87-1*) Kalimat.

Martyrdom of Women: A Study of Death Psychology in the Early Christian Church. 2nd ed. Arthur F. Ide. LC 98-23654. (Women in History Ser.). 1998. pap. 14.00 (*0-934667-12-8*) Tangelwuld.

Martyrdom of Women in the Early Christian Church. Arthur F. Ide. LC 85-14741. (Illus.). 100p. 1985. pap. 10.00 (*0-934667-00-4*) Tangelwuld.

Martyrdom Today. Edward Schillebeeckx & Johannes Baptist-Metz. (Concilium Ser.: Vol. 163). 128p. 1983. 6.95 (*0-8164-2443-8*) Harper SF.

Martyre de Pionios, Pretre de Smyrne. Ed. by Louis Robert. LC 93-24110. 152p. 1994. 35.00 (*0-88402-217-X*) Dumbarton Oaks.

Martyred Princes Boris & Gleb: A Social-Cultural Study of the Cult & the Texts. Gail Lenhoff. (UCLA Slavic Studies: Vol. 19). 168p. 1989. 18.95 (*0-89357-204-7*) Slavica.

Martyred Village: Commemorating the 1944 Massacre at Oradour-Sur-Glane. Sarah Farmer. LC 98-29646. 323p. 1998. 24.95 (*0-520-21186-3*, Pub. by U CA Pr) Cal Prin Full Svc.

***Martyred Village; Commemorating the 1944 Massacre at Oradour-Sur-Glane.** Sarah Farmer. LC 98-29646. (Illus.). 317p. 2000. pap. text 17.95 (*0-520-22483-3*, Pub. by U CA Pr) Cal Prin Full Svc.

Martyring. Thomas Sullivan. LC 97-29853. 1998. text 22.95 (*0-312-86361-6*) St Martin.

***Martyring.** Thomas Sullivan. 256p. 2000. pap. 13.95 (*0-312-87498-7*); pap. 24.95 (*0-8125-4543-5*) Tor Bks.

Martyrium, No. Betl 117. E. Peters. 1998. 93.95 (*90-6831-680-X*, Pub. by Peeters Pub) Bks Intl VA.

Martyrium Polycarpi - Eine Formkritische Studie: Ein Beitrag zur Frage Nach der Entstehung der Gattung Maertyrerakte. Gerd Buschmann. (Beiheft zur Zeitschrift fuer die Neuetestamentliche Wissenschaft Ser.: Band 70). (GER.). xiv, 366p. (C). 1993. lib. bdg. 118.70 (*3-11-014199-X*) De Gruyter.

Martyrologium: An Old English Martyrology. Ed. by G. Herzfeld. (EETS, OS Ser.: No. 116). 1969. reprint ed. 54.00 (*0-527-00115-5*) Periodicals Srv.

Martyrology of St. Aengus. Aengus. 1982. pap. 12.50 (*0-89981-057-8*) Eastern Orthodox.

Martyrology of Ukrainian Churches Vol. 1: Ukrainian Orthodox Church. Osyp Zinkewych & Oleksander Voronym. LC 85-50592. (Ukrainian Ser.). 1207p. 1987. 39.75 (*0-914834-36-3*) Smoloskyp.

Martyros Saryan, 1860-1972. Vera Razdolskaya. (Great Painters Ser.). (Illus.). 176p. 1997. 40.00 (*1-85995-320-4*) Parkstone Pr.

Martyrs. Francois-Rene De Chateaubriand. Ed. & Tr. by O. W. Wight from FRE. LC 76-15294. 1976. reprint ed. 48.00 (*0-86527-275-1*) Fertig.

Martyrs: Contemporary Writers on Modern Lives of Faith. Ed. by Susan Bergman. LC 96-14863. 1996. pap. 11.00 (*0-06-061121-9*) Harper SF.

Martyrs: Contemporary Writers on Modern Lives of Faith. Ed. by Susan Bergman. LC 97-466393. 334p. 1998. reprint ed. pap. 15.00 (*1-57075-161-7*) Orbis Bks.

Martyrs: Joan of Arc to Yitzhak Rabin. Norbert J. Gossman. LC 96-29471. 172p. 1996. pap. text 24.00 (*0-7618-0488-9*); lib. bdg. 44.00 (*0-7618-0487-0*) U Pr of Amer.

Martyrs - They Died for Christ. Bob Lord & Penny Lord. 320p. (Orig.). 1993. pap. 13.95 (*0-926143-14-X*) Journeys Faith.

Martyr's Chapel. Dudley J. Delffs. 32p. 1998. pap. 9.99 (*0-7642-2086-1*) Bethany Hse.

Martyr's Chapel. Dudley J. Delffs. LC 98-53617. 1999. 22.95 (*0-7862-1808-8*) Thorndike Pr.

Martyrs Grecs, IIe-VIIIe Siecles. Francois Halkin. (Collected Studies: No. CS30). 324p. (C). 1974. reprint ed. lib. bdg. 94.95 (*0-902089-66-8*, Pub. by Variorum) Ashgate Pub Co.

Martyrs Mirror. rev. ed. Thieleman J. Van Braght. (Illus.). 1158p. 1998. pap. 37.50 (*0-8361-9087-4*) Herald Pr.

Martyrs' Mirror. 15th ed. Thieleman J. Van Braght. (Illus.). 1157p. 1938. 45.00 (*0-8361-1390-X*) Herald Pr.

Martyrs of Charity: Christians & Jews. Ed. by Waclaw Zajaczkowski. (Christian & Jewish Response to the Holocaust Ser.). (Illus.). 336p. (Orig.). (C). 1988. pap. 9.95 (*0-945281-00-5*) St Maximilian Kolbe Found.

Martyrs of Cordoba: Community & Family Conflict in an Age of Mass Conversion. Jessica A. Coope. LC 94-30425. xvii, 115p. 1995. text 35.00 (*0-8032-1471-5*) U of Nebr Pr.

Martyrs of the Coliseum with Historical Records of the Great Amphitheater of Ancient Rome. A. J. O'Reilly. LC 82-50595. 450p. 1994. reprint ed. pap. 18.50 (*0-89555-192-6*) TAN Bks Pubs.

Martyrs of the English Reformation. Malcolm Brennan. 174p. (Orig.). 1991. pap. text 9.95 (*0-935952-85-3*) Angelus Pr.

Martyrs of Turon & Tarragona: The De La Salle Brothers in Spain, 1934-1939. Luke Salm. LC 90-81484. (Illus.). 84p. (Orig.). 1990. pap. 3.50 (*0-9623279-3-X*) Christian Brothers.

***Martyrs' Shrine: The Reform Movement of 1898 in China.** Lee Ao. (Illus.). 312p. 2000. 35.00 (*0-19-592438-X*) OUP.

***Martyrs to Madness: The Victims of the Nazis.** Ted Gottfried. LC 99-57587. 2000. lib. bdg. write for info. (*0-7613-1715-5*) TFC Bks NY.

***Martyrs' Torch.** Bruce Porter. 2000. pap. 12.99 (*0-7684-2046-6*) Destiny Image.

Martyrs, Traitors, & Patriots: Kurdistan after the Gulf War. Sheri Laizer. LC 95-25552. 240p. (C). 1996. text 62.50 (*1-85649-395-4*, Pub. by Zed Books); text 22.50 (*1-85649-396-2*, Pub. by Zed Books) St Martin.

***Martyr's Wine: Life in Pursuit of God.** (Illus.). 90p. 1999. 15.00 (*0-9679657-0-5*) Whitestone Pubg.

Marty's Microwave Mania. Marty Webster. (Illus.). 76p. 1992. spiral bd. 9.93 (*0-9644128-0-2*) Martys.

***Marty's Miraculous Monday.** Peter R. Bergethon. (Illus.). 36p. (J). (gr. k-4). 1999. pap. write for info. (*1-58447-004-6*) Symmetry Lrng.

Marty's Miraculous Monday Reader. Peter R. Bergethon. (Illus.). (J). (gr. k-3). Date not set. pap. text. write for info. (*1-58447-011-9*) Symmetry Lrng.

Marty's Missouri Meals. Marty Webster. (Illus.). 192p. (Orig.). 1994. spiral bd. 12.06 (*0-9644128-1-0*) Martys.

Marty's World. Watts & Wunderli. (J). 1986. pap. 5.95 (*0-88494-610-X*) Bookcraft Inc.

Maru. Bessie Head. (African Writers Ser.). 128p. (C). 1972. pap. 9.95 (*0-435-90718-2*, 90718) Heinemann.

Maru. Bessie Head. 1996. pap. 9.95 (*0-435-90963-0*) Heinemann.

Maru Cult of the Pomo Indians: A California Ghost Dance Survival. Clement W. Meighan & Francis A. Riddell. 134p. 1972. 12.50 (*0-916561-51-8*) Southwest Mus.

Maru Killer: The War Patrols of the USS Seahorse. LC 96-92073. (Illus.). 224p. 1996. 25.00 (*0-9651720-0-7*) Seahorse Bks.

Maruja & Other Tales. Bret Harte. LC 71-113671. (Short Story Index Reprint Ser.: Vol. 1). 1977. 30.95 (*0-8369-3400-8*) Ayer.

Marune: Alastor 933 see Alastor

Marus the Longneck & the Journey to Stone Mountain. Candace N. Bearden & Michael D. Bearden. (Marus the Longneck Ser.). (Illus.). 25p. (J). (ps-6). 1998. pap. 8.95 (*0-9667619-2-8*) Dino Tales.

Marus the Longneck & the Rescue at Moss Hill. Candace N. Bearden & Michael D. Bearden. (Marus the Longneck Ser.). (Illus.). 25p. (J). (ps-6). 1998. pap. 8.95 (*0-9667619-1-X*) Dino Tales.

Marus the Longneck Saves the Day. Michael D. Bearden & Candace N. Bearden. (Marus the Longneck Ser.). (Illus.). 25p. (J). (ps-6). 1998. pap. 8.95 (*0-9667619-0-1*) Dino Tales.

Marushka & the Month Brothers. Illus. & Retold by Anna Vojtech. LC 95-2973. 1996. 15.95 (*0-399-22793-8*, G P Putnam) Peng Put Young Read.

Marv Albert's Sports Quiz Book Marv Albert & Stan Fischler. LC 74-7549. 205p. 1976. write for info. (*0-448-11797-5*, G & D) Peng Put Young Read.

Marva Collins' Way: Returning to Excellence in Education. rev. ed. Marva Collins & Civia Tamarkin. LC 82-10516. 256p. 1990. pap. 10.95 (*0-87477-572-8*, Tarcher Putnam) Putnam Pub Group.

Marvel: Five Fabulous Decades of the World's Greatest Comics. Les Daniels. (Illus.). 288p. 1991. 49.50 (*0-8109-3821-9*) Abrams.

Marvel: Five Fabulous Decades of the World's Greatest Comics. Les Daniels. (Illus.). 288p. 1993. pap. 24.95 (*0-8109-2566-4*, Pub. by Abrams) Time Warner.

Marvel - DC Crossover Classics. Gerry Conway & Chris Claremont. (Illus.). 320p. 1991. pap. 24.95 (*0-87135-858-1*) Marvel Entrprs.

Marvel Massterworks: Thor. Stan Lee. (Illus.). 272p. 1999. 34.95 (*0-7851-0733-9*, Pub. by Marvel Entrprs) LPC Group.

Marvel Masterworks: The X-Men. Stan Lee & Jack Kirby. (Marvel Masterworks Ser.: Vol. 3). (Illus.). 232p. (YA). 1987. 34.95 (*0-87135-308-3*) Marvel Entrprs.

Marvel of the Desert: The Camel in Saudi Arabia. Angelo Pesce & Elvira G. Pesce. 112p. (C). 1995. 75.00 (*0-907151-21-3*, Pub. by IMMEL Pubng) St Mut.

Marvel Super Dice: Avengers 12. Michele Carter. 1998. 107.40 (*0-7869-0840-8*) TSR Inc.

An Asterisk (*) at the beginning of an entry indicates that the title is appearing for the first time.

Marvel Super Heroes: Secret Wars. 2nd ed. Jim Shooter. (Illus.). 336p. 1999. reprint ed. pap. 24.95 (*0-7851-0727-4*, Pub. by Marvel Entrprs) LPC Group.
Marvel Super Heroes Adventure Games. Olmesdahl et al. 1998. 24.95 (*0-7869-1227-8*, Pub. by TSR Inc) Random.
Marvel Team-Up Roster Book. Harold Johnson. (Marvel Super Heroes Dice Game Ser.). 1999. 18.95 (*0-7869-1409-2*, Pub. by TSR Inc) Random.
Marvel Try-Out Book. (Illus.). Date not set. pap. 24.95 (*0-7851-0274-4*) Marvel Entrprs.
Marvel Universe. Peter Sanderson. (Illus.). 288p. (J). 24.98 (*0-8109-8171-8*, Pub. by Abrams) Time Warner.
Marvel Universe. Peter Sanderson. LC 95-7151. (Illus.). 288p. 1996. 49.50 (*0-8109-4285-2*) Abrams.
Marveling at God's Mysteries: Creative Faith Experiences for Youth. Tracey Marx. 82p. 1997. pap. 12.95 (*1-57438-010-9*, 8368) Ed Ministries.
***Marvell: The Writer in Public Life.** Annabel Patterson. LC 99-39930. (Medieval & Renaissance Library Ser.). 280p. (C). 1999. pap. 33.86 (*0-582-35675-X*); text 85.95 (*0-582-35676-8*) Longman.
Marvell & Alchemy. Lindy Abraham. (Illus.). 384p. 1990. text 86.95 (*0-85967-774-5*, Pub. by Scolar Pr) Ashgate Pub Co.
Marvell & Liberty. Warren L. Chernaik & Martin Dzelzainis. LC 98-55451. 1999. text 59.95 (*0-312-22171-1*) St Martin.
Marvell, Nabokov: Childhood & Arcadia. Michael Long. 270p. (C). 1984. 55.00 (*0-19-812815-0*) OUP.
Marvellous Land of Snergs. E. A. Wyke-Smith. (Illus.). (J). (gr. 5-10). 1996. pap. 15.00 (*1-882968-04-2*) Old Earth Bks.
Marvellous Matter. Thomas-Cochran. (What a Wonderful World Intro Ser.). 1993. pap. text. write for info. (*0-582-91087-0*, Pub. by Addison-Wesley) Longman.
Marvellous Ministry. Charles Ray. 1985. pap. 6.00 (*1-56186-217-7*) Pilgrim Pubns.
Marvellous Moths of Nepal. M. Allen. (C). 1991. 60.00 (*0-7855-0194-0*, Pub. by Ratna Pustak Bhandar) St Mut.
Marvellous Party. John Wynne-Tyson. (Illus.). 112p. (Orig.). 1989. pap. 9.95 (*0-7145-4178-8*) Riverrun NY.
Marvell's Allegorical Poetry. Bruce King. (Language & Literature Ser.: Vol. 8). 1977. 25.00 (*0-902675-60-5*) Oleander Pr.
Marvelous Adventure of Cabeza de Vaca. Haniel Long. (Basket of Tolerance Ser.). (Illus.). 64p. (Orig.). 1992. 11.95 (*0-918801-46-X*) Dawn Horse Pr.
Marvelous Adventures of Pierre Baptiste. Patricia Eakins. LC 98-58147. 264p. 1999. 19.95 (*0-8147-2209-1*) NYU Pr.
Marvelous Arithmetics of Distance: Poems, 1987-1992. Audre Geraldine Lorde. LC 92-40859. 96p. 1993. 18.95 (*0-393-03513-1*) Norton.
Marvelous Arithmetics of Distance: Poems, 1987-1992. Audre Geraldine Lorde. 1994. pap. 8.95 (*0-393-31170-8*) Norton.
Marvelous Companion: Life Stories of the Buddha. Aryasura. LC 83-15023. (Tibetan Translation Ser.: Vol. 10). (Illus.). 250p. 1983. 40.00 (*0-913546-88-7*); pap. 19.95 (*0-913546-89-5*) Dharma Pub.
Marvelous Country: Three Years in Arizona & New Mexico, the Apaches Home. Samuel W. Cozzens. 1967. reprint ed. 20.00 (*0-87018-011-8*) Ross.
***Marvelous Crucifixion on Twin Peaks.** W. P. Byrnes. LC 99-91730. 2000. 25.00 (*0-7388-1206-4*); pap. 18.00 (*0-7388-1207-2*) Xlibris Corp.
Marvelous Freedom: Vigilance of Desire. Ed. by Franklin Rosemont. (Catalog of the 1976 World Surrealist Exhibition Ser.). (Illus.). 1976. pap. 15.00 (*0-941194-09-4*) Black Swan Pr.
Marvelous Garments of Brother Diego: And Other Short Stories. deluxe limited unabridged ed. Dan Rhea. 52p. 1994. pap. 15.00 (*0-9627171-2-6*) Hera Pub.
Marvelous Grace. Martha J. Doubledee. (Illus.). 327p. 1998. pap. 11.95 (*1-891635-13-1*) Moore Bks.
Marvelous Inventions of Alvin Fernald. Clifford B. Hicks. LC 97-50536. (Illus.). 128p. (J). (gr. 3-7). 1998. pap. 4.99 (*0-14-130038-8*, PuffinBks) Peng Put Young Read.
Marvelous Land of Oz. L. Frank Baum. 22.95 (*0-88411-773-1*) Amereon Ltd.
Marvelous Land of Oz. L. Frank Baum. (Illus.). 287p. (J). (gr. 4-6). 1985. pap. 7.95 (*0-486-20692-0*) Dover.
Marvelous Land of Oz. L. Frank Baum. LC 85-4856. (Books of Wonder). (Illus.). 294p. (J). (gr. 2 up). 1985. 22.95 (*0-688-05439-0*, Wm Morrow) Morrow Avon.
Marvelous Land of Oz. L. Frank Baum. 1990. 22.50 (*0-8446-6231-3*) Peter Smith.
Marvelous Land of Oz. large type ed. L. Frank Baum. (Large Print Heritage Ser.). 231p. (YA). 1998. lib. bdg. 28.95 (*1-58118-022-5*, 21999) LRS.
Marvelous Land of Oz. L. Frank Baum. LC 96-40055. (Illus.). 144p. (J). 1997. reprint ed. pap. text 1.50 (*0-486-29686-5*) Dover.
Marvelous Machines. Bobbie Kalman. Incl. Big Truck, Big Wheels. Petrina Gentile. LC 97-4091. (Illus.). 32p. (J). (ps-3). 1997. pap. 5.95 (*0-86505-742-7*); Big Truck, Big Wheels. Petrina Gentile. LC 97-4091. (Illus.). 32p. (J). (ps-3). 1997. lib. bdg. 19.96 (*0-86505-642-0*); Dirt Movers. Petrina Gentile. LC 94-932260. (Illus.). 32p. (J). (gr. k-7). 1994. lib. bdg. 19.96 (*0-86505-607-2*); Dirt Movers. Petrina Gentile. LC 94-34783. (Illus.). 32p. (J). (ps-3). 1994. pap. 5.95 (*0-86505-707-9*); Wings, Wheels & Sails. LC 94-932772. (Illus.). 32p. (J). (gr. k-7). 1995. lib. bdg. 19.96 (*0-86505-608-0*); Wings, Wheels & Sails. LC 94-43539. (Illus.). 32p. (J). (ps-3). 1995. pap. 5.95 (*0-86505-708-7*); (J). Set pap. 17.85 (*0-86505-743-5*) Crabtree Pub Co.
Marvelous Machines, 3 bks. Bobbie Kalman. Incl. Big Truck, Big Wheels. Petrina Gentile. LC 97-4091. (Illus.). 32p. (J). (ps-3). 1997. pap. 5.95 (*0-86505-742-7*); Big Truck, Big Wheels. Petrina Gentile. LC 97-4091. (Illus.). 32p. (J). (ps-3). 1997. lib. bdg. 19.96 (*0-86505-642-0*); Dirt Movers. Petrina Gentile. LC 94-932260. (Illus.). 32p. (J). (gr. k-7). 1994. lib. bdg. 19.96 (*0-86505-607-2*); Dirt Movers. Petrina Gentile. LC 94-34783. (Illus.). 32p. (J). (ps-3). 1994. pap. 5.95 (*0-86505-707-9*); Wings, Wheels & Sails. LC 94-932772. (Illus.). 32p. (J). (gr. k-7). 1995. lib. bdg. 19.96 (*0-86505-608-0*); Wings, Wheels & Sails. LC 94-43539. (Illus.). 32p. (J). (ps-3). 1995. pap. 5.95 (*0-86505-708-7*); (J). (ps-3). Set lib. bdg. 59.88 (*0-86505-644-7*) Crabtree Pub Co.
Marvelous Maps & Graphs. Ginger Wentrcek. (J). (gr. 1-3). pap. 5.99 (*0-8224-6332-6*) Fearon Teacher Aids.
Marvelous Marinades, Sauces & Salsa. (Cooking Companion Ser.). 1996. pap. 7.95 (*0-614-19356-7*) Cole Pub Co Inc.
Marvelous Market on Mermaid. Laura Krauss Melmed. LC 93-32621. (Illus.). 24p. (J). (ps-1). 1996. 15.00 (*0-688-13053-4*) Lothrop.
Marvelous Marvin & the Pioneer Ghost. Bonnie Pryor. LC 94-33237. (Illus.). 144p. (J). (gr. 2 up). 1995. 15.00 (*0-688-13886-1*, Wm Morrow) Morrow Avon.
Marvelous Marvin & the Wolfman Mystery. Bonnie Pryor. LC 93-49686. (Illus.). 144p. (YA). (gr. 7 up). 1994. 15.00 (*0-688-12866-1*, Wm Morrow) Morrow Avon.
Marvelous Math: A Book of Poems. Ed. by Lee Bennett Hopkins. LC 96-21597. (Illus.). 32p. (J). (gr. k up). 1997. per. 17.00 (*0-689-80658-2*) S&S Bks Yng.
Marvelous Math Masters. Linda Carbone. (J). (gr. 6-8). 1995. spiral bd. 17.95 (*1-881641-02-3*) Pencil Point.
Marvelous Maze. Maxine R. Schur. (Illus.). 48p. (J). (gr. 1-4). 1995. lib. bdg. 18.95 (*0-88045-132-7*) Stemmer Hse.
Marvelous Mazes. Juliet Snape. (Illus.). 32p. (J). (gr. 3-6). 1994. pap. 10.95 (*0-8109-2576-1*, Pub. by Abrams) Time Warner.
Marvelous Me. B. Liston & C. Choate. (Exploring Literature Theme Ser.: Bk. 4). (J). 1995. pap. text 44.28 (*0-201-59543-5*) Addison-Wesley.
Marvelous Me. Linda Schwartz. (Values & Feelings Ser.). (Illus.). 32p. (J). (gr. 1-3). 1979. pap., student ed. 4.95 (*0-88160-074-1*, LW 807) Learning Wks.
***Marvelous Memory Boosters.** Beth M. Ley. LC 99-47612. (Health Learning Handbook Ser.). 32p. 1999. pap. 3.95 (*1-890766-09-7*, Pub. by B L Pubns) Nutri-Books Corp.
Marvelous Microwave: Good Food in Practically No Time. Jane Trittipo. LC 96-85881. 264p. (Orig.). 1996. pap. 18.95 (*0-9621242-1-4*) Creat Cookery.
Marvelous Mini-Kites. Norman Schmidt. LC 98-25057. 1998. 19.95 (*1-895569-29-X*, Pub. by Tamos Bks) Sterling.
***Marvelous Mini Kites.** Norman Schmidt. 96p. 1999. pap. 13.95 (*1-895569-41-9*) Tamos Bks.
Marvelous Ministry: How the All-Round Ministry of C. H. Spurgeon Speaks to Us Today. Erroll Hulse et al. 147p. 1993. pap. 8.95 (*1-877611-59-X*) Soli Deo Gloria.
Marvelous Minnesota Recipes see License to Cook Minnesota Style: Land of 10,000 Recipes
***Marvelous Misadventures of Sebastian.** Lloyd Alexander. (Illus.). 224p. (YA). (gr. 5-9). 2000. pap. 4.99 (*0-14-130816-8*, PuffinBks) Peng Put Young Read.
Marvelous Mix-Up: And Other Tales of Reb Shalom. Rochama King-Feuerman. LC 97-74048. (Fun to Read Bks.). (Illus.). 112p. (Orig.). (J). (gr. 2-5). 1997. pap. 6.95 (*0-922613-86-9*) Hachai Pubng.
***Marvelous Money.** Annalisa McMorrow. (Illus.). (J). 1999. pap. 9.95 (*1-57612-113-5*) Monday Morning Bks.
***Marvelous Monikers: The People Behind More Than 400 Words & Expressions.** Tad Tuleja. 224p. 2000. 7.99 (*1-57866-101-3*) Galahad Bks.
***Marvelous Mosaics with Unusual Materials.** George Shannon & Pat Torlen. 2000. 27.95 (*1-895569-64-8*, Pub. by Tamos Bks) Sterling.
Marvelous Mud Washing Machine. Patty Wolcott. LC 84-40766. (Illus.). (J). 1974. 7.95 (*0-201-14246-5*) HarpC Child Bks.
***Marvelous Multiplication: Games & Activities That Make Math Easy & Fun.** Lynette Long. LC 00-20473. (Illus.). 128p. 2000. 12.95 (*0-471-36982-9*) Wiley.
***Marvelous Murals You Can Paint.** Gary Lord & David Schmidt. LC 00-37236. (Illus.). 128p. 2000. 27.99 (*0-89134-969-3*, North Lght Bks) F & W Pubns Inc.
Marvelous Musical Adventures for Developing Early Musicianship. Chris Patella & Eileen Oddo. (Musical Munchkins Presents Ser.). (Illus.). 50p. 1987. pap. 7.95 (*0-944333-00-1*); audio, lp 9.95 (*0-685-19315-2*) Musical Munchkins.
Marvelous Myth, Bk. 5. Regents. 32p. 1996. pap. text, student ed. 7.80 (*0-13-349804-2*) P-H.
***Marvelous Old Mansions: And Other Southern Treasures.** Sylvia Higginbotham. (Illus.). 216p. 2000. pap. 16.95 (*0-89587-227-7*) Blair.
Marvelous Orange see Naranja Maravillosa
Marvelous Playbill. Adapted by Tim Kelly. 1967. 3.50 (*0-87129-530-X*, M20) Dramatic Pub.
Marvelous Possessions: The Wonder of the New World. Stephen Greenblatt. LC 91-3447. (Illus.). xiv, 216p. 1992. pap. text 14.00 (*0-226-30652-6*) U Ch Pr.
Marvelous Possessions: The Wonder of the New World. Stephen Greenblatt. (Illus.). 216p. 1997. 28.95 (*0-226-30651-8*) U Ch Pr.
***Marvelous Reality: The Fascination of South America.** James Reid. (Illus.). 1999. write for info. (*0-9675934-0-9*) Alexandr Glob.
Marvelous Sauce. Joanna Scott. 10p. 1993. 9.00 (*1-880139-06-5*); pap. 60.00 (*1-880139-07-3*) French Broad.

***Marvelous Secrets: Stories by Marian Coe, No. 1.** Marian Coe. (Illus.). 240p. 2000. 16.95 (*0-9633341-8-2*, Pub. by SouthLore Pr) Enfield Pubs NH.

Marvelous Secrets is a collection of contemporary short stories, designed as a "gift of a good read" from southern novelist Marian Coe who is well reviewed for her sense-of-place. In these stories, a variety of voices deal with private hopes & challenges - from serious to the humorous. Celebrated southern author Lee Smith says, "Marvelous Secrets is a marvelous read." Gail Adams, a Flannery O'Connor award winner, says: "Marvelous Secrets gives us a voice full of grace & wisdom..shared with Southern charm & wit & a sense of wonder. These stories are fresh & insightful & each one speaks to us about the complexity of simple lives." Fred Chappel, novelist & poet laudreate of North Carolina, says: "There are no strident pages in Marian Coe's stories, none overblown or over wrought. ..but a wonderful variety of subtitle tones, sometimes wry, sometimes dismayed, sometimes foreboding--but always openhearted. The book is comfort to have & to keep. "Says social studies professor, Dr. Allen Speer: "A feast of stories to feed the soul." ***Publisher Paid Annotation.***

Marvelous Toy. Tom Paxton. LC 95-35384. (Illus.). 32p. (J). 1996. 15.93 (*0-688-13880-2*, Wm Morrow) Morrow Avon.
Marvelous Toy. Tom Paxton. LC 95-35384. (Illus.). 32p. (J). (gr. k up). 1996. 16.00 (*0-688-13879-9*, Wm Morrow) Morrow Avon.
***Marvelous Transforming Toys: With Complete Instructions & Plans.** Jim Makowicki. (Illus.). 2000. pap. 24.95 (*1-56158-381-2*) Taunton.
Marvelous Wooden Boxes You Can Make. Jeff Greef. LC 95-11068. (Illus.). 144p. 1995. 24.99 (*1-55870-374-8*, Betrwy Bks) F & W Pubns Inc.
Marvelous Work & a Wonder. LeGrand Richards. LC 76-2237. xv, 424p. 1976. 12.95 (*0-87747-161-4*); pap. 4.95 (*0-87579-171-9*) Deseret Bk.
Marvelous World, Poems. Benjamin Peret. Tr. by Elizabeth R. Jackson from FRE. LC 80-13631. 97p. 1985. text 25.00 (*0-8071-0664-X*) La State U Pr.
Marvelously Meaningful Maps. Madelyn W. Carlisle. LC 92-19788. (Let's Investigate Ser.). (Illus.). 32p. (J). (gr. 2-6). 1996. lib. bdg. 14.45 (*1-56674-133-5*) Forest Hse.
Marvelously Meaningful Maps. Madelyn Wood Carlisle. (Let's Investigate Ser.). 1992. 10.15 (*0-606-01639-2*, Pub. by Turtleback) Demco.
Marvels. Kurt Busiek. (Illus.). 216p. 1994. pap. 19.95 (*0-7851-0049-0*) Marvel Entrprs.
Marvels & Mysteries. Marie S. Bordner. 96p. (Orig.). 1986. pap. 4.95 (*0-912661-09-7*) Woodsong Graph.
Marvels Beyond Science (1910) Joseph Grasset. 414p. 1998. reprint ed. pap. 29.95 (*0-7661-0518-0*) Kessinger Pub.
Marvels of Charity: History of American Sisters & Nuns. George C. Stewart, Jr. LC 94-66024. 608p. 1994. 29.95 (*0-87973-648-8*) Our Sunday Visitor.
***Marvels of Kishangarh Paintings: From the Collection of the National Museum, New Delhi.** Mathur. 2000. 140.00 (*81-86050-43-4*, Pub. by Bharat Vidya) S Asia.
Marvels of Math: Fascinating Reads & Awesome Activities. Kendall Haven. LC 98-34084. 180p. 1998. pap., teacher ed. 21.50 (*1-56308-585-2*) Libs Unl.
Marvels of Prophecy. Howard B. Rand. 1959. 5.00 (*0-685-08810-3*) Destiny.
Marvels of Rigomer: Les Mervelles de Rigomer. Thomas E. Vesce. LC 88-10973. (Library of Medieval Literature).Tr. of Les/Mervelles De Rigomer. 337p. 1988. text 20.00 (*0-8240-1518-5*) Garland.
Marvels of Rome. rev. ed. Tr. by Francis M. Nichols from LAT. LC 86-45750. (Historical Travel Ser.). Orig. Title: Mirabilia Urbis Romae. (Illus.). 164p. 1986. pap. 12.50 (*0-934977-02-X*) Italica Pr.
Marvels of Science: Fifty Fascinating Five-Minute Reads. Kendall Haven. xxii, 238p. 1994. pap. text 20.00 (*1-56308-159-8*) Libs Unl.
Marvels of Science Fiction, Vol. 2. Isaac Asimov. 23.95 (*0-88411-586-0*) Amereon Ltd.
Marvels of the Molecule. L. Salem. Tr. by James Wuest. (FRE.). 88p. 1987. 20.00 (*0-89573-345-5*, Wiley-VCH) Wiley.
Marven of the Great North Woods. Kathryn Lasky. LC 96-2334. (Illus.). 48p. (J). (gr. 1-5). 1997. 16.00 (*0-15-200104-2*) Harcourt.
Marvena: Paintings & Works on Paper. Annabel Armstrong. (Illus.). 36p. 1990. pap. 15.00 (*0-8150-0015-4*) Wittenborn Art.
Marville: Paris. Photos by Charles Marville. (FRE., Illus.). 450p. 1998. pap. 55.00 (*2-85025-374-X*) Gingko Press.
Marvin: Poetry & Dialysis. William T. Burke et al. (Illus.). 48p. 1988. pap. 3.95 (*0-944231-03-9*) Slvr Wings CA.
***Marvin & Bailey's Junkyard Circus.** David H. Sparks. (Illus.). 32p. 2000. pap. write for info. (*0-9701951-0-9*) Keystone Pub Inc.
Marvin & the Mean Words. Suzy Kline. LC 96-1450. (Illus.). 80p. (J). 1997. 14.95 (*0-399-23009-2*, G P Putnam) Peng Put Young Read.
Marvin & the Mean Words. Suzy Kline. (Illus.). 96p. (J). (gr. 2-5). 1998. pap. 4.99 (*0-698-11657-7*, PapStar) Peng Put Young Read.
***Marvin & the Mean Words.** Suzy Kline. 1998. 10.09 (*0-606-13599-5*, Pub. by Turtleback) Demco.
Marvin & the Meanest Girl. Suzy Kline. LC 99-20925. (Illus.). 96p. (J). (gr. 2-6). 2000. 14.99 (*0-399-23409-8*, G P Putnam) Peng Put Young Read.
Marvin Composes a Tea: And Other Humorous Stories. Highlights for Children Staff. LC 90-85916. (Illus.). 96p. (J). (gr. 3-7). 1992. pap. 3.95 (*1-878093-40-1*) Boyds Mills Pr.
Marvin Gaye. Tom Stockdale. LC 99-24344. (Illus.). 48p. (gr. 4-7). 1999. 16.95 (*0-7910-5227-3*) Chelsea Hse.
Marvin Gaye Greatest Hits. 48p. 1996. per. 14.95 (*0-7935-7567-2*) H Leonard.
Marvin Gaye the Untold Chapter: Based on the Upcoming Feature Film "The Untold Chapter" Deborah Y. Anderson. LC 97-66302. x, 130p. (Orig.). 1997. pap. 16.95 (*0-9657332-0-3*) DeVonne Prod.
Marvin Hamlisch Songbook. 72p. 1986. otabind 12.95 (*0-7935-1061-9*, 00306910) H Leonard.
Marvin Jones: The Public Life of an Agrarian Advocate. Irvin M. May, Jr. LC 79-5282. (Centennial Series of the Association of Former Students: No. 8). (Illus.). 312p. 1980. 29.95 (*0-89096-093-3*) Tex A&M Univ Pr.
Marvin K. Mooney, Will You Please Go Now. Dr. Seuss, pseud. (Bright & Early Bks.: No. 13). (Illus.). (J). (ps-2). 1972. lib. bdg. 11.99 (*0-394-92490-8*, Pub. by Random Bks Yng Read) Random.
Marvin K. Mooney, Will You Please Go Now. Dr. Seuss, pseud. (Bright & Early Bks.: No. 13). (Illus.). 28p. (J). (ps-3). 1988. 7.99 (*0-394-82490-3*, Pub. by Random Bks Yng Read) Random.
Marvin K. Mooney, Will You Please Go Now. Dr. Seuss, pseud. (Bright & Early Bks.). (J). 1988. 7.99 (*0-606-03933-3*, Pub. by Turtleback) Demco.
***Marvin Measures Up.** Dave Browning. LC 99-38026. (Illus.). 12p. (YA). (ps-3). 2000. pap. 6.95 (*0-688-17734-4*, Wm Morrow) Morrow Avon.
Marvin One Too Many. Katherine Paterson. 48p. (gr. k-3). pap. 3.95 (*0-06-444279-9*) HarpC.
Marvin One Too Many. Katherine Paterson. (Illus.). 48p. (gr. k-3). 14.95 (*0-06-028769-1*) HarpC.
Marvin One Too Many. Katherine Paterson. (Illus.). 48p. (J). (gr. k-3). 14.89 (*0-06-028770-5*) HarpC Child Bks.
***Marvin Redpost.** Louis Sachar. 1999. pap. 11.10 (*0-7857-0343-8*) Econo-Clad Bks.
Marvin Redpost: A Flying Birthday Cake. Louis Sachar. LC 98-7204. Vol. 6. (Illus.). 80p. (J). (gr. 1-4). 1999. 3.99 (*0-679-89000-9*) Random.
Marvin Redpost: A Flying Birthday Cake. Louis Sachar. LC 98-7204. (J). (gr. 1-4). 1999. lib. bdg. 11.99 (*0-679-99000-3*) Random.
Marvin Redpost: Alone in His Teacher's House. Louis Sachar. LC 93-19791. (First Stepping Stone Bks.). (Illus.). 96p. (J). (gr. k-3). 1994. lib. bdg. 11.99 (*0-679-91949-X*, Pub. by Random Bks Yng Read) Random.
Marvin Redpost: Alone in His Teacher's House. Louis Sachar. LC 93-19791. (First Stepping Stone Bks.: Vol. 4). (Illus.). 96p. (J). (gr. 1-4). 1994. pap. 3.99 (*0-679-81949-5*, Pub. by Random Bks Yng Read) Random.
Marvin Redpost: Alone in His Teacher's House. Louis Sachar. LC 93-19791. (J). 1994. 9.09 (*0-606-07029-X*, Pub. by Turtleback) Demco.
Marvin Redpost: Class President. Louis Sachar. LC 98-14313. (J). 1999. 3.99 (*0-679-88999-X*) Random.
Marvin Redpost: Class President. Louis Sachar. LC 98-14313. (J). 1999. lib. bdg. 11.99 (*0-679-98999-4*) Random.
Marvin Redpost: Is He a Girl? Louis Sachar. (Illus.). 112p. (J). (gr. 3-7). 1993. pap. 3.99 (*0-679-81948-7*, Pub. by Random Bks Yng Read) Random.
Marvin Redpost: Is He a Girl? Louis Sachar. LC 92-40784. (First Stepping Stone Bks.). (Illus.). 80p. (J). (gr. 1-4). 1993. pap. 2.99 (*0-685-71893-X*); lib. bdg. 11.99 (*0-679-91948-1*, Pub. by Random Bks Yng Read) Random.
Marvin Redpost: Is He a Girl? Louis Sachar. (J). 1993. 9.19 (*0-606-05920-2*, Pub. by Turtleback) Demco.
Marvin Redpost: Kidnapped at Birth? Louis Sachar. LC 91-51105. (First Stepping Stone Bks.). (Illus.). 80p. (J). (gr. 1-4). 1992. pap. 3.99 (*0-679-81946-0*, Pub. by Random Bks Yng Read); lib. bdg. 11.99 (*0-679-91946-5*, Pub. by Random Bks Yng Read) Random.
Marvin Redpost: Kidnapped at Birth? Louis Sachar. (J). 1992. 9.19 (*0-606-02323-2*, Pub. by Turtleback) Demco.
Marvin Redpost: Why Pick on Me? Louis Sachar. LC 92-12858. (First Stepping Stone Bks.). (Illus.). 80p. (Orig.). (J). (gr. 1-4). 1993. pap. 3.99 (*0-679-81947-9*, Pub. by Random Bks Yng Read) Random.
Marvin Redpost: Why Pick on Me? Louis Sachar. LC 92-12858. (First Stepping Stone Bks.). (Illus.). 80p. (Orig.). (J). (gr. 1-4). 1993. lib. bdg. 11.99 (*0-679-91947-3*, Pub. by Random Bks Yng Read) Random.
Marvin Redpost: Why Pick on Me? Louis Sachar. (First Stepping Stone Bks.). (Orig.). (J). 1993. 9.19 (*0-606-12417-9*, Pub. by Turtleback) Demco.
Marvin the Red Frog. Michael T. Whittaker. (Illus.). 18p. (Orig.). (J). (ps-6). 1996. pap. 3.95 (*1-889832-00-6*) Auburn Pub.
Marvin the Tap Dancing Horse. Betty Paraskevas. LC 98-47939. (Illus.). (J). 2000. 20.01 (*0-689-82153-0*) S&S Childrens.
***Marvin Weighs In.** Dave Browning. LC 99-38022. (Illus.). 12p. (YA). (ps-3). 2000. pap. 6.95 (*0-688-17735-2*, Wm Morrow) Morrow Avon.
Marvin's Best Christmas Present Ever. Katherine Paterson. LC PZ7.P273Mar 1997. (I Can Read Bks.). (Illus.). 48p. (J). (gr. 2-4). 1997. 14.95 (*0-06-027159-0*) HarpC Child Bks.
Marvin's Best Christmas Present Ever. Katherine Paterson. LC 96-31692. (I Can Read Bks.). (Illus.). 48p. (J). (ps-3). 1997. lib. bdg. 14.89 (*0-06-027160-4*) HarpC Child Bks.

M

Marvin's Best Christmas Present Ever. Katherine Paterson. (I Can Read Bks.). (Illus.). 48p. (J). (gr. 2-4). 1999. pap. 3.95 (*0-06-444265-9*) HarpC Child Bks.

Marvin's Favorite Halloween Songs. 32p. 1985. pap. 6.95 (*0-7935-3945-5*) H Leonard.

Marvin's Favorite Halloween Songs. Ed. by Ron Middlebrook. 36p. (C). 1985. pap. text 5.95 (*0-931759-07-2*) Centerstream Pub.

Marvin's Mansion. Ken Wilkins. LC 98-60805. (Illus.). 128p. 1998. pap. 10.95 (*1-57921-129-1*, Pub. by WinePress Pub) BookWorld.

Marvin's Room. Scott McPherson. 1992. pap. 5.25 (*0-8222-1312-5*) Dramatists Play.

Marvin's Room. Scott Mcpherson. 128p. 1996. reprint ed. pap. 9.95 (*0-452-27819-8*, Plume) Dutton Plume.

Marwaris: From Traders to Industrialists. T. A. Timberg. 268p. 1978. 19.95 (*0-7069-0528-8*) Asia Bk Corp.

*__Marx.__ Gill Hands. (Guides for Beginners - Great Lives Ser.). 2000. pap. 11.95 (*0-340-78013-4*, Pub. by Headway) Trafalgar.

*__Marx.__ Meikle. LC 99-55612. 540p. 2000. 166.95 (*1-84014-707-5*) Ashgate Pub Co.

Marx. Edward Reiss. 192p. 1997. pap. 15.95 (*0-7453-1014-1*, Pub. by Pluto GBR) Stylus Pub VA.

*__Marx.__ Peter Singer. (Very Short Introductions Ser.). 96p. 2000. pap. 8.95 (*0-19-285405-4*) OUP.

Marx: A Clear Guide. Reiss. LC 96-28836. 1996. 44.95 (*0-7453-1015-X*, Pub. by Pluto GBR) Stylus Pub VA.

Marx: A Hundred Years On. Betty Matthews. LC 97-187380. 312 p. 1983. write for info. (*0-85315-565-8*) Lawrence & Wishart.

Marx: Early Political Writings. Karl Marx. Ed. by Joseph O'Malley. Tr. by Richard A. Davis. LC 93-31207. (Cambridge Texts in the History of Political Thought Ser.). 230p. (C). 1994. text 44.95 (*0-521-34241-4*) Cambridge U Pr.

Marx: Early Political Writings. Karl Marx. Ed. by Joseph O'Malley. Tr. by Richard A. Davis. LC 93-31207. (Cambridge Texts in the History of Political Thought Ser.). 230p. (C). 1994. pap. text 13.95 (*0-521-34994-X*) Cambridge U Pr.

Marx: Great Philosophers. Terry Eagleton. LC 99-24218. (Great Philosophers Ser.). 64p. 1999. pap. 6.00 (*0-415-92377-8*) Routledge.

Marx: Later Political Writing. Karl Marx. Ed. by Terrell Carver. (Cambridge Texts in the History of Political Thought Ser.). 297p. (C). 1996. text 44.95 (*0-521-36504-X*); pap. text 14.95 (*0-521-36739-5*) Cambridge U Pr.

Marx: Sociology-Social Change-Capitalism. Donald McQuarie. 15.95 (*0-7043-3221-3*, Pub. by Quartet); pap. 6.95 (*0-686-82876-3*, Pub. by Quartet) Charles River Bks.

Marx Against the Marxists: The Christian Humanism of Karl Marx. Jose P. Miranda. Tr. by John Drury from SPA. LC 80-14415. Orig. Title: El Christianism de Marx. 332p. (Orig.). reprint ed. pap. 103.00 (*0-7837-5517-1*, 204528700005) Bks Demand.

Marx & America. Earl Browder. LC 73-16734. 146p. 1974. reprint ed. lib. bdg. 65.00 (*0-8371-7218-7*, BRMA, Greenwood Pr) Greenwood.

Marx & Aristotle: Nineteenth-Century German Social Theory & Classical Antiquity. Ed. by George E. McCarthy. 260p. (C). 1992. text 67.50 (*0-8476-7713-3*); pap. text 27.95 (*0-8476-7714-1*) Rowman.

Marx & Contemporary Scientific Thought: Proceedings. Role of Karl Marx in the Development of Contempora. (Publications of the International Social Science Council: No. 13). 1970. 69.25 (*90-279-6276-6*) Mouton.

Marx & Contradiction. Lawrence Wilde. 126p. 1989. text 72.95 (*0-566-05662-3*, Pub. by Avebry) Ashgate Pub Co.

Marx & Education in Late Capitalism. R. F. Price. LC 86-3541. 318p. 1986. 53.00 (*0-389-20617-2*, N8175) B&N Imports.

*__Marx & Engels: Their Contribution to the Democratic Breakthrough.__ August H. Nimtz, Jr. LC 99-53178. (C). 2000. text 71.50 (*0-7914-4489-9*); pap. text 23.95 (*0-7914-4490-2*) State U NY Pr.

Marx & Engels & the English Workers & Other Essays. W. O. Henderson. (Illus.). 200p. 1989. text 42.00 (*0-7146-3334-8*, Pub. by F Cass Pubs) Intl Spec Bk.

Marx & Engels on Ecology, 8. Karl Marx & Friedrich Engels. Ed. by Howard L. Parsons. LC 77-71866. (Contributions in Philosophy Ser.: No.8). 262p. 1977. 65.00 (*0-8371-9538-1*, PME/, Greenwood Pr) Greenwood.

Marx & Engels on the Means of Communication: A Selection of Texts. Karl Marx & Friedrich Engels. Ed. by Yves De La Haye. 173p. (Orig.). 1980. pap. 13.95 (*0-88477-013-3*) Intl General.

Marx & Engels on the Trade Unions. Karl Marx & Friedrich Engels. LC 90-43327. xx, 240p. 1990. reprint ed. pap. 8.95 (*0-7178-0676-6*) Intl Pubs Co.

Marx & Engels on Trade Unions. Karl Marx & Friedrich Engels. Ed. by Kenneth Lapides. LC 86-25266. 264p. 1986. 55.00 (*0-275-92373-8*, C2373, Praeger Pubs) Greenwood.

Marx & Ethics. Philip J. Kain. 232p. 1991. reprint ed. pap. text 26.00 (*0-19-823932-7*) OUP.

Marx & His Legacy: A Centennial Appraisal. Ed. by Deb K. Banerjee. (C). 1988. 17.50 (*81-7074-012-6*, Pub. by KP Bagchi) S Asia.

Marx & Human Nature. Norman Geras. (C). 1985. pap. 15.00 (*0-86091-066-0*, Pub. by Verso) Norton.

Marx & Keynes: The Limits of the Mixed Economy. Paul Mattick. LC 69-15526. (Extending Horizons Ser.). 384p. (C). 1969. 6.95 (*0-87558-045-9*); pap. 3.45 (*0-87558-069-6*) Porter Sargent.

Marx & Keynes on Economic Recessions: The Theories of Unemployment & Effective Demand. Claudio Sardoni. 256p. (C). 1987. text 50.00 (*0-8147-7871-2*) NYU Pr.

Marx & Marxism. Ed. by Ajit Jain & Alexander J. Matejko. LC 84-3461. 309p. 1984. 55.00 (*0-275-91195-0*, C1195, Praeger Pubs) Greenwood.

Marx & Modern Economic Analysis, 2 vols., Set. Ed. by G. A. Caravale. (Illus.). 538p. 1991. text 215.00 (*1-85278-435-0*) E Elgar.

Marx & Modern Political Theory: From Hobbes to Contemporary Feminism. Philip J. Kain. (Studies in Social & Political Philosophy). 446p. (Orig.). (C). 1993. pap. text 31.95 (*0-8476-7866-0*); lib. bdg. 77.00 (*0-8476-7865-2*) Rowman.

Marx & Nature: A Red & Green Perspective. Paul Burkett. LC 98-42328. 336p. 1999. text 45.00 (*0-312-21940-7*) St Martin.

Marx & Nietzsche: The Record of an Encounter-the Reminiscences & Transcripts of a Nineteenth Century Journalist. David B. Myers. (Illus.). 186p. (Orig.). (C). 1986. pap. text 21.00 (*0-8191-5102-5*) U Pr of Amer.

Marx & Non-Equilibrium Economics. Ed. by Alan Freeman & Guglielmo Carchedi. LC 95-30784. 336p. 1996. 100.00 (*1-85898-268-5*) E Elgar.

Marx & Philosophy of Culture. Robert D'Amico. LC 80-24405. (University of Florida Humanities Monographs: No. 50). viii, 108p. (Orig.). 1981. pap. 15.95 (*0-8130-0689-9*) U Press Fla.

Marx & Philosophy of Culture. Robert D'Amico. LC 80-24405. (University of Florida Monographs: Vol. 50). 118p. (Orig.). 1981. reprint ed. pap. 36.60 (*0-608-04465-2*, 206521000001) Bks Demand.

Marx & Satan. Richard Wurmbrand. 1986. 7.00 (*0-88264-084-4*) Living Sacrifice Bks.

*__Marx & Sociobiology.__ George A. Huaco. LC 99-46843. 144p. 1999. 49.00 (*0-7618-1534-1*); pap. 27.50 (*0-7618-1535-X*) U Pr of Amer.

Marx & the Ancients. George McCarthy. 356p. (C). 1990. lib. bdg. 51.00 (*0-8476-7641-2*) Rowman.

Marx & the Bible: A Critique of the Philosophy of Oppression. Jose P. Miranda. Tr. by John Eagleson. LC 73-89053. Orig. Title: Marx y la Biblia: Critica a la filosofia de la oppresion. 360p. (Orig.). 1974. reprint ed. pap. 111.60 (*0-7837-9817-2*, 206054600005) Bks Demand.

Marx & the French Revolution. Francois Furet & Karl Marx. Ed. by Lucien Calvie. Tr. by Deborah K. Furet. 253p. 1988. 41.95 (*0-226-27338-5*) U Ch Pr.

Marx & the Gulag: Two Essays. Thomas G. West & Sanderson Schaub. (Claremont Paper: No. 8). 57p. (Orig.). 1987. pap. text 3.00 (*0-317-61647-1*) Claremont Inst.

Marx & the Marxists: The Ambiguous Legacy. Sidney Hook. LC 81-20921. (Anvil Ser.). 256p. 1982. reprint ed. pap. 12.50 (*0-89874-443-1*) Krieger.

Marx & the Missing Link: Human Nature. W. Peter Archibald. LC 89-1978. 292p. (C). 1992. pap. 18.50 (*0-391-03754-4*) Humanities.

Marx & the New Individual. Ian Forbes. 256p. (C). (gr. 13). 1990. text 59.95 (*0-04-445432-5*) Routledge.

*__Marx & the Postmodernism Debates: An Agenda for Critical Theory.__ Lorraine Y. Landry. LC 99-86107. 240p. 2000. 62.00 (*0-275-96889-8*, C6889, Praeger Pubs) Greenwood.

Marx & the Proletariat: A Study in Social Theory, 18. Timothy McCarthy. LC 78-4025. (Contributions in Political Science Ser.: No. 18). 102p. 1978. 49.95 (*0-313-20412-8*, MPL/, Greenwood Pr) Greenwood.

Marx & the Third World. Peter Hudis. 42p. 1983. pap. 1.00 (*0-914441-12-4*) News & Letters.

Marx at the Millennium. Smith. LC 95-52759. 1996. 54.95 (*0-7453-1001-X*, Pub. by Pluto GBR) Stylus Pub VA.

Marx at the Millennium. Cyril Smith. 196p. 1996. pap. 19.95 (*0-7453-1000-1*, Pub. by Pluto GBR) Stylus Pub VA.

Marx at 2000. Munck. LC 99-15594. 164p. 2000. text 65.00 (*0-312-22407-9*) St Martin.

Marx Beyond Marx. Negri. (C). 1996. 80.95 (*0-7453-0575-X*); pap. 23.00 (*0-7453-0576-8*) Westview.

Marx Beyond Marx: Lessons on the Grundrisse. Antonio Negri. Orig. Title: Marx Oltre Marx. 248p. 1991. pap. 10.00 (*0-936756-25-X*) Autonomedia.

Marx Brothers. Kate Stables. 1992. 10.98 (*1-55521-793-1*) Bk Sales Inc.

Marx Brothers: A Bio-Bibliography. Wes D. Gehring. LC 86-31823. 277p. 1987. lib. bdg. 57.95 (*0-313-24547-9*, Greenwood Pr) Greenwood.

Marx Brothers: Monkey Business, Duck Soup, A Day at the Races. S. J. Perelman et al. (Classic Screenplay Ser.). (Illus.). 224p. (Orig.). 1993. pap. 16.95 (*0-571-16647-4*) Faber & Faber.

Marx Brothers Encyclopedia. Glenn Mitchell. (Illus.). 256p. 1996. pap. 19.95 (*0-7134-7838-1*) Trafalgar.

Marx' Critique of Science & Positivism. George E. McCarthy. 233p. (C). 1988. lib. bdg. 140.50 (*90-277-2702-3*, Pub. by Kluwer Academic) Kluwer Academic.

Marx Demystifies Calculus. Paulus Gerdes. Tr. by Beatrice Lumpkin from POR. LC 85-8988. (Studies in Marxism: Vol. 16).Tr. of Karl Marx Arrancar O, Veu Misterioso A Matematica. 139p. 1985. 19.95 (*0-930656-39-3*); pap. 9.95 (*0-930656-40-7*) MEP Pubns.

Marx, Durkheim, Weber: Formations of Modern Social Thought. Kenneth Morrison. LC 95-235612. 352p. 1995. 69.95 (*0-8039-7562-7*); pap. 21.95 (*0-8039-7563-5*) Sage.

Marx-Engels Dictionary. James Russell. LC 80-786. (Illus.). 140p. 1980. lib. bdg. 59.95 (*0-313-22035-2*, RME/, Greenwood Pr) Greenwood.

Marx-Engels Reader. 2nd ed. Karl Marx. Ed. by David P. McLellan. 788p. (C). 1978. pap. 21.00 (*0-393-09040-X*) Norton.

*__Marx-Engels Reader.__ 2nd ed. Robert Tucker. (C). 1999. pap. text 17.25 (*0-393-98881-3*) Norton.

Marx et Keynes see Cahiers de l'Institut de Science Economique Appliquee: Bibliographie Marxologique. Liste Complementaire

Marx Family Saga. Juan Goytisolo. Tr. by Peter Bush from SPA. LC 98-30358. 185p. 1999. pap. 10.95 (*0-87286-349-2*) City Lights.

Marx for Beginners. Ed. by Tom Engelhardt. LC 78-20422. 186p. 1990. pap. 11.00 (*0-679-72512-1*) McKay.

Marx for Beginners. Errol Selkirk. LC 91-50560. (Writers & Readers Documentary Comic Bks.). (Illus.). 96p. 1991. pap. 9.00 (*0-86316-142-1*) Writers & Readers.

Marx, Hayek, & Utopia. Chris M. Sciabarra. LC 94-39676. (SUNY Series in the Philosophy of the Social Sciences). 178p. (C). 1995. text 59.50 (*0-7914-2615-7*); pap. text 19.95 (*0-7914-2616-5*) State U NY Pr.

Marx in Soho: A Play on History. Howard Zinn. LC 98-55072. 88p. 1999. 23.00 (*0-89608-594-5*); pap. 12.00 (*0-89608-593-7*) South End Pr.

Marx, Justice & History. Ed. by Marshall Cohen et al. LC 79-5478. (Philosophy & Public Affairs Reader Ser.). 325p. 1980. reprint ed. pap. 100.80 (*0-7837-9278-6*, 206001700004) Bks Demand.

Marx-Lexikon zur Politischen Oekonomie: Marx-Lexicon on Political Economy, 3 vols. S. Kuruma. (GER.). 1110p. 1973. pap. 95.00 (*0-8288-6318-0*, M-7549) Fr & Eur.

*__Marx, Marxism & Utopia.__ 190p. 2000. 64.95 (*0-7546-1178-7*, Pub. by Ashgate Pub) Ashgate Pub Co.

Marx, Method, & the Division of Labor. Rob Beamish. 208p. 1992. text 24.95 (*0-252-01878-8*) U of Ill Pr.

Marx Method, Epistemology, & Humanism. Philip J. Kain. 208p. 1986. text 118.00 (*90-277-2223-4*, D Reidel) Kluwer Academic.

Marx, Morality, & the Virtue of Beneficence. Robert T. Sweet. LC 90-19280. (American University Studies: Philosophy: Ser. V, Vol. 115). VI, 207p. (C). 1991. text 35.95 (*0-8204-1486-7*) P Lang Pubng.

Marx, Nietzsche, & Modernity. Nancy S. Love. 224p. 1986. text 57.50 (*0-231-06238-9*) Col U Pr.

Marx, Nietzsche, & Modernity. Nancy S. Love. 264p. 1996. pap. 18.50 (*0-231-06239-7*) Col U Pr.

Marx Not Madison: The Crisis of American Legal Education. Martha R. Martini. LC 96-3341. 180p. 1996. lib. bdg. 36.50 (*0-7618-0485-4*) U Pr of Amer.

Marx Oltre Marx see Marx Beyond Marx: Lessons on the Grundrisse

Marx on China. 1968. pap. 19.95 (*0-8464-4449-6*) Beekman Pubs.

Marx on China. Karl Marx. 1973. lib. bdg. 250.00 (*0-87968-352-X*) Gordon Pr.

Marx on Suicide. Karl Marx. Ed. & Tr. by Eric A. Plaut & Kevin Anderson from FRE. LC 99-19436. 152p. 1999. 49.95 (*0-8101-1632-4*); pap. 14.95 (*0-8101-1638-3*) Northwestern U Pr.

Marx One Hundred Years On. Ed. by Matthews. (C). 1983. pap. 19.50 (*0-85315-566-6*, Pub. by Lawrence & Wishart) NYU Pr.

Marx or Jesus: Two Men - Two Plans. Pearl Evans. LC 89-5866. (Illus.). 160p. 1989. 17.95 (*0-938453-03-3*) Small Helm Pr.

Marx, Reason & the Art of Freedom. Kevin M. Brien. LC 86-24048. 288p. 1987. 37.95 (*0-87722-466-8*) Temple U Pr.

Marx, Schumpeter & Keynes: A Centenary Celebration of Dissent. Ed. by Suzanne Helbrun & David Bramhall. LC 86-10069. 354p. (gr. 13). 1987. pap. text 39.95 (*0-87332-381-5*) M E Sharpe.

Marx, Schumpeter & Keynes: A Centenary Celebration of Dissent. Ed. by Suzanne W. Helburn & David F. Bramhall. LC 86-10069. 355p. 1986. reprint ed. pap. 110.10 (*0-7837-9988-8*, 206071500006) Bks Demand.

*__Marx Sisters.__ Barry Maitland. (Kathy & Brock Mysteries Ser.). 2000. pap. 6.99 (*0-14-029176-8*) Viking Penguin.

Marx Sisters: A Kathy Kolla & David Brock Mystery. Barry Maitland. LC 99-72640. 288p. 1999. 23.95 (*1-55970-474-8*, Pub. by Arcade Pub Inc) Time Warner.

Marx, the Young Hegelians & the Origins of Radical Social Theory. Warren Breckman. LC 98-15205. (Modern European Philosophy Ser.). 352p. (C). 1999. text 54.95 (*0-521-62440-1*) Cambridge U Pr.

Marx Toys: Robots, Space & Comic Characters. Maxine A. Pinsky. (Illus.). 176p. (YA). (gr. 10-13). 1995. 39.95 (*0-88740-936-9*) Schiffer.

*__Marx Toys Sampler: Playthings from an Ohio Valley Legend.__ Michelle Smith. (Illus.). 192p. 2000. pap. 26.95 (*0-87341-894-8*, MXTS) Krause Pubns.

Marx und die Verwirklichung der Philosophie. A. Wildermuth. 873p. 1971. pap. text 249.00 (*90-247-5032-6*) Kluwer Academic.

*__Marx und Engels in der Dr-Linguistik: Zur Herausbildung Einer Marxistisch-Leninistischen Sprachtheorie.__ Jens Wurche. (GER.). 188p. 1999. 38.00 (*3-631-34016-8*) P Lang Pubng.

Marx Versus Tolstoy: A Debate. Clarence S. Darrow & Arthur M. Lewis. LC 73-137537. (Peace Movement in America Ser.). 124p. 1972. reprint ed. lib. bdg. 22.95 (*0-89198-066-0*) Ozer.

Marx vs. Markets. Stanley W. Moore. 136p. 1993. 30.00 (*0-271-00865-2*) Pa St U Pr.

Marx-Weber Debate. Ed. by Norbert Wiley. LC 86-13909. (Key Issues in Sociological Theory Ser.: No. 2). 206p. reprint ed. pap. 63.90 (*0-7837-1134-4*, 204166400022) Bks Demand.

Marx Went Away - But Karl Stayed Behind: Karl Marx Collective: Economy, Society, & Religion in a Siberian Collective Farm. rev. ed. Caroline Humphrey. LC 98-8341. 640p. (C). 1999. text 70.00 (*0-472-09676-1*, 09676) U of Mich Pr.

Marx Went Away but Karl Stayed Behind. Caroline Humphrey. LC 98-8341. (Illus.). 640p. (C). 1999. pap. text 29.95 (*0-472-06676-5*, 06676) U of Mich Pr.

Marx y la Biblia see Marx & the Bible: A Critique of the Philosophy of Oppression

Marx y la Biblia: Critica a la filosofia de la oppresion see Marx & the Bible: A Critique of the Philosophy of Oppresion

Marxian & Christian Utopianism: Toward a Socialist Political Theology. Marsden. 236p. 33.00 (*0-85345-831-6*, Pub. by Monthly Rev); pap. 19.00 (*0-85345-832-4*, Pub. by Monthly Rev) NYU Pr.

Marxian Concept of Capital & the Soviet Experience: Essay in the Critique of Political Economy. Paresh Chattopadhyay. LC 93-37881. (Praeger Series in Political Economy). 208p. 1994. 59.95 (*0-275-94530-8*, Praeger Pubs) Greenwood.

Marxian Dilemma: Transformation of Values to Prices. Ed. by A. J. Fonseca. 1980. 10.00 (*0-8364-0654-0*, Pub. by Manohar) S Asia.

Marxian Economics, 3 vols., Set. Ed. by J. E. King. (Schools of Thought in Economics Ser.: No. 9). (Illus.). 1384p. 1990. text 520.00 (*1-85278-121-1*) E Elgar.

Marxian Economics Vol. 1: A Reappraisal - Essays on Volume III of Capital; Method, Value, & Money. Riccardo Bellofiore. LC 97-17608. 276p. 1998. text 79.95 (*0-312-17664-3*) St Martin.

Marxian Economics Vol. II: A Reappraisal - Profits, Prices, & Dynamics. R. Bellofiore. LC 97-17608. 304p. 1998. text 79.95 (*0-312-17665-1*) St Martin.

Marxian Hermeneutics of Fredric Jameson. Christopher A. Wise. LC 94-36372. (American University Studies: Ser. III, Vol. 49). VIII, 144p. (C). 1995. text 33.95 (*0-8204-2046-8*) P Lang Pubng.

Marxian Legal Theory. Ed. by Csaba Varga. LC 92-36109. (International Library of Essays in Law & Legal Theory: Vol. 9). (C). 1993. lib. bdg. 150.00 (*0-8147-8772-X*) NYU Pr.

Marxian Political Economy: An Outline. James F. Becker. LC 76-9172. 336p. reprint ed. pap. 95.80 (*0-608-18409-8*, 2030580) Bks Demand.

*__Marxian Political Economy: Theory History & Contemporary Relevance.__ Bob Milward. 2000. text 69.95 (*0-312-23417-1*) St Martin.

Marxian Science & the Colleges. 3rd ed. Daniel De Leon. 96p. 1944. 2.00 (*0-935534-19-9*) NY Labor News.

Marxian Science & the Colleges. 3rd ed. Daniel De Leon. 96p. 1966. pap. 0.75 (*0-935534-20-2*) NY Labor News.

Marxian Socialism in the United States. Daniel Bell & Michael Kazin. 280p. 1996. pap. text 16.95 (*0-8014-8309-3*) Cornell U Pr.

Marxian Socialism in the United States. Daniel Bell. LC 67-30481. 228p. reprint ed. pap. 70.70 (*0-608-18439-X*, 203263600080) Bks Demand.

Marxische Aufhebund der Philosophie und der Philosophische Marxismus. Joseph G. Fracchia. (American University Studies: Philosophy: Ser. V). (GER.). 438p. (C). 1987. text 55.90 (*0-8204-0346-6*) P Lang Pubng.

Marxism, 2 vols. Ed. by Margaret Levi. (Schools of Thought in Politics Ser.: No. 1). 1188p. 1991. text 385.00 (*1-85278-355-9*) E Elgar.

Marxism. Anson Rabinbach. 1998. 26.95 (*0-8057-8620-1*, Twyne); per. 14.95 (*0-8057-8621-X*, Twyne) Mac Lib Ref.

Marxism: A Historical & Critical Study. rev. ed. George Lichtheim. 432p. 1964. pap. 13.95 (*0-7100-4645-6*, Routledge Thoemms) Routledge.

Marxism: An Historical & Critical Study. George Lichtheim. LC 81-17066. 424p. 1982. reprint ed. pap. text 23.00 (*0-231-05425-4*) Col U Pr.

Marxism: Essential Writings. Ed. by David McLellan. 428p. 1988. pap. text 23.95 (*0-19-827517-X*) OUP.

Marxism: For & Against. Robert L. Heilbroner. (C). 1980. pap. text 14.00 (*0-393-95166-9*) Norton.

Marxism: Last Refuge of the Bourgeoisie? Ed. by Paul Mattick, Jr. LC 83-620. 333p. 1983. reprint ed. pap. 103.30 (*0-7837-9956-X*, 206068300006) Bks Demand.

Marxism: The Inner Dialogue. 2nd ed. Michael Curtis. LC 96-52289. 406p. 1997. pap. text 22.95 (*1-56000-945-4*) Transaction Pubs.

Marxism - Last Refuge of the Bourgeoisie? Ed. by Paul Mattick, Jr. LC 83-620. 336p. (gr. 13). 1983. pap. text 36.95 (*0-87332-261-4*) M E Sharpe.

Marxism, a Living Science. Kenneth N. Cameron. 264p. 1993. pap. 9.95 (*0-7178-0707-X*) Intl Pubs Co.

Marxism & African Literature. George M. Gugelberger. LC 85-72994. 240p. 1985. 29.95 (*0-86543-030-6*); pap. 9.95 (*0-86543-031-4*) Africa World.

Marxism & Alienation. Nicholas Churchich. LC 88-46151. 368p. 1990. 49.50 (*0-8386-3372-2*) Fairleigh Dickinson.

Marxism & Alternatives: Towards the Conceptual Interaction among Soviet Philosophy, NeoThomism, Pragmatism, & Phenomenology. Tom Rockmore et al. 325p. 1981. text 162.50 (*90-277-1285-9*) Kluwer Academic.

Marxism & Art: Essays Classic & Contemporary. Maynard Soloman. LC 79-2063. 694p. 1979. reprint ed. pap. 21.95 (*0-8143-1621-2*) Wayne St U Pr.

Marxism & Beyond. Sidney Hook. LC 82-20542. 238p. 1983. text 38.50 (*0-8476-7159-3*) Rowman.

Marxism & Christianity. Denys Turner. LC 82-22713. 268p. (C). 1983. text 53.00 (*0-389-20351-3*, N7211) B&N Imports.

Marxism & Christianity. Alasdair C. MacIntyre. LC 83-40600. 143p. 1984. reprint ed. pap. text 9.50 (*0-268-01358-6*) U of Notre Dame Pr.

Marxism & Class Theory: A Bourgeois Critique. Frank Parkin. LC 79-14222. 1983. pap. text 20.50 (*0-231-04881-5*) Col U Pr.

Marxism & Council Communism: Modern Revolutionary Thought. Peter Rachleff. 312p. 1974. 250.00 (*0-87700-227-4*) Revisionist Pr.

An Asterisk (*) at the beginning of an entry indicates that the title is appearing for the first time.

Marxism & Deconstruction: A Critical Articulation. Michael Ryan. LC 81-48185. 272p. (C). 1982. pap. 14.95 (*0-8018-3248-9*) Johns Hopkins.

Marxism & Democracy. Joseph V. Femia. LC 93-9236. (Marxist Introductions Ser.). 194p. 1993. pap. text 17.95 (*0-19-827921-3*) OUP.

Marxism & Democracy. Ed. by Barry D. Hunt. (C). 1980. pap. 19.50 (*0-85315-504-6*, Pub. by Lawrence & Wishart) NYU Pr.

Marxism & Domination: A Neo-Hegelian, Feminist, Psychoanalytic Theory of Sexual, Political, & Technological Liberation. Isaac D. Balbus. LC 82-47582. 432p. 1982. reprint ed. pap. 134.00 (*0-608-00002-7*, AU0046800006) Bks Demand.

Marxism & Ecology. Reiner Grundmann. (Marxist Introductions Ser.). 336p. 1991. 75.00 (*0-19-827314-2*) OUP.

***Marxism & Ecology: A Bibliography.** Ed. by Joan Nordquist. (Social Theory: Vol. 56). 1999. pap. 20.00 (*1-892068-11-7*) Ref Rsch Serv.

Marxism & Existentialism: The Political Philosophy of Satre & Merlean-Ponty. David Archard. (Modern Revivals in Philosophy Ser.). 142p. 1992. 56.95 (*0-7512-0051-4*, Pub. by Gregg Revivals) Ashgate Pub Co.

Marxism & Feminism. Charnie Guettel. 62p. pap. 3.95 (*0-88961-005-3*, Pub. by Womens Pr) LPC InBook.

Marxism & Form: 20th Century Dialectical Theories of Literature. Fredric Jameson. LC 71-155962. 454p. 1972. pap. text 19.95 (*0-691-01311-X*, Pub. by Princeton U Pr) Cal Prin Full Svc.

***Marxism & Freedom: From 1776 until Today.** Raya Dunayeskaya. LC 99-87116. 400p. 2000. pap. 24.95 (*1-57392-819-4*, Humanity Bks) Prometheus Bks.

Marxism & Historical Writing. Paul Q. Hirst. 194p. 1987. 19.95 (*0-7100-9925-8*, Routledge Thoemms) Routledge.

***Marxism & History: A Critical Introduction.** 2nd ed. S H Rigby. 314p. 1999. pap. 27.95 (*0-7190-5612-8*, Pub. by Manchester Univ Pr) St Martin.

Marxism & Human Nature. Sean Sayers. LC 98-11835. 216p. (C). 1998. 75.00 (*0-415-19147-5*) Routledge.

Marxism & Human Sociobiology: The Perspective of Economic Reforms in China. Boshu Zhang. LC 93-23450. (SUNY Series in Philosophy & Biology). 184p. (C). 1994. text 49.50 (*0-7914-2003-5*); pap. text 16.95 (*0-7914-2004-3*) State U NY Pr.

Marxism & Ideology. Jorge A. Larrain. (Modern Revivals in Philosophy Ser.). 272p. 1992. 58.95 (*0-7512-0013-1*, Pub. by Gregg Revivals) Ashgate Pub Co.

Marxism & Ideology. Ferruccio Rossi-Landi. Tr. by Roger Griffin. (Marxist Introductions Ser.). (Illus.). 384p. 1990. text 85.00 (*0-19-876127-9*) OUP.

Marxism & Law. Hugh Collins. LC 84-7199. (Marxist Introductions Ser.). (Illus.). 176p. 1996. pap. text 16.95 (*0-19-285144-6*) OUP.

Marxism & Leninism, Not Marxism-Leninism: An Essay in the Sociology of Knowledge, 335. John H. Kautsky. LC 93-25074. (Contributions in Political Science Ser.: No. 335). 160p. 1993. 57.95 (*0-313-29044-X*, GM9044, Greenwood Pr) Greenwood.

Marxism & Literary Criticism. Terry Eagleton. LC 76-6707. 1976. pap. 14.95 (*0-520-03243-8*, Pub. by U CA Pr) Cal Prin Full Svc.

Marxism & Literary Criticism Terry Eagleton. LC 76-381772. viii, 87 p. 1976. write for info. (*0-416-82420-X*, Methuen Drama) Methn.

Marxism & Literary History. John Frow. (Illus.). 304p. 1986. 32.00 (*0-674-55096-X*) HUP.

Marxism & Literature. Raymond Williams. (Marxist Introductions Ser.). 224p. 1978. pap. text 12.95 (*0-19-876061-2*) OUP.

Marxism & Modernism: An Historical Study of Lukacs, Brecht, Benjamin, & Adorno. Eugene Lunn. LC 81-23169. 344p. 1982. pap. 17.95 (*0-520-05330-3*, Pub. by U CA Pr) Cal Prin Full Svc.

Marxism & Nationalism: The Theoretical Origins of the Political Crisis. Nimni. 242p. (C). pap. 19.95 (*0-7453-0730-2*, Pub. by Pluto GBR) Stylus Pub VA.

Marxism & Nationalism: The Theoretical Origins of the Political Crisis. Nimni. 242p. (C). 54.95 (*0-7453-0358-7*, Pub. by Pluto GBR) Stylus Pub VA.

Marxism & Other Western Fallacies: An Islamic Critique. Ali Shariati. Ed. by Hamid Algar. Tr. by R. Campbell from PER. LC 79-29729. 1980. 19.95 (*0-933782-06-3*); pap. 9.95 (*0-933782-05-5*) Mizan Pr.

Marxism & Philosophy. Karl Korsch. Tr. & Intro. by Fred Halliday. LC 71-158921. (Modern Reader Ser.: No. PB-189). 175p. reprint ed. pap. 54.30 (*0-7837-3909-5*, 204375700010) Bks Demand.

Marxism & Philosophy in the Twentieth Century: A Defense of Vulgar Marxism. Richard Hudelson. LC 90-32302. 272p. 1990. 65.00 (*0-275-93593-0*, C3593, Praeger Pubs) Greenwood.

Marxism & Primitive Societies: Two Studies. Emmanuel Terray. Tr. by Mary Klopper. LC 75-178712. (Modern Reader Ser.: No. PB-214). 192p. 1972. reprint ed. pap. 59.60 (*0-7837-9610-2*, 206036700005) Bks Demand.

Marxism & "Really Existing Socialism" Alec Nove. (Fundamentals of Pure & Applied Economics Ser.: Vol. 8). viii, 56p. 1986. pap. text 35.00 (*3-7186-0330-6*) Gordon & Breach.

Marxism & Reform in China. Su Shaozhi. 173p. 1993. pap. 37.50 (*0-85124-547-1*, Pub. by Spkesman) Coronet Bks.

Marxism & Religion in Eastern Europe. Ed. by R. T. De George & James P. Scanlan. LC 75-33051. (Sovietica Ser.: No. 36). 199p. 1975. text 126.50 (*90-277-0636-0*, D Reidel) Kluwer Academic.

Marxism & Revolution. Moira Donald. LC 93-60569. 336p. 1993. 45.00 (*0-300-04390-2*) Yale U Pr.

Marxism & Science: Analysis of an Obsession. Gavin Kitching. LC 93-2304. 1994. 40.00 (*0-271-01026-6*); pap. 18.95 (*0-271-01027-4*) Pa St U Pr.

Marxism & Social Democracy: The Revisionist Debate, 1896-98. Ed. by Henry Tudor & J. M. Tudor. 400p. 1988. text 80.00 (*0-521-34049-7*) Cambridge U Pr.

Marxism & Social Life. Andrew Gamble. Ed. by David Marsh et al. LC 98-48308. 381p. 1999. pap. 19.95 (*0-252-06816-5*) U of Ill Pr.

Marxism & Social Science. Andrew Gamble. LC 98-48308. 384p. 1999. 42.50 (*0-252-02501-6*) U of Ill Pr.

Marxism & Socialist Theory: Socialism in Theory & Practice. Michael Albert & Robin Hahnel. LC 80-85407. 303p. (C). 1981. 35.00 (*0-89608-076-5*); pap. 8.50 (*0-89608-075-7*) South End Pr.

Marxism & Spirituality: An International Anthology. Ed. by Benjamin B. Page. LC 92-18499. 248p. 1993. 57.95 (*0-89789-291-7*, H291, Bergin & Garvey) Greenwood.

Marxism & Terrorism. 2nd ed. Leon Trotsky. 30p. 1995. pap. 3.50 (*0-87348-813-X*) Pathfinder NY.

Marxism & the Chinese Experience: Issues in Contemporary Chinese Socialism. Ed. by Arif Dirlik & Maurice Meisner. LC 89-4251. (Socialism & Social Movements Ser.). 396p. (gr. 13). 1989. pap. text 42.95 (*0-87332-546-X*, East Gate Bk) M E Sharpe.

Marxism & the Chinese Experience: Issues in Contemporary Chinese Socialism. Ed. by Arif Dirlik & Maurice Meisner. LC 89-4251. (Socialism & Social Movements). 396p. (C). (gr. 13). 1989. text 87.95 (*0-87332-515-X*) M E Sharpe.

Marxism & the City. Ira Katznelson. (Marxist Introductions Ser.). 336p. (C). 1994. reprint ed. pap. 17.95 (*0-19-827924-8*) OUP.

Marxism & the Crisis of Development in Prewar Japan. Germaine A. Hoston. LC 86-42846. 420p. reprint ed. pap. 130.20 (*0-608-06364-9*, 206672500008) Bks Demand.

Marxism & the French Left: Studies on Labour & Politics in France, 1830-1981. Tony Judt. (Illus.). 352p. 1986. text 38.00 (*0-19-821929-6*) OUP.

Marxism & the Interpretation of Culture. Ed. by Cary Nelson & Lawrence Grossberg. LC 87-5981. 752p. 1988. pap. text 21.95 (*0-252-01401-4*) U of Ill Pr.

Marxism & the Irrationalists. John Lewis. LC 72-6687. 141p. 1973. reprint ed. lib. bdg. 55.00 (*0-8371-6494-X*, LEMB, Greenwood Pr) Greenwood.

Marxism & the Leap to the Kingdom of Freedom: The Rise & Fall of the Communist Utopia. Andrzej Walicki. LC 94-32893. 654p. 1995. 75.00 (*0-8047-2384-2*) Stanford U Pr.

Marxism & the Leap to the Kingdom of Freedom: The Rise & Fall of the Communist Utopia. Andrzej Walicki. 654p. 1997. pap. 29.95 (*0-8047-3164-0*) Stanford U Pr.

Marxism & the Mass Media: Towards a Basic Bibliography, Vols. 1-2-3. rev. ed. Ed. by International Mass Media Research Center Staff. (Illus.). 105p. (Orig.). 1978. pap. 12.95 (*0-88477-009-5*) Intl General.

Marxism & the Mass Media: Towards a Basic Bibliography, Vols. 4-5. Ed. by International Mass Media Research Center Staff. (Illus.). 93p. (Orig.). 1986. pap. 12.95 (*0-88477-007-9*) Intl General.

Marxism & the Mass Media: Towards a Basic Bibliography, Vols. 6-7. Ed. by International Mass Media Research Center Staff. 122p. (Orig.). 1980. pap. 12.95 (*0-88477-008-7*) Intl General.

Marxism & the Muslim World. Maxime Rodinson. Tr. by Jean Matthews. LC 81-81695. 349p. reprint ed. pap. 108.20 (*0-7837-3910-9*, 204375800010) Bks Demand.

Marxism & the Open Mind. John Lewis. 222p. 1957. 34.95 (*0-87855-032-1*) Transaction Pubs.

Marxism & the Oppression of Women. Lise Vogel. 218p. 1987. pap. 17.00 (*0-8135-1234-4*) Rutgers U Pr.

Marxism & the Philosophy of Language. V. N. Volos. 216p. (C). 1986. pap. 15.95 (*0-674-55098-6*) HUP.

Marxism & the Philosophy of Language. V. N. Volosinov. Tr. by Ladislav Matejka & Irwin R. Titunik. 216p. 1986. pap. text 10.95 (*0-674-55125-7*) HUP.

Marxism & the Philosophy of Science: A Critical History. Helena Sheehan. LC 92-23094. 456p. (C). 1993. reprint ed. pap. 19.95 (*0-391-03780-3*) Humanities.

Marxism & the Proletariat: A Lukacsian Perspective. Perkins. LC 93-20550. (C). 54.95 (*0-7453-0492-3*, Pub. by Pluto GBR); pap. 19.95 (*0-7453-0499-0*, Pub. by Pluto GBR) Stylus Pub VA.

Marxism & the Question of the Asiatic Mode of Production. Marian Sawer. (Studies in Social History: Vol. 3). 1978. lib. bdg. 141.50 (*90-247-2027-3*) Kluwer Academic.

Marxism & the Theory of Human Personality. Lucien Seve. 1975. pap. 11.95 (*0-8464-1283-7*) Beekman Pubs.

Marxism & the Trade Unions. David North. (SEP Lecture Ser.). 38p. 1998. pap. 5.00 (*1-875639-29-2*) Mehring Bks.

Marxism & the Working Farmer. Doug Jenness et al. 62p. pap. 7.00 (*0-87348-688-9*) Pathfinder NY.

Marxism & Totality: The Adventures of a Concept from Lukacs to Habermas. Martin Jay. LC 83-17950. 576p. (C). 1984. pap. 22.50 (*0-520-05742-2*, Pub. by U CA Pr) Cal Prin Full Svc.

Marxism & Workers' Self-Management: The Essential Tension, 123. David L. Prychitko. LC 91-9152. (Contributions in Economics & Economic History Ser.: No. 123). 176p. 1991. 57.95 (*0-313-27854-7*, PPY, Greenwood Pr) Greenwood.

Marxism at Work: Ideology, Class & French Socialism During the Third Republic. Robert C. Stuart. 535p. (C). 1992. text 89.95 (*0-521-41526-8*) Cambridge U Pr.

Marxism Beyond Marxism. Saree Makdisi & Cesare Casarino. 290p. (C). 1995. pap. 21.99 (*0-415-91443-4*) Routledge.

Marxism Beyond Marxism. Ed. by Saree Makdisi & Cesare Casarino. 290p. (C). (gr. 13). 1996. 75.00 (*0-415-91442-6*) Routledge.

Marxism, Central Planning & the Soviet Economy: Economic Essays in Honor of Alexander Erlich. Ed. by Padma Desai. (Illus.). 352p. 1983. 42.50 (*0-262-04071-9*) MIT Pr.

Marxism, China, & Development: Reflections on Theory & Reality. A. James Gregor. 290p. (C). 1994. 39.95 (*1-56000-195-X*) Transaction Pubs.

Marxism, China & Development: Reflections on Theory & Reality. A. James Gregor. 294p. 1999. pap. 27.95 (*0-7658-0634-7*) Transaction Pubs.

Marxism, Class Analysis & Socialist Pluralism. Les Johnston. 1986. pap. text 15.95 (*0-04-301240-X*) Routledge.

Marxism, 1844-1990: Origins, Betrayal, Rebirth. Roger S. Gottlieb. (Revolutionary Thought & Radical Movements Ser.). 224p. (C). 1992. pap. 18.99 (*0-415-90654-7*, A7620) Routledge.

Marxism for Our Times: C. L. R. James on Revolutionary Organization. C. L. James. Ed. by Martin Glaberman. LC 99-17326. 192p. 1999. pap. 18.00 (*1-57806-151-2*) U Pr of Miss.

Marxism for Our Times: C. L. R. James on Revolutionary Organization. C. L. James. Ed. by Martin Glaberman. LC 99-17326. 192p. (C). 1999. text 45.00 (*1-57806-150-4*) U Pr of Miss.

Marxism, Freedom & the State. Michael Bakunin. 64p. (Orig.). 1984. reprint ed. pap. 3.50 (*0-900384-27-1*) Left Bank.

***Marxism, History & Intellectuals: Toward a Reconceptualized Transformative Socialism.** Suman Gupta. LC 99-47460. 272p. 2000. 44.50 (*0-8386-3852-X*) Fairleigh Dickinson.

Marxism, Ideology & Literary Criticism. P. Renga Ramanujam. ix, 199p. 1996. 20.00 (*81-85445-96-6*, Pub. by Manak Pubns Pvt Ltd) Nataraj Bks.

Marxism in Parliamentary Politics: Chile, 1932-1973. Julio Faundez. (C). 1988. 42.50 (*0-300-04024-5*) Yale U Pr.

Marxism in Power: The Rise & Fall of a Doctrine. Michael G. Kort. LC 92-15697. (Illus.). 176p. (YA). (gr. 7 up). 1993. lib. bdg. 23.90 (*1-56294-241-7*) Millbrook Pr.

Marxism in the Modern World. Milorad M. Drachkovitch. LC 65-13109. (Hoover Institution Publications). 308p. 1965. reprint ed. pap. 30.00 (*0-608-02957-2*, 206342200006) Bks Demand.

Marxism in the Postmodern Age: Confronting the New World Order. Ed. by Antonio Callari et al. LC 93-49636. (Critical Perspectives Ser.). 560p. 1994. pap. text 21.95 (*0-89862-424-X*); lib. bdg. 49.95 (*0-89862-423-1*, C2423) Guilford Pubns.

Marxism in the U. S. S. R. A Critical Survey of Current Soviet Thought. James P. Scanlan. LC 84-45802. 368p. (C). 1985. pap. 18.95 (*0-8014-9329-3*) Cornell U Pr.

Marxism in the United States: Remapping the History of the American Left. rev. ed. Paul Buhle. (Haymarket Ser.). 300p. (C). 1991. pap. 20.00 (*0-86091-547-6*, A5356, Pub. by Verso) Norton.

Marxism-Leninism As the Civil Religion of Soviet Society: God's Commissar. James Thrower. LC 92-30299. (Studies in Religion & Society: Vol. 30). 216p. 1992. text 89.95 (*0-7734-9180-5*) E Mellen.

Marxism-Leninism on War & Peace. V. Sobakin. (Library of Political Knowledge: No. 8). 158p. 1983. pap. 22.00 (*0-7855-1229-2*, Pub. by Collets) St Mut.

Marxism, Maoism & Utopianism: Eight Essays. Maurice Meisner. 276p. 1982. 17.95 (*0-299-08420-5*) U of Wis Pr.

Marxism, Morality, & Social Justice. Rodney G. Peffer. LC 89-38899. (Studies in Moral, Political, & Legal Philosophy). 540p. reprint ed. pap. 167.40 (*0-608-08019-5*, 206798400001) Bks Demand.

Marxism, Mysticism & Modern Theory. Ed. by Suke Wolton. 192p. 1996. text 65.00 (*0-312-15940-4*) St Martin.

Marxism of Regis Debray: Between Lenin & Guevara. Hartmut Ramm. LC 77-17915. xii, 240p. 1978. 25.00 (*0-7006-0170-8*) U Pr of KS.

Marxism, Opportunism & the Balkan Crisis: Statement of the International Committee of the Fourth International. International Committee of the Fourth Internationa. 56p. 1994. pap. 5.95 (*0-929087-69-0*) Mehring Bks.

Marxism Recycled. Philippe Van Parijs. LC 92-23166. (Studies in Marxism & Social Theory). (Illus.). 262p. (C). 1993. text 54.95 (*0-521-41802-X*) Cambridge U Pr.

***Marxism, Revisionism & Leninism: Explication, Assessment & Commentary.** Richard F. Hamilton. LC 99-55874. 288p. 2000. 59.95 (*0-275-96882-0*, Praeger Pubs) Greenwood.

Marxism, Revolution, & Democracy. John Hoffman. (Praxis Ser.: Vol. 9). xxviii, 151p. (Orig.). 1983. pap. 21.00 (*90-6032-236-3*, Pub. by B R Gruner) Humanities.

Marxism, Science, & the Movement of History. Ed. by Alan R. Burger et al. (Philosophical Currents Ser.: Vol. 127). vi, 298p. (Orig.). 1980. pap. 35.00 (*90-6032-186-3*, Pub. by B R Gruner) Humanities.

***Marxism, the Millenium & Beyond.** Mark Cowling & Paul Reynolds. LC 00-42062. .p. 2000. write for info. (*0-312-23597-6*) St Martin.

Marxism Today: Essays on Capitalism, Socialism, & Strategies for Social Change. Ed. by Chronis Polychroniou & Harry R. Targ. LC 95-14301. 232p. 1996. 62.95 (*0-275-94604-5*, Praeger Pubs) Greenwood.

Marxism vs. Ultraleftism: The Record of Healy's Break with Trotskyism. Joseph Hansen. 253p. pap. 15.00 (*0-87348-689-7*) Pathfinder NY.

Marxismo y Derecho. Eduardo De Acha. LC 84-72917. (Coleccion Cuba y sus Jueces). 158p. (Orig.). 1985. pap. 9.95 (*0-89729-364-9*) Ediciones.

Marxismo y la Liberacion de la Mujer. Dorothy Ballan. (Illus.). vii, 108p. 1986. pap. 4.95 (*0-89567-081-X*) World View Forum.

Marxism's Retreat from Africa. Ed. by Arnold Hughes. LC 92-28755. 164p. 1993. text 39.50 (*0-7146-4502-8*, Pub. by F Cass Pubs) Intl Spec Bk.

Marxismus-Leninismus in der CSR: Die tschechoslowakische Philosophie seit 1945. N. Lobkowicz. (Sovietica Ser.: No. 8). (GER.). 267p. 1962. lib. bdg. 85.50 (*90-277-0058-3*) Kluwer Academic.

Marxist Analyses & Social Anthropology. 2nd ed. Maurice Bloch. (ASA Studies). 256p. (C). 1984. pap. 15.95 (*0-422-79500-3*, 9278, Pub. by Tavistock) Routldge.

Marxist Approaches in Economic Anthropology. Ed. by Alice Littlefield & Hill Gates. (Monographs in Economic Anthropology: No. 9). 280p. 1991. 50.00 (*0-8191-7926-4*) U Pr of Amer.

Marxist Criticism of Shakespeare. Sier. 70.95 (*1-84014-270-7*) Ashgate Pub Co.

Marxist Defense of the L. A. Rebellion. Sam March. 1992. pap. 2.50 (*0-89567-106-9*) World View Forum.

Marxist Economic Theory, 2 vols., 2. Ernest Mandel. Tr. by Brian Pearce. LC 68-13658. 417p. reprint ed. pap. 129.30 (*0-8357-6204-1*, 203433600002) Bks Demand.

Marxist Economic Theory, 2 vols., Vol. 1. Ernest Mandel. Tr. by Brian Pearce. LC 68-13658. 383p. reprint ed. pap. 118.80 (*0-8357-6203-3*, 203433600001) Bks Demand.

Marxist Empire: Communist Dream - World Nightmare. James F. Nihan. 322p. 1990. pap. 12.80 (*0-89412-171-5*) Aegean Park Pr.

Marxist Ethical Theory in the Soviet Union. P. T. Grier. (Sovietica Ser.: No. 40). 293p. 1978. text 108.00 (*90-277-0927-0*) Kluwer Academic.

Marxist-Humanist Theory of State-Capitalism. Raya Dunayevskaya. 200p. (Orig.). 1992. pap. 8.50 (*0-914441-30-2*) News & Letters.

Marxist Ideology & Soviet Criminal Law. R. W. McCauley. 319p. 1980. 44.00 (*0-389-20099-9*, 06873) B&N Imports.

Marxist Ideology in the Contemporary World-Its Appeals & Paradoxes. Ed. by Milorad M. Drachkovitch. LC 72-13359. (Essay Index Reprint Ser.). 1977. reprint ed. 21.95 (*0-8369-8154-5*) Ayer.

Marxist Influences & South Asian Literature. Ed. by Carlo Coppola. (C). 1988. 38.50 (*81-7001-011-X*, Pub. by Chanakya) S Asia.

Marxist Inquiries: Studies of Labor, Class & States. Michael Burawoy. 338p. 1983. lib. bdg. 36.00 (*0-226-08039-0*) U Ch Pr.

Marxist Inquiries: Studies of Labor, Class & States (Supplement to the American Journal of Sociology) Ed. by Michael Burawoy & Theda Skocpol. 338p. (C). 1983. pap. text 18.00 (*0-226-08040-4*) U Ch Pr.

Marxist Intellectuals & the Chinese Labor Movement: A Study of Deng Zhongxia 1894-1933. Daniel Y. Kwan. LC 96-27538. (Jackson School Publications in International Studies). (Illus.). xiv, 309p. 1997. 45.00 (*0-295-97601-2*) U of Wash Pr.

Marxist Intellectuals & the Working-Class Mentality in Germany, 1887-1912. Stanley Pierson. LC 92-41089. 344p. 1993. text 49.95 (*0-674-55123-0*) HUP.

Marxist-Leninist Critique of Roy Innis on Community Self-Determination & Martin Kilson on Education. Henry Winston. 64p. 1973. pap. 0.75 (*0-87898-104-7*) New Outlook.

Marxist-Leninist Philosophy. A. P. Sheptulin. 520p. 1978. 60.00 (*0-7855-1230-6*, Pub. by Collets) St Mut.

Marxist-Leninist 'Scientific Atheism' & the Study of Religion & Atheism in the U. S. S. R. James Thrower. (GER.). 500p. 1983. 101.55 (*90-279-3060-0*) Mouton.

Marxist Literary & Cult Theory. Haslett. LC 99-29987. 2000. pap. 19.95 (*0-312-22674-8*) St Martin.

Marxist Literary & Cult Theory. Haslett. LC 99-29987. 2000. text 55.00 (*0-312-22673-X*) St Martin.

Marxist Literary Theory: A Reader. Ed. by Terry Eagelton & Drew Milne. 600p. (C). 1996. pap. 28.95 (*0-631-18581-X*) Blackwell Pubs.

Marxist Local Government in Western Europe & Japan. Bogdan Szajkowski. 1992. pap. text 17.50 (*0-86187-459-5*, Pub. by P P Pubs) Cassell & Continuum.

***Marxist Modern: An Ethnographic History of the Ethiopian Revolution.** Donald L. Donham. LC 98-43144. 284p. 1999. 45.00 (*0-520-21328-9*, Pub. by U CA Pr); pap. 17.95 (*0-520-21329-7*, Pub. by U CA Pr) Cal Prin Full Svc.

***Marxist Modern: An Ethnographic History of the Ethiopian Revolution** Donald L. Donham. LC 98-43144. xxvi, 236 p. 1999. pap. write for info. (*0-85255-264-5*) J Currey.

Marxist Perspectives on Imperialism: A Theoretical Analysis. Chronis Polychroniou. LC 90-45483. 200p. 1991. 49.95 (*0-275-93720-8*, C3720, Praeger Pubs) Greenwood.

Marxist Philosophy & Our Time. P. Redoseyev. (Social Science Today Problems of the Contemporary World Ser.: No.109). 256p. 1983. pap. 30.00 (*0-7855-1231-4*, Pub. by Collets) St Mut.

Marxist Philosophy & the Sciences. John Burdon Sanderson Haldane. LC 78-86757. (Essay Index Reprint Ser.). 1977. 18.95 (*0-8369-1137-7*) Ayer.

Marxist Policies Today in Socialist & Capitalist Countries. Ed. by Edwin Dowdy. LC 85-8481. 234p. 1986. text 44.95 (*0-7022-1927-4*, Pub. by Univ Queensland Pr) Intl Spec Bk.

Marxist Reading of Fuentes, Vargas Llosa & Puig. Victor M. Duran. 136p. (C). 1993. lib. bdg. 38.00 (*0-8191-9305-4*) U Pr of Amer.

Marxist Scholarship, Vol. 3, No. 2. Ed. by Tani E. Barlow. 390p. 1996. pap. 12.00 (*0-8223-6438-7*) Duke.

An Asterisk (*) at the beginning of an entry indicates that the title is appearing for the first time.

***Marxist Shakespeares.** Jean E. Howard & Scott C. Shershow. LC 00-30823. (Accents on Shakespeare Ser.). 2000. pap. write for info. (*0-415-20234-5*) Routledge.

Marxist Sociology. Tom Bottomore. LC 75-5986. 66p. (C). 1975. 12.00 (*0-8419-0201-1*) Holmes & Meier.

Marxist State Government in India: Politics, Economics & Society. T. J. Nossiter. 250p. 1992. 49.00 (*0-86187-456-0*, Pub. by P P Pubs) Cassell & Continuum.

Marxist State Government in India: Politics, Economics & Society. T. J. Nossiter. (Marxist Regimes Ser.). 250p. 1992. pap. 17.50 (*0-86187-457-9*) St Martin.

Marxist Study of Shakespeare's Comedies. Elliott Krieger. LC 79-55522. 181p. 1979. text 45.00 (*0-06-493970-7*, N6550) B&N Imports.

Marxist System: Economic, Political, & Social Perspectives. Robert Freedman. LC 86-23275. (Chatham House Series on Change in American Politics). 192p. (C). 1990. pap. text 17.95 (*0-934540-31-4*, Chatham House Pub) Seven Bridges.

Marxist Theories of Imperialism. Anthony Brewer. 320p. 1980. pap. 15.95 (*0-415-04307-7*, Routledge Thoemms) Routledge.

Marxist Theories of Imperialism: A Critical Survey. 2nd ed. Anthony Brewer. 320p. (C). (gr. 13). 1990. pap. 29.99 (*0-415-04469-3*, A5113) Routledge.

Marxist Theory. Ed. by Alex Callinicos et al. (Oxford Readings in Politics & Government Ser.). 288p. (C). 1989. 49.95 (*0-19-827294-4*); pap. text 15.95 (*0-19-827295-2*) OUP.

Marxist Theory & Nationalist Politics: The Case of Colonial India. Sanjay Seth. LC 94-42503. 268p. 1995. 25.95 (*0-8039-9207-6*) Sage.

Marxist Theory of Alienation. 2nd rev. ed. Ernest Mandel & George Novack. LC 72-96599. (Illus.). 94p. 1973. reprint ed. pap. 10.95 (*0-87348-230-1*); reprint ed. lib. bdg. 30.00 (*0-87348-229-8*) Pathfinder NY.

Marxist Theory of Ideology: A Conceptual Analysis. Luis A. Conde-Costas. (Studia Sociologica Upsaliensia: No. 33). 147p. (Orig.). 1991. pap. 35.00 (*91-554-2791-X*) Coronet Bks.

Marxist Thought on Imperialism: A Critical Survey. Charles A. Barone. LC 84-23556. 225p. (gr. 13). 1989. pap. text 40.95 (*0-87332-345-9*) M E Sharpe.

Marxist Thought on Imperialism: Survey & Critique. Charles A. Barone. LC 84-23556. 239p. 1985. reprint ed. pap. 74.10 (*0-7837-9961-6*, 206068800006) Bks Demand.

Marxistisch-Leninistisches Woerterbuch der Philosophie: Marxist-Leninist Dictionary of Philosophy, 3 vols. G. Klaus & M. Buhr. (GER.). 1280p. 1972. 95.00 (*0-8288-6414-4*, M-7550) Fr & Eur.

Marx's Alter Ego see Life of Friedrich Engels

Marx's Attempt to Leave Philosophy. Daniel Brudney. LC 97-38497. 480p. 1999. 45.00 (*0-674-55133-8*) HUP.

Marx's Capital. Karl Marx. Ed. by C. J. Arthur. 416p. (C). 1992. pap., student ed. 27.50 (*0-85315-777-4*, Pub. by Lawrence & Wishart) NYU Pr.

Marx's Capital. 3rd ed. Ben Fine. 112p. (C). 1989. text 45.00 (*0-333-49456-3*, Pub. by Macmillan) Humanities.

Marx's Capital & Capitalism Today, Vol. 1. Antony Cutler et al. 1977. pap. 13.95 (*0-7100-8746-2*, Routledge Thoemms) Routledge.

Marx's Capital & Today's Global Crisis. Raya Dunayevskaya. 108p. (Orig.). 1978. pap. 2.00 (*0-914441-11-6*) News & Letters.

Marx's Concept of Man. Erich Fromm. LC 61-11935. (Milestones of Thought Ser.). 276p. 1982. pap. 14.95 (*0-8044-6161-9*) Continuum.

Marx's Concept of Money: The God of Commodities. Anitra Nelson. LC 98-8109. 1998. 99.99 (*0-415-18200-X*) Routledge.

Marx's Crises Theory: Scarcity, Labor, Finance. Michael Perelman. LC 87-6936. 256p. 1987. 55.00 (*0-275-92372-X*, C2372, Praeger Pubs) Greenwood.

Marx's Critique of Politics, 1842-1847. Gary Teeple. 318p. 1984. text 40.00 (*0-8020-5631-8*) U of Toronto Pr.

Marx's Ecology: Materialism & Nature. John B. Foster. LC 99-38837. 1999. pap. 18.00 (*1-58367-012-2*, Pub. by Monthly Rev) NYU Pr.

***Marx's Ecology: Materialism & Nature.** John B. Foster. LC 99-38837. 200p. 1999. 48.00 (*1-58367-011-4*, Pub. by Monthly Rev) NYU Pr.

Marx's Fate: The Shape of a Life. Jerrold Seigel. LC 92-37354. 464p. (C). 1993. reprint ed. pap. 22.50 (*0-271-00935-7*) Pa St U Pr.

Marx's Method in Capital: A Reexamination. Ed. by Fred Moseley. LC 92-22220. 240p. (C). 1993. text 45.00 (*0-391-03785-4*) Humanities.

Marx's Proletariat: The Making of a Myth. David W. Lovell. 320p. (C). 1988. lib. bdg. 52.50 (*0-415-00116-1*) Routledge.

Marx's Religion of Revolution: Regeneration Through Chaos. Gary North. 280p. 1989. pap. 8.95 (*0-930464-15-X*) Inst Christian.

Marx's Theory of Alienation. 4th ed. Istvan Meszaros. (C). 1986. pap. write for info. (*0-85036-191-5*, Pub. by MRLN) Paul & Co Pubs.

Marx's Theory of Exchange. Paul C. Roberts. LC 83-19136. 127p. 1983. 49.95 (*0-275-91065-2*, C1065, Praeger Pubs) Greenwood.

Marx's Theory of History. William H. Shaw. LC 77-76154. xii, 202p. 1978. pap. 11.95 (*0-8047-1059-7*) Stanford U Pr.

Marx's Theory of History: The Contemporary Debate. Ed. by Paul Wetherly. (Avebury Series in Philosophy). 250p. 1992. 82.95 (*1-85628-157-4*, Pub. by Avebry) Ashgate Pub Co.

Marx's Theory of Ideology. Bhikhu C. Parekh. LC 81-13743. 255p. reprint ed. pap. 79.10 (*0-608-06180-8*, 206651200008) Bks Demand.

Marx's Theory of Social Formation. Zhongqiao Duan. (Avebury Series in Philosophy). 144p. 1995. 66.95 (*1-85972-015-3*, Pub. by Avebry) Ashgate Pub Co.

Marx's Theory of the Transcendence of the State: A Reconstruction. John F. Sitton. (American University Studies: Political Science: Ser. X, Vol. 19). X, 224p. (C). 1989. text 36.00 (*0-8204-0827-1*) P Lang Pubng.

Marx's Wage Theory in Historical Perspective: Its Origins, Development & Interpretation. Kenneth Lapides. LC 98-4941. 288p. 1998. 59.95 (*0-275-96271-7*, Praeger Pubs) Greenwood.

Marxsche Theorie: Eine Philosophische Untersuchung zu den Hauptschriften. Klaus Hartmann. 593p. (C). 1970. 93.10 (*3-11-002893-X*) De Gruyter.

Mary. (St. Joseph's Coloring Bks.). (Illus.). 32p. (J). (ps-3). 1988. pap. 0.99 (*0-89942-685-9*, 685/00) Catholic Bk Pub.

Mary. Mark Dunster. LC 78-112416. (Henry the Eighth Ser.: Pt. 3). 1978. pap. 4.00 (*0-89642-043-4*) Linden Pubs.

Mary. Mary E. Mebane. LC 98-49044. (Chapel Hill Book Ser.). 242p. (C). 1999. pap. 16.95 (*0-8078-4821-2*) U of NC Pr.

Mary. Harold F. Sorensen. 508p. 1992. 22.50 (*0-9622100-1-3*) Pawprint Pr.

Mary: A History of Devotion in Ireland. Peter O'Dwyer. 331p. 1999. reprint ed. text 25.00 (*0-7881-6130-X*) DIANE Pub.

Mary: A History of Irish Devotion. 356p. 1988. 39.50 (*1-85182-036-1*, Pub. by Four Cts Pr) Intl Spec Bk.

Mary: A Marian Anthology. Patrick Murray. 192p. 1989. pap. 22.00 (*0-905092-85-6*, Pub. by Veritas Pubns) St Mut.

Mary: A Mother Highly Favored. George W. Rice. 56p. 1994. pap. 2.99 (*0-8341-1524-7*) Beacon Hill.

Mary: A Novel. Vladimir Nabokov. Tr. by Michael Glenny. (Vintage International Ser.). 1989. pap. 12.00 (*0-679-72620-9*) Vin Bks.

Mary: Another Redeemer? James White. LC 98-220288. 16p. 1998. pap. 7.99 (*0-7642-2102-7*, 212102) Bethany Hse.

Mary: Art, Culture, & Religion Through the Ages. Caroline Ebertshauser et al. Tr. by Peter Heinegg from ENG. LC 98-15608. (Illus.). 272p. 1998. 59.95 (*0-8245-1760-1*, Herdr & Herdr) Crossroad NY.

Mary: Catechist at Fatima. Frederick L. Miller. 25p. 1991. 1.50 (*1-56036-010-0*, 38611) AMI Pr.

Mary: Choosing the Joy of Obedience. Ed. by Zondervan Publishing Staff. (Women of Faith Ser.: Vol. 3). 80p. Date not set. pap. 5.99 (*0-310-22664-3*) Zondervan.

Mary: Coredemptrix Mediatrix Advocate. Mark I. Miravalle. Tr. by Olga Pavisich-Ryan. LC 93-84470. (SPA.). 96p. 1993. pap. 1.00 (*1-882972-12-0*, 2000S) Queenship Pub.

Mary: Coredemptrix Mediatrix Advocate. Mark I. Miravalle. Tr. by Maria Rota. LC 93-87016. (ITA.). 77p. 1993. pap. 1.00 (*1-882972-16-3*, 20001) Queenship Pub.

Mary: Coredemptrix Mediatrix Advocate. Mark I. Miravalle. Tr. by Salwa Hamadi. LC 93-87014. (FRE.). 79p. 1993. pap. 1.00 (*1-882972-18-X*, 2000F) Queenship Pub.

Mary: Coredemptrix Mediatrix Advocate. Mark I. Miravalle. Tr. by Garte Hatzel. LC 93-87013. (GER.). 88p. 1993. pap. 1.00 (*1-882972-19-8*, 2000G) Queenship Pub.

Mary: Coredemptrix Mediatrix Advocate. Mark I. Miravalle. Tr. by Bridget Hooker. LC 93-87015. (POL.). 79p. 1994. pap. 1.00 (*1-882972-17-1*, 2000P) Queenship Pub.

Mary: Glimpses of the Mother of Jesus. Beverly R. Gaventa. Ed. by Moody D. Smith. LC 95-4424. (Studies on Personalities of New Testament). 250p. 1995. text 24.95 (*1-57003-072-3*) U of SC Pr.

Mary: Glimpses of the Mother of Jesus. Beverly Roberts Gaventa. LC 99-22806. (Personalities of the New Testament Ser.). 176p. 1999. pap. text 18.00 (*0-8006-3166-8*, 1-3166, Fortress Pr) Augsburg Fortress.

***Mary: Human & Holy.** Antonio Bello. Tr. by Paul Duggan. 96p. 2000. pap. 5.95 (*0-8198-4810-7*) Pauline Bks.

Mary: Icon of the Spirit & of the Church. Francois-Xavier Durrwell. 123p. (C). 1996. pap. 39.95 (*0-85439-364-1*, Pub. by St Paul Pubns) St Mut.

***Mary: Images of the Holy Mother.** Jacqueline Orsini. LC 00-22361. (Illus.). 2000. 19.95 (*0-8118-2850-6*) Chronicle Bks.

Mary: Model of Justice. Ed. by William F. Maestri. LC 86-22304. 92p. (Orig.). 1987. pap. 4.95 (*0-8189-0511-5*) Alba.

Mary: Mother of Jesus. C. MacKenzie. (BibleTime Bks.). (J). 1995. 2.99 (*0-906731-06-2*, Pub. by Christian Focus) Spring Arbor Dist.

***Mary: Or The Test of Honour.** Susanna Haswell Rowson. (Notable American Authors Ser.). 1999. reprint ed. lib. bdg. 125.00 (*0-7812-8836-3*) Rprt Serv.

Mary: Shadow of Grace. Megan McKenna. LC 94-46242. 176p. (Orig.). 1995. pap. 12.00 (*0-88344-996-X*) Orbis Bks.

Mary: The Lord's Servant. Douglas Connelly & Karen Connelly. (LifeGuide Bible Studies). 64p. 1996. pap., wbk. ed. 4.99 (*0-8308-1078-1*, 1078) InterVarsity.

Mary: The Mother of Jesus. Tomie De Paola. LC 92-54491. (Illus.). 32p. (J). (ps-3). 1995. lib. bdg. 16.95 (*0-8234-1018-8*) Holiday.

Mary: The Mother of Jesus. Wendy Virgo. LC 99-28709. 200p. 1999. pap. text 7.99 (*0-7814-3306-1*) Chariot Victor.

Mary: What the Bible Really Says. Douglas Connelly. LC 97-49088. 132p. 1998. pap. 9.99 (*0-8308-1950-9*, 1950) InterVarsity.

Mary: Yesterday, Today, Tomorrow. Edward Schillebeeckx & Catharina Halkes. Tr. by John Bowden from DUT. LC 93-19852.Tr. of Maria. 88p. (Orig.). 1993. pap. 9.95 (*0-8245-1371-1*) Crossroad NY.

Mary - God's Yes to Man: Encyclical Letter of John Paul II. Ed. by Hans Urs Von Balthasar. Tr. by Lothar Krauth from GER. LC 88-80726. 179p. (Orig.). 1988. pap. 9.95 (*0-89870-219-4*) Ignatius Pr.

Mary According to Women. Carol F. Jegen. LC 84-82550. 170p. (Orig.). 1985. pap. 7.95 (*0-934134-31-6*) Sheed & Ward WI.

Mary Adelaide Nutting: Pioneer of Modern Nursing. Helen E. Marshall. LC 72-174557. 410p. 1972. reprint ed. pap. 127.10 (*0-608-03668-4*, 206449400009) Bks Demand.

Mary, after the Queen: Memories of a Working Girl. Angela Hewins. 1985. 14.95 (*0-19-212242-8*) OUP.

Mary Alice Peale: Philadelphia, 1777. Kathleen Duey. LC 96-16052. (American Diaries Ser.: No. 4). 176p. (J). (gr. 4-6). 1996. per. 3.99 (*0-689-80387-7*) S&S Childrens.

Mary Alice Peale: Philadelphia, 1777. Kathleen Duey. (American Diaries Ser.: No. 4). (J). (gr. 4-6). 1996. 9.09 (*0-606-10739-8*, Pub. by Turtleback) Demco.

Mary Allen College: Its Rich History, Pioneering Spirit & Continuing Tradition. LC 95-92302. 104p. (Orig.). 1995. 24.95 (*0-614-30076-2*); pap. 16.95 (*0-614-30077-0*) NAAMAC.

Mary Allen College: Its Rich History, Pioneering Spirit, & Continuing Tradition. Naomi W. Lede. 104p. (YA). 1995. 24.95 (*0-9646839-0-3*) NAAMAC.

Mary Allen West: A Lady of Grit, Grace & Gumption. Martin Litvin. LC 96-62022. (Illus.). 160p. (Orig.). 1997. pap. 9.95 (*0-9654930-0-8*) Zephyr IL.

Mary & Human Liberation: The Story & the Text. Tissa Balasuriya. LC 97-23821. 256p. 1997. pap. 20.00 (*1-56338-225-3*) TPI PA.

***Mary & Joseph's Journey to Bethlehem.** Concordia Publishing Staff. (Folding Board Bks.). (Illus.). 10p. (J). (ps-k). 1998. bds. 3.99 (*0-570-05464-8*, 56-1964GJ) Concordia.

Mary & Maria. Mary Wollstonecraft Shelley. 1994. reprint ed. lib. bdg. 24.95 (*1-56849-365-7*) Buccaneer Bks.

Mary & Maria; Matilda. Mary Wollstonecraft Shelley. Ed. by Janet Todd. (Women's Classics Ser.). 250p. (C). 1992. text 55.00 (*0-8147-9252-9*) NYU Pr.

Mary & Martha: Pencil Fun Book. Sandi Verano. pap. 0.79 (*1-55513-998-1*) Chariot Victor.

Mary & Martha's Dinner Guest. Arch Books Staff. 16p. (J). (gr. k-4). 1998. pap. 1.99 (*0-570-07548-3*) Concordia.

***Mary & Martha's House.** Allia Zobel-Nolan. (My Bible Village Ser.). (Illus.). (J). 2000. 5.99 (*0-310-98254-5*, Zonderkidz) Zondervan.

Mary & Our Love. Zygmunt V. Szarnicki. 192p. 1995. pap. 15.95 (*0-939332-22-1*) J Pohl Assocs.

Mary & the Children of Medjugorje & You. Judith M. Albright. LC 89-62765. (Illus.). 32p. 1989. pap. 3.00 (*1-877678-05-8*) Queenship Pub.

Mary & the Empty Tomb. Alice J. Davidson. LC 98-182179. (My Bible Friends Ser.). (Illus.). 12p. 1998. 3.99 (*0-310-97455-0*, Zondervan Gifts) Zondervan.

Mary & the Eucharist. Richard Foley. LC 97-76925. 208p. 1997. pap. 10.95 (*1-891431-00-5*) Hope St Monica.

Mary & the Fundamentalist Challenge. Peter M. J. Stravinskas. LC 97-69276. 272p. 1998. pap. 12.95 (*0-87973-611-9*) Our Sunday Visitor.

Mary & the Kingdom of God: A Synthesis of Mariology. Joseph Paredes. 282p. (C). 1996. pap. 39.95 (*0-85439-379-X*, Pub. by St Paul Pubns) St Mut.

Mary & the Mystery Dog. Wolfram Hanel. Tr. by Alison James from GER. LC 98-42104. (Illus.). (J). (gr. 1-4). 1999. 13.95 (*0-7358-1043-5*, Pub. by North-South Bks NYC); lib. bdg. 13.88 (*0-7358-1044-3*, Pub. by North-South Bks NYC) Chronicle Bks.

***Mary & the Mystery Dog.** Wolfram Hanel. (Illus.). 48p. (gr. 1-4). 2000. pap. 5.95 (*0-7358-1337-X*) North-South Bks NYC.

Mary & the Wrongs of Woman. Mary Wollstonecraft Shelley. LC 99-228760. 272p. 1999. pap. 8.95 (*0-19-283536-X*) OUP.

Mary Ann & Bill. large type ed. Catherine Cookson. 1983. 15.95 (*0-7089-0984-1*) Ulverscroft.

Mary Ann Shadd Cary: The Black Press & Protest in the Nineteenth Century. Jane Rhodes. LC 98-19997. (Illus.). 304p. 1998. lib. bdg. 39.95 (*0-253-33446-2*) Ind U Pr.

***Mary Ann Shadd Cary: The Black Press & Protest in the Nineteenth Century.** Jane Rhodes. (Illus.). 304p. 2000. pap. 18.95 (*0-253-21350-9*) Ind U Pr.

Mary Anne. Daphne Du Maurier. LC 76-184729. 352p. 1971. reprint ed. lib. bdg. 20.00 (*0-8376-0411-7*) Bentley Pubs.

Mary Anne & Camp BSC. Ann M. Martin. (Baby-Sitters Club Ser.: No. 86). 192p. (gr. 4-6). 1995. pap. 3.50 (*0-590-48227-0*) Scholastic Inc.

Mary Anne & Camp BSC. Ann M. Martin. (Baby-Sitters Club Ser.: No. 86). 1995. 8.60 (*0-606-07228-4*, Pub. by Turtleback) Demco.

Mary Anne & Miss Priss. Ann M. Martin. (Baby-Sitters Club Ser.: No. 73). 192p. (J). (gr. 3-7). 1994. pap. 3.99 (*0-590-47011-6*) Scholastic Inc.

Mary Anne & Miss Priss. Ann M. Martin. (Baby-Sitters Club Ser.: No. 73). (J). 1994. 9.09 (*0-606-05738-2*, Pub. by Turtleback) Demco.

Mary Anne & the Great Romance. Ann M. Martin. (Baby-Sitters Club Ser.: No. 30). 192p. (J). (gr. 4-6). 1990. pap. 3.50 (*0-590-42498-X*) Scholastic Inc.

Mary Anne & the Great Romance. Ann M. Martin. (Baby-Sitters Club Ser.: No. 30). (J). 1990. 9.09 (*0-606-01876-X*, Pub. by Turtleback) Demco.

Mary Anne & the Great Romance, Vol. 30. Ann M. Martin. (Baby-Sitters Club Ser.: No. 30). 160p. (J). (gr. 3-7). 1997. pap. text 3.99 (*0-590-67398-X*) Scholastic Inc.

Mary Anne & the Haunted Bookstore. Ann M. Martin. (Baby-Sitters Club Mystery Ser.: No. 34). (J). 1998. pap. text 3.99 (*0-590-05974-2*, Apple Paperbacks) Scholastic Inc.

Mary Anne & the Library Mystery. Ann M. Martin. (Baby-Sitters Club Mystery Ser.: No. 13). 176p. (J). (gr. 3-7). 1994. pap. 3.50 (*0-590-47051-5*) Scholastic Inc.

Mary Anne & the Library Mystery. Ann M. Martin. (Baby-Sitters Club Mystery Ser.: No. 13). (J). 1994. 8.60 (*0-606-05740-4*, Pub. by Turtleback) Demco.

Mary Anne & the Little Princess. Ann M. Martin. LC 00-9331. (Baby-Sitters Club Ser.: No. 102). 142p. (J). (gr. 3-7). 1996. pap. 3.99 (*0-590-69208-9*) Scholastic Inc.

Mary Anne & the Little Princess. Ann M. Martin. (Baby-Sitters Club Ser.: No. 102). 1996. 9.09 (*0-606-10132-2*, Pub. by Turtleback) Demco.

Mary Anne & the Memory Garden. Ann M. Martin. (Baby-Sitters Club Ser.: No. 93). (J). 1996. pap. text 3.99 (*0-590-22877-3*) Scholastic Inc.

Mary Anne & the Memory Garden. Ann M. Martin. (Baby-Sitters Club Ser.: No. 93). (J). 1996. 9.09 (*0-606-08482-7*, Pub. by Turtleback) Demco.

Mary Anne & the Music Box Secret. Ann M. Martin. (Baby-Sitters Club Mystery Ser.: No. 31). (J). (gr. 3-7). 1997. mass mkt. 3.99 (*0-590-69179-1*) Scholastic Inc.

Mary Anne & the Music Box Secret. Ann M. Martin. (Baby-Sitters Club Mystery Ser.: No. 31). 1997. 9.09 (*0-606-11075-5*, Pub. by Turtleback) Demco.

Mary Anne & the Playground Fight. Ann M. Martin. (Baby-Sitters Club Ser.: No. 120). (J). 1998. pap. 3.99 (*0-590-05998-X*, Apple Paperbacks) Scholastic Inc.

***Mary Anne & the Playground Fight.** Ann M. Martin. (Baby-Sitters Club Ser.: No. 120). (J). 1998. 9.09 (*0-606-13164-7*, Pub. by Turtleback) Demco.

Mary Anne & the Search for Tigger. Ann M. Martin. (Baby-Sitters Club Ser.: No. 25). 192p. (J). (gr. 4-6). 1989. pap. 3.50 (*0-590-43347-4*) Scholastic Inc.

Mary Anne & the Search for Tigger. Ann M. Martin. (Baby-Sitters Club Ser.: No. 25). 160p. (J). (gr. 3-7). 1997. pap. text 3.99 (*0-590-67393-9*, Apple Paperbacks) Scholastic Inc.

Mary Anne & the Search for Tigger. Ann M. Martin. (Baby-Sitters Club Ser.: No. 25). (J). 1989. 8.60 (*0-606-04272-5*, Pub. by Turtleback) Demco.

Mary Anne & the Secret in the Attic. Ann M. Martin. (Baby-Sitters Club Mystery Ser.: No. 5). 176p. (J). (gr. 3-7). 1992. pap. 3.25 (*0-590-44801-3*, Apple Paperbacks) Scholastic Inc.

Mary Anne & the Silent Witness. Ann M. Martin. (Baby-Sitters Club Mystery Ser.: No. 24). (J). (gr. 3-7). 1996. pap. 3.99 (*0-590-22868-4*) Scholastic Inc.

Mary Anne & the Silent Witness. Ann M. Martin. (Baby-Sitters Club Mystery Ser.: No. 24). (YA). 1996. 9.09 (*0-606-09038-X*, Pub. by Turtleback) Demco.

Mary Anne & the Zoo Mystery. Ann M. Martin. (Baby-Sitters Club Mystery Ser.: No. 20). 176p. (J). (gr. 3-7). 1995. pap. 3.50 (*0-590-48309-9*) Scholastic Inc.

Mary Anne & the Zoo Mystery. Ann M. Martin. (Baby-Sitters Club Mystery Ser.: No. 20). (J). 1995. 8.60 (*0-606-07234-9*, Pub. by Turtleback) Demco.

Mary Anne & Too Many Boys. Ann M. Martin. (Baby-Sitters Club Ser.: No. 34). (J). (gr. 3-7). 1990. pap. text 3.99 (*0-590-73283-8*) Scholastic Inc.

Mary Anne & Too Many Boys. Ann M. Martin. (Baby-Sitters Club Ser.: No. 34). 192p. (J). (gr. 4-6). 1990. pap. 3.50 (*0-590-42494-7*) Scholastic Inc.

Mary Anne & Too Many Boys. Ann M. Martin. (Baby-Sitters Club Ser.: No. 34). (J). 1990. 8.60 (*0-606-04475-2*, Pub. by Turtleback) Demco.

Mary Anne & 2 Many Babies. Ann M. Martin. (Baby-Sitters Club Ser.: No. 52). (gr. 3-7). 1948. mass mkt. 3.99 (*0-590-92577-6*) Scholastic Inc.

Mary Anne & 2 Many Babies. Ann M. Martin. (Baby-Sitters Club Ser.: No. 52). 192p. (J). (gr. 4-6). 1992. pap. 3.50 (*0-590-44966-4*) Scholastic Inc.

Mary Anne & 2 Many Babies. Ann M. Martin. (Baby-Sitters Club Ser.: No. 52). (J). 1992. 9.09 (*0-606-01897-2*, Pub. by Turtleback) Demco.

Mary Anne Breaks the Rules. Ann M. Martin. (Baby-Sitters Club Ser.: No. 79). 192p. (J). (gr. 4-6). 1994. pap. 3.50 (*0-590-48223-8*) Scholastic Inc.

Mary Anne Breaks the Rules. Ann M. Martin. (Baby-Sitters Club Ser.: No. 79). 1994. 8.60 (*0-606-06205-X*, Pub. by Turtleback) Demco.

Mary Anne in the Middle. Ann M. Martin. (Baby-Sitters Club Ser.: No. 125). 1998. pap. text 3.99 (*0-590-50179-8*) Scholastic Inc.

Mary Anne Misses Logan. Ann M. Martin. LC 96-15213. (Baby-Sitters Club Ser.: No. 46). 144p. (J). (gr. 4 up). 1996. lib. bdg. 21.27 (*0-8368-1570-X*) Gareth Stevens Inc.

Mary Anne Misses Logan. Ann M. Martin. (Baby-Sitters Club Ser.: No. 46). 192p. (J). (gr. 4-6). 1991. pap. 3.50 (*0-590-43569-8*) Scholastic Inc.

Mary Anne Saves the Day. Ann M. Martin. (Baby-Sitters Club Ser.: No. 4). (J). (gr. 3-7). 1987. pap. 3.50 (*0-590-43512-4*) Scholastic Inc.

Mary Anne Saves the Day. Ann M. Martin. (Baby-Sitters Club Ser.: No. 4). 192p. (J). (gr. 3-7). 1995. pap. text 3.50 (*0-590-25159-7*) Scholastic Inc.

Mary Anne Saves the Day. Ann M. Martin. (Baby-Sitters Club Ser.: No. 4). (J). (gr. 3-7). 1987. 8.60 (*0-606-03085-9*, Pub. by Turtleback) Demco.

Mary Anne to the Rescue. Ann M. Martin. (Baby-Sitters Club Ser.: No. 109). 1997. pap. text 3.99 (*0-590-69215-1*, Apple Paperbacks) Scholastic Inc.

Mary Anne to the Rescue. Ann M. Martin. (Baby-Sitters Club Ser.: No. 109). 1997. 9.09 (*0-606-11069-0*, Pub. by Turtleback) Demco.

An Asterisk (*) at the beginning of an entry indicates that the title is appearing for the first time.

Mary Anne vs. Logan. Ann M. Martin. LC 96-17008. (Baby-Sitters Club Ser.: No. 41). 176p. (J). (gr. 4 up). 1996. lib. bdg. 21.27 (*0-8368-1565-3*) Gareth Stevens Inc.

Mary Anne vs. Logan. Ann M. Martin. (Baby-Sitters Club Ser.: No. 41). 192p. (J). (gr. 4-6). 1991. pap. 3.50 (*0-590-43570-1*) Scholastic Inc.

Mary Anne vs. Logan. Ann M. Martin. (Baby-Sitters Club Ser.: No. 41). (J). (gr. 4-7). 1997. pap. 3.99 (*0-590-74241-8*, Scholastic Ref) Scholastic Inc.

Mary Anne vs. Logan. Ann M. Martin. (Baby-Sitters Club Ser.: No. 41). (J). 1991. 8.60 (*0-606-04743-3*, Pub. by Turtleback) Demco.

Mary Anne's Bad-Luck Mystery. Ann M. Martin. (Baby-Sitters Club Ser.: No. 17). 192p. (J). (gr. 4-6). 1988. 3.50 (*0-590-43659-7*) Scholastic Inc.

Mary Anne's Bad-Luck Mystery. Ann M. Martin. (Baby-Sitters Club Ser.: No. 17). (J). (gr. 3-7). 1996. pap. text 3.99 (*0-590-60428-7*) Scholastic Inc.

Mary Anne's Bad-Luck Mystery. Ann M. Martin. (Baby-Sitters Club Ser.: No. 17). (J). 1988. 9.09 (*0-606-04090-0*, Pub. by Turtleback) Demco.

Mary Anne's Big Breakup. Ann M. Martin. (Baby-Sitters Club Friends Forever Ser.: No. 3). 1999. pap. text 54.00 (*0-439-11739-9*) Scholastic Inc.

***Mary Anne's Big Breakup.** Ann M. Martin. Vol. 3. 144p. (J). (gr. 3-7). 1999. mass mkt. 4.50 (*0-590-52326-0*) Scholastic Inc.

Mary Anne's Book. Ann M. Martin. (Baby-Sitters Club Portrait Collection). (J). (gr. 3-7). 1996. pap. 3.99 (*0-590-22865-X*) Scholastic Inc.

Mary Anne's Book. Ann M. Martin. (Baby-Sitters Club Portrait Collection). (YA). 1996. 9.09 (*0-606-09041-X*, Pub. by Turtleback) Demco.

Mary Anne's Makeover. Ann M. Martin. (Baby-Sitters Club Ser.: No. 60). 192p. (J). (gr. 3-7). 1993. pap. 3.99 (*0-590-92586-5*) Scholastic Inc.

Mary Anne's Makeover. Ann M. Martin. (Baby-Sitters Club Ser.: No. 60). 192p. (J). (gr. 4-6). 1993. pap. 3.50 (*0-590-45662-8*) Scholastic Inc.

Mary Anne's Makeover. Ann M. Martin. (Baby-Sitters Club Ser.: No. 60). (J). 1993. 9.09 (*0-606-02498-0*, Pub. by Turtleback) Demco.

***Mary Anne's Revenge.** Ann M. Martin. (Baby-Sitters Club Friends Forever Ser.: No. 8). (Illus.). 144p. (J). (gr. 3-7). 2000. mass mkt. 4.50 (*0-590-52340-6*) Scholastic Inc.

***Mary Anning: Fossil Hunter.** Sally M. Walker. LC 99-40094. (On My Own Biography Ser.). (Illus.). 64p. (J). (ps-3). 2000. 19.93 (*1-57505-425-6*, Carolrhoda) Lerner Pub.

Mary Anning & the Sea Dragon. Jeannine Atkins. LC 97-47547. (Illus.). 32p. (YA). (gr. k-3). 1999. 16.00 (*0-374-34840-5*) FS&G.

Mary Ann's & Gilligan's Island Cookbook. Dawn Wells et al. LC 93-32529. (Illus.). 256p. 1993. spiral bd. 12.95 (*1-55853-245-5*) Rutledge Hill Pr.

***Mary Ann's Funeral Guide: Stories & Advice from Northeast Ohio's Foremost Paranormal.** Mary Ann & Kathleen Carey. (Illus.). 40p. 1998. pap. 9.95 (*0-9675677-0-X*) Maka.

Mary Arden. Grace Livingston Hill. 1976. reprint ed. lib. bdg. 23.95 (*0-89190-021-7*, Rivercity Pr) Amereon Ltd.

Mary Arden's House & the Shakespeare Countryside Museum. Ed. by Levi Fox. (Shakespeare Travel Ser.). (Illus.). 32p. (Orig.). 1994. pap. 3.95 (*0-7117-0392-2*) Seven Hills Bk.

Mary Ashe. Barbara Sherrod. 1987. mass mkt. 2.95 (*0-446-34491-5*, Pub. by Warner Bks) Little.

Mary at My Side. Robert Guste. LC 85-51277. 70p. (Orig.). 1993. reprint ed. pap. 5.95 (*1-882972-00-7*, 3031) Queenship Pub.

Mary Austin: Song of a Maverick. Esther F. Lanigan. LC 96-42224. (Illus.). 285p. 1997. pap. 19.95 (*0-8165-1714-2*) U of Ariz Pr.

Mary Austin Holley: A Biography. Rebecca S. Lee. (Elma Dill Russell Spencer Foundation Ser.: No. 2). (Illus.). 480p. 1987. reprint ed. pap. 14.95 (*0-292-75098-6*) U of Tex Pr.

Mary Austin Reader. Ed. by Esther F. Lanigan. LC 95-41730. (Illus.). 271p. 1996. 40.00 (*0-8165-1619-7*); pap. 17.95 (*0-8165-1620-0*) U of Ariz Pr.

Mary Baker Eddy. Gillian Gill. 528p. 1998. write for info. (*0-201-62613-6*) Addison-Wesley.

Mary Baker Eddy. Gillian Gill. 776p. 1999. pap. text 22.50 (*0-7382-0227-4*, Pub. by Perseus Pubng) HarpC.

Mary Baker Eddy: A Life Size Portrait. Lyman P. Powell. LC 91-72519. (Twentieth-Century Biographers Ser.). (Illus.). 408p. 1992. 17.95 (*0-87510-260-3*) Writings of Mary Baker.

Mary Baker Eddy: A New Look. Helen M. Wright. 395p. 1980. pap. 15.50 (*0-9604648-0-8*) H M Wright.

Mary Baker Eddy: Christian Healer. 496p. 1997. 29.95 (*0-87510-374-X*, G61394) Writings of Mary Baker.

Mary Baker Eddy: God's Great Scientist, Vol. 1. 2nd ed. Helen M. Wright. 289p. 1995. pap. text 15.50 (*1-886505-01-2*) H M Wright.

Mary Baker Eddy: God's Great Scientist, Vol. 3. Helen M. Wright. 289p. 1987. 15.50 (*0-9604648-7-5*) H M Wright.

Mary Baker Eddy: Her Mission & Triumph. Julia M. Johnston. (Twentieth-Century Biographers Ser.). (Illus.). 168p. 1998. 26.95 (*0-87510-345-6*) Writings of Mary Baker.

Mary Baker Eddy: Her Spiritual Footsteps. Gilbert C. Carpenter, Sr. & Gilbert C. Carpenter, Jr. 281p. 1987. 10.95 (*1-878641-02-6*) Aequus Inst Pubns.

Mary Baker Eddy: Leader Forever. Helen M. Wright. 112p. 1992. pap. text 7.95 (*1-886505-03-9*) H M Wright.

Mary Baker Eddy a Life Size Portrait. Lyman P. Powell. 434p. 1998. reprint ed. pap. 29.95 (*0-7661-0460-5*) Kessinger Pub.

Mary Baker Eddy & Her Books. William D. Orcutt. (Twentieth-Century Biographers Ser.). (Illus.). 224p. 1992. 14.95 (*0-87510-274-3*) Writings of Mary Baker.

Mary Baker Eddy, Discoverer & Founder of Christian Science. Louise A. Smith. (Twentieth-Century Biographers Ser.). (Illus.). 142p. 1992. 12.95 (*0-87510-226-3*) Writings of Mary Baker.

Mary Baker Eddy, Discoverer & Founder of Christian Science. Louise A. Smith. Tr. by Dominique Tieche from ENG. (FRE., Illus.). 162p. 1992. pap. 17.95 (*0-87510-235-2*) Writings of Mary Baker.

Mary Baker Eddy, Discoverer & Founder of Christian Science. Louise A. Smith. Tr. by Lazar Shtaynmets from ENG. (GER., Illus.). 162p. 1992. pap. 17.95 (*0-87510-236-0*) Writings of Mary Baker.

Mary Baker Eddy, Discoverer & Founder of Christian Science. Louise A. Smith. Tr. by Ivone R. Harrison from ENG. (POR., Illus.). 158p. 1992. pap. 17.95 (*0-87510-237-9*) Writings of Mary Baker.

Mary Baker Eddy, Discoverer & Founder of Christian Science. Louise A. Smith. Tr. by Diana Dreyzin from ENG. (SPA., Illus.). 162p. 1992. pap. 17.95 (*0-87510-238-7*) Writings of Mary Baker.

Mary Baker Eddy God's Great Scientist, Vol. 1. Helen M. Wright. LC 85-178036. 289p. 1995. 15.50 (*0-9604648-2-4*) H M Wright.

Mary Baker Eddy God's Great Scientist, Vol. 2. Helen M. Wright. 146p. 1984. pap. text 13.20 (*0-9604648-3-2*) H M Wright.

Mary Baker Eddy God's Great Scientist: An Examination of the First Edition of Science & Health's Chapter II Imposition & Demonstration. 2nd ed. Helen M. Wright. 133p. 1996. pap. text 13.20 (*1-886505-05-5*) H M Wright.

Mary Baker Eddy Institute Letters. Helen M. Wright. (Mary Baker Eddy Institute Letters Ser.: Vol. 1). (Illus.). 344p. 1999. 18.20 (*1-886505-18-7*) H M Wright.

Mary Baker Eddy Reveals Your Divinity. Helen M. Wright. 270p. 1991. 15.50 (*0-8062-3849-6*) H M Wright.

Mary Baker Eddy's Church Manual & "Church Universal & Triumphant" Helen M. Wright. 342p. 1981. 18.20 (*0-9604648-1-6*) H M Wright.

Mary Baldwin College. Photos by Daniel Grogan. (Illus.). 112p. 1992. 39.95 (*0-916509-71-0*) Harmony Hse Pub.

Mary Barton. Elizabeth Gaskell. Ed. by Jennifer Foster. (Literary Texts Ser.). 520p. 2000. pap. 9.95 (*1-55111-169-1*) Broadview Pr.

Mary Barton. Elizabeth Gaskell. 1994. 17.00 (*0-679-43494-1*) Everymns Lib.

Mary Barton. Elizabeth Gaskell. Ed. & Intro. by Edgar Wright. (Oxford World's Classics Ser.). 530p. 1998. pap. 6.95 (*0-19-283510-6*) OUP.

Mary Barton. Elizabeth Gaskell. Ed. & Intro. by Macdonald Daly. LC 98-107431. 464p. 1997. pap. 7.95 (*0-14-043464-X*) Viking Penguin.

Mary Barton: A Tale of Manchester Life. Elizabeth Gaskell. Ed. by Angus Easson. LC 98-150828. 432p. 1998. 45.00 (*1-85331-020-4*, Pub. by Edinburgh U Pr) Col U Pr.

Mary, Behold Thy Son. Roxcy Jeppson. 1998. pap. 11.95 (*1-57734-230-5*, 01113356) Covenant Comms.

Mary Belle Barclay: Founder of Canadian Hostelling. Evelyn Edgeller. (Illus.). 91p. (Orig.). 1988. pap. 10.95 (*0-920490-79-4*) Temeron Bks.

Mary Bell's Complete Dehydrator Cookbook. Mary Bell. LC 93-38778. 556p. 1994. 15.00 (*0-688-13024-0*, Hearst) Hearst Commns.

***Mary Berry's New Aga Cookbook.** Mary Berry. 2000. pap. 24.95 (*0-7472-7358-8*, Pub. by Headline Bk Pub) Trafalgar.

Mary Betty Lizzie McNutt's Birthday. Felicia Bond. (Illus.). (J). 1983. 4.70 (*0-690-04255-8*) HarpC Child Bks.

Mary Black Songbook. Declan Sinnott. 1994. pap. 23.95 (*0-9522864-0-8*, AM92055) Music Sales.

Mary Blair's Hors D'Oeuvres Cookbook. Mary Blair. LC 84-25850. 433p. 1985. 25.00 (*0-88191-004-X*) Freundlich.

Mary Bloody Mary. Carolyn Meyer. LC 99-21185. 256p. 1999. 16.00 (*0-15-201906-5*) Harcourt.

Mary Bloody Mary. Carolyn Meyer. 2001. pap. write for info. (*0-15-201905-7*) Harcourt.

Mary Boykin Chesnut: A Biography. Elisabeth Muhlenfeld. LC 80-26610. (Southern Biography Ser.). (Illus.). 302p. (C). 1980. pap. 17.95 (*0-8071-1804-4*) La State U Pr.

Mary Boykin Chestnut: A Confederate Woman's Life. Mary A. Decredico. LC 95-11155. (American Profiles Ser.). (Illus.). 212p. (C). 1996. pap. text 14.95 (*0-945612-47-8*) Madison Hse.

Mary Boykin Chestnut: A Confederate Woman's Life. Mary A. Decredico. LC 95-11155. (American Profiles Ser.). (Illus.). 212p. (C). 1996. text 29.95 (*0-945612-46-X*) Madison Hse.

Mary Broome: A Comedy in Four Acts. Allan Monkhouse. LC 83-45818. reprint ed. 16.00 (*0-404-20181-4*) AMS Pr.

Mary Bunyan. unabridged ed. Sallie R. Ford. (Children's Heritage Ser.). (Illus.). 488p. (J). (gr. 4-6). 1996. pap. 17.95 (*1-58339-132-0*, D32) Triangle Press.

Mary Butts: Scenes from the Life. Nathalie Blondel. LC 97-41973. (Illus.). 600p. 1998. 35.00 (*0-929701-55-0*) McPherson & Co.

Mary by Myself. Jane Denitz Smith & Stephen Johnson. LC 93-47457. (Illus.). 160p. (YA). (gr. 3-7). 1999. pap. 4.95 (*0-06-440568-0*) HarpC Child Bks.

Mary Caper. Gene Detro. LC 81-51876. (Sunburst Originals Ser.: No. 10). (Illus.). 130p. (Orig.). 1982. pap. 4.65 (*0-934648-09-3*) Sunburst Pr.

Mary Carbery's West Cork Journals, 1898-1901. Mary Carbery. Ed. by Jeremy Sandford. LC 96-130570. (Illus.). 320p. 1998. pap. 29.95 (*1-874675-36-8*, Pub. by Lilliput Pr) Irish Bks Media.

Mary Carleton Narratives, 1663-73. Ernest Bernbaum. LC 76-164588. (Select Bibliographies Reprint Ser.). 1977. reprint ed. 17.95 (*0-8369-5872-1*) Ayer.

Mary Carter Smith: African-American Storyteller. Babs Bell Hajdusiewicz. LC 98-66953. (Illus.). 104p. (J). (gr. 4-10). 1998. pap. 9.95 (*0-9665568-0-1*, MCS-1) Read Realm.

***Mary Cassatt.** Abrams Staff. (Illus.). (J). 1998. pap. 8.80 (*0-8109-2766-7*, Pub. by Abrams) Time Warner.

***Mary Cassatt.** Ernestine Giesecke. LC 99-14557. (Life & Work of...Ser.). (Illus.). 32p. (J). (gr. k-3). 1999. lib. bdg. 13.95 (*1-57572-955-5*) Heinemann Lib.

***Mary Cassatt.** Georgette Gouveia. (Essential Ser.). 2000. pap. 12.95 (*0-8109-5814-7*, Pub. by Abrams) Time Warner.

***Mary Cassatt.** Georgette Gouveia. (Essential Ser.). (Illus.). 112p. 2000. 12.95 (*0-7407-0730-2*, Abrams Essential) Andrews & McMeel.

Mary Cassatt. Nancy M. Mathews. LC 86-17224. (Illus.). 160p. 1987. 45.00 (*0-8109-0793-3*, Pub. by Abrams) Time Warner.

Mary Cassatt. Nancy M. Mathews. LC 92-15548. (Rizzoli Art Ser.). (Illus.). 24p. 1992. pap. 7.95 (*0-8478-1611-7*, Pub. by Rizzoli Intl) St Martin.

Mary Cassatt. Susan E. Meyer. (First Impressions Ser.). (Illus.). 80p. (YA). (gr. 7 up). 1990. 19.95 (*0-8109-3154-0*, Pub. by Abrams) Time Warner.

Mary Cassatt. Mike Venezia. LC 90-2165. (Getting to Know the World's Greatest Artists Ser.). (Illus.). 32p. (J). (ps-4). 1990. pap. 6.95 (*0-516-42278-2*); lib. bdg. 21.00 (*0-516-02278-4*) Childrens.

Mary Cassatt: A Catalogue Raisonne of the Graphic Work. 2nd ed. Adelyn Breeskin. (Illus.). 190p. 1979. reprint ed. 150.00 (*1-55660-249-9*) A Wofsy Fine Arts.

Mary Cassatt: A Life. Nancy M. Mathews. LC 98-8028. (Illus.). 383p. 1998. pap. 18.00 (*0-300-07754-8*) Yale U Pr.

Mary Cassatt: An American Impressionist, 1. Gerhard Gruitrooy. 1998. pap. text 10.95 (*1-880908-67-0*) Todtri Prods.

Mary Cassatt: An American in Paris see First Books

Mary Cassatt: Impressionist at Home. Barbara Stern Shapiro. (Illus.). 80p. 1998. 19.95 (*0-7893-0246-2*, Pub. by Universe) St Martin.

Mary Cassatt: Modern Woman. Ed. by Judith A. Barter et al. LC 98-7306. (Illus.). 376p. 1998. 65.00 (*0-8109-4089-2*, Pub. by Abrams) Time Warner.

Mary Cassatt: Modern Woman. Judith A. Barter et al. LC 98-7306. (Illus.). 376p. 1998. pap. 29.95 (*0-86559-167-9*) Art Inst Chi.

Mary Cassatt: Painter of Modern Women. Griselda Pollock. LC 98-60039. (World of Art Ser.). (Illus.). 224p. 1998. pap. 14.95 (*0-500-20317-2*, Pub. by Thames Hudson) Norton.

Mary Cassatt: Reflections of Women's Lives. Debra N. Mancoff. 96p. 1998. 24.95 (*1-55670-852-1*) Stewart Tabori & Chang.

Mary Cassatt & Philadelphia. Suzanne G. Lindsay. LC 84-29623. (Illus.). 100p. 1985. pap. 18.95 (*0-87633-061-8*) Phila Mus Art.

Mary Cassatt Datebook. Mary Cassatt. (Illus.). 32p. 1998. 12.50 (*1-55595-006-X*, Pub. by Hudson Hills) Natl Bk Netwk.

Mary Cassatt, Modern Woman. Mary Cassatt et al. LC 98-7306. 1998. write for info. (*0-86559-166-0*) Abrams.

***Mary Cassatt Notebook.** Mary Cassata. (Illus.). (J). 1999. pap. 1.00 (*0-486-40836-1*) Dover.

Mary Cassatt Oils & Pastels. E. John Bullard. (Great Artists Ser.). (Illus.). 88p. 1984. pap. 16.95 (*0-8230-0570-4*) Watsn-Guptill.

Mary Cassatt-Postcards. Mary Cassatt. 1989. pap. 4.95 (*0-486-26135-2*) Dover.

Mary Cassatt, the Life of an Artist. Nancy Plain. LC 93-46578. (People in Focus Ser.). 112p. (J). (gr. 5). 1994. pap. 7.95 (*0-382-24720-5*); text, lib. bdg. write for info. (*0-87518-597-5*, Dillon Silver Burdett) Silver Burdett Pr.

Mary Celeste. Brian Freemantle. 208p. 1999. 26.00 (*0-7278-5411-9*, Pub. by Severn Hse) Chivers N Amer.

***Mary Celeste.** Brian Freemantle. 344p. 2000. 31.99 (*0-7089-4229-6*) Ulverscroft.

Mary Celeste: An Unsolved Mystery from History. Jane Yolen & Heidi E. Y. Stemple. LC 97-24613. (Illus.). 32p. (J). (gr. k-3). 1999. 16.00 (*0-689-81079-2*) S&S Bks Yung.

Mary-Chapin Carpenter: Come on Come On. (Piano-Vocal-Guitar Ser.). 64p. (Orig.). 1993. pap. 14.95 (*0-7935-1853-9*, HL00308165) H Leonard.

***Mary Chapin Carpenter: Party Doll.** 96p. 1999. otabind 16.95 (*1-57560-282-2*, Pub. by Cherry Lane) H Leonard.

Mary Chapin Carpenter: Stones in the Road. Ed. by Milton Okun. (Illus.). 92p. (Orig.). (YA). 1995. pap. 17.95 (*0-89524-901-4*, Pub. by Cherry Lane) H Leonard.

Mary Chesnut's Civil War. Ed. by C. Vann Woodward & Mary B. Chestnut. LC 80-36661. 886p. 1981. 50.00 (*0-300-02459-2*) Yale U Pr.

Mary Chesnut's Civil War. Ed. by C. Vann Woodward & Mary B. Chestnut. LC 80-36661. 886p. 1983. pap. 21.00 (*0-300-02979-9*, Y-450) Yale U Pr.

Mary Church Terrell: Leader for Equality. Patricia McKissack & Fredrick McKissack. LC 91-3083. (Great African Americans Ser.). (Illus.). 32p. (J). (gr. 1-4). 1991. lib. bdg. 14.95 (*0-89490-305-5*) Enslow Pubs.

Mary Coffin Starbuck & the Early History of Nantucket. Roland L. Warren. LC 87-61138. (Illus.). 300p. 1987. pap. 12.95 (*0-942861-01-9*) Pingry Pr.

Mary Colter: Builder upon the Red Earth. rev. ed. Virginia L. Grattan. (Illus.). 131p. 1995. reprint ed. pap. 14.95 (*0-938216-45-7*, 30284) GCA.

Mary Communes with the Saints see Saints Who Saw Mary

Mary Contrary. large type ed. Peggy O'More. 212p. 1994. pap. 18.99 (*1-85389-437-0*, Dales) Ulverscroft.

Mary, Coredemptrix, Mediatrix Advocate. Mark I. Miravalle. Tr. by Bridget Hooker. LC 94-67388. (RUS.). 80p. 1994. pap. 1.00 (*1-882972-38-4*, 2000R) Queenship Pub.

Mary, Coredemptrix, Mediatrix, Advocate Theological Foundation Vol. II: Papal, Pneumatological, Ecumenical. Mark I. Miravalle. 1996. pap. text 19.95 (*1-882972-92-9*) Queenship Pub.

Mary; Coredemptrix, Mediatrix, Advocate Theological Foundations: Towards a Papal Definition? Ed. by Mark I. Miravalle. LC 95-68326. 327p. 1995. text 25.00 (*1-882972-58-9*); pap. text 12.00 (*1-882972-57-0*) Queenship Pub.

Mary Day by Day. Intro. by Charles Fehrenbach. (Spiritual Life Ser.). (Illus.). 192p. 1988. vinyl bd. 6.25 (*0-89942-180-6*, 180/09) Catholic Bk Pub.

Mary Diana Dods: A Gentleman & a Scholar. Betty T. Bennett. LC 94-13170. 312p. 1994. reprint ed. pap. 15.95 (*0-8018-4984-5*) Johns Hopkins.

Mary, Did You Know? The Story of God's Great Plan. Mark Lowry. (Illus.). 32p. (J). (ps-2). 1998. 14.95 (*1-57856-179-5*) Waterbrook Pr.

Mary Donoho: New First Lady of the Santa Fe Trail. Marian Meyer. LC 90-56218. (Illus.). 150p. 1991. pap. 12.95 (*0-941270-69-6*) Ancient City Pr.

Mary Douglas: Critical Introduction. Richard Fardon. LC 98-25907. (Illus.). 320p. (C). 1999. 85.00 (*0-415-04092-2*); pap. 24.99 (*0-415-04093-0*) Routledge.

***Mary Downing Hahns Teacher's Guide.** (J). 2000. pap., teacher ed. write for info. (*0-06-449240-0*, HarpTrophy) HarpC Child Bks.

Mary Dugan's Dependable Home. Sam Cardonsky. 1988. 21.95 (*0-689-11937-2*) Atheneum Yung Read.

Mary Dyer: Biography of a Rebel Quaker. Ruth Plimpton. (Illus.). 247p. 1999. text 22.00 (*0-7881-5993-3*) DIANE Pub.

Mary Dyer: Biography of a Rebel Quaker. Ruth T. Plimpton. (Illus.). 300p. 1994. 21.95 (*0-8283-1964-2*) Branden Bks.

Mary E. Murphy's Contributions to Accountancy. Margaret Hoskins. LC 93-39174. (New Works in Accounting History). (Illus.). 384p. 1994. text 20.00 (*0-8153-1716-6*) Garland.

Mary E. Wilkins Freeman. Edward Foster. 238p. 1956. 22.95 (*0-87532-058-9*) Hendricks House.

Mary E. Wilkins Freeman: A Study of the Short Fiction. Mary R. Reichardt & Mary E. Wilkins Freeman. LC 97-18464. 1997. 29.00 (*0-8057-4626-9*, Twyne) Mac Lib Ref.

Mary Elizabeth Ryder - Grand Dame: Matriarch of Women. Sandra M. Brunsmann. 1997. pap. 14.95 (*0-9632178-1-X*) S M Brunsmann.

Mary Ellen Pleasant, 1817-1904: Mother of Human Rights in California. 2nd rev. ed. C. Susheel Bibbs. (Illus.). 20p. (J). (gr. 5-12). 1996. reprint ed. mass mkt. 7.95 (*1-892516-00-4*) MEP Publications.

Mary Ellen's Best of Helpful Hints, Bk. II. Mary E. Pinkham. (Illus.). 144p. (Orig.). 1981. 4.50 (*0-941298-00-0*) M E Pinkham.

Mary Ellen's Best of Helpful Hints, Bk. Two. Mary Ellen Pinkham. LC 81-10376. (Illus.). 144p. 1989. mass mkt. 6.95 (*0-446-38644-8*, Pub. by Warner Bks) Little.

Mary Ellen's Best of Helpful Hints Library. Mary E. Pinkham. 1981. pap. 12.50 (*0-941298-03-5*) M E Pinkham.

Mary Ellen's Best of Helpful Kitchen Hints. Mary E. Pinkham. (Illus.). 144p. (Orig.). 1980. pap. 4.50 (*0-941298-01-9*) M E Pinkham.

Mary Ellen's Best of Helpful Kitchen Hints. Mary Ellen Pinkham. (Illus.). (Orig.). 1980. mass mkt. 4.50 (*0-446-97212-6*, Pub. by Warner Bks) Little.

Mary Ellen's Clean House. Mary Ellen Pinkham. 1994. pap. 14.00 (*0-517-88185-3*) Crown Pub Group.

Mary Ellen's Giant Book of Helpful Hints, 3 bks. in 1. Mary E. Pinkham. LC 93-38935. 416p. 1994. 9.99 (*0-517-10179-3*) Random Hse Value.

Mary Ellen's Greatest Hints. Mary E. Pinkham. 352p. 1990. mass mkt. 5.99 (*0-449-21714-0*, Crest) Fawcett.

Mary Ellen's Wow! Ideas That Really Work. Mary E. Pinkham. 150p. 1992. 6.95 (*0-9631933-0-9*) M Ellen Bks.

Mary Emma. Ralph Moody. (J). 1976. 23.95 (*0-8488-1107-0*) Amereon Ltd.

Mary Emma & Company. Ralph Moody. (J). 1976. 26.95 (*0-8488-1513-0*) Amereon Ltd.

Mary Emma & Company. Ralph Moody. LC 93-43936. (Illus.). 235p. (J). 1994. pap. 9.95 (*0-8032-8211-7*, Bison Books) U of Nebr Pr.

Mary Emme. Date not set. write for info. (*0-517-80135-3*) Random Hse Value.

Mary Emmerling's American Country Cottages. Photos by Joshua Greene. LC 92-24897. (Illus.). 1993. 25.00 (*0-517-58365-8*) C Potter.

Mary Emmerling's American Country Decorating Details. Mary E. Emmerling & Carol S. Sheehan. LC 94-641. (Illus.). 208p. 1994. 25.00 (*0-517-58369-0*) C Potter.

Mary Emmerling's New Country Collecting. Photos by Joshua Greene. (Illus.). 1996. 40.00 (*0-614-96829-1*) C Potter.

Mary Emmerling's New Country Collecting. Photos by Joshua Greene. (Illus.). 1996. 40.00 (*0-614-96953-0*) Crown Pub Group.

Mary Emmerling's Quick Decorating. Mary E. Emmerling & Jill Kirchner. LC 96-29241. 1997. 27.50 (*0-517-70467-6*) C Potter.

***Mary Engelbreit, 4 vols.** Mary Engelbreit. 2000. boxed set 19.95 (*0-7407-0865-1*) Andrews & McMeel.

Mary Engelbreit: The Art & the Artist. Mary Engelbreit & Patrick Regan. (Illus.). 192p. 1996. 29.95 (*0-8362-2232-6*) Andrews & McMeel.

M

Mary Engelbreit Countdown to Christmas. Adventure House Staff. 1998. 14.95 (*0-8362-7225-0*) Andrews & McMeel.

Mary Engelbreit Cross-Stitch. Mary Engelbreit. LC 96-76684. (Illus.). 192p. 1996. 27.95 (*0-696-04665-2*, Meredith Pr) Meredith Bks.

Mary Engelbreit Cross-Stitch for All Seasons. Ed. by Carol Dahlstrom. LC 97-71327. (Illus.). 192p. 1998. 29.95 (*0-696-20707-9*, Meredith Pr) Meredith Bks.

Mary Engelbreit Photo Album: Christmas. Mary Engelbreit. 1996. 9.95 (*0-8362-2041-2*) Andrews & McMeel.

Mary Engelbreit Photo Albums: Motifs. Mary Engelbreit. (Illus.). 1995. 9.95 (*0-8362-0078-0*) Andrews & McMeel.

Mary Engelbreit's Autumn. Mary Engelbreit & Charlotte Lyons. LC 96-11116. (Illus.). 80p. 1996. 10.95 (*0-8362-2229-6*) Andrews & McMeel.

Mary Engelbreit's Children's Companion: The Mary Englebreit Look & How to Get It. Mary Engelbreit et al. LC 97-7261. (Illus.). 144p. 1997. 24.95 (*0-8362-3675-0*) Andrews & McMeel.

Mary Engelbreit's Christmas Companion: The Mary Engelbreit Look & How to Get It. Charlotte Lyons. (Illus.). 136p. 1995. 24.95 (*0-8362-4627-6*) Andrews & McMeel.

Mary Engelbreit's Cookies. Mary Engelbreit. LC 98-22460. (Illus.). 112p. 1998. 16.95 (*0-8362-6758-3*) Andrews & McMeel.

***Mary Engelbreit's Home Companion: Collections.** Mary Engelbreit. LC 99-462035. 2000. 12.95 (*0-7407-0684-5*) Andrews & McMeel.

Mary Engelbreit's Home Companion: The Mary Engelbreit Look & How to Get It. Charlotte Lyons. (Illus.). 128p. 1994. 24.95 (*0-8362-4621-7*) Andrews & McMeel.

Mary Engelbreits Journals. Mary Engelbreit. 1996. 9.95 (*0-8362-1297-5*) Andrews & McMeel.

Mary Engelbreit's Queen of the Kitchen Cookbook: Cooking for Family & Friends. Andrews & McMeel Staff. LC 98-22459. (Illus.). 144p. 1998. 24.95 (*0-8362-6761-3*) Andrews & McMeel.

Mary Engelbreit's Spring Craft Book. Mary Engelbreit & Charlotte Lyons. LC 96-38490. (Illus.). 80p. 1997. 10.95 (*0-8362-2885-5*) Andrews & McMeel.

Mary Engelbreit's Summer Craft Book. Mary Engelbreit & Charlotte Lyons. LC 96-34006. (Illus.). 80p. 1997. 10.95 (*0-8362-2768-9*) Andrews & McMeel.

Mary Engelbreit's Sweet Treats Dessert Cookbook, 1 vol. Mary Engelbreit. LC 99-32149. 1999. 24.95 (*0-7407-0319-6*) Andrews & McMeel.

Mary Engelbreit's the Snow Queen. Hans Christian Andersen. LC 93-11436.Tr. of Snedronningen. (Illus.). 48p. (J). (gr. k up). 1993. 16.95 (*1-56305-438-8*, 3438) Workman Pub.

***Mary Engelbreit's 'Tis the Season Holiday Cookbook.** Mary Engelbreit. LC 00-21313. (Illus.). 2000. 24.95 (*0-7407-0586-5*) Andrews & McMeel.

Mary Engelbreit's Winter. Mary Engelbreit & Charlotte Lyons. LC 96-11117. (Illus.). 80p. 1996. 10.95 (*0-8362-2231-8*) Andrews & McMeel.

Mary Fedden. Mel Gooding. (Illus.). 96p. 1995. 51.95 (*1-85928-149-4*, Pub. by Scolar Pr) Ashgate Pub Co.

Mary Fedden. limited ed. Mel Gooding. (Illus.). 96p. 1995. 393.95 (*1-85928-150-8*, Pub. by Scolar Pr) Ashgate Pub Co.

Mary, Ferrie & the Monkey Virus: The Story of an Underground Medical Laboratory. 3rd ed. Edward T. Haslam. (Illus.). 144p. (Orig.). 1997. 19.95 (*0-9643981-2-5*) Wrdswrth Communs.

Mary Fielding Smith: Daughter of Britain. Don C. Corbett. LC 66-29293. 310p. 1995. 17.95 (*0-87579-990-6*) Deseret Bk.

Mary Fielding Smith: Mother of a Prophet: Her Trek West. Myrth E. Burr. 36p. 1997. pap. text 8.95 (*1-57636-038-5*) SunRise Pbl.

***Mary, First Disciple: Reflections on Mary of Nazareth.** Thomas Grady. (Illus.). 72p. 1999. pap. 5.50 (*0-8198-4806-9*) Pauline Bks.

Mary Flagler Cary Music Collection. Ed. by H. Cahoon. LC 73-133290. (Illus.). 108p. 1970. pap. 6.00 (*0-87598-009-0*) Pierpont Morgan.

Mary Fletcher. Eglinton. Ed. by Greenhill. (Exeter Maritime Studies). (Illus.). 96p. 1990. text 35.00 (*0-85989-326-X*, Pub. by Univ Exeter Pr) Northwestern U Pr.

Mary Florence. Kathleen S. Tiffany. 254p. Date not set. 22.95 (*0-8488-2410-5*) Amereon Ltd.

Mary for All Christians. John Macquarrie. 160p. 1992. reprint ed. 21.95 (*0-00-599219-2*, Pub. by T & T Clark) Bks Intl VA.

Mary for Today. Hans Urs Von Balthasar & Hans U. Von Balthasar. LC 87-83506. 75p. pap. 9.95 incl. audio (*0-89870-190-2*, 120) Ignatius Pr.

Mary for Today. Hans U. Von Balthasar. (Orig.). (C). 1988. 39.00 (*0-85439-266-1*, Pub. by St Paul Pubns) St Mut.

Mary Ford Cake & Biscuit Recipes. Mary Ford. (Illus.). 192p. 1996. 22.50 (*0-946429-58-8*, Pub. by M OMara) Trans-Atl Phila.

Mary Ford One Hundred Easy Cake Designs. Mary Ford. (Illus.). 208p. 1995. 23.95 (*0-946429-47-2*, Pub. by M OMara) Trans-Atl Phila.

Mary Ford Writing in Icing. Mary Ford. (The Classic Step-by-Step Ser.). (Illus.). 96p. 1996. 18.95 (*0-946429-57-X*, Pub. by M OMara) Trans-Atl Phila.

Mary Ford's New Book of Cake Decorating. Mary Ford. (The Classic Step-by-Step Ser.). (Illus.). 224p. 1994. 24.95 (*0-946429-59-6*, Pub. by M OMara) Trans-Atl Phila.

Mary Frances Cook Book: Adventures among the People. Jane E. Fryer. (Illus.). 176p. 1998. 28.00 (*0-916896-96-X*, LE50) Lacis Pubns.

Mary Frances Garden Book: Adventures among the Garden People. Jane E. Fryer. (Illus.). 382p. (J). (gr. 5-8). 1998. reprint ed. 28.00 (*1-891656-01-5*, LE58) Lacis Pubns.

Mary Frances Housekeeper: Adventures among the Doll People. Jane E. Fryer. (Mary Frances Ser.: Vol. 3). (Illus.). 254p. (J). (gr. 3-8). 1998. pap. 28.00 (*0-916896-92-7*) Lacis Pubns.

Mary Frances Knitting & Crocheting Book: Adventures among the Knitting People. Jane E. Fryer. (Illus.). 270p. (J). (gr. 3-10). 1997. reprint ed. 28.00 (*0-916896-90-0*) Lacis Pubns.

Mary Frances Sewing Book. Jane E. Fryer. (Illus.). 280p. 1998. pap. 19.95 (*0-87588-537-3*) Hobby Hse.

Mary Francis Sewing Book: Adventures among the Thimble People. unabridged ed. Jane E. Fryer. (Illus.). 280p. 1997. 28.00 (*0-916896-85-4*) Lacis Pubns.

Mary Frank. Hayden Herrera. (Illus.). 144p. 1990. 55.00 (*0-8109-3301-2*, Pub. by Abrams) Time Warner.

***Mary Frank: Encounters.** Linda Nochlin. (Illus.). 120p. 2000. 34.95 (*0-8109-6723-5*, Pub. by Abrams) Time Warner.

Mary from Nazareth. Bruna Battistella. Tr. by Deana Basile from ITA. LC 94-2694. (Illus.). 128p. (Orig.). (J). (gr. 2-4). 1996. 12.95 (*0-8198-4772-0*) Pauline Bks.

Mary Fulstone: Recollections of a Country Doctor in Smith, Nevada. Intro. by Mary E. Glass. 110p. 1980. lib. bdg. 31.50 (*1-56475-183-X*); fiche. write for info. (*1-56475-184-8*) U NV Oral Hist.

Mary Garden. Michael Turnbull. Tr. by James M. McPherson. LC 96-21686. (Opera Biography Ser.: Vol. 8). (Illus.). 250p. 1997. 29.95 (*1-57467-017-4*, Amadeus Pr) Timber.

Mary Garden's Story. Mary Garden & Louis L. Biancolli. Ed. by Annette K. Baxter. LC 79-8794. (Signal Lives Ser.). (Illus.). 1980. reprint ed. lib. bdg. 39.95 (*0-405-12840-1*) Ayer.

Mary Geddy's Day: A Colonial Girl in Williamsburg. Kate Waters. LC 98-46274. (Illus.). 40p. (J). (gr. 1-4). 1999. 16.95 (*0-590-92925-9*, Pub. by Scholastic Inc) Penguin Putnam.

Mary Gilliatt's New Guide to Decorating. Mary Gilliatt. 1999. pap. text 27.95 (*1-85029-979-X*) Conran Octopus.

Mary Gilliatt's Room-By-Room Decorating. Mary Gilliatt. 1994. pap. write for info. (*0-316-31437-4*) Little.

Mary Gilliatt's Shortcuts to Great Decorating. Mary Gilliatt. 1991. 19.95 (*0-685-50991-5*) Little.

Mary Gilliatt's Shortcuts to Great Decorating. Mary Gilliatt. 160p. 1991. pap. 23.95 (*0-316-31422-6*) Little.

Mary-God's Supreme . . . Masterpiece. Bartholomew Gottemoller. LC 95-69784. 144p. 1996. pap. 5.95 (*1-882972-48-1*, 3361) Queenship Pub.

Mary Gordon. Alma Bennett. 1996. 32.00 (*0-8057-4024-4*, Twyne) Mac Lib Ref.

Mary Gregory Glassware, 1880-1990. Robert Truitt & Deborah Truitt. (Illus.). iv, 83p. 1992. pap. 19.95 (*0-9668376-0-6*) B&D Glass.

Mary Grew: Abolitionist & Feminist, 1813-1896. Ira V. Brown. LC 90-50769. 216p. 1991. 40.00 (*0-945636-20-2*) Susquehanna U Pr.

Mary Hackett: A Survey. Ed. by Christopher Busa. LC 96-70324. (Introductions Ser.: Vol. 1). (Illus.). 48p. 1996. pap. 20.00 (*0-944854-31-1*) Provincetown Arts.

***Mary Had A Little Ham.** Margie Palatini. 32p. (J). 2005. 15.99 (*0-7868-0566-8*, Pub. by Hyperion) Little.

Mary Had a Little Lamb see Extended Nursery Rhymes

***Mary Had a Little Lamb.** Sarah Josepha Hale. LC 94-24847. (Illus.). 32p. (J). (ps-1). 2000. pap. 5.95 (*0-531-07165-0*) Orchard Bks Watts.

Mary Had a Little Lamb. Sarah Josephbuell Hale. LC 94-24847. (Illus.). 32p. (J). (ps-1). 1995. 15.95 (*0-531-06875-7*); lib. bdg. 16.99 (*0-531-08725-5*) Orchard Bks Watts.

Mary Had a Little Lamb. Sarah Josephbuell Hale. LC 89-24391. (Illus.). 32p. (J). (ps-3). 1992. pap. 4.95 (*0-590-43774-7*, 045, Blue Ribbon Bks) Scholastic Inc.

Mary Had a Little Lamb. Sarah Josephbuell Hale. (Illus.). 32p. (J). (ps-3). 1993. 19.95 (*0-590-72755-9*) Scholastic Inc.

Mary Had a Little Lamb. Sarah Josephbuell Hale. (J). 1990. 10.15 (*0-606-07845-2*, Pub. by Turtleback) Demco.

***Mary Had a Little Lamb.** Linda Jennings. (Illus.). (J). 2000. 6.95 (*1-86233-122-7*) Levinson Bks.

Mary Had a Little Lamb. Linda Jennings. 1999. 10.95 (*1-86233-069-7*) Sterling.

Mary Had a Little Lamb. unabridged ed. Sarah Josephbuell Hale. (Illus.). (J). (ps-2). 1989. 22.95 incl. audio (*0-87499-125-0*); pap. 15.95 incl. audio (*0-87499-124-2*) Live Oak Media.

Mary Had a Little Lamb, 4 bks., Set. unabridged ed. Sarah Josephbuell Hale. (Illus.). (J). (ps-2). 1989. pap. 33.95 incl. audio (*0-87499-126-9*) Live Oak Media.

Mary Hallock Foote: Pioneer Woman Illustrator. Doris Bickford-Swarthout. LC 96-95072. (Illus.). 130p. 1996. 35.00 (*0-9646900-2-0*) Berry Hill NY.

Mary Heaton Vorse: The Life of an American Insurgent. Dee Garrison. (American Subjects Ser.). (Illus.). 400p. 1990. pap. 19.95 (*0-87722-781-0*) Temple U Pr.

Mary Heilmann Color & Passion. Christa Hausler. 1998. pap. text 14.95 (*3-89322-351-7*, Pub. by Edition Cantz) Dist Art Pubs.

Mary Herd Black, Her Story: Autobiography: Letterography: Pictography. Mary H. Black. (Illus.). 600p. (Orig.). (YA). (gr. 6-12). 1998. pap. 35.00 (*0-9657775-1-0*) EZ Print.

Mary Higgins Clark: A Critical Companion. Linda C. Pelzer. LC 95-4660. (Critical Companions to Popular Contemporary Writers Ser.). 192p. 1995. 29.95 (*0-313-29413-5*, Greenwood Pr) Greenwood.

***Mary Higgins Clark: A Reader's Checklist & Reference Guide.** CheckerBee Publishing Staff. 1999. pap. text 4.95 (*1-58598-012-9*) CheckerBee.

Mary Higgins Clark: Boxed Set, 3 vols. Mary Higgins Clark. 1990. pap., boxed set 14.85 (*0-440-36009-9*) Dell.

Mary Higgins Clark: Three Complete Novels. Mary Higgins Clark. 560p. 1991. 13.99 (*0-517-06462-6*) Random Hse Value.

Mary Higgins Clark: Three New York Times Bestselling Novels. Mary Higgins Clark. 704p. 1996. 13.99 (*0-517-18368-4*) Random Hse Value.

Mary Higgins Clark Audio Double Feature: While My Pretty One Sleeps; Weep No More, My Lady. abr. ed. Mary Higgins Clark. 1992. audio 25.00 (*0-671-77677-0*) S&S Audio.

***Mary Higgins Clark Presents: The Plot Thickens.** large type ed. Ed. by Mary Higgins Clark. 268p. 2000. lib. bdg. 25.95 (*1-58547-048-1*) Ctr Point Pubg.

Mary Howitt: An Autobiography, 2 vols. Mary B. Howitt. Ed. by Margaret Howitt. reprint ed. 65.00 (*0-404-56754-1*) AMS Pr.

Mary Howitt: Another Lost Victorian Writer. Joy Dunicliff. LC 93-168845. 264 p. 1992. write for info. (*1-85634-102-X*) Excalibur.

Mary Hunter Austin. T. M. Pearce. (Twayne's United States Authors Ser.). 1965. pap. text 4.95 (*0-8290-0003-8*); lib. bdg. 20.95 (*0-89197-837-2*) Irvington.

***Mary Hunt's Debt-Proof Living: The Complete Guide to Living Financially Free.** Mary Hunt. LC 99-42629. 320p. 1999. 14.99 (*0-8054-2078-9*) Broadman.

***Mary Hunt's Debt-Proof Your Holidays.** Mary Hunt. LC 98-24555. 192p. 1998. pap. 8.99 (*0-8054-1678-1*) Broadman.

Mary in an Adult Church: Beyond Devotion to Response. David M. Knight. 76p. 1988. pap. 5.00 (*0-942971-11-6*) His Way.

Mary in Modern Spirituality. Quentin Hakenewerth. 52p. (Orig.). 1966. pap. 1.25 (*0-9608124-2-3*) Marianist Com Ctr.

Mary in the Christian Tradition. Kathleen Coyle. LC 95-78539. 152p. (Orig.). 1996. pap. 12.95 (*0-89622-672-7*) Twenty-Third.

Mary in the Church. John Hyland. 160p. 1989. pap. 24.00 (*1-85390-043-5*, Pub. by Veritas Pubns) St Mut.

***Mary in the Church Today: Official Catholic Teachings on the Mother of God Since Vatican II.** Bill McCarthy & James Tibbets. (Illus.). 504p. 2000. pap. 14.95 (*1-891903-22-5*) St Andrew Prodns.

Mary in the Churches. Ed. by Hans Kung & Jurgen Moltmann. (Concilium Ser.: Vol. 168). 128p. (Orig.). 1983. 6.95 (*0-8164-2448-9*) Harper SF.

Mary in the Fathers of the Church. Luigi Gambero. 1998. pap. 19.95 (*0-89870-686-6*) Ignatius Pr.

Mary in the Mystery of the Convenant. Ignace De la Potterie. Tr. by Bertrand Buby. LC 91-43114. 306p. (Orig.). 1992. pap. 15.95 (*0-8189-0632-4*) Alba.

Mary in the New Testament. Ed. by Raymond E. Brown et al. LC 78-8797. 336p. 1978. pap. 14.95 (*0-8091-2168-9*) Paulist Pr.

Mary in Today's World. Peter Bourne. LC 97-17413. (Illus.). 90p. 1997. pap. 4.50 (*0-930887-29-8*) Wenzel Pr.

Mary Is for Everyone. Ed. by William McLoughlin & Jill Pinnock. 320p. 1998. pap. 23.95 (*0-85244-429-X*, 2493, Pub. by Gra1cewing) Morehouse Pub.

Mary Jane & Bud Wiser. Rock. LC 96-92297. 206p. (Orig.). 1996. pap. 11.95 (*0-9652562-0-0*) Rock.

Mary Jane Forbes Greene (1845-1910) Mother of the Japan Mission: An Anthropological Portrait. Marion Kilson. LC 91-29582. (Studies in Women & Religion: Vol. 30). (Illus.). 160p. 1991. lib. bdg. 69.95 (*0-7734-9728-5*) E Mellen.

Mary Jemison: White Woman of the Seneca. Rayna M. Gangi. LC 94-43546. (Illus.). 152p. 1995. 22.95 (*0-940666-57-X*); pap. 12.95 (*0-940666-58-8*) Clear Light.

Mary Joan Waid: Recent Works. Howard D. Spencer. (Illus.). 8p. 1988. pap. 3.00 (*0-939324-40-7*) Wichita Art Mus.

Mary Joe Fernandez. Melanie Cole. LC 97-43510. (Real-Life Reader Biographies Ser.). (Illus.). 32p. (J). (gr. 3-8). 1998. lib. bdg. 15.95 (*1-883845-63-7*) M Lane Pubs.

Mary Jones & Her Bible. M. E. R. (Victorian Children's Classics Ser.). 96p. 1985. pap. 5.99 (*1-85030-012-7*) Bridge-Logos.

***Mary Jones & Her Bible.** Mary Ropes. (Children's Victorian Classics Ser.). 1999. pap. 6.99 (*0-88270-789-2*) Bridge-Logos.

***Mary-Kate & Ashley.** Mary-Kate Olsen & Ashley Olsen. (Illus.). 32p. (ps-3). 1999. 13.95 (*0-06-107566-3*, HarpCollins) HarperTrade.

***Mary-Kate & Ashley Be My Valentine: Cards for You to Make.** HarperCollins Children Publishing Staff. (Illus.). 24p. (J). (gr. 2-5). 2000. pap. 10.99 (*0-06-107568-X*) HarpC Child Bks.

***Mary-Kate & Ashley Olsen.** Contrib. by Tamara L. Britton. LC 99-27235. (Young Profiles Ser.). (Illus.). 32p. (J). 2000. lib. bdg. write for info. (*1-57765-351-3*, Checkerboard Library) ABDO Pub Co.

***Mary-Kate & Ashley Our Story: Mary-Kate & Ashley Olsen's Official Biography.** Mary-Kate Olsen & Ashley Olsen. 96p. (gr. 3-7). 2000. mass mkt. 4.99 (*0-06-107569-8*) HarpC.

***Mary-Kate & Ashley Switching Goals.** Mary-Kate Olsen & Ashley Olsen. 128p. (J). (gr. 3-7). 2000. 4.99 (*0-06-107603-1*, HarpEntertain) Morrow Avon.

Mary-Kate & Ashley's Adventure at Walt Disney World. Nancy E. Krulik. LC 98-84798. (Illus.). 64p. (J). (ps-3). 1998. 14.45 (*0-7868-3205-3*, Pub. by Hyperion) Time Warner.

***Mary-Kate & Ashley's Passport to Paris Scrapbook.** Mary-Kate Olsen & Ashley Olsen. (Illus.). 48p. (gr. 3-7). 2000. mass mkt. 7.95 (*0-06-107570-1*, HarpEntertain) Morrow Avon.

***Mary Kay.** 3rd ed. Mary Kay Ash. 224p. 2005. pap. 8.00 (*0-06-092601-5*) HarpC.

Mary Kay: Cosmetics Queen. Laurie E. Rozakis. LC 92-45124. (Made in America Ser.). 48p. (J). (gr. 4-8). 1993. lib. bdg. 21.27 (*0-86592-040-0*) Rourke Enter.

Mary Kay: You Can Have It All. Mary Kay Ash. 1996. 16.95 (*0-7615-0342-0*) Prima Pub.

Mary Kay: You Can Have It All. Mary Kay Ash. 272p. 1996. pap., per. 13.00 (*0-7615-0647-0*) Prima Pub.

Mary Kay: You Can Have It All: Practical Advice for Doing Well by Doing Good. Mary Kay Ash. LC 95-12582. 272p. 1995. 22.95 (*0-7615-0162-2*) Prima Pub.

Mary Kay - You Can Have It All: Lifetime Wisdom from America's Foremost Woman Entrepreneur. Mary Kay Ash. 258p. 1998. text 23.00 (*0-7881-5294-7*) DIANE Pub.

Mary Kay on People Management. Mary Kay Ash. LC 84-40254. 208p. 1985. mass mkt. 3.95 (*0-446-32974-6*, Pub. by Warner Bks) Little.

Mary Kelly. Margaret Iversen. (Illus.). 160p. 1997. pap. 29.95 (*0-7148-3661-3*, Pub. by Phaidon Press) Phaidon Pr.

Mary Kelly: Gloria Patri. Klaus Ottmann. (Illus.). 38p. (Orig.). (C). 1992. 12.00 (*0-929687-11-6*) E & C Zilkha Gal.

Mary Kelly: Interim. Marcia Tucker et al. (Illus.). 67p. 1990. pap. 18.00 (*0-915557-67-3*) New Mus Contemp Art.

***Mary, la Ostra Timida (Mary, the Shy Oyster) Cuentos Bilingues (Bilingual Stories)** Tito Alberto Brovelli. Tr. by Kirk Anderson. (ENG & SPA., Illus.). 24p. (J). (ps-6). 2000. 14.00 (*0-9673032-1-4*, Pub. by Sweet Dreams Bilingual Pubs) IPG Chicago.

Mary Lamb. Anne Gilchrist. LC 78-148784. reprint ed. 37.50 (*0-404-07348-4*) AMS Pr.

Mary Lavin. Zack R. Bowen. LC 73-126002. (Irish Writers Ser.). 77p. 1975. 8.50 (*0-8387-7762-7*); pap. 1.95 (*0-8387-7701-5*) Bucknell U Pr.

Mary Lavin: Quiet Rebel. A. A. Kelly. 200p. 1997. 12.95 (*0-905473-46-9*, Pub. by Wolfhound Press); pap. 11.95 (*0-86327-123-5*, Pub. by Wolfhound Press) Irish Amer Bk.

Mary Leapor: A Study in Eighteenth Century Women's Poetry. Richard Greene. LC 92-29386. (Oxford English Monographs). 256p. 1993. text 55.00 (*0-19-811988-7*, Clarendon Pr) OUP.

Mary Lee Settle. Hill. 1997. 22.95 (*0-8057-4592-0*, Twyne) Mac Lib Ref.

Mary Lee Settle's Beulah Quintet: The Price of Freedom. Brian Rosenberg. LC 85-23683. (Southern Literary Studies). 203p. 1991. 30.00 (*0-8071-1674-2*) La State U Pr.

***Mary Lewis: The Golden Haired Beauty with the Golden Voice.** Alice F. Zeman. Ed. by Gale Stewart. (Illus.). 270p. 1999. write for info. (*0-914546-99-6*) Rose Pub.

Mary Lincoln: Wife & Widow. Carl Sandburg. LC 94-43071. (Illus.). 160p. 1995. pap. 12.95 (*1-55709-248-6*) Applewood.

Mary Lincoln's Dressmaker: Elizabeth Keckley's Remarkable Rise from Slave to White House Confidante. Becky Rutberg. LC 94-45839. (Illus.). 176p. (YA). (gr. 5 up). 1995. 15.95 (*0-8027-8224-8*); lib. bdg. 16.85 (*0-8027-8225-6*) Walker & Co.

***Mary Lou Likes Blue.** Lyn Hester. (Illus.). 46p. 1998. pap. 10.95 (*0-9676006-1-8*) Mktg Dyn Inc.

***Mary Lou Retton's Gateways to Happiness: 7 Ways to a More Peaceful, More Accomplished, More Satisfying Life.** Mary Lou Retton. LC 99-86417. (Illus.). 288p. 2000. 22.95 (*0-7679-0439-7*) Broadway BDD.

***Mary Lou Retton's Gateways to Happiness: 7 Ways to a More Peaceful, More Prosperous, More Satisfying Life with Others, 8 vols.** Mary Lou Retton. 2000. 183.60 (*0-7679-9899-5*) Broadway BDD.

***Mary Lou Retton's Gateways to Happiness: 8 Ways to a More Peaceful, More Prosperous, More Satisfying Life with Others.** Mary Lou Retton & David Bender. 2000. 22.95 (*1-57856-347-X*) Waterbrook Pr.

Mary Louise. Lyle Stuart. 128p. 6.00 (*0-8065-0282-7*) Barricade Bks.

***Mary Louise Loses Her Manners.** Diane Cuneo. (Illus.). (J). 2000. pap. 6.99 (*0-440-41445-8*) Dell.

Mary Louise Loses Her Manners. Diane Cuneo. LC 97-27875. (Illus.). 32p. (J). 1999. 15.95 (*0-385-32538-X*) Doubleday.

Mary Lu Walker's Songs for Young Children. Mary L. Walker. LC 73-82640. (Illus.). 64p. (Orig.). 1973. pap. 5.95 (*0-8091-1779-7*) Paulist Pr.

***Mary Lucier.** Melinda Barlow. LC 99-87601. 2000. 45.00 (*0-8018-6379-1*) Johns Hopkins.

***Mary Lucier.** Ed. by Melinda Barlow. LC 99-87601. 2000. pap. 19.95 (*0-8018-6380-5*) Johns Hopkins.

Mary Lyon & the Mount Holyoke Missionaries. Amanda Porterfield. LC 96-45425. (Religion in America Ser.). (Illus.). 192p. (C). 1997. text 39.95 (*0-19-511301-2*) OUP.

Mary M. Ruprecht Speaks on End-User Computing. Ruprecht. (KU - Office Procedures Ser.). (C). 1991. 385.50 (*0-538-70785-2*) S-W Pub.

Mary Mack - A Paper Doll Circa, 1985: Color Decorate Authentic Fashions & Ethnic Costumes. Judith M. Hough. (Original Mary Mack Collection: No. 1). (Illus.). 26p. (J). (gr. 2-6). 1992. pap. 7.95 (*0-9633769-1-8*) Touch The Sky.

Mary MacKillop: An Extraordinary Australian. Paul Gardiner. 1994. pap. 15.95 (*0-85574-038-8*, Pub. by E J Dwyer) Morehouse Pub.

An Asterisk (*) at the beginning of an entry indicates that the title is appearing for the first time.

Mary Magdalen. Edgar E. Saltus. LC 78-116002. reprint ed. 37.50 (*0-404-05517-6*) AMS Pr.

Mary Magdalene: Beyond the Myth. Esther De Boer. Tr. by John Bowden from DUT. LC 97-27069. Orig. Title: Maria Magdalena: De Mythe Voorbij; Op Zoek Naar Wie Zij Werkelijkis. 176p. (Orig.). 1997. pap. 15.00 (*1-56338-212-1*) TPI PA.

Mary Magdalene: The Disciple Jesus Loved. Stuart Ledwith. Ed. by Kathlyn J. LC 90-91795. (Illus.). 122p. (Orig.). 1990. pap. 6.95 (*0-9627250-0-5*) Soul Works Intl.

Mary Magdalene: The Image of a Woman Through the Centuries. Ingrid Maisch. Tr. by Linda M. Maloney from ENG. LC 98-5542. 1998. 19.95 (*0-8146-2471-5*) Liturgical Pr.

Mary Magdalene & Her Seven Devils. Alvin B. Kuhn. 1994. pap. 5.95 (*1-55818-299-3*, Sure Fire) Holmes Pub.

Mary Magdalene & Many Others: Women Who Followed Jesus. Carla Ricci. 240p. 1994. pap. 20.00 (*0-8006-2718-0*, Fortress Pr) Augsburg Fortress.

Mary Magdalene & Many Others: Women Who Followed Jesus. Carla Ricci. 240p. 1994. pap. 40.00 (*0-86012-208-5*, Pub. by Srch Pr) St Mut.

Mary Magdelene: God's New Covenant Woman. Janice A. Duseau. 16p. (Orig.). 1989. pap. write for info. (*0-318-65835-6*) Word Power Pub.

Mary Manatee: A Tale of Sea Cows. Suzanne Tate. LC 90-60102. (Suzanne Tate's Nature Ser.: No. 7). (Illus.). 28p. (J). (gr. k-4). 1990. pap. 4.95 (*0-9616344-9-9*) Nags Head Art.

Mary Manatee, a Tale of Sea Cows. Suzanne Tate. LC 90-60102. 1990. 9.15 (*0-606-10325-2*, Pub. by Turtleback) Demco.

Mary Mapes Dodge. Susan R. Gannon & Ruth A. Thompson. LC 92-24231. (United States Authors Ser.). 170p. 1993. 32.00 (*0-8057-3956-4*, Twyne) Mac Lib Ref.

Mary Margaret's Tree. Blair Drawson. LC 96-3998. (Illus.). 40p. (J). (ps-2). 1996. 15.95 (*0-531-09521-5*); lib. bdg. 16.99 (*0-531-08871-5*) Orchard Bks Watts.

Mary-Maria-Matilda. Mary Wollstonecraft Shelley et al. Ed. & Intro. by Janet Todd. 256p. 1993. pap. 18.99 (*0-14-043371-6*, Penguin Classics) Viking Penguin.

Mary-Marie. Eleanor H. Porter. 1976. lib. bdg. 14.25 (*0-89968-102-6*, Lghtyr Pr) Buccaneer Bks.

Mary Marony & the Chocolate Surprise. Suzy Kline. LC 94-23600. (Illus.). 80p. (J). (gr. 1-4). 1995. 13.95 (*0-399-22829-2*, G P Putnam) Peng Put Young Read.

Mary Marony & the Chocolate Surprise. Suzy Kline. 1997. 9.19 (*0-606-11002-X*, Pub. by Turtleback) Demco.

Mary Marony Hides Out. Suzy Kline. 1996. 8.70 (*0-606-09594-2*, Pub. by Turtleback) Demco.

Mary Marony Mummy. Sims Kline. (J). 1996. pap. 4.99 (*0-440-91146-X*) BDD Bks Young Read.

Mary Marony, Mummy Girl. Suzy Kline. LC 93-14348. (Illus.). 80p. (J). (gr. 1-4). 1994. 13.95 (*0-399-22609-5*, G P Putnam) Peng Put Young Read.

Mary Marony, Mummy Girl. Suzy Kline. 1996. 9.19 (*0-606-09595-0*, Pub. by Turtleback) Demco.

Mary Marston. George MacDonald. (George MacDonald Original Works Ser.: Series VI). 355p. 1995. reprint ed. 22.00 (*1-881084-37-X*) Johannesen.

Mary Martin: A Bio-Bibliography, 18. Barry Rivadue. LC 91-16233. (Bio-Bibliographies in the Performing Arts Ser.: No. 18). 272p. 1991. lib. bdg. 49.95 (*0-313-27345-6*, RMF, Greenwood Pr) Greenwood.

Mary Martin: A Double Life - Australia-India, 1915-1973. Julie Lewis. LC 98-146131. 280p. 1997. pap. 29.95 (*0-7022-2725-0*, Pub. by Univ Queensland Pr) Intl Spec Bk.

Mary, Mary see Best American Plays: Fifth Series, 1958-1963

Mary, Mary. Jean Kerr. 1965. pap. 5.25 (*0-8222-0737-0*) Dramatists Play.

Mary, Mary. Ed McBain, pseud. 384p. 1994. mass mkt. 5.99 (*0-446-60054-7*, Pub. by Warner Bks) Little.

Mary, Mary Julie Parsons. LC 99-175779. viii, 376p. 1998. write for info. (*1-86059-080-2*, Pub. by Town Hse) Roberts Rinehart.

***Mary, Mary.** Julie Parsons & Simon & Schuster Staff. 448p. 2000. mass mkt. 6.99 (*0-06-103049-X*) HarpC.

Mary, Mary. James Stephens. LC 70-131839. 1970. reprint ed. 19.00 (*0-403-00726-7*) Scholarly.

Mary, Mary: A Novel. Julie Parsons. LC 98-33753. 304p. 1999. 22.50 (*0-684-85324-8*) S&S Trade.

Mary, Mary Quite Contrary. John G. Ervine. 96p. 1923. 8.95 (*0-910278-18-0*) Boulevard.

Mary McCarthy. Irvin Stock. LC 68-64755. (University of Minnesota Pamphlets on American Writers Ser.: No. 72). 47p. (Orig.). reprint ed. pap. 30.00 (*0-7837-2861-1*, 205759400006) Bks Demand.

Mary McCarthy: An Annotated Bibliography. Joy Bennett & Gabriella Hochmann. LC 91-47702. 464p. 1992. text 15.00 (*0-8240-7028-3*, H#1251) Garland.

Mary McCleod Bethune. Milton Meltzer. (Women of Our Time Ser.). (Illus.). (J). (gr. 2-6). 1988. pap. 3.50 (*0-317-69647-5*, PuffinBks) Peng Put Young Read.

Mary McGreevy. Walter Keady. 1999. pap. 13.00 (*1-878448-93-5*) MacMurray & Beck.

Mary McLean & the St. Patrick's Day Parade. Steven Kroll. (Illus.). 32p. (J). (ps-3). 1991. 15.95 (*0-590-43701-1*, Scholastic Hardcover) Scholastic Inc.

Mary McLean & the St. Patrick's Day Parade. Steven Kroll. (J). 1991. 9.15 (*0-606-05454-5*, Pub. by Turtleback) Demco.

Mary McLeod Bethune see Read-&-Discover Photo-Illustrated Biographies Series

Mary McLeod Bethune. Eloise Greenfield. LC 76-11522. (Trophy Nonfiction Bk.). (Illus.). 40p. (J). (gr. k-4). 1994. pap. 6.95 (*0-06-446168-8*, HarpTrophy) HarpC Child Bks.

Mary McLeod Bethune. Eloise Greenfield. LC 79-11522. 1977. 11.15 (*0-606-06559-8*, Pub. by Turtleback) Demco.

***Mary McLeod Bethune.** Amy R. Jones. LC 99-45336. (J). 2000. lib. bdg. write for info. (*1-56766-722-8*) Childs World.

Mary McLeod Bethune. Ed. by Puffin Books Staff. (Women of Our Time Ser.). (J). (gr. 2-6). 1989. pap. 3.50 (*0-14-042219-6*, PuffinBks) Peng Put Young Read.

Mary McLeod Bethune: A Great Teacher. Patricia McKissack & Fredrick McKissack. LC 91-8818. (Great African Americans Ser.). (Illus.). 32p. (J). (gr. 1-4). 1991. lib. bdg. 14.95 (*0-89490-304-7*) Enslow Pubs.

***Mary McLeod Bethune: Building A Better World.** Audrey Thomas McCluskey. LC 99-43292. 1999. 39.95 (*0-253-33626-0*) Ind U Pr.

Mary McLeod Bethune: Educator. Malu Halasa. Ed. by Nathan I. Huggins. (Black Americans of Achievement Ser.). (Illus.). 124p. (YA). (gr. 5 up). 1989. lib. bdg. 19.95 (*1-55546-574-9*) Chelsea Hse.

Mary McLeod Bethune: Educator. Malu Halasa. Ed. by Nathan I. Huggins. (Black Americans of Achievement Ser.). (Illus.). 124p. (YA). (gr. 5 up). 1993. pap. 8.95 (*0-7910-0225-X*) Chelsea Hse.

Mary McLeod Bethune: Educator. Bernice A. Poole. (Black American Ser.). (Illus.). 208p. (Orig.). (YA). 1994. mass mkt. 3.95 (*0-87067-783-7*, Melrose Sq) Holloway.

Mary McLeod Bethune: Her Own Words of Inspiration. Florence J. Hicks. LC 75-18004. 96p. 1975. pap. 4.95 (*0-912444-00-2*) DARE Bks.

Mary McLeod Bethune: Teacher with a Dream see Discovery Biographies

Mary McLeod Bethune: Voice of Black Hope. Milton Meltzer. (Women of Our Time Ser.). (J). 1988. 10.19 (*0-606-03613-X*, Pub. by Turtleback) Demco.

Mary McLeod Bethune: Voice of Black Hope. Milton Meltzer. (Women of Our Time Ser.). (Illus.). 64p. (J). (gr. 2-6). 1988. reprint ed. pap. 4.99 (*0-14-032219-1*, PuffinBks) Peng Put Young Read.

Mary McLeod Bethune: We've Come This Far by Faith. AESOP Enterprises, Inc. Staff & Gwendolyn J. Crenshaw. (Heroes & Sheroes Ser.). 14p. (J). (gr. 3-12). 1991. pap. write for info. incl. audio (*1-880771-08-X*) AESOP Enter.

Mary McLeod Bethune Papers: The Bethune-Cookman College Collection, 1922-1955. Compiled by Randolph H. Boehm. LC 95-30841. (Black Studies Research Sources). (C). 1995. 1790.00 (*1-55655-554-7*) U Pubns Amer.

Mary Mcleod Bethune Papers: The Bethune Foundation Collection. Mary M. Bethune et al. LC 96-48361. 1996. 2620.00 (*1-55655-636-5*) U Pubns Amer.

Mary Meade's Country Cookbook: Traditional American Cooking. Ruth Ellen Church. 384p. 1998. pap. 14.95 (*0-88486-206-2*, Bristol Park Bks) Arrowood Pr.

Mary Meade's Magic Recipes for the Electric Blender. Ruth E. Church. LC 65-22932. 1952. 6.00 (*0-672-50745-5*, Bobbs) Macmillan.

Mary Mead's Country Cookbook. Ruth E. Church. 1993. 8.98 (*0-88365-816-X*) Galahad Bks.

***Mary Meditation, Vol. I.** Mary L. Hennessy. (Illus.). 24p. 1999. pap. 10.00 (*0-9676070-0-0*) Info Specialists.

Mary Mehan Awake. Jennifer Armstrong. LC 97-6465. 160p. (J). (gr. 5-9). 1997. 18.00 (*0-679-88276-6*, Pub. by Knopf Bks Yng Read) Random.

Mary Mehan Awake. Jennifer Armstrong. (J). (gr. 6-11). 1998. pap. 4.99 (*0-679-89265-6*, Pub. by Random Bks Yng Read) Random.

Mary Meigs Atwater Recipe Book for Weavers. 1969. 19.50 (*0-937512-01-X*) Wheelwright UT.

Mary Metzker's Cooking Plain & Fancy. Mary Metzker. Ed. by Charles AmBroc. (Illus.). 100p. (Orig.). 1988. pap. 8.95 (*0-317-91230-5*) Jam Prodns PA.

Mary, Michael, & Lucifer: Folk Catholicism in Central Mexico. John M. Ingham. LC 85-22703. (University of Texas at Austin, Institute of Latin American Studies: No. 69). (Illus.). 228p. reprint ed. pap. 70.70 (*0-608-20113-8*, 207138500011) Bks Demand.

Mary, Michael & Lucifer: Folk Catholicism in Central Mexico. John M. Ingham. (Latin American Monographs: No. 69). (Illus.). 228p. 1986. reprint ed. pap. 12.95 (*0-292-75110-9*) U of Tex Pr.

Mary Militant. Gene Detro. (Orig.). 1979. pap. 3.00 (*0-914974-24-6*) Holmgangers.

Mary Miracle see Milagro de Maria

Mary Miraculous: Extraordinary Stories of Ordinary People Touched by Our Lady. Tom Sheridan. 1998. pap. text 8.95 (*0-87946-176-4*) ACTA Pubns.

Mary, Mirror of the Church. Raniero Cantalamessa. Tr. by Frances L. Villa. 216p. (Orig.). 1992. pap. 11.95 (*0-8146-2059-0*) Liturgical Pr.

Mary Miss. Christian Zapatka. (Illus.). 96p. 1997. pap. 29.95 (*0-8230-3010-5*, Whitney Lib) Watsn-Guptill.

Mary Miss: Photo - Drawings. Nancy Princenthal. (Illus.). 68p. (C). 1991. pap. text 25.00 (*0-941972-12-7*) Freedman.

Mary Miss Photo/Drawings. I. Michael Danoff & M. Jessica Rowe. (Illus.). 31p. 1996. pap. 15.00 (*1-879003-15-5*) Edmundson.

Mary Moody Emerson & the Origins of Transcentalism: A Family History. Phyllis Cole. LC 97-1413. (Illus.). 400p. (C). 1998. 45.00 (*0-19-503949-1*) OUP.

***Mary Moon Is Missing.** Patricia Reilly Giff. (Adventures of Minnie & Max Ser.: Vol. 2). (Illus.). 80p. (J). (gr. 2-6). 2000. pap. 3.99 (*0-14-130823-0*, PuffinBks) Peng Put Young Read.

Mary Moon Is Missing. Patricia Reilly Giff. LC 98-15554. (Ballet Slippers Ser.: Vol. 2). (Illus.). 74p. (J). (gr. 2-6). 1998. 13.99 (*0-670-88182-1*, Viking) Viking Penguin.

***Mary Moon is Missing.** Patricia Reilly Giff. (Adventures of Minnie & Max Ser.). (Illus.). (J). 2000. 9.34 (*0-606-18385-X*) Turtleback.

Mary Morgan - Tarzanne - Frida & Diego: Three Plays. Greg Cullen. 180p. 1998. pap. 21.95 (*1-85411-223-6*) Seren Bks.

Mary Moses' Statement. William C. Brown et al. (Illus.). 70p. 1990. 17.95 (*0-87770-453-8*) Ye Galleon.

***Mary, Mother of All Nations.** Megan McKenna. (Illus.). 144p. 2000. pap. 20.00 (*1-57075-325-3*) Orbis Bks.

Mary, Mother of God, Mother of the Poor. Ivone Gebara & Maria C. Bingemer. 208p. 1994. pap. 27.00 (*0-86012-166-6*, Pub. by Srch Pr) St Mut.

Mary, Mother of Jesus. Mary Joslin. LC 99-207846. (Illus.). (J). (ps up). 1999. 15.95 (*0-8294-1380-4*) Loyola Pr.

***Mary, Mother of Jesus.** Ellyn Sanna. (Young Reader's Christian Library). (Illus.). 224p. (J). (ps-3). 1999. pap. 1.39 (*1-57748-653-6*) Barbour Pub.

Mary, Mother of My Lord. Christine Granger. (Illus.). 64p. (Orig.). (J). 1996. text 11.95 (*0-8146-2466-9*, Liturg Pr Bks) Liturgical Pr.

Mary, Mother of the Church: What Recent Popes Have Said about the Blessed Mother's Role in the Church. Francis J. Ripley. 1987. reprint ed. pap. 4.00 (*0-89555-094-6*) TAN Bks Pubs.

Mary, Mother of the Redeemer. Juan L. Bastero. 272p. 1999. pap. 39.50 (*1-85182-263-1*, Pub. by Four Cts Pr) Intl Spec Bk.

Mary, Mother or Sorrows, Mother of Defiance. Peter Daino. LC 92-34370. (Illus.). 102p. reprint ed. pap. 31.70 (*0-608-20200-2*, 207145900012) Bks Demand.

Mary Mulari Appliques with Style: Designs & Techniques with Fresh Attitude. Mary Mulari. LC 98-85566. (Illus.). 144p. 1998. pap. 15.95 (*0-87341-683-X*, MEAC) Krause Pubns.

Mary My Hope. large type ed. Lawrence G. Lovasik. (Illus.). 1977. 7.75 (*0-89942-364-7*, 365/00) Catholic Bk Pub.

Mary, My Mother. rev. ed. Lawrence G. Lovasik. (Saint Joseph Picture Bks.). (Illus.). 1978. pap. 1.25 (*0-89942-280-2*, 280-00) Catholic Bk Pub.

Mary Myth: On the Femininity of God. Andrew M. Greeley. 240p. 1984. 10.45 (*0-8164-0333-3*) Harper SF.

Mary N. Murfree. Richard Cary. LC 67-24762. (Twayne's United States Authors Ser.). 1967. pap. 20.95 (*0-89197-990-5*); lib. bdg. 20.95 (*0-89197-839-9*) Irvington.

Mary Neufeld & the Repphun Story: From the Molotschna to Manitoba. Herman A. Neufeld. LC 88-70276. (Illus.). 240p. 1988. 16.75 (*0-945608-07-1*) C Joyce Gall.

Mary Newcomb. Contrib. by Christopher Andreae. (Illus.). 200p. 1996. 80.00 (*0-85331-695-3*, Pub. by Lund Humphries) Antique Collect.

Mary Norton. Jon C. Stott. LC 93-27319. (Twayne's English Authors Ser.: No. 508). 158p. 1994. 22.95 (*0-8057-7054-2*, Twyne) Mac Lib Ref.

Mary of Galilee. Frances Woodard. LC 98-40275. 168p. 1998. pap. 14.95 (*1-885373-23-6*) Emerald Ink.

Mary of Galilee: The Marian Heritage of the Early Church. Bertrand Buby. (Trilogy of Marian Studies: Vol. 3). 346p. (Orig.). 1996. pap. 19.95 (*0-8189-0698-7*) Alba.

Mary of Galilee Vol. 1: Mary in the New Testament. Bertrand Buby. LC 94-10788. (Mary of Galilee Ser.). 193p. 1994. pap. 11.95 (*0-8189-0692-8*) Alba.

Mary of Galilee Vol. 2: Woman of Israel Daughter of Zion. Bertrand Buby. 318p. 1995. 17.95 (*0-8189-0697-9*) Alba.

Mary of Galilee Vol. 3: The Marian Heritage of the Early Church. Bertrand Buby. 346p. 1997. 39.95 (*0-8189-0699-5*) Alba.

Mary of Magdala: Apostle & Leader. Mary R. Thompson. LC 95-13887. 160p. (Orig.). 1995. pap. 12.95 (*0-8091-3573-6*) Paulist Pr.

Mary of Migdal. Madeline Tiger. Ed. by Shirley Warren. (Illus.). 44p. 1991. pap. 6.00 (*1-877801-13-5*) Still Waters.

Mary of Mile 18. Ann Blades. LC 74-179430. (Illus.). 40p. (J). (gr. 1-4). 1996. reprint ed. pap. 8.95 (*0-88776-059-7*) Tundra Bks.

Mary of Nazareth. Kenneth Howell. 160p. 1998. pap. 7.95 (*1-57918-061-2*, 3761) Queenship Pub.

Mary of Nazareth: A Dramatic Monologue for Lent or Easter. Lynda Pujado. 20p. (Orig.). 1995. pap. 4.50 (*0-7880-0332-1*) CSS OH.

Mary of Nazareth & the Hidden Life of Jesus. Eugene Kevane. 47p. 1989. 1.00 (*0-911988-92-0*, 38607) AMI Pr.

Mary of Nemmegen. Margaret M. Raferty. (Medieval & Renaissance Texts Ser.: No. 5). 85p. 1991. 42.00 (*90-04-09252-8*) Brill Academic Pubs.

Mary of Nimmegen: A Facsimile Reproduction of the Copy of the English Version in the Huntington Library. Harry M. Ayres. LC 32-31585. (Huntington Library Publications). 80p. reprint ed. pap. 30.00 (*0-608-14000-7*, 205554000028) Bks Demand.

***Mary of Plymouth.** James Otis. (Illus.). 160p. (YA). 1999. 10.00 (*1-889128-60-0*) Mantle Ministries.

Mary of Plymouth: A Story of the Pilgrim Settlement. James Otis. LC 97-71254. (Illus.). 178p. (J). (gr. 3-6). 1997. reprint ed. 14.95 (*0-9652735-9-8*) Lost Classics.

Mary of Scotland see Four Verse Plays

Mary of the Americas: Our Lady of Guadalupe. Christopher Rengers. LC 88-8155. 154p. (Orig.). 1988. pap. 8.95 (*0-8189-0543-3*) Alba.

***Mary on Horseback.** Rosemary Wells. (Illus.). (J). 1999. 16.99 (*0-670-88923-7*, Viking Child) Peng Put Young Read.

***Mary on Horseback.** Rosemary Wells. (Illus.). 64p. (J). (gr. 3-7). 2000. pap. 4.99 (*0-14-130815-X*, PuffinBks) Peng Put Young Read.

Mary Our Hope. John Wright. LC 84-80015. 227p. (Orig.). 1984. pap. 4.95 (*0-89870-046-9*) Ignatius Pr.

Mary Parker Follett-Prophet of Management: A Celebration of Writings from the 1920s. Ed. by Pauline Graham. 336p. 1995. 29.95 (*0-87584-563-0*) Harvard Busn.

Mary Parker Follett-Prophet of Management: A Celebration of Writings from the 1920s. Ed. by Pauline Graham. 336p. 1996. pap. 16.95 (*0-87584-736-6*) Harvard Busn.

Mary Parket Follet - Profit of Management: A Celebration of Writings from the 1920s. Harvard Business Review Staff. 352p. 1994. 14.95 (*0-07-103605-9*) McGraw.

Mary Parket Follet - Profit of Management: A Celebration of Writings from the 1920s. Harvard Business School Press Staff. 336p. 1996. pap. write for info. (*0-07-103846-9*) McGraw.

Mary Patten's Voyage. Richard Berleth. Ed. by Judith Mathews. LC 93-45919. (Illus.). 40p. (J). (gr. 3-6). 1994. lib. bdg. 14.95 (*0-8075-4987-8*) A Whitman.

Mary Pickford Rediscovered: Rare Pictures of a Hollywood Legend. Kevin Brownlow & Robert Cushman. LC 98-41302. (Illus.). 256p. 1999. 39.95 (*0-8109-4374-3*, Pub. by Abrams) Time Warner.

Mary Play: From the N. Town Manuscript. Peter Meredith. (Exeter Medieval English Texts & Studies Ser.). 196p. 1997. pap. 19.95 (*0-85989-547-5*, Pub. by Univ Exeter Pr) Northwestern U Pr.

M

Mary Poppins. Pamela L. Travers. LC 97-223987. (Illus.). (J). 1997. 18.00 (*0-15-252595-5*, Harcourt Child Bks) Harcourt.

Mary Poppins. Pamela L. Travers. 202p. (J). (gr. 3-5). pap. 6.00 (*0-8072-1536-8*) Listening Lib.

Mary Poppins. Pamela L. Travers. 1997. 11.35 (*0-606-12418-7*) Turtleback.

Mary Poppins. Pamela L. Travers. (J). (gr. 4-7). 1981. reprint ed. lib. bdg. 27.95 (*0-89966-390-7*) Buccaneer Bks.

Mary Poppins. rev. ed. Pamela L. Travers. LC 81-7273. (Illus.). 206p. 1981. 14.95 (*0-15-252408-8*) Harcourt.

Mary Poppins. 2nd ed. Pamela L. Travers. LC 97-223987. (Illus.). (J). 1997. pap. 6.00 (*0-15-201717-8*, Harcourt Child Bks) Harcourt.

Mary Poppins Comes Back. Pamela L. Travers. LC 74-17258. (Illus.). (J). 1997. pap. 6.00 (*0-15-201719-4*, Harcourt Child Bks) Harcourt.

Mary Poppins Comes Back. Pamela L. Travers. LC 97-223090. (Illus.). (J). (gr. 3-7). 1997. 18.00 (*0-15-201718-6*) Harcourt.

Mary Poppins Comes Back. Pamela L. Travers. (J). 1981. reprint ed. lib. bdg. 27.95 (*0-89966-392-3*) Buccaneer Bks.

Mary Poppins from A to Z. Pamela L. Travers. LC 62-15629. (Illus.). 56p. (J). (gr. 1-4). 1962. 10.95 (*0-15-252590-4*, Harcourt Child Bks) Harcourt.

Mary Poppins in Cherry Tree Lane. Pamela L. Travers. (J). 1982. 10.95 (*0-440-05137-1*) Delacorte.

Mary Poppins in the Kitchen: A Cookery Book with a Story. Pamela L. Travers & Maurice Moore-Betty. LC 75-10131. (Illus.). 128p. (J). (gr. k up). 1975. 6.95 (*0-15-252898-9*, Harcourt Child Bks) Harcourt.

Mary Poppins in the Park. Pamela L. Travers. LC 90-45523. (Illus.). 265 p. (J). 1952. 11.95 (*0-15-252947-0*, Harcourt Child Bks) Harcourt.

Mary Poppins in the Park. Pamela L. Travers. LC 75-30526. (Illus.). (J). (gr. 3-7). 1997. 18.00 (*0-15-201716-X*) Harcourt.

Mary Poppins in the Park. 2nd ed. Pamela L. Travers. LC 75-30526. (Illus.). (J). (gr. 3-7). 1997. pap. 6.00 (*0-15-201721-6*) Harcourt.

Mary Poppins Opens the Door. Pamela L. Travers. LC 75-30697. (Illus.). (J). (gr. 3-7). 1997. 18.00 (*0-15-201720-8*) Harcourt.

Mary Poppins Opens the Door. Pamela L. Travers. (J). 1981. reprint ed. lib. bdg. 27.95 (*0-89966-391-5*) Buccaneer Bks.

Mary Poppins Opens the Door. 2nd ed. Pamela L. Travers. LC 75-30697. (Illus.). (J). (gr. 3-7). 1997. pap. 6.00 (*0-15-201722-4*) Harcourt.

Mary Poppins Vocal Selections. Sherman. 44p. 1985. pap. 9.95 (*0-88188-603-3*, 00360439) H Leonard.

***Mary Potter: A Life of Painting.** Julian Potter & Mary Potter. LC 98-71509. 128p. 1998. 26.95 (*1-84014-640-0*, Pub. by Ashgate Pub) Ashgate Pub Co.

Mary, Prophetess & Model of Freedom of Responsibility. Virgilio P. Elizondo. 18p. 1983. write for info. (*0-614-04874-5*) Mex Am Cult.

Mary Queen of Scotland & the Isles: A Novel. 4th ed. Margaret George. 1997. pap. 15.95 (*0-312-15585-9*, St Martin Griffin) St Martin.

Mary Queen of Scots. (Scotland in Words & Pictures Ser.). (Illus.). 32p. 3.95 (*0-7117-0147-4*, Pub. by JARR UK) Seven Hills Bk.

Mary Queen of Scots. Ian B. Cowan. 31p. 1986. 30.00 (*0-85411-037-2*, Pub. by Saltire Soc) St Mut.

Mary, Queen of Scots. Antonia Fraser. 640p. 1993. pap. 18.95 (*0-385-31129-X*, Delta Trade) Dell.

Mary, Queen of Scots. Illus. by Rebecca Fraser. (C). 1990. 50.00 (*0-413-48550-1*, Pub. by Greville Pr) St Mut.

Mary Queen of Scots. Ed. by Tricia Hedge. (Illus.). 48p. 1993. pap. text 5.95 (*0-19-422703-0*) OUP.

Mary, Queen of Scots. Sally Stepanek. (World Leaders Past & Present Ser.). (Illus.). 120p. (YA). (gr. 5 up). 1987. lib. bdg. 19.95 (*0-87754-540-5*) Chelsea Hse.

Mary Queen of Scots: A Study in Failure. Jenny Wormald. pap. 14.95 (*1-86064-588-7*, Pub. by I B T) St Martin.

Mary Queen of Scots: Her Environment & Tragedy, 2 Vols, Set. Thomas F. Henderson. LC 68-25241. (English Biography Ser.: No. 31). 1969. reprint ed. lib. bdg. 150.00 (*0-8383-0163-0*) M S G Haskell Hse.

Mary Queen of Scots: Romance & Nation. Jayne E. Lewis. LC 98-17140. (Illus.). 256p. (C). 1998. 85.00 (*0-415-11480-2*); pap. 20.99 (*0-415-11481-0*) Routledge.

Mary Queen of Scots in Nineteenth & Twentieth Century Drama: Poetic License with History. Pearl J. Brandwein. (American University Studies: General Literature: Ser. XIX, Vol. 13). XXII, 268p. (C). 1989. text 42.95 (*0-8204-0628-7*) P Lang Pubng.

Mary, Queen of the Poor. Barnabas Ahern. (Queen of Apostles Ser.: Vol. VII). 19p. 1994. 0.65 (*0-911988-97-1*, 49736) AMI Pr.

*__Mary Quequesah's Love Story: A Pend D'Oreille Indian Tale.__ Pete Beaverhead et al. LC 00-24101. 2000. pap. write for info. (*0-917298-71-3*) MT Hist Soc.

Mary Reilly. Valerie Martin. 1994. pap. 10.00 (*0-671-50702-8*, WSP) PB.

Mary Reilly. Valerie Martin. 1996. mass mkt. 5.99 (*0-671-52113-6*) PB.

Mary Remembers. Mary C. Goni. 224p. 1990. text. write for info. (*0-9628340-0-9*) M C J Goni.

Mary Renault. Peter Wolfe. LC 70-98029. (Twayne's English Authors Ser.). 1969. lib. bdg. 20.95 (*0-8057-1458-8*) Irvington.

Mary Renault: A Biography. David Sweetman. LC 93-16391. 1993. 24.95 (*0-15-193110-0*) Harcourt.

Mary Ritter Beard: A Sourcebook. Ed. by Ann J. Lane. LC 99-13674. 272p. 2000. pap. 19.95 (*1-55861-219-X*, Pub. by Feminist Pr) Consort Bk Sales.

Mary Roberts Rinehardt. Mary Roberts Rinehart. 1995. pap. 13.00 (*1-57566-114-4*) Kensgtn Pub Corp.

Mary Roberts Rinehart: Mistress of Mystery. Frances H. Bachelder. LC 93-342. (Brownstone Mystery Guides Ser.: No. 15). 120p. 1993. pap. 17.00 (*0-8095-5175-6*) Millefleurs.

Mary Robinson: A Woman of Ireland & the World. John Horgan. (Illus.). 224p. 1998. 22.95 (*1-57098-200-7*) Roberts Rinehart.

*__Mary Robinson: Ireland's Citizen of the World.__ Gerald Colman Jones. (Contemporary Profiles & Policy Series for the Younger Reader). (YA). (gr. 8 up). 2000. write for info. (*0-934272-63-8*); pap. write for info. (*0-934272-64-6*) J G Burke Pub.

*__Mary Robinson: Selected Poems.__ Mary Robinson. Ed. by Judith Pascoe. 1999. text 24.95 (*1-55111-317-1*) Broadview.

Mary Robinson: Selected Poems. Mary Robinson. Ed. by Judith Pascoe. (Literary Texts Ser.). 450p. 1999. pap. 12.95 (*1-55111-201-9*) Broadview Pr.

Mary Rose & Other Plays see Works of J. M. Barrie: Peter Pan Edition

Mary Rose Museum. Christopher Alexander et al. LC 93-18221. (Illus.). 128p. 1995. 35.00 (*0-19-521017-4*) OUP.

Mary Sans Femme. Montfleury. Ed. by Forman. (Exeter French Texts Ser.: Vol. 59). (FRE.). 154p. Date not set. pap. text 19.95 (*0-85989-212-3*, Pub. by Univ Exeter Pr) Northwestern U Pr.

*__Mary Sarton: A Biography.__ 2nd ed. Lenora P. Blouin. LC 99-87233. (Scarecrow Author Bibliography Ser.: No. 104). (Illus.). 448p. 2000. 85.00 (*0-8108-3687-4*) Scarecrow.

Mary Schafer & Her Quilts. Gwen Marston & Joe Cunningham. Ed. by Ruth D. Fitzgerald & Sue Caltrider. (Illus.). 64p. (Orig.). 1990. pap. 19.95 (*0-944311-04-0*) MSU Museum.

Mary Shaw: Actress, Suffragist, Activist (1854-1929) John D. Irving. 1981. 27.95 (*0-405-14089-4*) Ayer.

Mary Shelley. Richard W. Church. 1977. 13.95 (*0-8369-6925-1*, 7806) Ayer.

*__Mary Shelley.__ John Williams. LC 99-40596. (Literary Lives Ser.). 210p. 2000. text 35.00 (*0-312-22832-5*) St Martin.

Mary Shelley. large type ed. Joanna M. Smith. 1996. 32.00 (*0-8057-7045-3*, Twayne) Mac Lib Ref.

Mary Shelley: A Biography. Rosalie G. Grylls. LC 76-95428. (English Biography Ser.: No. 31). 1969. reprint ed. lib. bdg. 75.00 (*0-8383-0978-X*) M S G Haskell Hse.

Mary Shelley: Collected Tales & Stories. Ed. by Charles E. Robinson. (Illus.). 399p. 1990. reprint ed. pap. text 19.95 (*0-8018-4062-7*) Johns Hopkins.

*__Mary Shelley: Frankenstein: Essays - Articles - Reviews.__ Ed. by Berthold Schoene-Harwood. 192p. 2000. text 39.50 (*0-231-12192-X*) Col U Pr.

Mary Shelley: Frankenstein's Creator - The First Science Fiction Writer. Joan K. Nichols. LC 98-27023. (Barnard Biography Ser.: No. 3). (Illus.). 150p. (YA). (gr. 8 up). 1998. pap. 6.95 (*1-57324-087-7*) Conari Press.

Mary Shelley: Her Life, Her Fiction, Her Monsters. Anne K. Mellor. (Illus.). 350p. 1988. 35.00 (*0-415-02591-5*) Routledge.

Mary Shelley: Her Life, Her Fiction, Her Monsters. Anne K. Mellor. (Illus.). 350p. (C). 1989. pap. 23.99 (*0-415-90147-2*) Routledge.

Mary Shelley: Romance & Reality. Emily W. Sunstein. 478p. 1989. 24.95 (*0-685-26672-9*) Little.

Mary Shelley: Romance & Reality. Emily W. Sunstein. LC 90-23541. (Illus.). 478p. 1991. reprint ed. pap. 16.95 (*0-8018-4218-2*) Johns Hopkins.

Mary Shelley & Frankenstein: The Fate of Androgyny. William Veeder. LC 85-14141. 288p. 1997. pap. text 17.95 (*0-226-85226-1*) U Ch Pr.

Mary Shelley, Author of Frankenstein. Elizabeth Nitchie. LC 72-100233. 255p. 1970. reprint ed. lib. bdg. 59.50 (*0-8371-3689-X*, NIMS, Greenwood Pr) Greenwood.

*__Mary Shelley Encyclopedia.__ Paula R. Feldman et al. LC 99-462062. 552p. 2000. lib. bdg. 95.00 (*0-313-30159-X*, GR0159, Greenwood Pr) Greenwood.

*__Mary Shelley, Frankenstein.__ Berthold Schoene. LC 00-26252. (Critical Guides Ser.). 2000. pap. 14.50 (*0-231-12193-8*) Col U Pr.

Mary Shelley Reader. Mary Wollstonecraft Shelley. Ed. by Betty T. Bennett & Charles E. Robinson. (Illus.). 450p. (C). 1990. pap. text 27.95 (*0-19-506259-0*) OUP.

Mary Shelley's Early Novels: This Child of Imagination & Misery. Jane Blumberg. LC 92-61803. 269p. 1993. text 27.95 (*0-87745-397-7*) U of Iowa Pr.

*__Mary Shelley's Fictions: From Frankenstein to Falkner.__ Michael Eberle-Sinatra. LC 00-33266. 2000. write for info. (*0-312-23718-9*) St Martin.

Mary Shelley's Frankenstein see Bloom's Notes

Mary Shelley's Frankenstein: A Classic Tale of Terror Reborn on Film. Kenneth Branagh et al. LC 94-22945. (Illus.). 192p. 1995. 29.95 (*1-55704-207-1*, Pub. by Newmarket); pap. 17.95 (*1-55704-208-X*, Pub. by Newmarket) Norton.

Mary Shelley's Monster: The Story of Frankenstein Martin Tropp. LC 75-44041. xii, 192p. 1976. write for info. (*0-395-24066-2*) HM.

Mary Shelley's Plays & Her Translation of the Cenci Story: Bodleian MSS Shelley Adds, Nos. d.2 & e.13. Mary Wollstonecraft Shelley. Ed. by Charles E. Robinson & Betty T. Bennett. LC 92-23188. (Bodleian Shelley Manuscripts Ser.: Vol. 10). 282p. 1992. text 65.00 (*0-8240-6986-2*) Garland.

Mary Sidney, Countess of Pembroke (1561-1621) & Sir Philip Sidney: The Sidney Psalms. Ed. & Selected by R. E. Pritchard. pap. write for info. (*0-85635-983-1*, Pub. by Carcanet Pr) Paul & Co Pubs.

*__Mary Slessor.__ Janet Benge. 1999. pap. text 8.99 (*1-57658-148-9*) YWAM Pub.

Mary Slessor. Basil Miller. LC 85-71477. 144p. 1985. reprint ed. mass mkt. 4.99 (*0-87123-849-7*) Bethany Hse.

Mary Slessor: Queen of Calabar. Sam Wellman. LC 99-162995. (Heroes of the Faith Ser.). 208p. 1998. pap. 3.97 (*1-57748-178-X*) Barbour Pub.

Mary Slessor of Calabar. W. P. Livingstone. LC 83-9286. 352p. 1984. 7.95 (*0-310-27451-6*, 9286P) Zondervan.

Mary Somerville & the Cultivation of Science, 1815-1840. Elizabeth C. Patterson. (International Archives of the History of Ideas Ser.: No. 102). 278p. 1983. lib. bdg. 126.50 (*90-247-2823-1*) Kluwer Academic.

Mary Somerville & the Cultivation of Science, 1815-1848. Elizabeth C. Patterson. 1983. lib. bdg. 39.50 (*90-247-2433-3*) Kluwer Academic.

Mary, Star of the New Millennium: Guiding Us to Renewal. David E. Rosage. LC 96-52394. (Celebrate 2000! Ser.). 200p. (Orig.). 1997. pap. 10.99 (*0-89283-994-5*, Charis) Servant.

Mary Stewart. Lenemaja Friedman. (English Authors Ser.: No. 474). 1990. text 21.95 (*0-8057-6985-4*, Twayne) Mac Lib Ref.

Mary Stewart: Rotary Exchange Student to London. Rennie Mae M. Hickman. 54p. pap. write for info. (*1-878096-32-X*, Epigram Pr) Best E TX Pubs.

*__Mary Stewart Omnibus: Price of a Princess; Lord in Waiting.__ Mary Stewart. (Illus.). 1999. pap. 16.95 (*0-340-71755-6*, Pub. by Hodder & Stought Ltd) Trafalgar.

Mary Stewarts Merlin Tri. Mary Stewart. LC 80-21019. 919p. 1980. 20.95 (*0-688-00347-8*, Wm Morrow) Morrow Avon.

Mary Stocks, 1891-1975: An Uncommonplace Life. Barbara Hooper. LC 96-8818. (Illus.). 248p. 1996. 49.95 (*0-485-11507-7*, Pub. by Athlone Pr) Humanities.

Mary Stuart. Friedrich Schiller. Tr. by Joseph Mellish from GER. 105p. 1990. pap. 7.95 (*0-936839-00-7*) Applause Theatre Bk Pubs.

Mary Stuart. Friedrich Schiller. Tr. & Notes by F. J. Lamport. LC 99-179743. 150p. 1999. pap. 10.95 (*0-14-044711-3*) Viking Penguin.

Mary Stuart: A Queen Betrayed. Leonard M. Trawick. 77p. (Orig.). 1991. pap. 6.00 (*0-914946-92-7*) Cleveland St Univ Poetry Ctr.

Mary Stuart, a Romantic Drama. Juliusz Slowacki. Tr. by Arthur P. Coleman & Marion M. Coleman from POL. LC 74-11993. 106p. 1978. reprint ed. lib. bdg. 49.50 (*0-8371-7712-X*, SLMS, Greenwood Pr) Greenwood.

Mary Stuart's Ravishment Descending Time: Prose Symphony. Georgiana Peacher. LC 75-35307. 117p. 1992. reprint ed. pap. 9.00 (*0-916384-01-2*) P Shedding.

Mary Sue Extrusion, Vol. 1. Dave Stone. (New Adventures Ser.). 1999. mass mkt. 6.95 (*0-426-20531-6*) Virgin Pubng.

Mary Summer Rain's Guide to Dream Symbols. Mary S. Rain & Alex Greystone. 608p. 1997. pap. 18.95 (*1-57174-100-3*) Hampton Roads Pub Co.

Mary Surratt: An American Tragedy. Elizabeth S. Trindal & Mary E. Trindal. LC 95-500031. (Illus.). 304p. 1996. 26.95 (*1-56554-185-5*) Pelican.

Mary Swartz Rose, 1874-1941: Pioneer in Nutrition. Juanita Eagles et al. LC 79-4342. 192p. reprint ed. pap. 59.60 (*0-608-14935-7*, 202600800048) Bks Demand.

Mary the Blessed Virgin of Islam. Aliah Schleifer. Ed. by Gray Heny. 160p. 1998. pap. 15.95 (*1-887752-02-1*) Fons Vitae.

Mary the Lamb Gets Lost. Thorpe Hunt. (J). 1998. 6.99 (*1-85608-285-7*, Pub. by Hunt GBR) Assoc Pubs Grp.

Mary, the Mother of God. Victor Hoagland. 1999. 8.95 (*0-88271-624-7*) Regina Pr.

Mary the Mother of Jesus. Lamberto Schiatti & Simona Cillario. (Illus.). 64p. 1996. pap. 39.95 (*0-85439-448-6*, Pub. by St Paul Pubns) St Mut.

Mary, the Mother of Jesus: God's Woman of Obedience. Janice A. Duseau. 16p. (Orig.). 1989. pap. write for info. (*0-318-65836-4*) Word Power Pub.

*__Mary, the Mouse & the Coal Mine.__ Illus. by Marrin Southcott & Thom Laz. 64p. (J). (gr. 2-4). 1999. 6.95 (*0-9651689-2-1*) K F Gross.

Mary, the Perfect Prayer Partner. Kenneth J. Roberts. Ed. by Anna M. Waters. LC 83-61151. (Illus.). 128p. (Orig.). 1983. pap. 3.95 (*0-9610984-1-4*) PAX Tapes.

Mary the Second Eve. John Henry Newman. 40p. 1991. reprint ed. pap. 3.00 (*0-89555-181-0*) TAN Bks Pubs.

Mary II, Queen of England. Hester W. Chapman. LC 75-17197. 279p. 1976. reprint ed. lib. bdg. 59.75 (*0-8371-8302-2*, CHMQ, Greenwood Pr) Greenwood.

Mary Thomas's Book of Knitting Patterns. Mary Thomas. (Illus.). 329p. 1972. reprint ed. pap. 7.95 (*0-486-22818-5*) Dover.

Mary Thomas's Embroidery Book. Mary Thomas. (Illus.). 304p. 1983. pap. 7.95 (*0-486-24530-6*) Dover.

Mary Thomas's Knitting Book. Mary Thomas. (Illus.). 256p. (YA). (gr. 6-12). 1972. reprint ed. pap. 6.95 (*0-486-22817-7*) Dover.

Mary Through the Centuries: Her Place in the History of Culture. Jaroslav J. Pelikan. LC 96-24726. (Illus.). 240p. 1998. 30.00 (*0-300-06951-0*); pap. 14.00 (*0-300-07661-4*) Yale U Pr.

Mary Todd Lincoln. Jean Baker. Date not set. reprint ed. pap. write for info. (*0-393-31599-1*) Norton.

Mary Todd Lincoln: A Biography. Jean H. Baker. LC 86-23757. (Illus.). 500p. 1989. pap. 17.95 (*0-393-30586-4*) Norton.

Mary Todd Lincoln: President's Wife see Discovery Biographies

Mary Todd Lincoln: Tragic First Lady of the Civil War. Mary E. Hull. LC 99-20080. (Historical American Biographies Ser.). (Illus.). 128p. (gr. 6 up). 2000. lib. bdg. 20.95 (*0-7660-1252-2*) Enslow Pubs.

Mary Todd Lincoln, Girl of the Bluegrass. Katharine E. Wilkie. LC 92-9782. (Childhood of Famous Americans Ser.). (Illus.). 192p. (J). (gr. 3-7). 1992. mass mkt. 4.95 (*0-689-71655-9*) Aladdin.

Mary Todd Lincoln, Girl of the Bluegrass. Katharine Elliott Wilkie. (Childhood of Famous Americans Ser.). (J). 1992. 10.34 (*0-606-07846-0*) Turtleback.

Mary Todd Lincoln, 1818-1882. Dan Santow. LC 98-45254. (Encyclopedia of First Ladies Ser.). 112p. (J). 1999. 32.00 (*0-516-20481-5*) Childrens.

Mary Told the Good News. John D. Horman. 1.25 (*0-687-07225-5*) Abingdon.

Mary Tyler Moore. Sylvia Stoddard. 1996. mass mkt. 5.99 (*0-312-95945-1*) St Martin.

Mary Tyler Moore: The Award-Winning Actress Who Has Diabetes. Intro. by Jerry Lewis. (Great Achievers Ser.). (Illus.). 120p. (YA). (gr. 5 up). 1996. lib. bdg. 19.95 (*0-7910-2416-4*) Chelsea Hse.

Mary Veronica's Egg. Mary Nethery. LC 98-35723. (Illus.). 32p. (J). (ps-2). 1999. 15.95 (*0-531-30134-6*); lib. bdg. 16.99 (*0-531-33134-2*) Orchard Bks Watts.

Mary-Verse in "Meistergesang" M. J. Schroeder. (Catholic University Studies in German: No. 16). 1970. reprint ed. 37.50 (*0-404-50236-9*) AMS Pr.

Mary-Verse of the Teutonic Knights. M. E. Goenner. LC 72-140022. (Catholic University of America. Studies in Romance Languages & Literatures: No. 19). reprint ed. 37.50 (*0-404-50239-3*) AMS Pr.

Mary Wanna Student Activity Book. Bill Moran. (Illus.). 23p. (J). (gr. 4-6). 1989. pap. 2.50 (*0-942493-10-9*) Woodmere Press.

Mary Wanna Student Activity Book: Based Upon: The Sad Story of Mary Wanna Or How Marijuana Harms You. rev. ed. Bill Moran & Peggy Mann. (Illus.). 26p. (J). (gr. 4-6). 1990. pap. text 2.95 (*0-942493-11-7*) Woodmere Press.

Mary Wanna Teacher's Guide. Peggy Mann. 20p. (gr. 3-6). 1989. pap. 4.50 (*0-318-50074-4*) Woodmere Press.

Mary Ward. Henrietta Peters. 658p. 1995. 40.00 (*0-85244-268-8*, 948, Pub. by Gracewing) Morehouse Pub.

Mary Ware in Texas. Mary F. Ware. 1982. 16.95 (*0-89201-040-1*) Zenger Pub.

Mary Ware's Promised Land. Mary F. Ware. 1982. 16.95 (*0-89201-041-X*) Zenger Pub.

Mary, Wayfarer. Mary E. Mebane. LC 98-46858. (Chapel Hill Book Ser.). 230p. 1999. pap. 17.95 (*0-8078-4822-0*) U of NC Pr.

Mary, We Never Knew You. James B. Ganong. 246p. (Orig.). 1982. pap. 6.50 (*0-9608620-0-5*) K Pillman.

Mary Webb. Gladys M. Coles. 160p. 1990. pap. 17.95 (*1-85411-035-7*) Dufour.

Mary Webb. Gladys M. Coles. 160p. 1990. 27.00 (*1-85411-034-9*, Pub. by Seren Bks) Dufour.

*__Mary Wells.__ James A. Franks. 1999. pap. 12.95 (*0-9657173-3-X*) Wld Goose Pr.

Mary Whitcher's Shaker House-Keeper. fac. ed. 32p. (Orig.). 1991. pap. 1.25 (*0-915836-18-1*) United Soc Shakers.

Mary Wilkins Freeman. Perry D. Westbrook. (Twayne's United States Authors Ser.). 1968. pap. 4.95 (*0-8290-0017-8*); lib. bdg. 20.95 (*0-89197-838-0*) Irvington.

Mary Wilkins Freeman. rev. ed. Perry D. Westbrook. (United States Authors Ser.: No. 122). 184p. 1988. 23.95 (*0-8057-7523-4*, Twayne) Mac Lib Ref.

Mary Wilkins Freeman: Great American Short Stories III. Illus. by James Balkovek. LC 95-76751. (Classic Short Stories Ser.). 80p. (YA). (gr. 6-12). 1995. pap. 5.95 (*0-7854-0626-3*, 40087) Am Guidance.

Mary Wilkins Freeman Reader. Mary E. Wilkins Freeman. Ed. & Intro. by Mary R. Reichardt. LC 96-20358. xxi, 428p. 1997. text 65.00 (*0-8032-1998-9*); pap. text 27.50 (*0-8032-6894-7*) U of Nebr Pr.

Mary Will Not Watch Moon. Brooks. 32p. (ps-1). 14.95 (*0-06-024491-7*) HarpC.

Mary Will Not Watch the Moon. Brooks. 32p. (ps-1). lib. bdg. 14.89 (*0-06-024492-5*) HarpC.

Mary with Us: Readings & Prayers. Joseph A. Viano. LC 89-33524. 1989. pap. 4.95 (*0-8189-0559-X*) Alba.

Mary Wolf. Cynthia D. Grant. LC 95-2128. 176p. (YA). (gr. 7 up). 1995. 16.00 (*0-689-80007-X*) Atheneum Yung Read.

Mary Wolf. Cynthia D. Grant. 224p. (J). 1997. per. 4.50 (*0-689-81251-5*) S&S Childrens.

Mary Wolf. Cynthia D. Grant. LC 95-2128. (YA). 1997. 9.60 (*0-606-11600-1*, Pub. by Turtleback) Demco.

*__Mary Wollstone Godwin: A Bibliography.__ John Windle. LC 99-55165. (Illus.). 90p. 1999. 37.50 (*1-58456-015-0*) Oak Knoll.

Mary Wollstonecraft. Moira Ferguson & Janet M. Todd. LC 83-18342. (English Authors Ser.: No. 381). 176p. 1984. 22.95 (*0-8057-6867-X*, Twyne) Mac Lib Ref.

*__Mary Wollstonecraft.__ Jane Moore. (Writers & Their Works Ser.). 112p. 1999. pap. text 19.00 (*0-7463-0747-0*, Pub. by Northcote House) U Pr of Miss.

Mary Wollstonecraft. Henry R. James. LC 73-181004. (Studies in Women's Rights: No. 51). 180p. 1972. reprint ed. lib. bdg. 75.00 (*0-8383-1373-6*) M S G Haskell Hse.

*__Mary Wollstonecraft: A Revolutionary Life.__ Janet Todd. LC 00-27352. (Oxford Portraits Ser.). 2000. 29.95 (*0-231-12184-9*) Col U Pr.

Mary Wollstonecraft: A Study in Economics & Romance. George Taylor. LC 68-24924. (English Biography Ser.: No. 31). (Illus.). 1969. reprint ed. lib. bdg. 75.00 (*0-8383-0246-7*) M S G Haskell Hse.

Mary Wollstonecraft: A Study in Economics & Romance. George R. Taylor. (BCL1-PR English Literature Ser.). 209p. 1992. reprint ed. lib. bdg. 79.00 (*0-7812-7636-5*) Rprt Serv.

Mary Wollstonecraft: Writer. Jump. 192p. (C). 1995. pap. text 29.95 (*0-13-320656-4*) P-H.

Mary Wollstonecraft & Feminism. Eileen J. Yeo. 1997. pap. text 18.50 (*1-85489-061-1*) Rivers Oram.

Mary Wollstonecraft & Feminism. Eileen J. Yeo. LC 97-180713. 1997. pap. 55.00 (*1-85489-060-3*, Pub. by Rivers Oram) NYU Pr.

Mary Wollstonecraft & the Language of Sensibility. Syndy McMillen Conger. LC 93-33718. 1994. 39.50 (*0-8386-3553-9*) Fairleigh Dickinson.

*__Mary Wollstonecraft & the Rights of Women.__ Calvin C. Miller. LC 99-13519. (World Writers Ser.). (Illus.). 112p. (YA). (gr. 5 up). 1999. lib. bdg. 18.95 (*1-883846-41-2*) M Reynolds.

Mary Wollstonecraft Shelley see Modern Critical Views Series

Mary Wollstonecraft Shelley. Betty T. Bennett. 192p. 1998. pap. text 13.95 (*0-8018-5976-X*) Johns Hopkins.

Mary Wollstonecraft Shelley, 2 vols. Percy Bysshe Shelley. Ed. by Alan M. Weinberg & Donald H. Reiman. LC 97-2254. (Bodleian Shelley Manuscripts Ser.: Vol. 22). 792p. 1997. text 330.00 (*0-8153-1157-5*) Garland.

Mary Wollstonecraft Shelley: An Introduction. Betty T. Bennett. LC 98-16237. 192p. 1998. 38.00 (*0-8018-5975-1*) Johns Hopkins.

Mary Wollstonecraft Shelley's Frankenstein see Modern Critical Interpretations

Mary Wollstonecraft to William Godwin see Library of Literary Criticism

Mary Wondrausch on Slipware. Mary Wondrausch. 1986. 23.50 (*1-889250-08-2*) Gentle Br.

Mary Wore Her Red Dress. Merle Peek. (Carry-Along Book & Cassette Favorites Ser.). (Illus.). 1p. (J). (ps-1). 1993. bds. 9.95 incl. audio (*0-395-61577-1*, Clarion Bks) HM.

Mary Wore Her Red Dress & Henry Wore His Green Sneakers. Merle Peek. LC 84-12733. 32p. (J). (ps-3). 1988. pap. 5.95 (*0-89919-701-9*, Clarion Bks) HM.

Mary Wore Her Red Dress & Henry Wore His Green Sneakers. Merle Peek. LC 84-12733. (Illus.). 22p. (ps). 1998. bds. 5.95 (*0-395-90022-0*, Clarion Bks) HM.

Mary Wore Her Red Dress Big Book: Black & White Nellie Edge I Can Read & Sing Big Book. Illus. by Melissa Saylor. (J). (ps-2). 1988. pap. text 21.00 (*0-922053-17-0*) N Edge Res.

Mary y las Campanas. Pablo Neruda. (SPA.). 80p. 1976. pap. 19.95 (*0-7859-5003-6*) Fr & Eur.

*__Mary Yoder's Candy & Confection Cookbook: Recipes to Satisfy Your Sweet Tooth Plus a Dash of Memories.__ Mary Yoder. (Illus.). 127p. 1999. spiral bd. 9.95 (*1-890050-36-9*) Carlisle Press.

Marya: A Life. Joyce Carol Oates. 320p. 1998. pap. 12.95 (*0-452-28020-6*, Truman Talley) St Martin.

Maryann & Her Baby. Noura Durkee. (Illus.). 22p. (J). (gr. 1-5). 1999. 10.00 (*1-879402-60-2*) Tahrike Tarsile Quran.

Maryanne & Camp. Martin. 1995. pap. 7.98 (*1-57042-265-6*) Warner Bks.

Maryan's Personages. Ed. by Michele Vishny. (Illus.). 60p. (Orig.). (C). 1983. pap. 10.00 (*0-935982-20-5*, SMJ-08) Spertus Coll.

Marya's Emmets. Clare Cooper. 151p. (J). (gr. 4-8). 1996. pap. 14.95 (*0-8464-4632-4*) Beekman Pubs.

Marya's Emmets Clare Cooper. LC 97-202606. 152p. (YA). (gr. 5-8). 1996. write for info. (*1-85902-289-8*) Gomer Pr.

*__Maryat Lee's Ecotheater: A Theater for the Twenty-first Century.__ William French. LC 98-61607. 1998. write for info. (*0-937058-46-7*) West Va U Pr.

Maryborough, Queensland: Spirit of Place Album. Eve Buscombe. (Practising History Ser.: No. 3). (Illus.). 80p. 1992. 50.00 (*0-646-08237-X*, Pub. by Eureka Res); pap. 20.00 (*0-646-08238-8*, Pub. by Eureka Res) Continental Bk.

*__Marye's Heights: Fredericksburg.__ Victor D. Brooks. 2000. pap. 16.95 (*1-58097-036-2*, 970362) Combined Pub.

Maryfield U. S. A. A Success Story. Joe E. Brown. LC 97-70101. (Illus.). 168p. 1997. write for info. (*0-9656718-0-1*) Maryfield Nursing.

*__Maryhill Museum of Art.__ Linda Brady Tesner. LC 00-101311. (Illus.). 120p. 2000. pap. 14.95 (*0-9642006-2-7*) Arcus Pubg.

An Asterisk (*) at the beginning of an entry indicates that the title is appearing for the first time.

Maryknoll in China: A History, 1918-1955. Jean-Paul Wiest. LC 87-32068. 650p. (gr. 13). 1988. text 88.95 (*0-87332-418-8*) M E Sharpe.

Maryknoll in China: A History, 1918-1955. Jean-Paul Wiest. 615p. 1997. pap. 26.00 (*1-57075-142-0*) Orbis Bks.

Maryland see From Sea to Shining Sea

***Maryland.** (Switched on Schoolhouse Ser.). (Illus.). (J). 2000. pap. 24.95 (*0-7403-0272-8*) Alpha AZ.

Maryland. Michael Burgan. LC 98-42164. (America the Beautiful Ser.). (Illus.). 144p. (YA). (gr. 5-8). 1999. 32.00 (*0-516-21039-4*) Childrens.

Maryland. Dennis B. Fradin. (From Sea to Shining Sea Ser.). 64p. (J). 1997. pap. 5.95 (*0-516-26126-6*) Childrens.

Maryland. Joyce Johnston. (Hello U. S. A. Ser.). (Illus.). 72p. (J). (gr. 3-6). 1991. lib. bdg. 19.93 (*0-8225-2713-8*, Lerner Publctns) Lerner Pub.

Maryland. Joyce Johnston. (Hello U. S. A. Ser.). (Illus.). 72p. (J). 1997. pap. text 5.95 (*0-8225-9764-0*) Lerner Pub.

Maryland. Paul Joseph. LC 97-23901. (United States Ser.). (Illus.). 32p. (J). 1998. lib. bdg. 19.93 (*1-56239-881-4*, Checkerboard Library) ABDO Pub Co.

Maryland. Patricia K. Kummer. LC 97-40818. (One Nation Ser.). (Illus.). 48p. (J). (gr. 3-7). 1998. lib. bdg. 19.00 (*1-56065-680-8*) Capstone Pr.

Maryland. Kathleen Thompson. LC 95-25727. (Portrait of America Library). 48p. (YA). (gr. 4-8). 1996. pap. 5.95 (*0-8114-7445-3*) Raintree Steck-V.

Maryland. Kathleen Thompson. LC 95-25727. (Portrait of America Library). (Illus.). 48p. (YA). (gr. 3-6). 1996. lib. bdg. 22.83 (*0-8114-7340-6*) Raintree Steck-V.

Maryland, 19. Capstone Press Geogra Staff. Vol. 19. (Illus.). 48p. (J). (gr. 3-7). 1998. 19.00 (*0-516-21303-2*) Childrens.

***Maryland, 5 vols. , Set.** Leslie Rauth. LC 98-43960. (Celebrate the States Ser.). (Illus.). 144p. (J). (gr. 4-7). 2000. lib. bdg. 35.64 (*0-7614-0671-9*, Benchmark NY) Marshall Cavendish.

Maryland: A Guide to the Old Line State. Federal Writers' Project Staff. (American Guidebook Ser.). 1940. reprint ed. 89.00 (*0-403-02171-5*) Somerset Pub.

Maryland: A Guide to the Old Line State. Federal Writers' Project Staff & Writers Program-WPA Staff. (American Guide Ser.). 1989. reprint ed. lib. bdg. 79.00 (*0-7812-1019-4*, 1019) Rprt Serv.

Maryland: A History of Its People. Suzanne E. Chapelle et al. LC 85-19888. (Illus.). 352p. (gr. 9-12). 1986. text 24.95 (*0-8018-3005-2*) Johns Hopkins.

Maryland: A Middle Temperament, 1634-1980. Robert J. Brugger. (Maryland Paperback Bookshelf Ser.). (Illus.). 864p. 1996. reprint ed. pap. 25.95 (*0-8018-5465-2*) Johns Hopkins.

Maryland: A New Guide to the Old Line State. Edward C. Papenfuse et al. LC 76-17224. (Illus.). 488p. 1976. 29.50 (*0-8018-1874-5*) Johns Hopkins.

Maryland: A New Guide to the Old Line State. 2nd ed. Earl Arnette et al. LC 98-46982. 631p. 1999. pap. 22.50 (*0-8018-5980-8*) Johns Hopkins.

Maryland: A New Guide to the Old Line State. 2nd ed. Earl Arnette et al. LC 98-46982. (Illus.). 631p. 1999. 45.00 (*0-8018-5979-4*) Johns Hopkins.

Maryland: A Portrait. 4th rev. ed. Roger Miller. (Illus.). 168p. 1998. 39.95 (*0-911897-45-3*) Image Ltd.

Maryland: Biographical Sketches. George Schaun & Virginia Schaun. 1984. 15.75 (*0-917882-15-6*) MD Hist Pr.

***Maryland: Facts & Symbols.** Muriel L. Dubois. LC 99-53463. (States & Their Symbols Ser.). (Illus.). 24p. (J). (ps-3). 2000. lib. bdg. 15.93 (*0-7368-0523-0*, Hilltop Bks) Capstone Pr.

Maryland: Its Past & Present. 5th ed. Richard Wilson et al. LC 99-27407. 234p. (J). (gr. 4). 1999. 24.50 (*0-917882-48-2*) MD Hist Pr.

Maryland: Old Line to New Prosperity. Joseph L. Arnold. LC 85-6416. 256p. 1985. 24.95 (*0-89781-147-X*) Am Historical Pr.

Maryland: The Federalist Years. L. Marx Renzulli. LC 70-149405. 354p. 1975. 39.50 (*0-8386-7903-X*) Fairleigh Dickinson.

Maryland: The Night the Harbor Lights Went Out. Elizabeth Massie. (American Chills Ser.: No. 1). 144p. 1995. pap. 3.50 (*0-8217-5059-3*, Zebra Kensgtn) Kensgtn Pub Corp.

Maryland: The Spirit of America State by State. Esther Wanning. Ed. by Diana Landau. LC 97-12017. (Art of the State Ser.). (Illus.). 96p. 1998. 12.95 (*0-8109-5551-2*, Pub. by Abrams) Time Warner.

Maryland - Collected Works of Federal Writers Project. Federal Writers' Project Staff. 1991. reprint ed. lib. bdg. 98.00 (*0-7812-5608-9*) Rprt Serv.

***Maryland Advance Legislative Service: Pamphlet Number 3.** 1000p. 1999. Price not set. (*0-327-09113-4*, 4401813) LEXIS Pub.

***Maryland Advance Legislative Service: Pamphlet Number 4.** 1000p. 1999. Price not set. (*0-327-09114-2*, 4401913) LEXIS Pub.

***Maryland Advance Legislative Service Pamphlet, No. 1.** 200p. 1999. pap. write for info. (*0-327-08728-5*, 44016-13) LEXIS Pub.

***Maryland Advance Legislative Service Pamphlet, No. 2.** 950p. 1999. Price not set. (*0-327-09105-3*, 4401713) LEXIS Pub.

***Maryland Advance Rules Service Issue 2: 99-2K Subscription.** 40p. 1999. pap. write for info. (*0-327-09890-2*, 4125811) LEXIS Pub.

***Maryland Advance Rules Service, 99-2K Subscription, Issue No. 1.** 40p. 1999. pap. Price not set. (*0-327-09626-8*, 4125711) LEXIS Pub.

Maryland Album: Quiltmaking Traditions, 1634-1934. Gloria S. Allen & Nancy G. Tuckhorn. LC 95-2387. (Illus.). 224p. 1995. 34.95 (*1-55853-341-9*) Rutledge Hill Pr.

Maryland & America, 1940-1980. George H. Callcott. LC 85-166. (Illus.). 392p. 1985. 39.95 (*0-8018-2492-3*) Johns Hopkins.

Maryland & Baltimore 1870 Census Index. 644p. lib. bdg. 130.00 (*1-877677-58-2*, Precision Index) Herit Quest.

Maryland & DC Birds. James Kavanagh. (Pocket Naturalist Ser.). (Illus.). 1999. 5.95 (*1-889903-86-8*, Pub. by Waterford WA) Falcon Pub Inc.

Maryland & Delaware: Off the Beaten Path: A Guide to Unique Places. 4th ed. Judy Colbert. LC 99-28880. (Off the Beaten Ser.). (Illus.). 225p. 1999. pap. text 12.95 (*0-7627-0458-6*) Globe Pequot.

Maryland & Delaware Canoe Trails: A Paddler's Guide to Rivers of the Old Line & First States. 4th rev. ed. Edward Gertler. (Illus.). 290p. 1996. pap. 13.95 (*0-9605908-7-0*) Seneca Pr MD.

Maryland & Delaware Genealogies & Family Histories. Donald O. Virdin. 120p. (Orig.). 1993. pap. text 15.50 (*1-55613-867-9*) Heritage Bk.

Maryland & District of Columbia Retirement & Relocation Guide. large type ed. (Retirement & Relocation Guides Ser.). (Illus.). 350p. Date not set. pap. 24.95 (*1-56559-153-4*) HGI-Over Fifty.

Maryland & North Carolina in the Campaign of 1780-1781, with a Preliminary Notice of the Revolution, in Which the Troops of the Two States Won Distinction. Edward G. Davis. LC 72-14418. (Maryland Historical Society. Fund-Publications: No. 33). reprint ed. 27.50 (*0-404-57633-8*) AMS Pr.

Maryland & Other State Greats (Biographies) Carole Marsh. (Carole Marsh Maryland Bks.). (Illus.). (J). (gr. 3-8). 1994. pap. 19.95 (*1-55609-637-2*); lib. bdg. 29.95 (*1-55609-636-4*); disk 29.95 (*1-55609-638-0*) Gallopade Intl.

Maryland & the Empire, 1773: The Antilon-First Citizen Letters. Daniel Dulany. Ed. by Peter S. Onuf. LC 73-8128. (Maryland Bicentennial Studies). 250p. reprint ed. pap. 77.50 (*0-7837-0047-4*, 204029400016) Bks Demand.

Maryland & the French & Indian War. 250th ed. Allan Powell. LC 97-41130. 1998. write for info. (*0-9619995-4-3*) A R Powell.

Maryland Anthology, 1608-1986. Ed. by Dora J. Ashe. 262p. (Orig.). (C). 1987. lib. bdg. 47.00 (*0-8191-6572-7*) U Pr of Amer.

Maryland As a Proprietary Province. Newton D. Mereness. xx, 530p. 1997. pap. 35.00 (*0-7884-0667-1*, M161) Heritage Bk.

Maryland Bandits, Bushwackers, Outlaws, Crooks, Devils, Ghosts, Desperadoes & Other Assorted & Sundry Characters! Carole Marsh. (Carole Marsh Maryland Bks.). (Illus.). (J). (gr. 3-8). 1994. pap. 19.95 (*0-7933-0550-0*); lib. bdg. 29.95 (*0-7933-0551-9*); disk 29.95 (*0-7933-0552-7*) Gallopade Intl.

Maryland Basic Mastery Test for Reading (BMT-R) Jack Rudman. (Admission Test Ser.: Vol. 63). 43.95 (*0-8373-5163-4*) Nat Learn.

Maryland Basic Mastery Test for Reading (BMT-R) Jack Rudman. (Admission Test Ser.: ATS-63). 1994. pap. 23.95 (*0-8373-5063-8*) Nat Learn.

Maryland Bed of Grass. Janet Dailey. (Janet Dailey Americana Ser.: No. 20). 1991. per. 3.59 (*0-373-89870-3*) Harlequin Bks.

Maryland "BIO" Bingo! 24 Must Know State People for Kids to Learn about While Having Fun! Carole Marsh. (Bingo! Ser.). (Illus.). (J). (gr. 2-8). 1998. pap. 14.95 (*0-7933-8582-2*) Gallopade Intl.

Maryland Bookstore Book: A Surprising Guide to Our State's Bookstores & Their Specialties for Students, Teachers, Writers & Publishers. Carole Marsh. (Carole Marsh Maryland Bks.). (Illus.). 1994. pap. 19.95 (*0-7933-2916-7*); lib. bdg. 29.95 (*0-7933-2915-9*); disk 29.95 (*0-7933-2917-5*) Gallopade Intl.

***Maryland Boy in Lee's Army: Personal Reminiscences of a Maryland Soldier in the War Between the States, 1861-1865.** George Wilson Booth. 177p. 2000. pap. 12.00 (*0-8032-6175-6*, Bison Books) U of Nebr Pr.

Maryland Business Almanac. rev. ed. Ed. by Gerald Merrell. (Illus.). 500p. 1996. pap. write for info. (*0-9649819-2-0*) Baltimore Sun.

***Maryland Business Directory, 1999-2000.** rev. ed. American Business Directories Staff. 1744p. 1999. boxed set 520.00 incl. cd-rom (*0-7687-0156-2*) Am Busn Direct.

Maryland Business Directory, 1999 Edition. 5th ed. CJS, Inc. Staff. 408p. 1998. pap. 65.00 (*1-882538-68-4*) CJS.

Maryland Calendar of Wills: Wills from 1635-1743; Vol. I: 1635-1685; Vol. II: 1685-1702; Vol. III: 1703-1713; Vol. IV: 1713-1720; Vol. V: 1720-1726; Vol. VI: 1726-1732; Vol. VII: 1732-1738: Vol. VIII: 1738-1743, 8 vols. in 4. Ed. by Jane B. Cotton. 2583p. 1997. reprint ed. pap. 175.00 (*0-8063-4744-9*) Clearfield Co.

Maryland Campaign of 1862 & Its Aftermath: No. 2, \. Mark Snell. (Civil War Regiments Ser.: Vol. 6, No. 2). 1998. pap. 12.00 (*1-882810-56-2*) Savas Pub.

Maryland Census Index, 1880. (Illus.). lib. bdg. write for info. (*0-89593-369-1*, Accel Indexing) Genealogical Srvcs.

Maryland Census Index 1880 Baltimore Co. (Illus.). lib. bdg. write for info. (*0-89593-370-5*, Accel Indexing) Genealogical Srvcs.

Maryland Census Index 1850 Slave Schedule. (Illus.). 1988. lib. bdg. 55.00 (*0-89593-363-2*, Accel Indexing) Genealogical Srvcs.

Maryland Census Index 1800. Ronald V. Jackson. LC 77-85953. (Illus.). lib. bdg. 95.00 (*0-89593-060-9*, Accel Indexing) Genealogical Srvcs.

Maryland Census Index 1810. Ronald V. Jackson. LC 77-85954. (Illus.). lib. bdg. 52.00 (*0-89593-061-7*, Accel Indexing) Genealogical Srvcs.

Maryland Census Index 1890 Vets & Widows. (Illus.). lib. bdg. 113.00 (*0-89593-371-3*, Accel Indexing) Genealogical Srvcs.

Maryland Census Index, 1870 (Excludes Baltimore County) (Illus.). 1993. lib. bdg. write for info. (*0-89593-367-5*, Accel Indexing) Genealogical Srvcs.

Maryland Census Index 1870 Baltimore Co. (Illus.). 1993. lib. bdg. write for info. (*0-89593-368-3*, Accel Indexing) Genealogical Srvcs.

Maryland Census Index 1860 Baltimore Co. (Includes City of Baltimore) Ed. by Ronald Vern Jackson. LC 99-197557. (Illus.). 1997. lib. bdg. 165.00 (*0-89593-365-9*, Accel Indexing) Genealogical Srvcs.

Maryland Census Index, 1860 (Excluding City of Baltimore) Ed. by Ronald Vern Jackson. LC 99-197551. (Illus.). 1996. lib. bdg. 165.00 (*0-89593-364-0*, Accel Indexing) Genealogical Srvcs.

Maryland Census Index 1860 Slave Schedule. (Illus.). 1990. lib. bdg. 55.00 (*0-89593-366-7*, Accel Indexing) Genealogical Srvcs.

Maryland Census Index, 1790 (1907) Ronald V. Jackson. (Illus.). 1978. lib. bdg. 35.00 (*0-89593-673-9*, Accel Indexing) Genealogical Srvcs.

Maryland Civil Jury Instructions & Commentary. Rosalyn B. Bell. 1232p. 95.00 (*0-327-01940-9*) LEXIS Pub.

Maryland Civil Jury Instructions & Commentary. Rosalyn B. Bell. 1232p. 1993. 95.00 (*1-55834-056-4*, MICHIE) LEXIS Pub.

Maryland Civil Procedure Forms, Issue 5. 300p. 1998. ring bd. write for info. (*0-327-00522-X*, 8155815) LEXIS Pub.

Maryland Civil Procedure Forms, 2 vols., Set. 2nd ed. Robert D. Klein. 1230p. 1994. spiral bd. 198.00 (*0-250-40725-6*, 81554-10, MICHIE) LEXIS Pub.

Maryland Classic Christmas Trivia: Stories, Recipes, Activities, Legends, Lore & More! Carole Marsh. (Carole Marsh Maryland Bks.). (Illus.). (J). (gr. 3-8). 1994. pap. 19.95 (*0-7933-0553-5*); lib. bdg. 29.95 (*0-7933-0554-3*); disk 29.95 (*0-7933-0555-1*) Gallopade Intl.

Maryland Coastales! Carole Marsh. (Carole Marsh Maryland Bks.). (J). 1994. lib. bdg. 29.95 (*0-7933-7285-2*) Gallopade Intl.

Maryland Coastales! Carole Marsh. (Carole Marsh Maryland Bks.). (Illus.). (J). (gr. 3-8). 1994. pap. 19.95 (*1-55609-631-3*); lib. bdg. 29.95 (*1-55609-630-5*); disk 29.95 (*1-55609-632-1*) Gallopade Intl.

Maryland Code of 1957, 37 vols., Set. Michie Company Editorial Staff. write for info. (*0-87215-129-8*, MICHIE) LEXIS Pub.

Maryland Colony. Dennis B. Fradin. LC 90-2210. (Thirteen Colonies Ser.). (Illus.). 160p. (J). (gr. 4 up). 1990. lib. bdg. 30.00 (*0-516-00394-1*) Childrens.

Maryland Commercial Financing Forms. John A. Stalfort & Michael S. Speas. LC 86-1173. 520p. 1994. spiral bd. 159.00 (*0-87189-052-6*, MICHIE); ring bd., suppl. ed. 85.00 (*0-614-03769-7*, MICHIE) LEXIS Pub.

Maryland Corporate Forms. Frank-John Hadley. 1994. ring bd. 60.00 incl. disk (*0-614-03770-0*, MICHIE) LEXIS Pub.

Maryland Corporate Forms, 3 vols. Sachs. 684p. 1997. ring bd. 239.00 (*0-327-03957-4*, 81567, MICHIE) LEXIS Pub.

Maryland Corporate Forms, 3 vols., No. 24. Sachs. 200p. 1998. ring bd. 239.00 (*0-327-00769-9*, 8157314) LEXIS Pub.

Maryland Corporate Forms, 3 vols., Set. Alan R. Sachs. 1100p. 1994. spiral bd. 239.00 incl. disk (*0-87189-278-2*, 81567-10, MICHIE) LEXIS Pub.

Maryland Corporation: Legal Aspects of Organization & Operation. Kenneth B. Abel & Guy W. Warfield. (Corporate Practice Ser.: No. 71). 1997. 95.00 (*1-55871-362-X*) BNAC.

Maryland Corporation Law. James J. Hanks, Jr. 828p. 1992. ring bd. 155.00 (*0-13-109331-2*) Aspen Law.

***Maryland Corporations & Associations: 1999 Replacement Volume.** 725p. 1999. write for info. (*0-327-09914-3*, 9413114) LEXIS Pub.

***Maryland Correctional Services 1999 Replacement Volume.** 480p. 1999. Price not set. (*0-327-09715-9*, 4390110) LEXIS Pub.

***Maryland Court Rules, June 1999 Supplement, 2 vols.** 150p. 1999. write for info. (*0-327-08733-1*, 44007-16) LEXIS Pub.

Maryland Court Rules September 1998 Interim Supplement. 30p. 1998. pap., suppl. ed. write for info. (*0-327-06406-4*, 4400915) LEXIS Pub.

Maryland Court Rules Update, 1998-99, Vol. 1, Issue 1, Sept. 98. 50p. Date not set. write for info. (*0-327-06204-5*, 41257-10) LEXIS Pub.

Maryland Court Rules Update, 1998-99, Vol. 1, Issue 2, Nov. 98. 50p. Date not set. write for info. (*0-327-06205-3*, 41258-10) LEXIS Pub.

Maryland Court Rules Update, 1998-99, Vol. 1, Issue 3, Jan. 99. 50p. Date not set. write for info. (*0-327-06206-1*, 41259-10) LEXIS Pub.

Maryland Court Rules Update, 1998-99, Vol. 1, Issue 4, Mar. 99. 50p. Date not set. write for info. (*0-327-06207-X*, 41260-10) LEXIS Pub.

Maryland Court Rules Update, 1998-99, Vol. 1, Issue 5, May 99. 50p. Date not set. write for info. (*0-327-06442-0*, 41261-10) LEXIS Pub.

Maryland Court Rules Update, 1998-99, Vol. 1, Issue 6, June 99. 50p. Date not set. write for info. (*0-327-06443-9*, 41262-10) LEXIS Pub.

***Maryland Crime in Perspective 2000.** Ed. by Kathleen O'Leary Morgan & Scott E. Morgan. 22p. 2000. spiral bd. 19.00 (*0-7401-0319-9*) Morgan Quitno Corp.

Maryland Crime Perspective, 1998. Ed. by Kathleen O'Leary Morgan & Scott E. Morgan. 20p. 1998. pap. 19.00 (*1-56692-919-9*) Morgan Quitno Corp.

Maryland Crime Perspectives, 1999. Kathleen O'Leary Morgan. 22p. 1999. spiral bd. 19.00 (*0-7401-0119-6*) Morgan Quitno Corp.

Maryland Criminal Jury Instructions & Commentary. 2nd ed. David F. Aaronson. 1,013p. 1988. 75.00 (*0-87473-335-9*, 60003-10, MICHIE) LEXIS Pub.

Maryland Criminal Law & Motor Vehicle Handbook. annuals Ed. by Gould Editorial Staff. 960p. (C). pap. 21.95 (*1-882476-04-2*) Gould.

***Maryland Criminal Laws Annotated, 1999 Edition.** 1006p. 1999. 42.00 (*0-327-09853-8*, 2635818, MICHIE) LEXIS Pub.

Maryland Criminal Laws Annotated, 1998 Edition. annot. ed. 993p. 1998. pap. write for info. (*0-327-06468-4*, 2635814) LEXIS Pub.

Maryland Criminal Procedure Forms. Jonathan S. Smith. LC 87-83520. 1988. 190.00 (*0-318-37612-1*) West Group.

Maryland Criminal Procedure Forms. Jonathan S. Smith. LC 87-83520. 1993. suppl. ed. 67.50 (*0-317-03326-3*) West Group.

Maryland "Crinkum-Crankum" A Funny Word Book about Our State. Carole Marsh. (Carole Marsh Maryland Bks.). (Illus.). (J). 1994. pap. 19.95 (*0-7933-4869-2*); lib. bdg. 29.95 (*0-7933-4868-4*); disk 29.95 (*0-7933-4870-6*) Gallopade Intl.

Maryland-D. C. Manufacturers Directory. 7th rev. ed. Ed. by Frank Lambing. 1999. 73.00 (*1-58202-053-1*) Manufacturers.

***Maryland Department of Natural Resources Laws: 1999 Edition.** 669p. 1999. pap. 65.00 (*0-327-09851-1*, 2633112) LEXIS Pub.

Maryland Dingbats! Bk. 1: A Fun Book of Games, Stories, Activities & More about Our State That's All in Code! for You to Decipher. Carole Marsh. (Carole Marsh Maryland Bks.). (Illus.). (J). (gr. 3-12). 1994. pap. 19.95 (*0-7933-3834-4*); lib. bdg. 29.95 (*0-7933-3833-6*); disk 29.95 (*0-7933-3835-2*) Gallopade Intl.

Maryland Domestic Relations Case Finder. John F. Fader, 2nd & Mark E. Smith. 583p. 1993. 75.00 (*1-55834-078-5*, MICHIE) LEXIS Pub.

Maryland Domestic Relations Forms. Ann M. Turnbul & Joseph J. Wase. 600p. 1994. spiral bd. 159.00 incl. disk (*0-87189-279-0*, 81578-10, MICHIE) LEXIS Pub.

Maryland Domestic Relations Forms. Ann M. Turnbull & Joseph J. Wase. 600p. 1993. ring bd., suppl. ed. 82.00 incl. disk (*1-56257-248-2*, MICHIE) LEXIS Pub.

Maryland Domestic Relations Forms. Turnbull & Wase. 1995. ring bd. 159.00 (*0-327-03929-9*, 81578-10, MICHIE) LEXIS Pub.

Maryland Domestic Relations Forms, Issue 20. 300p. 1998. ring bd. write for info. (*0-327-00520-3*, 8158114) LEXIS Pub.

Maryland During & after the Revolution: A Political & Economic Study. Phillip A. Crowl. LC 78-64189. (Johns Hopkins University. Studies in the Social Sciences. Thirtieth Ser. 1912: 1). reprint ed. 37.50 (*0-404-61296-2*) AMS Pr.

Maryland Early Census, Vol. 1. Ronald V. Jackson. (Illus.). 1980. lib. bdg. 34.00 (*0-89593-654-2*, Accel Indexing) Genealogical Srvcs.

Maryland Early Census, Vol. 2. Ronald V. Jackson. (Illus.). lib. bdg. 34.00 (*0-89593-726-3*, Accel Indexing) Genealogical Srvcs.

Maryland Education 1999 Replacement Volume. 905p. 1999. write for info. (*0-327-08427-8*, 43884-12) LEXIS Pub.

Maryland 1870 Census Index. Raeone C. Steuart. LC 99-170093. xix, 1590 p. 1997. 295.00 (*1-877677-66-3*) Herit Quest.

***Maryland Employer's Guide: A Handbook of Employment Laws & Regulations.** Ed. by Summers Press, Inc. Staff. 660p. 2000. 92.50 (*1-56759-059-4*) Summers Pr.

Maryland Employment Law. Stanley Mazaroff. 767p. 1990. 90.00 (*0-87473-658-7*, 64645-10, MICHIE) LEXIS Pub.

Maryland Employment Law, 1998 Cumulative Supplement. Stanley Mazaroff. 250p. 1998. write for info. (*0-327-00823-7*, 6464613) LEXIS Pub.

Maryland Environmental Law Handbook. 3rd rev. ed. Piper & Marbury Law Firm Staff. LC 98-170180. (State Environmental Law Ser.). 258p. 1997. pap. text 89.00 (*0-86587-555-3*) Gov Insts.

Maryland Estate Planning, Will Drafting & Estate Administration Forms. A. MacDonough Plant. 220p. 1993. spiral bd. 159.00 incl. disk (*0-87189-280-4*, MICHIE) LEXIS Pub.

Maryland Estate Planning, Will Drafting & Estate Administration Forms. Albin M. Plant. 220p. 1993. ring bd., suppl. ed. 79.00 incl. disk (*1-56257-795-6*, MICHIE) LEXIS Pub.

Maryland Estate Planning, Will Drafting & Estate Administration Forms, 2 vols. 2nd ed. Plant et al. 1995. ring bd. 229.00 (*0-327-03917-5*, 81584-10, MICHIE) LEXIS Pub.

Maryland Estate Planning, Will Drafting & Estate Administration Forms, Issue 3. Plant et al. 1998. ring bd. 229.00 (*0-327-00144-5*, 81587-14) LEXIS Pub.

Maryland Estate Planning, Will Drafting & Estate Administration Forms, Issue 4. 2nd ed. Albert S. Barr, III et al. 200p. 1999. ring bd. write for info. (*0-327-01264-1*, 8158715) LEXIS Pub.

Maryland Estate Planning, Wills & Trusts Library: Forms & Practice Manual, 2 vols. Aryeh Guttenberg. LC 98-30857. 1088p. 1998. ring bd. 239.90 (*1-57400-037-3*) Data Trace Pubng.

Maryland Evidence Handbook. 2nd ed. Joseph F. Murphy, Jr. 1009p. 1993. 90.00 (*1-55834-124-2*, 64905-11, MICHIE) LEXIS Pub.

M

***Maryland Evidence Handbook.** 3rd ed. Joseph F. Murphy, Jr. LC 99-64694. 735p. 1999. 120.00 (*0-327-01532-2*, 6490512) LEXIS Pub.

Maryland Evidence Handbook: 1989 Edition, 1992 Supplement. Joseph Murphy. 1989. text. write for info. (*0-87473-499-1*, 64905-10, MICHIE) LEXIS Pub.

Maryland Evidence Handbook: 1990 Supplement. Joseph F. Murphy. 1990. write for info. (*0-87473-727-3*, 64906-10, MICHIE) LEXIS Pub.

Maryland Evidence Handbook: 1991 Cumulative Supplement. Joseph Murphy. 1991. write for info. (*0-87473-855-5*, 64907-10, MICHIE) LEXIS Pub.

Maryland Evidence Handbook: 1998 Cumulative Supplement. 200p. 1998. suppl. ed. write for info. (*0-327-00246-8*, 64908-15) LEXIS Pub.

***Maryland Experience Pocket Guide.** Carole Marsh. (Maryland Experience! Ser.). (Illus.). (J). 2000. pap. 6.95 (*0-7933-9610-7*) Gallopade Intl.

Maryland Facts & Factivities. Carole Marsh. (Carole Marsh State Bks.). (Illus.). (J). (gr. 4-7). 1996. pap., teacher ed. 19.95 (*0-7933-7887-7*, C Marsh) Gallopade Intl.

Maryland Family Law. 2nd ed. Fader & Gilbert. 1,081p. 1995. text 95.00 (*1-55834-292-3*, 61903-11, MICHIE) LEXIS Pub.

Maryland Family Law: 1991 Supplement. Fader & Gilbert. 125p. 1991. pap. 25.00 (*0-87473-777-X*, 61904-10, MICHIE) LEXIS Pub.

Maryland Family Law, 1998 Cumulative Supplement. 2nd ed. John F. Fader, II & Richard J. Gilbert. 275p. 1998. suppl. ed. write for info. (*0-327-00557-2*, 6190215) LEXIS Pub.

Maryland Federal Census Index, 1820. Ronald V. Jackson. LC 77-85955. (Illus.). lib. bdg. 56.00 (*0-89593-062-5*, Accel Indexing) Genealogical Srvcs.

Maryland Federal Census Index, 1830. Ronald V. Jackson. LC 77-85956. (Illus.). lib. bdg. 62.00 (*0-89593-063-3*, Accel Indexing) Genealogical Srvcs.

Maryland Federal Census Index, 1840. Ronald V. Jackson. LC 77-85957. (Illus.). lib. bdg. 66.00 (*0-89593-064-1*, Accel Indexing) Genealogical Srvcs.

Maryland Federal Census Index, 1850. Ronald V. Jackson. LC 77-85959. (Illus.). lib. bdg. 99.00 (*0-89593-065-X*, Accel Indexing) Genealogical Srvcs.

Maryland Festival Fun for Kids! Carole Marsh. (Carole Marsh Maryland Bks.). (Illus.). (YA). (gr. 3-12). 1994. pap. 19.95 (*0-7933-3987-1*); lib. bdg. 29.95 (*0-7933-3986-3*); disk 29.95 (*0-7933-3988-X*) Gallopade Intl.

Maryland Folklore. George G. Carey. LC 89-40302. (Illus.). 175p. 1989. pap. 12.95 (*0-87033-396-8*, Tidewtr Pubs) Cornell Maritime.

Maryland Football Mystery. Carole M. Longmeyer. (Sportsmystery Ser.). (Illus.). 80p. (Orig.). (J). (gr. 3 up). 1994. pap. 19.95 (*0-935326-32-4*) Gallopade Intl.

Maryland Functional Math Practice Tests Workbook. 1996. teacher ed., wbk. ed. 14.95 (*0-9679929-1-5*) Learn Tog Ed Serv.

Maryland Gardening 1998 Calendar. Mike Klingaman. (Illus.). 28p. 1997. pap. 10.95 (*0-9649819-5-5*) Baltimore Sun.

Maryland Gazette, 1727-1761: Genealogical & Historical Abstracts. Karen M. Green. LC 89-82073. 352p. 1990. lib. bdg. 28.50 (*0-932231-07-1*) Frontier Pr.

Maryland Genealogical Library Guide. John W. Heisey. (Illus.). 59p. 1998. pap. 7.50 (*1-883294-61-4*) Masthof Pr.

Maryland Genealogical Research. George K. Schweitzer. 208p. 1998. pap. 15.00 (*0-913857-14-9*) Genealog Sources.

Maryland Genealogies: A Consolidation of Articles from the Maryland Historical Magazine, 2 vols. Maryland Genealogies Staff. LC 80-80064. 1097p. 1997. reprint ed. 75.00 (*0-8063-0887-7*) Genealog Pub.

Maryland "GEO" Bingo! 38 Must Know State Geography Facts for Kids to Learn While Having Fun! Carole Marsh. (Bingo! Ser.). (Illus.). (J). (gr. 2-8). 1998. pap. 14.95 (*0-7933-8583-0*) Gallopade Intl.

***Maryland German Church Records No. 13: St. John's Evangelical Lutheran Church 1770-1819, Hagerstown, Washington Co., MD.** LC 99-73764. 115p. 1999. pap. 18.00 (*1-886742-05-7*) Hist Soc Carroll.

Maryland German Church Records Vol. 1: Christ Reformed Church, Middletown. Ed. by Frederick S. Weiser. LC 86-61245. (Maryland German Church Records Ser.). 108p. (Orig.). 1986. pap. 15.00 (*0-913281-03-4*) Noodle-Doosey.

Maryland German Church Records Vol. 1: Christ Reformed Church, Middletown, Frederick Co., MD. Ed. & Tr. by Frederick S. Weiser from GER. LC 86-61245. 108p. (Orig.). 1989. reprint ed. pap. 15.00 (*0-9614125-4-2*) Hist Soc Carroll.

Maryland German Church Records Vol. 2: Zion Lutheran Church, Middletown. Ed. by Frederick S. Weiser. Tr. by Charles T. Zahn. LC 86-62419. (Maryland German Church Records Ser.). (Orig.). 1987. 15.00 (*0-913281-04-2*) Hist Soc Carroll.

Maryland German Church Records Vol. 3: Monacacy Lutheran Congregation & Evangelical Lutheran Church - Baptisms 1742-1779, Frederick. Ed. & Tr. by Frederick S. Weiser. LC 86-63901. (Maryland German Church Records Ser.). 118p. (Orig.). 1987. 18.00 (*0-913281-05-0*) Hist Soc Carroll.

Maryland German Church Records Vol. 4: Evangelical Lutheran Church Baptisms 1780-1811, Frederick Co., Maryland. Ed. & Tr. by Frederick S. Weiser from GER. LC 89-80494. (Orig.). 1989. pap. 18.00 (*0-9614125-5-0*) Hist Soc Carroll.

Maryland German Church Records Vol. 4: Evangelical Lutheran Church Baptisms, 1780-1811, Frederick, Maryland. Ed. & Tr. by Frederick S. Weiser. LC 87-60112. (Maryland German Church Records Ser.). 150p. (Orig.). 1987. pap. 20.00 (*0-913281-06-9*) Noodle-Doosey.

Maryland German Church Records Vol. 5: Evangelical Reformed Church 1746-1789, Frederick. Ed. by Frederick S. Weiser. Tr. by William J. Hinke. LC 87-60840. (Maryland German Church Records Ser.). (Orig.). 1987. pap. 20.00 (*0-913281-07-7*) Noodle-Doosey.

Maryland German Church Records Vol. 5: Evangelical Reformed Church 1746-1789, Frederick Co., Maryland. Ed. by Frederick S. Weiser. Tr. by William J. Hinke from GER. LC 89-80493. (Orig.). 1989. pap. 18.00 (*0-9614125-6-9*) Hist Soc Carroll.

Maryland German Church Records Vol. 6: Evangelical Reformed Church 1790-1835, Frederick. Ed. by Frederick S. Weiser. Tr. by William J. Hinke. LC 87-60841. (Maryland German Church Records Ser.). (Orig.). 1987. pap. 20.00 (*0-913281-08-5*) Noodle-Doosey.

Maryland German Church Records Vol. 6: Evangelical Reformed Church, 1790-1835, Frederick Co., Maryland. Ed. by Frederick S. Weiser. Tr. by William J. Hinke. LC 87-60841. (Orig.). 1989. pap. 18.00 (*0-9614125-7-7*) Hist Soc Carroll.

Maryland German Church Records Vol. 7: St. Mary's Reformed Church, Silver Run; St. Mary's Lutheran Church, Silver Run, Carroll County. Ed. & Tr. by Frederick S. Weiser. LC 87-60842. (Maryland German Church Records Ser.). (Orig.). 1987. 18.00 (*0-913281-09-3*) Hist Soc Carroll.

Maryland German Church Records Vol. 8: St. Luke's Evangelical Lutheran Church 1784-1884, Trinity Evangelical Lutheran Church 1788-1841, Emanual Church Lutheran & Reformed 1792-1849. Ed. & Tr. by Frederick S. Weiser. LC 94-72940. 182p. 1994. pap. 18.00 (*1-886742-00-6*) Hist Soc Carroll.

Maryland German Church Records Vol. 9: Benjamin's Reformed 1766-1835 & St. Benjamin's Lutheran 1767-1837, Near Westminster, Jerusalem Lutheran 1799-1881, Bachman's Valley. Ed. by Charles T. Zahn & Frederick S. Weiser. LC 89-80493. 1994. 18.00 (*0-614-15328-X*) Hist Soc Carroll.

Maryland German Church Records Vol. 9: The Pipe Creek Church, Benjamin's Reformed, 1766-1835 & St. Benjamin's Lutheran, 1767-1837, near Westminster; Jerusalem Lutheran, 1799-1881, Bachman's Valley. Ed. by Charles T. Zahn & Frederick S. Weiser. LC 93-61216. (Maryland German Church Records Ser.). 124p. 1994. pap. 18.00 (*1-886742-16-2*) Hist Soc Carroll.

Maryland German Church Records Vol. 10: Zion Church "The German Church", Manchester, Carroll County; Today - Trinity United Church of Christ Records, 1760-1836, Immanuel Lutheran Church, Records 1760-1853. Ed. & Tr. by Frederick S. Weiser. LC 95-77063. 133p. 1995. pap. 18.00 (*1-886742-01-4*) Hist Soc Carroll.

Maryland German Church Records Vol. 11: Apple's Church, Lutheran & Reformed Records, 1773-1849; Union Church, Lutheran & Reformed Records, 1789-1863. Ed. by Frederick S. Weiser. LC 95-80950. 100p. (Orig.). 1996. pap. 18.00 (*1-886742-02-2*) Hist Soc Carroll.

Maryland German Church Records Vol. 12: Zion Evangelical & Reformed Church, Hagerstown, Washington County, Maryland, 1771-1849. Ed. & Tr. by Frederick S. Weiser from GER. LC 97-78281. 106p. 1997. pap. 18.00 (*1-886742-03-0*) Hist Soc Carroll.

Maryland German Church Records Vol. 16: St. Peter's Lutheran Church, 1767-1854; Glade Reformed Church, 1769-1836; Mount Zion Lutheran & Reformed Church, 1798-1834. Ed. by Frederick S. Weiser & John P. Dern. LC 98-74019. 115p. 1998. pap. 18.00 (*1-886742-04-9*) Hist Soc Carroll.

Maryland Government! The Cornerstone of Everyday Life in Our State! Carole Marsh. (Carole Marsh Maryland Bks.). (Illus.). (J). (gr. 3-12). 1996. pap. 19.95 (*0-7933-6242-3*); lib. bdg. 29.95 (*0-7933-6241-5*); disk 29.95 (*0-7933-6243-1*) Gallopade Intl.

Maryland Guide to Zoning Decisions: 1991 Supplement. Stanley Abrams. 151p. 1998. pap. text 25.00 (*0-87473-854-7*, 60028-10, MICHIE) LEXIS Pub.

***Maryland Health - General Volume 2 2000 Replacement Volume.** 819p. 2000. write for info. (*0-327-13167-5*, 4397712) LEXIS Pub.

***Maryland Health - General 2000 Replacement Volume, Vol. 1.** 695p. 2000. write for info. (*0-327-13166-7*, 4397312) LEXIS Pub.

***Maryland Health Care in Perspective 2000.** Ed. by Kathleen O'Leary Morgan & Scott E. Morgan. 21p. 2000. spiral bd. 19.00 (*0-7401-0219-2*) Morgan Quitno Corp.

Maryland Health Care Perspective, 1998. Ed. by Kathleen O'Leary Morgan & Scott E. Morgan. 20p. 1998. pap. 19.00 (*1-56692-819-2*) Morgan Quitno Corp.

Maryland Health Care Perspective, 1999. Ed. by Kathleen O'Leary Morgan. 21p. 1999. spiral bd. 19.00 (*0-7401-0069-6*) Morgan Quitno Corp.

Maryland Health Laws & Regulations Annotated with Current Supplement: 1997 Edition. 1,137p. pap. 52.50 (*1-55834-706-2*) LEXIS Pub.

Maryland Health Laws & Regulations Annotated 1998 Supplement. 155p. 1999. pap. write for info. (*0-327-07230-X*, 2637510, MICHIE) LEXIS Pub.

***Maryland Health Occupations 2000 Replacement Volume.** 767p. 2000. write for info. (*0-327-13168-3*, 4388612) LEXIS Pub.

Maryland "HISTO" Bingo! 42 Must Know State History Facts for Kids to Learn While Having Fun! Carole Marsh. (Bingo! Ser.). (Illus.). (J). (gr. 2-8). 1998. pap. 14.95 (*0-7933-8584-9*) Gallopade Intl.

Maryland Historical & Biographical Index, Vol. 1. Ronald V. Jackson. LC 78-53702. (Illus.). 1984. lib. bdg. 30.00 (*0-89593-185-0*, Accel Indexing) Genealogical Srvcs.

Maryland History! Surprising Secrets about Our State's Founding Mothers, Fathers & Kids! Carole Marsh. (Carole Marsh Maryland Bks.). (Illus.). (J). (gr. 3-12). 1996. pap. 19.95 (*0-7933-6089-7*); lib. bdg. 29.95 (*0-7933-6088-9*); disk 29.95 (*0-7933-6090-0*) Gallopade Intl.

***Maryland History in Prints, 1752-1900.** Laura Rice. (Illus.). 320p. 2000. 65.00 (*0-938420-71-2*, Pub. by MD Hist) A C Hood.

Maryland Hot Air Balloon Mystery. Carole Marsh. (Carole Marsh Maryland Bks.). (Illus.). (J). (gr. 2-9). 1994. 29.95 (*0-7933-2498-X*); pap. 19.95 (*0-7933-2499-8*); disk 29.95 (*0-7933-2500-5*) Gallopade Intl.

Maryland Hot Zones! Viruses, Diseases, & Epidemics in Our State's History. Carole Marsh. (Hot Zones! Ser.). (Illus.). (J). (gr. 3-12). 1998. pap. 19.95 (*0-7933-8889-9*); lib. bdg. 29.95 (*0-7933-8888-0*) Gallopade Intl.

Maryland in Africa: The Maryland State Colonization Society, 1831-1857. Penelope Campbell. LC 75-131058. 272p. reprint ed. pap. 84.40 (*0-608-14869-5*, 202591500047) Bks Demand.

Maryland in Perspective, 1998. Ed. by Kathleen O'Leary Morgan & Scott E. Morgan. 24p. 1998. pap. 19.00 (*1-56692-869-9*) Morgan Quitno Corp.

***Maryland in Perspective, 1999.** Ed. by Kathleen O'Leary Morgan. 26p. 1999. spiral bd. 19.00 (*1-56692-969-5*) Morgan Quitno Corp.

***Maryland In Perspective 2000.** Ed. by Kathleen O'Leary Morgan & Scott E. Morgan. 26p. 2000. spiral bd. 19.00 (*0-7401-0269-9*) Morgan Quitno Corp.

Maryland in the Civil War. Robert I. Cottom & Mary E. Hayward. (Illus.). 128p. 1996. pap. text 24.95 (*0-938420-51-8*) MD Hist.

***Maryland Income Tax Laws & Regulations: 1999 Edition.** 206p. 1999. pap. 24.00 (*0-327-10168-7*, 2635613) LEXIS Pub.

Maryland Income Tax Laws & Regulations, 1998. Lexis Law Publishing Staff. 38p. 1998. suppl. ed. write for info. (*0-327-06585-0*) LEXIS Pub.

Maryland Indian Dictionary for Kids! Carole Marsh. (Carole Marsh State Bks.). (J). (gr. 2-9). 1996. 29.95 (*0-7933-7704-8*, C Marsh); pap. 19.95 (*0-7933-7705-6*, C Marsh) Gallopade Intl.

Maryland Interactive Distance Learning Network. Ronald A. Phipps & David Sumler. 1994. 10.00 (*0-614-13559-1*) SHEEO.

***Maryland Investment & Business Guide: Business, Investment, Export-Import Opportunities, 50 vols., Vol. 20.** Global Investment Center, USA Staff. (U. S. Regional Investment & Business Library-99: Vol. 20). (Illus.). 350p. (Orig.). 1999. pap. 59.95 (*0-7397-1119-9*) Intl Business Pubns.

***Maryland Jeopardy.** Carole Marsh. (Maryland Experience! Ser.). (Illus.). (J). (gr. 2-6). 2000. pap. 7.95 (*0-7933-9612-3*) Gallopade Intl.

Maryland Jeopardy! Answers & Questions about Our State! Carole Marsh. (Carole Marsh Maryland Bks.). (Illus.). (J). (gr. 3-12). 1994. pap. 19.95 (*0-7933-4140-X*); lib. bdg. 29.95 (*0-7933-4139-6*); disk 29.95 (*0-7933-4141-8*) Gallopade Intl.

***Maryland Jography.** Carole Marsh. (Maryland Experience! Ser.). (Illus.). (J). (gr. 2-6). 2000. 7.95 (*0-7933-9605-0*) Gallopade Intl.

Maryland "Jography" A Fun Run Thru Our State! Carole Marsh. (Carole Marsh Maryland Bks.). (Illus.). (J). (gr. 3-8). 1994. pap. 19.95 (*1-55609-620-8*); lib. bdg. 29.95 (*1-55609-619-4*); disk 29.95 (*1-55609-621-6*) Gallopade Intl.

Maryland Journal of International Law & Trade, 1975-1995, 21 vols., Set. 1975. 735.00 (*0-8377-9110-3*, Rothman) W S Hein.

Maryland Kid's Cookbook: Recipes, How-To, History, Lore & More! Carole Marsh. (Carole Marsh Maryland Bks.). (Illus.). (J). (gr. 3-8). 1994. pap. 19.95 (*0-7933-0562-4*); lib. bdg. 29.95 (*0-7933-0563-2*); disk 29.95 (*0-7933-0564-0*) Gallopade Intl.

***Maryland Labor & Employment: 1999 Replacement Volume.** 900p. 1999. write for info. (*0-327-09915-1*, 9413115) LEXIS Pub.

Maryland Landlord & Tenant: 1987 Supplement. Bregman & Evergam. 1987. pap. write for info. (*0-87473-326-X*, 60402-10, MICHIE) LEXIS Pub.

Maryland Landlord-Tenant Law: Practice & Procedure. Douglas M. Bregman & Gary G. Everngam. 481p. 1994. 70.00 (*1-55834-125-0*, MICHIE) LEXIS Pub.

Maryland Landlord-Tenant Law: Practice & Procedure. 2nd ed. Douglas M. Bregman & Gary G. Everngam. 481p. 70.00 (*0-327-01937-9*) LEXIS Pub.

Maryland Landlord-Tenant Law, 1998 Cumulative Supplement. 2nd ed. Douglas M. Bregman & Gary G. Everngam. 105p. 1998. pap., suppl. ed. write for info. (*0-327-00539-4*, 6040314) LEXIS Pub.

Maryland Landscapes of Eugene Leake. Craig Hankin. LC 86-45437. (Illus.). 112p. 1986. 39.95 (*0-8018-3366-3*) Johns Hopkins.

Maryland Law Forum, 1970-1985, 11 vols. 1970. 380.00 (*0-8377-9176-6*, Rothman) W S Hein.

Maryland Law Relating to Fair Election Practices, 1998 Edition. 43p. 1998. 7.00 (*0-327-06577-X*, 2632512) LEXIS Pub.

Maryland Law Review, 1936-1995, 56 vols., Set. 1996. 2660.00 (*0-8377-9111-1*, Rothman) W S Hein.

Maryland Lawyers' Rules of Professional Conduct & Attorney Trust Account: 1998 Edition. rev. ed. 104p. 1998. pap. write for info. (*0-327-05000-4*, 26333-14) LEXIS Pub.

***Maryland Lawyers' Rules of Professional Conduct & Attorney Trust Accounts: 2000 Edition.** 114p. 2000. write for info. (*0-327-10411-2*, 2633316) LEXIS Pub.

Maryland Lawyer's Rules of Professional Conduct & Attorney Trust Accounts, 1999 Edition. 101p. 1999. pap. 12.00 (*0-327-08411-1*, 26333-15) LEXIS Pub.

Maryland Library Book: A Surprising Guide to the Unusual Special Collections in Libraries Across Our State for Students, Teachers, Writers & Publishers - Includes Reproducible Mailing Labels Plus Activities for Young People! Carole Marsh. (Carole Marsh Maryland Bks.). (Illus.). 1994. pap. 19.95 (*0-7933-3066-1*); lib. bdg. 29.95 (*0-7933-3065-3*); disk 29.95 (*0-7933-3067-X*) Gallopade Intl.

Maryland Lighthouses of the Chesapeake Bay: An Illustrated History. F. Ross Holland, Jr. LC 96-42187. (Illus.). 200p. 1997. 32.95 (*1-878399-70-5*) Div Hist Cult Progs.

Maryland Limited Liability Company: Forms & Practice Manual, 2 vols. 3rd rev. ed. Robert M. Ercole et al. LC 94-47986. 768p. 1995. ring bd. 239.90 (*1-57400-000-4*) Data Trace Pubng.

Maryland Line in the Confederate Army. W. W. Goldsborough. 1976. 42.00 (*0-913419-00-1*, J M C & Co) Amereon Ltd.

Maryland Line in the Confederate Army. W. W. Goldsborough. 400p. 1987. reprint ed. 35.00 (*0-942211-49-9*) Olde Soldier Bks.

***Maryland Lost & Found... Again.** expanded rev. ed. Eugene L. Meyer. LC 99-89771. (Illus.). 240p. 2000. pap. write for info. (*1-891521-08-X*) Woodholme Hse.

Maryland Loyalists in the American Revolution. M. Christopher New. LC 96-47702. (Illus.). 200p. 1996. 26.95 (*0-87033-495-6*, Tidewtr Pubs) Cornell Maritime.

Maryland Math! How It All Adds up in Our State. Carole Marsh. (Carole Marsh Maryland Bks.). (Illus.). (YA). (gr. 3-12). 1996. pap. 19.95 (*0-7933-6548-1*); lib. bdg. 29.95 (*0-7933-6547-3*) Gallopade Intl.

Maryland Media Book: A Surprising Guide to the Amazing Print, Broadcast & Online Media of Our State for Students, Teachers, Writers & Publishers - Includes Reproducible Mailing Labels Plus Activities for Young People! Carole Marsh. (Carole Marsh Maryland Bks.). (Illus.). 1994. pap. 19.95 (*0-7933-3222-2*); lib. bdg. 29.95 (*0-7933-3221-4*); disk 29.95 (*0-7933-3223-0*) Gallopade Intl.

***Maryland Medical Practice Act & Related Regulations: 1999 Edition.** 210p. 2000. write for info. (*0-327-10210-1*, 2634316) LEXIS Pub.

Maryland Militia in the Revolutionary War. Ed. by Eugene Clements & Edward F. Wright. LC 87-81636. 280p. 1987. 20.00 (*0-940907-01-1*) Family Line Pubns.

***Maryland Motor Vechile Insurance.** 2nd ed. Andrew Janquitto. 1150p. 1999. 125.00 (*0-327-04921-9*, 6354511) LEXIS Pub.

Maryland Motor Vehicle Insurance. Andrew Janquitto. 935p. 1992. 85.00 (*0-87473-992-6*, 63545-10, MICHIE) LEXIS Pub.

Maryland Motor Vehicle Insurance, 1998 Cumulative Supplement. Andrew Janquitto. 411p. 1998. pap., suppl. ed. 45.00 (*0-327-00481-9*, 6354615) LEXIS Pub.

Maryland Mystery Van Takes Off! Bk. 1: Handicapped Maryland Kids Sneak off on a Big Adventure. Carole Marsh. (Carole Marsh Maryland Bks.). (Illus.). (J). (gr. 3-12). 1994. 29.95 (*0-7933-5021-2*); pap. 19.95 (*0-7933-5022-0*); disk 29.95 (*0-7933-5023-9*) Gallopade Intl.

Maryland 1998 Advance Code Service, No. 1. 80p. 1997. pap. write for info. (*0-327-05247-3*, 44011-14) LEXIS Pub.

Maryland 1998 Advance Code Service, No. 2. 122p. 1998. pap. write for info. (*0-327-05248-1*, 44012-14) LEXIS Pub.

Maryland 1998 Advance Code Service, No. 3. 175p. 1998. pap. write for info. (*0-327-05249-X*, 44013-14) LEXIS Pub.

Maryland 1998 Advance Code Service, 3 vols., Set. 1998. pap. write for info. (*0-327-05250-3*, 44010-14) LEXIS Pub.

Maryland 1998 Advance Legislative Service Set. 4200p. 1998. pap. write for info. (*0-327-05129-9*, 44015-12) LEXIS Pub.

Maryland 1998 Advance Legislative Service, No. 1. 850p. 1998. pap. write for info. (*0-327-05130-2*, 44016-12) LEXIS Pub.

Maryland 1998 Advance Legislative Service, No. 2. 850p. 1998. pap. write for info. (*0-327-05131-0*, 44017-12) LEXIS Pub.

Maryland 1998 Advance Legislative Service, No. 3. 850p. 1998. pap. write for info. (*0-327-05132-9*, 44018-12) LEXIS Pub.

Maryland 1998 Advance Legislative Service, No. 4. 850p. 1998. pap. write for info. (*0-327-05133-7*, 44019-12) LEXIS Pub.

Maryland 1998 Advance Legislative Service, No. 5. 850p. 1998. pap. write for info. (*0-327-05134-5*, 44020-12) LEXIS Pub.

Maryland 1998 Public Utility Companies Article. (Michie's Annotated Code of Maryland Ser.: No. PUC). 300p. 1998. write for info. (*0-327-06358-0*, 4390410) LEXIS Pub.

Maryland 1998 Replacement. (Michie's Annotated Code of Maryland Ser.: No. 4). 1250p. 1998. write for info. (*0-327-06357-2*, 4382612) LEXIS Pub.

Maryland 1998 Replacement Volume -- Business Regulation. 800p. 1998. write for info. (*0-327-06662-8*, 4399511) LEXIS Pub.

An Asterisk (*) at the beginning of an entry indicates that the title is appearing for the first time.

Maryland 1998 Replacement Volume -- Courts & Judicial Proceedings, Vol. CJ. 950p. 1998. write for info. (0-327-06663-6, 4397412) LEXIS Pub.

Maryland 1998 Rules Supplement, 2 vols., Set. 200p. 1998. pap. write for info. (0-327-05244-9, 44007-15) LEXIS Pub.

Maryland 1998 Rules Supplement, Vol. 1. 100p. 1998. pap. write for info. (0-327-05242-2, 52595-15) LEXIS Pub.

Maryland 1998 Rules Supplement, Vol. 2. 100p. 1998. pap. write for info. (0-327-05243-0, 52596-15) LEXIS Pub.

***Maryland 1999 Advance Code Service Pamphlet, No. 3.** 231p. 1999. pap. write for info. (0-327-08734-X, 44013-15) LEXIS Pub.

Maryland 1999 Advance Code Service, Issue No. 2. 183p. 1999. write for info. (0-327-07817-0, 4401215) LEXIS Pub.

Maryland 1999 Index, 2 vols. Incl. Vol. I-Z. Maryland 1999 Index. 1999. (0-327-09708-6, 43994-17); Vol. A-H. Maryland 1999 Index. 1999. (0-327-09707-8, 43990-17); 2302p. write for info. (0-327-09706-X, 44002-17) LEXIS Pub.

Maryland 1999 Index see Maryland 1999 Index

Maryland 1999 Replacement Volume Vol. AG: Agriculture. 550p. 1999. write for info. (0-327-07646-1, 4393811, MICHIE) LEXIS Pub.

Maryland 1999 Replacement Volume Vol. FL: Family Law. 500p. 1999. write for info. (0-327-07440-X, 4389511, MICHIE) LEXIS Pub.

Maryland 1999 Rules Vols. 1 & 2: Annotated Code of Maryland Court Rules, 1999 Edition. 2100p. 1998. write for info. (0-327-06593-1, 4400316) LEXIS Pub.

Maryland 1999 Transportation Replacement. 910p. 1999. write for info. (0-327-07965-7, 43910-12) LEXIS Pub.

Maryland 1970 Census Index: Heads of Families. pap. 21.00 (1-877677-44-2) Herit Quest.

Maryland One-Day Trip Book. 2nd rev. ed. Jane Ockershausen. (Illus.). 288p. 1999. pap. 14.95 (1-57427-089-3, EPM) Howell Pr VA.

Maryland Original Research Society of Baltimore, 3 vols. Maryland Original Research Society of Baltimore St. Ed. by Albert Levin Richardson. LC 67-28066. 1310p. 1999. reprint ed. pap. 16.50 (0-8063-0546-0) Genealog Pub.

Maryland Our Maryland, Vol. 7. Ed. by Virginia Geiger. LC 87-13261. (Illus.). 296p. (Orig.). (C). 1987. pap. text 25.00 (0-8191-6455-0); lib. bdg. 53.00 (0-8191-6454-2) U Pr of Amer.

Maryland Pet Profiles. Michelle S. Walters. LC 82-61528. (Illus.). 224p. 1982. pap. 10.95 (0-911071-00-8) Olde Maryland.

Maryland Political Behavior: Four Centuries of Political Culture. George H. Callcott. (Illus.). 64p. (Orig.). 1986. pap. 8.95 (0-938420-42-9) MD Hist.

***Maryland Public Utility Companies Article & Related Laws: 1999 Edition.** 506p. 1999. pap. 62.50 (0-327-10140-7, 2634912) LEXIS Pub.

Maryland Quiz Bowl Crash Course! Carole Marsh. (Carole Marsh Maryland Bks.). (Illus.). (J). (gr. 3-8). 1994. pap. 19.95 (1-55609-634-8); lib. bdg. 29.95 (1-55609-633-X); disk 29.95 (1-55609-635-6) Gallopade Intl.

Maryland Real Estate: Practice & Law. 9th ed. Donald Allen White. LC 98-33295. 1999. pap. 14.95 (0-7931-3181-2) Dearborn.

Maryland Real Estate Forms. Barry Hannah. 1994. ring bd., suppl. ed. 80.00 incl. disk (0-614-03771-9, MICHIE) LEXIS Pub.

Maryland Real Estate Forms, Issue 13. 100p. 1998. ring bd. write for info. (0-327-00503-3, 8160513) LEXIS Pub.

Maryland Real Estate Forms, No. 13. Russell R. Reno, Jr. et al. Ed. by Michael S. Kosmas. LC 84-149438. 100p. 1998. ring bd. write for info. (0-327-00318-9, 81605-13) LEXIS Pub.

***Maryland Real Estate Forms, No. 14.** Russell R. Reno, Jr. et al. 120p. 1999. ring bd. write for info. (0-327-01585-3, 8160514) LEXIS Pub.

Maryland Real Estate Forms, 2 vols., Set. Russell R. Reno, Jr. & Wilbur E. Simmons. 900p. 1986. spiral bd. 229.00 incl. disk (0-87189-281-2, MICHIE) LEXIS Pub.

Maryland Real Estate Leasing Forms. Charles T. Albert & Edward J. Levin. 1994. ring bd., suppl. ed. 85.00 (0-685-74616-X, MICHIE) LEXIS Pub.

Maryland Real Estate Leasing Forms, 2 vols., Set. Charles T. Albert & Edward J. Levin. 1020p. 1994. spiral bd. 269.00 incl. disk (0-87189-065-8, 81590-10, MICHIE) LEXIS Pub.

Maryland Real Estate Principles. Ralph A. Palmer & Joanne Bailey. 456p. (C). 1995. pap. text 32.67 (0-13-777624-1) P-H.

Maryland Records: Colonial, Revolutionary, County & Church from Original Sources, 2 vols., Set. Gaius M. Brumbaugh. (Illus.). 1201p. 1993. 75.00 (0-8063-0059-0, 750) Genealog Pub.

***Maryland Regulations: Containing Insurance Division Regulations, Notices & Orders, & Guidelines; & Selected Attorney General's Opinions.** LC 95-72440. 1998. write for info. (0-89246-443-7) NILS Pub.

Maryland Rent Rolls: Baltimore & Anne Arundel Counties, 1700-1707, 1705-1724. Reprinted with a New Index. 282p. 1996. reprint ed. pap. 25.00 (0-8063-0716-1, 3770) Clearfield Co.

Maryland Revolutionary Records: Data Obtained from 3,050 Pension Claims & Bounty Land Applications, Including 1,000 Marriages of Maryland Soldiers & a List of 1,200 Proved Services of Soldiers & Patriots of Other States. Harry W. Newman. LC 67-28367. 155p. 1993. reprint ed. 17.50 (0-8063-0257-7) Genealog Pub.

Maryland Rollercoasters! Carole Marsh. (Carole Marsh Maryland Bks.). (Illus.). (YA). (gr. 3-12). 1994. pap. 19.95 (0-7933-5285-1); lib. bdg. 29.95 (0-7933-5284-3); disk 29.95 (0-7933-5286-X) Gallopade Intl.

Maryland Rules Commentary. Paul V. Niemeyer & Linda M. Schuette. 610p. 1993. 85.00 (0-614-06185-7, MICHIE) LEXIS Pub.

Maryland Rules, 1994 Edition, 2 vols., Set. Michie Butterworth Editorial Staff. pap. 50.00 (1-55834-043-2, MICHIE) LEXIS Pub.

Maryland Sales & Use Tax Admissions & Amusement Tax Laws & Regulations, 1998 Supplement. 67p. 1999. pap. write for info. (0-327-07446-9, 2639110) LEXIS Pub.

Maryland Sales & Use Tax/Admissions & Amusement Tax Laws & Regulations,with Current Cumulative Supplement: 1997 Edition. The Publisher's Editorial Staff. 206p. pap. 15.00 (1-55834-795-X) LEXIS Pub.

Maryland School Laws & Regulations Annotated, 1998 Edition. 629p. 1999. 45.00 (0-327-07448-5, 2636110) LEXIS Pub.

Maryland School Trivia: An Amazing & Fascinating Look at Our State's Teachers, Schools & Students! Carole Marsh. (Carole Marsh Maryland Bks.). (Illus.). (J). (gr. 3-8). 1994. pap. 19.95 (0-7933-0559-4); lib. bdg. 29.95 (0-7933-0560-8); disk 29.95 (0-7933-0561-6) Gallopade Intl.

Maryland Seafood Cookbook, No. I. Maryland Department of Agriculture Staff. (Illus.). 48p. 1995. 6.95 (1-885457-00-6) Eastwind MD.

Maryland Seafood Cookbook, No. II. Maryland Department of Agriculture Staff. 72p. 1994. pap. 6.95 (1-885457-02-2) Eastwind MD.

Maryland Seafood Cookbook, No. III. Maryland Department of Agriculture Staff. 72p. 1994. pap. 6.95 (1-885457-03-0) Eastwind MD.

Maryland September: True Stories from the Antietam Campaign. (Illus.). 70p. 1997. pap. 7.95 (1-57747-014-1) Thomas Publications.

Maryland Silly Basketball Sportsmysteries, Vol. I. Carole Marsh. (Carole Marsh Maryland Bks.). (Illus.). (J). (gr. 3-8). 1994. pap. 19.95 (0-7933-0556-X); lib. bdg. 29.95 (0-7933-0557-8); disk 29.95 (0-7933-0558-6) Gallopade Intl.

Maryland Silly Basketball Sportsmysteries, Vol. II. Carole Marsh. (Carole Marsh Maryland Bks.). (Illus.). (J). (gr. 3-8). 1994. pap. 19.95 (0-7933-1697-9); lib. bdg. 29.95 (0-7933-1696-0); disk 29.95 (0-7933-1698-7) Gallopade Intl.

Maryland Silly Football Sportsmysteries, Vol. I. Carole Marsh. (Carole Marsh Maryland Bks.). (Illus.). (J). (gr. 3-8). 1994. pap. 19.95 (1-55609-625-9); lib. bdg. 29.95 (1-55609-624-0); disk 29.95 (1-55609-626-7) Gallopade Intl.

Maryland Silly Football Sportsmysteries, Vol. II. Carole Marsh. (Carole Marsh Maryland Bks.). (Illus.). (J). (gr. 3-8). 1994. pap. 19.95 (1-55609-628-3); lib. bdg. 29.95 (1-55609-627-5); disk 29.95 (1-55609-629-1) Gallopade Intl.

Maryland Silly Trivia! Carole Marsh. (Carole Marsh Maryland Bks.). (Illus.). (J). (gr. 3-8). 1994. pap. 19.95 (1-55609-042-0); lib. bdg. 29.95 (1-55609-617-8); disk 29.95 (1-55609-618-6) Gallopade Intl.

***Maryland Special Education Laws & Regulations: 1999 Edition.** 363p. 2000. write for info. (0-327-10423-6, 2638810) LEXIS Pub.

Maryland Spelling Bee! Score Big by Correctly Spelling Our State's Unique Names. Carole Marsh. (Carole Marsh Maryland Bks.). (Illus.). (YA). (gr. 3-12). 1996. pap. 19.95 (0-7933-6701-8); lib. bdg. 29.95 (0-7933-6700-X) Gallopade Intl.

Maryland State Court Rules Newsletter. Date not set. pap. write for info. (0-327-06203-7, 41250-10) LEXIS Pub.

***Maryland State Credit Directory, 2000 Edition.** rev. ed. American Business Directories Staff. 464p. 1999. boxed set 145.00 incl. cd-rom (0-7687-0306-9) Am Busn Direct.

***Maryland State Government: 1999 Replacement Volume.** 725p. 1999. write for info. (0-327-09919-4, 9413116) LEXIS Pub.

Maryland State Parks. Barbara McCaig & Boyce. (Illus.). 100p. (Orig.). 1989. pap. text 5.95 (0-935201-63-7) Affordable Adven.

Maryland State Rules of Evidence with Objections. Anthony J. Bocchino et al. 227p. 1995. pap. 25.95 (1-55681-466-6) Natl Inst Trial Ad.

Maryland Survival. Betty L. Hall & Mary B. Webb-Hernandez. 160p. (Orig.). (gr. 10-12). 1979. pap. text 5.84 (0-03-055501-9) Westwood Pr.

Maryland, the History of a Palatinate. enl. rev. ed. William H. Browne. LC 72-3758. (American Commonwealths Ser.: No. 3). reprint ed. 39.50 (0-404-57203-0) AMS Pr.

Maryland the Seventh State a History. 4th rev. ed. John T. Marck. (Illus.). 456p. 1998. 32.95 (1-884604-78-1) Creative Impress.

Maryland Time Exposures, 1840-1940. Mame Warren & Marion E. Warren. LC 84-47939. (Illus.). 360p. 1984. 37.50 (0-8018-2496-6) Johns Hopkins.

Maryland Timeline: A Chronology of Maryland History, Mystery, Trivia, Legend, Lore & More. Carole Marsh. (Carole Marsh Maryland Bks.). (Illus.). (J). (gr. 3-12). 1994. pap. 19.95 (0-7933-5936-8); lib. bdg. 29.95 (0-7933-5935-X); disk 29.95 (0-7933-5937-6) Gallopade Intl.

Maryland Title Searcher's Handbook. 2nd ed. Bayard H. Waterbury. 3339p. 1990. pap. 50.00 (0-87473-573-4, 68374-10, MICHIE) LEXIS Pub.

Maryland Title 10. Motor Fuel & Lubricants Business Regulation Article: 1998 Edition. 32p. pap. 7.00 (0-327-06654-7) LEXIS Pub.

Maryland Title 9, Fuel Taxes/title 13, Procedure/tax General Article: 1997 Edition. 121p. pap. 12.00 (1-55834-745-3) LEXIS Pub.

Maryland Today: A Geography. 3rd ed. Vera F. Rollo. LC 99-33419. 188p. (J). (gr. 4). 1999. 22.50 (0-917882-49-0) MD Hist Pr.

Maryland Tort Law: Includes 1998 Supplement. Pamela A. Jenrym et al. LC 97-31500. (Case Summaries Ser.). 1997. 90.00 (0-89059-080-X) Bernan Pr.

Maryland Tort Law Handbook. 2nd ed. Richard J. Gilbert & Paul T. Gilbert. 420p. 1992. 75.00 (1-55834-013-0, 62398-10, MICHIE) LEXIS Pub.

Maryland Tort Law Handbook: 1998 Cumulative Supplement. Richard J. Gilbert & Paul T. Gilbert. 150p. 1998. write for info. (0-327-00232-8, 62399-14) LEXIS Pub.

Maryland Tort Law Handbook, 1999 Cumulative Supplement. 2nd ed. Paul T. Gilbert & Richard J. Gilbert. 150p. 1999. write for info. (0-327-01513-6, 6239915) LEXIS Pub.

Maryland Trivia. Al Menendez & Shirley Menendez. LC 92-6746. 192p. (Orig.). 1992. pap. 6.95 (1-55853-164-5) Rutledge Hill Pr.

Maryland 2000! Coming Soon to a Calendar Near You - The 21st Century! - Complete Set of AL 2000 Items. Carole Marsh. (Two Thousand! Ser.). (Illus.). (J). (gr. 3-12). 1998. pap. 75.00 (0-7933-9349-3); lib. bdg. 85.00 (0-7933-9350-7) Gallopade Intl.

Maryland 2000! Coming Soon to a Calendar Near You-The 21st Century! Carole Marsh. (Two Thousand! Ser.). (Illus.). (J). (gr. 3-12). 1998. pap. 19.95 (0-7933-8736-1); lib. bdg. 29.95 (0-7933-8735-3) Gallopade Intl.

***Maryland 2000 Advance Code Service, Vol. 1.** 60p. 1999. pap. write for info. (0-327-09928-3, 4401116) LEXIS Pub.

***Maryland 2000 Rules, 2 vols.** 2082p. 1999. write for info. (0-327-09929-1, 4400317) LEXIS Pub.

Maryland UFO's & Extraterrestrials! A Look at the Sightings & Science in Our State. Carole Marsh. (Carole Marsh Maryland Bks.). (Illus.). (J). (gr. 3-12). 1997. pap. 19.95 (0-7933-6395-0); lib. bdg. 29.95 (0-7933-6394-2) Gallopade Intl.

Maryland under the Commonwealth: A Chronicle of the Years, 1649-1658. Bernard C. Steiner. LC 79-158209. reprint ed. 32.50 (0-404-06248-2) AMS Pr.

Maryland under the Commonwealth: A Chronicle of the Years, 1649-1658. Bernard C. Steiner. (BCL1 - United States Local History Ser.). 178p. 1991. reprint ed. lib. bdg. 69.00 (0-7812-6282-8) Rprt Serv.

Maryland Vehicle Law: 1993 Edition. American Academy of Pediatrics Staff. 25.00 (0-614-05893-7, MICHIE) LEXIS Pub.

Maryland Vehicle Law: 1998 Edition. annot. ed. Anne S. Ferro. LC 99-163228. 1998. write for info. (0-327-06296-7, 26335-16) LEXIS Pub.

***Maryland Vehicle Law: 1999 Edition.** 807p. 1999. pap. 32.00 (0-327-09825-2, 2633517) LEXIS Pub.

***Maryland Vehicle Law Advance Legislative Service.** 326p. 1999. pap. Price not set. (0-327-09790-6, 2639510) LEXIS Pub.

(Maryland) Washington Surburban Sanitary District Laws, 1998 Edition. 204p. 1998. 70.00 (0-327-06803-5, 3750512) LEXIS Pub.

Maryland Wits & Baltimore Bards: A Literary History with Notes on Washington Writers. Frank R. Shivers, Jr. LC 97-26678. (Illus.). 348p. 1998. reprint ed. pap. 14.95 (0-8018-5810-0) Johns Hopkins.

Maryland Women's History: Resource Packet. (Illus.). 268p. (Orig.). (C). 1996. pap. text 45.00 (0-7881-2682-2) DIANE Pub.

Maryland Workers' Compensation Handbook. 2nd ed. Richard P. Gilbert & Robert L. Humphreys, Jr. 590p. 1993. 85.00 (1-55834-034-3, 62402-10, MICHIE) LEXIS Pub.

Maryland Workers' Compensation Handbook: 1998 Cumulative Supplement. 2nd ed. Robert L. Humphreys, Jr. LC 93-77057. 1998. 40.00 (0-327-00116-X, 62403-14) LEXIS Pub.

Maryland Workers' Compensation Handbook, 1999 Cumulative Supplement. 2nd ed. Robert L. Humphreys, Jr. 200p. 1999. 45.00 (0-327-01153-X, 6240315) LEXIS Pub.

Maryland 1999: Advance Code Service, 001. Lexis Law Publishing Staff. 60p. 1998. pap. write for info. (0-327-06581-8) LEXIS Pub.

***Maryland 1999 Cumulative Supplement, 35 vols., Set.** 6000p. 1999. pap. write for info. (0-327-07399-3, 4400016) LEXIS Pub.

***Maryland/Delaware Atlas.** 2nd ed. Ed. by DeLorme Mapping Staff. (Illus.). 2000. pap. 19.95 (0-89933-279-X) DeLorme Map.

***Marylanders at Gettysburg.** 2nd ed. Daniel Carroll Toomey. (Illus.). 1998. pap. 11.95 (0-9612670-3-8) Toomey Pr.

***Marylanders in Blue: The Artillery & the Cavalry.** Daniel Carroll & Charles Albert Earp. LC 99-70879. (Illus.). 176p. 1999. 34.95 (0-9612670-8-9) Toomey Pr.

Marylanders in the Confederacy. Daniel D. Hartzler. LC 86-82702. 420p. 1986. 25.00 (0-940907-00-3) Family Line Pubns.

***Maryland's Big Activity Book.** Carole Marsh. (Maryland Experience! Ser.). (Illus.). (J). (gr. k-5). 2000. pap. 9.95 (0-7933-9614-X) Gallopade Intl.

Maryland's Blue & Gray: A Border State's Union & Confederate Junior Officer Corps. Kevin C. Ruffner. LC 97-7078. (Illus.). 464p. 1997. 34.95 (0-8071-2135-5) La State U Pr.

Maryland's Catoctin Mountain Parks: An Interpretive Guide to Catoctin Mountain Park & Cunningham Falls State Park. John Means. (Illus.). 174p. (Orig.). 1995. pap. text 14.95 (0-939923-38-6) M & W Pub Co.

***Maryland's Colonial Eastern Shore: Historical Sketches of Counties & of Some Notable Structures.** Ed. by Swepson Earle & Percy G. Skirven. 204p. 1999. reprint ed. pap. 22.50 (0-8063-4850-X) Clearfield Co.

Maryland's Colonial Eastern Shore: Historical Sketches of Counties & of Some Notable Structures. Ed. by Swepson Earle & Percy G. Skirven. (Illus.). xx, 215p. 1996. reprint ed. pap. 24.50 (0-7884-0555-1, E064) Heritage Bk.

Maryland's Colonial Eastern Shore: Historical Sketches of Counties & of Some Notable Structures. Ed. by Swepson Earle & Percy G. Skirven. (Illus.). 204p. 1997. reprint ed. lib. bdg. 29.00 (0-8328-5941-9) Higginson Bk Co.

Maryland's Conservation Laws, Licenses & Enforcement Officers. Paul M. Hanyok. LC 95-95296. 1996. pap. 14.95 (0-9651951-0-4) Old Line Pr.

Maryland's Eastern Shore: A Guide for Wanderers. Mary U. Coradry. 224p. (Orig.). 1997. pap. 14.95 (0-937692-14-X) Litrary Hse Pr.

Maryland's Eastern Shore: A Journey in Time & Place. John R. Wennersten. LC 91-50584. (Illus.). 310p. 1992. 23.95 (0-87033-428-X, Tidewtr Pubs) Cornell Maritime.

Maryland's Garrett County Graves. NSDAR Youghiogheny Glades Chapter Staff. LC 87-50355. (Illus.). 488p. 1987. 29.00 (0-9618240-0-X) N S D A R.

Maryland's Geology. Martin F. Schmidt, Jr. LC 92-16980. (Illus.). 175p. 1993. pap. 24.95 (0-87033-437-9, Tidewtr Pubs) Cornell Maritime.

Maryland's German Heritage: Daniel Wunderlich Nead's History. Ed. by Don H. Tolzmann. (Illus.). 304p. 1994. pap. text 24.00 (0-7884-0064-9) Heritage Bk.

Maryland's Great Outdoors. Middleton Evans. (Illus.). 224p. 1996. 45.00 (0-9620806-4-0) Middle Pr.

Maryland's Historic Restaurants & Their Recipes. 2nd ed. Dawn O'Brien & Rebecca Schenck. LC 95-24800. (Historic Restaurant Cookbooks Ser.). (Illus.). 206p. 1996. 15.95 (0-89587-137-8) Blair.

Maryland's Influence upon Land Cessions to the United States. Herbert B. Adams. LC 04-8520. 1885. 5.00 (0-403-00136-6) Scholarly.

Maryland's Influence upon Land Cessions to the United States. Herbert B. Adams. LC 77-97563. (Johns Hopkins University. Studies in the Social Sciences. Tenth Ser. 1892:10-11). reprint ed. 32.50 (0-404-00286-2) AMS Pr.

Maryland's (Most Devastating!) Disasters & (Most Calamitous!) Catastrophies! Carole Marsh. (Carole Marsh Maryland Bks.). (Illus.). (J). (gr. 3-8). 1994. pap. 19.95 (0-7933-0547-0); lib. bdg. 29.95 (0-7933-0548-9); disk 29.95 (0-7933-0549-7) Gallopade Intl.

Maryland's Museums & Preservation Organizations: A Historical & Cultural Directory. Ed. by Maryland Association of History Museums Staff. (Illus.). 155p. 1999. pap. 5.00 (1-878399-74-8) Div Hist Cult Progs.

Maryland's Ocean Fisheries: A Bioeconomic Assessment. Douglas W. Lipton & Ivar E. Strand. 1983. pap. 1.50 (0-943676-22-3) MD Sea Grant Col.

Maryland's Oyster Navy: The First Fifty Years. Norman H. Plummer. LC 93-26694. 1993. 19.95 (0-922249-05-9) Ches Bay Mus.

Maryland's Oysters: An Annotated Bibliography. Victor S. Kennedy & Linda L. Breisch. 1981. pap. 15.00 (0-943676-01-0) MD Sea Grant Col.

Maryland's Persistent Pursuit to End Slavery, 1850-1864: Antislavery Activity Between 1850 & 1864. rev. ed. Anita A. Guy. LC 96-44999. (Studies in African American History & Culture). 640p. 1996. text 83.00 (0-8153-2578-9) Garland.

Maryland's Unsolved Mysteries (And Their "Solutions") Includes Scientific Information & Other Activities for Students. Carole Marsh. (Carole Marsh Maryland Bks.). (Illus.). (J). (gr. 3-12). 1994. pap. 19.95 (0-7933-5783-7); lib. bdg. 29.95 (0-7933-5782-9); disk 29.95 (0-7933-5784-5) Gallopade Intl.

Maryland's Vanishing Lives. John Sherwood. (Maryland Paperback Bookshelf Ser.). (Illus.). 232p. 1995. reprint ed. pap. 25.95 (0-8018-5249-8) Johns Hopkins.

Maryland's Way Cook Book. 14th unabridged ed. Ed. by Hammond-Harwood House Staff et al. LC 64-25429. (Illus.). 364p. 1991. 22.00 (0-910688-01-X) Hammond-Harwood.

Marylou on Stage. Raymond Plante. (Early Readers Ser.). (Illus.). 62p. (J). (gr. 1-4). 1999. mass mkt. 3.99 (0-88780-480-2) Formac Publ Co.

Marynia, Don't Cry: Memoirs of Two Polish-Canadian Families. Kojder M. Apolonja. LC 96-132578. (Illus.). 208p. 1995. pap. 24.94 (0-919045-65-0) Multicult Hist.

Mary's Child. Elaine Cannon. 1997. 13.95 (1-57008-359-2) Bookcraft Inc.

Mary's Child. I. Carr. 1997. mass mkt. 13.95 (0-340-65433-3, Pub. by Hodder & Stought Ltd) Trafalgar.

Mary's Child. Terese Ramin. (Intimate Moments Ser.). 1998. per. 4.25 (0-373-07881-1, 1-07881-5) Silhouette.

Mary's Child. large type ed. Irene Carr. (Large Print Ser.). 656p. 1997. 27.99 (0-7089-3698-9) Ulverscroft.

Mary's Christmas Story. (Arch Bks.). (Illus.). (J). (ps-4). 1996. 1.99 (0-570-07526-2, 59-1499) Concordia.

Mary's City of David: A Pictorial History of the Israelite House of David As Reorganized by Mary Purnell. large type ed. R. James Taylor. (Illus.). 181p. 1996. 50.00 (0-9653055-0-3) Marys City of David.

Mary's Fiat. Robert D. Eimer & Sarah A. O'Malley. 32p. (J). 1994. pap. 2.95 (0-8198-4771-2) Pauline Bks.

Mary's First Christmas. Walker Wangerin, Jr. (J). 1998. 19.99 (0-310-22746-1) Zondervan.

Mary's First Christmas. Walter Wangerin, Jr. LC 97-51811. (Illus.). 48p. 1998. 19.99 (0-310-22216-8) Zondervan.

Mary's Flowers: Gardens, Legends & Meditations. Vincenzina Krymow. 192p. 1999. 29.95 (0-86716-349-6) St Anthony Mess Pr.

Mary's Grave. Malcolm McClintick. 224p. 1990. pap. 3.50 (0-380-70818-3, Avon Bks) Morrow Avon.

***Mary's House.** PUBLISHING Concordia Publishing. 1999. 8.00 (0-570-07049-X) Concordia.

M

Mary's House: Mary Pyle under the Spiritual Guidance of Padre Pio. Dorothy M. Gaudiose. LC 92-21401. 202p. (Orig.). 1992. pap. 9.95 (*0-8189-0646-4*) Alba.
Mary's Journal: A Mother's Story. Evelyn Bence. 2000. 4.99 (*0-310-21488-2*) Zondervan.
Mary's Land. Lucia St. Clair Robson. 1996. mass mkt. 5.99 (*0-345-40628-1*) Ballantine Pub Grp.
Mary's Light of Grace: Marian Lectures. Louise D'Angelo. (Illus.). 34p. (Orig.). 1973. pap. 3.00 (*1-878886-05-3*) Maryheart Crusaders.
Mary's Little Donkey: A Christmas Story for Young Children. Gunhild Sehlin. Tr. by Hugh Latham & Donald Mackan. (SWE., Illus.). 157p. (J). (gr. 3-6). 1992. pap. 10.95 (*0-86315-064-0*, Pub. by Floris Bks) Gryphon Hse.
Mary's Little Instruction Book: Learning from the Wisdom of the Blessed Mother. Eileen E. Freeman. LC 95-1885. 160p. (Orig.). 1995. mass mkt. 5.99 (*0-446-67181-9*, Pub. by Warner Bks) Little.
Mary's Memories. Phyllis Vos Wezeman & Colleen A. Wiessner. (Celebrate: A Creative Approach to Bible Studies). 38p. (Orig.). (J). (gr. 1-6). 1989. pap. 5.95 (*0-940754-72-X*) Ed Ministries.
Mary's Merry Chase. Darrell Wiskur. Ed. by Silver Dollar City, Inc. Staff. (City Stories Ser.). (Illus.). (J). (ps-1). 1977. 1.99 (*0-686-19126-9*) Silver Dollar.
Mary's Message of Hope: Volume I: As Sent By Mary, The Mother of Jesus, To Her Messenger. 3rd ed. Annie Kirkwood. LC 95-42600. (Illus.). 144p. (Orig.). 1996. pap. 10.95 (*0-931892-35-X*) B Dolphin Pub.
Mary's Message to the World. Annie O. Kirkwood. LC 91-11517. 304p. 1996. pap. 10.00 (*0-399-52200-X*, Perigee Bks) Berkley Pub.
Mary's Message to the World, Set. abr. ed. Annie Kirkwood. 17.95 incl. audio (*1-57453-106-9*) Audio Lit.
*__Mary's Monster.__ William Latham. 298p. 1999. pap. 9.95 (*0-9677280-0-2*) Powys.
Mary's Place in Christian Dialogue. Ed. by Alberic Stacpoole. (C). 1988. 60.00 (*0-85439-201-7*, Pub. by St Paul Pubns) St Mut.
Mary's Plan: The Madonna Comes to Santa Maria. J. Ridley Castro. LC 93-83223. 180p. 1993. pap. 2.00 (*1-882972-08-2*, 3011) Queenship Pub.
*__Mary's Pope: John Paul II, Mary & the Church since Vatican II.__ Antoine E. Nachef. LC 00-33883. 220p. 2000. write for info. (*1-58051-077-9*) Sheed & Ward WI.
Mary's Prayer. Maggie Swanson. (Maggie Swanson Board Books). 1999. 3.95 (*0-88271-710-3*) Regina Pr.
Mary's Recipe Box. Mary Gubser. (Illus.). 240p. 1996. pap. 18.95 (*1-57178-015-7*) Coun Oak Bks.
Mary's Rosary & the Living Word. Vincenza Genovese. 260p. 1987. 2.50 (*0-911988-83-1*, 50350) AMI Pr.
Mary's Spiritual Maternity. J. Patrick Gaffney. 1977. 4.95 (*0-910984-18-2*) Montfort Pubns.
*__Mary's Story.__ Sarah Boss. (Illus.). 48p. (J). (ps up). 1999. 16.95 (*1-901223-44-2*) Barefoot Bks NY.
Mary's Story. Linda Parry. LC 98-215204. (Illus.). 24p. (J). (ps-2). 1998. 12.99 (*0-8010-4359-X*) Baker Bks.
*__Mary's Story.__ Random House Staff. 176p. (J). (gr. 4-7). 1999. pap. 4.99 (*0-375-80332-7*, Pub. by Random Bks Yng Read) Random.
Mary's Story: Luke 1:5-2:18. M. M. Brem. (Arch Bks.: Set 4). 1967. pap. 1.99 (*0-570-06029-X*, 59-1140) Concordia.
Mary's Story of Christmas. Don J. Black. 1996. pap. 3.95 (*1-55503-343-1*, 29004764) Covenant Comms.
Mary's Testimony: A Christmas Story. S. Dilworth Young. 8p. (Orig.). 1991. write for info. (*0-318-68387-3*) Jackman Pubng.
Mary's Three Gifts to Her Beloved Priests. Albert J. Shamon. LC 97-67583. (Illus.). 100p. (Orig.). 1997. pap. 2.95 (*1-57918-005-1*, 3502) Queenship Pub.
Mary's Tiger. Rex Harley. LC 89-49009. (Illus.). 23p. (J). (ps-2). 1990. 13.95 (*0-15-200524-2*, Gulliver Bks) Harcourt.
Mary's Treasure Box. Carolyn W. Kramlich. LC 98-6487. 32p. (J). 1998. 12.99 (*0-8499-5834-2*) Tommy Nelson.
Mary's Vineyard: Daily Meditations, Readings & Revelations. Andrew Harvey. (Illus.). 208p. 1996. 20.00 (*0-8356-0745-3*, Quest) Theos Pub Hse.
*__Mary's Way: A Memoir of the Life of Mary Cooper Back.__ Ruth M. Lamb & Mary W. Cooper Back. (Illus.). vii, 280p. 1999. pap. 13.00i (*0-9671734-0-X*) FuturePrep Corp.
Mary's Way: A Universal Story of Spiritual Growth & Transformation. Peggy T. Millin. (Illus.). 144p. 1995. pap. 11.95 (*0-89087-644-4*) Celestial Arts.
Mary's Way of the Cross. Richard Furey. 32p. 1984. 0.99 (*0-89622-198-9*) Twenty-Third.
*__Mary's Wonder Kite.__ Dorothy S. Harding. (J). (gr. 2-5). 2000. pap. 5.95 (*0-533-13432-3*) Vantage.
*__Mary's World: Love, War & Family Ties in Nineteenth-Century Charleston.__ Richard N. Cote. Ed. by Elizabeth Burnett. (Illus.). 2000. 29.95 (*1-929175-19-1*, Corinthian Bks) Cote Lit Grp.
Marzio's Crucifix. Francis M. Crawford. LC 04-15090. 1887. 9.00 (*0-403-00014-9*) Scholarly.
Marzio's Crucifix. Francis M. Crawford. LC 79-80626. (BCL Ser. I). reprint ed. 31.50 (*0-404-01829-7*) AMS Pr.
Marzio's Crucifix. Francis M. Crawford. (Works of Francis Marion Crawford). 1990. reprint ed. lib. bdg. 79.00 (*0-7812-2532-9*) Rprt Serv.
Marzipan Moon. Nancy Willard. LC 80-24221. (Illus.). 48p. (J). (gr. 2-5). 1981. 9.95 (*0-15-252962-4*, Harcourt Child Bks) Harcourt.
Marzipan Moon. Nancy Willard. LC 80-24221. (Illus.). 48p. 1989. pap. 3.95 (*0-15-252963-2*) Harcourt.
Marzipan Pigeon. Alyssa Donati. 1994. 21.00 (*0-671-86889-6*) S&S Trade.
Mas Alla: Lab A - English, 2. Gallego. 1999. pap. text, wbk. ed. write for info. (*0-471-32337-3*) Wiley.
Mas Alla (Beyond Death) D. Winter. (SPA.). 1.95 (*0-685-74952-5*, 540478) Editorial Unilit.
Mas Alla de la Bella (In)Diferencia. Heidi Figueroa Sarriera et al. (SPA.). 250p. 1994. pap. write for info. (*0-929441-66-4*) Pubns Puertorriquenas.
Mas Alla de la Cumbre. Zig Ziglar.Tr. of Over the Top. (SPA.). 292p. 1995. 10.99 (*0-88113-332-9*, B001-3329) Caribe Betania.
Mas Alla de la Escuela Dominical. Editorial Caribe Staff.Tr. of Beyond Sunday School. (SPA.). 1997. pap. text 7.99 (*0-89922-384-2*) Caribe Betania.
Mas Alla de la Fe. Tr. of Moving Beyond Belief. (SPA.). 275p. 1995. 11.99 (*0-88113-108-3*, B046-1083) Caribe Betania.
Mas Alla de la Herrumbre I. Javier Avila. (Ciencia para Todos Ser.). (SPA.). pap. 6.99 (*968-16-2396-7*, Pub. by Fondo) Continental Bk.
Mas Alla de la Herrumbre III. Joan Genesca. (Ciencia para Todos Ser.). (SPA.). pap. 6.99 (*968-16-4370-4*, Pub. by Fondo) Continental Bk.
Mas Alla de la Herrumbre II. Javier Avila. (Ciencia para Todos Ser.). (SPA.). pap. 6.99 (*968-16-3153-6*, Pub. by Fondo) Continental Bk.
*__Mas Alla de la Inocencia (Beyond the Innocence)__ Catherine Spencer. (Bianca Ser.). (SPA.). 2000. mass mkt. 3.50 (*0-373-33565-2*, 1-33565-2) Harlequin Bks.
*__Mas Alla de la Ira.__ Robyn Donald. (Bianca Ser.: Bk. 207).Tr. of Beyond the Anger. (SPA.). 2000. per. 3.50 (*0-373-33557-1*, 1-33557-9) Harlequin Bks.
Mas Alla de la Oscuridad: Mi Viaje a la Muerte y Al Filo del Infierno. Angie Fenimore. 1997. pap. text 16.95 (*970-05-0647-9*) Grijalbo Edit.
Mas Alla de la Seduccion. David Hunt. (SPA.). 272p. 1995. pap. 8.99 (*0-8254-1324-9*, Edit Portavoz) Kregel.
Mas Alla de las Mascaras. Lucia Guerra. (SPA.). 87p. 1984. pap. 7.00 (*968-434-331-0*, 3016) Ediciones Norte.
Mas Alla de las Mascaras. 2nd ed. Lucia Guerra. Ed. by Yvette E. Miller. LC 86-15309. (SPA., Illus.). 87p. 1986. reprint ed. pap. 8.95 (*0-935480-23-4*) Lat Am Lit Rev Pr.
Mas Alla de Mis Fuerzas. William Arbelo. LC 88-82056. (Coleccion Cuba y sus Jueces). (SPA., Illus.). 100p. (Orig.). 1989. pap. 9.95 (*0-89729-502-1*) Ediciones.
Mas Alla del Horizonte. abr. ed. Walter Mercado. (SPA.). 272p. 1997. audio 12.98 (*1-57042-526-4*, Pub. by Warner Bks) Little.
Mas Alla del Horizonte: Visiones del Nuevo Milenio. Walter Mercado. 1997. 20.00 (*0-446-52077-2*) Warner Bks.
Mas Alla del Horizonte: Visiones del Nuevo Milenio. Walter Mercado. 304p. 1997. mass mkt. 9.99 (*0-446-67353-6*, Pub. by Warner Bks) Little.
Mas Alla del Jardin/Further from the Garden. Antonio Gala. 1997. pap. text 9.95 (*84-08-02012-9*) Planeta.
Mas Alla del Perdon. Donald Baker.Tr. of Beyond Forgiveness. (SPA.). 119p. 1984. pap. 4.99 (*958-95163-2-7*, 498520) Editorial Unilit.
Mas Alla del Recuerdo. Olga Rosado. LC 96-83697. (Coleccion Caniqui). (SPA.). 85p. (Orig.). 1996. pap. 9.95 (*0-89729-800-4*) Ediciones.
Mas Alla la Isla. Ramon Ferreira. LC 89-80762. (Coleccion Caniqui). (SPA.). 227p. (Orig.). 1991. pap. 15.00 (*0-89729-545-5*) Ediciones.
Mas Antes: Hispanic Folklore of the Rio Puerco Valley. Nasario Garcia. LC 97-27785. (Illus.). 200p. 1997. 24.95 (*0-89013-320-4*) Museum NM Pr.
Mas Antes: Voices from the Rio Puerco Valley. Nasario Garcia. LC 97-27785. (Illus.). 200p. 1997. pap. 12.95 (*0-89013-323-9*) Museum NM Pr.
Mas Bosquejos de Sermones para Dias y Ocasiones Especiales. Charles R. Wood. (SPA.). 64p. 1996. mass mkt. 2.99 (*0-8254-1903-4*, Edit Portavoz) Kregel.
Mas Cerca de la Llama. Tr. of Flying Closer to the Flame. (SPA.). 1994. pap. text 9.99 (*0-88113-186-5*) Caribe Betania.
Ma's Cookin Notes . . . And Other Things. unabridged ed. Robert F. Schissel. Ed. & Illus. by Krueger Graphics Staff. (Orig.). 1997. pap. 6.95 (*0-9653916-1-2*) Recipe Res Inst.
Mas Costura para el Hogar. Cy DeCosse Inc., Staff. (Singer Sewing Reference Library). (SPA., Illus.). 128p. 1992. 17.95 (*0-86573-271-X*) Creat Pub Intl.
Mas Cuentos Picantes de Rosendo Rosell. Rosendo Rosell. LC 79-5001. (Coleccion Caniqui). (Illus.). 138p. 1980. pap. 9.95 (*0-89729-219-7*) Ediciones.
Mas Cuentos y Juegos. 2nd rev. ed. Ed. by Ellen C. Lavroff et al. (SPA., Illus.). (C). 1982. pap. text 9.75 (*0-393-95108-1*) Norton.
Mas de 1000 Palabras (More Than 1000 Words) Jean M. Miscisin. (SPA.). 154p. (C). 1995. pap. text. write for info. (*0-9648585-0-9*) Pocasse Pr.
Mas Facil: A Concise Review of Spanish Grammar. Estelita Calderon-Young & Rodney M. Mebane. LC 92-35386. 256p. 1993. pap. text 27.40 (*0-13-178336-X*) P-H.
*__Mas Historias de Aguas Refrescantes.__ Alice Gray. (SPA.). 2000. pap. 9.99 (*0-7899-0657-0*) Spanish Hse Distributors.
Ma's in the Kitchen: You'll Know When It's Done. Carl R. McQueary & May N. Paulisen. (Illus.). 216p. 1994. 16.95 (*0-89015-953-X*) Sunbelt Media.
*__Mas Joven que Nunca (Age Erasers for Women) Recursos Rejuvenecedores para la Mujer (Actions You Can Take)__ Ed. by Prevention Magazine Editors. (SPA., Illus.). 656p. 2000. pap. 16.95 (*0-87596-470-2*) Rodale Pr Inc.
Mas Mierda! More of the Real You Were Never Taught in School. Frances de T. Berger & Kim W. Eversz. LC 94-25530. (Illus.). 1995. pap. 8.95 (*0-452-27185-1*, Plume) Dutton Plume.
Mas Objetos Que Ensenan de Dios: More Objects That Teach about God. Jose L. Martinez. (SPA.). 96p. (Orig.). 1992. pap. 7.99 (*0-311-44008-8*) Casa Bautista.
*__Mas Oyama: The Legend, the Legacy.__ Michael L. Larden. (Illus.). 184p. 2000. pap. 14.95 (*1-892515-24-5*, Pub. by Multi-Media Commns) Unique Pubns.
Mas Oyama's Complete Karate Course. Mas Oyama. LC 99-187442. (Illus.). 256p. 1998. pap. 14.95 (*0-8069-8845-2*) Sterling.
Mas Pequenos. David Wilkerson. (SPA.). pap. 5.99 (*0-8297-0377-2*) Vida Pubs.
Mas Proceedings 1991, Military Modeling & Management. Stanley A. Erickson, Jr. (Topics in Operations Research Ser.). 303p. 1992. pap. 22.00 (*1-877640-12-3*) INFORMS.
*__Mas Proyectos?__ Susan F. Tierno. Tr. by Ana M. Alvarado. (Think-Kids Book Collection).Tr. of I Hate Projects. (SPA., Illus.). 16p. (J). 2000. pap. 2.95 (*1-58237-041-9*) Creat Think.
Mas Puro Que el Diamante. J. C. Ferrieres. Orig. Title: Purer Than Diamond. (SPA.). 80p. 1963. mass mkt. 3.99 (*0-8254-1227-7*, Edit Portavoz) Kregel.
*__Mas Que Amante.__ 2000. per. 3.50 (*0-373-33553-9*) S&S Trade.
Mas Que Amigos: Courtship in Granite Ridge. Barbara McCauley. (Deseo Ser.: No. 139).Tr. of More Than Friends. 1999. mass mkt. 3.50 (*0-373-35269-7*, 1-35269-9) Harlequin Bks.
Mas Que Belleza. Elizabeth Bevarly. 1999. per. 3.50 (*0-373-35297-2*, 1352970) Harlequin Bks.
Mas Que Cajas see Homeplay: La Alegria de Aprender Entre Ninos y Adultos, Series I
Mas Que No Love It. Jim Sagel. (ENG & SPA.). 117p. (Orig.). 1990. pap. 9.95 (*0-931122-62-7*) West End.
*__Mas Que Un Banco: 40 Anos Banco Interamericano de Desarrollo.__ IDB Staff. (SPA.). 201p. 1999. 30.00 (*1-886938-68-7*) IADB.
Mas Que un Carpintero. Josh McDowell.Tr. of More Than a Carpenter. 1997. mass mkt. 3.99 (*0-7899-0356-3*, 497678) Editorial Unilit.
*__Mas Que un Recuerdo (More Than a Memory) Taming Tall, Dark Brandon.__ Joan Elliott Pickart. (Deseo Ser.: No. 195). (SPA.). 2000. per. 3.50 (*0-373-35325-1*, 1-35325-9) Silhouette.
Mas Que Vencedores. C. Jimenez.Tr. of More Than Winners. (SPA.). 10.99 (*0-7899-0206-0*, 550048) Editorial Unilit.
*__Mas Que Vencedores.__ Portavoz Editorial Staff. (Sabio & Prudente Ser.: Vol. 2). 96p. 1999. pap. 4.99 (*0-8254-0945-4*, Edit Portavoz) Kregel.
Mas Que Vencedores. 2nd ed. W. Hendrikson. (SPA.). 256p. 1984. pap. 9.00 (*0-939125-35-8*) CRC Wrld Lit.
Mas Que Vencedores: Secretos para Conquistar Actitudes Negativas. Gloria Ricardo. (SPA.). 56p. (Orig.). 1994. pap. 4.00 (*0-614-11599-X*) HLM Producciones.
*__Mas Que Vencedores Nuevo Testamento.__Tr. of RVA N. T. "More Than Conquers". (SPA., Illus.). 1999. pap. text 3.50 (*0-311-48766-1*, Edit Mundo) Casa Bautista.
Ma's Ram & Other Poems. Anne N. Carpenter. LC 85-1893. (Eileen W. Barnes Award Ser.). (Illus.). 80p. (Orig.). 1985. pap. 6.50 (*0-938158-06-6*) Saturday Pr.
Mas Sal Que Dulce Saltier Than Sweet: Bilingual English-Spanish Poetry. Ed. by Carlos Cumpian. LC 94-72876. 82p. (Orig.). 1995. pap. 7.95 (*1-877636-13-4*) March Abrazo.
Mas Tacticas Amorosas. W. Thomas. 1997. pap. text 9.98 (*968-38-0399-7*) Panorama Edit.
Mas Theotime. Henri Bosco. (FRE.). 448p. 1972. pap. 11.95 (*0-7859-1706-3*, 2070361683) Fr & Eur.
Masaccio. Ornella Casazza. (Grandes Maestros del Arte Ser.). (SPA., Illus.). 80p. 1993. pap. 12.99 (*1-878351-29-X*) Riverside NY.
Masaccio. John T. Spike. LC 95-47500. (Illus.). 256p. 1996. 125.00 (*0-7892-0090-2*) Abbeville Pr.
Masaccio: And the Brancacci Chapel. Ornella Casazza. (Library of Great Masters). (Illus.). 80p. (Orig.). 1990. pap. 14.99 (*1-878351-11-7*) Riverside NY.
Masaccio? Die Zuschreibung des Triptychons von San Giovenale. Anja-Silvia Going. (Studien Zur Kunstgeschichte Ser.: Bd. 102). (GER.). viii, 205p. 1996. 50.00 (*3-487-10235-8*) G Olms Pubs.
*__Masaccio: The Complete Paintings by the Master of Perspective.__ Richard Fremantle. LC 98-211613. (Master Artists Library). Orig. Title: Masaccio: Catalogo Completo (Biblioteca d'Arte Ser.). (Illus.). 160p. 1998. 8.98 (*0-7651-0866-6*) Smithmark.
Masaccio & Masolino: A Complete Catalogue. Paul Joannides. (Illus.). 490p. 1997. 195.00 (*0-7148-2398-8*, Pub. by Phaidon Press) Phaidon Pr.
Masaccio: Catalogo Completo (Biblioteca d'Arte Ser.) see Masaccio: The Complete Paintings by the Master of Perspective
Masaccio's "Trinity" Ed. by Rona Goffen. LC 97-27041. (Masterpieces of Western Painting Ser.). (Illus.). 176p. (C). 1998. text 49.95 (*0-521-46150-2*); pap. text 15.95 (*0-521-46709-8*) Cambridge U Pr.
Masada. Neil Waldman. LC 97-32912. (Illus.). 64p. (J). (gr. 5-9). 1998. 16.00 (*0-688-14481-0*, Wm Morrow) Morrow Avon.
Masada: Herod's Fortress & the Zealot's Last Stand. Yigael Yadin. (Illus.). 272p. 1998. pap. 22.95 (*1-56649-033-2*) Welcome Rain.
Masada: The Last Fortress. Gloria D. Miklowitz. LC 98-17756. 198p. (YA). (gr. 7-12). 1999. pap. 7.00 (*0-8028-5168-1*, Eerdmans Bks) Eerdmans.
Masada: The Last Fortress. Gloria D. Miklowitz. LC 98-17756. 198p. (YA). (gr. 7 up). 1999. 16.00 (*0-8028-5165-7*, Eerdmans Bks) Eerdmans.
Masada & the Dead Sea. 64p. text 10.95 (*88-7009-960-1*, Pub. by Bonechi) Eiron.
Masada & the World of the New Testament. John F. Hall & John W. Welch. LC 97-4715. (BYU Studies Monographs). 432p. 1997. pap. 16.95 (*0-8425-2344-8*, Friends of the Library) Brigham.
Masada Myth: Collective Memory & Mythmaking in Israel. Nachman Ben-Yehuda. LC 95-13543. 424p. 1995. 60.00 (*0-299-14830-0*); pap. 24.95 (*0-299-14834-3*) U of Wis Pr.
Masai. Rapp. LC 96-233554. 126p. (C). 1996. pap. 25.40 (*0-536-59707-3*) Pearson Custom.
Masai: Their Language & Folklore. Alfred C. Hollis. LC 71-157372. (Black Heritage Library Collection). 1977. 37.95 (*0-8369-8810-8*) Ayer.
Masai & I. Kroll. 1998. pap. 4.99 (*0-87628-558-2*) Ctr Appl Res.
Masai & I. Virginia L. Kroll. LC 91-24561. (Illus.). 32p. (J). (ps-2). 1992. lib. bdg. 16.00 (*0-02-751165-0*, Four Winds Pr) S&S Childrens.
Masai & I. Virginia L. Kroll. (J). 1997. 4.99 (*0-689-80454-7*) S&S Childrens.
Masai & I. Virginia L. Kroll. LC 91-24561. 1997. 10.19 (*0-606-11601-X*, Pub. by Turtleback) Demco.
Masai Dreaming. Justin Cartwright. LC 94-41335. 1995. 22.00 (*0-614-32177-8*) Random.
*__Masaje: Tecnica de Beard.__ 4th ed. Domenico. (C). 1998. text 20.50 (*84-8174-341-0*) Mosby Inc.
Masajid Allah Coloring Book. 2nd rev. ed. Sahebzada A. Khan. Ed. by Abidullah Ghazi & Tasneema Ghazi. (Fun in Islamic Learning Ser.). (Illus.). 26p. (Orig.). (J). (gr. 1-6). 1988. pap. 4.00 (*1-56316-351-9*) Iqra Intl Ed Fdtn.
Masami Teraoka: From Tradition to Technology, the Floating World Comes of Age. John Stevenson. Ed. by Lorna Price. LC 97-10396. (Illus.). 64p. 1997. pap. 22.50 (*0-295-97651-9*) U of Wash Pr.
Masao Abe: A Zen Life of Dialogue. Ed. by Donald W. Mitchell. LC 98-6073. 320p. 1998. pap. 24.95 (*0-8048-3123-8*) Tuttle Pubng.
Masaoka Shiki: Selected Poems. Masaoka Shiki. Tr. by Burton Watson from ENG. LC 97-25799. (Modern Asian Literature Ser.). 136p. 1998. pap. 17.50 (*0-231-11091-X*); lib. bdg. 47.50 (*0-231-11090-1*) Col U Pr.
Masardis Saga: Nineteenth Century Life in Aroostook County, Maine. Paul M. Maureau. LC 83-50686. (Illus.). 160p. (Orig.). 1985. pap. 10.95 (*0-931474-28-0*) TBW Bks.
Masaryk, a Biography. Paul Selver. LC 74-33506. (Illus.). 326p. 1975. reprint ed. lib. bdg. 38.50 (*0-8371-7972-6*, SEMA, Greenwood Pr) Greenwood.
Masaryks: The Making of Czechoslovakia. Zbynek Zeman. 230p. 1990. pap. 16.50 (*0-685-38704-6*, Pub. by I B T) St Martin.
Masaryk's Path & Legacy: Funeral Oration at the Burial of the President-Liberator, 21 September 1937. Edvard Benes. LC 77-135793. (Eastern Europe Collection). (Illus.). 1971. reprint ed. 15.95 (*0-405-02735-4*) Ayer.
Mascagni. Mario Pasi. (Portraits of Greatness Ser.). (Illus.). 48p. 1989. 17.50 (*0-918367-30-1*); pap. text 12.50 (*0-918367-31-X*) Elite.
Mascagni: An Autobiography Compiled, Edited & Translated from Original Sources. David Stivender. (Illus.). 388p. 1988. 35.00 (*0-912483-06-7*) Pro-Am Music.
Mascara Maldita. R. L. Stine, pseud. (Escalofrios Ser.: No. 11).Tr. of Haunted Mask. (SPA.). (J). 1998. pap. text 3.99 (*0-590-14927-X*, Little Apple) Scholastic Inc.
Mascara Maldita. R. L. Stine, pseud. (Escalofrios Ser.: No. 11).Tr. of Haunted Mask. 1998. 9.09 (*0-606-13554-5*, Pub. by Turtleback) Demco.
Mascara y el Maranon: La Identidad Nacional Cubana. Lucrecia Artalejo. LC 91-76552. (Coleccion Cuba y sus Jueces). (SPA.). 196p. (Orig.). 1992. pap. 19.95 (*0-89729-626-5*) Ediciones.
Mascaras de la Cueva de Santa Ana Teloxtoc. Ed. by Ernesto Vargas. 208p. 1989. pap. 7.00 (*968-36-1107-9*, UN027) UPLAAP.
Mascarones De Oliva. Ulises Prieto. LC 78-55925. (Coleccion Espejo de Paciencia). 1978. pap. 5.00 (*0-89729-195-6*) Ediciones.
Maschinelle Sprachanalyse. Ed. by Peter Eisenberg. (Grundlagen der Kommunikation Ser.). (C). 1976. pap. text 35.40 (*3-11-005722-0*) De Gruyter.
Mascot Book: An Encyclopedia of Bringers of Good Luck-Charms, Spells, Talismans & Colors. Elizabeth Villiers. 1991. lib. bdg. 79.95 (*0-8490-4959-8*) Gordon Pr.
Mascot Book: The Book That Brings Good Luck. Elizabeth Villiers. 192p. 1996. reprint ed. spiral bd. 16.00 (*0-7873-0908-7*) Hlth Research.
Mascot Catalogs. Robert L. Ames. LC 98-92429. 133 p. 1998. pap. write for info. (*0-9661017-0-7*, Pub. by R Ames) Gr Arts Ctr Pub.
Mascot Mayhem. John Vornholt. (Sabrina, the Teenage Witch Ser.: Vol. 14). 96p. (J). (gr. 2-6). 1909. mass mkt. 3.99 (*0-671-03837-0*, Minstrel Bks) PB.
Mascots: The History of Senior College & University Mascots/Nicknames. Roy E. Yarbrough. Ed. by Claudia S. Yarbrough. LC 98-229721. (Illus.). 350p. 1998. pap. 24.95 (*1-891248-25-1*) Bluff Univ Comm.
Mascots '96: 4th International Workshop on Modeling, Analysis & Simulation. LC 95-82376. 312p. 1996. 90.00 (*0-8186-7235-8*, PRO7235) IEEE Comp Soc.
Mascots 93. Ed. by Herb Schwetman et al. (Simulation Ser.: Vol. 25, No. 1). 396p. 1993. 80.00 (*1-56555-018-8*) Soc Computer Sim.
Mascoutens of Prairie Potawatomi Indians, Vol. 6, No. 1--1. Alanson B. Skinner. LC 79-111399. 262p. 1970. reprint ed. lib. bdg. 59.75 (*0-8371-4631-3*, SKMA, Greenwood Pr) Greenwood.

An Asterisk (*) at the beginning of an entry indicates that the title is appearing for the first time.

Masculine & Feminine: Gender Roles over the Life Cycle. 2nd ed. Marie Richmond-Abbott. 448p. (C). 1991. 50.31 (*0-07-052357-6*) McGraw.
Masculine Cross & Ancient Sex Worship. Sha Rocco. 65p. 1993. pap. 6.00 (*0-89540-210-6*, SB-210) Sun Pub.
Masculine Cross & Ancient Sex Worship (1874) Sha Rocco. 65p. 1996. reprint ed. pap. 5.00 (*1-56459-723-7*) Kessinger Pub.
Masculine Desire: The Sexual Politics of Victorian Aestheticism. Richard Dellamora. LC 89-16748. xii, 276p. (C). 1990. 45.00 (*0-8078-1882-8*); pap. 19.95 (*0-8078-4267-2*) U of NC Pr.
Masculine Identity in Hardy & Gissing. Annette Federico. LC 90-56171. 152p. 1991. 33.50 (*0-8386-3423-0*) Fairleigh Dickinson.
Masculine Journey Study Guide. Robert Hicks. 96p. 1993. pap. 5.00 (*0-89109-734-1*) NavPress.
Masculine Landscapes: Walt Whitman & the Homoerotic Text. Byrne R. Fone. LC 91-31153. 320p. (C). 1992. 36.95 (*0-8093-1761-3*) S Ill U Pr.
Masculine Marine: Homoeroticism in the U. S. Marine Corps. Steven Zeeland. LC 96-6803. (Illus.). 220p. 1996. 39.95 (*1-56024-982-X*); pap. 14.95 (*1-56023-874-7*, Harrington Park) Haworth Pr.
Masculine Masquerade: Masculinity & Representation. Andrew Perchuk et al. Ed. by Helaine Posner. (Illus.). 160p. 1995. pap. text 27.50 (*0-262-16154-0*) MIT Pr.
Masculine Migrations: Reading the Postcolonial Male in New Canadian Narratives. Daniel Coleman. LC 98-220236. (Theory/Culture Ser.). 216p. 1998. text 40.00 (*0-8020-4264-3*); pap. text 16.95 (*0-8020-8102-9*) U of Toronto Pr.
Masculine Self. 2nd ed. Kilmartin. LC 99-31663. 408p. 1999. pap. 44.05 (*0-07-303532-7*) McGraw.
Masculine Spirit: Resources for Reflective Living. Max Oliva. LC 97-20164. 160p. 1997. pap. 8.95 (*0-87793-630-7*) Ave Maria.
Masculine Wholeness & the Beatles. Joyce Rockwood Hudson. (Wisdom Ser.: Vol. 4). (Illus.). iii, 52p. 1998. pap. 2.00 (*1-893383-04-0*) JRH Pubns.
Masculinidad Ante las Encrucijadas. G. Oliver. (Hombres de Integridad Ser.).Tr. of Masculinity at the Crossroads. (SPA.). 53p. 1995. 2.99 (*1-56063-574-6*, 495677) Editorial Unilit.
Masculinites & Identities. David Buchbinder. LC 94-189135. (Interpretations Ser.). 160p. 1994. pap. 19.95 (*0-522-84545-2*, Pub. by Melbourne Univ Pr) Paul & Co Pubs.
Masculinities: An Anthropology of Football, Polo & Tango. Eduardo P. Archetti. LC 99-229403. 224p. 1999. pap. 19.50 (*1-85973-266-6*, Pub. by Berg Pubs) NYU Pr.
***Masculinities: An Anthropology of Football, Polo & Tango.** Eduardo P. Archetti. LC 99-229403. 224p. 1999. 55.00 (*1-85973-261-5*, Pub. by Berg Pubs) NYU Pr.
Masculinities: Knowledge, Power & Social Change. R. W. Connell. LC 94-36172. 1995. pap. 18.95 (*0-520-08999-5*, Pub. by U CA Pr) Cal Prin Full Svc.
Masculinities & Crime: Critique & Reconceptualization of Theory. James W. Messerschmidt. LC 93-7809. 248p. (C). 1993. text 66.00 (*0-8476-7868-7*); pap. text 26.95 (*0-8476-7869-5*) Rowman.
Masculinities & Violence. Lee H. Bowker. LC 97-33904. (Research on Men & Masculinities Ser.). 1997. 58.00 (*0-7619-0451-4*); pap. 26.00 (*0-7619-0452-2*) Sage.
***Masculinities at School.** Ed. by Nancy Lesko. LC 99-6785. (Research on Men & Masculinities Ser.: No. 11). 360p. 2000. 74.95 (*0-7619-1493-5*) Sage.
***Masculinities, Crime & Criminology: Men, Heterosexuality & the Criminalized Other** Richard Collier. LC 98-60954. xiv, 205 p. 1998. write for info. (*0-8039-7997-5*) Sage.
Masculinities in Organizations. Ed. by Cliff Cheng. LC 96-10041. (Research on Men & Masculinities Ser.: Vol. 9). 288p. 1996. 58.00 (*0-7619-0223-6*); pap. 26.00 (*0-7619-0224-4*) Sage.
Masculinities in Victorian Painting. John Kestner. (Illus.). 323p. 1995. 86.95 (*1-85928-108-7*, Pub. by Scolar Pr) Ashgate Pub Co.
***Masculinities, Sexualities & Child Sexual Abuse.** Anne Cossins. 316p. 2000. 93.00 (*90-411-1355-X*) Kluwer Law Intl.
Masculinity. Leo Braudy. 1999. pap. write for info. (*0-679-76830-0*) Knopf.
Masculinity. Robert Crawford. 68p. 1997. pap. 14.95 (*0-224-04371-4*, Pub. by Jonathan Cape) Trafalgar.
***Masculinity: Bodies, Movies, Culture.** Peter Lehman. 2000. 75.00 (*0-415-92323-9*) Routledge.
***Masculinity: Bodies, Movies, Culture.** Peter Lehman. (AFI Film Readers Ser.). (Illus.). 2000. pap. 21.00 (*0-415-92324-7*) Routledge.
Masculinity & Femininity: The Taboo Dimension of National Cultures. Geert H. Hofstede & Willem A. Arrindell. LC 98-9074. (Cross Cultural Psychology Ser.). 238p. 1998. 30.00 (*0-7619-1028-X*); pap. 13.99 (*0-7619-1029-8*) Sage.
Masculinity & Femininity: Their Psychological Dimensions, Correlates, & Antecedents. Janet T. Spence & Robert L. Helmreich. LC 77-10693. 309p. 1978. pap. text 9.95 (*0-292-75052-8*) U of Tex Pr.
Masculinity & Male Codes of Honor in Modern France. Robert A. Nye. LC 98-6520. 336p. 1998. pap. 17.95 (*0-520-21510-9*, Pub. by U CA Pr) Cal Prin Full Svc.
Masculinity & Morality. Larry May. LC 97-37785. 240p. 1998. pap. 15.95 (*0-8014-8442-1*); text 39.95 (*0-8014-3418-1*) Cornell U Pr.
***Masculinity & Sexuality: Selected Topics in the Psychology of Men.** Richard C. Friedman & Jennifer I. Downey. LC 99-26611. (Review of Psychiatry Ser.). 155p. 1999. 27.50 (*0-88048-962-6*) Am Psychiatric.
***Masculinity & Spirituality in Victorian Culture.** Andrew Bradstock. LC 00-33339. 2000. write for info. (*0-312-23561-5*) St Martin.
Masculinity at the Crossroads see Masculinidad Ante las Encrucijadas
***Masculinity Besieged? Issues of Modernity & Male Subjectivity in Chinese Literature of Late Twentieth Century.** Xueping Zhong. LC 99-50298. 224p. 2000. pap. 17.95 (*0-8223-2442-3*) Duke.
Masculinity Goes to School. Rob Gilbert & Pam Gilbert. 272p. 1998. pap. 29.95 (*1-86448-562-0*, Pub. by Allen & Unwin Pty) Paul & Co Pubs.
Masculinity Goes to School. Rob Gilbert & Pam Gilbert. LC 98-21286. 288p. (C). 1998. 75.00 (*0-415-19793-7*) Routledge.
Masculinity Goes to School. Rob Gilbert & Pam Gilbert. LC 98-21286. 288p. (C). 1998. pap. 24.99 (*0-415-19794-5*) Routledge.
Masculinity in Crisis: Myths, Fantasies & Realities. Roger Horrocks. LC 93-37500. 1994. pap. 18.95 (*0-312-12021-4*) St Martin.
***Masculinity in Medieval Europe.** Dawn Hadley. LC 98-30102. 296p. (C). 1998. pap. 34.60 (*0-582-31645-6*) Longman.
Masculinity in Medieval Europe. Dawn Hadley. LC 98-30102. 296p. (C). 1998. 73.50 (*0-582-31644-8*) Longman.
Masculinity, Law, & the Family. Richard Collier. LC 94-5591. 352p. (C). 1995. pap. 24.99 (*0-415-09195-0*, B2217) Routledge.
Masculinizing Hormonal Therapy for the Transgendered. Sheila Kirk. 64p. 1996. pap. 14.95 (*1-887796-02-9*) Together Lifeworks.
Maserati Heritage. David Sparrow & Iain Ayre. (Osprey Colour Library: No. 10). (Illus.). 128p. 1995. pap. 15.95 (*1-85532-441-5*) MBI Pubg.
Masers & Lasers: An Historical Approach. Mario Bertolotti. (Illus.). 268p. 1988. pap. 65.00 (*0-85274-437-4*) IOP Pub.
M*A*S*H: A Novel about Three Army Doctors. Richard Hooker. 188p. reprint ed. lib. bdg. 20.95 (*0-88411-198-9*) Amereon Ltd.
Mash: A Novel About Three Army Doctors. Richard Hooker. LC 96-49064. 224p. 1997. reprint ed. pap. 12.00 (*0-688-14955-3*, Quil) HarperTrade.
M*A*S*H: An Army Surgeon in Korea. Otto F. Apel & Pat Apel. LC 98-15170. (Illus.). 256p. 1998. 25.00 (*0-8131-2070-5*) U Pr of Ky.
M*A*S*H: The Exclusive Inside Story of the TV's Most Popular Show. rev. ed. David S. Reiss. LC 89-19743. 168p. 1983. pap. 9.95 (*0-672-52762-6*, Bobbs) Macmillan.
M*A*S*H: The First Five Years. Ed. by J. Clauss. reprint ed. pap. 12.95 (*0-88411-197-0*) Amereon Ltd.
M*A*S*H - Full: A Novel about Three Army Doctors. Richard Hooker. 1973. 5.50 (*0-87129-428-1*, M21) Dramatic Pub.
M*A*S*H - 1-Act: A Novel about Three Army Doctors. Richard Hooker & Tim Kelly. 1973. pap. 3.95 (*0-87129-382-X*, M46) Dramatic Pub.
***Mash = The Role Playing Game.** Tony W. Digiacomo. (Illus.). 25p. 2000. pap. 15.00 (*1-58265-016-0*, 00016) Orphan Press.
Mash & Smash Cookbook: Fun & Yummy Recipes Every Kid Can Make. Marian Buck-Murray. LC 97-10746. 124p. (J). 1997. pap. 12.95 (*0-471-17969-8*) Wiley.
Mash Goes to Hollywood. Richard Hooker & W. E. Butterworth. 20.95 (*0-89190-811-0*) Amereon Ltd.
Mash Goes to London. Richard Hooker & W. E. Butterworth. 21.95 (*0-89190-320-8*) Amereon Ltd.
Mash Goes to Maine. Richard Hooker & W. E. Butterworth. 21.95 (*0-89190-846-3*) Amereon Ltd.
Mash Goes to Montreal. Richard Hooker & W. E. Butterworth. 19.95 (*0-89190-812-9*) Amereon Ltd.
Mash Goes to Morocco. Richard Hooker & W. E. Butterworth. 20.95 (*0-89190-318-6*) Amereon Ltd.
Mash Goes to Paris. Richard Hooker & W. E. Butterworth. 21.95 (*0-89190-319-4*) Amereon Ltd.
Mash Goes to San Francisco. Richard Hooker & H. E. Butterworth. 20.95 (*0-89190-813-7*) Amereon Ltd.
***Masha & the Firebird.** Margaret Bateson-Hill. (Illus.). 32p. (J). 2000. 17.95 (*1-84089-134-3*, Pub. by Zero to Ten) IPG Chicago.
***Masha I Feliks.** Viktoriia Tokareva. 1999. pap. 9.95 (*5-237-01795-9*) Distribks Inc.
Mashairi Ya Vita Vya Kuduhu: War Poetry in Kiswahili Exchanged at the Time of Kuduhu. Ann Biersteker & Ibrahim N. Shariff. LC 92-35316. (African Historical Sources Ser.: Vol. 7). (ENG & SWA.). 1995. 26.95 (*0-87013-323-3*) Mich St U Pr.
Mashallah. Charles W. Stoddard. (Notable American Authors Ser.). 1999. reprint ed. lib. bdg. 125.00 (*0-7812-8941-6*) Rprt Serv.
Mashangu's Reverie. N. C. Manganyi. LC 78-386905. 106 p. 1977. write for info. (*0-86975-068-2*) Ohio U Pr.
Mashantucket Pequots. Jeff Benedict. 2000. pap. 15.00 (*0-06-093196-5*) HarpC.
Mashi. Rabindranath Tagore. 223p. 1985. 6.50 (*0-318-36925-7*) Asia Bk Corp.
Mashi, & Other Stories. Rabindranath Tagore. LC 70-37564. (Short Story Index Reprint Ser.). 1977. reprint ed. 18.95 (*0-8369-4123-3*) Ayer.
Mashiach: The Principle of Mashiach & the Messianic Era in Jewish Law & Tradition. 3rd expanded ed. Jacob I. Schochet. LC 92-90728. 112p. 1991. pap. 7.00 (*1-881400-00-X*) S I E.
Mashiach: Who? What? Why? How? Where? When? Chaim Kramer. Ed. by Avraham Sutton. 364p. 1994. 16.00 (*0-930213-54-8*) Breslov Res Inst.
Mashkiki: Old Medicine Nourishing the New. Edwin W. Haller & Larry P. Aitken. 214p. (Orig.). 1992. pap. text 24.50 (*0-8191-8557-4*); lib. bdg. 49.50 (*0-8191-8556-6*) U Pr of Amer.
Mashpee Indians: Tribe on Trial. Jack Campisi. (Iroquois & Their Neighbors Ser.). (Illus.). 176p. (C). 1991. pap. 17.95 (*0-8156-2595-2*) Syracuse U Pr.
Masini French-Rumanian Dictionary of Construction: Dictionar de Constructii de Masini, Francez-Roman. S. Enache. (FRE & RUM.). 1982. write for info. (*0-8288-1329-9*, M15842) Fr & Eur.
Mask see Kegginaquq
Mask. Eve Bunting. (Eve Bunting Collection). (Illus.). 40p. (J). (gr. 3-8). 1992. lib. bdg. 12.79 (*0-89565-769-4*) Childs World.
Mask. Ed. by Edward G. Craig. 1972. 52.95 (*0-405-08394-7*) Ayer.
Mask. Alan M. Hofmeister et al. (Reading for All Learners Ser.). (Illus.). pap. write for info. (*1-56861-139-0*) Swift Lrn Res.
Mask. Dean Koontz. 1988. 12.60 (*0-606-00939-6*, Pub. by Turtleback) Demco.
Mask. Dorothy R. Murphree. 1967. pap. 3.50 (*0-87129-231-9*, M22) Dramatic Pub.
Mask. Donna L. Poff. 368p. 1998. mass mkt. 4.99 (*0-8439-4416-1*, Leisure Bks) Dorchester Pub Co.
Mask. deluxe limited ed. John Arcudi. (Illus.). 1995. boxed set 99.95 (*1-56971-056-2*) Dark Horse Comics.
Mask. John Cournos. LC 74-26098. (Labor Movement in Fiction & Non-Fiction Ser.). reprint ed. 47.50 (*0-404-58416-0*) AMS Pr.
Mask. Dean Koontz. 320p. 1990. reprint ed. mass mkt. 7.50 (*0-425-12758-3*) Berkley Pub.
Mask, 16 vols., 14 bks., Set. Ed. by Edward G. Craig. LC 65-27911. 1965. reprint ed. 674.95 (*0-405-08382-3*, Pub. by Blom Pubns) Ayer.
Mask, Vol. 2. Ed. by Edward G. Craig. LC 65-27911. 1972. 52.95 (*0-405-08383-1*); 52.95 (*0-405-08384-X*) Ayer.
Mask, Vol. 3. Ed. by Edward G. Craig. LC 65-27911. 1972. 52.95 (*0-405-08385-8*) Ayer.
Mask, Vol. 4. Ed. by Edward G. Craig. LC 65-27911. 1972. 52.95 (*0-405-08386-6*) Ayer.
Mask, Vol. 5. Ed. by Edward G. Craig. LC 65-27911. 1972. 52.95 (*0-405-08387-4*) Ayer.
Mask, Vol. 6. Edward G. Craig. LC 65-27911. 1972. 52.95 (*0-405-08388-2*) Ayer.
Mask, Vol .11. Ed. by Edward G. Craig. LC 65-27911. 1972. 52.95 (*0-405-08393-9*) Ayer.
Mask, Vol. 13. Ed. by Edward G. Craig. LC 65-27911. 1972. 52.95 (*0-405-08395-5*) Ayer.
Mask, Vol. 14. Ed. by Edward G. Craig. LC 65-27911. 1972. 52.95 (*0-405-08396-3*) Ayer.
Mask, Vol. 15. Ed. by Edward G. Craig. LC 65-27911. 1972. 52.95 (*0-405-08397-1*) Ayer.
Mask, Vol. 16. Edward G. Craig. LC 65-27911. 1972. 30.95 (*0-405-08398-X*) Ayer.
Mask, vols. 7 & 8. Ed. by Edward G. Craig. LC 65-27911. 1972. 52.95 (*0-405-08389-0*) Ayer.
Mask, vols. 9 & 10. Ed. by Edward G. Craig. LC 65-27911. 1972. 52.95 (*0-405-08391-2*) Ayer.
Mask: A Mask for All Seasons. Dark Horse Comics Staff. (Illus.). 1997. pap. text 14.95 (*1-56971-177-1*) Dark Horse Comics.
Mask: A Periodical Performance by Edward Gordon Craig. Olga Taxidou. (Illus.). 216p. 1998. pap. text 18.00 (*90-5755-046-6*) Gordon & Breach.
Mask: A Periodical Performance by Edward Gordon Craig. Olgo Taxidou. (Illus.). 216p. 1998. text 32.00 (*90-5755-045-8*) Gordon & Breach.
Mask: A Weird New Adventure! Marc Cerasini. (J). (gr. 3-7). 1997. pap. 3.99 (*0-614-28923-8*) Random Bks Yng Read.
Mask: He's Gone from Zero to Hero! Madeline Dorr. (J). (gr. 3 up). 1994. pap. 3.99 (*0-679-87115-2*, Bullseye Bks) Random Bks Yng Read.
Mask: Mars Needs Chocolate. Scott Ciencin. (Tattoo Tales Ser.). (Illus.). (J). (ps-6). 1997. pap. 5.99 (*0-614-28930-0*) Random Bks Yng Read.
Mask: Strikes Back. unabridged ed. John Arcudi. (Illus.). 128p. (Orig.). (YA). (gr. 9 up). 1996. pap. 17.95 (*1-56971-168-2*) Dark Horse Comics.
Mask & Scene: An Introduction to a World View of Theatre. Diana Devlin. LC 89-33471. (Illus.). 227p. 1989. 34.50 (*0-8108-2234-2*) Scarecrow.
Mask & Sword: Two Plays for the Contemporary Japanese Theater. Ed. by J. Thomas Rimer. (Modern Asian Literature Ser.). (Illus.). 1980. text 55.50 (*0-231-04932-3*) Col U Pr.
Mask & the Sorceress. Dennis Jones. Date not set. pap. write for info. (*0-380-80618-5*) Morrow Avon.
***Mask & the Sorceress.** Dennis Jones. 2001. write for info. (*0-380-97802-4*) Morrow Avon.
Mask & Tragedy: Yeats & Nietzsche, 1902-10. Frances N. Oppel. LC 86-24652. 267p. reprint ed. pap. 82.80 (*0-7837-4366-1*, 204407600012) Bks Demand.
Mask Arts of Mexico. Ruth D. Lechuga & Chloe Sayer. (Illus.). 96p. 1995. pap. 17.95 (*0-8118-0811-4*) Chronicle Bks.
Mask at Ludlow Castle see Comus
Mask Beneath the Face: Reading about & with, Writing about & for Children. E. L. Kongsburg. LC 90-21319. 31p. 1990. 3.95 (*0-8444-0712-7*) Lib Congress.
***Mask Carver's Son.** Alyson Richman. 384p. 2000. 23.95 (*1-58234-063-3*) Bloomsbury Pubg.
Mask Characterization: An Acting Process. Libby Appel. LC 81-9157. 136p. (Orig.). (C). 1982. pap. 17.95 (*0-8093-1039-2*) S Ill U Pr.
Mask Collection. John Arcudi & Doug Mahnke. (Illus.). 152p. 1993. pap. 14.95 (*1-878574-50-7*) Dark Horse Comics.
Mask Conspiracy: An Environmental Fable for All Ages. Myke Feinman & Jim Ridings. Ed. & Illus. by Cathy Feinman. Illus. by Anthony Feinman. (Myke Feinman's Terry Freedom Ser.: Vol. 1). 96p. 1991. pap. 6.95 (*0-9664974-0-6*) Ink & Feathers.
Mask Dancing: Nigerian Novelists of the Eighties. Adewale Maja-Pearce. (New Perspectives on African Literature Ser.: No. 4). 216p. 1992. lib. bdg. 85.00 (*0-905450-92-2*, Pub. by H Zell Pubs) Seven Hills Bk.
Mask for a Diva. Grant Michaels. LC 95-39343. 304p. 1996. pap. 9.95 (*0-312-14120-3*) St Martin.
Mask for Janus. W. S. Merwin. LC 76-144755. (Yale Series of Younger Poets: No. 49). reprint ed. 18.00 (*0-404-53849-5*) AMS Pr.
Mask for Mayor. Nancy E. Krulik. 32p. (J). (gr. k-2). 1996. pap. text 2.99 (*0-590-50206-9*) Scholastic Inc.
Mask for Privilege: Anti-Semitism in America. Carey McWilliams. LC 78-26197. 299p. 1979. reprint ed. lib. bdg. 65.00 (*0-313-20880-8*, MCMP, Greenwood Pr) Greenwood.
Mask for Privilege: Anti-Semitism in America. 2nd ed. Carey McWilliams. LC 99-12370. 299p. 1999. pap. write for info. (*0-7658-0612-6*) Transaction Pubs.
Mask in School Spirits. Rick Geary. (Illus.). 1995. 10.95 (*1-56971-121-6*) Dark Horse Comics.
Mask Making. Book Sales Staff. 1998. 8.99 (*0-7858-1008-0*) Bk Sales Inc.
Mask Making. Gill Dickison. 1995. 7.98 (*0-7858-0314-9*) Bk Sales Inc.
Mask Making. Glynn McKay. 80p. 1994. 12.98 (*0-7858-0176-6*) Bk Sales Inc.
Mask of Aeschylus. Richard Ball. LC 81-66410. 88p. (Orig.). 1981. pap. 3.00 (*0-940066-00-9*) Dalmas & Ricour.
***Mask of Agamemnon: Poems by June Owens.** June Owens. 24p. 1999. pap. 7.00 (*0-916897-40-0*) Andrew Mtn Pr.
Mask of Anarchy: Written on the Occasion of the Massacre of Manchester. Percy Bysshe Shelley. LC 74-30281. (Extra Ser.: No. 4). reprint ed. 29.50 (*0-404-11522-5*) AMS Pr.
Mask of Apollo. Mary Renault. LC 86-46177. 400p. 1988. pap. 13.00 (*0-394-75105-1*) Vin Bks.
Mask of Art: Breaking the Aesthetic Contract, Film & Literature. Clyde R. Taylor. LC 97-50462. 368p. 1998. 45.00 (*0-253-33403-9*); pap. 22.95 (*0-253-21192-1*) Ind U Pr.
***Mask of Benevolence: Disabling the Deaf Community.** Harlan Lane. LC 99-13183. 1999. pap. 11.95 (*1-58121-009-4*) Dawn Sign.
Mask of Benevolence: Disabling the Deaf Community. Harlan Lane. LC 93-13107. 1993. pap. 14.00 (*0-679-73614-X*) Vin Bks.
Mask of Comedy: Aristophanes & the Intertextual Parabasis. Thomas K. Hubbard. LC 91-11953. (Cornell Studies in Classical Philology: Vol. 51). 264p. 1991. text 45.00 (*0-8014-2564-6*) Cornell U Pr.
Mask of Command. John Keegan. 1988. pap. 13.95 (*0-14-011406-8*, Penguin Bks) Viking Penguin.
Mask of Cthulhu. August Derleth. 256p. 1996. mass mkt. 4.95 (*0-7867-0337-7*) Carroll & Graf.
Mask of Deception: Postcards from Europe. Sara Wood. (Presents Ser.). 1994. per. 2.99 (*0-373-11628-4*, 1011628-4) Harlequin Bks.
Mask of Democracy: Labor Suppression in Mexico Today. Dan La Botz. 224p. (Orig.). 1992. 35.00 (*0-89608-438-8*); pap. 14.00 (*0-89608-437-X*) South End Pr.
Mask of Democracy: Labour Suppression in Mexico Today. Dan LaBotz. 223p. write for info. (*1-895431-59-X*); pap. write for info. (*1-895431-58-1*) Black Rose.
Mask of Enlightenment: Nietzsche's Zarathustra. Stanley Rosen. (Modern European Philosophy Ser.). 286p. (C). 1995. text 59.95 (*0-521-49546-6*); pap. text 21.95 (*0-521-49889-9*) Cambridge U Pr.
Mask of Evil. Anthony Tatlow. (European University Studies: Comparative Literature: Ser. 18, Vol. 12). 629p. 1977. 80.00 (*3-261-02905-6*) P Lang Pubng.
Mask of Fiction: Essays on W. D. Howells. John W. Crowley. LC 88-39866. 288p. 1989. 32.50 (*0-87023-674-1*) U of Mass Pr.
Mask of Fortune. large type ed. Sally James. 1991. 27.99 (*0-7089-2537-5*) Ulverscroft.
Mask of Fu Manchu. Sax Rohmer, pseud. LC 84-23983. 362 p. 1985. write for info. (*0-89621-588-1*) Chivers N Amer.
Mask of Fu Manchu. Sax Rohmer, pseud. 1976. reprint ed. lib. bdg. 21.95 (*0-89190-803-X*, Rivercity Pr) Amereon Ltd.
Mask of Gold. large type ed. Rachel Lindsay. 405p. 1981. 27.99 (*0-7089-0706-7*) Ulverscroft.
Mask of Keats: The Endeavour of a Poet. Thomas McFarland. 264p. 2000. text 49.95 (*0-19-818645-2*) OUP.
Mask of Loki. Roger Zelazny & Thomas T. Thomas. (Orig.). 1990. per. 4.95 (*0-671-72021-X*) Baen Bks.
Mask of Madusa. Sheryl St. Germain. Ed. by Stanley H. Barkan. (Review Women Writers Chapbook Ser.: No. 7). 48p. 1987. 15.00 (*0-89304-430-X*); pap. 5.00 (*0-89304-431-8*); pap. 5.00 (*0-89304-433-4*) Cross-Cultrl NY.
Mask of Madusa: Mini. Sheryl St. Germain. Ed. by Stanley H. Barkan. (Review Women Writers Chapbook Ser.: No. 7). 48p. 1987. 15.00 (*0-89304-432-6*) Cross-Cultrl NY.
Mask of Motherhood: How Becoming a Mother Changes Everything & Why We Pretend It Doesn't. Susan Maushart. LC 98-27830. 266p. 1999. 24.00 (*1-56584-483-1*, Pub. by New Press NY) Norton.
***Mask of Motherhood: How Becoming a Mother Changes Our Lives & Why We Never Talk about It.** Susan Maushart. 2000. pap. 12.95 (*0-14-029178-4*) Viking Penguin.
Mask of Motion. deluxe ed. Lyn Hejinian. (Burning Deck Poetry Ser.). 1977. pap. 20.00 (*0-930900-21-9*) Burning Deck.

M

An Asterisk (*) at the beginning of an entry indicates that the title is appearing for the first time.

Mask of Murder. large type ed. E. Radford & M. A. Radford. 320p. pap. 18.99 (0-7089-5447-2) Ulverscroft.
Mask of Nostradamus: The Prophecies of the World's Most Famous Seer. James Randi. LC 92-41554. (Illus.). 270p. (C). 1993. reprint ed. pap. 19.95 (0-87975-830-9) Prometheus Bks.
Mask of Reality: An Approach to Design for Theatre. Irene Corey. (Illus.). 1968. 37.50 (0-87602-007-4) Anchorage.
Mask of Religion. G. Peter Fleck. LC 79-9644. (Library of Liberal Religion). 216p. 1980. 27.95 (0-87975-125-8) Prometheus Bks.
Mask of Sanity: An Attempt to Clarify Some Issues about the So-Called Psychopathic Personality. 5th ed. Hervey Cleckley. 471p. (C). 1988. reprint ed. text 25.00 (0-9621519-0-4) E S Cleckley.
Mask of Sanity: The Bain Murders. James McNeish. LC 98-140451. (Illus.). 1997. 24.95 (0-908990-46-4) David Ling Pub.
Mask of Socrates: The Image of the Intellectual in Antiquity. Paul Zanker. Tr. by Alan Shapiro. LC 95-12409. (Sather Classical Lectures: Vol. 59). (Illus.). 376p. 1996. 48.00 (0-520-20105-1, Pub. by U CA Pr) Cal Prin Full Svc.
Mask of State: Watergate Portraits Including a Postscript on the Pardons. Mary McCarthy. LC 74-26953. 183p. 1975. pap. 2.65 (0-15-657302-4, Harvest Bks) Harcourt.
Mask of the King. Jwing-Ming Yang. Ed. by Alan Dougall. LC 90-71759. (YMAA Storybook Ser.: No. 2). (Illus.). 32p. (J). (gr. 4-7). 1990. mass mkt. 3.50 (0-940871-11-4, CB002/114) YMAA Pubn.
Mask of the Night. large type ed. Mary Ryan. LC 98-41388. 1998. 30.00 (0-7838-0380-X, G K Hall Lrg Type) Mac Lib Ref.
Mask of the Parasite: A Pathology of Roman Patronage. Cynthia Damon. LC 97-33297. 320p. (C). 1997. text 44.50 (0-472-10760-7, 10760) U of Mich Pr.
Mask of the Prophet: The Extraordinary Fictions of Jules Verne. Andrew Martin. (Illus.). 236p. 1990. text 59.00 (0-19-815798-3) OUP.
Mask of the Sun. Fred Saberhagen. 240p. 1991. mass mkt. 3.99 (0-8125-1357-6, Pub. by Tor Bks) St Martin.
Mask of the Wolf Boy: Jonathan & Rosalind Goforth. Dave Jackson & Neta Jackson. (Trailblazer Bks.). 144p. (J). (gr. 3-7). 1999. pap. 5.99 (0-7642-2011-X) Bethany Hse.
Mask of Treachery. John Costello. 1990. mass mkt. 5.95 (0-446-35783-9, Pub. by Warner Bks) Little.
Mask of Treason. large type ed. Anne Stevenson. 416p. 1982. 27.99 (0-7089-0875-6) Ulverscroft.
Mask of Zorro. Frank Lauria. (J). (gr. 3-7). 1998. mass mkt. 4.50 (0-671-51967-0) PB.
Mask of Zorro. James Luceno. 1998. 9.09 (0-606-13600-2, Pub. by Turtleback) Demco.
Mask of Zorro. John Whitman. LC 97-32936. (Mighty Chronicles Ser.). 320p. (J). 1999. 9.95 (0-8118-2036-X) Chronicle Bks.
Mask Prints. (Illus.). 1991. 29.95 (1-56290-087-0, 6015) Crystal.
Mask Punch Out Book. Created by Lucas Books & Random House Staff. 1999. pap. 4.99 (0-375-80019-0) Random.
Mask Returns. John Arcudi. (Illus.). pap. 14.95 (1-56971-021-X) Dark Horse Comics.
Mask Summer Vacation. Rick Geary. LC 96-154356. (Illus.). 32p. 1995. 10.95 (1-56971-102-X) Dark Horse Comics.
***Mask Technology for Integrated Circuits & Microcomponents '98.** Ed. by Uwe Behringer. 190p. 1999. pap. text 62.00 (0-8194-3139-7) SPIE.
Maske: The Earlier Versions. John Milton. Ed. by S. E. Sprott. LC 72-97784. 236p. reprint ed. pap. 73.20 (0-608-16710-X, 202638500049) Bks Demand.
Maske und Spiegel. Bernhard Gallistl. (Studien Zur Kunstgeschichte Ser.: Vol. 101). (GER.). viii, 74p. 1995. write for info. (3-487-10029-0) G Olms Pubs.
Masked Avenger. Douglas De Mars. 64p. 1986. pap. 5.00 (0-941452-18-2) Acheron Pr.
Masked Ball. Giuseppe Verdi. Ed. by Nicholas John. Tr. by Edmund Tracey from ITA. (English National Opera Guide Series: Bilingual Libretto, Articles: No. 40). (Illus.). 128p. (Orig.). 1989. pap. 9.95 (0-7145-4167-2) Riverrun NY.
Masked Ball: Dreams & Disguises. Judyl Mudfoot. 36p. (Orig.). 1986. pap. 10.00 (0-930012-47-X) J Mudfoot.
Masked Ball & Other Stories. Alexandre Dumas. Tr. & Intro. by A. Craig Bell. LC 98-115360. (Pocket Classics Ser.). 128p. 1997. pap. 12.95 (0-7509-1467-X, Pub. by Sutton Pub Ltd) Intl Pubs Mktg.
Masked Ball: Libretto see Ballo in Maschera: Libretto
Masked Bobwhite Rides Again. John Alcock. LC 93-15416. 186p. (Orig.). 1993. pap. 17.95 (0-8165-1405-4); lib. bdg. 36.00 (0-8165-1387-2) U of Ariz Pr.
Masked Culture: The Greenwich Village Halloween Parade. Jack Kugelmass et al. LC 93-29821. 215p. 1994. 47.50 (0-231-08400-5) Col U Pr.
Masked Dancers: A Mitch Bushyhead Mystery. Jean Hager. LC 97-34560. 288p. 1998. 22.50 (0-89296-641-6, Pub. by Mysterious Pr) Little.
Masked Dancers: A Mitch Bushyhead Mystery. Jean Hager. (Cloak & Dagger Ser.). 1998. 24.95 (0-7862-1485-6) Thorndike Pr.
Masked Deception. Mary Balogh. 1999. 25.00 (0-7278-5460-7, Pub. by Severn Hse) Chivers N Amer.
Masked Depression. Ed. by Stanley Lesse. LC 73-17744. 394p. 1983. 60.00 (0-87668-688-9) Aronson.
Masked Depression. Stanley Lesse. 1996. pap. text 60.00 (1-56821-871-0) Aronson.
Masked Dog. Raymond Obstfeld. 1986. pap. 3.50 (0-373-62101-9) Harlequin Bks.
Masked Gods: Navaho & Pueblo Ceremonialism. Frank Waters. LC 73-1799. 438p. 1950. pap. 12.95 (0-8040-0641-5) Swallow.
Masked Inversion in French. Paul M. Postal. (Illus.). 168p. 1989. 33.00 (0-226-67569-6) U Ch Pr.
Masked Ladies see Four Plays by Holberg
Masked Love. large type ed. Katrina Wright. (Linford Romance Library). 1991. pap. 16.99 (0-7089-6991-7) Ulverscroft.
Masked Marquis. Winifred Witton. (Regency Romance Ser.: No. 174). 1992. per. 2.99 (0-373-31174-5, 1-31174-5) Harlequin Bks.
Masked Media: Aymara Fiestas & Social Interaction in the Bolivian Highlands. Hans C. Buechler. (Approaches to Semiotics Ser.: No. 59). 400p. 1980. 69.25 (90-279-7777-1) Mouton.
Masked Men: Masculinity & the Movies in the Fifties. Steven Cohan. LC 96-29965. (Arts & Politics of the Everyday Ser.). (Illus.). 448p. 1997. pap. 18.95 (0-253-21127-1) Ind U Pr.
Masked Monkey. Franklin W. Dixon. LC 71-180994. (Hardy Boys Mystery Stories Ser.: No. 51). (Illus.). 196p. (J). (gr. 4-7). 1972. 5.95 (0-448-08951-3, G & D) Peng Put Young Read.
Masked Performance: The Play of Self & Other in Ritual & Theater. John Emigh. LC 96-17690. (Illus.). 352p. 1996. text 39.95 (0-8122-3058-2); pap. text 18.50 (0-8122-1336-X) U of Pa Pr.
Masked Spirits: New Work from the Institute of American Indian Arts. Ed. by Barbara Miller & Debra Yepa. (IAIA Anthology Ser.: No. 3). 72p. 1991. pap. 6.00 (1-881396-02-9) IOA Indian Arts.
Masked War: The Story of a Peril That Threatened the United States. William J. Burns. LC 76-90168. (Mass Violence in America Ser.). 1969. reprint ed. 31.95 (0-405-01303-5) Ayer.
Maskell. Thomas Maskell of Simsbury, Conn., His Son Thomas Maskell of Greenwich, New Jersey, & Some of Their Descendants. Compiled by Frank D. Andrews. 38p. 1995. reprint ed. pap. 8.00 (0-8328-4880-8); reprint ed. lib. bdg. 18.00 (0-8328-4879-4) Higginson Bk Co.
Maskerade. Terry Pratchett. 368p. 1998. mass mkt. 6.50 (0-06-105691-X, HarperPrism) HarpC.
Maskerade. large type ed. Terry Pratchett. (Isis Large Print Ser.). 1997. 25.95 (0-7531-5156-1) T T Beeler.
Masking & Unmasking the Female Mind: Disguising Romances in Feminine Fiction, 1713-1799. Mary A. Schofield. LC 89-40006. (Illus.). 224p. 1990. 38.50 (0-87413-365-3) U Delaware Pr.
Masking Selves, Making Subjects: Japanese American Women & the Poetics of Subjectivity. Traise Yamamoto. LC 98-14154. 1999. 45.00 (0-520-21033-6, Pub. by U CA Pr); 17.95 (0-520-21034-4, Pub. by U CA Pr) Cal Prin Full Svc.
Masking the Blow: The Scene of Representation in Late Prehistoric Egyptian Art. Whitney Davis. (California Studies in the History of Art: No. XXX). (C). 1992. 65.00 (0-520-07488-2, Pub. by U CA Pr) Cal Prin Full Svc.
Maskmaking. Carole Sivin. LC 86-70902. (Illus.). 138p. (YA). (gr. 7-12). 1986. 25.95 (0-87192-178-2) Davis Mass.
Masks. Krystyna Baker. 150p. 1981. pap. 20.00 (0-89672-085-3) Tex Tech Univ Pr.
Masks. Clare Beaton. LC 95-60779. (Fun to Do Ser.). (Illus.). 32p. (J). (gr. 2 up). 1995. lib. bdg. 15.95 (1-887238-02-6) Fitzgerald.
Masks. Kevin K. Casey. LC 96-11394. (Customs, Costumes, & Cultures Ser.). 32p. (J). (gr. 3-6). 1996. lib. bdg. 18.60 (0-86625-592-3) Rourke Pubns.
Masks! Sara Corbett & Alice K. Flanagan. LC 95-39672. (World of Difference Ser.). (Illus.). 32p. (J). (gr. 3-7). 1996. lib. bdg. 21.00 (0-516-08213-2) Childrens.
Masks. Meryl Doney. (World Crafts Ser.). (J). (gr. 4). 1997. pap. text 5.95 (0-531-15870-5) Watts.
Masks. Fumiko Enchi. LC 83-48033. 160p. 1983. pap. 11.00 (0-394-72218-3) Vin Bks.
Masks! Alice K. Flanagan. (J). 1996. pap. 6.95 (0-516-20079-8) Childrens.
Masks. R. Gibson & P. Borton. (How to Make Ser.). (Illus.). 32p. (J). (gr. 3-7). 1994. pap. 6.95 (0-7460-1443-0, Usborne); lib. bdg. 14.95 (0-88110-662-3, Usborne) EDC.
Masks. Kate Green. LC 94-4007. (Illus.). 32p. (J). (ps up). 1994. 22.60 (1-56846-097-X, Creat Educ) Creative Co.
Masks. Gloria Hatrick. LC 95-38070. 128p. (YA). (gr. 5 up). 1996. 15.95 (0-531-09514-2); lib. bdg. 16.99 (0-531-08864-2) Orchard Bks Watts.
Masks. Ruthann Robson. LC 98-25138. 160p. 1999. pap. 14.00 (0-9654578-5-0, Pub. by Leapfrog Pr) Consort Bk Sales.
Masks. Schaefer. LC 98-19939. (Fall Fun Ser.). (J). 1998. 9.95 (0-7368-0106-5, Pebble Bks) Capstone Pr.
Masks. Lola M. Schaefer. (Fall Fun Ser.). (J). 1998. 13.25 (0-516-21498-5) Childrens.
Masks. Danielle Sensier & Amanda Earl. (Traditions Around the World Ser.). (Illus.). 48p. (J). (gr. 4-6). 1994. 24.26 (1-56847-226-9) Raintree Steck-V.
Masks. Jaki Shelton-Green. 12p. 1981. pap. 2.00 (0-932112-25-0) Carolina Wren.
Masks. deluxe limited ed. Krystyna Baker. 150p. 1981. 50.00 (0-89672-086-1) Tex Tech Univ Pr.
Masks, No. 7. Vornholt. 1991. mass mkt. 5.50 (0-671-74139-X) PB.
Masks: A Love Story. Jay Bennett. LC 79-147396. 121 p. (J). 1971. write for info. (0-531-01979-9) Watts.
Masks: Asian Art Motifs from Korea. Weatherhill Staff. (Illus.). 200p. 1994. 42.50 (89-7059-016-1, Pub. by Ahn Graphics) Weatherhill.
Masks: Blackness, Race & the Imagination. Adams Lively. LC 99-88632. 304p. 2000. 30.00 (0-19-513370-6) OUP.
Masks: Faces of Culture. John W. Nunley & Cara McCarty. LC 98-53973. (Illus.). 344p. 1999. 60.00 (0-8109-4379-4, Pub. by Abrams) Time Warner.
***Masks: Faces of Culture.** John W. Nunley & Cara McCarty. (Illus.). 280p. 1999. pap. 39.95 (0-89178-078-5) St Louis Art Mus.
Masks: From Around the World. Vivien Frank. LC 96-75416. (Illus.). 32p. 1996. pap. 12.95 (0-15-201318-0) Harcourt.
Masks: Poems from Hollywood. Mark Dunster. 20p. 1998. pap. 5.00 (0-89642-404-9) Linden Pubs.
Masks: Six Plays. Plinio Prioreschi. LC 98-70675. 370p. 1998. text 35.00 (1-888456-25-6) Horatius Pr.
Masks & Faces. Ed. by Dan Garrett. (Drama Workshop Plays Ser.). (Illus.). 96p. (Orig.). (YA). 1990. pap. 15.00 (0-333-36056-7, Pub. by Macmillan Ed) Players Pr.
Masks & the Art of Expression. Ed. by John Mack. LC 93-48524. (Illus.). 224p. 1994. 49.50 (0-8109-3641-0, Pub. by Abrams) Time Warner.
Masks Anthropology on the Sinhalese Belief System. David S. Blundell. LC 91-36067. (American University Studies: Theology & Religion: Ser. VII, Vol. 88). XVII, 197p. (C). 1994. text 46.95 (0-8204-1427-1) P Lang Pubng.
***Masks Before the Altar.** James Lorenzo Wheaton. LC 99-91901. 181p. 1999. 25.00 (0-7388-1396-6); pap. 18.00 (0-7388-1397-4) Xlibris Corp.
Masks Book. Peter Linenthal. 1999. pap. 12.99 (0-525-45837-9) NAL.
Masks from Antiquity to the Modern Era: An Annotated Bibliography. Herbert Inhaber. LC 97-14942. 336p. 1997. 45.00 (0-8108-3360-3) Scarecrow.
Masks in a Pageant. William A. White. (BCL1 - U. S. History Ser.). 507p. 1991. reprint ed. lib. bdg. 99.00 (0-7812-6033-7) Rprt Serv.
Masks in a Pageant. William A. White. LC 79-145367. (Illus.). 1971. reprint ed. 39.00 (0-403-01272-4) Scholarly.
Masks, Modes, & Morals: The Art of Evelyn Waugh. William J. Cook, Jr. LC 73-118125. 352p. 1975. 39.50 (0-8386-7707-X) Fairleigh Dickinson.
Masks, Myths & Monsters: In Japanese Art. (Exotic Miniatures Ser.). (Illus.). 90p. 1995. 14.95 (981-00-6490-X) Heian Intl.
Masks of a Professional. Virginia Boyle. 160p. 1992. per. 9.95 (0-8403-8234-0, 40823401) Kendall-Hunt.
***Masks of Anarchy: The Destruction of Liberia & the Religious Dimension of an African Civil War.** Stephen Ellis. LC 99-37702. 1999. text 36.50 (0-8147-2211-3) NYU Pr.
Masks of Black Africa. Ladislas Segy. LC 74-15005. (Illus.). 248p. 1976. pap. 13.95 (0-486-23181-X) Dover.
Masks of Comedy. Ed. by Ann Boaden. LC 79-57417. (Augustana College Library Publications: No. 34). 102p. (Orig.). 1980. pap. 9.00 (0-910182-40-X) Augustana Coll.
Masks of Conquest: Literary Study & British Rule in India. Gauri Viswanathan. (Social Foundations of Aesthetic Forms Ser.). 224p. 1989. text 46.00 (0-231-07084-5) Col U Pr.
Masks of Conquest: Literary Study & British Rule in India. Gauri Viswanathan. 218p. 1998. pap. text 14.50 (0-19-564640-1) OUP.
Masks of Difference: Cultural Representations in Literature, Anthropology & Art. David Richards. (Cultural Margins Ser.: No. 2). (Illus.). 362p. (C). 1995. pap. text 22.95 (0-521-47972-X) Cambridge U Pr.
Masks of Dionysos: A Commentary on Plato's Symposium. Daniel E. Anderson. LC 91-48020. (SUNY Series in Ancient Greek Philosophy). 223p. (C). 1993. text 22.50 (0-7914-1315-2) State U NY Pr.
Masks of Dionysus. Thomas H. Carpenter & Christopher A. Faraone. LC 92-54965. (Myth & Poetics Ser.). (Illus.). 360p. 1993. text 52.50 (0-8014-2779-7); pap. text 19.95 (0-8014-8062-0) Cornell U Pr.
Masks of Fiction in Dream of the Red Chamber: Myth, Mimesis, & Persona. fac. ed. Lucien Miller. LC 75-23643. (Association for Asian Studies, Monographs & Papers: No. 28). 359p. 1994. pap. 111.30 (0-7837-7674-8, 204742700007) Bks Demand.
Masks of Flipside: A Novel Collection. Guichard Cadet. LC 97-52641. 1998. pap. 15.00 (0-9647635-4-0) La Caille-Nous.
Masks of God, 4 vols. Joseph Campbell. 1991. reprint ed. pap. 12.95 (0-685-72477-8, Arkana) Viking Penguin.
Masks of God, 4 vols., Vol. I: Primitive Mythology. Joseph Campbell. 520p. 1991. reprint ed. pap. 16.95 (0-14-019443-6, Arkana) Viking Penguin.
Masks of God, 4 vols., Vol. II: Oriental Mythology. Joseph Campbell. 576p. 1992. reprint ed. pap. 23.99 (0-14-019442-8, Arkana) Viking Penguin.
Masks of God, 4 vols., Vol. III: Occidental Mythology. Joseph Campbell. 576p. 1991. reprint ed. pap. 16.95 (0-14-019441-X, Arkana) Viking Penguin.
Masks of God, 4 vols., Vol. IV: Creative Mythology. Joseph Campbell. 752p. 1991. reprint ed. pap. 16.95 (0-14-019440-1, Arkana) Viking Penguin.
Masks of God: Occidental Mythology. Joseph Campbell. (Illus.). 564p. 1976. pap. 9.95 (0-14-004306-3, Penguin Bks) Viking Penguin.
Masks of Hamlet. Marvin Rosenberg. LC 92-22566. 992p. (C). 1993. 69.50 (0-87413-480-3) U Delaware Pr.
Masks of King Lear. Marvin Rosenberg. LC 74-115492. 440p. 1993. reprint ed. 30.00 (0-87413-482-X); reprint ed. pap. 15.00 (0-87413-485-4) U Delaware Pr.
Masks of Macbeth. Marvin Rosenberg. LC 76-14295. 816p. 1993. reprint ed. 30.00 (0-87413-483-8); reprint ed. pap. 15.00 (0-87413-486-2) U Delaware Pr.
Masks of Mexico. Barbara Mauldin. (Illus.). 128p. 1999. pap. 24.95 (0-89013-325-5) Museum NM Pr.
***Masks of Mexico.** Barbara Mauldin. (Illus.). 128p. 1999. 45.00 (0-89013-329-8) Museum NM Pr.
Masks of Misrule: The Horned God & His Cult in Europe. Nigel Jackson. (Illus.). (Orig.). 1996. pap. 21.95 (1-898307-67-9, Pub. by Capall Bann Pubng) Holmes Pub.
Masks of Mystery: Explorations in Christian Faith & Arts. J. Daniel Brown. LC 96-46098. 184p. 1996. 49.50 (0-7618-0596-6); pap. 27.50 (0-7618-0597-4) U Pr of Amer.
Masks of Odin: Wisdom of the Ancient Norse. Elsa-Brita Titchenell. LC 85-40652. (Illus.). 316p. 1999. 23.95 (0-911500-72-3) Theos U Pr.
Masks of Odin: Wisdom of the Ancient Norse. Elsa-Brita Titchenell. LC 85-40652. (Illus.). 316p. 1998. reprint ed. pap. 15.95 (0-911500-73-1) Theos U Pr.
Masks of Othello: The Search for the Identity of Othello, Iago, & Desdemona by Three Centuries of Actors & Critics. Marvin Rosenberg. LC 61-7521. 328p. 1993. reprint ed. 30.00 (0-87413-481-1); reprint ed. pap. 15.00 (0-87413-484-6) U Delaware Pr.
Masks of Play. Brian Sutton-Smith & Diana Kelly-Byrne. LC 83-80745. (Illus.). 200p. (Orig.). 1984. reprint ed. pap. 62.00 (0-608-07097-1, 206732400009) Bks Demand.
Masks of Proteus: Canadian Reflections on the State. Philip Resnick. 352p. (C). 1990. 65.00 (0-7735-0731-0, Pub. by McG-Queens Univ Pr) CUP Services.
Masks of Proteus: Canadian Reflections on the State. Philip Resnick. 352p. 1997. pap. text 24.95 (0-7735-1694-8, Pub. by McG-Queens Univ Pr) CUP Services.
Masks of Rome. large type ed. Caroline Llewellyn. (General Ser.). 432p. 1989. lib. bdg. 21.95 (0-8161-4752-3, G K Hall Lrg Type) Mac Lib Ref.
Masks of Satan: The Demonic in History. Christopher Nugent. 216p. 1984. 22.50 (0-89860-128-2) Eastview.
***Masks of the Darkest American Game.** Reginald Webster Carter. LC 99-97515. 243p. 2000. pap. 17.95 (0-9676268-0-3) Sire Pubng.
Masks of the Illuminati. Robert A. Wilson. 368p. 1990. pap. 13.95 (0-440-50306-X) Dell.
Masks of the Martyrs. Jack L. Chalker. (Rings of the Master Ser.: Bk. 4). 352p. 1988. mass mkt. 4.95 (0-345-34309-3, Del Rey) Ballantine Pub Grp.
Masks of the Martyrs. Jack L. Chalker. (Rings of the Master Ser.). 1988. pap. write for info. (0-318-62998-4) Random.
Masks of the Spirit: Image & Metaphor in Mesoamerica. Roberta H. Markman & Peter T. Markman. (Illus.). 276p. 1989. 75.00 (0-520-06418-6, Pub. by U CA Pr) Cal Prin Full Svc.
Masks of the Spirit: Image & Metaphor in Mesoamerica. Roberta H. Markman & Peter T. Markman. (Illus.). 276p. (C). 1994. pap. 32.50 (0-520-08654-6, Pub. by U CA Pr) Cal Prin Full Svc.
Masks of the World. Douglas Congdon-Martin. LC 99-29934. (Illus.). 160p. 1999. 49.95 (0-7643-0968-4) Schiffer.
Masks of the World. Josef Gregor. LC 68-18150. (Illus.). 1972. reprint ed. 36.95 (0-405-08579-6, Pub. by Blom Pubns) Ayer.
Masks of Tradition: Women & the Politics of Writing in Twentieth-Century France. Martha N. Evans. LC 87-6685. 256p. (C). 1987. 35.00 (0-8014-2028-8) Cornell U Pr.
Masks of Tradition: Women & the Politics of Writing in Twentieth-Century France. Martha N. Evans. LC 87-6685. 243p. reprint ed. pap. 75.40 (0-608-20887-6, 207198600003) Bks Demand.
Masks of Tragedy, Essays on Six Greek Dramas. Thomas G. Rosenmeyer. LC 78-150417. 261p. (C). 1971. reprint ed. 50.00 (0-87752-140-9) Gordian.
Masks of War: American Military Styles in Strategy & Analysis. Carl H. Builder. LC 88-13517. 240p. 1989. pap. 15.95 (0-8018-3776-6) Johns Hopkins.
Masks of Wedlock: Seventeenth-Century Dutch Marriage Portraiture. David R. Smith. Ed. by Linda Seidel. LC 82-8618. (Studies in the Fine Arts: No. 8). (Illus.). 304p. 1982. reprint ed. pap. 94.30 (0-8357-1353-9, 207001900063) Bks Demand.
Masks Outrageous & Austere: Culture, Psyche, & Persona in Modern Women Poets. Cheryl Walker. LC 91-6294. (Illus.). 244p. 1991. pap. 6.95 (0-253-20666-9, MB-666) Ind U Pr.
Masks Tell Stories. Carol Gelber. LC 92-15595. (Beyond Museum Walls Ser.). (Illus.). 72p. (J). (gr. 4-6). 1993. pap. 6.95 (1-56294-765-6); lib. bdg. 23.90 (1-56294-224-7) Millbrook Pr.
Masks Tell Stories. Houghton Mifflin Company Staff. 1992. pap. 6.70 (0-395-66817-4) HM.
Masks Tents Vessels Talismans. Janet Kardon. LC 79-92164. (Illus.). 1979. pap. 8.00 (0-88454-053-7) U of Pa Contemp Art.
Masks, Transformation, & Paradox. A. David Napier. 1986. pap. 18.95 (0-520-04533-5, Pub. by U CA Pr) Cal Prin Full Svc.
Maskwork. Jennifer Foreman. LC 99-35439. 2000. pap. 29.95 (0-325-00167-7) Heinemann.
Maslov Classes, Metaplectic Representation & Lagrangian Quantization. Maurice De Gosson. 188p. 1997. pap. 105.00 (3-527-40087-7) Wiley.
Maslov Classes, Metapletic Representation & Lagrangian Quantization. Maurice De Gosson. LC 97-154820. 188p. 1997. pap. 89.20 (3-05-501714-5) Wiley.
Maslow Business Reader. Abraham H. Maslow. Ed. by Deborah C. Stephens. LC 99-55086. 304p. 2000. text 29.95 (0-471-36008-2) Wiley.
Maslow on Management. Abraham H. Maslow et al. LC 98-21068. 336p. 1998. 27.95 (0-471-24780-4) Wiley.
Maslow's Motivation & Personality. 3rd ed. Robert Frager & James Fadiman. 336p. (C). 1997. pap. 32.48 (0-06-041987-3) Addson-Wesley Educ.

An Asterisk (*) at the beginning of an entry indicates that the title is appearing for the first time.

MASM: Tips & Techniques for Unisys 1100-2200 Systems. Mike Maddux. Ed. by Michele Drolet. 260p. 1990. student ed. 45.00 (*0-9627241-0-6*) PCI TX.
***Masnavi: A Study of Urdu Romance.** Anna A. Suvorova. Tr. by M. Osama Faruqi. 250p. 2000. text 14.95 (*0-19-579148-7*) OUP.
Masnavi Mawlana Rumi. Jalal Al-Din Rumi. Tr. by Reynold A. Nicholson. 1200p. 1996. 165.00 (*0-614-21309-6*, 758) Kazi Pubns.
Masnavi Ravayeh. Molana S. Ali. LC 89-16557. (ARA, FRE & PER.). 125p. (Orig.). 1990. pap. 15.00 (*0-8191-7676-1*) U Pr of Amer.
Masochism: A Jungian View. rev. ed. Lyn Barrett Cowan. LC 82-16957. 138p. (Orig.). (C). 1998. pap. 15.00 (*0-88214-367-0*) Spring Pubns.
Masochism: Coldness & Cruelty; Venus in Furs. Gilles Deleuze & Leopold Von Sacher-Masoch. Tr. by Jean McNeil from FRE. LC 88-20823. 293p. 1989. reprint ed. 25.95 (*0-942299-54-X*); reprint ed. pap. 13.50 (*0-942299-55-8*) Zone Bks.
Masochism: Current Psychoanalytic Perspectives. Ed. by Robert A. Glick & Donald I. Meyers. 248p. (C). 1993. reprint ed. pap. 24.95 (*0-88163-171-X*) Analytic Pr.
Masochism: Index of New Information & Research Reference Book. Haynes B. Goyer. 150p. 1996. 47.50 (*0-7883-1160-3*); pap. 44.50 (*0-7883-1161-1*) ABBE Pubs Assn.
Masochism: The Art of Power. Nick Mansfield. LC 96-26279. 128p. 1997. 52.95 (*0-275-95702-0*) Greenwood.
Masochism: The Treatment of Self-Inflicted Suffering. Ed. by Jill D. Montgomery & Ann C. Greif. 1989. 42.50 (*0-8236-3145-1*, BN#03145) Intl Univs Pr.
Masochism & the Emergent Ego. Esther Menaker. LC 96-10226. (Master Works). 1996. reprint ed. pap. 50.00 (*1-56821-837-0*) Aronson.
Masochism & the Self. Roy F. Baumeister. 256p. (C). 1989. text 59.95 (*0-8058-0486-2*) L Erlbaum Assocs.
***Masochistic Pleasures of Sentimental Literature.** Marianne Noble. LC 99-48831. 240p. 2000. text 55.00 (*0-691-00936-8*, Pub. by Princeton U Pr); pap. text 18.95 (*0-691-00937-6*, Pub. by Princeton U Pr) Cal Prin Full Svc.
Masocriticism. Paul Mann. LC 98-13738. (SUNY Series in Postmodern Culture). 224p. (C). 1998. text 59.50 (*0-7914-4031-1*); pap. text 19.95 (*0-7914-4032-X*) State U NY Pr.
Masomo Ya Kisasa: Contemporary Readings in Swahili. Ann Biersteker. 480p. (C). 1990. 29.95 (*0-300-04811-4*) Yale U Pr.
Mason. Jack Rudman. (Career Examination Ser.: C-473). 1994. pap. 23.95 (*0-8373-0473-3*) Nat Learn.
Mason: Ancestors & Descendants of Elisha Mason, Litchfield, Conn., 1759-1858, & His Wife Lucretia Webster, 1766-1853. G. W. Mason. 120p. 1992. reprint ed. pap. 23.00 (*0-8328-2685-5*); reprint ed. lib. bdg. 33.00 (*0-8328-2684-7*) Higginson Bk Co.
Mason & Dixon. Thomas Pynchon. LC 97-6467. 773p. 1995. 27.50 (*0-8050-3758-6*) H Holt & Co.
Mason & Dixon. Thomas Pynchon. 1998. write for info. (*0-8050-5850-8*, Owl) H Holt & Co.
Mason Co., Illinois Heritage Cookbook. 53p. (Orig.). 1988. pap. text 4.95 (*0-685-26556-0*) Mason Cnty Hist Proj.
Mason Co. VA/WV Marriages. Carrie Eldridge. (Illus.). 49p. 1992. reprint ed. spiral bd. 15.00i (*1-928979-14-9*) C Eldridge.
Mason County, Illinois: Lutheran Church Records to 1904. CJCLDS Mason County Staff. 53p. 1990. pap. 5.00 (*1-877869-23-6*) Mason Cnty Hist Proj.
Mason County, Kentucky, County Clerk Court Orders, 1789-1800: An Every-Name Index. 127p. 1995. spiral bd. 15.00 (*1-57445-012-3*) TLC Genealogy.
Mason County, Kentucky, Court Orders, 1800-1803. LC 98-185613. 162p. (Orig.). 1997. pap. 20.00 (*1-57445-030-1*) TLC Genealogy.
Mason County, Kentucky, Court Orders, 1803-1816: An Every-Name Index. T.L.C. Genealogy Staff. LC 95-122898. 107p. (Orig.). 1994. pap., spiral bd. 20.00 (*1-886633-05-3*) TLC Genealogy.
Mason County, Kentucky Taxpayers, 1790-1799. T.L.C. Genealogy Staff. 159p. (Orig.). 1993. pap., spiral bd. 10.00 (*1-886633-10-X*) TLC Genealogy.
Mason County Trees. J. W. Duffield. (Illus.). 92p. 1998. pap. 8.00 (*0-9635361-2-5*) Burton Bks.
Mason Decoys: A Pictorial Guide. Russ J. Goldberger & Alan G. Haid. LC 92-74942. (Illus.). 144p. 1993. 49.95 (*0-9631815-1-3*) Decoy Mag.
***Mason Dixon Line.** Tom Croft. 260p. 2000. pap. 10.95 (*0-9661994-1-3*) Palmer & Stewart.
***Mason Jars in the Flood: And Other Stories.** Gary N. Carden. LC 99-58227. 1999. 16.95 (*1-887905-22-7*) Pkway Pubs.
Mason Williams-F. C. C. Rapport. Mason Williams. LC 71-114380. 1970. pap. 2.95 (*0-87140-222-X*, Pub. by Liveright) Norton.
Mason Williams/Classical Gas: Guitar Personality Book. 48p. (Orig.). 1993. pap. 17.95 (*0-7692-0573-9*, P0961GTX) Wrner Bros.
Masoneria: Mas alla de la Luz. William Schnoebelen. (SPA., Illus.). 286p. (Orig.). 1997. pap. 9.95 (*0-937958-51-4*) Chick Pubns.
Masonic Addresses & Writings of Roscoe Pound. 3rd ed. (Illus.). xiii, 384p. 1978. reprint ed. text 15.95 (*0-88053-019-7*, M-68) Macoy Pub.
***Masonic & Occult Symbols Illustrated.** Cathy Burns. (Illus.). 552p. 1998. pap. 21.95 (*1-891117-12-2*) Sharing.
Masonic Antiquities of the Orient Unveiled. M. Wolcott Redding. 454p. 1997. reprint ed. pap. 35.00 (*0-7661-0016-2*) Kessinger Pub.
Masonic Apron: Its Traditions, History, & Secret Significances. Frank Higgens. 1990. pap. 5.95 (*1-55818-167-9*) Holmes Pub.
Masonic Baptism: Reception of a Louveteau & Adoption. Albert Pike. 221p. 1993. reprint ed. pap. 24.95 (*1-56459-348-7*) Kessinger Pub.
Masonic Burial Service. pap. 5.00 (*0-911164-20-0*) Powner.
Masonic Burial Service. Grand Lodge of Massachusetts Staff. 24p. 1997. reprint ed. pap. 9.95 (*0-7661-0070-7*) Kessinger Pub.
Masonic Charges & Lectures. John Yarker. 200p. 1993. reprint ed. pap. 16.95 (*1-56459-307-X*) Kessinger Pub.
Masonic Christian Conflict Explained. Keith Harris. 155p. 1993. pap. text 10.00 (*0-9636534-0-7*) Omega Pub KY.
Masonic Chronology in Context. Leon Zeldis. 100p. 1993. reprint ed. pap. 19.95 (*1-56459-382-7*) Kessinger Pub.
Masonic Compendium to the Sacred Books & Early Literature of the East (1918) George W. Plummer. 67p. 1996. reprint ed. pap. 12.00 (*1-56459-556-0*) Kessinger Pub.
***Masonic Death Records from the Grand Lodge of Arkansas, 1941-1990.** Desmond W. Allen. 315p. (Orig.). 1999. pap. 39.00 (*1-56546-153-3*) Arkansas Res.
Masonic Dictionary. 2nd enl. rev. ed. C. Bruce Hunter. LC 86-62666. xi, 105p. 1996. pap. 5.95 (*0-88053-083-9*, M329) Macoy Pub.
Masonic Funeral Services (6) Simons & Macoy. 1994. reprint ed. pap. 3.50 (*0-88053-009-X*, M029) Macoy Pub.
Masonic History of Unadilla, N. Y. George D. Raitt et al. Ed. by Shirley B. Goerlich. (Illus.). 59p. 1995. reprint ed. pap. 14.00 (*1-887530-00-2*) RSG Pub.
Masonic Initiation. W. L. Wilmshurst. 223p. 1996. pap. 17.00 (*0-89540-288-2*, SB-288) Sun Pub.
Masonic Initiation. W. L. Wilmshurst. 223p. 1992. reprint ed. pap. 15.95 (*1-56459-147-6*) Kessinger Pub.
Masonic Jurisprudence. Roscoe Pound. 120p. 1992. reprint ed. pap. 12.95 (*1-56459-048-8*) Kessinger Pub.
Masonic Ladder or the Nine Steps to Ancient Freemasonry. John Sherer. 274p. 1997. reprint ed. pap. 24.95 (*0-7661-0076-6*) Kessinger Pub.
Masonic Letter G. Paul F. Case. 96p. 1994. pap. 8.50 (*0-88053-066-9*, M-326) Macoy Pub.
Masonic Lifeline: Leadership. Allen E. Roberts. Orig. Title: More Light in Masonry. (Illus.). 160p. 1992. pap. 6.00 (*0-935633-11-1*) Anchor Comm.
Masonic Lodge see Logia Masonica
Masonic Lodge: What You Need to Know: Quick Reference Guide. Ron D. Rhodes & Decker. (Quick Reference Guide Ser.). 10p. 1997. pap. 1.99 (*1-56507-566-8*) Harvest Hse.
Masonic Lodge: Where Will It Take You? Carol Crook. 1998. pap. 5.25 (*0-939399-23-7*) Bks of Truth.
Masonic Manual: A Pocket Companion for the Initiated Containing the Rituals of Freemasonry. Robert Macoy. 322p. 1997. reprint ed. pap. 24.95 (*0-7661-0067-7*) Kessinger Pub.
Masonic Movement & the Fatima Message. Robert I. Bradley. (Queen of Apostles Ser.: Vol. X). 12p. 1990. 0.65 (*1-56036-004-6*, 49741) AMI Pr.
***Masonic Mysteries.** Perf. by John Thaw. (Inspector Morse Ser.). 1998. audio 14.95 (*1-56938-259-X*, AMP-8259) Acorn Media.
Masonic Orders of Fraternity. Manly P. Hall. (Adepts Ser.). pap. 12.95 (*0-89314-536-X*) Philos Res.
Masonic Poems. Masonic Service Association of the U. S. Staff. 91p. 1992. reprint ed. pap. 12.95 (*1-56459-039-9*) Kessinger Pub.
Masonic Proverbs, Poems & Sayings. 36p. 1998. reprint ed. pap. 12.95 (*0-7661-0218-1*) Kessinger Pub.
Masonic Quiz. William Petersen. 17.95 (*0-685-22032-X*) Wehman.
Masonic Quiz: Ask Me Another, Brother. pap. 17.00 (*0-911164-21-9*) Powner.
Masonic Rites & Wrongs: An Examination of Freemasonry. Steven Tsoukalas. 256p. (Orig.). 1995. pap. 12.99 (*0-87552-457-5*) P & R Pubng.
Masonic Ritual. rev. ed. M. C. Duncan. 21.95 (*0-685-22033-8*) Wehman.
Masonic Ritual & Monitor, 2 pts. Malcolm Duncan. 1946. pap. 13.00 (*0-911164-22-7*) Powner.
Masonic Sketches & Reprints. William J. Hughan. 228p. 1999. reprint ed. pap. 17.95 (*0-7661-0832-5*) Kessinger Pub.
Masonic Soldiers of Fortune (1928) William M. Stuart. 280p. 1998. reprint ed. pap. 19.95 (*0-7661-0723-X*) Kessinger Pub.
Masonic Symbolism. Charles C. Hunt. 512p. 1997. reprint ed. pap. 35.00 (*0-7661-0029-4*) Kessinger Pub.
Masonic Symbolism & the Mystic Way: A Series of Papers on the True Secrets of the Lost World (1923) Arthur Ward. 170p. 1998. reprint ed. pap. 19.95 (*0-7661-0431-1*) Kessinger Pub.
Masonic Thread in Mozart. Katharine Thomson. (C). text 29.95 (*0-85315-381-7*, Pub. by Lawrence & Wishart) NYU Pr.
Masonic Token: A Gift Book. William T. Anderson. 300p. 1997. reprint ed. pap. 19.95 (*0-7661-0044-8*) Kessinger Pub.
Masonic Trivia (And Facts) Allen E. Roberts. 209p. 1994. 18.00 (*0-935633-13-8*) Anchor Comm.
Masonry. (Home Repair & Improvement Ser.). (Illus.). 136p. 1976. 14.60 (*0-8094-2362-6*); lib. bdg. 20.60 (*0-8094-2363-4*) Time-Life.
Masonry. FHB Editors. LC 97-10637. (Builder's Library). (Illus.). 128p. 1997. 24.95 (*1-56158-214-X*, 070342) Taunton.
Masonry. FHB Editors. LC 96-30092. (Best of FHB Ser.). (Illus.). 128p. 1997. pap. 14.95 (*1-56158-169-0*, 070357) Taunton.
Masonry. G. Parkinson & G. Shaw. LC 96-136374. 162p. 1996. 57.00 (*0-7277-2055-4*) Am Soc Civil Eng.
Masonry. Jack Rudman. (Occupational Competency Examination (OCE) Ser.: Vol. 23). 47.95 (*0-8373-5773-X*) Nat Learn.
Masonry. Jack Rudman. (Occupational Competency Examination Ser.: OCE-23). 1994. pap. 27.95 (*0-8373-5723-3*) Nat Learn.
***Masonry.** Simon & Schuster Staff. 386p. (C). 1998. pap. 50.00 (*0-13-012268-8*) S&S Trade.
Masonry. Time-Life Books Editors. LC 96-43206. (Home Repair & Improvement Ser.). (Illus.). 128p. (gr. 11). 1999. 14.95 (*0-7835-3906-1*) Time-Life.
Masonry, Level 2. National Center for Construction Education & Reseach Staff. (Wheels of Learning Ser.). (C). 1996. teacher ed., ring bd. 75.00 (*0-13-265349-4*); student ed., ring bd. 55.00 (*0-13-265760-0*) P-H.
Masonry, Level 3. National Center for Construction Education & Reseach Staff. (Wheels of Learning Ser.). (C). 1996. teacher ed., ring bd. 75.00 (*0-13-265356-7*) P-H.
Masonry, Level 3. National Center for Construction Education & Reseach Staff. (Wheels of Learning Ser.). (C). 1996. student ed., ring bd. 55.00 (*0-13-265778-3*) P-H.
Masonry: Beyond the Light. William Schnoebelen. (Illus.). (Orig.). 1991. pap. 9.95 (*0-937958-38-7*) Chick Pubns.
Masonry: Components to Assemblages. Ed. by John H. Matthys. LC 90-36037. (Special Technical Publication (STP) Ser.: STP 1063). (Illus.). 450p. 1990. text 42.00 (*0-8031-1453-2*, STP1063) ASTM.
Masonry: Concrete, Brick & Stone. 2nd ed. Christine Beal. Ed. by Alexander Samuelson & David Schiff. LC 96-84686. (Illus.). 176p. 1998. pap. 14.95 (*1-880029-86-3*) Creative Homeowner.
Masonry: Conspiracy Against Christianity: Evidence That the Masonic Lodge Has a Secret Agenda. Ralph Epperson. (Illus.). 401p. 1998. pap. 16.95 (*0-9614135-4-9*) Publius Pr.
Masonry: Design & Construction, Problems & Repair. Ed. by John M. Melander & Lynn R. Lauersdorf. LC 93-1147. (STP Ser.: Vol. 1180). (Illus.). 430p. 1993. 47.00 (*0-8031-1492-3*, STP1180) ASTM.
Masonry: Esthetics, Engineering, & Economy. Donald H. Taubert et al. LC 96-9356. (Stp Ser.: Vol. 1246). 193p. 1996. 39.00 (*0-8031-2037-0*, STP1246) ASTM.
Masonry: Materials, Design, Construction, & Maintenance, STP 992. Ed. by Harry A. Harris. LC 88-15446. (Special Technical Publication (STP) Ser.). (Illus.). 304p. 1988. text 48.00 (*0-8031-1168-1*, STP992) ASTM.
Masonry: Materials, Properties & Performance - STP 778. Ed. by J. Borchelt. 277p. 1982. 39.00 (*0-8031-0610-6*, STP778) ASTM.
***Masonry: Materials, Testing & Applications.** J. H. Brisch et al. LC 99-36980. (STP Ser.: No. 1356). (Illus.). 170p. 1999. pap. text 46.00 (*0-8031-2600-X*) ASTM.
Masonry: Past & Present: A Symposium Presented at the Seventy-Seventh Annual Meeting, ASTM, Washington, DC, 23-28 June 1974. Symposium on Historical Review, Research, & New De. LC 75-13059. (ASTM Special Technical Publication: No. 589). 299p. reprint ed. pap. 92.70 (*0-7837-4789-6*, 204482600003) Bks Demand.
Masonry: Research, Application & Problems - STP 871. Ed. by John C. Grogan & John T. Conway. LC 85-3852. (Illus.). 253p. 1985. text 36.00 (*0-8031-0402-2*, STP871) ASTM.
***Masonry Level 2.** NCCER Staff. 1999. pap. text, teacher ed. 80.00 (*0-13-014830-X*); student ed., ring bd. 80.00 (*0-13-014839-3*) P-H.
***Masonry Level 2.** rev. ed. NCCER Staff. 1999. teacher ed., ring bd. 80.00 (*0-13-014841-5*) P-H.
***Masonry Level One.** rev. ed. Simon & Schuster Staff. 392p. (C). 1998. teacher ed., ring bd. 80.00 (*0-13-012269-6*) S&S Trade.
Masonry Level Three: Ttainee Guide, Level 3. (C). 1996. per. 55.00 (*0-13-245671-0*) P-H.
Masonry Level Two: Insructor's Guide, Level 2. (C). 1996. teacher ed., per. 75.00 (*0-13-245663-X*) P-H.
Masonry Level Two: Trainee Guide, Vol. 2. (C). 1996. student ed., per. 55.00 (*0-13-245655-9*) P-H.
Masonry - The Great Gift to Man. Albert G. Brice. 38p. 1995. reprint ed. pap. 7.00 (*1-887560-23-8*) M Poll Pub.
Masonry & Americanism. Masonic Service Association of the U. S. Staff. 145p. 1992. reprint ed. pap. 12.95 (*1-56459-038-0*) Kessinger Pub.
***Masonry & Concrete.** Christine Beall. (Complete Construction Ser.). (Illus.). 464p. 2000. pap. text 39.95 (*0-07-006706-6*) McGraw.
Masonry & Concrete Construction. rev. ed. Ken Nolan. LC 97-43739. (Illus.). 304p. (Orig.). 1998. pap. 28.50 (*1-57218-044-7*) Craftsman.
***Masonry & Concrete Industry.** 31p. 1998. pap. 3.25 (*0-16-062327-8*) USGPO.
Masonry & Its Symbols, in Light of "Thinking & Destiny" Harold W. Percival. LC 52-2237. 1991. reprint ed. pap. 5.95 (*0-911650-07-5*) Word Foun.
Masonry & Magic of Frater Rudyard Kipling. Vaughan Bateson. (Orig.). 1993. pap. 6.95 (*1-55818-238-1*) Holmes Pub.
Masonry & Medieval Mysticism: Traces of a Hidden Tradition. Isabal Cooper-Oakley. 192p. 1996. reprint ed. pap. 16.95 (*1-56459-643-5*) Kessinger Pub.
Masonry & Related Occupations. (Equipment Planning Guide for Vocational & Technical Training & Education Programmes Ser.: No. 12). v, 117p. (Orig.). 1986. pap. 36.00 (*92-2-105621-X*) Intl Labour Office.
Masonry & Steel Detailing Handbook. 218p. 1993. pap. 45.95 (*0-924659-48-3*, 4505) Hanley.
Masonry & the Flag. John W. Barry. 109p. 1992. reprint ed. pap. 12.95 (*1-56459-049-6*) Kessinger Pub.
Masonry Block Explained. Chuck Griffith. (Illus.). 21p. (YA). (gr. 10 up). 1989. pap., wbk. ed. 7.00 (*0-8064-1386-7*, M41) Bergwall.
Masonry Brick & Block, Vol. 6. H. Leslie Simmons. 1992. text. write for info. (*0-442-20619-4*) Chapman & Hall.
***Masonry Bridges, Viaducts & Aqueducts.** Rudock. 400p. 2000. 156.00 (*0-86078-751-6*) Ashgate Pub Co.
Masonry Codes & Specifications Handbook, 1994. James E. Amrhein. LC 94-78167. 441p. 1994. 10.00 (*0-940116-28-6*) Masonry Inst Am.
Masonry Codes & Specifications Handbook, 1997. John Chrysler & Thomas Escobar. 464p. 1997. per. 29.95 (*0-8493-7549-5*); boxed set 54.95 (*0-8493-7548-7*) CRC Pr.
Masonry Condemned. 1992. lib. bdg. 88.00 (*0-8490-5406-0*) Gordon Pr.
Masonry Construction. David L. Hunter. LC 96-28573. 496p. 1996. 85.00 (*0-13-235136-6*) P-H.
Masonry Construction: Structural Mechanics & Other Aspects. Ed. by C. R. Calladine. LC 92-18221. 100p. (C). 1992. text 154.50 (*0-7923-1846-3*) Kluwer Academic.
Masonry Defined: A Liberal Masonic Education That Every Mason Should Have, Compiled from the Writings of Albert G. Mackey & Many Other Eminent Authorities. enl. rev. ed. E. R. Johnston. 937p. 1993. pap. 75.00 (*1-56459-379-7*) Kessinger Pub.
Masonry Design & Detailing. 4th rev. ed. Christine Beall. LC 97-1066. (Illus.). 613p. 1997. 94.95 (*0-07-005844-X*) McGraw.
Masonry Designer's Guide. 880p. 1993. 99.65 (*0-685-72317-8*, MDG-1BOW6) ACI.
***Masonry Designers' Guide.** 2nd ed. Masonry Society Staff et al. (Illus.). 553p. 1999. write for info. (*0-87031-000-3*) ACI.
Masonry Dissected. Samuel Prichard. 50p. 1996. reprint ed. pap. 12.95 (*1-56459-982-5*) Kessinger Pub.
Masonry Essentials. (Black & Decker Quick Steps Ser.). (Illus.). 80p. (Orig.). 1997. pap. 9.95 (*0-86573-647-2*) Creat Pub Intl.
Masonry Estimating. Rynold V. Kolkoski. LC 95-13384. 1995. reprint ed. pap. 26.50 (*0-924659-74-2*, 560) Hanley.
Masonry in the Americas. 368p. 1994. pap. 38.25 (*0-614-02515-X*, SP147BOW6) ACI.
Masonry in the Formation of Our Government, 1761-1799. Philip A. Roth. 187p. 1996. reprint ed. pap. 17.95 (*1-56459-527-7*) Kessinger Pub.
Masonry Inspection & Maintenance: Trouble Shooting & Preserving Masonry Structures. (Illus.). 51p. (Orig.). 1994. pap. 11.95 (*0-924659-56-4*, 4525) Hanley.
***Masonry Level Three: 99 Review Perfect Bond Trainee Guide.** (C). 2000. pap. 80.00 (*0-13-017987-6*) P-H.
***Masonry Level 3 Instruction Guide 99 Review.** (C). 2000. per. 80.00 (*0-13-017986-8*) S&S Trade.
***Masonry Level Two, 1999.** rev. ed. NCCER Staff. 1999. pap. text, teacher ed. 80.00 (*0-13-014837-7*, Prentice Hall) P-H.
***Masonry Level 3 Binder Instrutor Guide 1999 Rev.** (C). 2000. ring bd. 80.00 (*0-13-017984-1*) Addison-Wesley.
***Masonry Level 3 Binder Trainee Guide 1999 Review.** (C). 2000. ring bd. 80.00 (*0-13-017985-X*) Addison-Wesley.
Masonry of Adoption: Albert Pike's Masonic Rituals for Women. Albert Pike. 220p. 1992. reprint ed. pap. 19.95 (*1-56459-286-3*) Kessinger Pub.
Masonry Problem Clinic. (Illus.). 123p. 1999. pap. 20.00 (*0-924659-25-4*, 4062) Hanley.
Masonry Reference Manual: Specifications for Masonry Structures. 300p. 1992. pap. 110.50 (*0-685-45548-3*, SP-115(92)BOW6) ACI.
Masonry Repair & Restoration: A Guide to Techniques & Materials. (Illus.). 54p. (Orig.). 1994. pap. 11.95 (*0-924659-60-2*, 4520) Hanley.
Masonry Simplified, Vol. 1. 3rd ed. James R. Dalzell & Gilbert Townsend. LC 72-93804. 414p. reprint ed. pap. 128.40 (*0-608-15392-3*, 202941100060) Bks Demand.
Masonry Skills. 3rd ed. Richard Kreh. (Masonry Trades Ser.). 328p. 1990. pap. text 30.50 (*0-8273-3775-2*) Delmar.
Masonry Skills. 3rd ed. Richard Kreh. (Masonry Trades Ser.). 328p. 1990. pap., teacher ed. 16.95 (*0-8273-3777-9*) Delmar.
Masonry Skills. 4th ed. Kreh. (Construction/Building Trades Ser.). 1997. teacher ed. 17.95 (*0-8273-7177-2*, VNR) Wiley.
Masonry Skills - Hardcover 3e. 3rd ed. Richard Kreh. (CONSTRUCTION/BUILDING TRADES). 328p. 1990. pap. 35.25 (*0-8273-3776-0*) Delmar.
Masonry Skills SC. 4th ed. R. T. Kreh. LC 96-47084. (Construction & Building Trades Ser.). 608p. (C). 1997. pap. 56.95 (*0-8273-7178-0*) Delmar.
Masonry Skills SC. 4th ed. Richard T. Kreh. LC 96-47084. (Construction & Building Trades Ser.). 608p. (C). 1997. mass mkt. 48.95 (*0-8273-7176-4*) Delmar.
Masonry Specification Sheets. Kenneth Thomas. LC 92-30669. 1992. write for info. (*0-419-17810-4*, E & FN Spon) Routledge.
Masonry Stone, Vol. 7. H. Leslie Simmons. 1992. text. write for info. (*0-442-20620-8*) Chapman & Hall.
Masonry Supervision: Playing the Game to Win, Not Just to Stay in the Game. Tom LaJaune. 116p. 1996. per. 21.95 (*0-7872-2387-5*) Kendall-Hunt.
Masonry Veneer. 2nd rev. ed. James E. Amrhein. (Illus.). 109p. (Orig.). 1994. pap. text 20.00 (*0-940116-23-5*) Masonry Inst Am.
***Masonry Wall Construction.** A. W. Hendry & F. M. Khalaf. LC 00-39499. (Illus.). 2000. pap. write for info. (*0-415-23282-1*) Routledge.
Masonry Walls: Design & Specification. Ken Thomas. (Illus.). 288p. 1995. 76.95 (*0-7506-2465-5*, Butterwrth Archit) Buttrwrth-Heinemann.

M

An Asterisk (*) at the beginning of an entry indicates that the title is appearing for the first time.

***Masonry 1 '98.** rev. ed. NCCER Staff. 1998. ring bd. 50.00 (*0-13-012260-2*) P-H.

***Masonry 98.** rev. ed. Simon & Schuster Staff. 332p. (C). 1998. pap. 50.00 (*0-13-012271-8*); ring bd. 80.00 (*0-13-012272-6*) S&S Trade.

Masons. H. Berry. 1990. pap. text 1.35 (*0-8474-0828-0*) Back to Bible.

Masons & Builders Libary Louis M. Dezettel. 1972. 17.95 (*0-672-23185-9*) Sams.

Masons & Builders Library, 2 vols, Set. 2nd ed. Louis M. Dezettel & Tom Philbin. LC 83-22352. (Illus.). 1984. text 29.95 (*0-672-23401-7*) Macmillan.

Masons & Methodists in Utica, Mississippi. James E. Price. 167p. 1998. pap. 17.00 (*1-885480-24-5*) Pioneer Pubng.

Masons & Sculptors. Nicola Coldstream. (Medieval Craftsmen Ser.). (Illus.). 72p. 1991. pap. text 19.95 (*0-8020-6916-9*) U of Toronto Pr.

Masons & Sculptors in Romanesque Burgundy: The New Aesthetic of Cluny III, 2 vols. C. Edson Armi. LC 82-42784. (Illus.). 384p. 1984. 87.50 (*0-271-00338-3*) Pa St U Pr.

Mason's Basic Medical-Surgical Nursing. 6th ed. Ed. by Grace F. Bates. LC 96-9332. (Illus.). 835p. 1996. text 45.00 (*0-07-105428-6*) McGraw-Hill HPD.

Mason's Helper. Jack Rudman. (Career Examination Ser.: C-474). 1994. pap. 23.95 (*0-8373-0474-1*) Nat Learn.

Mason's Manual of Legislative Procedure. rev. ed. American Society of Legislative Clerks & Secretari. 677p. 1989. reprint ed. 40.00 (*1-55516-729-2*, 7120) Natl Conf State Legis.

Mason's Retreat. Christopher Tilghman. Date not set. write for info. (*0-679-45240-0*) McKay.

Mason's Retreat. Christopher Tilghman. LC 97-2989. 304p. 1997. pap. 13.00 (*0-312-15586-7*) St Martin.

Mason's Retreat. Christopher Tilghman. 1997. pap. 13.00 (*0-614-27291-2*, Picador USA) St Martin.

Mason's Retreat. large type ed. Christopher Tilghman. LC 96-18641. 397p. 1996. 24.95 (*0-7838-1863-7*, G K Hall Lrg Type) Mac Lib Ref.

***Masons, Tricksters & Cartographers: Makers of Knowledge & Space.** David Turnbull. 224p. 2000. pap. 24.00 (*90-5823-001-5*, Harwood Acad Pubs); text 56.00 (*90-5702-499-3*, Harwood Acad Pubs) Gordon & Breach.

Masonville, Delaware County, New York: Early Records from the Past. Compiled & Transcribed by Shirley B. Goerlich. 220p. 1995. pap. 30.00 (*0-9614858-8-4*) RSG Pub.

Masorah of Biblia Hebraica Stuttgartensia: Introduction & Annotated Glossary. Page H. Kelley et al. LC 97-42457. 256p. (C). 1998. pap. 26.00 (*0-8028-4363-8*) Eerdmans.

Masoretic Chant of the Bible. Daniel Meir Weil. 447p. 1995. 58.00 (*965-09-0061-6*, 88040, Pub. by R Mass Ltd) Lambda Pubs.

Masoretische und Alexandrinische Sondergut des Jeremiabuches: Textgeschichtlicher Rang, Eigenarten, Triebkrafte. Hermann-Josef Stipp. (Orbis Biblicus et Orientalis Ser.: Vol. 136). (GER.). 186p. 1994. text 40.75 (*3-7278-0956-6*, Pub. by Presses Univ Fribourg) Eisenbrauns.

***Masory Level 1, '98.** NCCER Staff. 1998. teacher ed., ring bd. 50.00 (*0-13-012273-4*) P-H.

Masoud the Bedouin. Alfreda Carhart. LC 76-150541. (Short Story Index Reprint Ser.). (Illus.). 1977. reprint ed. 20.95 (*0-8369-3838-0*) Ayer.

Masque. F. Paul Wilson & Matthew J. Costello. LC 97-34571. 342p. 1998. 23.00 (*0-446-51977-4*, Pub. by Warner Bks) Little.

Masque. F. Paul Wilson & Matthew J. Costello. 352p. 1999. mass mkt. 6.99 (*0-446-60676-6*, Pub. by Warner Bks) Little.

Masque: Photographs of Halloween. Edward Reed. LC 80-54591. (Illus.). 60p. 1981. pap. 8.95 (*0-89822-012-2*) Visual Studies.

Masque de Fer. Marcel Pagnol. pap. 9.50 (*0-685-37005-4*) Fr & Eur.

Masque in Honor of the Marriage of Lord Hayes, 1607 see Old English Edition

Masque of Anarchy. Percy Bysshe Shelley. Ed. by Thomas J. Wise. LC 74-30293. (Shelley Society, Second Ser.: No. 13). reprint ed. 29.50 (*0-404-11511-X*) AMS Pr.

Masque of Anarchy. Percy Bysshe Shelley. LC 90-36266. 88p. 1990. reprint ed. 35.00 (*1-85477-055-1*) Continuum.

Masque of Beauty & the Beast. Michael E. Brill. (J). 1979. 6.00 (*0-87602-156-9*) Anchorage.

Masque of Betrayal. Andrea Kane. Ed. by Carolyn Tolley. 384p. 1993. mass mkt. 4.99 (*0-671-75532-3*) PB.

Masque of Femininity: The Presentation of Woman in Everyday Life. Efrat Tseelon. LC 95-69789. (Theory, Culture & Society Ser.). (Illus.). 160p. 1995. 45.00 (*0-8039-8806-0*); pap. 14.99 (*0-8039-8807-9*) Sage.

Masque of Pandora & Other Poems. Henry Wadsworth Longfellow. (Notable American Authors Ser.). 1999. reprint ed. lib. bdg. 125.00 (*0-7812-3843-9*) Rprt Serv.

Masque of Passion. Tesni Morgan. 1998. mass mkt. 5.95 (*0-352-33259-X*, Pub. by BLA4) London Brdge.

Masque of Poets. George P. Lathrop. 1999. reprint ed. lib. bdg. 125.00 (*0-7812-3757-2*) Rprt Serv.

Masque of Queens: A Play in Two Acts. Maxwell Anderson. Ed. by D. M. Anderson. (Illus.). vi, 76p. (Orig.). 1987. pap. 9.50 (*0-944075-00-2*) Anderson NY.

Masque of Stuart Culture. Jerzy Limon. LC 89-40475. (Illus.). 240p. 1990. 40.00 (*0-87413-396-3*) U Delaware Pr.

Masque of the Gods. Bayard Taylor. (Notable American Authors). 1999. reprint ed. lib. bdg. 125.00 (*0-7812-8990-4*) Rprt Serv.

***Masque of the Gonzagas.** Clare Colvin. 2000. pap. 13.99 (*1-900850-25-7*) Arcadia Bks.

Masque of the Red Death. Edgar Allan Poe. (Short Story Library). (Illus.). 32p. (YA). (gr. 4 up). 1991. lib. bdg. 18.60 (*0-88682-477-X*, Creat Educ) Creative Co.

Masque of the Red Death. Edgar Allan Poe. Ed. by Raymond Harris. (Classics Ser.). (Illus.). 48p. (YA). (gr. 6-12). 1982. teacher ed. 7.32 (*0-89061-272-2*, 477, Jamestwn Pub); pap. text 5.99 (*0-89061-271-4*, 475, Jamestwn Pub); audio 17.96 (*0-89061-273-0*, 476, Jamestwn Pub) NTC Contemp Pub Co.

Masque of the Red Death & Other Tales. William W. Connors et al. (Advanced Dungeons & Dragons, 2nd Edition: Ravenloft Campaign World Ser.). 1994. 25.00 (*1-56076-877-0*) TSR Inc.

Masque of the Swan. Rebecca Ashe. 320p. 1996. mass mkt. 4.99 (*0-7860-0212-3*, Pinncle Kensgtn) Kensgtn Pub Corp.

***Masqued Mysteries Unmasked: Early Modern Music Theater & Its Pythagorean Subtext.** Kristin Rygg. LC 00-23699. (Interplay Ser.). 2000. write for info. (*1-57647-035-0*) Pendragon NY.

Masquerade. Lowell Cauffiel. 1989. mass mkt. 4.95 (*0-8217-2833-4*, Zebra Kensgtn) Kensgtn Pub Corp.

Masquerade. Lowell Cauffiel. 480p. 1997. mass mkt. 5.99 (*0-7860-0468-1*, Pinncle Kensgtn) Kensgtn Pub Corp.

Masquerade. Janet Dailey. 384p. 1991. mass mkt. 5.95 (*0-316-17147-6*) Little.

***Masquerade.** Katherine Deauxville et al. 400p. 1999. mass mkt. 5.99 (*0-8439-4577-X*, Pub. by Dorchester Pub Co) CMG.

Masquerade. Caroline Gray. 288p. 1997. 25.00 (*0-7278-5119-5*) Severn Hse.

Masquerade. B. J. Hoff. LC 96-25287. (Portraits Ser.: No. 1). 224p. 1996. pap. 8.99 (*1-55661-860-3*) Bethany Hse.

Masquerade. Gayle Lynds. 464p. 1997. mass mkt. 6.99 (*0-425-16019-X*) Berkley Pub.

Masquerade. Walter Satterthwait. 336p. 1999. mass mkt. 5.99 (*0-312-96989-9*, Thomas Dunne) St Martin.

Masquerade. Alexa Smart. 512p. 1994. mass mkt. 4.99 (*0-7860-0080-5*, Pinncle Kensgtn) Kensgtn Pub Corp.

***Masquerade.** Michael A. Stackpole. (Star Wars: No. 7). (YA). (gr. 5 up). 2000. pap. text 12.95 (*1-56971-487-8*) Dark Horse Comics.

Masquerade. Ian Valz. LC 88-80156. (Illus.). 71p. (Orig.). 1988. pap. text 8.00 (*0-913441-06-6*) Hse of Nehesi.

***Masquerade.** Crystal Wilson-Harris. 2000. mass mkt. 5.99 (*1-58314-085-9*) BET Bks.

***Masquerade.** large type ed. Janet Cookson. 200p. 1999. pap. 18.99 (*0-7089-5612-2*, Linford) Ulverscroft.

***Masquerade.** large type ed. B. J. Hoff. LC 99-58240. (Christian Mystery Ser.). 2000. 24.95 (*0-7862-2376-6*) Thorndike Pr.

Masquerade. large type ed. Jean Ure. (Linford Romance Library). 1990. pap. 16.99 (*0-7089-6830-9*, Linford) Ulverscroft.

Masquerade. 2nd ed. Wolf White Wolf Publishing Staff et al. 192p. 1994. 18.00 (*1-56504-154-2*, 5200) White Wolf.

Masquerade, Vol. 1. Walter Satterthwait. LC 98-16932. Vol. 1. 272p. 1998. text 22.95 (*0-312-18629-0*) St Martin.

Masquerade: An Historical Novel. Oscar Micheaux. LC 73-18595. reprint ed. 49.50 (*0-404-11406-7*) AMS Pr.

Masquerade: The Complete Book with the Answer Explained. Kit Williams. LC 82-40502. (Illus.). 48p. 1983. pap. 3.95 (*0-89480-369-7*, 369) Workman Pub.

Masquerade: Unveiling Our Deadly Dance with Drugs & Alcohol. Milton Creagh. 32p. 1996. 28.99 incl. VHS (*1-56179-500-3*, VI190) Focus Family.

Masquerade & Civilization: The Carnivalesque in Eighteenth-Century English Culture & Fiction. Terry Castle. LC 86-1942. (Illus.). 416p. 1986. pap. 18.95 (*0-8047-1468-1*) Stanford U Pr.

Masquerade & Gender: Disguise & Female Identity in Eighteenth-Century Fictions by Women. Catherine Craft-Fairchild. LC 92-30851. 184p. 1993. 30.00 (*0-271-00918-7*); pap. 17.95 (*0-271-00919-5*) Pa St U Pr.

Masquerade at Sea House. Elizabeth Ogilvie. reprint ed. lib. bdg. 19.95 (*0-88411-333-7*) Amereon Ltd.

Masquerade for the King. large type ed. Marina Oliver. (Historical Romance Ser.). 272p. 1992. 27.99 (*0-7089-2679-7*) Ulverscroft.

Masquerade in Black. William T. Leonard. LC 86-6597. (Illus.). 443p. 1986. 50.00 (*0-8108-1895-7*) Scarecrow.

Masquerade in Blue. D. C. Brod. 208p. 1991. 19.95 (*0-8027-5792-8*) Walker & Co.

Masquerade in Oz. Bill Campbell & Irwin Terry. (Illus.). 125p. (J). (gr. 2 up). 1995. 34.95 (*0-929605-34-9*); pap. 9.95 (*0-929605-33-0*) Books of Wonder.

Masquerade in Port-Cros: A Romance of the Cote D'Azur. John Sampson. LC 84-18. (Illus.). 224p. 1984. 5.96 (*0-9613075-0-1*) Thornfield Pr.

Masquerade in the Moonlight. Kasey Michaels. 1994. mass mkt. 5.50 (*0-671-79339-X*) PB.

***Masquerade Journey.** Miriam Lee. LC 99-91812. 2000. 25.00 (*0-7388-1306-0*); pap. 18.00 (*0-7388-1307-9*) Xlibris Corp.

Masquerade Novels. Eliza F. Hayward. LC 86-13075. 380p. 1986. reprint ed. 50.00 (*0-8201-1412-X*) Schol Facsimiles.

Masquerade of Angels. Karla Turner & Ted Rice. 268p. (Orig.). 1994. pap. 16.95 (*0-9640899-1-2*) Kelt Works.

Masquerade of Monopoly. Frank A. Fetter. LC 66-22623. (Reprints of Economic Classics Ser.). (Illus.). xii, 512p. 1971. reprint ed. 49.50 (*0-678-00291-6*) Kelley.

Masquerade of Vengeance. large type ed. Alice C. Ley. (Large Print Ser.). 384p. 1996. 27.99 (*0-7089-3653-9*) Ulverscroft.

Masquerade on the Western Trail. Laurel J. Pamplin. Ed. by M. Roberts. (Illus.). 112p. (J). (gr. 6-7). 1991. 9.95 (*0-89015-755-3*) Sunbelt Media.

Masquerade Peace: America's U. N. Policy, 1944-1945. Thomas M. Campbell. LC 72-93328. 236p. reprint ed. pap. 73.20 (*0-7837-5076-5*, 204477400004) Bks Demand.

Masquerade Politics: Explorations in the Structure of Urban Cultural Movements. Abner Cohen. LC 92-26339. 1993. 40.00 (*0-520-07838-1*, Pub. by U CA Pr) Cal Prin Full Svc.

Masquerade Time. Cyprian O. Ekwensi. (Junior African Writers Ser.). (Illus.). 80p. (J). (gr. 3 up). 1992. pap. 3.88 (*0-7910-2911-5*) Chelsea Hse.

Masquerade Vision in Poe's Short Stories. James W. Gargano. 1977. pap. 2.50 (*0-910556-09-1*) Enoch Pratt.

Masquerade Waltz. Claudette Williams. 256p. 1995. mass mkt. 3.99 (*0-8217-4816-5*, Pinncle Kensgtn) Kensgtn Pub Corp.

Masqueraders. Georgette Heyer. 1980. pap. 2.25 (*0-449-23253-0*, Crest) Fawcett.

Masqueraders. Georgette Heyer. 256p. 1998. lib. bdg. 22.95 (*1-56723-052-0*) Yestermorrow.

Masquerades see Four Plays by Holberg

Masquerades of Nigeria & Touch. David Griffiths. (Mask Ser.). (Illus.). 73p. 1998. text 44.00 (*3-7186-5719-8*, Harwood Acad Pubs); pap. text 18.00 (*3-7186-5720-1*, Harwood Acad Pubs) Gordon & Breach.

Masques. Ru Emerson. (Beauty & the Beast Ser.: No. 2). 288p. 1990. pap. 3.95 (*0-380-76194-7*, Avon Bks) Morrow Avon.

Masques. Bill Pronzini. 272p. 1999. mass mkt. 4.99 (*0-8439-4501-X*) Dorchester Pub Co.

Masques No. 3: All-New Works of Horror & the Supernatural. Ed. by J. N. Williamson. 320p. 1989. 17.95 (*0-685-26917-5*) St Martin.

Masques Anglais. Paul Reyher. LC 64-14712. 1972. 36.95 (*0-405-08880-9*, Pub. by Blom Pubns) Ayer.

Masques IV: All-New Works of Horror & the Supernatural. Intro. by J. N. Williamson. LC 91-66380. 256p. 1991. 19.95 (*0-940776-26-X*) Maclay Assoc.

Masques in Jacobean Tragedy. Sarah P. Sutherland. LC 81-69122. (Studies in the Renaissance: No. 9). (Illus.). 1984. 34.50 (*0-404-62279-8*) AMS Pr.

Masques of Morality: Female in Fiction. Johan L. Aitken. 190p. pap. 12.95 (*0-88961-113-0*; Pub. by Womens Pr) LPC InBook.

Masques II: All-New Stories of Horror & the Supernatural. Ed. by J. N. Williamson. LC 87-60415. 224p. 1987. 19.95 (*0-940776-24-3*) Maclay Assoc.

Mass. (Illus.). 32p. (Orig.). (J). (ps-3). 1987. pap. 0.99 (*0-89942-683-2*, 683/00) Catholic Bk Pub.

Mass. 32p. (Orig.). 1998. pap. 9.90 (*0-88271-632-8*) Regina Pr.

Mass. Lucien Deiss. 110p. (Orig.). 1992. pap. 9.95 (*0-8146-2058-2*) Liturgical Pr.

Mass: A Biblical Prayer. Peter M. Stravinkas. (Illus.). 32p. 1989. pap. 1.50 (*0-87973-165-6*) Our Sunday Visitor.

Mass: Its Mysteries Revealed. George P. Morse. 61p. (YA). (gr. 4 up). pap. 7.95 (*0-9672595-0-9*) Caths Comitd Pope.

Mass: Remembering Our Story. Whitney Roberson. (Catholic Home Library). (Illus.). 128p. 1989. 4.95 (*1-55944-002-3*) Franciscan Comns.

Mass: Spirituality, History, & Practice. Guy-Marie Oury. Tr. by John Otto from FRE.Tr. of La/Messe: Spiritualite, Historie, Pratique. 126p. 1988. pap. 3.95 (*0-89942-126-1*, 126/04) Catholic Bk Pub.

***Mass: The Art of John Harris.** Ron Tiner. (Illus.). 2000. 29.95 (*1-85585-831-2*) Paper Tiger.

***Mass: Understanding What We Do & Say.** 2nd rev. ed. Michael C. Witczak. 30p. 1999. 1.95 (*0-937997-73-0*, 4560) Hi-Time Pflaum.

Mass Action in the Nervous System: Examination of the Neurophysiological Basis of Adaptive Behavior Through the EEG. Walter J. Freeman. 1975. text 83.00 (*0-12-267150-3*) Acad Pr.

Mass Activity Book. (J). 1996. pap. 1.49 (*0-88271-193-8*) Regina Pr.

Mass Advertising As Social Forecast: A Method for Futures Research. Robert B. Fowles. LC 75-35344. (Illus.). 156p. 1976. 35.00 (*0-8371-8595-5*, FMA/, Greenwood Pr) Greenwood.

Mass & Antimass (Positive & Negative Mass) in Five Dimensions. Ian McCrimmon. (C). 1992. text 19.00 (*1-874686-01-7*, Pub. by Cosmatom) St Mut.

Mass & Charge Transport in Ceramics. Ed. by Kunihito Koumoto et al. LC 96-32732. (Ceramic Transactions Ser.: No. 71). (Illus.). 1996. 95.00 (*1-57498-018-1*, CT071) Am Ceramic.

Mass & Elite in Democratic Athens: Rhetoric, Ideology, & the Power of the People. Josiah Ober. 408p. 1989. pap. text 18.95 (*0-691-02864-8*, Pub. by Princeton U Pr) Cal Prin Full Svc.

Mass & the Sacraments: The Mass, Seven Sacraments, Indulgences, Sacramentals. John Laux. LC 90-70439. (Course in Religion for Catholic High Schools & Academies Ser.: Bk. II). (Illus.). 199p. 1994. reprint ed. pap. text 10.00 (*0-89555-392-9*) TAN Bks Pubs.

***Mass & Volume Relationships.** 5th ed. James M. Postma et al. 2000. pap. text, lab manual ed. 1.95 (*0-7167-9411-X*) W H Freeman.

Mass Apathy & Voluntary Social Participation in the United States. Bernard Barber. Ed. by Harriet Zuckerman & Robert K. Merton. LC 79-8972. (Dissertations on Sociology Ser.). 1980. lib. bdg. 28.95 (*0-405-12949-1*) Ayer.

Mass Appeal. Bill C. Davis. 1982. pap. 5.25 (*0-8222-0738-9*) Dramatists Play.

***Mass Appraisal of Real Property.** Robert J. Gloudemans. LC 99-75328. 428p. 1999. text 100.00 (*0-88329-165-7*); pap. text 75.00 (*0-88329-166-5*) IAAO.

Mass at Dawn. 2nd rev. ed. Roy Campbell. 20p. (Orig.). 1991. pap. 20.00 (*0-930126-35-1*) Typographeum.

Mass Atrocity, Collective Memory & the Law. Mark Osiel. LC 96-50097. 310p. 1997. text 34.95 (*1-56000-322-7*) Transaction Pubs.

Mass Atrocity, Collective Memory & the Law. Mark Osiel. 317p. 1999. pap. 24.95 (*0-7658-0663-0*) Transaction Pubs.

Mass Attraction in Atomic Structure. John F. Johnson. (Illus.). 56p. (Orig.). (C). 1991. pap. text 50.00 (*0-931571-07-3*) RP Pubng.

Mass Audience. James G. Webster & Patricia Phalen. (Communication Ser.). 176p. (C). 1996. text 39.95 (*0-8058-2304-2*) L Erlbaum Assocs.

Mass Audience: Rediscovering the Dominant Model. James G. Webster & Patricia Phalen. (Communication Ser.). 168p. (C). 1996. pap. text 18.50 (*0-8058-2305-0*) L Erlbaum Assocs.

Mass Behaviour in Battle & Captivity: The Communist Soldier in the Korean War. William C. Bradbury. Ed. by Samuel M. Meyers. LC 68-16705. 407p. reprint ed. pap. 126.20 (*0-608-30735-1*, 202003400016) Bks Demand.

Mass Catering. Charles. (WHO Regional Publications, European Ser.: No. 15). 70p. 1983. pap. text 13.00 (*92-890-1106-8*) World Health.

Mass Central: Quabbin's Phantom RR. J. R. Greene. (Illus.). 104p. (Orig.). 1996. pap. 14.95 (*1-884132-04-9*) J R Greene.

Mass Choir Praise. D. Marsh. 1994. pap. 6.95 (*1-55897-768-6*) Brentwood Music.

Mass Communication, 5 vols. Defleur. (C). 1993. pap., teacher ed. 5.96 (*0-395-67405-0*) HM.

Mass Communication. Folkerts. 1997. write for info. (*0-205-26126-4*) Allyn.

Mass Communication. Godfrey. (C). 1999. pap. text. write for info. (*0-15-507261-7*, Pub. by Harcourt Coll Pubs) Harcourt.

Mass Communication. 2nd ed. Farrar. 1995. teacher ed. 14.06 (*0-697-17384-4*) McGraw.

Mass Communication. 2nd annot. ed. Farrar. 1995. teacher ed. 31.87 (*0-697-25987-0*, WCB McGr Hill) McGrw-H Hghr Educ.

Mass Communication. 3rd ed. Charles Wright. 224p. (C). 1985. pap. text 28.50 (*0-07-554465-2*) McGraw.

Mass Communication, 5 vols. 5th ed. Defleur. (C). 1995. pap. text 47.96 (*0-395-74681-7*) HM.

Mass Communication, 5 vols. 5th ed. Melvin L. Defleur. LC 93-78692. (C). 1993. pap. text 46.76 (*0-395-67404-2*) HM.

Mass Communication. 6th ed. Bittner. 1995. pap. text, teacher ed. write for info. (*0-205-17844-8*) Allyn.

Mass Communication. 6th ed. John R. Bittner. LC 95-10813. 514p. 1995. pap. text 61.00 (*0-13-560798-1*) Allyn.

Mass Communication. 6th annot. ed. John R. Bittner. 1995. text, teacher ed. write for info. (*0-205-17842-1*) Allyn.

Mass Communication see Communication As a Second Language

Mass Communication, Vol. 1. Hausman. 2000. pap. text. write for info. (*0-312-14511-X*) St Martin.

Mass Communication: An Introduction to the Field. 2nd ed. Ronald T. Farrar. 480p. (C). 1995. text. write for info. (*0-697-17383-6*) Brown & Benchmark.

Mass Communication: Issues & Perspectives. Robert Abelman. 230p. (C). 1990. text 28.40 (*0-536-57747-1*) Pearson Custom.

Mass Communication: Issues & Perspectives. 2nd ed. Robert Abelman. 354p. (C). 1992. 48.00 (*0-536-58182-7*) Pearson Custom.

Mass Communication & Journalism in India. D. S. Mehta. (C). 1992. pap. 14.00 (*81-7023-353-4*, Pub. by Allied Pubs) S Asia.

Mass Communication & Journalism in India. D. S. Mehta. 313p. 1979. 20.95 (*0-318-37284-3*) Asia Bk Corp.

Mass Communication & Journalism in the Pacific Islands: A Bibliography. Jim Richstad & Michael McMillan. LC 77-20695. 330p. reprint ed. pap. 102.30 (*0-7837-3975-3*, 204380500011) Bks Demand.

Mass Communication & Political Information Processing. Ed. by Sidney Kraus. 240p. 1990. 49.95 (*0-8058-0389-0*) L Erlbaum Assocs.

Mass Communication & Public Health. Ed. by Charles K. Atkin & Lawrence Wallack. (Focus Editions Ser.: Vol. 121). (Illus.). 250p. (C). 1990. 59.95 (*0-8039-3924-8*); pap. 26.00 (*0-8039-3925-6*) Sage.

Mass Communication & Society. Ed. by James Curran et al. LC 78-68700. 488p. 1979. reprint ed. pap. 151.30 (*0-608-02791-X*, 206385800007) Bks Demand.

Mass Communication, Culture & Society in West Africa. Ed. by Frank O. Ogboaja. 335p. 1990. 50.00 (*0-905450-18-3*, Pub. by H Zell Pubs) Seven Hills Bk.

Mass Communication Effects & Processes: A Comprehensive Bibliography, 1950-1975. Thomas F. Gordon & Mary E. Verna. LC 77-26094. 230p. reprint ed. pap. 71.30 (*0-608-11414-6*, 202190700026) Bks Demand.

Mass Communication in Canada. 3rd ed. Rowland Lorimer & Jean McNulty. 376p. 1996. pap. text 49.95 (*0-19-541208-7*) OUP.

***Mass Communication in Canada.** 4th ed. Rowland Lorimer & Michael Gasher. (Illus.). 400p. 2000. pap. text 35.00 (*0-19-541528-0*) OUP.

Mass Communication in Japan. Anne Cooper-Chen & Miiko Kodama. LC 97-9167. (Illus.). 1997. 39.95 (*0-8138-2710-8*) Iowa St U Pr.

Mass Communication in the Information Age. Ed. by W. David Sloan et al. (Illus.). 627p. (Orig.). 1996. pap. 29.95 (*1-885219-02-4*) Vision AL.

Mass Communication Law: Cases & Comments. 5th ed. Donald M. Gillmor & Jerome A. Barron. Ed. by Tubb. 947p. (C). 1989. mass mkt. 54.50 (*0-314-56267-2*) West Pub.

Mass Communication Law: Cases & Comments. 6th ed. Don Gillmor et al. LC 97-27920. (C). 1997. 92.95 (*0-314-20221-8*) Wadsworth Pub.

Mass Communication Law & Ethics. Moore. Ed. by Jennings Bryant & Dolf Zillmann. (Communication Ser.). 64p. 1994. teacher ed. write for info. (*0-8058-1460-4*) L Erlbaum Assocs.

Mass Communication Law & Ethics. Roy L. Moore. (Communication Ser.). 616p. (C). 1994. text 45.00 (*0-8058-0240-1*) L Erlbaum Assocs.

Mass Communication Law & Ethics. 2nd ed. Roy L. Moore. LC 98-36329. (LEA's Communication Ser.). 696p. 1999. 55.00 (*0-8058-2599-1*) L Erlbaum Assocs.

Mass Communication Law & Ethics: A Casebook. Roy L. Moore. LC 99-17431. (LEA's Communication Ser.). 344p. 1999. pap. 29.95 (*0-8058-3278-5*) L Erlbaum Assocs.

Mass Communication Law & Ethics: 1996 Update. Roy L. Moore. (LEA's Communication Ser.). 86p. 1995. text Not sold separately (*0-8058-2219-4*) L Erlbaum Assocs.

Mass Communication Law in Arkansas. Bruce L. Plopper. 105p. 1997. pap. 12.95 (*0-913507-83-0*) New Forums.

Mass Communication Law in Georgia. 2nd ed. Gregory C. Lisby. (State Law Ser.). 120p. (C). 1996. pap. text 14.95 (*0-913507-66-0*) New Forums.

Mass Communication Law in Hawaii. Jeffrey S. Portnoy. 122p. (C). 1994. pap. 14.95 (*0-913507-56-3*) New Forums.

Mass Communication Law in Idaho. Roy A. Atwood. (State Law Ser.). 112p. (C). 1992. pap. text 12.95 (*0-913507-35-0*) New Forums.

Mass Communication Law in Minnesota. Patricia H. Longstaff & John R. Finnegan, Sr. (State Law Ser.). 86p. (C). 1992. text 10.95 (*0-913507-23-7*) New Forums.

Mass Communication Law in Mississippi. Gene Wiggins. (State Law Ser.). 112p. (C). 1992. pap. text 11.95 (*0-913507-30-X*) New Forums.

Mass Communication Law in Nebraska. David A. Haberman. (State Law Ser.). 88p. 1992. pap. 10.95 (*0-913507-33-4*) New Forums.

***Mass Communication Law in New Mexico.** 2nd ed. Steve Pasternack. (State Law Ser.). 70p. 1999. pap. text 12.95 (*0-913507-82-2*) New Forums.

Mass Communication Law in North Carolina. Ruth Walden. (State Law Ser.). 54p. 1993. pap. text 14.95 (*0-913507-49-0*) New Forums.

Mass Communication Law in Oklahoma. Gregory Stefaniak. (State Law Ser.). 80p. (Orig.). 1990. pap. text 8.95 (*0-913507-14-8*) New Forums.

Mass Communication Law in Pennsylvania. Douglas S. Campbell et al. 104p. 1996. pap. 12.95 (*0-913507-68-7*) New Forums.

Mass Communication Law in Rhode Island. Linda L. Levin. (State Law Ser.). 114p. (Orig.). 1993. pap. text 12.95 (*0-913507-45-8*) New Forums.

***Mass Communication Law in Virginia.** 2nd ed. W. Wat Hopkins. (State Law Ser.). 70p. 1999. pap. text 14.95 (*1-58107-002-0*) New Forums.

Mass Communication Law in West Virginia. John H. Boyer. (State Law Ser.). 110p. 1992. pap. text 11.95 (*0-913507-36-9*) New Forums.

Mass Communication Law in Wisconsin. Gary Coll. 92p. 1996. pap. 12.95 (*0-913507-77-6*) New Forums.

Mass Communication Process: A Behavioral & Social Perspective. Keith R. Stamm & John E. Bowes. 256p. 1990. per. 25.95 (*0-8403-6045-2*) Kendall-Hunt.

Mass Communication Research: Contemporary Methods & Applications. Michael W. Singletary. LC 93-13973. 512p. (C). 1994. text 65.63 (*0-8013-0882-8*, 78984) Longman.

Mass Communication Research: Contemporary Methods & Applications. 2nd ed. Michael Singletary. (C). 1998. text. write for info. (*0-8013-1697-9*) Addison-Wesley.

Mass Communication Research: On Problems & Policies. Ed. by Cees J. Hamelink & Olga Linne. LC 93-46341. (Communication & Information Science Ser.). 438p. 1994. text 78.50 (*0-89391-738-9*) Ablx Pub.

Mass Communication Research: On Problems & Policies. Contrib. by Colin Seymour-Ure et al. LC 93-46341. (Communication & Information Science Ser.). 438p. 1994. pap. 39.50 (*0-89391-951-9*) Ablx Pub.

Mass Communication Research Methods. Ed. by Anders Hansen. LC 97-24755. 1997. text 55.00 (*0-8147-3571-1*); pap. text 20.00 (*0-8147-3572-X*) NYU Pr.

Mass Communication Review Yearbook, 3 vols., Vol. 1. Ed. by G. Cleveland Wilhoit. LC 81-643154. (Illus.). 751p. 1980. reprint ed. pap. 200.00 (*0-7837-4852-3*, 204408900001) Bks Demand.

Mass Communication Review Yearbook, 3 vols., Vol. 2. Ed. by G. Cleveland Wilhoit. LC 81-643154. (Illus.). 768p. 1981. reprint ed. pap. 200.00 (*0-7837-4853-1*, 204408900002) Bks Demand.

Mass Communication Review Yearbook, 3 vols., Vol. 3. Ed. by G. Cleveland Wilhoit. LC 81-643154. (Illus.). 766p. 1982. reprint ed. pap. 200.00 (*0-7837-4854-X*, 204408900003) Bks Demand.

Mass Communication Review Yearbook, Vol. 4. Mass Communication Review Yearbook Staff. LC 81-643154. (Illus.). 719p. 1984. reprint ed. pap. 200.00 (*0-608-01171-1*, 205947100004) Bks Demand.

Mass Communication Review Yearbook, Vol. 5, 1985. Mass Communication Review Yearbook Staff. LC 81-643154. (Illus.). 658p. 1985. reprint ed. pap. 200.00 (*0-608-01172-X*, 205947100005) Bks Demand.

Mass Communication Review Yearbook, Vol. 6, 1987. Mass Communication Review Yearbook Staff. LC 81-643154. (Illus.). 642p. 1987. reprint ed. pap. 199.10 (*0-608-01173-8*, 205947100006) Bks Demand.

Mass Communication Services: An Analysis (Puerto Rican Government: Radio, Television, & Community Education) Consuelo Rivera De Otero. LC 76-2025. 153p. (Orig.). 1976. pap. 5.00 (*0-8477-2731-9*) U of PR Pr.

Mass Communication Theory: An Introduction. 3rd ed. Denis McQuail. 448p. 1994. 65.00 (*0-8039-7784-0*); pap. 27.50 (*0-8039-7785-9*) Sage.

Mass Communication Theory: Foundations, Ferment & Future. Stanley J. Baran & Dennis K. Davis. LC 94-16637. 407p. 1994. pap. 36.25 (*0-534-17670-4*) Wadsworth Pub.

Mass Communication Theory: Foundations, Ferment, & Future. 2nd ed. Stanley J. Baran. LC 99-34363. (Mass Communication Ser.). 1999. pap. 56.95 (*0-534-56088-1*) Wadsworth Pub.

Mass Communications. Leslie. (C). 1999. pap. text 37.16 (*0-395-90490-0*) HM.

Mass Communications, 6 vols. 6th ed. Defleur. (C). Date not set. 54.76 (*0-395-89764-5*) HM.

Mass Communications: A Book of Readings. 2nd ed. Wilbur L. Schramm. LC 60-8343. (Illus.). 712p. 1970. reprint ed. pap. 200.00 (*0-7837-8087-7*, 204784000008) Bks Demand.

Mass Communications: A Comparative Introduction. Rowland Lorimer & Paddy Scanell. LC 94-19057. 1994. text 24.95 (*0-7190-3947-9*, Pub. by Manchester Univ Pr) St Martin.

Mass Communications: Freedom & Control of Print & Broadcast Media, Instruction Manual To. 7th ed. Dwight L. Tetter, Jr. & Don R. LeDuc. 132p. (C). 1992. pap. text. write for info. (*1-56662-041-4*) Foundation Pr.

Mass Communications & Youth: Some Current Perspectives. Ed. by F. Gerald Kline & Peter Clarke. LC 73-89939. (Sage Contemporary Social Science Issues Ser.: No. 5). 128p. reprint ed. pap. 39.70 (*0-608-10107-9*, 202191900026) Bks Demand.

Mass Communications in the Caribbean. John A. Lent. LC 90-33583. (Illus.). 412p. 1990. reprint ed. pap. 127.80 (*0-608-06886-1*, 206709400009) Bks Demand.

Mass Communications Law Casebook. 3rd ed. Ed. by Jo A. Smith. 250p. (Orig.). 1986. pap. text 10.95 (*0-89894-001-X*) Advocate Pub Group.

Mass Communications Law in a Nutshell. 4th ed. Harvey L. Zuckman et al. (Nutshell Ser.). 520p. (C). 1994. pap. 23.50 (*0-314-04081-1*) West Pub.

Mass Communications Research Methods: A Step-by-Step Approach. Ed. by H. J. Hsia. 648p. 1988. 49.95 (*0-89859-914-8*) L Erlbaum Assocs.

Mass Communications Research Methods: A Step-by-Step Approach - Instructor's Manual. H. J. Hsia. (Communication Textbook Ser.). 176p. 1988. pap. write for info. (*0-8058-0216-9*) L Erlbaum Assocs.

Mass Communications Research Methods: A Step-by-Step Approach - Workbook. H. J. Hsia. (Mass Communications - Rubin Ser.). 136p. 1988. pap. text, wbk. ed. 14.95 (*0-8058-0051-4*) L Erlbaum Assocs.

Mass Communications Research Resources: An Annotated Guide. Ed. by Christopher H. Sterling et al. LC 97-28441. (LEA's Communication Ser.). 224p. 1997. 49.95 (*0-8058-2024-8*) L Erlbaum Assocs.

Mass Communications Seminar: Proceedings of an Interdisciplinary Seminar Held under the Auspices of the Wenner-Gren Foundation for Anthropological Research, Inc., May 11-13, 1951. Ed. by Hortense Powdermaker. LC 65-27671. (Illus.). 157p. reprint ed. pap. 48.70 (*0-608-09185-5*, 205268900002) Bks Demand.

Mass Confusion: The Do's & Don'ts of Catholic Worship. 2nd expanded ed. James Akin. 244p. 1998. pap. 15.95 (*1-888992-05-0*) Catholic Answers.

***Mass Control: Engineering Human Consciousness.** Jim Keith. LC 99-40749. 256p. 1999. pap. 16.95 (*1-881532-20-8*) IllumiNet Pr.

Mass Culture & Everyday Life. Peter Gibian. LC 96-21130. 272p. (C). 1997. 75.00 (*0-415-91674-7*); pap. 18.99 (*0-415-91675-5*) Routledge.

Mass Culture & Modernism in Egypt. Walter Armbrust. (Studies in Social & Cultural Anthropology: No. 102). (Illus.). 286p. (C). 1996. pap. text 20.95 (*0-521-48492-8*) Cambridge U Pr.

Mass Culture & Modernism in Egypt. Walter Armbrust. (Cambridge Studies in Social & Cultural Anthropology: No. 102). (Illus.). 286p. (C). 1996. text 59.95 (*0-521-48147-3*) Cambridge U Pr.

Mass Culture in Soviet Russia: Tales, Poems, Songs, Movies, Plays, & Folklore, 1917-1953. Ed. by James von Geldern & Richard Stites. LC 94-47995. (Illus.). 624p. 1995. text 49.95 (*0-253-32893-4*); pap. text 24.95 (*0-253-20969-2*) Ind U Pr.

Mass Culture in the Age of Enlightenment: The Blindman's Ballads of Eighteenth-Century Spain. Madeline Sutherland. LC 90-6201. (American University Studies: Romance Languages & Literature: Ser. II, Vol. 149). XXIX, 274p. (C). 1991. text 44.95 (*0-8204-1338-0*) P Lang Pubng.

Mass Customization: The New Frontier in Business Competition. B. Joseph Pine, II. LC 92-17506. 368p. 1999. 32.50 (*0-87584-372-7*) Harvard Busn.

Mass Customization: The New Frontier in Business Competition. B. Joseph Pine, II. 368p. 1999. pap. 16.95 (*0-87584-946-6*) Harvard Busn.

Mass Customization: The New Frontier in Business Competition. B. Joseph Pine, II. 380p. 1992. 32.50 (*0-07-103385-8*) McGraw.

Mass Deacidification: An Update on Possibilities & Limitations. Henk Porck. LC 96-231763. 54p. (Orig.). 1996. pap. 15.00 (*1-887334-52-1*) Coun Lib & Info.

Mass Deacidification Systems: Planning & Managerial Decision Making. Karen Turko. 24p. 1990. pap. 15.00 (*0-918006-19-8*) ARL.

Mass Demonstrations Against Foreign Regimes, Vol. 10. Henry L. Mason. LC 66-8068. 1966. 11.00 (*0-930598-09-1*) Tulane Stud Pol.

Mass Demonstrations Against Foreign Regimes: A Study of Five Crises. Henry L. Mason. LC 66-8608. (Tulane Studies in Political Science: No. 10). 104p. Date not set. reprint ed. pap. 32.30 (*0-608-20656-3*, 207209300003) Bks Demand.

***Mass Determination.** R. P. Mahajan. 562p. 2000. 185.00 (*3-527-29614-X*) Wiley.

Mass Dreams of the Future. 2nd ed. Chet B. Snow. 368p. 1993. reprint ed. pap. 15.95 (*1-882530-10-1*) Deep Forest Pr.

Mass Ejection from Active Galactic Nuclei: Proceedings of a Workshop Held at the Carnegie Observatories in Pasadena, California, February 19-21, 1997. Ed. by N. Arav et al. (ASP Conference Series Proceedings: Vol. 128). 328p. 1997. 34.00 (*1-886733-48-1*) Astron Soc Pacific.

Mass Enlightenment: Critical Studies in Rousseau & Diderot. Julia Simon. LC 94-23757. (SUNY Series in Social & Political Thought). 236p. (C). 1995. pap. text 19.95 (*0-7914-2638-6*) State U NY Pr.

Mass Enlightenment: Critical Studies in Rousseau & Diderot. Julia Simon. LC 94-23757. (SUNY Series in Social & Political Thought). 236p. (C). 1995. text 59.50 (*0-7914-2637-8*) State U NY Pr.

Mass Entertainment. Harold Mendelsohn. 1966. pap. 14.95 (*0-8084-0218-8*) NCUP.

Mass Explained to Children. Maria Montessori. 116p. (J). (gr. 3-9). 1998. reprint ed. 14.95 (*0-912141-61-1*) Roman Cath Bks.

Mass Expulsion in Modern International Law & Practice. Jean-Marie Henckaerts. (International Studies in Human Rights: Vol. 41). 1995. lib. bdg. 90.50 (*90-411-0072-5*, Pub. by M Nijhoff) Kluwer Academic.

Mass-Extinction Debates: How Science Works in a Crisis. Ed. by William Glen. LC 93-26195. xvi, 370p. (C). 1994. 49.50 (*0-8047-2285-4*); pap. 17.95 (*0-8047-2286-2*) Stanford U Pr.

Mass Extinctions: Processes & Evidence. Donovan. 256p. 1991. pap. text 65.00 (*0-471-94524-2*) Wiley.

Mass Extinctions: Processes & Evidence. Ed. by Stephen K. Donovan. (Illus.). 266p. 1991. pap. text 32.50 (*0-231-07091-8*) Col U Pr.

Mass Extinctions & Their Aftermath. Anthony Hallam & Paul Wignall. LC 97-22349. (Illus.). 328p. 1997. pap. text 40.00 (*0-19-854916-4*) OUP.

Mass Extinctions & Their Aftermath. Anthony Hallam & Paul Wignall. LC 97-22349. (Illus.). 328p. (C). 1997. 85.00 (*0-19-854917-2*) OUP.

Mass Facing the People. Michael Davies. (Illus.). 43p. 1991. pap. 6.00 (*0-911845-25-9*) Neumann Pr.

***Mass Fatality & Casualty Incidents: A Field Guide.** Robert A. Jensen. LC 99-38116. 272p. 1999. otabind 39.95 (*0-8493-1295-7*) CRC Pr.

Mass Flights of Italo Balbo: The Flights of 1928, 1929, 1930 & 1933 - A History & Catalog of Their Postal Artifacts. Robert E. Lana. LC 95-83532. (Illus.). 144p. (Orig.). 1996. pap. 10.00 (*0-939429-15-2*) Am Air Mail.

Mass for Arras: A Novel. Andrzej Szczypiorski. Tr. by Richard Luorie from POL. LC 92-40176. 192p. 1994. pap. 12.00 (*0-8021-3402-5*, Grove) Grove-Atltic.

Mass for Children. Lawrence G. Lovasik. (Saint Joseph Picture Bks.). (Illus.). 1990. pap. text 1.25 (*0-89942-489-9*, 489-00) Catholic Bk Pub.

Mass for Children. Jude Winkler. (Illus.). (J). (ps-3). 1988. 3.50 (*0-89942-215-2*, 215/22) Catholic Bk Pub.

Mass for Hard Times. R. S. Thomas. 96p. 1993. 30.00 (*1-85224-228-0*, Pub. by Bloodaxe Bks); pap. 15.95 (*1-85224-229-9*, Pub. by Bloodaxe Bks) Dufour.

Mass for Jesse James. Fintan O'Toole. 1996. pap. 12.95 (*1-85186-078-9*) Dufour.

Mass for the Grace of a Happy Death. Frank X. Gaspar. Ed. by Rex West. (Anhinga Prize for Poetry Ser.). 72p. (Orig.). (C). 1995. pap. 10.00 (*0-938078-38-0*) Anhinga Pr.

Mass Graves & Other Atrocities in Bosnia: Hearing Before the Commission on Security & Cooperation in Europe, 104th Congress, 1st Session, December 6, 1995. USGPO Staff. LC 96-202479. iii, 116p. 1996. pap. write for info. (*0-16-052829-1*) USGPO.

Mass Hate: The Global Rise of Genocide & Terror. Neil J. Kressel. LC 96-148886. (Illus.). 350p. (C). 1996. 25.95 (*0-306-45271-5*, Plenum Trade) Perseus Pubng.

Mass Health Examinations. (Public Health Papers: No. 45). 1971. pap. text 6.00 (*92-4-130045-0*, 1110045) World Health.

Mass Hysteria: A Social History of the Strange. Robert E. Bartholomew. 250p. 1995. text 37.50 (*0-89341-751-3*) Hollowbrook.

Mass Immigration & the National Interest. Vernon Briggs, Jr. LC 92-16927. (Labor & Human Resources Ser.). 287p. (gr. 13). 1992. pap. text 34.95 (*1-56324-171-4*) M E Sharpe.

Mass Immigration & the National Interest. Vernon M. Briggs, Jr. LC 92-16927. (Labor & Human Resources Ser.). 287p. (C). (gr. 13). 1992. text 74.95 (*1-56324-170-6*) M E Sharpe.

Mass Immigration & the National Interest. 2nd ed. Vernon M. Briggs, Jr. LC 96-2929. (Labor & Human Resources Ser.). 296p. (gr. 13). 1996. pap. text 36.95 (*1-56324-830-1*) M E Sharpe.

Mass Immigration & the National Interest. 2nd ed. Vernon M. Briggs, Jr. LC 96-2929. (Labor & Human Resources Ser.). 296p. (YA). (gr. 13). 1996. text 77.95 (*1-56324-829-8*) M E Sharpe.

Mass in B Minor in Full Score. Johann Sebastian Bach. 320p. pap. 13.95 (*0-486-25992-7*) Dover.

Mass in C & Christ on the Mount of Olives in Full Score. Ludwig van Beethoven. 272p. pap. 16.95 (*0-486-29346-7*) Dover.

***Mass in D Minor.** Padre J. de Castro Lobo. (Music Archive Publications Ser.: Series E, Vol. 3). 147p. 1999. text 34.00 (*90-5755-027-X*, Harwood Acad Pubs) Gordon & Breach.

Mass in F: Deutsche Messe. Franz Schubert. (ENG & GER.). 24p. 1986. pap. 4.25 (*0-7935-4860-8*, 50324820) H Leonard.

Mass in G: Vocal Score. Franz Schubert. (LAT.). 64p. 1986. pap. 6.95 (*0-7935-5482-9*, 50324620) H Leonard.

Mass in Sweden: Its Development from the Latin Rite from 1531 to 1917. Ed. by Eric E. Yelverton. LC 83-45637. reprint ed. 34.50 (*0-404-19879-1*) AMS Pr.

Mass in Time of Doubt. Ralph Keifer. 1983. 9.95 (*0-912405-00-7*, Pastoral Press) OR Catholic.

Mass Internment of Japanese Americans & the Quest for Legal Redress. Charles J. McClain. LC 94-22630. (Asian Americans & the Law Ser.: No. 3). (Illus.). 485p. 1994. text 88.00 (*0-8153-1866-9*) Garland.

Mass Interviewing & the Marshalling of Ideas to Improve Performance: The Crawford Slip Method. Gilbert B. Siegel & Ross Clayton. 140p. (Orig.). (C). 1996. pap. text 24.00 (*0-7618-0166-9*); lib. bdg. 38.50 (*0-7618-0165-0*) U Pr of Amer.

Mass Is a Sacrifice. H. E. Calnan. (Compact Study Ser.). 20p. (Orig.). 1993. pap. 1.95 (*0-935952-91-8*) Angelus Pr.

Mass Land, Set. Bobrowski. 928p. 1994. 145.00 (*0-316-10185-0*) Little.

Mass Listeria. Theodore Dalrymple. 1998. 17.95 (*0-233-99137-9*, Pub. by Andre Deutsch) Trafalgar.

Mass Loss & Evolution of O-Type Stars. Ed. by Peter S. Conti & Camiel W. De Loore. (International Astronomical Union Symposia Ser.: No. 83). 1979. pap. text 82.50 (*90-277-0989-0*); lib. bdg. 158.50 (*90-277-0988-2*) Kluwer Academic.

Mass Loss from Red Giants. Ed. by Mark Morris & Ben Zuckerson. 1985. text 167.00 (*90-277-2075-4*) Kluwer Academic.

Mass Loss from the Stars: Proceedings of the Triest Colloquium on Astrophysics, 2nd, September 12-17, 1969. Trieste Colloquium on Astrophysics Staff. Ed. by M. Hack. (Astrophysics & Space Science Library: No.13). 345p. 1969. text 185.00 (*90-277-0118-0*) Kluwer Academic.

Mass Market Woman: Defining Yourself As a Person in a World That Defines You By. Linda McBryde. LC 98-96650. 224p. 1999. 19.95 (*1-893070-06-9*) Crowded Hour.

Mass, Measurement & Motion No. 2: A New Look at Maxwell's Equations & the Permittivity of Free Space. B. A. Soldano. Ed. by William H. Brantley. (Illus.). 50p. (Orig.). 1982. pap. 7.00 (*0-943410-00-2*) Grenridge Pub.

Mass Media. Ed. by John Coleman & Miklos Tomka. (Concilium Ser.). 1993. 15.00 (*0-88344-874-2*) Orbis Bks.

Mass-Media. Pierre Sorlin. LC 93-33671. (Key Ideas Ser.). 128p. (C). 1994. pap. 17.99 (*0-415-07209-3*, B3720) Routledge.

Mass Media. Byron L. Stay. LC 98-47722. (Opposing Viewpoints Ser.). 312p. 1999. lib. bdg. 27.45 (*0-7377-0055-6*) Greenhaven.

***Mass Media.** Byron L. Stay. LC 98-47722. (Opposing Viewpoints Ser.). (Illus.). 312p. (YA). (gr. 10-12). 1999. pap. 17.45 (*0-7377-0054-8*) Greenhaven.

Mass Media. 2nd ed. Gorham. 1995. 12.74 (*1-56134-340-4*) McGraw.

Mass Media: Aspen Guide to Communication Industry Trends. Christopher H. Sterling & Timothy R. Haight. LC 76-24370. (Special Studies). 457p. 1978. 79.50 (*0-275-90316-8*, C0316, Praeger Pubs) Greenwood.

Mass Media: Introduction to Modern Communication. 6th ed. (C). 1991. text. write for info. (*0-8013-0818-6*) Addison-Wesley Educ.

Mass Media: Past, Present, & Future. Dana R. Ulloth et al. (Illus.). 429p. (C). 1983. pap. text, teacher ed. write for info. (*0-314-71133-3*) West Pub.

Mass Media 1999-2000 Edition. 6th ed. Gorham. 1999. pap., student ed. 16.56 (*0-07-041133-6*) McGraw.

Mass Media - Mass Culture. 4th ed. Stan L. Wilson & James R. Jamesn. LC 97-25991. 480p. 1997. pap. 49.06 (*0-07-070828-2*) McGraw.

Mass Media - Mass Culture: An Introduction. 3rd ed. Stan L. Wilson. LC 94-24861. (C). 1994. pap. text 42.74 (*0-07-070826-6*) McGraw.

Mass Media & Adult Education. Ed. by John A. Niemi. LC 73-168491. 128p. 1971. pap. 24.95 (*0-87778-025-0*) Educ Tech Pubns.

Mass Media & American Foreign Policy: Insider Perspectives on Global Journalism & the Foreign Policy Process. Patrick O'Heffernan. 288p. 1991. pap. 39.50 (*0-89391-729-X*); text 73.25 (*0-89391-728-1*) Ablx Pub.

Mass Media & American Politics. 5th ed. Doris A. Graber. LC 96-32482. 428p. (YA). (gr. 11). 1996. pap. text 28.95 (*0-87187-768-6*) Congr Quarterly.

Mass Media & Education. Padma C. Mohanty. (C). 1992. 22.00 (*81-7024-439-0*, Pub. by Ashish Pub Hse) S Asia.

Mass Media & Environmental Conflict: America's Green Crusades. Mark Neuzil & William Kovarik. LC 96-10051. 372p. 1996. 45.95 (*0-7619-0332-1*); pap. 21.95 (*0-7619-0333-X*) Sage.

Mass Media & Environmental Issues. Ed. by Anders Hansen. LC 93-3392. (Studies in Communication & Society). 256p. 1993. text 59.00 (*0-7185-1444-0*) St Martin.

Mass Media & Farm Women. Ekha Bhagat. (C). 1989. 12.75 (*81-7076-019-4*, Pub. by Intellectual) S Asia.

Mass Media & Free Trade: NAFTA & the Cultural Industries. Ed. by Emile G. McAnany & Kenton T. Wilkinson. LC 96-10222. 1996. 45.00 (*0-292-75198-2*); pap. 24.95 (*0-292-75199-0*) U of Tex Pr.

M

Mass Media & Mass Communication. Ed. by Peter Davison et al. LC 77-90610. (Literary Taste, Culture & Mass Communication Ser.: Vol. 2). 348p. 1978. write for info. (0-85964-037-X) Chadwyck-Healey.

Mass Media & Media Policy in Western Europe. Peter Humphreys. LC 95-36975. (European Policy Research Unit Studies). 256p. 1996. text 79.95 (0-7190-3196-6); text 27.95 (0-7190-3197-4, Pub. by Manchester Univ Pr) St Martin.

Mass Media & Political Modernity. B. N. Mukharjee. 168p. 1971. 15.95 (0-318-37278-9) Asia Bk Corp.

Mass Media & Political Thought: An Information-Processing Approach. Ed. by Sidney Kraus & Richard M. Perloff. LC 85-14190. (Illus.). 350p. reprint ed. pap. 108.50 (0-7837-4577-X, 204410600003) Bks Demand.

Mass Media & Political Transition: The Hong Kong Press in China's Orbit. Joseph Man Chan & Chin-Chuan Lee. LC 91-8931. (Communication Ser.). 239p. 1991. lib. bdg. 38.95 (0-89862-313-8) Guilford Pubns.

Mass Media & Politics. Robert E. Denton & Gary C. Woodward. 432p. (C). 1997. 22.00 (0-02-328721-7, Macmillan Coll) P-H.

Mass Media & Politics. Ed. by James F. Fixx. LC 76-183137. (Great Contemporary Issues Ser.). (Illus.). 600p. 1971. 25.00 (0-685-00512-7) Ayer.

Mass Media & Politics. Ed. by James F. Fixx. 1972. pap. 27.95 (0-405-01291-8) Ayer.

Mass Media & Politics in Nigeria. L. U. Uche. (C). 1989. 26.00 (81-7022-232-X, Pub. by Concept) S Asia.

Mass Media & Power in Modern Britain. John Eldridge. (Illus.). 210p. 1997. pap. text 20.00 (0-19-878171-7) OUP.

Mass Media & Power in Modern Britain. John Eldridge et al. LC 96-32233. (Oxford Modern Britain). (Illus.). 210p. 1997. text 55.00 (0-19-878172-5) OUP.

Mass Media & Social Problems. Dennis Howitt. (International Series in Experimental Social Psychology: Vol. 2). 180p. 1982. text 101.00 (0-08-026759-9, J125, CRC Reprint) Franklin.

Mass Media & Society. Ed. by James Curran & Michael Gurevitch. LC 91-23441. 352p. 1995. pap. text 18.95 (0-340-51759-X, A6112, Pub. by E A) St Martin.

Mass Media & Society. Alan Wells & Ernest A. Hakanen. LC 96-32262. (Communication, Culture & Information Studies). 1997. pap. 49.50 (1-56750-289-X); text 82.50 (1-56750-288-1) Ablx Pub.

Mass Media & Society. 2nd ed. Ed. by James Curran & Michael Gurevitch. 384p. 1996. pap. text 19.95 (0-340-61418-8, Pub. by E A) OUP.

***Mass Media & Society.** 3rd ed. Ed. by James Curran & Michael Gurevitch. (An Arnold Publication). (Illus.). 432p. 2000. pap. 24.95 (0-340-73201-6, Pub. by E A) OUP.

Mass Media & the Caribbean, Vol. 6. Ed. by Stuart H. Surlin. (Caribbean Studies). 480p. 1991. text 110.00 (2-88124-447-5); pap. text 49.00 (2-88124-448-3) Gordon & Breach.

Mass Media & the Moral Imagination. Ed. by Philip J. Rossi & Paul A. Soukup. LC 93-30845. 300p. (Orig.). 1994. pap. 24.95 (1-55612-622-0) Sheed & Ward WI.

Mass Media & the School Newspaper. 2nd ed. DeWitt C. Reddick. (Mass Communication). 1986. mass mkt. 24.75 (0-534-03597-3) West Pub.

Mass Media & Tiananmen Square. Zhou He. (Illus.). 287p. (C). 1996. lib. bdg. 95.00 (1-56072-355-6) Nova Sci Pubs.

Mass Media & Village Life: An Indian Study. Paul Hartman et al. (Communication & Human Values Ser.). 276p. (C). 1989. text 52.00 (0-8039-9581-4); pap. text 24.95 (0-8039-9582-2) Sage.

Mass Media Between the Wars: Perceptions of Cultural Tension, 1918-1941. Ed. by Catherine L. Covert & John D. Stevens. LC 83-20329. 240p. 1984. text 39.95 (0-8156-2307-0) Syracuse U Pr.

Mass Media Bibliography: An Annotated Guide to Books & Journals for Research & Reference. Eleanor Blum & Frances M. Wilhoit. 352p. 1990. text 49.95 (0-252-01706-4) U of Ill Pr.

Mass Media Declaration of UNESCO. Kaarle Nordenstreng. LC 83-25818. (Communication & Information Science Ser.). 496p. (C). 1984. text 82.50 (0-89391-077-5) Ablx Pub.

Mass Media Education in Transition: Preparing for the 21st Century. Thomas Dickson. LC 99-23014. (Communication Ser.). 296p. 1999. 59.95 (0-8058-3097-9) L Erlbaum Assocs.

Mass Media Effects. 2nd ed. Leo W. Jeffres. LC 98-115510. ix, 494 p. (C). 1997. pap. text 25.95 (0-88133-962-8) Waveland Pr.

Mass Media Effects Across Cultures. Ed. by Felipe Korzenny et al. (International & Intercultural Communication Ser.: Vol. 16). (Illus.). 248p. (C). 1992. 59.95 (0-8039-4623-6); pap. 26.00 (0-8039-4624-4) Sage.

Mass Media for the Nineties: The South African Handbook of Mass Communication. A. S. De Beer. LC 93-215629. 426 p. 1993. write for info. (0-627-01837-8) J L Van Schaik.

Mass Media Images & Impact on Health: A Sourcebook. Nancy Signorielli. LC 92-35546. 240p. 1993. lib. bdg. 65.00 (0-313-27800-8, SYY, Greenwood Pr) Greenwood.

Mass Media in Adult Education. John Ohliger. LC 73-80717. (Occasional Papers: No. 18). 1968. pap. text 2.00 (0-685-76689-6, OCP 18) Syracuse U Cont Ed.

Mass Media in America. 6th ed. Donald R. Pember. LC 91-11193. (Illus.). 608p. (C). 1991. pap. text 67.00 (0-02-393780-7, Macmillan Coll) P-H.

Mass Media in Canada. rev. ed. Mary Vipond. 206p. 1992. pap. 21.95 (1-55028-388-X, Pub. by J Lorimer) Formac Dist Ltd.

Mass Media in China: The History & the Future. Won H. Chang. LC 88-34694. (Illus.). 320p. 1989. reprint ed. pap. 99.20 (0-608-00149-X, 206093000006) Bks Demand.

Mass Media in Greece: Power, Politics & Privatization. Thimios Zaharopoulos & Manny E. Paraschos. LC 92-18839. 240p. 1992. 59.95 (0-275-94106-X, C4106, Praeger Pubs) Greenwood.

Mass Media in India, 1981 to 83. Research & Reference Division Staff. 269p. 1984. 21.95 (0-318-37285-1) Asia Bk Corp.

Mass Media in Liberal Democratic Societies. Ed. by Stanley Rothman. LC 91-4048. 312p. 1992. 24.95 (0-943852-92-7); pap. text 14.95 (0-943852-93-5) Prof World Peace.

Mass Media in Modern Society. Ed. by Norman Jacobs. 212p. (C). 1992. pap. 24.95 (1-56000-612-9) Transaction Pubs.

Mass Media in Revolution & National Development: The Romanian Laboratory. Peter Gross. LC 96-22614. 224p. (C). 1996. text 42.95 (0-8138-2670-5) Iowa St U Pr.

Mass Media in Sub-Saharan Africa. Louise M. Bourgault. LC 94-27829. 320p. 1995. 35.00 (0-253-31250-7); pap. 14.95 (0-253-20938-2) Ind U Pr.

Mass Media in the Asian Pacific. Bryce T. McIntyre. LC 97-20525. (Monographs on Asian Pacific Communication Ser.). 101p. 1997. 49.00 (1-85359-397-4, Pub. by Multilingual Matters) Taylor & Francis.

Mass Media in the Middle East: A Comprehensive Handbook. Yahya R. Kamalipour. LC 93-50536. 352p. 1994. lib. bdg. 75.00 (0-313-28535-7) Greenwood.

***Mass Media in the New Millenium.** 2nd ed. 386p. (C). 2000. per. 48.75 (0-7872-7130-6) Kendall-Hunt.

Mass Media, International Relations & Non-Alignment. Regina Mulay. 536p. 1987. 48.50 (0-8364-2030-6, Pub. by Deep & Deep Pubns) S Asia.

Mass Media Issues. 5th ed. Denis Mercier. 512p. (C). 1995. pap. text, per. 35.95 (0-7872-0507-9) Kendall-Hunt.

Mass Media Issues. 6th ed. Denis Mercier. 500p. 1997. 36.95 (0-7872-4436-8) Kendall-Hunt.

Mass Media Law. 7th ed. Donald R. Pember. 656p. (C). 1995. text. write for info. (0-697-24600-0) Brown & Benchmark.

Mass Media Law. 7th ed. Donald R. Pember. 656p. (C). 1995. text, student ed. 16.87 (0-697-24603-5) Brown & Benchmark.

Mass Media Law. 8th ed. Donald R. Pember. 656p. (C). 1996. text. write for info. (0-697-28904-4) Brown & Benchmark.

Mass Media Law. 8th ed. Donald R. Pember & Jeremy Cohen. 128p. (C). 1996. text, student ed. 15.00 (0-697-28906-0) Brown & Benchmark.

Mass Media Law. 9th ed. Pember. 1997. 16.00 (0-697-35370-2) McGraw.

Mass Media Law. 9th ed. Donald R. Pember. 672p. (C). 1997. per. write for info. (0-697-32716-7, WCB McGr Hill) McGrw-H Hghr Educ.

Mass Media Law. 10th ed. Don R. Pember. 664p. 1998. pap. 52.19 (0-697-35371-0); pap., student ed. 17.19 (0-697-35372-9) McGraw.

Mass Media Law. 11th ed. Pember. 664p. 1999. pap. 58.75 (0-07-230009-4) McGraw.

Mass Media Law: Cases & Materials. 4th ed. Marc A. Franklin & David A. Anderson. (University Casebook Ser.). 951p. 1990. pap. text 42.95 (0-88277-778-5) Foundation Pr.

Mass Media Law: Cases & Materials, 1994 Supplement. 4th ed. Marc A. Franklin & David A. Anderson. (University Casebook Ser.). 223p. 1994. 10.95 (1-56662-220-4) Foundation Pr.

Mass Media Law & Ethics. (C). 1986. 20.00 (0-8087-5905-1) Pearson Custom.

Mass Media Law & Regulation. 6th rev. ed. William Francois. 651p. (C). 1994. text 45.95 (0-88133-746-3) Waveland Pr.

***Mass Media Law 2000.** 124p. (C). 1999. pap., student ed. 20.00 (0-07-230010-8) McGrw-H Hghr Educ.

Mass Media, Mass Culture. 3rd ed. Wilson. 1994. teacher ed. 10.31 (0-07-070827-4) McGraw.

Mass Media Mass Culture. 5th ed. Wilson. 2000. 36.50 (0-07-231462-1) McGraw.

Mass Media, Modernity, & Development: Arab States of the Gulf. Fayad E. Kazan. LC 92-36550. 320p. 1993. 62.95 (0-275-94533-2, C4533, Praeger Pubs) Greenwood.

Mass Media, 1996-1997. annuals 3rd ed. Joan Gorham. 256p. (C). 1996. text. write for info. (0-697-31611-4) Brown & Benchmark.

Mass Media, 98-99. 5th ed. Joan Gorham. (Annual Ser.). (Illus.). 240p. 1998. pap. text 12.25 (0-697-39178-7, Dshkn McG-Hill) McGrw-H Hghr Educ.

Mass Media Processes. 2nd ed. Leo W. Jeffres. (Illus.). 519p. (C). 1994. pap. text 26.95 (0-88133-760-9) Waveland Pr.

Mass Media Religion: The Social Sources of the Electronic Church. Stewart M. Hoover. (Communication & Human Values Ser.: Vol. 1). 240p. (C). 1988. text 52.00 (0-8039-2994-3); pap. text 24.95 (0-8039-2995-1) Sage.

Mass Media Religion: The Social Sources of the Electronic Church. Stewart M. Hoover. LC 87-36859. (Communication & Human Values Ser.). 251p. 1988. reprint ed. pap. 77.90 (0-608-03566-1, 205965100009) Bks Demand.

Mass Media Research: An Introduction. Roger D. Wimmer & Joseph R. Dominick. 416p. (C). 1983. mass mkt. 27.50 (0-534-01228-0) Wadsworth Pub.

Mass Media Research: An Introduction. 2nd ed. Roger D. Wimmer & Joseph R. Dominick. 514p. (C). 1986. pap. 34.00 (0-534-06702-6) Wadsworth Pub.

Mass Media Research: An Introduction. 3rd ed. Wimmer & Dominick. (Mass Communication Ser.). 1990. pap. text, teacher ed. write for info. (0-534-13963-9) Wadsworth Pub.

Mass Media Research: An Introduction. 3rd ed. Roger D. Wimmer & Joseph R. Dominick. 478p. (C). 1990. pap. 40.00 (0-534-13962-0) Wadsworth Pub.

Mass Media Research: An Introduction. 4th ed. Roger D. Wimmer & Joseph R. Dominick. 497p. (C). 1993. mass mkt. 47.50 (0-534-17472-8) Wadsworth Pub.

Mass Media Research: An Introduction. 5th ed. Roger D. Wimmer & Joseph R. Dominick. LC 96-197165. (Mass Communication & Journalism Ser.). (C). 1996. pap. 56.50 (0-534-24474-2) Wadsworth Pub.

Mass Media Research: An Introduction. 6th ed. Wimmer. LC 99-29037. (Mass Communication). 1999. pap. 88.95 (0-534-56007-5) Wadsworth Pub.

***Mass Media, Social Control & Social Change: A Macrosocial Perspective.** David P. Demers & K. Viswanath. LC 98-26143. 468p. 1999. text 59.95 (0-8138-2682-9) Iowa St U Pr.

Mass Media, Towards the Millennium: The South African Handbook of Mass Communication. 2nd ed. A. S. De Beer. LC 98-143264. vii, 530 p. 1998. write for info. (0-627-02324-X) J L Van Schaik.

Mass Media vs. the Italian Americans. Adolph Caso. 1984. pap. 11.95 (0-8283-1831-X) Branden Bks.

Mass Media Writing. Baker & Gail Baker Woods. 350p. (C). 1996. pap. text 53.00 (0-13-776444-8) P-H.

Mass Media Writing: An Introduction. Gail Baker-Woods et al. (C). 1996. pap. text, teacher ed. write for info. (0-13-776451-0, 77645-0) Allyn.

Mass Media 1996/97. 3rd annot. ed. Gorham. 1996. teacher ed. (0-697-31612-2, WCB McGr Hill) McGrw-H Hghr Educ.

***Mass Mediations.** Walter Armbrust. LC 99-43224. 325p. 2000. 55.00 (0-520-21925-2, Pub. by U CA Pr) Cal Prin Full Svc.

***Mass Mediations: New Approaches to Popular Culture in the Middle East & Beyond.** Walter Armbrust. LC 99-43224. 325p. 2000. pap. 24.95 (0-520-21926-0, Pub. by U CA Pr) Cal Prin Full Svc.

Mass Mediauras: Essays on Form, Technics & Media. Samuel Weber. Ed. by Alan Cholodenko. LC 95-70817. 245p. 1996. 39.50 (0-8047-2675-2); pap. 14.95 (0-8047-2676-0) Stanford U Pr.

Mass Medica 96/97. 3rd ed. Gorham. 1996. (0-697-31613-0, WCB McGr Hill) McGrw-H Hghr Educ.

Mass Merchandised Healthy Foods. BCC Staff. 241p. 1991. 2350.00 (0-89336-733-8, GA 047N) BCC.

Mass Merchant Distribution Channel: Challenges & Opportunities. Compiled by Andersen Consulting Logistics Strategy Group Staff. (Illus.). 31p. 1994. pap. 25.00 (1-892663-07-4) WERC.

Mass Migrations in Europe: The Legacy & the Future. Ed. by Russell King. LC 92-36700. 334p. 1993. 59.95 (1-85293-224-4, Belhaven) Halsted Pr.

Mass Migrations in Europe: The Legacy & the Future. Ed. by Russell King. 350p. 1995. pap. 65.00 (0-471-96113-2, GE11) Wiley.

Mass Militia System & Chinese Modernization. Chen-Ya Tien. 180p. 1994. pap. 14.95 (0-88962-162-4) Mosaic.

***Mass Moca: From Mill to Museum.** Nicholas Whitman. (Illus.). 300p. 2000. 35.00 (0-9700738-0-1) Mass Moca.

Mass, Model Atmospheres & Spectrum Synthesis, Vol. 108. Ed. by Saul J. Adelman et al. (ASP Conference Series Proceedings). 336p. 1996. 34.00 (1-886733-28-7) Astron Soc Pacific.

Mass Murder: America's Growing Menace. J. Levin & J. A. Fox. LC 84-26585. (Illus.). 270p. (C). 1985. 19.95 (0-306-41943-2, Plenum Trade) Perseus Pubng.

Mass Murder Is Liberty. Alan Ernest. LC 98-5604. (Illus.). 288p. (C). 1998. pap. 16.95 (0-9640104-3-7) Bridger Hse.

Mass Murderers. Time-Life Books Editors. Ed. by Laura Foreman. LC 92-37015. (True Crime Ser.). (Illus.). 92p. 1993. lib. bdg. 12.99 (0-7835-0005-X) Time-Life.

Mass Murderers. B. D. Wallace & M. J. Philippus. 53p. (YA). (gr. 7-12). 1992. pap. 6.95 (1-57515-018-2) PPI Pubng.

Mass of Glory. Seoirse Bodley. 1989. pap. 30.00 (0-86217-050-8, Pub. by Veritas Pubns); pap. 30.00 (0-86217-049-4, Pub. by Veritas Pubns) St Mut.

Mass of Joy: In Honour of St. John of God. Seoirse Bodley. 1989. pap. 30.00 (0-905092-78-3, Pub. by Veritas Pubns) St Mut.

***Mass of Saint Cyprian, 1.** Kenneth W. Louis. 1999. 15.95 (5-550-73196-7); pap. 10.95 (5-550-73197-5) Nairi.

Mass of St. James: Solemn Mass for the Feast of the Passion of St. James of Compostela. Paul Helmer. (Wissenschaftliche Abhandlungen-Musicological Studies: Vol. 49). (ENG.). 252p. 1988. 80.00 (0-931902-58-4) Inst Mediaeval Mus.

Mass of St. Martin de Porres (Choral Book) Composed by Leon Roberts. 79p. 1997. pap. 8.95 (0-915531-56-9) OR Catholic.

Mass of the Pilgrim Church Choral Book. Composed by John Foley. 1997. 9.95 (0-915531-67-4) OR Catholic.

Mass of the Pilgrim Church (Instrument Book) Composed by John Foley. 1997. pap. 3.95 (0-915531-82-8) OR Catholic.

Mass Ornament: Weimar Essays. Siegfried Kracauer. Ed. & Tr. by Thomas Y. Levin. (Illus.). 320p. 1995. text 54.00 (0-674-55162-1, KRAMAS); pap. text 26.50 (0-674-55163-X, KRAMAX) HUP.

Mass Outflows from Stars & Galactic Nuclei. Luciana Bianchi & Roberto Gilmozzi. (C). 1988. text 237.50 (90-277-2698-1) Kluwer Academic.

Mass-Participatory Economy: A Democratic Alternative for Korea. Kim D. Jung. 94p. (Orig.). 1985. pap. text 15.00 (0-8191-4921-7); lib. bdg. 36.00 (0-8191-4920-9) U Pr of Amer.

Mass Participatory Economy: Korea's Road to World Economic Power. Kim D. Jung. LC 95-15377. 280p. 1996. pap. 29.95 (0-8191-9960-5) U Pr of Amer.

Mass Participatory Economy: Korea's Road to World Economic Power. Kim D. Jung. LC 95-15377. 280p. 1996. 46.95 (0-8191-9959-1) U Pr of Amer.

Mass Persuasion: The Social Psychology of a War Bond Drive. Robert K. Merton. LC 77-136076. 210p. 1971. reprint ed. lib. bdg. 49.75 (0-8371-5226-7, MEMP, Greenwood Pr) Greenwood.

***Mass. Pharm. Laws & Regulations for Law 351.** Doug Pisano. (C). 1999. pap. text 22.54 (1-56870-368-6) RonJon Pub.

Mass Politics. Shea. 1999. text 35.00 (0-312-21949-0) St Martin.

***Mass Politics & Culture in Democratizing Korea.** Doh C. Shin. LC 98-49357. (Asia-Pacific Studies). (Illus.). 352p. (C). 1999. text 59.95 (0-521-65146-8); pap. text 22.95 (0-521-65823-3) Cambridge U Pr.

Mass Prayers for Children. Fitzpatrick, (J). 1980. pap. 2.50 (0-88271-150-4) Regina Pr.

Mass Production Justice & the Constitutional Ideal. Ed. by Charles H. Whitebread. LC 77-119994. (Virginia Legal Studies). 262p. reprint ed. pap. 81.30 (0-608-18116-1, 203276700081) Bks Demand.

Mass-Production Management, the Design & Operation of Production Flow-Line Systems. Ray Wild. LC 72-611. (Illus.). 247p. reprint ed. pap. 76.60 (0-608-17996-5, 202789300057) Bks Demand.

Mass Production, the Stock Market Crash & the Great Depression: The Macroeconomics of Electrification, 175. Bernard C. Beaudreau. LC 95-48363. (Contributions in Economics & Economic History: Vol. 175). 208p. 1996. 62.95 (0-313-29920-X, Greenwood Pr) Greenwood.

Mass Psychogenic Illness: A Social Psychological Analysis. Ed. by Michael J. Colligan et al. 288p. 1982. 49.95 (0-89859-160-0) L Erlbaum Assocs.

Mass Psychology of Ethnonationalism. Dusan Kecmanovic. LC 96-41872. (PATH in Psychology Ser.). (Illus.). 256p. (C). 1996. 47.00 (0-306-45442-4, Plenum Trade) Perseus Pubng.

Mass Psychology of Fascism. 3rd ed. Wilhelm Reich. Tr. by Vincent R. Carfagno from GER. 126p. 1980. pap. 18.00 (0-374-50884-4) FS&G.

Mass Rape: The War Against Women in Bosnia-Herzegovina. Ed. by Alexandra Stiglmayer. Tr. by Marion Faber. LC 93-45997. (Illus.). xxiii, 234p. 1994. pap. 14.95 (0-8032-9229-5, Bison Books); text 45.00 (0-8032-4239-5) U of Nebr Pr.

Mass-Reared Natural Enemies, Application, Regulation & Needs. Ed. by Richard L. Ridgway et al. (Proceedings, Thomas Say Publications in Entomology Ser.). 341p. 1998. pap. 35.00 (0-938522-66-3) Entomol Soc.

Mass Response & Individual Choice: The Sociology of Behavioral Trends. Gosta Carlsson. 154p. (Orig.). 1987. pap. 52.00 (91-22-01172-2) Coronet Bks.

Mass Scale Housing for Hot Climate. B. B. Puri. (C). 1993. 18.00 (81-204-0797-0, Pub. by Oxford IBH) S Asia.

Mass Society & Extremist Politics. Joseph R. Gusfield. (Reprint Series in Social Sciences). (C). 1993. reprint ed. pap. text 5.00 (0-8290-2752-1, S-588) Irvington.

Mass Society & Political Conflict: Toward a Reconstruction of Theory. Sandor Halebsky. LC 75-18118. 320p. reprint ed. pap. 91.20 (0-608-13574-7, 2022455) Bks Demand.

Mass Society & the Extension of Welfare, 1960-1970. Kirsten A. Gronbjerg. LC 76-8101. (Illus.). 1995. lib. bdg. 24.00 (0-226-30964-9) U Ch Pr.

***Mass Society, Pluralism, & Bureaucracy: Explication, Assessment & Commentary.** Richard Hamilton. LC 00-32374. 240p. 2000. 64.00 (0-275-96986-X, Praeger Pubs) Greenwood.

***Mass Spec Desk Reference.** O. David Sparkman. (Illus.). 136p. 2000. pap. text 29.95 (0-9660813-2-3) Global View Pub.

Mass Spectra & GC Data of Steroids: Androgens & Estrogens. Hugh L. J. Makin & David James Hamilton Trafford. (Lopkowski/Ross). 806p. 1999. 690.00 (3-527-29644-1) Wiley.

Mass Spectra of Prostaglandins & Related Products. Cecil Pace-Asciak. LC 83-645438. (Advances in Prostaglandin, Thromboxane, & Leukotriene Research Ser.: Vol. 18). 586p. 1989. reprint ed. pap. 181.70 (0-608-04669-8, 206539000004) Bks Demand.

***Mass Spectral & Gc Data, 4 vols., Set.** 2nd ed. K. Pfleger et al. 4700p. 2000. 1350.00 (3-527-29793-6) Wiley.

Mass Spectral & GC Data, Pt. 4. 2nd ed. K. Pfleger et al. 700p. 2000. 325.00 (3-527-28880-5) Wiley.

Mass Spectral & GC Data of Drugs, Poisons, Pesticides, Pollutants & Their Metabolites, Pts. I, II & III. 2nd enl. rev. ed. Karl Pfleger et al. LC 92-49331. 3000p. 1992. lib. bdg. 825.00 (0-89573-855-4, Wiley-VCH) Wiley.

Mass Spectral & GC Data of Drugs, Poisons, Pesticides, Pollutants & Their Metabolites, Vol. 1. 2nd rev. ed. K. Pfleger et al. 3409p. 1992. 1155.00 (3-527-26989-4) Wiley.

Mass Spectral Correlations. 2nd ed. Fred W. McLafferty. LC 81-205644. (Advances in Chemistry Ser.: No. 40). 124p. 1982. text 35.00 (0-8412-0702-X, Pub. by Am Chemical) OUP.

Mass Spectrometer. J. R. Majer. (Wykeham Science Ser.: No. 44). 160p. 1977. pap. 18.00 (0-85109-550-X) Taylor & Francis.

Mass Spectrometer. J. R. Majer & M. Berry. LC 77-15307. (Wykeham Science Ser.: No. 44). 159p. (C). 1977. 18.00 (0-8448-1171-8, Crane Russak) Taylor & Francis.

Mass Spectrometer Testing HM. American Society for Nondestructive Testing (ASNT). (Illus.). 51p. (Orig.). (C). 1996. pap. 31.25 (0-931403-40-5, 2033M) Am Soc Nondestructive.

An Asterisk (*) at the beginning of an entry indicates that the title is appearing for the first time.

Mass Spectrometric Characterization of Shale Oils. American Society for Testing & Materials Staff. LC 86-1203. (ASTM Special Technical Publication: No. 902). (Illus.). 155p. reprint ed. pap. 48.10 (0-7837-5977-0, 204578100007) Bks Demand.
Mass Spectrometric Characterization of Shale Oils STP 902. Ed. by Thomas Aczel. LC 86-1203. (Special Technical Publication Ser.). (Illus.). 149p. 1986. text 29.00 (0-8031-0467-7, STP902) ASTM.
Mass Spectrometry. Ed. by John N. Abelson et al. (Methods in Enzymology Ser.: Vol. 193). 890p. 1990. text 146.00 (0-12-182094-7) Acad Pr.
Mass Spectrometry. Edmond De Hoffmann et al. LC 96-6746. 352p. 1996. pap. 74.95 (0-471-96697-5) Wiley.
Mass Spectrometry. Charles Wilkins. (C). 2001. pap. 14.95 (0-13-149220-9) P-H.
Mass Spectrometry. Ed. by Charles Merritt, Jr. & Charles N. McEwen. LC 78-24085. (Practical Spectroscopy Ser.: No. 3). (Illus.). 415p. reprint ed. pap. 128.70 (0-7837-0670-7, 204100500002) Bks Demand.
Mass Spectrometry, Vol. 6. Malcolm E. Rose. 1990. 142.00 (0-85186-308-6) CRC Pr.
Mass Spectrometry, Vol. 7. Malcolm E. Rose. 1989. 175.00 (0-85186-318-3) CRC Pr.
Mass Spectrometry, Vol. 8. Malcolm E. Rose. 1989. 208.00 (0-85186-328-0) CRC Pr.
Mass Spectrometry, Vol. 9. Ed. by Malcolm E. Rose. (Specialist Periodical Reports). (Illus.). 502p. 1987. text 171.00 (0-85186-338-8, Pub. by Royal Soc Chem) Spr-Verlag.
Mass Spectrometry, Vol. 10. Malcolm E. Rose. 1989. 252.00 (0-85186-348-5) CRC Pr.
Mass Spectrometry, Vols. 1-4. Ed. by R. A. Johnstone. Incl. 1968-70 Literature. 1971. 34.00 (0-85186-258-6); 1970-72 Literature. 1973. 32.00 (0-85186-268-3); 1972-74 Literature. 1975. 43.00 (0-85186-278-0); Vol. 4. 1974-76 Literature. 1977. 57.00 (0-85186-288-8); write for info. (0-318-50473-1) Am Chemical.
Mass Spectrometry Pt. B. 2nd ed. J. Barker. LC 98-3127. 532p. 1999. pap. 79.95 (0-471-96762-9) Wiley.
Mass Spectrometry Vol. 1: Clinical & Biomedical Applications, Vol. 1. D. M. Desiderio. (Illus.). 368p. (C). 1993. text 79.50 (0-306-44261-2, Kluwer Plenum) Kluwer Academic.
Mass Spectrometry - Mass Spectrometry: Techniques & Applications of Tandem. K. L. Busch et al. 333p. 1989. 139.00 (0-471-18699-6) Wiley.
Mass Spectrometry - Mass Spectrometry: Techniques & Applications of Tandem Mass Spectrometry. Kenneth L. Busch et al. LC 88-33755. 333p. 1989. 90.00 (0-89573-275-0, Wiley-VCH) Wiley.
Mass Spectrometry for Biotechnology. Gary Siuzdak. LC 95-30593. (Illus.). 161p. 1996. pap. text 36.00 (0-12-647471-0) Acad Pr.
Mass Spectrometry for Chemists & Biochemists. 2nd ed. Robert A. Johnstone & Malcolm E. Rose. (Illus.). 523p. (C). 1996. text 125.00 (0-521-41466-0); pap. text 44.95 (0-521-42497-6) Cambridge U Pr.
Mass Spectrometry for the Characterization of Microorganisms: Developed from a Symposium Sponsored by the Division of Analytical Chemistry at the 204th Meeting of the American Chemical Society, Washington, D. C., August 23-28, 1992. Ed. by Catherine Fenselau. LC 93-39043. (Symposium Ser.: Vol. 541). 240p. 1994. text 74.00 (0-8412-2737-3, Pub. by Am Chemical) OUP.
*__Mass Spectrometry in Biology & Medicine.__ Ed. by A. L. Burlingame et al. LC 99-23633. 592p. 1999. 150.00 (0-89603-799-1) Humana.
Mass Spectrometry in Biomedical Research. fac. ed. Ed. by Simon J. Gaskell. LC 86-5601. (Illus.). 508p. 1986. reprint ed. pap. 157.50 (0-608-00995-4, 206185300012) Bks Demand.
Mass Spectrometry in Biomolecular Sciences: Proceedings of the NATO Advanced Study Institute, Lacco Ameno, Ischia, Italy, June 23 - July 5, 1993. Ed. by Richard M. Caprioli, III et al. (NATO Advanced Science Institute Ser.: Pt. C). 548p. (C). 1996. text 276.00 (0-7923-3946-0) Kluwer Academic.
Mass Spectrometry in Biotechnological Process Analysis & Control. Ed. by E. Heinzle & M. Reuss. LC 87-25935. (Illus.). 254p. 1988. 75.00 (0-306-42777-X, Plenum Trade) Perseus Pubng.
Mass Spectrometry in Cancer Research. Roboz. 1995. write for info. (0-8493-0167-X) CRC Pr.
Mass Spectrometry in Environmental Sciences. Ed. by Francis W. Karasek et al. LC 84-13469. (Illus.). 598p. (C). 1985. 174.00 (0-306-41552-6, Plenum Trade) Perseus Pubng.
Mass Spectrometry in Inorganic Chemistry: A Symposium Sponsored by the Division of Inorganic Chemistry at the 152nd Meeting of the American Chemical Society, New York, NY, Sept. 15-16, 1966. American Chemical Society Staff. LC 68-25995. (Advances in Chemistry Ser.: No. 72). (Illus.). 337p. 1968. reprint ed. pap. 104.50 (0-608-06804-7, 206700100009) Bks Demand.
Mass Spectrometry in Science & Technology. Frederick A. White. LC 68-19783. (Illus.). 368p. reprint ed. pap. 114.10 (0-608-30238-4, 200635900058) Bks Demand.
Mass Spectrometry in the Analysis of Large Molecules. Texas Symposium on Mass Spectrometry (3rd: 1986: T. Ed. by C. J. McNeal. LC 86-18927. (Illus.). 231p. 1986. reprint ed. pap. 71.70 (0-608-05904-8, 206623900007) Bks Demand.
Mass Spectrometry in the Biological Sciences. Ed. by A. L. Burlingame & Steven A. Carr. LC 95-38333. 584p. 1996. 175.00 (0-89603-340-6) Humana.
Mass Spectrometry of Biological Materials. 2nd ed. Ed. by Barbara Larsen & Charles McEwen. LC 97-52814. (Illus.). 488p. 1998. text 195.00 (0-8247-0157-7) Dekker.
Mass Spectrometry of Large Non-Volatile Molecules for Marine Organic Chemistry. Ed. by E. R. Hilf & W. Tuszynski. 248p. (C). 1990. text 81.00 (981-02-0250-4) World Scientific Pub.
Mass Spectrometry of Lipids. R. C. Murphy. (Handbook of Lipid Research Ser.: Vol. 7). (Illus.). 308p. (C). 1993. text 79.50 (0-306-44361-9, Kluwer Plenum) Kluwer Academic.
*__Mass Spectrometry of Natural Substances in Food.__ F. Mellon et al. 312p. 2000. 129.00 (0-85404-571-6, Pub. by Royal Soc Chem) Spr-Verlag.
Mass Spectrometry of Peptides. Ed. by Dominic M. Desidereo. 440p. 1990. lib. bdg. 239.00 (0-8493-6293-8, QP551) CRC Pr.
Mass Spectrometry of Polymers. Giorgio Montaudo & Robert P. Lattimer. 1999. 99.95 (0-8493-3127-7) CRC Pr.
Mass Spectrometry of Priority Pollutants. Brian S. Middleditch et al. LC 80-14953. 320p. 1981. 75.00 (0-306-40505-9, Plenum Trade) Perseus Pubng.
*__Mass Spectrometry of Proteins & Peptides.__ Ed. by John R. Chapman. LC 99-41621. (Methods in Molecular Biology Ser.: Vol. 146). 539p. 2000. 125.00 (0-89603-609-X) Humana.
Mass Spectrometry of Soils. Ed. by Thomas W. Boutton & Shin-ichi Yamasaki. (Books in Soils, Plants & the Environment: Vol. 49). (Illus.). 520p. 1996. text 199.00 (0-8247-9699-3) Dekker.
Mass Spectrometry 2e (acol) 2nd ed. James Barker et al. LC 98-3127. (Analytical Chemistry by Open Learning Ser.). 532p. 1999. 165.00 (0-471-96764-5) Wiley.
Mass Spectronomy, Pt. A. Merritt & McEwen. (Practical Spectroscopy Ser.: Vol. 3). (Illus.). 304p. 1979. text 180.00 (0-8247-6749-7) Dekker.
*__Mass Storage in the Year 2000.__ Jack Scott. 43p. 1999. 100.00 (0-89258-358-4, C204) Assn Inform & Image Mgmt.
Mass Supply & Flows in the Solar Corona: The 2nd SOHO Workshop. Ed. by Bernhard Fleck et al. LC 94-27705. 384p. (C). 1994. text 191.50 (0-7923-2999-6) Kluwer Academic.
Mass Terms: Some Philosophical Problems. Ed. by Francis Jeffry Pelletier. (Studies in Linguistics & Philosophy: No. 6). 316p. 1979. text 121.50 (90-277-0931-9) Kluwer Academic.
Mass That Made Padre Pio. large type ed. Paul Trinchard. LC 96-76325. 285p. 1997. pap. 14.95 (1-889168-01-7) MAETA.
Mass Tort Litigation: Cases & Materials (American Casebook Series) Linda S. Mullenix. (Paralegal). 1160p. (C). 1996. text 55.00 (0-314-06635-7) West Pub.
Mass Tort Litigation - Cases & Materials. Linda S. Mullenix. (American Casebook Ser.). 208p. 1995. pap. text, teacher ed. write for info. (0-314-09001-0) West Pub.
Mass Transfer: Fundamentals & Applications. Anthony L. Hines & Robert N. Maddox. LC 83-19140. (Illus.). 600p. (C). 1984. 105.00 (0-13-559609-2) P-H.
Mass Transfer & Absorbers. T. Hobler & P. Danckwerts. LC 65-27688. (International Series of Monographs in Chemical Engeering: Vol. 6). 1966. 239.00 (0-08-011002-9, Pub. by Pergamon Repr) Franklin.
Mass Transfer in Engineering Practice. Aksel Lydersen. LC 82-7086. (Illus.). 335p. 1983. reprint ed. pap. 103.90 (0-608-05288-4, 206582600001) Bks Demand.
Mass Transfer in Heterogeneous Catalysis. Charles N. Satterfield. LC 80-23432. 286p. (C). 1980. reprint ed. text 33.50 (0-89874-198-X) Krieger.
Mass-Transfer Induced Activity in Galaxies. Ed. by Isaac Shlosman. (Illus.). 524p. (C). 1994. text 90.00 (0-521-47195-8) Cambridge U Pr.
Mass Transfer Operations. 3rd ed. Robert E. Treybal. (Chemical Engineering Ser.). (Illus.). 800p. (C). 1980. 101.56 (0-07-065176-0) McGraw.
Mass Transfer Operations: A Self-Instructional Problem Workbook. Louis Theodore & James E. Barden. (Illus.). 361p. (Orig.). 1995. pap. text, wbk. ed. 60.00 (1-882767-17-9) ETS.
Mass Transit. Maniza Naqvi. LC 98-930644. 208p. 1998. 12.95 (0-19-577900-2) OUP.
Mass Transit: Actions Needed for the Bart Airport Extension. (Illus.). 53p. (Orig.). (C). 1996. pap. text 25.00 (0-7881-3402-7) DIANE Pub.
*__Mass Transport in Solids & Fluids.__ David S. Wilkinson. (Cambridge Solid State Science Ser.). (Illus.). 400p. 2000. write for info. (0-521-62409-6); pap. write for info. (0-521-62494-0) Cambridge U Pr.
Mass Transport Phenomena. Christie J. Geankoplis. LC 79-154348. 1984. reprint ed. 49.50 (0-9603070-0-1) Geankoplis.
Mass Transportation Problems Pt. I: Theory. S. T. Rachev & Ludger Rhschendorf. LC 97-34593. (Probability & Its Applications Ser.). 516p. 1998. 79.95 (0-387-98350-3) Spr-Verlag.
Mass Transportation Problems Pt. II: Applications. S. T. Rachev & Ludger Rhschendorf. LC 97-34593. (Probability & Its Applications Ser.). 516p. 1998. 79.95 (0-387-98352-X) Spr-Verlag.
Mass Unemployment: Plant Closings & Community Mental Health. Terry F. Buss & F. Stevens Redburn. LC 83-4450. (Sage Studies in Community Mental Health: No. 6). (Illus.). 224p. reprint ed. pap. 69.50 (0-8357-8481-9, 203474800091) Bks Demand.
Mass Violence in America, 43 vols., Set. Ed. by Robert M. Fogelson & Richard E. Rubenstein. 1969. 678.25 (0-405-01299-3) Ayer.
MASS-11: The Useable Portable Guide. Jon Haber & Herbert R. Haber. 32p. (Orig.). pap. 4.95 (0-945765-16-9) Useable Portable Pubns.
Massac Biographies. George May. (Illus.). 209p. 1998. 10.00 (0-9605566-2-1, 500) G W May.
Massac County, 1955 to 1982: Accompanies History of Massac County. George W. May. 1983. pap. 1.00 (0-9605566-6-4) G W May.
Massachusets Political Almanac, Vol. II, The Executive see Massachusetts Political Almanac, 1997 Edition
Massachusettensis. Daniel Leonard. LC 72-10246. (American Revolutionary Ser.). 1979. reprint ed. lib. bdg. 22.50 (0-8398-1180-2) Irvington.
Massachusetts see From Sea to Shining Sea
Massachusetts see One Nation Series
*__Massachusetts.__ (Illus.). (J). 2000. pap. 24.95 (0-7403-0273-6) Alpha AZ.
Massachusetts. Capstone Press Geography Department Staff. (One Nation Ser.). (Illus.). 48p. (J). (gr. 3-7). 1996. 19.00 (0-516-20264-2) Childrens.
Massachusetts. Mark Dunster. (John Brown Ser.: Pt. 2). 1978. pap. 4.00 (0-89642-041-8) Linden Pubs.
Massachusetts. Dennis B. Fradin. (From Sea to Shining Sea Ser.). (Illus.). 64p. (J). (gr. 3-5). 1994. pap. 7.95 (0-516-43821-2) Childrens.
Massachusetts. Gousha, H. M., Editors. 1995. 2.95 (0-671-55124-8, H M Gousha) Prntice Hall Bks.
Massachusetts. Paul Joseph. LC 97-18132. (United States Ser.). (Illus.). 32p. 1998. lib. bdg. 19.93 (1-56239-882-2, Checkerboard Library) ABDO Pub Co.
Massachusetts. Emily McAuliffe. (States & Their Symbols Ser.). 1998. 14.00 (0-531-11606-9) Childrens.
*__Massachusetts.__ Bryan Pezzi. (American States Ser.). (Illus.). 32p. (J). (gr. 3-7). 2000. write for info. (1-930954-35-2) Weigl Pubs.
Massachusetts. Kathleen Thompson. LC 85-11915. (Portrait of America Library). 48p. (J). (gr. 4-8). 1996. pap. text 5.95 (0-8114-7446-1) Raintree Steck-V.
Massachusetts. Kathleen Thompson. LC 85-11915. (Portrait of America Library). (Illus.). 48p. (J). (gr. 3-6). 1996. lib. bdg. 22.83 (0-8114-7341-4) Raintree Steck-V.
*__Massachusetts.__ Mary D. Wade. (Illus.). 64p. (gr. 1-5). 2000. pap. 5.95 (1-892920-47-6) G H B Pubs.
Massachusetts. J. F. Warner. LC 93-37203. (Hello U. S. A. Ser.). (Illus.). 72p. (J). (gr. 3-6). 1994. pap. 5.95 (0-8225-9666-0, Lerner Publctns); lib. bdg. 19.93 (0-8225-2737-5, Lerner Publctns) Lerner Pub.
Massachusetts. Steve Dunwell. Ed. by James B. Patrick. (Scenic Discovery Ser.). (Illus.). 120p. reprint ed. 30.00 (0-940078-04-X) Foremost Pubs.
Massachusetts. 2nd ed. Sylvia McNair. LC 97-40668. (America the Beautiful Ser.). (J). 1998. 32.00 (0-516-20635-4) Childrens.
*__Massachusetts, 5 vols. , Set.__ Suzanne LeVert. LC 98-52549. (Celebrate the States Ser.). 144p. (J). (gr. 4-7). 2000. 35.64 (0-7614-0666-2, Benchmark NY) Marshall Cavendish.
*__Massachusetts: A Concise History.__ Richard D. Brown & Jack Tager. (Illus.). 400p. 2000. 60.00 (1-55849-248-8); pap. 19.95 (1-55849-249-6) U of Mass Pr.
Massachusetts: A Guide to Its Places & People. Federal Writers' Project Staff. (American Guidebook Ser.). 675p. 1937. reprint ed. 95.00 (0-403-02150-2) Somerset Pub.
Massachusetts: A Guide to Its Places & People. Federal Writers' Project Staff & Writers Program-WPA Staff. (American Guide Ser.). 1989. reprint ed. lib. bdg. 89.00 (0-7812-1020-8, 1020) Rprt Serv.
Massachusetts: A Scenic Discovery. rev. ed. Photos by Steve Dunwell. LC 97-71381. (Illus.). 120p. 1997. 35.00 (0-9643015-3-9) Back Bay Boston.
Massachusetts: A View from Above. Charles Feil. LC 98-35380. (Illus.). 96p. 1998. 30.00 (0-89272-421-8) Down East.
*__Massachusetts: An Explorer's Guide.__ 3rd ed. Christina Tree & William Davis. LC 99-57817. 2000. pap. 18.95 (0-88150-439-4, Pub. by Countryman) Norton.
Massachusetts: An Explorer's Guide, Beyond Boston & Cape Cod. 2nd ed. Christina Tree & William Davis. LC 97-43869. (Explorer's Guide Ser.). (Illus.). 416p. 1998. pap. 18.00 (0-88150-405-X, Pub. by Countryman) Norton.
Massachusetts: From Colony to Commonwealth. Judith F. Clark. (Illus.). 328p. 1987. 32.95 (0-89781-216-6) Am Historical Pr.
Massachusetts: Its Historians & Its History, an Object Lesson. Charles F. Adams. (Works of Charles Frances Adams Jr. (1835- 1915)). 110p. reprint ed. lib. bdg. 49.00 (0-932051-10-3) Rprt Serv.
Massachusetts: Off the Beaten Path: A Guide to Unique Places. 3rd ed. Barbara Rogers & Stillman Rogers. LC 99-18078. (Off the Beaten Path Ser.). 224p. 1999. pap. 12.95 (0-7627-0398-9) Globe Pequot.
Massachusetts: Ten Poems. Thomas Lux. 15p. (C). 1981. pap. 5.00 (0-913219-32-0) Pym-Rand Pr.
Massachusetts: Ten Poems. deluxe ed. Thomas Lux. 15p. (C). 1981. 10.00 (0-913219-33-9) Pym-Rand Pr.
*__Massachusetts: The Spirit of America, State by State.__ Patricia Harris. Ed. by Diana Landau. LC 98-43099. (Art of the State Ser.). 1999. 12.95 (0-8109-5560-1, Pub. by Abrams) Time Warner.
Massachusetts - Collected Works of Federal Writers Project, Vol. 1. Federal Writers' Project Staff. 1991. reprint ed. lib. bdg. 98.00 (0-7812-5611-9) Rprt Serv.
Massachusetts - Collected Works of Federal Writers Project, Vol. 2. Federal Writers' Project Staff. 1991. reprint ed. lib. bdg. 98.00 (0-7812-5616-X) Rprt Serv.
Massachusetts Actions & Remedies: Family Law. Ed. by Marc G. Perlin. 480p. 1991. ring bd. 95.00 (0-88063-446-4, MICHIE) LEXIS Pub.
Massachusetts Alternative Dispute Resolution. David A. Hoffman & David E. Matz. LC 94-22974. 1994. spiral bd. 180.00 (1-56257-350-0, 81414-10, MICHIE) LEXIS Pub.
Massachusetts & Maine Families: In the Ancestry of Walter Goodwin Davis (1885-1966), 3 vols., Set. Walter Goodwin Davis. LC 95-81293. 2096p. 1996. reprint ed. 135.00 (0-8063-1496-6) Genealog Pub.
Massachusetts & Maine Families in the Ancestry of Walter Goodwin Davis (1885-1966) Vol. I: Allanson-French. Walter Goodwin Davis. 746p. 1996. text 50.00 (0-8063-1495-8) Genealog Pub.
Massachusetts & Maine Families in the Ancestry of Walter Goodwin Davis (1885-1966) Vol. II: Gardner-Moses. Walter Goodwin Davis. 732p. 1996. text 50.00 (0-8063-1494-X) Genealog Pub.
Massachusetts & Maine Families in the Ancestry of Walter Goodwin Davis (1885-1966) Vol. III: Neal-Wright. Walter Goodwin Davis. 732p. 1996. text 50.00 (0-8063-1493-1) Genealog Pub.
Massachusetts & Other State Greats (Biographies) Carole Marsh. (Carole Marsh Massachusetts Bks.). (Illus.). (J). (gr. 3-8). 1994. pap. 19.95 (1-55609-700-X); lib. bdg. 29.95 (1-55609-699-2); disk 29.95 (1-55609-701-8) Gallopade Intl.
Massachusetts & Rhode Island Trail Guide. 7th rev. ed. Appalachian Mountain Club Staff. (Illus.). 384p. 1995. pap. 16.95 (1-878239-39-2) AMC Books.
Massachusetts & the New Nation. Ed. by Conrad E. Wright. (Studies in American History & Culture: No. 2). xiv, 296p. 1992. 40.00 (0-934909-28-8, Pub. by Mass Hist Soc) NE U Pr.
Massachusetts & Western Connecticut. Elizabeth Dugger. (Adventure Guide Ser.). (Illus.). 400p. 1999. pap. 17.95 (1-55650-861-1) Hunter NJ.
Massachusetts Appellate Division Reports, 1980-1994. Ed. by Paul E. Lamoureux. 366p. 1984. 56.90 (0-318-03673-8) Lawyers Weekly.
Massachusetts Appellate Tax Board Reporter. Ed. by Borins. 75p. 1998. ring bd. 85.00 (0-327-00311-1, 8142426) LEXIS Pub.
Massachusetts Appellate Tax Board Reporter. Ed. by Jennifer Borins. 1981. ring bd. 85.00 (0-614-05894-5, MICHIE) LEXIS Pub.
Massachusetts Appellate Tax Board Reporter. Ed. by Stephen M. Politi. 85.00 (0-327-12433-4) LEXIS Pub.
Massachusetts Appellate Tax Board Reporter, 1986-1991. Ed. by Ruth Kleinfeld. 1991. ring bd. 85.00 (0-88063-006-X, MICHIE) LEXIS Pub.
Massachusetts Appellate Tax Board Reporter 21:3. Ed. by Borins. 75p. 1998. ring bd. 85.00 (0-327-00310-3, 8142425) LEXIS Pub.
Massachusetts Atlas: A Student's Guide to the Geography of the Bay State. Thomas E. Sherer, Jr. (Illus.). 108p. (Orig.). (J). (gr. 4-12). 1995. pap. text 19.95 (0-9647011-0-3); pap. text, teacher ed. 19.95 (0-9647011-1-1) Kilderatlas.
*__Massachusetts Atlas & Gazetteer: Topo Maps of the Entire State.__ DeLorme Mapping Co. Staff. LC 99-462942. (Illus.). 1998. pap. text. write for info. (0-89933-220-X) DeLorme Map.
Massachusetts Attorney Conduct Manual, 2 vols., Set. Gilda M. Tuoni. 900p. 1992. ring bd. 75.00 (0-88063-259-3, 81410-10, MICHIE) LEXIS Pub.
Massachusetts Attorney Discipline Reports, 14 vols., Set. Board of Bar Overseers, Superior Judicial Court St. 2370p. 1980. boxed set 420.00 (0-88063-027-2, 81427-10, MICHIE) LEXIS Pub.
Massachusetts Attorney Discipline Reports, 9 vols., Vol. 1. Massachusetts Board of Bar Overseers of the Suprem. 420p. 55.00 (0-685-42459-6, MICHIE) LEXIS Pub.
Massachusetts Attorney Discipline Reports, Vol. 2. Massachusetts Board of Bar Overseers of the Suprem. (Illus.). 420p. 55.00 (0-614-03140-0, MICHIE) LEXIS Pub.
Massachusetts Attorney Discipline Reports, 9 vols., Vol. 5. Massachusetts Board of Bar Overseers of the Suprem. 65.00 (0-685-42460-X, MICHIE) LEXIS Pub.
Massachusetts Attorney Discipline Reports, Vol. 7. Massachusetts Board of Bar Overseers of the Suprem. 420p. 1993. 70.00 (0-614-03147-8, MICHIE) LEXIS Pub.
Massachusetts Attorney Discipline Reports, Vol. 8. Massachusetts Board of Bar Overseers of the Suprem. 420p. 1993. 70.00 (0-614-03148-6, MICHIE) LEXIS Pub.
Massachusetts Attorney Discipline Reports, Vol. 9. Massachusetts Board of Bar Overseers of the Suprem. 420p. 1994. 70.00 (0-614-03149-4, MICHIE) LEXIS Pub.
*__Massachusetts Attorney Discipline Reports, Vol. 14.__ Ed. by Karen O'Toole. 850p. 1999. write for info. (0-327-04957-X, 8144110) LEXIS Pub.
Massachusetts Automotive Directory. Ed. by T. L. Spelman. 1985. 24.95 (1-55527-017-4) Auto Contact Inc.
Massachusetts Bandits, Bushwackers, Outlaws, Crooks, Devils, Ghosts, Desperadoes & Other Assorted & Sundry Characters! Carole Marsh. (Carole Marsh Massachusetts Bks.). (Illus.). (J). (gr. 3-8). 1994. pap. 19.95 (0-7933-0574-8); lib. bdg. 29.95 (0-7933-0575-6); disk 29.95 (0-7933-0576-4) Gallopade Intl.
*__Massachusetts Basic Practice Manual.__ 2000. write for info. (1-57589-117-4) Mass CLE.
Massachusetts Basic Practice Manual, 3 vols., Vol. I. LC 90-63087. 150p. 1992. ring bd. 35.00 (0-944490-31-X) Mass CLE.
Massachusetts Basic Practice Manual, Vol. II. LC 90-63087. 696p. 1998. ring bd., suppl. ed. 35.00 (1-57589-088-7, 98-11.02-SP) Mass CLE.
*__Massachusetts Basic Practice Manual: Buying & Selling a Home.__ Ruth A. Dillingham. (Massachusetts Basic Practice Ser.). 150p. 1999. pap. write for info. (1-57589-162-X) Mass CLE.
*__Massachusetts Basic Practice Manual: Drafting Simple Will & Trust Clauses.__ Janet W. Moore. (Massachusetts Basic Practice Ser.). 150p. 1999. pap. write for info. (1-57589-161-1) Mass CLE.

M

An Asterisk (*) at the beginning of an entry indicates that the title is appearing for the first time.

*Massachusetts Basic Practice Manual: Preparation, Negotiation & Trial of a Chapter 93A Case. James F. Kavanaugh. (Massachusetts Basic Practice Ser.). 150p. 1999. pap. write for info. (1-57589-163-8) Mass CLE.

*Massachusetts Basic Practice Manual: Preparing & Trying Your First Civil Case. Jeffrey C. Melick. (Massachusetts Basic Practice Ser.). 150p. 1999. pap. write for info. (1-57589-175-1) Mass CLE.

*Massachusetts Basic Practice Manual: Representing Clients in the United States Bankruptcy Court. Mark G. DeGiacomo. (Massachusetts Basic Practice Ser.). 150p. 1999. pap. write for info. (1-57589-164-6) Mass CLE.

Massachusetts Basic Practice Manual: 2001 Supplement. write for info. (1-57589-196-4) Mass CLE.

Massachusetts Basic Practice Manual, 1992 Supplement, Vol. I. LC 90-63087. 250p. 1992. ring bd. 35.00 (0-944490-20-4) Mass CLE.

Massachusetts Basic Practice Manual, 1994 Supplement. 1994. ring bd. 35.00 (0-944490-82-4) Mass CLE.

Massachusetts Basic Practice Manual, 1996 Supplement, 3 vols. LC 90-63087. 596p. 1996. ring bd., suppl. ed. 35.00 (1-57589-021-6, 96-11.06-SP) Mass CLE.

Massachusetts Basic Practice Manual, 1997 Supplement, 3 vols. LC 90-63087. 714p. 1997. ring bd., suppl. ed. 35.00 (1-57589-056-9, 97-11.05-SP) Mass CLE.

M

*Massachusetts Bay: An Historical Novel. Harry Birchard. LC 00-190966. 463p. 2000. 25.00 (0-7388-2027-X); pap. 18.00 (0-7388-2028-8) Xlibris Corp.

Massachusetts Bay Company & Its Predecessors. Frances Rose-Troup. LC 98-157379. 176p. 1998. reprint ed. pap. 18.50 (0-7884-0867-4, R574) Heritage Bk.

Massachusetts Bay Company & Its Predecessors. Frances Rose-Troup. LC 73-15804. xi, 176p. 1973. reprint ed. 35.00 (0-678-00871-X) Kelley.

Massachusetts "BIO" Bingo! 24 Must Know State People for Kids to Learn about While Having Fun! Carole Marsh. (Bingo! Ser.). (Illus.). (J). (gr. 2-8). 1998. pap. 14.95 (0-7933-8585-7) Gallopade Intl.

Massachusetts Birds. James Kavanagh. (Pocket Naturalist Ser.). (Illus.). 1997. 5.95 (1-889903-38-8, Pub. by Waterford WA) Falcon Pub Inc.

Massachusetts Bookstore Book: A Surprising Guide to Our State's Bookstores & Their Specialties for Students, Teachers, Writers & Publishers. Carole Marsh. (Massachuseets Bks.). (Illus.). 1994. pap. 19.95 (0-7933-2919-1); lib. bdg. 29.95 (0-7933-2918-3); disk 29.95 (0-7933-2920-5) Gallopade Intl.

*Massachusetts Business Directory, 1999-2000. rev. ed. American Business Directories Staff. 2496p. 1999. boxed set 520.00 incl. cd-rom (0-7687-0164-3) Am Busn Direct.

Massachusetts Business Lawyering, Vol. III. Stanley Keller et al. LC 90-63088. 882p. 1998. ring bd., suppl. ed. 59.50 (1-57589-044-5, 07-04.17-SP) Mass CLE.

Massachusetts Business Lawyering Supplement, 3 vols., Vol. I. Ed. by Stanley Keller. LC 90-63088. 500p. 1991. ring bd., suppl. ed. 29.50 (0-944490-18-2, 94-04.40-SP) Mass CLE.

Massachusetts Business Lawyering Supplement, 3 vols., Vol. II. Ed. by Stanley Keller. LC 90-63088. 670p. 1996. ring bd., suppl. ed. 39.50 (1-57589-013-5, 96-04.45-SP) Mass CLE.

Massachusetts Census Index, 1850 Mortality Schedule. (Illus.). lib. bdg. write for info. (0-89593-372-1, Accel Indexing) Genealogical Srvcs.

Massachusetts Census Index, 1890 Union Vets. (Illus.). lib. bdg. 113.00 (0-89593-378-0, Accel Indexing) Genealogical Srvcs.

Massachusetts Census Index, 1860 Boston & Suffolk County. Ed. by Ronald Vern Jackson. LC 99-197578. (Illus.). 1996. lib. bdg. 190.00 (0-89593-374-8, Accel Indexing) Genealogical Srvcs.

Massachusetts Census Index, 1870. (Illus.). lib. bdg. write for info. (0-89593-375-6, Accel Indexing) Genealogical Srvcs.

Massachusetts Civil Practice. Robert V. Greco et al. LC 96-77953. 800p. 1996. text. write for info. (0-7620-0101-1) West Group.

Massachusetts Civil Procedure. write for info. (1-57589-206-5) Mass CLE.

Massachusetts Classic Christmas Trivia: Stories, Recipes, Activities, Legends, Lore & More! Carole Marsh. (Carole Marsh Massachusetts Bks.). (Illus.). (J). (gr. 3-8). 1994. pap. 19.95 (0-7933-0577-2); lib. bdg. 29.95 (0-7933-0578-0); disk 29.95 (0-7933-0579-9) Gallopade Intl.

Massachusetts Coastales. Carole Marsh. (Massachuseets Bks.). (J). 1994. lib. bdg. 29.95 (0-7933-7286-0) Gallopade Intl.

Massachusetts Coastales. Carole Marsh. (Carole Marsh Massachusetts Bks.). (Illus.). (J). (gr. 3-8). 1994. pap. 19.95 (1-55609-694-1); lib. bdg. 29.95 (1-55609-693-3); disk 29.95 (1-55609-695-X) Gallopade Intl.

Massachusetts Code Research Guide. 1990. suppl. ed. write for info. (0-318-68086-6) West Group.

Massachusetts Code Research Guide 1999 Supplement. 450p. 1999. pap. write for info. (0-327-07474-4, 5674112) LEXIS Pub.

Massachusetts Collection Law. 2nd ed. Jordan L. Shapiro et al. LC 91-78333. (Massachusetts Practice Systems Library). 1984. ring bd. 120.00 (0-318-02975-8) West Group.

Massachusetts Collection Law. 2nd ed. Jordan L. Shapiro et al. LC 84-80874. (Massachusetts Practice Systems Library). 1993. suppl. ed. 40.00 (0-317-03248-8) West Group.

Massachusetts Collections Manual. Berman, Gold & West, PC Kamberg Staff. 250p. 1991. ring bd. 95.00 (0-614-05895-3, MICHIE) LEXIS Pub.

Massachusetts Collections Manual, 1990-1991. 2nd ed. Kamberg, Berman, Gold & West Staff et al. 250p. 1990. ring bd. 95.00 (0-88063-050-7, MICHIE) LEXIS Pub.

Massachusetts Colony. Dennis B. Fradin. LC 86-9753. (Thirteen Colonies Ser.). (Illus.). 144p. (YA). (gr. 4 up). 1986. lib. bdg. 30.00 (0-516-00386-0) Childrens.

Massachusetts Condominium Law, 2 vols. 2nd ed. Barry Brown et al. 1993. suppl. ed. 49.00 (0-685-74463-9, MICHIE) LEXIS Pub.

Massachusetts Condominium Law, 2 vols., Set. 2nd ed. Barry Brown & Douglas S. MacGregor. 800p. 1993. spiral bd. 180.00 (1-56257-311-X, 81442-10, MICHIE) LEXIS Pub.

Massachusetts Condominium Law, 1996 Supplement. Robert J. Galwin et al. LC 88-63516. 168p. 1996. ring bd., suppl. ed. 39.50 (0-944490-10-7, 96-19.24-SP) Mass CLE.

Massachusetts Condominium Law, 1991 Supplement. Robert J. Galvin et al. LC 88-63516. 1991. ring bd. 34.50 (0-944490-32-8) Mass CLE.

Massachusetts Condominium Law, 1994 Supplement. Robert J. Galvin et al. LC 88-63516. 1994. ring bd. 27.50 (0-944490-53-0) Mass CLE.

Massachusetts Congregationalist Political Thought, 1760-1790: The Design of Heaven. Dale S. Kuehne. 208p. (C). 1996. text 37.50 (0-8262-1057-0) U of Mo Pr.

Massachusetts Constitution: A Citizen's Guide. George M. Jarnis & Nicholas S. Racheotes. 200p. (Orig.). 1987. pap. text 25.00 (0-931684-10-2) Gov Res Pubns.

Massachusetts Constitution of 1780: A Social Compact. Ronald M. Peters, Jr. LC 77-90730. 256p. 1978. 30.00 (0-87023-143-X) U of Mass Pr.

Massachusetts Construction Law. James J. Myers. LC 98-65213. xxi, 698 p. 1998. 95.00 (1-55834-882-4) LEXIS Pub.

Massachusetts Conveyancers' Handbook. 3rd ed. Edward C. Mendler. LC 83-83043. 1984. 115.00 (0-318-01918-3) West Group.

Massachusetts Conveyancers' Handbook. 3rd ed. Edward C. Mendler. LC 83-83043. 1993. suppl. ed. 54.00 (0-317-03246-1) West Group.

Massachusetts Corporate Forms, 2 vols. Michael J. Bohnen & Dana Coggins. 1260p. 1994. suppl. ed. 35.00 (0-318-71301-2, MICHIE) LEXIS Pub.

Massachusetts Corporate Forms, Issue 11. Dana C. Coggins & Michael J. Bohnen. 100p. 1999. ring bd. 87.00 (0-327-01301-X, 8145516); ring bd. 85.00 incl. disk (0-327-01302-8, 8145516) LEXIS Pub.

Massachusetts Corporate Forms, 2 vols., Set. Michael J. Bohnen & Dana Coggins. 1260p. 1989. ring bd. 290.00 incl. disk (0-8342-0043-0, 81450-10, MICHIE) LEXIS Pub.

Massachusetts Corporate Tax Manual, 2 vols. 3rd ed. Ernest M. Dichele et al. 800p. 1993. suppl. ed. 60.00 (0-685-74464-7, MICHIE) LEXIS Pub.

Massachusetts Corporate Tax Manual, 2 vols., Set. 3rd ed. Ernest M. Dichele et al. 800p. 1993. ring bd. 160.00 (0-88063-817-6, MICHIE) LEXIS Pub.

Massachusetts Corporation: Legal Aspects of Organization & Operation. Jonathan C. Guest. (Corporate Practice Ser.: No. 64). (Illus.). 1995. ring bd. 95.00 (1-55871-314-X) BNA.

Massachusetts Corporation Law & Practice. Richard W. Southgate & Donald W. Glazer. (National Corporation Law Ser.). 1280p. 1998. ring bd. 165.00 (0-13-110454-3) Aspen Law.

Massachusetts Corporation Law with Federal Tax Analysis. James W. Smith & Zolman Cavitch. 1963. ring bd. 245.00 (0-8205-1378-4) Bender.

Massachusetts Corporation Laws: Reprinted from Massachusetts General Laws Annotated - Containing General Laws Enacted Through the 1982 Session of the General Court. Massachusetts Continuing Legal Education-New Engla. iii, 377p. 1983. write for info. (0-318-57764-X) West Pub.

Massachusetts Corporations. Douglas A. Muir & Michael J. Puzo. LC 79-92872. (Practice Systems Library Manual). 1993. suppl. ed. 69.50 (0-317-03187-2) West Group.

Massachusetts Corporations. Douglas A. Muir et al. LC 79-92872. (Practice Systems Library Manual). Date not set. ring bd. 140.00 (0-317-03186-4, 68820, MICHIE) LEXIS Pub.

Massachusetts Corporations: A Practice Systems Library Manual. Douglas A. Muir et al. 1981. ring bd. 140.00 (0-327-00971-3, 68820, MICHIE) LEXIS Pub.

*Massachusetts Corporations: 1999 Edition. Douglas A. Muir et al. 1000p. 1999. ring bd. 155.00 (0-327-04910-3, 6882011) LEXIS Pub.

Massachusetts Corporations, 1998 Supplement. Douglas A. Muir et al. 150p. 1998. ring bd., suppl. ed. write for info. (0-327-00550-5, 6883212) LEXIS Pub.

*Massachusetts Crime in Perspective 2000. Ed. by Kathleen O'Leary Morgan & Scott E. Morgan. 22p. 2000. spiral bd. 19.00 (0-7401-0320-2) Morgan Quitno Corp.

Massachusetts Crime Perspective, 1998. Ed. by Kathleen O'Leary Morgan & Scott E. Morgan. 20p. 1998. pap. 19.00 (1-56692-920-2) Morgan Quitno Corp.

Massachusetts Crime Perspectives, 1999. Kathleen O'Leary Morgan. 22p. 1999. spiral bd. 19.00 (0-7401-0120-X) Morgan Quitno Corp.

Massachusetts Criminal & Traffic Law Manual, 1998. 1102p. 1998. write for info. (0-327-05765-3, 25200-10) LEXIS Pub.

*Massachusetts Criminal & Traffic Law Manual, 2000 Edition. Ed. by LEXIS Law Publishing Editors. 880p. 2000. write for info. (0-327-10899-1, 2520011) LEXIS Pub.

Massachusetts Criminal Defense. Eric D. Blumenson et al. 270p. 1994. pap., student ed. 45.00 (0-88063-727-7, 10626-10, MICHIE) LEXIS Pub.

Massachusetts Criminal Defense, 2 vols., Set. Eric D. Blumenson. 1600p. 1993. ring bd., wbk. ed. 140.00 (0-614-05896-1, MICHIE) LEXIS Pub.

Massachusetts Criminal Defense, 2 vols., Set. Eric D. Blumenson et al. 1600p. 1990. boxed set 140.00 (0-88063-202-X, 81459-10, MICHIE) LEXIS Pub.

Massachusetts Criminal Jury Instructions. Homans. 1994. write for info. (1-56257-211-3, MICHIE) LEXIS Pub.

Massachusetts Criminal Law & Procedure. 928p. 1986. pap. 24.00 (0-317-52109-8) West Pub.

Massachusetts Criminal Law & Procedure: Annual Edition. Gould Editorial Staff. student ed. 6.00 (0-87526-275-9) Gould.

Massachusetts Criminal Law & Procedure: Annual Edition. Gould Editorial Staff. 860p. (C). ring bd. 21.95 (0-87526-320-8) Gould.

Massachusetts Criminal Law Sourcebook: 2001 Edition. write for info. (1-57589-126-3) Mass CLE.

Massachusetts Criminal Law Sourcebook, 1997 Edition. rev. ed. R. Marc Kautrowitz & Timothy E. Maguire. LC 97-70502. Orig. Title: Compendium of Massachusetts Criminal Law. 776p. 1997. pap. text 50.00 (1-57589-058-5, 97-06.10-BK) Mass CLE.

Massachusetts Criminal Practice see Massachusetts Criminal Practice

Massachusetts Criminal Practice, 2 vols., Vols. 1 & 2. 2nd ed. Blumenson. Incl. Vol. 1. Massachusetts Criminal Practice. 2nd ed. LC 98-89802. 1998. (0-327-00759-1); Vol. 2. Massachusetts Criminal Practice. 2nd ed. 1998. (0-327-00760-5); LC 98-89802. 1500p. 1998. 195.00 (0-327-00639-0, 8145911) LEXIS Pub.

Massachusetts Criminal Practice Forms. J. W. Carney. 1994. write for info. (1-56257-219-9, MICHIE) LEXIS Pub.

Massachusetts Criminal Practice, Student Edition 1998. Eric D. Blumenson & Stanley Z. Fisher. 800p. 1999. write for info. (0-327-01013-4, 1062611) LEXIS Pub.

Massachusetts "Crinkum-Crankum" A Funny Word Book about Our State. Carole Marsh. (Massachuseets Bks.). (Illus.). (J). 1994. pap. 19.95 (0-7933-4872-2); lib. bdg. 29.95 (0-7933-4871-4); disk 29.95 (0-7933-4873-0) Gallopade Intl.

*Massachusetts Deposition Practice Manual. 2000. pap. write for info. (1-57589-177-8) Mass CLE.

Massachusetts Deposition Practice Manual, 1996 Supplement. Ed. by Peter M. Lauriat et al. LC 92-64380. 330p. 1996. ring bd., suppl. ed. 39.50 (0-944490-42-5, 96-05.29-SP) Mass CLE.

Massachusetts Dingbats! A Fun Book of Games, Stories, Activities & More about Our State That's All in Code! for You to Decipher. Carole Marsh. (Massachuseets Bks.). (Illus.). (J). (gr. 3-12). 1994. pap. 19.95 (0-7933-3837-9) Gallopade Intl.

Massachusetts Dingbats! A Fun Book of Games, Stories, Activities & More about Our State That's All in Code! for You to Decipher, Bk. 1. Carole Marsh. (Massachuseets Bks.). (Illus.). (J). (gr. 3-12). 1994. lib. bdg. 29.95 (0-7933-3836-0); disk 29.95 (0-7933-3838-7) Gallopade Intl.

Massachusetts Directory of Manufacturers. 11th rev. ed. Ed. by Louise M. West & Frank Lambing. 1997. pap. 72.50 (1-58202-000-0) Manufacturers.

Massachusetts District Court Criminal Defense Manual. Andrew Silverman. LC 96-76071. 1996. ring bd. 35.00 (0-944490-91-3) Mass CLE.

Massachusetts Divorce: A Consumer Guide. 2nd rev. ed. Wendy Sibbison. LC 95-78280. x, 140p. (Orig.). 1996. pap. 14.95 (0-944490-89-1, 96-10.14-BK) Mass CLE.

Massachusetts Divorce Workbook, 1996. Sharyn T. Sooho & Steven L. Fuchs. 200p. 1996. pap. 19.95 (0-9650371-0-X) Fmly Law Pr.

Massachusetts Domestic Relations, 2 vols. (Practice Systems Library Manual). 1993. suppl. ed. 75.00 (0-317-03268-2) West Group.

Massachusetts Domestic Relations. Paul Kane. 176p. 1994. suppl. ed. 41.00 (0-614-03150-8, MICHIE) LEXIS Pub.

Massachusetts Domestic Relations. 2nd ed. Paul Kane. 200p. 1994. spiral bd. 95.00 (0-88063-751-X, MICHIE) LEXIS Pub.

Massachusetts Domestic Relations, 2 vols., Set. 2nd ed. Harvey et al. LC 82-82112. (Practice Systems Library Manual). Date not set. ring bd. 290.00 (0-318-11941-2, 68835, MICHIE) LEXIS Pub.

Massachusetts Domestic Relations: A Practice Systems Library Manual, 2 vols. 2nd ed. Harvey et al. 1996. ring bd. 290.00 (0-327-00969-1, 68835, MICHIE) LEXIS Pub.

Massachusetts Domestic Relations, 1998 Supplement, 2 vols. Harvey et al. 150p. 1998. ring bd. write for info. (0-327-00870-9, 6884212) LEXIS Pub.

Massachusetts Elder Law, 1998. William J. Brisk et al. LC 98-89532. 900p. 1998. 135.00 (0-327-00810-5, 8153411) LEXIS Pub.

*Massachusetts Elder Law, 1999 Supplement: Pocketpart. Margaret A. Hoag et al. 100p. 1999. suppl. ed. write for info. (0-327-01682-5, 8153521) LEXIS Pub.

Massachusetts Electric Vehicle Demonstration Program, Aug. 1995: First Year Program Results. Massachusetts Division of Energy Resources Staff. (Electric Vehicle Information Ser.: Vol. 10). (Illus.). 60p. 1996. pap. 55.00 (0-89934-259-0, BT037); lib. bdg. 105.00 (0-89934-260-4, BT937) Bus Tech Bks.

Massachusetts Environmental Law: 1996 Edition. Gregor I. McGregor. LC 90-63090. 1400p. 1996. ring bd. 125.00 (1-57589-014-3, 96-09-14-SP) Mass CLE.

Massachusetts Environmental Law Handbook. Gould Editorial Staff. 800p. ring bd. 34.95 (0-87526-426-3) Gould.

Massachusetts Environmental Law, 2001 Supplement. write for info. (1-57589-208-1) Mass CLE.

Massachusetts Estate Planning, Will Drafting & Estate Administration Forms, 2 vols., Vol. 1 & 2. 2nd ed. Clymer et al. 2000p. 1998. lib. bdg. 280.00 (0-327-00797-4, 8147311); lib. bdg. write for info. (0-327-00798-2, 8147311); lib. bdg. write for info. (0-327-00799-0, 8147311); lib. bdg. write for info. (0-327-00800-8, 8147311) LEXIS Pub.

Massachusetts Estate Planning, Will Drafting, & Estate Administration Forms; 1989-1993. John J. Clymer et al. 224p. 1994. ring bd., suppl. ed. 85.00 (0-614-03151-6, MICHIE) LEXIS Pub.

Massachusetts Estate Planning, Will Drafting, & Estate Administration Forms, 1989-1993, 2 vols., Set. John H. Clymer, Jr. et al. LC 92-43737. 1420p. 1994. spiral bd. 270.00 (0-8342-0061-9, 81473-10, MICHIE) LEXIS Pub.

Massachusetts Evidence. 6th ed. Paul J. Liacos. 947p. 1994. 145.00 (0-316-52410-7, Aspen Law & Bus) Aspen Pub.

Massachusetts Evidence Law, 1995. Paul J. Liacos. 1995. 65.00 (0-316-52416-6, Aspen Law & Bus) Aspen Pub.

Massachusetts Evidence, 1994. Paul J. Liacos. 1994. suppl. ed. 60.00 (0-316-52411-5, Aspen Law & Bus) Aspen Pub.

Massachusetts Evidence, 1997: A Courtroom Reference. rev. ed. J. Harold Flannery et al. LC 96-77820. 470p. 1997. ring bd. 95.00 (1-57589-036-4, 97-05.35-BK) Mass CLE.

*Massachusetts Eye & Ear Infirmary Handbook of Challenges in Phacoemulsification. Alejandro Espaillat et al. 200p. (C). 2000. text 95.00 (1-55642-486-8) SLACK Inc.

Massachusetts Eye & Ear Infirmary Illustrated Manual of Ophthalmology. Neil Friedman et al. LC 97-37851. (Illus.). 336p. (C). 1998. pap. text 49.95 (0-7216-7025-3, W B Saunders Co) Harcrt Hlth Sci Grp.

Massachusetts Eye & Ear Infirmary Residents' Guide to Ocular Antimicrobial Therapy. Ed. by Thomas A. Ciulla & Ann Sullivan Baker. 88p. (C). 1996. pap. text 9.95 (1-56881-062-8) AK Peters.

Massachusetts Eye & Ear Infirmary Review Manual for Ophthalmology. Jeffrey C. Lamkin. LC 92-49469. (Illus.). 672p. 1993. pap. text 76.00 (0-316-51293-1) Lppncott W & W.

Massachusetts Eye & Ear Infirmary Review Manual for Ophthalmology. 2nd ed. Jeffrey C. Lamkin & Massachusetts Eye & Ear Infirmary Staff. LC 98-27315. 1998. write for info. (0-7817-1763-9) Lppncott W & W.

Massachusetts Facts & Factivities. Carole Marsh. (Carole Marsh State Bks.). (Illus.). (J). (gr. 4-7). 1996. pap., teacher ed. 19.95 (0-7933-7889-3, C Marsh) Gallopade Intl.

Massachusetts Facts & Symbols. Emily McAuliffe. LC 98-3674. (States & Their Symbols Ser.). 24p. (J). 1999. write for info. (0-7368-0082-4, Hilltop Bks) Capstone Pr.

Massachusetts Family Law Guidebook: A View from the Bench. 2nd ed. Edward M. Ginsburg & Anita Robboy. LC 92-32853. 250p. 1992. spiral bd. 95.00 (1-56257-340-3, MICHIE) LEXIS Pub.

Massachusetts Family Law Handbook. 3rd ed. Gerald D. McLellan. 439p. (C). 99.05 (0-318-03672-X) Lawyers Weekly.

Massachusetts Family Law Handbook Supplement, 1995. Ed. by Gerald D. McLellan & Ellen Zack. 1995. 39.40 (0-318-18707-8) Lawyers Weekly.

Massachusetts Family Law Journal. Ed. by Alfred L. Podolski. 1628p. 1985. 125.00 (0-88063-029-9, 81489-10, MICHIE) LEXIS Pub.

Massachusetts Family Law Journal. Alfred L. Podolski et al. 140.00 (0-327-12441-5) LEXIS Pub.

Massachusetts Family Law Manual, 1997, 2 vols. rev. ed. Haskell A. Kassler et al. LC 96-78930. 1596p. 1996. ring bd. 125.00 (1-57589-045-3, 97-10.20-BK) Mass CLE.

*Massachusetts Family Law Sourcebook: 2000 Edition. 2000. write for info. (1-57589-128-X) Mass CLE.

Massachusetts Family Law Sourcebook: 2001 Edition. write for info. (1-57589-192-1) Mass CLE.

Massachusetts Family Law Sourcebook, 1997 Edition. rev. ed. Michael L. Leshin. LC 97-70501. Orig. Title: Compendium of Massachusetts Family Law. 450p. 1997. pap. text 50.00 (1-57589-057-7, 97-10.23-BK) Mass CLE.

Massachusetts Federal Census Index, 1870 Boston City. (Illus.). lib. bdg. write for info. (0-89593-376-4, Accel Indexing) Genealogical Srvcs.

Massachusetts Federal Census Index, 1790 (1908) Ronald V. Jackson. (Illus.). 1978. lib. bdg. 55.00 (0-89593-674-7, Accel Indexing) Genealogical Srvcs.

Massachusetts Federal Census Index, 1800. Ronald V. Jackson. LC 77-85960. (Illus.). 1973. lib. bdg. 58.00 (0-89593-066-8, Accel Indexing) Genealogical Srvcs.

Massachusetts Federal Census Index, 1810. Ronald V. Jackson. LC 77-85961. (Illus.). 1976. lib. bdg. 67.00 (0-89593-067-6, Accel Indexing) Genealogical Srvcs.

Massachusetts Federal Census Index, 1820. Ronald V. Jackson. LC 77-85967. (Illus.). 1976. lib. bdg. 79.00 (0-89593-068-4, Accel Indexing) Genealogical Srvcs.

Massachusetts Federal Census Index, 1830. Ronald V. Jackson. LC 77-85965. (Illus.). lib. bdg. 95.00 (0-89593-069-2, Accel Indexing) Genealogical Srvcs.

Massachusetts Federal Census Index, 1840. Ronald V. Jackson. LC 77-85964. (Illus.). 1978. lib. bdg. 110.00 (0-89593-070-6, Accel Indexing) Genealogical Srvcs.

Massachusetts Federal Census Index, 1850. Ronald V. Jackson. LC 77-85963. (Illus.). lib. bdg. 150.00 (0-89593-071-4, Accel Indexing) Genealogical Srvcs.

Massachusetts Federal Census Index, 1860 South (Barnstable, Bristol, Dukes, Nantucket, Norfolk, Plymouth Counties) Ed. by Ronald Vern Jackson. LC 99-197571. (Illus.). 1998. lib. bdg. 400.00 (0-89593-373-X, Accel Indexing) Genealogical Srvcs.

An Asterisk (*) at the beginning of an entry indicates that the title is appearing for the first time.

Massachusetts Federal Census Index, 1880. (Illus.). lib. bdg. write for info. (*0-89593-377-2*, Accel Indexing) Genealogical Srvcs.

Massachusetts Festival Fun for Kids! Carole Marsh. (Massachuseets Bks.). (Illus.). (YA). (gr. 3-12). 1994. pap. 19.95 (*0-7933-3990-1*); lib. bdg. 29.95 (*0-7933-3989-8*); disk 29.95 (*0-7933-3991-X*) Gallopade Intl.

Massachusetts First National Bank of Boston, 1784-1934. Norman S. Gras. LC 75-41759. (Companies & Men: Business Enterprises in America Ser.). (Illus.). 1976. reprint ed. 66.95 (*0-405-08075-1*) Ayer.

Massachusetts Foreclosures, 1997 Edition. rev. ed. Joseph P. Vrabel et al. LC 96-80043. 442p. 1997. ring bd. 75.00 (*1-57589-040-2*, 97-19.14-BK) Mass CLE.

Massachusetts Genealogical Research. George K. Schweitzer. 279p. 1999. pap. 15.00 (*0-913857-12-2*) Genealog Sources.

Massachusetts General Hopsital Handbook of Pain Management. Ed. by David Borsook et al. 400p. 1996. pap. text 35.95 (*0-316-54946-0*, Little Brwn Med Div) Lppncott W & W.

***Massachusetts General Hospital Comprehensive Psychiatry Update & Review.** Theodore Stern. 679p. 2000. pap. 65.00 (*0-07-135435-2*) McGraw.

Massachusetts General Hospital Guide to Menopause: What It Is, How to Treat It, How to Cope with It. Isaac Schiff & Ann B. Person. LC 95-15171. 336p. 1996. pap. 15.00 (*0-8129-2318-9*, Times Bks) Crown Pub Group.

Massachusetts General Hospital Guide to Psychiatry in Primary Care. Ed. by Theodore Stern et al. LC 97-48338. (Illus.). 552p. 1997. pap. text 45.00 (*0-07-061498-9*) McGraw-Hill HPD.

Massachusetts General Hospital Handbook of Neurology. Alice W. Flaherty. 208p. pap. text 24.95 (*0-683-30576-X*) Lppncott W & W.

Massachusetts General Hospital, 1935-1955. Nathaniel W. Faxon. LC 59-12968. 508p. reprint ed. pap. 157.50 (*0-7837-4471-4*, 204417900001) Bks Demand.

Massachusetts "GEO" Bingo! 38 Must Know State Geography Facts for Kids to Learn While Having Fun! Carole Marsh. (Bingo! Ser.). (Illus.). (J). (gr. 2-8). 1998. pap. 14.95 (*0-7933-8586-5*) Gallopade Intl.

Massachusetts Government! The Cornerstone of Everyday Life in Our State! Carole Marsh. (Carole Marsh Massachusetts Bks.). (Illus.). (J). (gr. 3-12). 1996. pap. 19.95 (*0-7933-6245-8*); lib. bdg. 29.95 (*0-7933-6244-X*); disk 29.95 (*0-7933-6246-6*) Gallopade Intl.

Massachusetts Governments Performance Standards, 1990. Ed. by Greg Michels. (Governments Performance Standards Ser.). (Illus.). 150p. 1990. text 125.00 (*1-55507-488-X*) Municipal Analysis.

Massachusetts Grantmakers. Associated Grantmakers of Massachusetts, Inc. Staf. LC 85-52426. 223p. (Orig.). 1993. pap. text 50.00 (*0-912427-05-1*) Assoc Grant.

Massachusetts Grantmakers Directory. Ed. by Gracelaw Simmons. 348p. 1999. pap. 50.00 (*0-912427-06-X*) Assoc Grant.

Massachusetts Guardianship & Conservatorship Practice. Christopher G. Mehne et al. LC 97-62773. 380p. 1997. ring bd. 125.00 (*1-57589-062-3*, 97-08.27-BK) Mass CLE.

***Massachusetts Health Care in Perspective 2000.** Ed. by Kathleen O'Leary Morgan & Scott E. Morgan. 21p. 2000. spiral bd. 19.00 (*0-7401-0220-6*) Morgan Quitno Corp.

Massachusetts Health Care Perspective, 1998. Ed. by Kathleen O'Leary Morgan & Scott E. Morgan. 20p. 1998. pap. 19.00 (*1-56692-820-6*) Morgan Quitno Corp.

Massachusetts Health Care Perspective, 1999. Ed. by Kathleen O'Leary Morgan. 21p. 1999. spiral bd. 19.00 (*0-7401-0070-X*) Morgan Quitno Corp.

Massachusetts Health Plan: The Right Prescription? Attiat F. Ott & Wayne B. Gray. LC 88-62773. (Pioneer Paper Ser.: No. 1). 123p. (Orig.). 1988. pap. 10.00 (*0-929930-00-2*) Pioneer Inst.

Massachusetts Help to Ireland During the Great Famine. H. A. Forbes & Henry Lee. LC 67-24085. (Illus.). 1967. 14.00 (*0-937650-00-5*) Mus Am China Trade.

Massachusetts "HISTO" Bingo! 42 Must Know State History Facts for Kids to Learn While Having Fun! Carole Marsh. (Bingo! Ser.). (Illus.). (J). (gr. 2-8). 1998. pap. 14.95 (*0-7933-8587-3*) Gallopade Intl.

Massachusetts Historical & Biographical Index, Vol. 1. Ronald V. Jackson. LC 78-53703. (Illus.). lib. bdg. 30.00 (*0-89593-186-9*, Accel Indexing) Genealogical Srvcs.

Massachusetts History! Surprising Secrets about Our State's Founding Mothers, Fathers & Kids! Carole Marsh. (Carole Marsh Massachusetts Bks.). (Illus.). (J). (gr. 3-12). 1996. pap. 19.95 (*0-7933-6092-7*); lib. bdg. 29.95 (*0-7933-6091-9*); disk 29.95 (*0-7933-6093-5*) Gallopade Intl.

Massachusetts Hot Air Balloon Mystery. Carole Marsh. (Carole Marsh Massachusetts Bks.). (Illus.). (J). (gr. 2-9). 1994. 29.95 (*0-7933-2507-2*); pap. 19.95 (*0-7933-2508-0*); disk 29.95 (*0-7933-2509-9*) Gallopade Intl.

Massachusetts Hot Zones! Viruses, Diseases, & Epidemics in Our State's History. Carole Marsh. (Hot Zones! Ser.). (Illus.). (J). (gr. 3-12). 1998. pap. 19.95 (*0-7933-8892-9*); lib. bdg. 29.95 (*0-7933-8891-0*) Gallopade Intl.

Massachusetts in Perspective, 1998. Ed. by Kathleen O'Leary Morgan & Scott E. Morgan. 24p. 1998. pap. 19.00 (*1-56692-870-2*) Morgan Quitno Corp.

***Massachusetts in Perspective, 1999.** Ed. by Kathleen O'Leary Morgan. 26p. 1999. spiral bd. 19.00 (*1-56692-970-9*) Morgan Quitno Corp.

***Massachusetts In Perspective 2000.** Ed. by Kathleen O'Leary Morgan & Scott E. Morgan. 26p. 2000. spiral bd. 19.00 (*0-7401-0270-2*) Morgan Quitno Corp.

Massachusetts in the Civil War. William Schouler. Orig. Title: A History of Massachusetts in the Civil War. xiv, 670p. 1998. reprint ed. pap. 29.95 (*1-58218-001-6*) Digital Scanning.

Massachusetts Indian Dictionary for Kids! Carole Marsh. (Carole Marsh State Bks.). (J). (gr. 2-9). 1996. 29.95 (*0-7933-7707-2*, C Marsh); pap. 19.95 (*0-7933-7708-0*, C Marsh) Gallopade Intl.

***Massachusetts Investment & Business Guide: Business, Investment, Export-Import Opportunities, 50 vols., Vol. 21.** Global Investment Center, USA Staff. (U. S. Regional Investment & Business Library-99: Vol. 21). (Illus.). 350p. (Orig.). 1999. pap. 59.95 (*0-7397-1120-2*) Intl Business Pubns.

Massachusetts, Its Historians & Its History: An Object Lesson. Charles F. Adams, Jr. LC 73-146849. (Select Bibliographies Reprint Ser.). 1977. reprint ed. 16.95 (*0-8369-5616-8*) Ayer.

Massachusetts Jeopardy! Answers & Questions about Our State! Carole Marsh. (Massachuseets Bks.). (Illus.). (J). (gr. 3-12). 1994. pap. 19.95 (*0-7933-4143-4*); lib. bdg. 29.95 (*0-7933-4142-6*); disk 29.95 (*0-7933-4144-2*) Gallopade Intl.

Massachusetts "Jography" A Fun Run Thru Our State! Carole Marsh. (Carole Marsh Massachusetts Bks.). (Illus.). (J). (gr. 3-8). 1994. pap. 19.95 (*1-55609-111-7*); lib. bdg. 29.95 (*1-55609-682-8*); disk 29.95 (*1-55609-683-6*) Gallopade Intl.

Massachusetts Jury Instruction - Civil. John M. Greaney et al. LC 97-71438. 100p. 1998. ring bd. 95.00 (*0-327-00659-5*, 6302511) LEXIS Pub.

Massachusetts Jury Instructions: Civil. John M. Greaney et al. 1997. text 95.00 (*1-55834-491-8*, 63022-10, MICHIE) LEXIS Pub.

Massachusetts Jury Instructions: Criminal. William P. Homans, Jr. LC 96-76790. 1996. spiral bd. 105.00 (*1-55834-375-X*, 63017, MICHIE) LEXIS Pub.

***Massachusetts Jury Instructions - Criminal, Issue 1.** 2nd ed. LC 99-63742. 450p. 1999. ring bd. 95.00 (*0-327-01365-6*, 6302010) LEXIS Pub.

Massachusetts Jury Trial Benchbook. Ed. by Peter M. Lauriat & Toni L. Pomeroy. xii, 238p. (Orig.). 1996. pap. 100.00 (*1-889916-00-5*) F N Flaschner.

Massachusetts Juvenile Court Bench Book, 2 vol. Marc Kantrowitz. LC 98-84887. 1998. write for info. (*1-57589-091-7*) Mass CLE.

Massachusetts Juvenile Law Sourcebook: 2001 Edition. write for info. (*1-57589-193-X*) Mass CLE.

Massachusetts Kid's Cookbook: Recipes, How-To, History, Lore & More! Carole Marsh. (Carole Marsh Massachusetts Bks.). (Illus.). (J). (gr. 3-8). 1994. pap. 19.95 (*0-7933-0586-1*); lib. bdg. 29.95 (*0-7933-0587-X*); disk 29.95 (*0-7933-0588-8*) Gallopade Intl.

***Massachusetts Labor & Employment, Issue 2.** 2nd ed. Jeffrey L. Hirsch. 100p. 1999. ring bd. write for info. (*0-327-01389-3*, 8153022) LEXIS Pub.

Massachusetts Labor & Employment: 1990 Edition, Issue 9. Jeffrey Hirsh. 1995. ring bd. 95.00 (*0-88063-392-1*, 81530-13, MICHIE) LEXIS Pub.

Massachusetts Land Bankers of 1740. George A. Billias. LC 59-63155. 1959. pap. 8.95 (*0-89101-005-X*) U Maine Pr.

Massachusetts Land Surveying Law: Questions & Answers. John E. Keen. 42p. (C). 1995. pap. text 25.00 (*1-56569-028-1*) Land Survey.

Massachusetts Land Use. Bobrowski. 1993. 145.00 (*0-316-10150-8*, Aspen Law & Bus) Aspen Pub.

Massachusetts Landlord & Tenant. Ward. 1994. ring bd. write for info. (*0-88063-832-X*, MICHIE) LEXIS Pub.

Massachusetts Landlord-Tenant Law. George Warshaw. LC 86-83061. Date not set. text 125.00 (*0-317-03801-X*, 68850, MICHIE) LEXIS Pub.

Massachusetts Landlord-Tenant Law. George Warshaw. 1987. text 125.00 (*0-327-00970-5*, 68850, MICHIE) LEXIS Pub.

Massachusetts Landlord-Tenant Law. George Warshaw. LC 86-83061. 1993. suppl. ed. 56.50 (*0-317-03802-8*) West Group.

***Massachusetts Landlord-Tenant Law, 1999 Cumulative Supplement.** George Warshaw. 415p. 1999. pap., suppl. ed. write for info. (*0-327-01713-9*, 6885513) LEXIS Pub.

Massachusetts Landlord-Tenant Practice: Law & Forms. G. Emil Ward. 649p. 90.00 (*0-327-12349-4*) LEXIS Pub.

Massachusetts Landlord-Tenant Practice: Law & Forms. G. Emil Ward. LC 96-75443. 649p. 1996. 90.00 (*1-55834-321-0*, 68410, MICHIE) LEXIS Pub.

Massachusetts Landlord-Tenant Practice: Law & Forms, 1998 Cumulative Supplement. G. Emil Ward. LC 96-75443. 1998. write for info. (*0-327-00220-4*, 68411-11) LEXIS Pub.

***Massachusetts Landlord-Tenant Practice: Law & Forms, 1999 Cumulative Supplement: Pocketpart.** G. Emil Ward. 200p. 1999. suppl. ed. write for info. (*0-327-01703-1*, 6841112) LEXIS Pub.

Massachusetts Law Finder: A New Topical Reference Guide for Co-Ordinated Research Providing Comprehensive References to the Following West Publications-Massachusetts General Laws Annotated, Massachusetts Digest, Massachusetts Practice Series, United States Code Annotated, Corpus Juris Secundum, Federal Publications, Key Number Publications, Texts & Treatises. West Publishing Company Editorial Staff. 1984. write for info. (*0-318-59238-X*) West Pub.

Massachusetts Legal Practice Library. write for info. (*0-327-12431-8*) LEXIS Pub.

Massachusetts Legal Services Plan for Action. 137p. 1987. 17.00 (*0-685-54047-2*, 43,150A); pap. 3.75 (*0-317-03738-2*, 43,150B) NCLS Inc.

Massachusetts Library Book: A Surprising Guide to the Unusual Special Collections in Libraries Across Our State for Students, Teachers, Writers & Publishers - Includes Reproducible Mailing Labels Plus Activities for Young People! Carole Marsh. (Massachusetts Bks.). (Illus.). 1994. pap. 19.95 (*0-7933-3069-6*); lib. bdg. 29.95 (*0-7933-3068-8*); disk 29.95 (*0-7933-3070-X*) Gallopade Intl.

Massachusetts Lighthouses: A Pictorial Guide. 2nd ed. Courtney Thompson. LC 98-70230. (Illus.). 122p. 1998. 24.95 (*0-9651786-6-8*, Pub. by Catnap Publns); pap. 19.95 (*0-9651786-5-X*, Pub. by Catnap Publns) Magazines Inc.

Massachusetts Limited Liability Company Forms & Practice Manual. Stanley Keller. LC 96-43496. 516p. 1996. ring bd. 219.90 (*1-57400-019-5*) Data Trace Pubng.

Massachusetts Litigation Forms & Analysis. Anthony M. Doniger. Ed. by Ronald E. Fleury. LC 95-76594. 1500p. 1995. text. write for info. (*0-7620-0010-4*) West Group.

Massachusetts Manufacturers Register. Ed. by Frank Lambing. 1998. 79.00 (*1-58202-077-9*) Manufacturers.

Massachusetts Math! How It All Adds up in Our State. Carole Marsh. (Carole Marsh Massachusetts Bks.). (Illus.). (YA). (gr. 3-12). 1996. pap. 19.95 (*0-7933-6551-1*); lib. bdg. 29.95 (*0-7933-6550-3*) Gallopade Intl.

Massachusetts Media Book: A Surprising Guide to the Amazing Print, Broadcast & Online Media of Our State for Students, Teachers, Writers & Publishers - Includes Reproducible Mailing Labels Plus Activities for Young People! Carole Marsh. (Massachuseets Bks.). (Illus.). 1994. pap. 19.95 (*0-7933-3225-7*); lib. bdg. 29.95 (*0-7933-3224-9*); disk 29.95 (*0-7933-3226-5*) Gallopade Intl.

Massachusetts Military Shoulder Arms, 1784-1877. George D. Moller. LC 88-60020. (Illus.). 124p. 1988. 24.00 (*0-917218-34-5*) A Mowbray.

Massachusetts' (Most Devastating!) Disasters & (Most Calamitous!) Catastrophies! Carole Marsh. (Carole Marsh Massachusetts Bks.). (Illus.). (J). (gr. 3-8). 1994. pap. 19.95 (*0-7933-0571-3*); lib. bdg. 29.95 (*0-7933-0572-1*); disk 29.95 (*0-7933-0573-X*) Gallopade Intl.

Massachusetts Motor Vehicle & Traffic Laws: Annual Edition. 8.95 (*0-87526-550-2*) Gould.

Massachusetts Motor Vehicle & Traffic Laws: Annual Edition. Gould Editorial Staff. 1989. 6.00 (*0-87526-281-3*) Gould.

Massachusetts Motor Vehicle & Traffic Laws: Annual Edition. Gould Editorial Staff. 710p. (C). 1989. ring bd. 21.95 (*0-87526-231-7*) Gould.

Massachusetts Motor Vehicle Offenses: 2001 Supplement. write for info. (*1-57589-198-0*) Mass CLE.

Massachusetts Motor Vehicle Offenses, 1997 Supplement. Ed. by William J. Teahan, Jr. et al. LC 93-80662. 616p. 1996. ring bd., suppl. ed. 75.00 (*1-57589-049-6*, 97-06.08-SP) Mass CLE.

Massachusetts Motor Vehicle Torts: Liability & Litigation. R. Marc Kantrowitz et al. LC 94-77483. 804p. 1994. ring bd. 75.00 (*0-944490-65-4*) Mass CLE.

Massachusetts Motor Vehicle Torts, 1996 Supplement. R. Marc Kantrowitz et al. LC 94-77483. 236p. 1996. ring bd., suppl. ed. 39.50 (*1-57589-029-1*, 96-17.15-SP) Mass CLE.

Massachusetts Municipal Law Manual. write for info. (*1-57589-184-0*) Mass CLE.

***Massachusetts Municipal Profiles 1999-2000.** 14th rev. ed. Ed. by Edith R. Hornor. 395p. 1999. pap. 84.00 (*0-931845-63-7*) Info Pubns.

Massachusetts Mystery Van Takes Off! Bk. 1: Handicapped Massachusetts Kids Sneak Off on a Big Adventure. Carole Marsh. (Massachuseets Bks.). (Illus.). (J). (gr. 3-12). 1994. 29.95 (*0-7933-5024-7*); pap. 19.95 (*0-7933-5025-5*); disk 29.95 (*0-7933-5026-3*) Gallopade Intl.

Massachusetts 1970 Census Index: Heads of Families. pap. 35.00 (*1-877677-49-3*) Herit Quest.

***Massachusetts Non-Profit Organizations.** 2000. write for info. (*1-57589-154-9*) Mass CLE.

Massachusetts Nonprofit Organizations, 1996 Supplement, 2 vols. Frederic J. Marx et al. LC 92-85281. 1414p. 1995. ring bd., suppl. ed. 125.00 (*1-57589-008-9*, 96-04.11-BK) Mass CLE.

Massachusetts Nonprofit Organizations, 1998 Supplement. Richard C. Allen et al. Ed. by Frederic J. Marx. LC 97-76388. 1998. ring bd. 145.00 (*1-57589-081-X*, 97-04.41-BK) Mass CLE.

Massachusetts Officers & Soldiers in the French & Indian Wars, 1755-1756. Ed. by K. David Goss & David Zarowin. LC 84-27224. 376p. 1985. pap. 14.95 (*0-88082-010-1*) New Eng Hist.

Massachusetts One Hundred Years Ago: The Northeast. Drake & Chadwick. (Historical Ser.). (Illus.). 1976. pap. 3.50 (*0-89540-017-0*, SB-017) Sun Pub.

Massachusetts One Hundred Years Ago: The Southeast. Nordhoff et al. (Historical Ser.). (Illus.). 1976. pap. 3.50 (*0-89540-018-9*, SB-018) Sun Pub.

Massachusetts Paper Money, 1690-1780: The Collection of the Massachusetts Historical Society. Leonard Travers. (Picture Bks.). 1988. pap. 5.00 (*0-934909-67-9*) Mass Hist Soc.

Massachusetts Paralegal Practice Manual. Ed. by Mary Jo Romano et al. LC 96-77822. 750p. 1997. ring bd. 125.00 (*1-57589-022-4*, 97-22.06-BK) Mass CLE.

Massachusetts Personal Injury Sourcebook. James E. Harvey, Jr. LC 97-70624. 544p. 1997. pap. text 50.00 (*1-57589-059-3*, 97-17.12-BK) Mass CLE.

Massachusetts Personal Injury Sourcebook. 2nd rev. ed. James E. Harvey, Jr. LC 97-76387. 1998. pap. text 50.00 (*1-57589-085-2*, 98-17.13-BK) Mass CLE.

***Massachusetts Personal Injury Sourcebook: 2000 Edition.** 2000. pap. write for info. (*1-57589-155-7*) Mass CLE.

Massachusetts Personal Injury Sourcebook: 2001 Edition. write for info. (*1-57589-207-3*) Mass CLE.

***Massachusetts Pharmacy Law Review.** Doug Pisano. 1998. pap. text 19.68 (*1-56870-342-2*) RonJon Pub.

Massachusetts Pleading & Practice: Forms & Commentary, 7 vols. Edward M. Swartz & Frederic A. Swartz. 1974. 680.00 (*0-8205-1379-2*) Bender.

Massachusetts Poems. Leo Connellan. (Hollow Spring Poetry Ser.). 60p. (Orig.). 1981. pap. 6.95 (*0-685-02322-2*) Hollow Spring Pr.

Massachusetts Political Almanac: The Legislature, 1998 Edition, Vol. 1. rev. ed. Ed. by Holly Burch. 359p. 1998. pap. 45.00 (*0-926766-21-X*) Ctr Leader Stu.

Massachusetts Political Almanac Vol. 2: 1998 Edition, The Executive. rev. ed. Ed. by Carolyn Barnes. 349p. 1998. pap. 45.00 (*0-926766-22-8*) Ctr Leader Stu.

Massachusetts Political Almanac, 1998, 2 vols., Set. rev. ed. Ed. by Holly Burch & Carolyn Barnes. 1998. pap. 75.00 (*0-926766-23-6*) Ctr Leader Stu.

Massachusetts Political Almanac, 1997 Edition, 2 vols. Incl. Massachusets Political Almanac Vol. II: The Executive. rev. ed. Ed. by Holly Burch. 352p. 1997. pap. 40.00 (*0-926766-19-8*); Vol. I: The Legislature. rev. ed. Ed. by Margaret E. Buckley. 368p. 1997. pap. 40.00 (*0-926766-18-X*); 75.00 (*0-926766-20-1*) Ctr Leader Stu.

Massachusetts Political Almanacs, 2 vols. Ed. by Barbara Talley. Incl. Vol. 1: The Legislature, 1996 Edition. rev. ed. 356p. 1996. 40.00 (*0-926766-15-5*); Vol. II: The Executive, 1996 Edition. rev. ed. 338p. 1996. 40.00 (*0-926766-16-3*); 65.00 (*0-926766-17-1*) Ctr Leader Stu.

Massachusetts Practice: Administrative Law & Practice, 3 vols. Alexander Cella. 2136p. 1986. 172.50 (*0-317-52113-6*) West Pub.

Massachusetts Practice Series - Taxation, 4 vols. Baily & Van Dorn. 1986. 147.50 (*0-317-52107-1*) West Pub.

Massachusetts Premises Liability: Includes Forms on Disk. Jeffrey A. Newman et al. LC 97-70630. 618p. 1997. ring bd. 95.00 incl. disk (*1-57589-065-8*, 98-17.05-BK) Mass CLE.

Massachusetts Probate Law & Rules. 448p. 1986. pap. 20.50 (*0-317-52111-X*) West Pub.

Massachusetts Probate Manual, 1997 Supplement. Ed. by Joseph Warner & Hanson Reynolds. LC 87-62744. 760p. 1997. ring bd., suppl. ed. 95.00 (*1-57589-054-2*, 97-08.13-BK) Mass CLE.

Massachusetts Quiz Bowl Crash Course! Carole Marsh. (Carole Marsh Massachusetts Bks.). (Illus.). (J). (gr. 3-8). 1994. pap. 19.95 (*1-55609-697-6*); lib. bdg. 29.95 (*1-55609-696-8*); disk 29.95 (*1-55609-698-4*) Gallopade Intl.

Massachusetts Real Estate, 2 vols. Robert Marzelli. LC 83-82338. (Massachusetts Practice Systems Library). Date not set. ring bd. 240.00 (*0-317-00786-6*, 68860, MICHIE) LEXIS Pub.

Massachusetts Real Estate. Robert L. Marzelli. LC 83-82338. (Massachusetts Practice Systems Library). 1993. suppl. ed. 70.00 (*0-317-03242-9*) West Group.

Massachusetts Real Estate: A Practice Systems Library Manual, 2 vols. Robert Marzelli. 1983. ring bd. 240.00 (*0-327-00972-1*, 68860, MICHIE) LEXIS Pub.

Massachusetts Real Estate: 1998 Supplement. 178p. 1998. ring bd., suppl. ed. write for info. (*0-327-00250-6*, 68867-11) LEXIS Pub.

***Massachusetts Real Estate: 1999 Edition.** Robert Marzelli. 1800p. 1999. write for info. (*0-327-04926-X*, 6886011) LEXIS Pub.

Massachusetts Real Estate Leasing Forms. James W. Hackett. 650p. 1991. ring bd. 159.00 incl. disk (*0-8342-0194-1*, MICHIE); disk 75.00 (*0-685-74617-8*, MICHIE) LEXIS Pub.

Massachusetts Real Estate Principles & Practices. 4th ed. Peter J. Regan & Arthur J. Neuner. 301p. (C). 1995. 27.00 (*0-9627396-1-8*) Nrth Shr Pr.

Massachusetts Retirement & Relocation Guide. large type ed. (Retirement & Relocation Guides Ser.). (Illus.). 350p. Date not set. pap. 24.95 (*1-56559-132-1*) HGI-Over Fifty.

Massachusetts, Rhode Island & South New Hampshire Pocket Guide. 7th ed. Richard Barnett. 192p. 1995. pap. 16.95 (*0-939430-39-8*) Scanner Master.

Massachusetts Rollercoasters! Carole Marsh. (Massachuseets Bks.). (Illus.). (YA). (gr. 3-12). 1994. pap. 19.95 (*0-7933-5288-6*); lib. bdg. 29.95 (*0-7933-5287-8*); disk 29.95 (*0-7933-5289-4*) Gallopade Intl.

Massachusetts Sales & Use Tax Manual. Joseph X. Donovan. 600p. 1994. ring bd., wbk. ed. 175.00 (*0-614-05897-X*, MICHIE) LEXIS Pub.

Massachusetts Sales & Use Tax Manual, 2 vols. rev. ed. Joseph X. Donovan. 586p. 1994. ring bd., suppl. ed. 49.00 (*0-685-73824-8*, MICHIE) LEXIS Pub.

Massachusetts Sales & Use Tax Manual, Issue 7. Joseph Donovan. 1995. ring bd. write for info. (*0-88063-356-5*, 83362-11, MICHIE) LEXIS Pub.

Massachusetts School Law. write for info. (*1-57589-186-7*) Mass CLE.

Massachusetts School Trivia: An Amazing & Fascinating Look at Our State's Teachers, Schools & Students! Carole Marsh. (Carole Marsh Massachusetts Bks.). (Illus.). (J). (gr. 3-8). 1994. pap. 19.95 (*0-7933-0583-7*); lib. bdg. 29.95 (*0-7933-0584-5*); disk 29.95 (*0-7933-0585-3*) Gallopade Intl.

Massachusetts Search & Seizure Manual. write for info. (*1-57589-187-5*) Mass CLE.

Massachusetts Service Directory, 1994-1995. pap. 64.00 (*0-614-14371-3*) G D Hall Co.

M

Massachusetts Silly Basketball Sportsmysteries, Vol. I. Carole Marsh. (Carole Marsh Massachusetts Bks.). (Illus.). (J). (gr. 3-8). 1994. pap. 19.95 (*0-7933-0580-2*); lib. bdg. 29.95 (*0-7933-0581-0*); disk 29.95 (*0-7933-0582-9*) Gallopade Intl.

Massachusetts Silly Basketball Sportsmysteries, Vol. II. Carole Marsh. (Carole Marsh Massachusetts Bks.). (Illus.). (J). (gr. 3-8). 1994. pap. 19.95 (*0-7933-1706-1*); lib. bdg. 29.95 (*0-7933-1705-3*); disk 29.95 (*0-7933-1707-X*) Gallopade Intl.

Massachusetts Silly Football Sportsmysteries, Vol. I. Carole Marsh. (Carole Marsh Massachusetts Bks.). (Illus.). (J). (gr. 3-8). 1994. pap. 19.95 (*1-55609-688-7*); lib. bdg. 29.95 (*1-55609-687-9*); disk 29.95 (*1-55609-689-5*) Gallopade Intl.

Massachusetts Silly Football Sportsmysteries, Vol. II. Carole Marsh. (Carole Marsh Massachusetts Bks.). (Illus.). (J). (gr. 3-8). 1994. pap. 19.95 (*1-55609-691-7*); lib. bdg. 29.95 (*1-55609-690-9*); disk 29.95 (*1-55609-692-5*) Gallopade Intl.

Massachusetts Silly Trivia! Carole Marsh. (Carole Marsh Massachusetts Bks.). (Illus.). (J). (gr. 3-8). 1994. pap. 19.95 (*1-55609-110-9*); lib. bdg. 29.95 (*1-55609-680-1*); disk 29.95 (*1-55609-681-X*) Gallopade Intl.

Massachusetts Silver Coinage. Sydney P. Noe. LC 88-72077. (Illus.). 210p. 1990. 35.00 (*0-942666-56-9*) S J Durst.

M

Massachusetts Silver Coinage No. 9: Handbook. Anthony Terranova. 20p. 1994. pap. 9.00 (*0-685-72031-4*); boxed set 30.00 incl. sl. (*0-685-72032-2*) Am Numismatic.

Massachusetts Society for Promoting Agriculture, 1942-1992. Charles P. Lyman & David W. Lynch. (Illus.). 128p. 1992. 20.00 (*0-938864-16-5*) Ipswich Pr.

Massachusetts Society of Mayflower Descendants, 1935, Vol. 33. Massachusetts Society of Mayflower Descendants Sta. (Illus.). x, 237p. 1997. reprint ed. 27.00 (*0-7884-0643-4*, MD33) Heritage Bk.

Massachusetts Spelling Bee! Score Big by Correctly Spelling Our State's Unique Names. Carole Marsh. (Carole Marsh Massachusetts Bks.). (Illus.). (YA). (gr. 3-12). 1996. pap. 19.95 (*0-7933-6704-2*); lib. bdg. 29.95 (*0-7933-6703-4*) Gallopade Intl.

Massachusetts (Springfield, Hamden) Federal Census, 1860. 1990. 160.00 (*0-89593-622-4*, Accel Indexing) Genealogical Srvcs.

Massachusetts Standardized Civil Practice Forms, 4 vols., Set. Paul G. Garrity & James A. Frieden. 4064p. 1986. 325.00 (*0-316-29368-7*, Aspen Law & Bus) Aspen Pub.

***Massachusetts State Credit Directory, 2000 Edition.** rev. ed. American Business Directories Staff. 640p. 1999. boxed set 175.00 incl. cd-rom (*0-7687-0307-7*) Am Busn Direct.

Massachusetts State Park. Barbara McCaig & Boyce. (Illus.). 100p. (Orig.). 1989. pap. text 5.95 (*0-935201-67-X*) Affordable Adven.

Massachusetts Student Pocket Part to Accompany Administration of Wills, Trusts, & Estates. Gordon W. Brown. 119p. 1993. 10.50 (*0-8273-6022-3*) Delmar.

Massachusetts Superior Court Civil Forms: Includes Forms on Disk. Ed. by Paul A. Chernoff et al. LC 96-80042. 782p. 1997. ring bd. 95.00 incl. disk (*1-57589-051-8*, 97-05.13-BK) Mass CLE.

***Massachusetts Superior Court Civil Practice Manual.** Ed. by Patrick F. Brady et al. LC 97-70625. 1998. write for info. (*1-57589-061-5*) Mass CLE.

Massachusetts Superior Court Civil Practice Manual. Ed. by Paul A. Chernoff et al. LC 96-80041. 616p. 1997. ring bd. 95.00 (*1-57589-050-X*, 97-05.12-BK) Mass CLE.

Massachusetts Supplement for Modern Real Estate Practice. 5th ed. David L. Kent. 96p. 1996. pap. 12.95 (*0-7931-1623-6*, 1510-1305, Real Estate Ed) Dearborn.

***Massachusetts Suppression Matters: A Guide to Search, Seizure, & Massachusetts Law.** Christine M. McEvoy & Joseph A. Grasso. 360p. 1999. 95.00 (*0-327-01658-2*, 6453010) LEXIS Pub.

Massachusetts Survival. Betty L. Hall & James F. McGuirk. 160p. (gr. 10-12). 1979. pap. text 5.84 (*0-03-046881-7*) Westwood Pr.

Massachusetts Tax Handbook. Joseph M. Flynn. 328p. 1988. 17.50 (*0-13-559220-8*) P-H.

Massachusetts Tax Handbook, 1985. Joseph M. Flynn. write for info. (*0-318-58202-3*) P-H.

Massachusetts Tax Valuation List of 1771. Ed. by Bettye H. Pruitt. LC 97-81345. 960p. 1998. reprint ed. 125.00 (*0-89725-318-3*, 1839) Picton Pr.

Massachusetts Taxation. Jacobs. 1982. 80.00 (*0-316-45539-3*, Aspen Law & Bus) Aspen Pub.

Massachusetts Taxation: The Law & the Lore. Mitchell H. Jacobs et al. LC 81-81903. 491p. 1982. suppl. ed. 80.00 (*0-316-45541-5*, Aspen Law & Bus) Aspen Pub.

Massachusetts Taxation & DOR Practice, 1996 Supplement. Frank J. Scharaffa et al. LC 88-62783. 616p. 1996. ring bd., suppl. ed. 95.00 (*1-57589-042-9*, 96-20.01-BK) Mass CLE.

Massachusetts Timeline: A Chronology of Massachusetts History, Mystery, Trivia, Legend, Lore & More. Carole Marsh. (Massachuseets Bks.). (Illus.). (J). (gr. 3-12). 1994. pap. 19.95 (*0-7933-5939-2*); lib. bdg. 29.95 (*0-7933-5938-4*); disk 29.95 (*0-7933-5940-6*) Gallopade Intl.

Massachusetts Tort Damages. Michael B. Bogdanow. 340p. 1994. spiral bd. 125.00 (*1-56257-276-8*, MICHIE); ring bd., suppl. ed. 48.00 (*0-614-03152-4*, MICHIE) LEXIS Pub.

Massachusetts Tort Damages. Michael B. Bogdanow. 1997. ring bd. 125.00 (*0-327-01047-9*, 81494-10, MICHIE) LEXIS Pub.

***Massachusetts Tort Damages.** 2nd ed. Michael B. Bogdanow. 1999. text 145.00 (*0-327-10662-X*, MICHIE) LEXIS Pub.

***Massachusetts Tort Damages.** 2nd ed. Michael B. Bogdanow. 700p. 1999. write for info. (*0-327-04938-3*, 8149411) LEXIS Pub.

Massachusetts Tort Damages, No. 5. Bogdanow. 150p. 1998. ring bd. write for info. (*0-327-00322-7*, 81495-11) LEXIS Pub.

Massachusetts Tort Law. Brody. 1993. 105.00 (*1-880637-99-5*, 81499-10, MICHIE) LEXIS Pub.

Massachusetts Tort Law. Alvin Brody & Betty Brody. LC 94-26585. 300p. 1994. spiral bd. 95.00 (*0-88063-799-4*, MICHIE) LEXIS Pub.

Massachusetts Towns & Counties. Michael J. Denis. (New England Towns & Counties Ser.). 46p. 1984. pap. 6.00 (*0-935207-03-1*) Danbury Hse Bks.

Massachusetts 2000! Coming Soon to a Calendar Near You - The 21st Century! - Complete Set of AL 2000 Items. Carole Marsh. (Two Thousand! Ser.). (Illus.). (J). (gr. 3-12). 1998. pap. 75.00 (*0-7933-9351-5*); lib. bdg. 85.00 (*0-7933-9352-3*) Gallopade Intl.

Massachusetts 2000! Coming Soon to a Calendar Near You-The 21st Century! Carole Marsh. (Two Thousand! Ser.). (Illus.). (J). (gr. 3-12). 1998. pap. 19.95 (*0-7933-8739-6*); lib. bdg. 29.95 (*0-7933-8738-8*) Gallopade Intl.

Massachusetts UFO's & Extraterrestrials! A Look at the Sightings & Science in Our State. Carole Marsh. (Carole Marsh Massachusetts Bks.). (Illus.). (J). (gr. 3-12). 1997. pap. 19.95 (*0-7933-6398-5*); lib. bdg. 29.95 (*0-7933-6397-7*) Gallopade Intl.

Massachusetts Unemployment Advocacy Guide, 1997 Edition. rev. ed. Allan Rodgers & Monica Halas. LC 96-79771. 108p. 1996. pap. text 5.00 (*1-57589-048-8*, 97-15.11-BK) Mass CLE.

***Massachusetts Vital Records.** Jay Mack Holbrook. LC 82-81851. 1998. write for info. (*0-931248-23-X*) Holbrook Res.

Massachusetts Wildlife Viewing Guide. William J. Davis. LC 96-36433. (Illus.). 96p. (Orig.). 1997. pap. 8.95 (*1-56044-426-6*) Falcon Pub Inc.

Massachusetts Woman's Divorce Handbook. rev. ed. Isabella Jancourtz. 100p. 1990. pap. 10.00 (*0-9618632-1-8*) I Jancourtz.

Massachusetts Woman's Divorce Handbook. rev. ed. Isabella Jancourtz. 104p. 1994. pap. 10.00 (*0-9618632-2-6*) I Jancourtz.

Massachusetts Woman's Divorce Handbook. 10th rev. ed. Isabella Jancourtz. 148p. 1998. pap. 19.95 (*0-9618632-3-4*) I Jancourtz.

Massachusetts Workers Compensation Guide. Standard Publishing Editors. 506p. 1998. ring bd. 124.00 (*0-923240-20-9*) Stndrd Publishing.

Massachusetts Workers' Compensation Practice Manual. 3rd ed. Paul A. Gargano. LC 93-35811. 1993. 170.00 (*0-562-57359-3*, MICHIE) LEXIS Pub.

Massachusetts Workers' Compensation Reports. annuals Department of Industrial Accidents, Reviewing Boar & Paul A. Gargano. 300p. 1990. boxed set 95.00 (*0-88063-401-4*, 81512-10, MICHIE) LEXIS Pub.

Massachusetts Workers' Compensation Reports, Vol. 12, No. 1. 200p. 1998. pap. text. write for info. (*0-327-00247-6*, 84594-10) LEXIS Pub.

Massachusetts Worker's Compensation Reports: Official Edition, Vol. 12, No. 3. 225p. 1998. pap. write for info. (*0-327-00628-5*, 8459310) LEXIS Pub.

***Massachusetts Worker's Compensation Reports Index.** 850p. 1999. write for info. (*0-327-04961-8*, 8144810) LEXIS Pub.

Massachusetts Workers' Compensation Reports, Official Edition, Vol. 12. 600p. 1999. write for info. (*0-327-01339-7*, 8151511) LEXIS Pub.

Massachusetts Worker's Compensation Reports, Official Edition, Vol. 13, No. 1. Ed. by Paul Ernest. 225p. 1999. pap. write for info. (*0-327-01358-3*, 8459510) LEXIS Pub.

***Massachusetts Worker's Compensation Reports, Official Edition, Vol. 13, No. 2.** Ed. by Paul Ernest. 200p. 1999. pap. write for info. (*0-327-01717-1*, 8459511) LEXIS Pub.

Massachusetts Zoning & Land Use Law. Levy. 1994. write for info. (*1-56257-217-2*, MICHIE) LEXIS Pub.

Massachusetts Zoning & Land Use Law: 1996 Edition. Ed. by Brian C. Levey. 417p. 1996. 95.00 (*1-55834-407-1*, 64525, MICHIE) LEXIS Pub.

Massachusetts Zoning & Land Use Law: 1998 Supplement. Ed. by Brian C. Levey. 50p. 1998. 29.50 (*0-327-00790-7*, 6452611) LEXIS Pub.

Massachusetts Zoning Manual, 1997 Supplement. Cynthia Barr. Ed. by Martin R. Healy. LC 97-75568. 388p. 1997. ring bd., suppl. ed. 49.50 (*1-57589-072-0*, 97-19.34-SP) Mass CLE.

***Massachusetts, 1860, North, U.S. Federal Census Index: Berkshire, Franklin, Hampshire, Worcester Counties.** Ronald Vern Jackson. LC 99-197565. (Illus.). 1999. write for info. (*0-89593-890-1*) Genealogical Srvcs.

Massachusetts's Unsolved Mysteries (& Their "Solutions") Includes Scientific Information & Other Activities for Students. Carole Marsh. (Massachuseets Bks.). (Illus.). (J). (gr. 3-12). 1994. pap. 19.95 (*0-7933-5786-1*); lib. bdg. 29.95 (*0-7933-5785-3*); disk 29.95 (*0-7933-5787-X*) Gallopade Intl.

Massachussetts State Police. Turner Publishing Company Staff. LC 97-61567. (Illus.). 304p. 1998. 39.95 (*1-56311-388-0*) Turner Pub KY.

Massacio the Documents with the Collaboration of Gino Corti. James Beck. LC 78-67679. 1978. 28.00 (*0-686-92649-8*) J J Augustin.

Massacre! Frank Laumer. LC 68-9812. (Illus.). 1968. pap. 15.95 (*0-8130-0479-9*) U Press Fla.

Massacre: A Survey of Today's American Indian. Robert Gessner. LC 72-38831. (Civil Liberties in American History Ser.). 418p. 1972. reprint ed. lib. bdg. 45.00 (*0-306-70445-5*) Da Capo.

Massacre: An Historical Perspective. Eric Carlton. LC 93-12373. 240p. (C). 1993. write for info. (*0-7185-1469-6*) St Martin.

Massacre - The Custer Cover-Up: The Original Maps of Custer's Battlefield. W. Kent King. LC 88-50601. (Custer Trails Ser.: Vol. 3). (Illus.). 310p. (C). 1989. 45.00 (*0-912783-15-X*) Upton & Sons.

Massacre Along the Medicine Road: A Social History of the Indian War of 1864 in Nebraska Territory. Ronald Becher. LC 98-48924. 1999. pap. 22.95 (*0-87004-387-0*) Caxton.

Massacre along the Medicine Road: A Social History of the Indian War of 1864 in Nebraska Territory. Ronald Becher. Ed. by Wayne Cornell. LC 98-48924. 500p. 1999. 32.95 (*0-87004-389-7*, 038970) Caxton.

Massacre & Retribution: Forgotten Colonial Wars of the 19th Century. Ian Hernon. LC 99-188380. (Illus.). 224p. 1998. 39.95 (*0-7509-1846-2*, Pub. by Sutton Pub Ltd) Intl Pubs Mktg.

Massacre at Bad Axe. Ed. by Crawford B. Thayer. (Black Hawk War Eye-Witness Ser.). (Illus.). 544p. (Orig.). 1984. pap. text 9.95 (*0-9611000-2-8*) Thayer Assocs.

Massacre at Cawnpore. large type ed. Vivian Stuart. 432p. 1995. 25.99 (*0-7089-3229-0*) Ulverscroft.

***Massacre at Cheyenne Hole: Lieutenant Austin Henely & the Sappa Creek Controversy.** John H. Monnett. LC 99-10853. (Illus.). 128p. 1999. 24.95 (*0-87081-527-X*) Univ Pr Colo.

Massacre at Fall Creek. Jessamyn West. 380p. 1986. pap. 12.00 (*0-15-657681-3*, Harvest Bks) Harcourt.

Massacre at Fort Mims. David P. Mason. 196p. 1989. pap. 14.95 (*0-926291-02-5*) Greenberry Pub.

Massacre at Glencoe. Ed. by John S. Keltie. 49p. 1994. pap. 12.95 (*1-886015-07-4*) Sandlins Bks.

Massacre at Glencoe. deluxe limited ed. Ed. by John S. Keltie. 49p. 1994. 85.00 (*1-886015-06-6*) Sandlins Bks.

Massacre at Goliad. Elmer Kelton & Frank H. Spearman. 1999. mass mkt. 5.99 (*0-8125-7489-3*, Pub. by Forge NYC) St Martin.

Massacre at Ludlow: Four Reports, 1914-1915. Ed. by Leon Stein & Philip Taft. LC 76-156431. (American Labor Ser., No. 2). 1974. 27.95 (*0-405-02957-8*) Ayer.

Massacre at Malmedy: The Story of Jochen Peiper's Battle Group - Ardennes, December, 1994. Charles Whiting. (Illus.). 244p. 1996. pap. 16.95 (*0-85052-512-8*, Pub. by Leo Cooper) Trans-Atl Phila.

Massacre at Myall Creek. John Summons. LC 93-21583. 1994. pap. 11.95 (*0-521-44763-1*) Cambridge U Pr.

Massacre at Paris see Complete Plays

Massacre at Paris: With the Death of the Duke of Guise. Christopher Marlowe. LC 73-25759. (English Experience Ser.: No. 335). 1971. reprint ed. 15.00 (*90-221-0335-8*) Walter J Johnson.

Massacre at Parit Sulong. Gilbert Mant. 1996. pap. text 16.95 (*0-86417-732-1*, Pub. by Kangaroo Pr) Seven Hills Bk.

Massacre at Powder River. G. Clifton Wisler. 1997. mass mkt. 5.99 (*0-425-15675-3*) Berkley Pub.

Massacre at Sand Creek: Narrative Voices. Bruce Cutler. LC 94-31306. (American Indian Literature & Critical Studies Ser.: Vol. 16). xi, 252p. 1997. pap. 11.95 (*0-8061-2990-5*) U of Okla Pr.

Massacre at the Yuma Crossing: Spanish Relations with the Quechans, 1779-1782. Mark Santiago. LC 98-8867. (Illus.). 240p. 1998. 35.00 (*0-8165-1824-6*) U of Ariz Pr.

Massacre at Waco: The Shocking True Story of Cult Leader David Koresh & the Branch Davidians. Clifford L. Linedecker. 1993. mass mkt. 4.99 (*0-312-95226-0*) St Martin.

Massacre in History. Ed. by Mark Levene & Penny Roberts. LC 97-38276. (Illus.). 320p. 1998. pap. 25.00 (*1-57181-935-5*) Berghahn Bks.

Massacre in History. Ed. by Mark Levene & Penny Roberts. LC 97-38276. (Illus.). 320p. 1999. 65.00 (*1-57181-934-7*) Berghahn Bks.

Massacre in Mexico. Elena Poniatowska. Tr. by Helen R. Lane. (Illus.). 352p. (C). 1991. pap. 18.95 (*0-8262-0817-7*) U of Mo Pr.

Massacre in Mexico: Killings & Cover-Up in the State of Guerrero. MN. Advocates for Human Rights Staff. 33p. (Orig.). 1995. pap. 5.00 (*0-929293-30-4*) MN Advocates.

Massacre in Milwaukee: The Macabre Case of Jeffrey Dahmer. Richard W. Jaeger & M. William Balousek. Ed. by Karen Faster. (Illus.). 235p. (Orig.). 1991. pap. 9.95 (*1-878569-09-0*) WI State Journal.

Massacre in Paradise: The Untold Story of the Fountain Valley Massacre. Harold Willocks. Ed. by Marvin Williams. (Illus.). 1997. pap. 25.00 (*1-891013-00-9*) H W L Willocks.

Massacre in Shansi. Nat Brandt. LC 93-41314. (Illus.). 358p. 1994. reprint ed. pap. 111.00 (*0-608-07596-5*, 205991100010) Bks Demand.

Massacre in the Pampas, 1872: Britain & Argentina in the Age of Migration. John Lynch. LC 97-35259. (Illus.). xiii, 256p. 1998. 28.95 (*0-8061-3018-0*) U of Okla Pr.

Massacre of El Mozote: A Parable of the Cold War. Mark Danner. LC 94-2637. 1994. pap. 13.00 (*0-679-75525-X*) Vin Bks.

***Massacre of Glencoe.** John Buchan. 176p. 1999. pap. 40.00 (*1-86227-062-7*, Pub. by Spellmnt Pubs) St Mut.

Massacre of Saint Bartholomew. Soman. 1975. lib. bdg. 135.00 (*90-247-1652-7*, Pub. by M Nijhoff) Kluwer Academic.

Massacre of the Dreamers: Essays on Xicanisma. Ana Castillo. LC 95-12412. 258p. 1995. pap. 14.95 (*0-452-27424-9*, Plume) Dutton Plume.

Massacre of the Innocents. Bin Ramke. LC 94-37407. (Iowa Poetry Prize Ser.). 95p. (Orig.). 1995. pap. 11.95 (*0-87745-492-2*) U of Iowa Pr.

Massacre of the Innocents: Infanticide in Britain, 1800-1939. Lionel Rose. (Illus.). 215p. (C). 1986. 45.00 (*0-7102-0339-X*, Routledge Thoemms) Routledge.

Massacre of Troops Near Fort Phil Kearney Secretary of Interior. 45p. 1987. pap. 6.95 (*0-87770-433-3*) Ye Galleon.

Massacre on the Gila: An Account of the Last Major Battle Between American Indians, with Reflections on the Origin of War. Clifton B. Kroeber & Bernard L. Fontana. LC 86-24974. 232p. 1993. reprint ed. pap. 17.95 (*0-8165-1359-7*) U of Ariz Pr.

Massacre on the Lordsburg Road: A Tragedy of the Apache Wars. Marc Simmons. LC 97-19530. (Elma Dill Russell Spencer Series in the West & Southwest: Vol. 15). (Illus.). 256p. 1997. 29.95 (*0-89096-772-5*) Tex A&M Univ Pr.

Massacres: A Historical Perspective. Eric Carlton. 207p. 1994. 67.95 (*1-85928-017-X*, Pub. by Scolar Pr) Ashgate Pub Co.

***Massacres of the Mountains: A History of the Indian Wars of the Far West.** J. P. Dunn, Jr. (Illus.). ix, 784p. 2000. write for info. (*1-58218-203-5*); pap. write for info. (*1-58218-204-3*) Digital Scanning.

Massage. Steven Berkoff. 10.00 (*0-929741-10-2*) Playsmith.

Massage. Denise Brown. (Headway Lifeguides Ser.). (Illus.). 88p. 1995. pap. 15.95 (*0-340-55949-7*, Pub. by Headway) Trafalgar.

Massage. Denise W. Brown. (Teach Yourself Ser.). 192p. 1996. pap. 9.95 (*0-8442-3108-8*, Teach Yrslf) NTC Contemp Pub Co.

Massage. Henry Flesh. LC 98-74034. 384p. 1999. pap. 15.95 (*1-888451-06-8*, AKB03, Pub. by Akashic Bks) SPD-Small Pr Dist.

***Massage.** Ed. by Harpercollins UK Staff. (Collins Gem Ser.). (Illus.). 256p. 2000. pap. 7.95 (*0-00-472469-0*, Pub. by HarpC) Trafalgar.

Massage. Nitya LaCroix. (101 Essential Tips Ser.). (Illus.). 72p. 1995. pap. 4.95 (*1-56458-990-0*) DK Pub Inc.

Massage. Lorenz Staff. 1998. 12.95 (*1-85967-753-3*) Anness Pub.

Massage. Rosalind Widdowson. 213p. 1995. write for info. (*1-57215-081-5*) World Pubns.

Massage: A Career at Your Fingertips. 3rd ed. Martin Ashley. (Illus.). 300p. 1998. pap. 22.00 (*0-9644662-6-0*) Enterprse Pub.

Massage: For Health, Relaxation & Vitality. Sarah Porter. 1998. pap. 12.95 (*1-85967-855-6*, Lorenz Bks) Anness Pub.

Massage: Index of Modern Information. Floyd J. Kazis. LC 88-47989. 150p. 1989. 47.50 (*1-55914-058-5*); pap. 44.50 (*1-55914-059-3*) ABBE Pubs Assn.

***Massage: Introductory Guide to the Healing Power of Touch.** Stewart Mitchell. (New Perspectives Ser.). 2000. pap. 9.95 (*1-86204-626-3*, Pub. by Element MA) Penguin Putnam.

***Massage: Learn the Healing Art of Touch.** Yvonne Worth. (Spa in a Box Ser.). 2000. 12.95 incl. audio (*1-86204-678-6*, Pub. by Element MA) Penguin Putnam.

Massage: The Healing Power of Touch. Andrews & McMeel Staff. (Little Bks.). 1998. 4.95 (*0-8362-5221-7*) Andrews & McMeel.

Massage: The Ultimate Illustrated Guide. Clare Maxwell-Hudson. LC 98-32293. 168p. 1999. 24.95 (*0-7894-4176-4*) DK Pub Inc.

Massage & Aromatherapy. Lorenz. 1999. 15.98 (*1-84038-204-X*, Pub. by Hermes Hse) Random.

Massage & Aromatherapy: A Guide for Health Professionals. A. Vickers. (Illus.). 328p. (Orig.). 1996. pap. 55.00 (*1-56593-349-4*, 0673) Singular Publishing.

Massage & Aromatherapy: A Practical Approach for NVQ Level 3. Lyn Goldberg. 216p. 1999. pap. 39.50 (*0-7487-2081-2*, Pub. by S Thornes Pubs) Trans-Atl Phila.

Massage & Loving. Anne Hooper. LC 88-82688. (Illus.). 128p. 1995. pap. 12.95 (*0-8050-1019-X*, Owl) H Holt & Co.

Massage & Other Plays. Michael Wilcox. (Methuen New Theatrescripts Ser.). 55p. (C). 1988. pap. 8.95 (*0-413-16080-7*, A0169) Heinemann.

***Massage, Aromatherapy & Yoga.** Nitya Lacroix. (Practical Handbook Ser.). 1999. pap. 12.95 (*0-7548-0023-7*, Lorenz Bks) Anness Pub.

Massage Basics. David Sechi. LC 99-170600. (Illus.). 160p. 1999. pap. 14.95 (*0-8069-4895-7*) Sterling.

Massage Book. George Downing. 1972. pap. 12.00 (*0-394-70770-2*) Random.

Massage Book. Hosler. (Runner's World Ser.). 1982. pap. 9.95 (*0-02-499560-6*, Macmillan Coll) P-H.

Massage Book. Barbara K. Koplan. (Runner's World Ser.). 1982. pap. 9.95 (*0-02-499550-9*, Macmillan Coll) P-H.

Massage Book. 25th anniversary ed. George Downing. LC 97-27511. 1998. pap. 14.95 (*0-679-77789-X*) Random.

Massage During Pregnancy. 2nd rev. ed. Bette Waters. (Illus.). 177p. 1995. pap. 16.95 (*0-9665584-0-5*) Bluwaters Pr.

Massage for Beginners. 4th ed. Marilyn Aslani. LC 97-2636. (Illus.). 96p. 1997. pap. 16.95 (*0-06-273398-2*, Harper Ref) HarpC.

Massage for Body & Soul. K. Schutte. LC 99-36725. 1999. pap. text 11.95 (*0-8069-2037-8*) Sterling.

Massage for Busy People: Five Minutes to a More Relaxed Body. Dawn Groves. LC 98-32404. (Illus.). 160p. 1999. pap. 10.95 (*1-57731-082-9*) New Wrld Lib.

Massage for Common Ailments. Sara Thomas. 1989. pap. 9.95 (*0-671-67552-4*, Fireside) S&S Trade Pap.

Massage for Cyclists. Rogen Pozeznik. LC 95-61678. 1997. pap. 14.95 (*0-941950-33-6*) Vitesse Pr.

***Massage for Dummies.** Steve Capellini. (For Dummies (Lifestyles) Ser.). (Illus.). 2000. 4.95 (*0-7624-0839-1*) Running Pr.

Massage for Dummies. Steve Capellini & Michel Van Welden. (For Dummies Ser.). (Illus.). 384p. 1999. pap. 19.99 (*0-7645-5172-8*, Dummies Trade Pr) IDG Bks.

An Asterisk (*) at the beginning of an entry indicates that the title is appearing for the first time.

Massage for Health & Healing: Ayurvedic & Spiritual Energy Approach. S. V. Govindan. (C). 1996. 40.00 (*81-7017-330-2*, Pub. by Abhinav) S Asia.

Massage for Healthier Children. Marybetts Sinclair. LC 92-11050. (Illus.). 110p. (Orig.). 1992. pap. 15.95 (*0-914728-76-8*) Wingbow Pr.

Massage for Horses, Vol. 38. Mary Bromiley. (Threshold Picture Guides Ser.). (Illus.). 24p. (YA). 1996. pap. 12.00 (*1-872082-87-4*, Pub. by Kenilworth Pr) Half Halt Pr.

*__Massage for Lovers: Touch Techniques for Enchancing Romance.__ Tim Freke. 128p. 1999. pap. text 14.95 (*0-8069-1807-1*) Sterling.

*__Massage for Nurses.__ Walker. 2001. pap. 15.95 (*0-7668-0692-8*) Delmar.

Massage for Pain Relief. Peijian Shen. LC 95-31371. 1996. pap. 14.95 (*0-679-76954-4*) Random.

*__Massage for Sports.__ Joan Watt. 1999. pap. 29.95 (*1-86126-160-8*, Pub. by Cro1wood) Trafalgar.

*__Massage for Sports Health Care Professionals.__ 72p. 1999. 69.00 (*0-7360-0208-1*) Human Kinetics.

Massage for Therapists. Margaret Hollis. 125p. 1987. pap. 23.50 (*0-632-01757-0*) Blackwell Sci.

Massage for Therapists. 2nd ed. Margaret Hollis. LC 98-15039. 208p. 1998. pap. text 34.95 (*0-632-04788-7*) Blackwell Sci.

*__Massage for Total Well-Being: A Hands-On Guide to Reviving Body, Mind & Spirit.__ Ann Kent Rush. (Illus.). 2000. 25.00 (*0-7893-0490-2*) Universe.

Massage in a Box: All the Tools You Need to Give & Receive Great Massages. (Illus.). 64p. 1999. 24.95 (*1-86204-571-2*, Pub. by Element MA) Penguin Putnam.

Massage Made Easy. Mario-Paul Cassar. 160p. 1995. pap. 16.95 (*1-882606-17-5*) Peoples Med Soc.

*__Massage Manual: Massage, Aromatherapy, Shiatsu, Reflexology.__ Mark Evans et al. (Illus.). 192p. 2000. 19.95 (*1-84038-227-9*) Hermes Hse.

*__Massage National Exam Questions & Answers.__ 3rd rev. ed. Daphna R. Moore. (Illus.). 202p. 2000. pap. 49.95 (*1-892693-08-9*) Hughes Henshaw Pubs.

Massage Parlor Prostitution. Paul Rasmussen. 163p. text. write for info. (*0-8290-1029-7*) Irvington.

Massage Therapist's Guide to Pathology. Ed. by Ruth Werner & Ben E. Benjamin. LC 98-4257. 489p. 1998. 37.00 (*0-683-30210-8*) Lppncott W & W.

Massage Therapy: Principles & Practice. Susan G. Salvo. Ed. by Maureen Pfeiffer. LC 98-8139. (Illus.). 590p. (C). 1999. pap. text. write for info. (*0-7216-7419-4*, W B Saunders Co) Harcrt Hlth Sci Grp.

Massage Therapy: Theory & Practice. Jean Loving. LC 98-3419. 300p. 1998. pap. text 42.95 (*0-8385-6161-6*) Appleton & Lange.

Massage Therapy Career Guide for Hands-On Success. Capellini. LC 98-24161. (MASSAGE). 288p. 1998. 22.95 (*1-56253-382-7*) Thomson Learn.

Massage Therapy Exam Questions. 2nd rev. ed. Daphna R. Moore & Gina Perrusquia. LC 99-12414. Orig. Title: How to Pass Your Massage Therapy Exams. 141p. 1999. pap. text 38.00 (*1-892693-02-X*) Hughes Henshaw Pubs.

Massage Therapy Healing Techniques Workbook. rev. ed. Julie Donnelly. (Illus.). 57p. 1996. pap., wbk. ed. 15.95 (*1-929632-00-2*) Julstro Pubns.

Massage Therapy in Ayurveda. Vaidya Bhagwan Dash. (Pancakarma Therapy of Ayurveda Ser.: No. 1). (C). 1992. 21.00 (*81-7022-380-6*, Pub. by Concept) S Asia.

Massaging with Essential Oils: The Complete Illustrated Guide to Aromatherapy. Clare Maxwell-Hudson. LC 94-16051. (Illus.). 112p. 1994. 19.95 (*1-56458-642-1*) DK Pub Inc.

Massarenes. Quida. LC 79-8186. reprint ed. 44.50 (*0-404-62087-6*) AMS Pr.

Massawomeck: Raiders & Traders into the Chesapeake Bay in the Seventeenth Century. James F. Pendergast. LC 90-56111. (Transactions Ser.: Vol. 81, Pt. 2). (Illus.). 93p. (C). 1991. pap. 15.00 (*0-87169-812-9*, T812-PEJ) Am Philos.

Massenarbeitslosigkeit Durch Politikversagen? Diskussionsbeitrage. Bremer Gesellschaft fur Wirtschaftsforschung e.V. (GER., Illus.). 206p. 1996. 24.95 (*3-631-30708-X*) P Lang Pubng.

Massena's Retreat, Fuentes de Onoro, Albuera, Tarragona, Dec. 1810-Dec. 1811 see History of the Peninsular War

Massenet. James Harding. (Music Ser.). 1990. 32.50 (*0-306-79713-5*) Da Capo.

Massenet: A Chronicle of His Life & Times. Demar Irvine. LC 93-24443. (Illus.). 380p. 1993. 32.95 (*0-931340-63-2*, Amadeus Pr) Timber.

Massenet: A Chronicle of His Life & Times. Demar B. Irvine. (Illus.). 400p. 1997. pap. 22.95 (*1-57467-024-7*, Amadeus Pr) Timber.

Massenet & His Operas. Henry T. Finck. 1976. reprint ed. 42.50 (*0-404-12912-9*) AMS Pr.

Massenet Compendium, 2. Otto T. Salzer. LC 84-60802. (Illus.). 327p. (Orig.). 1984. pap. 15.00 (*0-9615735-2-X*) Massenet Soc.

Massenet Compendium, Set. Otto T. Salzer. (Illus.). 327p. (Orig.). 1984. pap. 25.00 (*0-9615735-0-3*) Massenet Soc.

Massenet Compendium, Vol. 1. Otto T. Salzer. (Illus.). 327p. (Orig.). 1984. pap. 15.00 (*0-9615735-1-1*) Massenet Soc.

Massengill. R. Massengill. LC 96-6072. (Illus.). 64p. 1996. text 13.00 (*0-312-14367-2*) St Martin.

Masseni: A Novel. Tidiane Dem. Tr. by Frances Frenaye from FRE. LC 82-36. xvii, 174p. 1982. 16.95 (*0-8071-1011-6*) La State U Pr.

Massenmediale Aufklaerung: Eine Sprachwissenschaftliche Untersuchung Zu Ratgebenden Beitragen von Elektronischen und Printmedien. Wilhelm Franke. (GER., Illus.). 510p. 1997. pap. 82.95 (*3-631-31079-X*) P Lang Pubng.

Masserschmitt Rf110 Zerstorer Aces - Aircraft of the Aces 25: Aircraft of the Aces 25. John Weal. (Illus.). 96p. 1999. pap. 17.95 (*1-85532-753-8*, 128255AE, Pub. by Ospry) Motorbooks Intl.

Masses. Pietro D. Antoni & Giovanni B. Bassani. Ed. by Anne Schnoebelen. (Seventeenth-Century Italian Sacred Music Ser.: Vol. 10). 272p. 1999. 125.00 (*0-8153-2416-2*) Garland.

Masses. Jean Maillard. Ed. by R. Rosenstock. (Collected Works: Vol. XVI, Pt. 1). (ENG, FRE & LAT.). 282p. 1997. 70.00 (*1-896926-07-X*) Inst Mediaeval Mus.

Masses & Man: Nationalist & Fascist Perceptions of Reality. George L. Mosse. LC 80-15399. xi, 362p. 1980. 45.00 (*0-86527-334-0*) Fertig.

Masses & Man: Nationalist & Fascist Perceptions of Reality. George L. Mosse. LC 87-6131. 374p. 1987. reprint ed. pap. 18.95 (*0-8143-1895-9*) Wayne St U Pr.

Masses & Mixings of Quarks & Leptons: Shizuoka, Japan 19-21 March, 1997. Ed. by Yoshio Koide. LC 98-196733. 340p. 1998. 88.00 (*981-02-3363-9*) World Scientific Pub.

Masses & Motets. Giovanni P. Da Palestrina. 240p. 1993. pap. 11.95 (*0-486-27631-7*) Dover.

*__Masses Are Asses, Vol. 71.__ Pedro Pietri. 2000. pap. 8.95 (*1-892295-62-8*) Green Integer.

Masses by Alessandro Grandi, Giovanni Battista Chinelli, Tarquinio Merula, Giovanni Antonio Rigatti. Ed. by Anne Schnoebelen. (Seventeenth-Century Italian Sacred Music Ser.: No. 4). 324p. 1996. text 109.00 (*0-8153-2363-8*) Garland.

Masses by Carlo Milanuzzi, Leandro Gallerano, Alessandro Grandi. Ed. by Anne Schnoebelen. (Seventeenth-Century Italian Sacred Music Ser.: Vol. 3). 304p. 1996. text 109.00 (*0-8153-2168-6*) Garland.

Masses by Domenico Scorpione, Lorenzo Penna, Giovanni Paolo Colonna. Ed. by Anne Schnoebelen. (Seventeenth-Century Italian Sacred Music Ser.: Vol. 9). 218p. 1998. 125.00 (*0-8153-2415-4*) Garland.

Masses by Gasparo Villani, Allessandro Grandi, Pietro Lappi, Bentivoglio Leva. Ed. by Anne Schoebelen. LC 95-32690. (Seventeenth-Century Italian Sacred Music Ser.). 292p. 1995. text 99.00 (*0-8153-2166-X*) Garland.

Masses by Giovanni Andrea Florimi, Giovanni Francesco Mognossa, & Benifazio Graziani. Ed. by Anne Schnoebelen. (Seventeenth-Century Italian Sacred Music Ser.: Vol. 8). 288p. 1998. 110.00 (*0-8153-2414-6*) Garland.

Masses by Giovanni Francesco Capello, Amadio Freddi, Ercole Porta, Ignazio Donati. Ed. by Ann Schnoebelen. LC 95-32691. (Seventeenth-Century Italian Sacred Music Ser.: Vol. 2). 280p. 1995. text 109.00 (*0-8153-2167-8*) Garland.

Masses by Giovanni Pietro Finatti, Maurizio Cazzati, Giulio Cesare Arresti, Carlo Donato Cossoni. Ed. by Anne Schnoebelen. LC 56-5. (Seventeenth-Century Italian Sacred Music Ser.: Vol. 6). 328p. 1997. text 109.00 (*0-8153-2412-X*) Garland.

Masses by Giovanni Rovetta, Ortensio Polidori, Giovanni Battista Chinelli, Orazio Tarditi. Ed. by Anne Schnoebelen. (Seventeenth-Century Italian Sacred Music Ser.: Vol. 5). 280p. 1996. text 109.00 (*0-8153-2358-1*) Garland.

Masses by Maurizio Cazzati, Giovanni Antonio Grossi & Giovanni Legrenzi. Ed. by Anne Schnoebelen. LC 56-5. (Seventeenth-Century Italian Sacred Music Ser.: Vol. 7). 296p. 1997. text 105.00 (*0-8153-2413-8*) Garland.

*__Masses, Classes & the Public Sphere.__ Ed. by Mike Hill & Warren Montag. 288p. 2000. 30.00 (*1-85984-777-3*, Pub. by Verso) Norton.

Masses, Classes, Ideas: Studies on Politics & Philosophy before & after Marx. Etienne Balibar. Tr. by James Swenson. LC 93-19168. (ENG & FRE.). 272p. (C). 1994. pap. 20.99 (*0-415-90602-4*, A7328) Routledge.

Masses in Flight: The Global Crisis of Internal Displacement. Roberta Cohen & Francis M. Deng. LC 98-8939. 414p. 1998. text 52.95 (*0-8157-1512-9*); pap. text 22.95 (*0-8157-1511-0*) Brookings.

Masses Magazine, 1911-1917: Odyssey of an Era. Thomas A. Maik. LC 93-43979. (Modern American History Ser.). 272p. 1994. text 30.00 (*0-8153-1642-9*) Garland.

Masses Nos. 5 & 6 in Full Score. Franz Schubert. 336p. 1995. pap. 17.95 (*0-486-28832-3*) Dover.

Masses of Francesco Soriano: A Style-Critical Study. S. Philip Kniseley. LC 67-22198. (University of Florida Humanities Monographs: No. 26). 92p. reprint ed. pap. 30.00 (*0-7837-4934-1*, 204460000004) Bks Demand.

Masses of Fundamental Particles: Cargese 1996: Proceedings of a NATO ASI Held in Cargese, France, August 5-17, 1996. North Atlantic Treaty Organization Staff. Ed. by Maurice Levy et al. LC 97-31221. (NATO ASI Ser.: Vol. 363). 404p. (C). 1997. text 125.00 (*0-306-45694-X*, Kluwer Plenum) Kluwer Academic.

Masses with Children. Frwd. by Alan F. Detscher. (Liturgy Documentary Ser.: Vol. 12). 47p. (Orig.). 1996. pap. 5.95 (*1-57455-107-8*) US Catholic.

Massess Are Asses = Las masas son crasas. Pedro Pietri. Tr. & Prologue by Alfredo Matilla Rivas. LC 98-202585. xv, 197 p. 1997. write for info. (*0-86581-499-6*) Instituto de Cultura Puertorriquena.

Massey & Archie: A Study of Two Hopwellian Homesteads in the Western Illinois Uplands. Kenneth B. Farnsworth & Ann L. Koski. LC 85-13281. (Kampsville Archeological Center Research Ser.: No. 3). (Illus.). 280p. (Orig.). 1985. pap. 9.95 (*0-942118-20-0*) Ctr Amer Arche.

Massey Family of Worcester, Maryland. Barbara M. Horsoman. LC 96-132818. 596p. 1995. pap. 18.00 (*0-7884-0364-8*) Heritage Bk.

Massey-Ferguson Tractors. Michael Williams. (Illus.). 128p. 1987. 29.95 (*0-85236-203-X*, Pub. by Farming Pr) Diamond Farm Bk.

Massey-Ferguson/Ferguson Massey-Harris: I&T Shop Manual - Massey Ferguson Collection MF175, MF180 - MF205, MF210, MF220 - MF2675, MF2705 - MF2745, MF2775, MF2805. (Illus.). 272p. Date not set. reprint ed. pap. 29.95 (*0-87288-362-0*, MF-202) Intertec Pub.

Massey-Ferguson/Ferguson Massey-Harris: I&T Shop Manual - Massey Ferguson Collection MF65 - MF85, MF88, MF Super 90, MF Super 90WR - MF1100, MF1130 - MF1150, MF1105 - MF1135 - MF1155 - MF1080, MF1085. (Illus.). 408p. Date not set. reprint ed. pap. 29.95 (*0-87288-376-0*, MF-201) Intertec Pub.

Massey-Ferguson/Ferguson Massey-Harris: I&T Shop Manual - Minneapolis Moline Collection. (Illus.). 432p. Date not set. reprint ed. pap. 29.95 (*0-87288-377-9*, MM-201) Intertec Pub.

Massey-Ferguson/Ferguson Massey-Harris: I&T Shop Manual - Model MF285. (Illus.). 48p. Date not set. reprint ed. pap. 24.95 (*0-87288-136-9*, MF-36) Intertec Pub.

Massey-Ferguson/Ferguson Massey-Harris: I&T Shop Manual - Models MF1010 (Standard, Hydro), 1020 (Standard, Hydro) (Illus.). 104p. Date not set. pap. 24.95 (*0-87288-568-2*, MF-47) Intertec Pub.

Massey-Ferguson/Ferguson Massey-Harris: I&T Shop Manual - Models MF135, MF150, MF165. (Illus.). 96p. Date not set. reprint ed. pap. 24.95 (*0-87288-129-6*, MF-27) Intertec Pub.

Massey-Ferguson/Ferguson Massey-Harris: I&T Shop Manual - Models MF230, MF235, MF240, MF245, MF250. (Illus.). 96p. Date not set. reprint ed. pap. 24.95 (*0-87288-411-2*, MF-42) Intertec Pub.

Massey-Ferguson/Ferguson Massey-Harris: I&T Shop Manual - Models MF255, MF265, MF270, MF275, MF290. (Illus.). 96p. Date not set. reprint ed. pap. 24.95 (*0-87288-527-5*, MF-43) Intertec Pub.

Massey-Ferguson/Ferguson Massey-Harris: I&T Shop Manual - Models MF340, MF350, MF355, MF360, MF399. (Illus.). 216p. Date not set. pap. 24.95 (*0-87288-539-9*, MF-46) Intertec Pub.

Massey-Ferguson/Ferguson Massey-Harris: I&T Shop Manual - Models MF3505, MF3525, MF3545. (Illus.). 112p. Date not set. reprint ed. pap. 24.95 (*0-87288-391-4*, MF-44) Intertec Pub.

Massey-Ferguson/Ferguson Massey-Harris: I&T Shop Manual - Models MF670, MF690, MF698. (Illus.). 72p. Date not set. pap. 24.95 (*0-87288-438-4*, MF-41) Intertec Pub.

Massey-Ferguson/Ferguson Massey-Harris: I&T Shop Manual - Models TE20, TO20, TO30. (Illus.). 32p. Date not set. reprint ed. pap. 24.95 (*0-87288-118-0*, FE-2) Intertec Pub.

Massey-Ferguson/Ferguson Massey-Harris: I&T Shop Manual - Models TO35, TO35 Diesel, F40, MH50, MHF202, MF35, MF35 Diesel, MF50, MF202, MF204. (Illus.). 80p. Date not set. reprint ed. pap. 24.95 (*0-87288-124-5*, MF-14) Intertec Pub.

Massey Tractor Data Book. Keith Oltrogge. LC 99-43587. (Tractor Data Bks.). (Illus.). 160p. 1999. pap. text 11.95 (*0-7603-0599-4*, 128922AP, Pub. by MBI Pubg) Motorbooks Intl.

Massey Tractors. Andrew Morland & Charles H. Wendel. (Farm Tractor Color History Ser.). (Illus.). 128p. 1992. pap. 21.95 (*0-87938-618-5*) MBI Pubg.

Massillon Memories: The Inside Story of the Greatest Show in High School Football. Scott H. Shook. (Illus.). 288p. 1998. 19.95 (*0-9667027-0-0*); pap. 12.95 (*0-9667027-1-9*) Massillon Memories.

Massillon Tigers Story: The First 100 Years. John E. White, Jr. (Illus.). 272p. (Orig.). 1994. pap. 17.50 (*0-9642448-0-2*) Classic Pr AZ.

Massimiliano Fuksas. Massimiliano Fuksas. Ed. by Oscar R. Ojeda. (Contemporary World Architects Ser.). (Illus.). 132p. (Orig.). 1997. pap. 19.99 (*1-56496-361-6*) Rockport Pubs.

Massimiliano Fuksas: Recent Buildings & Projects. John Welsh. (Illus.). 128p. 1994. pap. 45.00 (*3-7643-5546-8*, Pub. by Birkhauser) Princeton Arch.

Massimilla Doni. Honore de Balzac. (FRE.). 264p. 1964. pap. 19.95 (*0-7859-5321-3*) Fr & Eur.

Massingham Butterfly, & Other Stories. Joseph S. Fletcher. LC 76-122699. (Short Story Index Reprint Ser.). 1977. 19.95 (*0-8369-3532-2*) Ayer.

Massive Action Marketing: How to Grow Your MLM Business Outside Your Warm Market. Randy Gage. 1996. 77.00 (*1-884667-12-0*) Prime Concepts Grp.

Massive Action Study Guide: How to Grow Your MLM Business Outside Your Warm Market. Randy Gage. 168p. 1996. pap. 17.00 (*1-884667-11-2*) Prime Concepts Grp.

Massive at Last! How to Build More Muscle Mass Than You Ever Thought Possible. Robert Kennedy & Dwayne Hines, II. LC 97-901067. (Illus.). 64p. 1997. pap. 10.50 (*1-55210-007-3*, Pub. by MuscleMag Intl) BookWorld.

*__Massive Entanglement, Marginal Influence: Carter & Korea in Crisis.__ William H. Gleysteen. LC 99-50593. 1999. 29.95 (*0-8157-3170-1*) Brookings.

Massive File on Zwetschkenbaum: A Novel. Albert Drach. Tr. by Harvey I. Dunkle from GER. LC 95-34150. (Studies in Austrian Literature, Culture, & Thought). Orig. Title: Das Grosse Protokoll Gegen Zwetschkenbaum. 285p. (Orig.). 1996. pap. 21.50 (*1-57241-003-5*) Ariadne CA.

Massive Mandate for Rajiv Gandhi. G. G. Mirachandani. 1985. 24.95 (*0-318-36588-X*) Asia Bk Corp.

Massive Myths with Simple Solutions: Revolutionary Breakthrough in Drug Dependencies Derived from Psychopharmacology. Paul M. D'Amico. (Illus.). 290p. (YA). 1987. 10.00 (*0-89288-163-1*) Damico.

Massive Neutrinos in Physics & Astrophysics. R. N. Mohapatra & Palash B. Pal. 336p. 1991. text 78.00 (*981-02-0434-5*); pap. text 41.00 (*981-02-0435-3*) World Scientific Pub.

Massive Neutrinos in Physics & Astrophysics. Rabindra N. Mohapatra & Palash B. Pal. 380p. 1998. 48.00 (*981-02-3373-6*) World Scientific Pub.

Massive Parallelism - Hardware, Software & Applications: Proceedings of the 2nd International Workshop. Ed. by Mario M. Furnari. LC 94-33392. 444p. 1994. text 109.00 (*981-02-2037-5*) World Scientific Pub.

Massive Stars in Starbursts: Proceedings of the Massive Stars in Starbursts Meeting, Baltimore, 1990 May 15-17. Ed. by Claus Leitherer et al. (Space Telescope Science Institute Symposium Ser.: No. 5). 349p. 1991. text 69.95 (*0-521-40465-7*) Cambridge U Pr.

*__Massive Swelling: Celebrity Re-Examined as a Grotesque, Crippling Disease & Other Cultural Revolutions.__ Cintra Wilson. LC 99-56496. 256p. 2000. 23.95 (*0-670-89162-2*, Viking) Viking Penguin.

Massive Transfusion. Ed. by Leigh C. Jefferies & Mark E. Brecher. (Illus.). 166p. (C). 1994. text 45.00 (*1-56395-031-6*) Am Assn Blood.

Massively Parallel Artificial Intelligence. Ed. by Hiroaki Kitano & James A. Hendler. (Illus.). 442p. 1994. pap. text 45.00 (*0-262-61102-3*) MIT Pr.

M

Massively Parallel, Optical, & Neural Computing in Japan. Ed. by Ulrich Wattenberg. LC 92-19767. 172p. (gr. 12). 1992. pap. 75.00 (*90-5199-098-7*, Pub. by IOS Pr) IOS Press.

Massively Parallel, Optical, & Neural Computing in the United States. Ed. by Gilbert Kalb & Robert Moxley. LC 92-19769. 216p. (gr. 12). 1992. pap. 85.00 (*90-5199-097-9*, Pub. by IOS Pr) IOS Press.

Massively Parallel Processing Applications & Development: Proceedings of the 1994 EUROSIM Conference on Massively Parallel Processing Applications & Development, Delft, The Netherlands, 21-23 June 1994. Ed. by L. Dekker et al. LC 94-33562. 996p. 1994. 241.50 (*0-444-81784-0*) Elsevier.

Massively Parallel Processing System Jump-1. Ed. by Hidehiko Tanaka et al. 235p. (YA). (gr. 12). 1996. 90.00 (*90-5199-262-9*, 262-9) IOS Press.

Massively Parallel Processing Using Optical Interconnections: Proceedings of the 4th International Conference on Massively Parallel Processing Using Optical Interconnections, Montreal, Canada, 1997. LC 97-72014. 500p. 1997. pap. 110.00 (*0-8186-7974-3*) IEEE Comp Soc.

Massively Parallel Processor. Ed. by J. L. Potter. (Scientific Computation Ser.). (Illus.). 320p. 1985. 37.50 (*0-262-16100-1*) MIT Pr.

Massively Parallel Processors Using Optical Interconnections, 3rd Workshop on. LC 96-78441. 500p. 1996. 100.00 (*0-8186-7591-8*) IEEE Comp Soc.

Massless Representations of the Poincare Group. R. Mirman. 1995. 75.00 (*1-56072-259-2*) Nova Sci Pubs.

Massry & Glassock's Textbook of Nephrology. 4th ed. Shaul G. Massry & Richard J. Glassock. 2,048p. text 299.00 (*0-683-30488-7*) Lppncott W & W.

Mast Cell Activation & Mediator Release. Ed. by K. Ishizaka. (Progress in Allergy Ser.: Vol. 34). (Illus.). xii, 336p. 1984. 172.25 (*3-8055-3713-1*) S Karger.

Mast Cell & Basophil Differentiation & Function in Health & Disease. Ed. by Stephen J. Galli & K. Frank Austen. LC 89-3576. 366p. 1989. reprint ed. pap. 113.50 (*0-608-04715-5*, 206543600004) Bks Demand.

Mast Cell Differentiation & Heterogeneity. Ed. by A. Dean Befus et al. LC 86-6589. 448p. 1986. reprint ed. pap. 138.90 (*0-608-03385-5*, 206408200008) Bks Demand.

Mast Cell in Health & Disease. Ed. by Michael A. Kaliner & Dean D. Metcalfe. LC 92-49151. (Lung Biology in Health & Disease Ser.: Vol. 62). (Illus.). 858p. 1992. text 255.00 (*0-8247-8732-3*) Dekker.

Mast Cell Proteases in Immunology & Biology, No. 6. George H. Caughey. (Clinical Allergy & Immunology Ser.: Vol. 6). (Illus.). 352p. 1995. text 170.00 (*0-8247-9484-2*) Dekker.

Mast Cells. Hans Selye. LC 65-19996. 540p. reprint ed. pap. 167.40 (*0-608-14433-9*, 205184300009) Bks Demand.

*__Mast Cells & Basophils.__ Gianni Marone et al. (Illus.). 450p. 2000. 99.95 (*0-12-473335-2*) Acad Pr.

Mast Farm Inn Family Style Cookbook: A Collection of Traditional & Contemporary Cuisine. Compiled by Wanda Henshaw & Kay Philipp. (Illus.). 148p. 1999. spiral bd. 22.95 (*1-879802-01-5*) Dancing Fish.

Mastabas de l'Ancien Empire. Auguste E. Mariette. 592p. 1976. reprint ed. write for info. (*3-487-05987-8*) G Olms Pubs.

Masted Structures in Architecture. James Harris & Kevin Li. (Illus.). 128p. 1996. pap. text 74.95 (*0-7506-1282-7*) Buttrwrth-Heinemann.

Master. Bryan MacMahon. (Illus.). 187p. 1994. 30.00 (*1-85371-222-1*, Pub. by Poolbeg Pr); pap. 14.95 (*1-85371-254-X*, Pub. by Poolbeg Pr) Dufour.

Master: A Life of Jesus. John Pollock. 240p. 1994. pap. 6.50 (*1-56476-241-6*, 6-3241, Victor Bks) Chariot Victor.

Master: A Life of Jesus. large type ed. John Pollock. (Large Print Inspirational Ser.). 1988. pap. 16.95 (*0-8027-2603-8*) Walker & Co.

Master: His Life & Teachings. John T. Ferrier. 622p. 1913. text 18.00 (*0-900235-05-5*) Order Of The Cross.

Master a Month. Deborah Christine & Stevie Mack. (Programs Ser.). 251p. (YA). (gr. 7-12). 1987. pap. 299.00 (*0-945666-61-6*) Crizmac.

*__Master Active Directory Visually.__ Simmons. 576p. 2000. pap. 34.99 (*0-7645-3425-4*) IDG Bks.

Master Album of Pictorial Calligraphy & Scrollwork: An Antique Copybook Rediscovered. Baldri Van Horicke. (Illus.). 64p. (Orig.). 1985. pap. 5.95 (*0-486-24974-3*) Dover.

Master Alienators: Perceptions of the Mind of the Minnesota Divorce Court. D. Alwyn Stivers. 1971. 4.95 (*0-9600666-0-8*) Family Pr.

*__Master Amateurs: The Story of Golf's Only Amateurs Who Have Won Both the United States Open & United States Amateur.__ Arthur-Walter J. Curtis, Sr. (Illus.). 160p. 2000. 24.95 (*0-9659419-1-4*) Curtis Pub.

Master & Commander. Patrick O'Brian. (Aubrey-Maturin Ser.). (Illus.). 411p. 1990. pap. 13.95 (*0-393-30705-0*) Norton.

Master & Commander. Patrick O'Brian. 1994. 24.00 (*0-393-03701-0*) Norton.

Master & Commander. large type ed. Patrick O'Brian. LC 99-26534. 1999. 28.95 (*0-7862-1932-7*) Thorndike Pr.

Master & Disciple: The Cultural Foundations of Moroccan Authoritarianism. Abdellah Hammoudi. LC 96-43270. 1997. pap. text 13.95 (*0-226-31528-2*); lib. bdg. 38.00 (*0-226-31527-4*) U Ch Pr.

Master & Fool. J. V. Jones. (Book of Words Ser.: Bk. 3). 544p. (Orig.). 1996. mass mkt. 12.99 (*0-446-67096-0*, Pub. by Warner Bks) Little.

Master & Fool. J. V. Jones. (Book of Words Ser.: Bk. 3). 656p. (Orig.). 1997. mass mkt. 6.99 (*0-446-60414-3*, Pub. by Warner Bks) Little.

Master & Man. Leo Tolstoy. 348p. Date not set. 25.95 (*0-8488-2496-2*) Amereon Ltd.

Master & Man & Other Stories. Leo Tolstoy. Tr. & Intro. by Paul Foote. (Classics Ser.). 272p. (Orig.). 1977. pap. 11.95 (*0-14-044331-2*, Penguin Classics) Viking Penguin.

Master & Margarita. Mikhail Afanasevich Bulgakov. Tr. by Diana Burgin & Katherine T. O'Connor from RUS. 367p. 1995. 35.00 (*0-87501-067-9*) Ardis Pubs.

Master & Margarita. Mikhail Afanasevich Bulgakov. Tr. by Mirra Ginsburg from RUS. LC 87-297. 416p. 1987. pap. 11.95 (*0-8021-3011-9*, Grove) Grove-Atltic.

Master & Margarita. Mikhail Afanasevich Bulgakov. 1992. 17.00 (*0-679-41046-5*) McKay.

Master & Margarita. Mikhail Afanasevich Bulgakov. 1974. pap. 12.95 (*0-452-00899-9*, Mer) NAL.

Master & Margarita. Mikhail Afanasevich Bulgakov. Tr. by Diana Burgin & Katherine O'Connor. LC 95-45873. 1996. pap. 13.00 (*0-679-76080-6*) Vin Bks.

Master & Margarita. Mikhail Afanasevich Bulgakov. 480p. 1999. reprint ed. pap. 12.95 (*0-14-118014-5*, Penguin Bks) Viking Penguin.

*__Master & Margarita.__ 10th ed. Mikhail Afanasevich Bulgakov. 1999. pap. 9.95 (*5-7684-0317-5*) Distribks Inc.

Master & Margarita: A Critical Companion. Mikhail Bulgakov. Ed. by Laura D. Weeks. (AATSEEL/ Northwestern Critical Companions to Russian Literature Ser.). 160p. (C). 1995. pap. text, student ed. 16.95 (*0-8101-1212-4*) Northwestern U Pr.

Master & Margarita: or The Devil Comes to Moscow. Mikhail Afanasevich Bulgakov. Ed. & Tr. by Jean-Claude Van Itallie. 1995. pap. 5.25 (*0-8222-1412-1*) Dramatists Play.

Master & Mastership: Wila Wa Wilayat. rev. ed. Murtaza Mutahhery. Tr. by Islamic Seminary Staff & M. A. Ansari from PER. 131p. (C). 1983. reprint ed. pap. 4.00 (*0-941724-15-8*) Islamic Seminary.

Master & Minerva: Disputing Women in French Medieval Culture. Helen Solterer. LC 93-47918. 325p. 1995. pap. 19.95 (*0-520-08835-2*, Pub. by U CA Pr) Cal Prin Full Svc.

Master & Minerva: Disputing Women in French Medieval Culture. Helen Solterer. LC 93-47918. (C). 1995. 55.00 (*0-520-08565-5*, Pub. by U CA Pr) Cal Prin Full Svc.

Master & the Apostle. 1995. text 12.99 (*0-88486-119-8*, Inspirational Pr) Arrowood Pr.

Master & the Disciple. Sri Chinmoy. LC 85-72172. 115p. (Orig.). 1985. pap. 5.95 (*0-88497-884-2*) Aum Pubns.

Master Angler. John Bailey. 1997. 29.95 (*0-00-218734-5*, Pub. by HarpC) Trafalgar.

*__Master AP Chemistry.__ 3rd ed. Brett Barker. 2000. pap. 15.99 (*0-7645-6182-0*, Arco) Macmillan Gen Ref.

*__Master AP English Literature & the Composition Test.__ Laurie E. Rozakis. 2000. pap. 15.99 (*0-7645-6184-7*, Arco) Macmillan Gen Ref.

*__Master AP European History.__ Nathan Barber. 2000. pap. 15.99 (*0-7645-6185-5*, Arco) Macmillan Gen Ref.

*__Master AP Spanish Language.__ Jill Rodriguez. 2000. pap. 19.99 (*0-7645-6187-1*, Arco) Macmillan Gen Ref.

Master Architect: Conversations with Frank Lloyd Wright. Frank Lloyd Wright. Ed. by Patrick J. Meehan. LC 84-11931. (Illus.). 330p. 1984. 54.95 (*0-471-80025-2*, Wiley-Interscience) Wiley.

Master Architects: Building the United States Foreign Service, 1890-1913. Richard H. Werking. LC 76-9509. 350p. reprint ed. pap. 108.50 (*0-7837-5785-9*, 204545100006) Bks Demand.

Master As I Saw Him. Sister Nivedita. 336p. 5.95 (*0-87481-088-4*, Pub. by Advaita Ashrama) Vedanta Pr.

*__Master Asker: Expect God to Answer Your Prayer!__ Charles Neiman. 2000. pap. 12.99 (*0-88419-694-1*) Creation House.

Master Assassin: Tales of Murder from the Shogun's City. Shotaro Ikenami. Tr. by Gavin Frew from JPN. 224p. 1992. 19.95 (*4-7700-1534-8*) Kodansha.

Master at Arms. Raphael Sabatini. 27.95 (*0-89190-746-7*) Amereon Ltd.

*__Master AutoCAD 2000 Visually.__ Ron Morin. (Illus.). 704p. 2000. pap. text 34.99 (*0-7645-3466-1*) IDG Bks.

Master Backwoodsman. Bradford Angier. 224p. 1984. pap. 5.95 (*0-449-90126-2*) Fawcett.

Master Bedroom Poems. Sandra Agricola. (Ohio Review Bks.). 72p. 1985. 9.95 (*0-942148-05-3*); pap. 5.95 (*0-942148-04-5*) Ohio Review.

Master Birding see Audubon Society Master Guide to Birding

Master Bladesmith: Advanced Studies in Steel. Jim Hrisoulas. (Illus.). 296p. 1991. 49.95 (*0-87364-612-6*) Paladin Pr.

Master Book of Astrology. Gayle Bachicha. 250p. (Orig.). 1997. pap. 29.95 (*1-885084-22-6*) Tickerwick.

Master Book of Candle Burning. Henry Gamache. 96p. 1998. pap. 5.95 (*0-942272-56-0*) Original Pubns.

Master Book of Herbalism. Paul Beyerl. (Illus.). 424p. 1984. pap. 14.95 (*0-919345-53-0*) Phoenix WA.

Master Book of Irish Placenames: Master Atlas & Book of Irish Placenames. Michael C. O'Laughlin. (Illus.). 270p. 1994. 19.95 (*0-940134-33-0*) Irish Genealog.

Master Book of Irish Surnames: Locations, Origins & Ethnicity. Michael C. O'Laughlin. (Illus.). 304p. 1993. 23.95 (*0-940134-32-2*) Irish Genealog.

Master Book of Mathematical Puzzles & Recreations. Fred Schuh. Ed. by T. H. O'Beirne. Tr. by F. Gobel. LC 68-28064. Orig. Title: Wonderlijke Problemen Leerzaam Tijoverdrijf Door Puzzle En Spel. (Illus.). 430p. 1968. reprint ed. pap. 9.95 (*0-486-22134-2*) Dover.

Master Book of Soups: A Complete Book of Soups. Henry Smith. 1974. lib. bdg. 250.00 (*0-685-51362-9*) Revisionist Pr.

Master Book of the Water Garden. Storey Publishing Staff. 1997. 49.95 (*0-676-57195-6*) Random.

Master Book of the Water Garden. Phillip Swindells. 1997. 49.95 (*1-56465-188-6*) Tetra Pr.

Master Book of Wedding & Bridal Photography. 2nd ed. J. C. Adamson & Piare Mohan. (Illus.). 165p. 1994. reprint ed. pap. 39.50 (*0-934420-17-3*, 1580) Studio Pr NE.

Master Breasts: Objectified, Aesthetisized, Fantasized, Eroticized, Feminized by Photography's Most Titillating Masters . . . Intro. by Francine Prose. LC 98-84498. (Illus.). 16p. 1998. 60.00 (*0-89381-803-8*) Aperture.

Master Brewer. rev. ed. James F. Willenbecher. (Illus.). 1994. pap. 49.95 (*0-9632514-8-1*) Crossfire Eng.

Master Builder. Henrik Ibsen. Tr. by Nicholas Rudall. (Plays for Performance Ser.). 111p. 1994. text 15.95 (*1-56663-043-6*, Pub. by I R Dee) Natl Bk Netwk.

Master Builder. Henrik Ibsen. Tr. by Nicholas Rudall from NOR. (Plays for Performance Ser.). 111p. 1994. pap. 7.95 (*1-56663-042-8*, Pub. by I R Dee) Natl Bk Netwk.

Master Builder. Henrik Ibsen. Tr. by Eve Le Gallienne. LC 55-26942. 222p. reprint ed. pap. 68.90 (*0-608-30789-0*, 205021700058) Bks Demand.

Master Builder. unabridged ed. Henrik Ibsen. Ed. by William-Alan Landes. LC 98-5628. 67p. 1997. pap. 7.00 (*0-88734-748-7*) Players Pr.

Master Builder & Other Plays. Incl. John Gabriel Borkman. Henrik Ibsen. Tr. by Una Ellis-Fermor. 1959. Little Eyoif. Henrik Ibsen. Tr. by Una Ellis-Fermor. 1959. Rosmersholm. (Classics Ser.). 384p. (Orig.). 1959. Set pap. 7.95 (*0-14-044053-4*, Penguin Classics) Viking Penguin.

Master Builders. Bob Gordon. 1990. pap. text 21.99 (*1-85240-042-0*) SOV5.

Master Builders. Peter Blake. LC 96-229682. (Illus.). 448p. 1996. reprint ed. pap. 16.95 (*0-393-31504-5*) Norton.

Master Builders. Henry J. Cowan. LC 84-19400. 314p. (C). 1986. reprint ed. lib. bdg. 42.50 (*0-89874-804-6*) Krieger.

Master Builders: A Guide to Famous American Architects. National Trust for Historic Preservation Staff. Ed. by Diane Maddex. LC 85-16982. (Building Watchers Ser.). (Illus.). 204p. 1995. pap. 12.95 (*0-471-14402-9*) Wiley.

Master Builders: A History of the Grand Lodge of Free & Accepted Masons of Pennsylvania, Vol. I: 1731-1873, 3 vols., Set. Wayne A. Huss. (Illus.). 35.95 (*0-9617310-3-6*) Grnd Lodge F&AMOP.

Master Builders: Structures of Empire in the New World - Spanish Initiatives & United States Invention. J. V. Fifer. LC 97-113893. (New Perspectives on American History Ser.). 320p. 1996. 22.50 (*1-900838-01-X*, Pub. by Durham Acad Pr) U of Wash Pr.

Master Builders Vol. I: A History of the Grand Lodge of Free & Accepted Masons of Pennsylvania, 1731-1873. Wayne A. Huss. (Illus.). xi, 327p. 1989. 21.50 (*0-9617310-0-1*) Grnd Lodge F&AMOP.

Master Builders Vol. II: A History of the Grand Lodge of Free & Accepted Masons of Pennsylvania, 1874-1985. Wayne A. Huss. (Illus.). xiii, 243p. 1988. 21.50 (*0-9617310-1-X*) Grnd Lodge F&AMOP.

Master Builders Vol. III: A History of the Grand Lodge of Free & Accepted Masons of Pennsylvania, Grand Master Biographies. Wayne A. Huss. (Illus.). xiii, 470p. 1989. 21.50 (*0-9617310-2-8*) Grnd Lodge F&AMOP.

*__Master Builders of Byzantium.__ Robert G. Ousterhout. LC 99-29652. 320p. 2000. 65.00 (*0-691-00535-4*, Pub. by Princeton U Pr) Cal Prin Full Svc.

Master Builders of Modern Psychology: From Freud to Skinner. J. D. Keehn. 216p. (C). 1996. text 40.00 (*0-8147-4685-3*) NYU Pr.

Master Builders of Opera. George C. Jell. LC 78-134102. (Essay Index Reprint Ser.). 1977. 21.95 (*0-8369-1964-5*) Ayer.

Master Builders of Opera. George C. Jell. (Essay Index Reprint Ser.). (Illus.). 267p. reprint ed. lib. bdg. 19.00 (*0-8290-0798-9*) Irvington.

Master Builders of Sixty Centuries. John A. Miller. LC 70-37524. (Essay Index Reprint Ser.). (Illus.). 1977. reprint ed. 23.95 (*0-8369-2566-1*) Ayer.

Master Building Menu: A Tool for Residential Construction. write for info. (*0-9636378-3-5*) Archi Pub.

Master Bun: The Baker's Boy. Allan Ahlberg. (Illus.). (J). 1988. pap. 6.95 (*0-14-032344-9*, Pub. by Pnguin Bks Ltd) Trafalgar.

Master C++ Let the PC Teach You Object-Oriented Programming. Rex Woollard et al. (Illus.). 380p. (Orig.). 1992. pap. 39.95 (*1-878739-07-7*) Sams.

Master C++ for Windows: Let the PC Teach You Object-Oriented Programming. Rex Wollard. (Illus.). 400p. 1995. pap. 34.95 (*1-57169-000-X*) Sams.

Master Carver's Legacy: Essentials of Wood Carving Techniques. Brieuc Bouche. (Illus.). 160p. 1986. 24.95 (*0-8306-0329-8*, 2629) McGraw-Hill Prof.

Master Catalog Eighty-Two: Precision Electro-Mechanical Components. rev. ed. Sterling Instrument Engineers Staff et al. 464p. 1985. pap. 4.95 (*0-686-18285-5*) Sterling Instru.

Master Catalogue Eighty. Sterling Instrument Engineers Staff et al. 1969. pap. 2.95 (*0-686-09561-8*) Sterling Instru.

Master Checkmate Strategy. Bill Robertie. LC 96-85084. (Road to Chess Mastery Ser.). (Illus.). 152p. 1997. pap. 9.95 (*0-940685-66-3*) Cardoza Pub.

Master Chef. Jean Conil. 256p. 1995. write for info. (*1-57215-136-6*) World Pubns.

Master Chef Cookbook. Camaro Editors. (Illus.). 1985. pap. 10.95 (*0-913290-63-7*) Camaro Pub.

Master Chef, 1997. Intro. by Loyd Grossman. 160p. 1997. pap. 19.95 (*0-09-185305-2*, Pub. by Ebury Pr) Trafalgar.

Master Chefs Cook Kosher. Judy Zeidler. LC 97-30795. (Illus.). 1998. 24.95 (*0-8118-1402-5*) Chronicle Bks.

Master Chefs of the World Vol. 1: U. S. A. Ed. by Garth Bishop. (Illus.). 1985. pap. 5.95 (*0-913290-57-2*) Camaro Pub.

Master Cheng's New Method of T'ai Chi Self-Cultivation. Cheng Man-ch'ing. Tr. by Mark Hennessy from CHI. LC 99-11813. 100p. 1999. pap. 11.95 (*1-883319-92-7*) Frog Ltd CA.

Master Cheng's Thirteen Chapters on T'ai-Chi Ch'uan. 12th ed. Cheng Man-Ch'ing. Tr. by Douglas Wile from CHI. (Illus.). 102p. (Orig.). 1985. pap. 8.95 (*0-912059-00-1*) Sweet Ch I Pr.

Master Chess: A Course in 21 Lessons. Daniel Kopec et al. (Chess Ser.). (Illus.). 200p. 1985. 27.95 (*0-08-029725-0*, Pub. by PPL); pap. 17.90 (*0-08-029724-2*, Pub. by PPL) Elsevier.

Master Chief: Diary of a Navy SEAL. Gary R. Smith & Alan Maki. LC 96-94326. 1996. mass mkt. 5.99 (*0-8041-1091-3*) Ivy Books.

Master Chohans of the Color Rays. John-Roger. LC 79-88974. 1979. pap. 8.00 (*0-914829-14-9*) Mandeville LA.

Master Chorus Book II: 100 Contemporary, Traditional & New Choruses, Words Only. Arranged by Ken Bible. 1994. 2.25 (*0-8341-9182-2*, BCMB-698A) Lillenas.

Master Christian (1900) Marie Corelli. 600p. 1998. reprint ed. pap. 36.00 (*0-7661-0161-4*) Kessinger Pub.

Master Class. Terrence McNally. 1996. pap. 5.25 (*0-8222-1521-7*) Dramatists Play.

Master Class. Terrence McNally. 96p. 1995. pap. 9.95 (*0-452-27615-2*, Plume) Dutton Plume.

*__Master Class.__ Morris West. 2001. write for info. (*0-15-100574-5*) Harcourt.

Master Class in Figure Drawing. Robert B. Hale. (Illus.). 144p. 1991. pap. 19.95 (*0-8230-3014-8*) Watsn-Guptill.

Master Class in Watermedia. Edward Betts. LC 93-3421. (Illus.). 144p. (Orig.). 1993. 29.95 (*0-8230-3017-2*) Watsn-Guptill.

*__Master Class in Watermedia: Techniques in Traditional & Experimental Painting.__ Edward Betts. (Illus.). 144p. 2000. pap. 19.95 (*0-8230-3040-7*) Watsn-Guptill.

Master Classes: Callas at Juilliard. John Ardoin. 1997. pap. text 16.00 (*1-880909-60-X*) Baskerville.

Master Classes 6. Maddox. 176p. 1997. 20.00 (*0-465-04517-0*, Pub. by Basic) HarpC.

Master Classes 7. Pagels. 176p. 1997. 20.00 (*0-465-04518-9*, Pub. by Basic) HarpC.

*__Master Classes 9.__ Turkle. 176p. 2000. 22.00 (*0-465-04520-0*, Pub. by Basic) HarpC.

Master Cleanser. (Illus.). 50p. 1976. pap. 5.95 (*0-9639262-0-9*) Burroughs Bks.

*__Master Clinicians Confront the Treatment of Borderline Personality Disorders.__ Henk-Jan Dalewijk. 2001. 45.00 (*0-7657-0294-0*) Aronson.

Master Clinicians on Treating the Regressed Patient, Vol. 1. Ed. by L. Bryce Boyer & Peter L. Giovacchini. LC 89-6975. 408p. 1990. 60.00 (*0-87668-834-2*) Aronson.

Master Comprehension. Carole Gerber. 1992. pap. text 5.95 (*1-56189-045-6*) Amer Educ Pub.

Master Comprehension: Grade Four. Carole Gerber. 1992. pap. text 5.95 (*1-56189-044-8*) Amer Educ Pub.

Master Comprehension: Grade Six. Carole Gerber. pap. text 5.95 (*1-56189-046-4*) Amer Educ Pub.

Master Comprehension Workbook. Carole Gerber. 1992. pap. text 5.95 (*1-56189-042-1*); pap. text 5.95 (*1-56189-043-X*) Amer Educ Pub.

Master Comprehension Workbook: Grade One. Carole Gerber. 1990. pap. 5.95 (*1-56189-041-3*) Amer Educ Pub.

Master Control Genes in Development & Evolution: The Homeobox Story. Walter J. Gehring. LC 98-19922. (Terry Lecture Ser.). (Illus.). 296p. 1998. 35.00 (*0-300-07409-3*) Yale U Pr.

Master Cook: Cooking Light. Sierra On-Line Staff. 1996. 29.54 (*0-87177-357-0*) Sierra Online.

Master Corkonata. Edmund C. Stedman. (Notable American Authors Ser.). 1999. reprint ed. lib. bdg. 125.00 (*0-7812-8911-4*) Rprt Serv.

Master Counting. Senior. pap. 3.95 (*0-575-04456-X*, Pub. by V Gollancz) Trafalgar.

Master Craft of the Medieval Free Masons & Sacred Builders. R. Christopher Abel & Hector St. Luke. 1997. reprint ed. pap. 6.95 (*1-55818-378-7*) Holmes Pub.

Master Criminals among the Gypsies. Jack Morris. (Illus.). 200p. 1994. text 20.00 (*0-912479-11-6*) Palmer Pr.

Master Dancer. Adi Da-Samraj. 176p. 1993. pap. 12.95 (*0-918801-74-5*) Dawn Horse Pr.

Master Dating: How to Meet & Attract Quality Men. unabridged ed. Felicia Rose Adler. Ed. by Virginia Iorio. LC 98-50194. (Illus.). 224p. 1999. pap. 12.95 (*0-911493-24-7*) Blue Sky.

Master Deceptive Plays. Reese. pap. 3.95 (*0-575-04384-9*, Pub. by V Gollancz) Trafalgar.

Master Dictionary of Food & Wine. 2nd ed. Joyce Rubash. (Culinary Arts Ser.). 458p. 1996. 41.95 (*0-442-02242-5*, VNR) Wiley.

Master Dictionary of Food & Wine. 2nd ed. Joyce Rubash. (Culinary Arts Ser.). 464p. 1996. 44.95 (*0-471-28756-3*, VNR) Wiley.

Master Discipleship: Jesus' Prayer & Plan for Every Believer. Don Hawkins. 192p. 1996. pap. 10.99 (*0-8254-2866-1*) Kregel.

Master Dogen's Shobogenzo, Bk. 1. Tr. by Gudo Nishijima & Chodo Cross from JPN. LC 94-220964. 358p. 1994. pap. 20.00 (*0-9523002-1-4*) Windbell Pubns.

Master Dogen's Shobogenzo, Bk. 2. Tr. by Gudo Nishijima & Chodo Cross from JPN. 400p. 1996. pap. 20.00 (*0-9523002-2-2*) Windbell Pubns.

Master Dogen's Shobogenzo, Bk. 3. Tr. by Gudo Nishijima & Chodo Cross from JPN. 350p. 1997. pap. 20.00 (*0-9523002-3-0*) Windbell Pubns.

Master Dogen's Shobogenzo, Bk. 4. Tr. by Gudo Nishijima & Chodo Cross from JPN. 1999. pap. 25.00 (*0-9523002-4-9*) Windbell Pubns.

Master Doubles. Ron Klinger. 8p. 1990. pap. 3.95 (*0-575-04130-7*, Pub. by V Gollancz) Trafalgar.

Master Drawings: From the National Portrait Gallery. Malcolm Rogers. (Illus.). 224p. 1993. 49.50 (*1-85514-134-5*) Antique Collect.

Master Drawings: Sterling & Francine Clark As Collectors. David S. Brooke. LC 95-18873. (Illus.). 40p. (Orig.). 1995. pap. 10.95 (*0-931102-34-0*) S & F Clark Art.

*__Master Drawings from the Cleveland Museum of Art.__ Ed. by de Grazia Diane. (Illus.). 288p. 2000. 75.00 (*0-8478-2296-6*) Rizzoli Intl.

Master Drawings from the Hermitage & Pushkin Museums. I. N. Novoselskia et al. LC 98-27216. 1998. 45.00 (*0-87598-125-9*) Pierpont Morgan.

Master Drawings from the Nelson-Atkins Museum of Art, Kansas City. Mark S. Weil & Roger Ward. LC 89-51232. (Illus.). 56p. (Orig.). 1989. pap. 10.00 (*0-936316-12-8*) Wash U Gallery.

*__Master Drawings from the Smith College Museum of Art.__ Ann H. Sievers et al. (Illus.). 336p. 2000. 75.00 (*1-55595-183-X*, Pub. by Hudson Hills) Natl Bk Netwk.

*__Master Drawings from the Smith College Museum of Art.__ Smith College Staff et al. LC 00-40909. (Illus.). 2000. write for info. (*1-55595-184-8*) Hudson Hills.

Master Drawings from the Worcester Art Museum. David Acton. LC 97-48740. (Illus.). 288p. 1998. 75.00 (*1-55595-146-5*, Pub. by Hudson Hills) Natl Bk Netwk.

Master Drawings in the Los Angeles County Museum of Art. Bruce Davis. LC 97-73596. (Illus.). 244p. 1998. 60.00 (*1-55595-152-X*, Pub. by Hudson Hills) Natl Bk Netwk.

Master Drawings of the Hudson River School. Tracie Felker. (Illus.). 14p. (Orig.). 1993. pap. 10.00 (*0-934483-12-4*) Gal Assn NY.

Master Drawings Rediscovered: Treasures from Prewar German Collections. Tatiana Ilatovskaya. LC 96-3545. (Illus.). 224p. 1997. 49.50 (*0-8109-3788-3*, Pub. by Abrams) Time Warner.

*__Master Dreams: A Memoir of Isaac Bashevis Singer.__ Deborah Telushkin. (Illus.). 350p. 2000. text 25.00 (*0-7881-9084-9*) DIANE Pub.

Master Duplicate Bridge. Husband. pap. 3.95 (*0-575-04367-9*, Pub. by V Gollancz) Trafalgar.

Master Dyers to the World: Technique & Trade in Early Indian Dyed Cotton Textiles. Mattiebelle Gittinger. Ed. by Caroline K. McEuen. LC 82-10695. (Illus.). 208p. 1982. pap. 20.00 (*0-87405-020-0*) Textile Mus.

Master Electrician. Jack Rudman. (Career Examination Ser.: C-475). 1994. pap. 29.95 (*0-8373-0475-X*) Nat Learn.

*__Master Electrician Exam.__ Tom Henry. (Illus.). 1999. pap. text 29.17 (*0-945495-61-7*) T Henrys CECB.

Master Electrician Exam Questions & Answers. Tom Henry. (Illus.). 227p. 1995. reprint ed. pap. text 21.00 (*0-945495-48-X*, 103) T Henrys CECB.

Master Electrician Examinations: Based on 1999 NEC. 6th rev. ed. Michael G. Owen. 60p. 1999. pap. text 19.95 (*1-888512-08-3*) Elect Trnging.

Master Electricians Exam Prep. 2nd ed. Holt. LC 99-13241. 544p. (C). 1999. 39.95 (*0-7668-0376-7*) Delmar.

Master Electrician's Exam Preparation. Michael Holt. 64p. (C). 1996. text, teacher ed. 17.00 (*0-8273-7624-3*) Delmar.

Master Electrician's Exam Preparation. Michael Holt. LC 95-49219. (Career Education Ser.). 576p. 1996. pap. 37.25 (*0-8273-7623-5*) Delmar.

Master Electrician's Exam Preparation. Richard E. Loyd. LC 94-174544. 305p. 1993. pap. 35.95 (*0-8273-5852-0*) Delmar.

Master Electrician's Review. 2nd ed. Richard Loyd. (Electrical Trades Ser). 432p. 1996. pap. 61.95 (*0-8273-6678-7*) Thomson Learn.

*__Master Electrician's Review.__ 3rd ed. Richard E. Loyd. LC 99-24747. 352p. 1999. 61.95 (*0-7668-1276-6*) Delmar.

Master Enciclopedia Universal Ilustrada Vox. Vox Staff. (SPA.). 912p. 1983. 49.95 (*0-8288-2021-X*, S39847) Fr & Eur.

An Asterisk (*) at the beginning of an entry indicates that the title is appearing for the first time.

Master English Workbook Grade K. Carole Gerber. 1992. pap. 5.95 (*1-56189-020-0*) Amer Educ Pub.

Master English Workbook Grade 1. Carole Gerber. 1992. pap. 5.95 (*1-56189-021-9*) Amer Educ Pub.

Master English Workbook Grade 2. Carole Gerber. 1992. pap. 5.95 (*1-56189-022-7*) Amer Educ Pub.

Master English Workbook Grade 3. Carole Gerber. 1992. pap. 5.95 (*1-56189-023-5*) Amer Educ Pub.

Master English Workbook Grade 4. Carole Gerber. 1992. pap. 5.95 (*1-56189-024-3*) Amer Educ Pub.

Master English Workbook Grade 5. Carole Gerber. 1992. pap. 5.95 (*1-56189-025-1*) Amer Educ Pub.

Master English Workbook Grade 6. Carole Gerber. 1992. pap. 5.95 (*1-56189-026-X*) Amer Educ Pub.

Master Essences: Daily Inspirations of Love & Light. Sage. LC 97-60618. 170p. 1997. pap. write for info. (*0-9645194-6-1*, Pub. by TrHse Pr) New Leaf Dist.

Master Eustace. Henry James. LC 74-157780. (Short Story Index Reprint Ser.). 1977. reprint ed. 21.95 (*0-8369-3892-5*) Ayer.

***Master Evangelist: How to Present the Gospel the Way Jesus Did.** Philip Delre. 112p. 2000. pap. text 10.00 (*0-9677520-0-0*) Voice Pubg IL.

Master Fard Muhammad: Detroit History. E. D. Benyon. Ed. by Prince Cuba. 19p. (Orig.). 1990. pap. 3.95 (*1-56411-109-1*) Untd Bros & Sis.

Master Feeding Program. Bernard Jensen. 1988. pap. 12.99 (*0-932615-12-0*) B Jensen.

Master Fiddler. Janet Dailey. 1991. mass mkt. 3.50 (*0-373-83230-3*) Harlequin Bks.

***Master Fiddler.** large type ed. Janet Dailey. LC 99-31431. 1999. pap. 28.95 (*0-7838-8678-0*, G K Hall Lrg Type) Mac Lib Ref.

Master File Containing References to Official Documents of the Third United Nations Conference on the Law of the Sea, Vol.9. (The Law of the Sea Ser.). 176p. pap. 19.50 (*92-1-133271-0*, E.85.V.9) UN.

Master Financial Statements (Who Murdered Savings & Loans?) Patrick G. Finegan, Jr. LC 90-61773. 203p. 1990. 21.95 (*1-878905-04-X*); pap. 14.95 (*1-878905-05-8*) Palindrome Pr.

Master Finessing. Kelsey. pap. 3.95 (*0-575-04188-9*, Pub. by V Gollancz) Trafalgar.

Master Fire Supression Piping Contractor. Rudman. (Career Examination Ser.: C-3765). 1985. pap. 23.95 (*0-8373-3765-8*) Nat Learn.

Master Flower Finder. Nature Guild Study Editors. 224p. 1986. mass mkt. 3.95 (*0-446-32934-7*, Pub. by Warner Bks) Little.

Master Franchising: Selecting, Negotiating & Operating a Master Franchise. Carl E. Zwisler. 180p. 1999. pap. text 70.00 (*0-8080-0368-2*) CCH INC.

Master Frequency File. James E. Tunnell & Robert Kelly. 1993. pap. 29.95 (*0-07-065486-7*) McGraw.

Master Frequency File. James E. Tunnell & Robert Kelty. LC 92-30650. 1993. text 39.95 (*0-8306-4132-7*); pap. text 29.95 (*0-8306-4131-9*) McGraw-Hill Prof.

Master Gemcutting Tips: A Complete Guide Containing Tips & Methods That Can Be Used by a First-Time or Professional Gemcutter. Gerald L. Wykoff. LC 93-28639. 1993. 14.95 (*0-9607892-7-8*) Adamas Pubs.

Master Georgie. Beryl Bainbridge. 190p. 1998. 21.00 (*0-7867-0563-9*) Carroll & Graf.

***Master Georgie.** Beryl Bainbridge. 190p. 1999. pap. text 11.95 (*0-7867-0697-X*) Carroll & Graf.

Master Georgie. large type ed. Beryl Bainbridge. LC 98-41988. 1999. 30.00 (*0-7862-1681-6*) Thorndike Pr.

Master Go in Ten Days. Yutopian Enterprises Staff. 1998. pap. text 17.50 (*0-9641847-8-8*) Yutopian Ent.

***Master Guide for Passing the Respiratory Care Credentialing Exams.** 4th ed. Rick Meyer. 566p. 1999. pap. text 53.33 (*0-13-013832-0*) P-H.

***Master Guide for Passing the Respiratory Care Credentialing Exams.** 4th ed. Rick Meyer et al. LC 99-43212. (Cancer Chemotherapy Annual Ser.). 632p. 2000. 195.00 (*0-444-50074-X*) Elsevier.

Master Guide for Passing the Respiratory Credentialing Exams. 2nd ed. Terrance M. Krider et al. 472p. 1989. pap. 29.95 (*0-931263-01-8*) Educ Res Consortium.

***Master Guide to Birds.** Audubon Society Staff. 2001. 29.95 (*0-679-45123-4*) Knopf.

Master Guide to Creative Financing of Real Estate Investments. Robert J. Eastgate. LC 82-9313. 243p. 1982. text 39.95 (*0-87624-366-9*, Inst Busn Plan) P-H.

Master Guide to Electronics Circuits. Harry L. Helms. (Illus.). 352p. 1988. text 39.00 (*0-13-559790-0*) P-H.

Master Guide to Meditation. Roy E. Davis. 1994. 6.95 (*0-87707-238-8*) CSA Pr.

Master Guide to the American History Videodisc & CD-ROM. 2nd ed. Constance B. Schulz. 360p. (Orig.). 1996. pap. text, teacher ed. 495.00 incl. vdisk, cd-rom (*0-923805-17-6*) Instruc Resc MD.

Master Guide to the Western Civilization Videodisc & CD-ROM. 2nd ed. James E. Straukamp. (Orig.). 1996. pap. text, teacher ed. 495.00 incl. vdisk, cd-rom (*0-923805-20-6*) Instruc Resc MD.

Master Guide to the World History. 2nd ed. 347p. 1996. 45.00 incl. vdisk, cd-rom (*0-923805-23-0*, 4111) Instruc Resc MD.

Master Guitar Builder John D'Angelico: What's in a Name? Frank Green. (Illus.). 20872p. 1998. pap. 35.00 (*1-57424-033-1*) Centerstream Pub.

Master Hand: A Study of the Origin & Meaning of Right & Left Sidedness & Its Relation to Personality & Language. Abram Blau. LC 78-72790. (Brainedness, Handedness, & Mental Abilities Ser.). reprint ed. 49.50 (*0-404-60854-X*) AMS Pr.

Master Handbook of Acoustics. 2nd ed. F. Alton Everest. (Illus.). 384p. 1988. 27.95 (*0-8306-9096-4*, 3096) McGraw-Hill Prof.

Master Handbook of Acoustics. 3rd ed. F. Alton Everest. (Illus.). 384p. pap. 21.95 (*0-8306-9396-3*, 3096) McGraw.

Master Handbook of Acoustics. 3rd ed. F. Alton Everest. 452p. 1994. pap. 29.95 (*0-07-019897-7*) McGraw.

Master Handbook of Acoustics. 3rd ed. F. Alton Everest. 1994. 32.95 (*0-07-019896-9*) McGraw.

Master Handbook of Acoustics. 3rd ed. F. Alton Everest. LC 93-17402. 1993. pap. 19.95 (*0-8306-4437-7*); text 32.95 (*0-8306-4438-5*) McGraw-Hill Prof.

***Master Handbook of Acoustics.** 4th ed. F. Alton Everest. (Illus.). 2000. pap. 34.95 (*0-07-136097-2*) McGraw.

Master Handbook of Electronic Tables & Formulas. 4th ed. Martin Clifford. LC 84-8529. (Illus.). 392p. 1984. 24.95 (*0-8306-0625-4*, 1625) McGraw-Hill Prof.

Master Handbook of Electronic Tables & Formulas. 5th ed. Martin Clifford. 576p. 1992. 39.95 (*0-8306-2192-X*); pap. 22.95 (*0-8306-2191-1*) McGraw-Hill Prof.

Master Handbook of High-Level Microcomputer Languages. Charles F. Taylor, Jr. 256p. (Orig.). 1984. 21.95 (*0-8306-0733-1*); pap. 15.15 (*0-8306-1733-7*, 1733) McGraw-Hill Prof.

Master Handbook of IC Circuit Applications. 3rd ed. Delton T. Horn. LC 97-7937. (Illus.). 448p. 1997. 49.95 (*0-07-030562-5*); pap. 34.95 (*0-07-030563-3*) McGraw.

Master Handbook of IC Circuits. Thomas R. Powers. pap. 18.60 (*0-8306-1370-6*) McGraw-Hill Prof.

Master Handbook of 1001 More Practical Electronic Circuits. Ed. by Michael L. Fair. (Illus.). 1979. 17.95 (*0-8306-8804-8*); pap. 21.95 (*0-8306-7804-2*, 804) McGraw-Hill Prof.

Master Handbook of 1001 Practical Electronic Circuits: Solid-State Edition. Kendall W. Sessions. (Illus.). 420p. 1988. 28.95 (*0-8306-0980-6*); pap. 19.95 (*0-8306-2980-7*) McGraw-Hill Prof.

Master Handicapping. Steven Davidowitz. 1987. 19.95 (*0-525-24291-0*, Dutt); pap. 8.95 (*0-525-48139-7*, Dutt) Dutton Plume.

Master Harold & the Boys. Athol Fugard. (Plays Ser.). 64p. 1984. pap. 8.95 (*0-14-048187-7*, Penguin Bks) Viking Penguin.

Master Harold & the Boys. Kirszne. 1997. mass mkt. 10.50 (*0-15-505483-X*) Dryden Pr.

Master Has Come. Tom Pilgrim. (Orig.). 1989. pap. 4.95 (*1-55673-102-7*, 9813) CSS OH.

***Master-Haunter.** 1998. 29.95 (*0-7459-3795-0*, Pub. by Lion Pubng) Trafalgar.

Master Hilarion. Hilda Charlton. Ed. by Golden Quest Staff. (Golden Quest Ser.: Vol. 1). (Illus.). 104p. (Orig.). 1990. pap. text 7.95 (*0-927383-02-0*) Golden Quest.

Master Homeowner. Larry Reavis. (Illus.). 256p. (Orig.). 1991. pap. 12.98 (*0-9617523-1-9*) Hathaway Pub.

***Master HTML 4 & Xhtml 1 Visually.** Kelly Murdock. (Illus.). 704p. 2000. pap. text 34.99 (*0-7645-3454-8*) IDG Bks.

Master Hua's Classic of the Central Viscera. Hua Tuo. Ed. by Bob Flaws. Tr. by Yang Shou-zhong from CHI. LC 93-71096. 250p. 1993. pap. 21.95 (*0-936185-43-0*) Blue Poppy Pr.

Master Humphrey's Clock & a Child's History of England see Oxford Illustrated Dickens

Master Humphrey's Clock & Other Stories. Ed. by Peter Mudford. (Everyman Paperback Classics). 224p. 1997. pap. 6.95 (*0-460-87654-6*, Everyman's Classic Lib) Tuttle Pubng.

Master i Margarita. Mikhail Afanasevich Bulgakov. Ed. by Ellendea C. Proffer. (Sobranie Sochineii Ser.: Vol. 8). (RUS., Illus.). 425p. 1988. 25.00 (*0-88233-345-3*) Ardis Pubs.

Master IC Cookbook. 2nd ed. Clayton L. Hallmark & Delton T. Horn. (Illus.). 390p. 1991. pap. 22.95 (*0-8306-3550-5*) McGraw-Hill Prof.

Master IC Cookbook. 3rd ed. Delton T. Horn. LC 96-40098. (Illus.). 464p. 1997. 49.95 (*0-07-030564-1*); pap. 34.95 (*0-07-030565-X*) McGraw.

Master Idea (1899) Raymond L. Bridgman. 354p. 1998. reprint ed. pap. 27.95 (*0-7661-0575-X*) Kessinger Pub.

Master Impression: A Clay Sealing from the Greek-Swedish Excavations at Kastelli, Khania. Erik Hallager. (Studies in Mediterranean Archaeology). (Illus.). 76p. (Orig.). 1985. pap. text 34.00 (*91-86098-28-4*) Coronet Bks.

Master Index see Civil War Series

Master Index. (Civil War Ser.). (Illus.). 176p. 1987. lib. bdg. 25.93 (*0-8094-4797-5*) Time-Life.

Master Index. LC 94-13272. 1989. ring bd. 215.00 (*0-87632-690-4*) West Group.

Master Index. (Clark Boardman Callaghan's Environmental Law Ser.). 1990. ring bd. 195.00 (*0-87632-707-2*) West Group.

Master Index: Of Spirits, Angels, Entities & Subjects of Magickal Significance, from the Following Sources. Compiled by Nelson H. White. 275p. 1999. pap. 100.00 (*1-877884-26-X*) Tech Group.

Master Index Vols. 1-10: The Forgotten Settlers of Kansas. 102p. 1998. pap. 12.00 (*1-877881-20-1*) KS Coun Geneal Soc.

Master Index Vols. 11-20: The Forgotten Settlers of Kansas. 105p. 1998. pap. 12.00 (*1-877881-21-X*) KS Coun Geneal Soc.

Master Index & Menu Planner. 2nd rev. ed. Sue Gregg. (Eating Better Cookbooks: Basic Set: Vol. 7). (Illus.). 316p. 1999. spiral bd. 20.00 (*1-878272-09-8*) S Gregg Cookbks.

Master Index II see Directory of Corporate Affiliations: Who Owns Whom

Master Index of Articles & Book Reviews, Vols. 1-50, Suppls. 1-5. xviii, 324p. 1990. 79.95 (*0-387-82251-8*) Spr-Verlag.

***Master Index of the Books of Alice A. Bailey.** Alice A. Bailey. 793p. 1998. pap. 25.00 (*0-85330-144-1*) Lucis.

Master Index I see Directory of Corporate Affiliations: Who Owns Whom

Master Index to More Summaries of Children's Books, 1980-1990. Eloise S. Pettus & Daniel D. Pettus. LC 98-11254. 1998. 198.00 (*0-8108-3269-0*) Scarecrow.

Master Index to 1907 Census of Alabama Confederate Soldiers. Compiled by Gregath Publishing Company Staff. 100p. 1985. lib. bdg. 20.00 (*0-944619-12-6*) Gregath Pub Co.

Master Index to Poetry. 2nd ed. Roth Publishing Editorial Board Staff. LC 85-81058. l, 1939p. 1992. 250.00 (*0-89609-309-3*) Roth Pub Inc.

Master Index to SAS System Documentation, Version 6. 4th ed. SAS Institute, Inc. Staff. 1096p. 1992. pap. 37.95 (*1-58025-352-0*, BR55770) SAS Publ.

Master Index to SAS System Documentation, Version 6, Vol. 6. 2nd ed. 304p. (C). 1993. pap. 9.95 (*1-55544-352-4*, BR56000) SAS Publ.

Master Index to SAS System Documentation, Version 6, Vol. 6. 3rd ed. 624p. (C). 1990. pap. 20.95 (*1-55544-423-7*, BR56003) SAS Publ.

Master Index to SAS System Documentation, Version 6, Vol. 6. 4th ed. 1096p. (C). 1992. pap. 36.95 (*1-55544-503-9*, BR56004) SAS Publ.

Master Index to SUGI Proceedings. 138p. (C). 1995. pap. 9.98 (*1-55544-268-4*, BR55344) SAS Publ.

Master Index to Summaries of Children's Books: Title & Subject Indexes, 2 vols. Eloise S. Pettus & Daniel D. Pettus. LC 85-1901. 1998. 94.00 (*0-8108-1795-0*) Scarecrow.

Master Initiate & the Maid. Marguerite Verdier & R. Swinburne Clymer. 287p. 1956. 9.95 (*0-932785-90-5*) Philos Pub.

Master Initiate & the Maid. deluxe ed. Marguerite Verdier & R. Swinburne Clymer. 287p. 1956. lthr. 20.00 (*0-932785-91-3*) Philos Pub.

***Master Instructs: or How to Wake up on Time.** Richard D. Kuslan. 64p. 2000. 8.95 (*0-9678669-0-1*, TUG-1001, Pellucid Pr) Lttle Red Tugboat.

Master Is Calling: Discovering the Wonders of Spirit-Led Prayer. Lynne Hammond. Ed. by Gina Jennings. 208p. 1998. 17.95 (*1-57399-006-X*) Mac Hammond.

Master It. A. Long. (C). 1997. 128.00 (*0-06-501599-1*) Addison-Wesley.

Master It Faster. Colin Rose. pap. 19.95 (*0-905553-62-4*) Acclrtd Learn.

***Master It Faster: How to Learn Faster, Make Good Decisions & Think Creatively.** Colin Rose. 192p. 2000. pap. 19.95 (*1-85835-806-X*, Indust Soc) Stylus Pub VA.

Master Key. L. Frank Baum. 22.95 (*0-8488-0734-0*) Amereon Ltd.

Master Key. L. Frank Baum. (Illus.). 160p. (YA). (gr. 3 up). 1997. 34.95 (*0-929605-68-3*) Books of Wonder.

Master Key. Lauron W. DeLaurence. 21.95 (*0-685-22037-0*) Wehman.

Master Key: A Growth Experience for Christian Media Professionals. Larry W. Poland. (Illus.). 160p. 1997. pap., wbk. ed. 19.95 (*0-9621692-1-8*) Mastermed Intl.

Master Key of the Scriptures. Lloyd K. Jones. 189p. 1996. reprint ed. spiral bd. 14.00 (*0-7873-0479-4*) Hlth Research.

Master Key of the Scriptures, 1926. Lloyd K. Jones. 190p. 1996. reprint ed. pap. 12.95 (*1-56459-880-2*) Kessinger Pub.

***Master Key System by Charles F. Haanel.** Ed. by Anthony R. Michalski. LC 98-88742. x, 195p. 2000. pap. 19.95 (*0-9678514-0-8*) Kallisti Pubng.

Master Key to Good Golf. Leslie King. (Illus.). 160p. 1979. pap. 16.95 (*0-9607140-0-6*) Golf Assoc.

Master Key to Psychic Unfoldment: A Physiological, Psychical & Philosophical Analysis. Delta Samadhi. 1996. reprint ed. spiral bd. 12.00 (*0-7873-0740-8*) Hlth Research.

Master Key to Riches. Napoleon Hill. 1986. mass mkt. 5.95 (*0-449-21350-1*) Fawcett.

Master Keys for Making Profits in Lapidary: A Complete Guide of Practical Tips & Methods That Can Help Hobbyists & Professionals Realize a Splendid, Dependable Income from Gemcutting. Gerald L. Wykoff. LC 93-28639. (Illus.). 204p. (Orig.). 1994. pap. 19.95 (*0-9607892-8-6*) Adamas Pubs.

Master Keys Getting Most Out of Employees, 1987. (C). 1990. pap. 6.85 (*0-13-807512-3*) P-H.

Master Letters. Lucie Brock-Broido. 96p. 1997. pap. 14.00 (*0-679-76599-9*) Knopf.

Master Letters. Lucie Brock-Broido. LC 95-30284. 96p. 1995. 21.00 (*0-679-44174-3*) Random.

Master Letters of Emily Dickinson. Ed. by R. W. Franklin. LC 86-1093. (Illus.). 52p. 1998. 11.95 (*1-55849-155-4*) U of Mass Pr.

Master Level Exercise: Psycho-Calisthenics. Oscar Ichazo. LC 93-85915. (Illus.). 97p. 1993. pap. 24.95 (*0-916554-25-2*) Arica Inst Pr.

Master Level Exercise: Psycho-Calisthenics. Oscar Ichazo. 97p. 1993. pap. 24.95 (*0-939033-00-3*) Sequoia NYC.

Master Lubrication Handbook. rev. ed. (Illus.). 900p. student ed. 90.00 (*0-88098-079-6*, H M Gousha) Prntice Hall Bks.

Master Lubrication Handbook Supplement. rev. ed. student ed. 74.25 (*0-88098-080-X*, H M Gousha) Prntice Hall Bks.

Master Lubrication Handbook Supplement, 1987. rev. ed. student ed. 76.50 (*0-88098-094-X*, H M Gousha) Prntice Hall Bks.

Master Lubrication Handbook, 1985. Chek-Chart Staff. (Illus.). 1000p. student ed. 90.00 (*0-88098-059-1*, H M Gousha); suppl. ed. 85.45 (*0-88098-075-3*, H M Gousha) Prntice Hall Bks.

Master Lubrication Handbook, 1987. rev. ed. student ed. 96.80 (*0-88098-095-8*, H M Gousha) Prntice Hall Bks.

Master Lubrication Handbook, 1990. 768p. 1990. 96.95 (*0-13-130626-X*, H M Gousha) Prntice Hall Bks.

Master Magician: An Action Book. Sandy Ransford. (Illus.). 18p. (J). (gr. 4-7). 1994. 19.95 (*1-56138-460-7*) Running Pr.

Master Man. large type ed. Ruby M. Ayres. 184p. 1989. 19.95 (*0-7451-0941-1*, G K Hall Lrg Type) Mac Lib Ref.

Master Man: A Tall Tale of Nigeria. Aaron Shepard. LC 99-48513. (Illus.). 32p. (J). 2000. 15.95 (*0-688-13783-0*, Wm Morrow) Morrow Avon.

Master Man: A Tall Tale of Nigeria. Aaron Shepard. LC 99-48513. (Illus.). 32p. (J). 2001. lib. bdg. 15.89 (*0-688-13784-9*, Wm Morrow) Morrow Avon.

***Master Mariner: Captain James Cook & the Peoples of the Pacific.** Daniel Conner & Lorraine Miller. 176p. 1999. pap. 18.95 (*1-55054-723-2*) DGL InfoWrite.

Master Mason Bible. 1992. pap. 39.95 (*1-55665-545-2*) Fireside Catholic Bibles.

Master Masons of Chartres. John James. (Illus.). 208p. 1991. reprint ed. 30.00 (*0-646-00805-6*) Boydell & Brewer.

Master Math: Algebra. Debra Ross. LC 96-22993. 192p. (Orig.). 1996. pap. 10.99 (*1-56414-194-2*) Career Pr Inc.

Master Math: Basic Mathg & Pre-Algebra. Debra Ross. LC 96-22992. 192p. 1996. pap. 10.99 (*1-56414-214-0*) Career Pr Inc.

Master Math: Calculus, Including Everything from the Derivative & the Integral to Partial Derivatives, Vector Calculus & Differential Equations. Debra Ross. LC 98-25769. 352p. 1998. pap. 12.99 (*1-56414-337-6*) Career Pr Inc.

Master Math: Pre-Calculus & Geometry. Debra Ross. LC 96-22994. 192p. (Orig.). 1996. pap. 10.99 (*1-56414-218-3*) Career Pr Inc.

Master Math Workbook Grade 4. Carole Gerber. (J). (gr. 4-7). 1992. pap., student ed. 5.95 (*1-56189-014-6*) Amer Educ Pub.

Master Math Workbook Grade K. Carole Gerber. 1992. pap. 5.95 (*1-56189-010-3*) Amer Educ Pub.

Master Math Workbook Grade 1. Carole Gerber. 1992. pap. 5.95 (*1-56189-011-1*) Amer Educ Pub.

Master Math Workbook Grade 2. Carole Gerber. 1992. pap. 5.95 (*1-56189-012-X*) Amer Educ Pub.

Master Math Workbook Grade 3. rev. exp. ed. Carole Gerber. (Master Skills Ser.). (Illus.). 127p. 1992. pap. 5.95 (*1-56189-013-8*) Amer Educ Pub.

Master Math Workbook Grade 5. Carole Gerber. 1992. pap. 5.95 (*1-56189-015-4*) Amer Educ Pub.

Master Math Workbook Grade 6. Carole Gerber. 1992. pap. 5.95 (*1-56189-016-2*) Amer Educ Pub.

Master Measurement Model of Employee Performance. Carl Thor. 1990. pap. text 15.00 (*0-9626880-1-0*) SITE.

Master Mercury. Daniel Defoe. LC 92-23722. (Augustan Reprints Ser.: No. 184). 1977. reprint ed. 14.50 (*0-404-70184-1*, DA490) AMS Pr.

***Master Microsoft Access 2000 Visually.** Curtis Frye. LC 99-43747. 700p. 2000. pap. 39.99 (*0-7645-6048-4*) IDG Bks.

***Master Microsoft Word 2000 Visually.** Shelley O'Hara. LC 99-26495. 704p. 2000. pap. 39.99 (*0-7645-6046-8*) IDG Bks.

***Master Microsoft's Windows Millenium Visually.** Ruth Maran. (Master Visually Ser.). (Illus.). 704p. 2000. pap. 34.99 (*0-7645-3496-3*) IDG Bks.

Master Mind: The Key to Mental Power, Development & Efficiency. Theron Q. Dumont. 276p. 1980. reprint ed. 15.00 (*0-911662-66-9*) Yoga.

Master-Minded: Ten Stories of Contemporary Servants. Melanie Smith. Ed. by Becky Nelson. (Illus.). 91p. (Orig.). (YA). (gr. 7-12). 1992. pap. text 4.95 (*1-56309-046-5*, N926101, New Hope) Womans Mission Union.

Master Minds. Richard Kostelanetz. LC 69-18246. 384p. 1981. reprint ed. text 75.00 (*0-932360-30-0*) Archae Edns.

Master Minds of Modern Science. Thomas C. Bridges & Hubert H. Tiltman. LC 68-57307. (Essay Index Reprint Ser.). 1977. 20.95 (*0-8369-0064-2*) Ayer.

Master Modellers. Robin Smith. Ed. by Tim Newark. LC 97-27072. (Brassey's Master Class Ser.). (Illus.). 143p. 1997. 29.95 (*1-85753-240-6*, Pub. by Brasseys) Brasseys.

Master Money the Millionaire: The Millionaire. Allan Ahlberg. 24p. (J). (gr. 3). 1981. pap. 6.95 (*0-14-031246-3*, Pub. by Pnguin Bks Ltd) Trafalgar.

Master Motivator: Secrets of Inspiring Leadership. Mark Victor Hansen & Joe Batten. 150p. 1995. pap. 9.95 (*1-55874-355-3*, 3553) Health Comm.

Master Motor Builders: The Inception, Design, Production & Uses of the Non-Automotive Engines of Packard. unabridged ed. Robert J. Neal. (Illus.). 384p. 1998. 65.00 (*0-9647483-1-2*) Aero-Marine Hist Pubng.

Master Moves. Moshe Feldenkrais. LC 84-61647. 1985. pap. 17.95 (*0-916990-15-X*) META Pubns.

Master Musician. Ed. by Debbie Cavalier. (YA). 1995. pap. text 24.95 (*1-57623-718-4*, BMR06101) Wrner Bros.

***Master-Myth of Modern Society: A Sketch of the Scientific Worldview & Its Psyco-Social Effects.** G. Martin Kinget. 90p. 1999. pap. 24.50 (*0-7618-1570-8*) U Pr of Amer.

Master Numbers: Cycles of Divine Order. Faith Javane. Ed. by Julie Lockhart. LC 88-60422. 204p. 1988. pap. 14.95 (*0-914918-81-8*, Whitford) Schiffer.

Master of Airpower: General Carl A. Spaatz. David R. Mets. LC 88-5427. (Illus.). 448p. 1997. pap. 17.95 (*0-89141-639-0*) Presidio Pr.

***Master of All Desires.** Judith M. Riley. LC 99-29828. 480p. 1999. 26.95 (*0-670-88450-2*, Viking) Viking Penguin.

***Master of All Desires.** Judith M. Riley. 2000. pap. 14.00 (*0-14-029653-0*) Penguin Putnam.

Master of Aysgarth. large type ed. Margaret Mayhew. 368p. 1983. 27.99 (*0-7089-1058-0*) Ulverscroft.

M

Master of Balantrae, Dr. Jekyll & Mr. Hyde, Kidnapped. Robert Louis Stevenson. (J). 1985. 15.45 (*0-671-52760-6*) S&S Trade.

Master of Ballantrae. Robert Louis Stevenson. (Classics Illustrated Study Guides Ser.). (Illus.). 1997. mass mkt. 4.99 (*1-57840-049-X*, Pub. by Acclaim Bks) Penguin Putnam.

Master of Ballantrae. Robert Louis Stevenson. (Airmont Classics Ser.). (YA). (gr. 8 up). 1964. mass mkt. 1.95 (*0-8049-0047-7*, CL-47) Airmont.

Master of Ballantrae. Robert Louis Stevenson. 22.95 (*0-89190-738-6*) Amereon Ltd.

Master of Ballantrae. Robert Louis Stevenson. (J). 1997. pap. 2.95 (*0-8167-0853-3*) Troll Communs.

Master of Ballantrae. large type ed. Robert Louis Stevenson. (Large Print Ser.). 393p. 1992. reprint ed. lib. bdg. 24.00 (*0-939495-35-X*) North Bks.

Master of Ballantrae. Robert Louis Stevenson. 247p. 1998. reprint ed. lib. bdg. 24.00 (*1-58287-047-0*) North Bks.

Master of Ballantrae: A Winter's Tale. Robert Louis Stevenson. Ed. & Intro. by Emma Letley. (World's Classics Paperback Ser.). 288p. 1983. pap. 7.95 (*0-19-281635-7*) OUP.

Master of Ballantrae: A Winter's Tale. Robert Louis Stevenson. Ed. & Intro. by Adrian Poole. LC 97-184669. xxx, 249p. 1997. pap. 9.95 (*0-14-043446-1*) Viking Penguin.

M

Master of Ballantrae & Weir of Hermiston. Robert Louis Stevenson. LC 92-52909. xlix, 373p. 1992. 17.00 (*0-679-41744-3*) Everymns Lib.

Master of Ballantrae, The Great North Road see Works of Robert Louis Stevenson, Valima Edition

Master of Blacktower. Barbara Michaels, pseud. 304p. 1995. mass mkt. 6.50 (*0-425-14941-2*) Berkley Pub.

Master of Bucklands. large type ed. Minka Jones. (Linford Romance Library). 1990. pap. 16.99 (*0-7089-6821-X*, Linford) Ulverscroft.

Master of Craigraven. large type ed. Jan Constant. LC 93-34649. 230p. 1994. lib. bdg. 16.95 (*0-8161-5844-4*, G K Hall Lrg Type) Mac Lib Ref.

Master of D.E.A.T.H. Jerry Ahern. 1985. pap. 2.50 (*0-373-62007-1*) Harlequin Bks.

Master of Death: The Lifeless Art of Pierre Remiet, Illuminator. Michael Camille. LC 95-9088. (Illus.). 286p. 1996. 45.00 (*0-300-06457-8*) Yale U Pr.

Master of Desert Nomads. David Cook. 1983. 5.50 (*0-394-53161-2*) Random.

Master of Desolation: The Reminiscences of Capt. Joseph J. Fuller. Ed. by Briton C. Busch. (American Maritime Library: Vol. 9). (Illus.). xxx, 349p. 1980. 19.95 (*0-913372-21-8*) Mystic Seaport.

***Master of Destiny.** Angela Drake. 320p. 1999. 26.00 (*0-7278-5502-6*, Pub. by Severn Hse) Chivers N Amer.

***Master of Diaster.** James Chiles. 2000. 27.00 (*0-06-662081-3*); pap. 16.00 (*0-06-662082-1*) HarpC.

Master of Disaster: A Tale of Manifestation, Mayhem, & Magic. Jan Longwell-Smiley. LC 98-71587. 328p. 1998. pap. 13.95 (*1-57174-105-4*) Hampton Roads Pub Co.

***Master of Disguise: My Secret Life in the CIA.** Antonio J. Mendez. (Illus.). 2000. pap. 14.00 (*0-06-095791-3*) HarpC.

***Master of Disguise: My Secret Life in the CIA.** Antonio J. Mendez & Malcolm McConnell. LC 99-23066. (Illus.). 368p. 1999. 25.00 (*0-688-16302-5*, Wm Morrow) Morrow Avon.

Master of Earth & Water. Diana L. Paxson & Adrienne Martine-Barnes. 416p. 1994. mass mkt. 4.99 (*0-380-75801-6*, Avon Bks) Morrow Avon.

Master of Earth & Water. Diana L. Paxson & Adrienne Martine-Barnes. 2000. 22.00 (*0-380-97219-0*, Avon Bks) Morrow Avon.

Master of El Corazon. Sandra Marton. (Presents Ser.: No. 1928). 1997. per. 3.50 (*0-373-11928-3*, 1-11928-8) Harlequin Bks.

Master of Fate. Gonzalo Munevar. 240p. 2000. 23.95 (*0-930773-55-1*) Black Heron Pr.

Master of Frinton Park. large type ed. Freda M. Long. (Dales Large Print Ser.). 321p. 1997. pap. 18.99 (*1-85389-672-1*) Ulverscroft.

Master of Game: Oldest English Book on Hunting. Duke Edward of Norwich. Ed. by William A. Baillie-Grohman & F. Baillie-Grohman. LC 78-178528. (Illus.). reprint ed. 62.50 (*0-404-56541-7*) AMS Pr.

Master of Glass: Charles Eamer Kempe, 1837-1907. Ed. by Margaret Stavridi. 172p. (C). 1988. 110.00 (*0-9513125-0-2*) St Mut.

Master of Go. Yasunari Kawabata. Orig. Title: Meijin. 1996. pap. 12.00 (*0-679-76106-3*) Random Hse Value.

Master of Gray Trilogy. Nigel Tranter. 612p. 1996. mass mkt. 19.95 (*0-340-66675-7*, Pub. by Hodder & Stought Ltd) Trafalgar.

Master of Guise. large type ed. Alex Stuart. 352p. 1993. 27.99 (*0-7089-2816-1*) Ulverscroft.

Master of Herringham. large type ed. Julia Murray. 1994. 27.99 (*0-7089-3152-9*) Ulverscroft.

Master of Hestviken. Sigrid Undset. LC 94-16662. 304p. 1994. pap. 13.00 (*0-679-75273-0*) Random.

Master of Hiddenness: A Practical Commentary on the Prayer Adon Olam for the Restoration of Our Original Connection to God. Jason Shulman. Ed. by Jan Bresnick. 56p. 1999. lib. bdg. 20.00 (*1-892192-03-9*) Soc of Souls.

Master of Hope: Selected Writings of Naphtali Imber. Ed. by Jacob Kabakoff. LC 84-48476. (Illus.). 344p. 1985. 39.50 (*0-8386-3238-6*) Fairleigh Dickinson.

Master of Horses. Katharine Kincaid. (Zebra Splendor Historical Romances Ser.). 352p. 1999. mass mkt. 4.99 (*0-8217-6224-9*) Kensgtn Pub Corp.

***Master of Ironwood.** Don Winslow. 192p. 1999. mass mkt. 7.95 (*1-56201-148-0*, Pub. by Blue Moon Bks) Publishers Group.

Master of Jalna. large type ed. Mazo De La Roche. (Whiteoak Chronicles Ser.). 1973. 27.99 (*0-85456-682-1*) Ulverscroft.

Master of Judo. Richard Brightfield. (Choose Your Own Adventure Ser.: No. 148). (J). (gr. 4-8). 1994. 8.60 (*0-606-06560-1*, Pub. by Turtleback) Demco.

Master of Knives. C. W. Truesdale & Lucas Johnson. (Illus.). 102p. lib. bdg. 20.00 (*0-912316-01-2*) Hamman Pub.

Master of Lies. Graham Masterton. 336p. 1995. 4.99 (*0-8125-1166-2*, Pub. by Tor Bks) St Martin.

Master of Light: Ansel Adams & His Influences. Therese Lichtenstein. 1998. 24.98 (*1-57717-059-8*) Todtri Prods.

Master of Line: John Winkler, American Etcher. Mary Millman & Dave Bohn. LC 94-5208. (Illus.). 192p. 1994. 58.00 (*0-88496-358-6*) Capra Pr.

Master of Liversedge. large type ed. Alice C. Ley. 1994. 11.50 (*0-7089-3203-7*) Ulverscroft.

Master of Love & Mercy: Cheng Yen. Yu-ing Ching Bezine. LC 95-1191. (Illus.). 288p. 1995. 24.95 (*0-931892-27-9*) B Dolphin Pub.

Master of Magic: Shadows of Time. Tom Alvarez & Michael Morga. Ed. by Michael Payne. (Illus.). 350p. (Orig.). (YA). (gr. 9-12). 1998. pap. text 6.95 (*1-880852-00-4*) Magical Pub FL.

Master of Magic: The Official Strategy Guide. Alan Emrich. 1995. pap. 19.95 (*1-55958-722-9*) Prima Pub.

Master of Mahogany: The Story of Tom Day, Free Black Cabinetmaker. Mary E. Lyons. LC 93-37900. (Illus.). 48p. (J). (gr. 3-6). 1994. mass mkt. 15.95 (*0-684-19675-1*, Scribners Ref) Mac Lib Ref.

Master of Malcarew. large type ed. Veronica Black. 272p. 1995. 27.99 (*0-7089-3233-9*) Ulverscroft.

Master of Many Treasures. Mary Brown. 384p. 1995. mass mkt. 5.99 (*0-671-87693-7*) Baen Bks.

Master of Marshlands. large type ed. Miriam Macgregor. 288p. 1991. reprint ed. lib. bdg. 18.95 (*0-263-12718-4*) Mac Lib Ref.

Master of Mary of Burgundy: A Book of Hours for Engelbert of Nassau. Ed. by J. J. G. Alexander. LC 78-128576. 194p. 1970. boxed set 45.00 (*0-8076-0578-6*) Braziller.

Master of Mary of Burgundy: A Book of Hours for Englebert of Nassau. J. J. G. Alexander. LC 78-128576. 194p. 1993. 25.00 (*0-8076-1332-0*) Braziller.

Master of Masters. Larry Townsend. Ed. by Victor Terry. (Illus.). 185p. (Orig.). 1997. pap. 14.95 (*1-881684-13-X*) L T Pubns CA.

Master of Masterton. large type ed. Kay Stephens. 385p. 1996. pap. 18.99 (*1-85389-631-4*, Dales) Ulverscroft.

Master of Men. fac. ed. Ed. by Thomas C. Clark. LC 72-116396. (Granger Index Reprint Ser.). 1977. 18.95 (*0-8369-6137-4*) Ayer.

Master of Middle-Earth: The Achievement of J. R. R. Tolkien. Paul H. Kocher. LC 75-306945. 247p. 1973. write for info. (*0-500-01095-1*) Thames Hudson.

Master of Midnight. Penelope Neri. 1995. pap. 4.99 (*0-8217-5035-6*) NAL.

Master of Modern French Criticism. Irving Babbitt. LC 76-56408. 427p. 1977. reprint ed. lib. bdg. 75.00 (*0-8371-9415-6*, BAMF, Greenwood Pr) Greenwood.

Master of Modern Physics: The Scientific Contributions of H. A. Kramers. D. Ter Haar. LC 97-22356. (Series in Physics). vi, 288p. 1998. text 39.50 (*0-691-02141-4*, Pub. by Princeton U Pr) Cal Prin Full Svc.

Master of Moonlight. Joyce Myrus. 384p. 1995. mass mkt. 4.99 (*0-8217-4900-5*, Pinncle Kensgtn) Kensgtn Pub Corp.

Master of Moonspell. Deborah Camp. 416p. (Orig.). 1993. mass mkt. 4.50 (*0-380-76736-8*, Avon Bks) Morrow Avon.

***Master of Moor House.** Anne Ashley. 320p. 2000. 26.99 (*0-263-16416-0*, Pub. by Mills & Boon) Ulverscroft.

Master of Morholm. large type ed. Timothy Wilson. 576p. 1987. 27.99 (*0-7089-8425-8*, Charnwood) Ulverscroft.

Master of Murder. Christopher Pike, pseud. Ed. by Pat MacDonald. (YA). (gr. 9 up). 1999. mass mkt. 3.99 (*0-671-69059-0*, Archway) PB.

Master of Murder. Christopher Pike, pseud. 1992. 9.09 (*0-606-02089-6*, Pub. by Turtleback) Demco.

Master of My Dreams. Danelle Harmon. 416p. (Orig.). 1993. mass mkt. 4.50 (*0-380-77227-2*, Avon Bks) Morrow Avon.

Master of Mysteries: Problems Solved by Astro, Seer of Secrets & His Love Affair with Valeska Wynne, His Assistant. Gelett Burgess. LC 75-32736. (Literature of Mystery & Detection Ser.). (Illus.). 1976. reprint ed. 40.95 (*0-405-07865-X*) Ayer.

Master of None: The Story of Me Life. Ben Wicks. (Illus.). 288p. 1995. 29.99 (*0-7710-8994-5*) McCland & Stewart.

Master of Orion II: Battle at Antares: The Official Strategy Guide. Dave Ellis. LC 95-72241. 336p. 1996. per. 19.99 (*0-7615-0273-4*) Prima Pub.

Master of Our Time. G. Grigson. LC 72-3175. (English Literature Ser.: No. 33). 1972. reprint ed. lib. bdg. 75.00 (*0-8383-1534-8*) M S G Haskell Hse.

Master of Our Time: Wyndham Lewis. Geoffrey Grigson. 1972. 250.00 (*0-87968-010-5*) Gordon Pr.

Master of Passion. Jacqueline Baird. (Presents Ser.). 1994. per. 2.99 (*0-373-11683-7*, 1-11683-9) Harlequin Bks.

Master of Petersburg. J. M. Coetzee. 256p. 1995. pap. 12.95 (*0-14-023810-7*, Penguin Bks) Viking Penguin.

Master of Precision: Henry M. Leland. Ottilie M. Leland & Minnie Dubbs Millbrook. LC 66-10501. (Great Lakes Bks.). (Illus.). 300p. 1996. pap. 17.95 (*0-8143-2665-X*) Wayne St U Pr.

Master of Putting. Al Barkow & George Low. LC 96-39940. (Illus.). 96p. 1997. reprint ed. pap. 12.95 (*1-58080-012-2*) Burford Bks.

Master of Putting. George Low & Al Barkow. LC 96-39940. (Illus.). 96p. 1997. reprint ed. pap. 12.95 (*1-55821-524-7*) Lyons Pr.

Master of Seapower: A Biography of Fleet Admiral Ernest J. King. Thomas B. Buell. (Classics of Naval Literature Ser.). (Illus.). 638p. 1995. 32.95 (*1-55750-092-4*) Naval Inst Pr.

***Master of Seduction.** Kenley MacGregor. 352p. 2000. mass mkt. 5.99 (*0-06-108712-2*) HarpC.

Master of Seduction. large type ed. Sarah Holland. 288p. 1995. 23.99 (*0-263-14317-1*, Pub. by Mills & Boon) Ulverscroft.

Master of Shilden. Lucinda Carrington. 256p. (Orig.). 1997. mass mkt. 5.95 (*0-352-33140-2*, Pub. by BLA4) London Brdge.

Master of Skelgale. large type ed. Muriel Howe. 416p. 1986. 27.99 (*0-7089-1460-8*) Ulverscroft.

Master of Song. Elsie S. Santos. (Stories for Young Grandchildren by Grandma Elsie Ser.). (Illus.). 44p. (Orig.). (J). (ps-2). 1984. pap. 4.25 (*0-914151-02-9*) E S Santos.

Master of Surprise: Mark Interpreted. Donald H. Juel. LC 94-6132. 160p. 1994. 16.00 (*0-8006-2594-3*, 1-2594) Augsburg Fortress.

Master of Tae Kwon Do. Richard Brightfield. (Choose Your Own Adventure Ser.: No. 102). (J). (gr. 4-8). 1990. 8.60 (*0-606-04553-8*, Pub. by Turtleback) Demco.

***Master of the Blade: Secrets of the Deadly Art of Knife Fighting.** Richard Ryan. (Illus.). 176p. 1999. pap. 20.00 (*1-58160-048-8*) Paladin Pr.

Master of the Century Past. R. S. Metzger. LC 93-37721. 288p. 1996. 17.95 (*0-913720-87-9*) Beil.

Master of the Chase. large type ed. Susan Macias. (Black Satin Romance Ser.). 287p. 1997. 27.99 (*1-86110-025-6*) Ulverscroft.

Master of the Courts. limited ed. Andrew J. Purdy. LC 72-96446. (Illus.). 44p. 1973. 20.00 (*0-912292-31-8*) Smith.

***Master of the Crossroads.** Madison Smartt Bell. 704p. 2000. 30.00 (*0-375-42056-8*) Knopf.

Master of the Day of Judgement. Leo Perutz. Tr. by Eric Mosbacher from GER. LC 94-14353. 148p. 1994. 19.45 (*1-55970-171-4*, Pub. by Arcade Pub Inc) Time Warner.

Master of the Day of Judgement: An Arcade Mystery. Leo Perutz. Tr. by Eric Mosbacher. 192p. 1996. pap. 10.45 (*1-55970-334-2*, Pub. by Arcade Pub Inc) Time Warner.

Master of the Forge: William F. Moran, Jr. & His Classic Blades. B. R. Hughes & C. Houston Price. LC 96-92166. (Illus.). 216p. 1996. 85.00 (*0-940362-48-1*) Knife World.

Master of the Game. Sidney Sheldon. 1986. mass mkt. 4.95 (*0-446-73325-3*, Pub. by Warner Bks) Little.

Master of the Game. Sidney Sheldon. 1991. 5.95 (*0-446-77481-2*) Warner Bks.

Master of the Game. Sidney Sheldon. 496p. 1988. reprint ed. mass mkt. 7.99 (*0-446-35545-3*, Pub. by Warner Bks) Little.

Master of the Grove. Victor Kelleher. (J). (gr. 5-9). 1988. pap. 3.95 (*0-317-69634-3*, PuffinBks) Peng Put Young Read.

Master of the Hohenfurth Alterpiece. Jaroslav Pesina. (Illus.). 260p. 1989. 95.00 (*0-85667-339-0*) Sothebys Pubns.

Master of the Inn see Collected Works of Robert Herrick

Master of the Inn. Robert Herrick. 274p. 1980. reprint ed. lib. bdg. 12.95 (*0-89968-188-3*, Lghtyr Pr) Buccaneer Bks.

Master of the Inn. Robert Herrick. LC 76-96886. reprint ed. pap. text 8.50 (*0-8290-1683-X*); reprint ed. lib. bdg. 19.50 (*0-8398-0779-1*) Irvington.

Master of the Inn. Robert Herrick. (Collected Works of Robert Herrick). 1988. reprint ed. lib. bdg. 59.00 (*0-7812-1269-3*) Rprt Serv.

Master of the Leaping Figures. Jeremy T. Hooker. 77p. 1987. reprint ed. pap. 12.95 (*0-905289-74-9*, Pub. by Enitha Pr) Dufour.

Master of the Lotus Garden: The Life & Art of Bada Shanren, 1626-1705. Wang Fangyu & Richard M. Barnhart. Ed. by Judith G. Smith. LC 90-70036. 300p. (C). 1990. pap. 40.00 (*0-89467-054-9*) Yale Art Gallery.

Master of the Lotus Garden: The Life & Art of Bada Shanren, 1626-1705. Wang Fangyu & Richard M. Barnhart. 304p. (C). 1990. 70.00 (*0-300-04933-1*) Yale U Pr.

Master of the Moor. Ruth Rendell. 256p. 1986. mass mkt. 5.95 (*0-345-34147-3*) Ballantine Pub Grp.

Master of the Mountain. Eunice A. Pennington. 1971. 4.50 (*0-685-47078-4*); pap. 2.50 (*0-685-47079-2*) Pennington.

***Master of the Return.** Tova Reich. LC 99-34313. 256p. 1999. pap. text 17.95 (*0-8156-0620-6*) Syracuse U Pr.

Master of the River. Felix Savard. Tr. by Richard Howard. LC 77-551736. (French Writers of Canada Ser.). 135p. reprint ed. pap. 41.90 (*0-608-14943-8*, 202612100048) Bks Demand.

Master of the Russian Ballet: The Memoirs of Cav. Enrico Cecchetti. Olga Racster. LC 78-18777. (Series in Dance). (Illus.). 1978. reprint ed. lib. bdg. 35.00 (*0-306-77589-1*) Da Capo.

Master of the Sacred Page: Essays & Articles in Honor of Roland E. Murphy, O. Carm., on the Occasion of His Eightieth Birthday. Roland E. Murphy. Ed. by Craig E. Morrison et al. LC 97-16137. (Illus.). 416p. (Orig.). 1997. pap. 24.00 (*0-9656910-0-4*) Carmelite Inst.

Master of the Sultan. Kevin McDermott. 148p. 1997. pap. 7.95 (*1-85371-706-1*, Pub. by Poolbeg Pr) Dufour.

***Master of the Sundown Shore.** Robert Campbell. 208p. 1999. pap. 15.95 (*1-58444-055-4*) DiscUs Bks.

Master of the Titanic. large type ed. Pat Lacey. (Magna Large Print Ser.). 574p. 1997. 27.99 (*0-7505-1067-6*) Ulverscroft.

Master of the Titanic: The Career of Captain Ted Smith. Pat Lacey. 359p. 1996. 22.50 (*1-85776-221-5*, Pub. by Book Guild Ltd) Trans-Atl Phila.

Master of the Unicorn: The Life & Work of Jean Duvet. Colin Eisler. (Illus.). 1978. lib. bdg. 70.00 (*0-913870-46-3*) Abaris Bks.

Master of the World. (J). (gr. 4-7). 1997. pap. 2.95 (*0-8167-0459-7*) Troll Communs.

Master of the World. Jules Verne. (Airmont Classics Ser.). (YA). (gr. 7 up). 1965. mass mkt. 1.25 (*0-8049-0073-6*, CL-73) Airmont.

Master of the World. Jules Verne. 20.95 (*0-89190-518-9*) Amereon Ltd.

Master of Timberland. 3rd ed. Sara H. French. (Orig.). 1997. mass mkt. 6.95 (*1-56333-595-6*) Masquerade.

Master of Tradition: The Art of Chang Ta-Ch'ien. Richard E. Strassberg. (Illus.). 109p. 1983. pap. 24.00 (*1-877921-23-8*) Pacific Asia.

Master of Uluru. large type ed. Helen Bianchin. (Linford Romance Library). 326p. 1984. pap. 16.99 (*0-7089-6038-3*, Linford) Ulverscroft.

Master of Villainy. Elizabeth S. Rohmer. 322p. Date not set. 24.95 (*0-8488-2383-4*) Amereon Ltd.

Master of Winterbourne. Francesca Shaw. (Historical Ser.: No. 8). 1998. pap. 4.99 (*0-373-30317-3*, 1-30317-1) Harlequin Bks.

Master of Wisdom: Writings of the Buddhist Master Nagarjuna. Tr. by Christian Lindtner from CHI. LC 86-29111. (Tibetan Translation Ser.: Vol. 14). 413p. 1986. 40.00 (*0-89800-139-0*) Dharma Pub.

Master of Wisdom: Writings of the Buddhist Master Nagarjuna. Tr. by Christian Lindtner from CHI. LC 86-29111. (Tibetan Translation Ser.: Vol. 14). 413p. 1997. pap. 19.95 (*0-89800-286-9*) Dharma Pub.

Master Office Manual. Wayne Wood. (Office Manual Ser.). 172p. 1992. 89.00 (*1-890018-01-5*) Anadem Pubng.

Master Office 97 Visually. Marangraphics Staff. LC HF5548.4.M525M38. 704p. 1998. pap. 39.99 (*0-7645-6036-0*) IDG Bks.

***Master Office 2000 Visually.** Maran. LC HF5548.4.M525M368. 704p. 1999. pap. 39.99 (*0-7645-6050-6*) IDG Bks.

Master Optical Techniques. Arthur S. De Vany. LC 80-24442. (Wiley Series in Pure & Applied Optics). 608p. reprint ed. pap. 188.50 (*0-7837-2368-7*, 204005400006) Bks Demand.

Master Pack. Deborah Christine & Stevie Mack. (Programs Ser.). 46p. 1987. pap. 209.00 incl. audio, VHS (*0-945666-00-4*) Crizmac.

Master Package. (Bowdoin Method Ser.). 1989. pap. write for info. (*1-55997-094-4*) Websters Intl.

Master Painter: Warner E. Sollman. Jack R. Lundbom. LC 99-18430. (Illus.). 260p. 1998. 29.95 (*0-86554-610-X*, H460) Mercer Univ Pr.

Master Painters' Biblical History & Destiny of the World. Denny L. Brown. LC 97-47719. 1998. 39.95 (*1-57345-371-4*, Shadow Mount) Deseret Bk.

Master Paintings from the Phillips Collection. Robert Hughes. LC 98-10763. (Illus.). 224p. Date not set. pap. 30.00 (*1-887178-78-3*, Pub. by Counterpt DC) HarpC.

Master Paintings in the Art Institute of Chicago. 2nd rev. ed. Sally Ruth May. LC 88-9367. (Illus.). 168p. 1999. 50.00 (*0-86559-175-X*, Pub. by Art Inst Chi) Hudson Hills.

Master Pairs Technique. Senior. pap. 3.95 (*0-575-04883-2*, Pub. by V Gollancz) Trafalgar.

Master Pastelists of the Pastel Society of America. Frank Getlein. (Illus.). 44p. (Orig.). 1987. pap. 10.00 (*0-911431-22-5*) Harmon-Meek Gal.

Master Patterns & Grading for Women's Outsizes: Pattern Sizing Technology. Gerry Cooklin. 228p. 1995. pap. 34.95 (*0-632-03915-9*) Blackwell Sci.

Master Percentages in Bridge. Kelsey. pap. 3.95 (*0-575-04570-1*, Pub. by V Gollancz) Trafalgar.

Master Photographer's Lith Printing Course: A Definitive Guide to Creative Lith Printing. Tim Rudman. 128p. 1999. pap. 24.95 (*0-8174-4539-0*) Watsn-Guptill.

***Master Photoshop 5 Visually.** Ken Milburn. LC 99-10950. 640p. 2000. pap. 39.99 (*0-7645-6045-X*) IDG Bks.

***Master Pieces: The Architecture of Chess.** Gareth Williams. (Illus.). 160p. 2000. 23.95 (*0-670-89381-1*, Viking) Viking Penguin.

Master Pieces: The Corning Painters Group. Rachael Sadinsky. (Illus.). 30p. (Orig.). 1990. pap. text 2.50 (*1-877885-06-1*) Arnot Art.

Master Pieces Vol. 1: The Art History of Jigsaw Puzzles. Chris McCann. LC 98-35401. Orig. Title: Masterpieces. (Illus.). 256p. 1999. 39.95 (*1-888054-24-7*, 54247) Collectors Pr.

Master Pieces from the Museum of Classical Furnitures. Shixiang Wang & Curtis Evarts. (Illus.). 264p. 1995. write for info. (*7-883662-02-8*) Chinese Arts.

Master Pipers. George Sand. Tr. by Rosemary Lloyd. LC 93-31046. (World's Classics Ser.). (Illus.). 356p. 1994. pap. 10.95 (*0-19-283097-X*) OUP.

Master Plan see Plan Supremo

Master Plan. John F. Avanzini & Patrick Ondrey. (Financial Freedom Ser.). 62p. 1993. pap. 5.95 (*1-878605-12-7*) HIS Pub Co.

Master Plan. Al Duncan. 1999. pap. text 12.95 (*0-9663533-3-1*) Ambassador Hse.

Master Plan. Cornel Lengyel. (Living Playwrights' Library). 1978. pap. 2.50 (*0-686-00548-1*) Dragons Teeth.

Master Plan. large type ed. Ian Stuart. (Linford Mystery Library). 496p. 1997. pap. 16.99 (*0-7089-5026-4*, Linford) Ulverscroft.

Master Plan for Financial Security. (How to Manage in a Depression & Recession Ser.). 1992. lib. bdg. 88.95 (*0-8490-8779-1*) Gordon Pr.

Master Plan for the City of Litchfield Park. Karen Apple et al. (Illus.). 105p. 1993. pap. text 100.00 (*1-884320-04-X*); pap. text 35.00 (*1-884320-03-1*) ASU Herberger Ctr.

An Asterisk (*) at the beginning of an entry indicates that the title is appearing for the first time.

Master Plan, General Studies, Preliminary Studies & Other Buildings & Projects. Ed. by Franz Schulze & George E. Danforth. LC 86-9980. Vol. 8. (Illus.). 488p. 1993. text 300.00 (*0-8240-5992-1*) Garland.

Master Plan of Discipleship. Robert E. Coleman. 160p. 1998. mass mkt. 4.99 (*0-8007-8655-6*) Revell.

Master Plan of Evangelism see Plan Supremo de Evangelizacion

Master Plan of Evangelism see Plan Maestro de la Evangelizacion

Master Plan of Evangelism. 2nd abr. ed. Robert E. Coleman. LC 93-6792. 144p. 1994. mass mkt. 4.99 (*0-8007-8624-6*, Spire) Revell.

Master Plan of Evangelism: Leader's Guide. Robert E. Coleman & Frank G. Tunstall. 1990. pap. 9.95 (*0-911866-24-8*) LifeSprings Res.

Master Plan of Evangelism: 30th Anniversary Edition. 2nd anniversary ed. Robert E. Coleman. LC 93-6792. 204p. (YA). (gr. 10). 1992. pap. 9.99 (*0-8007-5467-0*) Revell.

Master Plan Process for Parks & Recreation. Craig W. Kelsey et al. LC 85-161331. 83p. 1985. write for info. (*0-88314-298-8*) AAHPERD.

Master Plan Process for Parks & Recreation. 2nd rev. ed. Craig W. Kelsey & Howard Gray. (Illus.). 83p. 1996. pap. 20.00 (*0-88314-851-X*, 300-10007) AAHPERD.

Master Planning for Architecture: Theory & Practice of Designing Building Complexes as Development Frameworks. Keith Billings. 184p. 1993. 69.95 (*0-471-29086-6*) Wiley.

Master Planning Instructor Guide Kit. American Production & Inventory Control Society St. 1994. 600.00 (*1-55822-072-0*) Am Prod & Inventory.

Master Planning Reprints. Ed. by Appic Master Planning Committee. LC 86-72586. 164p. 1993. pap. 21.00 (*1-55822-040-2*) Am Prod & Inventory.

Master Planning Student Guide. American Production & Inventory Control Society St. 1994. 37.00 (*1-55822-073-9*) Am Prod & Inventory.

Master Planning the Aviation Environment. Ed. by Angelo J. Cerchione et al. LC 74-125171. 224p. reprint ed. pap. 69.50 (*0-608-13351-5*, 202555300044) Bks Demand.

Master Play at Trick, No. 1. Klinger. pap. 3.95 (*0-575-04351-2*, Pub. by V Gollancz) Trafalgar.

Master Play in Contract Bridge. Terence Reese. (Illus.). 144p. 1974. reprint ed. 5.95 (*0-486-20336-0*) Dover.

Master Players. Gretchen Reynolds & Elizabeth Jones. (Early Childhood Education Ser.: Vol. 60). 144p. (C). 1996. text 36.00 (*0-8077-3582-5*); pap. text 16.95 (*0-8077-3581-7*) Tchrs Coll.

Master Plays in a Single Suit. Terence Reese. 8p. 1988. pap. 3.95 (*0-575-04132-3*, Pub. by V Gollancz) Trafalgar.

Master Plot of the Bible. Robert L. Prall. 154p. 1997. pap. 9.95 (*0-9657835-0-2*, 001) Emmaus Bks.

Master Plots: Race & the Founding of an American Literature, 1787-1845. Jared Gardner. LC 97-40732. (Illus.). 288p. 1998. text 39.95 (*0-8018-5813-5*) Johns Hopkins.

***Master Plots: Race & the Founding of an American Literature, 1787-1845.** Jared Gardner. (Illus.). 262p. 2000. pap. 16.95 (*0-8018-6538-7*) Johns Hopkins.

Master Plumber. Jack Rudman. (Career Examination Ser.: C-476). 1994. pap. 29.95 (*0-8373-0476-8*) Nat Learn.

Master Plumber's Licensing Exam Guide. R. Dodge Woodson. 1995. pap. 34.95 (*0-07-071786-9*) McGraw.

Master Potter & His Clay. Deena D. Cashion. 62p. 1992. pap. text 5.00 (*1-882411-00-5*) Walk Faith Minist.

Master Printmakers of 3 Centuries: Durer, Rembrandt, & Beyond: From the Collection of Adolph Weil, Jr. Montgomery Museum of Fine Arts Staff. Ed. by Margaret L. Ausfeld. LC 94-11868. (Illus.). 1994. pap. 10.00 (*0-89280-033-X*) Montgomery Mus.

Master Prints from Upstate New York Museums. Nancy E. Green. (Illus.). 196p. 1995. 20.00 (*0-9646042-9-9*) Cornell U H F Johnson.

Master Procedures. rev. ed. Paul L. Simmons. 1997. ring bd. 99.00 (*1-880626-15-2*, YPS1455) FOI Services.

Master Production Scheduling: Principles & Practices. William Berry et al. LC 82-236025. 183p. 1983. 25.00 (*0-935406-21-2*) Am Prod & Inventory.

Master Production Scheduling: The Practical Guide for Managing World Class MPS. John F. Proud. LC 93-60667. 400p. 1994. 150.00 (*0-939246-36-8*, TM7638) Wiley.

Master Puppeteer. Katherine Paterson. (Illus.). 180p. (J). (gr. 5 up). 1981. pap. 2.95 (*0-380-53322-7*, Avon Bks) Morrow Avon.

Master Puppeteer. Katherine Paterson. (J). 1975. 10.05 (*0-606-04273-3*, Pub. by Turtleback) Demco.

Master Puppeteer. Katherine Paterson. LC 75-8614. (Trophy Bk.). (Illus.). 192p. (J). (gr. 7-12). 1989. reprint ed. pap. 4.95 (*0-06-440281-9*, HarpTrophy) HarpC Child Bks.

Master Puppeteer: A Study Guide. Estelle Kleinman. Ed. by J. Friedland & R. Kessler. (Novel-Ties Ser.). (J). (gr. 5-7). 1998. pap. text, student ed. 15.95 (*0-7675-0309-0*) Lrn Links.

***Master Puppeteer: Literature Unit.** Teacher Created Materials Staff & Michelle A. Breyer. Ed. by Rita Seho. (Illus.). 48p. 1999. pap., teacher ed. 7.95 (*1-57690-517-9*, TCM2517) Tchr Create Mat.

Master Puzzles. Woodham. 1993. pap. 3.99 (*1-85792-014-7*, Pub. by Christian Focus) Spring Arbor Dist.

Master Puzzles. R. Woodman. Date not set. pap. 1.75 (*0-906731-14-3*, Pub. by Christian Focus) Spring Arbor Dist.

***Master Quest Vol. 1: Pathways to Inward Journeys.** Stacey Schafer & Jane Berryhill-Johnson. (Illus.). 32p. (J). (gr. 1-8). 2000. pap. 49.95 incl. disk (*0-9701093-1-8*) Life Mgmnt.

***Master Quest Vol. 1: Pathways to Inward Journeys - Including Stress Cards.** Stacey Schafer & Jane Berryhill-Johnson. (Illus.). 32p. (J). (gr. 1-8). 2000. pap. 15.00 (*0-9701093-0-X*) Life Mgmnt.

Master Race. Troy L. Strother. i, 200p. 1997. pap. 10.99 (*0-9661905-0-5*) Symbolic Pr.

Master Race: What Every Jewish Child Should Know about Inherited Jewish Blood. Gilbert Lubin. Ed. by Charlotte St. John. LC 92-43704. 224p. 1998. 19.95 (*0-89896-492-X*) Larksdale.

Master Reading Workbook Grade K. Carole Gerber. 1990. pap. 5.95 (*1-56189-000-6*) Amer Educ Pub.

Master Reading Workbook Grade 1. Carole Gerber. 1990. pap. 5.95 (*1-56189-001-4*) Amer Educ Pub.

Master Reading Workbook Grade 2. Carole Gerber. 1990. pap. 5.95 (*1-56189-002-2*) Amer Educ Pub.

Master Reading Workbook Grade 3. Carole Gerber. 1990. pap. 5.95 (*1-56189-003-0*) Amer Educ Pub.

Master Reading Workbook Grade 4. Carole Gerber. 1990. pap. 5.95 (*1-56189-004-9*) Amer Educ Pub.

Master Reading Workbook Grade 5. Carole Gerber. 1990. pap. 5.95 (*1-56189-005-7*) Amer Educ Pub.

Master Reading Workbook Grade 6. Carole Gerber. 1990. pap. 5.95 (*1-56189-006-5*) Amer Educ Pub.

Master Recipes: A New Approach to the Fundamentals of Good Cooking. 2nd ed. Stephen Schmidt. LC 98-3303. 960p. 1998. 29.95 (*1-57416-013-3*) Clear Light.

***Master Red Hat Linux.** Michael Bellomo. 612p. 2000. pap. 34.99 incl. cd-rom (*0-7645-3436-X*) IDG Bks.

Master Revealed: A Journey with Tangrams. Barbara E. Ford. (Illus.). 118p. (Orig.). 1990. pap. 8.95 (*0-9627337-8-4*) Tandoras Box Pr.

Master Richard Quyny, Bailiff of Stratford-upon-Avon & Friend of William Shakespeare. Edgar I. Fripp. LC 74-153320. reprint ed. 38.00 (*0-404-02621-4*) AMS Pr.

***Master Richard's "Bestiary of Love" & "Response"** Richard De Fournival. Tr. by Jeanette Beer. (Illus.). 168p. 1999. reprint ed. pap. 16.95 (*1-55753-175-7*, NotaBell) Purdue U Pr.

Master Rigger. Jack Rudman. (Career Examination Ser.: C-477). 1994. pap. 27.95 (*0-8373-0477-6*) Nat Learn.

Master-Rogue. David C. Phillips. (Collected Works of David G. Phillips). 1988. reprint ed. lib. bdg. 59.00 (*0-7812-1325-8*) Rprt Serv.

Master-Rogue. David G. Phillips. (American Author Ser.). 1981. reprint ed. lib. bdg. 69.00 (*0-686-71931-X*) Scholarly.

Master Rogue: The Confessions of Croesus. David G. Phillips. LC 68-23724. (Americans in Fiction Ser.). (Illus.). reprint ed. pap. text 10.95 (*0-89197-841-0*); reprint ed. lib. bdg. 21.00 (*0-8398-1565-4*) Irvington.

Master Sales Management. 2nd ed. (C). 1992. pap. text, teacher ed. 34.00 (*0-03-074304-4*) Harcourt Coll Pubs.

Master Scale & Chord Guide - Piano Method. 48p. 1997. pap. 4.95 (*0-7935-7216-9*) H Leonard.

Master Scale & Chord Guide for Piano. 60p. 1982. pap. 5.95 (*0-7935-6944-3*) H Leonard.

Master Scheduling: A Practical Guide to Competitive Manufacturing. John F. Proud. 560p. 1995. 60.00 (*0-471-13219-5*) Wiley.

Master Scheduling: A Practical to Competitive Manufacturing. John F. Proud. LC 99-13999. (Oliver Wright Manufacturing Ser.). 640p. 1999. 74.95 (*0-471-24322-1*) Wiley.

Master Scheduling Training Aid. Romeyn Everdell. LC 83-73009. 34p. 1984. 35.00 (*0-935406-34-4*) Am Prod & Inventory.

Master Scheduling Training Aid. Romeyn Everdell. (SPA.). 65p. 1995. student ed. 35.00 (*1-55822-107-7*) Am Prod & Inventory.

Master Scratch Builders: Tips & Techniques from the Master Aircraft Modelers. John Alcorn. LC 98-89832. (Illus.). 224p. 1999. 45.00 (*0-7643-0795-9*) Schiffer.

Master Scribes: Qur'ans of the 10th to 14th Centuries. David James. (Nassar D. Khalili Collection of Islamic Art: Vol. II). (Illus.). 240p. 1992. text 340.00 (*0-19-727601-6*) OUP.

Master Secrets of Hypnosis & Self-Hypnosis. Kurt Tepperwein. Ed. by Christian Godefroy. Tr. by R. Sullivan from FRE. LC 91-73801. 535p. 1991. 38.00 (*0-941683-15-X*) Instant Improve.

Master Secrets of Prayer. Cameron V. Thompson. 112p. (Orig.). (YA). (gr. 8 up). 1990. pap. 5.95 (*0-9627630-0-4*) Light & Living.

Master Sign Hanger. Jack Rudman. (Career Examination Ser.: C-478). 1994. pap. 27.95 (*0-8373-0478-4*) Nat Learn.

Master Signals. Hugh Kelsey. (Mini Masters Ser.). 10p. 1989. pap. 3.95 (*0-575-04350-4*, Pub. by V Gollancz) Trafalgar.

Master SimCity-SimEarth. Dennis Derrick & Dan Derrick. 425p. 1991. 16.95 (*0-672-22787-8*) Sams.

Master Skylark. John Bennet. 20.95 (*0-88411-823-1*) Amereon Ltd.

Master Skylark. John Bennett. (Airmont Classics Ser.). (J). (gr. 5 up). 1965. mass mkt. 1.95 (*0-8049-0092-2*, CL-92) Airmont.

Master Slam Bidding. Hugh Kelsey. (Mini Masters Ser.). 8p. 1988. pap. 3.95 (*0-575-04131-5*, Pub. by V Gollancz) Trafalgar.

Master Smart Woman: A Portrait of Sarah Orne Jewett. Cynthia Keyworth et al. LC 87-23946. 179p. 1988. 21.95 (*0-945980-02-7*) Nrth Country Pr.

Master Smart Woman: A Portrait of Sarah Orne Jewett. Cynthia Keyworth et al. LC 87-23946. (Illus.). 179p. 1988. pap. 12.95 (*0-945980-03-5*) Nrth Country Pr.

Master Sniper. Stephen Hunter. 432p. 1996. mass mkt. 7.50 (*0-440-22187-0*, Island Bks) Dell.

***Master Solos: Intermediate Level.** 40p. 2000. pap. 12.95 (*0-7935-9551-7*); pap. 12.95 (*0-7935-9557-6*) H Leonard.

Master Sorai's Responsals: An Annotated Translation of Sorai Sensei Tomonsho. Samuel H. Yamashita. LC 94-15416. 264p. (C). 1994. text 23.00 (*0-8248-1570-X*) UH Pr.

Master Space: Film Images of Capra, Lubitsch, Sternberg, & Wyler, 31. Barbara Bowman. LC 91-33480. (Contributions to the Study of Popular Culture Ser.: No. 31). 192p. 1992. 49.95 (*0-313-28026-6*, BWQ, Greenwood Pr) Greenwood.

Master Speaks. Joel S. Goldsmith. 192p. 1984. pap. 7.95 (*0-8065-0912-0*, Citadel Pr) Carol Pub Group.

Master Speaks. Joel S. Goldsmith. LC 99-10132. 333p. 1999. reprint ed. 27.95 (*1-889051-43-8*); reprint ed. pap. 16.95 (*1-889051-42-X*) Acrpls Bks CO.

Master Speaks. 2nd ed. Intro. by Benjamin Creme. 256p. (Orig.). 1994. pap. 11.00 (*90-71484-10-6*) Share Intl.

Master Spelling & Writing Workbook. Carole Gerber. 1992. pap. text 5.95 (*1-56189-032-4*) Amer Educ Pub.

Master Spelling & Writing Workbook Grade 1. Carole Gerber. 1992. pap. 5.95 (*1-56189-031-6*) Amer Educ Pub.

Master Spelling & Writing Workbook Grade 3. Carole Gerber. 1992. pap. 5.95 (*1-56189-033-2*) Amer Educ Pub.

Master Spelling & Writing Workbook Grade 4. Carole Gerber. 1992. pap. 5.95 (*1-56189-034-0*) Amer Educ Pub.

Master Spelling & Writing Workbook Grade 5. Carole Gerber. 1992. pap., wbk. ed. 5.95 (*1-56189-035-9*) Amer Educ Pub.

Master Spelling & Writing Workbook Grade 6. Carole Gerber. 1992. pap., wbk. ed. 5.95 (*1-56189-036-7*) Amer Educ Pub.

Master Spirit of the Age: Canadian Engineers & the Politics of Professionalism, 1887-1922. Rodney J. Millard. 236p. 1988. text 37.50 (*0-8020-2652-4*) U of Toronto Pr.

Master Squeeze Play. Kelsey. pap. 3.95 (*0-575-04884-0*, Pub. by V Gollancz) Trafalgar.

Master Standard Data: The Economic Approach to Work, Measurement. rev. ed. Richard M. Crossan & Harold W. Nance. LC 80-11165. 268p. 1980. reprint ed. lib. bdg. 35.50 (*0-89874-133-5*) Krieger.

Master Stress. Malcolm Newell. 1995. pap. 17.95 (*0-949142-16-6*, Pub. by Stirling Pr) Intl Spec Bk.

Master Stroke. Elizabeth Gage. Ed. by Claire Zion. 480p. 1992. mass mkt. 5.99 (*0-671-74816-5*) PB.

Master Stroke. large type ed. Elizabeth Gage. LC 91-46123. 685p. 1992. reprint ed. 18.95 (*1-56054-353-1*) Thorndike Pr.

Master Stroke 1: Exploring the World of Power Billiards. Dick Jacobs. Ed. by Kathleen Jacobs. (Illus.). 175p. (YA). 1995. student ed. 19.95 (*0-9647523-0-1*) SGS Press.

Master Strokes: A Practical Guide to Decorative & Paint Techniques. Jennifer Bennell. (Illus.). 160p. 1997. pap. 22.99 (*1-56496-360-8*) Rockport Pubs.

Master Strokes: Golf Pros on the Game. Marc Anello. LC 99-162752. (Pocket Gift Editions Ser.). 1998. 4.95 (*0-88088-071-6*) Peter Pauper.

***Master Strokes: Spiritual Growth Through the Game of Golf.** Gary York & Ken Osness. 2000. 12.99 (*0-8423-3592-7*) Tyndale Hse.

Master Studies: Drum. J. Morello. 96p. 1986. pap. 12.95 (*0-88188-748-X*, 06631474) H Leonard.

Master Study Skills Grade 5. Carole Gerber. 1992. pap. 5.95 (*1-56189-055-3*) Amer Educ Pub.

Master Study Skills Grade 4. Carole Gerber. 1992. pap. 5.95 (*1-56189-054-5*) Amer Educ Pub.

Master Study Skills Grade 6. Carole Gerber. 1992. pap. 5.95 (*1-56189-056-1*) Amer Educ Pub.

Master Study Skills Workbook Grade 2. Carole Gerber. 1992. pap. 5.95 (*1-56189-052-9*) Amer Educ Pub.

Master Subject Index see Preacher's Outline & Sermon Bible - New Testament Set

***Master Success.** Bill Fitzpatrick. (Illus.). 288p. 1999. pap. 19.95 (*1-884864-12-0*) Am Success Inst.

***Master Sweep Theater Presents... The New Animal's Side of the Story.** A. Sylvia Seymour. (Illus.). 64p. 2000. pap., teacher ed. 11.95 (*0-9651396-2-X*) StoryLoft.

***Master Swing Trader: Tool & Techniques to Profit from Outstanding Short-Term Trading Opportunities.** Alan S. Farley. 2000. 55.00 (*0-07-136309-2*) McGraw.

Master Switch. William H. Stender, Jr. LC 96-14679. 448p. 1996. 24.95 (*1-56145-132-0*) Peachtree Pubs.

Master System: A Visual Guide to the Structure of Music on the Guitar & Bass Fretboards. Eric Brecker. (Illus.). 62p. 1992. pap. text 19.95 (*0-925191-10-8*) Omnitek.

Master Tara Singh No. 28: Political Thinkers of Modern India. Ed. by Verinder Grover. (C). 1995. 52.00 (*81-7100-574-8*) S Asia.

Master Teacher. Norvel Hayes. pap. 1.00 (*1-57794-093-8*) Harrison Hse.

Master Teachers. Ruth Hobbs. 80p. 1986. pap. 4.75 (*0-7399-0233-4*, 2326) Rod & Staff.

Master Teachers of Theatre: Observations on Teaching Theatre by Nine American Masters. Ed. by Burnet M. Hobgood. LC 88-4446. 222p. (C). 1988. text 31.95 (*0-8093-1464-9*) S Ill U Pr.

Master Teaching Techniques. 4th ed. Bernard F. Cleveland. LC 83-73524. (Illus.). 248p. 1987. pap. 17.95 (*0-9608678-3-X*) Connecting Link.

Master Techniques in Ophthalmic Surgery. Roy. (Illus.). 1277p. 1995. 225.00 (*0-683-07410-5*) Lppncott W & W.

Master Techniques in Orthopaedic Surgery: Trauma. Wiss. LC 98-15918. 700p. 1998. text 189.00 (*0-397-51703-3*) Lppncott W & W.

Master Techniques in Orthopaedic Surgery - The Spine: Master Techniques in Orthopaedic Surgery. Ed. by David S. Bradford. (Master Techniques in Orthopaedic Surgery Ser.: vol. 7). (Illus.). 400p. 1996. text 189.00 (*0-7817-0033-7*) Lppncott W & W.

Master Tells Stories. Ching Hai. (CHI, KOR & VIE., Illus.). 201p. 1997. pap. 10.00 (*1-886544-15-8*) Suma Ching Hai Intl.

***Master Tells Stories.** Ching Hai. (VIE., Illus.). 213p. 1998. pap. 10.00 (*1-886544-23-9*) Suma Ching Hai Intl.

Master Terrorist: The True Story Behind Abu-Nidal. Yossi Melman. Tr. by Shmuel Himmelstein. LC 86-10820. 216p. 1986. 16.95 (*0-915361-52-3*) Lambda Pubs.

Master Terrorist: The True Story Behind Abu-Nidal. Yossi Melman. 296p. 1987. pap. 3.95 (*0-380-70428-5*, Avon Bks) Morrow Avon.

***Master the ACT 2001.** Arco Publishing Staff. (Arco ACT Ser.). 608p. 2000. pap. 13.95 (*0-7645-6117-0*) IDG Bks.

Master the Art Masters. Frances S. Hall. Ed. by Fran Dykes. 144p. (C). 1991. write for info. (*0-318-68306-7*) Hmmngbird SC.

Master the Art of Carving Melon Centerpieces: Carving Watermelons. Lonnie T. Lynch. Ed. by Bob Barry. (Mastering the Art of Ser.). (Illus.). 112p. (C). 1992. reprint ed. pap. 9.95 (*0-9629277-0-8*) L Lynch.

Master the Art of Cold Reading: An Actors Guide to Making the Best of Cold Reading Workshop. 4th rev. ed. Angel Harper. Ed. by Shirley Jordon & Ken Sobel. 69p. (YA). (gr. 5 up). 1999. 20.00 (*0-9630551-1-9*) Heaven Sent Pubng.

Master the Art of Cold Reading: An Actor's Guide to Making the Best of Cold Reading Workshops. 4th rev. ed. 153p. Date not set. pap. 17.95 (*0-9630551-2-7*) Heaven Sent Pubng.

Master the Basics: English. Jean Yates. 320p. 1996. pap. text 11.95 (*0-8120-9720-3*) Barron.

Master the Basics: French. 2nd ed. Christopher Kendris. LC 94-49345. 290p. 1995. pap. 11.95 (*0-8120-9000-4*) Barron.

Master the Basics: Spanish. 2nd ed. Christopher Kendris. LC 94-49344. 290p. 1995. pap. 10.95 (*0-8120-9003-9*) Barron.

***Master the Catholic High School Entrance Examinations 2001.** Arco Publishing Staff. 408p. 2000. pap. 13.95 (*0-7645-6081-6*) IDG Bks.

Master the Dynamics of Innovation. Utterback. 256p. 1994. 29.95 (*0-07-103582-6*) McGraw.

***Master the GMAT 2001.** Arco Publishing Staff. 560p. 2000. pap. 13.95 (*0-7645-6118-9*) IDG Bks.

***Master the GRE 2001.** Arco Publishing Co. Staff. (Arco GRE). 704p. 2000. pap. 13.95 (*0-7645-6119-7*) IDG Bks.

***Master the GRE 2001.** IDG Books Worldwide Staff. 720p. 2000. pap. 16.95 (*0-7645-6084-0*) IDG Bks.

Master the LSAT. rev. ed. Jeff Kolby. (Illus.). 560p. (C). 1999. pap. 29.95 (*1-889057-11-8*) Nova Pr.

***Master the LSAT 2001.** Arco Publishing Co. Staff. (Arco LSAT Ser.). 448p. 2000. pap. 16.95 (*0-7645-6121-9*) IDG Bks.

***Master the LSAT 2001.** IDG Books Worldwide Staff. 702p. 2000. pap. 14.95 (*0-7645-6143-X*) IDG Bks.

Master the Manual: A Study Guide to Accompany the Ace Aerobics Instructor Manual. Guy Andrews. Ed. by Richard T. Cotton. (Illus.). 98p. (Orig.). 1995. pap. text. write for info. (*0-9618161-4-7*) Am Coun Exer.

Master the Manual: A Study Guide to Accompany the Ace Personal Trainer Manual. Richard J. Seibert. Ed. by Richard T. Cotton. (Illus.). 131p. 1996. pap. text 24.95 (*0-9618161-1-2*) Am Coun Exer.

***Master the MAT 2001: Miller Analogies Test.** ARCO Editorial Board Staff. 702p. 2000. pap. 15.95 (*0-7645-6144-8*) IDG Bks.

***Master the Math Monsters: Factors, Fractions, & Long Division.** 2nd rev. ed. Denise Gaskins. LC 00-190130. (Homeschool Math Manuals: Vol. 2). (Illus.). 100p. 2000. pap. 10.95 (*1-892083-12-4*) Tabletop Acad.

Master the Power of Self Hypnosis. C. Roy Hunter. LC 98-30850. 144p. 1999. pap. 12.95 (*0-8069-6351-4*) Sterling.

Master the SAT & PSAT. 2000th ed. Phil Pine. (Arco Preparation for the SAT & PSAT Ser.). (Illus.). 717p. 1999. pap. 12.95 (*0-02-863214-1*, Arc) IDG Bks.

***Master the SAT & PSAT 2001.** Arco Publishing Co. Staff. (Arco SAT & PSAT Ser.). 672p. 2000. pap. 12.95 (*0-7645-6120-0*) IDG Bks.

***Master the SAT & PSAT 2001.** IDG Books Worldwide Staff. 720p. 2000. pap. 14.95 (*0-7645-6085-9*) IDG Bks.

***Master the SSAT & ISEE 2001.** Arco Editorial Staff. (Illus.). 702p. 2000. pap. 13.95 (*0-7645-6145-6*) IDG Bks.

Master the Techniques of Ophthalmic Surgery. Ed. by F. Hampton Roy & Renee Tindall. LC 94-7614. (Illus.). 1994. write for info. (*0-8121-1679-8*) Lppncott W & W.

***Master the TOEFL 2001.** Arco Editorial Staff. 720p. 2000. pap. 16.95 (*0-7645-6146-4*) IDG Bks.

***Master the TOEFL 2001.** Patricia Noble Sullivan. (Arco TOEFL Ser.). 454p. 2000. pap. 12.95 (*0-7645-6122-7*) IDG Bks.

Master Theme of the Bible: A Comprehensive Study of the Lamb of God. J. Sidlow Baxter. LC 96-46397. 208p. 1997. pap. 10.99 (*0-8254-2147-0*) Kregel.

Master Thinking Skills Workbook: Grade 3. Carole Gerber. 1992. pap. text 5.95 (*1-56189-053-7*) Amer Educ Pub.

Master Thoughts, 4 vols., Set. Friend Stuart. 900p. 1991. vinyl bd. 69.95 (*0-912132-05-1*) Dominion Pr.

Master Thoughts of Master Minds in Poem, Prose & Pencil (1890) W. Harrison Starkey. 320p. 1998. reprint ed. pap. 24.95 (*0-7661-0149-5*) Kessinger Pub.

Master Tips. Ed. by Jon Winokur. 96p. (Orig.). 1985. pap. text 11.95 (*0-932373-00-3*) Potshot Pr.

An Asterisk (*) at the beginning of an entry indicates that the title is appearing for the first time.

Master Tong's Acupuncture: An Ancient Alternative Style in Modern Clinical Practice. Tr. & Comment by Miriam Lee. LC 92-73391. (Illus.). 240p. 1992. pap. 21.95 (0-936185-37-6) Blue Poppy Pr.

Master Track & Field Ranking Book, 1980: Men & Women Ages 30-89, U. S. A., Canada & Mexico. Haig E. Bohigian. 104p. (Orig.). 1981. pap. 4.00 (0-933390-07-6) Valian Assocs.

Master Trend: How the Baby Boom Generation Is Remaking America. Cheryl Russell. LC 93-11511. (Illus.). 284p. (C). 1993. 23.95 (0-306-44507-7, Plenum Trade) Perseus Pubng.

Master Trust: Simplifying Employee Benefits Trust Fund Administration. Michael J. Costa. LC 80-65872. 221p. reprint ed. pap. 68.60 (0-608-12158-4, 202391300034) Bks Demand.

Master Tung's Western Chamber Romance: A Chinese Chantefable. Tung Chieh-Yuan. LC 94-18056.Tr. of Hsi Hsiang Chi Chu Kung Tiao. 1994. pap. 20.50 (0-231-10119-8) Col U Pr.

Master Tung's Western Chamber Romance (Tung Hsi-Hsiang-Chu-Kung-Tiao: A Chinese Chantefable. Tung Chieh-Yuan. LC 75-12469. (Cambridge Studies in Chinese History, Literature & Institutions). 267p. reprint ed. pap. 76.10 (0-608-17056-9, 2027283) Bks Demand.

Master Tutor: A Guidebook for More Effective Tutoring. Ross B. MacDonald. (Illus.). 64p. (Orig.). (C). 1994. teacher ed. 64.95 (0-935637-20-6); student ed. 19.95 (0-935637-19-2); trans. 85.00 (0-935637-21-4) Cambridge Strat.

Master Type: A Teaching Aid for the Classroom. LC 80-84350. 55p. 1982. pap. 3.95 (0-89709-023-3) Liberty Pub.

Master Ultima. Sams Development Group Staff. 400p. 1991. 16.95 (0-672-22828-9) Sams.

Master Vinayak. M. W. Kelkar. (C). 1991. 12.00 (81-224-0112-0) S Asia.

Master Visual Basic 4. 2nd ed. Nathan Gurewich & Ori Gurewich. 1000p. 1995. 49.99 incl. cd-rom (0-672-30640-9) Sams.

Master Wace: His Chronicle of the Norman Conquest from the Roman De Rou. Henry Wace. LC 78-178501. (Illus.). reprint ed. 49.50 (0-404-56682-0) AMS Pr.

Master Watercolors & Drawings from the Norton Gallery of Art. Bruce Weber. (Illus.). 48p. 1988. pap. 9.95 (0-86528-039-8) Norton Gal Art.

Master Weaver from Ghana. Gilbert Ahiagble & Louise Meyer. LC 98-26514. (Illus.). 32p. (YA). (gr. 2-8). 1998. 18.00 (0-940880-61-X) Open Hand.

Master Weavers: Tapestry from the Dovecot Studios, 1912 to 1980. Cannongate Staff. (Illus.). 144p. 1982. pap. 15.95 (1-56554-620-2) Pelican.

***Master Windows 98 Visually.** Ruth Maran. LC 98-84747. 736p. 1998. pap. 39.99 (0-7645-6034-4) IDG Bks.

Master Windows 95 Visually. Marangraphics Staff & Ruth Maran. LC 97-80209. 800p. 1997. pap. 39.99 (0-7645-6024-7) IDG Bks.

***Master Windows 2000 Professional Visually.** Maran. 700p. 2000. pap. 39.99 (0-7645-3421-1) IDG Bks.

***Master Windows 2000 Server Visually.** IDG Books Staff. (Illus.). 702p. 2000. pap. 34.99 (0-7645-3426-2) IDG Bks.

Master Wolf. 1987. mass mkt. 3.95 (0-88038-280-5) TSR Inc.

Master Woodworker see Art of Woodworking Series

Master Works: How to Use Paint Finishes to Transform Your Surroundings. Jennifer Bennell. (Illus.). 176p. 1994. 29.95 (1-56496-125-7) Rockport Pubs.

Master Your Budget: Taming the Beast. Patrick G. Finegan, Jr. LC 90-63266. 208p. 1991. 21.95 (1-878905-08-2); pap. 14.95 (1-878905-09-0) Palindrome Pr.

Master Your Disaster. Kathy Alix. 1997. pap. text 18.95 (0-9646754-4-7) Assure Yourself.

Master Your Keyboard Typing, Vol. 1. unabridged rev. ed. 7p. 1994. pap. text 34.50 incl. audio (0-88432-750-7, S17080) Audio-Forum.

Master Your Keyboard Typing: Speed & Accuracy at Your Keyboard, Vol. 2. unabridged ed. 41p. 1994. pap. 34.50 incl. digital audio (0-88432-751-5, S17085) Audio-Forum.

***Master Your Memory with Dr. Amazing: How Not to Forget.** M. M. Teitelbaum. LC 99-21. 273p. 1999. spiral bd. 43.95 (1-55212-252-2, Pub. by Tra3fford) Trafford Pub.

Master Your Migraine: The Migraine Home Cure Manual. Ronald H. Lange. Ed. by Michael Reed. LC 95-83475. (Illus.). 75p. 1996. pap. 17.95 (0-9648931-0-X) Enigma Pub.

Master Your Money: A Step-by-Step Plan for Financial Freedom Revised & Updated for the Financial Realities of the 90s. Ron Blue. LC 97-27076. 1997. pap. 10.99 (0-7852-7061-2) Nelson.

***Master Your Money or It Will Master You.** unabridged ed. Arlo E. Moehlenpah. (Illus.). 158p. 1999. pap. 11.95 (0-9667054-1-6) Doing Good.

Master Your Money Workbook. Ron Blue. 1993. pap., wbk. ed. 16.99 (0-8407-3393-3) Nelson.

Master Your Panic . . . & Take Back Your Life! Twelve Treatment Sessions to Overcome High Anxiety. 2nd ed. Denise F. Beckfield. LC 97-51465. 304p. 1998. pap. 15.95 (1-886230-08-0) Impact Pubs CA.

Master Your PC Visually with Minimal Reading. Tehseen Naqvi. LC 97-90013. (Orig.). 1997. pap. 12.95 (0-533-12268-6) Vantage.

Master Your Psychic Powers. Billy Roberts. LC 98-194388. 128p. 1998. 12.95 (0-7137-2716-0, Pub. by Blandford Pr) Sterling.

Master Your Short Game in 16 Days: A How-To Guide for the Weekend Golfer. Walter Ostroske & John Devaney. LC 93-36213. (Illus.). 128p. (Orig.). 1994. pap. 9.95 (0-399-51861-4, Perigee Bks) Berkley Pub.

Master Your Stockbroker: Wall Street Secrets. Patrick G. Finegan, Jr. LC 90-61322. 416p. 1990. 39.95 (1-878905-00-7); pap. 34.95 (1-878905-01-5) Palindrome Pr.

***Master Your Whole Life: Foundation for an Art, Science & Technology of Human Development.** Bob Reed. 124p. 2000. pap. 12.95 (0-9686390-0-3, Pub. by New Vision) Hushion Hse.

Master Yourself: A Xuan Ming Oao Gigong Workbook. Yu Cheng Huang. Ed. by Laurie Manning & Elizabeth Morrill. LC 99-93881. (Illus.). 230p. Date not set. wbk. ed. 25.00 (1-892686-05-8) Ching Ying Assn.

Master Yunmen: From the Record of the Chan Master "Gate-of-the-Clouds" Urs App. Ed. by Paul De Angelis. LC 93-42824. (Illus.). 256p. 1994. pap. 13.00 (1-56836-005-3) Kodansha.

Master Zacharius: A Winter Amid the Ice. Jules Verne. reprint ed. lib. bdg. 19.95 (0-88411-916-5) Amereon Ltd.

Mastera: The Artists. Bella Ezerskaya. 1982. 5.95 (0-685-44309-4) RWCPH.

MasterBook. 20.00 (0-87431-370-8, 51000) West End Games.

MasterBook Companion. 18.00 (0-87431-371-6, 51003) West End Games.

Masterbook of Portraiture & Studio Management. 5th ed. Don Peterson. (Master Ser.: No. 1). (Illus.). 147p. 1989. reprint ed. pap. 29.97 (0-934420-07-6, 1127) Studio Pr NE.

***Masterbrand Mandate: The Management Strategy That Unifies Companies & Multiplies Value.** Lynn B. Upshaw & Earl Taylor. (Illus.). 304p. 2000. 29.95 (0-471-35659-X) Wiley.

Masterbuilder. Charlene S. McCadden. (Illus.). 14p. (Orig.). 1988. pap. 3.00 (0-9620794-0-5) King Realm Pubns.

Mastercam Book for Windows. S. C. Lin & F. C. Shiue. Ed. by Karen L. Sterzik. (Illus.). 900p. 1995. pap. 69.00 (1-886552-01-0) Scholars Intl.

Mastercam Post Processor User Guide. (Illus.). 1997. pap. 25.00 (1-883310-00-8) CNC Sftware.

***Mastercam Solids.** S. C. Jonathon Lin. Ed. by Karen L. Sterzik. (Illus.). 350p. (C). 1999. pap. 59.00 (1-886552-13-4) Scholars Intl.

***Mastercam Version 7.** S. C. Jonathon Lin & F. C. Tony Shiue. Ed. by Karen L. Sterzik. (Illus.). 1300p. (C). 1998. pap. 83.00 (1-886552-11-8) Scholars Intl.

Mastercam Version 7.0 Design Reference Manual. CNC Software Staff. (Illus.). 462p. 1998. pap. 25.00 (1-883310-05-9) CNC Sftware.

Mastercam Version 7.0 Mill Reference Manual. CNC Software Staff. (Illus.). 406p. 1998. pap. 25.00 (1-883310-04-0) CNC Sftware.

Mastercam Version 6 Quick Part Instructor Guide. (Illus.). 28p. 1997. teacher ed., spiral bd., wbk. ed. write for info. (1-883310-01-6) CNC Sftware.

Mastercam 4 Design Workbook. Leonard O. Nasman. (Illus.). 100p. 1994. student ed. 24.95 (1-880544-48-2, Pub. by Micro Educ) Tech Ed Concepts.

MasterCases: Orthopaedic Trauma. Perry. (Illus.). 456p. 1998. 95.00 (0-86577-782-9) Thieme Med Pubs.

***MasterCases: Orthopaedic Trauma.** Clayton R. Perry. 1998. write for info. (3-13-115121-8) Thieme Med Pubs.

***MasterCases in Neurosurgery: Peripheral Nerve Surgery.** Seth M. Zeidman. (Illus.). 320p. 2001. pap. 59.00 (0-86577-860-4) Thieme Med Pubs.

***MasterCases in Shoulder & Elbow Surgery.** Felix H. Savoie. (Illus.). 480p. 2000. 95.00 (0-86577-873-6) Thieme Med Pubs.

***MasterCases in Spine Surgery.** Alexander R. Vaccaro. (Illus.). 430p. 2000. 99.00 (0-86577-924-4) Thieme Med Pubs.

Masterclass: Learning, Teaching & Curriculum in Taught Master's Degrees. Ed. by Peter Knight. LC 98-112195. (Illus.). 208p. 1997. 90.00 (0-304-33983-0); pap. 25.95 (0-304-33984-9) Continuum.

Masterclass: The Actor's Audition Manual for Men. Ed. by Dean Carey. 246p. 1995. pap. 10.95 (0-435-08678-2, 08678) Heinemann.

Masterclass: The Actor's Audition Manual for Women. Ed. by Dean Carey. 246p. 1995. pap. 10.95 (0-435-08679-0, 08679) Heinemann.

***Masterclass: The Actor's Manuals for Men.** Dean Carey. (Nick Hern Bks.). (Illus.). 2000. pap. 27.95 (1-85459-233-5) Theatre Comm.

***Masterclass: The Actor's Manuals for Women.** Dean Carey. (Nick Hern Bks.). 2000. pap. 27.95 (1-85459-238-6) Theatre Comm.

Masterclass Golf. Peter D. Smith. (Illus.). 192p. 1994. 29.95 (1-85470-168-1) Collins & Br.

Mastercon: M6. Ed. & Photos by Francois Verlinden. (Illus.). 36p. 1997. 11.95 (1-930607-38-5, VPI 1304) Verlinden Prod.

Mastered by the Clock: Time, Slavery, & Freedom in the American South. Mark M. Smith. LC 97-7045. (Fred W. Morrison Series in Southern Studies). 328p. (gr. 13). 1997. pap. 17.95 (0-8078-4693-7); lib. bdg. 49.95 (0-8078-2344-9) U of NC Pr.

Masterful Coaching: Extraordinary Results by Impacting People & the Way They Think & Work Together. Robert Hargrove. LC 95-30092. 320p. 1995. 39.95 (0-89384-281-8, Pfiffr & Co) Jossey-Bass.

***Masterful Coaching Feedback Tool Facilitator's Guide: Grow Your Business, Multiply Your Profits.** Robert Hargrove. 2000. 99.95 (0-7879-4756-3) Jossey-Bass.

***Masterful Coaching Fieldbook: Grow Your Business, Multiply Your Profits, Win the Talent War!** Robert Hargrove. LC 99-37628. 240p. 1999. pap. 39.95 (0-7879-4755-5) Jossey-Bass.

Masterful Facilitation: Becoming a Catalyst for Meaningful Change. A. Glenn Kiser. LC 98-5786. 224p. 1998. 24.95 (0-8144-0398-0) AMACOM.

Masterful Man. Lindsay Armstrong. LC 96-255. 189p. 1995. per. 3.25 (0-373-11770-1, 1-11770-4) Harlequin Bks.

***Masterful Woodturning: Projects & Inspiration for the Skilled Turner.** S. Gary Roberts. LC 00-37290. (Illus.). 2000. write for info. (0-8069-8709-X) Sterling.

Mastergate & Power Failure: Two Political Satires for the Stage. Larry Gelbart. LC 94-1204. 160p. 1994. pap. 10.95 (1-55783-177-7) Applause Theatre Bk Pubs.

Masterharper of Pern. Anne McCaffrey. (Dragonriders of Pern Ser.). 422p. 1999. mass mkt. 6.99 (0-345-42460-3, Del Rey) Ballantine Pub Grp.

Mastering a New Role: Shaping Technology Policy for National Economic Performance. National Academy of Engineering Staff. (Prospering in a Global Economy Ser.). 144p. 1993. pap. text 22.95 (0-309-04646-7) Natl Acad Pr.

Mastering Access 97 for Windows 95/NT. 4th ed. Alan Simpson & Elizabeth Olson. LC 96-71646. 1184p. 1996. pap. text 44.99 incl. cd-rom (0-7821-1924-7) Sybex.

***Mastering Access 2000 Development.** Alison Balter. LC 98-87340. (Illus.). 1342p. 1999. pap. 49.99 incl. cd-rom (0-672-31484-3) Sams.

***Mastering Access 2000.** Alan Simpson & Celeste Robinson. (Mastering Ser.). 1200p. 1999. pap. text 44.99 (0-7821-2628-6) Sybex.

Mastering Access 2000: Premium Edition. Alan Simpson et al. (Mastering Ser.). 1440p. 1999. 49.99 (0-7821-2326-0) Sybex.

Mastering Acoustic Guitar. write for info. (0-7390-0429-8, 19340); write for info. (0-7390-0430-1, 19341) Alfred Pub.

***Mastering Active Directory.** Robert King. LC 99-60028. (Mastering Ser.). 512p. 1999. pap. 39.99 (0-7821-2423-2) Sybex.

***Mastering Active Directory.** 2nd ed. Robert King. (Mastering Computers Ser.). 608p. 2000. pap. 39.99 (0-7821-2659-6, Network Pr) Sybex.

***Mastering Active Server Pages X.** A. Russell Jones. (Illus.). 800p. 2000. pap. 49.99 (0-7821-2619-7) Sybex.

Mastering Activex. Owen Williams. 1997. pap. text 39.99 incl. cd-rom (0-7821-2112-8) Sybex.

***Mastering ADHD: Handbook for Parents & Clinicians.** Kenneth Aitken. 160p. 2000. pap. 18.95 (1-85302-800-2) Jessica Kingsley.

Mastering Adjusting Entries: Accruals & Deferrals. 10th unabridged ed. Gary F. Bulmash. 150p. 1989. pap. text 39.00 (1-884826-25-3) AIPB.

Mastering Adobe Illustrator PC. Deke McClelland & Craig Danuloff. 300p. 1989. pap. 28.00 (1-55623-158-X, Irwn Prfssnl) McGraw-Hill Prof.

Mastering Adobe InDesign. 3rd ed. Mike Cuenca. (Mastering Ser.). 864p. 1999. 39.99 (0-7821-2552-2) Sybex.

Mastering Advanced French. (Mastering Languages Ser.). (Orig.). 1995. audio 12.95 (0-7818-0313-6) Hippocrene Bks.

Mastering Advanced French. Erika Haber. (Mastering Languages Ser.). (Illus.). 348p. (Orig.). 1996. pap. 14.95 (0-7818-0312-8) Hippocrene Bks.

Mastering Advanced Italian. Davidovic Mladen. (Mastering Languages Ser.). (ITA., Illus.). 357p. (Orig.). 1995. pap. text 14.95 (0-7818-0333-0) Hippocrene Bks.

Mastering Advanced Math. (Illus.). 408p. (C). 1997. pap. text. write for info. (1-58059-905-2) Kaplan Educ.

Mastering Advanced Spanish. Robert Clarke. (Mastering Languages Ser.). (Illus.). 303p. 1993. pap. 14.95 (0-7818-0081-1); audio 12.95 (0-7818-0089-7) Hippocrene Bks.

***Mastering Aesop: Medieval Education, Chaucer & His Followers.** Edward W. Wheatley. LC 99-56399. 288p. (C). 2000. 55.00 (0-8130-1745-9) U Press Fla.

Mastering Algebra: An Introduction. Said Hamilton. Ed. by Pat Eblen. 525p. (YA). (gr. 8 up). 1997. pap. text 49.95 (0-9649954-1-7) Hamilton Assocs.

Mastering Algebra: Intermediate Level. Said Hamilton. Ed. by Pat Eblen. 590p. (YA). (gr. 9 up). 1998. pap. text 49.95 (0-9649954-2-5) Hmlton Assocs.

Mastering Algorithms with C. Kyle Loudon. Ed. by Andy Oram. (Illus.). 540p. 1999. pap. 34.95 (1-56592-453-3) OReilly & Assocs.

Mastering Algorithms with Perl. Jon Orwant et al. (Illus.). 684p. 1999. pap. 34.95 (1-56592-398-7) OReilly & Assocs.

Mastering American English. Grant Taylor. (Saxon Series in English As a Second Language). (C). 1956. pap. 25.31 (0-07-062942-0) McGraw.

Mastering American English: A Handbook-Workbook of Essentials. R. E. Hayden et al. (C). 1956. pap. text 21.20 (0-13-560045-6) P-H.

Mastering & Managing the FDA Maze: Medical Device Overview :.a Training & Management Desk Reference for Manufacturers Regulated by the Food & Drug Administration. Gordon Harnack. LC 99-19229. 1999. write for info. (0-87389-455-3) ASQ Qual Pr.

Mastering (& Succeeding with) the Job Hunt. MasterCard International Staff & College Student Editors. 149p. (C). 1994. write for info. (0-9642751-0-4) Mstercard Intl.

Mastering & Using Corel Word Perfect 8. Napier & Judd. (C). 1998. pap. text 56.95 (0-7600-5780-X) Course Tech.

Mastering & Using Corel WordPerfect 7. H. Albert Napier & Philip J. Judd. 640p. 1997. teacher ed. write for info. (0-7600-5005-8) Course Tech.

Mastering & Using Corel WordPerfect 7. H. Albert Napier & Philip J. Judd. 640p. (C). 1997. pap. 56.95 (0-7600-5004-X) Course Tech.

Mastering & Using in Workplace. Judd Napier. (C). 1997. text 7.95 (0-7600-5072-4) Course Tech.

Mastering & Using Lotus for DOS, Release 4.0. H. Albert Napier & Phillip J. Judd. (C). 1995. mass mkt., teacher ed. 50.50 (0-87709-549-3) Course Tech.

Mastering & Using Lotus for DOS, Release 4.0. H. Albert Napier & Phillip J. Judd. 656p. (C). 1995. pap., mass mkt. 43.95 incl. disk (0-87709-548-5) Course Tech.

Mastering & Using Lotus, Release 4.0 for Windows. H. Albert Napier. 640p. (C). 1994. pap. 44.95 (0-87709-169-2) Course Tech.

Mastering & Using Lotus 1-2-3 for Windows, Release 4.0. H. Albert Napier & Philip Judd. (C). 1995. mass mkt., teacher ed. 50.50 (0-87709-534-5) Course Tech.

Mastering & Using Lotus 1-2-3, Release 5.0 for Windows. H. Albert Napier & Philip Judd. 1995. mass mkt., teacher ed. 50.50 (0-7895-0596-7) Course Tech.

Mastering & Using Lotus 1-2-3, Release 5.0 for Windows. H. Albert Napier & Phillip J. Judd. 640p. 1995. pap. 30.00 incl. disk (0-7895-0039-6) Course Tech.

Mastering & Using Lotus 1-2-3 R3.4. Napier. 1994. 35.75 (0-87709-306-7) Course Tech.

***Mastering & Using Microsoft Access 2000.** H. Albert Napier & Philip J. Judd. (Office 2000 Ser.). 448p. 1999. pap. 34.95 (0-538-42611-X) Sth-Wstrn College.

Mastering & Using Microsoft Access 97. Al Napier & Philip Judd. (Illustrated Ser.). (Illus.). 208p. (C). 1997. pap. 30.95 (0-7600-5061-9) Course Tech.

Mastering & Using Microsoft Excel Version 5.0. H. Albert Napier & Philip J. Judd. (C). 1995. mass mkt., teacher ed. 31.50 (0-87709-309-1) Course Tech.

***Mastering & Using Microsoft Excel 2000.** H. Albert Napier & Philip J. Judd. LC 99-230211. (Office 2000 Ser.). 560p. 1999. pap. 42.95 (0-538-42615-2) Sth-Wstrn College.

Mastering & Using Microsoft Excel 7 for Windows 95. Al Napier & Philip Judd. 536p. (C). 1996. pap. 44.95 (0-7600-4598-4) Course Tech.

Mastering & Using Microsoft Excel 7 for Windows 95. Al Napier & Philip Judd. 536p. 1997. teacher ed. write for info. (0-7600-4600-X) Course Tech.

Mastering & Using Microsoft Excel 97. H. Albert Napier & Philip J. Judd. 512p. (C). 1997. pap. 44.95 (0-7600-5024-4) Course Tech.

Mastering & Using Microsoft Excel 97. 10th ed. H. Albert Napier & Philip J. Judd. 512p. (C). 1997. mass mkt., teacher ed. 1.00 (0-7600-5025-2) Course Tech.

***Mastering & Using Microsoft Frontpage 2000.** Judd Napier. 2000. pap. 28.95 (0-538-43151-2) Sth-Wstrn College.

Mastering & Using Microsoft Office for Windows 95: Professional Edition. Al Napier & Philip Judd. 880p. (C). 1996. pap. 59.95 (0-7600-4440-6) Course Tech.

Mastering & Using Microsoft Office for Windows 95 Professional Edition. Al Napier & Philip Judd. 1997. teacher ed. write for info. (0-7600-4594-1) Course Tech.

***Mastering & Using Microsoft Office 2000.** H. Albert Napier & Philip J. Judd. LC 99-218729. (Office 2000 Ser.). 896p. 1999. pap. 54.95 (0-538-42605-5) Sth-Wstrn College.

Mastering & Using Microsoft Office 97: Professional Business Simulations. Keith Mulbery. 96p. 1997. pap. write for info. (0-7600-5045-7) Course Tech.

Mastering & Using Microsoft Office 97: Professional Edition. H. Albert Napier & Philip J. Judd. 1024p. 1997. teacher ed. write for info. (0-7600-5021-X) Course Tech.

Mastering & Using Microsoft Office 97: Professional Edition. H. Albert Napier & Philip J. Judd. 1024p. (C). 1997. pap. 59.95 (0-7600-5020-1) Course Tech.

***Mastering & Using Microsoft Powerpoint 2000.** H. Albert Napier & Philip J. Judd. (Office 2000 Ser.). 480p. 1999. pap. 39.95 (0-538-42617-9) Sth-Wstrn College.

Mastering & Using Microsoft PowerPoint 97 for Business Presentations. H. Albert Napier et al. 320p. (C). 1997. pap. 41.95 (0-7600-5026-0) Course Tech.

Mastering & Using Microsoft PowerPoint 97 for Business Presentations. 10th ed. H. Albert Napier et al. 320p. (C). 1997. mass mkt., teacher ed. 1.00 (0-7600-5027-9) Course Tech.

Mastering & Using Microsoft Word for Windows 6.0. H. Albert Napier & Philip J. Judd. LC 94-23822. 664p. 1995. 46.95 (0-7895-0010-8) Course Tech.

***Mastering & Using Microsoft Word 2000.** H. Albert Napier & Philip J. Judd. (Office 2000 Ser.). 784p. 1999. pap. 54.95 (0-538-42608-X) Sth-Wstrn College.

***Mastering & Using Microsoft Word 2000: Advanced Course.** H. Albert Napier & Philip J. Judd. LC 99-233542. 304p. 1999. pap. 25.95 (0-538-42814-7) Sth-Wstrn College.

***Mastering & Using Microsoft Word 2000: Beginning Course.** H. Albert Napier & Philip J. Judd. 304p. 1999. pap. 25.95 (0-538-42812-0) Sth-Wstrn College.

***Mastering & Using Microsoft Word 2000: Intermediate Course.** H. Albert Napier & Philip J. Judd. 304p. 1999. pap. 25.95 (0-538-42813-9) Sth-Wstrn College.

Mastering & Using Microsoft Word 6, Windows 3.1. Napier. 1996. 23.95 (0-7600-4090-7) Course Tech.

Mastering & Using Microsoft Word 6.0 for Windows. H. Albert Napier & Philip J. Judd. 1995. mass mkt., teacher ed. 31.50 (0-7895-0011-6) Course Tech.

Mastering & Using Microsoft Word 7 for Windows 95. Al Napier & Philip Judd. 656p. (C). 1996. pap. 56.95 (0-7600-4595-X) Course Tech.

Mastering & Using Microsoft Word 7 for Windows 95. Al Napier & Philip Judd. 656p. 1997. teacher ed. write for info. (0-7600-4597-6) Course Tech.

Mastering & Using Microsoft Word 97. H. Albert Napier & Philip J. Judd. 704p. (C). 1997. pap. 56.95 (0-7600-5022-8) Course Tech.

Mastering & Using Microsoft Word 97. 10th ed. H. Albert Napier & Philip J. Judd. 704p. (C). 1997. mass mkt., teacher ed. 1.00 (0-7600-5023-6) Course Tech.

Mastering & Using Microsoft Word 97 to Create Web Pages. Napier. (C). 1998. pap. 14.95 (0-7600-7347-3) S-W Pub.

Mastering & Using the Internet for Office Professional: Netscape V. Napier & Judd. (C). 1997. pap. 17.95 (0-7600-5013-9) Course Tech.

An Asterisk (*) at the beginning of an entry indicates that the title is appearing for the first time.

Mastering & Using the Internet for Office Professional Using Netscape Communicator. Napier & Judd. (C). 1997. pap. text 22.95 (*0-7600-5779-6*) Course Tech.

Mastering & Using the Internet for Office Professionals: Netscape Navigator Software Version, Internet Explorer Version. H. Albert Napier. 96p. 1997. write for info. incl. disk (*0-7600-5015-5*) Course Tech.

Mastering & Using the Internet for Office Professionals Using Microsoft Internet Explorer 4.0. Al Napier. (Mastering & Using Ser.). 1997. pap. 22.95 (*0-7600-7184-5*) Course Tech.

Mastering & Using the Microsoft Office (Windows 3.1) Professional Edition. H. Albert Napier & Phillip J. Judd. 704p. 1996. pap., mass mkt. 36.75 incl. disk (*0-7895-0361-1*) Course Tech.

Mastering & Using Wordperfect 6.0. Napier. 1994. teacher ed. 35.75 (*0-87709-427-6*) Course Tech.

Mastering & Using WordPerfect 6.0 for Windows. H. Albert Napier & Philip J. Judd. LC 94-14819. 751p. (C). 1994. mass mkt. 46.95 (*0-87709-536-1*) Course Tech.

Mastering & Using WordPerfect 6.1 for Windows. Albert H. Napier & Philip J. Judd. 1995. mass mkt., teacher ed. 50.50 (*0-7895-0600-9*) Course Tech.

Mastering & Using Wordperfect 6.1 with Windows. H. Albert Napier. (DF - Computer Applications Ser.). 648p. 1995. mass mkt. 46.95 (*0-7895-0404-9*) Course Tech.

Mastering Anger - Resolving Conflict: Creating Peace & Harmony in Ourselves, Our Relationships & Our Communities, 3 vols. Constance H. Dembrowsky. Incl. Mastering Anger - Resolving Conflict: Teacher Manual. (Illus.). 402p. 1999. teacher ed., ring bd. 200.00 (*0-924609-23-0*); Mastering Anger - Resolving Conflict: Transparencies. (Illus.). 101p. 1999. ring bd. 425.00 (*0-924609-25-7*); Mastering Anger Resolving Conflicting: Blackline Master. (Illus.). 186p. 1999. ring bd. 699.00 (*0-924609-24-9*); (Illus.). 689p. (YA). (gr. 6-8). Set ring bd. 945.00 (*0-924609-26-5*) Inst Affect Skill.

Mastering Anger - Resolving Conflict: Teacher Manual see Mastering Anger - Resolving Conflict: Creating Peace & Harmony in Ourselves, Our Relationships & Our Communities

Mastering Anger - Resolving Conflict: Transparencies see Mastering Anger - Resolving Conflict: Creating Peace & Harmony in Ourselves, Our Relationships & Our Communities

***Mastering Anger - Resolving Conflicts: Creating Peace & Harmony in Ourselves, Our Relationships & Our Communities.** Constance H. Dembrowsky. (Illus.). 700p. (YA). (gr. 7-12). 1999. ring bd. 945.00 (*0-924609-21-4*) Life Mission.

Mastering Anger Resolving Conflicting: Blackline Master see Mastering Anger - Resolving Conflict: Creating Peace & Harmony in Ourselves, Our Relationships & Our Communities

Mastering Anxiety: The Nature & Treatment of Anxious Conditions. R. A. Kleinknecht. LC 91-2218. (Illus.). 292p. (C). 1991. 23.95 (*0-306-43769-4*, Plen Insight) Perseus Pubng.

Mastering APA Style: Student's Workbook & Training Guide. Harold Gelfand & Charles J. Walker. 238p. (Orig.). (C). 1990. pap. 19.95 (*1-55798-085-3*) Am Psychol.

Mastering Arabic. Jane Wightwick & Mahmoud Gaafar. (Language Studies - Mastering Language). (ARA., Illus.). 370p. 1991. pap. 14.95 (*0-87052-922-6*); audio 12.95 (*0-87052-984-6*) Hippocrene Bks.

Mastering AS/400 Performance. Alan Arnold et al. LC 96-25347. 259p. (Orig.). 1996. pap. 45.00 (*1-882419-49-9*) News Four-Hund.

Mastering Auditory Sequencing. Jean G. DeGaetano. 60p. (J). (gr. 2-4). 1993. pap. text 22.00 (*1-886143-19-6*) Grt Ideas Tching.

Mastering AutoCAD: Native Solids. Cheng. LC 97-30211. (General Engineering Ser.). 272p. (C). 1997. 43.95 (*0-534-95108-2*) PWS Pubs.

Mastering AutoCAD 14. George Omura. LC 97-67593. (Illus.). 1312p. 1997. pap. text 49.99 incl. cd-rom (*0-7821-2109-8*) Sybex.

Mastering AutoCAD14: Premium Edition. George Omara. LC 98-85873. (Mastering Ser.). (Illus.). 1440p. 1998. 59.99 (*0-7821-2338-4*) Sybex.

Mastering AutoCAD 14 for Mechanical Engineers. Stephen Keith & George Omura. LC 97-61716. 1168p. 1997. pap. text 59.99 incl. cd-rom (*0-7821-2108-X*) Sybex.

Mastering AutoCAD LT for Windows 95. George Omura. LC 96-69282. 896p. 1996. pap. text 34.99 incl. cd-rom (*0-7821-1855-0*) Sybex.

Mastering AutoCAD Release 13. Ron Cheng. LC 97-28667. 352p. (C). 1997. mass mkt. 53.95 (*0-534-95506-1*) Brooks-Cole.

Mastering AutoCAD 3D. George Omura. LC 96-67845. (Illus.). 1104p. (Orig.). 1996. pap. 49.99 incl. cd-rom (*0-7821-1850-X*) Sybex.

***Mastering Autocad 2000 Objects.** 4th ed. Dietmar Rudolph. 416p. 1999. 49.99 (*0-7821-2562-X*) Sybex.

Mastering AutoCAD 2000. George Omura. LC 99-61306. (Mastering Ser.). 1504p. 1999. pap. 49.99 (*0-7821-2501-8*) Sybex.

Mastering AutoCAD 2000: Premium Edition. 3rd ed. George Omura. (Mastering Ser.). 1664p. 1999. 59.99 (*0-7821-2499-2*) Sybex.

Mastering AutoCAD 2000 for Mechanical Engineers. 3rd ed. George Omura. (Mastering Ser.). 1376p. 1999. pap. 54.99 (*0-7821-2500-X*) Sybex.

Mastering Autosurf 3.0. Cheng. LC 97-29789. (General Engineering Ser.). 240p. (C). 1997. mass mkt. 43.95 (*0-534-95085-X*) PWS Pubs.

Mastering Bach Flower Therapies: A Guide to Diagnosis & Treatment. Mechthild Scheffer. LC 96-5716. (Illus.). 128p. 1996. pap. 12.95 (*0-89281-630-9*, Heal Arts VT) Inner Tradit.

Mastering Basic Concepts & Specific Words. Jean G. DeGaetano. 93p. (J). (gr. k-2). 1991. pap. text 26.00 (*1-886143-20-X*) Grt Ideas Tching.

Mastering Basics: Ephesians. Coleman. 1994. pap. 5.95 (*1-883419-30-1*) Serendipty Hse.

Mastering Basics: Ephesians. large type ed. Coleman. 1994. pap. 15.00 (*1-883419-40-9*) Serendipty Hse.

Mastering Basics: I & II Timothy. large type ed. Coleman. 1994. pap. 15.00 (*1-883419-42-5*) Serendipty Hse.

Mastering Basics: I Corinthian. large type ed. Coleman. 1994. pap. 15.00 (*1-883419-39-5*) Serendipty Hse.

Mastering Basics: I Corinthians. Coleman. 1994. pap. 5.95 (*1-883419-29-8*) Serendipty Hse.

Mastering Basics: I John. Coleman. 1994. pap. 5.95 (*1-883419-35-2*) Serendipty Hse.

Mastering Basics: I Peter. Coleman. 1994. pap. 5.95 (*1-883419-34-4*); pap. 15.00 (*1-883419-44-1*) Serendipty Hse.

Mastering Basics: James. Coleman. 1994. pap. 5.95 (*1-883419-33-6*); pap. 15.00 (*1-883419-43-3*) Serendipty Hse.

Mastering Basics: Philippians. large type ed. Coleman. 1994. pap. text 15.00 (*1-883419-41-7*) Serendipty Hse.

Mastering Basics: Phillipians. 1995. pap. 5.95 (*1-883419-77-8*) Serendipty Hse.

Mastering Basics: Romans. Coleman. 1995. pap. 5.95 (*1-883419-27-1*) Serendipty Hse.

Mastering Basics: Romans. large type ed. Coleman. 1994. pap. 15.00 (*1-883419-38-7*) Serendipty Hse.

Mastering Basics: 1 & 2 Timothy. Coleman. 1994. pap. 5.95 (*1-883419-32-8*) Serendipty Hse.

***Mastering Bible Study Skills - Student Edition: Tools for Investigating God's Word.** ACSI Staff. (Enabling Educators Ser.). (Illus.). 47p. (YA). (gr. 9-11). 1999. student ed. 13.00 (*1-58331-128-9*) Assn Christ Sch.

***Mastering Bible Study Skills - Teacher Edition: Tools for Investigating God's Word.** ACSI Staff. (Enabling Educators Ser.). (Illus.). xi, 193p. 1999. teacher ed. 50.00 (*1-58331-129-7*) Assn Christ Sch.

Mastering Black & White Photography: From Camera to Darkroom. Bernhard J. Suess. LC 94-72260. (Illus.). 240p. 1995. pap. 18.95 (*1-880559-23-4*) Allworth Pr.

Mastering Blues Guitar. Wayne Riker. Ed. by Workshop Arts Staff. (Complete Electric Blues Guitar Method Ser.). 144p. 1994. pap. 17.95 (*0-7390-0408-5*, 4482) Alfred Pub.

Mastering Blues Guitar. Wayne Riker. Ed. by Workshop Arts Staff. (Complete Electric Blues Guitar Method Ser.). 144p. 1994. pap. 28.90 incl. audio compact disk (*0-7390-0407-7*, 8234); audio compact disk 10.95 (*0-7390-0409-3*, 11280) Alfred Pub.

***Mastering Bookkeeping.** 4th ed. Peter Marshall. (Illus.). 192p. (Orig.). 1999. pap. 19.95 (*1-85703-495-3*, Pub. by How To Bks) Trans-Atl Phila.

Mastering Borland Latte. Marco Cantu. 848p. 1996. pap. text 49.99 (*0-7821-1989-1*) Sybex.

Mastering Brainwaves: An Instructor's Guide to Teaching Mental Training Skills. Keith T. Krotish. Ed. by Laurinda Krotish. 75p. (YA). (gr. 5 up). 1999. pap., teacher ed. 9.95 (*0-9670179-1-2*) Taekwondo Ctr.

***Mastering Business English: How to Sharpen up Your Communication Skills at Work.** 4th ed. Michael Bennie. (Illus.). 208p. (Orig.). 1998. pap. 19.95 (*1-85703-376-0*) How To Bks.

Mastering C. Date not set. teacher ed. write for info. incl. disk (*0-02-800451-5*) Glencoe.

Mastering C. Anthony Rudd. 371p. 1994. pap. 24.95 (*0-471-60820-3*) Wiley.

Mastering C++ Anthony Rudd. 486p. 1994. pap. 24.95 (*0-471-06565-X*) Wiley.

Mastering C. Herbert Schildt. LC 93-12200. 1993. write for info. (*0-02-800448-5*) Glencoe.

Mastering C++ Herbert Schildt. LC 93-10307. 1993. write for info. (*0-02-801000-0*) Glencoe.

Mastering C. large type ed. Herbert Schildt. 1993. 109.50 (*0-614-09558-1*, L-31413-00) Am Printing Hse.

Mastering C++ An Introduction to C++ & Object-Oriented Programming for C & Pascal Programmers. Cay S. Horstmann. 320p. 1997. text 75.95 (*0-471-29102-1*) Wiley.

Mastering C++ An Introduction to C++ & Object-Oriented Programming for C & Pascal Programmers. 2nd ed. Cay S. Horstmann. LC 95-34176. 320p. 1995. text 53.95 (*0-471-10427-2*) Wiley.

Mastering C Pointers: Tools for Programming Power. 2nd ed. Robert J. Traister. LC 93-10540. (Illus.). 163p. 1993. pap., pap. text 42.00 incl. disk (*0-12-697409-8*) Morgan Kaufmann.

Mastering Cadkey. Al Torizzo. 1993. pap. 38.95 (*0-02-677117-9*) Glencoe.

Mastering CADKEY: Version 6 & All Earlier Versions, Instructor's Guide. Al Torizzo & Greg Garguilo. 1999. teacher ed. 16.86 (*0-02-677118-7*) Glencoe.

Mastering Cadkey, Version 6 & All Earlier Versions. 2nd ed. Al Torizzo. 1995. pap. text 47.95 incl. disk (*0-02-677138-1*) Glencoe.

Mastering CDA Competencies. Judy Herr. 275p. (Orig.). (C). 1997. pap. text 22.64 (*1-56637-394-8*) Goodheart.

Mastering Change: Evolution to Success: Proceedings of the Thirty-Seventh International Conference. 759p. (Orig.). 1994. 35.00 (*1-55822-116-6*) Am Prod & Inventory.

Mastering Change: The Power of Mutual Trust & Respect in Personal Life, Family Life, Business & Society. Ichak Adizes. 240p. 1992. 19.95 (*0-937120-04-9*) Adizes Inst Inc.

Mastering Change: The Power of Mutual Trust & Respect in Personal Life, Family Life, Business & Society. Ichak Adizes. (Illus.). 243p. 1992. reprint ed. pap. write for info. (*0-937120-07-3*) Adizes Inst Inc.

Mastering Change: Winning Strategies for Effective City Planning. Bruce W. McClendon & Ray Quay. LC 87-70796. (Illus.). 282p. 1988. pap. 29.95 (*0-918286-48-4*, Planners Press) Am Plan Assn.

Mastering Change Management: A Practical Guide for Turning Obstacles into Opportunities. Richard Y. Chang. LC 93-74767. (Management Skills Ser.). Orig. Title: Managing in a Changing Environment. (Illus.). 108p. 1994. pap. 14.95 (*0-7879-5088-2*) R Chang Assocs.

Mastering Change Management: A Practical Guide for Turning Obstacles Into Opportunities. Richard Y. Chang. (Management Skills Ser.). 1994. pap. 14.95 (*1-883553-54-7*) R Chang Assocs.

Mastering Change Using Principles of Synergy: How to Solve Problems Together & Build Joyous, Lasting Relationships! rev. ed. Eileen L. Anderson. 320p. (Orig.). (C). 1994. pap. 28.95 (*0-9638150-9-1*) Tahirih Inst.

Mastering Chronic Pain: A Professional's Guide to Behavioral Treatment. Robert N. Jamison. LC 96-16713. 192p. (Orig.). 1996. pap. 33.95 (*1-56887-018-3*, MCPBP, Prof Resc Pr) Pro Resource.

***Mastering Cisco Routers.** Chris Brenton. (Illus.). 800p. 2000. 49.99 (*0-7821-2643-X*) Sybex.

***Mastering Client Access Express.** International Business Machines Staff. 2000. pap. 59.95 (*1-58304-072-2*) News Four-Hund.

Mastering Coaching & Supervision. Madeline C. Hunter. LC 95-7957. (Principals of Learning Ser.). 128p. 1982. pap. 19.95 (*0-8039-6315-7*) Corwin Pr.

Mastering COBOL. Carol Baroudi. LC 98-88951. (Mastering Ser.). 1024p. 1999. pap. 49.99 (*0-7821-2321-X*) Sybex.

Mastering COBOL: Let the PC Teach You Cobol Programming. Rex Woollard & Andrea Bonner. 1997. pap. 23.95 (*0-471-15974-3*) Wiley.

***Mastering Cold Fusion 4.** Arman Danesh. LC 99-61819. (Mastering Ser.). (Illus.). 880p. 1999. pap. 44.99 (*0-7821-2452-6*) Sybex.

***Mastering Coldfusion 4.5.** Arman Danesh. (Illus.). 1008p. 2000. pap. 49.99 (*0-7821-2773-8*) Sybex.

Mastering College Reading. Theodore O. Knight. LC 94-26923. 320p. (C). 1994. text 19.60 (*0-256-14565-2*, Irwn McGrw-H) McGrw-H Hghr Educ.

***Mastering Com & Com+** 4th ed. Ash Rofail & Yasser Shohoud. 720p. 1999. pap. 39.99 (*0-7821-2384-8*) Sybex.

Mastering Commodity Futures & Options: A Step-by-Step Guide to Successful Trading. George Kleinman. 250p. 1997. pap. text 55.00 (*0-273-62642-6*) F T P-H.

Mastering Communication. 2nd ed. Dennis S. Gouran et al. LC 93-21229. 528p. 1994. pap. text 52.00 (*0-205-15508-1*) Allyn.

Mastering Communication. 2nd annot. ed. Dennis S. Gouran et al. (C). 1994. pap. text, teacher ed. write for info. (*0-205-15509-X*, H5509-8) Allyn.

Mastering Communication in Contemporary America: Theory, Research & Practice. Melvin L. DeFleur et al. LC 92-4797. xii, 536p. (C). 1993. pap. text 46.95 (*1-55934-097-5*, 1097) Mayfield Pub.

Mastering Communication in Contemporary America, Instructor's Manual: Theory, Research & Practice. Melvin L. DeFleur et al. (C). 1993. pap. text, teacher ed. write for info. (*1-55934-319-2*, 1319) Mayfield Pub.

***Mastering Competitive Debate.** Dana Hensley & Diana Carlin. (YA). (gr. 10-12). 1999. pap., teacher ed. 8.00 (*0-931054-60-5*); pap. text 25.00 (*0-931054-59-1*) Clark Pub.

***Mastering Competitive Debate.** 5th ed. Dana Hensley & Diana Carlin. (YA). (gr. 10-12). 1999. text 38.00 (*0-931054-58-3*) Clark Pub.

***Mastering Component Development Using Atl 3.0.** 450p. 2000. 49.99 (*0-7897-2344-1*) Que.

Mastering Computer Applications. 2nd ed. Catherine Ricardo. 166p. (C). 1993. text 32.00 (*0-536-58447-8*) Pearson Custom.

Mastering Computer Applications. 3rd ed. Catherine Ricardo & Frances Bailie. 166p. (C). 1994. text 32.00 (*0-536-58661-6*) Pearson Custom.

Mastering Computer Communication. Michael J. Plonien & Stephanie J. Black. 1997. ring bd. 59.00 (*0-7646-0098-2*, QCCP97) Prctnrs Pub Co.

Mastering Computer Typing: Learning the ABCs of the Computer Keyboard. Sheryl Lindsell-Roberts. LC 94-41777. (Illus.). 208p. 1995. 14.00 (*0-395-71406-0*) HM.

Mastering Conducting Techniques. John Haberlen. LC 77-78469. (Illus.). 70p. (C). 1977. pap. text, spiral bd. 17.95 (*0-916656-01-2*, MFBK 01) Mark Foster Mus.

***Mastering Copperplate Calligraphy: A Step-by-Step Manual.** Eleanor Winters. (Illus.). 2000. pap. 12.95 (*0-486-40951-1*) Dover.

Mastering CorelDraw 8. 4th ed. Rick Altman. LC 97-81023. 960p. 1998. pap. text 49.99 (*0-7821-2208-6*) Sybex.

***Mastering CorelDraw 9.** Rick Altman. (Mastering Ser.). 944p. 1999. 39.99 (*0-7821-2520-4*) Sybex.

Mastering CorelDRAW 4. Chris Dickman et al. (Illus.). 776p. 1999. pap. 34.95 incl. disk (*1-56609-099-7*) Peachpit Pr.

Mastering Correction of Accounting Errors. 6th unabridged ed. Sharon H. Fettus & Mary D. Myers. 148p. 1994. pap. text 39.00 (*1-884826-26-1*) AIPB.

Mastering Cotton. Burton H. Pugh. (Illus.). 27p. (C). 1976. pap. 25.00 (*0-939093-14-6*) Lambert Gann Pub.

Mastering Craps. Tony Badillo. Ed. by Jose L. Badillo & Earl Chew. (Illus.). 192p. 1996. pap. 21.95 (*0-9700571-0-5*) L L David.

***Mastering Customer Service.** Michael E. Young. 2000. pap. 19.95 (*1-58790-001-7*) Regent Pr.

Mastering D. C. A Newcomer's Guide to Living in the Washington, D. C. Area. 4th ed. Kay Killingstad. Ed. by Sheila Donoghue & Dartha Dragnich. LC 98-70456. (Illus.). 288p. 1998. pap. 14.95 (*0-9631935-3-8*) Advent Pub.

Mastering Data Mining. Berry. 240p. (C). 1999. pap. 44.99 (*0-471-33123-6*) Wiley.

***Mastering Data Modeling Using Logical Data Structures.** John Carlisle & Joseph Maguire. 2000. 44.95 incl. cd-rom (*0-201-70045-X*) Addison-Wesley.

***Mastering Database Programming with Visual Basic 6.** 4th ed. Evangelos Petroutsos. 928p. 1999. pap. text 39.99 (*0-7821-2598-0*) Sybex.

Mastering dBASE III in Less Than a Day. Anthony K. Lima. (Illus.). 160p. 1986. 20.50 (*0-13-559816-8*) P-H.

Mastering DB2 400. Lin. 2000. text 46.92 (*0-13-262205-X*) P-H.

Mastering Death! Bill Panko & Margaret Panko. 175p. (Orig.). Date not set. pap. 14.95 (*1-885342-09-8*) Creative Ways.

Mastering Degrees of Homemaking. Marilynn Gazowsky. (Illus.). (Orig.). (C). 1989. pap. 6.00 (*0-926629-01-8*) Voice Pentecost Pub.

Mastering Delphi 4. Marco Cantu. LC 98-86254. (Mastering Ser.). 1280p. 1998. pap. 49.99 (*0-7821-2350-3*) Sybex.

***Mastering Delphi X.** 3rd ed. Marco Cantu. 1120p. 1999. 49.99 (*0-7821-2565-4*) Sybex.

Mastering Depreciation. unabridged ed. Garo Kalfayan & Denise Patterson. 212p. 1998. pap. text 49.00 (*1-884826-28-8*) AIPB.

***Mastering Depression Through Interpersonal Psychotherapy.** Myrna M. Weissman. 2000. pap., wbk. ed. 26.50 (*0-12-784453-8*) Acad Pr.

Mastering Derivative Markets: A Step-by-Step Guide to the Products, Applications & Risks. Francesca Taylor. LC 96-153648. (Market Editions). (Illus.). 256p. (Orig.). 1995. pap. text 39.95 (*0-273-62045-2*) F T P-H.

Mastering Design Patterns in C++ Luke Hohmann & Tim DeBruine. (C). 2000. 40.00 (*0-13-911173-5*, Macmillan Coll) P-H.

Mastering Design Patterns for Java. Hohmann & Debruine. 1999. pap. text 40.00 (*0-13-911165-4*) P-H.

Mastering Digital Electronics. (C). 2000. pap. 49.99 (*0-13-013986-6*) P-H.

Mastering Digital Signal Processing Using Matlab. Craig Borghesani. LC 97-28987. 72p. 1997. pap. 30.80 (*0-13-534976-1*) P-H.

***Mastering Direct Access Fundamentals: Understanding Market Information & Learning the Key Skills.** Jenny Bailly. (Direct Access Trader Ser.). 2001. 24.95 (*0-07-136249-5*) McGraw.

Mastering Discourse: The Politics of Intellectual Culture. Paul A. Bove. LC 91-41256. 269p. 1992. text 54.95 (*0-8223-1232-8*); pap. text 19.95 (*0-8223-1245-X*) Duke.

Mastering Diversity: Managing for Success under ADA & Other Anti-Discrimination Laws. James Walsh. LC 94-73598. (Taking Control Ser.). 474p. 1995. pap. 29.95 (*1-56343-102-5*) Silver Lake.

Mastering Documentation. Springhouse Publishing Company Staff et al. LC 94-29557. 416p. 1994. 39.95 (*0-87434-749-1*) Springhouse Corp.

Mastering Dollars & Sense on the Macintosh. James E. Richardson. 650p. (C). 1991. 27.66 (*0-673-38557-4*, Scott Frsmn) Addson-Wesley Educ.

***Mastering Domino R5.** Sandra Moulton. (Mastering Ser.). 704p. 2000. pap. 39.99 (*0-7821-2678-2*) Sybex.

Mastering DOS 5.0. Herbert Schildt. LC 92-43344. 1993. write for info. (*0-02-800460-4*) Glencoe.

Mastering DOS 5.0. large type ed. Herbert Schildt. 1993. 100.50 (*0-614-09559-X*, L-31409-00) Am Printing Hse.

Mastering DOS 6.0. Herbert Schildt. LC 93-34937. 1994. write for info. (*0-02-801905-9*) Glencoe.

Mastering Drawing the Human Figure from Life Memory Imagination. Jack Faragasso. Ed. by Karen Bonacorda. LC 98-90798. (Illus.). 256p. 1998. pap. 39.95 (*0-9667113-0-0*, Pub. by Stargarden Pr) BookMasters.

Mastering Dreamweaver 2. David L. Crowder & Rhonda Crowder. (Mastering Ser.). 912p. 1999. 39.99 (*0-7821-2553-0*) Sybex.

Mastering Dysrhythmias. Kevin R. Brown & Sheldon Jacobson. LC 87-15448. (Illus.). 295p. (C). 1987. pap. 20.00 (*0-8036-1251-6*) Delmar.

Mastering Electric Bass. David Overthrow. Date not set. pap. write for info. (*0-7390-0682-7*, 19355); pap. write for info. incl. audio compact disk (*0-7390-0683-5*, 19356) Alfred Pub.

Mastering Electrical Engineering. 2nd ed. Noel Morris. 1991. 30.00 (*0-07-043295-3*) McGraw-Hill Prof.

Mastering Electricity. Stuart Asser & Vincent Stigliano. 436p. 1993. mass mkt. 54.25 (*0-8273-4604-2*) Delmar.

Mastering Electricity: Comp TB IBM. Dwiggins. (Electronics Technology Ser.). 1993. 49.95 (*0-8273-5816-4*) Delmar.

Mastering Electricity: Instructor's Guide. Stuart Asser & Vincent Stigliano. LC 92-26598. 202p. 1993. pap. 28.00 (*0-8273-4605-0*) Delmar.

Mastering Electronics Math. 2nd ed. Jesse R. Phagan. (Illus.). 352p. 1991. pap. 17.95 (*0-8306-3589-0*) McGraw-Hill Prof.

***Mastering Electronics Workbench.** John Adams. (Illus.). 324p. 2000. pap. 39.95 (*0-07-134483-7*) McGraw-Hill Prof.

Mastering Elementary Algebra. Yoshiko Yamato & Mary J. Cordon. 623p. (C). 1987. VHS. write for info. (*0-318-61988-1*) Harcourt Coll Pubs.

M

Mastering Elliott Wave: Presenting the Neely Method. Glenn Neely. 223p. 1990. 95.00 (0-930233-44-1) Windsor.

***Mastering Engineer's Handbook.** Bobby Owsinski. 2000. pap. 29.95 (0-87288-741-3) Intertec Pub.

Mastering English: An Advanced Grammar for Non-Native & Native Speakers. Carl Bache & Niels Davidsen-Nielsen. LC 97-23493. 538p. 1997. text 112.00 (3-11-015535-4); pap. text 24.00 (3-11-015536-2) Mouton.

Mastering English: An Advanced Grammar for Non-Native & Native Speakers. Alex Klinge. 120p. 1997. pap. text, wbk. ed. 11.00 (3-11-015818-3) Mouton.

Mastering English Usage. Janet Whitcut & Robert Ilson. LC 93-41825. 1994. 10.50 (0-13-554171-9) P-H.

***Mastering Enterprise JavaBeans & the Java 2 Platform, Enterprise Edition: Proven Methods for Building Enterprise Applications.** Ed Roman. LC 99-49590. 752p. 1999. pap. 49.99 incl. cd-rom (0-471-33229-1) Wiley.

***Mastering Entrepreneurship.** Sue Birley & Daniel F. Muzyka. 448p. 2000. pap. 34.00 (0-273-64928-0) S&S Trade.

***Mastering ENVY/Developer.** Joseph Pelrine et al. (Advances in Object Technology Ser.: No. 25). 350p. (C). 2000. pap. text. write for info. (0-521-66650-3) Cambridge U Pr.

M

Mastering Essential Math Skills: 20 Minutes a Day to Success, 1. Richard W. Fisher. LC 98-67549. (Illus.). 127p. 1998. pap. 14.95 (0-9666211-0-7) Math Essentials.

Mastering Essential Mathematics: Preparing. Weingarden. (Academic Math Ser.). 1997. pap. 10.95 (0-538-68302-3); pap., teacher ed. 21.95 (0-538-68303-1) S-W Pub.

Mastering Excel: A Problem Solving Approach. 2nd ed. James Gips. LC 96-23076. 352p. 1996. pap. 43.95 (0-471-16372-4) Wiley.

Mastering Excel for Windows 95. 3rd ed. Thomas Chester. LC 95-70847. 1040p. 1995. 29.99 (0-7821-1785-6) Sybex.

Mastering Excel 2000: Premium Edition. Thomas Chester & Mindy Martin. LC 99-60015. (Mastering Ser.). 1328p. 1999. pap. 39.99 (0-7821-2317-1) Sybex.

***Mastering Exchange Server 5.5.** 2nd ed. Barry Gerber. (Mastering Computers Ser.). (Illus.). 1999. pap. 44.99 (0-7821-2658-8, Network Pr) Sybex.

Mastering Exchange Trades Equity Derivative: A Step-by-Step Guide to the Markets, Applications & Risks. David Ford. (Market Editions). (Illus.). 250p. (Orig.). 1996. pap. text 50.00 (0-273-61974-8) F T P-H.

Mastering Executive Arts & Skills. C. Parris. 1985. 14.95 (0-13-560086-3, Parker Publishing Co) P-H.

Mastering Expert Testimony: A Courtroom Handbook for Mental Health Professionals. William T. Tsushima & Robert M. Anderson, Jr. 224p. 1996. 45.00 (0-8058-1888-X); pap. 19.50 (0-8058-1889-8) L Erlbaum Assocs.

Mastering Fall Assortments. RSI Promotion Staff. 1997. pap. text 35.99 (0-7821-2217-5) Sybex.

Mastering Family Therapy: Journeys of Growth & Transformation. Salvador Minuchin et al. LC 96-22887. 272p. 1996. 59.95 (0-471-15558-6) Wiley.

Mastering Fear: The Ultimate Challenge. Steven Bisyak & Michael McDermott. LC 94-234825. 195p. (Orig.). (C). 1994. 9.95 (0-9640871-1-1) Frog & Latte.

Mastering Fee Management: All Factors Accounted For. Brett Behling & Bruce Harville. 86p. (Orig.). 1993. pap. 89.00 (1-889394-28-9) Credit Union Execs.

Mastering Finance & Accounting. David A. Farrow. LC 94-18518. 1994. write for info. (0-07-707833-0) McGraw.

Mastering Financial Calculations: A Step-by-Step Guide to the Mathematics of the Market. Bob Steiner. (FT Market Editions Ser.). (Illus.). 280p. (Orig.). 1997. pap. text 39.95 (0-273-62587-X) F T P-H.

Mastering Fine Decorative Paint Techniques. Sharon Ross. Ed. by Kathie Robitiz. LC 98-89443. (Illus.). 272p. 1999. pap. 24.95 (1-58011-064-9) Creative Homeowner.

***Mastering Finnish.** 2nd rev. ed. Borje Vahamaki. (Mastering Languages Ser.). 288p. 2000. pap. 16.95 (0-7818-0800-6) Hippocrene Bks.

Mastering Flash Photography: A Course in Basic to Advanced Lighting Techniques. Susan McCartney. LC 97-18999. (Illus.). 144p. 1997. pap. 24.95 (0-8174-4545-5, Amphoto) Watsn-Guptill.

Mastering for Skill. Illus. by Michael Anderson, Jr. 136p. (Orig.). (YA). (gr. 7-12). 1998. pap. 19.95 (1-928726-03-8) Positive Prods.

Mastering Foreign Exchange & Currency Options: A Practitioner's Guide to the Mechanics of the Market. Francesca Taylor. 250p. (Orig.). 1996. pap. text 45.00 (0-273-62537-3) F T P-H.

Mastering Foreign Exchange & Money Markets: A Step-by-Step Guide to the Products, Applications & Risks. Paul Roth. (FT Market Editions Ser.). (Illus.). 320p. (Orig.). 1997. pap. 75.00 (0-273-62586-1) F T P-H.

Mastering Fourth Dimension. Eric Hall. (Illus.). 304p. 1990. 29.95 (0-8306-8444-1, 3444); pap. 19.60 (0-8306-3444-4) McGraw-Hill Prof.

Mastering Fractions: The Most Complete Book on Fractions. Said Hamilton. Ed. by Melvin DeGree. 568p. (YA). (gr. 6 up). 1996. pap. text 49.95 (0-9649954-0-9) Hmlton Assocs.

Mastering French. (Mastering Ser.). (ENG & FRE.). 1992. pap. 15.95 (0-8120-1358-1) Barron.

Mastering French. Monique Cossard & Salazar. (Foreign Service Institute Language Ser.). (FRE & ENG.). 1985. 79.95 incl. audio (0-8120-7321-5) Barron.

Mastering French. Cossard & Salazar. (Foreign Service Institute Language Ser.). (FRE & ENG.). 1985. pap. 16.95 (0-8120-2204-1) Barron.

Mastering French, 13 CDs. Cossard & Salazar. (Mastering Ser.). (ENG & FRE.). 1992. pap. 110.00 incl. audio compact disk (0-8120-7874-8) Barron.

Mastering French. E. J. Neather. (Mastering Languages Ser.). (Illus.). 262p. (Orig.). 1991. pap. 14.95 (0-87052-055-5); audio 12.95 (0-87052-060-1) Hippocrene Bks.

Mastering French Business Vocabulary: A Thematic Approach. Bernard Gillman. LC 95-81522. (FRE.). 448p. 1996. pap. 10.95 (0-8120-9514-6) Barron.

Mastering French, Level II, 12 cassettes, Set. Barron's Educational Series Staff & Carolyn B. Mitchell. (Foreign Service Institute Mastering Series-Level II: Level 2). (FRE & ENG.). 1992. pap., boxed set 79.95 incl. audio (0-8120-7918-3) Barron.

Mastering French Vocabulary: A Thematic Approach. Reinhild Herrmann & Rainer Rauch. (Mastering Vocabulary Ser). 368p. 1995. pap. 8.95 (0-8120-9107-8) Barron.

Mastering Fundamental Analysis: How to Spot Trends & Pick Winning Stocks Like the Pros. Michael C. Thomsett. LC 98-8159. 256p. 1998. 26.95 (0-7931-2873-0, 56807701) Dearborn.

Mastering Geriatric Care. Ed. by Patricia Schull. LC 96-28895. (Illus.). 480p. (Orig.). 1996. 39.95 (0-87434-871-4) Springhouse Corp.

Mastering German. (Mastering Ser.). (ENG & GER.). 1992. pap. 16.95 (0-8120-1365-4) Barron.

Mastering German. Brown & Christoph. (Foreign Service Institute Language Ser.). (GER & ENG.). 1985. pap. 16.95 (0-8120-2210-6) Barron.

Mastering German. Contrib. by Brown & Christoph. (Foreign Service Institute Language Ser.). (GER & ENG.). 1985. 79.95 incl. audio (0-8120-7352-5) Barron.

Mastering German, 15 CD. Brown & Christoph. (Mastering Ser.). (ENG & GER.). 1992. pap. 120.00 incl. audio compact disk (0-8120-7869-1) Barron.

Mastering German. A. J. Peck. (Mastering Languages Ser.). (Illus.). 322p. 1991. pap. 11.95 (0-87052-056-3) Hippocrene Bks.

Mastering German, Level II, 12 cassettes, Set. Tessa Krailing. (Foreign Service Institute Mastering Series-Level II: Level 2). (GER & ENG.). 1992. pap., boxed set 79.95 incl. audio (0-8120-7920-5) Barron.

Mastering German Vocabulary: A Thematic Approach. Veronika Schnorr & Gabriele Forst. (Mastering Vocabulary Ser). 368p. 1995. pap. 8.95 (0-8120-9108-6) Barron.

Mastering Global Studies: An Interactive Textbook. 3rd ed. James Killoran et al. (Illus.). 340p. 1995. pap. text 11.95 (1-882422-04-X) Jarrett Pub.

***Mastering Gnome.** Bryan Pfaffenberger. 800p. 1999. pap. 34.99 (0-7821-2625-1) Sybex.

Mastering Government Securities: A Step-by-Step Guide to the Products, Applications & Risks. Stephan Mahony. 256p. (Orig.). 1996. pap. text 45.00 (0-273-62416-4) F T P-H.

Mastering Grammar I. Ed. by B. Schnek. 180p. 1988. pap. text 7.05 (0-8428-0175-8) Cambridge Bk.

Mastering Grammar II. Ed. by B. Schnek. 132p. 1988. pap. text 6.75 (0-8428-0177-4) Cambridge Bk.

Mastering Greek. P. Sapountzis & A. Sapountzis. (Foreign Service Institute Language Ser.). (GRE & ENG.). 1988. pap. 16.95 (0-8120-3987-4); pap. 79.95 incl. audio (0-8120-7477-7) Barron.

Mastering Greek Vocabulary. 2nd rev. ed. Thomas A. Robinson. 178p. (Orig.). 1991. pap. 9.95 (0-943575-85-0) Hendrickson MA.

Mastering Guerrilla Marketing: 100 Profit-Producing Insights That You Can Take to the Bank. Jay Conrad Levinson. LC 99-33627. 256p. 1999. pap. 14.00 (0-395-90875-2) HM.

Mastering Guitar Technique: Process & Essence. Christopher Berg. 144p. 1997. 19.95 (0-7866-2373-X, 96216) Mel Bay.

Mastering Hand Tool Techniques. Alan Bridgewater & Gill Bridgewater. (Illus.). 144p. 1997. 27.99 (1-55870-457-4, Betrwy Bks) F & W Pubns Inc.

Mastering Harvard Graphics 2.3. Campbell. 1993. teacher ed. write for info. incl. disk (0-02-802580-6) Glencoe.

Mastering Harvard Graphics 2.3. Mary V. Campbell & David R. Campbell. LC 92-42891. 1993. write for info. (0-02-802578-4) Glencoe.

Mastering Harvard Graphics 2.3. large type ed. Mary V. Campbell & David R. Campbell. 1993. 158.50 (0-614-09560-3, L-31423-00) Am Printing Hse.

Mastering Hebrew. Levinson. (Foreign Service Institute Language Ser.). (HEB & ENG.). 1988. pap. 16.95 (0-8120-3990-4) Barron.

Mastering Hebrew. Contrib. by Levinson. (Foreign Service Institute Language Ser.). (HEB & ENG.). 1988. pap. 79.95 incl. audio (0-8120-7478-5) Barron.

***Mastering Home Networking.** Mark Henricks. (Mastering Ser.). 496p. 2000. pap. 29.99 (0-7821-2630-8) Sybex.

Mastering Household Electrical Wiring. James L. Kittle. (Orig.). 1991. 24.95 (0-8306-5310-4) McGraw-Hill Prof.

Mastering Household Electrical Wiring. 2nd ed. James L. Kittle. (Illus.). 304p. (Orig.). 1988. 24.95 (0-8306-0987-3) McGraw-Hill Prof.

Mastering HTML for Help Authors. 2nd ed. Debbie Wilimek. 110p. (C). 1996. pap. 19.95 (0-9647236-3-8) Blue Sky Sftware.

***Mastering HTML 4.** 2nd ed. Deborah Ray & Eric J. Ray. LC 99-61309. (Mastering Ser.). (Illus.). 960p. 1999. 34.99 (0-7821-2523-9) Sybex.

***Mastering HTML 4: Premium Edition.** Deborah Ray. (Mastering Ser.). 1216p. 1999. 49.99 (0-7821-2524-7) Sybex.

Mastering HTML 4.0. Eric Ray & Deborah Ray. 1040p. 1997. pap. text 49.99 (0-7821-2102-0) Sybex.

***Mastering I-DEAS.** S. C. Jonathon Lin & F. C. Tony Shiue. Ed. by Karen L. Sterzik. (Illus.). 750p. (C). 1999. pap. 69.00 (1-886552-12-6) Scholars Intl.

Mastering IC Electronics see Electronic Devices

Mastering IC Electronics. Joseph J. Carr. 448p. 1991. 32.95 (0-8306-2185-7, 3502); pap. 19.95 (0-8306-2184-9) McGraw-Hill Prof.

Mastering Ideas in Psychology. Stephen B. Wilson. (Illus.). 160p. 1995. pap. 20.00 (0-614-08392-3) Minds Eye Illinois.

Mastering Information in the New Century. Marvin J. Cetron & Owen Davies. LC 94-208421. 100p. 1994. reprint ed. pap. 31.00 (0-608-03812-1, 206466200009) Bks Demand.

***Mastering Information Management: The Complete MBA Companion in Information Management.** Tom Davenport & Donald A. Marchand. 416p. 2000. pap. 34.00 (0-273-64352-5) F T P-H.

Mastering Instrument Flying. 2nd ed. Henry Sollman & Sherwood Harris. 1993. 32.95 (0-07-026891-6) McGraw.

***Mastering Instrument Flying.** 3rd ed. Henry Sollman. LC 98-52811. 371p. 1999. pap. 34.95 (0-07-059690-5) McGraw.

***Mastering Instrument Flying.** 3rd ed. Henry Sollman. LC 98-52811. 1999. write for info. (0-07-059691-3) McGraw.

Mastering Internet Explorer 4.0 for Macintosh. T. Kelley Boylan. 400p. 1996. pap. text 39.99 incl. cd-rom (1-56830-322-X) Hayden.

Mastering Inventory. 2nd unabridged ed. Philip E. Meyer. 218p. 1996. pap. text 49.00 (1-884826-29-6) AIPB.

Mastering Italian. Noemi Messora. (Mastering Languages Ser.). (Illus.). 341p. (Orig.). 1991. pap. 11.95 (0-87052-057-1); audio 12.95 (0-87052-066-0) Hippocrene Bks.

Mastering Italian. Zappala. (Foreign Service Institute Language Ser.). (ITA & ENG.). 1986. pap. 16.95 (0-8120-2222-X) Barron.

Mastering Italian. Ed. by Zappala. (Foreign Service Institute Language Ser.). (ITA & ENG.). 1987. 79.95 incl. audio (0-8120-7323-1) Barron.

Mastering Italian, 15 CDs. Zappala. (Mastering Ser.). (ENG & ITA.). 1992. pap. 120.00 incl. audio compact disk (0-8120-7867-5) Barron.

Mastering Italian Vocabulary: A Thematic Approach. Luciana Feinler-Torriani & Gunter H. Klemm. (Mastering Vocabulary Ser). 368p. 1995. pap. 8.95 (0-8120-9109-4) Barron.

Mastering Japanese, 8 cassettes. Foreign Service Language Institute Staff. (Foreign Service Institute Language Ser.). (JPN & ENG.). 464p. 1990. pap. 79.95 incl. audio (0-8120-7633-8) Barron.

Mastering Japanese. Foreign Service Language Institute Staff. 464p. 1990. 30.00 (0-8120-4411-8) Barron.

Mastering Japanese. Harry Guest. (Mastering Languages Ser.). (JPN., Illus.). 339p. (Orig.). 1991. pap. 14.95 (0-87052-923-4); audio 12.95 (0-87052-983-8) Hippocrene Bks.

Mastering Japanese, 10 CDs. Harz Jorden. (Mastering Ser.). (ENG & JPN.). 1992. pap. 120.00 incl. audio compact disk (0-8120-7865-9) Barron.

Mastering Japanese, Level II, 8 cassettes, Set. (Foreign Service Institute Mastering Series-Level II: Level 2). (JPN & ENG.). 1992. boxed set 79.95 incl. audio (0-8120-7921-3) Barron.

Mastering Java. DDC Publishing Staff. 1999. pap. text 50.00 (1-56243-841-7) DDC Pub.

Mastering Java Threads. DDC Publishing Staff. 1999. pap. text 45.00 (1-56243-842-5) DDC Pub.

Mastering Java 1.2. John Zukowski. 1280p. 1998. pap. text 49.99 (0-7821-2180-2) Sybex.

Mastering JavaBeans. Laurence Vanhelsuwe. LC 97-66375. 832p. 1997. pap. text 49.99 incl. cd-rom (0-7821-2097-0) Sybex.

Mastering JavaScript. James Jaworski. LC 96-71650. (Illus.). 1120p. 1997. pap. text 49.99 incl. cd-rom (0-7821-2014-8) Sybex.

Mastering JavaScript Part 1. DDC Publishing Staff. 1999. pap. text 18.00 (1-56243-836-0) DDC Pub.

Mastering JavaScript Part 2. DDC Publishing Staff. 1999. pap. text 18.00 (1-56243-837-9) DDC Pub.

Mastering JavaScript & JScript. James Jaworski. LC 99-60013. (Mastering Ser.). (Illus.). 928p. 1999. pap. 39.99 (0-7821-2492-5) Sybex.

***Mastering JavaScript with CD-ROM.** James Jaworski. (Mastering Ser.). 1104p. 2000. pap. 49.99 incl. cd-rom (0-7821-2819-X) Sybex.

Mastering Jazz Guitar - Chord/Melody. Jody Fischer. (FRE.). 64p. Date not set. pap. write for info. incl. audio compact disk (0-7390-0829-3, 19377) Alfred Pub.

Mastering Jazz Guitar Improv. Jody Fischer. (FRE.). Date not set. pap. write for info. incl. audio compact disk (0-7390-0828-5, 19376) Alfred Pub.

***Mastering Jazz Keyboard.** Noah Baerman. (National Guitar Workshop Arts Ser.). 1998. pap. 20.90 incl. audio compact disk (0-88284-914-X, 17861) Alfred Pub.

Mastering Joker Wild Video Poker: How to Play As an Expert & Walk Away a Winner. Bradley H. Davis. LC 90-82847. 144p. (Orig.). 1990. pap. 14.95 (0-9626766-5-9) Applied Tech Pr.

***Mastering K Office for Linux.** Arthur Griffith. (Illus.). 2000. pap. 34.99 (0-7821-2652-9) Sybex.

***Mastering KDE.** Bryan Pfaffenberger. (Mastering Ser.). (Illus.). 704p. 2000. pap. text 34.99 (0-7821-2629-4) Sybex.

***Mastering Kempo.** William Durbin. (Illus.). 192p. 2000. pap. 19.95 (0-7360-0350-9) Human Kinetics.

Mastering Keyboarding & Word Processing: An Applied Approach to Letters & Memos. 3rd ed. Bartholomew. (TA - Typing/Keyboarding Ser.). 1994. mass mkt. 11.00 (0-538-62000-5) S-W Pub.

Mastering Keyboarding & Word Processing: Applied Approach - Center & Table. 3rd ed. Bartholomew. (TA - Typing/Keyboarding Ser.). 1995. mass mkt. 11.00 (0-538-62004-8); mass mkt. 11.00 (0-538-62006-4) S-W Pub.

Mastering Keyboarding & Word Processing, Reports/Forms: An Applications Approach. 3rd ed. Bartholomew. (TA - Typing/Keyboarding Ser.). 1994. mass mkt. 11.00 (0-538-62002-1) S-W Pub.

Mastering Korean. (Foreign Service Institute Language Ser.). (KOR & ENG.). 1988. pap. 16.95 (0-8120-3375-2); pap. 79.95 incl. audio (0-8120-7480-7) Barron.

Mastering Largemouth Bass. Larry Larsen. LC 89-63111. (Complete Angler's Library). 261p. 1989. write for info. (0-914697-24-2) N Amer Outdoor Grp.

Mastering Law Studies & Law Exam Techniques. 2nd ed. R. Krever. 275p. 1990. pap. 32.00 (0-409-30121-3, AT, MICHIE) LEXIS Pub.

Mastering Layout: The Art of Eye Appeal. Michael R. Stevens. LC 85-61336. 1986. pap. 29.95 (0-911380-68-X) ST Pubns.

Mastering Leadership in the Christian Camp. David Burrow. (Illus.). 166p. (Orig.). 1996. pap. 14.95 (0-9622191-6-9) McElroy Pub.

Mastering Legal Environment. Miller. Date not set. pap. text 20.00 (0-314-02201-5) West Pub.

***Mastering Legends of the Five Rings.** George H. Baxter. LC 98-11887. 1998. pap. 16.95 (1-55622-626-8) Wordware Pub.

Mastering Life: Getting with God's Program for Your Future. Charles A. Kollar. LC 99-29664. 208p. 2000. pap. 12.99 (0-310-22775-5) Zondervan.

Mastering Life for Children. Illus. by Michael Anderson, Jr. (YA). (gr. 7-12). 1998. 69.95 (1-928726-00-3) Positive Prods.

Mastering Life Starter Kit. (YA). (gr. 7-12). 1998. write for info. (1-928726-02-X) Positive Prods.

Mastering Life Starter Kit Plus. (YA). (gr. 7-12). 39.95 (1-928726-01-1) Positive Prods.

***Mastering LightWave Modeler.** Bill Fleming. (Conquering 3D Graphics Ser.). 500p. 1999. pap. 49.95 incl. cd-rom (0-12-260501-2, Pub. by Morgan Kaufmann) Harcourt.

Mastering Linux. Arman Danesh. LC 98-86867. (Mastering Ser.). xxviii, 960p. 1998. pap. text 39.99 (0-7821-2341-4) Sybex.

Mastering Linux. Angie Hansen. 800p. 1997. pap. text 44.99 incl. cd-rom (0-7821-2164-0) Sybex.

Mastering Linux: Premium Edition. Arman Danesh. (Mastering Ser.). 1248p. 1999. 49.99 (0-7821-2555-7) Sybex.

Mastering Local Area Networks. Christa Anderson. (Mastering Ser.). 784p. 1999. pap. 39.99 (0-7821-2258-2) Sybex.

Mastering Lotus Approach 96 for Windows 95. 2nd ed. James E. Powell. 816p. 1996. pap. 34.99 (0-7821-1773-2) Sybex.

***Mastering Lotus Notes & Dominion R5: Premium Edition.** Scott Haberman. (Mastering Ser.). 2000. pap. 49.99 (0-7821-2635-9) Sybex.

Mastering Lotus Notes 4.5 & Domino. 2nd ed. Kenyon Brown et al. LC 97-65366. 1152p. 1997. pap. text 49.99 incl. cd-rom (0-7821-1996-4) Sybex.

Mastering Lotus Notes Release 5. 3rd ed. Kenyon Brown. LC 99-61234. (Mastering Ser.). 1168p. 1999. pap. text 39.99 (0-7821-2185-3) Sybex.

Mastering Lotus Notes 4.6. 3rd ed. Scott Haberman. (Mastering Ser.). 960p. 1998. pap. text 44.99 (0-7821-2342-2) Sybex.

Mastering Lotus Smartsuite: Millennium Edition. Sandra E. Eddy. LC 98-87091. (Mastering Ser.). 1998. pap. text 49.99 (0-7821-2410-0) Sybex.

***Mastering Lotus SmartSuite: Release 9.5.** 3rd ed. Sandra E. Eddy. 1024p. 1999. pap. 39.99 (0-7821-2620-0) Sybex.

Mastering Lotus SmartSuite - Millennium Edition. 2nd ed. Sandra E. Eddy. 1088p. 1998. pap. text 39.99 (0-7821-2238-8) Sybex.

Mastering Lotus SmartSuite 97 for Windows 95. 2nd ed. Sandra E. Eddy. LC 96-68126. (Illus.). 1136p. 1996. pap. text 39.99 (0-7821-1780-5) Sybex.

Mastering Lotus Word Pro 96 for Windows 95 Special Edition. Sheila S. Dienes. 928p. 1996. pap. 34.99 (0-7821-1390-7) Sybex.

***Mastering Mac OS X.** Todd Stauffer. (Mastering Ser.). 752p. 2000. pap. 39.99 (0-7821-2581-6) Sybex.

Mastering Machine Applique. Harriet Hargrave. Ed. by Jane P. Parkinson. LC 91-58593. (Illus.). 144p. (Orig.). 1995. pap. 21.95 (0-914881-45-0, 10054) C & T Pub.

Mastering Machine Code on Your ZX-81. Toni Baker. 176p. 1982. 18.41 (0-685-08667-4) P-H.

Mastering Macromedia Director 6. Chuck Henderson. LC 97-65910. 816p. 1997. pap. text 49.99 incl. cd-rom (0-7821-2084-9) Sybex.

Mastering Macros for Lotus 1-2-3. Bonnie Holloway & Donna Sarber. 112p. (C). 1995. spiral bd. write for info. (0-697-27780-1) Bus & Educ Tech.

Mastering Magic: 100 Secrets of the Great Magicians. deluxe ed. Walter B. Gibson. (Illus.). 256p. (YA). (gr. 5 up). 1995. 12.95 (0-8119-0825-9) F Fell Pubs Inc.

Mastering MAKE. Clovis L. Tondo et al. 150p. 1992. pap. text 22.00 (0-685-50513-8) P-H.

Mastering Management: Practical Procedures for Effective Business Control. A. Leslie Derbyshire. LC 80-83028. 300p. 1981. 19.98 (0-88290-159-1, 2046) Horizon Utah.

Mastering Management Education: Innovations in Teaching Effectiveness. Ed. by Charles M. Vance. (Illus.). 320p. 1993. 52.00 (0-8039-4951-0); pap. 24.00 (0-8039-4952-9) Sage.

Mastering Management Skills. (SWC-Management Ser.). 2001. pap. 55.00 (0-324-01330-2) Thomson Learn.

An Asterisk (*) at the beginning of an entry indicates that the title is appearing for the first time.

Mastering Market Data: An Approach to Analyzing & Applying Salary Survey Information. Jane A. Bjorndal & Linda K. Ison. (Building Blocks Ser.: Vol. 2). (Illus.). 24p. (Orig.). 1991. pap. 24.95 (*1-57963-005-7*, A0002) Am Compensation.

Mastering Marketing. 1988. 25.00 (*1-878604-18-X*) Briefings Pub Grp.

Mastering Markets in South America. Lawrence W. Turner. LC 94-90584. 239p. 1998. pap. 32.95 (*1-886188-23-8*) Fomalhaut Pr.

Mastering Martial Arts see New Action Sports

Mastering Mary Sue. 2nd ed. Mary Love. (Orig.). 1998. reprint ed. mass mkt. 6.95 (*1-56333-660-X*) Masquerade.

Mastering Math. (Illus.). 413p. (C). 1997. pap. text. write for info. (*1-58059-904-4*) Kaplan Educ.

Mastering Math: How to Be a Great Math Student. 3rd ed. Richard Manning Smith. LC 97-21749. (Mathematics Ser.). 215p. 1999. pap. 11.95 (*0-534-34947-1*) Brooks-Cole.

Mastering Math Basic Skills Workbook. Fabian Lacret-Subirat. (Illus.). 251p. (J). (gr. 7). 1987. pap. 8.48 (*0-943144-21-3*) Lacret Pub.

*__Mastering Math for the Building Trades.__ James Gerhart. (Illus.). 368p. 2000. pap. 24.95 (*0-07-136023-9*) McGraw.

Mastering Mathcad Version 7. Howard Keller & John G. Crandall. LC 97-51231. (Illus.). 256p. 1998. pap., pap. text 39.95 incl. cd-rom (*0-07-913136-0*) McGraw.

Mastering MathCad: Version 7. Howard Keller & John G. Crandall. LC 97-51231. 1998. write for info. (*0-07-034310-1*) McGraw.

Mastering Mathematica. John W. Gray. 1995. pap. text 20.00 (*0-12-784812-6*) Acad Pr.

Mastering Mathematica: Programming Methods & Applications. 2nd ed. John W. Gray. LC 97-30329. (Illus.). 629p. 1997. pap. text 44.95 (*0-12-296105-6*) Acad Pr.

Mastering Mathematical Skills. Antonios Gonis & Wayne Strand. LC 80-19989. (Illus.). 432p. (C). 1981. pap. text 28.75 (*0-201-03062-4*) Addison-Wesley.

Mastering Mathematics. Antonios Gonis & Wayne Strand. LC 80-19989. (Illus.). 432p. (C). 1981. suppl. ed. 12.75 (*0-201-03064-0*) Addison-Wesley.

Mastering Mathematics: How to Be a Great Math Student. Richard M. Smith. (Math). 157p. (C). 1990. mass mkt. 8.25 (*0-534-14628-7*) PWS Pubs.

Mastering Mathematics: How to Be a Great Math Student. 2nd ed. Richard M. Smith. 198p. 1993. mass mkt. 12.50 (*0-534-20838-X*) PWS Pubs.

Mastering MATLAB: A Comprehensive Tutorial & Reference. Duane C. Hanselman & Bruce Littlefield. (C). 1995. pap. text 50.67 (*0-13-191594-0*) P-H.

Mastering MATLAB 5: A Comprehensive Tutorial & Reference. Duane C. Hanselman & Bruce C. Littlefield. LC 97-47330. 638p. (C). 1997. pap. 56.00 (*0-13-858366-8*) P-H.

*__Mastering Maya Complete, No. 2.__ 4th ed. Perry Harovas. (Mastering Ser.). 608p. 2000. pap. 59.99 (*0-7821-2521-2*) Sybex.

Mastering McKim's Plan: Columbia's First Century on Morningside Heights. Barry Bergdoll et al. LC 97-74871. (Illus.). 249p. (C). 1997. 50.00 (*1-884919-05-7*); pap. 35.00 (*1-884919-04-9*) Wallach Art Gallery.

*__Mastering Mechanical Desktop.__ Cheng. LC 99-35674. (General Engineering Ser.). 1999. pap. text 63.95 (*0-534-95760-9*) PWS Pubs.

Mastering Mechanical Desktop. 11th ed. Howell. (Miscellaneous/Catalogs Ser.). 1998. pap. 45.95 (*0-534-95128-7*) PWS Pubs.

Mastering Mechanical Desktop: Parametric. Cheng. LC 97-29788. (General Engineering Ser.). 304p. (C). 1997. 43.95 (*0-534-95109-0*) PWS Pubs.

Mastering Mechanics I, Using Matlab: A Guide to Statistics & Strength of Materials. Hull. LC 98-41443. 384p. (C). 1998. pap., lab manual ed. 47.00 (*0-13-864034-3*) P-H.

Mastering Medical-Surgical Nursing. SPC Staff. LC 97-22241. 736p. 1997. 39.95 (*0-87434-909-5*) Springhouse Corp.

Mastering Medicine: The Most Current, Concise & Comprehensive Guide to Medical Education. Zia Hashemi. LC 95-94427. (Illus.). 135p. (Orig.). 1995. pap. 12.95 (*0-9645956-7-2*) Z Hashemi.

Mastering Meeting: Discovering the Hidden Potential of Effective Business Meetings. 2nd ed. Three M Meeting-Management Team. 1994. 24.95 (*0-07-031037-8*) McGraw.

Mastering Meetings. Robert L. DeBruyn & James M. Benjamin. LC 83-62444. 107p. (Orig.). 1984. pap. 5.95 (*0-914607-02-2*) Master Tchr.

Mastering Metrics in Minutes: Instructor's Guide. Thomas F. Gilbert & Marilyn B. Gilbert. 110p. 1992. ring bd. write for info. (*0-87425-169-9*) HRD Press.

Mastering Metrics in Minutes: Participant's Manual. Thomas F. Gilbert & Marilyn B. Gilbert. 24p. (Orig.). 1992. pap. write for info. (*0-87425-170-2*) HRD Press.

Mastering Microcaps: Strategies, Trends & Stock Selection. Daniel P. Coker. LC 98-46111. (Professional Library). (Illus.). 282p. 1999. 55.00 (*1-57660-062-9*, Pub. by Bloomberg NJ) Norton.

Mastering Microcomputer Applications: WordPerfect 6.0, Lotus 1-2-3 Release 2.4, dBase IV 2.0, & DOS 6. David R. Campbell & Mary V. Campbell. LC 93-12424. (Glencoe-Osborne Ser.). 1994. write for info. (*0-02-800419-1*) Glencoe.

Mastering Microcomputer Applications: WordPerfect 6.0, Lotus 1-2-3 Release 2.4, dBase IV 2.0, & DOS 6. large type ed. David R. Campbell & Mary V. Campbell. 1994. 209.50 (*0-614-09807-6*, L-31412-00) Am Printing Hse.

Mastering Microcomputers. William S. Davis et al. LC 92-41337. (C). 1993. pap. text 46.00 (*0-8053-1170-X*) Benjamin-Cummings.

Mastering Microcomputers: Applications & Core Concepts. William S. Davis et al. (Illus.). 640p. (C). 1992. pap. text. write for info. (*0-201-55583-2*) Addison-Wesley.

Mastering Microcomputers: Core Concept Appl. (C). 1994. pap. 12.33 (*0-8053-1172-6*); pap. 12.33 (*0-8053-1173-4*) Benjamin-Cummings.

Mastering Microcontrollers. Heiserman. (C). 2000. 49.00 (*0-7668-0073-3*) Thomson Learn.

Mastering Microsoft Access for Windows 95. 3rd ed. Alan Simpson & Elizabeth Olson. 1216p. 1995. pap. 39.99 (*0-7821-1764-3*) Sybex.

Mastering Microsoft Excel 5 for Windows 3.1. Al Napier & Philip Judd. 256p. 1996. pap. 23.95 (*0-7600-4091-5*) Course Tech.

Mastering Microsoft Excel 5 for Windows 3.1. Al Napier & Philip Judd. 256p. 1996. teacher ed. write for info. (*0-7895-0599-1*) Course Tech.

Mastering Microsoft Exchange Server 5.5. 3rd ed. Barry Gerber. LC 97-80779. 912p. 1997. pap. text 44.99 (*0-7821-2237-X*) Sybex.

Mastering Microsoft Foundation Classes. Shirley Wodtke. 1996. pap. text 44.99 incl. audio compact disk (*0-7821-1986-7*) Sybex.

Mastering Microsoft FrontPage 98. Daniel A. Tauber & Brenda Kienan. LC 97-61714. 960p. 1997. pap. text 49.99 incl. cd-rom (*0-7821-2144-6*) Sybex.

*__Mastering Microsoft Frontpage 2000.__ Daniel A. Tauber. (Mastering Ser.). 1008p. 1999. 75.00 (*0-7821-2456-9*) Sybex.

Mastering Microsoft FrontPage 2000. Daniel A. Tauber et al. LC 99-60020. (Mastering Ser.). (Illus.). 704p. 1999. pap. 34.99 (*0-7821-2455-0*) Sybex.

Mastering Microsoft HTML Help: The Ultimate Guide for Help Authors & Software Developers. rev. ed. 200p. (C). 1997. pap. 19.95 (*0-9647236-5-4*) Blue Sky Sftware.

Mastering Microsoft Internet Explorer 4. 2nd ed. Gene Weisskopf. (Mastering Ser.). 608p. 1998. pap. 29.99 (*0-7821-2339-2*) Sybex.

Mastering Microsoft Internet Information Server 4. Peter Dyson. LC 97-66376. (Illus.). 944p. 1997. pap. text 49.99 incl. cd-rom (*0-7821-2080-6*) Sybex.

Mastering Microsoft Office 97 Professional Edition. 2nd ed. Lonnie E. Moseley & David M. Boodey. LC 96-71022. 1216p. 1996. pap. text 39.99 (*0-7821-1925-5*) Sybex.

Mastering Microsoft Office 2000 Professional Edition. Gini Courter & Annette Marquis. LC 98-88950. (Mastering Ser.). (Illus.). 1200p. 1999. 39.99 (*0-7821-2313-9*) Sybex.

Mastering Microsoft Office 2000: Premium Edition. Gini Courter. (Mastering Ser.). 1488p. 1999. 49.99 (*0-7821-2312-0*) Sybex.

Mastering Microsoft Outlook 98. Gini Courter. LC 98-85470. (Illus.). 816p. 1998. pap. text 34.99 (*0-7821-2276-0*) Sybex.

Mastering Microsoft Outlook 2000. Gini Marquis Courter. LC 99-60017. (Mastering Ser.). 832p. 1999. 34.99 (*0-7821-2472-0*) Sybex.

*__Mastering Microsoft Outlook 2000: Premium Edition.__ Gini Courter. (Illus.). 1104p. 2000. 44.99 (*0-7821-2676-6*) Sybex.

Mastering Microsoft PhotoDraw 2000. Shane Hunt. LC 99-62856. (Mastering Ser.). (Illus.). 432p. 1999. 29.99 (*0-7821-2537-9*) Sybex.

*__Mastering Microsoft Project 2000.__ Gini Courter. (Mastering Ser.). 2000. pap. 34.99 (*0-7821-2656-1*) Sybex.

Mastering Microsoft SMS. 1008p. 1997. 49.99 (*0-7821-2009-1*) Sybex.

Mastering Microsoft SNA Server. 1008p. 1997. 49.99 (*0-7821-2008-3*) Sybex.

Mastering Microsoft Visual Interdev. Michael J. Young. 800p. 1997. pap. text 49.99 (*0-7821-1938-7*) Sybex.

*__Mastering Microsoft Works Suite 2000.__ Celeste Robinson. (Mastering Ser.). 608p. 2000. pap. 29.99 (*0-7821-2655-3*) Sybex.

Mastering MicroStation: Structured Projects Designed to Master MicroStation PC One Step at a Time. Kim H. Young. (Mastering MicroStation Ser.). (Illus.). 356p. (Orig.). (C). 1990. pap. 34.95 (*1-878789-00-7*) Chanimar Ace.

Mastering MicroStation Basics. 2nd ed. Kim H. Young. (Mastering MicroStation Ser.). (Illus.). (Orig.). (C). 1991. pap. 34.95 (*1-878789-02-3*) Chanimar Ace.

Mastering MicroStation Concepts. Kim H. Young. (Mastering MicroStatio Ser.). (Illus.). 128p. (Orig.). (C). 1991. pap. 19.95 (*1-878789-05-8*) Chanimar Ace.

Mastering MicroStation Implementation. Kim H. Young. (Mastering MicroStation Ser.). (Illus.). 128p. (Orig.). (C). 1991. pap. 19.95 (*1-878789-06-6*) Chanimar Ace.

Mastering MicroStation MDL. Kim H. Young. (Mastering MicroStation Ser.). (Illus.). 352p. (Orig.). (C). 1991. pap. 34.95 (*1-878789-04-X*) Chanimar Ace.

Mastering MicroStation PC Purchasing. Kim H. Young. (Mastering MicroStation Ser.). (Illus.). (Orig.). (C). 1991. pap. 19.95 (*1-878789-07-4*) Chanimar Ace.

Mastering Middle Earth, Strategies for Middle Earth - Wizards. Scott Langlinais. 250p. 1997. pap. 14.95 (*1-55622-559-8*) Wordware Pub.

Mastering Miracles see Healing Art of Qi Gong: Ancient Wisdom from a Modern Master

Mastering Modern English. Etherton. Date not set. pap. text. write for info. (*0-582-52573-X*, Pub. by Addison-Wesley) Longman.

Mastering Money. Dudley J. Delffs. LC 99-180919. 96p. 1998. pap. 6.50 (*1-57683-085-3*) NavPress.

*__Mastering Money in Your Marriage.__ Group Publishing Staff. (Homebuilders Couples Ser.). 2000. pap. 10.99 (*0-7644-2241-3*) Group Pub.

Mastering Movement, 1. Henrik Ibsen. Ed. by Emlyn Williams. 1998. pap. 1.95 (*0-87830-080-5*) Routledge.

*__Mastering MP3 & Digital Audio.__ Guy Hart-Davis. 2000. pap. text 29.99 (*0-7821-2792-4*) Sybex.

Mastering Mule Deer. Wayne Van Zwoll. LC 88-62840. (Hunter's Information Ser.). 282p. 1988. write for info. (*0-914697-16-1*) N Amer Outdoor Grp.

Mastering Multiple Sclerosis: A Guide to Management. 2nd ed. John K. Wolf et al. LC 87-70100. (Illus.). 432p. 1987. spiral bd. 22.95 (*0-914960-65-2*) Academy Bks.

Mastering NABPLEX. Kosegarten. (Essentials of Medical Imaging Ser.). 336p. 2000. 32.95 (*0-07-134538-8*) McGraw-Hill Prof.

Mastering NAUI Leadership. Ira Barocas & Michael Williams. 1994. pap. 39.95 (*0-916974-58-8*, 12901) NAUI.

Mastering Netrunner. Ben Matthews & Charles Schwope. LC 96-39506. 192p. 1996. pap. 9.95 (*1-55622-531-8*) Wordware Pub.

Mastering Netscape. 2nd ed. Greg Holden. 560p. 1997. pap. text 39.99 incl. cd-rom (*1-56830-312-2*) Hayden.

Mastering Netscape Communicator X. 2nd ed. Daniel A. Tauber. (Mastering Ser.). 880p. 1998. pap. 39.99 (*0-7821-2311-2*) Sybex.

Mastering NetWare 5. James E. Gaskin. LC 98-86253. 1600p. 1998. 69.99 (*0-7821-2268-X*) Sybex.

*__Mastering NetWare 5.1.__ James Gaskin. (Illus.). 2000. pap. 69.99 (*0-7821-2772-X*) Sybex.

Mastering Network Management. Valerie M. Swisher et al. (Self-Paced Learning Ser.). (Illus.). 230p. (Orig.). pap. 29.95 (*1-880548-13-5*) Numidia Pr.

Mastering Network Security. Chris Brenton. LC 98-87201. (Mastering Ser.). (Illus.). xxvi, 704p. 1998. pap. text 49.99 (*0-7821-2343-0*) Sybex.

Mastering New Architectural Techniques. Hiroaki Matsubara. (Illus.). 160p. (Orig.). 1996. pap. 49.95 (*4-7661-0820-5*, Pub. by Graphic-Sha) Bks Nippan.

Mastering New Medical Terminology. 2nd ed. Christine Stanfield & Pogorzala. (Nursing Ser.). 192p. 1995. pap., teacher ed. 10.00 (*0-86720-733-7*) Jones & Bartlett.

Mastering New Medical Terminology: Principles & Practices: (With Self-Instructional Modules) 2nd ed. Peggy S. Stanfield & Yiu H. Hui. LC 94-31116. 592p. 1995. pap. 47.50 (*0-86720-686-1*) Jones & Bartlett.

Mastering No-Load Mutual Funds: The Road Map to Investment Success. Christopher A. Lowry. 304p. 1996. pap. 24.95 (*1-888164-04-2*) No-Load Fund.

Mastering Norwegian. Eric Friis. (Hippocrene Mastering Languages Ser.). 179p. (Orig.). 1995. pap. 14.95 (*0-7818-0320-9*) Hippocrene Bks.

Mastering NT Server 4. 3rd ed. Mark Minasi. 1996. 49.99 (*0-614-20333-3*, Network Pr) Sybex.

Mastering NT Server 4. 4th ed. Mark Minasi. 1997. pap. 54.99 (*0-614-28534-8*, Network Pr) Sybex.

Mastering Object-Oriented Design in C++ Cay S. Horstmann. 464p. 1995. pap. 67.95 (*0-471-59484-9*) Wiley.

Mastering of Mexico. Kate Stephens. 1977. lib. bdg. 59.95 (*0-8490-2214-2*) Gordon Pr.

*__Mastering Office 2000 with CD-ROM.__ 2nd ed. Gini Courter & Annette Marquis. (Mastering Ser.). 1456p. 2000. pap. 39.99 incl. cd-rom (*0-7821-2823-8*) Sybex.

Mastering Ohio's 12th Grade Citizenship Test. James Killoran et al. (Illus.). 250p. (YA). (gr. 12). 1993. pap. text 8.95 (*1-882422-06-6*) Jarrett Pub.

Mastering Ohio's 9th Grade Citizenship Test. James Killoran et al. (Illus.). 134p. (YA). (gr. 9 up). 1993. pap. text 6.95 (*1-882422-05-8*) Jarrett Pub.

Mastering Olap: Practical Guide to Online. Kador. (ITCP-US Computer Science Ser.). (C). 1997. pap. 44.99 (*1-85032-912-5*) ITCP.

*__Mastering Online Investing: How to Use the Internet to Become a More Successful Investor.__ Michael C. Thomsett. 2001. pap. 19.95 (*0-7931-4150-8*) Dearborn.

Mastering Optics: Applications Guide to Optical Engineering. John Blackwell & Shane Thornton. LC 95-47412. 1996. pap. write for info. (*0-07-707875-6*) McGrw-H Intl.

Mastering Oracle 8. 4th ed. Jatinder Prem. (Mastering Ser.). 1008p. 2000. pap. 49.99 (*0-7821-2281-7*) Sybex.

Mastering Oracle7 & Client/Server Computing. 2nd ed. Steve M. Bobrowski. 752p. 1996. pap. 39.99 incl. disk (*0-7821-1840-2*) Sybex.

Mastering Oscillator Circuits Through Projects & Experiments. Joseph J. Carr. LC 92-42360. 1993. text 27.95 (*0-8306-4067-3*); pap. text 17.95 (*0-8306-4066-5*) McGraw-Hill Prof.

Mastering OSF: Motif Widgets. 2nd ed. Don McMinds. (C). 1993. pap. text. write for info. (*0-201-59470-6*) Addison-Wesley.

Mastering OSF-Motif Widgets. 2nd ed. Donald L. McMinds. LC 92-30994. 768p. (C). 1992. pap. text 58.95 (*0-201-63335-3*) Addison-Wesley.

Mastering OS/2 REXX. Gabriel Gargiulo. 417p. 1994. pap. 39.95 (*0-471-51901-4*) Wiley.

Mastering Overpower. George H. Baxter. 1997. pap. text 14.95 (*1-55622-576-8*) Wordware Pub.

Mastering Pain: A Twelve-Step Program for Coping with Chronic Pain. Richard A. Sternbach. 1988. mass mkt. 5.99 (*0-345-35428-1*) Ballantine Pub Grp.

Mastering Paradox X for Windows Special Edition. Alan Simpson. 950p. 1993. pap. 34.99 (*0-7821-1451-2*) Sybex.

Mastering Parts of Speech. Contemporary Book Editors. 30p. 1993. pap. 2.50 (*0-8092-3749-0*) NTC Contemp Pub Co.

Mastering Path-Based Patient Care. Patrice L. Spath. (Illus.). 210p. 1995. 50.00 (*1-929955-02-2*) Brown Spath.

Mastering Payroll. 8th unabridged ed. Debera J. Salam. 258p. 1991. pap. text 49.00 (*1-884826-27-X*) AIPB.

Mastering PerfectOffice for Windows 95. Alan Simpson. 1996. pap. text 39.99 (*0-7821-1892-5*) Sybex.

Mastering Perl 5. Eric Herrmann. LC 98-86868. (Mastering Ser.). 960p. 1999. pap. 57.00 (*0-7821-2200-0*) Sybex.

Mastering Personal Change! 71p. 1995. pap. 149.00 incl. audio, VHS (*1-56052-374-3*); pap. 24.95 incl. audio (*1-56052-375-1*) Crisp Pubns.

Mastering Photoshop 5 for the Web. Lise Depres. 704p. 1998. pap. text 49.99 (*0-7821-2230-2*) Sybex.

Mastering Piano Technique: A Guide for Students, Teachers & Performers. Seymour Fink. LC 91-48342. (Illus.). 192p. 1992. 24.95 (*0-931340-46-2*, Amadeus Pr) Timber.

*__Mastering Pixels: 3D: A Comprehensive Guide.__ R. Shamms Mortier. LC 00-101316. (Illus.). 450p. 2000. pap. 49.95 incl. audio compact disk (*0-12-508040-9*) Morgan Kaufmann.

Mastering Pointers & Complexity in C++ & C. Christopher J. Skelly. 400p. (C). 1996. text. write for info. (*0-201-59156-1*) Addison-Wesley.

Mastering Polish. Albert Juszczak. (Mastering Languages Ser.). (Illus.). 320p. 1993. pap. 14.95 (*0-7818-0015-3*) Hippocrene Bks.

Mastering Polish. Albert Juszczak. (Mastering Languages Ser.). (POL & ENG.). 288p. 1993. pap. 12.95 incl. audio (*0-7818-0016-1*) Hippocrene Bks.

Mastering Portal. George Baxter. LC 97-51726. 1997. pap. 14.95 (*1-55622-583-0*) Wordware Pub.

Mastering Portuguese. Ulsh. (Foreign Service Institute Language Ser.). (POR & ENG.). 1988. pap. 16.95 (*0-8120-3989-0*) Barron.

Mastering Portuguese. Contrib. by Ulsh. (Foreign Service Institute Language Ser.). (POR & ENG.). 1988. pap. 79.95 incl. audio (*0-8120-7479-3*) Barron.

Mastering Powerpoint for Windows X. 5th ed. Murray. 1996. pap. text 29.99 (*0-7821-1923-9*) Sybex.

Mastering PowerPoint 97. 3rd ed. Katherine Murray. LC 97-69204. 448p. 1997. pap. text 29.99 (*0-7821-2154-3*) Sybex.

Mastering Powerpoint 2000. Katherine Murray. (Mastering Ser.). 448p. 1999. pap. 29.99 (*0-7821-2356-2*) Sybex.

Mastering Practical Instrument Flight. Henry Sollman & Sherwood Harris. (Practical Flying Ser.). (Illus.). 256p. (Orig.). 1989. 24.95 (*0-8306-9433-1*); pap. 18.95 (*0-8306-0433-2*) McGraw-Hill Prof.

*__Mastering Priorities.__ (Illus.). 100p. 2000. reprint ed. spiral bd. 29.95 (*1-57431-174-3*, MP) Tech Trng Systs.

Mastering Project Management: Applying Advanced Concepts of Project Planning, Control & Evaluation. James P. Lewis. LC 97-38133. 319p. 1998. 45.00 (*0-7863-1188-6*, Irwn Prfssnl) McGraw-Hill Prof.

Mastering Prolog. Lucas. 224p. 1995. pap. 44.95 (*1-85728-400-3*, Pub. by UCL Pr Ltd) Taylor & Francis.

Mastering Psychology. 3rd ed. Lester A. Lefton. 680p. (C). 1988. pap. text 34.00 (*0-205-10626-9*, H0626-5) Allyn.

Mastering Psychology. 4th ed. Lester A. Lefton & Laura Valvatne. (C). 1992. teacher ed. write for info. (*0-205-13191-3*, H3191-7) Allyn.

Mastering Psychology: A Computer Assisted Laboratory Manual. 2nd ed. James G. Myers. (Illus.). 278p. (C). 1994. reprint ed. pap. text 32.00 (*1-879972-00-X*, NW Innovations) Chemeketa Coll.

Mastering Psychology, Critical Thinking, Study Skills, & Inside Psychology. 4th ed. (C). 1992. 57.00 (*0-205-13740-7*) Allyn.

*__Mastering Public Administration.__ 2nd ed. Brian R. Fry. 312p. (C). 2001. pap. text 24.95 (*1-889119-21-0*, Chatham House Pub) Seven Bridges.

Mastering Public Administration: From Max Weber to Dwight Waldo. Brian R. Fry. LC 89-624. (Chatham House Series on Change in American Politics). 272p. (C). 1989. pap. text 21.95 (*0-934540-56-X*, Chatham House Pub) Seven Bridges.

*__Mastering Public Speaking.__ 3rd ed. George L. Grice & John F. Skinner. 446p. 1999. pap. 0.00 (*0-205-29478-2*) Allyn.

Mastering Public Speaking. 3rd ed. George L. Grice & John F. Skinner. LC 97-18935. 446p. 1997. pap. 50.00 (*0-205-27092-1*) P-H.

Mastering Public Speaking. 3rd annot. ed. George L. Grice & John F. Skinner. (C). 1997. pap. text, teacher ed. write for info. (*0-205-27195-2*, T7195-5) Allyn.

*__Mastering Public Speaking.__ 4th ed. 512p. (C). 2000. write for info. (*0-205-32453-3*) Allyn.

*__Mastering Public Speaking.__ 4th ed. 512p. (C). 2000. pap. text 48.00 (*0-205-31808-8*) Allyn.

Mastering Public Speaking: How to Prepare & Deliver a Successful Speech or Presentation. 4th ed. Anne Nicholls. 144p. 1998. pap. 144.00 (*1-85703-256-X*, Pub. by How To Bks) Trans-Atl Phila.

*__Mastering Punctuation.__ Alvin Granowsky & Marjorie Merwin. 1999. write for info. (*0-8136-1456-2*) Modern Curr.

Mastering QBasic & QuickBasic. Bob Albrecht & Don Inman. LC 93-39036. 1993. write for info. (*0-02-802581-4*) Glencoe.

Mastering Quattro Pro for Windows 95. 4th ed. Gene Weisskopf. 1,072p. 1996. pap. text 34.99 (*0-7821-1772-4*, Strategies & Secrets) Sybex.

Mastering QuickBASIC & QBASIC. Date not set. teacher ed. write for info. incl. disk (*0-02-802582-2*) Glencoe.

Mastering Quicken 99. Steve Nelson. LC 98-87089. (Mastering Ser.). (Illus.). 736p. 1998. pap. 34.99 (*0-7821-2359-7*) Sybex.

*__Mastering Quicken 2000.__ 3rd ed. Stephen L. Nelson. 672p. 1999. pap. 29.99 (*0-7821-2596-4*) Sybex.

M

Mastering Quilt Marking: Marking Tools & Techniques - Choosing Stencils - Matching Borders & Corners. Pepper Cory. Ed. by Cyndy Rymer & Carolyn Aune. LC 99-6016. (Illus.). 80p. 1999. pap. text 19.95 (*1-57120-077-0*, 10197) C & T Pub.

Mastering Reading. Bernard Johnson & Lee. (Adult Education Ser.). 1991. 47.95 (*0-538-70981-2*) S-W Pub.

Mastering Reading. Robert Ventre. (Ya - Adult Education Ser.). 1991. 47.95 (*0-538-70993-6*) S-W Pub.

Mastering Reading: Comp. I. Ed. by Alexandra B. Drake. 156p. 1988. pap. text 7.35 (*0-8428-0189-8*) Cambridge Bk.

Mastering Reading: Comp. II. Ed. by Alexandra B. Drake. 156p. 1988. pap. text 7.05 (*0-8428-0191-X*) Cambridge Bk.

Mastering Reading Bk. 1: Office Work. Bernard Johnston & Lee. (YA - Adult Education Ser.). 1991. pap. 12.95 (*0-538-70991-X*) S-W Pub.

Mastering Reading & Language Skills with the Newspaper. International Herald Tribune Staff et al. (Illus.). 160p. 1995. pap. 26.95 (*0-8442-0791-8*, 07918, Natl Textbk Co) NTC Contemp Pub Co.

Mastering Reading, Commercial Truck Driving. Contemporary Perspectives Staff. (YA - Adult Education Ser.). 1991. pap. 12.95 (*0-538-70976-6*); pap. 12.95 (*0-538-70977-4*); pap. 12.95 (*0-538-70978-2*); pap. 12.95 (*0-538-70979-0*) S-W Pub.

M

Mastering Reading, Food Service Book, Bk. 1. Robert Ventre Assoc. Staff. (YA - Adult Education Ser.). 1991. pap. 12.95 (*0-538-70997-9*) S-W Pub.

Mastering Reading, Food Service Book, Bk. 2. Robert Ventre Assoc. Staff. (YA - Adult Education Ser.). 1991. pap. 12.95 (*0-538-70996-0*) S-W Pub.

Mastering Reading, Food Service Book, Bk. 3. Robert Ventre Assoc. Staff. (YA - Adult Education Ser.). 1991. pap. 12.95 (*0-538-70995-2*) S-W Pub.

Mastering Reading, Food Service Book, Bk. 4. Robert Ventre Assoc. Staff. (YA - Adult Education Ser.). 1991. pap. 12.95 (*0-538-70994-4*) S-W Pub.

Mastering Reading, Health Care Book, Bk. 1. Robert Ventre Assoc. Staff. (YA - Adult Education Ser.). 1990. pap. 12.95 (*0-538-71002-0*) S-W Pub.

Mastering Reading, Health Care Book, Bk. 2. Robert Ventre Assoc. Staff. (YA - Adult Education Ser.). 1990. pap. 12.95 (*0-538-71001-2*) S-W Pub.

Mastering Reading, Health Care Book, Bk. 3. Robert Ventre Assoc. Staff. (YA - Adult Education Ser.). 1990. pap. 12.95 (*0-538-71000-4*) S-W Pub.

Mastering Reading, Health Care Book, Bk. 4. Robert Ventre Assoc. Staff. (YA - Adult Education Ser.). 1990. pap. 12.95 (*0-538-70999-5*) S-W Pub.

Mastering Reading, Manufacturing. Bernard Johnson & Lee. (YA - Adult Education Ser.). 1991. pap. 12.95 (*0-538-70982-0*); pap. 12.95 (*0-538-70983-9*) S-W Pub.

Mastering Reading, Manufacturing, Bk. 1. Bernard Johnson & Lee. (YA - Adult Education Ser.). 1991. pap. 12.95 (*0-538-70985-5*) S-W Pub.

Mastering Reading, Manufacturing, Bk. 2. Bernard Johnson & Lee. (YA - Adult Education Ser.). 1991. pap. 12.95 (*0-538-70984-7*) S-W Pub.

Mastering Reading, Office Work Book, Bk. 2. Bernard Johnson & Lee. (YA - Adult Education Ser.). 1991. pap. 12.95 (*0-538-70990-1*) S-W Pub.

Mastering Reading, Office Work Book, Bk. 3. Bernard Johnson & Lee. (YA - Adult Education Ser.). 1991. pap. 12.95 (*0-538-70989-8*) S-W Pub.

Mastering Reading, Office Work Book, Bk. 4. Bernard Johnson & Lee. (YA - Adult Education Ser.). 1991. pap. 12.95 (*0-538-70988-X*) S-W Pub.

Mastering Real Estate Mathematics see Bienes Raices y los Numeros

Mastering Real Estate Mathematics. 6th ed. Ralph Tamper. 259p. 1995. pap. 26.95 (*0-7931-1142-0*, 1512-1006) Dearborn.

Mastering Real Estate Principles. 2nd ed. Gerald R. Cortesi. LC 98-39821. 552p. 1999. pap. 43.95 (*0-7931-2990-7*, 15108002, G&C Learning) Dearborn.

Mastering Records Completion: Successful Strategies from Medical Records Briefing. Rob Stuart. 140p. 1997. pap. text 87.00 (*1-57839-019-2*) Opus Communs.

***Mastering Red Hat Linux 6.** 3rd ed. Arman Danesh. (Mastering Ser.). (Illus.). 944p. 1999. pap. 39.99 (*0-7821-2613-8*) Sybex.

Mastering Regular Expressions. Jeffrey E. F. Friedl. Ed. by Andy Oram. LC 97-116815. (Illus.). 368p. (Orig.). 1996. reprint ed. pap. 34.95 (*1-56592-257-3*) Thomson Learn.

Mastering Repo Markets: A Step-by-Step Guide to the Products, Applications & Risks. Bob Steiner. (FT Market Editions Ser.). (Illus.). 280p. (Orig.). 1996. pap. text 59.95 (*0-273-62589-6*) F T P-H.

Mastering Resistance: A Practical Guide to Family Therapy. Carol M. Anderson & Susan Stewart. LC 82-21033. (Family Therapy Ser.). 259p. 1983. lib. bdg. 32.50 (*0-89862-044-9*) Guilford Pubns.

Mastering Risk: Environment, Markets & Politics in Australian Economic History. Colin J. White. (Illus.). 334p. 1992. pap. text 32.00 (*0-19-553351-8*) OUP.

Mastering Russian. Erika Haber. (Mastering Languages Ser.). 368p. (Orig.). 1994. pap. 14.95 (*0-7818-0270-9*); audio 12.95 (*0-7818-0271-7*) Hippocrene Bks.

Mastering SAP's ABAP-4. Tipton Cole. 1998. pap. text. write for info. (*0-7821-2253-1*) Sybex.

Mastering SCO Unix. Peter Dyson. 1998. pap. text 44.99 (*0-7821-2262-0*) Sybex.

Mastering Security Using Management Skills. ASIS Staff. LC 96-232356. 120p. 1996. pap. text, per. 19.95 (*0-7872-2566-5*, 41256601) Kendall-Hunt.

Mastering Security Using Technology. ASIS Staff. LC 96-210067. 122p. 1996. pap. text, per. 19.95 (*0-7872-2565-7*) Kendall-Hunt.

Mastering Self-Leadership: Empowering Yourself for Personal Excellence. Charles C. Manz. 168p. (C). 1991. pap. text 15.95 (*0-13-560863-5*) P-H.

***Mastering Self Leadership: Empowering Yourself for Personal Excellence.** 2nd ed. Charles C. Manz & Christopher P. Neck. LC 98-34044. 132p. (C). 1998. pap. text 21.00 (*0-13-011087-6*) P-H.

Mastering Show Biz... from the Heart: 10 Timeless Principles. J. Michael Dolan. LC 97-92654. (Illus.). 192p. 1998. pap. 16.95 (*1-880867-20-6*) Mulholland Pac.

Mastering Simulink, Vol. 2. James B. Dabney & Thomas L. Harman. LC 97-47332. Vol. 2. 345p. (C). 1997. pap. 56.00 (*0-13-243767-8*, Prentice Hall) P-H.

***Mastering Simulink 3.** James B. Dabney & Thomas L. Harman. 400p. 2000. write for info. (*0-13-017085-2*) P-H.

Mastering Skills: Study Supplement. Antonios Gonis. LC 81-12732. (Math-Mallion Ser.). (Illus.). 528p. 1981. 12.00 (*0-201-10145-9*) Addison-Wesley.

Mastering Skills: Study Supplement. Antonios Gonis. 1982. student ed. 12.00 (*0-201-10142-4*) Addison-Wesley.

Mastering Skills in Intermediate Algebra. Antonios Gonis. LC 81-12732. (Math-Mallion Ser.). (Illus.). 528p. 1981. pap. text 29.50 (*0-201-10143-2*) Addison-Wesley.

Mastering Slavery: Memory, Family, & Identity in Women's Slave Narratives. Jennifer Fleischner. LC 96-4519. 232p. (C). 1996. text 45.00 (*0-8147-2630-5*); pap. text 19.00 (*0-8147-2653-4*) NYU Pr.

Mastering SMT Manufacturing. Michael Brisky. 265p. (C). 1992. text 249.95 (*1-882812-08-5*) SMT Plus.

***Mastering Solaris 8 with CD-ROM.** Phyllis Romanski. (Mastering Ser.). 800p. 2000. pap. 49.99 incl. cd-rom (*0-7821-2816-5*) Sybex.

Mastering Solaris 2.6. Brent D. Heslop. 1008p. 1998. pap. text 39.99 (*0-7821-1889-5*) Sybex.

***Mastering Soldiers: Conflict, Emotions & the Enemy in an Israeli Military Unit.** Ben Ari. 2000. 18.95 (*1-57181-838-3*) Berghahn Bks.

Mastering Soldiers: Conflict, Emotions & the Enemy in an Israeli Military Unit. Eyal Ben-Ari. LC 97-42089. (New Directions in Anthropology Ser.). (Illus.). 157p. 1998. 35.00 (*1-57181-145-1*) Berghahn Bks.

Mastering Solid-State Amplifiers. Joseph J. Carr. LC 92-10488. (Illus.). 304p. 1992. 29.95 (*0-8306-3082-1*, 3976); pap. 19.95 (*0-8306-3081-3*, 3976) McGraw-Hill Prof.

Mastering Space: Hegemony, Territory & International Political Economy. John Agnew & Stuart Corbridge. LC 94-22292. (Illus.). 336p. (C). 1995. pap. 25.99 (*0-415-09434-8*, B0132) Routledge.

Mastering Spanish. (SPA & ENG.). 1992. pap. 16.95 (*0-8120-1360-3*) Barron.

Mastering Spanish, 11 CDs. Bowen et al. (Mastering Ser.). (ENG & SPA.). 1992. pap. 100.00 incl. audio compact disk (*0-8120-7871-3*) Barron.

Mastering Spanish. Robert Clarke. (Mastering Languages Ser.). (Orig.). 1991. audio 12.95 (*0-87052-067-9*) Hippocrene Bks.

Mastering Spanish. Robert Clarke. (Mastering Languages Ser.). (Illus.). 322p. (Orig.). 1991. pap. 11.95 (*0-87052-059-8*) Hippocrene Bks.

Mastering Spanish. Stockwell & Silva-Fuenzalida. (Foreign Service Institute Language Ser.). (SPA & ENG.). 1985. pap. 16.95 (*0-8120-2229-7*) Barron.

Mastering Spanish. Stockwell & Silva-Fuenzalida. (Foreign Service Institute Language Ser.). (SPA & ENG.). 1985. 79.95 incl. audio (*0-8120-7325-8*) Barron.

Mastering Spanish. 4th ed. Laurel H. Turk et al. (ENG & SPA.). 297p. (C). 1983. text 45.96 (*0-669-05395-3*); pap. text, student ed. 29.16 (*0-669-05396-1*); 2.66 (*0-669-05400-3*); 13.00 (*0-685-06173-6*); audio 31.16 (*0-669-05399-6*) HM Trade Div.

Mastering Spanish Business Vocabulary. Elena Meliveo. LC 96-78917. 1997. pap. text 11.95 (*0-8120-9826-9*) Barron.

Mastering Spanish, Level II, 12 cassettes, Set. (Foreign Service Institute Mastering Series-Level II: Level 2). (SPA & ENG.). 1992. pap., boxed set 79.95 incl. audio (*0-8120-7919-1*) Barron.

Mastering Spanish Vocabulary: A Thematic Approach. Jose M. Navarro & Ramil A. Navarro. (Mastering Vocabulary Ser). 368p. 1995. pap. 8.95 (*0-8120-9110-8*) Barron.

Mastering Spelling. Ed. by Marjorie P. Weiser. 204p. 1988. pap. text 7.05 (*0-8428-0183-9*) Cambridge Bk.

***Mastering Spelling Level C.** 1999. text. write for info. (*0-8359-4867-6*); text, teacher ed. write for info. (*0-8359-4877-3*) Globe Fearon.

***Mastering Spelling Level D.** 1999. text, teacher ed. write for info. (*0-8359-4878-1*); text, student ed. write for info. (*0-8359-4868-4*) Globe Fearon.

Mastering Spreadsheet Budgets & Forecasts: A Practical Guide. Malcolm Secrett. (Institute of Management Ser.). (Illus.). 230p. (Orig.). 1997. pap. 48.50 (*0-273-62684-1*, Pub. by Pitman Pub) Trans-Atl Phila.

***Mastering Spreadsheet Budgets & Forecasts: A Practical Guide to Preparing & Presenting Financial Information.** Malcolm Secrett. (Smarter Solutions Ser.). (Illus.). 262p. 2000. pap. 22.50 (*0-273-64491-2*, Pub. by F T P-H) Trans-Atl Phila.

Mastering SQL. 4th ed. Martin Gruber. 592p. 2000. pap. text 39.99 (*0-7821-2538-7*) Sybex.

***Mastering SQL Server 7 2000.** Mike Gunderloy & Joe Jorden. (Mastering Ser.). (Illus.). 1008p. 2000. pap. text 49.99 (*0-7821-2627-8*) Sybex.

Mastering SQL Server 7. Rick Pal. 1008p. 1998. pap. text 59.99 (*0-7821-2209-4*) Sybex.

***Mastering StarOffice 5.1 for Linux.** David D. Busch. 2000. pap. write for info. (*0-7821-2709-6*) Sybex.

Mastering Statistics: A Guide for Health Service Professionals & Researchers. Kelvin Jordan et al. 1998. pap. 42.50 (*0-7487-3325-6*, Pub. by S Thornes Pubs) Trans-Atl Phila.

***Mastering Strategy.** C. K. Prahalad et al. (Illus.). 488p. 2000. pap. 34.00 (*0-273-64930-2*, Pub. by F T P-H) Trans-Atl Phila.

Mastering Study Skills: A Student Guide. Thomas G. Devine & Linda D. Meagher. (Illus.). 320p. 1988. pap. text 26.20 (*0-13-560021-9*) P-H.

Mastering Successful Work: Skillful Means Wake-Up! Tarthang Tulku. LC 93-51511. (Business - Psychology Ser.). 288p. 1994. pap. 15.95 (*0-89800-262-1*) Dharma Pub.

***Mastering SWAPS Markets: A Step-By-Step Guide to Products, Applications & Risks.** Alan McDougal. 208p. 1999. pap. 59.95 (*0-273-62588-8*) F T P-H.

Mastering Sybase SQL Server II. Charles B. Clifford. LC 96-47146. (Illus.). 320p. 1997. pap. 44.95 (*0-07-011662-8*) McGraw.

Mastering Symphony. David Bolocan. (Illus.). 224p. 1985. pap. 16.95 (*0-8306-1948-8*, 1948P) McGraw-Hill Prof.

Mastering Symphony. 2nd ed. David Bolocan. (Illus.). 240p. 1986. 22.95 (*0-8306-1318-8*, NO. 2718) McGraw-Hill Prof.

Mastering Symphony. 3rd ed. David Bolocan. (Illus.). 260p. 1989. pap. 22.95 (*0-8306-9368-8*, 3068) McGraw-Hill Prof.

***Mastering Tactical Ideas.** Nikolay Minev. (Illus.). 200p. 2000. pap. 19.95 (*1-879479-83-4*) ICE WA.

Mastering TCP-IP for NT Server. Mark Minasi et al. LC 97-68480. 544p. 1997. pap. text 44.99 (*0-7821-2123-3*) Sybex.

***Mastering Technical Analysis.** Michael Thomsett. LC 99-37991. 288p. 1999. 27.00 (*0-7931-3359-9*) Dearborn.

Mastering Technical Mathematics. Norman H. Crowhurst. 512p. 1991. pap. 29.95 (*0-07-157586-3*) McGraw.

Mastering Technical Mathematics. Norman H. Crowhurst. (Illus.). 586p. 1991. 34.95 (*0-8306-6438-6*, 3438); pap. 24.95 (*0-8306-3438-X*) McGraw-Hill Prof.

Mastering Technical Writing. Joseph C. Mancuso. 1990. pap. 29.95 (*0-201-52350-7*) Addison-Wesley.

Mastering Technical Writing. Joseph C. Mancuso. 1995. reprint ed. pap. text 29.95 (*0-9643750-1-X*) Training Edge.

Mastering Television Technology: A Cure for the Common Video. Coleman C. Smith. (Illus.). 400p. 1988. 49.95 (*0-929549-02-3*) Newman-Smith.

Mastering Television Technology: A Cure for the Common Video - Instruction Manual. Coleman C. Smith. (Illus.). 82p. 1989. ring bd. 19.95 incl. disk (*0-929549-01-5*) Newman-Smith.

Mastering the Air. (Longman Biology Topics Ser.). Date not set. pap. text. write for info. (*0-582-32300-2*, Pub. by Addison-Wesley) Longman.

Mastering the Art of Carving Melon Centerpieces. large type ed. Lonnie T. Lynch. Ed. by Bob Barry. (Carving Melons Ser.: Vol. 2). (Illus.). 112p. 1997. pap. 9.95 (*0-9629277-1-6*) L Lynch.

Mastering the Art of Communication: Your Keys to Developing a More Effective Personal Style. Michelle F. Poley. Ed. by Kelly Scanlon. 132p. (Orig.). 1995. pap. 15.95 (*1-878542-34-6*, 13-0005) SkillPath Pubns.

Mastering the Art of Cooking Florida Seafood. Lonnie T. Lynch. (Illus.). 160p. (Orig.). 1996. pap. 9.95 (*0-9629277-2-4*) L Lynch.

Mastering the Art of Creative Collaboration. Robert Hargrove. LC 97-49712. (Illus.). 256p. 1997. 24.95 (*0-07-026409-0*) McGraw.

Mastering the Art of Florida Seafood. Lonnie T. Lynch. LC 99-26592. (Illus.). 200p. 1999. pap. 12.95 (*1-56164-176-6*) Pineapple Pr.

Mastering the Art of Fly-Tying. Richard W. Talleur. (Illus.). 224p. pap. 24.95 (*0-8117-2852-8*) Stackpole.

Mastering the Art of Fly-Tying. Richard W. Talleur. LC 78-32041. (Illus.). 224p. 1979. 34.95 (*0-8117-0907-8*) Stackpole.

Mastering the Art of French Cooking, 2 vols., 1. rev. ed. Julia Child et al. (Illus.). 1983. pap. 30.00 (*0-394-72178-0*) Knopf.

Mastering the Art of French Cooking, 2 vols., 1. rev. ed. Julia Child et al. (Illus.). 1983. 50.00 (*0-394-53399-2*) Knopf.

Mastering the Art of French Cooking, 2 vols., 2. rev. ed. Julia Child et al. (Illus.). 1983. pap. 30.00 (*0-394-72177-2*) Knopf.

Mastering the Art of French Cooking, 2 vols., Vol. 2. rev. ed. Julia Child et al. (Illus.). 1970. 50.00 (*0-394-40152-2*) Knopf.

Mastering the Art of Intercessory Prayer. Germaine Copeland. 144p. (Orig.). 1997. pap. 6.99 (*0-89274-988-1*, HH-988) Harrison Hse.

Mastering the Art of Pulled Thread Embroidery. Ilse Altherr. (Illus.). 132p. (Orig.). 1989. reprint ed. spiral bd. 24.50 (*0-9624090-0-6*) I Altherr.

Mastering the Art of Selling: Hopkins,&Tom. Tom Hopkins. 1995. audio 12.00 (*1-55994-467-6*) HarperAudio.

Mastering the Art of Substitute Teaching. S. Harold Collins. (Substitute Teaching Ser.). (Illus.). 69p. 1979. pap. 8.95 (*0-931993-02-4*, GP-002) Garlic Pr OR.

Mastering the Art of War. Zhuge Liang & Liu Ji. Ed. & Tr. by Thomas Cleary from CHI. LC 89-10264. (Dragon Editions Ser.). 152p. 1989. pap. 14.95 (*0-87773-513-1*, Pub. by Shambhala Pubns) Random.

Mastering the Art of War. Zhuge Liang et al. Tr. by Thomas Cleary. 208p. 1995. pap. 6.00 (*1-57062-081-4*, Pub. by Shambhala Pubns) Random.

Mastering the AS/400. 2nd ed. Jerry Fottral. LC 98-25502. 485p. 1998. pap. text 65.00 (*1-882419-77-4*) News Four-Hund.

***Mastering the AS/400: A Practical, Hands-On Guide.** 3rd ed. Jerry Fottral. (Illus.). 550p. 2000. pap. 67.00 (*1-58304-070-6*) News Four-Hund.

Mastering the AS/400 Control Language. George Lin. 432p. (C). 1995. pap. 50.00 (*0-13-461955-2*) P-H.

Mastering the Basics. Paulette Morrissey. (Fast, Fun & Easy Ser.: Bk. 1). (Illus.). 21p. 1996. spiral bd. 9.95 (*1-893502-00-7*) Morrissey Co.

Mastering the Basics of English for Spanish Speakers: Domine Lo Basico - Ingles. Jean Yates. (Illus.). 328p. 1997. pap. text 11.95 (*0-7641-0121-8*) Barron.

***Mastering the Basics of Photography.** Susan McCartney. (Illus.). 192p. 2000. pap. 19.95 (*1-58115-054-7*, Pub. by Allworth Pr) Watsn-Guptill.

***Mastering the Bishop Pair.** E. Borulia. (Illus.). 200p. 1999. pap. 19.95 (*1-879479-78-8*) ICE WA.

Mastering the Business of Remodeling. Linda W. Case & Victoria L. Downing. LC 97-69352. 300p. 1997. pap. 35.00 (*0-9648587-5-4*) Remodelers Advantage.

Mastering the Business of Writing: A Leading Literary Agent Reveals the Secrets of Success. Richard Curtis. LC 96-84618. 256p. (Orig.). 1996. pap. 18.95 (*1-880559-55-2*) Allworth Pr.

Mastering the Challenges of Change: Strategies for Each Stage in Your Organization's Life Cycle. LeRoy Thompson, Jr. LC 94-28683. 176p. 1994. 21.95 (*0-8144-0218-6*) AMACOM.

Mastering the Changing Information World. Anne W. Branscomb. Ed. by Martin L. Ernst & Anthony Oettinger. LC 92-21400. (Communication & Information Science Ser.). 352p. 1993. pap. 39.50 (*0-89391-989-6*) Ablx Pub.

Mastering the Changing Information World. Martin L. Ernst et al. LC 92-21400. (Communication & Information Science Ser.). 358p. 1993. text 78.50 (*0-89391-876-8*) Ablx Pub.

***Mastering the Chaos of Mergers & Acquisitions.** J. Garrett Ralls & Kimberly A. Webb. LC 99-36244. 1999. 24.95 (*0-87719-365-7*, 9365, Cashman Dud) Gulf Pub.

Mastering the Chess Opening. John Grefe. 103p. (Orig.). 1992. pap. 7.95 (*0-945470-23-1*) Chess Ent.

Mastering the City: North European City Planning, 1900-2000. Text by Koos Bosma & Helma Hellings. (Illus.). 480p. 1998. text 90.00 (*90-5662-061-4*, 810752, Pub. by NAi Uitgevers) Dist Art Pubs.

Mastering the College Experience. John W. Santrock & Jane S. Halonen. LC 97-47065. 1998. pap. 33.95 (*0-534-53352-3*) PWS Pubs.

***Mastering the Craft of Modern Trial Advocacy.** Michael E. Tigar. 1998. pap. 185.00 (*0-943380-57-X*); pap. 325.00 (*0-943380-58-8*) PEG MN.

***Mastering the Curve of Change.** J. Konrad Hole. 2000. pap. 11.99 (*1-890900-23-0*) Insight Intl.

***Mastering the Digital Marketplace: Practical Strategies for Competitiveness in the New Economy.** Douglas F. Aldrich. LC 99-26880. 336p. 1999. 29.95 (*0-471-34546-6*) Wiley.

Mastering the Diversity Challenge: Easy On-the-Job Applications for Measurable Results. Fern Lebo. LC 95-226112. 176p. 1995. boxed set 49.95 (*1-884015-35-2*) St Lucie Pr.

Mastering the Dynamics of Innovation. James M. Utterback. 288p. 1996. pap. 15.95 (*0-87584-740-4*) Harvard Busn.

Mastering the Dynamics of Innovation: How Companies Can Seize Opportunities in the Face of Technological Change. James M. Utterback. LC 93-38429. 256p. 1994. 29.95 (*0-87584-342-5*) Harvard Busn.

Mastering the Endgame. Mikhail I. Shereshevsky & Leonid M. Slutsky. Tr. by Kenneth P. Neat. LC 91-9970. (PECH Pergamon Chess Ser.: Vol. 1). (Illus.). 250p. 1991. 34.95 (*0-685-52580-5*, Pub. by CHES) Macmillan.

Mastering the Endgame. Mikhail I. Shereshevsky & L.M. Slutsky. Tr. by Kenneth P. Neat. LC 91-9970. (PECH Pergamon Chess Ser.: Vol. 1). (Illus.). 248p. 1991. pap. 24.95 (*0-08-037777-7*, Pub. by CHES) Macmillan.

Mastering the Endgame, Vol. I. Mikhail I. Shereshevsky & Leonid M. Slutsky. Tr. by Kenneth P. Neat. (Russian Chess Ser.). 250p. 1991. pap. 34.95 (*0-685-48776-8*, Pub. by CHES) Macmillan.

Mastering the Endgame: From the Closed Games. Mikhail I. Shereshevsky & Leonid M. Slutsky. (PECH Pergamon Chess Ser.: Vol. 2). 240p. 1992. pap. 24.95 (*0-08-037784-X*, Pub. by CHES) Macmillan.

Mastering the Endgame: From the Closed Games. Mikhail I. Shereshevsky & Leonid M. Slutsky. (PECH Pergamon Chess Ser.: Vol. 2). (Illus.). 250p. 1993. 34.95 (*0-685-52579-1*, Pub. by CHES) Macmillan.

Mastering the Essentials of Microsoft Excel for Windows: Version 7.0. Brian P. Favro. Ed. by Kiat Ang. (Illus.). 328p. (Orig.). 1996. pap. text 22.95 (*1-887281-19-3*) Labyrinth CA.

Mastering the Essentials of Microsoft Excel for Windows: Version 7.0 Quick Course. Brian P. Favro. (Illus.). 173p. (YA). 1996. pap. text 14.95 (*1-887281-06-1*) Labyrinth CA.

Mastering the Essentials of Microsoft Word for Windows: Version 7.0. Brian P. Favro. Ed. by Kiat Ang. (Illus.). 400p. (Orig.). 1996. pap. text 22.95 (*1-887281-13-4*) Labyrinth CA.

Mastering the Essentials of WordPerfect 6.1 for Windows. Brian P. Favro. (Illus.). 425p. 1995. pap. text 19.95 (*1-887281-04-5*) Labyrinth CA.

Mastering the Euromarkets: A Guide to International Bonds, the Instruments, the Players. Valerie Thompson. 232p. 1996. text 40.00 (*1-900717-00-X*, Irwn Prfssnl) McGraw-Hill Prof.

Mastering the Film & Other Essays. Charles T. Samuels. Ed. by Lawrence Graver. LC 77-642. 256p. reprint ed. pap. 79.40 (*0-8357-6545-8*, 203590900097) Bks Demand.

Mastering the Floral Classic. Robert Depalma & Roxanne Depalma. (Illus.). 50p. 1999. 19.95 (*0-9673044-0-7*) H I S C.

***Mastering the Fundamentals.** Robert Caldwell & Joan Wall. (Excellence in Singing Ser.: Vol. 2). (C). 2000. pap. 34.95 (*1-877761-17-6*) Pst.

Mastering the Fundamentals of Music. Herrold. 1997. pap. text 50.40 incl. cd-rom (*0-13-263229-2*) P-H.

Mastering the Fundamentals of Music. Rebecca M. Herrold. LC 96-34376. 276p. 1997. pap. 47.00 (*0-13-121872-7*) P-H.

Mastering the Game: THe Human Edge in Sales & Marketing. Kerry L. Johnson. 277p. 1988. 18.95 (*0-9618535-0-6*) Louis & Ford.

Mastering the Game of Caribbean Stud Poker. Stanley Ko. 45p. 1995. pap. 7.95 (*1-887929-01-0*) Gambology.

Mastering the Game of Let It Ride. Stanley Ko. 43p. 1995. pap. 7.95 (*1-887929-00-2*) Gambology.

***Mastering the Game of Three Card Poker.** Stanley Ko. 20p. 1999. pap. text 6.95 (*1-887929-02-9*) Gambology.

Mastering the GED. Ed. by Charles Herring. 112p. 1986. 5.00 (*0-317-45341-6*) GED Inst.

***Mastering the GMAT 2001.** IDG Books Worldwide Staff. 560p. 2000. pap. 16.95 (*0-7645-6083-2*) IDG Bks.

Mastering the Guitar, 3 bks. Mike Christiansen & William Bay. 440p. 1997. 26.95 (*0-7866-2894-4*, 96716BP) Mel Bay.

***Mastering the Guitar, Bk. 2A.** William Bay & Mike Christiansen. 184p. 1998. pap. 31.95 incl. audio compact disk (*0-7866-3651-3*, 97195CDP) Mel Bay.

***Mastering the Guitar, Bk. 2B.** William Bay & Mike Christiansen. 152p. 1999. pap. 29.95 incl. audio compact disk (*0-7866-3813-3*, 97196CDP); pap. 24.95 incl. audio compact disk (*0-7866-4448-6*, 97196BCD) Mel Bay.

***Mastering the Guitar, Bk. 2C.** William Bay & Mike Christiansen. 144p. 1999. pap. 24.95 incl. audio compact disk (*0-7866-4449-4*, 97197BCD); pap. 33.95 incl. audio compact disk (*0-7866-3815-X*, 97197CDP) Mel Bay.

Mastering the Guitar, Level 2A. William Bay & Mike Christiansen. 184p. 1998. pap. 14.95 (*0-7866-3507-X*, 97195); pap. 24.95 incl. audio compact disk (*0-7866-3650-5*, 97195BCD) Mel Bay.

Mastering the Guitar: A Comprehensive Method for Today's Guitarist!, Bk. 1A. William Bay & Mike Christiansen. 144p. 1996. pap. 9.95 (*0-7866-2804-9*, 96620) Mel Bay.

Mastering the Guitar: A Comprehensive Method for Today's Guitarist!, Bk. 1B. William Bay & Mike Christiansen. 144p. 1997. pap. 9.95 (*0-7866-2801-4*, 96621) Mel Bay.

Mastering the Guitar Bk. 1A: Beginning Level. William Bay & Mike Christiansen. 144p. 1997. spiral bd. 22.95 incl. audio compact disk (*0-7866-2927-4*, 96620BCD) Mel Bay.

Mastering the Guitar Bk. 1B: Beginning-Intermediate Level. William Bay & Mike Christiansen. 144p. 1997. spiral bd. 22.95 incl. audio compact disk (*0-7866-2928-2*, 96621BCD) Mel Bay.

***Mastering the Guitar - Class Method.** William Bay & Mike Christiansen. 136p. 2000. spiral bd. write for info. (*0-7866-5700-6*, 97121) Mel Bay.

Mastering the Guitar - Technique Studies. William Bay & Mike Christiansen. 152p. 1997. pap. 9.95 (*0-7866-2817-0*, 96622) Mel Bay.

***Mastering the Guitar Book, No. 2C.** William Bay. 144p. 1999. 14.95 (*0-7866-3510-X*, 97197) Mel Bay.

***Mastering the Guitar Book, Vol. 2B.** William Bay & Mike Christiansen. 152p. 1999. 14.95 (*0-7866-3509-6*, 97196) Mel Bay.

Mastering the Guitar Book IA CD Package. William Bay. 144p. 1997. 28.95 (*0-7866-2806-5*) Mel Bay.

Mastering the Guitar Book IB CD Package. William Bay & Mike Christiansen. 144p. 1997. 9.95 (*0-7866-2803-0*, 96621CDP) Mel Bay.

Mastering the Instructional Design Process: A Systematic Approach. 2nd ed. William J. Rothwell. 1997. 59.95 (*0-471-36513-0*) Wiley.

Mastering the Internet. Salley. 1995. write for info. (*0-201-41858-4*) Addison-Wesley.

Mastering the Machine Poverty, Aid & Technology. Ian Smillie. 360p. 1991. pap. write for info. (*0-921149-91-3*) Broadview Pr.

***Mastering the Machine Revisited: Poverty, Aid & Technology.** Ian Smillie. 2000. 60.00 (*1-85339-514-5*); pap. 25.00 (*1-85339-507-2*) Intermed Tech.

Mastering the Magic of Motivation: A Complete Education on Motivational Program Management. unabridged ed. Kimberly J. Smithson. Ed. by Linda A. Fetter & Debra Fini. (Illus.). 135p. 1996. 79.95 (*0-9655122-0-7*) Incentive Automation.

Mastering the Market: The State & the Grain Trade in Northern France, 1700-1860. Judith A. Miller. LC 98-20682. (Illus.). 288p. (C). 1998. text 49.95 (*0-521-62129-1*) Cambridge U Pr.

Mastering the Marketplace, 2 vols. Ross Clark. Incl. Taking Your Practice to the Top. LC 96-60136. 358p. 1996. pap. Not sold separately (*0-935078-57-6*); The Workbook. LC 96-60136. (Illus.). 158p. 1996. pap. Not sold separately (*0-935078-58-4*); Set pap. 89.95 (*0-935078-65-7*) Veterinary Med.

Mastering the Math Monsters: Factors, Fractions, & Long Division. Denise Gaskins. LC 98-90093. (Home School Basics Ser.). (Illus.). iv, 68p. 1998. pap. 5.95 (*1-892083-03-5*) Tabletop Acad.

Mastering the Math SAT 1 - PSAT. Paul Lawrence & Douglas J. Paul. LC 98-203040. 512p. (YA). (gr. 10-12). 1997. text, teacher ed. 26.60 (*0-669-45763-9*) Great Source.

***Mastering the Message: Media Writing with Substance & Style.** 2nd ed. Lauren Kessler & Duncan McDonald. 336p. (C). 1999. per. 33.95 (*0-7872-6403-2*) Kendall-Hunt.

Mastering the Morse Code. Martin Schwartz. LC 86-72231. 1988. pap. 3.00 (*0-912146-02-8*, 6-01) Ameco.

Mastering the Net with Netscape Communicator. John Buckley et al. Ed. by Jill McKenna. (Illus.). 370p. 1997. pap. 29.95 (*1-58143-000-0*) Prosoft I-net.

Mastering the News Media Interview: How to Do Successful Television, Radio & Print Interviews. Stephen C. Rafe. 204p. 1991. 24.95 (*0-88730-439-7*, HarpBusn) HarpInfo.

Mastering the Nimzo-Indian. Tony Kosten. 1998. pap. text 19.95 (*0-7134-8383-0*, Pub. by B T B) Branford.

Mastering the Nursing Process: A Case Method Approach. Jean D. Leuner et al. LC 89-71523. (Illus.). 494p. (Orig.). (C). 1990. pap. text 26.95 (*0-8036-5588-6*) Davis Co.

Mastering the Objective Structured Clinical Examination & Clinical Skills Assessment. Jo-Ann Reteguiz & Beverly Cornel-Avendano. LC 98-55698. (Illus.). 300p. 1999. pap. 39.95 (*0-07-135012-8*) McGraw-Hill HPD.

Mastering the Old Testament. Ed. by Lloyd J. Ogilvie & Brisco Stuart. LC 93-39330. (Mastering the Old & New Testament Ser.: Vol. 1). pap. 14.99 (*0-8499-3540-7*) Word Pub.

Mastering the Oral Boards: An Oral Board Review System. G. A. Smith. 250p. (Orig.). 1994. pap. text, per. 149.95 (*0-9635538-4-4*) MEDTEXT Med.

***Mastering the PalmPilot & Palm Organizers.** 4th ed. Gayle Ehrenmann. 608p. 2000. pap. 29.99 (*0-7821-2569-7*) Sybex.

Mastering the Politics of Planning: Crafting Credible Plans & Policies That Make a Difference. Guy Benveniste. LC 89-8189. (Public Administration-Management Ser.). 336p. 1989. 33.95 (*1-55542-167-9*) Jossey-Bass.

Mastering the Possibilities. R. Neal Shambaugh & Susan G. Magliaro. LC 97-152568. 320p. 1997. pap. text 36.00 (*0-205-19795-7*) Allyn.

Mastering the Possibilities: A Process Approach to Instructional Design. R. Neal Shambaugh & Susan G. Magliaro. (C). 1997. pap., teacher ed. write for info. (*0-205-26633-9*, T6633-6) Allyn.

Mastering the Power Dynamics of Career Interviewing: How to Be in the Best Form, Ask the Right Questions, & Get the Job You Want. Stephen C. Rafe. 224p. 1990. 18.95 (*0-88730-438-9*, HarpBusn) HarpInfo.

Mastering the Power of Persuasion. Roger Parker. 300p. 1990. pap. 28.00 (*1-55623-243-8*, Irwn Prfssnl) McGraw-Hill Prof.

Mastering the Power of Persuasion. Thomas L. Quick. 1990. pap. 29.95 (*0-685-59307-X*) Exec Ent Pubns.

Mastering the Powers of Your Inner Health. Nick Delgado. 150p. (Orig.). 1992. pap. 19.95 (*1-879084-03-1*) Delgado.

Mastering the Printed Page: Electronic Publishing with Quark XPress. Roger C. Parker. (Illus.). 224p. 1988. 29.95 (*0-8306-0223-2*, 3023); pap. 19.95 (*0-8306-9323-8*) McGraw-Hill Prof.

Mastering the Reimbursement Process. 2nd ed. American Medical Association. 200p. 1999. pap. 49.95 (*0-89970-762-9*, OP080095WE) AMA.

Mastering the Requirements Process. Suzanne Robertson. 416p. (C). 2000. 44.95 (*0-201-36046-2*) Addison-Wesley.

Mastering the Research Paper. (C). 1994. write for info. (*0-8087-7249-X*) Pearson Custom.

Mastering the Revels: The Regulation & Censorship of English Renaissance Drama. Richard Dutton. LC 90-72125. (Illus.). 327p. 1991. text 37.95 (*0-87745-335-7*) U of Iowa Pr.

Mastering the Secrets of True Love: How to Find True Love, How to Solve Love Problems, How to Keep Your Love Alive. Heidi Boyer. (Illus.). 240p. (Orig.). 1994. pap. write for info. (*0-9638452-0-9*) Lakewood Ent.

***Mastering the Sicilian: Openings.** Danny Kopec. (Chess Bks.). 1999. pap. text 18.95 (*0-7134-8482-9*) B T B.

Mastering the Sky: A History of Aviation from Ancient Times to the Present. James P. Harrison. LC 97-105018. (Illus.). 352p. 1996. 29.95 (*1-885119-23-2*) Sarpedon.

Mastering the Spanish. Daniel King. 1995. pap. write for info. (*0-8050-3278-9*, Pub. by Batsford Chess) H Holt & Co.

Mastering the Spring Creeks: A Fly Angler's Guide. John Shewey. (Illus.). 144p. 1995. 39.95 (*1-57188-001-1*); pap. 24.95 (*1-57188-000-3*) F Amato Pubns.

Mastering the Standard C++ Classes: A Complete Reference. Cameron Hughes & Tracey Hughes. LC 99-25757. (Illus.). 513p. 1999. pap. 44.99 incl. cd-rom (*0-471-32893-6*) Wiley.

Mastering the Systems: Air Traffic Control & Weather. Richard L. Collins. 256p. 1991. 24.95 (*0-02-527245-4*, Aude IN) IDG Bks.

Mastering the Tarot: Basic Lessons in an Ancient Mystic Art. Eden Gray. 224p. 1973. mass mkt. 5.99 (*0-451-16781-3*, Sig) NAL.

Mastering the Teaching of Adults. Jerold W. Apps. LC 91-3362. 160p. (C). 1991. lib. bdg. 22.50 (*0-89464-558-7*) Krieger.

Mastering the Techniques of Teaching. Joseph Lowman. LC 83-49265. (Jossey-Bass Higher Education Ser.). 267p. reprint ed. pap. 82.80 (*0-7837-2517-5*, 204267600006) Bks Demand.

Mastering the Techniques of Teaching. 2nd ed. Joseph Lowman. LC 95-12476. (Higher & Adult Education Ser.). 368p. 1995. text 34.45 (*0-7879-0127-X*) Jossey-Bass.

Mastering the THINK Class Library: Using Symantec C++ & Visual Architect. Richard O. Parker. LC 95-218. 496p. (C). 1995. pap. text 29.95 (*0-201-48356-4*) Addison-Wesley.

Mastering the TI-92: Explorations from Algebra Through Calculus. Lawrence Gilligan et al. (Illus.). 208p. (Orig.). (C). 1996. pap. 24.95 (*0-9626661-9-X*) Gilmar Pub.

***Mastering the Uncommon Common Sense.** Eleanor Conrad & Michael Hart. 120p. 2000. pap. 9.95 (*0-615-11754-6*) Off Beat Tours.

Mastering the Verbal SAT/PSAT. Larry S. Krieger & Douglas J. Paul. 456p. (gr. 10-12). 1998. pap. text 21.26 (*0-669-46825-8*); pap. text, teacher ed. 26.60 (*0-669-46826-6*) Great Source.

***Mastering the Zone.** B. Sears. 1999. 6.50 (*0-06-101124-X*) HarpC.

Mastering The Zone: Sears,&Barry, Set. abr. ed. Barry Sears. 1997. audio 18.00 (*0-694-51777-1*, CPN 10103, Pub. by HarperAudio) Lndmrk Audiobks.

Mastering the Zone: The Next Step in Achieving SuperHealth Permanent Fat Loss. Barry Sears & Mary Goodbody. LC 96-39111. 384p. 1997. 25.00 (*0-06-039190-1*, ReganBks) HarperTrade.

Mastering the Zone export edition. Barry Sears. 384p. 1997. pap. 14.00 (*0-06-092903-0*) HarpC.

***Mastering 3D Studio Viz 3.0.** George Omura. 656p. 2000. pap. text 39.99 (*0-7821-2775-4*) Sybex.

***Mastering 3D Texturing.** Bill Fleming. 1999. 49.95 (*0-12-260503-9*) Morgan Kaufmann.

***Mastering 3D Animation.** Peter Ratner. (Illus.). 480p. 2000. pap. 35.00 incl. cd-rom (*1-58115-068-7*, Pub. by Allworth Pr) Watsn-Guptill.

***Mastering 3D Graphics: Digital Botany & Creepy Insects.** Bill Fleming. LC 99-53031. 384p. 2000. pap. 49.99 incl. cd-rom (*0-471-38089-X*) Wiley.

***Mastering 3D Lighting.** Bill Fleming. (Conquering 3D Graphics Ser.). 350p. 1999. pap. 49.95 incl. cd-rom (*0-12-260497-0*, Pub. by Morgan Kaufmann) Harcourt.

Mastering 3D Studio Max R3. 4th ed. Chris Murray. 896p. 2000. pap. text 49.99 (*0-7821-2561-1*) Sybex.

Mastering Time. Gisbert L. Brunner. 1997. 100.00 (*2-908228-82-3*, Pub. by Assouline) Rizzoli Intl.

Mastering Today's Packaging Needs. Technical Association of the Pulp & Paper Industry. LC TS0198.3T3. 337p. reprint ed. pap. 104.50 (*0-608-14857-1*, 202617200048) Bks Demand.

***Mastering Today's Software.** Edward G. Martin & Charles S. Parker. LC 99-204127. (Illus.). 2000. write for info. (*0-03-026122-8*) Harcourt Coll Pubs.

Mastering Today's Software-Paradox 4.0. 2nd ed. Martin. LC 94-236560. (C). 1994. pap. text, lab manual ed. 22.50 (*0-03-097925-0*, Pub. by Harcourt Coll Pubs) Harcourt.

Mastering Today's Software: Access 2000. Martin. LC 99-217112. (C). 1999. pap. text 25.50 (*0-03-025992-4*) Harcourt.

Mastering Today's Software: Access 7.0 for Windows. Martin. LC 96-206076. (C). 1996. lab manual ed. write for info. (*0-03-017334-5*) Harcourt Coll Pubs.

Mastering Today's Software: Approach 97. Martin. (C). 1997. pap. write for info. (*0-03-019697-3*) Harcourt Coll Pubs.

Mastering Today's Software: Custom (Laurentian University) Martin. (C). 1995. lab manual ed. write for info. (*0-15-555582-0*) Harcourt Coll Pubs.

Mastering Today's Software: Database Management with dBase III Plus. 2nd ed. Edward G. Martin & Charles S. Parker. LC 94-211389. 191p. (C). 1994. pap. text 22.50 (*0-03-098226-X*) Dryden Pr.

Mastering today's software: Database Management with dBase IV version 1.5/2.0. 2nd ed. Edward G. Martin & Charles S. Parker. LC 94-211372. 232p. (C). 1993. pap. text 22.50 (*0-03-098227-8*) Dryden Pr.

Mastering Today's Software: Database Management with Microsoft Access 2.0 for Windows. 2nd ed. Edward G. Martin. 296p. (C). 1995. pap. text, student ed. 23.00 (*0-03-015537-1*) Dryden Pr.

Mastering Today's Software: DBase IV. 2nd ed. Martin. (C). 1994. lab manual ed. write for info. (*0-15-555422-0*) Harcourt Coll Pubs.

Mastering Today's Software: DOS 5.0 Module. 2nd ed. Edward G. Martin & Charles S. Parker. LC 94-211357. 85p. (C). 1993. pap. text 17.50 (*0-03-098588-9*) Dryden Pr.

Mastering Today's Software: DOS 6.0. 2nd ed. Edward G. Martin & Charles S. Parker. 88p. (C). 1994. pap. text 22.50 (*0-03-000638-4*) Dryden Pr.

Mastering Today's Software: Excel 2000. Martin. LC 99-217097. (C). 1999. pap. text 25.50 (*0-03-025993-2*) Harcourt.

Mastering Today's Software: Extended Microcomputer Concepts. 3rd ed. Martin. LC 97-126904. (C). 1996. pap. text 33.50 (*0-03-014067-6*) Harcourt.

Mastering Today's Software: Extended Microcomputer Concepts Module. 2nd ed. Edward G. Martin & Charles S. Parker. 264p. (C). 1994. pap. text 26.75 (*0-03-098587-0*) Dryden Pr.

Mastering Today's Software: Freelance Graphics. Martin. (C). 1996. pap. text 20.50 (*0-03-019674-4*) Harcourt Coll Pubs.

Mastering Today's Software: Internet Explorer. Martin. (C). 1998. pap. text 24.00 (*0-03-021307-X*) Harcourt Coll Pubs.

Mastering Today's Software: Lotus Smart Suite 97. Martin. (C). 1997. pap. write for info. (*0-03-019568-3*) Harcourt Coll Pubs.

Mastering Today's Software: Lotus 1-2-3/Windows. Martin. LC 95-135860. (C). 1994. pap. text, lab manual ed. 17.50 (*0-03-011073-4*) Harcourt.

Mastering Today's Software: Microcomputer Concepts. 2nd ed. Martin. (C). 1994. pap. text 22.75 (*0-03-098586-2*) Harcourt Coll Pubs.

Mastering Today's Software: Microsoft Access 7.0 for Windows 95. Edward G. Martin et al. LC 96-153449. 311p. (C). Date not set. pap. text, lab manual ed. 20.00 (*0-03-017338-8*) Dryden Pr.

Mastering Today's Software: Microsoft Office for Windows 95 Includes Word 7.0, Excel 7.0, Access 7.0, Power Point 7.0 & Windows 95. Edward Martin et al. 544p. (C). 1996. pap. text, teacher ed. 46.25 (*0-03-018139-9*) Harcourt Coll Pubs.

Mastering Today's Software: Microsoft Office Windows 95. Martin. (C). 1995. pap. text 59.00 (*0-03-018138-0*) Harcourt Coll Pubs.

Mastering Today's Software: Microsoft Powerpoint 2000. Edward G. Martin & Charles S. Parker. LC 99-212786. (C). 1999. pap. text 25.50 (*0-03-025996-7*) Harcourt.

Mastering Today's Software: Microsoft Windows 95. Edward Martin et al. 240p. (C). 1996. pap. text, lab manual ed. 24.00 (*0-03-016302-1*) Dryden Pr.

Mastering Today's Software: Outlook 2000. Martin. LC 99-229998. (C). 1999. pap. text 25.50 (*0-03-025994-0*) Harcourt.

Mastering Today's Software: PowerPoint 7.0 Windows 95. Martin. LC 96-153471. (C). 1996. lab manual ed. write for info. (*0-03-017339-6*) Harcourt Coll Pubs.

Mastering Today's Software: Spreadsheets with Lotus 1-2-3 2.2-2.3 & 2.4. 2nd ed. Edward G. Martin & Charles S. Parker. 132p. (C). 1994. pap. text 40.75 (*0-03-003607-0*) Dryden Pr.

Mastering Today's Software: Windows NT 4.0. Martin. (C). 1998. text 24.00 (*0-03-027304-8*) Harcourt Coll Pubs.

Mastering Today's Software: Windows 3.1. Martin. (C). 1994. pap. text, teacher ed. 66.50 (*0-03-004157-0*) Harcourt.

Mastering Today's Software: With DOS, WordPerfect, Lotus 1-2-3, & dBASE III Plus. Edward G. Martin & Charles S. Parker. LC 91-32925. 826p. (C). 1992. pap. text 42.75 (*0-03-073603-X*) Dryden Pr.

Mastering Today's Software: With DOS, WordPerfect, Lotus 1-2-3, dBASE III PLUS, & BASIC. Edward G. Martin & Charles S. Parker. LC 91-35016. 992p. (C). 1992. pap. text 46.75 (*0-03-076707-5*) Dryden Pr.

Mastering Today's Software: With DOS, WordPerfect, Lotus 1-2-3, dBASE IV, & BASIC. Edward G. Martin & Charles S. Parker. LC 91-34517. 992p. (C). 1992. pap. text 46.75 (*0-03-076706-7*) Dryden Pr.

Mastering Today's Software: Word Processing with Microsoft Word 6.0 for Windows. Edward G. Martin & Charles S. Parker. 304p. (C). 1995. pap. text 18.50 (*0-03-015444-8*) Dryden Pr.

Mastering Today's Software: Word Processing with WordPerfect 6.0 for Windows, 1995. 95th ed. Edward G. Martin & Charles S. Parker. LC 95-114089. 304p. (C). 1994. pap. text, lab manual ed. 20.50 (*0-03-011077-7*) Dryden Pr.

Mastering Today's Software: Word 2000. Martin. (C). 1999. pap. text 25.50 (*0-03-025991-6*) Harcourt.

Mastering Today's Software: WordPerfect 7.0 for Windows 95. 14th ed. Edward G. Martin & Charles S. Parker. LC 96-79306. 328p. (C). 1997. pap. text 40.00 (*0-15-503685-8*) Dryden Pr.

Mastering Today's Software: Work Pro. Martin. (C). 1997. pap. write for info. (*0-03-019684-1*) Harcourt Coll Pubs.

Mastering Today's Software, Database Management with DBase (III & IV) Instructor's Manual with Test Bank & Transparency Masters to Accompany. 2nd ed. Edward G. Martin & Charles S. Parker. 152p. (C). 1994. pap. text 42.00 (*0-03-002699-7*) Dryden Pr.

Mastering Today's Software, DOS (5.0 & 6.0) Instructor's Manual with Test Bank to Accompany. 2nd ed. Edward G. Martin & Charles S. Parker. 56p. (C). 1994. pap. text 40.75 (*0-03-003017-X*) Dryden Pr.

Mastering Today's Software, Microsoft Access 97. Edward G. Martin et al. LC 98-119367. 224p. (C). 1997. pap. text 25.50 (*0-03-024787-X*) Dryden Pr.

Mastering Today's Software, Microsoft Excel 97. Edward G. Martin et al. LC 98-164417. 240p. (C). 1997. pap. text 25.50 (*0-03-024788-8*) Dryden Pr.

Mastering Today's Software, Microsoft PowerPoint 97. Edward G. Martin & Charles S. Parker. 144p. (C). 1997. pap. text 25.50 (*0-03-024789-6*) Dryden Pr.

Mastering Today's Software, Microsoft Word 97. Edward G. Martin & Charles S. Parker. LC 98-212310. 256p. (C). 1997. pap. text 25.50 (*0-03-024791-8*) Dryden Pr.

Mastering Today's Software, Spreadsheets with Microsoft Excels 5.0 for Windows. Edward G. Martin. 312p. (C). 1995. pap. text, lab manual ed. 19.75 (*0-03-015539-8*) Dryden Pr.

Mastering Today's Software, Windows 3.1. 2nd ed. Edward G. Martin & Charles S. Parker. 189p. (C). 1994. pap. text, student ed. 17.50 (*0-03-004154-6*) Dryden Pr.

Mastering Today's Software, Word Processing with WordPerfect 5.1: Instructor's Manual with Test Bank & Transparency Masters to Accompany. 2nd ed. Edward G. Martin & Charles S. Parker. 136p. (C). 1994. pap. text 94.00 (*0-03-002907-4*) Dryden Pr.

Mastering Today's Software, 1995: Spreadsheets with Quattro Pro 6.0 for Windows. 95th ed. Edward G. Martin. 312p. (C). 1995. pap. text, lab manual ed. 22.50 (*0-03-010812-8*) Dryden Pr.

Mastering Tools, Taming Demons: UNIX for the Wizard Apprentice. Dean Brock. 350p. (C). 1995. pap. text 34.00 (*0-13-228016-7*) P-H.

Mastering Torts. Vincent R. Johnson. LC 95-70547. 304p. (Orig.). 1995. pap. text 24.95 (*0-89089-803-0*) Carolina Acad Pr.

Mastering Tournament Fighting: The Art of Winning the Game of Point Tournament Fighting. Gregory A. Price. LC 98-28367. (Illus.). ix, 174p. 1998. pap. 29.95 (*0-9665309-0-X*) Renshi Prince.

Mastering Turbo Assembler. 2nd ed. Tom Swan. (Illus.). 944p. (Orig.). 1995. 45.00 (*0-672-30526-7*) Sams.

Mastering U. S. History & Government: An Interactive Textbook. 2nd ed. James Killoran et al. (Illus.). 358p. 1995. pap. text 11.95 (*0-9624723-9-5*) Jarrett Pub.

M

M

Mastering UML with Rational Rose. Wendy Boggs & Michael D. Boggs. (Mastering Ser.). (Illus.). 957p. 1999. pap. 49.99 incl. cd-rom (0-7821-2453-4) Sybex.

Mastering Value at Risk. 1998. pap. text 39.95 (0-273-63752-5) F T P-H.

***Mastering VBA 6.** Guy Hart-Davis. 752p. 2000. pap. 39.99 incl. cd-rom (0-7821-2636-7) Sybex.

Mastering Viavoice Gold. large type ed. Peggy Caugtenvto. (Illus.). 110p. 1997. pap. 25.00 (0-9662486-0-0, BSI1297001.0) SunBeach Intl.

Mastering Virtual Teams: Strategies, Tools & Techniques That Succeed. Deborah L. Duarte. LC 98-53902. (Illus.). 256p. 1999. 28.95 (0-7879-4183-2) Jossey-Bass.

Mastering Visual Basic 5. Evangelos Petroutsos. LC 97-65358. 1104p. 1997. pap. text 49.99 incl. cd-rom (0-7821-1984-0) Sybex.

Mastering Visual Basic 6. Evangelos Petroutsos. 1312p. 1998. pap. text 49.99 incl. cd-rom (0-7821-2272-8) Sybex.

Mastering Visual Basic 4. Gerard Frantz. 1996. pap. text 39.99 incl. cd-rom (0-7821-1758-9) Sybex.

Mastering Visual C++ 6. Michael J. Young. LC 98-85538. (Illus.). 1424p. 1998. pap. text 54.99 (0-7821-2273-6) Sybex.

Mastering Visual FoxPro X. Rod Paddock. 1996. pap. text 39.99 incl. audio compact disk (0-7821-1940-9) Sybex.

Mastering Visual InterDev 6. Juan Llibre. (Mastering Ser.). 1999. pap. text 39.99 (0-7821-2454-2) Sybex.

Mastering Visual J++ 6.0. Steven Holzner. (Mastering Ser.). 1998. pap. 39.99 (0-7821-2361-9) Sybex.

Mastering Vocabulary I. Ed. by Marjorie P. Weiser. 32p. 1988. teacher ed. 1.00 (0-8428-0180-4); pap. text 7.05 (0-8428-0179-0) Cambridge Bk.

Mastering Vocabulary II. Ed. by Marjorie P. Weiser. 120p. 1988. pap. text 7.05 (0-8428-0181-2); pap. text, teacher ed. 1.40 (0-8428-0182-0) Cambridge Bk.

Mastering Voir Dire & Jury Selection: Gaining an Edge in Questioning & Selecting a Jury. LC 94-70877. 264p. 1995. pap. 89.95 (0-89707-981-7, 515-0241, ABA Genl Prac) Amer Bar Assn.

Mastering Wartime: A Social History of Philadelphia During the Civil War. J. Matthew Gallman. (Interdisciplinary Perspectives on Modern History Ser.). (Illus.). 368p. (C). 1990. text 85.00 (0-521-37474-X) Cambridge U Pr.

***Mastering Wartime: A Social History of Philadelphia During the Civil War.** J. Matthew Gallman. LC 00-25222. 2000. write for info. (0-8122-1744-6) U of Pa Pr.

Mastering Windows 98. 2nd ed. Robert Cowart. LC 98-84008. (Illus.). 1200p. 1996. 34.99 (0-7821-1961-1) Sybex.

***Mastering Windows 98.** 2nd ed. Robert Cowart. (Mastering Ser.). 928p. 1999. pap. 39.99 (0-7821-2618-9) Sybex.

Mastering Windows 98 - Premium Edition. Robert Cowart. LC 98-84032. 1664p. 1998. 59.99 (0-7821-2186-1) Sybex.

Mastering Windows 95: Special Edition. 3rd ed. Robert Cowart. LC 95-67727. 1216p. 1995. 34.99 (0-7821-1413-X) Sybex.

Mastering Windows 95 Help: The Official Book for Help Authoring. 2nd ed. LC 95-78124. 180p. 1995. pap. 29.95 (0-9647236-0-3) Blue Sky Sftware.

Mastering Windows NT Server 4. 6th ed. Mark Minasi. (Mastering Ser.). 1616p. 1999. 59.99 (0-7821-2445-3) Sybex.

***Mastering Windows NT Server 4.** 7th ed. Mark Minasi. (Illus.). 1696p. 2000. pap. 69.99 (0-7821-2693-6) Sybex.

Mastering Windows NT Workstation 4, Vol. 4. 2nd ed. Mark Minasi. LC 99-60025. (Mastering Ser.). 1152p. 1999. 49.99 (0-7821-2491-7) Sybex.

***Mastering Windows Registry 2000.** 4th ed. Peter D. Hipson. 896p. 2000. pap. 39.99 (0-7821-2615-4) Sybex.

***Mastering Windows 2000 Professional.** 4th ed. Mark Minasi. (Mastering Ser.). 1008p. 2000. pap. 39.99 (0-7821-2448-8) Sybex.

***Mastering Windows 2000 Programing with Visual C++** 4th ed. Ben Ezzell. (Mastering Ser.). 1008p. 2000. pap. 49.99 (0-7821-2642-1) Sybex.

Mastering Windows 2000 Server. Mark Minasi. (Mastering Ser.). 512p. 1999. pap. 39.99 (0-7821-2447-X) Sybex.

***Mastering Windows 2000 Server.** 2nd ed. Mark Minasi et al. (Illus.). 1632p. 2000. pap. 49.99 (0-7821-2774-6) Sybex.

***Mastering Windows 2000 Server.** 4th ed. Mark Minasi. (Mastering Ser.). 1344p. 1999. 49.99 (0-7821-2446-1) Sybex.

Mastering Windows 3.1. large type ed. Tom Sheldon. 1992. 110.00 (0-614-09868-8, L-31422-00) Am Printing Hse.

Mastering Windows 95 Help: A Preview of Law School & Legal Processing. 3rd rev. ed. Blue Sky Software Corporation Staff. LC 95-81226. 192p. 1996. pap. 24.95 incl. disk (0-9647236-1-1) Blue Sky Sftware.

Mastering Wine: A Learner's Manual. Tom Maresca. LC 92-8288. 320p. 1992. pap. 14.00 (0-8021-3298-7, Grove) Grove-Atltic.

Mastering Witchcraft. Paul Huson. 1980. pap. 13.00 (0-399-50442-7, Perigee Bks) Berkley Pub.

Mastering Women's Ministry: The Handbook for Organizing & Administering an Effective Ministry. Kathy Slamp. Ed. by Cindy Spear. 66p. 1998. ring bd. 39.95 incl. audio (1-57052-098-4) Chrch Grwth VA.

Mastering Woodworking Machines. Mark Duginske. (Illus.). 245p. 1992. pap. 24.95 (0-942391-98-5, 70136) Taunton.

Mastering Word Problems the Easy Way. Edmon Lindsey. 170p. 1991. pap. text 15.25 (0-9634346-0-8) S Paul Pub.

Mastering Word 2000: Premium Edition. Ron Mansfield & J. W. Olsen. LC 98-88913. (Mastering Ser.). 1088p. 1999. pap. text 39.99 incl. cd-rom (0-7821-2314-7) Sybex.

***Mastering Word 2000: Premium Edition.** 2nd ed. Michael Miller. 2000. pap. 39.99 (0-7821-2662-6) Sybex.

Mastering WordPerfect 8. 2nd ed. Alan Simpson. LC 97-67592. 1072p. 1997. pap. text 34.99 (0-7821-2088-1) Sybex.

Mastering WordPerfect 9. 3rd ed. Alan Simpson. LC 99-61815. 1056p. 1999. pap. text 39.99 (0-7821-2236-1) Sybex.

***Mastering Wordperfect 9 for Linux.** Alan Simpson. 832p. 1999. pap. 34.99 (0-7821-2595-6) Sybex.

Mastering WordPerfect Office 2000. Alan Simpson. (Mastering Ser.). 1200p. 1999. 49.99 (0-7821-2429-1) Sybex.

Mastering WordPerfect Office 2000. Celeste Robinson & Alan Simpson. LC 99-60026. (Mastering Ser.). (Illus.). 1067p. 1999. pap. 39.99 (0-7821-2198-5) Sybex.

Mastering WordPerfect 6 for DOS, Vol. 1. Alan Simpson. LC 98-88996. (Illus.). 706p. 1998. reprint ed. pap. 31.95 (1-58348-098-6) iUniversecom.

Mastering WordPerfect 6 for DOS, Vol. 2. Alan Simpson. LC 98-88996. (Illus.). 712p. 1998. reprint ed. pap. 31.95 (1-58348-099-4) iUniversecom.

Mastering Writing Essentials. Andrew MacDonald & Gina MacDonald. (Illus.). 464p. (C). 1996. pap. text 32.80 (0-205-15010-1) P-H.

Mastering Written Discovery: Interrogatories, Documents, & Admissions. 2nd ed. John H. Young & Terri A. Zall. LC 92-33925. 470p. 1993. spiral bd. 95.00 (1-56257-271-7, MICHIE) LEXIS Pub.

Mastering Written Discovery: Interrogatories, Documents, & Admissions. 2nd ed. John H. Young & Terri A. Zall. LC 92-33925. 1994. suppl. ed. 48.00 (0-685-74485-X, MICHIE) LEXIS Pub.

Mastering Written Discovery: Interrogatories, Documents & Admissions. 3rd ed. John Hardin Young & Terri A. Zall. LC 98-86261. 800p. 1998. write for info. (0-327-00253-0, 81549-11) LEXIS Pub.

***Mastering Written Discovery, 1999 Supplement: Procedures & Tactics.** 3rd ed. John H. Young & Terri A. Zall. 70p. 1999. pap. write for info. (0-327-01671-X, 8154810) LEXIS Pub.

Mastering Written English Level 1: The Comp-Lab Exercises. 5th ed. Mary T. Epes & Michael G. Southwell. LC 96-43545. 399p. (C). 1996. pap. text 37.00 (0-13-244526-3) P-H.

Mastering Written Sentences. Epes & Southwell. 266p. 1998. pap. text 18.80 (0-13-970774-3) P-H.

Mastering Written Sentences: Self-Teaching Exercises for College Writers. Mary Epes & Michael G. Southwell. LC 97-32614. 1997. pap. text 16.00 (0-13-628363-2) P-H.

***Mastering XHTML.** Eric J. Ray. 896p. 2000. pap. text 39.99 (0-7821-2820-3) Sybex.

***Mastering XMI: Java Programming with the XMI Toolkit, XML & UML.** Steven Brodsky. (Illus.). 416p. 2000. text 49.99 (0-471-38429-1) Wiley.

Mastering XML. 4th ed. Ann Navarro. (Mastering Ser.). 832p. 1999. pap. text 39.99 (0-7821-2266-3) Sybex.

Mastering Your Atari Through 8 BASIC Projects. Micro Magazine Staff. write for info. (0-318-58229-5) P-H.

Mastering Your Commodore 64 Through Eight BASIC Projects. Micro Magazine Staff. write for info. (0-318-58230-9) P-H.

Mastering Your Finances: Integrated Book & Software Designed to Develop Financial Mastery. Susan S. Isgar & Tom Isgar. (Illus.). 250p. 1997. pap. write for info. incl. disk (0-9623464-2-X) Seluera Pr.

Mastering Your Hidden Self: A Guide to the Huna Way. SergeK. King. LC 84-40509. (Illus.). 210p. 1996. pap. text 11.95 (0-8356-0591-4, Quest) Theos Pub Hse.

Mastering Your Influence Workbook. Shawn Kent. Ed. by Elizabeth DiCandilo. (Orig.). 1998. per., wbk. ed. 24.95 (0-9664623-0-0) Skills Mastery.

***Mastering Your Inner Game.** David Kauss. LC 00-31906. (Illus.). 272p. 2000. pap. write for info. (0-7360-0176-X) Human Kinetics.

Mastering Your Moods. Melvyn Kinder. 1994. 21.00 (0-671-78223-1) S&S Trade.

Mastering Your Moods. Frank Minirth et al. LC 98-53506. 288p. 1999. 18.99 (0-7852-7869-9) Nelson.

Mastering Your Professional Image: Dressing to Enhance Your Credibility. Diane Parente & Stephanie Petersen. Ed. by Karen Johnson. LC 95-77376. (Illus.). 130p. (Orig.). 1995. pap. 19.95 (0-9646688-0-7) Image Dev & Mgt.

Mastering 3D Studio. Jon M. Duff. (General Engineering Ser.). 1996. pap., teacher ed. 10.50 (0-534-95137-6) PWS Pubs.

***Mastering Macromedia Dreamweaver 3.** David L. Crowder & Rhonda Crowder. (Mastering Ser.). 2000. pap. 39.99 (0-7821-2624-3) Sybex.

Masterkey, Vol. VII:4. M. R. Harrington et al. (Illus.). 32p. (C). 1933. pap. text 3.75 (1-55567-741-X) Coyote Press.

Masterkey, Vol. VIII:1. M. R. Harrington et al. (Illus.). 32p. (C). 1934. pap. text 3.75 (1-55567-742-8) Coyote Press.

Masterkey, Vol. XVII:5. G. B. Grinnell et al. 40p. (C). 1943. pap. text 4.38 (1-55567-743-6) Coyote Press.

Masterkey, Vol. XXVI:4. M. N. Everett et al. (Illus.). 34p. (C). 1952. pap. text 3.75 (1-55567-744-4) Coyote Press.

Masterkey, Vol. XXVI:6. Ruth D. Simpson & M. R. Harrington. (Illus.). 36p. (C). 1952. pap. text 4.06 (1-55567-745-2) Coyote Press.

Masterkey II(4) fac. ed. A. V. Kidder & M. R. Harrington. (Southwest Museum, Los Angeles, California Ser.). (Illus.). 32p. (C). 1928. reprint ed. pap. text 3.75 (1-55567-801-7) Coyote Press.

Masterless: Self & Society in Modern America. Wilfred M. McClay. LC 93-9673. 380p. (C). 1994. pap. 22.50 (0-8078-4419-5); lib. bdg. 59.95 (0-8078-2117-9) U of NC Pr.

Masterless Man. Jules Verne. lib. bdg. 22.95 (0-8488-2052-5) Amereon Ltd.

Masterlife. Avery T. Willis, Jr. LC 98-12670. 256p. 1998. pap. 12.99 (0-8054-0165-2) Broadman.

MasterLife Bk. 1: The Disciple's Cross. Avery T. Willis, Jr. 144p. 1996. pap. text 7.95 (0-7673-2579-6, LifeWy Press) LifeWay Christian.

MasterLife Bk. 2: The Disciple's Personality. Avery T. Willis, Jr. 144p. 1996. pap. text 7.95 (0-7673-2580-X, LifeWy Press) LifeWay Christian.

MasterLife Bk. 3: The Disciple's Victory. Avery T. Willis, Jr. 144p. 1997. pap. text 7.95 (0-7673-2581-8, LifeWy Press) LifeWay Christian.

MasterLife Bk. 4: The Disciple's Mission. Avery T. Willis, Jr. 144p. 1997. pap. text 7.95 (0-7673-2582-6, LifeWy Press) LifeWay Christian.

MasterLife Leader Guide. Avery T. Willis, Jr. 224p. 1997. pap. text 15.95 (0-7673-2583-4, LifeWy Press) LifeWay Christian.

***Masterman.** Max Brand. 197p. 2000. 30.00 (0-7862-2099-6) Mac Lib Ref.

***Masterman.** large type ed. 2001. 30.00 (0-7838-8722-1, G K Hall Lrg Type) Mac Lib Ref.

Masterman Reader. Captain Marrtay. 390p. Date not set. 27.95 (0-8488-2364-8) Amereon Ltd.

MasterMate/JaquesMaestros Vol. 10: Complete Plays 10: The Marriage of Hippolyta; The Two Caballeros of Central Park West; Santiago; Las Bodas de Hipolita; Dos Caballeros Con Vista al Parque Central. Manuel P. Garcia. Tr. by Jose Corrales. (SPA.). 100p. 1998. 4.95 (1-885901-60-7, Liberts) Presbyters Peartree.

***Mastermind: A New World of Possibilities.** Isabelle Sennery. (Odyssey Empowerment Ser.). 150p. 2000. pap. 17.95 (0-9577945-0-9, Pub. by Odyssey Mind Inst) Dana Kerr.

***Mastermind: A New World of Possibilities.** deluxe ed. Isabelle Sennery. (Odyssey Empowerment Ser.). 150p. 2000. 39.95 (0-9577945-1-7, Pub. by Odyssey Mind Inst) Dana Kerr.

Mastermind: Exercises in Critical Thinking, Grades 4-6. Zacharie J. Clements & Richard R. Hawhes. (Illus.). 68p. (Orig.). 1985. pap. 9.95 (0-673-16653-8, GoodYrBooks) Addson-Wesley Educ.

Mastermind for the Primary Grades. Richard R. Hawkes et al. (Illus.). 120p. (Orig.). (J). (gr. k up). 1992. pap. 9.95 (0-673-36018-0, GoodYrBooks) Addson-Wesley Educ.

Mastermind Mazes. Patrick Merrell. (Illus.). 32p. (J). (gr. 3-7). 1997. pap. 3.95 (0-8167-4399-1) Troll Communs.

Masterminding the Store: Advertising, Sales Promotion & the New Marketing Reality. Donald Ziccardi. LC 96-30258. 336p. 1996. 27.95 (0-471-13910-6) Wiley.

Masterminding Tomorrow's Information: Creative Strategies for the '90s: Professional Papers from the 82nd Annual Conference of the Special Libraries Association, June 8-13, 1991, San Antonio, TX. Special Libraries Association, Conference Staff. LC Z 0674.4.S65. (Illus.). 143p. 1991. reprint ed. pap. 44.40 (0-608-04408-3, 206518900001) Bks Demand.

Masterminds - Pre-Algebra: Reproducible Skill Builders & Higher Order Thinking Activities Based on NCTM Standards. Brenda Opie. (Illus.). 96p. (Orig.). (J). (gr. 4-7). 1995. pap. text 10.95 (0-86530-338-X, IP 200-6) Incentive Pubns.

Masterminds Addition, Subtraction, Place Value, & Other Numeration Systems: Reproducible Skill Builders & Higher Order Thinking Activities Based on NCTM Standards. Brenda Opie et al. (Illus.). 96p. (Orig.). (J). (gr. 3-7). 1995. pap. text 10.95 (0-86530-303-7, 200-3) Incentive Pubns.

Masterminds Decimals, Percentages, Metric System, & Consumer Math: Reproducible Skill Builders & Higher Order Thinking Activities Based on NCTM Standards. Brenda Opie et al. (Illus.). 96p. (Orig.). (J). (gr. 4-8). 1995. pap. text 10.95 (0-86530-301-0, 200-1) Incentive Pubns.

Masterminds Fractions, Ratio, Probability, & Standard Measurement: Reproducible Skill Builders & Higher Order Thinking Activities Based on NCTM Standards. Brenda Opie et al. (Illus.). 96p. (Orig.). (J). (gr. 3-7). 1995. pap. text 10.95 (0-86530-302-9, 200-2) Incentive Pubns.

Masterminds Geometry & Graphing: Reproducible Skill Builders & Higher Order Thinking Activities Based on NCTM Standards. Brenda Opie et al. (Illus.). 96p. (Orig.). (J). (gr. 4-8). 1995. pap. text 10.95 (0-86530-305-3, 200-5) Incentive Pubns.

Masterminds Multiplication & Division: Reproducible Skill Builders & Higher Order Thinking Activities Based on NCTM Standards. Brenda Opie et al. (Illus.). 96p. (Orig.). (J). (gr. 4-7). 1995. pap. text 10.95 (0-86530-304-5, 200-4) Incentive Pubns.

Masterminds of Falkenstein: A Castle Falkenstein Novel. John DeChancie & Debbie Notkin. 312p. 1996. mass mkt., per. 5.99 (0-7615-0484-2) Prima Pub.

***Masterminds Skills Boosters for the Reluctant Math Student: Reproducible Skill Builders & Higher Order Thinking Activities Based on NCTM Standards.** Brenda Opie & Douglas McAvinn. (Masterminds Riddle Math Ser.). (Illus.). 96p. (J). (gr. 4-8). 2000. pap. text 10.95 (0-86530-448-3, IP 200-7) Incentive Pubns.

***Mastermyr Find: A Viking Age Tool Chest from Gotland.** Greta Arwidsson & Gosta Berg. (Illus.). 90p. 2000. reprint ed. pap. 17.95 (0-9650755-1-6) Larson Publng.

MasterPath: The Divine Science of Light & Sound. Gary Olsen. (Illus.). 230p. 1999. pap. 20.00 (1-885949-01-4) MasterPath.

***Masterpiece.** Anna Enquist. Tr. by Jeannette K. Ringold from DUT. 1999. 29.95 (1-902881-05-2, Pub. by Toby Pr Ltd) Toby Pr.

***Masterpiece.** Anna Enquist. 240p. 2000. pap. 15.95 (1-902881-21-4, Pub. by Toby Pr Ltd) Toby Pr.

***Masterpiece, 1.** Impact Productions Staff. 1999. 12.95 (0-9663325-3-9) Impact Prodns.

Masterpiece. Emile Zola. Ed. by Roger Pearson. Tr. by Thomas Walton. (Oxford World's Classics Ser.). 458p. 1999. pap. 10.95 (0-19-283963-2) OUP.

Masterpiece. Emile Zola. 368p. 1968. reprint ed. pap. 16.95 (0-472-06145-3, 06145, Ann Arbor Bks) U of Mich Pr.

Masterpiece, Vol. 1. Beverly Fox. 178p. (Orig.). 1997. pap. 16.50 (1-57502-518-3, P01540) Morris Pubng.

Masterpiece: Nostradamus, Branham & the "Little Book" Patricia Sunday. (Illus.). 1999. pap. text 19.95 (0-9665933-1-6) Sunday Ministries.

Masterpiece: Nostradamus, Branham & the "Little Book" Patricia A. Sunday. Ed. & Illus. by LeRoy Miller. 298p. 1998. spiral bd. 29.95 (0-9665933-0-8) Sunday Ministries.

Masterpiece: Short Stories. Ranjan Umapathy. 1993. text 15.95 (0-7069-6375-X, Pub. by Vikas) S Asia.

Masterpiece in Focus: Soap Bubbles by Jean-Simeon Chardin. Philip Consibee. LC 91-107248. (Illus.). 28p. 1990. pap. text 8.95 (0-87587-154-2) LA Co Art Mus.

Masterpiece in Progress. Jeff Steinberg. LC 90-61752. 290p. 1990. reprint ed. pap. 10.95 (0-89221-183-0) New Leaf.

Masterpiece Library of Buddhis, 10 vols. Print India Staff. 1996. 3700.00 (81-7305-106-2, Pub. by Print Hse) St Mut.

Masterpiece Me: Children's Activities in Anatomy & Development. Sally Wittman. LC 92-41497. 1993. 14.95 (1-56071-118-3) ETR Assocs.

***Masterpiece of Chinese Art.** Rhonda Cooper & Jeffrey Cooper. 128p. 1998. 16.98 (1-57717-060-1) Todtri Prods.

Masterpiece of Murder: A Gilded Age Mystery. Mary Kruger. 1997. mass mkt. 5.50 (1-57566-229-9) Kensgtn Pub Corp.

Masterpiece of Revenge: A Novel. J. J. Fiechter. LC 98-73500. 192p. 1998. 21.95 (1-55970-430-6, Pub. by Arcade Pub Inc) Time Warner.

Masterpiece of the Month. Jennifer Thomas. (Illus.). 96p. (J). (gr. k-5). 1990. student ed. 11.95 (1-55734-018-8) Tchr Create Mat.

***Masterpiece Paintings.** Theodore E. Stebbins, Jr. (Illus.). 148p. 2000. 45.00 (0-8109-1424-7) Abrams.

Masterpiece Recipes of the American Club. American Club Staff. (Illus.). 208p. 1993. write for info. (0-9635933-1-5); pap. 24.95 (0-9635933-0-7) Kohler Co.

Masterpiece Sex: The Art of Sexual Discovery. Elaine Kittredge. LC 95-125672. (Illus.). 180p. 1994. pap. 24.95 (0-9611266-3-9) Optext.

Masterpiece Showcase. Attic Annies. LC 98-66978. 1999. pap. 19.96 (1-57367-104-5) Needlecrft Shop.

Masterpiece Studies: Manet, Zola, Van Gogh, & Monet. Kermit S. Champa. LC 93-3547. (Illus.). 160p. (C). 1994. 32.50 (0-271-01088-6) Pa St U Pr.

Masterpiece Sweaters; Twelve Dramatic New Designs. Janice Wright. LC 94-71053. (Illus.). 120p. 1994. pap. 24.95 (0-89272-334-3) Down East.

Masterpiece Theatre: A Celebration of 25 Years of Outstanding Television. Terrence O'Flaherty. LC 95-38710. (Illus.). 256p. (Orig.). 1995. pap. 24.95 (0-912333-74-X) BB&T Inc.

Masterpiece Theatre: An Academic Melodrama. Sandra M. Gilbert & Susan Gubar. 200p. 1995. 40.00 (0-8135-2182-3); pap. 15.95 (0-8135-2183-1) Rutgers U Pr.

Masterpiece Theatre & the Politics of Quality: A Case Study. Laurence A. Jarvik. LC 98-34464. 261p. 1998. text 60.00 (0-8108-3204-6) Scarecrow.

Masterpieces see Master Pieces, Vol. 1, The Art History of Jigsaw Puzzles

Masterpieces. Arthur Bicknell. 1979. pap. 5.25 (0-8222-0739-7) Dramatists Play.

Masterpieces. Beth Dunlop. (Arts & Crafts Ser.). 1999. 19.95 (0-7148-3876-4) Phaidon Pr.

Masterpieces. 2nd ed. Sarah Daniels. (Methuen Modern Plays Ser.). 68p. (Orig.). (C). 1984. pap. write for info. (0-413-41260-1, A0432, Methuen Drama) Methn.

Masterpieces: The Best Loved Paintings from America's Museums. David Frankel. LC 95-939. 160p. 1995. 35.00 (0-684-80197-3) S&S Trade.

Masterpieces by Shibata Zeshin: Treasures of Imperial Japan. Joe Earle & Goke Tadaomi. (The Nasser D. Khalili Collection of Japanese Art). (Illus.). 228p. 1999. 490.00 (1-874780-08-0) OUP.

Masterpieces East & West: From the Collection of the Birmingham Museum of Art. LC 93-26353. 1993. write for info. (0-931394-38-4); pap. write for info. (0-931394-37-6) Birmingham Mus.

Masterpieces for 2 Guitars. Richard Pick. 68p. 1996. pap. 9.95 (0-7866-0405-0, 95428) Mel Bay.

Masterpieces from Central Africa: The Tervuren Museum. Ed. by Gustaaf Verswijver et al. LC 96-31058. (Illus.). 200p. 1996. 65.00 (3-7913-1683-4, Pub. by Prestel) te Neues.

Masterpieces from the Collections of the Prince of Liechtenstein: Sculpture, Decorative Arts, Weaponry. Uwe Wieczorek et al. LC 98-109938. 301 p. 1997. write for info. (3-7165-1046-7) Benteli Verlag.

Masterpieces from the House of Faberge. Alexander Von Solodkoff. Ed. by Christopher Forbes. LC 88-34349. (Illus.). 192p. 1989. pap. 19.98 (0-8109-8089-4, Pub. by Abrams) Time Warner.

Masterpieces from the House of Faberge. S. Von Solodkoff. (C). 1990. pap. 130.00 (0-7855-4435-6, Pub. by Collets) St Mut.

Masterpieces from the Los Angeles County Museum of Art Collection. Lorna Price. LC 87-36685. (Illus.). 154p. (Orig.). 1988. pap. text 9.95 (0-87587-146-1) LA Co Art Mus.

An Asterisk (*) at the beginning of an entry indicates that the title is appearing for the first time.

Masterpieces from the Metropolitan Museum of Art. Barbara Burn. 1997. 39.50 (0-87099-677-0) Metro Mus Art.

Masterpieces from the Norton Simon Museum. Sara Campbell et al. (Illus.). 207p. (Orig.). 1989. 35.00 (0-915776-05-7); pap. 20.00 (0-915776-04-9) NS Mus.

Masterpieces from the Shin-Enkan Collection: Japanese Painting of the Edo Period Los Angeles County Museum of Art Staff. LC 85-45953. 139 p. 1986. write for info. (0-87587-128-3) LA Co Art Mus.

Masterpieces from the Shin'enkan Collection: Japanese Painting of the Edo Period. Yuzo Yamane et al. LC 85-24152. (Illus.). 140p. (Orig.). 1986. 34.95 (0-87587-133-X) LA Co Art Mus.

***Masterpieces in Detail: What Great Paintings Say.** Rose-Marie Hagen. (Examining Paintings Ser.). (Illus.). 2000. 49.99 (3-8228-7047-1) Taschen Amer.

Masterpieces in Little Portrait Miniatures: From the Collection of Her Majesty Queen Elizabeth II. Christopher Lloyd & Vanessa Remington. LC 97-117011. (Illus.). 192p. 1997. 99.00 (0-85115-694-0) Boydell & Brewer.

***Masterpieces in Miniature: Dollhouses, 3 vols.** Nick Forder. 32p. 1999. boxed set 24.95 (0-7641-7269-7) Barron.

***Masterpieces in Miniature: Teddy Bears, 3 vols.** Garry Grey. 32p. 1999. boxed set 24.95 (0-7641-7270-0) Barron.

Masterpieces in the Barakat Collection. (Illus.). 64p. pap. 10.00 (0-685-37763-6) Barakat.

***Masterpieces of African-American Eloquence, 1818-1913: Descriptions, Analyses, Characters, Plots, Themes, Critical Evaluations & Significance of Major Works of Fiction, Non-Fiction, Drama & Poetry.** A. Dunbar. 2000. pap. 12.95 (0-486-41142-7) Dover.

***Masterpieces of American Furniture from the Munson-Williams-Proctor Institute.** Ed. by Anna Tobin D'Ambrosio. LC 98-45261. (Illus.). 171p. 1999. 50.00 (0-8156-8127-5) Syracuse U Pr.

***Masterpieces of American Furniture from the Munson-Williams-proctor Institute.** Munson-Williams-Proctor Institute Staff. 1999. 50.00 (0-915895-20-X) Munson Williams.

Masterpieces of American Indian Art: From the Eugene & Clare Thaw Collection. Photos by John B. Taylor. (Illus.). 96p. 1995. pap. 19.95 (0-8109-2628-8) Abrams.

Masterpieces of American Indian Literature. Ed. by Willis Regier. (Illus.). 624p. 1993. 12.98 (1-56731-035-4, MJF Bks) Fine Comms.

Masterpieces of American Literature. Ed. by Frank N. Magill. LC 93-15940. 640p. 1993. 47.50 (0-06-270072-3, Harper Ref) HarpC.

Masterpieces of American Literature. Ed. by Horace E. Scudder. LC 70-128156. (Granger Index Reprint Ser.). 1977. 29.95 (0-8369-6183-8) Ayer.

Masterpieces of American Literature. Ed. by Horace E. Scudder. LC 70-128156. (Granger Index Reprint Ser.). 504p. reprint ed. lib. bdg. 28.50 (0-8290-0519-6) Irvington.

Masterpieces of American Painting. Leonard Everett-Fisher. (Illus.). 224p. 1995. write for info. (1-57215-065-3) World Pubns.

Masterpieces of American Painting from Randolph-Macon Woman's College. Randolph Macon Woman's College Staff. 1990. pap. 3.95 (0-486-26384-3) Dover.

Masterpieces of American Painting from the Brooklyn Museum. Teresa A. Carbone. LC 96-78480. (Illus.). 103p. 1996. 25.00 (0-614-29364-2) V Jordan Fine Art.

Masterpieces of Americana: The Collection of Mr. & Mrs. Adolph Henry Meyer. Joan B. Treund. LC 97-178302. (Illus.). 96p. 1995. 35.00 (0-9622588-1-4) Sothebys Pubns.

Masterpieces of Americana: The Mr. & Mrs. Adolph Henry Meyer Collection. Sidney Long. 1995. 39.00 (0-614-15405-7) Antique Collect.

Masterpieces of Art at Great Museums - Text & Prints. (Illus.). 18p. 1992. pap. text 159.00 (0-935493-70-0) Modern Learn Pr.

Masterpieces of Art Nouveau Stained Glass Design. Arnold Lyongrun. (Illus.). 32p. 1989. pap. 7.95 (0-486-25953-6) Dover.

Masterpieces of Baroque Painting from the Collection of the Sarah Campbell Blaffer Foundation. George T. Shackelford. (Illus.). 132p. 1993. 35.00 (0-89090-055-8, ND 177.55 1992); pap. 35.00 (0-89090-056-6) Mus Fine TX.

Masterpieces of Bird Art: 700 Years of Ornithological Illustration. Roger F. Pasquier & John Farrand, Jr. (Illus.). 256p. 1991. 75.00 (1-55859-134-6) Abbeville Pr.

Masterpieces of British Literature. Ed. by Horace E. Scudder. LC 74-128157. (Granger Index Reprint Ser.). 1977. 29.95 (0-8369-6184-6) Ayer.

Masterpieces of British Literature. Ed. by Horace E. Scudder. LC 74-128157. (Granger Index Reprint Ser.). 480p. reprint ed. lib. bdg. 28.50 (0-8290-0507-2) Irvington.

Masterpieces of Calligraphy: 261 Examples, 1500-1800. Peter Jessen. (Illus.). 224p. 1981. reprint ed. pap. 10.95 (0-486-24100-9) Dover.

Masterpieces of Chinese & Japanese Art. LC 76-11656. (Illus.). 1976. pap. 5.00 (0-934686-32-7) Freer.

Masterpieces of Chinese & Japanese Art: Freer Gallery of Art Handbook. (Illus.). 142p. (Orig.). (C). 1997. reprint ed. pap. 15.00 (0-7881-5052-9) DIANE Pub.

Masterpieces of Costume Jewelry. J. Ball & Dorothy H. Torem. LC 95-31294. 208p. (gr. 10). 1996. 49.95 (0-88740-900-8) Schiffer.

Masterpieces of Early South Indian Bronzes. R. Nagaswamy. 172p. 1983. 52.95 (0-940500-90-6, Pub. by Natl Museum) Asia Bk Corp.

Masterpieces of Egyptian Museums. Casa Bonechi Staff. 64p. 10.95 (88-7009-235-6, Pub. by Bonechi) Eiron.

Masterpieces of English Furniture: The Gerstenfeld Collection. Ed. by Edward Lennox-Boyd. (Illus.). 272p. 1999. 125.00 (0-903432-56-0, Pub. by CMW Ltd) Antique Collect.

Masterpieces of Faberge: The Matilda Geddings Gray Foundation Collection. John W. Keefe. LC 93-83124. (Illus.). 160p. 1993. pap. 30.00 (0-89494-040-6) New Orleans Mus Art.

Masterpieces of Flower Painting. Cirker. 1998. pap. 4.95 (0-486-29531-1) Dover.

Masterpieces of Furniture in Photographs & Measured Drawings. rev. ed. Verna C. Salomonsky. (Illus.). 212p. 1953. pap. 10.95 (0-486-21381-1) Dover.

Masterpieces of George Sand, 20 vols., Set. George Sand. Tr. by George B. Ives. LC 76-7893. reprint ed. 750.00 (0-404-15200-7) AMS Pr.

Masterpieces of Glass: A World History from the Corning Museum of Glass. Robert J. Charleston. (Illus.). 240p. 1993. pap. 29.95 (0-8109-2557-5, Pub. by Abrams) Time Warner.

Masterpieces of Greek Drawing & Painting. Ernst Pfuhl. Tr. by John D. Beazley from GER. LC 79-83879. (Illus.). 1979. reprint ed. lib. bdg. 50.00 (0-87817-250-5) Hacker.

Masterpieces of Greek Literature. Ed. by John H. Wright. LC 72-132136. (Play Anthology Reprint Ser.). 1977. 29.95 (0-8369-8213-4) Ayer.

Masterpieces of Hebrew Literature: A Treasury of 2000 Years of Jewish Creativity. Curt Leviant. 1969. pap. 24.95 (0-87068-079-X) Ktav.

Masterpieces of Heeresgeschich. Bonechi. 64p. text 11.95 (88-7009-505-3, Pub. by Bonechi) Eiron.

Masterpieces of Impressionism & European Modernism from the Columbus Museum of Art, Columbus Museum of Art & TG Concepts, Inc. Norma J. Roberts. LC 92-83841. (Illus.). 1993. pap. 29.95 (0-685-72344-5) Columbus Mus Art.

Masterpieces of Indian Jewellery. Jamila Brijbhushan. (Illus.). 142p. 1979. 34.95 (0-318-36272-4) Asia Bk Corp.

Masterpieces of Indian Sculpture. Alice N. Heeramaneck. (Illus.). 133p. 1979. 90.00 (0-318-36250-3) Asia Bk Corp.

Masterpieces of Indian Textiles. Rustam J. Mehta. (Illus.). 132p. 1979. 42.95 (0-318-36266-X) Asia Bk Corp.

Masterpieces of Irish Crochet Lace: Technique, Patterns, Instructions. Therese De Dillmont. (Illus.). 64p. 1986. reprint ed. pap. 3.95 (0-486-25079-2) Dover.

Masterpieces of Japanese Prints: Ukiyo-E from the Victoria & Albert Museum. Rupert Faulkner. 1999. pap. 29.00 (4-7700-2387-1) Kodansha.

Masterpieces of Kunsthistorisc. Bonechi. 64p. text 14.95 (88-7009-500-2, Pub. by Bonechi) Eiron.

Masterpieces of Kunsthistorisches. 128p. text 14.95 (88-8029-550-0, Pub. by Bonechi) Eiron.

Masterpieces of Landeszeughaus. 64p. text 9.95 (88-7009-754-4, Pub. by Bonechi) Eiron.

Masterpieces of Louvre. Giovanna Magi. Tr. by Michael Hollingworth. 64p. pap. text 9.95 (88-7009-151-1, Pub. by Bonechi) Eiron.

***Masterpieces of Marquetry, Vols. 1-3.** Pierre Ramond. LC 99-86492. 2000. write for info. (0-89236-594-3, J P Getty Museum) J P Getty Trust.

Masterpieces of Modern Urdu Poetry K. C. Kanda. LC 98-908716. x, 357p. 1998. write for info. (81-207-2096-2) Sterling Pub.

Masterpieces of Negro Eloquence: African-American Women Writers, 1910-1940 by Dunbar-Nelson. Ed. by Alice M. Dunbar-Nelson. LC 96-44327. 1996. 30.00 (0-7838-1424-0, Hall Reference) Macmillan.

Masterpieces of Painting. Portland Museum of Art Staff. (Illus.). 1992. pap. 3.95 (0-486-27139-0) Dover.

***Masterpieces of Painting.** Thyssen-Bornemisza. (Illus.). 2000. pap. 29.99 (3-8228-6307-6) Taschen Amer.

Masterpieces of Persian Art. Arthur U. Pope. LC 76-97351. (Illus.). 204p. 1970. reprint ed. lib. bdg. 41.50 (0-8371-3013-1, POPA, Greenwood Pr) Greenwood.

Masterpieces of Photography from the Merrill Lynch Collection. Brian H. Peterson. (Illus.). 84p. 1997. pap. write for info. (1-879636-09-3) J A Michener.

Masterpieces of Piano Music. Franz Schubert. LC 87-751900. (Masterpieces of Piano Music Ser.). (Illus.). 192p. 1986. pap. 17.95 (0-8256-1087-7, AM65103) Music Sales.

Masterpieces of Piano Music. Ed. by Albert Wier. 536p. (Orig.). 1918. pap. 29.95 (0-8258-0006-4, 03619) Fischer Inc NY.

Masterpieces of Pinacoteca. Casa Bonechi. 96p. text 12.95 (88-7009-465-0, Pub. by Bonechi) Eiron.

Masterpieces of Renaissance & Baroque Sculpture from the Palazzo Venezia, Rome: Georgia Museum of Art, October 5-November 24, 1996. Museo di Palazzo Venezia Staff et al. LC 96-36152. (Illus.). 90p. 1996. pap. 25.00 (0-915977-29-X) Georgia Museum of Art.

***Masterpieces of Renaissance Sculpture.** Andrew Butterfield. (Illus.). (C). 1999. 45.00 (1-58821-001-4) Salander OReilly.

Masterpieces of Reporting. Ed. by William D. Sloan & Cheryl S. Wray. LC 97-447. 473p. (Orig.). 1997. pap. 24.95 (1-885219-04-0) Vision AL.

Masterpieces of Russian Literature, 7 bks. Ed. by Dover Staff. 880p. 1999. pap. text 9.50 (0-486-40665-2) Dover.

Masterpieces of Shaker Furniture. Edward Demin Andrews. LC 99-42700. 128p. 1999. pap. text 9.95 (0-486-40724-1) Dover.

Masterpieces of the Anthropology Collection. Richard M. Gramly. LC 81-66994. (Illus.). 55p. (Orig.). (C). 1981. pap. 2.50 (0-944032-46-X) Buffalo SNS.

Masterpieces of the Drama. 6th rev. ed. Alexander W. Allison et al. LC 90-43954. 1056p. (C). 1990. pap. text 72.00 (0-02-301975-1, Macmillan Coll) P-H.

Masterpieces of the English Short Novel. Intro. by Ken Brown. 896p. 1992. pap. 14.95 (0-88184-848-4) Carroll & Graf.

Masterpieces of the Grand Louvre. 128p. text 12.95 (88-7009-780-3, Pub. by Bonechi) Eiron.

Masterpieces of the Israel Museum. 64p. text 11.95 (88-7009-627-0, Pub. by Bonechi) Eiron.

Masterpieces of the J. Paul Getty Museum: Decorative Arts: Japanese-Language Edition. (Getty Trust Publications). (JPN., Illus.). 128p. 1997. pap. 22.50 (0-89236-462-9, Pub. by J P Getty Trust) OUP.

Masterpieces of the J. Paul Getty Museum: Drawings: Japanese-Language Edition. (JPN., Illus.). 128p. 1997. pap. 22.50 (0-89236-443-2, Pub. by J P Getty Trust) OUP.

Masterpieces of the J. Paul Getty Museum: Photographs. J. Paul Getty Museum Staff. LC 98-7456. 128p. 1999. 34.95 (0-89236-516-1, Pub. by J P Getty Trust) OUP.

Masterpieces of the J. Paul Getty Museum: Photographs. J. Paul Getty Museum Staff. LC 98-7456. (Illus.). 128p. 1999. pap. 22.50 (0-89236-517-X, Pub. by J P Getty Trust) OUP.

Masterpieces of the J. Paul Getty Museum: Photographs. Ed. by J. Paul Getty Museum Staff. (JPN., Illus.). 128p. 1999. pap. 22.50 (0-89236-524-2, Pub. by J P Getty Trust) OUP.

Masterpieces of the J. Paul Getty Museum: Sculpture. LC 98-13409. (Illus.). 128p. 1998. pap. 22.50 (0-89236-513-7, Pub. by J P Getty Trust) OUP.

Masterpieces of the J. Paul Getty Museum - Antiquities. LC 96-22653. 1997. pap. 22.50 (0-89236-421-1, Pub. by J P Getty Trust) OUP.

Masterpieces of the J. Paul Getty Museum - Antiquities. LC 96-22653. 128p. 1997. 34.95 (0-89236-420-3, Pub. by J P Getty Trust) OUP.

Masterpieces of the J. Paul Getty Museum - Antiquities: Japanese-Language Version. (JPN., Illus.). 128p. 1997. pap. 22.50 (0-89236-426-2, Pub. by J P Getty Trust) OUP.

Masterpieces of the J. Paul Getty Museum - Decorative Arts. J. Paul Getty Museum Staff. LC 96-26469. 1997. pap. 22.50 (0-89236-455-6, Pub. by J P Getty Trust) OUP.

Masterpieces of the J. Paul Getty Museum - Decorative Arts. J. Paul Getty Museum Staff. LC 96-26469. 128p. 1997. 34.95 (0-89236-454-8, Pub. by J P Getty Trust) OUP.

Masterpieces of the J. Paul Getty Museum - Drawings. J. Paul Getty Museum Staff. LC 96-23151. (Illus.). 128p. 1996. 34.95 (0-89236-437-8, Pub. by J P Getty Trust); pap. 22.50 (0-89236-438-6, Pub. by J P Getty Trust) OUP.

Masterpieces of the J. Paul Getty Museum - Illuminated Manuscripts. 128p. 1997. 34.95 (0-89236-445-9, Pub. by J P Getty Trust); pap. 22.50 (0-89236-446-7, Pub. by J P Getty Trust) OUP.

Masterpieces of the J. Paul Getty Museum - Illuminated Manuscripts: Japanese-Language Version. (JPN., Illus.). 128p. 1997. pap. 22.50 (0-89236-453-X, Pub. by J P Getty Trust) OUP.

Masterpieces of the J. Paul Getty Museum - Paintings. LC 97-70931. (Illus.). 128p. 1997. 34.95 (0-89236-427-0, Pub. by J P Getty Trust); pap. 22.50 (0-89236-428-9, Pub. by J P Getty Trust) OUP.

Masterpieces of the J. Paul Getty Museum - Paintings: Japanese-Language Version. (JPN., Illus.). 128p. 1997. 34.95 (0-89236-435-1, Pub. by J P Getty Trust); pap. 22.50 (0-89236-436-X, Pub. by J P Getty Trust) OUP.

Masterpieces of the J. Paul Getty Museum - Sculpture. LC 98-13409. (Illus.). 128p. 1998. 34.95 (0-89236-512-9, Pub. by J P Getty Trust) OUP.

Masterpieces of the Metropolitan Museum of Art. Ed. by Barbara Burn. LC 93-7966. (Illus.). 320p. 1993. 50.00 (0-8212-2047-0, Pub. by Bulfinch Pr) Little.

Masterpieces of the Metropolitan Museum of Art. Metropolitan Museum of Art Staff. (Illus.). 320p. 1998. pap. 35.00 (0-8212-2509-X, Pub. by Bulfinch Pr) Little.

Masterpieces of the Orient. expanded ed. Ed. by G. L. Anderson. (C). 1976. pap. text 46.00 (0-393-09196-1) Norton.

Masterpieces of the Peabody Museum. LC 78-67472. (Peabody Museum Press Ser.). (Illus.). 104p. 1978. pap. 6.50 (0-87365-797-7) Peabody Harvard.

Masterpieces of the Poster from the Belle Epoque: 48 Full-Color Plates from "Les Maitres de L'Affiche" Ed. by Hayward Cirker & Blanche Cirker. (Fine Art Ser.). 48p. 1984. reprint ed. pap. 6.95 (0-486-24549-7) Dover.

Masterpieces of the Twentieth Century: The Beyeler Collection. Ewen McDonald et al. LC 98-175470. 231p. 1996. write for info. (0-7310-9480-8) NSW.

Masterpieces of Time: Long-Case Clocks & Fine Furniture by Wendell Castle. Edward Lucie-Smith. (Illus.). 20p. (Orig.). 1985. pap. 5.00 (0-915577-07-0) Taft Museum.

Masterpieces of 20th-Century Art: From the Kunstsammlung Nordrhein-Westfalen, Duesseldorf. Werner Schmalenbach. (Illus.). 356p. 1994. pap. 29.95 (3-7913-1338-X, Pub. by Prestel) te Neues.

Masterpieces of Twentieth-Century Art at the Philadelphia Museum of Art. Rachel Arauz et al. (Illus.). 160p. 1999. write for info. (0-87633-133-9) Phila Mus Art.

Masterpieces of Twentieth-Century Canadian Painting. E. Robert Hunter. LC 83-63352. (Illus.). 63p. 1984. pap. 8.00 (0-943411-09-2) Norton Gal Art.

Masterpieces of Twentieth Century Canadian Painting: Catalogue of an Exhibition, March 18 to April 29, 1984. E. Robert Hunter. (Illus.). 64p. 1984. 17.50 (0-89062-193-4) Norton Gal Art.

Masterpieces of Urdu Ghazal from 17th to 20th Century. K. C. Kanda. (C). 1992. write for info. (81-207-1195-5) Sterling Pubs.

Masterpieces of Urdu Nazm. K. C. Kanda. 1996. 36.00 (81-207-1845-3, Pub. by Manohar) S Asia.

Masterpieces of Urdu Rubaiyat. K. C. Kanda. (C). 1994. write for info. (0-685-72915-X) Sterling Pubs.

Masterpieces of Vijayanarara Art. S. Rajasekhara. (Illus.). 100p. 1983. text 40.00 (0-86590-115-5) Apt Bks.

***Masterpieces of Western Art: A History of Art in 1900 Individual Studies.** Ingo F. Walther. (Jumbo Ser.). (Illus.). 1999. 49.99 (3-8228-7031-5) Taschen Amer.

Masterpieces of Women's Literature. Ed. by Frank N. Magill. LC 95-26601. (Masterpieces of...Ser.). 608p. 1996. 50.00 (0-06-270138-X, Harper Ref) HarpC.

Masterpieces of World Literature. Ed. by Frank N. Magill. LC 89-45052. 992p. 1991. 55.00 (0-06-270050-2) HarperTrade.

Masterpieces of World Philosophy: More Than 100 Classics of the World's Greatest Philosophers Analyzed & Explained. Ed. by Frank N. Magill & John Roth. LC 15-8176. 704p. 1991. 47.00 (0-06-270051-0, Harper Ref) HarpC.

Masterpieces of World Photography-Postcard: A Postcard Book. 1993. pap. 7.95 (1-55859-574-0) Abbeville Pr.

Masterpieces with Flair, Bk. 2. Ed. by Jane Magrath. 72p. 1993. pap. 8.95 (0-7390-0440-9, 6667) Alfred Pub.

Masterplan, Judaism: Its Program, Meanings, & Goals. Aryeh Carmell. 1991. pap. 17.95 (0-87306-581-6) Feldheim.

***Masterplan, Judaism: Its Program, Meanings, & Goals.** Aryeh Carmell. 1999. 11.95 (1-58330-369-3) Feldheim.

Masterplanning: A Complete Guide for Building a Strategic Plan for Your Business, Church, or Organization. Bobb Biehl. LC 97-958. 288p. (Orig.). 1997. pap. 16.99 (0-8054-6096-9) Broadman.

Masterplots, 12 vols. 2nd rev. ed. Ed. by Frank N. Magill & Laurence W. Mazzeno. 7680p. 1996. lib. bdg. 600.00 (0-89356-084-7) Salem Pr.

Masterplots: Revised Category Edition, 3 vols. rev. ed. Ed. by Frank N. Magill. (British Fiction Ser.). 1832p. 1985. lib. bdg. 120.00 (0-89356-504-0) Salem Pr.

***Masterplots Complete Cd-Rom (1999 Edition), 100 vols.** Ed. by Salem Press Staff. 1999. cd-rom 750.00 (0-89356-264-5) Salem Pr.

Masterplots Revised Category Edition: American Fiction, 3 vols., Set. rev. ed. Ed. by Frank N. Magill. LC 85-1936. 1532p. 1985. lib. bdg. 120.00 (0-89356-500-8) Salem Pr.

Masterplots Revised Category Edition: European Fiction, 3 vols., Set. rev. ed. Ed. by Frank N. Magill. LC 85-18297. 1482p. 1986. lib. bdg. 120.00 (0-89356-508-3) Salem Pr.

***Masterplots II.** Steven G. Kellman. LC 99-53295. 2000. write for info. (0-89356-872-4); write for info. (0-89356-873-2); write for info. (0-89356-874-0); write for info. (0-89356-875-9); write for info. (0-89356-876-7) Salem Pr.

***Masterplots II, 6 vols.** rev. ed. Ed. by Steven G. Kellman. LC 99-53295. (American Fiction Ser.). 3072p. 2000. lib. bdg. 425.00 (0-89356-871-6) Salem Pr.

Masterplots II: African American Literature, 3 vols., Set. Ed. by Frank N. Magill. LC 93-33876. 1568p. (YA). (gr. 9-12). 1994. lib. bdg. 275.00 (0-89356-594-6) Salem Pr.

Masterplots II: British & Commonwealth Fiction, 4 vols., Set. Frank N. Magill. LC 87-4639. 2024p. 1987. lib. bdg. 365.00 (0-89356-468-0) Salem Pr.

Masterplots II: Drama, 4 vols., Set. Ed. by Frank N. Magill. LC 89-10989. 1864p. 1990. lib. bdg. 365.00 (0-89356-491-5) Salem Pr.

Masterplots II: Juvenile & Young Adult Fiction, 4 vols., Set. Ed. by Frank N. Magill. LC 91-4509. 1792p. (YA). (gr. 6 up). 1991. lib. bdg. 365.00 (0-89356-579-2) Salem Pr.

Masterplots II: Juvenile & Young Adult Literature, Supplement, 1997, 3 vols. Frank N. Magill & Salem Press Editors. LC 96-39759. 1536p. (YA). (gr. 6-12). 1997. lib. bdg. 275.00 (0-89356-916-X) Salem Pr.

Masterplots II: Nonfiction, 4 vols., Set. Ed. by Frank N. Magill. LC 89-5877. 1810p. 1989. lib. bdg. 365.00 (0-89356-478-8) Salem Pr.

Masterplots II: Poetry, 6 vols., Set. Ed. by Frank N. Magill. LC 91-44341. 2630p. 1992. lib. bdg. 425.00 (0-89356-584-9) Salem Pr.

Masterplots II: Short Story, 6 vols., Set. Frank N. Magill. LC 86-22025. 2856p. 1986. lib. bdg. 425.00 (0-89356-461-3) Salem Pr.

Masterplots II: Short Story Series Supplement, 4 vols., Set. Ed. by Frank N. Magill. LC 88-6469. 1746p. (YA). (gr. 9-12). 1996. lib. bdg. 325.00 (0-89356-769-8) Salem Pr.

Masterplots II: Women's Literature, 6 vols. Ed. by Frank N. Magill. LC 94-25180. 2698p. 1995. lib. bdg. 500.00 (0-89356-898-8) Salem Pr.

***Masterplots II, Poetry Series Supplement, 3 vols.** Ed. by Salem Press Editors. 1344p. (YA). (gr. 9-12). 1998. lib. bdg. 225.00 (0-89356-625-X) Salem Pr.

Masters see Great Moments in Sports

Masters. Annie W. Besant. 54p. 1995. pap. 3.95 (81-7059-159-7) Theos Pub Hse.

Masters. Victor Terry. (Orig.). 1996. mass mkt. 5.95 (1-56333-418-6, Badboy) Masquerade.

Masters, Vol 2. Atrium. 1997. pap. 42.00 (84-8185-109-4) St. Martin.

Masters: Golf, Money & Power in Augusta, Georgia. Curt Sampson. LC 97-49143. 256p. 1998. 25.00 (0-679-45753-4) Villard Books.

M

An Asterisk (*) at the beginning of an entry indicates that the title is appearing for the first time.

***Masters: Golf, Money, & Power in Augusta, Georgia.** Curt Sampson. (Illus.). 320p. 1999. pap. 14.95 (*0-375-75337-0*) Villard Books.

Masters: Leonardo & Michelangelo - A Calendar Book, 1999. Beth Garbo. (Illus.). 106p. 1998. spiral bd. 12.95 (*1-892373-39-4*, 39-4) Especially Bks.

Masters: Leonardo & Michelangelo - A Calendar Book 2000. Beth Garbo. (Illus.). 106p. 1998. spiral bd. 12.95 (*1-892373-48-3*, 48-3) Especially Bks.

Masters & Friends. Paul Valery. Tr. by Martin Turnell. LC 56-9337. (Collected Works of Paul Valery: Vol. 9). 441p. 1968. reprint ed. pap. 136.80 (*0-608-02897-5*, 206396100008) Bks Demand.

Masters & Johnson on Sex & Human Loving. William H. Masters et al. 621p. 1988. pap. 21.95 (*0-316-50160-3*, Back Bay) Little.

Masters & Managers: The Study of Gender Relations in Urban Java. Norma Sullivan. 224p. 1995. pap. 24.95 (*1-86373-756-1*) Paul & Co Pubs.

Masters & Masterpieces of the Screen. C. W. Taylor. 1972. 300.00 (*0-87968-353-8*) Gordon Pr.

Masters & Men: The Human Story in the Mahatma Letters (A Fictional Account) Virginia Hanson. LC 79-3665. (Illus.). 1980. pap. 7.50 (*0-8356-0534-5*, Quest) Theos Pub Hse.

Masters & Servants. Pierre Michon. Tr. by Wyatt A. Mason from FRE. LC 97-24184. (Illus.). 192p. (Orig.). 1997. pap. 14.95 (*1-56279-103-6*) Mercury Hse Inc.

Masters & Servants on the Cape Eastern Frontier, 1760-1803. Susan Newton-King. LC 98-38423. (African Studies: No. 97). (Illus.). 275p. (C). 1999. text 64.95 (*0-521-48153-8*) Cambridge U Pr.

Masters & Slaves in the House of the Lord: Race & Religion in the American South, 1740-1870. John B. Boles. LC 88-6525. 264p. 1990. pap. 17.00 (*0-8131-0187-5*) U Pr of Ky.

Masters & Statesmen: The Political Culture of American Slavery. Kenneth S. Greenberg. LC 85-9786. (New Studies in American Intellectual & Cultural History). 207p. reprint ed. pap. 64.20 (*0-608-08806-4*, 206944500004) Bks Demand.

Masters & the Path. C. W. Leadbeater. 1998. pap. 24.95 (*81-7059-199-6*, Quest) Theos Pub Hse.

Masters & the Path. C. W. Leadbeater. 354p. 1998. reprint ed. pap. 27.50 (*0-7873-0545-6*) Hlth Research.

Masters & the Path. C. W. Leadbeater. 356p. 1996. reprint ed. pap. 24.95 (*1-56459-686-9*) Kessinger Pub.

Masters & the Path of Occultism see Mahatmas & Genuine Occultism

***Masters & the Way to Them (1912)** Annie W. Besant. 50p. 1998. reprint ed. pap. 9.95 (*0-7661-0166-5*) Kessinger Pub.

Masters & Their Music. William S. Mathews. LC 78-153364. reprint ed. 39.50 (*0-404-07209-7*) AMS Pr.

Master's Apprentice. James C. Perin & Joseph Sharp. 250p. 1996. 19.95 (*0-9644656-1-2*); pap. 5.95 (*0-9644656-2-0*) Deep Lingo.

Master's Assistant: A Complete Treatise on Freemasonry (1912) Delmar D. Darrah. 150p. 1998. reprint ed. pap. 17.95 (*0-7661-0192-4*) Kessinger Pub.

Masters' Book of Bonsai. Directors of the Japan Bonsai Association Staff. LC 67-12585. (Illus.). 144p. 1984. pap. 18.00 (*0-87011-453-0*) Kodansha.

Master's Book of Short Speeches. rev. ed. Walter E. Willets. xiii, 61p. 1993. reprint ed. pap. 6.50 (*0-88053-050-2*, M310) Macoy Pub.

Masters Book of Snook. Frank Sargeant. LC 97-70713. (Illus.). 160p. 1997. pap. 13.95 (*0-936513-48-9*) Larsens Outdoor.

Master's Bride. Suzannah Davis. 416p. (Orig.). 1993. mass mkt. 4.50 (*0-380-76821-6*, Avon Bks) Morrow Avon.

Masters Carpet. Edmond Ronayne. 15.95 (*0-685-41897-9*) Wehman.

Master's Carpet or Masonry & Baal-Worship Identical (1887) Edmond Ronayne. 280p. 1998. reprint ed. pap. 24.95 (*0-7661-0195-9*) Kessinger Pub.

Master's Cat: The Story of Charles Dickens as Told by His Cat. Eleanor Poe Barlow. (Illus.). 132p. (YA). (gr. 7 up). 1998. 24.00 (*0-9518525-3-1*) Dickens Bks.

Master's Cat: The Story of Charles Dickens as Told by His Cat. Eleanor Poe Barlow. (YA). 1999. pap. 16.50 (*1-880158-22-1*) J N Townsend.

Master's Choice: Mystery Stories by Today's Top Writers & the Masters Who Inspired Them. Ed. by Lawrence Block. LC 99-30270. 1999. 21.95 (*0-425-17031-4*, Prime Crime) Berkley Pub.

***Masters' Classroom! Apprentice Workbook.** Barbara Ann Rossi. (Illus.). 64p. 1999. pap. 13.95 (*0-9673957-1-2*) Lark Enter.

Masters' Counterpoints: A Suspense Novel. Larry Townsend. 216p. (Orig.). 1996. pap. 9.95 (*1-55583-394-2*) Alyson Pubns.

Masters Curricula in Educational Communications & Technology: A Descriptive Directory. 474p. 1985. 15.00 (*0-317-36898-2*); 10.00 (*0-317-36899-0*) Assn Ed Comm Tech.

Master's Degree. P. B. Wilson & Frank Wilson. LC 96-16556. 224p. (Orig.). 1996. pap. 9.99 (*1-56507-514-5*) Harvest Hse.

Master's Degree: Tradition, Diversity, Innovation. Judith S. Glazer. LC 86-72855. (ASHE-ERIC Higher Education Reports: No. 86-6). 129p. 1987. pap. 24.00 (*0-913317-33-0*) GWU Grad Schl E&HD.

Masters Family History, 1691 to 1989. Jack Masters. (Illus.). 576p. 1989. 37.50 (*0-9622761-0-3*) J Masters.

Masters for Classical Guitar - Bach. Ed. by Aaron Stang. 20p. (C). 1985. pap. text 7.50 (*0-7692-1291-3*, EL03081) Wrner Bros.

Master's Guide to Atlantic Salmon Fishing. Bill Cummings. LC 95-10516. (Illus.). 288p. 1995. pap. 34.95 (*0-07-015059-1*, Ragged Mntain) McGraw-Hill Prof.

Master's Guide to Basic Self-Defense: Progressive Retraining of the Reflexive Response. Hei Long. (Illus.). 124p. 1990. pap. 18.00 (*0-87364-574-X*) Paladin Pr.

Master's Guide to Building a Bamboo Fly Rod. 4th ed. Everett Garrison & Hoagy B. Carmichael. (Illus.). 296p. 1994. 75.00 (*0-9620609-7-6*) Meadow Run Pr.

***Master's Hand: Drawings & Manuscripts from the Morgan Library.** LC 98-36210. (Illus.). 335p. 1999. 65.00 (*3-7757-0754-9*, Pub. by Gerd Hatje) Dist Art Pubs.

Master's Hand: Drawings & Manuscripts from the Morgan Library, New York. Cara D. Denison et al. LC 98-36210. 1998. 29.95 (*0-87598-126-7*) Pierpont Morgan.

Master's Hand: Drawings & Manuscripts from the Pierpont Morgan Library, New York. Text by Cara Dufour Denison et al. (Illus.). 304p. 1999. 65.00 (*3-7757-0785-9*, Pub. by Gerd Hatje) Dist Art Pubs.

Master's Healing Touch. James W. Zackrison. LC 97-17258. 144p. 1997. pap. 8.99 (*0-8280-1298-9*) Review & Herald.

Masters in Early Childhood Education. Elkind. (C). 1998. 34.50 (*0-205-27113-8*) Allyn.

Masters in Modern Art. James W. Lane. LC 67-22100. (Essay Index Reprint Ser.). 1977. 19.95 (*0-8369-1332-9*) Ayer.

Masters in Modern German Literature. Otto E. Lessing. LC 67-23239. (Essay Index Reprint Ser.). 1977. 19.95 (*0-8369-0616-0*) Ayer.

Masters in Music, Set. Vols. 1-6, Nos. 1-36. reprint ed. 250.00 (*0-404-19532-6*) AMS Pr.

Masters in Pieces: The Art of Russell Connor. Russell Connor. LC 96-28289. 1997. pap. 49.95 (*1-885203-28-4*) Jrny Editions.

Master's Indwelling. Andrew Murray. 178p. 1983. mass mkt. 5.99 (*0-88368-121-8*) Whitaker Hse.

Master's Manual: A Handbook of Erotic Dominance. Jack Rinella. Ed. by Joseph Bean. LC 93-74629. 200p. (Orig.). 1994. pap. 14.95 (*1-881943-03-8*) Daedalus Pub.

Master's Memories. Cal Brown. LC 98-30971. 133p. 1998. 19.95 (*1-886947-46-5*) Sleepng Bear.

Master's Men. large type ed. William Barclay. LC 85-6395. 224p. 1985. reprint ed. pap. 8.95 (*0-8027-2496-5*) Walker & Co.

Master's Minstrel: The Christian Confession of a Soviet Singer. Yury Bogachev. Tr. by Barry Stronge from RUS. LC 95-158613. 144p. (Orig.). 1995. pap. 8.95 (*1-883893-03-8*) WinePress Pub.

Masters More Challenge. 1994. pap. 17.95 incl. audio compact disk (*0-7935-2438-5*, 00699392) H Leonard.

Masters Next to God. Bernard Edwards. 149p. (C). 1986. 30.00 (*0-86383-242-3*, Pub. by Gomer Pr); pap. 30.00 (*0-86383-427-2*, Pub. by Gomer Pr) St Mut.

***Masters of a Tired World.** 1998. pap. 26.95 (*0-273-63559-X*) F T P H.

***Masters of All They Surveyed: Exploration, Geography & a British El Dorado.** D. Graham Burnett. LC 99-98199. 1999. 45.00 (*0-226-08120-6*) U Ch Pr.

Masters of American Modernism: Vignettes from the Katz Collection. Jay Cantor et al. (Illus.). 48p. (Orig.). 1995. pap. 20.00 (*0-936270-34-9*) CA St U LB Art.

Masters of American Piano Music. Ed. by Maurice Hinson. 64p. 1992. pap. 8.50 (*0-88284-975-1*, 4603) Alfred Pub.

Masters of American Sculpture: The Figurative Tradition. Donald M. Reynolds. (Illus.). 276p. 1993. 67.50 (*1-55859-276-8*) Abbeville Pr.

Masters of Animals: Oral Traditions of the Tolupan Indians, Honduras. Anne Chapman. (Library of Anthropology). 312p. 1992. pap. text 26.00 (*2-88124-565-X*) Gordon & Breach.

Masters of Animals: Oral Traditions of the Tolupan Indians, Honduras, Vol. 10. Anne Chapman. LC 92-11055. (Library of Anthropology). 312p. 1992. text 58.00 (*2-88124-560-9*) Gordon & Breach.

Masters of Art. Ed. by Nal-Dutton Staff. 1999. pap. 22.50 (*0-525-45838-7*) NAL.

Masters of Art: The World's Great Artists, Their Lives & Works. Natalie Baker. 1987. 17.98 (*0-88365-716-3*) Galahad Bks.

***Masters of Atlantis.** Charles Portis. LC 99-86846. 272p. 2000. pap. 14.95 (*1-58567-021-9*, Pub. by Overlook Pr) Penguin Putnam.

Masters of Battle. John Wilcox. (Illus.). 224p. 1998. pap. 17.95 (*1-85409-454-8*, Pub. by Arms & Armour) Sterling.

Masters of Battle: Selected Great Warrior Classes. John Wilcox. (Illus.). 224p. 1996. 29.95 (*1-85409-269-3*, Pub. by Arms & Armour) Sterling.

Masters of Bedlam: The Transformation of the Mad-Doctoring Trade. Andrew T. Scull et al. 408p. 1996. 35.00 (*0-691-03411-7*, Pub. by Princeton U Pr) Cal Prin Full Svc.

Masters of Bedlam: The Transformation of the Mad-Doctoring Trade. Andrew Scull et al. 374p. 1996. pap. text 17.95 (*0-691-00251-7*, Pub. by Princeton U Pr) Cal Prin Full Svc.

Masters of Biology. 5th ed. Mader. 1995. 43.00 (*0-697-21831-7*, WCB McGr Hill) McGrw-H Hghr Educ.

Masters of British Painting, 1800 to 1950. Museum of Modern Art Library Staff & Andrew C. Ritchie. 1981. 24.95 (*0-405-12884-3*) Ayer.

Masters of Candlelight. Christopher Wright. LC 96-181552. (Illus.). 136p. 1997. 32.95 (*3-9803285-9-7*, Pub. by Art Bks Intl) Partners Pubs Grp.

Masters of Ceremony. Ray R. Cowdery & Josephine N. Cowdery. (Illus.). 128p. 1998. reprint ed. pap. 20.00 (*0-910667-38-1*) USM.

Masters of Change: How Great Leaders in Every Age Thrived in Turbulent Times. William M. Boast & Benjamin Martin. 168p. 1997. 22.95 (*1-890009-07-5*) Exec Excell.

Masters of Color & Light: Home, Sargent, & the American Watercolor Movement. Linda S. Ferber & B. Gallali. LC 98-10924. 240p. 1998. 55.00 (*1-56098-572-0*) Smithsonian.

Masters of Contemporary Brazilian Song: MPB, 1965-1985. Charles A. Perrone. (Illus.). 293p. 1989. 27.95 (*0-292-75102-8*) U of Tex Pr.

Masters of Contemporary Brazilian Song: MPB, 1965-1985. Charles A. Perrone. (Illus.). 293p. (C). 1993. pap. 15.95 (*0-292-76550-9*) U of Tex Pr.

Masters of Darkness, No. 3. Dennis Etchison. 1991. pap. 3.95 (*0-8125-1766-0*) Tor Bks.

Masters of Deceit. J. Edgar Hoover. 1994. reprint ed. lib. bdg. 35.95 (*1-56849-294-4*) Buccaneer Bks.

Masters of Deception: Gang That Ruled Cyberspace, The. Michelle Slatalla & Joshua Quittner. 240p. 1996. pap. 15.00 (*0-06-092694-5*) HarpC.

Masters of Deception: The Gang That Ruled Cyberspace. Michelle Slatalla & Joshua Quittner. 225p. 1999. reprint ed. text 23.00 (*0-7881-6265-9*) DIANE Pub.

Masters of Deception: The Worldwide White Collar Crime Crisis. Louis R. Mizell. LC 96-1921. 253p. 1996. 24.95 (*0-471-13355-8*) Wiley.

***Masters of Disasters: Irreverent Look at the Other Side of Americas Lifesavers.** Chris St. John & Lou Jordan. (Illus.). 200p. 2000. pap. write for info. (*1-887321-01-2*) Emerg Trng Assocs.

Masters of Disguise: A Natural History of Chameleons. James Martin. (Illus.). 192p. 1992. 24.95 (*0-8160-2618-1*) Facts on File.

***Masters of Dutch Art.** Pieter Brueghel. (Illus.). 140p. 1999. 19.95 (*3-8290-2579-3*) Konemann.

***Masters of Dutch Art.** Rogier Van Der Weyden. 1999. 19.95 (*3-8290-1626-3*) Konemann.

Masters of Enchantment: The Lives & Legends of the Mahasiddhas. Tr. by Keith Dowman. (Illus.). 192p. 1989. pap. 19.95 (*0-89281-224-9*, Destiny Bks) Inner Tradit.

Masters of English Literature. Edwin W. Chubb. LC 67-23194. (Essay Index Reprint Ser.). 1977. 23.95 (*0-8369-0303-X*) Ayer.

Masters of English Literature. Stephen L. Gwynn. LC 71-177958. (Essay Index Reprint Ser.). 1977. reprint ed. 23.95 (*0-8369-2552-1*) Ayer.

Masters of English Music. Charles Willeby. LC 72-5561. (Essay Index Reprint Ser.). 1977. reprint ed. 27.95 (*0-8369-7280-5*) Ayer.

Masters of Enterprise: Giants of American Business from John Jacob Astor & J. P. Morgan to Bill Gates & Oprah Winfrey. H. W. Brands. LC 98-51054. 368p. 1999. 24.50 (*0-684-85473-2*) Free Pr.

Masters of Eternal Night. Bruce R. Cordell. 1998. pap. 9.95 (*0-7869-1253-7*, Pub. by TSR Inc) Random.

Masters of Everon. Gordon Rupert Dickson. 1992. mass mkt. 3.99 (*0-8125-0394-5*, Pub. by Tor Bks) St Martin.

Masters of Fantasy. G. Carr. 1992. 9.98 (*0-88365-786-4*) Galahad Bks.

Masters of Fantasy: 31 Strange & Imaginative Tales from the Masters in the Art. Ed. by Martin H. Greenburg. 528p. 1994. pap. 12.95 (*0-88486-094-9*, Bristol Park Bks) Arrowood Pr.

Masters of Fear, Vol. 2. R. Mathews-Danzer. Ed. by Rinaldo Mathews. (Wizard, Ghost & Heroes Ser.). (Illus.). 165p. 2000. pap. 18.00 (*1-888417-03-X*) Dimefast.

***Masters of Fingerpicking Guitar Intermediate to Advanced Level.** Ed. by Stefan Grossman. 96p. 1998. spiral bd. 17.95 incl. audio compact disk (*0-7866-3455-3*) Mel Bay.

Masters of Flint. A. J. Forrest. 142p. 1990. 30.00 (*0-86138-015-0*, Pub. by T Dalton); pap. 24.00 (*0-86138-016-9*, Pub. by T Dalton) St Mut.

Masters of French Literature. George M. Harper. LC 68-22095. (Essay Index Reprint Ser.). 1977. 20.95 (*0-8369-0512-1*) Ayer.

Masters of French Literature. Horatio E. Smith. LC 69-17589. (Essay Index Reprint Ser.). 1977. 18.95 (*0-8369-0092-8*) Ayer.

Masters of French Music. Arthur Hervey. LC 72-13993. (Essay Index Reprint Ser.). (Illus.). 1977. reprint ed. 29.95 (*0-518-10014-6*) Ayer.

Masters of Greatness: The God-Mind Plan for Saving Both Planet & Man. Jean K. Foster. LC 90-90149. (God-Mind Bks.: Bk. 6). 162p. (Orig.). 1990. pap. 9.95 (*0-9626366-0-6*) Teamup.

Masters of Illusion. large type ed. Mary-Ann T. Smith. 282p. 1995. pap. 19.95 (*0-7838-1187-X*, G K Hall Lrg Type) Mac Lib Ref.

Masters of Illusion: The World Bank & the Poverty of Nations. Catherine Caufield. LC 96-16804. 384p. 1995. 27.50 (*0-8050-2875-7*) H Holt & Co.

Masters of Instrumental Blues Guitar. Donald Garwood. (Illus.). 78p. 1968. pap. 15.95 (*0-8256-0001-4*, OK61960, Oak) Music Sales.

Masters of International Thought. Kenneth W. Thompson. LC 79-20030. xii, 250p. 1980. text 35.00 (*0-8071-0580-5*); pap. text 18.95 (*0-8071-0581-3*) La State U Pr.

Masters of Italian Music. Richard A. Streatfield. LC 72-3381. (Essay Index Reprint Ser.). 1977. reprint ed. 27.95 (*0-8369-2929-2*) Ayer.

Masters of Italian Opera. Philip Gossett. 1997. pap. 16.95 (*0-393-30361-6*) Norton.

Masters of Japanese Calligraphy 8th-19th Century. Yoshiaki Shimizu & John M. Rosenfield. LC 84-82053. (Illus.). 340p. 1984. 75.00 (*0-913720-57-7*) Beil.

***Masters of Jazz Guitar: The Story of the Players & Their Music.** Ed. by Charles Alexander. (Illus.). 192p. 1999. 39.95 (*0-87930-592-4*) Miller Freeman.

***Masters of Jazz Saxophone: The Story of the Players & Their Music.** Ed. by Dave Gelly. (Illus.). 192p. 2000. pap. 39.95 (*0-87930-622-X*, M Freeman Bks) Miller Freeman.

Masters of Legalized Confusion & Their Puppets. Hans J. Schneider. LC 78-12609. 32p. 1979. pap. 2.95 (*0-930294-11-4*) World Wide OR.

Masters of Lens & Light: A Checklist of Major Cinematographers & Their Feature Films. William Darby. LC 91-20656. (Illus.). 1071p. 1991. 110.00 (*0-8108-2454-X*) Scarecrow.

Masters of Light: Conversations with Contemporary Cinematographers. Dennis Schaefer & Larry Salvato. LC 84-2512. 368p. 1985. pap. 19.95 (*0-520-05336-2*, Pub. by U CA Pr) Cal Prin Full Svc.

Masters of Madness: Social Origins of the American Psychiatric Profession. Constance M. McGovern. LC 85-40491. 278p. reprint ed. pap. 86.20 (*0-608-09090-5*, 206972400005) Bks Demand.

Masters of Mahamudra: Songs & Histories of the Eighty-Four Buddhist Siddhas. Keith Dowman. LC 85-20771. (SUNY Series in Buddhist Studies). 454p. (C). 1986. text 64.50 (*0-88706-158-3*); pap. text 21.95 (*0-88706-160-5*) State U NY Pr.

Masters of Medicine: An Historical Sketch of the College of Medical Sciences of the University of Minnesota, 1888-1966. J. Arthur Myers. LC 68-8890. (Illus.). 942p. 1968. 22.50 (*0-87527-058-1*); pap. 17.50 (*0-87527-140-5*) Green.

Masters of Meditation & Miracles: Lives of the Great Buddhist Masters of India & Tibet. Tulku Thondup. 400p. pap. 22.95 (*1-57062-509-3*, Pub. by Shambhala Pubns) Random.

Masters of Meditation & Miracles: The Longchen Nyingthig Lineage of Tibetan Buddhism. Tulku Thondup. 478p. 1996. 35.00 (*1-57062-113-6*, Pub. by Shambhala Pubns) Random.

Masters of Modern Art. Walter Pach. LC 72-5633. (Essay Index Reprint Ser.). 1977. reprint ed. 27.95 (*0-8369-7295-3*) Ayer.

Masters of Music. (YA). 1991. pap. 17.00 incl. audio (*0-89898-664-8*, BMR04075) Wrner Bros.

Masters of Music. Arvid C. Anderson. LC 70-117320. (Biography Index Reprint Ser.). 1977. 19.95 (*0-8369-8012-3*) Ayer.

***Masters of Music: Conversations with Berklee Greats.** Mark Smalley. (Illus.). 2000. pap. 24.95 (*0-634-00642-8*, Berklee Pr) H Leonard.

Masters of Music Series Assortment. Barron's Educational Editors. 1999. 14.95 (*0-7641-7314-6*) Barron.

Masters of Mystery & Detective Fiction. J. Randolph Cox. (Magill Bibliographies Ser.). 281p. 1989. 42.00 (*0-8108-2804-9*) Scarecrow.

***Masters of Networking: Building Relationships for Your Pocketbook & Soul.** Ivan R. Misner. 2000. pap. 18.95 (*1-885167-48-2*) Bard Press.

Masters of Old Time Fiddling. Miles Krassen. 1983. pap. 21.95 (*0-8256-0250-5*, Oak) Music Sales.

Masters of Orion: Ultimate Strategy Guide. Alan Emrich. LC 93-86920. (Illus.). 400p. 1994. pap. 19.95 (*1-55958-507-2*) Prima Pub.

Masters of Photography: H. Callahan. Contrib. by Jonathan Williams. LC 98-86908. 1999. text 12.50 (*0-89381-821-6*) Aperture.

***Masters of Photography: W. Smith.** Contrib. by Jim Hughes. LC 98-86912. 96p. 1999. text 12.50 (*0-89381-836-4*) Aperture.

Masters of Popular Painting. Holger Cahill et al. LC 66-26120. (Museum of Modern Art Publications in Reprint). 1967. reprint ed. 20.95 (*0-405-01524-0*) Ayer.

Masters of Science Fiction, Vol. I. Isaac Asimov. 23.95 (*0-88411-585-2*) Amereon Ltd.

Masters of Seventeenth-Century Dutch Genre Painting. Peter C. Sutton et al. LC 84-5798. (Illus.). 384p. 1984. pap. 26.95 (*0-87633-057-X*) Phila Mus Art.

Masters of Small Worlds: Yeoman Households, Gender Relations & the Political Culture of the Antebellum South Carolina Low Country. Stephanie McCurry. 344p. 1995. text 60.00 (*0-19-507236-7*) OUP.

Masters of Small Worlds: Yeoman Households, Gender Relations, & the Political Culture of the Antebellum South Carolina Low Country. Stephanie McCurry. (Illus.). 344p. 1997. reprint ed. pap. 19.95 (*0-19-511795-6*) OUP.

Masters of Social Psychology: Freud, Mead, Lewin, & Skinner. James A. Schellenberg. 152p. 1979. pap. text 17.95 (*0-19-502622-5*) OUP.

Masters of Sociological Thought: Ideas in Historical & Social Context. 2nd ed. Lewis A. Coser. (Illus.). 611p. (C). 1977. text 72.00 (*0-15-555130-2*, Pub. by Harcourt Coll Pubs); write for info. (*0-318-52970-X*) Harcourt Coll Pubs.

Masters of Soviet Cinema: Vsevolod Pudovkin, Dziga Vertov, Alexander Kovzhenko, Sergei Mikhailovich Eisenstein. Herbert Marshall. (Illus.). 280p. 1983. 35.00 (*0-7100-9287-3*, Routledge Thoemms) Routledge.

Masters of Space No. 2: The Alien Web. Robert E. Vardeman. 176p. 1987. pap. 2.95 (*0-380-75005-8*, Avon Bks) Morrow Avon.

Masters of Space No. 3: A Plague in Paradise. Robert E. Vardeman. 176p. (Orig.). 1987. pap. 2.95 (*0-380-75006-6*, Avon Bks) Morrow Avon.

Masters of Suspense. Ellery Queen. 1992. 9.98 (*0-88365-787-2*) Galahad Bks.

Masters of Tatoo. Gregor Von Glinski. (Illus.). 144p. 1998. 50.00 (*3-908161-38-X*) Abbeville Pr.

Masters of Teras Kasi: The Official Strategy Guide. Anthony James. LC 97-69793. 80p. 1997. per. 12.99 (*0-7615-1179-2*) Prima Pub.

***Masters of the Art.** Dierdre Brooks & Adam McCandliss. (Mage Ser.). (Illus.). 88p. 1999. pap. 13.95 (*1-56504-427-4*, 4017) White Wolf.

An Asterisk (*) at the beginning of an entry indicates that the title is appearing for the first time.

Masters of the Art of Command. Martin Blumenson & James L. Stokesbury. (Quality Paperbacks Ser.). (Illus.). 410p. 1990. reprint ed. pap. 14.95 (*0-306-80403-4*) Da Capo.
Masters of the Chicago Blues Harp. Transcribed by David Barrett. 88p. 1997. pap. 14.95 (*0-7866-2884-7*, 96476) Mel Bay.
Masters of the Crafts: Recipients of the Saidye Bronfman Award for Excellence in the Crafts, 1977-86. Stephen Inglis & Kristin Rothschild. (Illus.). 144p. 1989. 24.95 (*0-660-10788-0*, Pub. by CN Mus Civilization) U of Wash Pr.
Masters of the Dew. Jacques Roumain. LC 98-140605. (Caribbean Writers Ser.). 192p. (C). 1978. pap. 10.95 (*0-435-98745-3*, 98745) Heinemann.
Masters of the Diamond: Interviews with Players Who Began Their Careers More Than Fifty Years Ago. Rich Westcott. LC 94-179. (Illus.). 199p. 1994. pap. 25.95 (*0-7864-0020-X*) McFarland & Co.
Masters of the Dream: The Strength & Betrayal of Black America. Alan L. Keyes. 1996. pap. 12.00 (*0-688-14618-X*, Quil) HarperTrade.
Masters of the Dream: The Strength & Betrayal of Black America. Alan L. Keyes. LC 94-28840. 1995. 23.00 (*0-688-09599-2*, Wm Morrow) Morrow Avon.
Masters of the Drum: Black Literature Across the Continuum, 175. Robert E. Fox. LC 94-29836. (Contributions in Afro-American & African Studies: Vol. 175). 200p. 1995. 55.00 (*0-313-29296-5*, Greenwood Pr) Greenwood.
Masters of the English Novel. Richard Burton. LC 79-90620. (Essay Index Reprint Ser.). 1977. 23.95 (*0-8369-1252-7*) Ayer.
Masters of the French Art Song: Translations of the Complete Songs of Chausson, Debussy, Duparc, Favre & Ravel. Timothy LeVan. LC 91-41123. 457p. 1991. 50.00 (*0-8108-2522-8*) Scarecrow.
***Masters of the Futures: Top Players Reveal the Inside Story of the World's Futures Markets.** Scott Slutsky. LC 98-46144. 221p. 1999. 27.95 (*0-07-134111-0*) McGraw.
***Masters of the Graviton: Forgotten Futures Adventures for Log Of.** Marcus L. Rowland. (Illus.). 2000. pap. 18.00 (*0-9668926-5-8*) Heliograph Inc.
Masters of the House: A Novel of Suspense. Robert Barnard. LC 94-5853. 224p. 1994. 20.00 (*0-684-19728-6*, Scribners Ref) Mac Lib Ref.
Masters of the House: A Novel of Suspense. Robert Barnard. 224p. 1996. mass mkt. 4.99 (*0-380-72511-8*, Avon Bks) Morrow Avon.
Masters of the House: A Novel of Suspense. large type ed. Robert Barnard. 319p. 1994. lib. bdg. 22.95 (*0-7862-0329-3*) Thorndike Pr.
Masters of the House: Congressional Leadership over Two Centuries. Ed. by Roger H. Davidson et al. LC 98-11326. (Transforming American Politics Ser.). 360p. (C). 1998. pap. text 30.00 (*0-8133-6895-2*, Pub. by Westview) HarpC.
Masters of the Italian Art Song: Word-by-Word & Poetic Translations of the Complete Songs for Voice & Piano. Timothy LeVan. LC 90-8955. 333p. 1990. 45.00 (*0-8108-2363-2*) Scarecrow.
Masters of the Italic Letter: Twenty-Two Exemplars from the Sixteenth Century. Kathryn A. Atkins. LC 85-45968. (Illus.). 192p. 1988. 45.00 (*0-87923-594-2*) Godine.
Masters of the Japanese Print: Moronobu to Utamaro. Margaret Gentles. LC 74-27414. (Asia Society Ser.). (Illus.). 1976. reprint ed. lib. bdg. 36.95 (*0-405-06563-9*) Ayer.
Masters of the Keyboard. Donald Brook. LC 75-114479. 184p. 1971. reprint ed. lib. bdg. 45.00 (*0-8371-4768-9*, BRMK, Greenwood Pr) Greenwood.
Masters of the Keyboard. 2nd ed. Donald Brook. LC 76-148206. (Biography Index Reprint Ser.). 1977. 21.95 (*0-8369-8053-0*) Ayer.
Masters of the Keyboard: A Brief Survey of Pianoforte Music. Willi Apel. LC 47-12245. 335p. reprint ed. pap. 103.90 (*0-7837-4135-9*, 205795800011) Bks Demand.
Masters of the Keyboard: Individual Style Elements in the Piano Music of Bach, Haydn, Mozart, Beethoven, & Schubert. enl. ed. Konrad Wolff. LC 89-45570. (Illus.). 328p. 1990. 35.00 (*0-253-36458-2*); pap. 15.95 (*0-253-20567-0*, MB-567) Ind U Pr.
Masters of the Keyboard: Music Book Index. Donald Brook. 183p. 1993. reprint ed. lib. bdg. 69.00 (*0-7812-9571-8*) Rprt Serv.
Masters of the Links. Ed. by Geoff Shackelford. LC 97-35486. 250p. 1997. 24.95 (*1-886947-27-9*) Sleeping Bear.
***Masters of the Millennium.** Caroline Childers. (Illus.). 244p. 2000. 50.00 (*0-8478-2276-1*) Rizzoli Intl.
***Masters of the Millennium.** Robert Hartman. 256p. 1999. 20.00 (*1-58382-038-8*, Pub. by Sports Masters) Partners-West.
Masters of the Nyingma Lineage. unabridged ed. Leslie Bradburn. Ed. by Tarthang Tulku. LC 95-46695. (Crystal Mirror Ser.: Vol. 11). (Illus.). 500p. (Orig.). 1996. pap. 25.00 (*0-89800-275-3*) Dharma Pub.
Masters of the Ocean Realm: Whales, Dolphins, & Porpoises. John Heyning. LC 95-37435. (Illus.). 112p. (C). 1995. pap. 17.95 (*0-295-97487-7*) U of Wash Pr.
Masters of the Orchestra from Bach to Prokofieff. Louis L. Biancolli & Herbert F. Peyser. LC 70-94578. 481p. 1969. reprint ed. lib. bdg. 75.00 (*0-8371-2545-6*, BIMO, Greenwood Pr) Greenwood.
Masters of the Path: A History of the Nimatullahi Sufi Order. 2nd ed. Javad Nurbakhsh. LC 80-80902. (Illus.). 130p. 1980. pap. 8.95 (*0-933546-03-3*) KNP.
Masters of the Peaks. Joseph A. Altsheler. 1990. reprint ed. lib. bdg. 20.95 (*0-89968-464-5*) Buccaneer Bks.
Masters of the Peaks: A Story of the Great North Woods. Joseph A. Altsheler. 311p. reprint ed. lib. bdg. 24.95 (*0-88411-938-6*) Amereon Ltd.
Masters of the Plectrum Guitar. William Bay. 280p. 1995. pap. 29.95 (*0-7866-0267-8*, 95293) Mel Bay.
Masters of the Sea: British Marine Watercolors, 1650-1930. Roger Quarm & Scott Wilcox. (Illus.). 96p. 1990. text 29.95 (*0-7148-2490-9*) Phaidon Pr.
Masters of the Sonatina, Vol. 3. Ed. by Maurice Hinson. 64p. 1986. pap. 5.95 (*0-7390-0783-1*, 2208) Alfred Pub.
Masters of the Spiritual Life: St. Augustine to St. Therese of Lisieux. John A. Hardon. LC 89-81978. (Great Catholic Books Home Study Course). 80p. 1990. write for info. (*0-9625211-0-8*) Inter Mirifica.
Masters of the Spiritual Life, 1916. F. W. Drake. 169p. 1996. reprint ed. pap. 17.95 (*1-56459-559-5*) Kessinger Pub.
Masters of the Telecaster. (YA). 1996. pap. 34.95 incl. audio (*0-89724-806-6*, GF9512AT) Wrner Bros.
Masters of the Telecaster. Arlen Roth. Ed. by Aaron Stang. (Illus.). 188p. (Orig.). (YA). 1996. pap. 34.95 incl. audio compact disk (*0-89724-805-8*, GF9512CD) Wrner Bros.
Masters Of The Universe. Kadlec. text 32.00 (*0-471-62352-0*) Wiley.
***Masters Of The Universe.** Daniel J. Kadlec. 288p. 2000. pap. 15.00 (*0-88730-932-1*, HarpBusn) HarpInfo.
***Masters of the Universe? NATO's Balkan Crusade.** Tariq Ali. Ed. by Harold Pinter et al. 460p. 2000. 65.00 (*1-85984-752-8*, Pub. by Verso) Norton.
***Masters of the Universe: NATO's Balkan Crusade.** Tariq Ali. Ed. by Harold Pinter et al. 460p. 2000. pap. 20.00 (*1-85984-269-0*, Pub. by Verso) Norton.
Masters of the Universe: Winning Strategies of America's Greatest Deal Makers. Daniel Kadlec. LC HC102.5.A2K34 1999. (Illus.). 288p. 1999. 26.00 (*0-88730-933-X*, HarpBusn) HarpInfo.
Masters of Their Craft: Tradition & Innovation in the Australian Contemporary Decorative Arts. Noris Ioannou. (Illus.). 264p. 1997. text 85.00 (*90-5703-281-3*) Gordon & Breach.
Masters of Time: How Wormholes, Snakewood & Assaults on the Big Bang Have Brought Mystery Back to the Universe. John Boslough. (Illus.). 320p. 1992. write for info. (*0-318-68854-9*) Addison-Wesley.
***Masters of Traditional Arts: A Biographical Dictionary & Curriculum Guide, 2 Vols.** Documentary Arts Inc. 2001. lib. bdg. 175.00 (*1-57607-240-1*) ABC-CLIO.
***Masters of Truth in Archaic Greece.** Marcel Detienne. 1999. pap. 16.00 (*0-942299-86-8*) Zone Bks.
Masters of Truth in Archaic Greece. Marcel Detienne & Pierre Vidal-Naquet. Tr. by Janet Lloyd from FRE. 232p. 1996. 24.00 (*0-942299-85-X*) Zone Bks.
***Masters of War: Classical Strategic Thought.** 3rd rev. ed. Ed. by Michael I. Handel. 470p. 2000. 57.50 (*0-7146-5091-9*, Pub. by F Cass Pubs) Intl Spec Bk.
***Masters of War: Classical Strategic Thought.** 3rd rev. expanded ed. Michael I. Handel. LC 00-35874. 470p. 2000. pap. 26.50 (*0-7146-8132-6*) Intl Spec Bk.
Masters of War: Classical Strategic Thought: Sun Tzu, Clausewitz, Jomini & Machiavelli. 2nd enl. rev. ed. Michael I. Handel. LC 95-21167. (Illus.). 320p. (C). 1996. 49.50 (*0-7146-4674-1*, Pub. by F Cass Pubs); pap. 24.95 (*0-7146-4205-3*, Pub. by F Cass Pubs) Intl Spec Bk.
Masters of War: Military Dissent & Politics in the Vietnam Era. Robert Buzzanco. 400p. (C). 1996. text 39.95 (*0-521-48046-9*) Cambridge U Pr.
Masters of War: Military Dissent & Politics in the Vietnam Era. Robert Buzzanco. 384p. 1997. pap. 18.95 (*0-521-59940-7*) Cambridge U Pr.
Masters of Wisdom: An Esoteric History of the Spiritual Unfolding of Life on This Planet. John Bennett. 192p. 1996. pap. 18.00 (*0-614-21310-X*, 1455) Kazi Pubns.
Masters of Wisdom: An Esoteric History of the Spiritual Unfolding of Life on This Planet. 2nd ed. John G. Bennett. 192p. 1999. pap. 20.00 (*1-881408-01-9*) Bennett Bks.
Masters of World Painting in the Museums of the Soviet Union. E. Marchenko. (Illus.). 160p. 1975. 59.95 (*0-8464-0617-9*) Beekman Pubs.
Master's Perspective on Contemporary Issues, Vol. 2. Ed. by Robert L. Thomas. LC 98-27365. (Master's Perspective Ser.). 272p. 1998. pap. text 12.99 (*0-8254-3181-6*) Kregel.
Master's Perspective on Difficult Passages, Vol. 1. Ed. by Robert L. Thomas. LC 98-26787. (Master's Perspective Ser.). 288p. 1998. pap. text 12.99 (*0-8254-3180-8*) Kregel.
Master's Plan: As the Artist Sees It. Walt Crawford. (Illus.). 128p. (Orig.). 1989. pap. 6.95 (*0-317-93462-7*) HEPC Inc.
Master's Plan for Making Disciples: Every Christian an Effective Witness through an Enabling Church. 2nd ed. Win Arn & Charles Arn. LC 97-35109. 176p. 1998. pap. 10.99 (*0-8010-9051-2*) Baker Bks.
Master's Plan for the Church. John MacArthur, Jr. pap. 12.99 (*0-8024-7841-7*, 213) Moody.
Master's Plan of Prayer. Leslie B. Flynn. LC 95-7845. 192p. 1995. pap. 10.99 (*0-8254-2641-3*, 95-024) Kregel.
Masters Racewalking: American Coaches & Athletes Share Ideas on Technique, Training & Racing. Elaine P. Ward. LC 95-71241. (Illus.). 250p. (Orig.). 1996. pap. 14.95 (*1-884647-03-0*) N A R F.
Masters Repetition: Poetry, Culture, & Work in the Thomson, Wordsworth, Shelley & Emerson. Steinman. LC 98-5081. 288p. 1998. text 49.95 (*0-312-21141-4*) St Martin.
Masters Revealed: Madame Blavatsky & the Myth of the Great White Lodge. K. Paul Johnson. LC 93-47226. (SUNY Series in Western Esoteric Traditions). 288p. (C). 1994. pap. text 18.95 (*0-7914-2064-7*) State U NY Pr.
Masters Revealed: Madame Blavatsky & the Myth of the Great White Lodge. K. Paul Johnson. LC 93-47226. (SUNY Series in Western Esoteric Traditions). 288p. (C). 1994. text 54.50 (*0-7914-2063-9*) State U NY Pr.
Masters' Secrets of Bowhunting Deer: Secret Tactics from Master Bowmen. John E. Phillips. LC 93-78226. (Illus.). 160p. (Orig.). 1993. pap. text 9.95 (*0-936513-34-9*) Larsens Outdoor.
Masters' Secrets of Catfishing. John Phillips. LC 93-79799. (Illus.). 160p. (Orig.). 1993. pap. text 9.95 (*0-936513-44-6*) Larsens Outdoor.
Masters' Secrets of Crappie Fishing. John E. Phillips. LC 92-74324. (Fishing Library). (Illus.). 160p. (Orig.). (C). 1992. pap. text 9.95 (*0-936513-29-2*) Larsens Outdoor.
Masters' Secrets of Deer Hunting. John Phillips. LC 91-90327. (Deer Hunting Library). 160p. (Orig.). 1991. pap. 11.95 (*0-936513-14-4*) Larsens Outdoor.
Masters' Secrets of Turkey Hunting. John E. Phillips. LC 91-76443. (Turkey Hunting Ser.). (Illus.). 160p. (Orig.). 1991. pap. 11.95 (*0-936513-18-7*) Larsens Outdoor.
Masters Series, 6 vols. write for info. (*0-89381-837-2*) Aperture.
Masters, Slaves, & Subjects: The Culture of Power in the South Carolina Low Country, 1740-1790. Robert Olwell. LC 97-53061. (Illus.). 296p. 1998. text 49.95 (*0-8014-3488-2*) Cornell U Pr.
Masters, Slaves & Subjects: The Culture of Power in the South Carolina Low Country, 1740-1790. Robert Olwell. LC 97-53061. (Illus.). 296p. 1998. pap. 17.95 (*0-8014-8491-X*) Cornell U Pr.
Masters Speak. Ruth E. Norman. (Tesla Speaks Ser.: Vol. 8, Pt. 1). (Illus.). 320p. 1975. 16.00 (*0-932642-30-6*) Unarius Acad Sci.
Masters Speak. Ruth E. Norman et al. (Tesla Speaks Ser.: Vol. 8, Pt. 2). (Illus.). 285p. 1976. 16.00 (*0-932642-29-2*) Unarius Acad Sci.
Masters' Theses in Anthropology: A Bibliography of Theses from United States Colleges & Universities. David R. McDonald. LC 77-7867. (Bibliographies Ser.). 460p. 1977. 15.00 (*0-87536-217-6*) HRAFP.
Master's Theses in Library Science, 1970-1974. Shirley Magnotti. LC 75-8232. iii, 198p. 1976. 35.00 (*0-87875-100-9*) Whitston Pub.
Masters Theses in the Pure & Applied Sciences: Accepted by Colleges & Universities of the United States & Canada, Vol. 30. Ed. by Wade H. Shafer. LC 58-62673. (Illus.). 418p. (C). 1988. text 179.00 (*0-306-42790-7*, Kluwer Plenum) Kluwer Academic.
Masters Theses in the Pure & Applied Sciences: Accepted by Colleges & Universities of the United States & Canada, Vol. 31. Ed. by Wade H. Shafer. LC 58-62673. (Illus.). 390p. (C). 1988. text 179.00 (*0-306-43039-8*, Kluwer Plenum) Kluwer Academic.
Masters Theses in the Pure & Applied Sciences: Accepted by Colleges & Universities of the United States & Canada, Vol. 32. Ed. by Wade H. Shafer. LC 58-62673. (Illus.). 414p. (C). 1989. text 179.00 (*0-306-43504-7*, Kluwer Plenum) Kluwer Academic.
Masters Theses in the Pure & Applied Sciences: Accepted by Colleges & Universities of the United States & Canada, Vol. 33. Ed. by Wade H. Shafer. (Illus.). 430p. (C). 1990. text 179.00 (*0-306-43732-5*, Kluwer Plenum) Kluwer Academic.
Masters Theses in the Pure & Applied Sciences: Accepted by Colleges & Universities of the United States & Canada, Vol. 34. Ed. by Wade H. Shafer. (Illus.). 432p. (C). 1992. text 179.00 (*0-306-44239-6*, Kluwer Plenum) Kluwer Academic.
Masters Theses in the Pure & Applied Sciences: Accepted by Colleges & Universities of the United States & Canada, Vol. 35. W. H. Shafer. (Illus.). 382p. (C). 1992. text 149.50 (*0-306-44348-1*, Kluwer Plenum) Kluwer Academic.
Masters Theses in the Pure & Applied Sciences: Accepted by Colleges & Universities of the United States & Canada, Vol. 36. W. H. Shafer. (Illus.). 354p. (C). 1993. text 149.50 (*0-306-44495-X*, Kluwer Plenum) Kluwer Academic.
Masters Theses in the Pure & Applied Sciences: Accepted by Colleges & Universities of the United States & Canada, Vol. 37. W. H. Shafer. (Illus.). 394p. (C). 1994. text 149.50 (*0-306-44711-8*, Kluwer Plenum) Kluwer Academic.
Masters Theses in the Pure & Applied Sciences: Accepted by Colleges & Universities of the United States & Canada, Vol. 38. Ed. by Wade H. Shafer. LC 58-62673. (Illus.). 430p. 1995. 179.00 (*0-306-45061-5*, Kluwer Plenum) Kluwer Academic.
Masters Theses in the Pure & Applied Sciences: Accepted by Colleges & Universities of the United States & Canada, Vol. 40. Ed. by Wade H. Shafer. (Illus.). 344p. (C). 1997. text 215.00 (*0-306-45760-1*, Kluwer Plenum) Kluwer Academic.
Masters Thesis in the Pure & Applied Sciences: Accepted by Colleges & Universities of the United States & Canada, Vol. 39. Ed. by Wade H. Shafer. (Illus.). 430p. (C). 1996. text 179.00 (*0-306-45329-0*, Kluwer Plenum) Kluwer Academic.
Masters to Managers: Historical & Comparative Perspectives on American Employers. Sanford M. Jacoby. 1991. text 46.00 (*0-231-06802-6*) Col U Pr.
Master's Touch. Charles Mills. LC 93-6802. 1993. pap. 8.99 (*0-8280-0754-3*) Review & Herald.
Master's Touch, Vol. II. Mildred N. Smith. 336p. 1995. 16.00 (*1-890991-00-7*, MT2001) Paragon Pubns.
Master's Touch: Disciples' Stories. Compiled by Sita Bordow. LC 84-28857. 1984. pap. 8.95 (*0-932040-26-8*) Integral Yoga Pubns.
Master's Touch: On Being a Sacred Teacher for the New Age. Yogi Bhajan. LC 97-73614. (Illus.). x, 400p. (Orig.). 1997. pap. write for info. (*0-9639991-1-7*) KRI.
Master's Touch Psychic Massage. Ma Sagarpriya. (Illus.). 317p. 1995. pap. text 29.95 (*1-881445-52-6*) Sandvik Pub.
***Masters Track & Field: A History.** Leonard T. Olson. (Illus.). 320p. 2000. 65.00 (*0-7864-0889-8*) McFarland & Co.
Master's Way of Personal Evangelism: A Companion to "The Master Plan of Evangelism" Robert E. Coleman. LC 96-41251. 192p. 1997. pap. 10.99 (*0-89107-912-2*) Crossway Bks.
Masters Without Slaves. James L. Roark. (C). 1978. pap. 14.00 (*0-393-00901-7*) Norton.
Master's Word: A Short Treatise on the Word, the Light & the Self (1913) George W. Plummer. 120p. 1998. reprint ed. pap. 14.95 (*0-7661-0505-9*) Kessinger Pub.
Mastership: The Divine Law. R. Swinburne Clymer. 256p. 1949. 9.95 (*0-932785-30-1*) Philos Pub.
Mastership: The Divine Law. deluxe ed. R. Swinburne Clymer. 256p. 1949. lthr. 20.00 (*0-932785-92-1*) Philos Pub.
Mastersingers of Nuremberg. Richard Wagner. Ed. by Nicholas John. Tr. by F. Jameson & Feasey Kember from GER. (English National Opera Guide Series: Bilingual Libretto, Articles: No. 19). 128p. (Orig.). 1983. pap. 9.95 (*0-7145-3961-9*) Riverrun NY.
***Masterson.** Richard S. Wheeler. LC 99-38396. 256p. 1999. 24.95 (*0-312-87047-7*, Pub. by Forge NYC) St Martin.
***Masterson.** Richard S. Wheeler. 304p. 2000. mass mkt. 6.99 (*0-8125-6856-7*) Forge NYC.
Masterson & Roosevelt. Jack DeMattos. LC 84-17591. (Early West Ser.). (Illus.). 151p. 1984. 21.95 (*0-932702-31-7*) Creative Texas.
Masterstroke: Use the Power of Your Mind to Improve Your Golf with NLP. Harry Alder & Karl Morris. (Illus.). 176p. (Orig.). 1997. pap. text 13.95 (*0-7499-1715-6*, Pub. by Piatkus Bks) London Brdge.
Masterstrokes: Pastel. Hazel Harrison. LC 98-46792. 1999. 24.95 (*0-8069-2425-X*) Sterling.
Masterstrokes: Watercolor. Hazel Harrison. LC 98-47138. 1999. 24.95 (*0-8069-2427-6*) Sterling.
MasterSweep Theater Presents: The Animal's Side of the Story. Sylvia Seymour. (Illus.). 64p. (J). (gr. 1-6). 1996. pap. 6.95 (*0-9651396-8-9*) StoryLoft.
Masterthinker. Edward De Bono. (Illus.). 1990. student ed. 99.95 incl. audio (*0-9615400-3-6*) Intl Ctr Creat Think.
Masterthinker's Handbook. Edward De Bono. 160p. 1990. pap. 30.00 (*0-14-014594-X*) Intl Ctr Creat Think.
Master/Users Manual for WordPerfect 5.1 for DOS. H. Albert Napier. (DF - Computer Applications Ser.). 1995. text, suppl. ed. 37.95 (*0-7895-0067-1*) S-W Pub.
Masterwork. D. Kern Holoman. LC 96-24580. 1996. pap. 29.95 (*0-02-871106-8*) Macmillan.
***Masterwork: Master of Time.** Arnaud Maitland. 217p. 2000. pap. 15.95 (*0-89800-309-1*) Dharma Pub.
Masterwork in Music Vol. 2: A Yearbook, 1926. Heinrich Schenker. Ed. by William Drabkin. (Studies in Music Theory & Analysis: No. 8). (Illus.). 149p. (C). 1996. text 80.00 (*0-521-45542-1*) Cambridge U Pr.
Masterwork in Music Vol. 3, 1930: A Yearbook. Heinrich Schenker. Ed. by William Drabkin. (Cambridge Studies in Music Theory & Analysis: No. 9). 134p. (C). 1997. text 80.00 (*0-521-45543-X*) Cambridge U Pr.
Masterwork Technical Skills Level 3. Jane Magrath. 32p. 1992. pap. 6.50 (*0-7390-0494-8*, 6584) Alfred Pub.
Masterworks. D. Kern Holoman. LC 97-29876. 416p. (C). 1997. pap. text 37.80 (*0-13-226358-0*) P-H.
Masterworks: A Musical Directory. D. Kern Holoman. 401p. 1998. pap. text 84.00 (*0-13-226408-0*) P-H.
***Masterworks: A Musical Discovery.** 2nd ed. D. Kern Holoman. LC 00-37359. 2001. write for info. (*0-13-020543-5*) Aspen Law.
Masterworks at the Albright-Knox Art Gallery. rev. ed. Ed. by Karen Lee Spaulding. LC 99-12236. (Illus.). 304p. 1999. reprint ed. 50.00 (*1-55595-168-6*) Hudson Hills.
Masterworks Bible Study Syllabus. Contrib. by Hewitt Staff. 20p. (YA). (gr. 10-12). 1998. pap. text 3.50 (*1-57896-031-2*, 2532) Hewitt Res Fnd.
Masterworks by Pennsylvania Painters in Pennsylvania Collections: Exhibition Catalogue. Harold E. Dickson. (Illus.). 72p. 1972. pap. 6.00 (*0-911209-00-X*) Palmer Mus Art.
Masterworks Classics, Level 4. Ed. by Jane Magrath. 48p. 1988. pap. 7.50 (*0-7390-0754-8*, 168) Alfred Pub.
Masterworks for Clarinet & Piano. Weber & Clara (Wieck) Schumann. 152p. 1986. per. 14.95 (*0-7935-5405-5*, 50261350) H Leonard.
Masterworks from Stuttgart: The Romantic Age in German Art. Jeremy Strick et al. Ed. by Mary A. Steiner. LC 94-69686. (Illus.). 160p. 1995. text. write for info. (*0-89178-041-6*) St Louis Art Mus.
Masterworks from the Albertina: Italian Drawings, 1350-1800. Veronika Birke. 1992. pap. 45.00 (*0-89835-276-2*) Abaris Bks.
Masterworks from the David & Peggy Rockefeller Collection: Manet to Picasso. Kirk Varnedoe. LC 94-76018. (Illus.). 96p. 1994. 37.50 (*0-87070-155-X*); pap. 19.95 (*0-87070-156-8*) Mus of Modern Art.
Masterworks from the Louise Reinhardt Smith Collection. Kirk Varnedoe. (Illus.). 96p. 1995. 37.50 (*0-87070-148-7*); pap. 19.95 (*0-87070-149-5*) Mus of Modern Art.
Masterworks from the Musee des Beaux-Arts, Lille. LC 92-24688. (Illus.). 340p. 1992. 45.00 (*0-87099-649-5*, 0-8109-6417-1); pap. 35.00 (*0-87099-650-9*) Metro Mus Art.
Masterworks in Berlin: A City's Paintings Reunited. Colin Eisler. LC 95-17511. (Illus.). 704p. 1996. 135.00 (*0-8212-1951-0*, Pub. by Bulfinch Pr) Little.

M

An Asterisk (*) at the beginning of an entry indicates that the title is appearing for the first time.

Masterworks in Metal: A Millennium of Treasures from the State Art Museum of Georgia, U. S. S. R. T. Sanikidze et al. Ed. by Hal Fischer. (Illus.). 80p. (Orig.). 1989. pap. 8.95 (*0-9610866-8-8*) Putnam Found.

Masterworks of American Painting & Sculpture from the Smith College Museum of Art. Deborah Chotner et al. Ed. by Linda Muehlig. LC 99-35616. (Illus.). 308p. 1999. 65.00 (*1-55595-170-8*) Hudson Hills.

Masterworks of Asian Art. Cleveland Museum of Art Staff & Michael R. Cunningham. LC 97-45033. 1998. write for info. (*0-940717-42-5*); pap. 59.03 (*0-940717-43-3*) Cleveland Mus Art.

Masterworks of Asian Art. Michael R. Cunningham et al. LC 97-62327. (Illus.). 256p. 1998. 75.00 (*0-500-97466-7*, Pub. by Thames Hudson) Norton.

Masterworks of Asian Literature in Comparative Perspective: A Guide for Teaching. Ed. by Barbara S. Miller. LC 93-24473. (Columbia Project on Asia in the Core Curriculum Ser.). 616p. (C). (gr. 13). 1994. text 93.95 (*1-56324-257-5*, East Gate Bk); pap. text 31.95 (*1-56324-258-3*, East Gate Bk) M E Sharpe.

Masterworks of Autobiography. Ed. by Richard D. Mallery. LC 70-111848. (Essay Index Reprint Ser.). 1977. 40.95 (*0-8369-1760-X*) Ayer.

Masterworks of California Impressionism: The FFCA, Morton H. Fleischer Collection. Ed. by Jean Stern & Morton H. Fleischer. (Illus.). 180p. 1987. 45.00 (*0-9617882-0-8*) FFCA Pub.

***Masterworks of European Painting in Houston.** Museum of Fine Arts, Houston Staff et al. LC 99-39064. 2000. write for info. (*0-89090-093-0*) Mus Fine TX.

***Masterworks of European Painting in the California Palace of the Legion of Honor.** Steven A. Nash et al. LC 99-65341. (Illus.). 144p. 1999. 50.00 (*1-55595-182-1*, Pub. by Hudson Hills) Natl Bk Netwk.

***Masterworks of European Painting in the Museum of Fine Arts, Houston.** Edgar Peters Bowron & Mary G. Morton. (Illus.). 2000. 60.00 (*0-691-00460-9*) Princeton U Pr.

Masterworks of European Sculpture. Michael Conforti et al. (Mead Art Museum Monographs: Vol. 4). (Illus.). 36p. 1983. pap. 3.00 (*0-914337-00-9*) Mead Art Mus.

Masterworks of Impressionism. Arlene D. Kirkpatrick. LC 84-63016. (Illus.). 212p. 1985. 60.00 (*0-9615194-1-X*) Masterworks Art.

Masterworks of Impressionism. limited ed. Arlene D. Kirkpatrick. LC 84-63016. (Illus.). 212p. 1985. lthr. 200.00 (*0-9615194-0-1*) Masterworks Art.

Masterworks of Latin American Short Fiction: Eight Novellas. Ed. by Cass Canfield Cass. 416p. (C). 1997. pap. 16.00 (*0-06-430984-3*, Pub. by Westview) HarpC.

Masterworks of Man & Nature. Jim Thorsell. 1997. 39.95 (*1-57769-009-5*) Wrld Heritage.

Masterworks of Man & Nature. limited ed. Mark Swadling. 400p. 1994. 120.00 (*0-646-19264-7*) Wrld Heritage.

Masterworks of Man & Nature. 2nd ed. Mark Swadling. 400p. (gr. 9 up). 1994. 35.00 (*0-614-10619-2*) Wrld Heritage.

Masterworks of Man & Nature: Preserving Our World Heritage. Ed. by Mark Swadling. (Illus.). 448p. (C). 1992. 75.00 (*0-646-05376-0*, Pub. by IUCN) Elsevier.

Masterworks of Ming & Qing Painting from the Forbidden City: A Color Catalogue of Paintings from the Palace Museum in Bejing, China. Howard Rogers & Sherman E. Lee. (Illus.). 224p. (Orig.). 1989. 70.00 (*0-9621061-2-7*); pap. 65.00 (*0-9621061-1-9*) Intl Arts Coun.

Masterworks of Russian Painting from Soviet Museums. T. Lyina. (Illus.). 295p. (C). 1989. text 350.00 (*0-569-09218-3*, Pub. by Collets) St Mut.

Masterworks of the French Cinema. Intro. by John Weightman. LC 73-21853. 350p. 1974. 24.95 (*0-06-435331-1*) Boulevard.

Masterworks of Travel & Exploration. Ed. by Richard D. Mallery. LC 73-111849. (Essay Index Reprint Ser.). 1977. 34.95 (*0-8369-1761-8*) Ayer.

Masterworks on Paper from the Albright-Knox Art Gallery. Cheryl A. Brutvan et al. LC 87-3619. (Illus.). 176p. 1987. 50.00 (*0-933920-89-X*); pap. 30.00 (*0-933920-90-3*) Buffalo Fine-Albrght-Knox.

Mastery: A University Word List Reader. Gladys Valcourt & Linda Wells. LC 99-233238. 336p. 1999. pap. text 18.95 (*0-472-08588-3*, 08588); pap. text, teacher ed. 11.95 (*0-472-08592-1*, 08592) U of Mich Pr.

***Mastery: A University Word List Reader.** Gladys Valcourt & Linda Wells. (Illus.). 336p. (C). 1999. pap. text 32.50 (*0-472-08593-X*, 08593) U of Mich Pr.

Mastery: The Art of Mastering Life. E. Stanley Jones. (Abingdon Classics Ser.). 364p. 1992. reprint ed. pap. 5.95 (*0-687-23734-3*) Abingdon.

Mastery: The Keys to Long-Term Success & Fulfillment. George Leonard. LC 91-38072. 192p. 1992. reprint ed. pap. 12.95 (*0-452-26756-0*, Plume) Dutton Plume.

Mastery - Management. N. Stevenson. 26p. 1990. student ed. 5.95 (*0-941112-35-7*) Stevnson Lrn.

Mastery - Management. N. Stevenson & Ellen D'Agnenica. 13p. 1990. student ed. 14.95 (*0-941112-36-5*) Stevnson Lrn.

***Mastery Activities for Special Needs Students.** 2nd ed. Whitney Sizer-Webb. 1998. pap. 15.75 (*0-538-69063-1*) Thomson Learn.

Mastery & Elegance: Two Centuries of French Drawings from the Collection of Jeffrey E. Horvitz. Ed. by Alvin L. Clark, Jr. et al. LC 98-45920. (Illus.). 1998. pap. 40.00 (*1-891771-02-7*, Pub. by Harvard Art Mus) U of Wash Pr.

Mastery & Escape: T. S. Eliot & the Dialectic of Modernism. Jewel S. Brooker. LC 93-45634. 288p. 1996. pap. 18.95 (*1-55849-040-X*) U of Mass Pr.

Mastery & Management of Time. Sydney F. Love. (Illus.). 1978. 14.95 (*0-13-559971-7*, Busn) P-H.

Mastery Approach to Advanced WordPerfect Version 5.1, Desktop Publishing. Nita H. Rutkosky & Holly Yasui. (C). 1991. pap. text 31.95 (*1-56118-425-X*); pap. text, teacher ed. 14.00 (*1-56118-373-3*) Paradigm MN.

Mastery Approach to Lotus 1-2-3, Release 2.3, 2.4. Eileen B. Dlugoss et al. LC 92-47135. 1993. 27.95 (*1-56118-378-4*); teacher ed. 19.00 (*1-56118-379-2*) Paradigm MN.

Mastery Approach to Microsoft 3.1 IG & DK: Instructor's Guide with Instructor's Disk, 3.5. Edward J. Coburn. text 69.00 (*1-56118-495-0*) EMC-Paradigm.

Mastery Approach to Microsoft Windows, Version 3.1. 5th ed. Edward J. Coburn. LC 92-36634. 1993. pap. text 27.95 (*1-56118-496-9*) Paradigm MN.

Mastery Approach to Microsoft Word, Version 5.0. Nita H. Rutkosky. 446p. (C). 1990. pap. text 32.95 (*1-56118-109-9*) Paradigm MN.

Mastery Approach to Microsoft Word, Version 5.0. Nita H. Rutkosky. 352p. (C). 1990. pap. text, teacher ed. 19.00 (*1-56118-108-0*) Paradigm MN.

Mastery Approach to Microsoft Word, Version 5.0: Short Course. Nita H. Rutkosky. 208p. 1990. text 22.95 (*1-56118-112-9*) Paradigm MN.

Mastery Approach to Microsoft Word, Version 5.5. Nita H. Rutkosky & Cheryl L. Bruns. 544p. 1993. pap. text 32.95 (*1-56118-464-0*) Paradigm MN.

Mastery Approach to Microsoft Word, Version 5.5: Short Course. Nita H. Rutkosky & Cheryl L. Bruns. 256p. 1993. pap. text 22.95 (*1-56118-465-9*) Paradigm MN.

Mastery Approach to Microsoft Word 2.0 for Windows. Nita H. Rutkosky & Cheryl L. Bruns. 608p. 1993. text 33.95 (*1-56118-489-6*) Paradigm MN.

Mastery Approach to Microsoft Word 2.0 for Windows: Short Course. Nita H. Rutkosky & Cheryl L. Bruns. 300p. 1993. text 22.95 (*1-56118-490-X*) Paradigm MN.

Mastery Approach to MS - PC DOS, Version 5.0. Edward J. Coburn. LC 92-36635. 272p. 1993. pap. text 25.95 (*1-56118-647-3*) Paradigm MN.

Mastery Approach to MS - PC DOS, Version 5.0. 5th ed. Edward J. Coburn. LC 92-36635. 272p. 1993. pap. text 25.95 (*1-56118-612-0*); pap. text, teacher ed. 69.00 (*1-56118-613-9*) Paradigm MN.

Mastery Approach to MS-PC Dos, Version 6.2X. Edward J. Coburn. LC 94-20643. 300p. 1994. pap. text 27.95 (*1-56118-760-7*) Paradigm MN.

Mastery Approach to MS-PC Dos, Version 6.2X. 25th ed. Edward J. Coburn. LC 94-20643. 300p. 1994. pap. text 27.95 (*1-56118-761-5*) Paradigm MN.

Mastery Approach to MS/PC Dos, Version 6.2: Instructor's guide. Edward J. Coburn. 24.00 (*1-56118-846-8*) EMC-Paradigm.

Mastery Approach to Paradox 4.0. Michael Mocciola & Constantinos P. Karantzas. 416p. 1993. teacher ed. 8.00 (*1-56118-675-9*); text 26.95 incl. 5.25 hd (*1-56118-606-6*) Paradigm MN.

Mastery Approach to Paradox 4.0. 5th ed. Michael Mocciola & Constantinos P. Karantzas. 416p. 1993. text 26.95 incl. 3.5 hd (*1-56118-609-0*) Paradigm MN.

Mastery Approach to WordPerfect for Windows, Version 5.1. Nita H. Rutkosky. 688p. 1993. pap. text 33.95 (*1-56118-469-1*) Paradigm MN.

Mastery Approach to WordPerfect for Windows, Version 5.1: Short Course. Nita H. Rutkosky. 348p. 1993. pap. text 22.95 (*1-56118-470-5*) Paradigm MN.

Mastery Approach to WordPerfect for Windows, Version 5.2. Nita H. Rutkosky. LC 93-48952. 720p. 1993. pap. text 33.95 (*1-56118-650-3*) Paradigm MN.

Mastery Approach to WordPerfect for Windows, Version 5.2. Nita H. Rutkosky. 720p. 1993. pap. text, teacher ed. 19.00 (*1-56118-651-1*) Paradigm MN.

Mastery Approach to WordPerfect, Version 5.0: Short Course. Nita H. Rutkosky. 208p. (C). 1990. pap. text 17.80 (*1-56118-077-7*) Paradigm MN.

Mastery Approach to WordPerfect, Version 5.0: Short Course. Nita H. Rutkosky. 208p. (C). 1990. pap. text, teacher ed. 7.10 (*1-56118-078-5*) Paradigm MN.

Mastery Approach to WordPerfect, Version 5.0 with 5.1 Update. Nita H. Rutkosky. 587p. (C). 1989. pap. text 27.95 (*1-56118-075-0*) Paradigm MN.

Mastery Approach to WordPerfect, Version 5.0 with 5.1 Update. Nita H. Rutkosky. 587p. (C). 1989. teacher ed. 19.00 (*1-56118-076-9*) Paradigm MN.

Mastery Approach to WordPerfect, Version 5.1. Nita H. Rutkosky. 600p. (C). 1991. teacher ed. 19.00 (*1-56118-083-1*); pap. text 32.95 (*1-56118-082-3*) Paradigm MN.

Mastery Motivation Vol. 12: Origins, Conceptualizations & Applications. Robert H. MacTurk & George A. Morgan. Ed. by Gallaudet University Press Staff & Colorado State University Staff. LC 96-136371. (Advances in Applied Developmental Psychology Ser.: Vol. 12). (Illus.). 336p. 1995. text 73.25 (*1-56750-146-X*) Ablx Pub.

Mastery Motivation Vol. 12: Origins, Conceptualizations & Applications. Ed. by Robert H. MacTurk & George A. Morgan. LC 96-136371. (Advances in Applied Developmental Psychology: Vol. 12). (Illus.). 336p. 1995. pap. 39.50 (*1-56750-203-2*) Ablx Pub.

Mastery of Being. William W. Atkinson. 196p. 1996. reprint ed. spiral bd. 15.00 (*0-7873-0052-7*) Hlth Research.

Mastery of Being: A Study of the Ultimate Principle of Reality, & the Practical Application Thereof (1911) William W. Atkinson. 198p. 1996. reprint ed. pap. 14.25 (*1-56459-656-7*) Kessinger Pub.

Mastery of Cardiothoracic Surgery. Ed. by Larry R. Kaiser & Irving Kron. LC 97-23282. (Illus.). 1008p. 1997. text 175.00 (*0-316-48210-2*) Lppncott W & W.

Mastery of Cardiothoracic Surgery. Larry R. Kaiser & Irving L. Kron. LC 97-23282. 1053p. 1997. text. write for info. (*0-7817-1423-0*) Lppncott W & W.

Mastery of Conversational Spanish. Carolyn C. Thorburn. 431p. (Orig.). (C). 1992. pap. 45.00 (*0-9636198-0-2*) Educat Res Ctr.

Mastery of Conversational Spanish: Workbook. Carolyn Coles-Thorburn. 304p. (C). 1994. per. 32.95 (*0-8403-9542-6*) Kendall-Hunt.

Mastery of Destiny. James Allen. 120p. 1992. pap. 12.00 (*0-89540-209-2*, SB-209) Sun Pub.

Mastery of Destiny. James Allen. 120p. 1998. reprint ed. pap. 10.00 (*0-7873-0024-1*) Hlth Research.

Mastery of Destiny, 1909. James Allen. 120p. 1996. reprint ed. pap. 9.00 (*1-56459-850-0*) Kessinger Pub.

Mastery of Drawing, 2 vols., Set. Joseph Meder. Tr. by Winslow Ames from GER. LC 76-22300. (Illus.). 720p. lib. bdg. 115.00 (*0-913870-16-1*) Abaris Bks.

Mastery of Endoscopic & Laparoscopic Surgery. Eubanks et al. LC 98-32156. (Illus.). 800p. 1998. text 175.00 (*0-316-26865-8*) Lppncott W & W.

Mastery of English. Wheeler. 1991. pap. text. write for info. (*0-582-66251-6*, Pub. by Addison-Wesley) Longman.

Mastery of English Grammar & Mechanics: An Individualized Program. rev. ed. James Scott. 87p. (YA). (gr. 7-12). 1986. ring bd. 57.99 (*1-58049-701-2*, IT33) Prestwick Hse.

Mastery of Fate. Christian D. Larson. 95p. 1997. pap. 35.00 (*0-89540-383-8*) Sun Pub.

Mastery of Grief (1913) see Halo of Grief: A Companion on Your Journey Through Loss

Mastery of Hand Strength. John Brookfield. LC 95-78894. 120p. (Orig.). 1995. pap. 14.95 (*0-926888-03-X*) IronMind Enterprises.

Mastery of Joinery & Business. Ed. by G. Lister Sutcliffe. (Modern Carpenter Joiner & Cabinet-Maker Ser.: Vol. 8). (Illus.). 208p. 1990. reprint ed. 24.95 (*0-918678-62-5*) Natl Hist Soc.

Mastery of Love: A Practical Guide to the Art of Relationship. Don Miguel Ruiz. LC 99-18199. (Toltec Wisdom Ser.). 224p. 1999. pap. 14.00 (*1-878424-42-4*) Amber-Allen Pub.

Mastery of Mind: Perspectives on Time, Space, & Knowledge. LC 93-10597. (Perspectives on TSK Ser.). 416p. 1993. pap. 16.95 (*0-89800-245-1*) Dharma Pub.

Mastery of Nature: Aspects of Art, Science, & Humanism in the Renaissance. Thomas D. Kaufmann. (Essays on the Arts Ser.). (Illus.). 300p. 1993. text 47.50 (*0-691-03205-X*, Pub. by Princeton U Pr) Cal Prin Full Svc.

***Mastery of Obsessive Compulsive Disorder Client.** Michael J Kozak. 1999. pap. text, wbk. ed. 38.50 (*0-12-785051-1*) Acad Pr.

Mastery of Obsessive Compulsive Disorder Therapist Guide. Michael J Kozak. (Therapyworks Ser.). 1999. pap. text 36.50 (*0-12-785050-3*) Acad Pr.

Mastery of Plastic & Reconstructive Surgery. Ed. by Mimis Cohen. LC 93-33838. 2736p. 1994. text 357.00 (*0-316-15003-7*) Lppncott W & W.

Mastery of Reason: Cognitive Development & the Production of Rationality. Valerie Walkerdine. 240p. (C). 1988. 59.95 (*0-415-00696-1*) Routledge.

Mastery of Reason: Cognitive Development & the Production of Rationality. Valerie Walkerdine. LC 87-34840. 236p. reprint ed. pap. 73.20 (*0-608-20397-1*, 207165000002) Bks Demand.

Mastery of Self. Christian D. Larson. 87p. 1997. pap. 35.00 (*0-89540-384-6*) Sun Pub.

Mastery of Stress: Techniques for Relaxation in the Workplace. Paul Skye. LC 98-34005. (Illus.). 264p. 1999. 14.95 (*1-56718-630-0*, K630) Llewellyn Pubns.

Mastery of Submission: Inventions of Masochism. John K. Noyes. LC 96-51035. (Cornell Studies in the History of Psychiatry). (Illus.). 256p. 1997. text 29.95 (*0-8014-3345-2*) Cornell U Pr.

Mastery of Surgery, 2 vols. 3rd ed. Ed. by Lloyd M. Nyhus et al. (Illus.). 2400p. 1996. text 285.00 (*0-316-61746-6*) Lppncott W & W.

Mastery of Surgery. 3rd ed. Lloyd M. Nyhus et al. LC 96-9115. 1996. write for info. (*0-316-61751-2*, Little Brwn Med Div) Lppncott W & W.

Mastery of Surgery, 2 vols., Set. Lloyd M. Nyhus & Robert Baker. 1540p. 1984. 240.00 (*0-316-61742-3*, Little Brwn Med Div) Lppncott W & W.

Mastery of the Bow. Emery Erdlee. (Illus.). 169p. (C). 1988. pap. 14.95 (*0-942963-00-8*) Distinctive Pub.

Mastery of the Pacific. Archibald R. Colquhoun. LC 70-111750. (American Imperialism: Viewpoints of United States Foreign Policy, 1898-1941 Ser.). 1970. reprint ed. 29.95 (*0-405-02009-0*) Ayer.

Mastery of the Pacific. Frank Fox. LC 75-111757. (American Imperialism: Viewpoints of United States Foreign Policy, 1898-1941 Ser.: No. 1). 1970. reprint ed. 20.95 (*0-405-02020-1*) Ayer.

Mastery of Writing: An Individualized Program. rev. ed. James Scott. 117p. (YA). (gr. 7-12). 1993. ring bd. 57.99 (*1-58049-702-0*, IG34) Prestwick Hse.

***Mastery of Your Anxiety & Panic: Therapist Guide.** 3rd ed. Michelle G. Craske. 2000. pap. text 35.00 (*0-12-784464-3*) Acad Pr.

Mastery of Your Specific Phobia Client Workbook. Michelle G. Craske. 1998. pap. text 40.00 (*0-12-785034-1*) Acad Pr.

Mastery of Your Specific Phobia Therapist Guide. Michelle G. Craske. 1999. pap. text 35.50 (*0-12-785033-3*) Acad Pr.

Mastery Series. Alan C. Walter. Ed. by Beverly Miles. 27p. (Orig.). 1995. pap. text 2.89 (*1-57569-021-7*) Wisdom Pubng.

Mastery Teaching. Madeline C. Hunter. 118p. 1994. pap. 19.95 (*0-8039-6264-9*) Corwin Pr.

Mastery Tests. S. Harold Collins. (Straight Forward Math Ser.). (Illus.). 35p. (J). (gr. 3-6). 1992. pap. 3.95 (*0-931993-44-X*, GP-044) Garlic Pr OR.

Mastery Through Accomplishment: Developing Inner Strength for Life's Challenges. 2nd ed. Hazrat I. Khan. 320p. 1978. pap. 16.00 (*0-930872-40-1*) Omega Pubns NY.

Mastery Two: A University Word List Reader. Gladys Valcourt & Linda Wells. (Illus.). 230p. (C). 18.95 (*0-472-08659-6*, 08659); teacher ed. 13.95 (*0-472-08658-8*, 08658); pap. text 18.95 (*0-472-08657-X*, 08657) U of Mich Pr.

Mastery Workbook for Ann: Short "a" Sound. E. Reid et al. (Start Reading Ser.: No. A1). 12p. (J). (ps-3). 1986. pap., student ed. 2.99 (*1-56422-015-X*) Start Reading.

Mastery Workbook for Get Set: Short "e" Sound. E. Reid et al. (Start Reading Ser.: No. A5). 16p. (J). (ps-3). 1986. pap., student ed. 2.99 (*1-56422-019-2*) Start Reading.

Mastery Workbook for the Blue Boat: Long "o" Sound. E. Reid et al. (Start Reading Ser.: No. B2). 28p. (J). (ps-3). 1986. pap., student ed. 2.99 (*1-56422-023-0*) Start Reading.

Mastery Workbook for the Brown Mule: Long "u" Sound. E. Reid et al. (Start Reading Ser.: No. B5). 16p. (J). (ps-3). 1986. pap., student ed. 2.99 (*1-56422-024-9*) Start Reading.

Mastery Workbook for the Chimp: "Ch" Sound. E. Reid et al. (Start Reading Ser.: No. C3). 20p. (J). (ps-3). 1986. pap., student ed. 2.99 (*1-56422-027-3*) Start Reading.

Mastery Workbook for the Green Jeep: Long "e" Sound. E. Reid et al. (Start Reading Ser.: No. B3). 28p. (J). (ps-3). 1986. pap., student ed. 2.99 (*1-56422-021-4*) Start Reading.

Mastery Workbook for the Queen: "Qu" Sound. E. Reid et al. (Start Reading Ser.: No. C4). 20p. (J). (ps-3). 1986. pap., student ed. 2.99 (*1-56422-028-1*) Start Reading.

Mastery Workbook for the Red Plane: Long "a" Sound. E. Reid et al. (Start Reading Ser.: No. B1). 32p. (J). (ps-3). 1986. pap., student ed. 2.99 (*1-56422-020-6*) Start Reading.

Mastery Workbook for the Shark: "Sh" Sound. E. Reid et al. (Start Reading Ser.: No. C2). 20p. (J). (ps-3). 1986. pap., student ed. 2.99 (*1-56422-026-5*) Start Reading.

Mastery Workbook for the Thing: "Th" Sound. E. Reid et al. (Start Reading Ser.: No. C5). 20p. (J). (ps-3). 1986. pap., student ed. 2.99 (*1-56422-029-X*) Start Reading.

Mastery Workbook for the Whale: "Wh" Sound. E. Reid et al. (Start Reading Ser.: No. C1). 24p. (J). (ps-3). 1986. pap., student ed. 2.99 (*1-56422-025-7*) Start Reading.

Mastery Workbook for the White Bike: Long "i" Sound. E. Reid et al. (Start Reading Ser.: No. B4). 20p. (J). (ps-3). 1986. pap., student ed. 2.99 (*1-56422-022-2*) Start Reading.

Mastery Workbook for Tip: Short "i" Sound. E. Reid et al. (Start Reading Ser.: No. A2). 20p. 1986. pap., student ed. 2.99 (*1-56422-017-6*) Start Reading.

Mastery Workbook for Top Dog: Short "o" Sound. E. Reid et al. (Start Reading Ser.: No. A3). 24p. (J). (ps-3). 1986. pap., student ed. 2.99 (*1-56422-016-8*) Start Reading.

Mastery Workbook for up & Up: Short "u" Sound. E. Reid et al. (Start Reading Ser.: No. A4). 20p. (J). (ps-3). 1986. pap., student ed. 2.99 (*1-56422-018-4*) Start Reading.

Mastery Worksheets. E. Reid et al. (Start Reading Ser.: Set A). 72p. (J). (ps-3). 1989. 44.95 (*1-56422-032-X*) Start Reading.

Mastery Worksheets. E. Reid et al. (Start Reading Ser.: Set B). 86p. (J). (ps-3). 1989. 44.95 (*1-56422-033-8*) Start Reading.

Mastery Worksheets. E. Reid et al. (Start Reading Ser.: Set C). 73p. (J). (ps-3). 1989. 44.95 (*1-56422-034-6*) Start Reading.

Mastication & Swallowing: Biological & Chemical Correlates. Ed. by Barry J. Sessle & Alan G. Hannam. LC 75-38957. (Illus.). 204p. reprint ed. pap. 63.30 (*0-8357-3651-2*, 203637900003) Bks Demand.

Mastiff: An Owner's Guide to a Healthy Pet. John M. Becknell. (Owner's Guide to a Happy, Healthy Pet Ser.). 128p. 1998. 12.95 (*0-87605-609-5*) Howell Bks.

Mastiff: The Aristocratic Guardian. Dee Dee Andersson. Ed. by Luana Luther. LC 98-70320. (Pure-Bred Ser.). (Illus.). 312p. 1999. 28.50 (*0-944875-51-3*, Pub. by Doral Pub) Natl Bk Netwk.

Mastiff & Bullmastiff Handbook. Douglas B. Oliff. (Illus.). 230p. 1988. 25.95 (*0-85115-485-9*) Howell Bks.

Mastiff Champions, 1952-1988. Camino E. E. & Bk. Co. Staff. (Illus.). 175p. 1990. pap. 36.95 (*1-55893-004-3*) Camino E E & Bk.

Mastiff Champions, 1989-1993. Camino E. E. & Bk. Co. Staff. LC 95-136174. (Illus.). 138p. 1995. pap. 32.95 (*1-55893-032-9*) Camino E E & Bk.

Mastiffs. Marie A. Moore. (Illus.). 1997. pap. 9.95 (*0-7938-2317-X*, KW-180S) TFH Pubns.

***Mastiffs.** Kim Thornton. LC 98-49737. (Complete Pet Owner's Manual Ser.). (Illus.). 104p. 1999. pap. 6.95 (*0-7641-0762-3*) Barron.

Masting & Rigging: The Clipper Ship & Ocean Carrier. Ed. by Harold A. Underhill. (C). 1987. 126.00 (*0-85174-173-8*) St Mut.

Masting & Rigging of English Ships of War, 1625-1860. 2nd ed. James Lees. (Illus.). 212p. 1984. 59.95 (*0-87021-948-0*) Naval Inst Pr.

***Mastitis Control & Milk Quality.** American Dairy Science Association Staff. (ADSA Scientific Reader Ser.). (Illus.). 260p. (C). 2000. 40.00 (*1-884706-03-7*) Fed Animal Sci.

Mastitis Control in Dairy Herds. Roger Blowey & Peter Edmondson. (Illus.). 208p. 1995. 44.95 (*0-85236-314-1*, Pub. by Farming Pr) Diamond Farm Bk.

An Asterisk (*) at the beginning of an entry indicates that the title is appearing for the first time.

Mastitis Literature Survey, 1986. 68p. 1988. 34.00 (0-00-000099-X) C A B Intl.

Mastodon-Bearing & Late Quaternary Geochronology of the Lower Pomme de Terre Valley, Missouri. Caleb V. Haynes, Jr. LC 85-12546. (Geological Society of America Ser.: Vol. 204). (Illus.). 58p. 1985. reprint ed. pap. 30.00 (0-608-07733-X, 206782100010) Bks Demand.

Mastodon Hunters to Mound Builders: North American Archaeology. Peter Nichols & Belia Nichols. (Illus.). 112p. (J). (gr. 6-7). 1992. 12.95 (0-89015-748-0) Sunbelt Media.

Mastodons, Mammoths, & Modern-Day Elephants. Marianne Johnston. LC 98-3877. (Prehistoric Animals & Their Modern-Day Relatives Ser.). (J). 1999. 18.60 (0-8239-5202-9, PowerKids) Rosen Group.

Mastology--Breast Diseases: Proceedings of the 8th International Congress on Senology, Breast Diseases, 8-12 May, 1994, Rio de Janeiro, Brazil. Antonio S. S. Figueira Fo. LC 95-45214. (International Congress Ser.: No. 1067). 422p. 1995. 218.50 (0-444-82102-3, Excerpta Medica) Elsevier.

Mastro-Don Gesualdo. Giovanni Verga. Tr. by D. H. Lawrence from ITA. LC 75-11486. 454p. 1976. reprint ed. lib. bdg. 37.50 (0-8371-8198-4, VEMG, Greenwood Pr) Greenwood.

Mastro Don Gesualdo. 2nd ed. Giovanni Verga. Tr. by D. H. Lawrence from ITA. (European Classics). 356p. 1999. reprint ed. pap. 11.95 (1-873982-52-6) Dedalus.

Masts, Antennas & Service Planning. Geoff Wiskin et al. (Illus.). 233p. 1992. 125.00 (0-240-51336-3, Focal) Buttrwrth-Heinemann.

Masturbation Van Nec Stengers. 1999. text. write for info. (0-312-22443-5) St Martin.

Masturbation: From Infancy to Senescence. Ed. by Irwin M. Marcus & John J. Francis. LC 73-16855. 634p. 1975. 75.00 (0-8236-3150-8) Intl Univs Pr.

Masturbation, Tantra, & Self-Love. Margo Woods. 107p. (Orig.). 1981. pap. 10.95 (0-917320-15-8) Mho & Mho.

Masulipatnam & Cambay: A History of 2 Port-Towns, 1500-1800. Sinnappah Arasaratnam & Aniruddha Rya. LC 94-907524. (C). 1994. text 34.00 (81-215-0646-8, Pub. by M Manoharial) Coronet Bks.

***Masuto Investigates.** Howard Fast. 2000. 14.00 (0-7434-0022-4, Pub. by ibooks) S&S Trade.

Mat. Alan M. Hofmeister et al. (Reading for All Learners Ser.). (Illus.). pap. write for info. (1-56861-077-7) Swift Lrn Res.

MAT: Miller Analogies Test. 6th ed. Bader & Burt. 1995. pap. 11.95 (0-671-52112-8) PB.

MAT - The Miller Analogies Test. Research & Education Association Staff. 256p. 2000. pap. text 15.95 (0-87891-864-7) Res & Educ.

Mat & the Nut. Alan M. Hofmeister et al. (Reading for All Learners Ser.). (Illus.). (J). pap. write for info. (1-56861-109-9) Swift Lrn Res.

Mat at Bat. Alan M. Hofmeister et al. (Reading for All Learners Ser.). (Illus.). (J). pap. write for info. (1-56861-118-8) Swift Lrn Res.

Mat Cutting & Mat Decoration, Vol. 2. Vivian C. Kistler. LC 86-72676. (Library of Professional Picture Framing: Vol. 2). (Illus.). 96p. 1999. pap. text 19.00 (0-938655-01-9) Columba Pub.

Mat Did It. Alan M. Hofmeister et al. (Reading for All Learners Ser.). (Illus.). (J). pap. write for info. (1-56861-102-1) Swift Lrn Res.

Mat in the Hat. Alan M. Hofmeister et al. (Reading for All Learners Ser.). (Illus.). (J). pap. write for info. (1-56861-106-4) Swift Lrn Res.

Mat in the Sun. Alan M. Hofmeister et al. (Reading for All Learners Ser.). (Illus.). (J). pap. write for info. (1-56861-094-7) Swift Lrn Res.

Mat Irvin's Auto Modelling Masterclass. Matt Irvine. (Illus.). 128p. 1998. 29.95 (1-85915-089-6, Pub. by W & G) Motorbooks Intl.

Mat Is Wet. Alan M. Hofmeister et al. (Reading for All Learners Ser.). (Illus.). (J). pap. write for info. (1-56861-120-X) Swift Lrn Res.

Mat Mopped the Moon. Bobby L. Maslen. (Bob Books Activity Bks.: No. 1). 32p. (J). (ps up). 1997. pap. 3.99 (0-590-92172-X) Scholastic Inc.

Mat' (Mother) Nepridumannaia Istoriia. Alexander Khakhulin. LC 89-83898. (RUS.). 132p. (Orig.). (C). 1990. pap. 10.00 (0-911971-46-7) Effect Pub.

Mat Power: Lehigh Wrestling Highlights, 1910-1997. Dennis R. Diehl. Ed. by Gary Brownell. LC 97-91579. (Illus.). 250p. 1997. 38.00 (0-9656588-0-5) Roby Pub.

MAT Preparation Guide: Miller Analogies Test. 2nd ed. Michele Spence. LC 97-220277. (Cliffs Test Preparation Ser.). 101p. 1997. pap. text 12.95 (0-8220-2051-3, Cliff) IDG Bks.

MAT 7 English Pretest. Phychological Harcourt Staff. 1993. 24.00 (0-15-831407-7) Harcourt.

Mat the Rat. Alan M. Hofmeister et al. (Reading for All Learners Ser.). (Illus.). (J). pap. write for info. (1-56861-111-0) Swift Lrn Res.

Mata the Magician. Isabella Ingalese. 183p. 1996. reprint ed. spiral bd. 14.50 (0-7873-0461-1) Hlth Research.

Matabele Rebellion, 1896. Roberts Staff. (C). 1989. 95.00 (1-873058-05-5, Pub. by Roberts) St Mut.

Matachines Dance: Ritual Symbolism & Interethnic Relations in the Upper Rio Grande Valley. Sylvia Rodriguez. (Publications of the American Folklore Society). 193p. 1996. 45.00 (0-8263-1677-8); pap. 25.00 (0-8263-1678-6) U of NM Pr.

Matachines Dance of the Upper Rio Grande: History, Music, & Choreography. Flavia W. Champs. LC 82-10892. 121p. 1983. reprint ed. pap. 37.60 (0-608-01409-5, 206217200002) Bks Demand.

Mataco of the Gran Chaco: An Ethnographic Account of Change & Continuity in Mataco Socio-Economic Organization (Bolivia) Jan-Ake Alvarsson. (Uppsala Studies in Cultural Anthropology: No. 11). (Illus.). 314p. (Orig.). 1988. pap. 50.00 (91-554-2251-9, Pub. by Uppsala Univ Acta Univ Uppsaliensis) Coronet Bks.

Matador. Barbara Faith. (Intimate Moments Ser.: No. 432). 1992. per. 3.39 (0-373-07432-8, 5-07432-3) Harlequin Bks.

Matador of the 5 Towns & Other Stories. Arnold Bennett. LC 74-17074. (Collected Works of Arnold Bennett: Vol. 53). 1977. reprint ed. 34.95 (0-518-19134-6) Ayer.

Matador of the 5 Towns & Other Stories. Arnold Bennett. LC 79-144875. 1971. reprint ed. 25.00 (0-403-00862-X) Scholarly.

***Matadors: A Journey into the Heart of Modern Bullfighting.** Eamonn O'Neill. (Illus.). 224p. 1999. 35.00 (1-85158-932-5, Pub. by Mainstream Pubng) Trafalgar.

Matagorda. Louis L'Amour. 176p. 1985. mass mkt. 4.50 (0-553-28108-9) Bantam.

Matagorda. large type ed. Louis L'Amour. LC 96-36194. 1999. 20.00 (0-7862-0874-0) Thorndike Pr.

Matagorda Island: A Naturalist's Guide. Wayne H. McAlister & Martha K. McAlister. LC 92-13024. (Illus.). 380p. (Orig.). 1993. pap. 19.95 (0-292-75151-6) U of Tex Pr.

Matamora to Shohola. Matthew Osterberg. LC 98-87321. (Images of America Ser.). (Illus.). 128p. 1998. pap. 18.99 (0-7524-1297-3) Arcadia Publng.

Matamoros Mission. large type ed. Jeff Sadler. (Linford Western Library Ser.). 272p. 1995. pap. 16.99 (0-7089-7691-3, Linford) Ulverscroft.

Matamoros Trade: Confederate Commerce, Diplomacy, & Intrigue. James W. Daddysman. LC 81-72031. (Illus.). 216p. 1984. 32.50 (0-87413-215-0) U Delaware Pr.

Matanga-Lila of Nilakantha see Elephant-Lore of the Hindus

Matanuska Bard's Alaskan Verses. unabridged ed. Bob Klem. Ed. & Photos by Gus Klem. LC 96-94666. (Illus.). 108p. (Orig.). 1996. pap. 11.95 (0-9654189-0-1) G Klem.

Matanza. 2nd ed. Thomas Anderson. LC 92-24610. 220p. (C). 1992. pap. 12.95 (1-880684-04-7) Curbstone.

Matar Gigantes, a Sacar Espinas. Charles R. Swindoll.Tr. of Killing Giants, Pulling Thorns. (SPA.). 128p. 1995. pap. 6.99 (0-8297-2006-5) Vida Pubs.

Matar Un Ruisenor. Harper Lee. 1986. 16.60 (0-606-10483-6, Pub. by Turtleback) Demco.

Matarese Circle. Robert Ludlum. 544p. 1983. mass mkt. 7.99 (0-553-25899-0) Bantam.

Matarese Countdown. Robert Ludlum. 576p. 1998. mass mkt. 7.99 (0-553-57983-5) Bantam.

Matarese Countdown. large type ed. Robert Ludlum. LC 97-32902. 1997. pap. 27.95 (0-7838-8353-6, G K Hall Lrg Type) Mac Lib Ref.

***Matarese Countdown.** large type ed. Robert Ludlum. LC 97-32902. (Core Ser.). 794p. 1998. 29.95 (0-7838-8352-8, G K Hall & Co) Mac Lib Ref.

Matbakh Sayidata. Sonia Beiruti. Ed. by Ramzi Kaliffe.Tr. of Lady's Kitchen. (ARA., Illus.). 318p. 1990. 62.99 (1-58311-009-7) Eastern Corp.

***Match Books.** (Illus.). 1998. bds. 6.98 (1-58048-041-1) Sandvik Pub.

Match for Celia. Gina F. Wilkins. (Silhouette Romance Ser.). 1995. per. 3.75 (0-373-09967-3, 1-09967-0) Silhouette.

Match for Elizabeth. large type ed. Mira Stables. (Large Print Ser.). 336p. 1996. 27.99 (0-7089-3598-2) Ulverscroft.

Match for Melanie. large type ed. Carol Marsh. 1991. pap. 16.99 (0-7089-6981-X) Ulverscroft.

Match for Melissa. Kathryn Kirkwood. 224p. 1998. pap. 4.99 (0-8217-5932-9) Kensgtn Pub Corp.

Match for Mom: Guilty, a Man for Mom, the Fix-It Man. Anne Mather et al. 1997. per. 5.99 (0-373-20135-4, 1-20135-9) Harlequin Bks.

Match for Morgan (The Cutlers of the Shady Lady Ranch) Marie Ferrarella. (Yours Truly Ser.). 1999. per. 3.50 (0-373-52087-5, 1-52087-3) Harlequin Bks.

Match for Mother. Mona Gedney. 254p. 1999. mass mkt. 4.99 (0-8217-6185-4, Zebra Kensgtn) Kensgtn Pub Corp.

Match Holders: 100 Years of Ingenuity. Denis B. Alsford. LC 94-65852. (Illus.). 160p. 1994. pap. 29.95 (0-88740-633-5) Schiffer.

Match Labels In Japan. Hajime Miyoshi. (Arts Collection Ser.: Vol. 82). 1998. pap. 14.95 (4-7636-1582-3, Pub. by Kyoto Shoin) Bks Nippan.

Match Labels Postcard Book. (Arts Collection Ser.: Vol. 95). (Illus.). 48p. pap. 14.95 (4-7636-1595-5, Pub. by Kyoto Shoin) Bks Nippan.

Match Made in Heaven. Jeanne Carmichael. (Regency Romance Ser.). 1993. per. 2.99 (0-373-31199-0, 1-31199-2) Harlequin Bks.

Match Made in Heaven. Jeanne Carmichael. 1999. per. 3.75 (0-373-31222-9) Harlequin Bks.

Match Made in Heaven. Jane M. Choate. LC 96-95282. 192p. 1997. 18.95 (0-8034-9192-1, Avalon Bks) Bouregy.

Match Made in Heaven. Shari MacDonald. (Salinger Sisters Romantic Comedy Ser.: Bk. 2). 256p. 1999. pap. 6.95 (1-57856-137-X) Waterbrook Pr.

Match Made in Heaven: A Collection of Inspirational Love Stories. Susan Wales & Ann Platz. LC 98-46112. 268p. 1999. pap. text 10.99 (1-57673-393-9) Multnomah Pubs.

***Match Made in Heaven Vol. 2: More Inspirational Love Stories.** Susan Wales & Ann Platz. 267p. 1999. pap. 10.99 (1-57673-658-X, Pub. by Multnomah Pubs) GL Services.

Match Made in Texas. Ginger Chambers. LC 96-2343. (Superromance Ser.). 299p. 1996. per. 3.99 (0-373-70680-4, 1-70680-3) Harlequin Bks.

Match Made in Texas. Tina Leonard. (American Romance Ser.: No. 796). 1999. per. 3.99 (0-373-16796-2, 1-16796-4) Harlequin Bks.

Match Magic: More than 70 Impromptu Tricks with Matches. unabridged ed. Martin Gardner. Ed. by Bruce Fife. LC 98-49741. (Illus.). 48p. 1998. pap. 10.00 (0-941599-40-X, Pub. by Piccadilly Bks) Empire Pub Srvs.

Match Play & the Spin of the Ball. William T. Tilden & Asher Birnbaum. LC 75-33763. (Illus.). 1977. 11.95 (0-405-06679-1) Ayer.

Match Point. Robin Cruise. Ed. by Liz Parker. (Take Ten Bks.). (Illus.). 52p. (YA). (gr. 6-12). 1993. pap. text 3.95 (1-56254-093-9) Saddleback Pubns.

***Match Point.** rev. ed. Robin Cruise. (Take Ten Ser.). (Illus.). 52p. (YA). (gr. 4-12). 1999. pap. 3.95 (1-58659-035-9) Artesian.

Match Point Bridge. Hugh Kelsey. (Illus.). 240p. 1996. pap. 19.95 (0-575-04937-5, Pub. by V Gollancz) Trafalgar.

Match Pointers: Courtside with the Winningest Coach in Tennis History. Dan Magill. 192p. 1995. 19.95 (1-56352-194-6) Longstreet.

Match Shapes with Me. Reader's Digest Editors & Susan Hood. (Fisher Price Spin & Learn Bks.). (Illus.). 12p. (J). (gr. k-3). 1999. bds. 6.99 (1-57584-324-2, Pub. by Rdrs Digest) Random.

Match Success. 2nd rev. ed. Stanley Zaslau. 130p. 1996. pap. text 25.00 (1-886468-10-9) FMSG.

Match This, P. J. Funnybunny. Judith Conaway. 32p. (J). 1998. pap. 3.99 (0-679-88165-4, Pub. by Random Bks Yng Read) Random.

Match to the Heart: One Woman's Story of Being Struck by Lightning. Gretel Ehrlich. 240p. 1995. pap. 13.00 (0-14-017937-2, Penguin Bks) Viking Penguin.

Match Tournament at St. Petersburg, 1895-6. John C. Owen. (World's Greatest Chess Tournaments Ser.). (Illus.). 118p. 1989. 26.00 (0-939433-10-9) Caissa Edit.

***Match Wits with American Mensa: Test Your Trivia Smarts.** Peter Gordon. LC 99-39743. 96p. 1999. pap. text 6.95 (0-8069-1243-X) Sterling.

***Match Wits with Mensa: The Complete Quiz Book.** Marvin Grosswirth. (Mensa Genius Quiz Ser.). 646p. 1999. pap. text 19.95 (0-7382-0250-9, Pub. by Perseus Pubng) HarpC.

Match Wits with Sherlock Holmes. Murray Shaw. (J). 1993. 14.95 (0-87614-717-1, Lerner Publctns) Lerner Pub.

Match Wits with Sherlock Holmes, Vol. 3. Illus. by George Overlie. (Match Wits with Sherlock Holmes Ser.: Vol. III). (J). (gr. 4-7). 1993. pap. 4.95 (0-87614-530-6, Carolrhoda) Lerner Pub.

***Matchbook: A Little Collection of Flammable Poems.** Ed. by Suzanne Lummis. 33p. 1999. pap. 12.00 (1-889504-01-7) Red Wind Bks.

Matchbox & Lledo Toys: Price Guide & Variations List. Edward Force. LC 88-61034. (Illus.). 185p. 1988. pap. 14.95 (0-88740-127-9) Schiffer.

Matchbox Mountain: Stories Based on a Mountain Childhood. Amy A. Garza. LC 94-36115. (Illus.). 96p. (Orig.). 1994. pap. 6.95 (0-914875-24-8) Bright Mtn Bks.

***Matchbox Toys.** 5th rev. ed. Nancy N. Schiffer. (Illus.). 208p. 2000. pap. 19.95 (0-7643-0991-9) Schiffer.

Matchbox Toys: A Collector's Guide. Peter Mcmarco. 1993. 17.98 (1-55521-937-3) Bk Sales Inc.

Matchbox Toys: Revised, with Updated Price Guide. 4th enl. rev. ed. Nancy Schiffer. (Illus.). 208p. 1998. pap. 19.95 (0-7643-0495-X) Schiffer.

Matchbox Toys: The Universal Years, 1982-1992. Charlie Mack. (Illus.). 256p. 1993. pap. 19.95 (0-88740-550-9) Schiffer.

Matchbox Toys: The Universal Years, 1982-1992. 2nd rev. ed. Charlie Mack. (Illus.). 256p. 1999. pap. 19.95 (0-7643-0771-1) Schiffer.

Matchbox Toys, 1947-1998. 3rd ed. Dana Johnson. LC 99-195683. 240p. 1999. pap. text 19.95 (1-57432-115-3) Collector Bks.

Matchbox Toys, the Tyco Years, 1993-1994. Charlie Mack. LC 95-19425. (Illus.). 144p. (Orig.). 1995. pap. 19.95 (0-88740-865-6) Schiffer.

Matchcover Collector's Price Guide. 2nd rev. ed. Bill Retskin. LC 97-72680. (Illus.). 304p. 1998. pap. 21.95 (0-930625-77-3) Krause Pubns.

Matched Aymptotic Expansions. P. A. Lagerstrom. (Applied Mathematical Sciences Ser.: Vol. 76). (Illus.). xiii, 251p. 1988. 65.95 (0-387-96811-3) Spr-Verlag.

Matched by Mistake. Gina F. Wilkins et al. 1996. per. 5.99 (0-373-20123-0, 1-20123-5) Harlequin Bks.

Matched Colts. Don Bendell. 1997. mass mkt. 5.99 (0-451-19128-5, Sig) NAL.

Matched Field Processing for Underwater Acoustics. A. Tolstoy. 228p. 1993. text 74.00 (981-02-1059-0) World Scientific Pub.

Matched Mortality & Population Schedules of the 1860 Census of Albany City & County, NY. David P. Davenport. LC 93-182178. 133p. 1988. lib. bdg. 27.00 (1-56012-083-5, 82) Kinship Rhinebeck.

***Matched Pair: The Elys of Embassy Row.** Jarvis Harriman. (Illus.). 304p. 2000. 24.95 (0-9634323-2-X); pap. 14.95 (0-9634323-1-1) Pooh Stix Pr.

Matched Pairs. Elizabeth Mansfield. 224p. (Orig.). 1996. mass mkt. 4.99 (0-515-11785-4, Jove) Berkley Pub.

Matched Pearls. Grace Livingston Hill. 21.95 (0-8488-0081-8) Amereon Ltd.

Matched Pearls. Grace Livingston Hill. (Grace Livingston Hill Ser.: Vol. 30). 272p. 1996. pap. text 4.99 (0-8423-3895-0) Tyndale Hse.

Matches at Midnight. Sibyl J. Pischke. (Illus.). 365p. (Orig.). 1987. pap. 4.95 (0-9608532-1-9) S J Pischke.

Matches to Nitrosamines see Encyclopedia of Chemical Technology

Matching. (Look & Learn Ser.). (Illus.). 24p. (J). 1993. 7.98 (1-56173-905-7) Pubns Intl Ltd.

Matching. Barney Publishing Staff. 32p. (J). 1997. pap. text, wbk. ed. 2.95 (1-57064-124-2, Barney Publ) Lyrick Pub.

Matching. Istar Schwager. (Look & Learn Ser.). (Illus.). 24p. (J). (ps-2). 1993. lib. bdg. 13.95 (1-56674-068-1, HTS Bks) Forest Hse.

Matching: Similarities & Differences. (Home Workbooks Ser.). (Illus.). 64p. (Orig.). (J). (ps-1). 1995. pap., wbk. ed. 2.49 (0-88724-306-1, CD6803) Carson-Dellos.

Matching Books to Readers: A Leveled Book List for Guided Reading, K-3. Irene Fountas & Gay Su Pinnell. 416p. 1999. pap. text 27.50 (0-325-00193-6, E00193) Heinemann.

Matching Clients & Services: Information & Referral. R. Mark Mathews & Stephen B. Fawcett. LC 81-4337. (Sage Human Services Guide Ser.: No. 21). (Illus.). 160p. 1981. reprint ed. pap. 49.60 (0-608-01174-6, 205947200001) Bks Demand.

Matching Colors. Piers Baker. (Build-a-Block Bks.). (Illus.). 16p. (J). (ps-1). 1998. 9.99 (0-689-81568-9) Litle Simon.

Matching Consultation, Assessment, & Intervention. Donald J. Dickinson. LC 93-79581. (Illus.). 310p. (C). 1993. pap. text 18.00 (0-9637951-4-7) Hart-Whitlow Pubs.

Matching End Use Energy Needs to Source Possibilities. 101p. 1981. 20.00 (0-318-17713-7, DG 81-328) Pub Tech Inc.

Matching Gift Details Directory, 1997-98: The Guidebook to Corporate Matching Gift Programs. 1997. pap. 121.00 (0-89964-319-1, 21897) Coun Adv & Supp Ed.

Matching Law: A Research Review. Michael Davison & Dianne McCarthy. 296p. 1987. 59.95 (0-89859-923-7) L Erlbaum Assocs.

***Matching Law: Papers in Psychology & Economics.** Richard J. Herrnstein. 2000. pap. text 19.95 (0-674-00177-X) HUP.

Matching Metaphors: Companion Teaching Tales to Teaching Stress Management Skills. Frances K. Wiggins. 45p. (Orig.). (C). 1987. pap. 6.50 (0-942937-03-1) Rivijon Pr.

Matching Methodology. Prem K. Goel & T. Ramalingam. (Lecture Notes in Statistics Ser.: Vol. 52). (Illus.). viii, 152p. 1989. pap. 20.60 (0-318-41906-8) Spr-Verlag.

Matching of Asymptotic Expansions of Solutions of Boundary Value Problems. A. M. Ilin. Tr. by V. V. Minachin from RUS. LC 92-12324. (Translations of Mathematical Monographs: Vol. 102). 281p. 1992. text 169.00 (0-8218-4561-6, MMONO/102) Am Math.

Matching of Orbital Integrals on Gl(4) & GSP(2) Y. Z. Flicker. LC 98-46542. (Memoirs of the American Mathematical Society Ser.). 1999. 41.00 (0-8218-0959-8) Am Math.

Matching People with Services in Long-Term Care. Ed. by Zev Harel & Ruth Dunkle. LC 95-3183. (Illus.). 304p. 1995. 42.95 (0-8261-8950-4) Springer Pub.

Matching Research & Policy in Integrated Water Management. J. Wisserhof. (Studies in Integrated Water Management: No. 3). 200p. (Orig.). 1994. pap. 52.50 (90-407-1026-0, Pub. by Delft U Pr) Coronet Bks.

Matching Resources to Needs in Community Care. Bleddwyn Davies & David Challis. 350p. 1986. text 91.95 (1-85742-113-2, Pub. by Arena) Ashgate Pub Co.

Matching Revenues with Costs: An Analysis of Accounting Adaptation to Uncertainty. Reed K. Storey. LC 77-87305. (Development of Contemporary Accounting Thought Ser.). 1978. lib. bdg. 23.95 (0-405-10944-X) Ayer.

Matching Shapes. Piers Baker. (Build-a-Block Bks.). (Illus.). 16p. (J). (ps-1). 1998. 9.99 (0-689-81569-7) Litle Simon.

***Matching the Energy Source to the Clinical Need: Proceedings of a Conference Held 23-24 January, 2000, San Jose, California.** Thomas P. Ryan & Society of Photo-Optical Instrumentation Engineers Staff. LC 99-59974. (Critical Reviews of Optical Science & Technology Ser.). 2000. pap. write for info. (0-8194-3512-0) SPIE.

Matching the Hatch: Stillwater, River & Stream. Pat O'Reilly. (Illus.). 224p. 1998. 24.95 (1-85310-822-7) Swan Hill Pr.

Matching Theory. Laszlo Lovasz & M. D. Plummer. 544p. 1986. 161.50 (0-444-87916-1, North Holland) Elsevier.

Matching Up: Winning with Team Defense. Marnald Ostby. 57p. (Orig.). 1985. pap. 9.95 (0-932741-03-7) Championship Bks & Vid Prodns.

Matching Yourself with the World of Work. Melvin Fountain. 10p. 1986. pap. 1.00 (0-16-003789-1) USGPO.

Matching Yourself with the World of Work: Prospects & Earnings for 200 Occupations. 1991. lib. bdg. 75.00 (0-8490-5149-5) Gordon Pr.

***Matching Yourself with the World of Work, 1998.** Erik A. Savisaar. 19p. 1998. pap. 2.25 (0-16-061772-3) USGPO.

Matchless Altar of the Soul: Symbolized As a Shining Cube of Diamond, One Cubit in Dimensions, & Set Within the Holy of Holies in All Grand Esoteric Temples of Antiquity (1917) Edgar L. Larkin. 310p. 1996. reprint ed. pap. 24.95 (1-56459-525-0) Kessinger Pub.

Matchless Mice. Tony Hickey. 64p. (J). 1992. pap. 6.95 (0-947962-16-6) Dufour.

Matchless Mice in Space. Tony Hickey. 80p. (J). 1986. pap. 5.95 (0-947962-10-7) Dufour.

Matchless Mice's Adventure. Tony Hickey. 64p. (J). 1984. pap. 5.95 (0-900068-81-7) Dufour.

Matchless Model A, a Tour Through the Factory. Ford Motor Company Staff. Ed. by Dan R. Post. (Illus.). 64p. 1961. pap. 5.00 (0-911160-29-9) Post Group.

Matchless Weapon - Satyagraha. James K. Mathews. 210p. 1994. pap. 15.00 (0-934676-77-1) Greenlf Bks.

M

Matchlock Gun. Walter D. Edmonds. (Illus.). 64p. (J). (gr. 3-7). 1941. 16.95 (*0-399-21911-0*, G P Putnam) Peng Put Young Read.
Matchlock Gun. Walter D. Edmonds. (Illus.). 80p. (J). (gr. 3-7). 1998. pap. 4.99 (*0-698-11680-1*, PapStar) Peng Put Young Read.
Matchmaker see Best American Plays: Fourth Series, 1952-1957
***Matchmaker.** Rexanne Becnel. 2001. pap. write for info. (*0-312-97699-2*, St Martins Paperbacks) St Martin.
Matchmaker. Debra S. Cowan. 272p. (Orig.). 1995. mass mkt. 4.99 (*0-515-11711-0*, Jove) Berkley Pub.
Matchmaker & She Stoops to Conquer: Curriculum Unit. Center for Learning Network Staff et al. (Drama Ser.). 64p. (YA). (gr. 9-12). 1995. spiral bd. 18.95 (*1-56077-325-1*) Ctr Learning.
Matchmakers. Janet Dailey. (Janet Dailey Americana Ser.: No. 8). 1991. per. 3.50 (*0-373-89858-4*) Harlequin Bks.
Matchmakers. Janette Oke. LC 97-33830. 144p. 1997. pap. 12.99 (*0-7642-2020-9*); text 12.99 (*0-7642-2002-0*) Bethany Hse.
Matchmakers. large type ed. Audrey Blanshard. (Dales Large Print Ser.). 259p. 1997. pap. 18.99 (*1-85389-763-9*, Dales) Ulverscroft.
Matchmaker's Match. Nina Porter. 1992. mass mkt. 3.50 (*0-8217-3783-X*, Zebra Kensgtn) Kensgtn Pub Corp.
***Matchmakers.com.** Diana Burke. (Full House Sisters Ser.). (Illus.). 160p. (J). (gr. 4-6). 2000. per. 3.99 (*0-671-04091-X*, Minstrel Bks) PB.
Matchmaking Baby. Cathy G. Thacker. LC 96-2790. (American Romance Ser.). 247p. 1996. per. 3.50 (*0-373-16613-3*, 1-16613-1) Harlequin Bks.
Matchmaking Baby. Cathy Gillen Thacker. (Promo Ser.). 1999. per. 4.50 (*0-373-21981-4*, 1-21981-5) Harlequin Bks.
Matchmaking Ghost. Janice Bennett. (Zebra Romance Ser.). 256p. 1998. pap. 4.99 (*0-8217-5890-X*, Zebra Kensgtn) Kensgtn Pub Corp.
Matchmaking Mona. Diana Mars. (Desire Ser.: No. 1080). 1997. per. 3.50 (*0-373-76080-9*, 1-76080-0) Silhouette.
***Matchsafes.** Deborah Sampson Shinn. (Illus.). 112p. 2000. pap. 24.95 (*1-85759-237-9*, Pub. by Scala Books) Antique Collect.
***Matchstick Fun Book.** Dennis Patten. (Illus.). 48p. (J). 1999. pap. 9.95 (*0-7641-1215-5*) Barron.
Matchsticks. Phydella Hogan. LC 92-71896. 78p. 1992. pap. 9.95 (*0-9664290-2-8*) Lost Creek Pr.
Mate. Jack Rudman. (Career Examination Ser.: C-3156). 1994. pap. 29.95 (*0-8373-3156-0*) Nat Learn.
Mate Choice in Plants: Tactics, Mechanisms, & Consequences. Mary F. Willson & Nancy Burley. LC 83-42590. (Monographs in Population Biology: No. 19). (Illus.). 264p. reprint ed. pap. 81.90 (*0-608-06301-0*, 206666300008) Bks Demand.
Mate for Murder: And Other Tales from the Pulps. Russell Grey, pseud & Bruno Fischer. 1992. pap. 15.00 (*0-936071-26-5*) Gryphon Pubns.
Mate, Master & Extra Master, Vol. 11. Brown, Son & Ferguson Ltd. Staff. (C). 1987. 180.00 (*0-7855-6058-0*) St Mut.
***Mate Next Move.** Michael Jacob Rochlin. (Illus.). 80p. 2000. write for info. (*0-9648304-4-2*); pap. write for info. (*0-9648304-3-4*) Unreinforced Mason.
Mate of the Daylight & Friends Ashore. Sarah Orne Jewett. (Collected Works of Sarah Orne Jewett). 1988. reprint ed. lib. bdg. 59.00 (*0-7812-1305-3*) Rprt Serv.
Mate Relationship: Cross-Cultural Applications of a Rules Theory. Anne M. Nicotera. LC 97-500. (SUNY Series, Human Communication Processes). 183p. (C). 1997. text 59.50 (*0-7914-3543-1*); pap. text 19.95 (*0-7914-3544-X*) State U NY Pr.
Mate Selection: A Study of Complementary Needs. Robert F. Winch. (Reprint Series in Sociology). reprint ed. pap. text 16.95 (*0-89197-842-9*); reprint ed. lib. bdg. 39.50 (*0-697-00215-2*) Irvington.
Mate Selection: How to Make Things Start & Go Right. Roosevelt Gentry & William T. Henderson. Ed. by John Neel. LC 86-72012. 1987. pap. 10.00 (*0-938991-03-5*) Colonial Pr AL.
Matean Voghberkowtean: The Book of Lamentations, Gregory Narekatzi. Ed. by James R. Russell. LC 81-6177. 416p. 1982. 50.00 (*0-88206-029-5*) Caravan Bks.
Matemaker. Eli Glass. (Read-along Radio Dramas Ser.). (YA). (gr. 7-12). 1984. ring bd. 38.00 (*1-878298-09-7*) Balance Pub.
Matematica Aplicada: Aprendizaje de Tecnicas de Resolvcion de Problemas. Center for Occupational Research & Development Staff. (Illus.). 1993. teacher ed. write for info. (*1-55502-493-9*); pap. text. write for info. (*1-55502-492-0*) CORD Commns.
Matematica Aplicada: Conozca Su Calculadora. Center for Occupational Research & Development Staff. (Illus.). 1993. teacher ed. write for info. (*1-55502-487-4*); pap. text. write for info. (*1-55502-486-6*) CORD Commns.
Matematica Aplicada: Diferentes Formas de Llamar a los Numeros. Center for Occupational Research & Development Staff. (Illus.). 1993. teacher ed. write for info. (*1-55502-489-0*); pap. text. write for info. (*1-55502-488-2*) CORD Commns.
Matematica Aplicada: Encontramos Respuestas Con la Calculadora. Center for Occupational Research & Development Staff. (Illus.). 1993. teacher ed. write for info. (*1-55502-491-2*); pap. text. write for info. (*1-55502-490-4*) CORD Commns.
Matematica Aplicada: Estimacion y Calculo de Respuestas. Center for Occupational Research & Development Staff. (Illus.). 1993. teacher ed. write for info. (*1-55502-495-5*); pap. text. write for info. (*1-55502-494-7*) CORD Commns.
Matematica Aplicada: Medidas en Unidades Inglesas y Metricas. Center for Occupational Research & Development Staff. (Illus.). 1993. pap. text. write for info. (*1-55502-496-3*) CORD Commns.
Matematica Aplicada: Nos Ocupamos de los Datos. Center for Occupational Research & Development Staff. (Illus.). 1993. pap. text. write for info. (*1-55502-500-5*) CORD Commns.
Matematica Aplicada: Trabajo Con Dibujos a Escala. Center for Occupational Research & Development Staff. (Illus.). 1993. pap. text. write for info. (*1-55502-510-2*) CORD Commns.
Matematica Aplicada: Trabajo Con Formas en Tres Dimensiones. Center for Occupational Research & Development Staff. (Illus.). 1993. pap. text. write for info. (*1-55502-506-4*) CORD Commns.
Matematica Aplicada: Trabajo Con Formas on Dos Dimensiones. Center for Occupational Research & Development Staff. (Illus.). 1993. teacher ed. write for info. (*1-55502-505-6*); pap. text. write for info. (*1-55502-504-8*) CORD Commns.
Matematica Aplicada: Trabajo Con Rectas y Angulos. Center for Occupational Research & Development Staff. (Illus.). 1993. pap. text. write for info. (*1-55502-502-1*) CORD Commns.
Matematica Aplicada: Use de Notacion Cientifica. Center for Occupational Research & Development Staff. (Illus.). 1993. pap. text. write for info. (*1-55502-514-5*) CORD Commns.
Matematica Aplicada: Uso de Graficos, Cuadrosy Tablas. Center for Occupational Research & Development Staff. (Illus.). 1993. pap. text. write for info. (*1-55502-498-X*) CORD Commns.
Matematica Aplicada: Uso de Numeros Con Su Signoy Vectores. Center for Occupational Research & Development Staff. (Illus.). 1993. pap. text. write for info. (*1-55502-512-9*) CORD Commns.
Matematica Aplicada: Uso de Razones y Proporciones. Center for Occupational Research & Development Staff. (Illus.). 1993. pap. text. write for info. (*1-55502-508-0*) CORD Commns.
Matematica Basica. Diana Santos & Ramon L. Lopez. (SPA.). 481p. 1995. pap. write for info. (*0-929441-09-5*) Pubns Puertorriquenas.
Matematica para la Familia. Jean K. Stenmark et al. Tr. by Jorge M. Lopez. (Equals Ser.). Orig. Title: Family Math. (SPA., Illus.). 320p. (J). (gr. k-8). 1997. pap. 19.95 (*0-912511-08-7*, EQUALS) Lawrence Science.
Matematicas 5+ 1999. 19.95 (*3-8290-2505-X*, 541072) Konemann.
Matematicas de Addison-Wesley. 1990. 25.66 (*0-201-62939-9*) Addison-Wesley.
Matematicas de Addison-Wesley. (C). 1990. 25.67 (*0-201-62938-0*) Addison-Wesley.
Matematicas de Addison-Wesley. 2nd ed. Robert Eicholz. 1987. pap. text, student ed. 19.48 (*0-201-26050-6*) Addison-Wesley.
Matematicas de Addison-Wesley, Bk. 3. 2nd ed. Robert Eicholz. 1987. pap. text 45.96 (*0-201-26350-5*) Addison-Wesley.
Matematicas de Addison-Wesley, Bk. 4. 2nd ed. Robert Eicholz. (C). 1987. pap. text 43.66 (*0-201-26450-1*) Addison-Wesley.
Matematicas de Addison-Wesley, Bk. 5. 2nd ed. Robert Eicholz. (C). 1987. pap. text 43.66 (*0-201-26550-8*) Addison-Wesley.
Matematicas de Addison-Wesley, Bk. 6. 2nd ed. Robert Eicholz. (C). 1987. pap. text 43.66 (*0-201-26650-4*) Addison-Wesley.
Matematicas de Addison Wesley: Suplemento de Practica 1. Addison-Wesley Publishing Staff. (SPA.). 168p. (C). 1995. pap. text 8.00 (*0-201-51862-7*) Addison-Wesley.
Matematicas de Addison Wesley: Suplemento de Practica 2. Addison-Wesley Publishing Staff. (SPA.). 168p. (C). 1995. pap. text 8.00 (*0-201-51863-5*) Addison-Wesley.
Matematicas de Addison Wesley: Suplemento de Practica 3. Addison-Wesley Publishing Staff. (SPA.). 168p. (C). 1995. pap. text 8.00 (*0-201-51864-3*) Addison-Wesley.
Matematicas de Addison Wesley: Suplemento de Practica 4. Addison-Wesley Publishing Staff. (SPA.). 168p. (C). 1995. pap. text 8.00 (*0-201-51865-1*) Addison-Wesley.
Matematicas de Addison Wesley: Suplemento de Practica 5. Addison-Wesley Publishing Staff. 1995. pap. text. write for info. (*0-201-51866-X*) Addison-Wesley.
Matematicas de Addison Wesley: Suplemento de Practica 6. Addison-Wesley Publishing Staff. (SPA.). 168p. (C). 1995. pap. text 8.00 (*0-201-51867-8*) Addison-Wesley.
Matematicas Discretas Y Combinatorias. 3rd ed. 1056p. (C). 1997. pap. 21.33 (*0-201-65376-1*) HEPC Inc.
Matematicas Mentales en Espanol. Ellen Hechler.Tr. of Mental Math Brain Skills in Spanish. (SPA.). (Orig.). (YA). 1997. pap. text 6.00 (*0-9638483-0-5*) Midmath.
Matematicas Modernas en el Nivel Elemental: Guia Metodologica. Fe Acosta DeGonzalez & Isabel Freire DeMatos. (Illus.). 245p. 1971. 5.00 (*0-8477-2700-9*) U of PR Pr.
Matematicas para Ingenieira Electronica, Modelos & Aplicaciones. J. E. Szymanski. (SPA.). 240p. (C). 1994. pap. text 14.33 (*0-201-62553-9*) Addison-Wesley.
Matematicas Para Niveles Intermedios. Prentice-Hall Staff. (SPA.). 1997. 49.29 (*0-13-839689-2*); 52.63 (*0-13-839697-3*); 52.63 (*0-13-839705-8*) P-H.
Matematicas Sin Limites: Grade K. Fennell. (SPA.). (J). (gr. k). 1988. pap. 16.75 (*0-03-009138-1*) Harcourt Schl Pubs.
Matematicas Sin Limites: Grade Kindergarten. Fennell. (SPA.). 1988. pap., teacher ed. 33.00 (*0-03-009153-5*) Harcourt Schl Pubs.
Matematicas Sin Limites: Grade 1. Fennell. (SPA.). 1988. teacher ed. 74.50 (*0-03-009157-8*); pap. 22.00 (*0-03-009139-X*) Harcourt Schl Pubs.
Matematicas Sin Limites: Grade 2. Fennell. (SPA.). 1988. teacher ed. 74.50 (*0-03-009154-3*); pap. 22.00 (*0-03-009142-X*) Harcourt Schl Pubs.
Matematicas Sin Limites: Grade 3. Fennell. (SPA.). 1988. teacher ed. 84.25 (*0-03-009158-6*); pap. 22.00 (*0-03-009143-8*) Harcourt Schl Pubs.
Matematicas Sin Limites: Grade 4. Fennell. (SPA.). 1988. teacher ed. 84.25 (*0-03-009159-4*) Harcourt Schl Pubs.
Matematicas Sin Limites: Grade 5. Fennell. (SPA.). 1988. teacher ed. 84.25 (*0-03-009162-4*) Harcourt Schl Pubs.
Matematicas Sin Limites: Grade 6. Fennell. (SPA.). 1988. teacher ed. 84.25 (*0-03-009163-2*) Harcourt Schl Pubs.
Matematicas Sin Limites, 1988. Fennell. 1988. 42.00 (*0-03-009147-0*) Harcourt Schl Pubs.
Matematicas Sin Limites, 1988. Fennell. (J). (gr. k-4). 1988. 42.00 (*0-03-009144-6*) Harcourt Schl Pubs.
Matematicas Sin Limites, 1988: Grades 6. Fennell. 1988. 43.25 (*0-03-009148-9*) Harcourt Schl Pubs.
Matematicas 3+ 19.95 (*3-8290-0976-3*, 540683) Konemann.
Matematicas Y Metodos. Shao. (C). 1997. 27.00 (*0-673-19246-6*) Addison-Wesley.
Matematicas/Mathematics: Grades 1-6 Mathematics Handbook for Bilingual Education Teachers. Magdalena Laswell. (SPA., Illus.). 114p. 1998. spiral bd. 25.00 (*0-944551-33-5*) Sundance Pr TX.
Matematika - Priklady Na Prijimacie Skusky Na Stredne Skoly (Mathematics - Problems to Study for Admittance Examinations for Secondary Schools) L. Hrdina & M. Maxian. (SLO.). 192p. 1997. pap. write for info. (*80-08-02432-1*, Pub. by Slov Pegagog Naklad) IBD Ltd.
Matematika i Sport see Mathematics & Sports
Matematika V Poistovnictve (Mathematics in the System of Insurance) F. Lamos. (SLO.). 136p. 1997. pap. write for info. (*80-08-02552-2*, Pub. by Slov Pegagog Naklad) IBD Ltd.
Matengo Folk Tales. Joseph L. Mbele. 1999. pap. 13.95 (*0-7414-0028-6*) Buy Books.
Mateo. James Bartley et al. Ed. by Daniel Carro et al. (Comentario Biblico Mundo Hispano Ser.: Vol. 14). (SPA., Illus.). 379p. 1993. pap. 9.99 (*0-311-03114-5*, Edit Mundo) Casa Bautista.
Mateo. Arthur Robertson. (Comentario Biblico Portavoz Ser.). (SPA.). 168p. 1994. pap. 6.99 (*0-8254-1620-5*, Edit Portavoz) Kregel.
Mateo: El Rey y el Reino. Ronald Q. Leavell. Tr. by Alfredo Quezada from ENG. (Estudios Biblicos Basicos Ser.).Tr. of Matthew: the King & the Kingdom. (SPA.). 160p. 1988. pap. 7.99 (*0-311-04363-1*) Casa Bautista.
Mateo Aleman. Donald McGrady. LC 67-25196. (Twayne World Authors Ser.). 1968. lib. bdg. 20.95 (*0-8057-2028-6*) Irvington.
Mateo Atlas. Josep Lluis Mateo. 1998. pap. text 25.00 (*84-88258-25-9*) Colegio Arquit.
Mateo 1 (1:1 - 16:12) (Matthew 1 (1:1 - 16:12) Antonimo. (Biblia de Bosquejos y Sermones (The Preacher's Outline & Sermon Bible) Ser.). (SPA.). 336p. 1997. pap. 19.99 (*0-8254-1006-1*, Edit Portavoz) Kregel.
Mateo 2 (16:13 - 28:20) (Matthew 2 (16:13 - 28:20) Antonimo. (Biblia de Bosquejos y Sermones (The Preacher's Outline & Sermon Bible) Ser.). (SPA.). 272p. 1997. pap. 19.99 (*0-8254-1007-X*, Edit Portavoz) Kregel.
Mateo y la Grua de Medianoche. Allen Morgan. Tr. by Shirley Langer.Tr. of Matthew & the Midnight Tow Truck. (SPA., Illus.). 32p. (YA). (ps up). 1991. pap. 5.95 (*1-55037-190-8*, Pub. by Annick) Firefly Bks Ltd.
Mateo y los Pavos de Medianoche. Allen Morgan. Tr. by Shirley Langer.Tr. of Matthew & the Midnight Turkeys. (SPA., Illus.). 32p. (YA). (ps up). 1991. pap. 5.95 (*1-55037-188-6*, Pub. by Annick) Firefly Bks Ltd.
Mateo y los Reyes Magos. Alonso De Fernando. (SPA.). 1996. 24.95 (*84-372-2198-6*) Santillana.
Mateo y Mati. Rebecca C. Jones.Tr. of Matthew & Tilly. (J). 1995. 10.19 (*0-606-08567-X*, Pub. by Turtleback) Demco.
Mater Larum: Zum Wesen der Larenreligion. Ernst Tabeling. LC 75-10657. (Ancient Religion & Mythology Ser.). (GER.). 1976. reprint ed. 15.95 (*0-405-07265-1*) Ayer.
Mater Spiritualis: The Life of Adelheid of Vilich. Berta of Vilich. Tr. by Madelyn B. Dyck. (Translation Ser.). 152p. 1994. pap. 15.00 (*0-920669-48-4*, Pub. by Peregrina Pubng) Cistercian Pubns.
***Master the ACT 2001.** IDG Books Worldwide Staff. (Illus.). 702p. 2000. pap. 14.95 (*0-7645-6080-8*) IDG Bks.
Materada. Fulvio Tomizza. Tr. by Russell S. Valentino. LC 99-56050. 136p. 2000. 45.95 (*0-8101-1758-4*); pap. 15.95 (*0-8101-1759-2*) Northwestern U Pr.
Materia Critica. George J. Nathan. LC 75-120099. 242p. 1975. 24.50 (*0-8386-7966-8*) Fairleigh Dickinson.
Materia Dispuesta. Juan Villoro. 1998. pap. 19.95 (*968-19-0305-6*) Santillana.
Materia Indica, 2 vols., Set. W. Ainslie. (C). 1988. reprint ed. 100.00 (*0-7855-2257-3*, Pub. by Scientific) St Mut.
Materia Indica, Vol. 1. W. Ainslie. xxxiv, 654p. 1979. reprint ed. 300.00 (*0-7855-6645-7*, Pub. by Intl Bk Distr) St Mut.
Materia Inidica, Vol. 1. W. Ainslie. (C). 1979. text 325.00 (*0-89771-539-X*, Pub. by Intl Bk Distr) St Mut.
Materia Medica see Elsevier's Dictionary of Pharmaceutical Science & Techniques
***Materia Medica Lecture Notes of Carl A. Williams.** Jay Yasgur. LC 99-95094. (Illus.). 275p. 2000. pap. 22.00 (*1-886149-06-2*) Van Hoy Pubs.
Materia Medica of Ayureda. Bhagwan D. Vaidya. (C). 1991. text 18.50 (*0-8364-2781-5*) S Asia.
Materia Medica of Ayurveda. Bhagwan Dash & Lalitesh Kashyap. (C). 1988. 64.00 (*0-8364-2325-9*, Pub. by Concept) S Asia.
Materia Medica of Ayurveda. Bhagwan Dass. (C). 1988. 75.00 (*0-7855-2283-2*, Pub. by Scientific) St Mut.
Materia Medica of Human Mind. M. L. Aggarwal. 783p. 1985. 29.95 (*0-318-36364-X*) Asia Bk Corp.
Materia Medica of Indo-Tibetan Medicine. Vaidya B. Dash. 647p. (C). 1987. 64.00 (*81-85132-00-3*, Pub. by Classics India Pubns) S Asia.
Materia Medica of the Hindus. U. C. Dutt. 1989. reprint ed. 46.50 (*0-8364-2540-5*, Pub. by Mittal Pubs Dist) S Asia.
Materia Medica of the Hindus. U. C. Dutt. (C). 1995. reprint ed. 30.00 (*0-8364-2915-X*, Pub. by Mittal Pubs Dist) S Asia.
Materia Medica of Tibetan Medicine. Vaidya B. Dash. LC 93-908512. (C). 1994. 98.00 (*81-7030-387-7*, Pub. by Sri Satguru Pubns) S Asia.
Materia Medica of W. India. A. Dymock. (C). 1986. 140.00 (*0-7855-2264-6*, Pub. by Scientific) St Mut.
Materia Medica with Repertory. William Boericke. 1982. 25.00 (*0-685-76567-9*) Formur Intl.
Materia Solar-Solar Matter. Eugenio De Andrade. Tr. by Alexis Levitin from POR. LC 94-26801. (ENG & POR.). 128p. (Orig.). 1994. pap. 12.95 (*0-936609-34-6*) QED Ft Bragg.
Material & Capacity Requirements Planning Certification Review Course Instructor Guide Kit. LC 87-71851. 1994. 600.00 (*1-55822-076-3*) Am Prod & Inventory.
Material & Capacity Requirements Planning Reprints. Ed. by American Production & Inventory Control Society St. LC 86-70024. 332p. 1993. pap. 21.00 (*1-55822-042-9*) Am Prod & Inventory.
Material & Capacity Requirements Planning Student Guide. American Production & Inventory Control Society St. 1993. 37.00 (*1-55822-077-1*) Am Prod & Inventory.
Material & Energy Balances. Alois X. Schmidt & Harvey L. List. 1962. text 72.67 (*0-13-560219-X*) P-H.
Material & Energy Balances: A Self Instructional Problem Workbook. J. Reynolds. 240p. (C). 1992. pap. text 60.00 (*1-882767-07-1*) ETS.
Material & Energy Balancing in the Process Industries: From Microscopic Balances to Large Plants. Vladimir Veverka & Frantisek Madron. LC 96-49566. (Computer-Aided Chemical Engineering Ser.). 648p. 1996. 322.00 (*0-444-82409-X*) Elsevier.
Material & Interpretation: The Archaeology of Sjaelland in the Early Roman Iron Age. David Liversage. (Publications of the National Museum: No. 1; Pt. 20). (Illus.). 204p. (C). 1980. pap. 21.00 (*87-480-0311-5*, Pub. by Aarhus Univ Pr) David Brown.
Material & Methods for Contemporary Construction. 2nd ed. Caleb Hornbostel & William J. Hornung. 1982. write for info. (*0-318-56632-X*) P-H.
Material & Process Advances '82: National SAMPE Technical Conference, 14th, Sheraton Hotel, Atlanta, Georgia, October 12-14, 1982. National SAMPE Technical Conference Staff. LC 82-232953. (National SAMPE Technical Conference Ser.: No. 14). 584p. reprint ed. pap. 181.10 (*0-7837-1290-1*, 204143100020) Bks Demand.
Material & Process Applications - Land, Sea, Air Space, 26th, National SAMPE Symposium & Exhibition. National SAMPE Symposium & Exhibition Staff. LC 81-183027. (Science of Advanced Materials & Process Enginnering Ser.: No. 26). 893p. reprint ed. pap. 200.00 (*0-7837-1279-0*, 204142000020) Bks Demand.
Material & Social Determinants of Political Leadership in a Tojolabal Maya Community. J. S. Thomas. xiii, 97p. 1986. 8.00 (*0-913134-27-9*) Mus Anthro MO.
Material Anthropology: Contemporary Approaches to Material Culture. Barrie Reynolds & Margaret A. Stott. (Illus.). 242p. (Orig.). 1987. lib. bdg. 47.50 (*0-8191-6543-3*) U Pr of Amer.
Material Aspects of Pomo Culture. S. A. Barrett. (Public Museum of the City of Milwaukee, Bulletins Ser.: Vol. 20, Pt. 1). (Illus.). 194p. 1952. pap. text 20.63 (*1-55567-880-7*) Coyote Press.
Material Aspects of Pomo Culture. S. A. Barrett. (Public Museum of the City of Milwaukee, Bulletins Ser.: Vol. 20, Pt. 2). (Illus.). 281p. 1952. pap. text 29.38 (*1-55567-881-5*) Coyote Press.
Material Aspects of Pomo Culture, 2 pts. in 1 vol. Samuel A. Barrett. LC 76-43649. (Bulletin of the Public Museum of the City of Milwaukee Ser.: Vol. 20). reprint ed. 67.50 (*0-404-15483-2*) AMS Pr.
Material Beings. Peter Van Inwagen. LC 90-55125. (Illus.). 288p. 1990. text 47.50 (*0-8014-1969-7*) Cornell U Pr.
Material Child: Coming of Age in Japan & America. Merry White. 200p. 1993. 24.95 (*0-02-935035-2*) Free Pr.
Material Child: Coming of Age in Japan & America. Merry White. LC 94-10639. 1994. reprint ed. pap. 14.95 (*0-520-08940-5*, Pub. by U CA Pr) Cal Prin Full Svc.
Material Christianity: Religion & Popular Culture in America. Colleen McDannell. (Illus.). 384p. 1996. pap. 24.95 (*0-300-07499-9*) Yale U Pr.
Material Christianity: Religion & Popular Culture in America. Colleen McDannell. LC 95-18066. (Illus.). 384p. 1998. 40.00 (*0-300-06440-3*) Yale U Pr.
Material Concerns: From Profit & Pollution to Quality of Life. Tim Jackson. LC 95-36950. (Illus.). 240p. (C). 1996. pap. 24.99 (*0-415-13249-5*) Routledge.
Material Conflicts: Parades & Visual Displays in Northern Ireland. Neil Jarman. LC 97-199843. (Illus.). 290p. 1997. 55.00 (*1-85973-124-4*, Pub. by Berg Pubs); pap. 19.50 (*1-85973-129-5*, Pub. by Berg Pubs) NYU Pr.
Material Constitution: A Reader. Ed. by Michael Rea. LC 96-37532. 408p. 1997. 73.00 (*0-8476-8383-4*); pap. 24.95 (*0-8476-8384-2*) Rowman.
Material Control Clerk I. Jack Rudman. (Career Examination Ser.: C-3088). 1994. pap. 23.95 (*0-8373-3088-2*) Nat Learn.

M

Material Control Clerk II. Jack Rudman. (Career Examination Ser.: C-3089). 1994. pap. 27.95 (*0-8373-3089-0*) Nat Learn.

Material Control Clerk III. Jack Rudman. (Career Examination Ser.: C-3090). 1994. pap. 27.95 (*0-8373-3090-4*) Nat Learn.

Material Control Clerk IV. Jack Rudman. (Career Examination Ser.: C-3091). 1994. pap. 29.95 (*0-8373-3091-2*) Nat Learn.

Material Culture. Henry Glassie. LC 99-36047. 1999. 29.95 (*0-253-33574-4*) Ind U Pr.

Material Culture: A Research Guide. Ed. by Thomas J. Schlereth. LC 85-15643. xiv, 226p. 1985. pap. 14.95 (*0-7006-0275-5*) U Pr of KS.

***Material Culture: The J.S. Emerson Collection of Hawaiian Artifacts.** Catherine C. Summers. LC 99-26662. 142p. 1999. 40.00 (*1-58178-006-0*) Bishop Mus.

Material Culture & Medieval Drama. Clifford Davidson. LC 98-54791. (Early Drama, Art, & Music Monographic Ser. : Vol. 25). 11p. 1999. pap. 15.00 (*1-58044-021-5*) Medieval Inst.

Material Culture & People's Art among the Norwegians in America. Marion Nelson et al. (Special Publications). 228p. 1994. 30.00 (*0-87732-082-9*) Norwegian-Am Hist Assn.

Material Culture & Social Institutions of the Simpler Peoples: An Essay in Correlation. Leonard T. Hobhouse et al. LC 74-25759. (European Sociology Ser.). 304p. 1975. reprint ed. 25.95 (*0-405-06513-2*) Ayer.

Material Culture in Europe & China, 1400-1800: The Rise of Consumerism. Samuel A. Adshead. LC 96-45195. 256p. 1997. text 59.95 (*0-312-17285-0*) St Martin.

***Material Culture in the Social World: Values, Activities, Lifestyles.** Tim Dant. LC 99-14375. 1999. pap. 24.95 (*0-335-19821-X*) OpUniv Pr.

Material Culture of Gender - The Gender of Material Culture. Ed. by Katharine A. Martinez & Kenneth L. Ames. LC 97-29399. (Illus.). 465p. 1997. 40.00 (*0-912724-40-4*) Winterthur.

Material Culture of Kapingamarangi: Coordinated Investigation of Micronesian Anthropology. Peter H. Buck. (BMB Ser.: No. 200). 1969. reprint ed. 45.00 (*0-527-02308-6*) Periodicals Srv.

Material Culture of Key Marco, Florida. Marion S. Gilliland. (Illus.). 266p. 1989. pap. 19.95 (*0-912451-24-6*) Florida Classics.

***Material Culture of Steamboat Passengers: Archaeological Evidence from the Missouri River.** Annalies Corbin. LC 99-48649. (Series in Underwater Archaeology). 237p. 1999. write for info. (*0-306-46168-4*) Kluwer Academic.

Material Culture of the American Freemasons. John D. Hamilton. LC 94-47242. (Illus.). 320p. 1994. text 80.00 (*0-87451-971-3*) U Pr of New Eng.

Material Culture of the Blackfoot Indians. Clark Wissler. LC 74-9018. (Anthropological Papers of the American Museum of Natural History: Vol. 5, Pt. 1). reprint ed. 42.50 (*0-404-11915-8*) AMS Pr.

Material Culture of the Chumash Interaction Sphere Vol. 2: Food Preparation & Shelter. Travis Hudson & Thomas C. Blackburn. LC 82-13832. (Anthropological Papers: No. 27). (Illus.). 462p. 1983. pap. 24.95 (*0-87919-102-3*); text 39.95 (*0-87919-103-1*) Ballena Pr.

Material Culture of the Chumash Interaction Sphere Vol. III: Clothing, Ornamentation, & Grooming. Travis Hudson & Thomas C. Blackburn. LC 82-13832. (Anthropological Papers: No. 28). (Illus.). 375p. (C). 1985. text 39.95 (*0-87919-105-8*) Ballena Pr.

Material Culture of the Chumash Interaction Sphere Vol.1: Food Procurement & Transportation. Travis Hudson & Thomas C. Blackburn. LC 82-13832. (Anthropological Papers: No. 25). (Illus.). 392p. 1982. pap. 24.95 (*0-87919-097-3*) Ballena Pr.

Material Culture of the Cook Islands (Aitutaki) Peter H. Buck. LC 75-35178. reprint ed. 59.50 (*0-404-14206-0*) AMS Pr.

Material Culture of the Crow Indians. Robert H. Lowie. LC 74-7980. reprint ed. 27.50 (*0-404-11869-0*) AMS Pr.

Material Culture of the Formosan Aborigines. Chen Chi-lu. (Illus.). 422p. 1986. reprint ed. 65.00 (*0-89986-362-0*) Oriental Bk Store.

Material Culture of the Iglulik Eskimos. Therkel Mathiassen. LC 76-21671. (Thule Expedition. 5th. 1921-1924 Ser.: Vol. 6, No. 1). reprint ed. 67.50 (*0-404-58317-2*) AMS Pr.

Material Culture of the Klamath Lake & Modoc Indians of Northeastern California & Southern Oregon. fac. ed. Samuel A. Barrett. (University of California Publications in American Archaeology & Ethnology: Vol. 5: 4). (Illus.). 55p. (C). 1910. reprint ed. pap. text 6.56 (*1-55567-172-1*) Coyote Press.

Material Culture of the Numa: The John Wesley Powell Collection, 1867-1880. Don D. Fowler & John F. Matley. LC 78-22066. (Smithsonian Contributions to Anthropology Ser.: No. 26). 187p. reprint ed. pap. 58.00 (*0-608-13836-3*, 202030700016) Bks Demand.

Material Culture of the Wooden Age. Ed. by Brooke Hindle. LC 81-2332. 400p. 1981. 22.50 (*0-912882-45-X*) Sleepy Hollow.

Material Culture Studies in America. Ed. & Compiled by Thomas J. Schlereth. LC 82-8812. (American Association for State & Local History Book Ser.). 430p. 1982. pap. 25.95 (*0-7619-9160-3*) AltaMira Pr.

Material Cultures: Why Some Things Matter. Daniel Miller. LC 97-31175. 256p. 1998. pap. 22.00 (*0-226-52601-1*); lib. bdg. 45.00 (*0-226-52600-3*) U Ch Pr.

Material Data for Cyclic Loading, 5 vols., Set. C. Boller & T. Seeger. (Materials Science Monographs: No. 42 A-E). xxxvi,1856p. 1987. 824.00 (*0-444-42875-5*) Elsevier.

Material Data for Electrical Engineering. J. Villain. (Illus.). 400p. 1997. 99.00 (*3-540-62002-8*) Spr-Verlag.

Material Discourses of Health & Illness. Ed. by Lucy Yardley. 256p. (C). 1997. 75.00 (*0-415-13823-X*) Routledge.

Material Discourses of Health & Illness. Ed. by Lucy Yardley & Jane M. Ussher. 256p. (C). 1997. pap. 24.99 (*0-415-13824-8*) Routledge.

Material Dreams: Southern California Through the 1920s. Kevin Starr. (Americans & the California Dream Ser.). 496p. (C). 1990. 35.00 (*0-19-504487-8*) OUP.

Material Dreams: Southern California Through the 1920s. Kevin Starr. (Illus.). 472p. 1991. reprint ed. pap. 16.95 (*0-19-507260-X*) OUP.

Material Durability - Life Prediction Modeling, Materials for the 21st Century: Proceedings: International Mechanical Engineering Congress & Exposition (1994: Chicago, IL) Ed. by G. R. Halford & S. Y. Zamrik. LC 94-79730. (PVP Ser.: Vol. 290). 151p. 1995. pap. 68.00 (*0-7918-1394-0*, G00889) ASME Pr.

Material-Environment Interactions in Structural & Pressure Containment Service: Papers Presented at the Winter Annual Meeting of the American Society of Mechanical Engineers, Chicago, Illinois, November 16-21, 1980. American Society of Mechanical Engineers Staff. Ed. by George V. Smith. LC 80-69194. (MPC Ser.: No. 15). (Illus.). 166p. reprint ed. pap. 51.50 (*0-8357-2879-X*, 203911600011) Bks Demand.

Material Environmental Data Sheets. Karel Verschueren. 1996. 165.00 (*0-471-28658-3*, VNR) Wiley.

Material Facilities Needed in the Training of Intermediate Grade Teachers in Science. Harry A. Cunningham. LC 73-176684. (Columbia University. Teachers College. Contributions to Education Ser.: No. 812). reprint ed. 37.50 (*0-404-55812-7*) AMS Pr.

Material Faith: Thoreau on Science. Henry David Thoreau. Ed. by Laura D. Walls. LC 99-12267. (The Spirit of Thoreau Ser.). (Illus.). 112p. 1999. pap. 6.95 (*0-395-94800-2*) HM.

Material Fill Rate & Flow Characteristics - Student's Manual: Controlling Cavity Filling, Lesson 2. (Illus.). 1997. pap., student ed. write for info. (*1-58677-044-6*) Polymer Train.

Material Fluxes on the Surface of the Earth. National Research Council, Geophysics Study Commit. LC 94-20773. (Studies in Geophysics). 192p. (C). 1994. text 39.95 (*0-309-04745-5*) Natl Acad Pr.

Material for the History of Dor. George Dahl. (Connecticut Academy of Arts & Sciences Ser., Trans.: Vol. 20). 1915. pap. 75.00 (*0-685-22848-7*) Elliots Bks.

Material for Thought. Far West Eds. Staff. LC 92-81570. 76p. 1992. pap. 11.00 (*0-614-30602-7*) Far West Edns.

Material for Thought, No. 8. Far West Editions Staff. LC 79-56899. 88p. 1979. pap. 6.00 (*0-914480-05-7*) Far West Edns.

Material for Thought, No. 9. Far West Editions Staff. LC 81-68048. 94p. 1981. pap. 6.00 (*0-914480-07-3*) Far West Edns.

Material for Thought, No. 10. Far West Editions Staff. LC 73-94407. 96p. 1983. pap. 4.95 (*0-317-17277-8*) Far West Edns.

Material for Thought, No. 11. Far West Editions Staff. LC 86-81101. 110p. 1986. pap. 4.95 (*0-685-52039-0*) Far West Edns.

Material for Thought, No. 14. Far West Editions Staff. LC 92-81570. 103p. 1995. pap. 12.00 (*0-614-30603-5*) Far West Edns.

Material for Thought, No.7. Far West Editions Staff. LC 77-89507. 76p. 1977. pap. 4.95 (*0-914480-03-0*) Far West Edns.

Material for Thought, Vol.74 & 76, Nos. 7 & 8. Far West Editions Staff. pap. 7.95 (*0-686-47075-3*) Far West Edns.

Material for Thought, 1970. Far West Editions Staff. 31p. 1970. pap. 3.00 (*0-686-47079-6*) Far West Edns.

Material for Thought, 1974. Far West Editions Staff. LC 73-94407. 114p. 1974. pap. 6.00 (*0-914480-01-4*) Far West Edns.

Material for Thought, 1971. Far West Editions Staff. 47p. 1971. pap. 3.00 (*0-686-47081-8*) Far West Edns.

Material for Thought, 1972. Far West Editions Staff. 63p. 1972. pap. 2.00 (*0-686-47082-6*) Far West Edns.

Material for Thought, Spring 1976. Far West Editions Staff. LC 73-94407. 1976. pap. 4.95 (*0-914480-02-2*) Far West Edns.

Material Ghost: Films & Their Medium. Gilberto Perez. LC 97-16877. (Illus.). 482p. 1998. 29.95 (*0-8018-5673-6*) Johns Hopkins.

***Material Ghost: Films & Their Medium.** Gilberto Perez. (Illus.). 448p. 2000. reprint ed. pap. 18.95 (*0-8018-6523-9*) Johns Hopkins.

Material Girls: Making Sense of Feminist Cultural Theory. Suzanna D. Walters. LC 94-29007. 1995. pap. 15.95 (*0-520-08978-2*, Pub. by U CA Pr) Cal Prin Full Svc.

Material Goods. Janet Burroway. LC 80-12381. 77p. 1980. pap. 16.95 (*0-8130-0670-8*) U Press Fla.

***Material Handling Machinery Market in Poland: A Strategic Entry Report, 1998.** Compiled by Icon Group International Staff. (Country Industry Report). (Illus.). 183p. 1999. ring bd. 1830.00 incl. audio compact disk (*0-7418-0263-5*) Icon Grp.

***Material Handling Systems: Designing for Safety & Health.** Charles D. Reese. LC 99-57159. 2000. write for info. (*1-56032-868-1*) Taylor & Francis.

Material Handling Systems & Terminology. Ed. by Edward Frazelle. 1992. 29.95 (*0-9629217-3-4*) Lionheart Pub.

Material Handling Technologies in Japan: Executive Summary. Ed. by Edward H. Frazelle & Richard E. Ward. ii, 5p. 1992. pap. write for info. (*1-883712-03-3*, JTEC) Intl Tech Res.

Material Identification Using Mixed Numerical Experimental Methods: Proceedings of the EUROMECH Colloquium Held in Kerkrade, The Netherlands, 7-9 Ajpril 1997. Ed. by H. Sol & C. W. Oomens. LC 97-31343. 240p. 1997. text 130.50 (*0-7923-4779-X*) Kluwer Academic.

Material Inhomogeneities in Elasticity. Gerard A. Maugin. LC 93-6887. 280p. (gr. 13). 1993. ring bd. 78.95 (*0-412-49520-1*, Chap & Hall CRC) CRC Pr.

Material Instabilities in Solids. Renede Borst & E. Giessen. LC 98-8796. 576p. 1998. 140.00 (*0-471-97460-9*) Wiley.

Material Instabilities, Theory & Application: Proceedings: International Mechanical Engineering Congress & Exposition (1994: Chicago, IL) Ed. by R. C. Batra & Hussein M. Zbib. LC 94-78972. (AMD - MD Ser.: Vol. 183, Vol. 50). 369p. 1995. pap. 100.00 (*0-7918-1400-9*, G00895) ASME Pr.

Material Life in America, 1600-1860. Ed. by Robert B. St. George. 640p. 1988. text 55.00 (*1-55553-019-2*); pap. text 27.50 (*1-55553-020-6*) NE U Pr.

***Material Life of Human Beings: Artifacts, Behavior & Communication.** Michael B. Schiffer. LC 98-51397. 1999. 65.00 (*0-415-20032-6*) Routledge.

Material Life of Human Beings: Artifacts, Behavior & Communication. Michael Brian Schiffer. LC 98-51397. 1999. pap. 19.99 (*0-415-20033-4*) Routledge.

***Material London, C. A. 1600.** Lena Cowen Orlin. LC 99-54378. (New Cultural Studies). 2000. pap. 26.50 (*0-8122-1721-7*) U of Pa Pr.

***Material Man: Masculinity, Sexuality, Style.** Ed. by Giannino Malossi. LC 99-67946. (Illus.). 208p. 2000. pap. 39.95 (*0-8109-2709-8*, Pub. by Abrams) Time Warner.

Material, Materials, Recovery Of. Adriano Spatola. Tr. by Paul Vangelisti from ITA. 20p. (Orig.). 1994. pap. 5.00 (*1-55713-113-9*) Sun & Moon CA.

***Material Matters: The Conservation of Modern Sculpture.** Ed. by Jackie Heuman. (Illus.). 100p. 1999. pap. 24.95 (*1-85437-288-2*, Pub. by Tate Gallery) U of Wash Pr.

Material Matters: 7 Young Contemporary Artists. (Illus.). 1980. pap. 3.00 (*0-943411-11-4*) Norton Gal Art.

***Material Meanings: Critical Approaches to the Intepretation of Material Culture.** Ed. by Elizabeth S. Chilton. LC 99-15804. (Illus.). 208p. 1999. 55.00 (*0-87480-607-0*) U of Utah Pr.

***Material Meanings: Critical Approaches to the Interpretation of Material Culture.** Ed. by Elizabeth S. Chilton. LC 99-15804. (Illus.). 208p. 1999. pap. 25.00 (*0-87480-608-9*) U of Utah Pr.

Material Memories: Design & Evocation. Ed. by Marius Kwint & Christopher Breward. (Illus.). 256p. 1999. 65.00 (*1-85973-247-X*, Pub. by Berg Pubs) NYU Pr.

***Material Memories: Design & Evocation.** Ed. by Marius Kwint & Christopher Breward. (Illus.). 256p. 1999. pap. 19.50 (*1-85973-252-6*, Pub. by Berg Pubs) NYU Pr.

***Material Modification by Electronic Excitation.** Noriaki Itoh & Marshall L. Stoneham. (Illus.). 11/2000p. 2000. write for info. (*0-521-55498-5*) Cambridge U Pr.

Material of Invention: Materials & Design. Ezio Manzini. 250p. (C). 1989. text 150.00 (*0-85072-247-0*) St Mut.

Material on Light, Heat, Charged Particles, Radioactive Decay & Chemical Bonding Related to the Geostellar Shell Theory. 3rd rev. ed. Peter D. Hays. 68p. (C). 1994. pap. text 11.95 (*1-885554-01-X*) P D Hays.

Material Parameter Estimation for Modern Constitutive Equations. Ed. by L. A. Bertram et al. 289p. 1993. pap. 67.50 (*0-7918-1016-X*) ASME.

***Material Politics: Consumers, Citizenship & Political Cultures.** Ed. by Martin J. Daunton & Matthew Hilton. (Leisure, Consumption & Culture Ser.). (Illus.). 256p. 2001. 65.00 (*1-85973-466-9*, Pub. by Berg Pubs); pap. 19.50 (*1-85973-471-5*, Pub. by Berg Pubs) NYU Pr.

Material Processing by Non-Traditional Techniques: Proceedings of Harima International Symposium. Ed. by M. Terasawa et al. LC 97-111455. 191p. 1996. 65.00 (*4-906417-06-X*, Pub. by Jap Sci Soc Pr) Intl Spec Bk.

Material Processing with ND-Lasers. C. J. Nonhof. 259p. 1997. pap. 268.00 (*0-901150-23-1*) St Mut.

Material Queer: A Lesbigay Cultural Studies Reader. Donald Morton. (Queer Critique Ser.). 416p. (C). 1996. pap. 32.00 (*0-8133-1927-7*, Pub. by Westview) HarpC.

Material Recovery Facilities for Municipal Solid Waste. (Illus.). 156p. (Orig.). (C). 1995. pap. text 30.00 (*0-7881-2522-2*) DIANE Pub.

Material Recovery Facility Design Manual. PEER Consultants & CalRecovery, Inc. Staff. 176p. 1993. boxed set 94.95 (*0-87371-944-1*, TD794) CRC Pr.

Material Remains of Megiddo Cult. Herbert Gordon May. 1972. lib. bdg. 5.00 (*0-226-51177-4*) U Ch Pr.

Material Requirements Planning see Planeacion de los Requerimentos de Material

Material Requirements Planning: A Study of Implementation & Practice. Ed. by John C. Anderson et al. LC 81-68514. 57p. 1981. pap. 10.00 (*0-935406-03-4*) Am Prod & Inventory.

Material Requirements Planning: Integrating Material Requirement Planning & Modern Business. Terry Lunn & Susan A. Neff. (APICS Ser.). (Illus.). 275p. 1992. 47.50 (*1-55623-656-5*, Irwn Prfssnl) McGraw-Hill Prof.

Material Requirements Planning Training Aid. APICS Bucks-Mont. Chapter Staff. 62p. 1979. 40.00 (*0-935406-10-7*) Am Prod & Inventory.

Material Resources of Britain: An Economic Geography of the United Kingdom. Francis John Monkhouse. LC 72-185556. xi, 241 p. 1971. write for info. (*0-582-52633-7*) Longman.

Material Safety Data Sheet: Handbook for the Preparation of MSDS Worldwide. Michael L. Holcomb. 1997. 99.99 (*0-9644990-1-0*) Intl Toxicol.

Material Safety Data Sheets Collection. Genium Publishing Staff. 1840p. 1981. 449.00 (*0-931690-06-4*) Genium Pub.

Material Science. Matter. 1996. cd-rom 99.50 (*0-412-80080-2*, Chap & Hall CRC) CRC Pr.

Material Science. Russ. (General Engineering Ser.). (C). 1995. 29.95 (*0-534-95052-3*) PWS Pubs.

Material Science & Material Properties for Infrared Optoelectronics, Vol. 3182. Ed. by Fiodor F. Sizov & Vladimir V. Tetyorkin. LC 98-122041. 426p. 1997. 89.00 (*0-8194-2609-1*) SPIE.

Material Selection for Engineering Design. Mahmoud M. Farag. LC 96-51853. 320p. 1997. pap. 85.00 (*0-13-575192-6*) P-H.

Material Selection for Performance & Value: Regional Technical Conference, March 10-11, 1986, Parkview Hilton, Hartford, CT. Society of Plastics Engineers Staff. LC TP1140.. (Illus.). 227p. pap. 70.40 (*0-608-15526-8*, 202970700064) Bks Demand.

Material Substitution: Lessons from Tin-Using Industries. Ed. by John E. Tilton. LC 83-16164. 118p. 1983. pap. 17.50 (*0-8018-3161-X*) Resources Future.

Material Symbols: Culture & Economy in Prehistory. Ed. by John E. Robb. LC 97-77573. (Center for Archaeological Investigations Occasional Paper Ser.: Vol. 26). (Illus.). x, 414p. 1999. pap. 40.00 (*0-88104-083-5*) Center Archaeol.

M

Material Unconscious: American Amusement, Stephen Crane, & the Economies of Play. Bill Brown. LC 96-26028. (Illus.). 384p. 1996. 48.95 (*0-674-55380-2*) HUP.

Material Unconscious: American Amusement, Stephen Crane, & the Economies of Play. Bill Brown. LC 96-26028. (Illus.). 384p. 1997. reprint ed. pap. 23.95 (*0-674-55381-0*) HUP.

Material Wealth: Living with Luxurious Fabrics. deluxe ed. Jack L. Larsen. (Illus.). 240p. 1989. 125.00 (*1-55859-112-5*) Abbeville Pr.

Material Witness. Robert K. Tanenbaum. 416p. 1994. mass mkt. 7.50 (*0-451-18020-8*, Sig) NAL.

***Material Witness: Masters from California Crafts.** Janice Driesbach. LC 99-75841. (Illus.). 124p. 1999. 39.95 (*0-9674288-1-5*); pap. 19.95 (*0-9674288-0-7*) Creat Arts Sacramento.

Material Word: Literate Culture in the Restoration & Early Eighteenth Century. Richard W. Kroll. LC 90-30586. 464p. 1991. text 55.00 (*0-8018-4002-3*) Johns Hopkins.

Material World. Robert Friedel. (Business & Technology Ser.). (Illus.). 72p. 1988. pap. text 24.50 (*0-8026-0023-9*) Univ Pub Assocs.

Material World. Holman. (UK - Science Ser.). 1992. mass mkt. 31.95 (*0-17-438406-8*) S-W Pub.

Material World: A Global Family Portrait. Peter Menzel. LC 94-8588. (Illus.). 255p. 1994. 35.00 (*0-87156-437-8*, Pub. by Sierra) Random.

Material World: A Global Family Portrait. Peter Menzel & Sierra Club Staff. LC 94-8588. (Illus.). 256p. 1995. pap. 25.00 (*0-87156-430-0*, Pub. by Sierra) Random.

Material Writer's Guide: Write for Publication. Patricia Byrd. 240p. (J). 1994. mass mkt. 34.95 (*0-8384-4270-6*) Heinle & Heinle.

Materiales. Karen Bryant-Mole. (Images Ser.).Tr. of Materials. (SPA., Illus.). 24p. 1996. pap. text 4.95 (*0-382-39577-8*) Silver Burdett Pr.

Materiales Arqueologicos de Tlapacoya. Jesus Narez. 149p. 1990. pap. 9.00 (*968-6487-18-2*, IN030) UPLAAP.

Materiales de la Civilizacion. Carlos E. Rangel Nafaile. (Ciencia para Todos Ser.). (SPA.). pap. 6.99 (*968-16-2567-6*, Pub. by Fondo) Continental Bk.

Materiales del Futuro. 2nd ed. Ken Easterling. (SPA., Illus.). 176p. 1997. pap. 30.00 (*1-86125-023-1*, Pub. by Inst Materials) Ashgate Pub Co.

Materiales Dentales. 6th ed. Craig. (C). 1996. text 29.42 (*84-8174-188-4*) Mosby Inc.

Materiales Liticos y Ceramicos Encontrados en las Cercanias del Monolito Coyolxauhqui. Francisco G. Rul. (SPA., Illus.). 65p. 1997. pap. 10.00 (*968-29-5118-6*, IN88, Pub. by Dir Gen Pubicaiones) UPLAAP.

Materiales para Inegenieria. V. B. John. (SPA.). 240p. (C). 1994. pap. text 15.33 (*0-201-60145-1*) Addison-Wesley.

Materialien fur die Mittelstuffe, Lehrbuch see Deutsch Aktiv, Level 3

Materialism. Jorie Graham. 1993. 22.00 (*0-88001-342-7*) HarpC.

Materialism. Jorie Graham. 1995. pap. 13.00 (*0-88001-394-X*) HarpC.

Materialism. Jorie Graham. LC 93-27828. 160p. 1999. pap. 14.00 (*0-88001-617-5*) HarpC.

Materialism. M. N. Roy. 1982. reprint ed. 18.50 (*0-8364-0914-0*, Pub. by Ajanta) S Asia.

Materialism: An Affirmative History & Definition. Richard C. Vitzthum. LC 95-25149. 246p. 1995. 31.95 (*1-57392-027-4*) Prometheus Bks.

Materialism & Sensations. James W. Corman. LC 75-151570. 366p. reprint ed. pap. 113.50 (*0-608-30606-1*, 202199000024) Bks Demand.

***Materialism & the Mind-Body Problem.** Ed. by David M. Rosenthal. 296p. (C). 2000. lib. bdg. 34.95 (*0-87220-479-0*) Hackett Pub.

Materialism & the Mind-Body Problem. Ed. & Intro. by David M. Rosenthal. LC 87-23794. 249p. (C). 1987. reprint ed. pap. text 8.95 (*0-87220-023-X*); reprint ed. lib. bdg. 29.95 (*0-87220-024-8*) Hackett Pub.

***Materialism & the Mind-Body Problem.** 2nd ed. Ed. by David M. Rosenthal. 296p. (C). 2000. pap. 10.95 (*0-87220-478-2*) Hackett Pub.

An Asterisk (*) at the beginning of an entry indicates that the title is appearing for the first time.

M

Materialism & the Task of Anthroposophy. Rudolf Steiner. Tr. by Maria St. Goar from GER.Tr. of Perspektiven der Menschheitsentwicklung. 300p. 1987. 30.00 (*0-88010-177-6*); pap. 18.95 (*0-88010-176-8*) Anthroposophic.

Materialism in Indian Thought. K. L. Mittal. 336p. 1974. 19.95 (*0-318-37022-0*) Asia Bk Corp.

Materialism in Today's World. 2nd ed. Thrower. 1995. pap., student ed. 28.13 (*0-07-050711-2*) McGraw.

Materialism, Philosophical Examined: or The Immateriality of the Soul Asserted & Proved, on Philosophical Principles: 1778 Edition. John Whitehead. 198p. 1996. reprint ed. 58.00 (*1-85506-131-7*) Bks Intl VA.

Materialism Revisited. Chapman Cohen. 190p. 1998. reprint ed. 20.00 (*0-936128-88-7*) De Young Pr.

Materialisms. (New Critical Idiom Ser.). 152p. (C). Date not set. write for info. (*0-415-09810-6*); pap. write for info. (*0-415-09811-4*) Routledge.

Materialist Approaches to the Bible. Michel Clevenot. Tr. by William J. Nottingham. LC 84-14711. 160p. (Orig.). 1985. reprint ed. pap. 49.60 (*0-7837-9820-2*, 206054900005) Bks Demand.

Materialist Conception of History. John H. Kautsky. LC 87-32167. (C). 1988. 70.00 (*0-300-04168-3*) Yale U Pr.

Materialist Conception of History. abr. annot. ed. Karl Kautsky. Tr. by John H. Kautsky & Raymond Meyer. LC 87-34028. 628p. 1988. reprint ed. pap. 194.70 (*0-608-07827-1*, 205400300010) Bks Demand.

Materialist Conception of History: A Critical Analysis. Karl Federn. LC 75-114523. 262p. 1971. reprint ed. lib. bdg. 75.00 (*0-8371-4789-1*, FECH, Greenwood Pr) Greenwood.

Materialist Critique of English Romantic Drama. Daniel P. Watkins. LC 93-13776. 256p. 1993. 49.95 (*0-8130-1240-6*); pap. 18.95 (*0-8130-1241-4*) U Press Fla.

Materialist Feminism. Ed. by Toril Moi & Janice Radway. 200p. 1994. pap. 10.00 (*0-8223-6421-2*) Duke.

Materialist Feminism: Reader. Ed. by Rosemary Hennessy & Chrys Ingraham. LC 97-12406. 224p. (C). 1997. pap. 24.99 (*0-415-91634-8*) Routledge.

Materialist Feminism: Reader. Ed. by Rosemary Hennessy & Chrys Ingraham. LC 97-12406. 224p. (C). 1997. 75.00 (*0-415-91633-X*) Routledge.

Materialist Feminism & the Politics of Discourse. Rosemary Hennessy. LC 92-9689. (Thinking Gender Ser.). 312p. (C). 1992. pap. 20.99 (*0-415-90480-3*, A6335) Routledge.

Materialist Film. Peter Gidal. 236p. 1989. pap. text 16.95 (*0-415-00382-2*) Routledge.

Materialist Reading of the Gospel of Mark. Fernando Belo. Tr. by Matthew J. O'Connell from FRE. LC 80-24756.Tr. of Lectero Materialiste de L'evangele de Marc. 384p. (Orig.). reprint ed. pap. 119.10 (*0-8357-2666-5*, 204020200015) Bks Demand.

Materialist Shakespeare: A History. Ivo Kamps. 388p. (C). 1995. 65.00 (*0-86091-463-1*, C0527, Pub. by Verso); pap. 20.00 (*0-86091-674-X*, C0528, Pub. by Verso) Norton.

Materialist Theory of the Mind. 2nd ed. David M. Armstrong. LC 93-19013. (International Library of Philosophy). 400p. (C). 1993. pap. 27.99 (*0-415-10031-3*, B2456) Routledge.

Materialistisch-Dialektische Fundierung des Epischen Theaters Brechts Als eines Zweidimensionalen Theatralischen Kommunikationssystems. Seong-Kyun Oh. Ed. by Martin Bollacher et al. (Bochumer Schriften zur Deutschen Literatur Ser.: Bd. 49). 233p. 1998. pap. 39.95 (*3-631-32526-6*) P Lang Pubng.

Materialities of Communication. Ed. by Hans U. Gumbrecht & K. Ludwig Pfeiffer. LC 93-4911. xviii, 447p. 1994. 55.00 (*0-8047-2263-3*); pap. 18.95 (*0-8047-2264-1*) Stanford U Pr.

Materialized Apparitions. E. A. Brackett. 182p. 1996. reprint ed. spiral bd. 12.00 (*0-7873-0116-7*) Hlth Research.

Materialized Views: Techniques, Implementations, & Applications. Ed. by Ashish Gupta & Inderpal S. Mumick. LC 98-17338. (Illus.). 616p. 1999. pap. text 50.00 (*0-262-57122-6*) MIT Pr.

Materializing Art History. Gen Doy. LC 98-218568. (Materializing Culture Ser.). (Illus.). 256p. 1998. 55.00 (*1-85973-933-4*, Pub. by Berg Pubs); pap. 19.50 (*1-85973-938-5*, Pub. by Berg Pubs) NYU Pr.

***Materializing Bakhtin.** Craig Brandist & Galin Tikhanov. LC 99-40986. 2000. text 65.00 (*0-312-22860-0*) St Martin.

***Materializing Thailand.** Penny Van Esterik. (Materializing Culture Ser.). (Illus.). 244p. 2000. 65.00 (*1-85973-306-9*, Pub. by Berg Pubs); pap. 19.50 (*1-85973-311-5*, Pub. by Berg Pubs) NYU Pr.

Materials see Materiales

Materials. (Alpha Bks.). (Illus.). (J). 1997. write for info. (*0-237-51771-X*) EVN1 UK.

Materials. Karen Bryant-Mole. LC 95-51186. (Illus.). 24p. (J). 1996. pap. 4.95 (*0-382-39623-5*, Silver Pr NJ); lib. bdg. 10.95 (*0-382-39587-5*) Silver Burdett Pr.

Materials. Center for Occupational Research & Development Staff. (Mechanical Technology Ser.). (Illus.). 148p. (C). 1983. pap. text 22.00 (*1-55502-155-7*) CORD Commns.

Materials. Sally Morgan & Adrian Morgan. LC 93-31722. (Designs in Science Ser.). (Illus.). 48p. (J). (gr. 4-9). 1994. 16.95 (*0-8160-2985-7*) Facts on File.

Materials. Peter Riley. LC 97-44653. (Cycles in Science Ser.). (J). 1998. (*1-57572-619-X*) Heinemann Lib.

Materials see ICALEO "Eighty Four: Proceedings

Materials: A BBC Fact Finders Book. Martin Hollins. (Illus.). 48p. (J). (gr. 3-5). 1996. 14.95 (*0-563-39782-9*, BBC-Parkwest); pap. 8.95 (*0-563-39654-7*, BBC-Parkwest) Parkwest Pubns.

Materials: Performance & Prevention of Deficiencies & Failures: Proceedings of the Materials Engineering Congress. Ed. by Thomas D. White. LC 92-24011. 776p. 1992. 71.00 (*0-87262-880-9*) Am Soc Civil Eng.

Materials: Renewable & Nonrenewable Resources. Ed. by Philip H. Abelson & Allen L. Hammond. LC 76-7295. (AAAS Publication Ser.: No. 76-4). 208p. reprint ed. pap. 64.50 (*0-7837-0064-4*, 204031100016) Bks Demand.

Materials - Fabrication & Patterning at the Nanoscale. Ed. by F. Cerrina & Christie Marrian. (Symposium Proceedings Ser.: Vol. 380). 203p. 1995. text 83.00 (*1-55899-283-9*) Materials Res.

Materials - Pathway to the Future: International SAMPE Symposium & Exhibition, 33rd, Anaheim Convention Center, Anaheim, California, March 7-10, 1988. International SAMPE Symposium & Exhibition Staff et al. Ed. by Gilberto Carrillo. LC TA0401.3.S68. (Science of Advanced Materials & Process Enginnering Ser.: No. 21). 1833p. reprint ed. pap. 200.00 (*0-7837-1285-5*, 204142600020) Bks Demand.

Materials - The Star at the Center Stage: 30th International SAMPE Technical Conference, San Antonio Convention Center, San Antonio, TX, October 20-24, 1998. International SAMPE Technical Conference Staff. Ed. by Brian A. Wilson et al. LC TA0401.3.N37. (International SAMPE Technical Conference Ser.: Vol. 30). (Illus.). 712p. reprint ed. pap. 200.00 (*0-608-20281-9*, 207154000030) Bks Demand.

Materials Analysis by Ion Channeling: Submicron Crystallography. Leonard Feldman et al. 1982. text 124.00 (*0-12-252680-5*) Acad Pr.

Materials Analysis of Byzantine Pottery. Dumbarton Oaks Staff & Henry P. Maguire. LC 96-49564. 1998. 78.00 (*0-88402-251-X*) Dumbarton Oaks.

Materials Analysis Using a Nuclear Microprobe. Mark B. H. Breese et al. LC 95-11166. 460p. 1996. 124.00 (*0-471-10608-9*) Wiley.

Materials & Components of Interior Architecture. 5th ed. J. Rosemary Riggs. LC 98-4590. 240p. 1998. pap. text 61.00 (*0-13-923228-1*) P-H.

***Materials & Construction: Exploring the Connection.** Ed. by Lawrence C. Bank. LC 99-13265. 928p. 1999. 99.00 (*0-7844-0423-2*) Am Soc Civil Eng.

Materials & Corrosion Problems in Energy Systems. Ed. by W. J. Lochmann & M. Indig. (Illus.). 211p. 1980. pap. 10.00 (*0-915567-57-1*) NACE Intl.

Materials & Crystallographic Aspects of HTC-Superconductivity. Ed. by E. Kaldis. LC 94-7727. (NATO Advanced Study Institutes Series E, Applied Sciences: Vol. 263). 612p. (C). 1994. text 357.00 (*0-7923-2773-X*) Kluwer Academic.

Materials & Design Technology, 1995: Proceedings: The Energy & Environmental EXPO '95 - the Energy-Sources Technology Conference & Exhibition (1995: Houston, TX) Ed. by Thomas J. Kozik & Karen S. Surana. LC 93-74683. (PD Ser.: Vol. 71). 237p. 1995. pap. 92.00 (*0-7918-1295-2*, H00927) ASME.

***Materials & Development of Plastics Packaging for the Consumer Market.** Geoff A. Giles & David R. Bain. LC 00-21385. 2000. write for info. (*0-8493-0507-1*) CRC Pr.

Materials & Device Characterization in Micromachining. Ed. by Craig R. Freidrich & Yuli Vladimirsky. LC 99-200311. (Proceedings of SPIE Ser.: Vol. 3512). 454p. 1998. 89.00 (*0-8194-2971-6*) SPIE.

***Materials & Device Characterization in Micromachining II.** Ed. by Yuli Vladimirsky & Craig R. Friedrich. 266p. 1999. pap. text 72.00 (*0-8194-3472-8*) SPIE.

Materials & Devices for Electrical Engineers & Physicists. R. A. Colclaser & S. D. Nagle. 284p. (C). 1984. 97.50 (*0-07-011693-8*) McGraw.

Materials & Devices for Silicon-Based Optoelectronics Vol. 486: Materials Research Society Symposium Proceedings. Ed. by S. Coffa et al. LC 98-14958. 409p. 1998. text 68.00 (*1-55899-391-6*) Materials Res.

Materials & Engineering Design: The Next Decade. Ed. by B. F. Dyson & D. R. Hayhurst. 500p. 1989. text 110.00 (*0-901462-65-9*, Pub. by Inst Materials) Ashgate Pub Co.

Materials & Fluids under Low Gravity: Proceedings of the IX European Symposium on Gravity Dependent Phenomena in Physical Sciences, Held at Berlin, Germany, 2-5 May 1995. Ed. by Lorenz Ratke et al. LC 95-51687. (Lecture Notes in Physics Ser.: Vol. 464). 424p. 1996. 92.00 (*3-540-60677-7*) Spr-Verlag.

Materials & Human Resources for Teaching Ethnic Studies. Ed. by Francesco Cordasco. LC 77-17706. (Bilingual-Bicultural Education in the U. S. Ser.). 1978. reprint ed. lib. bdg. 29.95 (*0-405-11088-X*) Ayer.

Materials & Lighting: 3D Studio Tips & Tricks. Michele Bousquet. (3D Studio Tips & Tricks Ser.). (Illus.). 160p. 1994. pap. 14.95 (*0-8273-7012-1*) Delmar.

Materials & Measurements in Molecular Electronics: Proceedings of the International Symposium on Materials & Measurements in Molecular Electronics, Tsukuba, Japan, February 6-8, 1996, Vol. 81. K. L. Kajimura & S. Kuroda. LC 96-18854. (Springer Proceedings in Physics Ser.). 274p. 1996. 114.50 (*4-431-70185-0*) Spr-Verlag.

Materials & Member Behavior. Ed. by Duane S. Ellifritt. 708p. 1987. 9.00 (*0-87262-616-4*) Am Soc Civil Eng.

Materials & Methods for Landscape Architecture Construction. Harlow Landphair. (C). 2000. text 60.00 (*0-13-254954-9*) P-H.

Materials & Methods in ELT: A Teachers Guide. Jo McDonough & Christopher Shaw. (Applied Language Studies). 288p. 1993. pap. 25.95 (*0-631-18003-6*) Blackwell Pubs.

Materials & Methods of Sculpture. Jack C. Rich. (Illus.). 512p. pap. 13.95 (*0-486-25742-8*) Dover.

Materials & Methods Researching Information Resources & Developing a Learning Plan: Guidelines. Richard L. Crews. 110p. (C). 1988. student ed. write for info. (*0-945864-01-9*); pap. text. write for info. (*0-945864-00-0*) Columbia Pacific U Pr.

Materials & New Processing Technologies for Photovoltaics: Proceedings of the Symposia. Symposium on Materials & New Processing Technologi. Ed. by Erhard Sirtl et al. LC 81-66183. (Electrochemical Society Proceedings Ser.: Vol. 81-3). (Illus.). 358p. 1981. pap. 111.00 (*0-7837-9002-3*, 205926700002) Bks Demand.

Materials & New Processing Technologies for Photovoltaics: Proceedings of the Symposium, Held in San Francisco, CA, 1983. Symposium on Materials & New Processing Technologi. Ed. by James A. Amick et al. LC 83-82253. (Electrochemical Society, Proceedings Ser.: Vol. 83-11). 509p. 1983. reprint ed. pap. 157.80 (*0-608-04660-4*, 205257700002) Bks Demand.

Materials & New Processing Technologies for Photovoltaics: Proceedings of the Symposium, Held in 1984, New Orleans, LA. Symposium on Materials & New Processing Technologi. Ed. by Vijay K. Kapur et al. LC 85-81525. (Electrochemical Society Ser.: No. 85-9). (Illus.). 430p. 1985. reprint ed. pap. 133.30 (*0-608-05718-5*, 205261000007) Bks Demand.

***Materials & Process Affordability: Keys to the Future : Anaheim Convention Center, Anaheim, California, May 31-June 4, 1998.** International SAMPE Symposium and Exhibition et al. LC 99-230989. (Illus.). 1998. write for info. (*0-938994-79-4*) SAMPE.

Materials & Process Affordability: Keys to the Future, 43rd International SAMPE Symposium & Exhibition, Anaheim Convention Center, Anaheim, CA, May 31-June 4, 1998. International SAMPE Symposium & Exhibition Staff. Ed. by Howard S. Kliger et al. LC TA0401.3.S63. (Science of Advanced Materials & Process Engineering Ser.: Vol. 43). (Illus.). 1159p. reprint ed. pap. 200.00 (*0-608-20279-7*, 207153900001) Bks Demand.

Materials & Process Affordability Bk. 2: Keys to Future, 43rd International SAMPE Symposium & Exhibition, Anaheim Convention Center, Anaheim, CA, May 31-June 4, 1998. International SAMPE Symposium & Exhibition Staff. Ed. by Howard S. Kliger et al. LC TA0401.3.S63. (Science of Advanced Materials & Process Engineering Ser.: Vol. 43). (Illus.). 1178p. reprint ed. pap. 200.00 (*0-608-20280-0*, 207153900002) Bks Demand.

Materials & Process Challenges Bk. 1: Aging Systems, Affordability, Alternative Applications: 41st International SAMPE Symposium & Exhibition, Anaheim Convention Center, Anaheim, CA, March 24-28, 1996. International SAMPE Symposium & Exhibition Staff. Ed. by George Schmitt et al. LC TA0401.3.I57. (Science of Advanced Materials & Process Enginnering Ser.: No. 41). (Illus.). 968p. 1996. pap. 200.00 (*0-608-05006-7*, 206554700001) Bks Demand.

Materials & Process Characterization for VLSI: Proceedings of the International Conference. Ed. by X. F. Zong et al. 552p. 1988. text 125.00 (*9971-5-0688-2*) World Scientific Pub.

Materials & Processes. Peter Riley. LC 97-45602. (Straightforward Science Ser.). (J). 1998. 18.00 (*0-531-11514-3*) Watts.

Materials & Processes. Peter Riley. (Straightforward Science Ser.). (Illus.). 32p. (J). (gr. 3-6). 1999. pap. text 6.95 (*0-531-15369-X*) Watts.

Materials & Processes, Set, Pt. A. 3rd ed. Ed. by James F. Young & Shane. (Illus.). 888p. 1985. text 390.00 (*0-8247-7197-4*) Dekker.

Materials & Processes, Set, Pt. B. 3rd ed. Ed. by Young & Shane. (Illus.). 1688p. 1985. text 390.00 (*0-8247-7198-2*) Dekker.

Materials & Processes - Continuing Innovations: National SAMPE Symposium & Exhibition, 28th, Disneyland Hotel, Anaheim, California, April 12-14, 1983. National SAMPE Symposium & Exhibition Staff. LC 83-177138. (Science of Advanced Materials & Process Enginnering Ser.: No. 28). 1571p. reprint ed. pap. 200.00 (*0-7837-1281-2*, 204142200020) Bks Demand.

Materials & Processes for Environmental Protection Vol. 344: Materials Research Society Symposium Proceedings. Ed. by L. M. Quick et al. LC 94-36857. 343p. 1994. text 62.00 (*1-55899-244-8*) Materials Res.

Materials & Processes for NDT Technology. Ed. by Harry D. Moore. (Illus.). 204p. 1984. reprint ed. 44.50 (*0-931403-06-5*, 2250) Am Soc Nondestructive.

***Materials & Processes for Submicron Technologies.** J. M. Martinez-Duart. 1999. 127.00 (*0-08-043617-X*, Pub. by Elsevier) Elsevier.

Materials & Processes for Surface & Interface Engineering: Proceedings of the NATO Advanced Study Institute, Chateau de Bonas, Gers, France, July 18-29, 1994. Ed. by Yves Pauleau. LC 95-11665. (NATO ASI Ser.: Series E, Applied Sciences: Vol. 290). 660p. (C). 1995. text 327.50 (*0-7923-3458-2*) Kluwer Academic.

Materials & Processes for Wireless Communications: Proceedings: Symposium on Materials & Processes for Wireless Communication (1994: Boston, MA) Symposium on Materials & Processes for Wireless Co et al. Ed. by T. Negas & H. Ling. LC 95-12977. (Ceramic Transactions Ser.: Vol. 53). (Illus.). 230p. 1995. 88.00 (*0-944904-94-7*, CT053) Am Ceramic.

Materials & Processes in Manufacturing. 8th ed. E. Paul DeGarmo. 1272p. 1997. text 102.95 (*0-471-36679-X*) Wiley.

Materials & Processes in Manufacturing. 8th ed. E. Paul Degarmo & J. Temple Black. 1172p. (C). 1996. text 96.00 (*0-02-328621-0*, Macmillan Coll) P-H.

Materials & Processing Failures in the Electronics & Computer Industries. A. S. Brar & P. B. Narayan. 330p. 1993. 135.00 (*0-87170-468-4*) ASM.

Materials & Strategies for the Education of Trainable Mentally Retarded Learners. James P. White. LC 90-38465. (Source Books on Education: Vol. 24). 366p. 1990. text 50.00 (*0-8240-6345-7*) Garland.

Materials & Structures. 2nd ed. Whitlow. (C). 1991. pap. text 60.95 (*0-582-06698-0*, Pub. by Addison-Wesley) Longman.

Materials & Structures of Music, Vol. 1. 3rd ed. William B. Christ et al. 1980. text. write for info. (*0-318-54922-0*) P-H.

***Materials & Techniques.** LEMA PUBLICATIONS. 1999. 16.95 (*84-95323-09-5*) LEMA.

***Materials & Techniques in the Decorative Arts: An Illustrated Dictionary.** Lucy Trench. LC 00-29865. (Illus.). 2000. write for info. (*0-226-81200-6*) U Ch Pr.

Materials & Techniques of Medieval Painting. Daniel V. Thompson. Orig. Title: Materials of Medieval Painting. 239p. 1956. pap. 8.95 (*0-486-20327-1*) Dover.

Materials & Techniques of Painting. Jonathan Stephenson. LC 92-62134. (Illus.). 192p. 1993. reprint ed. pap. 19.95 (*0-500-27704-4*, Pub. by Thames Hudson) Norton.

Materials & Techniques of Twentieth-Century Music. 2nd ed. Stefan M. Kostka. LC 98-14766. 328p. (C). 1998. 58.00 (*0-13-924077-2*) P-H.

Materials & Their Uses. Bolton. 192p. 1996. pap. text 24.95 (*0-7506-2726-3*) Buttrwrth-Heinemann.

Materials & Their Uses. Snape & Rowlands. 1992. pap. text. write for info. (*0-582-07430-4*, Pub. by Addison-Wesley) Longman.

Materials Aspects of X-Ray Lithography. Ed. by G. K. Celler & J. R. Maldonado. (Symposium Proceedings Ser.: Vol. 306). 291p. 1993. text 30.00 (*1-55899-202-2*) Materials Res.

Materials at Low Temperature. Ed. by Richard P. Reed & Alan F. Clark. LC 82-73607. (Illus.). 608p. reprint ed. pap. 188.50 (*0-7837-1873-X*, 204207400001) Bks Demand.

Materials at Their Limits. 88p. 1986. pap. 31.50 (*0-904357-86-4*, Pub. by Inst Materials) Ashgate Pub Co.

Materials Beneficiation. C. B. Gill. (Materials Research & Engineering Ser.). (Illus.). x, 245p. 1991. 102.95 (*0-387-97336-2*) Spr-Verlag.

Materials, Bulk Processing & Bulk Applications: Proceedings of the 1992 TCSUH Workshop. C. W. Chu et al. 625p. 1992. text 137.00 (*981-02-1032-9*) World Scientific Pub.

Materials Challenge Diversification & the Future: 40th International SAMPE Symposium & Exhibition, Anaheim Convention Center, Anaheim, CA, May 8-11, 1995, Bk. 1. International SAMPE Symposium & Exhibition Staff. Ed. by Don Harmston et al. (Science of Advanced Materials & Process Engineering Ser.: No. 40). (Illus.). 1046p. 1995. reprint ed. pap. 200.00 (*0-608-16102-0*, 2061714) Bks Demand.

Materials Challenge Diversification & the Future: 40th International SAMPE Symposium & Exhibition, Anaheim Convention Center, Anaheim, CA, May 8-11, 1995, Bk. 2. International SAMPE Symposium & Exhibition Staff. Ed. by Don Harmston et al. LC TA0401.3.N36. (Science of Advanced Materials & Process Engineering Ser.: No. 40). (Illus.). 1059p. 1995. reprint ed. pap. 200.00 (*0-608-00921-0*, 206171400002) Bks Demand.

Materials Characterization & Optical Probes Techniques: Proceedings of a Conference Held 27-30 July 1997, San Diego, California. Roger A. Lessard et al. LC 97-23156. (Critical Reviews of Optical Science Technology Ser.). 1997. pap. write for info. (*0-8194-2600-8*) SPIE.

Materials Characterization Applied to Utilization, Immobilization & Disposal of Solid Wastes. McCarthy. write for info. (*0-444-00870-5*) Elsevier.

Materials Characterization by Thermomechanical Analysis, STP 1136. Ed. by Alan T. Riga & Michael Neag. (Special Technical Publication Ser.). (Illus.). 200p. 1991. text 61.00 (*0-8031-1434-6*, STP1136) ASTM.

Materials Characterization for Process Control & Product Conformity. Klaus Goebbels. LC 94-15307. 256p. 1994. boxed set 110.95 (*0-8493-8957-7*) CRC Pr.

Materials Characterization for Systems Performance & Reliability. Ed. by James W. McCauley & Volker Weiss. LC 85-19118. (Sagamore Army Materials Research Conference Proceedings Ser.: Vol. 31). 618p. 1986. 135.00 (*0-306-42095-3*, Plenum Trade) Perseus Pubng.

Materials Characterization Series. C. R. Brundle. 1993. 683.00 (*0-7506-9452-1*) Buttrwrth-Heinemann.

Materials Characterization Strategy for the Giga-Bit DRAM Era II. 1998. pap. write for info. (*1-892568-07-1*) Smicndctr Equip.

Materials Chemistry: An Emerging Discipline. Ed. by Leonard V. Interrante et al. LC 94-23580. (Advances in Chemistry Ser.: No. 245). (Illus.). 400p. 1995. text 83.95 (*0-8412-2809-4*, Pub. by Am Chemical) OUP.

Materials Chemistry at High Temperatures Vol. 1: Characterization. Ed. by John W. Hastie. (Illus.). 464p. 1990. 120.00 (*0-89603-186-1*) Humana.

Materials Chemistry at High Temperatures Vol. 2: Processing & Performance. Ed. by John W. Hastie. (Illus.). 536p. 1990. 120.00 (*0-89603-187-X*) Humana.

Materials Chemistry for Engineers. Fabes. text. write for info. (*0-471-14163-1*) Wiley.

Materials Considerations in Liquid Metal Systems in Power Generation. Ed. by N. J. Hoffman & G. A. Whitlow. LC 78-64965. (Illus.). 77p. 1979. pap. 10.00 (*0-915567-54-7*) NACE Intl.

Materials Construction. 2nd ed. G. D. Taylor. (C). 1994. pap. 49.95 (*0-582-21431-9*, Pub. by Addison-Wesley) Longman.

An Asterisk (*) at the beginning of an entry indicates that the title is appearing for the first time.

Materials Containing Natural Radionuclides in Enhanced Concentrations: EUR 17625. 1997. 20.00 (*92-828-0191-8*, CR-NA-17625-ENC, Pub. by Comm Europ Commun) Bernan Associates.

Materials Crystal Chemistry. Relva C. Buchanan & Taeun Park. LC 97-18615. (Illus.). 472p. 1997. text 185.00 (*0-8247-9798-1*) Dekker.

Materials Degradation & Its Control by Surface Engineering. Loh N. Lam & Andrew W. Batchelor. 500p. 1998. 68.00 (*1-86094-072-2*, Pub. by Imperial College) World Scientific Pub.

Materials Degradation & Its Control by Surface Engineering. Loh N. Lam & Andrew W. Batchelor. LC 99-17069. 500p. 1998. 78.00 (*1-86094-083-8*, Pub. by Imperial College) World Scientific Pub.

Materials Degradation Caused by Acid Rain. Ed. by Robert Baboian. LC 86-20560. (ACS Symposium Ser.: No. 318). (Illus.). ix, 438p. 1986. 87.95 (*0-8412-0988-X*) Am Chemical.

Materials Degradation Caused by Acid Rain. Ed. by Robert Baboian. LC 86-20560. (ACS Symposium Ser.: Vol. 318). 466p. 1986. reprint ed. pap. 144.50 (*0-608-03522-X*, 206424100008) Bks Demand.

Materials Degradation in Low Earth Orbit (LEO) Proceedings of a Symposium Sponsored by the TMS-ASM Joint Corrosion & Environmental Effects Committee, Held at the 119th Annual Meeting of the Minerals, Metals & Materials Society in Anaheim, California, February 17-22, 1990. Minerals, Metals & Materials Society Staff. Ed. by V. Srinivasan & Bruce A. Banks. LC 90-62097. (Illus.). 231p. 1990. reprint ed. pap. 71.70 (*0-608-01698-5*, 206235300002) Bks Demand.

***Materials Development for Direct Write Technologies: Materials Research Society Symposium Proceedings, Vol. 624.** Ed. by D. B. Chrisey et al. 2000. text 77.00 (*1-55899-532-3*) Materials Res.

Materials Development in Language Teaching. 382p. (C). 1998. pap. text 26.95 (*0-521-57419-6*) Cambridge U Pr.

Materials Development in Tubro-machinery. Taplin. 1989. 80.00 (*0-901462-60-8*) Institute of Management Consultants.

Materials Developments in Microelectronic Packaging: Performance & Reliability: Proceedings of the Fourth Electronic Materials & Processing Congress. Ed. by Prabjit Singh. LC 91-76343. (Illus.). 415p. 1991. reprint ed. pap. 128.70 (*0-608-02626-3*, 206328400004) Bks Demand.

Materials, Devices, & Systems for Optoelectronic Processing. Ed. by John A. Neff & Bahram Javidi. 206p. 1996. 56.00 (*0-8194-2236-3*) SPIE.

Materials Engineer. Jack Rudman. (Career Examination Ser.: C-1780). 1994. pap. 39.95 (*0-8373-1780-0*) Nat Learn.

Materials Engineering. Kutz. text 195.00 (*0-471-35924-6*) Wiley.

Materials Engineering. James P. Schaffer. LC 94-27232. 880p. (C). 1994. per. 39.95 (*0-256-17072-X*, Irwn McGrw-H) McGrw-H Hghr Educ.

Materials Engineering. Lawrence H. Van Vlack. 1982. pap. text 1.50 (*0-201-08069-9*) Addison-Wesley.

Materials Engineering in the Arctic: Proceedings of an International Conference, St. Jovite, Quebec, Canada, Sept. 27 - Oct. 1, 1976. American Society for Metals Staff. LC 77-4214. (Illus.). 343p. reprint ed. pap. 106.40 (*0-608-30313-5*, 201949900013) Bks Demand.

Materials Evaluation 50 Year Index. American Society for Nondestructive Testing (ASNT). 392p. (Orig.). 1994. pap. 59.00 (*1-57117-006-5*) Am Soc Nondestructive.

Materials Evaluation under Fretting Conditions - STP 780. Ed. by S. R. Brown. 189p. 1982. 24.75 (*0-8031-0829-X*, STP780) ASTM.

Materials Flows in the Post-Consumer Waste Stream of the EEC. H. C. Bailly & C. T. De Borms. 96p. 1977. pap. text 73.00 (*0-86010-080-4*) G & T Inc.

Materials for a Balance of the Soviet Economy, 1928-1930. Stephen G. Wheatcroft & Richard W. Davies. (Cambridge Russian, Soviet & Post-Soviet Studies: No. 48). (Illus.). 491p. 1985. text 85.00 (*0-521-26125-2*) Cambridge U Pr.

Materials for a Basic Course in Civil Procedure. 6th ed. (University Casebook Ser.). 1250p. 1990. text 47.95 (*0-88277-783-1*) Foundation Pr.

Materials for a Carcenological Fauna of India, 1895-1900, 6pts. in 1. A. Alcock. 1968. 160.00 (*3-7682-0544-4*) Lubrecht & Cramer.

Materials for a Classroom Presentation of the Constitution of the United States: Script, Props, & Activities for Elementary School Children. Janice Howes. LC 87-50154. (Illus.). 91p. (Orig.). 1987. pap. 7.00 (*0-942431-01-4*) Teachers Pub Hse.

Materials for a History of the Reign of Henry VII from Original Documents Preserved in the Public Record Office, 2 vols. Ed. by William Campbell, Jr. (Rolls Ser.: No. 60). 1969. reprint ed. 140.00 (*0-8115-1128-6*) Periodicals Srv.

Materials for a History of the Sessions Family in America: The Descendants of Alexander Sessions of Andover, MA, 1669. Francis C. Sessions. (Illus.). 252p. 1998. pap. 23.00 (*0-7884-0847-X*, S177) Heritage Bk.

Materials for a Motion Practice Workshop see Problems & Materials in Civil Procedure: Polisi v. Clark & Parker & Gould - Law School Edition

Materials for a Motion Practice Workshop see Problems & Materials in Civil Procedure: Polisi v. Clark & Parker & Gould - Library of Cases

Materials for Advanced Metalization, 1997 European Workshop on. LC 97-229275. 82.00 (*0-7803-3976-2*, TH8287-QOE) Inst Electrical.

Materials for Advanced Technology Applications. Ed. by M. Buggy & S. Hampshire. 704p. 1992. text 275.00 (*0-87849-646-7*, Pub. by Trans T Pub) Enfield Pubs NH.

Materials for Aerospace - Aircraft Propulsion Systems. 365p. 1990. 2950.00 (*0-685-49395-4*, GB124) BCC.

Materials for an Oirat-Mongolian to English Citation Dictionary, Pt. 1. John R. Krueger. (ENG & MON.). 1978. pap. 15.00 (*0-910980-42-X*) Mongolia.

Materials for an Oirat-Mongolian to English Citation Dictionary, Pt. 2. John R. Krueger. 15.00 (*0-910980-43-8*) Mongolia.

Materials for an Oirat-Mongolian to English Citation Dictionary, Pt. III. John R. Krueger. 20.00 (*0-910980-44-6*) Mongolia.

Materials for Architects & Builders. write for info. (*0-340-64556-3*, Pub. by E A) Routldge.

Materials for Built-Up Roof Coverings, UL 55A. 12th ed. (C). 1993. pap. text 95.00 (*1-55989-447-4*) Underwrtrs Labs.

Materials for Civil & Construction Engineers. Mamlouk. 400p. (C). 1998. 95.00 (*0-673-98187-8*, Prentice Hall) P-H.

Materials for Civil & Highway Engineers. 4th ed. Kenneth N. Derucher & George Korfiatis. LC 98-187494. 470p. (C). 1998. 95.00 (*0-13-905043-4*) P-H.

Materials for Coal Gasification: Proceedings of a Conference Held in Conjunction with ASM's Materials Week '87, Cincinnati, OH, 10-15 October 1987. Ed. by W. T. Bakker et al. LC 88-70075. (Illus.). 268p. reprint ed. pap. 83.10 (*0-8357-4090-0*, 203685600005) Bks Demand.

Materials for Conservation. C. V. Horie. (Conservation & Museology Ser.). (Illus.). 144p. 1987. pap. 44.95 (*0-7506-0881-1*) Buttrwrth-Heinemann.

Materials for Display & Printing Technologies. A. H. Land. write for info. (*0-444-00909-4*) Elsevier.

Materials for Electrochemical Energy Storage & Conversion II--Batteries, Capacitors & Fuel Cells Vol. 496: Materials Research Society Symposium Proceedings. Ed. by D. S. Ginley et al. LC 98-16666. 682p. 1998. text 76.00 (*1-55899-401-7*) Materials Res.

Materials for Electronic Packaging. Deborah D. Chung. 368p. 1995. text 155.00 (*0-7506-9314-2*) Buttrwrth-Heinemann.

Materials for Engineering. John Martin. (Illus.). 240p. 1997. pap. 29.00 (*1-86125-012-6*, Pub. by Inst Materials) Ashgate Pub Co.

***Materials for Engineering.** 2nd ed. W. Bolton. 192p. 2000. pap. 28.95 (*0-7506-4855-4*) Buttrwrth-Heinemann.

Materials for Engineering. 2nd ed. William Bolton. LC 93-51083. 2000. pap. text 29.95 (*0-7506-1838-8*) Buttrwrth-Heinemann.

Materials for Environmentally Acceptable Coatings, Inks, & Adhesives. 119p. 1992. 2450.00 (*0-89336-928-4*, C-161) BCC.

Materials for First Responders: Study Guide for Second Edition. Susan S. Walker. (Illus.). 260p. 1994. pap. text 17.00 (*0-87939-113-8*) IFSTA.

Materials for Future Energy Systems: Proceedings of a Conference. Conference on Materials for Future Energy Systems. LC 85-73249. (Conference Proceedings Ser.). (Illus.). 488p. reprint ed. pap. 151.30 (*0-608-15995-6*, 203306700083) Bks Demand.

Materials for High-Density Electronic Packaging & Interconnection. National Research Council Staff. 156p. (C). 1990. pap. text 19.00 (*0-309-04233-X*) Natl Acad Pr.

***Materials for High Temperature Engineering Applications: Introduction for Students & Engineers.** Marcel H. Van de Voorde & G. W. Meetham. LC 00-26198. (Engineering Materials Ser.). (Illus.). 150p. 2000. 39.95 (*3-540-66861-6*) Spr-Verlag.

Materials for High-Temperature Semiconductor Devices. National Research Council, Materials for High-Temp. 136p. (Orig.). (C). 1995. pap. text 34.00 (*0-309-05335-8*) Natl Acad Pr.

Materials for History. Frank Moore. (Notable American Authors Ser.). 1999. reprint ed. lib. bdg. 125.00 (*0-7812-4576-1*) Rprt Serv.

Materials for Infrared Detectors & Sources. Ed. by R. F. C. Farrow et al. (MRS Symposium Proceedings Ser.: Vol. 90). 1987. text 17.50 (*0-931837-55-3*) Materials Res.

Materials for Magneto-Optic Data Storage Vol. 150: Materials Research Society Symposium Proceedings. Ed. by T. Suzuki et al. 261p. 1989. text 17.50 (*1-55899-023-2*) Materials Res.

***Materials for Marine Propulsion Gearing.** AGMA Technical Committee. (ANSI/AGMA Standard Ser.: Vol. 6033-B98). 48p. 2000. pap. text 80.00 (*1-55589-711-8*) AGMA.

***Materials for Marine Propulsion Gearing.** AGMA Technical Committee. (ANSI/AGMA Standard Ser.: Vol. 6133-B98). 48p. 2000. pap. text 70.00 (*1-55589-712-6*) AGMA.

Materials for Mechanical & Optical Microsystems. Ed. by M. Elwenspoek et al. LC 97-6201. (Materials Research Society Symposium Proceedings Ser.: No. 444). 242p. 1997. text 75.00 (*1-55899-348-7*) Materials Res.

Materials for Microlithography: Radiation-Sensitive Polymers. Ed. by L. F. Thompson et al. LC 84-21744. (ACS Symposium Ser.: No. 266). 492p. 1984. lib. bdg. 60.95 (*0-8412-0871-9*) Am Chemical.

Materials for Microlithography: Radiation-Sensitive Polymers. Ed. by L. F. Thompson et al. LC 84-21744. (ACS Symposium Ser.: No. 266). 504p. 1984. reprint ed. pap. 156.30 (*0-608-03258-1*, 206377700007) Bks Demand.

Materials for Noise & Vibration Control: 1994 International Mechanical Engineering Congress & Exposition, Chicago, Illinois - November 6-11, 1994. (Noice Control & Acoustics - Design Engineering Ser.: Vol. 18, Vol. 80). 172p. 1994. 70.00 (*0-7918-1459-9*, G00954) ASME.

Materials for Nonlinear Optics: Chemical Perspectives. Ed. by Seth R. Marder et al. LC 90-25768. (ACS Symposium Ser.: No. 455). (Illus.). 740p. 1991. text 140.00 (*0-8412-1939-7*, Pub. by Am Chemical) OUP.

Materials for Occupational Education: An Annotated Source Guide. 2nd ed. Patricia G. Schuman. LC 83-8195. (Neal-Schuman Sourcebook Ser.). 384p. 1983. 39.95 (*0-918212-17-0*) Neal-Schuman.

Materials for Optical Information Processing Vol. 228: Materials Research Society Symposium Proceedings. Ed. by C. Warde et al. 373p. 1992. text 17.50 (*1-55899-122-0*) Materials Res.

Materials for Optical Limiting, Vol. 374. Ed. by R. Crane et al. (MRS Symposium Proceedings Ser.). 390p. 1995. 81.00 (*1-55899-276-6*) Materials Res.

Materials for Optical Limiting II: Materials Research Society Symposium Proceedings, Vol. 479. Ed. by P. Hood et al. LC 97-43582. 340p. 1997. text 71.00 (*1-55899-383-5*) Materials Res.

Materials for Optoelectronics. Ed. by Maurice Quillec. LC 95-25831. (International Series in Engineering & Computer Science, Natural Language Processing & Machine Translation: No. 346). 392p. (C). 1996. text 169.50 (*0-7923-9665-0*) Kluwer Academic.

Materials for Photonic Devices - Italy, 27-31 May 1991. Ed. by A. D'Andrea et al. 300p. (C). 1991. text 93.00 (*981-02-0648-8*) World Scientific Pub.

Materials for Refractories & Ceramics: A Study of Patents & Patent Applications. Ed. by Marten Terpstra. 282p. 1986. 84.75 (*1-85166-059-3*) Elsevier.

Materials for Semiconductor Devices: A Study of Patents & Patent Applications. Ed. by Marten Terpstra. 199p. 1986. 63.00 (*1-85166-060-7*) Elsevier.

Materials for Siding, Windows & Roofing. Business Communications Co., Inc. Staff. 141p. 1994. 2850.00 (*0-89336-748-6*, P-209R) BCC.

Materials for Smart Systems. Ed. by Easo P. George et al. (MRS Symposium Proceedings Ser.: Vol. 360). 557p. 1995. 67.00 (*1-55899-261-8*) Materials Res.

Materials for Smart Systems II. Ed. by K. Otsuka et al. LC 97-6489. (Materials Research Society Symposium Proceedings Ser.: No. 459). 588p. 1997. text 68.00 (*1-55899-363-0*) Materials Res.

***Materials for Smart Systems III Vol. 604: Materials Research Society Symposium Proceedings.** Ed. by M. Wun-Fogle et al. 2000. text 90.00 (*1-55899-512-9*) Materials Res.

Materials for Solid State Batteries: Proceedings of the Regional Workshop, Nus, Singapore, June 2-6, 1985. Ed. by B. V. Chowdari & S. Radhakrishna. 516p. 1986. text 113.00 (*9971-5-0149-X*) World Scientific Pub.

Materials for Spallation Neutron Sources: Proceedings, Symposium on Materials for Spallation Neutron Sources, Orlando, FL, 1997. Ed. by M. S. Wechsler et al. LC 97-71553. (Illus.). 155p. 1998. pap. 76.00 (*0-87339-361-9*, QC793) Minerals Metals.

Materials for the Engineering Technician. 3rd ed. Raymond A. Higgins. LC 97-163132. 384p. 1997. pap. text 34.95 (*0-340-67654-X*, VNR) Wiley.

Materials for the Engineering Technician. 3rd ed. Raymond A. Higgins. LC 97-163132. (Illus.). 384p. 1997. pap. 54.95 (*0-470-23626-4*) Wiley.

Materials for the History of the Text of the Qur'an. Ed. by Arthur Jeffery. LC 79-180350. reprint ed. 57.50 (*0-404-56282-5*) AMS Pr.

Materials for the History of Thomas Becket, 7 vols. Ed. by James C. Robertson & J. B. Sheppard. (Rolls Ser.: No. 67). 1969. reprint ed. 490.00 (*0-8115-1135-9*) Periodicals Srv.

Materials for the Life of Shakespeare. Pierce Butler. LC 71-113568. reprint ed. 34.50 (*0-404-01248-5*) AMS Pr.

Materials for the New Millennium: Proceedings of the Fourth Materials Engineering Conference, Washington, D. C., November 10-14, 1996, 2 vols. American Society of Civil Engineers Staff. Ed. by K. P. Chong. LC 96-44714. 1776p. 1996. 175.00 (*0-7844-0210-8*) Am Soc Civil Eng.

Materials for the Physical Anthropology of the Eastern European Jews. Maurice Fishberg. LC 06-2111. (American Anthropological Association Memoirs Ser.). 1905. 25.00 (*0-527-00500-2*) Periodicals Srv.

Materials for the Study of Inheritance in Man. Franz Boas. LC 71-82349. (Columbia Univ. Contributions to Anthropology Ser.: No. 6). 1969. reprint ed. 49.50 (*0-404-50556-2*) AMS Pr.

Materials for the Study of Navya-Nyaya Logic. Daniel H. Ingalls. (Harvard Oriental Ser.: No. 40). (C). 1988. reprint ed. 21.00 (*81-208-0384-1*, Pub. by Motilal Bnarsidass) S Asia.

Materials for the Study of the Apostolic Gnosis. Thomas S. Lea et al. 130p. 1997. reprint ed. pap. 19.95 (*0-7661-0098-7*) Kessinger Pub.

Materials for the Study of the 15th-Century Basse Danse. Frederick Crane. (Wissenschaftliche Abhandlungen-Musicological Studies: Vol. 16). 128p. 1970. lib. bdg. 40.00 (*0-912024-86-0*) Inst Mediaeval Mus.

Materials for the Study of Variation: Treated with Especial Regard to Discontinuity in the Origin of Species. William Bateson. (Foundations of Natural History Ser.). (Illus.). 652p. 1992. reprint ed. pap. text 32.50 (*0-8018-4420-7*) Johns Hopkins.

Materials for Tomorrow's Infrastructure: A Ten-Year Plan for Using High-Performance Construction Materials & Systems. Civil Engineering Research Foundation Staff. LC 94-44437. 55p. 1994. 43.00 (*0-7844-0066-0*) Am Soc Civil Eng.

Materials for Tribology. W. A. Glaeser. (Tribology Ser.: Vol. 20). xiv, 260p. 1992. 147.00 (*0-444-88495-5*) Elsevier.

Materials for Wormgear Drives. C. H. Bierbaum. (Technical Papers: Vol. P195). (Illus.). 14p. 1939. pap. text 30.00 (*1-55589-337-6*) AGMA.

Materials for 1988 Training on New Nursing Home Admission Agreement Law. 76p. 1988. pap. 10.75 (*0-685-30146-X*, 44,220) NCLS Inc.

Materials Foresight on the Electronics Industry: A Report of a Working Party of the Institute of Materials. Institute of Materials Staff. (Materials Strategy Commission Ser.). (Illus.). 104p. 1998. pap. 90.00 (*1-86125-078-9*, Pub. by Inst Materials) Ashgate Pub Co.

***Materials from Nature.** Ed. by Blackbirch Press Staff. LC 99-38940. (Crafts for All Seasons Ser.). (Illus.). 32p. (J). (gr. 3-7). 2000. lib. bdg. 18.95 (*1-56711-433-4*) Blackbirch.

Materials Fundamentals of Molecular Beam Epitaxy. Jeffrey Y. Tsao. (Illus.). 301p. 1992. pap. text 59.00 (*0-12-701625-2*) Acad Pr.

Materials Futures: Strategies & Opportunities. Ed. by R. Byron Pipes & Rune Lagneborg. (MFSO Conference Proceedings Ser.). 1988. text 17.50 (*1-55899-000-3*) Materials Res.

Materials Guide Scienceplus. HRW Staff. 1997. pap. text 7.00 (*0-03-095682-X*) Harcourt.

Materials Handbook. 14th ed. George S. Brady et al. (Illus.). 1136p. 1996. 99.00 (*0-07-007084-9*) McGraw.

***Materials Handbook: A Concise Desktop Reference.** Franpcois Cardarelli. LC 99-20194. 510p. 2000. 116.00 (*1-85233-168-2*, Pub. by Spr-Verlag) Spr-Verlag.

Materials Handbook for Hybrid Microelectronics. Ed. by Joseph A. King. LC 88-19333. (Illus.). 628p. 1988. reprint ed. pap. 194.70 (*0-608-00574-6*, 206145700009) Bks Demand.

Materials Handling. Robert M. Eastman. (Industrial Engineering Ser.: Vol.15). (Illus.). 416p. 1987. text 165.00 (*0-8247-7596-1*) Dekker.

Materials Handling. Keller, J. J., & Associates, Inc. Staff. LC 95-81790. (Workplace Safety in Action Ser.). 220p. 1995. spiral bd. 49.00 (*1-877798-50-9*, 1-SLM-6) J J Keller.

Materials Handling: Principles & Practice. Theodore H. Allegri, Sr. LC 91-35559. 542p. (C). 1992. reprint ed. 69.50 (*0-89464-672-9*) Krieger.

Materials Handling & Storing. 27p. 1992. pap. 1.75 (*0-16-037935-0*) USGPO.

***Materials Handling & Storing.** Government Printing Office Staff. 37p. 1998. pap. text 2.00 (*0-16-049481-8*) USGPO.

Materials Handling Engineering Division 75th Anniversary Commemorative Volume: 1994 International Mechanical Engineering Congress & Exposition, Chicago, Illinois - November 6-11, 1994. (MH Ser.: Vol. 2). 200p. 1994. 74.00 (*0-7918-1415-7*, G00910) ASME.

***Materials Handling Equipment in Argentina: A Strategic Entry Report, 1998.** Compiled by Icon Group International Staff. (Country Industry Report). (Illus.). 146p. 1999. ring bd. 1460.00 incl. audio compact disk (*0-7418-0264-3*) Icon Grp.

***Materials Handling Equipment in Colombia: A Strategic Entry Report, 1999.** Compiled by Icon Group International. (Illus.). 201p. 1999. ring bd. 2010.00 incl. audio compact disk (*0-7418-1851-5*) Icon Grp.

***Materials Handling for the Printer.** 2nd ed. A. John Geis & Paul L. Addy. LC 99-71814. (Illus.). 190p. (C). 1999. pap. 65.00 (*0-88362-245-9*, 15362) GATFPress.

Materials Handling Handbook. Ed. by David E. Mulcahy. LC 98-22675. (Illus.). 768p. 1998. 99.50 (*0-07-044014-X*) McGraw.

Materials Handling Handbook 2. 2nd ed. International Material Management Society Staff & American Society of Mechanical Engineers Staff. LC 84-10443. 1488p. 1985. 275.00 (*0-471-09782-9*, Wiley-Interscience) Wiley.

Materials Handling Machinery in Hong Kong: A Strategic Entry Report, 1997. Compiled by Icon Group International Staff. (Illus.). 117p. 1999. ring bd. 1170.00 incl. audio compact disk (*0-7418-1054-9*) Icon Grp.

Materials Handling Machinery in Netherlands: A Strategic Entry Report, 1997. Compiled by Icon Group International Staff. (Illus.). 122p. 1999. ring bd. 1220.00 incl. audio compact disk (*0-7418-1055-7*) Icon Grp.

Materials Handling Machinery in Thailand: A Strategic Entry Report, 1997. Compiled by Icon Group International Staff. (Illus.). 148p. 1999. ring bd. 1480.00 incl. audio compact disk (*0-7418-1056-5*) Icon Grp.

***Materials Handling Machinery in Turkey: A Strategic Entry Report, 1998.** Compiled by Icon Group International Staff. (Country Industry Report). (Illus.). 149p. 1999. ring bd. 1490.00 incl. audio compact disk (*0-7418-0265-1*) Icon Grp.

Materials-Handling Technologies Used at Hazardous Waste Sites. Majid Dosani & John Miller. LC 91-46546. (Pollution Technology Review Ser.: No. 208). (Illus.). 214p. 1992. 69.00 (*0-8155-1299-6*) Noyes.

Materials in Action: Principles & Practice. Charles Newey & Graham Weaver. (Illus.). 405p. 1990. pap. text 56.95 (*0-7506-0390-9*) Buttrwrth-Heinemann.

Materials in Art & Technology. Rohit Trivedi. Ed. by Susan Knowlton. LC 97-74317. (Illus.). 400p. (C). 1998. pap. text 59.95 (0-9659790-0-8) Taylor Knowlton.

Finally, a serious knowledgeable book explaining the world of materials & their technologies without requiring formal mathematics or previous background in the subject. The book has a broad-based appeal to anyone who has an interest in working with metals, ceramics & polymers. The author, a material scientist, is internationally known in the area of materials processing. Scientific

properties & principles are clearly explained while the "how-to" shape materials are illustrated, step-by-step. This book would be of special interest to: LIBRARIANS as an excellent scientifically-grounded reference book that introduces the reader to materials, their properties & shaping techniques, while tracing the historical development of materials from early to modern times. ARCHAEOLOGISTS, ANTHROPOLOGISTS & HISTORIANS as a guide to the history of materials & their related technologies that have impacted cultures from ancient time to the present. Chinese bronzes, glassmaking & the secrets of Damascus steel are examined. SCULPTORS, JEWELRY MAKERS & MATERIAL PROCESSORS as a definitive guide to the understanding & shaping of materials. The reader will learn how to identify problems in shaping materials & how to correct them. Techniques from casting, welding, soldering to electroforming, integrated circuits & vapor deposition are discussed. Order directly from the publisher: Taylor Knowlton, 3213 Maplewood Circle, Ames, IA 50014. phone: 515-268-8141, fax: 515-268-8131, e-mail: editor@taylorknowlton.com. ***Publisher Paid Annotation.***

Materials in Clinical Dentistry. D. F. Williams & J. Cunningham. (Illus.). 1980. pap. text 21.95 (*0-19-267006-9*) OUP.

Materials in Dentistry: Principles & Applications. Jack L. Ferracane. (Illus.). 352p. (C). 1994. pap. text 37.00 (*0-397-54955-5*, Lippncott) Lppncott W & W.

Materials in Design & Technology. John Fulton. 140p. (C). 1992. pap. text 100.00 (*0-85072-289-6*) St Mut.

Materials in Electronics. C. E. Jowett. 321p. 1971. 39.95 (*0-8464-1426-0*) Beekman Pubs.

Materials in Industry. 3rd ed. William J. Patton. (Illus.). 480p. (C). 1986. text 52.00 (*0-13-560749-3*) P-H.

*__Materials in Industry Solutions Manual.__ 3rd ed. 1999. write for info. (*0-13-560756-6*) P-H.

Materials in Marine Technology. Robert Reuben. LC 93-15462. 1994. 315.95 (*0-387-19789-3*) Spr-Verlag.

Materials in Microelectronic & Optoelectronic Packaging. Ed. by Hung C. Ling et al. LC 93-11050. (Ceramic Transactions Ser.: Vol. 33). 471p. 1993. 74.00 (*0-944904-63-7*, CT033) Am Ceramic.

Materials in Nuclear Energy, 2 vols., I. Ed. by C. K. Gupta. 296p. 1989. 161.00 (*0-8493-6772-7*, TK9185, CRC Reprint) Franklin.

Materials in Nuclear Energy, 2 vols., II. Ed. by C. K. Gupta. 240p. 1989. 134.00 (*0-8493-6773-5*, TK9185, CRC Reprint) Franklin.

Materials in Nuclear Energy: Proceedings of an International Conference, Huntsville, Ontario, Canada, 29 September - 2 October 1982. American Society for Metals Staff. LC 83-71303. 280p. reprint ed. 86.80 (*0-608-17156-5*, 202698900053) Bks Demand.

Materials in Pretrial Litigation: Problems & Cases. Thomas A. Mauet. 800p. 1992. teacher ed. write for info. (*0-316-55106-6*, 51066) Aspen Law.

Materials in Pretrial Litigation: Problems & Cases. Thomas A. Mauet. 800p. 1992. pap. 31.00 (*0-316-55102-3*, 51023) Aspen Law.

Materials in Space--Science, Technology & Exploration Vol. 551: Materials Research Society Symposium Proceedings. Ed. by A. F. Hepp et al. 312p. 1999. text 81.00 (*1-55899-457-2*) Materials Res.

Materials in the Law of Business Contracts. 3rd ed. Leonard Lakin & Leona Beane. 368p. (C). 1995. pap. text, per. 30.95 (*0-8403-9236-2*) Kendall-Hunt.

Materials in the Law of Business Corporations: With Special Reference to the Law of New York. James V. Sullivan. LC 74-78634. (Quality Paperback Ser.: No. 236). 245p. (Orig.). 1977. reprint ed. pap. 15.00 (*0-8226-0236-9*) Littlefield.

Materials in Today's World. 2nd rev. ed. Peter Thrower. (Illus.). 352p. (C). 1992. text. write for info. (*0-07-050698-1*) McGraw.

Materials in Trial Advocacy: Problems & Cases. Thomas A. Mauet & Warren D. Wolfson. 992p. 1994. teacher ed. write for info. (*0-316-55069-8*, 50698) Aspen Law.

Materials in Trial Advocacy: Problems & Cases. 4th ed. Thomas A. Mauet & Warren D. Wolfson. LC 97-46974. 1998. pap. text 40.00 (*1-56706-693-3*) Aspen Law.

Materials in World Perspective. D. G. Altenpohl et al. (Materials Research & Engineering Ser.: Vol. 1). (Illus.). 208p. 1980. 51.95 (*0-387-10037-7*) Spr-Verlag.

*__Materials Instabilities.__ Ed. by Daniel Walgraef et al. 400p. 2000. 88.00 (*981-02-4265-4*) World Scientific Pub.

Materials Interactions Relevant to the Pulp, Paper, & Wood Industries. Ed. by D. Caulfield et al. (Symposium Proceedings Ser.: Vol. 197). 357p. 1990. text 17.50 (*1-55899-086-0*) Materials Res.

*__Materials Issues & Modeling for Device Nanofabrication Vol. 584: Materials Research Society Symposium Proceedings.__ Ed. by L. Merhari et al. (Materials Research Society Symposium Proceedings Ser.). 2000. text 93.00 (*1-55899-492-0*) Materials Res.

Materials Issues for Advanced Electronic & Opto-Electronic Connectors. Ed. by J. Crane et al. LC 91-61921. (Illus.). 157p. 1991. pap. 48.70 (*0-608-04891-7*, 206558300004) Bks Demand.

*__Materials Issues for Tunable RF & Microwave Devices Vol. 603: Materials Research Society Symposium Proceedings.__ Ed. by Q. Jia et al. 2000. text 90.00 (*1-55899-511-0*) Materials Res.

Materials Issues in Amorphous-Semiconductor Technology. Ed. by D. Adler et al. (MRS Symposium Proceedings Ser.: Vol. 70). 1986. text 17.50 (*0-931837-36-7*) Materials Res.

Materials Issues in Applications of Amorphous Silicon Technology, Vol. 49. Ed. by M. J. Thompson et al. 1985. text 17.50 (*0-931837-14-6*) Materials Res.

Materials Issues in Art & Archaeology. Ed. by E. V. Sayre et al. (Symposium Proceedings Ser.: Vol. 123). 1988. text 17.50 (*0-931837-93-6*) Materials Res.

Materials Issues in Art & Archaeology III. Ed. by J. R. Druzik et al. (Materials Research Society Symposium Proceedings Ser.: Vol. 267). 1097p. 1992. text 62.00 (*1-55899-162-X*) Materials Res.

Materials Issues in Art & Archaeology V. Ed. by P. B. Vandiver et al. (Materials Research Society Symposium Proceedings Ser.: No. 462). 427p. 1997. text 71.00 (*1-55899-366-5*) Materials Res.

Materials Issues in Heat Exchangers & Boilers Conference: Proceedings 17-18 October 1995. Fred Starr & Barry Meadowcroft. (Illus.). 380p. 1997. 150.00 (*1-86125-046-0*, Pub. by Inst Materials) Ashgate Pub Co.

Materials Issues in Machining: Proceedings of a Symposium & the Physics of Machining Processes: Proceedings of a Symposium. Minerals, Metals & Materials Society Staff. Ed. by Robin Stevenson & David A. Stephenson. LC 92-85453. (Illus.). 233p. 1992. reprint ed. pap. 72.30 (*0-608-05690-1*, 206620500007) Bks Demand.

Materials Issues in Machining & the Physics of Machining Pt. II: 1994 International Mechanical Engineering Congress & Exposition, Chicago, Illinois - November 6-11, 1994. Greg Evans. 424p. 1994. 100.00 (*0-614-05620-9*, 392426) ASME.

Materials Issues in Machining II & the Physics of Machining Processes. Ed. by David A. Stephenson & Robin Stevenson. LC 94-78112. 419p. 1994. reprint ed. pap. 129.90 (*0-608-00770-6*, 206156800010) Bks Demand.

Materials Issues in Machining III & the Physics of Machining Processes III. Ed. by D. A. Stephenson & R. A. Stevenson. LC 96-77726. (Illus.). 227p. 1996. 20.00 (*0-87339-345-7*, 3457) Minerals Metals.

Materials Issues in Microcrystalline Semiconductors: Materials Research Society Symposium Proceedings, Vol. 164. Ed. by P. M. Fauchet et al. 393p. 1990. text 17.50 (*1-55899-052-6*) Materials Res.

Materials Issues in Silicon Integrated Circuit Processing. Ed. by M. Wittmer et al. (MRS Symposium Proceedings Ser.: Vol. 71). 1986. text 17.50 (*0-931837-37-5*) Materials Res.

Materials Issues in Vacuum Microelectronics Vol. 509: Proceedings Materials Research Society Symposium. Ed. by W. Zhu et al. LC 98-33480. 207p. 1998. text 79.00 (*1-55899-415-7*) Materials Res.

Materials Management. Gilian Beekman-Love & L. Neiger. (Applied Business Logistics Ser.: Vol. 1). 1978. pap. text 78.50 (*90-207-0748-5*) Kluwer Academic.

Materials Management: Emerging Professional Excellence, 1986 Annual Conference Proceedings. 73p. 1986. 30.00 (*0-318-35037-8*) AHRMM.

Materials Management Handbook. Theodore H. Allegri, Sr. (Illus.). 448p. 1991. 34.95 (*0-8306-3513-0*, 3513) McGraw-Hill Prof.

Materials Management Handbook. Theodore H. Allegri. 1991. 49.95 (*0-07-157602-9*) McGraw.

Materials Management Handbook. Peter Baily & David Farmer. 300p. (C). 1988. 220.00 (*0-7855-3765-1*, Pub. by Inst Pur & Supply) St Mut.

Materials Management Handbook. Peter Baily & David Farmer. 300p. (C). 1989. 450.00 (*0-7855-4616-2*, Pub. by Inst Pur & Supply) St Mut.

Materials Management in Clothing Production. David J. Tyler. (Illus.). 176p. 1991. pap. 34.95 (*0-632-02896-3*) Blackwell Sci.

Materials Management in the Operating Room. Mary Starr. (Illus.). 122p. (Orig.). 1993. pap. 55.00 (*0-87258-644-8*, 142901) Am Hospital.

Materials Management Systems. Robert G. Brown. LC 83-19978. 448p. (C). 1984. reprint ed. lib. bdg. 46.50 (*0-89874-707-4*) Krieger.

Materials Manager. Jack Rudman. (Career Examination Ser.: C-3395). 1994. pap. 34.95 (*0-8373-3395-4*) Nat Learn.

Materials, Manufacturing & Measurement for Synchrotron Radiation Mirrors, Vol. 3047. Ed. by Peter Z. Takacs & Thomas W. Tonnessen. LC 98-122054. 274p. 1997. 69.00 (*0-8194-2574-5*) SPIE.

Materials Modelling: From Theory to Technology. Ed. by C. A. English et al. (Illus.). 240p. 1992. 124.00 (*0-7503-0196-1*) IOP Pub.

Materials Modification & Growth Using Ion Beams. Ed. by Ursula Gibson et al. (MRS Symposium Proceedings Ser.: Vol. 93). 1987. text 17.50 (*0-931837-60-X*) Materials Res.

Materials Modification & Synthesis by Ion Beam Processing. Ed. by D. E. Alexander et al. LC 97-811. (Materials Research Society Symposium Proceedings Ser.: No. 438). 727p. 1997. text 78.00 (*1-55899-342-8*) Materials Res.

Materials Modification by Energetic Atoms & Ions. Ed. by K. S. Grabowski et al. (Materials Research Society Symposium Proceedings Ser.: Vol. 268). 403p. 1992. text 30.00 (*1-55899-163-8*) Materials Res.

Materials Modification by High-Fluence Ion Beams. Ed. by Roger Kelly & M. Fernanda Da Silva. (C). 1988. text 299.00 (*0-7923-0035-1*) Kluwer Academic.

Materials Modification by Ion Irradiation. Ed. by Emile J. Knystautas. LC 98-226763. (Proceedings of SPIE Ser.: Vol. 3413). 274p. 1998. 59.00 (*0-8194-2867-1*) SPIE.

Materials of Construction. Frank R. Dagostino. (Construction & Building Trades Ser.). 1997. teacher ed. 13.95 (*0-8273-7118-7*); text 55.95 (*0-8273-7117-9*) Delmar.

Materials of Construction. James Lai. 368p. (C). 1997. 53.90 (*0-7872-4404-X*) Kendall-Hunt.

*__Materials of Construction.__ 2nd ed. James Lai. 308p. (C). 1999. per. 61.95 (*0-7872-6108-4*, 41610801) Kendall-Hunt.

Materials of Construction. 4th ed. R. C. Smith. 1987. pap. 53.85 (*0-07-058504-0*) McGraw.

Materials of Construction for Steam Power Plant. L. M. Wyatt. (Illus.). 312p. 1976. 79.25 (*0-85334-661-5*) Elsevier.

Materials of Construction for Use in an LNG Pipeline. J. Dainora et al. 130p. 1968. 7.00 (*0-318-12652-4*, L40000) Am Gas Assn.

Materials of Construction of Fluid Machinery & Their Relationship to Design & Performance: Presented at the Winter Annual Meeting of the American Society of Mechanical Engineers, Washington, D.C., November 15-20, 1981. American Society of Mechanical Engineers Staff. Ed. by R. C. Cherry et al. LC 81-69017. (Illus.). 111p. reprint ed. pap. 34.50 (*0-8357-2863-3*, 203909900011) Bks Demand.

Materials of Construction, Their Manufacture & Properties. Adelbert P. Mills. LC 55-73681. (Illus.). 662p. reprint ed. pap. 200.00 (*0-608-30319-4*, 205513200008) Bks Demand.

Materials of Dance As a Creative Art Activity. 5th ed. Ed. by Barbara Mettler. 1979. 18.50 (*0-912536-10-1*) Mettler Studios.

Materials of Interior Design. Dennis G. Murphy. Ed. by Gladys N. Murphy. (Interior Furnishings & Products Ser.). (Illus.). 208p. (Orig.). (C). 1978. 14.00 (*0-938614-00-2*, 211-196) Stratford Hse.

Materials of Medieval Painting see Materials & Techniques of Medieval Painting

Materials of Sculpture. Nicholas Penny. 1996. pap. 32.50 (*0-300-06581-7*) Yale U Pr.

Materials of the Artist & Their Use in Painting with Notes of the Techniques of the Old Masters. rev. ed. Max Doerner. Tr. by Eugen Neuhaus. LC 84-10888. (Illus.). 458p. 1949. pap. 16.00 (*0-15-657716-X*, Harvest Bks) Harcourt.

Materials on Accounting for Lawyers. 2nd ed. David R. Nerwitz & Matthew J. Barrett. LC 97-25345. (University Casebook Ser.). 749p. 1997. text. write for info. (*1-56662-451-7*) Foundation Pr.

Materials on Corporate Political Activity, 3 vols., Set, No. 006. 1100p. 1981. ring bd. 245.00 (*0-929576-22-5*) Busn Laws Inc.

Materials on Housing Issues. 253p. 1988. 28.50 (*0-685-30168-0*, 43,610) NCLS Inc.

Materials on International Human Rights & U. S. Constitutional Law. Hurst Hannum & Richard B. Lillich. (Procedural Aspects of International Law Ser.). iii, 116p. (Orig.). (C). 1985. pap. text 32.50 (*0-9615124-0-7*, 306150) W S Hein.

Materials on International Human Rights & U. S. Criminal Law Procedure. Hurst Hannum. (Procedural Aspects of International Law Ser.). ii, 152p. (Orig.). 1989. pap. 25.00 (*0-9615124-2-3*, 306650) W S Hein.

Materials on Japanese Social & Economic History: Tokugawa, Japan. Neil S. Smith. LC 78-65370. (Studies in Japanese History & Civilization). 176p. 1979. reprint ed. lib. bdg. 62.50 (*0-313-26994-7*, U6994, Greenwood Pr) Greenwood.

Materials on Left Dislocation. Ed. by Elena Anagnostopoulou et al. LC 97-4489. (Linguistik Aktuell/Linguistics Today Ser.: Vol. 14). viii, 349p. 1997. lib. bdg. 86.00 (*1-55619-233-9*) J Benjamins Pubng Co.

Materials on Legislation. 4th ed. Horace E. Read et al. LC 81-17479. (University Casebook Ser.). 953p. (C). 1981. text 38.00 (*0-88277-045-4*) Foundation Pr.

Materials on Legislation: Political Language & the Political Process. William D. Popkin. (University Casebook Ser.). 718p. (C). 1993. text 40.50 (*1-56662-051-1*) Foundation Pr.

Materials on Legislation: Political Language & the Political Process. 2nd ed. William D. Popkin. LC 97-1097. (University Casebook Ser.). 940p. 1997. text 48.50 (*1-56662-519-X*) Foundation Pr.

Materials on Legislation: Political Language & the Political Process, Teacher's Manual For. 2nd ed. William D. Popkin. (University Casebook Ser.). 237p. 1997. pap. text. write for info. (*1-56662-540-8*) Foundation Pr.

Materials on Legislation: Political Language & the Political Process, 1994 Supplement. William D. Popkin. (University Casebook Ser.). 129p. 1994. 8.50 (*1-56662-210-7*) Foundation Pr.

Materials on the Americans with Disabilities Act, 3 vols., Set, No. 86. Ed. by William A. Hancock. 800p. 1991. ring bd. 155.00 (*0-929576-65-9*) Busn Laws Inc.

Materials on the Law of Insider Trading. C. Edward Fletcher. LC 91-73518. 647p. 1991. 49.95 (*0-89089-418-3*) Carolina Acad Pr.

Materials on the Law of the European Communities, 1983. D. J. Gijstra & Edmond L. Volker. 550p. 1983. pap. 66.00 (*90-6544-069-0*) Kluwer Law Intl.

Materials on the Move: The Sixth National SAMPE Technical Conference, Dayton, OH, October 8-10, 1974. National SAMPE Technical Conference Staff. LC 74-194771. (National SAMPE Technical Conference Ser.: No. 6). 477p. reprint ed. pap. 147.90 (*0-7837-1286-3*, 204142700020) Bks Demand.

Materials on Trial Advocacy. 3rd ed. Thomas A. Mauet. LC 93-80974. 992p. 1994. lib. bdg. 36.00 (*0-316-55110-4*, Aspen Law & Bus) Aspen Pub.

Materials Overview for 1982: National SAMPE Symposium & Exhibition, 27th, Town & Country Hotel, San Diego, California, May 4-6, 1982. National SAMPE Symposium & Exhibition Staff. LC 82-179801. (Science of Advanced Materials & Process Enginnering Ser.: No. 27). 1080p. reprint ed. pap. 200.00 (*0-7837-1280-4*, 204142100020) Bks Demand.

Materials Performance & the Deep Sea-STP 445. 146p. 1969. pap. 9.50 (*0-8031-0706-4*, STP445) ASTM.

Materials Performance in Waste Incineration Systems. Ed. by G. Y. Lai & G. Sorrell. (Illus.). 538p. 1992. 32.00 (*1-877914-31-2*) NACE Intl.

Materials Performance Maintenance: Proceedings of the International Symposium on Materials Performance Maintenance, Ottawa, Ontario, Canada, August 18-21, 1991. Ed. by R. W. Revie et al. (Proceedings of Metallurgical Society of the Canadian Institute of Mining & Metallurgy Ser.: No. 25). (Illus.). 360p. 1991. 137.25 (*0-08-041441-9*, Pergamon Pr) Elsevier.

Materials Problem Solving with the Transmission Electron Microscope, Vol. 62. Ed. by L. W. Hobbs et al. (Materials Research Society Symposium Proceedings Ser.). 1986. text 17.50 (*0-931837-27-8*) Materials Res.

Materials Processes: A Short Introduction. I. Minkoff. (Illus.). 160p. (C). 1992. 82.95 (*0-387-18895-9*) Spr-Verlag.

Materials Processing. Bradley R. Thode. (Tech & Industrial Education Ser.). 1981. teacher ed. 11.95 (*0-8273-1768-9*) Delmar.

Materials Processing: A Multimedia Approach. Constant. (General Engineering Ser.). (C). 1909. pap. 50.00 (*0-534-95111-2*) PWS Pubs.

Materials Processing & Design: Grain-Boundary-Controlled Properties of Fine Ceramics II. Ed. by Koichi Niihara et al. (Ceramic Transactions Ser.: Vol. 44). 1994. 88.00 (*0-944904-78-5*, CT044) Am Ceramic.

Materials Processing & Performance: Bk. H00162, MD2 see Advances in Materials Technology in the Americas

Materials Processing Defects. Ed. by S. K. Ghosh & M. Predeleanu. LC 95-3186. (Studies in Applied Mechanics: No. 43). 446p. 1995. 187.50 (*0-444-81706-9*) Elsevier.

Materials Processing in High Gravity. L. L. Regel & W. R. Wilcox. LC 94-40006. (Illus.). 230p. (C). 1994. 85.00 (*0-306-44862-9*, Plenum Trade) Perseus Pubng.

Materials Processing in Space. Ed. by V. Laxmanan et al. (Materials Science Forum Ser.). 450p. 1989. text 106.00 (*0-87849-592-4*, Pub. by Trans T Pub) Enfield Pubs NH.

Materials Processing in Space: Theory, Experiments, & Technology, Vol. 1. L. L. Regel. LC 89-7222. (Illus.). 248p. (C). 1990. 85.00 (*0-306-11026-1*, Kluwer Plenum) Kluwer Academic.

Materials Processing in the Computer Age: Proceedings of an International Symposium Sponsored by TMS Synthesis & Analysis in Materials Processing Committee Held in New Orleans, Louisiana, USA, February 17 Through February 21, 1991 at the 120th TMS Annual Meeting & Exhibit. fac. ed. Minerals, Metals & Materials Society Staff. Ed. by V. R. Voller et al. LC 90-64039. 474p. 1991. reprint ed. pap. 147.00 (*0-7837-8298-5*, 204908400010) Bks Demand.

Materials Processing in the Computer Age, II: Proceedings: International Symposium Sponsored by TMS Synthesis, Control, & Analysis in Materials Processing Committee, TMS Solidification: Proceedings. Ed. by N. El-Kaddah et al. LC 94-73533. (Illus.). 488p. 1995. 10.00 (*0-87339-282-5*, 2825) Minerals Metals.

Materials Processing in the Computer Age III. Ed. by Vaughan R. Voller & Hani Henein. (Illus.). 244p. pap. 62.00 (*0-87339-467-4*) Minerals Metals.

Materials Processing in the Reduced Gravity Environment of Space. Ed. by R. H. Doremus et al. (MRS Symposium Proceedings Ser.: Vol. 87). 1987. text 17.50 (*0-931837-52-9*) Materials Res.

Materials, Properties & Preparation, 2 vols. enl. rev. ed. Ed. by S. Mahajan. LC 93-732. (Handbook on Semiconductors Ser.: Vol. 3). 2398p. 1994. 771.75 (*0-444-88835-7*, North Holland) Elsevier.

Materials Properties Handbook: Stainless Steels. Ed. by R. Lula. 500p. 1996. 192.00 (*0-87170-588-5*, 6195) ASM.

Materials Properties Handbook: Titanium Alloys. Ed. by E. W. Collings et al. 1169p. 1994. 290.00 (*0-87170-481-1*, 6005) ASM.

Materials Recovery & Utilization: Bk. H00161, MD1 see Advances in Materials Technology in the Americas

Materials Recovery from Municipal Waste: Unit Operations in Practice. H. Alter. (Illus.). 280p. 1983. text 155.00 (*0-8247-7134-6*) Dekker.

Materials Recycling: The Virtue of Necessity. William U. Chandler. 1983. pap. write for info. (*0-916468-55-0*) Worldwatch Inst.

Materials Reliability in Microelectronics II. Ed. by C. V. Thompson & J. R. Lloyd. (Materials Research Society Symposium Proceedings Ser.: Vol. 265). 327p. 1992. text 17.50 (*1-55899-160-3*) Materials Res.

Materials Reliability in Microelectronics III. Ed. by P. S. Ho et al. (Symposium Proceedings Ser.: Vol. 309). 495p. 1993. text 30.00 (*1-55899-205-7*) Materials Res.

Materials Reliability in Microelectronics IV Vol. 338: Materials Research Society Symposium Proceedings. Ed. by Peter Borgesen et al. 629p. 1994. text 30.00 (*1-55899-238-3*) Materials Res.

Materials Reliability in Microelectronics IX Vol. 563: Materials Research Society Symposium Proceedings. Ed. by C. A. Volkert et al. 311p. 1999. text 72.00 (*1-55899-470-X*) Materials Res.

An Asterisk (*) at the beginning of an entry indicates that the title is appearing for the first time.

Materials Reliability in Microelectronics V: Materials Research Society Symposium Proceedings. Ed. by Anthony S. Oates et al. (MRS Symposium Proceedings Ser.: Vol. 391). 523p. 1995. text 82.00 (*1-55899-294-4*, 391) Materials Res.

Materials Reliability in Microelectronics VI. Ed. by Robert Rosenberg et al. (MRS Symposium Proceedings Ser.: Vol. 428). 583p. 1996. 76.00 (*1-55899-331-2*, 428) Materials Res.

Materials Reliability in Microelectronics VII: Materials Research Society Symposium Proceedings, Vol. 473. Ed. by J. J. Clement et al. 457p. 1997. text 75.00 (*1-55899-377-0*) Materials Res.

Materials Reliability in Microelectronics VIII Vol. 516: Proceedings Materials Research Society Symposium. Ed. by T. Marieb et al. 365p. 1998. text 79.00 (*1-55899-422-X*) Materials Res.

Materials Reliability Issues in Microelectronics Vol. 225: Materials Research Society Symposium Proceedings. Ed. by J. R. Lloyd et al. 354p. 1991. text 70.00 (*1-55899-119-0*) Materials Res.

Materials Research Agenda for the Automobile & Aircraft Industries. National Research Council Staff. 83p. 1993. pap. text 25.00 (*0-309-04985-7*) Natl Acad Pr.

Materials Research Centres. 4th ed. 1991. text 475.00 (*0-582-08124-6*) Longman.

Materials Research in European Laboratories. (Illus.). 38p. (Orig.). (C). 1993. pap. text 30.00 (*0-7881-0035-1*) DIANE Pub.

Materials Research in Low Gravity. Ed. by Narayanan Ramachandran. LC 98-125244. 23p. 1997. pap. 69.00 (*0-8194-2545-1*) SPIE.

***Materials Research Using Cold Neutrons at Pulsed Neutron Sources: Argonne National Laboratory, USA 25 - 26 August 1997.** Ed. by C-K Loong et al. 250p. 1999. 56.00 (*981-02-3748-0*) World Scientific Pub.

Materials Research with Ion Beams. Ed. by H. Schmidt-Bocking et al. (Research Reports in Physics). (Illus.). 180p. 1992. 82.95 (*0-387-55774-1*) Spr-Verlag.

Materials Review, '75: National SAMPE Technical Conference, 7th, Hilton Inn, Albuquerque, New Mexico, October 14-16, 1975. National SAMPE Technical Conference Staff. LC 75-332485. (National SAMPE Technical Conference Ser.: No. 7). 548p. reprint ed. pap. 169.90 (*0-7837-1287-1*, 204142800020) Bks Demand.

Materials Revolution: Superconductors, New Materials, & the Japanese Challenge. Ed. by Tom Forester. 300p. (Orig.). 1988. 40.00 (*0-262-06116-3*); pap. text 25.00 (*0-262-56043-7*) MIT Pr.

Materials Science. (Quick Study Academic Ser.). 4p. pap. 3.95 (*1-57222-257-3*) Barcharts.

Materials Science. (Basic Academics Ser.: Module 9). (Illus.). 120p. 1982. spiral bd. 39.50 (*0-87683-233-8*) GP Courseware.

Materials Science. 172p. 1998. pap. 34.50 (*0-7487-1807-9*) St Mut.

Materials Science. Charles A. Wert. LC 78-58666. (Opportunities In . . . Ser.). (Illus.). 160p. pap. 12.95 (*0-8442-6582-9*, 297OIMS, VGM Career) NTC Contemp Pub Co.

Materials Science. Charles A. Wert. (Opportunities in...Ser.). 160p. 1995. pap. 10.95 (*0-614-95839-3*) NTC Contemp Pub Co.

Materials Science: A Multimedia Approach-Win. Russ. (General Engineering Ser.). (C). 1996. pap. 29.95 (*0-534-95736-6*) Wadsworth Pub.

Materials Science: Japanese Research on Polymers, Ceramics & Mechanical Properties of Materials at High Temperatures. 23p. (Orig.). (C). 1993. pap. text 30.00 (*1-56806-301-6*) DIANE Pub.

Materials, Science & Engineering. Jeff Perkins. (C). 2000. text. write for info. (*0-201-53848-2*) Addison-Wesley.

Materials Science & Engineering: A Self-Instructional Problem Workbook. Joseph P. Reynolds. 224p. 1994. pap. text 60.00 (*1-882767-11-X*) ETS.

Materials Science & Engineering: An Introduction. William D. Callister. LC 96-18784. 880p. 1996. text 105.95 (*0-471-13459-7*) Wiley.

Materials Science & Engineering: An Introduction. 5th ed. William D. Callister. LC 99-17182. 896p. 1999. text 109.95 (*0-471-32013-7*) Wiley.

***Materials Science & Engineering: An Introduction.** 5th ed. William D. Callister. 86p. 2000. pap., student ed. 26.95 (*0-471-38912-9*) Wiley.

***Materials Science & Engineering: Forging Stronger Links to Users.** National Research Council Staff. 124p. 1999. pap. 29.00 (*0-309-06826-6*) Natl Acad Pr.

Materials Science & Engineering for Manufacturing. Ed. by Lawrence E. Murr. (Illus.). 375p. (C). 1990. text 89.00 (*1-878907-37-9*) TechBooks.

Materials Science & Engineering of Rigid-Rod Polymers Vol. 134: Materials Research Society Symposium Proceedings. Ed. by W. W. Adams et al. 699p. 1989. text 17.50 (*1-55899-007-0*) Materials Res.

Materials Science & Engineering Serving Society: Proceedings of the Third Okinaga Symposium on Materials Science & Engineering Serving Society, Chiba, Japan, 3-5 September 1997. Ed. by S. Somiya et al. LC 98-52810. 356p. 1998. 181.00 (*0-444-82793-5*) Elsevier.

Materials Science & Implant Orthopedic Surgery. Ram Kossowsky & Nir Kossovsky. 1986. text 218.00 (*90-247-3409-6*) Kluwer Academic.

Materials Science & Metallurgy. 4th ed. Herman W. Pollack. (Illus.). 560p. 1988. text 24.00 (*0-13-560814-7*) P-H.

Materials Science & Technology: A Comprehensive Treatment, 22 vols. Incl. Vol. 1, Structure of Solids. Materials Science & Technology: A Comprehensive Treatment, Vol. 1, Structure of Solids. Ed. by V. Gerold. (Illus.). 621p. 1992. 398.00 (*3-527-26814-6*, Wiley-VCH); Vol. 2A, Characterization of Materials, Pt. I. Materials Science & Technology: A Comprehensive Treatment, Vol. 2A, Characterization of Materials, Pt. I. Ed. by E. Lifshin. 725p. 1992. 395.00 (*3-527-26815-4*, Wiley-VCH); Vol. 2B, Characterization of Materials, Pt. II. Characterization of Materials. Ed. by E. Lifshin. 776p. 1994. 495.00 (*3-527-28265-3*, Wiley-VCH); Vol. 3A, Electronic and Magnetic Properties of Met. Materials Science & Technology: A Comprehensive Treatment, Vol. 3A, Electronic & Magnetic Properties of Metals & Ceramics, Pt. I. Ed. by Jurgen Buschow. (Illus.). 642p. 1991. 398.00 (*3-527-26816-2*, Wiley-VCH); Vol. 3B, Electronic and Magnetic Properties of Met. Electronic & Magnetic Properties of Metals & Ceramics Pt. II. Ed. by Jurgen Buschow. (Illus.). 625p. 1993. 495.00 (*3-527-28264-5*, Wiley-VCH); Vol. 4, Electronic Structure and Properties of Sem. Materials Science & Technology: A Comprehensive Treatment, Vol. 4, Electronic Structure & Properties of Semiconductors. Ed. by Wolfgang Schroter. (Illus.). 603p. 1991. 398.00 (*3-527-26817-0*, Wiley-VCH); Vol. 5, Phase Transformation in Materials. Materials Science & Technology: A Comprehensive Treatment, Vol. 5, Phase Transformation in Materials. Ed. by P. Haasen. (Illus.). 649p. 1990. 398.00 (*3-527-26818-9*, Wiley-VCH); Vol. 6, Plastic Deformation and Fracture of Materi. Materials Science & Technology: A Comprehensive Treatment, Vol. 6, Plastic Deformation & Fracture of Materials. Ed. by H. Mughrabi. (Illus.). 698p. 1992. 398.00 (*3-527-26819-7*, Wiley-VCH); Vol. 7, Constitution and Properties of Steels. Materials Science & Technology: A Comprehensive Treatment, Vol. 7, Constitution & Properties of Steels. Ed. by F. B. Pickering. 824p. 1991. 398.00 (*3-527-26820-0*, Wiley-VCH); Vol. 8, Structure and Properties of Nonferrous All. Materials Science & Technology: A Comprehensive Treatment, Vol. 8, Structure & Properties of Nonferrous Alloys. Ed. by K. H. Matucha. (Illus.). 837p. 1995. 495.00 (*3-527-26821-9*, Wiley-VCH); Vol. 9, Glasses and Amorphous Materials. Materials Science & Technology: A Comprehensive Treatment, Vol. 9, Glasses & Amorphous Materials. Ed. by J. Zarzycki. 798p. 1991. 398.00 (*3-527-26822-7*, Wiley-VCH); Vol. 10A, Nuclear Materials, Pt. I. Materials Science & Technology: A Comprehensive Treatment, Vol. 10A, Nuclear Materials, Pt. I. Ed. by B. R. Frost. 557p. 1994. 495.00 (*3-527-26823-5*, Wiley-VCH); Vol. 10B, Nuclear Materials, Pt. II. Materials Science & Technology: A Comprehensive Treatment, Vol. 10B, Nuclear Materials, Pt. II. Ed. by B. R. Frost. 455p. 1994. 495.00 (*3-527-29236-5*, Wiley-VCH); Vol. 11, Structure and Properties of Ceramics. Materials Science & Technology: A Comprehensive Treatment, Vol. 11, Structure & Properties of Ceramics. Ed. by Micahel Swain. (Illus.). 842p. 1993. 495.00 (*3-527-26824-3*, Wiley-VCH); Vol. 12, Structure and Properties of Polymers. Materials Science & Technology: A Comprehensive Treatment, Vol. 12, Structure & Properties of Polymers. Ed. by E. L. Thomas. (Illus.). 785p. 1993. 495.00 (*3-527-26825-1*, Wiley-VCH); Vol. 13, Structure and Properties of Composites. Materials Science & Technology: A Comprehensive Treatment, Vol. 13, Structure & Properties of Composites. Ed. by T. W. Chou. 626p. 1993. 495.00 (*3-527-26826-X*, Wiley-VCH); Vol. 14, Medical and Dental Materials. Materials Science & Technology: A Comprehensive Treatment, Vol. 14, Medical & Dental Materials. Ed. by D. F. Williams. (Illus.). 469p. 1992. 390.00 (*3-527-26827-8*, Wiley-VCH); Vol. 15, Processing of Metals and Alloys. Materials Science & Technology: A Comprehensive Treatment, Vol. 15, Processing of Metals & Alloys. Ed. by R. W. Cahn. 629p. 1991. 398.00 (*3-527-26828-6*, Wiley-VCH); Vol. 16, Processing of Semiconductors. Materials Science & Technology: A Comprehensive Treatment, Vol. 16, Processing of Semiconductors. Ed. by K. A. Jackson. (Illus.). 715p. 1997. 495.00 (*3-527-26829-4*, Wiley-VCH); Vol. 17A, Processing of Ceramics, Pt. I. Materials Science & Technology: A Comprehensive Treatment, Vol. 17A, Processing of Ceramics, Pt. I. Ed. by R. J. Brook. 406p. 1995. 495.00 (*3-527-26830-8*, Wiley-VCH); Vol. 17B, Processing of Ceramics, Pt. II. Materials Science & Technology: A Comprehensive Treatment, Vol. 17B, Processing of Ceramics, Pt. II. Ed. by R. J. Brook. 379p. 1995. 495.00 (*3-527-29356-6*, Wiley-VCH); Vol. 18, Synthesis of Polymers. Materials Science & Technology: A Comprehensive Treatment, Vol. 18, Processing of Polymers. Ed. by H. E. Meijer. 906p. 1997. 495.00 (*3-527-26831-6*, Wiley-VCH); 4230.00 (*0-614-20067-9*, Wiley-VCH) Wiley.

Materials Science & Technology: A Comprehensive Treatment, 18 Vols. R. W. Cahn et al. LC 90-21936. 999p. 1997. 7349.00 (*3-527-26813-8*) Wiley.

Materials Science & Technology: A Comprehensive Treatment, Vol. 1, Structure of Solids see Materials Science & Technology: A Comprehensive Treatment

Materials Science & Technology: A Comprehensive Treatment, Vol. 10A, Nuclear Materials, Pt. I see Materials Science & Technology: A Comprehensive Treatment

Materials Science & Technology: A Comprehensive Treatment, Vol. 10B, Nuclear Materials, Pt. II see Materials Science & Technology: A Comprehensive Treatment

Materials Science & Technology: A Comprehensive Treatment, Vol. 11, Structure & Properties of Ceramics see Materials Science & Technology: A Comprehensive Treatment

Materials Science & Technology: A Comprehensive Treatment, Vol. 12, Structure & Properties of Polymers see Materials Science & Technology: A Comprehensive Treatment

Materials Science & Technology: A Comprehensive Treatment, Vol. 13, Structure & Properties of Composites see Materials Science & Technology: A Comprehensive Treatment

Materials Science & Technology: A Comprehensive Treatment, Vol. 14, Medical & Dental Materials see Materials Science & Technology: A Comprehensive Treatment

Materials Science & Technology: A Comprehensive Treatment, Vol. 15, Processing of Metals & Alloys see Materials Science & Technology: A Comprehensive Treatment

Materials Science & Technology: A Comprehensive Treatment, Vol. 16, Processing of Semiconductors see Materials Science & Technology: A Comprehensive Treatment

Materials Science & Technology: A Comprehensive Treatment, Vol. 17A, Processing of Ceramics, Pt. I see Materials Science & Technology: A Comprehensive Treatment

Materials Science & Technology: A Comprehensive Treatment, Vol. 17B, Processing of Ceramics, Pt. II see Materials Science & Technology: A Comprehensive Treatment

Materials Science & Technology: A Comprehensive Treatment, Vol. 18, Processing of Polymers see Materials Science & Technology: A Comprehensive Treatment

Materials Science & Technology: A Comprehensive Treatment, Vol. 2A, Characterization of Materials, Pt. I see Materials Science & Technology: A Comprehensive Treatment

Materials Science & Technology: A Comprehensive Treatment, Vol. 3A, Electronic & Magnetic Properties of Metals & Ceramics, Pt. I see Materials Science & Technology: A Comprehensive Treatment

Materials Science & Technology: A Comprehensive Treatment, Vol. 4, Electronic Structure & Properties of Semiconductors see Materials Science & Technology: A Comprehensive Treatment

Materials Science & Technology: A Comprehensive Treatment, Vol. 5, Phase Transformation in Materials see Materials Science & Technology: A Comprehensive Treatment

Materials Science & Technology: A Comprehensive Treatment, Vol. 6, Plastic Deformation & Fracture of Materials see Materials Science & Technology: A Comprehensive Treatment

Materials Science & Technology: A Comprehensive Treatment, Vol. 7, Constitution & Properties of Steels see Materials Science & Technology: A Comprehensive Treatment

Materials Science & Technology: A Comprehensive Treatment, Vol. 8, Structure & Properties of Nonferrous Alloys see Materials Science & Technology: A Comprehensive Treatment

Materials Science & Technology: A Comprehensive Treatment, Vol. 9, Glasses & Amorphous Materials see Materials Science & Technology: A Comprehensive Treatment

Materials Science & Technology: Comprehensive Treatment, Index of Vol. 1-18. Ed. by R. W. Cahn et al. (Materials Science & Technology). 412p. 1998. 398.00 (*3-527-29504-6*) Wiley.

Materials Science & Technology: 1996 Annual Report. Ed. by Michael Janssen. (Illus.). 273p. 1997. pap. 45.00 (*90-407-1537-8*, Pub. by Delft U Pr) Coronet Bks.

Materials Science & the Physics of Non-Conventional Energy Sources (1987) G. Furlan et al. 584p. (C). 1989. text 161.00 (*9971-5-0906-7*) World Scientific Pub.

Materials Science & the Physics of Non-Conventional Energy Sources (1989) Proceedings of the Workshop ICTP, Trieste, 11-29 September 1989. Ed. by G. Furlan et al. 600p. (C). 1991. text 118.00 (*981-02-0752-2*) World Scientific Pub.

Materials Science Applications of Ion Beam Techniques: Proceedings of the International Symposium on Materials Science Applications of Ion Beam Techniques Incorporating the 1st German-Australian Workshop on Ion Beam Analysis, Seeheim, Germany, September 1996. A. G. Balogh & G. Walter. (Materials Science Forum Ser.: Vols. 248 & 249). (Illus.). 512p. (C). 1997. text 176.00 (*0-87849-767-6*, Pub. by Trans T Pub) Enfield Pubs NH.

Materials Science for Energy Conversion Systems. Ed. by C. G. Granqvist. (Renewable Energy Ser.: No. 1). (Illus.). 210p. 1991. 87.75 (*0-08-040937-7*, Pergamon Pr) Elsevier.

Materials Science for Engineers. Lawrence H. Van Vlack. LC 74-91151. (Metallurgy & Materials Engineering Ser.). (C). 1970. text. write for info. (*0-201-08074-5*) Addison-Wesley.

Materials Science for High Technologies - MASHTEC '90. Ed. by J. Barthel. 880p. 1990. text 283.00 (*0-87849-612-2*, Pub. by Trans T Pub) Enfield Pubs NH.

Materials Science in Microelectronics Vol. I: The Relationships Between Thin Film Processing & Structure. E. S. Machlin. (Materials Science Ser.). (Illus.). 240p. (C). 1995. text 65.00 (*1-878857-07-X*) Giro Pr.

Materials Science in Microelectronics Vol. II: Effects of Structure on Properties in Thin Films. Eugene S. Machlin. (Illus.). 240p. (C). 1998. 75.00 (*1-878857-10-X*) Giro Pr.

Materials Science in Space. Ed. by A. Bewersdorff. (Advances in Space Research Ser.: Vol. 1, No. 5). (Illus.). 171p. 1981. pap. 25.00 (*0-08-027161-8*, Pergamon Pr) Elsevier.

Materials Science in Space: Proceedings of the Topical Meeting of the COSPAR Interdisciplinary Scientific Commission G (Meeting G1) of the COSPAR Twenty-Fifth Plenary Meeting Held in Graz, Austria, 25th June - 7th July 1984. Ed. by A. Bewersdorff. (Illus.). 116p. 1985. pap. 54.00 (*0-08-032733-8*, Pergamon Pr) Elsevier.

Materials Science of Carbides, Nitrides & Borides: Proceedings of the NATO Advanced Study Institute on Materials Science of Carbides, Nitrides & Borides, St. Petersburg, Russia, August 12-22, 1998. NATO Advanced Study Institute on Materials Science of Carbides & Nitrides Staff et al. LC 99-25783. (NATO Science Ser.). 1999. write for info. (*0-7923-5706-X*) Kluwer Academic.

Materials Science of Concrete III. Ed. by Jan P. Skalny. 362p. 1992. 90.00 (*0-944904-55-6*, MSC03) Am Ceramic.

Materials Science of Concrete IV. Ed. by Sidney Mindess & Jan P. Skalny. 1995. 90.00 (*0-944904-75-0*, MSC04) Am Ceramic.

Materials Science of Concrete I. Ed. by Jan P. Skalny. 1989. 90.00 (*0-944904-01-7*, MSC01) Am Ceramic.

Materials Science of Concrete, Special Volume: Sulfate Attack Mechanisms. Ed. by Jacques Marchand & Jan Skalny. (Illus.). 200p. 1999. 85.00 (*1-57498-074-2*, MSCUL) Am Ceramic.

Materials Science of Concrete II. Ed. by Sidney Mindess & Jan P. Skalny. 281p. 1991. 90.00 (*0-944904-37-8*, MSC02) Am Ceramic.

Materials Science of Concrete V, No. 5. Ed. by Jan Skalny & Sidney Mindess. 579p. 1998. 110.00 (*1-57498-027-0*, MSC05) Am Ceramic.

Materials Science of High-Temperature Polymers for Microelectronics Vol. 227: Materials Research Society Symposium Proceedings. Ed. by D. Y. Yoon et al. 400p. 1991. text 72.00 (*1-55899-121-2*) Materials Res.

Materials Science of Microelectromechanical Systems (MEMS) Devices Vol. 546: Materials Research Society Symposium Proceedings. Ed. by Arthur H. Heuer & S. Joshua Jacobs. LC 99-51976. 246p. 1999. text 85.00 (*1-55899-452-1*) Materials Res.

***Materials Science of Microelectromechanical Systems (MEMS) Devices II Vol. 605: Materials Research Society Symposium Proceedings.** Ed. by M. P. DeBoer et al. 2000. text 90.00 (*1-55899-513-7*) Materials Res.

Materials Science of Microelectronics. K. J. Bachmann. 541p. 1994. 110.00 (*0-471-18544-2*) Wiley.

Materials Science of Microelectronics. Klaus J. Bachmann. LC 93-7878. (Illus.). xiv, 530p. 1994. 79.95 (*0-89573-280-7*, Wiley-VCH) Wiley.

***Materials Science of Novel Oxide-Based Electronics: Materials Research Society Sympsium Proceedings, Vol. 623.** Ed. by D. S. Ginley et al. 2000. 79.00 (*1-55899-531-5*) Materials Res.

Materials Science of Polymers for Engineers. Tim A. Osswald & Georg Menges. LC 95-33357. 512p. (C). 1995. pap. 49.95 (*1-56990-192-9*) Hanser-Gardner.

Materials Science of Synthetic Membranes. Ed. by Douglas R. Lloyd. LC 84-21652. (ACS Symposium Ser.: No. 269). 494p. 1984. lib. bdg. 87.95 (*0-8412-0887-5*) Am Chemical.

Materials Science of Synthetic Membranes. Ed. by Douglas R. Lloyd. LC 84-21652. (ACS Symposium Ser.: No. 269). 504p. 1985. reprint ed. pap. 156.30 (*0-608-03261-1*, 206378000007) Bks Demand.

Materials Science of the Cell Vol. 489: Materials Research Society Symposium Proceedings. Ed. by B. Mulder et al. (Materials Research Society Symposium Proceedings Ser.). 226p. 1998. text 80.00 (*1-55899-394-0*) Materials Res.

Materials Science of the Earth's Interior. Ed. by Ichiro Sunagawa. 1984. text 398.00 (*90-277-1649-8*) Kluwer Academic.

Materials Science of Thin Films. Milton Ohring. (Illus.). 704p. 1991. text 93.00 (*0-12-524990-X*) Acad Pr.

Materials Science Progress: Anniversary Vol. - Progress in Materials Science. Ed. by J. W. Christian et al. (Illus.). 330p. 1981. 61.00 (*0-08-027147-2*, Pergamon Pr) Elsevier.

Materials Science Progression, ser. vol. 24. Christian. (Progress in Materials Science Ser.). 1980. pap. 39.00 (*0-08-026014-4*, no. 3, Pergamon Pr) Elsevier.

Materials Science Research: Proceedings of the Research Conference on Structure & Property of Engineering Materials, North Carolina State University, Raleigh, Nov. 16-18, 1964. Research Conference on Structure & Property of Engineering Materials Staff. Ed. by Hayne Palmour & W. Wurth Kriegel. LC 63-17645. (Illus.). 645p. reprint ed. pap. 200.00 (*0-608-30329-1*, 201940900003) Bks Demand.

Materials Science Research Vol. 2: The Proceedings of the 1964 Southern Metals/Materials Conference on Advances in Aerospace Materials, Held April 16-17, 1964, at Orlando, Florida, Hosted by the Orlando Chapter of the American Society of Metals. Southern Metals/Materials Conference on Advances i. Ed. by Henry M. Otte & Saul R. Locke. LC 63-17645. (Illus.). 332p. 1965. reprint ed. pap. 103.00 (*0-608-05464-X*, 206593300002) Bks Demand.

Materials Science Research in Japan: High-Performance Plastics, Metal Matrix Composites, & 21st Century Applications. (Illus.). 58p. (Orig.). (C). 1994. pap. text 30.00 (*0-7881-0708-9*) DIANE Pub.

Materials Science, Testing, & Properties for Technicians. William O. Fellers. 350p. (C). 1989. text 69.80 (*0-13-560764-7*) P-H.

Materials Science Using Synchrotron Radiation. Eisenberger. write for info. (*0-444-00893-4*) Elsevier.

Materials Sciences, ser. vol. 6. Legros. (Advances in Space Research Ser.). 1988. pap. 56.00 (*0-08-036640-6*, Pergamon Pr) Elsevier.

Materials Sciences for the Future: 31st International SAMPE Symposium & Exhibition, Los Angeles, California, 1986. International SAMPE Symposium &

M

Exhibition Staff. Ed. by Jerome L. Bauer & Robert Dunaetz. LC TA0401.3.S68. (Science of Advanced Materials & Process Enginnering Ser.: Vol. 31). 1897p. reprint ed. pap. 200.00 (*0-608-15342-7*, 202962700061) Bks Demand.

Materials Selection Deskbook. Nicholas P. Cheremisinoff. LC 96-10911. 191p. 1996. 79.00 (*0-8155-1400-X*) Noyes.

Materials Selection for Corrosion Control. Sohan L. Chawla & R. K. Gupta. LC 93-38047. 508p. 1993. 153.00 (*0-87170-474-9*, 6189) ASM.

Materials Selection for Design & Manufacturing: Theory & Practice. Joseph Datsko. LC 96-50430. (Illus.). 392p. 1997. text 145.00 (*0-8247-9844-9*) Dekker.

Materials Selection for Hydrocarbon & Chemical Plants. David A. Hansen & Robert B. Puyear. LC 96-27760. (Illus.). 448p. 1996. text 190.00 (*0-8247-9778-7*) Dekker.

Materials Selection in Mechanical Design. Michael F. Ashby. (Illus.). 360p. 1992. pap. text 44.95 (*0-7506-2727-1*, Prgamon Press) Buttrwrth-Heinemann.

Materials Selection in Mechanical Design. Marriott. 80p. (C). 1994. 48.00 (*0-02-376251-9*, Macmillan Coll) P-H.

Materials Selection in Mechanical Design. 2nd ed. Michael F. Ashby. LC 98-55392. 502p. 2000. pap. text 49.95 (*0-7506-4357-9*) Buttrwrth-Heinemann.

Materials Selection Wallchart. Ashby. ring bd. 40.00 (*0-412-61300-X*) Chapman & Hall.

Materials Selections for Petroleum Refineries & Gathering Facilities. R. A. White. (Illus.). 203p. 1998. 127.00 (*1-57590-032-7*, 37563) NACE Intl.

Materials Selector for Hazardous Chemicals: Concentrated Sulfuric Acid & Oleum. C. P. Dillon. Ed. by Warren I. Pollock. (MS Ser.: Vol. 1). (Illus.). 276p. 1997. 89.00 (*1-57698-008-1*) Matrls Tech Inst.

Materials Selector for Hazardous Chemicals: Formic, Acetic & Other Organic Acids. C. P. Dillon. Ed. by Warren I. Pollock. (MS Ser.: Vol. 2). (Illus.). 184p. 1997. 69.00 (*1-57698-012-X*) Matrls Tech Inst.

Materials Source Book. (Pathways Through Science Ser.). 1992. pap. text. write for info. (*0-582-09417-8*, Pub. by Addison-Wesley) Longman.

Materials Stability & Environmental Degradation. Ed. by A. Barkatt et al. (Symposium Proceedings Ser.: Vol. 125). 1988. text 17.50 (*0-931837-95-2*) Materials Res.

Materials Standards for P-M Self-Lubricating Bearings. Metal Powder Staff. (Illus.). 20p. 1998. pap. 20.00 (*1-878954-66-0*) Metal Powder.

Materials Standards for P-M Self-Lubricating Bearings, 1991-1992. 16p. 1991. 10.00 (*1-878954-05-9*) Metal Powder.

Materials Standards for P-M Structural Parts. Metal Powder Staff. 1997. pap. 20.00 (*1-878954-62-8*, 1023) Metal Powder.

Materials Symposium Vol. 3: Materials Symposium. Ed. by S. C. Liu et al. LC 82-70515. (1995 Offshore Mechanics & Arctic Engineering Conference Ser.: Vol. III). 604p. 1995. 180.00 (*0-7918-1309-6*, H00940) ASME.

Materials Synthesis & Characterization: Based on the Proceedings of an American Chemical Society Symposium Held in San Diego, California, March 13-17, 1994. D. L. Perry. LC 97-31218. 226p. (C). 1997. 95.00 (*0-306-45377-0*, Kluwer Plenum) Kluwer Academic.

Materials Synthesis & Processing Using Ion Beams Vol. 316: Materials Research Society Symposium Proceedings. Ed. by Karen Maex et al. LC 94-3152. 1077p. 1994. text 80.00 (*1-55899-215-4*) Materials Res.

Materials Synthesis Utilizing Biological Processes Vol. 174: Materials Research Society Symposium Proceedings. Ed. by P. C. Rieke et al. 294p. 1990. text 17.50 (*1-55899-062-3*) Materials Res.

Materials, Techknowledge Reference Series. Hutchinson. (TP - Technology Education Ser.). (J). (gr. k-12). 1997. 19.95 (*0-538-64482-6*) S-W Pub.

Materials Technology, Level 2. Timing. (I). 1984. pap. text. write for info. (*0-582-41339-7*, Pub. by Addison-Wesley) Longman.

Materials Technology, Level 2. Roger L. Timings. LC 85-72. (Longman Technician Series, Mechanical & Production Engineering). (Illus.). 180p. reprint ed. pap. 55.80 (*0-8357-2973-7*, 203923500011) Bks Demand.

Materials Technology, Level 3. Timings. 1985. pap. text. write for info. (*0-582-41338-9*, Pub. by Addison-Wesley) Longman.

Materials Technology: Proceedings. American Physical Society Conference, New York Cit. Ed. by A. G. Chynoweth & W. M. Walsh. LC 76-27967. (AIP Conference Proceedings Ser.: No. 32). 1976. 18.00 (*0-88318-131-2*) Am Inst Physics.

Materials Technology & Development: Materials Technology & Development. (ATAS Bulletin Ser.: No. 5). 156p. pap. 15.00 (*92-1-104196-1*, E.87.II.A.2) UN.

***Materials, Technology & Reliability for Advanced Interconnects & Low-k Dielectrics: Materials Research Society Symposium Proceedings, Vol. 612.** Ed. by K. Maex et al. 2000. text 82.00 (*1-55899-520-X*) Materials Res.

Materials Technology for Electrical Appliances: Magnetic & Electrical Properties of Metals & Alloys. G. N. Dubinin & Yu S. Avraamov. Tr. by T. S. Patel from RUS. (Illus.). 282p. (C). 1987. 21.00 (*81-205-0030-X*, Pub. by Oxford IBH) S Asia.

Materials Technology for Semiconductor Technicians. TEEX Staff. (Illus.). xiv, 246p. 1996. student ed., spiral bd. 185.00 incl. cd-rom (*1-58257-019-1*, 8029B/M); spiral bd. 59.95 (*1-58257-018-3*, 8029B) TX Eng Extsn Servs.

Materials Technology Foresight for the U. K. Power Generation Industry. Materials Strategy Commission. 78p. 1995. pap. 40.00 (*0-901716-86-3*, Pub. by Inst Materials) Ashgate Pub Co.

Materials Technology Foresight in Biomaterials. Institute of Materials, Materials Strategy Commiss. 38p. 1995. pap. 40.00 (*0-901716-87-1*, Pub. by Inst Materials) Ashgate Pub Co.

Materials Technology Foresight on Aerospace Structural Materials. Report of a Working Party Staff. (Materials Strategy Commission Ser.: Bk. 624). 37p. 1995. pap. 40.00 (*0-901716-88-X*, Pub. by Inst Materials) Ashgate Pub Co.

Materials Testing & Biocompatibility: Index of New Information & Medical Research Bible. rev. ed. Steve K. Martinez. 183p. 1997. 47.50 (*0-7883-1564-1*); pap. 44.50 (*0-7883-1565-X*) ABBE Pubs Assn.

Materials Testing for the Metal Forming Industry. K. Pohlandt. (Illus.). 240p. 1989. 94.95 (*0-387-50651-9*) Spr-Verlag.

Materials Testing Technician. Jack Rudman. (Career Examination Ser.: C-1834). 1994. pap. 34.95 (*0-8373-1834-3*) Nat Learn.

Materials Theory & Modelling. Ed. by P. D. Bristowe et al. (Materials Research Society Symposium Proceedings Ser.: Vol. 291). 663p. 1993. text 30.00 (*1-55899-186-7*) Materials Res.

Materials Theory, Simulations, & Parallel Algorithms: Materials Research Society Symposium Proceedings, Vol. 408. Ed. by E. Kaxiras et al. 611p. 1996. 65.00 (*1-55899-311-8*) Materials Res.

Materials Thermochemistry. 6th enl. rev. ed. Ortrud Kubaschewski et al. LC 92-31280. 376p. 1993. text 175.00 (*0-08-041889-9*, Prgamon Press) Buttrwrth-Heinemann.

Materials to Supply the Energy Demand: Proceedings of an International Conference. American Society for Metals Staff et al. Ed. by E. B. Hawbolt & A. Mitchell. LC 81-66630. 918p. reprint ed. pap. 200.00 (*0-608-17187-5*, 202699500053) Bks Demand.

Materials Toward a History of the Baptists, Vol. 2. Morgan Edwards. 1984. 28.00 (*0-317-38301-9*) Church History.

Materials Toward a History of Witchcraft, 3 vols. Ed. by Henry C. Lea & George L. Burr. LC 79-8109. reprint ed. 265.00 (*0-404-18420-0*) AMS Pr.

Materials under Irradiation. A. Dunlop et al. (Solid State Phenomena Ser.: Vols. 30-31). 512p. 1992. text 192.00 (*0-87849-651-3*, Pub. by Trans T Pub) Enfield Pubs NH.

Materials Used at the Embalming of King Tut-Ankh-Amun No. 10: Metropolitan Museum of Art Papers. Herbert E. Winlock. LC 79-168412. (Metropolitan Museum of Art Publications in Reprint). (Illus.). 30p. 1980. reprint ed. 18.95 (*0-405-02248-4*) Ayer.

Materials Used in Pharmaceutical Formulation. A. T. Florence. LC 85-210857. (Critical Reports on Applied Chemistry Ser.). 35.00 (*0-632-01257-9*) Blackwell Sci.

Materials Used to Write upon Before the Invention of Printing. fac. ed. Albert Maire. (Shorey Lost Arts Ser.). (Illus.). 44p. 1904. reprint ed. pap. 10.00 (*0-8466-6006-7*, U-6) Shoreys Bkstore.

Materials with Memory: Initial-Boundary Value Problems for Constitutive Equations with Internal Variablees. Hans D. Alber. Ed. by A. Dold & F. Takens. LC 98-9337. (Lecture Notes in Mathematics Ser.: Vol. 1682). x, 166p. 1998. pap. 33.00 (*3-540-64066-5*) Spr-Verlag.

Materials Working for You in the 21st Century: 37th International SAMPE Symposium & Exhibition, Anaheim, Convention Center, Anaheim, CA, March 9-12, 1992. International SAMPE Symposium & Exhibition Staff. Ed. by Glenn C. Grimes et al. LC TA0401.3.I85. (Science of Advanced Materials & Process Enginnering Ser.: No. 37). (Illus.). 1521p. 1992. reprint ed. pap. 200.00 (*0-7837-9623-4*, 206037800005) Bks Demand.

Materialtool. 2nd ed. Wroblewski. 1998. cd-rom 77.00 (*0-13-934316-4*) P-H.

Materialy Do Biografii, Genealogii I Heraldyki Polskiej, 9 vols., Set. Ed. by Konarski Szymon. (POL.). 1963. pap. 1075.00 (*0-318-23350-9*) Szwede Slavic.

Materialy O Russkoi Emigratsii, 1920-1930-KH GG. V Sobranii Baronessy M. D. Vrangel' Arkhiv Guverovskogo Instituta V Stenforde. Irina Sjevelenko. (Stanford Slavic Studies: Vol. 9). (RUS., Illus.). 228p. (Orig.). 1993. pap. 25.00 (*1-57201-010-X*) Berkeley Slavic.

Materiaux d'Une Theorie du Proletariat: Materials for a Theory of the Proletariat. Georges Sorel. LC 74-25788. (European Sociology Ser.). 466p. 1975. reprint ed. 39.95 (*0-405-06540-X*) Ayer.

Materiaux en Design D'Interieur: Les Revetements de Sol. Jean Therrien. LC 98-940952. (FRE., Illus.). ix, 188p. 1998. write for info. (*2-89105-692-2*) GME.

Materie und Organismus Bei Leibniz. Hans L. Koch. (Abhandlungen Zur Philosophie und Ihrer Geschichte Ser.: Vol. 30). (GER.). 1980. reprint ed. write for info. (*3-487-06785-4*) G Olms Pubs.

Materiel Distribution: Improving Support to Army Operations in Peace & War. Nancy Y. Moore & Arroyo Center Staff. LC 96-9515. 1997. pap. text 9.00 (*0-8330-2424-8*, MR-642-A) Rand Corp.

Maternal - Infant Nursing Care Plans. unabridged ed. Karla Luxner. (Nursing Care Plans Ser.). 309p. 1999. pap. 39.95 (*1-56930-099-2*) Skidmore Roth Pub.

Maternal & Child Health: Programs, Problems, & Policy in Public Health. Jonathan B. Kotch. LC 96-48785. 400p. 1997. 45.00 (*0-8342-0771-0*, 20771) Aspen Pub.

Maternal & Child Health in Kenya: A Study of Poverty, Disease & Malnutrition in Samia. Richard N. K'Okul. (Monographs of the Finnish Society for Development Studies: No. 4). 214p. 1991. 23.95 (*91-7106-320-X*, Pub. by Nordic Africa) Transaction Pubs.

Maternal & Child Health in the U. S. S. R. WHO Staff. (Public Health Papers: No. 11). 70p. 1962. 3.00 (*92-4-130011-6*) World Health.

Maternal & Child Health Legislation, 1991. Martha P. King. 113p. 1991. pap. text 15.00 (*1-55516-696-2*, 6633) Natl Conf State Legis.

Maternal & Child Health Legislation, 1994. NCSL Health Program Staff. 75p. 1995. 15.00 (*1-55516-609-1*, 6650) Natl Conf State Legis.

Maternal & Child Health Nurse. Jack Rudman. (Certified Nurse Examination Ser.: CN-9). 1994. pap. 23.95 (*0-8373-6109-5*) Nat Learn.

Maternal & Child Health Nursing. 2nd ed. Joyce Y. Johnson. 352p. 1994. pap. text, student ed. 16.95 (*0-397-55112-6*) Lppncott W & W.

Maternal & Child Health Nursing. 4th ed. A. Joy Ingalls & M. Constance Salerno. 1987. pap. text 15.95 (*0-8016-2412-6*) Mosby Inc.

Maternal & Child Health Nursing: Care of the Childbearing & Childrearing Family. 2nd ed. Adele Pillitteri. LC 94-16338. 1,936p. 1994. text 72.95 (*0-397-55113-4*) Lppncott W & W.

Maternal & Child Health Nursing: Care of the Childbearing & Childrearing Family. 3rd ed. Joyce Young Johnson & Edna Boyd-Davis. pap. text, student ed. 17.95 (*0-7817-1849-X*) Lppncott W & W.

Maternal & Child Health Nursing: Care of the Childbearing & Childrearing Family. 3rd ed. Adele Pillitteri. LC 98-22348. 1775p. 1998. text 73.95 (*0-7817-1547-4*) Lppncott W & W.

Maternal & Child Health on the U. S.-Mexico Border. Linda S. Chan et al. (Special Project Reports). 296p. 1988. pap. 10.00 (*0-89940-687-4*) LBJ Sch Pub Aff.

Maternal & Child Health Research Program: Active Projects Fiscal Year 1994 & Fiscal Year 1995. Ed. by Gontran Lamberty. (Illus.). 192p. (C). 1998. pap. text 40.00 (*0-7881-7376-6*) DIANE Pub.

Maternal & Child Health Research Program: Active Projects FY1993 & FY1992. Prod. by National Center for Education in Maternal and Child Health (U.S.). LC 95-71143. 264p. 1995. pap. write for info. (*1-57285-019-1*) Nat Ctr Educ.

Maternal & Child Health Research Program: Active Projects FY1994 & FY1995. Prod. by National Center for Education in Maternal and Child Health (U.S.). LC 97-69797. 210p. 1997. pap. write for info. (*1-57285-045-0*) Nat Ctr Educ.

***Maternal & Child Health Research Program: Active Projects FY1996 & FY1997.** Prod. by National Center for Education in Maternal and Child Health (U.S.). LC 98-68259. 204p. 1998. pap. write for info. (*1-57285-054-X*) Nat Ctr Educ.

Maternal & Child Health Research Program: Completed Projects 1992 & 1993. Prod. by National Center for Education in Maternal and Child Health (U.S.). LC 95-71142. 200p. 1995. pap. write for info. (*1-57285-020-5*) Nat Ctr Educ.

***Maternal & Child Health Research Program: Completed Projects, 1994-96.** Prod. by National Center for Education in Maternal and Child Health (U.S.). LC 98-67519. 320p. 1998. pap. write for info. (*1-57285-053-1*) Nat Ctr Educ.

Maternal & Child Health Statistics: Russian Federation & United States, Selected Years 1985-1995. National Center for Health Statistics Staff. LC 98-15066. (International Vital & Health Statistics Series 5). 120p. 1998. write for info. (*0-8406-0545-5*) Natl Ctr Health Stats.

Maternal & Child Nursing. 9th ed. Novak. LC 99-10442. 1999. text 45.95 (*0-323-00322-2*) Mosby Inc.

Maternal & Child Nursing - Associate. Jack Rudman. (Regents College Proficiency Examination Ser.: Vol. 22). 43.95 (*0-8373-5472-2*) Nat Learn.

Maternal & Child Nursing - Baccalaureate. Jack Rudman. (Regents College Proficiency Examination Ser.: Vol. 23). 43.95 (*0-8373-5473-0*) Nat Learn.

Maternal & Child Nursing, Associate. Jack Rudman. (Regents College Proficiency Examination Ser.: CPEP-22). 1994. pap. 23.95 (*0-8373-5422-6*) Nat Learn.

Maternal & Child Nursing, Associate Degree. Jack Rudman. (ACT Proficiency Examination Program (PEP) Ser.: Vol. 37). 43.95 (*0-8373-5587-7*) Nat Learn.

Maternal & Child Nursing, Associate Degree. Jack Rudman. (ACT Proficiency Examination Program Ser.: PEP-37). 1994. pap. 23.95 (*0-8373-5537-0*) Nat Learn.

Maternal & Child Nursing, Baccalaureate. Jack Rudman. (Regents College Proficiency Examination Ser.: CPEP-23). 1994. pap. 23.95 (*0-8373-5423-4*) Nat Learn.

Maternal & Child Nursing, Baccalaureate Degree. Jack Rudman. (ACT Proficiency Examination Program (PEP) Ser.: Vol. 38). 43.95 (*0-8373-5588-5*) Nat Learn.

Maternal & Child Nursing, Baccalaureate Degree. Jack Rudman. (ACT Proficiency Examination Program Ser.: PEP-38). 1994. pap. 23.95 (*0-8373-5538-9*) Nat Learn.

Maternal & Child Oral Health Regional Workshops: Summary Report. Jane E. Steffensen. 52p. 1994. pap. text. write for info. (*1-57285-002-7*) Nat Ctr Educ.

Maternal & Fetal Thyroid Function in Pregnancy. Ed. by J. G. Thorpe Beeston & K. H. Nicolaides. (Illus.). 128p. 1995. text 65.00 (*1-85070-611-5*) Prthnon Pub.

Maternal & Infant Health Care. Ed. by Mary J. Houston. LC 96-6398. (Illus.). 205p. 1984. pap. 8.50 (*0-443-02813-3*) Church.

Maternal & Infant Nursing Care. 3rd ed. Elizabeth J. Dickason. LC 97-10756. (Illus.). 928p. (C). (gr. 13). 1997. text 55.00 (*0-8151-2517-8*, 29925) Mosby Inc.

Maternal & Infant Nursing Care. 3rd ed. Elizabeth J. Dickason. (Illus.). 128p. (C). (gr. 13). 1997. pap. text, student ed. 14.95 (*0-8151-2518-6*, 29926) Mosby Inc.

Maternal & Neonatal Nursing. Aileen MacLaren. LC 93-37753. (Concepts & Activities Ser.). (Illus.). 448p. 1993. pap. 23.95 (*0-87434-576-6*) Springhouse Corp.

Maternal & Neonatal Nursing: Family-Centered Care. 3rd ed. Kathryn A. May & Laura R. Mahlmeister. (Illus.). 1232p. (C). 1993. text 61.95 (*0-397-54953-9*, Lippncott) Lppncott W & W.

Maternal & Newborn Nursing. 3rd ed. Martha A. Auvenshine & Martha G. Enriquez. (Illus.). 656p. 1997. pap. text. write for info. (*0-316-06293-6*) Lppncott W & W.

Maternal & Perinatal Infections: Report of a WHO Consultation. 122p. 1991. pap. text 13.50 (*0-614-08044-4*, 1930033) World Health.

Maternal Anthropometry & Pregnancy Outcomes: A WHO Collaborative Study. (WHO Bulletin Supplement Ser.: No. 73). 98p. 1995. pap. text 20.00 (*92-4-068730-0*) World Health.

Maternal Attachment & Mothering Disorders, No. 1. rev. ed. Marshall H. Klaus et al. (PTR Ser.). 81p. 1982. pap. text 10.00 (*0-931562-04-X*) J & J Consumer Prods.

Maternal Care for the Reduction of Perinatal & Neonatal Mortality: A Joint WHO-UNICEF Statement. 22p. 1986. pap. text 2.70 (*92-4-156099-1*, 1150248) World Health.

Maternal Child Health Nursing Research Digest. Ed. by Joyce J. Fitzpatrick & Kristen S. Montgomery. LC 99-23404. 244p. 1999. text 34.95 (*0-8261-1294-3*) Springer Pub.

Maternal-Child Home Health Aide Training Manual. Mary Ann Chestnut. LC 97-25842. 208p. 1997. pap. text 36.95 (*0-7817-1204-1*) Lppncott W & W.

Maternal Child Nursing. Littleton. (C). 2001. 50.50 (*0-7668-0121-7*) Delmar.

Maternal-Child Nursing. Emily S. McKinney et al. Ed. by Thomas Eoyang. LC 99-31878. (Illus.). 1945p. (C). 1999. text. write for info. (*0-7216-8138-7*, W B Saunders Co) Harcrt Hlth Sci Grp.

Maternal-Child Nursing Care. Shannon E. Perry & Donna L. Wong. LC 97-8667. (Illus.). 1848p. (C). (gr. 13). 1997. text 79.00 (*0-8151-2837-1*, 29893) Mosby Inc.

Maternal-Child Nursing Care. Donna L. Wong. (Illus.). 448p. (C). (gr. 13). 1998. student ed. write for info. (*0-8151-2473-2*, 31054) Mosby Inc.

***Maternal-Child Nursing Care: Includes Testbank.** Donna L. Wong & Shannon E. Perry. (Illus.). 1998. teacher ed. write for info. (*0-8151-2537-2*) Mosby Inc.

Maternal Deprivation. Michael Rutter. 1991. pap. 19.95 (*0-14-013526-X*, Pub. by Pnguin Bks Ltd) Trafalgar.

Maternal Deprivation. Child Welfare League of America Staff. LC 61-18462. 76p. reprint ed. pap. 30.00 (*0-608-11297-6*, 200366800038) Bks Demand.

Maternal Drug Abuse & Drug Exposed Children: Understanding the Problem. (Illus.). 82p. (Orig.). (C). 1994. pap. text 25.00 (*0-7881-1480-8*) DIANE Pub.

Maternal Education & Child Survival: Pathways & Evidence. Ed. by Leela Visaria. LC 97-905318. xx, 254 p. 1998. 28.00 (*81-259-0382-8*, Pub. by Vikas) S Asia.

Maternal Effects as Adaptations. Ed. by Timothy A. Mousseau & Charles W. Fox. (Illus.). 400p. 1998. text 65.00 (*0-19-511163-X*) OUP.

Maternal Employment & Children's Development: Longitudinal Research. A. E. Gottfried & A. W. Gottfried. LC 88-15167. (Studies in Work & Industry). (Illus.). 316p. (C). 1988. 52.50 (*0-306-42867-9*, Plenum Trade) Perseus Pubng.

Maternal Ethics & Other Slave Moralities. Cynthia Willett. LC 95-35111. 256p. (C). 1995. pap. 20.99 (*0-415-91210-5*) Routledge.

Maternal Ethics & Other Slave Moralities. Cynthia Willett. LC 95-35111. 256p. (C). (gr. 13). 1995. 70.00 (*0-415-91209-1*) Routledge.

Maternal, Fetal & Neonatal Physiology: A Clinical Perspective. Blackburn. (Illus.). 735p. 1991. text 95.00 (*0-7216-2936-9*, W B Saunders Co) Harcrt Hlth Sci Grp.

Maternal-Fetal Endocrinology. 2nd ed. Ed. by Dan Tulchinsky & Brian A. Little. LC 93-9931. (Illus.). 448p. 1994. text 79.00 (*0-7216-4232-2*, W B Saunders Co) Harcrt Hlth Sci Grp.

Maternal Fetal Interface. Ed. by Anthony Carter et al. LC 98-30167. (Trophoblast Research Ser.: Vol. 12). (Illus.). 448p. 1998. 120.00 (*1-58046-043-7*) Univ Rochester Pr.

Maternal-Fetal Medicine. 4th ed. Robert K. Creasy & Robert Resnick. Ed. by Lisette Bralow. LC 98-12044. (Illus.). 1152p. (C). 1998. text 139.00 (*0-7216-7605-7*, W B Saunders Co) Harcrt Hlth Sci Grp.

Maternal-Fetal Medicine: Principles & Practice. 3rd ed. Ed. by Robert K. Creasy & Robert Resnik. LC 92-48215. (Illus.). 1168p. (C). 1993. text 135.00 (*0-7216-6590-X*, W B Saunders Co) Harcrt Hlth Sci Grp.

Maternal-Fetal Toxicology: A Clinician's Guide. 2nd expanded rev. ed. Ed. by Gideon Koren. (Medical Toxicology Ser.: Vol. 2). (Illus.). 848p. 1994. text 190.00 (*0-8247-8841-9*) Dekker.

Maternal Fictions: Stendhal, Sand, Rachilde & Bataille. Maryline Lukacher. LC 93-38693. 192p. 1994. text 49.95 (*0-8223-1432-0*); pap. text 16.95 (*0-8223-1436-3*) Duke.

Maternal Fitness: Preparing for Healthy Pregnancy. Julie Tupler & Andrea Thompson. (Illus.). 160p. 1996. per. 12.00 (*0-684-80295-3*) S&S Trade Pap.

Maternal Genetic Disease. Nelson Isada & Evans Johnson. 272p. (C). 1996. pap. text 95.00 (*0-8385-6164-0*, A6164-6, Apple Lange Med) McGraw.

Maternal Health & Infant Survival. 2nd ed. C. Arden Miller. LC 91-62010. 52p. 1991. reprint ed. pap. text 7.50 (*0-943657-14-8*) ZERO TO THREE.

An Asterisk (*) at the beginning of an entry indicates that the title is appearing for the first time.

Maternal Health Services: Index of New Information with References. Maurice K. Hobden. 160p. 1997. 47.50 (*0-7883-1542-0*); pap. 44.50 (*0-7883-1543-9*) ABBE Pubs Assn.

Maternal-Infant Care Planning. 3rd ed. Melson et al. LC 98-36726. 368p. 1998. 34.95 (*0-87434-951-6*) Springhouse Corp.

Maternal-Infant Nursing Care, Includes Testbank. 3rd ed. Elizabeth J. Dickason & Martha O. Schultz. (Illus.). 1998. teacher ed. write for info. (*0-8151-2563-1*) Mosby Inc.

***Maternal-Infant Nursing Care: Text, Student Learning Guide Package, Set.** 3rd ed. Elizabeth J. Dickason et al. (Illus.). (C). 1998. text, student ed. write for info. (*0-8151-2521-6*) Mosby Inc.

Maternal-Infant Nursing Care Pocket Handbook. 3rd ed. Elizabeth J. Dickason. (Illus.). 400p. (C). (gr. 13). 1998. pap. text 14.95 (*0-8151-2519-4*, 29927) Mosby Inc.

Maternal Influence: The Search for Social Universals. Marion J. Levy, Jr. 263p. (C). 1992. pap. 24.95 (*1-56000-614-5*) Transaction Pubs.

***Maternal Instincts.** Beth Henderson. (Special Edition Ser.: Bk. 1338). 2000. mass mkt. 4.50 (*0-373-24338-3*, 1-24338-5) Silhouette.

Maternal Instincts, 1875-1925. Claudia Nelson. Ed. by Ann S. Holmes. LC 96-30027. 240p. 1997. text 59.95 (*0-312-17412-8*) St Martin.

Maternal Journal. Matthew Bennett. (Illus.). 28p. 1992. pap. 10.00 (*0-88166-185-6*) Meadowbrook.

Maternal Journal. Linda Schwartz et al. LC 82-4736. (Illus.). 80p. (Orig.). 1982. pap. 5.95 (*0-912800-99-2*) Woodbridge Pr.

***Maternal Journal: Your Personal Pregnancy Guide.** Matthew Bennett. (Illus.). 28p. 1999. per. 10.00 (*0-671-31798-9*) S&S Trade.

Maternal Journal: Your Personal Pregnancy Guide. Don Parker & Matthew Bennett. (Illus.). 27p. 1992. 10.00 (*0-671-76031-9*) S&S Trade.

Maternal Justice. Estelle B. Freedman. 458p. 1998. lib. bdg. 19.00 (*0-226-26150-6*) U Ch Pr.

Maternal Justice: Miriam Van Waters & the Female Reform Tradition, 1887-1974. Estelle B. Freedman. LC 95-49171. 456p. 1996. 34.95 (*0-226-26149-2*) U Ch Pr.

Maternal Legacy: A Mother-Daughter Anthology. Ed. by Susan L. Aglietti. LC 85-50065. 104p. (Orig.). 1985. pap. text 7.95 (*0-9614375-0-2*) Vintage Forty-Five.

***Maternal Measures: Figuring Caregiving in the Early Modern Period.** Ed. by Naomi Miller & Naomi Yavneh. LC 99-55005. (Women & Gender in Early Modern England, 1500-1750 Ser.). (Illus.). 400p. 2000. text 70.95 (*0-7546-0031-9*, Pub. by Ashgate Pub) Ashgate Pub Co.

Maternal Mortality: A Global Factbook. Compiled by C. AbouZahr & E. Royston. 608p. 1991. pap. text 50.00 (*92-4-159001-7*, 1930024) World Health.

Maternal, Neonatal & Women's Health Nursing Student's Activity Book. MacLaren et al. 304p. 1991. pap., student ed. 17.95 (*0-87434-360-7*) Springhouse Corp.

Maternal-Neonatal Nursing. 3rd ed. Lynne Conrad. LC 96-29145. (Springhouse Notes Ser.). (Illus.). 192p. (Orig.). 1996. 22.95 incl. disk (*0-87434-860-9*) Springhouse Corp.

Maternal Neonatal Nursing: A Holistic Approach. Staley. (Professional Reference - Nursing Ser.). 1996. 60.95 (*0-8273-7785-1*); 18.95 (*0-8273-7786-X*); 10.50 (*0-8273-7787-8*); 10.50 (*0-8273-7788-6*) Delmar.

Maternal Newborn. 2nd ed. Patricia A. Ladewig et al. Ed. by Debra Hunter. 889p. (C). 1990. pap. text 9.95 (*0-201-53238-7*) Addison-Wesley.

Maternal-Newborn Home Care Manual. Mary A. Chestnut. LC 97-25845. 320p. 1997. pap. text 36.95 (*0-397-55474-5*) Lppncott W & W.

Maternal-Newborn Nursing. Francine H. Nichols. (C). 1997. text 82.00 (*0-7216-7574-3*, W B Saunders Co) Harcrt Hlth Sci Grp.

Maternal-Newborn Nursing. Georgiana M. Stamps & Gasparis. LC 91-5208. (Nursetest: A Review Ser.). 272p. 1991. pap. 21.95 (*0-87434-304-6*) Springhouse Corp.

***Maternal-Newborn Nursing.** 2nd ed. Springhouse Corporation Staff. LC 99-30079. 1999. pap. 24.95 (*1-58255-002-6*) Springhouse Corp.

Maternal-Newborn Nursing. 2nd ed. Barbara R. Stright & Lee-Olive Harrison. LC 95-25938. (Lippincott's Review Ser.). 320p. 1996. pap. text 21.95 (*0-397-55214-9*) Lppncott W & W.

Maternal Newborn Nursing. 4th ed. Sally B. Olds. Ed. by Patti Cleary. 1328p. (C). 1992. pap. text 18.75 (*0-8053-5581-2*) Addison-Wesley.

Maternal Newborn Nursing. 5th ed. Sally B. Olds et al. LC 95-38372. 1142p. (C). 1995. 84.00 (*0-8053-5612-6*) Addison-Wesley.

***Maternal Newborn Nursing.** 6th ed. Sally Olds. (C). 2000. pap. text, student ed., wbk. ed. 25.31 (*0-8053-8074-4*) Benjamin-Cummings.

Maternal Newborn Nursing: Clinical Handbook. 6th ed. Sally B. Olds. (C). 2000. pap. text 25.31 (*0-8053-8076-0*) Benjamin-Cummings.

Maternal-Newborn Nursing: Theories. Francine H. Nichols. 1997. pap. text, student ed. 17.95 (*0-7216-6258-7*, W B Saunders Co) Harcrt Hlth Sci Grp.

Maternal-Newborn Nursing: Theory & Practice. Francine H. Nichols & Elaine Zwelling. Ed. by Ilze Rader. LC 96-15371. 1344p. 1997. text 66.95 (*0-7216-6777-5*, W B Saunders Co) Harcrt Hlth Sci Grp.

Maternal-Newborn Nursing: Theory & Practice. Francine H. Nichols & Elaine Zwelling. 1997. teacher ed. write for info. (*0-7216-6249-8*, W B Saunders Co) Harcrt Hlth Sci Grp.

Maternal-Newborn Nursing Care: A Family-Centered Approach. 2nd ed. Sally B. Olds et al. 1168p. 1984. write for info. (*0-201-12797-0*, Health Sci) Addison-Wesley.

Maternal-Newborn Nursing Care: A Workbook. 2nd ed. Sally B. Olds et al. 1984. pap. write for info. (*0-201-12799-7*) Addison-Wesley.

Maternal-Newborn Nursing Care: The Nurse, the Family & the Community. 4th ed. Patricia W. Ladewig. 288p. (C). 1997. pap. text, wbk. ed. 27.19 (*0-8053-5628-2*) Addison-Wesley.

Maternal-Newborn Plans of Care: Guidelines for Planning & Documenting Client Care. 3rd ed. Marilynn E. Doenges & Mary F. Moorhouse. (Illus.). 592p. (C). 1999. pap. text 36.95 (*0-8036-0320-7*) Davis Co.

Maternal Nutrition & Pregnancy Outcome. Ed. by Carl L. Keen et al. LC 93-21708. (Annals Ser.: Vol. 678). 1993. write for info. (*0-89766-753-0*); pap. 110.00 (*0-89766-754-9*) NY Acad Sci.

Maternal Nutrition & Pregnancy Outcomes: Anthropometric Assessment. Ed. by K. Krasovec et al. (PAHO Scientific Publications: No. 529). (ENG & SPA.). ix, 214p. 1991. pap. text 50.00 (*92-75-11529-X*, 1610529) World Health.

Maternal Overprotection. David M. Levy. (C). 1966. pap. 3.50 (*0-393-00349-3*) Norton.

Maternal Pasts, Feminist Futures: Nostalgia, Ethics, & the Question of Difference. Lynne Huffer. LC 97-41231. 216p. 1998. 45.00 (*0-8047-3025-3*); pap. 16.95 (*0-8047-3026-1*) Stanford U Pr.

Maternal Personality, Evolution, & the Sex Ratio: Do Mothers Control the Sex of the Infant? Valerie J. Grant. LC 97-14825. 240p. (C). 1998. write for info. (*0-415-15879-6*); pap. 24.99 (*0-415-15880-X*) Routledge.

Maternal Physician: A Treatise on the Nurture & Management of Infants from the Birth until Two Years Old Being the Result of Sixteen Years' Experience in the Nursery. 2nd ed. American Matron. LC 70-180581. (Medicine & Society in America Ser.). 294p. 1972. reprint ed. 20.95 (*0-405-03958-1*) Ayer.

Maternal Serum Screening for Fetal Genetic Disorders. Ed. by Sherman Elias & Joe L. Simpson. LC 92-16757. (Illus.). 139p. 1992. text 68.00 (*0-443-08867-5*) Church.

Maternal Substance Abuse & the Developing Nervous System. Ed. by Ian S. Zagon & Theodore A. Slotkin. (Illus.). 377p. 1992. text 73.00 (*0-12-775225-0*) Acad Pr.

Maternal Thinking: Toward a Politics of Peace. 2nd rev. ed. Sara Ruddick. 320p. 1994. pap. 18.00 (*0-8070-1409-5*) Beacon Pr.

Maternal Ties: A Selection of Programs for Female Offenders. Cynthia L. Blinn. LC 97-12521. 191p. 1997. 29.95 (*1-56991-068-5*) Am Correctional.

Maternal Voice in Victorian Fiction: Rewriting the Patriarchal Family. Barbara Z. Thaden. Ed. by Sally Mitchell. LC 97-12364. (Literature & Society in Victorian Britain Ser.: No. 2). 176p. 1997. text 45.00 (*0-8153-2777-3*) Garland.

Maternal/Pediatric Nursing for Practical Nursing. Shapiro. (LPN/LVN Nursing Ser.). 1994. teacher ed. 16.95 (*0-8273-4994-7*) Delmar.

Maternidades. Virginnia Maitax. 1999. pap. text 9.95 (*84-08-02429-9*) Planeta.

Maternities & Modernities: Colonial & Postcolonial Experiences in Asia & the Pacific. Ed. by Kalpana Ram & Margaret Jolly. LC 97-6813. (Illus.). 320p. (C). 1998. text 64.95 (*0-521-58428-0*); pap. text 23.95 (*0-521-58614-3*) Cambridge U Pr.

Maternity - Women's Health Nursing. Paulette D. Rollant & Karen A. Piotrowski. (Mosby's Review Ser.). (Illus.). 560p. (C). (gr. 13). 1995. pap. text 24.95 incl. 3.5 hd (*0-8151-7246-X*, 24859) Mosby Inc.

Maternity & Gynecologic Care: The Nurse & the Family. 4th ed. Irene M. Bobak et al. (Illus.). 1408p. (C). 1988. trans. 75.00 (*0-8016-0470-2*) Mosby Inc.

Maternity & Parental Benefits & Leaves: An International Review. Sheila B. Kamerman. LC 80-69763. (Impact on Policy Monograph: No. 1). (Illus.). 80p. (Orig.). 1980. pap. text 6.00 (*0-938436-00-7*) Columbia U Ctr Soc Sci.

Maternity & Reproductive Health in Asian Societies. Pranee L. Rice & Lenore Manderson. 320p. 1996. text 39.00 (*90-5702-021-1*, Harwood Acad Pubs) Gordon & Breach.

***Maternity & Woman's Health.** 7th ed. LOWDERMILK. 2000. pap. text. write for info. (*0-323-01180-2*) Mosby Inc.

Maternity & Women's Health Care. 6th ed. Deitra L. Lowdermilk & Irene M. Bobak. (Illus.). 328p. (C). (gr. 13). 1996. pap. text, student ed. 19.95 (*0-8151-5579-4*, 28012) Mosby Inc.

Maternity & Women's Health Care. 6th ed. Deitra L. Lowdermilk et al. (Illus.). 1997. teacher ed. write for info. (*0-8151-5578-6*) Mosby Inc.

***Maternity & Women's Healthcare.** 6th ed. C. V. Mosby Company Staff. 1999. 66.00 (*0-323-01063-6*) Mosby Inc.

Maternity & Work: Conditions of Work Digest. (Conditions of Work Digest Ser.: Vol. 13). xi, 482p. 1995. pap. 45.50 (*92-2-109199-6*) Intl Labour Office.

Maternity Bride. Maureen Child. 1998. per. 3.75 (*0-373-76138-4*, 1-76138-6) Silhouette.

Maternity Care. 2nd ed. Helen Farrer. (Illus.). 224p. 1990. pap. text 30.00 (*0-443-04209-8*) Church.

Maternity Care: Science, Guidelines, & Medical Practice. 1995. lib. bdg. 251.95 (*0-8490-6841-X*) Gordon Pr.

Maternity Care - Resources for Family-Centered Practice: Family-Centered Care: Changing Practice, Changing Attitudes, 3 vols. Beveryl H. Johnson et al. (Family-Centered Care Ser.). 140p. 1997. ring bd. 40.00 (*0-9642014-9-6*) Inst Fmly Ctr.

Maternity Fashion. Doretta D. Poli. (Twentieth Century-Histories of Fashion Ser.). (Illus.). 119p. 1996. 29.95 (*0-89676-208-4*, Costume & Fashion Pr) QSMG Ltd.

Maternity Leave: Tabloid Baby; The Nine-Month Knight; The Paternity Test. Candace Camp et al. 1998. per. 5.99 (*0-373-48366-X*) Harlequin Bks.

Maternity Leave: The Working Woman's Practical Guide to Combining Pregnancy, Motherhood & Career. Eileen Casey. LC 94-32059. 144p. (Orig.). 1995. pap. 10.00 (*0-380-77810-6*, Avon Bks) Morrow Avon.

Maternity Leave: The Working Woman's Practical Guide to Combining Pregnancy, Motherhood & Career. Eileen L. Casey. Ed. by Buff Lindau. LC 91-45065. (Illus.). 144p. 1992. 19.95 (*0-9631555-1-2*); pap. 12.95 (*0-9631555-0-4*); lib. bdg. 19.95 (*0-685-51619-9*) Green Mtn Pub.

Maternity Massage: A Healthy Indulgence a Welcome Relief. Connie Cox. LC 94-66358. 98p. 1994. pap. 12.95 (*1-885044-01-1*) Stress Less.

Maternity, Morality, & the Literature of Madness. Marilyn Yalom. LC 84-43061. 176p. 1985. 28.50 (*0-271-00398-7*) Pa St U Pr.

Maternity Nursing. (ACT Proficiency Examination Program Ser.: PEP-58). 1994. 39.95 (*0-8373-5933-3*, PEP-58); pap. 23.95 (*0-8373-5908-2*) Nat Learn.

Maternity Nursing. 2nd ed. Janice Holmes. (Nursing Education Ser.). 1995. text 57.50 (*0-8273-5531-9*) Delmar.

Maternity Nursing. 3rd ed. Connolly-Lauder & Schwartz. 222p. (C). 1998. per. 44.95 (*0-7872-4568-2*, 41456801) Kendall-Hunt.

Maternity Nursing. 3rd ed. Van Hoozer. (Illus.). 154p. 1999. write for info. (*0-8385-7087-9*, A7087-8) Appleton & Lange.

Maternity Nursing. 3rd ed. Zimbler. (Illus.). 154p. 1999. pap. text, student ed. 24.95 (*0-8385-7113-1*, Medical Exam) Appleton & Lange.

Maternity Nursing. 4th ed. Irene M. Bobak et al. (Illus.). teacher ed. write for info. (*0-8151-0615-7*) Mosby Inc.

Maternity Nursing. 5th ed. Deitra Leonard Lowdermilk et al. LC 98-33732. 1998. 54.00 (*0-323-00215-3*) Mosby Inc.

***Maternity Nursing.** 5th ed. Deitra L. Lowdermilk et al. (Illus.). 1998. teacher ed. write for info. (*0-323-00217-X*) Mosby Inc.

***Maternity Nursing.** 5th ed. Karen A. Piotrowski. (Illus.). 224p. 1998. student ed. write for info. (*0-323-00216-1*) Mosby Inc.

Maternity Nursing: An Introductory Text. 6th ed. Arlene Burroughs. (Illus.). 1992. pap., teacher ed. write for info. (*0-7216-4507-0*, W B Saunders Co) Harcrt Hlth Sci Grp.

Maternity Nursing: An Introductory Text. 7th ed. Burroughs. (C). text. write for info. (*0-8089-2119-3*, Grune & Strat) Harcrt Hlth Sci Grp.

Maternity Nursing: An Introductory Text. 7th ed. Arlene Burroughs. (Illus.). 1997. pap., teacher ed. write for info. (*0-7216-2496-0*, W B Saunders Co) Harcrt Hlth Sci Grp.

Maternity Nursing: An Introductory Text. 7th ed. Arlene Burroughs. Ed. by Ilze Rader. LC 97-7111. (Illus.). 608p. 1997. pap. text 31.50 (*0-7216-2473-1*, W B Saunders Co) Harcrt Hlth Sci Grp.

Maternity Nursing: Care of the Childbearing Family. 3rd rev. ed. Mary A. Scoloveno et al. LC 98-31091. (Illus.). 1219p. (C). 1999. boxed set 62.95 (*0-8385-7083-6*) Appleton & Lange.

Maternity Nursing: Family, Newborn & Women's Health Care. 18th ed. Sharon J. Reeder et al. LC 96-15970. 1,312p. 1996. text 59.95 (*0-397-55166-5*) Lppncott W & W.

Maternity Nursing: Quick Reference. 4th ed. Deitra L. Lowdermilk. (Illus.). 64p. (C). (gr. 13). 1994. pap. text 8.95 (*0-8151-0612-2*, 24708) Mosby Inc.

Maternity Nursing: Student Workbook. 2nd ed. Barbara Connolly-Lauder & Linda Schwartz. 208p. (C). 1996. pap. text, student ed., spiral bd. 20.95 (*0-8403-9496-9*) Kendall-Hunt.

Maternity Nursing IRK. Janice Holmes. (Nursing Education Ser.). 1997. teacher ed. 51.50 (*0-8273-7216-7*); student ed. 20.95 (*0-8273-7217-5*) Delmar.

Maternity Rights at Work. Ruth Evans et al. 1986. 20.00 (*0-946088-24-1*, Pub. by NCCL) St Mut.

***Maternity Rights 1999.** Hammond Suddards. 48p. 2000. pap. 89.99 (*0-8464-5120-4*) Beekman Pubs.

***Maternity Ward: Final Flight of a WWII Liberator.** Marguerite Aronowitz. LC 98-91721. (Illus.). 164p. 1998. pap. 14.95 (*0-9666615-0-8*) Pine Castle.

Mates Don't Grow on Trees: How to Meet the Man or Woman for You. Todd Landen. LC 94-74071. (Illus.). 208p. (Orig.). 1995. pap. 14.95 (*0-9644671-4-3*) Dancing Hearts.

Mates Don't Grow on Trees: How to Meet the Man or Woman for You. Todd Landen. (Illus.). 208p. (Orig.). 1996. pap. 14.95 (*0-9644671-9-4*) Dancing Hearts.

***Mate's Log, Level A, Bk. 1.** Brenda K. Murphy. (Sail Away Ser.). 104p. (J). (gr. k-5). 1999. pap. text 16.95 (*1-58504-004-5*) UTW Res Inc.

***Mate's Log, Level A, Bk. 2.** Brenda K. Murphy. (Sail Away Ser.). 124p. (J). (gr. k-5). 1999. pap. text 16.95 (*1-58504-005-3*) UTW Res Inc.

***Mate's Log, Level A, Bk. 3.** Brenda K. Murphy. (Sail Away Ser.). 124p. (J). (gr. k-5). 1999. pap. text 16.95 (*1-58504-006-1*) UTW Res Inc.

Mateship in Local Organization: A Study of Egalitarianism, Stratification, Leadership & Amenities Projects in a Semi-industrial Community of Inland New South Wales. H. G. Oxley. LC 74-174424. xvi, 240p. 1974. write for info. (*0-7022-0820-5*) Intl Spec Bk.

Math. (C). 1977. text (*0-201-13422-5*) Addison-Wesley.

***Math.** (C). 1998. pap. text 23.00 (*0-201-44461-5*) Addison-Wesley.

Math. (Illus.). 352p. (J). (gr. 1-2). 14.95 (*1-56189-504-0*) Amer Educ Pub.

Math. (Illus.). 352p. (J). (gr. 3-4). 14.95 (*1-56189-505-9*) Amer Educ Pub.

Math. (Jr. Academic Ser.). (Illus.). 80p. (J). (gr. k). 1998. wbk. ed. 2.99 (*1-57768-200-9*) MG-Hill OH.

Math. (Jr. Academic Ser.). (Illus.). 80p. (J). (gr. 1). 1998. wbk. ed. 2.99 (*1-57768-201-7*) MG-Hill OH.

Math. (Jr. Academic Ser.). (Illus.). 80p. (J). (gr. 2). 1998. wbk. ed. 2.99 (*1-57768-202-5*) MG-Hill OH.

Math. (Jr. Academic Ser.). (Illus.). 80p. (J). (ps-k). 1998. wbk. ed. 2.99 (*1-57768-209-2*) MG-Hill OH.

Math. (Spectrum Trade Ser.). (Illus.). 128p. (J). (-2). 1999. pap., wbk. ed. 6.95 (*1-57768-402-8*) MG-Hill OH.

Math. 1993. 6.95 (*1-55708-389-4*, MCC920) McDonald Pub Co.

Math. (Fisher-Price First Grade Workbooks Ser.). (Illus.). 72p. (J). (gr. 1). 1997. pap. write for info. (*1-56144-927-X*, Honey Bear Bks) Modern Pub NYC.

Math. ASP Staff. (Building Skills Ser.). (Illus.). 48p. (J). (gr. 3). 1997. pap., wbk. ed. 2.49 (*1-57768-053-7*) MG-Hill OH.

Math. ASP Staff. (Building Skills Ser.). (Illus.). 48p. (J). (gr. 4). 1997. pap., wbk. ed. 2.49 (*1-57768-054-5*) MG-Hill OH.

Math. ASP Staff. (Building Skills Ser.). (Illus.). 48p. (J). (gr. 5). 1997. pap., wbk. ed. 2.49 (*1-57768-055-3*) MG-Hill OH.

Math. ASP Staff. (Building Skills Ser.). (Illus.). 48p. (J). (gr. 6). 1997. pap., wbk. ed. 2.49 (*1-57768-056-1*) MG-Hill OH.

Math. ASP Staff. (Building Skills Ser.). (Illus.). 48p. (J). (gr. 7). 1997. pap., wbk. ed. 2.49 (*1-57768-057-X*) MG-Hill OH.

Math. ASP Staff. (Building Skills Ser.). (Illus.). 48p. (J). (gr. 8). 1997. pap., wbk. ed. 2.49 (*1-57768-058-8*) MG-Hill OH.

Math. Sue Boulais. 1994. 6.95 (*1-55708-418-1*, MCC900) McDonald Pub Co.

Math. Bryan H. Bunch. (Step Ahead Plus Workbks.). (Illus.). (J). (gr. 3-4). 1984. pap., wbk. ed. 2.09 (*0-307-23578-5*, 03578, Goldn Books) Gldn Bks Pub Co.

Math. Bryan H. Bunch. (Step Ahead Plus Workbks.). (Illus.). 32p. (J). (gr. 4-5). 1984. pap., wbk. ed. 2.09 (*0-307-23579-3*, 03579, Goldn Books) Gldn Bks Pub Co.

Math. Bryan H. Bunch & Iris Finklestein. (Step Ahead Plus Workbks.). (Illus.). 32p. (J). (gr. 5-6). 1984. pap., wbk. ed. 2.09 (*0-307-23580-7*, 03580) Gldn Bks Pub Co.

***Math.** Dalmatian Press Staff. (Tools Ser.). (J). (gr. 2). 1999. pap. text 2.29 (*1-57759-152-6*) Dalmatian Pr.

Math. Vincent Douglas. (Spectrum Ser.). (Illus.). 128p. (J). (gr. 1). 1997. pap., wbk. ed. 6.95 (*1-57768-111-8*) MG-Hill OH.

Math. Vincent Douglas. (Spectrum Ser.). (Illus.). 128p. (J). (gr. 2). 1997. pap., wbk. ed. 6.95 (*1-57768-112-6*) MG-Hill OH.

Math. Vincent Douglas. (Spectrum Ser.). (Illus.). 176p. (J). (gr. 3). 1997. pap., wbk. ed. 6.95 (*1-57768-113-4*) MG-Hill OH.

Math. Vincent Douglas. (Spectrum Ser.). (Illus.). 176p. (J). (gr. 4). 1997. pap., wbk. ed. 6.95 (*1-57768-114-2*) MG-Hill OH.

Math. Vincent Douglas. (Spectrum Ser.). (Illus.). 176p. (J). (gr. 5). 1997. pap., wbk. ed. 6.95 (*1-57768-115-0*) MG-Hill OH.

Math. Vincent Douglas. (Spectrum Ser.). (Illus.). 176p. (J). (gr. 6). 1997. pap., wbk. ed. 6.95 (*1-57768-116-9*) MG-Hill OH.

Math. Vincent Douglas. (Spectrum Ser.). (Illus.). 208p. (J). (gr. 7). 1997. pap., wbk. ed. 6.95 (*1-57768-117-7*) MG-Hill OH.

Math. Vincent Douglas. (Spectrum Ser.). (Illus.). 208p. (J). (gr. 8). 1997. pap., wbk. ed. 6.95 (*1-57768-118-5*) MG-Hill OH.

Math. Frank Schaffer Publications, Inc. Staff. (Back-to-Basics Ser.). 32p. (J). (gr. k). 1996. wbk. ed. 3.95 (*0-86734-997-2*, FS-30100) Schaffer Pubns.

Math. Frank Schaffer Publications, Inc. Staff. (Back-to-Basics Ser.). 32p. (J). (gr. 1). 1996. wbk. ed. 3.95 (*0-86734-998-0*, FS-30101) Schaffer Pubns.

Math. Frank Schaffer Publications, Inc. Staff. (Back-to-Basics Ser.). 32p. (J). (gr. 2). 1996. wbk. ed. 3.95 (*0-86734-999-9*, FS-30102) Schaffer Pubns.

Math. Frank Schaffer Publications, Inc. Staff. (Back-to-Basics Ser.). 32p. (J). (gr. 3). 1996. wbk. ed. 3.95 (*0-7647-0000-6*, FS-30103) Schaffer Pubns.

Math. Frank Schaffer Publications, Inc. Staff. (Back-to-Basics Ser.). 32p. (J). (gr. 4). 1996. wbk. ed. 3.95 (*0-7647-0001-4*, FS-30104) Schaffer Pubns.

Math. Jacobs. 1994. pap. text, student ed. 14.95 (*0-7167-2539-8*) W H Freeman.

Math. Teri C. Jones. (Homework Survival Guide Ser.). (Illus.). 64p. (J). (gr. 4-6). 1998. pap. 6.95 (*0-8167-4815-2*) Troll Communs.

Math. Elizabeth McGovern. 1997. 4.95 (*1-55708-574-9*, MCJ801) McDonald Pub Co.

Math. Scholastic, Inc. Staff. (NBA Slam & Jam Skills Ser.). (J). (gr. 7-8). 1997. pap. text 3.50 (*0-590-06385-5*) Scholastic Inc.

Math. Scholastic, Inc. Staff. (NBA Slam & Jam Skills Ser.). (gr. 7-12). 1997. pap. text 3.50 (*0-590-18847-X*) Scholastic Inc.

Math. Steck-Vaughn Co., Staff. (Pre-GED Ser.). 1994. pap. text 9.96 (*0-8114-4486-4*) Raintree Steck-V.

Math. Linda Thompson & Joan Ebbens. Ed. by Shirley Ryan. (Step Ahead Workbooks Ser.). (Illus.). 36p. (J). (gr. 2). 1985. wbk. ed. 2.09 (*0-307-23548-3*, 03548) Gldn Bks Pub Co.

Math. 3rd ed. Jacobs. 1994. 16.00 (*0-7167-2569-X*) W H Freeman.

Math. 3rd ed. Johnson. LC 97-35495. (Mathematics Ser.). 1997. mass mkt. 77.95 (*0-534-35075-5*) Brooks-Cole.

***Math.** 10th ed. Bob Alexander. 2000. text. write for info. (*0-201-68484-5*) Addison-Wesley.

M

Math, Bk. II. Martha Cheney. (Gifted & Talented Ser.). (Illus.). 64p. (J). (gr. 1-3). 1998. pap. 4.95 (*1-56565-666-0*, 06660W, Pub. by Lowell Hse Juvenile) NTC Contemp Pub Co.

Math, Grade 3. 85th ed. Nichols. 1985. text 45.75 (*0-03-064203-5*) Holt R&W.

Math, Grade 4. 85th ed. Nichols. 1985. text 45.75 (*0-03-064208-6*) Holt R&W.

Math, Grade 6. 85th ed. Nichols. 1985. text 46.50 (*0-03-064216-7*) Holt R&W.

Math, Grade 7. 85th ed. Nichols. 1985. text 51.75 (*0-03-064219-1*) Holt R&W.

Math, Grade 8. 85th ed. Nichols. 1985. text 51.75 (*0-03-064223-X*, q) Holt R&W.

Math: Addition & Subtraction 1-10. Schaffer, Frank, Publications Staff. (Reproducible Workbooks Ser.). (Illus.). 48p. (J). (gr. 1-2). 1983. student ed. 4.98 (*0-86734-041-X*, FS-2670) Schaffer Pubns.

Math: Addition & Subtraction 11-20. Schaffer, Frank, Publications Staff. (Reproducible Workbooks Ser.). (Illus.). 48p. (J). (gr. 1-2). 1983. 4.98 (*0-86734-042-8*, FS-2671) Schaffer Pubns.

Math: Addition & Subtraction 2-3 Digits. Schaffer, Frank, Publications Staff. (Reproducible Workbooks Ser.). (Illus.). 48p. (J). (gr. 2-3). 1983. student ed. 4.98 (*0-86734-043-6*, FS-2672) Schaffer Pubns.

Math: An Exploratory Approach. Stein. (Adaptable Courseware-Softside Ser.). Date not set. pap. 35.00 (*0-534-15929-X*) Wadsworth Pub.

Math: An Informal Approach. 2nd ed. Albert B. Bennett, Jr. & Leonard T. Nelson. 680p. (C). 1985. text 47.81 (*0-697-06853-6*, WCB McGr Hill) McGrw-H Hghr Educ.

Math! Encounters with High School. Serge A. Lang. (Illus.). 150p. 1995. 34.95 (*0-387-96129-1*) Spr-Verlag.

Math: Facing an American Phobia. Marilyn Burns. LC 97-45225. (Illus.). 164p. 1998. pap. 14.95 (*0-941355-19-5*) Math Solns Pubns.

Math: Grade K. Frank Schaffer Publications, Incorporated Staff. (J). 1997. pap. text 3.95 (*0-7647-0223-8*) Schaffer Pubns.

Math: Grade 1. (Home Workbooks Ser.). (Illus.). 64p. (Orig.). (J). (gr. 1). 1995. pap., wbk. ed. 2.49 (*0-88724-354-1*, CD-6851) Carson-Dellos.

Math: Grade 1. Roberta Bannister. Ed. by Joan Hoffman. (I Know It! Book Ser.). (Illus.). 32p. (J). (ps-3). 1979. student ed. 2.25 (*0-938256-28-9*, 02028) Sch Zone Pub Co.

Math: Grade 1. Frank Schaffer Publications, Incorporated Staff. (J). 1997. pap. text 3.95 (*0-7647-0224-6*) Schaffer Pubns.

*__Math: Grade 11, 11 vols.__ (Illus.). (YA). (gr. 11). 2000. teacher ed., student ed., boxed set 50.95 (*1-58095-743-9*, MAT1115, Lifepac) Alpha AZ.

*__Math: Grade 12, 11 vols.__ (Illus.). (YA). (gr. 11). 2000. teacher ed., student ed., boxed set 50.95 (*1-58095-746-3*, MAT1215, Lifepac) Alpha AZ.

Math: Grade 2. (Home Workbooks Ser.). (Illus.). 64p. (Orig.). (J). (gr. 2). 1995. pap., wbk. ed. 2.49 (*0-88724-355-X*, CD-6852) Carson-Dellos.

Math: Grade 2. Roberta Bannister. Ed. by Joan Hoffman. (I Know It! Book Ser.). (Illus.). 32p. (J). (ps-3). 1979. student ed. 2.49 (*0-938256-30-0*, 02030) Sch Zone Pub Co.

Math: Grade 2. Frank Schaffer Publications, Incorporated Staff. (J). 1997. pap. text 3.95 (*0-7647-0225-4*) Schaffer Pubns.

Math: Grade 3. (Home Workbooks Ser.). (Illus.). 64p. (Orig.). (J). (gr. 3). 1995. pap., wbk. ed. 2.49 (*0-88724-356-8*, CD-6853) Carson-Dellos.

Math: Grade 3. Roberta Bannister. Ed. by Joan Hoffman. (I Know It! Book Ser.). (Illus.). 32p. (J). (ps-3). 1979. student ed. 2.49 (*0-938256-31-9*, 02031) Sch Zone Pub Co.

Math: Grade 4. Roberta Bannister. Ed. by Joan Hoffman. (I Know It! Book Ser.). (Illus.). 32p. (J). (ps-3). 1979. student ed. 2.25 (*0-938256-33-5*, 02033) Sch Zone Pub Co.

Math: Grade 5. Nichols. 1985. 40.00 (*0-03-064212-4*) Harcourt Schl Pubs.

Math: Grades 5-6. Roberta Bannister. Ed. by Joan Hoffman. (I Know It! Book Ser.). (Illus.). 32p. (J). (ps-3). 1980. student ed. 2.49 (*0-938256-35-1*, 02035) Sch Zone Pub Co.

Math: Multiplication & Division. Schaffer, Frank, Publications Staff. (Reproducible Workbooks Ser.). (Illus.). 48p. (J). (gr. 3-4). 1983. student ed. 4.98 (*0-86734-044-4*, FS-2673) Schaffer Pubns.

Math: Seeing Is Believing. Frank Schaffer Publications, Inc. Staff. (Middle School Bks.). (Illus.). 1996. wbk. ed. 9.99 (*0-7647-0060-X*, FS-10212) Schaffer Pubns.

Math: Skill Enhancement. Lloyd D. Brooks. LC 92-44949. 224p. 1994. 10.95 (*1-56118-261-3*) Paradigm MN.

Math: Time & Money. Schaffer, Frank, Publications Staff. (Reproducible Workbooks Ser.). (Illus.). 48p. (J). (gr. 2-3). 1983. student ed. 4.98 (*0-86734-045-2*, FS-2674) Schaffer Pubns.

Math-a-Day: A Book of Days for Your Mathematical Year. Theoni Pappas. LC 99-88313. (Illus.). 288p. 1999. pap. 12.95 (*1-884550-20-7*) Wide World-Tetra.

Math! A Four Letter Word: The Self-Help Handbook for People Who Hate Or Fear Math. Angela Sembera & Michael Hovis. (Illus.). 100p. (Orig.). 1990. pap. 8.95 (*0-9627036-0-5*) Wimberly Pr.

Math-a-Magic: Number Tricks for Magicians. Laurence B. White. (Albert Whitman Prairie Book Ser.). (J). (gr. 3-6). 1994. pap. 4.95 (*0-8075-4995-9*) A Whitman.

*__Math-a-Magic Grade 1.__ Brighter Vision Publishing Staff. (Illus.). (J). 1999. pap. text 2.25 (*1-55254-110-X*) Brighter Vision.

*__Math-a-Magic Grade 3.__ Brighter Vision Publishing Staff. (Illus.). (J). (gr. 3). 1999. pap. 2.25 (*1-55254-112-6*) Brighter Vision.

*__Math-a-Magic Grade 2.__ Brighter Vision Publishing Staff. (Illus.). (J). 1999. pap. text 2.25 (*1-55254-111-8*) Brighter Vision.

*__Math-a-Magic Grades 3-4.__ Brighter Vision Publishing Staff. (Illus.). (J). (gr. 3-4). 1999. pap. 2.25 (*1-55254-113-4*) Brighter Vision.

*__Math-a-Magic Kindergarten.__ Brighter Vision Publishing Staff. (Illus.). (J). (gr. k). 2000. pap. 2.25 (*1-55254-156-8*) Brighter Vision.

*__Math-a-Magic Phonics Magic.__ Brighter Vision Publishing Staff. (Illus.). (J). (gr. k). 2000. pap. 2.25 (*1-55254-157-6*) Brighter Vision.

*__Math-a-Magic Phonics Magic.__ Brighter Vision Publishing Staff. (Illus.). (J). (gr. 3). 2000. pap. 2.25 (*1-55254-160-6*) Brighter Vision.

*__Math-a-Magic Phonics Magic.__ Brighter Vision Publishing Staff. (Illus.). (J). (ps-3). 2000. pap. 2.25 (*1-55254-158-4*); pap. 2.25 (*1-55254-159-2*) Brighter Vision.

Math about Me. Bob DeWeese. (Math Is Everywhere Ser.). (Illus.). 48p. (J). (gr. 2-3). 1994. pap. text, teacher ed. 6.45 (*1-55799-336-X*, EMC 088) Evan-Moor Edu Pubs.

Math Activities. Frank Schaffer Publications, Inc. Staff. (Homework Helpers Ser.). (Illus.). 56p. (J). (gr. 1). 1996. wbk. ed. 2.29 (*0-86734-900-X*, FS-11027) Schaffer Pubns.

Math Activities. Frank Schaffer Publications, Inc. Staff. (Homework Helpers Ser.). (Illus.). 56p. (J). (gr. 2). 1996. wbk. ed. 2.29 (*0-86734-902-6*, FS-11029) Schaffer Pubns.

Math Activities. Frank Schaffer Publications, Inc. Staff. (Homework Helpers Ser.). (Illus.). 56p. (J). (gr. 3). 1996. wbk. ed. 2.29 (*0-86734-904-2*, FS-11031) Schaffer Pubns.

Math Activities. Frank Schaffer Publications, Inc. Staff. (Homework Helpers Ser.). (Illus.). 56p. (J). (gr. 4). 1996. wbk. ed. 2.29 (*0-86734-906-9*, FS-11033) Schaffer Pubns.

Math Activities. Frank Schaffer Publications, Inc. Staff. (Homework Helpers Ser.). (Illus.). 56p. (J). (gr. 5). 1996. wbk. ed. 2.29 (*0-86734-908-5*, FS-11035) Schaffer Pubns.

Math Activities for Every Month of the School Year. Sonia M. Helton. 288p. (C). 1990. pap. text 27.95 (*0-87628-567-1*) P-H.

Math Activities for Preschool. Margaret Noraas. 93p. (J). (ps). pap. text 12.95 (*0-9637985-0-2*) Penguin Family.

Math Activities for Young Children: A Resource Guide for Parents & Teachers. Robert Gamble & Julia Wilkins. 1994. pap. 25.63 (*0-07-022812-4*) McGraw.

Math Activities on the Computer: Grades 1-3. Jill Norris. Ed. by Marilyn Evans. (Teaching & Learning with the Computer Ser.: Vol. 3). (Illus.). 80p. 1998. pap., teacher ed. 16.95 (*1-55799-675-X*, 063) Evan-Moor Edu Pubs.

Math Activities with Dominoes. Sandy Oringel & Helene Silverman. 80p. (J). (gr. k-3). 1997. pap. text 9.95 (*0-938587-97-8*) Cuisenaire.

Math Activities with Dominoes. Sandy Oringel & Helene Silverman. 80p. (J). (gr. 3-8). 1997. pap. text 9.95 (*1-57452-027-X*) Cuisenaire.

Math Adventure, Grade 3: Math Integrated with Science & Playground Activities. Peter Gray & Neil Gray. (Illus.). 112p. 1996. teacher ed., spiral bd. 15.95 (*1-889639-13-3*, 0103) AMSC.

*__Math Advancement.__ Marilyn Simon. 154p. 1998. per. 15.95 (*0-7872-5539-4*, 41555901) Kendall-Hunt.

Math Adventure, Grade 5-8: Math Integrated with Science & Playground Activities. Peter Gray & Neil Gray. (Illus.). 112p. 1996. teacher ed., spiral bd. 15.95 (*1-889639-09-5*, 0105) AMSC.

Math Adventure, Grade 4: Math Integrated with Science & Playground Activities. Peter Gray & Neil Gray. (Illus.). 112p. 1996. teacher ed., spiral bd. 15.95 (*1-889639-04-4*, 0104) AMSC.

Math Adventure, Grade 1: Math Integrated with Science & Playground Activities. Peter Gray & Neil Gray. (Illus.). 112p. 1996. teacher ed., spiral bd. 15.95 (*1-889639-00-1*, 0101) AMSC.

Math Adventure, Grade 2: Math Integrated with Science & Playground Activities. Peter Gray & Neil Gray. (Illus.). 112p. 1996. teacher ed., spiral bd. 15.95 (*1-889639-05-2*, 0102) AMSC.

Math Alive! unabridged ed. Linda C. Foreman & Albert B. Bennett. (Illus.). 450p. 1998. spiral bd. 145.00 (*1-886131-45-7*, MAC3) Math Lrning.

Math Amazement. Ronn Yablun. 208p. 1996. 25.00 (*1-56565-454-4*, 04544W, Pub. by Lowell Hse) NTC Contemp Pub Co.

Math America. Lynn Embry & Betty Bobo. (Illus.). 128p. (J). (gr. 4-6). 1987. pap. 12.99 (*0-86653-378-8*, GA1015) Good Apple.

Math America: Florida, Level 1. Houghton Mifflin Company Staff. 1991. pap., wbk. ed. write for info. (*0-395-49983-6*) HM.

Math America: Florida, Level 2. Houghton Mifflin Company Staff. 1991. pap., wbk. ed. write for info. (*0-395-49981-X*) HM.

Math America: Florida, Level 3. Houghton Mifflin Company Staff. 1991. pap., wbk. ed. write for info. (*0-395-49982-8*) HM.

Math America: Florida, Level 4. Houghton Mifflin Company Staff. 1991. pap., wbk. ed. write for info. (*0-395-49985-2*) HM.

Math America: Florida, Level 5. Houghton Mifflin Company Staff. 1991. pap., wbk. ed. write for info. (*0-395-49986-0*) HM.

Math America: Florida, Level 6. Houghton Mifflin Company Staff. 1991. pap., wbk. ed. write for info. (*0-395-49987-9*) HM.

Math America: Florida, Level 7. Houghton Mifflin Company Staff. 1991. pap., wbk. ed. write for info. (*0-395-49988-7*) HM.

Math America: Florida, Level 8. Houghton Mifflin Company Staff. 1991. pap., wbk. ed. write for info. (*0-395-49989-5*) HM.

Math America: Indiana, Level 1. Houghton Mifflin Company Staff. 1991. pap., wbk. ed. write for info. (*0-395-60024-3*) HM.

Math America: Indiana, Level 2. Houghton Mifflin Company Staff. 1991. pap., wbk. ed. write for info. (*0-395-60025-1*) HM.

Math America: Indiana, Level 3. Houghton Mifflin Company Staff. 1991. pap., wbk. ed. write for info. (*0-395-60026-X*) HM.

Math America: Indiana, Level 4. Houghton Mifflin Company Staff. 1991. pap., wbk. ed. write for info. (*0-395-60027-8*) HM.

Math America: Indiana, Level 5. Houghton Mifflin Company Staff. 1991. pap., wbk. ed. write for info. (*0-395-60028-6*) HM.

Math America: Indiana, Level 6. Houghton Mifflin Company Staff. 1991. pap., wbk. ed. write for info. (*0-395-60030-8*) HM.

Math America: Indiana, Level 7. Houghton Mifflin Company Staff. 1991. pap., wbk. ed. write for info. (*0-395-60031-6*) HM.

Math America: Indiana, Level 8. Houghton Mifflin Company Staff. 1991. pap., wbk. ed. write for info. (*0-395-60032-4*) HM.

Math America: Level 5: West Virginia. Houghton Mifflin Company Staff. 1991. pap., wbk. ed. write for info. (*0-395-60055-3*) HM.

Math America: North Carolina, Level 1. Houghton Mifflin Company Staff. 1991. pap., wbk. ed. write for info. (*0-395-60033-2*) HM.

Math America: North Carolina, Level 2. Houghton Mifflin Company Staff. 1991. pap., wbk. ed. write for info. (*0-395-60034-0*) HM.

Math America: North Carolina, Level 3. Houghton Mifflin Company Staff. 1991. pap., wbk. ed. write for info. (*0-395-60035-9*) HM.

Math America: North Carolina, Level 4. Houghton Mifflin Company Staff. 1991. pap., wbk. ed. write for info. (*0-395-60036-7*) HM.

Math America: North Carolina, Level 5. Houghton Mifflin Company Staff. 1991. pap., wbk. ed. write for info. (*0-395-60037-5*) HM.

Math America: North Carolina, Level 6. Houghton Mifflin Company Staff. 1991. pap., wbk. ed. write for info. (*0-395-60038-3*) HM.

Math America: North Carolina, Level 7. Houghton Mifflin Company Staff. 1991. pap., wbk. ed. write for info. (*0-395-60039-1*) HM.

Math America: North Carolina, Level 8. Houghton Mifflin Company Staff. 1991. pap., wbk. ed. write for info. (*0-395-60040-5*) HM.

Math America: Oklahoma, Level 1. Houghton Mifflin Company Staff. 1991. pap., wbk. ed. write for info. (*0-395-60042-1*) HM.

Math America: Oklahoma, Level 2. Houghton Mifflin Company Staff. 1991. pap., wbk. ed. write for info. (*0-395-60043-X*) HM.

Math America: Oklahoma, Level 3. Houghton Mifflin Company Staff. 1991. pap., wbk. ed. write for info. (*0-395-60044-8*) HM.

Math America: Oklahoma, Level 4. Houghton Mifflin Company Staff. 1991. pap., wbk. ed. write for info. (*0-395-60045-6*) HM.

Math America: Oklahoma, Level 5. Houghton Mifflin Company Staff. 1991. pap., wbk. ed. write for info. (*0-395-60046-4*) HM.

Math America: Oklahoma, Level 6. Houghton Mifflin Company Staff. 1991. pap. write for info. (*0-395-60047-2*) HM.

Math America: Oklahoma, Level 7. Houghton Mifflin Company Staff. 1991. pap. write for info. (*0-395-60048-0*) HM.

Math America: Oklahoma, Level 8. Houghton Mifflin Company Staff. 1991. pap. write for info. (*0-395-60049-9*) HM.

Math America: U. S. A., Level 1. Houghton Mifflin Company Staff. 1991. pap., wbk. ed. write for info. (*0-395-49972-0*) HM.

Math America: U. S. A., Level 2. Houghton Mifflin Company Staff. 1991. pap., wbk. ed. write for info. (*0-395-49973-9*) HM.

Math America: U. S. A., Level 3. Houghton Mifflin Company Staff. 1991. pap., wbk. ed. write for info. (*0-395-49974-7*) HM.

Math America: U. S. A., Level 4. Houghton Mifflin Company Staff. 1991. pap., wbk. ed. write for info. (*0-395-49975-5*) HM.

Math America: U. S. A., Level 5. Houghton Mifflin Company Staff. 1991. pap., wbk. ed. write for info. (*0-395-49976-3*) HM.

Math America: U.S.A. Houghton Mifflin Company Staff. 1991. pap., wbk. ed. write for info. (*0-395-49977-1*) HM.

Math America: West Virginia, Level 1. Houghton Mifflin Company Staff. 1991. pap., wbk. ed. write for info. (*0-395-60051-0*) HM.

Math America: West Virginia, Level 2. Houghton Mifflin Company Staff. 1991. pap., wbk. ed. write for info. (*0-395-60052-9*) HM.

Math America: West Virginia, Level 3. Houghton Mifflin Company Staff. 1991. pap., wbk. ed. write for info. (*0-395-60053-7*) HM.

Math America: West Virginia, Level 4. Houghton Mifflin Company Staff. 1991. pap., wbk. ed. write for info. (*0-395-60054-5*) HM.

Math America: West Virginia, Level 6. Houghton Mifflin Company Staff. 1991. pap., wbk. ed. write for info. (*0-395-60056-1*) HM.

Math America: West Virginia, Level 7. Houghton Mifflin Company Staff. 1991. pap., wbk. ed. write for info. (*0-395-60057-X*) HM.

Math America: West Virginia, Level 8. Houghton Mifflin Company Staff. 1991. pap., wbk. ed. write for info. (*0-395-60058-8*) HM.

Math Analysis For Business & Economics. 2nd ed. Charles W. Schelin & David W. Bange. (Math). 672p. (C). 1988. pap. 65.95 (*0-534-91493-4*) PWS Pubs.

Math Analysis in Business & Economy. Allyn. 1999. text 12.32 (*0-205-13780-6*) P-H.

Math & Classroom Pets. Jo E. Moore. (Math Is Everywhere Ser.). (Illus.). 48p. (J). (gr. k-1). 1994. pap. text, teacher ed. 6.45 (*1-55799-322-X*, EMC 094) Evan-Moor Edu Pubs.

Math & Computing. 4th ed. Cheney. LC 98-49447. (Mathematics). 671p. 1999. pap. 88.95 (*0-534-35184-0*) Brooks-Cole.

Math & Dosage Calculations for Health Occupations. Renee A. Dawe. (Illus.). 240p. (gr. 6-12). 1993. text, student ed. 29.90 (*0-02-800677-1*) Glencoe.

Math & Dosage Calculations for Health Occupations: Instructor's Guide. Dawe. 1999. teacher ed. 12.21 (*0-02-800678-X*) Glencoe.

*__Math & Following Directory.__ (Little Books for Little Hands). (Illus.). 80p. (J). (ps-2). 2000. pap. 9.95 (*1-58273-377-5*) Newbridge Educ.

Math & Graphing Skills. Daniel K. Apple & Cyndie Merten. 89p. (C). 1992. 20.00 incl. 3.5 hd (*0-87843-721-5*) Pac Crest Soft.

Math & Graphing Skills. Cyndie Marten. Ed. by Daniel K. Apple. (Illus.). 89p. (C). 1992. pap. text 20.00 (*1-878437-21-6*) Pac Crest Soft.

Math & Literature for Grades K-6. Rusty Bresser. (Illus.). 1995. pap. text 15.95 (*0-941355-14-4*) Math Solns Pubns.

Math & Literature (K-3), Bk. 1. Marilyn Burns. 73p. 1995. pap. text 14.95 (*0-941355-07-1*) Math Solns Pubns.

Math & Literature (K-3), Bk. 2. Stephanie Sheffield. 13p. 1995. pap. text 14.95 (*0-941355-11-X*) Math Solns Pubns.

Math & Logic Puzzles for PC Enthusiasts. J. J. Clessa. LC 96-5615. Orig. Title: Micropuzzles. 1996. reprint ed. pap. 5.95 (*0-486-29192-8*) Dover.

*__Math & Mathematicians: The History of Math Discoveries Around the World, 2 vols.__ Leonard C. Bruno. Ed. by Lawrence W. Baker. LC 99-32424. 420p. (J). (gr. 6-10). 1999. text 63.00 (*0-7876-3812-9*) Gale.

*__Math & Mathematicians: The History of Math Discoveries Around the World__ Leonard C. Bruno & Lawrence W. Baker. LC 99-32424. 1999. write for info. (*0-7876-3814-5*) Visible Ink Pr.

Math & Meds for Nurses. Delores F. Saxton. LC 97-44437. (Student Material TV). 304p. (C). 1998. pap. 44.95 (*0-8273-7331-7*) Thomson Learn.

Math & Money Management. Thomas Camilli. (Math Is Everywhere Ser.). 48p. (J). (gr. 4-6). 1994. pap. text 6.45 (*1-55799-328-9*, EMC 101) Evan-Moor Edu Pubs.

Math & More: Grade 1. ECS Learning Systems Staff. (ECS Home Study Bk.). (Illus.). 64p. (Orig.). (J). 1995. pap., wbk. ed. 4.95 (*1-57022-033-6*) ECS Lrn Systs.

Math & More: Grade 2. ECS Learning Systems Staff. (ECS Home Study Bk.). (Illus.). 64p. (Orig.). (J). 1995. pap., wbk. ed. 4.95 (*1-57022-034-4*) ECS Lrn Systs.

Math & More: Grade 3. ECS Learning Systems Staff. (ECS Home Study Bk.). (Illus.). 64p. (Orig.). (J). 1995. pap., wbk. ed. 4.95 (*1-57022-035-2*) ECS Lrn Systs.

Math & More: Grade 4. ECS Learning Systems Staff. (ECS Home Study Bk.). (Illus.). 64p. (Orig.). (J). 1995. pap., wbk. ed. 4.95 (*1-57022-036-0*) ECS Lrn Systs.

Math & More: Grade 5. ECS Learning Systems Staff. (ECS Home Study Bk.). (Illus.). 64p. (Orig.). (J). 1995. pap., wbk. ed. 4.95 (*1-57022-037-9*) ECS Lrn Systs.

Math & More: Grade 6. ECS Learning Systems Staff. (ECS Home Study Bk.). (Illus.). 64p. (Orig.). (J). 1995. pap., wbk. ed. 4.95 (*1-57022-038-7*) ECS Lrn Systs.

Math & More: Home Study Collection, 6 bks. Lori Mammen. 56p. (J). (gr. 1-6). 1995. 29.70 (*1-57022-186-3*) ECS Lrn Systs.

Math & More Directed Activities: Fifth Grade. large type ed. Kathy J. French. Ed. by Michele Hollister. 200p. (J). (gr. 5). 2001. pap. text. write for info. (*1-893632-10-5*, 300-113) Math Con.

Math & More Directed Activities: First Grade. large type ed. Kathy J. French. Ed. by Michele Hollister. 200p. (J). (gr. 1). 2001. pap. text. write for info. (*1-893632-06-7*, 300-109) Math Con.

Math & More Directed Activities: Fourth Grade. large type ed. Kathy J. French. Ed. by Michele Hollister. 200p. (J). (gr. 4). 2001. pap. text. write for info. (*1-893632-09-1*, 300-112) Math Con.

Math & More Directed Activities: Kindergarten. large type ed. Kathy J. French. Ed. by Michele Hollister. 200p. (J). (gr. k). 2001. pap. text. write for info. (*1-893632-05-9*, 300-108) Math Con.

Math & More Directed Activities: Second Grade. large type ed. Kathy J. French. Ed. by Michele Hollister. 200p. (J). (gr. 2). 2001. pap. text. write for info. (*1-893632-07-5*, 300-110) Math Con.

Math & More Directed Activities: Third Grade. large type ed. Kathy J. French. Ed. by Michele Hollister. 200p. (J). (gr. 3). 2001. pap. text. write for info. (*1-893632-08-3*, 300-111) Math Con.

Math & Music: Harmonious Connections. Trudi H. Garland & Charity V. Kahn. Ed. by Katarina Stenstedt. (Illus.). 168p. (Orig.). (YA). (gr. 6-12). 1994. pap. text, teacher ed. 11.95 (*0-86651-829-0*, 21335); pap. text, teacher ed. 19.95 (*0-86651-831-2*, 21336 (poster)); pap. text, teacher ed. 9.95 (*0-86651-830-4*, 37304 (poster)) Seymour Pubns.

Math & Science for Young Children. Charlesworth. (Early Childhood Education Ser.). 1990. pap. 35.00 (*0-8273-3402-8*, VNR) Wiley.

Math & Science for Young Children. Charlesworth. (Early Childhood Education Ser.). 1995. pap., teacher ed. 12.00 (*0-8273-5870-9*, VNR) Wiley.

Math & Science for Young Children. 2nd ed. Rosalind Charlesworth. LC 94-34419. (Illus.). 559p. (C). 1995. pap. 37.50 (*0-8273-5869-5*) Delmar.

Math & Science for Young Children. 3rd ed. Charlesworth-Lind. (Early Childhood Education Ser.). 592p. (C). 1998. pap. text 58.95 (*0-8273-8635-4*) Delmar.

Math & Science for Young Children: Instructor's Guide. Rosalind Charlesworth. 1990. pap., teacher ed. 10.00 (*0-8273-3403-6*) Delmar.

Math & Stories. Marian R. Bartch. (J). (gr. k-3). 1996. 13.95 (*0-614-09791-6*, GoodYrBooks) Addson-Wesley Educ.

Math & Stories. Marian R. Bartch. 184p. (gr. k-3). 1996. pap. 13.95 (*0-673-36317-1*, GoodYrBooks) Addson-Wesley Educ.

Math & Stories. Marian R. Bartch. 1997. pap. text 13.95 (*0-673-36321-X*) Addson-Wesley Educ.

Math & Students with Learning Disabilities: A Practice Guide to Course Substitution. Paul Nolting. 120p. 1993. pap. 19.95 (*0-940287-24-2*) Acad Success Pr.

***Math & Test Taking Grade 8.** Dawn Talluto Jacobi. (Kelley Wingate Ser.). 128p. (YA). (gr. 8). 2000. pap. 10.95 (*0-88724-539-0*, CD-3758) Carson-Dellos.

***Math & Test Taking Grade 5.** Dawn Talluto Jacobi. (Kelley Wingate Ser.). 128p. (J). (gr. 5). 2000. pap. 10.95 (*0-88724-536-6*, CD-3755) Carson-Dellos.

***Math & Test Taking Grade 4.** Patricia Pedigo & Roger DeSanti. (Kelley Wingate Ser.). 128p. (J). (gr. 4). 2000. pap. 10.95 (*0-88724-535-8*, CD-3754) Carson-Dellos.

***Math & Test Taking Grade 1.** Patricia Pedigo & Roger DeSanti. (Kelley Wingate Ser.). 128p. (J). (gr. 1). 2000. pap. 10.95 (*0-88724-532-3*, CD-3751) Carson-Dellos.

***Math & Test Taking Grade 7.** Dawn Talluto Jacobi. (Kelley Wingate Ser.). 128p. (YA). (gr. 7). 2000. pap. 10.95 (*0-88724-538-2*, CD-3757) Carson-Dellos.

***Math & Test Taking Grade 6.** Dawn Talluto Jacobi. (Kelley Wingate Ser.). 128p. (J). (gr. 6). 2000. pap. 10.95 (*0-88724-537-4*, CD-3756) Carson-Dellos.

***Math & Test Taking Grade 3.** Patricia Pedigo & Roger DeSanti. (Kelley Wingate Ser.). 128p. (J). (gr. 3). 2000. pap. 10.95 (*0-88724-534-X*, CD-3753) Carson-Dellos.

***Math & Test Taking Grade 2.** Patricia Pedigo & Roger DeSanti. (Kelley Wingate Ser.). 128p. (J). (gr. 2). 2000. pap. 10.95 (*0-88724-533-1*, CD-3752) Carson-Dellos.

Math & the Learning Disabled Student: A Practical Guide for Accommodations. Paul D. Nolting. 1991. pap. 14.95 (*0-940287-23-4*) Acad Success Pr.

Math Anxiety: What It Is & What to Do about It. rev. ed. Charlie R. Mitchell. 1987. pap. 8.95 (*0-9610794-3-6*) Action Pr.

Math Applications. Balch. 1995. 47.95 (*0-02-824625-X*) McGraw.

Math Applied to Space Science: Interesting Problems & Their Solutions. Research Education Association Staff. LC 97-69458. 1998. pap. text 14.95 (*0-87891-217-7*) Res & Educ.

Math Approach to Chemistry. Michels. (Chemistry Ser.). 1997. 36.25 (*0-534-49836-1*) Brooks-Cole.

Math Around the House: Basic Mathematics Skills. Jo Ellen Moore. (Illus.). 31p. (J). (ps-k). 1995. pap., wbk. ed. 2.50 (*1-58610-059-6*, Learn on the Go) Learn Horizon.

Math Around the World. Beverly Braxton et al. Ed. by Lincoln Bergman et al. (Great Explorations in Math & Science (GEMS) Ser.). (Illus.). 200p. (Orig.). (J). (gr. 5-8). 1995. teacher ed., spiral bd. 25.50 (*0-912511-94-X*, GEMS) Lawrence Science.

Math Around the World. Lynn Embry & Betty Bobo. 144p. (J). (gr. 4-6). 1991. 13.99 (*0-86653-600-0*, GA1319) Good Apple.

Math Art Activities. Carolyn Brunetto. 1997. pap. 12.95 (*0-590-96371-6*) Scholastic Inc.

Math As a Way of Knowing. Susan Ohanian. LC 96-45740. (Strategies for Teaching & Learning Ser.). 96p. (C). 1996. reprint ed. pap. text 15.00 (*1-57110-051-2*) Stenhse Pubs.

Math at a Glance: A Month-by-Month Celebration of the Numbers Around Us. Susan Ohanian. LC 94-46723. 115p. 1995. pap. 13.95 (*0-435-08364-3*, 08364) Heinemann.

Math at Bat: Baseball, Statistics, & Everyday Life. Abigail Silver. (Textworks Ser.). (Illus.). ix, 120p. (J). (gr. 4-8). 1995. ring bd. 29.95 (*1-58284-010-5*, Thoughtful Educ) Silver Strong.

Math at Hand: A Mathematics Handbook. Great Source Education Group Staff. (Illus.). 548p. (gr. 4-6). 1999. text 20.66 (*0-669-46807-X*); pap. text 16.66 (*0-669-46922-X*) Great Source.

Math at Playtime. Jo E. Moore. (Math Is Everywhere Ser.). (Illus.). 48p. (J). (gr. k-1). 1994. pap. text, teacher ed. 6.45 (*1-55799-323-8*, EMC 095) Evan-Moor Edu Pubs.

Math at the Mall. Bob DeWeese. (Math Is Everywhere Ser.). (Illus.). 48p. (J). (gr. 2-3). 1994. pap. text, teacher ed. 6.45 (*1-55799-326-2*, EMC 098) Evan-Moor Edu Pubs.

Math at Work. Clifford E. Martin. 1989. pap. 6.95 (*0-87813-924-9*) Christian Light.

***Math at Work.** Jocelyn Riley. (Women in Nontraditional Careers Ser.: Vol. 8). 114p. (J). (gr. 6-12). 2000. teacher ed. 45.00 (*1-877933-85-6*, 25002) Her Own Words.

Math at Work, Bk. 1. Robert B. Angus & Claudia Clark. LC 97-45052. 592p. 1998. pap. text 54.00 (*0-13-860388-X*) P-H.

Math at Work, Bk. 2. Robert B. Angus & Claudia Clark. LC 97-45052. Vol. 2. 528p. 1998. pap. text 54.00 (*0-13-857442-1*) P-H.

***Math Attack: How to Reduce Math Anxiety in the Classroom, at Work & in...** Marilyn Curtain-Phillips. 120p. 1999. 15.00 (*0-9673997-1-8*) Curtain-Phillips.

Math Bag: Includes: Mini-Manual, 104-Piece Block Set, in a Roll Bag. Katherine S. Koonce & Susan S. Simpson. (Illus.). 8p. 1996. 26.00 (*1-880892-71-5*) Com Sense FL.

***Math Behind Wall Street: How the Market Works & How to Make It Work for You.** Nicholas Teebagy. 128p. 2000. pap. 14.95 (*1-56858-160-2*, Pub. by FWEW) Publishers Group.

Math Behind Wall Street: How the Market Works & How to Make It Work for You. Nick Teebagy. LC 98-37942. 176p. 1998. 18.00 (*1-56858-111-4*) FWEW.

Math Blaster Adventures & Activities: Danger in the Dark Nebula. Roger Stewart. LC 96-68915. (Illus.). 64p. 1996. pap., per. 9.99 (*0-7615-0730-2*) Prima Pub.

***Math Book for Girls & Other Beings Who Count.** Valerie Wyatt & Pat Cupples. (Illus.). 64p. (J). (gr. 3-7). 2000. 14.95 (*1-55074-830-0*, Pub. by Kids Can Press) Genl Dist Srvs.

***Math Book for Girls & Other Beings Who Count.** Valerie Wyatt & Patricia Cupples. (Illus.). 64p. (J). (gr. 3-7). 2000. pap. 9.95 (*1-55074-584-0*, Pub. by Kids Can Press) Genl Dist Srvs.

Math Brain Teasers: Basic Mathematics Skills. Thomas Camilli. Ed. by Bob DeWeese. (Illus.). 32p. (J). (gr. 4-6). 1995. pap., wbk. ed. 2.50 (*1-58610-093-9*, Learn on the Go) Learn Horizon.

Math Brainbusters Grades 3-4. Thomas Camilli. (Daily Problem Solving Ser.). (Illus.). 44p. (J). (gr. 3-4). 1994. pap. text 14.95 (*1-55799-281-9*, EMC 385) Evan-Moor Edu Pubs.

Math Brainbusters Grades 5-6. Thomas Camilli. (Daily Problem Solving Ser.). (Illus.). 44p. (J). (gr. 5-6). 1994. pap. text 14.95 (*1-55799-282-7*, EMC 386) Evan-Moor Edu Pubs.

Math Brainstorms. Becky Daniel. 80p. (J). (gr. 1-4). 1990. 10.99 (*0-86653-565-9*, GA1170) Good Apple.

Math Brainteasers. April Blakely. (Illus.). 96p. (YA). (gr. 6 up). 1996. pap. 9.95 (*0-673-36318-X*, GoodYrBooks) Addson-Wesley Educ.

***Math Bridge: First Grade.** Carla Dawn Fisher. 2000. pap. text 9.95 (*1-887923-55-1*, Pub. by Rainbow UT) Midpt Trade.

***Math Bridge: Second Grade.** Carla Dawn Fisher. 2000. pap. text 9.95 (*1-887923-54-3*, Pub. by Rainbow UT) Midpt Trade.

***Math Bridge: Third Grade.** Carla Dawn Fisher. 2000. pap. text 9.95 (*1-887923-53-5*, Pub. by Rainbow UT) Midpt Trade.

***Math Bridge: 4th Grade.** Jennifer Moore et al. Ed. by Kirsten Willie et al. (Illus.). 96p. (J). (gr. 4). 1999. pap., wbk. ed. 9.95 (*1-887923-16-0*, Pub. by Rainbow UT) Midpt Trade.

***Math Bridge: 5th Grade.** Jennifer Moore et al. Ed. by Kirsten Willie et al. (Illus.). 96p. (J). (gr. 5). 1999. pap., wbk. ed. 9.95 (*1-887923-17-9*, Pub. by Rainbow UT) Midpt Trade.

***Math Bridge: 6th Grade.** Tracy Dankberg & Leland Graham. Ed. by Kirsten Willie et al. (Illus.). 96p. (J). (gr. 6). 1999. pap., wbk. ed. 9.95 (*1-887923-18-7*, Pub. by Rainbow UT) Midpt Trade.

***Math Bridge: 7th Grade.** Leland Graham & Tracy Dankberg. Ed. by Kirsten Willie et al. (Illus.). 96p. (YA). (gr. 7). 1999. pap., wbk. ed. 9.95 (*1-887923-19-5*, Pub. by Rainbow UT) Midpt Trade.

***Math Bridge: 8th Grade.** Tracy Dankberg & Leland Graham. Ed. by Kirsten Willie et al. (Illus.). 96p. (YA). (gr. 8). 1999. pap., wbk. ed. 9.95 (*1-887923-20-9*, Pub. by Rainbow UT) Midpt Trade.

Math Builder for Standardized Tests. rev. ed. Research & Education Association Staff. LC 97-69309. (Illus.). 1998. pap. 15.95 (*0-87891-876-0*) Res & Educ.

Math Bulletin Boards. Marjorie Frank. (Easy-To-Make-&-Use Ser.). (Illus.). 64p. (J). (gr. k-6). 1986. pap. text 7.95 (*0-86530-133-6*, IP 112-2) Incentive Pubns.

Math Bulletin Boards That Teach. Jacqueline Howes. (Illus.). 80p. 1999. pap. 10.95 (*0-590-02905-3*) Scholastic Inc.

Math by Kids: A Collection of Word Problems Written by Kids for Kids of All Ages. Ed. by Susan P. Richman. (J). (gr. k-12). 1996. wbk. ed. 6.95 (*0-929446-04-6*) PA Homeschoolers.

Math By-Lines. Carol Greenes. 1997. pap. text 8.50 (*0-86651-132-6*) Seymour Pubns.

Math Cad Intro to Introductory Physics. Addison-Wesley Publishing Staff. 386p. (C). 1992. pap. 39.40 (*0-201-54736-8*) Addison-Wesley.

Math Calculations in Respiratory Therapy. Ray Sibberson. 200p. 1994. write for info. (*0-683-07732-5*) Lppncott W & W.

Math Can Be a Dangerous Thing! Bob Knauff. (Illus.). 120p. 1997. 11.95 (*0-89278-004-5*) Carolina Biological.

Math Can Be Easy. Sheinfeld. (C). 1992. pap. text 16.74 (*0-07-056844-8*) McGraw.

Math Card Games: 340 Games for Learning & Enjoying Math. 2nd ed. Joan A. Cotter. (Illus.). 156p. 1987. pap. 18.00 (*0-9609636-3-4*) Activities Learning.

Math Challenges: Puzzles, Tricks & Games. Glen Vecchione. LC 96-43526. (Illus.). 96p. (YA). (gr. 6 up). 1997. 14.95 (*0-8069-8114-8*) Sterling.

***Math Chat Book.** Frank Morgan. LC 99-67970. 124p. 2000. pap. 19.95 (*0-88385-530-5*) Math Assn.

Math Chef: Over 60 Math Activities & Recipes for Kids. Joan D'Amico & Karen E. Drummond. LC 96-22143. (Illus.). 180p. (J). (gr. 3-9). 1996. pap. 12.95 (*0-471-13813-4*) Wiley.

Math Color by Number: Grades K-2. Avaril Wedemeyer & Joyce Cejka. 1988. 5.95 (*0-89108-186-0*, 8812) Love Pub Co.

Math Combo Story Problems: Combo GR 1. J. Hoffman & B. Gregorich. Ed. by Lorie De Young. (Math Combo Bks.: No. 02201). (Illus.). 64p. (Orig.). (gr. 1). 1997. pap., wbk. ed. 3.25 (*0-88743-137-2*, 02201) Sch Zone Pub Co.

Math Combo Story Problems: Grade 4. Susan Loughrin et al. (Math Combo Bks.: No. 02204). (Illus.). 64p. (Orig.). (J). (gr. 4-4). 1997. pap., wbk. ed. 3.25 (*0-88743-140-2*, 02204) Sch Zone Pub Co.

Math Companion for Computer Science. Zamir Bavel. (Illus.). 1992. pap. 35.00 (*0-9623885-4-8*) ZB Pub Indus.

Math Competencies for Everyday Living. Powell. (MA - Academic Math Ser.). 1989. mass mkt. 22.95 (*0-538-13072-5*) S-W Pub.

Math Concepts. Gordon Staff. Date not set. 59.95 (*0-02-824314-5*) Glencoe.

***Math Concepts for Algebra Preparation.** 376p. (C). 1999. text 34.00 (*0-536-02172-4*) Pearson Custom.

Math Concepts for Algebra Preparation. 2nd ed. 424p. (C). 1999. pap. text 37.00 (*0-536-02444-8*) Pearson Custom.

***Math Concepts for Algebra Preparation.** 3rd ed. 490p. (C). 2000. 40.00 (*0-536-60938-1*) Pearson Custom.

Math Concepts for Food Engineering. Ed. by R. W. Hartel et al. LC 97-60545. 187p. 1997. pap. text 34.95 (*1-56676-564-1*) Technomic.

Math Connection. Dolciani. (C). 1991. pap., student ed., suppl. ed. 29.28 (*0-395-56993-1*) HM.

Math Connection. Dolciani. (C). 1991. pap., student ed., suppl. ed. 29.28 (*0-395-57016-6*) HM.

Math Connection. Gardella. (C). 1991. pap., student ed. 11.80 (*0-395-58558-9*); pap., student ed., suppl. ed. 13.84 (*0-395-58559-7*); pap., suppl. ed. 27.72 (*0-395-58557-0*) HM.

Math Connection. Gardella. 1991. pap., teacher ed., suppl. ed. 7.32 (*0-395-47024-2*) HM.

Math Connection. Gardella. (C). 1992. pap., student ed. 11.80 (*0-395-47025-0*) HM.

Math Connection. Gardella. (C). 1993. pap., suppl. ed. 20.04 (*0-395-66939-1*) HM.

Math Connection. Lockwood. (C). 1991. pap. text, teacher ed. 2.76 (*0-395-57742-X*) HM.

Math Connections. Fraze. 1991. text, teacher ed. 87.80 (*0-395-47020-X*); text, student ed. 58.88 (*0-395-46150-2*) HM.

Math Connections. Fraze. 1991. pap., suppl. ed. 644.36 (*0-395-56777-7*) HM.

Math Connections. Gardella. 1993. text 58.88 (*0-395-66937-5*) HM.

Math Connections. David J. Glatzer. 64p. (J). (gr. 4-6). 1997. pap. text 10.95 (*0-86651-634-4*) Seymour Pubns.

Math Connections. David J. Glatzer. (J). (gr. 7-9). 1997. pap. text 10.95 (*0-86651-463-5*) Seymour Pubns.

Math Connections. David J. Glatzer. 72p. (J). (gr. 9-12). 1997. pap. text 10.95 (*0-86651-633-6*) Seymour Pubns.

Math Connections: Linking Manipulatives & Critical Thinking. David J. Glatzer & Joyce Glatzer. Ed. by Catherine Anderson et al. (Illus.). 80p. (Orig.). (J). (gr. k-3). 1996. pap. text 10.95 (*1-57232-268-3*, 21806) Seymour Pubns.

***Math Connections Excel.** Cabral & Hay. 220p. 1999. pap. text 13.75 (*0-536-02548-7*) Pearson Custom.

Math Consumable, 1985. Nichols. 1985. pap. 28.75 (*0-03-064206-X*) Harcourt Schl Pubs.

Math Contests - Grades 4, 5, & 6 Vol. 3: School Years: 1991-92 Through 1995-96. Steven R. Conrad & Daniel Flegler. (Math Contests Ser.). 154p. (Orig.). (J). (gr. 3-7). 1996. pap. 12.95 (*0-940805-09-X*) Math Leagues.

Math Contests - Grades 7 & 8 Vol. 3: School Years: 1991-92 Through 1995-96. Steven R. Conrad & Daniel Flegler. (Math Contests Ser.). 136p. (Orig.). (YA). (gr. 6-12). 1996. pap. 12.95 (*0-940805-10-3*) Math Leagues.

Math Contests - Grades 4, 5, & 6 Vol. 1: School Years: 1979-80 Through 1985-86. rev. ed. Steven R. Conrad & Daniel Flegler. 94p. 1992. pap. 12.95 (*0-940805-06-5*) Math Leagues.

Math Contests - Grades 4, 5, & 6 Vol. 2: School Years: 1986-87 Through 1990-91. Steven R. Conrad & Daniel Flegler. (Math Contests Ser.). 102p. (Orig.). (J). (gr. 3-8). 1991. pap. 12.95 (*0-940805-03-0*) Math Leagues.

Math Contests - Grades 7 & 8: Surival, Vol. 1. rev. ed. Steven R. Conrad & Daniel Flegler. 94p. 1992. pap. 12.95 (*0-940805-07-3*) Math Leagues.

Math Contests - Grades 7 & 8 Vol. 2: School Years: 1982-83 Through 1990-91. Steven R. Conrad & Daniel Flegler. (Math Contests Ser.). 166p. (Orig.). (J). (gr. 5-8). 1992. pap. 12.95 (*0-940805-05-7*) Math Leagues.

Math Contests - High School Vol. 1: School Years: 1977-78 Through 1981-82. rev. ed. Steven R. Conrad & Daniel Flegler. 70p. 1992. pap. 12.95 (*0-940805-08-1*) Math Leagues.

Math Contests - High School Vol. 2: School Years: 1982-83 Through 1990-91. Steven R. Conrad & Daniel Flegler. (Math Contests Ser.). 118p. (Orig.). (YA). (gr. 9-12). 1992. pap. 12.95 (*0-940805-04-9*) Math Leagues.

Math Contests - High School Vol. 3: School Years: 1991-92 Through 1995-96. Steven R. Conrad & Daniel Flegler. (Math Contests Ser.). 70p. (Orig.). (YA). (gr. 9-12). 1996. pap. 12.95 (*0-940805-11-1*) Math Leagues.

***Math Core Assignment: Multiplication, Grade 4, Student Edition.** (Math Ser.). 67p. (J). 1999. pap., student ed. 5.00 (*1-889630-03-9*) Natl Ctr & Econ.

***Math Core Assignment: Proportionality, Grade 8, Student Edition.** (Math Ser.). 69p. (YA). 1999. pap., student ed. 6.00 (*1-889630-11-X*) Natl Ctr & Econ.

***Math Core Assignments: Division, Grade 5, Student Edition.** (Math Ser.). 97p. (J). 1999. pap., student ed. 5.00 (*1-889630-05-5*) Natl Ctr & Econ.

***Math Core Assignments: Division, Grade 5, Teachers Edition.** (Math Ser.). 117p. 1999. pap., teacher ed. 25.00 (*1-889630-04-7*) Natl Ctr & Econ.

***Math Core Assignments: Exponential Growth High School, Teacher's Edition.** (Math Ser.). 194p. 1999. pap., teacher ed. 25.00 (*1-889630-14-4*) Natl Ctr & Econ.

***Math Core Assignments: Exponential Growth, Student Edition.** (Math Ser.). 96p. (YA). 1999. pap., student ed. 5.00 (*1-889630-15-2*) Natl Ctr & Econ.

***Math Core Assignments: From Addition to Subtraction, Grade 3, Student Edition.** (Math Ser.). 75p. (J). 1999. pap., student ed. 5.00 (*1-889630-01-2*) Natl Ctr & Econ.

***Math Core Assignments: From Addition to Subtraction, Teacher's Edition.** (Math Ser.). 194p. 1999. pap., teacher ed. 25.00 (*1-889630-00-4*) Natl Ctr & Econ.

***Math Core Assignments: Geometric Measurement, Grade 7, Student Edition.** (Math Ser.). 65p. (J). 1999. pap., student ed. 6.00 (*1-889630-09-8*) Natl Ctr & Econ.

***Math Core Assignments: Geometric Measurement, Teacher's Edition.** (Math Ser.). 130p. 1999. pap., teacher ed. 25.00 (*1-889630-08-X*) Natl Ctr & Econ.

***Math Core Assignments: Numbers from 0-1, Grade 6, Student Edition.** (Math Ser.). 97p. (J). 1999. pap., student ed. 6.00 (*1-889630-07-1*) Natl Ctr & Econ.

***Math Core Assignments: Numbers from 0-1, Teacher's Edition.** (Math Ser.). 150p. 1999. pap., teacher ed. 25.00 (*1-889630-06-3*) Natl Ctr & Econ.

***Math Core Assignments: Proportionality, Teacher's Edition.** (Math Ser.). 142p. 1999. pap., teacher ed. 25.00 (*1-889630-10-1*) Natl Ctr & Econ.

***Math Core Assignments: Slope High School, Student's Edition.** (Math Ser.). 84p. (YA). 1999. pap., student ed. 6.00 (*1-889630-13-6*) Natl Ctr & Econ.

***Math Core Assignments: Slope High School, Teacher's Edition.** (Math Ser.). 168p. 1999. pap., teacher ed. 25.00 (*1-889630-12-8*) Natl Ctr & Econ.

***Math Core Assignments: Volume High School, Student Edition.** (Math Ser.). 115p. (YA). 1999. pap., student ed. 6.00 (*1-889630-17-9*) Natl Ctr & Econ.

Math Cue for College Graph(MAC) 5th ed. Barker. (C). 1995. student ed. 276.50 (*0-03-010197-2*, Pub. by Harcourt Coll Pubs) Harcourt.

Math Curse. Jon Scieszka. LC 95-12341. (Illus.). 32p. (J). (ps-3). 1995. 16.99 (*0-670-86194-4*, Viking Child) Peng Put Young Read.

Math Dictionary for Young People. William Bennet. 176p. (YA). (gr. 5 up). 1998. lib. bdg. 19.95 (*0-382-39629-4*) Silver Burdett Pr.

Math Dictionary with Solutions: A Math Review. 2nd ed. Chris Kornegay. LC 98-55316. 570p. 1999. 75.00 (*0-7619-1784-5*) Sage.

Math Dictionary with Solutions: A Math Review. 2nd ed. Chris Kornegay. LC 98-55316. 532p. 1999. write for info. (*0-7619-1785-3*) Sage.

***Math Doctor.** Der Meer Ron Van. 1999. 29.95 (*90-76048-22-3*) Abbeville Pr.

Math DoodleLoops. Sandy Baker. (DoodleLoops Ser.). 96p. 1996. teacher ed. 11.99 (*1-56417-842-0*, GA1549) Good Apple.

Math Drillsters. Bob Bernstein. (Illus.). 224p. 1992. 16.99 (*0-86653-660-4*, GA1392) Good Apple.

Math Easy As Apples & Bananas: Multimedia CD-Rom with Animations for Win 95 or Higher. Yasmin Khan. (Math Easy As Apples & Bananas). (Illus.). 70p. 1998. ring bd. 49.99 incl. audio compact disk (*0-9669624-0-0*) Alivebooksnet.

Math Education at Its Best: The Potsdam Model. Dilip K. Datta. LC 93-85952. 235p. 1993. pap. 9.95 (*0-9638605-1-8*) RI Desktop.

***Math 87 Syllabus & Tests.** 10p. 1999. ring bd. 1.50 (*1-57896-064-9*, 1964, Hewitt Homeschl Res) Hewitt Res Fnd.

Math Electronics. Myers. Date not set. pap. text, student ed. write for info. (*0-314-02809-9*) West Pub.

Math Elementary Teaching Activity Approach. Bennett. 1997. pap., lab manual ed. 57.19 (*0-07-913259-6*) McGraw.

Math Equals, Biographies of Women Mathematicians & Related Activities. Teri Perl. 1978. text 18.95 (*0-201-05709-3*) Addison-Wesley.

Math Essentials. Steve Slavin. LC 97-39196. (Basics Made Easy Ser.). (Illus.). 208p. 1998. pap. 13.95 (*1-57685-094-3*) LrningExprss.

***Math Essentials: Learn to Conquer Fractions, Decimals & Percentages.** Steven L. Slavin. (Illus.). 208p. 2000. pap. text 14.95 (*1-57685-305-5*) LrningExprss.

Math Excursions No. 1: Project-Based Mathematics for First Graders. Donna Burk et al. LC 91-46272. (Illus.). 259p. (C). 1992. pap. text 29.50 (*0-435-08331-7*, 08331) Heinemann.

Math Excursions No. 2: Project-Based Mathematics for Second Graders. Donna Burk et al. LC 91-15387. 218p. (C). 1991. pap. text 29.50 (*0-435-08321-X*, 08321) Heinemann.

Math Excursions No. K: Project-Based Mathematics for Kindergarteners. 2nd rev. ed. Donna Burk et al. LC 92-16735. (Math Excursions Ser.). 299p. (YA). 1993. pap. text 25.00 (*0-435-08345-7*, 08345) Heinemann.

Math Exercise Book. (J). (gr. 5-8). 8.33 (*0-8092-0932-2*) NTC Contemp Pub Co.

Math Exercises: Algebra. Mitchell. 1994. pap. 2.50 (*0-8092-3653-2*) NTC Contemp Pub Co.

Math Exercises: Decimals. Mitchell. 1993. pap. 2.50 (*0-8092-3826-8*) NTC Contemp Pub Co.

Math Exercises: Fractions. Mitchell. 1993. pap. 2.50 (*0-8092-3827-6*) NTC Contemp Pub Co.
Math Exercises: Geometry. Mitchell. 1994. pap. 2.50 (*0-8092-3652-4*) NTC Contemp Pub Co.
Math Exercises: Percents. Mitchell. 1993. pap. 2.50 (*0-8092-4168-4*) NTC Contemp Pub Co.
Math Exercises: Pre Algebra. Mitchell. 1994. pap. 2.50 (*0-8092-3654-0*) NTC Contemp Pub Co.
Math Exercises: Problelm Solving & Applications. Mitchell. 1993. pap. 2.50 (*0-8092-4171-4*) NTC Contemp Pub Co.
Math Exercises: Whole Numbers & Money. Mitchell. 1993. pap. 2.50 (*0-8092-3828-4*) NTC Contemp Pub Co.
Math Exercises for Nonreaders. Anne M. Johnson. 203p. (J). 1994. spiral bd. 24.00 (*1-884135-11-0*) Mayer-Johnson.
Math Exercises (in Division) Larry D. Andrew & Patricia Andrew. 1980. pap. 3.00 (*0-931992-39-7*) Penns Valley.
Math Exercises (in Multiplication) Larry D. Andrew & Patricia Andrew. 1980. pap. 3.00 (*0-931992-38-9*) Penns Valley.
Math Exercises (in Subtraction) Larry D. Andrew & Patricia Andrew. 1980. pap. 3.00 (*0-931992-37-0*) Penns Valley.
Math Explorations. Tina Tucker. (J). (gr. 1-3). 1997. pap. 12.95 (*1-57690-007-X*) Tchr Create Mat.
Math Facts: Survival Guide to Basic Mathematics. Theodore J. Szymanski. (Mathematics Ser.). 149p. (C). 1991. pap. 8.95 (*0-534-17154-0*) PWS Pubs.
Math Facts: Survival Guide to Basic Mathematics. 2nd ed. Theodore J. Szymanski. 160p. 1995. mass mkt. 6.95 (*0-534-94734-4*) PWS Pubs.
Math Finder Source Book: A Collection of Resources for Mathematics Reform. Laurie Kreindler & Barbara Zahm. 128p. (Orig.). (C). 1992. pap. text 12.95 (*0-9624352-1-X*) Learning Team.
*__Math 5.__ deluxe ed. School Zone Publishing Staff. (Illus.). (J). 2000. pap. 3.79 (*0-88743-141-0*) Sch Zone Pub Co.
Math Flashcards for Middle School: Math Facts Including Square Roots, Exponents, Greater & Less Than Signs. 40p. (J). (gr. 4-10). 1997. pap. text 5.00 (*0-9638483-9-9*) Midmath.
Math Flip-Over Series, 12 vols., Set. Kathy Knoblock. 48p. 1998. teacher ed. 27.00 (*1-58232-012-8*, BH 90157512); teacher ed. 27.00 (*1-58232-016-0*, BH 90151512) Bryan Hse.
Math Flipper: A Guide to Basic Mathematics. Jack L. Cushman. (Illus.). 49p. (J). (gr. 6 up). 1989. reprint ed. 6.95 (*1-878383-02-7*) C Lee Pubns.
Math Floormat. 1994. 28.48 (*0-395-67942-7*) HM.
Math Fluency Games. Jock Gunter et al. (Technical Notes Ser.: No. 8). 25p. (Orig.). 1974. pap. 2.00 (*0-932288-18-9*); pap. 2.00 (*0-932288-19-7*) Ctr Intl Ed U of MA.
Math for Automotive Trade. 3rd ed. Peterson. 320p. (C). 1995. mass mkt. 43.95 (*0-8273-6712-0*) Delmar.
Math for Autumn: Grades 1-2. (Daily Problem Solving Ser.). (Illus.). 88p. (J). (gr. 1-2). 1993. pap. text 14.95 (*1-55799-259-2*, EMC 359) Evan-Moor Edu Pubs.
Math for Autumn 2-3. Jo E. Moore. (Daily Problem Solving Ser.). (Illus.). 44p. (J). (gr. 2-3). 1996. pap., teacher ed. 14.95 (*1-55799-584-2*, 478) Evan-Moor Edu Pubs.
Math for Boys: A Book with the Number or Getting Boys to Love & Excel in Math! Carole Marsh. (Quantum Leap Ser.). (Illus.). (J). (gr. 4-12). 1994. pap. 19.95 (*1-55609-830-8*); lib. bdg. 29.95 (*1-55609-806-5*); disk 29.95 (*1-55609-878-2*) Gallopade Intl.
Math for Business. Baylor. 632p. 1998. pap. text 45.71 (*0-536-01386-1*) Pearson Custom.
*__Math for Business Applications.__ 2nd ed. 2000. teacher ed. write for info. (*0-201-61447-2*) Addison-Wesley.
Math for Business Applications. 2nd ed. Margaret L. MacLaughlin. 400p. (Orig.). 2000. pap. 59.95 (*0-201-61446-4*) Addison-Wesley.
Math for Calculus: Study Guide. 2nd ed. James Stewart & Lothar Redlin. (Mathematics Ser.). 1993. mass mkt., student ed. 20.75 (*0-534-20252-7*) Brooks-Cole.
Math for College Students: Arithmetic with Introduction to Algebra & Geometry. 5th ed. Ronald Staszkow. 600p. (C). 1996. pap. text, per. 44.95 (*0-7872-2448-0*, 41244801) Kendall-Hunt.
Math for Computer Science. 2nd ed. Arnold. 350p. 1996. pap. 61.00 (*0-13-234717-2*) P-H.
Math for Economics. Hoy. (C). 1996. pap. text, student ed. 23.70 (*0-201-55367-8*) Addison-Wesley.
*__Math for Electricity & Electronics.__ 2nd ed. Kramer. (C). 2001. pap. 63.75 (*0-7668-2701-1*) Delmar.
Math for Electronic Technology. Arthur Kramer. (Electronics Technology Ser.). 160p. 1995. student ed. 19.50 (*0-8273-5808-3*); student ed. 21.00 (*0-8273-5806-7*) Delmar.
Math for Elementary School Teachers. 4th ed. Swenson. 1996. pap. text, student ed. 29.33 (*0-13-259177-4*) P-H.
Math for Elementary School Teachers. 5th ed. Billstein. (C). 1996. text 45.00 (*0-201-40241-6*) Addison-Wesley.
Math for Elementary Teachers. Thomas A. Sonnabend. (C). 1993. pap. text, teacher ed., suppl. ed. 24.50 (*0-03-020714-2*, Pub. by Harcourt Coll Pubs) Harcourt.
Math for Elementary Teachers. Thomas A. Sonnabend. (C). 1993. pap. text, teacher ed. 34.00 (*0-03-020712-6*) Harcourt Coll Pubs.
Math for Elementary Teachers. 2nd ed. Thomas A. Sonnabend. (C). 1996. pap. text, teacher ed. 28.00 (*0-03-018362-6*) Harcourt.
Math for Elementary Teachers. 2nd ed. Thomas A. Sonnabend. (C). 1997. text 92.00 (*0-03-018367-7*) Harcourt.
Math for Elementary Teachers. 2nd ed. Thomas A. Sonnabend. (C). 1997. pap. text, teacher ed. 33.50 (*0-03-019523-3*) Harcourt.
Math for Elementary Teachers. 5th ed. Bennett. 2000. 34.50 (*0-07-232653-0*) McGraw.
Math For Elementary Teachers. 5th ed. Bennett. 1032p. 2000. 72.50 (*0-07-234681-7*) McGraw.
Math for Fun Projects. Andrew King. (Math for Fun Ser.). (Illus.). 224p. 1999. pap. 16.95 (*0-7613-0789-3*) Millbrook Pr.
Math for Girls: The Book with the Number to Get Girls to Love & Excel in Math! Carole Marsh. (Quantum Leap Ser.). (Illus.). 60p. (J). (gr. 3-9). 1994. pap. 19.95 (*1-55609-344-6*); lib. bdg. 29.95 (*1-55609-343-8*); disk 29.95 (*1-55609-345-4*) Gallopade Intl.
Math for Girls & Other Problem Solvers. Diane Downie et al. (Equals Ser.). (Illus.). 108p. (J). (gr. k-8). 1997. pap. 11.95 (*0-912511-01-X*, EQUALS) Lawrence Science.
Math for Health Occupations. Richard Harms & Margaret Rooney. 192p. (C). 1995. pap. text, spiral bd. 40.95 (*0-7872-1028-5*) Kendall-Hunt.
Math for Health Professionals. 3rd ed. B. Louise Whisler. 320p. (C). 1992. pap. text 37.50 (*0-86720-447-8*) Jones & Bartlett.
Math for Humans: Teaching Math Through 7 Intelligences. Mark Wahl. (Illus.). 256p. (J). (gr. 3-7). 1995. pap. 29.95 (*0-9656414-7-3*, Pub. by LivnLern Pr) M Wahl.
*__Math for Humans: Teaching Math Through 8 Intelligences.__ 2nd rev. ed. Mark Wahl. LC 99-94575. (Illus.). 256p. (Orig.). (J). (gr. 3-7). 1999. pap. 29.95 (*0-9656414-8-1*, Pub. by LivnLern Pr) M Wahl.
Math for Kids - And Other People Too. Theoni Pappas. LC 97-43091. (Illus.). 132p. (YA). (gr. 2 up). 1997. pap. 10.95 (*1-884550-13-4*) Wide World-Tetra.
*__Math for Liberal Arts.__ Richman. 394p. (C). 1998. pap. text 26.00 (*0-536-01588-0*) Pearson Custom.
Math for Life Sciences. Adler. 1998. pap., student ed. 30.95 (*0-534-35231-6*) Brooks-Cole.
Math for Life Scientists. Adler. LC 97-38657. (Mathematics Ser.). 1998. mass mkt. 96.95 (*0-534-34816-5*) Wadsworth Pub.
Math for Life Scientists: Preliminary Edition. Adler. LC 96-100817. (Mathematics Ser.). 1995. mass mkt. 58.95 (*0-534-34059-8*) Brooks-Cole.
Math for Logical Minds. Huong Nguyen. (Illus.). 382p. (J). (gr. 1-4). 1997. spiral bd. 50.00 (*0-9655937-1-1*) Logical Connect.
Math for Managerial, Life, & Social Sciences. Soo T. Tan. (Math Ser.). 1996. pap., teacher ed. 27.25 (*0-534-95186-4*) Brooks-Cole.
Math for Managerial, Life, & Social Sciences. Soo T. Tan. (Adaptable Courseware Ser.). 1998. 42.00 (*0-534-50123-0*) Brooks-Cole.
*__Math for Meds: Dosages & Solutions.__ 8th rev. ed. Laurie D. Munday. LC 76-43259. (Illus.). 306p. 2000. pap. text 34.95 (*0-918082-09-9*, 30,000) WI Pubns Inc.
Math for Meds - Dosages & Solutions. 7th rev. ed. Anna M. Curren & Laurie D. Munday. (Illus.). 336p. (C). 1995. pap. text 28.95 (*0-918082-07-2*) WI Pubns Inc.
Math for Merchandising: A Step-by-Step Approach. Evelyn C. Moore. LC 97-25438. 308p. 1997. pap. text 54.00 (*0-13-268723-2*) P-H.
*__Math for Merchandising: A Step-by-step Approach.__ 2nd ed. Evelyn C. Moore. 352p. 2000. pap. 40.00 (*0-13-018202-8*) P-H.
Math for Nurses: A Pocket Guide to Dosage Calculation & Drug Administration. 4th ed. Mary Jo Boyer. LC 97-42716. 320p. 1998. spiral bd. 15.95 (*0-7817-1021-9*) Lppncott W & W.
Math for Nurses: A Problem Solving Approach. Sally I. Lipsey & Donna D. Ignatavicius. (Illus.). 256p. 1993. pap. text 28.00 (*0-7216-6481-4*, W B Saunders Co) Harcrt Hlth Sci Grp.
Math for Nurses: A Problem Solving Approach. Sally I. Lipsey & Donna D. Ignatavicius. (Illus.). (C). 1993. pap. text, teacher ed. write for info. (*0-7216-6496-2*, W B Saunders Co) Harcrt Hlth Sci Grp.
Math for Plumbers & Pipefitters. 4th ed. Darchangelo. (Trade/Tech Math Ser.). 1989. pap., teacher ed. 16.00 (*0-8273-3954-2*) Delmar.
Math for Smarty Pants. Marilyn Burns. (Brown Paper School Bks.). (J). 1982. 17.05 (*0-606-04019-6*, Pub. by Turtleback) Demco.
Math for Smarty Pants: or Who Says Mathematicians Have Little Pig Eyes. Marilyn Burns. (Brown Paper School Bks.). (Illus.). 128p. (YA). (gr. 7 up). 1982. pap. 12.95 (*0-316-11739-0*) Little.
Math for Spring. (Daily Problem Solving Ser.). (Illus.). 88p. (J). (gr. 1-2). 1993. pap. text 14.95 (*1-55799-261-4*, EMC 362) Evan-Moor Edu Pubs.
Math for Spring 2-3. Jo E. Moore. (Daily Problem Solving Ser.). (Illus.). 44p. (J). (gr. 2-3). 1996. pap., teacher ed. 14.95 (*1-55799-582-6*, 476) Evan-Moor Edu Pubs.
Math for Summer, Grades 1-2. (Daily Problem Solving Ser.). (Illus.). 88p. (J). (gr. 1-2). 1993. pap. text 14.95 (*1-55799-262-2*, EMC 363) Evan-Moor Edu Pubs.
Math for Summer 2-3. Jo E. Moore. (Daily Problem Solving Ser.). (Illus.). 44p. (J). (gr. 2-3). 1996. pap., teacher ed. 14.95 (*1-55799-583-4*, 477) Evan-Moor Edu Pubs.
Math for the Automotive Trade. Peterson. (Trade/Tech Math Ser.). 1983. pap. 16.95 (*0-538-33020-1*) S-W Pub.
Math for the Automotive Trade. 2nd ed. Peterson. (Trade/Tech Math Ser.). 1989. pap., teacher ed. 14.00 (*0-8273-3555-5*) Delmar.
Math for the Brighter Child. (Illus.). (J). mass mkt. 6.95 (*0-340-72243-6*, Pub. by Hodder & Stought Ltd) Trafalgar.
Math for the Computer User. Danny P. Clark. 60p. (Orig.). 1989. pap. 12.95 (*0-317-93653-0*) Questar CA.
Math for the Real World, Bk. 1. 1993. 10.00 (*0-88336-838-2*) New Readers.
Math for the Real World, Bk. 2. 1993. 10.00 (*0-88336-839-0*) New Readers.
Math for the Real World, Bks. 1 & 2. 1993. teacher ed. 7.95 (*0-88336-837-4*) New Readers.
Math for the Very Young: A Handbook of Activities for Parents & Children. Lydia Polonsky et al. LC 94-20861. 210p. 1995. 29.95 (*0-471-01671-3*); pap. 14.95 (*0-471-01647-0*) Wiley.
*__Math for Welders.__ Nino Marion. LC 00-34077. (Illus.). 2000. write for info. (*1-56637-740-4*) Goodheart.
Math for Welders 2-3. Nino Marion. LC 95-2199. (Illus.). 224p. (YA). (gr. 9-12). 1995. text 26.00 (*1-56637-194-5*) Goodheart.
Math for Winter, Grades 1-2. (Daily Problem Solving Ser.). (Illus.). 88p. (J). (gr. 1-2). 1993. pap. text 14.95 (*1-55799-260-6*, EMC 361) Evan-Moor Edu Pubs.
Math for Winter 2-3. Jo E. Moore. (Daily Problem Solving Ser.). (Illus.). 44p. (J). (gr. 2-3). 1996. pap., teacher ed. 14.95 (*1-55799-581-8*, 475) Evan-Moor Edu Pubs.
Math for Workplace Success. Lloyd D. Brooks. 363p. (C). 1991. pap. text 17.95 (*1-56118-257-5*); pap. text, teacher ed. 8.00 (*1-56118-258-3*) Paradigm MN.
Math for Young Children. Jean M. Shaw & Sally S. Blake. LC 97-1900. 288p. 1997. pap. text 36.00 (*0-02-409764-0*) Macmillan.
*__Math for Young Children.__ 4th ed. Charlesworth. LC 99-17401. (Early Childhood Education Ser.). 400p. (C). 1999. pap. 46.95 (*0-7668-0233-7*) Delmar.
Math for Your First & Second Grader. Steven L. Slavin. 288p. 1995. pap. 12.95 (*0-471-04242-0*) Wiley.
Math Formulas Handbook. Alan K. Garinger. Ed. by Terry Tucker. 50p. 1984. student ed. 1.75 (*0-910475-24-5*) KET.
Math Foundations in Computer Science. Barrington. 2000. 60.50 (*0-07-006276-5*) McGraw.
Math Foundations Instructor's Resource Guide. (Foundations TV Ser.). 238p. 1990. ring bd. 180.00 (*0-910475-90-3*) KET.
Math Foundations Student's Guide. (Foundations TV Ser.). 181p. 1990. spiral bd. 20.00 (*0-685-51659-8*) KET.
Math Fun: Test Your Luck. Rose Wyler & Mary Elting. LC 91-3919. (Math Fun Ser.). (Illus.). 64p. (J). (gr. 4-7). 1992. pap. 5.95 (*0-671-74312-0*, Julian Messner); lib. bdg. 10.95 (*0-671-74311-2*, Julian Messner) Silver Burdett Pr.
Math Fun: With Pocket Calculator. Rose Wyler & Mary Elting. LC 91-16265. (Math Fun Ser.). (Illus.). 64p. (J). (gr. 4-7). 1992. pap. 5.95 (*0-671-74309-0*, Julian Messner); lib. bdg. 10.95 (*0-671-74308-2*, Julian Messner) Silver Burdett Pr.
Math Fun Grade 4. Dawn T. Jacobi. Ed. by Patricia Pedigo & Roger DeSanti. (Kelley Wingate Ser.). (Illus.). 127p. (J). (gr. 4). 1996. pap. text 10.95 (*0-88724-442-4*, CD-3724) Carson-Dellos.
Math Fun Grade 1. Dawn T. Jacobi. Ed. by Patricia Pedigo & Roger DeSanti. (Kelley Wingate Ser.). (Illus.). 125p. (J). (gr. 1). 1996. pap. text 10.95 (*0-88724-439-4*, CD-3721) Carson-Dellos.
Math Fun Grade 3. Dawn T. Jacobi. Ed. by Patricia Pedigo & Roger DeSanti. (Kelley Wingate Ser.). (Illus.). 129p. (J). (gr. 3). 1996. pap. text 10.95 (*0-88724-441-6*, CD-3723) Carson-Dellos.
Math Fun Grade 2. (Kelley Wingate Ser.). (Illus.). 127p. (J). (gr. 2). 1996. pap. text 10.95 (*0-88724-440-8*, CD-3722) Carson-Dellos.
Math Fun with Money Puzzlers. Rose Wyler. LC 92-351. (Math Fun Ser.). 64p. (J). (gr. 4-7). 1992. pap. 5.95 (*0-671-74314-7*, Julian Messner) Silver Burdett Pr.
Math Fun with Tricky Lines & Shapes. Rose Wyler. LC 92-351. (Math Fun Ser.). (J). (gr. 4-7). 1992. pap. 5.95 (*0-671-74316-3*, Julian Messner) Silver Burdett Pr.
Math Function Handbook. Louis Baker. 1991. pap. text 49.95 incl. disk (*0-07-911158-0*) McGraw.
Math Fundamentals. Freedman. 1995. 10.25 (*0-07-021933-8*) McGraw.
*__Math Games.__ Vicky Shiotsu. (Illus.). 64p. (J). (gr. 1-3). 2000. pap. 5.95 (*0-7373-0483-9*, 04839W, Pub. by Lowell Hse Juvenile) NTC Contemp Pub Co.
Math Games & Activities for the Primary Grades. Bill Bentley. 64p. (J). (gr. k-2). 8.99 (*0-86653-883-6*, FE0883) Fearon Teacher Aids.
Math Games & Activities from Around the World. Claudia Zaslavsky. LC 97-46918. (Illus.). 160p. (J). (gr. 3-7). 1998. pap. 14.95 (*1-55652-287-8*) Chicago Review.
Math Games & Centers. Morgan & Moore. (Illus.). 112p. (J). (ps-1). 1998. pap., teacher ed. 14.95 (*1-55799-660-1*, 735) Evan-Moor Edu Pubs.
Math Games for Adult & Child: Math Games for 2 Through 7-Year-Olds. rev. ed. Agnes Azzolino. LC 93-7994. (Illus.). 90p. (Orig.). (J). (ps-2). 1993. spiral bd. 20.00 (*0-9623593-4-3*) Mathematical.
Math Games for Fun & Practice. Alan Barson. 1993. pap. 16.75 (*0-201-29106-1*) Addison-Wesley.
Math Games for Middle School: Challenges & Skill-Builders for Students at Every Level. Mario Salvadori & Joseph P. Wright. LC 97-51422. (Illus.). 128p. (J). (gr. 6-9). 1998. pap. 14.95 (*1-55652-288-6*) Chicago Review.
*__Math Gene.__ Devlin. 2000. pap. 16.00 (*0-465-01619-7*, Pub. by Basic) HarpC.
*__Math Gene: How Mathematical Thinking Evolved & Why Numbers Are Like Gossip.__ Keith J. Devlin. 2000. 25.00 (*0-465-01618-9*, Pub. by Basic) HarpC.
*__Math Handbook-English: Algebra.__ 2nd ed. Robert K. Gerver et al. 2000. pap. 15.95 (*0-538-69538-2*) Thomson Learn.
*__Math Handbook-Spanish: Algebra 2.__ 2nd ed. Robert K. Gerver et al. 2000. pap. 15.95 (*0-538-69539-0*) Thomson Learn.
*__Math Homework That Counts: Grades 4-6.__ Annette Raphel. LC 00-40187. (Illus.). (J). (gr. 4-6). 2000. write for info. (*0-941355-27-6*) Math Solns Pubns.
*__Math Hooks.__ Robyn Silbey. (Illus.). (J). (gr. 1). 1999. pap. 10.95 (*0-673-58916-1*, GoodYrBooks) Addson-Wesley Educ.
*__Math Hooks 2.__ Robyn Silbey. (Illus.). (J). (gr. 2). 1999. pap. 10.95 (*0-673-58917-X*, GoodYrBooks) Addson-Wesley Educ.
Math in a Bag. Silva. (Illus.). 80p. (J). (gr. 1-3). 1995. pap. text, wbk. ed. 9.95 (*1-55734-199-0*) Tchr Create Mat.
Math in a Bath & in Other Fun Places, Too: Everywhere, Everyday Math Concept Book. Sara Atherlay. LC 94-30264. (Illus.). (J). (ps-3). 1995. 15.95 (*0-02-707601-6*) Macmillan.
Math in a Snap: Super Simple Beginning Math Experiences for Home & School. Deborah March & Nancy Canull. Ed. by Leslie Britt & Diane Hamstra. (Illus.). 64p. (Orig.). (J). (ps). 1996. pap. text 8.95 (*0-86530-329-0*, IP 329-0) Incentive Pubns.
Math in Action Subtraction. Fearon. 1991. pap. text 8.95 (*0-8224-4493-3*) Fearon Teacher Aids.
Math in American History. Don Blattner & Myrl Shireman. (Illus.). 96p. 1997. pap. text 10.95 (*1-58037-117-5*, Pub. by M Twain Media) Carson-Dellos.
Math in Astronomy. Robert Sadler. (Illus.). 128p. (YA). (gr. 5). 1997. pap. text 11.95 (*1-58037-038-1*, Pub. by M Twain Media) Carson-Dellos.
Math in Context 7. Nelson. (UM - International Math Ser.). 1992. teacher ed. 106.95 (*0-538-62698-4*) S-W Pub.
Math in Context 7. Nelson Canada Staff. (UM - International Math Ser.). 1992. pap., suppl. ed. 106.95 (*0-538-62699-2*); pap., suppl. ed. 106.95 (*0-538-62700-X*); mass mkt., student ed. 53.95 (*0-538-62697-6*) S-W Pub.
Math in Context 8. Nelson Canada Staff. (UM - International Math Ser.). 1992. teacher ed. 106.95 (*0-538-62704-2*); pap., suppl. ed. 106.95 (*0-538-62705-0*); mass mkt., student ed. 53.95 (*0-538-62703-4*) S-W Pub.
Math in Context 9. Ebos. (UM - International Math Ser.). 1995. pap., teacher ed. 106.95 (*0-538-64664-0*) S-W Pub.
Math in Context 9. Ebostalo. (UM - International Math Ser.). 1995. text, student ed. 53.95 (*0-538-64663-2*) S-W Pub.
Math in Context 9, Resource Masters. Ebos. (UM - International Math Ser.). 1995. pap. 93.95 (*0-538-64665-9*) S-W Pub.
Math in Geography. Don Blattner & Myrl Shireman. (Illus.). 96p. 1997. pap. text 10.95 (*1-58037-139-6*, Pub. by M Twain Media) Carson-Dellos.
Math in Geography. Tom Nelson. (Math Is Everywhere Ser.). (Illus.). 48p. (J). (gr. 4-6). 1994. pap. text, teacher ed. 6.45 (*1-55799-331-9*, EMC 115) Evan-Moor Edu Pubs.
Math in Space. Thomas Camilli. (Math Is Everywhere Ser.). (Illus.). 48p. (J). (gr. 4-6). 1994. pap. text, teacher ed. 6.45 (*1-55799-330-0*, EMC 114) Evan-Moor Edu Pubs.
Math in Stories That Rhyme. Story Time Stories That Rhyme Staff. (Illus.). 50p. (Orig.). (J). (gr. 4-7). 1992. ring bd. 19.95 (*1-56820-017-X*) Story Time.
Math in Stride, Bk. 1. Clara E. Clark & Betty J. Sternberg. (Illus.). 166p. (Orig.). (J). (gr. k-2). 1980. teacher ed. 19.95 (*0-934734-12-7*); pap. 5.95 (*0-934734-06-2*) Construct Educ.
Math in Stride, Bk. 2. Clara E. Clark & Betty J. Sternberg. (Illus.). 203p. (Orig.). (J). (gr. 1-3). 1980. teacher ed. 19.95 (*0-934734-13-5*); pap. 6.50 (*0-934734-07-0*) Construct Educ.
Math in Stride, Bk. 3. Clara E. Clark & Betty J. Sternberg. (Illus.). 219p. (Orig.). (J). (gr. 2-4). 1980. pap. 6.95 (*0-934734-08-9*) Construct Educ.
Math in Stride, Bk. 3. 3rd ed. Clare E. Clarke. (C). 1988. text, student ed., wbk. ed. 10.95 (*0-201-22371-6*) Addison-Wesley.
Math in Stride, No. 4. Clare E. Clark. 1989. pap. text, wbk. ed. 11.50 (*0-201-23653-2*) Addison-Wesley.
Math in Stride, No. 5. Clare E. Clark. 1989. pap. text, wbk. ed. 12.95 (*0-201-23657-5*) Addison-Wesley.
Math in Stride, No. 6. Clare E. Clark. 1989. pap. text, wbk. ed. 12.95 (*0-201-23661-3*) Addison-Wesley.
Math in the Bath: And Other Fun Places Too! Sara Atherlay. LC 94-30264. (Illus.). 32p. (J). (ps-1). 1995. 12.00 (*0-689-80318-4*) S&S Bks Yung.
Math in the Garden. Laura Mackey. (Math Is Everywhere Ser.). (Illus.). 48p. (J). (gr. k-1). 1994. pap. text, teacher ed. 6.45 (*1-55799-320-3*, EMC 092) Evan-Moor Edu Pubs.
Math in the Kitchen. Laura Mackey. (Math Is Everywhere Ser.). (Illus.). 48p. (J). (gr. 2-3). 1994. pap. text, teacher ed. 6.45 (*1-55799-327-0*, EMC 099) Evan-Moor Edu Pubs.
Math in the Real World of Architecture: Dimensions, Quantities, Shapes, & Patterns. Shirley Cook. Ed. by Catherine Aldy. (Illus.). 96p. (Orig.). (J). (gr. 5-8). 1996. pap. text 10.95 (*0-86530-342-8*, IP 343-5) Incentive Pubns.
Math in the Real World of Business & Living: Probability, Graphing, & Statistics. Shirley Cook. Ed. by Anna Quinn. (Illus.). 96p. (Orig.). (J). (gr. 5-8). 1996. pap. text 10.95 (*0-86530-343-6*, IP 343-6) Incentive Pubns.
Math in the Real World of Design & Art: Geometry, Measurements, & Projections. Shirley Cook. Ed. by Anna Quinn. (Illus.). 96p. (Orig.). (J). (gr. 5-8). 1996. pap. text 10.95 (*0-86530-344-4*, IP 344-4) Incentive Pubns.
Math in Weather. Don Blattner & Myrl Shireman. (Illus.). 96p. 1997. pap. text 10.95 (*1-58037-113-2*, Pub. by M Twain Media) Carson-Dellos.
Math in Your World. Weinberger & Roux. 98p. (C). 1998. spiral bd. 10.95 (*0-7872-5269-7*) Kendall-Hunt.

An Asterisk (*) at the beginning of an entry indicates that the title is appearing for the first time.

*Math into LaTeX. 3rd ed. George Gratzer. (Illus.). 520p. 1999. pap. 39.50 (0-8176-4131-9, Pub. by Birkhauser) Spr-Verlag.

*Math into Latex. 3rd ed. George A. Gratzer. LC 00-36088. 2000. write for info. (3-7643-4131-9) Birkhauser.

Math into LaTex: An Introduction to LaTex & AMS-LaTex. George Gratzer. 451p. 1995. text 54.50 (0-8176-3805-9) Birkhauser.

Math into Tex: A Simple Introduction to Ams-Latex George A. Gratzer. LC 92-6320. xxix, 294 p. 1993. write for info. (3-7643-3637-4) Birkhauser.

Math into TeX: A Simplified Introduction Using AMS-LaTeX. G. Gratzer. (Illus.). xiv, 187p. 1993. pap. 42.50 (0-8176-3637-4) Birkhauser.

Math Intro Kit: 4 Individual Sets. Marion W. Stuart. text. write for info. (0-943343-81-X) Lrn Wrap-Ups.

Math Invaders Jewel Window /95. Ssi. 1997. 6.00 (0-671-58007-8) S&S Trade.

Math Is Easy. Stephen Scarpitta. 320p. 1992. pap. text 28.50 (1-878038-01-X) Multi-Services.

*Math Is Language Too: Talking & Writing in the Mathematics Classroom. Phyllis Whitin & David J. Whitin. LC 99-87801. (Illus.). 118p. 2000. pap. 19.95 (0-8141-2134-9) NCTE.

Math Jingo. Gary Grimm & Phoebe Wear. 32p. (J). (gr. k-6). 1995. 12.00 (1-56490-010-X) G Grimm Assocs.

Math Journal. Sharon Vogt. (Illus.). 80p. (YA). (gr. 5). 1995. pap. text 9.95 (1-58037-028-4, Pub. by M Twain Media) Carson-Dellos.

Math Journal 2 Fall 90 5PK. 2nd ed. 1990. pap. 74.75 (0-201-59932-5) Addison-Wesley.

Math Journal1 Sum 90 5PK. 1990. pap. 74.75 (0-201-59931-7) Addison-Wesley.

Math K: An Incremental Development. Larson. (J). (gr. k). 1991. 175.00 (0-939798-90-5); teacher ed. 125.00 (0-939798-84-0) Saxon Pubs OK.

Math K: An Incremental Development, Manipulative kit. Larson. 1991. 340.00 (1-56577-001-3) Saxon Pubs OK.

*Math K: And Thinking Activities. Brighter Vision Publishing Staff. (Primary Skills Ser.). (Illus.). (J). 1999. pap. 2.25 (1-55254-114-2) Brighter Vision.

Math Kit. Ron Van Der Meer. (Illus.). 1994. 35.00- (0-02-621535-7, Scribners Ref) Mac Lib Ref.

Math Kit: A Three Dimensional Tour Through Mathematics. Ron Van Der Meer. 1994. 6.00 (0-684-19774-X) S&S Trade.

Math Lab. Frank Schaffer Publications, Inc. Staff. (Middle School Bks.). (Illus.). 1996. wbk. ed. 10.95 (0-7647-0012-X, FS-10188) Schaffer Pubns.

Math Lab. Ron Marson. (Task Cards Ser.: No. 7). (Illus.). 56p. 1994. teacher ed. 9.50 (0-941008-77-0) Tops Learning.

Math Leads the Way: Perspectives on Math Reform. 18p. (Orig.). 1993. pap. 7.50 (1-889483-17-6) Public Agenda.

Math Learning Centers for the Primary Grades. Carole Cook. 224p. 1991. pap. text 27.95 (0-87628-574-4) Ctr Appl Res.

Math Lessons K-5 for Teacher Appraisal Success. Amanda C. Gonzales & Dianne V. Shannon. Ed. by John Gonzales. (Illus.). 107p. (Orig.). (C). 1987. pap. 12.95 (0-9618511-0-4) Teachers Two.

Math Liberal Arts. Richard Billstein & Johnny W. Lott. (Illus.). 646p. (C). 1986. text 52.75 (0-8053-0863-6) Addison-Wesley.

Math Libs. Amy M. Burke. (Illus.). 93p. (J). (gr. 4-6). 1996. pap., wbk. ed. 14.99 (0-89824-223-1) Royal Fireworks.

Math Life. Parks. 1996. pap. text, student ed. 29.33 (0-13-259417-X) P-H.

Math Logic Puzzles. Kurt Smith. LC 95-48475. (Illus.). 96p. 1996. pap. 5.95 (0-8069-3864-1) Sterling.

Math Logic with Applications. Rubin. (C). 1990. pap. text, teacher ed. 34.00 (0-03-012809-9) Harcourt Coll Pubs.

Math Made Easy. (Illus.). 64p. 1993. spiral bd. 5.98 (1-56173-738-0, 3615100) Pubns Intl Ltd.

Math Made Easy. Carol Vorderman. LC 97-39622. 48p. (J). (gr. 2-6). 1998. 15.95 (0-7894-2799-0) DK Pub Inc.

Math Magic: The Human Calculator. Scott Flansburg & Victoria Hay. LC 94-7373. 352p. 1994. reprint ed. pap. 13.00 (0-06-097619-5, Perennial) HarperTrade.

Math Magic for Your Kids: Hundreds of Games & Exercises from the Human Calculator to Make Math Fun & Easy. annuals Scott Flansburg. LC 97-34764. 352p. (YA). (ps). 1998. pap. 13.00 (0-06-097731-0) HarpC.

Math Magic for Your Kids: Hundreds of Games & Exercises from the Human Calculator to Make Math Fun & Easy. Scott Flansburg. LC 96-17227. (J). 1997. 19.00 (0-688-13548-X, Wm Morrow) Morrow Avon.

Math Majors. Stephen Lambert & Ruth DeCotis. LC 98-7868. (Great Jobs for... Ser.). 304p. 1998. pap. 11.95 (0-8442-6422-9, 64229, VGM Career) NTC Contemp Pub Co.

Math Makes Sense: Teaching & Learning in Context. Rachel Griffiths & Margaret Clyne. LC 94-29523. 165p. 1994. pap. text 17.50 (0-435-08362-7) Heinemann.

Math Master Activity Book. David Williams. (Illus.). 144p. 1996. pap. text 14.95 (0-914534-15-7, 118) Stokes.

Math Master One: Strategies for Computation & Problem Solving. Jerry Howett. 1989. pap. text 6.00 (0-13-943960-9) P-H.

Math Master Two: Strategies for Computation & Program. Jerry Howett. 176p. (C). 1989. pap. text 6.00 (0-13-943978-1) P-H.

Math Masters, Lv. 3. 1994. 13.92 (0-395-67981-8) HM.

Math Masters, Lv. 4. 1994. 13.92 (0-395-67982-6) HM.

Math Masters, Lv. 5. 1994. 15.12 (0-395-67983-4) HM.

Math Masters, Lv. 6. 1994. 15.12 (0-395-67984-2) HM.

Math Mastery. 5th ed. Marilyn K. Simon. 128p. 1996. text 18.69 (0-7872-2112-0) Kendall-Hunt.

Math Mastery in 41 Steps on Your Scientific Calculator. John L. Stedl. 60p. (Orig.). 1988. student ed. 7.00 (0-685-33044-3); pap. 7.00 (0-9623913-0-1) Inst Advan Ed.

Math Mates: Linking Math & Literature. Petty Hoerner & Caroline Street. 96p. 1996. teacher ed. 10.99 (1-56417-851-X, GA1558) Good Apple.

Math Matters!, 13 vols. LC 98-7404. (J). 1999. lib. bdg. 335.00 (0-7172-9294-0) Grolier Educ.

Math Matters. Lynch. (MA - Academic Math Ser.: Bk. 2). 1994. text, teacher ed. 72.95 (0-538-63730-7) S-W Pub.

Math Matters. Lynch. (MA - Academic Math Ser.: Bk. 2). (SPA.). 1996. mass mkt., suppl. ed. 12.95 (0-538-65888-6) S-W Pub.

Math Matters. H. Lynch. 1993. teacher ed. 350.00 (0-538-61941-4) Sth-Wstrn College.

Math Matters. Olmstead Lynch. 1997. pap. 43.75 (0-538-68107-1) Sth-Wstrn College.

Math Matters. Olmstead. (Academic Math Ser.: Bk. 3). 1994. text 221.95 (0-538-61131-6) S-W Pub.

Math Matters. Olmstead. (MA - Academic Math Ser.: Bk. 2). 1995. teacher ed. 191.95 (0-538-63955-5) S-W Pub.

Math Matters. James V. Rauff. LC 94-42054. 512p. 1995. pap. 55.95 (0-471-30452-2) Wiley.

Math Matters. 3rd ed. Olmstead Lynch. 1994. pap. text 9.75 (0-538-61126-X) Sth-Wstrn College.

Math Matters, Bk. 1. Ebos. (UM - International Math Ser.). 1981. 61.95 (0-538-95000-5) S-W Pub.

Math Matters, Bk. 1. 2nd ed. Olmstead Lynch. (Academic Math Ser.). 2000. mass mkt. 43.95 (0-538-68659-6) S-W Pub.

Math Matters, Bk. 2. Ebos. (UM - International Math Ser.). 1983. teacher ed. 63.95 (0-538-95003-X) S-W Pub.

Math Matters, Bk. 2. Ebos. (UM - International Math Ser.). 1989. 60.95 (0-538-95002-1) S-W Pub.

Math Matters, Bk. 2. Lynch. (MA - Academic Math Ser.). (C). 1997. reprint ed. 38.95 (0-538-68109-8) S-W Pub.

Math Matters, Bk. 2. 2nd ed. Olmstead Lynch. (Academic Math Ser.). 2000. mass mkt. 43.95 (0-538-68661-8) S-W Pub.

Math Matters, Bk. 3. Olmstead. (MA - Academic Math Ser.). (C). 1997. mass mkt. 52.95 (0-538-68111-X) S-W Pub.

Math Matters, Bk. 3. 2nd ed. Olmstead Lynch. (Academic Math Ser.). 2000. mass mkt. 43.95 (0-538-68663-4) S-W Pub.

Math Matters: Alternate Assessment. Olmstead. (Academic Math Ser.: Bk. 3). 1994. text 72.95 (0-538-63389-1) S-W Pub.

Math Matters: An Integrated Approach. Lynch. (MA - Academic Math Ser.: Bk. 1). 1992. mass mkt. 12.95 (0-538-61101-4) S-W Pub.

Math Matters: An Integrated Approach. Lynch. (MA - Academic Math Ser.: Bk. 2). 1993. pap., wbk. ed. 12.95 (0-538-61113-8) S-W Pub.

Math Matters: An Integrated Approach. Lynch. (MA - Academic Math Ser.: Bk. 1). 1993. 221.95 (0-538-61107-3) S-W Pub.

Math Matters: An Integrated Approach. Lynch. (MA - Academic Math Ser.: Bk. 3). 1995. pap. 52.95 (0-538-61124-3) S-W Pub.

Math Matters: An Integrated Approach. Olmstead & Lynch. (MA - Academic Math Ser.: Bk. 3). 1994. mass mkt., wbk. ed. 12.95 (0-538-61125-1) S-W Pub.

Math Matters: An Integrated Approach, Vol. 1. Olmstead. (Academic Math Ser.). 1994. mass mkt. 29.95 (0-538-63968-7) S-W Pub.

Math Matters: An Integrated Approach, Vol. 2. Olmstead. (Academic Math Ser.). 1995. text 29.95 (0-538-63969-5) S-W Pub.

Math Matters: Integral Approach, Copyright Update. Lynch. (MA - Academic Math Ser.: Bk. 2). 1997. text 52.95 (0-538-63952-0) S-W Pub.

Math Matters: Spanish. (Ma - Academic Math Ser.). 1994. pap., suppl. ed. 12.95 (0-538-63959-8) S-W Pub.

Math Matters: Tests, 1. Lynch & Olmstead. (Academic Math Ser.). 1992. 2.50 (0-538-61102-2) S-W Pub.

*Math Matters: Understanding the Math You Teach, Grades K-6. Suzanne H. Chapin & Art Johnson. LC 00-32423. 2000. pap. write for info. (0-941355-26-8) Math Solns Pubns.

Math Matters Bk. 1: Assessment Options. Lynch. 1994. text 53.95 (0-538-63729-3) S-W Pub.

Math Matters Bk. 1: Copyright Update. Lynch. (Academic Math Ser.). 1995. text 59.95 (0-538-63953-9) S-W Pub.

Math Matters Bk. 2: Copyright Update. Olmstead. (Academic Math Ser.). 1995. text 59.95 (0-538-63954-7) S-W Pub.

Math Medley: Activities for Teaching Beginning Math Skills & Concepts. Sylvia Gay & Janet Hoelker. (Illus.). 64p. (Orig.). (J). (ps-3). 1992. pap. text 8.95 (0-86530-216-2, 195-0) Incentive Pubns.

Math Medley II: 200 Quick & Easy Beginning Math Activities for Home & School. Sylvia Gay. LC 96-75604. (Illus.). 64p. (Orig.). (J). (ps). 1995. pap. text 8.95 (0-86530-319-3, IP 319-3) Incentive Pubns.

Math Method Programming Number. John F. Leblanc et al. (Mathematics Ser.). (Illus.). 128p. (C). 1976. pap. text 4.00 (0-201-14624-X) Addison-Wesley.

Math Mind Benders A1: Deductive Reasoning in Mathematics. Anita Harnadek. 32p. (YA). (gr. 7 up). 1989. pap. 8.95 (0-89455-375-5) Crit Think Bks.

Math Mind Benders B1: Deductive Reasoning in Mathematics. Anita Harnadek. 32p. (YA). (gr. 9 up). 1989. pap. 8.95 (0-89455-376-3) Crit Think Bks.

Math Mind Benders C1: Deductive Reasoning in Mathematics. Anita Harnadek. 32p. (YA). (gr. 11 up). 1989. pap. 8.95 (0-89455-377-1) Crit Think Bks.

Math Mind Benders Warm Up: Deductive Reasoning in Mathematics. 2nd rev. ed. Anita Harnadek. 32p. (YA). (gr. 5 up). 1996. pap. 8.95 (0-89455-649-5) Crit Think Bks.

Math Mini-Mysteries. Sandra Markle. LC 92-11217. (Illus.). 64p. (J). (gr. 3-7). 1993. 14.95 (0-689-31700-X) Atheneum Yung Read.

Math Mini-Tests. Educational Solutions Staff & Caleb Gattegno. Incl. Elementary. 157.50 (0-87825-165-0); Elementary. 105.00 (0-87825-171-5); Elementary. teacher ed. 7.90 (0-87825-206-1); Elementary. 60.50 (0-87825-200-2); Elementary. teacher ed. 4.20 (0-87825-209-6); Intermediate. 126.00 (0-87825-172-3); Intermediate. teacher ed. 6.85 (0-87825-207-X); Intermediate. 52.50 (0-87825-201-0); Intermediate. teacher ed. 3.15 (0-87825-210-X); Multiplication. 14.70 (0-87825-202-9); Multiplication. teacher ed. 2.10 (0-87825-211-8); Primary 1. 89.25 (0-87825-162-6); Primary 1. 57.75 (0-87825-168-5); Primary 1. teacher ed. 5.80 (0-87825-203-7); Primary 3. 126.00 (0-87825-164-2); Primary 3. 84.00 (0-87825-170-7); Primary 3. teacher ed. 6.85 (0-87825-205-3); Primary 2. 99.75 (0-87825-163-4); Primary 2. 65.10 (0-87825-169-3); Primary 2. teacher ed. 5.80 (0-87825-204-5); 1981p. (gr. k-9). write for info. (0-318-58111-6) Ed Solutions.

Math Modeling. 2nd ed. Helen Christensen. 148p. (C). 1995. pap. text, per. 37.95 (0-7872-1575-9) Kendall-Hunt.

Math Modeling in Social & Biomedical Sciences. Edward Beltrami. (C). 1992. 50.00 (0-86720-292-0) Jones & Bartlett.

Math Motivators! Investigations in Geometry. Alfred S. Posamentier. 1982. text 12.95 (0-201-05583-X) Addison-Wesley.

Math Motivators! Investigations in Pre-Algebra. Alfred S. Posamentier. 1982. text 12.95 (0-201-05581-3) Addison-Wesley.

Math Motivators! Investigations in Pre-Algebra & Geometry. Alfred S. Posamentier. 1983. text 15.95 (0-201-05582-1) Addison-Wesley.

Math Munchies: A Collection of Math-Inspiring Recipes. Renee Ewing. (Illus.). 100p. (Orig.). pap. 19.95 (1-884340-01-6) MathAmer Math.

Math Mysteries. Barbara Helwig & Susan Stewart. (Little Books for Kids). (Illus.). 40p. (J). (gr. 2-5). 1991. spiral bd. 4.95 (1-881285-00-6) Arbus Pub.

Math Mysteries. rev. ed. Barbara Helwig & Susan Stewart. (Little Books for Kids). (Illus.). 90p. (J). (gr. 2-6). 1992. spiral bd. 4.95 (1-881285-03-0) Arbus Pub.

Math Mysteries: Basic Mathematics Skills. Jo Ellen Moore. (Illus.). 30p. (J). (gr. 3-5). 1995. pap., wbk. ed. 2.50 (1-58610-087-4, Learn on the Go) Learn Horizon.

Math Mysteries: Stories & Activities to Build Problem-Solving Skills. Jack Silbert. 1996. pap. text 14.95 (0-590-60337-X) Scholastic Inc.

Math Mysteries (Math) Jo E. Moore. (Mathematics Ser.). (Illus.). 32p. (J). (gr. 3-5). 1996. pap., teacher ed. 2.95 (1-55799-466-8, 4068) Evan-Moor Edu Pubs.

Math, 1985. Nichols. 1985. pap. 21.75 (0-03-064196-9); pap. 21.75 (0-03-064199-3); pap., wbk. ed. 12.75 (0-03-068827-2); pap., wbk. ed. 12.75 (0-03-068841-8); pap., wbk. ed. 12.75 (0-03-068854-X); pap., wbk. ed. 12.75 (0-03-068868-X); pap., wbk. ed. 14.75 (0-03-068881-7); pap., wbk. ed. 14.75 (0-03-068892-2) Harcourt Schl Pubs.

Math, 1985. Eugene D. Nichols. 1985. pap. 16.75 (0-03-064192-6) Harcourt Schl Pubs.

*Math 91: Practice Answer Key. 5th ed. 1999. (0-673-33155-5, Scott Frsmn) Addison-Wesley Educ.

Math Odyssey 2000: Puzzles, Mysteries, Unsolved Problems, Breakthroughs, & the People of Mathematics. Clement E. Falbo. 219p. (Orig.). (C). 1994. pap. text 24.80 (0-87563-477-X) Stipes.

Math of Astrology. Peter Murphy & Beth H. Koch. 1996. spiral bd. 14.95 (0-86690-456-5, K3590-014) Am Fed Astrologers.

Math of Money. Clayton. (MA - Academic Math Ser.). 1994. text, teacher ed. 107.95 (0-538-63497-9) S-W Pub.

Math of Money. 2nd ed. Austin. Date not set. pap. text, teacher ed. write for info. (0-314-09464-4) West Pub.

Math of Money. 2nd ed. Austin. 1994. mass mkt., wbk. ed. 26.75 (0-314-04648-8) West Pub.

Math of Money: With Algebra. Clayton. (Ma - Academic Math Ser.). 1994. pap. 93.95 (0-538-63472-3) S-W Pub.

Math of Money with Algebra - Extension Activities. Clayton. (MA - Academic Math Ser.). 1994. mass mkt. 11.95 (0-538-63496-0) S-W Pub.

Math Olympiad Contest Problems for Elementary & Middle Schools. 2nd expanded rev. ed. George Lenchner. Ed. by Gilbert W. Kessler & Lawrence J. Zimmerman. LC 96-77380. Orig. Title: Mathematical Olympiad Contest Problems for Children. (Illus.). 280p. (Orig.). (J). (gr. 4-8). 1997. pap. 24.95 (0-9626662-1-1) Glenwood Pubns.

Math on a Trip. Bob DeWeese. (Math Is Everywhere Ser.). (Illus.). 48p. (J). (gr. 4-6). 1994. pap. text, teacher ed. 6.45 (1-55799-324-6, EMC 096) Evan-Moor Edu Pubs.

Math on Call. Great Source Education Group Staff. (Illus.). 480p. (J). (gr. 5-9). 1997. text 20.66 (0-669-45771-X); pap. text 16.66 (0-669-45770-1) Great Source.

Math on File. Diagram Group Staff. (Illus.). 288p. 1995. ring bd. 165.00 (0-8160-2936-9) Facts on File.

Math on the Internet 1997-1998. 2nd ed. (C). 1997. write for info. (0-13-889833-2, Macmillan Coll) P-H.

Math on the Job: Graphic Designer. National Center for Research in Vocational Educati. (Orig.). 1987. pap. text 14.95 (0-923325-88-3) Conover Co.

Math on the Menu. Jaine Kopp & Denise Davila. (Illus.). 116p. (J). (gr. 3-5). Date not set. pap. 16.00 (0-924886-16-1, Pub. by Lawrence Science) Consort Bk Sales.

Math 1. (C). 1976. text, wbk. ed. write for info. (0-201-13301-6) Addison-Wesley.

Math 1, Vol. 2. (C). 1976. text. write for info. (0-201-13302-4) Addison-Wesley.

Math 1, Vol. 3. (C). 1976. text. write for info. (0-201-13303-2) Addison-Wesley.

Math 1, Vol. 4. (C). 1976. text. write for info. (0-201-13304-0) Addison-Wesley.

*Math-1: And Thinking Activities. Brighter Vision Publishing Staff. (Primary Skills Ser.). (Illus.). (J). 1999. pap. 2.25 (1-55254-116-9) Brighter Vision.

Math 113 College Algebra with Applications: Resource Manual. Jacqueline Stone. 132p. (C). 1998. per. 7.00 (0-7872-4759-6) Kendall-Hunt.

MATH PAC W/3.5"DSK(ST KEY DSK) Graves. (C). 1989. 32.00 incl. 3.5 hd (0-15-517703-6) Harcourt Coll Pubs.

MATH PAC W/(5.25") DISK. 3rd ed. Charles P. McKeague. 542p. (C). 1989. 32.00 (0-15-555254-6) SCP.

Math Pack: Includes: Complete Manual, 104-Piece Block Set, in a Back Pack. Katherine S. Koonce & Susan S. Simpson. (Illus.). 68p. 1996. spiral bd. 38.00 (1-880892-72-3) Com Sense FL.

Math Pack Bilingual English, Haitian Creole: PakMat. Henock Vilsaint. (Illus.). 64p. (J). (gr. 1-3). Date not set. wbk. ed. 5.50 (1-881839-64-8) Educa Vision.

Math Palette. Ronald Staszkow. (C). 1991. pap. text, teacher ed. 54.75 (0-03-047129-X) Harcourt Coll Pubs.

Math Palette. 2nd ed. Ronald Staszkow. LC 94-65398. (C). 1994. text 77.50 (0-03-000897-2) Harcourt Coll Pubs.

Math Palette. 2nd ed. Ronald Staszkow. (C). 1994. pap. text, teacher ed. 28.00 (0-03-000898-0) Harcourt Coll Pubs.

Math Palette. 2nd ed. Ronald Staszkow. (C). 1994. pap. text, teacher ed., suppl. ed. 40.00 (0-03-000902-2, Pub. by Harcourt Coll Pubs) Harcourt.

Math Panic. Laurie Buxton. LC 90-28874. 260p. (C). (gr. 9). 1991. pap. text 22.50 (0-435-08313-9, 08313) Heinemann.

Math Patterns. Ed. by Christine J. Dillon. 70p. 1995. pap. 5.95 (0-913717-73-8, 2155) Hewitt Res Fnd.

Math Phonics - Addition: Quick Tips & Alternative Techniques for Math Mastery. Marilyn B. Hein. Ed. by Judy Mitchell. (Illus.). 96p. (Orig.). (J). (gr. 1-3). 1997. pap., teacher ed. 9.95 (1-57310-085-4) Teachng & Lrning Co.

*Math Phonics - Decimals: Quick Tips & Alternative Techniques for Math Mastery. Marilyn B. Hein. Ed. by Judy Mitchell. 96p. (J). (gr. 3-6). 1999. 9.95 (1-57310-200-8) Teachng & Lrning Co.

Math Phonics - Division: Quick Tips & Alternative Techniques for Math Mastery. Marilyn B. Hein. Ed. by Judy Mitchell. (Illus.). 96p. (J). (gr. 3-6). 1997. pap. 9.95 (1-57310-095-1) Teachng & Lrning Co.

Math Phonics - Multiplication: Quick Tips & Alternative Techniques for Math Mastery. Marilyn B. Hein. Ed. by Judy Mitchell. (Illus.). 96p. (Orig.). (J). (gr. 3-6). 1996. pap. 9.95 (1-57310-069-2) Teachng & Lrning Co.

Math Phonics - Subtraction: Quick Tips & Alternative Techniques for Math Mastery. Marilyn B. Hein. Ed. by Judy Mitchell. (Illus.). 96p. (J). (gr. 1-3). 1997. pap. 9.95 (1-57310-096-X) Teachng & Lrning Co.

Math Phonics-Fractions: Quick Tips & Alternative Techniques for Math Mastery. Marilyn B. Hein. Ed. by Judy Mitchell. (Illus.). 96p. (Orig.). (J). (gr. 3-6). 1998. pap., teacher ed. 9.95 (1-57310-112-5) Teachng & Lrning Co.

Math Plans. Patricia Marshall. 432p. (C). 1997. pap. 32.00 (0-205-16270-3) Allyn.

Math Plausibles. 1988. 105.00 (0-8176-1986-0) Birkhauser.

Math Play! 80 Ways to Count & Learn. Diane McGowan & Mark Schrooten. Ed. by Susan Williamson. LC 96-37806. (Little Hands Ser.: Vol. 6). (Illus.). 141p. (Orig.). (J). (ps-1). 1997. pap. 12.95 (1-885593-08-2) Williamson Pub Co.

Math Playbook: A Math Skill Development System. Martin N. Mooney. (Illus.). 176p. (Orig.). (YA). 1997. per. 24.95 (0-9656857-0-5) Alexandrian Schl.

Math Plus. (J). (gr. k). 1992. pap. text, student ed. 18.50 (0-15-300137-2) Harcourt Schl Pubs.

Math Plus. (J). (gr. 1). 1992. pap. text, teacher ed., wbk. ed. 18.00 (0-15-300954-3); pap. text, student ed. 24.00 (0-15-300138-0); pap. text, wbk. ed. 10.00 (0-15-300945-4) Harcourt Schl Pubs.

Math Plus. (J). (gr. 2). 1992. pap. text, teacher ed., wbk. ed. 18.00 (0-15-300955-1); pap. text, student ed. 24.00 (0-15-300139-9); pap. text, wbk. ed. 10.00 (0-15-300946-2) Harcourt Schl Pubs.

Math Plus. (J). (gr. 3). 1992. pap. text, wbk. ed. 11.00 (0-15-300947-0) Harcourt Schl Pubs.

Math Plus. 1994. pap. text, wbk. ed. 18.00 (0-15-305110-8); pap. text, wbk. ed. 18.25 (0-15-305113-2); pap. text, wbk. ed. 20.00 (0-15-305117-5); pap. text, wbk. ed. 20.00 (0-15-305116-7) Harcourt Schl Pubs.

Math Plus. (J). (gr. 2). 1994. pap. text, wbk. ed. 10.00 (0-15-305102-7) Harcourt Schl Pubs.

Math Plus. (J). (gr. 3). 1994. pap. text, wbk. ed. 11.00 (0-15-305103-5) Harcourt Schl Pubs.

Math Plus. (J). (gr. 4). 1994. pap. text, wbk. ed. 11.00 (0-15-305104-3) Harcourt Schl Pubs.

Math Plus. (J). (gr. 5). 1994. pap. text, wbk. ed. 11.00 (0-15-305105-1) Harcourt Schl Pubs.

Math Plus. (J). (gr. 6). 1994. pap. text, wbk. ed. 11.25 (0-15-305106-X) Harcourt Schl Pubs.

Math Plus. (J). (gr. 7). 1994. pap. text, wbk. ed. 12.00 (0-15-305107-8) Harcourt Schl Pubs.

Math Plus. (J). (gr. 8). 1994. pap. text, wbk. ed. 12.00 (0-15-305108-6) Harcourt Schl Pubs.

Math Plus, 1994: Grade K, vol. 1. (J). (ps up). 1994. text, teacher ed. 63.25 (0-15-301870-4) H Holt & Co.

Math Plus, 1994: Grade K, vol. 2. (J). (ps up). 1994. text, teacher ed. 63.25 (0-15-301871-2) H Holt & Co.

M

An Asterisk (*) at the beginning of an entry indicates that the title is appearing for the first time.

Math Plus, 1994: Grade 1. (J). (gr. 1 up). 1994. text, teacher ed. 80.50 (0-15-301872-0); text, teacher ed. 80.50 (0-15-301873-9) H Holt & Co.

Math Plus, 1994: Grade 1. Holt Staff. (J). (gr. 1 up). 1994. text, student ed. 24.00 (0-15-301862-3) H Holt & Co.

Math Plus, 1994: Grade 2. (J). (gr. 2 up). 1994. text, teacher ed. 80.50 (0-15-301874-7); text, teacher ed. 80.50 (0-15-301875-5) H Holt & Co.

Math Plus, 1994: Grade 2. Holt Staff. (J). (gr. 2 up). 1994. text, student ed. 24.00 (0-15-301863-1) H Holt & Co.

Math Plus, 1994: Grade 3. (J). (gr. 3 up). 1994. text, teacher ed. 121.75 (0-15-301876-3); text, student ed. 41.00 (0-15-301864-X) H Holt & Co.

Math Plus, 1994: Grade 4. (J). (gr. 4 up). 1994. text, teacher ed. 126.50 (0-15-301877-1); text, student ed. 42.00 (0-15-301865-8) H Holt & Co.

Math Plus, 1994: Grade 5. (YA). (gr. 5 up). 1994. text, teacher ed. 126.50 (0-15-301878-X); text, student ed. 42.00 (0-15-301866-6) H Holt & Co.

Math Plus, 1994: Grade 6. (YA). (gr. 6 up). 1994. text, teacher ed. 136.25 (0-15-301879-8); text, student ed. 43.25 (0-15-301867-4) H Holt & Co.

Math Plus, 1994: Grade 7. 1994. text, teacher ed. 150.75 (0-15-301880-1) H Holt & Co.

Math Plus, 1994: Grade 7. (YA). (gr. 7 up). 1994. text, student ed. 47.50 (0-15-301868-2) H Holt & Co.

Math Plus, 1994: Grade 8. 1994. text, teacher ed. 150.75 (0-15-301881-X) H Holt & Co.

Math Plus, 1994: Grade 8. (YA). (gr. 8 up). 1994. text, student ed. 47.50 (0-15-301869-0) H Holt & Co.

Math Plus, 1992: Grade 3. Harcourt Brace Staff. 1989. student ed. 41.00 (0-15-300140-2) Harcourt Schl Pubs.

Math Plus, 1992: Grade 3. Harcourt Brace Staff. 1992. teacher ed. 126.50 (0-15-300150-X) Harcourt Schl Pubs.

Math Plus, 1992: Grade 3. 92nd ed. Harcourt Brace Staff. 1992. text, teacher ed. 128.50 (0-15-300149-6) Holt R&W.

Math Plus, 1992: Grade 4. Harcourt Brace Staff. 1989. student ed. 42.00 (0-15-300141-0) Harcourt Schl Pubs.

Math Plus, 1992: Grade 5. Harcourt Brace Staff. 1989. student ed. 42.00 (0-15-300142-9) Harcourt Schl Pubs.

Math Plus, 1992: Grade 5. Harcourt Brace Staff. 1992. 126.50 (0-15-300151-8) Harcourt Schl Pubs.

Math Plus, 1992: Grade 6. Harcourt Brace Staff. 1989. student ed. 43.25 (0-15-300143-7) Harcourt Schl Pubs.

Math Plus, 1992: Grade 6. Harcourt Brace Staff. 1992. teacher ed. 136.25 (0-15-300152-6) Harcourt Schl Pubs.

Math Plus, 1992: Grade 7. 92nd ed. Harcourt Brace Staff. 1992. text, student ed. 50.50 (0-15-300145-3) Holt R&W.

Math Plus, 1992: Grade 8. Harcourt Brace Staff. 1992. 150.75 (0-15-300154-2) Harcourt Schl Pubs.

Math Plus Science: A Solution. Judith Hillen et al. (J). (gr. 5-9). 1987. 16.95 (1-881431-06-1, 1302) AIMS Educ Fnd.

Math Power. Patricia C. Kenschaft. LC 97-16812. 272p. 1997. pap. 15.00 (0-201-77289-2) Addison-Wesley.

Math Power Set, 2 vols. World Book Staff. LC 96-60607. (Illus.). 848p. (J). (gr. 5-12). 1997. write for info. (0-7166-3897-5) World Bk.

Math Practice 1-2. (Kelley Wingate Ser.). (Illus.). 129p. (J). (gr. 1-2). 1995. pap. text 10.95 (0-88724-423-8, CD-3705) Carson-Dellos.

Math Practice Games. 1998. pap. text 4.95 (1-56822-749-3) Instruct Fair.

***Math Practice Grades 5-6.** Ed. by Aaron Uri Levy. (Kelley Wingate Ser.). (Illus.). vii, 128p. (J). (gr. 5-6). 1999. pap. 10.95 (0-88724-529-3, CD-3748) Carson-Dellos.

***Math Practice Grades 4-5.** Ed. by Aaron Uri Levy. (Kelley Wingate Ser.). (Illus.). vii, 128p. (J). (gr. 4-5). 1999. pap. 10.95 (0-88724-528-5, CD-3747) Carson-Dellos.

***Math Practice Grades K-1.** Ed. by Aaron Uri Levy. (Kelley Wingate Ser.). (Illus.). iii, 128p. (J). (gr. k-1). 1999. pap. 10.95 (0-88724-527-7, CD-3746) Carson-Dellos.

***Math Practice Grades 7-8.** Ed. by Aaron Uri Levy. (Kelley Wingate Ser.). (Illus.). vi, 128p. (YA). (gr. 7-8). 1999. pap. 10.95 (0-88724-531-5, CD-3750) Carson-Dellos.

***Math Practice Grades 6-7.** Ed. by Aaron Uri Levy. (Kelley Wingate). (Illus.). vii, 128p. (YA). (gr. 6-7). 1999. pap. 10.95 (0-88724-530-7, CD-3749) Carson-Dellos.

Math Practice 3-4. (Kelley Wingate Ser.). (Illus.). 130p. (J). (gr. 3-4). 1995. pap. text 10.95 (0-88724-425-4, CD-3707) Carson-Dellos.

Math Practice 2-3. (Kelley Wingate Ser.). (Illus.). 128p. (J). (gr. 2-3). 1995. pap. text 10.95 (0-88724-424-6, CD-3706) Carson-Dellos.

Math Preparation for Biology. Jacobson & Nicolaz. 1997. 15.00 (0-697-34124-0, WCB McGr Hill) McGrw-H Hghr Educ.

Math Preparation for General Chemistry PB 2E. 2nd ed. William L. Masterton & Emil J. Slowinski. 260p. (C). 1982. pap. text 32.00 (0-03-060119-3) SCP.

Math Primer: Economic Principles & Policy. 6th ed. Toutkoushian. (HB - Economics Ser.). 1994. mass mkt. 10.95 (0-538-85360-3) S-W Pub.

Math Principles & Practice: Preparing for Health Career Success. Michele Benjamin-Chung. LC 98-28717. 176p. 1998. pap. text 33.33 (0-8359-5272-X) P-H.

Math Principles for Food Service Occupations. 2nd ed. Robert G. Haines. 1988. pap. 24.95 (0-8273-3131-2) Delmar.

Math Principles for Food Service Occupations. 3rd ed. Haines. (Food & Hospitality Ser.). 32p. 1996. teacher ed. 14.00 (0-8273-6650-7) Delmar.

Math Principles for Food Service Occupations. 3rd ed. Robert G. Haines. LC 95-6003. 384p. (C). 1995. mass mkt. 41.95 (0-8273-6649-3) Delmar.

***Math Principles for Food Service Occupations.** 4th ed. Anthony J. Strianese. (Illus.). 384p. 2000. pap. text. write for info. (0-7668-1317-7) Delmar.

Math-Pro: Preparation for Real World Medical Administration. Cynthia R. Butters. 129p. 1992. pap. 17.95 (0-397-54904-0) Lppncott W & W.

Math Problem Solver. Ed. by Myrna Manly. 1993. pap., teacher ed. 8.95 (0-8092-3763-6) NTC Contemp Pub Co.

Math Problem Solver: Reasoning Skills for Application. Myrna Manly. LC 92-38293. 1993. pap. 11.93 (0-8092-3764-4) NTC Contemp Pub Co.

Math Problem-Solving Brain Teasers. Sylvia Connolly. (Brain Teasers Ser.). (Illus.). 80p. (J). (gr. 5-8). 1998. pap. 9.95 (1-57690-219-6, TCM2219) Tchr Create Mat.

Math Problem Solving for Grades 4 Through 8. James L. Overholt et al. 428p. (gr. 4-8). 1983. pap. text 36.00 (0-205-08024-3, H80245) Allyn.

Math Problem Visual Masters: With BASIC Program Solutions. Donald D. Spencer. 96p. 1988. pap. 15.96 (0-89218-154-0, NO. 3053) Camelot Pub.

Math Problem Visual Masters: With Pascal Program Solutions. Donald D. Spencer. 96p. 1988. pap. 15.95 (0-89218-155-9, NO. 3054) Camelot Pub.

Math Problems. J. Glasthal. 64p. (J). (ps-3). 1997. pap. 9.95 (0-590-96568-9) Scholastic Inc.

Math Professor: To Pass 185 Math Tests & Quizzes, Bk. 4. Alton D. Rison. (Illus.). 280p. (J). (gr. 2-12). 1997. pap. text 25.00 (0-9635870-4-8, Book 4) Sunbelt Theatre.

Math Projects: Organization, Implementation, & Assessment. Katie DeMeulemeester. Ed. by Joan Gideon. (Illus.). 73p. 1995. teacher ed. 12.95 (0-86651-836-3, 21340) Seymour Pubns.

Math Projects & Investigations. Ferguson. (UM - International Math Ser.). 1990. text 45.95 (0-538-62778-6) S-W Pub.

Math Projects for Young Students. Thomas. (J). 1991. pap. text 6.95 (0-516-95133-5) Childrens.

Math Projects in the Computer Age. David A. Thomas. (Projects for Young Scientists Ser.). (Illus.). 176p. (YA). (gr. 9-12). 1995. lib. bdg. 24.00 (0-531-11213-6) Watts.

Math Puzzlers. Sonya Kimble-Ellis. 64p. (J). 1998. 9.95 (0-590-20943-4) Scholastic Inc.

Math Puzzles. (Math Sticker Work Bk.). 16p. (J). 1998. pap. 4.95 (0-7894-3727-9) DK Pub Inc.

Math Puzzles & Games: A Workbook for Ages 6-8. Martha Cheney. (Gifted & Talented Ser.). (Illus.). 64p. (J). 1998. pap. 4.95 (1-56565-835-3, 08353W, Pub. by Lowell Hse Juvenile) NTC Contemp Pub Co.

Math Puzzles, Riddles & Dot-to-Dots: Basic Mathematics Skills. Jo Ellen Moore. (Illus.). 30p. (J). (gr. 2-3). 1995. pap., wbk. ed. 2.50 (1-58610-074-2, Learn on the Go) Learn Horizon.

Math Quest 1. Addison-Wesley Publishing Staff. 1985. pap. text, student ed. 15.00 (0-201-19100-8) Addison-Wesley.

Math Quest 3. Addison-Wesley Publishing Staff. LC 85-98688. (Illus.). 360p. 1986. pap. text, student ed. 26.56 (0-201-19300-0) Addison-Wesley.

***Math Rashes: And Other Classroom Tales.** Douglas Evans. (Illus.). 132p. (J). (gr. 4-7). 2000. 15.95 (1-886910-66-9, Front Street) Front Str.

Math Reasoning for Elementary Teachers. Long & Detemple. (C). 1997. pap. text 66.00 (0-201-30472-4) Addison-Wesley.

Math Refresher for Scientists & Engineers. John R. Fanchi. LC 97-18910. 272p. 1997. pap. 29.95 (0-471-19101-9) Wiley.

***Math Refresher for Scientists & Engineers.** 2nd ed. John R. Franchi. 320p. 2000. 34.95 (0-471-38457-7) Wiley.

Math Regrouping Games: Apple Set, Set. John E. Haugo. (Math Drill & Practice Ser.). 32p. (J). (gr. 4-6). 1982. 71.92 (0-07-079118-X) McGraw.

Math Regrouping Games: TRS-80 Model III, Set. John E. Haugo. (Math Drill & Practice Ser.). (Illus.). 32p. (J). (gr. 4-6). 1982. 71.92 (0-07-079224-0) McGraw.

Math Renaissance Teacher's Handbook: A Practical Guide to Getting the Most Out of Accelarated Mat. School Renaissance Institute Staff. (Reading Renaissance Library). (Illus.). 72p. 1998. pap., teacher ed. 14.95 (0-9646404-9-X) Schl Ren Inst.

***Math Renaissance Teacher's Handbook: A Practical Guide to Getting the Most Out of Accelerated Math in Your Classroom.** rev. ed. 75p. 1998. pap., teacher ed. 14.95 (1-893751-78-3, 5001) Schl Ren Inst.

Math Resource Guide, Vol. 3499. Linda Benton et al. Ed. by Jeanne Corker & Rozanne L. Williams. (Learn to Read Resource Guide Ser.). (Illus.). 80p. 1996. pap. text 25.98 (1-57471-146-6, 3499) Creat Teach Pr.

Math Review. (Quick Study Academic Ser.). 4p. pap. 3.95 (1-57222-137-2) Barcharts.

Math Review. Frank Schaffer Publications, Inc. Staff. (Homework Helpers Ser.). (Illus.). 56p. (J). (gr. 1). 1996. wbk. ed. 2.29 (0-86734-901-8, FS-11028) Schaffer Pubns.

Math Review. Frank Schaffer Publications, Inc. Staff. (Homework Helpers Ser.). (Illus.). 56p. (J). (gr. 2). 1996. wbk. ed. 2.29 (0-86734-903-4, FS-11030) Schaffer Pubns.

Math Review. Frank Schaffer Publications, Inc. Staff. (Homework Helpers Ser.). (Illus.). 56p. (J). (gr. 3). 1996. wbk. ed. 2.29 (0-86734-905-0, FS-11032) Schaffer Pubns.

Math Review. Frank Schaffer Publications, Inc. Staff. (Homework Helpers Ser.). (Illus.). 56p. (J). (gr. 4). 1996. wbk. ed. 2.29 (0-86734-907-7, FS-11034) Schaffer Pubns.

Math Review. Frank Schaffer Publications, Inc. Staff. (Homework Helpers Ser.). (Illus.). 56p. (J). (gr. 5). 1996. wbk. ed. 2.29 (0-86734-909-3, FS-11036) Schaffer Pubns.

Math Review Exerc CB. Hornsby. (C). 1997. pap. text 5.40 (0-201-33886-6) Addison-Wesley.

Math Review for Standardized Tests. Jerry Bobrow et al. (Cliffs Test Preparation Ser.). (Illus.). 422p. (Orig.). (C). 1985. pap. text 8.95 (0-8220-2033-5, Cliff) IDG Bks.

Math Riddles. Jo E. Moore. (Mathematics Ser.). (Illus.). 32p. (J). (gr. 2-3). 1996. pap., teacher ed. 2.95 (1-55799-454-4, 4056) Evan-Moor Edu Pubs.

Math Riddles. Harriet Ziefert. (Puffin Math Easy-To-Read Level 2 Ser.). 1997. 8.70 (0-606-11603-6, Pub. by Turtleback) Demco.

Math Riddles. Harriet Ziefert. (Illus.). 32p. (J). (gr. 1-4). 1997. pap. 3.50 (0-14-038541-X) Viking Penguin.

Math Riddles. Harriet Ziefert. LC 96-61641. (Illus.). 32p. (J). (gr. 2-4). 1997. 13.99 (0-670-87498-1) Viking Penguin.

Math Riddles: Basic Mathematics Skills. Jo Ellen Moore. Ed. by Joy Evans. (Illus.). 30p. (J). (gr. 2-3). 1995. pap., wbk. ed. 2.50 (1-58610-075-0, Learn on the Go) Learn Horizon.

Math Sci User's Guide. 2nd ed. 624p. 1990. pap. text 93.00 (0-8218-0233-X, USERSGUIDE) Am Math.

Math Seatwork Without Dittos. Amanda C. Gonzales & Dianne V. Shannon. Ed. by John Gonzales. (Illus.). 87p. (Orig.). (C). 1987. pap. 9.95 (0-9618511-1-2) Teachers Two.

Math Sense Manual. Katherine S. Koonce & Susan S. Simpson. (Illus.). 68p. 1996. spiral bd. 16.00 (1-880892-70-7) Com Sense FL.

Math Set A, 4 bks. Incl. Nickels & Pennies. large type ed. Deborah Williams. (Illus.). 12p. (Orig.). (J). (gr. k-2). 1997. text 4.95 (1-879835-87-8); Quarter Story. large type ed. Deborah Williams. (Illus.). 16p. (Orig.). (J). (gr. k-2). 1997. text 4.95 (1-879835-95-9); Robert Makes a Graph. Mia Colton. (Illus.). 16p. (Orig.). (J). (gr. k-2). 1997. text 4.95 (1-879835-89-4); We Like to Graph. large type ed. Mia Colton. (Illus.). 8p. (Orig.). (J). (gr. k-2). 1997. text 4.95 (1-879835-88-6); Set pap. 19.25 (1-879835-86-X) Kaeden Corp.

Math Set "B" Includes "In the Hen House," "The Bird Feeder," "How to Make Snack Mix," "How Much Does This Hold?", 4 vols. Meredith Oppenlander & Mia Coulton. (Illus.). (J). (gr. k-2). Date not set. pap. 19.25 (1-57874-071-1) Kaeden Corp.

Math, '77: Mathematical Subprograms for Fortran 77. Advanced Computing Applications Group, JPL Section. 1994. pap. write for info. (1-885644-00-0) Fortner Sftware.

***Math 76 Syllabus & Tests.** 10p. 1999. ring bd. 1.00 (1-57896-074-6, 1960, Hewitt Homeschl Res) Hewitt Res Fnd.

Math Shortcuts to Ace the SAT (New SAT) & the New PSAT/NMSQT. Kurt Trenkmann. 1996. 12.95 (1-882228-00-6) Achieve Pub Inc.

Math Shown Here! Illustrations from Math Spoken Here. Agnes Azzolino. LC 96-94236. (Illus.). 200p. 1996. pap. 20.00 (0-9623593-6-X, MSHH) Mathematical.

Math Simulations. Karen Hall. (Simulations Ser.). 144p. (J). (gr. 3-5). 1997. pap. 11.95 (1-57734-192-9) Tchr Create Mat.

Math Sin Limits, 1988: Grade 8. Fennell. 1987. 40.75 (0-03-009164-0) Harcourt Schl Pubs.

***Math 6.** deluxe ed. School Zone Publishing Staff. (Illus.). (J). 2000. pap. 3.79 (0-88743-142-9) Sch Zone Pub Co.

***Math 65 Syllabus & Tests.** 10p. (YA). 1999. ring bd. 1.00 (1-57896-073-8, 1959, Hewitt Homeschl Res) Hewitt Res Fnd.

Math 65 Teacher's Edition. 2nd ed. Nancy Larson. 1994. teacher ed. 85.00 (1-56577-037-4) Saxon Pubs OK.

Math Skill Games: Apple, Set. John E. Haugo. (Math Drill & Practice Ser.). (Illus.). 40p. (J). (gr. 4-6). 1982. 71.92 (0-07-079116-3) McGraw.

Math Skill Games: TRS-80 Model III, Set. John E. Haugo. (Math Drill & Practice Ser.). (Illus.). 40p. (J). (gr. 4-6). 1982. 71.92 (0-07-079222-4) McGraw.

Math Skillbuilders. Stephen R. Covey. (Step Ahead Plus Workbooks). (Illus.). 64p. (J). (gr. 3-4). 1995. pap., wbk. ed. 3.50 (0-307-03657-X, 03657) Gldn Bks Pub Co.

Math Skillbuilders. Golden Staff. (Step Ahead Plus Workbks.). (Illus.). 64p. (J). (ps-3). pap. 3.49 (0-307-03653-7, 03653, Goldn Books); pap., wbk. ed. 3.49 (0-307-03655-3, 03655, Goldn Books) Gldn Bks Pub Co.

Math Skills. Dalmatian Press Staff. (Precious Moments Workbooks Ser.). (J). 1998. pap. 2.99 (1-57759-116-X) Dalmatian Pr.

Math Skills. Myrl Shireman. (Illus.). 80p. (YA). (gr. 5). 1994. pap. text 9.95 (1-58037-060-8, Pub. by M Twain Media) Carson-Dellos.

Math Skills by Objectives. Ed. by Louise Keston. (Skills by Objectives Ser.: Bk. 2). 240p. (J). (gr. 7-9). 1985. pap. text 5.25 (0-317-46527-9) Cambridge Bk.

Math Skills by Objectives. Ed. by E. Speiser. (Skills by Objectives Ser.: Bk. 1). 288p. (J). (gr. 7-9). 1988. pap. text 8.00 (0-8428-0200-2) Cambridge Bk.

Math Skills by Objectives. Ed. by E. Speiser & Marjorie P. Weiser. (Skills by Objectives Ser.: Bk. 3). 352p. (J). (gr. 7-9). 1988. pap. text 8.00 (0-8428-0202-9) Cambridge Bk.

Math Skills for College Students. Judith Robinovitz. LC 97-43600. (Learning Express Basic Skills for College Students Ser.). 212p. 1997. pap. text 20.40 (0-13-080257-3) P-H.

Math Skills for Trips: Basic Mathematics Skills. Jo Ellen Moore. Ed. by Bob DeWeese. (Illus.). 30p. (J). (gr. 4-6). 1995. pap., wbk. ed. 2.50 (1-58610-099-8, Learn on the Go) Learn Horizon.

***Math Skills Made Easy.** Myrl Shireman. (Illus.). 96p. (YA). (gr. 5). 1999. pap. text 10.95 (1-58037-094-2, Pub. by M Twain Media) Carson-Dellos.

Math Skills Made Fun: Dazzling Math Line Designs, 1 vol. Cindi Mitchell. (Illus.). 64p. 1999. pap. text 9.95 (0-590-00088-8) Scholastic Inc.

***Math Skills Made Fun Dazzling Math Line Designs; Dozens of Reproducible Activities That Build Skills & Working Fractions, Decimals, Percents, Integers & Prime Numbers.** Cindi Mitchell. 1999. pap. 9.95 (0-590-00085-3) Scholastic Inc.

***Math Skills Made Fun: Great Graph Art Decimals & Fractions.** Cindi Mitchell. (Illus.). (J). 2000. pap. 10.95 (0-590-64375-4) Scholastic Inc.

***Math Skills Made Fun: Great Graph Art Multiplication & Division.** Cindi Mitchell. (Illus.). 64p. (J). (gr. 3-11). 2000. pap. 15.99 (0-590-64374-6) Scholastic Inc.

***Math Skills Practice & Apply: Grade 4.** Steve Davis. (Illus.). 128p. 2000. pap. text 10.95 (1-58037-127-2, Pub. by M Twain Media) Carson-Dellos.

***Math Skills Practice & Apply: Grade 5.** Steve Davis. (Illus.). 128p. 2000. pap. text 10.95 (1-58037-128-0, Pub. by M Twain Media) Carson-Dellos.

***Math Skills Practice & Apply: Grade 6.** Steve Davis. (Illus.). 128p. 2000. pap. text 10.95 (1-58037-129-9, Pub. by M Twain Media) Carson-Dellos.

***Math Skills Practice & Apply: Grade 7.** Steve Davis. (Illus.). 128p. 2000. pap. text 10.95 (1-58037-130-2, Pub. by M Twain Media) Carson-Dellos.

Math Skills That Work: A Functional Approach for Life & Work, Bk. 1. Robert Mitchell. 1991. pap. 11.93 (0-8092-4124-2) NTC Contemp Pub Co.

***Math Skills Worksheets.** HRW Staff. (Science Spectrum). 2000. 10.20 (0-03-055604-X) Harcourt Schl Pubs.

Math Smart: Essential Math for These Numeric Times. Marcia Lerner & Princeton Review Publishing Staff. LC 93-18543. (Princeton Review Ser.). 304p. 1993. pap. 12.00 (0-679-74616-1) Villard Books.

Math Smart for Businesses: Essentials of Managerial Finance. Rajiv Dev. LC 97-208384. (Princeton Review Ser.). 1997. pap. 12.00 (0-679-77356-8) Villard Books.

Math Smart II. Marcia Lerner. LC 98-132835. (Princeton Review Ser.). 288p. 1997. pap. 12.00 (0-679-78383-0) Random.

Math Smart Jr. II: More Math Made Easy. Princeton Rev Staff. LC 98-229112. (Princeton Review Ser.). (J). 1998. pap. 10.00 (0-679-78377-6) Random.

Math Smart Junior: Grade School Math Made Easy. Princeton Review Publishing Staff & Marcia Lerner. (J). (gr. 6-8). 1995. pap. 12.00 (0-679-75935-2) Villard Books.

***Math Snacks: Problem-Solving Fun with Food Manipulatives.** Eliza Anne Sorte. (Illus.). 144p. (J). 1999. pap., teacher ed. 14.95 (1-57690-323-0, TCM2323) Tchr Create Mat.

Math Spoken Here! Math Dictionary for Arithmetic & Algebra. Agnes Azzolino. LC 95-94794. (Illus.). 140p. (Orig.). 1995. pap., spiral bd. 10.00 (0-9623593-5-1) Mathematical.

Math Sponges. Leigh Childs & Nancy Adams. 112p. 1997. pap. text 8.95 (0-86651-248-9) Seymour Pubns.

Math Standards in Action: Professional Guide. Amy S. Flint. LC 96-226290. 1997. pap. text 9.95 (1-55734-886-3) Tchr Create Mat.

***Math Start-Ups.** Scott McMorrow. (Illus.). (J). 1999. pap. 11.95 (1-57612-114-3) Monday Morning Bks.

***Math Starters! Five-to-Ten Minute Activities That Make Students Think.** Judith A. Muschla. LC 98-28657. (Illus.). (YA). (gr. 6-12). 1999. pap. 29.95 (0-87628-566-3) Ctr Appl Res.

Math Statistics with Applications. 3rd ed. Mendenhall. (Statistics Ser.). 1986. teacher ed. 3.00 (0-87150-942-3) PWS Pubs.

Math Statistics with Applications. 4th ed. Wackerly-Sheaffer Mendenhall. (Adaptable Courseware-Hardside Ser.). 26.00 (0-534-32032-5) Brooks-Cole.

Math Stories. Kari Jenson Gold. (Early Math Big Bks.). (Illus.). 16p. (J). (ps-2). Date not set. pap. 16.95 (1-58273-280-9) Newbridge Educ.

Math Stories: Reading, Level 3-4. 1993. 9.00 (0-88336-746-7); 9.00 (0-88336-747-5); 9.00 (0-88336-748-3); teacher ed. 5.95 (0-88336-749-1) New Readers.

Math Stories for Problem Solving Success: Ready-to-Use Activities for Grades 7-12. James L. Overholt et al. 256p. 1989. pap. text 28.95 (0-87628-570-1) Ctr Appl Res.

Math Structures for Computer Science. 2nd ed. Judith L. Gersting. LC 86-9974. (Computer Science Ser.). (Illus.). 618p. (C). 1986. teacher ed. 5.60 (0-7167-1803-0) W H Freeman.

Math Structures for Computer Science. 4th ed. Gersting. LC 98-29149. xix, 748p. 1998. text 79.95 (0-7167-8306-1) W H Freeman.

Math Study Skills Workbook: Your Guide to Reducing Test Anxiety & Improving Study Strategies. Paul Nolting. 112p. 1998. pap., wbk. ed. 9.95 (0-940287-28-5) Acad Success Pr.

Math Study Skills Workshop Kit. Catherine Tobin. Ed. by Daniel Marshak & Kiyo Morimoto. 1981. pap. text 16.50 (0-88210-122-6) Natl Assn Principals.

***Math Success Series.** (Illus.). (YA). (gr. 4-10). 2000. lib. bdg. write for info. (0-7660-1601-3) Enslow Pubs.

MATH SUPPL - ECONOMICS, 6/E (B. 6th ed. Denise Kummer. 33p. (C). 1994. pap. text 14.00 (0-03-004754-4) Dryden Pr.

Math Survival Guide: Tips for Science Students. Jeffrey R. Appling. LC 94-223785. 140p. 1994. pap. 28.95 (0-471-03103-8) Wiley.

Math TAAS Cross Number/Crossword Puzzles for Exit Level. Margaret Dominguez & Marissa Dominguez. (Illus.). 50p. (YA). (gr. 9-12). 1997. ring bd. 19.95 (1-889684-07-4) Texas Testing.

Math TAAS Cross Number/Crossword Puzzles for 8th & 9th Grades. Margaret Dominguez & Marissa Dominguez. (Illus.). 63p. (YA). (gr. 8-9). 1997. ring bd. 19.95 (1-889684-06-6) Texas Testing.

An Asterisk (*) at the beginning of an entry indicates that the title is appearing for the first time.

Math TAAS Study Guide. Margaret Dominguez & Marissa Dominguez. (Illus.). 208p. (Orig.). (YA). (gr. 9-12). 1995. pap. text 9.99 (*0-9650840-0-0*) Texas Testing.

Math Talk. Mathematical Association Staff. 66p. (C). (gr. k). 1990. pap. text 16.50 (*0-435-08307-4*, 08307) Heinemann.

Math Talk. Theoni Pappas. LC 90-25380. (Illus.). 72p. (Orig.). 1991. pap. 8.95 (*0-933174-74-8*) Wide World-Tetra.

***Math Talks for Undergraduates.** Serge Lang. LC 98-55410. 112p. 1999. 29.95 (*0-387-98749-5*) Spr-Verlag.

Math Teachers Problem Solving Study Guide. 4th ed. Miller. 488p. 1997. pap., student ed. 31.95 (*0-471-36868-7*) Wiley.

Math Teacher's Book of Lists. Judith A. Muschla & Gary R. Muschla. LC 94-36753. 432p. (C). 1994. spiral bd. 29.95 (*0-13-180357-3*) P-H.

Math Teacher's Book of Lists. Judith A. Muschla & Gary R. Muschla. LC 94-36753. 432p. (C). 1996. pap., teacher ed. 29.50 (*0-13-255910-2*) P-H.

Math Teachers Press: Using Models to Learn Addition & Subtraction Facts. rev. ed. Caryl K. Pierson. 52p. (J). (gr. 1-2). 1991. pap. 4.95 (*0-933383-10-X*) Math Teachers Pr.

Math Teachers Press: Using Models to Learn Multiplication & Division Facts. rev. ed. Caryl K. Pierson. (Illus.). 52p. 1991. pap. 4.95 (*0-933383-11-8*) Math Teachers Pr.

Math Teachers Student Research Handbook. 5th ed. Swenson. write for info. (*0-471-37720-1*) Wiley.

Math Teaching Handbook: For Tutors, Parents & Teachers. Persis J. Herold & Elizabeth Sampson. (Illus.). 236p. 1992. pap. 27.50 (*0-9633701-0-3*) Hypatia Pr.

Math Teaching Manual: Individual Book. Marion W. Stuart. text. write for info. (*0-943343-70-4*) Lrn Wrap-Ups.

Math Tensor: A System for Doing Tensor Analysis by Computer. Leonard Parker & Steven M. Christensen. 1994. write for info. (*0-318-72530-4*) Addison-Wesley.

Math Text Academic Skills. Juelg. 1990. pap. 3.00 (*0-13-915711-5*, Prentice Hall) P-H.

Math the Easy Way: Your Key to Learning. 3rd ed. Anthony Prindle & Katie Prindle. Ed. by Eugene J. Farley. LC 95-20390. (Barron's Easy Way Ser.). (Illus.). 232p. 1996. pap. 11.95 (*0-8120-9139-6*) Barron.

Math, the Exciting Language. James O. Morrison. 120p. 1986. pap. text 6.50 (*0-935920-42-0*, Ntl Pubs Blck) P-H.

Math Theory Hole. S. Chandrasekhar. (Illus.). 672p. 1993. pap. text 60.00 (*0-19-852050-6*) OUP.

Math Thinker Sheets. Becky Daniel. 64p. (J). (gr. 4-8). 1988. student ed. 8.99 (*0-86653-429-6*, GA1036) Good Apple.

Math Thinking Motivators. Bob Bernstein. 96p. (J). (gr. 2-7). 1988. student ed. 11.99 (*0-86653-431-8*, GA1049) Good Apple.

***Math-3: And Thinking Activities.** Brighter Vision Publishing Staff. (Primary Skills Ser.). (Illus.). (J). 1999. pap. 2.25 (*1-55254-120-7*) Brighter Vision.

Math Three Home Study Kit. Nancy Larson. 1994. 90.00 (*1-56577-039-0*) Saxon Pubs OK.

Math Through Children's Literature: Making the NCTM Standards Come Alive. Kathryn L. Braddon et al. LC 91-34286. xviii, 218p. 1993. pap. text 23.50 (*0-87287-932-1*) Teacher Ideas Pr.

Math Ties A1: Problem Solving, Logic Teasers & Math Puzzles. Terri Santi. (Illus.). 84p. (J). (gr. 4-6). 1998. pap. 14.95 (*0-89455-670-3*, MP4101) Crit Think Bks.

Math Ties B1 Vol. 2: Problem Solving, Logic Teasers & Math Puzzles. Terri Santi. (Illus.). 79p. (YA). (gr. 6-8). 1998. pap. 14.95 (*0-89455-671-1*, MP4102) Crit Think Bks.

Math Time: The Learning Environment. Kathy Richardson. Ed. by Karen Antell. (Illus.). 143p. (Orig.). 1996. pap. 19.95 (*1-888117-01-X*) Educ Enrich.

Math to Build On: A Book for Those Who Build. Johnny E. Hamilton & Margaret S. Hamilton. LC 93-10890. (Illus.). 240p. (C). 1993. text 24.95 (*0-9624197-1-0*) Constrctn Trades.

***Math To-Go Books & Hands-On Library, Set.** Irene D. H. Sasman. (Illus.). (J). (gr. 1-2). 1999. pap. 99.95 (*1-56831-517-1*) Lrning Connect.

***Math To-Go Books & Hands-On Library, Set.** Irene D. H. Sasman. (Illus.). (J). (gr. 3-5). 1999. pap. 99.95 (*1-56831-519-8*) Lrning Connect.

***Math To-Go Books & Hands-On Library, Set.** Irene D. H. Sasman. (Illus.). (J). (ps-1). 1999. pap. 99.95 (*1-56831-515-5*) Lrning Connect.

***Math to Know: A Mathematics Handbook.** Great Source Ed. Group Staff. (Illus.). 483p. (J). (gr. 3-4). 2000. text 20.67 (*0-669-47154-2*); pap. text 16.67 (*0-669-47153-4*) Great Source.

***Math Together: Green Books.** Jez Alborough. (Illus.). (YA). (ps up). 2000. pap. 19.99 (*0-7636-0954-4*) Candlewick Pr.

***Math Together: Yellow Books.** Jez Alborough. (Illus.). (YA). (ps up). 2000. 19.99 (*0-7636-0947-1*) Candlewick Pr.

Math Toolkit C++ Williamson. 1995. pap. text 43.00 (*0-02-428101-8*) P-H.

***Math Toolkit for Real-Time Development.** Jack Crenshaw. 416p. 2000. pap. 44.95 incl. cd-rom (*1-929629-09-5*, Pub. by C M P Books) Publishers Group.

Math Trailblazers. Tims Project Inc. Staff. 264p. (J). (gr. 2 up). 1996. pap. text, student ed. 17.90 (*0-7872-0244-4*) Kendall-Hunt.

Math Trailblazers: Adventure Book Big Book. Tims Project. 136p. (J). (gr. 3). 1996. student ed., spiral bd. 15.90 (*0-7872-0249-5*) Kendall-Hunt.

Math Trailblazers: Adventure Book Big Book, Vol. 1. Tims Project, Inc. Staff. 60p. (J). (gr. 1 up). 1996. 114.90 (*0-7872-0241-X*) Kendall-Hunt.

Math Trailblazers: Adventure Book Big Book, Vol. 11. Tims Project, Inc. Staff. 56p. (J). (gr. 1 up). 1996. 114.90 (*0-7872-1191-5*) Kendall-Hunt.

Math Trailblazers: Student Guide. Tims Project Inc. Staff. 344p. (J). (gr. 3 up). 1996. text, student ed. 29.90 (*0-7872-0248-7*) Kendall-Hunt.

***Math Trek: Adventures in the Mathzone.** Ivars Peterson. LC 99-25900. 128p. 1999. pap. 12.95 (*0-471-31570-2*) Wiley.

***Math Trek 2: A Mathematical Space Odyssey.** Ivars Peterson & Nancy Henderson. 128p. 2000. pap. 12.95 (*0-471-31571-0*) Wiley.

Math Tricks, Puzzles & Games. Raymond Blum. LC 93-46750. (Illus.). 128p. (J). 1994. 14.95 (*0-8069-0582-4*) Sterling.

Math Tricks, Puzzles & Games. Raymond Blum. (Illus.). 128p. 1995. pap. 5.95 (*0-8069-0583-2*) Sterling.

Math Trivial Pursuit - Intermediate Level. Patricia Dunn. (Illus.). 64p. (J). (gr. 4-6). 1989. student ed. 12.99 (*0-86653-468-7*, GA1073) Good Apple.

Math Trivial Pursuit - Junior High Level. Patricia Dunn. (Illus.). 64p. (J). (gr. 7-9). 1989. student ed. 12.99 (*0-86653-469-5*, GA1074) Good Apple.

Math Two. Carolyn A. Maher. 1981. 20.00 (*0-07-039595-0*) McGraw.

***Math-2: And Thinking Activities.** Brighter Vision Publishing Staff. (Primary Skills Ser.). (Illus.). (J). 1999. pap. 2.25 (*1-55254-118-5*) Brighter Vision.

Math Two Home Study Kit. Nancy Larson. 1994. 87.50 (*1-56577-038-2*) Saxon Pubs OK.

***Math Uab Mathonwy: Text from the Diplomatic Edition of the White Book of Rhydderch, by J. Gwenogvryn Evans.** Patrick K. Ford. LC 99-55813. 102p. 1999. 15.95 (*0-926689-06-1*) Ford & Bailie Pubs.

Math Unit & MMX Programming. unabridged ed. Julio Sanchez. (Professional Programming Ser.). (Illus.). xix, 608p. (Orig.). 1999. pap. 49.95 (*0-9665088-3-1*) Skipanon SW Assocs.

Math Unlimited, 1987: Grade 5. Fennell. 1987. 40.50 (*0-03-006437-6*) Harcourt Schl Pubs.

Math Unlimited, 1991. Harcourt Brace Staff. 1991. 45.25 (*0-15-351569-4*) Harcourt Schl Pubs.

Math Unlimited, 1991: Grade K. 1991. pap. text, teacher ed. 68.00 (*0-15-351570-8*); pap. text, student ed. 17.50 (*0-15-351560-0*) Harcourt Schl Pubs.

Math Unlimited, 1991: Grade 1. 1991. pap. text, teacher ed. 73.00 (*0-15-351571-6*); pap. text, student ed. 23.00 (*0-15-351561-9*) Harcourt Schl Pubs.

Math Unlimited, 1991: Grade 2. 1991. pap. text, teacher ed. 73.00 (*0-15-351572-4*); pap. text, student ed. 23.00 (*0-15-351562-7*) Harcourt Schl Pubs.

Math Unlimited, 1991: Grade 3. 1991. pap. text, teacher ed. 85.75 (*0-15-351573-2*) Harcourt Schl Pubs.

Math Unlimited, 1991: Grade 3. Harcourt Brace Staff. 1991. student ed. 40.00 (*0-15-351563-5*) Harcourt Schl Pubs.

Math Unlimited, 1991: Grade 7. Harcourt Brace Staff. 1991. teacher ed. 95.50 (*0-15-351577-5*) Harcourt Schl Pubs.

Math Unlimited, 1991: Grade 8. Harcourt Brace Staff. 1991. teacher ed. 95.50 (*0-15-351578-3*) Harcourt Schl Pubs.

Math Verses to Stretch Minds, Vol. II. 1989. pap. write for info. (*0-88092-009-2*) Trillium Pr.

Math Verses to Stretch Minds, Vol. III. 1989. pap. write for info. (*0-88092-010-6*) Trillium Pr.

Math Verses to Stretch Minds, Vol. IV. 1989. pap. write for info. (*0-88092-011-4*) Trillium Pr.

Math Verses with Twists, Vol. I. Sidney R. Levine. 30p. 1989. pap. write for info. (*0-88092-008-4*, Kav Bks) Royal Fireworks.

Math War! (High Q Ser.). (Illus.). 60p. (J). (ps-6). 1998. pap. 2.99 (*0-7681-0071-2*, McClanahan Book) Learn Horizon.

***Math War-Multiplication.** 56p. (gr. 3-7). 1998. pap. text 2.79 (*0-88743-287-5*) Sch Zone Pub Co.

Math Warm-Up for Grades 2 & 3: Short Exercises for Review & Exploration. Karen M. Higgins et al. Ed. by Joan Gideon. (Math Warm-Ups Ser.). (Illus.). 90p. (Orig.). (J). (gr. 2-3). 1996. pap., teacher ed. 11.95 (*1-57232-283-7*, 21811) Seymour Pubns.

Math Warm-Ups. Scott McFadden. 96p. (J). (gr. 4-6). 1997. pap. text 11.95 (*0-86651-612-3*) Seymour Pubns.

Math Warm-Ups. Scott McFadden. (J). (gr. 7-9). 1997. pap. text 11.50 (*0-86651-107-5*) Seymour Pubns.

***Math We Need to "Know" & "Do" Content Standards for Elementary & Middle Grades.** Pearl G. Solomon. LC 00-9203. 2000. write for info. (*0-7619-7577-2*) Corwin Pr.

Math Whiz Kids, 4 vols. Arlene Brown. Ed. by Shirley Durst. (Illus.). 80p. (J). 1997. pap., wbk. ed. 43.80 (*1-57022-132-4*, ECS1324) ECS Lrn Systs.

Math Whiz Kids: Math Whiz Kids at Home. Arlene Brown. Ed. by Shirley J. Durst. (Illus.). 80p. (J). (gr. 3-5). 1997. pap., wbk. ed. 10.95 (*1-57022-105-7*, ECS1057) ECS Lrn Systs.

Math Whiz Kids: Math Whiz Kids at the Amusement Park. Arlene Brown. Ed. by Shirley J. Durst. (Illus.). 80p. (J). (gr. 3-5). 1997. pap. 10.95 (*1-57022-103-0*, ECS1030) ECS Lrn Systs.

Math Whiz Kids: Math Whiz Kids at the Mall. Arlene Brown. Ed. by Shirley J. Durst. (Illus.). 80p. (J). (gr. 3-5). 1997. pap. 10.95 (*1-57022-106-5*, ECS1065) ECS Lrn Systs.

Math Whiz Kids: Math Whiz Kids at the Zoo. Arlene Brown. Ed. by Shirley J. Durst. (Illus.). 80p. (J). (gr. 3-5). 1997. pap., wbk. ed. 10.95 (*1-57022-104-9*, ECS1049) ECS Lrn Systs.

Math Wise: Hands-On Activities & Worksheets for Elementary Students. James L. Overholt. LC 95-6989. 251p. 1995. pap. text 29.95 (*0-87628-555-8*) Ctr Appl Res.

Math with Applications. 4th ed. Lial & Miller. (C). 1987. pap. text 14.33 (*0-673-18469-2*) Addison-Wesley Educ.

Math with Charts & Graphs: Basic Mathematics Skills. Jo Ellen Moore. Ed. by Marilyn Evans. (Illus.). 32p. (J). (gr. 2-3). 1995. pap., wbk. ed. 2.50 (*1-58610-076-9*, Learn on the Go) Learn Horizon.

Math with Computers. Karl Barksdale et al. (Illus.). 240p. 1998. spiral bd. 30.60 (*1-57426-056-1*) Computer Lit Pr.

Math with Connecting People. Rosamond Welchman-Tischler. 72p. (J). (gr. k-3). 1995. pap. text 9.50 (*0-938587-80-3*) Cuisenaire.

Math with Games. Bob DeWeese. (Math Is Everywhere Ser.). (Illus.). 48p. (J). (gr. 2-3). 1994. pap. text, teacher ed. 6.45 (*1-55799-325-4*, EMC 097) Evan-Moor Edu Pubs.

Math with Nursery Rhymes. Kathy Darling. (Math Is Everywhere Ser.). (Illus.). 48p. (J). (gr. k-1). 1994. pap. text, teacher ed. 6.45 (*1-55799-321-1*, EMC 093) Evan-Moor Edu Pubs.

Math Without Fear. Joseph G. Martinez. 167p. (C). 1996. pap. text 33.00 (*0-205-16021-2*) Allyn.

Math Wiz. Betsy Duffey. (Illus.). (J). (gr. 2-5). 1990. 13.99 (*0-670-83422-X*, Viking Child) Peng Put Young Read.

Math Wiz. Betsy Duffey. (Illus.). 80p. (J). (gr. 2-5). 1997. pap. 3.99 (*0-14-038647-5*, PuffinBks) Peng Put Young Read.

Math Wiz. Betsy Duffey. (J). 1993. 9.19 (*0-606-05455-3*, Pub. by Turtleback) Demco.

Math Wizardry for Kids. Margaret E. Kenda & Phyllis S. Williams. LC 94-31243. (Illus.). 336p. (J). (gr. 3-7). 1995. pap. 13.95 (*0-8120-1809-5*) Barron.

Math Wizardry for Kids, Incl. math accessories in pkg. Margaret E. Kenda & Phyllis S. Williams. (Illus.). 336p. (J). (gr. 3 up). 1995. pap. 21.95 (*0-8120-8363-6*) Barron.

Math Word Problems. Anita Harnadek. 312p. (Orig.). (J). (gr. 3 up). 1996. pap., student ed. 32.95 (*0-89455-646-0*) Crit Think Bks.

***Math Workbook.** Landoll. (Beginners Bible Ser.). 2000. pap. text 14.95 (*1-56189-622-5*) Amer Educ Pub.

***Math Workbook: Grades 1-2.** Golden Books Staff. (Step Ahead Ser.). (Illus.). (J). (gr. 1-2). 1999. pap. 2.09 (*0-307-03541-7*, Goldn Books) Gldn Bks Pub Co.

Math Workbook for FDSER 3D Answer. M. McDowell. 1997. pap. 9.95 (*0-442-31830-8*, VNR) Wiley.

Math Workbook for Foodservice-Lodging. 3rd ed. Milton C. McDowell & Hollie W. Crawford. (Illus.). 288p. 1988. pap. 44.95 (*0-442-21872-9*, VNR) Wiley.

Math Workbook for Foodservice/Lodging. M. C. McDowell & H. W. Crawford. (Hospitality, Travel & Tourism Ser.). 265p. 1988. pap. 39.95 (*0-471-28875-6*, VNR) Wiley.

***Math Workbook for the SAT I.** 2nd ed. Lawrence S. Leff. 432p. 2000. pap. text 13.95 (*0-7641-0768-2*) Barron.

Math Workshop: Algebra. Deborah Hughes-Hallett. (Illus.). (C). 1980. text 44.50 (*0-393-09030-2*) Norton.

Math Workshop: Algebra. Deborah Hughes-Hallett. (Illus.). (C). 1980. pap. text, teacher ed. write for info. (*0-393-09024-8*) Norton.

Math Workshop: Elementary Functions. Deborah Hughes-Hallett. (Illus.). (C). 1980. text 40.50 (*0-393-09033-7*) Norton.

Math Workshop: Elementary Functions. Deborah Hughes-Hallett. (Illus.). (C). 1981. pap. text, teacher ed. write for info. (*0-393-09028-0*) Norton.

Math Worlds: Philosophical & Social Studies of Mathematics & Mathematics Education. Ed. by Sal P. Restivo et al. LC 92-4252. (SUNY Series in Science, Technology, & Society). 292p. (C). 1993. text 22.50 (*0-7914-1329-2*) State U NY Pr.

Math, Writing & Games in the Open Classroom. Herbert R. Kohl. (New York Review Bks.). 1974. 6.95 (*0-394-48841-5*) Random.

Math Yellow Pages for Students & Teachers. LC 87-82071. (Yellow Pages Ser.). 64p. (J). (gr. 2-8). 1988. pap. text 8.95 (*0-86530-008-9*, 89-0) Incentive Pubns.

Math 1: An Incremental Development. Larson. (J). (gr. 1). 1991. 568.00 (*0-939798-26-3*); 465.00 (*0-939798-85-9*); teacher ed. 125.00 (*0-939798-27-1*); student ed. 22.75 (*0-939798-81-6*); 365.00 (*0-939798-68-9*); 468.00 (*0-939798-67-0*); 320.00 (*1-56577-002-1*) Saxon Pubs OK.

Math 2: An Incremental Development. Larson. (J). (gr. 2). 1991. teacher ed. 125.00 (*0-939798-29-8*); student ed. 475.00 (*0-939798-86-7*); student ed. 584.00 (*0-939798-28-X*); student ed. 23.00 (*0-939798-82-4*); 375.00 (*0-939798-69-7*); 484.00 (*0-939798-88-3*); 360.00 (*1-56577-003-X*) Saxon Pubs OK.

Math 3: An Incremental Development. Larson. (J). (gr. 3). 1991. 592.00 (*0-939798-30-1*); 480.00 (*0-939798-87-5*); teacher ed. 125.00 (*0-939798-31-X*); student ed. 23.50 (*0-939798-83-2*); 380.00 (*0-939798-70-0*); 492.00 (*0-939798-89-1*); 265.00 (*1-56577-004-8*) Saxon Pubs OK.

Math 54: An Incremental Development. Hake & John H. Saxon. (J). (gr. 4-6). 1990. 39.00 (*0-939798-23-9*); disk 150.00 (*0-939798-91-3*) Saxon Pubs OK.

Math 54: An Incremental Development. Hake & John H. Saxon. (J). (gr. 4-6). 1994. text 27.00 (*0-939798-21-2*); teacher ed. 27.00 (*0-939798-22-0*) Saxon Pubs OK.

Math 65. Hake & John H. Saxon. 305p. (YA). (gr. 5-12). 1987. 39.00 (*0-939798-60-3*); disk 150.00 (*0-939798-92-1*) Saxon Pubs OK.

Math 65. Hake & John H. Saxon. 305p. (YA). (gr. 5-12). 1994. teacher ed. 27.00 (*0-939798-19-0*); text 27.00 (*0-939798-18-2*) Saxon Pubs OK.

Math 65-An Incremental Development. 2nd ed. Stephen Hake & John Saxon. 1994. 41.33 (*1-56577-036-6*) Saxon Pubs OK.

Math 76: An Incremental Development. 2nd ed. Hake & John H. Saxon. (YA). (gr. 6-12). 1992. teacher ed. 27.75 (*0-939798-75-1*); student ed. 27.75 (*0-939798-74-3*); 39.00 (*0-939798-76-X*); disk 150.00 (*0-939798-93-X*) Saxon Pubs OK.

Math 87. Hake & John H. Saxon. (J). (gr. 7-9). 1991. teacher ed. 30.00 (*0-939798-55-7*); student ed. 30.00 (*0-939798-54-9*); 39.00 (*0-939798-56-5*); disk 150.00 (*0-939798-94-8*) Saxon Pubs OK.

Mathagrams. Robert Stark. (YA). (gr. 7 up). 1996. pap. 19.95 (*0-939765-72-1*) Janson Pubns.

Mathamatics for Consumers. 2nd ed. Dezilwa & Mansour. 1990. pap. text. write for info. (*0-582-86900-5*, Pub. by Addison-Wesley) Longman.

Mathamatics Problem Solving. Hook & Ingram. 1989. pap. text. write for info. (*0-582-86966-8*, Pub. by Addison-Wesley) Longman.

Mathamusements. Blum. LC 98-7678. 1998. pap. 5.95 (*0-8069-9784-2*) Sterling.

Mathamusements. Raymond Blum. (J). Date not set. 5.95 (*0-8069-3190-6*) Sterling.

Mathamusements. Raymond Blum. LC 96-49196. (Illus.). 96p. (J). 1997. 14.95 (*0-8069-9783-4*) Sterling.

Mathamusic: Children's Book. Barbara Kronau-Sorensen & Paul Sorensen. Ed. by Elizabeth Byrne. (Illus.). 56p. (J). (ps-12). 1994. pap. text, wbk. ed. 20.00 (*1-892185-03-2*) Emerald City Mus.

Mathamusic: Teacher's Edition. Barbara Kronau-Sorensen. Ed. by Paul Sorensen. (Illus.). 36p. (J). (ps-12). 1998. pap. text, teacher ed., wbk. ed. 15.00 (*1-892185-04-0*) Emerald City Mus.

MathArts: Exploring Math Through Art for 3 to 6 Year Olds. MaryAnn F. Kohl & Cindy Gainer. LC 96-17571. (Illus.). 276p. (Orig.). 1996. pap. 19.95 (*0-87659-177-2*) Gryphon Hse.

MathCAD: A Tool for Engineering Problem Solving. Philip J. Pritchard. LC 97-47318. 336p. 1998. pap. 28.75 (*0-07-012189-3*) McGraw.

MathCad Electronic Materials Science Handbook. Shackelford. 1992. lib. bdg. 189.00 (*0-8493-7470-7*, TK) CRC Pr.

MATHCAD-FUND ANAL CHE6E&ANAL C. 6th ed. Douglas A. Skoog. (C). 1994. pap. text 28.00 (*0-03-076017-8*) Harcourt Coll Pubs.

MathCAD Lab Manual. (C). 1996. pap. text 25.16 (*0-669-41839-0*) HM Trade Div.

Mathcad Manual for Statistics. 160p. (C). 1999. 21.00 (*0-13-794124-2*, Macmillan Coll) P-H.

MathCad Plus 6.0 for Engineers. 2nd ed. Joe King. (C). 1997. pap. text. write for info. (*0-8053-6484-6*) Benjamin-Cummings.

***MathCAD Primer for Physical Chemistry.** M. P. Cady & C. A. Trapp. LC 99-15225. 1999. write for info. (*0-19-850359-8*) OUP.

Mathcad 6.0 for Engineers: Toolkit. 2nd ed. Joe King. 128p. 1997. pap. text 21.33 (*0-8053-6485-4*) Benjamin-Cummings.

MATHCUE SOL FNDR BASIC ALG 3E+ 3rd ed. Barker. (C). 1991. 28.50 (*0-03-055237-0*) Harcourt Coll Pubs.

MATHCUE SOL FNDR INTM ALG 3E+ 3rd ed. Barker. (C). 1991. 49.50 (*0-03-055234-6*) Harcourt Coll Pubs.

Mathdroid, Addition. Tom Strelich. 1988. pap. 14.00 (*0-201-20102-X*) Addison-Wesley.

Mathdroid, Division. Tom Strelich. 1988. pap. 14.00 (*0-201-20108-9*) Addison-Wesley.

Mathdroid, Multiplication. Tom Strelich. 1988. pap. 14.00 (*0-201-20106-2*) Addison-Wesley.

Mathdroid, Subtraction. Tom Strelich. 1988. pap. 14.00 (*0-201-20104-6*) Addison-Wesley.

Mathemactivities. Bob Bernstein. 112p. (J). (gr. 2-7). 1991. 12.99 (*0-86653-617-5*, GA1336) Good Apple.

Mathemagic. Raymond Blum. LC 91-22523. (Illus.). 128p. (YA). (gr. 8 up). 1991. pap. 4.95 (*0-8069-8355-8*) Sterling.

Mathemagic: Magic, Puzzles & Games with Numbers. Royal V. Heath. (Illus.). 128p. (J). (gr. 2 up). 1953. pap. 4.95 (*0-486-20110-4*) Dover.

Mathemagician & Pied Puzzler: A Collection in Tribute to Martin Gardner. Ed. by Elwyn R. Berlekamp & Tom Rodgers. LC 98-51744. (Illus.). 266p. 1999. 34.00 (*1-56881-075-X*) AK Peters.

Mathemagics. Margaret Ball. 352p. 1996. mass mkt. 5.99 (*0-671-87755-0*) Baen Bks.

Mathemagics: How to Look Like a Genius Without Really Trying. Arthur Benjamin & Michael B. Shermer. 228p. 1993. 22.95 (*0-929923-54-5*) Lowell Hse.

Mathemagics: How to Look Like a Genius Without Really Trying. 2nd rev. ed. Arthur Benjamin & Michael B. Shermer. 240p. 1998. pap. 18.00 (*0-7373-0008-6*, 00086W) NTC Contemp Pub Co.

Mathematic Elements. 4th ed. Maurer. 1996. pap. text, student ed. 29.33 (*0-13-259185-5*) P-H.

Mathematic Structure. 3rd ed. Judith L. Gersting. LC 92-732. 784p. (C). 1992. pap. text 77.95 (*0-7167-8259-6*) W H Freeman.

Mathematic Structures. Judith L. Gersting. (C). 1993. text 20.00 (*0-7167-8276-6*) W H Freeman.

Mathematica. Date not set. text, teacher ed. 49.95 (*3-540-62736-7*) Spr-Verlag.

Mathematica. 2nd ed. Wolfram Research Inc. Staff. (JPN.). (C). 1991. pap. text. write for info. (*0-201-55601-4*) Addison-Wesley.

Mathematica: A Practical Approach. Nancy Blachman. 384p. 1992. pap. text 38.20 (*0-13-563826-7*) P-H.

Mathematica: A Practical Approach. 2nd ed. Nancy Blachman & Colin Williams. LC 98-44766. 640p. (C). 1998. pap. 58.00 (*0-13-259201-0*) P-H.

Mathematica: A System for Doing Mathematics by Computer. Stephen Wolfram. 600p. 1988. 44.25 (*0-201-19334-5*); pap. 26.95 (*0-201-19330-2*) Addison-Wesley.

An Asterisk (*) at the beginning of an entry indicates that the title is appearing for the first time.

Mathematica: A System for Doing Mathematics by Computer. 2nd ed. Stephen Wolfram. (Illus.). 992p. (C). 1991. 51.95 (*0-201-51502-4*) Addison-Wesley.

Mathematica: Operation Research. Joyce Nakamura. (C). 1995. pap. text. write for info. (*0-201-42731-1*) Addison-Wesley.

Mathematica als Werkzeug see Mathematica As a Tool: An Introduction with Practical Examples

***Mathematica Approach to Calculus.** Gresser. 285p. 1998. pap. text 20.00 (*0-13-010586-4*, Prentice Hall) P-H.

Mathematica As a Tool: An Introduction with Practical Examples. Stephan Kaufmann. LC 94-23460. Orig. Title: Mathematica als Werkzeug. (ENG & GER.). 1994. write for info. (*3-7643-5031-8*) Birkhauser.

Mathematica As a Tool: An Introduction with Practical Examples. Stephan Kaufmann. LC 94-23460. Orig. Title: Mathematica als Werkzeug. (ENG & GER., Illus.). 429p. 1994. 40.50 (*0-8176-5031-8*) Birkhauser.

Mathematica Book. 3rd ed. Stephen Wolfram. LC 96-14076. (Illus.). 1400p. (C). 1996. text 59.95 (*0-521-58889-8*); pap. text 44.95 (*0-521-58888-X*) Cambridge U Pr.

Mathematica Book. 3rd ed. Stephen Wolfram. LC 96-7218. (Illus.). 1996. write for info. (*0-9650532-0-2*); pap. write for info. (*0-9650532-1-0*) Wolfram Media.

"Mathematica" Book: Version 4. 4th ed. Stephen Wolfram. 1400p. (C). 1999. text 49.95 (*0-521-64314-7*) Cambridge U Pr.

Mathematica Book 4.0. Stephen Wolfram. LC 98-37600. (Illus.). 1999. 49.95 (*1-57955-004-5*) Wolfram Media.

Mathematica by Example. 2nd ed. Martha Abell & James Braselton. LC 96-43815. (Illus.). 603p. 1997. pap. text 44.00 (*0-12-041552-6*) Morgan Kaufmann.

Mathematica for Calculus-Based Physics. Marvin L. DeJong. LC 98-53298. 257p. (C). 1999. pap. text 21.40 (*0-201-60339-X*) Addison-Wesley.

Mathematica for Mathematics Teachers. Ed Packel. (Illus.). 96p. 1996. pap. 25.00 (*0-9631678-4-7*) Inst Computation.

Mathematica for Physicists. Robert L. Zimmerman et al. 436p. (C). 1994. pap. 63.00 (*0-201-53796-6*) Addison-Wesley.

Mathematica for Science & Engineering: Using Mathematia to do Science. Richard Gass. LC 97-19709. 498p. 1997. pap. 51.00 (*0-13-227612-7*) P-H.

Mathematica for Sciences. Mark Toppan. (C). 1991. pap. text. write for info. (*0-201-55604-9*) Addison-Wesley.

Mathematica for Scientists & Engineers. Thomas B. Bahder. (Illus.). 359p. 1993. pap. write for info. (*0-318-70293-2*) Addison-Wesley.

Mathematica for Scientists & Engineers. Thomas B. Bahder. 864p. (C). 1994. pap. text 51.95 (*0-201-54090-8*) Addison-Wesley.

Mathematica for the Sciences. Richard E. Crandall. (Illus.). 320p. (C). 1991. 40.95 (*0-201-51001-4*) Addison-Wesley.

Mathematica 4.0 Standard Add-On Packages. Wolfram Research, Inc. Staff. LC 99-20671. 1999. 49.95 (*1-57955-006-1*); pap. 49.95 (*1-57955-007-X*) Wolfram Media.

Mathematica Graphics Guidebook. Cameron Smith. (Illus.). 368p. (C). 1993. pap. text 41.95 (*0-201-53280-8*) Addison-Wesley.

***Mathematica Guidebook: Graphics.** M. William Trott. Ed. by Springer-Verlag Publishing Staff. (Illus.). 1000p. 2000. 79.95 incl. cd-rom (*0-387-95010-9*) Spr-Verlag.

***Mathematica Guidebook: Mathematics & Physics.** Michael Trott. (Illus.). 1000p. 2000. 79.95 incl. cd-rom (*0-387-95011-7*) Spr-Verlag.

Mathematica Guidebook: Programming. Michael Trott. LC 98-24057. (Illus.). 904p. 2000. 79.95 incl. cd-rom (*0-387-94282-3*, Telos) Spr-Verlag.

Mathematica in Action. Stan Wagon. (Illus.). 352p. (C). 1991. pap. text 34.95 (*0-7167-2202-X*) W H Freeman.

***Mathematica in Action.** 2nd ed. Stan Wagon. (Illus.). 616p. 1999. pap. 45.00 incl. cd-rom (*0-387-98684-7*) Spr-Verlag.

Mathematica in the Laboratory. Samuel Dick et al. (Illus.). 338p. 1997. text 74.95 (*0-521-58137-0*); pap. text 30.95 (*0-521-49906-2*) Cambridge U Pr.

Mathematica in Theoretical Physics. Gerd Baumann. (Electronic Library of Science). (Illus.). 348p. 1996. 59.00 incl. disk (*0-387-94424-9*) Spr-Verlag.

Mathematica, Introductory Differential. Lee Wayand. 96p. (C). 1997. pap. text, lab manual ed. 17.00 (*0-201-31128-3*) Addison-Wesley.

Mathematica Lab Manual. (C). 1996. pap. text 26.36 (*0-669-32795-6*) HM Trade Div.

Mathematica Lab Manual Reform Calculus. Stewart. (Mathematics Ser.). (C). 1997. pap. 18.75 (*0-534-34967-6*) Brooks-Cole.

Mathematica Labs for Linear Algebra. Terry Lawson & William D. Emerson. LC 97-104051. 161p. 1996. pap., lab manual ed. 23.95 (*0-471-14952-7*) Wiley.

Mathematica Navigator: Graphics & Methods of Applied Mathematics. A. Heikki Ruskeep. LC 98-22863. (Illus.). 848p. 1998. pap. text 44.95 incl. cd-rom (*0-12-603640-3*) Acad Pr.

Mathematica Primer. Kevin R. Coombes et al. LC 97-51989. (Illus.). 256p. (C). 1998. text 64.95 (*0-521-63130-0*); pap. text 24.95 (*0-521-63715-5*) Cambridge U Pr.

Mathematica Programmer - Mathematica Programmer II. Roman Maeder. 1997. pap. text 59.95 incl. cd-rom, disk (*0-12-799060-7*) Acad Pr.

Mathematica Programmer II. Roman E. Maeder. (Illus.). 296p. 1996. pap. text 44.95 (*0-12-464992-0*) Acad Pr.

Mathematica Programs for Physical Chemistry. William H. Cropper. LC 97-34136. (Illus.). 168p. 1998. pap. text 42.00 incl. cd-rom (*0-387-98337-6*) Spr-Verlag.

Mathematica Projects for Vector Calculus. 176p. (C). 1996. pap. text, per. 25.95 (*0-7872-2858-3*, 41285801) Kendall-Hunt.

Mathematica to Accompany Advanced Engineering Mathematics. Erwin Kreyszig. 389p. 1995. pap. text 26.00 (*0-471-11719-6*) Wiley.

Mathematica 2.2 for Engineers: Toolkit. Henry Shapiro. 128p. 1995. pap. text 21.33 (*0-8053-6404-8*) Benjamin-Cummings.

Mathematica 3.0 Standard Add-On Packages. Wolfram Research, Inc. Staff. LC 96-22327. 1996. pap. write for info. (*0-9650532-2-9*) Wolfram Media.

Mathematica 3.0 Standard Add-On Packages. Wolfram Research, Inc. Staff. 516p. 1996. pap. text 29.95 (*0-521-58585-6*) Cambridge U Pr.

Mathematical Activities. Brian Bolt. 224p. 1982. pap. 20.95 (*0-521-28518-6*) Cambridge U Pr.

Mathematical Activities for Elementary School Teachers, a Problem Solving Approach, to Accompany Long & Detemple's Mathematical Reasoning for Elementary Teachers. 3rd ed. Dolan. 352p. (C). 1996. pap. text 26.00 (*0-201-85754-5*) Addison-Wesley.

Mathematical Aesthetic Principles/Nonintegrable Systems. M. Muraskin. 232p. 1995. text 55.00 (*981-02-2200-9*) World Scientific Pub.

Mathematical Algorithms in Visual BASIC for Scientists & Engineers. Namir C. Shammas. LC 95-32896. 1995. pap. 45.00 (*0-07-912003-2*) McGraw.

Mathematical Analysis. G. Klambauer. (Pure & Applied Mathematics Ser.: Vol. 31). (Illus.). 512p. 1975. text 165.00 (*0-8247-6329-7*) Dekker.

Mathematical Analysis. 4th ed. Jagdish C. Arya & Robin W. Lardner. 1993. pap. text, student ed. 22.00 (*0-13-564295-7*) P-H.

Mathematical Analysis see Progress in Mathematics

Mathematical Analysis: A Modern Approach to Advanced Calculus. 2nd ed. Tom M. Apostol. LC 72-11473. 492p. (C). 1974. 106.00 (*0-201-00288-4*, Health Sci) Addison-Wesley.

Mathematical Analysis: A Special Course. G. Y. Shilov & J. Davis. LC 65-18619. (International Series of Monographs on Pure & Applied Mathematics: Vol. 77). 1965. 222.00 (*0-08-010796-6*, Pub. by Pergamon Repr) Franklin.

Mathematical Analysis: A Straightforward Approach. 2nd ed. K. G. Binmore. LC 81-21728. 376p. 1983. pap. text 32.95 (*0-521-28882-7*) Cambridge U Pr.

Mathematical Analysis: An Introduction. Andrew Browder. Ed. by S. Axler et al. LC 95-44877. (Undergraduate Texts in Mathematics Ser.). (Illus.). 333p. (C). 1996. 39.95 (*0-387-94614-4*) Spr-Verlag.

Mathematical Analysis: Differentiation & Integration. I. G. Aramanovic & Ian N. Sneddon. LC 64-8051. (International Series of Monographs on Pure & Applied Mathematics: No. 81). 1965. 152.00 (*0-08-011011-8*, Pub. by Pergamon Repr) Franklin.

Mathematical Analysis: Functions Limits Series Continued Fractions. L. Lyusternik & A. Yanpol'skii. LC 63-19330. (International Series of Monographs on Pure & Applied Mathematics: Vol. 69). 1965. 185.00 (*0-08-010133-X*, Pub. by Pergamon Repr) Franklin.

Mathematical Analysis & Numerical Methods for Science & Technology, Vol. 1. R. Dautray & J. L. Lions. (Illus.). 670p. 1990. 139.95 (*0-387-50207-6*) Spr-Verlag.

Mathematical Analysis & Numerical Methods for Science & Technology: Evolution Problems II - the Navier-Stokes & Transport Equations & Numerical Methods, Vol. 6. R. Dautray & J. L. Lions. Tr. by A. Craig from FRE. (Illus.). 500p. 1993. 145.00 (*0-387-50206-8*) Spr-Verlag.

Mathematical Analysis & Numerical Methods for Science & Technology: Functional & Variational Methods, Vol. 2. R. Dautray. (Illus.). 580p. 1988. 139.95 (*0-387-19045-7*) Spr-Verlag.

***Mathematical Analysis & Numerical Methods for Science & Technology Vol. 1: Physical Origins & Classical Methods.** R. Dautray & J. L. Lions. 695p. 2000. pap. 49.95 (*3-540-66097-6*) Spr-Verlag.

***Mathematical Analysis & Numerical Methods for Science & Technology Vol. 2: Functional & Variational Methods.** R. Dautray & J. L. Lions. (Illus.). 560p. 2000. pap. 49.95 (*3-540-66098-4*) Spr-Verlag.

Mathematical Analysis & Numerical Methods for Science & Technology Vol. 3: Spectral Theory & Applications, 6 vols. R. Dautray & J. L. Lions. Tr. by J. C. Amson from FRE. (Illus.). 536p. 1990. 139.95 (*0-387-50208-4*) Spr-Verlag.

***Mathematical Analysis & Numerical Methods for Science & Technology Vol. 3: Spectral Theory & Applications.** R. Dautray & J. L. Lions. (Illus.). 515p. 2000. pap. 49.95 (*3-540-66099-2*) Spr-Verlag.

Mathematical Analysis & Numerical Methods for Science & Technology Vol. 4: Integral Equations & Numerical Methods, 6 vols. R. Dautray & J. L. Lions. Tr. by J. C. Amson from FRE. (Illus.). 488p. 1990. 149.95 (*0-387-50209-2*) Spr-Verlag.

***Mathematical Analysis & Numerical Methods for Science & Technology Vol. 4: Integral Equations & Numerical Methods.** R. Dautray & J. L. Lions. (Illus.). 465p. 2000. pap. 49.95 (*3-540-66100-X*) Spr-Verlag.

Mathematical Analysis & Numerical Methods for Science & Technology Vol. 5: Evolution Problems I. R. Dautray & J. L. Lions. Tr. by A. Craig from FRE. (Illus.). 728p. 1992. 149.95 (*0-387-50205-X*) Spr-Verlag.

***Mathematical Analysis & Numerical Methods for Science & Technology Vol. 5: Evolution Problems I.** R. Dautray & J. L. Lions. (Illus.). 710p. 2000. pap. 49.95 (*3-540-66101-8*) Spr-Verlag.

***Mathematical Analysis & Numerical Methods for Science & Technology Vol. 6: Evolution Problems II.** R. Dautray & J. L. Lions. (Illus.). 485p. 2000. pap. 49.95 (*3-540-66102-6*) Spr-Verlag.

Mathematical Analysis & Proof. David S. Stirling. 250p. 1997. pap. 35.00 (*1-898563-36-5*, Pub. by Horwood Pub) Paul & Co Pubs.

Mathematical Analysis Explained. Neil A. Watson. 192p. 1993. text 44.00 (*981-02-1591-6*) World Scientific Pub.

Mathematical Analysis for Business, Economics & the Life & Social Sciences. 4th ed. Jagdish C. Arya & Robin W. Lardner. 880p. (C). 1992. 70.00 (*0-13-564287-6*) P-H.

Mathematical Analysis for Modeling. Judah Rosenblatt. LC 98-40054. (Mathematical Modelling Ser.). 880p. 1998. boxed set 74.95 (*0-8493-8337-4*) CRC Pr.

Mathematical Analysis in Engineering: How to Use the Basic Tools. Chiang C. Mei. (Illus.). 478p. (C). 1995. text 85.00 (*0-521-46053-0*) Cambridge U Pr.

Mathematical Analysis in Engineering: How to Use the Basic Tools. Chiang C. Mei. (Illus.). 478p. 1997. pap. text 37.95 (*0-521-58798-0*) Cambridge U Pr.

Mathematical Analysis of Biomedical Images, 1996 Workshop On. LC 96-77115. 350p. 1996. pap. 70.00 (*0-8186-7367-2*, PRO7367) IEEE Comp Soc.

Mathematical Analysis of Bluffing in Poker. R. Christensen. LC 80-67727. 60p. 9.50 (*0-938876-33-3*) Entropy Ltd.

Mathematical Analysis of Fish Stock Dynamics. Ed. by E. F. Edwards & B. A. Megrey. LC 89-81885. (Symposium Ser.: No. 6). 214p. 1989. text 40.00 (*0-913235-63-6*, 540.06) Am Fisheries Soc.

Mathematical Analysis of Groundwater Resources. Bruce Hunt. (Illus.). 288p. 1983. text 89.95 (*0-408-01399-0*) Buttrwrth-Heinemann.

Mathematical Analysis of Logic: Being an Essay Towards a Calculus of Deductive Reasoning. George Boole. (Key Issues Ser.). 82p. 1998. reprint ed. pap. 14.00 (*1-85506-583-5*) Thoemmes Pr.

Mathematical Analysis of Physical Problems. Philip R. Wallace. (Physics Ser.). 616p. 1984. reprint ed. pap. 15.95 (*0-486-64676-9*) Dover.

Mathematical Analysis of Spectra Orthogonality. Ed. by John H. Kalivas & Patrick Lang. (Practical Spectroscopy Ser.: Vol. 17). (Illus.). 344p. 1993. text 195.00 (*0-8247-9155-X*) Dekker.

Mathematical Analysis of the Electrical Activity of the Brain. Ed. by M. N. Livanov & V. S. Rusinov. Tr. by John S. Barlow. LC 68-17621. (Illus.). 113p. 1968. 22.95 (*0-674-55400-0*) HUP.

Mathematical Analysis of Thin Plate Models, Vol. 24. P. Destuynder & M. Salaun. Ed. by Jean-Michel Ghidaglia & P. Lascaux. LC 96-201278. (Mathematics & Its Applications Ser.). viii, 238p. 1996. pap. 59.95 (*3-540-61167-3*) Spr-Verlag.

***Mathematical Analysis of Viscoelastic Flows.** Michael Renardy. (CBMS-NSF Regional Conference Ser.: Vol. 73). 2000. pap. 35.00 (*0-89871-457-5*) Soc Indus-Appl Math.

Mathematical Analysis, Wavelets, & Signal Processing: An International Conference on Mathematical Analysis & Signal Processing, January 3-9, 1994, Cairo University, Cairo, Egypt. Ed. by Mourad E. Ismail. LC 95-21409. (Contemporary Mathematics Ser.: Vol. 190). 354p. 1995. pap. 59.00 (*0-8218-0384-0*, CONM/190) Am Math.

Mathematical & Biological Interrelations. Brian A. Dudley. LC 77-7284. (Illus.). 329p. reprint ed. pap. 102.00 (*0-608-17693-1*, 203041300069) Bks Demand.

***Mathematical & Computational Analysis of Natural Language: Selected Papers from the 2nd International Conference on Mathematical Linguistics, Tarragona, 1996.** Ed. by Carlos Martin-Vide. LC 98-26169. (Studies in Functional & Structural Linguistics: No. 45). xviii, 391p. 1998. 79.00 (*1-55619-896-5*) J Benjamins Pubng Co.

Mathematical & Computational Aspects. Ed. by Carlos A. Brebbia. (Boundary Elements X Ser.: Vol. 1). 480p. 1988. 190.95 (*0-387-50091-X*) Spr-Verlag.

Mathematical & Computational Biology: Computational Morphogenesis, Hierarchical Complexity & Digital Evolution: An International Workshop on Mathematical & Computational Biology, October 21-25, 1997, University of Aizu, Aizu-wakamatsu City, Japan. International Workshop on Mathematical & Computational Staff & Chrystopher L. Nehaniv. LC 98-54449. (Lectures on Mathematics in the Life Sciences). 1999. write for info. (*0-8218-0941-5*) Am Math.

Mathematical & Computational Methods in Nuclear Physics. Ed. by J. S. Dehesa et al. (Lecture Notes in Physics Ser.: Vol. 209). vi, 276p. 1984. 33.95 (*0-387-13392-5*) Spr-Verlag.

Mathematical & Computational Methods in Seismic Exploration & Reservoir Modeling. Ed. & Pref. by William E. Fitzgibbon. LC 86-60091. (Proceedings in Applied Mathematics Ser.: No. 23). (Illus.). xiv, 277p. 1986. text 38.75 (*0-89871-205-X*) Soc Indus-Appl Math.

Mathematical & Computational Techniques for Multilevel Adaptive Methods. Ulrich Ruede. LC 93-28379. (Frontiers in Applied Mathematics Ser.: No. 13). xii, 140p. 1993. pap. 29.00 (*0-89871-320-X*) Soc Indus-Appl Math.

Mathematical & Control Applications in Agriculture & Horticulture: Proceedings of the IFAC Workshop, Matsuyama, Japan, 30 September - 3 October, 1991. Ed. by Y. Hashimoto & W. Day. (IFAC Workshop Ser.: No. 9101). 462p. 1991. 181.50 (*0-08-041273-4*, Pergamon Pr) Elsevier.

Mathematical & Control Applications in Agriculture & Horticulture, 1997: Proceedings of the 3rd IFAC Workshop, Hannover, Germany, 28 September-2 October 1997. Ed. by A. Munack & H. J. Tantau. 322p. 1998. pap. 76.50 (*0-08-043037-6*, Pergamon Pr) Elsevier.

Mathematical & Numerical Modelling in Electrical Engineering: Theory & Applications. Pekka Neittaanmaki & Michael Krizek. LC 96-35769. (Mathematical Modelling Ser.). 316p. (C). 1996. text 169.00 (*0-7923-4249-6*) Kluwer Academic.

Mathematical & Numerical Techniques in Physical Geodesy. Ed. by Hans Sunkel. (Lecture Notes in Earth Sciences Ser.: Vol. 7). ix, 548p. 1986. 70.95 (*0-387-16809-5*) Spr-Verlag.

Mathematical & Philosophical Dictionary, 2 vols., Set. Charles Hutton. 1416p. 1973. reprint ed. 388.70 (*3-487-04758-6*) G Olms Pubs.

Mathematical & Philosophical Works, 2 vols. in one. John Wilkins. 572p. 1970. reprint ed. 47.50 (*0-7146-1618-4*, BHA-01618, Pub. by F Cass Pubs) Intl Spec Bk.

Mathematical & Physical Aspects of Stochastic Mechanics. P. Blanchard et al. (Lecture Notes in Physics Ser.: Vol. 281). 171p. 1987. 29.95 (*0-387-18036-2*) Spr-Verlag.

Mathematical & Physical Modeling of Materials Processing Operations. Olusegun J. Ilegbusi & Manabu Iguchi. LC 99-24511. (Mechanical Engineering Ser.). 1998. 89.95 (*0-8493-9662-X*) CRC Pr.

***Mathematical & Physical Modeling of Materials Processing Operations.** Olusegun J. Ilegbusi et al. (Mechanical Engineering Ser.). 512p. 1999. boxed set 89.95 (*1-58488-017-1*, Chap & Hall CRC) CRC Pr.

***Mathematical & Physical Simulation of the Properties of Hot Rolled Products.** J. G. Lenard et al. 376p. 1999. 140.00 (*0-08-042701-4*) Elsevier.

***Mathematical & Quantum Aspects of Relativity & Cosmology: Proceedings of the Second Samos Meeting on Cosmology, Geometry & Relativity, Held at Pythagoreon, Samos, Greece, 31 August-4 September 1998.** Ed. by Spiro Cotsakis & G. W. Gibbons. LC 99-59222. (Lecture Notes in Physics Ser.). xii, 251p. 2000. 58.00 (*3-540-66865-9*) Spr-Verlag.

Mathematical & Statistical Approaches to AIDS Epidemiology. C. Castillo-Chavez. (Lecture Notes in Biomathematics Ser.: Vol. 83). ix, 405p. 1990. 69.95 (*0-387-52174-7*) Spr-Verlag.

Mathematical & Statistical Developments of Evolutionary Theory: Proceedings of the NATO Advanced Study Institute Dordrecht, The Netherlands & Seminaire de Mathematiques Superleures Held in Montreal, Canada, August 3-21, 1987. Ed. by Sabin Lessard. (C). 1990. text 207.50 (*0-7923-0595-7*) Kluwer Academic.

Mathematical & Statistical Methods for Genetic Analysis. Kenneth Lange. LC 96-49533. (Statistics for Biology & Health Ser.). (Illus.). 288p. 1997. 54.95 (*0-387-94909-7*) Spr-Verlag.

***Mathematical & Statistical Methods for Sensitivity Analysis.** A. Saltelli et al. LC 00-23093. (Series in Probability & Statistics). 2000. write for info. (*0-471-99892-3*) Wiley.

Mathematical & Statistical Methods in Artificial Intelligence: Proceedings of the ISSEK94 Workshop. Ed. by G. Della Riccia et al. (International Centre for Mechanical Sciences Ser.: No.363). 256p. 1995. 86.95 (*3-211-82713-7*) Spr-Verlag.

Mathematical & Statistical Methods in Nuclear Safeguards, Vol. 2. Ed. by F. Argentesi et al. (Ispra Courses on Nuclear Engineering & Technology Ser.). xii, 446p. 1983. text 404.00 (*3-7186-0124-9*) Gordon & Breach.

Mathematical Applications for Business CB. Ed. by Lial. (C). 1997. text 68.00 (*0-673-67530-0*) Addison-Wesley.

Mathematical Applications for the Management, Life & Social Sciences. 4th ed. Ronald J. Harshbarger & James J. Reynolds. 823p. (C). 1992. 24.36 (*0-669-28202-2*) HM Trade Div.

Mathematical Applications for the Management, Life & Social Sciences. 5th ed. Ronald J. Harshbarger & James J. Reynolds. LC 95-68036. 980p. (C). 1996. pap. text 81.16 (*0-669-39840-3*); pap. text, teacher ed. 2.66 (*0-669-39841-1*) HM Trade Div.

Mathematical Applications for the Management, Life & Social Sciences: Study & Solutions Guide. 5th ed. Ronald J. Harshbarger & James J. Reynolds. (C). 1996. pap. text 28.36 (*0-669-39842-X*) HM Trade Div.

Mathematical Applications in Political Science, Vol. 6. Ed. by James F. Herndon & Joseph L. Bernd. LC 67-28023. 151p. reprint ed. pap. 46.90 (*0-608-13786-3*, 202031800006) Bks Demand.

Mathematical Applications of Category Theory. Ed. by John W. Gray. LC 84-9371. (Contemporary Mathematics Ser.: Vol. 30). 307p. 1984. pap. 40.00 (*0-8218-5032-6*, CONM/30) Am Math.

Mathematical Approach to Fluctuations, Vol. II. T. Hida. 392p. 1995. text 86.00 (*981-02-1756-0*) World Scientific Pub.

Mathematical Approach to Fluctuations: Proceedings of the Kyoto Workshop. T. Hida. 192p. 1994. text 78.00 (*981-02-1288-7*) World Scientific Pub.

Mathematical Approach to Glass. M. B. Volf. (Glass Science & Technology Ser.: Vol. 9). 408p. 1988. 240.75 (*0-444-98951-X*, BTHO0175) Elsevier.

Mathematical Approach to Proportional Representation: Duncan Black on Lewis Carroll. Ed. by Iain McLean et al. 240p. (C). 1995. lib. bdg. 78.50 (*0-7923-9620-0*) Kluwer Academic.

Mathematical Approaches in Hydrodynamics. Ed. by T. Miloh. (Miscellaneous Bks.: No. 24). xxi, 517p. 1991. pap. 79.75 (*0-89871-277-7*) Soc Indus-Appl Math.

Mathematical Approaches to Biomolecular Structure & Dynamics. L. Sumners et al. LC 96-24164. (IMA Volums in Mathematics & Its Applications Ser.). 264p. 1996. 65.95 (*0-387-94838-4*) Spr-Verlag.

Mathematical Approaches to Neural Networks. Ed. by J. G. Taylor. LC 93-34573. (Mathematical Library: No. 52). 390p. 1993. 127.00 (*0-444-81692-5*, North Holland) Elsevier.

An Asterisk (*) at the beginning of an entry indicates that the title is appearing for the first time.

Mathematical Approaches to Problems in Resource Management & Epidemiology. Ed. by C. Castillo-Chavez et al. (Lecture Notes in Biomathematics Ser.: Vol. 81). vii, 327p. 1989. 60.95 (0-387-51820-7) Spr-Verlag.

Mathematical Approximations of Special Functions: Ten Papers on Chebyshev Expansions. Geza Nemeth. 185p. (C). 1992. pap. text 165.00 (1-56072-052-2) Nova Sci Pubs.

Mathematical Aspects of Artificial Intelligence. Ed. by Frederick Hoffman. LC 98-4693. (Proceedings of Symposia in Applied Mathematics Ser.: Vol. 55). 288p. 1998. 49.00 (0-8218-0611-4, PSAPM/55) Am Math.

***Mathematical Aspects of Boundary Element Methods: Dedicated to Vladimir Maz'ya on the Occasion of His 60th Birthday** V. G. Maz'kila et al. LC 99-38269. 312p. 1999. per. 69.95 (1-58488-006-6) CRC Pr.

Mathematical Aspects of Chemical & Biochemical Problems & Quantum Chemistry: Proceedings of the SIAM-AMS Seminar, New York, 1974. Ed. by Donald S. Cohen. LC 74-26990. (SIAM-AMS Proceedings Ser.: Vol. 8). 153p. 1974. text 45.00 (0-8218-1328-5, SIAMS-8) Am Math.

Mathematical Aspects of Classical & Celestial Mechanics. 2nd ed. V. I. Arnold. 291p. 1997. pap. text 54.50 (3-540-61224-6) Spr-Verlag.

Mathematical Aspects of Classical Field Theory. Ed. by Mark Gotay et al. LC 92-19389. (Contemporary Mathematics Ser.: No. 132). 644p. 1992. pap. 79.00 (0-8218-5144-6, CONM/132) Am Math.

Mathematical Aspects of Computer Science: Proceedings of a Symposium, New York City, Apr. 1966. Ed. by J. T. Schwartz. LC 67-16554. (Proceedings of Symposia in Applied Mathematics Ser.: Vol. 19). 224p. 1968. reprint ed. pap. 30.00 (0-8218-1319-6, PSAPM/19) Am Math.

Mathematical Aspects of Conformal & Topological Field Theories & Quantum Groups. Ed. by Paul J. Sally, Jr. et al. LC 94-27537. (Contemporary Mathematics Ser.: Vol. 175). 267p. 1994. 50.00 (0-8218-5186-1, CONM/175C) Am Math.

Mathematical Aspects of Electrical Network Analysis: Proceedings of the Society for Industrial & Applied Mathematics-American Mathematical Society Symposia-New York-April, 1969. Ed. by Frank Harary & Herbert S. Wilf. LC 79-167683. (SIAM-AMS Proceedings Ser.: Vol. 3). 206p. 1971. text 37.00 (0-8218-1322-6, SIAMS/3) Am Math.

Mathematical Aspects of Fluid Plasma Dynamics: Proceedings of an International Workshop Held in Salice Terme, Italy 26-30 September 1988. Ed. by Giuseppe Toscani et al. (Lecture Notes in Mathematics Ser.: Vol. 1460). v, 221p. 1991. 41.95 (0-387-53545-4) Spr-Verlag.

Mathematical Aspects of Geometric Modeling. Charles A. Micchelli. LC 94-10478. (CBMS-NSF Regional Conference Series in Applied Mathematics: Vol. 65). ix, 256p. 1994. pap. 42.50 (0-89871-331-5) Soc Indus-Appl Math.

Mathematical Aspects of Hodgkin-Huxley Neural Theory. Jane Cronin. (Cambridge Studies in Mathematical Biology: NO. 7). (Illus.). 288p. 1987. text 74.95 (0-521-33482-9) Cambridge U Pr.

Mathematical Aspects of Natural & Formal Languages. Ed. by Gheorghe Paun. LC 94-30230. (Series in Computer Science: Vol. 43). 500p. 1994. text 124.00 (981-02-1914-8) World Scientific Pub.

Mathematical Aspects of Numerical Grid Generation. Ed. by Jose E. Castillo. LC 91-14973. (Frontiers in Applied Mathematics Ser.: No. 8). xiv, 157p. 1991. pap. 33.00 (0-89871-267-X) Soc Indus-Appl Math.

***Mathematical Aspects of Numerical Solution of Hyperbolic Systems.** A. G. Kulikovskiy et al. 1999. 94.95 (0-8493-0608-6) CRC Pr.

Mathematical Aspects of Physiology. Ed. by Frank C. Hoppensteadt. LC 81-1315. (Lectures in Applied Mathematics: No. 19). 394p. 1981. text 60.00 (0-8218-1119-3, LAM/19) Am Math.

Mathematical Aspects of Physiology. Ed. by Frank C. Hoppensteadt. LC 81-1315. (Lectures in Applied Mathematics: Vol. 19). (Illus.). 400p. reprint ed. pap. 124.00 (0-608-09612-1, 205277000007) Bks Demand.

Mathematical Aspects of Production & Distribution of Energy. Ed. by Peter D. Lax. LC 77-7174. (Proceedings of Symposia in Applied Mathematics Ser.: No. 21). 137p. 1977. reprint ed. pap. 26.00 (0-8218-0121-X, PSAPM/21) Am Math.

Mathematical Aspects of Reacting & Diffusing Systems. P. C. Fife. LC 79-10216. (Lecture Notes in Biomathematics Ser.: Vol. 28). 1979. pap. text 23.00 (0-387-09117-3) Spr-Verlag.

Mathematical Aspects of Scheduling & Applications. Richard Ernest Bellman et al. LC 81-15809. (International Series in Modern Applied Mathematics & Computer Science: Vol. 4). (Illus.). 329p. 1982. text 155.00 (0-08-026477-8, Pub. by Pergamon Repr) Franklin.

Mathematical Aspects of Scientific Software. Ed. by J. R. Rice. (IMA Volumes in Mathematics & Its Applications Ser.: Vol. 14). (Illus.). xi, 208p. 1988. 45.95 (0-387-96706-0) Spr-Verlag.

Mathematical Aspects of Spin Glasses & Neural Networks. Ed. by Anton Bovier et al. LC 97-20693. (Progress in Probability Ser.: No. 41). 400p. 1997. 98.50 (0-8176-3863-6) Birkhauser.

Mathematical Aspects of Spin Glasses & Neural Networks. Anton Bovier & Pierre Picco. LC 97-20693. (Progress in Probability Ser.). 1997. write for info. (3-7643-3863-6) Birkhauser.

Mathematical Aspects of Statistical Mechanics: Proceedings of the SIAM-AMS Symposia, New York, April, 1971. Ed. by J. C. Pool. LC 72-321. (SIAM-AMS Proceedings Ser.: Vol. 5). 89p. 1972. text 33.00 (0-8218-1324-2, SIAMS/5) Am Math.

Mathematical Aspects of String Theory: Proceedings of the Conference, California, August 1986. S. T. Yau. (Advanced Series in Mathematical Physics: Vol. 1). 664p. 1987. text 117.00 (9971-5-0273-9); pap. text 59.00 (9971-5-0274-7) World Scientific Pub.

Mathematical Aspects of Superspace. Ed. by H. J. Seifert. 240p. 1984. text 122.00 (90-277-1805-9) Kluwer Academic.

Mathematical Aspects of Vortex Dynamics. Ed. by Russell E. Caflisch. LC 89-6182. (Proceedings in Applied Mathematics Ser.: No. 37). xii, 220p. 1989. pap. 34.00 (0-89871-235-1) Soc Indus-Appl Math.

Mathematical Astronomy in Copernicus' de Revolutionibus, 2 pts., Set. N. M. Swerdlow & O. Neugebauer. (Studies in the History of Mathematics & Physical Sciences: Vol. 10). (Illus.). 736p. 1984. 179.00 (0-387-90939-7) Spr-Verlag.

Mathematical Astronomy in Medieval Yemen: A Biobibliographical Survey. David A. King. (American Research Center in Egypt, Catalogs Ser.: Vol. 4). (Illus.). xiv, 98p. 1983. pap. text 18.50 (0-89003-098-7, Pub. by Amer Res Ctr Egypt) Eisenbrauns.

Mathematical Astronomy in Medieval Yemen: A Biobibliographical Survey. David A. King. (American Research Center in Egypt, Catalogs Ser.: Vol. 4). (Illus.). xiv, 98p. 1983. text 28.50 (0-89003-099-5, Pub. by Amer Res Ctr Egypt) Eisenbrauns.

Mathematical Astronomy Morsels. Jean H. Meeus. LC 97-22651. 1997. 24.95 (0-943396-51-4) Willmann-Bell.

Mathematical Bafflers. rev. ed. Angela Dunn. (Illus.). 217p. 1980. reprint ed. pap. 6.95 (0-486-23961-6) Dover.

Mathematical Basis of Finite Element Methods: With Application to Partial Differential Equations. Ed. by David F. Griffiths. (Institute of Mathematics & Its Applications Conference Series, New Ser.). (Illus.). 250p. 1985. 39.95 (0-19-853605-4) OUP.

Mathematical Basis of the Arts. Joseph Schillinger. LC 76-8189. (Music Reprint Ser.). 696p. 1976. reprint ed. 65.00 (0-306-70781-0) Da Capo.

Mathematical Beauty of Physics: A Memorial Volume of Claude Itzykson. LC 97-3545. 400p. 1997. lib. bdg. 62.00 (981-02-2807-4) World Scientific Pub.

Mathematical Beginnings. Janine Blinko. 1995. pap. text 20.95 (1-871098-00-9, Pub. by Claire Pubns) Parkwest Pubns.

Mathematical Bioeconomics: The Optimal Management of Renewable Resources. 2nd ed. Colin Clark. LC 89-22599. (Pure & Applied Mathematics: A Wiley-Interscience Series of Texts, Monographs & Tracts). 400p. 1990. 135.00 (0-471-50883-7) Wiley.

Mathematical Biofluiddynamics. J. Lighthill. (CBMS-NSF Regional Conference Ser.: No. 17). vi, 281p. 1975. reprint ed. pap. text 53.00 (0-89871-014-6) Soc Indus-Appl Math.

Mathematical Biology. J. D. Murray. (Biomathematics Ser.: Vol. 19). (Illus.). 760p. 1989. 64.95 (0-387-19460-6) Spr-Verlag.

Mathematical Biology. 2nd rev. ed. J. D. Murray. Ed. by S. A. Levin. (BIOMED Ser.: Vol. 19). (Illus.). xiv, 767p. 1997. 43.95 (0-387-57204-X) Spr-Verlag.

Mathematical Book Review Index, 1800-1940. Louise S. Grinstein. LC 91-37397. 480p. 1992. text 86.00 (0-8240-4114-3, 527) Garland.

Mathematical Brain-Benders: Second Miscellany of Puzzles. Stephen Barr. (Illus.). 224p. (YA). (gr. 6 up). 1982. pap. 6.95 (0-486-24260-9) Dover.

Mathematical Brain-Teasers. J. A. Hunter. 1976. pap. 4.95 (0-486-23347-2) Dover.

Mathematical Buds, Vol. I. Ed. by Harry Ruderman. (Illus.). 1978. pap. text 2.50 (0-940790-01-7) Mu Alpha Theta.

Mathematical Buds, Vol. II. Mu Alpha Theta Staff. 126p. 1981. 2.50 (0-940790-02-5) Mu Alpha Theta.

Mathematical Buds, Vol. III. 93p. 1984. 2.50 (0-940790-03-3) Mu Alpha Theta.

Mathematical Buds, Vol. IV. 109p. 1988. 2.50 (0-940790-04-1) Mu Alpha Theta.

Mathematical Buds, Vol. V. Ed. by Harry Ruderman. 1992. 2.50 (0-940790-05-X) Mu Alpha Theta.

Mathematical Career of Pierre de Fermat, 1601-1665. Michael S. Mahoney. 438p. (C). 1994. pap. text 19.95 (0-691-03666-7, Pub. by Princeton U Pr) Cal Prin Full Svc.

Mathematical Career of Pierre de Fermat, 1601-1665. Michael S. Mahoney. LC 72-733. 439p. reprint ed. pap. 136.10 (0-608-30734-3, 201601700006) Bks Demand.

Mathematical Cavalcade. Brian Bolt. (Illus.). 130p. (C). 1992. pap. 19.95 (0-521-42617-0) Cambridge U Pr.

Mathematical Challenge. A. Gardiner. 144p. (C). 1996. pap. 13.95 (0-521-55875-1) Cambridge U Pr.

Mathematical Challenges: Puzzles & Problems in Secondary School Mathematics. Ed. by Peter Giblin. (Illus.). 59p. (YA). (gr. 9 up). 1989. pap. 19.95 (0-939765-28-4, G118) Janson Pubns.

Mathematical Challenges for the Middle Grades: From the "Arithmetic Teacher" Compiled by William D. Jamski. LC 90-37386. (Illus.). 48p. 1990. pap. 12.95 (0-87353-296-1) NCTM.

Mathematical Challenges for the Middle Grades: From the "Mathematics Teacher" Calendar Problems. Ed. by William D. Jamski. LC 91-33263. (Illus.). 46p. 1991. pap. 12.95 (0-87353-340-2) NCTM.

Mathematical Challenges from Theoretical/Computational Chemistry. National Research Council Staff. 144p. 1995. pap. text 25.00 (0-309-05097-9) Natl Acad Pr.

Mathematical Circles: Russian Experience. Dmitry Fomin et al. Tr. by Mark Saul from RUS. LC 96-17683. (Mathematical World Ser.: Vol. 7). 272p. 1996. pap. 29.00 (0-8218-0430-8, MAWRLD/7) Am Math.

Mathematical Circus. Martin Gardner. LC 92-60996. (MAA Spectrum Ser.). 296p. 1992. pap. 9.60 (0-88385-506-2, CIRCUS) Math Assn.

Mathematical Classification & Clustering. Boris G. Mirkin. LC 96-28669. (Nonconvex Optimization & Its Applications Ser.). 448p. (C). 1996. text 228.00 (0-7923-4159-7) Kluwer Academic.

Mathematical Computation with Maple V - Ideas & Applications: Proceedings of the Maple Summer Workshop & Symposium, University of Michigan, Ann Arbor, June 28-30, 1993. Maple Summer Workshop & Symposium Staff. Ed. by Thomas Lee. LC 93-21604. viii, 199p. 1993. 39.50 (0-8176-3724-9) Birkhauser.

Mathematical Concepts in Nonlinear Gas Dynamics. Liviu Dinu. 1994. write for info. (0-318-70229-0) Longman.

Mathematical Concepts in Nursing: A Workbook. H. Readey & W. Readey. 1980. pap. text 17.56 (0-201-06166-X, Health Sci) Addison-Wesley.

Mathematical Concepts in Organic Chemistry. I. Gutman & O. E. Polansky. (Illus.). 230p. 1986. 169.95 (0-387-16235-6) Spr-Verlag.

Mathematical Connections: A Modeling Approach to Business Calculus, Vol. 1. Bruce Pollack-Johnson & Audrey F. Borchardt. LC 97-34502. Vol. 1. 553p. (C). 1998. pap. text 38.33 (0-13-576398-3) P-H.

Mathematical Connections: Integrated & Applied. Robert B. Ashlock et al. 1996. teacher ed. 56.51 (0-02-824796-5); student ed. 46.50 (0-02-824795-7); wbk. ed. 8.15 (0-02-824803-1) Glencoe.

***Mathematical Connections Chapter 5: Statistics.** (C). 1999. write for info. (0-536-02249-6) Pearson Custom.

Mathematical Connections Vol. 2: A Modeling Approach to Finite Mathematics, Vol. 2. Bruce Pollack-Johnson & Audrey F. Borchardt. 850p. (C). 1997. pap. text 38.33 (0-13-576687-7) P-H.

Mathematical Connections 1. 124p. (C). 1995. text 25.80 (0-536-58855-4) Pearson Custom.

Mathematical Connections Revised. 2nd ed. Alverno. 280p. (C). 1999. 39.00 (0-536-02295-X) Pearson Custom.

Mathematical Connections 2. 202p. (C). 1995. text 25.80 (0-536-58856-2) Pearson Custom.

Mathematical Control Theory: An Introduction. Jerzy Zabczyk. LC 92-12101. x, 260p. 1995. 69.50 (0-8176-3645-5) Birkhauser.

Mathematical Control Theory: Deterministic Finite Dimensional Systems. E. D. Sontag. (Texts in Applied Mathematics Ser.: Vol. 6). (Illus.). xiii, 396p. 1990. 49.95 (0-387-97366-4) Spr-Verlag.

Mathematical Control Theory: Deterministic Finite Dimensional Systems. 2nd ed. E. D. Sontag. Ed. by J. E. Marsden et al. LC 98-13182. (Texts in Applied Mathematics Ser.: Vol. 6). 530p. 1998. 49.95 (0-387-98489-5) Spr-Verlag.

Mathematical Cranks. Underwood Dudley. LC 92-69179. (MAA Spectrum Ser.). 384p. 1992. pap. 33.95 (0-88385-507-0, CRANKS) Math Assn.

Mathematical Cryptology for Computer Scientists & Mathematicians. Wayne Patterson. 336p. 1987. 68.00 (0-8476-7438-X) Rowman.

Mathematical Crystallography. G. V. Gibbs & M. Boisen. (Reviews in Mineralogy Ser.: Vol. 15). 450p. 1990. per. 24.00 (0-939950-19-7) Mineralogical Soc.

Mathematical Cuneiform Texts. O. Neugebauer & A. Sachs. (American Oriental Ser.: Vol. 29). x, 177p. 1945. 32.00 (0-940490-29-3) Am Orient Soc.

Mathematical Curiosities 1: 9 Curious Models. Gerald Jenkins & Anne Wild. (Illus.). 60p. 1985. pap. 6.50 (0-906212-13-8, Pub. by Tarquin Pubns) Parkwest Pubns.

Mathematical Curiosities 3. Gerald Jenkins & Anne Wild. (Tarquin Mathematical Curiosities Ser.). (Illus.). 60p. (J). (gr. 5-9). 1986. pap. 6.50 (0-906212-25-1, Pub. by Tarquin Pubns) Parkwest Pubns.

Mathematical Curiosities 2: Another 9 Curious Models. Gerald Jenkins & Anne Wild. (Illus.). 60p. 1985. pap. 6.50 (0-906212-14-6, Pub. by Tarquin Pubns) Parkwest Pubns.

Mathematical Definition of Dimensioning & Tolerancing Principles: ASME Y14.51M-1994. 1994. pap. 49.00 (0-7918-2252-4, N13294) ASME Pr.

Mathematical Demography: Selected Readings. D. P. Smith & Nathan Keyfitz. (Biomathematics Ser.: Vol. 6). 1977. 54.00 (0-387-07899-1) Spr-Verlag.

Mathematical Description of Linear Systems. Wilson J. Rugh. LC 75-1684. (Control & Systems Theory Ser.: No. 2). (Illus.). 191p. reprint ed. pap. 59.30 (0-7837-0697-9, 204103000019) Bks Demand.

Mathematical Description of Shape & Form. E. A. Lord & C. B. Wilson. LC 83-26685. (Mathematics & Its Applications Ser.: 1-176). 323p. 1986. pap. text 37.95 (0-470-20254-8) P-H.

Mathematical Design: Building Reliable Complex Computer Systems. J. Paul Roth. LC 98-17152. 144p. 1998. 69.95 (0-7803-3430-2, PC5706-QOE) Inst Electrical.

Mathematical Developments Arising from Linear Programming: Proceedings of the Conference. J. Lagarias & M. Todd. LC 90-22942. (Contemporary Mathematics Ser.: Vol. 114). 341p. 1991. pap. 61.00 (0-8218-5121-7, CONM/114) Am Math.

Mathematical Developments Arising from the Hilbert Problems: Proceedings, 2 pts, Set. Pure Mathematics Symposium Staff. LC 76-20437. (Proceedings of Symposia in Pure Mathematics Ser.: Vol. 28). 628p. 1976. reprint ed. pap. 34.00 (0-8218-1428-1, PSPUM/28) Am Math.

Mathematical Dictionary for Schools. Brian Bolt & David Hobbs. 160p. (C). 1998. pap. 10.95 (0-521-55657-0) Cambridge U Pr.

Mathematical Difficulties of Students of Educational Statistics. Ralph Brown. LC 70-176599. (Columbia University. Teachers College. Contributions to Education Ser.: No. 569). reprint ed. 37.50 (0-404-55569-1) AMS Pr.

Mathematical Disabilities: A Cognitive Neuropsychological Perspective. Ed. by G. Deloche & X. Seron. (Harry Whitaker's Neuropsychology & Neurolinguistics Ser.). 304p. 1987. text 59.95 (0-89859-891-5) L Erlbaum Assocs.

Mathematical Discovery Combined Volume. George Polya. 464p. (C). 1981. pap. 92.95 (0-471-08975-3) Wiley.

Mathematical Doodling. Margaret J. Kenney. (Motivated Math Project Activity Booklets). 86p. (Orig.). (YA). (gr. 6-12). 1976. pap. text 2.50 (0-917916-17-4) Boston Coll Math.

Mathematical Ecology: Proceedings of the Autumn Course Research Seminars Int'l Centre for Theoretical Physics. Ed. by T. G. Hallam et al. 792p. (C). 1988. pap. 55.00 (9971-5-0557-6); text 125.00 (9971-5-0556-8) World Scientific Pub.

Mathematical Ecology: Proceedings of the Autumn Research Seminar, Held at the International Centre for Theoretical Physics, Miramare-Trieste, Italy, November 29-December 10, 1982. Ed. by S. A. Levin & T. G. Hallam. (Lecture Notes in Biomathematics Ser.: Vol. 54). xii, 513p. 1984. 59.95 (0-387-12919-7) Spr-Verlag.

Mathematical Ecology of Plant Species Competition. Anthony G. Pakes & R. A. Maller. (Cambridge Studies in Mathematical Biology). (Illus.). 207p. (C). 1990. text 69.95 (0-521-37388-3) Cambridge U Pr.

M

Mathematical Economic Theory: Pure & Mixed Types of Economic Mechanisms. Valery L. Makarov et al. LC 94-33657. (Advanced Textbooks in Economics Ser.: Vol. 33). 632p. 1994. 95.00 (0-444-89443-8) Elsevier.

Mathematical Economics. Baldani. (C). 1996. pap. text, student ed. write for info. (0-03-011579-5) Harcourt Coll Pubs.

Mathematical Economics. Jeffrey Baldani. (C). 1995. text 91.50 (0-03-098145-X, Pub. by Harcourt Coll Pubs) Harcourt.

Mathematical Economics, 3 vols. Ed. & Intro. by Graciela Chichilnisky. LC 98-15017. (International Library of Critical Writings in Economics Ser.: Vol. 93). 1644p. 1998. 590.00 (1-85898-260-X) E Elgar.

Mathematical Economics. Kelvin Lancaster. xiii, 411p. 1987. reprint ed. pap. text 12.95 (0-486-65391-9) Dover.

Mathematical Economics. J. E. Woods. LC 77-1660. (Modern Economics Ser.). 378p. reprint ed. pap. 117.20 (0-608-13537-2, 202252300027) Bks Demand.

Mathematical Economics. 2nd ed. Akira Takayama. 768p. 1985. pap. text 39.95 (0-521-31498-4) Cambridge U Pr.

Mathematical Economics: 20 Papers of Gerard Debreu. Gerard Debreu. LC 82-12875. (Econometric Society Monographs). 262p. 1986. pap. text 26.95 (0-521-33561-2) Cambridge U Pr.

Mathematical Economics & Game Theory: Essays in Honor of Oskar Morgenstern. Ed. by R. Hehn & O. Moeschlin. LC 76-30791. (Lecture Notes in Economics & Mathematical Systems Ser.: Vol. 141). 1977. 46.00 (0-387-08063-5) Spr-Verlag.

Mathematical Economics of Multi-Level Optimisation: Theory & Application. Sadar M. Islam. LC 97-42018. (Contributions to Economics Ser.). (Illus.). xviii, 284p. 1997. pap. 73.00 (3-7908-1050-9) Spr-Verlag.

Mathematical Education of Engineers. Leslie R. Mustoe & Stephen Hibberd. (Institute of Mathematics & Its Applications Conference Ser.; New Ser.: No. 57). (Illus.). 406p. (C). 1996. text 120.00 (0-19-851191-4) OUP.

Mathematical Elasticity Vol. 1: Three-Dimensional Elasticity. P. G. Ciarlet. (Studies in Mathematics & Its Applications: Vol. 20). 496p. 1994. pap. 98.50 (0-444-81776-X, North Holland) Elsevier.

Mathematical Elasticity Vol. II: Theory of Plates. P. G. Ciarlet. 262p. 1997. 166.50 (0-444-82570-3, North Holland) Elsevier.

Mathematical Elements for Computer Graphics. 2nd ed. David F. Rogers & J. Alan Adams. 512p. (C). 1989. pap. 54.69 (0-07-053530-2) McGraw.

Mathematical Encounters of the Second Kind. Philip J. Davis. LC 96-22131. 1996. write for info. (3-7643-3939-X) Birkhauser.

Mathematical Encounters of the Second Kind. Philip J. Davis. (Illus.). 304p. 1996. 24.95 (0-8176-3939-X) Birkhauser.

Mathematical Enculturation: A Cultural Perspective on Mathematics Education. Alan J. Bishop. (C). 1991. pap. text 49.00 (0-7923-1270-8) Kluwer Academic.

Mathematical Enrichment Exercises: A Teacher's Book. Dennis Thyer. 224p. 1993. pap. text 33.95 (0-304-32591-0) Continuum.

Mathematical Environmental Modeling. Uchrin. 1997. 49.95 (0-87371-447-4, L447) Lewis Pubs.

***Mathematical Epidemiology of Infectious Diseases: Model Building, Analysis & Interpretation.** O. Diekmann. (Illus.). 320p. 2000. 150.00 (0-471-98682-8) Wiley.

***Mathematical Epidemiology of Infectious Diseases: Model Building, Analysis & Interpretation.** O. Diekmann & J. A. Heesterbeek. LC 99-52964. (Series in Mathematical & Computational Biology). 2000. pap., boxed set. write for info. (0-471-49241-8) Wiley.

Mathematical Epistomology & Psychology. E. W. Beth & J. Piaget. Tr. by W. Mays from FRE. (Synthese Library: No. 12). 326p. 1974. text 182.50 (90-277-0071-0) Kluwer Academic.

Mathematical Essays: In Honor of Buchin Su. Ed. by C. C. Hsiung. 292p. 1983. text 55.00 (9971-950-98-7) World Scientific Pub.

Mathematical Essays in Honor of Gian-Carlo Rota. B. E. Sagan & R. Stanley. LC 98-15395. 300p. 1997. 69.50 (0-8176-3872-5) Birkhauser.

Mathematical Evolutionary Theory. Ed. by Marcus W. Feldman. LC 88-15591. (Illus.). 351p. reprint ed. pap. 108.90 (0-608-06320-7, 206668200008) Bks Demand.

M

Mathematical Experience. Philip J. Davis. 464p. 1999. pap. 18.00 (0-395-92968-7) HM.

Mathematical Experience. Philip J. Davis et al. 460p. 1987. 29.95 (0-8176-3018-X) Birkhauser.

Mathematical Experience. Philip J. Davis et al. 487p. 1995. student ed. 38.50 (0-8176-3739-7) Birkhauser.

Mathematical Exploration of the Environment. Istvan Ban. LC 95-236915. 115p. 1995. pap. 75.00 (963-05-6820-9, Pub. by Akade Kiado) St Mut.

Mathematical Explorations with MATLAB. Ke Chen et al. LC 99-19617. (Illus.). 320p. (C). 1999. text 64.95 (0-521-63078-9); pap. text 24.95 (0-521-63920-4) Cambridge U Pr.

Mathematical Exposition of Some Doctrines of Political Economy in 1829, 1831 & 1850: A Series of Papers Reprinted from the Transactions of the Cambridge Philosophical Society. William Whewell. LC 66-21700. (Reprints of Economic Classics Ser.). 1971. reprint ed. lib. bdg. 35.00 (0-678-00302-5) Kelley.

Mathematical Facts & Processes Prerequisite to the Study of Calculus. William H. Fagerstrom. LC 76-176761. (Columbia University. Teachers College. Contributions to Education Ser.: No. 572). reprint ed. 37.50 (0-404-55572-1) AMS Pr.

Mathematical Fallacies & Paradoxes. Marcia Ascher & Robert Ascher. LC 97-15386. 224p. 1997. reprint ed. pap. text 7.95 (0-486-29664-4) Dover.

***Mathematical Fallacies, Flaws & Filmflam.** Edward J. Barbeau. LC 99-67971. 152p. 1999. pap. 24.95 (0-88385-529-1) Math Assn.

Mathematical Finance. Ed. by Mark H. Davis et al. LC 94-44431. (IMA Volumes in Mathematics & Its Applications Ser.: Vol. 65). 1996. 59.95 (0-387-94439-7) Spr-Verlag.

Mathematical Footprints: Discovering Mathematical Impressions All Around Us. Theoni Pappas. LC 99-58173. (Illus.). 224p. 1999. pap. 10.95 (1-884550-21-5) Wide World-Tetra.

Mathematical Formula. S. Barnett. 1996. pap. write for info. (0-582-44758-5, Pub. by Addison-Wesley) Longman.

Mathematical Formula. 2nd ed. J. O. Bird. 1994. pap. 7.95 (0-582-22910-3, Pub. by Addison-Wesley) Longman.

Mathematical Formulae for Reference. Royal Society of Chemistry Staff. 1989. write for info. (0-85404-006-4) CRC Pr.

Mathematical Foundation of Parallel Computing. V. V. Voevodin. (Series on Soviet & East European Mathematics: Vol. 7). 364p. (C). 1992. text 74.00 (981-02-0820-0) World Scientific Pub.

Mathematical Foundation of Structural Mechanics. Francis X. Hartmann. (Illus.). 400p. 1985. 136.95 (0-387-15002-1) Spr-Verlag.

Mathematical Foundations see Elements of Hadronic Mechanics

Mathematical Foundations for Electromagnetic Theory. Donald G. Dudley. LC 94-3159. (Electromagnetic Waves Ser.). 264p. 1994. 59.95 (0-7803-1022-5, PC03715) Inst Electrical.

Mathematical Foundations for Electromagnetic Theory. Donald G. Dudley. (IEEE/OUP Series on Electromagnetic Wave Theory). (Illus.). 264p. (C). 1997. text 65.00 (0-19-859216-7) OUP.

Mathematical Foundations in Engineering & Science see Applied Algebra & Functional Analysis

Mathematical Foundations of Classical Statistical Mechanics, Vol. 6. D. Y. Petrina et al. xviii, 338p. 1989. text 383.00 (2-88124-681-8) Gordon & Breach.

Mathematical Foundations of Computer Science Vol. 1: Sets, Relations, & Induction. P. A. Fejer & D. A. Simovici. Ed. by David Gries. (Texts & Monographs in Computer Science). (Illus.). x, 428p. 1990. 79.95 (0-387-97450-4) Spr-Verlag.

Mathematical Foundations of Computer Science, 1976. Ed. by A. Mazurkiewicz. (Lecture Notes in Computer Science Ser.: Vol. 45). (Illus.). 1976. 33.95 (0-387-07854-1) Spr-Verlag.

Mathematical Foundations of Computer Science, 1977: Proceedings, 6th Symposium, Tatranska Lmnica, Sept. 5-9, 1977. Ed. by J. Gruska. LC 77-10135. (Lecture Notes in Computer Science Ser.: Vol. 53). 1977. 29.95 (0-387-08353-7) Spr-Verlag.

Mathematical Foundations of Computer Science, 1978: Proceedings, 7th Symposium Zakopane, Poland, Sept. 4-8, 1978. Ed. by J. Winkowski. (Lecture Notes in Computer Science Ser.: Vol. 64). 1978. 31.95 (0-387-08921-7) Spr-Verlag.

Mathematical Foundations of Computer Science, 1981. M. P. Chytil. Ed. by J. Gruska. (Lecture Notes in Computer Science Ser.: Vol. 118). 589p. 1981. 43.00 (0-387-10856-4) Spr-Verlag.

Mathematical Foundations of Computer Science, 1984: Praha, Czechoslovakia, September 3-8, 1984. M. P. Chytil et al. (Lecture Notes in Computer Science Ser.: Vol. 176). xi, 581p. 1984. 55.00 (0-387-13372-0) Spr-Verlag.

Mathematical Foundations of Computer Science, 1986. Ed. by J. Gruska et al. (Lecture Notes in Computer Science Ser.: Vol. 233). ix, 650p. 1986. 73.00 (0-387-16783-8) Spr-Verlag.

Mathematical Foundations of Computer Science, 1988. Ed. by M. P. Chytil et al. (Lecture Notes in Computer Science Ser.: Vol. 324). ix, 562p. 1988. 61.00 (0-387-50110-X) Spr-Verlag.

Mathematical Foundations of Computer Science, 1989. Ed. by A. Kreczmar & G. Mirkowska. (Lecture Notes in Computer Science Ser.: Vol. 379). viii, 605p. 1989. 65.00 (0-387-51486-4) Spr-Verlag.

Mathematical Foundations of Computer Science, 1990: Banska Bystrica, Czechoslovakia, August 27-31, 1990 Proceedings. Ed. by B. Rovan et al. (Lecture Notes in Computer Science Ser.). viii, 544p. 1990. 50.95 (0-387-52953-5) Spr-Verlag.

Mathematical Foundations of Computer Science, 1991: 16th International Symposium, Kazimierz Dolny, Poland, September 9-13, 1991 Proceedings. Ed. by Andrzej Tarlecki et al. (Lecture Notes in Computer Science Ser.: Vol. 520). xi, 435p. 1991. 44.95 (0-387-54345-7) Spr-Verlag.

Mathematical Foundations of Computer Science, 1992: 17th International Symposium, Prague, Czechoslovakia, August 24-28, 1992: Proceedings. Ed. by I. M. Havel & V. Koubek. LC 92-25414. (Lecture Notes in Computer Science Ser.: Vol. 629). ix, 521p. 1992. 74.00 (0-387-55808-X) Spr-Verlag.

Mathematical Foundations of Computer Science, 1993: 18th International Symposium, MFCS '93, Gdansk, Poland, August 30-September 3, 1993: Proceedings. Ed. by Andrzej M. Borzyszkowski & Stefan Sokolowski. LC 93-11820. (Lecture Notes in Computer Science Ser.: Vol. 711). 1993. pap. 107.00 (0-387-57182-5) Spr-Verlag.

Mathematical Foundations of Computer Science, 1994, 841. Ed. by I. Privara et al. (Lecture Notes in Computer Science Ser.: Vol. 841). 628p. 1994. pap. text 82.00 (0-387-58338-6) Spr-Verlag.

Mathematical Foundations of Computer Science, 1995: 20th International Symposium, MFCS'95, Prague, Czech Republic, August 28-September 1, 1995, Proceedings, Vol. XIII. Ed. by J. Wiedermann et al. (Lecture Notes in Computer Science Ser.: Vol. 969). 588p. 1995. pap. 87.00 (3-540-60246-1) Spr-Verlag.

Mathematical Foundations of Computer Science, 1996: 21st International Symposium, MFCS '96, Crakow, Poland, September 2-6, 1996: Proceedings. Ed. by Wojciech Penczek & Andrzej Szaas. LC 96-27444. (Lecture Notes in Computer Science Ser.: Vol. 111). 592p. 1996. pap. 94.00 (3-540-61550-4) Spr-Verlag.

Mathematical Foundations of Computer Science, 1997: 22nd International Symposium, MFCS'97, Bratislava, Slovakia, August 25-29, 1997, Proceedings. Ed. by I. Privara et al. (Lecture Notes in Computer Science Ser.: Vol. 1295). x, 519p. 1997. pap. 79.00 (3-540-63437-1) Spr-Verlag.

***Mathematical Foundations of Computer Science, 1998: 23rd International Symposium, MFCS '98, Brnmo, Czech Republic August 24-28, 1998.** Ed. by L. Brim et al. (Lecture Notes in Computer Science Ser.: Vol. 1450). xvii, 846p. 1998. pap. 90.00 (3-540-64827-5) Spr-Verlag.

***Mathematical Foundations of Computer Science, 1999: Proceedings, 24th International Symposium, MFCS'99, Szklarsaka Poreba, Poland, September 6-10, 1999.** Ed. by M. Kutylowski et al. xii, 455p. 1999. pap. 73.00 (3-540-66408-4) Spr-Verlag.

Mathematical Foundations of Elasticity. Jerrold E. Marsden & Thomas J. Hughes. (Illus.). 576p. 1994. reprint ed. pap. text 14.95 (0-486-67865-2) Dover.

Mathematical Foundations of Gauge Theories. Kishore B. Marathe & G. Martucci. LC 92-18717. (Studies in Mathematical Physics: Vol. 5). xxii, 372p. 1992. 136.00 (0-444-89708-9, North Holland) Elsevier.

Mathematical Foundations of Information Theory. Alexander I. Khinchin. 120p. 1957. pap. text 5.95 (0-486-60434-9) Dover.

Mathematical Foundations of Learning Machines. Nils J. Nilsson et al. 1998. pap. text 28.95 (1-55860-123-6) Morgan Kaufmann.

Mathematical Foundations of Neural Networks. Ellacott. (C). 1990. mass mkt. 88.00 (0-412-41460-0) Chapman & Hall.

Mathematical Foundations of Programming. Frank S. Beckman. LC 79-1453. 1980. text. write for info. (0-201-14462-X) Addison-Wesley.

Mathematical Foundations of Programming Language Semantics. Ed. by D. A. Schmidt et al. (Lecture Notes in Computer Science Ser.: Vol. 298). viii, 637p. 1988. 65.00 (0-387-19020-1) Spr-Verlag.

Mathematical Foundations of Programming Semantics. Michael G. Main et al. (Lecture Notes in Computer Science Ser.: Vol. 802). 648p. 1994. 93.95 (0-387-58027-1) Spr-Verlag.

Mathematical Foundations of Programming Semantics. Ed. by A. C. Melton. (Lecture Notes in Computer Science Ser.: Vol. 239). vi, 395p. 1986. 42.00 (0-387-16816-8) Spr-Verlag.

Mathematical Foundations of Programming Semantics: Ninth International Conference, New Orleans, LA, U. S. A., April 1993. Ed. by Stephen D. Brookes. No. 802. 1994. write for info. (0-318-72717-X) Spr-Verlag.

Mathematical Foundations of Programming Semantics: Seventh International Conference, Pittsburgh, PA, March 25-28, 1991, Proceedings. Ed. by D. A. Schmidt et al. LC 92-15320. (Lecture Notes in Computer Science Ser.: Vol. 598). viii, 506p. 1992. 69.95 (0-387-55511-0) Spr-Verlag.

Mathematical Foundations of Programming Semantics: 5th International Conference, Tulane University, New Orleans, Louisiana, USA, March 29 - April 1, 1989 Proceedings. Ed. by G. Goos et al. (Lecture Notes in Computer Science Ser.: Vol. 442). vi, 439p. 1990. 58.95 (0-387-97375-3) Spr-Verlag.

Mathematical Foundations of Quantum Mechanics. John Von Neumann. (Investigations in Physics Ser.: Vol. 2). 472p. 1955. text 89.50 (0-691-08003-8, Pub. by Princeton U Pr) Cal Prin Full Svc.

Mathematical Foundations of Quantum Mechanics. Newmann J. Von. 472p. 1955. pap. text 24.95 (0-691-02893-1, Pub. by Princeton U Pr) Cal Prin Full Svc.

Mathematical Foundations of Quantum Scattering Theory for Multiparticle Systems. I. M. Sigal. LC 78-10154. (Memoirs Ser.: No. 16/209). 147p. 1978. pap. 22.00 (0-8218-2209-8, MEMO/16/209) Am Math.

Mathematical Foundations of Quantum Statistical Mechanics: Continuous Systems. D. Y. Petrina. LC 94-39303. (Mathematics Physics Studies: Vol. 15). 1995. text 250.00 (0-7923-3258-X) Kluwer Academic.

Mathematical Foundations of Quantum Statistics. Aleksandr I. Khinchin. LC 97-47143. 232p. 1998. 8.95 (0-486-40025-5) Dover.

Mathematical Foundations of Software Development. Hartmut Ehrig. (Lecture Notes in Computer Science Ser.: Vol. 185). xiv, 418p. 1986. 42.00 (0-387-15198-2) Spr-Verlag.

Mathematical Foundations of Statistical Mechanics. Alexander I. Khinchin. Tr. by George Gamow. 179p. 1949. pap. text 6.95 (0-486-60147-1) Dover.

Mathematical Foundations of the Lie-Santilli Theory. Dimitri S. Sourlas & Grigorios T. Tsagas. (Monographs in Mathematics). 232p. 1994. pap. text 75.00 (0-911767-65-7) Hadronic Pr Inc.

Mathematical Foundations of the State Lumping of Large Systems. Vladimir S. Korolyuk. (Mathematics & Its Applications Ser.). 288p. (C). 1993. text 196.50 (0-7923-2413-7) Kluwer Academic.

Mathematical Foundations of Thermodynamics. R. Giles & Ian N. Sneddon. LC 63-10126. (International Series of Monographs on Pure & Applied Mathematics: Vol. 53). 1964. 111.00 (0-08-010071-6, Pub. by Pergamon Repr) Franklin.

Mathematical Frontiers in Computational Chemical Physics. Ed. by Donald G. Truhlar. (IMA Volumes in Mathematics & Its Applications Ser.: Vol. 15). (Illus.). xiii, 349p. 1988. 62.95 (0-387-96782-6) Spr-Verlag.

Mathematical Fun, Games & Puzzles. Jack Frohlichstein. (Illus.). (Orig.). 1962. pap. 7.95 (0-486-20789-7) Dover.

Mathematical Fundamentals for Microeconomics. C. Barry Pfitzner. LC 92-72588. 150p. (C). 1992. pap. text 25.95 (1-878975-13-7) Blackwell Pubs.

Mathematical Funfair. Brian Bolt. (Illus.). 128p. (C). 1990. pap. 18.95 (0-521-37743-9) Cambridge U Pr.

Mathematical Games & Pastimes. A. Domoryad & H. Moss. LC 63-16860. (Popular Lectures in Mathematics: Vol. 10). 1963. 142.00 (0-08-013673-7, Pub. by Pergamon Repr) Franklin.

Mathematical Gardner see Mathematical Recreations: A Collection in Honor of Martin Gardner

***Mathematical Gems from the Bolyai Chests.** Elemer Kiss. LC 99-236795. (Illus.). 200p. 1999. 48.00 (963-9132-21-7) Intl Spec Bk.

Mathematical Gems from the Bolyai Chests: Janos Bolyai's Discoveries in Number Theories & Algebra as Recently Deciphered from His Manuscripts. Elemer Kiss. LC 99-236795. (Illus.). 200p. 1999. 48.00 (963-05-7563-9, Pub. by Akade Kiado) Intl Spec Bk.

Mathematical Gems III. Ross Honsberger. LC 85-61842. (Dolciani Mathematical Expositions Ser.: No. 9). 260p. 1985. pap. 12.00 (0-88385-318-3, DEP-09) Math Assn.

Mathematical Gems II. Ross Honsberger. LC 76-15927. (Dolciani Mathematical Expositions Ser.: No. 2). 192p. 1976. pap. 12.00 (0-88385-319-1, DEP-02) Math Assn.

Mathematical Geography & Global Art: The Mathematics of David Barr's "Four Corners Project" Sandra L. Arlinghaus & John D. Nystuen. (Monographs: No. 1). (Illus.). 78p. (Orig.). (C). 1986. pap. 15.95 (1-877751-02-2); pap. text 15.95 (1-877751-03-0) Inst Math Geo.

Mathematical Geology & Geoinformatics see Proceedings of the 30th International Geological Congress

Mathematical Geology & Geological Information: Proceedings of the 27th International Geological Congress, Vol. 20. International Geological Congress Staff. 306p. 1984. lib. bdg. 87.50 (90-6764-029-8, Pub. by VSP) Coronet Bks.

Mathematical Geophysics: A Survey of Recent Developments in Seismology & Geodynamics Ser. Ed. by N. J. Vlaar et al. (C). 1987. text 132.50 (90-277-2620-5) Kluwer Academic.

Mathematical Go: Chilling Gets the Last Point. Elwyn R. Berlekamp & David Wolfe. LC 93-46609. (Illus.). 256p. 1994. 39.00 (1-56881-032-6) AK Peters.

Mathematical Grammar of English. George Hemphill. (Janua Linguarum, Series Practica: No. 153). 1973. text 25.40 (90-279-2433-3) Mouton.

Mathematical Graphics Cookbook. Cameron Smith. (C). 1995. pap. text. write for info. (0-201-60975-4) Addison-Wesley.

***Mathematical Handbook for Scientist & Engineer.** G. Korneck & T. W. Korner. 2000. pap. 26.95 (0-486-41147-8) Dover.

Mathematical Heritage of C. F. Gauss. G. M. Rassias. 550p. (C). 1991. text 118.00 (981-02-0201-6) World Scientific Pub.

Mathematical Heritage of Henri Poincare, 2 Pts., Pt. 1. Ed. by Felix E. Browder. LC 83-2774. (Proceedings of Symposia in Pure Mathematics Ser.: Vol. 39). 435p. 1984. reprint ed. pap. 58.00 (0-8218-1448-6, PSPUM/39.2) Am Math.

Mathematical Heritage of Henri Poincare, 2 Pts., Pt. 2. Ed. by Felix E. Browder. LC 83-2774. (Proceedings of Symposia in Pure Mathematics Ser.: Vol. 39). 470p. 1984. reprint ed. pap. 58.00 (0-8218-1449-4, PSPUM/39.1) Am Math.

Mathematical Heritage of Henri Poincare, 2 Pts., Set. Ed. by Felix Browder. LC 83-2774. (Proceedings of Symposia in Pure Mathematics Ser.: Vol. 39). 905p. 1984. reprint ed. pap. 49.00 (0-8218-1442-7, PSPUM/39) Am Math.

Mathematical Heritage of Hermann Weyl. R. O. Wells. LC 88-19367. (Proceedings of Symposia in Pure Mathematics Ser.: No. 48). 344p. 1988. pap. 39.00 (0-8218-1482-6, PSPUM/48) Am Math.

Mathematical Hierarchies & Biology: DIMACS Workshop, November 13-15, 1996. B. G. Mirkin et al. LC 97-26706. (DIMACS Series in Discrete Mathematics & Theoretical Computer Science). 388p. 1997. text 79.00 (0-8218-0762-5) Am Math.

Mathematical History: Activities, Puzzles, Stories & Games. Merle Mitchell. LC 78-26206. (Illus.). 74p. 1978. pap. 12.95 (0-87353-138-8) NCTM.

Mathematical History of the Golden Number. Roger Herz-Fischler. LC 97-52729. 1998. pap. 13.95 (0-486-40007-7) Dover.

***Mathematical Ideas.** (C). 2000. 29.00 (0-536-61113-0) Pearson Custom.

Mathematical Ideas. 7th ed. Charles D. Miller et al. LC 93-1955. 828p. (C). 1993. 14.50 (0-673-99095-8) Addson-Wesley Educ.

Mathematical Ideas. 8th ed. (C). 1997. text. write for info. (0-321-40184-0) Addison-Wesley.

Mathematical Ideas. 8th ed. Charles D. Miller et al. LC 96-25478. 928p. (C). 1997. 86.00 (0-673-99893-2) Addson-Wesley Educ.

***Mathematical Ideas.** 9th ed. (C). 2000. pap. 26.40 (0-321-07606-0, Celebration); pap. text 0.00 (0-321-07603-6, Celebration); pap. text 0.00 (0-321-07604-4, Celebration); pap. text 0.00 (0-321-07602-8, Celebration); pap. text 0.00 (0-321-07607-9, Celebration); pap. text 0.00 (0-321-07608-7, Celebration) Addson-Wesley Educ.

***Mathematical Ideas.** 9th ed. (C). 2000. text. write for info. (0-321-04324-3) Addison-Wesley.

***Mathematical Ideas.** 9th ed. (C). 2000. text. write for info. (0-321-07666-4); text. write for info. (0-321-07667-2) Addison-Wesley.

Mathematical Ideas: Custom Book (8th Edition) 8th ed. Miller. 970p. (C). 1997. pap. text 75.00 (0-321-01303-4) Addson-Wesley Educ.

Mathematical Ideas: Solutions Manual. 8th ed. Charles D. Miller. 464p. (C). 1997. pap. text, student ed. 25.00 (0-673-98371-4) Addison-Wesley.

***Mathematical Ideas Alt Edtn Florida Version.** 9th ed. (C). 2000. pap. text 0.00 (0-321-07610-9, Celebration) Addson-Wesley Educ.

Mathematical Ideas & Sociological Theory: Current State & Prospects, A Special Issue of the Journal of Mathematical Sociology. Thomas J. Fararo. iv, 188p. 1984. pap. text 64.00 (0-677-16635-4) Gordon & Breach.

Mathematical Impressions. Anatolii T. Fomenko. LC 90-47514. 184p. 1990. text 19.00 (0-8218-0162-7, MATIMP) Am Math.

Mathematical Intelligent Learning Environments. Hyacinth S. Nwana. 272p. (Orig.). 1993. pap. text 29.95 (1-871516-29-3, Pub. by Intellect) Cromland.

Mathematical Introduction to Conformal Field Theory: Lectures at the Mathematisches Institut der Universit at Hamburg. Martin Schottenloher. LC 97-7263. (Lecture Notes in Physics Ser.). 1997. write for info. (3-540-61753-1) Spr-Verlag.

Mathematical Introduction to Fluid Mechanics. 2nd ed. Alexandre J. Chorin & Jerrold E. Marsden. (Texts in Applied Mathematics Ser.: Vol. 4). (Illus.). ix, 168p. 1990. 29.00 (0-387-97300-1) Spr-Verlag.

Mathematical Introduction to Fluid Mechanics. 3rd ed. Alexandre J. Chorin & Jerrold E. Marsden. LC 92-26645. (Texts in Applied Mathematics Ser.: Vol. 4). (Illus.). 170p. 1994. 41.95 (0-387-97918-2) Spr-Verlag.

Mathematical Introduction to Linear Programming & Game Theory. L. Brickman. (Undergraduate Texts in Mathematics Ser.). (Illus.). ix, 130p. 1989. 42.95 (0-387-96931-4) Spr-Verlag.

Mathematical Introduction to Logic. Herbert B. Enderton. 1972. text 48.00 (0-12-238450-4) Acad Pr.

Mathematical Introduction to Robotic Manipulation. Zexiang Li & Richard M. Murray. 480p. (C). 1994. boxed set 104.95 (0-8493-7981-4, TJ211) CRC Pr.

Mathematical Introduction to Wavelets. P. Wojtaszczyk. LC 96-37157. (London Mathematical Society Student Texts Ser.: No. 37). 272p. 1997. text 64.95 (0-521-57020-4); pap. text 24.95 (0-521-57894-9) Cambridge U Pr.

Mathematical Intuition. Richard L. Tieszen. (Synthese Library: No. 203). 224p. 1989. lib. bdg. 138.50 (0-7923-0131-5, Pub. by Kluwer Academic) Kluwer Academic.

Mathematical Intuitionism & Intersubjectivity: A Critical Exposition of Arguments for Intuitionism. Tomasz Placek. LC 99-18111. (Synthese Library). 1999. write for info. (0-7923-5630-6) Kluwer Academic.

Mathematical Intuitionism, Introduction to Proof Theory. A. Dragalin. LC 87-32766. (Translations of Mathematical Monographs: Vol. 67). 228p. 1988. text 93.00 (0-8218-4520-9, MMONO/67) Am Math.

Mathematical Investigation of the Effect of Machinery on the Wealth of a Community & On the Effect Of the Non-Residence of Landlords On the Wealth of a Community. John Tozer. LC 66-21696. (Reprints of Economic Classics Ser.). xxi, 24p. 1968. 27.50 (0-678-00300-9) Kelley.

Mathematical Investigations, Bk. 1. R. Souviney et al. 168p. 1997. 18.95 (0-86651-502-X) Seymour Pubns.

Mathematical Investigations, Bk. 2. R. Souviney et al. 240p. 1997. 18.95 (0-86651-541-0) Seymour Pubns.

Mathematical Investigations: An Introduction to Algebraic Thinking. alternate ed. 320p. (C). 1997. text, teacher ed. write for info. (0-06-502382-X) Addson-Wesley Educ.

An Asterisk (*) at the beginning of an entry indicates that the title is appearing for the first time.

Mathematical Investigations: An Introduction to Algebraic Thinking. alternate ed. DeMarios & McGowen. 144p. (C). 1997. pap., student ed. 25.00 (*0-06-502383-8*) Addson-Wesley Educ.

***Mathematical Investigations: An Introduction to Algebraic Thinking.** 2nd ed. Phil DeMarois et al. LC 00-21999. 624p. 2000. pap. text 75.00 (*0-321-06931-5*) Addson-Wesley Educ.

Mathematical Investigations in the Theory of Value & Prices: Appreciation & Interest. Irving Fisher. LC 90-4603. (Reprints of Economic Classics Ser.). 226p. 1991. reprint ed. lib. bdg. 35.00 (*0-678-01456-6*) Kelley.

Mathematical Jamboree. Brian Bolt. (Illus.). 111p. (C). 1995. pap. 19.95 (*0-521-48589-4*) Cambridge U Pr.

Mathematical Journals: An Annotated Guide. Compiled by Diana F. Liang. LC 92-18459. 246p. 1992. 36.00 (*0-8108-2585-6*) Scarecrow.

Mathematical Journey. 2nd ed. Gudder. 1993. text, teacher ed. 32.50 (*0-07-025131-2*) McGraw.

Mathematical Journey. 2nd ed. Stanley P. Gudder. LC 93-1359. (C). 1994. text 67.50 (*0-07-025130-4*); pap. text, student ed. 17.25 (*0-07-025133-9*) McGraw.

Mathematical Kaleidoscope: Applications in Industry, Business & Science. Brian Conolly & Steven Vajda. (Illus.). 256p. 1995. pap. 25.00 (*1-898563-21-7*) Paul & Co Pubs.

Mathematical Knowledge: Its Growth Through Teaching. Ed. by Alan J. Bishop. 200p. (C). 1991. lib. bdg. 126.50 (*0-7923-1344-5*) Kluwer Academic.

Mathematical Knowledge for Primary Teachers. Jennifer Suggate. 1998. pap. 28.95 (*1-85346-559-3*) Taylor & Francis.

Mathematical Learning Models - Theory & Algorithms. Ed. by U. Herkenrath et al. (Lecture Notes in Statistics Ser.: Vol. 20). 226p. 1983. 56.95 (*0-387-90913-3*) Spr-Verlag.

Mathematical Legacy of Eduard Cech. Peter Simon. Ed. by Miroslav Katetov. LC 93-3188. 448p. 1993. 112.00 (*0-8176-2861-4*, Pub. by Birkhauser) Princeton Arch.

Mathematical Legacy of Hanno Rund. Ed. by J. Vladimir Kadeisvili. 440p. 1994. pap. text 90.00 (*0-911767-80-0*) Hadronic Pr Inc.

***Mathematical Legacy of Harish-Chandra: A Celebration of Representation Theory & Harmonic Analysis.** Ed. by Robert S. Doran & V. S. Varadarajan. (PSPUM Ser.: Vol. 68). 549p. 2000. 110.00 (*0-8218-1197-5*) Am Math.

Mathematical Legacy of Wilhelm Magnus: Groups, Geometry, & Special Functions. Ed. by William Abikoff et al. LC 94-11625. (Contemporary Mathematics Ser.: Vol. 169). 499p. 1994. pap. 80.00 (*0-8218-5156-X*, CONM/169) Am Math.

Mathematical Linguistics in the Soviet Union. Ferenc Papp. (Janua Linguarum, Ser. Minor: No. 40). (Orig.). 1966. pap. text 20.80 (*0-686-22446-9*) Mouton.

Mathematical Location & Land Use Theory: An Introduction. Tonu Puu. LC 96-52372. (Advances in Spatial Science Ser.). (Illus.). 294p. 1997. 109.00 (*3-540-61819-8*) Spr-Verlag.

Mathematical Logic. H. D. Ebbinghaus et al. Tr. by A. S. Ferebee from GER. (Undergraduate Texts in Mathematics Ser.). (Illus.). 280p. 1990. 36.00 (*0-387-90895-1*) Spr-Verlag.

Mathematical Logic. Ed. by P. P. Petkov. (Illus.). 420p. (C). 1990. 144.00 (*0-306-43511-X*, Plenum Trade) Perseus Pubng.

Mathematical Logic. Daniel Ponasse. LC 72-136738. (Notes on Mathematics & Its Applications Ser.). Orig. Title: Logique Mathematique. x, 126p. (C). 1973. text 160.00 (*0-677-30390-4*) Gordon & Breach.

Mathematical Logic. Jan T. Srzednicki. 84.95 (*1-84014-182-4*) Ashgate Pub Co.

Mathematical Logic. rev. ed. Willard V. Quine. LC 51-7541. 358p. 1979. pap. 16.95 (*0-674-55451-5*) HUP.

Mathematical Logic. 2nd ed. Heinz-Dieter Ebbinghaus et al. LC 93-50621. (Under Graduate Texts in Mathematics Ser.). 289p. 1996. 49.95 (*0-387-94258-0*) Spr-Verlag.

Mathematical Logic 2nd ed. Heinz-Dieter Ebbinghaus et al. LC 97-108485. (Undergraduate Texts in Mathematics Ser.). x, 289 p. 1996. write for info. (*3-540-94258-0*) Spr-Verlag.

Mathematical Logic: An Introduction to Model Theory. A. H. Lightstone. LC 77-17838. (Mathematical Concepts & Methods in Science & Engineering Ser.: Vol. 9). (Illus.). 352p. 1978. 55.00 (*0-306-30894-0*, Plenum Trade) Perseus Pubng.

Mathematical Logic: Application & Theory. Jean Rubin. 417p. (C). 1990. text 81.50 (*0-03-012808-0*) SCP.

Mathematical Logic: Proceedings of the First Brazilian Conference, Held 1977. Brazilian Conference on Mathematical Logic Staff. Ed. by Ayda I. Arruda et al. LC 78-14488. (Lecture Notes in Pure & Applied Mathematics Ser.: No. 39). 319p. 1978. reprint ed. pap. 98.90 (*0-608-01331-5*, 206207400001) Bks Demand.

***Mathematical Logic : A Course with Exercises Part 1: Propositional Calculus.** Rene Cori & Daniel Lascar. Tr. by Donald H. Pelletier. 352p. 2000. pap. text 39.95 (*0-19-850048-3*) OUP.

***Mathematical Logic : A Course with Exercises Part 1: Propositional Calculus.** Rene Cori & Daniel Lascar. Tr. by Donald H. Pelletier. 352p. 2000. text 70.00 (*0-19-850049-1*) OUP.

Mathematical Logic & Applications. Ed. by J. Shinoda et al. (Lecture Notes in Mathematics Ser.: Vol. 1388). v, 222p. 1989. 36.95 (*0-387-51527-5*) Spr-Verlag.

Mathematical Logic & Formal Systems. L. P. De Alcantara. (Lecture Notes in Pure & Applied Mathematics Ser.: Vol. 94). (Illus.). 320p. 1985. pap. text 155.00 (*0-8247-7330-6*, 7330-6) Dekker.

Mathematical Logic & Hilbert's E-Symbol. A. C. Leisenring. x, 142p. 1969. text 249.00 (*0-677-61790-9*) Gordon & Breach.

Mathematical Logic & Its Applications. Ed. by D. G. Skordev. LC 87-20243. (Illus.). 386p. 1987. 95.00 (*0-306-42599-8*, Plenum Trade) Perseus Pubng.

Mathematical Logic & Theoretical Computer Science. Ed. by David W. Kueker & Edgar G. K. Lopez-Escobar. (Lecture Notes in Pure & Applied Mathematics Ser.: Vol. 106). (Illus.). 408p. 1986. pap. text 165.00 (*0-8247-7746-8*) Dekker.

Mathematical Logic for Computer Science. Ed. by Z. W. Lu. (Series in Computer Science: Vol. 13). 260p. (C). 1989. text 60.00 (*9971-5-0251-8*) World Scientific Pub.

Mathematical Logic for Computer Science, 47. 2nd ed. 250p. 1997. text 33.00 (*981-02-3091-5*) World Scientific Pub.

Mathematical Logic, the Theory of Algorithms & the Theory of Sets: Dedicated to Academician Petr Sergeevic Novikov. Ed. by S. I. Adjan. LC 77-3359. (Proceedings of the Steklov Institute of Mathematics Ser.: No. 133). 274p. 1977. pap. 90.00 (*0-8218-3033-3*, STEKLO/133) Am Math.

Mathematical Look at the Calendar. Richard L. Francis. (Hi Map Ser.: No. 5610). (Illus.). 60p. pap. text 9.99 (*0-614-05316-1*, HM 5610) COMAP Inc.

Mathematical Magic. William Simon. LC 93-15007. (Illus.). 192p. 1993. reprint ed. pap. 6.95 (*0-486-27593-0*) Dover.

Mathematical Magic Show. Martin Gardner. (MAA Spectrum Ser.). 312p. 1990. pap. 8.00 (*0-88385-449-X*, MAGIC) Math Assn.

Mathematical Magpie: Being More Stories, Mainly Transcendental, Plus Subsets of Essays, Rhymes, Music, Anecdotes, Epigrams, & Other Prime Oddments & Diversions, Rational or Irrational, All Derived from the Infinite Domain of Mathematics. 2nd ed. Clifton Fadiman. LC 97-1187. (Copernicus Ser.). 320p. 1997. pap. 19.95 (*0-387-94950-X*) Spr-Verlag.

***Mathematical, Management, & Statistical Sciences--The Index to the 20th Century, Prologue to the 21st Century.** Ed. by Joo O. Koo. LC 00-131646. (American Series in Mathematical & Management Sciences: Vol. 42). (Illus.). 200p. 2000. 195.00 (*0-935950-46-X*) Am Sciences Pr.

Mathematical Medley: Gleanings from the Globe & Beyond. Winton Laubach. Ed. by Norma Frey & Janet Laubach. LC 99-94703. (Illus.). 146p. 1999. pap. 13.75 (*0-9670087-0-0*) Aftermath Pubng.

Mathematical Method: A Transition to Advanced Mathematics. Murray Eisenberg. LC 95-650. 1995. text 57.00 (*0-13-127002-8*) P-H.

***Mathematical Method Algorithm Signl Process.** (C). 2000. write for info. (*0-13-016561-1*) S&S Trade.

Mathematical Methods. School Mathematics Project Staff. (Mathematics Series: Ages 16-19). 160p. (C). 1990. pap. text 11.95 (*0-521-40894-6*) Cambridge U Pr.

Mathematical Methods. 2nd ed. Merle C. Potter. 1978. 69.95 (*1-881018-11-3*) Grt Lks Pr.

***Mathematical Methods: For Students of Physics & Related Fields.** Sadri Hassani. LC 99-52788. (Undergraduate Texts in Contemporary Physics Ser.). (Illus.). 672p. 2000. 69.95 (*0-387-98958-7*) Spr-Verlag.

Mathematical Methods: Unit Guide. School Mathematics Project Staff. (School Mathematics Project 16-19 Ser.). 160p. 1990. pap. text 13.95 (*0-521-40885-7*) Cambridge U Pr.

***Mathematical Methods: With Applications.** M. Rahman. 450p. 2000. 155.00 (*1-85312-847-3*, Pub. by WIT Pr) Computational Mech MA.

***Mathematical Methods & Algorithms for Signal Processing.** Todd K Moon. LC 99-31038. 937p. (C). 1999. text 105.00 incl. cd-rom, audio compact disk (*0-201-36186-8*, Prentice Hall) P-H.

Mathematical Methods & Models for Economists. Angel de la Fuente. LC 98-52086. (Illus.). 848p. (C). 2000. text 90.00 (*0-521-58512-0*); pap. text 39.95 (*0-521-58529-5*) Cambridge U Pr.

Mathematical Methods & Theory in Games, Programming, & Economics. Samuel Karlin. xxii, 819p. 1992. reprint ed. pap. 24.95 (*0-486-67020-1*) Dover.

Mathematical Methods for Artificial Intelligance & Autonomous Systems. Charles R. Giardina & Edward R. Dougherty. (Illus.). 512p. 1988. text 61.40 (*0-13-560913-5*) P-H.

Mathematical Methods for CAD. J. J. Risler. (Illus.). 198p. (C). 1993. text 100.00 (*0-521-43100-X*) Cambridge U Pr.

Mathematical Methods for Construction of Queueing Models. Vladimir V. Kalashnikov & S. T. Rachev. LC 89-70639. (Illus.). 325p. (C). 1990. text 69.95 (*0-534-13254-5*) Chapman & Hall.

Mathematical Methods for Curves & Surfaces II: Lillehammer, 1997. Ed. by Morten Daehlen et al. LC 98-15040. (Innovations in Applied Mathematics Ser.). (Illus.). 576p. (C). 1998. text 55.00 (*0-8265-1315-8*) Vanderbilt U Pr.

Mathematical Methods for Digital Computers, Vol. 1. Ed. by Anthony Ralston & Herbert S. Wilf. LC QA0076.5.R34. 305p. 1960. reprint ed. pap. 94.60 (*0-608-08272-4*, 205566900030) Bks Demand.

Mathematical Methods for Digital Computers, Vol. 3. Ed. by Anthony Ralston & Herberts Wilf. LC 60-6509. 464p. reprint ed. pap. 143.90 (*0-608-08273-2*, 205655400003) Bks Demand.

Mathematical Methods for DNA Sequences. Ed. by Michael S. Waterman. 288p. 1988. lib. bdg. 215.95 (*0-8493-6664-X*, QP624) CRC Pr.

***Mathematical Methods for Economic Theory 1.** J. C. Moore. Ed. by C. D. Aliprantis & N. C. Yannelis. LC 99-46807. (Studies in Economic Theory: Vol. 9). (Illus.). xii, 414p. 1999. 64.95 (*3-540-66235-9*) Spr-Verlag.

***Mathematical Methods for Economic Theory 2.** James C. Moore. Ed. by C. D. Aliprantis & N. C. Yannelis. LC 99-46807. (Studies in Economic Theory: Vol. 10). (Illus.). x, 339p. 1999. 64.95 (*3-540-66242-1*) Spr-Verlag.

Mathematical Methods for Economics. Michael Klein. LC 97-21670. 562p. (C). 1997. 92.00 (*0-201-85572-0*) Addison-Wesley.

Mathematical Methods for Economics. Michael Klein. (C). 1998. pap. text. write for info. (*0-201-33900-5*) Addison-Wesley.

Mathematical Methods for Economists. 3rd ed. Stephen Glaister. 216p. 1984. pap. 32.95 (*0-631-13712-2*) Blackwell Pubs.

Mathematical Methods for Engineers. R. K. Livesley. 1989. text 74.95 (*0-470-21468-6*) P-H.

Mathematical Methods for Industrial Problems: Proceedings of the International Workshop, Bari, Italy, 1988. Ed. by V. Capasso & R. Caselli. 344p. 1989. 199.00 (*90-6764-122-7*, Pub. by VSP) Coronet Bks.

Mathematical Methods for Introductory Physics with Calculus. 3rd ed. Ronald C. Davidson. LC 94-5656. (C). 1994. pap. text 29.50 (*0-03-009128-4*, Pub. by SCP) Harcourt.

Mathematical Methods for Neural Network Analysis & Design. Richard M. Golden. LC 96-25116. (Illus.). 435p. (C). 1996. 67.50 (*0-262-07174-6*, Bradford Bks) MIT Pr.

Mathematical Methods for Oceanographers: An Introduction. Edward Laws. LC 96-31998. 343p. 1997. 90.00 (*0-471-16221-3*) Wiley.

Mathematical Methods for Physicists. 4th ed. Ed. by George B. Arfken & Hans-Jurgen Weber. (Illus.). 1029p. 1995. text 73.00 (*0-12-059815-9*) Acad Pr.

Mathematical Methods for Physicists & Engineers. 2nd unabridged ed. Royal E. Collins. LC 98-28913. 15p. 1998. pap. 14.95 (*0-486-40229-0*) Dover.

Mathematical Methods for Physics. H. W. Wyld. (Lecture Notes & Supplements in Physics Ser.: Vol. 15). 628p. (C). 1976. pap. 50.00 (*0-8053-9857-0*) Addison-Wesley.

Mathematical Methods for Physics. 4th ed. George B. Arfken. 1995. pap. text 42.00 (*0-12-059816-7*) Acad Pr.

Mathematical Methods for Physics & Engineering: A Comprehensive Guide. K. F. Riley et al. LC 96-52942. (Illus.). 1028p. (C). 1998. pap. text 49.95 (*0-521-55529-9*) Cambridge U Pr.

Mathematical Methods for Scientists & Engineers: Linear & Nonlinear Systems. Peter B. Kahn. LC 89-32383. 469p. 1990. 120.00 (*0-471-62305-9*) Wiley.

Mathematical Methods for Scientists & Engineers: Linear & Nonlinear Systems. Peter B. Kahn. LC 89-32383. 496p. 1996. pap. 59.95 (*0-471-16611-1*) Wiley.

Mathematical Methods for System Theory. F. Gentili et al. LC 98-2575. 550p. 1998. 88.00 (*981-02-3334-5*) World Scientific Pub.

Mathematical Methods in Artificial Intelligence. Edward A. Bender. LC 95-24708. 664p. 1996. 59.00 (*0-8186-7200-5*, BP07200) IEEE Comp Soc.

Mathematical Methods in Chemical Engineering. Arvind Varma & Massimo Morbidelli. (Topics in Chemical Engineering Ser.). (Illus.). 704p. (C). 1997. text 88.00 (*0-19-509821-8*) OUP.

Mathematical Methods in Chemical Engineering. 2nd ed. Ed. by V. G. Jenson & G. V. Jeffreys. 1978. pap. text 59.00 (*0-12-384456-8*) Acad Pr.

Mathematical Methods in Chemistry & Physics. M. E. Starzak. (Illus.). 662p. (C). 1989. text 95.00 (*0-306-43066-5*, Kluwer Plenum) Kluwer Academic.

Mathematical Methods in Classical Mechanics. V. I. Arnold. (Graduate Texts in Mathematics Ser.: Vol. 60). (Illus.). 1978. 39.00 (*0-387-90314-3*) Spr-Verlag.

Mathematical Methods in Clinical Practice. Ed. by Gurii I. Marchuk & N. I. Nisevich. (Illus.). 150p. 1980. 50.00 (*0-08-025493-4*, Pub. by Pergamon Repr) Franklin.

Mathematical Methods in Contemporary Chemistry. Ed. by S. I. Kuchanov. 456p. 1995. text 132.00 (*2-88449-125-2*) Gordon & Breach.

Mathematical Methods in Defense Analyses. 2nd ed. J. S. Przemieniecki. LC 94-25921. (Illus.). 425p. 1994. 74.95 (*1-56347-092-6*, 92-6) AIAA.

***Mathematical Methods in Defense Analyses.** 3rd ed. J. S. Przemieniecki. LC 00-33138. 2000. write for info. (*1-56347-397-6*) AIAA.

***Mathematical Methods in Dynamic Economics.** Andras Simonovits. LC 99-42139. 2000. text 69.95 (*0-312-22940-2*) St Martin.

Mathematical Methods in Economics. Ed. by Frederick Van der Ploeg. LC 84-2327. (Handbook of Applicable Mathematics Ser.: Vol. 6). 608p. 1984. reprint ed. pap. 188.50 (*0-608-04604-3*, 206537400003) Bks Demand.

Mathematical Methods in Electrical Engineering. Thomas B. Senior. (Illus.). 288p. 1986. text 57.95 (*0-521-30661-2*) Cambridge U Pr.

Mathematical Methods in Electromagnetism: Linear Theory & Applications. M. Cessenat. (Series on Advances in Mathematics for Applied Sciences). 384p. 1996. text 68.00 (*981-02-2467-2*, Ma-B2938) World Scientific Pub.

Mathematical Methods in Energy Research. Ed. by Kenneth I. Gross. LC 84-52185. (Proceedings in Applied Mathematics Ser.: No. 15). (Illus.). ix, 242p. 1984. text 38.75 (*0-89871-199-1*) Soc Indus-Appl Math.

Mathematical Methods in Geophysical Imaging IV, Vol. 2822. Ed. by Siamak Hassanzadeh. 224p. 1996. 46.00 (*0-8194-2210-X*) SPIE.

Mathematical Methods in Geophysical Imaging V, Vol. 3453. Ed. by Siamak Hassanzadeh. LC 99-192663. 1998. 59.00 (*0-8194-2908-2*) SPIE.

Mathematical Methods in Human Geography & Planning. Alan G. Wilson & R. J. Bennett. LC 85-6435. (Handbook of Applicable Mathematics, Guidebook Ser.: No. 7). 427p. reprint ed. pap. 132.40 (*0-8357-2609-6*, 203992900014) Bks Demand.

Mathematical Methods in Hydrodynamics & Integrability in Dynamical Systems: La Jolla Institute, 1981. American Institute of Physics. Ed. by Michael Tabor & Yvain M. Treve. LC 82-72462. (AIP Conference Proceedings Ser.: No. 88). 352p. 1982. lib. bdg. 34.00 (*0-88318-187-8*) Am Inst Physics.

Mathematical Methods in Kinetic Theory. 2nd ed. C. Cercignani. (Illus.). 263p. (C). 1990. 59.50 (*0-306-43460-1*, Plenum Trade) Perseus Pubng.

Mathematical Methods in Linguistics. Barbara H. Partee et al. 684p. (C). 1990. pap. text 35.00 (*90-277-2245-5*, D Reidel); lib. bdg. 185.00 (*90-277-2244-7*, D Reidel) Kluwer Academic.

Mathematical Methods in Management. Geoffrey Gregory. LC 82-23836. (Handbook of Applicable Mathematics, Guidebook Ser.: No. 2). 166p. reprint ed. pap. 51.50 (*0-8357-3397-1*, 203965400013) Bks Demand.

Mathematical Methods in Medicine. Richard Ernest Bellman. (Series in Modern Applied Mathematics: Vol. 1). 268p. 1983. text 52.00 (*9971-950-20-0*); pap. text 30.00 (*9971-950-21-9*) World Scientific Pub.

Mathematical Methods in Medicine Pt. I: Statistical & Analytical Techniques. fac. ed. Ed. by D. Ingram & R. F. Bloch. LC 83-17044. (Handbook of Applicable Mathematics, Guidebook Ser.: No. 3-4). (Illus.). 476p. 1984. reprint ed. pap. 147.60 (*0-608-00994-6*, 206185100001) Bks Demand.

Mathematical Methods in Optimization of Differential Systems. Viorel Barbu. LC 94-37359. (Mathematics & Its Applications Ser.: Vol. 310).Tr. of Methode Matematice in Optimizarea Sistemelor Diferentiale. 259p. (C). 1994. text 178.50 (*0-7923-3176-1*) Kluwer Academic.

Mathematical Methods in Physics. Samuel D. Lindenbaum. LC 96-31604. 450p. 1996. write for info. (*981-02-2760-4*) World Scientific Pub.

Mathematical Methods in Physics & Engineering. John W. Dettman. (Illus.). 448p. 1988. reprint ed. pap. text 10.95 (*0-486-65649-7*) Dover.

Mathematical Methods in Queueing Theory. Vladimir V. Kalashnikov. LC 93-43035. (Mathematics & Its Applications Ser.: Vol. 271). 388p. (C). 1994. text 205.50 (*0-7923-2568-0*) Kluwer Academic.

Mathematical Methods in Risk Theory. 2nd ed. H. Buhlmann. Ed. by M. Berger et al. (Grundlehren der Mathematischen Wissenschaften Ser.: Vol. 172). xii, 210p. 1996. pap. 69.95 (*3-540-61703-5*) Spr-Verlag.

Mathematical Methods in Sample Surveys. LC 98-29452. 206p. 1998. 24.00 (*981-02-2617-9*) World Scientific Pub.

Mathematical Methods in Scattering Theory & Biomedical Technology. Ed. by G. Dassios et al. (Pitman Research Notes in Mathematics Ser.: No. 390). 248p. 1998. pap. 51.00 (*0-582-36804-9*) Addison-Wesley.

Mathematical Methods in Science. George Polya. Ed. by Leon Bowden. LC 76-25863. (New Mathematical Library: No. 26). 234p. 1977. pap. text 6.00 (*0-88385-626-3*, NML-26) Math Assn.

Mathematical Methods in Small Group Processes. Ed. by Joan Criswell et al. viii, 361p. 1962. 47.50 (*0-8047-0116-4*) Stanford U Pr.

Mathematical Methods in Small Group Processes: Papers. fac. ed. Symposium on Mathematical Methods in Small Group P. Ed. by Joan H. Criswell et al. LC 62-8660. (Stanford Mathematical Studies in the Social Sciences: No. 8). 371p. 1962. reprint ed. pap. 30.00 (*0-7837-7918-6*, 204767400008) Bks Demand.

Mathematical Methods in Social Science. David J. Bartholomew. LC 80-41593. (Handbook of Applicable Mathematics, Guidebook Ser.: No. 1). 163p. reprint ed. pap. 50.60 (*0-7837-6367-0*, 204607900010) Bks Demand.

Mathematical Methods in Statistics: A Workbook. David Freedman & David Love. (C). 1981. pap. text, wbk. ed. 18.00 (*0-393-95223-1*) Norton.

Mathematical Methods in the Physical Sciences. 2nd ed. Mary L. Boas. LC 83-1226. 816p. 1983. text 102.95 (*0-471-04409-1*) Wiley.

Mathematical Methods in the Physical Sciences. 2nd ed. Mary L. Boas. 616p. (C). 1984. pap., teacher ed. 49.95 (*0-471-09920-1*) Wiley.

Mathematical Methods in the Physical Sciences. 3rd ed. Boas. text (*0-471-19826-9*) Wiley.

Mathematical Methods in the Social & Managerial Sciences. Patrick Hayes. LC 74-22361. 478p. reprint ed. 148.20 (*0-8357-9930-1*, 201741300007) Bks Demand.

Mathematical Methods in the Social Sciences, 1959: Proceedings. Stanford Symposium on Mathematical Methods in the. Ed. by Kenneth Joseph Arrow et al. LC 60-9048. (Stanford Mathematical Studies in the Social Sciences: No. 4). 273p. 1960. reprint ed. pap. 30.00 (*0-7837-1096-8*, 204162800021) Bks Demand.

Mathematical Methods in Tomography: Proceedings of a Conference Held in Oberwolfach, 5-11 June, 1990. Ed. by G. T. Herman et al. (Lecture Notes in Mathematics Ser.: Vol. 1497). x, 268p. 1992. 47.00 (*0-387-54970-6*) Spr-Verlag.

Mathematical Methods of Airfoil Design: Inverse Boundary Value Problems of Aerohydrodynamics. Alexander M. Elizarov & Nikolay B. Ilinskiy. 292p. 1997. 136.50 (*3-05-501701-3*) Wiley.

Mathematical Methods of Airfoil Design: Inverse Boundary-Value Problems of Aerohydrodynamics. Alexander M. Elizarov et al. 292p. 1997. 149.95 (*3-527-40080-X*) Wiley.

Mathematical Methods of Analysis of Biopolymer Sequences. Ed. by Simon G. Gindikin. Tr. by Oksana Khleborodova from RUS. LC 92-30834. (DIMACS Series in Discrete Mathematics & Theoretical Computer Science: Vol. 8). 150p. 1992. text 48.00 (*0-8218-6601-X*, DIMACS/8) Am Math.

Mathematical Methods of Classical Mechanics. 2nd ed. V. I. Arnold. (Graduate Texts in Mathematics Ser.: Vol. 60). (Illus.). 520p. 1997. text 49.95 (*0-387-96890-3*) Spr-Verlag.

Mathematical Methods of Game & Economic Theory. 2nd ed. Jean P. Aubin. (Studies in Mathematics & Its Applications: Vol. 7). 616p. 1980. 257.50 (*0-444-85184-4*, North Holland) Elsevier.

Mathematical Methods of Physics. Joseph J. Kyame. (Illus.). 460p. 1979. pap. text 29.95 (*0-89641-017-X*) American Pr.

Mathematical Methods of Physics. H. W. Wyld. LC 99-60036. 656p. 1999. pap. text 45.00 (*0-7382-0125-1*, Pub. by Perseus Pubng) HarpC.

Mathematical Methods of Physics. 2nd ed. Jon Mathews & Robert L. Walker. 501p. (C). 1971. pap. text 101.00 (*0-8053-7002-1*) Addison-Wesley.

Mathematical Methods of Population Biology. Frank C. Hoppensteadt. (Cambridge Studies in Mathematical Biology: No. 4). (Illus.). 144p. 1982. pap. text 23.95 (*0-521-28256-X*) Cambridge U Pr.

***Mathematical Methods of Quantum Physics: 2nd Jagna International Workshop: Essays in Honor of Professor Hiroshi Ezawa.** Ed. by C. C. Bernido et al. 362p. 1999. text 120.00 (*90-5699-211-2*) Gordon & Breach.

Mathematical Methods of Specification & Synthesis of Software Systems '85. Ed. by Wolfgang Bibel & K. P. Jantke. (Lecture Notes in Computer Science Ser.: Vol. 215). 245p. 1986. 33.00 (*0-387-16444-8*) Spr-Verlag.

Mathematical Methods of Statistical Mechanics of Model Systems. 288p. 1993. 100.00 (*0-8493-7744-7*) CRC Pr.

Mathematical Methods of Statistics. H. Cramer. (Mathematical Ser.: Vol. 9). 592p. 1946. text 89.50 (*0-691-08004-6*, Pub. by Princeton U Pr) Cal Prin Full Svc.

***Mathematical Methods of Statistics.** Harald Cramer. LC 99-12156. 1999. pap. text 24.95 (*0-691-00547-8*, Pub. by Princeton U Pr) Cal Prin Full Svc.

Mathematical Methods with Special Functions. B. D. Gupta. x, 906p. (C). 1992. pap. 25.00 (*81-220-0268-4*, Pub. by Konark Pubs Pvt Ltd) Advent Bks Div.

Mathematical Metrological & Chronological Tablets from the Temple Library of Nippur. Hermann V. Hilprecht. LC 08-33648. (University of Pennsylvania, Babylonian Expedition, Series A: Cuneiform Texts: Vol. 20, Pt. 1). 135p. reprint ed. pap. 41.90 (*0-608-13647-6*, 205201900027) Bks Demand.

Mathematical Model Building: An Introduction to Engineering. 2nd rev. ed. Charles R. Mischke. LC 79-25436. (Illus.). 408p. 1980. reprint ed. pap. 126.50 (*0-608-00076-0*, 206083900006) Bks Demand.

Mathematical Model of Aggregate Plant Production. Donn E. Hancher & John A. Havers. 115p. 1974. pap. 3.00 (*0-87262-071-9*) Am Soc Civil Eng.

Mathematical Modeling. Mark M. Meerschaert. (Illus.). 287p. 1993. text 53.00 (*0-12-487650-1*) Acad Pr.

Mathematical Modeling. 2nd ed. Meerschaer. LC 98-19869. 351p. (C). 1998. text 59.95 (*0-12-487652-8*) Acad Pr.

Mathematical Modeling: A Chemical Engineer's Perspective. Rutherford Aris. LC 98-89644. (Illus.). 479p. 1999. text 99.95 (*0-12-604585-2*) Acad Pr.

Mathematical Modeling: Applications in Emergency Health Services. Ralph B. D'Agostino et al. LC 84-12917. (Emergency Health Services Review Ser.: Vol. 2, Nos. 2-3). 118p. 1984. 29.95 (*0-86656-373-3*) Haworth Pr.

Mathematical Modeling & Computer Simulation of Biomechanical Systems. A. V. Zinkovsky & V. A. Sholuha. LC 97-139934. 200p. 1997. text 42.00 (*981-02-2395-1*) World Scientific Pub.

Mathematical Modeling & Computer Simulation of Processes in Energy Systems. Ed. by Kemal Hanjalic. (International Centre for Heat & Mass Transfer Ser.). 1000p. 1990. 297.00 (*0-89116-875-3*) Hemisp Pub.

Mathematical Modeling & Estimation Techniques in Computer Vision, Vol. 3457. Ed. by Francoise Preteux et al. LC 99-193800. 1998. 69.00 (*0-8194-2912-0*) SPIE.

Mathematical Modeling & Numerical Techniques in Drying Technology. Ed. by Ian Turner & Arun S. Mujumdar. LC 96-18672. (Illus.). 688p. 1996. text 215.00 (*0-8247-9818-X*) Dekker.

Mathematical Modeling & Scale-Up of Liquid Chromatography. T. Y. Gu. (Illus.). 130p. 1995. 85.95 (*3-540-58884-1*) Spr-Verlag.

Mathematical Modeling & Scale-Up of Liquid Chromatography. Tingyue Gu. LC 95-15162. 1995. write for info. (*0-387-58884-1*) Spr-Verlag.

Mathematical Modeling & Simulation in Hydrodynamic Stability. D. N. Riahi. 350p. 1996. text 86.00 (*981-02-2308-0*) World Scientific Pub.

Mathematical Modeling Courses. John S. Berry. (Mathematics & Its Applications Ser.). 340p. 1987. text 104.00 (*0-470-20836-8*) P-H.

Mathematical Modeling Courses for Engineering Education. Ed. by Yasar Esrby et al. (NATO ASI Series F: Computer & Systems Science: Vol. 132). 246p. 1994. 71.95 (*0-387-58010-7*) Spr-Verlag.

Mathematical Modeling for Design. Bhonsle. LC 98-13195. 448p. (C). 1998. pap. text 52.00 (*0-13-727231-6*, Prentice Hall) P-H.

Mathematical Modeling for Flow & Transport Through Porous Media. Ed. by Gedeon Dagan et al. (C). 1992. text 186.00 (*0-7923-1616-9*) Kluwer Academic.

Mathematical Modeling for Industry. Thomas P. Svobodny. LC 97-35547. 534p. (C). 1997. 90.67 (*0-13-260894-4*) P-H.

Mathematical Modeling for Industry, Science & Government. C. R. MacCluer. LC 99-27073. 308p. 1999. 76.00 (*0-13-949199-6*) P-H.

Mathematical Modeling in Combustion & Related Topics. Ed. by Claude-Michel Brauner & Claudine Schmidt-Laine. (C). 1988. text 211.50 (*90-247-3656-0*) Kluwer Academic.

Mathematical Modeling in Combustion Science. Ed. by John D. Buckmaster & Tadeo Takeno. (Lecture Notes in Physics Ser.: Vol. 299). vi, 168p. 1988. 34.95 (*0-387-19181-X*) Spr-Verlag.

Mathematical Modeling in Ecology: A Workbook for Students. Clark Jeffries. (Mathematical Modeling Ser.: No. 3). 193p. 1988. 48.50 (*0-8176-3421-5*) Birkhauser.

Mathematical Modeling in Epidemiology. J. C. Frauenthal. (Universitext Ser.). 118p. 1980. 53.95 (*0-387-10328-7*) Spr-Verlag.

Mathematical Modeling in Experimental Nutrition: Proceedings of a Conference Held in Davis, California, August 17-20, 1997. Ed. by Andrew J. Clifford. LC 98-8315. (Advances in Experimental Medicine & Biology Ser.: Vol. 445). (Illus.). 436p. (C). 1998. text 125.00 (*0-306-46020-3*, Kluwer Plenum) Kluwer Academic.

Mathematical Modeling in the Environment. Charles Hadlock. LC 98-86932. (Classroom Resource Materials). 302p. 1998. pap. text 55.00 (*0-88385-709-X*) Math Assn.

Mathematical Modeling in the Life Sciences. Paul Doucet & Peter B. Sloep. LC 92-36766. (Ellis Horwood Series in Mathematics & Its Applications). 450p. 1993. pap. text 45.00 (*0-13-562018-X*, Pub. by Tavistock-E Horwood) Chapman & Hall.

Mathematical Modeling in the Secondary School Curriculum: A Resource Guide of Classroom Exercises. Ed. by Frank J. Swetz & J. S. Hartzler. LC 90-25644. (Illus.). 136p. 1991. pap. 14.95 (*0-87353-306-2*) NCTM.

Mathematical Modeling in the Undergraduate Curriculum: Proceedings of the 1994 Conference. Ed. by Helen Skala. (1994 Ser.). (Illus.). 156p. (Orig.). (C). 1995. pap. 10.00 (*0-9647164-0-2*) U WI Math Dept.

Mathematical Modeling in the Undergraduate Curriculum: Proceedings of the 1996 Conference. Ed. by Helen Skala. 404p. (Orig.). (C). 1997. pap. 15.00 (*0-9647164-1-0*) U WI Math Dept.

Mathematical Modeling in the Undergraduate Curriculum: Proceedings of the 1998 Symposium. Ed. by Helen Skala. (Nineteen Ninety-Eight Ser.). 229p. (C). 1999. pap. 15.00 (*0-9647164-2-9*) U WI Math Dept.

Mathematical Modeling in Tumor Growth & Progression. Ed. by Seth Michelson. (Invasion & Metastasis Ser.: Vol. 16, No. 4-5, 1997). (Illus.). 100p. 1997. pap. 48.75 (*3-8055-6548-8*) S Karger.

Mathematical Modeling of Cell Proliferation: Stem Cell Regulation in Hemopoiesis, 2 vols. Ed. by H. E. Wichmann & M. Loeffler. Incl. Vol. I. Model Description, Irradiation, Erythropoietic Stimulation. 248p. 1985. 141.00 (*0-8493-5503-6*, QP91); Vol. II. Erythropoietic Suppression, Combined Stresses, Drug Effects. 224p. 1985. 126.00 (*0-8493-5504-4*, QP91, CRC Reprint); 1985. write for info. (*0-318-59107-3*) CRC Pr.

Mathematical Modeling of Chemical Processes. Ostrovsky. 1991. 104.00 (*0-8493-7132-5*, TP155) CRC Pr.

Mathematical Modeling of Convective Heat & Mass Transfer on the Basis of Navier Stokes Equations. Ed. by V. S. Avduevsky et al. 200p. 1991. 115.00 (*1-56032-005-2*) CRC Pr.

Mathematical Modeling of Creep & Shrinkage of Concrete. fac. ed. Ed. by Zdenek P. Bazant. LC 88-17422. (Wiley Series in Numerical Methods in Engineering). (Illus.). 485p. 1988. reprint ed. pap. 150.40 (*0-608-00985-7*, 206184100012) Bks Demand.

Mathematical Modeling of Energy Systems. Ed. by Ibbrahim Kavrakoglu. (NATO Advanced Study Institute Ser.: Applied Science, No. 37). 490p. 1981. text 155.50 (*90-286-0690-4*) Kluwer Academic.

Mathematical Modeling of Fire, Vol. STP 983. Ed. by J. R. Mehaffey. 140p. 1988. pap. 26.00 (*0-8031-0992-X*, STP983) ASTM.

Mathematical Modeling of Hydrologic Series. G. G. Svanidze. LC 79-57578. 1980. 35.00 (*0-918334-32-2*) WRP.

Mathematical Modeling of Materials Processing Operations: Proceedings of Symposium Held in Palm Springs, California, U. S. A., November 29-December 2, 1987 at the Fifth Extractive & Process Metallurgical Fall Meeting. Metallurgical Society of AIME Staff. Ed. by J. Szekely et al. LC 87-42884. 1212p. reprint ed. pap. 200.00 (*0-7837-1437-8*, 205241100016) Bks Demand.

Mathematical Modeling of Melting & Freezing Processes. V. Alexiades & Alan D. Solomon. 275p. 1992. 57.95 (*1-56032-125-3*) Hemisp Pub.

Mathematical Modeling of Metabolic & Endocrine Systems: Model Formulation, Identification & Validation. Ewart R. Carson et al. LC 82-13402. (Biomedical Engineering & Health Systems Ser.). 418p. reprint ed. pap. 129.60 (*0-7837-2834-4*, 205763800006) Bks Demand.

Mathematical Modeling of Pharmacokinetic Data. David W. Bourne. LC 94-61269. 142p. 1995. text 104.95 (*1-56676-204-9*) Technomic.

Mathematical Modeling of the Immune Response. Daniela Prikrylova. 224p. 1992. boxed set 125.00 (*0-8493-6753-0*, QR186) CRC Pr.

Mathematical Modelling. J. Berry. (Plastics Ser.). 1995. pap. 17.95 (*0-340-61404-8*, VNR) Wiley.

Mathematical Modelling: Classroom Notes in Applied Mathematics. Ed. by Murray S. Klamkin. LC 86-60090. (Miscellaneous Bks.: No. 15). (Illus.). xiv, 338p. 1987. pap. text 41.50 (*0-89871-204-1*) Soc Indus-Appl Math.

***Mathematical Modelling: Concepts & Case Studies** J. Caldwell & Y. M. Ram. LC 99-29973. (Mathematical Modelling Ser.). 1999. write for info. (*0-7923-5820-1*) Kluwer Academic.

***Mathematical Modelling: Teaching & Assessment in a Technology-Rich World.** P. Galbraith et al. LC 99-208374. 368p. 1999. 75.00 (*1-898563-42-X*, Pub. by Horwood Pub) Paul & Co Pubs.

Mathematical Modelling & Differential Equations. A. M. Blokhin. 217p. (C). 1996. lib. bdg. 135.00 (*1-56072-310-6*) Nova Sci Pubs.

Mathematical Modelling & Simulation of Electrical Circuits & Semiconductor Devices. Ed. by R. E. Bank et al. LC 94-21583. (International Numerical Mathematics Ser.: Vol. 117). 336p. 1994. 99.50 (*0-8176-5053-9*) Birkhauser.

Mathematical Modelling & Simulation of Electrical Circuits & Semiconductor Devices: Proceedings of a Conference Held at the Mathematisches Forschunginstitut, Oberwolfach, Oct. 30-Nov. 5, 1988. Ed. by R. E. Bank et al. (International Series of Numerical Mathematics: Vol. 93). 312p. 1990. 87.50 (*0-8176-2439-2*) Birkhauser.

Mathematical Modelling Courses for Engineering Education. Ed. by Yasar Esroy & A. O. Moscardini. LC 94-22842. (NATO ASI Series F: Computer & Systems Science: Vol. 132). 1994. write for info. (*3-540-58010-7*) Spr-Verlag.

Mathematical Modelling for Materials Processing. Ed. by Mark Cross et al. (Institute of Mathematics & Its Applications Conference Series, New Ser.: New Series 42). (Illus.). 576p. (C). 1993. text 125.00 (*0-19-853687-9*) OUP.

Mathematical Modelling in Biology & Ecology: Proceedings of a Symposium Held at the CSIR, Pretoria, July 1979. Ed. by W. M. Getz. (Lecture Notes in Biomathematics Ser.: Vol. 33). viii, 355p. 1980. pap. 28.00 (*3-540-09735-X*) Spr-Verlag.

Mathematical Modelling in Biomedicine. Y. Cherruault. 1986. text 144.00 (*90-277-2149-1*) Kluwer Academic.

***Mathematical Modelling in Continuum Mechanics.** Roger Temam & Alain Miranville. LC 99-86300. (Illus.). 350p. (C). 2000. 54.95 (*0-521-64362-7*) Cambridge U Pr.

Mathematical Modelling in Economics: Essays in Honor of Wolfgang Eichhorn, Vol. XVIII. Ed. by W. Erwin Diewert et al. LC 93-34005. 713p. 1993. 159.00 (*0-387-57224-4*) Spr-Verlag.

Mathematical Modelling in Non-Destructive Testing. Ed. by Michael Blakemore & George A. Georgiou. (Institute of Mathematics & Its Applications Conference Series, New Ser.: New Series 16). (Illus.). 378p. 1988. 79.00 (*0-19-853622-4*) OUP.

Mathematical Modelling in Science & Technology: Proceedings of 6th International Conference, St Louis, MO, August 1987. Ervin Y. Rodin & Xavier J. Avula. (Mathematical Modeling Ser.). 1300p. 1989. pap. 315.00 (*0-08-036380-6*, Pergamon Pr) Elsevier.

Mathematical Modelling in the Theory of Multivelocity Continuum. A. M. Blokhin & V. N. Dorovsky. 192p. (C). 1995. lib. bdg. 165.00 (*1-56072-240-1*) Nova Sci Pubs.

Mathematical Modelling Methodology, Models & Micros. Berry. (Mathematics & Its Applications Ser.). 350p. 1986. text 97.95 (*0-470-20717-5*) P-H.

Mathematical Modelling of Flow through Porous Media. LC 96-137329. 528p. 1995. 79.00 (*981-02-2483-4*) World Scientific Pub.

Mathematical Modelling of Groundwater Pollution. Ne-Zheng Sun. LC 94-10680. 1995. 84.95 (*0-387-94212-2*) Spr-Verlag.

Mathematical Modelling of Heat & Mass Transfer Processes. V. G. Danilov et al. (Mathematics & Its Applications Ser.: Vol. 348). 316p. (C). 1995. text 173.50 (*0-7923-3789-1*) Kluwer Academic.

Mathematical Modelling of Immune Response in Infectious Diseases, Vol. 395. G. I. Marchuk. LC 97-12156. (Mathematics & Its Applications Ser.). 1997. text 187.00 (*0-7923-4528-2*) Kluwer Academic.

Mathematical Modelling of Industrial Processes: Lectures Given at the 3rd Session of the Centro Internazionale Matematico Estive Held in Bari, Italy, Sept. 24-29, 1990. Stavros N. Busenberg et al. Ed. by Vincenzo Capasso & A. P. Fasano. LC 92-16917. 1992. 40.95 (*0-387-55595-1*) Spr-Verlag.

Mathematical Modelling of Inelastic Deformation. J. F. Besseling & E. Van Der Giessen. LC 93-32189. 328p. (gr. 13). 1994. ring bd. 78.95 (*0-412-45280-4*, Chap & Hall CRC) CRC Pr.

Mathematical Modelling of Planar Flame Propagation. Henri Berestycki & Bernard Larrouturou. LC 93-4716. (Pitman Monographs & Surveys in Pure & Applied Mathematics). 1996. pap. write for info. (*0-582-03332-2*) Longman.

Mathematical Modelling of Solids with Nonregular Boundaries. A. B. Movchan & N. V. Movchan. Ed. by N. Bellomo. LC 95-23090. (Mathematical Modelling Ser.). 352p. 1995. boxed set 99.95 (*0-8493-8338-2*, 8338) CRC Pr.

Mathematical Modelling of Tides & Estuarine Circulation. P. B. Crean et al. (Lecture Notes on Coastal & Estuarine Studies: Vol. 30). xv, 471p. 1988. pap. 65.00 (*0-387-96897-0*) Spr-Verlag.

Mathematical Modelling of Trace Elements in Biological Systems. Johnathan L. Kiel. LC 94-36841. 234p. 1995. lib. bdg. 189.95 (*0-8493-4576-6*) CRC Pr.

Mathematical Modelling of Turbulent Diffusion in the Environment. C. J. Harris. LC 79-50301. (Institute of Mathematics & Its Applications Conference Series, New Ser.). 1980. text 150.00 (*0-12-328350-7*) Acad Pr.

Mathematical Modelling of Weld Phenomena. Ed. by H. Cerjak & K. E. Easterling. 370p. 1992. 170.00 (*0-901716-16-2*, Pub. by Inst Materials) Ashgate Pub Co.

Mathematical Modelling of Weld Phenomena 2. 2nd ed. Ed. by H. Cerjak & H. K. Bhadeshia. 287p. 1995. 170.00 (*0-901716-63-4*, Pub. by Inst Materials) Ashgate Pub Co.

Mathematical Modelling of Weld Phenomena 3. Ed. by H. Cerjak. (Illus.). 960p. 1997. 240.00 (*1-86125-010-X*, Pub. by Inst Materials) Ashgate Pub Co.

Mathematical Modelling of Weld Phenomena 4. Ed. by H. Cerjak. (Materials Modelling Ser.). (Illus.). 708p. 1998. 200.00 (*1-86125-060-6*, Pub. by Inst Materials) Ashgate Pub Co.

Mathematical Modelling Techniques. Rutherford Aris. (Illus.). 288p. 1995. reprint ed. pap. 9.95 (*0-486-68131-9*) Dover.

Mathematical Modelling with Chernobyl Registry Data: Registry & Concepts. Ed. by W. Morgenstern et al. 110p. 1995. 21.95 (*3-540-60411-1*) Spr-Verlag.

Mathematical Models. 458p. (C). 1998. pap. text 33.50 (*0-536-02051-5*) Pearson Custom.

Mathematical Models. H. M. Cundy & A. P. Rollett. 1996. pap., teacher ed. 18.95 (*0-906212-20-0*, Pub. by Tarquin Pubns) Parkwest Pubns.

Mathematical Models: Mechanical Vibrations, Population Dynamics, & Traffic Flow. Richard Haberman. LC 97-62401. (Classics in Applied Mathematics Ser.: Vol. 21). (Illus.). xvii, 402p. (C). 1998. pap. text 40.00 (*0-89871-408-7*, CL21) Soc Indus-Appl Math.

Mathematical Models: Preliminary Edition. Robert L. Kimball. (Illus.). 209p. (C). 1996. pap. text 18.67 (*0-13-271297-0*) P-H.

Mathematical Models & Design Methods in Solid-Liquid Separation. Ed. by Albert Rushton. 1985. text 184.00 (*90-247-3140-2*) Kluwer Academic.

Mathematical Models & Methods of Localized Interaction Theory. A. I. Bunimovich & A. V. Dubinskii. (Series on Advances in Mathematics). 244p. 1995. text 86.00 (*981-02-1743-9*) World Scientific Pub.

Mathematical Models & Simulation in Solar Energy Research for Buildings. Ed. by A. V. Sebald. 237p. 1980. pap. 36.00 (*0-08-025453-5*, Pergamon Pr) Elsevier.

Mathematical Models As a Tool for Social Sciences. Bruce J. West. xii, 120p. 1980. text 157.00 (*0-677-10390-5*) Gordon & Breach.

***Mathematical Models for Biological Pattern Formulation: Frontiers in Biological Mathematics.** Philip K. Maini & H. G. Othmer. LC 00-44018. (IMA Volumes in Mathematics & Its Applications Ser.). 2000. write for info. (*0-387-95103-2*) Spr-Verlag.

Mathematical Models for Decision Support. Ed. by G. Mitra et al. LC 88-30718. (NATO Asi Series F: Vol. 48). ix, 756p. 1988. 180.95 (*0-387-50084-7*) Spr-Verlag.

Mathematical Models for Elastic Structures. Piero Villaggio. (Illus.). 692p. (C). 1997. text 150.00 (*0-521-57324-6*) Cambridge U Pr.

Mathematical Models for Handling Partial Knowledge in Artificial Intelligence: Proceedings of the International School of Mathematics "G Stampacchia" 18th Workshop Held in Erice, Italy, June 19-25, 1994. G. Coletti et al. LC 95-34723. (Illus.). 318p. (C). 1995. text 110.00 (*0-306-45076-3*, Kluwer Plenum) Kluwer Academic.

Mathematical Models for Particle Dissolution in Extrudable Aluminum Alloys. Fred Vermolen. (Illus.). 284p. 1998. pap. 57.50 (*90-407-1697-8*, Pub. by Delft U Pr) Coronet Bks.

Mathematical Models for Phase Change Problems. J. F. Rodrigues. (International Series of Numerical Mathematics: No. 88). 408p. 1989. 137.00 (*0-8176-2309-4*) Birkhauser.

Mathematical Models for Structural Reliability Analysis. Fabio Casciati & J. B. Roberts. LC 96-28018. 384p. 1996. lib. bdg. 95.00 (*0-8493-9631-X*) CRC Pr.

Mathematical Models for the Semantics of Parallelism. Ed. by Zilli Venturini. (Lecture Notes in Computer Science Ser.: Vol. 280). v, 231p. 1987. 33.00 (*0-387-18419-8*) Spr-Verlag.

Mathematical Models in Applied Mechanics. A. B. Tayler. (Oxford Applied Mathematics & Computing Science Ser.). (Illus.). 280p. 1986. pap. 29.95 (*0-19-853541-4*) OUP.

Mathematical Models in Biology. Leah Edelstein-Keshet. 600p. (C). 1988. 86.56 (*0-07-554950-6*) McGraw.

***Mathematical Models in Boundary Layer Theory.** O. A. Oleinik & V. N. Samokhin. LC 99-25191. 528p. 1999. boxed set 74.95 (*1-58488-015-5*, Chap & Hall CRC) CRC Pr.

***Mathematical Models in Boundary Layer Theory.** O. A. Oleinik & V. N. Samokhin. 528p. 1999. 74.95 (*0-8493-0840-2*) CRC Pr.

Mathematical Models in Computer Systems. M. Arato & L. Varga. 1981. pap. 170.00 (*963-05-2945-9*, Pub. by Akade Kiado) St Mut.

Mathematical Models in Economics: Oxford University Mathematical Economic Seminar 25th Anniversary. anniversary ed. Ed. by M. O. L. Bacharach et al. (Illus.). 476p. 2000. text 55.00 (*0-19-823296-9*) OUP.

Mathematical Models in Electrical Circuits: Theory & Applications. Pekka Neittaanmaki & C. A. Marinov. (C). 1991. text 118.00 (*0-7923-1155-8*) Kluwer Academic.

Mathematical Models in Environmental Policy. L. A. Petrosjan & V. V. Zakharov. LC 98-112188. 207p. 1997. 95.00 (*1-56072-515-X*) Nova Sci Pubs.

An Asterisk (*) at the beginning of an entry indicates that the title is appearing for the first time.

Mathematical Models in Finance. S. D. Howison et al. 1995. ring bd. 64.95 (*0-412-63070-2*) Chapman & Hall.

Mathematical Models in Immunology. Gurii I. Marchuk. Ed. by A. V. Balakrishnan. LC 83-8269. (Translations Series in Mathematics & Engineering). (Illus.). 378p. 1983. pap. text 98.00 (*0-911575-01-4*) Optimization Soft.

Mathematical Models in Immunology. G. I. Mnarchuk. (Illus.). xxv, 351p. 1983. pap. 89.00 (*0-387-90901-X*) Spr-Verlag.

Mathematical Models in Marketing. P. S. Leeflang. lib. bdg. 24.00 (*0-685-02820-8*) Kluwer Academic.

Mathematical Models in Marketing. P. S. Leeflang. 1974. pap. text 78.50 (*90-207-0436-2*, Pub. by Kluwer Academic) Kluwer Academic.

Mathematical Models in Medical & Health Science. Ed. by Mary Ann Horn et al. LC 98-38746. (Innovations in Applied Mathematics Ser.). (Illus.). 496p. 1998. text 60.00 (*0-8265-1310-7*) Vanderbilt U Pr.

Mathematical Models in Medical Diagnosis. M. C. Miller, III et al. LC 81-5170. 187p. 1981. 62.95 (*0-275-91349-X*, C1349, Praeger Pubs) Greenwood.

Mathematical Models in Medicine, Vol. 2. M. Witten. (Computers & Mathematics with Applications Ser.: No. 301). 310p. 1988. 95.00 (*0-08-036377-6*, Pergamon Pr) Elsevier.

Mathematical Models in Medicine: Diseases & Epidemics, Vol. 7, Nos. 5-12. Ed. by M. Witten. 1100p. 1987. 215.00 (*0-08-034692-8*, Pergamon Pr) Elsevier.

Mathematical Models in Microbial Population Dynamics. Ed. by Richard B. Philp. 288p. 1981. 164.00 (*0-8493-6110-9*, RM340, CRC Reprint) Franklin.

Mathematical Models in Microbial Population Dynamics, Vol. I. Ed. by Michael J. Bazin. 216p. 1982. 122.00 (*0-8493-5951-1*, QR86, CRC Reprint) Franklin.

Mathematical Models in Statistical Mechanics. Ed. by M. Fannes & A. Verbeure. (Leuven Notes in Mathematical & Theoretical Physics Ser.: No. 1). 200p. (Orig.). 1989. pap. 37.50 (*90-6186-306-6*, Pub. by Leuven Univ) Coronet Bks.

Mathematical Models in the Applied Sciences. A. C. Fowler. LC 97-10390. (Texts in Applied Mathematics Ser.: Vol. 17). (Illus.). 416p. (C). 1997. text 85.00 (*0-521-46140-5*); pap. text 37.95 (*0-521-46703-9*) Cambridge U Pr.

Mathematical Models in the Earth Sciences: Proceedings of the 7th Geochautauqua, Syracuse University, Oct. 1978. Ed. by J. M. Cubitt. 90p. 1980. pap. 50.00 (*0-08-025305-9*, Pergamon Pr) Elsevier.

Mathematical Models in the Social Management & Life Sciences. D. N. Burghes & A. D. Wood. LC 79-40989. (Mathematics & Its Applications Ser.). 287p. 1980. pap. text 41.95 (*0-470-27073-X*) P-H.

Mathematical Models in Water Pollution Control. Ed. by A. James. LC 77-7214. (Wiley-Interscience Publications). 436p. reprint ed. pap. 135.20 (*0-608-12458-3*, 202520000042) Bks Demand.

Mathematical Models of Chemical Reactions: Theory & Application. Erdi. 284p. 85.00 (*0-471-93515-8*) Wiley.

Mathematical Models of Conception & Birth. Mindel C. Sheps & Jane Menken. 1994. lib. bdg. 25.00 (*0-226-75245-3*) U Ch Pr.

Mathematical Models of Financial Derivatives. Y. K. Kwok. LC 98-2950. (Illus.). 250p. (C). 1998. 69.50 (*981-3083-25-5*) Spr-Verlag.

Mathematical Models of Group Structure. Thomas F. Mayer. LC 74-1031. (Studies in Sociology). (C). 1975. pap. text 3.00 (*0-672-61212-7*, Bobbs) Macmillan.

Mathematical Models of Morphogenesis. Reane F. Thom. (Mathematics & Its Applications Ser.). 305p. 1983. text 78.95 (*0-470-27499-9*) P-H.

Mathematical Models of Soviet Foreign Trade Optimization. Gene Davidovich. Ed. by Melissa Dawson. 247p. (Orig.). 1989. pap. text 75.00 (*1-55831-106-8*) Delphic Associates.

Mathematical Models of the Circadian Sleep-Wake Cycle. Ed. by Martin C. Moore-Ede & Charles A. Czeisler. LC 83-19054. (Illus.). 224p. 1984. reprint ed. pap. 69.50 (*0-608-00639-4*, 206122700007) Bks Demand.

Mathematical Models of Thermal Conditions in Buildings. Yuri A. Tabunshchikov. 240p. 1992. lib. bdg. 139.00 (*0-8493-9310-8*, TH6025) CRC Pr.

*__Mathematical Morphology.__ Ed. by J. Goutsias & H. J. A. M. Heijmans. 266p. 2000. pap. 98.00 (*1-58603-056-6*) IOS Press.

Mathematical Morphology: Theory & Hardware. Ed. by Robert M. Haralick. LC 96-17718. (Oxford Series on Optical & Imaging Sciences: No. 12). (Illus.). 672p. 2000. text 75.00 (*0-19-508187-0*) OUP.

*__Mathematical Morphology & Its Applications to Image & Signal Processing.__ John Goutsias et al. LC 00-30174. (International Series in Engineering & Computer Science). 2000. write for info. (*0-7923-7862-8*) Kluwer Academic.

Mathematical Morphology & Its Applications to Image & Signal Processing. Henk J. Heijmans & Jos B. Roerdink. LC 98-8190. (Computational Imaging & Vision Ser.). 1998. 195.00 (*0-7923-5133-9*) Kluwer Academic.

Mathematical Morphology & Its Applications to Image & Signal Processing. Ed. by Petros Maragos et al. LC 96-14893. (Computational Imaging & Vision Ser.). 488p. (C). 1996. text 180.50 (*0-7923-9733-9*) Kluwer Academic.

Mathematical Morphology & Its Applications to Image & Signal Processing. Ed. by Pierre Soille & Jean Serra. LC 94-32857. (Computational Imaging & Vision Ser.: 2). 1994. text 204.50 (*0-7923-3093-5*) Kluwer Academic.

Mathematical Morphology in Image Processing. Ed. by Edward Dougherty. LC 92-25560. (Optical Engineering Ser.: Vol. 34). (Illus.). 552p. 1992. text 215.00 (*0-8247-8724-2*) Dekker.

Mathematical Mosaic: Patterns & Problem Solving. Ravi Vakil. 253p. 16.95 (*1-895997-04-6*, Pub. by BREN) IPG Chicago.

Mathematical Mysteries: The Beauty & Magic of Numbers. Calvin C. Clawson. (Illus.). 310p. (C). 1996. 27.95 (*0-306-45404-1*, Plenum Trade) Perseus Pubng.

*__Mathematical Mysteries: The Beauty & Magic of Numbers.__ Calvin C. Clawson. LC 99-66854. 328p. 1999. pap. text 17.00 (*0-7382-0259-2*, Pub. by Perseus Pubng) HarpC.

Mathematical Mystery Tour: Discovering the Truth & Beauty of the Cosmos. A. K. Dewdney. LC 98-36470. 218p. 1999. 22.95 (*0-471-23847-3*) Wiley.

Mathematical Mystery Tour: Higher-Thinking Math Tasks. Mark H. Wahl. (Illus.). 264p. 1988. pap. text, teacher ed. 35.00 (*0-913705-26-8*) Zephyr Pr AZ.

Mathematical Mystery Tour "Tour Guide Newspapers" Higher-Thinking Math Tasks, 5 vols. Mark H. Wahl. (Illus.). 16p. (J). (gr. 5-12). 1988. 9.95 (*0-913705-27-6*) Zephyr Pr AZ.

Mathematical Nonlinear Image Processing: A Special Issue of the Journal of Mathematical Imaging & Vision. Ed. by Edward R. Dougherty & Jaakko Astola. LC 92-40136. 184p. (C). 1992. text 179.00 (*0-7923-9314-7*) Kluwer Academic.

Mathematical Nonparametric Statistics. Edward B. Manoukian. xvi, 326p. 1986. text 252.00 (*2-88124-093-3*) Gordon & Breach.

Mathematical Notes & Examples for Second Mates. A. C. Gardner. (C). 1987. 59.00 (*0-85174-242-4*) St Mut.

Mathematical Objects & Mathematical Knowledge. Ed. by Michael D. Resnik. LC 95-5672. (International Research Library of Philosophy). (Illus.). 672p. 1995. text 235.95 (*1-85521-638-8*, Pub. by Dartmth Pub) Ashgate Pub Co.

*__Mathematical Olympiad Challenges.__ T. Andreescu & R. Gelca. (Illus.). 240p. (C). 2000. text 59.95 (*0-8176-4190-4*, Pub. by Birkhauser) Spr-Verlag.

*__Mathematical Olympiad Challenges.__ T. Andreescu & R. Gelca. LC 99-86229. (Illus.). 280p. 2000. 24.95 (*0-8176-4155-6*, Pub. by Birkhauser) Spr-Verlag.

*__Mathematical Olympiad Challenges.__ Titu Andreescu & Riazvan Gelca. LC 99-86229. 2000. write for info. (*3-7643-4155-6*) Birkhauser.

Mathematical Olympiad Contest Problems for Children see Math Olympiad Contest Problems for Elementary & Middle Schools

Mathematical Olympiad Handbook: An Introduction to Problem Solving Based on the First 32 British Mathematical Olympiads, 1965-1996. Anthony D. Gardiner. LC 97-17647. (Illus.). 242p. 1997. pap. text 27.95 (*0-19-850105-6*) OUP.

Mathematical Origami: Geometrical Shapes by Paper Folding. David Mitchell. 1997. pap. 12.95 (*1-899618-18-X*, Pub. by Tarquin Pubns) Parkwest Pubns.

Mathematical Palette. Ronald Staszkow & Robert Bradshaw. 534p. (C). 1991. teacher ed. write for info. (*0-03-054988-4*) SCP.

Mathematical Palette: Prepared Tests. Ronald Staszkow. (C). 1991. pap. text 24.50 (*0-03-047134-6*, Pub. by Harcourt Coll Pubs) Harcourt.

Mathematical Pamphlets of Charles Lutwidge Dodgson & Related Pieces. Ed. by Francine F. Abeles. (Pamphlets of Lewis Carroll Ser.: Vol. 2). (Illus.). 440p. (C). 1994. text 65.00 (*0-930326-08-3*) L Carroll Soc.

Mathematical Pamphlets of Charles Lutwidge Dodgson & Related Pieces Vol. 2: The Pamphlets. Francine F. Abeles. 1995. 65.00 (*0-930326-09-1*) L Carroll Soc.

Mathematical Pandora's Box. Brian Bolt. LC 92-45680. (Illus.). 126p. (C). 1993. pap. 18.95 (*0-521-44619-8*) Cambridge U Pr.

Mathematical Papers. George Green. LC 70-92316. 25.00 (*0-8284-0229-9*) Chelsea Pub.

Mathematical Papers. William K. Clifford. LC 67-28488. 1968. reprint ed. 49.50 (*0-8284-0210-8*) Chelsea Pub.

*__Mathematical Papers, Vol. IV.__ William Rowan Hamilton, (Illus.). 900p. 2000. write for info. (*0-521-59216-X*) Cambridge U Pr.

Mathematical Papers in Honor of Yuri Ivanovich Manin. Ed. by M. Reid et al. 650p. (C). 1987. text 143.00 (*0-8223-0798-7*) Duke.

Mathematical Papers, 1683-1684, Vol. 5. Sir Isaac Newton. Ed. by D. T. Whiteside et al. LC 65-11203. (Illus.). 649p. 1972. text 235.00 (*0-521-08262-5*) Cambridge U Pr.

Mathematical Perspectives of Theoretical Physics. N. Prakash. 300p. 1997. text 61.00 (*981-02-2160-6*) World Scientific Pub.

Mathematical Perspectives on Neural Networks. Paul Smolensky et al. (Developments in Connectionist Theory Ser.). 864p. 1996. 225.00 (*0-8058-1201-6*); pap. text 90.00 (*0-8058-1202-4*) L Erlbaum Assocs.

Mathematical Philosophy of Bertrand Russell: Origins & Development. Francisco A. Rodriguez-Consuegra. xiv, 236p. 1991. 100.00 (*0-8176-2656-5*) Birkhauser.

Mathematical Physics. E. Butkov. 35p. (C). 1968. 76.00 (*0-201-00727-4*) Addison-Wesley.

Mathematical Physics. L. Faddeev. 690p. 1998. pap. 85.00 (*5-85270-304-4*) Intl Scholars.

Mathematical Physics. Robert Geroch. (Chicago Lectures in Physics Ser.). 358p. 1985. pap. text 26.00 (*0-226-28862-5*) U Ch Pr.

Mathematical Physics. Robert Geroch. (Chicago Lectures in Physics Ser.). 310p. 1985. lib. bdg. 35.00 (*0-226-28861-7*) U Ch Pr.

Mathematical Physics. F. Hussain & Asghar Qadir. 576p. (C). 1990. text 123.00 (*981-02-0159-1*) World Scientific Pub.

Mathematical Physics. Donald H. Menzel. 412p. 1961. pap. text 11.95 (*0-486-60056-4*) Dover.

Mathematical Physics. N. J. Vlaar. 1900. pap. text. write for info. (*90-277-2621-3*) Kluwer Academic.

Mathematical Physics: A Modern Introduction to Its Foundations. S. Hassani. (Illus.). 152p. 1998. 89.00 (*0-387-98579-4*) Spr-Verlag.

Mathematical Physics: Applied Mathematics for Scientists & Engineer. Bruce Kusse & Erik Westwig. LC 98-13436. 680p. 1998. 89.95 (*0-471-15431-8*) Wiley.

Mathematical Physics: Eighth International Congress. M. Meldehout & R. Seneor. 892p. 1987. pap. 43.00 (*9971-5-0209-7*); text 148.00 (*9971-5-0208-9*) World Scientific Pub.

*__Mathematical Physics: Mathematical Methods for Scientists & Engineers.__ Tai L. Chow. LC 99-44592. 2000. write for info. (*0-521-65227-8*); write for info. (*0-521-65544-7*) Cambridge U Pr.

Mathematical Physics & Complex Analysis: A Collection of Survey Papers on the 50th Anniversary of the Institute. L. Faddeev. LC 88-7667. (Proceedings of the Steklov Institute of Mathematics Ser.: No. 176). 326p. 1988. pap. 179.00 (*0-8218-3120-8*, STEKLO/176) Am Math.

Mathematical Physics & Physical Mathematics. Ed. by Krzysztof Maurin & R. Raczka. LC 74-34289. (Mathematical Physics & Applied Mathematics Ser: No. 2). 1976. text 176.50 (*90-277-0537-2*) Kluwer Academic.

Mathematical Physics, Applied Mathematics & Informatics. Ed. by Yu I. Koptev. 374p. (C). 1993. text 145.00 (*1-56072-083-2*) Nova Sci Pubs.

*__Mathematical Physics of Quantum Wire & Devices: From Spectral Resonances to Anderson Localization.__ Norman Hurt. LC 00-37086. (Mathematics & Its Applications Ser.). (Illus.). 2000. write for info. (*0-7923-6288-8*, Kluwer Plenum) Kluwer Academic.

Mathematical Physics Reviews, Vol. 2. Ed. by S. P. Novikov. (Soviet Scientific Reviews Ser.: Section C). x, 268p. 1981. text 600.00 (*3-7186-0069-2*) Gordon & Breach.

Mathematical Physics Reviews, Vol. 3. Ed. by S. P. Novikov. x, 312p. 1982. text 516.00 (*3-7186-0107-9*) Gordon & Breach.

Mathematical Physics Reviews, Vol. 4. Ed. by S. P. Novikov. Tr. by Morton Hamermesh from RUS. (Soviet Scientific Reviews Ser.: Section C). x, 280p. 1984. text 552.00 (*3-7186-0146-X*) Gordon & Breach.

Mathematical Physics Reviews, Vol. 7. S. P. Novikov. (Soviet Scientific Reviews Ser.: Section C). xiv, 338p. 1988. text 483.00 (*3-7186-0455-8*) Gordon & Breach.

Mathematical Physics Reviews, Vol.1. Ed. by S. P. Novikov. (Soviet Scientific Reviews Ser.). xiv, 208p. 1980. text 552.00 (*3-7186-0019-6*) Gordon & Breach.

Mathematical Physics Reviews: Integrable & Non-Integrable Hamiltonian Systems, Vol. 8. Valery V. Kozlov. Ed. by S. P. Novikov & Y. G. Sinai. (Soviet Scientific Reviews Ser.: Vol. 8, Pt. 1). ii, 86p. 1989. pap. text 96.00 (*3-7186-4864-4*) Gordon & Breach.

Mathematical Physics Reviews: Soviet Scientific Reviews, Section C, Vol. 5. Ed. by S. P. Novikov. xii, 272p. 1985. text 440.00 (*3-7186-0198-2*) Gordon & Breach.

Mathematical Physics Reviews: Soviet Scientific Reviews, Section C, Vol. 6. Ed. by S. P. Novikov. Tr. by Morton HAmermesh from RUS. xii, 272p. 1987. text 457.00 (*3-7186-0292-X*) Gordon & Breach.

Mathematical Physics Reviews: Weak Chaos & Structures, Vol. 8. A. A. Chernikov et al. Ed. by S. P. Novikov & Ya G. Sinai. (Soviet Scientific Reviews Ser.: Vol. 8, Pt. 2). ii, 94p. 1989. pap. text 59.00 (*3-7186-4865-2*) Gordon & Breach.

Mathematical Physics Reviews Vol. 9, Pt. 1: Geometric Integration Theory on Super-Manifolds, Vol. 9. T. Voronov. (Soviet Scientific Reviews Ser.: Section C). 138p. 1991. pap. text 145.00 (*3-7186-5199-8*, Harwood Acad Pubs) Gordon & Breach.

Mathematical Physics Reviews Vol. 9, Pt. 2: Peturbation Theory in Periodic Problems for Two-Dimensional Integrable Systems, Vol. 9. I. M. Krichever. (Soviet Scientific Reviews Ser.: Section C). 106p. 1992. pap. text 134.00 (*3-7186-5218-8*, Harwood Acad Pubs) Gordon & Breach.

Mathematical Physics Reviews Vol. 9, Pt. 4: Hydrodynamics of Soliton Lattices, Vol. 9. B. Dubrovin. (Soviet Scientific Reviews Ser.: Section C). 136p. 1993. pap. text 240.00 (*3-7186-5454-7*, Harwood Acad Pubs) Gordon & Breach.

*__Mathematical Physics 2000: Proceedings of the XIII International Congress on Mathematical Physics, Imperial College, London, 17-22 July, 2000.__ International Conference on Mathematical Physics Staff & A. S. Fokas. LC 00-37042. 336p. 2000. 94.00 (*1-86094-230-X*) Imperial College.

Mathematical Physics X: Proceedings of the Tenth Congress on Mathematical Physics Held at Leipzig, Germany, 30 July-9 August, 1991. Ed. by Konrad Schmudgen. xx, 447p. 1992. 114.95 (*0-387-55166-2*) Spr-Verlag.

Mathematical Physiology. J. Keener et al. LC 98-14499. (Interdisciplinary Applied Mathematics Ser.: Vol. 8). (Illus.). 750p. 1998. 69.95 (*0-387-98381-3*) Spr-Verlag.

Mathematical Population Dynamics: Proceedings of the Second International Conference. Ed. by Ovide Arino et al. (Lecture Notes in Pure & Applied Mathematics Ser.: Vol. 131). (Illus.). 808p. 1991. pap. text 215.00 (*0-8247-8424-3*) Dekker.

Mathematical Power: Lessons from a Classroom. Ruth E. Parker. LC 92-46283. 48p. 1993. pap. text 19.00 (*0-435-08339-2*, 08339) Heinemann.

Mathematical Practitioners. E. G. Taylor. xi, 442p. 1985. reprint ed. lib. bdg. 59.00 (*0-7812-0323-6*) Rprt Serv.

*__Mathematical Preface to the Elements of Geometry of Euclid of Megara.__ John Dee. 60p. 1999. reprint ed. pap. 17.95 (*0-7661-0766-3*) Kessinger Pub.

Mathematical Primer on Groundwater Flow. John F. Hermance. LC 98-30038. 230p. 1998. pap. text 32.67 (*0-13-896499-8*) P-H.

Mathematical Principles in Mechanics & Electromagnetism. C. C. Wang. Incl. Part A: Analytical & Continuum Mechanics. LC 79-11862. 218p. 1979. 42.50 (*0-306-40211-4*, Kluwer Plenum); Part B: Electromagnetism & Gravitation. LC 79-11862. 208p. 1979. 42.50 (*0-306-40212-2*, Kluwer Plenum); LC 79-11862. (Mathematical Concepts & Methods in Science & Engineering Ser.: Vols. 16 & 17). (Illus.). 1979. write for info. (*0-318-55331-7*, Plenum Trade) Perseus Pubng.

Mathematical Principles of Economics. W. Laonhardt. Ed. by John Creedy. (Classics in the History of Economics Ser.). 208p. 1992. 90.00 (*1-85278-723-6*) E Elgar.

*__Mathematical Principles of Fuzzy Logic.__ Vilbem Novbak et al. LC 99-37210. (International Series in Engineering & Computer Science). 1999. write for info. (*0-7923-8595-0*) Kluwer Academic.

Mathematical Problem Solving & New Information Technologies: Research in Contexts of Practice. Ed. by J. P. Ponte et al. (NATO ASI Series F: Computer & Systems Science: Vol. 89). xv, 346p. 1992. 98.95 (*0-387-55735-0*) Spr-Verlag.

Mathematical Problem-Solving with the Microcomputer: Projects to Increase Your Programming Skill. Stephen L. Snover & Mark A. Spikell. 188p. 1985. pap. 19.95 incl. digital audio (*0-685-09443-X*) P-H.

Mathematical Problems: An Anthology. E. G. Dynkin et al. (Pocket Mathematical Library). viii, 70p. 1967. text 128.00 (*0-677-20710-7*) Gordon & Breach.

Mathematical Problems & Methods in Hydrodynamic Weather Forecasting. Vladimir Gordin. (Illus.). 812p. 1999. text 250.00 (*90-5699-164-7*) Gordon & Breach.

Mathematical Problems & Proofs: Combinatorics, Number Theory & Geometry. Branislav Kisacanin. 214p. 1998. 55.00 (*0-306-45967-1*, Kluwer Plenum) Kluwer Academic.

Mathematical Problems & Puzzle Polish Mathematical Olympiad. S. Straszewicz & J. Smolska. LC 63-22366. (Popular Lectures in Mathematics: Vol. 12). 1965. 164.00 (*0-08-010556-4*, Pub. by Pergamon Repr) Franklin.

Mathematical Problems from Combustion Theory. J. Bevernes & D. Eberly. (Applied Mathematical Sciences Ser.: Vol. 83). (Illus.). x, 177p. 1989. 58.95 (*0-387-97104-1*) Spr-Verlag.

Mathematical Problems in Elasticity. Ed. by Remigio Russo. LC 95-48843. 200p. 1996. write for info. (*981-02-2576-8*) World Scientific Pub.

Mathematical Problems in Elasticity & Homogenization. O. A. Oleinik et al. LC 92-15390. (Studies in Mathematics & Its Applications: Vol. 26). 412p. 1992. 169.50 (*0-444-88441-6*, North Holland) Elsevier.

Mathematical Problems in Linear Viscoelasticity. Mauro Fabrizio & Angelo Morro. LC 92-4050. (Studies in Applied Mathematics: No. 12). ix, 203p. 1992. text 64.00 (*0-89871-266-1*) Soc Indus-Appl Math.

Mathematical Problems in Semiconductor Physics. P. Marcati. 1995. pap. 55.00 (*0-582-28704-9*, Pub. by Addison-Wesley) Longman.

Mathematical Problems in Shape Optimization & Shape Memory Materials. Antoni Zochowski. LC 92-20254. (Methoden und Verfahren der Mathematischen Physik Ser.: Bd. 38). (Illus.). 120p. 1992. 34.00 (*3-631-45085-0*) P Lang Pubng.

Mathematical Problems in the Biological Sciences. Sol I. Rubinow. (CBMS-NSF Regional Conference Ser.: No. 10). vii, 90p. 1973. pap. text 21.00 (*0-89871-008-1*) Soc Indus-Appl Math.

Mathematical Problems in the Biological Sciences: Proceedings. Ed. by R. Bellman. LC 50-1183. (Proceedings of Symposia in Applied Mathematics Ser.: Vol. 14). 250p. 1962. text 34.00 (*0-8218-1314-5*, PSAPM/14) Am Math.

Mathematical Problems in the Geophysical Sciences Vol. 2: Inverse Problems, Dynamo Theory & Tides. Summer Seminar on Applied Mathematics, 6th, 1970,. Ed. by William H. Reid. LC 70-31351. (Lectures in Applied Mathematics: No. 14, Vol. 2). 378p. reprint ed. pap. 117.20 (*0-608-09195-2*, 205269900002) Bks Demand.

Mathematical Problems in the Geophysical Sciences I: Geophysical Fluid Dynamics. Ed. by William H. Reid. LC 62-21481. (Lectures in Applied Mathematics). 383p. 1972. text 66.00 (*0-8218-1113-4*, LAM/13) Am Math.

Mathematical Problems in the Geophysical Sciences, No. 2: Inverse Problems, Dynamo Theory & Tides. Ed. by William H. Reid. LC 62-21481. (Lectures in Applied Mathematics: Vol. 14). 370p. 1972. text 62.00 (*0-8218-1114-2*, LAM/14) Am Math.

Mathematical Problems in the Theory of Water Waves: A Workshop on the Problems in the Theory of Nonlinear Hydrodynamic Waves, May 15-19, 1995, Luminy, France, Vol. 197. F. Dias & Jean-Michel Ghidaglia. LC 96-22083. (Contemporary Mathematics Ser.: Vol. 200). 235p. 1996. pap. 55.00 (*0-8218-0510-X*, CONM/200) Am Math.

Mathematical Problems of Relativistic Physics. I. E. Segal & G. W. Mackey. LC 62-21480. (Lectures in Applied Mathematics: Vol. 2). 131p. 1963. pap. 23.00 (*0-8218-1102-9*, LAM/2) Am Math.

Mathematical Problems of Statistical Hydromechanics. M. J. Vishik & A. V. Fursikov. (C). 1988. text 321.00 (*90-277-2336-2*) Kluwer Academic.

M

An Asterisk (*) at the beginning of an entry indicates that the title is appearing for the first time.

Mathematical Problems of Statistical Mechanics. Ed. by Ya G. Sinai. 364p. (C). 1993. text 74.00 (*981-02-0552-X*); pap. text 40.00 (*981-02-0553-8*) World Scientific Pub.

Mathematical Problems of Tomography. I. Gelfand & S. Gindikin. LC 90-845. (Translations of Mathematical Monographs). 267p. 1990. text 100.00 (*0-8218-4534-9*, MMONO/81) Am Math.

Mathematical Problems Relating to the Navier-Stokes Equation. Giovanni P. Galdi. (Series on Advances in Mathematics for Applied Sciences: Vol. 10). 250p. 1992. text 81.00 (*981-02-0846-4*) World Scientific Pub.

Mathematical Proceedings: Nonsmooth Optimization: Methods & Applications: Proceedings of a Meeting Held in Erice, Sicily, at "E. Majorana" Centre for Scientific Culture, "G. Stampacchia International School of Mathematics," June 19-30, 1991. Ed. by F. Giannessi. LC 92-19711. 445p. 1992. text 235.00 (*2-88124-878-0*) Gordon & Breach.

Mathematical Programming. Claude McMillan. LC 74-23273. (Wiley Management & Administration Ser.). 664p. (C). reprint ed. 200.00 (*0-8357-9931-X*, 201700000005) Bks Demand.

Mathematical Programming: A Tool for Engineers. M. Save. 234p. 1991. text 631.00 (*2-88124-829-2*) Gordon & Breach.

M

Mathematical Programming: An Introduction to Optimization. Melvyn Jeter. (Pure & Applied Mathematics Ser.: Vol. 102). (Illus.). 360p. 1986. text 155.00 (*0-8247-7478-7*) Dekker.

Mathematical Programming: Recent Developments & Applications. Ed. by Masao Iri & Kunio Tanabe. (C). 1989. text 309.00 (*0-7923-0490-X*) Kluwer Academic.

Mathematical Programming - Bonn, 1982: The State of the Art. Ed. by Achim Bachem et al. (Illus.). 660p. 1983. 180.00 (*0-387-12082-3*) Spr-Verlag.

Mathematical Programming & Competitive Equilibrium in the Location of Agricultural Production. David Pines & Benjamin H. Stevens. (Discussion Papers: No. 23). 1968. pap. 10.00 (*1-55869-073-5*) Regional Sci Res Inst.

Mathematical Programming & Games. Edward L. Kaplan. LC 81-2990. 608p. reprint ed. pap. 188.50 (*0-7837-2822-0*, 205765000006) Bks Demand.

Mathematical Programming Essays in Honor of George B. Dantzig, 2 pts., Set. Ed. by R. W. Cottle. 1985. pap. 50.00 (*0-317-44633-9*, North Holland) Elsevier.

Mathematical Programming for Industrial Engineers. Ed. by Mordecai Avriel & Boaz Golany. (Industrial Engineering Ser.: Vol. 20). (Illus.). 656p. 1996. text 190.00 (*0-8247-9620-9*) Dekker.

Mathematical Programming for Operations Researchers & Computer Scientists. Holzman. (Industrial Engineering Ser.: Vol. 6). (Illus.). 392p. 1981. text 165.00 (*0-8247-1499-7*) Dekker.

Mathematical Programming in Practice. Evelyn M. Beale. LC 68-95780. (Illus.). 207p. reprint ed. pap. 64.20 (*0-608-11447-2*, 205189800013) Bks Demand.

Mathematical Programming in Statistics. T. S. Arthanari & Yadolah Dodge. LC 80-21637. 431p. reprint ed. pap. 133.70 (*0-7837-2840-9*, 205763200006) Bks Demand.

Mathematical Programming in Statistics Paper. T. S. Arthanari & Yadolah Dodge. (Wiley Classics Library). 432p. 1993. pap. 84.95 (*0-471-59212-9*) Wiley.

Mathematical Programming Methods in Structural Plasticity. Ed. by D. L. Smith. (CISM International Centre for Mechanical Sciences Ser.: Vol. 299). (Illus.). viii, 435p. 1990. 107.95 (*0-387-82191-0*) Spr-Verlag.

Mathematical Programming with Data Perturbations. Anthony V. Fiacco. LC 97-35930. (Lecture Notes in Pure & Applied Mathematics). (Illus.). 464p. 1997. pap. text 175.00 (*0-8247-0059-7*) Dekker.

Mathematical Programming with Data Perturbations, Pt. II. 2nd ed. Anthony V. Fiacco. (Lecture Notes in Pure & Applied Mathematics Ser.: Vol. 85). (Illus.). 168p. 1983. pap. text 125.00 (*0-8247-1789-9*) Dekker.

Mathematical Programming with Parameters & Multi-Level Constraints. J. E. Falk & Anthony V. Fiacco. 100p. 1981. pap. 46.00 (*0-08-023621-9*, Pergamon Pr) Elsevier.

Mathematical Programs with Equilibrium Constraints. Zhi Quan Luo et al. LC 96-19428. (Illus.). 425p. (C). 1996. text 59.95 (*0-521-57290-8*) Cambridge U Pr.

Mathematical Projects in Physics. 2nd ed. Varley. 1996. pap. text, student ed. 31.20 (*0-13-231739-7*) P-H.

Mathematical Psychology: Current Developments. Ed. by J. P. Doignon & Jean-Claude Falmagne. (Recent Research in Psychology Ser.). ix, 453p. 1991. 96.95 (*0-387-97665-5*) Spr-Verlag.

Mathematical Psychology & Psychophysiology. Ed. by Stephen Grossberg. LC 81-3500. (SIAM-AMS Proceedings Ser.: 13). 318p. 1981. text 49.00 (*0-8218-1333-1*, SIAMS/13) Am Math.

Mathematical Psychology & Psychophysiology. Ed. by Stephen Grossberg. 330p. 1981. 59.95 (*0-89859-182-1*) L Erlbaum Assocs.

Mathematical Psychology in Progress. Ed. by E. E. Roskam. (Recent Research in Psychology Ser.). viii, 385p. 1989. 79.95 (*0-387-51686-7*) Spr-Verlag.

Mathematical Puzzles for Beginners & Enthusiasts. 2nd ed. Geoffrey Mott-Smith. (Illus.). 248p. 1954. pap. 7.95 (*0-486-20198-8*) Dover.

Mathematical Puzzling. A. Gardiner. LC 99-45604. 160p. 1999. pap. text 7.95 (*0-486-40920-1*) Dover.

Mathematical Quantum Field Theory & Related Topics. J. Feldman & Lon M. Rosen. LC 88-1274. (Canadian Mathematical Society Conference Proceedings Ser.: Vol. 9). 261p. 1988. pap. 41.00 (*0-8218-6014-3*, CMSAMS/9) Am Math.

Mathematical Quantum Theory I: Field Theory & Many-Body Theory. Ed. by Joel S. Feldman et al. LC 94-37710. (CRM Proceedings & Lecture Notes: Vol. 7). 234p. 1994. pap. 57.00 (*0-8218-0365-4*, CRMP/7) Am Math.

Mathematical Quantum Theory II: Schrodinger Operators. Ed. by J. Feldman et al. LC 95-6092. (CRM Proceedings & Lecture Notes Ser.: No. 8). 304p. 1995. pap. 79.00 (*0-8218-0366-2*, CRMP/8) Am Math.

Mathematical Questions from the Classroom, Pt. 1 & Pt. 2. rev. ed. Richard J. Crouse & Clifford W. Sloyer. LC 86-27502. (Illus.). (Orig.). (C). 1987. pap. text 32.50 (*0-939765-04-7*, G107) Janson Pubns.

Mathematical Questions from the Classroom, Pts. 1 & 2. rev. ed. Richard J. Crouse & Clifford W. Sloyer. LC 86-27502. (Illus.). 208p. (Orig.). (C). 1987. pap. text 18.00 (*0-939765-02-0*, G108); pap. text 18.00 (*0-939765-03-9*, G109) Janson Pubns.

Mathematical Questions in the Theory of Wave Diffraction I: Proceedings. Ed. by V. M. Babic. LC 74-2362. (Proceedings of the Steklov Institute of Mathematics Ser.: No. 115). 167p. 1974. pap. 82.00 (*0-8218-3015-5*, STEKLO/115) Am Math.

Mathematical Questions of Quantum Statistics. Ed. by V. S. Vladimirov. LC 78-6757. (Proceedings of the Steklov Institute of Mathematics Ser.: Vol. 136). 450p. 1982. reprint ed. pap. 125.00 (*0-8218-3036-8*, STEKLO/136) Am Math.

Mathematical Quickies: 270 Stimulating Problems with Solutions. Charles W. Trigg. 224p. 1985. reprint ed. pap. 6.95 (*0-486-24949-2*) Dover.

Mathematical Reasoning 2nd ed. Long. 192p. (C). 1999. pap. text 26.40 (*0-321-04325-1*) Addison-Wesley.

Mathematical Reasoning. 4th ed. Long. (C). 2000. pap., lab manual ed. 27.40 (*0-321-04328-6*) Addson-Wesley Educ.

Mathematical Reasoning: Analogies, Metaphors, & Images. Ed. by Lyn D. English. LC 96-48234. 336p. 1997. 79.95 (*0-8058-1978-9*) L Erlbaum Assocs.

Mathematical Reasoning: Analogies, Metaphors, & Images. Ed. by Lyn D. English. LC 96-48234. 336p. 1997. pap. 39.95 (*0-8058-1979-7*) L Erlbaum Assocs.

Mathematical Reasoning: Nature, Form & Development: A Special Issue of the Journal Mathematica. Lyn D. English. 80p. 1999. pap. 34.95 (*0-86377-603-5*) L Erlbaum Assocs.

***Mathematical Reasoning Elem School Teachers.** 2nd ed. (C). 2000. pap. text 25.20 (*0-321-06836-X*, Celebration); pap. text 0.00 (*0-321-07609-5*, Celebration) Addson-Wesley Educ.

***Mathematical Reasoning for Elementary School Teachers.** 2nd ed. Calvin T. Long & Duane DeTemple. LC 99-22166. 962p. (C). 1999. 92.00 (*0-321-04333-2*) Addison-Wesley.

Mathematical Reasoning for Elementary Teachers. Calvin T. Long & Detemple. 1124p. (C). 1997. text 86.00 (*0-321-01330-1*) Addison-Wesley.

***Mathematical Reasoning For Elementary Teachers.** 2nd ed. 432p. (C). 1999. 25.20 (*0-321-04327-8*); 71.00 (*0-321-04329-4*) Addison-Wesley.

***Mathematical Reasoning For Elementary Teachers.** 2nd ed. (C). 2000. 25.20 (*0-321-04326-X*) Addison-Wesley.

***Mathematical Reasoning for Elementary Teachers.** 2nd ed. (C). 2000. write for info. (*0-321-07781-4*) Addson-Wesley Educ.

***Mathematical Reasoning for Elementary Teachers.** 2nd ed. (C). 2000. 153.00 (*0-201-43641-8*) S&S Trade.

***Mathematical Reasoning for Elementary Teachers: Marketing Walk Through.** 2nd ed. 1999. write for info. (*0-321-07748-2*) Addison-Wesley.

Mathematical Reasoning for Elementary Teachers: Student's Solutions Manual. Calvin T. Long & Duane W. DeTemple. (C). 1997. pap. text, student ed. 25.00 (*0-673-99391-4*) Addison-Wesley Educ.

Mathematical Reasoning, Sets, Logic & Probability. Eiki Satake. (C). 1998. pap. text 24.01 (*1-56870-289-2*) RonJon Pub.

Mathematical Reasoning Through Verbal Analysis Book 1. Warren Hill & Ronald Edwards. 143p. (Orig.). 1988. pap., teacher ed. 12.95 (*0-89455-359-3*) Crit Think Bks.

Mathematical Reasoning Through Verbal Analysis Book 1. Warren Hill & Ronald Edwards. 282p. (Orig.). (J). (gr. 2-4). 1988. pap., student ed. 22.95 (*0-89455-347-X*) Crit Think Bks.

Mathematical Reasoning through Verbal Analysis Book 2. Warren Hill & Ronald Edwards. 183p. (Orig.). 1991. pap., teacher ed. 12.95 (*0-89455-403-4*) Crit Think Bks.

Mathematical Reasoning through Verbal Analysis Book 2. Warren Hill & Ronald Edwards. 283p. (Orig.). (J). (gr. 4-8). 1991. pap., student ed. 22.95 (*0-89455-402-6*) Crit Think Bks.

Mathematical Recreations: A Collection in Honor of Martin Gardner. unabridged ed. Ed. by David A. Klarner. LC 98-23750. Orig. Title: The Mathematical Gardner. (Illus.). 382p. 1998. pap. 12.95 (*0-486-40089-1*) Dover.

Mathematical Recreations & Essays. W. W. Rouse Ball & H. S. M. Coxeter. 448p. 1987. reprint ed. pap. 8.95 (*0-486-25357-0*) Dover.

Mathematical Reflections: In a Room with Many Mirrors. Jean J. Pedersen et al. LC 96-14274. (Undergraduate Texts in Mathematics Ser.). 351p. 1996. 34.00 (*0-387-94770-1*) Spr-Verlag.

Mathematical Research in Materials Science: Opportunities & Perspectives. National Research Council, Commission on Physical. 144p. (Orig.). (C). 1993. pap. text 23.00 (*0-309-04930-X*) Natl Acad Pr.

Mathematical Research Today & Tomorrow: Viewpoints of 7 Fields Medalists - Lectures Given at the Institut d'Estudis Catalans, Barcelona, Spain, June, 1991. Ed. by C. Casacuberta et al. (Lecture Notes in Mathematics Ser.). vii, 112p. 1993. 36.95 (*0-387-56011-4*) Spr-Verlag.

Mathematical Research Today & Tomorrow: Viewpoints of 7 Fields Medalists - Lectures Given at the Institut d'Estudis Catalans, Barcelona, Spain, June, 1991. Ed. by C. Casacuberta & M. Castellet. LC 92-32541. 1992. write for info. (*3-540-56011-4*) Spr-Verlag.

Mathematical Results in Quantum Mathematics: International Conference in Blossin, Germany,May 17-21, 1993. Ed. by M. Demuth. LC 94-4710. (Operator Theory, Advances & Applications Ser.). 1994. 111.00 (*0-8176-5025-3*) Birkhauser.

Mathematical Results in Quantum Mechanics: Qmath 7th Conference, Prague, June 22-26, 1998. Ed. by J. Dittrich et al. LC 99-20181. (Operator Theory Ser.). 408p. 1999. 125.00 (*3-7643-6097-6*) Birkhauser.

***Mathematical Results in Quantum Mechanics: Qmath7 Conference, Prague, June 22-26, 1998.** Jaroslav Dittrich et al. LC 99-20181. (Operator Theory, Advances & Applications Ser.). x, 393p. 1999. 125.00 (*0-8176-6097-6*) Birkhauser.

Mathematical Results in Statistical Mechanics: Proceedings of the Satellite Colloquium Statphys. J. Ruiz. 450p. 1999. 98.00 (*981-02-3863-0*) World Scientific Pub.

Mathematical Reviews Annual Index, 1978. 1979. pap. 561.00 (*0-8218-4013-4*, IMP/10) Am Math.

Mathematical Reviews Annual Index, 1979. 1980. pap. 561.00 (*0-8218-4014-2*, IMP/11) Am Math.

Mathematical Reviews Annual Index, 1980. pap. 561.00 (*0-8218-4016-9*, IMP/12) Am Math.

Mathematical Reviews Annual Indexes, 1989. 1989. pap. 812.00 (*0-685-70677-X*, IMP/21C) Am Math.

Mathematical Reviews Annual Indexes, 1990, Vol. 22. 1990. pap. 877.00 (*0-685-70678-8*, IMP/22C) Am Math.

Mathematical Reviews Annual Indexes, 1991. 1991. pap. 802.00 (*0-685-70679-6*, IMP/23C) Am Math.

Mathematical Reviews Annual Indexes, 1992. 1992. pap. 866.00 (*0-685-70680-X*, IMP/24C) Am Math.

Mathematical Reviews Annual Indexes, 1993. 1994. pap. 918.00 (*0-685-70681-8*, IMP/25C) Am Math.

Mathematical Revolution Inspired by Computing. Ed. by J. H. Johnson & Martin J. Loomes. (Institute of Mathematics & Its Applications Conference Series, New Ser.: New Series 30). (Illus.). 340p. 1991. 80.00 (*0-685-40492-7*) OUP.

Mathematical Scandals. Theoni Pappas. LC 97-12297. (Illus.). 192p. 1997. pap. 10.95 (*1-884550-10-X*) Wide World-Tetra.

Mathematical Scattering Theory. Hellmut Baumgartel & Manfred Wollenberg. (Operator Theory, Advances & Applications Ser.: Vol. 9). 1983. text 68.95 (*3-7643-1519-9*) Birkhauser.

Mathematical Scattering Theory: General Theory. D. R. Yafaev. LC 92-803. (Translations of Mathematical Monographs: No. 105). 341p. 1992. pap. 59.00 (*0-8218-0951-2*) Am Math.

Mathematical Scattering Theory: General Theory. D. R. Yafaev. LC 92-803. (Translations of Mathematical Monographs: Vol. 105). 341p. 1992. 59.00 (*0-8218-4558-6*, MMONO/105) Am Math.

Mathematical Science, Technology & Economic Competition. Ed. by National Research Council Staff. 128p. (C). 1991. pap. text 22.00 (*0-309-04483-9*) Natl Acad Pr.

Mathematical Sciences Professional Directory. annuals 220p. 1997. pap. 50.00 (*0-8218-0192-9*, PRODIR/97C) Am Math.

Mathematical Sciences Professional Directory. 224p. 1998. pap. 50.00 (*0-8218-0934-2*) Am Math.

Mathematical Sciences Professional Directory 1999. 225p. 1999. pap. 50.00 (*0-8218-1090-1*) Am Math.

***Mathematical Sciences Professional Directory, 2000.** (PRODIR Ser.: No. 2000). 232p. 2000. 50.00 (*0-8218-2043-5*) Am Math.

Mathematical Scientists at Work. 21p. 1993. pap. 3.00 (*0-88385-458-9*, MSW) Math Assn.

Mathematical Simulation in Electrometallurgy, Vol. 6, Issue 2. 2nd ed. Zhadkevick. 137p. 1997. pap. text 81.00 (*90-5702-112-9*, Harwood Acad Pubs) Gordon & Breach.

Mathematical Skills Primer. John M. Martin. Ed. & Illus. by Davies Group Staff. 142p. (C). 1996. pap. 12.25 (*1-888570-06-7*) Davies Grp.

Mathematical Snapshots. H. Steinhart. LC 99-33052. 320p. 1999. pap. text 12.95 (*0-486-40914-7*) Dover.

Mathematical Sociology: An Introduction to Fundamentals. Thomas J. Fararo. LC 78-2379. 830p. 1978. reprint ed. lib. bdg. 59.50 (*0-88275-664-8*) Krieger.

Mathematical Software for the P. C. & Work Stations: A Collection of Fortran 77 Programs. Ed. by T. Watanabe et al. 402p. 1994. text 178.50 (*0-444-82000-0*, North Holland) Elsevier.

Mathematical Software Tools in C++ Alain Reverchon & Marc Ducamp. LC 93-13741. 520p. 1993. pap. 90.00 (*0-471-93792-4*) Wiley.

Mathematical Solitaires & Games. Ed. by Benjamin L. Schwartz. LC 79-55714. (Excursions in Recreational Mathematics Ser.). (Illus.). 160p. 1968. pap. text 17.95 (*0-89503-017-9*) Baywood Pub.

Mathematical Sorcery: Revealing the Secrets of Numbers. C. C. Clawson. LC QA93.C62 1999. (Illus.). 294p. (C). 1999. 26.95 (*0-306-46003-3*, Kluwer Plenum) Kluwer Academic.

Mathematical Statistical Mechanics. Colin J. Thompson. LC 77-150071. 288p. reprint ed. pap. 89.30 (*0-8357-3710-1*, 203643200003) Bks Demand.

Mathematical Statistics. Peter J. Bickel et al. 492p. 1991. 105.00 (*0-13-564147-0*) P-H.

Mathematical Statistics. A. A. Borokov. Tr. by A. Moullagaliev from RUS. 592p. 1998. text 140.00 (*90-5699-018-7*) Gordon & Breach.

***Mathematical Statistics.** K. Knight. 1999. 49.95 (*0-8493-0318-4*) CRC Pr.

Mathematical Statistics. Wiebe R. Pestman. LC 98-18771. 546p. 1998. pap. 49.00 (*3-11-015356-4*) De Gruyter.

***Mathematical Statistics.** Jun Shao. LC 98-45794. 1998. 74.95 (*0-387-98674-X*) Spr-Verlag.

Mathematical Statistics. B. L. Van Der Waerden. LC 72-84145. (Grundlehren der Mathematischen Wissenschaften Ser.: Vol. 156). (Illus.). 1969. 86.95 (*0-387-04507-4*) Spr-Verlag.

Mathematical Statistics. 2nd ed. P. J. Bickel & Kjell A. Doksum. 500p. (C). 2000. 93.33 (*0-13-850363-X*, Macmillan Coll) P-H.

Mathematical Statistics: A Decision Theoretic Approach. Thomas S. Ferguson. (Probability & Mathematical Statistics Ser.: Vol. 1). 1967. text 78.00 (*0-12-253750-5*) Acad Pr.

Mathematical Statistics: A Unified Introduction. G. R. Terrell. Ed. by G. Casella et al. LC 98-30565. (Springer Texts in Statistics Ser.). 456p. 1999. 79.95 (*0-387-98621-9*) Spr-Verlag.

Mathematical Statistics: An Introduction. Wiebe R. Pestman. LC 98-18771. 545p. 1997. 80.00 (*3-11-015357-2*) De Gruyter.

Mathematical Statistics: Basic Ideas & Selected Topics. P. J. Bickel & K. A. Doksum. LC 76-8724. 1977. 49.95 (*0-8162-0784-4*) Holden-Day.

Mathematical Statistics: Problems & Detailed Solutions. Wiebe R. Pestman & Ivo B. Alberink. LC 98-20084. 325p. 1998. 80.00 (*3-11-015359-9*) De Gruyter.

Mathematical Statistics: Problems & Detailed Solutions. Wiebe R. Pestman & Ivo B. Alberink. LC 98-20084. 326p. 1998. pap. 49.00 (*3-11-015358-0*) De Gruyter.

Mathematical Statistics & Applications. Ed. by Imre Vincze et al. 1986. text 168.00 (*90-277-2088-6*) Kluwer Academic.

Mathematical Statistics & Data Analysis. John A. Rice. (Statistics). 595p. (C). 1987. pap. 56.00 (*0-534-08247-5*) Wadsworth Pub.

Mathematical Statistics & Data Analysis. 2nd ed. John A. Rice. 602p. 1994. pap. 106.95 (*0-534-20934-3*) Wadsworth Pub.

Mathematical Statistics & Its Applications. 3rd ed. Larsen. 640p. (C). 2000. 106.67 (*0-13-922303-7*, Macmillan Coll) P-H.

***Mathematical Statistics & Its Applications.** 3rd ed. Larsen & Marx. 2000. pap., student ed. write for info. (*0-13-031015-8*) P-H.

Mathematical Statistics & Probability Theory: Proceedings. Ed. by W. Klonecki et al. (Lecture Notes in Statistics Ser.: Vol. 2). 373p. 1980. pap. 54.00 (*0-387-90493-X*) Spr-Verlag.

Mathematical Statistics & Probability Theory: Statistical Inference & Methods, Vol. B. Ed. by P. Bauer et al. (C). 1987. text 166.50 (*90-277-2581-0*) Kluwer Academic.

Mathematical Statistics & Probability Theory: Theoretical Aspects, Vol. A. Ed. by Madan L. Puri et al. (C). 1987. lib. bdg. 154.50 (*90-277-2580-2*) Kluwer Academic.

Mathematical Statistics for Economics & Business. Ron Mittelhammer. LC 95-37686. 723p. 1996. 54.95 (*0-387-94587-3*) Spr-Verlag.

Mathematical Statistics W/ Applications. 4th ed. William Mendenhall et al. (Statistics Ser.). 752p. (C). 1989. pap. 60.75 (*0-534-92026-8*) PWS Pubs.

Mathematical Statistics with Applications. Mendenhall. (Statistics Ser.). 1973. 25.00 (*0-87872-047-2*) PWS Pubs.

Mathematical Statistics with Applications. 2nd ed. William Mendenhall & Richard L. Scheaffer. (C). 1981. pap. 28.25 (*0-87150-410-3*) PWS Pubs.

Mathematical Statistics with Applications. 3rd ed. Dennis D. Wackerly et al. (C). 1986. pap. 38.25 (*0-87150-939-3*, 36G8300) PWS Pubs.

Mathematical Statistics with Applications. 5th ed. William Mendenhall & Dennis D. Wackerly. (Statistics Ser.). 1996. pap., student ed. 17.95 (*0-534-20918-1*) Wadsworth Pub.

Mathematical Statistics with Applications. 5th ed. Dennis D. Wackerly et al. LC 95-34340. (C). 1995. pap. 106.95 (*0-534-20916-5*) PWS Pubs.

Mathematical Statistics with Applications. 5th ed. Wackerly & Mendenhall. 1996. 28.00 (*0-534-20917-3*) Brooks-Cole.

***Mathematical Statistics with Applications.** 6th ed. Dennis D. Wackerly et al. 2000. pap. 60.00 (*0-534-37741-6*) Thomson Learn.

***Mathematical Structure for Emergent Computation.** Victor Korotkich. LC 99-47043. (Nonconvex Optimization & Its Applications Ser.). 1999. write for info. (*0-7923-6010-9*) Kluwer Academic.

Mathematical Structure of the Human Sleep-Wake Cycle. Steven H. Strogatz. (Lecture Notes in Biomathematics Ser.: Vol. 69). viii, 239p. 1986. 46.95 (*0-387-17176-2*) Spr-Verlag.

Mathematical Structures & Mathematical Modeling. I. M. Yaglom. x, 218p. 1986. text 274.00 (*2-88124-044-5*) Gordon & Breach.

Mathematical Structures for Software Engineering: Based on the Proceedings of a Conference Organized by the Systems & Software Engineering Specialist Group of the Institute of Mathematics & Its Applications Held Manchester Polytechnic in July 1988. Ed. by Bernard De Neumann et al. (Institute of Mathematics & Its Applications Conference Series, New Ser.: New Series 27). (Illus.). 376p. 1991. text 105.00 (*0-19-853627-5*, 8993) OUP.

Mathematical Structures in Continuous Dynamical Systems: Poisson Systems & Complete Integrability with Applications from Fluid Dynamics. E. Van Groesen & E. M. De Jager. LC 95-153751. (Studies in Mathematical Physics: Vol. 6). 632p. 1994. 187.50 (*0-444-82151-1*) Elsevier.

Mathematical Structures in Population Genetics. Y. I. Lyubich. Ed. by E. Akin & S. A. Levin. (Biomathematics Ser.: Vol. 22). (Illus.). x, 373p. 1992. 149.95 (*0-387-53337-0*) Spr-Verlag.

Mathematical Structures of Epidemic Systems. Vincenzo Capasso. LC 93-10042. (Lecture Notes in Biomathematics Ser.: Vol. 97). 1993. 64.95 (*0-387-56526-4*) Spr-Verlag.

Mathematical Structures of Language. Zellig S. Harris. LC 79-4568. 240p. 1979. reprint ed. lib. bdg. 21.50 (*0-88275-958-2*) Krieger.

Mathematical Structures of Nonlinear Science. M. S. Berger. (C). 1990. text 226.50 (*0-7923-0728-3*) Kluwer Academic.

Mathematical Studies of Information Processing: Proceedings, International Conference, Kyoto, Japan, August 23-26, 1978. Ed. by E. K. Blum et al. (Lecture Notes in Computer Science Ser.: Vol. 75). 1979. 46.00 (*0-387-09541-1*) Spr-Verlag.

Mathematical Submodels in Water Quality Systems. Ed. by S. E. Jorgenson & M. J. Gromiec. (Developments in Environmental Modelling Ser.: No. 14). 408p. 1989. 199.00 (*0-444-88030-5*) Elsevier.

*** Mathematical Supplement for Statistics.** Ed. by Prentice-Hall Staff. (C). 1999. text 21.00 (*0-13-794132-3*) P-H.

Mathematical Support for Molecular Biology: Special Year Workshops, 1994-1998. DIMACS "Special Year" in Mathematical Support for Molecular Biology Staff & Martin Farach-Colton. LC 98-32095. (DIMACS Series in Discrete Mathematics & Theoretical Computer Science). 1999. write for info. (*0-8218-0826-5*) Am Math.

Mathematical Systems Theory: The Influence of R. E. Kalman. Ed. by A. C. Antoulas. (Illus.). 528p. 1991. 228.95 (*0-387-52994-2*) Spr-Verlag.

Mathematical Tables & Formulas. Robert D. Carmichael & Edwin R. Smith. 269p. (C). 1962. pap. 6.95 (*0-486-60111-0*) Dover.

Mathematical Talent, Discovery, Description & Development Proceedings: Hyman Blumberg Symposium on Research in Early Childhood Education, 3rd, 1973, Johns Hopkins University. Ed. by Julian C. Stanley et al. LC 73-19342. 242p. reprint ed. pap. 75.10 (*0-7837-6427-8*, 204642500012) Bks Demand.

*** Mathematical Techniques.** 442p. (C). 1999. 29.50 (*0-536-02727-7*) Pearson Custom.

Mathematical Techniques: An Introduction for the Engineering, Physical & Mathematical Science. 2nd ed. D. W. Jordan & P. Smith. LC 97-222942. (Illus.). 806p. (C). 1997. text 95.00 (*0-19-856462-7*) OUP.

Mathematical Techniques: An Introduction for the Engineering, Physical & Mathematical Sciences. 2nd ed. D. W. Jordan & P. Smith. LC 97-222942. (Illus.). 806p. 1997. pap. text 30.00 (*0-19-856461-9*) OUP.

Mathematical Techniques for Biology & Medicine. William Simon. 320p. 1987. reprint ed. pap. 10.95 (*0-486-65247-5*) Dover.

Mathematical Techniques for Water Waves. Ed. by B. N. Mandal. LC 96-83306. (Advances in Fluid Mechanics Ser.: Vol. 8). 368p. 1997. 168.00 (*1-85312-413-3*, 4133) Computational Mech MA.

Mathematical Techniques in Crystallography & Materials Science. E. Prince. (Illus.). 192p. 1982. 54.00 (*0-387-90627-4*) Spr-Verlag.

Mathematical Techniques in Crystallography & Materials Science. 2nd ed. Edward Prince. LC 94-17913. 1994. 99.95 (*0-387-58115-4*) Spr-Verlag.

*** Mathematical Technology: Resource Manual to Accompany Lay's Linear Algebra & Its applications.** 2nd ed. 2000. 21.00 (*0-201-87489-X*) Addison-Wesley.

Mathematical Terms in Computer Science: A Glossary. T. S. Blyth. 200p. 1993. 20.00 (*0-387-19611-0*) Spr-Verlag.

Mathematical Theories of Economic Growth. Burmeister. 464p. 1993. 79.95 (*0-7512-0177-4*) Ashgate Pub Co.

Mathematical Theories of Plastic Deformation under Impulsive Loading. John A. Simmons & F. Hauser. LC 62-63111. (University of California Publications in Social Welfare: Vol. 5, No. 7). 58p. reprint ed. pap. 30.00 (*0-608-11076-0*, 202118900022) Bks Demand.

Mathematical Theories of Populations: Demographics, Genetics & Epidemics. Frank Hoppensteadt. LC 97-19735. (CBMS-NSF Regional Conference Ser.: No. 20). vii, 72p. 1975. pap. text 21.50 (*0-89871-017-0*) Soc Indus-Appl Math.

Mathematical Theory in Fluid Mechanics. G. P. Galdi. (Pitman Research Notes in Mathematics Ser.). 1996. pap. 47.95 (*0-582-29810-5*, Pub. by Addison-Wesley) Longman.

Mathematical Theory of Black Holes. S. Chandrasekhar. (Oxford Classic Texts in the Physical Sciences Ser.). 668p. 1998. pap. text 29.95 (*0-19-850370-9*) OUP.

Mathematical Theory of Communication. Claude Shannon. LC 98-230924. 144p. 1999. 30.00 (*0-252-72546-8*) U of Ill Pr.

Mathematical Theory of Communication. Claude Shannon & Warren Weaver. LC 49-11922. 136p. 1963. pap. text 11.95 (*0-252-72548-4*) U of Ill Pr.

Mathematical Theory of Control. Ed. by Mohan C. Joshi & A. V. Balakrishnan. LC 92-26047. (Lecture Notes in Pure & Applied Mathematics Ser.: Vol. 142). (Illus.). 448p. 1992. pap. text 165.00 (*0-8247-8750-1*) Dekker.

Mathematical Theory of Control Systems Design. V. R. Nosov et al. LC 95-20901. (Mathematics & Its Applications Ser.: Vol. 341). 1996. text 309.00 (*0-7923-3724-7*) Kluwer Academic.

Mathematical Theory of Creep & Creep Ruptures. Folke K. Odqvist. LC 75-306213. (Oxford Mathematical Monographs). (Illus.). 213p. reprint ed. pap. 66.10 (*0-608-30321-6*, 205183400008) Bks Demand.

Mathematical Theory of Design: Foundations, Algorithms & Applications. Dan Braha & Oded Z. Maimon. LC 98-7545. (Applied Optimization Ser.). 680p. 1998. write for info. (*0-7923-5079-0*) Kluwer Academic.

Mathematical Theory of Diffusion & Reaction in Permeable Catalysts, 2 vols., Set. Rutherford Aris. Incl. Vol. 1. Theory of the Steady State. (Illus.). 460p. 1975. text 95.00 (*0-19-851931-1*); Vol. 2. Questions of Uniqueness, Stability, & Transient Behaviour. 232p. 1975. 85.00 (*0-19-851942-7*); (Illus.). 692p. (C). 1975. 150.00 (*0-19-519829-8*) OUP.

Mathematical Theory of Dilute Gases. Carlo Cercignani et al. LC 94-10086. (Applied Mathematical Sciences Ser.). (Illus.). vii, 347p. 1994. 64.95 (*0-387-94294-7*) Spr-Verlag.

Mathematical Theory of Dislocations. Ed. by Toshio Mura. LC 70-88019. 215p. reprint ed. pap. 66.70 (*0-608-30982-6*, 200472200046) Bks Demand.

Mathematical Theory of Dislocations & Fracture. Ring Lardner, Jr. LC 75-190346. (Mathematical Expositions Ser.: No. 17). 375p. reprint ed. pap. 116.30 (*0-608-30067-5*, 202049800018) Bks Demand.

Mathematical Theory of Domains. E. R. Griffor et al. (Cambridge Tracts in Theoretical Computer Science Ser.: No. 22). (Illus.). 361p. (C). 1994. text 52.95 (*0-521-38344-7*) Cambridge U Pr.

Mathematical Theory of Elastic Structures. K. Q. Feng & Z. Shi. 397p. 1995. 126.95 (*0-387-51326-4*) Spr-Verlag.

Mathematical Theory of Elastic Structures. Feng Kang & Shi Zhongci. 1995. write for info. (*3-540-51326-4*) Spr-Verlag.

Mathematical Theory of Elasticity. 2nd ed. Ivan S. Sokolnikoff. LC 82-14844. 496p. (C). 1983. reprint ed. lib. bdg. 56.50 (*0-89874-555-1*) Krieger.

Mathematical Theory of Electrophoresis. V. G. Babskii et al. (Illus.). 250p. (C). 1988. 110.00 (*0-306-11018-0*, Kluwer Plenum) Kluwer Academic.

Mathematical Theory of Evidence. Glenn Shafer. LC 75-30208. 302p. 1976. reprint ed. pap. 93.70 (*0-608-02508-9*, 206315200004) Bks Demand.

Mathematical Theory of Finite & Boundary Element Methods. A. H. Schatz et al. (DMV Seminar Ser.: Vol. 15). 280p. 1990. 57.50 (*0-8176-2211-X*) Birkhauser.

Mathematical Theory of Finite Element Methods. Susanne Brenner & L. Ridgway Scott. LC 93-40882. (Texts in Applied Mathematics Ser.: Vol.15). (Illus.). 294p. 1996. 47.95 (*0-387-94193-2*) Spr-Verlag.

Mathematical Theory of Hemivariational Inequalities & Applications. Z. Naniewicz & P. D. Panagiotopoulos. LC 94-35419. (Pure & Applied Mathematics Ser.: Vol. 188). (Illus.). 296p. 1994. text 145.00 (*0-8247-9330-7*) Dekker.

Mathematical Theory of Hints: An Approach to the Dempster-Shafer Theory of Evidence. Jurg Kohlas & Paul-Andre Monney. LC 95-12080. (Lecture Notes in Economics & Mathematical Systems Ser.: Vol. 425). 1995. write for info. (*0-387-59176-1*) Spr-Verlag.

Mathematical Theory of Hints: An Approach to the Dempster-Shafer Theory of Evidence. Jurg Kohlas & Paul-Andre Monney. (Lecture Notes in Economics & Mathematical Systems Ser.: Vol. 425). 419p. 1995. 84.00 (*3-540-59176-1*) Spr-Verlag.

Mathematical Theory of Huygens Principle. Bevan B. Baker & E. T. Copson. LC 50-8926. 200p. reprint ed. pap. 62.00 (*0-608-30952-4*, 205116600080) Bks Demand.

Mathematical Theory of Huygens Principle. 3rd ed. Bevan B. Baker & E. T. Copson. vii, 195p. 1987. text 17.95 (*0-8284-0329-5*, 329) Chelsea Pub.

Mathematical Theory of Incompressible Non-Viscous Fluids. Carlo Marchioro & Mario Pulvirenti. LC 93-4683. (Applied Mathematical Sciences Ser.: Vol. 96). (Illus.). 312p. 1993. 65.95 (*0-387-94044-8*) Spr-Verlag.

Mathematical Theory of Infectious Diseases. 2nd ed. write for info. (*0-85264-231-8*) Lubrecht & Cramer.

Mathematical Theory of Kinetic Equations. A.A. Arseniev. 1999. 55.00 (*981-02-3717-0*) World Scientific Pub.

Mathematical Theory of Nonblocking Switching Networks. F. Hwang. LC 98-28569. (Series on Applied Mathematics). 180p. 1998. 32.00 (*981-02-3311-6*) World Scientific Pub.

Mathematical Theory of Nonlinear Elasticity. A. Hanyga. LC 83-9140. (Mathematics & Its Applications Ser.). 400p. 1985. text 97.95 (*0-470-27493-X*, 1-176) P-H.

Mathematical Theory of Oil & Gas Recovery: With Applications to Ex-U. S. S. R. Oil & Gas Fields. Pavel Bedrikovetsky. LC 93-14525. (Petroleum Engineering Studies & Development Ser.). 600p. (C). 1993. text 313.00 (*0-7923-2381-5*) Kluwer Academic.

Mathematical Theory of Optimal Processes. Lev S. Pontryagin & V. Boltyanskii. LC 63-15354. 1964. 154.00 (*0-08-010176-3*, Pub. by Pergamon Repr) Franklin.

Mathematical Theory of Plasticity. R. Hill. LC 99-172404. (Oxford Classic Texts in the Physical Sciences Ser.). (Illus.). 366p. 1998. pap. text 29.95 (*0-19-850367-9*) OUP.

Mathematical Theory of Population, of Its Character & Fluctuations, & of the Factors Which Influence Them. Australia Bureau of Census & Statistics Staff. LC 75-38132. (Demography Ser.). (Illus.). 1976. reprint ed. 44.95 (*0-405-07985-0*) Ayer.

*** Mathematical Theory of Quantum Fields.** Huzihiro Araki. LC 99-41253. 101. 248p. 2000. text 100.00 (*0-19-851773-4*) OUP.

Mathematical Theory of Relativity. 3rd ed. Arthur S. Eddington. LC 74-1458. ix, 270p. 1975. text 19.95 (*0-8284-0278-7*) Chelsea Pub.

Mathematical Theory of Reliability. Richard Barlow & Frank Proschan. LC 96-13952. (Classics in Applied Mathematics Ser.: No. 17). xv, 258p. 1996. pap. 37.00 (*0-89871-369-2*, CL17) Soc Indus-Appl Math.

Mathematical Theory of Reliability of Time Dependent Systems with Practical Applications. Igor N. Kovalenko et al. LC 97-11253. 316p. 1997. 135.00 (*0-471-95060-2*) Wiley.

Mathematical Theory of Statistics: Statistical Experiments & Asymptotic Decision Theory. Helmut Strasser. (Studies in Mathematics: Vol. 7). xii, 491p. 1985. 109.95 (*3-11-010258-7*) De Gruyter.

Mathematical Theory of Stellar Eclipses. Zdenek Kopal. (C). 1990. text 114.50 (*0-7923-0661-9*) Kluwer Academic.

Mathematical Theory of the Dynamics of Biological Populations, No. 2. Ed. by R. W. Hiorns & D. Cooke. LC 73-1468. (Institute of Mathematics & Its Applications Conference Series, New Ser.). 1981. text 116.00 (*0-12-348780-3*) Acad Pr.

Mathematical Theory of the Top see Congruence of Sets, & Other Monographs

Mathematical Theory of Thermodynamic Limits: Thomas--Fermi Type Models. Isabelle Catto et al. (Oxford Mathematical Monographs). (Illus.). 292p. 1998. text 115.00 (*0-19-850161-7*) OUP.

Mathematical Theory of Turbulence. M. M. Stanisic. (Universitext Ser.). (Illus.). 501p. 1990. 69.95 (*0-387-96685-4*) Spr-Verlag.

Mathematical Theory of Viscous Incompressible Flow, Vol. 2. 2nd ed. O. A. Ladyzhenskaya. (Mathematics & Its Applications Ser.). (Illus.). xviii, 224p. 1969. text 332.00 (*0-677-20760-3*) Gordon & Breach.

*** Mathematical Thinking: Problem-Solving & Proofs.** 2nd ed. John P. D'Angelo. LC 99-50074. 412p. 1999. 81.33 (*0-13-014412-6*) P-H.

Mathematical Thinking & Problem-Solving. Ed. by Alan H. Schoenfeld. (Studies in Mathematical Thinking & Learning). 360p. 1994. pap. 32.50 (*0-8058-0990-2*); text 69.95 (*0-8058-0989-9*) L Erlbaum Assocs.

Mathematical Thinking & Quantitative Reasoning. 2nd ed. Sons et al. 342p. 1998. 41.95 (*0-7872-5103-8*, 41510301) Kendall-Hunt.

Mathematical Thinking at Grade 5: Introduction & Landmarks in the Number System. Marlene Kilman et al. Ed. by Catherine Anderson et al. (Investigations in Number, Data, & Space Ser.). (Illus.). 170p. (Orig.). 1995. teacher ed. 22.95 (*0-86651-989-0*, DS21425) Seymour Pubns.

Mathematical Thinking at Grade 5: Introduction & Landmarks in the Number System. rev. ed. Marlene Kliman et al. Ed. by Catherine Anderson & Beverly Cory. LC 97-185339. (Investigations in Number, Data, & Space Ser.). (Illus.). 169p. (YA). (gr. 5 up). 1997. pap. text 32.95 (*1-57232-796-0*, 47043) Seymour Pubns.

Mathematical Thinking at Grade 4: Introduction. Cornelia Tierney. Ed. by Priscilla C. Samii et al. LC 94-223949. (Investigations in Number, Data, & Space Ser.). (Illus.). 154p. (Orig.). 1994. pap., teacher ed. 22.95 (*0-86651-809-6*, DS21247) Seymour Pubns.

Mathematical Thinking at Grade 4: Introduction. rev. ed. Cornelia Tierney. Ed. by Catherine Anderson & Beverly Cory. (Investigations in Number, Data, & Space Ser.). (Illus.). 148p. (Orig.). (J). (gr. 4 up). 1997. pap. text 22.95 (*1-57232-743-X*, 43890) Seymour Pubns.

Mathematical Thinking at Grade 1: Introduction. Marlene Kilman et al. Ed. by Catherine Anderson et al. LC 97-114628. (Investigations in Number, Data, & Space Ser.). (Illus.). 184p. (Orig.). 1996. teacher ed. 22.95 (*1-57232-466-X*, 43702) Seymour Pubns.

Mathematical Thinking at Grade 3: Introduction. Susan J. Russell et al. Ed. by Priscilla C. Samii et al. (Investigations in Number, Data, & Space Ser.). (Illus.). 144p. (Orig.). 1994. pap., teacher ed. 22.95 (*0-86651-800-2*, DS21238) Seymour Pubns.

Mathematical Thinking at Grade 2: Introduction. Karen Economopoulos et al. Ed. by Catherine Anderson et al. (Investigations in Number, Data, & Space Ser.). (Illus.). 218p. (Orig.). 1996. pap., teacher ed. 32.95 incl. disk (*1-57232-214-4*, DS21645) Seymour Pubns.

Mathematical Thinking at Grade 2: Introduction. rev. ed. Karen Economopoulos et al. Ed. by Catherine Anderson et al. (Investigations in Number, Data, & Space Ser.). (Illus.). 220p. (Orig.). (J). (gr. 2 up). 1997. pap. text 32.95 (*1-57232-653-0*, 43800) Seymour Pubns.

*** Mathematical Thinking at Grade 3: Introduction.** Susan Jo Russell et al. LC 97-172739. (Illus.). 1998. write for info. (*1-57232-694-8*) Seymour Pubns.

Mathematical Thinking in Kindergarten: Introduction. Karen Economopoulos & Megan Murray. Ed. by Catherine Anderson & Beverly Cory. (Investigations in Number, Data, & Space Ser.). (Illus.). 89p. (Orig.). (J). (gr. k). 1997. pap. text 22.95 (*1-57232-926-2*, 47103) Seymour Pubns.

Mathematical Thought: An Introduction to the Philosophy of Mathematics. E. W. Beth. xii, 207p. 1965. text 252.00 (*0-677-00600-4*) Gordon & Breach.

Mathematical Thought: An Introduction to the Philosophy of Mathematics. E. W. Beth. (Synthese Library: No. 11). 220p. 1965. text 126.50 (*90-277-0070-2*, D Reidel) Kluwer Academic.

Mathematical Thought from Ancient to Modern Times, Vol. 1. Morris Kline. (Illus.). 432p. 1990. pap. text 18.95 (*0-19-506135-7*) OUP.

Mathematical Thought from Ancient to Modern Times, Vol. 2. Morris Kline. (Illus.). 480p. 1990. pap. 18.95 (*0-19-506136-5*) OUP.

Mathematical Thought from Ancient to Modern Times, Vol. 3. Morris Kline. (Illus.). 448p. 1990. pap. 18.95 (*0-19-506137-3*) OUP.

Mathematical Toolbox. Rosamond Welchman-Tischler. (Illus.). 90p. (J). (gr. 1-8). 1995. pap. write for info. (*0-938587-27-7*) Cuisenaire.

Mathematical Toolkit: Numerical Routines with Applications in Engineering, Mathematics & the Sciences. R. D. Harding. (Illus.). 208p. 1986. disk 51.00 (*0-85274-405-6*); disk 51.00 (*0-85274-406-4*) IOP Pub.

Mathematical Tools - Changing Spatial Scales. Anton Leijnse. 256p. 1993. boxed set 72.95 (*0-8493-8934-8*) CRC Pr.

Mathematical Tools for Applied Multivariate Analysis. 2nd rev. ed. J. Douglas Carroll & Paul E. Green. (Illus.). 376p. 1997. text 69.95 (*0-12-160954-5*) Morgan Kaufmann.

Mathematical Tools for Applied Multivariate Analysis. 2nd rev. ed. J. Douglas Carroll et al. LC 97-74470. (Illus.). 376p. 1997. pap. text 39.95 (*0-12-160955-3*) Morgan Kaufmann.

Mathematical Tools in Crystallography Tutorial. (American Crystallographic Association Lecture Notes Ser.: No. 5). 98p. 1980. pap. 15.00 (*0-686-47113-X*) Polycrystal Bk Serv.

Mathematical Tools in Production Management. J. M. Proth & H. P. Hillion. (Competitive Methods in Operations Research & Data Analysis Ser.). (Illus.). 400p. (C). 1990. 110.00 (*0-306-43358-3*, Plenum Trade) Perseus Pubng.

*** Mathematical Topics Between Classical & Quantum Mechanics.** N. P. Landsman. LC 98-18391. (Monographs in Mathematics). xix, 529p. 1998. 64.95 (*0-387-98318-X*) Spr-Verlag.

Mathematical Topics in Fluid Mechanics. Ed. by J. F. Rodrigues & A. Sequeira. 280p. 1992. 65.95 (*0-582-20954-4*, LM0954, Chap & Hall CRC) CRC Pr.

Mathematical Topics in Fluid Mechanics: Compressible Models, Vol. 2. Pierre-Louis Lions. (Oxford Lecture Series in Mathematics & Its Applications: No. 10). 362p. 1998. text 75.00 (*0-19-851488-3*) OUP.

Mathematical Topics in Fluid Mechanics Vol. 3: Incompressible Models, Vol. 1. Pierre-Louis Lions. LC 96-4085. (Oxford Lecture Series in Mathematics & Its Applications). 252p. 1996. text 55.00 (*0-19-851487-5*, Clarendon Pr) OUP.

Mathematical Topics in Neutron Transport Theory: New Aspects. LC 97-21755. 300p. 1997. lib. bdg. 40.00 (*981-02-2869-4*) World Scientific Pub.

Mathematical Topics in Nonlinear Kinetic Theory. N. Bellomo et al. 240p. 1989. text 61.00 (*9971-5-0702-1*) World Scientific Pub.

Mathematical Topics in Nonlinear Kinetic Theory II. N. Bellomo et al. (Series on Advances in Mathematics for Applied Sciences: Vol. 1). 224p. 1991. text 55.00 (*981-02-0447-7*); pap. text 32.00 (*981-02-0448-5*) World Scientific Pub.

Mathematical Topics in Population Biology, Morphogenesis & Neurosciences. Ed. by E. Teramoto & M. Yamaguti. (Lecture Notes in Biomathematics Ser.: Vol. 71). ix, 348p. 1987. pap. 58.00 (*0-387-17875-9*) Spr-Verlag.

Mathematical Tourist: Snapshots, Vol. 1. Ivars Peterson. LC 98-2697. 266p. 1998. pap. text 14.95 (*0-7167-3250-5*) W H Freeman.

Mathematical Traveller: Exploring the Grand History of Numbers. C. C. Clawson. (Illus.). 318p. (C). 1994. 25.95 (*0-306-44645-6*, Plenum Trade) Perseus Pubng.

Mathematical Undecidability, Quantum Nonlocality & the Question of the Existence of God. Alfred Driessen & Antoine Suarez. LC 96-36621. 1997. text 107.00 (*0-7923-4306-9*) Kluwer Academic.

Mathematical Understanding of Chemical Engineering Systems: Selected Papers of Neal R. Amundson. Ed. by Rutherford Aris & Arvind Varma. LC 79-40686. (Illus.). 1980. 370.00 (*0-08-023836-X*, Pub. by Pergamon Repr) Franklin.

Mathematical Universe. William W. Dunham. LC 93-48720. (Illus.). 320p. 1997. pap. 19.95 (*0-471-17661-3*) Wiley.

Mathematical Universe: An Alphabetical Journey Through the Great Proofs, Problems, & Personalities. William Dunham. LC 93-48720. (Illus.). 314p. 1994. 24.95 (*0-471-53656-3*) Wiley.

Mathematical Utility Theory: Utility Functions, Models & Applications in the Social Sciences. Ed. by Gerhard Herden et al. LC 99-14446. (Illus.). 260p. 1999. pap. 119.00 (*3-211-83223-8*) Spr-Verlag.

Mathematical Value Problems of Mathematical Physics: Proceedings. Steklov Institute of Mathematics, Academy of Scien. Ed. by Olga A. Ladyzhenskaja. LC 67-6187. (Proceedings of the Steklov Institute of Mathematics Ser.: No. 110). 210p. 1972. pap. 58.00 (*0-8218-3010-4*, STEKLO/110) Am Math.

Mathematical Value Problems of Mathematical Physics: Proceedings. Steklov Institute of Mathematics Staff. Ed. by Olga A. Ladyzhenskaja. LC 67-6187. (Proceedings of the Steklov Institute of Mathematics Ser.: No. 116). 245p. 1973. pap. 84.00 (*0-8218-3016-3*, STEKLO/116) Am Math.

Mathematical Visualization: Algorithms, Applications, & Numerics. Ed. by H. C. Hege & K. Polthier. LC 98-36657. (Illus.). 430p. 1998. 99.00 (*3-540-63991-8*) Spr-Verlag.

Mathematical Word Search Puzzle Book. Ellen Hechler. 50p. (Orig.). (J). (gr. 3-10). 1996. pap. text 9.95 (*0-9638483-4-8*) Midmath.

Mathematical Work of John Wallis. 2nd ed. Joseph F. Scott. LC 80-85524. (Illus.). xii, 240p. 1981. text 16.50 (*0-8284-0314-7*) Chelsea Pub.

M

M

Mathematical Works, 2 vols. in 1. Isaac Barrow. Ed. by W. Whewell. (Illus.). xix, 734p. 1973. reprint ed. 225.00 (*3-487-04788-8*) G Olms Pubs.

Mathematical Works of J. H. C. Whitehead, 4 vols., Set. I. James. LC 62-11568. 1962. 731.00 (*0-08-009873-8*, Pub. by Pergamon Repr) Franklin.

Mathematical Works of J. H. C. Whitehead Vol. 2: Complexes & Manifolds. I. James. LC 62-11568. 1962. 195.00 (*0-08-009870-3*, Pub. by Pergamon Repr) Franklin.

Mathematical Works of J. H. C. Whitehead Vol. 3: Homotopy Theory. I. James. LC 62-11568. 1962. 202.00 (*0-08-009871-1*, Pub. by Pergamon Repr) Franklin.

Mathematical Works of J. H. C. Whitehead Vol. 4: Algebraic & Classical Topology. I. James. LC 62-11568. 1962. 160.00 (*0-08-009872-X*, Pub. by Pergamon Repr) Franklin.

Mathematical World of Walter Noll: A Scientific Biography. Yurie A. Ignatieff. 206p. 1996. 49.00 (*3-540-59440-X*) Spr-Verlag.

Mathematical Writing. rev. ed. Donald Knuth et al. LC 89-62390. (MAA Notes Ser.: Vol. 14). 128p. 1989. pap. text 21.00 (*0-88385-063-X*, NTE-14) Math Assn.

Mathematicall Iewell. John Blagrave. LC 74-171735. (English Experience Ser.: No. 294). 1971. reprint ed. 45.00 (*90-221-0294-7*) Walter J Johnson.

Mathematically Speaking: A Dictionary of Quotations. C. C. Gaither & A. E. Cavazos-Gaither. LC 98-6351. (Illus.). 500p. 1998. pap. 24.99 (*0-7503-0503-7*) IOP Pub.

Mathematica(r) in Action. 2nd ed. S. Wagon. LC 97-48853. 560p. 1998. 49.95 incl. disk (*0-387-98252-3*) Spr-Verlag.

Mathematician. Jack Rudman. (Career Examination Ser.: C-479). 1994. pap. 29.95 (*0-8373-0479-2*) Nat Learn.

Mathematician & Administrator, Shirley Mathis McBay. Mary E. Verheyden-Hilliard. LC 84-25983. (American Women in Science Biographies Ser.). (Illus.). 32p. (Orig.). (J). (gr. 1-4). 1985. pap. 8.50 (*0-932469-04-3*) Equity Inst.

Mathematician & Computer Scientist, Caryn Navy. Mary E. Verheyden-Hilliard. LC 87-82595. (American Women in Science Biographies Ser.). (Illus.). 32p. (Orig.). (J). (gr. 1-4). 1988. pap. 8.50 (*0-932469-12-4*) Equity Inst.

Mathematician & His Mathematical Work - Selected Papers of S. S. Chern. Ed. by P. Li et al. (World Scientific Series in 20th Century Mathematics: Vol. 4). 700p. 1996. text 86.00 (*981-02-2385-4*) World Scientific Pub.

Mathematician Reads the Newspaper. John A. Paulos. LC 94-48206. (Illus.). 212p. 1995. 18.00 (*0-465-04362-3*, Pub. by Basic) HarpC.

Mathematician Reads the Newspaper. John A. Paulos. LC 95-46049. (Illus.). 224p. 1996. pap. 12.95 (*0-385-48254-X*, Anchor NY) Doubleday.

Mathematicians & Education Reform. Ed. by H. Keynes et al. LC 89-18601. (CBMS Issues in Mathematics Education Ser.: Vol. 1). 217p. 1990. pap. 41.00 (*0-8218-3500-9*, CBMATH/1) Am Math.

Mathematicians & Education Reform, 1989-1990. Ed. by Naomi D. Fisher et al. LC 91-15768. (CBMS Issues in Mathematics Education Ser.: Vol. 2). 176p. 1991. pap. 42.00 (*0-8218-3502-5*, CBMATH/2) Am Math.

Mathematicians & Education Reform, 1990-1991. Ed. by Naomi D. Fisher et al. (CBMS Issues in Mathematics Education Ser.: Vol. 3). 185p. 1993. pap. 62.00 (*0-8218-3503-3*, CBMATH/3C) Am Math.

Mathematician's Apology. Godfrey H. Hardy. (Canto Book Ser.). 153p. (C). 1992. pap. 10.95 (*0-521-42706-1*) Cambridge U Pr.

Mathematicians Are People, Too: Stories from the Lives of Great Mathematicians, Vol. 1. Luetta Reimer & Wilbert Reimer. (Illus.). 143p. (Orig.). (J). (gr. 3-10). 12.95 (*0-86651-509-7*, 2001) Seymour Pubns.

Mathematicians Are People, Too: Stories from the Lives of Great Mathematicians, Vol. 2. Luetta Reimer & Wilbert Reimer. (Illus.). 150p. (Orig.). (J). (gr. 3 up). 11.95 (*0-86651-823-1*, 2004) Seymour Pubns.

Mathematician's Coloring Book. Richard L. Francis. (Illus.). 60p. pap. text 11.99 (*0-614-05313-7*, HM 5613) COMAP Inc.

Mathematician's Mind: The Psychology of Invention in the Mathematical Field. Jacques Hadamard. 166p. 1945. pap. 12.95 (*0-691-02931-8*, Pub. by Princeton U Pr) Cal Prin Full Svc.

Mathematician's Toolbox: Proof, Logic, & Conjecture. Wolf. 1998. teacher ed. 16.00 (*0-7167-3247-5*) W H Freeman.

Mathematician's Toolbox: Proof, Logic, & Conjecture. Robert S. Wolf. LC 97-31940. 400p. 1997. pap. text 68.95 (*0-7167-3050-2*) W H Freeman.

***Mathematics.** (Switched on Schoolhouse Ser.). (Illus.). (J). 2000. 61.95 (*0-7403-0225-6*) Alpha AZ.

Mathematics. (J). (gr. k). 1994. pap., teacher ed. 221.76 (*0-395-67914-1*) HM.

Mathematics. (J). (gr. 1). 1994. pap., teacher ed. 221.76 (*0-395-67915-X*) HM.

Mathematics. (J). (gr. 2). 1994. pap., teacher ed. 221.76 (*0-395-67916-8*) HM.

Mathematics. (J). (gr. 3). 1994. pap., teacher ed. 104.72 (*0-395-67917-6*) HM.

Mathematics. (J). (gr. 4). 1994. pap., teacher ed. 104.72 (*0-395-67918-4*) HM.

Mathematics. (J). (gr. 5). 1994. pap., teacher ed. 104.72 (*0-395-67919-2*) HM.

Mathematics. (J). (gr. 6). 1994. pap., teacher ed. 104.72 (*0-395-67920-6*) HM.

Mathematics. 35.95 (*0-8373-5297-5*, ATS-9C); pap. 23.95 (*0-8373-5247-9*, ATS-9C); pap. 23.95 (*0-8373-8416-8*, NT-6) Nat Learn.

Mathematics. (Regents Competency Test Ser.). 1997. pap. 23.95 (*0-8373-6401-9*, RCT-1) Nat Learn.

Mathematics. (Building Strategies Ser.). (J). (gr. 4-6). 1997. pap. 11.00 (*0-8114-6504-7*) Raintree Steck-V.

Mathematics. Ed. by Robert W. Deutsch & J. W. Whitney. (Academic Program for Nuclear Power Plant Personnel Ser., BWR Version: Vol. I). (Illus.). 372p. 1972. teacher ed. 195.00 (*0-87683-153-6*); ring bd. 39.95 (*0-87683-146-3*, A 326517); 25.00 (*0-87683-160-9*); 35.00 (*0-87683-167-6*) GP Courseware.

Mathematics. Susan Echaore-Yoon. Ed. by Kathy Osmus. LC 93-20197. (Foundations Ser.). 1993. pap. 11.26 (*0-8092-3830-6*) NTC Contemp Pub Co.

Mathematics. John Edeen. 1997. pap. 8.95 (*0-86651-455-4*) Seymour Pubns.

Mathematics. Innovative Learning Staff et al. (The Rivers Curriculum Ser.). (Illus.). 243p. 1997. pap. 23.95 (*0-201-49372-1*) Addison-Wesley.

Mathematics. Contrib. by Instructional Fair Staff. (Illus.). (J). (gr. 4). 1996. pap. 2.99 (*0-88012-455-5*) Instruct Fair.

Mathematics. Thomas J. Miles. LC 96-29496. 650p. 1997. mass mkt. 76.95 (*0-314-09576-4*) West Pub.

Mathematics. Jack Rudman. (Graduate Record Examination (GRE) Ser.: Vol. 12). 43.95 (*0-8373-5262-2*) Nat Learn.

Mathematics. Jack Rudman. (Undergraduate Program Field Tests (UPFT) Ser.: Vol. 15). 43.95 (*0-8373-6065-X*) Nat Learn.

Mathematics. Jack Rudman. (Graduate Record Examination Ser.: GRE-12). 1994. pap. 23.95 (*0-8373-5212-6*) Nat Learn.

Mathematics. Jack Rudman. (Teachers License Examination (TLE) Ser.: Vol. G-4). 1994. pap. 27.95 (*0-8373-8194-0*) Nat Learn.

Mathematics. Jack Rudman. (Undergraduate Program Field Tests (UPFT) Ser.: Vol. UPFT-15). 1994. pap. 23.95 (*0-8373-6015-3*) Nat Learn.

***Mathematics.** Schwager. (C). 1999. 10.95 (*0-07-135249-X*) McGraw.

Mathematics. Stein. 288p. 1999. pap. 16.95 (*0-471-32974-6*) Wiley.

Mathematics. Abraham P. Sperling & Monroe Stuart. LC 89-49249. (Illus.). 285p. reprint ed. pap. 88.40 (*0-608-09069-7*, 206970300005) Bks Demand.

Mathematics. rev. ed. (GED Exercise Bks.). (YA). (gr. 8-12). 1997. pap. 7.96 (*0-8114-7369-4*) Raintree Steck-V.

Mathematics. 2nd ed. Black. 1980. pap. text 38.95 (*0-471-27660-X*) Wiley.

Mathematics. 2nd ed. David B. Johnson. (Mathematics Ser.). 1994. mass mkt., student ed. 18.25 (*0-534-94375-6*) PWS Pubs.

Mathematics. 2nd ed. Wolfram. (C). 1992. text. write for info. (*0-201-55670-7*) Addison-Wesley.

Mathematics. 7th ed. Mizrahi. Date not set. pap. text. write for info. (*0-471-35547-X*) Wiley.

***Mathematics.** 8th ed. Erwin Kreyszig. 311p. (C). 1998. pap., teacher ed. 25.00 (*0-471-31797-7*) Wiley.

Mathematics, No. 11. Anthony Nicolaides. (C). 1990. pap. 39.95 (*1-872684-11-4*, Pub. by P A S S Pubns) St Mut.

Mathematics see Mathematics & Physical Science

Mathematics, Vol. 1. rev. ed. (NAVEDTRA Rate Training Manual Ser.: No. 10069-D1). (Illus.). 240p. 1985. reprint ed. pap. text 8.50 (*0-16-002077-8*, S/N 008-047-00377-3) USGPO.

Mathematics: A Concise History & Philosophy. W. S. Anglin. LC 94-8075. (Undergraduate Texts in Mathematics Ser.). (Illus.). 275p. 1996. 42.95 (*0-387-94280-7*) Spr-Verlag.

***Mathematics: A Discrete Introduction.** Edward R. Scheinerman. LC 99-53837. (Mathematics Ser.). 2000. 83.95 (*0-534-35638-9*) Brooks-Cole.

Mathematics: A Good Beginning. 2nd ed. Andria P. Troutman & Betty K. Lichtenberg. LC 81-17997. (Mathematics Ser.). (C). 1982. mass mkt. 26.75 (*0-8185-0492-7*) Brooks-Cole.

Mathematics: A Good Beginning. 5th ed. Troutman & Lichtenberg. 1995. pap. text, teacher ed. write for info. (*0-534-21949-7*) S-W Pub.

Mathematics: A Good Beginning: Strategies for Teaching Children. 5th ed. Andrai P. Troutman & Betty K. Lichtenberg. LC 94-23428. 600p. 1994. mass mkt. 83.95 (*0-534-21948-9*) Brooks-Cole.

Mathematics: A Historical & Integrated Approach. John E. Sasser. 240p. 1989. per. 45.95 (*0-8403-5211-5*) Kendall-Hunt.

Mathematics: A Human Endeavor. Harold R. Jacobs. LC 81-17499. (Illus.). (C). 1982. text 28.00 (*0-7167-1326-8*) W H Freeman.

Mathematics: A Human Endeavor. 2nd ed. Harold R. Jacobs. LC 81-17499. (Illus.). (C). 1982. teacher ed. 10.40 (*0-7167-1327-6*); trans. 48.00 (*0-7167-1329-2*) W H Freeman.

Mathematics: A Practical Approach. Kenneth Kalmanson & Patricia C. Kenschaft. LC 77-81755. (Illus.). 1978. text 59.95 (*0-87901-085-1*) Worth.

Mathematics: A Practical Odyssey. 2nd ed. David B. Johnson & Thomas A. Mowry. LC 94-35421. 672p. 1996. mass mkt. 55.00 (*0-534-94374-8*) PWS Pubs.

***Mathematics: A Practical Odyssey.** 3rd ed. David B. Johnson & Thomas A. Mowry. 1998. pap. 22.00 (*0-534-35077-1*) Thomson Learn.

***Mathematics: A Practical Odyssey.** 4th ed. Johnson & Mowry. (Mathematics Ser.). (C). 2000. text 49.00 (*0-534-37891-9*) Brooks-Cole.

Mathematics: A Second Start. J. Berry et al. 1995. write for info. (*0-13-149857-6*) Prntice Hall Bks.

Mathematics: A Second Start. S. G. Page. (Mathematics & Its Applications Ser.). 409p. 1986. pap. text 29.95 (*0-470-20752-3*) P-H.

Mathematics: A Simple Tool for Geologists. David Waltham. (Illus.). 1994. pap. 35.95 (*0-412-49210-5*, Chap & Hall NY) Chapman & Hall.

***Mathematics: A Simple Tool for Geologists.** 2nd ed. David Waltham. LC 99-53787. 2000. pap. 32.95 (*0-632-05345-3*) Blackwell Sci.

Mathematics: An Applied Approach. 7th ed. Abe Mizrahi & Michael Sullivan. LC 99-29010. 1080p. 1999. text 102.95 (*0-471-32203-2*) Wiley.

***Mathematics: An Applied Approach.** 7th ed. Abe Mizrahi & Michael Sullivan. 470p. 1999. pap. 33.95 (*0-471-34939-9*) Wiley.

Mathematics: An Interactive Approach. Thomas A. Sonnabend. (C). 1993. text 76.50 (*0-03-094905-X*) Harcourt Coll Pubs.

***Mathematics: Applications Graphing Tech.** 192p. (C). 1998. 23.00 (*0-321-04315-4*) Addison-Wesley.

Mathematics: Attainment Tests. S. Burndred. (National Curriculum 11-14 Year Olds Ser.). 192p. (C). 1991. 60.00 (*1-870941-63-2*) St Mut.

Mathematics: Book 2. John Edeen. 1997. pap. 8.95 (*0-86651-456-2*) Seymour Pubns.

Mathematics: Calculus AB/BC. (Advanced Placement (AP) Test Ser.: Vol. AP-14). 1997. pap. 23.95 (*0-8373-6214-8*, AP-2) Nat Learn.

Mathematics: For Business, Life Sciences, & Social Sciences. 5th ed. A. Mizahi et al. 144p. 1993. pap., suppl. ed. 25.95 (*0-471-59097-5*) Wiley.

Mathematics: Form & Function. S. Mac Lane. (Illus.). xi, 476p. 1985. 59.95 (*0-387-96217-4*) Spr-Verlag.

Mathematics: From the Birth of Numbers. Jan Gullberg. LC 96-13428. (Illus.). 1120p. 1997. 50.00 (*0-393-04002-X*) Norton.

***Mathematics: Frontiers & Perspectives.** International Mathematical Union Staff. Ed. by Vladimir I. Arnold et al. LC 99-47980. 433p. 2000. 49.00 (*0-8218-2070-2*) Am Math.

Mathematics: Fundamentals for Managerial Decision-Making. 2nd ed. Michael L. Kovacic. LC 74-34212. xiv, 626 p. 1975. write for info. (*0-87150-178-3*) PWS Pubs.

Mathematics: Good Beginning Strategies for Teaching Children. 4th ed. Andria P. Troutman & Betty K. Lichtenberg. 560p. (C). 1991. pap. 47.95 (*0-534-15144-2*) Brooks-Cole.

Mathematics: Human Endeavor: A Book for Those Who Think They Don't Like the Subject. Harold R. Jacobs. LC 93-37458. (C). 1994. text, teacher ed. 52.00 (*0-7167-2423-5*) W H Freeman.

Mathematics: Human Endeavor: A Book for Those Who Think They Don't Like the Subject. 3rd ed. Harold R. Jacobs. LC 93-37458. 704p. (C). 1994. pap. text 58.95 (*0-7167-2426-X*) W H Freeman.

Mathematics: Human Endeavor: A Book for Those Who Think They Don't Like the Subject. 3rd ed. Harold R. Jacobs. LC 93-37458. (C). 1994. text, teacher ed. 11.20 (*0-7167-2422-7*) W H Freeman.

Mathematics: Its Content, Methods & Meaning. A. D. Aleksandrov. LC 99-33023. 1120p. 1999. pap. text 29.95 (*0-486-40916-3*) Dover.

Mathematics: Its Power & Utility. 4th ed. Karl J. Smith. LC 93-28515. 1994. text 46.75 (*0-534-20484-8*) Brooks-Cole.

Mathematics: Its Power & Utility. 5th ed. Karl J. Smith. (C). 1996. mass mkt., teacher ed. write for info. (*0-534-34463-1*) Brooks-Cole.

Mathematics: Its Power & Utility. 5th ed. Karl J. Smith. LC 96-32205. (Mathematics Ser.). 608p. (C). 1997. mass mkt. 50.50 (*0-534-34462-3*) Brooks-Cole.

Mathematics: Its Power & Utility. 6th ed. Smith. LC 99-34743. (Mathematics Ser.). 1999. 72.95 (*0-534-36455-1*) Brooks-Cole.

Mathematics: Language Development Through Content, Bk. A. Anna U. Chamot & J. Michael O'Malley. (ESOL Secondary Supplements Ser.). (Illus.). 96p. 1988. pap. text 16.57 (*0-201-12931-0*); pap. text, teacher ed. 14.50 (*0-201-12935-3*) Addison-Wesley.

Mathematics: Modeling Our World. Comap. 1997. pap. 43.75 (*0-538-68210-8*) Thomson Learn.

***Mathematics: Modeling Our World.** Comap. 1998. pap. 43.75 (*0-538-68224-8*) Thomson Learn.

***Mathematics: Modeling Our World Course.** COMAP Inc. Staff. 2000. pap. text, teacher ed. write for info. (*0-7167-4114-8*, Pub. by W H Freeman) VHPS.

***Mathematics: Modeling Our World Course.** COMAP, Inc. Staff. 2000. pap. text, student ed. write for info. (*0-7167-4115-6*, Pub. by W H Freeman) VHPS.

***Mathematics: Modeling Our Worldarise Crs 2.** Comap. 1998. pap. 43.75 (*0-538-68218-3*) Thomson Learn.

Mathematics: Models & Applications. Laurence C. Eggan & Charles L. Vanden Eynden. 525p. (C). 1979. text 61.96 (*0-669-01051-0*) HM Trade Div.

Mathematics: One of the Liberal A. Thomas J. Miles. (Mathematics Ser.). (C). 1997. pap., student ed. 21.95 (*0-314-20973-5*) Brooks-Cole.

Mathematics: Principles & Process. Ebos & Tuck. (UM - International Math Ser.). 1989. 45.95 (*0-538-95009-9*) S-W Pub.

Mathematics: Principles & Process 10. Ebos et al. (UM - International Math Ser.). 1987. teacher ed. 77.95 (*0-538-95008-0*) S-W Pub.

Mathematics: Principles & Process 10. Ebos et al. (UM - International Math Ser.). 1989. 48.95 (*0-538-95007-2*) S-W Pub.

Mathematics: Principles & Process 9. Ebos. (UM - International Math Ser.). 1981. teacher ed. 78.95 (*0-538-95001-3*) S-W Pub.

Mathematics: Principles & Process 9. Ebos et al. (UM - International Math Ser.). 1988. teacher ed. 76.95 (*0-538-95006-4*) S-W Pub.

Mathematics: Principles & Process 9. Ebos et al. (UM - International Math Ser.). 1989. 45.95 (*0-538-95005-6*) S-W Pub.

Mathematics: Problem Solving Activities. Dale Seymour Staff. 1997. text 10.25 (*0-86651-255-1*) Seymour Pubns.

Mathematics: Queen & Servant of Science. E. T. Bell, pseud. LC 87-62937. (MAA Spectrum Ser.). 454p. 1987. reprint ed. pap. text 5.00 (*0-88385-447-3*, QAS) Math Assn.

Mathematics: Report of the Project 2061 Phase I Mathematics Panel. David Blackwell & Leon Henkin. LC 89-103. 48p. 1989. pap. 8.00 (*0-87168-344-X*, 89-03S) AAAS.

Mathematics: The Islamic Legacy. Q. Mushtaq & A. L. Tan. 1995. pap. text 12.95 (*0-934905-59-2*) Kazi Pubns.

Mathematics: The Loss of Certainty. Morris Kline. (Illus.). 376p. 1982. pap. 15.95 (*0-19-503085-0*) OUP.

***Mathematics: The New Golden Age.** Keith J. Devlin. LC 99-23438. 312p. 1999. 24.95 (*0-231-11638-1*) Col U Pr.

***Mathematics Course 1, Teacher's Wraparound Edition: Applications & Connections.** Collins et al. 1999. teacher ed. 62.69 (*0-02-833053-6*) Glencoe.

***Mathematics Course 2, Teacher's Wraparound: Applications & Connections.** Collins et al. 1999. teacher ed. 62.69 (*0-02-833054-4*) Glencoe.

***Mathematics Course 3, Teacher's Wraparound Edition: Applications & Connections.** Collins et al. 1999. teacher ed. 62.69 (*0-02-833055-2*) Glencoe.

***Mathematics no.93.** 3rd ed. 384p. (C). 1999. 39.96 (*0-536-02891-5*) Pearson Custom.

Mathematics Vol. 2: Its Content, Methods, & Meaning, 3 vols. 2nd ed. Ed. by A. D. Aleksandrov et al. Tr. by S. H. Gould. 1969. reprint ed. pap. text 16.00 (*0-262-51004-9*) MIT Pr.

Mathematics Vol. 3: Its Content, Methods, & Meaning, 3 vols. 2nd ed. Ed. by A. D. Aleksandrov et al. Tr. by S. H. Gould. 1969. reprint ed. pap. text 16.00 (*0-262-51003-0*) MIT Pr.

Mathematics - Level I. (College Board SAT II Subject Test Ser.). 1997. pap. 23.95 (*0-8373-6311-X*, SATII-11) Nat Learn.

Mathematics - Level II. (College Board SAT II Subject Test Ser.). 1997. pap. 23.95 (*0-8373-6312-8*, SATII-12) Nat Learn.

Mathematics - Mechanics & Probability. L. Bostock & S. Chandler. 672p. (C). 1994. pap. 39.00 (*0-85950-141-8*, Pub. by S Thornes Pubs) Trans-Atl Phila.

Mathematics - the Basic Skills. 5th ed. S. Llewellyn & A. Greer. 320p. 1996. pap. 27.50 (*0-7487-2509-1*, Pub. by S Thornes Pubs) Trans-Atl Phila.

Mathematics - The Music of Reason: With Forty-One Figures. Jean A. Dieudonne. Tr. by J. Dales & H. G. Dales from FRE. LC 92-27390. (Illus.). 300p. 1992. 39.00 (*3-540-53346-X*); 42.95 (*0-387-53346-X*) Spr-Verlag.

Mathematics - The Science of Patterns: The Search for Order in Life, Mind & the Universe. Keith J. Devlin. (Illus.). 224p. 1996. pap. text 19.95 (*0-7167-6022-3*) W H Freeman.

Mathematics: A Good Beginning. 3rd ed. Andria P. Troutman & Betty K. Lichtenberg. LC 86-14802. (Math). 532p. (C). 1987. mass mkt. 36.00 (*0-534-06984-3*) Brooks-Cole.

Mathematics: A Practical Odyssey. David B. Johnson & Thomas A. Mowry. (Math). 722p. (C). 1992. mass mkt. 59.75 (*0-534-12924-2*) PWS Pubs.

Mathematics-A Good Beginning. Troutman. (Math). 1977. mass mkt. 18.50 (*0-8185-0222-3*) Brooks-Cole.

Mathematics, a Good Beginning: Strategies for Teaching Children. Andria P. Troutman & Betty K. Lichtenberg. LC 94-23428. 1994. 410.95 (*0-534-16693-8*) Brooks-Cole.

Mathematics Achievement in Missouri & Oregon in an International Context: 1997 TIMSS Benchmarking. Ina V. Mullis & Michael O. Martin. LC 98-86204. 200p. 1998. write for info. (*1-889938-10-6*) Intl Study Ctr.

Mathematics Achievement in the Middle School Years: IEA's 3rd International Mathematics. Albert E. Beaton et al. LC 96-71251. (Illus.). 244p. (Orig.). 1996. pap. 30.00 (*1-889938-02-5*) Intl Study Ctr.

Mathematics Achievement in The Middle School Years: Third International Mathematics & Science Study. Albert E. Beaton. 248p. 1997. per. 21.00 (*0-16-063627-2*) USGPO.

Mathematics Achievement in the Primary School Years: IEA's 3rd International Mathematics. Ina V. Mullis et al. LC 97-67235. 200p. (Orig.). 1997. pap. write for info. (*1-889938-04-1*) Intl Study Ctr.

Mathematics Across the Curriculum. Ohio Math Project, Inc. Staff. Ed. by Edward F. Anthony. (Illus.). 575p. (YA). (gr. 8-10). 1992. text 37.80 (*1-880251-06-X*) EFA & Assocs.

Mathematics Across the Curriculum. Ohio Math Project, Inc. Staff. Ed. by Edward F. Anthony. (Illus.). 575p. (YA). (gr. 8-10). 1992. teacher ed. 70.00 (*1-880251-08-6*) EFA & Assocs.

***Mathematics Across the Disciplines.** Dan H. Wishnietsky. LC 98-89289. vii, 83p. 1999. pap. 9.50 (*0-87367-736-6*) Phi Delta Kappa.

Mathematics Activities for Elementary School Teachers. 10th ed. Wheeler & Barnard. 374p. 1998. spiral bd. 28.95 (*0-7872-5128-3*) Kendall-Hunt.

Mathematics Activities for Elementary School Teachers: A Problem Solving Appproach. 4th ed. Dan Dolan & Jim Williamson. 300p. (C). 1990. pap. text 13.95 (*0-8053-0392-8*) Addison-Wesley.

Mathematics Activities for Elementary School Teachers: A Problem Solving Approach. 3rd ed. Dan Dolan. Ed. by Karen Guardino. LC 96-26206. 352p. (C). 1996. pap. text 28.00 (*0-201-44096-2*) Addison-Wesley.

Mathematics Activities for Elementary School Teachers: A Problem Solving Approach. 3rd ed. Dan Dolan. (C). 1997. pap. text 23.66 (*0-201-84846-5*) Addison-Wesley.

Mathematics Activities for Elementary Teachers. Melfried Olson. 168p. (C). 1996. pap. text, spiral bd. 20.95 (*0-8403-9930-8*) Kendall-Hunt.

An Asterisk (*) at the beginning of an entry indicates that the title is appearing for the first time.

*Mathematics Activities Handbook. Douglas K. Brumbaugh. 208p. 2000. write for info. (1-58692-006-5) Copyright Mgmt.

Mathematics Aide. Jack Rudman. (Career Examination Ser.: C-480). 1994. pap. 27.95 (0-8373-0480-6) Nat Learn.

*Mathematics All Around. (C). 1999. text. write for info. (0-201-43643-4) Addison-Wesley.

*Mathematics All Around. (C). 1999. text. write for info. (0-201-61134-1) S&S Trade.

Mathematics All Around. Thomas Pirnot. 736p. (C). 2000. text. write for info. (0-201-30815-0) Addison-Wesley.

Mathematics & Applications: Student's Solution Manual. 6th ed. Margaret L. Lial et al. LC 94-13576. (C). 1995. pap. text, student ed. 29.06 (0-673-46944-1) Addison-Wesley Educ.

Mathematics & Calculus with Applications. 2nd ed. Marvin L. Bittinger & J. Conrad Crown. (Illus.). 928p. (C). 1989. text 61.25 (0-201-05941-X) Addison-Wesley.

Mathematics & Chess. Miodrag Petkovic. LC 97-8398. 1997. pap. 5.95 (0-486-29432-3) Dover.

Mathematics & Choice. John Mayer. 156p. (C). 1996. pap. text, spiral bd. 18.95 (0-7872-1348-9) Kendall-Hunt.

Mathematics & Computer Science in Medical Imaging. Ed. by Max A. Viergever & Andrew E. Todd-Pokropek. (NATO Asi Series F: Vol. 39). viii, 546p. 1988. 142.95 (0-387-18672-7) Spr-Verlag.

Mathematics & Computers in Archaeology. James E. Doran & Frank R. Hodson. (Illus.). 382p. 1975. 42.00 (0-674-55455-8) HUP.

*Mathematics & Control in Smart Structures. Ed. by Vasundara V. Varadan. 862p. 1999. pap. text 136.00 (0-8194-3141-9) SPIE.

Mathematics & Development: Methodologoical Problems, Essays. Ljubomir Iliev. 122p. (C). 1985. 40.00 (0-7855-4983-8, Pub. by Collets) St Mut.

Mathematics & Elementary Teaching Concept. 4th ed. Bennett. 1997. pap. 74.31 (0-07-561354-9) McGraw.

Mathematics & Gender. Ed. by Elizabeth Fennema & Gilah C. Leder. 224p. (C). 1990. text 37.00 (0-8077-3002-5); pap. text 17.95 (0-8077-3001-7) Tchrs Coll.

Mathematics & Global Survival. 2nd rev. ed. Richard Schwartz. (C). 1990. pap. text 38.60 (0-536-57842-7) Pearson Custom.

Mathematics & Global Survival. 4th ed. 250p. (C). 1997. text 39.20 (0-536-00708-X) Pearson Custom.

Mathematics & Graphics. Taj M. Bakhshi. (Orig.). 1995. pap. 19.13 (1-56870-175-6) RonJon Pub.

Mathematics & Humor. John A. Paulos. LC 80-12742. 124p. 1982. pap. 12.95 (0-226-65025-1) U Ch Pr.

Mathematics & Its History. John C. Stillwell. Ed. by J. H. Ewing et al. LC 99-461876. (Undergraduate Texts in Mathematics Ser.). (Illus.). x, 371p. 1997. reprint ed. 49.95 (0-387-96981-0) Spr-Verlag.

Mathematics & Logic. Mark Kac & Stanislaw M. Ulam. Orig. Title: Mathematics & Logic: Retrospect & Prospects. (Illus.). 192p. 1992. reprint ed. pap. 7.95 (0-486-67085-6) Dover.

Mathematics & Logic: Retrospect & Prospects see Mathematics & Logic

Mathematics & Mathematica for Economists. Cliff J. Huang & Philip S. Crooke. LC 96-37456. (Illus.). 584p. (C). 1997. text 73.95 (1-57718-034-8) Blackwell Pubs.

Mathematics & Mathematicians: Mathematics in Sweden Before 1950. Lars Garding. LC 97-27619. (History of Mathematics Ser.: Vol. GARDING). 268p. 1997. text 75.00 (0-8218-0612-2) Am Math.

Mathematics & Measurement. O. A. Dilke. (Reading the Past Ser.: Vol. 2). (Orig.). (C). 1987. pap. 13.95 (0-520-06072-5, Pub. by U CA Pr) Cal Prin Full Svc.

Mathematics & Medicine: How Serious Is the Injury? William Sacco et al. (Contemporary Applied Mathematics Ser.). (Illus.). 61p. (Orig.). (YA). (gr. 9 up). 1987. pap. text 11.95 (0-939765-06-3, G103) Janson Pubns.

Mathematics & Mind. Ed. by Alexander L. George. LC 92-39900. (Logic & Computation in Philosophy Ser.). (Illus.). 216p. (C). 1994. text 49.95 (0-19-507929-9) OUP.

Mathematics & Modelling. Ed. by A. D. Bazykin & Yu G. Zarkhin. 310p. 1993. lib. bdg. 165.00 (1-56072-104-9) Nova Sci Pubs.

Mathematics & Music: Some Intersections. Joan Reinthaler. 1990. 2.50 (0-940790-08-4) Mu Alpha Theta.

Mathematics & Music: The Deeper Links. Edward Rothstein. 1988. write for info. (0-318-61943-1) Knopf.

Mathematics & Natural Science Dictionary: Mathematisch-Narurwissenschaftliches Woerterbuch. G. Englander. 249p. 1983. 49.95 (0-8288-1901-7, M15446) Fr & Eur.

*Mathematics & Necessity: Essays in the History of Philosophy. Ed. by Timothy Smiley. (Proceedings of the British Academy Ser.: Vol. 103). (Illus.). 100p. 2000. text 25.00 (0-19-726215-5) OUP.

Mathematics & Optimal Form. Stefan Hildebrandt & Anthony J. Tromba. LC 84-23461. (Scientific American Library). (Illus.). 215p. 1984. text 26.40 (0-7167-5009-0) W H Freeman.

Mathematics & Physical Science, 2 vols. W. J. Eresian et al. Incl. Vol. 2-Physical Science. 318p. 1979. ring bd. 79.95 (0-87683-027-0); Vol. 2-Physical Science. 318p. 1979. teacher ed. 350.00 (0-87683-030-0); Vol. 1. Mathematics. (Illus.). 370p. 1979. ring bd. 295.00 (0-87683-026-2); Vol. 1. Mathematics. (Illus.). 370p. 1979. teacher ed. 350.00 (0-87683-029-7); (Illus.). 688p. 1979. 295.00 (0-87683-028-9) GP Courseware.

Mathematics & Physical Science, 2 vols., Set. W. J. Eresian et al. Incl. Vol. 2-Physical Science. 318p. 1979. ring bd. 79.95 (0-87683-027-0); Vol. 2-Physical Science. 318p. 1979. teacher ed. 350.00 (0-87683-030-0); Vol. 1. Mathematics. (Illus.). 370p. 1979. ring bd. 295.00 (0-87683-026-2); Vol. 1. Mathematics. (Illus.). 370p. 1979. teacher ed. 350.00 (0-87683-029-7); (Illus.). 688p. 1979. 149.50 (0-87683-025-4) GP Courseware.

Mathematics & Physics for Aviation Personnel. 2nd ed. (Illus.). 97p. 1987. pap. text 7.95 (0-9614216-8-1) Jeppesen Sanderson.

Mathematics & Physics for Aviation Personnel. 3rd ed. Charles E. Dole. LC 91-24823. (Illus.). 94p. 1991. pap. text 12.45 (0-89100-399-1, JS312619) Jeppesen Sanderson.

Mathematics & Physics of Disordered Media: Percolation, Random Walk, Modeling & Simulation. B. D. Hughes & B. W. Ninham. (Lecture Notes in Mathematics Ser.: Vol. 1035). vii, 431p. 1983. 49.95 (0-387-12707-0) Spr-Verlag.

Mathematics & Physics of Emerging Biomedical Imaging. National Research Council Staff. 260p. (Orig.). 1996. pap. text 29.00 (0-309-05387-0) Natl Acad Pr.

Mathematics & Physics of Neutron Radiography. A. A. Harms & D. R. Wyman. 1986. text 107.50 (90-277-2191-2) Kluwer Academic.

Mathematics & Plausible Reasoning, 1. George Polya. (Illus.). 296p. 1954. pap. text 19.95 (0-691-02509-6, Pub. by Princeton U Pr) Cal Prin Full Svc.

Mathematics & Plausible Reasoning, 2. George Polya. (Illus.). 200p. 1954. pap. text 19.95 (0-691-02510-X, Pub. by Princeton U Pr) Cal Prin Full Svc.

Mathematics & Politics. A. D. Taylor. 304p. 1995. 47.95 (0-387-94500-8) Spr-Verlag.

Mathematics & Politics: Strategy, Voting, Power & Proof. Alan Taylor. LC 94-23399. 1995. 27.95 (0-387-94391-9) Spr-Verlag.

Mathematics & Science. Ed. by Ronald E. Mickens. 352p. (C). 1990. pap. 32.00 (981-02-0234-2); text 101.00 (981-02-0233-4) World Scientific Pub.

Mathematics & Science Achievement in the Final Year of Secondary School: IEA's Third International Mathematics & Science Study. Ina V. Mullis & Michael O. Martin. LC 97-81365. 1998. pap. write for info. (1-889938-08-4) Intl Study Ctr.

*Mathematics & Science Achievement State by State, 1998. 292p. 1998. pap. 18.00 (0-16-063666-3) USGPO.

Mathematics & Science Curriculum Change in the People's Republic of China. Xiufeng Liu. LC 95-42603. (Mellen Studies in Education: Vol. 27). 204p. 1996. 89.95 (0-7734-8863-4) E Mellen.

Mathematics & Science Education Around the World: What Can We Learn from the Survey of Mathematics & Science Opportunities (SMSO) & the Third International Mathematics & Science Study (TIMSS) National Research Council Staff. LC 97-105406. 32p. (C). 1996. pap. text 10.00 (0-309-05631-4) Natl Acad Pr.

Mathematics & Sports. L. E. Sadovskii & A. L. Sadovskii. Tr. by S. Makar-Limanov from RUS. LC 93-23024. (Mathematical World Ser.: Vol. 3).Tr. of Matematika i Sport. 152p. 1993. pap. 19.00 (0-8218-9500-1, MAWRLD/3) Am Math.

Mathematics & Statistics see Comprehensive Dissertation Index: Ten Year Cumulation, 1973-1982

Mathematics & Statistics. 2nd ed. Saunders. 1971. 12.50 (0-85369-077-4, Pub. by Pharmaceutical Pr) Rittenhouse.

Mathematics & Statistics see Comprehensive Dissertation Index 1861-1972

Mathematics & Statistics for the Bio-Sciences. G. Eason et al. LC 79-41815. (Mathematics & Its Applications Ser.). 578p. 1983. pap. text 46.95 (0-470-27400-X) P-H.

Mathematics & Statistics in Anaesthesia. Steven Cruickshank. (Illus.). 268p. 1998. text (0-19-262313-3) OUP.

Mathematics & Statistics in Anaesthesia. Steven Cruickshank. LC 97-53170. (Illus.). 268p. 1998. pap. text 49.50 (0-19-262312-5) OUP.

Mathematics & Statistics, Physics see Comprehensive Dissertation Index: Five-Year Cumulation, 1983-1987

Mathematics & the Image of Reason. Mary Tiles. LC 90-8971. (Philosophical Issues in Science Ser.). 208p. (C). 1991. 75.00 (0-415-03318-7, A5475) Routledge.

Mathematics & the Medieval Ancestry of Physics. George Molland. (Collected Studies: Vol. CS481). 352p. 1995. 113.95 (0-86078-470-3, Pub. by Variorum) Ashgate Pub Co.

Mathematics & the Physical World. Morris Kline. (Illus.). 496p. 1981. reprint ed. pap. 11.95 (0-486-24104-1) Dover.

Mathematics & the Sciences of the Heavens & the Earth see Science & Civilisation in China

Mathematics & the Search for Knowledge. Morris Kline. LC 84-14809. (Illus.). 263p. 1986. pap. 10.95 (0-19-504230-1) OUP.

Mathematics & the Unexpected. Ivar Ekeland. LC 87-30230. (Illus.). xiv, 160p. 1990. pap. 9.95 (0-226-19990-8) U Ch Pr.

Mathematics & the Unexpected. Ivar Ekeland. (Illus.). 176p. 1992. 19.95 (0-226-19989-4) U Ch Pr.

Mathematics Applied to Continuum Mechanics. Lee A. Segel & G. H. Handelman. 608p. 1987. reprint ed. pap. text 14.95 (0-486-65369-2) Dover.

Mathematics Applied to Deterministic Problems in the Natural Sciences. C. C. Lin & Lee A. Segel. LC 88-62304. (Classics in Applied Mathematics Ser.: No. 1). xxi, 609p. 1988. pap. 39.50 (0-89871-229-7) Soc Indus-Appl Math.

Mathematics Applied to Electronics. 4th ed. James H. Harter & Wallace D. Beitzel. LC 96-37946. 742p. 1997. 86.00 (0-13-602061-5) P-H.

*Mathematics Applied to Electronics. 5th ed. James H. Harter & Wallace D. Beitzel. 768p. 2000. 80.00 (0-13-017184-0) P-H.

Mathematics Applied to Fluid Mechanics & Stability: Proceedings of a Conference Dedicated to Richard C. DiPrima. Ed. by Donald A. Drew & Joseph E. Flaherty. LC 86-61597. (Proceedings in Applied Mathematics Ser.: No. 24). (Illus.). xii, 295p. 1986. text 42.50 (0-89871-208-4) Soc Indus-Appl Math.

Mathematics Applied to Physics. Ed. by E. Roubine et al. (Illus.). 1970. 86.95 (0-387-04965-7) Spr-Verlag.

Mathematics Appreciation. McLoughlin & James Magliano. 450p. (C). 1998. per. 49.95 (0-7872-5639-0, 41563903) Kendall-Hunt.

Mathematics Appreciation. Theoni Pappas. 154p. 1987. pap. 10.95 (0-933174-28-4) Wide World-Tetra.

Mathematics As a Cultural System. Raymond J. Wilder. (Foundations & Philosophy of Science & Technology Ser.). 170p. 1981. 84.00 (0-08-025796-8, Pub. by Pergamon Repr) Franklin.

Mathematics As a Science of Patterns. Michael D. Resnik. LC 96-51610. (Illus.). 298p. 1997. text 45.00 (0-19-823608-5) OUP.

Mathematics As a Science of Patterns. Michael D. Resnik. (Illus.). 304p. 2000. pap. text 19.95 (0-19-825014-2) OUP.

Mathematics as a Science of Quantities. Hippocrates G. Apostle. LC 91-91162. 95p. 1991. text 25.00 (0-911589-12-0) Peripatetic.

Mathematics As a Second Language. 4th ed. Joseph Newmark. LC 85-30646. (Mathematics Ser.). (C). 1987. text. write for info. (0-201-05885-5) Addison-Wesley.

Mathematics As a Second Language. 4th rev. ed. Joseph Newmark. 1987. 51.75 (0-201-19297-7) Addison-Wesley.

Mathematics As a Service Subject. Ed. by A. G. Howson et al. (International Commission on Mathematical Instruction Study Ser.). 96p. 1988. pap. text 25.95 (0-521-35703-9) Cambridge U Pr.

Mathematics As an Educational Task. Hans Freudenthal. LC 72-77874. (Illus.). 680p. 1972. pap. text 64.50 (90-277-0322-1) Kluwer Academic.

Mathematics As Known to the Vedic Samhitas. M. D. Pandit. (Sri Garib Dass Oriental Ser.: No. 169). (C). 1993. text 22.00 (81-7030-368-0) S Asia.

Mathematics As Problem Solving. Alexander Soifer. LC 86-72215. (Illus.). viii, 117p. (YA). (gr. 8-12). 1987. pap. 19.95 (0-940263-00-9) Ctr Excel Math.

*Mathematics as Sign: Writing, Imagining, Counting. B. Rotman. LC 00-23291. 2000. pap. write for info. (0-8047-3684-7) Stanford U Pr.

*Mathematics Assessment: A Practical Handbook for Grades 9-12. Ed. by William S. Bush & Anja S. Greer. LC 99-45423. (Classroom Assessment for School Mathematics Ser.). (Illus.). 144p. (YA). (gr. 9-12). 1999. pap. 20.95 (0-87353-476-X) NCTM.

Mathematics Assessment: Alternative Approaches: A Viewer's Guide. Therese M. Kuhs. 20p. 1993. pap. 5.50 (0-87353-355-0) NCTM.

Mathematics Assessment: Myths, Models, Good Questions, & Practical Suggestions. Ed. by Jean K. Stenmark. LC 91-41156. (Illus.). 67p. 1991. pap. 14.95 (0-87353-339-9) NCTM.

Mathematics Assessment: What Works in the Classroom. Gerald Kulm. (Education Ser.). 198p. 1994. pap. 29.95 (0-7879-0040-0) Jossey-Bass.

Mathematics Assessment & Evaluation: Imperatives for Mathematics Educators. Ed. by Thomas A. Romberg. LC 91-11157. (SUNY Series, Reform in Mathematics Education). 369p. (C). 1992. pap. text 23.95 (0-7914-0900-7) State U NY Pr.

Mathematics, Astronomy & Biology in Indian Tradition: Some Conceptual Preliminaries. Ed. by D. P. Chattopadhyaya & Ravinder Kumar. LC 95-905857. (C). 1995. 14.00 (81-215-0688-3, Pub. by M Manoharial) S Asia.

Mathematics at Work. 3rd ed. Holbrook Norton & Henry H. Ryffel. (Illus.). 624p. 1990. pap. text 20.95 (0-8311-3029-6) Indus Pr.

*Mathematics at Work: Practical Applications of Arithmetic, Algebra, Geometry, Trigonometry & Logarithms to the Step-by-Step Solutions of Mechanical Problems, with Formulas Commonly Used in Engineering Practice & a Concise Review of Basic Mathematical Principles. 4th ed. Holbrook L. Horton et al. LC 99-14606. 687p. 1999. text 22.95 (0-8311-3083-0) Indus Pr.

Mathematics Basic Facts. Harper Collins Staff. (Collins Gem Ser.). 1998. 8.00 (0-00-472154-3) Collins.

*Mathematics Behind Fuzzy Logic. E. Turunen. LC 99-44345. (Advances in Soft Computing Ser.). x, 191p. 1999. pap. 44.00 (3-7908-1221-8) Spr-Verlag.

Mathematics Beyond Measure: Essays on Nature, Myth & Number. Jay Kappraff. (Illus.). 320p. 1996. text 22.95 (0-07-034254-7) McGraw.

*Mathematics Beyond the Numbers. George T. Gilbert & Rhonda L. Hatcher. 212p. 2000. pap., student ed. 34.95 (0-471-29397-0) Wiley.

Mathematics Beyond the Numbers. Rhonda L. Hatcher & George T. Gilbert. LC 99-32789. 704p. (C). 1999. text 84.95 (0-471-13934-3) Wiley.

Mathematics Can Be Fun. Yakov Perelman. 400p. (C). 1985. 50.00 (0-7855-4982-X, Pub. by Collets) St Mut.

Mathematics Chemistry. G. Doggett. (C). 1996. pap. text 46.00 (0-582-21970-1) Addison-Wesley.

Mathematics Classroom Management Guide, Grade 1-8. Gary G. Bitter et al. (Mathematics Ser.). (J). (gr. 2). 1981. pap. text 2.80 (0-07-006092-4) McGraw.

Mathematics Classroom Management Guide, Grade 1-8. Gary G. Bitter et al. (Mathematics Ser.). (J). (gr. 3). 1981. pap. text 2.80 (0-07-006093-2) McGraw.

Mathematics Classroom Management Guide, Grade 1-8. Gary G. Bitter et al. (Mathematics Ser.). (J). (gr. 4). 1981. pap. text 2.80 (0-07-006094-0) McGraw.

Mathematics Classroom Management Guide, Grade 1-8. Gary G. Bitter et al. (Mathematics Ser.). (J). (gr. 5). 1981. pap. text 2.80 (0-07-006095-9) McGraw.

Mathematics Classroom Management Guide, Grade 1-8. Gary G. Bitter et al. (Mathematics Ser.). (J). (gr. 6). 1981. pap. text 2.80 (0-07-006096-7) McGraw.

Mathematics Classroom Management Guide, Grade 1-8. Gary G. Bitter et al. (Mathematics Ser.). (J). (gr. 7). 1981. pap. text 2.80 (0-07-006097-5) McGraw.

Mathematics Classroom Management Guide, Grade 1-8. Gary G. Bitter et al. (Mathematics Ser.). (J). (gr. 8). 1981. pap. text 2.80 (0-07-006098-3) McGraw.

Mathematics Classrooms That Promote Understanding. Ed. by Elizabeth Fennema & Thomas A. Romberg. LC 99-17343. (Studies in Mathematical Thinking & Learning). 304p. 1999. pap. 22.50 (0-8058-3028-6) L Erlbaum Assocs.

Mathematics Classrooms That Promote Understanding. Ed. by Elizabeth Fennema & Thomas A. Romberg. LC 99-17343. (Studies in Mathematical Thinking & Learning). 216p. 1999. 49.95 (0-8058-3027-8) L Erlbaum Assocs.

Mathematics Competency. 2nd ed. (C). 1992. suppl. ed. write for info. (0-8087-9355-1) Pearson Custom.

*Mathematics Competency, 2000: Algebra & Geometry Refresher Course. R. Caprice-Konstantine. (C). 2000. pap. 8.50 (0-7442-0105-5) Montezuma.

Mathematics Contests: A Guide for Involving Students & Schools. Frederick O. Flener. LC 89-28855. (Illus.). 115p. 1990. pap. 15.50 (0-87353-282-1) NCTM.

Mathematics Cubed. Rod Bramald et al. 64p. (J). (gr. 3-11). pap. 12.50 (1-871098-08-4, Pub. by Claire Pubns) Parkwest Pubns.

Mathematics Dictionary. 5th ed. Robert C. James. 1992. 47.50 (0-412-99031-8, Chap & Hall NY); pap. 29.95 (0-442-01241-1); pap. 53.95 (0-412-99041-5, Chap & Hall NY); text 42.95 (0-442-00741-8) Chapman & Hall.

Mathematics Dictionary, 2 vols., Set. Ralf Sube & Gunther Eisenreich. (ENG, FRE, GER & RUS.). 1460p. 1992. 275.00 (0-8288-1902-5, M6983) Fr & Eur.

Mathematics Dictionary & Handbook. Eugene D. Nichols & Sharon Schwartz. 464p. (J). (gr. 5-10). 1999. text 29.95 (1-882269-09-8) N Schwartz Pub.

Mathematics Dictionary & Handbook. 3rd rev. ed. Sharon Schwartz & Eugene Nicols. (Illus.). 464p. (J). (gr. 5-12). 1998. pap. 14.95 (1-882269-07-1) N Schwartz Pub.

Mathematics Education: A Wider Perspective. J. Pottage. 197p. 1995. pap. 66.00 (0-7300-1585-8, Pub. by Deakin Univ) St Mut.

Mathematics Education: Models & Processes. Lyn D. English & Graeme Halford. 376p. 1995. pap. 39.95 (0-8058-1458-2); text 69.95 (0-8058-1457-4) L Erlbaum Assocs.

Mathematics Education & Culture. Ed. by Alan J. Bishop. (C). 1988. lib. bdg. 98.50 (90-277-2802-X) Kluwer Academic.

Mathematics Education & Language: Interpreting Hermeneutics & Post-Structuralism. Tony Brown. LC 97-11134. (Mathematics Education Library). 1997. lib. bdg. 113.50 (0-7923-4554-1) Kluwer Academic.

Mathematics, Education & Philosophy. Ed. by Paul Ernest. (Studies in Mathematics Education Ser.). 260p. 1996. pap. 27.95 (0-7507-0569-8, Falmer Pr) Taylor & Francis.

Mathematics, Education & Philosophy: An International Perspective. Ed. by Paul Ernest. LC 94-16902. (Studies in Mathematics Education Ser.: Vol. 3). 230p. 1994. 75.00 (0-7507-0290-7, Falmer Pr) Taylor & Francis.

Mathematics Education as a Research Domain: A Search for Identity, 2 vols. Ed. by Anna Sierpinska & Jeremy Kilpatrick. LC 97-20240. (New ICMI Studies: No. 4). 240p. 1997. 250.00 (0-7923-4599-1); pap. 99.00 (0-7923-4600-9) Kluwer Academic.

Mathematics Education for a Changing World. Stephen S. Willougby. 103p. 1990. pap. 14.95 (0-87120-175-5, 611-90100) ASCD.

Mathematics Education for Students with Learning Disabilities: Theory to Practice. Diane P. Rivera. LC 97-38019. 318p. 1998. write for info. (0-89079-710-2) PRO-ED.

Mathematics Education in China: Its Growth & Development. Frank J. Swetz. 350p. 1974. 27.50 (0-262-19121-0) MIT Pr.

*Mathematics Education in the Middle Grades: Teaching to Meet the Needs of Middle Grades Learners & to Maintain High Expectations : Proceedings of a National Convocation & Action Conferences. National Research Council Staff. LC 99-50765. 270p. 1999. pap. 29.00 (0-309-06797-9) Natl Acad Pr.

*Mathematics Education Research: A Guide for the Research Mathematician. C. McKnight et al. 106p. 2000. 20.00 (0-8218-2016-8) Am Math.

Mathematics Electrified! Susan Bassein. (Illus.). 93p. (Orig.). (YA). (gr. 12 up). 1996. wbk. ed. 15.00 (0-9654724-0-X) Grant Pub.

Mathematics Elementary Teaching Concept. 4th ed. Bennett. 256p. 1998. pap. 20.63 (0-07-006300-1) McGraw.

Mathematics English-Japanese/Japanese-English Dictionary. (ENG & JPN.). 95.00 (0-7859-9412-2) Fr & Eur.

*Mathematics Every Elementary Teacher Should Know. Derek Haylock & Douglas McDougall. (Springboards for Teaching Ser.). (Illus.). 224p. 1999. pap., teacher ed. 25.95 (1-55244-012-5, Pub. by Trifolium Inc) ACCESS Pubs Network.

Mathematics Explained for Primary Teachers. Derek Haylock. 144p. 1995. pap. 19.95 (1-85396-261-9, Pub. by P Chapman) Taylor & Francis.

*Mathematics for Agriculture. 2nd ed. Betty C. Rogers & Clifford M. Hokanson. xiv, 317p. 2000. 43.75 (0-8134-3174-3) Interstate.

***Mathematics for Agriculture: Answer Key.** 2nd ed. Betty C. Rogers & Clifford M. Hokanson. 2000. 1.00 (0-8134-3196-4) Interstate.

Mathematics for All: An Interactive Approach Within Level 1. 2nd ed. Pam Aherne & Ann Thornber. 32p. 1993. pap. 16.00 (1-85346-255-1, Pub. by David Fulton) Taylor & Francis.

Mathematics for Auto Mechanics. T. G. Hendrix & C. S. LaFevor. LC 77-72431. (C). 1978. pap. 24.95 (0-8273-1630-5) Delmar.

Mathematics for Basic Electronics. 3rd ed. Bernard Grob. 1989. pap. 34.12 (0-07-024921-0) McGraw.

Mathematics for Beginners, 1. David Corfield. LC 98-75004. 176p. 1999. pap. 10.95 (1-84046-011-3) Icon Bks.

Mathematics for Business see College Mathematics with Business Applications

Mathematics for Business. Brechne. (C). 1995. pap. text 37.50 (0-03-096610-8) Harcourt Coll Pubs.

Mathematics for Business. Karl J. Smith. 752p. (C). 1989. text 56.25 (0-697-05944-8, WCB McGr Hill) McGrw-H Hghr Educ.

Mathematics for Business. Karl J. Smith. 752p. (C). 1990. text, student ed. 21.25 (0-697-06248-1, WCB McGr Hill) McGrw-H Hghr Educ.

Mathematics for Business. 2nd ed. David R. Peterson & Kathleen N. Miller. 1989. text 40.23 (0-07-049630-7) McGraw.

Mathematics for Business. 4th ed. Jay Diamond & Gerald Pintel. (C). 1990. pap. text, wbk. ed. 19.20 (0-13-563081-9) P-H.

Mathematics for Business. 6th ed. Stanley Salzman et al. LC 97-21401. 747p. (C). 1997. 83.00 (0-321-01598-3) Addison-Wesley Educ.

***Mathematics for Business.** 7th ed. 2000. 28.00 (0-201-71947-9) P-H.

***Mathematics For Business: Annotated Instr Ed.** 7th ed. 2000. text. write for info. (0-321-08097-1) P-H.

Mathematics for Business: College Course. 6th ed. Kathleen N. Miller. 1987. text 37.95 (0-07-042061-0) McGraw.

Mathematics for Business: Solution Manual & Study Guide. 5th ed. Stanley A. Salzman et al. LC 93-14230. (C). 1997. pap. text, student ed. 33.00 (0-673-99010-9) Addison-Wesley Educ.

Mathematics for Business Careers. 4th ed. Jack Cain & Robert A. Carman. LC 96-49152. 895p. 1997. pap. text 80.00 (0-13-849258-1) P-H.

Mathematics for Business Careers. 4th ed. Harry Huffman et al. 1974. text 28.56 (0-07-031121-8) McGraw.

***Mathematics for Business Careers.** 5th ed. Jack Cain & Robert A. Carman. 816p. 2000. pap. 72.00 (0-13-019749-1) P-H.

Mathematics for Business Decisions. Coyle. 1971. 50.95 (0-442-30727-6, VNR) Wiley.

Mathematics for Business, Economics & Management. Marvin L. Bittinger & J. Conrad Crown. 1982. write for info. (0-201-10104-1) Addison-Wesley.

Mathematics for Business, Finance & Economics. F. M. Wilkes. LC 94-7554. (Illus.). 432p. (C). 1994. pap. 82.95 (0-415-11488-8, B4233); pap. 36.95 (0-415-11489-6, B4265) Thomson Learn.

Mathematics for Business, Finance & Economics. 2nd ed. F. M. Wilkes. LC 99-194038. 450p. 1999. pap. 25.99 (1-86152-241-X) Thomson Learn.

Mathematics for Business, Management & Economics: A Systems Modelling Approach. (Prentice Hall College Titles Ser.). (C). 1985. text 25.95 (0-13-563743-0, Macmillan Coll) P-H.

Mathematics for Business, Management & Economics: A Systems Modelling Approach. D. J. Harris. LC 85-898. (Mathematics & Its Applications Ser.). 392p. 1985. text 89.95 (0-470-20186-X) P-H.

Mathematics for Business Occupations. Dennis Bila et al. 567p. (gr. 10-12). 1986. reprint ed. 18.36 (0-935115-01-3) Instruct Tech.

Mathematics For Calculus. James Stewart et al. (Math). 589p. (C). 1989. mass mkt. 46.00 (0-534-10080-5) Brooks-Cole.

Mathematics For Calculus. 2nd ed. James Stewart et al. LC 92-42810. (Math). 1993. mass mkt. 57.00 (0-534-20250-0) Brooks-Cole.

Mathematics for Careers: Consumer Applications. Saint Paul Technical Vocational Institute Curricul. LC 80-67550. (Trade/Tech Math Ser.). 144p. (Orig.). 1981. pap. 10.00 (0-8273-2056-6) Delmar.

Mathematics for Carpenters. Robert Bradford. LC 75-19525. (C). 1975. teacher ed. 16.00 (0-8273-1117-6); mass mkt. 24.75 (0-8273-1116-8) Delmar.

Mathematics for Carpentry & the Construction. Alfred Webster & Kathryn Judy. 240p. 1989. pap. text 53.20 (0-13-562331-6) P-H.

Mathematics for Chemists. P. G. Francis. 176p. (Orig.). 1984. text 42.50 (0-412-24980-4, 9193) Chapman & Hall.

Mathematics for Communication: Number Relations. Ralph C. Williams. LC 70-123614. 311p. reprint ed. pap. 96.50 (0-608-30849-8, 200773400064) Bks Demand.

Mathematics for Communications Engineering. Harold B. Wood. 335p. 1988. text 64.95 (0-470-21245-4) P-H.

Mathematics for Computer Algebra. M. Mignotte. xiv, 346p. 1991. 62.95 (0-387-97675-2) Spr-Verlag.

Mathematics for Computer Graphics Applications: An Introduction to the Mathematics & Geometry Of Cad/cam, Geometric Modeling, Scientific Visualization, & Other CG Applications. 2nd ed. Michael E. Mortenson. LC 99-10096. (Illus.). 416p. 1999. text 39.95 (0-8311-3111-X) Indus Pr.

Mathematics for Computer Programmers. Christine B. Kay. (Illus.). 304p. (C). 1984. text 46.00 (0-13-562140-2) P-H.

Mathematics for Computer Studies. James T. Sedlock. (Illus.). 448p. (C). 1991. reprint ed. text 85.00 (1-878907-49-2) TechBooks.

Mathematics for Computer Technology. Paul Calter. (Illus.). 608p. (C). 1986. text 47.00 (0-13-562190-9) P-H.

Mathematics for Cosmetology. Fleck. (Career Development Ser.). 1990. pap. 21.75 (0-87350-128-4) Thomson Learn.

Mathematics for Daily Living. rev. ed. Harold Lewis. 1979. 21.96 (0-8009-1552-6); text, teacher ed. 23.92 (0-8009-1549-6) Random.

Mathematics for Data Processing & Computer Programming. Fernand Tessier. 640p. 1989. boxed set 37.00 (0-13-562356-1) P-H.

Mathematics for Data Processing & Computing. Maria Shopay-Kolatis. (C). 1985. teacher ed. write for info. (0-201-14956-7); text. write for info. (0-201-14955-9) Addison-Wesley.

Mathematics for Derivatives: Self-Study Workbook. John Marshall. (D. C. Gardner Self-Study Workbook Ser.). 1998. pap., wbk. ed. 295.00 (1-85564-642-0) Am Educ Systs.

Mathematics for Dynamic Modeling. 2nd ed. Edward A. Beltrami. LC 97-16264. (Illus.). 219p. 1997. text 55.00 (0-12-085566-6) Morgan Kaufmann.

Mathematics for Dyslexics: A Teaching Handbook. Stephen J. Chinn & J. Richard Ashcroft. 246p. 1993. 29.99 (1-56593-250-1, 0547) Thomson Learn.

Mathematics for Dyslexics: A Teaching Handbook. 2nd ed. S. J. Chinn & J. R. Ashcroft. 250p. 1999. 39.95 (1-56593-887-9, 1738) Singular Publishing.

Mathematics for Dyslexics: A Teaching Handbook. 2nd ed. Stephen J. Chinn & J. Richard Ashcroft. LC 98-184658. xiv, 268p. 1998. write for info. (1-86156-043-5) Whurr Pub.

Mathematics for Econometrics. 2nd ed. P. J. Dhrymes. 150p. 1990. 48.95 (0-387-90988-5) Spr-Verlag.

***Mathematics for Econometrics.** 3rd ed. Phoebus J. Dhrymes. LC 00-30761. (Illus.). 264p. 2000. pap. 44.95 (0-387-98995-1) Spr-Verlag.

Mathematics for Economic Analysis. Knut Sydsaeter & Peter J. Hammond. LC 94-4225. 800p. (C). 1994. text 57.80 (0-13-583600-X) P-H.

Mathematics for Economics & Business. 2nd ed. Ian Jacques. LC 94-42144. (C). 1995. pap. text 21.25 (0-201-42769-9) Addison-Wesley.

Mathematics for Economics & Business. 3rd ed. Ian Jacques. LC 98-38622. (C). 1999. pap. text. write for info. (0-201-36066-7) Addison-Wesley.

Mathematics for Economics & Finance: Methods & Modelling. Norman L. Biggs & M. H. Anthony. (Illus.). 394p. (C). 1996. text 74.95 (0-521-55113-7); pap. text 27.95 (0-521-55913-8) Cambridge U Pr.

Mathematics for Economics & Business: An Interactive Introduction. Jean Soper. LC 98-35150. 256p. 1998. 64.95 (0-631-21189-6); pap. 32.95 (0-631-20781-3) Blackwell Pubs.

Mathematics for Economist Problems. Simon Blume. pap. text 0.00 (0-393-95734-9) Norton.

Mathematics for Economists. 100p. (C). 1991. pap. 36.00 (0-7855-6609-0, Pub. by HLT Pubns) St Mut.

Mathematics for Economists. William Novshek. LC 93-16696. (Economic Theory, Econometrics & Mathematical Economics Ser.). (Illus.). 308p. 1993. text 69.95 (0-12-522575-X) Acad Pr.

Mathematics for Economists. Pemberton. 240p. Date not set. pap. 24.95 (0-7190-3341-1, Pub. by Manchester Univ Pr); text 79.95 (0-7190-3340-3, Pub. by Manchester Univ Pr) St Martin.

Mathematics for Economists. Carl P. Simon & Lawrence E. Blume. LC 93-24962. (C). 1994. 93.25 (0-393-95733-0) Norton.

Mathematics for Economists: A First Course. J. M. Pearson. LC 81-14309. (Illus.). 220p. reprint ed. pap. 68.20 (0-8357-2971-0, 203923300011) Bks Demand.

Mathematics for Economists: Answers Pamphlet. Carl P. Simon & Lawrence E. Blume. LC 93-24962. (C). 1994. pap. text 12.95 (0-393-96083-8) Norton.

Mathematics for Electrical & Telecommunications Engineers: Level 2. J. O. Bird & A. J. May. LC TA0330.. (Longman Technician Series, Methematics & Sciences). (Illus.). 383p. reprint ed. pap. 118.80 (0-608-18736-4, 203033300068) Bks Demand.

Mathematics for Electrical Technicians. 2nd ed. J. O. Bird. 1996. pap. (0-582-23421-2) Addison-Wesley.

Mathematics for Electricians & Electronics Technicians. Rex Miller & Martin R. Miller. 1985. text 14.95 (0-8161-1700-4) Macmillan.

Mathematics for Electricity/Electronics. Kramer. (Electronic Technology Ser.). 1995. 49.95 (0-8273-5807-5, VNR) Wiley.

Mathematics for Electronic Technology. D. P. Howson. 280p. (C). 1975. 123.00 (0-08-018219-4, Pub. by Pergamon Repr) Franklin.

Mathematics for Electronic Technology. Arthur D. Kramer. (Illus.). 576p. (C). 1995. mass mkt. 82.95 (0-8273-5804-0) Delmar.

Mathematics for Electronics. Harry Forster. LC 97-152371. 160p. 1997. text 17.66 (0-02-802001-4) Glencoe.

Mathematics for Electronics. Nancy Myers. Ed. by Pullins. LC 92-25704. 450p. (C). 1993. mass mkt. 37.25 (0-314-01266-4) West Pub.

Mathematics for Electronics. Edward J. Pasahow. (Electronics Technology Ser.). 1984. text 52.95 (0-8273-3920-8) Delmar.

Mathematics for Electronics. 2nd ed. Donald P. Leach. (Illus.). 448p. (C). 1987. text. write for info. (0-318-61354-9) P-H.

Mathematics for Elementary School Teachers. (C). 1997. text 67.00 (0-201-32304-4) Addison-Wesley.

Mathematics for Elementary School Teachers. 384p. (C). 1997. text 24.00 (0-201-46146-3) Addison-Wesley.

***Mathematics for Elementary School Teachers.** (C). 1999. 26.00 (0-536-60275-1) Pearson Custom.

Mathematics for Elementary School Teachers. Randall Charles et al. Ed. by Karen Guardino. LC 97-7647. 914p. (C). 1997. 92.00 (0-201-53979-9) Addison-Wesley.

Mathematics for Elementary School Teachers. Phares G. O'Daffer. Ed. by Karen Guardino. 928p. (C). 1997. pap. text. write for info. (0-201-62099-5) Addison-Wesley.

Mathematics for Elementary School Teachers: A Problem Solving Approach. 5th ed. Billstein. 1995. pap. text 165.00 (0-201-52718-9) Addison-Wesley.

Mathematics for Elementary School Teachers: A Problem Solving Approach. 5th ed. Richard Billstein. 176p. (C). 1992. pap. text, student ed. 23.00 (0-201-52778-2) Addison-Wesley.

Mathematics for Elementary School Teachers: A Problem Solving Approach. 5th ed. Richard Billstein et al. (Illus.). 976p. (C). 1992. text 63.00 (0-201-52565-8) Addison-Wesley.

Mathematics for Elementary Teachers. Tom Bassarear. (C). 1997. text, teacher ed. 11.96 (0-395-66961-8) HM.

Mathematics for Elementary Teachers. 5th ed. (C). 2000. pap. text 28.00 (0-13-017020-8) HEPC Inc.

Mathematics for Elementary Teachers: A Balanced Approach. 2nd ed. Eugene F. Krause. LC 90-83094. 896p. (C). 1991. text 69.56 (0-669-24882-7); teacher ed. 2.66 (0-669-24883-5); student ed. 25.96 (0-669-24884-3); 2.66 (0-669-27639-1) HM Trade Div.

Mathematics for Elementary Teachers: A Conceptual Approach. 4th ed. Albert B. Bennett & Leonard T. Nelson. LC 97-16757. 1008p. (C). 1997. 65.31 (0-07-006295-1) McGraw.

Mathematics for Elementary Teachers: A Contemporary Approach. 4th ed. Gary L. Musser. (Illus.). 1997. teacher ed. 119.90 (0-471-37478-4); pap., teacher ed. 119.90 (0-471-37508-X) Wiley.

Mathematics for Elementary Teachers: A Contemporary Approach. 4th ed. Herb Trimpe. (Illus.). 1994. pap., teacher ed. 28.95 (0-471-36861-X) Wiley.

***Mathematics for Elementary Teachers A Contemporary Approach.** 5th ed. Miller. 2000. pap. text 31.95 (0-471-36862-8) Wiley.

***Mathematics for Elementary Teachers: A Contemporary Approach.** 5th ed. Gary L. Musser. 367p. 1999. pap. 26.95 (0-471-36636-6) Wiley.

***Mathematics for Elementary Teachers A Contemporary Approach.** 5th ed. Gary L. Musser. 408p. 1999. pap. 31.95 (0-471-36654-4) Wiley.

***Mathematics for Elementary Teachers: A Contemporary Approach.** 5th ed. Gary L. Musser et al. 1056p. 1999. text 87.95 (0-471-36858-X) Wiley.

***Mathematics for Elementary Teachers: A Contemporary Approach, A Guide to Problem Solving.** 5th ed. Musser. 118p. 1999. pap. 26.95 (0-471-37803-8) Wiley.

Mathematics for Elementary Teachers: A Content Approach. Ruth Heintz. LC 79-18727. (Illus.). 512p. 1980. text. write for info. (0-201-03227-9) Addison-Wesley.

Mathematics for Elementary Teachers: An Activity Approach. 3rd ed. Albert B. Bennett, Jr. & Leonard T. Nelson. 336p. (C). 1992. text 41.88 (0-697-05917-0, WCB McGr Hill) McGrw-H Hghr Educ.

Mathematics for Elementary Teachers: An Activity Approach. 4th ed. Albert B. Bennett & Leonard T. Nelson. LC 97-5914. 1998. write for info. (0-07-006298-6) McGraw.

Mathematics for Elementary Teachers: Contemporary Approach. 3rd ed. (C). 1994. 80.00 (0-02-385465-0, Macmillan Coll); 80.00 (0-02-385466-9, Macmillan Coll) P-H.

Mathematics for Elementary Teachers: Explorations Manual. Tom Bassarear. 256p. (C). 1997. pap. text 23.96 (0-395-66960-X) HM.

Mathematics for Elementary Teachers Via Problem Solving, Preliminary ed. Joanna Masingila. 394p. 1997. pap. text 38.20 (0-13-888488-9) P-H.

***Mathematics for Engineering.** 2nd ed. W. Bolton. 352p. 2000. pap. 28.95 (0-7506-4931-3) Buttrwrth-Heinemann.

Mathematics for Engineers, Vol. 2. L. J. Nicolescu & M. Stoka. (Illus.). 412p. 1974. text 110.00 (0-85626-004-5, Abacus) Gordon & Breach.

Mathematics for Engineers: A Modern Interactive Approach. Tony Croft. LC 98-48541. (C). 1999. pap. text. write for info. (0-201-87752-X) Addison-Wesley.

Mathematics for Engineers: Examination Subjects for Technical Students. 2nd ed. S. F. Hancock. LC TA0332.5. 240p. reprint ed. pap. 74.40 (0-608-12188-6, 202527700043) Bks Demand.

Mathematics for Engineers - Toolkit. Henry Shapiro. (C). 1995. pap. text 13.66 (0-8053-6403-X) Addison-Wesley.

Mathematics for Engineers & Scientists. K. Weltner et al. 512p. (Orig.). (C). 1986. pap. 54.00 (0-85950-120-5, Pub. by S Thornes Pubs) Trans-Atl Phila.

Mathematics for Engineers & Scientists. 4th ed. Jeffrey. (Mechanical Engineering Ser.). 1991. text 16.95 (0-412-34310-X) Chapman & Hall.

Mathematics for Engineers & Scientists. 4th ed. Jeffrey. (Illus.). 896p. (C). (gr. 13). 1992. mass mkt. 51.95 (0-412-44540-9, Chap & Hall NY) Chapman & Hall.

Mathematics for Engineers Problem Solver. rev. ed. Research & Education Association Staff. (Illus.). 816p. 1996. pap. text 29.95 (0-87891-838-8) Res & Educ.

Mathematics for Every Young Child. Karen Schultz & Ron Colarusso. 384p. (C). 1990. pap. text 40.60 (0-675-20425-9, Merrill Coll) P-H.

Mathematics for Everyday Living: The Mathematics of Buying. Roland E. Larson et al. (Illus.). 119p. (J). (gr. 9-12). 1996. pap. text 19.95 (1-887050-21-3) Meridian Creative.

Mathematics for Everyday Living: The Mathematics of Investment. Roland E. Larson et al. (Illus.). 135p. (J). (gr. 9 up). 1997. pap. text 19.95 (1-887050-29-9) Meridian Creative.

Mathematics for Everyday Living: The Mathematics of Saving. Roland E. Larson et al. (Illus.). 134p. (J). (gr. 9-12). 1997. pap. text 19.95 (1-887050-24-8) Meridian Creative.

Mathematics for Finance. Robert J. Elliott & P. E. Kopp. LC 98-8540. (Springer Finance Ser.). xii, 288p. 1998. 59.95 (0-387-98553-0) Spr-Verlag.

Mathematics for Financial Analysis. Michael Gartenberg & Barry Shaw. 240p. 1976. 95.00 (0-08-019599-7, Pub. by Pergamon Repr) Franklin.

Mathematics for Freshman in the Life Sciences. Erik A. Lippa. (Illus.). 319p. (Orig.). (C). 1977. pap. text 30.00 (0-9607980-0-5) E A Lippa.

Mathematics for Geologists. L. D. Knoring & V. N. Dech. Ed. by Ryszard B. Zeidler. LC 99-226646. (Geotechnika 10: Selected Translations of Russian Geotechnical Literature Ser.). 210p. 1993. text 91.00 (90-5410-253-5, Pub. by A A Balkema) Ashgate Pub Co.

Mathematics for Grob Basic Electronics. 5th ed. Bernard Grob. 144p. 1997. text, suppl. ed. 20.54 (0-02-802254-8) Glencoe.

Mathematics for Health Careers. Carol Castellon et al. LC 93-15623. (C). 1993. pap. 26.50 (0-8273-5569-6) Delmar.

Mathematics for Health Careers: Instructor's Guide. Carol Castellon et al. 52p. 1994. teacher ed. 12.95 (0-8273-6357-5) Delmar.

Mathematics for Health Occupations. Kathi Dunlap. 200p. (C). 1991. mass mkt. 28.50 (0-8273-4173-3) Delmar.

Mathematics for Health Occupations. Dennis Bila et al. 526p. 1986. reprint ed. student ed. write for info. (0-935115-04-8); reprint ed. pap. text 18.36 (0-87626-570-0) Instruct Tech.

Mathematics for Health Sciences. Keith Roberts & Leo Michels. LC 81-12234. (Mathematics Ser.). 423p. (C). 1996. mass mkt. 41.25 (0-8185-0478-1) Brooks-Cole.

Mathematics for Higher National Certificate, Vol. II. 3rd ed. S. W. Bell et al. (Illus.). 504p. reprint ed. pap. 143.70 (0-608-30996-6, 2050773); reprint ed. pap. 156.30 (0-608-10686-0, 2050773) Bks Demand.

Mathematics for Innumerate Economists. Gavin Kennedy. LC 81-13337. 134p. (C). 1982. 39.75 (0-8419-0777-3) Holmes & Meier.

Mathematics for Introductory Statistics: A Programmed Review. Andrew R. Baggaley. LC 69-19103. 185p. reprint ed. pap. 57.40 (0-608-30001-2, 205527100011) Bks Demand.

Mathematics for Large Scale Computing. J. C. Diaz. (Lecture Notes in Pure & Applied Mathematics Ser.: Vol. 120). (Illus.). 368p. 1989. pap. text 155.00 (0-8247-8122-8) Dekker.

Mathematics for Liberal Arts. (C). 2000. write for info. (0-13-014920-9) S&S Trade.

Mathematics for Liberal Arts. Rueger Johnson. (Mathematics Ser.). 1999. pap. 35.25 (0-534-21870-9) Brooks-Cole.

Mathematics for Liberal Arts. Frederick K. Richmond et al. (C). 2000. 20.00 (0-13-014932-2) S&S Trade.

***Mathematics for Life.** 1999. write for info. (0-13-014285-9) P-H.

Mathematics for Life: Preliminary. Donald Pierce & Edward B. Wright. 552p. (C). 1997. pap. text 44.00 (0-13-493859-3) P-H.

Mathematics for Life Sciences. (C). 2001. pap. text 0.00 (0-13-017001-1) HEPC Inc.

***Mathematics for Linear Circuits & Filters.** Wai-Kai Chen. LC 99-43798. 263p. 1999. boxed set 59.95 (0-8493-0052-5) CRC Pr.

Mathematics for Little Ones: How to Make Your Child Successful in Math. Dina Migachyov. (Illus.). viii, 183p. (J). (gr. k-3). 1999. pap. 19.95 (0-9672535-0-0) Quaternion.

Mathematics for Machine Technology. 3rd ed. Smith. (Trade/Tech Math Ser.). 1990. pap., teacher ed. 16.00 (0-8273-4043-5) Delmar.

Mathematics for Machine Technology. 3rd ed. Robert D. Smith. (Trade/Tech Math Ser.). 408p. (C). 1990. pap. 32.25 (0-8273-4042-7) Delmar.

Mathematics for Machine Technology. 4th ed. Robert D. Smith. LC 98-6660. 496p. (C). 1998. text 53.95 (0-8273-7942-0) Delmar.

Mathematics for Machine Technology - IML. 4th ed. Robert D. Smith. 160p. (C). 1998. teacher ed. 16.95 (0-8273-7943-9) Delmar.

Mathematics for Management. Richard C. Lucking. LC 80-40127. (Illus.). 340p. reprint ed. pap. 105.40 (0-7837-6388-3, 204610100010) Bks Demand.

Mathematics for Management & Finance. 7th ed. Stephen P. Shao & Lawrence P. Shao. LC 94-23342. 864p. (C). 1995. mass mkt. 60.50 (0-538-82980-X) S-W Pub.

Mathematics for Management Science. Gordon Bancroft. (C). 1998. pap. text. write for info. (0-201-17846-X) Addison-Wesley.

Mathematics for Managerial Decisions. 2nd ed. Robert L. Childress et al. 704p. (C). 1989. text 66.80 (0-13-563024-X) P-H.

***Mathematics for Mechanical Engineers.** William F. Ames. 221p. 2000. 49.95 (0-8493-0056-8) CRC Pr.

Mathematics for Nurses with Clinical Applications. Mary K. Miller. LC 80-26040. 390p. (Orig.). (C). 1981. pap. 31.00 (0-8185-0429-3) Brooks-Cole.

Mathematics for Operations Research. W. H. Marlow. LC 93-24974. (Illus.). 483p. 1993. reprint ed. pap. 12.95 (0-486-67723-0) Dover.

Mathematics for Physical Chemistry. 2nd ed. Robert G. Mortimer. LC 98-89310. (Illus.). 456p. (C). 1999. pap. 35.00 (0-12-508340-8) Acad Pr.

An Asterisk (*) at the beginning of an entry indicates that the title is appearing for the first time.

Mathematics for Physicists. unabridged ed. Philippe Dennery & Andre Krzywicki. LC 96-10774. (Illus.). 400p. 1996. reprint ed. pap. text 12.95 (0-486-69193-4) Dover.

Mathematics for Plumbers & Pipefitters. 5th ed. Bartholomew D'Arcangelo et al. LC 95-34211. (Trade/Tech Math Ser.). 288p. 1995. mass mkt. 40.95 (0-8273-7061-X) Delmar.

Mathematics for Plumbers & Pipefitters. 5th ed. Bartholomew D'Arcangelo et al. (Trade/Tech Math Ser.). 64p. 1996. text, teacher ed. 16.95 (0-8273-7062-8) Delmar.

***Mathematics for Primary Teachers.** Valsa Koshy et al. LC 99-33554. 226p. 2000. write for info. (0-415-20090-3) Routledge.

Mathematics for Principles of Technology. Ralph E. Blake. 1988. ring bd. 39.95 (0-945035-01-2) Ctrl UT Pub.

Mathematics for Real Estate Appraisers. C. E. Fisher, Jr. 1996. pap. 110.00 (0-922154-27-9, Pub. by R-I-C-S Bks) St Mut.

Mathematics for Retail Buying. 4th rev. ed. Bette K. Tepper & Newton Godnick. 333p. (Orig.). 1996. pap. text 47.00 (1-56367-088-7) Fairchild.

Mathematics for Retail Buying: The Newly Revised Answer Manual/Instructor's Guide. Bette K. Tepper & Newton E. Godnick. 219p. 1998. pap., teacher ed. write for info. (1-56367-089-5) Fairchild.

Mathematics for Science Technicians, Level 2. J. O. Bird & A. J. May. LC TA0330.. (Longman Technician Series, Mathematics & Sciences). (Illus.). 330p. reprint ed. pap. 102.30 (0-8357-2979-6, 203924100011) Bks Demand.

Mathematics for Semiconductor Technicians. TEEX Staff. (Illus.). ix, 180p. 1997. student ed., spiral bd. 185.00 incl. cd-rom (1-58257-021-3, 8081B/M); spiral bd. 49.95 (1-58257-020-5, 8081B) TX Eng Extsn Servs.

Mathematics for Sheet Metal Fabrication. LC 79-118846. 1970. teacher ed. 16.00 (0-8273-0296-7) Delmar.

Mathematics for Sheet Metal Fabrication. LC 79-118846. (C). 1970. pap. text 27.50 (0-8273-0295-9) Delmar.

Mathematics for Statistics. W. L. Bashaw. LC 84-11228. 344p. (C). 1984. reprint ed. lib. bdg. 40.50 (0-89874-761-9) Krieger.

Mathematics for Technical & Vocational Students. Boyce. 1997. pap. text, student ed. 25.00 (0-13-253915-2) P-H.

Mathematics for Technical & Vocational Students. 10th ed. John G. Boyce et al. LC 99-22852. (Illus.). 644p. (C). 1999. 83.00 (0-13-010432-9) P-H.

Mathematics for Technical & Vocational Students: A Worktext. 2nd ed. Richard C. Spangler. LC 99-23324. 736p. 1999. pap. text 68.00 (0-13-011417-0) P-H.

Mathematics for Technical Education. 3rd ed. Dale Ewen et al. LC 97-35563. 669p. (C). 1998. 76.00 (0-13-895517-4) P-H.

Mathematics for Technical Occupations. Dennis Bila et al. 606p. (gr. 10-12). 1985. reprint ed. 18.36 (0-935115-02-1) Instruct Tech.

Mathematics for Technician Engineers: Levels 4 & 5. G. E. Dyball. 384p. 1983. write for info. (0-07-084664-2) McGraw.

***Mathematics for Technologists in Electronics.** (C). 2000. 42.00 (0-536-61109-2) Pearson Custom.

Mathematics for the Analysis of Algorithms. 2nd ed. Daniel H. Greene & Donald Ervin Knuth. LC 82-17718. (Progress in Computer Science Ser.). 123 p. 1982. write for info. (3-7643-3102-X) Birkhauser.

Mathematics for the Analysis of Algorithms. 3rd ed. Ed. by D. Greene & Donald E. Knuth. (Progress in Computer Science Ser.: Vol. 1). 127p. 1990. 36.50 (0-8176-3515-7) Birkhauser.

Mathematics for the Analysis of Algorithms. 3rd ed. Daniel H. Greene & Donald E. Knuth. LC 90-517. (Progress in Computer Science & Applied Logic Ser.). viii, 132p. 1990. write for info. (3-7643-3515-7) Birkhauser.

Mathematics for the Automotive Trades. 3rd ed. Peterson. (Trade/Tech Math Ser.). 1996. teacher ed. 15.00 (0-8273-6713-9) Delmar.

Mathematics for the Biological Sciences. Jagdish C. Arya & Robin W. Lardner. LC 78-13424. (Illus.). 705p. 1979. 96.00 (0-13-562439-8) P-H.

Mathematics for the Biological Sciences. A. Menell & Michael J. Bazin. 200p. 1988. text 41.95 (0-470-21167-9) P-H.

Mathematics for the Biosciences. Michael R. Cullen. (Illus.). 783p. (C). 1992. reprint ed. text 89.00 (1-878907-57-3) TechBooks.

Mathematics for the Clinical Laboratory. Lorraine J. Doucette & Selma Kaszczuk. LC 96-21902. 352p. 1997. pap. text 31.50 (0-7216-4458-9, W B Saunders Co) Harcrt Hlth Sci Grp.

Mathematics for the Curious. Peter M. Higgins. (Illus.). 232p. 1998. pap. 12.95 (0-19-288072-1) OUP.

Mathematics for the Fundamentals-of-Engineering Examination. Max Kurtz. 1996. text 45.00 (0-07-046022-1) McGraw.

Mathematics for the Fundamentals-of-Engineering Examination. Max Kurtz. 247p. 1997. 45.00 (0-07-036022-7) McGraw.

Mathematics for the Health Sciences. Paul T. Olsen & Sandra Murrell. (Developmental & Precalculus Math Ser.). (Illus.). 432p. 1981. pap. text. write for info. (0-201-04647-4) Addison-Wesley.

Mathematics for the Health Sciences. John B. Scott & E. L. Hutton. 205p. 1978. pap. text 19.95 (0-89641-009-9) American Pr.

Mathematics for the Heating, Ventilating & Cooling Trades. David L. Goetsch et al. (Illus.). 176p. (C). 1988. pap. text 22.00 (0-13-562521-1) P-H.

Mathematics for the Liberal Arts Student. Lawrence H. Hufendick. 163p. (C). 1971. 5.00 (0-910268-03-7); pap. 3.00 (0-910268-04-5) Books.

***Mathematics for the Liberal Arts Student.** Fred Richman et al. LC 99-26057. 386p. 1999. pap. 44.00 (0-13-014547-5) P-H.

Mathematics for the Machine Trades. David L. Goetsch et al. (Illus.). 192p. (C). 1988. pap. text 23.00 (0-13-563008-8) P-H.

Mathematics for the Management, Life & Social Sciences (Custom Pub) John Costello. (C). 1994. pap. text. write for info. (0-07-047138-X) McGraw.

Mathematics for the Manager. Tennant. 1973. pap. 41.95 (0-442-30786-1) Chapman & Hall.

***Mathematics for the Managerial, Life & Social Sciences.** 2nd ed. Tan. 2001. pap. 56.00 (0-534-36593-0) Thomson Learn.

Mathematics for the Managerial Lifestyle & the Social Sciences. Soo T. Tan. (Mathematics Ser.). 1995. pap. 105.95 (0-534-95184-8) PWS Pubs.

Mathematics for the Managerial Lifestyle & the Social Sciences. Soo T. Tan. (Mathematics Ser.). 1996. mass mkt., student ed. 25.50 (0-534-95187-2) PWS Pubs.

***Mathematics for the Million: How to Master the Magic of Numbers.** Lancelot Hogben. (Illus.). 649p. 1999. reprint ed. pap. 19.95 (0-85036-380-2, Pub. by MRLN) Paul & Co Pubs.

Mathematics for the Millions: How to Master the Magic of Numbers. Lancelot Hogben. 656p. 1993. pap. 16.95 (0-393-31071-X) Norton.

Mathematics for the Minority: Some Historical Perspectives of School Mathematics in Victoria. M. A. Clements. 94p. (C). 1989. pap. 44.00 (0-7300-0663-8, ECS807, Pub. by Deakin Univ) St Mut.

***Mathematics for the Modern World.** 640p. (C). 2000. text 24.00 (0-201-61132-5); pap. text 25.00 (0-201-61133-3) Addison-Wesley.

***Mathematics for the Modern World.** Dale K. Hathaway. LC 99-14099. 718p. (C). 1999. pap. 63.00 (0-201-61129-5) Addison-Wesley.

Mathematics for the Non-Mathematician. Morris Kline. (Popular Science Ser.). 641p. 1998. reprint ed. pap. 11.95 (0-486-24823-2) Dover.

Mathematics for the Sheet Metal Technician, Pt. 1. Claude J. Zinngrabe. LC QA0040.Z5. 152p. 1969. reprint ed. pap. 47.20 (0-608-11685-8, 200456300043) Bks Demand.

Mathematics for the Sheet Metal Technician, Pt. 2. Claude J. Zinngrabe. LC QA0040.Z5. 202p. 1969. reprint ed. pap. 62.70 (0-608-11686-6, 200456300044) Bks Demand.

Mathematics for the Trades: A Guided Approach. 5th ed. Robert A. Carman & Hal M. Saunders. LC 98-18951. 617p. (C). 1998. pap. text 71.00 (0-13-907783-9) P-H.

Mathematics for the Traffic Accident Investigator & Reconstructionist. Nathan S. Shigemura. (Illus.). 157p. (Orig.). 1996. pap. text 29.95 (1-884566-23-5) Inst Police Tech.

Mathematics for the Young Child. Ed. by Joseph N. Payne. LC 90-42418. (Illus.). 306p. 1990. 38.50 (0-87353-288-0) NCTM.

Mathematics for Tomorrow's Young Children: International Perspectives on Curriculum. Ed. by Helen Mansfield et al. LC 96-10933. (Mathematics Education Library: Vol. 16). 1996. lib. bdg. 128.00 (0-7923-3998-3) Kluwer Academic.

Mathematics for Young Children: An Active Thinking Approach. Marion H. Bird. (Illus.). 176p. (C). (gr. 13). 1991. text 79.95 (0-415-06479-1, A6270) Routledge.

Mathematics Framework for California Public Schools, K-12. California Department of Education Staff. (Illus.). 234p. 1992. pap. 8.00 (0-8011-1033-5) Calif Education.

Mathematics from Leningrad to Austin: George G. Lorentz's Selected Works in Real, Functional & Numerical Analysis. G. G. Lorentz & Rudolph A. Lorentz. LC 96-16946. (Contemporary Mathematicians Ser.). 1996. write for info. (3-7643-3710-9); write for info. (3-7643-3922-5, Pub. by Birkhauser); write for info. (3-7643-3923-3) Birkhauser.

Mathematics from Leningrad to Austin: George G. Lorentz's Selected Works in Real, Functional, & Numerical Analysis, 2 vols., Set. Ed. by Rudolph A. Lorentz. LC 96-16946. (Contemporary Mathematicians Ser.). 1167p. 1996. 189.00 (0-8176-3923-3) Birkhauser.

Mathematics from Leningrad to Austin: George G. Lorentz's Selected Works in Real, Functional, & Numerical Analysis, Vol. 1. Ed. by Rudolph A. Lorentz. LC 96-16946. (Contemporary Mathematicians Ser.). 538p. 1997. 110.00 (0-8176-3710-9) Birkhauser.

Mathematics from Leningrad to Austin: George G. Lorentz's Selected Works in Real, Functional, & Numerical Analysis, Vol. 2. Ed. by Rudolph A. Lorentz. LC 96-16946. (Contemporary Mathematicians Ser.). 629p. 1996. 120.00 (0-8176-3922-5) Birkhauser.

Mathematics from Manuscript to Print, 1300-1600. Ed. by Cynthia Hay. (Illus.). 284p. 1988. text 69.00 (0-19-853909-6) OUP.

Mathematics Getting in Touch: Grades K-3, Bk. 1. Fredda Friederwitzer. 1997. pap. text 10.95 (0-914040-44-8) Cuisenaire.

Mathematics Getting in Touch: Grades 4-5, Bk. 2. Fredda Friederwitzer. 1997. pap. text 10.95 (0-914040-45-6) Cuisenaire.

Mathematics Grade 3: Pupil Edition. Bolster. (Illus.). (J). pap. 6.59 (0-673-11812-6) Addson-Wesley Educ.

Mathematics-Grade 7. (YA). (gr. 7). 1996. pap. text 2.95 (0-88012-484-9) Instruct Fair.

Mathematics Handbook for Science & Engineering. Lennart Rade & Bertil Westergren. 531p. 1995. 45.00 (0-8176-3858-X, QA1) Birkhauser.

Mathematics Handbook for Science & Engineering. 4th ed. L. Rade & B. Westergren. LC 99-26578. 540p. 1999. 49.95 (3-540-65569-7) Spr-Verlag.

Mathematics Human Endeavor. 3rd ed. Jacobs. 1994. wbk. ed. 48.00 (0-7167-2611-4) W H Freeman.

Mathematics in a Cultural Context: Aboriginal Perspectives on Space, Time, & Money. Pam Harris. 168p. 1995. pap. 46.00 (0-7300-1293-X, Pub. by Deakin Univ) St Mut.

Mathematics in a Cultural Context: Aboriginal Perspectives on Space, Time & Money. Pam Harris. 168p. (C). 1991. pap. 69.00 (0-7300-1209-3, ECS807, Pub. by Deakin Univ) St Mut.

***Mathematics in a World of Data.** 2000. write for info. (1-57232-402-3) Seymour Pubns.

Mathematics in Action. 496p. (C). 1998. pap. text, teacher ed. 54.00 (0-201-34032-1) Addison-Wesley.

Mathematics in Action. Hatcher. 300p. (C). 2000. pap. text, teacher ed. write for info. (0-471-29399-7) Wiley.

***Mathematics in Action: An Introduction to Algebraic, Graphical & Trigonometric Problem Solving.** Consortium for the Foundation of Mathematics Staff. LC 00-25664. (Illus.). 2000. write for info. (0-201-66043-1) Addison-Wesley.

***Mathematics in Action 2.** Pre-Precalculus Grou SUNY Staff et al. 504p. (C). 1998. pap. text 61.00 (0-201-38318-7) Addison-Wesley.

Mathematics in Action 1. Pre-Precalculus Grou SUNY Staff & CUNY Staff. 512p. (C). 1998. pap. text 61.00 (0-201-38317-9) Addison-Wesley.

Mathematics in Aristotle: 1949 Edition. Thomas Heath. (Key Texts Ser.). (Illus.). 320p. 1998. pap. 22.00 (1-85506-564-9) Thoemmes Pr.

Mathematics in Berlin. Heinrich G. Begehr. LC 98-21860. 1998. 32.00 (0-8176-5943-9) Birkhauser.

Mathematics in Berlin. Ed. by Heinrich G. Begehr et al. LC 98-21860. (Illus.). 200p. 1998. pap. 22.00 (3-7643-5943-9) Spr-Verlag.

Mathematics in Certain Elementary Social Studies in Secondary Schools & Colleges. Eugene W. Hellmich. LC 12-32085. (Columbia University. Teachers College. Contributions to Education Ser.: No. 706). reprint ed. 37.50 (0-404-55706-6) AMS Pr.

Mathematics in Civilization. H. L. Resnikoff & R. O. Wells, Jr. (Popular Science Ser.). (Illus.). 448p. 1999. reprint ed. pap. 11.95 (0-486-24674-4) Dover.

Mathematics in Civilization. H. L. Resnikoff & R. O. Wells. LC 72-83805. (Illus.). reprint ed. 29.50 (0-03-085035-5) Irvington.

Mathematics in Clinical Dietetics. 2nd ed. Helen Sanders & Polly Bittle. 85p. (C). 1988. pap. 24.00 (1-880864-01-0) F S H.

Mathematics in Communication Theory. R. H. Jones & N. C. Steele. 1990. text 59.95 (0-470-21246-2) P-H.

Mathematics in Economics: Critical Readings. Ed. & Intro. by David R. Grossman. 300p. (Orig.). 1990. pap. 19.95 (0-9621435-1-0) Political Econ Pr.

Mathematics in Economics: Models & Methods. Adam Ostaszewski. LC 92-32454. 1993. 64.95 (0-631-18055-9); pap. 31.95 (0-631-18056-7) Blackwell Pubs.

***Mathematics in Engineering & Science.** L. Mustoe & M. D. Barry. 768p. 1998. pap. 44.95 (0-471-97093-X) Wiley.

Mathematics in General Relativity. J. Isenberg. LC 88-9685. (Contemporary Mathematics Ser.: No. 71). 367p. 1988. pap. 44.00 (0-8218-5079-2, CONM/71) Am Math.

Mathematics in Industrial Problems. A. Friedman. (IMA Volumes in Mathematics & Its Applications Ser.: Vol. 16). (Illus.). x, 174p. 1988. 19.80 (0-387-96860-1) Spr-Verlag.

Mathematics in Industrial Problems. A. Friedman. Ed. by W. B. Miller, Jr. (IMA Volumes in Mathematics & Its Applications Ser.: Vol. 38, Pt. 4). (Illus.). xiv, 197p. 1991. 43.95 (0-387-97680-9) Spr-Verlag.

Mathematics in Industrial Problems. Ed. by A. Friedman. (Mathematics & Its Applications Ser.: Vol. 88). (Illus.). 226p. 1997. 49.95 (0-387-94945-3) Spr-Verlag.

Mathematics in Industrial Problems. Ed. by A. Friedman & W. B. Miller, Jr. (IMA Volumes in Mathematics & Its Applications Ser.: Vol. 83). (Illus.). 200p. 1996. 54.95 (0-387-94865-1) Spr-Verlag.

Mathematics in Industrial Problems, Pt. 3. Ed. by A. Friedman & W. B. Miller, Jr. (IMA Volumes in Mathematics & Its Applications Ser.: Vol. 31). (Illus.). xiii, 187p. 1990. 43.95 (0-387-97436-9) Spr-Verlag.

Mathematics in Industrial Problems, Pt. 5. A. Friedman. Ed. by W. B. Miller, Jr. & George R. Sell. (IMA Volumes in Mathematics & Its Applications Ser.: Vol. 49). (Illus.). xvi, 216p. 1992. 69.95 (0-387-97937-9) Spr-Verlag.

Mathematics in Industrial Problems, Pt. 6. A. Friedman. (IMA Volumes in Mathematics & Its Applications Ser.: Vol. 57). 229p. 1993. 63.95 (0-387-94157-6) Spr-Verlag.

Mathematics in Industrial Problems, Pt. 10. Ed. by A. Friedman & R. Gulliver. (IMA Volumes in Mathematics & Its Applications Ser.: Vol. 100). (Illus.). 203p. 1998. 59.95 (0-387-98518-2) Spr-Verlag.

Mathematics in Industrial Problems, Vol. 2. A. Friedman. (IMA Volumes in Mathematics & Its Applications Ser.: Vol. 24). (Illus.). xii, 183p. 1989. 43.95 (0-387-97139-4) Spr-Verlag.

Mathematics in Industrial Problems Pt. 7, Pt. 7. Ed. by A. Friedman. (IMA Volumes in Mathematics & Its Applications Ser.: 67). 264p. 1995. 59.95 (0-387-94444-3) Spr-Verlag.

Mathematics in Industry, 1st European Symposium: Proceedings. Ed. by Michiel Hazewinkel et al. (C). 1988. text 140.50 (90-277-2730-9) Kluwer Academic.

Mathematics in Industry, 2nd European Symposium: Proceedings. Ed. by Helmut Neunzert. (C). 1988. text 195.50 (90-277-2732-5) Kluwer Academic.

Mathematics in Language: Language Factors in Mathematics Learning. Nerida F. Ellerton & M. A. Clements. 170p. 1995. pap. 46.00 (0-7300-1356-1, ECT403, Pub. by Deakin Univ) St Mut.

Mathematics in Life Society & the World. Musser. 1997. pap. text, teacher ed. write for info. (0-13-259367-X) Allyn.

Mathematics in Life Society & the World. 2nd ed. (C). 2000. write for info. (0-13-014926-8); write for info. (0-13-014927-6); pap. 29.33 (0-13-014928-4) S&S Trade.

***Mathematics in Life, Society, & the World.** 2nd ed. 2000. write for info. (0-13-014273-5) P-H.

***Mathematics in Life, Society & the World.** 2nd ed. Harold B. Parks. LC 99-43379. 814p. 1999. 86.00 (0-13-011690-4) P-H.

Mathematics in Major Accident Risk Assessment. Ed. by R. A. Cox. (Institute of Mathematics & Its Applications Conference Series, New Ser.: New Series 19). (Illus.). 272p. 1989. text 75.00 (0-19-853616-X) OUP.

Mathematics in Marketing. 2nd ed. William B. Logan. Ed. by Eugene L. Dorr. (Occupational Manuals & Projects in Marketing Ser.). (Illus.). (gr. 11-12). 1978. text 12.28 (0-07-038462-2) McGraw.

Mathematics in Medicine & the Life Sciences. Frank C. Hoppensteadt & C. S. Peskin. Ed. by F. John et al. (Texts in Applied Mathematics Ser.: Vol. 10). (Illus.). 288p. 1996. 43.95 (0-387-97536-9) Spr-Verlag.

Mathematics in Modern Life: Sixth Yearbook. NCTM Staff. Ed. by W. D. Reeve. 195p. 1995. reprint ed. pap. 15.95 (0-87353-398-4) NCTM.

Mathematics in Nursery Education. Ann Montague-Smith. LC 97-199883. 160p. 1997. pap. 24.95 (1-85346-472-4, Pub. by David Fulton) Taylor & Francis.

Mathematics in Our World. 1981. write for info. (0-201-16136-2); write for info. (0-201-16135-4) Addison-Wesley.

Mathematics in Our World. 1983. write for info. (0-201-18101-0) Addison-Wesley.

Mathematics in Our World, Vol. 3. 1983. write for info. (0-201-18134-7) Addison-Wesley.

Mathematics in Philosophy: Selected Essays. Charles Parsons. LC 83-45153. 368p. 1983. text 55.00 (0-8014-1471-7) Cornell U Pr.

Mathematics in Process. Ann Baker & Johnny Baker. LC 90-34373. 170p. (C). (gr. k). 1990. pap. text 21.50 (0-435-08306-6, 08306) Heinemann.

Mathematics in Review. Eleanor S. Young & Billie Stacy. 324p. 1996. 38.80 (4-00-031787-3) Tichenor Pub.

Mathematics in St. Petersburg. A. A. Bolibruch et al. LC 91-640741. (American Mathematical Society Translations Ser.: Series 2, Vol. 174). 273p. 1996. text 99.00 (0-8218-0559-2, TRANS2/174) Am Math.

Mathematics in Signal Processing, No. II. Ed. by J. G. McWhirter. (Institute of Mathematics & Its Applications Conference Series, New Ser.: New Series 26). (Illus.). 840p. 1990. 175.00 (0-19-853641-0) OUP.

Mathematics in Signal Processing IV. Ed. by J. G. McWhirter & I. K. Proudler. (Institute of Mathematics & Its Applications Conference Ser.: No. 67). (Illus.). 352p. 1999. text 175.00 (0-19-850202-8) OUP.

Mathematics in Signal Processing III. J. G. McWhirter. (Institute of Mathematics & Its Applications Conference Series, New Ser.: No. 49). (Illus.). 460p. 1994. text 110.00 (0-19-853480-9) OUP.

Mathematics in Society & History: Sociological Inquiries. Sal P. Restivo. LC 92-13695. 208p. (C). 1992. lib. bdg. 127.50 (0-7923-1765-3, Pub. by Kluwer Academic) Kluwer Academic.

Mathematics in Sport. Stewart Townsend. LC 84-6639. (Mathematics & Its Applications Ser.: 1-176). 202p. (C). 1984. pap. text 29.95 (0-470-20082-0) P-H.

Mathematics in the Automotive Industry. Ed. by James R. Smith. (Institute of Mathematics & Its Applications Conference Series, New Ser.: New Series 36). (Illus.). 352p. 1992. text 110.00 (0-19-853660-7) OUP.

Mathematics in the Early Years. Ed. by Juanita V. Copley. LC 99-34458. (Illus.). 226p. 1999. pap. 30.95 (0-87353-469-7) NCTM.

Mathematics in the Making: Supporting Authors in Primary Classrooms. Heidi Mills & Timothy O'Keefe. LC 96-14198. 197p. 1996. pap. text 25.00 (0-435-07100-9) Heinemann.

Mathematics in the Making in Ancient India. G. Thibaut. Ed. by Debiprasad Chattopadhyay. 1985. reprint ed. 15.00 (0-8364-1435-7, Pub. by KP Bagchi) S Asia.

Mathematics in the Middle. Ed. by Larry Leutzinger. LC 98-52986. (Illus.). 218p. 1998. pap. 28.50 (0-87353-460-3) NCTM.

Mathematics in the Nineteenth Century: Mathematical Logic, Algebra, Number Theory, Probability Theory. Ed. by A. P. Yushkevich & Andrei N. Kolmogorov. LC 92-15980. xiv, 308p. 1992. 193.00 (0-8176-2552-6) Birkhauser.

Mathematics in the Primary Classroom: A Sense of Progression. Christine Hopkins et al. LC 96-210906. (Roehampton Teaching Studies). 200p. 1996. pap. text 24.95 (1-85346-384-1, Pub. by David Fulton) Taylor & Francis.

***Mathematics in the Primary School: A Sense of Progression.** 2nd ed. Christine Hopkins. (Roehampton Studies in Education). (Illus.). 1999. pap. 29.95 (1-85346-592-5) David Fulton.

Mathematics in the Social & Life Sciences: Theories, Models & Methods. M. A. Ball. (Mathematics & Its Applications Ser.). 1985. text 69.95 (0-470-20191-6) P-H.

Mathematics in the Time of the Pharaohs. Richard Gillings. (Illus.). 286p. (C). 1982. reprint ed. pap. 8.95 (0-486-24315-X) Dover.

Mathematics in Transport Planning & Control: Based on the Proceedings of a Conference on Mathematics in Transport Planning & Control, Organized by the Institute of Mathematics & Its Applications & Held at the University of Wales College of Cardiff in

M

September 1989. Ed. by J. D. Griffiths. LC 92-18095. (Institute of Mathematics & Its Applications Conference Series, New Ser.: New Series 38). (Illus.). 480p. 1992. text 145.00 (*0-19-853650-X*, Clarendon Pr) OUP.

***Mathematics in Transport Planning & Control: Proceedings of the Third Ima International Conference on Mathematics in Transport & Planning Control.** J.D. Griffths. LC 98-44516. 1998. write for info. (*0-08-043430-4*) Elsevier.

Mathematics in Western Culture. Morris Kline. (Illus.). 512p. 1964. reprint ed. pap. text 17.95 (*0-19-500714-X*) OUP.

***Mathematics Inspired by Biology: Lectures Given at the 1st Session of the Centro Internazionale Matematico Estivo (C.I.M.E.), Held in Martina Franca, Italy, June 13-20, 1997.** O. Diekmann et al. LC 99-48772. (Lecture Notes in Mathematics Ser.). vii, 268p. 1999. pap. 52.80 (*3-540-66522-6*) Spr-Verlag.

Mathematics Instruction: A Model Program for Elementary Teachers. unabridged ed. Clifford Russell et al. 468p. (C). 1998. ring bd. 62.00 (*0-9657270-3-3*) Germane Pubs.

Mathematics into the Twenty-First Century. Ed. by Felix E. Browder. LC 91-22093. (Centennial Publications: Vol. II). 491p. 1992. text 165.00 (*0-8218-0167-8*, HMBROWDER) Am Math.

Mathematics into Type Ellen Swanson & Arlene A. O'Sean. LC 99-25448. 1999. pap. write for info. (*0-8218-1961-5*) Am Math.

Mathematics into Type. rev. ed. Ellen Swanson. LC 72-170708. 90p. 1994. reprint ed. pap. 22.00 (*0-8218-0053-1*, MIT) Am Math.

Mathematics Is .... Kaufmann. (Mathematics Ser.). 1979. 16.00 (*0-87150-263-1*) PWS Pubs.

Mathematics Is Elementary (Guide) AIT/General Learning Corp./Wisconsin Educational C. 96p. (Orig.). (J). (gr. 2-4). 1996. pap. text 7.95 (*0-7842-0814-X*) Agency Instr Tech.

Mathematics Is for Solving Problems: A Volume in Honor of Julian Cole on his 70th Birthday. Ed. by L. Pamela Cook et al. (Proceedings in Applied Mathematics Ser.: No. 84). xxxiv, 249p. 1996. pap. 52.50 (*0-89871-371-4*, PR84) Soc Indus-Appl Math.

Mathematics is More Than Counting. Kristina Leeb-Lundberg. LC 85-5967. 23p. 1985. 5.00 (*0-87173-110-X*) ACEI.

Mathematics: Its Power & Utility. 2nd ed. Karl J. Smith. LC 85-9687. (Math). 512p. (C). 1985. mass mkt. 34.50 (*0-534-05268-1*) Brooks-Cole.

Mathematics: Its Power & Utility. 3rd ed. Karl J. Smith. (Math). 544p. (C). 1989. mass mkt. 52.25 (*0-534-11538-1*) Brooks-Cole.

Mathematics, Jr. H.S. Jack Rudman. (Teachers License Examination Ser.: T-40). 1994. pap. 27.95 (*0-8373-8040-5*) Nat Learn.

Mathematics, Machines & Godel's Proof. Natarajan Shankar. (Cambridge Tracts in Theoretical Computer Science Ser.: No. 38). 218p. 1997. pap. text 26.95 (*0-521-58533-3*) Cambridge U Pr.

Mathematics Made Simple. 5th ed. Abraham P. Sperling. 272p. 1991. pap. 12.95 (*0-385-26584-0*) Doubleday.

Mathematics, Magic, & Mystery. Martin Gardner. (Illus.). 176p. 1956. pap. 5.95 (*0-486-20335-2*) Dover.

Mathematics Masterclasses: Stretching the Imagination. Ed. by Michael J. Sewell. (Illus.). 250p. 1997. text 65.00 (*0-19-851494-8*); pap. text 28.00 (*0-19-851493-X*) OUP.

***Mathematics, Mechanization & Applications.** Dongming Wang & Xiao-Shan Gao. 520p. 2000. 120.00 (*0-12-734760-7*) Acad Pr.

***Mathematics Methods for Elementary & Middle School Teacher.** 4th ed. Mary M. Hatfield et al. 480p. 1999. pap. text 54.00 (*0-205-30548-2*) Allyn.

Mathematics Methods for Elementary & Middle School Teachers. 3rd ed. Mary M. Hatfield. (Illus.). 480p. 1997. pap., teacher ed. 65.95 incl. cd-rom (*0-471-36728-1*) Wiley.

***Mathematics Methods for Elementary & Middle School Teachers.** 4th ed. Mary M. Hatfield. LC 99-40457. 430p. 1999. pap. 73.95 (*0-471-36544-0*) Wiley.

Mathematics Methods Program: Rational Numbers with Integers & Reals. John F. LeBlanc et al. (Mathematics Ser.). (Illus.). 240p. 1976. write for info. (*0-201-14613-4*) Addison-Wesley.

Mathematics Model Curriculum Guide, K-8. California Department of Education Staff. 112p. 1987. pap. 7.50 (*0-8011-0664-8*) Calif Education.

Mathematics 1999-2000. Kaplan. 352p. 1999. pap. 18.00 (*0-684-85662-X*) S&S Trade.

Mathematics of Adaptive Control Processes. Sidney J. Yakowitz. LC 68-26813. (Modern Analytic & Computational Methods in Science & Mathematics Ser.: No. 14). 174p. reprint ed. pap. 54.00 (*0-608-16314-7*, 202626100049) Bks Demand.

Mathematics of Biology. Ed. by G. Koch & Michiel Hazewinkel. LC 85-18279. 1985. text 134.50 (*90-277-2069-X*) Kluwer Academic.

Mathematics of Business. 4th ed. Jay Diamond & Gerald Pintel. 368p. (C). 1990. text 45.80 (*0-13-563057-6*) P-H.

***Mathematics Of Business: Study Wizard.** 2000. text. write for info. (*0-13-017342-8*) Prentice-Hall.

Mathematics of Cell Electrophysiology. Cronin. (Lecture Notes in Pure & Applied Mathematics Ser.: Vol. 63). (Illus.). 144p. 1981. pap. text 125.00 (*0-8247-1157-2*) Dekker.

Mathematics of Choice. Ivan Niven. LC 65-17470. (New Mathematical Library: No. 15). 202p. 1965. pap. text 18.50 (*0-88385-615-8*, NML-15) Math Assn.

Mathematics of Ciphers: Number Theory & RSA Cryptography. S. C. Coutinho. LC 98-49611. Orig. Title: Numeros Inteiros e Criptografia. (Illus.). 198p. 1998. 30.00 (*1-56881-082-2*) AK Peters.

Mathematics of Classical & Quantum Physics. Frederick W. Byron, Jr. & Robert W. Fuller. (Illus.). xii, 665p. 1992. reprint ed. pap. 18.95 (*0-486-67164-X*) Dover.

Mathematics of Classical & Quantum Physics, 2 vols., 1. Frederick W. Byron & Robert W. Fuller. LC 69-18006. (Addison-Wesley Advanced Physics Ser.). (Illus.). 320p. pap. 99.20 (*0-608-15550-0*, 205637800001) Bks Demand.

Mathematics of Classical & Quantum Physics, 2 vols., 2. Frederick W. Byron & Robert W. Fuller. LC 69-18006. (Addison-Wesley Advanced Physics Ser.). (Illus.). 368p. pap. 114.10 (*0-608-15551-9*, 205637800002) Bks Demand.

Mathematics of Climate Modeling. V. Dymnikov & A. H. Filatov. LC 96-47912. 346p. 1997. write for info. (*3-7643-3915-2*) Birkhauser.

Mathematics of Climate Modelling. V. P. Dymnikov & A. N. Filatov. LC 96-47912. 300p. 1996. 64.50 (*0-8176-3915-2*) Birkhauser.

Mathematics of Combustion. Ed. by John D. Buckmaster. LC 85-50339. (Frontiers in Applied Mathematics Ser.: No. 2). xii, 254p. 1985. 48.00 (*0-89871-053-7*) Soc Indus-Appl Math.

Mathematics of Compound Interest. 6th ed. Marjorie V. Butcher & Cecil J. Nesbitt. (Illus.). xii, 324p. (C). 1991. reprint ed. text 22.50 (*0-9603000-1-5*) Butcher & Nesbitt.

Mathematics of Computation, 1943-1993, 3 pts. Ed. by Walter Gautschi. LC 94-31835. (Proceedings of Symposia in Applied Mathematics Ser.: Vol. 48). 644p. 1994. text 90.00 (*0-8218-0291-7*, PSAPM/48) Am Math.

Mathematics of Conflict. Frank C. Zagare. (Hi Map Ser.: No. 3). (Illus.). 60p. pap. text 9.99 (*0-614-05324-2*, HM 5603) COMAP Inc.

Mathematics of Control Theory: Based on the Proceedings of a Conference on Control Theory, Organized by the Institute of Mathematics & Its Applications, & Held at the University of Strathclyde in September 1988. Ed. by N. K. Nichols & D. H. Owens. LC 92-23022. (Institute of Mathematics & Its Applications Conference Series, New Ser.: New Series 37). (Illus.). 496p. 1992. text 115.00 (*0-19-853640-2*, Clarendon Pr) OUP.

Mathematics of Data Fusion. LC 97-26122. 1997. text 264.50 (*0-7923-4674-2*) Kluwer Academic.

Mathematics of Data/Image Coding, Compression & Encryption, Vol. 3456. Ed. by Mark S. Schmalz. LC 99-211213. 1998. 59.00 (*0-8194-2911-2*) SPIE.

***Mathematics of Data/Image Coding, Compression & Encryption II.** Ed. by Mark S. Schmalz. 1999. pap. text 50.00 (*0-8194-3300-4*) SPIE.

Mathematics of Deforming Surfaces. Ed. by David G. Dritschel & R. J. Perkins. (Institute of Mathematics & Its Applications Conference Ser.; New Ser.: Vol. 56). (Illus.). 260p. (C). 1996. text 140.00 (*0-19-853643-7*) OUP.

Mathematics of Dependable Systems. Ed. by Christopher J. Mitchell & Victoria Stavridou. (Institute of Mathematics & Its Applications Conference Ser.: No. 55). (Illus.). 312p. 1995. text 95.00 (*0-19-853491-4*) OUP.

Mathematics of Dependable Systems II. Ed. by V. Stavridou. (The Institute of Mathematics & Its Applications Conference Ser.: No. 64). (Illus.). 270p. 1998. text 165.00 (*0-19-852382-3*) OUP.

Mathematics of Derivative Securities. Ed. by M. A. Dempster & Stanley R. Pliska. LC 97-3027. (Publications of the Newton Institute: No. 15). 600p. 1997. text 85.00 (*0-521-58424-8*) Cambridge U Pr.

Mathematics of Diffusion. 2nd ed. John Crank. (Illus.). 424p. 1980. pap. text 65.95 (*0-19-853411-6*) OUP.

Mathematics of Drugs & Solutions with Clinical Applications. 5th ed. Judith Knight Richardson & Lloyd I. Richardson. (Illus.). 188p. (C). (gr. 13). 1993. pap. text 27.00 (*0-8016-7895-1*, 07895) Mosby Inc.

Mathematics of Everday Living: The Mathematics of Borrowing. Roland E. Larson et al. (Illus.). 157p. (J). (gr. 9-12). 1997. pap. text 19.95 (*1-887050-27-2*) Meridian Creative.

***Mathematics of Evolution.** Fred Hoyle. Ed. by Diane Nesin. 160p. 1999. 36.00 (*0-9669934-0-3*) Acorn Ent.

Mathematics of Finance. 2nd ed. Joe D. Austin et al. LC 93-42967. 1994. mass mkt. 44.95 (*0-314-02947-8*) West Pub.

***Mathematics of Finance.** 2nd ed. Steven Roman. (Illus.). 66p. (C). 1999. pap. text. write for info. (*1-878015-23-0*) Innov Textbooks.

Mathematics of Finance, 8 vols. 8th ed. Robert Cissell et al. (C). 1989. pap. text 3.96 (*0-395-52652-3*) HM.

Mathematics of Finance, 8 vols. 8th ed. Robert Cissell et al. (C). 1990. text 69.96 (*0-395-43324-X*) HM.

***Mathematics of Finance with Canadian Applications.** 4th ed. 2000. teacher ed. write for info. (*0-13-030426-3*) P-H.

Mathematics of Financial Derivatives: A Student Introduction. P. Wilmott et al. (Illus.). 333p. (C). 1995. pap. text 29.95 (*0-521-49789-2*) Cambridge U Pr.

Mathematics of Finite Elements & Application II: Mafelap 1977. Ed. by John R. Whiteman. 1977. text 209.00 (*0-12-747252-5*) Acad Pr.

Mathematics of Finite Elements & Applications: Highlights-1993. Ed. by J. R. Whitman. 438p. 1994. 260.00 (*0-471-93996-X*) Wiley.

Mathematics of Fractals. Masaya Yamaguti et al. Tr. by Kiki Hudson from JPN. LC 97-11489. (Translations of Mathematical Monographs: Vol. 167). 96p. 1997. text 29.00 (*0-8218-0537-1*, MMONO/168) Am Math.

***Mathematics of Fuzzy Sets: Logic, Topology & Measure Theory.** Ulrich Hohle. LC 98-45584. (Handbooks of Fuzzy Sets Ser.). 1998. 200.00 (*0-7923-8388-5*) Kluwer Academic.

Mathematics of Gambling. Edward Thorp. (Illus.). (Orig.). 1984. pap. 7.95 (*0-89746-019-7*) Gambling Times.

Mathematics of Games & Gambling. Edward W. Packel. LC 80-85037. (New Mathematical Library: No. 28). 141p. 1981. pap. text 22.00 (*0-88385-628-X*, NML-28) Math Assn.

Mathematics of Games of Strategy: Theory & Applications. Pref. by Melvin Dresher. viii, 184p. (C). 1981. reprint ed. pap. 6.95 (*0-486-64216-X*) Dover.

Mathematics of Generalization: The Proceedings of the SFI - CNLS Workshop on Formal Approaches to Supervised Learning. Ed. by David H. Wolpert. LC 94-42868. (Santa Fe Institute Studies in the Sciences of Complexity: Vol. 20). 464p. (C). 1995. pap. 38.00 (*0-201-40983-6*) Addison-Wesley.

Mathematics of Genetic Diversity. J. F. Kingman. LC 80-51290. (CBMS-NSF Regional Conference Ser.: No. 34). vii, 70p. 1980. pap. text 27.00 (*0-89871-166-5*) Soc Indus-Appl Math.

***Mathematics of Genome Analysis.** Jerome K. Percus. (Cambridge Studies in Mathematical Biology: Vol. 17). 200p. 2001. write for info. (*0-521-58517-1*); pap. write for info. (*0-521-58526-0*) Cambridge U Pr.

Mathematics of Great Amateurs. 2nd ed. Julian L. Coolidge. (Illus.). 236p. 1990. pap. text 45.00 (*0-19-853939-8*) OUP.

Mathematics of Heat Transfer. Ed. by G. E. Tupholme & A. S. Wood. LC 98-19459. (The Institute of Mathematics & Its Applications Conference Ser.: No. 66). (Illus.). 358p. 1998. text 155.00 (*0-19-850358-X*) OUP.

Mathematics of Horse Racing: A Guide to Better Handicapping. David B. Fogel. 144p. 1988. pap. 9.95 (*0-89709-173-6*) Liberty Pub.

Mathematics of Information Coding, Extraction & Distribution. Ed. by G. Cybenko et al. LC 98-31464. (IMA Volumes in Mathematics & Its Applications Ser.: Vol. 107). (Illus.). 143p. 1999. 59.95 (*0-387-98665-0*) Spr-Verlag.

Mathematics of Information Processing. Ed. by Michael Anshel & W. Gewirtz. LC 85-26693. (Proceedings of Symposia in Applied Mathematics Ser.: Vol. 34). 233p. 1986. pap. 37.00 (*0-8218-0086-8*, PSAPM/34) Am Math.

Mathematics of Inheritance Systems. David S. Touretzky. LC 86-2954. (Research Notes in Artificial Intelligence Ser.). (Illus.). 220p. (Orig.). 1986. pap. text 34.95 (*0-934613-06-0*) Morgan Kaufmann.

Mathematics of Investing: Complete Reference Guide. Michael C. Thomsett. LC 89-16458. 256p. 1989. 49.95 (*0-471-50664-8*) Wiley.

Mathematics of Investment. Paul R. Rider & Carl H. Fischer. (C). 1951. text 9.95 (*0-914004-02-6*) Ulrich.

Mathematics of Investment & Credit. 2nd ed. Samuel A. Broverman. (Illus.). 391p. (C). 1996. pap. text 55.00 (*1-56698-218-9*) Actex Pubns.

Mathematics of Kalman-Bucy Filtering. P. A. Ruymgaart & T. T. Soong. (Information Sciences Ser.: Vol. 14). (Illus.). 190p. 1985. 35.00 (*0-387-13508-1*) Spr-Verlag.

Mathematics of Kalman-Bucy Filtering. P. A. Ruymgaart & T. T. Soong. (Information Sciences Ser.: Vol. 14). (Illus.). 180p. 1988. 53.95 (*0-387-18781-2*) Spr-Verlag.

Mathematics of Language: Proceedings of a Conference Held at the University of Michigan, Ann Arbor, October, 1984. Ed. by Alexis Manaster-Ramer. LC 87-9183. ix, 401p. (C). 1988. 83.00 (*1-55619-032-8*) J Benjamins Pubng Co.

Mathematics of Life Insurance. 2nd ed. Walter O. Menge & Carl H. Fischer. LC 65-12855. (C). 1965. text 12.95 (*0-914004-00-X*) Ulrich.

Mathematics of Long-Range Aperiodic Order: Proceedings of the NATO Advanced Study Institute on the Mathematics of Long-Range Aperiodic Order Held in the Fields Institute, Waterloo, Ontario, Canada, 1995. LC 97-12166. (NATO ASI Ser.: Vol. 489). 555p. 1997. text 281.00 (*0-7923-4506-1*) Kluwer Academic.

Mathematics of Manpower Planning. S. Vajda. LC 77-26104. (Illus.). 216p. reprint ed. pap. 67.00 (*0-8357-3087-5*, 203934400012) Bks Demand.

Mathematics of Meaning. Svend Ostergaard. 224p. (C). 1997. pap. 27.00 (*87-7288-515-7*, Pub. by Aarhus Univ Pr) David Brown.

Mathematics of Measurement. J. Roche. (Illus.). 422p. 1998. 79.95 (*0-387-91581-8*) Spr-Verlag.

Mathematics of Measurement: A Critical History. Roche. (C). Date not set. text. write for info. (*0-485-11473-9*, Pub. by Athlone Pr) Humanities.

Mathematics of Microcirculation Phenomena. Symposium on Mathematics of Microcirculation Pheno. Ed. by Joseph F. Gross & Aleksander Popel. LC 79-5321. 186p. 1980. reprint ed. pap. 57.70 (*0-608-00418-9*, 206113300007) Bks Demand.

Mathematics of Microstructure Evolution. Ed. by L. Q. Chen & Brent Fultz. (Illus.). 380p. 1996. 50.00 (*0-87339-351-1*, 3511) Minerals Metals.

Mathematics of Microstructure Evolution: Proceedings of a Symposium on Mathematics of Microstructure Evolution, Cleveland, OH, 1995. Ed. by Long-Qing Chen et al. LC 96-78157. (Proceedings in Applied Mathematics Ser.: No. 90). (Illus.). x, 391p. 1996. pap. 53.50 (*0-89871-386-2*, PR90) Soc Indus-Appl Math.

Mathematics of Modality. Robert Goldblatt. LC 93-13522. (CSLI Lecture Notes Ser.: No. 43). 1993. 54.95 (*1-881526-24-0*); pap. 23.95 (*1-881526-23-2*) CSLI.

***Mathematics of Modeling Dynamic Systems.** Kurt Kreith & G. D. Chakerian. LC 98-55409. (Textbooks in Mathematical Sciences Ser.). (Illus.). 320p. 1999. 49.95 (*0-387-98758-4*) Spr-Verlag.

Mathematics of Models for Climatology & Environment. J. I. Diaz & North Atlantic Treaty Organization Staff. LC 96-46904. (NATO ASI Ser.: Vol. 48). 478p. 1996. 239.00 (*3-540-61879-1*) Spr-Verlag.

Mathematics of Money. Cheryl Clayton. (MA - Academic Math Ser.). 1991. mass mkt. 55.95 (*0-538-61450-1*) S-W Pub.

Mathematics of Money. 21st ed. Austin & Howard. (Um - International Math Ser.). 1994. pap. 56.25 (*0-314-02948-6*) West Pub.

Mathematics of Money Management: Risk Analysis Techniques for Traders. Ralph Vince. LC 91-33547. (Finance Editions Ser.: No. 1935). 400p. 1992. 69.95 (*0-471-54738-7*) Wiley.

Mathematics of Money with Algebra. Clayton. (MA - Academic Math Ser.). 1994. mass mkt. 51.95 (*0-538-63471-5*) S-W Pub.

Mathematics of Multidimensional Fourier Transform Algorithms. 2nd ed. Richard Tolimieri et al. LC 97-16669. (Signal Processing & Digital Filtering Ser.). 1997. 59.95 (*0-387-98260-4*) Spr-Verlag.

Mathematics of Multidimensional Fourier Transforms. Richard Tolimieri et al. Ed. by C. S. Burrus. LC 93-29029. (Signal Processing & Digital Filtering Ser.). 1993. 65.95 (*0-387-94105-3*); write for info. (*3-540-94105-3*) Spr-Verlag.

***Mathematics of Multidimensional Seismic Inversion.** Norman Bleistein et al. LC 00-41971. (Interdisciplinary Applied Mathematics Ser.). 2000. write for info. (*0-387-95061-3*) Spr-Verlag.

Mathematics of Multiscale Materials. Ed. by K. M. Golden et al. LC 98-18394. (IMA Volumes in Mathematics & Its Applications Ser.: Vol. 99). (Illus.). 301p. 1998. 59.95 (*0-387-98528-X*) Spr-Verlag.

Mathematics of Natural Catastrophes. G. C. Woo. LC 99-16721. 300p. 1999. 58.00 (*1-86094-182-6*) World Scientific Pub.

Mathematics of Networks. Ed. by Stefan A. Burr. LC 82-18469. (Proceedings of Symposia in Applied Mathematics Ser.: No. 26). 142p. 1983. reprint ed. pap. 25.00 (*0-8218-0031-0*, PSAPM/26) Am Math.

Mathematics of Neural Networks: Models, Algorithms, & Applications. Steve Ellacott et al. LC 97-5274. (Operations Research - Computer Science Interface Ser.). 1997. text 154.00 (*0-7923-9933-1*) Kluwer Academic.

Mathematics of Nonlinear Programming. A. L. Peressini et al. (Undergraduate Texts in Mathematics Ser.). (Illus.). x, 325p. 1996. 49.95 (*0-387-96614-5*) Spr-Verlag.

Mathematics of Nonlinear Programming. 2nd ed. A. L. Peressini et al. (Undergraduate Texts in Mathematics Ser.). x, 273p. 1993. write for info. (*3-540-96614-5*) Spr-Verlag.

Mathematics of Nonlinear Science. M. Berger. LC 90-574. (Contemporary Mathematics Ser.: Vol. 108). 153p. 1990. pap. 33.00 (*0-8218-5114-4*, CONM/108) Am Math.

Mathematics of Numerical Analysis: 1995 Summer Seminar on Mathematics of Numerical Analysis, July 17-August 11, 1995, Park City, Utah, Vol. 32. Ed. by James Renegar et al. LC 96-14611. (Lectures in Applied Mathematics). 929p. 1996. pap. 125.00 (*0-8218-0530-4*, LAM/32) Am Math.

Mathematics of Oil Recovery. Ed. by P. R. King. (Institute of Mathematics & Its Applications Conference Series, New Ser.: New Series 31). (Illus.). 846p. 1992. 195.00 (*0-19-853645-3*) OUP.

Mathematics of Oil Recovery: Second European Conference on the Mathematics of Oil Recovery, Aries, 1989. Ed. by D. Guerillot & O. Guilllon. (Illus.). 376p. (C). 1990. 605.00 (*2-7108-0589-8*, Pub. by Edits Technip) Enfield Pubs NH.

Mathematics of Optimization. Giorgi et al. 1999. pap. text. write for info. (*0-08-042022-2*, Pergamon Pr) Elsevier.

Mathematics of Paul Erdos I. R. L. Graham & J. Nesetril. 420p. 1996. 105.00 (*3-540-61032-4*) Spr-Verlag.

Mathematics of Paul Erdos II. R. L. Graham & J. Nesetril. 420p. 1996. 105.00 (*3-540-61031-6*) Spr-Verlag.

Mathematics of Personal Finance: Using Calculators & Computers. Garman & Xiao. LC 97-67118. 1998. pap. 46.95 (*0-87393-533-0*) Dame Pubns.

Mathematics of Physics & Modern Engineering. 2nd ed. Ivan S. Sokolnikoff & Raymond M. Redheffer. 752p. (C). 1966. 100.63 (*0-07-059625-5*) McGraw.

***Mathematics of Plato's Academy: A New Reconstruction.** 2nd expanded ed. David H. Fowler. LC 98-44339. (Illus.). 466p. 1999. text 110.00 (*0-19-850258-3*) OUP.

Mathematics of Program Construction. Ed. by Jan L. Van de Snepscheut. (Lecture Notes in Computer Science Ser.: Vol. 375). vi, 421p. 1989. 47.00 (*0-387-51305-1*) Spr-Verlag.

Mathematics of Program Construction: Proceedings of the 2nd International Conference, Oxford, U. K., June-July 1992. Ed. by R. S. Bird et al. LC 93-16952. (Lecture Notes in Computer Science Ser.: Vol. 669). 1993. 55.95 (*0-387-56625-2*) Spr-Verlag.

Mathematics of Program Construction: 3rd International Conference, MPC '95, Kloster Irsee, Germany, July 17-21, 1995, Proceedings, Vol. VIII. Ed. by Bernhard Moller et al. LC 97-51978. (Lecture Notes in Computer Science Ser.: Vol. 947). 472p. 1995. 75.00 (*3-540-60117-1*) Spr-Verlag.

Mathematics of Program Construction: 4th International Conference, MPC '98, Marstrand, Sweden, June 15-17, 1998, Proceedings, Vol. 142. Ed. by Johan Jeuring et al. LC 98-25680. (Lecture Notes in Computer Science Ser.: Vol. 1422). x, 383p. 1998. pap. 59.00 (*3-540-64591-8*) Spr-Verlag.

Mathematics of Projectiles in Sport. Neville De Mestre. (Australian Mathematical Society Lecture Ser.: No. 6). 187p. (C). 1990. pap. text 31.95 (*0-521-39857-6*) Cambridge U Pr.

Mathematics of Radiology & Nuclear Medicine. rev. ed. Herbert L. Jackson. LC 70-107201. (Illus.). 167p. 1991. reprint ed. 10.20 (*0-87527-019-0*) Green.

An Asterisk (*) at the beginning of an entry indicates that the title is appearing for the first time.

Mathematics of Ramsey Theory. Ed. by J. Nesetril et al. (Algorithms & Combinatorics Ser.: Vol. 5). (Illus.). 281p. 1990. 135.95 (*0-387-18191-1*) Spr-Verlag.

Mathematics of Random Media: (Proceedings of the AMS-SIAM Summer Seminar) W. Kohler & B. White. LC 90-27442. (Lectures in Mathematics: Vol. 27). 499p. 1991. pap. 191.00 (*0-8218-1133-9*, LAM/27) Am Math.

Mathematics of Random Phenomena: Random Vibrations of Mechanical Structures. Paul Kree & Christian Soize. 1986. text 222.50 (*90-277-2355-9*) Kluwer Academic.

Mathematics of Reservoir Simulation. Ed. by R. E. Ewing. LC 83-51501. (Frontiers in Applied Mathematics Ser.: No. 1). (Illus.). xii, 186p. 1984. text 40.50 (*0-89871-192-4*) Soc Indus-Appl Math.

***Mathematics of Soap Films: Explorations with Maple.** John Oprea. LC 00-41614. (Student Mathematical Library: Vol. 10). (Illus.). 277p. (J). 2000. pap. 29.00 (*0-8218-2118-0*) Am Math.

***Mathematics of Social Science.** 3rd ed. Steven Roman. (Illus.). 93p. (C). 1999. pap. text. write for info. (*1-878015-20-6*) Innov Textbooks.

Mathematics of Solitons. T. Miwa et al. (Tracts in Mathematics Ser.: No. 135). 120p. (C). 1999. text 39.95 (*0-521-56161-2*) Cambridge U Pr.

Mathematics of Sonya Kovalevskaya. R. Cooke. (Illus.). 275p. 1984. 87.95 (*0-387-96030-9*) Spr-Verlag.

Mathematics of Stochastic Manufacturing Systems: AMS-Siam Summer Seminar in Applied Mathematics, June 17-22, 1996, Williamsburg, Virginia. Yin, George, M.E.R. Seminar in Applied Mathematics & Qing Zhang. LC 97-12175. (Lectures in Applied Mathematics). 399p. 1997. pap. 69.00 (*0-8218-0755-2*) Am Math.

Mathematics of Surfaces No.6, Vol. VI. Ed. by Glen Mullineux. LC 97-108428. (Institute of Mathematics & Its Applications Conference Series, New Ser.: No. 58). (Illus.). 584p. 1996. text 145.00 (*0-19-851198-1*) OUP.

Mathematics of Surfaces VII. Ed. by Tim Goodman & Ralph Martin. 528p. 1997. 245.00 (*1-874728-12-7*, Pub. by Info Geometers) St Mut.

Mathematics of Surfaces III. Ed. by D. C. Handscomb. (Institute of Mathematics & Its Applications Conference Series, New Ser.: New Series 23). (Illus.). 504p. 1990. 98.00 (*0-19-853629-1*) OUP.

Mathematics of Surfaces II. Ed. by Ralph Martin. (Institute of Mathematics & Its Applications Conference Series, New Ser.: New Series 11). (Illus.). 528p. 1987. text 89.00 (*0-19-853619-4*) OUP.

Mathematics of Syntactic Structure: Trees & Their Logics. Hans-Peter Kolb & Uwe Mhonnich. LC 99-24939. (Studies in Generative Grammar). viii, 348p. 1999. 132.00 (*3-11-016273-3*) De Gruyter.

Mathematics of Technical Analysis: Applying Statistics to Trading Stocks, Options & Futures. Clifford J. Sherry. 300p. 1992. text 55.00 (*1-55738-462-2*, Irwn Prfssnl) McGraw-Hill Prof.

Mathematics of the Cosmic Mind. L. Gordon Plummer. (Illus.). 240p. 1982. 24.95 (*0-913004-84-7*) Point Loma Pub.

Mathematics of the Decision Sciences, Pt. 1. Ed. by G. Dantzig & A. F. Veinott, Jr. LC 62-21481. (Lectures in Applied Mathematics: Vol. 11). 429p. 1969. reprint ed. text 57.00 (*0-8218-1111-8*, LAM/11) Am Math.

Mathematics of the Decision Sciences, Pt. 2. Ed. by G. B. Dantzig & A. F. Veinott, Jr. LC 62-21481. 443p. 1969. reprint ed. text 59.00 (*0-8218-1112-6*, LAM 12) Am Math.

Mathematics of the Elementary Grades. William P. Berlinghoff & Robert Washburn. (Illus.). 602p. 1990. text 48.95 (*0-912675-80-2*); pap. text, teacher ed. write for info. (*0-912675-81-0*) Ardsley.

Mathematics of the Energy Crisis. Ed. by Richard L. Gagliardi & Samuel W. Valenza. 1978. 7.95 (*0-936918-01-2*) Intergalactic NJ.

Mathematics of the Ideal Villa & Other Essays. Colin Rowe. (Illus.). 233p. (C). 1982. pap. text 17.50 (*0-262-68037-8*) MIT Pr.

Mathematics of the Incas: Code of the Quipu. Marcia Ascher & Robert Ascher. LC 96-47494. (Illus.). 176p. 1997. reprint ed. pap. text 11.95 (*0-486-29554-0*) Dover.

Mathematics of the 19th Century: Function Theory According to Chebyshev, Ordinary Differential Equations, Calculus of Variations, & Theory of Finite Differences. A. N. Kolmogorov & A. P. Ushkevich. Tr. by Roger Cooke from RUS. LC 97-46763. 1998. write for info. (*0-8176-5845-9*) Birkhauser.

Mathematics of the 19th Century: Function Theory According to Chebyshev, Ordinary Differential Equations, Calculus of Variations, & Theory of Finite Differences. Ed. by A. N. Kolmogorov & A. P. Yushkevich. Tr. by Roger Cooke from RUS. LC 97-46763. (Mathematics of the 19th Century: Vol. 3). 363p. 1998. 98.00 (*3-7643-5845-9*) Birkhauser.

Mathematics of the 19th Century: Geometry, Analytic Function Theory. Ed. by A. P. Yushkevich & Andrei N. Kolmogorov. Tr. by Roger Cooke from RUS. 291p. 1996. 94.50 (*0-8176-5048-2*); 94.50 (*3-7643-5048-2*) Birkhauser.

Mathematics of the Rubik's Cube Design. Hana M. Bizek. LC 98-137444. (Illus.). 332p. 1996. pap. 20.00 (*0-8059-3919-9*) Dorrance.

Mathematics of the Shop. 4th ed. Frank J. McMackin et al. LC 76-6726. 628p. (C). 1978. teacher ed. 14.00 (*0-8273-1298-9*); mass mkt. 43.00 (*0-8273-1297-0*) Delmar.

Mathematics of the Universe: The Universe of the Mind. Philip Francis. (Mathematics Ser.: Vol. 1). (Illus.). 1977. pap. 9.95 (*0-902675-75-3*) Oleander Pr.

Mathematics of Time. Stephen Smale. (Illus.). 151p. 1990. 40.95 (*0-387-90519-7*) Spr-Verlag.

***Mathematics of Turfgrass Maintenance.** 3rd ed. Nick Christians & Michael Agnew. LC 99-462014. (Illus.). 150p. 2000. text 34.95 (*1-57504-147-2*, Ann Arbor Press) Sleepng Bear.

Mathematics of Turfgrass Maintenance, Vol. 2. Nick Christians & Michael Agnew. 150p. (C). 1997. pap. text 34.95 (*1-57504-059-X*, 059-X, Ann Arbor Press) Sleepng Bear.

Mathematics of Unit Root Econometrics. Karim Abadir. 1998. text 90.00 (*0-471-96650-9*) Wiley.

Mathematics of Vortex Methods & Vortex Motion. K. Gustafson & J. Sethian. LC 91-4781. (Miscellaneous Bks.: No. 19). viii, 212p. 1991. pap. 64.50 (*0-89871-258-0*) Soc Indus-Appl Math.

***Mathematics on the Internet: A Resource for K-12 Teachers.** Jerry A. Ameis & Jazlin V. Ebenezer. LC 99-14010. 129p. 1999. pap. 15.00 (*0-13-011061-2*) P-H.

***Mathematics on the Internet, 1999.** Ed. by Prentice-Hall Staff. 48p. (C). 1998. text, student ed. write for info. (*0-13-083998-1*) P-H.

Mathematics I. (Basic Mathematics Ser.: Module 3). (Illus.). 100p. 1982. spiral bd. 22.50 (*0-87683-227-3*) GP Courseware.

Mathematics 1: A Textbook for Grade 10. Kunihiko Kodaira. LC 96-23129. (Mathematical World Ser.: Vol. 8). 247p. 1996. pap. 29.00 (*0-8218-0583-5*, MAWRLD/8) Am Math.

Mathematics 118: Finite Mathematics & Its Applications 300p. (C). 1996. text 27.40 (*0-536-59576-3*) Pearson Custom.

Mathematics Past & Present: Fourier Integral Operators. Ed. by James L. Bruning & Victor W. Guillemin. LC 93-38405. 300p. 1994. 86.95 (*0-387-56741-0*) Spr-Verlag.

Mathematics, Pedagogy & Secondary Teacher Education. Cooney. 1998. pap. text 23.00 (*0-325-00115-4*) Heinemann.

Mathematics, Pedagogy & Secondary Teacher Education: An Introduction. Cooney & Wittman. 1996. text. write for info. (*0-435-07113-0*) Heinemann.

Mathematics, Pedagogy & Secondary Teacher Education: Reweaving the Frayed Braid. 2nd ed. Thomas J. Cooney & Brown. LC 96-19145. 1997. text, teacher ed. 100.00 (*0-435-07101-7*) Heinemann.

Mathematics, Physics & Reality: Two Essays. Arthur M. Young. LC 90-81337. (Illus.). 146p. 1990. pap. 12.95 (*1-892160-07-2*, 07-2) Anodos Found.

Mathematics Placement Examination Review. 2nd ed. Colorado State University Staff. Ed. & Illus. by Davies Group Staff. 96p. (C). 1997. pap. 4.25 (*1-888570-07-5*) Davies Grp.

Mathematics Plus Physics, Vol. 1. Ludwig Streit. 338p. 1985. text 55.00 (*9971-966-63-8*); pap. text 36.00 (*9971-966-64-6*) World Scientific Pub.

Mathematics Plus Physics, Vol. 3. Ed. by Ludwig Streit. 228p. 1989. text 67.00 (*9971-5-0771-4*) World Scientific Pub.

Mathematics Plus Physics: Lectures on Recent Results, Vol. 2. Ed. by Ludwig Streit. 350p. 1986. text 108.00 (*9971-978-40-7*); pap. text 52.00 (*9971-978-60-1*) World Scientific Pub.

Mathematics Portfolios for Elementary & Middle Grades. T. Kuhs. LC 96-49303. 1997. pap. text 18.00 (*0-435-07135-1*, 07135) Heinemann.

Mathematics Power Learning for Children, 3 vols., Bk. I. Everard Barrett. 1993. pap. text, teacher ed. write for info. (*1-883324-01-7*) Prof B Ent.

Mathematics Power Learning for Children, 3 vols., Bk. II. Everard Barrett. 1993. pap. text, teacher ed. write for info. (*1-883324-02-5*) Prof B Ent.

Mathematics Power Learning for Children, 3 vols., Bk. III. Everard Barrett. 1993. pap. text, teacher ed. write for info. (*1-883324-03-3*) Prof B Ent.

Mathematics Power Learning for Children, 3 vols., Set. Everard Barrett. 1993. pap. text, teacher ed. write for info. (*1-883324-00-9*) Prof B Ent.

Mathematics Program in Japan to Upper Secondary School. Eizo Nagasaki. 49p. 1997. pap. 5.50 (*0-16-063631-0*) USGPO.

Mathematics Programs: A Guide to Evaluation. George W. Bright et al. (Essential Tools for Educators Ser.). 144p. 1993. pap. 27.95 (*0-8039-6044-1*) Corwin Pr.

Mathematics Projects Handbook. 4th ed. Glenn D. Allinger et al. LC 99-32453. 93p. 1999. pap. 13.95 (*0-87353-472-7*) NCTM.

Mathematics Recovered for the Natural & Medical Sciences. Dennis Rosen. (Illus.). 224p. (C). (gr. 13). 1992. ring bd. 49.95 (*0-412-41040-0*, A6503, Chap & Hall CRC) CRC Pr.

Mathematics Resource Center: Level A, Boxed Kit. P-H Learning Systems Staff. 1976. 84.00 (*0-685-03880-7*) P-H.

Mathematics Resource Center: Level A, Boxed Kit, Set. P-H Learning Systems Staff. 1976. 120.00 (*0-13-565291-X*) P-H.

Mathematics Resource Center: Level B, Boxed Kit, Set. P-H Learning Systems Staff. 1976. 120.00 (*0-685-03881-5*) P-H.

Mathematics Review. Pamela Cohen & Walter Antoniotti. (Quick Notes Learning System Ser.). (Illus.). 20p. (Orig.). (YA). (gr. 4-12). 1998. pap. text 4.95 (*0-9632772-7-8*) Twen Frst Cent Lrn.

***Mathematics Review.** Peter Schiavone. 141p. (C). 1999. pap. 21.33 (*0-13-011501-0*) P-H.

Mathematics Review for Health Physics Technicians. K. Paul Steinmeyer et al. 412p. 1994. pap. text 35.00 (*0-9630191-1-2*) RSA Pubns.

Mathematics Sampler: Topics for the Liberal Arts. 4th rev. ed. William P. Berlinghoff et al. (Illus.). 592p. (C). 1996. text 53.95 (*1-880157-23-3*, 7-23-3) Ardsley.

Mathematics, Science, & Postclassical Theory. Ed. by Arkady Plotnitsky & Barbara H. Smith. (Special Issue of SAQ Ser.: Vol. 94, No. 2). 230p. 1995. pap. 10.00 (*0-8223-6426-3*) Duke.

Mathematics, Science, & Postclassical Theory. Ed. by Barbara H. Smith & Arkady Plotnitsky. LC 96-13178. 288p. 1997. pap. text 16.95 (*0-8223-1863-6*); lib. bdg. 49.95 (*0-8223-1857-1*) Duke.

***Mathematics, Science & Technology Connections.** Peel Board of Education Teachers Staff & Bob Corney. 148p. (YA). (gr. 6-9). 2000. pap., teacher ed. 31.95 (*1-895579-37-6*, Pub. by Trifolium Inc) ACCESS Pubs Network.

Mathematics, Science & Technology Education Programs That Work. 1997. lib. bdg. 252.99 (*0-8490-8113-0*) Gordon Pr.

Mathematics, Science & Technology Education Programs That Work: A Collection of Exemplary Educational Programs & Practices in the National Diffusion Network. Ed. by Luna Levinson. 145p. (Orig.). (C). 1994. pap. text 30.00 (*0-7881-1525-1*) DIANE Pub.

Mathematics, Science & Technology Education Programs That Work & Promising Practices in Mathematics & Science Education, 2 vols., Set. 1994. lib. bdg. 575.95 (*0-8490-5834-1*) Gordon Pr.

Mathematics Sin Limits, 1988: Grade 8. Fennell. 1987. 40.75 (*0-03-009167-5*) Harcourt Schl Pubs.

Mathematics, Sr. H.S. Jack Rudman. (Teachers License Examination Ser.: T-41). 1994. pap. 27.95 (*0-8373-8041-3*) Nat Learn.

Mathematics, Statistics & Systems for Health. Norman T. Bailey. LC 77-1307. (Wiley Series in Probability & Mathematical Statistics). 232p. reprint ed. pap. 72.00 (*0-608-17855-1*, 203265300080) Bks Demand.

Mathematics Study Aid. Thomas J. Finnegan et al. (J). 1975. pap. 2.50 (*0-87738-036-8*) Youth Ed.

Mathematics Success - & Failure among African American Youth: The Roles of Sociohistorical Context, Community Forces, School Influence, & Individual Agency. Danny B. Martin. LC 99-34928. (Studies in Mathematical Thinking & Learning). 202p. 1999. write for info. (*0-8058-3042-1*) L Erlbaum Assocs.

Mathematics Survey with Applications. 508p. (C). 1996. text 56.00 (*0-536-59506-2*) Pearson Custom.

Mathematics Teacher Education: Critical International Perspectives. Ed. by Barbara Jaworski et al. LC 99-220444. (Studies in Mathematics Education). 240p. 1999. 85.00 (*0-7507-0809-3*, Falmer Pr); pap. 29.95 (*0-7507-0808-5*, Falmer Pr) Taylor & Francis.

Mathematics Teacher Resource Handbook: A Practical Guide for Teaching K-12 Mathematics. LC 93-16939. (Teacher Resource Handbook Ser.). (Illus.). 468p. 1993. pap. 34.95 (*0-8039-6372-6*) Corwin Pr.

Mathematics Teacher's Complete Calculator Handbook. David E. Williams. LC 83-19164. 318p. 1984. 24.95 (*0-13-563296-X*, Busn) P-H.

Mathematics Teacher's Guide. (Spanish Storybooks Ser.). (ENG & SPA.). 36p. (Orig.). 1992. 12.00 (*1-56334-148-4*) Hampton-Brown.

Mathematics Teachers in Transition. Elizabeth Fennema & Barbara S. Nelson. LC 96-37791. 1997. pap. 39.95 (*0-8058-2688-2*) L Erlbaum Assocs.

Mathematics Teachers in Transition. Ed. by Elizabeth Fennema & Barbara S. Nelson. LC 96-37791. (Studies in Mathematical Thinking & Learning). 352p. 1997. 89.95 (*0-8058-2583-5*) L Erlbaum Assocs.

Mathematics Teachers' Views on Certain Issues in the Teaching of Mathematics. Homer Howard. LC 76-176883. (Columbia University. Teachers College. Contributions to Education Ser.: No. 827). reprint ed. 37.50 (*0-404-55827-5*) AMS Pr.

Mathematics Teaching: Theory in Practice. T. H. Brissenden. 192p. (C). 1980. pap. 45.00 (*0-7855-2375-8*) St Mut.

Mathematics Teaching in the Early Years: An Investigation of Teachers' Subject Knowledge. Carol Aubrey. LC 97-144803. 192p. 1996. pap. 27.95 (*0-7507-0597-3*, Falmer Pr) Taylor & Francis.

Mathematics Tests & Reviews. Ed. by Oscar K. Buros. LC 75-8113. (Tests in Print Ser.). xxv, 435p. 1975. text 35.00 (*0-910674-18-3*) U of Nebr Pr.

Mathematics Textbooks, 7 bks. Caleb Gattegno. Incl. Bk. 1. Study of Numbers up to 20. 102p. pap. text 1.65 (*0-87825-011-5*); Bk. 2. Study of Numbers up to 1,000. 147p. pap. text 2.50 (*0-87825-012-3*); Bk. 3. Applied Arithmetic. 53p. pap. text 1.65 (*0-87825-013-1*); Bk. 4. Fractions, Decimals, Percentages. 65p. pap. text 1.65 (*0-87825-014-X*); Bk. 5. Study of Numbers. 83p. pap. text 1.65 (*0-87825-015-8*); Bk. 6. Applied Mathematics. 104p. pap. text 4.50 (*0-87825-016-6*); Bk. 7. Algebra & Geometry. 92p. pap. text 4.75 (*0-87825-017-4*); pap. write for info. (*0-318-51805-8*) Ed Solutions.

Mathematics-The Basic Skills. S. Llewellyn & D. A. Greer. 304p. (C). 1991. 32.00 (*0-7478-0598-9*, Pub. by S Thornes Pubs) Trans-Atl Phila.

Mathematics, the Gas Laws & the Respiratory Practitioner. C. Peters. 33p. (C). 1988. pap. 15.00 (*0-933195-37-0*) CA College Health Sci.

Mathematics the Write Way: Activities for Every Elementary Classroom. Marilyn S. Neil. LC 96-3313. 200p. 1996. pap. 29.95 (*1-883001-19-6*) Eye On Educ.

Mathematics Their Way. Mary Baratta-Lorton. 1976. pap. text 38.95 (*0-201-04320-3*) Addison-Wesley.

Mathematics Their Way: 20th Anniversary Edition. anniversary ed. Mary Baratta. 1995. pap. 39.95 (*0-201-86149-6*) Addison-Wesley.

Mathematics Their Way Summary Newsletter. Cynthia Garland. (Illus.). 280p. (Orig.). 1989. pap. text 9.46 (*0-9614646-2-3*) Ctr Innovation.

Mathematics Through Measurement, Pt. I. rev. ed. Barbara Berman & Fredda J. Friederwitzer. (Project S.I.T.E. Ser.). 63p. (C). 1983. pap. text 15.00 (*1-880744-02-3*) Educ Support.

Mathematics Through Measurement, Pt. II. rev. ed. Barbara Berman & Fredda J. Friederwitzer. 48p. (C). 1983. pap. text 15.00 (*1-880744-03-1*) Educ Support.

Mathematics Through Paper Folding. Alton T. Olson. LC 75-16115. (Illus.). 60p. 1975. pap. 8.95 (*0-87353-076-4*) NCTM.

Mathematics Today, Level 1. Abbott. 1987. pap., student ed. 21.75 (*0-15-350031-X*) Harcourt Schl Pubs.

Mathematics Today, Level 2. Abbott. 1987. pap., student ed. 21.75 (*0-15-350032-8*) Harcourt Schl Pubs.

Mathematics Today, Level 3. Abbott. 1987. pap., student ed. 40.00 (*0-15-350033-6*); pap., student ed. 28.75 (*0-15-350034-4*) Harcourt Schl Pubs.

Mathematics Today, Level 8. Abbott. 1987. text, teacher ed. 134.60 (*0-15-350048-4*) Harcourt.

Mathematics Today, Level K. Abbott. 1987. pap., student ed. 16.75 (*0-15-350030-1*) Harcourt Schl Pubs.

Mathematics Today: Level 5. Abbott. 1987. teacher ed. 91.00 (*0-15-350045-X*) Harcourt Schl Pubs.

Mathematics Today: Level 6. Abbott. 1987. teacher ed. 91.00 (*0-15-350046-8*) Harcourt Schl Pubs.

Mathematics Today: Level 7. Janet S. Abbott. 1987. 45.25 (*0-15-350038-7*) Harcourt Schl Pubs.

Mathematics Today: Level 8. Janet S. Abbott. 1987. 45.25 (*0-15-350039-5*) Harcourt Schl Pubs.

Mathematics Today, 1985. Abbott. (SPA.). 1985. 50.00 (*0-15-351094-3*); 30.50 (*0-15-351091-9*); 30.50 (*0-15-351092-7*); 50.00 (*0-15-351093-5*); pap. 21.75 (*0-15-350702-0*); pap. 21.75 (*0-15-350703-9*); pap. 16.75 (*0-15-350701-2*); pap. 20.25 (*0-15-351090-0*); pap., wbk. ed. 12.25 (*0-15-350738-1*); pap., wbk. ed. 9.75 (*0-15-350764-0*); pap., wbk. ed. 9.75 (*0-15-350765-9*); pap., wbk. ed. 11.25 (*0-15-350766-7*); pap., wbk. ed. 11.25 (*0-15-350768-3*); pap., wbk. ed. 11.25 (*0-15-350769-1*); pap., wbk. ed. 11.25 (*0-15-350767-5*) Harcourt Schl Pubs.

Mathematics Today, 1987. Abbott. (SPA.). 1987. pap., student ed. 31.50 (*0-15-350412-9*) Harcourt Schl Pubs.

Mathematics Today, 1987, Level 1. Abbott. (SPA.). 1987. pap., student ed. 31.50 (*0-15-350411-0*) Harcourt Schl Pubs.

Mathematics Today, 1987, Level 1. Abbotts. 1987. 76.00 (*0-15-350041-7*) Harcourt Schl Pubs.

Mathematics Today, 1987, Level 2. Abbott. 1987. teacher ed. 76.00 (*0-15-350042-5*); teacher ed. 84.00 (*0-15-350043-3*) Harcourt Schl Pubs.

Mathematics Today, 1987, Level 4. Barrera. 1987. 43.25 (*0-15-331030-8*); 40.00 (*0-15-350035-2*) Harcourt Schl Pubs.

Mathematics Today, 1987, Level 5. Abbott. 1987. student ed. 40.00 (*0-15-350036-0*) Harcourt Schl Pubs.

Mathematics Today, 1987, Level 6. Abbott. 1987. student ed. 40.50 (*0-15-350037-9*) Harcourt Schl Pubs.

Mathematics Today, 1987, Level K. Abbott. 1987. 68.00 (*0-15-350040-9*) Harcourt Schl Pubs.

Mathematics Today, 1987: Level 4. Abbott. 1987. 84.00 (*0-15-350044-1*) Harcourt Schl Pubs.

Mathematics Today, 1995. Abbott. (SPA.). 1985. 50.00 (*0-15-351095-1*) Harcourt Schl Pubs.

Mathematics Today-Twelve Informal Essays. Ed. by Lynn A. Steen. LC 78-7594. (Illus.). 1984. 55.95 (*0-387-90305-4*) Spr-Verlag.

Mathematics II. (Basic Academics Ser.: Module 4). (Illus.). 110p. 1982. spiral bd. 16.95 (*0-87683-228-1*) GP Courseware.

Mathematics 2: A Textbook for Grade 11. Kunihiko Kodaira. Tr. by Hiromi Nagata from ENG. LC 96-18853. (Mathematical World Ser.: Vol. 9). 262p. 1996. pap. 29.00 (*0-8218-0582-7*, MAWRLD/9) Am Math.

Mathematics Unlimited: Grade 8. Fennell. 1987. 45.25 (*0-03-006452-X*) Harcourt Schl Pubs.

***Mathematics Unlimited - 2001 & Beyond.** Ed. by B. Engquist & W. Schmid. 800p. 2000. 44.95 (*3-540-66913-2*) Spr-Verlag.

***Mathematics Unlimited - 2001 & Beyond: Special Edition.** Ed. by B. Engquist & W. Schmid. 800p. 2000. 44.95 (*3-540-67099-8*) Spr-Verlag.

Mathematics Unlimited, 1987: Grade 6. Fennell. 1987. 40.50 (*0-03-006442-2*) Harcourt Schl Pubs.

Mathematics Unraveled: A New Commonsense Approach. James Kyle. LC 83-23855. 280p. (C). 1984. reprint ed. 17.50 (*0-89874-714-7*) Krieger.

Mathematics Versus the National Curriculum. Ed. by Paul Dowling & Richard Noss. 258p. 1990. 79.95 (*1-85000-891-4*, Falmer Pr); pap. 39.95 (*1-85000-892-2*, Falmer Pr) Taylor & Francis.

***Mathematics With Appl: Mgmt Natrl Soc Sci.** 7th ed. (C). 1999. pap. text 0.00 (*0-321-03960-2*, Celebration) Addson-Wesley Educ.

Mathematics with Applications. (C). 1997. text 177.00 (*0-673-55865-7*, GoodYrBooks) Addson-Wesley Educ.

***Mathematics with Applications.** (C). 1999. text 73.50 (*0-536-60536-X*) Pearson Custom.

***Mathematics with Applications.** 7th ed. (C). 1998. 25.00 (*0-321-03953-X*); 18.00 (*0-321-03959-9*) Addison-Wesley.

***Mathematics with Applications.** 7th ed. (C). 1999. 67.00 (*0-321-03562-3*) Addison-Wesley.

***Mathematics with Applications.** 7th ed. (C). 1999. 67.00 (*0-321-03561-5*) Addison-Wesley.

***Mathematics with Applications.** 7th ed. 304p. (C). 1999. 24.00 (*0-321-03956-4*) Addison-Wesley.

Mathematics with Applications: A Graphing Approach. Ed. by Margaret L. Lial. LC 98-21684. 864p. (C). 1998. 103.00 (*0-321-01621-1*) Addson-Wesley Educ.

M

An Asterisk (*) at the beginning of an entry indicates that the title is appearing for the first time.

Mathematics with Applications: Answer Book. 7th ed. Lial & Hungerford. 192p. 1998. 23.00 (*0-321-03955-6*) Addson-Wesley Educ.

Mathematics with Applications: In the Management, Natural & Social Sciences. 4th ed. Margaret L. Lial et al. (C). 1995. teacher ed. write for info. (*0-673-55304-3*) Addson-Wesley Educ.

Mathematics with Applications: In the Management, Natural & Social Sciences. 7th ed. Margaret L. Lial. LC 98-21682. 880p. (C). 1998. 103.00 (*0-321-02294-7*) Addson-Wesley Educ.

Mathematics with Applications: Management of Natural Social Science. 7th ed. Margaret Lial. 1999. text 22.50 (*0-321-03954-8*) Addison-Wesley.

***Mathematics with Applications Graphing Tech.** (C). 1998. 28.00 (*0-321-03957-2*) Addison-Wesley.

***Mathematics with Applications Graphing Tech.** (C). 1999. 67.00 (*0-321-03563-1*) Addison-Wesley.

***Mathematics With Applications: Graphing Technology Version Instructors' Resource Guide & Solutions Manual With Explorations In Finite Math & Visual Calculus DOS Disk.** Thomas W. Hungerford. 1998. text 24.00 (*0-321-03958-0*) Addison-Wesley.

Mathematics with Applications in Management & Economics. 7th rev. ed. Gordon D. Prichett & John C. Saber. LC 92-36042. 1088p. (C). 1993. text 72.75 (*0-256-09237-0*, Irwn McGrw-H) McGrw-H Hghr Educ.

***Mathematics with Business Applications.** rev. ed. Lange et al. 1998. student ed. 39.00 (*0-02-814730-8*) Glencoe.

***Mathematics with Business Applications: Teacher's Wraparound Edition.** Lange et al. 1998. teacher ed. 52.50 (*0-02-814731-6*) Glencoe.

Mathematics with Calculus & Its Applications to Management, Life & Social Sciences. Margaret B. Cozzens & Richard D. Porter. LC 86-81262. 893p. (C). 1987. text 77.96 (*0-669-09366-1*) HM Trade Div.

Mathematics with Cubes: Problem Solving Activities for Older Children. Janine Blinko & Noel Graham. 64p. (J). (gr. 3-7). pap. 12.50 (*1-871098-14-9*, Pub. by Claire Pubns) Parkwest Pubns.

***Mathematics with Excel.** Piascik. 2001. pap. 15.00 (*0-534-37059-4*) Thomson Learn.

Mathematics with Maple. David Hough. (C). 1997. pap. text. write for info. (*0-201-40379-X*) Addison-Wesley.

Mathematics with Reason: The Emergent Approach to Primary Maths. Ed. by Sue Atkinson. LC 92-35837. 176p. (C). (gr. k). 1992. pap. text 21.50 (*0-435-08333-3*, 08333) Heinemann.

Mathematics with Teddy Bears. Elizabeth Graham. 64p. (J). (gr. k-4). pap. 12.50 (*1-871098-09-2*, Pub. by Claire Pubns) Parkwest Pubns.

Mathematics with Understanding, 1. H. Fletcher & A. A. Howell. (C). 1972. 92.00 (*0-08-015657-6*, Pub. by Pergamon Repr) Franklin.

Mathematics with Vision. Ed. by V. Keranen & P. Mitic. 416p. 1995. 169.00 (*1-85312-386-2*) Computational Mech MA.

Mathematics with Vision. Ed. by V. Keranen & P. Mitic. LC 95-68883. 416p. 1995. 210.00 (*1-56252-310-4*, 3862) Computational Mech MA.

Mathematics Without Borders: A History of the International Mathematical Union. Olli E. Lehto. LC 97-37950. (Illus.). 368p. 1997. 35.00 (*0-387-98358-9*) Spr-Verlag.

Mathematics Without Numbers: Towards a Modal-Structural Interpretation. Geoffrey Hellman. 156p. (C). 1994. reprint ed. pap. text 17.95 (*0-19-824034-1*) OUP.

Mathematics Workbook for the GED. Johanna Holm. LC 96-35819. 1997. pap. 12.95 (*0-8120-9707-6*) Barron.

***Mathematics Workshop: Math on the Job (Teacher's Edition) 2000.** 1999. write for info. (*0-13-023362-5*) P-H.

***Mathematics Workshop: Math on the Job 2000c.** (gr. 6-12). 1999. student ed. write for info. (*0-13-023361-7*) P-H.

***Mathematics Workshop: Problem Solving.** 2nd ed. 1999. write for info. (*0-13-023358-7*) S&S Trade.

***Mathematics Workshop: Problem Solving Book.** 1999. write for info. (*0-13-023356-0*) S&S Trade.

***Mathematics Workshop: SE 2000c.** (gr. 6-12). 1999. student ed. write for info. (*0-13-023363-3*) P-H.

***Mathematics Workshop 2000C.** (gr. 6-12). 1999. teacher ed., student ed. write for info. (*0-13-023364-1*) P-H.

Mathematics Write Now! Ed. by Peggy House & Nancy Desmond. LC 96-157089. 129p. 1994. pap. 13.95 (*0-939765-65-9*, G162) Janson Pubns.

Mathematics 7: Teacher's Edition, 1 & 2. 1995. teacher ed. write for info. (*0-201-27722-0*) Addison-Wesley.

Mathematics 7: Texas Vol. 1 & 2. 1995. teacher ed. write for info. (*0-201-27724-7*) Addison-Wesley.

Mathematics...a Way of Thinking. Mary Baratta-Lorton. 1977. text 28.00 (*0-201-04322-X*) Addison-Wesley.

Mathematics/Science Education & Technology, 1994: Proceedings of the 1994 International Symposium on Mathematics/Science Education & Technology. Ed. by Gary H. Marks. (Illus.). 254p. (Orig.). 1994. pap. 25.00 (*1-880094-12-6*) Assn Advan Comput Educ.

Mathematik: Deutsch-Russisches Woerterbuch: Mathematics, German-Russian Dictionary. L. A. Kaluzhnin. (GER & RUS.). 559p. 1980. 69.95 (*0-8288-1899-1*, M15445) Fr & Eur.

Mathematik Lernen - Lehrbar? Die Mathematiklernende Person Im Zyklus Ihrer Lebensumwelt. Hans Bussmann. (GER., Illus.). 491p. 1997. 82.95 (*3-631-31201-6*) P Lang Pubng.

Mathematik und Plausibles Schliessen, 2 vols. George Polya. Incl. Vol. 2. Typen und Strukturen Plausibler Folgerung. 326p. 1980. 97.00 (*0-8176-0715-3*); (Science & Civilization Ser.: Nos. 14 & 15). write for info. (*0-318-51087-1*) Birkhauser.

Mathematiques Mentales en Francais. Ellen Hechler.Tr. of Mental Math Brain Skills in French. (FRE.). (Orig.). (YA). 1997. pap. text 6.00 (*0-9638483-5-6*) Midmath.

Mathematisch Begabte Kinder: Modelle, Empirische Studien und Forderungsprojekte Fur das Grundschulalter. (Greifswalder Studien zur Erziehungswissenschaft: Bd. 5). (GER., Illus.). 332p. 1998. 45.95 (*3-631-33395-1*) P Lang Pubng.

Mathematische Abhandlungen see Festschrift Schwarz

Mathematische Abhandlungen, 3 vols. Helmut Hasse. Ed. by Heinrich W. Leopoldt & Peter Roquette. xxxvi, 1592p. (C). 1975. 603.85 (*3-11-005931-2*) De Gruyter.

Mathematische Analyse des Raumproblems see Kontinuum und Andere Monographien

Mathematische Beitrage Zum Kulturleben der Volker. Moritz Cantor. xii, 432p. 1964. reprint ed. 110.00 (*0-318-70731-4*) G Olms Pubs.

Mathematische Grundbegriffe Bei Sextus Empiricus. Wolfgang Freytag. (Spudasmata Ser.: Vol. 57). (GER.). viii, 258p. 1995. write for info. (*3-487-10033-9*) G Olms Pubs.

Mathematische Logik Von 1847 Bis Zur Gegenwart: Eine Bibliometrische Untersuchung. Roland Wagner-Doebler & Jan Berg. (Grundlagen der Kommunikation & Kognition (Foundations of Communication & Cognition) Ser.). (GER.). x, 271p. 1993. lib. bdg. 113.85 (*3-11-013987-1*) De Gruyter.

Mathematische Schriften, 7 vols., Set. Gottfried Wilhelm Leibniz. xxviii, 3401p. 1971. reprint ed. write for info. (*0-318-71368-3*); reprint ed. pap. write for info. (*0-318-71369-1*) G Olms Pubs.

***mathematische Weltbild der Maya.** Andrea C. Schalley. 2000. 45.95 (*3-631-35091-0*) P Lang Pubng.

Mathematische Werke, 2 vols. 2nd ed. Gotthold F. Eisenstein. LC 75-17855. xxiii, 940p. 1988. 125.00 (*0-8284-1280-4*) Chelsea Pub.

Mathematische Werke - Mathematical Works Vol. 2: Linear Algebra & Analysis. Helmut Wielandt. Ed. by Bertram Huppert & Hans Schneider. xx, 632p. (C). 1996. lib. bdg. 209.95 (*3-11-012453-X*) De Gruyter.

Mathematische Werke (Mathematical Works) Vol. 1: Group Theory. Helmut Wielandt. Ed. by Bertram Huppert & Hans Schneider. LC 93-48652. (ENG & GER.). xix, 802p. (C). 1994. lib. bdg. 209.95 (*3-11-012452-1*, 1-94) De Gruyter.

Mathematisches Vokabular. 4th ed. E. Berthold Klaften. (ENG & GER.). 1971. 39.95 (*0-8288-6471-3*, M-7551) Fr & Eur.

Mathematisme de Descartes. Jean-Louis Allard. LC 65-53234. (Publications Seriees de l'Universite d'Ottawa: Vol. 68). (FRE.). 232p. 1963. reprint ed. pap. 72.00 (*0-608-02188-1*, 206285700003) Bks Demand.

Mathemtca Quik Ref&Begnn. Nancy Blackman. (C). 1995. pap. text 39.95 (*0-201-82085-4*) Addison-Wesley.

***Mathemtcs with Applications: Management.** (C). 1999. pap. text 71.00 (*0-321-03564-X*) Addison-Wesley Educ.

Mather: Lineage of Rev. Richard Mather. H. E. Mather. (Illus.). 540p. 1990. reprint ed. pap. 81.00 (*0-8328-1613-2*); reprint ed. lib. bdg. 89.00 (*0-8328-1612-4*) Higginson Bk Co.

Mather (P. E.) on Sheriff & Execution Law. 3rd ed. C. R. Wigan & Dougall Meston. LC 90-55184. xci, 702p. 1990. reprint ed. 160.00 (*0-912004-85-1*) Gaunt.

Mather Papers: History of Larue County, Kentucky. Otis M. Mather. 57p. 1995. pap. 7.00 (*1-889221-26-0*) Ancestral Trails.

Mathercise Classroom Warm-Up Exercises, A. rev. ed. Michael Serra. 62p. 1992. pap. text 9.95 (*1-55953-059-6*) Key Curr Pr.

Mathercise Classroom Warm-Up Exercises, B. rev. ed. Michael Serra. 62p. 1992. pap. text 9.95 (*1-55953-060-X*) Key Curr Pr.

Mathercise Classroom Warm-Up Exercises, C. rev. ed. Michael Serra. 62p. 1992. pap. text 9.95 (*1-55953-061-8*) Key Curr Pr.

Mathercise Classroom Warm-Up Exercises, D. rev. ed. Michael Serra. 62p. 1992. pap. text 9.95 (*1-55953-062-6*) Key Curr Pr.

Mathercise Classroom Warm-Up Exercises, E. rev. ed. Michael Serra. 62p. 1992. pap. text 9.95 (*1-55953-063-4*) Key Curr Pr.

Mathers: Three Generations of Puritan Intellectuals,1596-1728. Robert Middlekauff. LC 98-50840. 450p. 1999. pap. 16.95 (*0-520-21930-9*, Pub. by U CA Pr) Cal Prin Full Svc.

Matheson. History of the Mathesons, with Genealogies of the Various Familes (with 1998 Index by Marlene Sue Van Horne) enl. ed. Alexander MacKenzie. Ed. by Alexander MacBain. (Illus.). 201p. 1998. reprint ed. pap. 32.00 (*0-8328-9681-0*); reprint ed. lib. bdg. 42.00 (*0-8328-9680-2*) Higginson Bk Co.

Matheus Millers' Memoir: A Merchant's Life in the Seventeenth Century. Thomas Max Safley. LC 99-15613. 240p. 1999. text 59.95 (*0-312-22646-2*) St Martin.

Mathevasion: Exercises Trav aux Pratiques 2e-1re Terminales. Philippe De Sablet. (FRE., Illus.). vii, 71p. (Orig.). 1997. pap. 11.95 (*0-9652357-0-X*) Mathevasion.

Mathew Brady: Civil War Photographer. Elizabeth Van Steenwyk. (First Bks). (J). 1997. pap. text 6.95 (*0-531-15851-9*) Watts.

Mathew Brady: Civil War Photographer. Elizabeth Van Steenwyk. LC 96-35102. (First Bk.). (J). 1997. lib. bdg. 22.00 (*0-531-20264-X*) Watts.

Mathew Brady & the Image of History. Mary Panzer et al. LC 97-9493. 232p. 1997. 39.95 (*1-56098-793-6*) Smithsonian.

Mathew Carey: Editor, Author & Publisher. Earl L. Bradsher. LC 78-181915. (BCL Ser. I). reprint ed. 31.50 (*0-404-00969-7*) AMS Pr.

Mathew Carey, a Study in American Economic Development. Kenneth W. Rowe. LC 78-64151. (Johns Hopkins University. Studies in the Social Sciences. Thirtieth Ser. 1912: 4). 144p. 1982. reprint ed. 37.50 (*0-404-61261-X*) AMS Pr.

Mathew Carey, Editor, Author & Publisher: A Study in American Literary Development. Earl L. Bradsher. (BCL1-PS American Literature Ser.). 144p. 1992. reprint ed. lib. bdg. 69.00 (*0-7812-6659-9*) Rprt Serv.

Mathew Carey, Publisher & Patriot. James N. Green. (Illus.). iv, 32p. (Orig.). 1985. pap. 5.00 (*0-914076-74-4*) Lib Co Phila.

Mathew Henry's Commentary on the Whole Bible. Matthew Henry. Ed. by Leslie F. Church. 1981. 239.60 (*0-310-26358-1*) Zondervan.

Mathew Henry's Commentary on the Whole Bible. Matthew Henry. Ed. by Leslie F. Church. 1986p. 1988. 29.99 (*0-310-26018-3*) Zondervan.

Mathew Henry's Commentary on the Whole Bible. Matthew Henry. 1986p. 1988. 30.95 (*0-310-53008-3*) Zondervan.

Mathew Henry's Commentary on the Whole Bible. Matthew Henry. Ed. by Leslie F. Church. 1986p. 1990. 35.99 (*0-310-26019-1*) Zondervan.

***Mathews Light Artillery: Penick's Pittsylvania Artillery; Young's Halifax Light Artillery & Johnson's Jackson Flying Artillery.** George L. Sherwood. (Virginia Regimental Histories Ser.). (Illus.). 108p. 1999. 19.95 (*1-56190-114-8*) H E Howard.

Mathias J. Alten: Journey of an American Painter. M. Alten et al. LC 98-71838. 175 p. 1998. write for info. (*0-942159-22-5*) Grnd Rpds Art Mus.

Mathias Sandorf, 2 vols. Jules Verne. 8.95 (*0-685-73300-9*) Fr & Eur.

Mathias Sandorf. 2nd ed. Jules Verne. (FRE.). 192p. 1978. pap. 10.95 (*0-7859-1363-7*, 2070330567) Fr & Eur.

***Mathilda's Journey: The Life of Clara Mathilda Glasrud Lee.** Robert E. A. Lee. LC 99-76009. (Illus.). 288p. 2000. pap. 16.95 (*0-9675900-0-0*, Pub. by Real World Comm) ACCESS Pubs Network.

Mathis at Colmar: A Visual Confrontation. Linda Nochlin. LC 63-2298. (Illus.). 1963. 5.00 (*0-87376-002-6*) Red Dust.

Mathis Photosynthesis, Vol. 2. 1995. lib. bdg. write for info. (*0-7923-3858-8*) Kluwer Academic.

Mathis Photosynthesis, Vol. 3. 1995. lib. bdg. write for info. (*0-7923-3859-6*) Kluwer Academic.

Mathis Photosynthesis, Vol. 4. 1995. lib. bdg. write for info. (*0-7923-3860-X*) Kluwer Academic.

Mathis Photosynthesis, Vol. 5. 1995. lib. bdg. write for info. (*0-7923-3861-8*) Kluwer Academic.

Mathland: The Expert Version. L. C. Norman. (Illus.). 80p. (J). 1994. pap. 8.50 (*0-521-46802-7*) Cambridge U Pr.

Mathland: The Novice Version. L. C. Norman. (Illus.). 88p. (J). 1994. pap. 8.50 (*0-521-46801-9*) Cambridge U Pr.

Mathletics: Gold Medal Problems. Carole Greenes et al. (Illus.). 149p. (YA). (gr. 8-10). 1989. pap. 19.95 (*0-939765-31-4*, G119) Janson Pubns.

***MathLink Network Programming in Mathematica.** Chikara Miyaji & Paul Abbott. 400p. (C). 1999. write for info. (*0-521-64172-1*); pap. 24.95 (*0-521-64598-0*) Cambridge U Pr.

Mathmagic with Flexagons. Donovan A. Johnson. Ed. by Diane Kaz. (Illus.). 43p. (Orig.). (J). (gr. 4-12). 1974. pap. 8.50 (*0-918932-30-0*, AE-1238) Activity Resources.

Mathmagical Fun. Stuart A. Kallen. LC 92-14777. 32p. (J). (gr. 3-8). 1992. lib. bdg. 13.98 (*1-56239-129-1*) ABDO Pub Co.

Mathmagical Moments. Sue Heckler & Christine Weber. (Illus.). 128p. 1995. pap. 11.95 (*1-880505-14-2*, CLC0193) Pieces of Lrning.

Mathmaker. Bob Bernstein. 112p. teacher ed. 12.99 (*0-86653-741-4*, GA1456) Good Apple.

Mathmaster No. 3. Contrib. by Bob Gardner & Ron Van der Meer. (Illus.). 336p. 1998. 19.95 (*3-8290-1432-5*, 520683) Konemann.

***MathMaster 5+** Koneman Staff. (Illus.). (gr. 4-7). 1999. 19.95 (*3-8290-3044-4*) Konemann.

MathMate Activity Book, Level 1. David E. Williams. (Illus.). 1992. pap. text 10.95 (*0-914534-04-1*) Stokes.

MathMate Activity Book, Level 2. David E. Williams. (Illus.). 1992. pap. text 10.95 (*0-914534-05-X*) Stokes.

MathMate Activity Book, Level 3. David E. Williams. (Illus.). 1992. pap. text 10.95 (*0-914534-06-8*) Stokes.

Mathmedia. AIT Staff. (YA). (gr. 7-12). 1995. teacher ed. 24.95 (*0-7842-0815-8*) Agency Instr Tech.

Mathnawi of Jalalu'ddin Rimi Vols. 7 & 8: Commentary. Incl. Vol. 7. 77.00 (*0-906094-15-1*, Pub. by Aris & Phillips); Vol. 8. 77.00 (*0-7189-0206-8*, Pub. by Aris & Phillips); 144.00 (*0-906094-28-3*) David Brown.

Mathnawi of Jalalu'ddin Rumi Vols. 1,3, & 5: Persian. Incl. Vol. 1. 77.00 (*0-906094-24-0*, Pub. by Aris & Phillips); Vol. 3. 88.00 (*0-906094-25-9*, Pub. by Aris & Phillips); Vol. 5. 88.00 (*0-7189-0205-X*, Pub. by Aris & Phillips); 237.00 (*0-906094-26-7*) David Brown.

***Mathnotes: Every Student's Handy Homework Notebook.** Barney Quinn. (Panterra Notes Ser.). 220p. (YA). 1999. pap. 18.95 (*1-892680-00-9*) Panterra Pubng.

Mathographics. Robert Dixon. (General Science Ser.). (Illus.). 224p. 1991. pap. 10.95 (*0-486-26639-7*) Dover.

Mathpack User's Guide. Date not set. pap. write for info. (*0-395-82826-0*) HM.

***Mathpass: Lial Basic College Mathematics.** 5th ed. Lial. 1998. 29.00 (*0-201-44073-3*) Addison-Wesley.

***Mathpass: Lial Basic College Mathematics.** 6th ed. Lial. 2001. 29.00 (*0-201-44077-6*) Addison-Wesley.

***Mathpass for Intermediate Algebra.** 8th ed. Marvin Bittinger. (C). 1999. pap. text 82.00 (*0-201-43402-4*) Addison-Wesley.

Mathpass Interactive Cd Paper Instructions. Wesley Addison. 1p. (C). 1998. pap. text Price not set. (*0-201-43692-2*) Addison-Wesley.

Mathpass System Administrator Booklet. Ed. by Addison-Wesley Publishing Staff. 34p. (C). 1998. ring bd. write for info. (*0-201-44045-8*) Addison-Wesley.

Maths - A Students' Survival Guide: A Self-Help Workbook for Science & Engineering Students. Jenny Olive. LC 97-28653. (Illus.). 584p. (C). 1998. text, student ed., wbk. ed. 74.95 (*0-521-57306-8*); pap. text, student ed., wbk. ed. 29.95 (*0-521-57586-9*) Cambridge U Pr.

Maths Alive! Inset Mathematics for the National Curriculum (Key States 1, 2, & 3) Edith Biggs & Kathleen Shaw. (Cassell Education Ser.). (Illus.). 144p. 1995. 110.00 (*0-304-32994-0*); pap. 33.95 (*0-304-32990-8*) Continuum.

Math's & Music's Metasonics see Psycho-Mathematics: The Key to the Universe

Maths & Statistics for Business. M. Lawson. 1995. pap. 18.95 (*0-582-23187-6*) Addison-Wesley.

Maths & Statistics for the Built Environment. J. Bacon. 1997. pap. write for info. (*0-582-23188-4*) Longman.

Maths for Computing & Information Technology. F. Giannasi. 1996. pap. 20.95 (*0-582-23654-1*) Addison-Wesley.

***Maths for Map Makers.** Arthur L. Allan. (Illus.). 320p. 1999. pap. text 50.00 (*0-7881-8121-1*) DIANE Pub.

Maths for the Dyslexic: A Practical Guide. Anne Henderson. LC 98-184556. 1998. pap. 24.95 (*1-85346-534-8*, Pub. by David Fulton) Taylor & Francis.

Maths in Context: A Thematic Approach. Deidre Edwards. 148p. (C). (gr. k). 1990. pap. text 21.50 (*0-435-08308-2*, 08308) Heinemann.

Maths in the Mind: A Process Approach to Mental Strategies. Ann Baker & Johnny Baker. LC 91-7547. (Illus.). 120p. (Orig.). (C). (gr. k). 1991. pap. text 16.50 (*0-435-08316-3*) Heinemann.

Maths Made Easy. Dexter J. Booth. 280p. 1995. ring bd. 32.95 (*0-412-71870-7*) CRC Pr.

Math's Problem Solving & Modelling. Lovitt. (UM - International Math Ser.). 1991. text 47.95 (*0-538-62776-X*) S-W Pub.

Maths Problem Solving & Modelling. Lovitt. (Um - International Math Ser.). 1991. text 38.95 (*0-538-62777-8*) S-W Pub.

Maths Workbook. 250p. 1987. 39.50 (*1-85313-003-6*, Pub. by Checkmate Pubns) St Mut.

Mathscore. M. Rosen. Date not set. pap. text. write for info. (*0-582-18393-6*, Pub. by Addison-Wesley) Longman.

MathTensor: A System for Doing Tensor Analysis by Computer. Leonard Parker & Steven M. Christensen. 400p. (C). 1994. 54.95 (*0-201-56990-6*) Addison-Wesley.

MathTivities! Classroom Activities for Grades One Through Six. Creative Publications Staff. LC 97-104172. 240p. 1996. 27.95 (*0-534-52740-X*) Wadsworth Pub.

***MathType: The Mathematical Equation Editor: Version 3.5 for Windows.** Ed. by Design Science Inc. Staff. 150p. 1998. 150.00 incl. cd-rom (*3-540-14713-6*) Spr-Verlag.

Mathura: A District Memori. F. S. Growse. (Illus.). 460p. 1986. reprint ed. 73.50 (*0-8364-1753-4*, Pub. by Manohar) S Asia.

Mathura: A Gazetteer. D. L. Drake-Brockman. 1985. reprint ed. 32.00 (*0-8364-1324-5*, Pub. by Usha) S Asia.

Mathura: The Cultural Heritage. Ed. by Doris Srinivasan. (Illus.). 405p. (C). 1989. text 64.00 (*0-685-33230-6*) South Asia Pubns.

Mathura: The Cultural Heritage. Ed. by Doris M. Srinivasan. (C). 1988. 72.50 (*81-85054-37-1*, Pub. by Manohar) S Asia.

Mathura: The Cultural Heritage. Ed. by Doris M. Srinivasan. (C). 1989. 67.50 (*0-945921-05-5*) S Asia.

Mathura & Its Society: The Saka Pahlava Phase. B. N. Mukherjee. 1981. 14.00 (*0-8364-1589-2*) S Asia.

Mathware: A Math Workshop for Home Use Kit. Caleb Gattegno. 1973. 40.00 (*0-87825-010-7*) Ed Solutions.

Mathwise: Teaching Mathematical Thinking & Problem Solving. Arthur A. Hyde & Pamela R. Hyde. LC 90-47046. 232p. (Orig.). (C). (gr. 3). 1991. pap. text 25.00 (*0-435-08311-2*, 08311) Heinemann.

Mathwords: A Word Book for Mathematics. Language Studies Centre Staff & Carol Jenkins. (Illus.). 62p. (C). 1994. 20.95 (*0-521-45527-8*) Cambridge U Pr.

Matias Montes Huidobro: Acercamientos a Su Obra Literaria. Jorge M. Febles. Ed. by Armando Gonzalez-Perez. LC 96-45645. (Hispanic Literature Ser.: Vol. 35). 256p. 1997. text 89.95 (*0-7734-8723-9*) E Mellen.

Matiere Derobee: L'Appropriation Critique de l'Objet de la Physique Contemporaine. M. Paty. 442p. 1988. pap. text 61.00 (*2-88124-186-7*) Gordon & Breach.

Matiere et Memoire: Essai sur la Relation du Corps a l'Esprit. 3rd ed. Henri Bergson. (FRE.). 1990. pap. 18.95 (*0-7859-3013-2*) Fr & Eur.

Matigari. Ngugi wa Thiong'o. Tr. by Wangui wa Goro. (African Writers Ser.). 175p. (C). 1989. 17.95 (*0-435-90654-2*, 90654); pap. 9.95 (*0-435-90546-5*, 90546) Heinemann.

Matigari: A Novel. Ngugi wa Thiong'o. LC 96-44440. 160p. 1996. 21.95 (*0-86543-360-7*) Africa World.

***Matilda.** 1999. 9.95 (*1-56137-589-6*) Novel Units.

Matilda. Blackwell North America Staff. (Illus.). (J). pap. text 6.95 (*2-07-033555-0*) Gallimard Edns.

Matilda. Roald Dahl. (Illus.). 224p. (J). (gr. 3-7). 1988. 15.99 (*0-670-82439-9*, Viking Child) Peng Put Young Read.

Matilda. Roald Dahl. LC 89-10604. (Illus.). 240p. (J). (gr. 3-7). 1998. pap. 4.99 (*0-14-130106-6*, PuffinBks) Peng Put Young Read.

Matilda. Roald Dahl. (J). 1995. pap. text 12.95 (*84-204-4638-6*) Santillana.

An Asterisk (*) at the beginning of an entry indicates that the title is appearing for the first time.

Matilda. Roald Dahl. (J). 1989. 18.05 (*0-606-10484-4*, Pub. by Turtleback) Demco.

Matilda. Roald Dahl. (J). 1996. 10.09 (*0-606-02745-9*, Pub. by Turtleback) Demco.

***Matilda.** Roald Dahl & Quentin Blake. 1999. 16.95 (*0-7540-6060-8*) Chivers N Amer.

Matilda. Mary Wollstonecraft Shelley. 1994. reprint ed. lib. bdg. 18.95 (*1-56849-335-5*) Buccaneer Bks.

***Matilda.** 6th ed. Roald Dahl. (J). 1998. pap. 17.95 (*2-07-051784-5*) Distribks Inc.

Matilda: A Study Guide. Duncan Searl. Ed. by J. Friedland & R. Kessler. (Novel-Ties Ser.). (J). (gr. 4-6). 1994. pap. text, student ed. 15.95 (*1-56982-065-1*) Lrn Links.

Matilda: Literature Unit. Jasmine. (Literature Units Ser.). (Illus.). 48p. 1996. pap., wbk. ed. 7.95 (*1-55734-819-7*) Tchr Create Mat.

***Matilda Bone.** Karen Cushman. (Illus.). 176p. (J). (gr. 4-7). 2000. 15.00 (*0-395-88156-0*, Clarion Bks) HM.

Matilda Infantry Tank, 1988-94. Christopher F. Foss. (New Vanguard Ser.). (Illus.). 48p. 1994. pap. 12.95 (*1-85532-457-1*, 9346, Pub. by Ospry) Stackpole.

Matilda the Dream Bear. Nicholas Heller. LC 88-3830. (Illus.). 32p. (J). (ps up). 1989. lib. bdg. 12.88 (*0-688-08239-4*, Grenwillow Bks) HarpC Child Bks.

Matilda the Moocher. Diana Cain Bluthenthal. LC 96-42288. (Illus.). 32p. (J). (ps-2). 1997. 15.95 (*0-531-30003-X*); lib. bdg. 16.99 (*0-531-33003-6*) Orchard Bks Watts.

Matilda's Bloomers: Prairie School Stories. Marjorie Northcutt. Ed. by Sue Williams. LC 93-61048. (Illus.). 112p. (Orig.). 1994. pap. 9.95 (*1-882420-09-8*) Hearth KS.

Matilda's Game. large type ed. Denis Kilcommons. 467p. 1993. 27.99 (*0-7505-0549-4*, Pub. by Mgna Lrg Print) Ulverscroft.

***Matilda's Last Waltz.** Tamara McKinley. 448p. 2000. text 25.95 (*0-312-26202-7*) St Martin.

Matilda's Story: A Biographical Novel. Jacquelyn Hanson. LC 97-73356. (Illus.). 672p. 1997. 24.95 (*0-9637265-3-6*, 9704); pap. 12.95 (*0-9637265-4-4*, 9704) Glenhaven Pr.

***Matilda's Wedding: White Weddings.** 2000. per. 3.50 (*0-373-03601-9*) S&S Trade.

***Matilda's Wedding: White Weddings.** large type ed. 2000. per. 3.50 (*0-373-15847-5*) S&S Trade.

Matin des Magiciens. Jacques Bergier. (FRE.). 640p. 1972. pap. 13.95 (*0-7859-1701-2*, 2070361292) Fr & Eur.

Matin Latin, Vol. I. Karen Craig. (Illus.). 144p. (J). (gr. 3-6). 1998. pap. text 25.00 (*1-885767-46-3*) Canon Pr ID.

Matin Latin, Vol. II. Karen Craig. (Illus.). 144p. (J). (gr. 3-6). 1998. pap. text 30.00 (*1-885767-48-X*) Canon Pr ID.

***Matin Latin 1: Teacher's Edition.** Karen L. Craig. (Mars Hill Textbook Ser.). 144p. 1998. teacher ed., spiral bd. 28.00 (*1-885767-47-1*) Canon Pr ID.

***Matin Latin 2.** Karen L. Craig. (Mars Hill Textbook Ser.). 208p. 1999. teacher ed., spiral bd. 33.00 (*1-885767-49-8*) Canon Pr ID.

Martin Luther King Jr. Marcia Gresko. (Easy Reader Ser.). (Illus.). (J). 1997. pap., teacher ed. 2.49 (*1-57690-267-6*, TCM2267) Tchr Create Mat.

***Matin Nouveau.** 1999. 7.95 (*0-7407-0136-3*) Andrews & McMeel.

Matinaux. Rene Char. (Poesie Ser.). (FRE.). 156p. 1950. 11.95 (*2-07-030066-8*) Schoenhof.

Matinaux, Parole en Archipel. Rene Char. (FRE.). 1969. pap. 10.95 (*0-8288-3821-6*, F93260) Fr & Eur.

Matinee. Robert Steiner. 288p. 1990. 21.95 (*0-932511-13-9*); pap. 10.95 (*0-932511-14-7*) Fiction Coll.

Matinee Idylls: Reflections on the Movies. Richard Schickel. LC 99-21111. 304p. 1999. 26.50 (*1-56663-260-9*, Pub. by I R Dee) Natl Bk Netwk.

***Matinee Idylls: Reflections on the Movies.** Richard Schickel. 320p. 2000. reprint ed. pap. 15.95 (*1-56663-318-4*, Pub. by I R Dee) Natl Bk Netwk.

***Matinees.** Ange Mlinko. LC 98-54199. 128p. 1999. pap. 13.00 (*1-58195-005-5*, Pub. by Zoland Bks) Consort Bk Sales.

Mating. M. Ronald Minge et al. 352p. 1982. pap. 9.95 (*0-940162-01-6*) Red Lion.

Mating. Norman Rush. LC 92-50106. 480p. 1992. pap. 13.00 (*0-679-73709-X*) Vin Bks.

Mating & Marriage. Ed. by Vernon Reynolds & John Kellett. (Biosocial Society Ser.: No. 3). (Illus.). 176p. 1991. 57.00 (*0-19-858406-7*) OUP.

Mating Behavior of Iguana. Gordon H. Rodda. LC 92-2499. (Smithsonian Contributions to Zoology Ser.: No. 534). (Illus.). 44p. reprint ed. pap. 30.00 (*0-7837-3877-3*, 204371900010) Bks Demand.

Mating, Conservation, & Bison. Joel Berger & Carol Cunningham. LC 93-46571. (Methods & Cases in Conservation Science Ser.). 1994. 34.50 (*0-231-08456-0*) Col U Pr.

Mating Cries. Conrad Bishop & Elizabeth Fuller. 70p. 1998. pap. 5.00 (*0-9624511-6-9*) WordWorkers.

Mating Cry of the Dodo. Ed. by G. Giannito. (C). 1988. pap. 30.00 (*0-948466-02-2*, Pub. by Gibraltar Bks) St Mut.

Mating Dance. Eleanor H. Howard & Helen McAvity. 1966. pap. 5.25 (*0-8222-0740-0*) Dramatists Play.

Mating Dance. Bernice L. Webb. LC 96-92926. xi, 52p. 1996. pap. 12.00 (*0-9631384-2-1*) Spider Pr.

Mating for Life. Laura Abbot. LC 95-6888. (Superromance Ser.). 296p. 1995. per. 3.75 (*0-373-70639-1*, 1-70639-9) Harlequin Bks.

Mating Game. Susan Crosby. 1994. per. 2.99 (*0-373-05888-8*, 1-05888-2) Harlequin Bks.

Mating Game. Anita Lawson. 360p. pap. 13.95 (*0-9647410-4-0*) After Words Ink.

Mating Game: What Every Woman Should Know. Lyndon McGill. LC 91-91486. (Illus.). 208p. 1992. pap. 12.95 (*0-9631771-0-9*) Sundial Pr.

Mating in Captivity. Genni Gunn. 72p. 1993. pap. 12.95 (*1-55082-067-2*, Pub. by Quarry Pr) LPC InBook.

Mating, Marriage & the Status of Women. James Corin. LC 72-9633. reprint ed. 39.50 (*0-404-57432-7*) AMS Pr.

***Mating Mind: How the Sexual Choice Shaped the Evolution of Human Nature.** Geoffrey F. Miller. LC 00-22673. 352p. 2000. 27.50 (*0-385-49516-1*) Doubleday.

Mating Reflex. Jim Hall. LC 80-70563. (Poetry Ser.). 55p. 1980. pap. 9.95 (*0-915604-42-6*) Carnegie-Mellon.

Mating Season. P. G. Wodehouse. 22.95 (*0-8488-0677-8*) Amereon Ltd.

Matinicus Isle, Maine, Its Story & Its People, in Two Parts. Charles A. Long. (Illus.). 245p. 1996. reprint ed. lib. bdg. 35.00 (*0-8328-5202-3*) Higginson Bk Co.

Matins, Lauds & Vespers for St. David's Day: The Medieval Office of the Welsh Patron Saint in National Library of Wales MS. 20541 E. Owain T. Edwards. (Illus.). 240p. (C). 1990. 75.00 (*0-85991-293-0*) Boydell & Brewer.

Matisse. Mila Boutan. (Art Activity Packs Ser.). (Illus.). 13p. (J). (ps-5). 1996. pap. 9.95 (*0-8118-1310-X*) Chronicle Bks.

Matisse, 11 vols. Volkmar Essers. (Thunder Bay Artists Ser.). (Illus.). 96p. 1997. pap. text 7.98 (*1-57145-127-7*, Thunder Bay) Advantage Pubs.

Matisse. Volkmar Essers. 1994. pap. 9.99 (*3-8228-9640-3*) Taschen Amer.

Matisse. Volkmar Essers. 1995. pap. 8.99 (*3-8228-9496-6*) Taschen Amer.

Matisse. Volkmar Essers. (SPA.). 1996. pap. 9.99 (*3-8228-0213-1*) Taschen Amer.

Matisse. Jose M. Faerna. Ed. by Teresa S. Waldes. LC 94-36573. (Great Modern Masters Ser.). (Illus.). 64p. 1995. pap. 11.98 (*0-8109-4685-8*, Pub. by Abrams) Time Warner.

Matisse. Laurence Gowing. LC 87-50517. (World of Art Ser.). (Illus.). 216p. 1985. pap. 14.95 (*0-500-20170-6*, Pub. by Thames Hudson) Norton.

Matisse. Laurence Gowing. LC 87-50517. (World of Art Ser.). (Illus.). 216p. 1985. 19.95 (*0-500-18171-3*, Pub. by Thames Hudson) Norton.

Matisse. John Jacobus. (Masters of Art Ser.). (Illus.). 1983. 24.95 (*0-8109-1326-7*, Pub. by Abrams) Time Warner.

Matisse. Antony Mason. (Famous Artists Ser.). 1995. 12.15 (*0-606-08815-6*, Pub. by Turtleback) Demco.

Matisse. Antony Mason & Andrew S. Hughes. (Famous Artists Ser.). (Illus.). 32p. (J). (gr. 5 up). 1995. 11.95 (*0-8120-6534-4*) Barron.

Matisse. Antony Mason et al. (Famous Artists Ser.). (Illus.). 32p. (J). (gr. 5 up). 1995. pap. 6.95 (*0-8120-9426-3*) Barron.

Matisse. Henri Matisse. 1998. 1.00 (*0-486-40394-7*) Dover.

Matisse. Gilles Neret. (Big Ser.). 1997. pap. 19.99 (*3-8228-8276-3*) Taschen Amer.

***Matisse.** Gilles Neret. 1999. 19.99 (*3-8228-6543-5*) Taschen Amer.

Matisse. Taschen Staff. (SPA.). 1997. 9.99 (*3-8228-8010-8*, Pub. by Benedikt Taschen) Bks Nippan.

Matisse. Sarah Wilson. LC 91-50997. (Twentieth Century Masters Ser.). (Illus.). 128p. 1992. 27.50 (*0-8478-1509-9*, Pub. by Rizzoli Intl) St Martin.

Matisse. Nicholas Watkins. (Color Library). (Illus.). 128p. (C). 1993. reprint ed. pap. 14.95 (*0-7148-2709-6*, Pub. by Phaidon Press) Phaidon Pr.

Matisse: A Portrait. Hayden Herrera. (Illus.). 232p. 1995. pap. 16.00 (*0-15-600204-3*) Harcourt.

Matisse: A Portrait of the Man & His Art. Hayden Herrera. (Illus.). 1993. 29.95 (*0-15-158183-5*) Harcourt.

Matisse: A Postcard Book. Ed. by Running Press Staff. (Postcard Bks.). (Illus.). 64p. (Orig.). 1989. pap. text 8.95 (*0-89471-711-1*) Running Pr.

Matisse: A Way of Life in the South of France. Photos by Jean-Bernard Naudin. (Illus.). 192p. 1998. 40.00 (*0-8478-2088-2*, Pub. by Rizzoli Intl) St Martin.

Matisse: Artist Speaks, The. Ed. by Genevieve Morgan. LC 95-25200. 96p. 1996. 16.95 (*0-00-255458-5*) Collins SF.

Matisse: Drawings & Sculpture. Ed. & Intro. by Ernst-Gerhard Guse et al. (Illus.). 224p. 1991. 39.95 (*3-7913-1133-6*, Pub. by Prestel) te Neues.

Matisse: Father & Son. John Russell. LC 98-29571. (Illus.). 464p. 1999. 39.95 (*0-8109-4378-6*, Pub. by Abrams) Time Warner.

Matisse: Fifty Years of His Graphic Art. William S. Lieberman. 150p. 1981. pap. 12.95 (*0-8076-1022-4*) Braziller.

Matisse: His Art & His Public. Alfred H. Barr, Jr. LC 66-26118. (Museum of Modern Art Publications in Reprint). 1967. reprint ed. 36.95 (*0-405-01525-9*) Ayer.

Matisse: Image into Sign. Jack D. Flam. Ed. by Mary A. Steiner. (Illus.). 48p. (Orig.). 1993. pap. text 10.00 (*0-89178-037-8*) St Louis Art Mus.

***Matisse: Jazz.** Henri Matisse. (Pegasus Library). (Illus.). 136p. 2000. 25.00 (*3-7913-2392-X*) Prestel Pub NY.

Matisse: Master of Pure Color-His Life in Paintings. DK Publishing Staff. LC 98-86755. 1999. pap. text 12.95 (*0-7894-4136-5*) DK Pub Inc.

Matisse: Painter of the Essential see Art for Children

Matisse: Selected Works. Anette Robinson. 1999. pap. 12.95 (*2-86656-199-6*) Scala Edit.

Matisse: Spanish. Taschen Staff. (SPA.). 1997. 19.99 (*3-8228-8538-X*, Pub. by Benedikt Taschen) Bks Nippan.

Matisse: The Dance. Jack D. Flam. (Illus.). 88p. 1994. pap. 12.95 (*0-8109-2583-4*, Pub. by Abrams) Time Warner.

Matisse: The Wonder of Color. Xavier Girard. (Discoveries Ser.). (Illus.). 176p. 1994. pap. 12.95 (*0-8109-2820-5*, Pub. by Abrams) Time Warner.

Matisse: 50 Years of His Graphic Art. William S. Lieberman. 152p. 1956. reprint ed. 30.00 (*0-8076-0037-7*, Pub. by Braziller) Norton.

Matisse & Fauvism. Diana Vowels. (Illus.). 64p. 1994. write for info. (*0-9640034-4-9*) World Pubns.

Matisse & Picasso. Yve-Alain Bois. LC 98-44307. (Illus.). 272p. 1999. 50.00 (*2-08-013548-1*, Pub. by Flammarion) Abbeville Pr.

Matisse & Picasso. Yve-Alain Bois & Kimbell Art Museum Staff. LC 98-44307. 1998. write for info. (*0-912804-34-3*) Kimbell Art.

Matisse & Teriade: Collaborative Works by the Artist & Art Publisher. Casimiro Di Crescenzo. Ed. by Charles A. Riley, 2nd. Tr. by Christian Fournier from ITA. (FRE.). 141p. 1997. 35.00 (*1-887054-02-2*) Yoshii Gallery.

Matisse Cut-Outs. Gilles Neret. (Illus.). 95p. 1997. pap. 9.99 (*3-8228-8658-0*) Taschen Amer.

Matisse Cut-Outs Postcard Book. Henri Matisse. (Illus.). 1995. pap. 5.99 (*3-8228-9443-5*) Benedikt Taschen.

Matisse for Kids. Margaret E. Hyde. LC 95-80610. (Great Art for Kids Ser.). (Illus.). 12p. (J). (ps). 1996. 12.95 (*1-888108-05-3*) Budding Artists.

Matisse from A to Z. Marie Sellier. Tr. by Claudia Z. Bedrick. LC 95-10869. (Artists from A to Z Ser.). (Illus.). 60p. (YA). (gr. 4 up). 1995. lib. bdg. 14.95 (*0-87226-475-0*, 64750B, P Bedrick Books) NTC Contemp Pub Co.

Matisse in Morocco: Paintings & Drawings, 1912-1913. Jack Cowart et al. LC 89-13676. (Illus.). 300p. 1990. pap. 11.99 (*0-89468-140-0*) Natl Gallery Art.

Matisse in Nice. Xavier Girard. (Illus.). 80p. 1996. text 18.95 (*0-7893-0061-3*) St Martin.

Matisse Jazz. 1995. pap. 8.99 (*3-8228-9354-4*) Taschen Amer.

***Matisse, la Dance.** Federico Zeri. (One Hundred Paintings Ser.). (Illus.). 48p. 2000. 14.95 (*1-55321-010-7*, Pub. by NDE Pub) IPG Chicago.

Matisse Line Drawings & Prints. Henri Matisse. (Fine Art Ser.). (Illus.). 48p. 1980. pap. 3.95 (*0-486-23877-6*) Dover.

Matisse, 1904-1917. (Illus.). 57p. (C). 1997. reprint ed. pap. text 15.00 (*0-7881-5159-2*) DIANE Pub.

Matisse on Art. Henri Matisse. Ed. & Intro. by Jack D. Flam. (Documents of Twentieth-Century Art Ser.). (Illus.). 300p. 1995. pap. 18.95 (*0-520-20032-2*, Pub. by U CA Pr) Cal Prin Full Svc.

Matisse on Art. rev. ed. Henri Matisse. Ed. & Intro. by Jack D. Flam. (Documents of Twentieth-Century Art Ser.). (Illus.). 300p. 1995. 35.00 (*0-520-20037-3*, Pub. by U CA Pr) Cal Prin Full Svc.

Matisse Stories. A. S. Byatt. 1996. pap. 10.00 (*0-679-76223-X*) Random.

Matisse Stories. A. S. Byatt. Date not set. 1.99 (*0-517-19704-9*) Random Hse Value.

Matisse Stories. A. S. Byatt. 1996. pap. 10.00 (*0-614-99274-5*) Vin Bks.

Matisse's Notes of a Painter: Criticism, Theory, & Context, 1891-1908. Roger Benjamin. LC 86-25056. (Studies in the Fine Arts: Criticism: No. 21). (Illus.). 367p. reprint ed. pap. 113.80 (*0-8357-1743-7*, 207061500005) Bks Demand.

Matkailualan Ammattisanasto. Honelin. (ENG & FIN.). 130p. 1987. pap. 95.00 (*0-8288-7813-7*) Fr & Eur.

Matlab & Simulink for Control Systems. Robert H. Bishop. LC 96-46978. 250p. (C). 1996. pap. text 19.80 (*2-01-049846-4*) Addison-Wesley.

Matlab Companion Prob & Stats F/Eng & The Sci 5th ed. Devore. 2000. pap. text 14.00 (*0-534-37474-3*) Thomson Learn.

***Matlab 5.0 for Engineers.** 2nd ed. Adrian Biran. LC 98-44898. 672p. (C). 1999. pap. 56.00 (*0-201-36043-8*) Addison-Wesley.

MATLAB 5.0 for Engineers. 2nd ed. Joe King. 128p. (C). 1997. 17.00 (*0-201-35094-7*, Prentice Hall) P-H.

MATLAB for Engineering Applications. William J. Palm. LC 98-40456. 552p. 1998. pap. 40.94 (*0-07-047330-7*) McGraw.

***MATLAB Guide.** Desmond J. Higham & Nicholas J. Higham. (Miscellaneous Bks.: Vol. 75). 282p. 2000. 42.00 (*0-89871-469-9*) Soc Indus-Appl Math.

Matlab Handbook. Darren Redfern. LC 96-10769. 520p. 1997. pap. 29.95 (*0-387-94200-9*) Spr-Verlag.

***MATLAB in Mechanical Engineering.** Edward B. Magrab. 512p. 2000. pap. 81.00 (*0-13-011335-2*) P-H.

Matlab Manual: Computer Laboratory Excercises. 5th ed. Grossma. (C). 1993. pap. text, lab manual ed. 24.00 (*0-03-094896-7*) Harcourt Coll Pubs.

MATLAB Primer. 4th ed. Kermitt Sigmon. LC 94-28934. 112p. 1994. lib. bdg. 15.95 (*0-8493-9440-6*) CRC Pr.

MATLAB Primer. 5th ed. Kermit N. Sigmon et al. LC 97-44381. 144p. 1997. per. 15.95 (*0-8493-1305-8*, 1305) CRC Pr.

MATLAB Supplement to Fuzzy & Neural Approaches in Engineering. J. Wesley Hines & Lefteri H. Tsoukalas. LC 97-154014. (Adaptive & Learning Systems for Signal Processing, Communications & Control Ser.). (Illus.). 210p. 1997. pap. write for info. incl. disk (*0-471-19247-3*) Wiley.

MATLAB Tools for Control Systems & Design for MS-DOS Personal Computers. 2nd ed. Duane C. Hanselman & Benjamin C. Kuo. LC 94-40850. (MATLAB Curriculum Ser.). (C). 1995. text 54.00 P-H.

***Matlab Version 5.3.** The\Mathworks. (C). 1999. pap. text, student ed. 100.00 incl. audio compact disk (*0-13-022598-3*) P-H.

Matlab 5 Handbook. 2nd ed. Eva Dart-Enander. 32p. (C). 1999. pap. text 51.95 (*0-201-39845-1*) Addison-Wesley.

Matlab 5.0 Programming for Engineers. Stephen J. Chapman. LC 99-54392. (Electrical Engineering Ser.). 444p. (C). 1999. 61.95 (*0-534-95151-1*) PWS Pubs.

Matlack: Colonel Timothy Matlack, Patriot & Soldier, Haddonfield, NJ. A. M. Stackhouse. (Illus.). 105p. 1994. reprint ed. pap. 19.00 (*0-8328-4225-7*); reprint ed. lib. bdg. 29.00 (*0-8328-4224-9*) Higginson Bk Co.

Matlatzincas: Epoca Prehispanica y Epoca Colonial Hasta 1650. Noemi Quezada. (SPA., Illus.). 143p. 1996. pap. 18.50 (*968-36-4665-4*, UN057, Pub. by Instit de Invest) UPLAAP.

Matlock Paper. Robert Ludlum. 384p. 1989. mass mkt. 7.99 (*0-553-27960-2*) Bantam.

Matlock's System. large type ed. Reginald Hill. (Ulverscroft Large Print Ser.). 400p. 1997. 27.99 (*0-7089-3792-6*) Ulverscroft.

***Matpro, a Library of Materials Properties for Light-Water- Reactor Accident Analysis: SCDAP/RELAP5/MOD 3.2 Code Manual.** R. Y. Lee. 736p. 1998. per. 61.00 (*0-16-062937-3*) USGPO.

Matralaksanam. Wayne Howard. (C). 1988. 26.00 (*81-208-0585-2*, Pub. by Motilal Bnarsidass) S Asia.

Matrceta's Hymn to the Buddha. Tr. by S. Dhammika. 48p. 1989. 3.00 (*955-24-0050-3*, Pub. by Buddhist Pub Soc) Vipassana Res Pubns.

Matres Lectionis in Ancient Hebrew Epigraphs. Ziony Zevit. LC 80-19652. (American Schools of Oriental Research Monographs: Vol. 2). x, 43p. (C). 1980. text 30.00 (*0-89757-402-8*, Pub. by Sheffield Acad) CUP Services.

Matriarch: Selected Poems (1968-1992) Glenna Luschei. LC 92-80450. 96p. (Orig.). 1992. pap. 10.95 (*0-912292-98-9*) Smith.

Matriarch of Conspiracy: Ruth Von Kleist, 1867-1945. 2nd ed. Jane Pejsa. LC 90-92033. (Illus.). 432p. 1998. pap. 22.95 (*0-9612776-9-6*) Kenwood Pub.

Matriarchs: Great Mares of the 20th Century. Edward L. Bowen. 1999. 35.00 (*1-58150-022-X*, Pub. by Blood-Horse) IPG Chicago.

***Matriarchs: Great Mares of the 20th Century.** limited ed. Edward L. Bowen. (Illus.). 224p. 1999. 195.00 (*1-58150-036-X*) Blood-Horse.

***Matriarchs of England's Cooperative Movement: Female Leadership & Gender Politics Within the English Cooperative Movement, 56.** Barbara J. Blaszak. LC 99-4303. (Contributions in Labor Studies: No. 56). 224p. 1999. 59.95 (*0-313-30995-7*, Greenwood Pr) Greenwood.

Matriarch's Power: A Cross Cultural Literary Study. Beth A. Bassein. LC 93-17015. (American University Studies: Feminist Studies: Ser. XXVII, Vol. 4). XII, 168p. (C). 1993. text 39.95 (*0-8204-2205-3*) P Lang Pubng.

Matriarchy: Freedom in Bondage. Malcolm McKesson. LC 96-77595. (Illus.). 208p. 1997. pap. 14.95 (*0-9638129-7-1*, 620221) Heck Editions.

Matriarchy: Freedom in Bondage. deluxe limited ed. Malcolm McKesson. LC 96-77595. (Illus.). 208p. 1996. 34.95 (*0-9638129-8-X*, 620222) Heck Editions.

Matriarchy in the Malay Peninsula & Neighbouring Countries. George A. De Moubray. LC 77-87025. 304p. reprint ed. 54.50 (*0-404-16810-8*) AMS Pr.

Matrice de Comptabilite Sociale pour Madagascar: Methodologie et Resultats. Paul A. Dorosh et al. (Working Papers). (C). 1991. pap. text 7.00 (*1-56401-200-X*) Cornell Food.

Matricentric Narratives: Recent British Women's Fiction in a Postmodern Mode. Daniel Dervin. LC 97-14786. (Women's Studies: Vol. 16). 290p. 1997. text 89.95 (*0-7734-8644-5*) E Mellen.

Matrices: Methods & Applications. Stephen Barnett. (Oxford Applied Mathematics & Computing Science Ser.). (Illus.). 466p. 1990. pap. text 45.00 (*0-19-859680-4*) OUP.

Matrices & Graphs: Stability Problems in Mathematical Ecology. Dmitrii O. Logofet. 320p. 1993. lib. bdg. 89.95 (*0-8493-4246-5*, QH541) CRC Pr.

Matrices & Graphs: Theory & Applications to Economics. LC 97-140815. 250p. 1996. 36.00 (*981-02-3038-9*) World Scientific Pub.

Matrices & Indefinite Scalar Products. I. Gohberg et al. (Operator Theory Ser.: Vol. 8). 302p. (C). 1983. text 70.95 (*3-7643-1527-X*) Birkhauser.

Matrices & Linear Algebra. Hans Schneider. 432p. 1989. pap. 10.95 (*0-486-66014-1*) Dover.

Matrices & Linear Programming with Business Applications. Toshinori Munakata. LC 78-54198. 1979. teacher ed. 6.00 (*0-8162-6167-9*); text 36.95 (*0-8162-6166-0*) Holden-Day.

Matrices & Linear Transformations. Charles G. Cullen. 336p. 1990. pap. 9.95 (*0-486-66328-0*) Dover.

Matrices & Matlab: A Tutorial. Marvin Marcus. 736p. (C). 1992. text 53.00 (*0-13-562901-2*) P-H.

***Matrices & Matroids for Systems Analysis.** Kazuo Murota. LC 99-52231. (Algorithms & Combinatorics Ser.: Vol. 20). (Illus.). xii, 483p. 2000. 112.00 (*3-540-66024-0*) Spr-Verlag.

***Matrices & Quadratic Forms.** John Bowers. (Modular Mathematics Series). 280p. 2000. pap. text 19.95 (*0-340-69138-7*) E A.

Matrices & Simplex Algorithms. A. R. Heesterman. 1982. lib. bdg. 272.50 (*90-277-1514-9*) Kluwer Academic.

Matrices & Systems Linear Equations. (C). 1994. 9.60 (*0-8087-7987-7*) Pearson Custom.

Matrices & Tensors in Physics. 3rd ed. A. W. Joshi. LC 94-21798. 342p. 1995. 102.00 (*0-470-23438-5*) Wiley.

Matrices & Their Roots - A Textbook of Matrix Algebra. A. R. Heesterman. 468p. 1990. text 97.00 incl. disk (*981-02-0395-0*); pap. text 55.00 incl. disk (*981-02-0396-9*) World Scientific Pub.

Matrices & Transformations. Anthony J. Pettofrezzo. 133p. 1978. reprint ed. pap. text 6.95 (*0-486-63634-8*) Dover.

Matrices & Vector Spaces. William C. Brown. (Pure & Applied Mathematics Ser.: Vol. 145). (Illus.). 328p. 1991. text 69.75 (*0-8247-8419-7*) Dekker.

Matrices, Etymons, Racines. E. Peters. 1998. 43.95 (*90-6831-917-5*, Pub. by Peeters Pub) Bks Intl VA.

Matrices for Statistics. M. J. Healy. (Illus.). 100p. 1991. reprint ed. pap. text 35.00 (*0-19-852248-7*) OUP.

***Matrices for Statistics.** 2nd ed. Michael Healy. (Illus.). 160p. 2000. text 60.00 (*0-19-850703-8*) OUP.

***Matrices For Statistics.** 2nd ed. Michael Healy. (Illus.). 160p. 2000. pap. text 29.95 (*0-19-850702-X*) OUP.

***Matrices in Combinatorics & Graph Theory.** Bolian Liu & Hong-Jian Lai. LC 00-42808. (Network Theory & Applications Ser.). 2000. write for info. (*0-7923-6469-4*) Kluwer Academic.

Matrices in Control Theory. rev. ed. Stephen Barnett. LC 82-21321. 206p. (C). 1984. lib. bdg. 24.50 (*0-89874-590-X*) Krieger.

***Matrices of Genre: Authors, Canons & Society.** Mary Depew. 352p. 2000. 50.00 (*0-674-00338-1*) HUP.

Matrices of Sign-Solvable Linear Systems. Richard A. Brualdi & Brian L. Shader. (Tracts in Mathematics Ser.: No. 116). (Illus.). 312p. (C). 1995. text 54.95 (*0-521-48296-8*) Cambridge U Pr.

Matrices over Commutative Rings. William C. Brown. LC 92-29098. (Pure & Applied Mathematics Ser.: Vol. 169). (Illus.). 296p. 1992. text 155.00 (*0-8247-8755-2*) Dekker.

Matricide: The Tragedy on Prospect Hill. Vincent L. Lombardi. 345p. 1998. pap. 20.94 (*0-07-154153-5*) McGraw.

***Matricide: The Tragedy on Prospect Hill.** Vincent L. Lombardi. 287p. 2000. pap. 15.95 (*1-892590-31-X*, Fifth Way Pr) Out Your Bk.

Matricide at St. Martha's. large type ed. Ruth D. Edwards. LC 94-45641. 320p. 1995. pap. 20.95 (*0-7862-0400-1*) Thorndike Pr.

Matricula de Tributos: or Codice de Moctezuma. fac. ed. Comment by J. De Durand-Forest & F. Berdan. (Codices Selecti C Ser.: Vol. LXVIII). 1980. 159.00 (*3-201-01130-4*, Pub. by Akademische Druck-und) Balogh.

Matrifocal Family: Power, Pluralism, & Politics. Raymond T. Smith. LC 95-13171. 250p. (C). 1995. pap. 20.99 (*0-415-91215-6*) Routledge.

Matrifocal Family: Power, Pluralism, & Politics. Raymond T. Smith. LC 95-13171. 250p. (C). (gr. 13). 1995. 75.00 (*0-415-91214-8*) Routledge.

Matrikel der Universitat Wurzburg, 1582-1830, 2 vols., Pt. 1. Ed. by Sebastian Merkle. (Alumni of German Universities Ser.). 1990. reprint ed. 130.00 (*0-8115-3811-7*) Periodicals Srv.

Matrilineal Complex. fac. ed. Robert H. Louie. (University of California Publications in American Archaeology & Ethnology: Vol. 16: 2). 16p. (C). 1919. reprint ed. pap. text 2.19 (*1-55567-222-1*) Coyote Press.

Matrilineal Kinship & the Question of Its Priority. Edwin S. Hartland. LC 18-15715. (American Anthropological Association Memoirs Ser.: No. 17). 1917. 25.00 (*0-527-00516-9*) Periodicals Srv.

Matrilineal Peoples of Eastern Tanzania (Zaramo, Luguru, Kaguru, Ngulu, Etc.) Thomas O. Beidelman. LC 67-112486. (Ethnographic Survey of Africa - East Central Africa Ser.: Pt. 16). (Illus.). 96p. reprint ed. pap. 30.00 (*0-8357-3212-6*, 205708300010) Bks Demand.

Matriliny & Modernity: Sexual Politics & Social Change in Rural Malaysia. Maila Stivens. 336p. 1996. pap. 29.95 (*1-86373-892-4*, Pub. by Allen & Unwin Pty) Paul & Co Pubs.

Matriliny to Patriliny: A Study of the Rabha Society. Manis K. Raha. (C). 1989. 49.00 (*81-212-0244-2*, Pub. by Gian Publng Hse) S Asia.

***Matriliny Transformed: Family, Law & Ideology in 20th Century Travancore.** Ed. by K. Saradamoni. LC 99-36548. 184p. 1999. 39.95 (*0-7619-9342-8*) Sage.

Matrimonial Advocacy & Litigation. 2nd ed. Richard Greenslade. 220p. 1993. pap. text 60.00 (*0-406-02090-6*, UK, MICHIE) LEXIS Pub.

Matrimonial & Commercial Injunctions. Richard Matthews & Mark Hoyle. 130p. 1994. 175.00 (*0-85459-823-5*, Pub. by Tolley Pubng) St Mut.

Matrimonial & Family Law, MFL: Covering Domestic Relations, General Obligations, Family Court, with Practice Commentaries. Joseph L. Marino. Vol. 9A: 10. write for info. (*0-318-58376-3*) West Pub.

Matrimonial & Family Law Update. 382p. 1995. pap. 30.00 (*0-614-26683-1*, 1058); pap. 175.00 incl. VHS (*0-614-26684-X*, 30581); pap. 92.00 incl. audio (*0-614-26685-8*, 20581) NYS Bar.

Matrimonial Appellate Practice. 1997. 99.00 incl. audio PA Bar Inst.

Matrimonial Causes & Proceedings. 4th ed. A. K. Biggs & J. Strong. 265p. (C). 1992. 150.00 (*1-85190-164-7*, Pub. by Tolley Pubng) St Mut.

Matrimonial Education in Islam. Ahmad Sakr. 92p. 1996. pap. 7.50 (*0-614-21516-1*, 761) Kazi Pubns.

Matrimonial Finance & Taxation. 5th ed. Joseph Jackson et al. 584p. 1992. 150.00 (*0-406-11381-5*, UK, MICHIE) LEXIS Pub.

Matrimonial Proceedings. A. K. Biggs. 1980. 100.00 (*0-7855-7332-1*, Pub. by Fourmat Pub) St Mut.

Matrimonial Proceedings. A. K. Biggs. 174p. 1984. 90.00 (*0-906840-78-3*, Pub. by Fourmat Pub) St Mut.

Matrimonial Proceedings. A. K. Biggs. 240p. (C). 1989. 110.00 (*1-85190-064-0*, Pub. by Fourmat Pub) St Mut.

Matrimonial Property Law in India. B. Sivaramayya. LC 99-932097. (Law in India Ser.). 148p. 1999. text 17.95 (*0-19-564447-6*) OUP.

Matrimonial Trials of Henry VIII. Henry A. Kelly. LC 75-7483. 347p. reprint ed. pap. 107.60 (*0-608-09160-X*, AU0049900001) Bks Demand.

Matrimonie. Herve Bazin. (FRE.). 1984. pap. 12.95 (*0-7859-3062-0*) Fr & Eur.

Matrimonio a Ciegas: Instant Husband. Judith McWilliams. 1997. per. 3.50 (*0-373-35178-X*, 1-35178-2) Harlequin Bks.

Matrimonio a Prueba de Infidelidad. J. Allan Petersen. (Serie Guia de Bolsillo - Pocket Guides Ser.).Tr. of High Fidelity Marriage. (SPA.). 78p. 1987. pap. 2.79 (*0-8423-6513-3*, 498043) Editorial Unilit.

Matrimonio a Prueba de Infidelidad. Kay Thorpe. (Bianca Ser.: No. 169). (SPA.). 1999. per. 3.50 (*0-373-33519-9*) Harlequin Bks.

Matrimonio Al Maximo: Como Complementarse y No Fastidiarse. Victor Ricardo & Gloria Ricardo. 36p. 1993. pap. 1.15 (*1-885630-06-9*) HLM Producciones.

Matrimonio Bendecido por Dios. Ricardo M. Pugliese. (Serie Guia de Bolsillo - Pocket Guides Ser.).Tr. of Marriage Blessed by God. (SPA.). 1990. pap. 2.79 (*1-56063-011-6*, 498053) Editorial Unilit.

Matrimonio, Cosas Que las Mujeres Preguntan. Gloria Gaither et al.Tr. of Marriage: Questions Women Ask. (SPA.). 170p. 1995. 8.99 (*0-88113-235-7*, B026-2357) Caribe Betania.

Matrimonio Cristocentrico. N. Anderson & Charles Mylander.Tr. of Christ Centered Marriage. 12.99 (*0-7899-0287-7*, 497505) Editorial Unilit.

***Matrimonio de Amor (Marriage of Love)** Kate Walker. (Bianca Ser.). (SPA.). 2000. mass mkt. 3.50 (*0-373-33580-6*, 1-33580-1) Harlequin Bks.

Matrimonio de Conveniencia: The Rancher & the Redhead. Suzannah Davis. (Deseo Ser.). (SPA.). 1996. per. 3.50 (*0-373-35163-1*, 1-35163-4) Harlequin Bks.

***Matrimonio de Papel.** Kathryn Ross.Tr. of Marriage on Paper. (ENG & SPA.). 2000. per. 3.50 (*0-373-33541-5*) Harlequin Bks.

Matrimonio, Divorcio y Nuevo Matrimonio. Theodore H. Epp. Orig. Title: Marriage, Divorce & Remarriage. (SPA.). 96p. 1989. mass mkt. 3.99 (*0-8254-1208-0*, Edit Portavoz) Kregel.

***Matrimonio en Perspectiva: Incluye la Misa de la Boda.** (SPA.). 88p. 1998. pap. 4.95 (*0-7648-0216-X*, Libros Liguori) Liguori Pubns.

Matrimonio en Toda Su Excelencia. James C. Dobson. (Serie Enriquezca a la Familia - Enriching the Family Ser.).Tr. of Marriage at Its Best. (SPA.). 229p. 1995. 1.99 (*0-7899-0056-4*, 498203) Editorial Unilit.

Matrimonio es una Promesa de Amor. Ed. by Susan Polis Schutz. LC 95-37574.Tr. of Marriage Is a Promise of Love. (ENG & SPA.). 64p. 1995. pap. 7.95 (*0-88396-415-5*) Blue Mtn Art.

Matrimonio Feliz (A Happy Marriage), No. 133. Sharon Kendrick. (Harlequin Bianca Ser.). (SPA.). 1998. mass mkt. 3.50 (*0-373-33483-4*, 1-33483-8) Harlequin Bks.

Matrimonio Intimidad Romance. Donald C. Hocking. (Serie Actualidades - Actualities Ser.).Tr. of Intimate Marriage. (SPA.). 51p. 1986. pap. 2.29 (*1-56063-165-1*, 498122) Editorial Unilit.

Matrimonio por Amor - Marriage by Love. Sharon Kendrick. (SPA.). 1997. per. 3.50 (*0-373-33425-7*, 1-33425-9) Harlequin Bks.

Matrimonio Prohibido (Forbidden Marriage) Margaret Mayo. (Bianca Ser.). (SPA.). 1999. per. 3.50 (*0-373-33496-6*, 1-33496-0) Harlequin Bks.

***Matrimonio Roto.** Lee Wilkinson. (Bianca Ser.: Bk. 206).Tr. of Broken Marriage. (SPA.). 156p. 2000. per. 3.50 (*0-373-33556-3*, 1-33556-1) Harlequin Bks.

Matrimonio Triunfante. N. C. Warren.Tr. of Triumphant Marriage. 8.99 (*0-7899-0199-4*, 497457) Editorial Unilit.

Matrimonio y la Familia en la Vida Cristiana: Marriage & the Family in the Christian Life. Guillermo Goff. (SPA.). 240p. 1985. pap. 12.99 (*0-311-46097-6*) Casa Bautista.

Matrimono y Familia Cristiana. P. Pedro Rodriguez. 116p. 1984. pap. 4.95 (*0-915388-20-0*, 171) ACTA Pubns.

***Matrimonsio por un Ano: Instant Mother.** Emma Richmond. (Bianca Ser.: No. 152).Tr. of Marriage for a Year. (SPA.). 1999. per. 3.50 (*0-373-33502-4*, 1-33502-5) Harlequin Bks.

Matrimony. Beverly Cohn & Jack Nadel. (Nit-Wits Ser.). 80p. (Orig.). 1997. pap. 4.95 (*0-922658-08-0*) MMS Pub.

Matrimony in Christ, the New Rite. M.A.C.C. Team Staff. (SPA.). 20p. 1970. write for info. (*0-614-04880-X*) Mex Am Cult.

Matrix. Spencer Lamm. pap. 24.95 (*1-55704-432-5*, Pub. by Newmarket) Norton.

***Matrix.** Robert Perry. (Doctor Who Ser.). (Illus.). 1998. mass mkt. 5.95 (*0-563-40596-1*) BBC Bks.

***Matrix, Vol. 10.** Michael Muevihill. (Shadowrun Ser.). 2000. pap. 22.00 (*1-55560-401-3*) FASA Corp.

Matrix: Computer Networks & Conferencing Systems Worldwide. John S. Quarterman. (Illus.). 719p. 1989. pap. 64.95 (*1-55558-033-5*, EY C176E-DP, Digital DEC) Buttrwrth-Heinemann.

Matrix: Computer Networks & Conferencing Systems Worldwide. John Quaterman. 400p. 1999. pap. 39.95 (*1-55558-137-4*, Digital DEC) Buttrwrth-Heinemann.

Matrix Vol. 23: Anthology of the Red Herring Poets. Ed. by L. D. Smith. 88p. 1998. pap. 6.00 (*0-932884-79-2*) Red Herring.

Matrix Algebra. David J. Winter. (Illus.). 560p. (C). 1991. teacher ed. write for info. (*0-318-69530-8*) Macmillan.

Matrix Algebra: An Introduction. Krishnan Namboodiri. (Quantitative Applications in the Social Sciences Ser.: Vol. 38). 96p. (Orig.). (C). 1984. pap. text 10.95 (*0-8039-2052-0*) Sage.

Matrix Algebra & Its Applications to Statistics & Econometrics. C. R. Rao & M. B. Rao. LC 98-5596. 600p. 1998. 86.00 (*981-02-3268-3*) World Scientific Pub.

Matrix Algebra as a Tool. Ali S. Hadi. 212p. (C). 1995. pap. 37.95 (*0-534-23712-6*) Wadsworth Pub.

Matrix Algebra from a Statistician's Perspective. David A. Harville. LC 97-9854. 640p. 1997. text. write for info. (*0-387-94978-X*) Spr-Verlag.

Matrix Algebra Useful for Statistics. Shayle R. Searle. LC 82-4862. (Probability & Mathematical Statistics Ser.). 464p. 1982. 99.95 (*0-471-86681-4*) Wiley.

Matrix Algebra Using MINImal MATlab. Joel W. Robbin. LC 93-39372. (Illus.). 560p. (C). 1994. text 68.00 incl. disk (*1-56881-024-5*) AK Peters.

Matrix Algorithms: Basic Decompositions. G. W. Stewart. LC 98-22445. (Miscellaneous Titles in Applied Mathematics Ser.: Vol. 60). (Illus.). xix, 458p. 1998. pap. 32.00 (*0-89871-414-1*, BKOT0060) Soc Indus-Appl Math.

Matrix Analyis for Statistics. James R. Schott. LC 96-12133. (Wiley Series in Probability & Statistics). 426p. 1996. 79.95 (*0-471-15409-1*) Wiley.

***Matrix Analysis.** Cowen. 1999. pap. text. write for info. (*0-7167-3206-8*) W H Freeman.

Matrix Analysis. Roger A. Horn & Charles R. Johnson. 576p. 1985. text 90.00 (*0-521-30586-1*) Cambridge U Pr.

Matrix Analysis. Roger A. Horn & Charles R. Johnson. (Illus.). 575p. (C). 1990. pap. text 32.95 (*0-521-38632-2*) Cambridge U Pr.

Matrix Analysis, Vol. 169. Rajendra Bhatia. LC 96-32217. (Graduate Texts in Mathematics Ser.). 347p. 1996. 49.95 (*0-387-94846-5*) Spr-Verlag.

***Matrix Analysis & Applied Linear Algebra.** Carl Meyer. (Miscellaneous Titles in Applied Mathematics Ser.: No. 71). (Illus.). 695p. 2000. 75.00 incl. audio compact disk (*0-89871-454-0*, OT0071) Soc Indus-Appl Math.

Matrix Analysis of Circuits Using Matlab. James G. Gottling. LC 95-193460. 144p. 1994. pap., lab manual ed. 22.60 (*0-13-127044-3*) P-H.

Matrix Analysis of Electrical Machinery. 2nd ed. Norman N. Hancock. LC 74-3286. 1974. 155.00 (*0-08-017898-7*, Pub. by Pergamon Repr) Franklin.

***Matrix Analysis of Structures.** Robert E. Sennett. 228p. 2000. pap. 29.95 (*1-57766-143-5*) Waveland Pr.

Matrix-Analytic Methods in Stochastic Models. Ed. by Srinivas R. Chakravarthy & Attahiru S. Alfa. LC 96-31577. (Lecture Notes in Pure & Applied Mathematics Ser.: Vol. 183). (Illus.). 398p. 1996. pap. text 165.00 (*0-8247-9766-3*) Dekker.

Matrix & Line: Derrida & the Possibilities of Postmodern Social Theory. Bill Martin, Jr. LC 91-20980. (SUNY Series in Radical Social & Political Theory). 255p. (C). 1992. text 59.50 (*0-7914-1049-8*); pap. text 19.95 (*0-7914-1050-1*) State U NY Pr.

Matrix & Matrix Regulation: Basis for a Holistic Theory in Medicine. Alfred Pischinger. Ed. by Hartmut Heine. Tr. by Norman Mac Lean from GER. (Illus.). 221p. (C). 1991. text 39.95 (*2-8043-4000-7*, Pub. by Edits Haug Intl) Medicina Bio.

Matrix & Operator Valued Functions: The Vladimir Petrovich Potapov Memorial Volume, 72. I. Gohberg & Lev A. Sakhnovich. (Advances & Applications Ser.). 240p. 1994. 86.00 (*0-8176-5091-1*) Birkhauser.

Matrix & Space - Phasor Theory of Electrical Machines. G. J. Retter. 412p. (C). 1987. 335.00 (*0-569-09003-2*, Pub. by Collets) St Mut.

Matrix Calculus & Kronecker Product with Applications & C++ Programs. W. H. Steeb & Tan K. Shi. LC 97-26420. 250p. 1997. 38.00 (*981-02-3241-1*) World Scientific Pub.

Matrix Computations. 3rd ed. Gene H. Golub & Charles F. Van Loan. LC 96-14291. 664p. (C). 1996. text 65.00 (*0-8018-5413-X*); pap. text 29.95 (*0-8018-5414-8*) Johns Hopkins.

Matrix Computations on Systolic-Type Arrays. Jaime H. Moreno & Tomas Lang. LC 92-9868. (Kluwer International Series in Engineering & Computer Science: No. SECS 174). 320p. (C). 1992. text 139.50 (*0-7923-9237-X*) Kluwer Academic.

Matrix-Computer Methods in Engineering. Louis A. Pipes & Shahen A. Hovanessian. LC 77-23111. 346p. 1978. reprint ed. 34.50 (*0-88275-591-9*) Krieger.

Matrix Derivatives. Gerald S. Rogers. LC 80-24248. (Lecture Notes in Statistics Ser.). 221p. reprint ed. pap. 68.60 (*0-7837-3548-0*, 204338500009) Bks Demand.

***Matrix Diagonal Stability in Systems & Computation.** Eugenius Kaszkurewicz & Amit Bhaya. LC 99-23774. 272p. 1999. 69.95 (*0-8176-4088-6*, Pub. by Birkhauser) Spr-Verlag.

***Matrix Differential Calculus with Applications in Statistics & Econometrics.** 2nd ed. J. R. Magnus & H. Neudecker. LC QA188.M345 1999. 422p. 1999. pap. 64.95 (*0-471-98633-X*) Wiley.

Matrix Eigensystem Routines-Eispack Guide. B. T. Smith et al. (Lecture Notes in Computer Science Ser.: Vol. 6). 1990. 58.95 (*0-387-07546-1*) Spr-Verlag.

Matrix Eigensystem Routines-Eispack Guide Extension. B. S. Garbow. (Lecture Notes in Computer Science Ser.: Vol. 51). 1990. 34.00 (*0-387-08254-9*) Spr-Verlag.

Matrix 18: Anthology of Red Herring Poets. 18th ed. Ed. by Ruth S. Walker. 56p. 1993. pap. 5.00 (*0-932884-75-X*) Red Herring.

Matrix 11: Anthology of Red Herring Poets. 11th ed. Ed. by John W. Edwards. 31p. 1986. pap. 3.95 (*0-932884-41-5*) Red Herring.

Matrix 15: Anthology of Red Herring Poets. 15th ed. Ed. by Carmen M. Pursifull & Ruth S. Walker. 156p. 1990. pap. 7.95 (*0-932884-45-8*) Red Herring.

Matrix 14: Anthology of Red Herring Poets. 14th ed. Ed. by Kenneth E. Gale & Ruth S. Walker. 103p. 1989. pap. 4.95 (*0-932884-44-X*) Red Herring.

Matrix Games: Matrix Games. Sivasailam Thiagarajan. 48p. (Orig.). 1995. pap. text 25.00 (*0-87425-264-4*) HRD Press.

Matrix-Geometric Solutions in Stochastic Models: An Algorithmic Approach. Marcel F. Neuts. LC 80-8872. (Johns Hopkins Series in the Mathematical Sciences: No. 2). 348p. reprint ed. pap. 107.90 (*0-7837-5378-0*, 204514200005) Bks Demand.

Matrix-Geometric Solutions in Stochastic Models: An Algorithmic Approach. unabridged ed. Marcel F. Neuts. 332p. 1995. pap. text 9.95 (*0-486-68342-7*) Dover.

Matrix Groups. Dimitri A. Suprunenko. LC 75-45115. (Translations of Mathematical Monographs: Vol. 45). 252p. 1976. text 77.00 (*0-8218-1595-4*, MMONO/45) Am Math.

Matrix Groups. 2nd ed. M. L. Curtis. (Universitext Ser.). (Illus.). xiii, 210p. 1987. 42.95 (*0-387-96074-0*) Spr-Verlag.

Matrix Heparan Sulphate Proteoglycan: Structure, Assembly, & Core Protein Binding Interactions. A. Heremans. No. 41. 120p. (Orig.). 1991. pap. 32.50 (*90-6186-443-7*, Pub. by Leuven Univ) Coronet Bks.

Matrix Isolation Spectroscopy. Ed. by Austin Barnes et al. x, 606p. 1981. text 226.00 (*90-277-1328-6*) Kluwer Academic.

Matrix-Isolation Techniques: A Practical Approach. Ian R. Dunkin. (The Practical Approach Ser.). (Illus.). 252p. 1998. text 105.00 (*0-19-855863-5*) OUP.

***Matrix Iterative Analysis.** 2nd rev. expanded ed. Richard S. Varga. LC 99-50196. (Computational Mathematics Ser.: Vol. 27). vi, 358p. 2000. 89.95 (*3-540-66321-5*) Spr-Verlag.

Matrix Logic & Mind. A. Stern. 290p. 1992. 106.25 (*0-444-88798-9*, North Holland) Elsevier.

Matrix Management. Kenneth Knight. LC 78-1516. 1978. text 20.00 (*0-89433-082-9*) Petrocelli.

***Matrix Metalloproteinase Inhibitors in Cancer Therapy.** Ed. by Neil J. Clendeninn & Krysztof Appelt. (Cancer Drug Discovery & Development Ser.). 250p. 2000. 135.00 (*0-89603-668-5*) Humana.

Matrix Metalloproteinase Protocols. Ed. by Ian M. Clark. LC 99-87618. (Methods in Molecular Biology Ser.: Vol. 151). 600p. 2000. 99.50 (*0-89603-733-9*) Humana.

Matrix Metalloproteinases. Ed. by William C. Parks et al. LC 98-133584. (Biology of Extracellular Matrix Ser.). (Illus.). 362p. 1998. text 89.95 (*0-12-545090-7*) Morgan Kaufmann.

Matrix Metalloproteinases & Inhibitors: Proceedings of the Matrix Metalloproteinase Conference, Held Sept. 11-15, 1989, Sandestin Beach, Florida. Ed. by Hennig Birkedal-Hansen et al. (Illus.). 650p. 1992. 275.00 (*1-56081-309-1*, Pub. by Gustav Fischer) Balogh.

***Matrix Metalloproteinases & TIMPs.** 2nd ed. Fred Woessner & Hideaki Nagase. LC 99-49877. (Protein Profile Ser.). (Illus.). 240p. 2000. pap. text 55.00 (*0-19-850268-0*) OUP.

Matrix Methods: An Introduction. 2nd ed. Richard Bronson. 503p. (C). 1991. text 48.00 (*0-12-135251-X*) Acad Pr.

Matrix Methods & Engineering Dynamics. A. R. Collar & A. Simpson. (Engineering Science Ser.). 513p. 1987. text 179.00 (*0-470-20271-8*) P-H.

Matrix Methods Applied to Engineering Rigid Body Mechanics. T. Crouch. LC 80-41186. 385p. 1981. 159.00 (*0-08-024245-6*, Pub. by Pergamon Repr) Franklin.

Matrix Methods for Structural Analysis. Cameron West. 496p. text. write for info. (*0-471-13084-2*) Wiley.

Matrix Methods in Analysis. P. Antosik & C. Schwartz. (Lecture Notes in Mathematics Ser.: Vol. 1113). iv, 114p. 1985. 29.95 (*0-387-15185-0*) Spr-Verlag.

Matrix Methods in Finite Mathematics: An Introduction with Applications to Business & Industry. Steven C. Althoen & Robert J. Bumcrot. 350p. (C). 1976. text 40.50 (*0-393-09192-9*) Norton.

Matrix Methods of Structural Analysis. 2nd ed. R. K. Livesley. 208p. 1975. 176.00 (*0-08-018888-5*, Pub. by Pergamon Repr) Franklin.

Matrix Methods of Structural Analysis. 2nd enl. ed. M. B. Kanchi. 561p. 1994. text 59.95 (*0-470-21859-2*) Halsted Pr.

Matrix 9: Anthology of Red Herring Poets, 9th. Ed. by Michael Spooner & Kathryn Kerr. 40p. 1984. pap. 3.95 (*0-932884-39-3*) Red Herring.

Matrix 19: Anthology of Red Herring Poets. 19th ed. Ed. by Ruth S. Walker. 60p. 1994. pap. 5.00 (*0-932884-49-0*) Red Herring.

Matrix Norms & Their Applications. G. R. Belitskii & Y. I. Lyubich. (Operator Theory Ser.: No. 36). 216p. 1988. 156.00 (*0-8176-2220-9*) Birkhauser.

Matrix of Change. Michael R. Bradley & Weldon Payne. 162p. (C). 1996. pap. text, per. 24.95 (*0-7872-2756-0*) Kendall-Hunt.

Matrix of Community Based Initiatives: Violence & Delinquency Prevention. Ed. by Shay Bilchik. (Illus.). 49p. (C). 1997. reprint ed. pap. text 30.00 (*0-7881-4037-X*) DIANE Pub.

Matrix of Language: Contemporary Linguistic Anthropology. Ed. by Donald Brenneis & Ronald K. Macaulay. LC 95-43947. 352p. (C). 1996. pap. 35.00 (*0-8133-2321-5*, Pub. by Westview) HarpC.

Matrix of Life. J. C. Collins. (Illus.). 104p. (Orig.). 1992. pap. 14.95 (*0-9629719-0-1*) Molecular Present.

Matrix of Lyric Transformation: Poetic Modes & Self-Presentation in Early Chinese Pentasyllabic Poetry. Zong-qi Cai. LC 96-9730. (Michigan Monographs in Chinese Studies: No. 75). 320p. 1997. text 50.00 (*0-89264-111-8*) Ctr Chinese Studies.

Matrix of Modernism: Pound, Eliot, & Early Twentieth-Century Thought. Sanford Schwartz. LC 85-42702. 246p. 1985. reprint ed. pap. 76.30 (*0-608-02587-9*, 206324400004) Bks Demand.

An Asterisk (*) at the beginning of an entry indicates that the title is appearing for the first time.

Matrix of Narrative: Family Systems & the Semiotics of Story. Denis Jonnes. (Approaches to Semiotics Ser.: No. 91). vi, 293p. (C). 1990. lib. bdg. 82.50 (*0-89925-624-4*) De Gruyter.

Matrix of Narrative: Family Systems & the Semiotics of Story. Denis Jonnes. (Approaches to Semiotics Ser.: No. 91). vi, 293p. (C). 1990. lib. bdg. 98.50 (*3-11-012252-9*) Mouton.

Matrix of the Gods. John Nelson. LC 95-128580. 288p. 1994. pap. 10.95 (*1-878901-97-4*) Hampton Roads Pub Co.

Matrix of the Mind: Object Relations & the Psychoanalytic Dialogue. Thomas H. Ogden. LC 85-13404. 288p. 1990. 40.00 (*0-87668-742-7*) Aronson.

Matrix of the Mind: Object Relations & the Psychoanalytic Dialogue. Thomas H. Ogden. LC 85-13404. 288p. 1994. reprint ed. pap. 40.00 (*1-56821-051-5*) Aronson.

***Matrix of Understanding: Thoughts about New Age & Science.** Vern Wiltse. Ed. by Eleanor F. Brockman & Tom Torrans. 66p. 2000. 4.00 (*1-930421-06-0*) BullFrog Pr.

Matrix Perturbation Theory. G. W. Stewart & Ji-guang Sun. (Computer Science & Scientific Computing Ser.). 365p. 1990. text 71.00 (*0-12-670230-6*) Acad Pr.

Matrix Polynomials. I. Gohberg et al. (Computer Science & Applied Mathematics Ser.). 1982. text 124.00 (*0-12-287160-X*) Acad Pr.

Matrix Population Models. 2nd rev. ed. Hal Caswell. 328p. (Orig.). (C). 1999. text 49.95 (*0-87893-096-5*) Sinauer Assocs.

Matrix Principle: Drug-Free Training for Sport & Bodybuilding a Revolutionary Approach to Muscle Development. Ronald S. Laura & Kenneth R. Dutton. Ed. by Richard J. McDermott & Gai Gardner. LC 92-60316. (Illus.). 238p. (Orig.). 1992. pap. 19.95 (*0-910944-02-4*) Magee.

Matrix 17: Anthology of Red Herring Poets. 17th ed. Ed. by Ruth S. Walker. 128p. 1992. pap. 8.00 (*0-932884-47-4*) Red Herring.

Matrix 16: Anthology of Red Herring Poets. 16th ed. Ed. by Carmen M. Pursifull & Ruth S. Walker. 72p. 1991. pap. 8.00 (*0-932884-46-6*) Red Herring.

Matrix Structural Analysis. J. J. Azar. 1972. 109.00 (*0-08-016781-0*, Pub. by Pergamon Repr) Franklin.

Matrix Structural Analysis. Lewis P. Felton & Richard B. Nelson. LC 96-19454. 700p. (C). 1996. text 103.95 (*0-471-12324-2*) Wiley.

Matrix Structural Analysis. Aslam Kassimali. LC 98-52798. (General Engineering Ser.). 1999. pap. 90.95 (*0-534-20670-0*) PWS Pubs.

Matrix Structural Analysis. Ronald L. Sack. (Illus.). 327p. (C). 1994. pap. text 36.95 (*0-88133-824-9*) Waveland Pr.

Matrix 10: Anthology of Red Herring Poets, 10th. Ed. by Michael Spooner & Kathryn Kerr. 30p. 1985. pap. 3.95 (*0-932884-40-7*) Red Herring.

Matrix-Tensor Methods in Continuum Mechanics. rev. ed. S. F. Borg. 356p. (C). 1990. text 71.00 (*981-02-0166-4*); pap. text 37.00 (*981-02-0167-2*) World Scientific Pub.

Matrix Theory. D. Lewis. 300p. (C). 1991. text 44.00 (*981-02-0689-5*) World Scientific Pub.

Matrix Theory: A Second Course. J. M. Ortega. LC 86-30312. (University Series in Mathematics). (Illus.). 274p. (C). 1987. text 49.50 (*0-306-42433-9*, Kluwer Plenum) Kluwer Academic.

Matrix Theory: Basic Results & Techniques. Fuzhen Zhang. Ed. by S. Axler et al. LC 98-51754. (Universitext Ser.). 278p. 1999. 49.95 (*0-387-98696-0*) Spr-Verlag.

Matrix Theory & Applications. Ed. by C. R. Johnson. LC 90-30584. (Proceedings of Symposia on Applied Mathematics Ser.: Vol. 40). 260p. 1990. text 62.00 (*0-8218-0154-6*, PSAPM/40) Am Math.

Matrix Theory & Its Applications: Selected Topics. N. J. Pullman. LC 75-40845. (Pure & Applied Mathematics Ser.: Vol. 35). 252p. reprint ed. pap. 78.20 (*0-608-16666-9*, 202781600054) Bks Demand.

Matrix Theory for Physicists. J. Heading. LC 58-3702. 254p. reprint ed. pap. 78.80 (*0-608-30443-3*, 200364100038) Bks Demand.

Matrix Theory of Photoelasticity. P. S. Theocaris & E. E. Gdoutos. (Optical Sciences Ser.: Vol. 11). (Illus.). 1979. 75.95 (*0-387-08899-7*) Spr-Verlag.

Matrix Theory with Applications. Jack L. Goldberg. 572p. (C). 1991. 78.75 (*0-07-557200-1*) McGraw.

Matrix 13: Anthology of Red Herring Poets. 13th ed. Ed. by Kenneth E. Gale. 36p. 1988. pap. 3.95 (*0-932884-43-1*) Red Herring.

Matrix 12: Anthology of Red Herring Poets. 12th ed. Ed. by Kenneth E. Gale. 35p. 1987. pap. 3.95 (*0-932884-42-3*) Red Herring.

Matrix Twenty: Anthology of the Red Herring Poets. Ed. by Ruth S. Walker. 48p. (Orig.). 1995. pap. 5.00 (*0-932884-76-8*) Red Herring.

***Matrix 24.** Workshop Members. Ed. by Heather Winters. 50p. 1999. pap. 6.00 (*0-932884-80-6*) Red Herring.

Matrix 21: Anthology of the Red Herring Poets. Red Herring Staff. Ed. by Ray Olsen. 48p. (Orig.). 1996. pap. 6.00 (*0-932884-77-6*) Red Herring.

Matrix 22, Vol. 22. Red Herring Poets Staff et al. (Illus.). 58p. 1997. pap. 6.00 (*0-932884-78-4*) Red Herring.

***Matrix Variate Distributions, 104.** A. K. Gupta & D. K. Nagar. LC 99-40291. 384p. 1999. boxed set 64.95 (*1-58488-046-5*, Chap & Hall CRC) CRC Pr.

Matrix With Linear Programming. Dittmore. (C). 1997. pap. 13.00 (*0-06-501266-6*) Addson-Wesley Educ.

***Matro of Pitane & the Tradition of Epic Parody in the Fourth Century BCE: Text, Translation & Commentary.** S. Douglas Olson & Alexander Sens. LC 99-50172. (American Philological Association American Classical Studies). 174p. 1999. 34.95 (*0-7885-0614-5*, 400444); pap. 19.95 (*0-7885-0615-3*, 400444) OUP.

Matroid Applications. Neil White. (Encyclopedia of Mathematics & Its Applications Ser.: No. 40). (Illus.). 375p. (C). 1992. text 99.95 (*0-521-38165-7*) Cambridge U Pr.

Matroid Theory. James G. Oxley. LC 92-20802. (Oxford Graduate Texts in Mathematics Ser.). (Illus.). 544p. (C). 1993. text 98.00 (*0-19-853563-5*) OUP.

Matroid Theory: AMS-IMS-SIAM Joint Summer Research Conference on Matroid Theory, July 2-6, 1995, University of Washington, Seattle. Ed. by Joseph E. Bonin et al. LC 96-18251. (Contemporary Mathematics Ser.: Vol. 196). 418p. 1996. pap. 72.00 (*0-8218-0508-8*, CONM/197) Am Math.

Matroid Theory & Its Applications in Electric Network Theory & Statics. A. Recski. (Algorithms & Combinatorics Ser.: Vol. 6). 350p. 1989. 135.95 (*0-387-15285-7*) Spr-Verlag.

Matrology: A Bibliography of Writings by Christian Women from the First to the Fifteenth Centuries. Andrew Kadel. LC 78-20945. 200p. (C). 1994. 29.50 (*0-8264-0676-9*) Continuum.

Matron of Honor. Sallie Bingham. LC 93-33845. 192p. 1996. reprint ed. pap. 10.95 (*0-944072-63-1*) Zoland Bks.

Matrona Docta: Educated Women in the Roman Elite from Cornelia to Julia Domna. Emily Ann Hemelrijk. LC 98-53036. 400p. 1999. 90.00 (*0-415-19693-0*) Routledge.

Matrons & Marginal Women in Medieval Society. Ed. by Robert R. Edwards & Vickie L. Ziegler. (Illus.). 139p. 1995. 60.00 (*0-85115-380-1*) Boydell & Brewer.

Mats. Francisco Arcellana. LC 98-35719. (Illus.). 32p. (J). (ps-4). 1999. 13.95 (*0-916291-86-3*) Kane-Miller Bk.

Mats Sundin. Kerry Banks. (Hockey Heroes Ser.). 1998. pap. text 6.95 (*1-55054-642-2*, Pub. by DGL) Sterling.

***Mats und die Wundersteine.** Marcus Pfister.Tr. of Milo & the Magical Stones. (GER., Illus.). (J). 1998. 18.95 (*3-314-00780-9*, Pub. by North-South Bks NYC) Chronicle Bks.

Matsuo Basho. Makoto Ueda. LC 82-48165. 192p. 1983. pap. 12.00 (*0-87011-553-7*) Kodansha.

Matsuri: Festival Japanese American Celebrations & Activities. Nancy K. Araki & Jane Horii. (Illus.). (Orig.). (J). 1985. reprint ed. pap. 9.95 (*0-89346-019-2*) Heian Intl.

Matsuri: Festivals of a Japanese Town. Michael Ashkenazi. LC 92-31751. 208p. (C). 1993. text 36.00 (*0-8248-1385-5*); pap. text 14.95 (*0-8248-1421-5*) UH Pr.

Matsuri: The Festivals of Japan: With a Selection from P. G. O'Neill's Photographic Archive of Matsuri. Herbert E. Plutschow. (Japan Library). 320p. (C). 1996. text 52.00 (*1-873410-63-8*, Pub. by Curzon Pr Ltd) UH Pr.

Matsuri: World of Japanese Festivals. Gorazd Vilhar & Charlotte Anderson. (Illus.). 160p. 1995. 39.95 (*4-07-976066-3*, Pub. by Shufunotomo) Weatherhill.

Matsushita. John P. Kotter. LC 96-44863. 320p. 1997. 24.50 (*0-684-83460-X*) Free Pr.

Matsutake Mushroom: The White Gold Rush of the 1990s. Jerry Guin. LC 97-17015. (Illus.). 96p. (Orig.). 1997. pap. 9.95 (*0-87961-248-7*) Naturegraph.

Matsya Puranam, 2 vols., Set. Bhagavatapurana Puranas. LC 73-3808. reprint ed. 74.50 (*0-404-57817-9*) AMS Pr.

Matt: The Story of Lewis Edward Mattingly. 4th ed. Duane Hutchinson. 96p. (Orig.). 1995. pap. 9.95 (*0-934988-37-4*, MAT323) Foun Bks.

Matt & Shawn: Backcourt Duo. Dave Ocorr. LC 98-91433. (Coach's Choice Ser.). 155p. (J). (gr. 4-9). 1998. pap. 8.95 (*0-9660758-2-X*) Perth Pubns.

Matt & Shawn: Baseball Battery. Dave Ocorr. LC 97-92505. (Coach's Choice Ser.). (J). (gr. 4-9). 1997. pap. 8.95 (*0-9660758-1-1*) Perth Pubns.

Matt Braun. Robert L. Gale. LC 90-80257. (Western Writers Ser.: No. 92). (Illus.). 55p. (Orig.). 1990. pap. 4.95 (*0-88430-091-9*) Boise St U W Writ Ser.

Matt Braun's Western Cooking. Matt Braun. (Illus.). 185p. (Orig.). 1996. reprint ed. pap. 17.95 (*0-87004-374-9*, 037490) Caxton.

***Matt Caldwell: Texas Tycoon.** Diana Palmer. (Special Edition Ser.: No. 1297). 2000. per. 4.50 (*0-373-24297-2*, 1-24297-3) Harlequin Bks.

Matt Christopher's All-Star Lineup: "The Kid Who Only Hits Homers," "Return of the Home Run Kid," "Baseball Pals", "Catcher with a Glass Arm," "Challenge at Second Base" Matt Christopher. LC 96-52601. (Illus.). 704p. (J). (gr. 3-7). 1997. 9.98 (*1-884822-68-1*) Blck Dog & Leventhal.

Matt Christopher's Book of Baseball Jokes & Riddles. Matt Christopher. (Illus.). (J). (ps-3). 1996. pap. 3.95 (*0-614-15671-8*) Little.

Matt Cohen & His Works. George Woodcock. (Canadian Author Studies). 60p. (C). 1987. pap. text 9.95 (*0-920763-29-4*, Pub. by ECW) Genl Dist Srvs.

***Matt Damon.** Meg Greene. (Galaxy of Superstars Ser.). 2000. 17.95 (*0-7910-5779-8*); pap. 9.95 (*0-7910-5780-1*) Chelsea Hse.

Matt Damon. Patricia Cronin Marcello. LC 98-85158. (Little Bks.). (Illus.). 80p. (J). (gr. 4-7). 1998. 4.95 (*0-8362-6992-6*) Andrews & McMeel.

***Matt Damon.** Contrib. by Miniature Book Collection Staff. LC 99-189488. (Pocket Romeos Ser.). (Illus.). 48p. (gr. 5 up). 1998. 4.98 (*0-7651-0940-9*) Smithmark.

Matt Damon. Kathleen Tracy. LC 98-217136. 192p. 1998. mass mkt. 4.99 (*0-312-96857-4*) St Martin.

Matt Damon, Scene 3. Kieran Scott. (Illus.). 32p. (J). (gr. 4-9). 1998. pap. 6.99 (*0-689-82405-X*) Aladdin.

Matt Damon: A Biography. Maxine Diamond & Harriet Hemmings. LC 99-195303. (J). 1998. per. 4.99 (*0-671-02649-6*) S&S Childrens.

***Matt Damon: An Illustrated Story.** Ian Calcutt. (Illustrated Story Ser.). (Illus.). 80p. 2000. pap. 9.95 (*0-600-59750-4*, Pub. by P HM) Trafalgar.

Matt Damon: An Unauthorized Biography. Chris Nickson. LC 99-18745. (Illus.). 256p. 1999. pap. 16.95 (*1-58063-072-3*, Pub. by Renaissance) St Martin.

Matt Damon Album. Brian J. Robb. (Illus.). pap. 16.95 (*0-85965-278-5*) Plexus.

Matt Damon & Ben Affleck: On & Off Screen. Altman. LC 98-73303. (Illus.). 128p. (J). (gr. 3 up). 1998. pap. 4.50 (*0-06-107145-5*) HarpC.

Matt Dennis Pop & Jazz Piano Styles. pap. 12.95 (*0-943748-69-0*) Ekay Music.

Matt Dennis Super Chords for the Great Standards. pap. 12.95 (*0-943748-50-X*) Ekay Music.

Matt Dillon Scrap Book. Cheryl Mead. (Illus.). 96p. 1984. pap. 7.95 (*0-312-52301-7*) St Martin.

Matt Field on the Santa Fe Trail. Matt Field. Ed. by John E. Sunder. LC 94-38313. (American Exploration & Travel Ser.: Vol. 29). (Illus.). 368p. 1995. pap. 16.95 (*0-8061-2716-3*) U of Okla Pr.

Matt Gray: Frosh Phenom. Dave Ocorr. (Coach's Choice Ser.). 152p. (J). (gr. 4-9). 1997. pap. 8.95 (*0-9660758-0-3*) Perth Pubns.

Matt Groening's Big Book of Hell. Matt Groening. 1990. pap. 20.00 (*0-679-72759-0*) Pantheon.

Matt Lamb: Obsessive Spirit (Wrestling with the Angels) Michael D. Hall. (Illus.). 34p. 1997. pap. 10.00 (*0-9652065-2-1*) Fassbender Gallery.

Matt Mahurin: Japan & America. Matt Mahurin. Ed. by Maya Ishiwata & Theresa Luisotti. (ENG & JPN., Illus.). 48p. 1993. 49.95 (*4-947671-01-7*) RAM Publications.

Matt Mahurin: Photographs. Photos by Matt Mahurin. (Illus.). 96p. 1998. 60.00 (*0-944092-60-8*) Twin Palms Pub.

Matt Mahurin: Photographs. limited ed. Photos by Matt Mahurin. (Illus.). 96p. 1998. 750.00 (*0-944092-61-6*) Twin Palms Pub.

***Matt Makes a Run for the Border: Recipes & Tales from a Tex-Mex Chef.** Matt Martinez, Jr. & Steve Pate. (Illus.). 192p. 2000. 29.95 (*0-86730-768-4*) Lebhar Friedman.

Matt Mattox - Jazz Dance: Mattox' Jazz-Art-Technik in Wort und Bild. 2nd ed. Elisabeth Frich. Tr. by Regine Popp. (ENG & GER., Illus.). 128p. (C). 1988. 41.00 (*3-8170-4002-4*, Pub. by Knstvrlag Weingrtn) Intl Bk Import.

Matt Mullican. Matt Mullican. 1994. 75.00 (*3-88375-189-8*, Pub. by Walther Konig) Dist Art Pubs.

Matt Mullican: Banners, Monuments, & the City: An Exhibition of Work for Public Spaces. Holland Cotter. Ed. by Elsa Longhauser. LC 89-84230. (Illus.). 24p. 1987. pap. 25.00 (*1-58442-032-4*) Galleries at Moore.

Matt Mullican: The MIT Project. Michael Tarantino. Ed. by Kline Katy. LC 90-61252. (Illus.). 60p. (Orig.). 1990. pap. 15.00 (*0-938437-32-1*) MIT List Visual Arts.

Matt Mullican World Frame. Matt Mullican. (Illus.). 222p. (Orig.). 1992. pap. text 35.00 (*1-879293-04-8*) Contemp Art Mus.

Matt Phillips: The Graphic Work. Sandra Phillips. 1976. pap. 7.50 (*0-686-24037-5*) Bellevue Pr.

Matt Talbot: His Life & Times. Mary Purcell. 238p. 1977. pap. 8.95 (*0-8199-0657-3*, Frncscn Herld) Franciscan Pr.

Matt Talbot: His Struggle, His Victory over Alcoholism. Susan H. Wallace. LC 92-33298. (Illus.). 87p. 1992. pap. 6.95 (*0-8198-4766-6*) Pauline Bks.

Matt Talbot: Hope for Addicts. Morgan Costelloe. 1989. pap. 25.00 (*0-86217-229-2*, Pub. by Veritas Pubns) St Mut.

Matt Urban Story: Life & World War Two Experiences. Matt Urban & Charles F. Conrad. (Illus.). 546p. 1989. 20.00 (*0-9624621-0-1*) M Urban Story.

Matt W. Ransom, Confederate General from North Carolina. Clayton C. Marlow. LC 96-26521. (Illus.). 198p. 1996. lib. bdg. 28.50 (*0-7864-0273-3*) McFarland & Co.

Matta. (Illus.). 264p. 1991. 55.00 (*3-8030-3195-8*) Dist Art Pubs.

Matta. D. Bozo et al. (Classiques du XX Siecle Ser.). (FRE., Illus.). 339p. 1985. pap. 75.00 (*2-85850-303-6*, Pub. by Centre National D'art) Beacon Pr.

Matta: Surrealism & Beyond. Curtis L. Carter et al. LC 97-74576. 80 p. 1997. write for info. (*0-945366-03-5*) MU Haggerty Mus.

Matta Battistini: Il Re Dei Baritoni. Francesco Palmegiani. Ed. by Andrew Farkas. LC 76-29960. (Opera Biographies Ser.).Tr. of Mattia Battistini: the Kind of Baritones. (ITA., Illus.). 1977. reprint ed. lib. bdg. 23.95 (*0-405-09700-X*) Ayer.

Mattachine Review, 5 vols., Set. Mattachine Society Staff. LC 75-12336. (Homosexuality Ser.). 1975. reprint ed. 242.95 (*0-405-07373-9*) Ayer.

Mattanawcook Observer. Ed. by Alan H. Hawkins. (Illus.). 100p. (Orig.). 1985. pap. 15.00 (*0-318-04472-2*) Mattanawcook Obs.

***Mattanza: Love & Death in the Sea of Sicily.** Theresa Maggio. (Illus.). 288p. 2000. text 25.00 (*0-7382-0269-X*) Perseus Pubng.

Mattanza: The Sicilian Madness. Charles Carmello. LC 86-22965. 407p. 1986. 17.95 (*0-88191-040-6*) Freundlich.

Matta's Graphic Work, 1943-74. Roland Sabatier. (FRE., Illus.). 156p. 1975. 200.00 (*1-55660-210-3*) A Wofsy Fine Arts.

Matte Paint: Its History & Technology, Analysis, Properties, Deterioration, & Treatment. Ed. by Eric F. Hansen et al. 600p. 1994. pap. 50.00 (*0-89236-262-6*, Pub. by J P Getty Trust) OUP.

Matteo Carcassi's 25 Estudios, Op. 60. David Tanenbaum. Ed. & Intro. by Jim Ferguson. LC 95-141389. (Essential Studies). (Illus.). 49p. (Orig.). (C). 1992. pap. text 16.95 (*0-9627832-2-6*) Guitar Solo.

Matteo Maria Boiardo: A Bibliography of Works & Criticism from 1487-1980. Julius A. Molinaro. (CFH-FCEH Ser.: No. 5). (Illus.). 100p. (Orig.). (C). 1984. pap. 10.00 (*0-920050-94-8*, Pub. by Can Fed Human) Speedimpex.

Matteo Thun. Ed. by Alex Buck & Matthias Vogt. (Designer Monographs: No. 2). (Illus.). 160p. 1994. 35.00 (*1-85490-902-9*) Academy Ed UK.

Matter. Gilda Berger. (Smart Science Ser.). (Illus.). 16p. (J). (gr. 2-5). Date not set. pap. 5.95 (*1-58273-506-9*) Newbridge Educ.

Matter. Dan Brown. LC 95-90583. 64p. 1996. 14.00 (*0-9647581-0-5*); pap. 9.00 (*0-9647581-1-3*) Crosstown Bks.

Matter. Karen Bryant-Mole. (Science All Around Me Ser.). 1998. 11.95 (*1-57572-110-4*) Heinemann Lib.

Matter. Chris Cooper. LC 92-6928. (Eyewitness Books). (Illus.). 64p. (J). (gr. 4-7). 1992. 15.95 (*1-879431-88-2*) DK Pub Inc.

***Matter.** DK Publishing Staff. (Eyewitness Books). 64p. (J). (gr. 4-7). 1999. 15.95 (*0-7894-4886-6*, D K Ink) DK Pub Inc.

***Matter.** Ann Fullick. LC 98-11589. (Science Topics Ser.). (Illus.). 32p. (J). 1999. write for info. (*1-57572-767-6*) Heinemann Lib.

***Matter.** Rebecca M. Hunter. LC 00-28041. (Discovering Science Ser.). (Illus.). 2000. 25.69 (*0-7398-2969-6*) Raintree Steck-V.

***Matter.** Peter Riley & Robert Snedden. LC 98-49823. (Smart Science Ser.). 32p. (YA). 1999. write for info. (*1-57572-871-0*) Heinemann Lib.

Matter see Ideas & Investigations in Science: Physical Science

Matter: Building Block. 2nd ed. Prentice-Hall Staff. 1901. text, student ed. write for info. (*0-13-402082-0*, Prentice Hall) P-H.

Matter & Consciousness. rev. ed. Paul M. Churchland. (Illus.). 194p. 1988. pap. text 14.95 (*0-262-53074-0*, Bradford Bks) MIT Pr.

Matter & Energy. DeWeese. (Illus.). 32p. (J). (gr. 4-6). 1997. pap., teacher ed. 2.95 (*1-55799-521-4*, 4123) Evan-Moor Edu Pubs.

Matter & Energy. Daniel J. Spero. (Science Mini-Unit Intermediate Ser.: Vol. 5). (Illus.). 16p. (J). (gr. 3-6). 1994. pap. text 5.95 (*1-55799-296-7*, EMC836) Evan-Moor Edu Pubs.

Matter & Energy see Macmillan Encyclopedia of Science

Matter & Energy: Big Book. Ed. by Susan Evento. (Early Science Ser.). 16p. (J). (ps-2). 1997. pap. 16.95 (*1-56784-323-9*) Newbridge Educ.

***Matter & Energy: Hands on Elementary School Science.** (Illus.). 50p. 2000. teacher ed. 35.00 (*1-883410-47-9*) L Poore.

Matter & Energy: Mini Book. Ed. by Susan Evento. (Early Science Ser.). 16p. (J). (ps-2). 1997. pap. 16.95 (*1-56784-348-4*) Newbridge Educ.

Matter & Energy: Physics in Action. Ed. by John Clark. (New Encyclopedia of Science Ser.). (Illus.). 160p. 1995. 39.95 (*0-19-521085-9*) OUP.

Matter & Gravity in Newton's Physical Philosophy. A. J. Snow. LC 74-26293. (History, Philosophy & Sociology of Science Ser.). 1979. reprint ed. 23.95 (*0-405-06619-8*) Ayer.

***Matter & Interaction.** Chabay. 1999. pap. text 10.00 (*0-471-37388-5*) Wiley.

Matter & Interactions. Chabay. pap. text. write for info. (*0-471-35491-0*) Wiley.

Matter & Manner of Praise: The Controversial Evolution of Hymnody in the Church of England, 1760-1820. Thomas K. McCart. LC 97-39136. (Drew Studies in Liturgy: No. 5). 176p. 1998. 49.50 (*0-8108-3450-2*) Scarecrow.

Matter & Memory. Henri Bergson. Tr. by N. M. Paul & W. S. Palmer from FRE. LC 87-37124. 284p. 1988. 28.95 (*0-942299-04-3*); pap. 14.95 (*0-942299-05-1*) Zone Bks.

Matter & Method. Rom Harre. x, 124p. (C). 1977. reprint ed. pap. text 11.00 (*0-917930-08-8*); reprint ed. lib. bdg. 24.00 (*0-917930-28-2*) Ridgeview.

Matter & Methods at Low Temperatures. F. Pobell. 319p. 1992. 79.00 (*0-387-53751-1*) Spr-Verlag.

Matter & Methods at Low Temperatures. 3rd ed. Seth Luth. (Illus.). 352p. 1996. pap. text 69.95 (*3-540-58572-9*) Spr-Verlag.

Matter & Motion. James Clerk Maxwell. 176p. 1991. reprint ed. pap. 6.95 (*0-486-66895-9*) Dover.

Matter at High Densities in Astrophysics: Compact Stars & the Equation of State. H. Herold et al. (Tracts in Modern Physics Ser.: Vol. 133). (Illus.). 200p. 1996. text 129.00 (*3-540-60605-X*) Spr-Verlag.

Matter, Energy, & Life: An Introduction to Chemical Concepts. 4th ed. Jeffrey J. Baker & Garland E. Allen. LC 80-17946. (Life Sciences Ser.). 256p. (C). 1981. pap. text 23.00 (*0-201-00169-1*) Addison-Wesley.

Matter in Mind: A Study of Kant's Transcendental Deduction. Richard E. Aquila. LC 88-45387. (Studies in Phenomenology & Existential Philosophy). 262p. 1989. 36.95 (*0-253-33712-7*) Ind U Pr.

Matter Is Life. J. California Cooper. LC 92-15970. 240p. 1992. pap. 12.00 (*0-385-41174-X*, Anchor NY) Doubleday.

Matter, Life & Generation: Eighteenth Century Embryology & the Haller-Wolff Debate. Shirley A. Roe. LC 80-19611. (Illus.). 225p. 1981. text 59.95 (*0-521-23540-5*) Cambridge U Pr.

***Matter Materiality & Modern Culture.** P. Graves-Brown. LC 99-56410. (Illus.). 192p. 2000. pap. 27.99 (*0-415-16705-1*) Routledge.

An Asterisk (*) at the beginning of an entry indicates that the title is appearing for the first time.

***Matter Materiality & Modern Culture.** Ed. by P. M. Graves-Brown. LC 99-56410. 176p. (C). 2000. text 85.00 (*0-415-16704-3*) Routledge.

Matter Matters. Thomas-Cochran. (What a Wonderful World 1 Ser.). 1991. pap. text. write for info. (*0-582-90953-8*, Pub. by Addison-Wesley) Longman.

Matter Matters? Vol. X: On the Material Basis of the Cognitive Activity of Mind. Ed. by Peter Arhem et al. LC 96-52744. (Illus.). 240p. 1997. 44.95 (*3-540-61776-0*) Spr-Verlag.

Matter, Mind & Meaning. Whately Carington. LC 78-111818. (Essay Index Reprint Ser.). 1977. 23.95 (*0-8369-1596-8*) Ayer.

Matter Mind Spirit: Twelve Contemporary Indiana Women Artists. Jean Robertson. LC 98-48198. (Distributed for the Indiana Committee, National Museum of Women in the Arts Ser.). (Illus.). 56p. 1999. pap. 19.95 (*0-253-21322-3*); text. write for info. (*0-253-33556-6*) Ind U Pr.

Matter, Morals & Medicine: The Ancient Greek Origins of Science, Ethics & the Medical Profession. Michael J. Carella. (American University Studies: Philosophy: Ser. V, Vol. 110). (Illus.). XIV, 361p. 1991. 43.95 (*0-8204-1432-8*) P Lang Pubng.

M

Matter, Motion, & Machines. Joan S. Gottieb. (Wonders of Science Ser.). 1997. pap., teacher ed. 10.55 (*0-8114-7494-1*) Raintree Steck-V.

Matter, Motion, & Machines. Joan S. Gottlieb. (Wonders of Science Ser.). 1997. pap., student ed. 11.16 (*0-8114-7488-7*) Raintree Steck-V.

Matter Myth: Dogmatic Discoveries That Challenge Our Understanding of Physical Reality. Paul Davies & John Gribbin. (Illus.). 320p. (Orig.). 1992. per. 13.00 (*0-671-72841-5*, Touchstone) S&S Trade Pap.

Matter of Allegiances: Maryland from 1850 to 1861. William J. Evitts. LC 73-19336. (Johns Hopkins University Studies in Historical & Political Science: 92nd Series, No. 1). 224p. 1974. reprint ed. pap. 69.50 (*0-608-03728-1*, 206455300009) Bks Demand.

Matter of Angels: Deborah Ruth's Christmas Journey. Jeannette Clift George. 50p. 1993. pap. 8.31 (*0-9616513-3-4*) Manor of Grace.

Matter of Araby in Medieval England. Dorothee Metlitzki. LC 76-23678. 1977. 47.50 (*0-300-02003-1*) Yale U Pr.

Matter of Balance. Margaret Mooney. LC 93-26222. (Illus.). (J). 1994. 4.25 (*0-383-03759-X*) SRA McGraw.

Matter of Balance: Personal Strategies for Alcohol & Other Drugs. Holstein et al. (Illus.). 180p. (C). 1995. pap. text 23.00 (*0-926544-12-8*) CNS.

Matter of Black & White: The Autobiography of Ada Lois Sipuel Fisher. Ada L. Fisher & Danney Goble. LC 95-38775. (Illus.). 224p. 1996. 21.95 (*0-8061-2819-4*) U of Okla Pr.

Matter of Britain & the Matter of England. Rees & Davies. 28p. 1996. pap. text 8.95 (*0-19-951377-5*) OUP.

Matter of Chance. D. H. Mellor. LC 70-152629. 203p. reprint ed. pap. 57.90 (*0-608-13305-1*, 2025592) Bks Demand.

Matter of Choice. Kenneth Copeland. 19p. 1994. pap. 1.00 (*0-88114-971-3*) K Copeland Pubns.

Matter of Choice: A Critique of Comparable Worth by a Skeptical Feminist - A Twentieth Century Fund Paper. Jennifer Roback. 53p. (Orig.). (C). 1986. pap. text 7.00 (*0-87078-172-3*) Century Foundation.

Matter of Choice: Abortion Law Reform in Apartheid South Africa. June Cope. 190p. 1994. pap. 40.00 (*0-86980-887-7*, Pub. by Univ Natal Pr) Intl Spec Bk.

Matter of Choices: Memoirs of a Female Physicist. Fay Ajzenberg-Selove. LC 93-28136. (Lives of Women in Science Ser.). (Illus.). 238p. (C). 1994. pap. text 20.00 (*0-8135-2035-5*) Rutgers U Pr.

***Matter of Circumstance.** Heather Graham. LC 00-30293. 2001. write for info. (*0-7862-2623-4*) Thorndike Pr.

Matter of Circumstance. Heather G. Pozzessere. 256p. 1994. per. 4.99 (*1-55166-005-9*, 1-66005-9, Mira Bks) Harlequin Bks.

Matter of Circumstance. Heather G. Pozzessere. 1994. mass mkt. 4.50 (*0-373-48281-7*, 5-48281-5) Silhouette.

Matter of Comfort: Ethnic Maintenance & Ethnic Style among Third-Generation Japanese Americans. Kaoru O. Kendis. LC 88-36700. (Immigrant Communities & Ethnic Minorities in the U. S. & Canada Ser.: No. 32). 1989. 45.00 (*0-404-19442-7*) AMS Pr.

Matter of Compromise. Judith Yoder. (American Romance Ser.: No. 432). 1992. per. 3.39 (*0-373-16432-7*, 1-16432-6) Harlequin Bks.

Matter of Concealment. Dewitt S. Copp. 384p. 1991. mass mkt. 4.50 (*0-8217-3269-2*, Zebra Kensgtn) Kensgtn Pub Corp.

***Matter of Conscience.** Rosemarie E. Bishop. LC 99-64381. (Moral Vampire Ser.: Bk. 2). 1999. 25.00 (*0-7388-0452-5*); pap. 18.00 (*0-7388-0453-3*) Xlibris Corp.

Matter of Conscience. Maurus E. Mallon. LC 89-64249. 112p. (Orig.). (C). 1990. pap. 6.95 (*0-88100-067-1*) Natl Writ Pr.

Matter of Conscience. large type ed. Palma Harcourt. 400p. 1987. 27.99 (*0-7089-1589-2*) Ulverscroft.

Matter of Conscience: Court-Martialed for his Faith. P.Harold Perris & Norma Jean Lutz. LC 97-47005. 164p. (Orig.). 1997. pap. 9.99 (*0-8280-1087-0*) Review & Herald.

Matter of Conscience: The Trial of Anne Hutchinson. Joan K. Nichols. LC 92-18087. (Stories of America Ser.). (Illus.). 101p. (J). (gr. 2-5). 1992. pap. 4.95 (*0-8114-8073-9*); lib. bdg. 25.68 (*0-8114-7233-7*) Raintree Steck-V.

Matter of Convenience. Dale M. Marsh. LC 97-60421. 192p. (Orig.). 1997. pap. 12.25 (*1-57921-011-2*) WinePress Pub.

***Matter of Critique: Readings in Kant's Philosophy.** Ed. by Andrea Rehberg. 296p. 2000. pap. 29.95 (*1-903083-11-7*, Pub. by Clinamen Pr) Paul & Co Pubs.

Matter of Degree: Playscript. rev. ed. Anson Campbell. 1985. pap. 6.00 (*0-88734-203-5*) Players Pr.

***Matter of Degree: The Hartford Circus Fire & the Mystery of Little Miss 1565.** Don Massey & Rick Davey. (Illus.). 320p. 2000. 26.95 (*1-930601-24-7*); pap. 19.95 (*1-930601-23-9*) Willow Brook.

Matter of Destiny. Gene Baldwin. LC 98-89479. 375p. 1998. text 25.00 (*0-7388-0271-9*); pap. text 15.00 (*0-7388-0272-7*) Xlibris Corp.

***Matter of Diamonds.** David Manuel. (Faith Abbey Mystery Ser.: Vol. 2). 350p. 2000. 23.00 (*1-55725-258-0*, 930-059, Pub. by Paraclete MA) BookWorld.

Matter of Difference: Materialist Feminist Criticism of Shakespeare. Ed. by Valerie Wayne. LC 91-11163. 312p. 1991. text 49.95 (*0-8014-2678-2*); pap. text 19.95 (*0-8014-9965-8*) Cornell U Pr.

Matter of Diplomacy. Agnes Adam. 32p. (Orig.). 1996. pap. 5.00 (*0-88734-356-2*) Players Pr.

Matter of Discourse: Community & Communication in Contemporary Philosophies. Ed. by Amos Nascimento. LC 97-77554. (Avebury Series in Philosophy). 248p. 1998. text 67.95 (*1-85972-681-X*, Pub. by Ashgate Pub) Ashgate Pub Co.

***Matter of Ethics: Facing the Fear of Doing the Right Thing.** Teri J. Traaen. LC 00-32260. (Contemporary Studies in Applied Behavioral Science). 2000. write for info. (*0-7623-0666-1*) Jai Pr.

Matter of Fact. Joe Weasel. (Illus.). 163p. 1995. 12.95 (*1-57074-290-1*) Greyden Pr.

Matter of Fact: A Digest of Current Facts, with Citations Sources, 1986, Vol. 4. Ed. by C. Edward Wall. 324p. 1986. pap. 45.00 (*0-87650-225-7*) Pierian.

Matter of Fact: A Digest of Current Facts, with Citations to Sources, 1986, Vol. 5. Ed. by C. Edward Wall. 304p. 1986. pap. 45.00 (*0-87650-234-6*) Pierian.

Matter of Fact: Statements Containing Statistics on Current Social Economic & Political Issues, 1987, Vols. 6 & 7. 1990. pap. 74.50 (*0-87650-242-7*) Pierian.

***Matter of Fact: Statements Containing Statistics on Current Social, Economic & Political Issues, 1998, Vol. 28.** Ed. by C. Edward Wall. 1998. 70.00 (*0-87650-377-6*) Pierian.

***Matter of Fact: Statements Containing Statistics on Current Social, Economic & Political Issues, 1998, Vol. 29.** Ed. by C. Edward Wall. 1999. 70.00 (*0-87650-378-4*) Pierian.

***Matter of Fact: Statements Containing Statistics on Current Social, Economic & Political Issues, 1999, Vol. 30.** C. Edward Wall. 1999. 75.00 (*0-87650-381-4*) Pierian.

Matter of Fact: Using Factual Texts in the Classroom. Pamela Green. Ed. by Ruth Siems. (Illus.). 144p. (Orig.). 1992. teacher ed. 16.00 (*1-875327-13-4*, Pub. by E Curtain) Peguis Pubs Ltd.

Matter of Fact Vol. 1: A Digest of Current Facts, with Citation Sources, 1984. 1985. pap. 45.00 (*0-87650-197-8*) Pierian.

Matter of Fact Vol. 2: A Digest of Current Facts, with Citation Sources, 1985. 1986. pap. 45.00 (*0-87650-200-1*) Pierian.

Matter of Fact Vol. 3: A Digest of Current Facts, with Citation Cources, 1985. 1986. pap. 45.00 (*0-87650-221-4*) Pierian.

Matter of Fact Vol. 16: Statements Containing Statistics on Current Social, Economic, & Political Issues, 1992. 1992. pap. 45.00 (*0-87650-307-5*) Pierian.

Matter of Fact Vol. 17: Statements Containing Statistics on Current Social, Economic, & Political Issues, 1992. 1993. pap. 45.00 (*0-87650-308-3*) Pierian.

Matter of Fact Vol. 18: Statements Containing Statistics on Current Social, Economic, & Political Issues, 1993. 432p. 1993. pap. 50.00 (*0-87650-312-1*) Pierian.

Matter of Fact Vol. 19: Statements Containing Statistics on Current Social, Economic, & Political Issues, 1993. 432p. 1994. pap. 50.00 (*0-87650-313-X*) Pierian.

Matter of Fact Vol. 20: Statements Containing Statistics on Current Social, Economic, & Political Issues, 1994. 469p. 1994. pap. 50.00 (*0-87650-333-4*) Pierian.

Matter of Fact Vol. 21: Statements Containing Statistics on Current Social, Economic, & Political Issues, 1994. 544p. 1995. pap. 50.00 (*0-87650-334-2*) Pierian.

Matter of Fact Vol. 22: Statements Containing Statistics on Current Social, Economic, & Political Issues, 1995. 1995. 70.00 (*0-87650-315-6*) Pierian.

Matter of Fact Vol. 23: Statements Containing Statistics on Current Social, Economic, & Political Issues, 1995. 1996. 70.00 (*0-87650-316-4*) Pierian.

Matter of Fact Vol. 24: Statements Containing Statistics on Current Social, Economic, & Political Issues. 744p. 1996. 70.00 (*0-87650-321-0*) Pierian.

Matter of Fact Vol. 25: Statements Containing Statistics on Current Social, Economic, & Political Issues. 1997. 70.00 (*0-87650-322-9*) Pierian.

Matter of Fact Vol. 26: Statements Containing Statistics on Current Social, Economic, & Political Issues, 1997. Ed. by C. Edward Wall. 1998. 70.00 (*0-87650-375-X*) Pierian.

Matter of Fact Vol. 27: Statements Containing Statistics on Current Social, Economic, & Political Issues, 1997. Ed. by C. Edward Wall. 1998. 70.00 (*0-87650-376-8*) Pierian.

***Matter of Fact Vol. 31: Statements Containing Statistics on Current Social, Economic & Political Issues.** Ed. by C. Edward Wall. 500p. 2000. 75.00 (*0-87650-382-2*) Pierian.

Matter of Fact Vols. 8 & 9: Statements Containing Statistics on Current Social, Economic, & Political Issues, 1988. 1991. pap. 74.50 (*0-87650-243-5*) Pierian.

Matter of Fact Vols. 10 & 11: Statements Containing Statistics on Current Social, Economic, & Political Issues, 1989. 1991. pap. 74.50 (*0-87650-295-8*) Pierian.

Matter of Fact Vols. 12 & 13: Statements Containing Statistics on Current Social, Economic, & Political Issues, 1990. 1991. pap. 74.50 (*0-87650-301-6*) Pierian.

Matter of Fact Vols. 14 & 15: Statements Containing Statistics on Current Social, Economic, & Political Issues, 1991. 1992. pap. 74.50 (*0-87650-305-9*) Pierian.

Matter of Faith: The Fiction of Brian Moore, 69. Robert Sullivan. LC 95-50457. (Contributions to the Study of World Literature Ser.: Vol. 69). 160p. 1996. 55.00 (*0-313-29871-8*, Greenwood Pr) Greenwood.

***Matter of Fate: The Concept of Fate in the Arab World As Reflected in Modern Arabic Literature.** Dalya Cohen-Mor. LC 99-30401. 288p. 2000. write for info. (*0-19-513398-6*) OUP.

Matter of Glory: A New Preface to "Paradise Lost" John P. Rumrich. LC 87-40158. 220p. 1987. reprint ed. pap. 68.20 (*0-608-00911-3*, 206170500010) Bks Demand.

Matter of Habit. Dennis Barone. (Chapbook Ser.). (Orig.). 1995. pap. 6.00 (*0-945112-21-1*) Generator Pr.

Matter of Heart. Cindy Hawn. 76p. 1998. pap. 4.00 (*1-55630-825-3*) Brentwood Comm.

Matter of Heart: One Woman's Story of Triumph. Nancy Shank Pedder. Ed. by Erica Orloff. Tr. by Pam Morrell. LC 98-61118. 192p. 1998. 19.95 (*1-885843-08-9*) Saturn Press.

Matter of History: Selected Work by Annette Lemieux. Judith H. Fox. LC 94-70431. (Illus.). 20p. (Orig.). 1994. pap. text 10.00 (*1-881894-03-7*) WC Davis Mus & Cult.

Matter of Honor. Jeffrey Archer. 368p. 1993. mass mkt. 6.50 (*0-06-100713-7*, Harp PBks) HarpC.

Matter of Honor. Eugene Izzi. LC 96-46830. 432p. 1997. mass mkt. 24.00 (*0-380-97342-1*, Avon Bks) Morrow Avon.

Matter of Honor. Eugene Izzi. 544p. 1998. mass mkt. 6.99 (*0-380-78842-X*, Avon Bks) Morrow Avon.

Matter of Honor. Mandalyn Kaye. 416p. 1996. mass mkt. 4.99 (*0-7860-0328-6*, Pinncle Kensgtn) Kensgtn Pub Corp.

Matter of Honor. Thomas K. Martin. 224p. (Orig.). 1994. mass mkt. 4.99 (*0-441-00107-6*) Ace Bks.

Matter of Honor. Christopher Ogden. 1999. 29.95 (*0-316-04491-1*) Little.

Matter of Hours: Treason at Harper's Ferry. Paul R. Teetor. LC 80-65575. (Illus.). 312p. 1982. 39.50 (*0-8386-3012-X*) Fairleigh Dickinson.

Matter of Images: Essays on Representations. Richard Dyer. LC 92-37765. (Illus.). 240p. (C). 1993. pap. 20.99 (*0-415-05719-1*, A9988) Routledge.

Matter of Infinite Moment. Manoah Bodman. 32p. 1998. reprint ed. pap. 4.00 (*1-893032-00-0*) Jensen Daniels.

Matter of Inheritance. large type ed. Margaret Stewart. (Lythway Adult Ser.). 248p. 1991. 20.50 (*0-7451-1388-5*, G K Hall Lrg Type) Mac Lib Ref.

Matter of Interest: Reexamining Money, Debt, & Real Economic Growth. William F. Hixson. LC 91-4628. 304p. 1991. 65.00 (*0-275-93895-6*, C3895, Praeger Pubs) Greenwood.

Matter of Interpretation: Federal Courts & the Law. Antonin Scalia. Ed. by Amy Gutmann. 176p. 1997. pap. 12.95 (*0-691-00400-5*, Pub. by Princeton U Pr) Cal Prin Full Svc.

Matter of Interpretation: Federal Courts & the Law. Antonin Scalia. LC 96-40969. 128p. 1997. 19.95 (*0-691-02630-0*, Pub. by Princeton U Pr) Cal Prin Full Svc.

Matter of Just Treatment: Substance Abuse & the Courts. 77p. 1996. reprint ed. pap. text 25.00 (*0-7881-3316-0*) DIANE Pub.

Matter of Justice. Robin Buhrke. 320p. (Orig.). (C). 1996. pap. 20.99 (*0-415-91469-8*) Routledge.

Matter of Justice. Robin A. Buhrke. 320p. (C). 1996. 70.00 (*0-415-91468-X*) Routledge.

Matter of Justice & Compassion: Addressing the Needs of Gay & Lesbian Youth Series, 4 vols. Karen M. Harbeck. (Illus.). 1997. pap. write for info. (*1-889393-10-X*, 0592) Amethyst Pr & Prod.

Matter of Justice & Compassion Vol. I: Addressing the Needs of Gay & Lesbian Youth - Overview for Advocacy. Karen M. Harbeck. (Illus.). 150p. 1997. pap. 29.95 (*1-889393-46-0*, 0151) Amethyst Pr & Prod.

Matter of Justice & Compassion Vol. II: Addressing the Needs of Gay & Lesbian Youth - Approaches for Change. Karen M. Harbeck. (Illus.). 160p. 1997. pap. 19.95 (*1-889393-40-1*, 0555) Amethyst Pr & Prod.

Matter of Justice & Compassion Vol. III: Addressing the Needs of Gay & Lesbian Youth - Legal & Policy Leverage. Karen M. Harbeck. (Illus.). 180p. 1997. pap. write for info. (*1-889393-81-9*, 0581) Amethyst Pr & Prod.

Matter of Justice & Compassion Vol. IV: Addressing the Needs of Gay & Lesbian Youth - Model for State Change-Kansas. Karen M. Harbeck. (Illus.). 150p. 1997. pap. 29.95 (*1-889393-32-0*, 0636) Amethyst Pr & Prod.

Matter of Justice (The Legal System in Ferment) Michael Zender. (C). 1988. 462.00 (*0-7855-4762-2*) St Mut.

***Matter of Life.** Robin Bayne. 278p. 2000. pap. 18.99 (*1-58365-031-8*, Indigo Publicatns) BT Pub.

Matter of Life. W. Coda Martin. 1965. 6.95 (*0-8159-6202-9*) Devin.

Matter of Life. Ed. by Clara Urquhart. LC 72-9052. 255p. 1973. reprint ed. lib. bdg. 65.00 (*0-8371-6561-X*, URML, Greenwood Pr) Greenwood.

Matter of Life: Philosophical Problems of Biology. Michael A. Simon. LC 74-158142. 270p. reprint ed. pap. 83.70 (*0-8357-8215-8*, 203388900087) Bks Demand.

Matter of Life & Death. Ian Christie. 80p. 2000. pap. 10.95 (*0-85170-479-4*, Pub. by British Film Inst) Ind U Pr.

Matter of Life & Death. Leonard Ingram. 172p. 1998. pap. 19.95 (*1-893745-03-1*) Royal House.

Matter of Life & Death. Robert P. Sikking. 112p. 1978. pap. 8.95 (*0-87516-256-8*) DeVorss.

Matter of Life & Death: A Study of the Baal-Mot Epic (CTA 4-5-6) Baruch Margalit. (Alter Orient und Altes Testament Ser.: Vol. 206). vii, 271p. 1980. text 29.50 (*3-7887-0608-2*) NeukirchenerV.

Matter of Life & Death: Bioethics & the Christians. Albert L. Truesdale. (Contemporary Social Issues Ser.). 128p. (Orig.). 1990. pap. 8.99 (*0-8341-1328-7*) Beacon Hill.

Matter of Life & Death: Health, Illness & Medicine in McLean County. Lucinda M. Beier. (Illus.). 312p. (Orig.). 1996. 40.00 (*0-943788-09-9*); pap. 15.00 (*0-943788-08-0*) McLean County.

Matter of Life & Death: Health-Seeking Behavior of Guatemalan Refugees in South Florida. Maria A. Miralles. LC 88-36497. (Immigrant Communities & Ethnic Minorities in the U. S. & Canada Ser.: No. 52). 1989. 42.50 (*0-404-19462-1*) AMS Pr.

Matter of Life & Death: Recent Death Rates among the South Dakotan Elderly. Joyce I. Nelson. (Studies in Historical Demography). 225p. 1990. reprint ed. text 50.00 (*0-8240-3361-2*) Garland.

Matter of Life & Death: Surviving Loss & Finding Hope. Thomas Hartman. LC 94-1172. 208p. 1994. 14.95 (*0-89243-639-5*, Liguori Triumph) Liguori Pubns.

Matter of Life & Deth Death. Anne Ridler. (C). 1990. 60.00 (*0-906887-07-0*, Pub. by Greville Pr) St Mut.

Matter of Loyalty: The Los Angeles School Board vs. Frances Eisenberg. Martha Kransdorf. LC 94-25186. 140p. (Orig.). 1994. pap. 14.95 (*1-880192-11-X*) Caddo Gap Pr.

Matter of Luck see Cuestion de Suerte

Matter of Mischief. large type ed. Evelyn Hood. 1990. 11.50 (*0-7089-2334-8*) Ulverscroft.

Matter of Oaths. Helen S. Wright. 1990. mass mkt. 4.50 (*0-445-20983-6*, Pub. by Warner Bks) Little.

Matter of People: Co-operative Dairying in India & Zimbabwe. Shanti George. (Illus.). 560p. (C). 1994. text 32.00 (*0-19-563166-8*) OUP.

Matter of Personal Protection: The Weapons & Self-Defense Laws of Texas. 3rd ed. Doug Briggs. (Illus.). 256p. 1994. pap. 12.95 (*1-881287-07-6*) Beverly Bk.

Matter of Perspective. Kevin Robinson. LC 93-15674. (Stick Foster Mystery Ser.). 1993. 19.95 (*0-8027-3242-9*) Walker & Co.

Matter of Possession. G. C. Scott. 1999. pap. 11.95 (*0-7867-0630-9*) Carroll & Graf.

Matter of Precedents. Berl Falbaum. LC 98-65519. 240p. 1998. 19.95 (*1-882792-65-3*) Proctor Pubns.

Matter of Pride. Dorothy Simpson. 192p. Date not set. 20.95 (*0-8488-2619-1*) Amereon Ltd.

Matter of Pride: Horsemanship for Riders of Gaited Horses. Nicole H. Carswell. (Illus.). 112p. 1998. pap. 25.00 (*0-9663262-0-2*) Seventh Heaven.

Matter of Pride & Other Stories. Nicholasa Mohr. LC 96-39826. 164p. 1997. 19.95 (*1-55885-163-1*); pap. 11.95 (*1-55885-177-1*) Arte Publico.

Matter of Principal. Hanoch Teller. LC 93-21938. 1993. 15.95 (*1-881939-03-0*) NYC Pub Co.

Matter of Principal. large type ed. Leigh Michaels. 277p. 1996. 11.50 (*0-7505-0856-6*, Pub. by Mgna Lrg Print) Ulverscroft.

Matter of Principle. Ronald M. Dworkin. LC 84-25122. 480p. 1985. 39.00 (*0-674-55460-4*) HUP.

Matter of Principle. Ronald M. Dworkin. 480p. 1985. pap. 19.50 (*0-674-55461-2*) HUP.

Matter of Principle. Leigh Michaels. (Romance Ser.: No. 3070). 1990. per. 2.50 (*0-373-03070-3*) Harlequin Bks.

Matter of Principles? Ferment in U. S. Bioethics. Ed. by Edwin R. DuBose et al. LC 94-33. 400p. (C). 1994. 30.00 (*1-56338-081-1*) TPI PA.

Matter of Record. large type ed. Malcolm Gray. 1990. pap. 16.99 (*0-7089-6998-4*, Linford) Ulverscroft.

Matter of Record: Documentary Sources in Social Research. John Scott. 200p. 1990. pap. text 31.95 (*0-7456-0070-0*) Blackwell Pubs.

Matter of Representative Newt Gingrich: Report of the Select Committee on Ethics. Date not set. per. 61.00 (*0-16-063278-1*) USGPO.

Matter of Revolution: Science, Poetry, & Politics in the Age of Milton. John Rogers. 288p. 1996. 45.00 (*0-8014-3238-3*) Cornell U Pr.

Matter of Revolution: Science, Poetry, & Politics in the Age of Milton. John Rogers. 280p. 1998. pap. text 16.95 (*0-8014-8525-8*) Cornell U Pr.

Matter of Right: The Rich, the Poor, & the U. N. Ross Stevens. pap. 3.50 (*0-685-16479-9*, CS1005) General Board.

Matter of Roses. David Manuel. LC 99-39525. 330p. 1999. 23.00 (*1-55725-234-3*, 930-006, Pub. by Paraclete MA) BookWorld.

Matter of Sacco & Vanzetti, an Ethical Dilemma. Intro. by James W. Jeans, Sr. (Classics of the Courtroom: Vol. XXIII). 78p. 1991. pap. 15.00 (*0-943380-29-4*) PEG MN.

Matter of Scotland: Historical Narrative in Medieval Scotland. James R. Goldstein. LC 92-16416. (Regents Studies in Medieval Culture). (Illus.). xvi, 386p. 1993. text 55.00 (*0-8032-2144-4*) U of Nebr Pr.

***Matter of Self-Esteem & Other Stories.** Carme Riera. Ed. by Roser Caminals-Heath. Tr. by Holly Cashman from SPA. Orig. Title: Contra l'Amor en Companyia i Altrer Relats. 160p. 2000. 21.95 (*0-8419-1411-7*) Holmes & Meier.

Matter of Shiva. Gabrielle O'Day. 226p. 1991. 24.95 (*0-8191-8202-8*) U Pr of Amer.

Matter of Speculation: The Case of Lord Cochrane see Henry Cecil Reprint Series

An Asterisk (*) at the beginning of an entry indicates that the title is appearing for the first time.

Matter of Style: Women in the Fashion Industry. Linda Leuzzi. LC 96-33960. (Women Then - Women Now Ser.). 160p. (YA). (gr. 8-12). 1996. lib. bdg. 24.00 (*0-531-11303-5*) Watts.

Matter of Style: Women in the Fashion Industry. Linda Leuzzi. (Women Then - Women Now Ser.). 160p. (J). 1997. pap. 9.95 (*0-531-15831-4*) Watts.

Matter of Survival - Burglary. Randolf Martinez. (Illus.). 109p. 1994. write for info. (*0-9644652-0-5*) Chico Pub.

Matter of Taste. Fred Saberhagen. 288p. 1992. mass mkt. 3.99 (*0-8125-2575-2*, Pub. by Tor Bks) St Martin.

Matter of Taste. rev. ed. William R. Cagle & Lisa K. Stafford. LC 99-19304. (Gernon Collection on Food & Drink). (Illus.). 1205p. (C). 1999. 95.00 (*1-884718-86-8*, 53908RB) Oak Knoll.

***Matter of Taste: How Names, Fashions & Culture Change.** Stanley Lieberson. (Illus.). 352p. 2000. 29.95 (*0-300-08385-8*) Yale U Pr.

Matter of Taste: Selected Chinese Art from California Collections. Terese T. Bartholomew et al. (Illus.). 52p. 1986. pap. 7.50 (*0-9609784-5-3*) CCF San Francisco.

***Matter of Time.** Terri Brisbin. 1999. mass mkt. 5.99 (*0-515-12683-7*, Jove) Berkley Pub.

Matter of Time. Shashi Deshpande. LC 98-52896. 272p. 1999. 21.95 (*1-55861-214-9*, Pub. by Feminist Pr) Consort Bk Sales.

Matter of Time. Bud Egeland. LC 98-90026. 1998. 19.95 (*0-533-12689-4*) Vantage.

Matter of Time. Sheri Cooper Sinykin. LC 97-3433. 207p. (J). (gr. 5-9). 1998. lib. bdg. write for info. (*0-7614-5019-X*) Marshall Cavendish.

Matter of Time: From Work Sharing to Temporal Flexibility in Belgium, France & Britain. Jens Bastian. 304p. 1994. 79.95 (*1-85628-911-7*, Pub. by Avebry) Ashgate Pub Co.

Matter of Time: Rhythm in Your Music: Developing Temporal-Tchythmic Awareness & Response. Charlotte L. Warren. (Illus.). 28p. (Orig.). (YA). (gr. 9 up). 1992. mass mkt. 14.95 (*0-614-30045-2*) Decision Pt.

Matter of Time: Risk & Opportunity in the Nonschool Hours. Carnegie Council on Adolescent Development Staff. Ed. by Jane Quinn & Ruby Takanishi. LC 92-37832. (Illus.). (Orig.). 1992. pap. text 9.00 (*0-9623154-3-5*) CCAD DC.

Matter of Timing: Alzheimer's - A Carer's Journey. Audrey Brown. (Illus.). 166p. 1998. 29.50 (*1-85776-331-9*, Pub. by Book Guild Ltd) Trans-Atl Phila.

Matter of Trust. T. Elizabeth Renich. (Shadowcreek Chronicles Ser.: Bk. 2). 1995. pap. 8.99 (*1-883002-14-1*) Emerald WA.

***Matter of Trust.** Deb Stover. (Zebra Bouquet Ser.: Vol. 31). 256p. 2000. mass mkt. 3.99 (*0-8217-6460-8*, Zebra Kensgtn) Kensgtn Pub Corp.

Matter of Trust. Cheryl Wolverton. (Love Inspired Ser.). 1997. per. 4.50 (*0-373-87011-6*, 1-87011-2) Harlequin Bks.

Matter of Trust. large type ed. Penny Jordan. (Harlequin Ser.). 1993. reprint ed. lib. bdg. 18.95 (*0-263-13277-3*) Mac Lib Ref.

Matter of Trust: (Presents Plus) Penny Jordan. LC 95-4578. (Presents Ser.). 186p. 1995. pap. 3.25 (*0-373-11719-1*, 1-11719-1) Harlequin Bks.

Matter of Trust: The Guide to Gestational Surrogacy. Gail Dutton. LC 96-93105. 230p. (Orig.). 1997. pap. 21.95 (*0-9655966-0-5*) Clouds Pub.

Matter of Two Chinas: The China-Taiwan Issue in U. S. Foreign Policy. William R. Kintner & John Franklin Copper. LC 79-4254. 127p. 1979. pap. 6.00 (*0-910191-04-2*) For Policy Res.

Matter of Two Chinas: The China-Taiwan Issue in U. S. Foreign Policy. William R. Kintner & John Franklin Copper. LC 79-4254. 140p. reprint ed. pap. 43.40 (*0-7837-1780-6*, 204197800001) Bks Demand.

Matter of Will. Robyn Donald. (Presents Ser.: No. 1343). 1991. per. 2.75 (*0-373-11343-9*) Harlequin Bks.

Matter Physics: Optical Spectroscopy of Glasses. Ed. by I. Zschokke. (C). 1986. text 206.50 (*90-277-2231-5*) Kluwer Academic.

Matter Really Matters. John M. Patten, Jr. LC 94-47601. (Read All about Let's Wonder about Science Ser.). 24p. (J). (gr. 1-4). 1995. lib. bdg. 18.60 (*1-55916-124-8*) Rourke Bk Co.

Matter, Space, & Motion: Theories in Antiquity & Their Sequel. Richard Sorabji. LC 87-47984. 392p. 1988. text 57.50 (*0-8014-2194-2*) Cornell U Pr.

Matter, Space, & Motion: Theories in Antiquity & Their Sequel. Richard Sorabji. LC 87-47984. 392p. 1992. pap. text 21.95 (*0-8014-8057-4*) Cornell U Pr.

Matter under Extreme Conditions: Proceedings of the 33th Internationale Universit Atswochen fur Kern - und Teilchenphysik, Schladming, Austria, 27 February - 5 March 1994. Ed. by Heimo Latal & Wolfgang Schweiger. (Lecture Notes in Physics Ser.: Vol. 440). 1995. 72.95 (*3-540-58689-X*) Spr-Verlag.

Matter with Stairs. Mitchell Toney. LC 86-7367. 73p. 1986. pap. 7.00 (*0-89924-048-8*) Lynx Hse.

Mattering: A Journey with Rural Youth. Loren Coleman & Dan Porter. 1992. 25.00 incl. VHS (*0-939561-13-1*) Univ South ME.

Matter's End. deluxe limited ed. Gregory Benford. (Illus.). 84p. 1990. boxed set 115.00 (*0-941826-20-1*) Cheap St.

Matters Mathematical. 2nd ed. I. N. Herstein & Irving Kaplansky. LC 77-16091. 1978. 18.95 (*0-8284-0300-7*) Chelsea Pub.

Matters of Chance: A Novel. Jeantte Haien. LC 97-15073. 448p. 1998. pap. 13.00 (*0-06-092952-9*, Perennial) HarperTrade.

Matters of Choice. Noah Gordon. 1996. pap. 12.95 (*0-452-27635-7*) NAL.

Matters of Choice. Noah Gordon. 1997. mass mkt. 6.99 (*0-451-18726-1*, Sig) NAL.

Matters of Composition & the Environment. Greg Jacob. 140p. 1998. pap. text 19.95 (*1-56226-403-6*) CAT Pub.

Matters of Conscience: Conversations with Sterling M. McMurrin on Philosophy, Education & Religion. Sterling M. McMurrin & L. Jackson Newell. LC 96-18068. 424p. 1996. 28.95 (*1-56085-087-6*) Signature Bks.

Matters of Fact: Reading Nonfiction over the Edge. Daniel W. Lehman. LC 97-26663. (Theory & Interpretation of Narrative Ser.). 234p. 1998. text 47.50 (*0-8142-0760-X*); pap. text 18.95 (*0-8142-0761-8*) Ohio St U Pr.

Matters of Intelligence. Ed. by Lucia M. Vaina. (C). 1987. lib. bdg. 203.00 (*90-277-2460-1*) Kluwer Academic.

Matters of Interpretation: Mutual Transformation in the Counseling Relationship. Michael J. Nakkula. LC 97-29503. 1997. 39.00 (*0-7879-0957-2*) Jossey-Bass.

Matters of Life & Death. John Cairns. LC 96-18026. 260p. 1997. text 29.95 (*0-691-02872-9*, Pub. by Princeton U Pr) Cal Prin Full Svc.

Matters of Life & Death. John B. Cobb, Jr. 120p. (Orig.). 1991. pap. 13.95 (*0-664-25169-2*) Westminster John Knox.

Matters of Life & Death. Jay G. Williams. 57p. 1993. pap. 4.95 (*0-9629662-1-5*) G Santes.

Matters of Life & Death. 3rd ed. Ed. by Tom Regan. LC 92-23158. 416p. (C). 1992. pap. 23.13 (*0-07-051330-9*) McGraw.

Matters of Life & Death: Jewish Bio-Ethics. Elliot N. Dorff. LC 97-36295. 474p. 1998. 34.95 (*0-8276-0647-8*) JPS Phila.

Matters of Life & Death: New American Stories. Ed. by Tobias Wolff. LC 82-70441. 256p. 1983. 14.95 (*0-931694-14-0*); pap. 9.95 (*0-931694-17-5*) Wampeter Pr.

Matters of Life & Death: Perspectives on Public Health, Molecular Biology, Cancer, & the Prospects for the Human Race. John Cairns. 272p. 1997. pap. text 14.95 (*0-691-00250-9*, Pub. by Princeton U Pr) Cal Prin Full Svc.

***Matters of Light & Depth.** Ross Lowell. 1999. pap. 28.95 (*0-9662504-0-0*) Lowel-Light.

Matters of Metaphysics. David H. Mellor. (Illus.). 315p. (C). 1991. text 54.95 (*0-521-41117-3*) Cambridge U Pr.

Matters of Mind: The University in Ontario, 1791-1951. A. B. McKillop. (Ontario Historical Studies). 776p. (C). 1994. text 75.00 (*0-8020-0424-5*); pap. text 35.00 (*0-8020-7216-X*) U of Toronto Pr.

Matters of Principle: Legal Argument & Constitutional Interpretation. Richard S. Markovits. LC 98-19602. 352p. 1998. text 50.00 (*0-8147-5513-5*) NYU Pr.

Matters of Proportion: The Portland Residential Architecture of Whidden & Lewis. Richard Marlitt. (Illus.). 96p. (Orig.). 1989. pap. 12.95 (*0-87595-177-5*) Oregon Hist.

Matters of Reality: Body, Mind & Soul. C. Liegh McInnis. LC 96-9260. (Illus.). viii, 88p. (Orig.). 1997. per. 15.00 (*0-9655775-1-1*) Psychedelic Lit.

***Matters of State: A Political Excursion.** Philip Hamburger. 240p. 2001. 25.00 (*1-58243-084-5*, Pub. by Counterpt DC) HarpC.

Matters of the Heart. Nate Collins. LC 96-90791. (Orig.). 1997. pap. 10.95 (*0-533-12177-9*) Vantage.

Matters of the Heart. C. Thom Duncan. 1997. pap. 4.00 (*1-57514-304-6*, 1010) Encore Perform Pub.

Matters of the Heart. Mayo Lucas. 368p. 1988. pap. 3.95 (*0-380-75537-8*, Avon Bks) Morrow Avon.

***Matters of the Heart.** Terry Z. McDermid. LC 99-90716. 192p. 1999. 18.95 (*0-8034-9373-8*, Avalon Bks) Bouregy.

Matters of the Heart. Charlotte Vale Allen. 1998. reprint ed. pap. 22.00 (*1-892738-05-8*) Isld Nation.

Matters of the Heart. Charlotte Vale Allen. 460p. 1999. reprint ed. 24.95 (*1-892738-20-1*, Pub. by Isld Nation) Brodart.

***Mattes & More: Step-by-Step Designs for Scrapbookers.** Christine Smith. (Illus.). 13p. 1998. pap. 4.95 (*1-929420-00-5*) Teeny Pr.

***Mattes & More: Step-by-Step Designs for Scrapbookers.** rev. ed. Christine Smith. (Illus.). 33p. 1999. pap. 10.95 (*1-929420-02-1*) Teeny Pr.

***Mattes & More Vol. 2: More Step-by-Step Designs for Scrapbookers.** Christine Smith. (Illus.). 20p. 1999. pap. 5.95 (*1-929420-01-3*) Teeny Pr.

Matthaei Parisiensis, Monachi Sancti Albani: Chronica Majora, 7 vols., Set. Ed. by Henry R. Luard. Incl. Vol. 1. Creation-1066. 1969. (*0-8115-1119-7*); Vol. 2. 1067-1216. Henry R. Luard. 1969. (*0-8115-1120-0*); Vol. 6. Additamenta. 1969. (*0-8115-1124-3*); Vol. 7. Index Glossary. 1969. (*0-8115-1125-1*); Vol. 3. 1216-1239. 1969. (*0-8115-1121-9*); 1240-1247. 1969. (*0-8115-1122-7*); 1248-1259. 1969. (*0-8115-1123-5*); (Rolls Ser.: No. 57). 1969. reprint ed. 490.00 (*0-685-10006-5*) Periodicals Srv.

Matthaei Parisiensis, Monachi Sancti Albani, Historia Anglorum Sive, ut Vulgo Dicitur, Historia Minor, 3 vols. Ed. by Frederic Madden. (Rolls Ser.: No. 44). 1969. reprint ed. 210.00 (*0-8115-1103-0*) Periodicals Srv.

Matthaeus: De Criminibus, Vol. 1. M. L. Hewett et al. 313p. 1987. 27.50 (*0-7021-1854-0*, Pub. by Juta & Co) Gaunt.

Matthaeus: De Criminibus, Vol. 4. M. L. Hewett & B. Stoop. 454p. 1996. 49.00 (*0-7021-3549-6*, Pub. by Juta & Co) Gaunt.

Matthaeus-Evangelium see Gospel of St. Matthew

Matthaeus-Evangelium see Itala: Das Neue Testament in Altlateinischer Ueberlieferung

Matthean Parables: A Literary & Historical Commentary. Ivor H. Jones. LC 95-18707. (Supplements to Novum Testamentum Ser.: Vol. 80). x, 602p. 1995. 191.50 (*90-04-10181-0*) Brill Academic Pubs.

Mattheus le Maistre: Catechesis Numeris Musicis Inclusa & Schone und Auserlesene Deudsche und Pateinische Geistliche Gesenge. Ed. by Donald Gresch. (Recent Researches in Music of the Renaissance Ser.: Vol. RRR39). (Illus.). xxiii, 90p. 1982. pap. 40.00 (*0-89579-160-9*) A-R Eds.

Matthew see Commentaries on the New Testament

Matthew see IVP New Testament Commentary

Matthew. (People's Bible Commentary Ser.). 454p. pap. 12.99 (*0-570-04963-6*, 12-8047) Concordia.

Matthew. (Ancient Christian Commentary on Scripture Ser.). 1999. lib. bdg. 40.00 (*1-57958-038-6*) Fitzroy Dearborn.

Matthew. (Life Application Bible Study Guide Ser.). 160p. 1992. pap. 5.99 (*0-8423-2883-1*) Tyndale Hse.

Matthew. Michael Albrecht. (People's Bible Teachings Ser.). 275p. 1996. pap. 13.99 (*0-8100-0582-4*, 15N0576) Northwest Pub.

Matthew. Ed. by William F. Albright & C. S. Mann. LC 77-150875. (Anchor Bible Ser.: Vol. 26). 576p. 1971. 37.50 (*0-385-08658-X*, Anchor NY) Doubleday.

Matthew. M. Augsburger. (Mastering the Old & New Testament Ser.: Vol. 1). pap. 14.99 (*0-8499-3317-X*) Word Pub.

Matthew. David R. Bauer. (NIV Application Commentary Ser.). 464p. 24.99 (*0-310-49310-2*) Zondervan.

Matthew. Craig L. Blomberg. LC 92-13777. (New American Commentary Ser.: Vol. 22). 1992. 27.99 (*0-8054-0122-9*) Broadman.

Matthew. Larry Chouinard. LC 97-43055. (College Press NIV Commentary Ser.). 1997. 21.99 (*0-89900-628-0*) College Pr Pub.

Matthew. Concordia Publishing Staff. (God's Word for Today Ser.). 1994. pap. 5.50 (*0-570-09486-0*, 20-2643) Concordia.

Matthew. Margaret Davies. (Readings Ser.). 224p. 1993. 57.50 (*1-85075-392-X*, Pub. by Sheffield Acad); pap. 19.50 (*1-85075-432-2*, Pub. by Sheffield Acad) CUP Services.

***Matthew.** Stephen D. Eyre. (LifeGuide Bible Studies). 2000. pap. 4.99 (*0-8308-3003-0*) InterVarsity.

Matthew. Richard France. Ed. by Leon Morris. (Tyndale New Testament Commentaries Ser.). 416p. (Orig.). 1986. pap. 15.00 (*0-8028-0063-7*) Eerdmans.

Matthew. Richard B. Gardner. Ed. by S. David Garber. LC 91-12048. (Believers Church Bible Commentary Ser.). 448p. (Orig.). 1991. pap. 21.99 (*0-8361-3555-5*) Herald Pr.

Matthew. Dana Gould. LC 97-25012. (Shepherd's Notes). 1997. pap. 5.95 (*1-55819-688-9*) Broadman.

Matthew. Ed. by William M. Greathouse & Williard H. Taylor. (Bible Exposition Ser.: Vol. 1). 223p. 1975. 14.99 (*0-8341-0312-5*) Beacon Hill.

Matthew. Douglas R. Hare. LC 92-17838. (Interpretation: A Bible Commentary for Teaching & Preaching Ser.). 320p. 1993. 25.00 (*0-8042-3126-5*) Westminster John Knox.

Matthew. William Hendriksen. LC 54-924. (New Testament Commentary Ser.). 1016p. 1973. 39.99 (*0-8010-4066-3*) Baker Bks.

Matthew. Henry A. Ironside. LC 93-8057. (Ironside Commentaries). 249p. 1993. pap. 9.99 (*0-87213-425-3*) Loizeaux.

Matthew. Irving L. Jensen. (Bible Self-Study Guides Ser.). pap. 6.99 (*0-8024-4459-8*, 439) Moody.

Matthew. Thomas G. Long. LC 97-16942. (Bible Companion Ser.). 1997. pap. 20.00 (*0-664-25257-5*) Westminster John Knox.

Matthew. Alyce M. Mckenzie. LC 98-11626. (Interpretation Bible Studies). 112p. 1998. pap. 7.95 (*0-664-50022-6*) Geneva Press.

Matthew. M. Meier. 1989. pap. 30.00 (*0-7855-6987-1*, Pub. by Veritas Pubns) St Mut.

Matthew. Robert H. Mounce. (New International Biblical Commentary Ser.). 288p. 1991. pap. 11.95 (*0-943575-18-4*) Hendrickson MA.

Matthew. NavPress Staff. (LifeChange Ser.). 1996. pap. text 7.00 (*0-89109-996-4*) NavPress.

Matthew. C. Price. 1997. pap. 10.99 (*1-85792-285-9*, Pub. by Christian Focus) Spring Arbor Dist.

Matthew. John E. Riches. (New Testament Guides Ser.: Vol. 1). 112p. 1996. pap. 12.50 (*1-85075-741-0*, Pub. by Sheffield Acad) CUP Services.

Matthew. Donald W. Senior. LC 98-13827. (Abingdon New Testament Commentaries Ser.). 384p. 1998. pap. 24.95 (*0-687-05766-3*) Abingdon.

Matthew. Ed. by Manlio Simonetti. (Ancient Christian Commentary on Scripture Ser.). 350p. Date not set. 39.99 (*0-8308-1486-8*, 1486) InterVarsity.

Matthew. Robert Spira. (GRE.). 49p. (Orig.). 1986. pap. 4.95 (*0-911455-02-7*) Quartz Pr.

Matthew. J. Arthur Springer. (Survey of the Scriptures Study Guides Ser.). 1995. pap. 8.99 (*1-56570-001-5*) Meridian MI.

***Matthew.** Jim Starr. (Illus.). 266p. (Orig.). 1999. pap. 2.79 (*1-930264-00-3*) True Jesus.

Matthew. Tyndale House Publishers Staff. (Life Application Bible Studies). 138p. 1999. pap. 5.99 (*0-8423-3418-1*) Tyndale Hse.

Matthew. Ronald D. Witherup. (Spiritual Commentaries on the New Testament Ser.). 216p. 2000. pap. 10.95 (*1-56548-123-2*) New City.

Matthew. J. C. Ryle. (Expository Thoughts on the Gospel Ser.). 368p. 1986. reprint ed. pap. 9.99 (*0-85151-483-9*) Banner of Truth.

Matthew see Preacher's Outline & Sermon Bible - New Testament Set

Matthew. 3rd rev. ed. Jack D. Kingsbury. LC 98-72656. x, 134p. 1998. pap. 12.00 (*0-916035-80-8*) Evangel Indiana.

Matthew, No. 1. William Barclay. 416p. 1993. pap. 30.00 (*0-7152-0270-7*, Pub. by St Andrew) St Mut.

Matthew, No. 2. William Barclay. 392p. 1993. pap. 22.00 (*0-7152-0271-5*, Pub. by St Andrew) St Mut.

Matthew, Pt. 1. J. Vernon McGee. (Thru the Bible Commentary Ser.: Vol. 34). 1997. pap. 6.97 (*0-7852-0637-X*) Nelson.

Matthew, Pt. II. J. McGee. (Thru the Bible Commentary Ser.: Vol. 35). 1997. pap. text 6.97 (*0-7852-0640-X*) Nelson.

Matthew, Vol. 1. STUART WEBER. (Holman New Testament Commentary Ser.). 2000. 16.99 (*0-8054-0201-2*) Broadman.

Matthew, Vol. 1. abr. ed. J. C. Ryle. LC 92-47006. (Classic Commentaries Ser.). 320p. 1993. pap. 15.99 (*0-89107-726-X*) Crossway Bks.

Matthew see Layman's Bible Commentary

Matthew: A Bible Study Commentary. Howard F. Vos. (Study Guide Commentary Ser.). 1979. pap. 6.99 (*0-310-33883-2*, 11152P) Zondervan.

Matthew: A Commentary on His Handbook for a Mixed Church under Persecution. Robert H. Gundry. 744p. 1994. pap. text 38.00 (*0-8028-0735-6*) Eerdmans.

Matthew: A Scribe Trained for the Kingdom of Heaven. O. Lamar Cope. LC 75-36778. (Catholic Biblical Quarterly Monographs: No. 5). 142p. 1976. pap. 4.50 (*0-915170-04-3*) Catholic Bibl Assn.

Matthew: A Simplified Version of the Gospel of Matthew, Pt. 1. Ed. by Laurie Penner. (Illus.). 76p. 1993. reprint ed. pap. text 5.95 (*1-893916-02-2*, 1004) Project Pr.

Matthew: A Simplified Version of the Gospel of Matthew, Pt. 2. Ed. by Laurie Penner. (Illus.). 76p. 1994. reprint ed. pap. text 5.95 (*1-893916-03-0*, 1005) Project Pr.

Matthew: Behold Your King. William MacDonald. 1988. pap. 9.00 (*0-937396-26-5*) Walterick Pubs.

Matthew: Being Discipled by Jesus. Stephen D. Eyre & Jacalyn Eyre. (LifeGuide Bible Studies). 64p. (Orig.). 1987. mass mkt., wbk. ed. 4.99 (*0-8308-1003-X*, 1003) InterVarsity.

Matthew: Evangelist & Teacher see New Testament Profiles

Matthew: Evangelist & Teacher. R. T. France. 345p. 1997. reprint ed. pap. 16.99 (*0-85364-480-2*, Pub. by Paternoster Pub) OM Literature.

Matthew: From the Last Days Bible. 75p. 1994. pap. 2.95 (*0-9642470-0-3*) Life Messengers.

Matthew: Gospel of God's King. Keith L. Brooks. (Teach Yourself the Bible Ser.). pap. 5.99 (*0-8024-5212-4*, 519) Moody.

Matthew: Moody Gospel Commentary. 640p. 1993. pap. 30.00 (*1-881256-23-5*) Wrld Outreach Church.

Matthew: Moody Gospel Commentary. Lawrence E. Glasscock. (Gospel Commentary Ser.). 640p. 1997. pap. 23.99 (*0-8024-5623-5*, 7) Moody.

Matthew: Our Healing God-with-Us. Robert Knopp. (Gospel Images for Prayer Ser.). 248p. 1998. pap. 7.95 (*0-8198-3086-0*) Pauline Bks.

Matthew: People of the Kingdom. Larry Sibley. (Fisherman Bible Studyguide Ser.). 64p. 1988. pap. 4.99 (*0-87788-537-0*, H Shaw Pubs) Waterbrook Pr.

Matthew: People of the Kingdom - Chinese Edition. Larry Sibley. Tr. by John Zheng. (CHI.). 64p. 1995. pap. 5.00 (*1-56582-007-X*) Christ Renew Min.

Matthew: Spirituality for the 80s & 90s. Leonard Doohan. LC 85-70838. (Scripture for Worship Ser.). 214p. (C). 1993. pap. text 10.95 (*0-89390-260-8*) Resource Pubns.

Matthew: Storyteller, Interpreter, Evangelist. Warren Carter. 322p. 1996. pap. 19.95 (*1-56563-153-6*) Hendrickson MA.

Matthew: The King & His Kingdom. David E. Schroeder. LC 95-68989. (Deeper Life Pulpit Commentary Ser.). 298p. (Orig.). 1995. pap. 12.99 (*0-87509-605-0*, 0016050) Chr Pubns.

Matthew: Thy Kingdom Come. John F. Walvoord. 264p. 1998. pap. 13.99 (*0-8254-3969-8*) Kregel.

Matthew Bk. 1, Chapters 1-16: God's Promise Fulfilled. rev. ed. Marilyn Kunz & Catherine Schell. 72p. 1995. pap. 5.99 (*1-880266-18-0*) Neighborhood Bible.

Matthew Bk. 2, Chpts. 17-28: God's Purpose Fulfilled. rev. ed. Marilyn Kunz & Catherine Schell. 85p. 1995. pap. 5.99 (*1-880266-19-9*) Neighborhood Bible.

Matthew Pt. 1: Pupil's Book. Vivian D. Gunderson. (Bible Learn & Do Ser.). (Illus.). 48p. (J). (gr. 6-9). 1993. pap. text, wbk. ed. 2.00 (*0-915374-20-X*) Rapids Christian.

Matthew Pt. I, Chapters 1-13: To Be a Disciple. Frank G. Carver. Ed. by Earl C. Wolf. (Beacon Small-Group Bible Studies). 88p. (Orig.). 1984. pap. 4.99 (*0-8341-0870-4*) Beacon Hill.

Matthew Pt. 2: Pupil's Book. Vivian D. Gunderson. (Bible Learn & Do Ser.). (Illus.). 48p. (Orig.). (J). (gr. 6-9). 1994. pap. text, wbk. ed. 2.00 (*0-915374-21-8*) Rapids Christian.

Matthew Pt. 2: Pupil's Book. Vivian D. Gunderson & Wilfred E. Gunderson. (Bible Learn & Do Ser.). (Illus.). 48p. (Orig.). (J). (gr. 3-8). 1994. pap., wbk. ed. 2.00 (*0-915374-95-1*, 94-4) Rapids Christian.

Matthew Pt. 2, Chapters 13-28: Come & Learn from Me. Earl C. Wolf. Ed. by Frank G. Carver. (Beacon Small-Group Bible Studies). 84p. 1986. pap. 4.99 (*0-8341-1076-8*) Beacon Hill.

Matthew - A Devotional Commentary: Meditations on the Gospel According to St. Matthew. Leo Zanchettin. LC 98-104684. 320p. 1997. pap. 22.95 (*0-8091-3775-5*, 3775-5) Paulist Pr.

Matthew - the Gospel of the Kingdom (Commentary) Charles H. Spurgeon. 1974. pap. 12.00 (*1-56186-202-9*) Pilgrim Pubns.

Matthew & Mark: A Relational Paraphrase. Ben C. Johnson. LC 78-59463. 154p. (Orig.). (C). 1993. reprint ed. pap. text 7.95 (*0-929263-07-3*) Great Love Church Intl.

***Matthew & Mark Bible 2000.** 1999. 24.95 (*5-550-00791-6*) Nairi.

M

An Asterisk (*) at the beginning of an entry indicates that the title is appearing for the first time.

***Matthew & the Margins: A Socio-Political & Religious Reading.** Warren Carter. (Bible & Liberation Ser.). 500p. 2000. pap. 35.00 (*1-57075-324-5*) Orbis Bks.

Matthew & the Midnight Ball Game. unabridged ed. Allen Morgan. LC 96-990105. (Illus.). 32p. (J). (ps-4). 1997. pap. 6.95 (*0-7737-5853-4*) STDK.

Matthew & the Midnight Flood. Allen Morgan. LC 99-235869. (Matthew & the Midnight Ser.). (Illus.). 32p. (J). (ps up). 1998. pap. 6.95 (*0-7737-5941-7*) STDK.

***Matthew & the Midnight Hospital.** Allen Morgan & Michael Martchenko. 32p. (J). (gr. k-3). 1999. pap. 6.95 (*0-7737-6014-8*) Genl Dist Srvs.

Matthew & the Midnight Money Van. Allen Morgan. (Illus.). 24p. (J). (ps-3). 1987. pap. 4.95 (*0-920303-72-2*, Pub. by Annick); lib. bdg. 14.95 (*0-920303-75-7*, Pub. by Annick) Firefly Bks Ltd.

Matthew & the Midnight Money Van. Allen Morgan. (Annikins Ser.: Vol. 11). (Illus.). 32p. (J). (ps-2). 1991. pap. 0.99 (*1-55037-194-0*, Pub. by Annick) Firefly Bks Ltd.

Matthew & the Midnight Pilot. unabridged ed. Allen Morgan. LC 96-990104. (Illus.). 32p. (J). (ps-4). 1997. pap. 6.99 (*0-7737-5852-6*) STDK.

***Matthew & the Midnight Pirates.** Allen Morgan. LC 99-235877. (Matthew & the Midnight Ser.). (Illus.). 32p. (ps-3). 1998. pap. 6.99 (*0-7737-5940-9*) STDK.

Matthew & the Midnight Tow Truck see Mateo y la Grua de Medianoche

Matthew & the Midnight Tow Truck. Allen Morgan. (Illus.). 32p. (J). (ps-3). 1984. pap. 5.95 (*0-920303-01-3*, Pub. by Annick); lib. bdg. 14.95 (*0-920303-00-5*, Pub. by Annick) Firefly Bks Ltd.

Matthew & the Midnight Tow Truck. Allen Morgan. (Annikins Ser.: Vol. 11). (Illus.). 24p. (J). (ps-2). 1991. pap. 0.99 (*1-55037-192-4*, Pub. by Annick) Firefly Bks Ltd.

Matthew & the Midnight Turkeys see Mateo y los Pavos de Medianoche

Matthew & the Midnight Turkeys. Allen Morgan. (Illus.). 24p. (J). (ps-3). 1985. pap. 4.95 (*0-920303-37-4*, Pub. by Annick); lib. bdg. 14.95 (*0-920303-36-6*, Pub. by Annick) Firefly Bks Ltd.

Matthew & the Midnight Turkeys. Allen Morgan. (Annikins Ser.: Vol. 11). (Illus.). 24p. (J). (ps-2). 1991. pap. 0.99 (*1-55037-193-2*, Pub. by Annick) Firefly Bks Ltd.

***Matthew & the Midnight Wrestlers.** Allen Morgan & Michael Martchenko. (Illus.). 32p. (J). 2000. pap. 6.99 (*0-7737-6053-9*, Stoddart Kids) Stoddart Publ.

Matthew & the Sea Singer. Jill Paton Walsh. LC 92-53467. (Illus.). 48p. (J). (ps-3). 1993. 13.00 (*0-374-34869-3*) FS&G.

Matthew & Tilly see Mateo y Mati

Matthew & Tilly. Rebecca C. Jones. 1995. 10.19 (*0-606-08568-8*, Pub. by Turtleback) Demco.

Matthew & Tilly. Rebecca J. Jones. (Illus.). 32p. (J). (ps-3). 1995. pap. 5.99 (*0-14-055640-0*, PuffinBks) Peng Put Young Read.

Matthew Arnold. Lionel Trilling. LC 79-10653. 480p. 1978. 12.95 (*0-15-158202-5*) Harcourt.

Matthew Arnold. Lionel Trilling. LC 79-10653. 493p. 1979. pap. 6.95 (*0-15-657734-8*, Harvest Bks) Harcourt.

Matthew Arnold. George W. Russell. LC 71-130250. (English Literature Ser.: No. 33). 1970. reprint ed. lib. bdg. 75.00 (*0-8383-1140-7*) M S G Haskell Hse.

Matthew Arnold: A Biography. Ian Hamilton. 1999. write for info. (*0-201-48398-X*) Addison-Wesley.

Matthew Arnold: A Life. Park Honan. 512p. 1983. pap. 21.50 (*0-674-55465-5*) HUP.

Matthew Arnold: A Literary Life. Clinton MacHann. LC 97-18187. 1998. text 35.00 (*0-312-21031-0*) St Martin.

Matthew Arnold: Poet & Prophet. A. L. Rowse. (Illus.). 210p. (C). 1986. reprint ed. lib. bdg. 36.00 (*0-8191-5120-3*) U Pr of Amer.

Matthew Arnold: Prose Writings. Ed. by J. Hepburn. (Critical Heritage Ser.). 574p. 1979. 65.00 (*0-7100-0244-0*, Routledge Thoemms) Routledge.

Matthew Arnold: Selected Poetry. Ed. by Keith Silver. 175p. 1995. pap. 14.95 (*1-85754-018-2*, Pub. by Carcanet Pr) Paul & Co Pubs.

Matthew Arnold: The Poet As Humanist. G. Robert Stange. LC 78-17747. 300p. 1979. reprint ed. 50.00 (*0-87752-202-2*) Gordian.

Matthew Arnold, Vol. 1, Prose Writings see Victorian Thinkers

Matthew Arnold, Vol. 2, The Poetry see Victorian Thinkers

Matthew Arnold - Poems. 1998. mass mkt. 3.50 (*0-460-87961-8*, Everyman's Classic Lib) Tuttle Pubng.

Matthew Arnold & Goethe. James Orrick. LC 70-179267. (Studies in Comparative Literature: No. 35). 1972. reprint ed. lib. bdg. 75.00 (*0-8383-1368-X*) M S G Haskell Hse.

Matthew Arnold & His Poetry. Francis L. Bickley. LC 77-120977. (Poetry & Life Ser.). reprint ed. 16.00 (*0-404-52501-6*) AMS Pr.

Matthew Arnold & the Betrayal of Language. David G. Riede. LC 87-13693. (Virginia Victorian Studies). 253p. reprint ed. pap. 78.50 (*0-7837-4347-5*, 204405700012) Bks Demand.

Matthew Arnold & the Education of the New Order: A Selection of Arnold's Writings on Education. Matthew Arnold. Ed. by Peter Smith & Geoffrey Summerfield. LC 69-10433. (Cambridge Texts & Studies in the History of Education). 268p. reprint ed. pap. 76.40 (*0-608-12175-4*, 2024533) Bks Demand.

Matthew Arnold, How to Know Him. Stuart P. Sherman. (BCL1-PR English Literature Ser.). 326p. 1992. reprint ed. lib. bdg. 89.00 (*0-7812-7426-5*) Rprt Serv.

Matthew Arnold in His Time & Ours: Centenary Essays. Ed. by Clinton Machann & Forrest D. Burt. LC 87-25271. 220p. 1988. text 35.00 (*0-8139-1173-7*) U Pr of Va.

Matthew Arnold the Ethnologist. Frederic E. Faverty. LC 68-54264. (Northwestern University. Humanities Ser.: No. 27). reprint ed. 36.50 (*0-404-50727-1*) AMS Pr.

***Matthew Arnold's Critical Legacy.** Laurence W. Mazzeno. LC 99-38102. (Studies in English & American Literature). 256p. 1999. 55.00 (*1-57113-278-3*) Camden Hse.

Matthew Arnold's Letters: A Descriptive Checklist. Arthur K. Davis. LC 68-14092. 478p. reprint ed. pap. 148.20 (*0-608-11327-1*, 201142400078) Bks Demand.

Matthew Arnold's Prose: Three Essays in Literary Enlargement. William E. Buckler. LC 83-45276. (Studies in the Nineteenth Century: No. 3). 116p. 1984. 29.50 (*0-404-61481-7*) AMS Pr.

Matthew As Story. 2nd enl. rev. ed. Jack D. Kingsbury. LC 88-3718. 192p. 1988. pap. 18.00 (*0-8006-2099-2*, 1-2099, Fortress Pr) Augsburg Fortress.

***Matthew B. Ridgway: Soldier, Statesman, Scholar, Citizen.** George C. Mitchell. LC 99-41830. (Illus.). 252p. 1999. pap. 15.95 (*1-887969-10-1*) Cathedral PA.

***Matthew Barney: Cremaster 2.** Matthew Barney. 160p. 1999. pap. 45.00 (*0-935640-64-9*, Pub. by Walker Art Ctr) Dist Art Pubs.

Matthew Barney: Drawing Restraint 7. Klaus Kertess. (Illus.). 76p. 1996. pap. 40.00 (*3-89322-792-X*, Pub. by Edition Cantz) Dist Art Pubs.

Matthew Calbraith Perry: A Typical American Naval Officer. William E. Griffis. (Notable American Authors Ser.). 1992. reprint ed. lib. bdg. 75.00 (*0-7812-2960-X*) Rprt Serv.

Matthew 8-18, Vol. 1. 1991. 69.95 (*0-567-09545-2*, Pub. by T & T Clark) Bks Intl VA.

Matthew 8-15. John MacArthur, Jr. 1986. 23.99 (*0-88469-172-1*) BMH Bks.

Matthew 8-15. John J. MacArthur, Jr. (MacArthur New Testament Commentaries Ser.). 23.99 (*0-8024-0763-3*, 501) Moody.

***Matthew 8-20: Hermeneia.** Ulrich Luz. 2000. 62.00 (*0-8006-6034-X*, Fortress Pr) Augsburg Fortress.

Matthew Fairlesse & Other Works. unabridged ed. Natalie McKelvy. 500p. 1999. pap. 9.00 (*0-944771-24-6*) Dunery Pr.

Matthew Fontaine Maury. Charles L. Lewis. LC 79-6116. (Navies & Men Ser.). (Illus.). 1980. reprint ed. lib. bdg. 31.95 (*0-405-13045-7*) Ayer.

Matthew Fontaine Maury, the Pathfinder of the Seas. Charles L. Lewis. LC 72-98638. reprint ed. 34.50 (*0-404-03984-7*) AMS Pr.

Matthew 4:1-11/Psalm 91. Ed. by David Meyer & Alice Meyer. 16p. (Orig.). 1997. pap. 12.95 (*1-879099-27-6*) Thy Word.

Word Biblical Commentary: Matthew 14-28, 33B. Donald A. Hagner. (Biblical Commentary Ser.: Vol. 33B). 1995. 29.99 (*0-8499-1096-X*) Word Pub.

Matthew G. Lewis, Charles Robert Maturin & the Germans: An Interpretative Study of the Influence of German Literature on Two Gothic Novels. Syndy M. Conger. Ed. by Devendra P. Varma. LC 79-8448. (Gothic Studies & Dissertations). 1980. reprint ed. lib. bdg. 35.95 (*0-405-12652-2*) Ayer.

Matthew Henry Commentary on the Whole Bible. Matthew Henry. LC 97-25241. 1200p. 1997. 24.99 (*0-7852-1247-7*) Nelson.

Matthew Henry Commentary on the Whole Bible Vol. 1: Genesis to Deuteronomy, Vol. 1. Matthew Henry. (Reference Library Edition). 912p. 1986. text 14.99 (*0-529-06365-4*) World Publng.

Matthew Henry Commentary on the Whole Bible Vol. 2: Joshua to Esther, Vol. 2. Matthew Henry. (Reference Library Edition). 1160p. 1986. reprint ed. text 14.99 (*0-529-06366-2*) World Publng.

Matthew Henry Commentary on the Whole Bible Vol. 3: Job to Song of Solomon, Vol. 3. Matthew Henry. (Reference Library Edition). 1112p. 1986. reprint ed. text 14.99 (*0-529-06367-0*) World Publng.

Matthew Henry Commentary on the Whole Bible Vol. 4: Isaiah to Malachi, Vol. 4. Matthew Henry. (Reference Library Edition). 1520p. 1986. reprint ed. text 14.99 (*0-529-06368-9*) World Publng.

Matthew Henry's Commentary on the Whole Bible. Matthew Henry. Ed. by Leslie F. Church. 1986p. 1961. 29.99 (*0-310-26010-8*, 9802) Zondervan.

Matthew Henry's Commentary on the Whole Bible, 6 vols., Set. Matthew Henry. 5290p. 1991. 99.95 (*0-943575-51-6*) Hendrickson MA.

Matthew Henry's Commentary on the Whole Bible: Complete & Unabridged. Matthew Henry. 2528p. 1991. 34.95 (*0-943575-32-X*) Hendrickson MA.

Matthew Henry's Concise Commentary. Matthew Henry. 1024p. 1995. 34.99 (*1-884543-04-9*) O M Lit.

Matthew Henry's Concise Commentary Whole Bible see Comentario Biblia Matthew Henry en un Solo Tomo

Matthew Henson. LaVerne C. Johnson. LC 92-35253. (Empak Heritage Kids: An Empak "Black History" Publication). (Illus.). (J). 1992. 3.95 (*0-922162-94-8*) Empak Pub.

Matthew Henson: Explorer. Michael Gilman. Ed. by Nathan I. Huggins. (Black Americans of Achievement Ser.). (Illus.). 124p. (Orig.). (YA). (gr. 5 up). 1987. lib. bdg. 19.95 (*1-55546-590-0*) Chelsea Hse.

Matthew Henson: Explorer. Michael Gilman. Ed. by Nathan I. Huggins. (Black Americans of Achievement Ser.). (Illus.). 124p. (Orig.). (YA). (gr. 5 up). 1989. pap. 8.95 (*0-7910-0207-1*) Chelsea Hse.

Matthew Henson: North Pole Explorer. Michael Gilman. (Black American Ser.). (Illus.). 192p. (YA). 1990. mass mkt. 3.95 (*0-87067-556-7*, Melrose Sq) Holloway.

Matthew Henson: Polar Adventurer. Jean Williams. LC 93-6101. (First Bks.). (Illus.). 64p. (J). (gr. 5-8). 1994. lib. bdg. 22.00 (*0-531-20006-X*) Watts.

Matthew Henson: Polar Adventurer. large type ed. Jean William. (First Bks.). (Illus.). 64p. (J). (gr. 4-6). 1994. pap. 6.95 (*0-531-15724-5*) Watts.

***Matthew Hilton: Furniture for Our Time.** Catherine McDermott. (Illus.). 80p. 2000. pap. 33.00 (*0-85331-807-7*) Lund Humphries.

Matthew Jackson Meets the Wall. Patricia Reilly Giff. 96p. (J). (gr. 4-7). 1991. pap. 3.50 (*0-440-40547-5*, YB BDD) BDD Bks Young Read.

Matthew Jackson Meets the Wall. Patricia Reilly Giff. (J). 1990. 8.60 (*0-606-00588-9*, Pub. by Turtleback) Demco.

Matthew Kenney's Mediterranean Cooking: Dishes from Tangiers to Toulon for the American Kitchen. Matthew Kenney & Sam Gugino. LC 97-12218. (Illus.). 168p. 1997. 24.95 (*0-8118-1443-2*) Chronicle Bks.

Matthew Looney & the Space Pirates. Jerome Beatty. LC 84-40767. (Young Scott Bks.). (Illus.). (J). 1972. 9.95 (*0-201-09282-4*) HarpC Child Bks.

Matthew-Luke. 2nd ed. Ed. by Albert F. Harper & W. T. Purkiser. (Bible Commentary Ser.: Vol. 6). 623p. 1964. 32.99 (*0-8341-0305-2*) Beacon Hill.

Matthew-Luke Commentary of Philoxenus: Text, Translation & Critical Analysis. Douglas J. Fox. LC 78-12852. (Society of Biblical Literature. Dissertation Ser.: No. 43). 327p. reprint ed. pap. 101.40 (*0-7837-5442-6*, 204520700005) Bks Demand.

Matthew, Mark. Jim Allen. Vol. 2. 588p. 1996. 24.99 (*0-946351-02-3*, Pub. by John Ritchie) Loizeaux.

Matthew, Mark & Luke. Ed. by Michael E. Williams. (Storyteller's Companion to the Bible Ser.: Vol. 9). 18.00 (*0-687-00101-3*) Abingdon.

Matthew, Mark & Luke: Torrance Edition. John Calvin. (Calvin's New Testament Commentaries Ser.: Vol. 1). 1994. pap. 22.00 (*0-8028-0801-8*) Eerdmans.

Matthew, Mark & Luke: Torrance Edition. John Calvin. (Calvin's New Testament Commentaries Ser.: Vol. 2). 1995. pap. 22.00 (*0-8028-0802-6*) Eerdmans.

Matthew, Mark, Luke, & You: Unraveling the Gospel. William J. O'Malley. 264p. (Orig.). 1996. pap. 13.95 (*0-88347-286-4*, 7286) Res Christian Liv.

Matthew, Mark, Luke, James & Jude: Torrance Edition. John Calvin. (Calvin's New Testament Commentaries Ser.: Vol. 3). 1995. pap. 22.00 (*0-8028-0803-4*) Eerdmans.

Matthew McCaslin: Ausstellungen = Exhibitions: Sprengel Museum Hannover, Stadtische Ausstellungs. Matthew McCaslin. (Reihe Cantz Ser.). (Illus.). 1994. pap. text 14.95 (*3-89322-270-7*, Pub. by Edition Cantz) Dist Art Pubs.

Matthew 19-28, Vol. 3. W. D. Davies & Dale C. Allison. Ed. by J. A. Emerton. (International Critical Commentary Ser.). 800p. 1997. 69.95 (*0-567-08518-X*, Pub. by T & T Clark) Bks Intl VA.

Matthew One - Seven: A Continental Commentary. Ulrich Luz. Tr. by Wilhelm C. Linss from GER. LC 92-23792. 416p. 1992. text 49.50 (*0-8006-9600-X*, 1-9600, Fortress Pr) Augsburg Fortress.

Matthew One-Seven. John F. MacArthur, Jr. 1985. 23.99 (*0-88469-168-3*) BMH Bks.

Matthew 1-7. John J. MacArthur, Jr. (MacArthur New Testament Commentaries Ser.). 23.99 (*0-8024-0755-2*, 500) Moody.

Matthew 1-17, Vol. 1. W. D. Davies & Dale C. Allison. (International Critical Commentary Ser.). 780p. 1997. 69.95 (*0-567-09481-2*, Pub. by T & T Clark) Bks Intl VA.

Matthew 1-13. Donald A. Hagner. (Biblical Commentary Ser.: Vol. 33A). 1993. 29.99 (*0-8499-0232-0*) Word Pub.

Matthew Parker & His Books: Sandars Lectures in Bibliography Delivered on 14, 16, & 18 May 1990 at the University of Cambridge. R. I. Page. LC 93-1097. (Illus.). (C). 1990. boxed set 40.00 (*1-879288-20-6*) Medieval Inst.

Matthew Passion: A Lenten Journey to the Cross & Resurrection. John Fenton. LC 97-104370. (Young Reader Ser.). 160p. 1996. pap. 13.99 (*0-8066-2986-X*, 9-2986) Augsburg Fortress.

Matthew Poole's Commentary on the Holy Bible, 3 vols. Matthew Poole. 3104p. 1985. 19.95 (*0-917006-28-3*) Hendrickson MA.

Matthew-Revelation see Clarke's Commentary

Matthew 16-23. John J. MacArthur, Jr. (MacArthur New Testament Commentaries Ser.). 23.99 (*0-8024-0764-1*, 502) Moody.

Matthew Sweet Special: Guitar Section. 112p. 1994. otabind 16.95 (*0-7935-3074-1*, 00308222) H Leonard.

Matthew the Cowboy. Ruth Hooker. (Albert Whitman Prairie Book Ser.). (J). (ps-2). 1994. pap. 5.95 (*0-8075-4998-3*) A Whitman.

Matthew: the King & the Kingdom see Mateo: El Rey y el Reino

Matthew the Magician, Vol. 4148. Kimberlee Graves. (Science Ser.). (Illus.). 16p. (J). (gr. k-1). 1997. pap. 2.75 (*1-57471-311-6*, 4148) Creat Teach Pr.

Matthew to Acts. Gordon Jones. LC 96-1096. (New Sermon Outlines Ser.). 112p. 1998. pap. 7.99 (*0-87213-452-0*) Loizeaux.

Matthew to John see Numerical Bible

Matthew Traveled Around the World. Connie K. McHugh. (Illus.). 32p. (Orig.). (J). (ps-4). 1997. pap. 12.95 incl. audio (*0-9657351-3-3*, Pub. by Music Fantasy) Penton Overseas.

Matthew 24: First Century Fulfillment or End-Time Expectation. Stanley W. Paher. (Illus.). 192p. (Orig.). 1996. pap. 10.95 (*0-913814-40-7*) Nevada Pubns.

Matthew 24-28. John J. MacArthur, Jr. (MacArthur New Testament Commentary Ser.). 1989. 21.99 (*0-8024-0765-X*) Moody.

Matthew 2 see Preacher's Outline & Sermon Bible - New Testament Set

Matthew's Brew. Gina C. Erickson & Kelli C. Foster. (Get Ready...Get Set...Read! Ser.). (Illus.). 26p. (J). (gr. k-3). 1994. pap. 3.50 (*0-8120-1922-9*) Barron.

Matthew's Brew. Kelli C. Foster & Gina C. Erickson. (Get Ready...Get Set...Read! Ser.: Set 5). (Illus.). 26p. (J). 1995. lib. bdg. 11.95 (*1-56674-116-5*) Forest Hse.

Matthew's Christian-Jewish Community. Anthony J. Saldarini. LC 93-5607. (Chicago Studies in the History of Judaism). 326p. 1994. pap. text 17.95 (*0-226-73421-8*); lib. bdg. 55.00 (*0-226-73419-6*) U Ch Pr.

Matthews Collection, African Art: Old & New. Mary Goodwin. (Illus.). 32p. (Orig.). 1992. pap. 20.00 (*0-945486-09-X*) CSU SBRVFAM.

Matthew's Community: The Evidence of his Special Sayings Material. Stephenson H. Brooks. (JSNTS Ser.: Vol. 16). 1987. pap. 23.75 (*1-85075-108-0*, Pub. by Sheffield Acad) CUP Services.

Matthew's Dragon. Susan Cooper. LC 90-31532. (Illus.). 32p. (J). (ps-3). 1991. 14.95 (*0-689-50512-4*) McElderry Bks.

Matthew's Dragon. Susan Cooper. (J). 1994. 11.19 (*0-606-05921-0*, Pub. by Turtleback) Demco.

Matthew's Dragon. Susan Cooper. LC 93-26574. (Illus.). 32p. (J). (gr. k-3). 1994. reprint ed. mass mkt. 5.99 (*0-689-71794-6*) Aladdin.

Matthew's Dream. Bobbi. (Illus.). 51p. (J). 1993. pap. 5.95 (*0-9626608-6-8*) Magik NY.

Matthew's Dream. Leo Lionni. (Illus.). 1995. pap. 5.99 (*0-679-87318-X*) Random.

Matthew's Dream. Leo Lionni. (J). 1995. 11.44 (*0-606-07847-9*) Turtleback.

Matthew's Emmanuel: Divine Presence & God's People in the First Gospel. David D. Kupp. LC 96-373. (Society for New Testament Studies Monographs: No. 90). 311p. 1997. text 64.95 (*0-521-57007-7*) Cambridge U Pr.

Matthew's Gospel & the History of Biblical Interpretation, Bk. 1. Sean P. Kealy. LC 97-22267. (Biblical Press Ser.: Vols. 55a & 55b). 496p. 1997. text 109.95 (*0-7734-2431-8*) E Mellen.

Matthew's Gospel & the History of Biblical Interpretation, Bk. 2. Sean P. Kealy. LC 97-22267. (Biblical Press Ser.: Vols. 55a & 55b). 500p. 1997. text 109.95 (*0-7734-2433-4*) E Mellen.

Matthew's Gospel of Peace & Salvation. Daniel G. Samuels. 84p. 1989. pap. 7.50 (*1-887621-10-5*) Found Ch Divine Truth.

Matthew's Inclusive Story: A Study in the Narrative Rhetoric of the First Gospel. David B. Howell. (JSNT Supplement Ser.: No. 42). 292p. 1990. 80.00 (*1-85075-236-2*, Pub. by Sheffield Acad) CUP Services.

Matthew's Jesus: Gospel Invitations to Believing, Hoping & Loving. William G. Thompson. 32p. 1989. pap. text 2.95 (*1-55612-314-0*) Sheed & Ward WI.

Matthew's Journey into the Deep. Gwen L. Johnson. (Illus.). 144p. (J). (gr. 3-9). 1993. pap. 6.99 (*0-9639527-0-6*) Triton Enter.

Matthew's Majestic Gospel. Ivor C. Powell. LC 86-10401. (Ivor Powell Commentaries Ser.). 526p. 1993. pap. 18.99 (*0-8254-3544-7*) Kregel.

Matthew's Meadow. Corinne D. Bliss. LC 91-10840. (Illus.). 40p. 1997. pap. 7.00 (*0-15-201500-0*) Harcourt.

Matthew's Meadow. Corinne Demas Bliss. 1997. 12.20 (*0-606-11604-4*, Pub. by Turtleback) Demco.

Matthew's Meadow. Corrine D. Bliss. LC 91-10840. (Illus.). 40p. (J). (gr. 1-5). 1992. 15.00 (*0-15-200759-8*, Harcourt Child Bks) Harcourt.

Matthew's Message: Good News for the New Millennium. Grace Imathiu. 72p. 1998. pap. 5.00 (*0-687-02183-9*) Abingdon.

Matthew's Missionary Discourse: A Literary-Critical Analysis. Dorothy Jean Weaver. (JSNT Supplement Ser.: No. 38). 250p. 1990. 75.00 (*1-85075-232-X*, Pub. by Sheffield Acad) CUP Services.

Matthews Municipal Ordinances, 7 vols., Set. Bruce Heskett. 1994. 700.00 (*0-614-06135-0*) West Group.

Matthews Municipal Ordinances, 1963-1992, 7 Vols. Thomas Matthews & Byron Matthews. LC 72-80615. 700.00 (*0-685-09238-0*) West Group.

Matthew's Narrative Portrait of Disciples: How the Text-Connoted Reader Is Informed. Richard A. Edwards. LC 97-1708. 160p. (Orig.). 1997. pap. 15.00 (*1-56338-205-9*) TPI PA.

Matthew's Narrative Use of Galilee in the Multicultural & Missiological Journeys of Jesus. Paul Hertig. LC 98-16139. (Mellen Biblical Press Ser.; Series 46). 204p. 1998. text 89.95 (*0-7734-2444-X*, Mellen Biblical Pr) E Mellen.

Matthew's Narrative Web: Over, & Over, & Over Again. Janice Capel Anderson. (JSNT Supplement Ser.: No. 91). 262p. 1994. 75.00 (*1-85075-450-0*, Pub. by Sheffield Acad) CUP Services.

Matthews, Page, Wilson, Dean, Bartlett & Related Families. Kermit D. Matthews. (Illus.). 290p. 1993. pap. 45.00 (*0-8328-3616-8*); lib. bdg. 55.00 (*0-8328-3615-X*) Higginson Bk Co.

Matthew's Parables: Audience-Oriented Perspectives. Warren Carter & John P. Heil. LC 97-44677. (Catholic Biblical Quarterly Monograph Ser.). 1998. write for info. (*0-915170-29-9*) Catholic Bibl Assn.

Matthew's Piano Book. Andre Previn. 1979. pap. 9.95 (*0-685-69091-1*, HC00103) Shawnee Pr.

Matthews Religions. 2nd ed. Date not set. pap. text, teacher ed. write for info. (*0-314-05378-6*) West Pub.

Matthews Religions. 2nd ed. 1995. student ed. 16.50 (*0-314-05426-X*) West Pub.

Matthew's Transfiguration Story & Jewish-Christian Controversy. A. D. Moses. LC 96-132445. (JSNT Supplement Ser.: No. 122). 294p. 1996. 85.00 (*1-85075-576-0*, Pub. by Sheffield Acad) CUP Services.

An Asterisk (*) at the beginning of an entry indicates that the title is appearing for the first time.

Matthias Claudius: Language as "Infamous Funnel" & Its Imperatives. Herbert Rowland. LC 96-29134. (Illus.). 335p. 1997. 48.50 *(0-8386-3686-1)* Fairleigh Dickinson.

Matthias Erzberger & the Dilemma of German Democracy. Klaus W. Epstein. LC 75-80546. 1971. reprint ed. 47.50 *(0-86527-123-2)* Fertig.

Matthias Grunewald. 3rd ed. Wilhelm Fraenger. (Illus.). 356p. 1995. text 70.00 *(3-364-00107-3)*; pap. text 37.00 *(3-364-00324-6)* Gordon & Breach.

Matthias Scheeben on Faith: The Doctoral Dissertation of John Courtney Murray. Ed. by D. Thomas Hughson. LC 87-5812. (Toronto Studies in Theology: Vol. 29). 256p. 1987. lib. bdg. 89.95 *(0-88946-773-0)* E Mellen.

Matthias Weckmann: Four Sacred Concertos. Matthias Weckmann. Ed. by Alexander Silbiger. (Recent Researches in Music of the Baroque Era Ser.: Vol. RRB46). (Illus.). xxx, 124p. 1984. pap. 50.00 *(0-89579-197-8)* A-R Eds.

Matthieu de Vendome, ars Versificatoria. Roger P. Parr. Ed. by James Robb. LC 80-84768. 1981. pap. 15.00 *(0-87462-222-0)* Marquette.

Mattia Battistini: the Kind of Baritones see Matta Battistini: Il Re Dei Baritoni

Mattie. Judy Alter. 192p. 1997. reprint ed. mass mkt. 3.99 *(0-8439-4156-1)* Dorchester Pub Co.

Mattie: A Woman's Journey West. Nan Weber. LC 95-81342. (Illus.). 160p. (Orig.). 1996. pap. 14.95 *(0-943972-42-6)* Homestead WY.

Mattie: In Search of God. Glenda P. Kuhn. 74p. 1994. 22.50 *(0-9643029-1-8)*; pap. 5.99 *(0-9643029-0-X)* SpritSBo.

Mattie Mae. Edna Beiler. LC 67-24800. (Illus.). 128p. (J). (gr. 3-7). 1967. pap. 5.99 *(0-8361-1789-1)* Herald Pr.

***Mattie Mae.** 2nd ed. Edna Beiler. LC 99-58469. (Illus.). (J). 2000. 6.99 *(0-8361-9143-9)* Herald Pr.

***Mattie Mae.** 2nd ed. Edna Beiler. (Illus.). 112p. (J). (ps-4). 2000. pap. 6.99 *(0-8361-9141-2)* Herald Pr.

Mattie's Hats: Won't Wear That. Elaine Greenstein. LC 96-31233. (Illus.). 40p. (J). (ps-2). 1997. 16.00 *(0-679-88349-5)* Knopf.

***Mattimeo.** Brian Jacques. (Redwall Ser.: Vol. 11). (Illus.). 432p. (J). (gr. 4-7). 1999. mass mkt. 6.50 *(0-441-00610-8)* Ace Bks.

Mattimeo. Brian Jacques. LC 89-37005. (Redwall Ser.: Vol. 3). (Illus.). 448p. (J). (gr. 4-7). 1991. mass mkt. 5.99 *(0-380-71530-9*, Avon Bks) Morrow Avon.

Mattimeo. Brian Jacques. (Redwall Ser.). (Illus.). 448p. (J). (gr. 4-8). 1990. 21.99 *(0-399-21741-X*, Philomel) Peng Put Young Read.

Matting & Framing Made Easy. Janean Thompson. (Illus.). 144p. 1996. pap. text 24.95 *(0-8230-3047-4)* Watsn-Guptill.

Matting & Hinging of Works of Art on Paper. 1991. pap. 10.00 *(0-913069-11-6)* Consultant Pr.

Matting, Mounting & Framing Art. Max Hyder. (Illus.). 144p. 1986. 29.95 *(0-8230-3027-X)* Watsn-Guptill.

Mattino: An Intermediate Italian Grammar Book. A. J. Masciello. 280p. 1995. pap. 16.95 *(0-88962-323-6)* Mosaic.

Mattoon: A Genealogy of the Descendants of Philip Mattoon of Deerfield, Mass. L. G. Mattoon & D. P. Mattoon. (Illus.). 339p. 1995. reprint ed. pap. 52.50 *(0-8328-4800-X)*; reprint ed. lib. bdg. 62.50 *(0-8328-4799-2)* Higginson Bk Co.

Mattress Factory: Installation & Performance, 1982-1989. Ed. by Susan Blackman. (Illus.). 223p. (Orig.). 1991. pap. 35.00 *(0-9623290-0-2)* Mattress Factory.

Mattress Testing. John McAuley. 1979. pap. 3.00 *(0-916696-09-X)* Cross Country.

***Matt's Best Christmas Ever.** large type ed. LC 00-130191. (Illus.). 40p. (J). (gr. 1-5). 2001. lib. bdg. 14.95 *(1-893595-06-4)* Four Seasons Bks.

Matt's Bike. Sharon Wohl. 8p. (J). (gr. k-2). 1998. mass mkt. 4.95 *(0-9665443-9-0)* A Better Way.

***Matt's Family.** Lynnette Kent. (Superromance Ser.: Vol. 938). 2000. mass mkt. 4.50 *(0-373-70938-2*, 1-70938-5) Harlequin Bks.

Matt's Hat. Rhyk Gilbar. LC 96-92291. (Illus.). 32p. (J). (ps-3). 1996. pap. 6.95 *(1-888588-17-9)*; lib. bdg. 14.95 *(1-888588-16-0)* Positive Press.

Matt's Mitt & Fleet-Footed Florence. Marilyn Sachs. 80p. (J). 1991. pap. 2.95 *(0-380-70963-5*, Avon Bks) Morrow Avon.

***Matt's Story.** Random House Staff. 176p. (J). (gr. 4-7). 1999. pap. 4.99 *(0-375-80333-5)* Random Hse Chldrns.

Matty & Patty. Cheryl Christian. LC 97-25375. (Domino Readers Ser.). (Illus.). 24p. (J). (ps-1). 1998. pap. 5.95 *(1-887734-30-9)* Star Brght Bks.

***Matty Doolin.** Cookson. 2000. 17.95 *(0-385-40138-8*, Pub. by Transworld Publishers Ltd) Trafalgar.

Matty's Heart: A Child's & Parents' Guide to Open Heart Surgery. Jean Clabough. Ed. by Debbie Polk & M. W. Cocalis. LC 94-71677. (Child's & Parent's Medical Storybooks Ser.: Vol. 1). (Illus.). 55p. (J). (gr. k-6). 1995. lib. bdg. 14.95 *(0-9638662-3-0)* Aletheia CA.

Matty's Heart Cath: Story & Coloring Book. Jean Clabough. (Illus.). 20p. (J). (gr. k-6). 1995. pap., wbk. ed. 3.99 *(0-9638662-0-6)* Aletheia CA.

Matura: Six Plays. Mustapha Matura. 374p. (C). 1992. pap. 13.95 *(0-413-66070-2*, A0631, Methuen Drama) Methn.

Maturation Factors & Cancer. Malcolm A. Moore. LC 80-5836. (Progress in Cancer Research & Therapy Ser.: Vol. 23). 405p. 1982. reprint ed. pap. 125.60 *(0-608-00323-9*, 206104000007) Bks Demand.

Maturation of Fetal Body Systems: Proceedings of the WHO Scientific Group, Geneva, 1973. WHO Staff. (Technical Reports: No. 540). 1974. pap. text 5.00 *(92-4-120540-7*, 1100540) World Health.

Maturation of Neurotransmission: Proceedings of the Satellite Symposium, Sainte-Vincent, August, 1977. Satellite Symposium on Maturational Aspects of Neu. Ed. by Antonia Vernadakis et al. (Illus.). 1978. 68.00 *(3-8055-2833-7)* S Karger.

Maturation of the Prophetic Life. Michael Lattiboudeaire. LC 98-91111. 100p. 1999. pap. 14.95 *(1-889448-51-6)* NBN Publishers Group.

Maturation of the Therapeutic Community: An Organic Approach to Health & Mental Health. Maxwell Jones. LC 75-11002. 169p. 1976. 32.95 *(0-87705-264-6*, Kluwer Acad Hman Sci) Kluwer Academic.

Maturation Phenomenon in Cerebral Ischemia: Proceedings of the Satelite Symposium of the International Congress on Neuropathology, 11th, Tokyo, September 11-12, 1990. Ed. by Umeo Ito et al. (Illus.). 192p. 1992. 82.95 *(0-387-54871-8)* Spr-Verlag.

Maturation Phenomenon in Cerebral Ischemia Vol. II: Neuronal Recovery & Plasticity, No. II. Ed. by Umeo Ito et al. LC 96-36379. (Illus.). 193p. 1997. pap. 78.00 *(3-540-61673-X)* Spr-Verlag.

Maturation Phenomenon in Cerebral Ischemia III: Defense Mechanisms Versus Apoptosis. Neuronal Recovery & Protection in Cerebral Infarction. Ed. by U. Ito et al. LC 98-44835. (Illus.). 320p. 1999. pap. 89.00 *(3-540-65023-7)* Spr-Verlag.

Maturational Processes & the Facilitating Environment: Studies in the Theory of Emotional Development. Donald Woods Winnicott. 296p. 1965. 45.00 *(0-8236-3200-8)* Intl Univs Pr.

Maturational Windows & Adult Cortical Plasticity. B. Julesz. (C). 1995. pap. 38.00 *(0-201-48370-X)* Addison-Wesley.

Mature Advertising: A Handbook of Effectiveness in Print. Robert B. Parker. 1981. 19.95 *(0-201-05714-X)* Addison-Wesley.

Mature Audiences: Television & the Elderly. Karen E. Riggs. LC 97-49866. (Communications, Media & Culture Ser.). 224p. (C). 1998. pap. text 18.00 *(0-8135-2540-3)* Rutgers U Pr.

Mature Audiences: Television in the Lives of Elders. Karen E. Riggs. LC 97-49866. (Communications, Media & Culture Ser.). xiv, 197p. (C). 1998. text 48.00 *(0-8135-2539-X)* Rutgers U Pr.

Mature Christianity in the 21st Century: The Recognition & Repudiation of the Anti-Jewish Polemic of the New Testament. rev. ed. Norman A. Beck. LC 93-46884. (Shared Ground among Jews & Christians Ser.: Vol. 5). 320p. 1994. 26.95 *(0-8245-1358-4)* Crossroad NY.

Mature Christians Are Boring People: And Other Myths about Maturity in Christ - A Daily Devotional for Teens. Ron Luce. LC 98-208051. 208p. (YA). 1997. pap. 9.99 *(1-57778-037-X*, Pub. by Albury Pub) Appalach Bk Dist.

Mature Elegance: Styles & Techniques for Mature Clients. Sara Ringler & Louise Cotter. LC 97-14863. 160p. (C). 1997. pap. 31.95 *(1-56253-339-8)* Thomson Learn.

Mature Faith: Spiritual Direction & Anthropology in a Theology of Pastoral Care & Counseling. D. J. Louw. (Louvain Theological & Pastoral Monographs). 323p. 1999. pap. 30.00 *(0-8028-4670-X)* Eerdmans.

Mature Gravida. Virginia A. Passero. Ed. by Karla Damus et al. LC 95-33586. 1995. write for info. *(0-86525-067-7)* March of Dimes.

***Mature Imagination: Dynamics of Identity in Midlife & Beyond.** Simon Biggs. LC 98-33196. 224p. 1999. pap. 26.95 *(0-335-20102-4)* OpUniv Pr.

***Mature Imagination: Dynamics of Identity in Midlife & Beyond: Dynamics of Identity in Midlife & Beyond.** Simon Biggs. LC 98-33196. 1999. 85.00 *(0-335-20103-2)* Taylor & Francis.

Mature Laurel: Essays on Modern Polish Poetry. Ed. by Adam Czerniawski. LC 90-24814. 320p. 1990. 35.00 *(0-8023-1292-6)* Dufour.

Mature Market. LC 99-171286. 162p. 1996. write for info. *(1-56241-376-7)* FIND-SVP.

Mature Market: A Gold Mine of Ideas for Tapping the 50 Plus Market. Robert S. Menchin. 265p. 1991. per. 24.95 *(1-55738-236-0*, Irwn Prfssnl) McGraw-Hill Prof.

Mature Modification & Dimorphism in Selected Late Paleozoic Ammonoids see Bulletins of American Paleontology: Vol. 62

Mature Money: Marketing Financial Services to the Booming Maturity Market. Joan M. Gruber. 288p. 1996. text 40.00 *(0-7863-0971-7*, Irwn Prfssnl) McGraw-Hill Prof.

Mature Stuff. 1990. 35.00 *(0-88314-433-6)* AAHPERD.

Mature Traveler's Book of Deals. 3rd rev. ed. Malloc. 144p. 1998. pap. 7.95 *(0-9629034-9-3)* GEM Pub Group.

Mature Traveler's Guide to Walt Disney World: And Other Orlando Attractions. Kerry Smith. LC 97-93608. (Illus.). 320p. 1997. pap. 13.95 *(0-9658189-1-8)* Mercurial Pr.

Mature Woman. Saiichi Maruya. Tr. by Dennis Keene. 328p. 1995. 28.00 *(4-7700-1864-9)* Kodansha.

Mature Woman. Saiichi Maruya. 1997. pap. text 12.00 *(4-7700-2183-6*, Pub. by Kodansha Intl) Kodansha.

Mature Women Students: Separating or Connecting Family & Education. Rosalind Edwards. (Gender & Society Ser.). 192p. 1993. 89.95 *(0-7484-0086-9)*; pap. 29.95 *(0-7484-0087-7)* Taylor & Francis.

Maturing Christian. Douglas J. Simpson. 1977. pap. 1.95 *(0-89265-047-8)* Randall Hse.

Maturing in a Changing World. E. Shipton et al. 1971. text 5.60 *(0-13-566166-8)* P-H.

Maturing in Hard Times: Canada's Department of Finance through the Great Depression. Robert B. Bryce. (Canadian Public Administration Ser.). 320p. 1986. 65.00 *(0-7735-0555-5*, Pub. by McG-Queens Univ Pr) CUP Services.

***Maturing Marketplace: Buying Habits of Baby Boomers & Their Parents.** George P. Moschis et al. LC 99-36602. (Illus.). 320p. 2000. 67.50 *(1-56720-344-2*, Q344, Quorum Bks) Greenwood.

Maturing of Multinational Enterprise: American Business Abroad from 1914 to 1970. Mira Wilkins. LC 73-88499. (Studies in Business History: No. 27). 590p. (C). 1974. 49.95 *(0-674-55475-2)* HUP.

Maturing Process. Barbara H. Seguin. 94p. 1987. pap. 3.95 *(0-88144-102-3)* Christian Pub.

Maturing Sun. large type ed. Rowan Edwards. (Dales Romance Ser.). 1992. pap. 13.95 *(1-85389-305-6*, Pub. by Mgna Lrg Print) Ulverscroft.

Maturing Weapon Systems for Improved Availability at Lower Costs. John Dumond et al. LC 94-6662. 1994. pap. 13.00 *(0-8330-1513-3*, MR-338-A) Rand Corp.

Maturity. Warren W. Wiersbe. LC 94-7624. (Thirty-Day Devotional Ser.). 72p. (Orig.). 1994. pap. 3.50 *(1-56476-261-0*, 6-3261, Victor Bks) Chariot Victor.

***Maturity: Evolution of the Self.** Justin L. Petaelio. LC 00-190513. 276p. 2000. 15.95 *(0-9700245-0-9)* DualGems.

Maturity: The Responsibilty of Being Oneself. Osho. LC 99-32893. 208p. 1999. pap. 11.95 *(0-312-20561-9*, St Martins Paperbacks) St Martin.

Maturity & Modernity: Nietzsche, Weber, Foucault, & the Ambivalence of Reason. David Owen. 272p. 1997. pap. 18.95 *(0-415-15343-3)* Routledge.

Maturity & Modernity: Nietzsche, Weber, Foucault, & the Ambivalence of Reason. David Owen. 272p. (C). 1997. pap. 24.99 *(0-415-15352-2)* Routledge.

Maturity & Stagnation in American Capitalism. Josef Steindl. LC 73-90077. 1978. pap. 10.00 *(0-85345-429-9*, Pub. by Monthly Rev) NYU Pr.

Maturity & the Quest for Spiritual Meaning. Ed. by Charles C. Kao. LC 88-9609. 224p. (Orig.). (C). 1988. lib. bdg. 45.00 *(0-8191-6972-2)* U Pr of Amer.

Maturity Is a Choice: Not Everyone Who Grows Old, Chooses to Grow Up! Karol Hess & Doug McCulley. 283p. (Orig.). (C). 1994. pap. 12.99 *(0-89900-679-5)* College Pr Pub.

Maturity Is a Paper Tiger. Illus. by Robin Shaw. 38p. 1987. pap. 6.00 *(0-9616570-2-2)* J G Bruhn.

Maturity Market. Ed. by Peter Allen. 222p. 1988. pap. 995.00 *(0-941285-28-6)* FIND-SVP.

Maturity Market: Americans 55 & Over. Ed. by Peter Allen. 200p. 1985. pap. 995.00 *(0-931634-47-4)* FIND-SVP.

Matutu. Sally Ash. Ed. by Pamela R. Goodfellow. 384p. 1997. pap. 12.99 *(0-9639882-9-8)* Goodfellow Pr.

Matvei Petrovich Bronstein & Soviet Theoretical Physics in the Thirties. Gennady E. Gorelik & Victor Y. Frenkel. Tr. by Valentina M. Levina. LC 93-34473. (Science Networks: Historical Studies Ser.: Vol. 12). (Illus.). 208p. 1994. 139.00 *(0-8176-2752-9)* Birkhauser.

Mat/women Health. Matteson. 2001. text. write for info. *(0-323-00915-8)* Harcourt.

Matza 101: An Innovative Cookbook Containing "101" Creative Recipes Simply Made with Matza! 2nd rev. ed. Jenny Kdoshim & Debbie Bevans. (Illus.). 141p. 1995. 29.99 *(0-9646564-1-8)* Matza One-Hund One.

Matza 101: An Innovative Cookbook Containing "101" Creative Recipes Simply Made with Matza. 3rd ed. Jenny Kdoshim. 1997. 29.99 *(0-9646564-2-6)* Matza One-Hund One.

***Matza 101: An Innovative Cookbook Containing 101 Creative Recipes Simply Made with Matza!** Jenny Kdoshim. 1998. 27.95 *(0-9646564-3-4)* Matza One-Hund One.

Matzah Ball. Mindy A. Portnoy. LC 93-39402. (Illus.). (J). (gr. 1-5). 1994. pap. 6.95 *(0-929371-69-0)* Kar-Ben.

Matzah Ball Fairy. Carla Heymsfeld. (Illus.). 32p. (J). (ps-3). 1996. 11.95 *(0-8074-0600-7*, 101070) UAHC.

***Matzah Ball Soup Book Club Edition.** Joan Rothenberg. (J). 1999. 14.99 *(0-7868-0574-9*, Pub. by Disney Pr) Little.

Matzah That Papa Brought Home. Fran Manushkin. LC 94-9952. (Illus.). 32p. (J). (ps-2). 1995. 14.95 *(0-590-47146-5)* Scholastic Inc.

Matzah's Favorite Thing. Dorothy Fish & Betty Cohen. (Illus.). 20p. (J). (ps-3). 1998. spiral bd. 5.99 *(0-914080-09-1)* Shulsinger Sales.

Matzo Ball Moon. Newman. 1998. 15.00 *(0-395-71519-9)* Ticknor & Fields.

Matzo Ball Moon. Leslea Newman. LC 95-49577. (Illus.). 32p. (J). (gr. k-3). 1998. 15.00 *(0-395-71530-X*, Clarion Bks) HM.

Matzo Ball Soup. Joan Rothenberg. LC 95-24432. (Illus.). 32p. (J). (ps-3). 1999. 14.99 *(0-7868-0202-2*, Pub. by Hyprn Child); lib. bdg. 15.49 *(0-7868-2170-1*, Pub. by Hyprn Child) Little.

Matzo Ball Soup: The Balls That Bobbed in the Broth That Bubbe Brewed. Jennifer Littman. (Illus.). 32p. (Orig.). (J). (ps-2). 1997. pap. 7.95 (0-9656431-0-7) Brickford Ln.

It is a cumulative story written with the rhythm, rhyme & repetition that children love. It is beautifully illustrated, & it is designed to support multicultural programs, family studies, Grandparents' Day, Shabbat, & cooking activities. In the book Bubbe prepares for Shabbat (Jewish Sabbath) dinner by making her family's favorite soup. First, Bubbe makes a broth, & with each new page she adds something else to her soup. Finally, dinner is ready, & all of her grandchildren are there to eat her special soup. The book includes a children's recipe for matzo ball soup & a glossary for Yiddish words. Pre-K to Grade 2. *Publisher Paid Annotation.*

Matzo Bunny. Nancy P. Ross. (Illus.). 20p. (Orig.). (J). (ps-4). 1995. pap. 8.95 *(0-9645964-0-7)* Powerhse Advert.

Matzo Mitzvah: Even More Tales My Great-Great-Grandfather Might Tell about Life in a Ghetto of Russia in the Time of the Czars. Herman I. Kantor & Eric Larson. LC 96-8331. (Illus.). 192p. 1996. 18.95 *(1-56474-179-6)*; pap. 9.95 *(1-56474-178-8)* Fithian Pr.

Matzoh Mouse. Lauren L. Wohl. LC 90-31976. (Charlotte Zolotow Bk.). (Illus.). 32p. (J). (gr. k-3). 1993. pap. 4.95 *(0-06-443323-4*, HarpTrophy) HarpC Child Bks.

Mau Mau & Kenya: An Analysis of a Peasant Revolt. Wunyabari O. Maloba. LC 92-31421. (Blacks in the Diaspora Ser.). (Illus.). 244p. (C). 1998. pap. 11.95 *(0-253-21166-2)*; text 36.95 *(0-253-33664-3)* Ind U Pr.

Mau Mau Detainee: The Account by a Kenya African of His Experiences in Detention Camps 1953-1960. Josiah M. Kariuki. LC DT0434. (Illus.). 222p. reprint ed. pap. 68.90 *(0-608-11628-9*, 20023110012) Bks Demand.

Mau Mau from Below. Greet Kershaw. LC 96-41339. (Eastern African Studies). (Illus.). 383p. (C). 1996. text 39.95 *(0-8214-1154-3)*; pap. text 19.95 *(0-8214-1155-1)* Ohio U Pr.

M

Mau Mau from Within: Autobiography & Analysis of Kenya's Peasant Revolt. Donald L. Barnett & Karari Njama. LC 65-24519. (Illus.). 510p. reprint ed. pap. 158.10 *(0-7837-3911-7*, 204375900010) Bks Demand.

Mau Mau Memoirs: History, Memory, & Politics. Marshall S. Clough. LC 97-36869. 284p. 1997. lib. bdg. 25.00 *(1-55587-537-8)* L Rienner.

Mau Mau War in Perspective. Frank Furedi. LC 89-32962. 239p. 1989. text 29.95 *(0-8214-0940-9)*; pap. text 15.95 *(0-8214-0941-7)* Ohio U Pr.

Mau Mau's Daughter: The Life History of Wambui Waiyaki Otieno. Wambui Otieno. Ed. & Intro. by Cora A. Presley. LC 98-10980. 255p. 1998. lib. bdg. 49.95 *(1-55587-722-2)* L Rienner.

***Mauch Chunk/Jim Thorpe.** Drury. (Images of America Ser.). 128p. 1999. pap. 18.99 *(0-7524-1325-2)* Arcadia Publng.

Mauchline Ware. John Baker. (Album Ser.: No. 140). (Illus.). 32p. 1998. pap. 6.25 *(0-85263-734-9*, Pub. by Shire Pubns) Parkwest Pubns.

Maud Gonne. Nancy Cardozo. Orig. Title: Lucky Eyes & a High Heart. (Illus.). 468p. (C). 1990. reprint ed. pap. 16.95 *(0-941533-95-6*, NAB) I R Dee.

Maud Gonne: Ireland's Joan of Arc. Margaret Ward. 232p. 1990. pap. 16.95 *(0-685-33058-3*, Pub. by Pandora) Routldge.

Maud Hart Lovelace. Ken Berg. LC 94-3389. (Tribute to the Young at Heart). (J). 1994. pap. 4.95 *(1-56239-372-3)* ABDO Pub Co.

Maud Hart Lovelace. Ken Berg. LC 94-3389. (Tribute to the Young at Heart). (Illus.). 32p. (J). 1994. lib. bdg. 14.98 *(1-56239-361-8)* ABDO Pub Co.

Maud Humphrey: Her Permanent Imprint on American Illustration. Karen Choppa & Paul Humphrey. LC 93-85279. (Illus.). 160p. 1993. 59.95 *(0-88740-540-1)*; pap. 29.95 *(0-88740-546-0)* Schiffer.

Maud in France. Alain Cheneviere. Tr. by Lisa Davidson. LC 95-30976. (My Future Ser.). (J). 1996. lib. bdg. 22.60 *(0-8225-2828-2*, Lerner Publctns) Lerner Pub.

Maud Latimer: Patience & Impatience, 10 vols. Ed. by Chris Zarate. (Rays of Sunshine Ser.: Vol. 3). (Illus.). 185p. 1998. reprint ed. pap. 10.50 *(1-893645-03-7)* Born Again.

Maud Martha. Gwendolyn Brooks. LC 92-63012. 192p. 1993. reprint ed. pap. 9.95 *(0-88378-061-5)* Third World.

Maud Morgan: A Retrospective Exhibition, 1927-1977. (Illus.). 60p. (Orig.). 1977. pap. write for info. *(1-879886-22-7)* Addison Gallery.

Maud of Llangibbi. Bob Murray & Alicia Fortinberry. 376p. (Orig.). 1996. pap. 9.95 *(1-885610-02-5)* European Amer.

Maud Powell, Legendary American Violinist. Karen A. Shaffer. (Women in Music Ser.). 24p. (J). (gr. 3-9). 1994. pap. 5.95 *(1-885824-00-9)* M Powell Fnd.

Maude. Suzanne Jacob. Tr. by Luise Von Flotow from FRE. LC 96-80175. 126p. 1997. pap. 10.00 *(1-55071-049-4)* Guernica Editions.

Maude. Christina Georgina Rossetti & Dinah M. Craik. Ed. by Elaine Showalter. LC 92-38333. (Women's Classics Ser.). 223p. (C). 1993. text 55.00 *(0-8147-7442-3)* NYU Pr.

Maude. Christina Georgina Rossetti & Dinah M. Craik. Ed. by Elaine Showalter. LC 92-38333. (Women's Classics Ser.). 223p. (C). 1995. pap. text 19.50 *(0-8147-7451-2)* NYU Pr.

Maude & Walter. Zibby O'Neal. LC 84-48357. (Illus.). 32p. (J). (ps-2). 1985. 11.95 *(0-397-32150-3)* HarpC Child Bks.

Maude (1883-1993) She Grew up with the Country. Mardo Williams. (Illus.). 335p. 1996. 22.95 *(0-9649241-2-9)* Calliope NY.

Maude's Ice Cream. deluxe ed. Darrell Rubel. (Set 1 Ser.: Vol. 3). (Illus.). 20p. (J). (ps-3). 1997. pap. 2.50 *(1-890567-02-7)* Berry Bks Ltd.

Maudie: A Positive Nursing Home Experience. Ricca L. Metz. (Illus.). 144p. 1999. 9.95 *(0-8158-0535-7)* Chris Mass.

Maudie: An Oregon Trail Childhood. Maude S. Maple. Ed. by Will Muller. (Illus.). 169p. (Orig.). (YA). 1993. pap. write for info. *(0-9637370-0-7)* Lincoln Sq.

Maudie & Me & the Dirty Book. Betty Miles. 140p. (J). (gr. 4-7). 1981. pap. 2.95 *(0-380-55541-7*, Avon Bks) Morrow Avon.

M

Maudie & the Green Children. Adrian Mitchell. (Illus.). 32p. (J). (gr. k-4). 1996. pap. 14.95 (*1-896580-06-8*, Pub. by T1rad Bks) Tricycle Pr.

Maudie in the Middle. Phyllis Reynolds Naylor & Lura Schield Reynolds. LC 87-3470. (Illus.). 176p. (J). (gr. 2-6). 1988. lib. bdg. 16.00 (*0-689-31395-0*) Atheneum Yung Read.

Maudite. Guy Des Cars. (FRE.). 320p. 1971. pap. 10.95 (*0-7859-4797-3*) Fr & Eur.

Maudlin Scourge. Mary Denis Reidy. 228p. mass mkt. 4.99 (*1-896329-43-8*) Picasso Publ.

Maud's House. Sherry Roberts. LC 94-715. 216p. 1994. 18.00 (*0-918949-32-7*) Roberts.

Maud's House. Sherry Roberts. LC 94-715. 216p. 1995. pap. 11.00 (*0-918949-28-9*) Roberts.

Maudslay's Central America: A Strategic View in 1887 see Studies in Middle American Economics

Maudsley & Burn's Land Law - Cases & Materials. 6th ed. E. H. Burn. 960p. 1992. pap. 58.00 (*0-406-60988-8*, UK, MICHIE) LEXIS Pub.

Maudsley & Burn's Trusts & Trustees: Cases & Materials. E. H. Burn. 1996. pap. write for info. (*0-406-01445-0*, MBTT5SC, MICHIE) LEXIS Pub.

Maudsley Handbook of Practical Psychiatry. 3rd ed. Ed. by David P. Goldberg & Bethlem Royal Hospital & the Maudsley Hospital Sta. LC 97-3039. (Oxford Medical Publications). (Illus.). 294p. 1997. pap. 27.50 (*0-19-262853-4*) OUP.

Maududi, Thought & Movements. A. Gilani. 1992. 25.00 (*1-56744-130-0*) Kazi Pubns.

Mauet's Trial Notebook. Thomas A. Mauet. pap. 80.00 incl. disk (*0-316-55111-2*, 51090) Aspen Law.

Mauet's Trial Notebook. 2nd ed. Thomas A. Mauet. LC 98-9798. 1998. write for info. (*1-56706-942-8*); ring bd. 89.00 (*1-56706-941-X*) Aspen Law.

Maugham. Ted Morgan. LC 80-26890. (Touchstone Book Ser.). xxi, 711p. 1981. 9.95 (*0-671-42811-X*) S&S Trade.

Maugham's Choice of Kipling's Best. Rudyard Kipling. Ed. by W. Somerset Maugham. reprint ed. lib. bdg. 27.95 (*0-88411-822-3*) Amereon Ltd.

Maughan & Webb: Lawyering Skills & the Legal Process. Caroline Maughan & Julian Webb. 1995. pap. write for info. (*0-406-04466-X*, WMLS, MICHIE) LEXIS Pub.

Maui. 42.95 (*0-528-81537-7*) Rand McNally.

Maui: Making the Most of Your Family Vacation. 5th ed. Greg Stilson & Christie Stilson. (Paradise Family Guides Ser.). (Illus.). 224p. (Orig.). 1992. pap. 12.95 (*1-55958-234-0*) Prima Pub.

Maui: Notes from a Private Guidebook. Hupi Paitson & Lloyd Paitson. (Illus.). (Orig.). 1970. pap. 1.50 (*0-941200-01-9*) Aquarius.

Maui: The Mischief Maker. Dietrich Varez & Pua K. Kanahele. 84p. 1991. 16.00 (*0-930897-53-6*) Bishop Mus.

Maui - How It Came to Be. Will Kyselka & Ray Lanterman. LC 80-10743. (Illus.). 168p. (J). (gr. 5-10). 1980. pap. 12.95 (*0-8248-0530-5*) UH Pr.

*__Maui & Hawaii Islands.__ Ecomae Baunach. LC 99-90857. (Travel Book for Kids Ser.: No. 3). (Illus.). 32p. (J). (ps-3). 2000. pap. 8.95 (*0-9651202-7-9*) Park Publishing.

Maui & His Magical Deeds. Kats Kajiyama. LC 97-71683. (Illus.). (J). 19.95 (*0-940350-27-0*) Barnaby Bks.

Maui & His Magical Deeds. Kats Kajiyama. Ed. by Donivee M. Laird. Tr. by Ahahui Olelo Hawaii Staff. (Illus.). 36p. (J). (gr. 2-4). 1997. 19.95 (*0-940350-28-9*) Barnaby Bks.

Maui & Lanai: Making the Most of Your Family Vacation. 7th ed. Christie Stilson. (Paradise Family Guides Ser.). (Illus.). 448p. 1996. pap., per. 15.00 (*0-7615-0655-1*) Prima Pub.

Maui & Lanai: Making the Most of Your Family Vacation. 8th ed. Christie Stilson & Greg Stilson. LC 99-180929. (Illus.). 456p. 1998. pap. 15.00 (*0-7615-1480-5*) Prima Pub.

Maui & the Secret of Fire. Suelyn C. Tune. LC 90-27175. (Illus.). 32p. (J). (ps-4). 1991. 9.95 (*0-8248-1391-X*, Kolowalu Bk) UH Pr.

Maui Art & Creative People. Ed. by Paul D. Wood. LC 96-204553. 168p. 1987. 8.95 (*0-9614443-2-0*) Jungle Pr.

Maui Art Thoughts: Expressions & Visions. Victor C. Pellegrino. LC 88-92541. (Illus.). 112p. 1988. pap. 9.95 (*0-945045-01-8*) Maui Arthoughts.

Maui Booklet. Hupi Paitson. (Illus.). 1970. pap. 0.50 (*0-941200-00-0*) Aquarius.

Maui Cooks Again. Maui Cooks Inc. Staff. (Illus.). pap. 15.95 (*0-9639120-0-3*) Maui Cooks.

Maui Dreams, 1975-95. Ken Hess. pap. 11.95 (*0-9614443-7-1*) Jungle Pr.

Maui Goes Fishing. Julie S. Williams. LC 90-27176. (Illus.). 32p. (J). (ps-4). 1991. 9.95 (*0-8248-1390-1*, Kolowalu Bk) UH Pr.

Maui-Maui. Stephen Cosgrove. LC 94-21449. (Serendipity Bks.). (Illus.). 32p. (J). (gr. k-4). 1995. pap. 4.99 (*0-8431-3829-7*, Price Stern) Peng Put Young Read.

Maui Millie's Famous Cheesecakes. Millie Slawson & Phyllis McElroy. 77p. (Orig.). 1995. pap. 12.95 (*0-9648054-0-5*) Slawson McElroy.

Maui Mouse's Supper. Marilyn Kahalewai. LC 87-92276. (Illus.). 16p. (Orig.). (J). (ps-3). 1989. pap. 4.95 (*1-880188-68-6*) Bess Pr.

Maui, '90: With Complete Hotel & Restaurant Reviews. 160p. 1990. 7.95 (*0-685-31375-1*) McKay.

Maui Now. Jack H. Stephens et al. (Illus.). (Orig.). 1969. pap. 1.70 (*0-941200-02-7*) Aquarius.

Maui-of-a-Thousand-Tricks: His Oceanic & European Biographers. K. Luomala. (BMB Ser.: No. 198). 1969. reprint ed. 45.00 (*0-527-02306-X*) Periodicals Srv.

Maui on My Mind. Rita Ariyoshi. (Illus.). 256p. 1988. 39.95 (*0-935180-16-8*) Mutual Pub HI.

Maui Onion Cookbook. Barbara Santos. LC 96-83235. (Illus.). 96p. 1996. pap. 5.95 (*0-89087-802-1*) Celestial Arts.

Maui Remembers: A Local History. Gail Bartholomew & Bren Bailey. (Illus.). 178p. 1994. pap. 22.95 (*1-56647-070-6*) Mutual Pub HI.

Maui Rose. Annette Mahon. LC 96-97003. 192p. 1996. 18.95 (*0-8034-9182-4*, Avalon Bks) Bouregy.

Maui Street Names: The Hawaiian Dictionary & History of Maui Street Names. Rich Budnick & Hokulani Holt-Padilla. LC 90-84607. (Illus.). 142p. (Orig.). 1991. pap. 10.95 (*0-944081-01-0*) Aloha HI.

Maui the Valley Isle. rev. ed. Allan Seiden. 64p. 1986. pap. 9.95 (*0-89610-053-7*) Island Heritage.

Maui the Whale: Coloring & Activity Book. Mark A. Wagenman. (Illus.). 24p. (J). (ps). 1989. pap. 2.95 (*0-89610-147-9*) Island Heritage.

Maui Trails: Walks, Strolls & Treks on the Valley Isle. 2nd ed. Kathy Morey. LC 96-6853. (Orig.). 1996. pap. 12.95 (*0-89997-196-2*) Wilderness Pr.

Maui Traveler's Guide. Bill Gleasner & Diana Gleasner. pap. 7.95 (*0-9651185-0-9*) B & D Gleasner.

Maui's Floral Splendor. Angela K. Kepler. (Illus.). 144p. (Orig.). 1995. pap. 12.95 (*1-56647-057-9*) Mutual Pub HI.

Maui's Hana Highway: A Vistor's Guide. Kay Kepler. (Illus.). 80p. 1988. pap. 9.95 (*0-935180-62-1*) Mutual Pub HI.

Maui's Mittee & the General. Irma G. Burns. 15.95 (*0-914916-90-4*) Ku Paa.

Maul. Mark Dunster. 32p. (Orig.). (YA). 1995. pap. 5.00 (*0-89642-233-X*) Linden Pubs.

Maul & the Pear Tree. P. D. James & T. A. Critchley. 240p. 1986. 17.95 (*0-89296-152-X*, Pub. by Mysterious Pr) Little.

Maul & the Pear Tree. P. D. James & T. A. Critchley. 256p. 1987. mass mkt. 5.99 (*0-445-40562-7*, Pub. by Warner Bks) Little.

"Maul" the Wilderness Creature. unabridged ed. Richard Robinson. 82p. 1998. pap. 10.95 (*0-9665678-7-0*) Buy Books.

Maulana Abul Kalam Azad: Unfulfilled Dreams. P. N. Chopra. 188p. (C). 1990. 195.00 (*81-85017-43-3*, Pub. by Interprint) St Mut.

Maulana Azad. V. N. Datta. 1990. 31.00 (*81-85054-98-3*, Pub. by Manohar) S Asia.

Maulana Azad, Vol. 1. Sai A. Tirmizi. (C). 1991. 21.50 (*81-7169-104-8*, Pub. by Commonwealth) S Asia.

Maulever Hall. Jane A. Hodge. Date not set. lib. bdg. 21.95 (*0-8488-1376-6*) Amereon Ltd.

Maulever Hall. Jane A. Hodge. 1987. lib. bdg. 21.95 (*0-89968-236-7*, Lghtyr Pr) Buccaneer Bks.

Mauleverer. A. C. Fox-Davies. 1976. lib. bdg. 14.95 (*0-89968-163-8*, Lghtyr Pr) Buccaneer Bks.

Maull. B. Maull. Ed. by R. F. Bailey. 241p. 1991. reprint ed. pap. 43.00 (*0-8328-2054-7*); reprint ed. lib. bdg. 53.00 (*0-8328-2053-9*) Higginson Bk Co.

Maullido de la Gata. Gary Soto. (SPA., Illus.). 80p. (J). (gr. 2-5). 1995. pap. 2.99 (*0-590-50208-5*) Scholastic Inc.

Maum Guinea: Holiday-Week on a Louisana Plantation. Metta V. Victor. 1999. pap. text 10.00 (*1-55709-550-7*, Pub. by Applewood) Consort Bk Sales.

Maum Guinea, & Her Plantation "Children": or Holiday-Week on a Louisiana Estate: A Slave Romance. Metta V. Victor. LC 72-3199. (Black Heritage Library Collection). 1977. reprint ed. 25.95 (*0-8369-9087-0*) Ayer.

Maumort. Roger Martin du Gard. (FRE.). 1983. lib. bdg. 110.00 (*0-8288-3555-1*, M5107) Fr & Eur.

Mauna Loa Macadamia Cookbook. Leslie Mansfield. LC 98-72530. 96p. 1998. pap. 4.95 (*0-89087-879-X*) Celestial Arts.

Mauna Loa Macadamia Cooking Treasury. Leslie Mansfield. LC 98-16925. (Illus.). 188p. 1998. 29.95 (*0-89087-885-4*); pap. 19.95 (*0-89087-880-3*) Celestial Arts.

Mauna Loa Revealed: Its Structure, Composition, History, & Hazards. Ed. by J. Michael Rhodes & John P. Lockwood. (Geophysical Monographs: Vol. 92). 348p. 1995. 70.00 (*0-87590-049-6*) Am Geophysical.

Maupassant: A Lion in the Path. Francis Steegmuller. LC 76-39210. (Select Bibliographies Reprint Ser.). 1977. reprint ed. 23.95 (*0-8369-6812-3*) Ayer.

Maupassant: The Semiotics of Text: Practical Exercises. Algirdas Julien Greimas & Guy de Maupassant. Tr. by Paul J. Perron from FRE. LC 88-9542. (Semiotic Crossroads Ser.: Vol. 1). xxxiv, 258p. (C). 1988. 83.00 (*1-55619-039-5*); pap. 24.95 (*1-55619-063-8*) J Benjamins Pubng Co.

Maupassant & the American Short Story: The Influence of Form at the Turn of the Century. Richard Fusco. LC 93-20350. 248p. (C). 1994. 45.00 (*0-271-01081-9*) Pa St U Pr.

Maupassant the Novelist. Edward D. Sullivan. LC 78-6859. 199p. 1978. reprint ed. lib. bdg. 69.50 (*0-313-20497-7*, SUMN, Greenwood Pr) Greenwood.

Mauprat. George Sand. Ed. by Claude Sicard. (FRE.). 480p. 1981. pap. 11.95 (*0-7859-1375-0*, 2070373118) Fr & Eur.

Mauprat. George Sand. Tr. by Sylvia Raphael. LC 97-16248. (Oxford World's Classics Ser.). (Illus.). 330p. 1998. pap. 9.95 (*0-19-282434-1*) OUP.

Mauprat. George Sand. (Folio Ser.: No. 1311). (FRE.). 476p. 1981. pap. 10.95 (*2-07-037311-8*) Schoenhof.

Mauprat. George Sand. LC 77-23992. (Quality Paperbacks Ser.). (Illus.). 1977. reprint ed. pap. 9.95 (*0-306-80077-2*) Da Capo.

Maura B. Jacobson's New York Magazine Crossword Puzzles, Vol. 1. Maura B. Jacobson. 64p. 1995. pap. 9.99 (*1-884910-08-4*, Story Press) F & W Pubns Inc.

Maura B. Jacobson's New York Magazine Crossword Puzzles, Vol. 2. Maura B. Jacobson. 64p. 1995. pap. 9.99 (*1-884910-09-2*, Story Press) F & W Pubns Inc.

Maura B. Jacobson's New York Magazine Crossword Puzzles, Vol. 3. Maura B. Jacobson. 64p. 1995. pap. 9.99 (*1-884910-10-6*, Story Press) F & W Pubns Inc.

Maura B. Jacobson's New York Magazine Crossword Puzzles, Vol. 4. Maura B. Jacobson. 64p. 1995. pap. 9.99 (*1-884910-11-4*, Story Press) F & W Pubns Inc.

Maura B. Jacobson's New York Magazine Crossword Puzzles, Vol. 5. Maura B. Jacobson. 64p. 1996. pap. 9.99 (*1-884910-13-0*, Story Press) F & W Pubns Inc.

Maura B. Jacobson's New York Magazine Crossword Puzzles, Vol. 6. Maura B. Jacobson. 64p. 1996. pap. 9.99 (*1-884910-14-9*, Story Press) F & W Pubns Inc.

Maurai & Kith. Poul Anderson. 240p. 1992. mass mkt. 3.99 (*0-8125-1397-5*, Pub. by Tor Bks) St Martin.

Maura's Angel. Lynne Reid Banks. LC 97-50350. (Little Women Journals). 128p. (J). (gr. 3-7). 1998. 14.00 (*0-380-97590-4*, Avon Bks) Morrow Avon.

Maura's Angel. Lynne Reid Banks. LC 97-50350. 160p. (YA). (gr. 3-7). 1999. mass mkt. 4.99 (*0-380-79514-0*, Avon Bks) Morrow Avon.

Maura's Boy: A Cork Childhood. Christy Kenneally. LC 96-227753. 128p. 1997. pap. 10.95 (*1-85635-151-3*, Pub. by Mercier Pr) Irish Amer Bk.

Maureen Birnbaum, Barbarian Swordsperson. George A. Effinger. (Illus.). 144p. (Orig.). 1993. pap. 10.00 (*1-883722-01-2*) Swan Pr TX.

Maureen McNaughton's Potpourri. Maureen McNaughton. (Illus.). 54p. 1991. pap. 8.95 (*0-941284-85-9*) J Shaw Studio.

Maureen O'Sullivan: A Bio-Bibliography, 13. Connie J. Billips. LC 90-31763. (Bio-Bibliographies in the Performing Arts Ser.: No. 13). 224p. 1990. lib. bdg. 45.00 (*0-313-26470-8*, BMF, Greenwood Pr) Greenwood.

Maureen Sangster: Out of the Urn. Scottish Cultural Press Staff. 1990. pap. 21.00 (*1-898218-65-X*) St Mut.

Maureen Stapleton: A Bio-Bibliography, 34. Jeannie M. Woods. LC 92-23787. (Bio-Bibliographies in the Performing Arts Ser.: No. 34). 176p. 1992. lib. bdg. 49.95 (*0-313-27761-3*, WMT, Greenwood Pr) Greenwood.

Maureen's Fairing. Jane Barlow. LC 72-4418. (Short Story Index Reprint Ser.). (Illus.). 1977. reprint ed. 21.95 (*0-8369-4169-1*) Ayer.

Maurice. E. M. Forster. 1976. 22.95 (*0-8488-0490-2*) Amereon Ltd.

Maurice. E. M. Forster. 256p. 1990. reprint ed. lib. bdg. 25.95 (*0-89966-751-1*) Buccaneer Bks.

Maurice: A Novel. E. M. Forster. LC 92-41161. 256p. 1993. pap. 13.00 (*0-393-31032-9*) Norton.

Maurice A.Gibbs: Japan. Alberta R. Metz. (Missionary Hero Ser.). (Illus.). 80p. (J). (gr. 4-7). 1980. pap. 3.99 (*0-89827-008-1*, BKD46) Wesleyan Pub Hse.

Maurice & Therese: The Story of a Love. Patrick Ahern. LC 98-13268. (Illus.). 304p. 1998. 19.95 (*0-385-49261-8*) Doubleday.

*__Maurice & Therese: The Story of a Love.__ Patrick Ahern. 2001. reprint ed. pap. 12.95 (*0-385-49740-7*) Doubleday.

Maurice Bishop Speaks: The Grenada Revolution & Its Overthrow, 1979-83. Maurice Bishop. LC 83-63309. 352p. 1983. reprint ed. pap. 20.95 (*0-87348-612-9*); reprint ed. lib. bdg. 55.00 (*0-87348-611-0*) Pathfinder NY.

Maurice Blanchot: Extreme Contemporary. Leslie Hill. LC 97-212722. (Warwick Studies in European Philosophy Ser.). 320p. (C). 1997. 85.00 (*0-415-09173-X*) Routledge.

Maurice Blanchot: Extreme Contemporary. Leslie Hill. LC 97-212722. (Warwick Studies in European Philosophy Ser.). 320p. (C). 1997. pap. 25.99 (*0-415-09174-8*) Routledge.

Maurice Blanchot: The Demand of Writing. Ed. by Carolyn B. Gill. LC 95-38890. (Warwick Studies in European Philosophy Ser.). 256p. (C). 1996. 80.00 (*0-415-12595-2*); pap. 25.99 (*0-415-12596-0*) Routledge.

Maurice Blanchot: The Refusal of Philosophy. Gerald L. Bruns. LC 96-34860. 384p. 1997. text 39.95 (*0-8018-5471-7*) Johns Hopkins.

Maurice Blanchot & the Literature of Transgression. John Gregg. LC 93-30911. 256p. 1994. text 37.50 (*0-691-03329-3*, Pub. by Princeton U Pr) Cal Prin Full Svc.

Maurice Brazil Prendergast - Charles Prendergast: A Catalogue Raisonne. Carol Clark et al. (Illus.). 812p. 1990. 285.00 (*3-7913-0965-X*, Pub. by Prestel) te Neues.

Maurice Chevalier: Up on Top of a Rainbow. David Bret. (Illus.). 242p. 1993. 26.95 (*0-86051-789-6*, Robson-Parkwest) Parkwest Pubns.

Maurice Chevalier: Up on Top of a Rainbow. 2nd large type ed. David Bret. (Illus.). 336p. 1993. 24.95 (*1-85695-165-0*, Pub. by ISIS Lrg Prnt) Transaction Pubs.

Maurice Denis et le Comte Kessler (1902-1913) Carina Schafer. (Publications Universitaires Europeennes: Vol. 309). (Illus.). 321p. 1997. 52.00 (*3-631-32150-3*) P Lang Pubng.

Maurice Greene: Voluntaries & Suites for Organ & Harpsichord. Maurice Greene. Ed. by Gwilym Beechey. (Recent Researches in Music of the Baroque Era Ser.: Vol. RRB19). xiv, 88p. 1975. pap. 35.00 (*0-89579-057-2*) A-R Eds.

*__Maurice Guest__ Henry Handel Richardson et al. LC 98-215770. (Academy Editions of Australian Literature Ser.). lxxi, 799p. 1998. write for info. (*0-7022-3028-6*, Pub. by Univ Queensland Pr) Intl Spec Bk.

Maurice Guest. Henry Handel Richardson. LC 82-12844. (Virago Modern Classic). 562 P. ;p. 1983. reprint ed. 9.95 (*0-385-27787-3*) Delacorte.

Maurice LeGrand LeSueur Sullins, Paintings, 1970-1986. Kent J. Smith & Michael Bonesteal. Ed. by Lynda K. Martin. (Illus.). x, 30p. (Orig.). 1988. pap. 10.00 (*0-89792-114-3*) Ill St Museum.

Maurice Logan Artist & Designer: A Retrospective of Painting from the "Society of Six" Years to the 1960s. Marvin A. Schenck. (Illus.). 16p. 1991. pap. 9.95 (*1-886091-02-1*) Hearst Art Gal.

Maurice Maeterlinck. Patrick F. Mahony. 1985. 20.00 (*0-941694-22-4*) Inst Study Man.

Maurice Maeterlinck. Edward Thomas. LC 73-21707. (Studies in French Literature: No. 45). 1974. lib. bdg. 75.00 (*0-8383-1826-6*) M S G Haskell Hse.

Maurice Maeterlinck: A Study of His Life & Thought. W. D. Halls. LC 78-16379. 1978. reprint ed. lib. bdg. 55.00 (*0-313-20574-4*, HAMM, Greenwood Pr) Greenwood.

Maurice Maeterlinck & the Making of Modern Theatre. Patrick McGuinness. LC 99-40052. 240p. 2000. text 70.00 (*0-19-815977-3*) OUP.

*__Maurice Merleau-Ponty: A Bibliography.__ Ed. by Joan Nordquist. (Social Theory: Vol. 57). 72p. 2000. pap. 20.00 (*1-892068-13-3*) Ref Rsch Serv.

Maurice, or the Fisher's Cot. Mary Wollstonecraft Shelley. Ed. & Intro. by Claire Tomalin. LC 98-88124. (Illus.). 192p. 1998. 20.00 (*0-375-40473-2*) Knopf.

*__Maurice: or The Fisher's Cot: A Tale.__ Mary Wollstonecraft Shelley & Claire Tomalin. LC 00-37789. (Illus.). 2000. pap. write for info. (*0-226-75228-3*) U Ch Pr.

Maurice Prendergast. Nancy M. Mathews et al. (Illus.). 196p. 1990. 65.00 (*3-7913-0966-8*, Pub. by Prestel) te Neues.

Maurice Prendergast. Richard J. Wattenmaker. LC 93-46816. (Illus.). 160p. 1994. 45.00 (*0-8109-3726-3*, Pub. by Abrams) Time Warner.

Maurice Prendergast: The Large Boston Public Garden Sketchbook. Intro. by George Szabo. LC 87-14601. (Illus.). 44p. 1987. 60.00 (*0-8076-1184-0*) Braziller.

Maurice Ravel. Gerald Larner. (20th Century Composers Ser.). (Illus.). 240p. (Orig.). 1996. pap. 19.95 (*0-7148-3270-7*, Pub. by Phaidon Press) Phaidon Pr.

Maurice Ravel. Victor I. Seroff. LC 77-126327. (Biography Index Reprint Ser.). 1977. reprint ed. 23.95 (*0-8369-8033-6*) Ayer.

*__Maurice Ravel: A Life.__ Benjamin Ivry. 2000. 24.95 (*1-56649-152-5*) Welcome Rain.

Maurice Ravel: Music Book Index. Roland Manuel. 152p. 1993. reprint ed. lib. bdg. 69.00 (*0-7812-9616-1*) Rprt Serv.

*__Maurice Ravels Schlusselwerk L'Enfant Et Les Sortileges: Eine Asthetisch-Analytische Studie.__ Mathias Schillmoller. (GER.). 267p. 1999. 45.95 (*3-631-34593-3*) P Lang Pubng.

Maurice Sceve. Ruth Mulhauser. LC 76-28722. (Twayne's World Authors Ser.). 138p. (C). 1977. lib. bdg. 20.95 (*0-8057-6264-7*) Irvington.

Maurice Sceve, the Entry of Henri II into Lyon, September 1548. Ed. by Richard Cooper. (Medieval & Renaissance Texts & Studies: Vol. 160). (Illus.). 328p. 1997. 36.00 (*0-86698-200-0*, MR160) MRTS.

Maurice Sendak. Julie Berg. LC 93-15738. (Young at Heart Ser.). (J). 1993. pap. 4.95 (*1-56239-365-0*) ABDO Pub Co.

Maurice Sendak. Julie Berg. LC 93-15738. (Young at Heart Ser.). (Illus.). 32p. (J). 1993. lib. bdg. 14.98 (*1-56239-225-5*) ABDO Pub Co.

Maurice Sendak. Amy Sonheim. (Twayne's United States Authors Ser.: No. 598). 180p. 1992. 32.00 (*0-8057-7628-1*, Twyne) Mac Lib Ref.

*__Maurice Sendak.__ Mae Woods. LC 99-89169. (Children's Authors Ser.). 2000. write for info. (*1-57765-112-X*) ABDO Pub Co.

Maurice Sendak Audio Collection, Set. abr. ed. Maurice Sendak. (J). (ps-1). 1992. audio 24.95 (*1-55994-674-1*, 393506) HarperAudio.

Maurice Sendak in the Classroom. Thomas J. Palumbo. 176p. teacher ed. 14.99 (*0-86653-713-9*, GA1430) Good Apple.

Maurice Sendak's Christmas Mystery. Maurice Sendak. (Illus.). 8p. (J). (ps-2). 1995. write for info. (*0-614-05332-3*, HarpFestival) HarpC Child Bks.

Maurice Sendak's Christmas Mystery. Maurice Sendak. (Michael di Capua Bks.). (Illus.). 8p. (J). (ps up). 1995. 12.95 (*0-06-205112-1*, HarpFestival) HarpC Child Bks.

Maurice Sendak's Really Rosie. Maurice Sendak. (Trophy Picture Bk.). (Illus.). 48p. (J). (gr. k-4). 1986. pap. 11.95 (*0-06-443138-X*, HarpTrophy) HarpC Child Bks.

Maurice Sendak's Really Rosie: Starring the Nutshell Kids. Maurice Sendak. (J). 1975. 16.15 (*0-606-00518-8*, Pub. by Turtleback) Demco.

Maurice Sendak's Really Rosie Audio: Starring the Nutshell Kids. unabridged ed. Maurice Sendak. LC 81-740022. (Share a Story Bks.). (Illus.). (J). (ps-3). 1998. bds. 14.95 incl. audio (*0-89845-879-X*, CPN 368, Caedmon) HarpC Child Bks.

Maurice Stern see Three American Modernist Painters

Maurice Strong: Working for Planet Earth. Hugh Westrup. LC 93-41528. (Gateway Greens Ser.). (Illus.). 48p. (J). (gr. 2-4). 1994. lib. bdg. 20.90 (*1-56294-414-2*) Millbrook Pr.

Maurice Sugar: Law, Labor, & the Left in Detroit 1912-1950. Christopher H. Johnson. LC 87-34636. 336p. 1988. 49.95 (*0-8143-1851-7*); pap. 19.95 (*0-8143-1852-5*) Wayne St U Pr.

Maurice the Hippo. Maarten Bos & Claire Bos. LC 97-76056. (Illus.). 20p. (J). (ps-k). 1998. 8.95 (*0-531-30098-6*) Orchard Bks Watts.

Maurice the Snake & Gaston the Near-Sighted Turtle: Louisiana Crawfish Man's Tales from the Atchafalaya. Louisiana Crawfish-Man. (Louisiana

An Asterisk (*) at the beginning of an entry indicates that the title is appearing for the first time.

Crawfish-Man's Tales from the Atchafalaya Ser.). (Illus.). 36p. (J). (gr. k-8). 1977. spiral bd. 8.00 (*0-931108-00-4*) Little Cajun Bks.

***Maurice Tierney.** Charles Lever. 252p. 2000. pap. 9.95 (*0-594-03101-X*) Eightn Hundrd.

Maurice Vellekoop's ABC Book: A Homoerotic Primer. Maurice Kellekoop. (Illus.). 64p. 1998. 12.95 (*1-889539-04-X*) Gates of Heck.

Maurice's Room. Paula Fox. LC 87-19504. (Illus.). 64p. (J). (gr. 2-6). 1988. reprint ed. mass mkt. 3.95 (*0-689-71216-2*) Aladdin.

Maurice's Room. 3rd ed. Paula Fox. LC 85-7200. (Illus.). 64p. (J). (gr. 2-6). 1985. lib. bdg. 13.95 (*0-02-735490-3*, Mac Bks Young Read) S&S Childrens.

Maurice's Room: A Study Guide. Dina Claydon. Ed. by Joyce Friedland & Rikki Kessler. (Novel-Ties Ser.). (J). (gr. 2-4). 1991. pap. text 15.95 (*0-88122-569-X*) Lrn Links.

Maurice's Tropical Fruit Cookbook. Maurice De Verteuil. 80p. 1979. pap. 2.95 (*0-8200-0806-0*) Great Outdoors.

***Maurin Keys to Success: How to Achieve Your Goals.** 2nd ed. 2000. write for info. (*0-13-019668-1*) P-H.

Maurine & Other Poems (1888) Ella Wheeler Wilcox. 260p. 1998. reprint ed. pap. 18.95 (*0-7661-0633-0*) Kessinger Pub.

Mauritania. Delia Cortese. LC 93-189401. (World Bibliographical Ser.). 184p. 1992. lib. bdg. 71.50 (*1-85109-152-1*) ABC-CLIO.

Mauritania. Kathleen Trayte. LC 95-22463. (Oles Country Guide Ser.). 1996. 20.00 (*0-929851-53-6*) Am Assn Coll Registrars.

Mauritania. James Webb. (Profiles of Africa Ser.). 1996. text 36.50 (*0-8133-8205-X*) Westview.

Mauritania: A Country Study. 2nd ed. Robert E. Handloff. LC 89-600361. (Area Handbook Ser.). (Illus.). 244p. 1996. boxed set 18.00 (*0-16-019797-X*, S/N 008-020-01197-5) USGPO.

***Mauritania: A Country Study Guide.** Global Investment & Business Center, Inc. Staff. (World Country Study Guides Library: Vol. 110). (Illus.). 350p. 2000. pap. 59.00 (*0-7397-2408-8*) Intl Business Pubns.

Mauritania - A Country Study Guide: Basic Information for Research & Pleasure. Global Investment Center, USA Staff. (World Country Study Guide Library: Vol. 110). (Illus.). 350p. 1999. pap. 59.00 (*0-7397-1507-0*) Intl Business Pubns.

Mauritania - Campaign of Terror: State Sponsored Repression of Black Africans. Human Rights Watch Africa Staff. LC 94-75822. 168p. (Orig.). 1994. pap. 15.00 (*1-56432-133-9*) Hum Rts Watch.

Mauritania - The Other Apartheid? Garba Diallo. (Current African Issues Ser.: No. 16). 57p. 1993. 4.95 (*91-7106-339-0*, Pub. by Nordic Africa) Transaction Pubs.

***Mauritania Business Intelligence Report, 190 vols.** Global Investment & Business Center, Inc. Staff. (World Business Intelligence Library: Vol. 110). (Illus.). 350p. 2000. pap. 99.95 (*0-7397-2608-0*) Intl Business Pubns.

***Mauritania Business Law Handbook, 190 vols.** Global Investment & Business Center, Inc. Staff. (Global Business Law Handbooks Library: Vol. 110). (Illus.). 350p. 2000. pap. 99.95 (*0-7397-2008-2*) Intl Business Pubns.

***Mauritania Business Opportunity Yearbook.** Global Investment & Business Center, Inc. Staff. (Global Business Opportunity Yearbooks Library: Vol. 110). (Illus.). 2000. pap. 99.95 (*0-7397-2208-5*) Intl Business Pubns.

***Mauritania Business Opportunity Yearbook: Export-Import, Investment & Business Opportunities.** International Business Publications, U. S. A. Staff & Global Investment Center, U. S. A. Staff. (Global Business Opportunity Yearbooks Library: Vol. 110). (Illus.). 350p. 1999. pap. 99.95 (*0-7397-1308-6*) Intl Business Pubns.

***Mauritania Country Review 2000.** Robert C. Kelly et al. (Illus.). 60p. 1999. pap. 39.95 (*1-58310-534-4*) CountryWatch.

***Mauritania Foreign Policy & Government Guide.** Contrib. by Global Investment & Business Center, Inc. Staff. (World Foreign Policy & Government Library: Vol. 106). (Illus.). 350p. 1999. pap. 99.00 (*0-7397-3604-3*) Intl Business Pubns.

***Mauritania Foreign Policy & Government Guide.** Global Investment & Business Center, Inc. Staff. (World Foreign Policy & Government Library: Vol. 106). (Illus.). 350p. 2000. pap. 99.95 (*0-7397-3808-9*) Intl Business Pubns.

***Mauritania in Photographs.** Joseph E. Murphy. (Illus.). 160p. 1999. pap. 25.00 (*1-892277-04-2*) Crossgar Pr.

***Mauritania Investment & Business Guide.** Global Investment & Business Center, Inc. Staff. (Global Investment & Business Guide Library: Vol. 110). (Illus.). 2000. pap. 99.95 (*0-7397-1808-8*) Intl Business Pubns.

***Mauritania Investment & Business Guide: Export-Import, Investment & Business Opportunities.** International Business Publications, USA Staff & Global Investment Center, USA Staff. (World Investment & Business Guide Library-99: Vol. 110). (Illus.). 350p. 1999. pap. 99.95 (*0-7397-0305-6*) Intl Business Pubns.

Mauritian Voices: New Writing in English. Ed. by Ron Butlin. (Illus.). 192p. 1997. pap. 15.95 (*1-873226-24-1*, Pub. by Flambard Pr) Firebird Dist.

Mauritius. P. Ramgulam. LC 93-180475. (World Bibliographical Ser.). 179p. 1992. lib. bdg. 70.00 (*1-85109-153-X*) ABC-CLIO.

***Mauritius.** 2nd ed. New Holland Publishing Staff. (Globetrotter Travel Maps Ser.). 2000. pap. 8.95 (*1-85974-416-8*) New5 Holland.

***Mauritius.** 2nd ed. Martine Self. (Globetrotter Travel Guides Ser.). (Illus.). 128p. 2000. pap. 10.95 (*1-85974-365-X*) New5 Holland.

***Mauritius: A Country Study Guide.** Global Investment & Business Center, Inc. Staff. (World Country Study Guides Library: Vol. 111). (Illus.). 350p. 2000. pap. 59.00 (*0-7397-2409-6*) Intl Business Pubns.

***Mauritius: A Visual Souvenir.** (Illus.). 80p. 2000. 19.95 (*1-86872-275-9*, Pub. by New Holland) BHB Intl.

Mauritius: Globetrotter Travel Guide. Globetrotter Staff. (Globetrotter Travel Guide Ser.). (Illus.). 128p. 1995. pap. text 17.95 (*1-85368-418-X*, Pub. by New5 Holland) Globe Pequot.

Mauritius - A Country Study Guide: Basic Information for Research & Pleasure. Global Investment Center, USA Staff. (World Country Study Guide Library: Vol. 111). (Illus.). 350p. 1999. pap. 59.00 (*0-7397-1508-9*) Intl Business Pubns.

***Mauritius Business Intelligence Report, 190 vols.** Global Investment & Business Center, Inc. Staff. (World Business Intelligence Library: Vol. 111). (Illus.). 350p. 2000. pap. 99.95 (*0-7397-2609-9*) Intl Business Pubns.

***Mauritius Business Law Handbook, 190 vols.** Global Investment & Business Center, Inc. Staff. (Global Business Law Handbooks Library: Vol. 111). (Illus.). 350p. 2000. pap. 99.95 (*0-7397-2009-0*) Intl Business Pubns.

***Mauritius Business Opportunity Yearbook.** Global Investment & Business Center, Inc. Staff. (Global Business Opportunity Yearbooks Library: Vol. 111). (Illus.). 2000. pap. 99.95 (*0-7397-2209-3*) Intl Business Pubns.

***Mauritius Business Opportunity Yearbook: Export-Import, Investment & Business Opportunities.** International Business Publications, U. S. A. Staff & Global Investment Center, U. S. A. Staff. (Global Business Opportunity Yearbooks Library: Vol. 111). (Illus.). 350p. 1999. pap. 99.95 (*0-7397-1309-4*) Intl Business Pubns.

Mauritius Command. Patrick O'Brian. 1991. pap. 13.95 (*0-393-30762-X*) Norton.

Mauritius Command. Patrick O'Brian. 1994. 24.00 (*0-393-03704-5*) Norton.

Mauritius Command. large type ed. Patrick O'Brian. 1950. 30.00 (*0-7862-1935-1*) Mac Lib Ref.

***Mauritius Country Review 2000.** Robert C. Kelly et al. (Illus.). 60p. 1999. pap. 39.95 (*1-58310-535-2*) CountryWatch.

***Mauritius Foreign Policy & Government Guide.** Contrib. by Global Investment & Business Center, Inc. Staff. (World Foreign Policy & Government Library: Vol. 107). (Illus.). 350p. 1999. pap. 99.00 (*0-7397-3605-1*) Intl Business Pubns.

***Mauritius Foreign Policy & Government Guide.** Global Investment & Business Center, Inc. Staff. (World Foreign Policy & Government Library: Vol. 107). (Illus.). 350p. 2000. pap. 99.95 (*0-7397-3809-7*) Intl Business Pubns.

Mauritius from the Air. Genvieve Dormann. 136p. 1999. 29.95 (*1-86812-455-X*) Menasha Ridge.

***Mauritius Investment & Business Guide.** Global Investment & Business Center, Inc. Staff. (Global Investment & Business Guide Library: Vol. 111). (Illus.). 2000. pap. 99.95 (*0-7397-1809-6*) Intl Business Pubns.

Mauritius Investment & Business Guide: Economy, Export-Import, Business & Investment Climate, Business Contacts. Contrib. by Russian Information & Business Center, Inc. Staff. (Russia, NIS & Emerging Markets Investment & Business Library-98). (Illus.). 350p. 1998. pap. 99.00 (*1-57751-906-X*) Intl Business Pubns.

***Mauritius Investment & Business Guide: Export-Import, Investment & Business Opportunities.** International Business Publications, USA Staff & Global Investment Center, USA Staff. (World Investment & Business Guide Library-99: Vol. 111). (Illus.). 350p. 1999. pap. 99.95 (*0-7397-0306-4*) Intl Business Pubns.

Mauritius, Reunion & Seychelles. 3rd ed. Sarina Singh et al. (Illus.). 416p. 1998. pap. 17.95 (*0-86442-498-1*) Lonely Planet.

Mauritius Rodriguez & Reunion: The Mascarene Isles. 4th ed. Royston Ellis & Derek Schuurman. LC 99-18507. 288p. 1999. pap. 17.95 (*1-898323-87-9*, Pub. by Bradt Pubns) Globe Pequot.

***Mauritius, Seychelles & Reunion.** James Penrith. (Travellers Survival Kit Ser.). 2000. pap. 18.95 (*1-85458-240-2*) Vac Wrk Pubns.

***Mauritius with Map.** (Illus.). 128p. 2000. pap. 14.95 (*1-85974-246-7*) New5 Holland.

Mauritshuis, The Hague. Museum Senior Curators Staff. LC 95-166231. (Illus.). 128p. 1994. 30.00 (*1-85759-031-7*) Scala Books.

***Maurizio Cattelan.** Nancy Spector. (Contemporary Artists Ser.). 2000. pap. 29.95 (*0-7148-3866-7*) Phaidon Pr.

***Maurizio Cattelan.** expanded rev. ed. Giorgio Verzotti. (Illus.). 2000. pap. 19.95 (*88-8158-267-8*) Charta.

Maurizius Case. Jacob Wasserman. 548p. 1985. pap. 9.95 (*0-88184-164-1*) Carroll & Graf.

Maurizius Case. Jacob Wassermann. 1959. 6.95 (*0-87140-816-3*, Pub. by Liveright) Norton.

Mauro Giuliani: Virtuoso Guitarist & Composer. 2nd ed. Thomas F. Heck. LC 95-17327. (Illus.). 304p. 1997. pap. 39.95 (*1-882612-00-0*, 497-00362) Edit Orphee.

***Mauru Investment & Business Guide: Export-Import, Investment & Business Opportunities.** International Business Publications, USA Staff & Global Investment Center, USA Staff. (World Investment & Business Guide Library-99: Vol. 121). (Illus.). 350p. 1999. pap. 99.95 (*0-7397-0316-1*) Intl Business Pubns.

***Maury County Remembered: The Gilbert MacWilliams Orr Family Collection.** Ed. by Lois Harlan Orr & Gilbert MacWilliams Orr, Jr. (Tennessee Heritage Library Bicentennial Collection). (Illus.). 192p. 1999. 32.95 (*1-57736-164-4*, Hillsboro Pr) Providence Hse.

Maury County, Tennessee, Deed, 1807-1817, Bks. A to F. Virginia W. Alexander. 248p. 1981. reprint ed. 27.50 (*0-89308-185-X*) Southern Hist Pr.

Maury County, Tennessee, Will, 1807-1832, Bks. A, B, C-1, D, & E. Jill K. Garrett & Marise P. Lightfoot. 288p. 1985. reprint ed. pap. 30.00 (*0-89308-362-3*) Southern Hist Pr.

***Maury Had a Little Lamb.** Janette Oke. (Oke Children's Classics Ser.). (Illus.). 144p. (Orig.). (J). (gr. 3 up). 1998. pap. 5.99 (*0-934998-34-5*) Bethany Hse.

***Maury Island U. F. O. The Crisman Conspiracy.** Kenn Thomas. LC 99-29419. (Illus.). 1999. pap. 14.95 (*1-881532-19-4*) IllumiNet Pr.

Maury, Williamson, Rutherford, Wilson, Bedford & Marshall Counties, History of Tennessee Illustrated, Historical & Biographical Sketches of the Counties Of. 536p. 1988. reprint ed. 42.50 (*0-89308-629-0*, TN 106) Southern Hist Pr.

Maury Yeston - December Songs. Ed. by Milton Okun. pap. 16.95 (*0-89524-679-1*) Cherry Lane.

***Maury Yeston Songbook.** 1998. otabind 19.95 (*1-57560-116-8*, Pub. by Cherry Lane) H Leonard.

Mauryan Polity. Ramachandra Dikshitar. (C). 1993. reprint ed. text 24.00 (*81-208-1023-6*, Pub. by Motilal Bnarsidass) S Asia.

Maus. (Meyers Klien Kinderbibliothek). (GER.). 24p. (J). 13.25 (*3-411-08551-7*) Langenscheidt.

Maus, Set, Vols. 1 & 2. Art Spiegelman. (Illus.). 1993. pap. 28.00 (*0-679-74840-7*) Pantheon.

Maus: A Survivor's Tale, 2 vols. Art Spiegelman. LC 96-32796. 1996. 35.00 (*0-679-40641-7*) Pantheon.

Maus: A Survivor's Tale I: My Father Bleeds History, Vol. I. Art Spiegelman. 1991. 22.00 (*0-394-54155-3*) Pantheon.

Maus: A Survivor's Tale II: And Here My Troubles Began, Vol. 2. Art Spiegelman. LC 91-52739. (Illus.). 144p. 1992. reprint ed. pap. 14.00 (*0-679-72977-1*) Pantheon.

MAUS: And Other German Armored Projects. Michael Sawodny & Kai Bracker. LC 89-84176. (Illus.). 48p. 1989. pap. 9.95 (*0-88740-186-4*) Schiffer.

Maus I. Art Spiegelman. 1986. pap. 12.00 (*0-394-24125-8*) Pantheon.

Mauser Automatic Pistol 6.35mm Calibre. reprint ed. 10.00 (*1-877704-05-9*) Pioneer Pr.

***Mauser Military Rifles of the World.** 2nd rev. ed. Robert W. D. Ball. LC 95-82422. (Illus.). 304p. 2000. 44.95 (*0-87341-828-X*) Krause Pubns.

Mauser Parabellum. Francis C. Allan. Ed. by Joseph P. Koss, Jr. (Illus.). 76p. (Orig.). 1985. pap. 14.95 (*0-9614814-0-4*) AK Enterprises.

Mauser Rifles & Pistols. Smith. (World's Great Gun Bks.). 1990. 30.00 (*0-935632-94-8*) Wolfe Pub Co.

Mauser Self-Loading Pistol. James N. Belford & Jack Dunlop. (Illus.). 208p. 1969. 29.95 (*0-87505-108-1*) Pioneer Pr.

Mausner & Bahn Epidemiology: An Introductory Text. 2nd ed. Judith S. Mausner & Shira Kramer. (Illus.). 361p. 1985. pap. text 40.95 (*0-7216-6181-5*, W B Saunders Co) Harcrt Hlth Sci Grp.

Mausoleum of Henry & Arabella Huntington. Diana G. Wilson. (Illus.). 36p. 1989. pap. 7.95 (*0-87328-125-X*) Huntington Lib.

Maussolleion at Halikarnassos, Reports of the Danish Archaeological Expedition to Bodrum Vol. 1: The Sacrificial Deposit. Kristian Jeppesen et al. (Jutland Archaeological Society Publications: No. 15). (Illus.). 110p. (C). 1981. 23.00 (*87-00-67291-2*, Pub. by Aarhus Univ Pr) David Brown.

Maussolleion at Halikarnassos, Reports of the Danish Archaeological Expedition to Bodrum Vol. 2: The Written Sources & Their Archaeological Background. Kristian Jeppesen & Anthony Luttrell. (Jutland Archaeological Society Publications: No. 15). (Illus.). 224p. (C). 1986. 39.00 (*87-7288-042-2*, Pub. by Aarhus Univ Pr) David Brown.

Maussolleion at Halikarnassos, Reports of the Danish Archaeological Expedition to Bodrum Vol. 3: The Maussolleion Terrace & Accessory Structures, 2 vols., Set. Poul O. Pedersen. (Jutland Archaeological Society Publications: No. 15). (Illus.). 342p. (C). 1992. 54.00 (*87-7288-563-7*, Pub. by Aarhus Univ Pr) David Brown.

***Mauswara Fish.** Cheri Floyd & Yago Kotabe. (Illus.). 15p. (J). (gr. 1-3). 2000. pap. text 5.99 (*0-89827-209-2*) Wesleyan Pub Hse.

Maute, Quelbe & Ting: A Calabash of Stories. Richard A. Schrader, Sr. LC 94-92150. (Illus.). 108p. (Orig.). (YA). (gr. 6-12). 1994. pap. text 22.50 (*0-9622987-4-3*) R A Schrader.

Mauthner Cells & Their Auditory Interactions: Proceedings of a Symposium Entitled "Interactions Between the Auditory & Mauthner Cell Systems", Vol. 46. Ed. by Arthur N. Popper & R. C. Eaton. (Journal Ser.: Vol. 46, No. 3, 1995). (Illus.). 60p. 1995. pap. 68.00 (*3-8055-6227-6*) S Karger.

Mauvais Garcon. Henri Pourrat. (FRE.). 1979. pap. 10.95 (*0-7859-4113-4*) Fr & Eur.

Mauvais Jars. Marcel Ayme. (Folio - Cadet Bleu Ser.: No. 236). (FRE., Illus.). 72p. (J). (gr. 1-5). 1990. pap. 10.95 (*2-07-031236-4*) Schoenhof.

Mauvais Lieu. Julien Green. (FRE.). 1988. pap. 16.95 (*0-7859-2711-5*) Fr & Eur.

Mauvais Oeil Suivi de au Bois Dormant. Boileau-Narcejac. (FRE.). 1978. pap. 10.95 (*0-7859-1823-X*, 2070367819) Fr & Eur.

Mauvais Reputation. Georges Brassens. (FRE.). 210p. 1986. pap. 10.95 (*0-7859-2051-X*, 2070377784) Fr & Eur.

Mauvais Reve. Georges Bernanos. (FRE.). 1988. pap. 10.95 (*0-7859-3218-6*, 2266022776) Fr & Eur.

Mauvais Temps. Paul Guimard. (FRE.). 150p. 1977. pap. 10.95 (*0-7859-2390-X*, 2070369277) Fr & Eur.

Mauvaises Pensees et Autre see Oeuvres

Mauvaises Pensees et Autres. Paul Valery. pap. 6.95 (*0-685-36618-9*) Fr & Eur.

***Mauve & Murder.** Barbara Burnett Smith. LC 00-41109. (First Edition Mystery Ser.). 2000. write for info. (*0-7862-2690-0*) Five Star.

Mauve Decade. Thomas Beer. LC 97-17485. 272p. 1997. pap. 11.95 (*0-7867-0501-9*) Carroll & Graf.

Mauve Gloves & Madmen, Clutter & Vine. Tom Wolfe. 240p. 1999. pap. 14.95 (*0-553-38059-1*) Bantam.

Mauve Gloves & Madmen, Clutter & Vine. Tom Wolfe. 243p. 1988. 18.95 (*0-374-20424-1*); pap. 9.95 (*0-374-52092-5*) FS&G.

***Mauzy's Comprehensive Handbook of Depression Glass Prices.** Barbara E. Mauzy & Jim Mauzy. LC 98-83095. 192 p. 1999. write for info. (*0-7643-0827-0*) Schiffer.

Mauzy's Comprehensive Handbook of Depression Glass Prices. Barbara Mauzy & Jim Mauzy. (Illus.). 160p. (Orig.). 1999. pap. 9.95 (*0-7643-0834-3*) Schiffer.

***Mauzy's Comprehensive Handbook of Depression Glass Prices.** 2nd rev. ed. Barbara Mauzy & Jim Mauzy. (Illus.). 192p. (Orig.). 2000. pap. 9.95 (*0-7643-0992-7*) Schiffer.

***Maveric Tumbleweed.** Fred H. Salter. (Illus.). 437p. 1998. pap. 18.95 (*0-9622429-7-7*) Big Mtn.

***Maverick.** S. S. Augustithis. LC 99-76193. 2000. pap. 13.95 (*1-57197-197-1*, Pub. by Pentland Pr) Assoc Pubs Grp.

Maverick. Garrett Flagg. pap. 18.95 (*0-9616326-8-2*) Bolton Pr.

Maverick. Dennis J. Marvicsin. 320p. 1991. mass mkt. 5.99 (*0-515-10662-3*, Jove) Berkley Pub.

Maverick. large type ed. Verne Athanas. LC 93-25507. 1993. pap. 15.95 (*0-8161-5838-X*, G K Hall Lrg Type) Mac Lib Ref.

Maverick. large type ed. Elliot Conway. (Linford Western Library). 1991. pap. 16.99 (*0-7089-7038-9*) Ulverscroft.

Maverick. large type ed. L. D. Tetlow. (Linford Western Large Print Ser.). 272p. 1998. pap. 17.99 (*0-7089-5201-1*, Linford) Ulverscroft.

Maverick: Legend of the West. Ed Robertson. (Illus.). 208p. (Orig.). 1994. pap. 17.95 (*0-938817-35-3*) Pomegranate Pr.

Maverick: The Success Story Behind the World's Most Unusual Workplace. Ricardo Semler. 352p. 1995. mass mkt. 14.99 (*0-446-67055-3*, Pub. by Warner Bks) Little.

Maverick American. Maury Maverick. 1993. reprint ed. lib. bdg. 75.00 (*0-7812-5969-X*) Rprt Serv.

Maverick Cats: Encounters with Feral Cats. Ellen P. Berkeley. LC 87-60370. (Illus.). 144p. 1987. reprint ed. pap. 12.95 (*0-933050-45-3*) New Eng Pr VT.

Maverick Column. Blandine Beaulieu. 1996. 25.95 (*0-9660181-1-7*) Concept Arts.

Maverick Column. large type ed. Blandine Beaulieu. 545p. 1996. 24.95 (*0-9660181-0-9*) Concept Arts.

Maverick Executive. Robert N. McMurry. LC 73-85189. 205p. reprint ed. pap. 63.60 (*0-608-11909-1*, 202357100033) Bks Demand.

Maverick Guide to Australia. 11th rev. ed. Len Ruttedge. (Maverick Guides Ser.). (Illus.). 416p. 1999. pap. 17.95 (*1-56554-151-0*) Pelican.

***Maverick Guide to Australia.** 12th ed. Len Rutledge. (Maverick Guides Ser.). (Illus.). 416p. 2000. pap. 17.95 (*1-56554-772-1*) Pelican.

Maverick Guide to Barcelona. Richard Scweid. (Illus.). 160p. 1999. pap. 14.95 (*1-56554-191-X*) Pelican.

Maverick Guide to Berlin. 2nd ed. Jay Brunhouse. (Maverick Guides Ser.). 400p. 1993. pap. text 15.95 (*1-56554-314-9*) Pelican.

***Maverick Guide to Bermuda.** Catherine Harriott. (Illus.). 192p. 2000. pap. 17.95 (*1-56554-690-3*) Pelican.

Maverick Guide to Hawaii. 20th ed. Robert W. Bone. (Maverick Guides Ser.). 432p. 1998. pap. text 15.95 (*1-56554-312-2*) Pelican.

Maverick Guide to Hong Kong, Macau, & South China. Len Rutledge. LC 95-190277. (Maverick Guides Ser.). (Illus.). 296p. (Orig.). 1995. pap. 15.95 (*1-56554-071-9*) Pelican.

Maverick Guide to Malaysia & Singapore. 2nd ed. Len Rutledge. (Maverick Guides Ser.). (Illus.). 488p. 1994. pap. 14.95 (*0-88289-990-2*) Pelican.

Maverick Guide to Morocco. Susan Searight. 288p. 1999. pap. 19.95 (*1-56554-348-3*) Pelican.

Maverick Guide to New Zealand. 10th rev. ed. Ed. by Susan Buckland. (Maverick Guides Ser.). (Illus.). 368p. 1999. pap. 17.95 (*1-56554-140-5*) Pelican.

***Maverick Guide to New Zealand.** 11th ed. Robert W. Bone. 368p. 2000. pap. text 17.95 (*1-56554-778-0*) Pelican.

Maverick Guide to Oman. Peter J. Ochs, 2nd. LC 98-145143. (Illus.). 84p. 1999. pap. 19.95 (*1-56554-241-X*) Pelican.

Maverick Guide to Oman. 2nd ed. Peter J. Ochs, 3rd. (Maverick Guides Ser.). (Illus.). 382p. 1999. pap. 19.95 (*1-56554-687-3*) Pelican.

Maverick Guide to Scotland. June S. Sawyers. LC 00-502901. (Maverick Guides Ser.). (Illus.). 608p. 1998. pap. text 19.95 (*1-56554-227-4*) Pelican.

Maverick Guide to Thailand. 3rd ed. Len Rutledge. (Illus.). 384p. 1999. pap. 15.95 (*1-56554-288-6*) Pelican.

Maverick Guide to the Great Barrier Reef. Len Rutledge. LC 97-135064. (Illus.). 224p. 1997. pap. 14.95 (*1-56554-193-6*) Pelican.

Maverick Guide to Vietnam, Laos, & Cambodia. 3rd rev. ed. Len Rutledge. (Maverick Guides Ser.). (Illus.). 392p. 1999. pap. 17.95 (*1-56554-126-X*) Pelican.

M

*Maverick Gun. large type ed. M. Lemartine. 264p. 1999. pap. 18.99 (0-7089-5620-3, Linford) Ulverscroft.
Maverick Guns. Jack Ballas. 208p. (Orig.). 1993. pap. 4.99 (0-515-11162-7, Jove) Berkley Pub.
Maverick Heart. Joan Johnston. 448p. (Orig.). 1995. mass mkt. 6.99 (0-440-21762-8) Dell.
*Maverick Heart: The Further Adventures of Zane Grey. Stephen J. May. (Illus.). 272p. 2000. 29.95 (0-8214-1316-3, Ohio U Ctr Intl); pap. 16.95 (0-8214-1317-1, Ohio U Ctr Intl) Ohio U Pr.
*Maverick Hearts. 1999. per. 9.99 (0-373-65210-0) Harlequin Bks.
Maverick Maestro Mrinal Sen. Deepankar Mukhopadhyay. (C). 1995. 28.00 (81-7223-213-6, Pub. by Indus Pub) S Asia.
Maverick Management: An Unconventional Guide to Success. John W. Hartman & Harvey Mackay. LC 97-68808. 192p. 1998. 15.95 (1-885884-03-6) Cormorant Pr.
Maverick Mania. Sigmund Brouwer. LC 98-14576. (Sigmund Brouwer's Sports Mystery Ser.). 128p. (J). 1998. 5.99 (0-8499-5813-X) Tommy Nelson.
Maverick Marine: General Smedley D. Butler & the Contradictions of American Military History. Hans Schmidt. (Illus.). 320p. 1998. reprint ed. pap. 18.00 (0-8131-0957-4) U Pr of Ky.
Maverick Marriage. Cathy G. Thacker. (American Romance Ser.). 1996. per. 3.75 (0-373-16633-8, 1-16633-9) Harlequin Bks.
Maverick Marshall. Nelson Nye. 1978. mass mkt. 1.75 (0-451-08356-3, E8356, Sig) NAL.
Maverick Marshall. large type ed. Nelson Nye. 1991. 8.95 (1-55504-588-X, 2127) Chivers N Amer.
Maverick Moon. Jane Archer. 1997. per. 5.99 (0-671-53708-3, Pocket Books) PB.
Maverick Poets: An Anthology. Sharon Olds et al. (Illus.). 146p. (Orig.). 1988. 18.50 (0-9610454-3-4); pap. 12.00 (0-9610454-2-6) Gorilla Pr.
Maverick Preacher. large type ed. M. Duggan. (Linford Western Library). 272p. 1997. pap. 16.99 (0-7089-5005-1, Linford) Ulverscroft.
Maverick Sea Fare: A Caribbean Cook Book. Dee Carstarphen. LC 78-107177. (Illus.). 60p. 1982. pap. 7.95 (0-9607544-2-3) Pen & Ink.
Maverick Sea Fare Caribbean Checkbook. Carstarphen. 1983. pap. 6.95 (0-916224-74-0) Banyan Bks.
Maverick Spirit: Building the New Nevada. Ed. by Richard Davies. LC 98-21144. (History & Humanities Ser.). (Illus.). 296p. 1998. pap. 17.95 (0-87417-327-2) U of Nev Pr.
Maverick State: Libya & the New World Order. Guy Arnold. LC 96-7827. (Global Issues Ser.). 224p. 1997. 89.50 (0-304-33366-2); pap. 18.95 (0-304-33367-0) Continuum.
Maverick Takes a Wife. Charlotte Moore. (Romance Ser.). 1996. per. 2.99 (0-373-19129-4, 1-19129-5) Silhouette.
Maverick Tales: True Stories of Early Texas. Jack D. Rittenhouse. 22.95 (0-89190-867-6) Amereon Ltd.
Maverick the Lucky Longhorn. David McKelvey. (Illus.). 32p. (J). (gr. k-3). 1986. pap. 3.95 (0-931722-47-0); lib. bdg. 10.95 (0-931722-48-9) Corona Pub.
Maverick Touch. Clyde M. Brundy. 224p. 1988. pap. 3.95 (0-380-89600-1, Avon Bks) Morrow Avon.
Maverick Town: The Story of Old Tascosa. John L. McCarty. LC 87-5946. (Illus.). 320p. 1988. pap. 15.95 (0-8061-2089-4) U of Okla Pr.
*Maverick Way: Profiting from the Power of the Corporate Misfit. Richard E. Cheverton. (Illus.). 288p. 2000. 22.95 (0-9668226-1-7, Maverick Way) Waypoint Bks.
Maverick Women: 19th Century Women Who Kicked over the Traces. Frances Laurence. LC 97-74353. (Illus.). 290p. 1998. pap. 18.50 (0-9627896-0-7) Manifest Pubns.
Mavericks: English Football When Flair Wore Flares. Rob Steen. (Illus.). 188p. 1995. pap. 22.95 (1-85158-740-3, Pub. by Mainstream Pubng) Trafalgar.
Mavericks: Ten Uncorralled Westerners. Dale L. Walker. LC 89-23338. (Illus.). 120p. (Orig.). 1989. pap. 5.00 (0-914846-42-6) Golden West Pub.
Mavericks: The Lives & Battles of Montana's Political Legends. John Morrison & Catherine W. Morrison. LC 96-52420. 310p. 1997. 34.95 (0-89301-199-1) U of Idaho Pr.
*Mavericks: The Story of Big-Wave Surfing. Matt Warshaw. LC 99-88228. (Illus.). 2000. 24.95 (0-8118-2652-X) Chronicle Bks.
Mavericks: What a Crying Shame. 56p. 1994. otabind 14.95 (0-7935-3909-9, 00306003) H Leonard.
Maverick's Bride: Rodeo Man. Doreen Roberts. (Intimate Moments Ser.: No. 945). 1999. per. 4.25 (0-373-07945-1, 1-07945-8) Silhouette.
Maverick's Guide to Poker. 176p. (Orig.). 1994. pap. 5.95 (0-8048-3032-0) Tuttle Pubng.
Mavericks in American Politics. Edward N. Kearny. 288p. (C). 1976. 8.95 (0-912084-09-X) Mimir.
Mavericks in the Workplace: Harnessing the Genius of American Workers. William G. Lee. LC 98-23710. 208p. 1998. 25.00 (0-19-511656-9) OUP.
*Mavericks on the Border: The Early Southwest in Historical Fiction & Films. J. Douglas Canfield. LC 00-28310. 256p. (C). 2000. 27.50 (0-8131-2180-9) U Pr of Ky.
Maverick's Progress: An Autobiography. James T. Flexner. xi, 510p. 1996. pap. 19.95 (0-8232-1661-6) Fordham.
Maverick's Progress: An Autobiography. James T. Flexner. LC 95-10132. (Illus.). xi, 510p. 1996. 29.95 (0-8232-1660-8) Fordham.
Mavis Gallant. Schaub. LC 98-21554. 230p. 1998. 32.00 (0-8057-4553-X, Twyne) Mac Lib Ref.
Mavis Gallant & Her Works. Judith S. Grant. (Canadian Author Studies). 58p. (C). 1989. pap. text 9.95 (1-55022-033-0, Pub. by ECW) Genl Dist Srvs.
Mavis Jukes Series. Mavis Jukes. (Illus.). 1994. 9.97 (0-679-87017-2) Random.
Mavreen. large type ed. Claire Lorrimer. (Charnwood Large Print Ser.). 832p. 1996. 27.99 (0-7089-8895-4) Ulverscroft.
Maw on Corporate Governance. Nigel G. Maw et al. Ed. by Alison Alsbury. LC 93-41372. 208p. (C). 1994. 48.95 (1-85521-378-8, Pub. by Dartmth Pub) Ashgate Pub Co.
Mawaed Al Aalam. Sonia Beiruti. Ed. by Ramzi Kaliffe.Tr. of Meals of the World. (ARA., Illus.). 463p. 1991. 73.50 (1-58311-010-0) Eastern Corp.
Mawaqif & Mukhatabat. Al-Niffari. (Gibb Memorial New Ser.: Vol. 9). 1935. 64.50 (0-906094-22-4, Pub. by Aris & Phillips) David Brown.
Mawarannabr Book Painting. Olimpiada Galerkina. 1980. 96.00 (0-569-08658-2) St Mut.
Mawlana Mawdudi & the Making of Islamic Revivalism. Seyyed V. Nasr. 1996. 42.50 (0-614-21493-9, 1429) Kazi Pubns.
Mawlana Mawdudi & the Making of Islamic Revivalism. Seyyed V. Nasr. (Illus.). 232p. 1996. text 52.00 (0-19-509695-9) OUP.
Maws. Erd Noswat, pseud. (Illus.). 36p. 1976. pap. 1.50 (0-939748-11-8) Cave Bks MO.
Mawson's Antarctic Diaries. Ed. by Fred Jacka & Eleanor Jacka. (Illus.). 464p. 1991. pap. 34.95 (1-86373-022-2, Pub. by Allen & Unwin Pty) Paul & Co Pubs.
Mawson's Antarctic Diaries. Ed. by Fred Jacka & Eleanor Jacka. (Illus.). 414p. 1990. text 45.00 (0-04-320209-8) Routledge.
Mawson's Diseases of the Ear. 5th ed. Harold Ludman. 688p. pap. text. write for info. (0-7131-4580-3, Pub. by E A) Routldge.
*Mawson's Will. unabridged deluxe ed. Lennard Bickel. LC 99-66364. (Illus.). 292p. 1999. reprint ed. lib. bdg. 35.00 (1-885283-18-0) Advent Library.
*Mawson's Will: The Greatest Polar Survival Story Ever Written. 2nd ed. Lennard Bickel. LC 99-59210. (Illus.). 272p. 2000. pap. 15.00 (1-58642-000-3, Pub. by Steerforth Pr) Publishers Group.
Mawsouat Al Mawsouaa. Nicola Nahed. Ed. by Saleam Diyraney.Tr. of Encyclopedia of Encyclopedias. (ARA., Illus.). 3864p. 1985. 985.00 (1-58311-000-3) Eastern Corp.
Mawsouat Al Tabekh. Sonia Beiruti. Ed. by Ramzi Kaliffe.Tr. of Cooking Encyclopedia. (ARA., Illus.). 2880p. 1990. 699.00 (1-58311-001-1) Eastern Corp.
Mawsouat Al Toubiya. Hamad A. Saamak. Ed. by Youssef Farhat.Tr. of Medical Encyclopedia. (ARA., Illus.). 2880p. 1990. 699.00 (1-58311-002-X) Eastern Corp.
*Max. Bob Graham. LC 99-43704. (Illus.). 32p. (J). (ps-2). 2000. 15.99 (0-7636-1138-7) Candlewick Pr.
Max. Romy Greer. Date not set. pap. 7.95 (0-9664868-2-X) Rags Inc.
Max. Rachel Isadora. LC 84-7649. (Illus.). 32p. (J). (gr. k-3). 1984. mass mkt. 3.95 (0-02-043800-1) Macmillan.
Max. Rachel Isadora. LC 76-9088. (Illus.). 32p. (J). (gr. k-3). 1976. lib. bdg. 13.95 (0-02-747450-X, Mac Bks Young Read) S&S Childrens.
Max. Richard Manton. 192p. 1999. mass mkt. 7.95 (1-56201-121-9) Blue Moon Bks.
Max. Harry Pollock. LC 98-101057. 1997. 12.95 (0-88962-636-7) Mosaic.
Max. Maurice Sendak. (J). 1994. 10.95 (0-694-00613-0, HarpFestival) HarpC Child Bks.
*Max. Ken Wilson-Max. LC 97-81289. (Illus.). 14p. (J). (ps-1). 1998. 12.95 (0-7868-0412-2, Pub. by Disney Pr) Time Warner.
MAX: A Personal Financial Management System. Alan Ramsay & Leslie Ramsay. 72p. 1983. vinyl bd. 15.00 (0-932925-00-6) Cactus Max.
Max: The Life & Music of Peter Maxwell Davies. Mike Seabrook. LC 96-160436. (Illus.). 281p. 1995. 35.00 (0-575-05672-X, Pub. by V Gollancz) Trafalgar.
Max: The Life & Music of Peter Maxwell Davies. Mike Seabrook. (Illus.). 281p. 1996. pap. 29.95 (0-575-05883-8, Pub. by V Gollancz) Trafalgar.
Max: The Story of a Simple Soul. A. B. West. 1891. 40.00 (0-7223-1371-3, Pub. by A H S Ltd) St Mut.
*Max & Emmy. Irene Trimble. 24p. (J). 2001. mass mkt. 3.25 (0-375-81156-7) Random Bks Yng Read.
Max & Felix. Larry D. Brimner. LC 91-77611. (Illus.). 32p. (J). (ps-1). 1995. pap. 5.95 (1-56397-519-X) Boyds Mills Pr.
*Max & Friends. Susan Surman. (Illus.). 150p. 1999. pap. 9.99 (0-88092-388-1) Royal Fireworks.
Max & Grandma & Grandpa Winky. Danielle Steel. (Illus.). 32p. (J). (ps-3). 1991. 9.95 (0-385-30165-0) Delacorte.
*Max & Jane. Elizabeth Craft. (Love Stories Ser.). 192p. (YA). (gr. 7-12). 2000. mass mkt. 4.50 (0-553-49318-3) BDD Bks Young Read.
Max & Jax in Second Grade. Jerdine Nolen. LC 98-5544. (Easy Reader Ser.). (Illus.). (J). 2000. 14.00 (0-15-201668-6) Harcourt.
Max & Jax in Second Grade. Jerdine Nolen. 2002. write for info. (0-15-201672-4) Harcourt.
Max & Maggie in Spring. Janet Craig. (Nice Mice Ser.). (J). 1995. 7.70 (0-606-07848-7, Pub. by Turtleback) Demco.
Max & Maggie in Winter. Janet Craig. LC 94-34183. (Illus.). 32p. (J). (ps-3). 1996. pap. 3.50 (0-8167-3355-4) Troll Communs.
Max & Maggie in Winter. Janet Craig. (Nice Mice Ser.). (J). 1995. 7.70 (0-606-07849-5, Pub. by Turtleback) Demco.
*Max & Marjorie: The Correspondence Between Maxwell E. Perkins & Marjorie Kinnan Rawlings. Maxwell E. Perkins & Marjorie Kinnan Rawlings. Ed. by Rodger L. Tarr. LC 99-34772. (Illus.). 625p. 1999. 34.95 (0-8130-1691-6) U Press Fla.
Max & Martha: The Twins of Fredericksburg. Marjorie Von Rosenberg. (ENG & GER., Illus.). 56p. (J). 1997. pap. 7.95 (0-89015-999-8, Eakin Pr) Sunbelt Media.
Max & Maxie. James McLure. 1989. pap. 5.25 (0-8222-0741-9) Dramatists Play.
Max & Me see Mingo y Yo
Max & Me. Karen M. Rogers. LC 98-71338. (Think-Kids Book Collection). (Illus.). 16p. (J). (gr. 1-4). 1998. pap. 2.95 (1-58237-013-3) Creat Think.
Max & Me: The Abuse of Power in Florida Community Colleges. Marion Brady. 254p. (Orig.). 1995. pap. 5.00 (0-614-03904-5) M Brady.
Max & Me & the Time Machine. Gery Greer. (J). 1983. 10.05 (0-606-03614-8, Pub. by Turtleback) Demco.
Max & Me & the Time Machine. Gery Greer & Robert Ruddick. LC 82-48762. 140p. (J). (gr. 4-7). 1983. 13.95 (0-15-253134-3, Harcourt Child Bks) Harcourt.
Max & Me & the Time Machine. Gery Greer et al. LC 87-45284. (Trophy Bk.). 128p. (J). (gr. 4-7). 1988. reprint ed. pap. 4.95 (0-06-440222-3, HarpTrophy) HarpC Child Bks.
Max & Me & the Wild West. Gery Greer & Robert Ruddick. LC 87-12066. (Illus.). 144p. (J). (gr. 3-7). 1988. 12.95 (0-15-253136-X) Harcourt.
*Max & Molly & the Mystery of the Missing Honey. Jurg Obrist. (Illus.). 48p. (J). (gr. 1-4). 2000. 13.95 (0-7358-1266-7, Pub. by North-South Bks NYC) Chronicle Bks.
Max & Moritz. Wilhelm Busch. Ed. by H. Arthur Klein. 216p. (J). (gr. 3-6). 1962. pap. 6.95 (0-486-20181-3) Dover.
Max & Moritz. Wilhelm Busch. Tr. by Walter Arndt. LC 85-1241. (Illus.). (J). (gr. 4 up). 1985. 9.95 (0-915361-19-1) Lambda Pubs.
Max & Moritz Buch. Wilhelm Busch. (GER., Illus.). 104p. 1994. pap. 10.63 (0-8442-2252-6, 22526, Natl Textbk Co) NTC Contemp Pub Co.
Max & Ruby in Pandora's Box. Rosemary Wells. (Picture Puffin Ser.). (Illus.). 32p. (J). (ps-3). 1998. pap. 5.99 (0-14-056415-2, PuffinBks) Peng Put Young Read.
Max & Ruby in Pandora's Box. Rosemary Wells. (Picture Puffin Ser.). (J). 1998. 11.19 (0-606-13601-0, Pub. by Turtleback) Demco.
Max & Ruby's Midas: Another Greek Myth. Rosemary Wells. LC 94-11181. (Max & Ruby Bks.). (Illus.). 32p. (J). (gr. k-2). 1995. 12.99 (0-8037-1782-2, Dial Yng Read) Peng Put Young Read.
Max & Sally & the Phenomenal Phone. Milos Macourek. Tr. by Dagmar Herrmann from CZE. LC 88-33871. (Illus.). 82p. (J). (gr. 2-4). 1989. 16.95 (0-922984-00-X) Wellington IL.
Max & the Baby-Sitter. Danielle Steel. (Illus.). 32p. (J). (ps-2). 1989. 8.95 (0-385-29796-3) Delacorte.
Max & the Big Fat Lie. Michael P. Waite. LC 87-35511. (Christian Character Builders Ser.). (Illus.). 32p. (J). (ps-2). 1988. 9.99 (1-55513-617-6, Chariot Bks) Chariot Victor.
Max & the Great Blueness. Lou Alpert. LC 92-23313. (Illus.). 32p. (J). (ps-3). 1993. 13.95 (1-879085-38-0, Whispering Coyote) Charlesbridge Pub.
Max & the Jayhawks: 50 Years on & off the Air with KU Sports. Max Falkenstien. (Illus.). 304p. (Orig.). 1996. pap. 19.95 (1-880652-55-2) Wichita Eagle.
*Max & the Missing Pony. Irene Trimble. (Dragon Tales Ser.). (Illus.). 24p. (J). (ps). 2000. 2.99 (0-375-80323-8, Pub. by Random Bks Yng Read) Random.
Max & the School Dinners. Colin Hawkins. (Illus.). 28p. (J). pap. 9.95 (0-14-055591-9, Pub. by Piguin Bks Ltd) Trafalgar.
Max & the Very Rare Bird. Graham Percy. (Meg & Max Bks.). (Illus.). 32p. (J). (ps-3). 1991. lib. bdg. 22.79 (0-89565-786-4) Childs World.
Max & Will: Max Beerbohm & William Rothenstein, Their Friendship & Letters, 1893-1945. Ed. by Mary M. Lago & Karl Beckson. LC 74-30853. (Illus.). 200p. 1976. 31.00 (0-674-55661-5) HUP.
*Max Baur: In the Bauhaus Spirit, Photographs, 1925-1960. Ed. by Stephan Steins. (Illus.). 2000. 65.00 (3-908163-23-4, Pub. by Edit Stemmle) Abbeville Pr.
Max Beckmann. Max Beckman. Ed. by Peter H. Selz et al. 1981. 24.95 (0-405-12888-6) Ayer.
Max Beckmann. F. Erpel. (GER.). 70p. 1981. 60.00 (0-7855-1639-5) St Mut.
Max Beckmann. Peter H. Selz. (Modern Masters Ser.). (Illus.). 128p. 1996. pap. 14.95 (0-7892-0119-4) Abbeville Pr.
Max Beckmann. Peter H. Selz. (Modern Masters Ser.). (Illus.). 128p. 1996. 35.00 (1-55859-889-8) Abbeville Pr.
Max Beckmann: A Retrospective. Carla Schilz-Hoffmann. 1990. pap. 39.95 (0-393-30684-4) Norton.
Max Beckmann: Paintings, Drawings, Sculpture & Works on Paper. Siegfried Gohr. 1994. 25.00 (1-885013-00-0) M Werner.
Max Beckmann: Prints from the Museum of Modern Art. Wendy Weitman & James Fisher. (Illus.). 112p. 1992. pap. 19.95 (0-87070-169-X) Mus of Modern Art.
*Max Beckmann: Zeichnungen. Max Beckmann. (Illus.). 256p. 2000. 60.00 (3-87909-613-9, Pub. by Wienand) Nazraeli Press.
Max Beckmann & Paris. Tobia Bezzola et al. (Illus.). 240p. 1998. 39.95 (0-89178-076-9) St Louis Art Mus.
Max Beckmann & Paris: The Exhibition Catalogue. Tobia Bezzola. (Jumbo Ser.). 1998. 39.99 (3-8228-7203-2) Taschen Amer.
Max Beckmann, 1948: Retrospective Exhibition Organized by City Art Museum of St. Louis. St. Louis City Art Museum Staff. LC 83-45798. reprint ed. 55.00 (0-404-20225-X) AMS Pr.
Max Beckmann Prints: From the Museum of Modern Art. Wendy Weitman & James L. Fisher. LC 92-60097. (Illus.). 104p. (Orig.). 1992. pap. 17.95 (0-929865-07-3) Mod Art Mus Ft Worth.
Max Beckmann's Triptychs. Charles S. Kessler. LC 78-88806. 207p. 1970. reprint ed. pap. 64.20 (0-7837-2286-9, 205737400004) Bks Demand.
Max Beerbohm: Collected Verse. Max Beerbohm. Ed. & Notes by J. G. Riewald. LC 93-36129. (Illus.). xxx, 222p. (C). 1994. lib. bdg. 42.50 (0-208-02390-9, Archon Bks) Shoe String.
Max Beerbohm & the Act of Writing. Lawrence Danson. (Illus.). 276p. 1991. reprint ed. pap. text 22.00 (0-19-811227-0) OUP.
Max Beerbohm & the Mirror of the Past. Lawrence Danson. (Illus.). 96p. 1982. 15.00 (0-87811-031-3) Princeton Lib.
Max Beerbohm Caricatures. N. John Hall. LC 97-13693. 224p. 1997. 45.00 (0-300-07217-1) Yale U Pr.
Max Beerbohm in Perspective. John Lynch. LC 73-21682. (English Biography Ser.: No. 31). 1974. lib. bdg. 75.00 (0-8383-1788-X) M S G Haskell Hse.
Max Beerbohm: or The Dandy Dante: Rereading with Mirrors. Robert Viscusi. LC 85-45044. (Illus.). 287p. reprint ed. pap. 89.00 (0-608-06161-1, 206649400008) Bks Demand.
Max Benjamin, 1964-1980. Matthew Kangas. LC 84-72831. (Illus.). 30p. (Orig.). 1984. pap. 9.95 (0-942342-04-6) Bellevue Art.
Max Bernstein Kritiker, Schriftsteller, Rechtsanwalt (1854-1925) Ein Beitrag Zur Literatur-, Rechts-, Zensur-, Kultur-, Sozial- und Allgemeinen Geschichte Zwischen 1878 & 1925 Mit Ausfuhrungen Zum Naturlismus, Zur Praktischen Anwendung des Sozialistengesetzes, Zu Ibsen, Conrad, Gerhart Hauptmann & Anderen Zeitgenossen. Jurgen Joachimsthaler. (GER., Illus.). X, 954p. 1995. 115.95 (3-631-48427-5) P Lang Pubng.
Max Bil see Sam's Car
Max Bodenheimer (1865-1940) Henriette H. Bodenheimer. 125p. (C). 1989. text 39.00 (0-946270-86-4, Pub. by Pentland Pr) St Mut.
Max Bohm: Romantic American Visionary. Susanna J. Fichera. 48p. 1994. pap. text. write for info. (0-9640289-0-5) A J Walker.
Max Bonker & the Howling Thieves. Scott Weidensaul. LC 95-54103. (Illus.). (J). 1996. 16.95 (1-55591-244-3) Fulcrum Pub.
Max Brand. William A. Bloodworth, Jr. (Twayne's United States Authors Ser.). 208p. 1993. 22.95 (0-8057-7646-X, Twyne) Mac Lib Ref.
Max Brand: Western Giant the Life & Times of Frederick Schiller Faust. William F. Nolan. 175p. 1986. pap. 10.95 (0-87972-292-4) Bowling Green Univ Popular Press.
Max Brand: Western Giant the Life & Times of Frederick Schiller Faust. William F. Nolan. LC 86-70192. 175p. 1986. 22.95 (0-87972-291-6) Bowling Green Univ Popular Press.
Max Brand Companion. Ed. by Jon Tuska & Vicki Piekarski. LC 96-18207. 576p. 1996. lib. bdg. 79.95 (0-313-29750-9, Greenwood Pr) Greenwood.
Max Brand's Best Poems: Verses from a Master of Popular Prose - A Centennial Selection. Max Brand. Ed. by Martin H. Greenberg. LC 91-16615. (Illus.). 104p. 1992. 14.95 (0-931832-96-9) Fithian Pr.
Max Brand's Best Western Stories, Vol. II. Ed. by William F. Nolan. 192p. 1986. mass mkt. 2.95 (0-446-34170-3, Pub. by Warner Bks) Little.
Max Brod, 1884 to 1984: Untersuchungen Zu Max Brods Literarischen und Philosophischen Schriften. Ed. by Margarita Pazi. (New Yorker Studien zur Neueren Deutschen Literaturgeschichte Ser.: Vol. 8). 268p. 1987. 52.00 (0-8204-0571-X) P Lang Pubng.
Max Brodel: The Man Who Put Art into Medicine. R. W. Crosby & J. Cody. (Illus.). ix, 352p. 1993. 65.00 (0-387-97563-2) Spr-Verlag.
Max City Guides: Berlin. 1999. pap. 10.95 (3-8238-9899-X) te Neues.
Max City Guides: London. 1999. pap. 10.95 (3-8238-9402-1) te Neues.
Max City Guides: New York. 1998. pap. 10.95 (3-8238-9400-5) te Neues.
*Max Cleans Up. Rosemary Wells. LC 99-462098. (Illus.). 32p. (J). (ps-3). 2000. 15.99 (0-670-89218-1, Viking Child) Peng Put Young Read.
Max D. Steuer: Trial Lawyer. Aron Steuer. LC 96-75318. (3) 301p. 1996. reprint ed. 65.00 (1-57588-070-9, 310490) W S Hein.
Max Danger: The Adventures of an Expat in Tokyo. Robert J. Collins. LC 87-51178. 206p. 1987. pap. 9.95 (0-8048-1531-3) Tuttle Pubng.
Max Doll. Maira Kalman. (ps-3). 1995. pap. 19.99 (0-670-86619-9) Viking Penguin.
*Max e-Marketing for the Net Future: How to Outsmart the Competition in the Battle for the Internet. Stan Rapp. 2000. 24.95 (0-07-136472-2) McGraw.
Max Eastman. Milton Cantor. LC 71-120012. (Twayne's United States Authors Ser.). 1970. lib. bdg. 20.95 (0-89197-844-5) Irvington.
Max Ehrmann: A Poet's Life. Bertha P. Ehrmann. LC 51-11422. 130p. reprint ed. pap. 40.30 (0-7837-5588-0, 204538100005) Bks Demand.
Max Ernst. (Prestel Postcard Bks.). (Illus.). 18p. 1993. pap. 8.95 (3-7913-1313-4, Pub. by Prestel) te Neues.
Max Ernst. Edward Quinn. (Art & Architecture Ser.). (Illus.). 444p. 1997. boxed set 39.95 (3-89508-930-3, 880035) Konemann.

An Asterisk (*) at the beginning of an entry indicates that the title is appearing for the first time.

Max Ernst. Karin Von Maur et al. Ed. by Werner Spies. (Illus.). 384p. 1991. 75.00 (*3-7913-1140-9*, Pub. by Prestel) te Neues.

Max Ernst. William S. Lieberman. LC 72-169307. (Museum of Modern Art Publications in Reprint). (Illus.). 66p. 1972. reprint ed. 15.95 (*0-405-01566-6*) Ayer.

Max Ernst: A Retrospective. Ed. & Intro. by Werner Spies et al. (Illus.). 384p. 1995. pap. 29.95 (*3-7913-1621-4*, Pub. by Prestel) te Neues.

Max Ernst: Dada & the Dawn of Surrealism. William Camfield. (Illus.). 376p. 1998. pap. text 35.00 (*3-7913-1944-2*) Prestel.

Max Ernst: Dada & the Dawn of Surrealism. William Camfield et al. (Illus.). 376p. 1993. 75.00 (*3-7913-1260-X*, Pub. by Prestel) te Neues.

Max Ernst: Inside the Sight. Werner Hofmann et al. LC 77-125283. (Illus.). 1973. pap. 14.95 (*0-914412-06-X*, Inst Arts Catalogues) Menil Found.

Max Ernst: Sculptures. Jurgen Pech. 1996. pap. 45.00 (*88-8158-070-5*, Pub. by Charta) Dist Art Pubs.

Max Ernst: The Late Lithographs. (Illus.). 32p. (Orig.). 1989. pap. 15.00 (*0-9624615-0-4*) Nahan Editions.

Max Ernst: The Psychoanalytic Sources. Elizabeth M. Legge. Ed. by Stephen Foster. LC 89-31850. (Studies in the Fine Arts: The Avant-Garde: No. 67). 245p. reprint ed. 76.00 (*0-8357-1964-2*, 207073100004) Bks Demand.

***Max Ernst & Alchemy: A Magician in Search of Myth.** M. E. Warlick. (Surrealist Revolution Ser.). (Illus.). 320p. 2001. 50.00 (*0-292-79135-6*); pap. 24.95 (*0-292-79136-4*) U of Tex Pr.

***Max Et La Poule En Chocolat.** Rosemary Wells. 1999. pap. 12.95 (*2-211-02083-6*) Distribks Inc.

Max Et Le Maximonsters. Maurice Sendak. 1996. pap. 9.95 (*2-211-01965-X*) Distribks Inc.

Max Factor: The Man Who Changed the Face of the World. Marianne Morino & Robert Salvatore. 300p. 1989. 19.95 (*0-942139-08-9*) Tale Weaver.

***Max Ferguson's Digital Darkroom Masterclass.** Max Ferguson. (Illus.). 224p. 2000. pap. 44.95 (*0-240-51569-2*, Focal) Buttrwrth-Heinemann.

Max Found Two Sticks. Brian Pinkney. (J). 1997. mass mkt. 5.99 (*0-689-81593-X*) Aladdin.

Max Found Two Sticks. Brian Pinkney. LC 93-12525. (Illus.). 40p. (J). (ps-3). 1994. pap. 16.00 (*0-671-78776-4*) S&S Bks Yung.

Max Found Two Sticks. Brian Pinkney. 1997. 11.19 (*0-606-11605-2*, Pub. by Turtleback) Demco.

***Max Friedman: No Pasaran.** Vittorio Giardino. 2000. pap. 13.95 (*1-56163-261-9*) NBM.

Max Frisch. Ulrich Weisstein. 192p. 1967. 49.50 (*0-685-63206-7*) Elliots Bks.

Max Frisch: Homo Faber. (Lekture Durchblick Ser.). (GER.). 64p. 1996. student ed. 8.95 (*3-580-63304-X*) Langenscheidt.

Max Frisch: Novels, Plays & Essays. Max Frisch. Ed. by Rolf Kieser. LC 62-12960. (German Library: Vol. 90). 350p. 1989. pap. 19.95 (*0-8264-0322-0*) Continuum.

Max Frisch: Novels, Plays & Essays. Max Frisch. Ed. by Rolf Kieser. LC 78-20945. (German Library: Vol. 90). 350p. 1989. 39.50 (*0-8264-0321-2*) Continuum.

***Max Frisch Romancier: Son Evolution de Mein Name Sei Gantenbein a Der Mensch Erscheint Im Holozan.** Regine Battiston-Zuliani. (Publications Universitaires Europeennes: Vol. 1732). xii, 300p. 1999. 46.95 (*3-906763-54-4*, Pub. by P Lang) P Lang Pubng.

Max Frisch, the Reluctant Modernist. Alfred D. White. 1995. write for info. (*0-7734-9133-3*) E Mellen.

Max Gets a Horse. Margaret Kandies. LC 96-27277. (J). 1997. write for info. (*1-56763-259-9*); pap. write for info. (*1-56763-260-2*) Ozark Pub.

Max Grunhut (1893-1964) Leben und Wissenschaftliches Wirken Eines Deutschen Strafrechtlers Juedischer Herkunft. Ulrike Fontaine. Ed. by Manfred Maiwald. (Schriften zum Strafrecht und Strafprozessrecht Ser.: Vol. 31). (GER., Illus.). 176p. 1998. pap. 39.95 (*3-631-32638-6*) P Lang Pubng.

Max Havelaar: Or the Coffee Auctions of the Dutch Trade. Tr. by Roy Edwards. 352p. 1995. pap. 13.95 (*0-14-044516-1*, Penguin Classics) Viking Penguin.

Max Havelaar: Or the Coffee Auctions of the Dutch Trading Company. Multatuli, pseud. Tr. by Roy Edwards from DUT. LC 82-2043. (Library of the Indies). 400p. 1982. lib. bdg. 40.00 (*0-87023-359-9*) U of Mass Pr.

Max Helfman: A Biographical Sketch. Cantor P. Moddel. 1974. 10.00 (*0-943376-04-1*) Magnes Mus.

Max Horkheimer: A Bibliography. Ed. by Joan Nordquist. (Social Theory: A Bibliographic Ser.: No. 18). 64p. (Orig.). (C). 1990. pap. 20.00 (*0-937855-35-9*) Ref Rsch Serv.

Max Horkheimer: A New Introduction. Peter M. Stirk. 288p. (C). 1993. text 59.50 (*0-389-21000-5*) B&N Imports.

Max Horkheimer Als Moralphilosoph: Studie Zur Kritischen Theorie. Dieter Sattler. (GER.). 243p. 1996. 44.95 (*3-631-49715-6*) P Lang Pubng.

***Max Horkheimer Zwischen Sozialphilosophie und Empirischer Sozialforschung.** Barbara Loffler-Erxleben. 104p. 1999. 26.95 (*3-631-34442-2*) P Lang Pubng.

Max in America Pt. 2: Communcating in the Culture. Ed. by Raymond C. Clark. (Illus.). 128p. 1987. pap. text 2.00 (*0-86647-025-5*) Pro Lingua.

Max in America, Posters: Communcating in the Culture. Ed. by Raymond C. Clark. (Illus.). 26p. 1987. pap. text 12.50 (*0-86647-027-1*) Pro Lingua.

Max in America, Teacher's Handbook: Communcating in the Culture. Ed. by Raymond C. Clark. (Illus.). 160p. 1987. pap. text, teacher ed. 2.00 (*0-86647-026-3*) Pro Lingua.

Max in Hollywood, Baby. Maira Kalman. 1999. pap. 5.99 (*0-14-054842-4*) NAL.

Max in Hollywood, Baby. Maira Kalman. LC 91-48200. (Illus.). 32p. (J). (gr. 2 up). 1992. 16.99 (*0-670-84479-9*, Viking Child) Peng Put Young Read.

Max Jacob: Lettres a Nino Frank. Anne S. Kimball. (American University Studies: Romance Languages & Literature: Ser. II, Vol. 64). 219p. (C). 1988. text 42.50 (*0-8204-0507-8*) P Lang Pubng.

Max Karant: My Flights & Fights. Max Karant & Charles F. Spence. LC 98-34956. (Illus.). 224p. 1998. 29.95 (*0-07-034928-2*) McGraw.

Max Klinger - The Late Graphic Work: Das Graphische Werk, 1909-1919. Carl Beyer. (ENG & GER., Illus.). 224p. 1997. 150.00 (*1-55660-170-0*) A Wofsy Fine Arts.

Max Klinger's Graphic Work: Radierungen, Stiche und Steindrucke. Hans Singer. (ENG & GER., Illus.). 400p. 1991. 150.00 (*1-55660-078-X*) A Wofsy Fine Arts.

Max Lakeman & the Beautiful Stranger. large type ed. Jon Cohen. 323p. 1990. reprint ed. 17.95 (*1-56054-028-1*) Thorndike Pr.

Max Leo: An Uncommon Cat. Nona Hengen. (Illus.). 113p. 1983. pap. 9.95 (*0-931474-20-5*) TBW Bks.

Max Lerner: Pilgrim in the Promised Land. Sanford Lakoff. LC 97-52640. (Illus.). 308p. 1998. 25.00 (*0-226-46831-3*) U Ch Pr.

Max Liebermann: The Graphic Work, 1876-1923. 4th ed. Gustav Schiefler. (ENG & GER.). 304p. 1991. 150.00 (*1-55660-077-1*) A Wofsy Fine Arts.

Max Loves Sunflowers. Ken Wilson-Max. LC 97-81288. (Illus.). 14p. (J). (ps-k). 1998. 12.95 (*0-7868-0413-0*, Pub. by Disney Pr) Time Warner.

Max Machinery. R. A. Hill. 124p. 1984. pap. 16.00 (*0-409-49114-4*, NZ, MICHIE) LEXIS Pub.

Max Makes a Million. Maira Kalman. 1999. pap. 5.99 (*0-14-054345-7*) NAL.

Max Malone & the Great Cereal Rip-Off. Charlotte Herman & Charlotte B. Smith. LC 89-26920. (Illus.). 64p. (J). (gr. 2-4). 1995. 12.95 (*0-8050-1069-6*, Redfeather BYR); pap. 4.95 (*0-8050-1843-3*, Redfeather BYR) H Holt & Co.

Max Malone Makes a Million. Charlotte Herman. LC 90-46373. (Illus.). 80p. (J). (gr. 2-4). 1995. 13.95 (*0-8050-1374-1*, Redfeather BYR); pap. 4.95 (*0-8050-2328-3*, Redfeather BYR) H Holt & Co.

Max Malone Makes a Million. Charlotte Herman. (Redfeather Bks.). (J). 1991. 11.15 (*0-606-02738-6*, Pub. by Turtleback) Demco.

Max Malone, Superstar. Charlotte Herman. LC 91-25191. (Illus.). 64p. (J). (gr. 2-4). 1995. 14.95 (*0-8050-1375-X*, Redfeather BYR) H Holt & Co.

Max Malone the Magnificent. Charlotte Herman. LC 92-14123. (Illus.). 64p. (J). (gr. 2-4). 1995. 14.95 (*0-8050-2282-1*, Bks Young Read); pap. 4.95 (*0-8050-3548-6*) H Holt & Co.

Max Morath: The Road to Ragtime. Max Morath et al. LC 99-19509. 1999. write for info. (*1-57864-068-7*) Donning Co.

Max Morath - Cripple Creek. Max Morath. pap. text 8.95 (*0-89524-748-8*) Cherry Lane.

Max Moves In Vol. 4: A Book about Obeying. Linda Porter Carlyle. Ed. by Aileen Sox. (Child's Steps to Jesus Ser.). (Illus.). 24p. (J). 1992. 7.99 (*0-8163-1095-5*, 0-8163-1095-5) Pacific Pr Pub Assn.

Max Muller & the Science of Language: A Criticism. William D. Whitney. (Notable American Authors Ser.). 1999. reprint ed. lib. bdg. 125.00 (*0-7812-9967-5*) Rprt Serv.

Max Muller's Encyclopaedia of Languages, 2 vols., Set. Prints India Staff. (C). 1988. 395.00 (*0-7855-0060-X*, Pub. by Print Hse) St Mut.

Max Nettlau Chronology. V. Munoz. 1973. 250.00 (*0-87700-179-0*) Revisionist Pr.

Max Nettlau, Rudolf Rocker, Han Ryner, Rodolfo Gonzalez Pacheco, Joseph Ishill & Other Essays in Anarchism, Humanism, Libertarianism & Freedom. Eugene Relgis. (History of Anarchism Ser.). 1984. lib. bdg. 250.00 (*0-8490-3234-2*) Gordon Pr.

Max Neuhaus: The Collection. Pier L. Tazzi. (Illus.). 40p. 1997. pap. 16.95 (*88-8158-114-0*) Dist Art Pubs.

Max Notes - A Raisin in the Sun. Research & Education Association Staff. (Illus.). 96p. 1994. pap. text 3.95 (*0-87891-945-7*) Res & Educ.

Max Notes - A Tale of Two Cities. Research & Education Association Staff. LC 94-65957. (Illus.). 128p. 1994. pap. text 3.95 (*0-87891-949-X*) Res & Educ.

Max Notes - Gone with the Wind. Research & Education Association Staff. (Illus.). 128p. 1994. pap. text 3.95 (*0-87891-955-4*) Res & Educ.

Max Notes - Hamlet. Research & Education Association Staff. LC 94-65964. (Illus.). 128p. 2000. pap. text 3.95 (*0-87891-952-X*) Res & Educ.

Max Notes - Huckleberry Finn. Research & Education Association Staff. (Illus.). 128p. 1994. pap. text 3.95 (*0-87891-953-8*) Res & Educ.

Max Notes - I Know Why the Caged Bird Sings. Research & Education Association Staff. (Illus.). 128p. 1994. pap. text 3.95 (*0-87891-956-2*) Res & Educ.

Max Notes - Julius Caesar. Research & Education Association Staff. 1500p. 1994. pap. text 3.95 (*0-87891-948-1*) Res & Educ.

Max Notes - Les Miserables. Research & Education Association Staff. (Illus.). 128p. 1994. pap. text 3.95 (*0-87891-951-1*) Res & Educ.

Max Notes - Macbeth. Research & Education Association Staff. (Illus.). 128p. 1994. pap. text 3.95 (*0-87891-944-9*) Res & Educ.

Max Notes - The Grapes of Wrath. Research & Education Association Staff. (Illus.). 128p. 1994. pap. text 3.95 (*0-87891-947-3*) Res & Educ.

Max Notes - The Great Gatsby. Research & Education Association Staff. (Illus.). 128p. 1994. pap. text 3.95 (*0-87891-942-2*) Res & Educ.

Max Notes - The Odyssey. Research & Education Association Staff. (Illus.). 100p. 2000. pap. text 3.95 (*0-87891-943-0*) Res & Educ.

Max Notes - To Kill a Mockingbird. Research & Education Association Staff. (Illus.). 128p. 1994. pap. text 3.95 (*0-87891-946-5*) Res & Educ.

Max-O-Narr, a Modern Fable. Lynne Guerra. LC 95-90955. 42p. 1996. 15.95 (*0-9649666-0-3*) T Green Pr.

***Max of Palm Beach.** Beverly J. Myers. (J). (gr. k-3). 2000. pap. 5.95 (*0-533-13107-3*) Vantage.

Max of Skamania. Suzanne Taylor-Moore. 1980. pap. 14.95 (*0-938758-07-1*) MTM Pub Co.

Max on View: An Exhibition. John O. Kirkpatrick. (Illus.). 80p. 1978. 12.00 (*0-87959-124-2*); pap. 7.50 (*0-87959-088-2*) U of Tex H Ransom Ctr.

MaX-1: A Visual Electromagnetics Platform for PCs. Christian Hafner. LC 98-36222. 64p. 1998. 875.00 incl. cd-rom (*0-471-98097-8*) Wiley.

Max Ophuls & the Cinema of Desire. abr. ed. Alan L. Williams. Ed. by Garth S. Jowett. LC 79-6693. (Dissertations on Film, 1980 Ser.). 1980. lib. bdg. 27.95 (*0-405-12924-6*) Ayer.

Max Ophuls in the Hollywood Studios. Lutz Bacher. LC 95-52726. (Illus.). 400p. (C). 1996. text 72.00 (*0-8135-2291-9*) Rutgers U Pr.

***Max Paints the House.** Ken Wilson-Max. LC 99-39884. 32p. (J). 2000. 14.99 (*0-7868-0537-4*, Pub. by Disney Pr) Time Warner.

Max Paints the House. Ken Wilson-Max. LC 99-39884. (Illus.). 32p. 2000. lib. bdg. 15.49 (*0-7868-2468-9*, Pub. by Hyprn Child) Little.

Max Perkins. A. Scott Berg. 1989. pap. 6.95 (*0-671-68174-5*, WSP) PB.

Max Perkins: Editor of Genius. A. Scott Berg. LC 96-52584. 512p. 1997. pap. 15.00 (*1-57322-621-1*, Riverhd Trade) Berkley Pub.

Max Planck Yearbook of United Nations Law, 001. Ed. by Jochen A. Frowein. 641p. 1998. 180.00 (*90-411-0700-2*) Kluwer Law Intl.

Max Planck Yearbook of United Nations Law, Vol. 3. text 162.00 (*90-411-9753-2*) Kluwer Law Intl.

Max Potta see Sam's Potty

Max Reger: A Bio-Bibliography, 7. William E. Grim. LC 87-25253. (Bio-Bibliographies in Music Ser.: No. 7). 281p. 1988. lib. bdg. 55.00 (*0-313-25311-0*, GMR/, Greenwood Pr) Greenwood.

Max Reinhardt & His Theatre. Ed. by Oliver M. Sayler. LC 68-20245. 381p. 1972. reprint ed. 30.95 (*0-405-08926-0*, Pub. by Blom Pubns) Ayer.

Max Runs Away. Danielle Steel. (Illus.). 32p. (J). 1990. 9.95 (*0-385-30213-4*) Delacorte.

Max Sackheim's Billion Dollar Marketing Concepts & Applications: The Man Who Revolutionized 20th Century Direct Response Advertising. Maxwell Sackheim. Ed. by Jerry Buchanan & David Reecher. LC 95-60017. (Illus.). 232p. (Orig.). 1995. pap. text 29.95 (*0-930668-11-1*) Towers Club.

Max Scheler: A Concise Introduction into the World of a Great Thinker. 2nd rev. ed. Manfred Frings. 1996. pap. 20.00 (*0-87462-605-6*) Marquette.

Max Scheler: The Man & His Work. John H. Nota. 213p. 1983. 5.95 (*0-8199-0852-5*, Frncscn Herld) Franciscan Pr.

Max Schling Book of Indoor Gardening. Dorothy Brandon & Alfred F. Scheider. (Illus.). 1963. 20.00 (*0-8392-1065-5*) Astor-Honor.

Max Schmeling: An Autobiography. Ed. & Tr. by George B. Von Der Lippe from GER. LC 98-24533.Tr. of Erinnerungen. (Illus.). 320p. 1998. 28.95 (*1-56625-108-7*) Bonus Books.

Max Schwimmer, Leben und Werk. Magdalena George. (GER.). 256p. 1981. 135.00 (*0-7855-1577-1*) St Mut.

Max Shachtman & His Left: A Socialist's Odyssey Through the American Century. Peter Drucker. LC 93-12763. (Revolutionary Studies). 336p. (C). 1993. pap. 18.50 (*0-391-03816-8*) Humanities.

Max Shachtman & His Left: A Socialist's Odyssey Through the American Century. Peter Drucker. LC 93-12763. (Revolutionary Studies). 336p. (C). 1993. text 49.95 (*0-391-03815-X*) Humanities.

Max Slevogt: The Graphic Work, 1890-1914. Johannes Sievers & Emil Waldmann. (ENG & GER.). 240p. 1991. reprint ed. 125.00 (*1-55660-075-5*) A Wofsy Fine Arts.

Max Stirner: A Chronology. V. Munoz. Tr. by W. Scott Johnson. (Libertarian & Anarchist Chronology Ser.). 1979. lib. bdg. 59.95 (*0-8490-3045-5*) Gordon Pr.

Max Stirner Versus Karl Marx: Individuality & the Social Organism. Phillip Dematteis. 1975. lib. bdg. 250.00 (*0-87700-239-8*) Revisionist Pr.

Max Stirner's Egoism. John P. Clark. 111p. (Orig.). 1976. pap. 5.00 (*0-900384-14-X*) Left Bank.

Max Stirner's Paradigmenwechsel. Filadelfo Linares. (Studien & Materialien zur Geschichte der Philosophie Ser.: Vol. 41). viii, 82p. 1996. pap. write for info. (*3-487-10053-3*) G Olms Pubs.

Max Strategy: How a Businessman Got Stuck at an Airport & Learned to Make His Career Take Off. Dale Dauten. 116p. 1998. text 20.00 (*0-7881-5974-7*) DIANE Pub.

Max Strategy: How a Businessman Got Stuck at an Airport & Learned to Make His Career Take Off. Dale A. Dauten. LC 95-14308. 160p. 1996. 19.95 (*0-688-14402-0*, Wm Morrow) Morrow Avon.

Max, the Apartment Cat. Mauro Magellan. LC 88-32067. (Illus.). 32p. (J). 1989. 10.95 (*0-89334-117-7*) Humanics Ltd.

Max the Bear. Joanne Wall. (Christmas Ornaments Ser.). (Illus.). 34p. (Orig.). (J). (ps up). 1996. pap. 12.95 (*0-9644283-3-4*) M J Wall.

Max the Man Mountain. Peter McFarlane. 1998. pap. 5.95 (*0-207-19116-6*) HarpC.

Max the Mighty. Rodman Philbrick. (J). 1998. pap. text 47.88 (*0-590-65859-X*, Blue Sky Press) Scholastic Inc.

Max the Mighty. Rodman Philbrick. LC 97-11762. 176p. (YA). (gr. 7 up). 1998. pap. 3.99 (*0-590-57964-9*) Scholastic Inc.

Max the Mighty. Rodman Philbrick & W. R. Philbrick. LC 97-11762. 166p. (J). (gr. 7-12). 1998. 16.95 (*0-590-18892-5*, Blue Sky Press) Scholastic Inc.

***Max the Muddy Puppy.** Jenny Dale. (Puppy Friends Ser.: No. 5). (Illus.). 64p. (J). (ps-3). 2000. pap. 3.99 (*0-689-83553-1*) Aladdin.

***Max the Rodeo Mouse.** large type ed. Herb Marlow & Lynn Marlowe. (Max Ser.). (Illus.). 32p. (J). (gr. k-5). 2000. lib. bdg. 7.95 (*1-893595-07-2*, MAX-2) Four Seasons Bks.

Max the School House Mouse. large type ed. Herb Marlow. (Illus.). 32p. (J). (gr. k-5). 1998. lib. bdg. 7.95 (*0-9666858-5-7*, MAX-1) Four Seasons Bks.

Max the Superhero. Sylvain Trudel. (First Novels Ser.). 59p. (J). 1996. mass mkt. 3.99 (*0-88780-376-8*, Pub. by Formac Publ Co); bds. 14.95 (*0-88780-377-6*, Pub. by Formac Publ Co) Formac Dist Ltd.

Max Trueblood & the Jersey Desperado. Teri White. 240p. 1988. mass mkt. 3.95 (*0-445-40685-2*, Pub. by Mysterious Pr) Little.

Max Weber see Three American Modernist Painters

Max Weber, 8 vols. Ed. by Peter Hamilton. (Critical Assessments of Leading Sociologists Ser.). 3264p. (C). 1998. 1235.00 (*0-415-12733-5*) Routledge.

Max Weber. Frank Parkin. (Key Sociologists Ser.). 128p. (C). 1982. pap. 16.99 (*0-415-03462-0*) Routledge.

Max Weber. Frank Parkin. (Key Sociologists Ser.). 123p. 1982. pap. 8.95 (*0-85312-409-4*, NO. 3676, Pub. by Tavistock-E Horwood) Routldge.

Max Weber: A Bibliography. Compiled by Joan Nordquist. (Social Theory: A Bibliographic Ser.: No. 13). 60p. (Orig.). 1989. pap. 20.00 (*0-937855-24-3*) Ref Rsch Serv.

Max Weber: A Bio-Bibliography, 2. Peter Kivisto & William H. Swatos, Jr. LC 88-24656. (Bio-Bibliographies in Sociology Ser.). 267p. 1988. lib. bdg. 65.00 (*0-313-25794-9*, KMX, Greenwood Pr) Greenwood.

Max Weber: A Biography. Marianne Weber. Ed. & Tr. by Harry Zohn from GER. 740p. 1987. 29.95 (*0-88738-702-0*) Transaction Pubs.

Max Weber: An Intellectual Portrait. Reinhard Bendix. LC 98-26542. (Max Weber Classic Monographs). 1998. write for info. (*0-415-17453-8*) Routledge.

Max Weber: An Intellectual Portrait. Reinhard Bendix. 1978. pap. 19.95 (*0-520-03194-6*, Pub. by U CA Pr) Cal Prin Full Svc.

Max Weber: An Introduction to His Life & Work. Dirk Kasler. Tr. by Philippa Hurd from GER. LC 88-19618. (Illus.). xiv, 288p. 1989. pap. text 17.95 (*0-226-42560-6*) U Ch Pr.

Max Weber: An Introduction to His Life & Work. Dirk Kasler. Tr. by Philippa Hurd from GER. LC 88-19618. (Illus.). xiv, 302p. 1997. lib. bdg. 54.00 (*0-226-42559-2*) U Ch Pr.

Max Weber: Classic Monographs, 8 vols. Ed. & Intro. by Bryan Turner. LC 98-26542. 1872p. (C). (gr. 13). 1998. reprint ed. 785.00 (*0-415-17451-1*, D5979) Routledge.

Max Weber: Critical Assessments, 4 vols., Set. Ed. by Peter Hamilton. LC 90-94918. (Illus.). 1664p. (C). (gr. 13). 1991. 700.00 (*0-415-01743-2*, A6271) Routledge.

Max Weber: Critical Assessments, 4 vols., Set. Ed. by Peter Hamilton. (Illus.). 1600p. (C). 1992. 700.00 (*0-415-06211-X*) Routledge.

Max Weber: Critical Responses see Max Weber: Critical Responses

Max Weber: Critical Responses, 3 vols. Ed. by Bryan S. Turner. Incl. Max Weber: Critical Responses. LC 98-11642. 1999. (*0-415-18474-6*); Vol. 3. Max Weber: Critical Responses. LC 98-11642. 1999. (*0-415-18476-2*); Vol. 2. LC 98-11642. 1999. (*0-415-18475-4*); LC 98-11642. 1999. 535.00 (*0-415-18473-8*) Routledge.

Max Weber: Essays in Reconstruction. Wilhelm Hennis. Tr. by Keith Tribe. 240p. 1987. text 65.00 (*0-04-301301-5*) Routledge.

Max Weber: From History to Modernity. Bryan S. Turner. 288p. (C). 1993. pap. 24.99 (*0-415-10387-8*) Routledge.

Max Weber: Pioneer of American Modernism. Howard E. Wooden. LC 83-60745. (Illus.). 16p. 1983. pap. 3.00 (*0-939324-10-5*) Wichita Art Mus.

Max Weber: Politics & the Spirit of Tragedy. John P. Diggins. 352p. 1996. pap. 16.00 (*0-465-01751-7*, Pub. by Basic) HarpC.

Max Weber: The Lawyer As Social Thinker. Stephen P. Turner & Regis A. Factor. LC 93-50670. 224p. 1994. 60.00 (*0-415-06751-0*, Pub. by Manchester Univ Pr); pap. 17.95 (*0-415-11452-7*, Pub. by Manchester Univ Pr) St Martin.

Max Weber & Culture Anarchy. Whimster. LC 97-42334. 235p. 1999. text 65.00 (*0-312-21302-6*) St Martin.

Max Weber & Democratic Politics. Peter Breiner. 1996. text 39.95 (*0-8014-3147-6*) Cornell U Pr.

Max Weber & German Politics. J. P. Mayer. LC 98-26544. (Max Weber Classic Monographs). 1998. write for info. (*0-415-17455-4*) Routledge.

Max Weber & German Politics. 3rd rev. ed. J. P. Mayer. LC 78-67371. (European Political Thought Ser.). 1979. reprint ed. lib. bdg. 17.95 (*0-405-11717-5*) Ayer.

Max Weber & German Politics, 1890-1920. Wolfgang J. Mommsen. Tr. by Michael S. Steinberg. LC 84-16274. xxii, 528p. 1990. pap. text 24.00 (*0-226-53399-9*) U Ch Pr.

Max Weber & German Politics, 1890-1920. Wolfgang J. Mommsen. Tr. by Michael S. Steinberg. LC 84-16274. 520p. 1997. lib. bdg. 60.00 (*0-226-53397-2*) U Ch Pr.

M

An Asterisk (*) at the beginning of an entry indicates that the title is appearing for the first time.

Max Weber & Islam. Ed. by Toby E. Huff & Wolfgang Schluchter. LC 99-24272. 264p. 2000. 34.95 (*1-56000-400-2*) Transaction Pubs.

Max Weber & Karl Marx. Karl Lowith. LC 93-18705. (Classics in Sociology Ser.). 144p. (C). 1993. pap. 22.99 (*0-415-09381-3*) Routledge.

Max Weber & Michel Foucault: Parallel Life-Works. Arpad Szakolczai. LC 97-13792. (Studies in Social & Political Thought). 336p. (C). 1998. 85.00 (*0-415-16681-0*) Routledge.

Max Weber & Modern Sociology. Arun Sahay & British Association for the Advancement of Science. LC 98-26545. (Max Weber Classic Monographs). 1998. write for info. (*0-415-17456-2*) Routledge.

Max Weber & the Destiny of Reason. Franco Ferrarotti. Tr. by John Fraser. LC 80-5457. Orig. Title: Max Weber e il Destino Ragione. 151p. reprint ed. pap. 46.90 (*0-608-18126-9*, 203277900081) Bks Demand.

Max Weber & the Fate of Politics. Irving Velody & Peter Lassman. 224p. (C). 1998. 75.00 (*0-415-13634-2*) Routledge.

Max Weber & the Idea of Economic Sociology. Richard Swedberg. LC 98-5129. 352p. 1998. text 29.95 (*0-691-02949-0*, Pub. by Princeton U Pr) Cal Prin Full Svc.

***Max Weber & the Idea of Economic Sociology.** Richard Swedberg. (Illus.). 352p. 2000. pap. 18.95 (*0-691-07013-X*) Princeton U Pr.

Max Weber & the Jewish Question: A Study of the Social Outlook of His Sociology. Gary A. Abraham. 336p. 1992. text 34.95 (*0-252-01841-9*) U of Ill Pr.

Max Weber & the Methodology of the Social Sciences. Toby E. Huff. 96p. 1983. pap. 21.95 (*0-87855-945-0*) Transaction Pubs.

Max Weber & the Problems of Value-Free Social Science: A Critical Examination of the "Werturteilsstreit" Jay A. Ciaffa. LC 97-51645. 192p. 1998. 34.50 (*0-8387-5395-7*) Bucknell U Pr.

Max Weber & the Sociology of Culture. Ralph Schroeder. (Theory, Culture & Society Ser.). (Illus.). 192p. (C). 1992. 55.00 (*0-8039-8549-5*); pap. 19.95 (*0-8039-8550-9*) Sage.

Max Weber, Democracy & Modernization. Schroeder. LC 97-38682. 1998. text 65.00 (*0-312-21244-5*) St Martin.

Max Weber e il Destino Ragione see Max Weber & the Destiny of Reason

Max Weber on Charisma & Institution Building. Samuel N. Eisenstadt & Max M. Weber. LC 68-54202. (Heritage of Sociology Ser.). (Orig.). 1968. 15.95 (*0-226-87722-1*); pap. text 22.00 (*0-226-87724-8*) U Ch Pr.

Max Weber on Economy & Society. Robert J. Holton & Bryan S. Turner. 224p. 1989. 37.50 (*0-415-02916-3*, A3497) Routledge.

Max Weber on Power & Social Stratification: An Interpretation & Critique. Catherine Brennan. LC 97-73613. 336p. 1997. text 78.95 (*1-85628-435-2*, Pub. by Ashgate Pub) Ashgate Pub Co.

Max Weber, Rationality & Modernity. Ed. by Sam Whimster & Scott Lash. 320p. 1987. text 55.00 (*0-04-301234-5*); pap. text 21.95 (*0-04-301235-3*) Routledge.

Max Weber Today - An Introduction to a Living Legacy: Selected Bibliography. Intro. by Vatro Murvar. 159p. 1983. pap. 9.00 (*0-931633-00-1*) Fnd Soc Stdy.

Max Weber und die Judische Ethik. Michael Spottel. 151p. 1997. pap. 38.95 (*3-631-32310-7*) P Lang Pubng.

Max Weber's Comparative & Historical Sociology: An Interpretation & Critique. Stephen Kalberg. LC 93-10012. 241p. 1994. pap. text 18.95 (*0-226-42303-4*); lib. bdg. 47.50 (*0-226-42302-6*) U Ch Pr.

Max Weber's Construction of Social Theory. Martin Albrow. LC 90-33088. 300p. 1991. pap. 16.95 (*0-312-04754-1*) St Martin.

Max Weber's Insights & Errors. Stanislav Andreski. (International Library of Sociology Ser.). 164p. 1985. 27.50 (*0-7102-0051-X*, Routledge Thoemms) Routledge.

***Max Weber's Methodology: The Unification of the Cultural & Social Sciences.** Fritz Ringer. 2000. pap. text 18.95 (*0-674-00183-4*) HUP.

Max Weber's Methodology: The Unification of the Cultural & Social Sciences. Fritz K. Ringer. LC 97-21685. (Illus.). 256p. 1998. 35.00 (*0-674-55657-7*) HUP.

Max Weber's Political Sociology: A Pessimistic Vision of a Rationalized World, 45. Ed. by Ronald M. Glassman & Vatro Murvar. LC 83-1678. (Contributions in Sociology Ser.: No. 45). (Illus.). 295p. 1984. 65.00 (*0-313-23642-9*, GMW/) Greenwood.

Max Weber's "Science As a Vocation" Ed. by Peter Lassman et al. 240p. 1988. 55.00 (*0-04-301211-6*) Routledge.

Max Weber's Sociology of Intellectuals. Ahmad Sadri. (Illus.). 192p. 1994. reprint ed. pap. text 19.95 (*0-19-509398-4*) OUP.

Max Weber's Theory of Concept Formation: History, Laws, & Ideal Types. 2nd ed. Thomas Burger. LC 74-31592. xx, 293p. 1986. pap. text 23.95 (*0-8223-0736-7*) Duke.

Max Webers Wissenschaftslehre: Max Webers Theory of Science. Alexander Von Schelting. LC 74-25796. (European Sociology Ser.). 432p. 1975. reprint ed. 35.95 (*0-405-06547-7*) Ayer.

Max Wehrli: Humanismus und Barock. Fritz Wagner & Wolfgang Maaz. (Spolia Berolinensia Ser.: Band 3). (GER.). x, 242p. 1994. 78.00 (*3-615-00094-3*, Pub. by Weidmann) Lubrecht & Cramer.

Maxcy-Rosenau-Last Public Health & Preventive Medicine. 13th ed. John M. Last. (Illus.). 1257p. (C). 1991. pap. text 135.00 (*0-8385-6188-8*, A6188-5) Appleton & Lange.

Maxdata. W. A. Hennerkes. xiii, 151p. 1990. 44.95 (*0-387-52209-3*) Spr-Verlag.

***Maxed Out! How Old Testament Personalities Handled the Stress.** Gary Wilde. (Generation Why Ser.: Vol. 5.1). 46p. (gr. 9-12). 1999. pap. 14.95 (*0-87303-384-1*) Faith & Life.

Maxewell: The Rise & Fall of Robert Maxewell & His Empire. Roy Greenslade. 1992. 18.95 (*1-55972-123-5*, Birch Ln Pr) Carol Pub Group.

Maxfield Parrish. Collectors Press Staff. (Edison Mazda Collection). (Illus.). 40p. 1995. pap. 17.50 (*0-9635202-3-7*, 20237) Collectors Pr.

Maxfield Parrish. Random House Value Publishing Staff. 1999. 9.99 (*0-517-16122-2*) Random Hse Value.

Maxfield Parrish. Coy Ludwig. LC 73-5691. (Illus.). 224p. 1993. reprint ed. 39.95 (*0-88740-527-4*) Schiffer.

Maxfield Parrish: A Price Guide. 2nd rev. ed. (Illus.). 114p. 1996. pap. 12.95 (*0-89538-014-5*) L-W Inc.

Maxfield Parrish: A Retrospective. Laurence S. Cutler & Judy G. Cutler. LC 95-71810. 176p. 1996. 45.00 (*0-87654-599-1*) Pomegranate Calif.

Maxfield Parrish: A Treasury of Art & Children's Literature. Compiled by Alma M. Gilbert. LC 95-60385. (Illus.). 96p. (J). (gr. 3 up). 1995. 23.00 (*0-689-80300-1*) Atheneum Yung Read.

Maxfield Parrish: Early & New Poems. Eileen Myles. LC 95-8852. 229p. (Orig.). (C). 1995. 25.00 (*0-87685-975-9*); pap. 14.00 (*0-87685-974-0*) Black Sparrow.

Maxfield Parrish: Early & New Poems, signed ed. deluxe ed. Eileen Myles. LC 95-8852. 229p. (Orig.). (C). 1995. 35.00 (*0-87685-976-7*) Black Sparrow.

Maxfield Parrish: Identification & Price Guide. 3rd rev. ed. Erwin Flacks. LC 98-36341. (Illus.). 256p. (Orig.). 1999. pap. 19.95 (*1-888054-18-2*, 54182) Collectors Pr.

Maxfield Parrish: Postcard Book. Maxfield Parrish. (Illus.). 1992. pap. text 9.95 (*0-87654-942-3*) Pomegranate Calif.

Maxfield Parrish: Price & Identification Guide. 11th rev. ed. Denis C. Jackson. (Illus.). 56p. 2000. pap. 9.95 (*1-888687-08-8*) Illust Collectors.

Maxfield Parrish: The Masterworks. Alma M. Gilbert. LC 92-11656. (Illus.). 224p. 1992. text 250.00 (*0-89815-483-9*) Ten Speed Pr.

Maxfield Parrish: The Masterworks. 2nd rev. ed. Alma M. Gilbert. (Illus.). 248p. 1995. 85.00 (*0-89815-784-6*) Ten Speed Pr.

***Maxfield Parrish: The Poster Book.** rev. ed. Ed. by Alma Gilbert. LC 99-86480. (Illus.). 2000. pap. 24.95 (*1-58008-199-1*) Ten Speed Pr.

***Maxfield Parrish & the Illustrators of the Golden Age.** Margaret E. Wagner. LC 99-50086. 2000. 30.00 (*0-7649-1257-7*) Pomegranate Calif.

***Maxfield Parrish, 1870-1966.** Sylvia Yount & Mark F. Bocknath. (Illus.). 160p. 1999. pap. 24.95 (*0-943836-19-0*) Penn Acad Art.

Maxfield Parrish, 1870-1966. Sylvia Yount et al. LC 98-40691. (Illus.). 160p. 1999. 39.95 (*0-8109-4367-0*, Pub. by Abrams) Time Warner.

Maxfield Parrish Prints. Marian S. Sweeney. LC 73-81165. 1975. pap. 15.00 (*0-87233-029-X*) Bauhan.

Maxfield Parrish Treasury for Children. Gilbert. (J). 1995. 22.95 (*0-684-19747-2*) Atheneum Yung Read.

***Maxfield Parrish 1870-1966.** Abrams Staff. 1999. pap. 12.50 (*0-8109-2931-7*, Pub. by Abrams) Time Warner.

Maxi, the Hero. Debra Barracca. 32p. (J). (ps-3). 1994. pap. 5.99 (*0-14-055497-1*, PuffinBks) Peng Put Young Read.

Maxi, the Hero. Debra Barracca. (J). 1994. 11.19 (*0-606-07850-9*) Turtleback.

Maxi, the Hero. Debra Barracca & Sal Barracca. LC 90-38329. (Illus.). 30p. (J). (ps-3). 1991. 14.99 (*0-8037-0939-0*, Dial Yng Read) Peng Put Young Read.

Maxi, the Star. Debra Barracca. 32p. 1999. pap. 5.99 (*0-14-056557-4*, PuffinBks) Peng Put Young Read.

Maxi, the Ultimate Racing Experience. Preben Nyeland. 1990. 50.00 (*0-393-03340-6*) Norton.

Maxibules. Marcel Ayme. (FRE.). 224p. 1962. pap. 19.95 (*0-7859-0369-0*, F8400) Fr & Eur.

Maxie. Betty B. Barboza. LC 97-77339. (Illus.). 80p. 1998. pap. 12.95 (*0-944851-12-6*) Earth Star.

Maxie & Chase. Denise Davis-Pack. (Illus.). 20p. (J). (gr. k-4). 1997. pap. 5.99 (*0-9660637-0-8*) D D Pack.

Maxie, Rosie & the Earl Partners in Crime. Barbara Park. 1991. 10.09 (*0-606-04974-6*, Pub. by Turtleback) Demco.

Maxillary & Trimalar Fractures: Applied Pathophysiology & Repair: Self-Instructional Package. 2nd ed. Arnold Komisar et al. LC 94-31838. (Self-Instructional Package Ser.). (Illus.). 75p. 1994. pap. text 25.00 (*1-56772-015-3*) AAO-HNS.

Maxillofacial & Dental Emergencies. John Hawkesford & James G. Banks. (Oxford Handbooks in Emergency Medicine Ser.: Vol. 7). (Illus.). 196p. 1994. 65.00 (*0-19-262391-5*); pap. text 29.50 (*0-19-261997-7*) OUP.

Maxillofacial Injuries, 2 vols. 2nd ed. Ed. by N. L. Rowe & J. L. Williams. (Illus.). 1067p. (C). 1994. text 315.00 (*0-443-04591-7*) Church.

Maxillofacial Injuries, 2 vols., Set. Ed. by N. L. Rowe & J. L. Williams. (Illus.). 1080p. 1985. text 320.00 (*0-443-01509-0*) Church.

Maxillofacial Rehabilitation: Prosthodontic & Surgical Considerations. John Beumer, 3rd et al. (Illus.). xii, 546p. 1996. text 195.00 (*1-56386-036-8*, Ishiyaku EuroAmerica) Med Dent Media.

Maxillofacial Trauma: An International Perspective. Ed. by John R. Jacobs. LC 82-18116. 303p. 1983. 79.50 (*0-275-91398-8*, C1398, Praeger Pubs) Greenwood.

Maxim Gorky. Barry P. Scherr. (World Authors Ser.: No. 781). 176p. 1988. 32.00 (*0-8057-6636-7*, Twyne) Mac Lib Ref.

Maxim Gorky: A Political Biography. Tovah Yedlin. LC 99-14383. 280p. 1999. 59.95 (*0-275-96605-4*, C6605, Praeger Pubs) Greenwood.

Maxim Gorky & His Russia. Alexander S. Kaun. LC 67-13330. 640p. 1972. reprint ed. 31.95 (*0-405-08686-5*, Pub. by Blom Pubns) Ayer.

Maxima & Minima: Theory & Economic Applications. R. Frisch. 176p. 1966. lib. bdg. 142.00 (*90-277-0093-1*) Kluwer Academic.

Maxima & Minima of Long Period Variables, 1949-1975. Compiled by Janet A. Mattei et al. 128p. 1990. pap. text 15.00 (*1-878174-09-6*) Am Assn Var Star.

***Maxima & Minima with Applications: Practical Optimization & Duality, 1.** Wilfred Kaplan. LC 98-7318. (Discrete Mathematics & Optimization Ser.). 284p. 1998. 79.95 (*0-471-25289-1*, Wiley-Interscience) Wiley.

Maximal Cohen-Macaulay Modules over Henselian Local Rings. Y. Yoshino. (London Mathematical Society Lecture Note Ser.: No. 146). 192p. (C). 1990. pap. text 38.95 (*0-521-35694-6*) Cambridge U Pr.

Maximal Factorizations of the Finite Simple Groups & Their Automorphism Groups. Martin W. Liebeck et al. LC 90-31827. (Memoirs Ser.: Vol. 86/432). 151p. 1990. pap. 22.00 (*0-8218-2494-5*, MEMO/86/432) Am Math.

Maximal Functions & Approach Regions in Theorems of Fatou Type. F. Di Biase. Ed. by H. Bass et al. LC 97-30694. (Progress in Mathematics Ser.). 160p. 1997. 38.50 (*0-8176-3976-4*) Birkhauser.

Maximal Functions Measuring Smoothness. Ronald A. DeVore & Robert C. Sharpley. LC 83-21494. (Memoirs Ser.: No. 47/293). 116p. 1984. pap. 18.00 (*0-8218-2293-4*, MEMO/47/293) Am Math.

Maximal Myocardial Perfusion As a Measure of the Functional Significance of Coronary Artery Disease: From a Pathoanatomic to a Pathophysiologic Interpretation of the Coronary Arteriogram. Nico H. Pijls. (Developments in Cardiovascular Medicine Ser.). 208p. 1991. text 137.50 (*0-7923-1430-1*) Kluwer Academic.

Maximal Subgroups of Classical Algebraic Groups. Gary M. Seitz. LC 87-1161. (Memoirs of the American Mathematical Society Ser.: No. 67/365). 286p. 1987. pap. 36.00 (*0-8218-2427-9*, MEMO/67/365) Am Math.

Maximal Subgroups of Exceptional Algebraic Groups. Gary M. Seitz. LC 90-26491. (Memoirs Ser.: Vol. 90/441). 197p. 1991. pap. 27.00 (*0-8218-2504-6*, MEMO/94/441) Am Math.

Maximality Properties in Numerical Semigroups & Applications to One-Dimensional Analytically Irreducible Local Domains. Valentina Barucci et al. LC 96-44757. (Memoirs of the American Mathematical Society Ser.: Vol. 125/598). 78p. 1997. pap. 36.00 (*0-8218-0544-4*, MEMO/125/598) Am Math.

Maxime Weygand & Civil-Military Relations in Modern France. Philip C. Bankwitz. LC 67-22860. (Historical Studies: No. 81). 458p. 1967. 30.00 (*0-674-55701-8*) HUP.

Maximes. unabridged ed. Francois de La Rochefoucauld. (FRE.). pap. 5.95 (*2-87714-203-5*, Pub. by Bookking Intl) Distribks Inc.

Maximes et Pensees. Honore de Balzac. 159p. 19.95 (*0-686-53894-3*) Fr & Eur.

Maximes et Pensees. Francois-Rene de Chateaubriand. 8.95 (*0-686-54369-6*) Fr & Eur.

Maximes et Pensees. Jean De La Bruyere. 9.95 (*0-686-54264-9*) Fr & Eur.

Maximes et Pensees. Denis Diderot. (FRE.). 1993. pap. 13.95 (*0-7859-3305-0*, 2850552453) Fr & Eur.

Maximes et Pensees. Francois de La Rochefoucauld. pap. 16.95 (*0-685-34232-8*) Fr & Eur.

Maximes et Pensees. Blaise Pascal. (FRE.). 9.95 (*0-686-54848-5*) Fr & Eur.

Maximes et Pensees: Caracteres et Anecdotes. Sebastien R. De Chamfort. (FRE.). 448p. 1982. pap. 11.95 (*0-7859-1953-8*, 2070373568) Fr & Eur.

Maximes et Reflexions Diverses. Francois de La Rochefoucauld. 1976. write for info. (*0-318-63490-2*) Fr & Eur.

Maximes et Reflexions Diverses. Francois de La Rochefoucauld & Jean Lafond. (Folio Ser.: No. 728). (FRE.). 286p. 1976. 8.95 (*2-07-036728-2*) Schoenhof.

Maximi Tyri. Ed. by Trapp. (GRE.). 1994. 100.00 (*3-8154-1535-7*, T1535, Pub. by B G Teubner) U of Mich Pr.

Maximianus: Concordantiae in Maximianum. Paolo Mastandrea et al. (GER., Illus.). vi, 196p. 1995. write for info. (*3-487-10019-3*) G Olms Pubs.

***Maximiliam & Carlota, Emperor & Empress of Mexico.** Elizar Torres. Ed. by Anna Marie Torres. (Illus.). 65p. (YA). (gr. 3-7). 2000. pap. 7.49 (*0-9678599-1-3*) E P Pubns.

Maximilian in Queretaro. Bilddokumentation Ueber Den Untergang Des Zweiten Mexikanischen Kaiserreiches. fac. ed. Konrad Ratz. (GER., Illus.). 424p. 1992. 57.00 (*3-201-01551-2*, Pub. by Akademische Druck-und) Balogh.

Maximilian in Queretaro. Bilddokumentation Ueber Den Untergang des Zweiten Mexikanischen Kaiserreiches (Maximilian in Queretaro. Pictorial Atlas of the Second Mexican Empire) fac. ed. Konrad Ratz. (GER., Illus.). 424p. 1992. 57.00 (*3-201-01474-5*, Pub. by Akademische Druck-und) Balogh.

Maximilian Kolbe: Authentic Franciscan. Anselm W. Romb. (Illus.). 192p. (Orig.). 1990. pap. 7.95 (*0-913382-56-6*, 101-37) Marytown Pr.

Maximilian Kolbe: Saint of Auschwitz. Elaine M. Stone. LC 96-46700. (Illus.). 128p. (Orig.). (J). (gr. 3-7). 1997. pap. 6.95 (*0-8091-6637-2*) Paulist Pr.

Maximilian Kolbe: The Apostle of Auschwitz. Demond Forristal. 1989. pap. 29.00 (*0-86217-220-9*, Pub. by Veritas Pubns) St Mut.

Maximilian, Prince of Wieds, Travel in the Interior of North America, 1832-34 see Early Western Travels, 1748-1846

***Maximilian the Great.** Lisa Funari Willever & Lorraine Funari. LC 00-90880. (Illus.). 32p. (J). (ps-3). 2000. 9.95 (*0-9679227-3-9*) Frank Mason.

Maximilian und Juarez. Das Zweite Mexikanische Kaiserreich und die Republik (Maximilian & Juarez. The Second Mexican Empire & the Republic); Die Augenblicke der Gefahr ("Queretaro-Chronik") (The Moment of Danger ("Queretaro-Chronicles")), 2 vols. fac. ed. Konrad Ratz. (GER.). 940p. 1998. 47.00 (*3-201-01679-9*, Pub. by Akademische Druck-und) Balogh.

Maximilian's Lieutenant: A Personal History of the Mexican Campaign, 1864-67. E. Pitner. LC 92-44670. 206p. 1994. 18.95 (*0-8263-1425-2*) U of NM Pr.

Maximilien Robespierre: Nationalist Dictator. James M. Eagan. LC 70-127439. (Columbia University. Studies in the Social Sciences: No. 437). reprint ed. 29.00 (*0-404-51437-5*) AMS Pr.

Maximilion's Treasure, 209. J. R. Roberts. (Gunsmith Ser.). 1999. mass mkt. 4.99 (*0-515-12534-2*, Jove) Berkley Pub.

***Maximising Performance in Insurance Operations** Julia Prichard & Louis Jordan. LC 99-33737. 1999. write for info. (*0-8493-0688-4*) CRC Pr.

Maximising the Impact of Industrial Engineering. Robert H. Schaffer. LC 66-5530. (American Management Association's Management Bulletins Ser.: No. 82). 23p. reprint ed. pap. 30.00 (*0-608-10871-5*, 200010000025) Bks Demand.

Maximising Your Memory: How to Train Yourself to Remember More. Peter Marshall. 128p. 2000. pap. 14.95 (*1-85703-234-9*, Pub. by How To Bks) Midpt Trade.

Maximize the Moment: God's Action Plan for Your Life. T. D. Jakes. 224p. 2000. 19.95 (*0-399-14565-6*, G P Putnam) Peng Put Young Read.

***Maximize Your Benefits.** Neil Downing. 2000. pap. 17.95 (*0-7931-3700-4*) Dearborn.

Maximize Your Day ... God's Way. Marilyn Hickey. pap. 7.95 (*1-56441-013-7*) M Hickey Min.

***Maximize Your Inheritance: For Widows, Widowers & Heirs.** Jarratt G. Bennett. LC 99-30539. 320p. 1999. pap. 22.95 (*0-7931-3330-0*) Dearborn.

Maximize Your IRA. Neil Downing. LC 98-13650. 200p. 1998. pap. text 18.95 (*0-7931-2853-6*) Dearborn.

Maximize Your Martial Arts Training: The Martial Arts Training Diary. Art Brisacher. (Illus.). 256p. 1996. otabind 14.95 (*1-880336-09-X*) Turtle CT.

***Maximize Your Memory.** Jonathan Hancock. LC 99-55958. 2000. 24.95 (*0-7621-0242-X*, Pub. by RD Assn) Penguin Putnam.

Maximize Your Ministry: How You As a Lay Person Can Impact Your World for Jesus Christ. Robert E. Slocum. LC 90-61783. 290p. (Orig.). 1990. pap. 12.00 (*0-89109-368-0*) NavPress.

***Maximize Your Moments with the Masters.** Dick Biggs. 48p. 2000. mass mkt. 8.00 (*0-9635977-0-1*) Chattahoo Pubs.

Maximize Your Training: Insights from Top Strength & Fitness Professionals. Matt Brzycki. LC 99-13968. (Illus.). 464p. 1999. 19.95 (*0-8442-8317-7*, 83177, Mstrs Pr) NTC Contemp Pub Co.

Maximize Your Vitality & Potency: For Men over 40. Jonathan Wright & Lane Lenard. LC 97-65917. (Illus.). 256 p. 1999. pap. 14.95 (*0-9627418-1-7*) Smart Pubns CA.

Maximized Manhood see Hombria Al Maximo

Maximized Manhood: A Guide To Family Survival. Edwin L. Cole. 176p. 1982. mass mkt. 5.99 (*0-88368-107-2*) Whitaker Hse.

Maximizing Access '97. Virginia Andersen. 1998. pap. 39.99 (*0-07-882473-7*) Intl Marine.

Maximizing, Action, & Market Adjustment: An Inquiry into the Theory of Economic Disequilibrium. Jack High. (International Carl Menger Library). (Illus.). 184p. (C). 1990. lib. bdg. 48.00 (*3-88405-029-X*) Philosophia Pr.

Maximizing Agency Value: A Guide for Buying, Selling & Perpetuating Insurance Agencies. John Persky. 190p. 1998. pap. text 55.00 (*1-878204-57-2*) APIS Inc.

Maximizing AutoCAD Release 13. Rusty Gesner. (Illus.). 832p. (C). 1996. mass mkt. 70.95 (*0-8273-7993-5*) Delmar.

Maximizing AutoCAD R13 for Windows: Release 14. Rusty Gesner et al. 832p. 1998. pap. 54.95 incl. cd-rom (*0-7668-0590-5*, AutoDesk Pr) Delmar.

Maximizing AutoLISP Release 13 & 14. Mark Middlebrook & Tony Tanzillo. 960p. (C). 1997. pap. 44.95 incl. cd-rom (*0-8273-7994-3*) Delmar.

Maximizing Baseball Practice. John Winkin et al. LC 94-14633. (Illus.). 144p. 1994. pap. 17.95 (*0-87322-430-2*, PWIN0430) Human Kinetics.

Maximizing Baseball Practice Indoors. John Winkin et al. 152p. 1995. pap. 44.95 incl. VHS (*0-88011-496-7*, MWIN0446) Human Kinetics.

Maximizing Benefits of Tourism in Guerrero, Mexico. Chandler Stolp et al. (Policy Research Project Report Ser.: No. 93). 124p. 1991. pap. 11.50 (*0-89940-701-3*) LBJ Sch Pub Aff.

Maximizing Call Center Performance: 136 Innovative Ideas for Increasing Productivity & Customer Satisfaction. Madeline Bodin. (Illus.). 110p. 1998. per. 19.95 (*1-57820-026-1*) Telecom Bks.

Maximizing Corel WordPerfect Suite 8. Scott Larsen & Gayle Humpherys. LC 98-150466. 800p. 1997. pap. text 39.99 incl. cd-rom (*0-07-882451-6*) Osborne-McGraw.

Maximizing Coverage Minimizing Costs. Richard G. Clarke. 52p. 1993. pap. 20.00 (*0-614-05731-0*) CPCU Society.

Maximizing Crop Yields. Ed. by N. A. Fageria. (Books in Soils, Plants & the Environment: Vol. 23). (Illus.). 288p. 1992. text 135.00 (*0-8247-8642-4*) Dekker.

An Asterisk (*) at the beginning of an entry indicates that the title is appearing for the first time.

Maximizing Customer Contact: Turning Customer Representatives into Sales Achievers. Judy McKee. 164p. 1996. write for info. (0-614-22081-5) Tech Marketing.

Maximizing Damages in Small Personal Injury Cases. Ellsworth T. Rundlett. 344p. 1991. ring bd. 119.00 (0-938065-55-6) James Pub Santa Ana.

Maximizing Employee Productivity: A Managers Guide. Robert E. Sibson. LC 93-41638. 192p. 1994. 22.95 (0-8144-5094-6) AMACOM.

***Maximizing Forest Product Resources for the 21st Century.** Richard F. Baldwin. LC 99-43322. 232p. 1999. pap. 49.00 (0-87930-599-1) Miller Freeman.

Maximizing Hospitality Sales. Patrick Forsyth. LC 78-57692. 160p. (C). 1999. pap. 21.50 (0-304-70428-8) Continuum.

Maximizing Law Firm Profitability: Hiring Training & Developing Productive Lawyers. Joel Henning. 500p. 1991. ring bd. 90.00 (0-317-05400-7, 00614) NY Law Pub.

Maximizing Leadership Effectiveness. Alexander W. Astin & Rita A. Scherrei. LC 79-9665. (Jossey-Bass Series in Higher Education). 256p. reprint ed. pap. 79.40 (0-8357-4930-4, 203786000009) Bks Demand.

Maximizing Management Effectiveness. Anthony J. Pansini. LC 77-85653. (Illus.). 1977. pap. 15.00 (0-911876-04-9, 0-911976-04) Greenvale.

Maximizing Manhood. Malcolm Carruthers. 1998. pap. 13.00 (0-7225-3532-5) Thorsons PA.

Maximizing Media. Bruce Fredericksen. (Family Life Issues Ser.). 1994. pap. 4.50 (0-570-09511-5, 20-2709) Concordia.

Maximizing Mind Power: The Art of Managing Your Greatest Asset. Timothy Clark. 197p. 1993. pap. 15.95 (0-9638625-0-2) Mind Power.

Maximizing Minimal Space. Cy DeCosse Incorporated Staff & Black & Decker Incorporated Staff. LC 96-18878. (Portable Workshop Ser.). (Illus.). 96p. 1996. spiral bd. 14.95 (0-86573-670-7) Creat Pub Intl.

Maximizing Mobility after Stroke: Nursing the Acute Patient. George I. Turnbull & Patricia A. Bell. LC 85-71509. (Illus.). 84p. 1985. pap. text 16.95 (0-914783-10-6) Charles.

***Maximizing Office.** Ellsworth. 1999. 39.99 (0-07-212117-3) McGraw.

Maximizing Outlook 2000. Simon. 696p. 2000. text 39.99 (0-07-212156-4) McGraw.

Maximizing Paraprofessional Potential. Joye A. Norris & Susan S. Baker. LC 98-17871. (Professional Practices in Adult Education & Human Resource Development Ser.). (Illus.). 144p. (C). 1999. text 24.50 (1-57524-027-0) Krieger.

Maximizing People Power in Schools: Motivating & Managing Teachers & Staff. Larry E. Frase. LC 92-4896. 160p. 1992. pap. 21.95 (0-8039-6015-8) Corwin Pr.

Maximizing Performance in Insurance Operations. Julia Prichard & Louis Jordan. 192p. 1999. 120.00 (1-85573-438-9) Am Educ Systs.

Maximizing Psychotherapeutic Gains & Preventing Relapse in Emotionally Distressed Clients. John W. Ludgate. LC 95-20029. (Practitioner's Resource Ser.). 81p. (Orig.). 1995. pap. 16.45 (1-56887-014-0, MPGBP, Prof Resc Pr) Pro Resource.

Maximizing Quality Performance in Health Care Facilities. Addison C. Bennett & Samuel J. Tibbitts. (Health Care Administration Ser.). 267p. 1989. 75.00 (0-8342-0025-2) Aspen Pub.

Maximizing School Guidance Program Effectiveness: A Guide for School Administrators & Program Directors. Ed. by Cass Dykeman. 156p. (C). 1998. pap. text 15.00 (1-56109-083-2, EC233) CAPS Inc.

Maximizing Small Business Growth: Developing a Bank's Game Plan. Jennifer Warner et al. Ed. by Shelley W. Geehr & Elaine Svenson. 150p. 1996. pap. text 48.00 (1-57070-014-1) Robt Morris Assocs.

Maximizing Small Business Profits: With Precision Management. William H. Day. LC 78-9407. 1979. 13.95 (0-13-566257-5, Spectrum IN); pap. 6.95 (0-13-566240-0, Spectrum IN) Macmillan Gen Ref.

Maximizing Surfcam. S. C. Jonathon Lin & Behrooz Lahidji. Ed. by Karen L. Sterzik. (Illus.). 900p. (C). 1997. pap. 79.00 (1-886552-05-3) Scholars Intl.

Maximizing the Arthritis Cure: A Step-by-Step Program to Faster, Stronger Healing During Any Stage of the Cure. Jason Theodosakis et al. LC 97-47099. (Illus.). 224p. 1998. text 22.95 (0-312-18134-5) St Martin.

Maximizing the Arthritis Cure: A Step-by-Step Program to Faster, Stronger Healing During Any Stage of the Cure. Jason Theodosakis et al. (Illus.). 302p. 1999. mass mkt. 6.50 (0-312-96916-3) St Martin.

Maximizing the Impact of Recognition: An Approach to Rewarding Employee Contributions. Contrib. by Donald W. Hay. LC 98-184048. (Building Blocks Ser.: Vol. 44). (Illus.). 1998. pap. 24.95 (1-57963-055-3) Am Compensation.

Maximizing the Odds: An Attorney's Guide to the Diversity Visa Lottery. Ed. by Stephanie Marks & John Assadi. 74p. (Orig.). 1995. pap. text 25.00 (0-934143-77-3) Lawyers Comm Human.

Maximizing the Profitability of Law Firms. Robert Mowbray. 134p. 1997. pap. 44.00 (1-85431-597-8, Pub. by Blackstone Pr) Gaunt.

Maximizing the Role of Nutrition in Diabetes Management. American Diabetes Association. 64p. 1994. pap. 24.95 (0-945448-42-2, 5607-01) Am Diabetes.

Maximizing the Value of Your Audit Reports: Managing Quality & Timeliness. Angela J. Maniak. 100p. 1991. text 95.00 (0-9629337-0-8) A J Maniak.

Maximizing the Value of 360-Degree Feedback: A Process for Successful Individual & Organizational Development. Walter W. Tornow & Manuel London. LC 97-45460. (Jossey-Bass Business & Management Ser.). 1998. 42.95 (0-7879-0958-0) Jossey-Bass.

Maximizing Third-Party Reimbursement in Your Mental Health Practice. 2nd ed. Richard F. Small. LC 93-5859. 148p. 1993. ring bd. 23.95 (0-943158-96-6, MTP2BP, Prof Resc Pr) Pro Resource.

Maximizing U. S. Interests in Science & Technology Relations with Japan. National Research Council Staff. 148p. (C). 1997. pap. text 28.00 (0-309-05884-8) Natl Acad Pr.

Maximizing Voting. Ed. by William Crotty. (Orig.). 1990. pap. 15.00 (0-944285-20-1) Pol Studies.

Maximizing Windows 98. Lenny Bailes. LC 98-235191. 912p. 1998. pap. text 34.99 (0-07-882539-3) Osborne-McGraw.

Maximizing Your Business Online: A 3.5.7 Method for Internet Success. Craig Settles. (Illus.). 302p. 1999. pap. 59.00 (0-86587-637-1, 637) Gov Insts.

Maximizing Your Church's Potential. Neil Wiseman. (Pastoral Quick Read Ser.). 96p. 1999. pap. text 8.99 (0-8341-1806-8) Beacon Hill.

Maximizing Your Effectiveness: How to Discover & Develop Your Divine Design. Aubrey Malphurs. LC 94-40064. (Illus.). 256p. 1995. pap. 14.99 (0-8010-6317-5) Baker Bks.

Maximizing Your Health Insurance Benefits: A Consumer's Guide to New & Traditional Plans. Richard Epstein. LC 97-8861. 224p. 1997. 35.00 (0-275-95510-9, Praeger Pubs) Greenwood.

Maximizing Your Impact in Contract Education: A Handbook for Community Colleges. Catherine Ayers. 256p. (Orig.). 1995. pap. 59.95 (0-938075-59-4) Ocean View Bks.

***Maximizing Your Leadership Potential: Syllabus.** Frank Damazio. 2000. pap. 13.00 (1-886849-42-0) City Bible Pub.

Maximizing Your Learning Potential. Jacqueline Frischknect & Glenn Capelli. 288p. (C). 1995. spiral bd. 36.95 (0-7872-0130-8, 41013001) Kendall-Hunt.

Maximizing Your Mac. Amy Laskin. 1995. pap. 24.95 (1-55828-244-0, MIS Pr) IDG Bks.

Maximizing Your Marriage. Chris Wilkes. 32p. 1998. pap. 8.00 (1-56411-200-4) Untd Bros & Sis.

Maximizing Your Media Dollars. Herbert Zeltner. 117p. 1996. 39.95 (1-56318-023-5) Assn Natl Advertisers.

Maximizing Your Memory Power. 2nd rev. ed. Danielle C. Lapp. LC 98-16506. (Barron's Business Success Ser.). 160p. 1998. pap. 6.95 (0-7641-0400-4) Barron.

Maximizing Your Nutrition. Dennis Nelson. (Illus.). 128p. (Orig.). 1988. pap. 3.50 (0-9612188-3-5) Nelsons Bks.

Maximizing Your Potential. Robert Heller. LC 99-15781. (Essential Managers Handbks.). 72p. 1999. pap. 6.95 (0-7894-4863-7) DK Pub Inc.

Maximizing Your Potential. Munroe. 196p. 1996. 10.99 (1-56043-182-2) Destiny Image.

Maximizing Your Potential. Myles Munroe. 196p. 1996. pap. 10.99 (1-56043-105-9) Destiny Image.

Maximizing Your Supervisory Performance. Philip C. Grant. 552p. (C). 1996. pap. text, per. 52.95 (0-8403-8844-6) Kendall-Hunt.

***Maximizing Your Vision Potential: Syllabus.** Frank Damazio. 2000. pap. 13.00 (1-886849-45-5) City Bible Pub.

***Maximizing Your Warfare Potential: Syllabus.** Frank Damazio. 2000. pap. 13.00 (1-886849-47-1) City Bible Pub.

Maximo Gomez, Caudillo o Dictador? Florencio G. Cisneros. (SPA.). 185p. (Orig.). 1987. pap. 9.95 (0-9617456-0-6) F Garcia-Cisneros.

Maximova & Vasiliev at the Bolshoi. Roberta Lazzarini. (Illus.). 176p. 1995. 45.00 (0-903102-62-5, Pub. by Dance Bks) Princeton Bk Co.

Maximov's Companion to Gold & Diamonds in the Russian Federation. 300p. 1996. 350.00 (1-900418-01-0) Maximov.

Maximov's Companion to the 1996 Presidential Elections. 250p. 1996. 49.00 (1-900418-04-5) Maximov.

Maximov's Companion to Who Governs Moscow City. 500p. 1996. 95.00 (1-900418-03-7) Maximov.

***Maxims.** Francois de La Rochefoucauld. 200p. 2000. 19.00 (1-890318-42-6, Pub. by St Augustines Pr) U Ch Pr.

Maxims. Francois de La Rochefoucauld. Tr. & Intro. by Leonard W. Tancock. (Classics Ser.). 128p. 1982. pap. 10.95 (0-14-044095-X, Penguin Classics) Viking Penguin.

Maxims. Theodore Roosevelt. LC 79-104554. reprint ed. lib. bdg. 20.00 (0-8398-1764-9) Irvington.

Maxims & Reflections. Johann Wolfgang Von Goethe. Ed. & Tr. by Simona Draghici from GER. LC 97-19671. (Illus.). 168p. 1997. pap. 7.95 (0-943045-09-6) Plutarch Pr OR.

Maxims & Reflections. Francesco Guicciardini. LC 64-23752. 150p. 1972. pap. 17.95 (0-8122-1037-9) U of Pa Pr.

Maxims Concerning Patriotism (Berkeley) George Berkeley. Ed. by Malachi McCormick. 24p. 1985. 7.00 (0-943984-22-X) Stone St Pr.

Maxims for the Issue Manager. Randall L. Scheel. 85p. (Orig.). 1991. pap. 14.95 (0-913869-02-3) Issue Action Pubns.

Maxims from My Mother's Milk: Hymns to Him: A Dialogue. Douglas Messerli. 72p. 1989. 12.95 (1-55713-031-0); pap. 8.95 (1-55713-047-7) Sun & Moon CA.

***Maxims in Old English Poetry.** Paul Cavill. LC 98-46866. 256p. 1999. 75.00 (0-85991-541-7) Boydell & Brewer.

Maxims in the Novels of Duclos. B. G. Silverblatt. (Archives Internationales D'Histoire des Idees Ser.: No. 2). 166p. 1973. pap. text 57.00 (90-247-1938-0, Pub. by M Nijhoff) Kluwer Academic.

Maxims of Ali. J. Chapman. 1991. pap. 4.50 (1-56744-131-9) Kazi Pubns.

Maxims of Chanakya: Kautilya. V. K. Subramanian. 1980. 14.00 (0-8364-0616-8, Pub. by Abhinav) S Asia.

Maxims of George Washington. Frederick Schroeder. 34.99 (0-87377-176-1) GAM Pubns.

Maxims of George Washington. 2nd ed. George Washington. Ed. by John F. Schroeder. LC 89-2964. (Illus.). 260p. 1989. pap. 7.95 (0-931917-16-6) Mt Vernon Ladies.

Maxims of la Rochefoucauld. Francois de La Rochefoucauld. Tr. by John Heard. 1982. pap. 5.95 (0-8283-1448-9) Branden Bks.

Maxims of Madness. Michael A. Roybal. 137p. (Orig.). 1993. pap. 8.00 (0-9639456-0-2) Maximedia NM.

Maxims of Sa'di. Sa'di. Tr. & Intro. by Mehdi K. Nakosteen. LC 77-608281. 126p. 1977. 25.00 (0-936347-47-3) IBEX.

Maxims of Vidur G. N. Das. LC 97-905685. 148p. 1997. write for info. (81-7017-353-1) S Asia.

Maxims of Washington: Political, Social, Moral & Religious. 455p. 1999. 29.95 (1-928596-02-9) Am Fndt Pubns.

Maximum Achievement: Strategies & Skills That Will Unlock Your Hidden Powers to Succeed. Brian S. Tracy. 352p. 1995. per. 13.00 (0-684-80331-3, Fireside) S&S Trade Pap.

Maximum Bob. Elmore Leonard. 352p. 1992. mass mkt. 6.99 (0-440-21218-9) Dell.

Maximum Bob. Elmore Leonard. 304p. 1998. pap. 9.95 (0-385-32396-4, Delta Trade) Dell.

Maximum Boost: Designing, Testing, & Installing Turbocharger Systems. Corky Bell. LC 97-9087. (Illus.). 256p. 1997. 34.95 (0-8376-0160-6) Bentley Pubs.

Maximum Calves. Health for Life Staff. (Illus.). 64p. 1987. pap. 14.95 (0-944831-16-8) Health Life.

Maximum Challenge. Franklin W. Dixon. (Hardy Boys Mystery Stories Ser.: No. 132). (Illus.). (J). (gr. 3-6). 1995. pap. 3.99 (0-671-87216-8, Minstrel Bks) PB.

Maximum Challenge. Franklin W. Dixon. (Hardy Boys Mystery Stories Ser.: No. 132). (J). (gr. 3-6). 1995. 9.09 (0-606-07611-5, Pub. by Turtleback) Demco.

Maximum Challenge. Linda K. Sibley et al. (Next Level Preteen Electives). (Illus.). 128p. 1997. teacher ed. 14.99 (0-7847-0648-4, 42108) Standard Pub.

Maximum Coverage: Wearables by Contemporary American Artists. (Illus.). 68p. 1980. pap. 13.50 (0-932718-07-8) Kohler Arts.

Maximum Damage. Tony Lee. Ed. by Duane Maxwell. 32p. 1998. pap. write for info. (1-892519-08-9, AAE-1020) Archangel Ent.

Maximum Digital Value. Croninm. (Business Technology Ser.). 1998. pap. 29.95 (0-442-02672-2, VNR) Wiley.

Maximum Distrust: Unusual Stories of Injustice, Unbalanced Thinking & Mob Psychology in America. Michael Cook. LC 96-25970. (Illus.). 181p. (Orig.). 1998. pap. 18.95 (1-56072-341-6, Nova Kroshka Bks) Nova Sci Pubs.

Maximum Energy: Top Ten Foods Never to Eat: Top Ten Health Strageties to Feel Great. Ted Broer. 1999. 19.99 (0-88419-643-7) Creation House.

Maximum Entropy & Bayesian Methods: Boise, Idaho, U. S. A., 1997: Proceedings of the 17th International Workshop of Statistical Analysis. Gary J. Erickson et al. LC 98-34657. (Fundamental Theories of Physics Ser.). 1998. 133.00 (0-7923-5047-2) Kluwer Academic.

Maximum Entropy & Bayesian Methods: Cambridge, England, 1988. Ed. by J. L. Skilling. (C). 1989. text 250.00 (0-7923-0224-9) Kluwer Academic.

Maximum Entropy & Bayesian Methods: Dartmouth, U. S. A., 1989. Ed. by P. F. Fougere. (C). 1990. text 226.50 (0-7923-0928-6) Kluwer Academic.

Maximum Entropy & Bayesian Methods: Laramie, Wyoming, 1990. Ed. by Walter T. Grandy, Jr. & L. H. Schick. (C). 1991. text 166.50 (0-7923-1140-X) Kluwer Academic.

Maximum Entropy & Bayesian Methods: Proceedings of the 11th International Workshop on Maximum Entropy & Bayesian Methods of Statistical Analysis, Seattle, 1991. Ed. by C. Ray Smith et al. LC 92-36593. (Fundamental Theories of Physics Ser.: Vol. 50). 1992. text 226.50 (0-7923-2031-X) Kluwer Academic.

Maximum Entropy & Bayesian Methods: Proceedings of the 14th International Workshop on Maximum Entropy & Bayesian Methods, Cambridge, England, 1994. J. L. Skilling & Sibusiso Sibisi. LC 96-28677. (Fundamental Theories of Physics Ser.). 1996. text 195.00 (0-7923-3452-3) Kluwer Academic.

Maximum Entropy & Bayesian Methods: Proceedings of the 15th International Workshop, Santa Fe, New Mexico, U. S. A., 1995. Ed. by Kenneth Hanson. LC 96-48823. (Fundamental Theories of Physics Ser.). 480p. (C). 1996. text 242.50 (0-7923-4311-5) Kluwer Academic.

Maximum Entropy & Bayesian Methods: Santa Barbara, California, U. S. A., 1993: Proceedings of the Thirteenth International Workshop on Maximum Entropy & Bayesian Methods. Ed. by Glenn R. Heidreder. (Fundamental Theories of Physics Ser.: Vol. 62). 424p. (C). 1996. text 206.00 (0-7923-2851-5) Kluwer Academic.

***Maximum Entropy & Bayesian Methods, Garching, Germany 1998: Proceedings of the 18th International Workshop on Maximum Entropy & Bayesian Methods of Statistical Analysis.** Wolfgang Von Der Linden. LC 99-27057. (Fundamental Theories of Physics Ser.). 360p. 1999. write for info. (0-7923-5766-3) Kluwer Academic.

Maximum-Entropy & Bayesian Methods in Inverse Problems. Ed. by C. Ray Smith & Walter T. Grandy, Jr. 1985. text 162.50 (90-277-2074-6) Kluwer Academic.

Maximum Entropy & Bayesian Methods in Paris, France, 1992: Proceedings of the 12th International Workshop on Maximum Entropy & Bayesian Methods. Ed. by Ali Mohammad-Djafari. LC 93-2024. (Fundamental Theories of Physics Ser.). 452p. (C). 1993. text 264.50 (0-7923-2280-0) Kluwer Academic.

Maximum-Entropy & Bayesian Spectral Analysis: Vol. 1: Foundations & Vol. 2: Applications, 2 vols., Vols. 1 & 2. Ed. by Gary J. Erickson & C. Ray Smith. (C). 1900. text 179.00 (90-277-2792-9) Kluwer Academic.

Maximum-Entropy & Bayesian Spectral Analysis & Estimation Problems. Ed. by C. Ray Smith & Gary J. Erickson. (C). 1987. text 168.00 (90-277-2579-9) Kluwer Academic.

Maximum Entropy Econometrics: Robust Estimation with Limited Data. George Judge et al. LC 95-41281. (Series in Financial Economics & Quantitative Analysis). 324p. 1996. 99.00 (0-471-95311-3) Wiley.

Maximum Entropy in Action: A Collection of Expository Essays. Ed. by Brian Buck & Vincent A. Macaulay. (Illus.). 248p. 1991. pap. text 39.95 (0-19-853963-0) OUP.

***Maximum Entropy, Information Without Probability & Complex Fractals: Classical & Quantum Approach.** Guy M. Jumarie. LC 00-38627. (Fundamental Theories of Physics Ser.). (Illus.). 2000. write for info. (0-7923-6330-2, Kluwer Plenum) Kluwer Academic.

Maximum Entropy Method. Nailong Wu. LC 96-54843. (Information Sciences Ser.). (Illus.). xii, 327p. 1997. write for info. (3-540-61965-8) Spr-Verlag.

Maximum Entropy Models in Science Engineering. J. N. Kapur. LC 89-8911. 635p. 1990. text 110.00 (0-470-21459-7) Halsted Pr.

***Maximum Fitness: The Complete Guide to Cross Training.** Stewart Smith. (Illus.). 160p. 2000. pap. 16.95 (1-57826-060-4, Pub. by Hatherleigh) Norton.

***Maximum Food Power for Women.** Julia VanTine & Debra Gordon. 2001. pap. 17.95 (1-57954-411-8) Rodale Pr Inc.

Maximum Friendship: Devotions for Students. Jeff Tucker. LC 98-54291. 1999. pap. text 8.99 (0-87788-583-4, H Shaw Pubs) Waterbrook Pr.

***Maximum Friendship: Devotions for Students.** Jeff Tucker & Ramona Cramer Tucker. LC 98-54291. 120p. 1999. pap. write for info. (0-87788-834-5, H Shaw Pubs) Waterbrook Pr.

***Maximum Furby Fun.** (Furby Coloring & Activity Pad Ser.). (Illus.). 48p. 1999. pap. write for info. (0-7666-0411-X, Honey Bear Bks) Modern Pub NYC.

Maximum Gifts by Return Mail: An Expert Tells How to Write Highly Profitable Fund-Raising Letters. Roland E. Kuniholm. (Illus.). 261p. 1989. 36.95 (0-930807-08-1, 600173) Fund Raising.

Maximum Happiness: Jack & Jill Discover True Love. Steve Castillo. (Illus.). 58p. (Orig.). (YA). (gr. 9). 1989. 5.95 (0-317-93187-3) Paisley Bks.

Maximum Healing. Mark Dana Mincolla. 1998. pap. 19.95 (0-9632811-2-7) Pennyroyal Pr.

***Maximum Hoof Power: A Horseowner's Guide to Shoeing & Soundness.** Cherry Hill & Richard Klimesh. LC 00-26403. (Illus.). 2000. reprint ed. pap. 19.95 (1-57076-168-X, Trafalgar Sq Pub) Trafalgar.

Maximum Hoof Power: How to Improve Your Horse's Performance Through Proper Hoof Management. Cherry Hill & Richard Klimesh. LC 93-14578. (Illus.). 288p. 1994. 30.00 (0-87605-964-7) Howell Bks.

Maximum Impact. Jean Heller. 640p. 1995. 5.99 (0-8125-1619-2, Pub. by Forge NYC) St Martin.

Maximum Impact. Tim Storey. LC 97-214724. 304p. 1997. pap. 12.99 (1-57794-008-3, HH2-008) Harrison Hse.

Maximum Insecurity. P. J. Grady. LC 98-52320. 200p. 1999. pap. 12.95 (0-9661072-4-1) Avocet Pr.

Maximum Java 1.1. Glenn Vanderburg. LC 96-72407. 892p. 1997. pap. text 49.99 incl. cd-rom (1-57521-290-0) Sams.

Maximum Leadership. Farkas. 1996. text 7.25 (0-13-259995-3) P-H.

Maximum Leadership: Five Strategies for Success from the World's Leading CEOs. Charles M. Farkas & Philippe De Backer. LC 97-28379. 304p. 1998. pap. 15.00 (0-399-52385-5, Perigee Bks) Berkley Pub.

Maximum Learning in Minimum Time. Dorcey Smith. LC 77-175235. 96p. 1972. pap. 8.00 (0-8315-0181-2) Speller.

Maximum Life Span. Roy L. Walford. 272p. 1984. mass mkt. 4.50 (0-380-65524-1, Avon Bks) Morrow Avon.

Maximum Light. Nancy Kress. LC 97-29850. 1997. text 22.95 (0-312-86535-X) St Martin.

Maximum Light. Nancy Kress. 1999. mass mkt. 5.99 (0-8125-4037-9, Pub. by Tor Bks) St Martin.

Maximum-Likelihood Deconvolution. J. M. Mendel. (Illus.). xiv, 227p. 1989. 89.95 (0-387-97208-0) Spr-Verlag.

Maximum Likelihood Estimation: Logic & Practice, No. 96. Scott R. Eliason. (Quantitative Applications in the Social Sciences Ser.: Vol. 96). (Illus.). 96p. (C). 1993. pap. text 10.95 (0-8039-4107-2) Sage.

Maximum Likelihood Estimation in Small Samples. Leonard R. Shenton & K. O. Bowman. 1977. 25.00 (0-85264-238-5) Lubrecht & Cramer.

***Maximum Likelihood Estimation with Stata: Release 6.0.** 169p. 1999. pap. text 35.00 (1-881228-41-X) Stata Corp.

M

An Asterisk (*) at the beginning of an entry indicates that the title is appearing for the first time.

Maximum Linux Security: A Hacker's Guide to Protecting Your Linux Server & Network. 800p. 1999. pap. text 39.99 (*0-672-31670-6*) Sams.

Maximum Linux Security Secure Server Kit. Sams Staff. 800p. 1920. pap. text 79.99 (*0-672-31840-7*) Sams.

***Maximum Marriage: Men on a Mission (Hunter's Prey; Bachelor Father; Hawk's Flight), 3 bks.** Annette Broadrick. (Thirty-Six Hours Ser.). 2000. mass mkt. 6.99 (*0-373-48411-9*) Silhouette.

Maximum Metabolism: The Diet Breakthrough for Permanent Weight Loss. Robert M. Giller. 1990. pap. 12.95 (*0-425-12180-1*) Berkley Pub.

Maximum Metal. Mark Colborn et al. (Cyberpunk Ser.). (Illus.). 104p. (Orig.). 1993. pap. 12.00 (*0-937279-34-X*, CP3191) Talsorian.

Maximum MIDI: Music Applications in C++ Paul Messick. LC 97-23268. (Illus.). 479p. 1997. pap. text 49.99 incl. cd-rom (*1-884777-44-9*) Manning Pubns.

Maximum Performance: A Golf Fitness Program. Sam Frattalone. Ed. by Michelle Barry. LC 99-94882. 112p. Date not set. pap. 19.95 (*1-892903-10-5*) Rockett Pubns.

Maximum Performance Management: How to Manage & Compensate People to Meet World Competition. 2nd rev. ed. Joseph H. Boyett & Henry P. Conn. LC 94-73144. (Illus.). 323p. 1994. 24.95 (*0-944435-25-4*) Glenbridge Pub.

Maximum Permissible Body Burdens & Maximum Permissible Concentrations of Radionuclides in Air & in Water for Occupational Exposures. (Report Ser.: No. 22). 1959. pap. 20.00 (*0-913392-06-5*) NCRP Pubns.

Maximum Power: The Ideas & Applications of H. T. Odum. Ed. by Charles A. Hall. LC 94-39093. (Illus.). 454p. (C). 1995. text 49.95 (*0-87081-362-5*) Univ Pr Colo.

Maximum Principles in Differential Equations. M. Protter & Hans F. Weinberger. (Illus.). 1984. 60.95 (*0-387-96068-6*) Spr-Verlag.

Maximum RPM. Ed Bailey. LC 97-66201. 450p. 1997. 39.99 (*0-672-31105-4*) Sams.

***Maximum Security.** 3rd ed. 900p. 2000. 49.99 (*0-672-31871-7*, Waite Grp Pr) Sams.

Maximum Security: A Hacker's Guide to Protecting Your Internet Site & Network. SamsNet Publishing. LC 96-71997. 928p. 1997. 49.99 incl. cd-rom (*1-57521-268-4*) Sams.

Maximum Security: A Hacker's Guide to Protecting Your Internet Site & Network. 2nd ed. LC 98-85046. 1000p. 1998. pap. 49.99 (*0-672-31341-3*) Sams.

Maximum Security: The Culture of Violence in Inner-City Schools. John Devine. LC 96-8910. (Illus.). 256p. 1996. pap. text 15.95 (*0-226-14387-2*) U Ch Pr.

Maximum Security: The Culture of Violence in Inner-City Schools. John Devine. LC 96-8910. (Illus.). 256p. 1997. lib. bdg. 40.00 (*0-226-14386-4*) U Ch Pr.

Maximum Security Ward & Selected Poems. Ramon Guthrie. LC 83-22067. (Lamplighter Ser.). 216p. 1983. pap. 9.95 (*0-89255-080-5*) Persea Bks.

Maximum Self-Esteem: The Handbook for Reclaiming Your Sense of Self-Worth. Jerry A. Minchinton. LC 92-76034. 254p. (Orig.). 1993. pap. 14.95 (*0-9635719-7-4*) Arnford MO.

Maximum Statistical Benefits from Higher-Level Values. Darrell Franken. 800p. 1995. pap. 250.00 (*0-934957-61-4*) Wellness Pubns.

Maximum Style: Look Sharp & Feel Confident in Every Situation. Men's Health Books Editors et al. LC 97-3799. (Men's Health Life Improvement Guides Ser.). (Illus.). 176p. 1997. 14.95 (*0-87596-379-X*) Rodale Pr Inc.

***Maximum Success: Changing the 12 Behavior Patterns That Keep You from Getting Ahead.** Timothy Butler & James Waldroop. 320p. 2000. 24.95 (*0-385-49849-7*) Doubleday.

Maximum Surveillance Society. Clive Norris & Gary Armstrong. 224p. 1999. pap. 19.50 (*1-85973-226-7*, Pub. by Berg Pubs) NYU Pr.

***Maximum Surveillance Society: The Rise of CCTV.** Clive Norris & Gary Armstrong. 224p. 1999. 55.00 (*1-85973-221-6*, Pub. by Berg Pubs) NYU Pr.

Maximum Tech! FASA Corp. Staff. (Battletech Ser.). 128p. 1997. pap. text 15.00 (*1-55560-295-9*, 02959F) NTC Contemp Pub Co.

***Maximum Tech.** rev. ed. Bryan Nystul. (Battletech Ser.). 1999. pap. 15.00 (*1-55560-381-5*) FASA Corp.

Maximum Travel Per Diem Allowances for Foreign Areas. Government Printing Office Staff. 1984. pap. 33.00 (*0-16-011665-1*) USGPO.

Maximum Volume. Siro. Ed. by Deb Rabas. Tr. by Michael Noris from FRE. (Illus.). 48p. 1994. reprint ed. 14.95 (*0-87816-281-X*) Kitchen Sink.

Maximum Wage: A Common-Sense Prescription for Revitalizing America by Taxing the Very Rich. Sam Pizzigati. LC 91-33410. (Illus.). 144p. (Orig.). 1992. pap. 11.95 (*0-945257-45-7*) Apex Pr.

Maximum Weights in Load Lifting & Carrying. (Occupational Safety & Health Ser.: No. 59). v, 38p. (Orig.). 1988. pap. 9.00 (*92-2-106271-6*) Intl Labour Office.

Maximum Windows 2000 Security. 800p. 1900. 49.99 (*0-672-31965-9*) Sams.

Maximum Windows 2000 Security. MacMillian Publishing Company Staff. 1000p. 1999. 39.99 (*0-672-31581-5*) Macmillan.

Maximus I. von Turin: Die Verkndigung Eines Bischofs der Frhen Reichskirche im Zeitgeschichtlichen, Gesellschaftlichen und Liturgischen Kontext. Andreas Merkt. (GER.). 336p. 1997. 118.00 (*90-04-10864-5*) Brill Academic Pubs.

Maximus of Tyre: The Philosophical Orations. Maximus of Tyre. Tr. & Intro. by M. B. Trapp. LC 96-21022. 458p. (C). 1997. text 98.00 (*0-19-814989-1*) OUP.

Maximus Poems. Charles Olson. Ed. by George F. Butterick. LC 79-65759. 664p. 1995. pap. 37.50 (*0-520-05595-0*, Pub. by U CA Pr) Cal Prin Full Svc.

Maximus the Confessor. Ed. by George C. Berthold. (Classics of Western Spirituality Ser.: Vol. 45). 1985. pap. 26.95 (*0-8091-2659-1*) Paulist Pr.

Maximus the Confessor. Andrew Louth. LC 95-20531. (Early Church Fathers Ser.). 240p. (C). 1996. 75.00 (*0-415-11845-X*); pap. 22.99 (*0-415-11846-8*) Routledge.

Maximus to Gloucester: The Letters & Poems of Charles Olson to the Editor of the Gloucester Daily Times, 1962-1969. Charles Olson. Ed. by Peter Anastas. (Illus.). 161p. (Orig.). 1992. pap. 15.00 (*0-938459-07-4*) Ten Pound Isl Bk.

Maximus Tyrius: Philosophumena. Ed. by George L. Koniaris. (Texte und Kommentare Ser.: No. 17). (LAT.). 610p. 1994. lib. bdg. 300.00 (*3-11-012833-0*) De Gruyter.

Maxine Hong Kingston. Diane Simmons. LC 99-14329. 1999. 28.95 (*0-8057-4621-8*, Twyne) Mac Lib Ref.

***Maxine Hong Kingston: A Critical Companion.** E. D. Huntley. (Critical Companions to Popular Contemporary Writers Ser.). 208p. 2000. 30.00 (*0-313-30877-2*, Greenwood Pr) Greenwood.

Maxine Hong Kingston's The Woman Warrior: A Casebook. Ed. by Say-ling Cynthia Wong. LC 98-11577. (Casebooks in Contemporary Fiction Ser.). (Illus.). 208p. 1999. pap. 14.95 (*0-19-511655-0*) OUP.

***Maxine Presents the Crabbiest of Crabby Road: Observations Guaranteed to Help You Learn to Love.** John Wagner. LC 99-72689. 128p. 1999. pap. 9.95 (*0-7407-0014-6*) Andrews & McMeel.

Maxine Sommers Presents Savory Soups: A Celebration of Exquisite Flavors! Ed. by Kaye Reid. (Illus.). 6p. (Orig.). 1993. pap. 3.00 (*0-943991-29-3*) Pound Sterling Pub.

Maxine Sommers Presents Tantalizing Texas Appetizers: The Best of the Best! Maxine S. Sommers. Ed. by Thomas Tagliabue. (Illus.). 6p. (Orig.). 1993. pap. 4.00 (*0-943991-34-X*) Pound Sterling Pub.

***Maxine's Guide to Aging Gracelessly.** John Wagner. 80p. 1999. 4.95 (*0-7407-0082-0*) Andrews & McMeel.

Maxine's Tree. Diane C. Leger & Dar Churcher. (Illus.). 32p. (Orig.). (J). (gr. 1-4). 1990. pap. 5.95 (*0-920501-38-9*) Orca Bk Pubs.

Maxing Out: Total Strength Training for Athletes. Gordon Scoles. 64p. (C). 1985. pap. 8.95 (*0-932741-02-9*) Championship Bks & Vid Prodns.

Maxing Out: Why Women Sabotage Their Financial Security. Colette Dowling. LC 97-49409. 304p. (gr. 8). 1998. 23.95 (*0-316-19120-5*) Little.

Maxi's Big Adventure. Jane Norman & Frank Beazley. 24p. (J). (ps-3). 1993. pap. write for info. (*1-883585-04-X*) Pixanne Ent.

Maxium Adverse Excursion: Analyzing Price Fluctuations for Trading Management. John Sweeney. LC 96-29431. (Wiley Trader's Advantage Ser.). (Illus.). 176p. 1996. 49.95 (*0-471-14152-6*) Wiley.

Maxnotes: Sula. Illus. by Karen Pica. LC 98-66564. v, 111 p. 1999. pap. 3.95 (*0-87891-229-0*) Res & Educ.

MaxNotes - Animal Farm. Joseph Scalia. (MaxNotes Ser.). 96p. 1995. pap. text 3.95 (*0-87891-988-0*) Res & Educ.

MaxNotes - Beowulf. Gail Rosensfit. (MaxNotes Ser.). 128p. 1999. pap. text 3.95 (*0-87891-998-8*) Res & Educ.

MaxNotes - Brave New World. S. Yunker. (MaxNotes Ser.). (Illus.). 128p. 1995. pap. text 3.95 (*0-87891-751-9*) Res & Educ.

MaxNotes - Canterbury Tales. Sarah Voelker. (MaxNotes Ser.). 128p. 1999. pap. text 3.95 (*0-87891-994-5*) Res & Educ.

MaxNotes - Death of a Salesman. Nick Yasinski. (MaxNotes Ser.). 128p. 1995. pap. text 3.95 (*0-87891-995-3*) Res & Educ.

MaxNotes - Great Expectations. Research & Education Association Staff. 128p. 1994. pap. text 3.95 (*0-87891-954-6*) Res & Educ.

MaxNotes - Iliad. Beth Tannis. (MaxNotes Ser.). 128p. 1999. pap. text 3.95 (*0-87891-993-7*) Res & Educ.

MaxNotes - King Lear. Corinna S. Ruth. (MaxNotes Ser.). 144p. 1999. pap. text 3.95 (*0-87891-989-9*) Res & Educ.

MaxNotes - Moby Dick. Naomi Shaw. (MaxNotes Ser.). 128p. 1995. pap. text 3.95 (*0-87891-986-4*) Res & Educ.

MaxNotes - Of Mice & Men. Lena Shamblin. (MaxNotes Ser.). 128p. 1995. pap. text 3.95 (*0-87891-997-X*) Res & Educ.

MaxNotes - Paradise Lost. Corinna S. Ruth. (MaxNotes Ser.). 128p. 1995. pap. text 3.95 (*0-87891-992-9*) Res & Educ.

MaxNotes - Plato's Republic. Research & Education Association Staff. LC 98-66192. (MaxNotes Ser.). (Illus.). 128p. 1999. pap. text 3.95 (*0-87891-987-2*) Res & Educ.

MaxNotes - The Crucible. Beth Tannis. (MaxNotes Ser.). (Illus.). 128p. 1995. pap. text 3.95 (*0-87891-753-5*) Res & Educ.

MaxNotes a Midsummer Night's Dream. Research & Education Association Staff. (MaxNotes Ser.). (Illus.). 128p. (Orig.). 1996. pap. 3.95 (*0-87891-030-1*) Res & Educ.

MaxNotes a Passage to India. Research & Education Association Staff. (MaxNotes Ser.). (Illus.). 128p. (Orig.). 1996. pap. 3.95 (*0-87891-039-5*) Res & Educ.

MaxNotes a Portrait of the Artist. Research & Education Association Staff. (MaxNotes Ser.). (Illus.). 128p. (Orig.). 1996. pap. 3.95 (*0-87891-041-7*) Res & Educ.

MaxNotes Absalom, Absalom. Research & Education Association Staff. (MaxNotes Ser.). (Illus.). 128p. (Orig.). 1996. pap. 3.95 (*0-87891-000-X*) Res & Educ.

MaxNotes Antony & Cleopatra. Research & Education Association Staff. LC 96-67443. (MaxNotes Ser.). (Illus.). 128p. (Orig.). 1996. pap. 3.95 (*0-87891-002-6*) Res & Educ.

MaxNotes As I Lay Dying. Research & Education Association Staff. LC 96-67417. (MaxNotes Ser.). (Illus.). 128p. (Orig.). 1996. pap. 3.95 (*0-87891-059-X*) Res & Educ.

MaxNotes As You Like It. Research & Education Association Staff. LC 96-67405. (MaxNotes Ser.). (Illus.). 128p. (Orig.). 1996. pap. 3.95 (*0-87891-003-4*) Res & Educ.

MaxNotes Beloved. Research & Education Association Staff. LC 95-71345. (MaxNotes Ser.). (Illus.). 128p. 1999. pap. 3.95 (*0-87891-006-9*) Res & Educ.

MaxNotes Billy Budd. Research & Education Association Staff. (MaxNotes Ser.). (Illus.). 128p. (Orig.). 1996. pap. 3.95 (*0-87891-007-7*) Res & Educ.

MaxNotes Death in Venice. Research & Education Association Staff. LC 96-67419. (MaxNotes Ser.). (Illus.). 128p. (Orig.). 1996. pap. 3.95 (*0-87891-010-7*) Res & Educ.

MaxNotes Divine Comedy Vol. I: Inferno. Research & Education Association Staff. (MaxNotes Ser.). (Illus.). 128p. (Orig.). 1996. pap. 3.95 (*0-87891-991-0*) Res & Educ.

MaxNotes Dubliners. Research & Education Association Staff. (MaxNotes Ser.). (Illus.). 128p. (Orig.). 1996. pap. 3.95 (*0-87891-011-5*) Res & Educ.

MaxNotes Emma. Research & Education Association Staff. (MaxNotes Ser.). (Illus.). 128p. (Orig.). 1996. pap. 3.95 (*0-87891-012-3*) Res & Educ.

MaxNotes Euripedes' Electra & Medea. Research & Education Association Staff & Tamara L. Underiner. LC 95-72125. (MaxNotes Ser.). (Illus.). 128p. (Orig.). 1996. pap. 3.95 (*0-87891-013-1*) Res & Educ.

MaxNotes Frankenstein. Research & Education Association Staff. (MaxNotes Ser.). (Illus.). 128p. (Orig.). 1996. pap. 3.95 (*0-87891-014-X*) Res & Educ.

MaxNotes Gulliver's Travels. Research & Education Association Staff. LC 96-67403. (MaxNotes Ser.). (Illus.). 128p. (Orig.). 1996. pap. 3.95 (*0-87891-015-8*) Res & Educ.

MaxNotes Hard Times. Research & Education Association Staff. (MaxNotes Ser.). (Illus.). 128p. (Orig.). 1996. pap. 3.95 (*0-87891-016-6*) Res & Educ.

MaxNotes Heart of Darkness. Research & Education Association Staff. (MaxNotes Ser.). (Illus.). 128p. (Orig.). 1996. pap. 3.95 (*0-87891-017-4*) Res & Educ.

MaxNotes Henry V. Research & Education Association Staff. LC 96-67445. (MaxNotes Ser.). (Illus.). 128p. 1996. pap. 3.95 (*0-87891-019-0*) Res & Educ.

MaxNotes Henry IV, Pt. I. Research & Education Association Staff. (MaxNotes Ser.). (Illus.). 128p. (Orig.). 1996. pap. 3.95 (*0-87891-018-2*) Res & Educ.

MaxNotes Invisible Man. Research & Education Association Staff. LC 96-67424. (MaxNotes Ser.). (Illus.). 128p. (Orig.). 1996. pap. 3.95 (*0-87891-021-2*) Res & Educ.

MaxNotes Jane Eyre. Research & Education Association Staff. (MaxNotes Ser.). (Illus.). 128p. (Orig.). 1996. pap. 3.95 (*0-87891-022-0*) Res & Educ.

MaxNotes Jazz. Research & Education Association Staff. (MaxNotes Ser.). (Illus.). 128p. (Orig.). 1996. pap. 3.95 (*0-87891-023-9*) Res & Educ.

MaxNotes Lord of the Flies. W. Freeman. (MaxNotes Ser.). (Illus.). 128p. 1995. pap. text 3.95 (*0-87891-754-3*) Res & Educ.

MaxNotes Metamorphosis. Research & Education Association Staff. LC 96-67406. (MaxNotes Ser.). (Illus.). 128p. (Orig.). 1996. pap. 3.95 (*0-87891-028-X*) Res & Educ.

MaxNotes Middlemarch. Research & Education Association Staff. LC 96-67451. (MaxNotes Ser.). (Illus.). 128p. (Orig.). 1996. pap. 3.95 (*0-87891-029-8*) Res & Educ.

MaxNotes Moll Flanders. Research & Education Association Staff. (MaxNotes Ser.). (Illus.). 128p. (Orig.). 1996. pap. 3.95 (*0-87891-031-X*) Res & Educ.

MaxNotes Mrs. Dalloway. Research & Education Association Staff. (MaxNotes Ser.). (Illus.). 128p. (Orig.). 1996. pap. 3.95 (*0-87891-032-8*) Res & Educ.

MaxNotes Much Ado about Nothing. Research & Education Association Staff. (MaxNotes Ser.). (Illus.). 128p. (Orig.). 1996. pap. 3.95 (*0-87891-033-6*) Res & Educ.

MaxNotes My Antonia. Research & Education Association Staff. (MaxNotes Ser.). (Illus.). 128p. (Orig.). 1996. pap. 3.95 (*0-87891-034-4*) Res & Educ.

MaxNotes Native Son. Research & Education Association Staff. LC 96-67428. (MaxNotes Ser.). (Illus.). 128p. (Orig.). 1996. pap. 3.95 (*0-87891-035-2*) Res & Educ.

MaxNotes 1984. Karen Brodeur. (MaxNotes Ser.). 128p. 1995. pap. text 3.95 (*0-87891-996-1*) Res & Educ.

MaxNotes Oedipus Trilogy. Research & Education Association Staff. (MaxNotes Ser.). (Illus.). 128p. (Orig.). 1996. pap. 3.95 (*0-87891-036-0*) Res & Educ.

MaxNotes on the Road. Research & Education Association Staff. (MaxNotes Ser.). (Illus.). 128p. (Orig.). 1996. pap. 3.95 (*0-87891-037-9*) Res & Educ.

MaxNotes Othello. Research & Education Association Staff. (MaxNotes Ser.). (Illus.). 128p. 2000. pap. 3.95 (*0-87891-038-7*) Res & Educ.

MaxNotes Pride & Prejudice. Research & Education Association Staff. (MaxNotes Ser.). (Illus.). 128p. (Orig.). 1996. pap. 3.95 (*0-87891-042-5*) Res & Educ.

MaxNotes Richard II. Research & Education Association Staff. LC 96-67421. (MaxNotes Ser.). (Illus.). 128p. (Orig.). 1996. pap. 3.95 (*0-87891-043-3*) Res & Educ.

MaxNotes Romeo & Juliet. Judy Clamon. (MaxNotes Ser.). 104p. 1999. pap. text. write for info. (*0-87891-990-2*) Res & Educ.

MaxNotes Sir Gawain & the Green Knight. Research & Education Association Staff. (MaxNotes Ser.). (Illus.). 128p. (Orig.). 1996. pap. 3.95 (*0-87891-044-1*) Res & Educ.

MaxNotes Slaughterhouse-Five. Research & Education Association Staff. LC 96-67404. (MaxNotes Ser.). (Illus.). 128p. (Orig.). 1996. pap. 3.95 (*0-87891-045-X*) Res & Educ.

MaxNotes Song of Solomon. Research & Education Association Staff. LC 96-67449. (MaxNotes Ser.). (Illus.). 128p. (Orig.). 1996. pap. 3.95 (*0-87891-046-8*) Res & Educ.

MaxNotes "Tar Baby" Contrib. by Research & Education Staff. LC 98-66563. (MaxNotes Ser.). 1999. pap. text 3.95 (*0-87891-230-4*) Res & Educ.

MaxNotes the Aeneid of Virgil. Research & Education Association Staff. (MaxNotes Ser.). (Illus.). 128p. (Orig.). 1996. pap. 3.95 (*0-87891-001-8*) Res & Educ.

MaxNotes the Autobiography of Malcolm X. Research & Education Association Staff et al. (MaxNotes Ser.). (Illus.). 128p. 1996. pap. 3.95 (*0-87891-004-2*) Res & Educ.

MaxNotes the Awakening. Research & Education Association Staff. (MaxNotes Ser.). (Illus.). 128p. (Orig.). 1996. pap. 3.95 (*0-87891-005-0*) Res & Educ.

MaxNotes the Bluest Eye: A Novel. Research & Education Association Staff. LC 96-67418. (MaxNotes Ser.). (Illus.). 128p. (Orig.). 1996. pap. 3.95 (*0-87891-008-5*) Res & Educ.

MaxNotes the Catcher in the Rye. R. Holzman & G. Perkins. (MaxNotes Ser.). (Illus.). 128p. 2000. pap. text 3.95 (*0-87891-752-7*) Res & Educ.

MaxNotes the Color Purple. Research & Education Association Staff. (MaxNotes Ser.). (Illus.). 128p. (Orig.). 1996. pap. 3.95 (*0-87891-009-3*) Res & Educ.

MaxNotes the House on Mango Street. Research & Education Association Staff. (MaxNotes Ser.). (Illus.). 128p. (Orig.). 1996. pap. 3.95 (*0-87891-020-4*) Res & Educ.

MaxNotes the Joy Luck Club. Research & Education Association Staff. (MaxNotes Ser.). (Illus.). 128p. (Orig.). 1996. pap. 3.95 (*0-87891-024-7*) Res & Educ.

MaxNotes the Merchant of Venice. Research & Education Association Staff. (MaxNotes Ser.). (Illus.). 128p. (Orig.). 1996. pap. 3.95 (*0-87891-026-3*) Res & Educ.

MaxNotes the Metamorphoses of Ovid. Research & Education Association Staff. LC 96-67410. (MaxNotes Ser.). (Illus.). 128p. (Orig.). 1996. pap. 3.95 (*0-87891-027-1*) Res & Educ.

MaxNotes the Portrait of a Lady. Research & Education Association Staff. LC 96-67450. (MaxNotes Ser.). (Illus.). 128p. (Orig.). 1996. pap. 3.95 (*0-87891-040-9*) Res & Educ.

MaxNotes the Scarlet Letter. Research & Education Association Staff. (Illus.). 128p. 1994. pap. text 3.95 (*0-87891-950-3*) Res & Educ.

MaxNotes the Sound & the Fury. Research & Education Association Staff. (MaxNotes Ser.). (Illus.). 128p. (Orig.). 1996. pap. 3.95 (*0-87891-047-6*) Res & Educ.

MaxNotes the Stranger. Research & Education Association Staff. (MaxNotes Ser.). (Illus.). 128p. (Orig.). 1996. pap. 3.95 (*0-87891-048-4*) Res & Educ.

MaxNotes "The Sun Also Rises" Contrib. by Research & Education Staff. (MaxNotes Ser.). (Illus.). 128p. 1996. pap. text 3.95 (*0-87891-049-2*) Res & Educ.

MaxNotes the Taming of the Shrew. Research & Education Association Staff. LC 96-67412. (MaxNotes Ser.). (Illus.). 128p. (Orig.). 1996. pap. 3.95 (*0-87891-050-6*) Res & Educ.

MaxNotes the Tempest. Research & Education Association Staff. (MaxNotes Ser.). (Illus.). 128p. (Orig.). 1996. pap. 3.95 (*0-87891-052-2*) Res & Educ.

MaxNotes Their Eyes Were Watching God. Research & Education Association Staff. (MaxNotes Ser.). (Illus.). 128p. (Orig.). 1996. pap. 3.95 (*0-87891-053-0*) Res & Educ.

MaxNotes to the Lighthouse. Research & Education Association Staff. LC 96-67414. (MaxNotes Ser.). (Illus.). 128p. (Orig.). 1996. pap. 3.95 (*0-87891-054-9*) Res & Educ.

MaxNotes Twelfth Night. Research & Education Association Staff. (MaxNotes Ser.). (Illus.). 128p. (Orig.). 1996. pap. 3.95 (*0-87891-055-7*) Res & Educ.

MaxNotes Uncle Tom's Cabin. Research & Education Association Staff. (MaxNotes Ser.). (Illus.). 128p. (Orig.). 1996. pap. 3.95 (*0-87891-056-5*) Res & Educ.

MaxNotes Waiting for Godot. Research & Education Association Staff. LC 96-67420. (MaxNotes Ser.). (Illus.). 128p. (Orig.). 1996. pap. 3.95 (*0-87891-057-3*) Res & Educ.

MaxNotes Wuthering Heights. Research & Education Association Staff. (MaxNotes Ser.). (Illus.). 128p. (Orig.). 1996. pap. 3.95 (*0-87891-058-1*) Res & Educ.

Maxon's Poe: Seven Short Stories & Poems. limited ed. Edgar Allan Poe. LC 98-105667. (Cottage Classics Ser.). (Illus.). 88p. 1997. 40.00 (*0-9642922-5-4*); pap. 17.95 (*0-9642922-4-6*) Word Play Calif.

MAXO2. Jerry Robinson & Frank Carrino. LC 93-73083. (Illus.). 222p. 1993. pap. 19.95 (*0-944831-30-3*) Health Life.

Max's Birthday. Rosemary Wells. LC 97-5453. (Max Board Bks.). (Illus.). 12p. (J). 1998. pap. 5.99 (*0-8037-2268-0*, Dial Yng Read) Peng Put Young Read.

Max's Breakfast. Rosemary Wells. LC 97-12859. (Max Board Bks.). (Illus.). 12p. (J). 1998. pap. 5.99 (*0-8037-2273-7*, Dial Yng Read) Peng Put Young Read.

***Max's Chocolate Chicken.** Rosemary Wells. (Max & Ruby Bks.). (Illus.). (J). (gr. k-2). 1999. 15.99 (*0-670-88713-7*, Viking Child) Peng Put Young Read.

Max's Christmas. Rosemary Wells. LC 85-27547. (Max & Ruby Bks.). (Illus.). 32p. (J). (gr. k-2). 1986. 12.99 (*0-8037-0289-2*, Dial Yng Read) Peng Put Young Read.

***Max's Christmas.** Rosemary Wells. (Max & Ruby Bks.). (Illus.). 32p. (J). (gr. k-2). 2000. pap. 5.99 (*0-14-056751-8*, PuffinBks) Peng Put Young Read.

Max's Christmas. Rosemary Wells. LC 85-27547. (Max & Ruby Bks.). (J). (gr. k-2). 1986. 9.19 (*0-606-06564-4*, Pub. by Turtleback) Demco.

Max's Christmas. Rosemary Wells. (Max & Ruby Bks.). (J). (gr. k-2). pap. text 8.95 incl. audio (*0-89719-968-5*, RAC322) Weston Woods.

Max's Daddy Goes to the Hospital. Danielle Steel. (Illus.). 32p. (J). (ps-2). 1989. 8.95 (*0-385-29797-1*) Delacorte.

***Max's Dragon Shirt.** Rosemary Wells. (Max & Ruby Bks.). (Illus.). (J). (gr. k-2). 2000. 15.99 (*0-670-88727-7*, Viking Child) Peng Put Young Read.

***Max's Dragon Shirt.** Rosemary Wells. (Max & Ruby Bks.). (Illus.). 32p. (J). (gr. k-2). 2000. pap. 5.99 (*0-14-056727-5*, PuffinBks) Peng Put Young Read.

Max's Dragon Shirt. Rosemary Wells. (Max & Ruby Bks.). (Illus.). (J). (gr. k-2). 1997. 10.19 (*0-606-11606-0*, Pub. by Turtleback) Demco.

Max's First Word. Rosemary Wells. LC 97-12856. (Max Board Bks.). 12p. (J). 1998. pap. 5.99 (*0-8037-2269-9*, Dial Yng Read) Peng Put Young Read.

Max's Letter. Ken Wilson-Max. LC 98-83292. (Illus.). 12p. (J). (ps-k). 1999. 6.99 (*0-7868-0525-0*, Pub. by Hyprn Ppbks) Little.

Max's Money. Teddy Slater. LC 98-23333. (Hello Reader! Math Ser.: Level 4). (Illus.). 32p. (J). (gr. 2-4). 1999. pap. 3.99 (*0-590-12010-7*, Pub. by Scholastic Inc) Penguin Putnam.

Max's Money. Ken Wilson-Max. LC 98-83291. (Illus.). 12p. (ps-k). 1999. 6.99 (*0-7868-0526-9*, Pub. by Hyprn Ppbks) Little.

Max's New Suit. Rosemary Wells. LC 97-12857. (Max Board Bks.). 12p. (J). 1998. pap. 5.99 (*0-8037-2270-2*, Dial Yng Read) Peng Put Young Read.

Max's Potty. Harriet Ziefert & Emilie Boon. LC 98-5467. (Harriet Ziefert's Potty Sticker Book Ser.). (Illus.). 18p. (J). (ps). 1999. 8.95 (*0-7894-2838-5*) DK Pub Inc.

Max's Train Ride: A Squeaky Storybook with a Surprise Ending. Fisher-Price Staff & Susan Hood. (Fisher-Price Playbks.). (Illus.). 12p. (J). (ps-k). 1997. bds. 6.99 (*1-57584-183-5*, Pub. by Rdrs Digest) Random.

Max's Wacky Taxi Day. Max Grover. LC 96-2333. (Illus.). 32p. (J). (gr. k-3). 1997. 15.00 (*0-15-200989-2*, Harcourt Child Bks) Harcourt.

***Max's Wild Goose Chase.** Sandra Philipson. (Illus.). (J). (gr. k-4). 1999. 17.95 (*1-929821-01-8*) Chagrin River.

***MAXScript for Advanced Users.** Alexander Bicalho. 2000. pap. 49.99 (*0-7821-2794-0*) Sybex.

Maxwell Anderson. 200p. 1977. 18.95 (*0-8369-5568-4*) Ayer.

Maxwell Anderson. Alfred S. Shivers. 1976. 21.95 (*0-8057-7179-4*, Twyne) Mac Lib Ref.

Maxwell Anderson: A Research & Production Sourcebook, 10. Barbara L. Horn. LC 96-1200. (Modern Dramatists Research & Production Sourcebooks Ser.). 208p. 1996. lib. bdg. 67.95 (*0-313-29070-9*, Greenwood Pr) Greenwood.

Maxwell Anderson & the New York Stage. Ed. by Nancy J. Hazelton & Kenneth Krauss. LC 90-20680. (Illus.). 177p. (C). 1991. 29.95 (*0-912526-51-3*) Lib Res.

Maxwell Anderson (1888-1959) & the Playwrights' Producing Company. Stephan S. Hadley et al. LC 88-208619. (Illus.). 20p. 1988. pap. 4.00 (*0-911183-46-9*) Rockland County Hist.

Maxwell Anderson on the European Stage, 1929-1992. Ron Engle. LC 95-38784. (Illus.). 454p. 1996. 35.00 (*0-912526-67-X*) Lib Res.

Maxwell G. The Racehorse's Racehorse. L. M. Schorsch. LC 77-933824. (Illus.). 1977. 5.95 (*0-686-26463-0*) Kukla Pr.

Maxwell History & Genealogies Many Lines: 1970 to Northern Ireland Then Back to 12th Century Scotland. Fay Maxwell. 165p. 1977. 35.00 (*1-885463-17-0*) Ohio Genealogy.

Maxwell History & Genealogy, Including Allied Families. Houston et al. (Illus.). 642p. 1991. reprint ed. pap. 96.50 (*0-8328-1881-X*); reprint ed. lib. bdg. 106.50 (*0-8328-1880-1*) Higginson Bk Co.

Maxwell House Coffee Drinks & Desserts Cookbook: From Lattes & Muffins to Decadent Cakes & Midnight Treats. Maxwell House Staff. Ed. by Barbara Albright. 208p. 1999. 22.50 (*0-609-60542-9*) Potrero Meadow Pub.

Maxwell Jewelry: Manual with Source Documentation. 4th ed. Swanson & Ross. (BA - Accounting - First Year Ser.). 1986. student ed. 12.50 (*0-538-02424-0*) S-W Pub.

Maxwell Land Grant: A New Mexico Item. William A. Keleher. LC 83-21638. 188p. reprint ed. pap. 58.30 (*0-7837-1635-4*, 204192800024) Bks Demand.

Maxwell Macmillan California Tax Handbook. Herbert K. Frentz. 1990. pap. 25.95 (*0-02-081142-X*) Macmillan.

Maxwell Macmillan Federal Tax Handbook: Professional & Business Reference Division. James A. Maxwell. 1991. pap. 27.95 (*0-02-081141-1*) Macmillan.

Maxwell Macmillan Preparing the 1040 Return. Franklyn E. Lee. 1991. pap. 49.50 (*0-02-081143-8*) Macmillan.

Maxwell on Heat & Statistical Mechanics: On "Avoiding All Personal Enquiries" of Molecules. Ed. by Elizabeth Garber et al. LC 94-25234. 1995. 59.50 (*0-934223-34-3*) Lehigh Univ Pr.

Maxwell on Molecules & Gases. James Clerk Maxwell. Ed. by Elizabeth Garber et al. (Illus.). 650p. 1986. 70.00 (*0-262-07094-4*) MIT Pr.

Maxwell on the Electromagnetic Field: A Guided Study. Thomas K. Simpson. LC 96-8341. (Masterworks of Discovery Ser.). (Illus.). 320p. (C). 1997. text 48.00 (*0-8135-2362-1*); pap. text 19.95 (*0-8135-2363-X*) Rutgers U Pr.

Maxwell Quick Medical Reference. Robert W. Maxwell. (Illus.). 32p. (Orig.). (C). 1995. pap. text 7.95 (*0-9645191-0-0*) Mxwll Pub.

Maxwell Quick Medical Reference. 3rd rev. ed. Robert W. Maxwell. (Illus.). 32p. (Orig.). (C). 1996. pap. text 7.95 (*0-9645191-1-9*) Mxwll Pub.

Maxwell Stories. Sam Jaffa. (Illus.). 190p. (Orig.). 1993. pap. 12.50 (*0-86051-829-9*, Robson-Parkwest) Parkwest Pubns.

***Maxwell 3-in-1: Becoming a Person of Influence, Winning Attitude, Developing the Leaders Around You.** John Maxwell & Jim Dornan. 672p. 2000. 16.99 (*0-7852-6840-5*) Nelson.

Maxwellians. Bruce J. Hunt. LC 91-13310. (History of Science Ser.). (Illus.). 280p. 1991. 42.50 (*0-8014-2641-3*) Cornell U Pr.

Maxwellians. Bruce J. Hunt. LC 91-13310. (History of Science Ser.). (Illus.). 280p. 1995. pap. text 17.95 (*0-8014-8234-8*) Cornell U Pr.

Maxwell's Equations & Their Consequences see Elementary Electromagnetic Theory

***Maxwell's Ghost: An Epilogue to Gavin Maxwell's Camusfearna.** Richard Frere. (Illus.). 256p. 1999. pap. 15.95 (*1-84158-003-1*, Pub. by Birlinn Ltd) Dufour.

Maxwell's Handbook for AACR2R: Explaining & Illustrating the Anglo-American Cataloging Rules & the 1993 Amendments. Robert L. Maxwell & Margaret F. Maxwell. LC 97-1449. 456p. 1997. 60.00 (*0-8389-0704-0*) ALA.

Maxwell's House. large type ed. M. J. Trow. LC 95-5312. 370p. 1995. pap. 20.95 (*0-7862-0423-0*) Thorndike Pr.

Maxwell's Train. Christopher Hyde. 288p. 1986. pap. 3.50 (*0-685-11842-8*) Bantam.

Maxx, Vol. I. Sam Kieth. (Illus.). 156p. (Orig.). (YA). 1995. pap. 12.95 (*1-887279-00-8*) Image Comics.

Maxx, Vol. I. 3rd ed. Sam Kieth. (Illus.). 156p. (Orig.). (YA). 1996. reprint ed. pap. 12.95 (*1-887279-37-7*) Image Comics.

Maxx, Vol. 2. Sam Keith & William Loebs. (Illus.). 136p. (Orig.). (YA). 1997. pap. 12.95 (*1-887279-43-1*) Image Comics.

Maxxam Inc. A Report on the Company's Environmental Policies & Practices. (Illus.). 69p. (C). 1994. reprint ed. pap. text 40.00 (*0-7881-0963-4*, Coun on Econ) DIANE Pub.

May. (J). 1992. pap. text 5.95 (*0-516-95638-8*) Childrens.

***May.** (Monthly Patterns & Projects Ser.). (Illus.). 80p. (J). (ps-2). 2000. pap. 7.95 (*1-58273-133-0*) Newbridge Educ.

May. Daniel Parker. LC 99-14012. (Countdown Ser.: No. 5). 128p. (YA). (gr. 7-12). 1999. per. 3.99 (*0-689-81823-8*) Aladdin.

May: Charles May & His Descendants, Who Settled at Mays Cross Roads in Old Edgefield County, S.C. Ed. by H. Woodson. 287p. 1993. reprint ed. pap. 43.00 (*0-8328-3718-0*); reprint ed. lib. bdg. 53.00 (*0-8328-3717-2*) Higginson Bk Co.

May All Be Fed: Diet for a New World. John Robbins. 416p. 1993. reprint ed. pap. 14.00 (*0-380-71901-0*, Avon Bks) Morrow Avon.

May All Creatures Live. Daniel Berrigan. (Illus.). 105p. 1984. 100.00 (*0-933861-05-2*) H Berliner.

May All Your Fences Have Gates: Essays on the Drama of August Wilson. Ed. by Alan Nadel. LC 93-34628. (Illus.). 282p. 1993. pap. text 16.95 (*0-87745-439-6*) U of Iowa Pr.

May Basket Quilt. Eleanor Burns. (Illus.). 62p. (Orig.). 1987. pap. 8.95 (*0-922705-07-0*) Quilt Day.

May Bell's Daughter. Eva W. Self & Lisa Harper. LC 99-20415. 224p. 1999. 16.99 (*0-7852-7047-7*) Nelson.

May Brook Site, Jackson County, Missouri. Larry J. Schmit et al. Ed. by Robert T. Bray. LC 44-14131. (Missouri Archaeologist Ser.: Vol. 43). (Illus.). 120p. 1982. pap. 6.00 (*0-943414-05-9*) MO Arch Soc.

May Christ Lift Thee up: Selections from the 1998 Women's Conference Sponsored by Brigham Young University & the Relief Society. LC 99-11518. 371 p. 1999. 21.95 (*1-57345-522-9*) Deseret Bk.

May Contain and/Or: A BS Poetry Drop-in Centre Anthology. Ed. by Joe Blades. 1995. pap. text 3.00 (*0-921411-39-1*) Genl Dist Srvs.

May Day: A Short History of the International Workers' Holiday, 1886-1986. Philip S. Foner. LC 85-23823. (Illus.). 200p. 1986. 14.00 (*0-7178-0633-2*); pap. 6.95 (*0-7178-0624-3*) Intl Pubs Co.

May Day & 8 Hours' Struggle in India. Sukomal Sen. (C). 1988. 22.00 (*81-7074-033-9*) S Asia.

May Day & Other Pieces (Poems) Ralph Waldo Emerson. (Notable American Authors Ser.). 1992. reprint ed. lib. bdg. 75.00 (*0-7812-2813-1*) Rprt Serv.

***May Day in Town: or New York in & Uproar.** Royall Tyler. (Notable American Authors Ser.). 1999. reprint ed. lib. bdg. 125.00 (*0-7812-9859-8*) Rprt Serv.

May Days. Samuel F. Pickering, Jr. LC 87-34292. 208p. 1988. reprint ed. pap. 14.95 (*0-87745-522-8*) U of Iowa Pr.

May Days Dialogues: A Selection from the Royal Court Season. (Royal Court Writers Ser.). 111p. (Orig.). (C). 1990. pap. write for info. (*0-413-64700-5*, AO505, Methuen Drama) Methn.

May Days of Barcelona, 1937. Augustin Souchy et al. 127p. (Orig.). (C). 1987. pap. 5.50 (*0-900384-39-5*) Left Bank.

May 18: What Your Birth Date Reveals about You. (Birth Date Book Ser.). (Illus.). 80p. 1999. 4.95 (*0-8362-6060-0*) Andrews & McMeel.

May 18, 1741-July 10, 1742 see Journal of the Commons House of Assembly: Series One

May 8: What Your Birth Date Reveals about You. (Birth Date Book Ser.). (Illus.). 80p. 1999. 4.95 (*0-8362-6048-1*) Andrews & McMeel.

May 11: What Your Birth Date Reveals about You. (Birth Date Book Ser.). (Illus.). 80p. 1999. 4.95 (*0-8362-6053-8*) Andrews & McMeel.

May Essentials: Idea Booklet & Pocket Folder Organizer. Karen Sevaly. (Illus.). 16p. 1997. pap., teacher ed., wbk. ed. 3.99 (*1-57882-005-7*, TF-1255) Teachers Friend Pubns.

May Eve: A Festival of Supernatural Poems. Ed. by Brett Rutherford. 1975. 5.00 (*0-318-64158-5*) Poets Pr.

May Fault. Theodore Enslin. 24p. 1979. pap. 5.00 (*0-686-30871-9*) Great Raven Pr.

May 15: What Your Birth Date Reveals about You. (Birth Date Book Ser.). (Illus.). 80p. 1999. 4.95 (*0-8362-6057-0*) Andrews & McMeel.

May 15, 1868-Sept 29, 1868 see Germans to America: Lists of Passengers Arriving at U. S. Ports, 1850-1893

May 5: What Your Birth Date Reveals about You. (Birth Date Book Ser.). (Illus.). 80p. 1999. 4.95 (*0-8362-6045-7*) Andrews & McMeel.

May 5, 1854-August 4, 1854 see Germans to America: Lists of Passengers Arriving at U. S. Ports, 1850-1893

May 1: What Your Birth Date Reveals about You. (Birth Date Book Ser.). (Illus.). 80p. 1999. 4.95 (*0-8362-6041-4*) Andrews & McMeel.

May 1, 1888-Nov. 30, 1888 see Germans to America: Lists of Passengers Arriving at U. S. Ports, 1850-1893

May 1, 1886-Jan. 3, 1887 see Germans to America: Lists of Passengers Arriving at U. S. Ports, 1850-1893

May 1, 1890-Nov. 28, 1890 see Germans to America: Lists of Passengers Arriving at U. S. Ports, 1850-1893

May 1st to September 18, 1777 see Letters of Delegates to Congress, 1774-1789, Vol. 25, March 1, 1788-July 25, 1789, with Supplement, 1774-87

May Flower & Miscellaneous Writings. Harriet Beecher Stowe. 471p. 1977. 25.95 (*0-8369-4189-6*) Ayer.

May 14: What Your Birth Date Reveals about You. (Birth Date Book Ser.). (Illus.). 80p. 1999. 4.95 (*0-8362-6056-2*) Andrews & McMeel.

May 4: What Your Birth Date Reveals about You. (Birth Date Book Ser.). (Illus.). 80p. 1999. 4.95 (*0-8362-6044-9*) Andrews & McMeel.

May Fourth Movement: Intellectual Revolution in Modern China. Chow Tse-Tsung. (East Asian Monographs: Vol. No. 6). 501p. (C). 1960. pap. 21.50 (*0-674-55751-4*) HUP.

May God Have Mercy: A True Story of Crime & Punishment. John C. Tucker. 368p. 1998. pap. 11.95 (*0-385-33294-7*) Delacorte.

May God Have Mercy: A True Story of Crime & Punishment. John C. Tucker. LC 96-51516. (Illus.). 384p. 1997. 27.50 (*0-393-04032-1*) Norton.

May Goes to England. Bonnie Bryant. (Pony Tails Ser.: No. 11). (Illus.). 112p. (J). (gr. 3-5). 1997. pap. 3.50 (*0-553-48481-8*, Skylark BDD) BDD Bks Young Read.

May I Bring a Friend? Beatrice Schenk De Regniers. 1964. 10.15 (*0-606-01049-1*, Pub. by Turtleback) Demco.

May I Bring a Friend? Beatrice S. De Regniers. LC 64-19562. (Illus.). 48p. (J). (ps-2). 1971. lib. bdg. 16.00 (*0-689-20615-1*) Atheneum Yung Read.

***May I Bring A Friend.** Beatrice S. De Regniers. 1999. pap. 13.40 (*0-88103-362-6*) Econo-Clad Bks.

May I Bring a Friend? 2nd ed. Beatrice S. De Regniers. LC 89-15087. (Illus.). 48p. (J). (gr. k-3). 1989. reprint ed. mass mkt. 4.95 (*0-689-71353-3*) Aladdin.

May I Bring a Friend: A Study Guide. Garrett Christopher. Ed. by J. Friedland & R. Kessler. (Little Novel-Ties Ser.). (J). (gr. k-2). 1994. pap. text, student ed. 14.95 (*1-56982-081-3*) Lrn Links.

May I Call You Brother? Messages from "A Course in Miracles" Thomas L. Davies. LC 95-92300. 128p. (Orig.). 1995. pap. 10.00 (*0-9646896-0-X*) Awaken The Genius.

May I Divorce & Remarry? First Corinthians 7. rev. ed. Spiros Zodhiates. (First Corinthians Commentary Ser.). 445p. 1992. pap. 8.99 (*0-89957-600-1*) AMG Pubs.

May I Feel Said He: Poem. E. E. Cummings. (Illus.). 32p. 1995. 17.95 (*1-55670-422-4*) Stewart Tabori & Chang.

May I Feel Said He: Poem. E. E. Cummings. Ed. by Linda Sunshine. LC 95-30234. (Illus.). 32p. 1995. reprint ed. 17.95 (*0-941807-00-2*) Welcome Enterprises.

***May I Go Out?** (Books to Go Ser.). 1998. pap. write for info. (*0-8136-8302-5*) Modern Curr.

May I Hate God? Pierre Wolff. LC 78-70815. 76p. 1979. pap. 4.95 (*0-8091-2180-8*) Paulist Pr.

May I Have the Pleasure? Belinda Quirey. 124p. 1976. reprint ed. pap. 17.95 (*1-85273-000-5*, Pub. by Dance Bks) Princeton Bk Co.

May I Have This Dance? Joyce Rupp. LC 92-71817. (Illus.). 184p. (Orig.). 1992. pap. 11.95 (*0-87793-480-0*) Ave Maria.

May I Help You? Diamond Jim Halter. 104p. (Orig.). 1989. pap. 9.95 (*0-685-27873-5*) Diamond Jim.

May I Help You? Heide S. Wrigley. (English for the Workplace Ser.). (Illus.). 160p. (YA). (gr. 9-12). 1987. teacher ed. 18.22 (*0-201-09898-9*) Addison-Wesley.

May I Help You Understand: Information to Improve Racial & Cultural Relations Between White & Black America. Darrell D. Simms. (Illus.). 250p. 1999. mass mkt. 16.95 (*0-9630776-7-8*) Mgmt Aspects.

***May I Kiss You On The Lips, Miss Sandra.** Sandra Bernhard. LC 98-47725. 256p. 1998. 24.00 (*0-688-16471-4*, Wm Morrow) Morrow Avon.

***May I Kiss You On The Lips, Miss Sandra.** Sandra Bernhard. 224p. 1999. pap. 14.00 (*0-688-17163-X*, Wm Morrow) Morrow Avon.

May I Quote You, General Chamberlain? Ed. by Randall Bedwell. (May I Quote You Ser.). (Illus.). 96p. 1998. pap. 7.95 (*1-888952-96-2*) Cumberland Hse.

May I Quote You, General Forrest? Ed. by Randall Bedwell. LC 96-51932. (May I Quote You Ser.). (Illus.). 96p. (Orig.). 1997. pap. 7.95 (*1-888952-35-0*) Cumberland Hse.

May I Quote You, General Grant? Randall Bedwell. (May I Quote You Ser.). (Illus.). 96p. 1998. pap. 7.95 (*1-888952-95-4*) Cumberland Hse.

May I Quote You, General Lee? Ed. by Randall Bedwell. LC 96-51927. (May I Quote You Ser.). (Illus.). 96p. 1997. pap. 7.95 (*1-888952-34-2*) Cumberland Hse.

May I Quote You, General Lee?, Vol. 2. Ed. by Randall Bedwell. (May I Quote You Ser.). (Illus.). 96p. 1998. pap. 7.95 (*1-888952-94-6*) Cumberland Hse.

May I Quote You, General Longstreet? Ed. by Randall Bedwell. LC 96-51928. (May I Quote You Ser.). (Illus.). 96p. (Orig.). 1997. pap. 7.95 (*1-888952-37-7*) Cumberland Hse.

May I Quote You, Stonewall Jackson? Ed. by Randall Bedwell. LC 96-52697. (May I Quote You Ser.). (Illus.). 96p. (Orig.). 1997. pap. 7.95 (*1-888952-36-9*) Cumberland Hse.

May I Say Nothing. Gregory Woods. LC 99-203181. 80p. 1999. pap. 14.95 (*1-85754-384-X*, Pub. by Carcanet Pr) Paul & Co Pubs.

May I See You a Moment? unabridged ed. M. J. Kitt. (Illus.). 1999. pap. 5.00 (*0-9663307-1-4*) M J Kitt.

May I Share Something with You Someone Once Shared with Me? Clarence L. Blasier. (Illus.). 96p. (Orig.). 1994. pap. 6.95 (*0-9625444-2-6*) Matthew OH.

May I Take Your Order? American Menu Design, 1920-1960. Jim Heimann. LC 97-46569. 1998. pap. 18.95 (*0-8118-1783-0*) Chronicle Bks.

May I Touch You Now . . . Joanne N. Hoey. LC 83-70553. (Illus.). 60p. (Orig.). 1983. 10.00 (*0-940538-03-2*) Blackbird Pr Pubns.

May I Touch You Now... Joanne N. Hoey. LC 83-70553. (Illus.). 60p. (Orig.). 1983. pap. 6.00 (*0-940538-02-4*) Blackbird Pr Pubns.

May I Try It? Barbara L. McCombs & Linda Brannan. (Skills for Job Success Ser.). (Illus.). 32p. (Orig.). (YA). (gr. 7-12). 1990. teacher ed. 1.95 (*1-56119-054-3*); disk 39.95 (*1-56119-127-2*) Educ Pr MD.

May I Try It? Barbara L. McCombs & Linda Brannan. (Skills for Job Success Ser.). (Illus.). 32p. (Orig.). 1990. pap., student ed. 5.95 (*1-56119-053-5*) Educ Pr MD.

May I Try It?, Set. Barbara L. McCombs & Linda Brannan. (Skills for Job Success Ser.). (Illus.). 32p. (Orig.). (YA). (gr. 7-12). 1990. teacher ed. 54.95 (*1-56119-085-3*) Educ Pr MD.

May I Visit? Charlotte Zolotow. LC 75-25405. (Ursula Nordstrom Bk.). (Illus.). 32p. (J). (gr. k-3). 1976. 13.00 (*0-06-026932-4*) HarpC Child Bks.

May I Walk You Home: Courage & Comfort for Caregivers of the Very Ill. Joyce Hutchison & Joyce Rupp. LC 98-42005. 160p. 1999. pap. 9.95 (*0-87793-670-6*) Ave Maria.

May I Wash Your Feet. Joy Haney. LC 91-21855. (Illus.). 100p. (Orig.). (YA). 1991. pap. 6.99 (*0-932581-87-0*) Word Aflame.

May Idea Book: A Creative Idea Book for the Elementary Teacher, Ps-6. rev. ed. Karen Sevaly. (Illus.). 144p. (Orig.). 1997. pap. 10.95 (*0-943263-08-5*, TF-0500) Teachers Friend Pubns.

May Isang Sundalo: Limang Maikling Dula. Rene O. Villanueva. (TAG.). 87p. (Orig.). (C). 1988. pap. 8.75 (*971-10-0268-X*, Pub. by New Day Pub) Cellar.

May It Fill Your Soul: Experiencing Bulgarian Music. Timothy Rice. LC 93-34083. (Chicago Studies in Ethnomusicology). 386p. (C). 1994. pap. text 27.50 (*0-226-71122-6*); lib. bdg. 65.00 (*0-226-71121-8*) U Ch Pr.

May It Please the Court. James M. Beck. Ed. by O. R. McGuire. LC 75-121447. (Essay Index Reprint Ser.). 1977. 30.95 (*0-8369-1694-8*) Ayer.

***May It Please the Court.** Ed. & Narrated by Peter H. Irons. LC 00-28247. 2000. 59.95 incl. audio (*1-56584-613-3*, Pub. by New Press NY) Norton.

May It Please the Court. Irving R. Segal. LC 98-169781. 232p. 1997. pap. 15.00 (*0-8059-4228-9*) Dorrance.

May It Please the Court. James M. Beck. Ed. by O. R. McGuire. xx, 511p. 1996. reprint ed. 132.00 (*1-56169-203-4*) Gaunt.

May It Please the Court: A Biography of Judge Robert R. Merhige, Jr. Ronald J. Bacigal. LC 92-16325. 332p. (Orig.). (C). 1992. lib. bdg. 49.50 (*0-8191-8757-7*) U Pr of Amer.

May It Please the Court: A Collection of Legal Episodes. Bob Daniels. LC 98-91750. 188p. 1998. write for info. (*0-9666068-0-9*) B Daniels Ink.

***May It Please the Court! From Auto Accidents to Agent Orange - Building a Storefront Practice into America's Largest Suburban Law Firm.** Leonard L. Rivkin & Jeffrey Silberfeld. LC 99-69959. 444p. 2000. 30.00 (*0-89089-915-0*) Carolina Acad Pr.

***May it Please the Court: Judicial Processes & Politics in America.** Brian L. Porto. LC 00-35482. 2000. pap. write for info. (*0-321-03683-2*) Longman.

May It Please the Court . . . Live Recordings & Transcripts of the Supreme Court in Session. Ed. by Peter H. Irons & Stephanie Guitton. 400p. 1994. pap. 16.00 (*1-56584-052-6*, Pub. by New Press NY) Norton.

May It Please the Court: The First Amendment. Ed. by Peter H. Irons. 1997. 59.95 incl. audio (*1-56584-330-4*, Pub. by New Press NY) Norton.

May It Please the Court . . . The Most Significant Oral Arguments Made Before the Supreme Court Since 1955. Ed. by Peter H. Irons & Stephanie Guitton. LC 92-50702. (Illus.). 240p. 1993. 45.00 (*1-56584-035-6*, Pub. by New Press NY) Norton.

May It Please the Court - The First Amendment: Transcripts of the Oral Arguments Made Before the Supreme Court in Sixteen Key First Amendment Cases. Ed. by Peter Irons. (May It Please the Court Ser.: Vol. III). 272p. 1998. pap. 14.95 (*1-56584-487-4*, Pub. by New Press NY) Norton.

M

May It Please the Court Arguments on Abortion: Live Recordings & Transcripts of Supreme Court Oral Arguments on Reproductive Rights. Ed. by Stephanie Guitton & Peter H. Irons. (Illus.). 224p. 1995. pap. 27.50 incl. audio (*1-56584-223-5*, Pub. by New Press NY) Norton.

May Iverson-Her Book. Elizabeth G. Jordan. LC 75-103521. (Short Story Index Reprint Ser.). 1977. 20.95 (*0-8369-3263-3*) Ayer.

***May Maisey Moo's Cowllection of Moo Tales Vol. I: The Convention.** Vin Esoldi. (Illus.). 48p. 1999. 17.95 (*1-929745-00-1*, MMM 001, May Maisey Moo) Paula Pr Pubs.

***May Maisey Moo's Cowllection of Moo Tales Vol. I: The Convention.** aut. ed. Vin Esoldi. (Illus.). 99p. 1999. 29.95 (*1-929745-01-X*, MM 001, May Maisey Moo) Paula Pr Pubs.

May Mann Jennings: Florida's Genteel Activist. Linda D. Vance. LC 85-17963. (Illus.). 208p. 1986. pap. 24.95 (*0-8130-0750-X*) U Press Fla.

May Massee Collection: Creative Publishing for Children, 1923-1963, a Checklist. Ed. by George V. Hodowanec. (Illus.). 1979. 25.00 (*0-686-25585-2*) Emporia State.

May Monthly Activities. Janet Hale. (Monthly Activities Ser.). (Illus.). 80p. (J). (gr. 1-5). 1990. student ed. 9.95 (*1-55734-159-1*) Tchr Create Mat.

May Monthly Activities. Rice. (J). (ps). 1996. pap. text, wbk. ed. 9.95 (*1-55734-868-5*) Tchr Create Mat.

May Monthly Activities. Dona H. Rice. (Illus.). 80p. 1996. pap., teacher ed. 9.95 (*1-55734-878-2*, TCM878) Tchr Create Mat.

May 1983 Agreement over Lebanon. Laura Blum & Barry Rubin. (Pew Case Studies in International Affairs). 50p. (C). 1992. pap. text 3.50 (*1-56927-312-X*) Geo U Inst Dplmcy.

May 1990 in Romania. National Democratic Institute for International Af. 133p. 1991. pap. 6.00 (*1-880134-05-5*) Natl Demo Inst.

May 1991 Direct Mail Catalog. 1991. text. write for info. (*1-55623-611-5*, Irwn Prfssnl) McGraw-Hill Prof.

May 19: What Your Birth Date Reveals about You. (Birth Date Book Ser.). (Illus.). 80p. 1999. 4.95 (*0-8362-6061-9*) Andrews & McMeel.

May 19, 1882-Aug. 9, 1882 see Germans to America: Lists of Passengers Arriving at U. S. Ports, 1850-1893

May 9: What Your Birth Date Reveals about You. (Birth Date Book Ser.). (Illus.). 80p. 1999. 4.95 (*0-8362-6050-3*) Andrews & McMeel.

May Out West: Poems of May Swenson. May Swenson. 72p. 1996. 4.95 (*0-87421-200-6*) Utah St U Pr.

May Patterns, Projects & Plans: To Perk up Early Learning Programs. Imogene Forte. Ed. by Sally D. Sharpe. (Illus.). 80p. (Orig.). (J). (gr. 1-6). 1990. pap. text 9.95 (*0-86530-140-9*, IP 167-5) Incentive Pubns.

May Peace Be with You: Messages from "The Spoken Word" Lloyd D. Newell. LC 94-22202. xi, 263p. 1994. 13.95 (*0-87579-866-7*) Deseret Bk.

May Peace I Leave with You. Clare Shakespeare. 60p. (C). 1988. 30.00 (*0-7212-0749-9*) St Mut.

May Rides A New Pony. Bonnie Bryant. (Pony Tails Ser.: No. 8). (Illus.). 96p. (J). (gr. 4-7). 1996. pap. 3.50 (*0-553-48380-3*, Skylark BDD) BDD Bks Young Read.

May Rides a New Pony. Bonnie Bryant. (Pony Tails Ser.: No. 8). (Illus.). 96p. (J). (gr. 3-5). 1996. 8.60 (*0-606-09759-7*, Pub. by Turtleback) Demco.

May Sarton. Margot Peters. 1998. pap. 14.95 (*0-449-90798-8*) Fawcett.

May Sarton. Margot Peters. LC 96-25557. (Illus.). 474p. 1997. 30.00 (*0-679-41521-1*) Knopf.

May Sarton: A Self Portrait. May Sarton. Ed. by Marita Simpson & Martha Wheelock. (Illus.). 82p. 1988. pap. 7.95 (*0-393-30535-X*) Norton.

May Sarton: Among the Usual Days: a Portrait: Unpublished Poems, Letters, Journals & Photographs. Selected by Susan Sherman. LC 92-16082. (Illus.). 416p. 1993. 25.00 (*0-393-03451-8*) Norton.

May Sarton: Selected Letters, 1916-1954, Vol. 1. May Sarton. LC 96-43614. (Illus.). 512p. 1997. 35.00 (*0-393-03954-4*) Norton.

May Sarton: Woman & Poet. Ed. by Constance Hunting. LC 82-81944. (Man & Poet Ser.). (Illus.). 344p. 1982. 27.50 (*0-915032-55-4*); pap. 14.95 (*0-915032-56-2*) Natl Poet Foun.

May Sarton, Revisited. Elizabeth Evans. (United States Authors Ser.: No. 551). 160p. 1989. 32.00 (*0-8057-7542-0*, Twyne) Mac Lib Ref.

May 2: What Your Birth Date Reveals about You. (Birth Date Book Ser.). (Illus.). 80p. 1999. 4.95 (*0-8362-6042-2*) Andrews & McMeel.

May 2, 1872-July 31, 1872 see Germans to America: Lists of Passengers Arriving at U. S. Ports, 1850-1893

May 17: What Your Birth Date Reveals about You. (Birth Date Book Ser.). (Illus.). 80p. 1999. 4.95 (*0-8362-6059-7*) Andrews & McMeel.

May 17, 1988: One Day in an American Community. Ed. by Carol Kamman. Orig. Title: One Day in Ithica. 242p. 1989. 30.00 (*1-55787-053-5*, NY55017) Hrt of the Lakes.

May 7: What Your Birth Date Reveals about You. (Birth Date Book Ser.). (Illus.). 80p. 1999. 4.95 (*0-8362-6047-3*) Andrews & McMeel.

May 7, 1989 Panamanian Elections. National Democratic Institute for International Af. 126p. 1989. pap. 6.00 (*1-880134-01-2*) Natl Demo Inst.

May Sinclair. Hrisey D. Zegger. Ed. by Sylvia E. Bowman. (Twayne's English Authors Ser.). 176p. (C). 1976. lib. bdg. 20.95 (*0-8057-6666-9*) Irvington.

***May Sinclair: A Modern Victorian.** Suzanne Raitt. LC 99-55119. 320p. 2000. write for info. (*0-19-812298-5*) OUP.

May 16: What Your Birth Date Reveals about You. (Birth Date Book Ser.). (Illus.). 80p. 1999. 4.95 (*0-8362-6058-9*) Andrews & McMeel.

May 16th to August 15th, 1776 see Letters of Delegates to Congress, 1774-1789, Vol. 25, March 1, 1788-July 25, 1789, with Supplement, 1774-87

May 6: What Your Birth Date Reveals about You. (Birth Date Book Ser.). (Illus.). 80p. 1999. 4.95 (*0-8362-6046-5*) Andrews & McMeel.

***May '68 in French Fiction & Film: Rethinking Society, Rethinking Representation.** Margaret Atach. (Illus.). 192p. 2000. text 60.00 (*0-19-871514-5*); pap. text 24.95 (*0-19-871515-3*) OUP.

May Sky: There's Always Tomorrow: A History & Anthology of Haiku. Violet K. De Cristoforo. LC 96-49284. 200p. 1996. 29.95 (*1-55713-253-4*) Sun & Moon CA.

May Swenson: A Poet's Life in Photos. R. R. Knudson & Suzzanne F. Bigelow. LC 96-35686. (Illus.). 192p. 1996. 10.95 (*0-87421-218-9*) Utah St U Pr.

May Takes the Lead. Bonnie Bryant. (Pony Tails Ser.: No. 5). (Illus.). 96p. (J). (gr. 3-5). 1995. pap. 3.50 (*0-553-48360-9*, Skylark BDD) BDD Bks Young Read.

May Takes the Lead. Bonnie Bryant. (Pony Tails Ser.: No. 5). (Illus.). 96p. (J). (gr. 3-5). 1996. pap. 4.75 (*0-553-54248-6*) BDD Bks Young Read.

May Takes the Lead. Bonnie Bryant. (Pony Tails Ser.: No. 5). (Illus.). 96p. (J). (gr. 3-5). 1996. 8.60 (*0-606-08588-2*, Pub. by Turtleback) Demco.

May 10: What Your Birth Date Reveals about You. (Birth Date Book Ser.). (Illus.). 80p. 1999. 4.95 (*0-8362-6051-1*) Andrews & McMeel.

May The Best Man Lose. Oinstrin. 1999. text. write for info. (*0-312-00224-6*) St Martin.

May the Circle Be Unbroken: An Intimate Journey into the Heart of Adoption. Lynn C. Franklin. LC 98-7418. 288p. 1998. 24.00 (*0-517-70755-1*) Harmony Bks.

***May the Circle Be Unbroken: An Intimate Journey into the Heart of Adoption.** Lynn C. Franklin & Elizabeth Ferber. 304p. 1999. pap. 14.00 (*0-609-80480-4*) Crown Pub Group.

May the Devil Walk Behind Ye! Scottish Traveller Tales. Duncan Williamson. 188p. 1995. pap. 12.95 (*0-86241-245-5*, Pub. by Canongate Books) Interlink Pub.

May the Farce Be with You. David Rogers. 96p. 1978. pap. 5.25 (*0-87129-614-4*, M43) Dramatic Pub.

May the Fires of Revival Consume America. David A. Felts. 96p. (Orig.). 1996. pap. 7.99 (*1-888887-00-1*) Dynamic Gospel.

May the Force Be with Us, Please. Bill Amend. (Illus.). 128p. 1994. pap. 9.95 (*0-8362-1741-1*) Andrews & McMeel.

May the Light & Love Flow. Raah-ne-ah. 160p. (C). 1988. pap. write for info. (*0-7212-0767-7*, Pub. by Regency Pr GBR) St Mut.

May the Lord in His Mercy Be Kind to Belfast. Tony Parker. LC 93-40754. 1995. 25.00 (*0-8050-3053-0*); pap. 13.95 (*0-8050-3806-X*, Owl) H Holt & Co.

***May the People Live: Maori Health Development, 1900-1920.** Raeburn Lange. 300p. 2000. pap. 29.95 (*1-86940-214-6*, Pub. by Auckland Univ) Paul & Co Pubs.

May the Road Rise to Meet You: Everything You Need to Know about Irish American History. Michael Padden. LC 98-42360. 320p. 1999. pap. 13.95 (*0-452-27853-8*) NAL.

May 3: What Your Birth Date Reveals about You. (Birth Date Book Ser.). (Illus.). 80p. 1999. 4.95 (*0-8362-6043-0*) Andrews & McMeel.

May 3, 1783-February 20, 1784 see Papers of James Madison

May 3, 200 Is Coming . . . Look Busy!! Aubrey Weldon. 123p. (Orig.). 1996. pap. 6.95 (*0-9638392-1-7*) Aubre Pubng.

May 13: What Your Birth Date Reveals about You. (Birth Date Book Ser.). (Illus.). 80p. 1999. 4.95 (*0-8362-6055-4*) Andrews & McMeel.

May 30: What Your Birth Date Reveals about You. (Birth Date Book Ser.). (Illus.). 80p. 1999. 4.95 (*0-8362-6073-2*) Andrews & McMeel.

May 30 Movement. Rigby. (Australian National University Press Ser.). 1980. 37.00 (*0-08-033001-0*, Pergamon Pr) Elsevier.

May 31: What Your Birth Date Reveals about You. (Birth Date Book Ser.). (Illus.). 80p. 1999. 4.95 (*0-8362-6074-0*) Andrews & McMeel.

May This House Be Safe from Tigers. Alexander King. Date not set. lib. bdg. 22.95 (*0-8488-2151-3*) Amereon Ltd.

May 12: What Your Birth Date Reveals about You. (Birth Date Book Ser.). (Illus.). 80p. 1999. 4.95 (*0-8362-6054-6*) Andrews & McMeel.

May 20: What Your Birth Date Reveals about You. (Birth Date Book Ser.). (Illus.). 80p. 1999. 4.95 (*0-8362-6062-7*) Andrews & McMeel.

May 28: What Your Birth Date Reveals about You. (Birth Date Book Ser.). (Illus.). 80p. 1999. 4.95 (*0-8362-6071-6*) Andrews & McMeel.

May 28, 1853-Oct. 24, 1853 see Germans to America: Lists of Passengers Arriving at U. S. Ports, 1850-1893

May 25: What Your Birth Date Reveals about You. (Birth Date Book Ser.). (Illus.). 80p. 1999. 4.95 (*0-8362-6068-6*) Andrews & McMeel.

May 21: What Your Birth Date Reveals about You. (Birth Date Book Ser.). (Illus.). 80p. 1999. 4.95 (*0-8362-6063-5*) Andrews & McMeel.

May 24: What Your Birth Date Reveals about You. (Birth Date Book Ser.). (Illus.). 80p. 1999. 4.95 (*0-8362-6067-8*) Andrews & McMeel.

May 24,1851-June 5,1852 see Germans to America: Lists of Passengers Arriving at U. S. Ports, 1850-1893

May 29: What Your Birth Date Reveals about You. (Birth Date Book Ser.). (Illus.). 80p. 1999. 4.95 (*0-8362-6072-4*) Andrews & McMeel.

May 22: What Your Birth Date Reveals about You. (Birth Date Book Ser.). (Illus.). 80p. 1999. 4.95 (*0-8362-6064-3*) Andrews & McMeel.

May 27, 1787-March 3, 1788 see Papers of James Madison

May 27: What Your Birth Date Reveals about You. (Birth Date Book Ser.). (Illus.). 80p. 1999. 4.95 (*0-8362-6070-8*) Andrews & McMeel.

May 26: What Your Birth Date Reveals about You. (Birth Date Book Ser.). (Illus.). 80p. 1999. 4.95 (*0-8362-6069-4*) Andrews & McMeel.

May 23: What Your Birth Date Reveals about You. (Birth Date Book Ser.). (Illus.). 80p. 1999. 4.95 (*0-8362-6065-1*) Andrews & McMeel.

May We All Remember Well: A Journal of the History & Cultures of Western North Carolina. Ed. by Robert S. Brunk. (Illus.). 288p. (Orig.). 1997. pap. 40.00 (*0-9656461-0-6*) R S Brunk.

May We Sleep Here Tonight? Tan Koide. LC 99-34963. (Illus.). 32p. (ps-3). 2000. reprint ed. per. 12.95 (*0-689-83288-5*) McElderry Bks.

May Week Was in June. large type ed. Clive James. 328p. 1991. 24.95 (*1-85089-551-1*, Pub. by ISIS Lrg Prnt) Transaction Pubs.

May You Always. Stuart Isacoff & Michele Baumann. pap. 14.95 (*0-943748-80-1*) Ekay Music.

May You Be the Mother of a Hundred Sons: A Journey among the Women of India. Elisabeth Bumiller. 320p. 1991. pap. 12.00 (*0-449-90614-0*) Fawcett.

***May You Grow in Grace.** C. R. Gibson. 2000. 7.95 (*0-7667-4843-X*) Gibson.

May You Live in Interesting Times. Loa Dee. 964p. 1998. write for info. (*0-7541-0285-8*) Communs Plus.

May You Live in Interesting Times. Tereze Gluck. LC 95-9444. (Iowa Short Fiction Award Ser.). 177p. 1995. 22.95 (*0-87745-519-8*) U of Iowa Pr.

May You Never Stop Dancing: A Professor's Letters to His Daughter. John D. Lawry. LC 98-230569. 136p. (C). 1998. pap. 13.95 (*0-88489-535-1*) St Marys.

May Your Days Be Merry & Bright: And Other Christmas Stories by Women. Ed. & Intro. by Susan Koppelman. 272p. 1991. mass mkt. 5.99 (*0-451-62837-3*, Ment) NAL.

May Your Days Be Merry & Bright: And Other Christmas Stories by Women. Compiled by Susan Koppelman. LC 88-21784. 260p. (C). 1988. 21.95 (*0-8143-2124-0*) Wayne St U Pr.

May Your Marriage Be a Happy One. rev. ed. John M. Drescher. 16p. 1989. pap. text 2.99 (*0-8361-3484-2*) Herald Pr.

Maya. Ed. by Robert Adkinson. LC 95-61825. (Sacred Symbols Ser.). (Illus.). 80p. 1996. 10.00 (*0-500-06022-3*, Pub. by Thames Hudson) Norton.

Maya. Peter Chrisp. LC 93-46604. (Look into the Past Ser.). (Illus.). 32p. (J). (gr. 4-6). 1994. 22.83 (*1-56847-170-X*) Raintree Steck-V.

Maya. Alexander Cockburn. (Illus.). 160p. 1999. 19.95 (*0-8478-2176-5*) Rizzoli Intl.

Maya. Kathryn Ellis. (Degrassi Book Ser.). 150p. (J). (gr. 7-9). 1995. mass mkt. 4.95 (*1-55028-361-8*); bds. 16.95 (*1-55028-363-4*) Formac Dist Ltd.

Maya. Jacqueline D. Greene. Ed. by Iris Rosoff. LC 91-29433. (First Bks.). (Illus.). 64p. (J). (gr. 3-5). 1992. lib. bdg. 22.00 (*0-531-20067-1*) Watts.

Maya. Patricia McKissack. LC 85-9927. (New True Books Ser.). (Illus.). 45p. (J). (gr. 2-3). 1985. pap. 5.50 (*0-516-41270-1*); lib. bdg. 21.00 (*0-516-01270-3*) Childrens.

Maya. Nirmala Moorthy. LC 97-904976. 1997. write for info. (*0-14-026533-3*) Penguin Books.

Maya. Robert Nicholson. LC 94-43691. (Illus.). 32p. (J). (gr. 4-7). 1994. lib. bdg. 15.95 (*0-7910-2705-8*) Chelsea Hse.

Maya. Robert Nicholson. LC 94-43691. (Illus.). 32p. (J). (gr. 4-7). 1994. pap. 7.95 (*0-7910-2729-5*) Chelsea Hse.

Maya. Robert Nicholson. (Journey into Civilization Ser.). (J). 1994. 13.15 (*0-606-07852-5*) Turtleback.

***Maya.** Henri Stierlin. 1998. 38.99 (*3-8228-7563-5*) Benedikt Taschen.

Maya. D. N. Stuefloten. 138p. 1992. 18.95 (*0-932511-58-9*); pap. 8.95 (*0-932511-59-7*) Fiction Coll.

Maya. 5th rev. ed. Michael D. Coe. LC 92-63273. (Illus.). 224p. 1993. pap. 16.95 (*0-500-27716-8*, Pub. by Thames Hudson) Norton.

Maya. 6th rev. expanded ed. Michael D. Coe. LC 98-60191. (Illus.). 256p. 1999. pap. 18.95 (*0-500-28066-5*, Pub. by Thames Hudson) Norton.

Maya: An Introduction. (Peabody Museum Press Ser.). (Illus.). 8p. 1974. pap. 2.00 (*0-87365-995-3*) Peabody Harvard.

Maya: Life, Myth, & Art. Timothy Laughton. (Illus.). 144p. 1998. 27.50 (*1-55670-823-8*) Stewart Tabori & Chang.

Maya: The Most Comprehensive Illustrated Survey of Mayan Culture. Palazzo Crassi Metropolitan Museum of Art. (Illus.). 695p. 2000. 85.00 (*0-8478-2129-3*, Pub. by Rizzoli Intl) St Martin.

Maya & Spaniard in Yucatan, 1648-1812. Robert W. Patch. LC 92-25923. 344p. 1993. 49.50 (*0-8047-2062-2*) Stanford U Pr.

Maya & the Town That Loved a Tree. Kiki Shaw & Kathryn Shaw. (Illus.). 32p. (J). (ps-1). 1993. 14.95 (*0-87663-796-9*, Pub. by Universe) St Martin.

Maya Angelou. Ed. by Harold Bloom. LC 97-50357. (Modern Critical Views Ser.). 300p. (YA). 1999. 34.95 (*0-7910-4782-2*) Chelsea Hse.

***Maya Angelou.** Harold Bloom. (Major Poets Ser.). 2000. 19.95 (*0-7910-5937-5*) Chelsea Hse.

***Maya Angelou.** Terrasita A. Cuffie. LC 99-20045. (Importance of Ser.). (Illus.). 80p. (YA). (gr. 4-9). 1999. lib. bdg. 23.70 (*1-56006-532-X*) Lucent Bks.

Maya Angelou. Judith E. Harper. LC 98-45559. (Journey to Freedom Ser.). (Illus.). 32p. (J). (gr. 2-6). 1999. lib. bdg. 24.21 (*1-56766-570-5*) Childs World.

***Maya Angelou.** Patricia L. Kite. LC 98-15763. (A&E Biography Ser.). 112p. (YA). (gr. 6-9). 1999. 25.26 (*0-8225-4944-1*) Lerner Pub.

Maya Angelou. Nancy Shuker. Ed. by Emily Easton. (Genius! The Artist & the Process Ser.). (Illus.). 128p. (J). (gr. 7-9). 1990. pap. 4.95 (*0-382-24267-X*) Silver Burdett Pr.

Maya Angelou. Nancy Shuker. (Genius! The Artist & the Process Ser.). 128p. (J). 1996. pap. 4.95 (*0-382-24647-0*) Silver Burdett Pr.

Maya Angelou. Ed. by Mary E. Williams. LC 96-36473. (Literary Companion Ser.). 1997. lib. bdg. 26.20 (*1-56510-631-8*) Greenhaven.

Maya Angelou. Ed. by Mary E. Williams. LC 96-36473. (Literary Companion Ser.). (YA). (gr. 9-12). 1997. pap. 16.20 (*1-56510-630-X*) Greenhaven.

Maya Angelou: A Critical Companion. Mary Jane Lupton. LC 98-17489. (Critical Companions to Popular Contemporary Writers Ser.). 200p. 1998. 29.95 (*0-313-30325-8*, Greenwood Pr) Greenwood.

Maya Angelou: Author. Pamela Loos. LC 99-19890. (Overcoming Adversity Ser.). (Illus.). 128p. (YA). (gr. 4-7). 1999. pap. 9.95 (*0-7910-4947-7*) Chelsea Hse.

Maya Angelou: Author. Pamela Loos. LC 99-19890. (Overcoming Adversity Ser.). (Illus.). 128p. (YA). (gr. 5 up). 1999. lib. bdg. 19.95 (*0-7910-4946-9*) Chelsea Hse.

Maya Angelou: Author. Miles Shapiro. Ed. by Nathan I. Huggins. (Black Americans of Achievement Ser.). (Illus.). 124p. (YA). (gr. 5 up). 1993. pap. 8.95 (*0-7910-1891-1*) Chelsea Hse.

Maya Angelou: Author. Miles Shapiro. Ed. by Nathan I. Huggins. (Black Americans of Achievement Ser.). (Illus.). 124p. (YA). (gr. 5 up). 1994. lib. bdg. 19.95 (*0-7910-1862-8*) Chelsea Hse.

Maya Angelou: Greeting the Morning. Sarah E. King. LC 93-4572. (Gateway Biographies Ser.). 48p. (J). (gr. 2-4). 1994. pap. 7.95 (*1-56294-725-7*) Millbrook Pr.

Maya Angelou: Greeting the Morning. Sarah E. King. LC 93-4572. (Gateway Biographies Ser.). (Illus.). 48p. (J). (gr. 2-4). 1994. lib. bdg. 20.90 (*1-56294-431-2*) Millbrook Pr.

Maya Angelou: Greeting the Morning. Sarah E. King. 1994. 12.15 (*0-606-12420-9*, Pub. by Turtleback) Demco.

Maya Angelou: Journey of the Heart. Jayne Pettit. 80p. 1998. pap. 4.99 (*0-14-038359-X*, PuffinBks) Peng Put Young Read.

Maya Angelou: Journey of the Heart. Jayne Pettit. 1998. 9.19 (*0-606-12991-X*, Pub. by Turtleback) Demco.

Maya Angelou: More Than a Poet. Elaine S. Lisandrelli. (African-American Biographies Ser.). 128p. (YA). (gr. 6 up). 1996. lib. bdg. 20.95 (*0-89490-684-4*) Enslow Pubs.

Maya Angelou: Poems. Maya Angelou. 1986. 10.60 (*0-606-03854-X*, Pub. by Turtleback) Demco.

***Maya Angelou: The Poetry of Living.** Margaret Courtney-Clarke. LC 99-34225. 132p. 1999. 22.50 (*0-609-60458-9*) C Potter.

Maya Angelou: Woman of Words, Deeds, & Dreams. Stuart A. Kallen. Ed. by Rosemary Wallner. LC 93-13877. (I Have a Dream Ser.). 1993. lib. bdg. 15.98 (*1-56239-257-3*) ABDO Pub Co.

***Maya Angelou: Writer & Documentary Filmmaker.** Lucia Raatma. LC 00-37582. (Career Biographies Ser.). (Illus.). 2000. write for info. (*0-89434-336-X*) Ferguson.

Maya Angelou's I Know Why the Caged Bird Sings see Bloom's Notes

Maya Angelou's I Know Why the Caged Bird Sings. Maya Angelou. Ed. & Intro. by Harold Bloom. 1997. pap. text 4.95 (*0-7910-4129-8*) Chelsea Hse.

Maya Angelou's I Know Why the Caged Bird Sings: A Casebook. Joanne M. Braxton & Maya Angelou. LC 98-13295. (Casebooks in Contemporary Fiction Ser.). (Illus.). 176p. 1998. pap. 13.95 (*0-19-511607-0*) OUP.

Maya Archaeologist. Eric S. Thompson. LC 63-8994. (Illus.). 302p. 1994. pap. 14.95 (*0-8061-1206-9*) U of Okla Pr.

Maya Architecture of the Central Yucatan Peninsula, Mexico. David F. Potter. (Publications: No. 44). (Illus.). xi, 118p. 1977. 20.00 (*0-939238-49-7*) Tulane MARI.

Maya Art & Architecture. Mary Ellen Miller. LC 99-70938. (World of Art Ser.). (Illus.). 240p. (Orig.). 1999. pap. 14.95 (*0-500-20327-X*, Pub. by Thames Hudson) Norton.

***Maya Arts & Crafts of Guatemala: Artes y Artesanias de Guatemala.** Marilyn Anderson. (SPA.). 64p. 2000. pap. 9.95 (*1-886502-36-6*) Yax Te Found.

Maya-Atlantis: Queen Moo & the Egyptian Sphinx. Augustus LePlongeon & Paul M. Allen. LC 73-186768. (Illus.). 424p. 1991. reprint ed. pap. 16.95 (*0-89345-238-6*, Steinerbks) Garber Comm.

Maya Atlas: Fighting for Land Rights in Southern Belize. Toledo Maya Cultural Council Staff & Toledo Alcaldes Association Staff. LC 97-15801. (Illus.). 150p. (Orig.). 1997. pap. text 25.00 (*1-55643-256-9*) North Atlantic.

Maya, Aztecs & Incas Pop-Up. Duncan Birmingham. (Tarquin Pop-up Ser.). (Illus.). 32p. (J). (gr. 3 up). 1985. pap. 8.95 (*0-906212-37-5*, Pub. by Tarquin Pubns) Parkwest Pubns.

Maya Ball Court: Sacred Ritual, Ultimate Game. Victoria Sauers. 194p. 1999. pap. 14.95 (*0-9666294-1-8*) Blue Bear Pr.

Maya Calendar: Voice of the Galaxy. Raymond Mardyks & Stacia Alana-Leah. (Illus.). 126p. (Orig.). 1999. pap. 13.00 (*0-9644180-2-9*, Pub. by Star Heart) New Leaf Dist.

M

An Asterisk (*) at the beginning of an entry indicates that the title is appearing for the first time.

Maya Chronicles. Ed. by Daniel G. Brinton. LC 70-83457. (Library of Aboriginal American Literature: No. 1). reprint ed. 37.50 (*0-404-52181-9*) AMS Pr.

Maya Civilization. John M. Weeks. LC 92-22798. (Research Guide to Ancient Civilizations Ser.: Vol. 1). (Illus.). 440p. 1993. text 30.00 (*0-8153-0095-6*, H1796) Garland.

Maya Civilization. George W. Brainerd. LC 76-43669. reprint ed. 39.50 (*0-404-15503-0*) AMS Pr.

Maya Civilization. George W. Brainerd. (Illus.). 93p. 1963. reprint ed. 3.00 (*0-916561-52-6*) Southwest Mus.

Maya Civilization, 1990-1995: A Research Guide. Ed. by John M. Weeks. (Research Guides to Ancient Civilizations Ser.: Vol. 2). (Illus.). 332p. 1997. 30.00 (*0-911437-70-3*) Labyrinthos.

Maya Color: The Painted Villages of Mesoamerica. Jeffrey Becom & Sally J. Aberg. LC 97-8347. (Illus.). 180p. 1997. 50.00 (*0-7892-0215-8*) Abbeville Pr.

Maya Conquistador. Matthew Restall. LC 98-15751. (Illus.). 272p. 1998. 25.00 (*0-8070-5506-9*) Beacon Pr.

Maya Conquistador. Matthew Restall. LC 98-15751. (Illus.). 272p. 1999. pap. 18.00 (*0-8070-5507-7*) Beacon Pr.

Maya Cosmogensis 2012: The True Meaning of the Maya Calendar End Date. John M. Jenkins. (Illus.). 464p. 1998. pap. 20.00 (*1-879181-48-7*) Bear & Co.

Maya Cosmos: 3000 Years on the Shaman's Path. David Freidel et al. (Illus.). 560p. 1995. pap. 16.00 (*0-688-14069-6*, Quil) HarperTrade.

Maya Cultural Activism in Guatemala. Edward F. Fischer. LC 96-28480. 1996. 30.00 (*0-292-70850-5*); pap. text 16.95 (*0-292-70851-3*) U of Tex Pr.

Maya Culture & Costume: A Catalogue of the Taylor Museum's E. B. Ricketson Collection of Guatemalan Textiles. Christine Conte. LC 84-40115. (Illus.). 120p. (Orig.). 1984. pap. 15.00 (*0-916537-00-5*, Taylor Museum) CO Springs Fine Arts.

Maya Designs. Wilson G. Turner. (Illus.). 48p. 1980. pap. 4.95 (*0-486-24047-9*) Dover.

***Maya Diaspora: Guatemalan Roots, New American Lives.** Ed. by James Loucky & Marilyn M. Moors. (Illus.). 248p. 2000. 64.50 (*1-56639-794-4*); pap. 22.95 (*1-56639-795-2*) Temple U Pr.

Maya Divine & Human. Teun Goudriaan. 1978. 28.00 (*0-89684-040-9*, Pub. by Motilal Bnarsidass) S Asia.

Maya Epic. Evan Bennett & Robert Somerlott. 135p. 1974. 12.95 (*0-686-27297-8*) U Wisc-River Falls Pr.

Maya Ethnohistory: A Guide to Spanish Colonial Documents at Tozzer Library, Harvard University. John M. Weeks. Ed. by Ronald M. Spores & Paula M. McNutt. (Vanderbilt University Publications in Anthropology: No. 34). 121p. (Orig.). 1987. pap. text 9.75 (*0-935462-25-2*) VUPA.

Maya for Travelers & Students: A Guide to Language & Culture in Yucatan. Gary Bevington. LC 93-48159. (Illus.). 168p. 1995. text 37.50 (*0-292-70838-6*); pap. text 14.95 (*0-292-70812-2*) U of Tex Pr.

Maya Glyphs. S. D. Houston. 1989. pap. 13.95 (*0-520-06771-1*, Pub. by U CA Pr) Cal Prin Full Svc.

Maya Glyphs: The Verbs. Linda Schele. 439p. (C). 1982. text 65.00 (*0-292-75066-8*) U of Tex Pr.

Maya Grammar. Alfred M. Tozzer. (HU PMP Ser.: Vol. 9). 1921. 30.00 (*0-527-01215-7*) Periodicals Srv.

Maya History & Religion. J. Eric Thompson. LC 72-88144. (Civilization of the American Indian Ser.: Vol. 99). 446p. 1990. pap. 21.95 (*0-8061-2247-1*) U of Okla Pr.

Maya Iconography. Ed. by Elizabeth P. Benson & Gillett G. Griffin. LC 87-26372. (Illus.). 395p. reprint ed. pap. 122.50 (*0-608-06307-X*, 206666900008) Bks Demand.

Maya in Exile: Guatemalans in Florida. Allan F. Burns. LC 92-22774. (Illus.). 224p. 1993. 59.95 (*1-56639-035-4*); pap. 18.95 (*1-56639-036-2*) Temple U Pr.

Maya in Physics: 6 Meanings Other Than Illusion. N. C. Panda. (C). 1991. 32.00 (*81-208-0698-0*, Pub. by Motilal Bnarsidass) S Asia.

Maya in Radhakrishnan's Thought: Six Meanings Other Than Illusion. Donald A. Braue. 1985. 15.00 (*0-8364-1129-3*) S Asia.

Maya in Sankara: Measuring the Immeasurable. L. Thomas O'Neal. 1980. 16.00 (*0-8364-0611-7*) S Asia.

Maya Indians see Junior Library of American Indians

Maya Indians of Southern Yucatan & Northern British Honduras. Ed. by Thomas W. Gann. (Bureau of American Ethnology Bulletins Ser.). 146p. 1995. lib. bdg. 79.00 (*0-7812-4064-6*) Rprt Serv.

Maya Indians of Southern Yucatan & Northern British Honduras. Thomas W. Gann. (Smithsonian Institution, Annual Reports of the Board of Regents: Vol. 64). (Illus.). 290p. 1918. pap. text 30.63 (*1-55567-885-8*) Coyote Press.

Maya Indians of Southern Yucatan & Northern British Honduras. Thomas W. Gann. 1988. reprint ed. lib. bdg. 79.00 (*0-7812-0057-1*) Rprt Serv.

Maya Indians of Yucatan. Morris Steggerda. LC 77-11524. (Carnegie Institution of Washington. Publications: No. 531). reprint ed. 64.50 (*0-404-16283-5*) AMS Pr.

***Maya-K'iche' und Spanisch - Sprachkontakt und Sprachkonflikt in Guatemala: Eine Soziolinguistische Beschreibung der Comunidad de Zunil.** Renate B. Grotehusmann. (GER.). 248p. 1999. 39.95 (*3-631-34671-9*) P Lang Pubng.

Maya Lin. Bettina Ling. LC 96-45935. (Contemporary Asian Americans Ser.). (Illus.). 48p. (J). 1997. lib. bdg. 24.26 (*0-8172-3992-8*) Raintree Steck-V.

***Maya Lin: American Academy in Rome, 10 Dicembre 1998-21 Febbraio 1999.** Maya Y. Lin et al. LC 99-197257. 99p. 1998. write for info. (*88-435-6832-9*, Pub. by Electa) Gingko Press.

Maya Lin: Architect & Artist. Mary Malone. LC 94-5333. (People to Know Ser.). (Illus.). 112p. (YA). (gr. 6 up). 1995. lib. bdg. 20.95 (*0-89490-499-X*) Enslow Pubs.

Maya Lin: Topologies. Maya Ying Lin et al. LC 98-60066. 56 p. 1998. write for info. (*1-888826-05-3*) SEC Contemp Art.

Maya Lin, Architect. Lynn Yokoe. (Illus.). (J). (gr. 1-4). 1995. pap. 4.95 (*0-8136-5735-0*); lib. bdg. 10.60 (*0-8136-5729-6*) Modern Curr.

Maya Maritime Trade, Settlement, & Populations on Ambergris Caye, Belize. Ed. by Thomas H. Guderjan et al. LC 93-85954. (Maya Research Program Ser.). (Illus.). 212p. (Orig.). (C). 1995. pap. text 25.00 (*0-911437-21-5*) Labyrinthos.

Maya Missions: Exploring the Spanish Colonial Churches of Yucatan. Richard Perry & Rosalind W. Perry. (Illus.). 256p. (Orig.). 1988. pap. 12.95 (*0-9620811-0-8*) Espadana Pr.

Maya Monuments: Sculptures of Unknown Provenance in Europe. Karl H. Mayer. Tr. by Sandra L. Brizee from GER. (Illus.). 1978. pap. 20.00 (*0-916552-11-X*) Acoma Bks.

Maya Monuments: Sculptures of Unknown Provenance in the U. S. Karl H. Mayer. (Illus.). 1980. pap. 30.00 (*0-916552-16-0*) Acoma Bks.

Maya Moon. Marianne Mitchell. (Illus.). (J). (gr. k-2). 1995. pap. 8.95 incl. audio (*0-7608-0494-X*); pap. 4.95 (*1-56801-794-4*); pap. 8.95 incl. audio (*0-7608-0499-0*); pap. 4.95 (*1-56801-358-2*) Sundance Pub.

Maya Moon, Big bk. Marianne Mitchell. (Illus.). (J). (gr. k-2). 1995. pap. 17.95 (*1-56801-793-6*); pap. 17.95 (*1-56801-335-3*) Sundance Pub.

Maya of Central America see Cultures of the Past - Group 2

Maya of East Central Quintana Roo. Rojas A. Villa. LC 77-11527. (Carnegie Institution of Washington Publications: No. 559). reprint ed. 47.50 (*0-404-16286-X*) AMS Pr.

Maya of Guatemala: Their Life & Dress. Carmen L. Pettersen. LC 76-42102. (Illus.). 276p. 1977. 60.00 (*0-295-95537-6*) U of Wash Pr.

***Maya Prophecy.** Ronald A. Bonewitz. (Guides Ser.). 144p. 2000. pap. 6.95 (*0-7499-1959-0*, Pub. by Piatkus Bks) London Brdge.

Maya Red. J. R. Humphreys. LC 88-63898. 254p. (Orig.). (C). 1989. pap. 9.95 (*0-943433-01-0*) Cane Hill Pr.

Maya Resistance to Spanish Rule: Time & History on a Colonial Frontier. Grant D. Jones. LC 89-36041. 383p. reprint ed. pap. 118.80 (*0-7837-5859-6*, 204557800006) Bks Demand.

Maya Resurgence in Guatemala: Qeqchi Experiences. Richard Wilson. LC 94-36177. (Illus.). 392p. 1995. 34.95 (*0-8061-2690-6*) U of Okla Pr.

***Maya Resurgence in Guatemala: Q'eqchi' Experiences.** Richard Wilson. (Illus.). 392p. 1999. pap. 17.95 (*0-8061-3195-0*) U of Okla Pr.

Maya Rulers of Time: A Study of Architectural Sculpture at Tikal, Guatemala. Arthur G. Miller. LC 86-7010. (Illus.). 96p. reprint ed. pap. 30.00 (*0-608-18330-X*, 203161100075) Bks Demand.

Maya Saints & Souls in a Changing World. John M. Watanabe. (Illus.). 296p. (Orig.). (C). 1992. pap. 15.95 (*0-292-75141-9*) U of Tex Pr.

Maya Salt Production & Trade. Anthony P. Andrews. LC 83-9306. 173p. 1983. 25.95 (*0-8165-0813-5*) U of Ariz Pr.

Maya Sculpture of Copan: The Iconography. Claude-Francois Baudez. LC 93-43681. (Illus.). 320p. 1994. 65.00 (*0-8061-2594-2*) U of Okla Pr.

Maya Settlement in Northwestern Belize: The 1988 & 1990 Seasons of the Rio Bravo Archaeological Project. Ed. by Thomas H. Guderjan. LC 91-75725. (Illus.). 130p. (Orig.). (C). 1991. pap. text 28.00 (*0-911437-13-4*) Labyrinthos.

Maya Skull from Uloa Valley, Honduras see Studies in Middle America

Maya Society under Colonial Rule: The Collective Enterprise of Survival. Nancy M. Farriss. LC 83-43071. (Illus.). 584p. 1984. pap. text 35.00 (*0-691-10158-2*, Pub. by Princeton U Pr) Cal Prin Full Svc.

Maya-Spanish Crosses in Yucatan. George D. Williams. (HU PMP Ser.: Vol. 13, No. 1). 1931. 25.00 (*0-527-01228-9*) Periodicals Srv.

Maya Stone Tools of Dzibilchaltun, Yucatan, & Becau & Chicanna, Campedie. Irwin Rovner & Suzanne H. Lewenstein. LC 97-19488. (Publication Ser.: No. 65). 1997. write for info. (*0-939238-95-0*) Tulane MARI.

Maya Subsistence. Ed. by Kent V. Flannery. (Studies in Archaeology). 1982. text 85.00 (*0-12-259780-X*) Acad Pr.

Maya Textile Tradition. Ed. & Text by Margot B. Schevill. LC 96-30451. (Illus.). 232p. 1997. 49.50 (*0-8109-4291-7*, Pub. by Abrams) Time Warner.

Maya Textiles of Guatemala: The Gustavus A. Eisen Collection, 1902. Margot B. Schevill. LC 92-18640. (Illus.). 320p. (C). 1993. pap. 29.95 (*0-292-77665-9*); text 65.00 (*0-292-75143-5*) U of Tex Pr.

***Maya, Tiger Cub.** Theresa Radcliffe. 32p. (J). 1999. 14.99 (*0-670-87894-4*, Viking Child) Peng Put Young Read.

Maya Trilogy: Plays about Augustus & Alice Le Plongeon. 2nd rev. ed. Martha Keltz. LC 99-70769. (Illus.). 64p. 1994. pap. 14.00 (*1-893592-04-9*, TC Pubs) Studio Eds.

Maya Two: Characters Animation. 450p. 1999. 59.99 (*0-7357-0866-5*) Macmillan Tech.

Maya Vase Book Vol. 4: A Corpus of Rollout Photographs of Maya Vases. Ed. by Barbara Kerr. (Illus.). 183p. 1994. pap. 45.00 (*0-9624208-3-2*) Kerr NY.

Maya Vase Book Vol. 5: A Corpus of Rollout Photographs of Maya Vases. Ed. by Barbara Kerr. (Illus.). 186p. 1997. spiral bd. 45.00 (*0-9624208-4-0*) Kerr NY.

Maya Vase Book Vol. 6: A Corpus of Rollout Photographs of Maya Vases. Justin Kerr et al. Ed. by Barbara Kerr. (Illus.). 186p. (C). 2001. spiral bd. 45.00 (*0-9624208-5-9*) Kerr NY.

Maya World. Peter Eltringham. 468p. 1999. pap. 19.95 (*1-85828-406-6*) Penguin Putnam.

Maya World: Yucatec Culture & Society, 1550-1850. Matthew Restall. LC 96-26167. 1997. 66.00 (*0-8047-2745-7*) Stanford U Pr.

Maya World: Yucatec Culture & Society, 1550-1950. Matthew Restall. 1999. pap. text 24.95 (*0-8047-3658-8*) Stanford U Pr.

Maya y el Truco Para Hacer la Tarea. Jo Pestum. (SPA.). (J). (gr. 3-4). 1995. pap. 5.99 (*968-16-4727-0*, Pub. by Fondo) Continental Bk.

Maya Year. Cyrus Thomas. (Bureau of American Ethnology Bulletins Ser.). 64p. 1995. lib. bdg. 79.00 (*0-7812-4018-2*) Rprt Serv.

Maya Year. Ed. by Cyrus Thomas. 1988. reprint ed. lib. bdg. 49.00 (*0-7812-0030-X*) Rprt Serv.

Maya/Atlantis: Queen Moo & the Egyptian Sphinx. Augustus Le Plongeon. 418p. 1997. reprint ed. pap. 29.95 (*0-7661-0102-9*) Kessinger Pub.

Mayaguez Institute of Tropical Agriculture, Puerto Rico: A Bibliography of Publications. Mayaguez Institute of Tropical Agriculture Staff. (Studies in Tropical Agriculture). 1980. lib. bdg. 59.95 (*0-8490-3072-2*) Gordon Pr.

Mayakovsky--Plays. Vladimir Mayakovsky. Tr. by Guy Daniels. (European Drama Classics Ser.). 276p. 1995. pap. 15.95 (*0-8101-1339-2*) Northwestern U Pr.

Mayakovsky Centennial, 1893-1993: A Commemoration of the Life, Work, & Times of Vladimir Mayakovsky: Proceedings of a Symposium. Ed. by Anne D. Perryman & Patricia J. Thompson. 196p. (C). Date not set. write for info. (*0-9640564-0-2*) Lehman College.

Mayamatam: Treatise of Housing, Architecture & Iconography, 2 vols., Set. Ed. by Bruno Dagens. (C). 1995. 98.50 (*81-208-1026-0*, Pub. by Motilal Bnarsidass); 98.50 (*0-614-09993-5*, Pub. by Motilal Bnarsidass) S Asia.

Mayan. La Loca. Ed. by Pamala Karol. (Illus.). 39p. 1988. pap. 10.00 (*0-9619965-0-1*) Bone Scan Pr.

***Mayan & Aztec Mythology.** Michael Schuman. LC 00-28779. (Mythology Ser.). 2000. write for info. (*0-7660-1409-6*) Enslow Pubs.

***Mayan Astronomer in Hell's Kitchen: Poems.** Martin Espada. LC 99-52626. 88p. 2000. 21.00 (*0-393-04888-8*) Norton.

Mayan Birthday Decoding Kit: Decoder, Guidebook & Galactic Signature Pad. Holly Davison. (Illus.). 72p. 1998. pap. 20.00 (*1-892102-03-X*) Design Mat.

Mayan Calendar Birthday Book: Ephemeris/Guide, Easy Reference Handbook for Finding & Understanding Your Birthday Solar Glyph & Tone. Mary F. Koppa. LC 96-94576. (Illus.). 144p. 1996. pap. write for info. (*1-889965-03-0*) Mayan Cal Art.

Mayan Calendar Guidebook. Rich Eagle. Ed. by Will Palmer & Krishna Gopa. (Illus.). 106p. (Orig.). 1995. pap. 17.99 (*0-9649098-7-1*) Sacred Earth.

Mayan Cooking: Classic Recipes from Sun Kingdoms of the Yucatan. Cherry Hamman. LC 97-41256. (Illus.). 250p. 1998. 24.95 (*0-7818-0580-5*) Hippocrene Bks.

Mayan Darpan & Other Stories. Nirmal Verma. 248p. 1986. pap. 8.95 (*0-19-561872-6*) OUP.

Mayan Design Book. Caren Caraway. (International Design Library). (Illus.). 56p. 1981. pap. 6.95 (*0-916144-80-1*) Stemmer Hse.

Mayan Drifter: Chicano Poet in the Lowlands of America. Juan F. Herrera. LC 96-16324. 330p. 1997. 69.95 (*1-56639-481-3*); pap. 22.95 (*1-56639-482-1*) Temple U Pr.

Mayan Factor: Path Beyond Technology. Jose Arguelles. LC 87-960. (Illus.). 224p. 1987. pap. 16.00 (*0-939680-38-6*) Bear & Co.

Mayan Folktale: An Introduction. Fernando Penalosa. 128p. (Orig.). 1996. pap. 9.95 (*1-886502-09-9*) Yax Te Found.

Mayan Folktales: Folklore from Lake Atitlban, Guatemala. Ed. & Tr. by James D. Sexton. LC 98-48990. 302p. (gr. 4-7). 1999. pap. 14.95 (*0-8263-2104-6*) U of NM Pr.

Mayan, Incan & Aztec Civilizations. Michael Kramme. (Illus.). 128p. (YA). (gr. 5). 1996. pap. text 11.95 (*1-58037-051-9*, Pub. by M Twain Media) Carson-Dellos.

Mayan Languages: A Comparative Vocabulary, 3 vols., Set. John M. Dienhart. 1010p. 1989. 225.00 (*87-7492-722-1*) Coronet Bks.

Mayan Life. Gaspar P. Gonzalez. Tr. by Elaine Elliott from ENG. LC 95-199716. 230p. (Orig.). 1995. pap. 9.95 (*1-886502-01-3*) Yax Te Found.

Mayan Life: Source & Symbol: The Paintings of Nicolas Reanda Quieju. Margaret Archuleta et al. LC 96-28449. 1996. write for info. (*0-934351-55-4*) Heard Mus.

Mayan Oracle: Return Path to the Stars. Ariel Spilsbury & Michael Bryner. LC 91-41670. (Illus.). 336p. 1992. 34.95 (*0-939680-86-6*) Bear & Co.

***Mayan People Within & Beyond Boundaries: Social Categories & Lived Identity in Yucatan.** Peter Hervik. (Studies in Anthropology & History: Vol. 25). 195p. 1999. text 48.00 (*90-5702-340-7*, Harwood Acad Pubs) Gordon & Breach.

Mayan Prophecies see Profecias Mayas

Mayan Prophecies. Adrian Gilbert. 352p. 1996. pap. 14.95 (*1-85230-906-7*, Pub. by Element MA) Penguin Putnam.

Mayan Prophecies: Unlocking the Secrets of a Lost Civilization. Adrian Gilbert. (Illus.). 352p. 1995. pap. 24.95 (*1-85230-692-0*, Pub. by Element MA) Penguin Putnam.

Mayan Safari. Aubrey Smith-Carter. (SPA.). 158p. (Orig.). 1992. pap. text 14.20 (*0-8013-0401-6*, 78209) Longman.

***Mayan Script: A Civilization Revealed Through the Signs.** Maria Longhena. LC 00-22495. (Illus.). 2000. 35.00 (*0-7892-0653-6*) Abbeville Pr.

Mayan Struggle: Portrait of a Guatemalan People in Danger. Vince Heptig & Rigoberta M. Tum. LC 97-219236.Tr. of Lucha Maya. (ENG & SPA., Illus.). x, 128p. (Orig.). 1997. pap. 24.95 (*0-9656144-0-9*) MayaMedia Pub.

Mayan Tales from Zinacantan: Dreams & Stories from the People of the Bat. Ed. by Carol Karasik. Tr. by Robert M. Laughlin. (Illus.). 282p. 1996. pap. 16.95 (*1-56098-727-8*) Smithsonian.

***Mayan Treasure.** Clarica Burns. 225p. 1999. pap. 4.95 (*0-9645041-5-4*) Cntryside Pub.

***Mayan Weaving: A Living Tradition.** Ann Stalcup. (Crafts of the World Ser.). (Illus.). 24p. (J). (gr. k-4). 1999. 18.00 (*0-8239-5331-9*) Rosen Group.

Mayans, Aztecs & Incas: Thematic Unit. Larsen. 80p. (J). (gr. 5-8). 1996. pap., wbk. ed. 9.95 (*1-55734-595-3*) Tchr Create Mat.

Mayas. Pamela Odijk. (Ancient World Ser.). (Illus.). 48p. (J). (gr. 5-8). 1990. 11.00 (*0-382-24265-3*); teacher ed. 4.50 (*0-382-24280-7*); lib. bdg. 14.95 (*0-382-09890-0*) Silver Burdett Pr.

Mayas. deluxe ed. Patricia Linehan & Patrick Landreth. 160p. 1995. 25.00 (*0-614-04527-4*) Donald R Hoflin.

***Mayas: Culture & Civilization.** Konemann Inc. Staff. (Illus.). 2001. 39.95 (*3-8290-4150-0*) Konemann.

Mayas: Los Historia Arte y Cu. Demetrio Sodi M. (SPA.). 1995. pap. 21.95 (*968-38-0286-9*) Panorama Edit.

Mayas: 3000 Years of Civilization. 128p. text 14.95 (*88-8029-020-7*) Bonechi.

Mayas, Aztecs & Incas. Mary Strohl. (Illus.). (J). 1996. pap. 15.95 (*0-590-49504-6*) Scholastic Inc.

***Mayas, Aztecs & Incas: Mysteries of Ancient Civilizations of Central & South America.** Mark J. Dworkin. (Illus.). 144p. (gr. 10-12). 1999. reprint ed. pap. text 17.00 (*0-7881-6589-5*) DIANE Pub.

Maya's Children: The Story of La Llorona. Rudolfo A. Anaya. LC 95-41973. (Illus.). 32p. (J). (gr. k-4). 1997. 14.95 (*0-7868-0152-2*, Pub. by Hyprn Child); lib. bdg. 14.89 (*0-7868-2124-8*, Pub. by Hyprn Child) Little.

Maya's Divided World. Gloria Velasquez. LC 94-33573. 125p. (YA). (gr. 6-12). 1995. 12.95 (*1-55885-126-7*, Pinata Bks) Arte Publico.

Maya's First Rose. Martin S. Kosins. LC 92-61948. (Illus.). 104p. 1992. 15.95 (*0-9634380-0-X*) Open Sky.

Maya's First Rose: Diary of a Very Special Love. large type ed. Martin S. Kosins. LC 94-32197. 168p. 1994. lib. bdg. 19.95 (*0-8161-7419-9*, G K Hall Lrg Type) Mac Lib Ref.

Maya's First Rose: Diary of a Very Special Love. Martin S. Kosins. (Illus.). 128p. 1996. reprint ed. pap. 10.00 (*0-425-15306-1*) Berkley Pub.

***Maya's Magic.** Kim Dulaney. (Fuzzy-Feeling Bks.). (Illus.). (J). (ps-3). 1999. pap. 8.25 (*1-891636-04-9*, 1003) Unique Exp.

***Mayas of the Classic Period.** A. Arellano Hernandez et al. (Illus.). 256p. 1999. 95.00 (*88-16-69002-X*, Pub. by Jaca) Antique Collect.

Maya's Own Words: An Anthology Comprising Abridgements of the Popol-Vuh, Warrior of Rabinal, & Selections from the Memorial of Solola, the Book of Chilam Balam of Chumayel, & the Title of the Lords Of Totonicapan. Ed. by Thomas B. Irving. LC 84-81822. (Illus.). 120p. (Orig.). 1985. pap. 18.00 (*0-911437-14-2*) Labyrinthos.

Mayasauria (Maiasaura) Janet Riehecky. LC 89-22076. (Libros Sobre Dinosaurios! Ser.). (SPA., Illus.). 32p. (J). (gr. k-4). 1994. lib. bdg. 21.36 (*1-56766-147-5*) Childs World.

***Maybe: Incidentally: The Satire of Federico Mangahas: Essays** Federico Mangahas & Ruby K. Mangahas. LC 98-947832. xxxi, 653p. 1998. write for info. (*971-542-189-X*, Pub. by U of Philippines Pr) UH Pr.

Maybe . . . Maybe Not Again! Ralf Konig. Tr. by Jeff Krell from GER.Tr. of Pretty Baby. (Illus.). 120p. (Orig.). 1999. pap. write for info. (*0-9656323-3-4*, Pub. by Ignite Ent) Bookazine Co Inc.

Maybe . . . Maybe Not (Der Bewegte Mann) Ralf Konig. Tr. by Jeff Krell from GER. LC 98-70081. (Illus.). 128p. (Orig.). 1998. pap. 14.95 (*0-9656323-2-6*) Ignite Ent.

Maybe by Then I'll Understand. Jane McFann. 192p. (Orig.). 1987. pap. 2.50 (*0-380-75221-2*, Avon Bks) Morrow Avon.

Maybe Four Steps: or The Shame of Our Cities. William Keisling. (Illus.). 175p. 1991. 15.95 (*0-9620251-8-6*); pap. 9.95 (*0-9620251-7-8*) Yardbird Bks.

Maybe Garden. Kimberly Burke-Weiner. Ed. by Michelle Roehm. (Illus.). 36p. (J). (gr. 1-4). 1992. 14.95 (*0-941831-56-6*); pap. 7.95 (*0-941831-57-4*) Beyond Words Pub.

Maybe I'll Be A . . . Nancy Kaufman. (Illus.). 29p. 1997. write for info. (*0-9653649-4-1*) Thirteenth Bomb Sqndrn.

***Maybe I'll Be (Tal Vez Sere)** Greta Quezada. (SPA & ENG., Illus.). 22p. (J). (ps-5). 1998. pap. 14.95 incl. audio (*0-9677193-0-5*) Ninos Del Mundo.

Maybe I'll Call Anna. William B. Spencer. LC 89-62518. 216p. 1989. pap. 16.00 (*1-57962-054-X*) Permanent Pr.

Maybe I'll Grow up to Be a Bullfrog. Wilma C. Erwin. Ed. by Sandra D. Romashko. LC 95-61806. (Illus.). 24p. (Orig.). (J). (gr. 1-3). 1995. pap. 3.95 (*0-89317-043-7*) Windward Pub.

Maybe I'll Pitch Forever. LeRoy S. Paige. LC 92-35221. xiv, 298p. 1993. text 45.00 (*0-8032-3702-2*) U of Nebr Pr.

Maybe I'll Pitch Forever. LeRoy S. Paige. LC 92-35221. (Illus.). xiv, 299p. 1993. pap. 12.95 (*0-8032-8732-1*, Bison Books) U of Nebr Pr.

Maybe in Missoula. Toni Volk. LC 93-48027. 280p. 1994. 22.00 (*1-56947-007-3*) Soho Press.

M

An Asterisk (*) at the beginning of an entry indicates that the title is appearing for the first time.

Maybe It Should Have Been a Three Iron: My Years As Caddy for the World's 438th Best Golfer. Lawrence Donegan. LC 98-6152. 256p. 1998. text 21.95 (*0-312-18584-7*) St Martin.

Maybe It Should Have Been a Three Iron: My Years As Caddy for the World's 438th Best Golfer. 2nd ed. Lawrence Donegan. 1999. pap. 12.95 (*0-312-20422-1*) St Martin.

Maybe It Was So. Reginald Gibbons. (Phoenix Poets Ser.). 78p. 1991. pap. 9.95 (*0-226-29056-5*) U Ch Pr.

Maybe It Was So. Reginald Gibbons. (Phoenix Poets Ser.). 78p. 1996. lib. bdg. 25.00 (*0-226-29055-7*) U Ch Pr.

***Maybe It's Me: A Holistic Point of View to Conquering Stress.** Russell Kirkman. 152p. 2000. pap. 16.95 (*0-9632857-2-6*) Collins Pubns.

Maybe It's My Heart. Abigail Stone. LC 89-12846. 164p. (Orig.). 1989. pap. 10.95 (*0-9617589-4-5*) Lincoln Springs Pr.

Maybe It's Not Your Fault, but You Can Do Something about It: The Blue Book for Personal Survival. Shale Paul. 64p. (Orig.). 1993. pap., per. 4.95 (*0-913787-08-6*) Delta G Pr.

Maybe Luck Isn't Just Chance. Ruth Liepman. Tr. by John Broadwin. LC 97-39708. 150p. 1998. 39.95 (*0-8101-1294-9*); pap. 15.95 (*0-8101-1295-7*) Northwestern U Pr.

Maybe (Maybe Not) Robert Fulghum. 1997. pap. 11.00 (*0-449-00097-4*) Fawcett.

Maybe (Maybe Not) Robert Fulghum. LC 92-56811. 1995. mass mkt. 6.99 (*0-8041-1115-4*) Ivy Books.

***Maybe, Molly & Must-Be-Red.** Joan Arlette. (Illus.). 8p. (J). (ps-5). 1998. mass mkt. 7.00 (*0-9700121-0-1*, 001) Light Years.

Maybe Mother Did Know Best: Old-Fashioned Parenting the Modern Way. Linda L. Small. LC 99-11098. 176p. 1999. pap. 12.00 (*0-380-79803-4*, Eos) Morrow Avon.

Maybe My Baby. Irene O'Book. LC 96-35921. (Illus.). 14p. (J). (ps up). 1998. 5.95 (*0-694-00872-9*) HarpC Child Bks.

Maybe No, Maybe Yes. Cait London. (Desire Ser.). 1993. pap. 2.89 (*0-373-05782-2*, 5-05782-3) Silhouette.

Maybe One: A Case for Smaller Families. Bill McKibben. 256p. 1999. pap. 12.95 (*0-452-28092-3*, Plume) Dutton Plume.

Maybe One: An Environmental & Personal Argument for Single-Child Families. Bill McKibben. LC 98-5417. 240p. 1998. 23.00 (*0-684-85281-0*) S&S Trade.

Maybe Right, Maybe Wrong: A Guide for Young Thinkers. Dan Barker. LC 92-416. (Young Readers Ser.). (Illus.). 76p. (J). 1992. pap. 14.95 (*0-87975-731-0*) Prometheus Bks.

Maybe She Is. Stacey Donovan. 1999. 14.99 (*0-525-45628-7*) NAL.

Maybe Stories of Uncle Dan. D. S. Barnes. 93p. (J). 1996. per. 7.95 (*0-614-24784-5*) Tesseract SD.

Maybe the Moon: A Novel. Armistead Maupin. LC 92-52596. 320p. 1993. reprint ed. pap. 13.00 (*0-06-092434-9*, Perennial) HarperTrade.

Maybe This Time. Victoria Barrett. 480p. 1996. mass mkt. 4.99 (*0-7860-0291-3*, Pinncle Kensgtn) Kensgtn Pub Corp.

Maybe This Time. Barbara Bretton. 352p. (Orig.). 1995. mass mkt. 5.99 (*0-425-14724-X*) Berkley Pub.

Maybe This Time. Kathleen G. Sidel. 1990. pap. 4.95 (*0-671-66216-3*) S&S Trade.

Maybe This Time. large type ed. Daoma Winston. 1990. 27.99 (*0-7089-2147-7*) Ulverscroft.

Maybe Tomorrow. Joan Hohl. 384p. 1998. mass mkt. 5.99 (*0-8217-6054-8*, Zebra Kensgtn) Kensgtn Pub Corp.

Maybe Tomorrow. large type ed. Joan Hohl. LC 98-56291. 1999. pap. 30.00 (*0-7862-1860-6*) Thorndike Pr.

Maybe Tomorrow: A Hidden Child of the Holocaust. Eric Cahn & Marilyn Saltzman. (Illus.). 210p. (Orig.). 1995. pap. 11.95 (*0-9645410-0-9*) Casan Pub.

Maybe Tomorrow I'll Have a Good Time. Mary Soderstrom. LC 80-25357. (Illus.). 32p. (J). (ps-3). 1981. 16.95 (*0-89885-012-6*, Kluwer Acad Hman Sci) Kluwer Academic.

***Maybe We Do Love Our Parents.** Stuwart Starr. 2000. pap. write for info. (*0-9668850-2-3*) CNC Pubg.

Maybe Yes, Maybe No: A Guide for Young Skeptics. Dan Barker. LC 90-43058. (Young Readers Ser.). (Illus.). 80p. (Orig.). (J). (gr. 8-12). 1990. pap. 14.95 (*0-87975-607-1*) Prometheus Bks.

Maybe Yes, Maybe No, Maybe Maybe. Susan Patron. LC 92-34067. (Richard Jackson Bk.). (Illus.). 96p. (J). (gr. 3-5). 1993. 15.95 (*0-531-05482-9*) Orchard Bks Watts.

Maybe You Know My Kid. Mary C. Fowler. 1990. 18.95 (*1-55972-022-0*, Birch Ln Pr) Carol Pub Group.

Maybe You Know My Kid: A Parent's Guide to Identifying, Understanding & Helping Your Child with Attention Deficit Hyperactivity Disorder. Mary C. Fowler. 240p. 1991. reprint ed. pap. 12.00 (*1-55972-097-2*, Birch Ln Pr) Carol Pub Group.

Maybe You Know My Kid: A Parent's Guide to Identifying, Understanding & Helping Your Child with Attention Deficit Hyperactivity Disorder. rev. ed. Mary Fowler. 240p. 1993. pap. 12.95 (*1-55972-209-6*) Carol Pub Group.

Maybe You Will Survive: The True Story of Aron Goldfarb. Aron Goldfarb. 208p. 1992. 24.95 (*0-89604-153-0*, Holocaust Library); pap. 12.95 (*0-89604-154-9*, Holocaust Library) US Holocaust.

Maybelle, the Cable Car. Virginia L. Burton. LC 96-9845. (Illus.). 48p. (J). (ps-4). 1997. 16.00 (*0-395-82847-3*) HM.

Maybelle the Cable Car. Virginia Lee Burton. LC 96-9845. (Illus.). 48p. (ps-4). 1997. pap. 5.95 (*0-395-84003-1*) HM.

Maybelle the Cable Car. Virginia Lee Burton. LC 96-9845. 1996. 11.15 (*0-606-11607-9*, Pub. by Turtleback) Demco.

Maybelleen: A Novel. Kathleen W. King. LC 94-31879. 1995. 20.00 (*0-8050-3600-8*) H Holt & Co.

Mayberry Humor Across the U. S. A. Jeanne Robertson. 349p. 1995. 19.95 (*0-927577-02-X*) Rich Pub Co.

***Mayberry Memories.** Ken Beck & Jim Clark. (Illus.). 2000. 34.99 (*1-55853-830-5*) Rutledge Hill Pr.

Mayberry, My Hometown: The Ultimate Guidebook to America's Favorite TV Small Town. Stephen J. Spignesi. Ed. by Thomas Schultheiss. (Illus.). 300p. 1991. reprint ed. pap. 26.50 (*1-56075-023-5*) Popular Culture.

Mayberry 101, 3 vols., vol. 1. Neal Brower. LC 98-28733. (Behind the Scenes of a TV Classic Ser.: Vol. 1). (Illus.). 507p. 1998. pap. 14.95 (*0-89587-218-8*) Blair.

Maybole, Carrick's Capital. Jas. T. Gray. (C). 1988. 80.00 (*0-907526-09-8*, Pub. by Alloway Pub) St Mut.

***Mayday.** Nelson DeMille. LC 98-33102. 1999. 29.95 (*0-7862-1792-8*) Thorndike Pr.

Mayday. Nelson DeMille & Thomas Block. LC 98-33102. 621p. 1999. write for info. (*0-7540-2194-7*) Chivers N Amer.

Mayday. William Faulkner. LC 76-22410. (Illus.). 1980. text 9.50 (*0-268-01339-X*) U of Notre Dame Pr.

Mayday! Edward Packard & Andrea Packard. (Choose Your Own Adventure Ser.: No. 184). (Illus.). 112p. (J). (gr. 3-7). 1998. mass mkt. 2.99 (*0-553-56758-6*, Choose) BDD Bks Young Read.

Mayday. Nelson DeMille & Thomas H. Block. 480p. 1998. reprint ed. mass mkt. 6.99 (*0-446-60476-3*, Pub. by Warner Bks) Little.

Mayday: The History of a Village Holocaust. Grant Parker. 260p. 1992. reprint ed. pap. 8.95 (*0-9604958-0-0*) Parker Pr MI.

Mayday! Yachts in Distress. Joachim Schult. Tr. by Detlef Jens. LC 97-18385. (Illus.). 192p. 1997. pap. 23.50 (*1-57409-039-9*) Sheridan.

Mayday from Malaga. large type ed. Bill Knox. (Ulverscroft Large Print Ser.). 416p. 1998. 29.99 (*0-7089-3893-0*) Ulverscroft.

Mayday! Mayday! Eastern Airlines in a Tailspin! Joan L. Mazauskas. LC 89-84208. (Illus.). 352p. 1990. pap. 9.95 (*0-9623740-0-8*) Mazauskas Pubns.

Mayday! Mayday! Mayday! This Is the Haleakala. Charles Coleman. LC 92-27856. 264p. 1997. 24.95 (*0-9634022-1-8*); pap. 17.95 (*0-9634022-0-X*) Word Prof.

Mayday Rampage. Clayton Bess. LC 92-74268. (Illus.). 208p. (YA). (gr. 9-12). 1993. 14.95 (*1-882405-00-5*); pap. 7.95 (*1-882405-01-3*) Lookout Pr.

Maydays. David Edgar. (Methuen Modern Plays Ser.). 148p. (C). 1988. pap. write for info. (*0-413-57080-0*, A0171, Methuen Drama) Methn.

Maydays & Mermaids. William A. Davis. 152p. 1983. 10.00 (*0-89540-133-9*, SB-133) Sun Pub.

Maye & Faye's Building & Loan: The Story of a Remarkable Sisterhood. large type ed. Maye Smith et al. LC 96-6540. 1997. 23.95 (*0-7862-1040-0*) Five Star.

***Mayer - International Auction Records, 1998: 120,000 Auction Prices,Prints, Drawings, Watercolors, Paintings, Sculpture, 2 vols.** Unknown. 6000p. 1998. 195.00 (*2-940033-27-7*, Pub. by Acatos Edit) Antique Collect.

Mayer & Thalberg: The Make-Believe Saints. Samuel Marx. LC 88-31081. (Illus.). 274p. 1988. pap. 12.95 (*0-573-60695-1*) S French Trade.

Mayer Boulding Dialogue on Peace Research. Kenneth E. Boulding & Milton Mayer. Ed. by Carol R. Murphy. LC 67-23313. (Orig.). 1967. pap. 1.00 (*0-87574-153-3*) Pendle Hill.

Mayer International Auction Records 1999. Acatos Publishing Staff. 6000p. 1999. 195.00 (*2-940033-49-8*, Pub. by Acatos Edit) Antique Collect.

Mayer, Ivanowski, Beijerinck, Baur. Tr. by J. Johnson. (Phytopathological Classics Ser.). 62p. 1942. 22.00 (*0-89054-008-X*) Am Phytopathol Soc.

Mayer on the Media: Issues & Arguments. Henry Mayer. Ed. by Rodney Tiffen. 208p. 1995. pap. 22.95 (*1-86373-625-5*, Pub. by Allen & Unwin Pty) Paul & Co Pubs.

Mayer Sulzberger - Alexander Marx Correspondence, 1904-1923. Herman Dicker. x, 206p. (Orig.). 1990. 29.50 (*0-87203-133-0*) Hermon.

Mayeroni Myth. large type ed. Daoma Winston. 259p. 1992. reprint ed. lib. bdg. 19.95 (*1-56054-279-9*) Thorndike Pr.

Mayeros: A Yucatec Maya Family. George Ancona. LC 96-2309. (Illus.). 40p. (J). (gr. 1 up). 1997. 16.00 (*0-688-13465-3*); lib. bdg. 15.93 (*0-688-13466-1*) Lothrop.

Mayer's Best of Vermont: A Pictorial Collection of the Green Mountain State. Alois Mayer. (Illus.). 80p. (Orig.). 1997. pap. 13.95 (*0-9657583-0-3*, 51395) Mayer Photo-graphics.

Maye's Midwifery. 12th ed. Betty R. Sweet. (Illus.). 915p. 1996. pap. text 55.00 (*0-7020-1757-4*, Pub. by W B Saunders) Saunders.

Mayfair. large type ed. Nancy Fitzgerald. 1990. 27.99 (*0-7089-2134-5*) Ulverscroft.

Mayfair, 1818-1824, Letters, 1180-1354 see Journals of Fanny Burney (Madam D'Arblay)

Mayfair, 1825-1840, Letters, 1355-1521 see Journals of Fanny Burney (Madam D'Arblay)

Mayfield Anthology of Western Philosophical Classics. Daniel Kolak & Mayfield Publishing Company Staff. LC 97-27184. xv, 1117p. 1997. pap. text 39.95 (*1-55934-972-7*, 1972) Mayfield Pub.

Mayfield Crossing. Vaunda M. Nelson. LC 92-10564. 96p. (YA). (gr. 4-7). 1994. mass mkt. 4.50 (*0-380-72179-1*, Avon Bks) Morrow Avon.

Mayfield Crossing. Vaunda M. Nelson. LC 92-10564. (Illus.). 96p. (J). (gr. 4-7). 1993. 14.95 (*0-399-22331-2*, G P Putnam) Peng Put Young Read.

Mayfield Crossing. Vaunda M. Nelson. (J). 1993. 9.70 (*0-606-05922-9*, Pub. by Turtleback) Demco.

Mayfield Handbook of Technical & Scientific Writing. Leslie C. Perelman et al. LC 97-20849. xxvii, 508p. 1997. spiral bd. 29.95 (*1-55934-647-7*, 1647) Mayfield Pub.

***Mayfield Quick Guide to the Internet for Communication Students.** John A. Courtright & Elizabeth M. Perse. LC 99-187313. (Illus.). iv, 84p. (C). 1998. pap. text 7.95 (*0-7674-0029-1*, 0029-1) Mayfield Pub.

***Mayfield Quick View Guide to the Internet for Students of Health, Physical Education & Exercise Science Version 2.0.** Jennifer Campbell Koella & Michael Keene. LC 00-36146. (Illus.). 2000. pap. write for info. (*0-7674-2062-4*) Mayfield Pub.

***Mayfield Quick View Guide to the Internet for Students of Research, Statistics & Measurement.** John S. Wilkerson. LC 99-207888. 64p. 1999. 7.95 (*0-7674-0731-8*) Mayfield Pub.

Mayfield's Quick View Guide to the Internet for Students of Anthropology. John Hoopes et al. 80p. 1997. pap. 7.95 (*0-7674-0179-4*) Mayfield Pub.

Mayfield's Quick View Guide to the Internet for Students of Anthropology. 2nd ed. John Hoopes et al. 80p. 1999. pap. 7.95 (*0-7674-1121-8*) Mayfield Pub.

Mayfield's Quick View Guide to the Internet for Students of English. 2nd ed. Jennifer Campbell Koella. 1997. pap. text 7.95 (*0-7674-1146-3*) Mayfield Pub.

Mayfield's Quick View Guide to the Internet for Students of Health & Physical Education. Jennifer Campbell Koella & Michael Keene. 64p. 1997. pap. 7.95 (*0-7674-0237-5*, 0237-5) Mayfield Pub.

Mayflies: An Angler's Study of Trout Water Ephemeroptera. Malcolm Knopp & Robert Cormier. LC 97-23765. (Illus.). 384p. 1997. 49.95 (*0-9626663-8-6*) Greycliff Pub.

***Mayflies: New Poems & Translations.** Richard Wilbur. LC 99-45452. 96p. 2000. 22.00 (*0-15-100469-2*) Harcourt.

Mayflies & Stoneflies: Proceedings of the 5th International Epheropters Conference & the 9th International Plecopters Conference. Ed. by Ian C. Campbell. (C). 1990. text 320.50 (*0-7923-0289-3*) Kluwer Academic.

Mayflies of Florida. rev. ed. Lewis Berner & Manuel L. Pescador. LC 87-16005. (Illus.). 431p. 1988. 49.95 (*0-8130-0845-X*) U Press Fla.

Mayflies of Michigan Trout Streams. Justin W. Leonard & Fannie A. Leonard. LC 62-9726. (Bulletin Ser.: No. 43). 139p. 1962. pap. 8.50 (*0-87737-020-6*) Cranbrook.

Mayflies of North & Central America. George F. Edmunds et al. LC 75-39446. 340p. reprint ed. pap. 105.40 (*0-608-14651-X*, 205585900039) Bks Demand.

Mayflies of the World: A Catalog of the Family & Genus Group Taxa (Insecta: Ephemeroptera) Michael D. Hubbard. LC 90-48456. (Flora & Fauna Handbook Ser.: No. 8). viii, 119p. 1990. lib. bdg. 49.95 (*1-877743-06-2*) Sandhill Crane.

Mayflies, or Ephemeroptera, of Illinois. B. D. Burks. LC 75-2296. (Illus.). viii, 216p. 1975. reprint ed. 15.00 (*0-911836-06-3*) Entomological Repr.

Mayflower Adventure. Betty McPherson. (Pocket Tales Ser.: Bk. 1). (Illus.). 32p. (J). (ps-1). 1985. 6.00 (*0-918823-00-5*) Boyce-Pubns.

***Mayflower Adventure.** Colleen L. Reece. (American Adventure Ser.: No. 1). (J). (gr. 3-6). 1998. 3.97 (*1-57748-059-7*) Barbour Pub.

Mayflower Adventure. Colleen L. Reece. LC 98-7226. (American Adventure Ser.: No. 1). 144p. (J). (gr. 3-7). 1999. lib. bdg. 15.95 (*0-7910-5041-6*) Chelsea Hse.

Mayflower Ancestral Index: Descendants of the Families: Brewster, Chilton, Eaton, Samuel Fuller, More, Rogers, Soule, White, Vol. 1. Milton E. Terry & Anne B. Harding. LC 80-28265. 717p. 1981. 15.00 (*0-930270-25-8*) Mayflower.

Mayflower & Her Log: July 15, 1620 - May 6, 1621. Azel Ames. LC 99-203408. (Illus.). 230p. 1999. reprint ed. pap. 36.00 (*0-7884-1070-9*, A516) Heritage Bk.

Mayflower & the Pilgrim Fathers. Richard Tames. 1991. student ed. 39.00 (*1-56696-089-4*) Jackdaw.

Mayflower Births & Deaths: From the Files of George Ernest Bowman, at the Massachusetts Society of Mayflower Descendants, 2 vols., Set. Susan E. Roser. 1075p. 1997. reprint ed. pap. 75.00 (*0-8063-1340-4*, 4999) Genealog Pub.

Mayflower Deeds & Probates: From the Files of George Ernest Bowman, at the Massachusetts Society of Mayflower Descendants. Susan E. Roser. LC 94-77222. 660p. 1994. pap. 44.95 (*0-8063-1423-0*, 4994) Genealog Pub.

Mayflower Descendant. Massachusetts Society of Mayflower Descendants Sta. ix, 245p. 1996. reprint ed. 27.00 (*0-7884-0581-0*, MD30) Heritage Bk.

Mayflower Descendant, Vol. 7, 1905. Ed. by George E. Bowman. (Illus.). 301p. 1995. reprint ed. text 25.00 (*0-7884-0178-5*) Heritage Bk.

Mayflower Descendant, Vol. 8, 1906. Ed. by George E. Bowman. (Illus.). 300p. 1995. reprint ed. text 25.00 (*0-7884-0179-3*) Heritage Bk.

Mayflower Descendant, Vol. 12. Massachusetts Society of Mayflower Descendants Sta. (Illus.). 299p. 1995. reprint ed. pap. 25.00 (*0-7884-0250-1*) Heritage Bk.

Mayflower Descendant, Vol. 13. Ed. by George E. Bowman. (Illus.). 327p. 1995. reprint ed. text 25.00 (*0-7884-0317-6*) Heritage Bk.

Mayflower Descendant, Vol. 14. Ed. by George E. Bowman. (Illus.). 328p. 1995. reprint ed. text 25.00 (*0-7884-0318-4*) Heritage Bk.

Mayflower Descendant, Vol. 17, 1915. MA Soc. of the Mayflower Desc. Staff. (Illus.). 315p. 1996. 27.00 (*0-7884-0377-X*, MD17) Heritage Bk.

Mayflower Descendant, Vol. 18, 1916. MA Soc. of the Mayflower Desc. Staff. (Illus.). x, 295p. 1996. 27.00 (*0-7884-0378-8*, MD18) Heritage Bk.

Mayflower Descendant, Vol. 19. Mass. Society of Mayflower Descendants Staff. (Illus.). 1996. 27.00 (*0-7884-0402-4*, MD19) Heritage Bk.

Mayflower Descendant, Vol. 20. Mass. Society of Mayflower Descendents Staff. (Illus.). 218p. 1996. 27.00 (*0-7884-0403-2*, MD20) Heritage Bk.

Mayflower Descendant, Vol. 21. Massachusetts Society of Mayflower Descendants Sta. (Illus.). 222p. 1996. 25.00 (*0-7884-0450-4*, MD21) Heritage Bk.

Mayflower Descendant, Vol. 22. Massachusetts Society of Mayflower Descendants Sta. (Illus.). 224p. 1996. 25.00 (*0-7884-0451-2*, MD22) Heritage Bk.

Mayflower Descendant, Vol. 25, 1923. Massachusetts Society of Mayflower Descendants Sta. (Illus.). xii, 222p. 1996. reprint ed. 27.00 (*0-7884-0523-3*, MD25) Heritage Bk.

Mayflower Descendant, Vol. 26, 1924. MA Society of Mayflower Descendants Staff. (Illus.). viii, 224p. 1996. reprint ed. 27.00 (*0-7884-0524-1*, MD26) Heritage Bk.

Mayflower Descendant, Vol. 29, 1931. Massachusetts Soc. of Mayflower Descendants Staff. x, 234p. 1996. reprint ed. 27.00 (*0-7884-0580-2*, MD29) Heritage Bk.

Mayflower Descendant: 1907, Vol. 9. Ed. by George E. Bowman. (Illus.). 302p. 1995. 25.00 (*0-7884-0201-3*) Heritage Bk.

Mayflower Descendant Vol. 1: 1899. Ed. by George E. Bowman. (Illus.). 281p. 1994. reprint ed. text 25.00 (*0-7884-0053-3*) Heritage Bk.

Mayflower Descendant Vol. 2: 1900. Ed. by George E. Bowman. (Illus.). 283p. 1994. reprint ed. text 25.00 (*0-7884-0054-1*) Heritage Bk.

Mayflower Descendant Vol. 3: 1901. Ed. by George E. Bowman. (Illus.). 286p. 1995. text 25.00 (*0-7884-0092-4*) Heritage Bk.

Mayflower Descendant Vol. 4: 1902. Ed. by George E. Bowman. 284p. 1995. text 25.00 (*0-7884-0093-2*) Heritage Bk.

Mayflower Descendant Vol. 5: 1903. Ed. by George E. Bowman. (Illus.). 292p. 1995. reprint ed. text 25.00 (*0-7884-0131-9*) Heritage Bk.

Mayflower Descendant Vol. 6: 1904. Ed. by George E. Bowman. (Illus.). 287p. 1994. reprint ed. text 25.00 (*0-7884-0132-7*) Heritage Bk.

Mayflower Descendant Vol. 10: 1908. Ed. by George E. Bowman. (Illus.). 305p. 1995. reprint ed. text 25.00 (*0-7884-0202-1*) Heritage Bk.

Mayflower Descendant, 1909, Vol. 11. Massachusetts Society of Mayflower Descendants Sta. (Illus.). 306p. 1995. reprint ed. pap. 25.00 (*0-7884-0249-8*) Heritage Bk.

Mayflower Descendant, 1913, Vol. 15. MA Society of Mayflower Descendants Staff. 301p. 1995. reprint ed. 25.00 (*0-7884-0334-6*, MD15) Heritage Bk.

Mayflower Descendant, 1914, Vol. 16. MA Society of Mayflower Descendants Staff. 300p. 1995. reprint ed. 25.00 (*0-7884-0335-4*, MD16) Heritage Bk.

Mayflower Descendant, 1925, Vol. XXVII. Massachusetts Society of Mayflower Descendants Sta. Ed. by George E. Bowman. (Illus.). x, 230p. 1996. reprint ed. 27.00 (*0-7884-0547-0*, MD27) Heritage Bk.

Mayflower Descendant, 1930, Vol. XXVIII. Massachusetts Society of Mayflower Descendants Sta. Ed. by George E. Bowman. (Illus.), viii, 237p. 1996. reprint ed. 27.00 (*0-7884-0548-9*, MD28) Heritage Bk.

Mayflower Descendant, 1937, Vol. 34. Massachusetts Society of Mayflower Descendants Sta. (Illus.). xii, 252p. 1997. 27.00 (*0-7884-0644-2*, MD34) Heritage Bk.

Mayflower Descendants & Their Marriages for Two Generations after the Landing. John T. Landis. LC 72-158139. 37p. 1998. reprint ed. pap. 8.00 (*0-8063-0206-2*) Clearfield Co.

Mayflower Descendants, 1921, Vol. 23. Massachusetts Society of Mayflower Descendants Sta. (Illus.). 230p. 1996. reprint ed. 27.00 (*0-7884-0482-2*, MD23) Heritage Bk.

Mayflower Descendants, 1922, Vol. 24. Massachusetts Society of Mayflower Descendants Sta. 221p. 1996. reprint ed. 27.00 (*0-7884-0483-0*, MD24) Heritage Bk.

Mayflower Essays: On the Story of the Pilgrim Fathers, As Told in Governor Bradford's Ms. History of the Plymouth Plantation. G. Cuthbert Blaxland. LC 78-39713. (Essay Index Reprint Ser.). 1977. reprint ed. 16.95 (*0-8369-2748-6*) Ayer.

Mayflower Families Through Five Generations: Family of George Soule, Vol. 3. John E. Soule & Milton E. Terry. LC 75-30145. xi, 486p. 1980. 25.00 (*0-930270-02-9*); pap. 3.00 (*0-685-05531-0*) Mayflower.

Mayflower Families Through Five Generations-Descendants of the Pilgrims Who Landed at Plymouth, Mass. December, 1620: Families Francis Eaton, Samuel Fuller, William White, Vol. 1. Ed. by Lee D. Van Antwerp et al. LC 75-30145. 261p. 1975. 20.00 (*0-930270-00-2*); pap. 3.00 (*0-685-03324-4*) Mayflower.

Mayflower Families Through Five Generations-Descendants of the Pilgrims Who Landed at Plymouth, Mass. December, 1620: Families Francis Eaton, Samuel Fuller, William White, Vol. 1. rev. ed. Ed. by Lee D. Van Antwerp et al. LC 75-30145. 52p. 1975. pap. 4.00 (*0-685-03323-6*) Mayflower.

Mayflower Families Through Five Generations-Descendants of the Pilgrims Who Landed at Plymouth, Mass. December 1620: Families James Chilton, Richard More, Thomas Rogers, Vol. 2. Ed. by Robert M. Sherman et al. LC 75-30145. 424p. 1978. 25.00 (*0-930270-01-0*); 3.00 (*0-685-03325-2*) Mayflower.

M

An Asterisk (*) at the beginning of an entry indicates that the title is appearing for the first time.

Mayflower Hotel: Grande Dame of Washington, D. C. Judith R. Cohen. (Illus.). 160p. 1987. 29.95 (0-940577-00-3, Balance Hse Ltd) Intl Archive Art.

Mayflower Increasings. 2nd ed. Susan E. Roser. LC 95-76482. 170p. 1996. reprint ed. pap. 20.00 (0-8063-1479-6) Genealog Pub.

Mayflower Madam: The Secret Life of Sydney Biddle Barrows. large type ed. Sydney B. Barrows & William Novak. 457p. 1987. reprint ed. lib. bdg. 19.95 (1-55736-007-3) BDD LT Grp.

Mayflower Murder. Paul Kemprecos. 1996. 22.95 (0-312-14852-6, Thomas Dunne) St Martin.

Mayflower People: Triumphs & Tragedies. Anna W. Hale. LC 95-17355. (Illus.). 96p. (Orig.). (J). (gr. 5-9). 1995. 15.95 (1-57140-002-8); pap. 9.95 (1-57140-003-6) Roberts Rinehart.

Mayflower Pilgrims. Edmund J. Carpenter. (Illus.). 256p. (YA). (gr. 7-12). 1993. pap. text 3.95 (1-930092-17-2, CLP29995) Christian Liberty.

Mayflower Reader: A Selection of Articles from the Mayflower Descendant. George E. Bowman. LC 77-99092. (Illus.). 537p. 1996. reprint ed. pap. 39.95 (0-8063-0797-8) Clearfield Co.

Mayflower Secret: Governor William Bradford. Dave Jackson & Neta Jackson. LC 97-45439. (Trailblazer Bks.). (Illus.). 16p. (J). (gr. 3-7). 1998. pap. 5.99 (0-7642-2010-1) Bethany Hse.

Mayflower Source Records: Primary Data Concerning Southeastern Massachusetts, Cape Cod, & the Islands of Nantucket & Martha's Vineyard, from the New England Historical & Genealogical Register. New England Historical & Genealogical Register Sta. 832p. 1997. reprint ed. 33.50 (0-8063-1145-2) Genealog Pub.

Mayflower II: On Buddhist Voyage to Liberation. C. T. Shen. LC 83-81198. (Basic Buddhism Ser.). (Illus.). 1983. pap. 4.95 (0-915078-03-1, P-02) Inst Adv Stud Wld.

Mayg-shem Fish. limited ed. Anne Tardos. 56p. 1995. 18.00 (0-937013-62-5) Potes Poets.

Mayhawk's Law. Robert Mayhawk. (Illus.). 128p. 1986. write for info. (0-940959-00-3) Murre Co.

Mayhaws. Billy Craft et al. 125p. (Orig.). 1996. pap. 12.95 (1-57502-235-4, P0906) Morris Pubng.

Mayhem. J. Robert Janes. LC 98-31949. (Crime Ser.). 272p. 1999. pap. 12.00 (1-56947-158-4) Soho Press.

Mayhem! More from the Master of Malice. George Hayduke. 208p. 1992. pap. 7.95 (0-8184-0565-1, L Stuart) Carol Pub Group.

Mayhem: Violence As Public Entertainment. Sissela Bok. LC 97-48620. 208p. 1998. 32.00 (0-201-48979-1) Perseus Pubng.

Mayhem: Violence As Public Entertainment. Sissela Bok. 208p. 1999. pap. text 13.00 (0-7382-0145-6, Pub. by Perseus Pubng) HarpC.

Mayhem & Miranda. Carola Dunn. 224p. 1997. mass mkt. 4.99 (0-8217-5766-0, Zebra Kensgtn) Kensgtn Pub Corp.

***Mayhem & Murder: Narrative & Moral Issues in the Detective Story.** Heta Pyrhienen. 1999. pap. text 21.95 (0-8020-8267-X) U of Toronto Pr.

Mayhem at the Marina: A Lexy Hyatt Mystery. Carlene Miller. LC 99-25699. 200p. 1999. pap. 11.95 (1-892281-05-8) New Victoria Pubs.

Mayhem in B-Flat: A Homer Evans Murder Mystery. Elliot Paul. 320p. 1988. reprint ed. pap. 6.95 (0-486-25621-9) Dover.

Mayhem in Mayville: A Whodunit in 2 Acts. Dean Kephart. 79p. 1993. 8.99 (0-8341-9712-X, MP-694) Lillenas.

Mayhem in Motion. Franklin W. Dixon. Ed. by Anne Greenberg. (Hardy Boys Casefiles Ser.: No. 69). 160p. (YA). (gr. 6 up). 1992. pap. 3.75 (0-671-73105-X, Archway) PB.

Mayhem in Motion. Franklin W. Dixon. (Hardy Boys Casefiles Ser.: No. 69). (YA). (gr. 6 up). 1992. 8.85 (0-606-02665-7, Pub. by Turtleback) Demco.

Mayhem in the Catskills. Norman J. Van Valkenburgh. LC 94-45461. 158p. 1994. 25.00 (0-935796-60-6) Purple Mnt Pr.

Mayhem in the Catskills. 2nd ed. Norman J. Van Valkenburgh. LC 94-45461. 158p. 1994. pap. 12.50 (0-935796-59-2) Purple Mnt Pr.

Mayhem on Maui. Susan Murray. (KC Flanagan Girl Detective Ser.). 1999. pap. 5.99 (1-55207-022-0) Genl Dist Srvs.

Mayhem Was Our Business: Memorias de un Veternao. Sabine R. Ulibarri. LC 96-43060. (SPA.). 96p. (Orig.). 1996. pap. 9.00 (0-927534-64-9) Biling Rev-Pr.

Mayi: Some Bush Fruits of Dampierland. Ed. by Merrilee Lands. (C). 1990. 30.00 (0-7855-6627-9, Pub. by Pascoe Pub) St Mut.

Mayim. Nachman & Nathan. Ed. by Moshe Mykoff. 64p. (Orig.). 1987. pap. 3.00 (0-930213-28-9) Breslov Res Inst.

Maylasia's Demographic Transition: Rapid Development, Culture, & Politics. Richard Leete. (South-East Asian Social Science Monographs). (Illus.). 246p. 1996. text 39.95 (967-65-3109-X) OUP.

Mayn Folk Vol. 2: Beyz. Jack Noskowitz.Tr. of My People. (YID., Illus.). 190p. (YA). (gr. 4-11). 1994. pap. 10.00 (1-877909-62-9) Jwsh Bk Ctr Wrkmns Cir.

Mayn Folk ALEF. Jack Noskowitz.Tr. of My People. 167p. 1962. pap. 10.00 (0-318-22121-7) Jwsh Bk Ctr Wrkmns Cir.

May'naise Sandwiches & Sunshine Tea. Sandra Belton. LC 93-46781. (Illus.). 32p. (J). (ps-4). 1994. mass mkt. 14.95 (0-02-709035-3) S&S Bks Yung.

***Maynard.** Lewis Halprin. (Images of America Ser.). 128p. 1999. pap. 18.99 (0-7385-0074-7) Arcadia Publng.

Maynard: Humor Through the Years with Maynard Speece. Marigold Speece. (Illus.). 144p. (Orig.). 1981. pap. 7.95 (0-911506-14-4) Thueson.

Maynard Keynes: An Economists' Biography. Don Moggridge. (Illus.). 968p. 1995. pap. 19.95 (0-415-12676-2, C0539) Routledge.

Maynard Keynes: An Economists' Biography. Don Moggridge. (Illus.). 976p. (C). 1995. pap. 32.99 (0-415-12711-4) Routledge.

Maynard's Industrial Engineering Handbook. 4th ed. William K. Hodson. LC 92-13512. 1872p. 1992. 125.00 (0-07-041086-0) McGraw.

***Maynard's Industrial Engineering Handbook.** 5th ed. Kjell B. Zandin. (Illus.). 2000. 150.00 (0-07-041102-6) McGraw.

Maynard's Mermaid. Robin James. LC 92-63051. (Serendipity Bks.). (Illus.). 32p. (J). (ps-3). 1993. pap. 3.95 (0-8431-3495-X, Price Stern) Peng Put Young Read.

Maynard's Mermaid. Robin James. (Serendipity Ser.). (J). 1993. 9.15 (0-606-05457-X, Pub. by Turtleback) Demco.

Maynaud Features, Acrocyanosis, Cryoimmunoproteins. Ed. by E. Davis. (Advances in Microcirculation Ser.: Vol. 10). (Illus.). viii, 116p. 1982. 85.25 (3-8055-2790-X) S Karger.

Mayne Inheritance. Rosamond Sieman. LC 98-115306. (Illus.). 160p. 1997. 32.95 (0-7022-2934-2, Pub. by Univ Queensland Pr) Intl Spec Bk.

***Mayne Inheritance.** Rosamond Siemon. 248p. 1999. pap. 16.95 (0-7022-3142-8, Pub. by Univ Queensland Pr) Intl Spec Bk.

***Maynerd the Australian Cockatiel.** Frederick Spain. (Illus.). i, 36p. (J). (ps-6). 1999. 13.95 (1-929792-01-8) Roehm Pubs.

Mayo Brothers: Doctors to the World. Lucile Davis. LC 97-35783. (Community Builders Ser.). (J). 1998. 23.00 (0-516-20965-5) Childrens.

Mayo Brothers: Doctors to the World. Lucile Davis. (Community Builders Ser.). (Illus.). 48p. (J). (gr. 3-5). 1999. pap. text 6.95 (0-516-26347-1) Childrens.

Mayo Clinic Diet Manual: A Handbook of Nutrition Practices. 7th ed. Jennifer K. Nelson et al. LC 93-43747. (Illus.). 912p. (C). (gr. 13). 1994. pap. text 75.00 (0-8151-6348-7, 23782) Mosby Inc.

Mayo Clinic Examinations in Neurology. 7th ed. Mayo Clinic Staff. LC 97-26131. (Illus.). 528p. (C). (gr. 13). 1997. text 62.95 (0-8151-9319-X, 26881) Mosby Inc.

Mayo Clinic Guide to Self-Care see Clinica Mayo Guia de Autocuidados

Mayo Clinic Guide to Self-Care. Ed. by Philip T. Hagen. 272p. 1999. pap. 19.95 (0-9627865-7-8) Mayo Fndtn Med Ed & Res.

Mayo Clinic Heart Book. Mayo Clinic Staff. LC 93-25353. 368p. 1993. 26.00 (0-688-09972-6, Wm Morrow) Morrow Avon.

***Mayo Clinic Heart Book.** 2nd rev. ed. Ed. by Bernard J. Gersh. LC 99-53785. (Illus.). 416p. 2000. 30.00 (0-688-17642-9, Wm Morrow) Morrow Avon.

Mayo Clinic Manual of Nuclear Medicine. Ed. by Michael K. O'Connor. LC 96-11649. 592p. 1996. pap. text 89.00 (0-443-07765-7) Church.

Mayo Clinic Manual of Pelvic Surgery. 2nd ed. Maurice J. Webb et al. 224p. text 99.00 (0-7817-2592-5) Lppncott W & W.

Mayo Clinic on Arthritis. Ed. by Gene G. Hunder. (Mayo Clinic on Health Ser.). (Illus.). 200p. 1999. pap. 14.95 (1-893005-00-3) Mayo Fndtn Med Ed & Res.

***Mayo Clinic on Chronic Pain.** Ed. by David Swanson. (Mayo Clinic on Health Ser.). 198p. 1999. pap. 14.95 (1-893005-02-X) Mayo Fndtn Med Ed & Res.

***Mayo Clinic on Digestive Health.** John E. King. (Illus.). 2000. pap. 14.95 (1-893005-04-6) Mayo Fndtn Med Ed & Res.

Mayo Clinic on High Blood Pressure. Sheldon G. Sheps. (Mayo Clinic on Health Ser.). 192p. 1999. pap. text 14.95 (1-893005-01-1) Mayo Fndtn Med Ed & Res.

***Mayo Clinic on Prostate Disease.** Ed. by David M. Barrett. 2000. pap. 14.95 (1-57566-541-7, Knsington) Kensgtn Pub Corp.

***Mayo Clinic on Prostate Health.** David M. Barrett. (Mayo Clinic on Health Ser.). 188p. 2000. pap. 14.95 (1-893005-03-8) Mayo Fndtn Med Ed & Res.

Mayo Clinic Williams - Sonoma Cookbook: Simple Solutions for Eating Well. Mayo Clinic Staff. LC 98-22188. (Illus.). 272p. (gr. 11). 1999. 29.95 (0-7370-0008-2) T-L Custom Pub.

***Mayo Clinic W/S Cookbook** John Phillip & Carroll. (gr. 11). 1999. pap. 18.95 (0-7370-2035-0) T-L Custom Pub.

***Mayo Clinic's Complete Guide for Family Physicians & Residents in Training.** Robert L. Bratton. (Illus.). 550p. 1999. pap. text 111.25 (0-07-134683-X) McGraw-Hill HPD.

Mayo Internal Medicine Board Review, 1996-1997. Ed. by Udaya B. Prakash. 100p. 1996. text 89.95 (0-9627865-2-7) Mayo Fndtn Med Ed & Res.

Mayo Internal Medicine Board Review, 1994-1995. Ed. by Udaya B. Prakash. 100p. 1994. text 89.95 (0-9627865-1-9) Mayo Fndtn Med Ed & Res.

Mayo Internal Medicine Board Review, 1998-1999. Udaya B. Prakash. LC 97-34817. 1000p. 1998. pap. text 89.95 (0-7817-1477-X) Lppncott W & W.

Mayo Internal Medicine Board Review, 2000-2001. Mayo Clinic Department of Internal Medicine Staff & Udaya B.S. Prakash. 1006p. pap. text 89.95 (0-7817-2393-0) Lppncott W & W.

Mayombe. Pepetela & Michael Wolfers. (African Writers Ser.). 1996. pap. 11.95 (0-435-90595-3) Heinemann.

Mayonnaise & the Origin of Life: Thoughts of Minds & Molecules. Harold J. Morowitz. LC 90-25713. vii, 244p. 1991. reprint ed. pap. 14.95 (0-918024-82-X) Ox Bow.

Mayor: An Inside View of San Antonio Politics, 1981-1995. Nelson W. Wolff & Henry Cisneros. LC 97-3280. 1997. 22.95 (1-890346-00-4); pap. 16.95 (1-890346-01-2) San Antonio Express-News.

Mayor & Assembly for London. (Command Papers: No. 3897). 1998. 30.00 (0-10-138972-8, HM389728, Pub. by Statnry Office) Bernan Associates.

Mayor & His Council. Desmond P. Corcoran. 168p. 1998. 24.95 (0-944551-32-7) Sundance Pr TX.

Mayor Consejero del Mundo. Lloyd J. Ogilvie.Tr. of Greatest Counselor in the World. (SPA.). 1996. pap. 7.99 (0-8297-0370-5) Vida Pubs.

Mayor Corning: Albany Icon, Albany Enigma. Paul Grondahl. LC 97-25477. (Illus.). 508p. 1997. 36.00 (1-881324-02-8) Wash Park.

Mayor for a Day. Carl Sommer. LC 99-35276. (Another Sommer-Time Story Ser.). (Illus.). 48p. (J). (ps-4). 1999. 9.95 (1-57537-013-1); lib. bdg. 14.95 (1-57537-057-3) Advance Pub.

Mayor Harding of New York. Walter A. Roberts. LC 73-18602. reprint ed. 42.50 (0-404-11412-1) AMS Pr.

Mayor Is Black. Robert W. Blakely. 156p. (Orig.). (C). 1996. pap. 19.95 (1-877858-42-0, TMIB) Amer Focus Pub.

Mayor Monstruo del Mundo. Pedro Calderon de la Barca. Ed. by Jose M. Ruano De La Haza. (Nueva Austral Ser.: Vol. 81). (SPA.). 1991. pap. text 12.95 (84-239-1881-5) Elliots Bks.

Mayor Monstruo del Mundo. Pedro Calderon de la Barca. Ed. by Angel J. Valbuena-Briones. (Ediciones Criticas Ser.: Vol. 8). (SPA., Illus.). 176p. 1995. pap. 16.00 (0-936388-74-9) Juan de la Cuesta.

Mayor Monstruo del Mundo - Principe Constante. Pedro Calderon de la Barca. 284p. 1989. pap. write for info. (0-7859-5164-4) Fr & Eur.

***Mayor of Aln.** James Rourke. LC 99-215243. 1999. pap. text 12.95 (0-9521558-9-3) Parthian Bks.

***Mayor of Casterbridge.** (YA). 1999. 9.95 (1-56137-350-8) Novel Units.

Mayor of Casterbridge. Thomas Hardy. 1991. pap. text. write for info. (0-17-556573-2) Addison-Wesley.

Mayor of Casterbridge. Thomas Hardy. 1994. pap. text. write for info. (0-582-22586-8, Pub. by Addison-Wesley) Longman.

Mayor of Casterbridge. Thomas Hardy. 336p. (gr. 9-12). 1981. mass mkt. 4.95 (0-553-21024-6, Bantam Classics) Bantam.

Mayor of Casterbridge. Thomas Hardy. Ed. by Norman Page. LC 96-932349. (Literary Texts Ser.). 411p. (C). 1997. pap. 9.95 (1-55111-122-5) Broadview Pr.

Mayor of Casterbridge. Thomas Hardy. LC 92-54297. 1993. 17.00 (0-679-42035-5) Everymns Lib.

Mayor of Casterbridge, 001. Thomas Hardy. Ed. by Robert B. Heilman. LC 62-1552. (gr. 9 up). 1962. pap. 13.96 (0-395-05158-4, RivEd) HM.

Mayor of Casterbridge. Thomas Hardy. Ed. by Richard Adams. (Study Texts Ser.). 1988. pap. text 4.29 (0-582-33171-4, 72064) Longman.

Mayor of Casterbridge. Thomas Hardy. LC 98-52872. (Signet Classics Ser.). 370p. 1999. mass mkt. 5.95 (0-451-52735-6, Sig Classics) NAL.

Mayor of Casterbridge. Thomas Hardy. Ed. by James K. Robinson. LC 76-57983. (Critical Editions Ser.). (Illus.). 436p. (C). 1977. pap. text 14.75 (0-393-09174-0) Norton.

Mayor of Casterbridge. Thomas Hardy. Ed. & Intro. by Dale Kramer. (Oxford World's Classics Ser.). (Illus.). 456p. 1998. pap. 6.95 (0-19-283441-X) OUP.

Mayor of Casterbridge. Thomas Hardy. Ed. by Pamela Norris. 448p. 1993. pap. 4.95 (0-460-87279-6, Everyman's Classic Lib) Tuttle Pubng.

Mayor of Casterbridge. Thomas Hardy. Ed. & Intro. by Keith Wilson. LC 98-134189. li, 393p. 1998. pap. 7.95 (0-14-043513-1) Viking Penguin.

Mayor of Casterbridge. Thomas Hardy. (Classics Library). 352p. 1998. pap. 3.95 (1-85326-098-3, 0983WW, Pub. by Wrdsworth Edits) NTC Contemp Pub Co.

***Mayor of Casterbridge.** Julian Wolfreys. 2000. text 49.95 (0-312-23386-8) St Martin.

Mayor of Casterbridge. large type ed. Thomas Hardy. LC 98-34553. 512p. 1998. 30.00 (0-7838-0351-6, G K Hall Lrg Type) Mac Lib Ref.

Mayor of Casterbridge. large type ed. Thomas Hardy. LC 97-34946. 492p. 1999. 27.95 (1-56000-518-1) Transaction Pubs.

Mayor of Casterbridge. large type ed. Thomas Hardy. 468p. 1997. reprint ed. lib. bdg. 24.00 (0-939495-14-7) North Bks.

Mayor of Casterbridge. Thomas Hardy. reprint ed. lib. bdg. 25.95 (0-88411-560-7) Amereon Ltd.

Mayor of Casterbridge. Thomas Hardy. 326p. 1990. reprint ed. lib. bdg. 24.95 (0-89966-719-8) Buccaneer Bks.

Mayor of Casterbridge. Thomas Hardy. 265p. 1998. reprint ed. lib. bdg. 24.00 (1-58287-048-9) North Bks.

***Mayor of Casterbridge.** 2nd ed. Thomas Hardy. LC 00-37986. 1999. pap. 18.00 (0-393-97498-7, Norton Paperbks) Norton.

Mayor of Casterbridge. 2nd ed. Thomas Hardy. (Illus.). 126p. 1993. pap. text 5.95 (0-19-585118-8) OUP.

Mayor of Casterbridge: A Unit Plan. Mary B. Collins. 75p. 1990. teacher ed., ring bd. 16.95 (1-58337-112-5) Teachers Pet Pubns.

Mayor of Casterbridge Notes. David C. Gild. (Cliffs Notes Ser.). 88p. 1959. pap. 4.95 (0-8220-0816-5, Cliff) IDG Bks.

Mayor of Heaven. Lynn Kanter. LC 97-7030. 224p. 1997. 22.95 (1-879427-29-X) Third Side Pr.

Mayor of Heaven. Lynn Kanter. LC 97-7030. 224p. 1998. pap. 12.95 (1-879427-30-3) Third Side Pr.

Mayor of New Orleans: Just Talking Jazz. Fatima Shaik. LC 87-71147. 160p. 1989. 13.95 (0-88739-050-1); pap. 9.95 (0-88739-071-4) Creat Arts Bk.

***Mayor of West Duluth.** Rick Fournier. 56p. 2000. pap. 4.00 (1-886895-23-6, Ming Ling Pr) Poetry Harbor.

Mayor of Zalamea. adapted ed. Pedro Calderon de la Barca. 1994. pap. 5.50 (0-87129-296-3, M83) Dramatic Pub.

Mayor Regalo Para Ti (Greatest Gift for You) (SPA.). 1.00 (0-685-74953-3, 490281) Editorial Unilit.

***Mayor Regalo (The Greatest Gift) His Woman, His Child.** Beverly Barton. (Deseo Ser.: No. 193). (SPA.). 2000. per. 3.50 (0-373-35323-5, 1-35323-4) Silhouette.

Mayor Who Cleaned up Chicago: A Political Biography of William E. Dever. John R. Schmidt. (Illus.). 255p. 1989. 30.00 (0-87580-144-7) N Ill U Pr.

Mayor Who Made Milwaukee Famous: An Autobiography. Henry W. Maier. LC 92-30042. 304p. 1993. 24.95 (0-8191-8621-X) Madison Bks UPA.

Mayordomia. Gary Teja. (SPA.). 1986. pap. 5.95 (1-55955-094-5) CRC Wrld Lit.

Mayordomo: Chronicle of an Acequia in Northern New Mexico. Stanley Crawford. LC 87-24487. (Illus.). 231p. (C). 1993. reprint ed. pap. 13.95 (0-8263-1445-7) U of NM Pr.

Mayores Estan Locos, Locos, Locos. Jordi S. Fabra.Tr. of Adults Are Crazy, Crazy, Crazy. (SPA., Illus.). 123p. (J). (gr. 5-7). 1994. 11.99 (84-348-4264-5, Pub. by Santillana) T R Bks.

Mayors: The Chicago Political Tradition. rev. ed. Ed. by Paul M. Green & Melvin G. Holli. LC 94-5734. (Illus.). 336p. (C). 1994. pap. 16.95 (0-8093-1961-6) S Ill U Pr.

Mayor's Alley. Mike Polovitz. Ed. by Eileen Zygarlicke. LC 97-222674. 160p. 1997. pap. 14.95 (1-890939-00-5) Century Creations.

Mayors & Money: Fiscal Policy in New York & Chicago. Ester R. Fuchs. (American Politics & Political Economy Ser.). (Illus.). 376p. 1992. pap. text 18.95 (0-226-26791-1); lib. bdg. 52.50 (0-226-26790-3) U Ch Pr.

Mayor's Mandate: Municipal Statecraft & Political Trust. Ann L. Greer. 200p. 1974. pap. 11.95 (0-87073-165-3) Schenkman Bks Inc.

Mayors of Cedar City. York F. Jones & Evelyn Jones. LC 86-61476. (Illus.). 537p. (Orig.). 1998. 10.95 (0-935615-01-6) S Utah U Pr.

***Mayotte: A Country Study Guide, 110 vols.** International Business Publications, USA Staff & Global Investment Center, USA Staff. (World Country Study Guides Library Ser.: Vol. 212). (Illus.). 350p. 2000. pap. 69.95 (0-7397-1035-4) Intl Business Pubns.

***Maypole in the Strand.** George E. Wellworth. LC 99-96674. 2000. pap. 11.95 (0-533-13309-2) Vantage.

***Maypole Traditions: Make-Your-Own Maypole.** Emma Zerik. (Illus.). 16p. 1999. pap. 25.00 (1-929624-01-8) Circle Creative.

Maypole Warriors. Fernando Alegria. Ed. by Yvette E. Miller. Tr. by Carlos Lozano from SPA. LC 92-21222. (Discoveries Ser.). 192p. 1992. pap. 16.95 (0-935480-58-7) Lat Am Lit Rev Pr.

***Maypoles from Around the World.** Emma Zerik. (Illus.). 76p. 1999. pap. 25.00 (1-929624-02-6) Circle Creative.

Mayrig. Henri Verneuil. Tr. by Elise A. Bayizian. LC 95-21411. 1995. 20.00 (0-934728-28-3) D O A C.

Mays: Summary Case Procedure in the Sheriff Court. Richard Mays. 1995. pap. write for info. (0-406-04657-3, MSCP1, MICHIE) LEXIS Pub.

May's Manual of the Diseases of the Eye. James H. Allen. LC 74-10746. 442p. 1974. reprint ed. 48.50 (0-88275-190-5) Krieger.

May's Riding Lesson. Bonnie Bryant. (Pony Tails Ser.: No. 2). (Illus.). (J). (gr. 3-5). 1995. pap. 4.50 (0-553-54207-9) BDD Bks Young Read.

May's Riding Lesson. Bonnie Bryant. (Pony Tails Ser.: No. 2). (Illus.). (J). (gr. 3-5). 1995. 8.60 (0-606-08030-9) Turtleback.

Mayson, French & Ryan on Company Law. Ed. by Derek French et al. 704p. (C). 1991. 58.00 (1-85431-145-X, Pub. by Blackstone Pr) Gaunt.

Mayson, French & Ryan on Company Law. 13th ed. Stephen W. Mayson et al. 709p. 1996. pap. 56.00 (1-85431-549-8, Pub. by Blackstone Pr) Gaunt.

Mayson, French & Ryan on Company Law: 1997-98. 14th ed. Stephen W. Mayson et al. 719p. 1998. pap. 56.00 (1-85431-652-4, Pub. by Blackstone Pr) Gaunt.

Mayson, French & Ryan on Company Law, 1998-99. 15th ed. Stephen W. Mayson et al. 745p. 1998. pap. 58.00 (1-85431-758-X) Gaunt.

***Mayson, French & Ryan on Company Law 1999-2000.** 16th ed. Stephen W. Mayson et al. 771p. 1999. 49.00 (1-85431-884-5, 18417, Pub. by Blackstone Pr) Gaunt.

Mayson on Revenue Law. Susan Blake & Stephen W. Mayson. 728p. (C). 1991. 90.00 (1-85431-146-8, Pub. by Blackstone Pr) Gaunt.

Maytag Corporation--Understanding Financial Statements. 2nd ed. (C). 1998. teacher ed. write for info. (0-13-080640-4, Macmillan Coll) P-H.

Maytag Handbook of Good Cooking. Maytag Staff. Ed. by Trudy Settel. (Illus.). (Orig.). 1985. pap. 3.95 (0-932523-00-5) Briarcliff Pr.

***Maytag Heights.** unabridged ed. Brendan Constantine & Janet Buck. Ed. by R. D. Armstrong. (Little Red Books Ser.). 56p. 1999. pap. 5.00 (1-929878-15-X) Lummox.

Mayuralria. large type ed. Loddie Jones & Marie Nicolai. (ESK., Illus.). 12p. (J). (gr. k-3). 1997. pap. text 6.00 (1-58084-008-6) Lower Kuskokwim.

Maz & the '60 Bucs: When Pittsburgh & Its Pirates Went All the Way. Jim O'Brien. (Pittsburgh Proud Ser.). (Illus.). 512p. 1993. 24.95 (0-916114-12-0) J P OBrien.

Mazacote see Homeplay: La Alegria de Aprender Entre Ninos y Adultos, Series I

Mazamir Hagh & Golzar Omid: Psalms of Truth & Garden of Hope. Shah Maghsoud Sadegh Angha. (PER.). 195p. 1981. 110.00 (0-910735-09-3) MTO Printing & Pubn Ctr.

M

Mazarin. Arthur Hassall. LC 73-137379. (Select Bibliographies Reprint Ser.). 1977. 19.95 (*0-8369-5580-3*) Ayer.

Mazarin: Crisis of Absolutism. Geoffrey Treasure. (Illus.). 432p. (C). 1997. pap. 29.99 (*0-415-16211-4*) Routledge.

Mazaris' Journey to Hades. Mazaris. (Arethusa Monographs: No. 5). xxxviii, 134p. (C). 1975. pap. 8.00 (*0-930881-02-8*) Dept Classics.

Mazda Miata 1800: Enthusiast Shop Manual. Rod Grainger. (Enthusiast Shop Manual Ser.). (Illus.). 300p. 1998. pap. 29.95 (*1-901295-38-9*, 127258AE, Pub. by Vloce Pub) Motorbooks Intl.

Mazda Miata Enthusiasts Manual. Rod Grainger. (Illus.). 600p. 1995. pap. text 29.95 (*1-874105-59-6*, Pub. by Vloce Pub) Motorbooks Intl.

Mazda Miata MX5 Performance Portfolio, 1989-1996. R. M. Clarke. (Performance Portfolio Ser.). (Illus.). 140p. 1997. pap. 19.95 (*1-85520-355-3*, Pub. by Brooklands Bks) Motorbooks Intl.

Mazda Miata Performance Handbook. Norman Garrett. LC 98-48733. (Illus.). 160p. 1998. pap. 21.95 (*0-7603-0437-8*) Motorbooks Intl.

***Mazda MX-5 & Miata, 1989-1999.** James Taylor. (Illus.). 128p. 2000. pap. 19.95 (*1-899870-42-3*, Pub. by Motor Racing) Motorbooks Intl.

Mazda 323/626/929/Glc/Mx-6/Rx-7 1978-1989. Chilton Automotive Editorial Staff. 632p. (C). 1995. pap. 22.95 (*0-8019-8581-1*) Thomson Learn.

Mazda 1978-89 Repair & Tune-Up Guide. Chilton Automotive Editorial Staff. LC 88-43189. (Illus.). 512p. (C). 1989. pap. 16.95 (*0-8019-7945-5*) Thomson Learn.

Mazda Pick-Ups, 1972-89 Repair & Tune up Guide. Chilton Automotive Editorial Staff. LC 88-43190. (Illus.). 448p. (C). 1989. pap. 17.95 (*0-8019-7946-3*) Thomson Learn.

Mazda RX-7. John L. Matras. (Sports Car Color History Ser.). (Illus.). 128p. 1994. pap. 21.95 (*0-87938-938-9*) MBI Pubg.

Mazda RX-7: The 1st Generation, 1979-1985. John F. Ball. (Illus.). 218p. 1990. 19.95 (*0-929214-04-8*) Goldstar Enterprises.

Mazda RX-7, 1986-91 Automotive Repair Manual. rev. ed. Mike Stubblefield & John Haynes. LC 91-75878. (Illus.). 308p. 1991. pap. 17.95 (*1-56392-007-7*) Haynes Manuals.

***Mazda RX-7 Performance Handbook.** Mike Ancas. (Illus.). 160p. 2000. pap. 21.95 (*0-7603-0802-0*, 129797AP, Pub. by MBI Pubg) Motorbooks Intl.

Mazda 626/MX-6 FWD, 1983-91. (Automobile Repair Manuals Ser.). (Illus.). pap. 17.95 (*1-56392-049-2*, MBI 110313AM) Haynes Manuals.

***Mazda 323/Mx-3/626/Mx-6/Millenia/Protege/Probe 1990-1998.** Chilton Automotive Editorial Staff. (Chilton's Total Car Care Ser.). (C). 1999. 22.95 (*0-8019-9130-7*) Thomson Learn.

***Mazda-Trucks, 1994-98.** Chilton Automotive Editorial Staff. LC 98-71363. (Chilton's Total Car Care Ser.). (Illus.). 550p. (C). 1999. pap. text 22.95 (*0-8019-9097-1*) Thomson Learn.

Mazda Trucks, 1972-1986. Chilton Automotive Editorial Staff. 512p. (C). 1997. pap. 22.95 (*0-8019-9057-2*) Thomson Learn.

***Mazda Trucks 1987-1993.** Chilton Designs Publishers Staff. (C). 1999. pap. 22.95 (*0-8019-8964-7*) Thomson Learn.

Mazda Wankel Rotary Aviation Conversion Resource Book. Steve Lafontaine. Ed. by Monique Lafontaine. (Illus.). 32p. (Orig.). 1990. pap. text 10.00 (*0-9625685-0-3*) Lafontaine Pr.

Mazdak: Geschichte einer sozialen Bewegung im sassanidischen Persien. Otakar Klima. Ed. by Moses Finley. LC 79-4986. (Ancient Economic History Ser.). (GER.). 1979. reprint ed. lib. bdg. 30.95 (*0-405-12371-X*) Ayer.

Maze. Catherine Coulter. 1997. mass mkt. 7.50 (*0-515-12249-1*, Jove) Berkley Pub.

Maze. Peter David. LC 98-66418. (Dinotopia Ser.). (YA). (gr. 5-8). 1998. pap. 3.99 (*0-679-88264-2*) Random.

Maze. Mick Fedullo. LC 84-81136. 55p. (Orig.). 1985. 6.50 (*0-913123-06-4*); pap. 4.50 (*0-913123-04-8*) Galileo.

Maze. Will Hobbs. LC 98-10791. 192p. (YA). (gr. 7-12). 1998. 15.95 (*0-688-15092-6*, Wm Morrow) Morrow Avon.

***Maze.** Will Hobbs. LC 98-10791. 256p. (YA). (gr. 5-9). 1999. mass mkt. 4.95 (*0-380-72913-X*, Avon Bks) Morrow Avon.

Maze. large type ed. Catherine Coulter. LC 98-26429. (Large Print Book Ser.). 1998. 26.95 (*1-56895-578-2*) Wheeler Pub.

***Maze: A Desert Journey.** Lucy Rees. 2000. 22.95 (*0-593-03858-4*, Pub. by Transworld Publishers Ltd) Trafalgar.

Maze: A Desert Journey. Lucy Rees. LC 97-26251. 189p. 1997. pap. 15.95 (*0-8165-1831-9*) U of Ariz Pr.

Maze: A Riddle in Words & Pictures. Christopher Manson. (Illus.). 96p. 1995. pap. 8.95 (*0-8050-1088-2*, Owl) H Holt & Co.

Maze: How Not to Go into Business. Elizabeth Petersen. LC 82-62505. 160p. 1983. 14.95 (*0-9610200-0-8*); pap. 9.95 (*0-9610200-1-6*) MEDA Pubns.

Maze Book. Paul McCreary. (Ann Arbor Educational Ser.). (Illus.). (J). (gr. 2-4). 1979. pap. 8.00 (*0-87879-712-2*, Ann Arbor Div) Acad Therapy.

Maze Bright. Carolyn Reed. 54p. 1986. pap. 6.00 (*0-912549-12-2*) Bread & Butter.

Maze Comes to Life. Irene Leland. LC 95-90293. (Illus.). 199p. 1995. 19.95 (*0-9646386-1-4*) Uplifting Pr.

Maze Craze: 46 Puzzles. A. Zipfel. (Illus.). (J). 1994. pap. text 3.95 (*0-486-28080-2*) Dover.

Maze Craze 1. Ruth Heller. (Illus.). 40p. (Orig.). (J). (gr. 1 up). 1988. pap. 4.99 (*0-8431-1732-X*, Price Stern) Peng Put Young Read.

Maze Fun. Mike Artell. (Illus.). (J). 1995. pap. 1.00 (*0-486-28788-2*) Dover.

***Maze Golf.** David Schneiderman. (Illus.). 80p. 2000. mass mkt. 7.95 (*0-9676061-1-X*) Tallfellow.

Maze in the Mind & the World: Labyrinths in Modern Literature. Donald Gutierrez. LC 85-70152. xii, 197p. 1985. 39.00 (*0-87875-293-5*) Whitston Pub.

Maze in the Mirror. Jack L. Chalker. (G. O. D. Inc. Ser.: Bk. 3). 416p. 1992. mass mkt. 3.99 (*0-8125-2069-6*) Tor Bks.

Maze Madness. Elvira Gamiello. (Illus.). 64p. (Orig.). (J). (gr. 4-6). 1988. pap. 1.95 (*0-942025-93-8*) Kidsbks.

Maze Madness. Robert Schnek. (Illus.). (J). 1996. pap. 3.95 (*0-486-29381-5*) Dover.

Maze Madness! Great Explorer Mazes & Mountain Mazes. Roger Moreau. 1997. pap. text 95.20 (*0-8069-9879-2*) Sterling.

Maze Mania. Patrick Merrell. (Illus.). 64p. (Orig.). (J). (gr. 3-7). 1996. pap. 3.95 (*0-8167-4111-5*) Troll Communs.

Maze of Death. Philip K. Dick. LC 93-42196. 1994. pap. 11.00 (*0-679-75298-6*) Random.

Maze of Grace: Claiming Your Twelve Powers. Dianne J. Moore. 220p. Date not set. pap. write for info. (*1-880670-05-4*) Write On Servs.

Maze of Ingenuity: Ideas & Idealism in the Development of Technology. Arnold Pacey. LC 74-18380. 337p. 1975. 37.95 (*0-8419-0181-3*) Holmes & Meier.

Maze of Ingenuity: Ideas & Idealism in the Development of Technology. 2nd ed. Arnold Pacey. (Illus.). 320p. 1992. 35.00 (*0-262-16128-1*); pap. text 17.50 (*0-262-66075-X*) MIT Pr.

Maze of Justice: Diary of a Country Prosecutor. Tawfiq Al-Hakim & A. S. Eban. 160p. 1989. text 25.00 (*0-292-75112-5*) U of Tex Pr.

Maze of Murders. Roderic Jeffries. LC 98-21924. 176p. 1997. text 19.95 (*0-312-18135-3*) St Martin.

Maze of Murders. large type ed. Roderic Jeffries. LC 97-52116. 1998. 21.95 (*0-7862-1381-7*) Thorndike Pr.

Maze of Peril. John E. Holmes. LC 86-15520. (Illus.). 160p. (Orig.). 1986. pap. 6.95 (*0-917053-05-2*) Space And.

***Maze of Secrets.** Mary Apple. 2000. mass mkt. 9.96 (*1-55279-004-5*) Picasso Publ.

Maze of the Fire Dragon: Tales of the Empty-Handed Masters. Terrence Webster-Doyle. (Martial Arts for Peace Ser.). (Illus.). 112p. (YA). (gr. 5-12). 1992. 19.95 (*0-942941-27-6*) Atrium Soc Educ.

Maze of the Fire Dragon: Tales of the Empty-Handed Masters. Terrence Webster-Doyle. LC 92-70338. (Martial Arts for Peace Ser.). (Illus.). 107p. (J). (gr. 5-12). 1996. pap. 14.95 (*0-942941-26-8*) North Atlantic.

Maze of Urban Housing Markets: Theory, Evidence, & Policy. Jerome Rothenberg et al. LC 90-22756. (Illus.). 558p. 1991. 69.95 (*0-226-72951-6*) U Ch Pr.

Maze of Worlds. Brian Lumley. LC 98-11451. 384p. 1998. 25.95 (*0-312-86604-6*, Pub. by Tor Bks) St Martin.

Maze of Worlds. Brian Lumley. 512p. 1999. mass mkt. 6.99 (*0-8125-7780-9*, Pub. by Tor Bks) St Martin.

Maze Puzzles. K. Blundell & Jenny Taylor. (Maze Fun Ser.). (Illus.). 72p. (J). (gr. k-2). 1994. pap. 10.95 (*0-7460-1327-2*, Usborne) EDC.

Maze Puzzles: Early Learning Workbooks. Peter M. Spizzirri. Ed. by Linda Spizzirri. (Illus.). 32p. (J). (ps-2). 1997. pap. 2.95 (*0-86545-236-9*) Spizzirri.

MazeCraze 3 see Nature's Mazes: Maze Funbook

Mazel & Shlimazel: or The Milk of a Lioness. Isaac Bashevis Singer. Tr. by Elizabeth Shub. 48p. pap. 6.95 (*0-374-44786-1*) FS&G.

Mazel & Shlimazel or The Milk of a Lioness. Isaac Bashevis Singer. 1995. 12.15 (*0-606-09602-7*, Pub. by Turtleback) Demco.

Mazel Tov Y'all: The Ultimate Southern-Jewish Bake Book. rev. ed. Sara Kasdan. LC 98-2870. (Illus.). 186p. 1998. pap. 14.95 (*1-57090-080-9*) Alexander Dist.

Mazeland. K. Kishida. 100p. 1985. 9.95 (*0-13-566612-0*) P-H.

Mazemaster 3: The Mazemaster Returns. David A. Russo. 96p. 1993. pap. 9.95 (*0-671-73020-7*, Fireside) S&S Trade Pap.

Mazengarb's Employment Law, 2 vols., Set. Moira Thompson & Robert Mackay. ring bd. 378.00 (*0-409-66770-6*, NZ, MICHIE) LEXIS Pub.

Mazenod, 1782-1864: Founder of the Oblates of Mary Immaculate. Jean Leflon. Tr. by Francis D. Flanagan from FRE. LC 94-11821. 394p. (Orig.). 1994. pap. 17.50 (*1-56518-062-3*) Coun Res Values.

Mazepa the Cossack: Mazepa Hetman of the Ukraine. S. C. Mazepa. (Illus.). 250p. 19.95 (*0-9636099-0-4*) S C Mazepa.

Mazepists: Ukrainian Separatism in the Eighteenth Century. Orest Subtelny. (East European Monographs: No. 87). 280p. 1981. text 60.00 (*0-914710-81-8*, Pub. by East Eur Monographs) Col U Pr.

Mazes. Adrian Fisher & Diana Kingham. (Album Ser.: No. 264). (Illus.). 32p. 1989. pap. 5.25 (*0-7478-0116-9*, Pub. by Shire Pubns) Parkwest Pubns.

Mazes. Barbara Gregorich. Ed. by Joan Hoffman. (Get Ready! Bks.). (Illus.). 32p. (J). (ps-3). 1983. student ed. 2.49 (*0-938256-57-2*, 02057) Sch Zone Pub Co.

Mazes. Illus. by Margeaux Lucas. (Home Workbooks Ser.). 64p. (Orig.). (J). (ps-1). 1997. pap., wbk. ed. 2.49 (*0-88724-369-X*, CD-6866) Carson-Dellos.

Mazes. D. Phillips. 1994. pap. text 1.00 (*0-486-27859-X*) Dover.

Mazes. Ross. (Illus.). 32p. (J). pap. 1.00 (*0-486-29565-6*) Dover.

Mazes: Essays. Hugh Kenner. LC 94-40314. 336p. 1995. pap. 17.95 (*0-8203-1720-9*) U of Ga Pr.

Mazes & Labyrinths. 2nd ed. Walter Shepherd. Orig. Title: For Amazement Only. 1961. pap. 4.95 (*0-486-20731-5*) Dover.

Mazes & Labyrinths: Their History & Development. W. H. Matthews. (Illus.). 254p. 1970. reprint ed. pap. 8.95 (*0-486-22614-X*) Dover.

Mazes Around the World. Mary D. Lankford. (J). 1924. write for info. (*0-688-16519-2*, Wm Morrow); lib. bdg. write for info. (*0-688-16520-6*, Wm Morrow) Morrow Avon.

Mazes, Mazes, Mazes. Ed. by Jody Taylor. LC 93-72343. (Illus.). 64p. (J). (gr. 2-7). 1994. pap. 6.95 (*1-56397-334-0*) Boyds Mills Pr.

***Mazes on Mars: An Astronishing Assortment of Astronomical Mazes.** Patrick Merrell. 1999. pap. 3.95 (*0-8167-5945-6*) Troll Communs.

***Mazilli's Shoes.** Darlene Madott. (Drama Ser.: Vol. 17). (ENG & ITA.). 128p. 1999. pap. 13.00 (*1-55071-097-4*, Pub. by Guernica Editions) Paul & Co Pubs.

***Mazing of the Text: The Search for Signification in the Labyrinth of French Poetics.** Margaret M. Bolovan. LC 98-48969. (Currents in Comparative Romance Languages & Literatures Ser.: Vol. 75). 208p. (C). 1999. text 48.95 (*0-8204-4069-8*) P Lang Pubng.

Maziva a Specialni Oleje see Lubricants & Special Fluids

Mazoezi Ya Kiswahili: Kitabu Cha Wanafunzi Wa Mwaka Wa Kwanza: Swahili Exercises: A Workbook for First Year Students. Lioba J. Moshi. LC 88-27671. 244p. (Orig.). (C). 1989. pap. text 26.50 (*0-8191-7215-4*) U Pr of Amer.

Mazruiana Collection: A Comprehensive Annotated Bibliography of the Published Works of Ali A. Mazrui, 1962-1997. Abdul S. Benath. LC 98-909224. xiii, 348p. 1998. write for info. (*81-207-2119-5*) Sterling Pubs.

Mazungumzo: Interviews with East African Writers, Publishers, Editors & Scholars. Ed. by Bernth Lindfors. LC 80-25684. (Papers in International Studies: Africa Ser.: No. 41). 187p. reprint ed. pap. 58.00 (*0-7837-1327-4*, 204147500001) Bks Demand.

Mazurca para Dos Muertos see Mazurka for Two Dead Men

Mazurca para Dos Muertos. Camilo J. Cela. (SPA.). 1983. pap. 8.50 (*84-322-0484-6*, 3014) Ediciones Norte.

Mazurca Para dos Muertos. 18th ed. C. Jose Cela. (SPA.). 267p. 1990. pap. 29.95 (*0-7859-0579-0*, S40349) Fr & Eur.

***Mazurka.** Frederic Chopin. (Music Scores Ser.). 1998. pap. 7.98 (*963-8303-31-X*) Kone Music.

Mazurka for Two Dead Men. Camilo Jose Cela. Tr. by Patricia Haugaard from SPA. LC 92-12618. Tr. of Mazurca para Dos Muertos. 272p. 1992. 21.95 (*0-8112-1222-X*, Pub. by New Directions) Norton.

Mazurka for Two Dead Men. Camilo Jose Cela. Tr. by Patricia Haugaard from SPA. LC 92-12618. Tr. of Mazurca para Dos Muertos. 272p. 1994. reprint ed. pap. 10.95 (*0-8112-1277-7*, NDP789, Pub. by New Directions) Norton.

Mazurkas. Frederic Chopin. 160p. 1987. pap. 8.95 (*0-486-25548-4*) Dover.

Mazurkas, 1. Alexander Skrjabin. 1998. pap. text 7.98 (*963-9059-71-4*, NIPI Bks) Natl Intermedia.

Mazurkas: Poems from Hollywood. Mark Dunster. 11p. 1998. pap. 5.00 (*0-89642-567-3*) Linden Pubs.

***Mazurkas Collection.** Matthew Ardizzone. 72p. 1999. 10.95 (*0-7866-4937-2*, 98096) Mel Bay.

Mazurkas Poemes Impromptus & Other Pieces for Piano. Alexander Scriabin. 336p. 1991. pap. 15.95 (*0-486-26555-2*) Dover.

***Maz'ya Anniversary Collection, 2 vols.** Ed. by J. Rossmann et al. 744p. 1999. 268.00 (*3-7643-6203-0*) Birkhauser.

***Maz'ya Anniversary Collection Vol. 1: On Maz'yas's Work in Functional Analysis, Partial Differential Equations & Applications.** Ed. by J. Rossmann et al. (Operator Theory Ser.: Vol. 109). 376p. 1999. 149.00 (*3-7643-6201-4*) Birkhauser.

***Maz'ya Anniversary Collection Vol. 2: Rostock Conference on Functional Analysis, Partial Differential Equations & Applications.** Ed. by J. Rossmann et al. (Operator Theory Ser.: Vol. 110). 368p. 1999. 149.00 (*3-7643-6202-2*) Birkhauser.

Mazzini. Denis Mack Smith. LC 93-38313. (Illus.). 352p. 1994. 37.50 (*0-300-05884-5*) Yale U Pr.

Mazzini. Denis M. Smith. (Illus.). 352p. 1996. pap. 17.00 (*0-300-06884-1*) Yale U Pr.

Mazzini: A Life for the Religion of Politics. Roland Sarti. LC 96-37112. 264p. 1997. 59.95 (*0-275-95080-8*, Praeger Pubs) Greenwood.

Mazzini: Prophet of Modern Europe. Gwilym O. Griffith. LC 78-80552. 1970. reprint ed. 45.00 (*0-86527-124-0*) Fertig.

Mazzini: The Story of a Great Italian. Edyth Hinkley. LC 73-114883. (Select Bibliographies Reprint Ser.). 1977. 23.95 (*0-8369-5287-1*) Ayer.

MBA: The First Century. Carter A. Daniel. LC 97-25110. 336p. 1998. 48.50 (*0-8387-5362-0*) Bucknell U Pr.

MBA - Management by Auerbach: Management Tips from the Leader of One of America's Most Successful Organizations. Red Auerbach & Ken Dooley. 256p. 1991. text 19.95 (*0-02-504481-8*) Macmillan.

MBA Answer Book: A Career Guide for the Person Who Means Business. Mark O'Brien. (Illus.). 240p. 1984. 15.50 (*0-13-566779-8*) P-H.

MBA Concepts for Lawyers. Edward S. Adams. 202p. 1997. pap. 35.00 (*0-943380-53-7*) PEG MN.

MBA Distance Learning Programs: The Best New Way to Earn an MBA 1999. Peterson's Guides Staff. (Peterson's Guides). 240p. 1998. pap. text 18.95 (*0-7689-0125-1*) Petersons.

***MBA Distance Learning Programs: The Hottest New Way to Earn a Graduate Business Degree.** 2nd ed. Petersons. 264p. 1999. pap. text 18.95 (*0-7689-0282-7*) Petersons.

MBA Economics. Mark Jackson. (Illus.). 200p. (C). 1995. pap. text 37.95 (*1-55786-631-7*) Blackwell Pubs.

MBA Field Studies: A Guide for Students & Faculty. Ed. by E. Raymond Corey. 80p. 1990. pap. 5.95 (*0-87584-251-8*) Harvard Busn.

MBA Golf: The Book for MBAs Who Love Golf. Richard J. Nolan, Jr. (Illus.). ix, 150p. (Orig.). (C). 1996. pap. 16.95 (*0-9653401-0-4*) MBA Golf.

MBA Handbook: Study Skills for Managers. 3rd ed. Sheila Cameron. vii, 337p. 1997. 57.50 (*0-273-62346-X*, Pub. by Pitman Pub) Trans-Atl Phila.

***MBA Management.** Harding & Long. 240p. 1998. pap. 27.95 (*0-566-08137-7*) Ashgate Pub Co.

MBA Programs. ETS Staff. 1986. pap. 9.95 (*0-446-38437-2*, Pub. by Warner Bks) Little.

MBA Programs, Vol. 1. 1988. pap. 9.95 (*0-446-38850-5*, Pub. by Warner Bks) Little.

***MBA Programs 2001: U.S., Canadian, & International Business Schools 2001.** 6th ed. Peterson's Guides Staff. 1275p. 2000. pap. text 29.95 (*0-7689-0441-2*) Petersons.

MBA Programs 92-94. 1994. 13.95 (*0-446-77748-X*) Warner Bks.

MBA's Guide to Microsoft Excel 2000: The Essential Reference for Business Professionals. Stephen L. Nelson. (Illus.). 512p. 1999. pap. 39.99 (*0-9672981-0-5*) Redmond Technology Pr.

***MBA's Guide to the Internet: The Essential Internet Reference for Business Professionals.** Stephen L. Nelson et al. 624p. 2000. pap. 39.95 (*0-9672981-6-4*) Redmond Technology Pr.

***MBA's Guide to Windows 2000: The Essential Windows 2000 Reference for Business Professionals.** Stephen L. Nelson et al. 624p. 2000. pap. 39.95 (*0-9672981-5-6*) Redmond Technology Pr.

MBAs on the Fast Track: Career Mobility of Young Managers. Phyllis A. Wallace. LC 88-34180. 224p. 1989. text 34.95 (*0-88730-120-7*, HarpBusn) HarpInfo.

MBD: The Family Book about Minimal Brain Dysfunction. Richard A. Gardner. LC 72-96533. (Illus.). 192p. 1973. 40.00 (*0-87668-853-9*) Aronson.

MBE Survival Kit: Guide to Success on the Multi-State Bar Exam. Jeff Adachi & Soloman Wallack. 443p. (Orig.). (C). 1998. pap. 29.95 (*1-882278-08-9*) Survival Series.

Mbeere in Kenya Vol. I: Changing Rural Ecology. Bernard W. Riley & David Brokensha. LC 88-12108. (Illus.). 384p. (Orig.). (C). 1988. pap. text 29.00 (*0-8191-6998-6*); lib. bdg. 55.00 (*0-8191-6997-8*) U Pr of Amer.

MBL Suite: 2 Flutes, String Quartet, Score & Parts. E. Laderman. 80p. 1993. pap. 35.00 (*0-7935-2363-X*) H Leonard.

MBO II: A System of Managerial Leadership. George S. Odiorne. LC 78-72336. 17.95 (*1-56103-977-2*) Ctr Effect Perf.

MBONE: Interactive Multimedia on the Internet. 2nd ed. Macmillan Technical Publishing Staff. 350p. 44.99 (*1-57870-019-1*) Macmillan Tech.

MBONE: Multicasting Tomorrow's Internet. Kevin Savetz. 264p. 1996. pap. 24.99 (*1-56884-723-8*) IDG Bks.

Mbongi: An African Traditional Political Institution. Kia B. Fu-Kiau. 98p. (Orig.). 1985. pap. 9.95 (*0-943324-14-9*) Omenana.

Mbundu. Onwuka N. Njoku. LC 96-32811. (Heritage Library of African Peoples: Set 3). (Illus.). 64p. (YA). (gr. 7-12). 1997. lib. bdg. 16.95 (*0-8239-2004-6*, D2004-6) Rosen Group.

Mbuti, 14 vols. Onukaba Adinoyi-ojo. Ed. by George Bond & Gary V. Wyck. LC 94-22789. (Heritage Library of African Peoples). (Illus.). 64p. (YA). (gr. 7-12). 1995. lib. bdg. 16.95 (*0-8239-1998-6*) Rosen Group.

Mbuti Design: Paintings by Pygmy Women of the Ituri Rainforest. Georges Meurant & Robert F. Tho. LC 95-78910. (Illus.). 224p. 1996. 60.00 (*0-500-97430-6*, Pub. by Thames Hudson) Norton.

Mbuti Pygmies: Adaptation & Change in Ituri Forest. Colin M. Turnbull. (Case Studies in Cultural Anthropology). 161p. (C). 1983. pap. text 23.50 (*0-03-061537-2*) Harcourt Coll Pubs.

Mbwa Wa Familia Ya Baskerville: The Hound of the Baskervilles (Kiswahili) Arthur Conan Doyle. Tr. by Zachary Mumbo Mosotf & Hassan O. Ali. (Sherlockian Scholarship Ser.). Tr. of Hound of the Baskervilles. (SWA.). pap. 12.00 (*1-55246-059-2*) Battered Silicon.

MC & AC Cable Guide. James G. Stallcup. Ed. by James W. Stallcup. LC 94-73592. (Illus.). 137p. (C). 1995. pap. 14.95 (*1-885341-04-0*) Thomson Learn.

Mc Carroll: The Family of Simon Mc Carroll & Ann Cosky Glenn of County Derry, Ulster, Ireland to America 1775-1993. Mabel R. Love. (Illus.). 278p. (Orig.). 1993. 38.00 (*0-9632429-1-1*) Love Pubs.

Mc Carthyism. 3rd ed. Ed. by Thomas C. Reeves. LC 88-13666. 154p. (C). 1989. pap. 11.50 (*0-89464-289-8*) Krieger.

Mc Clure Press. limited ed. Lewis McClure. (Illus.). 32p. 1984. 95.00 (*0-915998-21-1*) Lime Rock Pr.

MC Guide to Freshwater Fishing in New England. Brian R. Kologe. LC 91-9522. (Illus.). 288p. 1991. pap. 14.95 (*1-878239-07-4*) AMC Books.

MC95: Proceedings of the International Metallographic Conference Held in Colmar, France 10-12 May. LC 96-83615. 456p. 1996. 113.00 (*0-87170-569-9*, 6359) ASM.

MC 68HC11 an Introduction: Software & Hardware Interfacing. Han-Uei Huang. 500p. (C). 1998. pap. 58.95 (*0-314-06735-3*) West Pub.

MC68 HC11 Laboratory Manual: Software & Hardware Interfacing. Charles V. Melfi. LC 98-6997. (C). 2000. pap. 22.50 (*0-7668-0482-8*) Delmar.

An Asterisk (*) at the beginning of an entry indicates that the title is appearing for the first time.

MC68000 8- 16- 32-Bit Microprocessor User's Manual. 7th ed. Motorola, Inc. Staff. 368p. 1989. pap. 22.95 (*0-13-567074-8*) P-H.

MC 68020 32-Bit Microprocessor User's Manual. Motorola, Inc. Staff. (Illus.). 448p. 1984. pap. 18.95 (*0-13-541467-9*) P-H.

MC-Tools for PC XT/AT Using the Microcontroller SAB80C535: Board HEX-LOAD, Debugger & OSCI-Programs for Development & Training. O. Feger & A. Reith. 254p. 1992. 99.95 (*3-8009-4131-7*) Wiley.

MCA Code of Safe Working Practices for Merchant Seamen, 1998. 2nd ed. 350p. 1998. ring bd. 40.00 (*0-11-551836-3*, HM18363, Pub. by Statnry Office) Balogh.

MCAD Buyer's Guide: Solids-Based Systems for Mechanical CAD/CAM. 3rd rev. ed. John MacKrell & David Albert. (Illus.). 600p. 1999. ring bd. 795.00 (*1-889760-06-4*) CIMdata Inc.

McAdoo about Nothing: Selections from "The Rusty Saber" Joe McAdoo. (Illus.). 150p. 1997. pap. 8.95 (*0-9638648-1-5*) Barnabs Pub.

McAfee Anti-Virus for Beginners. Brian Howard. LC 97-128656. 1997. pap. text 19.95 incl. cd-rom (*1-55755-318-1*) Abacus MI.

McAfee County: A Chronicle. Mark Steadman. LC 97-31431. 1998. pap. 16.95 (*0-8203-2014-5*) U of Ga Pr.

McAfee County: A Chronicle. Mark S. Steadman, Jr. LC 83-46031. reprint ed. 37.50 (*0-404-19941-0*) AMS Pr.

McAlister's Car Care Organizer. Marcia McAlister. 12p. (Orig.). 1985. pap. 3.00 (*0-9615587-0-9*) M McAlister Enterps.

McAllen, Texas. San Antonio Cartographers Staff. 1995. 2.95 (*0-671-56289-4*) Macmillan.

McAllister: Die-Hard. large type ed. Matt A. Chisholm. (Linford Western Library). 336p. 1985. pap. 16.99 (*0-7089-6134-7*, Linford) Ulverscroft.

McAllister: Quarry. large type ed. Matt A. Chisholm. (Linford Western Library). 304p. 1985. pap. 16.99 (*0-7089-6141-X*, Linford) Ulverscroft.

McAllister: Scottish Law of Leases. Angus McAllister. 208p. 1989. pap. 44.00 (*0-406-10589-8*, MICHIE) LEXIS Pub.

McAllister & Cheyenne Death. large type ed. Matt A. Chisholm. (Linford Western Library). 304p. 1985. pap. 16.99 (*0-7089-6138-X*, Linford) Ulverscroft.

McAllister & Guthrie: Scottish Property Law - an Introduction. Angus McAllister & T. G. Guthrie. 304p. 1992. pap. 44.00 (*0-406-00105-7*, MICHIE) LEXIS Pub.

McAllister & His Double. Arthur C. Train. LC 76-110220. (Short Story Index Reprint Ser.). 1977. 23.95 (*0-8369-3372-9*) Ayer.

McAllister & the Spanish Gold. large type ed. Matt A. Chisholm. (Linford Western Library). 320p. 1985. pap. 16.99 (*0-7089-6090-1*, Linford) Ulverscroft.

McAllister. Descendants of Archibald McAllister of W. Pennsboro Township, Cumberland Co., Pa., 1730-1898. Mary C. McAllister. 105p. 1996. reprint ed. pap. 19.50 (*0-8328-5324-0*); reprint ed. lib. bdg. 29.50 (*0-8328-5323-2*) Higginson Bk Co.

McAllister Family Records: Compiled for the Descendants of Abraham Addams McAllister & His Wife Julia Ellen Stratton McAllister of Covington, Virginia. J. Gray McAllister. (Illus.). 88p. 1994. reprint ed. pap. 17.50 (*0-8328-4227-3*); reprint ed. lib. bdg. 27.50 (*0-8328-4226-5*) Higginson Bk Co.

McAllister Never Surrenders. large type ed. Matt A. Chisholm. (Linford Western Library). 320p. 1985. pap. 16.99 (*0-7089-6094-4*, Linford) Ulverscroft.

McAllister on the Comanche Crossing. large type ed. Matt A. Chisholm. (Linford Western Library). 320p. 1985. pap. 16.99 (*0-7089-6086-3*, Linford) Ulverscroft.

McAllister's Baby. Trisha David. 1997. per. 3.25 (*0-373-03472-5*, 1-03472-7) Harlequin Bks.

McAllister's Baby. large type ed. David. 1997. per. 3.25 (*0-373-15718-5*) Harlequin Bks.

McAlpine's Multiple Sclerosis. 2nd ed. W. B. Matthews et al. (Illus.). 401p. 1990. text 131.00 (*0-443-04047-8*) Church.

McAlpine's Multiple Sclerosis. 3rd ed. D. A. Compston et al. (Illus.). 440p. 1998. text. write for info. (*0-443-05008-2*) Church.

Mcarandy Was Hanged Under Tyburn Tree. Elanor Berry. LC 98-105686. 254p. 1997. 0.00 (*0-7223-3120-7*) A H Stockwell.

McArdel Diary: Saga of an Irish American. H. Dean Baugh. 308p. mass mkt. 4.99 (*1-55197-035-X*) Picasso Publ.

MCAT - Medical College Admission Test: Comprehensive Manual Self Study. 2nd rev. ed. David M. Tarlow. (Illus.). 135p. (C). 1999. pap. text 19.95 (*1-57732-089-1*) Datar Pub.

MCAT - Medical College Admission Test: For Comprehensive Review. 7th rev. ed. David M. Tarlow. (Illus.). 140p. (Orig.). (C). 1996. pap., student ed. 19.95 (*1-57732-000-X*) Datar Pub.

MCAT - Medical College Admission Test No. 1: Practice Exam Annotated Answers. 2nd rev. ed. David M. Tarlow. 20p. (C). 1999. pap. text 6.95 (*1-57732-091-3*) Datar Pub.

MCAT - Medical College Admission Test No. 1: Practice Examination. 2nd rev. ed. David M. Tarlow. 40p. (C). 1999. pap. text 18.95 (*1-57732-090-5*) Datar Pub.

MCAT - Medical College Admission Test No. 2: Practice Exam Annotated Answers. 2nd rev. ed. David M. Tarlow. 20p. (C). 1999. pap. text 6.95 (*1-57732-093-X*) Datar Pub.

MCAT - Medical College Admission Test No. 2: Practice Examination. 2nd rev. ed. David M. Tarlow. 40p. (C). 1999. pap. text 18.95 (*1-57732-092-1*) Datar Pub.

MCAT - Medical College Admission Test No. 3: Practice Exam Annotated Answers. 2nd rev. ed. David M. Tarlow. 20p. (C). 1999. pap. text 6.95 (*1-57732-095-6*) Datar Pub.

MCAT - Medical College Admission Test No. 3: Practice Examination. 2nd rev. ed. David M. Tarlow. 40p. (C). 1999. pap. text 18.95 (*1-57732-094-8*) Datar Pub.

MCAT - Medical College Admission Test No. 4: Practice Exam Annotated Answers. 2nd rev. ed. David M. Tarlow. (C). 1999. pap. text 6.95 (*1-57732-097-2*) Datar Pub.

MCAT - Medical College Admission Test No. 4: Practice Examination. 2nd rev. ed. David M. Tarlow. 40p. (C). 1999. pap. text 18.95 (*1-57732-096-4*) Datar Pub.

MCAT - Medical College Admission Test No. 5: Practice Exam Annotated Answers. 2nd rev. ed. David M. Tarlow. (C). 1999. pap. text 6.95 (*1-57732-099-9*) Datar Pub.

MCAT - Medical College Admission Test No. 5: Practice Examination. 2nd rev. ed. David M. Tarlow. 40p. (C). 1999. pap. text 18.95 (*1-57732-098-0*) Datar Pub.

MCAT - Medical College Admission Test - Core Content. 2nd rev. ed. David M. Tarlow. (Illus.). 400p. 1999. pap. text 49.95 (*1-57774-029-7*) Educ Tsting Cnslts.

MCAT Biology Book. Nancy Morvillo & Matthew Schmidt. (Illus.). 416p. (C). 2000. pap. 29.95 (*1-889057-08-8*) Nova Pr.

MCAT Chemistry Book. Ajikumar Aryangat. (Illus.). 496p. (C). 1999. pap. 29.95 (*1-889057-12-6*) Nova Pr.

***MCAT Complete Review.** Stefan Bosworth. 960p. 1999. pap. text 54.95 (*0-02-863562-0*, Arco) Macmillan Gen Ref.

***MCAT Comprehensive Review, 2000 Ed.** Kaplan. LC 98-657630. 1088p. 1999. pap. text 65.00 incl. cd-rom (*0-684-86746-X*) S&S Trade.

MCAT Comprehensive Review 1999. Kaplan Staff. (Illus.). 1088p. 1998. pap. 60.00 incl. cd-rom (*0-684-85357-4*) Kaplan.

MCAT Essentials. Daniel Roth. LC 97-16631. (Illus.). 125p. 1997. pap. 14.95 (*0-683-30105-5*) Lppncott W & W.

MCAT Exam No. 5 Annotated Answers (Medical College Admissions Test) 7th ed. David M. Tarlow. (Orig.). (C). 1996. pap. 5.95 (*1-57732-010-7*) Datar Pub.

MCAT Exam No. 4 Annotated Answers (Medical College Admissions Test) 7th ed. David M. Tarlow. (Orig.). 1996. pap. 5.95 (*1-57732-009-3*) Datar Pub.

MCAT Exam No. 4 (Medical College Admission Test) 7th ed. David M. Tarlow. 40p. (Orig.). (C). 1996. pap. 19.95 (*1-57732-004-2*) Datar Pub.

MCAT Exam No. 1 Annotated Answers (Medical College Admissions Test) David M. Tarlow. 1996. pap. 5.95 (*1-57732-006-9*) Datar Pub.

MCAT Exam No. 1 (Medical College Admission Test) 7th ed. David M. Tarlow. 40p. (Orig.). 1996. pap. 19.95 (*1-57732-001-8*) Datar Pub.

MCAT Exam No. 3 Annotated Answers (Medical College Admission Test) 7th ed. David M. Tarlow. (Orig.). 1996. pap. 5.95 (*1-57732-008-5*) Datar Pub.

MCAT Exam No. 3 (Medical College Admission Test) 7th ed. David M. Tarlow. (Illus.). 1996. pap. 19.95 (*1-57732-003-4*) Datar Pub.

MCAT Exam No. 2 Annotated Answers (Medical College Admission Test) 7th ed. David M. Tarlow. (Orig.). 1996. pap. 5.95 (*1-57732-007-7*) Datar Pub.

MCAT Exam No. 2 (Medical College Admission Test) 7th rev. ed. David M. Tarlow. 40p. (Orig.). 1996. pap. 19.95 (*1-57732-002-6*) Datar Pub.

MCAT Exam No. 5 (Medical College Admission Test) 7th ed. David M. Tarlow. (Orig.). 1996. pap. 19.95 (*1-57732-005-0*) Datar Pub.

MCAT (Medical College Admission Test) David M. Tarlow. (Practice Examination Ser.: No. 4). 40p. 1992. pap. 16.95 (*0-931572-10-X*) Datar Pub.

MCAT Medical College Admission Test. rev. ed. Research & Education Association Staff. LC 98-67276. (Illus.). 1008p. 2000. pap. 44.95 (*0-87891-872-8*) Res & Educ.

MCAT (Medical College Admission Test) Practice Examination, No. 1. David M. Tarlow. (Practice Examination Ser.). 40p. (Orig.). 1992. pap. 16.95 (*0-931572-07-X*) Datar Pub.

MCAT (Medical College Admission Test) Practice Examination, No. 2. David M. Tarlow. (Practice Examination Ser.). 40p. (Orig.). 1992. pap. 16.95 (*0-931572-08-8*) Datar Pub.

MCAT (Medical College Admission Test) Practice Examination, No. 3. David M. Tarlow. (Practice Examination Ser.). 40p. (Orig.). 1992. pap. 16.95 (*0-931572-09-6*) Datar Pub.

MCAT (Medical College Admission Test) Practice Examination, No. 5. David M. Tarlow. (Practice Examination Ser.). 40p. (Orig.). 1992. pap. 16.95 (*0-931572-11-8*) Datar Pub.

MCAT, 1998. Kaplan Staff. 1997. 20.00 (*0-684-83673-4*) S&S Trade.

MCAT, 1998: Complete Review. Kaplan Staff. 1997. 60.00 incl. cd-rom (*0-684-83672-6*) S&S Trade.

MCAT Physics. 5th ed. Giancoli. (C). 1998. pap. text, student ed. 22.20 (*0-13-627951-1*) S&S Trade.

MCAT Physics Book. Garrett Biehle. 444p. 2000. pap. 29.95 (*1-889057-00-2*) Nova Pr.

***MCAT Practice Book.** Ajikumar Aryangat. (Illus.). 450p. (C). 2000. 29.95 (*1-889057-16-9*) Nova Pr.

MCAT Practice Examination: Annotated Master Answer Guide, No. 1. David M. Tarlow. 1992. 4.95 (*0-931572-32-0*) Datar Pub.

MCAT Practice Examination: Annotated Master Answer Guide, No. 2. David M. Tarlow. 1992. 4.95 (*0-931572-33-9*) Datar Pub.

MCAT Practice Examination: Annotated Master Answer Guide, No. 3. David M. Tarlow. 1992. 4.95 (*0-931572-34-7*) Datar Pub.

MCAT Practice Examination: Annotated Master Answer Guide, No. 4. David M. Tarlow. 1992. 4.95 (*0-931572-35-5*) Datar Pub.

MCAT Practice Examination: Annotated Master Answer Guide, No. 5. David M. Tarlow. 1992. 4.95 (*0-931572-36-3*) Datar Pub.

MCAT Preparation Guide. Miriam S. Willey' & Barbara M. Jarecky. 144p. 1995. pap. text 17.50 (*0-8131-0847-0*) U Pr of Ky.

MCAT Sample Exams. 2nd ed. Stefan Bosworth et al. LC 96-209878. 240p. 1996. pap. 13.95 (*0-02-861312-0*, Arco) Macmillan Gen Ref.

MCAT Sample Exams. 3rd ed. Stefan Bosworth. 240p. 1998. pap. text 13.95 (*0-02-862501-3*, Arc) IDG Bks.

MCAT Sample Tests with CD. Stefan Bosworth et al. (Illus.). 256p. 1999. pap. 34.95 incl. cd-rom (*0-02-863253-2*, Arco) Macmillan Gen Ref.

***MCAT Subject Review with Tests.** Stefan Bosworth. (Illus.). 464p. 1999. pap. text 39.95 incl. audio compact disk (*0-02-863255-9*, Arco) Macmillan Gen Ref.

MCAT Success. Peterson's Guides Staff. LC 96-39646. (Test Success Ser.). 352p. 1996. pap. 12.95 (*1-56079-685-5*); pap. 24.95 incl. disk (*1-56079-689-8*) Petersons.

***MCAT Success.** 4th ed. Petersons. 364p. 1999. pap. text 16.95 (*0-7689-0297-5*) Petersons.

MCAT Success 1999. Peterson's Guides Staff. (Peterson's Guides). 356p. 1998. pap. text 16.95 (*0-7689-0149-9*) Petersons.

MCAT SuperCourse. 4th ed. Stefan Bosworth et al. 720p. 1997. 39.95 (*0-02-861711-8*, Arc) IDG Bks.

MCAT Supercourse. 22nd ed. Stefan Bosworth et al. 720p. 1996. 35.00 (*0-02-861083-0*) Macmillan.

MCAT: The Answer Key: In Plain English. Nilanjan Sen. 1999. pap. text 29.95 (*1-890838-05-5*) Indus Pub.

***MCAT Verbal Reasoning Review.** Stefan Bosworth. 256p. 2000. pap. text 14.95 (*0-02-863561-2*, Arco) Macmillan Gen Ref.

Mcat with Testware: Book Plus Software. Research & Education Associaton Staff. 1997. pap. text 52.95 (*0-87891-807-8*) Res & Educ.

MCAT Workbook. Kaplan Educational Centres Staff. LC 97-30259. 304p. 1997. 20.00 (*0-684-84535-0*) S&S Trade.

McBain's Ladies: The Women of the 87th Precinct. Ed McBain, pseud. LC 87-40389. 272p. 1988. 16.45 (*0-89296-284-4*, Pub. by Mysterious Pr) Little.

McBain's Ladies: The Women of the 87th Precinct. Ed McBain, pseud. 1989. mass mkt. 4.95 (*0-445-40334-9*, Pub. by Warner Bks) Little.

McBroom & the Big Wind. Sid Fleischman. (Illus.). 48p. (J). (gr. 3 up). 1982. mass mkt. 3.95 (*0-316-28544-7*) Little.

McBroom Tells a Lie. Sid Fleischman. LC 98-56266. (Adventures of McBroom Ser.). (Illus.). 64p. (J). (gr. 2-5). 1999. pap. 3.99 (*0-8431-7497-8*, Price Stern) Peng Put Young Read.

McBroom Tells the Truth. Sid Fleischman. LC 98-26699. (Adventures of McBroom Ser.). (Illus.). 64p. (J). (gr. 2-5). 1998. 13.89 (*0-8431-7898-1*, Price Stern); pap. 3.99 (*0-8431-7947-3*, Price Stern) Peng Put Young Read.

McBroom Tells the Truth. Sid Fleischman. LC 81-1035. (Illus.). 48p. (J). (gr. 2-5). 1981. reprint ed. 12.95i (*0-316-28550-1*) Little.

McBroom the Rainmaker. Sid Fleischman. LC 98-56264. (Adventures of McBroom Ser.). (Illus.). 64p. (J). (gr. 2-5). 1999. pap. 3.99 (*0-8431-7496-X*, Price Stern) Peng Put Young Read.

McBroom the Rainmaker. Sid Fleischman. LC 98-56264. (Adventures of McBroom Ser.). (J). 1999. 13.89 (*0-8431-7518-4*) Putnam Pub Group.

McBroom's Camera Bluebook: A Complete, Up-to-Date Price & Buyer's Guide for New & Used Cameras, Lenses & Accessories. 6th ed. Michael McBroom. (Illus.). 323p. 1999. pap. 29.95 (*1-58428-013-1*, Pub. by Amherst Media) IPG Chicago.

McBroom's Ghost. Sid Fleischman. LC 98-26695. (Adventures of McBroom Ser.). (Illus.). 64p. (J). (gr. 2-5). 1998. pap. 3.99 (*0-8431-7948-1*, Price Stern) Peng Put Young Read.

McBroom's Wonderful One-Acre Farm: 3 Tall Tales. Sid Fleischman. LC 91-31906. (Beech Tree Chapter Books Ser.). (Illus.). 64p. (gr. 1-4). 1997. mass mkt. 4.95 (*0-688-15595-2*, Wm Morrow) Morrow Avon.

McBroom's Wonderful One-Acre Farm, Three Tall Tales. Sid Fleischman. (Beech Tree Chapter Bks.). 1997. 10.15 (*0-606-11608-7*, Pub. by Turtleback) Demco.

MCC Masterclass: The New MCC Coaching Book. Tony Lewis. (Illus.). 192p. 1995. 39.95 (*0-297-81431-1*, Pub. by Weidenfeld & Nicolson) Trafalgar.

***McCaffertys: Thorne.** Lisa Jackson. 2001. mass mkt. 3.50 (*0-373-24364-2*, 1-24364-1) Silhouette.

McCain's Memories. Maggie Simpson. 1997. per. 3.99 (*0-373-07785-8*, 1-07785-8) Silhouette.

***McCall.** Robert H. Redding. LC 99-90986. 192p. 1999. 18.95 (*0-8034-9391-6*, Avalon Bks) Bouregy.

McCall Crabbs: Standard Test Lessons in Reading. 3rd ed. William A. McCall & Lelah M. Crabbs. 1979. pap. text, teacher ed. 1.50 (*0-8077-5552-4*) Tchrs Coll.

McCall Crabbs Bk. C: Standard Test Lessons in Reading. 3rd ed. William A. McCall & Lelah M. Crabbs. (J). (gr. 5-7). 1979. pap. text 2.95 (*0-8077-5544-3*) Tchrs Coll.

McCall Crabbs Bk. D: Standard Test Lessons in Reading. 3rd ed. William A. McCall & Lelah M. Crabbs. (J). (gr. 6-8). 1979. pap. text 2.95 (*0-8077-5546-X*) Tchrs Coll.

McCall Crabbs Bk. A: Standard Test Lessons in Reading. 3rd ed. William A. McCall & Lelah M. Crabbs. (J). (gr. 3-5). 1979. pap. text 2.95 (*0-8077-5540-0*) Tchrs Coll.

McCall Crabbs Bk. B: Standard Test Lessons in Reading. 3rd ed. William A. McCall & Lelah M. Crabbs. (J). (gr. 4-6). 1979. pap. text 2.95 (*0-8077-5542-7*) Tchrs Coll.

McCall Crabbs Bk. E: Standard Test Lessons in Reading. 3rd ed. William A. McCall & Lelah M. Crabbs. (YA). (gr. 7-12). 1979. pap. text 2.95 (*0-8077-5548-6*) Tchrs Coll.

McCall Crabbs Bk. F: Standard Test Lessons in Reading, Bk. F. 3rd ed. William A. McCall & Lelah M. Crabbs. 1979. pap. text 2.95 (*0-8077-5550-8*) Tchrs Coll.

McCall Smith & Sheldon: Scots Criminal Law. R. Alexander Smith & David Sheldon. 328p. 1992. pap. 51.00 (*0-406-25269-6*, MICHIE) LEXIS Pub.

McCall's Creates: A Country Home. Margaret Chapman. LC 97-33084. 1998. write for info. (*1-56799-621-3*, Friedman-Fairfax) M Friedman Pub Grp Inc.

McCalls Needlework: 150 Best Loved Christmas Ornaments. Symbol of Excellence Staff. 160p. 1995. pap. 14.95 (*0-8487-1466-0*) Oxmoor Hse.

McCallum Family & Descendants of Duncan McCallum: Colonial Ancestors of the John McCallum Branch, & Other Allied Lines. I. F. Johnson. (Illus.). 77p. 1994. reprint ed. pap. 15.00 (*0-8328-4229-X*); reprint ed. lib. bdg. 25.00 (*0-8328-4228-1*) Higginson Bk Co.

McCallum Saga: The Story of the Founding of Palm Springs. Katherine Ainsworth. LC 96-52785. 1996. 28.00 (*0-9618724-1-1*) Palm Springs CA.

McCallum/Multivariable Calculus: Exploring Multivariable Calculus with Mathematica. Cheung. 234p. 1996. pap. text, suppl. ed. 28.95 (*0-471-13754-5*) Wiley.

McCampbell's Heroes: The True Story of Navy Air Group 15, the Most Celebrated Pilots of World War II, Popularly Chronicled. Edwin P. Hoyt. 296p. 1984. pap. 3.95 (*0-380-68841-7*, Avon Bks) Morrow Avon.

McCance & Widdowson: A Scientific Partnership of Sixty Years. Ed. by M. Ashwell. (Illus.). 264p. 1993. pap. 37.50 (*0-907667-07-4*) ILSI.

McCandlish - Black Family History. Elizabeth Black. 201p. 1995. reprint ed. pap. 30.00 (*0-8328-4926-X*); reprint ed. lib. bdg. 40.00 (*0-8328-4925-1*) Higginson Bk Co.

McCandlish Family History. David B. McCandlish. (Illus.). 1991. 50.00 (*0-9619300-0-4*) D McCandlish.

McCandlish Family History. 3rd ed. David B. McCandlish. (Illus.). 1993. 49.00 (*0-9619300-2-0*) D McCandlish.

McCarthy. John T. Flynn. 1987. lib. bdg. 79.00 (*0-8490-3957-6*) Gordon Pr.

McCarthy & the Communists. James Rorty. LC 78-138179. 163p. 1972. reprint ed. lib. bdg. 69.50 (*0-8371-5636-X*, ROCO, Greenwood Pr) Greenwood.

McCarthy & the Fear of Communism in American History. Karen Zeinert. LC 97-43162. (In American History Ser.). 128p. (YA). (gr. 5 up). 1998. lib. bdg. 20.95 (*0-89490-987-8*) Enslow Pubs.

McCarthy on Trademarks & Unfair Competition. 3rd ed. J. Thomas McCarthy. LC 92-33247. (IP Ser.). 1992. ring bd. 625.00 (*0-87632-900-8*) West Group.

McCarthy on Trademarks & Unfair Competition. 4th ed. J. Thomas McCarthy. LC 96-40294. 1996. write for info. (*0-8366-1108-X*) West Group.

McCarthyism: A Documentary History. Albert Fried. 240p. (C). 1996. pap. text 20.95 (*0-19-509701-7*) OUP.

McCarthyism: The Fight for America. Joseph R. McCarthy. LC 76-46087. (Anti-Movements in America Ser.). 1977. lib. bdg. 22.95 (*0-405-09960-6*) Ayer.

McCarthyism: The Seed Is in Us. James E. Bristol. LC 54-9201. (C). 1954. pap. 4.00 (*0-87574-076-6*) Pendle Hill.

McCarthyism & Consensus? William B. Ewald, Jr. Ed. by Kenneth W. Thompson. LC 86-9233. (Credibility of Institutions, Policies & Leadership Ser.: Vol. 13). 76p. (Orig.). (C). 1986. pap. text 13.50 (*0-8191-5434-2*, Pub. by White Miller Center); lib. bdg. 32.00 (*0-8191-5433-4*, Pub. by White Miller Center) U Pr of Amer.

McCarthyism & New York's Hearst Press: A Study of Roles in the Witch Hunt. Jim Tuck. 240p. (Orig.). (C). 1995. pap. text 29.00 (*0-8191-9878-1*); lib. bdg. 52.00 (*0-8191-9877-3*) U Pr of Amer.

McCarthy's Americans: Red Scare Politics in State & Nation, 1935-1965. M. J. Heale. LC 97-41118. xvii, 370p. 1998. 40.00 (*0-8203-2026-9*) U of Ga Pr.

McCarthy's Desk Encyclopedia of Intellectual Property. 2nd ed. J. Thomas McCarthy. LC 95-37468. 505p. 1995. 75.00 (*0-87179-899-9*) BNA Books.

McCartney: Yesterday . . . And Today. Ray Coleman. (Illus.). 194p. 1998. pap. text 17.00 (*0-7881-5935-6*) DIANE Pub.

McCartney: Yesterday & Today, 2 cass. abr. ed. Ray Coleman. (Illus.). 1996. audio. write for info. (*0-7871-1003-5*, Dove Audio) NewStar Media.

McCaslin Works-Sites. Konrad Bitterli. 1998. 45.00 (*3-89322-416-5*, Pub. by Edition Cantz) Dist Art Pubs.

McClairen's Isle. Connie Brockway. 400p. 1999. mass mkt. 6.50 (*0-440-22629-5*) Dell.

***McClairen's Isle: The Ravishing One.** Connie Brockway. 400p. 2000. mass mkt. 6.50 (*0-440-22630-9*) Bantam Dell.

***McClairen's Isle: The Reckless One.** Connie Brockway. 384p. 2000. mass mkt. 6.50 (*0-440-22627-9*) Dell.

McClane's Field Guide to Freshwater Fishes of North America. A. J. McClane. LC 77-11967. (Illus.). 232p. 1995. pap. 15.95 (*0-8050-0194-8*, Owl) H Holt & Co.

McClane's Field Guide to Saltwater Fishes of North America. A. J. McClane. LC 77-14417. (Illus.). 304p. 1995. pap. 15.95 (*0-8050-0733-4*, Owl) H Holt & Co.

McClane's Field Guide to Saltwater Fishes of North America: A Project of the Gamefish Research Association. A. J. McClane. 1978. pap. 13.95 (*0-03-021121-2*) Holt R&W.

McClane's Fishing Encyclopedia. Random House Value Publishing Staff. LC 98-6833. 1168p. 1998. 29.99 (*0-517-20336-7*) Random Hse Value.

McClane's New Standard Fishing Encyclopedia & International Angling Guide. rev. ed. A. J. McClane. LC 74-6108. (Illus.). 88p. 1995. 75.00 (*0-8050-1117-X*) H Holt & Co.

McClane's Secrets of Successful Fishing. A. J. McClane. LC 78-24367. (Owl Bks.). (Illus.). 288p. 1995. pap. 11.95 (*0-8050-0707-5*, Owl) H Holt & Co.

McClaughry. Genealogy of the MacClaughry Family: A Scoto-Irish Family from Galloway, Scotland, Appearing in Ireland about 1600, & Emigrants to N.Y. in 1765. C. C. McClaughry. 459p. 1991. reprint ed. pap. 71.00 (*0-8328-1994-8*); reprint ed. lib. bdg. 81.00 (*0-8328-1993-X*) Higginson Bk Co.

*__McClellan Legacy.__ LeeAnn Doherty. LC 99-65323. 192p. 2000. pap. 11.95 (*1-56315-213-4*, Pub. by SterlingHse) Natl Bk Netwk.

McClellan, Sherman & Grant. T. Harry Williams. (Illus.). 120p. 1991. reprint ed. pap. text 7.95 (*0-929587-70-7*, Elephant Paperbacks) I R Dee.

McClellanville Coast Cookbook: Recipes, Oral Histories, Poetry, Prose, Prints, Photographs & Paintings. McClellanville Arts Council Staff. 1992. pap. 17.95 (*1-882966-00-7*) McClellanville Arts.

McClellanville Coast Seafood Cookbook. Ed. by Susan Williams. (Illus.). 255p. 1996. pap., spiral bd. 17.95 (*1-882966-03-1*) McClellanville Arts.

McClenahan: The John McClenahan Folk: Biography & Genealogy. J. M. Henderson. 125p. 1993. reprint ed. pap. 19.00 (*0-8328-3372-X*); reprint ed. lib. bdg. 29.00 (*0-8328-3371-1*) Higginson Bk Co.

McClintock Piano Course: A New Experience in Learning, 11 vols., Set. Lorene McClintock. 2198p. (YA). 1992. spiral bd., boxed set 388.00 (*1-880556-70-7*) McClintock Ent.

McClure: Selected Poems. Michael McClure. (J). 1999. pap. write for info. (*0-14-058705-5*) NAL.

*__McColl: The Man with America's Money.__ Ross Yockey. LC 99-61753. 512p. 1999. 24.00 (*1-56352-539-9*) Longstreet.

McCollough Effect: An Indicator of Central Neurotransmitter Activity. Charles C. Shute. LC 78-15609. 157p. reprint ed. pap. 44.80 (*0-608-16864-5*, 2027242) Bks Demand.

*__McComb City Moments: Selections from the Newspaper of McComb, Mississippi over the Past 125 Years.__ Ed. & Compiled by Carl Lazenby. 206p. 1999. pap. 10.00 (*0-9677048-0-4*) LazArt.

*__McCone & Friends.__ Marcia Muller. 202p. 2000. pap. 16.00 (*1-885941-38-2*) Crippen & Landru.

*__McCone & Friends.__ limited ed. Marcia Muller. 202p. 2000. 40.00 (*1-885941-37-4*) Crippen & Landru.

McCone Files. Marcia Muller. 248p. 1995. pap. 15.00 (*1-885941-05-6*) Crippen & Landru.

McConey Vol. 2: The Hoodoodad. Lewis Trondheim. (Illus.). 48p. (YA). (gr. 10 up). 1998. pap. 10.95 (*1-56097-338-2*) Fantagraph Bks.

McConnell's Bride. Naomi Horton. (Here Come the Grooms Ser.: No. 15). 1996. per. 3.99 (*0-373-30115-4*, 1-30115-9) Harlequin Bks.

McCord Family: A Passionate Vision. Pamela Miller et al. (Illus.). 144p. 1993. pap. 44.95 (*0-7735-0971-2*, Pub. by McG-Queens Univ Pr) CUP Services.

McCord Family Reunion Cookbook: Pontotoc County, Mississippi. Ed. by Mary V. Golding. 120p. 1994. pap. 9.95 (*1-881576-31-0*) Providence Hse.

McCord Museum Archives. Pamela Miller. (Illus.). 32p. 1993. pap. 29.95 (*0-7735-0965-8*, Pub. by McG-Queens Univ Pr) CUP Services.

McCord of Alaska. John Long & Grace D. McCord. LC 74-28612. (Illus.). 150p. 1975. 7.95 (*0-913228-15-X*) Dillon-Liederbach.

McCormick-DeLapa Family Cookbook: A Collection of Receipes form Four Generations. Ed. by Judith A. DeLapa. 275p. 1997. 19.95 (*0-9638432-1-4*) High-Impact.

McCormick Family Record & Biography. L. J. McCormick. (Illus.). 490p. 1989. reprint ed. pap. 73.50 (*0-8328-0861-X*); reprint ed. lib. bdg. 81.50 (*0-8328-0860-1*) Higginson Bk Co.

*__McCormick Genealogies & Reminiscences.__ fac. rev. ed. Henrietta H. McCormick. (Illus.). 211p. 1999. reprint ed. 43.00 (*0-8328-9960-7*); reprint ed. pap. 33.00 (*0-8328-9961-5*) Higginson Bk Co.

*__McCormick of Rutgers: Scholar, Teacher, Public Historian, 6.__ Michael J. Birkner. Vol. 6. 2000. write for info. (*0-313-30356-8*, Greenwood Pr) Greenwood.

McCormick on Evidence, 1. 4th ed. John W. Strong. (Practitioner Treatise Ser.). 1500p. (C). 1991. text. write for info. (*0-314-89311-3*) West Pub.

McCormick on Evidence, 2. 4th ed. John W. Strong. (Practitioner Treatise Ser.). 1500p. (C). 1991. text. write for info. (*0-314-89312-1*) West Pub.

McCormick on Evidence, Set, Vols. 1 & 2. 4th ed. John W. Strong. (Practitioner Treatise Ser.). 1500p. (C). 1991. 162.00 (*0-314-05429-4*) West Pub.

*__McCormick on Evidence 2000.__ 5th ed. John W. Strong. 1999. 42.50 (*0-314-23238-9*) West Pub.

McCoy Cookie Jars. Harold Nichols. 1988. 15.95 (*0-9617912-1-7*) Nichols Wrestling.

McCoy Cookie Jars from the 1st to the Last. 2nd ed. Harold Nichols. LC 91-68550. (Illus.). 198p. (Orig.). 1992. pap. 18.95 (*0-9617912-2-5*) Nichols Wrestling.

McCoy Pottery. Jeffrey B. Snyder. LC 98-89369. (Illus.). 208p. 1999. 29.95 (*0-7643-0804-1*) Schiffer.

McCoy Pottery - Collectors Reference & Value Guide: Identification & Values. Bob Hanson & Graig Nissen. LC 96-232395. (Illus.). 336p. 1996. 19.95 (*0-89145-729-1*, 4722) Collector Bks.

McCoy Pottery Collector's Reference & Value Guide. 2nd ed. Bob Hanson et al. 304p. 1999. 24.95 (*1-57432-116-1*) Collector Bks.

McCracken: The Banker's Remedy of Set-Off. Sheelagh McCracken. 1997. write for info. (*0-406-99613-X*, MBRS1, MICHIE) LEXIS Pub.

McCracken in Command. large type ed. James Keene. (Linford Western Library). 400p. 1995. pap. 16.99 (*0-7089-7759-6*, Linford) Ulverscroft.

*__McCracken's Removable Partial Prosthodontics.__ 10th ed. Glen P. McGivney & Alan B. Carr. LC 99-37063. (Illus.). 576p. (C). 1999. text. write for info. (*0-323-00678-7*) Mosby Inc.

McCracken's Removable Partial Prosthodontics, No. 9. 9th ed. Glenn P. McGivney & Castleberry. (Illus.). 544p. (C). (gr. 13). 1994. text 79.00 (*0-8016-7964-8*, 07964) Mosby Inc.

McCrave: A Mental Operations Manual for the Seemingly Hopeless. unabridged ed. William L. McRobb. LC 97-95129. (Illus.). xx, 178p. 1998. spiral bd. 21.95 (*0-9662533-0-2*, ALK1.101) McCrave.

McCraw & Arnold's Atlas of Muscle & Musculocutaneour Flaps. John B. McCraw & Phillip G. Arnold. LC 86-82307. (Illus.). 748p. 1986. text 291.50 (*0-939789-00-0*) Lppncott W & W.

McCrays of America. 2nd ed. Philip R. McCray. (Illus.). xiv, 441p. (Orig.). 1993. pap. 43.00 (*1-55613-829-6*) Heritage Bk.

McCulloch's Wonder: The Story of the Kettle Valley Railway. 20th anniversary ed. Barrie Sanford. (Illus.). 260p. pap. write for info. (*1-55110-761-9*) Whitecap Bks.

McCullough's Bride. Anne Peters. (Silhouette Romance Ser.). 1994. pap. 2.75 (*0-373-19031-X*, 1-19031-3) Harlequin Bks.

McCully Historical Fiction. Emily Arnold McCully. (I Can Read Bks.). (Illus.). 64p. (ps-3). 14.95 (*0-06-028728-4*) HarpC.

McCully Historical Fiction. Emily Arnold McCully. (I Can Read Bks.). (Illus.). 64p. (ps-3). 14.89 (*0-06-028729-2*) HarpC Child Bks.

*__McCully Train: Iowa to Oregon 1852.__ Sanford R. Wilbur & Sally H. Wilbur. (Illus.). 204p. 2000. pap. 14.95 (*0-9651263-2-3*) Symbios.

McCurdy & the Silver Dart. Les Harding. 110p. 1999. pap. 10.95 (*0-920336-69-8*) Genl Dist Srvs.

McCutcheon's Emulsifiers & Detergent: International Edition. rev. ed. Michael Allured. LC 82-644576. 308p. 1998. pap. 72.00 (*0-944254-56-X*) MC Pub Co NJ.

McCutcheon's Emulsifiers & Detergents: North American Edition. Ed. by Michael Allured. 330p. 1997. pap. 72.00 (*0-944254-48-9*) MC Pub Co NJ.

McCutcheon's Emulsifiers & Detergents: North American Edition. Michael Allured. 330p. 1998. pap. 72.00 (*0-944254-55-1*) MC Pub Co NJ.

McCutcheon's Emulsifiers & Detergents: North American Edition & International Edition. rev. ed. Michael Allured. 588p. 1998. 176.00 (*0-944254-57-8*) MC Pub Co NJ.

McCutcheon's Functional Materials: International Edition. Michael Allured. LC 82-644577. 132p. 1998. pap. 61.00 (*0-944254-59-4*) MC Pub Co NJ.

McCutcheon's Functional Materials: North American & International Edition. rev. ed. MC Pub. Co. Staff. Ed. by Michael Allured. LC 82-64457. 475p. 1998. 165.00 (*0-944254-60-8*) MC Pub Co NJ.

McCutcheon's Functional Materials: North American Edition. rev. ed. Michael Allured. LC 82-644577. 354p. 1998. pap. 72.00 (*0-944254-58-6*) MC Pub Co NJ.

McD. Alexander Lesley. (Illus.). 1989. pap. 9.95 (*0-317-93841-X*) Palm Tree Words.

McDaniel Report: On the Failure of Executive, Congressional, & Scientific Responsibility in Investigating Possible Evidence of Artificial Structures on the Surface of Mars & in Setting Mission Priorities for NASA's Mars Exploration Program. Stanley V. McDaniel. (Illus.). 174p. (Orig.). (C). 1994. pap. 20.00 (*1-55643-088-4*) North Atlantic.

MCDBA SQL Server 7 Administration Study Guide: Exam No. 70-28. Syngress Media Inc. Staff. LC 99-222911. (Illus.). 686p. 1999. student ed. 49.99 incl. cd-rom (*0-07-211904-7*) Osborne-McGraw.

MCDBA SQL Server 7 Book P/N. Syngress Media, Inc. Staff. write for info. (*0-07-212090-8*) McGraw.

*__MCDBA SQL Server 7 Certification Boxed Set.__ Media Incorporated Syngress Media Incorporated Staff. 2064p. 2000. pap. text 119.99 (*0-07-212182-3*) Osborne-McGraw.

MCDBA SQL Server 7 Database Design Study Guide: (Exam 70-29) Syngress Media Incorporated Staff. (Illus.). 557p. 1999. pap. 49.99 (*0-07-212078-9*) McGraw.

*__MCDBA SQL Server 7 Test Yourself Practice Exams: (exams 70-28 & 70-29)__ Media Incorporated Syngress Media Incorporated Staff. 604p. 2000. pap. text 39.99 (*0-07-212181-5*) Osborne-McGraw.

*__MCDBA Training Guide: 5-in-1.__ Dennis Maione. 3000p. 1999. pap. 199.99 incl. cd-rom (*0-7357-0943-2*) New Riders Pub.

McDermott & McGough: A History of Photography. Photos by David McDermott & Peter McGough. (Illus.). 144p. 1998. text 100.00 (*0-9657280-2-1*, 810081) Arena Editions.

McDermott's Handbook of Ohio Real Estate Law. 2nd ed. Thomas J. McDermott. 304p. 1980. 15.00 (*0-614-05898-8*, MICHIE); pap. 15.00 (*0-87473-130-5*, MICHIE) LEXIS Pub.

McDermott's Ohio Real Property Law & Practice with 1991 Cumulative Supplements, 3 vols., Set. 4th ed. Sherman S. Hollander et al. 1988. 255.00 (*0-87473-377-4*, 62949-10, MICHIE) LEXIS Pub.

MCDM - Past Decade & Future Trends: A Source Book of Multiple Criteria Decision Making. Milan Zelany. LC 84-15405. (Decision Research: Vol. 2). 375p. 1986. 73.25 (*0-89232-439-2*) Jai Pr.

MCDMU Paradox for Windows. James Pratt & Last. (C). 1994. text. write for info. (*0-318-70354-8*, BF4012) S-W Pub.

McDonald Texas Civil Practice, 1981-1990, 5 vols. Roy W. McDonald. Ed. by Frank W. Elliott. LC 80-28736. 337.00 (*0-8321-0051-X*) West Group.

McDonaldization of Society. George Ritzer. 240p. 1994. 29.95 (*0-8039-9046-4*) Sage.

McDonaldization of Society: An Investigation into the Changing Character of Contemporary Social Life. rev. ed. George Ritzer. LC 95-16950. (Orig.). 1995. write for info. (*0-8039-9076-6*) Pine Forge.

McDonaldization of Society: An Investigation into the Changing Character of Contemporary Social Life. 2nd rev. ed. George Ritzer. LC 95-16950. (Orig.). 1995. pap. 17.95 (*0-8039-9077-4*) Pine Forge.

McDonaldization Revisited: Critical Essays on Consumer Culture. Mark S. Alfino et al. LC 97-21852. 232p. 1998. 59.95 (*0-275-95819-1*, Praeger Pubs) Greenwood.

McDonaldization Revisited: Critical Essays on Consumer Culture. Robin Wynyard. Ed. by Mark S. Alfino & John Caputo. LC 97-21852. 232p. 1998. pap. 19.95 (*0-275-96104-4*, Praeger Pubs) Greenwood.

McDonaldization Thesis: Explorations & Extensions. George Ritzer. LC 97-68493. 256p. 1997. 75.00 (*0-7619-5539-9*); pap. 32.00 (*0-7619-5540-2*) Sage.

McDonald's. William Gould. LC 96-10230. (VGM Business Portraits Ser.). (Illus.). 48p. (J). 1996. 14.95 (*0-8442-4778-2*, 47782, Natl Textbk Co) NTC Contemp Pub Co.

McDonald's: Behind the Arches. rev. ed. John F. Love. LC 95-11540. 496p. 1995. pap. 14.95 (*0-553-34759-4*) Bantam.

McDonald's Blood Flow in Arteries. 3rd ed. write for info. (*0-340-52944-X*, Pub. by E A) Routldge.

McDonald's Blood Flow in Arteries: Theoretical, Experimental & Clinical Principles. 4th ed. Wilmer W. Nichols & Michael F. O'Rourke. LC 97-21356. (Illus.). 576p. 1997. text 150.00 (*0-340-64614-4*) OUP.

McDonald's Collectibles. Richardson. (Illus.). 1997. 22.98 (*0-7858-0803-5*) Bk Sales Inc.

McDonald's Collectibles: Identification & Value Guide. Gary Henriques & Audre DuVall. LC 97-192517. (Illus.). 224p. 1997. pap. 19.95 (*0-89145-783-6*, 4871) Collector Bks.

McDonald's Collectibles: Illustrated Price Guide. Gary A. Henriques & D. Audre DuVall. LC 91-91553. (Illus.). 480p. (Orig.). 1992. pap. 26.95 (*0-9631785-6-3*) Piedmont Pub.

McDonald's Glassware. Joyce Losonsky & Terry Losonsky. (Illus.). 192p. 1999. pap. 16.95 (*0-7643-0879-3*) Schiffer.

McDonald's Happy Meal Toys: Around the World. Terry M. Losonsky & Joyce Losonsky. LC 95-37442. (Illus.). 270p. (Orig.). 1995. pap. 24.95 (*0-88740-835-4*) Schiffer.

McDonald's Happy Meal Toys: In the U. S. A. Terry Lasonsky & Joyce Lasonsky. LC 95-9054. (Illus.). 224p. (Orig.). 1995. pap. 24.95 (*0-88740-853-2*) Schiffer.

McDonald's Happy Meal Toys Around the World, 1996-Present. Joyce Losonsky & Terry Losonsky. (Illus.). 192p. 1999. pap. 24.95 (*0-7643-0960-9*) Schiffer.

McDonald's Happy Meal Toys from the Eighties. Joyce Losonsky & Terry Losonsky. LC 98-21473. 192p. 1998. pap. 24.95 (*0-7643-0322-8*) Schiffer.

McDonald's Happy Meal Toys from the Nineties. Joyce Losonsky & Terry Losonsky. LC 98-24944. 240p. 1998. pap. 24.95 (*0-7643-0673-1*) Schiffer.

McDonald's Pre-Happy Meal Toys from the Fifties, Sixties & Seventies. Joyce Losonsky & Terry Losonsky. LC 98-17409. 224p. 1998. pap. 24.95 (*0-7643-0599-9*) Schiffer.

McDonald's Veterinary Endocrinology & Reproduction. 5th ed. M. H. Pineda & M. P. Dooley. LC 98-9931. 1999. write for info. (*0-683-06920-9*) Lppncott W & W.

*__Mcdonnell Douglas Aircraft Cutaways.__ Mike Badrocke & Bill Gunston. (Illus.). 144p. 1999. 34.95 (*1-85532-924-7*, Pub. by Ospry) Motorbooks Intl.

McDonnell Douglas Aircraft since 1920, Vol. I. Rene J. Francillon. LC 88-61448. (Putnam Aviation Ser.). (Illus.). 640p. 1988. 55.00 (*0-87021-428-4*) Naval Inst Pr.

McDonnell Douglas Aircraft since 1920, Vol. II. Rene J. Francillon. (Putnam Aviation Ser.). (Illus.). 416p. 1990. 55.00 (*1-55750-550-0*) Naval Inst Pr.

McDonnell Douglas Corp. A Report on the Company's Environmental Policies & Practices. (Illus.). 35p. (C). 1994. reprint ed. pap. text 40.00 (*0-7881-0906-5*, Coun on Econ) DIANE Pub.

Mcdonnell Douglas DC-10. Gunter Endres. LC TL686.M25E53 1998. (Illus.). 128p. 1998. pap. 24.95 (*0-7603-0617-6*) MBI Pubg.

*__McDonnell Douglas DC-10.__ Terry Waddington. (Illus.). 144p. 2000. pap. 27.95 (*1-892437-04-X*, 130442AE, Pub. by World Transport) Motorbooks Intl.

*__McDonnell Douglas DC-10 & KC-10 Extender.__ Arthur A. C. Steffen. (Illus.). 128p. 1998. pap. 34.95 (*1-85780-051-6*, Pub. by Midland Pubng) Specialty Pr.

McDonnell Douglas DC-9. Terry Waddington. (Great Airliners Ser.). 1998. 27.95 (*0-9626730-9-9*) World Transport.

McDonnell Douglas F-15 Eagle. Dennis Jenkins. (Warbird Tech Ser.: Vol. 9). (Illus.). 100p. (Orig.). 1997. pap. 16.95 (*0-933424-72-8*) Specialty Pr.

McDonnell Douglas F-4 Gun Nosed Phantoms. Chris Hughes. (Warbird Tech Ser.: Vol. 8). (Illus.). 100p. (Orig.). 1997. pap. 16.95 (*0-933424-71-X*) Specialty Pr.

McDonnell Douglas F-15 Eagle: Supreme Heavy-Weight Fighter. Dennis R. Jenkins. 1998. pap. text 24.95 (*1-85780-081-8*) Midland Pubng.

McDonnell Douglas F/A-18 Hornet: A Photo Chronicle. Bill Holder & Mike Wallace. LC 96-71815. (Illus.). 80p. 1997. pap. 19.95 (*0-7643-0243-4*) Schiffer.

McDonnell Douglas Jetliners. Robbie Shaw. (Illus.). 128p. 1998. pap. 21.95 (*1-85532-752-X*, Pub. by Ospry) Motorbooks Intl.

McDonnell Douglas MD-80 & MD-90. Arthur Pearcy. LC 99-32255. (Illus.). 128p. 1999. pap. 24.95 (*0-7603-0698-2*, 128432AP) MBI Pubg.

McDonnell FH-1 Phantom. Steven J. Ginter. (Naval Fighters Ser.: No. 3). 34p. 1981. pap. 4.25 (*0-942612-03-5*) Naval Fighters.

McDonogh School, 1972-1997: Years of Challenge & Resolution. Lawrence Johnston. 256p. 1998. write for info. (*1-56167-446-X*) Am Literary Pr.

McDougall Health-Supporting Cookbook, Vol. 1. Mary A. McDougall. LC 85-5056. 122p. (Orig.). 1985. pap. 9.95 (*0-8329-0393-0*) New Win Pub.

McDougall Health-Supporting Cookbook, Vol. II. Mary A. McDougall. LC 86-5606. (Orig.). 1986. pap. 9.95 (*0-8329-0422-8*) New Win Pub.

McDougall Plan. John A. McDougall & Mary A. McDougall. LC 83-19412. (Illus.). 352p. 1985. pap. 11.95 (*0-8329-0392-2*) New Win Pub.

McDougall Program. John A. Mcdougall. 448p. 1998. pap. 15.95 (*0-452-27266-1*, Plume) Dutton Plume.

McDougall Program: Twelve Days to Dynamic Health. John A. McDougall. 448p. 1991. reprint ed. pap. 14.95 (*0-452-26639-4*, Plume) Dutton Plume.

McDougall Program for a Healthy Heart: A Life-Saving Approach to Preventing & Treating Heart Disease. John A. McDougall. (Illus.). 430p. 1998. text 25.00 (*0-7881-5356-0*) DIANE Pub.

McDougall Program for a Healthy Heart: A Life-Saving Approach to Preventing & Treating Heart Disease. large type ed. John A. McDougall. LC 96-46142. (Spec-Hall Ser.). 1997. lib. bdg. 25.95 (*0-7838-2013-5*, G K Hall Lrg Type) Mac Lib Ref.

McDougall Program for Maximum Weight Loss. John A. McDougall. 336p. 1995. pap. 13.95 (*0-452-27380-3*, Plume) Dutton Plume.

*__McDougall Program for Women: What Every Woman Needs to Know to Be Healthy for Life.__ John A. McDougall. 2000. pap. 14.95 (*0-452-27697-7*) NAL.

McDougall Quick & Easy Cookbook: Over 300 Delicious Low-Fat Recipes You Can Prepare in Fifteen Minutes or Less. John McDougall & Mary McDougall. 336p. 1999. pap. 19.95 (*0-452-27696-9*, Plume) Dutton Plume.

McDougall Quick & Easy Cookbook: Over 300 Quick & Easy Recipes for Delicious Low-Fat Meals. John A. McDougall & Mary McDougall. 1997. 25.95 (*0-614-27971-2*) NAL.

McDougall's Medicine: A Challenging Second Opinion. John A. McDougall. LC 85-21686. 298p. 1986. pap. 12.95 (*0-8329-0448-1*) New Win Pub.

McDowell County, NC Cemeteries. Bryan Aldridge et al. 252p. 1995. pap. 25.00 (*1-888549-00-9*) Appalachan Pr.

McDowell County North Carolina Land Entry Abstracts, 1843-1869, Vol. 1. Judson O. Crow. LC 82-20499. 509p. 1982. pap. 25.00 (*0-87152-365-5*) Reprint.

McDuff. Rosemary Wells. (J). 1998. pap. 8.95 (*0-7868-1297-4*, Pub. by Hyperion) Time Warner.

McDuff & the Baby. Rosemary Wells. LC 96-38220. (Illus.). 24p. (J). (ps-k). Date not set. pap. 4.95 (*0-7868-1191-9*, Pub. by Hyprn Ppbks) Little.

McDuff & the Baby, Bk. 3. Rosemary Wells. LC 96-38220. (Illus.). 24p. (J). (ps-k). 1997. lib. bdg. 12.89 (*0-7868-2258-9*, Pub. by Hyprn Child) Little.

McDuff & the Baby, Bk. 3. Rosemary Wells. LC 96-38220. Vol. 3. (Illus.). 24p. (J). (ps-k). 1997. 12.95 (*0-7868-0316-9*, Pub. by Hyprn Child) Time Warner.

McDuff Comes Home. Rosemary Wells. LC 96-38202. (Illus.). 32p. (J). 1997. lib. bdg. 12.89 (*0-7868-2259-7*, Pub. by Hyprn Child) Little.

McDuff Comes Home. Rosemary Wells. LC 96-38202. (Illus.). 32p. (J). (ps-k). 1997. 12.95 (*0-7868-0317-7*, Pub. by Hyprn Child) Time Warner.

McDuff Comes Home. Rosemary Wells. LC 96-38202. (Illus.). 24p. (J). (ps-k). 2000. pap. 4.95 (*0-7868-1192-7*, Pub. by Hyprn Ppbks) Little.

McDuff Moves In. Rosemary Wells. LC 96-38221. (Illus.). 32p. (J). (ps-k). 1997. 12.95 (*0-7868-0318-5*, Pub. by Hyprn Child); lib. bdg. 12.89 (*0-7868-2257-0*, Pub. by Hyprn Child) Little.

McDuff Moves In. Rosemary Wells. (Illus.). 24p. (J). (ps-k). 2000. pap. 4.95 (*0-7868-1190-0*, Pub. by Hyprn Ppbks) Little.

McDuff Plush Fall, 1997. Rosemary Wells. (J). 1997. 8.95 (*0-7868-1268-0*, Pub. by Hyprn Ppbks) Little.

*__McDuff Treasury.__ Rosemary Wells. (Illus.). 112p. (J). (ps-k). 2000. 19.99 (*0-7868-0697-4*, Pub. by Hyprn Child) Time Warner.

McDuff's Birthday. Rosemary Wells. 12p. 2000. 6.99 (*0-7868-0513-7*, Pub. by Hyprn Child) Little.

McDuff's New Friend. Rosemary Wells. LC 97-33232. (Illus.). 24p. (J). (ps-2). 1998. 12.95 (*0-7868-0386-X*, Pub. by Hyprn Child) Time Warner.

McDuff's New Friend. Rosemary Wells. LC 97-33232. (Illus.). 24p. (J). (ps-2). 1998. lib. bdg. 13.49 (*0-7868-2337-2*, Pub. by Hyprn Child) Little.

McDuff's New Friend: Christmas Bag. Rosemary Wells. 1998. 8.95 (*0-7868-0493-9*, Pub. by Hyprn Child) Little.

*__McDuff's New Friend: Includes Stuffed Toy Puppy.__ Rosemary Wells. (Illus.). (J). 1998. 219.00 (*0-7868-2825-0*) Hyperion.

M

An Asterisk (*) at the beginning of an entry indicates that the title is appearing for the first time.

McDurfee: Billy's Special Pal. Nell Klas. (Illus.). 20p. (Orig.). (J). (gr. k-3). 1991. pap. 4.00 (*0-9628560-0-2*) N Klas.

McDurfee Looked Bedraggled. Nell Klas. (Illus.). 20p. (J). (gr. k-3). 1993. pap. 5.00 (*0-9628560-1-0*) N Klas.

McDurfee Meets Ding-a-Ling. Nell Klas. (McDurfee Ser.). (Illus.). 24p. (J). (ps-3). 1997. 11.00 (*0-9628560-2-9*) N Klas.

McElhaney's Litigation. LC 93-74905. 433p. 1995. pap. 39.50 (*0-89707-954-X*, 531-0121, ABA Litigation) Amer Bar Assn.

McElhaney's Trial Notebook. 3rd expanded ed. LC 93-72490. 710p. 1994. pap. 44.50 (*0-89707-903-5*, 531-0096, ABA Litigation) Amer Bar Assn.

McElhiney's Guidebook: Historic St. Charles, Missouri. Richard G. Sperandio & Edna M. Olson. (Illus.). (Orig.). 1993. teacher ed. 10.95 (*0-9636679-1-2*); pap. 14.95 (*0-9636679-0-4*) McElhiney Pub.

McElligot's Pool. Dr. Seuss, pseud. (Illus.). (J). (gr. k-3). 1947. lib. bdg. 15.99 (*0-394-90083-9*, Pub. by Random Bks Yng Read) Random.

McElligot's Pool. Dr. Seuss, pseud. (Illus.). (J). (gr. k-3). 1966. 14.00 (*0-394-80083-4*, Pub. by Random Bks Yng Read) Random.

McElligot's Pool. Dr. Seuss, pseud. (J). 1947. 14.00 (*0-606-03944-9*, Pub. by Turtleback) Demco.

McElroy: The Scotch-Irish McElroys in America, 1717-1900 A.D. J. M. McElroy. 183p. 1992. reprint ed. pap. 28.00 (*0-8328-2687-1*); reprint ed. lib. bdg. 38.00 (*0-8328-2686-3*) Higginson Bk Co.

McElroy: World's Champion Radio Telegrapher. Tom French. (Illus.). 156p. (Orig.). 1993. pap. 19.95 (*1-890024-03-1*, MCE) Artifax Bks.

McEwen. Descendants of William McEwen (1775-1840) Rachel S. Tefft. 113p. 1997. pap. 18.00 (*0-8328-9469-9*); lib. bdg. 28.00 (*0-8328-9468-0*) Higginson Bk Co.

McFadden American Bank Directory, Spring 1994. Thomson Financial Publishing Inc. Staff. 1994. 249.00 (*1-56310-081-9*) Amer Bank Bond Buyer.

McFadden American Financial Directory, Spring 1994. Thomson Financial Publishing Inc. Staff. 1994. 375.00 (*1-56310-080-0*) Amer Bank Bond Buyer.

***McFadden American Financial Institutions Directory, January-June 2000, 5 vols.** Ed. by Thomson Financial Publishing Staff. 1999. 455.00 (*1-56310-302-8*) Thomson Fin Pub.

***McFadden Golden States Financial Directory, January-June 2000.** 1999. 119.00 (*1-56310-306-0*) Thomson Fin Pub.

***McFadden Southern Bankers Directory, January-June 2000.** 1999. 129.00 (*1-56310-307-9*) Thomson Fin Pub.

McFadden Southern Bankers Directory, Spring 1994, 2 vols. Thomson Financial Publishing Inc. Staff. 1994. 79.00 (*1-56310-083-5*) Amer Bank Bond Buyer.

***McFadden Upper Midwest Financial Directory, Spring 1999.** Ed. by Thomson Financial Publishing Staff. 1999. spiral bd. 105.00 (*1-56310-281-1*) Thomson Fin Pub.

***McFadden's Funnies, Vol. 101.** David McFadden. (Illus.). 36p. 1999. 2.95 (*0-9675254-0-3*) D McFadden.

McFaddin, 1730-1930. A. L. Blanding. (Illus.). 99p. 1992. reprint ed. pap. 19.00 (*0-8328-2689-8*); reprint ed. lib. bdg. 29.00 (*0-8328-2688-X*) Higginson Bk Co.

McFaddin Ward House: Life-Style & Legacy in Oil-Boom Beaumont, Texas. Jessica Foy & Judith Linsley. (Texas State Historical Association Popular History Ser.: No. 6). (Illus.). 60p. 1992. pap. 7.95 (*0-87611-117-7*) Tex St Hist Assn.

***McFarland Baseball Quotations Dictionary.** David H. Nathan. 304p. 2000. 45.00 (*0-7864-0888-X*) McFarland & Co.

McFarlane Boils the Sea. James Meek. 1989. 18.00 (*0-7486-6006-2*, Pub. by Polygon) Subterranean Co.

McFarlane Legacy: Studies in Late Medieval Politics & Society. R. H. Britnell & A. J. Pollard. LC 95-12671. 1995. text 59.95 (*0-312-12590-9*) St Martin.

McFarlane Legacy: Studies in Late Medieval Politics & Society. Ed. by R. H. Britnell & A. J. Pollard. (Fifteenth Century Ser.: No. 1). 240p. 1997. 72.00 (*0-7509-0626-X*, Pub. by Sutton Pub Ltd) Intl Pubs Mktg.

McFarlane's Customs Law Handbook, 1989-90. Gavin McFarlane. 320p. (C). 1990. 275.00 (*1-85431-057-7*) St Mut.

McFarlane's Customs Law Handbook, 1990-1991. Gavin McFarlane. 494p. (C). 1991. 64.00 (*1-85431-147-6*, Pub. by Blackstone Pr) Gaunt.

McGaffey Legal Forms with Tax Analysis, 1977-1990, 6 vols. Jere McGaffey. LC 77-12085. 495.00 (*0-317-11955-9*) West Group.

McGavock Family: A Genealogical History of James McGavock & His Descendants, from 1760 to 1903. Robert Gray. (Illus.). 175p. 1992. reprint ed. pap. 28.00 (*0-8328-2427-5*); reprint ed. lib. bdg. 38.00 (*0-8328-2426-7*) Higginson Bk Co.

McGee & Me see McGee y Yo

McGee Skills in Information Technology 1. (C). 1989. pap. text. write for info. (*0-201-41634-4*) Addison-Wesley.

McGee y Yo. Tr. of McGee & Me. (SPA.). write for info. (*0-318-72876-1*, 490608) Editorial Unilit.

McGee's New Media Kids' Bible. Date not set. cd-rom 39.99 (*0-8423-7601-1*) Tyndale Hse.

McGehee Papers: Southside Virginia in the 1850's. W. V. Ligon. (Illus.). 120p. (Orig.). 1984. pap. 9.95 (*0-930051-00-9*) Green Creek Pub Co.

McGill: A Celebration. Witold Rybczynski et al. (Illus.). 224p. (C). 1991. text 49.95 (*0-7735-0795-7*, Pub. by McG-Queens Univ Pr) CUP Services.

McGill Law Journal, 1952-1995/96, 42 vols., Set. 1952. 2275.00 (*0-8377-9108-1*, Rothman) W S Hein.

McGill Medicine: The First Half Century, 1829-1885. Joseph Hanaway. (Illus.). 288p. 1996. 55.00 (*0-7735-1324-8*, Pub. by McG-Queens Univ Pr) CUP Services.

McGill University: For the Advancement of Learning, 1801-1895, Vol. I: 1801-1895. Stanley B. Frost. (Illus.). 334p. 1980. 65.00 (*0-7735-0353-6*, Pub. by McG-Queens Univ Pr) CUP Services.

McGill University: For the Advancement of Learning, 1895-1971. Stanley B. Frost. 512p. 1984. 65.00 (*0-7735-0422-2*, Pub. by McG-Queens Univ Pr) CUP Services.

McGill University Collection of Greek & Roman Coins, Vols. 1-3. G. Michael Woloch. 1985. 85.00 (*90-6032-046-8*, Pub. by B R Gruner) Humanities.

McGill University Thesis Directory Vol. 1: 1881-1959. McGill University, Graduate Studies & Research Sta. Ed. by Frank Spitzer & Elizabeth Silvester. LC 78-317433. 776p. reprint ed. pap. 200.00 (*0-7837-1166-2*, 204169500022) Bks Demand.

McGill University Thesis Directory Vol. 2: 1960-1973. rev. ed. McGill University, Graduate Studies & Research Sta. Ed. by Frank Spitzer & Elizabeth Silvester. LC 78-317433. 871p. reprint ed. pap. 200.00 (*0-7837-4724-1*, 204169500002) Bks Demand.

McGillicuddy the Bookseller: A BiblioFantasy. H. C. Tidian. 160p. (C). 1997. 20.00 (*0-9658598-0-0*) Sam Johns.

***McGillivray & McIntosh Traders: On the Old Southwest Frontier, 1716-1815.** Albert J. Pickett. 450p. 2000. pap. 23.95 (*1-57966-025-8*, Black Belt) Black Belt Communs.

McGilloway's Ireland. Olly McGilloway. (Illus.). 288p. 1995. pap. 29.00 (*0-85640-540-X*, Pub. by Blackstaff Pr) Dufour.

McGills: Celts, Ulstermen, & American Pioneers: History, Heraldry, & Tradition. A. McGill. (Illus.). 345p. 1989. reprint ed. pap. 52.00 (*0-8328-0863-6*); reprint ed. lib. bdg. 60.00 (*0-8328-0862-8*) Higginson Bk Co.

McGill's Legal Aspects of Life Insurance. 2nd ed. Ed. by Edward E. Graves & Burke A. Christensen. LC 96-86473. 360p. (C). 1996. text 50.00 (*0-943590-85-X*) Amer College.

McGill's Life Insurance. 2nd ed. Ed. by Edward E. Graves. LC 98-71412. 900p. 1998. text 71.00 (*1-57996-004-9*) Amer College.

***McGill's Life Insurance.** 3rd ed. Ed. by Edward E. Graves. 975p. (C). 2000. text 71.00 (*1-57996-024-3*, Pub. by Amer College) Maple-Vail Bk.

Mcgillycuddy Could. Pamela Duncan Edwards. 32p. (ps-1). 14.95 (*0-06-029001-3*); pap. 5.95 (*0-06-443688-8*); lib. bdg. 14.89 (*0-06-029002-1*) HarpC.

***McGinty & the Dragon.** Rilda Humphrey. (Illus.). 39p. 1999. pap. 8.95 (*0-7414-0191-6*) Buy Books.

Mcglamry's Comprehensive Textbook of Foot Surgery. 3rd ed. Alan S. Banks et al. 2,256p. text 325.00 (*0-683-30471-2*) Lppncott W & W.

Mcgonagall: A Selection. William Mcgonagall. LC 99-164629. 1998. pap. text 9.95 (*1-874744-11-4*, Pub. by Birlinn Ltd) Dufour.

McGoonys Have a Party. Brian Schatell. LC 85-40095. (Illus.). 32p. (J). (gr. k-3). 1985. lib. bdg. 12.89 (*0-397-32124-4*) HarpC Child Bks.

***McGoorty: A Pool Room Hustler.** Robert Byrne. (Illus.). 240p. 2000. pap. 12.95 (*1-892129-49-3*) Total Sprts.

McGraw Electric Railway Directory, 1924. 1970. reprint ed. 10.50 (*0-914196-08-1*); reprint ed. pap. 6.60 (*0-914196-17-0*) JAS Pubng.

McGraw-Hill Anthology of German Literature, Vol. II. Vivian et al. (C). 1993. pap. text 47.50 (*0-07-036808-2*) McGraw.

McGraw-Hill Author Guide. 2nd ed. LC 94-11551. 1994. write for info. (*0-07-063138-7*) McGraw.

McGraw-Hill Big Book of Science Activities: Fun & Easy Experiments for Kids. Robert W. Wood. (Illus.). 512p. 1998. pap. text 15.95 (*0-07-071873-3*) McGraw.

McGraw-Hill Book of Drama. Compiled by James Howe & William A. Stephany. LC 94-37960. 1350p. (C). 1994. pap. 41.88 (*0-07-061224-2*) McGraw.

McGraw-Hill Book of Drama. Jerry Stephany. 1993. 46.00 (*0-07-061225-0*) McGraw.

McGraw-Hill Book of Fiction. Robert DiYanni & Kraft Rompf. LC 94-11559. 1264p. (C). 1994. pap. 41.88 (*0-07-016949-7*) McGraw.

McGraw-Hill Book of Poetry. Robert Diyanni & Kraft Rompf. LC 92-37243. 1268p. (C). 1993. pap. 41.88 (*0-07-016944-6*) McGraw.

McGraw-Hill Circuit Encyclopedia & Troubleshooting Guide. Michael Robin & Michel Poulin. (Illus.). 448p. 1997. pap. 39.95 (*0-07-038117-8*) McGraw.

McGraw-Hill Circuit Encyclopedia & Troubleshooting Guide, Vol. 2. John D. Lenk. (Illus.). 707p. 1996. pap. 39.95 (*0-07-037611-5*) McGraw.

McGraw-Hill Circuit Encyclopedia & Troubleshooting Guide, Vol. 3. John D. Lenk. (Illus.). 706p. 1996. 59.50 (*0-07-037716-2*); pap. 36.95 (*0-07-037717-0*) McGraw.

McGraw-Hill Circuit Encyclopedia & Troubleshooting Guide, Vol. 4. Michael Robin & Michel Poulin. (Illus.). 448p. 1997. 69.50 (*0-07-038116-X*) McGraw.

McGraw-Hill Circuit Encyclopedia & Troubleshooting Guide, Vol. No. 1. John D. Lenk. (Illus.). 647p. 1996. pap. 39.95 (*0-07-038076-7*) McGraw.

***McGraw-Hill Civil Engineering PE Exam Guide: Breadth & Depth.** James T. Ball. (Illus.). 2000. 99.95 (*0-07-136177-4*) McGraw.

McGraw-Hill College Handbook. 4th ed. Richard Marius & Harvey S. Wiener. LC 93-29714. 640p. (C). 1994. 39.06 (*0-07-040481-X*) McGraw.

McGraw-Hill Complete Book of Purchasing Forms & Agreements. Cliff Roberson. LC 97-39552. 371p. 1998. pap. 79.95 (*0-07-053117-X*) McGraw-Hill Prof.

McGraw-Hill Complete RBRVS: The Resource Based Relative Value Scale. Relative Value Studies, Inc. Staff. 1996. pap. 189.95 incl. disk (*0-07-810222-7*) McGraw.

McGraw-Hill Complete RBRVS: The Resource Based Relative Value Scale. Relative Value Studies, Inc. Staff. 1996. 89.95 (*0-07-600823-1*) McGraw.

McGraw-Hill Computing Essentials: Annual Edition, 1994-1995. annuals Timothy J. O'Leary & Linda I. O'Leary. (C). 1993. pap. text 34.25 (*0-07-048984-X*) McGraw.

McGraw-Hill Computing Essentials: Annual Edition 1995-1996. annuals Timothy J. O'Leary & Linda I. O'Leary. (C). 1995. text 32.00 (*0-07-049045-7*) McGraw.

McGraw-Hill Computing Essentials: Annual Edition 1995-1996, Brief Version. annuals Timothy J. O'Leary & Linda I. O'Leary. 1994. pap. text 24.50 (*0-07-049033-3*) McGraw.

McGraw-Hill Computing Essentials, 1996-1997. annuals Timothy J. O'Leary & Linda I. O'Leary. (C). 1995. pap. text 35.50 (*0-07-049091-0*) McGraw.

McGraw-Hill Computing Essentials, 1996-1997 Edition. annuals Timothy J. O'Leary & Linda I. O'Leary. (C). 1995. pap. text 24.50 (*0-07-049090-2*) McGraw.

McGraw-Hill Computing Essentials, 1997-1998: Brief Version. 3rd ed. Linda I. O'Leary & Timothy J. O'Leary. LC 96-48402. (C). 1997. pap. text 34.25 (*0-07-913062-3*) McGraw.

McGraw-Hill Concise Encyclopedia of Science & Technology. 4th ed. Sybil P. Parker. LC 98-3875. (Illus.). 2450p. 1998. 150.00 (*0-07-052659-1*) McGraw.

McGraw-Hill Data Communications Dictionary. William F. Potts. 268p. 1992. 34.50 (*0-07-003154-1*) McGraw.

McGraw-Hill Diccionario de Ciencias. 1992. text 65.00 (*0-07-104139-7*) McGraw.

McGraw-Hill Dictionary of Business Acronyms, Initials & Abbreviations. Ed. by Jerry M. Rosenberg. 336p. 1992. 29.95 (*0-07-053734-8*) McGraw.

McGraw-Hill Dictionary of Earth Science. McGraw-Hill Staff. (Mcgraw-Hill Dictionary Ser.). 480p. 1996. pap. 17.95 (*0-07-052427-0*) McGraw.

McGraw-Hill Dictionary of Electronics. 6th ed. John Markus & Neil J. Sclater. LC 97-16168. (Illus.). 544p. 1997. 55.00 (*0-07-057837-0*) McGraw.

McGraw-Hill Dictionary of Physics. 2nd ed. McGraw-Hill Staff. LC 96-46186. (Mcgraw-Hill Dictionary Ser.). 656p. 1996. pap. 16.95 (*0-07-052429-7*) McGraw.

McGraw-Hill Dictionary of Scientific & Technical Terms. 5th ed. S. Parker. (Illus.). 2200p. 1994. 150.00 (*0-07-042333-4*) McGraw.

McGraw-Hill Dictionary of Scientific & Technical Terms: English-Arabic, 4 vols., Set. McGraw Hill Staff. 1985. 295.00 (*0-86685-562-9*) Intl Bk Ctr.

McGraw-Hill Directory of Management Faculty, 1995-1996. James R. Hasselback. 1996. pap. text. write for info. (*0-07-027019-8*) McGraw.

McGraw-Hill Electrical Engineering Report. Donald G. Fink & H. Wayne Beaty. 48p. 1988. pap. text 95.00 (*0-07-020977-4*) McGraw.

McGraw-Hill Encyclopedia of Astronomy. 2nd ed. Ed. by Sybil P. Parker & Jay M. Pasachoff. LC 92-40523. 544p. 1993. 85.00 (*0-07-045314-4*) McGraw.

McGraw-Hill Encyclopedia of Environmental Science & Engineering. 3rd ed. Sybil P. Parker. 1993. 105.00 (*0-07-051396-1*) McGraw.

McGraw-Hill Encyclopedia of Geological Sciences. 2nd ed. (Illus.). 950p. 1988. 105.00 (*0-07-045500-7*) McGraw.

***McGraw-Hill Encyclopedia of Networking: Electronic Edition.** Sheldon. 1998. write for info. (*0-07-882350-1*) Osborne-McGraw.

McGraw-Hill Encyclopedia of Quality Terms & Concepts. James Cortada & John Woods. 392p. 1995. 34.95 (*0-07-024099-X*) McGraw.

McGraw-Hill Encyclopedia of Science & Technology, 20 vols. 8th ed. McGraw-Hill Staff. LC 96-52375. (Illus.). 15108p. (YA). (gr. 9). 1997. 1995.00 (*0-07-911504-7*) McGraw.

McGraw-Hill Encyclopedia of Science & Technology, 20 vols. 8th ed. Ed. by Sybil P. Parker. (Illus.). 15108p. 1997. 125.00 (*0-07-052418-1*) McGraw.

McGraw-Hill Encyclopedia of World Drama, 5 vols., Vol. 99. 2nd ed. McGraw-Hill Editors. LC 83-9919. (Illus.). 2900p. 1984. 450.00 (*0-07-079169-4*) McGraw.

McGraw-Hill Essential ISDN Sourcebook. Martin A. Nemzow. (Illus.). 366p. 1997. pap. 39.95 (*0-07-046384-0*) McGraw.

Mcgraw-Hill Finance Literature Index. 5th ed. Jean L. Heck. 1996. text. write for info. (*0-07-027790-7*) McGraw.

McGraw-Hill Financial Analyst, Software Version. Joel G. Siegel et al. 1995. 69.95 (*0-07-852806-2*) McGraw.

McGraw-Hill French Connaissances. Conrad J. Schmitt & Jo Helstrom. 384p. 1985. text, student ed. 29.84 (*0-07-041801-2*); student ed. 5.48 incl. audio (*0-07-041814-4*) McGraw.

McGraw-Hill Guide to Acquiring & Divesting Businesses. Edward E. Shea. (Illus.). 597p. 1998. 95.00 (*0-07-058030-8*) McGraw.

McGraw-Hill Guide to Clothing. Theodora Faiola & J. A. Pullen. Ed. by Sandra MacGowan. (Illus.). 384p. 1982. text 29.04 (*0-07-019855-1*) McGraw.

McGraw-Hill Guide to English Literature: Beowulf to Jane Austen, Vol. 1. Ed. by Karen Lawrence et al. 497p. (C). 1985. pap. 9.95 (*0-07-036704-3*) McGraw.

McGraw-Hill Guide to Passing the CLAST: Logic & Geometry. Salak & Dameron. (C). 1993. pap. text 9.25 (*0-07-054570-7*) McGraw.

McGraw-Hill Guide to Passing the CLAST: The Essay. 2nd ed. Luck & Markus. (C). 1993. pap. text 8.74 (*0-07-040473-9*) McGraw.

McGraw-Hill Guide to Starting Your Own Business: A Step-by-Step Blueprint for the First Time Entrepreneur. Stephen C. Harper. 203p. 1992. pap. 12.95 (*0-07-026687-5*) McGraw.

McGraw-Hill Guide to Writing a High-Impact Business Plan: A Proven Blueprint for First-Time Entrepreneurs. James B. Arkebauer. LC 94-21739. 1994. 32.95 (*0-07-003059-6*); pap. 17.95 (*0-07-003060-X*) McGraw.

McGraw-Hill Handbook of American Depository Receipts. Ed. by Richard J. Coyle. 392p. 1995. 59.95 (*0-07-013333-6*) McGraw.

McGraw-Hill Handbook of Business Letters. 3rd ed. Ray W. Poe. 400p. 1993. 59.50 (*0-07-911700-7*) McGraw.

McGraw-Hill Handbook of Business Letters. 3rd ed. Roy W. Poe. LC 93-24986. 384p. 1992. 59.50 (*0-07-050425-3*) McGraw.

McGraw-Hill Handbook of Business Letters. 3rd ed. Roy W. Poe. LC 93-24986. 363p. 1994. pap. 19.95 (*0-07-050451-2*) McGraw.

McGraw-Hill Handbook of Distance Learning. Alan Chute et al. (Illus.). 300p. 1998. 39.95 (*0-07-012028-5*) McGraw-Hill Prof.

McGraw-Hill Handbook of English. 4th ed. Harry Shaw. (Illus.). (gr. 9-12). 1978. text 15.96 (*0-07-056506-6*) McGraw.

McGraw-Hill Handbook of More Business Letters. Ann Poe. LC 98-24855. 416p. 1998. pap. 19.95 (*0-07-050517-9*) McGraw.

McGraw-Hill High-Speed LAN's Handbook. Stephen Saunders. 1996. text 60.00 (*0-07-057119-8*) McGraw.

McGraw-Hill High-Speed LAN's Handbook. Stephen Saunders. 460p. 1996. 60.00 (*0-07-057199-6*) McGraw.

McGraw-Hill Homebook. Sweet's Division Staff. (Illus.). 1980. 8.95 (*0-07-062606-5*) McGraw.

McGraw-Hill Illustrated Telecom Dictionary. Jade Clayton. LC 98-7686. 501p. 1998. pap. 29.95 (*0-07-012063-3*) McGraw.

***Mcgraw-Hill Illustrated Telecom Dictionary.** 2nd ed. Jade Clayton. (Illus.). 600p. 2000. pap. 29.95 (*0-07-136037-9*) McGraw-Hill Prof.

McGraw-Hill Internetworking Command Reference. D. Edgar Taylor. LC 95-45332. 1995. 60.00 (*0-07-063301-0*) McGraw.

McGraw-Hill Internetworking Handbook. Ed Taylor. LC 94-24060. 1995. 79.50 (*0-07-063263-4*) McGraw.

McGraw-Hill Internetworking Handbook. 2nd ed. D. Edgar Taylor, Jr. LC 97-20198. (Taylor Networking Ser.). (Illus.). 800p. 1997. 89.95 (*0-07-063334-7*); pap. 69.95 (*0-07-063399-1*) McGraw.

McGraw-Hill Introduction to Literature. 2nd ed. Intro. by Gilbert H. Muller & John A. Williams. LC 94-17019. 1200p. (C). 1994. pap. 39.38 (*0-07-044246-0*) McGraw.

***McGraw-Hill Investor's Desk Reference.** Ellie Williams. (Illus.). 600p. 2000. 29.95 (*0-07-135945-1*) McGraw.

McGraw-Hill Junior Academic Enrichment Series: Math. (Illus.). 80p. 1999. 2.99 (*1-57768-436-2*); wbk. ed. 2.99 (*1-57768-434-6*); wbk. ed. 2.99 (*1-57768-433-8*) MG-Hill OH.

McGraw-Hill Junior Academic Enrichment Series: Math. (Illus.). 80p. (J). (gr. 5). 1999. wbk. ed. 2.99 (*1-57768-435-4*) MG-Hill OH.

McGraw-Hill Junior Academic Enrichment Series: Reading. (Illus.). 80p. 1999. wbk. ed. 2.99 (*1-57768-443-5*); wbk. ed. 2.99 (*1-57768-444-3*); wbk. ed. 2.99 (*1-57768-445-1*); wbk. ed. 2.99 (*1-57768-446-X*) MG-Hill OH.

McGraw-Hill Junior Academic Series: Math. (Illus.). 80p. 1999. 2.99 (*1-57768-414-1*); wbk. ed. 2.99 (*1-57768-413-3*); wbk. ed. 2.99 (*1-57768-415-X*); wbk. ed. 2.99 (*1-57768-416-8*) MG-Hill OH.

McGraw-Hill Junior Academic Series: Reading. (Illus.). 80p. 1999. wbk. ed. 2.99 (*1-57768-423-0*); wbk. ed. 2.99 (*1-57768-424-9*); wbk. ed. 2.99 (*1-57768-425-7*); wbk. ed. 2.99 (*1-57768-426-5*) MG-Hill OH.

McGraw-Hill LAN Communications Handbook. Fred Simonds. LC 93-48540. (McGraw-Hill Series on Computer Communications). 444p. 1994. 54.50 (*0-07-057442-1*) McGraw.

McGraw-Hill Machining & Metalworking Handbook. Ronald A. Walsh. (Illus.). 1518p. 1994. 74.95 (*0-07-067958-4*, 6507U) McGraw.

McGraw-Hill Machining & Metalworking Handbook. 2nd ed. Ronald A. Walsh. LC 98-20537. 1683p. 1998. 99.95 (*0-07-068059-0*) McGraw.

McGraw-Hill Microcomputing Labs: Annual Edition 1992-1993. Timothy J. O'Leary et al. 1992. pap. text, teacher ed. 9.68 (*0-07-048834-7*) McGraw.

McGraw-Hill Microcomputing Labs: Edition B. Timothy J. O'Leary & Linda I. O'Leary. (C). 1993. spiral bd. 34.00 (*0-07-048904-1*) McGraw.

McGraw-Hill Microcomputing, 1992-1993 Edition. annuals Timothy J. O'Leary & Brian K. Williams. 1992. pap. text, teacher ed. 37.18 (*0-07-048833-9*) McGraw.

McGraw-Hill Multimedia Encyclopedia of Science & Technology: Release 1.1. McGraw-Hill Staff. 1996. 1300.00 (*0-07-852753-8*) McGraw.

McGraw-Hill Multimedia Handbook. Jessica Keyes. 1994. 69.50 (*0-07-911806-2*) McGraw.

McGraw-Hill Multimedia Handbook (1994) Ed. by Jessica Keyes. (Illus.). 800p. 1998. text 40.00 (*0-7881-5673-X*) DIANE Pub.

McGraw-Hill 1999 Yearbook of Science & Technology. McGraw-Hill Encyclopedia of Science & Technology E. (Illus.). 500p. 1998. 125.00 (*0-07-052625-7*) McGraw.

Mcgraw-Hill PC Programmer's Desk Reference. Maria P. Canton & Julio Sanchez. 470p. 1996. 50.00 (*0-07-057203-8*) McGraw.

McGraw-Hill Pocket Guide to Business Finance: 201 Decision-Making Tools for Managers. Joel G. Siegel. 354p. 1992. pap. 14.95 (*0-07-057576-2*) McGraw.

McGraw-Hill Pocket Guide to Managed Care. John La Puma & David L. Schiedermayer. 200p. 1996. reprint ed. pap. text 14.95 (*1-57066-105-7*, ME108) Practice Mgmt Info.

M

McGraw-Hill Reader. 4th ed. Muller. 1991. teacher ed. 28.12 (*0-07-044029-8*) McGraw.
McGraw-Hill Reader. 7th ed. Muller. LC 99-33123. 672p. 1999. pap. 37.81 (*0-07-229294-6*) McGraw.
McGraw-Hill Reader: Issues Across the Disciplines. 6th ed. Ed. by Gilbert H. Muller. 752p. (C). 1996. pap. 31.25 (*0-07-044009-3*) McGraw.
McGraw-Hill Real Estate Handbook. 2nd ed. Ed. by Robert Irwin. LC 92-34533. 641p. 1991. 69.50 (*0-07-032149-3*) McGraw.
***McGraw-Hill Recycling Handbook.** 2nd ed. Herbert F. Lund. LC 00-28382. (Illus.). 1152p. 2000. 99.95 (*0-07-039156-4*) McGraw.
McGraw-Hill Reference Book on Acquiring & Divesting Businesses. Edward E. Shea. LC 98-13577. 1998. 85.00 (*0-7863-0801-X*, Irwn Prfssnl) McGraw-Hill Prof.
McGraw-Hill Software Reliability Engineering Handbook. Michael R. Lyu. 850p. 1996. 79.99 (*0-07-039400-8*) McGraw.
McGraw-Hill Spanish 1. Conrad J. Schmitt et al. 432p. 1985. text, student ed. 28.24 (*0-07-056136-2*) McGraw.
McGraw-Hill Spanish 2. Conrad J. Schmitt et al. 400p. 1985. text 29.96 (*0-07-056156-7*) McGraw.
McGraw-Hill Spectrum Series: Dolch Sight Word Activities. (Illus.). 160p. 1999. wbk. ed. 9.95 (*1-57768-429-X*); wbk. ed. 9.95 (*1-57768-439-7*) MG-Hill OH.
McGraw-Hill Spectrum Series: Test Prep. (Illus.). 168p. 1999. wbk. ed. 8.95 (*1-57768-101-0*); wbk. ed. 8.95 (*1-57768-102-9*) MG-Hill OH.
McGraw-Hill Spectrum Trade Series: Math. (Illus.). 128p. 1999. wbk. ed. 6.95 (*1-57768-400-1*); wbk. ed. 6.95 (*1-57768-401-X*); wbk. ed. 6.95 (*1-57768-403-6*); wbk. ed. 6.95 (*1-57768-404-4*); wbk. ed. 6.95 (*1-57768-405-2*); wbk. ed. 6.95 (*1-57768-406-0*); wbk. ed. 6.95 (*1-57768-407-9*); wbk. ed. 6.95 (*1-57768-408-7*) MG-Hill OH.
McGraw-Hill Spectrum Trade Series: Phonics. (Illus.). 128p. 1999. wbk. ed. 6.95 (*1-57768-450-8*); wbk. ed. 6.95 (*1-57768-451-6*); wbk. ed. 6.95 (*1-57768-452-4*); wbk. ed. 6.95 (*1-57768-453-2*); wbk. ed. 6.95 (*1-57768-454-0*); wbk. ed. 6.95 (*1-57768-455-9*); wbk. ed. 6.95 (*1-57768-456-7*) MG-Hill OH.
McGraw-Hill Spectrum Trade Series: Reading. (Illus.). 152p. 1999. wbk. ed. 6.95 (*1-57768-460-5*); wbk. ed. 6.95 (*1-57768-461-3*); wbk. ed. 6.95 (*1-57768-462-1*); wbk. ed. 6.95 (*1-57768-463-X*); wbk. ed. 6.95 (*1-57768-464-8*); wbk. ed. 6.95 (*1-57768-465-6*); wbk. ed. 6.95 (*1-57768-466-4*) MG-Hill OH.
McGraw-Hill Telecommunications Factbook. Joseph A. Pecar et al. LC 92-24340. (Illus.). 1993. pap. 29.95 (*0-07-049183-6*) McGraw.
McGraw-Hill Thirty-Six Hour Accounting Course. 3rd ed. Robert L. Dixon. 448p. 1993. 50.00 (*0-07-017093-2*); pap. 19.95 (*0-07-017094-0*) McGraw.
McGraw-Hill 36-Hour Course: Business Presentations. Lani Arredondon. 337p. 1994. 39.95 (*0-07-002840-0*) McGraw.
McGraw-Hill Thirty-Six Hour Course in Finance for Non-Financial Managers. Robert A. Cooke. 266p. 1993. pap. 19.95 (*0-07-012538-4*) McGraw.
McGraw-Hill 36-Hour Negotiating Course. Mark K. Schoenfield & Rick M. Schoenfield. 352p. 1992. pap. 19.95 (*0-07-055517-6*) McGraw.
McGraw-Hill Thirty-Six Hour Real Estate Investing Course. Jack Cummings. 358p. 1992. pap. 19.95 (*0-07-015048-6*) McGraw.
***McGraw-Hill 2000 Yearbook of Science & Technology.** McGraw-Hill Publishing Staff. (Illus.). 1999. write for info. (*0-07-052771-7*) McGraw.
McGraw-Hill Vocabulary, Bk. 1. 2nd ed. Gene Stanford. Ed. by Hester E. Weeden. (Illus.). 128p. (gr. 7-12). 1981. pap. text 6.80 (*0-07-060771-0*) McGraw.
McGraw-Hill Vocabulary, Bk. 3. 2nd ed. Gene Stanford. (Illus.). 128p. (J). 1981. pap. text 6.80 (*0-07-060773-7*) McGraw.
McGraw-Hill Vocabulary, Bk. 4. 2nd ed. Gene Stanford. (Illus.). 128p. (gr. 10). 1981. pap. text 6.80 (*0-07-060774-5*) McGraw.
McGraw-Hill Vocabulary, Bk. 5. 2nd ed. Gene Stanford. 1982. 6.80 (*0-07-060775-3*) McGraw.
McGraw-Hill Vocabulary, Bk. 6. 2nd ed. Gene Stanford. 1981. 6.80 (*0-07-060776-1*) McGraw.
McGraw-Hill Warner Bros. Junior Academic Series: A Wakko Pursuit. (Illus.). 24p. (J). (gr. 2). 1999. pap. 2.99 (*1-57768-542-3*) MG-Hill OH.
McGraw-Hill Workbook. Mark Connelly. 480p. (C). 1994. pap., wbk. ed. 18.13 (*0-07-012498-1*) McGraw.
McGraw-Hill Workbook. Mark Connelly. 1994. pap. text, teacher ed. write for info. (*0-07-012499-X*) McGraw.
McGraw-Hill World Wide Web Training Manual. Ronald L. Wagner. 304p. 1996. pap. 32.95 (*0-07-966538-1*) McGraw.
***McGraw-Hill Yearbook of Science & Technology.** Ed. by McGraw-Hill Staff. (Illus.). 450p. 2000. 125.00 (*0-07-135867-6*) McGraw.
McGraw-Hill Zanichelli see Encyclopedic Dictionary of Science & Technology: English-Italian--Italian-English
McGraw-Hill Zanichelli see Encyclopedic Dictionary of Science & Technology
***McGraw-Hill's Chemical Safety Guide for the Plastics Industry.** Richard Pohanish. (Illus.). 1000p. 2000. 125.00 (*0-07-135607-X*) McGraw-Hill Prof.
McGraw-Hill's Compilation of Data Communications Standards. 2nd rev. ed. Ed. by Harold C. Folts. 1923p. 1983. 295.00 (*0-07-606775-0*) McGraw.
McGraw-Hill's Compilation of Open Systems Standards, 6 vols. 4th ed. Harold C. Folts. 10000p. 1991. 775.00 (*0-07-607030-1*) McGraw.
McGraw-Hill's Compound Interest & Annuity Tables. 2nd ed. Jack C. Estes. 256p. 1992. pap. 7.95 (*0-07-019686-9*) McGraw.
McGraw-Hill's Handbook of Electrical Construction Calculations. J. F. McPartland et al. LC 93-3994. (Illus.). 368p. 1993. 54.50 (*0-07-045682-8*) McGraw.
McGraw-Hill's Handbook of Electrical Construction Calculations. 2nd ed. Joseph F. McPartland & McGraw-Hill Book Company Staff. LC 97-29144. 464p. 1998. 59.95 (*0-07-046641-6*) McGraw.
McGraw-Hill's Illustrated Index to the 1996 National Electrical Code. John E. Traister. (Illus.). 1996. 47.50 (*0-07-065305-4*) McGraw.
McGraw-Hill's Illustrated Index to the 1999 National Electrical Code. John E. Traister & Dale Brickner. LC 99-20157. (Illus.). 480p. 1999. 49.95 (*0-07-065539-1*) McGraw.
McGraw-Hill's Interest Amortization Tables. 2nd ed. J. Estes. 311p. 1993. pap. 7.95 (*0-07-019696-6*) McGraw.
***McGraw-Hill's National Electrical Code Handbook.** Joseph F. McPartland. 1300p. 1999. 115.00 (*0-07-134598-1*) McGraw.
McGraw-Hill's National Electrical Code Handbook. 23rd ed. Joseph F. McPartland & Brian J. McPartland. (Illus.). 1360p. 1998. 92.95 (*0-07-047234-3*) McGraw-Hill Prof.
McGraw-Hill's National Electrical Code Handbook: Based on the 1996 National Electrical Code. 22nd ed. J. F. McPartland. (Illus.). 1264p. 1996. 65.00 (*0-07-045992-4*) McGraw.
McGraw-Hill's Programmer's Desk Reference. Maria P. Canton & Julio Sanchez. (Illus.). 452p. 1996. text 50.00 incl. disk (*0-07-912176-4*); pap. text 34.95 (*0-07-912177-2*) McGraw.
McGraw-Hill/Warner Bros. Jr. Academic Series: Key Skills. (Illus.). 320p. 1998. wbk. ed. 11.95 (*1-57768-241-6*); wbk. ed. 11.95 (*1-57768-249-1*); wbk. ed. 8.95 (*1-57768-248-3*); wbk. ed. 11.99 (*1-57768-240-8*); wbk. ed. 11.95 (*1-57768-242-4*) MG-Hill OH.
McGraw-Hill/Warner Bros. Junior Academic Series: A Flag on Mars. (Illus.). 24p. (J). (gr. k). 1999. pap. 2.99 (*1-57768-530-X*) MG-Hill OH.
McGraw-Hill/Warner Bros. Junior Academic Series: A Nap in Sand Land. (Illus.). 24p. (J). (gr. 1). 1999. pap. 2.99 (*1-57768-521-0*) MG-Hill OH.
McGraw-Hill/Warner Bros. Junior Academic Series: A Trip by Truck & Train. (Illus.). 24p. (J). (gr. k). 1999. pap. 2.99 (*1-57768-540-7*) MG-Hill OH.
McGraw-Hill/Warner Bros. Junior Academic Series: Beanstalk Bunny. (Illus.). 16p. (J). (gr. k-2). 1999. pap. 3.99 (*1-57768-216-5*) MG-Hill OH.
McGraw-Hill/Warner Bros. Junior Academic Series: Brain's Grand Plan. (Illus.). 24p. (J). (gr. 2). 1999. pap. 2.99 (*1-57768-512-1*) MG-Hill OH.
McGraw-Hill/Warner Bros. Junior Academic Series: Bugs' Puzzle Book. (Illus.). 32p. (J). (gr. k-2). 1999. 5.95 (*1-57768-236-X*) MG-Hill OH.
McGraw-Hill/Warner Bros. Junior Academic Series: Bugsilocks & the Three Bears. (Illus.). 16p. (J). (gr. k-2). 1999. pap. 3.99 (*1-57768-215-7*) MG-Hill OH.
McGraw-Hill/Warner Bros. Junior Academic Series: Daffy's Puzzle Book. (Illus.). 32p. (J). (gr. k-2). 1999. 2.25 (*1-57768-235-1*) MG-Hill OH.
McGraw-Hill/Warner Bros. Junior Academic Series: Enrichment Math. (Illus.). 80p. 1999. wbk. ed. 2.99 (*1-57768-281-5*) MG-Hill OH.
***McGraw-Hill/Warner Bros. Junior Academic Series: Enrichment Math.** (Illus.). 80p. 1999. wbk. ed. 2.99 (*1-57768-280-7*); wbk. ed. 2.99 (*1-57768-282-3*) MG-Hill OH.
McGraw-Hill/Warner Bros. Junior Academic Series: Enrichment Math & Reading. (Illus.). 160p. 1999. wbk. ed. 5.95 (*1-57768-500-8*); wbk. ed. 5.95 (*1-57768-501-6*); wbk. ed. 5.95 (*1-57768-502-4*) MG-Hill OH.
McGraw-Hill/Warner Bros. Junior Academic Series: Enrichment Reading. (Illus.). 80p. 1999. wbk. ed. 2.99 (*1-57768-290-4*); wbk. ed. 2.99 (*1-57768-291-2*); wbk. ed. 2.99 (*1-57768-292-0*) MG-Hill OH.
McGraw-Hill/Warner Bros Junior Academic Series: Get a Pet. (Illus.). 24p. (J). (gr. 1). 1999. pap. 2.99 (*1-57768-541-5*) MG-Hill OH.
McGraw-Hill/Warner Bros. Junior Academic Series: Go for a Spin. (Illus.). 24p. (J). (gr. 1). 1999. pap. 2.99 (*1-57768-511-3*) MG-Hill OH.
McGraw-Hill/Warner Bros. Junior Academic Series: Here's Lunch with Taz. (Illus.). 24p. (J). (gr. k). 1999. pap. 2.99 (*1-57768-520-2*) MG-Hill OH.
McGraw-Hill/Warner Bros. Junior Academic Series: Munch a Lunch with Wakko. (Illus.). 24p. (J). (gr. 2). 1999. pap. 2.99 (*1-57768-532-6*) MG-Hill OH.
McGraw-Hill/Warner Bros. Junior Academic Series: My First Picture Word Book. (Illus.). 64p. 1999. pap. 3.99 (*1-57768-206-8*) MG-Hill OH.
McGraw-Hill/Warner Bros. Junior Academic Series: My First Picture Word Book. (Illus.). 64p. (J). (gr. k-1). 1999. 7.99 (*1-57768-205-X*) MG-Hill OH.
McGraw-Hill/Warner Bros. Junior Academic Series: Phonics Bindup. (Illus.). 320p. 1999. wbk. ed. 11.95 (*1-57768-203-3*); wbk. ed. 11.95 (*1-57768-204-1*) MG-Hill OH.
McGraw-Hill/Warner Bros. Junior Academic Series: Phonics Readers Collection. (Illus.). 96p. (J). (gr. k). 1999. pap. 9.99 (*1-57768-550-4*) MG-Hill OH.
McGraw-Hill/Warner Bros. Junior Academic Series: Phonics Readers Collection. (Illus.). 96p. (J). (gr. 1). 1999. pap. 9.99 (*1-57768-551-2*) MG-Hill OH.
McGraw-Hill/Warner Bros. Junior Academic Series: Phonics Readers Collection. (Illus.). 96p. (J). (gr. 2). 1999. pap. 11.95 (*1-57768-552-0*) MG-Hill OH.
McGraw-Hill/Warner Bros. Junior Academic Series: Plotzo. (Illus.). 24p. (J). (gr. 2). 1999. pap. 2.99 (*1-57768-522-9*) MG-Hill OH.
McGraw-Hill/Warner Bros. Junior Academic Series: Shuttle Buggy. (Illus.). 24p. (J). (gr. 1). 1999. pap. 2.99 (*1-57768-531-8*) MG-Hill OH.
McGraw Hill/Warner Bros. Junior Academic Series: Taz's Puzzle Book. (Illus.). 32p. (J). (gr. k-2). 1999. 2.25 (*1-57768-233-5*) MG-Hill OH.
McGraw-Hill/Warner Bros. Junior Academic Series: The Gingerbread Fudd. (Illus.). 16p. (J). (gr. k-2). 1999. pap. 3.99 (*1-57768-214-9*) MG-Hill OH.
McGraw-Hill/Warner Bros. Junior Academic Series: The Lion & the Mouse. (Illus.). 16p. (J). (gr. k-2). 1999. pap. 3.99 (*1-57768-213-0*) MG-Hill OH.
***McGraw-Hill/Warner Bros. Junior Academic Series: The Park.** (Illus.). 24p. (J). (gr. k). 1999. pap. 2.99 (*1-57768-510-5*) MG-Hill OH.
McGraw-Hill/Warner Bros. Junior Academic Series: Tweety's Puzzle Book. (Illus.). 32p. (J). (gr. k-2). 1999. 2.25 (*1-57768-234-3*) MG-Hill OH.
McGraw's Emporium. Jim Aylesworth. (Illus.). 88p. (J). 1995. 15.95 (*0-8050-3192-8*) H Holt & Co.
McGraw's Emporium. Jim Aylesworth. (Illus.). (J). (ps-2). 1998. pap. 5.95 (*0-8050-5797-8*) H Holt & Co.
McGregor on Damages. H. McGregor. (C). 1988. 1125.00 (*0-7855-4080-6*, Pub. by Witherby & Co) St Mut.
McGregor Renewal & the Current Air Defense Mission. David Rubenson et al. LC 98-47603. (Illus.). 108p. 1998. pap. 15.00 (*0-8330-2669-0*, MR-1010-A) Rand Corp.
McGregor's Who Owns Whom, 1993: The Southern African Edition. Ed. by R. McGregor. 1100p. (C). 1993. lib. bdg. 480.00 (*1-85333-908-3*) Kluwer Academic.
McGruff's Drug Abuse Prevention Kit. Ed. by Jean O'Neil. 1989. 44.95 (*0-934513-83-X*) Natl Crime DC.
McGruff's Elementary Drug Prevention Activity Book. Ed. by Jean O'Neil. (Illus.). 64p. 1992. pap. 19.95 (*0-934513-29-5*, K8) Natl Crime DC.
MCGs in Paediatrics. 2nd ed. Jagdish M. Gupta & John Beveridge. 280p. 1996. pap. text 14.95 (*0-412-73340-4*, Pub. by E A) OUP.
McGuffey Eclectic Readers see Christian Eclectic Readers
McGuffey Eclectic Readers: Primer Through 6th Edition, 7 vols. William H. McGuffey. 1997. 59.95 (*0-471-29428-4*) Wiley.
McGuffey Reader: Selections from the 1879 Edition. Elliot J. Gorn. LC 97-81287. 120p. 1998. text 35.00 (*0-312-17766-6*) St Martin.
McGuffey Readers, 9 vols., Set. William H. McGuffey. 1973. lib. bdg. 2500.00 (*0-8490-0571-X*) Gordon Pr.
McGuffey's Eclectic Primer. rev. ed. William H. McGuffey. 64p. 1997. 9.95 (*0-471-28888-8*, VNR) Wiley.
McGuffeys Eclectic Spelling Book. William H. McGuffey. 1997. 9.95 (*0-317-64211-1*, VNR) Wiley.
McGuffey's Eclectic Spelling Book. rev. ed. William H. McGuffey. 144p. 1997. 9.95 (*0-471-28943-4*, VNR); text 9.95 (*0-442-26446-1*, VNR) Wiley.
McGuffey's Fifth Eclectic Reader. rev. ed. William H. McGuffey. 352p. (J). 1997. 12.95 (*0-471-28892-6*, VNR) Wiley.
McGuffey's First Eclectic Reader. William H. McGuffey. 96p. 1997. 9.95 (*0-471-28889-6*, VNR) Wiley.
McGuffey's Fourth Eclectic Reader. rev. ed. William H. McGuffey. 256p. (J). 1997. 10.95 (*0-471-28984-1*, VNR) Wiley.
McGuffey's Illustrated Address Book. William H. McGuffey. 1980. text 15.95 (*0-442-21257-7*, VNR) Wiley.
McGuffey's New High School Reader. William H. McGuffey. 1974. 250.00 (*0-87968-147-0*) Gordon Pr.
McGuffey's Revised Eclectic Readers, 7 bks. Incl. Fifth Reader. 1920. text 9.95 (*0-442-23565-8*, VNR); First Reader. 1920. text 9.95 (*0-442-23561-5*, VNR); Fourth Reader. 1920. text 9.95 (*0-442-33564-4*, VNR); McGuffey's Second Eclectic Reader. rev. ed. McGuffey. 160p. 1997. 9.95 (*0-442-23562-3*, VNR); Primer. 1920. text 9.95 (*0-442-23560-7*, VNR); Sixth Reader. 1920. text 10.95 (*0-442-23566-6*, VNR); Third Reader. 1920. text 9.95 (*0-442-23563-1*, VNR); write for info. (*0-318-56318-5*, VNR) Wiley.
McGuffey's Second Eclectic Reader see McGuffey's Revised Eclectic Readers
McGuffey's Second Eclectic Reader. rev. ed. William H. McGuffey. 160p. 1997. 9.95 (*0-471-28890-X*, VNR) Wiley.
McGuffey's Sixth Eclectic Reader. William H. McGuffey. 480p. (J). 1997. 12.95 (*0-471-28893-4*, VNR) Wiley.
McGuffey's Third Eclectic Reader. rev. ed. William H. McGuffey. 208p. (J). 1997. 10.95 (*0-471-28891-8*, VNR) Wiley.
McGuire's Irish Pub Cookbook. Jessie Tirsch. LC 97-44575. (Illus.). 280p. 1996. 22.50 (*1-56554-299-1*) Pelican.
***McGuire's Irish Pub Postcard Book.** McGuire's Irish Pub Staff. (Illus.). 30p. 1999. pap. text 9.95 (*1-56554-692-X*) Pelican.
McGuire's Turkey. Peaches Smith. LC 96-33895. (Illus.). 23p. (J). 1996. 2.95 (*1-56763-186-X*) Ozark Pub.
***McGwire & Sosa: A Season to Remember.** James Preller. (J). 1998. pap. 6.99 (*0-689-82871-3*) S&S Childrens.
McHenry Mansion Mystery. Colleen S. Bare. (Illus.). 24p. (Orig.). (J). (gr. 1-6). 1996. 2.95 (*0-9654556-0-2*) McHenry Mansion.
***McHenry's Quips, Quotes & Other Notes.** Raymond McHenry. 2000. 17.97 (*1-56563-462-4*) Hendrickson MA.
Mcheshi Goes on a Journey: Mcheshi Aenda Safari. Judy Wanjiku Mathenge. 1993. 13.15 (*0-606-08816-4*, Pub. by Turtleback) Demco.
McHeshi Goes on a Journey: McHeshi Aenda Safari. J. Wanjiko. 1995. pap. text 7.95 (*9966-884-25-4*) Jacaranda.
Mcheshi Goes to School. Carrie J. Williams. 1995. pap. text 7.95 (*9966-884-64-5*) Nocturnal Sun.
Mcheshi Goes to School: Mcheshi Aenda Shuleni. Judy Wanijiku Mathenge. 1995. 13.15 (*0-606-08817-2*, Pub. by Turtleback) Demco.
Mcheshi Goes to the Game Park: Mcheshi Aenda Hifadhi Ya Wanyama. Phyllis Koinange. 1992. 13.15 (*0-606-08818-0*, Pub. by Turtleback) Demco.
Mcheshi Goes to the Market: Mcheshi Aenda Sokoni. James Okello. 1991. 13.15 (*0-606-08819-9*, Pub. by Turtleback) Demco.
MCI: Failure Is Not an Option: How MCI Invented Competition in Telecommunications. Lorraine Spurge. LC 97-21903. (Illus.). 356p. 1998. pap. 16.95 (*1-888232-41-2*) Spurge ink.
MCI Classic - the Heritage of Golf: A Tournament Retrospective. Vance Fowler. (Illus.). 90p. 1995. 29.95 (*0-9645831-0-0*) Heritage Class Found.
MCI Directory of Management Information, 1998. MCI Staff. LC 99-219125. 161p. 1999. text 95.00 (*0-7506-3812-5*) Buttrwrth-Heinemann.
MCI/in Focus: Profiles of Global Telecommunications Carrier. Karen Furbish. (Illus.). 116p. 1998. pap. 795.00 (*0-938866-04-4*) Tele Rprts Intl.
McIllvanney on Racing. H. McIllvaney. 1992. 24.95 (*0-09-158430-2*, Pub. by Random) Trafalgar.
McIlvanney on Boxing. Hugh McILvanney. 320p. 1997. 35.00 (*1-85158-732-2*, Pub. by Mainstream Pubng) Trafalgar.
McIlvanney on Boxing. Hugh McIlvanney. 320p. 1997. pap. 19.95 (*1-84018-005-6*, Pub. by Mainstream Pubng) Trafalgar.
McIlvanney on Horseracing. Hugh McIlvanney. 288p. 1996. 34.95 (*1-85158-733-0*, Pub. by Mainstream Pubng); pap. 19.95 (*1-85158-877-9*, Pub. by Mainstream Pubng) Trafalgar.
McIlwraith & Turner's Equine Surgery: Advanced Techniques. 2nd ed. C. Wayne McIlwraith et al. LC 98-15576. 440p. 1998. 99.00 (*0-683-05770-7*) Lppncott W & W.
McIndoe's Army. large type ed. Peter Williams & Ted Harrison. 223p. 1981. 11.50 (*0-7089-8016-3*, Charnwood) Ulverscroft.
Mcintosh & Weatherford, Creek Indian Leaders. Benjamin W. Griffith. LC 98-160691. 336p. 1998. pap. 19.95 (*0-8173-0914-4*) U of Ala Pr.
***Mckay World Soc Sg V1.** 5th ed. McKay. 1999. pap. text 17.97 (*0-395-94494-5*) HM.
***Mckay World Soc Sg V2.** 5th ed. McKay. 1999. pap. text 17.97 (*0-395-94496-1*) HM.
***Mckay World Soc Va 5e.** 5th ed. McKay. 1999. pap. text 35.07 (*0-395-94492-9*) HM.
***Mckay World Soc Vb.** 5th ed. McKay. 1999. pap. text 35.07 (*0-395-94493-7*) HM.
***Mckay World Soc Vc.** 5th ed. McKay. 1999. pap. text 35.07 (*0-395-94495-3*) HM.
***Mckay World Soc V1.** 5th ed. McKay. 1999. pap. text 41.07 (*0-395-94490-2*) HM.
MCKAY WORLD SOC V1 (W/ATLAS), 4 vols. 4th ed. John P. McKay et al. 600p. (C). 1995. pap. text 49.16 (*0-395-74072-X*) HM.
***Mckay World Soc V2.** 5th ed. McKay. 1999. pap. text 41.07 (*0-395-94491-0*) HM.
MCKAY WORLD SOC V2 (W/ATLAS), 4 vols. 4th ed. John P. McKay et al. 675p. (C). 1995. pap. text 49.16 (*0-395-74073-8*) HM.
McKay's English-Polish - Polish-English Dictionary. J. Stanislawski. 1988. 19.00 (*0-8129-1691-3*, Times Bks) Crown Pub Group.
McKay's English-Polish Polish-English Dictionary. rev. ed. Fodor's Staff. (ENG & POL.). (YA). (gr. 9 up). 14.95 (*0-679-51209-8*) McKay.
McKee of Centre Street. Helen Reilly. 299p. 1980. reprint ed. lib. bdg. 14.25 (*0-89968-214-6*, Lghtyr Pr) Buccaneer Bks.
Mckendree. Belton. (J). 1999. mass mkt. 16.00 (*0-689-80204-8*) S&S Bks Yung.
McKendree. Sandra Belton. LC 99-24456. 144p. (YA). (gr. 5-9). 2000. 15.95 (*0-688-15950-8*, Greenwillow Bks) HarpC Child Bks.
McKendree. Douglas Hirt. 192p. 1997. reprint ed. mass mkt. 3.99 (*0-8439-4184-7*) Dorchester Pub Co.
McKennas. Virgil S. Cross. LC 97-675. (Orig.). 1997. pap. 22.50 (*1-880664-22-4*) E M Pr.
McKenna's Bartered Bride: Bachelor Gulch. Sandra Steffen. (Romance Ser.: No. 1398). 1999. per. 3.50 (*0-373-19398-X*, 1-19398-6) Silhouette.
McKenna's Bride. Judith E. French. 1998. mass mkt. 5.99 (*0-345-40873-X*) Ballantine Pub Grp.
McKenna's Fortune. Lauren Wilde. 320p. 1996. mass mkt. 4.99 (*0-8217-5231-6*, Zebra Kensgtn) Kensgtn Pub Corp.
McKenzie River Journal. Meyer Deke. (River Journal Ser.: Vol. 3, No. 3). 1997. pap. text 15.95 (*1-57188-053-4*) F Amato Pubns.
McKeown's Price Guide to Antique & Classic Cameras. 11th ed. Jim McKeown & Joan McKeown. (Illus.). 672p. 1998. pap. text 69.95 (*0-931838-32-0*) Watsn-Guptill.
McKim, Mead & White. Charles H. Reilly. LC 71-180028. (Illus.). 1972. reprint ed. 17.95 (*0-405-08877-9*) Ayer.
McKinley, Bryan, & the People. Paul W. Glad. 228p. 1991. reprint ed. pap. text 9.95 (*0-929587-49-9*, Pub. by I R Dee) Natl Bk Netwk.
McKinley Official Internet Yellow Pages. 3rd ed. Christine Maxwell et al. (Illus.). 900p. (Orig.). 1995. pap. 29.99 (*1-56205-440-6*) New Riders Pub.

An Asterisk (*) at the beginning of an entry indicates that the title is appearing for the first time.

McKinney: History of the Families of McKinney-Brady-Quigley. B. M. Swope. (Illus.). 326p. 1994. reprint ed. lib. bdg. 59.50 (*0-8328-4801-8*) Higginson Bk Co.

McKinney: History of the Families of McKinney-Brady-Quigley. B. M. Swope. (Illus.). 326p. 1995. reprint ed. pap. 49.50 (*0-8328-4802-6*) Higginson Bk Co.

McKinney Act: Education Homeless Children. 8p. 1990. 4.00 (*0-317-05347-7*) NASBE.

McKinney Act Programs in Nonmetro Areas: How Far Do They Reach? Case Studies, 2 Pts. Housing Assistance Council Staff. 66p. 1995. 5.50 (*1-58064-038-9*) Housing Assist.

McKinney Act Programs in Nonmetro Areas - How Far Do They Reach? Pt. 1: Distribution of Funds, 1987-1991. Housing Assistance Council Staff. 55p. 1995. 5.00 (*1-58064-037-0*) Housing Assist.

McKinney Falls: The Ranch Home of Thomas F. McKinney, Pioneer Texas Entrepreneur. Margaret S. Henson. LC 98-51738. (Fred Rider Cotten Popular History Ser.: No. 12). 64p. 1998. pap. 7.95 (*0-87611-172-X*) Tex St Hist Assn.

McKinney, Texas: The First 150 Years. Julia L. Vargo. LC 97-29774. 192p. 1997. write for info. (*1-57864-007-5*) Donning Co.

***McKinney's Law.** large type ed. Mike Stotter. 288p. 1999. pap. 18.99 (*0-7089-5476-6*, Linford) Ulverscroft.

McKinney's Revenge. large type ed. Mike Stotter. 272p. pap. 18.99 (*0-7089-5427-8*) Ulverscroft.

McKinnon's Machine. Wolf. 1993. mass mkt. write for info. (*0-312-92966-8*) Tor Bks.

McKinsey & Co. The WetFeet.com Insider Guide. 4th ed. WetFeet.com Staff. (Insider Guides Ser.). 60p. 1999. per. 25.00 (*1-58207-041-5*) WetFeet.

McKinsey Way: Using the Techniques of the World's Top Strategic Consultants to Help You & Your Business. Ethan M. Rasiel. LC 98-51500. 187p. 1999. 21.95 (*0-07-053448-9*) McGraw.

McKnight Genealogy, 1754-1981. Lilla M. Licht & William B. Moore. LC 81-85782. (Illus.). 476p. 1981. 25.00 (*0-9607184-0-0*); pap. 22.00 (*0-9607184-1-9*) Licht Pubns.

McLain v. Barber (Pretrial Edition) Anthony J. Bocchino & Ronald L. Beal. 120p. 1994. pap. 22.95 (*1-55681-393-7*) Natl Inst Trial Ad.

McLain vs. Barber. 2nd ed. Anthony J. Bocchina & Ronald L. Beal. 200p. 1997. pap. 22.95 (*1-55681-540-9*) Natl Inst Trial Ad.

***McLain's Law.** Kylie Brant. 2000. mass mkt. 4.50 (*0-373-82236-7*, 1-82236-0) Harlequin Bks.

McLain's Law: Premiere. Kylie Brant. (Intimate Moments Ser.). 1993. per. 3.50 (*0-373-07528-6*, 5-07528-8) Silhouette.

McLaren - Formula 1 Racing Team. (Illus.). 160p. 1999. pap. 24.95 (*1-85960-425-0*) Haynes Manuals.

McLaren - The Epic Years. Alan Henry. (Illus.). 224p. 1998. 36.95 (*1-85260-593-6*, Pub. by J H Haynes & Co) Motorbooks Intl.

McLaren-Formula 1. Koneman. 1999. 39.95 (*3-8290-0945-3*) Konemann.

McLaren Race Cars 1965-1996 Photo Album. Norman Hayes. LC 97-70618. (Photo Album Ser.). (Illus.). 112p. 1997. pap. 19.95 (*1-882256-74-3*) Iconografix.

***McLaren Sports Racing Cars.** Dave Friedman. LC 99-86486. (Illus.). 192p. 2000. 39.95 (*0-7603-0724-5*, Pub. by MBI Pubg) Motorbooks Intl.

***MCLE.** LC 99-189456. (New York Practice Skills Course Handbook Ser.). 904 p. 1999. write for info. (*0-87224-570-5*) PLI.

MCLE Bridge the Gap. LC 98-221898. (New York Practice Skills Course Handbook Ser.). 944 p. 1998. write for info. (*0-87224-515-2*) PLI.

MCLE Compulsories 1994. Practising Law Institute Staff. LC 95-122392. 472 p. 1994. write for info. (*0-87224-159-9*) PLI.

MCLE Compulsories, 1995: Ethics & Law Practice Management; Elimination of Bias, Substance Abuse & Emotional Distress. (Litigation & Administrative Practice Course Handbook, 1983-84 Ser.). Date not set. pap. 99.00 (*0-614-17266-7*, H4-5221) PLI.

MCLE Compulsories 1995: Ethics & Law Practice Management : Elimination of Bias, Substance Abuse & Emotional Distress. Jerome Fishkin et al. LC 96-169767. (Litigation Course Handbook Ser.). 336p. 1995. write for info. (*0-87224-218-8*) PLI.

McLean at the Golden Owl. large type ed. George Goodchild. (Large Print Ser.). 416p. 1997. 27.99 (*0-7089-3665-2*) Ulverscroft.

Mclean Disposes. large type ed. George Goodchild. (Linford Mystery Library). 1994. pap. 16.99 (*0-7089-7638-7*, Linford) Ulverscroft.

McLean Investigates. large type ed. George Goodchild. (Linford Mystery Library). 464p. 1995. pap. 16.99 (*0-7089-7799-5*, Linford) Ulverscroft.

McLean P. O. W. Camp. 2nd ed. Delbert Trew. (Illus.). 51p. 1997. reprint ed. pap. 13.50 (*0-9659677-0-0*) DRM Pub.

McLean to the Dark Tower Came. large type ed. George Goodchild. 416p. 1998. 29.99 (*0-7089-3989-9*) Ulverscroft.

McLellan & Stocks: VAT: Input Tax Recovery. Dermot McLellan & Barry Stocks. 300p. 1993. boxed set 133.00 (*0-406-01139-7*, U.K., MICHIE) LEXIS Pub.

Mclibel: Burger Culture on Trial. John Vidal. (Illus.). 352p. 1997. 24.00 (*1-56584-411-4*, Pub. by New Press NY) Norton.

McLoughlin: Commercial Leases & Insolvency. 2nd ed. Patrick McLoughlin. 1996. pap. write for info. (*0-406-08189-1*, MCLI02, MICHIE) LEXIS Pub.

McLuhan & Baudrillard: Masters of Implosion. Gary Genosko. LC 98-48297. 1999. pap. 20.99 (*0-415-19062-2*) Routledge.

Mcluhan & Baudrillard: The Masters of Implosion. Gary Genosko. LC 98-48297. 1999. write for info. (*0-415-19061-4*) Routledge.

Mcluhan for Beginners. W. Terrence Gordon & Susan Willmarth. (The For Beginners Ser.). (Illus.). 176p. 11.00 (*0-86316-231-2*) Writers & Readers.

McLuhan or Modernism in Reverse. Glenn Willmott. (Theory/Culture Ser.). 288p. 1996. text 55.00 (*0-8020-0801-1*); pap. text 19.95 (*0-8020-7163-5*) U of Toronto Pr.

MCM Assembly Technology. R. Jones. (Electrical Engineering & Electronics Ser.). Date not set. write for info. (*0-8247-9973-9*) Dekker.

MCM C-Mixed Technologies & Thick Film Sensors: Proceedings of the NATO Advanced Research Workshop on Advances in Ceramic Multi-Chip Modules (MCM) & High Performance Electronic Materials, Islamorada, Florida, U.S.A., May 23 - 25, 1994. Ed. by W. Kinzy Jones. (NATO Advanced Science Institutes - Partnership Sub Series 3). 328p. (C). 1995. text 176.50 (*0-7923-3460-4*) Kluwer Academic.

***MCM-Y2K.** Amy N. Worthen. 1999. pap. 5.00 (*1-879003-27-9*) Edmundson.

McMahon Chronicles: The Story of an Irish-American Family in Rhode Island, 1870-1994. Timothy E. McMahon. (Illus.). 115p. 1994. 35.00 (*0-9643509-9-8*) Taurus Hse Pubns.

McManus Treasury, No. 2. McManus. 1995. pap. 29.96 (*0-8050-4709-3*, M&T Bks) IDG Bks.

McManus Treasury I, 4 bks., Set. Patrick F. McManus. 1995. pap. 27.50 (*0-8050-0112-3*, Owl) H Holt & Co.

McManus Treasury 1 & 2 Special Offer. Patrick F. McManus. 1993. pap. 55.00 (*0-8050-3081-6*) H Holt & Co.

McManus Treasury II, 4 bks., Set. Patrick F. McManus. 1995. pap. 27.50 (*0-8050-2970-2*) H Holt & Co.

McMaster Family Workbook. Richard Archambault. 110p. (Orig.). 1996. pap. text 14.95 (*0-940139-38-3*) Consortium RI.

***McMaster Family Workbook.** 2nd rev. ed. Richard Archambault. 178p. (Orig.). 2000. pap. text, wbk. ed. 18.95 (*0-940139-54-5*) Consortium RI.

McMaster Family Workbook: One-Parent Family. rev. ed. Richard Archambault. 154p. 1997. pap. text, wbk. ed. 17.95 (*0-940139-48-0*) Consortium RI.

McMaster Family Workbook: Two-Parent Family. rev. ed. Richard Archambault. 154p. 1997. pap. text, wbk. ed. 17.95 (*0-940139-47-2*) Consortium RI.

McMaster Meighen History. 1989. text 49.95 (*0-7735-0419-2*) McG-Queens Univ Pr.

McMaster Reader on Gerontology. 3rd ed. 262p. (C). 1995. text 43.00 (*0-536-58766-3*) Pearson Custom.

McMaster University: The Early Years in Hamilton, 1930-1957, Vol. 2. Charles M. Johnston. LC 75-33006. (Illus.). 346p. 1981. reprint ed. pap. 107.30 (*0-7837-4291-6*, 204398300002) Bks Demand.

McMaster University Vol. 1: The Toronto Years, 2 vols. Charles M. Johnston. LC 75-33006. (Illus.). 365p. 1975. text 30.00 (*0-8020-3332-6*) U of Toronto Pr.

McMasters. Lee Morgan. 320p. (Orig.). 1995. mass mkt. 4.99 (*0-515-11632-7*, Jove) Berkley Pub.

McMasters No. 2: Silver Creek Showdown. Lee Morgan. 192p. (Orig.). 1995. mass mkt. 3.99 (*0-515-11682-3*, Jove) Berkley Pub.

McMasters No. 4: Big 70. Lee Morgan. 192p. (Orig.). 1995. mass mkt. 4.50 (*0-515-11765-X*, Jove) Berkley Pub.

McMasters No. 6: Violent Sunday. Lee Morgan. 192p. (Orig.). 1996. mass mkt. 4.99 (*0-515-11842-7*, Jove) Berkley Pub.

McMath: Collections for a History of the Ancient Family of McMath. F. M. McMath. (Illus.). 272p. 1992. reprint ed. pap. 43.00 (*0-8328-2324-4*); reprint ed. lib. bdg. 53.00 (*0-8328-2323-6*) Higginson Bk Co.

***McMeen Acoustic Guitar Treasures.** El McMeen. 64p. 1999. pap. 26.95 incl. audio compact disk (*0-7866-4354-4*, 97883CDP) Mel Bay.

McMeen Acoustic Guitar/Playing Favorites: Intermediate Level. El McMeen. 40p. 1997. pap. 8.95 (*0-7866-2095-1*, 95973) Mel Bay.

McMillan Lectures: The First 25 Years. 250p. 1992. pap. 34.95 (*0-912452-81-1*, APTA-12) Am Phys Therapy Assn.

McMillen's Texas Gardening: Vegetables. Sam Cotner. (Illus.). 160p. 1998. pap. 15.95 (*0-88415-895-0*, 5895) Gulf Pub.

McMinn County Tennessee, Marriages, 1820-1870. Reba B. Boyer. (Orig.). 1983. reprint ed. pap. 25.00 (*0-89308-330-5*) Southern Hist Pr.

McMinn's Color Atlas of Human Anatomy. 4th ed. Peter Abrahams. (Illus.). 1998. pap. text 40.00 (*0-7234-2772-0*, Pub. by Wolfe Pub) Mosby Inc.

McMiuen's Texas Garden Almanac 1998 Edition, Vol. 1. Mike Peters et al. (Illus.). 256p. 1997. pap. 12.95 (*0-9654378-1-7*, TX Grdn Almanac) McMillen Pubng.

MCML: Mary Cole Mason Lord, 1887-1988 - A Sampler of Stories from a Turn-of-the-Century Girlhood in Marblehead, Massachusetts. Compiled & Intro. by Martha M. Getchell. LC 92-75702. (Illus.). 80p. (Orig.). 1993. pap. 15.50 (*0-9625429-5-4*) Hardscratch Pr.

McMullen: Business Transfers & Employee Rights. 3rd ed. John Mullen. 1997. write for info. (*0-406-04467-8*, MBTE3, MICHIE) LEXIS Pub.

McMummy. Betsy C. Byars. LC 93-16717. 160p. (J). (gr. 5-9). 1993. 14.99 (*0-670-84995-2*, Viking Child) Peng Put Young Read.

McMummy. Betsy C. Byars. (Illus.). 160p. (J). (gr. 4-7). 1995. pap. 4.99 (*0-14-036439-0*, PuffinBks) Peng Put Young Read.

McMummy. Betsy C. Byars. (J). 1995. 9.09 (*0-606-07854-1*, Pub. by Turtleback) Demco.

McNae's Essential Law for Journalists. 12th ed. Walter Greenwood. Ed. by Tom Welsh. 262p. 1992. pap. 30.00 (*0-406-57920-2*, UK, MICHIE) LEXIS Pub.

McNair, McNear & McNeir Genealogies: Second Supplement. J. B. McNair. (Illus.). 457p. 1991. reprint ed. pap. 71.00 (*0-8328-1718-X*); reprint ed. lib. bdg. 81.00 (*0-8328-1717-1*) Higginson Bk Co.

McNair, McNear & McNeir Genealogies: Third Supplement. J. B. McNair. (Illus.). 314p. 1991. reprint ed. pap. 46.50 (*0-8328-1720-1*); reprint ed. lib. bdg. 56.50 (*0-8328-1719-8*) Higginson Bk Co.

McNally's Caper. Lawrence Sanders. 352p. 1995. mass mkt. 7.50 (*0-425-14530-1*) Berkley Pub.

McNally's Caper. large type ed. Lawrence Sanders. LC 94-6498. 384p. 1994. reprint ed. lib. bdg. 24.95 (*0-8161-5974-2*, G K Hall Lrg Type) Mac Lib Ref.

McNally's Caper. large type ed. Lawrence Sanders. LC 94-6498. 384p. 1995. reprint ed. pap. 18.95 (*0-8161-5975-0*, G K Hall Lrg Type) Mac Lib Ref.

***McNally's Dilemma.** Lawrence Sanders. 336p. 2000. mass mkt. 7.99 (*0-425-17536-7*) Berkley Pub.

McNally's Dilemma. Lawrence Sanders. LC 99-20988. 320p. 1999. 24.95 (*0-399-14490-0*, G P Putnam) Peng Put Young Read.

***McNally's Dilemma, Set.** abr. ed. Lawrence Sanders. 1999. audio 18.00 (*0-671-57692-5*) S&S Audio.

***McNally's Folly: An Archy McNally Novel by Vincent Lardo.** Lawrence Sanders. 320p. 2000. 24.95 (*0-399-14618-0*) Putnam Pub Group.

McNally's Gamble. Lawrence Sanders. 358p. 1998. mass mkt. 7.50 (*0-425-16259-1*) Berkley Pub.

McNally's Gamble. Lawrence Sanders. LC 96-50369. 1997. 24.95 (*0-399-14248-7*, G P Putnam) Peng Put Young Read.

McNally's Gamble. large type ed. Lawrence Sanders. LC 97-34313. 1997. 26.95 (*1-56895-487-5*) Wheeler Pub.

McNally's Luck. Lawrence Sanders. 352p. 1993. mass mkt. 7.50 (*0-425-13745-7*) Berkley Pub.

McNally's Luck. large type ed. Lawrence Sanders. LC 92-45884. 350p. 1993. 24.95 (*0-8161-5677-8*, G K Hall Lrg Type) Mac Lib Ref.

McNally's Luck. large type ed. Lawrence Sanders. LC 92-45884. 350p. 1994. pap. 19.95 (*0-8161-5678-6*, G K Hall Lrg Type) Mac Lib Ref.

McNally's Luck, Set. abr. ed. Lawrence Sanders. (Archy McNally Mystery Ser.). 1992. audio 17.00 (*0-671-76989-8*, Pub. by S&S Audio) Lndmrk Audiobks.

McNally's Price Guide for Collectible Soundtrack Records. Keith McNally & Dorie McNally. LC 94-96474. (Illus.). 240p. (Orig.). 1995. pap. 29.95 (*0-9643539-1-1*) W Pt Recs.

McNally's Puzzle. large type ed. Lawrence Sanders. 1997. mass mkt. 7.50 (*0-425-15746-6*) Berkley Pub.

McNally's Puzzle. large type ed. Lawrence Sanders. LC 96-5398. 1997. pap. 24.95 (*0-7838-1713-4*, G K Hall Lrg Type) Mac Lib Ref.

McNally's Risk. large type ed. Lawrence Sanders. 1993. 26.95 (*1-56895-042-X*) Wheeler Pub.

McNally's Risk. Lawrence Sanders. 336p. 1994. reprint ed. mass mkt. 7.50 (*0-425-14286-8*) Berkley Pub.

McNally's Secret. Lawrence Sanders. 352p. 1993. mass mkt. 7.50 (*0-425-13572-1*) Berkley Pub.

McNally's Trial. Lawrence Sanders. 352p. 1996. mass mkt. 7.50 (*0-425-14755-X*) Berkley Pub.

McNally's Trial. large type ed. Lawrence Sanders. LC 95-5417. (Large Print Bks.). 1995. 26.95 (*1-56895-208-2*) Wheeler Pub.

***McNally's Trial: Evidence Dismissed Soundvalue.** Lawrence Sanders. 1999. pap. 9.98 (*0-671-04455-9*) PB.

McNamara-O'Hara Service Contract Act: Prevailing Wage Conference, 1995. Government Printing Office Staff. 464p. 1995. pap. text 39.00 (*0-16-048304-2*) USGPO.

McNamara O'Hara Service Contract Act (SCA) Conformance Guide. 74p. 1998. ring bd. 6.00 (*0-16-049653-5*) USGPO.

McNamara Strategy & the Vietnam War: Program Budgeting in the Pentagon, 1960-1968, 13. Gregory Palmer. LC 77-94744. (Contributions in Political Science Ser.: Vol. 13). 169p. 1978. 55.00 (*0-313-20313-X*, PMS/, Greenwood Pr) Greenwood.

McNamara Years at the World Bank: Major Policy Addresses of Robert S. NcNamara, 1968-1981. Robert S. McNamara. LC 81-3743. 691p. reprint ed. pap. 200.00 (*0-7837-4266-5*, 204395800012) Bks Demand.

McNamara's Old Bronx. John McNamara. Ed. by Lloyd Ultan. (Illus.). 254p. (Orig.). 1989. pap. 19.00 (*0-941980-25-1*) Bronx County.

McNamara's Vietnam War & the Untold Truth. Pham K. Vinh. 250p. (Orig.). 1995. 12.00 (*1-882273-27-3*) P K Vinh Res.

McNary of Oregon: A Political Biography. Steve Neal. LC 85-13692. 1985. 17.95 (*0-87595-173-2*) Oregon Hist.

McNary Reservoir: A Study in Plateau Archaeology, Vol. 23. fac. ed. Joel Shiner. (Smithsonian Institution, Bureau of American Ethnology Ser.: Bulletin 179). (Illus.). 135p. (C). 1961. reprint ed. pap. text 15.00 (*1-55567-674-X*) Coyote Press.

McNear: The William McNear Family, 1770-1990. John D. McNair. 63p. 1993. reprint ed. pap. 13.00 (*0-8328-3373-8*) Higginson Bk Co.

McNeill - Beginning in Belfast: Descendants of Sampson Stuart McNeill. Carolyn Chapman. (Illus.). 82p. 1995. lib. bdg. 29.50 (*0-8328-4579-5*) Higginson Bk Co.

McNeill's Rangers. Roger U. Delauter. (Illus.). 130p. 1986. 19.95 (*0-930919-34-3*) H E Howard.

McNeills' SR Ranch: 100 Years in Blanco Canyon. J. C. McNeill, III. LC 88-2204. (Centennial Series of the Association of Former Students: No. 28). (Illus.). 224p. 1988. 19.95 (*0-89096-340-1*) Tex A&M Univ Pr.

McNeil's Mount Hood: Wyeast the Mountain Revisited. rev. ed. Freed H. McNeil. (Illus.). 224p. 1990. reprint ed. pap. 12.95 (*0-9614498-7-X*) Zig Zag Paper.

McNeil's Travels. Samuel McNeil. 57p. 1989. 14.95 (*0-87770-467-8*) Ye Galleon.

McOmber Adult Book 5 - Ben (Short e) Rachel McOmber & Perry Kassing. (Illus.). 78p. 1994. pap. 10.00 (*1-56861-008-4*) Swift Lrn Res.

McOmber Adult Book 4 - Muff (Short u) Rachel McOmber & Perry Kassing. (Illus.). 78p. 1994. pap. 10.00 (*1-56861-007-6*) Swift Lrn Res.

McOmber Adult Book 1 - Max (Short a) Rachel McOmber & Perry Kassing. (Illus.). 78p. 1994. pap. 10.00 (*1-56861-004-1*) Swift Lrn Res.

McOmber Adult Book 6 - Ben & Peggy (Review) Rachel McOmber & Perry Kassing. (Illus.). 78p. 1994. pap. 10.00 (*1-56861-009-2*) Swift Lrn Res.

McOmber Adult Book 3 - Rob (Short o) Rachel McOmber & Perry Kassing. (Illus.). 78p. 1994. pap. 10.00 (*1-56861-006-8*) Swift Lrn Res.

McOmber Adult Book 2 - Kim (Short i) Rachel McOmber & Perry Kassing. (Illus.). 78p. 1994. pap. 10.00 (*1-56861-005-X*) Swift Lrn Res.

McOmber Phonics Storybooks. rev. ed. Ed. by Rachel B. McOmber. (Illus.). (J). write for info. (*0-944991-72-6*) Swift Lrn Res.

McOmber Phonics Storybooks: A Box. rev. ed. Ed. by Rachel B. McOmber. (Illus.). (J). write for info. (*0-944991-13-0*) Swift Lrn Res.

McOmber Phonics Storybooks: A Game for Champions. rev. ed. Ed. by Rachel B. McOmber. (Illus.). (J). write for info. (*0-944991-68-8*) Swift Lrn Res.

McOmber Phonics Storybooks: A Hum-Bug. rev. ed. Ed. by Rachel B. McOmber. (Illus.). (J). write for info. (*0-944991-20-3*) Swift Lrn Res.

McOmber Phonics Storybooks: A Nifty Ball of String. rev. ed. Ed. by Rachel B. McOmber. (Illus.). (J). write for info. (*0-944991-50-5*) Swift Lrn Res.

McOmber Phonics Storybooks: A Night to Celebrate. rev. ed. Ed. by Rachel B. McOmber. (Illus.). (J). write for info. (*0-944991-71-8*) Swift Lrn Res.

McOmber Phonics Storybooks: A Package from Hong Kong. rev. ed. Ed. by Rachel B. McOmber. (Illus.). (J). write for info. (*0-944991-61-0*) Swift Lrn Res.

McOmber Phonics Storybooks: A Red Hen. rev. ed. Ed. by Rachel B. McOmber. (Illus.). (J). write for info. (*0-944991-25-4*) Swift Lrn Res.

McOmber Phonics Storybooks: A Trip to China. rev. ed. Ed. by Rachel B. McOmber. (Illus.). (J). write for info. (*0-944991-70-X*) Swift Lrn Res.

McOmber Phonics Storybooks: At the Fair. rev. ed. Ed. by Rachel B. McOmber. (Illus.). (J). write for info. (*0-944991-60-2*) Swift Lrn Res.

McOmber Phonics Storybooks: Ben Has a Pet. rev. ed. Ed. by Rachel B. McOmber. (Illus.). (J). write for info. (*0-944991-26-2*) Swift Lrn Res.

McOmber Phonics Storybooks: Ben in Bed. rev. ed. Ed. by Rachel B. McOmber. (Illus.). (J). write for info. (*0-944991-29-7*) Swift Lrn Res.

McOmber Phonics Storybooks: Ben Will Get Well. rev. ed. Ed. by Rachel B. McOmber. (Illus.). (J). write for info. (*0-944991-30-0*) Swift Lrn Res.

McOmber Phonics Storybooks: Boe E. Toad. rev. ed. Ed. by Rachel B. McOmber. (Illus.). (J). write for info. (*0-944991-54-8*) Swift Lrn Res.

McOmber Phonics Storybooks: Boyer's Toy Store. rev. ed. Ed. by Rachel B. McOmber. (Illus.). (J). write for info. (*0-944991-69-6*) Swift Lrn Res.

McOmber Phonics Storybooks: Bug. rev. ed. Ed. by Rachel B. McOmber. (Illus.). (J). write for info. (*0-944991-19-X*) Swift Lrn Res.

McOmber Phonics Storybooks: Chatsworth. rev. ed. Ed. by Rachel B. McOmber. (Illus.). (J). write for info. (*0-944991-74-2*) Swift Lrn Res.

McOmber Phonics Storybooks: Choose Which One - 1. rev. ed. Ed. by Rachel B. McOmber. (Illus.). (J). write for info. (*0-944991-67-X*) Swift Lrn Res.

McOmber Phonics Storybooks: Everyone Knows a Pitcher. rev. ed. Ed. by Rachel B. McOmber. (Illus.). (J). write for info. (*0-944991-79-3*) Swift Lrn Res.

McOmber Phonics Storybooks: Fizz in the Pit. rev. ed. Ed. by Rachel B. McOmber. (Illus.). (J). write for info. (*0-944991-12-2*) Swift Lrn Res.

McOmber Phonics Storybooks: Fizz Mix. rev. ed. Ed. by Rachel B. McOmber. (Illus.). (J). write for info. (*0-944991-11-4*) Swift Lrn Res.

McOmber Phonics Storybooks: Fizz Mud. rev. ed. Ed. by Rachel B. McOmber. (Illus.). (J). write for info. (*0-944991-21-1*) Swift Lrn Res.

McOmber Phonics Storybooks: Hello Again. rev. ed. Ed. by Rachel B. McOmber. (Illus.). (J). write for info. (*0-944991-84-X*) Swift Lrn Res.

McOmber Phonics Storybooks: Hen Pox. rev. ed. Ed. by Rachel B. McOmber. (Illus.). (J). write for info. (*0-944991-28-9*) Swift Lrn Res.

McOmber Phonics Storybooks: Humps & Lumps. rev. ed. Ed. by Rachel B. McOmber. (Illus.). (J). write for info. (*0-944991-62-9*) Swift Lrn Res.

McOmber Phonics Storybooks: In the Dell. rev. ed. Ed. by Rachel B. McOmber. (Illus.). (J). write for info. (*0-944991-32-7*) Swift Lrn Res.

McOmber Phonics Storybooks: Jud & Nell. rev. ed. Ed. by Rachel B. McOmber. (Illus.). (J). write for info. (*0-944991-33-5*) Swift Lrn Res.

McOmber Phonics Storybooks: Kim. rev. ed. Ed. by Rachel B. McOmber. (Illus.). (J). write for info. (*0-944991-07-6*) Swift Lrn Res.

McOmber Phonics Storybooks: Max. rev. ed. Ed. by Rachel B. McOmber. (Illus.). (J). write for info. (*0-944991-01-7*) Swift Lrn Res.

McOmber Phonics Storybooks: Max Is Six. rev. ed. Ed. by Rachel B. McOmber. (Illus.). (J). write for info. (*0-944991-43-2*) Swift Lrn Res.

McOmber Phonics Storybooks: Max Ran. rev. ed. Ed. by Rachel B. McOmber. (Illus.). (J). write for info. (*0-944991-02-5*) Swift Lrn Res.

McOmber Phonics Storybooks: Max the Grand. rev. ed. Ed. by Rachel B. McOmber. (Illus.). (J). write for info. (*0-944991-57-2*) Swift Lrn Res.

McOmber Phonics Storybooks: Me & the Bee. rev. ed. Ed. by Rachel B. McOmber. (Illus.). (J). write for info. (*0-944991-46-7*) Swift Lrn Res.

McOmber Phonics Storybooks: Miss Vie. rev. ed. Ed. by Rachel B. McOmber. (Illus.). (J). write for info. (*0-944991-48-3*) Swift Lrn Res.

McOmber Phonics Storybooks: Mom & Dad Hop-Jig. rev. ed. Ed. by Rachel B. McOmber. (Illus.). (J). write for info. (*0-944991-16-5*) Swift Lrn Res.

McOmber Phonics Storybooks: Number Fun. rev. ed. Ed. by Rachel B. McOmber. (Illus.). (J). write for info. (*0-944991-58-0*) Swift Lrn Res.

McOmber Phonics Storybooks: On TV. rev. ed. Ed. by Rachel B. McOmber. (Illus.). (J). write for info. (*0-944991-17-3*) Swift Lrn Res.

McOmber Phonics Storybooks: Pete's Bike Ride. rev. ed. Ed. by Rachel B. McOmber. (Illus.). (J). write for info. (*0-944991-40-8*) Swift Lrn Res.

M

McOmber Phonics Storybooks: Razz. rev. ed. Ed. by Rachel B. McOmber. (Illus.). (J). write for info. (*0-944991-06-8*) Swift Lrn Res.

McOmber Phonics Storybooks: Razz Visits Raz in Israel. rev. ed. Ed. by Rachel B. McOmber. (Illus.). (J). write for info. (*0-944991-75-0*) Swift Lrn Res.

McOmber Phonics Storybooks: Robin Hood's Cook. rev. ed. Ed. by Rachel B. McOmber. (Illus.). (J). write for info. (*0-944991-64-5*) Swift Lrn Res.

McOmber Phonics Storybooks: Snores & More. rev. ed. Ed. by Rachel B. McOmber. (Illus.). (J). write for info. (*0-944991-59-9*) Swift Lrn Res.

McOmber Phonics Storybooks: Tale of the Green Glob. rev. ed. Ed. by Rachel B. McOmber. (Illus.). (J). write for info. (*0-944991-65-3*) Swift Lrn Res.

McOmber Phonics Storybooks: Teacher's Manual. rev. ed. Ed. by Rachel B. McOmber. (Illus.). teacher ed. write for info. (*0-944991-00-9*) Swift Lrn Res.

McOmber Phonics Storybooks: Ten in the Hut. rev. ed. Ed. by Rachel B. McOmber. (Illus.). (J). write for info. (*0-944991-27-0*) Swift Lrn Res.

McOmber Phonics Storybooks: The Bag. rev. ed. Ed. by Rachel B. McOmber. (Illus.). (J). write for info. (*0-944991-03-3*) Swift Lrn Res.

McOmber Phonics Storybooks: The Big Deal. rev. ed. Ed. by Rachel B. McOmber. (Illus.). (J). write for info. (*0-944991-47-5*) Swift Lrn Res.

McOmber Phonics Storybooks: The Big Hole. rev. ed. Ed. by Rachel B. McOmber. (Illus.). (J). write for info. (*0-944991-38-6*) Swift Lrn Res.

McOmber Phonics Storybooks: The Bon-Bon Box. rev. ed. Ed. by Rachel B. McOmber. (Illus.). (J). write for info. (*0-944991-14-9*) Swift Lrn Res.

McOmber Phonics Storybooks: The Box Mix. rev. ed. Ed. by Rachel B. McOmber. (Illus.). (J). write for info. (*0-944991-15-7*) Swift Lrn Res.

McOmber Phonics Storybooks: The Cake. rev. ed. Ed. by Rachel B. McOmber. (Illus.). (J). write for info. (*0-944991-44-0*) Swift Lrn Res.

McOmber Phonics Storybooks: The Confection Connection. rev. ed. Ed. by Rachel B. McOmber. (Illus.). (J). write for info. (*0-944991-73-4*) Swift Lrn Res.

McOmber Phonics Storybooks: The Cove of Gloom. rev. ed. Ed. by Rachel B. McOmber. (Illus.). (J). write for info. (*0-944991-83-1*) Swift Lrn Res.

McOmber Phonics Storybooks: The Fumes. rev. ed. Ed. by Rachel B. McOmber. (Illus.). (J). write for info. (*0-944991-39-4*) Swift Lrn Res.

McOmber Phonics Storybooks: The Gal Pals. rev. ed. Ed. by Rachel B. McOmber. (Illus.). (J). write for info. (*0-944991-42-4*) Swift Lrn Res.

McOmber Phonics Storybooks: The Haircut. rev. ed. Ed. by Rachel B. McOmber. (Illus.). (J). write for info. (*0-944991-53-X*) Swift Lrn Res.

McOmber Phonics Storybooks: The Hum-Bug Hop. rev. ed. Ed. by Rachel B. McOmber. (Illus.). (J). write for info. (*0-944991-31-9*) Swift Lrn Res.

McOmber Phonics Storybooks: The Invisible Crocodiles. rev. ed. Ed. by Rachel B. McOmber. (Illus.). (J). write for info. (*0-944991-80-7*) Swift Lrn Res.

McOmber Phonics Storybooks: The Kit. rev. ed. Ed. by Rachel B. McOmber. (Illus.). (J). write for info. (*0-944991-08-4*) Swift Lrn Res.

McOmber Phonics Storybooks: The Land of Morning. rev. ed. Ed. by Rachel B. McOmber. (Illus.). (J). write for info. (*0-944991-82-3*) Swift Lrn Res.

McOmber Phonics Storybooks: The Lemonade Sale. rev. ed. Ed. by Rachel B. McOmber. (Illus.). (J). write for info. (*0-944991-41-6*) Swift Lrn Res.

McOmber Phonics Storybooks: The Magic "E" rev. ed. Ed. by Rachel B. McOmber. (Illus.). (J). write for info. (*0-944991-37-8*) Swift Lrn Res.

McOmber Phonics Storybooks: The Map. rev. ed. Ed. by Rachel B. McOmber. (Illus.). (J). write for info. (*0-944991-05-X*) Swift Lrn Res.

McOmber Phonics Storybooks: The Neat Trick. rev. ed. Ed. by Rachel B. McOmber. (Illus.). (J). write for info. (*0-944991-55-6*) Swift Lrn Res.

McOmber Phonics Storybooks: The Pit Kit. rev. ed. Ed. by Rachel B. McOmber. (Illus.). (J). write for info. (*0-944991-09-2*) Swift Lrn Res.

McOmber Phonics Storybooks: The Prime Time Trick. rev. ed. Ed. by Rachel B. McOmber. (Illus.). (J). write for info. (*0-944991-56-4*) Swift Lrn Res.

McOmber Phonics Storybooks: The Prize. rev. ed. Ed. by Rachel B. McOmber. (Illus.). (J). write for info. (*0-944991-49-1*) Swift Lrn Res.

McOmber Phonics Storybooks: The Quiz Is (1) rev. ed. Ed. by Rachel B. McOmber. (Illus.). (J). write for info. (*0-944991-34-3*) Swift Lrn Res.

McOmber Phonics Storybooks: The Quiz Is (2) rev. ed. Ed. by Rachel B. McOmber. (Illus.). (J). write for info. (*0-944991-35-1*) Swift Lrn Res.

McOmber Phonics Storybooks: The Rope. rev. ed. Ed. by Rachel B. McOmber. (Illus.). (J). write for info. (*0-944991-45-9*) Swift Lrn Res.

McOmber Phonics Storybooks: The Sub. rev. ed. Ed. by Rachel B. McOmber. (Illus.). (J). write for info. (*0-944991-22-X*) Swift Lrn Res.

McOmber Phonics Storybooks: The Tan Cab. rev. ed. Ed. by Rachel B. McOmber. (Illus.). (J). write for info. (*0-944991-04-1*) Swift Lrn Res.

McOmber Phonics Storybooks: The Time Box. rev. ed. Ed. by Rachel B. McOmber. (Illus.). (J). write for info. (*0-944991-52-1*) Swift Lrn Res.

McOmber Phonics Storybooks: The Tin Lid. rev. ed. Ed. by Rachel B. McOmber. (Illus.). (J). write for info. (*0-944991-10-6*) Swift Lrn Res.

McOmber Phonics Storybooks: The Tub. rev. ed. Ed. by Rachel B. McOmber. (Illus.). (J). write for info. (*0-944991-24-6*) Swift Lrn Res.

McOmber Phonics Storybooks: The TV Box. rev. ed. Ed. by Rachel B. McOmber. (Illus.). (J). write for info. (*0-944991-18-1*) Swift Lrn Res.

McOmber Phonics Storybooks: The Video Show. rev. ed. Ed. by Rachel B. McOmber. (Illus.). (J). write for info. (*0-944991-63-7*) Swift Lrn Res.

McOmber Phonics Storybooks: The Wizz Kid. rev. ed. Ed. by Rachel B. McOmber. (Illus.). (J). write for info. (*0-944991-23-8*) Swift Lrn Res.

McOmber Phonics Storybooks: Tid Bits. rev. ed. Ed. by Rachel B. McOmber. (Illus.). (J). write for info. (*0-944991-36-X*) Swift Lrn Res.

McOmber Phonics Storybooks: Under the Rainbow. rev. ed. Ed. by Rachel B. McOmber. (Illus.). (J). write for info. (*0-944991-81-5*) Swift Lrn Res.

McOmber Phonics Storybooks: Yellow Crocodile. rev. ed. Ed. by Rachel B. McOmber. (Illus.). (J). write for info. (*0-944991-76-9*) Swift Lrn Res.

McOmber Phonics Storybooks: You Can Make It. rev. ed. Ed. by Rachel B. McOmber. (Illus.). (J). write for info. (*0-944991-51-3*) Swift Lrn Res.

McOmber Phonics Storybooks Vol. 1: Writing Book. rev. ed. Ed. by Rachel B. McOmber. (Illus.). (J). write for info. (*0-944991-93-9*) Swift Lrn Res.

McOmber Phonics Storybooks Vol. 2: Writing Book. rev. ed. Ed. by Rachel B. McOmber. (Illus.). (J). write for info. (*0-944991-94-7*) Swift Lrn Res.

M'Connachie & J. M. B. Speeches. J. M. Barrie. LC 78-156611. (Essay Index Reprint Ser.). 1977. reprint ed. 23.95 (*0-8369-2343-X*) Ayer.

M'Connachie & J. M. B., Etc. see Works of J. M. Barrie: Peter Pan Edition

MCP Complete + Internet Specialist. New Riders Development Group. 1998. pap. 75.00 (*1-56205-897-5*) New Riders Pub.

McPherson: The Law of Company Liquidation. 3rd ed. James O'Donovan. lxxxii, 501p. 1987. 110.50 (*0-455-20741-0*, Pub. by LawBk Co) Gaunt.

McPherson Goes to Church. John McPherson. (Illus.). 128p. 1994. pap. 8.99 (*0-310-48181-3*) Zondervan.

McPherson's Law of Company Liquidation. James O'Donovan. 250p. 1994. pap. 39.00 (*0-455-21232-5*, Pub. by LawBk Co) Gaunt.

McPherson's Marriage Album. John McPherson. 112p. 1991. pap. 7.99 (*0-310-53901-3*) Zondervan.

McPherson's Respiratory Care Equipment. 6th ed. Cairo Pilbeam. LC 98-55692. (Illus.). 787p. (gr. 13). 1999. text 55.00 (*0-8151-2148-2*, 30759) Mosby Inc.

MCQ Companion to Anaesthesia in Clinical Practice. A. W. Crossley & R. P. Mahajan. LC 99-28932. 288p. 2000. pap. write for info. (*0-443-05311-1*, W B Saunders Co) Harcrt Hlth Sci Grp.

MCQ Companion to General & Systematic Pathology. Simon S. Cross. 208p. (Orig.). 1992. pap. text 19.95 (*0-443-04367-1*) Church.

MCQ Companion to General & Systematic Pathology. 2nd ed. S. S. Cross. 216p. 1998. pap. write for info. (*0-443-05281-6*) Church.

MCQ Companion to Grainger & Allison's Diagnostic Radiology, Vol. 1. J. Cockburn & A. Mitchell. Ed. by R. G. Grainger & D. V. Allison. 320p. 1998. pap. write for info. (*0-443-05941-1*) Church.

MCQ Companion to the Textbook of Anaesthesia. 2nd ed. D. Fell et al. 300p. 1998. pap. write for info. (*0-443-05346-4*) Church.

MCQ Examinations in Psychiatry. John M. Eagles & David A. Alexander. 272p. 1986. pap. text 22.00 (*0-08-032472-X*, Pub. by Aberdeen U Pr) Macmillan.

MCQ in Obstetrics Gynecology & Contraception. D. Dawn. (C). 1985. 35.00 (*0-7855-4656-1*, Pub. by Current Dist) St Mut.

MCQ Tutor for Principles & Practice of Surgery. Diamond. 1996. pap. text 21.00 (*0-443-05192-5*) Harcourt.

MCQ Tutor in Anaesthesia: Clinical Practice. Colin A. Pinnock & Robert M. Haden. 304p. (Orig.). 1993. pap. text 27.95 (*0-443-04610-7*) Church.

MCQ Tutor in Anaesthesia Pt. 1: FRCA. Colin A. Pinnock & Robert P. Jones. LC 93-29089. 1993. write for info. (*0-443-04963-7*) Church.

MCQ Tutor in Basic Sciences for Anaesthesia. Colin A. Pinnock & Robert P. Jones. 240p. (Orig.). 1993. pap. text 27.95 (*0-443-04611-5*) Church.

MCQ Tutor in Radiology. Brown. 1996. pap. text 25.00 (*0-443-05464-9*, W B Saunders Co) Harcrt Hlth Sci Grp.

MCQs & OSCEs for the Primary FRCA. Edward Doyle & Paul Goggin. LC 96-39853. 168p. 1997. pap. text 35.00 (*0-7506-2338-1*) Buttrwrth-Heinemann.

MCQ's for MRCOG, Pt. 2. K. Khaled. 144p. 1998. pap. write for info. (*0-443-06122-X*) Church.

MCQs for MRCP Pt. 1: General Medicine. 2nd ed. M. J. Ford & D. M. Matthews. 225p. 1995. pap. write for info. (*0-443-05083-X*) Church.

MCQ's for MRCP Pt. 1: General Medicine. 2nd rev. ed. Michael J. Ford & David M. Matthews. LC 94-34014. 1995. write for info. (*0-663-05083-9*) Silver.

MCQs for MRCP part 1, Pt. 1. N. I. Johnson & A. Pozniak. 95p. 1992. 21.95 (*0-387-16215-1*) Spr-Verlag.

MCQs for Psychiatric Studies. Chris Freeman. 162p. (Orig.). 1988. pap. text 22.00 (*0-443-03230-0*) Church.

MCQs for the DRCOG. Matthew Hoghton & Patrick Hogston. 160p. (Orig.). 1991. pap. text 28.95 (*0-443-04469-4*) Church.

MCQs for the Final FRCA. Henderson. (C). 1998. pap. text 39.95 (*0-7020-2347-7*) Bailliere Tindall.

***MCQS for the MRCPsych Pt. II: Basic Sciences Examination.** Gin S. Malhi. LC 99-58726. 181p. 2000. pap. text 40.00 (*0-7506-4089-8*) Buttrwrth-Heinemann.

MCQs for the Paediatric MRCP. A. P. Winrow & G. Supramaniam. LC 96-6477. 188p. 1996. pap. text 24.00 (*0-443-05354-5*) Church.

MCQs for the PLAB Examination. Kavita Dutta. 288p. 1998. pap. text 32.50 (*0-7506-4004-9*) Buttrwrth-Heinemann.

MCQS for the Primary FRCA. C. R. Bailey & A. Pearce. LC 98-45216. 260p. (C). 1999. pap. text 39.00 (*0-7020-2160-1*, Pub. by W B Saunders) Saunders.

MCQ's in Anaesthesia. Ganado. 1998. pap. text. write for info. (*0-443-05915-2*) Church.

MCQ's in Anatomy. 2nd ed. Lumley. 272p. 1988. pap. 26.00 (*0-443-03574-1*) Church.

MCQ's in Anatomy: A Self-Testing Supplement to Essential Anatomy. 3rd ed. J. S. Lumley & J. L. Craven. LC 95-40796. 1996. pap. text 17.95 (*0-443-04977-7*) Church.

MCQS in Anatomy for Undergraduate & Medical Students. Jamil & Mitchell. 192p. 1997. pap. text 27.50 (*0-7506-3591-6*) Buttrwrth-Heinemann.

MCQs in Applied Basic Sciences for the Primary FRCS. K. M. Mokbel. (C). 1992. pap. text 22.50 (*0-7923-8994-8*) Kluwer Academic.

MCQs in Basic & Clinical Physiology. Dom Colbert. 350p. 1996. pap. text 29.95 (*0-19-262736-8*) OUP.

MCQ's in Clinical Imaging. Asif Saifuddin. LC 92-49566. 400p. (gr. 13). 1993. pap. text 45.50 (*0-412-47970-2*) Chapman & Hall.

MCQs in Clinical Medicine. 2nd ed. Baliga. LC 99-29016. 1999. pap. text 16.00 (*0-7020-2296-9*, W B Saunders Co) Harcrt Hlth Sci Grp.

MCQS in Clinical Nuclear Medicine. David Scullion et al. 230p. 1997. text 45.00 (*90-5702-146-3*, Harwood Acad Pubs); pap. text 29.00 (*90-5702-109-9*, Harwood Acad Pubs) Gordon & Breach.

MCQS in Clinical Pathology. Bint. 1995. pap. text 21.00 (*0-7020-1782-5*, W B Saunders Co) Harcrt Hlth Sci Grp.

MCQS in Clinical Pharmacology. 2nd ed. Laurence. 1988. pap. text 27.95 (*0-443-03416-8*, W B Saunders Co) Harcrt Hlth Sci Grp.

MCQs in General Medicine. Ed. by J. R. Lawrence & J. D. Hunter. 216p. (Orig.). 1989. pap. text 26.00 (*0-443-03425-7*) Church.

MCQs in General Pathology. 2nd ed. F. G. Smiddy & J. L. Turk. LC 96-25829. 1996. pap. text 25.95 (*0-443-05419-3*) Church.

MCQs in Gynaecology & Obstetrics. 3rd ed. Richard J. Lilford & Marcus E. Setchell. 88p. pap. text 14.95 (*0-340-58896-9*, Pub. by E A) Routldge.

MCQs in Integrated Sciences. Wai-Ching Leung. LC 99-11697. 1999. write for info. (*0-443-06239-0*) Church.

MCQ's in Medicine for MRCP, Pt. 1. A. Provan. 208p. 1989. pap. write for info. (*0-443-04220-9*) Church.

MCQs in Obstetrics & Gynaecology. D. M. Gibb & John W. Studd. LC 82-14694. 310p. (C). 1983. pap. text 29.00 (*0-443-02283-6*) Church.

MCQs in Optometry. Robert Fletcher & Katherine M. Oliver. LC 95-39175. (Illus.). 192p. 1996. pap. text 37.50 (*0-7506-2187-7*) Buttrwrth-Heinemann.

MCQS in Otolaryngology. 2nd ed. R. S. Dhillon et al. 257p. 1999. pap. text 32.50 (*0-7506-2165-6*) Buttrwrth-Heinemann.

MCQS in Paediatrics. T. G. Marshall et al. LC 98-46987. 410p. 1999. pap. text 25.00 (*0-7020-2249-7*, Pub. by W B Saunders) Saunders.

MCQS in Paediatrics. Speight. 1984. pap. text 27.95 (*0-443-03653-5*, W B Saunders Co) Harcrt Hlth Sci Grp.

MCQs in Pediatrics. 2nd ed. Speight. (C). 1998. pap. text 25.00 (*0-443-05777-X*) Church.

MCQs in Pharmacology. Bryan V. Robinson. 286p. 1980. reprint ed. pap. text 26.00 (*0-443-03873-2*) Church.

MCQs in Physiology. C. A. Browne & R. Luff. 176p. 1996. text 11.50 (*0-412-75640-4*, Pub. by E A) OUP.

MCQS in Physiology. Jennett. 1986. pap. text 21.00 (*0-443-03620-9*, W B Saunders Co) Harcrt Hlth Sci Grp.

MCQs in Science & Mathematics for Engineering: Intermediate GNVQ. J. O. Bird. LC 95-45355. 64p. 1995. spiral bd. write for info. (*0-7506-2664-X*) Buttrwrth-Heinemann.

***MCQS in Sports Medicine.** Conor O'Brien. 151p. 1999. pap. text 32.50 (*0-7506-2949-5*) Buttrwrth-Heinemann.

MCQS in Surgery. D. Das. (C). 1987. 60.00 (*0-8110-0134-2*, Pub. by Current Dist) St Mut.

MCQS in Surgery: Student Self-Assessment. C. P. Shearman & N. C. Hickey. 220p. 1994. pap. text 23.00 (*0-7020-1761-2*, Pub. by W B Saunders) Saunders.

Mcqs in the Basic Sciences: For the Mrcp. 4th ed. S. Elborn. (Illus.). 192p. pap. text. write for info. (*0-412-79280-X*) Chapman & Hall.

MCQs in the Physics of Diagnostic Imaging. D. J. Dowsett et al. (An Arnold Publication). 368p. 1999. pap. text 24.50 (*0-340-74088-4*, Pub. by E A) OUP.

MCQ's in Undergraduate Obstetrics & Gynaecology. 2nd ed. Ian Johnson & Ken Dowell. LC 94-4028. 1994. pap. text 19.95 (*0-443-04959-9*) Church.

***MCQS in Veterinary Nursing, Pt. 1.** 2nd ed. Ed. by College of Animal Welfare Staff. 128p. 2000. pap. 18.00 (*0-7506-4699-3*) Buttrwrth-Heinemann.

***MCQS in Veterinary Nursing, Pt. 2.** 2nd ed. Ed. by College of Animal Welfare Staff. 128p. 2000. pap. 18.00 (*0-7506-4700-0*) Buttrwrth-Heinemann.

McQuaid's Justice: The/Cowboy Code. Carly Bishop. 1998. per. 3.99 (*0-373-22497-4*, 1-22497-1, Mira Bks) Harlequin Bks.

McQuillan Law of Municipal Corporations, 1939-1992, 28 vols. 3rd ed. 1850.00 (*0-685-14560-3*) West Group.

McQuillin Municipal Law Report. 1982. 250.00 (*0-685-44922-X*) West Group.

McQuillken Finds His Purpose. large type ed. Sharon S. Current. (Illus.). 24p. (J). (gr. k-2). 1998. pap. 9.95 (*0-9668072-0-0*) Sunshine Pr CO.

McQuiston-McCuiston-McQuesten Families, 1620-1937. L. B. McQuiston. 750p. 1991. reprint ed. lib. bdg. 119.00 (*0-8328-1929-8*) Higginson Bk Co.

Mcrosoft PowerPoint 97. Adams. (C). 1998. pap. text 22.50 (*0-03-023726-2*) Harcourt Coll Pubs.

MCRP Pt. 1: A System Based Tutorial. C. A, O'Callaghan. (Illus.). 1997. pap. 27.95 (*0-632-04781-X*) Blackwell Sci.

***Mcsc Visual Basic Test Yourself Personal Exam.** Syngress Media, Inc. Staff. 512p. 2000. pap. text 39.99 (*0-07-212366-4*) McGraw.

MCSD: Access 95 Study Guide. Peter Vogel. xxxii, 704p. 1998. pap. text 44.99 (*0-7821-2282-5*) Sybex.

***MCSD: Designing & Implementing Web Site Using Microsoft FrontPage 98.** David Karlins. LC 99-40533. (Microsoft Technology Ser.). 512p. 1999. 49.99 incl. cd-rom (*0-13-014117-8*) P-H.

MCSD: Visual Basic 6 Distrubuted Applications Study Guide. Michael Lee & Clark Christensen. LC 98-83173. 752p. 1999. 44.99 (*0-7821-2433-X*) Sybex.

MCSD Analyzing Requirements: Study Guide Exam No. 70-100. Syngress Media, Inc. Staff. 656p. 1999. student ed. 49.99 incl. cd-rom (*0-07-211955-1*) Osborne-McGraw.

***MCSD Analyzing Requirements Test Yourself Personal Exam.** Syngress Media, Inc. Staff. 512p. 2000. pap. text 39.99 (*0-07-212365-6*) McGraw.

MCSD Architectures Exam Cram. Certification Insider Press Staff. LC 99-23865. (Exam Cram / Coriolis' Certification Insi Ser.). 328p. 1999. pap. text 29.99 (*1-57610-378-1*) Coriolis Grp.

***MCSD Architectures Exam Prep.** Keith Morneau. LC 99-32121. 1999. write for info. (*1-57610-413-3*) W S Hein.

MCSD Architectures Study Guide: Analyzing Requirements & Defining Solution. Ben Ezzell. LC 99-61301. 720p. 1999. pap. 44.99 (*0-7821-2431-3*) Sybex.

MCSD: Designing & Implementing Desktop Applications with Visual Basic 6. Steven Holzner. LC 99-41256. 1024p. (C). 1999. pap. text 49.99 incl. audio compact disk (*0-13-013988-2*) P-H.

MCSD Fast Track: Solution Architectures. Duncan Mackenzie. (Fast Tracks Ser.). 400p. 1999. pap. text 44.95 (*0-7357-0029-X*) New Riders Pub.

MCSD Fast Track: Visual Basic 6, Exam 70-175. Lyle A. Brant. LC 98-89052. 300p. 1999. pap. 19.99 (*0-7357-0018-4*) New Riders Pub.

MCSD Fast Track: Visual Basic 6, Exam 70-176. Kent Sharkey & Lyle A. Bryant. LC 98-89021. 300p. 1999. pap. 19.99 (*0-7357-0019-2*) New Riders Pub.

***MCSD Fast Track: 4-in-1 Set.** Lyle A. Bryant. (Fast Tracks Ser.). 1500p. 1999. pap. text 119.95 (*0-7357-0913-0*) New Riders Pub.

***MCSD Front Page 98 Study Guide: (Exam 70-55)** Syngress Media Incorporated Staff. (MCSD Certification Ser.). (Illus.). 715p. 1999. student ed. 49.99 (*0-07-211994-2*) Osborne-McGraw.

***MCSD FrontPage 2000 Study Guide: Exam 70-0XX.** Syngress Media Incorporated Staff. (Certification Press Study Guides Ser.). 1999. 49.99 (*0-07-212235-8*) Osborne-McGraw.

McSd Guide to Analyzing Requirements & Defining Solutions Architecture. Marneau. (Programming Ser.). (C). 1999. text 43.25 (*0-7600-1178-8*) Course Tech.

MCSD Test Success: Sql Server 7 Database Design. 1999. 24.99 (*0-7821-2399-6*) Sybex.

MCSD TestPrep: Visual Basic 6 Exam 70-175. David Panagrosso. LC 98-88002. (TestPrep (New Riders') Ser.). (Illus.). 450p. 1999. pap. 29.99 (*0-7357-0032-X*) New Riders Pub.

MCSD Training Guide: Microsoft Access. rev. ed. New Riders Staff. 1998. 49.99 (*1-56205-928-9*, New Riders Sftwre) MCP SW Interactive.

MCSD Training Guide: MS Access 97. Kevin Marlowe. LC 98-123566. 1997. 59.99 (*1-56205-771-5*) New Riders Pub.

MCSD Training Guide: Solution Architectures. New Riders Staff. (Training Guides Ser.). 800p. 1999. 74.95 incl. cd-rom (*0-7357-0026-5*) New Riders Pub.

MCSD Training Guide: Wosa I & Wosa II. New Riders Development Staff. 1997. 90.00 (*1-56205-765-0*) New Riders Pub.

***MCSD Training Guide: 4-in-1 Set.** Howard Hawhee. (Training Guides Ser.). (Illus.). 2700p. 1999. 223.95 (*0-7357-0912-2*) New Riders Pub.

An Asterisk (*) at the beginning of an entry indicates that the title is appearing for the first time.

MCSD VB6 Distributed Exam Cram. Michael Lane Thomas. LC 98-52821. 1999. pap. text 29.99 (*1-57610-375-7*) Coriolis Grp.

MCSD Visual Basic Desktop Applications Training Kit. Associate Inc Training. LC 99-13775. 700p. 1999. pap. 69.99 (*0-7356-0620-X*) Microsoft.

***MCSD Visual Basic 6 Core Requirements, 3 vols.** Sybex, Inc. Staff. 2096p. 1999. boxed set 109.97 (*0-7821-2582-4*) Sybex.

***MCSD Visual Basic 6 Desktop Applications.** Luisa Cesana. LC 98-88946. (Microsoft Certified Professional Ser.). (Illus.). 592p. 1999. student ed. 44.99 incl. cd-rom (*0-7821-2438-0*) Sybex.

MCSD Visual Basic 6 Desktop Exam Cram. Michael D. MacDonald. LC 98-33444. (Exam Cram Ser.). 1999. pap. 29.99 (*1-57610-376-5*) Coriolis Grp.

MCSD Visual Basic 5 Exam Guide. Howard Hawhee. LC 97-80543. 1376p. 1997. 99.99 (*0-7897-1478-7*) Que.

MCSD Visual Basic 6 Desktop Applications: Study Guide Exam 70-176. Syngress Media, Inc. Staff. 767p. 1999. student ed. 49.99 incl. cd-rom (*0-07-211930-6*) Osborne-McGraw.

MCSD Visual Basic 6 Distributed Applications: Study Guide Exam 70-175. Syngress Media, Inc. Staff. LC 99-200326. 656p. 1999. student ed. 49.99 incl. cd-rom (*0-07-211932-2*) Osborne-McGraw.

MCSD Visual Basic 6 Exam Prep. Michael Ekedahl. LC 99-38513. (Exam Prep Ser.). 700p. 1998. pap. 49.99 (*1-57610-260-2*) Coriolis Grp.

***MCSD Visual Basic 6.0 Desktop Exam Cram.** MacDonald. (Programming Ser.). (C). 1999. pap. 15.60 (*0-619-01607-8*) Course Tech.

***MCSD Visual Basic 6.0 Distributed Exam Cram.** Thomas Lane. (Programming Ser.). (C). 1999. pap. 15.60 (*0-619-01608-6*) Course Tech.

***MCSD Visual C++ 6 Desktop.** James Lacey. LC 99-38873. (Exam Cram Ser.). 601p. 1999. pap. 29.99 (*1-57610-373-0*) Coriolis Grp.

***MCSD Visual C++ 6 Distributed Applications Study Guide: Exam 70-015.** Syngress Media, Inc. Staff. 687p. 2000. pap. 49.99 (*0-07-212137-8*) Osborne-McGraw.

***MCSD Visual C++ 6 Desktop Exam Cram.** Lacey. (Programming Ser.). (C). 1999. pap. 15.60 (*0-619-01610-8*) Course Tech.

***MCSD Visual C++ 6 Distributed Exam Cram.** Lacey. (Programming Ser.). (C). 2000. pap. 15.60 (*0-619-01611-6*) Course Tech.

***MCSD Visual C++6 Distributed Exam Cram.** James Lacey. LC 99-55320. (C). 1999. 29.99 (*1-57610-372-2*) Coriolis Grp.

***MCSD/MCP+SB Frontpage 98 Exam Cram.** Tittel & Hudson. (Networking Ser.). (C). 1999. pap. 29.99 (*0-619-01612-4*) Course Tech.

***MCSE: Accelerated Windows 2000 Exam Notes.** James Chellis. 2000. pap. 29.99 (*0-7821-2770-3*) Sybex.

***MCSE: Accelerated Windows 2000 Study Guide.** James Chellis. 2000. 69.99 (*0-7821-2760-6*) Sybex.

MCSE: Implementing & Supporting Microsoft Exchange Server 5.5. Marcus Goncalves. (MCSE Ser.). (Illus.). 432p. 1998. 49.99 (*0-13-923525-6*) P-H.

MCSE: NT Workstation Study Guide. Charles Perkins. 1996. 39.99 incl. cd-rom (*0-614-20334-1*, Network Pr) Sybex.

***MCSE: The Core Exams in a Nutshell.** 2nd ed. Michael Moncur. Ed. by Tim O'Reilly. (Illus.). 450p. 2000. pap. 24.95 (*1-56592-721-4*) OReilly & Assocs.

MCSE: The Electives in a Nutshell. Michael Moncur. (Illus.). 372p. 1998. pap. 19.95 (*1-56592-482-7*) OReilly & Assocs.

***MCSE: Windows 2000 Core Requirements Exam Notes, 3 vols.** James Chellis. 2000. pap. 79.96 (*0-7821-2764-9*) Sybex.

***MCSE: Windows 2000 Directory Services Administration Exam Notes.** Anil Desai. 2000. pap. 24.99 (*0-7821-2762-2*) Sybex.

***MCSE: Windows 2000 Directory Services Design Exam Notes.** Gary Govanus. (MCSE Exam Notes Ser.). (Illus.). 2000. pap. text 24.99 (*0-7821-2765-7*) Sybex.

***MCSE: Windows 2000 Directory Services Design Study Guide.** Gary Govanus. (Illus.). 2000. 49.99 (*0-7821-2757-6*) Sybex.

***MCSE: Windows 2000 Network Administration Exam Notes.** Paul Robichaux. 2000. pap. 24.99 (*0-7821-2761-4*) Sybex.

***MCSE: Windows 2000 Network Design Exam Notes.** Bill Heldman. 2000. pap. 24.99 (*0-7821-2767-3*) Sybex.

***MCSE: Windows 2000 Network Design Study Guide.** Bill Heldman. (Illus.). 2000. 49.99 (*0-7821-2759-2*) Sybex.

***MCSE: Windows 2000 Network Security Design Exam Notes.** Gary Govanus. (MCSE Exam Notes Ser.). 2000. pap. text 24.99 (*0-7821-2766-5*) Sybex.

***MCSE: Windows 2000 Network Security Design Study Guide.** Gary Govanus. (Illus.). 2000. 49.99 (*0-7821-2758-4*) Sybex.

***MCSE: Windows 2000 Professional Study Guide.** James Chellis. (Illus.). 2000. pap. 49.99 (*0-7821-2751-7*) Sybex.

***MCSE: Windows 2000 Server Study Guide.** James Chellis. (Illus.). 2000. pap. 49.99 (*0-7821-2752-5*) Sybex.

***MCSE: Windows 2000 Upgrade Exam Notes.** Sybex, Inc. Staff. 2000. pap. 24.99 (*0-7821-2769-X*) Sybex.

***MCSE: Windows 2000 Upgrade Study Guide.** James Chellis. 2000. 49.99 (*0-7821-2768-1*) Sybex.

***MCSE Accelerated Exams: TestTaker's Guide.** Timothy L. Warner. (Illus.). 300p. 2000. pap. 31.95 (*1-58450-027-1*) Chrles River Media.

MCSE Administering SQL Server 7. 10th ed. Jeffrey R. Garbus et al. LC 98-50747. (Exam Cram Ser.). xxiv, 346p. (C). 1999. pap. 29.99 (*1-57610-227-0*) Coriolis Grp.

***MCSE Administering SQL Server 7 Exam Cram.** Jeffrey Garbus et al. (Networking Ser.). (C). 1999. pap. 29.99 (*0-619-01613-2*) Course Tech.

MCSE & Internet Complete V1.2. Jason Sirockman. 1999. 199.99 (*0-7357-0072-9*) New Riders Pub.

MCSE Certification Press Core Four Set. Syngress Media, Inc. Staff. boxed set 159.99 (*0-07-882568-7*) Osborne-McGraw.

MCSE Certification Press Internet Expert. Syngress Inc. Staff. 1998. 124.99 (*0-07-211844-X*) Osborne-McGraw.

MCSE Certification Study Guide. Anthony Gatlin. (Illus.). 908p. 1997. pap., pap. text 69.95 incl. cd-rom (*0-07-913176-X*) McGraw.

MCSE Certification Test Yourself Practice Exams. Syngress Media, Inc. Staff. LC 99-229770. 718p. 1998. pap. 39.99 (*0-07-211854-7*) Osborne-McGraw.

***MCSE Complete: Core Requirements.** 1024p. 1999. 19.99 (*0-7821-2583-2*) Sybex.

***MCSE Complete: Electives.** 1072p. 1999. 19.99 (*0-7821-2584-0*) Sybex.

MCSE Complete: V 1.1. 1998. 99.99 (*0-7897-1564-3*, Que New Media) MCP SW Interactive.

MCSE Complete NT 4 Certification Exam Guide. Brian Langan et al. (Illus.). 1200p. 1998. 99.00 incl. cd-rom (*0-07-913714-8*) McGraw.

MCSE Core Essential Reference: Core NT Exams. Matthew Shepker. LC 98-87234. 1998. pap. 19.99 (*0-7357-0006-0*) New Riders Pub.

***MCSE Core Exams Examgear: Exams 70-067, 70-068, 70-073, 70-098, 70-058, Vol. 1.** New Riders Staff. 100p. 1999. 299.99 (*0-7357-0863-0*) New Riders Pub.

MCSE Core Exams Test Yourself Personal Testing Center. Osborne. (MCSE Certification Press Ser.). 1998. 99.00 (*0-07-211926-8*) Osborne-McGraw.

MCSE Core Exams Test Yourself Personal Testing Center. Syngress Media, Inc. Staff. 69p. 1998. pap. 129.00 (*0-07-211925-X*) McGraw.

***MCSE Core Four Exam Cram, Vol. 1.** adapted ed. Ed Tittel. (Exam Cram / Coriolis' Certification Insi Ser.). 1999. pap. 99.99 (*1-57610-449-4*) Coriolis Grp.

***MCSE Core-Four Exam Cram Pack: The New Interactive Study System Designed for Microsoft Certification : Microsoft Certified Systems Engineer.** 3rd ed. Ed Tittel. (Exam Cram / Coriolis' Certification Insi Ser.). 2000. pap. text 119.99 (*1-57610-622-5*) Coriolis Grp.

MCSE Core Four for Dummies, 4 vols. Dummies Technical Press Staff. (For Dummies Ser.). 1900p. 1998. pap. 99.99 incl. cd-rom (*0-7645-0526-2*) IDG Bks.

MCSE Core Four for Dummies. 2nd ed. Dummies Technical Press Staff. 1900p. 1999. pap. 99.99 incl. cd-rom (*0-7645-0627-7*) IDG Bks.

***MCSE Core Four Practice Test Exam Cram.** Ed Tittel et al. LC 99-24319. (Exam Cram (Coriolis' Certification Insider Press) Ser.). (Illus.). 299p. 1999. pap. 29.99 (*1-57610-475-3*) Coriolis Grp.

***MCSE Core+15-in-1 Certification Exam Guide.** Dan York. (MCSE Certification Ser.). (Illus.). 600p. 2000. pap. 49.99 (*0-7897-2259-3*) Que.

***MCSE Core Requirements.** 3rd ed. Microsoft Certified Trainers Staff. (MCSE Exam Preparation Guide Ser.). (Illus.). 1999. pap. 149.96 (*0-7821-2699-5*) Sybex.

MCSE Core Requirements: Covers Exams: 70-058, 10-067, 70-068, 70-073. abr. ed. Sybex, Inc. Staff. (MCSE Ser.). 3200p. 1998. boxed set 149.96 incl. cd-rom (*0-7821-2245-0*) Sybex.

MCSE Core Study Guide. 428p. 1997. pap. write for info. (*1-884486-16-9*) Wave Tech.

***MCSE Core Windows 2000 Test Yourself Practice Exams: Exams 70-210, 70-215, 70-216, 70-217, 70-24.** Snygress Media, Inc. Staff. (Global Knowledge Certification Ser.). (Illus.). 2000. 39.99 (*0-07-212610-8*) Osborne-McGraw.

***MCSE Core 4 Exam Cram.** Kurt Hudson. (Microsoft Certified Systems Engineer Ser.). 2000. audio 39.99 (*1-57610-631-4*) Coriolis Grp.

MCSE CP/IP for Dummies Flash Cards. Dummies Technical Press Staff. (For Dummies Ser.). 250p. 1999. pap. 24.99 incl. cd-rom (*0-7645-0552-1*) IDG Bks.

***MCSE Database Design on SQL Server 7.** Jeffrey Garbus et al. LC 99-13166. (Exam Cram (Coriolis' Certification Insider Press) Ser.). (Illus.). 464p. 1999. pap. 29.99 (*1-57610-228-9*) Coriolis Grp.

***MCSE Database Design on SQL Server 7 Exam Prep.** Christopher Leonard. LC 99-42704. (Exam Prep Ser.). 1999. pap. 44.99 (*1-57610-519-9*) Coriolis Grp.

***MCSE Designing a Windows 2000 Directory Services Infrastructure Study Guide (Exam 70-219)** Ed. by Syngress Media Staff. (Certification Press Study Guides Ser.). (Illus.). 752p. 2000. 49.99 (*0-07-212503-9*) Osborne-McGraw.

***MCSE Designing a Windows 2000 Network Infrastructure Study Guide: Exam 70-221.** Syngress Media, Inc. Staff. (Global Knowledge Certification Ser.). (Illus.). 2000. 49.99 (*0-07-212494-6*) Osborne-McGraw.

***MCSE Designing Security for Windows 2000 Network Study Guide (Exam 70-200)** Ed. by Syngress Media Staff. (Global Knowledge Certification Bks.). (Illus.). 752p. 2000. 49.99 (*0-07-212497-0*) Osborne-McGraw.

MCSE Elective Exam Cram. Ed Tittel. 1998. pap. 99.99 (*1-57610-285-8*) Coriolis Grp.

MCSE Elective Study Guide. 295p. 1997. pap. write for info. (*1-884486-15-0*) Wave Tech.

***MCSE Electives.** Sybex, Inc. Staff. (Illus.). 3200p. 1998. boxed set 149.96 incl. cd-rom (*0-7821-2512-3*) Sybex.

MCSE Exam Notes: Core Requirements, 4 vols. Sybex, Inc. Staff. 1600p. 1998. boxed set 64.96 (*0-7821-2288-4*) Sybex.

MCSE Exam Notes: Exchange Server 5.5, No. 70-081. Ed. by Robert King. LC 98-85933. (MCSE Exam Notes Ser.). 368p. 1998. pap. 19.99 (*0-7821-2302-3*) Sybex.

MCSE Exam Notes: Networking Essentials. Glenn Madow. LC 98-85670. (Illus.). 368p. 1998. pap. 19.99 (*0-7821-2291-4*) Sybex.

MCSE Exam Notes: NT Server 4. Gary Govanus. LC 98-85463. 1998. 19.99 (*0-7821-2289-2*) Sybex.

MCSE Exam Notes: NT Server 4 in the Enterprise. Robert King. LC 98-85466. 416p. 1998. pap. text 19.99 (*0-7821-2292-2*) Sybex.

MCSE Exam Notes: NT Workstation 4. Gary Govanas. 352p. 1998. pap. text 19.99 (*0-7821-2290-6*) Sybex.

MCSE Exam Notes: Proxy Server 2. Scott Richardson. LC 98-87585. (MCSE Exam Notes Ser.). 352p. 1998. pap. text 19.99 (*0-7821-2304-X*) Sybex.

***MCSE Exam Notes: Systems Management Server 2.** Frank Jewett. LC 99-49135. 624p. 1999. 49.99 (*0-13-017857-8*) P-H.

MCSE Exam Notes - Internet Information Server 4. Strebe. LC 98-85869. 320p. 1998. pap. 19.99 (*0-7821-2303-1*, 887284Q) Sybex.

***MCSE Exam Notes: Electives: Covers 5 Exams: 70-059, 70-081, 70-087, 70-088, 70-028, 5 vols.** Sybex, Inc. Staff. (MCSE Exam Notes Ser.). 1808p. 1999. boxed set 79.95 (*0-7821-2576-X*) Sybex.

***MCSE Exam Notes SMS 2.** David Schaer. (MCSE Exam Notes Ser.). 352p. 1999. pap. 24.99 (*0-7821-2368-6*) Sybex.

MCSE Exam Notes SQL Server 7 Administration. Rick Sawtell et al. LC 99-62867. (Illus.). 368p. 1999. pap. 19.99 (*0-7821-2477-1*) Sybex.

MCSE Exam Notes TCP/IP for NT Server 4, No. 70-059. Gary Govanus. LC 98-86627. (MCSE Exam Notes Ser.). 352p. 1998. pap. 19.99 (*0-7821-2307-4*) Sybex.

***MCSE Exam 70-240: Microsoft Windows 2000 Accelerated Exam for MCPS Certified on Microsoft Window.** Emmett Dulaney. 600p. 2000. pap. text 39.99 (*0-7897-2387-5*) Que.

***MCSE Exam 70-217: Implementing & Administering a Microsoft Windows 2000 Directory Services Information.** Brian Myers. 600p. 2000. pap. 39.99 (*0-7897-2382-4*) Que.

***MCSE Exam 70-216: Implementing & Adminstering a Microsoft Windows 2000 Network Infrastructure.** Roger Abell. 600p. 2000. pap. 39.99 (*0-7897-2383-2*) Que.

***Mcse Examgear: Windows 2000 Core Exams.** 2000. write for info. (*0-7357-0954-8*) Cisco Press.

MCSE Exams: Test Taker's Guide. Timothy Warner. (TestTaker's Guide Ser.). (Illus.). 300p. 1999. pap. 29.95 (*1-58450-052-2*) Chrles River Media.

MCSE Exchange 5.5: Study Guide Exam 70-81. Syngress Media, Inc. Staff. LC 98-167577. (MCSE Certification Press Ser.). 531p. 1998. student ed. 49.99 incl. cd-rom (*0-07-882488-5*) Osborne-McGraw.

MCSE Exchange Server 5 Exam Cram. 10th ed. Ed Tittel. LC 98-25782. (Exam Cram Ser.). xxvi, 496p. (C). 1998. mass mkt. 29.99 (*1-57610-229-7*) Coriolis Grp.

***MCSE, Exchange Server 5.5 Study Guide.** 2nd ed. Richard L. Easlick & James Chellis. 2000. pap. 49.99 (*0-7821-2726-6*) Sybex.

MCSE Exchange Server 5.5. Glenn. LC QA76.3.G56 1999. (Ace It Ser.). 416p. 1999. pap. 24.99 (*0-7645-3296-0*) IDG Bks.

MCSE Exchange Server 5.5 Exam Prep. James M. Stewart. LC 98-22449. (Exam Prep Ser.). 1998. pap. text 44.99 (*1-57610-263-7*) Coriolis Grp.

MCSE Exchange Server 5.5 for Dummies. Dummies Press Staff & Scott Rachui. LC 99-62292. (Illus.). 496p. 1999. pap. 29.99 incl. cd-rom (*0-7645-0481-9*) IDG Bks.

***MCSE Exchange Server 5.5 For Dummies Flash Cards.** Dummies Technical Press Staff. (For Dummies Ser.). 250p. 2000. pap. 24.99 incl. cd-rom (*0-7645-0631-5*) IDG Bks.

***MCSE Exchange Server 5.5 for Dummies Training Kit.** Dummies Technical Press Staff. (For Dummies Ser.). 568p. 1999. pap. 49.99 incl. cd-rom (*0-7645-0619-6*) IDG Bks.

MCSE Fast Track: Internet Information Server 4. Emmett Dulaney. LC 98-86319. 1998. pap. 19.99 (*1-56205-936-X*) New Riders Pub.

MCSE Fast Track: Networking Essentials. Emmett Dulaney. LC 98-86325. 1998. pap. 19.99 (*1-56205-939-4*) New Riders Pub.

Mcse Fast Track: Security Design. 400p. 1900. 29.99 (*0-7357-0987-4*) New Riders Pub.

MCSE Fast Track: TCP/IP. Emmett Dulaney. LC 98-86320. 1998. pap. 19.99 (*1-56205-937-8*) New Riders Pub.

MCSE Fast Track: WIndows NT Server 4. Emmett Dulaney. LC 98-86318. 1998. pap. 19.99 (*1-56205-935-1*) New Riders Pub.

MCSE Fast Track: Windows NT Server 4 Enterprise. Emmett Dulaney. LC 98-86322. 1998. pap. 19.99 (*1-56205-940-8*) New Riders Pub.

MCSE Fast Track: Windows NT Workstation 4. Emmett Dulaney. LC 98-86321. 1998. pap. 19.99 (*1-56205-938-6*) New Riders Pub.

MCSE Fast Track: Windows 2000 Accelerated Exam. 400p. 1900. 39.99 (*0-7357-0981-5*) New Riders Pub.

Mcse Fast Track: Windows 2000 Core Exams. 1600p. 1900. 99.99 (*0-7357-0989-0*) New Riders Pub.

MCSE Fast Track: Windows 2000 Directory Services Administration. 400p. 1900. 29.99 (*0-7357-0980-7*) New Riders Pub.

***Mcse Fast Track: Windows 2000 Network Infrastructure Admin.** 400p. 2000. 29.99 (*0-7357-0962-9*) New Riders Pub.

***MCSE Fast Track: Windows 2000 Professional.** 400p. 2000. 29.99 (*0-7357-0963-7*) New Riders Pub.

***Mcse Fast Track: Windows 2000 Server.** 400p. 2000. 29.99 (*0-7357-0964-5*) New Riders Pub.

***MCSE Guide to Frontpage 2000.** Hank Carbeck. (Networking Ser.). (C). 2000. text 45.00 (*0-619-01568-3*) Course Tech.

***MCSE Guide to Internet Explorer 5.0.** Course Technology Staff. (Networking Ser.). (C). 2000. text 45.00 (*0-7600-1146-X*) Course Tech.

MCSE Guide to Microsoft Proxy Server 2.0. Andy Ruth. 560p. per. 60.95 (*0-7600-1144-3*, Pub. by Course Tech) Thomson Learn.

MCSE Guide to Microsoft Exchange Server 5.5. Ed Tittel et al. 612p. per. write for info. (*0-7600-1143-5*, Pub. by Course Tech) Thomson Learn.

MCSE Guide to Microsoft Internet Information Server 4.0. J. Michael Stewart. 615p. per. 60.95 (*0-7600-1081-1*, Pub. by Course Tech) Thomson Learn.

***MCSE Guide to Microsoft Windows 2000 Active Directory.** Hudson. (Networking Ser.). (C). 2000. pap. 45.00 (*0-619-01600-0*) Course Tech.

MCSE Guide to Microsoft Windows 2000 Professional. 704p. per. 60.95 (*0-619-01513-6*, Pub. by Course Tech) Thomson Learn.

***MCSE Guide to MS Exchange Server 5.5.** (Networking Ser.). (C). 1999. text 45.00 incl. audio compact disk (*0-619-01551-9*) Course Tech.

***Mcse Guide to MS Windows 2000 Networking.** Cannon. (Networking Ser.). (C). 2000. pap. 45.00 (*0-619-01645-0*) Course Tech.

***MCSE Guide to MS Windows 2000 Server.** Palmer. (Networking Ser.). (C). 2000. pap. 60.95 (*0-619-01517-9*) Course Tech.

***MCSE Guide to Networking Essentials.** Johnson Tittel. (Networking Ser.). (C). 1999. text 60.95 incl. audio compact disk (*0-619-01552-7*) Course Tech.

***MCSE Guide to SQL Server Administration.** TBD Coriolis Group Staff. (Networking Ser.). (C). 2000. text 45.00 (*0-619-01572-1*) Course Tech.

***MCSE Guide to TCP/IP on Microsoft Windows NT 4.0.** Richard Burke. (Illus.). 4000p. 1999. pap. 60.95 incl. cd-rom (*0-619-01577-2*) Course Tech.

***MCSE Guide/MS NT Server 4.0 in the Enterprise-CD Version.** Williams & Johnson. (Networking Ser.). (C). 1999. pap. 60.95 (*0-619-01651-5*) Course Tech.

MCSE IIS 4 Ace It! David Iseminger. LC QA76.3.I83 1999. (Ace It Ser.). 416p. 1999. pap. text 24.99 (*0-7645-3276-6*) IDG Bks.

***MCSE IIS 4 Exam Cram.** 3rd ed. Libby Chovanec et al. LC 00-21533. (Illus.). 385p. 2000. pap. write for info. (*1-57610-678-0*) Coriolis Grp.

***MCSE IIS 4.0.** Gilster. (SLE Ser.). 1999. 24.99 (*0-07-212174-2*) McGraw.

***MCSE Implementing & Administering a Windows 2000 Directory Services Infrastructure Study Guide.** Syngress Media Staff. (Microsoft Certified Systems Engineer Ser.). (Illus.). 752p. 2000. student ed. 49.99 (*0-07-212380-X*) Osborne-McGraw.

***MCSE Implementing & Administering a Windows 2000 Network Infrastructure Study Guide (Exam 70-216)** (Microsoft Certified Systems Engineer Ser.). 752p. 2000. 49.99 (*0-07-212383-4*) Osborne-McGraw.

***Mcse Installing, Configuring, & Administering: Microsoft Windows 2000 Profess.** 600p. 2000. 39.99 (*0-7897-2371-9*) Que.

***MCSE Installing, Configuring & Administering Windows 2000 Professional Study Guide: Exam 70-21.** Syngress Media Staff. (Microsoft Certified Systems Engineer Ser.). (Illus.). 752p. 2000. student ed. 49.99 (*0-07-212389-3*) Osborne-McGraw.

***MCSE Installing, Configuring & Administering Windows 2000 Professional Study Guide: Exam 70-215.** 600p. 2000. 39.99 (*0-7897-2078-7*) Que.

***MCSE Installing, Configuring & Administering Windows 2000 Server Study Guide (Exam 70-215)** (Microsoft Certified Systems Engineer Ser.). 752p. 2000. 49.99 (*0-07-212386-9*) Osborne-McGraw.

MCSE Internet Explorer Administration Kit: Exam 70-79. Syngress Media Incorporated Staff. (MCSE Certification Press Ser.). 1999. pap. text, student ed. 49.99 (*0-07-211931-4*) Osborne-McGraw.

MCSE Internet Explorer 4 Exam Cram. James M. Stewart. LC 98-25773. (Exam Cram Ser.). xxiv, 309 p. 1998. pap. 29.99 (*1-57610-286-6*) Coriolis Grp.

***MCSE Internet Explorer 5 for Dummies.** Dummies Press Staff. 496p. 2000. pap. 29.99 incl. cd-rom (*0-7645-0522-X*) IDG Bks.

***MCSE Internet Information Server 4 Examgear.** 100p. 1999. 75.00 (*0-7357-0862-2*) New Riders Pub.

***MCSE, Internet Information Server 4 Study Guide.** 3rd ed. Matthew Strebe & Charles Perkins. 2000. pap. 49.99 (*0-7821-2727-4*) Sybex.

***MCSE Internet Information Server 3 Exam Cram.** 10th ed. Ed Tittel. LC 98-3699. xxvii, 336 p. (C). 1998. pap. 29.99 (*1-57610-194-0*) Coriolis Grp.

MCSE Internet Information Server 4. James M. Stewart. LC 98-8182. (Exam Prep Ser.). 615p. 1998. pap. 44.99 (*1-57610-267-X*) Coriolis Grp.

MCSE Internet Information Server 4 for Dummies. Iseminger. LC QA76.3.I84 1998. (For Dummies Ser.). 512p. 1998. pap. 29.99 incl. cd-rom (*0-7645-0482-7*) IDG Bks.

***MCSE Internet Information Server 4 for Dummies Flash Cards.** Dummies Technical Press Staff. (For Dummies Ser.). 250p. 1999. pap. 24.99 incl. cd-rom (*0-7645-0555-6*) IDG Bks.

MCSE JumpStart. Lisa Donald. LC 98-83172. (Illus.). 384p. 1999. pap. 19.99 (*0-7821-2462-3*) Sybex.

***MCSE Network Infrastructure Design.** 650p. 2000. student ed. 49.99 (*0-7357-0982-3*) Macmillan Tech.

***MCSE Network Training Course: Student Edition.** abr. ed. Keogh. 1999. pap. 71.93 (*0-13-014305-7*) P-H.

MCSE Networking Essentials: Study Guide Exam 70-58. Syngress Media, Inc. Staff & Syngress Knowledge Network Staff. 512p. 1998. 49.99 incl. cd-rom (*0-07-882493-1*) McGraw.

M

M

MCSE Networking Essentials Ace It! IDG Books Staff. LC QA73.3.N367 1998. 384p. 1998. pap. 24.99 (*0-7645-3257-X*) IDG Bks.

***MCSE Networking Essentials Certification Exam Guide.** Dan York. 1999. pap. 39.99 (*0-7897-2265-8*) Que.

***MCSE Networking Essentials Exam Cram, 1vol.** 3rd ed. Ed Tittel. LC 99-58382. (Microsoft Certified Systems Engineer Ser.). 1999. pap. text 29.99 (*1-57610-621-7*) Coriolis Grp.

MCSE Networking Essentials Exam Cram: Adaptive ed. Ed Tittel. LC 99-10840. (Exam Cram / Coriolis' Certification Insi Ser.). 1999. pap. text 29.99 (*1-57610-445-1*) Coriolis Grp.

***MCSE Networking Essentials Exam Cram Personal Trainer.** 3rd ed. Ed. by Coriolis Group Staff. (Illus.). 2000. pap. 69.99 incl. cd-rom (*1-57610-644-6*) Coriolis Grp.

MCSE Networking Essentials Exam Prep. Ed Tittel. 528p. 1998. pap. text 49.99 (*1-57610-237-8*) Coriolis Grp.

***MCSE Networking Essentials for Dummies.** 2nd ed. Arla Aschermann. LC 99-63442. (For Dummies Ser.). 384p. 1999. pap. 29.99 incl. cd-rom (*0-7645-0614-5*) IDG Bks.

***MCSE Networking Essentials for Dummies Flash Cards.** Dummies Technical Press Staff. (For Dummies Ser.). 250p. 1999. pap. 24.99 incl. cd-rom (*0-7645-0554-8*) IDG Bks.

***MCSE Networking Essentials for Dummies Training Kit.** Dummies Technical Press Staff. (For Dummies Ser.). 448p. 1999. pap. 49.99 incl. cd-rom (*0-7645-0621-8*) IDG Bks.

***Mcse Networking Essentials Interactive Training Course.** Jim Keogh. 1999. pap. 49.33 (*0-13-015494-6*, Prentice Hall) P-H.

MCSE NT Server 4. Michael J. Palmer. LC 98-4254. (Exam Prep Ser.). (Illus.). 640p. 1998. pap. text 49.99 (*1-57610-252-1*) Coriolis Grp.

***MCSE NT Server 4 Exam Cram Personal Trainer.** 3rd ed. Ed. by Coriolis Group Staff. (Illus.). 2000. pap. text 69.99 incl. cd-rom (*1-57610-645-4*) Coriolis Grp.

***MCSE NT Server 4 in the Enterprise Exam Cram Personal Trainer.** 3rd ed. Ed. by Coriolis Group Staff. (Illus.). 2000. pap. text 69.99 incl. cd-rom (*1-57610-646-2*) Coriolis Grp.

MCSE NT Server 4 in the E-W/CD. Linthic. LC 98-25127. 456p. 1998. 49.99 (*1-57610-253-X*) Coriolis Grp.

MCSE NT Server 4 in the Enterprise Study Guide. 2nd ed. Ed. by Lisa Donald. LC 97-81015. 800p. 1998. student ed. 54.99 incl. cd-rom (*0-7821-2221-3*) Sybex.

***MCSE NT Server 4.0 Ace It!** IDG Books Staff. LC 99-169231. 496p. 1998. pap. 24.99 (*0-7645-3266-9*) IDG Bks.

***MCSE NT Server 4.0 in the Enterprise Ace It! Exam 70-68.** IDG Books Staff. LC QA76.3.C6584 1999. (MCSE NT Ace It Ser.). (Illus.). 512p. 1998. pap. 24.99 (*0-7645-3265-0*) IDG Bks.

***MCSE NT Server 4 Prep & Cram Pack: Customized MCSE Training System for the Busy NT 4 Professional.** Certification Insider Press Staff. (Illus.). 1998. pap. 64.99 (*1-57610-307-2*) Coriolis Grp.

MCSE NT Server 4 Study Guide. 2nd ed. Matthew Strebe. 800p. 1998. student ed. 54.99 incl. cd-rom (*0-7821-2222-1*) Sybex.

***MCSE NT Server 4 in the Enterprise Exam Cram.** 3rd ed. Ed Tittel. LC 99-58380. (Microsoft Certified Systems Engineer Ser.). 2000. pap. text 29.99 (*1-57610-619-5*) Coriolis Grp.

***MCSE NT Server 4 Exam Cram.** 3rd ed. Ed Tittel. LC 99-58381. (Microsoft Certified Systems Engineer Ser.). 2000. pap. text 29.99 (*1-57610-618-7*) Coriolis Grp.

MCSE NT Server 4 Exam Cram: Adaptive ed. Ed Tittel. LC 99-10776. (Exam Cram / Coriolis' Certification Insi Ser.). 1999. pap. text 29.99 (*1-57610-446-X*) Coriolis Grp.

MCSE NT Server 4 in the Enterprise Exam Cram: Adaptive ed. Ed Tittel. LC 99-10770. (Exam Cram / Coriolis' Certification Insi Ser.). 1999. pap. text 29.99 (*1-57610-447-8*) Coriolis Grp.

MCSE NT Workstation 4 Exam Prep. 10th ed. Ed Tittel. LC 98-16106. (Exam Prep Ser.). 600p. (C). 1998. mass mkt. 59.99 (*1-57610-238-6*) Coriolis Grp.

***MCSE NT Workstation 4.0 Ace It!** IDG Books Staff. LC QA76.3.C66 1998. 480p. 1998. pap. 24.99 (*0-7645-3264-2*) IDG Bks.

***MCSE NT Workstation 4 Study Guide.** 2nd ed. Charles Perkins. LC 97-81249. 800p. 1998. student ed. 54.99 incl. cd-rom (*0-7821-2223-X*) Sybex.

***MCSE NT Workstation 4 Exam Cram.** 3rd ed. Ed Tittel. LC 99-58379. 2000. pap. text 29.99 (*1-57610-620-9*) Coriolis Grp.

MCSE NT Workstation 4 Exam Cram: Adaptive ed. Ed Tittel. LC 99-10775. (Exam Cram / Coriolis' Certification Insi Ser.). 1999. pap. text 29.99 (*1-57610-448-6*) Coriolis Grp.

MCSE NT 4 Certification Exam Guide. Total Seminars Staff & Brian Schwarz. 750p. 1999. 79.99 incl. cd-rom (*0-07-913739-3*) McGraw.

***MCSE Online Training Kit, Microsoft Windows Network Infrastructure Administration 2000.** Microsoft Corporation Staff. 2000. pap. text 99.99 (*0-7356-0952-7*) Microsoft.

***MCSE Online Training Kit, Microsoft Windows Professional 2000.** Microsoft Corporation Staff. (IT-Training Kits Ser.). 2000. pap. text 99.99 (*0-7356-0953-5*) Microsoft.

***MCSE Online Training Kit, Microsoft Windows Server 2000.** Microsoft Corporation Staff. (IT-Training Kits Ser.). 2000. pap. 99.99 (*0-7356-0954-3*) Microsoft.

***MCSE Online Training Kit, Networking Essentials Plus.** Microsoft Press Staff. 1999. pap. 99.99 incl. cd-rom (*0-7356-0881-4*) Microsoft Pr.

***MCSE Online Training Kit Windows Active Directory Services 2000.** Microsoft Corporation Staff. (IT-Training Kits Ser.). (Illus.). 2000. pap. text 99.99 (*0-7356-1008-8*) Microsoft.

***MCSE Prep Kit: 70-222 Upgrading from Windows NT 4.0 to Windows 2000.** Joe Habraken. 2000. pap. 39.99 (*0-7897-2391-3*) Que.

MCSE Proxy Server 2 Exam Cram. 10th ed. Ed Tittel. LC 98-16420. (Exam Cram Ser.). 350p. (C). 1998. mass mkt. 29.99 (*1-57610-230-0*) Coriolis Grp.

MCSE Proxy Server 2 Study Guide. James Chellis. LC 97-80847. 672p. 1998. pap. text 49.99 (*0-7821-2194-2*) Sybex.

MCSE Proxy Server 2. Michael Stewart. LC 98-21688. (Exam Prep Ser.). 700p. 1998. pap. text 44.99 (*1-57610-264-5*) Coriolis Grp.

***MCSE Readiness Exam 70-217 Implementing & Administering a Microsoft Windows Directory Services.** Jill Spealman. (MCSE Readiness Review Ser.). 2000. pap. text 24.99 (*0-7356-1000-2*) Microsoft.

MCSE Readiness Review; Designing & Implementing Databases with Microsoft SQL Serve: Exam 70-026. Microsoft Corporation Staff. LC 99-45690. 1999. pap. text 29.99 (*0-7356-0673-0*) Microsoft.

MCSE Readiness Review Exam 70-058 Networking Essentials. Microsoft Corporation Staff. LC 98-39270. 350p. 1998. 29.99 incl. cd-rom (*0-7356-0536-X*) Microsoft.

MCSE Readiness Review Exam 70-073 Windows NT Workstation 4.0. Microsoft Corporation Staff. LC 98-39269. 350p. 1998. 29.99 incl. cd-rom (*0-7356-0537-8*) Microsoft.

MCSE Readiness Review Exam 70-067 Windows NT Server 4.0. Microsoft Corporation Staff. LC 98-39271. 350p. 1999. 29.99 incl. cd-rom (*0-7356-0538-6*) Microsoft.

MCSE Readiness Review Exam 70-059 TCP/IP. Microsoft Corporation Staff. LC 99-20169. 350p. 1999. 29.99 incl. cd-rom (*0-7356-0540-8*) Microsoft.

***MCSE Readiness Review Exam 70-210 Installing, Configuring & Administering Microsoft Windows Pr.** Microsoft Corporation Staff. (MCSE Readiness Review Ser.). 2000. pap. text 24.99 (*0-7356-0949-7*) Microsoft.

***MCSE Readiness Review--Exam 70-019: Designing & Implementing Data Warehouses with Microsoft SQL Server 7.0.** Jill Spealman. 2000. pap. 29.99 (*0-7356-0774-5*) Microsoft.

Microsoft Internet Information Server 4.0: Exam 70-087. Microsoft Corporation Staff & James Semick. LC 99-13776. (MCSE Readiness Review Ser.). (Illus.). 463p. 1999. pap. 29.99 (*0-7356-0541-6*) Microsoft.

***MCSE Readiness Review Exam 70-216: Implementing & Administrating a Microsoft Windows Network I.** Microsoft Corporation Staff. 2000. pap. 24.99 (*0-7356-0950-0*) Microsoft.

***MCSE Readiness Review Exam 70-215: Installing, Configuring & Administering Microsoft Windows SE.** Microsoft Corporation Staff. 2000. pap. 24.99 (*0-7356-0948-9*) Microsoft.

MCSE Readiness Review Exam 70-068 Windows NT Server 4.0 in the Enterprise: MCSE Readiness Review, Exam 70-068. Microsoft Corporation Staff et al. LC 99-21358. 350p. 1999. 29.99 incl. cd-rom (*0-7356-0539-4*) Microsoft.

MCSE Readiness Review Exam 70-028: Administering Microsoft SQL Server 7.0. Jill Spealman. LC 99-33262. (MCSE Ser.). 1999. pap. text 29.99 (*0-7356-0672-2*) Microsoft.

***MCSE Readiness Review Holiday.** Microsoft Corporation Staff. 1999. pap. text 99.99 (*0-7356-0923-3*) Microsoft.

MCSE Silmulation Guide: Windows NT Server 4 & Enterprise. Dave Bixler. LC 98-87236. 1998. pap. 29.99 (*1-56205-914-9*) New Riders Pub.

MCSE Six Pack. Barry Meinster. (Certification Study Guides Ser.). 600p. 1999. 49.99 incl. cd-rom (*0-7645-3274-X*) IDG Bks.

***MCSE SMS 2 Exam Cram.** Ian Turek. LC 99-32816. 392p. 1999. 29.99 (*1-57610-424-9*) Coriolis Grp.

MCSE SQL Server 6.5 Administration Study Guide. Lance Mortensen et al. LC 97-80468. 672p. 1997. pap. text 49.99 (*0-7821-2172-1*) Sybex.

MCSE Stimulation Guide: WIndows NT Workstaion 4. Luther Stanton. LC 98-87272. 1998. pap. 29.99 (*1-56205-925-4*) New Riders Pub.

MCSE Study Guide: Windows NT Server & Workstation 4. Joe Casad. LC 97-112048. (Illus.). 1272p. (Orig.). 1997. pap. 75.00 (*1-56205-549-6*) New Riders Pub.

MCSE Study Guide: Windows 95 & Networking Essentials. Stephen Myers & Tim McLaren. LC 96-24486. 900p. 1996. student ed. 75.00 (*1-56205-568-2*) New Riders Pub.

MCSE Study Tips for Dummies. Neal. LC 99-474246. (For Dummies Ser.). 288p. 1998. pap. 16.99 (*0-7645-0484-3*) IDG Bks.

MCSE System Administration for SQL Server 7 Exam Prep. Bobbie Hagwood & Carolyn Jones. 700p. 1998. 49.99 incl. cd-rom (*1-57610-269-6*) Coriolis Grp.

MCSE: System Administrator for SQL Server 7. Jeffrey Byrne. LC 98-42435. (MCSE Ser.). 352p. 1998. pap. text 49.99 (*0-13-010795-6*) P-H.

***MCSE TCP/ IP for Dummies.** 2nd ed. Brandon. LC 99-63114. (For Dummies Ser.). 448p. 1999. pap. 29.99 incl. cd-rom (*0-7645-0613-7*) IDG Bks.

***MCSE TCP/IP Ace It!** IDG Books Staff. LC QA76.3.N3673 1998. 464p. 1998. pap. 24.99 (*0-7645-3258-8*) IDG Bks.

MCSE TCP/IP Exam Cram. Gary Novosel et al. LC 99-26464. (Exam Cram (Coriolis' Certification Insider Press) Ser.). (Illus.). 426p. 1999. pap. 29.99 (*1-57610-476-1*) Coriolis Grp.

***MCSE TCP/IP Exam Cram.** 3rd ed. Gary Novosel. (Illus.). 2000. pap. text. write for info. (*1-57610-677-2*) Coriolis Grp.

MCSE TCP/IP Exam Prep. 10th ed. Richard Burke. LC 98-16108. (Exam Prep Ser.). 376p. (C). 1998. mass mkt. 49.99 (*1-57610-239-4*) Coriolis Grp.

***MCSE TCP/IP Examgear.** 100p. 1999. 75.00 (*0-7357-0861-4*) New Riders Pub.

MCSE TCP/IP for Dummies. Cameron Brandon. (For Dummies Ser.). 480p. 1998. 29.99 incl. cd-rom (*0-7645-0404-5*) IDG Bks.

***MCSE Tcp/IP for Dummies Training Kit.** Dummies Technical Press Staff. (For Dummies Ser.). 512p. 1999. pap. 49.99 incl. cd-rom (*0-7645-0620-X*) IDG Bks.

***MCSE TCP/IP for NT 4.** Gilster. (SLE Ser.). 1999. 24.99 (*0-07-212175-0*) McGraw.

***MCSE, TCP/IP for NT Server 4 Study Guide.** 4th ed. Todd Lammle. 2000. pap. write for info. (*0-7821-2725-8*) Sybex.

MCSE TCP/IP for NT Server 4 Study Guide. 2nd ed. Todd Lammle & James Chellis. LC 97-61719. 640p. 1997. pap. text, student ed. 49.99 (*0-7821-2173-X*) Sybex.

MCSE Test Prep: Networking Essentials. Michael Barry et al. LC 98-136920. 1997. 29.99 (*1-56205-826-6*) New Riders Pub.

***MCSE Test Prep for MS Windows 2000 Professional.** Lanwrights. (Networking Ser.). (C). 2000. pap. 45.00 (*0-619-01511-X*) Course Tech.

***MCSE Test Prep Networking Essentials.** Lanwrights. (Networking Ser.). (C). 2000. pap. 45.00 (*0-619-01507-1*) Course Tech.

***MCSE Test Success: Core Requirements (With CD Rom)** Sybex, Inc. Staff. 1408p. 1998. pap. 79.96 (*0-7821-2296-5*) Sybex.

***MCSE Test Success: Electives.** Sybex, Inc. Staff. 1888p. 1999. pap. text 99.95 (*0-7821-2577-8*) Sybex.

MCSE Test Success: Internet Explorer 4 Administration Kit. Allen Jones. LC 98-87587. (MCSE Test Success Ser.). (Illus.). 416p. 1998. pap. 24.99 (*0-7821-2333-3*) Sybex.

MCSE Test Success: Internet Information Server 4. Lisa Donald. LC 98-86621. (MCSE Test Success Ser.). 400p. 1998. pap. 24.99 (*0-7821-2334-1*) Sybex.

MCSE Test Success: SQL 7 Administration. Michael Lee. LC 99-61297. 400p. 1999. pap. 24.99 (*0-7821-2375-9*) Sybex.

MCSE Test Success: Windows 98. VFX Technologies Staff. LC 98-86635. (MCSE Test Success Ser.). 416p. 1998. pap. 24.99 (*0-7821-2369-4*) Sybex.

MCSE Test Success - Exchange Server 5.5. Maria Aurelia Tapia-Ruddy Staff. (MCSE Ser.). 432p. 1998. pap. text 24.99 (*0-7821-2250-7*) Sybex.

MCSE Test Success - Networking Essentials. Todd Lammle et al. LC 98-84010. 384p. 1998. pap. text 24.99 incl. cd-rom (*0-7821-2146-2*, Network Pr) Sybex.

MCSE Test Success - NT Server 4. Lisa Donald et al. LC 97-61721. 368p. 1998. pap. text 39.99 incl. cd-rom (*0-7821-2148-9*) Sybex.

MCSE Test Success - NT Server 4 in the Enterprise. Lisa Donald et al. LC 97-61722. 464p. 1998. pap. text 39.99 (*0-7821-2147-0*, Network Pr) Sybex.

MCSE Test Success - NT Workstation 4. Todd Lammle et al. LC 98-84012. 384p. 1998. pap. text 24.99 incl. cd-rom (*0-7821-2149-7*, Network Pr) Sybex.

MCSE Test Success - TCP/IP for NT4. Sybex, Inc. Staff. LC 98-85462. 304p. 1998. pap. text 24.99 (*0-7821-2251-5*) Sybex.

MCSE Testing Guide. Cabiroy. 800p. 1997. pap. text 74.99 incl. cd-rom (*0-7821-2049-0*) Sybex.

MCSE TestPrep: Core Exams. 2nd ed. Grant Jones et al. 1500p. pap. 89.99 incl. cd-rom (*0-7357-0030-3*) New Riders Pub.

MCSe TestPrep: Networking Essentials. 2nd ed. Jay Adamson. LC 98-87716. 400p. 1999. pap. 19.99 (*0-7357-0010-9*) New Riders Pub.

MCSE Testprep: SQL Server 6.5 Design & Implementation. Owen Williams. LC 98-85228. 1998. 24.99 (*1-56205-915-7*, New Riders Sftwre) MCP SW Interactive.

MCSE TestPrep: SQL Server 7 Database Design. Rob Scrimger. Ed. by Mary Foote & Nancy Warner. (MCSE Ser.). 1999. pap. 19.99 (*0-7357-0042-7*) New Riders Pub.

MCSE TestPrep: TCP/IP. 2nd ed. Erik Rozell & Mary Pablo. LC 98-88578. 400p. 1998. pap. 19.99 (*0-7357-0025-7*) New Riders Pub.

MCSE TestPrep: Windows NT Server 4. 2nd ed. Edward Tetz. LC 98-88004. 400p. 1999. pap. 19.99 (*0-7357-0012-5*) New Riders Pub.

MCSE TestPrep: Windows NT Server 4 Enterprise. New Riders Development Staff. LC 98-88512. 1999. pap. 19.99 (*0-7357-0009-5*) New Riders Pub.

MCSE TestPrep: Windows NT Workstation 4. Emmett Dulaney et al. 400p. 1997. 24.99 (*1-56205-848-7*) New Riders Pub.

MCSE TestPrep: Windows NT Workstation 4. 2nd ed. Luther Stanton. LC 99-207381. 400p. 1999. pap. 29.99 (*0-7357-0008-7*) New Riders Pub.

MCSE TestPrep: Windows 95. 2nd ed. Edward Tetz. LC 98-87717. 1999. pap. text 29.99 (*0-7357-0011-7*) New Riders Pub.

MCSE TestPrep: Windows 98. Alain Guilbault. LC 98-87246. 1998. pap. 24.99 (*1-56205-922-X*) New Riders Pub.

MCSE TestPrep Software: Core Exam. New Riders Staff. 1998. pap. text 69.99 (*1-56205-868-1*) New Riders Pub.

***Mcse Testprep Software: Elective Exams.** Zahn Brown. 48p. 1998. pap. text 49.99 (*1-56205-900-9*) Pearson Educ.

MCSE Top Score Software: Core Exams. Grant Jones et al. 50p. student ed. 49.99 incl. cd-rom (*0-7357-0033-8*) New Riders Pub.

MCSE Training: Windows 98. Joseph Phillips. LC 98-88580. (Training Guides). 1998. 49.99 (*1-56205-890-8*) New Riders Pub.

MCSE Training Guide: Exchange Server 5.0. Macmillan General Reference Staff. 1998. 49.99 (*0-02-865274-6*, Pub. by Macmillan) S&S Trade.

MCSE Training Guide: Internet Explorer 4. Macmillan General Reference Staff. 1998. 49.99 (*0-02-865277-0*, Pub. by Macmillan) S&S Trade.

MCSE Training Guide: Internet Information Sever 4. Macmillan General Reference Staff. 1998. 49.99 (*0-02-865271-1*, Pub. by Macmillan) S&S Trade.

MCSE Training Guide: Microsoft Exchange Server 5.5. Macmillan General Reference Staff. 1998. 49.99 (*0-02-865278-9*, Pub. by Macmillan) S&S Trade.

MCSE Training Guide: Microsoft Exchange Server 5.5. Robert Wallingsford. (MCSE Training Guide Ser.). 1998. 49.99 (*1-56205-899-1*) New Riders Pub.

MCSE Training Guide: Networking Essentials. Macmillan General Reference Staff. 1998. 49.99 (*0-02-865266-5*, Pub. by Macmillan) S&S Trade.

MCSE Training Guide: SQL Server 6.5 Administration. Macmillan General Reference Staff. 1998. 49.99 (*0-02-865275-4*, Pub. by Macmillan) S&S Trade.

MCSE Training Guide: SQL Server 6.5 Design & Implementation. Sean Baird. LC 98-129835. 1997. 49.99 (*1-56205-830-4*) New Riders Pub.

MCSE Training Guide: SQL Server 6.5 Design & Implementation. Macmillan General Reference Staff. 1998. 49.99 (*0-02-865276-2*, Pub. by Macmillan) S&S Trade.

MCSE Training Guide: SQL Server 7 Design & Implementation. New Riders Staff. 1999. pap. 49.99 (*0-7357-0004-4*) New Riders Pub.

MCSE Training Guide: Systems Management Server 1. 2. Macmillan General Reference Staff. 1998. 49.99 (*0-02-865272-X*, Pub. by Macmillan) S&S Trade.

MCSE Training Guide: TCP/IP. 2nd ed. Kelli Adam. LC 98-86323. (Training Guides). 1998. 49.99 (*1-56205-920-3*) New Riders Pub.

MCSE Training Guide: WIndows NT Essentials. 2nd ed. Glenn Berg. LC 98-86317. (Training Guides). 1998. 49.99 (*1-56205-919-X*) New Riders Pub.

MCSE Training Guide: WIndows NT Server $ 2nd ed. Dennis Maione. 1998. 49.99 (*1-56205-916-5*) New Riders Pub.

MCSE Training Guide: Windows NT Server 4. Macmillan General Reference Staff. 1998. 49.99 (*0-02-865267-3*, Pub. by Macmillan) S&S Trade.

MCSE Training Guide: WIndows NT Server 4 Enterprise. 2nd ed. Jason Sirockman. (Training Guides). 1998. 49.99 (*1-56205-917-3*) New Riders Pub.

MCSE Training Guide: Windows NT Workstation. 2nd ed. Dennis Maione. (Training Guides). 1998. 49.99 (*1-56205-918-1*) New Riders Pub.

MCSE Training Guide: Windows NT Workstation 4. Macmillan General Reference Staff. 1998. 49.99 (*0-02-865269-X*, Pub. by Macmillan) S&S Trade.

***MCSE Training Guide: Windows 2000 Accelerated Exam.** 900p. 2000. 59.99 (*0-7357-0979-3*) Macmillan Tech.

***MCSE Training Guide: Windows 2000 Directory Services Administration.** 650p. 2000. 49.99 (*0-7357-0976-9*) Macmillan Tech.

MCSE Training Guide: Windows 2000 Network Infrastructure Administration. 800p. 1900. 49.99 (*0-7357-0966-1*) Macmillan Tech.

***MCSE Training Guide: Windows 2000 Professional.** 650p. 2000. 49.99 (*0-7357-0965-3*) Macmillan Tech.

***MCSE Training Guide: Windows 2000 Server.** 700p. 2000. 49.99 (*0-7357-0968-8*) Macmillan Tech.

MCSE Training Guide: Windows 95. 2nd ed. Macmillan General Reference Staff. 1998. 49.99 (*0-02-865273-8*, Pub. by Macmillan) S&S Trade.

MCSE Training Guide Internet Explorer 4.0. Kenrick Rawlings. LC 98-85226. (MCSE Training Guide Ser.). 1998. pap. text 49.99 (*1-56205-889-4*) New Riders Pub.

MCSE Training Guide Internet Specialist Exams. New Riders Staff. (MCSE Training Guides). 1998. pap. text 99.99 (*1-56205-879-7*) New Riders Pub.

***Mcse Training Guide Windows 2000 Exams.** 1500p. 2000. 89.99 (*0-7357-0967-X*) New Riders Pub.

MCSE Training Guide Windows 95. 2nd ed. Joseph Phillips. (MCSE Training Guides). 700p. 1998. 49.99 (*1-56205-880-0*) New Riders Pub.

MCSE Training Guides: Core Exams. 2nd ed. Dennis Maione. (Training Guides). 1998. 149.99 (*1-56205-926-2*) New Riders Pub.

***MCSE Training Kit: Microsoft Windows 2000 Infrastructure Administration.** Microsoft Corporation Staff. LC 00-24946. (Illus.). 520p. 2000. pap. 59.99 (*1-57231-904-6*) Microsoft.

***MCSE 2000 Exams: TestTaker's Guide.** Timothy L. Warner. (Illus.). 320p. 2000. pap. 31.95 (*1-58450-046-8*) Chrles River Media.

***MCSE 2000 Jumpstart.** Lisa Donald et al. (Illus.). 416p. 2000. pap. text 19.99 (*0-7821-2749-5*, Network Pr) Sybex.

***MCSE Upgrading from Microsoft Windows NT 4.0 to Microsoft Windows 2000 Study Guide: Exam 70-222.** Syngress Media, Inc. Staff. (Global Knowledge Certification Ser.). (Illus.). 2000. 49.99 (*0-07-212711-2*) Osborne-McGraw.

***MCSE Upgrading from NT 4 to 2000 Exam Prep.** Glenn Bergen. (Exam Prep Ser.). 700p. 2000. pap. 49.99 (*1-57610-691-8*) Coriolis Grp.

***MCSE Windows Network Server 4 for Dummies.** 2nd ed. MCSE Majors Staff. (For Dummies Ser.). 504p. 1999. pap. 29.99 incl. cd-rom (*0-7645-0611-0*) IDG Bks.

An Asterisk (*) at the beginning of an entry indicates that the title is appearing for the first time.

***MCSE Windows Network Workstation 4 for Dummies.** 2nd ed. Mike Kendzierski. (For Dummies Ser.). (Illus.). 464p. 1999. pap. 29.99 incl. cd-rom (*0-7645-0612-9*) IDG Bks.

***MCSE Windows Networking Server 4 for Dummies Training Kit.** Dummies Technical Press Staff. (For Dummies Ser.). 568p. 1999. pap. 49.99 incl. cd-rom (*0-7645-0616-1*) IDG Bks.

***MCSE Windows Networking Server 4 in the Enterprise for Dummies.** 2nd ed. Kenneth Majors & Jeffrey E. Ferris. (For Dummies Ser.). (Illus.). 540p. 1999. pap. 29.99 incl. cd-rom (*0-7645-0615-3*) IDG Bks.

***MCSE Windows Networking Server 4 in the Enterprise for Dummies Training Kit.** Dummies Technical Press Staff. (For Dummies Ser.). 604p. 1999. pap. 49.99 incl. cd-rom (*0-7645-0617-X*) IDG Bks.

***MCSE Windows Networking Workstation 4 for Dummies Training Kit.** Dummies Technical Press Staff. (For Dummies Ser.). 528p. 1999. pap. 49.99 incl. cd-rom (*0-7645-0618-8*) IDG Bks.

***MCSE Windows 98 Ace It!** IDG Books Staff. LC QA76.3.S558 1999. (Illus.). 448p. 1998. pap. 24.99 (*0-7645-3297-9*) IDG Bks.

MCSE Windows 98: Study Guide Exam 70-98. Syngress Media, Inc. Staff. Ed. by Duncan Anderson. LC 98-224237. 590p. 1998. student ed. 49.99 incl. cd-rom (*0-07-882532-6*) Osborne-McGraw.

MCSE Windows 95 Exam Cram. Ed Tittel. LC 98-28585. (Exam Cram Ser.). 400p. 1998. pap. 29.99 (*1-57610-287-4*) Coriolis Grp.

MCSE Windows 95 for Dummies. Brian Frederick. (For Dummies Ser.). 448p. 1998. 29.99 incl. cd-rom (*0-7645-0403-7*) IDG Bks.

MCSE Windows NT Server 4 for Dummies. Ken Majors & Bendan MacTague. LC QA76.3.M324 1998. (For Dummies Ser.). 512p. 1998. 29.99 incl. cd-rom (*0-7645-0400-2*) IDG Bks.

MCSE Windows NT Server 4.0: Study Guide Exam 70-67. Syngress Media, Inc. Staff et al. LC 99-462696. (Illus.). 699p. 1998. 49.99 incl. cd-rom (*0-07-882491-5*) Osborne-McGraw.

MCSE Windows NT Server 4.0 in the Enterprise: Study Guide Exam 70-68. Syngress Media, Inc. Staff & Global Knowledge Network Staff. LC 98-160287. (Illus.). 527p. 1998. 49.99 incl. cd-rom (*0-07-882490-7*) Osborne-McGraw.

***MCSE Windows NT Server in the Enterprise 4.0 Certification Exam Guide.** Steve Kaczmarek. (MCSE Certification Ser.). (Illus.). 600p. 1999. pap. 39.99 (*0-7897-2263-1*) Que.

***Mcse Windows Nt Server 4 in the Enterprise For Dummies Flash Cards.** Dummies Technical Press Staff. 250p. 1999. pap. 24.99 incl. cd-rom (*0-7645-0551-3*) IDG Bks.

***MCSE Windows NT Server 4.0 Certification Exam Guide.** 2nd ed. Steve Kaczmarek. (MCSE Certification Ser.). (Illus.). 600p. 1999. pap. 39.99 (*0-7897-2264-X*) Que.

***MCSE Windows NT Workstation Certification Exam Guide.** Steve Kaczmarek. (MCSE Certification Ser.). (Illus.). 1999. pap. 39.99 (*0-7897-2262-3*) Que.

MCSE Windows NT Workstation 4.0 Study Guide: Exam 70-73. Syngress Media, Inc. Staff & Global Knowledge Network Staff. 608p. 1998. 49.99 incl. cd-rom (*0-07-882492-3*) McGraw.

***MCSE Windows NT Workstation 4 for Dummies Flash Cards.** Dummies Technical Press Staff. (For Dummies Ser.). 250p. 1999. pap. 24.99 incl. cd-rom (*0-7645-0553-X*) IDG Bks.

***MCSE Windows NT 4 Server for Dummies Flash Cards.** Dummies Technical Press Staff. (For Dummies Ser.). 250p. 1999. pap. 24.99 incl. cd-rom (*0-7645-0550-5*) IDG Bks.

***MCSE Windows 2000 Directory Services Design Exam Prep.** J. Peter Bruzzese. LC 00-29490. (Exam Prep Ser.). 700p. 2000. pap. write for info. (*1-57610-668-3*) Coriolis Grp.

***MCSE Windows 2000 Accelerated Exam Prep.** Lance Cockcroft et al. (Exam Prep Ser.). (Illus.). 1000p. 2000. pap. 59.99 (*1-57610-690-X*) Coriolis Grp.

***MCSE Windows 2000 Network Design Exam Prep.** Anoop Jalan et al. (Exam Prep Ser.). (Illus.). 800p. 2000. pap. 49.99 (*1-57610-725-6*) Coriolis Grp.

***MCSE Windows 2000 Server Exam Prep.** David Johnson. (Exam Prep Ser.). (Illus.). 2000. pap. 49.99 (*1-57610-696-9*) Coriolis Grp.

***MCSE Windows 2000 Security Design Exam Prep.** Richard Alan McMahon. (Exam Prep Ser.). (Illus.). 800p. 2000. pap. 49.99 (*1-57610-707-8*) Coriolis Grp.

***MCSE Windows 2000 Server for Dummies.** Curt Simmons. (For Dummies Ser.). (Illus.). 504p. 2000. pap. 29.99 incl. cd-rom (*0-7645-0655-2*) IDG Bks.

***MCSE Windows 2000 Network Exam Prep.** Tammy Smith. (Exam Prep Ser.). 700p. 2000. pap. 49.99 (*1-57610-643-8*) Coriolis Grp.

***MCSE Windows 2000 Professional Exam Prep.** Michael D. Stewart et al. (Exam Prep Ser.). (Illus.). 700p. 2000. pap. 49.99 (*1-57610-703-5*) Coriolis Grp.

***MCSE Windows 2000 Master Course.** Ed Tittel et al. (Illus.). 650p. 2000. pap. 49.99 (*1-57610-679-9*) Coriolis Grp.

***MCSE Windows 2000 Accelerated Study Guide: Exam 70-240.** Syngress Media Staff. (Microsoft Certified Systems Engineer Ser.). (Illus.). 752p. 2000. student ed. 49.99 (*0-07-212500-4*) Osborne-McGraw.

***MCSE Windows 2000 Accelerated: Exam 70-240, Set.** Syngress Media, Inc. Staff. (Global Knowledge Certification Ser.). (Illus.). 2000. boxed set 79.99 (*0-07-212690-6*) Osborne-McGraw.

***MCSE Windows 2000 Certification Headstart: (With CD-ROM)** Syngress Media Staff et al. 1141p. 1999. pap., student ed. 59.99 incl. cd-rom (*0-07-212250-1*) McGraw.

***MCSE Windows 2000 Core: Exam 70-210, 70-215, 70-216, 70-217, 4 vols.** Syngress Media, Inc. Staff. (Global Knowledge Certification Ser.). 2000. 159.99 (*0-07-212615-9*) Osborne-McGraw.

***MCSE Windows 2000 Core 4 Exam Guide Kit: Covers Exams 70-210, 70-215, 70-216, 70-217.** Emmett Dulany. (Illus.). 2000. pap. 120.00 (*0-7897-2415-4*) Que.

***MCSE Windows 2000 Core Four Exam Prep Pack.** Ed Tittel. (Illus.). 2000. 159.99 (*1-57610-771-X*) Coriolis Grp.

***MCSE Windows 2000 Directory Services for Dummies.** Marcia Loughry. (For Dummies Ser.). (Illus.). 504p. 2000. pap. 29.99 incl. cd-rom (*0-7645-0710-9*) IDG Bks.

***MCSE Windows 2000 Directory Services Exam Prep.** William Willis. (Exam Prep Ser.). 2000. pap. 49.99 (*1-57610-624-1*) Coriolis Grp.

***MCSE Windows 2000 Network Infrastructure for Dummies.** Glenn Weadock. (For Dummies Ser.). (Illus.). 456p. 2000. pap. 29.99 incl. cd-rom (*0-7645-0711-7*) IDG Bks.

***MCSE Windows 2000 Professional for Dummies.** Glenn Weadock. (For Dummies Ser.). (Illus.). 504p. 2000. pap. 29.99 incl. cd-rom (*0-7645-0653-6*) IDG Bks.

***MCSE Windows 2000 Directory Services Design: Directory Services Design.** 650p. 2000. 49.99 (*0-7357-0983-1*) Macmillan Tech.

***MCSE Windows 2000 Network Security Design: Security Design.** 650p. 2000. 49.99 incl. cd-rom (*0-7357-0984-X*) Macmillan Tech.

***MCSE Windows 95 for Dummies Flash Cards.** Dummies Technical Press Staff. (For Dummies Ser.). 250p. 1999. pap. 24.99 incl. cd-rom (*0-7645-0549-1*) IDG Bks.

MCSE Windows 95 Testing Guide. Sybex, Inc. Staff. LC 98-84539. 368p. 1998. pap. text 39.99 (*0-7821-2252-3*) Sybex.

MCSE Windows 98 Exam Cram. J. Michael Stewart. 400p. 1998. pap. 29.99 (*1-57610-289-0*) Coriolis Grp.

MCSE Windows 98 Exam Prep. Ed Tittel. (Exam Prep Ser.). 700p. 1998. pap. 44.99 (*1-57610-290-4*) Coriolis Grp.

***MCSE Windows 98 for Dummies.** 464p. 1999. pap. 29.99 incl. cd-rom (*0-7645-0483-5*) IDG Bks.

***MCSE Windows 98 for Dummies Flash Cards.** Dummies Technical Press Staff. (For Dummies Ser.). 250p. 2000. pap. 24.99 incl. cd-rom (*0-7645-0630-7*) IDG Bks.

***MCSE Workstation 4 Exam Cram Personal Trainer.** 3rd ed. Ed. by Coriolis Group Staff. (Illus.). 2000. pap. text 69.99 incl. cd-rom (*1-57610-647-0*) Coriolis Grp.

***MCSEMCSE Database Design on SQL Server 7.** Jeffrey Garbus et al. (Exam Cram Ser.). (C). 1999. pap. 29.99 (*0-619-01614-0*) Course Tech.

MCSETraining Guide: SQL Server 7 Administration. New Riders Staff. LC 98-83055. 1999. pap. text 49.99 (*0-7357-0003-6*) New Riders Pub.

MC68020 32-Bit Microprocessor User's Manual. 2nd ed. Motorola, Inc. Staff. 464p. 1986. 21.95 (*0-13-566860-3*) P-H.

MC68HC11: An Introduction, 2E. 2nd ed. Han-Uei Huang & Paula Collins. 720p. 72.95 (*0-7668-1600-1*, Pub. by Delmar) Thomson Learn.

McSpadden. "Way Back When . . ." Happenings We Remember & Genealogies (Descendants of Samuel McSpadden of Tenn. & Related Families) Anna B. McSpadden. (Illus.). 160p. 1998. reprint ed. pap. 14.00 (*0-8328-9683-7*); reprint ed. lib. bdg. 24.00 (*0-8328-9682-9*) Higginson Bk Co.

McSpot's Hidden Spots: A Puppyhood Secret. Laura L. Seeley. LC 93-40514. (Illus.). 32p. (J). (ps-3). 1993. 16.95 (*1-56145-087-1*) Peachtree Pubs.

McSpot's Hidden Spots: A Puppyhood Secret. Laura L. Seeley. (Illus.). (J). (gr. 1-4). 1997. pap. 6.95 (*1-56145-148-7*) Peachtree Pubs.

McTavish & Twins. Trisha David. (Romance Ser.: No. 3494). 1998. per. 3.50 (*0-373-03494-6*, 1-03494-1) Harlequin Bks.

McTavish & Twins. large type ed. Trisha David. (Kids & Kisses Ser.). 1998. per. 3.50 (*0-373-15740-1*, Harlequin) Harlequin Bks.

McTeague. Frank Norris. 1976. lib. bdg. 18.95 (*0-89968-071-2*, Lghtyr Pr) Buccaneer Bks.

McTeague. Frank Norris. Ed. by Carvel Collins. 343p. (C). 1950. pap. text 25.00 (*0-03-009250-7*, Pub. by Harcourt Coll Pubs) Harcourt.

McTeague. unabridged ed. Frank Norris. 201p. 1997. reprint ed. pap. 14.95 (*1-57002-056-6*) Univ Publng Hse.

McTeague: A Story of California. Frank Norris. LC 72-184736. 1971. lib. bdg. 20.00 (*0-8376-0406-0*) Bentley Pubs.

McTeague: A Story of San Francisco. Frank Norris. LC 96-26012. 1996. 17.50 (*0-679-60238-0*) Fodors Travel.

McTeague: A Story of San Francisco. Frank Norris. 1964. mass mkt. 6.95 (*0-451-52421-7*, Sig Classics) NAL.

McTeague: A Story of San Francisco. Frank Norris. Ed. by Donald Pizer. LC 77-479. (C). 1978. pap. text 14.00 (*0-393-09136-8*) Norton.

McTeague: A Story of San Francisco. Frank Norris. Ed. & Intro. by Jerome Loving. 372p. 1996. pap. 9.95 (*0-19-282356-6*) OUP.

McTeague: A Story of San Francisco. Frank Norris. LC 72-184736. 1981. 12.05 (*0-606-03855-8*, Pub. by Turtleback) Demco.

McTeague: A Story of San Francisco. Frank Norris. Ed. & Intro. by Kevin Starr. 496p. 1994. pap. 10.95 (*0-14-018769-3*, Penguin Classics) Viking Penguin.

***Mcteague: A Story of San Francisco.** Frank Norris. Ed. by Jerome Loving. (Oxford World's Classics Ser.). 388p. 2000. pap. 10.95 (*0-19-284059-2*) OUP.

McTeague: A Story of San Francisco. Frank Norris. (BCL1-PS American Literature Ser.). 442p. 1992. reprint ed. lib. bdg. 99.00 (*0-7812-6809-5*) Rprt Serv.

McTeague: A Story of San Francisco: an Authoritative Text, Contexts, Criticism. 2nd ed. Frank Norris. Ed. by Donald Pizer. LC 96-16305. (Critical Editions Ser.). (C). 1996. pap. text 12.50 (*0-393-97013-2*) Norton.

McTeague Vocal Score. 304p. 1995. per. 50.00 (*0-7935-5032-7*, 00313024) H Leonard.

McVeigh is Innocent. Max. (Illus.). 45p. 1997. pap. 35.00 (*0-922070-93-8*) M Tecton Pub.

McVeys. Joseph Kirkland. 1888. reprint ed. 69.00 Somerset Pub.

Mcveys. Joseph Kirkland. (Collected Works of Joseph Kirkland). 1988. reprint ed. lib. bdg. 79.00 (*0-7812-1318-5*) Rprt Serv.

McWhorter History of the Henry McWhorter Family of N. J. & W. Va. Minnie S. McWhorter. (Illus.). 248p. 1995. reprint ed. pap. 39.00 (*0-8328-4804-2*); reprint ed. lib. bdg. 49.00 (*0-8328-4803-4*) Higginson Bk Co.

McWillie & Cunningham Families. R. B. Johnson. 219p. 1991. reprint ed. pap. 33.50 (*0-8328-1931-X*); reprint ed. lib. bdg. 43.50 (*0-8328-1930-1*) Higginson Bk Co.

MD-MBA: Physicians on the New Frontier of Medical Management. Ed. by Arthur Lazarus. LC 97-78156. 240p. 1998. pap. 45.00 (*0-924674-61-X*) Am Coll Phys Execs.

MD Natural Resources 1998 Cumulative Supplement. 167p. 1998. pap. write for info. (*0-327-06459-5*, 2633815, MICHIE) LEXIS Pub.

MDC Shay Handbook. Jeff Johnston. LC 97-23947. 1997. pap. 17.95 (*0-9647521-1-5*) Oso Pubng.

***MDD Compliance Using Quality Management Techniques.** Ray Tricker. LC 99-51579. 590p. 2000. text 115.00 (*0-7506-4441-9*) Buttrwrth-Heinemann.

***MDI, Multiaxial Diagnostic Inventory: Professional Manual.** rev. ed. William F. Doverspike. LC 99-27193. 100p. 1999. pap. 44.45 (*1-56887-051-5*, Prof Resc Pr) Pro Resource.

MDK: The Official Strategy Guide. PCS Staff. 128p. 1997. per. 12.99 (*0-7615-1063-X*) Prima Pub.

***MDK 2 Official Strategies & Secrets.** (Official Strategies & Secrets Ser.). 256p. 2000. pap. text 19.99 (*0-7821-2675-8*) Sybex.

***MDMA - Methylenedioxymethamphetamine.** Ed. by A. C. Parrott. (Neuropsychobiology Ser.: Vol. 42). (Illus.). 50p. 2000. pap. 25.25 (*3-8055-7110-0*) S Karger.

***MDR Domestic 2000, 2 vols. rev. ed. Ed. by Medical Economics Staff. (Illus.). 3500p. 2000. 325.00 (*1-56363-348-5*) Med Econ.**

The only single-source listing of every medical supplier licensed to sell products in the U.S. - with over 1,000 new companies added this year. Fast access to the facts on over 12,000 companies & more than 65,000 products. The 2000 edition contains more ISO 9000 Series Registration & CE-marked device data as well as e-mail & WWW addresses than ever before. Two fully cross-referenced volumes: Volume I - Product Directory: every medical device & supply & diagnostic available in the U.S. Unique 5-character FDA code identifying the medical specialty & the device name; Full company name, address & telephone number for every manufacturer of the product. Prices & product specifications (when available) to help compare products from different suppliers. Volume II - Supplier Profiles: complete background on each company including number of employees, ownership, method of distribution, sales volume, revenue & net income. Handy indexes include Keyword Index, Trade Name Index, Supplier Geographical Index & OEM (Original Equipment Manufacturer) Index. 3,200 pages. Available: January 2000. (Special combo package of WinMDR & MDR print edition also available. ISBN: 1-56363-351-5, $499.00. Call for details.) ***Publisher Paid Annotation.***

MDR Guide to 3D Accelerators: Chips & Companies. Ed. by Peter Glaskowsky. 160p. 1998. spiral bd. 1995.00 (*1-885330-15-4*) MicroDes Res.

***MDR International, 2001.** 1,100p. 2001. 275.00 (*1-56363-384-1*, PDR) Med Econ.

***MDR International, 2000. rev. ed. Ed. by Medical Economics Staff. (Illus.). 1100p. 2000. 275.00 (*1-56363-349-3*, PDR) Med Econ.**

For those interested in medical supplies & companies outside the U.S., this invaluable resource covers more than 7,000 suppliers & 25,000 products from over 70 countries including Canada. Organized in the same easy format as the U.S. edition, the MDR International Edition saves valuable research time. Detailed supplier profile directory includes manufacturer's address & telephone numbers, contracts, financial data, number of employees, method of distribution, a complete list of products available & more. Also includes Trade Name Index & Supplier Geography Index, all cross-referenced, making it easy to quickly find the right companies & products. 1,100 pages. Available: January 2000. ***Publisher Paid Annotation.***

***MDR's School Directories, 1999-2000: Arizona.** 1999. 41.00 (*1-57953-110-5*) Market Data Ret.

***MDR's School Directories, 1999-2000: Arkansas.** 1999. 56.00 (*1-57953-111-3*) Market Data Ret.

***MDR's School Directories, 1999-2000: California.** 1999. 81.00 (*1-57953-112-1*) Market Data Ret.

***MDR's School Directories, 1999-2000: Colorado.** 1999. 56.00 (*1-57953-113-X*) Market Data Ret.

***MDR's School Directories, 1999-2000: Connecticut.** 1999. 56.00 (*1-57953-114-8*) Market Data Ret.

***MDR's School Directories, 1999-2000: Delaware.** 1999. 41.00 (*1-57953-115-6*) Market Data Ret.

***MDR's School Directories, 1999-2000: District of Columbia.** 1999. 41.00 (*1-57953-116-4*) Market Data Ret.

MDR's School Directories, 1998-99: Oregon. 1998. 53.00 (*1-57953-090-7*) Market Data Ret.

***MDR's School Directories, 1999-2000: Alaska.** 1999. 41.00 (*1-57953-109-1*) Market Data Ret.

***MDR's School Directories 1999-2000: Alabama.** 1999. 56.00 (*1-57953-108-3*) Market Data Ret.

***MDR's School Directories, 199-2000: Nevada.** 1999. 41.00 (*1-57953-136-9*) Market Data Ret.

***MDR's School Directories, 1999-2000: Florida.** 1999. 67.00 (*1-57953-117-2*) Market Data Ret.

***MDR's School Directories, 1999-2000: Georgia.** 1999. 56.00 (*1-57953-118-0*) Market Data Ret.

***MDR's School Directories, 1999-2000: Hawaii.** 1999. 41.00 (*1-57953-119-9*) Market Data Ret.

***MDR's School Directories, 1999-2000: Idaho.** 1999. 41.00 (*1-57953-120-2*) Market Data Ret.

***MDR's School Directories, 1999-2000: Illinois.** 1999. 81.00 (*1-57953-121-0*) Market Data Ret.

***MDR's School Directories, 1999-2000: Indiana.** 1999. 56.00 (*1-57953-122-9*) Market Data Ret.

***MDR's School Directories, 1999-2000: Iowa.** 1999. 56.00 (*1-57953-123-7*) Market Data Ret.

***MDR's School Directories, 1999-2000: Kansas.** 1999. 56.00 (*1-57953-124-5*) Market Data Ret.

***MDR's School Directories, 1999-2000: Kentucky.** 1999. 56.00 (*1-57953-125-3*) Market Data Ret.

***MDR's School Directories, 1999-2000: Louisiana.** 1999. 56.00 (*1-57953-126-1*) Market Data Ret.

***MDR's School Directories, 1999-2000: Maine.** 1999. 41.00 (*1-57953-127-X*) Market Data Ret.

***MDR's School Directories, 1999-2000: Maryland.** 1999. 56.00 (*1-57953-128-8*) Market Data Ret.

***MDR's School Directories, 1999-2000: Massachusetts.** 1999. 67.00 (*1-57953-129-6*) Market Data Ret.

***MDR's School Directories, 1999-2000: Michigan.** 1999. 67.00 (*1-57953-130-X*) Market Data Ret.

***MDR's School Directories, 1999-2000: Minnesota.** 1999. 67.00 (*1-57953-131-8*) Market Data Ret.

***MDR's School Directories, 1999-2000: Mississippi.** 1999. 56.00 (*1-57953-132-6*) Market Data Ret.

***MDR's School Directories, 1999-2000: Missouri.** 1999. 56.00 (*1-57953-133-4*) Market Data Ret.

***MDR's School Directories, 1999-2000: Montana.** 1999. 41.00 (*1-57953-134-2*) Market Data Ret.

***MDR's School Directories, 1999-2000: National Set, 51 vols.** 1999. 1260.00 (*1-57953-160-1*) Market Data Ret.

***MDR's School Directories, 1999-2000: Nebraska.** 1999. 56.00 (*1-57953-135-0*) Market Data Ret.

***MDR's School Directories, 1999-2000: New Hampshire.** 1999. 41.00 (*1-57953-137-7*) Market Data Ret.

***MDR's School Directories, 1999-2000: New Jersey.** 1999. 67.00 (*1-57953-138-5*) Market Data Ret.

***MDR's School Directories, 1999-2000: New Mexico.** 1999. 41.00 (*1-57953-139-3*) Market Data Ret.

***MDR's School Directories, 1999-2000: New York.** 1999. 81.00 (*1-57953-140-7*) Market Data Ret.

***MDR's School Directories, 1999-2000: North Carolina.** 1999. 56.00 (*1-57953-141-5*) Market Data Ret.

***MDR's School Directories, 1999-2000: North Dakota.** 1999. 41.00 (*1-57953-142-3*) Market Data Ret.

***MDR's School Directories, 1999-2000: Ohio.** 1999. 67.00 (*1-57953-143-1*) Market Data Ret.

***MDR's School Directories, 1999-2000: Oklahoma.** 1999. 56.00 (*1-57953-144-X*) Market Data Ret.

***MDR's School Directories, 1999-2000: Oregon.** 1999. 56.00 (*1-57953-145-8*) Market Data Ret.

***MDR's School Directories, 1999-2000: Pennsylvania.** 1999. 67.00 (*1-57953-146-6*) Market Data Ret.

***MDR's School Directories, 1999-2000: Rhode Island.** 1999. 41.00 (*1-57953-147-4*) Market Data Ret.

***MDR's School Directories, 1999-2000: Sales Manager's Guide.** rev. ed. 400p. 1999. 130.00 (*1-57953-159-8*) Market Data Ret.

***MDR's School Directories, 1999-2000: South Carolina.** 1999. 56.00 (*1-57953-148-2*) Market Data Ret.

***MDR's School Directories, 1999-2000: South Dakota.** 1999. 41.00 (*1-57953-149-0*) Market Data Ret.

***MDR's School Directories, 1999-2000: Tennessee.** 1999. 56.00 (*1-57953-150-4*) Market Data Ret.

***MDR's School Directories, 1999-2000: Texas.** 1999. 81.00 (*1-57953-151-2*) Market Data Ret.

***MDR's School Directories, 1999-2000: Utah.** 1999. 41.00 (*1-57953-152-0*) Market Data Ret.

***MDR's School Directories, 1999-2000: Vermont.** 1999. 41.00 (*1-57953-153-9*) Market Data Ret.

***MDR's School Directories, 1999-2000: Virginia.** 1999. 56.00 (*1-57953-154-7*) Market Data Ret.

***MDR's School Directories, 1999-2000: Washington.** 1999. 56.00 (*1-57953-155-5*) Market Data Ret.

***MDR's School Directories, 1999-2000: West Virginia.** 1999. 41.00 (*1-57953-156-3*) Market Data Ret.

***MDR's School Directories, 1999-2000: Wisconsin.** 1999. 56.00 (*1-57953-157-1*) Market Data Ret.

M

***MDR's School Directories, 1999-2000: Wyoming.** 1999. 41.00 (*1-57953-158-X*) Market Data Ret.

MDRT Annuity Sales Manual. 2nd rev. ed. MDRT Annuity Task Force Staff. 220p. 1998. ring bd. 225.00 (*1-891042-00-9*) Million Dollar.

MDS Gold: Resident Assessment Instrument Training Manual - Colorado Edition. Eliot Press Staff. (C). (gr. 13). 1994. 16.95 (*0-9628976-2-0*, 26934) Eliot Pr.

Mds+ Multistate Nursing Home Case Mix & Quality Demo Training Manual (Dk Blue) Eliot Press Staff. (C). (gr. 13). 1991. 31.95 (*0-9628976-1-2*, 25278) Eliot Pr.

Mds+ Multistate Nursing Home Case Mix & Quality Demo Training Manual (Green) Eliot Press Staff. (YA). (gr. 12). 1992. pap. text 31.95 (*0-9628976-3-9*, 25279) Eliot Pr.

Mds+ Reference Manual (Lt Blue) Eliot Press Staff. (C). (gr. 13). 1993. 34.95 (*0-9628976-4-7*, 25281) Eliot Pr.

MDT Innovation: Machine Scoring of Fill-in-the-Blank Tests. Paul S. Anderson. (Illus.). 198p. 1987. pap. text 9.95 (*0-940387-01-8*); pap. text 14.95 (*0-317-60239-X*) Multi Digit Tech.

Me. Barbara J. Crane. (Crane Reading System-English Ser.). (Illus.). (gr. k-2). 1977. pap. text 4.85 (*0-89075-092-0*) Bilingual Ed Serv.

Me. Ed. by Christine J. Dillon. (My First Report Ser.). (Illus.). 44p. (J). (gr. 1-3). 1993. ring bd. 5.95 (*1-57896-002-9*, 1766) Hewitt Res Fnd.

Me. Katharine Hepburn. 1996. pap. 15.00 (*0-345-41009-2*) Ballantine Pub Grp.

Me. Abel Telles. 1997. pap. write for info. (*1-57553-504-1*) Watermrk Pr.

Me. Brenda Ueland. Ed. by Annette K. Baxter. LC 79-8819. (Signal Lives Ser.). (Illus.). 1980. reprint ed. lib. bdg. 40.95 (*0-405-12863-0*) Ayer.

Me: A Book of Remembrance. LC 96-52517. 1997. 45.00 (*0-87805-991-1*); pap. 17.00 (*0-87805-992-X*) U Pr of Miss.

Me: A Memoir. Brenda Ueland. 364p. 1994. pap. 14.95 (*0-930100-56-5*) Holy Cow.

Me! A Photo Memory Album. 1997. 15.99 (*1-57977-208-0*) Havoc Pub.

Me: By Jimmy (Big Boy) Valente. Told to Garrison Keillor. LC 99-19813. (Illus.). 152p. 1999. 15.95 (*0-670-88796-X*, Viking) Viking Penguin.

Me: Five Years from Now - The Life-Planning Book You Write Yourself. Sheree Bykofsky. 224p. 1999. pap. 12.95 (*0-7868-8391-X*, Pub. by Hyperion) Time Warner.

***Me: Jimmy (Big Boy) Valente, 2.** abr. ed. Garrison Keillor. 1999. audio 18.95 (*1-56511-327-6*, Pub. by HighBridge) Penguin Putnam.

Me: Stories of My Life. large type ed. Katharine Hepburn. 1992. pap. 22.00 (*0-679-74245-X*) Random Hse Lrg Prnt.

Me: Understanding Myself & Others. Audrey Riker. 1977. 11.96 (*0-02-665070-3*) Glencoe.

Me: Understanding Myself & Others. Audrey Riker. 1977. teacher ed. 14.85 (*0-02-665080-0*); student ed. 7.37 (*0-02-665090-8*) Glencoe.

***Me? A Missionary?** Millie Crouch. (Illus.). 123p. 1999. pap. 8.95 (*1-888796-17-0*) ABWE Pubng.

Me? Marry You? Lori Herter. 1997. per. 3.50 (*0-373-52035-2*, 1-52035-2) Silhouette.

Me , Minerva & the Flying Flora see Me, Minerva & the Flying Car: Going to Washington, D. C.

Me? Obey Him see Yo? Obedecer a Mi Marido?

Me, a Gourmet Cook? Carolyn Coats. (Illus.). 136p. 1985. 10.00 (*1-878722-02-6*) C Coats Bestsellers.

"Me" a Personal Journal: Journals Unlimited. Barbara Morina. (Write It down Ser.: Vol. 8). (Illus.). 202p. 1998. 19.95 (*1-892033-07-0*) Jrnls Unltd.

Me, a Submissive Wife. Glover Shipp. pap. 7.95 (*1-56794-206-7*) Star Bible.

***Me Against My Brother: At War in Somalia, Sudan & Rwanda.** Scott Peterson. LC 99-56411. (Illus.). 352p. 2000. 27.50 (*0-415-92198-8*) Routledge.

Me Ah P'Amin V'Echad - Aside (1,000 Times & 1 Future Tense) Dikduk L'Talmidim (Grammar for Students) Kalman Bachrach. (HEB.). 46p. (J). (gr. 1-3). 1937. pap. text 1.00 (*1-878530-21-6*) K Bachrach Co.

Me All Over: Memoirs of a Misfit. James Kirkup. 239p. 1994. 37.00 (*0-7206-0902-X*, Pub. by P Owen Ltd) Dufour.

***Me, Amazon Woman: What Every Woman Needs to Know about LCIS Breast Cancer.** Kim Davies. LC 00-103196. 208p. 2000. pap. 18.95 (*1-886289-24-7*) Three Pyramids.

Me, An Evangelist? Every Christian's Guide to Caring Evangelism. William J. McKay. 1992. pap. text 11.95 (*0-9633831-0-8*) Stephen Minist.

Me an' Shorty. Clarence E. Mulford. 1976. 23.95 (*0-88411-223-3*) Amereon Ltd.

Me & Adolf. Sherman E. Keller. LC 95-68444. (Illus.). 1996. 14.95 (*0-8158-0515-2*) Chris Mass.

Me & Alves: A Japanese Journey. Terumasa Akio. Tr. by Susan Matsui. (Illus.). 24p. (J). 1993. pap. 4.95 (*1-55037-222-X*, Pub. by Annick); lib. bdg. 14.95 (*1-55037-223-8*, Pub. by Annick) Firefly Bks Ltd.

Me & Bear: Finding a Best Friend. Jacqueline Joyce. (Illus.). 40p. (J). (ps-4). 1998. pap. 7.95 (*0-614-31256-6*, 11149) Bear Path.

***Me & Belinda Gillis.** Amanda Isaacs. 22p. (J). (gr. 5-9). 1999. 12.95 (*1-929409-04-4*) Blade Pubg.

***Me & Big Joe.** Michael Bloomfield & Scott Summerville. (Illus.). 60p. 1999. reprint ed. pap. 5.99 (*1-889307-05-X*, Pub. by RE Search) Subterranean Co.

Me & Bigfoot. Les Smith. (Western Americana Bks.). (Illus.). (Orig.). 2000. pap. 15.00 (*0-913626-20-1*) S S S Pub Co.

Me & Brenda. Philip Israel. 224p. 1992. reprint ed. pap. 9.00 (*0-380-71537-6*, Avon Bks) Morrow Avon.

Me & Brother Jesus: A Manic Depressive's Story. Olivia W. Cross. LC 88-71869. 200p. (Orig.). 1988. pap. 5.00 (*0-685-44502-X*) Cross Pubns.

Me & Buck. Dave Sargent. Ed. by Debbie Bowen. (Illus.). (J). (gr. k-8). pap. text 8.95 (*1-56763-070-7*); lib. bdg. 18.95 (*1-56763-069-3*) Ozark Pub.

Me & Dad. Mouse Works Staff. (J). 1995. 6.98 (*1-57082-191-7*, Pub. by Mouse Works) Little.

Me & DiMaggio: A Baseball Fan Goes in Search of His Gods. Christopher Lehmann-Haupt. LC 97-30433. 304p. 1998. reprint ed. pap. 14.95 (*1-55821-623-5*) Lyons Pr.

Me & Effie. Susan Rose. 47p. Date not set. pap. 8.95 (*1-879934-09-4*) St Andrews NC.

Me & Einstein: Breaking Through the Reading Barrier. Rose Blue. (Illus.). (J). (gr. 3 up). 1984. 16.95 (*0-87705-388-X*, Kluwer Acad Hman Sci); pap. 10.95 (*0-89885-185-8*, Kluwer Acad Hman Sci) Kluwer Academic.

***Me & Hank: A Boy & His Hero, Twenty Five Years Later.** Sandy Tolan. LC 00-26484. (Illus.). 224p. 2000. 23.50 (*0-684-87130-0*) Free Pr.

Me & Hitch. Evan Hunter. LC 98-120299. 86p. 1997. pap. 12.95 (*0-571-19306-4*) Faber & Faber.

***Me & Jeshua.** Eleanor Spence. LC 00-9084. (J). 2000. pap. write for info. (*0-88489-671-4*) St Marys.

Me & Jezebel: 1-Person & 2-Person Version. Elizabeth L. Fuller. LC 96-129374. 1995. pap. 5.25 (*0-8222-1498-9*) Dramatists Play.

***Me & Johnny Blue: A Novel of the American West.** Joseph West. 352p. 2000. mass mkt. 5.99 (*0-451-20017-9*, Sig) NAL.

Me & Juliet. (Vocal Score Ser.). 184p. 1981. per. 45.00 (*0-88188-033-7*, 00312255) H Leonard.

Me & Juliet: Vocal Selections. (Illus.). 40p. 1986. pap. 8.95 (*0-88188-601-7*, 00312256) H Leonard.

Me & Kev. Simon Black. LC 93-70995. 263p. 1993. 20.00 (*1-880909-08-1*) Baskerville.

Me & Mario Cuomo: Conversations in Candor. Alan S. Chartock. LC 95-706. 304p. 1995. pap. 14.00 (*1-56980-056-1*) Barricade Bks.

Me & Me. Jane Seymour & James Keach. (This One 'n That One Bks.). (Illus.). 20p. (J). (ps). 1999. 3.99 (*0-399-23376-8*) Putnam Pub Group.

Me & Mine. Daniel Brewster. 31p. 1997. pap. 15.95 (*0-9666484-0-4*) Dimby Co.

Me & Mine: The Life Story of Helen Sekaquaptewa As Told to Louise Udall. Louise Udall. LC 68-54714. (Illus.). 262p. 1969. pap. 13.95 (*0-8165-0270-6*) U of Ariz Pr.

***Me & Mr. Mah.** Andrea Spalding. LC 99-63059. (Illus.). 32p. (J). (ps-3). 2000. 14.95 (*1-55143-168-8*) Orca Bk Pubs.

Me & Morton. Sylvia Cassedy. LC 85-48251. (Trophy Bk.). 320p. (J). (gr. 4-7). 1989. pap. 3.95 (*0-06-440306-8*, HarpTrophy) HarpC Child Bks.

Me & Mr. Stenner. Evan Hunter & Ed McBain. LC 76-24810. (J). (gr. 4-7). 1976. 11.95 (*0-397-31689-5*) HarpC Child Bks.

Me & My Amazing Body. Joan Sweeney. LC 98-34628. (Illus.). 32p. (J). (gr. k-3). 1999. 13.00 (*0-517-80053-5*, Pub. by Crown Bks Yng Read); lib. bdg. 14.99 (*0-517-80054-3*, Pub. by Crown Bks Yng Read) Random.

***Me & My Amazing Body.** Joan Sweeney. (Illus.). 32p. (J). (gr. k-3). 2000. pap. 6.99 (*0-375-80623-7*, Pub. by Knopf Bks Yng Read) Random.

Me & My Baby View the Eclipse. Lee Smith. 1997. pap. 11.00 (*0-345-41910-3*) Ballantine Pub Grp.

Me & My Bean Bag. (J). 10.95 incl. audio (*0-937124-21-4*, KIM 9111C) Kimbo Educ.

Me & My Bear. Margaret Miller. (Illus.). 14p. (J). (ps-3). 1999. bds. 4.99 (*0-689-82355-X*, 076714004993) Litle Simon.

Me & My Big Mouth! Larry Adler. 1996. mass mkt. 5.99 (*1-85782-087-8*, Pub. by Blake Publng) Seven Hills Bk.

Me & My Big Mouth! Your Answer Is Right under Your Nose. Joyce Meyer. LC 97-141734. 288p. pap. 13.99 (*0-89274-969-5*) Harrison Hse.

***Me & My Big Mouth Study Guide.** Joyce Meyer. 2000. pap. 12.99 (*1-57794-218-3*) Harrison Hse.

Me & My Black Angels. Jeffery G. Sylvester. LC 96-70313. 160p. (Orig.). 1996. pap. 12.95 (*0-9653943-0-1*) Empty Wagon.

Me & My Body. Rosie McCormick & Anthony Lewis. LC 97-39705. (Fun Finding Out Ser.). (Illus.). 32p. (J). (ps-3). 1998. 12.95 (*0-7534-5126-3*) LKC.

Me & My Body. Rosie Mccormick & Anthony Lewis. LC 97-39705. (Fun Finding Out Ser.). (J). (ps-1). 1998. pap. 9.95 (*0-7534-5127-1*) LKC.

***Me & My Body.** rev. ed. (Ladders Ser.). (Illus.). (J). 2000. 4.95 (*1-58728-614-9*); pap. 4.95 (*1-58728-603-3*) Two Can Pub.

Me & My Bubby, My Zeidy & Me. Yaffa Gauz. (J). 1991. 12.95 (*0-87306-543-3*) Feldheim.

***Me & My Cat?** Satoshi Kitamura. LC 99-16598. (Illus.). 40p. (J). (ps-3). 2000. 16.00 (*0-374-34906-1*) FS&G.

Me & My Cat: A Feline Family Album. Stephen Baker. (Illus.). 144p. 1992. mass mkt. 12.99 (*0-446-39455-6*, Pub. by Warner Bks) Little.

Me & My Dad. LC 96-124461. (Storybook Ser.). (Illus.). 32p. (J). 1994. 6.98 (*1-57082-154-2*, Pub. by Mouse Works) Time Warner.

***Me & My Dad.** Stuart Hample. LC 99-21249. (Illus.). 96p. 1999. pap. 7.95 (*0-7611-1574-9*) Workman Pub.

Me & My Dad. Ed. by Debby Slier. (Baby Photo Board Bks.). (Illus.). 28p. (J). (ps). 1990. 2.95 (*1-56288-380-1*) Checkerboard.

***Me & My Dog.** Barbara Henning. (Poetry New York Pamphlet Ser.: No. 23). 23p. 1999. pap. 5.00 (*0-923389-39-3*) Meet Eyes Bind.

Me & My Family Tree. Joan Sweeney. (Illus.). 32p. (J). (gr. k-3). 1998. lib. bdg. 14.99 (*0-517-70967-8*, Pub. by Crown Bks Yng Read) Random.

Me & My Family Tree. Joan Sweeney. (Illus.). 32p. (J). (gr. k-3). 1999. 13.00 (*0-517-70966-X*, Pub. by Crown Bks Yng Read) Random.

***Me & My Family Tree.** Joan Sweeney. (Illus.). 32p. (J). (gr. k-3). 2000. pap. 6.99 (*0-517-88597-2*, Pub. by Crown Bks Yng Read) Random.

Me & My Family Tree. Carole B. Weatherford. (Illus.). 12p. (J). (ps-k). 1996. 5.95 (*0-86316-251-7*) Writers & Readers.

Me & My Friend. Gillian Plowman. 1990. pap. 5.95 (*0-87129-140-1*, M78) Dramatic Pub.

Me & My Friends. Carole Rollins. (Illus.). 36p. (J). (gr. k-3). 1996. 14.95 (*1-889862-00-2*); pap. 9.95 (*1-889862-01-0*) ECF.

Me & My Grandma. Ed. by Debby Slier. (Baby Photo Board Bks.). (Illus.). 28p. (J). (ps). 1992. bds. 2.95 (*1-56288-183-3*) Checkerboard.

Me & My Grandpa. Ed. by Debby Slier. (Baby Photo Board Bks.). (Illus.). 28p. (J). (ps). 1992. bds. 2.95 (*1-56288-182-5*) Checkerboard.

Me & My Job: A Career Awareness Program for Grades 2-4. rev. ed. Arden Martenz. LC 96-79716. (Illus.). (Orig.). (J). (gr. 2-4). 1997. pap. 10.95 (*1-57543-017-7*) Mar Co Prods.

Me & My Little Brain. John D. Fitzgerald. 144p. (J). (gr. 4-7). 1972. pap. 3.99 (*0-440-45533-2*, YB BDD) BDD Bks Young Read.

***Me & My Little Brain.** John D. Fitzgerald. (Illus.). (J). 2000. 6.99 (*0-8037-2592-2*, Dial Yng Read) Peng Put Young Read.

Me & My Little Brain. John D. Fitzgerald. (J). 1971. 9.09 (*0-606-03953-8*, Pub. by Turtleback) Demco.

Me & My Million. Clive King. LC 78-22501. (J). (gr. 5 up). 1979. lib. bdg. 12.89 (*0-690-03972-7*) HarpC Child Bks.

Me & My Mom. Marianne Hauser. (Sun & Moon Classics Ser.: No. 36). 78p. (Orig.). 1993. pap. 9.95 (*1-55713-175-9*) Sun & Moon CA.

Me & My Mom. Ed. by Debby Slier. (Baby Photo Board Bks.). (Illus.). 28p. (J). (ps). 1990. 2.95 (*1-56288-379-8*) Checkerboard.

Me & My Monkey. David Morrison. Date not set. write for info. (*0-385-48274-4*) Doubleday.

Me & My Pain: The Challenges of Chronic Pain. Abbey Strauss. 139p. 1998. pap. text 16.00 (*0-9663168-0-0*) A Strauss.

Me & My Pet, 4 vols., Set. (J). 1998. write for info. (*0-7166-7513-7*) World Bk.

Me & My Pet Cat. Christine Morley & Carole Orbell. LC 96-60459. (Me & My Pet Ser.). (Illus.). 32p. (J). (gr. 1-5). 1997. 10.00 (*0-7166-1749-8*) World Bk.

Me & My Pet Dog. Christine Morley & Carole Orbell. LC 96-60458. (Me & My Pet Ser.). (Illus.). 32p. (J). (gr. 1-5). 1997. write for info. (*0-7166-1747-1*) World Bk.

Me & My Pet Fish. Christine Morley & Carole Orbell. LC 96-50421. (Me & My Pet Ser.). (Illus.). 32p. (J). (gr. k-4). 1997. write for info. (*0-7166-1795-1*) World Bk.

Me & My Pet Rabbit. Christine Morley & Carole Orbell. LC 96-50420. (Me & My Pet Ser.). (Illus.). 32p. (J). (gr. 1-4). 1997. write for info. (*0-7166-1797-8*) World Bk.

Me & My Place in Space. Joan Sweeney. 1999. pap. 6.99 (*0-517-88590-5*) Crown Pub Group.

Me & My RC. Paul Bates et al. (Illus.). 84p. (Orig.). 1989. pap. 8.00 (*1-56046-128-4*) Interact Pubs.

Me & My Shadow. Devra Newberger Speregen. (J). 1995. pap. 3.99 (*0-590-85310-4*) Scholastic Inc.

***Me & My Shadow: Living with Multiple Sclerosis.** Carole Mackie & Sue Brattle. 224p. 1999. 24.95 (*1-85410-627-9*, Pub. by Aurum Press Ltd) London Brdge.

Me & My Shadows. large type ed. Lorna Luft. LC 98-35559. 1998. 26.95 (*0-7862-1623-9*) Thorndike Pr.

Me & My Shadows. unabridged ed. Lorna Luft. 1998. pap. 25.00 incl. audio (*0-671-58243-7*, Audioworks) S&S Trade.

Me & My Shadows: A Family Memior - Living with the Legacy of Judy Garland. Lorna Luft. 352p. 1998. 25.00 (*0-671-01899-X*, PB Hardcover) PB.

Me & My Shadows: A Family Memoir. rev. ed. Lorna Luft. (Illus.). 432p. 2000. pap. 14.00 (*0-671-01900-7*, PB Trade Paper) PB.

***Me & My Sister.** Mary Rodio. (J). (gr. k-3). 1999. pap. 5.95 (*0-533-13125-1*) Vantage.

Me & My Veggies. Issac Whitlatch. LC 87-2920. (Books for Students by Students). (Illus.). 24p. (J). (gr. 1-7). 1987. lib. bdg. 15.95 (*0-933849-16-8*) Landmark Edns.

Me & My World. 88p. 1996. pap. 11.23 (*0-8442-9000-9*) NTC Contemp Pub Co.

Me & My World. Rosie McCormick & Anthony Lewis. LC 97-39704. (Fun Finding Out Ser.). (J). (ps-1). 1998. pap. 9.95 (*0-7534-5129-8*) LKC.

Me & My World. Alexandra Parsons. LC 95-37521. (Life Education Ser.). (Illus.). 32p. (J). (gr. 5-8). 1996. lib. bdg. 19.00 (*0-531-14375-9*) Watts.

Me & My World: Literature Set, 6 stories. Ed. by L. Johnson. (Graphic Learning Integrated Social Studies Ser.). (ENG & SPA., Illus.). (J). 1993. 260.00 (*0-87746-318-2*) Graphic Learning.

Me & My World: Teachers Manual. Beth Lyons. (Graphic Learning Integrated Social Studies Ser.). 200p. 1997. teacher ed. 125.00 (*0-87746-364-6*) Graphic Learning.

Me & My World Multimedia Picture Dictionary with CD-ROM. (Illus.). 16p. (J). 1995. pap. 39.95 incl. cd-rom (*0-8442-0885-X*, 0885x, Passprt Bks) NTC Contemp Pub Co.

Me & Nana. Leslie Kimmelman. LC 89-29411. (Illus.). 32p. (J). (ps-3). 1990. 12.95 (*0-06-023166-1*) HarpC Child Bks.

Me & Nu: Childhood at Coole. Anne Gregory. (Illus.). 128p. 1990. pap. 12.95 (*0-86140-010-0*, Pub. by Smyth) Dufour.

Me & Other Great Hunters. Ted Knuckey. LC 98-85964. 325p. 1998. 25.00 (*0-7388-0005-8*); pap. 15.00 (*0-7388-0038-4*) Xlibris Corp.

Me & Rupert Goody. Barbara O'Connor. LC 98-30235. 112p. (YA). (gr. 4-7). 1999. 15.00 (*0-374-34904-5*, Frances Foster) FS&G.

***Me & Ted Against the World: The Unauthorized Story of the Founding of CNN.** Reese Schonfeld. (Illus.). 288p. 2000. 25.00 (*0-06-019746-3*, Cliff Street) HarperTrade.

***Me & the Education of Johnnie Negro.** 393p. 1999. per. 16.00 (*0-9671244-1-7*) Chicago Ave Pubns.

***Me & the Education of Johnnie Negro.** John F. Coffey. LC 00-190845. 372p. 2000. 25.00 (*0-7388-2018-0*); pap. 18.00 (*0-7388-2019-9*) Xlibris Corp.

Me & the End of the World. William Corbin. LC 90-2355. 256p. (YA). (gr. 5-9). 1991. pap. 15.00 (*0-671-74223-X*) S&S Bks Yung.

Me And The Fat Man. Julie Myerson. LC 98-37747. 224p. 1999. 23.95 (*0-88001-649-3*) HarpC.

Me & the Geezer: A True Story about Growing up in Little League Style. Ron Carter. LC 95-51021. 176p. (Orig.). (J). 1996. pap. write for info. (*0-9643672-2-X*) Harbour Bks.

Me & the Jolly Green Giant. Donal L. White & David Burrows. (J). (gr. 6-9). 1995. pap. 9.99 (*0-88092-293-1*) Royal Fireworks.

Me & the Law. Lindell Cline. 504p. 1995. 24.95 (*0-9644042-0-6*) Voice Common People.

Me & the Model T. Roscoe Sheller. Ed. by Dorothy Churchill. (Illus.). 217p. 1988. reprint ed. pap. 9.95 (*0-8323-0410-7*) Binford Mort.

***Me & the Time of My Life.** Joan Sweeney. LC 99-22311. (Illus.). 32p. (J). (gr. k-3). 2000. lib. bdg. 14.99 (*0-517-80056-X*) Crown Pub Group.

Me & Thee. Charles Horine. 1966. pap. 5.25 (*0-8222-0742-7*) Dramatists Play.

Me & Uncle Mike & the 3-Toed Bear. Dannel Roberts. (Illus.). 36p. (J). (gr. k-5). 1999. 14.95 (*1-893459-00-4*) Lions & Tigers.

Me & You. Margaret Diehl. LC 89-21958. 265p. 1990. 18.95 (*0-939149-31-1*) Soho Press.

Me & You. Ed. by John Robson. (Illus.). 48p. (Orig.). (J). (gr. 6-9). 1982. pap. 2.50 (*0-936098-33-3*) Intl Marriage.

***Me & You: Mother-Daughter Album.** Lisa Thiesing. 32p. (J). (ps-k). 2000. pap. 4.99 (*0-7868-1433-0*, Pub. by Disney Pr) Time Warner.

Me & You: Mother-Daughter Album. Lisa Thiesing. LC 97-27986. 32p. (J). (ps-k). 1998. lib. bdg. 15.49 (*0-7868-2338-0*, Pub. by Hyprn Child) Little.

Me & You: Mother-Daughter Album. Lisa Thiesing. LC 97-27986. 32p. (J). (ps-4). 1998. 14.95 (*0-7868-0358-4*, Pub. by Hyprn Child) Time Warner.

Me & You & the Hits of Kenny Chesney. Ed. by Jennette DeLisa. (Illus.). 44p. (Orig.). 1997. pap. text 16.95 (*1-57623-972-1*, PF9714) Wrner Bros.

Me 'ayin U-Le'An: Whence & Whither. R A Braudes. (Literaria Judaica Section Ser.: No. 7). 47.50 (*0-404-13860-8*) AMS Pr.

Me Book: An Illustrated Manual for Being Human. Susan Collins. LC 84-60763. (Illus.). 226p. 1986. pap. 9.95 (*0-915677-24-5*) Roundtable Pub.

Me (Boy) Bridiging School to Home Series C. large type ed. Terry Tonon. (Illus.). 8p. (J). (gr. k-1). 1998. pap. 3.95 (*1-57874-016-9*, Kaeden) Kaeden Corp.

Me, Candido! Walt Anderson. 1958. pap. 5.25 (*0-8222-0743-5*) Dramatists Play.

Me Case Con un Principe: (I Married a Prince) Kathryn Jensen. (Deseo Ser.: Bk. 145). (SPA.). 1999. per. 3.50 (*0-373-35275-1*, 1-35275-6) Harlequin Bks.

***Me Com' Back.** Magnolia Holiday. LC 99-66235. 69p. 1999. pap. 6.95 (*0-9611952-8-2*, 122P) Magnolia Prodns.

***Me, Cookie!** Naomi Kleinberg. (Sesame Street Pop-up Ser.). 1999. 2.99 (*0-375-80404-8*) Random.

Me Counting Time: From Seconds to Centuries. Joan Sweeney. LC 99-22311. (Illus.). 32p. (J). (gr. k-3). 2000. 12.95 (*0-517-80055-1*, Pub. by Crown Bks Yng Read) Random.

Me, Dad & Number Six. Dana A. Jennings. LC 93-43640. (Illus.). 32p. (J). 1997. 15.00 (*0-15-200085-2*, Gulliver Bks) Harcourt.

Me Darlin' Dublin's Dead & Gone. Bill Kelly. 180p. 1987. pap. 8.95 (*1-85371-002-4*, Pub. by Poolbeg Pr) Dufour.

Me Dijo Que No Se Lo Contara a Nadie: He Told Me Not to Tell: A Parent's Guide in Spanish for Talking to Children about Sexual Abuse. KCRR Staff & Jennifer Fay. Tr. by Sam Mark. (Illus.). 28p. (Orig.). 1979. pap. 2.50 (*0-941953-01-7*) KCSA Res Ctr.

Me Dying Trial. Patricia Powell. (Caribbean Writers Ser.). 192p. 1993. pap. 9.95 (*0-435-98935-9*, 98935) Heinemann.

Me Esteem Creates We Esteem: A Meland " Do It" Book. Eva Thayer. (Illus.). 65p. (Orig.). (J). (gr. 5-12). 1990. pap., student ed. 8.00 (*0-9616432-3-4*) Tes Pub.

Me Fecit Solingen. Albert W. Greenwade. LC 87-91043.Tr. of Soligen Made Me. 270p. 1988. 24.95 (*0-9618873-0-3*) Johnson Ref Bks.

Me First. Helen Lester. LC 91-45808. (Illus.). 32p. (J). (ps up). 1992. 15.00 (*0-395-58706-9*) HM.

Me First. Helen Lester. LC 91-45808. (Illus.). 32p. (J). (gr. k-3). 1995. pap. 5.95 (*0-395-72022-2*, Sandpiper) HM.

Me First. Helen Lester. (J). 1992. 11.15 (*0-606-07855-X*) Turtleback.

Me First, Me First. Stan Berenstain & Jan Berenstain. (Board Bks.). 7p. (J). 1999. pap. 3.99 (*0-679-89332-6*, Pub. by Random Bks Yng Read) Random.

An Asterisk (*) at the beginning of an entry indicates that the title is appearing for the first time.

Me Gusta Sonar. Jack Perricone. (Illus.). 16p. (J). (ps-2). 1993. lib. bdg. 10.95 (*1-879567-17-2*, Valeria Bks) Wonder Well.
*__Me Gustaria Tener...__ Alma Flor Ada. (SPA.). (gr. k-3). 2000. pap. 5.95 (*1-58105-194-8*) Santillana.
Me Gustaria Tener (How Happy I Would Be) Alma F. Ada. (Libros para Contar/Stories for the Telling Ser.). (SPA., Illus.). (J). (gr. k-1). 1989. pap. 5.95 (*0-88272-795-8*); pap. 5.95 (*0-88272-804-0*) Santillana.
Me Gustaria Tener (How Happy I Would Be), Big Book. Alma F. Ada. (Libros para Contar/Stories for the Telling Ser.). (SPA., Illus.). (J). (gr. k-1). 1989. 18.95 (*0-88272-796-6*); 18.95 (*0-88272-805-9*) Santillana.
Me Gusto Como Soy. Nancy Carlson. LC 96-39622.Tr. of I Like Me!. (SPA.). 32p. (J). (ps-2). 1997. 14.99 (*0-670-86960-0*) Penguin Putnam.
Me Ha Tocado! Los Milagros de Jesus. Ariel Zambrano. (SPA.). 112p. 1996. pap. 7.00 (*0-8358-0744-4*) Upper Room Bks.
Me Han Defraudado! G. Campbell Morgan. Orig. Title: Wherein!. (SPA.). 96p. 1992. mass mkt. 3.99 (*0-8254-1497-0*, Edit Portavoz) Kregel.
Me I Know: A Study of Adult Identity. S. Krauss Whitbourne. (Illus.). 288p. 1986. 78.95 (*0-387-96261-1*) Spr-Verlag.
Me I See. Ed. by Everett Leadingham. 128p. 1994. pap., student ed. 6.50 (*0-8341-1520-4*) Beacon Hill.
Me I See: A Christian Approach to Self-Esteem. Ed. by Everette Leadingham. (Dialog Ser.). 48p. 1994. pap., teacher ed. 5.50 (*0-8341-1519-0*) Beacon Hill.
Me I See: Answering Life's Questions. Warren Wiard & Wood & Barnes Staff. (Illus.). 120p. (YA). 1998. pap. 24.95 (*1-885473-25-7*) Wood N Barnes.
Me I'm Learning to Be. Imogene Forte. (Illus.). 80p. (J). (gr. 4-7). 1983. pap. text 9.95 (*0-86530-061-5*, IP61-5) Incentive Pubns.
Me in Ministry? Jack Eason. 66p. 1998. pap. 6.95 (*1-57502-741-0*, PO2060) Morris Pubng.
Me in the Mirror. Connie Panzarino. LC 93-41623. 272p. (Orig.). 1994. pap. 12.95 (*1-878067-45-1*) Seal Pr WA.
Me in the Universe. Joan Sweeney. LC 97-16169. 32p. (J). (ps-2). 1998. 13.00 (*0-517-70968-6*, Pub. by Crown Bks Yng Read) Random.
*__Me, Inc: The Business of Me Playbook.__ Jane Flagells. (Illus.). 110p. 1999. pap. 21.00 (*0-7392-0493-9*, PO3851) Morris Pubng.
Me Inside of Me. Agnes Robertson. 72p. 1987. pap. 6.00 (*0-940584-14-X*) Gull Bks.
Me Jane: Masculinity, Movies, & Women. Ed. by Pat Kirkham & Janet Thumin. LC 95-17088. 256p. 1995. pap. 18.95 (*0-312-12768-5*); text 49.95 (*0-312-12767-7*) St Martin.
Me Llamo Maria Isabel. Alma F. Ada. (SPA., Illus.). 64p. (J). (gr. 4-7). 1994. mass mkt. 15.00 (*0-689-31963-0*) Atheneum Yung Read.
Me Llamo Maria Isabel. Alma Flor Ada. 1996. 10.19 (*0-606-10485-2*, Pub. by Turtleback) Demco.
*__Me Llamo Rigoberta Menchu y As.__ Elizabeth Burgos-Debray. (SPA.). 1998. pap. 19.98 (*968-23-1315-5*) Siglo XXI.
Me Llamo Rigoberta Menchu/Rigoberta Menchu. Elizabeth Burogs. 1997. pap. text 21.95 (*84-322-4688-3*) Continental Bk.
Me! Me! Magnificent Me! large type ed. Judy Mullican. (HRL Little Bks.). (Illus.). 8p. (J). (ps-k). 1998. pap. text 10.95 (*1-57332-108-7*); pap. text 10.95 (*1-57332-109-5*) HighReach Lrning.
Me Me Me Me Me: Not a Novel. M. E. Kerr. LC 82-48521. (Charlotte Zolotow Bk.). 224p. (YA). (gr. 7 up). 1983. 13.00 (*0-06-023192-0*) HarpC Child Bks.
Me, Minerva & the Flying Car: Going to Washington, D. C. E. R. Emmer. Orig. Title: Me , Minerva & the Flying Flora. (Illus.). 96p. (Orig.). 2000. pap. 7.95 (*1-893577-03-1*) Four Corners Pubg.
Me, Molly Midnight, the Artist's Cat. Nadja Maril. LC 77-22708. (Illus.). 40p. (J). (gr. k up). 1977. 12.95 (*0-916144-15-1*); pap. 5.95 (*0-916144-16-X*) Stemmer Hse.
Me-Momma & the Try Cake see Me-Momma Tales Collection
Me-Momma Tales Collection, 4 vols. Illus. by Marie E. Tomlinson. Incl. Angels in the Snow. (Illus.). 18p. (J). (gr. k-6). 1995. pap. 10.00 (*1-888459-01-8*); Daddy's Part-Time Job. (Illus.). (Orig.). (J). (gr. k-6). 1996. pap. 10.00 (*1-888459-03-4*); Dried Apples on the Roof. (Illus.). (J). (gr. k-6). 1996. pap. 10.00 (*1-888459-02-6*); Me-Momma & the Try Cake. (Illus.). 18p. (J). (gr. k-3). 1995. pap. 10.00 (*1-888459-00-X*); 26.50 (*1-888459-04-2*) Smart Prods.
Me, Mop & the Moondance Kid. Walter Dean Myers. (J). 1995. pap. 4.99 (*0-440-91071-4*) BDD Bks Young Read.
Me, Mop & the Moondance Kid. Walter Dean Myers. (J). 1996. pap. 4.99 (*0-440-91093-5*) BDD Bks Young Read.
Me, Mop & the Moondance Kid. Walter Dean Myers. Ed. by Scoot Foresmman. 160p. (J). 1994. pap. 3.50 (*0-440-91005-6*) Dell.
Me, Mop, & the Moondance Kid. Walter Dean Myers. (J). 1988. 9.60 (*0-606-04745-X*, Pub. by Turtleback) Demco.
Me, Mop & the Moondance Kid. large type ed. Walter Dean Myers. (Illus.). 1995. pap. 41.50 (*0-614-09601-4*, L-34842-00) Am Printing Hse.
Me, Mop & the Moondance Kid. Walter Dean Myers. LC 88-6503. 160p. (J). (gr. 4-7). 1990. reprint ed. pap. 4.99 (*0-440-40396-0*) Dell.
Me Mum Sez: Outrageous Truths about Life & People. Meg Salty. 1994. pap. 5.95 (*0-9615390-9-7*) Aspen West Pub.
Me, My Sister, & I. Mary E. Ryan. LC 92-368. 160p. (YA). (gr. 5-9). 1992. pap. 15.00 (*0-671-73851-8*) S&S Bks Yung.
Me, Myself & I. (Wipe-Off Book Ser). (Illus.). 24p. (J). (ps-k). 1998. 4.99 (*0-7681-0091-7*, McClanahan Book) Learn Horizon.
*__Me, Myself & I.__ Sarah Albee. (Illus.). (J). 2000. pap. 3.99 (*0-307-45451-7*) Gldn Bks Pub Co.
Me, Myself & I. Redge Mahaffey. (Illus.). 54p. (Orig.). 1990. pap. 3.95 (*0-9622546-1-4*) Ramsgate MD.
Me, Myself, & I: A Program on Alcoholism & Its Effect on Family for Older Students. Grace Marinello. LC 93-79192. 16p. (YA). (gr. 6-12). 1993. 1.00 (*1-884063-06-3*) Mar Co Prods.
Me, Myself & I! Big Book, Theme 1. large type ed. Selected by Lee B. Hopkins. (Worlds of Poetry Ser.). (Illus.). 16p. (J). (gr. k-3). 1998. pap. text 28.95 (*0-8215-0500-9*) Sadlier.
Me, Myself & I: How Children Build Their Sense of Self 18-36 Months. Kyle D. Pruett. LC 99-60433. (Goddard Parenting Guides Ser.). 256p. 1999. pap. 19.95 (*0-9666397-5-8*) Goddard Pr.
Me, Myself & I: How Children Build Their Sense of Self 18-36 Months. Kyle D. Pruett. LC 99-60433. (Goddard Parenting Guides Ser.). 216p. 1999. 24.95 (*0-9666397-4-X*) Goddard Pr.
Me, Myself & I: Journal. Raquel Benatar. (Illus.). 24p. (YA). (gr. 3 up). 1997. pap., wbk. ed. 6.95 (*1-56492-146-8*) Laredo.
Me, Myself & I: Overcoming Inner Struggles. Gerald J. Beard. Ed. by Tracie L. Beard. 71p. 1998. pap. 9.99 (*1-57502-999-5*, PO2722) Morris Pubng.
Me, Myself & I! Theme Pack, Theme 1. large type ed. Selected by Lee B. Hopkins. (Worlds of Poetry Ser.). (Illus.). 16p. (J). (gr. k-3). 1998. pap. text 90.00 (*0-8215-0507-6*) Sadlier.
Me, Myself, & I, Inc. 10 Steps to Career Independence. Shirley Porter. LC 98-9771. 1998. pap. text 17.95 (*1-57023-093-5*) Impact VA.
*__Me, Myself, & Irene.__ St. Martin's Press Staff. 256p. 2000. mass mkt. 5.99 (*0-312-97636-4*, St Martins Paperbacks) St Martin.
*__Me Myself I.__ Pip Karmel. 224p. 2000. per. 12.95 (*0-7434-0652-4*) PB.
*__Me, Myself, My Team: How to Become an Effective Team Player Using NLP.__ Angus McLeod. 300p. 2000. pap. 19.95 (*1-899836-38-1*, Pub. by Crown Hse) LPC Group.
Me 'n Elvis. Charlie Hodge & Charles Goodman. 196p. 1984. pap. 9.95 (*0-916693-00-7*) Castle Bks.
Me 'n' George: A Story of George Corley Wallace & His Number One Crony Oscar Harper. Sandra B. Taylor. 162p. 1988. 15.95 (*0-926291-00-9*) Greenberry Pub.
Me 'n God in the Coffee Shop. Rene Donovan. 264p. 1998. pap. 10.95 (*1-881542-49-1*) Blue Star Prodns.
Me 'n God 'n Maybe You. 3rd ed. David W. Bouton. 112p. 1993. pap., spiral bd. 14.95 (*1-881494-08-X*, MP393C) Continuum Pubs.
*__Me 'n Paul & Old Hueneme.__ Ted Moranda. (Illus.). vi, 221p. 1999. pap. write for info. (*0-9671590-0-8*) T Moranda.
Me n' Pete. Ron Fowler. (Illus.). 256p. (Orig.). 1996. pap. 9.95 (*0-9654479-0-1*) Fowlers Creations.
Me Nobody Knew: A Story of Triumph for All Girls. Shannon McLinden. LC 97-35025. 112p. (J). 1997. lib. bdg. 26.95 (*0-8225-2688-3*) Lerner Pub.
Me Nobody Knows: A Guide for Teen Survivors. Barbara Bean & Shari Bennett. LC 97-26365. 1997. pap. 12.95 (*0-7879-3960-9*) Jossey-Bass.
Me Nobody Knows: Vocal Selections. (Illus.). 40p. 1983. pap. 8.95 (*0-88188-492-8*, 00360472) H Leonard.
Me Obey Him. Handfor. 1995. pap. 3.95 (*0-87398-551-6*) Sword of Lord.
Me on the Map. Joan Sweeney. (J). 1998. pap. 6.99 (*0-517-88557-3*, Pub. by Crown Bks Yng Read) Random.
Me on the Map. Joan Sweeney. (Illus.). 32p. (J). 1996. lib. bdg. 13.99 (*0-517-70096-4*) Random.
Me on the Map. Joan Sweeney. (Illus.). 32p. (J). (ps-2). 1996. 12.00 (*0-517-70095-6*) Random.
Me-ow: A Book of Pur-rific Cat Cartoons. Philip J. Rodano. LC 90-90370. (Illus.). 144p. (Orig.). 1990. pap. text 8.95 (*0-9627648-1-7*) Top Cat.
Me Plus Math Equals Headache. Lee Wardlaw. LC 86-20305. (Illus.). (Orig.). (J). (gr. 1-3). 1986. reprint ed. pap. 3.50 (*0-931093-07-4*) Red Hen Pr.
*__Me Que Huong Viet Nam D. V. D.__ Paul Van Chi Chu.Tr. of Mother of Vietnam Country D. V. D.. (VIE & ENG., Illus.). 15p. 1999. pap. 20.00 (*0-9663150-5-7*) P V C Chu.
*__Me Que Huong Vietnam.__ Paul Van Chi Chu.Tr. of Mother of Vietnam Country. (VIE & ENG., Illus.). 94p. 1999. 15.00 (*0-9663150-6-5*); pap. 5.00 (*0-9663150-4-9*) P V C Chu.
Me Querrias Tu? Andrea Wayne von Konigslow.Tr. of Would You Love Me?. (SPA., Illus.). 32p. (YA). (ps up). 1997. pap. 5.95 (*1-55037-449-4*, Pub. by Annick) Firefly Bks Ltd.
Me Quiere Mucho un Poquito Nada. Luis Palau. (Serie Cruzada - Crusade Ser.).Tr. of You Love Me a Lot a Little, Not at All. (SPA.). 20p. 1993. pap. 1.99 (*1-56063-541-X*, 498028) Editorial Unilit.
Me Quieres, Mama? Barbara Joosse. Tr. by Diego Lasconi. (SPA., Illus.). 32p. (J). (ps-1). 1998. 14.95 (*0-8118-2076-9*) Chronicle Bks.
Me Run Fast Good: Biographies of Tewanima (Hopi), Carlos Montezuma (Apache) & John Horse (Seminole) Beatrice Levin & Marjorie Vanderveld. 32p. (J). (gr. 5-9). 1983. pap. 3.95 (*0-89992-087-X*) Coun India Ed.
Me, Stressed Out. gif. ed. Charles M. Schulz. LC 96-16592. (Peanuts Wisdom Bks.). (Illus.). 32p. 1996. 7.95 (*0-00-225173-6*) Collins SF.
*__Me Talk Pretty One Day.__ David Sedaris. LC 00-25052. 288p. (gr. 8). 2000. 22.95 (*0-316-77772-2*) Little.
Me Tarzan. Betsy C. Byars. LC 99-34512. 96p. (gr. 2-5). mass mkt. 4.25 (*0-06-442119-8*) HarpC.
*__Me Tarzan.__ Betsy C. Byars. LC 99-34512. 96p. (J). (gr. 2-5). 2000. lib. bdg. 14.89 (*0-06-028707-1*) HarpC Child Bks.
*__Me Tarzan.__ Betsy C. Byars. LC 99-34512. (Illus.). 96p. (J). (gr. 2-5). 2000. 14.95 (*0-06-028706-3*) HarpC Child Bks.
Me, the People. Harry Smith. LC 79-63451. 116p. 1979. 12.50 (*0-912292-61-X*) Smith.
Me-Time Machine: Student Activity Book. Marcia Sohl & Gerald Dackerman. (Now Age Illustrated Ser.). (Illus.). 16p. (J). (gr. 4-10). 1976. pap. 1.25 (*0-88301-186-7*) Pendulum Pr.
Me Too see Yo Tambien
Me Too! Randy Brooks. (Chapbks.: No. 17). 40p. 1985. 10.00 (*0-913719-83-8*, High Coo Pr); pap. 3.50 (*0-913719-82-X*, High Coo Pr) Brooks Books.
Me Too. Vera Cleaver & Bill Cleaver. 160p. (YA). (gr. 7-9). 1973. 13.95 (*0-397-31485-X*) HarpC Child Bks.
Me Too. Vera Cleaver & Bill Cleaver. LC 85-42745. (Trophy Bk.). 160p. (J). (gr. 5-7). 1985. pap. 2.95 (*0-06-440161-8*, HarpTrophy) HarpC Child Bks.
Me Too! Mercer Mayer. (J). 1985. 7.45 (*0-606-12422-5*, Pub. by Turtleback) Demco.
Me Too. Susan Winter. LC 92-53483. (Illus.). 24p. (J). (ps-1). 1993. 9.95 (*1-56458-198-5*) DK Pub Inc.
Me Too! Mercer Mayer. (Look-Look Bks.). (Illus.). 24p. (J). (ps-3). 1985. reprint ed. pap. 3.29 (*0-307-11941-6*, 11941) Gldn Bks Pub Co.
Me Too. 2nd ed. Carter D. Thompkins. (Illus.). v, 64p. 1997. pap. 11.95 (*1-890667-02-1*) Introspect Bks.
*__Me Too! Two Small Stories about Small Animals.__ Katya Arnold. LC 99-16696. (Illus.). 32p. (J). (ps-1). 2000. 15.95 (*0-8234-1483-3*) Holiday.
Me, Too! Creative Crafts for Preschoolers. Ed. by Sarah H. Healton & Kay H. Whiteside. (Anytime Crafts Bk.). 112p. 1992. 13.95 (*0-8306-4041-X*, 4183); pap. 9.95 (*0-8306-4042-8*, 4183) McGraw-Hill Prof.
Me Too! Me Too! Harriet Ziefert. LC 87-11937. (Illus.). 36p. (J). (ps-1). 1988. 11.95 (*0-06-026880-8*) HarpC Child Bks.
Me Too, Zacchaeus: Conversations with the Man in the Tree & Other Bible Personalities. Carol S. Uecker & Betty W. Skold. LC 95-67099. (Illus.). 100p. (Orig.). 1995. pap. 9.00 (*0-9645240-0-7*) Porch Light Pr.
Me Two. Mary C. Ryan. 192p. (J). 1993. pap. 3.50 (*0-380-71826-X*, Avon Bks) Morrow Avon.
*__Me 262A Schwalbe: A Peregrine Photo Essay.__ Steve Muth. (Illus.). 12p. (YA). 2000. pap. 7.95 (*1-930432-02-X*, 1-Luftwaffe) Peregrine Pubng.
Me-won-i-toc: A Tale of Frontier Life & Indian Character. Solon Rovinson. (Notable American Authors Ser.). 1999. reprint ed. lib. bdg. 125.00 (*0-7812-8806-1*) Rprt Serv.
Me, You, Us & Them. Katz & Zakes. 280p. 1992. pap. text 42.00 (*0-536-58228-9*) Pearson Custom.
Mea Cuba. Guillermo C. Infante. Tr. by Kenneth Hall. LC 94-30856. 320p. 1994. 23.00 (*0-374-20497-7*) FS&G.
Mea Cuba. Guillermo C. Infante. Tr. by Kenneth Hall. 512p. 1995. pap. 15.00 (*0-374-52446-7*, Noonday) FS&G.
*__Mea Cuba.__ Guillermo Cabrena Infante. (SPA.). 2000. pap. 21.95 (*84-204-8271-4*) Santillana.
Mea Culpa: A Sociology of Apology & Reconciliation. Nicholas Tavuchis. LC 91-16463. 180p. 1991. 37.50 (*0-8047-1936-5*) Stanford U Pr.
Mea Culpa: A Sociology of Apology & Reconciliation. Nicholas Tavuchis. 180p. (C). 1993. pap. 12.95 (*0-8047-2223-4*) Stanford U Pr.
Mea Culpa: Money, Lies & the Killing of Democracy. Edmund G. Brown. 144p. 1994. pap. 7.95 (*1-882206-05-3*) Argonaut Pr.
Mea Culpa: Tales of Resurrection. Colette Aboulker-Muscat. 177p. 1997. 35.00 (*1-883148-05-7*); pap. 20.00 (*1-883148-06-5*) ACMI Pr.
Meacham, a Wide Spot on the Oregon Trail: Where the Meadowlark Still Sings. Betty Stewart. (Illus.). 198p. (Orig.). 1996. pap. 12.95 (*0-9653021-0-5*) Crossrd Bks.
Meachums of Van Buren Co., Michigan. Virginia M. Gerstman. (Illus.). 190p. 1989. text 28.00 (*0-9616538-8-4*); pap. text 22.00 (*0-9616538-7-6*) Heritage Val Pub.
Mead: Analog VLSI Systems. 1988. 39.95 (*0-318-32964-6*) Addison-Wesley.
Mead & Merleau-Ponty: Toward a Common Vision. Sandra B. Rosenthal & Patrick L. Bourgeois. LC 90-20226. 231p. (C). 1991. text 64.50 (*0-7914-0789-6*); pap. text 21.95 (*0-7914-0790-X*) State U NY Pr.
Mead Corp. A Report on the Company's Environment Policies & Practices. (Illus.). 39p. (C). 1994. reprint ed. pap. text 40.00 (*0-7881-0964-2*, Coun on Econ) DIANE Pub.
Meade County, Kentucky Births, 1852-1859, 1861, 1874-1878, 1894, 1900-1901, 1904 & 1906-1909. Wathena K. Miller. 167p. 1987. pap. 17.00 (*1-889221-27-9*) Ancestral Trails.
Meade County, Kentucky, 1880 Census. Jane M. Newton & Wathena K. Miller. 239p. 1996. pap. 22.00 (*1-889221-31-7*) Ancestral Trails.
Meade County, Kentucky, 1850 Census. Shelly Sims. 104p. 1984. pap. 12.00 (*1-889221-28-7*) Ancestral Trails.
Meade County, Kentucky, 1870 Census. Wathena K. Miller & Jane M. Newton. 204p. 1991. pap. 20.00 (*1-889221-30-9*) Ancestral Trails.
Meade County, Kentucky, 1860 Census. Avery Boucher. 118p. 1981. pap. 16.00 (*1-889221-29-5*) Ancestral Trails.
Meade County, Kentucky Marriages, 1824-1884. Wathena K. Miller. 239p. 1988. pap. 22.00 (*1-889221-33-3*) Ancestral Trails.
Meade County, Kentucky Marriages, 1885-1934. Wathena K. Miller. 262p. 1990. pap. 24.00 (*1-889221-34-1*) Ancestral Trails.
Meade of Gettysburg. Freeman Cleaves. LC 60-7735. (Illus.). 416p. 1991. pap. 16.95 (*0-8061-2298-6*) U of Okla Pr.
Meade Solution. Robert J. Conley. LC 97-48703. 144p. 1998. 19.95 (*0-87081-479-6*) Univ Pr Colo.
Meade's Headquarters, 1863 to 1865: Letters of Colonel Theodore Lyman from the Wilderness to Appomattox. Theodore Lyman. Ed. by George R. Agassiz. LC 71-137381. (Select Bibliographies Reprint Ser.). 1977. reprint ed. 32.95 (*0-8369-5582-X*) Ayer.
Meade's Headquarters, 1863-1865: Letters of Colonel Theodore Lyman from the Wilderness to Appomattox. Theodore Lyman. (American Biography Ser.). 371p. 1991. reprint ed. lib. bdg. 79.00 (*0-7812-8256-X*) Rprt Serv.
Meadow. (J). 1998. 4.95 (*0-7894-3476-8*) DK Pub Inc.
Meadow. James Galvin. 240p. 1995. pap. 12.00 (*0-8050-2703-3*) H Holt & Co.
Meadow. James Galvin. (Illus.). 192p. 1995. 19.95 (*0-8050-1684-8*) H Holt & Co.
Meadow. Tom Raworth. LC 99-19058. 41p. 1999. pap. 7.00 (*0-942996-34-8*, Pub. by Post Apollo Pr) SPD-Small Pr Dist.
Meadow. Barbara Taylor. LC 92-52821. (Look Closer Ser.). (Illus.). 32p. (J). (gr. 1-4). 1992. 9.95 (*1-56458-129-2*) DK Pub Inc.
Meadow Boy. Reed Parsley. (Illus.). 40p. (J). 1997. 18.00 (*0-9660288-0-5*) Penultimate.
Meadow City Milestones: A Collection of Historical Sketches. Alice H. Manning. (Illus.). 94p. (Orig.). 1987. pap. 4.95 (*0-9618052-1-8*) Daily Hampshire.
Meadow-Grass: Tales of New England Life. Alice Brown. 1972. reprint ed. lib. bdg. 18.00 (*0-8422-8011-1*) Irvington.
Meadow-Grass: Tales of New England Life, Vol. 1. Alice Brown. LC 72-4456. (Short Story Index Reprint Ser.). 1977. reprint ed. 23.95 (*0-8369-4172-1*) Ayer.
Meadow in the Sky: A History of Yosemite's Tuolumne Meadows Region. 3rd ed. Elizabeth S. O'Neill. LC 86-60495. (Illus.). 176p. (Orig.). 1984. pap. 12.95 (*0-914330-67-5*) Albicaulis Pr.
Meadow Lane. William Mulvihill. 142p. 1998. pap. 9.00 (*1-891380-01-X*) Brickiln Pr.
Meadow Mouse Seasons. 2nd ed. Annie J. Lang. 1997. pap. text. write for info. (*1-57377-012-4*) Easl Pubns.
*__Meadow Muffins Vol. 1: Cowboy Rhymes & Other B. S.__ Mike Puhallo. (Illus.). 64p. 1999. pap. 7.95 (*0-88839-436-5*) Hancock House.
Meadow Mystery. Lauren L. Young. 20p. (J). (ps-3). 1995. pap. text 7.95 (*0-9649057-0-1*) Laurens Lyrics.
Meadow Prospect Revisited. Gwyn Thomas. Ed. by Michael Parnell. 212p. 1993. pap. 14.95 (*1-85411-065-9*, Pub. by Seren Bks) Dufour.

*__Meadowland.__ Alison Giles. 384p. 1998. pap. 11.95 (*1-85702-609-8*, Pub. by Fourth Estate) Trafalgar.
Meadowland. Ray Mortenson. LC 83-80569. (Illus.). 80p. 1983. 25.00 (*0-912810-40-8*) Lustrum Pr.
Meadowlands. Louise Gluck. 72p. 1996. 22.00 (*0-88001-452-0*) HarpC.
Meadowlands. Louise Gluck. LC 95-33526. 72p. 1997. pap. 13.00 (*0-88001-506-3*) HarpC.
Meadowlands: Wilderness Adventures at the Edge of a city. Robert Sullivan. LC 99-23159. 224p. 1999. pap. 12.95 (*0-385-49508-0*) Doubleday.
Meadowlands: Wilderness Adventures at the Edge of a city. Robert Sullivan. LC 97-39656. 224p. 1998. 23.00 (*0-684-83285-2*, Scribner Pap Fic) S&S Trade Pap.
Meadowlark. Sheila Simonson. (Worldwide Library Mysteries: No. 240). 1997. per. 4.99 (*0-373-26240-X*, 1-26240-1, Wrldwide Lib) Harlequin Bks.
Meadowlark Economics: Work & Leisure in the Ecosystem. James Eggert. LC 92-17735. (Illus.). 140p. (C). (gr. 13). 1992. pap. 34.95 (*1-56324-163-3*) M E Sharpe.
Meadowlark West. Philip Lamantia. 104p. (Orig.). 1986. pap. 6.95 (*0-87286-176-7*) City Lights.

M

Meadowood Phase Settlement Pattern in the Niagara Frontier Region of Western New York State. Joseph E. Granger, Jr. (Anthropological Papers Ser.: No. 65). (Illus.). (Orig.). 1978. pap. 4.00 (*0-932206-76-X*) U Mich Mus Anthro.

Meadow's End. large type ed. Hilda A. Durman. 1990. pap. 16.99 (*0-7089-6876-7*, Linford) Ulverscroft.

Meadows in the Sierra Nevada of California: State of Knowledge. Raymond D. Ratliff. (Illus.). 64p. 1998. reprint ed. 13.40 (*0-89904-517-0*, Bear Meadows Resrch Grp); reprint ed. pap. 7.40 (*0-89904-518-9*, Bear Meadows Resrch Grp) Crumb Elbow Pub.

***Meadows Museum: A Handbook of Spanish Painting & Sculpture.** Pamela Patton. Ed. by John Lunsford & Jackson L. Powers. (Illus.). 100p. 2000. pap. write for info. (*0-935937-14-5*) Meadows Mus.

Meadows of Gold. Masudi. Tr. by Paul Lunde & Catherine Stone. 320p. 1987. 65.00 (*0-7103-0246-0*, A0086) Routledge.

***Meadows of Howling: or Abortion, Feminism & the Culture of Death.** Terris Wade Bradley. 180p. 2000. 21.95 (*0-7541-1362-0*, Pub. by Minerva Pr) Unity Dist.

Meadows of Memory: Images of Time & Tradition in American Art & Culture. Michael G. Kammen. LC 91-27637. (Tandy Lectures: No. 11). (Illus.). 220p. 1992. 39.95 (*0-292-75139-7*) U of Tex Pr.

Meadowsong. Phyllis Ann Karr. 224p. 1981. pap. 1.50 (*0-449-50209-0*, Coventry) Fawcett.

Mead's Other Manus: Phenomenology of the Encounter. Lola E. Romanucci-Ross. (Illus.). 256p. 1985. 34.95 (*0-89789-064-7*, H064, Bergin & Garvey) Greenwood.

Meagre Harvest: The Australian Women's Movement, 1950-1990s. Gisela Kaplan. LC 96-218295. 256p. 1997. pap. 29.95 (*1-86448-062-9*, Pub. by Allen & Unwin Pty) Paul & Co Pubs.

Meah Shaerim Centennial: A Study of the Neturei Karta. 1980. lib. bdg. 59.95 (*0-686-68746-9*) Revisionist Pr.

Meal Barrel Mystery. Theda Hagan. (Illus.). 64p. 1998. pap. 5.00 (*1-57502-837-9*, PO2301) T Hagan.

Meal Consumption Behavior. rev. ed. 60p. 1996. pap. 50.00 (*0-317-57908-8*, CS100) Natl Restaurant Assn.

Meal for the Road: 14 Sermons on the Lord's Prayer. Charles E. Link. LC 93-30840. 92p. 1994. pap. 9.75 (*1-55673-702-5*) CSS OH.

Meal Magic: Meals for the Food Combining Conscious. Farid Zarif. Ed. & Illus. by Victory Lee. 220p. (Orig.). 1996. pap. 14.95 (*1-888611-02-2*, 88863) Victry Pub.

Meal Manager Cookbook: A Guide to Healthy Living. Healthway, Inc. Staff. (Illus.). 160p. (Orig.). 1995. pap., per. 14.95 (*1-57102-504-9*) Hambleton-Hill.

Meal Pattern. Helen N. Sanders. 88p. (Orig.). (C). 1987. pap. 18.00 (*1-880864-02-9*) F S H.

Meal Planner. Ann M. Bramer. 168p. 1993. spiral bd. 15.95 (*0-9643906-0-4*) Menus & More.

Meal Planning for Diabetes in Pregnancy: Practical Applications. Johanna C. Burani. 60p. 1990. spiral bd. 29.95 (*1-879339-13-7*) Infinity Impress.

Meal Preparation: Teaching Individuals with Developmental Disabilities to Cook. Linda R. Harper. (Illus.). 104p. 1998. pap. 14.95 (*1-928752-07-1*) Mc Gowan Pubns.

Meal Preparation & Training: The Health Care Professional's Guide. Judith L. Klinger. LC 97-16055. (Illus.). 352p. (Orig.). 1997. pap. text 28.00 (*1-55642-343-8*, 33438) SLACK Inc.

***Meal Scenes in Luke-Acts: An Audience-Oriented Approach.** John Paul Heil. LC 99-56091. (Monograph Ser.). 384p. 2000. 45.00 (*0-88414-013-X*, 060052) Soc Biblical Lit.

Meal Service Study Course. 2nd ed. Iowa Dietetic Association Staff et al. LC 91-24467. (Illus.). 104p. 1991. pap. text, per. 24.95 (*0-8138-0866-9*) Iowa St U Pr.

Meal System for the Elderly: Conventional Food in Novel Form. Jurgen Schmandt. (Policy Research Project Report Ser.: No. 16). 150p. 1977. pap. 3.00 (*0-89940-609-2*) LBJ Sch Pub Aff.

Mealey's Insurance Law Review, 1996. David R. Anderson et al. 484p. 1997. pap. 125.00 (*0-9657810-2-X*) Mealey Pubns.

Mealey's International Arbitration Review, 1996. S. Hassan Amin et al. 218p. 1996. pap. 95.00 (*0-9657810-1-1*) Mealey Pubns.

***Mealey's Toxic Tort Expert Witnesses: A Compendium of Experts Who Have Testified in Recent Cases Reported by Mealey Publications.** 294p. 2000. pap. 395.00 (*1-930146-03-5*) Mealey Pubns.

MealLeaniYumm! All That's Missing Is the Fat! Norene Gilletz. Ed. by Elaine Kaplan. LC 99-193059. (Illus.). 414p. 1998. 33.95 (*0-9697972-2-2*) GOUR.

***Meals & Memories: How to Create Keepsake Cookbooks.** Kathy Steligo. LC 99-90018. (Illus.). 112p. 1999. pap. 18.95 (*0-9669799-0-7*) Carlo Press.

Meals for All Seasons. Georgina Campbell. LC 92-253154. (Illus.). 250p. 1997. 24.95 (*0-86327-322-X*, Pub. by Wolfhound Press) Irish Amer Bk.

Meals in a Social Context: Aspects of the Communal Meal in the Hellenistic & Roman World. Ed. by Inge Nielsen & Hanne S. Nielsen. LC 99-163706. (Aarhus Studies in Mediterranean Antiquity: Vol. 1). (Illus.). 248p. 1998. 34.95 (*87-7288-697-8*, Pub. by Aarhus Univ Pr) David Brown.

Meals in Minutes. Carolyn Humphries. (Quick & Easy Ser.). 160p. 1996. pap. text 17.95 (*0-572-02183-6*, Pub. by W Foulsham) Trans-Atl Phila.

Meals in Minutes: From Freezer to Table. 3rd ed. Sue Gregg. (Eating Better Cookbooks: Vol. 2). 98p. 1997. spiral bd. 8.00 (*1-878272-12-8*) S Gregg Cookbks.

Meals-in-Minutes: From theHome Library Test Kitchen. Home Library Editors. (Cole's Home Library Cookbooks). (Illus.). 118p. 1999. pap. 11.95 (*1-56426-150-6*, Pub. by Cole Group) ACCESS Pubs Network.

Meals in Minutes: Robert Rose's Favorites. Compiled by Robert Rose. (Illus.). 96p. (Orig.). 1999. pap. 7.95 (*0-7788-0008-3*, Pub. by R Rose Inc) Firefly Bks Ltd.

Meals in 30 Minutes: Health Food That Is Quick & Easy. 2nd ed. Cheryl Townsley. 220p. 1992. pap. 12.00 (*0-9644566-2-1*) Lifestyle for Hlth.

Meals of the World see Mawaed Al Aalam

Meals on the Go: Meals in Minutes. rev. ed. American Diabetes Association. (Month of Meals Ser.). Orig. Title: Month of Meals 3. (Illus.). 64p. 1998. pap. 14.95 (*1-58040-016-7*, 00167Q, Pub. by Am Diabetes) NTC Contemp Pub Co.

***Meals on the Move: Rush Hour Recipes.** Holly B. Clegg. LC 99-96229. (Trim & Terrific Ser.: Vol. 4). (Illus.). 256p. 2000. 19.95 (*0-9610888-6-9*, Pub. by H B Clegg) Wimmer Bk Dist.

Meals That Heal: A Nutraceutical Approach to Diet & Health. Lisa Turner. LC 96-21027. (Illus.). 224p. 1996. pap. 19.95 (*0-89281-625-2*, Heal Arts VT) Inner Tradit.

Meals That Heal: For Babies & Toddlers. Eileen Behan. 1999. pap. write for info. (*0-671-52985-4*) S&S Trade.

Meals That Heal for Babies & Toddlers. Eileen Behan. 304p. 1996. pap. 12.00 (*0-671-52986-2*) S&S Trade.

Meals Without Squeals: Child Care Feeding Guide & Cookbook. 2nd rev. ed. Christine Berman & Jacki Fromer. LC 97-29116. (Illus.). 288p. 1997. pap. 16.95 (*0-923521-39-9*) Bull Pub.

Mealtime. (Look at Me Ser.). (Illus.). (J). bds. 5.95 (*0-590-24863-4*) Scholastic Inc.

Mealtime for Zoo Animals. Caroline Arnold. LC 97-43099. (Illus.). 32p. (J). (gr. k-2). 1999. 21.27 (*1-57505-286-5*, Carolrhoda) Lerner Pub.

Mealtime for Zoo Animals. Caroline Arnold. LC 97-43099. 32p. (J). (gr. k-2). 1999. 9.95 (*1-57505-389-6*, Carolrhoda) Lerner Pub.

Mealtime Fun. Walter Elias Disney. (Illus.). 10p. (J). 1997. 7.98 (*1-57082-677-3*, Pub. by Mouse Works) Time Warner.

Mealtime Manual for People with Disabilities & the Aging. Judith L. Klinger. LC 97-16056. (Illus.). 256p. 1997. pap. text 26.00 (*1-55642-341-1*, 33411) SLACK Inc.

***Mealtime Moments: 164 Faith-Filling Entrees to Stir Family Discussion.** Tyndale House Publishers Staff. (Heritage Builders Ser.). 192p. 2000. pap. 13.99 (*1-56179-801-0*) Focus Family.

Mealtime Prayers. Alan Parry & Linda Parry. LC 94-5435. (Little Prayers Ser.). (Illus.). 12p. (J). (ps-k). 1995. 3.99 (*0-8499-1149-4*) Tommy Nelson.

Mealtimes & Memories: Fond Reflections of Family, Friends & Food. Thelma Carlile. 430p. 1995. pap. 16.95 (*0-9644579-0-3*) Sunline.

***Mealworms: Life Cycles.** Donna Schaffer. LC 98-53031. (Life Cycles Ser.). (Illus.). 24p. (J). 1999. 15.93 (*0-7368-0209-6*, Bridgestone Bks) Capstone Pr.

Mealworms: Raise Them, Watch Them, See Them Change. unabridged ed. Adrienne Mason. (Illus.). 24p. (J). (gr. 2-4). 1998. pap. 12.95 (*1-55074-448-8*, Pub. by Kids Can Pr) Genl Dist Srvs.

Mealworms & Silkworms. Sarah Clark. (Thematic Units Ser.). 80p. (J). (gr. 1-3). 1997. pap. 9.95 (*1-57690-371-0*) Tchr Create Mat.

Mealybugs of Central & South America. D. Williams & M. Christina Granara De Willink. (Illus.). 630p. 1992. text 175.00 (*0-85198-791-5*) OUP.

Mean. Ken Babstock. LC 99-235421. 96p. 1999. pap. text 14.95 (*0-88784-634-3*, Pub. by Hse1 of Anansi) Genl Dist Srvs.

Mean As Hell: The Life of a New Mexico Lawman. 2nd ed. Dee Harkey. LC 89-81746. (Illus.). 239p. 1990. reprint ed. pap. 15.95 (*0-941270-60-2*) Ancient City Pr.

Mean Business: How I Save Bad Companies & Make Good Companies Great. Albert J. Dunlap & Bob Andleman. 1996. 25.00 (*0-614-19862-3*, Times Bks) Crown Pub Group.

Mean Business: How I Save Bad Companies & Make Good Ones Great. Albert J. Dunlap. 304p. 1997. per. 14.00 (*0-684-84406-0*, Fireside) S&S Trade Pap.

***Mean Business: The Insiders Guide to Winning Any Political Election.** Matt Towery & Pierre Howard. LC 99-68605. 256p. 2000. 24.00 (*1-56352-608-5*) Longstreet.

Mean Clean Giant Canoe. Joseph Slate. (J). 1983. lib. bdg. 11.89 (*0-690-04294-9*) HarpC Child Bks.

Mean-Field Magnetohydrodynamics & Dynamo Theory. F. Krause & K-H. Radler. (Illus.). 270p. 1980. 126.00 (*0-08-025041-6*, Pub. by Pergamon Repr) Franklin.

***Mean Genes: From Sex to Money to Food--Taming Our Primal Instincts.** Terry Burnham & Jay Phelan. 224p. 2000. text 24.00 (*0-7382-0230-4*, Pub. by Perseus Pubng) HarpC.

Mean High Tide. James W. Hall. 448p. 1995. mass mkt. 6.99 (*0-440-21355-X*) Dell.

Mean High Tide. large type ed. James W. Hall. LC 94-10926. 545p. 1994. lib. bdg. 23.95 (*0-8161-7441-5*, G K Hall Lrg Type) Mac Lib Ref.

***Mean Illustrated Construction Dictionary.** 3rd ed. R. S. Means Company Staff. (Illus.). 2000. 99.95 (*0-87629-574-X*) R S Means.

Mean Jeans Manufacturing Co. A Business Community Simulation. 2nd ed. Boyer. 1990. text 160.00 (*0-538-60282-1*) Thomson Learn.

Mean Jean's Manufacturing Company, Reference Manual: Business Communication Simulation. 2nd ed. Boyer. (GB - Basic Business Ser.). 1990. mass mkt. 12.95 (*0-538-60283-X*) S-W Pub.

Mean Jean's Manufacturing Company Simulation: A Business. Boyer. (GB - Basic Business Ser.). 1983. 190.95 (*0-538-07100-1*) S-W Pub.

Mean Justice: A Town's Terror, a Prosecutor's Power, a Betrayal of Innocence. Edward Humes. 1999. per. 7.99 (*0-671-03427-8*) PB.

Mean Justice: A Town's Terror, a Prosecutor's Power, a Betrayal of Innocence. Edward Humes. LC 98-43801. 491p. 1999. 24.50 (*0-684-83174-0*) Scribner.

Mean Margaret. Tor Seidler. LC 97-71566. (Michael di Capua Bks.). (Illus.). 176p. (J). (gr. k-3). 1997. 15.95 (*0-06-205090-7*) HarpC Child Bks.

Mean Margaret. Tor Seidler. (Michael di Capua Bks.). (Illus.). 192p. (J). (gr. 2 up). 1997. lib. bdg. 14.89 (*0-06-205091-5*) HarpC Child Bks.

Mean Mary Jean. Mary J. Fielder. LC 96-23007. 1996. 18.00 (*1-881320-51-0*, Black Belt) Black Belt Communs.

Mean Mean Madeleen - Sweet Sweet Angeleen. unabridged ed. Elizabeth Burton. Ed. by Adolph Caso. LC 97-24767. (Illus.). 32p. (J). (gr. 2-6). 1997. pap. 12.95 (*0-8283-2043-8*) Branden Bks.

***Mean, Mean Maureen Green.** Judy Cox. LC 99-11935. (Illus.). 80p. (J). (gr. 1-5). 1999. 15.95 (*0-8234-1502-3*) Holiday.

Mean Monthly & Extreme Discharges, 1969-1972 see Discharge of Selected Rivers of the World

Mean on Sunday: The Autobiography of Ray Nitschke. 2nd ed. Told to Robert W. Wells. LC 98-37872. (Illus.). 329p. 1998. reprint ed. pap. 14.95 (*1-879483-54-8*) Prairie Oak Pr.

***Mean Rooms: A Short Story Collection.** Julie Smith. LC PS3569.M537553M4. (Mystery Ser.). 158p. 2000. 21.95 (*0-7862-2364-2*) Five Star.

Mean Soup. B. Everitt. LC 91-15244. (Illus.). 32p. (J). (ps-1). 1992. 16.00 (*0-15-253146-7*, Harcourt Child Bks) Harcourt.

Mean Soup. Betsy Everitt. (J). 1992. 12.45 (*0-606-07856-8*) Turtleback.

Mean Soup. abr. ed. Betsy Everitt. LC 91-15244. (Illus.). 32p. (J). (ps-1). 1995. pap. 7.00 (*0-15-200227-8*, Voyager Bks) Harcourt.

Mean Soup. large type ed. Betsy Everitt. LC 91-15244. (Illus.). 32p. (C). (ps-1). 1995. pap. 24.95 (*0-15-200231-6*, Red Wagon Bks) Harcourt.

Mean Spirit. Linda Hogan. 384p. 1992. mass mkt. 5.99 (*0-8041-0863-3*) Ivy Books.

Mean Streak. Carolyn Wheat. LC 95-38213. 240p. 1996. pap. 19.95 (*0-425-15317-7*, Prime Crime) Berkley Pub.

Mean Streak. Carolyn Wheat. 240p. 1997. mass mkt. 5.99 (*0-425-15577-3*, Prime Crime) Berkley Pub.

Mean Streets. (Bloodshadows Ser.). 15.00 (*0-87431-380-5*, 33050) West End Games.

Mean Streets. Terrance Dicks. (New Adventures Ser.). 1998. mass mkt. 5.95 (*0-426-20519-7*, Pub. by Virgin Bks) London Brdge.

Mean Streets: Youth Crime & Homelessness. John Hagan & Bill McCarthy. (Criminology Ser.). (Illus.). 315p. (C). 1997. text 54.95 (*0-521-49743-4*) Cambridge U Pr.

Mean Streets: Youth Crime & Homelessness. John Hagan & Bill McCarthy. (Cambridge Criminology Ser.). (Illus.). 317p. (C). 1998. pap. 19.95 (*0-521-64626-X*) Cambridge U Pr.

Mean Streets & Dark Deeds: The He-Man's Guide to Mysteries: Critical Evaluations of a Thousand Best Private Eye, Detective, Murder, Spy & Thriller Novels of Recent Times Philip H. Gray. LC 98-70575. x, 338 p. 1998. write for info. (*0-9663734-0-5*) Badger Pr MT.

Mean Streets & Raging Bulls: The Legacy of Film Noir in Contemporary American Cinema. Richard Martin. LC 97-11136. 208p. 1997. 29.50 (*0-8108-3337-9*) Scarecrow.

Mean Streets & Raging Bulls: The Legacy of Film Noir in Contemporary American Cinema. Richard Martin. LC 99-17309. 224p. 1999. reprint ed. pap. 22.50 (*0-8108-3642-4*) Scarecrow.

Mean Tears & In the Blue. Peter Gill. (Oberon Bks.). 96p. 1997. pap. 12.95 (*1-870259-05-X*) Theatre Comm.

Mean Things Happening in This Land: The Life & Times of H. L. Mitchell, Cofounder of the Southern Tenant Farmer's Union. H. L. Mitchell. LC 78-65660. 372p. 1979. text 17.50 (*0-916672-25-5*) Rowman.

Mean Time. Carol A. Duffy. 52p. 1993. pap. 14.95 (*0-85646-247-0*, Pub. by Anvil Press); pap. 17.95 (*0-85646-303-5*, Pub. by Anvil Press) Dufour.

Mean Time, 1. Jerry Sykes. 1999. pap. text 14.95 (*1-899344-40-3*) Do-Not Pr.

Mean Value Theorems & Functional Equations. P. K. Sahoo & T. Riedel. 240p. 1998. 38.00 (*981-02-3544-5*) World Scientific Pub.

***Mean Variance Analysis in Portfolio Choice & Capital Markets.** Harry M. Markowitz. 2000. 65.00 (*1-883249-75-9*) F J Fabozzi.

Mean Waters. Susannah Brin. (Orig.). 1992. 9.40 (*0-606-11609-5*) Turtleback.

Mean Waters. Frank Woodson. Ed. by Liz Parker. (Take Ten Bks.). (Illus.). 45p. (J). (gr. 6-12). 1992. pap. text 3.95 (*1-56254-059-9*) Saddleback Pubns.

***Mean Waters.** rev. ed. Frank Woodson. (Take Ten Ser.). (Illus.). 54p. (YA). (gr. 4-12). 1999. pap. 3.95 (*1-58659-015-4*) Artesian.

Mean Woman (Mina Cruel) Alicia Borinsky. Tr. & Intro. by Cola Franzen. LC 92-37129. (Latin American Women Writers Ser.: Vol. 2). xiv, 179p. (C). 1993. pap. 10.95 (*0-8032-6112-8*, Bison Books); text 42.00 (*0-8032-1234-8*) U of Nebr Pr.

Meandering. Joanne E. Nydegger. 1998. pap. write for info. (*1-57553-875-X*) Watermrk Pr.

Meandering Streams. Marvin Cameron. (Illus.). 108p. (Orig.). 1994. pap. 7.95 (*0-944653-02-2*) Silver State Pub.

Meanderings of a Fly Fisherman. Seth Norman. LC 96-60840. 234p. 1996. 29.95 (*1-885106-34-3*) Wild Adven Pr.

Meanderings of a Fly Fisherman. limited ed. Seth Norman. LC 96-60840. 1996. lthr. 95.00 (*1-885106-35-1*) Wild Adven Pr.

Meanderings Through the Soul of a Mother - Daughter: A Poetic Journal. 2nd rev. ed. Norma Harris-Hagan & Tracey D. Hagan. (Illus.). viii, 100p. 1997. pap. 14.95 (*0-9658125-0-2*) Carolina Charles.

***Meandthesedreamingeyesofmine.** Tajh Eldridge. 151p. 2000. 14.95 (*0-9701070-0-5*) Mile Seven.

Meanest Man in West Texas. H. B. Broome. 192p. 1988. pap. 2.95 (*0-671-66184-1*) PB.

Meanest Man on Death Row: A Life of Crime - From Black Ghetto to Drugs to Murder to Execution. J. Edward Cherryholmes & Roy Demouchette. 256p. Date not set. pap. 19.95 (*0-89896-322-2*) Larksdale.

Meanest Thing to Say. Bill Cosby. LC 96-32791. (Little Bill Books for Beginning Readers Ser.). (Illus.). 40p. (J). (gr. 1-5). 1997. 13.95 (*0-590-13754-9*); pap. 3.99 (*0-590-95616-7*) Scholastic Inc.

Meanest Thing to Say. Bill Cosby. (Little Bill Books for Beginning Readers Ser.). (J). (gr. k-3). 1997. 9.19 (*0-606-11610-9*, Pub. by Turtleback) Demco.

Meaning. Paul Horwich. 254p. 1999. text 55.00 (*0-19-823728-6*); pap. text 19.95 (*0-19-823824-X*) OUP.

Meaning. Michael Polanyi & Harry Prosch. LC 75-5067. 260p. 1977. reprint ed. pap. text 15.95 (*0-226-67295-6*, P740) U Ch Pr.

***M/E/A/N/I/N/G: An Anthology of Artists' Writing, Theory & Criticism.** Ed. by Susan Bee & Mira Schor. 2000. pap. 21.95 (*0-8223-2566-7*) Duke.

***M/E/A/N/I/N/G: An Anthology of Artists' Writings, Theory & Criticism.** Susan Bee. 2000. 64.95 (*0-8223-2534-9*) Duke.

Meaning: An Odyssey in Medicine. Rudi Binder. 291p. (YA). 1998. per. 11.95 (*1-893309-01-0*, 2) Red Maple Pubg.

***Meaning - The Secret of Being Alive.** Cliff Havener. LC 99-61136. 192p. (Orig.). 1999. pap. 16.95 (*1-890676-34-9*, Pub. by Beavers Pond) Bookman Bks.

Meaning a Life. Mary Oppen. LC 78-6223. (Illus.). 214p. 1990. reprint ed. 25.00 (*0-87685-375-0*); reprint ed. pap. 12.50 (*0-87685-374-2*) Black Sparrow.

Meaning & Acquisition of Wealth. Walter Russell. 25p. 1993. pap. 2.00 (*1-879605-41-4*) U Sci & Philos.

Meaning & Action: A Critical History of Pragmatism. H. Standish Thayer. LC 80-20890. 638p. (C). 1981. reprint ed. 39.95 (*0-915144-73-5*); reprint ed. pap. text 19.95 (*0-915144-74-3*) Hackett Pub.

Meaning & Action: A Study of American Pragmatism. Horace S. Thayer. LC 75-150861. (Orig.). (C). 1973. pap. write for info. (*0-672-61227-5*, 61227, Bobbs) Macmillan.

Meaning & Argument: A Theory of Meaning Centered on Immediate Argumental Role. Cesare Cozzo. LC 96-141811. (Stockholm Studies in Philosophy: Vol. 17). 208p. 1994. pap. 46.50 (*91-22-01648-1*, Pub. by Almqvist Wiksell) Coronet Bks.

***Meaning & Argument: An Introduction to Logic.** Ernest Lepore. 300p. 1999. 62.95 (*0-631-20581-0*); pap. 29.95 (*0-631-20582-9*) Blackwell Pubs.

Meaning & Authenticity: Further Work in the Sociology of Art. Cesar Grana. 320p. 1988. 44.95 (*0-88738-226-6*) Transaction Pubs.

Meaning & Being in Myth. Norman Austin. LC 89-34186. 256p. 1990. lib. bdg. 35.00 (*0-271-00681-1*) Pa St U Pr.

Meaning & Categorization. R. M. Frumkina & A. V. Mikhejev. 203p. 1996. 95.00 (*1-56072-143-X*) Nova Sci Pubs.

Meaning & Change of Meaning. Gustaf Stern. LC 75-2125. (Indiana University Studies in the History & Theory of Linguistics). 456p. 1975. reprint ed. lib. bdg. 75.00 (*0-8371-7938-6*, STME, Greenwood Pr) Greenwood.

***Meaning & Cognition: A Multidisciplinary Approach.** Liliana Albertazzi. LC 00-40314. (Converging Evidence in Language & Communication Research Ser.). 2000. write for info. (*1-55619-681-4*) J Benjamins Pubng Co.

Meaning & Cognitive Structure: Issues in the Computational Theory of Mind. Ed. by Zenon W. Pylyshyn & William Demopoulos. LC 86-10801. (Theoretical Issues in Cognitive Science Ser.: Vol. 3). 264p. (C). 1986. text 78.50 (*0-89391-372-3*) Ablx Pub.

Meaning & Context: A Introduction to the Psychology of Language. Ed. by H. Hermann. (Cognition & Language Ser.). (Illus.). 308p. (C). 90.00 (*0-306-42197-6*, Kluwer Plenum) Kluwer Academic.

Meaning & Context: An Introduction to the Psychology of Language. H. Hormann. (Cognition & Language). (Illus.). 308p. (C). 1986. pap. 37.50 (*0-306-42296-4*, Kluwer Plenum) Kluwer Academic.

Meaning & Creativity. Ronald E. Puhek. 118p. 1998. pap. 10.00 (*1-892590-06-9*) Out Your Bk.

Meaning & Demeaning of Routine Work: Restoring Meaning to the Workplace? 1991. lib. bdg. 79.95 (*0-8490-4634-3*) Gordon Pr.

Meaning & End of Religion: With a Revised Foreword from John Hick. Wilfred C. Smith. LC 90-44628. 352p. (Orig.). 1990. pap. 24.00 (*0-8006-2475-0*, 1-2475, Fortress Pr) Augsburg Fortress.

Meaning & Existence. Gustav Bergmann. LC 60-5036. 286p. (Orig.). reprint ed. pap. 88.70 (*0-608-09846-9*, 206923400003) Bks Demand.

Meaning & Existence in Mathematics. C. Castonguay. LC 72-96052. (Library of Exact Philosophy: Vol. 9). 159p. 1973. 52.95 (*0-387-81110-9*) Spr-Verlag.

Meaning & Experience of Happiness in Islam. Syed Muhammad Naquib al-Attas. 28p. (C). 1997. pap. 4.00 (*0-934905-90-8*, Library of Islam) Kazi Pubns.

An Asterisk (*) at the beginning of an entry indicates that the title is appearing for the first time.

Meaning & Expression: Toward a Sociology of Art. Hanna Deinhard. LC 83-18526. (Illus.). 120p. 1984. reprint ed. lib. bdg. 49.50 (*0-313-24252-6*, DEMX, Greenwood Pr) Greenwood.

Meaning & Form: Systemic Functional Interpretations; Meaning & Choice in Language: Studies for Michael Halliday. M. Halliday. (Advances in Discourse Processes Ser.: Vol. 57). 659p. 1996. pap. 42.50 (*1-56750-255-5*); text 78.50 (*1-56750-254-7*) Ablx Pub.

Meaning & Geography: The Social Conception of the Region in Northern Greece. Alexandros P. Lagopoulos & Karin Boklund-Lagopoulou. LC 91-43000. (Approaches to Semiotics Ser.: No. 104). xiv, 453p. (C). 1992. lib. bdg. 183.10 (*3-11-012956-6*) Mouton.

Meaning & Grammar: An Introduction to Semantics. 2nd ed. Gennaro Chierchia & Sally McConnell-Ginet. LC 99-20030. (Illus.). 522p. 2000. 75.00 (*0-262-03269-4*); pap. 32.50 (*0-262-53164-X*) MIT Pr.

Meaning & Grammar: Cross-Linguistic Perspectives. Ed. by Michael Kefer & Johan Van Der Auwera. LC 91-45131. (Empirical Approaches to Language Typology Ser.: No. 10). x, 427p. (C). 1992. lib. bdg. 153.85 (*3-11-012805-5*, 48-92) Mouton.

***Meaning & Ideology in Historical Archaeology: Style, Social Identity & Capitalism in an Australian Town.** Heather Burke. LC 99-37715. (Contributions to Global Historical Archaeology Ser.). 276p. 1999. 79.95 (*0-306-46066-1*) Kluwer Academic.

Meaning & Importance of the Jewish Holidays: The Feasts of the Lord. John Fischer. 24p. (Orig.). 1987. pap. 1.50 (*0-915775-06-9*) Love Song Mess Assn.

Meaning & Inference in Medieval Philosophy. Ed. by Norman Kretzmann. (Synthese Library: No. 32). 420p. (C). 1988. text 271.50 (*90-277-2577-2*) Kluwer Academic.

Meaning & Interpretation: Wittgenstein, Henry James, & Literary Knowledge. G. L. Hagberg. LC 93-36146. 200p. (C). 1994. text 32.50 (*0-8014-2926-9*) Cornell U Pr.

Meaning & Lexicography. Ed. by Jerzy Tomaszczyk & Barbara Lewandowska-Tomaszczyk. LC 90-23251. (Linguistic & Literary Studies in Eastern Europe: Vol. 28). xxv, 340p. 1990. 133.00 (*90-272-1533-2*) J Benjamins Pubng Co.

Meaning & Meaningfulness: Studies in the Analysis & Interpretation of Texts. Ross Chambers. LC 79-50280. (French Forum Monographs: No. 15). 197p. (Orig.). 1979. pap. 12.95 (*0-917058-14-3*) French Forum.

Meaning & Measurement of Moral Development. Ed. by L. Hohlberg. (Heinz Werner Lectures: No. 13). 1979. pap. 6.00 (*0-914206-18-4*) Clark U Pr.

Meaning & Measurement of Social Support. Ed. by Hans O. Veiel & Urs Baumann. 360p. 1991. 73.95 (*1-56032-220-9*) Hemisp Pub.

Meaning & Mental Representation. Robert Cummins. 173p. 1989. 25.00 (*0-262-03139-6*, Bradford Bks) MIT Pr.

Meaning & Mental Representation. Robert Cummins. 173p. 1991. reprint ed. pap. text 15.00 (*0-262-53096-1*, Bradford Bks) MIT Pr.

Meaning & Mental Representations. Ed. by Umberto Eco et al. LC 88-9251. (Advances in Semiotics Ser.). 238p. (Orig.). 1988. 31.95 (*0-253-33724-0*); pap. 13.95 (*0-253-20496-8*, MB-496) Ind U Pr.

Meaning & Message of the Traditions, 2 vols., Set. M. M. Nomani. 1990. 45.00 (*1-56744-132-7*) Kazi Pubns.

Meaning & Method in Information Studies. Ian V. Cornelius. LC 96-17290. (Information Management & Policy Ser.). 300p. 1996. pap. 39.50 (*1-56750-228-8*) Ablx Pub.

Meaning & Method in Information Studies. Ian V. Cornelius. LC 96-17290. (Information Management & Policy Ser.). 300p. 1996. text 73.25 (*1-56750-227-X*) Ablx Pub.

Meaning & Method in the Social Sciences: A Case for Methodological Pluralism. Paul A. Roth. LC 87-47718. 272p. 1987. text 42.50 (*0-8014-1941-7*); pap. text 15.95 (*0-8014-9605-5*) Cornell U Pr.

Meaning & Mind: An Intrapersonal Approach to Human Communication. Leonard Shedletsky. LC 89-25992. (C). 1989. pap. 12.95 (*0-927516-07-1*) ERIC-REC.

Meaning & Mode of Baptism. Jay Edward Adams. 63p. 1975. pap. 4.99 (*0-87552-043-X*) P & R Pubng.

Meaning & Modernity: Social Theory in Pragmatic Attitude. Eugene Rochberg-Halton. LC 86-7060. (Illus.). 320p. (C). 1995. lib. bdg. 48.00 (*0-226-72330-5*) U Ch Pr.

Meaning & Modernity: Social Theory in Pragmatic Attitude. Eugene Rochberg-Halton. LC 86-7060. (Illus.). 314p. (C). 2000. pap. text 18.00 (*0-226-72331-3*) U Ch Pr.

Meaning & Moral Order: Explorations in Cultural Analysis. Robert Wuthnow. LC 86-14668. 450p. 1987. pap. 17.95 (*0-520-06621-9*, Pub. by U CA Pr) Cal Prin Full Svc.

Meaning & Necessity: A Study in Semantics & Modal Logic. 2nd ed. Rudolf Carnap. 272p. 1988. pap. text 22.00 (*0-226-09347-6*, Midway Reprint) U Ch Pr.

Meaning & Negation. Steven B. Smith. (Janua Linguarum, Ser. Minor: No. 206). (Illus.). 91p. 1978. pap. text 27.70 (*90-279-3277-8*) Mouton.

***Meaning & Occupation: Essentials for Life.** Betty R. Hasselkus. 250p. (C). 2000. pap. text 32.00 (*1-55642-398-5*) SLACK Inc.

Meaning & Partiality. Reinhard Muskens. (Studies in Logic, Language & Information: No. 2). 152p. 1995. pap. 22.95 (*1-881526-79-8*) CSLI.

Meaning & Power in a Southeast Asian Realm. Shelly Errington. LC 88-39412. (Illus.). 344p. reprint ed. pap. 106.70 (*0-608-06333-9*, 206669400008) Bks Demand.

Meaning & Reading: A Philosophical Essay On Language & Literature. Michel Meyer. (Pragmatics & Beyond Ser.: Vol. IV: 3). ix, 176p. 1983. 53.00 (*90-272-2515-X*) J Benjamins Pubng Co.

Meaning & Reference. Ed. by A. W. Moore. LC 92-27073. (Oxford Readings in Philosophy Ser.). (Illus.). 308p. 1993. pap. text 22.00 (*0-19-875125-7*) OUP.

Meaning & Reliability of Economic Summit Undertakings, 1975-1989. Joseph P. Daniels. LC 92-40358. (Foreign Economic Policy of the United States Ser.). 320p. 1993. text 10.00 (*0-8153-1253-9*) Garland.

Meaning & Structure of Language. Wallace L. Chafe. LC 79-114855. x, 360p. 1975. pap. text 11.00 (*0-226-10056-1*) U Ch Pr.

Meaning & Style: Collected Papers. Stephen Ullmann. LC 73-76036. (Language & Style Series, Fourteen Ser.). x, 175p. 1973. write for info. (*0-631-08300-6*) Blackwell Pubs.

Meaning & Textuality. Francois Rastier. LC 98-145906. (Toronto Studies in Semiotics). (Illus.). 352p. 1997. pap. text 24.95 (*0-8020-8029-4*) U of Toronto Pr.

Meaning & Truth: The Essential Readings in Modern Semantics. Jay L. Garfield & Murray Kiteley. (Issues in Philosophy Ser.). 370p. (C). 1990. pap. text 19.95 (*1-55778-300-4*) Paragon Hse.

Meaning & Truth in the Arts. John Hospers. LC 47-2307. (Chapel Hill Bks.: No. 8). 262p. reprint ed. pap. 81.30 (*0-7837-2079-3*, 204235300004) Bks Demand.

Meaning & Truth in Wittgenstein's Tractatus. James C. Morrison. LC 68-15536. (Janua Linguarum, Series Minor: No. 64). 1968. pap. text 35.40 (*90-279-0592-4*) Mouton.

Meaning & Understanding. Ed. by Jacques Bouveresse & Herman H. Parret. 442p. (C). 1981. 106.15 (*3-11-008116-4*) De Gruyter.

Meaning & Use. Ed. by A. Margalit. (Synthese Language Library: No. 3). 319p. 1979. text 160.50 (*90-277-0888-6*, D Reidel) Kluwer Academic.

Meaning & Uses of Polish History. Adam Bromke. (East European Monographs: No. 212). 244p. 1987. text 46.50 (*0-88033-109-7*, Pub. by East Eur Monographs) Col U Pr.

Meaning & Validity of Economic Theory. Leo Rogin. LC 78-134129. (Essay Index Reprint Ser.). 1977. 42.95 (*0-8369-2126-7*) Ayer.

Meaning & Value of Mysticism. E. Herman. 1977. lib. bdg. 59.95 (*0-8490-2216-9*) Gordon Pr.

Meaning & Value of Mysticism. 3rd ed. E. Herman. LC 72-164607. (Select Bibliographies Reprint Ser.). 1977. reprint ed. 24.95 (*0-8369-5891-8*) Ayer.

Meaning & Value of the Sacraments. 2nd ed. Flower A. Newhouse. LC 77-186123. 123p. 1971. 13.00 (*0-910378-07-X*) Christward.

Meaning & Void: Inner Experience & the Incentives in People's Lives. Eric Klinger. LC 77-73546. (Illus.). 426p. 1978. pap. 19.95 (*0-8166-0856-3*) U of Minn Pr.

Meaning As Explanation: Advances in Linguistic Sign Theory. Ed. by Ellen Contini-Morava & Barbara S. Goldberg. (Trends in Linguistics, Studies & Monographs: No. 84). xii, 487p. (C). 1995. lib. bdg. 190.80 (*3-11-014122-1*) Mouton.

Meaning-Based Translation: A Guide to Cross-Language Equivalence. Mildred L. Larson. 548p. 1985. pap. text 36.00 (*0-8191-4301-4*) U Pr of Amer.

Meaning-Based Translation: A Guide to Cross-Language Equivalence. 2nd ed. Mildred L. Larson. LC 97-44626. 596p. (C). 1997. text 69.00 (*0-7618-0970-8*); pap. text 38.50 (*0-7618-0971-6*) U Pr of Amer.

Meaning-Based Translation Workbook: Biblical Exercises. Mildred L. Larson et al. LC 97-41214. 328p. (C). 1997. pap., wbk. ed. 39.50 (*0-7618-0948-1*) U Pr of Amer.

Meaning Built Environment: A Nonverbal Communication Approach. Rapoport. LC 90-10742. 253p. 1990. reprint ed. pap. 18.50 (*0-8165-1176-4*) U of Ariz Pr.

Meaning by All Means: A Vocabulary Text & Workbook for Students of ESL. Charles Mason. 144p. (C). 1986. pap. text 19.20 (*0-13-567058-6*) P-H.

Meaning by Shakespeare. Terence Hawkes. LC 92-7226. 176p. (C). 1992. pap. 24.99 (*0-415-07451-7*, A9652) Routledge.

***Meaning-Centered Marital & Family Therapy: Learning to Bear the Beams of Love.** James E. Lantz. LC 99-42368. (Illus.). 166p. 1999. pap. text 23.95 (*0-398-07017-2*) C C Thomas.

***Meaning-Centered Marital & Family Therapy: Learning to Bear the Beams of Love.** James E. Lantz. LC 99-42368. (Illus.). 166p. 2000. text 36.95 (*0-398-07016-4*) C C Thomas.

Meaning, Communication, & Understanding in the Classroom. Marian Sainsbury. (Avebury Series in Philosophy). 139p. 1992. 82.95 (*1-85628-352-6*, Pub. by Avebry) Ashgate Pub Co.

Meaning, Creativity, & the Partial Inscrutability of the Human Mind. Julius Moravcsik. LC 98-13456. (CSLI Lecture Notes Ser.: No. 79). 350p. (C). 1998. pap. 21.95 (*1-57586-126-7*); text 59.95 (*1-57586-127-5*) CSLI.

Meaning Detachment. Benoit De Cornulier. (Pragmatics & Beyond Ser.: Vol. I:7). vi, 124p. 1980. pap. 29.00 (*90-272-2502-8*) J Benjamins Pubng Co.

***Meaning First: A Functional Handbook of Fifty Ways to Polish Your Writing.** Carolyn G. Hartnett. 112p. 2000. pap. text 19.95 (*0-9644636-7-9*) Parlay Enter.

Meaning for a Life Entire. Charles A. Moser & P. Rollberg. LC 99-169956. 510 p. 1997. write for info. (*0-89357-249-7*) Slavica.

Meaning, Form, & Use in Context: Linguistic Applications. fac. ed. Georgetown University Round Table on Languages & L. Ed. by Deborah Schiffrin. LC 58-31607. (Illus.). 341p. 1984. reprint ed. pap. 105.80 (*0-7837-7796-5*, 204755200007) Bks Demand.

Meaning in Anthropology. Ed. by Keith H. Basso & Henry A. Selby. LC 75-21189. (School of American Research Advanced Seminar Ser.). 267p. reprint ed. pap. 82.80 (*0-608-15775-9*, 203099500073) Bks Demand.

Meaning in Anthropos: Anthropography As an Interdisciplinary Science of Culture. Kevin Shepherd. 255p. (C). 1989. 59.00 (*0-9508680-6-X*, Pub. by Anthropographia) St Mut.

Meaning in Comedy: Studies in Elizabethan Romantic Comedy. John S. Weld. LC 74-30168. 255p. (C). 1975. text 29.50 (*0-87395-278-2*) State U NY Pr.

Meaning in Culture. F. Allan Hanson. 127p. 1975. 19.95 (*0-7100-8132-4*, Routledge Thoemms) Routledge.

Meaning in Dreams & Dreaming. Maria F. Mahoney. 1966. reprint ed. pap. 9.95 (*0-8065-0095-6*, Citadel Pr) Carol Pub Group.

Meaning in English: An Introduction to Language Study. Jeffries. LC 97-48938. 280p. 1998. pap. 22.95 (*0-312-21380-8*); text 59.95 (*0-312-21379-4*) St Martin.

Meaning in Henry James. Millicent Bell. 400p. 1991. pap. 20.50 (*0-674-55763-8*) HUP.

Meaning in Henry James. Millicent Bell. 400p. (C). 1991. 55.00 (*0-674-55762-X*) HUP.

Meaning in History: The Theological Implications of the Philosophy of History. Karl Lowith. LC 57-7900. 266p. 1957. pap. text 15.00 (*0-226-49555-8*, P16) U Ch Pr.

Meaning in Language: An Introduction to Semantics & Pragmatics. D. Alan Cruse. LC 99-34409. (Oxford Textbooks in Linguistics Ser.). (Illus.). 416p. 2000. pap. text 24.95 (*0-19-870010-5*) OUP.

***Meaning in Legal Interpretation, Vol. 1.** Ed. by Graham Bradfield & Derek van der Merwe. 347p. 2000. pap. 55.50 (*0-7021-4799-0*, Pub. by Juta & Co) Gaunt.

Meaning in Life: The Creation of Value. Irving Singer. 220p. 1991. 24.95 (*0-02-928905-X*) Free Pr.

Meaning in Mayan Languages: Ethnolinguistic Studies. Ed. by Munro S. Edmonson. (Janua Linguarum, Series Practica: No. 158). 1973. pap. text 67.70 (*90-279-2489-9*) Mouton.

Meaning in Mid-Life Transitions. Edmund Sherman. LC 86-5999. (Illus.). 267p. (C). 1987. text 24.50 (*0-88706-384-5*) State U NY Pr.

Meaning in Mind: Fodor & His Critics. Ed. by Barry Loewer & Georges Reys. (Philosophers & Their Critics Ser.). 384p. 1993. pap. 31.95 (*0-631-18701-4*) Blackwell Pubs.

Meaning in Motion: New Cultural Studies of Dance. Jane C. Desmond. LC 96-43776. (Post-Contemporary Interventions Ser.). (Illus.). 392p. 1997. pap. 18.95 (*0-8223-1942-X*); lib. bdg. 54.95 (*0-8223-1936-5*) Duke.

Meaning in Myth. Thomas M. Casey. LC 89-61931. 160p. (Orig.). (C). 1989. pap. 14.95 (*1-55612-253-5*) Sheed & Ward WI.

Meaning in Suffering: Comfort in Crisis Through Logotherapy. Elisabeth Lukas. Tr. by Joseph Fabry from GER.Tr. of Auch Dein Leiden hat Sinn. 160p. (Orig.). 1986. pap. 9.95 (*0-917867-05-X*) V Frankl Inst.

Meaning in Technology. Arnold Pacey. LC 98-49287. (Illus.). 264p. 1999. 27.50 (*0-262-16182-6*) MIT Pr.

Meaning in Texts: The Historical Shaping of a Narrative. Edgar V. Mcknight. LC 77-15238. 344p. reprint ed. pap. 106.70 (*0-608-16333-3*, 202688500053) Bks Demand.

Meaning in the Visual Arts. Erwin Panofsky. LC 82-13600. (Right Brain - Whole Brain Learning Ser.). (Illus.). xx, 384p. (C). 1983. pap. text 18.95 (*0-226-64551-7*) U Ch Pr.

Meaning in Therapy. James Yoder. 192p. (Orig.). 1988. pap. text. write for info. (*0-932281-05-2*) Quill Pubns GA.

Meaning, Knowledge, & Reality. John H. McDowell. LC 98-19801. 448p. 1999. text 39.95 (*0-674-55777-8*) HUP.

Meaning Makers: Children Learning Language & Using Language to Learn. Gordon Wells. LC 85-21969. 235p. (Orig.). (C). 1985. pap. 28.00 (*0-435-08247-7*, 08247) Heinemann.

Meaning Making: A Special Issue of Discourse Processes. Ed. by Timothy Koschmann. 144p. 1999. pap. 32.50 (*0-8058-9805-0*) L Erlbaum Assocs.

Meaning-Making: Therapeutic Processes in Adult Development. Mary B. Carlsen. (Professional Bks.). 1988. 25.95 (*0-393-70049-6*) Norton.

Meaning of a Disability: The Lived Experience of Paralysis. Albert B. Robillard. LC 98-36637. 208p. 1999. 59.50 (*1-56639-675-1*); pap. 19.95 (*1-56639-676-X*) Temple U Pr.

Meaning of Addiction: An Unconventional View. Stanton Peele. LC 98-19896. (Psychology Ser.). 224p. 1998. reprint ed. pap. 24.95 (*0-7879-4382-7*) Jossey-Bass.

Meaning of Addiction: Compulsive Experience & Its Interpretations. Stanton Peele. LC 79-4750. 203p. 1985. pap. 27.95 (*0-669-13835-5*) Jossey-Bass.

Meaning of Adult Education. Eduard Lindeman. LC 89-61231. 150p. (C). 1989. pap. 24.95 (*0-9622488-1-9*) U OK PMC.

Meaning of Agapao & Phileo in the Greek New Testament. Roy F. Butler. 1977. pap. 7.50 (*0-87291-089-X*) Coronado Pr.

Meaning of AIDS: Implications for Medical Science, Clinical Practice, & Public Health Policy. Ed. by Eric T. Juengst & Barbara Koenig. LC 88-25464. 218p. 1989. 57.95 (*0-275-92646-X*, C2646, Praeger Pubs) Greenwood.

Meaning of Akita. John M. Haffert. 64p. 1989. pap. 3.25 (*1-890137-05-7*) One Hund-One Fnd.

Meaning of American Federalism: Constituting a Self-Governing Society. Vincent Ostrom. 301p. 1991. 24.95 (*1-55815-076-5*); pap. 19.95 (*1-55815-393-4*) ICS Pr.

Meaning of Anxiety. Rollo May. 448p. 1996. pap. 15.95 (*0-393-31456-1*, Norton Paperbks) Norton.

Meaning of Aphrodite. Paul Friedrich. LC 78-3177. (Illus.). 1993. lib. bdg. 13.95 (*0-226-26482-3*) U Ch Pr.

Meaning of Aphrodite. Paul Friedrich. LC 78-3177. (Illus.). 256p. 2000. pap. text 11.00 (*0-226-26483-1*) U Ch Pr.

Meaning of Beauty a Theory of Aesthetics. W. T. Stace. 256p. 1997. reprint ed. pap. 24.95 (*0-7661-0078-2*) Kessinger Pub.

Meaning of Biblical Sacrifice. unabridged ed. Bezalel. 280p. 1998. pap. 16.95 (*1-892896-04-4*) Buy Books.

Meaning of Blindness: Attitudes Toward Blindness & Blind People. Michael E. Monbeck. LC 73-77853. 224p. reprint ed. pap. 69.50 (*0-8357-9225-0*, 201763000007) Bks Demand.

Meaning of CAPHE: A Report on the First Five Years of the Consortium for the Advancement of Private Higher Education. J. Robert Moskin. ix, 147p. (Orig.). 1990. 3.00 (*1-879994-01-1*) Consortium Advan.

Meaning of Christ: A Mahayana Theology. John P. Keenan. LC 89-37873. (Faith Meets Faith Ser.). 320p. reprint ed. pap. 99.20 (*0-608-20190-1*, 207144900012) Bks Demand.

Meaning of Christian Brotherhood. 2nd ed. Joseph C. Ratzinger. Tr. by W. A. Glen-Doepfe from GER. LC 92-65064. 115p. 1993. pap. 9.95 (*0-89870-446-4*) Ignatius Pr.

Meaning of Christianity. Peter Nemeshegyi. 128p. 1982. pap. 3.95 (*0-8091-2464-5*) Paulist Pr.

Meaning of Christianity: An Expose of the Religious Rite of Circumcision. Garry De Young. 1988. pap. 17.95 (*0-936128-36-4*) De Young Pr.

Meaning of Church Membership. Wayne C. Clark. 1950. pap. 11.00 (*0-8170-0103-4*) Judson.

Meaning of Company Accounts. 6th ed. Walter Reid & David R. Myddelton. 360p. 1996. 43.95 (*0-566-07821-X*, Pub. by Gower) Ashgate Pub Co.

***Meaning of Company Accounts.** 7th ed. Walter Reid & David R. Myddelton. LC 00-42972. 368p. 2000. pap. 54.95 (*0-566-08378-7*, Pub. by Ashgate Pub) Ashgate Pub Co.

Meaning of Conscientizacao: The Goal of Paulo Freire's Pedagogy. William A. Smith. 170p. (Orig.). (C). 1976. spiral bd. 6.00 (*0-932288-35-9*) Ctr Intl Ed U of MA.

Meaning of Consciousness. Andrew Lohrey. LC 97-4581. 320p. (C). 1997. text 42.50 (*0-472-10821-2*, 10821) U of Mich Pr.

Meaning of Consecration Today: A Marian Model for a Secularized Age. Rene Laurentin. LC 91-77302. 208p. (Orig.). 1992. pap. 11.95 (*0-89870-403-0*) Ignatius Pr.

Meaning of Conservatism. 2nd ed. Roger Scruton. LC 98-18475. Date not set. pap. write for info. (*1-890318-40-X*) St Augustines Pr.

Meaning of Constitution. Countryman. LC 98-87526. 1999. pap. 11.95 (*0-312-18262-7*) St Martin.

Meaning of Contemporary Realism. Lukacs. (C). 1979. text. write for info. (*0-85036-069-2*, Pub. by MRLN) Paul & Co Pubs.

Meaning of Contemporary Realism. Georg Lukacs. 137p. (C). 1979. pap. write for info. (*0-85036-250-4*, Pub. by MRLN) Paul & Co Pubs.

Meaning of Conversion in Buddhism. Sangharakshita. (Illus.). 80p. (Orig.). (C). 1996. pap. 8.95 (*0-904766-67-5*) Windhorse Pubns.

Meaning of Costume. Dan Urian. (Illus.). 37p. (Orig.). 1984. pap. 1.00 (*0-932456-03-0*, TX 1-469-568) Personabks.

Meaning of Courtly Love: Papers of the First Annual Conference of the Center for... Ed. by F. X. Newman. LC 68-25571. 102p. (C). 1968. text 59.50 (*0-87395-038-0*, Pub. by State U NY Pr) Pegasus Pr.

Meaning of Courtly Love: Papers of the First Annual Conference of the Center for Medicine. Ed. by F. X. Newman. LC 68-25571. 102p. (C). 1968. pap. text 19.95 (*0-87395-222-7*, Pub. by State U NY Pr) Pegasus Pr.

Meaning of Culture. Morris Freilich. 325p. 1972. pap. 11.95 (*0-536-00699-7*) Schenkman Bks Inc.

Meaning of Culture: Moving the Postmodern Critique Forward. Kenneth Allan. LC 98-9941. 208p. 1998. 59.95 (*0-275-96124-9*, Praeger Pubs) Greenwood.

Meaning of Culture in Pediatric Rehabilitation & Health Care. Ed. by Suzann K. Campbell & Irma J. Wilhelm. LC 91-35397. (Physical & Occupational Therapy in Pediatrics Ser.). 72p. 1992. pap. text 19.95 (*1-56024-262-0*) Haworth Pr.

Meaning of Democracy & the Vulnerability of Democracies: A Response to Tocqueville's Challenge. Vincent Ostrom. LC 96-51299. 360p. (C). 1997. text 44.50 (*0-472-10797-6*, 10797); pap. text 19.95 (*0-472-08456-9*, 08456) U of Mich Pr.

Meaning of Difference: American Constructions of Race, Sex, & Gender, Social Class, & Sexual Orientation. Karen E. Rosenblum & Toni-Michelle C. Travis. LC 95-36974. (C). 1995. pap. text 29.74 (*0-07-053962-6*) McGraw.

Meaning of Difference: American Constructions of Race, Sex & Gender, Social Class & Sexual Orientation. 2nd ed. Karen Rosenblum & Toni-Michelle Travis. LC 99-34828. 480p. 1999. pap. 38.13 (*0-07-229602-X*) McGraw.

Meaning of Dreams. Isador H. Coriat. 194p. 1996. pap. 17.00 (*0-89540-313-7*, SB-313) Sun Pub.

***Meaning of Dreams.** Franklin D. Martini. 368p. 2001. 9.99 (*0-517-16250-4*) Crown Pub Group.

Meaning of Dreams for Sleeping Man. Vern Hansen. LC 93-42373. 256p. 1994. pap. 16.95 (*0-9634250-2-1*) J & L Pubns.

Meaning of Education: Contributions to a Philosophy of Education. enl. rev. ed. Nicholas M. Butler. LC 72-142611. (Essay Index Reprint Ser.). 1977. reprint ed. 23.95 (*0-8369-2219-0*) Ayer.

Meaning of Europe: Geography & Geopolitics. Michael Heffernan. (Arnold Publications). (Illus.). 304p. 1998. pap. text 24.95 (*0-340-58018-6*) OUP.

M

Meaning of Evolution: The Morphological Construction & Ideological Reconstruction of Darwin's Theory. Robert J. Richards. LC 91-19017. (Science & Its Conceptual Foundations Ser.). (Illus.). 222p. 1992. lib. bdg. 22.50 (*0-226-71202-8*) U Ch Pr.

Meaning of Evolution: The Morphological Construction & Ideological Reconstruction of Darwin's Theory. Robert J. Richards. LC 91-19017. (Science & Its Conceptual Foundations Ser.). (Illus.). xvi, 222p. (C). 1993. pap. text 10.95 (*0-226-71203-6*) U Ch Pr.

*__Meaning of Faith: Spirituality for Adult Christians.__ Center for Learning Network Staff. (Religion Ser.). 52p. 1999. pap. text 3.95 (*1-56077-580-7*) Ctr Learning.

Meaning of Famine. O'Sullivan. LC 96-44980. 1997. write for info. (*0-7185-1426-2*) St Martin.

Meaning of Fiction. Albert S. Cook. LC 60-9591. 330p. reprint ed. pap. 102.30 (*0-7837-3793-9*, 204361300010) Bks Demand.

Meaning of Flowers: Myth, Language & Love. Gretchen Scoble & Ann Field. LC 97-30802. (Illus.). 108p. 1998. 14.95 (*0-8118-1931-0*) Chronicle Bks.

Meaning of Fossils: Episodes in the History of Palaeontology. 2nd ed. Martin J. Rudwick. LC 84-28080. (Illus.). 304p. (C). 1985. pap. text 19.00 (*0-226-73103-0*) U Ch Pr.

Meaning of Freedom. Philip Drew. (Illus.). 500p. (C). 1985. pap. text 16.50 (*0-08-032450-9*, Pub. by Aberdeen U Pr) Macmillan.

Meaning of Freedom. Philip Drew. 460p. 1982. text 32.00 (*0-08-025743-7*, Pergamon Pr) Elsevier.

*__Meaning of Freedom: A Study of Secular, Muslim & Christian Views.__ J. Andrew Kirk. vii, 262p. 1998. reprint ed. pap. 20.00 (*0-85364-844-1*, Pub. by Paternoster Pub) OM Literature.

Meaning of Freedom: Economics, Politics, & Culture after Slavery. Ed. by Frank McGlynn, Jr. & Seymour Drescher. LC 91-26606. (Latin American Ser.). (Illus.). 352p. 1992. pap. 19.95 (*0-8229-5479-6*); text 49.95 (*0-8229-3695-X*) U of Pittsburgh Pr.

Meaning of Freedom of Speech, 15. Paul Murphy. LC 72-133500. (Contributions in American History Ser.: No. 15). 401p. 1972. 39.95 (*0-8371-5176-7*, MCLB, Greenwood Pr) Greenwood.

Meaning of Gandhi. Ed. by Paul F. Power. LC 72-170180. 205p. reprint ed. pap. 63.60 (*0-608-18714-3*, 202703200053) Bks Demand.

Meaning of Gardens. Ed. by Mark Francis & Randolph T. Hester, Jr. (Illus.). 294p. 1992. reprint ed. pap. text 32.50 (*0-262-56061-5*) MIT Pr.

Meaning of Gaulism. Cogan. 243p. 1995. pap. 15.95 (*0-312-10790-0*) St Martin.

Meaning of Gender in Theology: Problems & Possibilities. Anne-Louise Eriksson. LC 96-218483. (Uppsala Women's Studies: No. 6). 168p. (Orig.). 1995. pap. 39.50 (*91-554-3655-2*) Coronet Bks.

Meaning of General Education: The Emergence of a Curriculum Paradigm. Gary E. Miller. LC 87-26739. 224p. reprint ed. pap. 69.50 (*0-7837-0988-9*, 204129400020) Bks Demand.

Meaning of General Theoretical Sociology: Tradition & Formalization. Thomas J. Fararo. (American Sociological Assn. Rose Monographs). (Illus.). 401p. (C). 1989. text 65.00 (*0-521-37258-5*) Cambridge U Pr.

Meaning of General Theoretical Sociology: Tradition & Formalization. Thomas J. Fararo. (American Sociological Assn. Rose Monographs). (Illus.). 403p. (C). 1992. pap. text 25.95 (*0-521-43795-4*) Cambridge U Pr.

Meaning of God in Modern Jewish Religion. Mordecai Menaheim Kaplan. 1975. reprint ed. pap. 16.95 (*0-935457-19-4*) Reconstructionist Pr.

Meaning of God in Modern Jewish Religion. Mordecai Menaheim Kaplan. LC 94-39779. 412p. 1995. reprint ed. pap. text 17.95 (*0-8143-2552-1*) Wayne St U Pr.

Meaning of Grief: A Dramaturgical Approach to Understanding Emotion, 8. Larry Cochran & Emily Claspell. LC 86-27156. (Contributions in Psychology Ser.: No. 8). 189p. 1987. 49.95 (*0-313-25607-1*, CMG/, Greenwood Pr) Greenwood.

Meaning of Health. Paul Tillich. Ed. by Perry D. LeFevre. LC 83-83035. 251p. 1984. text 28.95 (*0-913552-21-6*) Exploration Pr.

Meaning of Heidegger. Thomas D. Langan. LC 59-9976. 258p. (C). reprint ed. 80.00 (*0-8357-9067-3*, 200611400061) Bks Demand.

Meaning of Heidegger: A Critical Study of an Existentialist Phenomenology. Thomas Langan. LC 83-12737. 247p. (C). 1983. reprint ed. lib. bdg. 55.00 (*0-313-24124-4*, LAMH, Greenwood Pr) Greenwood.

Meaning of History: A Dictionary of Quotations. N. Gordon Carper & Joyce Carper. LC 90-13977. 392p. 1990. lib. bdg. 65.00 (*0-313-26835-5*, CQH/, Greenwood Pr) Greenwood.

Meaning of Hitler. Sebastian Haffner. Tr. by Ewald Osers from GER. 180p. 1983. pap. 14.00 (*0-674-55775-1*) HUP.

*__Meaning of Hope: Spirituality for adult Christians.__ Center for Learning Network Staff. (Religion Ser.). 46p. 1999. pap. text 3.95 (*1-56077-581-5*) Ctr Learning.

Meaning of Human Existence. Leslie A. Paul. LC 73-148642. 1971. reprint ed. lib. bdg. 65.00 (*0-8371-6008-1*, PAHE, Greenwood Pr) Greenwood.

Meaning of Human Suffering. Ed. by Flavian Dougherty. LC 81-6267. 349p. 1982. 45.95 (*0-89885-011-8*, Kluwer Acad Hman Sci) Kluwer Academic.

Meaning of Icons. rev. ed. Vladimir Lossky & Leonid Ouspensky. Tr. by G. E. Palmer & E. Kadloubovsky from RUS. LC 82-22979. (Illus.). 224p. (C). 1982. reprint ed. pap. 39.95 (*0-913836-99-0*); reprint ed. text 49.95 (*0-913836-77-X*) St Vladimirs.

Meaning of Illness. Mark Kidel & Susan Rowe-Leete. 224p. 1988. text 39.95 (*0-415-00191-9*); pap. text 13.95 (*0-415-00192-7*) Routledge.

Meaning of Illness. Ed. by Mark Kidel & Susan Rowe-Leete. LC 87-28601. 176p. reprint ed. pap. 54.60 (*0-608-20356-4*, 207160900002) Bks Demand.

Meaning of Illness: A Phenomenological Account of the Different Perspectives of Physician & Patient. S. Kay Toombs. (Philosophy & Medicine Ser.). 184p. (C). 1993. pap. text 29.90 (*0-7923-2443-9*, Pub. by Kluwer Academic) Kluwer Academic.

Meaning of Illness: Anthropology, History & Sociology of Illness, No. 5. M. Auge. 270p. 1995. text 53.00 (*3-7186-5207-2*) Gordon & Breach.

Meaning of Illness: Selected Psychoanalytic Writings. Georg Groddeck. LC 76-46813. 290p. 1977. 42.50 (*0-8236-3205-9*) Intl Univs Pr.

Meaning of Immortality in Human Experience: Including Thoughts on Death & Life. rev. ed. William E. Hocking. LC 72-10697. 263p. 1973. reprint ed. lib. bdg. 65.00 (*0-8371-6621-7*, HOMI, Greenwood Pr) Greenwood.

Meaning of Independence: John Adams, George Washington, Thomas Jefferson. Edmund S. Morgan. LC 76-8438. (Richard Lectures for 1975, University of Virginia Ser.). 95p. reprint ed. pap. 30.00 (*0-7837-4227-4*, 204391400012) Bks Demand.

Meaning of India Flowering Plants Name. M. P. Nayar. (C). 1988. text 60.00 (*0-7855-3157-2*, Pub. by Scientific) St Mut.

Meaning of Information. Doede Nauta. LC 79-173382. (Approaches to Semiotics Ser.: No. 20). (Illus.). 314p. 1972. text 66.15 (*90-279-1996-8*) Mouton.

Meaning of International Experience for Schools. Angene H. Wilson. LC 92-38233. 184p. 1993. 55.00 (*0-275-94508-1*, C4508, Praeger Pubs) Greenwood.

Meaning of Irish Place Names. James O'Connell. 90p. 1979. pap. 5.95 (*0-685-25952-8*, Pub. by Blackstaff Pr) Dufour.

Meaning of Irish Place Names. James O'Connell. 90p. 1986. pap. 5.95 (*0-85640-175-7*) Dufour.

Meaning of Irony: A Psychoanalytic Investigation. Frank Stringfellow, Jr. LC 93-35583. (SUNY Series, The Margins of Literature). 177p. (C). 1994. text 49.50 (*0-7914-1977-0*); pap. text 16.95 (*0-7914-1978-9*) State U NY Pr.

Meaning of It All: Thoughts of a Citizen Scientist. Richard Phillips Feynman. LC 97-48250. 160p. 1998. 22.00 (*0-201-36080-2*) Addison-Wesley.

*__Meaning of It All: Thoughts of a Citizen Scientist.__ Richard Phillips Feynman. 144p. 1999. pap. text 13.00 (*0-7382-0166-9*, Pub. by Perseus Pubng) HarpC.

*__Meaning of It All in Everyday Speech.__ Don Cupitt. 1998. pap. 16.00 (*0-334-02786-1*) TPI PA.

Meaning of Jesus: Two Visions. Marcus J. Borg & N. T. Wright. LC 98-30672. 304p. 1999. 24.00 (*0-06-060875-7*, Pub. by Harper SF) HarpC.

Meaning of Jesus: Two Visions. Marcus J. Borg & N. T. Wright. LC 98-30672. 304p. 2000. pap. 15.00 (*0-06-060876-5*, Pub. by Harper SF) HarpC.

Meaning of Jewish Existence: Theological Essays, 1930-1939. Alexander Altmann. Ed. by Alfred L. Ivry. Tr. by Edith Ehrlich & Leonard H. Ehrlich from GER. LC 90-28748. (Tauber Institute Ser.: No. 12). 219p. 1991. text 45.00 (*0-87451-554-8*) U Pr of New Eng.

Meaning of Kahlil Gibran. M. S. Daoudi. 160p. 1982. 9.95 (*0-8065-0804-3*, Citadel Pr) Carol Pub Group.

Meaning of Language. Robert M. Martin. 239p. 1987. pap. text 16.50 (*0-262-63108-3*, Bradford Bks) MIT Pr.

*__Meaning of Liberalism: East & West.__ Ed. by Jiri Musil & Zdenek L. Suda. LC 00-24117. 2000. pap. text 22.95 (*963-9116-54-8*) Ctrl Europ Univ.

*__Meaning of Liberalism - East & West.__ Ed. by Jeri Musil & Zdenek L. Suda. LC 00-24117. 280p. (C). 2000. 49.95 (*963-9116-53-X*) Ctrl Europ Univ.

Meaning of Life. Jonathan Gabay. 144p. 1995. 19.95 (*1-85227-592-8*, Pub. by Virgin Bks) London Brdge.

Meaning of Life. 2nd ed. E. D. Klemke. LC 98-47102. 304p. (C). 1999. pap. 21.95 (*0-19-512703-X*) OUP.

*__Meaning of Life: And Other Lectures on Fundamental Issues.__ Rudolf Steiner. 176p. 1999. pap. 16.95 (*1-85584-092-8*, Pub. by R Steiner Pr) Anthroposophic.

*__Meaning of Life: Buddhist Perspectives on Cause & Effect.__ Dalai Lama. Ed. & Tr. by Jeffrey Hopkins. 164p. 2000. pap. 15.95 (*0-86171-173-4*) Wisdom MA.

Meaning of Life: Revelations, Reflections & Insights from all Walks of Life. Ed. by Jonathan Gabay. (Illus.). 144p. 1999. text 20.00 (*0-7881-6138-5*) DIANE Pub.

*__Meaning of Life: Spiritual Insights & Practical Advice on the Big Questions We All Ask.__ Tom Gregory. 2000. pap. 18.95 (*0-9672776-7-1*) Living Spirit.

Meaning of Life & Other Awesome Cosmic Revelations. Darrell Schweitzer. (Booklet Ser.: No. 30). 49p. 1988. pap. text 2.75 (*0-936055-35-9*) C Drumm Bks.

Meaning of Life & Other Awesome Cosmic Revelations. deluxe ed. Darrell Schweitzer. (Booklet Ser.: No. 30). 49p. 1988. pap. 6.00 (*0-936055-36-7*) C Drumm Bks.

Meaning of Life at the Edge of the Third Millennium. Leonard Swidler. LC 92-10911. 128p. 1992. pap. 8.95 (*0-8091-3315-6*) Paulist Pr.

Meaning of Life from a Buddhist Perspective. Dalai Lama XIV. Ed. & Tr. by Jeffrey Hopkins from TIB. LC 91-30315. (Illus.). 114p. 1993. pap. 12.50 (*0-86171-096-7*) Wisdom MA.

*__Meaning of Life in the World Religions.__ Nancy Martin. 256p. 1999. pap. 23.95 (*1-85168-200-7*) One Wrld.

Meaning of Literature. Timothy J. Reiss. LC 91-23344. 408p. 1992. pap. text 17.95 (*0-8014-9947-X*) Cornell U Pr.

Meaning of Lives: Biography, Autobiography & the Spiritual Quest. Richard A. Hutch. LC 96-52894. (Religious Studies). 256p. 1997. 79.50 (*0-304-33917-2*) Continuum.

Meaning of Love. Lori-Ann Desetto. 1999. pap. 7.95 (*0-533-12840-4*) Vantage.

Meaning of Love. Ed. by Ashley Montagu. LC 72-11335. 248p. 1974. reprint ed. lib. bdg. 35.00 (*0-8371-6656-X*, MOML, Greenwood Pr) Greenwood.

Meaning of Love. rev. ed. Vladimir Solovyov. 118p. 1985. pap. 12.95 (*0-940262-18-5*, Lindisfarne) Anthroposophic.

Meaning of Love. rev. ed. Vladimir Solovyov. 128p. 1992. 21.95 (*0-940262-55-X*, Lindisfarne) Anthroposophic.

Meaning of Ludwig von Mises: Contributions in Economics, Sociology, Epistemology, & Political Philosophy. Intro. by Jeffrey M. Herbener. LC 92-34816. (Studies in Austrian Economics). 349p. (C). 1993. 19.95 (*0-945466-12-9*) Ludwig von Mises.

*__Meaning of Lunch.__ Dan Leone. LC 99-65036. 257p. (YA). 2000. pap. 14.95 (*0-9666028-7-0*, Pub. by Mammoth Press) SPD-Small Pr Dist.

Meaning of Lunch: The Collected Restaurant Ramblings of San Francisco's Cheapest Eater. Dan Leone. 1998. pap. text 13.95 (*0-9653524-9-8*) Russn Hill Pr.

Meaning of Mannerism. Ed. by Franklin W. Robinson & Stephen G. Nichols, Jr. LC 71-189512. (Illus.). 142p. reprint ed. pap. 44.10 (*0-608-11309-3*, 202232700026) Bks Demand.

Meaning of Market Process: Essays in the Development of Modern Austrian Economics. Eric Kirzner. 272p. (C). 1996. pap. 29.99 (*0-415-13738-1*) Routledge.

Meaning of Masonry. W. L. Wilmhurst. 216p. 1995. 7.99 (*0-517-33194-2*) Random Hse Value.

Meaning of Masonry. Albert Pike. 66p. 1992. reprint ed. pap. 12.95 (*1-56459-050-X*) Kessinger Pub.

Meaning of Masonry. 2nd ed. Lynn Perkins. Ed. by Von Seggern Enterprises Staff. 188p. 1993. reprint ed. pap. 11.95 (*0-9639283-0-9*) Von Seggern.

Meaning of Mind: Language, Morality, & Neuroscience. Thomas Szasz. LC 96-2207. 200p. 1996. 19.95 (*0-275-95603-2*, Praeger Pubs) Greenwood.

Meaning of Mllarme: A Bilingual Edition of His Poesie & Un Coup de Des. Stephane Mallarme. 256p. 1990. pap. 30.00 (*1-898218-23-3*) St Mut.

Meaning of Modern Art: A Philosophical Interpretation. Karsten Harries. LC 68-17733. (Studies in Phenomenology & Existential Philosophy). 166p. 1968. pap. 15.95 (*0-8101-0593-4*) Northwestern U Pr.

Meaning of Modern Sculpture. Reginald H. Wilenski. LC 75-41297. reprint ed. 32.50 (*0-404-14757-7*) AMS Pr.

Meaning of Movement: Developmental & Clinical Perspectives of the Kestenberg Movement Profile. Janet K. Amighi et al. 336p. 1998. 65.00 (*90-5700-528-X*, ECU54, Harwood Acad Pubs) Gordon & Breach.

Meaning of Munich 50 Years Later. Ed. by Kenneth M. Jensen & David Wurmser. LC 89-26869. 1990. pap. text 10.95 (*1-878379-03-8*) US Inst Peace.

Meaning of Myriad Good Deeds: A Study of Yung-ming Yen-shou & the Wan-shan t'ungkuei Chi. Albert Welter. LC 91-41197. (Asian Thought & Culture Ser.: Vol. 13). X, 266p. (C). 1994. text 59.95 (*0-8204-1796-3*) P Lang Pubng.

Meaning of Mysticism. Lazar Puhalo. 48p. Date not set. pap. write for info. (*1-879038-63-3*, 9033) Synaxis Pr.

Meaning of Nolan Ryan. Nick Trujillo. LC 93-28038. (Illus.). 176p. 1994. 29.95 (*0-89096-574-9*); pap. 14.95 (*0-89096-575-7*) Tex A&M Univ Pr.

Meaning of Nouns: Semantic Theory in Classical & Medieval India. Namartha-nirnaya of Kaundabhatta. LC 92-17009. (Studies of Classical India: Vol. 13). 308p. (C). 1992. lib. bdg. 273.50 (*0-7923-1847-1*, Pub. by Kluwer Academic) Kluwer Academic.

Meaning of Nucleocytoplasmic Transport. Philip L. Taylor & Paul S. Agutter. LC 96-22042. (Molecular Biology Intelligence Unit Ser.). 207p. 1996. 99.00 (*1-57059-363-9*) Landes Bioscience.

Meaning of Persons. Paul Tournier. 1993. reprint ed. lib. bdg. 35.95 (*1-56849-248-0*) Buccaneer Bks.

Meaning of Prayer. Harry E. Fosdick. 1987. pap. 10.95 (*0-687-23962-1*) Abingdon.

Meaning of Prayer. Harry E. Fosdick. 1997. pap. 9.95 (*1-886158-08-8*) Macalester.

Meaning of Quantum Chemistry: A Guide for Students of Chemistry & Physics. Jim Baggott. (Illus.). 244p. 1992. pap. text 29.95 (*0-19-855575-X*) OUP.

Meaning of Quantum Gravity. H. H. Von Borzeszkowski & H. J. Treder. (C). 1987. text 107.50 (*90-277-2518-7*) Kluwer Academic.

Meaning of Race. Kenan Malik. (C). 1996. text 55.00 (*0-8147-5552-6*); pap. text 19.00 (*0-8147-5553-4*) NYU Pr.

Meaning of Redemption. Beverly F. Brandt. LC 99-90569. (Consciousness of Commitment Ser.: Vol. 8, Bk. 7). 600p. pap. write for info. (*1-929064-07-1*, 2007-1, Pub. by Brandt Pubns) First Bks.

Meaning of 'Relationship' in Interpersonal Communication. Ed. by Richard L. Conville & L. Edna Rogers. LC 97-14472. 216p. 1998. 59.95 (*0-275-95211-8*, Praeger Pubs) Greenwood.

Meaning of Relativity. Albert Einstein. 176p. 1996. reprint ed. 6.98 (*1-56731-136-9*, MJF Bks) Fine Comms.

Meaning of Relativity. 5th ed. Albert Einstein. 176p. 1956. pap. text 10.95 (*0-691-02352-2*, Pub. by Princeton U Pr) Cal Prin Full Svc.

Meaning of Religious Conversion: The Case of the Igbo of Nigeria. Cyril C. Okoroche. (Avebury Series in Philosophy). 354p. 1987. text 101.95 (*0-566-05030-7*, Pub. by Avebury) Ashgate Pub Co.

Meaning of Religious Freedom: Modern Politics & the Democratic Resolution. Franklin I. Gamwell. LC 94-15524. (SUNY Series in Religious Studies). 251p. (C). 1995. text 57.50 (*0-7914-2389-1*); pap. text 18.95 (*0-7914-2390-5*) State U NY Pr.

Meaning of Reminiscence & Life Review. Ed. by Jon Hendricks. LC 94-16680. (Perspectives on Aging & Human Development Ser.). 227p. 1995. pap. 25.95 (*0-89503-170-1*) Baywood Pub.

Meaning of Righteousness in Paul: A Linguistic & Theological Enquiry. John A. Ziesler. LC 75-164455. (Society for New Testament Studies,: Vol. 20). 267p. reprint ed. pap. 76.10 (*0-608-12477-X*, 2024567) Bks Demand.

Meaning of Ritual. Leonel L. Mitchell. LC 87-28282. 136p. 1977. reprint ed. pap. 7.95 (*0-8192-1451-5*) Morehouse Pub.

Meaning of Salvation. Michael Green. 256p. 1992. reprint ed. pap. 22.95 (*1-57383-003-8*) Regent College.

Meaning of San Rafael. Henry Winston. 1971. pap. 0.20 (*0-87898-070-9*) New Outlook.

Meaning of Sanctification. Charles E. Brown. 1980. pap. 7.99 (*0-88019-079-5*) Schmul Pub Co.

Meaning of Shakespeare, 2 vols., 1. Harold C. Goddard. LC 51-2288. 407p. 1960. pap. text 17.00 (*0-226-30041-2*, P50) U Ch Pr.

Meaning of Shakespeare, 2 vols., 2. Harold C. Goddard. LC 51-2288. 305p. 1960. pap. text 15.00 (*0-226-30042-0*, P51) U Ch Pr.

*__Meaning of Slavery in the North.__ Eastern National Park Staff. Ed. by Martin Blatt et al. LC 97-25042. (Labor in America Ser.: Vol. 4). 224p. 1998. text 40.00 (*0-8153-2345-X*, SS1184) Garland.

Meaning of Social Interaction: An Introduction to Social Psychology. Jeffrey E. Nash & James M. Calonico. LC 96-75605. 376p. (Orig.). 1996. text 39.95 (*1-882289-30-7*); pap. text 25.95 (*1-882289-29-3*) Gen Hall.

Meaning of Sociology. 6th ed. Charon. LC 98-33680. 376p. 1998. pap. text 32.20 (*0-13-906066-9*) P-H.

Meaning of Sociology. 6th ed. Joel M. Charon. LC 98-20626. 229p. 1998. pap. text 30.80 (*0-13-798042-6*) P-H.

Meaning of Star Trek: An Excursion into the Myth & Marvel of Star Trek Universe. Thomas Richards. LC 97-6845. 208p. 1999. pap. 12.95 (*0-385-48439-9*) Doubleday.

Meaning of Stoicism. Ludwig Edelstein. LC 66-23463. (Martin Classical Lectures: No. 21). 120p. 1966. 8.95 (*0-674-55850-2*) HUP.

Meaning of Suffering: An Interpretation of Human Existence from the Viewpoint of Time, 22. Adrian C. Moulyn. LC 82-6171. (Contributions in Philosophy Ser.: No. 22). (Illus.). 336p. 1982. 65.00 (*0-313-22233-9*, MOS/, Greenwood Pr) Greenwood.

Meaning of Suffering & Strife & Reconciliation, 2 vols. in 1. Archimandrite S. Alekseiv. Tr. by Ralitsa Doynova. LC 94-69053. (Spiritual Writings of Archimandrite Seraphim Alekseiv Ser.). (BUL., Illus.). 112p. 1996. pap. 8.95 (*0-938635-86-7*) St Herman Pr.

Meaning of Symbolism. Clair C. Boulton. Ed. by Paul L. Wilcox. 192p. (C). 1989. write for info. (*0-318-65066-5*) Placer Acad Pr.

Meaning of Syntax: A Study of Adjectives of English. Connor Ferris. LC 92-36946. (Linguistics Library). 1993. boxed set. write for info. (*0-582-21013-5*) Longman.

Meaning of the City. Jacques Ellul. (Biblical & Theological Classics Library: Vol. 15). xviii, 209p. 1997. reprint ed. pap. 9.99 (*0-85364-791-7*, Pub. by Paternoster Pub) OM Literature.

Meaning of the Constitution. 3rd ed. Angela R. Holder. LC 97-74678. 120p. 1997. pap. text 11.95 (*0-7641-0099-8*) Barron.

*__Meaning of the Famine.__ Patrick O'Sullivan. (Irish Worldwide Ser.). 2000. pap. text 24.95 (*0-7185-0232-9*) Leicester U Pr.

Meaning of the Finite Verb Forms in the Old Church Slavonic Codex Suprasliensis: A Synchronic Study. Tine H. Amse-De Jong. (Slavistic Printings & Reprintings Ser.: No. 319). 228p. (Orig.). 1974. pap. text 103.10 (*90-279-3012-0*) Mouton.

Meaning of the Glorious Quran. M. M. Pickthal. 810p. 1995. 14.95 (*81-7151-106-6*) Asia Bk Corp.

Meaning of the Glorious Quran. Pickthall. 1982. pap. 5.95 (*1-56744-133-5*) Kazi Pubns.

Meaning of the Glorious Quran. Tr. by Marmaduke Pickthall. 464p. 1997. pap. 8.95 (*1-879402-51-3*) Tahrike Tarsile Quran.

Meaning of the Glorious Quran, 2 vols., Set. Abdullah Y. Ali. 24.00 (*0-686-37146-1*) New World Press NY.

Meaning of the Glorious Quran: Text & Explanatory Translation. rev. ed. M. M. Pickthall. Ed. & Rev. by Arafat K. El-Ashi. LC 94-24009. 744p. (Orig.). 1996. pap. 12.00 (*0-915957-22-1*) amana pubns.

Meaning of the Holy Quran. Tr. by Abdullah Y. Ali. 1800p. 1996. 95.00 (*0-614-21061-5*, 766) Kazi Pubns.

Meaning of the Holy Quran. Tr. by Abdullah Yusef Ali. 1824p. 1998. 14.95 (*0-915957-32-9*) amana pubns.

Meaning of the Holy Quran. M. M. Pickthall. 464p. 1992. 12.95 (*81-85274-00-2*) Asia Bk Corp.

Meaning of the Holy Quran. Mohammed M. Pickthall. (C). 1995. 10.00 (*81-7476-005-9*, Pub. by UBS Pubs Dist) S Asia.

Meaning of the Holy Qur'an. 8th ed. Abdullah Y. Ali. LC 97-37495. (ARA.). 1824p. (Orig.). 1998. 21.95 (*0-915957-76-0*) Amana Corp.

Meaning of the Holy Qur'an. 9th rev. ed. Comment by Abdullah Y. Ali. LC 97-37495. 1824p. (Orig.). 1995. pap. 12.50 (*0-915957-77-9*) Amana Corp.

An Asterisk (*) at the beginning of an entry indicates that the title is appearing for the first time.

Meaning of the Idylls of the King. Conde B. Pallen. LC 65-26453. (Studies in Tennyson: No. 27). (C). 1969. reprint ed. lib. bdg. 75.00 (0-8383-0607-1) M S G Haskell Hse.

Meaning of the Illustrious Quran. Tr. by Abdullah Y. Ali. 990p. (Orig.). 1995. text 7.50 (1-56744-507-1) Kazi Pubns.

Meaning of the Liturgy: Memorial of Our Salvation & Divine Praise. Ed. by Angelus A. Haussling et al. Tr. by Linda M. Maloney. LC 94-7507. 152p. 1994. pap. 11.95 (0-8146-2273-9) Liturgical Pr.

Meaning of the Mark: Leonardo & Titian. David Rosand. (Franklin D. Murphy Lectures: No. 8). 1988. 12.00 (0-913689-01-7) Spencer Muse Art.

Meaning of the Medium: Perspectives of the Art of Television. Ed. by Katherine U. Henderson & Joseph A. Mazzeo. LC 89-16171. (Media & Society Ser.). 215p. 1990. 57.95 (0-275-93390-3, C3390, Praeger Pubs) Greenwood.

Meaning of the Microcosm. George Gilder. 1997. 29.95 (0-9659578-0-2); pap. 9.95 (0-9659578-1-0) Progress & Freedom.

Meaning of the Millennium. Robert G. Clouse. 212p. 1978. pap. 12.99 (0-88469-099-7) BMH Bks.

Meaning of the Millennium: Four Views. Ed. by Robert G. Clouse. LC 76-55556. 223p. (Orig.). 1977. pap. 12.99 (0-87784-794-0, 794) InterVarsity.

Meaning of the Millennium - Four Views see Que Es el Milenio? - Cuatro Enfoques Para una Respuesta

Meaning of the Mind: Language, Morality, & Neuroscience. Thomas Szasz. Date not set. write for info. (0-614-21941-8, Praeger Pubs) Greenwood.

Meaning of the Nuclear Revolution: Statecraft & the Prospect of Armageddon. Robert Jervis. LC 88-43443. (Cornell Studies in Security Affairs). 272p. 1989. reprint ed. text 35.00 (0-8014-2304-X); reprint ed. pap. text 15.95 (0-8014-9565-2) Cornell U Pr.

Meaning of the Prohibition on Taking An Endangered Species. John C. Nagle. LC 99-161327. (Briefly--Perspectives on Legislation, Regulation, & Litigation Ser.). 33p. 1998. write for info. (0-937299-74-X) Natl Legal Ctr Pub Interest.

Meaning of the Quran, 6 vols., Set. S. Abul Ala Maududi. (ARA & ENG.). 1991. 160.00 (1-56744-134-3) Kazi Pubns.

Meaning of the Sacramental Symbols: Answers to Today's Questions. Klemens Richter. Tr. by Linda M. Maloney from GER. 132p. 1990. pap. 11.95 (0-8146-1882-0) Liturgical Pr.

Meaning of the Salzburg Festival: Austria As Theater & Ideology, 1890-1938. Michael P. Steinberg. LC 89-42881. (Illus.). 288p. 1990. text 32.50 (0-8014-2362-7) Cornell U Pr.

Meaning of the Sanskrit Term Dhaman. J. Gonda. (Verhandelingen der Koninklijke Nederlandse Akademie van Wetenschappen, Afd. Letterkunde, Nieuwe Reeks Ser.: No. 72(3)). 100p. pap. 17.25 (0-7204-8366-2) Elsevier.

Meaning of the Sentence in Its Semantic & Pragmatic Aspects. Peter Sgall et al. 1986. text 176.50 (90-277-1838-5) Kluwer Academic.

Meaning of the Separation of Powers: An Analysis of the Doctrine from Its Origin to the Adoption of the United States Constitution. William B. Gwyn. LC 66-4274. (Tulane Studies in Political Science: Vol. 9). 169p. 1965. reprint ed. pap. 52.40 (0-608-00823-0, 206161200010) Bks Demand.

Meaning of the Term "Moral" in St. Thomas Aquinas. Brian T. Mullady. 144p. 1996. pap. 69.95 (1-57309-190-1, Cath Scholar Pr) Intl Scholars.

Meaning of the Times & Other Speeches. Albert J. Beveridge. LC 68-54327. (Essay Index Reprint Ser.). 1977. 23.95 (0-8369-0208-4) Ayer.

Meaning of the West (C). 2000. pap. write for info. (0-13-016088-1) P-H.

Meaning of the West (C). 2000. pap. write for info. (0-13-016089-X) S&S Trade.

Meaning of the West , Vol. 1. (C). 2000. pap. 18.67 (0-13-014810-5) S&S Trade.

Meaning of the West , Vol. 2. 196p. (C). 2000. pap. 18.67 (0-13-014821-0) S&S Trade.

Meaning of Things: Symbols in the Development of the Self. Mihaly Csikszentmihalyi & Eugene Rochberg-Halton. LC 81-1443. 330p. 1981. pap. text 27.95 (0-521-28774-X) Cambridge U Pr.

Meaning of This Life. Tr. by B. A. Reichenbach from GER. LC 98-67456. 63p. 1998. pap. 12.00 (0-915034-06-9) Kober Pr.

*Meaning of Total Fitness for Children. James H. Humphrey. 2000. pap. 13.00 (1-55279-007-X) Picasso Publ.

Meaning of Truth. William James. LC 97-4501. 326p. 1997. pap. 11.95 (1-57392-138-6) Prometheus Bks.

Meaning of Truth. William James. (Notable American Authors Ser.). 1992. reprint ed. lib. bdg. 75.00 (0-7812-3480-8) Rprt Serv.

Meaning of Vocation: In the Words of John Paul II. 40p. 1997. pap. 2.95 (0-933932-99-5) Scepter Pubs.

Meaning of Words: Analyzed into Words & Universal Things, & Universal Things Classified into Intellections, Sensations & Emotions. Alexander B. Johnson. 1948. 30.00 (0-686-30224-9) R S Barnes.

Meaning of Work & Retirement. Eugene A. Friedmann et al. Ed. by Leon Stein. LC 77-70496. 1977. reprint ed. lib. bdg. 23.95 (0-405-10166-X) Ayer.

Meaning of Work in Israel: Its Nature & Consequences. Itzhak Harpaz. LC 89-48748. 272p. 1990. 65.00 (0-275-92475-0, C2475, Greenwood Pr) Greenwood.

*Meaning of Yiddish. Benjamin Harshav. 1999. 17.95 (0-8047-3575-1) Stanford U Pr.

Meaning of Yiddish. Benjamin Harshav. 235p. 1990. 48.00 (0-520-05947-6, Pub. by U CA Pr) Cal Prin Full Svc.

*Meaning of Your Dreams: An Interactive Guide. David F. Melbourne & Keith Heaine. 224p. 2000. pap. 12.95 (0-7137-2778-0, Pub. by Blandford Pr) Sterling.

Meaning over Memory: Recasting the Teaching of Culture & History. Peter N. Stearns. LC 92-50815. (H. Eugene & Lillian Youngs Lehman Ser.). xvi, 254p. (C). 1994. pap. 19.95 (0-8078-4485-3) U of NC Pr.

Meaning, Reference, & Necessity: New Studies in Semantics. Ed. by Simon Blackburn. LC 74-31785. 220p. reprint ed. pap. 62.70 (0-608-12281-5, 2024425) Bks Demand.

Meaning Scepticism. Ed. by Klaus Puhl. (Foundations of Communication & Cognition Ser.). ix, 258p. (C). 1991. lib. bdg. 109.25 (3-11-011833-5) De Gruyter.

Meaning Syntax. Connor Ferris. LC 92-36946. (Linguistics Library). 1995. pap. text 32.28 (0-582-21012-7) Addison-Wesley.

Meaning the Lord's Prayer. Wild Goose Publications Staff. (C). 1990. 20.00 (0-947988-30-0, Pub. by Wild Goose Pubns) St Mut.

Meaning, Truth & God. Ed. by Leroy S. Rouner. LC 82-7023. (Boston University Studies in Philosophy & Religion: Vol. 3). (C). 1994. reprint ed. pap. text 13.00 (0-268-01415-9) U of Notre Dame Pr.

Meaning, Truth & Predication. Sukharanjan Saha. (C). 1991. 22.00 (81-7074-083-5, Pub. by KP Bagchi) S Asia.

*Meaning, Understanding & Practice: Philosophical Essays. Barry Stroud. LC 99-59017. 232p. 2000. 35.00 (0-19-825034-7) OUP.

Meaning, Use, & Interpretation of Language. Ed. by Rainer Bauerle et al. 1983. 150.00 (3-11-008901-7) De Gruyter.

Meaning Without Words: Philosophy & Non-Verbal Communication. Peter Gilroy. LC 96-83832. (Avebury Series in Philosophy). 224p. 1996. 69.95 (1-85972-254-7, Pub. by Avebury) Ashgate Pub Co.

Meaningful & Manageable Assessment Through Cooperative Learning. David W. Johnson & Roger T. Johnson. (Illus.). 304p. (Orig.). 1996. pap. text 25.00 (0-939603-25-X) Interaction Bk Co.

Meaningful Architecture: Social Interpretations of Buildings. Ed. by Martin Locock. (Worldwide Architecture Ser.: Vol. 9). 320p. 1994. 87.95 (1-85628-708-4, Pub. by Avebury) Ashgate Pub Co.

*Meaningful Care: A Multidisciplinary Approach to the Meaning of Care for People with Mental Retardation. Joop Stolk et al. LC 00-39110. 2000. write for info. (0-7923-6291-8) Kluwer Academic.

Meaningful Connections: A Personal Retrospective. Harry W. Stonecipher. (Illus.). 240p. 1995. boxed set 16.95 (1-879776-08-1) JEM Commns.

Meaningful Counseling: A Guide for Students, Counselors, & Clergy. Marian D. Robinson. 204p. 1988. 32.95 (0-89885-385-0, Kluwer Acad Hman Sci) Kluwer Academic.

Meaningful Differences: The Poetry & Prose of David Ignatow. Ed. by Virginia R. Terris. LC 93-19442. 288p. (C). 1994. text 39.95 (0-8173-0700-1) U of Ala Pr.

Meaningful Differences in the Everyday Experience of Young American Children. Betty Hart & Todd R. Risley. 304p. 1995. boxed set 29.00 (1-55766-197-9) P H Brookes.

Meaningful First Communion Liturgies: The Complete Planning Guide for Catechists & Teachers. Nick Wagner. LC 97-52019. (Celebrating the Sacraments Ser.). 128p. 1998. pap. 21.95 (0-89390-432-5) Resource Pubns.

Meaningful Life. Richard L. Gage & Nikkyo Niwano. Orig. Title: Ningen No Ikigai. 126p. 1982. pap. 4.95 (4-333-01027-6, Pub. by Kosei Pub Co) Tuttle Pubng.

Meaningful Living. Paul H. Dunn. LC 98-33634. 2000. 19.95 (1-882723-33-3) Gold Leaf Pr.

*Meaningful Math: Creating an Environment with Math-Rich Experiences: Grades PS-2. Jeri A. Carroll. Ed. by Judy Mitchell. (Illus.). 128p. 1999. pap., teacher ed. 12.95 (1-57310-191-5) Teachng & Lrning Co.

Meaningful Play, Playful Meaning. Association for the Anthropological Study of Play,. Ed. by Gary A. Fine. LC 86-21513. (Association for the Anthropological Study of Play Ser.: No. 11). 255p. 1987. reprint ed. pap. 79.10 (0-608-06445-9, 206728100009) Bks Demand.

*Meaningful Print: Creating an Environment with Print-Rich Experiences: Grades PS-2. Jeri A. Carroll. Ed. by Judy Mitchell. (Illus.). 128p. 1999. pap., teacher ed. 12.95 (1-57310-192-3) Teachng & Lrning Co.

Meaningful Relationships: Talking, Sense & Relating. Steve Duck. (Series on Close Relationships: Vol. 8). 240p. (C). 1994. text 42.00 (0-8039-5702-5) Sage.

Meaningful Relationships: Talking, Sense & Relating, No. 8. Steve Duck. (Series on Close Relationships: Vol. 8). 240p. (C). 1994. pap. text 17.95 (0-8039-5703-3) Sage.

Meaningful Thought Rhyming Poems. 2nd rev. ed. Thomas H. Stephens. 37p. 1988. pap. text, spiral bd. 10.00 (1-890556-02-5) T Stephens Pub.

Meaningful Tone: A Study of Tonal Morphology in Compounds, Form Classes, & Expressive Phrases in White Hmong. Martha Ratliff. (Special Reports: No. 27). 275p. 1992. pap. 19.95 (1-877979-77-5) SE Asia.

*Meaningful Work: Rethinking Professional Ethics. Mike W. Martin. LC 99-27536. (Practical & Professional Ethics Ser.). 272p. 2000. 35.00 (0-19-513325-0) OUP.

Meaningful Worship: A Guide to the Lutheran Service. James L. Brauer. LC 94-6861. 96p. 1994. 10.00 (0-570-04642-4, 12-3223) Concordia.

*Meanings - Biblical Commentaries. Stephen Allott. 1999. pap. 23.00 (1-85072-155-6, Pub. by W Sessions) St Mut.

Meanings & Situations. Arthur Brittan. (International Library of Sociology Ser.). 222p. 1973. 19.95 (0-7100-7509-X, Routledge Thoemms) Routledge.

Meanings for Manhood: Constructions of Masculinity in Victorian America. Ed. by Mark C. Carnes & Clyde Griffen. LC 90-32943. 288p. 1990. pap. text 17.95 (0-226-09365-4) U Ch Pr.

Meanings for Manhood: Constructions of Masculinity in Victorian America. Ed. by Mark C. Carnes & Clyde Griffen. LC 90-32943. 288p. 1990. lib. bdg. 48.00 (0-226-09364-6) U Ch Pr.

Meanings in Madagascar: Cases of Intercultural Communication. Oyvind Dahl. LC 98-41386. 216p. 1999. 59.95 (0-89789-642-4, Bergin & Garvey) Greenwood.

Meanings in Texts & Actions: Questioning Paul Ricoeur. Ed. by David E. Klemm & William Schweiker. LC 92-34072. (Studies in Religion & Culture). 380p. reprint ed. pap. 117.80 (0-608-20046-8, 207131800011) Bks Demand.

Meanings, Models & Metaphors: A Study in Lexical Semantics in English. Gunnar Persson. (Umea Studies in the Humanities: No. 92). (Illus.). 205p. (Orig.). 1990. pap. 43.50 (91-7174-478-9) Coronet Bks.

Meanings of Age: Selected Papers. Bernice L. Neugarten. Ed. & Frwd. by Dail A. Neugarten. LC 96-14865. (Illus.). 440p. 1996. pap. text 24.95 (0-226-57384-2); lib. bdg. 68.00 (0-226-57383-4) U Ch Pr.

Meanings of Agriculture: Essays in South Asian History & Economics. Ed. by Peter Robb. LC 96-902126. (S. O. A. S. Studies on South Asia). (Illus.). 400p. 1996. text 29.95 (0-19-563981-2) OUP.

Meanings of Black Power: A Comparison of White & Black Interpretations of a Political Slog. Joel D. Aberbach & Jack L. Walker. (Reprint Series in Political Science). (C). 1993. reprint ed. pap. text 5.00 (0-8290-2764-5, PS-421) Irvington.

Meanings of Death see Significados de la Muerte

Meanings of Death. John Bowker. (Canto Book Ser.). 257p. (C). 1993. pap. 11.95 (0-521-44773-9) Cambridge U Pr.

Meanings of Death in Rabbinic Judaism. David C. Kraemer. LC 99-20720. 1999. pap. 29.99 (0-415-21184-0) Routledge.

*Meanings of Death in Rabbinic Judaism. David Charles Kraemer. LC 99-20720. 208p. (C). 1999. text. write for info. (0-415-21183-2) Routledge.

Meanings of Faust & the Devil: Philosophical & Social Thought in Faustian Literature Precursory to Goethe's Faust. John E. Westburg. Ed. by Mildred W. Westburg. LC 90-12064. 170p. 1990. pap. 16.50 (0-87423-058-6) Westburg.

Meanings of Life. Roy F. Baumeister. LC 91-17859. 426p. 1991. lib. bdg. 45.00 (0-89862-763-X) Guilford Pubns.

Meanings of Life. Roy F. Baumeister. LC 91-17859. 426p. 1992. reprint ed. pap. text 25.00 (0-89862-531-9) Guilford Pubns.

Meanings of Love: An Introduction to Philosophy of Love. Robert E. Wagoner. LC 96-37115. 160p. 1997. 55.00 (0-275-95839-6, Praeger Pubs); pap. 18.95 (0-275-95840-X, Praeger Pubs) Greenwood.

Meanings of Macho: Being a Man in Mexico City. Matthew Gutmann. LC 95-49535. (Men & Masculinity Ser.: Vol. 3). (Illus.). 318p. (C). 1996. 50.00 (0-520-20234-1, Pub. by U CA Pr); pap. 17.95 (0-520-20236-8, Pub. by U CA Pr) Cal Prin Full Svc.

Meanings of Madness: Readings in Culture & Mental Illness. Richard L. Castillo. LC 97-19078. (Miscellaneous/Catalogs Ser.). 240p. (C). 1997. pap. 49.95 (0-534-34560-3) Brooks-Cole.

Meanings of Masonry. W. L. Wilmshurst. 216p. 1993. reprint ed. pap. 17.95 (1-56459-373-8) Kessinger Pub.

Meanings of Mass Higher Education. Peter Scott. LC 95-10593. 208p. 1995. 123.00 (0-335-19443-5); pap. 34.95 (0-335-19442-7) OpUniv Pr.

Meanings of Menopause: Historical, Medical, & Clinical Perspectives. Ed. by Ruth Formanek. 352p. 1990. text 59.95 (0-88163-080-2) Analytic Pr.

Meanings of Multiethnicity: A Case-Study of Ethnicity & Ethnic Relations in Singapore. Lai A. Eng. (South-East Asian Social Science Mongoraphs). (Illus.). 240p. 1995. text 69.00 (967-65-3087-5) OUP.

Meanings of Sex Difference in the Middle Ages: Medicine, Science, & Culture. Joan Cadden. (History of Medicine Ser.). (Illus.). 326p. (C). 1995. pap. text 20.95 (0-521-48378-6) Cambridge U Pr.

Meanings of Teaching: An International Study of Secondary Teachers' Work Lives. Allen Menlo & Pam Poppleton. LC 98-51219. 272p. 1999. 65.00 (0-89789-586-X, Bergin & Garvey) Greenwood.

Meanings of the Gene: Determination, Discrimination & Perfectionism in U.S. Public Discourse. Celeste Michelle Condit. LC 99-6274. (Rhetoric of the Human Sciences Ser.). 256p. 1999. text 49.95 (0-299-16360-1) U of Wis Pr.

Meanings of the Gene: Public Debates about Human Heredity. Celeste M. Condit. LC 99-6274. (Rhetoric of the Human Sciences Ser.). 256p. 1999. pap. text 19.95 (0-299-16364-4) U of Wis Pr.

Meanings of the Market. Ed. by James G. Carrier. LC 97-202478. 1997. 55.00 (1-85973-144-9, Pub. by Berg Pubs); pap. 19.50 (1-85973-149-X, Pub. by Berg Pubs) NYU Pr.

Meanings of Things: Material Culture & Symbolic Expression. Ed. by Ian Hodder. LC 88-17663. (One World Archaeology Ser.: No. 6). 265p. 1989. 60.95 (0-04-445017-6) Routledge.

*Meanings of Violence: A Cross-Cultural Perspective. Ed. by Goran Aijmer & Jon Abbink. 256p. 2000. 65.00 (1-85973-435-9, Pub. by Berg Pubs); pap. 24.50 (1-85973-440-5, Pub. by Berg Pubs) NYU Pr.

Meanings of Work: Considerations for the Twenty-First Century. Ed. by Frederick C. Gamst. LC 94-3370. (SUNY Series in the Anthropology of Work). 299p. (C). 1995. text 59.50 (0-7914-2413-8); pap. text 19.95 (0-7914-2414-6) State U NY Pr.

Meanjin: New Critical Essays, Fiction & Poetry. Jenny Lee. 846p. (C). 1990. 50.00 (0-7855-6618-X, Pub. by Pascoe Pub) St Mut.

Means & Their Inequalities. Dragoslav S. Mitrinovic et al. (C). 1987. text 211.50 (90-277-2629-9) Kluwer Academic.

*Means Concrete & Masonry Cost Data 2000. 18th ed. R. S. Means Company Staff. 1999. pap. 79.95 (0-87629-554-5) R S Means.

Means Electrical Estimating Methods. 2nd ed. Means, R. S., Staff. 1995. boxed set 64.95 (0-87629-358-5, 67230A) R S Means.

Means Estimating Handbook. Means, R. S., Co., Inc. Staff. (Illus.). 900p. 1990. 99.95 (0-87629-177-9, 67276) R S Means.

Means Facilities Maintenance Standards. Roger W. Liska. (Illus.). 600p. (C). 1988. 159.95 (0-87629-096-9, 67246) R S Means.

Means Family of America. Ed. by Elizabeth C. Foglesong. (Illus.). 1004p. 1972. 75.00 (0-686-32458-7) C V Barnes.

Means Forms for Building Construction Professionals. 2nd ed. Means, R. S., Staff. 325p. 1986. ring bd. 94.95 (0-911950-87-7, 67231) R S Means.

Means Forms for Contractors. Means, R. S., Staff. 1991. ring bd. 79.95 (0-87629-214-7, 67288) R S Means.

Means Heavy Construction Handbook. Richard Ringwald. 1993. pap. 74.95 (0-87629-283-X, 67148) R S Means.

*Means Illustrated Construction Dictionary. 3rd ed. Ed. by R S Means Staff. (Illus.). 2000. 99.95 (0-87629-538-3) R S Means.

*Means Interior Cost Data 2000. 17th ed. R. S. Means Company Staff. 1999. pap. 89.95 (0-87629-548-0) R S Means.

Means Mechanical Estimating Methods. 2nd ed. Means, R. S., Staff. 1992. 64.95 (0-87629-213-9, 67294) R S Means.

Means of Ascent: The Years of Lyndon Johnson. Robert A. Caro. 1990. 30.00 (0-394-52835-2) Knopf.

Means of Ascent: The Years of Lyndon Johnson. Robert A. Caro. LC 90-50483. Vol. 2. 592p. 1991. pap. 18.00 (0-679-73371-X) Vin Bks.

*Means of Escape: Stories. Penelope Fitzgerald. 224p. 2000. 20.00 (0-618-07994-7) HM.

Means of Grace. Edward M. Matthews. 58p. 1946. pap. 3.00 (0-935461-08-6) St Alban Pr CA.

Means of Grace. Edith Pargeter. 311p. 1996. mass mkt. 11.95 (0-7472-4679-3, Pub. by Headline Bk Pub) Trafalgar.

Means of Grace. large type ed. Edith Pargeter. LC 96-3375. 1996. pap. 20.95 (0-7862-0684-5) Thorndike Pr.

Means of Naming: A Social History. Stephen Wilson. LC 97-130690. 1999. pap. text 24.95 (1-85728-245-0) Taylor & Francis.

Means of Naming: A Social History. Stephen Wilson. LC 97-130690. 1999. 85.00 (1-85728-244-2) UCL Pr Ltd.

Means of Our Salvation: Public Education in Brazil, 1930-1995. David N. Plank. 208p. (C). 1996. pap. 69.00 (0-8133-8982-8, Pub. by Westview) HarpC.

Means Productivity Standards. 3rd ed. LC 95-109499. Orig. Title: Man-Hour Standards. 1994. 159.95 (0-87629-314-3, 67236A) R S Means.

*Means Repair & Remodeling Cost Data 2000. 23rd ed. R. S. Means Company Staff. LC 88-641537. 650p. 1999. pap. 79.95 (0-87629-544-8) R S Means.

Means Repair & Remodeling Estimating Methods. 3rd ed. Edward B. Wetherill. LC 97-182437. 1997. boxed set 69.95 (0-87629-454-9, 67265A) R S Means.

Means Scheduling Manual. 3rd ed. F. William Horsley. 1991. spiral bd. 62.95 (0-87629-220-1, 67291) R S Means.

Means Something Else--"Not Literally" Figures-of-Speech Writing Book. Jim DeWitt. (Figurative Expressions (for Schools, Libraries, School Libraries) Ser.: Vol. 6). (Illus.). 64p. (Orig.). 1987. student ed. 6.00 (0-915199-55-6) Pen-Dec.

Means Something Else--"The Doubles" Figures-of-Speech Writing Book. Jim DeWitt. (Figurative Expressions (for Schools, Libraries, School Libraries) Ser.: Vol. 3). (Illus.). 64p. (Orig.). 1987. pap., student ed. 6.00 (0-915199-52-1) Pen-Dec.

Means Something Else--"The Doubles" Figures-of-Speech Writing Book. Jim DeWitt. (Figurative Expressions (for Schools, Libraries, School Libraries) Ser.: Vol. 4). (Illus.). 64p. (Orig.). 1987. pap., student ed. 6.00 (0-915199-53-X) Pen-Dec.

Means Something Else--"The Doubles" Figures of Speech Writing Book, No. 2. Jim DeWitt. (Figurative Expressions (for Schools, Libraries, School Libraries) Ser.). (Illus.). 64p. (Orig.). (YA). (gr. 6-12). 1987. student ed. 6.00 (0-915199-51-3) Pen-Dec.

Means to an End: The Biological Basis of Aging & Death. William R. Clark. LC 98-18878. (Illus.). 256p. 1999. 27.50 (0-19-512593-2) OUP.

Means to an End: The Role of Nonprofit/Government Contracting in Sustaining the Social Contract. Jenice L. View. 90p. (Orig.). 1995. pap. 15.00 (1-886949-01-8) Union Inst.

Means to Christian Maturity. Ray Van Tassell, Jr. 352p. 1996. pap. 10.95 (1-57502-208-7, P0846) Morris Pubng.

Means to Message. Stanley L. Jaki. LC 98-53408. 241p. 1999. pap. 22.00 (0-8028-4651-3) Eerdmans.

Means to Revival. David Ward. 52p. (Orig.). (C). 1989. pap. 2.95 (1-877917-04-4) Alpha Bible Pubns.

Means to Revival. David Ward. (Orig.). (C). 1989. pap. write for info. (0-318-65603-5) D Ward.

Means to the End. large type ed. O. O'Banion. 297p. (C). 1996. reprint ed. write for info. (0-9637174-1-3) Two O Bks.

*Means to Win: Strategies for Success in Business & Politics. Tr. by William Bodri. 176p. 2000. pap. 15.00 (0-87573-083-3) Jain Pub Co.

M

Means Unit Price Estimating Methods. 2nd ed. Means, R. S., Staff. 432p. 1993. pap. 59.95 (*0-87629-315-1*, 67303) R S Means.

Means Which Guarantee Leadership. Brown Landone. 299p. 1996. reprint ed. spiral bd. 20.00 (*0-7873-0530-8*) Hlth Research.

Means Which Guarantee Leadership: How to Become a Leader. Brown Landone. 1991. lib. bdg. 79.95 (*0-8490-4993-8*) Gordon Pr.

***Means Without End: Notes on Politics.** Giorgio Agamben. LC 00-8712. (Theory Out of Bounds Ser.). 2000. write for info. (*0-8166-3036-4*) U of Minn Pr.

Meant. John Byrum. (Chapbook Ser.). 31p. 1987. 5.00 (*0-945112-03-3*) Generator Pr.

Meant for Each Other: The Blaines & the McCalls of Crockett/Texas. Ginna Gray. 1998. per. 4.25 (*0-373-24221-2*, 1-24221-3, Mira Bks) Harlequin Bks.

***Meant to Be.** Jill R. Lenes. LC 99-96803. 2000. pap. 7.95 (*0-533-13349-1*) Vantage.

***Meant to Be.** Jeanne Sumerix. 2000. pap. 8.95 (*1-58571-020-2*, 909-097, Pub. by Genesis Press) BookWorld.

***Meant to Be: Miraculous Stories to Inspire a Lifetime of Love.** Joyce Vissell & Barry Vissell. 264p. 2000. pap. 14.95 (*1-57324-161-X*) Conari Press.

Meant to Be Married. Ruth Wind. (Special Edition Ser.). 1998. per. 4.25 (*0-373-24194-1*, 1-24194-2) Silhouette.

Meant to Be Read Out Loud. Susan Hauser. (Illus.). 112p. (Orig.). 1988. pap. 7.95 (*0-926147-00-5*) Loonfeather.

Meant to Be Wild: The Struggle to Save Endangered Species Through Captive Breeding. Jan DeBlieu. (Illus.). 305p. 1993. pap. 12.95 (*1-55591-166-8*) Fulcrum Pub.

Meant to Marry. Robyn Donald. (Presents Ser.). 1997. per. 3.50 (*0-373-11871-6*, 1-11871-0) Harlequin Bks.

Meant to Marry. large type ed. Robyn Donald. (Harlequin Ser.). 1997. 20.95 (*0-263-14966-8*) Mac Lib Ref.

Meanwhile... Jules Feiffer. LC 97-70129. (Michael di Capua Bks.). (Illus.). 32p. (J). (gr. k up). 1997. 15.95 (*0-06-205155-5*) HarpC Child Bks.

Meanwhile... Jules Feiffer. LC 97-70129. (Michael di Capua Bks.). (Illus.). 32p. (J). (ps-3). 1997. lib. bdg. 15.89 (*0-06-205156-3*) HarpC Child Bks.

Meanwhile... Jules Feiffer. LC 97-70129. (Illus.). 32p. (YA). 1999. pap. 5.95 (*0-06-205933-5*) HarpC Child Bks.

Meanwhile, Back at the Ranch. Amory Cleveland. 1996. write for info. (*0-316-03766-4*) Little.

Meanwhile Back at the Ranch. Trinka Hakes Noble. (Illus.). 32p. (J). (ps-3). 1992. pap. 5.99 (*0-14-054564-6*, PuffinBks) Peng Put Young Read.

Meanwhile Back at the Ranch. Trinka Hakes Noble. (Reading Rainbow Bks.). (J). 1987. 11.19 (*0-606-01722-4*, Pub. by Turtleback) Demco.

Meanwhile, Back at the Ranch. Verdelle. 1999. 25.00 (*0-8050-5954-7*) H Holt & Co.

Meanwhile Back at the Ranch: The Stories, the Anecdotes, the Travelogues of 50 Adventurous Years in Sports. Ray Franks. Ed. by Floy Franks. LC 96-93001. (Illus.). 312p. (Orig.). 1996. pap. 12.95 (*0-943976-06-5*) R Franks Ranch.

Meanwhile, in Other News: A Graphic Look at Politics in the Empire of Money, Sex & Scandal. Matt Wuerker. (Illus.). 120p. 1998. pap. 10.95 (*1-56751-142-2*) Common Courage.

Meanwhile, in Other News . . . A Graphic Look at Politics in the Empire of Money, Sex & Scandel. Matt Wuerker. (Illus.). 128p. 1998. lib. bdg. 29.95 (*1-56751-143-0*) Common Courage.

Meaori Family Violence in Aotearoa. Roma Belzer et al. LC 98-180392. 92 p. 1997. write for info. (*0-478-09124-9*) Manaaki Whenua.

Measles: A History. Andrew Cliff et al. (Illus.). 500p. 1994. text 184.95 (*0-631-16235-6*) Blackwell Pubs.

Measles & Poliomyelitis: Vaccines, Immunization, & Control. Ed. by Eduard Kurstak. (Illus.). 416p. 1993. 158.00 (*0-387-82436-7*) Spr-Verlag.

Measles & Rubella. Alvin Silverstein et al. LC 97-3785. (Diseases & People Ser.). (Illus.). 128p. (YA). (gr. 6 up). 1997. lib. bdg. 20.95 (*0-89490-714-X*) Enslow Pubs.

Measles Virus, No. 191. Ed. by V. Ter Meulen & M. A. Billeter. (Currents Topics in Microbiology & Immunology Ser.: Vol. 191). 319p. 1995. 124.00 (*0-387-57389-5*) Spr-Verlag.

Measly Middle Ages. Terry Deary. (Horrible History Ser.). (J). (gr. 7-12). 1998. pap. text 3.99 (*0-590-49848-7*) Scholastic Inc.

Measurable, Continuous & Smooth Vectors for Semigroups & Group Representations. R. T. Moore. LC 52-42839. (Memoirs Ser.: No. 1/78). 80p. 1968. pap. 16.00 (*0-8218-1278-5*, MEMO/1/78) Am Math.

Measurable Outcomes of Individual Laboratory Work in High School Chemistry. Ralph E. Horton. LC 70-176879. (Columbia University. Teachers College. Contributions to Education Ser.: No. 303). reprint ed. 37.50 (*0-404-55303-6*) AMS Pr.

Measurable Parameters to Profile Child Development from "Slow & Steady, Get Me Ready" The How-to Book That Grows with the Child. June R. Oberlander. Ed. by Clyde G. Oberlander. 8p. (Orig.). 1993. pap. 3.95 (*0-9622322-3-8*) Bio-Alpha.

Measurable Selectors of PCA Multifunctions with Applications. Marian Srebrny. LC 84-18464. (Memoirs Ser.: No. 52/311). 50p. 1984. pap. 16.00 (*0-8218-2299-3*, MEMO/52/311) Am Math.

Measurable World: A Novel. Katharine Coles. LC 95-17114. (Western Literature Ser.). 320p. 1995. 23.00 (*0-87417-273-X*) U of Nev Pr.

Measure. Ivan Bulloch et al. LC 96-49797. (Action Math Ser.). (Illus.). 32p. (J). (gr. k-3). 1997. 10.00 (*0-7166-4906-3*) World Bk.

***Measure.** rev. ed. Ivan Bulloch. (Action Math Ser.). (Illus.). (J). 2000. pap. 4.95 (*1-58728-051-5*) Two Can Pub.

Measure Algebras. Joseph L. Taylor. LC 73-5930. (CBMS Regional Conference Series in Mathematics: No. 16). 108p. 1973. reprint ed. pap. 18.00 (*0-8218-1666-7*, CBMS/16) Am Math.

Measure & Category: A Survey of the Analogies Between Topological & Measure Spaces. 2nd rev. ed. J. C. Oxtoby. LC 73-149248. (Graduate Texts in Mathematics Ser.: Vol. 2). (C). 1996. 47.95 (*0-387-90508-1*) Spr-Verlag.

Measure & Construction of the Japanese House. Heinrich Engel. LC 84-51859. (Illus.). 152p. 1985. pap. 21.95 (*0-8048-1492-9*) Tuttle Pubng.

Measure & Integral, Vol. 1. J. L. Kelley & T. P. Srinivasan. (Graduate Texts in Mathematics Ser.: Vol. 116). 295p. 1987. 53.95 (*0-387-96633-1*) Spr-Verlag.

Measure & Integral: An Introduction to Real Analysis. Richard Wheeden & Antoni Zygmund. (Pure & Applied Mathematics Ser.: Vol. 43). (Illus.). 288p. 1977. text 59.75 (*0-8247-6499-4*) Dekker.

Measure & Integration: An Advanced Course in Basic Procedure & Applications. Heinz Konig. LC 96-46182. 260p. 1996. 79.95 (*3-540-61858-9*) Spr-Verlag.

Measure & Integration for Use. H. R. Pitt. (Institute of Mathematics & Its Applications Conference Series, New Ser.). 150p. 1985. text 29.95 (*0-19-853608-9*) OUP.

Measure & Manage Cap-Prof Seires. Klammer. 1998. pap. 35.00 (*0-07-039313-3*) McGraw.

Measure & Manage Stress. Herbert S. Kindler & Marilyn Ginsburg. Ed. by Chris Carrigan. LC 93-74715. 155p. (Orig.). 1994. pap. 15.95 (*1-56052-288-7*) Crisp Pubns.

Measure & Measurable Dynamics. R. Mauldin et al. LC 89-14914. (Contemporary Mathematics Ser.: Vol. 94). 326p. 1989. pap. 57.00 (*0-8218-5099-7*, CONM/94) Am Math.

Measure & Music: Enjambement & Sentence Structure in the Iliad. Carolyn Higbie. (Illus.). 240p. 1991. text 75.00 (*0-19-814387-7*) OUP.

Measure by Measure: A History of New England Conservatory from 1867. Bruce McPherson & James Klein. (Illus.). 152p. 1995. text 45.00 (*0-9648857-0-0*) New Eng Conser.

Measure for Measure. Arden. 1985. pap. 8.95 (*0-416-49630-X*) Routledge.

Measure for Measure. Ed. by Cookson. 1991. pap. text. write for info. (*0-582-07576-9*, Pub. by Addison-Wesley) Longman.

Measure for Measure. Harriet Hawkins. xxvii, 152 p. 1988. pap. 13.95 (*0-8057-8703-8*, Twyne) Mac Lib Ref.

Measure for Measure. M.H. Publications Staff. 1990. 95.00 (*1-872680-15-1*, Pub. by M H Pubns) St Mut.

Measure for Measure. G. Nicholls. (Text & Performance Ser.). (Illus.). 96p. (C). 1986. pap. 10.95 (*0-333-34982-2*, Pub. by Macmillan) Humanities.

Measure for Measure. William Shakespeare. Ed. by Brian Gibbons. (New Cambridge Shakespeare Ser.). (Illus.). 226p. (C). 1991. text 44.95 (*0-521-22227-3*); pap. text 11.95 (*0-521-29401-0*) Cambridge U Pr.

Measure for Measure. William Shakespeare. Ed. by Jane Coles & Rex Gibson. (Cambridge School Shakespeare Ser.). (Illus.). 192p. (C). 1993. pap. 11.95 (*0-521-42506-9*) Cambridge U Pr.

Measure for Measure. William Shakespeare. LC 99-29893. (Dover Thrift Editions Ser.). 96p. 1999. pap. text 1.50 (*0-486-40889-2*) Dover.

Measure for Measure. William Shakespeare. Ed. by Mark Eccles. (New Variorum Edition of Shakespeare Ser.: Vol. 29). xxvii, 555p. 1980. lib. bdg. 40.00 (*0-87352-284-2*, Z3600) Modern Lang.

Measure for Measure. William Shakespeare. Ed. by N. W. Bawcutt. (Oxford World's Classics Ser.). (Illus.). 264p. 1998. pap. 7.95 (*0-19-283422-3*) OUP.

***Measure for Measure.** William Shakespeare. (Big Works Collection). (Illus.). 1p. 1999. 29.95 (*1-929142-16-1*) One Page Bk.

Measure for Measure. William Shakespeare. Ed. by Grace Ioppolo. LC 96-2525. (Shakespearean Originals Ser.). 176p. (C). 1996. pap. text 12.95 (*0-13-355397-3*) P-H.

Measure for Measure. William Shakespeare. LC 99-166275. 1997. per. 3.99 (*0-671-72276-X*) PB.

Measure for Measure. William Shakespeare. 1997. mass mkt. 3.99 (*0-671-49612-3*) S&S Trade.

Measure for Measure. William Shakespeare. Ed. by John Andrews. (Everyman Shakespeare Ser.). 256p. 1994. pap. 3.95 (*0-460-87454-3*, Everyman's Classic Lib) Tuttle Pubng.

Measure for Measure. William Shakespeare. Ed. by Robert C. Bald. (Pelican Shakespeare Ser.). 140p. 1956. pap. 5.95 (*0-14-071403-0*, Pelican Bks) Viking Penguin.

Measure for Measure. William Shakespeare. Ed. by J. M. Nosworthy. (New Penguin Shakespeare Ser.). 192p. 1981. pap. 5.95 (*0-14-070715-8*, Penguin Classics) Viking Penguin.

***Measure for Measure.** William Shakespeare. (Pelican Shakespeare Ser.). 144p. 2000. pap. 4.95 (*0-14-071479-0*, Pelican Bks) Viking Penguin.

Measure for Measure. William Shakespeare. (English Ser.). (C). 2002. mass mkt. 9.95 (*0-17-443526-6*) Wadsworth Pub.

Measure for Measure. William Shakespeare. (Classics Library). 112p. pap. 3.95 (*1-85326-251-X*, 251XWW, Pub. by Wrdsworth Edits) NTC Contemp Pub Co.

Measure for Measure. William Shakespeare. Ed. by John R. Brown. (Shakespeare Library). 192p. 2000. pap. 7.95 (*1-55783-387-7*) Applause Theatre Bk Pubs.

Measure for Measure. Ed. by Nigel Wood. LC 95-32168. xiv, 210p. (C). 1995. pap. 28.95 (*0-335-19236-X*) OpUniv Pr.

Measure for Measure. Richard A. Young & Thomas J. Glover. LC 96-79884. 864p. 1996. pap. 14.95 (*1-889796-00-X*) Sequoia Pub Inc.

Measure for Measure. annot. ed. William Shakespeare. LC 97-9575. 170p. 1999. pap. 12.95 (*1-55783-291-9*) Applause Theatre Bk Pubs.

Measure for Measure. large type ed. William Shakespeare. (Charnwood Large Print Ser.). 1991. pap. 24.95 (*0-7089-4528-7*, Charnwood) Ulverscroft.

Measure for Measure. rev. ed. William Shakespeare. Ed. by Davis Harding. LC 54-5286. (Yale Shakespeare Ser.). 139p. reprint ed. pap. 43.10 (*0-8357-8216-6*, 203374500087) Bks Demand.

Measure for Measure. 2nd ed. William Shakespeare. Ed. by J. W. Lever. (Arden Shakespeare Ser.). 1965. pap. 45.00 (*0-416-47530-2*, NO. 2478) Thomson Learn.

Measure for Measure. 2nd ed. William Shakespeare. (English). 1997. 11.95 (*0-17-443477-4*) Thomson Learn.

Measure for Measure. 3rd ed. William Shakespeare. (English Ser.). (C). 2002. mass mkt. 45.00 (*0-17-443559-2*) Wadsworth Pub.

Measure for Measure, Set. unabridged ed. William Shakespeare. LC 67-741. 92p. 1984. pap. 18.00 incl. audio (*0-694-50652-4*, SWC 204, Caedmon) HarperAudio.

Measure for Measure, Set. unabridged ed. William Shakespeare. 1995. audio 18.00 (*1-55994-816-7*, CPN 204) HarperAudio.

Measure for Measure: A Musical History of Science. Thomas Levenson. LC 97-19859. 1997. write for info. (*0-19-288049-7*) OUP.

Measure for Measure: An Annotated Bibliography. James Mckenna. Ed. by William L. Godshalk. (Garland Shakespeare Bibliographies Ser.). 400p. Date not set. text 60.00 (*0-8153-1500-7*) Garland.

Measure for Measure: Casuistry & Artistry. Melvin Seiden. LC 89-22295. 218p. 1990. 34.95 (*0-8132-0716-9*) Cath U Pr.

Measure for Measure: Fascinating Facts about Length, Weight, Time & Temperature. Sally Dugan. (Illus.). 128p. 1995. pap. 14.95 (*0-563-36900-0*, Pub. by BBC) Parkwest Pubns.

Measure for Measure: Modern Text with Introduction. William Shakespeare. Ed. by A. L. Rowse. LC 86-11033. 122p. (Orig.). (C). 1986. pap. text 3.45 (*0-8191-3930-0*) U Pr of Amer.

Measure for Measure: With a New & Updated Critical Essay & a Revised Bibliography. 2nd rev. ed. William Shakespeare & S. Nagarajan. LC 98-24316. (Signet Classic Shakespeare Ser.). 1998. mass mkt. 4.95 (*0-451-52715-1*, Sig Classics) NAL.

Measure for Measure, All's Well that Ends Well, & Troilus & Cressida. William Shakespeare. Ed. by David Bevington et al. (Classics Ser.). 496p. 1988. mass mkt. 4.95 (*0-553-21287-7*, Bantam Classics) Bantam.

Measure for Measure Notes. L. L. Hillegass. (Cliffs Notes Ser.). 48p. 1962. pap. 4.95 (*0-8220-0049-0*, Cliff) IDG Bks.

Measure for Measure, the Law & the Convent. Darryl J. Gless. LC 79-83990. 303p. reprint ed. pap. 94.00 (*0-8357-4648-8*, 203757800008) Bks Demand.

Measure for Measures: A Manifesto for Empirical Sociology. Ray Pawson. 272p. 1989. 49.95 (*0-415-02870-1*) Routledge.

Measure, Integral, & Probability. Marek Capinski & P. E. Kopp. LC 98-34763. (Undergraduate Mathematics Ser.). 1999. pap. 29.95 (*3-540-76260-4*) Spr-Verlag.

Measure, Integration & Function Spaces. Charles W. Swartz. 292p. 1994. text 61.00 (*981-02-1610-6*) World Scientific Pub.

Measure It, Manage It: Laying the Foundation for Benchmarking Health Care Foodservice Operations. Lynne M. Richards. LC 97-33559. 1997. write for info. (*0-88091-157-3*) Am Dietetic Assn.

Measure Me. Harriet Ziefert. (Illus.). 12p. (J). (ps-3). 1991. 12.95 (*0-694-00322-0*) HarpC Child Bks.

Measure of a Church. Gene A. Getz. LC 75-17160. 1975. pap. 3.50 (*0-8307-0398-5*, 5014700, Regal Bks) Gospel Lght.

***Measure of a Different Greatness: The Intensive Infinite, 1250-1650** Anne Davenport. LC 99-29174. (Studien und Texte zur Geistesgeschichte des Mittelalters). 1999. write for info. (*90-04-11481-5*) Brill Academic Pubs.

Measure of a Family. Gene A. Getz. LC 76-46872. 1977. pap. 3.95 (*0-8307-0445-0*, 5015006, Regal Bks) Gospel Lght.

Measure of a Heart. Janette Oke. (Women of the West Ser.: No. 6). 224p. 1992. pap. 8.99 (*1-55661-296-6*) Bethany Hse.

Measure of a Heart. Janette Oke. LC 98-13840. (Women of the West Ser.: Bk. 6). 288p. 1998. mass mkt. 5.99 (*0-7642-2100-0*, 202100) Bethany Hse.

Measure of a Heart. large type ed. Janette Oke. (Women of the West Ser.: No. 6). 224p. 1992. pap. 10.99 (*1-55661-297-4*) Bethany Hse.

Measure of a Heart. large type ed. Janette Oke. LC 93-36155. 293p. 1994. 19.95 (*0-8161-5850-9*, G K Hall Lrg Type) Mac Lib Ref.

***Measure of a Hero.** Blaine Lee Pardoe. (Battletech Ser.: Vol. 48). 2000. mass mkt. 5.99 (*0-451-45794-3*, ROC) NAL.

Measure of a Man. Daniel Gillis. LC 81-83809. (Columban Celtic Ser.: Vol. 1). 64p. (Orig.). 1982. pap. 5.95 (*0-941638-00-6*) Iona Phila.

Measure of a Man. Martin Luther King, Jr. LC 87-45898. (Illus.). 64p. 1988. 12.00 (*0-8006-0877-1*, 1-877, Fortress Pr) Augsburg Fortress.

***Measure of a Man: A Spiritual Autobiography.** Sidney Poitier. LC 99-88322. (Illus.). 272p. 2000. 26.00 (*0-06-251607-8*, Pub. by Harper SF) HarpC.

***Measure of a Man: A Spiritual Autobiography.** large type ed. Sidney Poitier. 352p. 2000. 26.00 (*0-06-019717-X*) HarpC.

Measure of a Man: Becoming the Father You Wish Your Father Had Been. Jerrold L. Shapiro. LC 94-41668. 1995. pap. 14.95 (*0-399-51935-1*, Perigee Bks) Berkley Pub.

Measure of a Mountain. Bruce Barcott. 288p. 1998. pap. 12.95 (*0-345-42633-9*) Ballantine Pub Grp.

Measure of a Mountain: Beauty & Terror on Mount Rainier. Bruce Barcott. LC 97-22029. 288p. 1997. 23.95 (*1-57061-074-6*) Sasquatch Bks.

Measure of All Things: On the Relationship Between Photography & Objects. Ed. by Peter Weiermair. (Illus.). 1999. 39.95 (*3-908161-48-7*) Abbeville Pr.

Measure of Cognitive-Linguistic Abilities (MCLA) Wendy Ellmo et al. (Illus.). 64p. 1995. pap. text 89.00 (*0-937857-57-2*, 1450) Speech Bin.

Measure of Conduct. Barry Wallenstein. 78p. (C). 1999. pap. 12.50 (*1-56439-103-5*, Pub. by Ridgeway) Partners Pubs Grp.

Measure of Corrugated Productivity, 1991. Technical Association of the Pulp & Paper Industry. 80p. reprint ed. pap. 25.00 (*0-7837-1644-3*, 2041938) Bks Demand.

Measure of Days. Flower A. Newhouse. LC 85-72907. 63p. 1985. pap. 9.00 (*0-910378-20-7*) Christward.

Measure of Democracy: Polling, Market Research, & Public Life, 1930-1945. Daniel J. Robinson. LC 99-222936. 272p. 1999. text 55.00 (*0-8020-4274-0*) U of Toronto Pr.

Measure of Democracy: Polling, Market Research, & Public Life, 1930-1945. Daniel J. Robinson. LC 99-222936. (Illus.). 272p. 1999. pap. text 21.95 (*0-8020-8109-6*) U of Toronto Pr.

Measure of Emptiness: Grain Elevators in the American Landscape. Frank Gohlke. (Creating the North American Landscape Ser.). (Illus.). 112p. 1992. pap. 29.95 (*0-8018-3949-1*); text 59.95 (*0-8018-3928-9*) Johns Hopkins.

Measure of Excellence. 1992. write for info. (*0-9631868-0-9*) Inter-Tribal Indian.

***Measure of Freedom.** Ian Carter. LC 98-37478. 322p. 1999. text 70.00 (*0-19-829453-0*) OUP.

Measure of Heaven. Nance Van Winckel. Ed. by Peter Pereira et al. 34p. (Orig.). 1996. pap. 6.00 (*0-9647199-1-6*) Floating Bridge Pr.

***Measure of Her Powers: An M. F. K. Fisher Reader.** M. F. K. Fisher. Ed. by Dominique Gioia. 2000. reprint ed. pap. 20.00 (*1-58243-104-3*, Pub. by Counterpt DC) HarpC.

Measure of Islands. Mark Halperin. LC 89-36079. (Wesleyan Poetry Ser.). (Illus.). 72p. 1990. pap. 12.95 (*0-8195-1179-X*, Wesleyan Univ Pr); text 25.00 (*0-8195-2177-9*, Wesleyan Univ Pr) U Pr of New Eng.

Measure of Justice. Steven Linder. LC 92-11520. 194p. 1992. 19.95 (*0-8027-4134-7*) Walker & Co.

***Measure of Life: Virginia Woolf's Last Years.** Herbert Marder. LC 00-20957. (Illus.). 416p. 2000. 35.00 (*0-8014-3729-6*) Cornell U Pr.

***Measure of Love.** Christopher Wilkins. 208p. 2000. 21.00 (*0-7867-0758-5*, Pub. by Carroll & Graf) Publishers Group.

Measure of Love. large type ed. Jeanne Bowman. (Linford Romance Library). 272p. 1993. pap. 16.99 (*0-7089-7449-X*, Linford) Ulverscroft.

Measure of Malpractice: Medical Injury, Malpractice Litigation, & Patient Compensation. Paul C. Weiler et al. LC 92-1705. 200p. (C). 1993. 36.50 (*0-674-55880-4*) HUP.

***Measure of Man.** Suzanne Simmons. 2001. mass mkt. write for info. (*0-312-97299-7*) St Martin.

Measure of Man: Incursions in Philosophical & Political Anthropology. David J. Levy. 248p. (C). 1993. text 34.95 (*0-8262-0899-1*) U of Mo Pr.

Measure of Man: On Freedom, Human Values, Survival & the Modern Temper. Joseph Wood Krutch. 1990. 23.00 (*0-8446-0749-5*) Peter Smith.

Measure of Man & Woman: Human Factors in Design. Dreyfuss, Henry, Associates Staff. (Illus.). 96p. 1993. 60.00 (*0-8230-3031-8*, Whitney Lib) Watsn-Guptill.

Measure of Management: Designing Organizations for Human Effectiveness. Eliot D. Chapple & Leonard R. Sayles. LC 60-6654. (Illus.). 224p. 1961. reprint ed. pap. 69.50 (*0-608-08274-0*, AU0036300080) Bks Demand.

Measure of Memory: Storytelling & Identity in American Jewish Fiction. Victoria Aarons. LC 95-13362. 1996. 35.00 (*0-8203-1773-X*) U of Ga Pr.

Measure of My Days. Anne S. DiBartolo. 1998. pap. write for info. (*1-57553-863-6*) Watermrk Pr.

Measure of My Days. Florida Scott-Maxwell. LC 78-27682. 150p. 1979. reprint ed. pap. 11.95 (*0-14-005164-3*, Penguin Bks) Viking Penguin.

Measure of My Days: The Journal of a Country Doctor. David Loxterkamp. LC 96-54704. 333p. 1997. 35.00 (*0-87451-799-0*); pap. 15.95 (*0-87451-885-7*) U Pr of New Eng.

Measure of Our Days: A Spiritual Exploration of Illness. Jerome Groopman. 256p. 1998. pap. 13.95 (*0-14-026972-X*, 97011693) Viking Penguin.

Measure of Our Success: A Letter to My Children & Yours. Marian W. Edelman. LC 91-42743. 128p. 1992. 15.00 (*0-8070-3102-X*) Beacon Pr.

Measure of Our Success: A Letter to My Children & Yours. Marian W. Edelman. LC 92-54846. 112p. 1993. pap. 10.00 (*0-06-097546-6*, Perennial) HarperTrade.

***Measure of Our Torment.** A. H. Felman. 190p. 2000. 12.00 (*0-9669018-1-9*) Ally.

Measure of Party Strength in the 50 States. Frederick W. Zuercher. 1968. 1.00 (*1-55614-063-0*) U of SD Gov Res Bur.

Measure of Party Strength in the 50 States: A Reassessment. Frederick W. Zuercher. 1977. 1.00 (*1-55614-062-2*) U of SD Gov Res Bur.

Measure of Perfection: Phrenology & the Fine Arts in America. Charles Colbert. LC 97-8449. (Cultural Studies of the United States). 464p. 1998. pap. 27.50 (*0-8078-4673-2*); lib. bdg. 59.95 (*0-8078-2370-8*) U of NC Pr.

Measure of Reality: Quantification & Western Society, 1250-1600. Alfred W. Crosby. LC 96-3092. (Illus.). 257p. 1996. text 29.95 (*0-521-55427-6*) Cambridge U Pr.

Measure of Reality: Quantification & Western Society, 1250-1600. Alfred W. Crosby. (Illus.). 250p. (C). 1997. reprint ed. pap. 14.95 (*0-521-63990-5*) Cambridge U Pr.

Measure of Success: From Assignment to Assessment in Language Arts. Mary Claggett. LC 95-33583. 215p. 1996. pap. text 21.50 (*0-86709-373-0*, 0373, Pub. by Boynton Cook Pubs) Heinemann.

Measure of Success: Protestants & Public Culture in Antebellum Cleveland. Michael J. McTighe. LC 93-26789. 283p. (C). 1994. text 74.50 (*0-7914-1825-1*); pap. text 24.95 (*0-7914-1826-X*) State U NY Pr.

Measure of Tax Paying Ability of Local School Administrative Units. Francis G. Cornell. LC 71-176670. (Columbia University. Teachers College. Contributions to Education Ser.: No. 698). reprint ed. 37.50 (*0-404-55698-1*) AMS Pr.

Measure of Thatcherism: A Sociology of Britain. Stephen Edgell & Vic Duke. LC 90-22649. 1991. pap. 19.95 (*0-04-301248-5*) Routledge.

Measure of the Moon. Ralph B. Baldwin. LC 62-20025. 546p. reprint ed. pap. 169.30 (*0-608-30856-0*, 202002300016) Bks Demand.

Measure of the Moon: Proceedings of the International Conference on Selenodesy & Lunar Topography, 2nd, University of Manchester, England, May 30-June 4, 1966. International Conference on Selenodesy & Lunar Top. Ed. by Zdenek Kopal & C. L. Goudas. (Astrophysics & Space Science Library: No.8). 479p. 1967. lib. bdg. 152.00 (*90-277-0125-3*) Kluwer Academic.

Measure of the Universe: A History of Modern Cosmology. J. D. North. 480p. 1990. pap. 12.95 (*0-486-66517-8*) Dover.

*__Measure of the World.__ Denis Guedj. 1998. 25.00 (*0-226-31030-2*) U Ch Pr.

Measure of the Year. Roderick L. Haig-Brown. LC 79-142637. (Essay Index Reprint Ser.). 1977. 20.95 (*0-8369-2191-7*) Ayer.

Measure of the Year. Roderick L. Haig-Brown. 1990. pap. text 14.95 (*0-88894-696-1*, Pub. by DGL) Sterling.

Measure of the Year. Roderick L. Haig-Brown. LC 92-13080. 256p. 1990. pap. 14.95 (*1-55821-088-1*) Lyons Pr.

*__Measure of Time.__ Terece Murry. 64p. 1999. pap. 7.95 (*1-56167-485-0*, Five Star Spec Ed) Am Literary Pr.

Measure of Time Vol. 2: Collected Longer Poems. James Kirkup. 202p. 1997. pap. 19.95 (*3-7052-0070-4*, Pub. by Poetry Salzburg) Intl Spec Bk.

Measure of Times Past: Pre-Newtonian Chronologies & the Rhetoric of Relative Time. Donald J. Wilcox. LC 87-1669. 302p. (C). 1989. pap. text 20.50 (*0-226-89722-2*) U Ch Pr.

Measure of Times Past: Pre-Newtonian Chronologies & the Rhetoric of Relative Time. Donald J. Wilcox. LC 87-1669. 304p. (C). 1994. 27.50 (*0-226-89721-4*) U Ch Pr.

Measure of Uncertainty: The Effects of the MASS Media. Guy Cumberbatch & Dennis Howitt. LC 90-116011. vii, 88 p. 1989. 15.00 (*0-86196-231-1*) J Libbey Med.

Measure of Value Stated & Illuminated. Thomas Robert Malthus. LC 87-17246. (Reprints of Economic Classics Ser.). v, 81p. 1989. reprint ed. 25.00 (*0-678-00603-2*) Kelley.

Measure of Vengeance. Jerry Jellison. 295p. 2000. 24.95 (*1-885173-72-5*, Pub. by Write Way) Midpt Trade.

Measure of Wealth: The English Land Tax in Historical Analysis. Donald E. Ginter. (Illus.). 744p. 1992. 85.00 (*0-7735-0729-9*, Pub. by McG-Queens Univ Pr) CUP Services.

Measure Once, Kill Twice. Kathleen Anne Barrett. LC 99-475199. (Thumbprint Mysteries Ser.). 128p. (gr. 1). 1999. pap. 5.95 (*0-8092-0644-7*, 064470) NTC Contemp Pub Co.

Measure the Possibilities with Omnigrid. Nancy Johnson-Srebro. 64p. 1993. 9.95 (*0-9638764-0-6*) Omnigrid.

Measure Theory. Donald Cohn. 276p. 1997. 49.50 (*0-8176-3003-1*) Birkhauser.

Measure Theory. J. J. Doob. (Graduate Texts in Mathematics Ser.: Vol. 143). 240p. 1993. text. write for info. (*3-540-94055-3*) Spr-Verlag.

Measure Theory. P. R. Halmos. LC 74-10690. (Graduate Texts in Mathematics Ser.: Vol. 18). 305p. 1997. 46.95 (*0-387-90088-8*) Spr-Verlag.

Measure Theory & Fine Properties of Functions. Lawrence C. Evans & Ronald F. Gariepy. (Studies in Advanced Mathematics). 288p. 1991. boxed set 115.95 (*0-8493-7157-0*, PA325) CRC Pr.

Measure Theory & Its Applications. Ed. by J. M. Belly et al. (Lecture Notes in Mathematics Ser.: Vol. 1033). 317p. 1983. 42.95 (*0-387-12703-8*) Spr-Verlag.

Measure Theory & Probability. Malcolm Adams & Victor W. Guillemin. LC 95-46511. 1995. write for info. (*3-7643-3884-9*) Birkhauser.

Measure Theory & Probability. Malcolm Adams & Victor W. Guillemin. LC 95-46511. 205p. 1996. 29.50 (*0-8176-3884-9*) Birkhauser.

Measure Theory & Probability. Joseph L. Doob. LC 93-17497. (Graduate Texts in Mathematics Ser.: Vol. 143). 210p. 1994. 53.95 (*0-387-94055-3*) Spr-Verlag.

Measure, Topology & Fractal Geometry. Gerald A. Edgar. Ed. by J. H. Ewing et al. (Undergraduate Texts in Mathematics Ser.). (Illus.). xi, 230p. 1995. 36.95 (*0-387-97272-2*) Spr-Verlag.

Measure Twice, Cut Once. rev. ed. Jim Tolpin. LC 96-10780. (Illus.). 144p. 1996. pap. 22.99 (*1-55870-428-0*, Betrwy Bks) F & W Pubns Inc.

Measure Twice, Cut Once: Construction Debris & Nonhazardous Industrial Waste Report. Cathy Latham. (Illus.). 89p. (Orig.). (C). 1994. pap. text 35.00 (*0-7881-1067-5*) DIANE Pub.

Measure Twice, Cut Once: Lessons from a Master Carpenter. Norm Abram. (Illus.). 208p. (gr. 8). 1996. 18.00 (*0-316-00494-4*) Little.

Measure Up! Margie Burton et al. Ed. by Alison Adams. (Early Connections Ser.). 16p. (J). (gr. k-2). 1999. pap. text 4.50 (*1-58344-073-9*) Benchmark Educ.

Measure Up! Yardsticks for Continuous Improvement. 2nd ed. Richard L. Lynch & Kelvin F. Cross. LC 95-1580. 1995. pap. 30.95 (*1-55786-718-6*) Blackwell Pubs.

Measure up with Science, 6 bks. Brenda Walpole. Incl. Counting. LC 95-21856. (Illus.). 32p. (J). (gr. 3 up). 1995. lib. bdg. 21.27 (*0-8368-1359-6*); Distance. LC 95-21851. (Illus.). (J). 1995. lib. bdg. 21.27 (*0-8368-1360-X*); Size. LC 95-21852. (Illus.). 32p. (J). 1995. lib. bdg. 21.27 (*0-8368-1361-8*); Speed. LC 95-21853. (Illus.). 32p. (J). (gr. 3 up). 1995. lib. bdg. 21.27 (*0-8368-1362-6*); Temperature. LC 95-21854. (Illus.). 32p. (J). (gr. 3 up). 1995. lib. bdg. 21.27 (*0-8368-1363-4*); Time. LC 95-21855. (Illus.). 32p. (J). (gr. 3 up). 1995. lib. bdg. 21.27 (*0-8368-1364-2*); (Illus.). (J). Set lib. bdg. 127.60 (*0-8368-1358-8*) Gareth Stevens Inc.

Measure-Valued Processes, Stochastic Partial Differential Equations, & Interacting Systems. Ed. by D. A. Dawson. LC 93-48193. (CRM Proceedings & Lecture Notes Ser.: Vol. 5). 241p. 1994. pap. 59.00 (*0-8218-6992-2*, CRMP/5) Am Math.

Measure with Metric. Franklyn M. Branley. LC 74-4056. (Young Math Ser.). (Illus.). 40p. (J). (gr. k-3). 1975. lib. bdg. 12.89 (*0-690-01117-2*) HarpC Child Bks.

*__Measure Your EQ Factor: Discover & Develop Your Emotional Potential.__ Gilles Dambra. 2000. pap. 11.95 (*0-572-02538-6*) W Foulsham.

Measure Your IQ. Gilles Azzopardi. 160p. (Orig.). 1993. pap. 12.95 (*0-572-01935-1*, Pub. by W Foulsham) Trans-Atl Phila.

Measured Air Leakage of Building, STP 904. Ed. by P. L. Lagus & Heinz R. Trechsel. LC 86-10953. (Special Technical Publication Ser.). (Illus.). 428p. 1986. text 54.00 (*0-8031-0469-3*, STP904) ASTM.

Measured Drawings of Early American Furniture. Burl N. Osburn & Bernice B. Osburn. LC 74-79936. (Illus.). 82p. 1975. reprint ed. pap. 7.95 (*0-486-23057-0*) Dover.

Measured Drawings of 18th-Century American Furniture. Ejner Handberg. LC 93-22381. (Illus.). 80p. 1993. pap. 10.95 (*0-936399-46-5*) Berkshire Hse.

Measured Drawings of Old English Oak Furniture. John W. Hurrell. 1984. 16.75 (*0-8446-6106-6*) Peter Smith.

Measured Drawings of Old English Oak Furniture. John W. Hurrell. (Woodworking Ser.). viii, 110p. 1983. reprint ed. pap. 8.95 (*0-486-24521-7*) Dover.

Measured Drawings of Shaker Furniture & Woodenware. Ejner Handberg. LC 80-87765. (Illus.). 96p. 1992. pap. 12.95 (*0-936399-20-1*) Berkshire Hse.

*__Measured Excess: Status, Gender, & Consumer Nationalism in South Korea.__ Laura C. Nelson. LC 00-21051. 2000. pap. 18.50 (*0-231-11617-9*) Col U Pr.

*__Measured Excess: Status, Gender, & Consumer Nationalism in South Korea.__ Laura C. Nelson. 224p. 2000. text 45.00 (*0-231-11616-0*) Col U Pr.

Measured Lies: The Bell Curve Examined. 464p. 1997. pap. 17.95 (*0-312-17228-1*, St Martin Griffin) St Martin.

Measured Life: The Times & Places of an Orphaned Intellectual. Richard Hoggart. 753p. (C). 1993. text 44.95 (*1-56000-135-6*) Transaction Pubs.

Measured Pace. William Coleman. LC 86-11750. 144p. (Orig.). 1986. pap. 6.99 (*0-87123-671-0*) Bethany Hse.

Measured Pace: Toward a Philosophical Understanding of the Arts of Dance. Francis Sparshott. (Studies in Philosophy). 384p. 1995. text 65.00 (*0-8020-0510-1*); pap. text 22.95 (*0-8020-6946-0*) U of Toronto Pr.

Measured Performance of Shallow Foundations. Ed. by Miguel Picornell. (Sessions Proceedings Ser.). 116p. 1988. 17.00 (*0-87262-643-1*) Am Soc Civil Eng.

Measured Response. Intro. by H. Palmer Hall. (Orig.). 1993. pap. 10.00 (*1-877603-16-3*) Pecan Grove.

Measured Shop Drawings for American Furniture. Thomas Moser. LC 84-26872. (Illus.). 328p. 1988. pap. 21.95 (*0-8069-6792-7*) Sterling.

Measured Silence. Joseph Coulson. LC 86-82129. 68p. 1986. pap. 5.00 (*0-939483-00-9*) Hundred Pound Pr.

Measured Tones: The Interplay of Physics & Music. Ian Johnston. (Illus.). 408p. 1989. pap. 40.00 (*0-85274-236-3*) IOP Pub.

Measured Words: Applied Linguistic. Bernard Spolsky. 416p. 1995. pap. text 24.95 (*0-19-437201-4*) OUP.

Measurement. Susan Benhoff. (Basic Skills Ser.). (Illus.). 32p. (J). (gr. k-1). 1998. pap. text 4.95 (*0-88724-465-3*, CD-2133) Carson-Dellos.

Measurement. Christopher Carrie. (Crayola Kinder Art BKs.). (Illus.). 12p. (Orig.). (J). (gr. 3-6). 1987. pap. 4.70 (*0-86696-206-9*) Binney & Smith.

Measurement, Vol. 2653. Ed. by Janet Bruno. (Child-Centered Math Ser.: Vol. 3). (Illus.). 80p. 1997. pap. 4.98 (*1-57471-236-5*, 2653) Creat Teach Pr.

Measurement: A "Hands On" Approach to Teaching . . . Andy Heidemann et al. (Illus.). 217p. (J). (gr. k-9). 1988. teacher ed. 17.95 (*0-927726-01-7*) Hands On CA.

Measurement: Area, Perimeter see Learn Math Quickly Series: Videotapes & Workbooks

Measurement: Circles, Volume see Learn Math Quickly Series: Videotapes & Workbooks

Measurement: Its Concepts, Theories & Problems. Karel Berka. 256p. 1982. text 171.00 (*90-277-1416-9*, D Reidel) Kluwer Academic.

Measurement: The Basic Science. John R. Amend. LC 96-178718. (Chemistry Ser.). 104p. (Orig.). 1997. pap. 13.75 (*0-7637-0187-4*) Jones & Bartlett.

Measurement, Accounting, & Organizational Information. Theodore J. Mock & Hugh D. Grove. LC 78-10536. (Wiley Series in Accounting & Information Systems). (Illus.). 256p. reprint ed. pap. 79.40 (*0-7837-3458-1*, 205778400008) Bks Demand.

*__Measurement Analysis: An Introduction to the Statistical Analysis of Laboratory Data In Physics, Chemistry & the Life Sciences.__ Mario Caria. 280p. 2000. 48.00 (*1-86094-231-8*, Pub. by Imperial College) World Scientific Pub.

Measurement &... 8th ed. Linn. 1999. pap. text, student ed. 14.25 (*0-13-878976-2*) P-H.

Measurement & Accounting Information Criteria. Theodore J. Mock. (Studies in Accounting Research: Vol. 13). 116p. 1976. 12.00 (*0-86539-025-8*) Am Accounting.

Measurement & Analysis in Psychosocial Research: The Failing & Saving of Theory. Sheying Chen. 336p. 1997. text 83.95 (*1-85972-571-6*, Pub. by Avebry) Ashgate Pub Co.

Measurement & Analysis of Gear Noises. R. S. Davidson & L. J. Collins. (Technical Papers: Vol. P185). (Illus.). 22p. 1938. pap. text 30.00 (*1-55589-378-3*) AGMA.

Measurement & Analysis of Job Vacancies: An International Comparison. Ed. by Joan Muysken. LC 94-9578. 304p. 1994. 69.95 (*1-85628-617-7*, Pub. by Avebry) Ashgate Pub Co.

Measurement & Analysis of Political Systems: A Science of Social Behavior. Stephen Coleman. LC 75-8704. (Comparative Studies in Behavioral Science). (Illus.). 231p. reprint ed. pap. 71.70 (*0-608-20295-9*, AU0050700002) Bks Demand.

Measurement & Analysis of Vapor Sensors Used at Underground Storage Tank Sites. Marc A. Portnoff et al. (Illus.). 50p. (C). 1998. reprint ed. pap. text 20.00 (*0-7881-4892-3*) DIANE Pub.

Measurement & Applications see Basic Mathematics

Measurement & Assessment in Teaching. 8th ed. Linn. LC 98-51928. (Illus.). 574p. 1999. 72.00 (*0-13-878356-X*) P-H.

*__Measurement & Assessment in Teaching.__ 8th ed. Simon & Schuster Staff. (C). 1999. write for info. (*0-13-013740-5*) S&S Trade.

*__Measurement & Assessment in Teaching: Mac Ph Custom Test.__ 8th ed. 1999. write for info. (*0-13-013816-9*, Prentice Hall) P-H.

Measurement & Authentic Assess. 7th ed. Linn. 1999. 81.60 (*0-13-012487-7*, Pub. by P-H) S&S Trade.

Measurement & Behavior of Unemployment. (Universities-National Bureau Conference Ser.: No. 8). 615p. 1957. 40.00 (*0-691-04144-X*) Natl Bur Econ Res.

Measurement & Behavior of Unemployment: A Conference of the Universities-National Bureau Committee for Economic Research. National Bureau of Economic Research Staff. LC 57-5442. (National Bureau of Economic Research Ser.: Vol. 8). (Illus.). 615p. reprint ed. pap. 190.70 (*0-608-11576-2*, 201964100013) Bks Demand.

Measurement & Calculation of Radon Releases from Uranium Mill Tailings. IAEA Staff. (Technical Reports: No. 333). 59p. 1992. pap. 30.00 (*92-0-101092-3*, STI/DOC/333, Pub. by IAEA) Bernan Associates.

Measurement & Calibration Requirements for Quality Assurance to ISO 9000. Alan S. Morris. LC 97-22234. (Series in Quality & Reliability Engineering). 404p. 1998. 94.95 (*0-471-97685-7*) Wiley.

Measurement & Control - MECO '85: Proceedings, IASTED Symposium, Istanbul, Turkey, July 23-25, 1985. Ed. by A. T. Dinibutun et al. 226p. 1985. 80.00 (*0-88986-089-0*, 094) Acta Pr.

Measurement & Control Basics. 2nd ed. Thomas A. Hughes. LC 95-36232. (Resources for Measurement & Control Ser.). 315p. 1995. 76.00 (*1-55617-541-8*) ISA.

Measurement & Control for Batch Manufacturing: Presented at the Winter Annual Meeting of the American Society of Mechanical Engineers, Phoenix, Arizona, November 14-19, 1982. American Society of Mechanical Engineers Staff. Ed. by D. E. Hardt. LC 82-73180. (Illus.). 201p. reprint ed. pap. 62.40 (*0-8357-2856-0*, 203909100010) Bks Demand.

Measurement & Control in Agriculture. S. W. Cox. LC 98-55556. 1997. 99.95 (*0-632-04114-5*) Blackwell Sci.

Measurement & Control of Cardiovascular Risk Factors. fac. ed. Ed. by Ruth J. Hegyeli. LC 76-604124. (Atherosclerosis Reviews Ser.: No. 7). (Illus.). 352p. pap. 109.20 (*0-7837-7162-2*, 204713500005) Bks Demand.

Measurement & Control of Liquid Level. Chun H. Cho. LC 82-48156. (Independent Learning Module from the Instrument Society of America Ser.). (Illus.). 279p. 1982. reprint ed. pap. 86.50 (*0-7837-9046-5*, 204979700003) Bks Demand.

Measurement & Control of Paper Stock Consistency. Michael H. Waller. LC 82-48598. (Instrument Society of America Monographs: No. 5). 129p. reprint ed. pap. 40.00 (*0-8357-4426-4*, 203725700008) Bks Demand.

Measurement & Correction of Electrolyte Resistance in Electrochemical Tests. Ed. by L. L. Scribner & S. R. Taylor. LC 89-18322. (Special Technical Publication Ser.: No. 1056). (Illus.). 250p. 1990. text 65.00 (*0-8031-1283-1*, STP1056) ASTM.

Measurement & Data Analysis. Robert P. Mitchell. LC 96-4931. (Smart Solutions Ser.). 1996. pap. 9.64 (*1-56420-122-8*) New Readers.

Measurement & Design: Measuring in an Interdisciplinary Research Environment. Ed. by H. Kanis et al. 150p. 1994. pap. 46.50 (*90-407-1085-6*, Pub. by Delft U Pr) Coronet Bks.

Measurement & Detection of Radiation. 2nd ed. Nicholas Tsoulfanidis. LC 94-24270. 605p. 1995. 85.00 (*1-56032-317-5*) Hemisp Pub.

Measurement & Evaluation. 4th ed. (C). 1995. 15.84 (*0-8087-7262-7*) Pearson Custom.

Measurement & Evaluation: Basic Concepts. Sarah A. Lutterodt & Deborah J. Grafinger. (Instructor Training Ser.). (Illus.). 40p. (Orig.). 1985. pap. text 16.50 (*0-87683-686-4*) GP Courseware.

Measurement & Evaluation: Strategies for School Improvement. James F. McNamara et al. LC 99-22301. (School Leadership Library). 1999. 29.95 (*1-883001-78-1*) Eye On Educ.

Measurement & Evaluation in Early Childhood Education. 2nd ed. Wortham Sue C. LC 94-3594. 1994. pap. text 44.00 (*0-02-430033-0*, Macmillan Coll) P-H.

Measurement & Evaluation in Education & Psychology. 4th ed. William A. Mehrens & Irvin J. Lehmann. 672p. (C). 1991. text 70.50 (*0-03-030407-5*, Pub. by Harcourt Coll Pubs) Harcourt.

Measurement & Evaluation in Physical Education & Exercise Science. 3rd ed. Douglas N. Hastad & Alan C. Lacy. LC 97-43905. 575p. 1998. pap. text 53.00 (*0-205-27977-5*) Allyn.

M

Measurement & Evaluation in Psychology & Education. 6th ed. Robert M. Thorndike. LC 96-33590. 583p. 1996. 81.00 (*0-13-254178-5*, Merrill Coll) P-H.

Measurement & Evaluation in Schools. 2nd ed. Blaine Worthen. LC 98-8743. 544p. (C). 1998. 81.00 (*0-8013-1660-X*) Addison-Wesley.

Measurement & Evaluation of Health Education. 3rd ed. Mark Dignan. LC 94-30631. (Illus.). 210p. (C). 1995. pap. 35.95 (*0-398-05958-6*) C C Thomas.

Measurement & Evaluation of Health Education. 3rd ed. Mark B. Dignan. LC 94-30631. (Illus.). 210p. (C). 1994. text 51.95 (*0-398-05935-7*) C C Thomas.

Measurement & Evaluation of Library Services. 2nd ed. F. Wilfrid Lancaster & Sharon L. Baker. LC 91-72908. xviii, 411p. 1991. text 49.95 (*0-87815-061-7*) Info Resources.

Measurement & Evaluation of Musical Experiences. David J. Boyle & Rudolf E. Radocy. 332p. 1987. 45.00 (*0-02-870300-6*, Schirmer Books) Mac Lib Ref.

Measurement & Geometry. Nerisa B. Bryant. (Mathematics in Daily Living Ser.). 1997. pap., student ed. 10.32 (*0-8114-1515-5*) Raintree Steck-V.

Measurement & Geometry. Karen Lassiter. (Mathematics Skill Bks.). 1997. pap., student ed. 3.00 (*0-8114-4320-5*) Raintree Steck-V.

Measurement & Geometry: Answer Key. Jocelyn Walton & Cheryl Klein. 220p. 1995. text, teacher ed. 19.95 (*1-886292-16-7*) CEO Sftware.

Measurement & Geometry: Series E. Jocelyn C. Walton & Sheryl Klein. 220p. (J). (gr. 7-10). 1995. text, wbk. ed. 19.95 (*1-886292-11-6*) CEO Sftware.

Measurement & Geometry by Design. Russell F. Jacobs. Ed. by Janette M. Smidt & Erika D. Jacobs. (Illus.). 49p. (YA). (gr. 7-10). 1997. pap. text, wbk. ed. 17.95 (*0-918272-28-9*, 164) Jacobs.

Measurement & Instrumentations in Engineering Principles & Basic Laboratory Experiments. Ivan E. Morse & Francis L. Tse. (Mechanical Engineering Ser.: Vol. 67). (Illus.). 784p. 1989. text 85.00 (*0-8247-8086-8*) Dekker.

Measurement & Interpretation in Accounting: A Living Systems Theory Approach. G. A. Swanson & James G. Miller. LC 89-3857. 235p. 1989. 69.50 (*0-89930-422-2*, SMJ/, Greenwood Pr) Greenwood.

Measurement & Interpretation of Job Vacancies. National Bureau of Economic Research Staff. (Other Conferences Ser.: No. 5). 603p. 1966. reprint ed. 156.80 (*0-87014-471-5*) Natl Bur Econ Res.

Measurement & Interpretation of Productivity. Assembly of Behavioral & Social Sciences. LC 79-22715. (Illus.). 457p. reprint ed. pap. 141.70 (*0-8357-3184-7*, 203945300012) Bks Demand.

Measurement & Interpretation of School Building Utilization. Edgar L. Morphet. LC 75-177084. (Columbia University. Teachers College. Contributions to Education Ser.: No. 264). reprint ed. 37.50 (*0-404-55264-1*) AMS Pr.

Measurement & Management of Clinical Outcomes in Mental Health. John S. Lyons et al. LC 96-42269. 304p. 1997. 75.00 (*0-471-15429-6*) Wiley.

Measurement & Modeling Millimeter-Wave Response from Soil Surfaces. Adib Y. Nashashibi et al. LC QC0973.. (University of Michigan Reports: No. 029721-2-T). 60p. reprint ed. pap. 30.00 (*0-7837-6779-X*, 204660900003) Bks Demand.

Measurement & Modeling of Environmental Flows, 1992. Ed. by S. A. Sherif et al. (FED Series, Vol. 143: HTD: Vol. 232). 252p. 1992. 62.50 (*0-7918-1128-X*, G00772) ASME.

Measurement & Perspective: Del Modo Di Misurare, 1564. Cosimo Bartoli. (Printed Sources of Western Art Ser.). (ITA.). 294p. 1981. reprint ed. pap., boxed set 50.00 (*0-915346-67-2*) A Wofsy Fine Arts.

Measurement & Prediction of Judgment & Choice. Richard D. Bock & Lyle V. Jones. LC 66-17897. (Holden-Day Series in Psychology). 384p. reprint ed. pap. 119.10 (*0-608-13403-1*, 205574300034) Bks Demand.

Measurement & Predictions of Plastic Gear Transmission Errors with Comparison to the Measured Noise of Plastic & Steel Gears. Leonard Liauwnardi et al. (Technical Papers: Vol. 97FTM4). (Illus.). 11p. 1977. pap. text 30.00 (*1-55589-698-7*) AGMA.

Measurement & Synthesis in the Chemistry Laboratory. 2nd ed. Larry Peck & Kurt Irgolic. 478p. (C). 1997. pap. text 56.00 (*0-13-905050-7*) P-H.

Measurement & Use of Shear Wave Velocity for Evaluating Dynamic Soil Properties: Proceedings of a Session Sponsored by the Geotechnical Engineering Division. Ed. by Richard D. Woods. 78p. 1985. 16.00 (*0-87262-456-0*) Am Soc Civil Eng.

Measurement & Valuation of Unpaid Contribution: Accounting Through Time & Output. 124p. pap. 15.00 (*92-1-127007-3*) UN.

Measurement As a Powerful Software Management Tool. Nicholas Ashley. LC 94-27967. (International Software Quality Assurance Ser.). 1994. 29.95 (*0-07-707902-7*) McGraw.

Measurement Benchmarks: Estimating & Measuring. Cornelia Tierney et al. Ed. by Catherine Anderson et al. (Investigations in Number, Data, & Space Ser.). (Illus.). 133p. (Orig.). 1995. pap., teacher ed. 22.95 (*0-86651-991-2*, DS21427) Seymour Pubns.

Measurement Benchmarks: Estimating & Measuring. rev. ed. Cornelia Tierney et al. Ed. by Catherine Anderson & Beverly Cory. LC 97-184756. (Investigations in Number, Data, & Space Ser.). (Illus.). 137p. (Orig.). (YA). (gr. 5 up). 1997. pap. text 22.95 (*1-57232-801-0*, 47048) Seymour Pubns.

Measurement by the Physical Educator: Why & How. 2nd ed. David K. Miller. 400p. (C). 1993. text. write for info. (*0-697-16621-X*) Brown & Benchmark.

Measurement by the Physical Educator: Why & How. 3rd ed. David K. Miller. LC 97-187893. 352p. (C). 1997. text. write for info. (*0-697-29488-9*) Brown & Benchmark.

Measurement Challenges in Atmospheric Chemistry. Ed. by Leonard Newman. LC 92-38528. (Advances in Chemistry Ser.: No. 232). 408p. 1993. text 105.00 (*0-8412-2470-6*, Pub. by Am Chemical) OUP.

Measurement, Design, & Analysis: An Integrated Approach. E. Pedhazur & L. Schmelkin. 849p. (C). 1991. pap., student ed. 49.95 (*0-8058-1063-3*) L Erlbaum Assocs.

Measurement Error & Banks' Reported Earnings. Reed McKnight. LC 83-1393. (Research for Business Decisions Ser.: No. 61). 128p. 1983. reprint ed. pap. 39.70 (*0-8357-1411-X*, 207040700088) Bks Demand.

Measurement Error & Latent Variables in Econometrics. A. Kapteyn & T. Wansbeek. 1999. text. write for info. (*0-444-88100-X*, North Holland) Elsevier.

Measurement Error in Nonlinear Models. R. J. Carroll et al. (Illus.). 312p. (C). (gr. 13). 1995. boxed set 59.95 (*0-412-04721-7*, Chap & Hall CRC) CRC Pr.

Measurement Error Models. 9th ed. Wayne A. Fuller. LC 86-28186. (Probability & Mathematical Statistics Ser.). 464p. 1987. 174.95 (*0-471-86187-1*) Wiley.

Measurement Errors: Theory & Practice. Semyon Rabinovich. Tr. by M. E. Alferieff from RUS. LC 92-28122.Tr. of Pogreshnosti Izmerenii. 1992. 109.00 (*0-88318-866-X*) Spr-Verlag.

Measurement Errors: Theory & Practice. Semyon Rabinovich. Tr. by M. E. Alferieff from RUS. LC 92-28122.Tr. of Pogreshnosti Izmerenii. (Illus.). 271p. (C). 1994. pap. text 44.95 (*1-56396-323-X*, AIP Pr) Spr-Verlag.

Measurement Errors & Uncertainties: Theory & Practice. 2nd ed. S. G. Rabinovich. LC 99-20534. 312p. 1999. pap. 44.95 (*0-387-98835-1*) Spr-Verlag.

Measurement Errors in Surveys. Paul Biemer et al. LC 91-20598. (Probability & Mathematical Statistics: Applied Probability & Statistics Section Ser.). 800p. 1991. 135.00 (*0-471-53405-6*) Wiley.

Measurement Evaluation. 6th ed. Baumgartner & Jack. LC 98-23747. 1998. 42.50 (*0-697-29484-6*, WCB McGr Hill) McGrw-H Hghr Educ.

Measurement Evaluation in P. E. 5th ed. Baumgartner. 1994. teacher ed. 9.68 (*0-697-15219-7*) McGraw.

Measurement for Educational Evaluation. 2nd ed. Clinton I. Chase. LC 77-79456. (Illus.). 1978. teacher ed. write for info. (*0-201-01006-2*); student ed. write for info. (*0-201-01029-1*) Addison-Wesley.

Measurement for Evaluation in Physical Education & Exercise Science. 2nd ed. Ted A. Baumgartner & Andrew S. Jackson. 480p. (C). 1995. text, per. write for info. incl. 3.5 ld (*0-697-27971-5*) Brown & Benchmark.

Measurement for Evaluation in Physical Education & Exercise Science. 5th ed. Ted A. Baumgartner & Andrew S. Jackson. 465p. (C). 1994. text 49.80 (*0-697-15218-9*); text. write for info. (*0-697-24971-9*) Brown & Benchmark.

Measurement in Contract Control. Martin Barnes. 304p. 1977. 23.75 (*0-7277-0040-5*, Pub. by T Telford) RCH.

Measurement in Direct Practice. Betty J. Blythe & Tony Tripodi. (Human Services Guides Ser.: Vol. 59). 160p. (C). 1989. pap. text 18.95 (*0-8039-3080-1*) Sage.

Measurement in Economics. Ed. by Wolfgang Eichhorn. xii, 830p. 1987. 119.00 (*0-387-91321-1*) Spr-Verlag.

Measurement in Elderly Chronic Care Populations. Ed. by M. Powell Lawton et al. LC 97-28766. (Illus.). 272p. 1997. 43.95 (*0-8261-9990-9*) Springer Pub.

Measurement in Geometry see Basic Mathematics

Measurement in Health Promotion & Protection. T. Abelin & Z. Brzezinski. (WHO Regional Publications, European Ser.: No. 22). 682p. 1987. text 80.00 (*92-890-1113-0*) World Health.

Measurement in Hearing & Balance. Ed. by S. D. Stephens. (Advances in Audiology Ser.: Vol. 5). (Illus.). xx, 220p. 1988. 191.50 (*3-8055-4714-5*) S Karger.

Measurement in Information Science. Bert R. Boyce et al. (Illus.). 283p. 1994. text 64.95 (*0-12-121450-8*) Acad Pr.

Measurement in Laboratory Medicine: A Primer on Control & Interpretation. P. W. Strike. LC 95-36225. (Illus.). 360p. 1995. pap. text 75.00 (*0-7506-2259-8*) Buttrwrth-Heinemann.

Measurement in Neurological Rehabilitation. Derick T. Wade. 408p. 1992. pap. text 62.50 (*0-19-261954-3*) OUP.

Measurement in Nursing Research. 2nd ed. Carolyn F. Waltz et al. LC 90-14072. (Illus.). 533p. (C). 1991. 59.00 (*0-8036-9047-9*) Davis Co.

Measurement in Pediatric Exercise Science. Ed. by David Docherty. LC 96-23786. (Illus.). 360p. 1995. text 47.00 (*0-87322-960-6*, BDOC0960) Human Kinetics.

Measurement in Polyphase Flows: Papers Presented at the Winter Annual Meeting of the American Society of Mechanical Engineers, San Francisco, California, December 10-15, 1978. American Society of Mechanical Engineers Staff. Ed. by David E. Stock. LC 78-68328. 131p. reprint ed. pap. 40.70 (*0-608-30896-X*, 205171200005) Bks Demand.

Measurement in Psychology: A Critical History of a Methodological Concept. Joel Michell. LC 98-39566. (Ideas in Context Ser.: No. 53). 256p. (C). 1999. text 54.95 (*0-521-62120-8*) Cambridge U Pr.

Measurement in Radio. Frederick H. Lumley. LC 71-161164. (History of Broadcasting: Radio to Television Ser.). 1977. reprint ed. 28.95 (*0-405-03576-4*) Ayer.

Measurement in the Elementary School: Workbook Manual for Teachers. rev. ed. Barbara Berman & Fredda J. Friederwitzer. (Project S.I.T.E. Ser.). 102p. (C). 1991. student ed. 15.00 (*1-880744-00-7*) Educ Support.

Measurement in the Middle Grades. Dorothy Geddes et al. Ed. by Frances R. Curcio. LC 93-45338. (Curriculum & Evaluation Standards for School Mathematics Addenda Series, Gr. 5-8). (Illus.). 87p. 1994. pap. 16.95 (*0-87353-367-4*) NCTM.

***Measurement, Instrumentation & Sensors Handbook.** John Webster. 1999. 129.95 (*0-7803-4725-0*) Inst Electrical.

Measurement, Instrumentation & Sensors Handbook. John G. Webster. LC 98-31681. (Electrical Engineering Handbook Ser.). 2608p. 1998. boxed set 139.95 (*0-8493-8347-1*) CRC Pr.

Measurement, Instrumentation & Sensors Handbook, 001. John G. Webster. 1999. cd-rom 129.00 (*0-8493-2145-X*) CRC Pr.

Measurement Investigations. Tamara Drean & Randall Souviney. 152p. 1997. 13.50 (*0-86651-591-7*) Seymour Pubns.

Measurement Issues & Behavior of Productivity Variables. Ed. by Ali Dogramaci. (C). 1986. lib. bdg. 115.50 (*0-89838-171-1*) Kluwer Academic.

Measurement Issues in Criminology. Ed. by K. L. Kempf. (Illus.). xviii, 275p. 1990. 61.95 (*0-387-97260-9*) Spr-Verlag.

Measurement Judgment & Decision Making. 2nd ed. Ed. by Michael Birnbaum et al. (Handbook of Perception & Cognition Ser.). (Illus.). 367p. 1997. text 85.00 (*0-12-099975-7*) Morgan Kaufmann.

***Measurement Mania: Games & Activities That Make Math Easy & Fun.** Lynette Long. 128p. 2001. pap. 12.95 (*0-471-36980-2*) Wiley.

Measurement Methods in Rotating Components of Turbomachinery: Proceedings of the Joint Fluids Engineering Gas Turbine Conference & Products Show, New Orleans, LA, 1980. Joint Fluids Engineering Gas Turbine Conference & Products Show. Ed. by B. Lakshiminarayana & P. Runstadler. LC 79-57425. 349p. reprint ed. pap. 108.20 (*0-608-11878-8*, 202314900032) Bks Demand.

Measurement Motivators. Tom Palumbo. 96p. (J). (gr. 3-7). 1989. 11.99 (*0-86653-500-4*, GA1095) Good Apple.

Measurement Mysteries, Vol. 4475. Marcia S. Gresko. Ed. by Joel Kupperstein. (Learn to Read Math Ser.). (Illus.). 16p. (J). 1998. pap. 2.75 (*1-57471-382-5*, 4475) Creat Teach Pr.

Measurement Nightmare: How the Theory of Constraints Can Resolve Conflicting Strategies, Policies & Measures. Debra Smith. (APICS Constraints Management Ser.). 208p. 1999. boxed set 39.95 (*1-57444-246-5*) St Lucie Pr.

Measurement of Absorbed Dose in a Phantom Irradiated by a Single Beam of X or Gamma Rays, No. 23. International Commission on Radiation Units & Meas. LC 72-97332. 1973. 40.00 (*0-913394-16-5*) Intl Comm Rad Meas.

Measurement of Absorbed Dose of Neutrons & Mixtures of Neutrons & Gamma - Rays. (Report Ser.: No. 25). 1961. pap. 20.00 (*0-913392-08-1*) NCRP Pubns.

Measurement of Air Flow: In SI-Metric Units. 5th ed. Ernest Ower & F. C. Pankhurst. 1977. 167.00 (*0-08-021282-4*, Pub. by Pergamon Repr) Franklin.

Measurement of Air Pollutants: Guide to the Selection of Methods. Morris Katz. 123p. 1969. pap. text 23.00 (*92-4-154006-0*, 1150099) World Health.

Measurement of Appearance. 2nd ed. Richard S. Hunter & Richard W. Harold. LC 86-34034. 432p. 1987. 139.00 (*0-471-83006-2*) Wiley.

Measurement of Appreciation in Poetry, Prose, & Art, & Studies in Appreciation. Robert K. Speer. LC 78-177756. (Columbia University. Teachers College. Contributions to Education Ser.: No. 362). reprint ed. 37.50 (*0-404-55362-1*) AMS Pr.

Measurement of Association in Industrial Geography. Harold H. McCarty et al. LC 81-23752. 143p. 1982. reprint ed. lib. bdg. 65.00 (*0-313-23442-6*, MCME, Greenwood Pr) Greenwood.

Measurement of Atmospheric Emissions. Heikki Torvela. LC 93-31101. 1994. 158.95 (*0-387-19848-2*) Spr-Verlag.

Measurement of Attitudes Toward People with Disabilities: Methods, Psychometrics & Scales. Richard F. Antonak & Hanoch Livneh. (Illus.). 326p. 1988. pap., spiral bd. 40.95 (*0-398-06008-8*) C C Thomas.

Measurement of Attitudes Toward People with Disabilities: Methods, Psychometrics & Scales. Richard F. Antonak & Hanoch Livneh. (Illus.). 326p. (C). 1988. text 62.95 (*0-398-05404-5*) C C Thomas.

Measurement of Audition & Vision in the First Year of Postnatal Life: A Methodological Overview. Ed. by Norman A. Krasnegor & Gilbert Gottlieb. LC 84-28222. 484p. 1985. text 82.50 (*0-89391-130-5*) Ablx Pub.

Measurement of Behavior, Pt. 1. rev. ed. R. Vance Hall & Ron Van Houten. (Managing Behavior Ser.). 106p. 1983. pap. 13.00 (*0-89079-072-8*, 1045) PRO-ED.

Measurement of Biodegradable Organic Matter with Biofilm Reactors. Louis A. Kaplan et al. LC 96-153690. (Illus.). 69p. 1996. pap. 115.00 (*0-89867-853-6*, 90691) Am Water Wks Assn.

Measurement of Biological Shape & Shape Change. Fred L. Bookstein. LC 78-15923. (Lecture Notes in Biomathematics Ser.: Vol. 24). 1978. pap. 28.00 (*0-387-08912-8*) Spr-Verlag.

Measurement of Blast Fragmentation: Proceedings of a Workshop Held Parallel with FRAGBLAST-5, Montreal, 26-29 August 1996. Ed. by John A. Franklin & T. Katsabanis. (Illus.). 300p. (C). 1996. 142.00 (*90-5410-845-2*, Pub. by A A Balkema) Ashgate Pub Co.

Measurement of Business Inventories. Murray F. Foss. LC 80-607163. (Economic Research Report Ser.: No. 3). 227p. reprint ed. pap. 70.40 (*0-608-15351-6*, 205636800061) Bks Demand.

Measurement of Capital. Ed. by Dan Usher. LC 79-18893. (Studies in Income & Wealth: No. 45). (Illus.). 568p. 1980. lib. bdg. 71.00 (*0-226-84300-9*) U Ch Pr.

Measurement of Cardiac Function. Ed. by John H. McNeill. LC 96-31525. (Methods in Pharmacology Ser.). 144p. 1996. spiral bd. 74.95 (*0-8493-3332-6*) CRC Pr.

Measurement of Cardiovascular Function. Ed. by John H. McNeill. LC 96-31524. (Methods in the Life Sciences - Methods in Pharmacology Ser.). (Illus.). 128p. 1996. spiral bd. 74.95 (*0-8493-3331-8*) CRC Pr.

Measurement of Community Health: The Social Health Index. Yoku Shaw-Taylor. LC 99-26122. 112p. 1999. 33.00 (*0-7618-1414-0*) U Pr of Amer.

Measurement of Corporate Social Performance: Determining the Impact of Business Actions on Areas of Social Concern - Issued by the Committee on Social Measurement, AICPA. American Institute of Certified Public Accountants. LC HF5343.A54. 365p. reprint ed. pap. 113.20 (*0-608-17997-3*, 202657500050) Bks Demand.

Measurement of Corporate Sources & Uses of Funds. David Meiselman & Eli Shapiro. (Technical Papers: No. 18). 301p. 1964. reprint ed. 78.30 (*0-87014-424-3*) Natl Bur Econ Res.

Measurement of Delinquency. Marvin E. Wolfgang & Thorsten D. Sellin. (Criminology, Law Enforcement, & Social Problems Ser.: No. 209). 433p. 1975. reprint ed. 30.00 (*0-87585-209-2*) Patterson Smith.

Measurement of Dielectric Properties under Space Conditions. American Society for Testing & Materials Staff. LC 67-17472. No. 420. 106p. reprint ed. pap. 30.30 (*0-317-08047-4*, 2001119) Bks Demand.

Measurement of Dose Equivalents from External Photon & Electron Radiations. LC 92-9903. (ICRU Reports: No. 47). 1992. 55.00 (*0-913394-42-4*) Intl Comm Rad Meas.

Measurement of Durable Goods Prices. Robert J. Gordon. (Illus.). 742p. 1990. lib. bdg. 99.50 (*0-226-30455-8*) U Ch Pr.

Measurement of Economic & Social Performance. Ed. by Milton Moss. (Studies in Income & Wealth: No. 38). 615p. 1973. 159.90 (*0-87014-259-3*) Natl Bur Econ Res.

Measurement of Economic & Social Performance. Conference on the Measurement of Economic & Social. Ed. by Milton Moss. LC 72-97766. (Studies in Income & Wealth: No. 38). (Illus.). 615p. reprint ed. pap. 190.70 (*0-8357-7669-7*, 205699700001) Bks Demand.

Measurement of Economic Growth. Dan Usher. LC 79-14908. (Illus.). 316p. reprint ed. pap. 98.00 (*0-8357-4588-0*, 203751900008) Bks Demand.

Measurement of Efficiency of Production. Rolf Fare et al. 1985. lib. bdg. 110.50 (*0-89838-155-X*) Kluwer Academic.

Measurement of Efficiency of Scientific Research. Ben-Ami Lipetz. LC 65-23581. 1965. 20.00 (*0-910788-01-4*) Intermedia.

Measurement of Electric Utility Cost Performance: A Proposed Methodology. 425p. 1976. 15.00 (*0-318-15006-9*) NARUC.

Measurement of Electric Utility Efficiency. 386p. 1975. 14.00 (*0-318-15007-7*) NARUC.

Measurement of Environmental & Resource Values: Theory & Methods. A. Myrick Freeman, III. LC 93-36099. 516p. 1993. 45.00 (*0-915707-68-3*); pap. 32.95 (*0-915707-69-1*) Resources Future.

Measurement of Equity in School Finance: Conceptual, Methodological & Empirical Dimensions. Robert Berne & Leanna Stiefel. LC 83-24394. (Illus.). 317p. reprint ed. pap. 98.30 (*0-7837-4784-5*, 204454000003) Bks Demand.

Measurement of Fairmindedness. Goodwin B. Watson. LC 75-177660. (Columbia University. Teachers College. Contributions to Education Ser.: No. 176). reprint ed. 37.50 (*0-404-55176-9*) AMS Pr.

Measurement of Fiscal Impact: Methodological Issues. Ed. by Mario I. Blejer & Ke-Young Chu. (Occasional Papers: No. 59). 70p. 1988. pap. 7.50 (*1-55775-016-5*) Intl Monetary.

Measurement of Food Preferences. D. M. H. Thomson & H. J. H. Macfie. 301p. 1994. 135.00 (*0-8342-1679-5*) Aspen Pub.

Measurement of Free Radicals in Human Disease Process. Dalal. 1992. write for info. (*0-8493-0173-4*, CRC Reprint) Franklin.

Measurement of Gas Law Deviations with Bean & Burnett Apparatus. O. T. Bloomer. (Research Bulletin Ser.: No. 13). iv, 12p. 1952. pap. 25.00 (*1-58222-030-1*) Inst Gas Tech.

Measurement of Geometric Tolerances in Manufacturing. Meadows. LC 98-17836. (Illus.). 496p. 1998. text 175.00 (*0-8247-0163-1*) Dekker.

Measurement of Grain Boundary Geometry. V. Randle. (Electron Microscopy in Materials Science Ser.). (Illus.). 184p. 1993. 147.00 (*0-7503-0235-6*) IOP Pub.

Measurement of Grassland Vegetation. Ed. by L. T. Mannetje. 260p. (Orig.). 1978. pap. text 40.00 (*0-85198-404-5*) OUP.

Measurement of Health: Concepts & Indicators, 31. James S. Larson. LC 90-44840. (Contributions in Medical Studies: No. 31). 192p. 1991. 52.95 (*0-313-27339-1*, LMH, Greenwood Pr) Greenwood.

Measurement of Household Welfare. Ed. by Richard W. Blundell et al. LC 93-5717. (Illus.). 293p. (C). 1994. text 59.95 (*0-521-45195-7*) Cambridge U Pr.

Measurement of Human Resources. Ed. by W. T. Singleton. LC 74-14848. 68p. 1975. 44.00 (*0-85066-068-8*) Taylor & Francis.

Measurement of Hydrographic Parameters in Large Sand-Bed Streams from Boats. ASCE Task Committee on Hydrographic Investigations. 84p. 1983. pap. 14.00 (*0-87262-354-8*) Am Soc Civil Eng.

Measurement of Image Accuracy. Constance Manning. (C). 1991. pap. text 11.11 (*0-913412-58-9*) Brandon Hse.

Measurement of Image Velocity. David J. Fleet. (International Series in Engineering & Computer Science, VLSI, Computer Architecture, & Digital Screen Processing). 224p. (C). 1992. text 105.00 (*0-7923-9198-5*) Kluwer Academic.

Measurement of Intelligence. Lewis M. Terman. LC 74-21431. (Classics in Child Development Ser.). 376p. 1979. reprint ed. 41.95 (*0-405-06480-2*) Ayer.

Measurement of Intelligence. Edward Lee Thorndike et al. LC 73-2993. (Classics in Psychology Ser.). 1976. reprint ed. 38.95 (*0-405-05165-4*) Ayer.

Measurement of Intelligence by Drawings. Florence L. Goodenough. LC 74-21410. (Classics in Child Development Ser.). 196p. 1976. reprint ed. 26.95 (*0-405-06462-4*) Ayer.

Measurement of Intergenerational Relations. Ed. by David J. Mangen et al. LC 87-28466. (Sage Focus Editions Ser.: No. 92). 253p. reprint ed. pap. 78.50 (*0-7837-6579-7*, 204614400011) Bks Demand.

Measurement of Intrapersonal Space by Grid Technique, Vol. 2 Dimensions of Intrapersonal Space. Patrick Slater. LC 76-8908. 282p. reprint ed. pap. 87.50 (*0-608-12342-0*, 202437800002) Bks Demand.

Measurement of Intrapersonal Space by Grid Technique Vol. 1: Explorations of Intrapersonal Space. Ed. by Patrick Slater. LC 76-8908. (Illus.). 264p. reprint ed. pap. 81.90 (*0-8357-3111-1*, 203936700001) Bks Demand.

Measurement of Ion Transport & Metabolic Rate in Insects. Ed. by T. J. Bradley & T. A. Miller. (Experimental Entomology Ser.). (Illus.). 290p. 1983. 145.00 (*0-387-90855-2*) Spr-Verlag.

Measurement of Joint Motion. 2nd ed. Cynthia C. Norkin et al. (CHI., Illus.). 272p. 1996. write for info. (*962-356-018-4*) Lppncott W & W.

Measurement of Joint Motion: A Guide to Goniometry. 2nd ed. Cynthia C. Norkin & Joyce White. (Illus.). 241p. 1994. text 24.95 (*0-8036-6579-2*) Davis Co.

Measurement of Labor Cost. Ed. by Jack E. Triplett. LC 83-5920. (National Bureau of Economic Research Studies in Income & Wealth: Vol. 48). 562p. (C). 1983. lib. bdg. 72.00 (*0-226-81256-1*) U Ch Pr.

Measurement of Lead in the Atmosphere, Sampling Stacks for Particulates, & Determination of Oxides of Nitrogen in Combustion Products - DS 55-S5, S6, S8. 343p. 1975. pap. 18.00 (*0-8031-0387-5*, DS55S5) ASTM.

Measurement of Levels of Health: Published under Joint Sponsorship of WHO & IEA. W. W. Holland et al. (WHO Regional Publications, European Ser.: No. 7). 456p. 1979. 50.00 (*92-9020-107-X*, 1310007) World Health.

Measurement of Levels of Health: Report of a Study Group. (Technical Report Ser.: No. 137). 29p. 1957. pap. text 3.00 (*92-4-120137-1*) World Health.

Measurement of Locomotion. Vladimir Medved. 208p. 1999. 95.00 (*0-8493-7675-0*) CRC Pr.

Measurement of Love & Intimate Relations: Theories, Scales, & Applications for Love Development, Maintenance, & Dissolution. Oliver C. Tzeng. LC 92-41605. 328p. 1993. 75.00 (*0-275-94273-2*, C4273, Praeger Pubs) Greenwood.

Measurement of Low-Level Radioactivity, No. 22. International Commission on Radiation Units & Meas. LC 71-186876. (Illus.). v, 66p. 1972. 30.00 (*0-913394-40-8*) Intl Comm Rad Meas.

Measurement of Meaning. Charles E. Osgood et al. LC 56-5684. (Illus.). 356p. 1967. reprint ed. pap. text 23.95 (*0-252-74539-6*) U of Ill Pr.

Measurement of Metabolic Bone Disease. Ed. by F. I. Tovey & T. C. Stamp. LC 95-3667. (Medical Measurement Ser.: Vol. 1). 160p. 1995. 58.00 (*1-85070-465-1*) Prthnon Pub.

Measurement of Microbial Activities in the Carbon Cycle in Aquatic Ecosystems: Proceedings of the Third International Workshop, 18-21 Aug., 1986. Ed. by T. E. Cappenberg & C. L. Steenbergen. (Advances in Limnology Ser.: Vol. 31). (GER., Illus.). xii, 390p. 1988. pap. text 103.00 (*3-510-47029-X*, Pub. by E Schweizerbartsche) Balogh.

An Asterisk (*) at the beginning of an entry indicates that the title is appearing for the first time.

Measurement of Modernism: A Study of Values in Brazil & Mexico. Joseph A. Kahl. LC 68-63239. (Latin American Monographs: No. 12). 228p. reprint ed. pap. 70.70 (*0-8357-7749-9*, 203610600002) Bks Demand.

Measurement of Monetary Policy. M. Ray Perryman. 1983. lib. bdg. 73.50 (*0-89838-117-7*) Kluwer Academic.

Measurement of Nervous Habits in Normal Children, Vol. 3. Willard C. Olson. LC 73-9228. 97p. 1970. reprint ed. lib. bdg. 45.00 (*0-8371-6991-7*, CWOH, Greenwood Pr) Greenwood.

Measurement of Nontariff Barriers. Alan V. Deardorff & Robert M. Stern. 152p. (C). 1998. text 47.50 (*0-472-10931-6*, 10931) U of Mich Pr.

Measurement of Nursing Outcomes Vol. 1: Measuring Client Outcomes, Vol. 1. Carolyn F. Waltz & Ora L. Strickland. 592p. (C). 1988. 65.95 (*0-8261-5271-6*) Springer Pub.

Measurement of Nursing Outcomes Vol. 2: Measuring Nursing Performance, Practice, Education & Research. Ora L. Strickland & Carolyn F. Waltz. 512p. (C). 1988. 89.00 (*0-8261-5272-4*) Springer Pub.

Measurement of Nursing Outcomes Vol. 3: Measuring Clinical Skills & Professional Development in Education & Practice, Vol. 3. Ed. by Carolyn F. Waltz & Ora L. Strickland. 432p. (C). 1990. 62.95 (*0-8261-5273-2*) Springer Pub.

Measurement of Nursing Outcomes Vol. 4: Measuring Client Self-Care & Coping Skills, Vol. 4. Ed. by Ora L. Strickland & Carolyn F. Waltz. 368p. (C). 1991. 59.95 (*0-8261-5274-0*) Springer Pub.

Measurement of Occupational Performance: A Guide to Best Practice. Mary Law et al. 250p. 2000. pap. 38.00 (*1-55642-298-9*, 32989) SLACK Inc.

Measurement of Organic Pollutants in Water & Wastewater - STP 686. Ed. by C. E. Van Hall. 356p. 1982. 36.50 (*0-8031-0508-8*, STP686) ASTM.

Measurement of Oxygen by Membrane-Covered Probes. V. Linek et al. (Analytical Chemistry Ser.). 328p. 1988. text 92.00 (*0-470-21061-3*) P-H.

Measurement of Oxygen Transfer in Clean Water. 2nd ed. American Society of Civil Engineers Staff. LC 93-9407. 56p. 1993. 34.00 (*0-87262-885-X*) Am Soc Civil Eng.

Measurement of Pain in Infants & Children. Ed. by G. Allen Finley & Patrick J. McGrath. LC 98-44901. (Progress in Pain Research & Management Ser.: Vol. 10). (Illus.). 224p. 1998. 67.00 (*0-931092-20-5*) Intl Assn Study Pain.

Measurement of Pavement Surface Condition, 1990. (Transportation Research Record Ser.: No. 1260). 255p. 1990. 38.00 (*0-309-05013-8*) Transport Res Bd.

Measurement of Photosynthetic Pigments in Freshwaters & Standardization of Methods: Proceedings of the Workshop Held at Ploen, West Germany, July 28-29, 1978, Vol. 1. Ed. by Hakumat Rai. (Advances in Limnology Ser.: Vol. 14). (GER., Illus.). 106p. (Orig.). 1980. 33.00 (*3-510-47012-5*, Pub. by E Schweizerbartsche) Balogh.

Measurement of Photosynthetic Pigments in Freshwaters & Standardization of Methods: Proceedings of the 2nd Workshop Held at Plon, July 17-18, 1980, Vol. 2. Ed. by Hakumat Rai & A. F. Marker. (Advances in Limnology Ser.: Vol. 16). (GER., Illus.). 130p. (Orig.). 1982. 36.00 (*3-510-47014-1*, Pub. by E Schweizerbartsche) Balogh.

Measurement of Population Distribution. Otis D. Duncan. (Reprint Series in Social Sciences). (C). 1993. reprint ed. pap. text 2.30 (*0-8290-2663-0*, S-378) Irvington.

Measurement of Population Growth, Methods & Result, Vol. 6. P. Kuczynski. (Demographic Monographs). viii, 256p. 1969. text 160.00 (*0-677-02220-4*) Gordon & Breach.

Measurement of Production Movements. Charles F. Carter et al. LC 50-7304. (University of Cambridge, Dept. of Applied Economics, Occasional Papers: 1). 143p. reprint ed. pap. 40.80 (*0-608-12257-2*, 2024435) Bks Demand.

Measurement of Productive Efficiency: Techniques & Applications. Ed. by Harold O. Fried et al. (Illus.). 440p. 1993. text 70.00 (*0-19-507218-9*) OUP.

Measurement of Radon & Radon Daughters in Air. Intro. by Warren K. Sinclair. LC 88-15155. (Report Ser.: No. 97). 174p. (Orig.). 1988. pap. text 40.00 (*0-913392-97-9*) NCRP Pubns.

Measurement of Readability. George R. Klare. LC 62-9125. 340p. reprint ed. pap. 105.40 (*0-608-12978-X*, 202386300034) Bks Demand.

Measurement of Residual & Applied Stress Using Neutron Diffraction: Proceedings of the NATO Advanced Research Workshop, Oxford, U. K., 18-22 March, 1992. Ed. by Michael T. Hutchings. (NATO Advanced Science Institutes Series C: Mathematical & Physical Sciences). 608p. (C). 1992. text 321.50 (*0-7923-1809-9*) Kluwer Academic.

Measurement of Residual Radioactive Surface Contamination By 2-D Laser Heated TLD. S. C. Jones. 101p. 1997. per. 9.00 (*0-16-062849-0*) USGPO.

Measurement of Returns to Adult Health: Morbidity Effects on Wage Rates in Cote d'Ivoire & Ghana. T. Paul Schultz & Aysit Tansel. LC 93-9458. (Living Standards Measurement Study Working Papers: No. 95). 71p. 1993. 6.95 (*0-8213-2379-2*, 12379) World Bank.

Measurement of Rock Properties at Elevated Pressures & Temperatures-STP 869. Ed. by Howard J. Pincus & Earl R. Hoskins. LC 84-24558. (Illus.). 162p. 1985. text 30.00 (*0-8031-0237-2*, STP869) ASTM.

Measurement of Saving, Investment, & Wealth. Ed. by Robert E. Lipsey & Helen S. Tice. LC 88-4669. (National Bureau of Economic Research Studies in Income & Wealth: Vol. 52). (Illus.). 874p. 1989. lib. bdg. 99.50 (*0-226-48468-8*) U Ch Pr.

Measurement of Scientific & Technical Activities: Proposed Standard Practice for Surveys of Research & Development - Frascati Manual, 1993. 5th ed. OECD Staff. 262p. 1994. pap. 71.00 (*92-64-14202-9*) OECD.

Measurement of Segregation in the Labor Force. Y. Fluckiger & J. Silber. LC 99-34904. (Illus.). x, 170p. 1999. 56.00 (*3-7908-1214-5*) Spr-Verlag.

Measurement of Sensation. Donald Laming. LC 97-3966. (Oxford Psychology Ser.: No. 30). (Illus.). 276p. 1997. text 120.00 (*0-19-852342-4*) OUP.

Measurement of Short-Range Radiations. IAEA Staff. (Technical Reports: No. 150). (Illus.). 114p. 1973. pap. 30.00 (*92-0-125173-4*, IDC150, Pub. by IAEA) Bernan Associates.

Measurement of Starlight: Two Centuries of Astronomical Photometry. J. B. Hearnshaw. (Illus.). 522p. (C). 1996. text 95.00 (*0-521-40393-6*) Cambridge U Pr.

Measurement of Static & Dynamic Parameters of Structures & Materials. Ed. by K. Havrilla & T. Kemeny. (Illus.). 399p. (C). 1988. text 175.00 (*0-941743-40-3*) Nova Sci Pubs.

Measurement of Stress, Trauma, & Adaptation. Ed. by B. Hudnall Stamm. LC 96-9819. x, 445p. (Orig.). 1996. pap. 55.00 (*1-886968-02-0*, STMS) Sidran Pr.

Measurement of Supply & Demand in Freight Transport. Brian Bayliss. 140p. 1988. text 78.95 (*0-566-05526-0*, Pub. by Avebry) Ashgate Pub Co.

Measurement of Suspended Particles by Quasi-Elastic Light Scattering. Ed. by Barton E. Dahneke. LC 82-17334. (Wiley-Interscience Publications). 584p. 1983. reprint ed. pap. 181.10 (*0-7837-2393-8*, 204007800006) Bks Demand.

Measurement of the Dynamic Properties of Elastomers & Elastomeric Mounts. Symposium on the Measurement of Dynamic Properties. Ed. by B. M. Hillberry. LC 72-96457. (ASTM Special Technical Publication: No. 535). 138p. 1973. reprint ed. pap. 42.80 (*0-8357-2534-0*, 205715600014) Bks Demand.

Measurement of the Industrial Economy. Frederick M. Zimmerman. (Illus.). 114p. 1995. 25.00 (*0-9624229-8-3*) St Thomas Tech.

Measurement of the Intelligence of Young Children by an Object-Fitting Test, Vol. 5. Ruth E. Atkins. LC 75-12673. (University of Minnesota Institute of Child Welfare Monographs: No. 5). (Illus.). 89p. 1970. reprint ed. lib. bdg. 45.00 (*0-8371-8083-X*, CWAI) Greenwood.

Measurement of the Need for Transporting Pupils: Basis for State Equalization of Transportation Costs. Robert L. Burns. LC 72-176614. (Columbia University. Teachers College. Contributions to Education Ser.: No. 289). reprint ed. 37.50 (*0-404-55289-7*) AMS Pr.

Measurement of the Nucleon Structure Functions F2 & R in Deep Inelastic Muon Scattering. Ed. by Peter B. Bjorkholm. (Uppsala Dissertations from the Faculty of Science Ser.: No. 7). (Illus.). 124p. 1995. pap. 37.50 (*91-554-3570-X*) Coronet Bks.

Measurement of the Public Health Importance of Bilharziasis: Report of a WHO Scientific Group, 1967. (Technical Report Ser.). 93p. 1967. pap. text 5.00 (*92-4-120349-8*, 1100349) World Health.

Measurement of the Secondary School As a Part of the Pupil's Environment. John T. Wade. LC 70-177672. (Columbia University. Teachers College. Contributions to Education Ser.: No. 647). reprint ed. 37.50 (*0-404-55647-7*) AMS Pr.

Measurement of Thought: A Heuristic Approach to This Development. 2nd ed. Richard E. Popovich. LC 81-90419. 180p. (C). 1982. 19.95 (*0-9604876-0-3*) REP Pubs.

Measurement of Turbulent Fluctuations: An Introduction to Hot-Wire Anemometry & Related Transducers. A. V. Smolyakov & V. M. Tkachenko. Tr. by S. Chomet from RUS. (Illus.). 298p. 1983. 91.95 (*0-387-12144-7*) Spr-Verlag.

Measurement of Ultraviolet Radiation from Light Sources: LM-55-96. IESNA Staff. (Illus.). 6p. 1996. pap. 20.00 (*0-87995-137-0*, LM-55-96) Illum Eng.

Measurement of Urban Home Environments: Validation & Standardization of the Minnesota Home Status Index, Vol. 11. Alice M. Leahy. LC 79-142314. (Monograph: No. 11). (Illus.). 70p. 1975. reprint ed. lib. bdg. 45.00 (*0-8371-5902-4*, CWLM) Greenwood.

***Measurement of USMC Logistics Processes: Creating a Baseline to Support Precision Logistics Implementation.** Marc L. Robbins et al. LC 98-168088. xx, 139p. 1998. pap. 10.00 (*0-8330-2613-5*) Rand Corp.

Measurement of Utility. Tapas Majumdar. LC 74-14113. (Illus.). 149p. 1975. reprint ed. lib. bdg. 35.00 (*0-8371-7785-5*, MAMUT, Greenwood Pr) Greenwood.

Measurement of Values. Louis L. Thurstone. LC 58-11960. (Midway Reprint Ser.). 330p. reprint ed. pap. 102.30 (*0-608-16382-1*, 202674800051) Bks Demand.

Measurement of Voting Power: Theory & Practice, Problems & Paradoxes. Dan S. Felsenthal & Mosheh Mahover. LC 98-8603. 352p. 1998. 90.00 (*1-85898-805-5*) E Elgar.

Measurement of Weak Forces in Physics Experiments. Vladimir B. Braginsky & A. B. Manukin. Ed. by David H. Douglass. LC 76-22953. (Illus.). 1977. lib. bdg. 11.00 (*0-226-07070-0*) U Ch Pr.

Measurement of Weak Forces in Physics Experiments. Vladimir B. Braginsky. Ed. by David H. Douglass. LC 76-22953. (Illus.). 166p. Date not set. reprint ed. pap. 51.50 (*0-608-20604-0*, 205456900003) Bks Demand.

Measurement of Weak Radioactivity. P. Theodorsson. LC 96-38855. 250p. 1996. text 48.00 (*981-02-2315-3*) World Scientific Pub.

Measurement of Welfare Changes Caused by Large Price Shifts: An Issue in the Power Sector. Robert Bacon. LC 94-45701. (Discussion Paper Ser.: No. 273). 40p. 1995. pap. 22.00 (*0-8213-3155-8*, 13155) World Bank.

Measurement of Writing Ability. Fred I. Godshalk et al. LC 66-15921. (Research Monographs: No. 6). 92p. 1966. pap. 6.50 (*0-87447-060-9*, 251700) College Bd.

Measurement Readings for Marketing Research. Ed. by Michael L. Ray. LC 84-9385. 382p. reprint ed. pap. 118.50 (*0-7837-2492-6*, 204265700005) Bks Demand.

Measurement, Realism & Objectivity. Ed. by John Forge. 348p. (C). 1987. text 191.50 (*90-277-2542-X*, D Reidel) Kluwer Academic.

Measurement, Regression, & Calibration. P. J. Brown. (Oxford Statistical Science Ser.: No. 12). (Illus.). 210p. 1994. text 55.00 (*0-19-852245-2*) OUP.

Measurement, Signal Processing & Control - MECO '86: Proceedings IASTED Symposium, Taormina, Italy, September 3-5, 1986. Ed. by G. Messina & M. H. Hamza. 323p. 1986. 91.00 (*0-88986-096-3*, 105) Acta Pr.

Measurement, Statistics, & Research Design in Physical Education & Exercise Science - Current Issues & Trends: A Special Issue of Measurement in Physical Education & Exercise Science. Ed. by Terry M. Wood. 104p. 1997. pap. 20.00 (*0-8058-9870-0*) L Erlbaum Assocs.

Measurement Support for the U. S. Electric-Power Industry in the Era of Deregulation. Gerald J. Fitzpatrick et al. (Illus.). 64p. (C). 1998. pap. text 30.00 (*0-7881-4853-2*) DIANE Pub.

Measurement Systems. 4th ed. Ernest O. Doebelin. 992p. (C). 1989. 102.19 (*0-07-017338-9*) McGraw.

Measurement Techniques in Plant Science. Ed. by Yasushi Hashimoto et al. (Illus.). 431p. 1990. text 83.00 (*0-12-330585-3*) Acad Pr.

Measurement Techniques in Space Plasmas: Fields. Robert F. Pfaff et al. LC 98-18385. (Geophysical Monograph Ser.: Vol. 103). 1998. 80.00 (*0-87590-086-0*) Am Geophysical.

Measurement Techniques in Space Plasmas: Particles. Robert F. Pfaff et al. Ed. by Joseph E. Borovsky & David T. Young. LC 98-18386. (Geophysical Monographs: Vol. 102). 1998. 90.00 (*0-87590-085-2*) Am Geophysical.

Measurement Technology/Carcinogenic Agents/Workplace Air. Royal Society of Chemistry Staff. 1989. 83.00 (*0-85186-098-2*) CRC Pr.

Measurement Theory for the Behavioral Sciences. Edwin E. Ghiselli et al. LC 80-27069. (Psychology Ser.). (Illus.). 494p. (C). 1981. pap. text 23.20 (*0-7167-1252-0*) W H Freeman.

Measurement Tools in Patient Education. Barbara K. Redman. LC 97-29477. (Illus.). 408p. 1997. 59.95 (*0-8261-9860-0*) Springer Pub.

Measurement Uncertainty: Methods & Applications. Ronald H. Dieck. LC 92-24674. (An Independent Learning Module from the Instrument Society of America Ser.). (Illus.). 238p. reprint ed. pap. 73.80 (*0-608-08597-9*, 206912000003) Bks Demand.

Measurement Uncertainty: Methods & Applications : A Guide to Estimating & Understanding the Accuracy of Test & Experimental Data. 2nd ed. Ronald H. Dieck. LC 97-22013. 1997. 76.00 (*1-55617-628-7*) ISA.

***Measurement Uncertainty for Pitch & Runout Artifacts.** B. Cox. (Technical Papers: Vol. 99FTM3). 14p. 1999. pap. 30.00 (*1-55589-741-X*) AGMA.

Measurement Units for Use in Construction: Snip 528-80. Russia's Minstroy Staff. (Snip Building Codes of Russia Ser.). (Illus.). iv, 40p. (Orig.). 1996. ring bd. 399.95 (*1-57937-022-5*) Snip Register.

Measurements see Discovering Geography

Measurements. (Number Power Ser.: Vol. 9). 1995. pap. 10.60 (*0-8092-3414-9*) NTC Contemp Pub Co.

Measurements & Conversions: A Complete Guide. (Gem Ser.). (Illus.). 256p. (Orig.). (YA). 1994. pap. 5.95 (*1-56138-466-6*) Running Pr.

Measurements & Correlation Functions. Paul C. Martin. x, 98p. 1968. text 195.00 (*0-677-02440-1*) Gordon & Breach.

Measurements & Estimations of Forest Stand Parameters Using Remote Sensing. D. A. Stellingwerf & Y. A. Hussin. (Illus.). 280p. 1997. 125.00 (*90-6764-251-7*, Pub. by VSP) Coronet Bks.

Measurements & Landmarks in Physical Anthropology. Frederick W. Jones. (BMB Ser.: No. 63). (Illus.). 1969. reprint ed. 25.00 (*0-527-02169-5*) Periodicals Srv.

Measurements & Modelling in Environmental Pollution: Proceedings of the First International Conference. Ed. by R. San Jose & C. A. Brebbia. LC 97-65935. 560p. 1997. 238.00 (*1-85312-461-3*, 4613, Pub. by WIT Pr) Computational Mech MA.

Measurements for Competitiveness in Electronics. (Illus.). 448p. (C). 1994. pap. text 95.00 (*0-7881-0508-6*) DIANE Pub.

Measurements for Competitiveness in Electronics, 2 vols. 1995. lib. bdg. 633.99 (*0-8490-8367-2*) Gordon Pr.

Measurements for Effective Decision Making: A Guide for Manufacturing Companies. Mokshagundam L. Srikanth & Scott A. Robertson. LC 95-9547. (Illus.). 177p. (Orig.). 1995. pap. 24.95 (*0-943953-04-9*) Spectrum CT.

Measurements for Long-Term Care. Sarah R. Beaton & Susan A. Voge. LC 97-33870. 1998. pap. 47.95 (*0-8039-5388-7*) Sage.

Measurements for Terrestrial Vegetation. Charles Bonham. LC 88-14269. 352p. 1989. 125.00 (*0-471-04880-1*) Wiley.

Measurements in Cardiology. Ed. by P. M. Sutton. (Measurements in Medicine Ser.). (Illus.). 276p. 1999. 68.00 (*1-85070-463-5*) Prthnon Pub.

Measurements in Pediatric Radiology. H. Pettersson & Hans Ringertz. (Illus.). 192p. 1991. 96.95 (*0-387-19665-X*) Spr-Verlag.

Measurements in Polyphase Flows, 1982: Presented at the 1982 AIAA-ASME Joint Fluids, Plasma, Thermophysics & Heat Transfer Conference, St. Louis, Missouri, June 7-11, 1982. American Society of Mechanical Engineers Staff. Ed. by T. R. Heidrick & B. R. Patel. LC 78-68328. (Illus.). 135p. reprint ed. pap. 41.90 (*0-8357-2847-1*, 203908200010) Bks Demand.

Measurements in the Rheology of Foodstuffs. Ed. by J. H. Prentice. (Illus.). 200p. 1984. 63.00 (*0-85334-248-2*, I-221-84) Elsevier.

***Measurements 1999c: Globe Fearon Math.** 45p. 1998. write for info. (*0-13-023249-1*) S&S Trade.

Measurements of Fluorescent Lamps & Ballasts in Luminaires: LM-65-91. (Lighting Measurements Ser.). (Illus.). 5p. 1991. pap. 18.00 (*0-87995-050-1*, LM-62-91) Illum Eng.

Measurements of Indoor Toxic VOC Concentrations Attributed to the Residential Storage of Household Products. Clyde W. Sweet et al. (Illus.). 52p. (Orig.). (C). 1995. pap. text 20.00 (*0-7881-1957-5*) DIANE Pub.

Measurements of Iron Status. Thomas H. Bothwell et al. Ed. by Edouard M. DeMaeyer & Samuel G. Kahn. (Illus.). 78p. (Orig.). 1985. pap., student ed. 18.00 (*0-935368-47-7*) ILSI.

Measurements of Mechanical Ability. John L. Stenquist. LC 73-177744. (Columbia University. Teachers College. Contributions to Education Ser.: No. 130). reprint ed. 37.50 (*0-404-55130-0*) AMS Pr.

Measurements of Neutron Flux & Spectra for Physical & Biological Applications. (Report Ser.: No. 23). 1960. pap. 20.00 (*0-913392-07-3*) NCRP Pubns.

Measurements of Newtonian Gravitation. Ed. by George T. Gillies. (Illus.). 96p. 1992. pap. 26.00 (*0-917853-46-6*, RB-60) Am Assn Physics.

Measurements of Optical Fibers & Devices: Theory & Experiments. Giovanni Cancellieri & Umberto Ravaioli. LC 83-72775. (Artech House Telecommunications Library). 515p. reprint ed. pap. 159.70 (*0-7837-3016-0*, 204292400006) Bks Demand.

Measurements of Secondary Stresses in Pipeline: Report 1, Additional Data. T. J. Atterbury et al. 80p. 1959. pap. 3.00 (*0-318-12653-2*, L00220) Am Gas Assn.

Measurements of Some Achievements in Arithmetic. Clifford Woody. LC 73-177622. (Columbia University. Teachers College. Contributions to Education Ser.: No. 80). reprint ed. 37.50 (*0-404-55080-0*) AMS Pr.

Measurements of the Impacts of Materials Substitution: A Case Study in the Automobile Industry: Presented at the Winter Annual Meeting of ASME, San Francisco, CA, December 10-15, 1978. American Society of Mechanical Engineers Staff. Ed. by Andrew L. Bleloch. LC 78-59892. 72p. reprint ed. pap. 30.00 (*0-8357-8737-0*, 203363900087) Bks Demand.

Measurements of the Transport Properties. W. A. Wakeham. 1991. 149.00 (*0-632-02997-8*) CRC Pr.

Measurements of Time Reversal in Objective Quantum Theory. F. J. Belinfante. 1975. 62.00 (*0-08-018152-X*, Pub. by Pergamon Repr) Franklin.

Measures Against Sound & Audiovisual Piracy (Recommendation & Explanatory Memorandum), No. R(95)1. 1995. 12.00 (*92-871-2864-2*, Pub. by Council of Europe) Manhattan Pub Co.

Measures & Differential Equations in Infinite-Dimensional Space. Yu. L. Dalecky & S. V. Fomin. (C). 1991. text 215.00 (*0-7923-1517-0*) Kluwer Academic.

Measures & Hilbert Lattices. G. Kalmbach. 240p. 1986. text 33.00 (*9971-5-0009-4*) World Scientific Pub.

Measures & Offices of Friendship. Jeremy Taylor. LC 84-27516. 128p. 1985. reprint ed. 50.00 (*0-8201-1401-4*) Schol Facsimiles.

Measures & Probabilities. M. Simonnet. LC 95-49230. (Universitext Ser.). 498p. 1996. pap. 48.95 (*0-387-94644-6*) Spr-Verlag.

Measures & Space. David Kirkby. LC 95-33560. (Math Live Ser.). (Illus.). (J). 1998. 19.92 (*1-57572-045-0*) Heinemann Lib.

Measures for Clinical Practice: A Sourcebook. Kevin Corcoran & Joel Fischer. 576p. 1987. 45.00 (*0-02-906681-6*) Free Pr.

***Measures for Clinical Practice: A Sourcebook: Couples, Families & Children, Vol. 1.** 3rd ed. Kevin Corcoran. LC 00-37132. Vol. 1. 704p. 2000. 44.95 (*0-684-84830-9*) S&S Trade.

Measures for Clinical Practice Vol. 1: Couples, Families, & Children, I. 2nd ed. Joel Fischer & Kevin Corcoran. LC 93-32384. 1994. 39.95 (*0-02-906685-9*) Free Pr.

Measures for Clinical Practice Vol. 2: Adults, II. 2nd ed. Joel Fischer & Kevin Corcoran. LC 93-32384. 1994. 49.95 (*0-02-906686-7*) Free Pr.

***Measures For Clinical Practice A Sourcebook: Volume 2 Adults Third Edition.** 3rd ed. Corcoran. LC 00-37132. Vol. 2. 960p. 2000. 54.95 (*0-684-84831-7*) S&S Trade.

Measures for Evaluating Community Practice. Latting J. Kantambu & Patrick Leung. (C). 1999. pap. text 69.95 (*0-205-26595-2*, Macmillan Coll) P-H.

Measures for Excellence: Reliable Software on Time, Within Budget. Lawrence Putnam. 400p. 1991. 77.00 (*0-13-567694-0*, Pub. by P-H) S&S Trade.

Measures for Manufacturing Excellence. Kaplan. 425p. 1990. 45.00 (*0-07-103245-2*) McGraw.

Measures for Manufacturing Excellence. Ed. by Robert S. Kaplan. 400p. 1992. 39.95 (*0-87584-350-6*) Harvard Busn.

Measures for Progress: A History of the National Bureau of Standards. Rexmond C. Cochrane. LC 75-22808. (America in Two Centuries Ser.). (Illus.). 1976. reprint ed. 62.95 (*0-405-07679-7*) Ayer.

Measures in Science & Engineering: Their Expression, Relation & Interpretation. B. S. Massey. (Mathematics & Its Applications Ser.). 1986. text 48.95 (*0-470-20331-5*) P-H.

M

An Asterisk (*) at the beginning of an entry indicates that the title is appearing for the first time.

Measures in the College Admissions Process: A College Board Colloquium. Intro. by Robert C. Wood & George H. Hanford. 160p. (Orig.). (C). 1986. pap. 13.95 (*0-87447-276-8*) College Bd.

Measures of Association. Albert M. Liebetrau. LC 83-60229. (Quantitative Applications in the Social Sciences Ser.: Vol. 32). 95p. 1983. 10.95 (*0-8039-1974-3*) Sage.

Measures of Complexity. Ed. by L. Peliti & Angelo Vulpiani. (Lecture Notes in Physics Ser.: Vol. 314). vii, 150p. 1988. 45.95 (*0-387-50316-1*) Spr-Verlag.

Measures of Complexity & Chaos. Ed. by N. B. Abraham et al. LC 89-37104. (NATO ASI Series B, Physics: Vol. 208). (Illus.). 486p. (C). 1989. 174.00 (*0-306-43387-7*, Plenum Trade) Perseus Pubng.

Measures of Complexity & Chaos (Ii) - Proceedings of the 2nd Workshop. N. B. Abraham et al. 400p. 1994. text 109.00 (*981-02-1446-4*) World Scientific Pub.

Measures of Credit Risk & Experience. Edgar R. Fiedler. (General Ser.: No. 95). 367p. 1971. reprint ed. 95.50 (*0-87014-228-3*) Natl Bur Econ Res.

Measures of Educational Equity for Women. Kathleen L. Williams et al. (Orig.). 1977. pap. 13.00 (*0-89785-563-9*) Am Inst Res.

***Measures of Effectiveness for the Information-Age Army.** Richard E. Darilek. LC 00-36615. 2000. write for info. (*0-8330-2847-2*) Rand Corp.

Measures of Environmental Performance & Ecosystem Condition. National Academy of Engineering Staff. Ed. by Peter Schulze. LC 98-43781. 180p. 1998. text 32.95 (*0-309-05441-9*) Natl Acad Pr.

Measures of Exports of the United States. Dudley J. Cowden. LC 68-58561. (Columbia University. Studies in the Social Sciences: No. 356). reprint ed. 20.00 (*0-404-51356-5*) AMS Pr.

Measures of Family Function for Research & Practice. Kathleen J. Sawin & Marcia Harrigan. Ed. by Pierre Woog. (Illus.). 144p. 1994. 27.95 (*0-8261-8900-8*) Springer Pub.

Measures of Grace. Lawana Blackwell. LC 95-36082. (Victorian Serenade Ser.: No. 2). (Illus.). 368p. 1996. pap. 10.99 (*0-8423-7956-8*) Tyndale Hse.

Measures of High Quality & Performance: Simple Tools & Lessons Learned from America's Most Successful Corporations. Richard M. Hodgetts. LC 97-35583. 224p. 1997. 27.95 (*0-8144-0377-8*) AMACOM.

Measures of Info & Their Applications. J. N. Kapur. (C). 1994. 48.00 (*81-224-0484-7*, Pub. by Wiley Estrn) Franklin.

Measures of Information & Their Applications in Science & Engineering. J. N. Kapur. 572p. 1994. text 64.95 (*0-470-22064-3*) Halsted Pr.

Measures of Interlibrary Reference: A Manual. Thomas Childers. 120p. 1991. pap. text 22.50 (*0-929722-50-7*) CA State Library Fndtn.

Measures of Leadership. Ed. by Kenneth E. Clark & Miriam B. Clark. LC 90-32042. 636p. 1990. 59.50 (*1-878435-00-0*) Leadership Lib Amer.

Measures of Man: Methodologies in Biological Anthropology. Ed. by Eugene Giles & Jonathan S. Friedlaender. LC 76-28638. (Museum Press Ser.). (Illus.). 696p. 1976. 42.00 (*0-87365-800-0*); pap. 27.00 (*0-87365-782-9*) Peabody Harvard.

Measures of Medicine: Benefits, Harms & Costs. S. Schoth & Richard K. Riegelman. 320p. 1994. pap. 39.95 incl. disk (*0-86542-280-X*) Blackwell Sci.

Measures of Men. Harold Cummins et al. (Publications: No. 7). 331p. 1936. 25.00 (*0-939238-08-X*) Tulane MARI.

Measures of Noncompactness & Condensing Operators. R. R. Akhmerov et al. (Operator Theory: Advances & Applications Ser.: Vol. 55). 260p. 1992. 129.00 (*0-8176-2716-2*) Birkhauser.

Measures of Noncompactness in Banach Spaces. Jozef Banas & Goebel. (Lecture Notes in Pure & Applied Mathematics Ser.: Vol. 60). (Illus.). 112p. 1980. pap. text 115.00 (*0-8247-1248-X*) Dekker.

Measures of Noncompactness in Metric Fixed Point Theory. J. M. Ayerbe et al. LC 97-38052. (Operator Theory, Advances & Applications Ser.: Vol. 99). vii, 211p. 1997. text 90.00 (*3-7643-5794-0*) Birkhauser.

Measures of Noncompactness in Metric Fixed Point Theory. J. M. Ayerbe Toledano et al. LC 97-38052. (Operator Theory, Advances & Applications Ser.). 1997. write for info. (*0-8176-5794-0*) Birkhauser.

Measures of Personality & Social Psychological Attitudes, Vol. 1. Ed. by John P. Robinson et al. LC 90-91. (Measure of Social Psychological Changes Ser.). 753p. 1990. pap. text 69.95 (*0-12-590244-1*) Acad Pr.

Measures of Political Attitudes. John P. Robinson et al. LC 98-84427. (Measures of Social Psychological Attitudes Ser.). (Illus.). 816p. (C). 1999. text 125.00 (*0-12-590242-5*); pap. text 75.00 (*0-12-590245-X*) Acad Pr.

Measures of Protection: Methodology, Economic Interpretation & Policy Relevance. 96p. 1989. 12.00 (*92-5-102859-1*, F8591, Pub. by FAO) Bernan Associates.

Measures of Psychological, Vocational, & Educational Functioning in the Blind & Visually Handicapped. Ronald Schnur & Geraldine T. Scholl. LC 76-13905. 103p. reprint ed. pap. 32.00 (*0-7837-2756-9*, 204313700006) Bks Demand.

Measures of Religiosity. Ed. by Peter C. Hill & Ralph W. Hood. LC 99-10330. 534p. 1999. 99.95 (*0-89135-106-X*) Religious Educ.

Measures of Science: Theological & Technological Impulses in Early Modern Thought. James Barry. LC 96-26448. (Northwestern University Studies in Phenomenology & Existential Philosophy). 236p. 1996. 69.95 (*0-8101-1424-0*); pap. 19.95 (*0-8101-1425-9*) Northwestern U Pr.

Measures of Self-Concept. Ruth C. Wylie. LC 88-28038. x, 153p. 1989. text 40.00 (*0-8032-4751-6*) U of Nebr Pr.

Measures of Success: Creating a High Performing Organization. Carl G. Thor. 240p. 1995. 27.95 (*0-471-13180-6*) Wiley.

Measures of Success: Creating a Quality Driven Organisation. Carl G. Thor. (Illus.). 224p. (C). 1994. 75.00 (*0-939246-64-3*) Wiley.

Measures of Success: Designing, Monitoring & Managing Conservation & Development Projects. Richard Margoluis & Nick Salafsky. LC 98-13588. 363p. 1998. pap. text 35.00 (*1-55963-612-2*) Island Pr.

Measures of Wisdom: The Cosmic Dance in Classical & Christian Antiquity. James Miller. 672p. 1986. text 60.00 (*0-8020-2553-6*) U of Toronto Pr.

Measures on Infinite Dimensional Spaces. Y. Yamasaki. (Series in Pure Mathematics: Vol. 5). 268p. 1985. text 41.00 (*9971-978-52-0*) World Scientific Pub.

Measures Short of War: The George F. Kennan Lectures at the National War College 1946-47. Ed. by Giles D. Harlow & George C. Maerz. 326p. (Orig.). (C). 1994. pap. text 45.00 (*0-7881-1118-3*) DIANE Pub.

***Measures Taken & Other Lehrstucke.** Bertolt Brecht. 2001. reprint ed. pap. 9.95 (*1-55970-544-2*, Pub. by Arcade Pub Inc) Time Warner.

Measures to Combat Piracy in the Field of Copyright & Neighbouring Rights (Recommendation & Explanatory Memorandum), No. R(88)2. Council of Europe Staff. 1989. 12.00 (*92-871-1674-1*, Pub. by Council of Europe) Manhattan Pub Co.

Measures to Deal with Youth Unemployment in the Federal Republic of Germany. rev. ed. FESC. 1983. 24.00 (*0-907659-19-5*) St Mut.

Measures to Enhance the Capacity of Management. 65p. pap. 12.50 (*92-1-123116-7*) UN.

Measures to Promote Media Transparency (Recommendation & Explanatory Memorandum), No. R(94)13. 1995. 12.00 (*92-871-2735-2*, Pub. by Council of Europe) Manhattan Pub Co.

Measuring. Sheila Cato. LC 98-16123. (Question of Math Bks.). (Illus.). 32p. (J). (gr. 1-4). 1999. 25.26 (*1-57505-323-3*, Carolrhoda) Lerner Pub.

Measuring. Fearon Globe Staff. 1989. pap. 8.95 (*0-8224-4513-1*) Fearon Teacher Aids.

Measuring. Sally Hewitt. LC 95-18461. (Take off With Ser.). (Illus.). 32p. (J). 1996. lib. bdg. 21.40 (*0-8172-4113-2*) Raintree Steck-V.

Measuring. David Kirkby. LC 95-38706. (Mini Math Ser.). (Illus.). (J). 1998. (*1-57572-004-3*) Heinemann Lib.

Measuring. Peter Patilla. LC 99-20367. (Math Links Ser.). 1999. 19.92 (*1-57572-965-2*) Heinemann Lib.

***Measuring a Changing Nation: Modern Methods for the 2000 Census.** National Research Council Staff. LC 99-213866. 124p. 1999. pap. 28.75 (*0-309-06444-9*) Natl Acad Pr.

Measuring a Meridian. Jules Verne. lib. bdg. 22.95 (*0-8488-2066-5*) Amereon Ltd.

Measuring a Vision: The Mapping of Chicago's Waterways. Cheryl Hahn & Maureen Flanaghan. (Illus.). 36p. 1988. pap. 5.00 (*0-911028-39-0*) Newberry.

Measuring Academic Library Performance: A Practical Approach. Nancy A. Van House et al. LC 89-77253. (Illus.). 140p. 1990. pap. text 34.00 (*0-8389-0529-3*) Assn Coll & Res Libs.

Measuring Access to Care. Laura Summer. Ed. by Karen Glass. 48p. (Orig.). 1994. pap. 15.00 (*1-55877-189-1*) Natl Governor.

Measuring Advertising Effectiveness. Ed. by William Wells. (Advertising & Consumer Psychology Ser.). 400p. 1997. 89.95 (*0-8058-1901-0*) L Erlbaum Assocs.

Measuring Advertising Effectiveness. Ed. by William D. Wells. (Advertising & Consumer Psychology Ser.). 440p. 1997. pap. 39.95 (*0-8058-2812-5*) L Erlbaum Assocs.

Measuring Airport Landside Capacity. (Special Reports: No. 215). 190p. 1987. 20.00 (*0-309-04457-X*) Transport Res Bd.

Measuring Alcohol Consumption: Psychosocial & Biochemical Methods. Ed. by Raye Z. Litten & John P. Allen. LC 92-1536. 256p. 1992. 99.50 (*0-89603-231-0*) Humana.

Measuring an Enemy's War Intentions. (Analysis Ser.: No. 23). 12.50 (*0-686-45492-8*) Inst Analysis.

Measuring & Calculating: Basic Mathematics Skills. Thomas Camilli. Ed. by Bob DeWeese. (Illus.). 32p. (J). (gr. 4-6). 1995. pap., wbk. ed. 2.50 (*1-58610-096-3*, Learn on the Go) Learn Horizon.

Measuring & Controlling Interest Rate Risk. Frank J. Fabozzi. 300p. 1996. 55.00 (*1-883249-09-0*) F J Fabozzi.

Measuring & Controlling Volatile Organic Compound & Particulate Emissions from Wood Processing Operations & Wood-Based Products. 91p. 1995. 40.00 (*0-935018-72-7*, 7301) Forest Prod.

Measuring & Enhancing the Productivity of Service & Government Organizations. 3rd ed. Marvin E. Mundel. (Illus.). 296p. 1980. pap. text 22.25 (*92-833-1030-6*, 310306) Productivity Inc.

Measuring & Evaluating Pupil Progress. Ed. by Richard R. DeBlassie. LC 74-8974. 210p. 1974. 32.00 (*0-8422-5184-7*) Irvington.

Measuring & Evaluating School Learning. 2nd ed. Lou M. Carey. LC 93-35571. 480p. 1993. 76.00 (*0-205-12865-3*) Allyn.

Measuring & Evaluating School Learning. 2nd ed. Lou M. Carey. 480p. 1994. pap. text, student ed. 23.00 (*0-205-16094-8*, H6094-0) Allyn.

***Measuring & Evaluating School Learning.** 3rd ed. 2000. teacher ed. write for info. (*0-205-32731-1*) Allyn.

***Measuring & Evaluating School Learning.** 3rd ed. Lou M. Carey. 560p. 2000. 44.25 (*0-205-32388-X*) Allyn.

Measuring & Evaluating School Learning 1987. 2nd ed. Lou M. Carey. 1994. pap., teacher ed. write for info. (*0-205-12866-1*, H2866-5) Allyn.

Measuring & Evaluating the Radiography Student's Educational Achievement. Robert J. Parelli. 28p. (Orig.). 1997. pap., wbk. ed. 10.00 (*1-880359-10-3*) Par Rad.

Measuring & Funding Corporate Liabilities for Retiree Health Benefits. Employee Benefit Research Institute Staff. LC 87-24534. 1987. pap. 24.95 (*0-86643-054-7*) Empl Benefit Res Inst.

Measuring & Gaging in the Machine Shop. National Tooling & Machining Assn. Staff. 178p. (Orig.). 1981. pap. 18.25 (*0-910399-27-1*, 5023) Natl Tool & Mach.

Measuring & Gauging Geometric Tolerances. Gary K. Griffith. LC 93-25571. 315p. (C). 1993. text 92.00 (*0-13-374042-0*) Prntice Hall Bks.

***Measuring & Improving Cost, Cost-Effectiveness & Cost-Benefit for Substance Abuse Treatment Programs: A Manual.** Brian T. Yates. LC 99-489369. 133p. 1999. write for info. (*0-16-050141-5*) USGPO.

Measuring & Improving Infrastructure Performance. National Research Council (U. S.) Staff. LC 95-68207. (Studies in Infrastructure Technology & Policy). 132p. reprint ed. pap. 41.00 (*0-608-06196-4*, 206652800008) Bks Demand.

Measuring & Improving Organizational Productivity: A Practical Guide. Robert D. Pritchard. LC 90-34680. 264p. 1990. 65.00 (*0-275-93668-6*, C3668, Praeger Pubs) Greenwood.

Measuring & Improving Patient Satisfaction. Patrick J. Shelton. 300p. 2000. 59.00 (*0-8342-1074-6*, 10746) Aspen Pub.

Measuring & Improving the Efficiency of Boilers. D. Dyer et al. Ed. by Elias P. Gyftopoulos & Karen C. Cohen. (Industrial Energy-Conservation Manuals Ser.: No. 3). 120p. 1982. 20.00 (*0-262-04067-0*) MIT Pr.

Measuring & Improving the Health Status of the Elderly, Poor & Disabled. 175p. pap. text 35.00 (*0-7881-8681-7*) DIANE Pub.

Measuring & Interpreting Business Cycles. Ed. by Villy Bergstrom & Anders Vredin. LC 94-13283. (FIEF Studies in Labor Markets & Economic Policy). (Illus.). 282p. 1995. text 55.00 (*0-19-828859-X*, Clarendon Pr) OUP.

Measuring & Magnets. Thomas-Cochran. (What a Wonderful World Intro Ser.). 1993. pap. text. write for info. (*0-582-91088-9*, Pub. by Addison-Wesley) Longman.

Measuring & Managing Ambulatory Care Outcomes. Jean Carroll. 1996. 199.00 (*0-8342-0776-1*, S194) Aspen Pub.

Measuring & Managing Customer Satisfaction: Going for the Gold. Sheila Kessler. LC 96-19579. (Illus.). 228p. 1996. text 32.00 (*0-87389-364-6*, H0926) ASQ Qual Pr.

Measuring & Managing Customer Satisfaction: Going for the Gold. Sheila Kessler. (Illus.). 150p. 1995. pap. 29.00 (*1-879404-16-8*) Cmpetitive Edge.

Measuring & Managing Derivative Market Risk. David Lawrence. LC 96-38892. 208p. 1996. pap. 55.00 (*1-86152-006-9*) Thomson Learn.

Measuring & Managing Environmental Costs. Shahid L. Ansari et al. 32p. (C). 1996. text 7.50 (*0-256-23781-6*, Irwn McGrw-H) McGrw-H Hghr Educ.

Measuring & Managing Healthcare Quality: Procedures, Techniques, & Protocols, 2 vols., Set. Norbert Goldfield et al. ring bd. 189.00 (*0-8342-0265-4*) Aspen Pub.

Measuring & Managing IT Costs & Benefits. Dan Remnyi. LC 96-115805. 350p. 1995. pap. 51.95 (*0-7506-2432-9*) Buttrwrth-Heinemann.

Measuring & Managing Patient Satisfaction. 2nd rev. ed. William J. Krowinski & Steven R. Steiber. LC 96-22064. (Illus.). 278p. 1996. pap. 56.00 (*1-55648-157-8*, 136108) AHPI.

Measuring & Managing Performance in Organizations. Robert D. Austin. LC 96-9146. 216p. 1996. pap. 24.95 (*0-932633-36-6*) Dorset Hse Pub Co.

Measuring & Managing Quality Costs. Shahid L. Ansari et al. 32p. (C). 1996. text 7.50 (*0-256-23785-9*, Irwn McGrw-H) McGrw-H Hghr Educ.

Measuring & Managing the Value of Companies: Teacher's Manual to Valuation. 2nd ed. Copeland. 232p. 1996. pap. write for info. (*0-471-13989-0*) Wiley.

Measuring & Marking Metals. Ivan Law. (Workshop Practice Ser.: No. 6). (Illus.). 110p. 1985. pap. 21.50 (*0-85242-841-3*, Pub. by Nexus Special Interests) Trans-Atl Phila.

Measuring & Modeling Time Dependent Soil Behavior: Proceedings of Sessions. Thomas C. Sheahan et al. LC 96-36647. (Geotechnical Special Publications). 288p. 1997. 37.00 (*0-7844-0205-1*) Am Soc Civil Eng.

Measuring & Modelling Investigation of Environmental Processes. Ed. by Roberto San Jose. LC 98-87997. (Environmental Engineering Ser.: Vol. 2). 361p. 1999. 185.00 (*1-85312-566-0*, Pub. by WIT Pr) Computational Mech MA.

***Measuring & Modelling Sustainable Development: Principles, Analysis & Policies.** I. Moffatt & N. Hanley. (Illus.). 300p. 2001. pap. write for info. (*1-84214-008-6*) Prthnon Pub.

Measuring & Monitoring Biological Diversity: Standard Methods for Amphibians. Ed. by W. Ronald Heyer et al. LC 92-44743. (Biological Diversity Handbooks Ser.). (Illus.). 384p. (C). 1993. pap. text 22.50 (*1-56098-284-5*) Smithsonian.

Measuring & Monitoring Biological Diversity: Standard Methods for Mammals. Ed. by Don E. Wilson et al. LC 96-1554. (Biodiversity Handbook Ser.). (Illus.). 480p. 1996. text 55.00 (*1-56098-636-0*); pap. text 24.95 (*1-56098-637-9*) Smithsonian.

***Measuring & Monitoring Plant Populations.** Caryl L. Elzinga. 487p. 1999. per. 39.00 (*0-16-061714-6*) USGPO.

Measuring & Recording of Joint Motion: Instrumentation & Techniques. 2nd ed. Ed. by John J. Gerhardt et al. LC 89-7515. 140p. 1990. 37.00 (*0-920887-33-3*) Hogrefe & Huber Pubs.

Measuring & Scoring North American Big Game. William H. Nesbitt & Philip L. Wright. Ed. by C. Randall Byers & Jack Reneau. (Illus.). 160p. 1997. ring bd. 34.95 (*0-940864-32-0*) Boone & Crockett.

Measuring & Understanding Coastal Processes. National Research Council Staff. 130p. 1989. pap. text 15.00 (*0-309-04129-5*) Natl Acad Pr.

Measuring Angles: Poems. Fred Johnston. 80p. pap. 6.95 (*1-874700-11-7*, Pub. by Clo Iar-Chonnachta) Dufour.

Measuring Avoidable Deaths & Diseases in New York State. Willine Carr et al. (Paper Ser.: No. 8). 56p. 1988. 5.00 (*0-934459-40-1*) United Hosp Fund.

Measuring Behavioral Health Outcomes. R. P. Hawkins et al. LC 98-47605. (Clinical Child Psychology Library). (Illus.). 200p. (C). 1999. 75.00 (*0-306-46080-7*, Plenum Trade); pap. 24.95 (*0-306-46081-5*, Plenum Trade) Perseus Pubng.

Measuring Behaviour: An Introductory Guide. 2nd ed. Paul Martin & Patrick Bateson. (Illus.). 238p. (C). 1993. pap. text 18.95 (*0-521-44614-7*) Cambridge U Pr.

Measuring Benefits of Government Investments. Ed. by Robert Dorfman. LC 79-28577. (Brookings Institution, National Committee on Government Finance, Studies of Government Finance). (Illus.). 429p. 1980. reprint ed. lib. bdg. 79.50 (*0-313-22307-6*, DOMB) Greenwood.

Measuring Benefits of Government Investments: Papers Presented at a Conference of Experts: November 7-9, 1963. Ed. by Robert Dorfman. LC 65-18313. (Brookings Institution Studies of Government Finance). 445p. reprint ed. pap. 138.00 (*0-608-12176-2*, 202537200043) Bks Demand.

Measuring Bias on Television. Lutton Staff. LC 98-201470. 1997. 29.95 (*1-86020-526-7*, Pub. by U of Luton Pr) Bks Intl VA.

Measuring Business Cycles. Arthur F. Burns & Wesley C. Mitchell. LC 46-6004. (National Bureau of Economic Research, Studies in Business Cycles: No. 2). 590p. reprint ed. pap. 182.90 (*0-8357-3244-4*, 205713800011) Bks Demand.

Measuring Business Cycles. Arthur F. Burns & Wesley C. Mitchell. (Business Cycles Ser.: No. 2). 590p. 1946. reprint ed. 153.40 (*0-87014-085-X*) Natl Bur Econ Res.

Measuring Business Value in Health & Safety. S. Deacon. (Financial Times Management Briefings Ser.). 1997. pap. 89.50 (*0-273-63228-0*) F T P-H.

Measuring Business Value in Health Safety. S. Deacon. 1996. pap. 129.00 (*1-85953-095-8*, Pub. by Tech Comm) St Mut.

Measuring Business's Social Performance: Corporate Social Audit. John J. Corson & George A. Steiner. LC 74-19382. 1975. pap. 4.00 (*0-87186-239-5*) Comm Econ Dev.

Measuring Change in Nutritional Status: Guidelines for Assessing the Nutritional Impact of Supplementary Feeding Programme. (Nonserial Publication). 101p. 1983. pap. text 14.00 (*92-4-154166-0*, 1150208) World Health.

Measuring Changes in Alaska's Labor Market: Hours Worked vs. People Employed. Theodore Lane. (Occasional Papers: No. 16). 13p. 1982. pap. write for info. (*0-88353-035-X*) U Alaska Inst Res.

Measuring Changes in Consumption & Production Patterns: A Set of Indicators. LC 99-172473. 57p. 1998. pap. write for info. (*92-1-104483-9*) UN.

Measuring Church Growth: A Research-Based Tool for Evaluating & Planning. John W. Ellas. LC 97-69006. (Illus.). 120p. 1997. pap. text 12.95 (*0-9642447-2-1*) Ctr for Church.

Measuring Circuits. Rudolf F. Graf. LC 96-36495. 240p. 1996. pap. text 24.95 (*0-7506-9882-9*) Buttrwrth-Heinemann.

Measuring Clinical Care: A Guide for Physician Executives. Stephen Schoenbaum. LC 95-77379. 174p. (C). 1995. pap. text 48.00 (*0-924674-36-9*) Am Coll Phys Execs.

Measuring Cognitive Impairment. Folstein. (Illus.). 320p. (C). 2000. pap. text 34.95 (*0-8151-2931-9*, 31820) Mosby Inc.

Measuring Colour. R. W. Hunt. LC 87-21441. (Applied Science & Industrial Technology Ser.). 221p. 1987. text 69.95 (*0-470-20986-0*) P-H.

Measuring Commercial Damages. Patrick A. Gaughan. LC 99-38747. 403p. 1999. 105.00 (*0-471-35730-8*) Wiley.

Measuring Community Indicators: A Systems Approach to Drug & Alcohol Problems. Ed. by Paul J. Gruenewald et al. (Applied Social Research Methods Ser.: Vol. 45). 112p. 1996. pap. 18.95 (*0-7619-0685-1*) Sage.

Measuring Community Indicators: A Systems Approach to Drug & Alcohol Problems. Paul J. Gruenewald et al. (Applied Social Research Methods Ser.: Vol. 45). 112p. 1996. 42.00 (*0-7619-0684-3*) Sage.

***Measuring Computer Performance: A Practitioner's Guide.** David J. Lillja. LC 99-57225. (Illus.). 300p. (C). 2000. 44.95 (*0-521-64105-5*) Cambridge U Pr.

Measuring Corporate Environmental Performance: Best Practices for Costing & Managing an Effective Environmental Strategy. Marc Epstein. Ed. by Claire Barth. 322p. 1995. pap. 40.00 (*0-86641-238-7*, 95301) Inst Mgmt Account.

Measuring Corporate Environmental Performance: Best Practices for Costing & Managing an Effective Environmental Strategy. Marc J. Epstein. 175p. 1995. text 40.00 (*0-7863-0230-5*, Irwn Prfssnl) McGraw-Hill Prof.

*Measuring Country Performance on Health: Selected Indicators for 115 Countries. Jian Wang. LC 98-50177. (Health, Nutrition, & Population Ser.). 368p. 1999. pap. 30.00 (0-8213-4409-9) World Bank.

Measuring Credit Risk. Alastair Graham. (Risk Management Ser.: Vol. 6). 140p. 1999. 45.00 (0-8144-0537-1) AMACOM.

*Measuring Credit Risk. Ed. by Alastair Graham. 150p. 1999. 45.00 (1-57958-104-8) Fitzroy Dearborn.

*Measuring Credit Risk. Alastair Graham. (The Glenlake Risk Management Ser.). 140p. 2000. 45.00 (1-888998-74-1, 98-74-1) Glenlake Pub.

*Measuring Credit Risk: Credit Risk Management. 1999. pap. 120.00 (0-85297-450-7, Pub. by Chartered Bank) St Mut.

Measuring Culture: A Paradigm for the Analysis of Social Organization. Jonathan L. Gross & Steve Rayner. 144p. 1985. text 64.50 (0-231-06032-7) Col U Pr.

*Measuring Current, Voltage & Power. Kaj Iwansson et al. LC 99-29584. (Handbook of Sensors & Actuators Ser.). 232p. 1999. 177.50 (0-444-72001-4) Elsevier.

Measuring Customer & Service Profitability in the Finance Sector. Roger Connell. (Illus.). 272p. 1996. mass mkt. 89.95 (0-412-63180-6) Chapman & Hall.

Measuring Customer Satisfaction: A Guide to Managing Quality Service. Richard F. Gerson. Ed. by Brenda Machosky. LC 92-54368. (Fifty-Minute Ser.). 112p. (Orig.). 1993. pap. 10.95 (1-56052-178-3) Crisp Pubns.

*Measuring Customer Satisfaction: Hot Buttons & Other Measurement Issues James H. Myers. LC 99-32740. 1999. write for info. (0-87757-276-3) Am Mktg.

Measuring Customer Satisfaction: Survey Design, Use, & Statistical Analysis Methods. 2nd ed. Bob E. Hayes. LC 97-3240. (Illus.). 278p. 1997. 32.00 (0-87389-362-X, H0925) ASQ Qual Pr.

Measuring Delinquency. Michael J. Hindelang et al. LC 81-2522. (Sage Library of Social Research: No. 123). 248p. 1981. reprint ed. pap. 76.90 (0-608-01175-4, 205947300001) Bks Demand.

Measuring Delinquency: A Study of Probation Department Referrals. Joseph W. Eaton & Kenneth Polk. LC 85-30551. (Illus.). 111p. 1986. reprint ed. lib. bdg. 57.50 (0-313-25047-2, EAMD, Greenwood Pr) Greenwood.

Measuring Dinosaurs. Nancy Cook & Christine V. Johnson. Ed. by Cathy Anderson & Katarina Stenstedt. (Real-World Mathematics Through Science Ser.). 127p. (Orig.). (J). (gr. 6-8). 1995. pap. 24.95 (0-201-49312-8) Addison-Wesley.

Measuring Disease. Ann Bowling. LC 94-28081. 17.99p. 1994. pap. text 36.95 (0-335-19225-4) OpUniv Pr.

*Measuring Dispute Resolution Outcomes: A Literature Review with Implications for Workers Compensation. Duncan Ballantyne & Christopher Mazingo. LC 99-26092. 140p. 1999. 75.00 (0-935149-78-3, WC-99-1) Workers Comp Res Inst.

Measuring Diversity Results, No. 1. Edward E. Hubbard. (Illus.). 217p. 1997. 34.95 (1-883733-17-0) Global Insghts.

Measuring Drought & Drought Impacts in Red Sea Province, Sudan: Oxfam Research Discussion Papers. Roy Cole. (Oxfam Research Discussion Papers). 304p. (C). 1989. 15.95 (0-85598-168-7, Pub. by Oxfam Pub) Stylus Pub VA.

Measuring Earthquakes. Nancy Cook. Ed. by Katarina Stenstedt. (Real-World Mathematics Through Science Ser.). 87p. (Orig.). (YA). (gr. 6-8). 1994. pap. 18.95 (0-201-86122-4) Supplementary Div.

Measuring Economic Benefits for Water Investments & Policies. Robert A. Young. LC 96-34710. (Technical Papers: No. 338). 136p. 1996. pap. 22.00 (0-8213-3745-9) World Bank.

Measuring Economic Benefits of Water Pollution Abatement in an Irrigated River Basin. (Illus.). 29p. (Orig.). (C). 1993. pap. text 20.00 (1-56806-724-0) DIANE Pub.

Measuring Economic Welfare: New Methods. George McKenzie. LC 82-4422. 208p. 1983. text 74.95 (0-521-24862-0) Cambridge U Pr.

Measuring Ego Development. 2nd ed. Le-Xuan Hy & Jane Loevinger. (Personality & Clinical Psychology Ser.). 300p. 1995. pap. 30.00 (0-8058-2061-2) L Erlbaum Assocs.

Measuring Ego Development. 2nd abr. ed. Le-Xuan Hy & Jane Loevinger. (Personality & Clinical Psychology Ser.). 300p. 1995. text 49.95 (0-8058-2060-4) L Erlbaum Assocs.

Measuring Ego Development, Vol. 1. Jane Loevinger et al. LC 71-92891. (Jossey-Bass Behavioral Science Ser.). 265p. pap. 82.20 (0-7837-0179-9, 204047600001) Bks Demand.

Measuring Ego Development, Vol. 2. Jane Loevinger et al. LC 71-92891. (Jossey-Bass Behavioral Science Ser.). 477p. pap. 147.90 (0-7837-0180-2, 204047600002) Bks Demand.

Measuring Emotional Intelligence: The Ground-Breaking Guide to Applying the Principles of the New York Times Best Seller, "Emotional Intelligence" Steve Simmons. LC 97-33879. 308p. 1997. 22.99 (1-56530-268-0, Pub. by Summit TX) BookWorld.

Measuring Emotions in Infants & Children. Ed. by Carroll E. Izard. LC 81-10032. (Studies in Social & Emotional Development: No. 3). (Illus.). 352p. 1982. text 69.95 (0-521-24171-5) Cambridge U Pr.

Measuring Emotions in Infants & Children, Vol. 2. Ed. by Carroll E. Izard & Peter B. Read. (Studies in Social & Emotional Development: No. 7). (Illus.). 288p. 1986. text 69.95 (0-521-32367-3) Cambridge U Pr.

Measuring Employment & Training Program Impacts with Data on Program Applicants. Stephen H. Bell et al. LC 95-37399. 184p. (C). 1995. text 34.00 (0-88099-158-5) W E Upjohn.

Measuring Employment Effects in the Regulatory Process: Recommendations & Background Study. Nancy A. Bord et al. (Illus.). 78p. (Orig.). (C). 1994. pap. text 25.00 (0-7881-0694-5) DIANE Pub.

Measuring Environment Across the Life Span: Emerging Methods & Concepts. Ed. by Sarah L. Friedman & Theodore D. Wachs. LC 98-49321. (Illus.). 419p. 1999. 49.95 (1-55798-561-8); pap. 34.95 (1-55798-567-7) Am Psychol.

Measuring Environmental Quality in Asia. Peter Rogers et al. 386p. 1998. pap. 15.00 (971-561-104-4, Pub. by Asian Devel Bank) Paul & Co Pubs.

Measuring Excellence: The History of Correctional Standards & Accreditation. Paul W. Keve. LC 95-52084. 225p. 1996. pap. 21.00 (1-56991-040-5) Am Correctional.

Measuring Executive Effectiveness. Ed. by Frederic R. Wickert & Dalton E. McFarland. LC 67-18987. (Illus.). 1967. 36.50 (0-89197-298-6) Irvington.

Measuring Expenditures for Essential Public Health Services. Kay W. Eilbert et al. (Illus.). 98p. (C). 1998. reprint ed. pap. text 25.00 (0-7881-4205-4) DIANE Pub.

Measuring Fiscal Capacity. Ed. by H. Clyde Reeves. LC 85-30979. (Lincoln Institute of Land Policy Bk.). 221p. reprint ed. pap. 68.60 (0-7837-5754-9, 204541600006) Bks Demand.

Measuring Forensic Psychiatric & Mental Health Nursing Interactions. David K. Robinson & Val Reed. LC 96-84008. (Developments in Nursing & Health Care Ser.). 252p. 1996. 72.95 (1-85972-221-0, Pub. by Avebry) Ashgate Pub Co.

Measuring Functional Capacity & Work Requirements: Summary of a Workshop. National Research Council Staff & Institute of Medicine Staff. LC 99-184679. 124p. (C). 1999. pap. text 28.75 (0-309-06385-X) Natl Acad Pr.

Measuring Functioning & Well-Being: The Medical Outcomes Study Approach. Ed. by Anita L. Stewart & John E. Ware, Jr. LC 91-34579. 479p. 1991. text 64.95 (0-8223-1212-3) Duke.

Measuring Global Values: The Ranking of 162 Countries. Michael J. Sullivan, III. LC 90-25209. 440p. 1991. lib. bdg. 75.00 (0-313-27649-8, SJJ/, Greenwood Pr) Greenwood.

Measuring Health: A Guide to Rating Scales & Questionnaires. 2nd ed. Ian McDowell & Claire Newell. (Illus.). 544p. (C). 1996. text 62.50 (0-19-510371-8) OUP.

Measuring Health: A Practical Approach. Ed. by George Teeling-Smith. LC 88-7762. (Wiley-Medical Publication). 278p. reprint ed. pap. 86.20 (0-7837-5876-6, 204559600006) Bks Demand.

Measuring Health: A Review of Quality of Life Measurement Scales. 2nd ed. D. Bowling. LC 96-50373. 1997. pap. 30.95 (0-335-19754-X) OpUniv Pr.

Measuring Health: Lessons for Ontario. Anthony J. Culyer. LC 78-321436. (Ontario Economic Council Research Studies: No. 14). (Illus.). 197p. reprint ed. pap. 61.10 (0-8357-4020-X, 203671100005) Bks Demand.

Measuring Health & Medical Outcomes. Jenkinson. LC 94-12568. (Social Research Today Ser.: Vol. 3). 224p. 1994. 65.00 (1-85728-083-0, Pub. by UCL Pr Ltd); pap. 27.50 (1-85728-084-9, Pub. by UCL Pr Ltd) Taylor & Francis.

*Measuring Health Performance in the Public Sector: A Summary of Two Reports. National Research Council Staff. 48p. 1999. pap. 12.00 (0-309-06583-6) Natl Acad Pr.

Measuring Health-Related Quality of Life in Children & Adolescents: Implications for Research & Practice. Ed. by Dennis Drotar. LC 97-34793. 350p. 1998. write for info. (0-8058-2479-0); pap. write for info. (0-8058-2480-4) L Erlbaum Assocs.

Measuring HR & the Impact on the Bottom Line. P. Kearns. 1996. pap. 129.00 (1-85953-045-1, Pub. by Tech Comm) St Mut.

Measuring HR & the Impact on the Bottom Line. Phil Kearns. (Financial Times Management Briefings Ser.). 1997. pap. 89.50 (0-273-63185-3, Pub. by F T P-H) Trans-Atl Phila.

Measuring Human Problems: A Practical Guide to the Assessment of Adult Psychological Problems. Peck. 418p. 1992. pap. text 113.95 (0-471-93482-8) Wiley.

Measuring Immortality: Social Inquiry & the Problem of Illegitimacy. Gail Reekie. LC 98-26653. 284p. (C). 1998. 64.95 (0-521-62034-1); pap. 19.95 (0-521-62974-8) Cambridge U Pr.

*Measuring Inflation in Public Libraries: A Comparison of Two Approaches, the Input Cost Index & Cost of Services Index. Jay G. Chambers. 100p. 1999. pap. text 8.50 (0-16-050001-X) USGPO.

*Measuring Inflation in Public Libraries: A Comparison of Two Approcahes, the Input Cost & the Cost of Services Index. Jay C. Chambers et al. 88p. 2000. pap. text 20.00 (0-7881-8400-8) DIANE Pub.

Measuring Information Technology Investment Payoff: Contemporary Approaches. Ed. by Mo A. Mahmood & Edward J. Szewczak. LC 98-42507. (Series in Information Technology Management). (Illus.). 568p. 1998. 139.95 (1-878289-42-X) Idea Group Pub.

Measuring Institutional Performance in Higher Education. Ed. by Joel Meyerson. LC 93-6403. 141p. (C). 1993. 29.95 (1-56079-331-7) Petersons.

Measuring Instructional Results. 2nd ed. Robert F. Mager. LC 83-60502. 1984. pap. 18.95 (1-56103-340-5) Ctr Effect Perf.

Measuring Instructional Results: How to Find Out If Your Instructional Objectives Have Been Achieved see Mager Six-Pack

Measuring Instrument Calibration Pt. I: Involute Measurement. AMGA Technical Committee. (ANSI/AGMA Standard Ser.: Vol. 2010-A94). (Illus.). 39p. 1994. pap. text 55.00 (1-55589-630-8) AGMA.

Measuring Instrument Calibration Pt. I: Involute Measurement (Metric Edition) AGMA Technical Committee. (ANSI/AGMA Standard Ser.: Vol. 2110-A94). (Illus.). 39p. 2000. pap. text 55.00 (1-55589-631-6) AGMA.

*Measuring Instrument Calibration, Gear Pitch & Runout Measurements. AGMA Technical Committee. (ANSI/AGMA Standard Ser.: Vol. 2114-A98). 33p. 2000. pap. text 64.00 (1-55589-732-0) AGMA.

Measuring Instrument Calibration, Gear Tooth Alignment Measurement. AGMA Technical Committee. (ANSI/AGMA Standard Ser.: Vol. 2113-A97). (Illus.). 33p. 1997. pap. text 55.00 (1-55589-687-1) AGMA.

Measuring International Capital Movements. Walther P. Michael. LC 74-160315. (National Bureau of Economic Research, Occasional Paper Ser.: No. 114). 160p. reprint ed. pap. 49.60 (0-608-30153-1, 200622000055) Bks Demand.

Measuring International Capital Movements. Walther P. Michael. (Occasional Papers: No. 114). 160p. 1971. reprint ed. 40.00 (0-87014-229-1) Natl Bur Econ Res.

Measuring International Price Competitiveness: A Preliminary Report. Irving B. Kravis et al. (Occasional Papers: No. 94). 48p. 1965. reprint ed. 20.00 (0-87014-408-1) Natl Bur Econ Res.

Measuring Investment Performance: Calculating & Evaluating Investment Risk & Return. David Spaulding. LC 97-13946. 1997. 50.00 (0-7863-1177-0, Irwn Prfssnl) McGraw-Hill Prof.

Measuring Jerusalem: The Palestine Exploration Fund & British Interests in the Holy Land John J. Moscrop. LC 99-29412. 1999. 74.95 (0-7185-0220-5) Leicester U Pr.

Measuring Leadership: A Guide to Assessment for Development of School Executives. Larry Lashway. LC 99-19446. 1999. pap. 9.75 (0-86552-140-9) U of Oreg ERIC.

*Measuring Learning & Performance. Ed. by Jack J. Phillips & Toni K. Hodges. LC 99-72120. (In Action Ser.). 320p. 1999. pap. 50.00 (1-56286-123-9) Am Soc Train & Devel.

Measuring Learning in Organizations. Blair. 300p. 1998. 39.95 (0-88415-476-9, 5476) Gulf Pub.

Measuring Legislative Committee Performance. Alan L. Clem. 1975. 1.00 (1-55614-064-9) U of SD Gov Res Bur.

Measuring Length. Ron Marson. (Task Cards Ser.: No. 2). (Illus.). 48p. 1991. teacher ed. 8.00 (0-941008-72-X) Tops Learning.

Measuring Lives: A Thriller. Thomas Foley. LC 96-21041. 352p. 1996. 24.00 (1-56980-091-X) Barricade Bks.

Measuring Low Incomes: Self-Employment & Family Credit. R. Boden & A. Corden. 134p. 1994. pap. 25.00 (0-11-701787-6, HM17876, Pub. by Statnry Office) Bernan Associates.

*Measuring Mamma's Milk: Fascism & the Medicalization of Maternity in Italy. Elizabeth D. Whitaker. LC 99-50436. (Illus.). 368p. (C). 2000. text 49.50 (0-472-11078-0, 11078) U of Mich Pr.

Measuring Man & Other Poems. Harry Brown. Ed. by Patricia Schultz. LC 89-33519. (Poetry Ser.: Vol. 3). 72p. 1989. pap. 14.95 (0-88946-888-5) E Mellen.

Measuring Management Quality Cost V. Ansari. 1997. pap., student ed. 5.00 (0-256-27143-7) McGraw.

Measuring Managerial & Business Performance. R. Pettinger. (Financial Times Management Briefings Ser.). 1997. pap. 89.50 (0-273-63186-1, Pub. by F T P-H) Trans-Atl Phila.

Measuring Managerial & Business Performance. R. Pettinger. 1996. pap. 129.00 (1-85953-067-2, Pub. by Tech Comm) St Mut.

Measuring, Managing, & Maximizing Performance. Will Kaydos. (Illus.). 284p. 1991. 40.00 (0-915299-98-4) Productivity Inc.

*Measuring Market Risk with Value-at-Risk. Pietro Penza & Vipul K. Bansal. LC 00-38207. (Series in Financial Engineering). (Illus.). 336p. 2000. 79.95 (0-471-39313-4) Wiley.

Measuring, Marking & Layout: A Builder's Guide. John Carroll. LC 98-18115. 1998. 34.95 (1-56158-226-3) Taunton.

Measuring Mass. Norman E. Griswold. Ed. by Conrad L. Stanitski. (Modular Laboratory Program in Chemistry Ser.). 12p. (C). 1996. pap. text 1.50 (0-87540-485-5, TECH 485-5) Chem Educ Res.

Measuring Media Audiences. Ed. by Raymond Kent. LC 93-43868. 224p. (C). (gr. 13). 1994. pap. 61.95 (0-415-08289-7) Thomson Learn.

Measuring Military Power: The Soviet Air Threat to Europe. Joshua M. Epstein. LC 83-43070. 317p. 1984. reprint ed. pap. 98.30 (0-608-03312-X, 206402400008) Bks Demand.

Measuring Minds: Henry Herbert Goddard & the Origins of American Intelligence Testing. Leila Zenderland. (Studies in the History of Psychology). (Illus.). 464p. (C). 1998. text 64.95 (0-521-44373-3) Cambridge U Pr.

Measuring Minimum Wage Effects in the United States. J. St. O'Herlihy. 83p. 1969. 5.40 (92-2-100018-4) Intl Labour Office.

Measuring, Modelling, & Control, Vol. 4. Ed. by K. Schiigerl. xii, 658p. 1991. write for info. (1-56081-154-4, Wiley-VCH) Wiley.

Measuring Morality: A Comparison of Ethical Systems. Erwin W. Lutzer. LC 89-29503. Orig. Title: The Necessity of Ethical Absolutes. 120p. (C). 1989. reprint ed. pap. 8.99 (0-945241-04-6) Probe Bks.

Measuring Mortality, Fertility, & Natural Increase: A Self-Teaching Guide to Elementary Measures. rev. ed. James A. Palmore & Robert W. Gardner. 1994. pap. 15.00 (0-86638-165-1) EW Ctr HI.

Measuring Movement & Locomotion: From Invertebrates to Humans. Klaus-Peter Ossenkopp. Ed. by Martin Kavaliers & Paul R. Sanberg. (Neuroscience Intelligence Unit Ser.). 261p. 1996. 99.00 (1-57059-322-1) Landes Bioscience.

Measuring Museum Based Learning: Experimental Studies of the Education of Children in a Museum of Science. Arthur W. Melton et al. (Illus.). 106p. 1996. reprint ed. pap. 13.50 (0-931201-33-0) Am Assn Mus.

Measuring My World: Student Science Journal. Peter R. Bergethon. (Illus.). Date not set. pap. text. write for info. (1-58447-006-2) Symmetry Lrng.

Measuring My World: Teacher Manual. Peter R. Bergethon. (Illus.). Date not set. pap. text, teacher ed. write for info. (1-58447-005-4) Symmetry Lrng.

*Measuring National Power in the Postindustrial Age. Ashley J. Tellis et al. xvii, 157p. 2000. pap. 15.00 (0-8330-2792-1, MR-1110-A) Rand Corp.

*Measuring National Power in the Postindustrial Age: Analyst's Handbook. Ashley J. Tellis et al. LC 99-59380. (Illus.). 55p. 2000. pap. 7.50 (0-8330-2803-0, MR-1110/1-A) Rand Corp.

Measuring Numbers System. Paul H. Fejer. Ed. by Barbara Jones. (Illus.). 53p. (C). 1975. 100.00 (0-9607422-1-2, A-661691) P H Fejer.

Measuring Offender Risk: A Criminal Justice Sourcebook. Dean J. Champion. LC 93-1651. 352p. 1993. lib. bdg. 79.50 (0-313-28593-4, Greenwood Pr) Greenwood.

Measuring Organizational Improvement Impact: A Practical Guide to Measuring Tracking Against the Right Targets. Richard Y. Chang. 1996. pap. 14.95 (0-7879-5101-3) Jossey-Bass.

Measuring Outcome in the Public Sector. Ed. by Peter Smith. LC 95-48128. 224p. 1996. pap. 29.95 (0-7484-0404-X); text 89.95 (0-7484-0403-1) Taylor & Francis.

Measuring Outcomes. Deborah K. Wall. LC 97-17398. (Illus.). 96p. 1997. pap. 40.00 (0-944496-52-0) Precept Pr.

Measuring Outcomes: Desktop Reference for Behavioral Healthcare Providers. 3rd rev. ed. Ed. by Anne M. Christner. 550p. 1998. 149.00 (1-884937-51-9) Manisses Communs.

Measuring Outcomes in Ambulatory Care. Dale S. Benson. LC 92-49961. 192p. (Orig.). 1992. pap. 49.95 (1-55648-094-6, 169106) AHPI.

Measuring Outcomes in Children's Services. John Mordock. 1998. 75.00 (1-884937-47-0) Manisses Communs.

Measuring Outcomes in Speech-Language Pathology. Carol M. Frattali. LC 97-26377. (Illus.). 500p. 1997. 55.00 (0-86577-718-7) Thieme Med Pubs.

Measuring Outcomes in Speech-Language Pathology. Carol Frattali. LC 97-26377. 1997. write for info. (3-13-109731-0, Pub. by G Thieme) Thieme Med Pubs.

Measuring Outcomes of College: Fifty Years of Findings & Recommendations for the Future. Charles R. Pace. LC 79-88774. (Jossey-Bass Series in Higher Education). 200p. reprint ed. pap. 62.00 (0-8357-4957-6, 203788900009) Bks Demand.

Measuring Patient Changes in Mood, Anxiety, & Personality Disorders: Toward a Core Battery. Ed. by Hans H. Strupp et al. LC 97-7469. 544p. 1997. 49.95 (1-55798-414-X, 431-8590) Am Psychol.

Measuring Patient Reported Health Status in Advanced HIV Disease: HIV-PARSE Survey Instrument. Sandra H. Berry et al. LC 94-32313. 1994. pap. 9.00 (0-8330-1584-2, MR-342-NIAID) Rand Corp.

Measuring Penny. Loreen Leedy. LC 97-19108. (Illus.). 32p. (J). (gr. 1-4). 1998. 16.95 (0-8050-5360-3) H Holt & Co.

*Measuring Penny. Loreen Leedy. (Illus.). 32p. (gr. 2-4). 2000. pap. 6.95 (0-8050-6572-5) H Holt & Co.

*Measuring Performance: Using the New Metrics to Deploy Strategy & Improve Performance. Bob Frost. 94p. 1998. pap. text 9.95 (0-7880-1407-2) CSS OH.

*Measuring Performance & Demong Results of Information Technology Investments. Christopher W. Hoenig. (Illus.). 82p. (C). 2000. reprint ed. pap. text 20.00 (0-7881-8596-9) DIANE Pub.

Measuring Performance in Human Service Systems: Planning, Organization, & Control. James F. Budde. LC 79-19551. 221p. reprint ed. pap. 63.00 (0-608-12832-5, 2023557) Bks Demand.

Measuring Performance to Increase Total Productivity. Will Kaydos. LC 98-19227. 272p. 1998. boxed set 44.95 (1-57444-099-3, SL0993) St Lucie Pr.

Measuring Personality Adjustment in Children 9 to 13 Years of Age. Carl Ransom Rogers. LC 76-177202. (Columbia University. Teachers College. Contributions to Education Ser.: No. 458). reprint ed. 37.50 (0-404-55458-X) AMS Pr.

Measuring Physical Activity & Energy Expenditure. Han C. Kemper et al. LC 94-38604. (Illus.). 200p. 1995. text 35.00 (0-87322-500-7, BMON0500) Human Kinetics.

Measuring Police Corruption. Janet E. Fishman. (Criminal Justice Center Monographs). 1978. pap. text 3.50 (0-318-37487-0) John Jay Pr.

Measuring Poverty: A New Approach. National Research Council, Panel on Poverty & Fami. Ed. by Robert T. Michael & Constance F. Citro. 536p. (C). 1995. text 44.95 (0-309-05128-2) Natl Acad Pr.

Measuring Price & Quality Competitiveness: A Study of 18 British Product Markets. Peter Swann & Majid Taghavi. 225p. 1992. 82.95 (1-85628-328-3, Pub. by Avebry) Ashgate Pub Co.

M

An Asterisk (*) at the beginning of an entry indicates that the title is appearing for the first time.

M

Measuring Process Capability: Techniques & Calculations for Quality & Manufacturing Engineers. Davis R. Bothe. LC 96-30087. (Illus.). 897p. 1997. 99.95 (*0-07-006652-3*) McGraw.

Measuring Productivity in Word Formation: The Case of Israeli Hebrew. Shmuel Bolozky. LC 98-36385. (Studies in Semitic Languages & Linguistics). 1999. 54.50 (*90-04-11252-9*) Brill Academic Pubs.

Measuring Profitability & Capital Costs: An International Study. Daniel M. Holland. LC 82-48491. (Lincoln Institute of Land Policy Bk.). 503p. reprint ed. pap. 156.00 (*0-7837-3266-X*, 204328500007) Bks Demand.

Measuring Program Efficiency & Effectiveness in Local Government. Mark Glover. 128p. 1992. 23.95 (*1-882403-03-7*) The Innovation Grps.

Measuring Programmer Productivity & Software Quality. Lowell J. Arthur. LC 84-13176. (Wiley-Interscience Publications). 310p. reprint ed. pap. 96.10 (*0-7837-2381-4*, 204006700006) Bks Demand.

Measuring Progress: Is Life Getting Better? Ed. by R. M. Eckersley. (Illus.). 382p. (Orig.). pap. 34.95 (*0-643-06296-3*, Pub. by CSIRO) Accents Pubns.

Measuring Progress & Results in Early Childhood System Development. Nina S. O'Donnell & Ellen Galinsky. 28p. 1998. pap. 9.00 (*1-888324-12-0*) Families & Work.

Measuring Psychological Responses to Media Messages. Ed. by Annie Lang. (LEA's Communication Ser.). 256p. 1994. text 49.95 (*0-8058-0717-9*) L Erlbaum Assocs.

Measuring Quality: International Guidelines for Performance Measurement in Academic Libraries. Roswitha Poll & Peter te Boekhorst. (IFLA Publications: Vol. 76). 171p. 1996. 55.00 (*3-598-21800-1*) K G Saur Verlag.

Measuring Quality: Linking Customer Satisfaction to Process Improvement. David Wilkerson et al. 160p. 1993. pap. 24.95 (*0-944533-05-1*) Coopers Total Qlty.

Measuring Quality - Education Indicators: United Kingdom & International Perspectives. Ed. by Katheryn A. Riley & Desmond L. Nuttall. LC 94-2854. 176p. 1994. 85.00 (*0-7507-0260-5*, Falmer Pr); pap. 29.95 (*0-7507-0261-3*, Falmer Pr) Taylor & Francis.

Measuring Quality Improvement in Healthcare: A Guide to Statistical Process Control Applications. Raymond G. Carey & Robert C. Lloyd. LC 95-5101. 208p. 1995. pap. 26.95 (*0-527-76293-8*) Productivity Inc.

Measuring Range of Motion with the ORTHO RANGER II Inclinometer: An Illustrated Guide. John J. Gerhardt & Andrew V. Linial. Ed. by Philip King. (Illus.). 154p. (Orig.). 1990. ring bd. 29.95 (*0-9621736-2-2*) Isomed.

Measuring Reading Competence: A Theoretical-Prescriptive Approach. Steven Schwartz. LC 84-17953. (Illus.). 355p. (C). 1984. 78.00 (*0-306-41749-9*, Plenum Trade) Perseus Pubng.

Measuring Recessions. Geoffrey H. Moore. (Occasional Papers: No. 61). 64p. 1958. reprint ed. 20.00 (*0-87014-375-1*) Natl Bur Econ Res.

Measuring Recreation Supply. Winston Harrington. LC 87-9569. 77p. 1987. pap. 9.95 (*0-915707-31-4*) Resources Future.

Measuring Results: Successful Human Resources Management. 135p. 1997. pap. 20.00 (*1-57744-053-6*) Nat Acad Public Admin.

Measuring Return on Investment. Ed. & Pref. by Jack J. Phillips. LC 94-78503. (In Action Ser.). 271p. 1994. pap. 50.00 (*1-56286-008-9*) Am Soc Train & Devel.

Measuring Return on Investment. Ed. by Jack J. Phillips. LC 94-78503. (In Action Ser.: Vol. 2). 282p. 1997. pap. 50.00 (*1-56286-065-8*) Am Soc Train & Devel.

*__Measuring Risk in Complex Stochastic Systems.__ Ed. by J. Franke et al. (Lecture Notes in Statistics Ser.). 272p. 2000. pap. 44.95 (*0-387-98996-X*) Spr-Verlag.

Measuring Risks of Deposit Institutions. rev. ed. Frank M. Song. LC 93-41569. (Financial Sector of the American Economy Ser.). 152p. 1994. text 15.00 (*0-8153-1684-4*) Garland.

Measuring Road Roughness & Its Effects on User Cost & Comfort STP 884. Ed. by Thomas D. Gillespie & Michael W. Sayers. LC 85-17206. (Illus.). 200p. 1985. text 29.00 (*0-8031-0428-6*, STP884) ASTM.

Measuring Scale for Ability in Spelling. Leonard P. Ayres. 1986. pap. 5.99 (*0-88062-039-0*) Mott Media.

Measuring School Climate: Questions & Considerations. Bruce L. Wilson & Janet McGrail. 16p. 1987. pap. 5.95 (*1-56602-013-1*) Research Better.

Measuring Second Language Performance. T. F. McNamara. LC 95-26148. (Applied Linguistics & Language Ser.). 1996. pap. 35.70 (*0-582-08907-7*, Pub. by Addison-Wesley) Longman.

Measuring Security in Personal Adjustment. Mary D. Ainsworth & Leonard H. Ainsworth. LC 58-37947. 112p. reprint ed. pap. 34.80 (*0-608-30643-6*, 201411000094) Bks Demand.

Measuring Self-Concept Across the Life Span: Issues & Instrumentation. Barbara M. Byrne. LC 95-45591. (Measurement & Instrumentation in Psychology Ser.). 297p. 1996. 39.95 (*1-55798-332-1*); pap. text 29.95 (*1-55798-346-1*) Am Psychol.

Measuring Sex, Age & Death in the Roman Empire: Explorations in Ancient Demography. Walter Scheidel. (Journal of Roman Archaeology Supplementary Ser.: No. 21). 184p. 1996. 59.50 (*1-887829-21-0*) Jour Roman Arch.

Measuring Sex Stereotypes: A Thirty-Nation Study. rev. ed. John E. Williams & Deborah L. Best. (Cross-Cultural Research & Methodology Ser.: Vol. 6). (Illus.). 376p. (C). 1990. 46.00 (*0-8039-3815-2*); pap. 22.95 (*0-8039-3814-4*) Sage.

Measuring 6 Sigma & Beyond. R. Lawson. 1997. pap. 10.00 (*1-56946-023-X*) Motorola Univ.

Measuring Sizes. Andrew King. LC 98-4230. (Math for Fun Ser.). 32p. (J). (gr. 2-4). 1998. pap. 5.95 (*0-7613-0747-8*, Copper Beech Bks) Millbrook Pr.

Measuring Sizes. Andrew King. LC 98-4230. (Math for Fun Ser.). (Illus.). 32p. (J). (gr. 2-4). 1998. 20.90 (*0-7613-0853-9*, Copper Beech Bks) Millbrook Pr.

Measuring Social Life Feelings. Karl F. Schuessler. LC 82-48063. (Jossey-Bass Social & Behavioral Science Ser.). 203p. reprint ed. pap. 63.00 (*0-8357-4922-3*, 203785200009) Bks Demand.

Measuring Software Reuse: Principles, Practices & Economic Models. Jeffrey S. Poulin. 224p. (C). 1996. 39.95 (*0-201-63413-9*) Addison-Wesley.

Measuring Spokane: A Numerical Look at a City & Its Region. Shaun Higgins. LC 98-215251. x, 99 p. 1998. pap. 11.95 (*0-923910-13-1*) NMV.

Measuring State & Local Government Labor Productivity: Examples from Eleven Services. Donald M. Disk & Mary M. Greiner. (Labor Statistics Bureau Bulletin Ser.: No. 2495). (Illus.). 206p. 1998. pap. 18.00 (*0-16-049663-2*) USGPO.

Measuring Stress: A Guide for Health & Social Scientists. Ed. by Sheldon Cohen et al. LC 94-13307. (Illus.). 256p. 1995. text 60.00 (*0-19-508641-4*) OUP.

Measuring Stress: A Guide for Health & Social Scientists. Ed. by Sheldon Cohen et al. (Illus.). 256p. 1997. reprint ed. pap. text 29.50 (*0-19-512120-1*) OUP.

*__Measuring Student Knowledge & Skills: A New Framework for Assessment.__ Andreas Schleicher. 84p. (Orig.). 1999. pap. 26.00 (*92-64-17053-7*, 96-1999-05-1P, Pub. by Org for Econ) OECD.

*__Measuring Student Knowledge & Skills: The PISA 2000 Assessment of Reading, Mathematical & Scientific Literacy.__ OECD Staff. 108p. 2000. pap. 20.00 (*92-64-17646-2*, 96 2000 05 1 P, Pub. by Org for Econ) OECD.

Measuring Success in Bilingual Education Programs: Case Studies of Bilingual Practices. Angela Carrasquillo & Judy Rodriguez. 78p. (C). 1998. pap. text 17.00 (*1-883514-02-9*) Bastos Bk.

Measuring Suspended Sediment in Small Mountain Streams. Robert B. Thomas. (Illus.). 20p. 1998. reprint ed. pap. 3.00 (*0-89904-516-2*, Bear Meadows Resrch Grp) Crumb Elbow Pub.

Measuring Sustainable Development: Macroeconomics & the Environment. Giles Atkinson et al. LC 96-39592. 272p. 1997. 95.00 (*1-85898-572-2*) E Elgar.

Measuring Sustainable Development: Macroeconomics & the Environment. Giles Atkinson et al. LC 96-39592. 272p. 1999. pap. 30.00 (*1-84064-198-3*) E Elgar.

Measuring Systems see **Standard Instrumentation Questions & Answers: For Production Processes Control**

Measuring Systems & Transducers for Industrial Applications. D. F. Horne. (Illus.). 176p. 1988. 95.00 (*0-85274-391-2*) IOP Pub.

Measuring Team Performance: A Practical Guide to Tracking Team Success. Gloria E. Bader et al. LC 94-94045. (High Performance Team Ser.). (Illus.). 120p. 1994. pap. 12.95 (*1-883553-29-6*) R Chang Assocs.

*__Measuring Team Performance: A Step-By-Step, Customizable Approach for Managers, Facilitators.__ Steven D. Jones. 2000. write for info. (*0-7879-4569-2*) Jossey-Bass.

*__Measuring Team Performance Vol. 47: A Seven Step Guide to Team Success.__ American Compensation Association Staff. (Building Blocks Ser.). (Illus.). 1999. pap. 24.95 (*1-57963-063-4*) Am Compensation.

Measuring Techniques in Hydraulic Research: Proceedings of the International Symposium Techniques in Hydraulic Research, IAHR SEction, Delft, 22-24 April 1985. Ed. by A. C. Wessels. 288p. (C). 1986. text 123.00 (*90-6191-645-3*, Pub. by A A Balkema) Ashgate Pub Co.

Measuring the Benefits & Costs of Section 936. Norman B. Ture. 29p. (Orig.). 1985. pap. 5.95 (*0-922623-02-3*) IRET.

Measuring the Benefits of Clean Air & Water. Allen V. Kneese. LC 84-17899. 159p. (C). 1984. pap. text 14.95 (*0-915707-09-8*) Resources Future.

Measuring the Benefits of Federal Wetland Programs. Paul F. Scodari & Environmental Law Institute. LC 97-133033. 104p. 1997. 29.95 (*0-911937-71-4*) Environ Law Inst.

Measuring the Book Circulation Use of a Small Academic Library Collection: A Manual. Mary Kane Trochim. 73p. 1985. pap. 20.00 (*0-918006-50-3*) Assn Res Lib.

Measuring the Burden of Disease & the Cost-Effectiveness of Health Interventions: A Case Study in Guinea. Prabhat Jha. LC 96-31866. (Technical Papers: No. 333). 48p. 1996. pap. 22.00 (*0-8213-3727-0*) World Bank.

Measuring the Condition of the World's Poor: The Physical Quality of Life Index. Morris D. Morris. LC 79-16613. 190p. 1979. pap. 5.95 (*0-08-023889-0*) Overseas Dev Council.

Measuring the Condition of the World's Poor: The Physical Quality of Life Index Published for the Overseas Development Council. (Policy Studies). 1979. pap. 5.95 (*0-685-04007-0*, Pergamon Pr) Elsevier.

*__Measuring the Correlates of War.__ Ed. by J. David Singer & Paul F. Diehl. (Illus.). 285p. (C). 2000. reprint ed. text 25.00 (*0-7881-9423-2*) DIANE Pub.

Measuring the Correlates of War. J. David Singer & Paul F. Diehl. (Illus.). 308p. (C). 1991. reprint ed. text 52.50 (*0-472-10166-8*, 10166) U of Mich Pr.

Measuring the Cost of Protection in China. Shu-Kuang Chang et al. LC 97-20114. 1998. pap. 15.95 (*0-88132-247-4*) Inst Intl Eco.

China was steeped in the concepts & ideology of a planned economy for 30 years until reforms began in 1978. Although the country is now well on its way to becoming a market economy, its trading system remains shackled by its centrally planned past. Measuring the Costs of Protection in China analyzes some of the costs of trade protection & corresponding benefits of liberalization for 25 highly protected sectors in China. The book begins with a description of the development of China's trade administration system, sketching the obstacles to & prospects for further liberalization. The authors analyze the structure of Chinese trade protection & present their estimates of its static costs. They then offer an in-depth analysis of the country's trade regime & of the administrative barriers to rationalization & liberalization. The final chapter present the authors' recommendations for improving China's trade system. They conclude that the short-term costs of trade liberalization for goods examined in the study will be substantial in terms of lost domestic output & lost jobs. The long-term benefits, however, would provide some 35 billion worth of consumer benefits. Five appendices provide greater technical detail on the modeling & methodology applied in this study, as well as a brief description of some peculiarities of the Chinese trade regime-including copious levels of smuggling & monopolistic market structures. *Publisher Paid Annotation.*

---

*__Measuring the Costs of Protection in Europe.__ Patrick A. Messerlin. 100p. 2000. pap. 15.95 (*0-88132-273-3*) Inst Intl Eco.

Measuring the Costs of Protection in Japan. Yoko Sazanami et al. 76p. (Orig.). (C). 1995. pap. text 25.00 (*0-88132-211-3*) Inst Intl Eco.

Measuring the Costs of Protection in the United States. Gary C. Hufbauer & Kimberly A. Elliott. LC 93-5022. 125p. 1994. pap. 15.95 (*0-88132-108-7*) Inst Intl Eco.

Measuring the Demand for Environmental Quality. Ed. by J. B. Braden & C. D. Kolstad. (Contributions to Economic Analysis Ser.: No. 198). xii,370p. 1991. 128.50 (*0-444-88877-2*, North Holland) Elsevier.

*__Measuring the Democratic Prospect of Mediating Structures.__ Richard A. Conto. 27p. 1999. pap. 10.00 (*0-929556-16-X*) Ind Sector.

Measuring the Dynamics of Contraceptive Use. 1991. 25.00 (*92-1-151226-3*, E 91.XIII.7) UN.

Measuring the Dynamics of Technological Change. Ed. by Jon Sigurdson. 220p. 1992. 49.00 (*0-86187-842-6*) St Martin.

*__Measuring the Economy.__ C. Agwan Johnson. 1998. pap. 19.95 (*0-14-024092-6*, Pub. by Pnguin Bks Ltd) Trafalgar.

Measuring the Effect of Benefits & Taxes on Income & Poverty. (Illus.). 154p. (C). 1994. pap. text 40.00 (*0-7881-0239-7*) DIANE Pub.

Measuring the Effect of Benefits & Taxes on Income & Poverty. 1992. lib. bdg. 79.99 (*0-8490-5538-5*) Gordon Pr.

Measuring the Effect of Benefits & Taxes on Income & Poverty. 1994. lib. bdg. 250.00 (*0-8490-5765-5*) Gordon Pr.

Measuring the Effectiveness of Competitive Intelligence: Assessing & Communicating CI's Value to Your Organization. Jan P. Herring. 66p. (Orig.). 1996. pap. 35.00 (*0-9621241-2-5*) SCIP.

Measuring the Effectiveness of Image & Linkage Advertising: The Nitty-Gritty of Maxi-Marketing. Arch G. Woodside. LC 95-50739. 280p. 1996. 65.00 (*0-89930-984-4*, Quorum Bks) Greenwood.

Measuring the Effectiveness of Organized Crime Control Efforts. Michael D. Maltz. 132p. 1990. pap. 11.95 (*0-942511-38-7*) OICJ.

Measuring the Effects of Benefits & Taxes on Income & Poverty. 1996. lib. bdg. 250.96 (*0-8490-5993-3*) Gordon Pr.

Measuring the Effects of Geographic Targeting on Poverty Reduction. Judy L. Baker & Margaret E. Grosh. LC 93-33092. (Living Standards Measurement Study Working Papers: No. 99). 42p. 1994. pap. 22.00 (*0-8213-2666-X*, 12666) World Bank.

Measuring the Effects of Hazardous Materials Contamination on Real Estate Values: Techniques & Applications. 165p. 1992. 25.00 (*0-922154-09-0*) Appraisal Inst.

Measuring the Employment Effects of Regulation: Where Did the Jobs Go? Neal S. Zank. LC 96-911. 160p. 1996. 49.95 (*1-56720-070-2*, Quorum Bks) Greenwood.

Measuring the Extent of Domestic Violence. Anna Ferrante et al. 105p. 1995. 10.00 (*0-86422-581-4*, Pub. by Blackstone Pr) Gaunt.

Measuring the Flow of Time: The Works of James A. Ford, 1935-1941. Michael J. O'Brien & R. Lee Lyman. LC 99-6142. (Classics in Southeastern Archaeology Ser.). (Illus.). 600p. 1999. 39.95 (*0-8173-0991-8*) U of Ala Pr.

Measuring the Government Sector of the U. S. Economic Accounts. National Research Council Staff. Ed. by Courtenay M. Slater & Martin H. David. 40p. 1998. pap. text 10.00 (*0-309-06135-0*) Natl Acad Pr.

Measuring the Health Behavior of Adolescents: The Youth Risk Behavior Surveillance System & Recent Reports on High Risk Adolescents. (Illus.). 96p. (Orig.). (C). 1995. pap. text 30.00 (*0-7881-2321-1*) DIANE Pub.

Measuring the Health of Persian Gulf Veterans: Workshop Summary. Institute of Medicine Staff. LC 99-175490. 42p. 1998. pap. text 10.00 (*0-309-06245-4*) Natl Acad Pr.

Measuring the Impact of Climate Change on Indian Agriculture. Ariel Dinar et al. LC 98-14309. (Technical Paper Ser.: No. 402). 280p. 1998. pap. 22.00 (*0-8213-4192-8*, 14192) World Bank.

Measuring the Impact of Manpower Programs: A Primer. Michael E. Borus & William R. Tash. LC 73-633548. (Policy Papers in Human Resources & Industrial Relations Ser.: No. 17). (Orig.). 1970. pap. 5.00 (*0-87736-117-7*) U of Mich Inst Labor.

Measuring the Impact of Training. Richard Y. Chang & P. Keith Kelly. (Practical Guidebks.). 14.95 (*0-7879-5094-7*, Pfffr & Co) Jossey-Bass.

Measuring the Impact of Training: A Practical Guide to Calculating Measurable Results. 2nd ed. Pamela A. Wade. LC 98-71079. (Illus.). 120p. 1998. pap. 12.95 (*1-883553-36-9*) R Chang Assocs.

Measuring the Impact of Training & Development on the Bottom Line. Paul Kearns & Tony Miller. (Financial Times Management Briefings Ser.). 1997. pap. 89.50 (*0-273-63187-X*, Pub. by F T P-H) Trans-Atl Phila.

Measuring the Impact of Training & Development on the Bottom Line. R. Kearns & T. Miller. 1996. pap. 129.00 (*1-85953-087-7*, Pub. by Tech Comm) St Mut.

Measuring the Impact of Your Web Site. Robert W. Buchanan & Charles Lukaszewski. LC 96-47396. 316p. 1997. pap. 29.95 (*0-471-17249-9*) Wiley.

Measuring the Information Society: The Texas Studies. Ed. by Frederick Williams. (Focus Editions Ser.: Vol. 97). 320p. 1988. text 59.95 (*0-8039-3155-7*); pap. text 26.00 (*0-8039-3156-5*) Sage.

Measuring the Intentional World: Realism, Naturalism, & Quantitative Methods in the Behavioral Sciences. J. D. Trout. 304p. 1998. text 45.00 (*0-19-510766-7*) OUP.

Measuring the Leverage: Assessing Military Contributions to Drug Interdiction. Carl H. Builder. LC 93-7134. 1993. pap. 13.00 (*0-8330-1338-6*, MR-158-A/AF) Rand Corp.

Measuring the Locational Efficiency of the Urban Hospital. Jerry B. Schneider. (Discussion Papers: No. 11). 1967. pap. 10.00 (*1-55869-074-3*) Regional Sci Res Inst.

Measuring the Marketplace: An Approach to Designing & Conducting a Salary Survey. James R. McMahon & Janice S. Hand. (Building Blocks Ser.: Vol. 1). (Illus.). 19p. (Orig.). 1991. pap. 24.95 (*1-57963-004-9*, A0001) Am Compensation.

Measuring the Melting Points of Compounds & Mixtures. Joseph W. LeFevre. Ed. by J. Jeffers. (Modular Laboratory Program in Chemistry Ser.). 12p. (C). 1997. pap. text 1.75 (*0-87540-701-3*) Chem Educ Res.

Measuring the Metric Way. Richard A. Lay. (Illus.). 76p. 1975. pap. text 2.50 (*0-88323-123-9*, 211) Pendergrass Pub.

Measuring the Mind: Psychological Theory & Educational Controversy in England, C. 1860-C. 1990. Adrian Wooldridge. LC 93-29889. 458p. (C). 1995. text 74.95 (*0-521-39515-1*) Cambridge U Pr.

Measuring the Moment: Strategies of Protest in Eighteenth-Century Afro-English Writing. Keith A. Sandiford. LC 86-63364. 1988. 32.50 (*0-941664-79-1*) Susquehanna U Pr.

*__Measuring the Music: Another Look at the Contemporary Christian Music Debate.__ John Makujin. 304p. 2000. pap. 14.99 (*0-88019-403-0*) Schmul Pub Co.

Measuring the Nation's Wealth: Proceedings. Conference on Research in Income & Wealth. LC 75-19737. (National Bureau of Economic Research Ser.). (Illus.). 1975. reprint ed. 70.95 (*0-405-07614-2*) Ayer.

*__Measuring the Natural Environment.__ Ian C. Strangeways. LC 99-18381. (Illus.). 374p. (C). 2000. 74.95 (*0-521-57310-6*) Cambridge U Pr.

*__Measuring the Night Vol. 1: Evolutionary Astrology & the Keys to the Soul.__ Steven Forrest & Jeffrey W. Green. Ed. by Jodie Forrest. (Illus.). 396p. 2000. pap. 19.95 (*0-9649113-3-7*) Seven Paws.

*__Measuring the Night Vol. 2: Evolutionary Astrology & the Keys to the Soul.__ Steven Forrest & Jeffrey Wolf Green. Ed. by Jodie Forrest. (Illus.). 400p. 2001. pap. 19.95 (*0-9649113-4-5*) Seven Paws.

Measuring the Performance of Human Service Programs. Lawrence L. Martin & Peter M. Kettner. LC 95-41794. (Human Services Guides Ser.: Vol. 71). 139p. 1996. 42.00 (*0-8039-7134-6*); pap. 18.95 (*0-8039-7135-4*) Sage.

*__Measuring the Performance of Interlibrary Loan Operations in North America Research & College Libraries.__ Mary Jackson. (Illus.). 122p. 1998. reprint ed. pap. 45.00 (*0-918006-33-3*) Assn Res Lib.

Measuring the Prices of Medical Treatments. Jack E. Triplett. LC 99-6229. 1999. 54.95 (*0-8157-8344-2*); pap. text 22.95 (*0-8157-8343-4*) Brookings.

Measuring the Productivity of Commercial Banks: Algorithms & PC Programs, Marvin E. Mundel. 100p. 1987. pap. 23.95 (*0-527-91641-2*, 916412) Productivity Inc.

Measuring the Quality of Education. Ed. by Paul Vedder. vi, 167p. 1992. pap. 38.00 (*90-265-1259-7*) Swets.

*__Measuring the Quality of Health Care.__ 42p. 1999. 12.00 (*0-309-06387-6*) Natl Acad Pr.

Measuring the Quality of Schools. (ENG & FRE.). 240p. (Orig.). 1995. pap. 29.00 (*92-64-04355-1*, Pub. by Org for Econ) OECD.

Measuring the Quantum State of Light. Ulf Leonhardt. LC 96-44409. (Studies in Modern Optics: Vol. 22). (Illus.). 202p. (C). 1997. text 59.95 (*0-521-49730-2*) Cambridge U Pr.

An Asterisk (*) at the beginning of an entry indicates that the title is appearing for the first time.

Measuring the Real World: A Textbook in Applied Statistical Methods. Heiner Thiessen. LC 96-21458. 296p. 1996. pap. 54.95 (*0-471-96874-9*) Wiley.

Measuring the Risk of Financial Institutions' Portfolios: Some Suggestions for Alternative Techniques Using Stock Prices. fac. ed. S. G. Hall & D. K. Miles. LC HG0136.D57. (Bank of England, Discussion Papers: No. 33). 48p. 1994. pap. 30.00 (*0-7837-7645-4*, 204739800007) Bks Demand.

*__Measuring the Science & Engineering Enterprise: Priorities for the Division of Science Resources Studies.__ National Research Council Staff. 160p. 2000. pap. 34.75 (*0-309-06892-4*) Natl Acad Pr.

*__Measuring the Size of Things in the Universe: HBT Interferometry & Heavy Ion Physics.__ Ed. by S. Costa et al. 500p. 1999. 128.00 (*981-02-4038-4*) World Scientific Pub.

Measuring the Social Impact of Natural Resource Policies. William R. Burch & Donald R. DeLucca. LC 83-12378. 232p. reprint ed. pap. 72.00 (*0-7837-5858-8*, 204557700006) Bks Demand.

Measuring the Software Process: A Practical Guide to Functional Measurements. David Garmus & David Herron. 235p. (C). 1995. 53.33 (*0-13-349002-5*) P-H.

Measuring the Universe: Cosmic Dimensions from Aristarchus to Halley. Albert Van Helden. LC 84-16397. (Illus.). viii, 212p. 1986. pap. text 12.95 (*0-226-84882-5*) U Ch Pr.

Measuring the Universe: Cosmic Dimensions from Aristarchus to Halley. Albert Van Helden. LC 84-16397. (Illus.). 211p. reprint ed. pap. 65.50 (*0-8357-8947-0*, 205675500085) Bks Demand.

Measuring the Universe: Our Historic Quest to Chart the horizons of Space & Time. Kitty Ferguson. LC 99-19476. (Illus.). 272p. 1999. 24.00 (*0-8027-1351-3*) Walker & Co.

*__Measuring the Universe: Our Historic Quset to Chart the Horizons of Space & Time.__ Kitty Ferguson. 2000. pap. 14.95 (*0-8027-7592-6*) Walker & Co.

Measuring the Universe: The Cosmological Distance Ladder. Stephen Webb. LC 98-43764. (Series in Astronomy & Astrophysics). xvi, 360p. 1999. 44.95 (*1-85233-106-2*) Spr-Verlag.

Measuring the Unmeasurable: Analysis of Qualitative Spatial Data. Ed. by Peter Nijkamp & Helga Leitner. Tr. by Neil Wrigley. 1985. lib. bdg. 306.50 (*90-247-3124-0*) Kluwer Academic.

Measuring the Value of Information Technology. John Hares & Duncan Royle. 280p. 1994. 120.00 (*0-471-94307-X*) Wiley.

Measuring the Water Status of Plants & Soils. John S. Boyer. LC 95-10872. (Illus.). 178p. 1995. 32.00 (*0-12-122260-8*) Acad Pr.

Measuring the Wealth of Nations: The Political Economy of National Accounts. Anwar M. Shaikh & E. Ahmet Tonak. LC 93-37399. (Illus.). 400p. (C). 1994. text 69.95 (*0-521-41424-5*) Cambridge U Pr.

Measuring the Wealth of Nations: The Political Economy of National Accounts. Anwar M. Shaikh & E. Ahmet Tonak. LC 97-106415. (Illus.). 400p. 1996. pap. text 28.95 (*0-521-56479-4*) Cambridge U Pr.

Measuring the Yield Strength of Pipe in the Mill Expander. Battelle Columbus Laboratories Staff et al. 62p. 1973. pap. 4.00 (*0-318-12654-0*, L22273) Am Gas Assn.

Measuring Thinking Skills in the Classroom. Richard J. Stiggins et al. 32p. 1988. pap. 8.95 (*0-8106-0211-3*) NEA.

Measuring Time. Margie Burton et al. Ed. by Susan Evento. (Early Connections Ser.). 16p. (J). (gr. k-2). 1998. pap. 4.25 (*1-892393-42-5*) Benchmark Educ.

Measuring Time. David Chorlton. (Dog River Review Poetry Ser.: No. 8). 30p. (Orig.). 1990. pap. 4.00 (*0-916155-12-9*) Trout Creek.

Measuring Time: Complete Unit. National Science Resources Center Staff. (Science & Technology for Children Ser.). (Illus.). (Orig.). (YA). (gr. 6 up). 1994. pap. text. write for info. (*0-89278-706-6*) Carolina Biological.

Measuring Time Student Activity Book. National Science Resources Center Staff. (Science & Technology for Children Ser.). (Illus.). 65p. (YA). (gr. 6 up). 1994. pap. text, student ed. write for info. (*0-89278-708-2*) Carolina Biological.

Measuring Time Teacher's Guide. National Science Resources Center Staff. (Science & Technology for Children Ser.). 179p. (YA). (gr. 6 up). 1994. pap. text, teacher ed. write for info. (*0-89278-707-4*) Carolina Biological.

*__Measuring to the Nearest Inch.__ Robert W. Skarlinski. 25p. (J). 1998. 6.95 (*1-58532-080-3*) Basic Ed Materials.

*__Measuring to the Nearest 1/8 Inch.__ Robert W. Skarlinski. 25p. (J). 1998. 6.95 (*1-58532-083-8*) Basic Ed Materials.

*__Measuring to the Nearest 1/2 Inch.__ Robert W. Skarlinski. 25p. (J). 1998. 6.95 (*1-58532-081-1*) Basic Ed Materials.

*__Measuring to the Nearest 1/4 Inch.__ Robert W. Skarlinski. 25p. (J). 1998. 6.95 (*1-58532-082-X*) Basic Ed Materials.

*__Measuring to the Nearest 1/16 Inch.__ Robert W. Skarlinski. 25p. (J). 1998. 6.95 (*1-58532-084-6*) Basic Ed Materials.

Measuring Tools Explained. Leo Rizzo. LC 73-732668. 1972. student ed. 7.00 (*0-8064-0223-7*, 503) Bergwall.

Measuring Total Productivity in Manufacturing Organization: Algorithms & PC Programs. Marvin E. Mundel. 155p. 1987. pap. 27.95 (*0-527-91625-0*, 916250) Productivity Inc.

Measuring Tourism Performance. Tzung-Cheng Huan & Joseph O'Leary. (Advances in Tourism Applications Ser.: Vol. 1). (Illus.). 224p. 1999. pap. 16.95 (*1-57167-260-5*) Sagamore Pub.

Measuring Transactions Between World Areas. Herbert B. Wooley. LC 75-19739. (National Bureau of Economic Research Ser.). (Illus.). 1975. reprint ed. 18.95 (*0-405-07616-9*) Ayer.

Measuring Transactions Between World Areas. Herbert B. Woolley. (Studies in International Economic Relations: No. 3). 175p. 1966. reprint ed. 45.50 (*0-87014-155-4*) Natl Bur Econ Res.

Measuring Trees & Forests. 2nd ed. M. S. Philip. 336p. (Orig.). 1994. pap. text 55.00 (*0-85198-883-0*) OUP.

Measuring Trends in U. S. Income Inequality: Theory & Applications. Ed. by H. K. Ryu & D. J. Slottje. LC 98-3099. (Lecture Notes in Economics & Mathematical Systems Ser.: Vol. 459). (Illus.). xi, 195p. 1998. pap. 61.00 (*3-540-64229-3*) Spr-Verlag.

Measuring, Understanding, & Predicting Exposures in the 21st Century. Ed. by Edo Pellizzari et al. (Journal of Exposure Analysis & Environmental Epidemiology Ser.: Vol. 2, Suppl. 1). (Illus.). 244p. 1992. 65.00 (*0-911131-84-1*) Specialist Journals.

Measuring, Understanding, & Predicting Exposures in the 21st Century. Ed. by Edo Pellizzari et al. (Journal of Exposure Analysis & Environmental Epidemiology Ser.: Vol. 2, Suppl. 2). (Illus.). 204p. 1992. 65.00 (*0-911131-83-3*) Specialist Journals.

Measuring Union Climate. Shervin Freed & Joseph Lichko. LC 81-66402. 332p. 1981. 10.95 (*0-910436-20-7*) Conway Data.

Measuring Up. J. E. Osborne. (Early Math Big Bks.). (Illus.). 16p. (J). (ps-2). Date not set. pap. 16.95 (*1-56784-428-6*) Newbridge Educ.

Measuring Up: Assessment Tools for Volunteer Programs. Steve McCurley & Sue Vineyard. 72p. (Orig.). 1997. pap. 17.95 (*0-911029-48-6*) Heritage Arts.

*__Measuring Up: Challenges Minorities Face in Educational Assessment__ Arie L. Nettles & Michael T. Nettles. LC 99-12925. (Evaluation in Education & Human Services Ser.). xvi, 266p. 1999. write for info. (*0-7923-8401-6*) Kluwer Academic.

Measuring Up: Experiments, Puzzles & Games Exploring Measurement. Sandra Markle. LC 94-19240. (Illus.). 48p. (J). (gr. 3-7). 1995. 17.00 (*0-689-31904-5*) Atheneum Yung Read.

Measuring Up: Governing's Guide to Performance Measurement for Geniuses (And Other Public Managers) Jonathan Walters. LC 98-40498. 1998. pap. 14.95 (*1-56802-458-4*) Congr Quarterly.

Measuring Up: Prototypes for Mathematics Assessment. Mathematical Sciences Education Board Staff & National Research Council Staff. LC 92-62904. (Illus.). 176p. (Orig.). 1993. pap. text 10.95 (*0-309-04845-1*) Natl Acad Pr.

Measuring Up: Standards, Assessment, & School Reform. Robert Rothman. LC 94-43300. (Education Ser.). 240p. 1995. 27.95 (*0-7879-0055-9*) Jossey-Bass.

Measuring Up: The Performance Ethic in American Culture. James Mannon. LC 97-16789. 176p. (C). 1997. pap. text 18.00 (*0-8133-3297-4*, Pub. by Westview) HarpC.

Measuring Up: The Promises & Pitfalls of Performance Indicators in Higher Education. Gerald Gaither et al. Ed. & Frwd. by Jonathan D. Fife. LC 95-79711. (ASHE-ERIC Higher Education Reports: No. 94-5). 100p. (C). 1995. pap. 24.00 (*1-878380-61-3*) GWU Grad Schl E&HD.

Measuring Up: Toward a Common Framework for Tracking Corporate Environmental Performance. Daryl Ditz & Janet Ranganathan. LC 97-80030. 48p. 1997. pap. 20.00 (*1-56973-225-6*) World Resources Inst.

Measuring up to the Baldrige: A Quick & Easy Self-Assessment Guide for Organizations of All Sizes. Donald C. Fisher. LC 94-22220. 240p. 1994. 26.95 (*0-8144-0256-9*) AMACOM.

Measuring up to the Challenge: What Standards & Assessment Can Do for Arts Education. Ed. by Ruth Mitchell. LC 94-31023. 200p. 1994. pap. 19.95 (*1-879903-20-2*) Am for the Arts.

*__Measuring Violence Related Attitudes, Beliefs & Behaviors Among Youths: Assessment Tools.__ Linda L. Dahlberg. 272p. 1998. per. 21.00 (*0-16-061505-4*) USGPO.

Measuring Water Quality. Vinvent Kerry Smith. 1986. lib. bdg. 171.50 (*0-89838-181-9*) Kluwer Academic.

Measuring Weight & Time. Andrew King. LC 98-4229. (Math for Fun Ser.). 32p. (J). (gr. 2-4). 1998. 20.90 (*0-7613-0854-7*, Copper Beech Bks); pap. 5.95 (*0-7613-0748-6*, Copper Beech Bks) Millbrook Pr.

Measuring Welfare Changes & Tax Burdens. John Creedy. LC 98-17082. 221p. 1998. 80.00 (*1-85898-921-3*) E Elgar.

Measuring What Counts: A Conceptual Guide for Mathematics Assessment. National Research Council, Mathematical Sciences E. 236p. 1993. pap. text 17.95 (*0-309-04981-4*) Natl Acad Pr.

Measuring What Counts: A Policy Brief. National Research Council, Mathematical Sciences E. 32p. 1993. pap. text 3.95 (*0-309-04986-5*) Natl Acad Pr.

Measuring What People Know: Human Capital Accounting for the Knowledge Economy. OECD Staff. LC 96-181863. 114p. (Orig.). 1996. pap. 29.00 (*92-64-14778-0*, Pub. by Org for Econ) OECD.

Measuring What Students Learn. LC 95-223640. 231p. (Orig.). 1995. pap. 27.00 (*92-64-04358-6*, Pub. by Org for Econ) OECD.

Measuring Your Media Profile. Dermot McKeone. 250p. 1996. 78.95 (*0-566-07578-4*, Pub. by Gower) Ashgate Pub Co.

Measuring Your Performance see Designing & Applying Recognised Technologies

*__Measurit: Achieving Profitable Training.__ Marsha Mondschein. 280p. 1999. pap. 39.95 (*1-58597-006-9*) Leathers Pub.

*__Meat: Le Cordon Bleu: Techniques & Recipes.__ Jeni Wright & Eric Treuille. 54p. 2000. reprint ed. pap. 15.00 (*0-7881-9289-2*) DIANE Pub.

Meat: Proceedings. Easter School in Agricultural Science (21st: 1974:. Ed. by D. J. Cole & R. A. Lawrie. LC 76-375957. 608p. reprint ed. pap. 188.50 (*0-608-14847-4*, 202574200046) Bks Demand.

Meat: True Homosexual Experiences from S. T. H., Vol. 1. Ed. by Boyd McDonald. (STH Ser.). (Illus.). 192p. 1994. reprint ed. pap. 14.95 (*0-917342-78-X*) Gay Sunshine.

Meat & Dairy. E. Rosenberg. 1991. 18.99 (*0-89906-898-7*); pap. 15.99 (*0-89906-899-5*) Mesorah Pubns.

Meat & Game: Sauces & Base, Planning, Execution, Display & Decoration for Buffets & Receptions. Denis Ruffel. (Professional Caterer Ser.). 320p. 1997. text 69.95 (*0-470-25010-0*) Halsted Pr.

Meat & Health: Index of Modern Information with Bibliography. Thomas W. Pollock. LC 88-47788. 150p. (Orig.). 1988. 47.50 (*0-88164-900-7*); pap. 44.50 (*0-88164-901-5*) ABBE Pubs Assn.

Meat & Potatoes. Judith Choate. 128p. 1992. 15.00 (*0-385-25306-0*) Doubleday.

Meat & Potatoes: Home-Cooked Favorites from Perfect Pot Roast to Chocolate Cream Pie. Judith Choate. (American Kitchen Classics Ser.). (Illus.). 128p. 1992. 20.00 (*0-671-73548-9*) S&S Trade.

Meat & Potatoes: The Essential Cookbook. Luisa M. Scott. 1993. 10.98 (*0-88365-811-9*) Galahad Bks.

Meat & Potatoes of Breastfeeding: Easy Nutritional Guidelines for Breastfeeding Moms. Jill Dally. Ed. by Nicholas S. Dalley. LC 97-141808. (Illus.). 220p. (Orig.). 1997. pap. 14.95 (*0-9652008-0-9*) Footprint Pr.

Meat & Poultry. (French Delicacies Ser.). 1999. 29.95 (*3-8290-2744-3*) Konemann.

Meat & Poultry. Fabien Bellahsen & Daniel Rouche. (Eurodelices Ser.). (Illus.). 330p. 1998. 29.95 (*3-8290-1132-6*, 520377) Konemann.

Meat & Poultry Inspection Directory. Government Printing Office Staff. per. 33.00 (*0-16-009370-8*, Agriculture Dept) USGPO.

Meat & Poultry Inspection Regulations: Meat Inspection, Poultry Inspection, Rabbit Inspection, Voluntary Inspection & Certification Service of Meat & Poultry Inspection, Administrative Procedure. Government Printing Office Staff. 1986. ring bd. 258.00 (*0-16-016434-6*, Agriculture Dept) USGPO.

*__Meat & Protein Group.__ Helen Frost. LC 99-47744. (Food Guide Pyramid Ser.). 24p. (J). (ps-2). 2000. lib. bdg. 13.25 (*0-7368-0539-7*, Pebble Bks) Capstone Pr.

Meat Business: Devouring a Hungry Planet. Ed. by Joyce D'Silva & Geoff Tansey. LC 99-30053. 249p. 1999. text 45.00 (*0-312-22686-1*) St Martin.

Meat Buyers Guide. North American Meat Processors Association Staff. (Illus.). 218p. (Orig.). (C). 1991. reprint ed. pap. text 49.00 (*1-878154-00-1*) N Am Meat Process.

Meat Click. Robin Crozier & John M. Bennett. 1980. pap. 2.00 (*0-935350-02-0*) Luna Bisonte.

*__Meat Cuts & Muscle Foods: An International Glossary.__ Howard J. Swatland. 250p. 2000. pap. 120.00 (*1-897676-30-1*, Pub. by Nottingham Univ Pr) St Mut.

Meat Cutter. Jack Rudman. (Career Examination Ser.: C-516). 1994. pap. 27.95 (*0-8373-0516-0*) Nat Learn.

Meat Cutting: Testbook, Pt. 1. California Department of Education Staff. (Apprenticeship Instructional Materials Ser.). 88p. 1981. pap. 3.50 (*0-8011-0578-1*) Calif Education.

Meat Cutting: Testbook, Pt. 2. California Department of Education Staff. (Apprenticeship Instructional Materials Ser.). 96p. 1982. pap. 3.75 (*0-8011-0581-1*) Calif Education.

Meat Cutting: Workbook, Pt. 1. California Department of Education Staff. (Apprenticeship Instructional Materials Ser.). (Illus.). 160p. 1981. pap. 4.75 (*0-8011-0577-3*) Calif Education.

Meat Cutting: Workbook, Pt. 2. California Department of Education Staff. (Apprenticeship Instructional Materials Ser.). (Illus.). 144p. 1982. pap. 5.25 (*0-8011-0580-3*) Calif Education.

Meat Dictionary in Four Languages: English, French, German & Spanish. 2nd ed. Werner Frey. (ENG, FRE, GER & SPA.). 1995. 295.00 (*0-320-03692-8*) Fr & Eur.

Meat Dip: Fifteen Labels. John M. Bennett. 1976. pap. 3.00 (*0-935350-79-9*) Luna Bisonte.

Meat Eaters Arrive. Suzan Reid. (Illus.). 32p. (J). (ps-3). 1996. pap. 4.95 (*1-55209-004-3*) Firefly Bks Ltd.

Meat Eaters Arrive. Suzan Reid & Linda Hendry. (Tell Me a Story Ser.). (Illus.). 32p. (J). pap. 12.99 incl. audio (*0-590-24540-6*) Scholastic Inc.

Meat-Eating: A Cause of Disease. Raymond W. Bernard. 1996. spiral bd. 10.00 (*0-7873-1007-7*) Hlth Research.

*__Meat-Eating Dinosaurs: The Theropods.__ Thom Holmes & Laurie Holmes. LC 00-9329. (Dinosaur Library). (Illus.). (J). 2001. write for info. (*0-7660-1452-5*) Enslow Pubs.

Meat-Eating Plants. Nathan Aaseng. LC 95-3827. (Weird & Wacky Science Ser.). (Illus.). 48p. (J). (gr. 4-10). 1996. lib. bdg. 18.95 (*0-89490-617-8*) Enslow Pubs.

Meat Freezing: A Source Book. B. W. Berry et al. (Developments in Food Science Ser.: No. 20). viii,386p. 1989. 218.50 (*0-444-87463-1*) Elsevier.

Meat Goats of Caston Creek: A Tale of Whimsy & Wisdom Gleaned from Raising Meat Goats under Range Conditions. Sylvia Tomlinson. (Illus.). 200p. 1999. pap. write for info. (*0-7392-0236-7*, PO3278) Morris Pubng.

Meat Hygiene. 4th ed. James A. Libby. LC 73-14959. 670p. reprint ed. pap. 200.00 (*0-608-16680-4*, 205618900055) Bks Demand.

Meat Hygiene. 10th ed. Ed. by J. F. Gracey et al. (Illus.). 550p. 1999. text 69.00 (*0-7020-2253-5*, Pub. by W B Saunders) Saunders.

Meat Industry Safety Guidelines. 2nd ed. National Safety Council Staff. LC 78-52082. (Illus.). 112p. reprint ed. pap. 34.80 (*0-7837-0579-4*, 204092300019) Bks Demand.

Meat Inspector. Jack Rudman. (Career Examination Ser.: C-517). 1994. pap. 27.95 (*0-8373-0517-9*) Nat Learn.

Meat Inspector-Poultry Inspector. Jack Rudman. (Career Examination Ser.: C-513). 1994. pap. 29.95 (*0-8373-0513-6*) Nat Learn.

Meat Inspector Trainee. Jack Rudman. (Career Examination Ser.: C-518). 1994. pap. 23.95 (*0-8373-0518-7*) Nat Learn.

Meat Is Murder! An Illustrated Guide to Cannibal Culture. Mikita Brottman. (Creation Cinema Collection: Vol. 9). (Illus.). 224p. 1998. pap. 19.95 (*1-871592-90-9*) Creation Books.

Meat Loaf: Bat Out of Hell. (Piano-Vocal-Guitar Ser.). (Illus.). 80p. 1991. per. 14.95 (*0-7935-0765-0*, 00308103) H Leonard.

Meat Loaf: Bat Out of Hell II. 96p. 1993. otabind 16.95 (*0-7935-3024-5*, 00308217) H Leonard.

Meat Lovers: Step-by-Step Guide for the Meat Connoisseur. Brice Peterson. LC 94-65052. 320p. (Orig.). 1998. 29.95 (*1-884573-02-9*); pap. 19.95 (*1-884573-17-7*) S-By-S Pubns.

Meat Lover's Vegetarian Cookbook. Steven Ferry & Tanya Petrovna. LC 96-42379. 192p. (Orig.). 1997. pap. 12.95 (*0-87573-070-1*) Jain Pub Co.

Meat Management & Operations. Edward M. Harwell et al. LC 74-21115. (Illus.). 366p. 1990. pap. 29.95 (*0-912016-45-0*) Lebhar Friedman.

Meat Market: The Inside Story of the NFL Draft. Richard Whittingham. LC 92-13411. 1992. write for info. (*0-00-262766-3*) Macmillan.

*__Meat Market Man.__ George Wilson. 2000. reprint ed. pap. 5.95 (*1-930535-04-X*) Star Dists.

*__Meat, Metal & Fire: The Legendary Australian Barbecue.__ Mark Thompson. (Illus.). 208p. 2000. pap. 15.95 (*0-207-19768-7*) CARP.

Meat Microbiology. Ed. by M. H. Brown. (Illus.). 528p. 1982. 88.25 (*0-85334-138-9*, I-305-82) Elsevier.

Meat Pies & Puddings. Anne Chamberlain. (Illus.). 96p. (Orig.). 1979. pap. 9.95 (*0-572-01039-7*) Trans-Atl Phila.

Meat Preservation: Preventing Losses & Assuring Safety. Robert G. Cassens. LC 94-70368. (Publications in Food & Nutrition). 133p. 1994. 72.00 (*0-917678-34-6*) Food & Nut Pr.

*__Meat Processing Equipment in Australia: A Strategic Entry Report, 1996.__ Compiled by Icon Group International Staff. (Illus.). 139p. 1999. ring bd. 1390.00 incl. audio compact disk (*0-7418-1230-4*) Icon Grp.

*__Meat Processing Equipment in Canada: A Strategic Entry Report, 1999.__ Compiled by Icon Group International. (Illus.). 150p. 1999. ring bd. 1500.00 incl. audio compact disk (*0-7418-1826-4*) Icon Grp.

*__Meat Processing Equipment in Colombia: A Strategic Entry Report, 1996.__ Compiled by Icon Group International Staff. (Illus.). 182p. 1999. ring bd. 1820.00 incl. audio compact disk (*0-7418-1231-2*) Icon Grp.

*__Meat Processing Equipment in Poland: A Strategic Entry Report, 1996.__ Compiled by Icon Group International Staff. (Illus.). 184p. 1999. ring bd. 1840.00 incl. audio compact disk (*0-7418-1232-0*) Icon Grp.

Meat Rack. Ed. by John W. Dagion. (True Revelations & Strange Happenings Ser.: Vol. 6). 160p. (Orig.). 1992. pap. 12.95 (*0-943595-34-7*) Leyland Pubns.

Meat Refrigeration: Why & How. Ed. by S. J. James & C. James. 512p. Date not set. pap. 270.00 (*1-85573-442-7*) Am Educ Systs.

Meat Science. R. A. Lawrie. (C). 1985. text 74.00 (*0-08-030790-6*, Pergamon Pr); pap. text 42.00 (*0-08-030789-2*, Pergamon Pr) Elsevier.

Meat Science. 5th ed. R. A. Lawrie. (Food Science Ser.). (Illus.). 312p. (C). 1991. text 66.95 (*0-08-040824-9*, Prgamon Press); pap. text 62.95 (*0-08-040825-7*, Prgamon Press) Buttrwrth-Heinemann.

*__Meat Science: An Introductory Text.__ P. D. Warriss. LC 99-48373. 240p. 2000. write for info. (*0-85199-424-5*) OUP.

Meat Science & Processing. Joseph Sebranek. 1994. spiral bd. 26.00 (*0-88252-151-9*) Paladin Hse.

Meat Science & Technology Proceedings: An International Symposium. Ed. by Kenneth R. Franklin & H. Russell Cross. 398p. 1983. 7.00 (*0-88700-000-2*) Natl Live Stock.

Meat Science, Milk Science & Technology. Ed. by H. R. Cross & A. J. Overby. (World Animal Science Ser.: Vol. B3). xiv,458p. 1988. 344.00 (*0-444-42578-0*) Elsevier.

Meat Substitution Cookbook: Nutritional Foods that Can Be Prepared to Taste Like Meat. rev. ed. Ed. by Bibliotheca Press Staff. 50p. 1998. ring bd. 25.95 (*0-939476-60-6*) Prosperity & Profits.

Meat, Trilingual Dictionary. Werner Frey. (ENG, FRE & GER.). 293p. 1989. 295.00 (*0-7859-9995-7*) Fr & Eur.

Meat Watch. John M. Bennett. 1977. pap. 3.00 (*0-935350-80-2*) Luna Bisonte.

Meat Watch. deluxe limited ed. John M. Bennett. 1977. pap. 5.00 (*0-935350-81-0*) Luna Bisonte.

*__Meat We Eat.__ 14th ed. John R. Romans et al. (Illus.). xvi, 1200p. 2001. 93.25 (*0-8134-3175-1*) Interstate.

Meatball. Phyllis Hoffman. LC 89-49425. (Charlotte Zolotow Bk.). (Illus.). 32p. (J). (ps-2). 1991. 14.95 (*0-06-022563-7*) HarpC Child Bks.

Meatball. Phyllis Hoffman. LC 89-49425. (Charlotte Zolotow Bk.). (Illus.). 32p. (J). (ps-2). 1991. lib. bdg. 14.89 (*0-06-022564-5*) HarpC Child Bks.

Meatiest Corpse in Town. Mike Halchin. (Illus.). 45p. (Orig.). 1996. pap. 4.00 (*1-886206-17-1*) Venom Pr.

Meatless Burgers. Louise Hagler. LC 99-40523. (Illus.). 96p. 1999. pap. text 9.95 (*1-57067-087-0*) Book Pub Co.

*****Meatless Cuisine: Over 60 Simple Recipes for Elegant Home Cooking.** Time-Life Books Staff. LC 00-23458. (Culinary Classics). (Illus.). 96p. 2000. 12.95 (*0-7370-2056-3*) Time-Life Educ.

Meatless Days. Sara Suleri. LC 88-29517. (Illus.). vi, 192p. 1991. pap. 12.00 (*0-226-77981-5*) U Ch Pr.

Meatless Days. Sara Suleri. LC 88-29517. (Illus.). vi, 192p. 1998. 21.95 (*0-226-77980-7*) U Ch Pr.

Meatless Diabetic Cookbook: Over 100 Easy Recipes Combining. Barbara Grunes. LC 97-19463. 224p. 1997. per. 14.00 (*0-7615-1019-2*) Prima Pub.

Meatless Dishes in Twenty Minutes. Karen A. Levin. 144p. 1993. pap. 9.95 (*0-8092-3810-1*, 381010, Contemporary Bks) NTC Contemp Pub Co.

Meatless Galley Cookbook. Anne Carlson. LC 95-30807. (Illus.). 192p. 1995. pap. 16.95 (*0-9639566-2-0*) Seaworthy WI.

Meatless Gourmet: Easy Lowfat Favorites. Bobbie Hinman. 512p. 1996. pap. 18.95 (*0-7615-0059-6*) Prima Pub.

Meatless Gourmet: Favorite Recipes from Around the World. Bobbie Hinman. LC 94-21794. (Illus.). 496p. 1994. pap. 16.00 (*1-55958-559-5*) Prima Pub.

Meatless Indian Cooking from the Curry Club: Over 150 Delicious Dishes. Pat Chapman. LC 94-39442. (Illus.). 192p. 1995. pap. 26.95 (*1-55958-690-7*) Prima Pub.

Meatless Main Dishes. Time-Life Books Editors. Ed. by Catherine Hackett. LC 96-33475. (Great Taste, Low Fat Ser.). (Illus.). 160p. (gr. 7). 1999. spiral bd. 14.95 (*0-7835-4562-2*) Time-Life.

Meatless Meals. large type ed. pap. 5.50 (*0-317-01856-6*) Cath Guild Blind.

Meatless Meals for Working People: Quick & Easy Vegetarian Recipes. 2nd rev. ed. Debra Wasserman. (Illus.). 192p. 1998. pap. 12.00 (*0-931411-19-X*) Vegetarian Resc.

Meatless Mexican Home Cooking. Zaslavsky. 240p. 1998. pap. 15.95 (*0-312-20078-1*) St Martin.

Meatless Mexican Home Cooking. Nancy Zaslavsky. 1996. 25.95 (*0-614-19385-0*) St Martin.

Meatless Mexican Home Cooking. Nancy Zaslavsky. LC 96-27461. (Illus.). 224p. 1997. text 25.95 (*0-312-15170-5*) St Martin.

Meatmen: An Anthology of Gay Male Comics. Ed. by Winston Leyland. (Meatmen Comics Ser.: Vol. 16). (Illus.). 160p. 1995. pap. 15.95 (*0-943595-44-4*) Leyland Pubns.

Meatmen: An Anthology of Gay Male Comics. Ed. by Winston Leyland. (Comics Antholoby Ser.: Vol. 17). (Illus.). 160p. 1995. pap. 16.95 (*0-943595-50-9*) Leyland Pubns.

Meatmen: An Anthology of Gay Male Comics, 5. Ed. by Winston Leyland. (Illus.). 1989. pap. 14.95 (*0-943595-15-0*) Leyland Pubns.

Meatmen: An Anthology of Gay Male Comics, 6. Ed. by Winston Leyland. (Illus.). 1989. pap. 14.95 (*0-943595-20-7*) Leyland Pubns.

Meatmen: An Anthology of Gay Male Comics, 8. Ed. by Winston Leyland. (Illus.). 1990. pap. 13.95 (*0-943595-23-1*) Leyland Pubns.

Meatmen: An Anthology of Gay Male Comics, 9. Ed. by Winston Leyland. (Illus.). 1990. pap. 14.95 (*0-943595-24-X*) Leyland Pubns.

Meatmen: An Anthology of Gay Male Comics, 10. Ed. by Winston Leyland. (Illus.). 1991. pap. 14.95 (*0-943595-27-4*) Leyland Pubns.

Meatmen: An Anthology of Gay Male Comics, 11. Ed. by Winston Leyland. (Illus.). 1991. pap. 14.95 (*0-943595-28-2*) Leyland Pubns.

Meatmen: An Anthology of Gay Male Comics, 12. Ed. by Winston Leyland. (Illus.). 1991. pap. 15.95 (*0-943595-29-0*) Leyland Pubns.

Meatmen: An Anthology of Gay Male Comics, Vol. 1. 2nd ed. Ed. by Winston Leyland. (Illus.). 192p. 1996. reprint ed. pap. 16.95 (*0-917342-23-2*) Leyland Pubns.

Meatmen: An Anthology of Gay Male Comics, Vol. 14. Ed. by Winston Leyland. (Illus.). 160p. 1993. pap. 15.95 (*0-943595-35-5*) Leyland Pubns.

Meatmen: An Anthology of Gay Male Comics, Vol. 15. Ed. by Winston Leyland. (Illus.). 160p. 1993. pap. 15.95 (*0-943595-38-X*) Leyland Pubns.

Meatmen: An Anthology of Gay Male Comics, Vol. 18. Ed. by Winston Leyland. (Illus.). 160p. 1996. pap. 16.95 (*0-943595-53-3*) Leyland Pubns.

Meatmen: An Anthology of Gay Male Comics, Vol. 21. Ed. by Winston Leyland. (Illus.). 160p. 1997. pap. 16.95 (*0-943595-68-1*) Leyland Pubns.

Meatmen: An Anthology of Gay Male Comics, Vol. 23. Winston Leyland. 1999. pap. text 16.95 (*0-943595-76-2*) Leyland Pubns.

Meatmen: Anthology of Gay Male Comics, Vol. 2. Winston Leyland. (Anthology of Gay Male Comics Ser.). 1996. pap. text 16.95 (*0-943595-04-5*) Leyland Pubns.

Meatmen: Anthology of Gay Male Comics, Vol. 19. Ed. by Winston Leyland. (Anthology of Gay Male Comics Ser.). 1996. pap. text 16.95 (*0-943595-60-6*) Leyland Pubns.

Meatmen: Anthology of Gay Male Comics, Vol. 20. Ed. by Winston Leyland. (Illus.). 160p. 1997. pap. 16.95 (*0-943595-63-0*) Leyland Pubns.

Meatmen: Special Edition, Vol. 24. Winston Leyland. 2000. pap. text 16.95 (*0-943595-77-0*) Leyland Pubns.

Meatmen Vol. 22: An Anthology of Gay Male Comics. Ed. by Winston Leyland. (Illus.). 160p. 1998. pap. 16.95 (*0-943595-75-4*) Leyland Pubns.

Meatpackers: An Oral History of Black Packinghoue Workers & Their Struggle for Racial & Economic Equality. Rick Halpern & Roger Horowitz. 1996. 28.95 (*0-614-25359-4*) Macmillan.

Meatpackers: An Oral History of Black Packinghouse Workers & Their Struggle for Racial & Economic Equality. Rick Halpern & Roger Horowitz. LC 96-25096. 176p. (gr. 8 up). 1996. 29.95 (*0-8057-9120-5*, Twyne) Mac Lib Ref.

Meatpackers: An Oral History of Black Packinghouse Workers & Their Struggle for Racial & Economic Equality. Rick Halpern & Roger Horowitz. LC 98-48875. 1999. 19.00 (*1-58367-005-X*, Pub. by Monthly Rev) NYU Pr.

Meats see Charaeh Allahem

Meats: Cook Books from Amish Kitchens. Phyllis Pellman Good & Rachel T. Pellman. (From Amish Kitchens Ser.). 32p. 1996. mass mkt. 2.95 (*1-56148-200-5*) Good Bks PA.

Meats, Poultry, & Game. Yves Thuries. 1996. text 89.95 (*0-442-01691-3*, VNR) Wiley.

*****Mebasha Justice-Ordeal by Fire.** Joseph Ginat. 192p. 1999. (*1-898723-15-X*) Intl Spec Bk.

MEC Shotshell Reloading Secrets. Date not set. write for info. (*0-9700392-0-4*) Answer Works.

*****Meca & the Black Oracle.** Paul Masters. LC 98-90911. 1999. pap. 15.95 (*0-533-12983-4*) Vantage.

Mecanica de Fluidos. G. Boxer. (SPA.). 208p. (C). 1994. pap. text 13.66 (*0-201-62550-4*) Addison-Wesley.

Mecanica de Fluidos. 2nd ed. Phillip M. Gerhart. (SPA.). 1120p. (C). 1995. pap. text 31.00 (*0-201-60105-2*) Addison-Wesley.

Mecanica Ingenieria Estatica. 624p. (C). 1995. pap. 31.33 (*0-201-65367-2*) HEPC Inc.

Mecanica Relacional see Relational Mechanics

Mecanicien Anobli Pierre-Joseph Laurent 1713-1773: Des Mines d'Anzin au Canal de Saint Quentin. Louis Thbaut. Ed. by Stuart Bruchey. LC 80-2831. (Dissertations in European Economic History Ser.).Tr. of One Enobled Engineer: Pierre-Joseph Laurent 1713-1773: from the Anzin Coal Mining Company to the Saint-Quentin Underground Canal. (Illus.). 1981. lib. bdg. 60.95 (*0-405-14014-2*) Ayer.

Mecanisme du Fluteur Automate. J. Vaucanson. (FRE.). 75p. 1985. pap. text 29.00 (*2-903928-23-1*) Gordon & Breach.

Mecanismos de las Reacciones Organicas. (Serie de Quimica: No. 4). (SPA.). 1977. pap. 2.00 (*0-8270-6420-9*) OAS.

Mecanografia Al Dia. Maria D. Andujar et al. 96p. (C). 1993. pap. text 7.80 (*0-13-568684-9*) Prentice ESL.

Mecanografia Al Dia. rev. ed. Maria D. Andujar & Jose L. Iglesias. (YA). (gr. 10 up). 1977. pap. text 3.50 (*0-88345-306-1*, 18482) Prentice ESL.

Mecanografia Seglo 21: Curso Avanzado. (SPA.). (C). 1997. pap. 29.00 (*0-673-19299-7*) Addison-Wesley.

Mecanoo: Map 6. Ed. by Annette W. LeCuyer. (Illus.). 1999. pap. 16.50 (*1-891197-05-3*) U Mich Arch.

Mecca. Shahrukh Husain. (Holy Cities Ser.). (Illus.). 47p. (J). (gr. 5-8). 1998. text 15.00 (*0-7881-5853-8*) DIANE Pub.

Mecca. Donald Rawley. LC 91-10123. 108p. (Orig.). 1991. pap. 12.50 (*0-941749-24-X*) Black Tie Pr.

Mecca: A Literary History of the Muslim Holy Land. F. E. Peters. 500p. 1996. 29.95 (*0-614-21159-X*, 769) Kazi Pubns.

Mecca: A Literary History of the Muslim Holy Land. F. E. Peters. LC 94-20923. 504p. 1994. text 35.00 (*0-691-03267-X*, Pub. by Princeton U Pr) Cal Prin Full Svc.

Mecca - The Blessed Medina - The Radiant: The Holiest Cities of Islam. Seyyed Hossein Nasr. (Illus.). 192p. 1997. 76.00 (*0-89381-752-X*) Aperture.

MECCA Factor: 5 Imperatives for a Successful Life. 2nd ed. Tom Ruddell. LC 96-96446. (Illus.). 288p. 1996. 14.95 (*0-9649284-1-8*) Capstar.

Mecca, 1911 Double-Folder Baseball Cards: The Complete Set of 50 in Full Color, Vol. 181. Ed. by Bert R. Sugar. (Sports Ser.). (Illus.). 24p. (Orig.). 1991. pap. 5.95 (*0-486-26756-3*) Dover.

Meccan Trade & Islam: Problems of Origin & Structure. Robert Simon. Tr. by Feodora Sos from HUN. (Bibliotheca Orientalis Hungarica Ser.: Vol. 32). 205p. (C). 1989. 75.00 (*963-05-5292-2*, Pub. by Akade Kiado) St Mut.

Meccan Trade & the Rise of Islam. Patricia Crone. LC 86-42858. 309p. reprint ed. pap. 95.80 (*0-608-06345-2*, 206670700008) Bks Demand.

MECCAnize! Personal Planner. (Illus.). 60p. 1996. ring bd. 12.95 (*0-9649284-2-6*) Capstar.

Meccano Magazine: Anthology. Ed. by Allen Levy. (Hornby Companion Ser.: Vol. 7A). 1072p. 1992. 75.00 (*1-872727-80-8*) Pincushion Pr.

Meccano Magazine, 1916-1981. Joseph Manduca. (Hornby Companion Ser.: Vol. 7). 484p. 1992. 60.00 (*0-904568-37-7*) Pincushion Pr.

Meccano System. Bert Love & Jim Gamble. (Hornby Companion Ser.: Vol. 6). 432p. 1992. 60.00 (*0-904568-36-9*) Pincushion Pr.

Mech. Behavior of Salt. 3rd ed. 75.00 (*0-87849-100-7*, Pub. by Trans T Pub) Enfield Pubs NH.

Mech. Behavior of Salt. 4th ed. 100.00 (*0-87849-103-1*, Pub. by Trans T Pub) Enfield Pubs NH.

Mech-Check. 1996. write for info. (*0-614-16704-3*) ASME.

Mech E for Dynamics Utility & Tutorial Software for IBM Computers to Accompany Engineering Mechanics: Dynamics. I. C. Jong. (Illus.). 1995. text. write for info. incl. disk (*0-03-032604-4*, W B Saunders Co) Harcrt Hlth Sci Grp.

Mech E for Statics: Utility & Tutorial Software for IBM Computers to Accompany Engineering Mechanics: Statics: Disks 1 & 2. I. C. Jong. (Illus.). 1995. text. write for info. (*0-03-032603-6*, W B Saunders Co) Harcrt Hlth Sci Grp.

MECH '91 Australia: Engineering for a Competitive World, Conference 1: Improving the Manufacturing Environment. Intro. by Ian B. Lin. (Illus.). 58p. (Orig.). 1991. pap. 38.50 (*0-85825-525-1*, Pub. by Inst Engrs Aust-EA Bks) Accents Pubns.

MECH '91 Australia: Engineering for a Competitive World, Conference 2: Mechanical Engineering Design - It's Role in Innovation, Quality & Value. Intro. by Noel Svensson. (Illus.). 147p. (Orig.). 1991. pap. 48.00 (*0-85825-526-X*, Pub. by Inst Engrs Aust-EA Bks) Accents Pubns.

MECH '91 Australia: Engineering for a Competitive World, Conference 3: Competitive Manufacturing. Intro. by Frank Swinkels. (Illus.). 118p. (Orig.). 1991. pap. 43.25 (*0-85825-527-8*, Pub. by Inst Engrs Aust-EA Bks) Accents Pubns.

MECH '91 Australia: Engineering for a Competitive World, Conference 5: Cost Effective Bulk Materials Handling. Intro. by John Planner. (Illus.). 107p. (Orig.). 1991. pap. 38.50 (*0-85825-529-4*, Pub. by Inst Engrs Aust-EA Bks) Accents Pubns.

MECH '91 Australia: Engineering for a Competitive World, Conference 6: Maintenance Engineering: Emerging Technologies & a New Professionalism. Intro. by Bertha E. Mahony. (Illus.). 105p. (Orig.). 1991. pap. 38.50 (*0-85825-530-8*, Pub. by Inst Engrs Aust-EA Bks) Accents Pubns.

MECH '91 Australia: Engineering for a Competitive World, Conference 7: Occupational Health & Safety: Engineering the Work Environment. Intro. by Mike Stevenson. (Illus.). 89p. (Orig.). 1991. pap. 43.25 (*0-85825-531-6*, Pub. by Inst Engrs Aust-EA Bks) Accents Pubns.

MECH '91 Australia: Engineering in a Competitive World, Conference 4: Energy: Resources, Usage, Conservation & the Environment. Intro. by Brian Milton. (Illus.). 163p. 1991. pap. 48.00 (*0-85825-528-6*, Pub. by Inst Engrs Aust-EA Bks) Accents Pubns.

Mech Warrior 2: The Official Strategy Guide, Vol. 1. Joe G. Bell. 1995. pap. text 19.95 (*1-55958-723-7*) Prima Pub.

Mecham, Arizona's Fighting Governor: A Constitutional Conflict "Freedom of the Press" or Political Assassination. Sammy S. Jenkins, Sr. 302p. (C). 1988. 17.95 (*0-317-91290-9*); pap. 10.95 (*0-317-91291-7*) All States Pub.

Mechancial Engineering Problems & Solutions. 6th rev. ed. Richard K. Pefley. Orig. Title: Mechanical Engineering License Review Problems & Solutions. (Illus.). 378p. 1996. 39.50 (*1-57645-008-2*) Engineering.

Mechanic: Graphic Novel. Joe Chiodo & Jonathan Peterson. (Illus.). 48p. 1998. pap. 5.95 (*1-58240-024-5*) Image Comics.

Mechanic Accents: Dime Novels & Working Class Culture of America. 2nd ed. Michael Demming. (Haymarket Ser.). 288p. 1998. pap. 18.00 (*1-85984-250-X*) Routledge.

Mechanic Exercises: or The Doctrine of Handy-Works. Joseph Moxon. (Illus.). 352p. 1989. reprint ed. pap. 25.00 (*1-879335-85-9*) Astragal Pr.

Mechanical Ability of Deaf Children. Mildred B. Stanton. LC 74-177747. (Columbia University. Teachers College. Contributions to Education Ser.: No. 751). reprint ed. 37.50 (*0-404-55751-1*) AMS Pr.

Mechanical Action of Light on Atoms. A. P. Kazantsev et al. 392p. (C). 1990. text 48.00 (*9971-5-0575-4*) World Scientific Pub.

Mechanical Activation of Silicates by Grinding: Pulverizing & Morphology of Particles. Z. A. Juhasz & L. Opoczky. (Ellis Horwood Series in Mineral Resource). 1990. text 81.95 (*0-470-21518-6*) P-H.

Mechanical Alloying. Li Lu & Man O. Lai. LC 97-35207. xv, 276p. 1998. text 135.00 (*0-7923-8066-5*) Kluwer Academic.

Mechanical Alloying. Ed. by P. H. Shingu. 840p. 1992. text 250.00 (*0-87849-633-5*, Pub. by Trans T Pub) Enfield Pubs NH.

*****Mechanical Alloying: Fundamentals & Applications.** P. R. Soni. 290p. 1998. boxed set 99.00 (*1-898326-56-8*, Pub. by CISP) Balogh.

Mechanical Alloying for Structural Applications: Proceedings of the 2nd International Conference on Structural Applications of Mechanical Alloying, September 20-22, 1993, Vancouver, British Columbia, Canada. Ed. by J. J. De Barbadillo et al. LC 93-79328. (Illus.). 482p. 1993. reprint ed. pap. 149.50 (*0-608-02614-X*, 206327200004) Bks Demand.

Mechanical Analysis & Design. A. H. Burr. 640p. 1981. teacher ed. write for info. (*0-318-51819-8*) Elsevier.

Mechanical Analysis & Design. 2nd ed. Arthur H. Burr & John B. Cheatham, Jr. LC 94-25342. 832p. (C). 1995. 100.00 (*0-02-317265-7*, Macmillan Coll) P-H.

*****Mechanical Analysis of Electronic Pakaging Systems.** Stephen A. McKeown. LC 99-22027. (Mechanical Engineering Ser.). (Illus.). 376p. 1999. text 165.00 (*0-8247-7033-1*) Dekker.

*****Mechanical & Corrosion-Resistant Properties of Plastics & Elastomers.** Philip A. Schweitzer. LC 00-28053. (Corrosion Technology Ser.). 2000. write for info. (*0-8247-0348-0*) Dekker.

Mechanical & Electrical Building Construction. Robert M. Hettema. (Illus.). 400p. (C). 1984. text 54.00 (*0-13-569608-9*) P-H.

Mechanical & Electrical Equipment for Buildings. 9th ed. Benjamin Stein & John Reynolds. LC 99-24973. 1824p. 1999. 99.95 (*0-471-15696-5*) Wiley.

Mechanical & Electrical Systems in Buildings. William K. Tao & Richard R. Janis. LC 95-51717. 538p. (C). 1997. 88.00 (*0-13-086729-2*) P-H.

*****Mechanical & Electrical Systems in Buildings.** 2nd ed. William K. Y. Tao & Richard R. Janis. LC 00-39948. (Illus.). 608p. 2000. 78.67 (*0-13-013711-1*) P-H.

Mechanical & Electrical Systems in Construction. 3rd ed. Frank R. Dagostino. 450p. 1995. 91.00 (*0-13-181462-1*) P-H.

Mechanical & Fluid Devices & Systems. Center for Occupational Research & Development Staff. (EUTEC Instrumentation & Control Curriculum Ser.). (Illus.). 222p. (C). 1985. pap. text. write for info. (*1-55502-184-0*) CORD Commns.

Mechanical & Structural Vibrations. Demeter G. Fertis. LC 94-33121. 832p. 1995. 150.00 (*0-471-10600-3*) Wiley.

Mechanical & Thermal Problems of Fusion Reactors. Ed. by Folker H. Wittmann. (Structural Mechanics in Reactor Technology Ser.: Vol. N). 190p. (C). 1987. text 168.00 (*90-6191-775-1*, Pub. by A A Balkema) Ashgate Pub Co.

Mechanical & Thermophysical Properties of Polymer Liquid Crystals. Ed. by Brostow. (Polymer Liquid Crystals Ser.). (Illus.). 448p. 1998. 169.95 (*0-412-60900-2*, Chap & Hall NY) Chapman & Hall.

Mechanical Aptitude & Spatial Relations Tests. 2nd ed. Norman Levy & Joan U. Levy. 256p. 1991. pap. 12.00 (*0-13-568692-X*, Arco) Macmillan Gen Ref.

Mechanical Aptitude & Spatial Relations Tests. 4th ed. 288p. 1999. 14.95 (*0-02-862816-0*, Arc) IDG Bks.

Mechanical Behavior in Composites & Laminates. W. A. Green. 1988. 77.50 (*1-85166-144-1*) Elsevier.

Mechanical Behavior of Advanced Materials: Proceedings International Mechanical Engineering Congress & Exposition 1998, Anaheim, CA. Ed. by Daniel C. Davis et al. LC 98-74433. (MD Ser.: Vol. 84). 362p. 1998. 200.00 (*0-7918-1609-5*) ASME.

Mechanical Behavior of Anisotropic Solids. Ed. by J. P. Boehler. 1983. text 389.50 (*90-247-2813-4*) Kluwer Academic.

Mechanical Behavior of Ceramics. R. W. Davidge. LC 77-90206. (Illus.). 173p. (C). 1988. reprint ed. text 55.00 (*1-878907-04-2*, RAN) TechBooks.

Mechanical Behavior of Crustal Rocks. Ed. by N. L. Carter et al. (Geophysical Monograph Ser.: Vol. 24). 326p. 1981. 42.00 (*0-87590-024-0*) Am Geophysical.

Mechanical Behavior of Diamond & Other Forms of Carbon. Ed. by M. D. Drory et al. (Symposium Proceedings Ser.: Vol. 383). 474p. 1995. text 77.00 (*1-55899-286-3*) Materials Res.

Mechanical Behavior of High Performance Concretes Vol. 1: Summary Report. Paul Zia et al. 98p. (C). 1993. pap. text 10.00 (*0-309-05619-5*, SHRP-C-361) SHRP.

Mechanical Behavior of High Performance Concretes Vol. 2: Production of High Performance Concrete. Paul Zia et al. 92p. (C). 1993. pap. text 15.00 (*0-309-05621-7*, SHRP-C-362) SHRP.

Mechanical Behavior of High Performance Concretes Vol. 2: Very Early Strength Concrete. Paul Zia et al. 116p. (C). 1993. pap. text 10.00 (*0-309-05623-3*, SHRP-C-363) SHRP.

Mechanical Behavior of High Performance Concretes Vol. 4: High Early Strength Concrete. Michael Leming et al. 179p. (C). 1993. pap. text 15.00 (*0-309-05756-6*, SHRP-C-364) SHRP.

Mechanical Behavior of High Performance Concretes Vol. 5: Very High Strength Concrete. Paul Zia et al. 101p. (C). 1993. pap. text 10.00 (*0-309-05624-1*, SHRP-C-365) SHRP.

Mechanical Behavior of Material. 2nd ed. Courtney. LC 99-31791. (Series in Materials Science & Engineering). 752p. 1999. 108.44 (*0-07-028594-2*) McGraw.

Mechanical Behavior of Materials. Thomas H. Courtney. (Electrical Engineering Ser.). 710p. (C). 1990. 101.56 (*0-07-013265-8*); pap. text 23.75 (*0-07-013266-6*) McGraw.

Mechanical Behavior of Materials. Dominique Francois et al. LC 97-45958. (Solid Mechanics & Its Applications Ser.). 1997. lib. bdg. write for info. (*0-7923-4894-X*); lib. bdg. write for info. (*0-7923-4895-8*); lib. bdg. write for info. (*0-7923-4896-6*) Kluwer Academic.

Mechanical Behavior of Materials. Marc A. Meyers & Krishan K. Chawla. LC 98-22454. 680p. (C). 1998. 105.00 (*0-13-262817-1*) P-H.

Mechanical Behavior of Materials. Frank A. McClintock & A. S. Argon. 784p. (C). 1993. reprint ed. text 138.00 (*1-878907-71-9*) TechBooks.

Mechanical Behavior of Materials: Engineering Methods for Deformation, Fracture & Fatigue. 2nd ed. Dowling. LC 98-33811. 830p. 1998. 105.00 (*0-13-905720-X*) P-H.

Mechanical Behavior of Materials: Invited Papers Presented at the 7th International Conference, the Hague, the Netherlands, May 28-June 2, 1995. Ed. by A. Bakker. (Illus.). 164p. (Orig.). 1996. pap. 77.50 (*90-407-1126-7*, Pub. by Delft U Pr) Coronet Bks.

Mechanical Behavior of Materials & Structures in Microelectronics Vol. 226: Materials Research Society Symposium Proceedings. Ephraim Suhir. Ed. by R. C. Cammarata et al. 468p. 1991. text 85.00 (*1-55899-120-4*) Materials Res.

Mechanical Behavior of Materials: Proceedings. F. A. McClintock & A. S. Argon. 1966. text 44.75 (*0-201-04545-1*) Addison-Wesley.

Mechanical Behavior of Metal-Matrix Composites: Proceedings of a Symposium Sponsored by the Composite Materials Committee of the Metallurgical Society of AIME...Held at the 111th AIME Annual Meeting, Dallas, TX, February 16-18, 1982. Metallurgical Society of AIME Staff. Ed. by John E. Hack & Maurice F. Amateau. LC 83-61431. (Conference Proceedings Ser.). (Illus.). 363p. reprint ed. pap. 112.60 (*0-8357-6599-7*, 203599700097) Bks Demand.

Mechanical Behavior of Metals at Extremely High Strain Rates. Z. Buchar et al. (Materials Science Surveys Ser.: Vol. 4). (Illus.). 250p. (C). 1986. text 96.00 (*0-87849-528-2*, Pub. by Trans T Pub) Enfield Pubs NH.

An Asterisk (*) at the beginning of an entry indicates that the title is appearing for the first time.

Mechanical Behavior of Rapidly Solidified Materials: Proceedings of a Symposium Held at the AIME Annual Meeting, New York City, NY, February 24-28, 1985. Metallurgical Society of AIME Staff. Ed. by Shankar M. Sastry & Bruce A. MacDonald. LC 85-30989. 319p. reprint ed. pap. 98.90 (*0-8357-2509-X*, 205238900013) Bks Demand.

Mechanical Behavior of Salt: Proceedings of the Second Conference. H. R. Hardy, Jr. & M. Langer. (Series on Rock & Soil Mechanics: Vol. 14). 900p. 1987. text 45.00 (*0-87849-071-X*, Pub. by Trans T Pub) Enfield Pubs NH.

Mechanical Behavior of UV-Degraded HDPE: Consequences for Designers. Hielke Hoekstra. (Illus.). 133p. 1997. pap. 45.00 (*90-407-1535-1*, Pub. by Delft U Pr) Coronet Bks.

Mechanical Behaviour & Nuclear Application of Stainless Steel at Elevated Temperatures. 264p. 1982. text 24.00 (*0-904357-41-4*, Pub. by Inst Materials) Ashgate Pub Co.

***Mechanical Behaviour of Engineering Materials, 2 vols.** Y. M. Haddad. LC 00-30177. 2000. write for info. (*0-7923-6355-8*) Kluwer Academic.

Mechanical Behaviour of Materials. K. J. Miller & R. F. Smith. 1980. 781.00 (*0-08-024739-3*, Pub. by Pergamon Repr) Franklin.

Mechanical Behaviour of Materials: Proceedings of the 4th International Conference on Mechanical Behaviour of Materials, Stockholm, Sweden August 15-19, 1983, 2 vols., No. IV. Ed. by J. Carlsson. (International Series of Monographs on the Strength & Fracture of Materials & Structures). (Illus.). 1175p. 1984. 559.00 (*0-08-029340-9*, Pub. by Pergamon Repr) Franklin.

Mechanical Behaviour of Materials Vol. 1: Proceedings of the 6th International Conference, Kyoto, Japan, 29 July - 2 August 1991, 4 vols., Set. Ed. by M. Jono & T. Inoue. (Illus.). 3452p. 1992. 520.00 (*0-08-040176-7*) Elsevier.

Mechanical Behaviour of Materials Vol. 1: Proceedings of the 6th International Conference, Kyoto, Japan, 29 July-2 August 1991, 4 vols., Set. Ed. by M. Jono & T. Inoue. (International Series on the Strength & Fracture of Materials). (Illus.). 3452p. 1992. 831.50 (*0-08-037890-0*, Pergamon Pr) Elsevier.

Mechanical Behaviour of Materials at High Temperature. C. Branco et al. LC 96-18755. (ASI NATO Ser.). 1996. text 364.50 (*0-7923-4113-9*) Kluwer Academic.

Mechanical Behaviour of Nanostructured Materials. Ed. by D. G. Morris. (Materials Science Foundation Ser.: Vol. 2). (Illus.). 100p. (C). 48.00 (*0-87849-797-8*, Pub. by Trans T Pub) Enfield Pubs NH.

***Mechanical Behaviour of Rocks under High Pressure Conditions.** Mitsuhiko Shimada. (Geomechanics Research Ser.: Vol. 2). (Illus.). 180p. 2000. text 85.00 (*90-5809-316-6*, Pub. by A A Balkema) Ashgate Pub Co.

Mechanical Behaviour of Salt: Proceedings of the 1st Conference. H. R. Hardy & M. Langer. (Rock & Soil Mechanics Ser.: Vol. 9). 910p. 1984. 140.00 (*0-87849-045-0*, Pub. by Trans T Pub) Enfield Pubs NH.

Mechanical (Boilers Fuel & Ash-Handling Plant) see Modern Power Station Practice

Mechanical Brides: Women & Machines from Home to Office. Ellen Lupton. Ed. by Nancy Aakre. LC 93-22169. (Illus.). 64p. (Orig.). 1993. pap. 17.95 (*1-878271-97-0*) Princeton Arch.

Mechanical Cardiac Assistance. Wayne E. Richenbacher. LC 99-33746. (Vademecum Ser.). 1999. spiral bd. 45.00 (*1-57059-530-5*) Landes Bioscience.

Mechanical Characterisation of Load Bearing Fibre Composite Laminates: Proceedings of the European Mechanics Colloquium 182, Mechanical Characterisation of Load Bearing Fibre Composite Laminates Brussels, Belgium, August 29-31, 1984. Ed. by A. H. Cardon & G. Verchery. 264p. 1985. 66.75 (*0-85334-379-9*) Elsevier.

Mechanical Circulatory Support. 1997. 58.00 (*3-7985-1046-6*) Spr-Verlag.

Mechanical Circulatory Support. Ed. by Terence Lewis et al. (An Arnold Publication). 416p. 1995. text 135.00 (*0-340-57602-2*, Pub. by E A) OUP.

Mechanical Composition of Wind Deposits. Johan A. Udden. LC 06-31217. (Augustana College Library Publications: No. 1). 69p. 1898. pap. 1.00 (*0-910182-00-0*) Augustana Coll.

Mechanical Connections in Wood Structures. American Society of Civil Engineers Staff. (Manuals & Reports on Engineering Practice: Vol. 84). 248p. 1995. 43.00 (*0-7844-0110-1*) Am Soc Civil Eng.

Mechanical Conveyers: Selection & Operation. Mohammed E. Fayed & Thomas S. Skocir. LC 96-60867. 490p. 1996. text 189.95 (*1-56676-416-5*) Technomic.

***Mechanical Cost Data: 2000 Edition.** 23rd ed. R. S. Means Company Staff. 1999. pap. text 89.95 (*0-87629-542-1*) R S Means.

Mechanical Damage & Crack Growth in Concrete. Alberto Carpinteri. (Engineering Application of Fracture Mechanics Ser.). 1986. text 186.00 (*90-247-3233-6*) Kluwer Academic.

Mechanical Deburring & Surface Finishing Technology. Alfred F. Scheider. (Manufacturing Engineering & Materials Processing Ser.: Vol. 35). (Illus.). 168p. 1990. text 95.00 (*0-8247-8157-0*) Dekker.

***Mechanical Design: A Rotary Component Approach.** Peter R. Childs. LC 98-50988. 240p. 1998. pap. 59.95 (*0-470-32740-5*) Wiley.

Mechanical Design: Theory & Methodology. Ed. by Manjula B. Waldron & Kenneth J. Waldron. LC 95-37685. 400p. 1996. 69.95 (*0-387-94589-X*) Spr-Verlag.

Mechanical Design & Manufacturing of Hydraulic Machinery. Ed. by Zu-yan Mei. (Hydraulic Machinery Bks.). 574p. 1991. 119.95 (*1-85628-820-X*, Pub. by Avebury Technical) Ashgate Pub Co.

Mechanical Design Data Book. 4th rev. ed. William E. Rybolt. (Illus.). 60p. (C). 1999. pap. 8.95 (*0-941801-17-9*) Rybolt Pubns.

Mechanical Design Failure Analysis with Analysis System Software for the IBM PC. David G. Ullman. (Illus.). 184p. 1986. text 135.00 (*0-8247-7534-1*) Dekker.

Mechanical Design Handbook. Ed. by Harold A. Rothbart. (Illus.). 1472p. 1995. 125.00 (*0-07-054038-1*) McGraw.

Mechanical Design Heating. Singe. 1992. 255.95 (*0-387-16510-X*) Spr-Verlag.

Mechanical Design Manual. 1995. lib. bdg. 250.00 (*0-8490-5865-1*) Gordon Pr.

Mechanical Design of Heat Exchangers & Pressure Vessel Components. Krishna Singh & Alan Soler. LC 84-70460. (Illus.). 1100p. (C). 1984. 89.50 (*0-916877-00-0*) Arcturus Pubs.

Mechanical Design of Process Systems: Piping & Pressure Vessels, Vol. 1. fac. ed. A. Keith Escoe. LC 85-22005. (Illus.). 339p. pap. 105.10 (*0-7837-7431-1*, 204722600001) Bks Demand.

Mechanical Design of Process Systems: Piping & Pressure Vessels, Vol. 1. 2nd rev. ed. A. Keith Escoe. LC 85-22005. 300p. 1994. 125.00 (*0-88415-186-7*, 5186) Gulf Pub.

Mechanical Design of Process Systems Vol. 2: Heat Exchanges, Rotating Equipment & Machinery, Vol. 2. 2nd ed. A. Keith Escoe. LC 93-38415. (Illus.). 240p. 1995. 125.00 (*0-88415-195-6*, 5195) Gulf Pub.

Mechanical Design of Process Systems Vol. 2: Shell & Tube Heat Exchangers, Rotating Equipment, Bins, Silos, Stacks. A. Keith Escoe. LC 85-22005. 254p. 1986. reprint ed. pap. 78.80 (*0-608-00783-8*, 204722600002) Bks Demand.

Mechanical Design Process. Ullman. 1991. teacher ed. 27.50 (*0-07-065751-3*) McGraw.

Mechanical Design Process. David G. Ullman. (C). 1992. text 52.25 (*0-07-065739-4*) McGraw.

Mechanical Design Process. 2nd ed. David G. Ullman. LC 96-30987. 340p. (C). 1996. 62.50 (*0-07-065756-4*) McGraw.

Mechanical Design Synthesis: Creative Design & Optimization. 2nd ed. Ray C. Johnson. LC 77-10974. 468p. 1978. lib. bdg. 49.50 (*0-88275-612-5*) Krieger.

***Mechanical Desktop 4: Applying Designer & Assembly Modules.** Daniel T. Banach. LC 99-53881. (Student Material TV Ser.). (Illus.). 536p. (C). 1999. text 59.95 (*0-7668-1946-9*) Delmar.

***Mechanical Desktop 4: Surface Modeling.** Laura Martz et al. (Illus.). 548p. 2000. pap., student ed. 75.00 (*1-891502-71-9*, MDT4SURFSTUD) Tech Learn Co.

***Mechanical Desktop 4: Surface Modeling.** 3rd ed. Laura Martz et al. (Illus.). 253p. 2000. pap., teacher ed. 105.00 (*1-891502-72-7*) Tech Learn Co.

***Mechanical Desktop 4.0 - Advanced.** 2nd ed. Laura Martz et al. Ed. by Richard Allen. (Illus.). 260p. 1999. pap. text, student ed. 75.00 (*1-891502-69-7*, MDT4099) Tech Learn Co.

***Mechanical Desktop 4.0 - Advanced.** 2nd ed. Laura Martz et al. Ed. by Richard Allen. (Illus.). 260p. 1999. pap. text, teacher ed. 105.00 incl. cd-rom (*1-891502-70-0*, MDT4099) Tech Learn Co.

***Mechanical Desktop 4.0 Fundamentals.** 2nd ed. Laura Martz et al. Ed. by Richard Allen. (Illus.). 507p. 1999. pap. text, teacher ed. 125.00 incl. cd-rom (*1-891502-68-9*, MDT4099); pap. text, student ed. 95.00 (*1-891502-67-0*, MDT4099) Tech Learn Co.

***Mechanical Desktop 4.0 Update.** 2nd ed. Laura Martz. Ed. by Richard Allen. (Illus.). 179p. 1999. pap. text, teacher ed. 75.00 incl. cd-rom (*1-891502-66-2*, MDT4099) Tech Learn Co.

***Mechanical Desktop 4.0 Update.** 2nd unabridged ed. Laura Martz. Ed. by Richard Allen. (Illus.). 179p. 1999. pap. text, student ed. 105.00 (*1-891502-65-4*, MDT4099U) Tech Learn Co.

Mechanical Desktop 3.0: Assembly Modeling: Instructor Manual. 2nd ed. Laura Martz & Richard Allen. 1998. pap. text, teacher ed. 105.00 (*1-891502-38-7*, MDT30ASMI) Tech Learn Co.

Mechanical Desktop 3.0: Surface Modeling - Student Manual. 2nd large type unabridged ed. Richard L. Allen & Laura Martz. (Illus.). 200p. 1998. pap. text 95.00 (*1-891502-33-6*, MDT30SUR) Tech Learn Co.

Mechanical Desktop 3.0: Surface Modeling: Instructor Manual. 2nd ed. Laura Martz & Richard Allen. 1998. pap. text, teacher ed. 125.00 (*1-891502-39-5*, MDT30SURI) Tech Learn Co.

Mechanical Desktop 3.0 Part Modeling: Student Manual. 2nd ed. Laura Martz & Richard Allen. (Illus.). 300p. 1998. pap. text, student ed. 95.00 (*1-891502-31-X*, MDT30SOLI) Tech Learn Co.

Mechanical Desktop 3.0 Update - Student Manual. 2nd large type unabridged ed. Richard L. Allen & Laura Martz. (Illus.). 200p. 1998. pap. text 75.00 (*1-891502-30-1*, MDT30UPD) Tech Learn Co.

Mechanical Desktop 3.0 Update: Instructor Manual. 2nd ed. Laura Martz & Richard Allen. 1998. pap., teacher ed. 105.00 incl. cd-rom (*1-891502-36-0*, MDT30UPDI) Tech Learn Co.

Mechanical Desktop Training Material. Autodesk Press Staff. 752p. 1997. pap. text, teacher ed. write for info. (*0-7668-0056-3*) Delmar.

Mechanical Desktop Training Material. Autodesk Press Staff. 752p. 1997. text, student ed. 75.00 (*0-7668-0054-7*) Delmar.

***Mechanical Desktop Tutorial R4.** Jacob K. Halim. (Illus.). 340p. 2000. pap. 69.95 (*1-877928-12-7*) Orange Fortune.

Mechanical Desktop 2.0 Update Technical Training - Student Guide. Steven Hader et al. (Illus.). 1997. pap. text, student ed., spiral bd. 150.00 (*1-890484-46-6*, KnowledgeWorks) HTR Inc.

Mechanical Desktop 2.0: Applying Designer & Assembly Modules. abr. rev. ed. Daniel T. Banach. LC 98-14979. 700p. (C). 1998. pap. 70.95 (*0-7668-0068-7*, AutoDesk Pr) Delmar.

Mechanical Desktop 2.0: Assembly Modeling - Instructor Manual. 2nd large type unabridged ed. Richard L. Allen & Laura Martz. (Illus.). 300p. 1998. pap. text 95.00 (*1-891502-28-X*, MDT20SOLI) Tech Learn Co.

Mechanical Desktop 2.0: Assembly Modeling - Instructor Manual. 2nd large type unabridged ed. Laura Martz et al. (Illus.). 200p. 1998. pap. text, teacher ed. 75.00 (*1-891502-29-8*, MDJ20ASMI) Tech Learn Co.

Mechanical Desktop 2.0: Assembly Modeling - Student Workbook. 2nd unabridged ed. Mel Hoagland et al. (Illus.). 200p. 1998. pap. text 75.00 incl. disk (*1-891502-25-5*, MDT20ASM) Tech Learn Co.

Mechanical Desktop 2.0: Solid Modeling - Student Manual. 2nd unabridged ed. Laura Martz et al. (Illus.). 300p. 1998. pap. text, student ed. 95.00 incl. disk (*1-891502-23-9*, MDT20SOL) Tech Learn Co.

Mechanical Desktop 2.0 Update. 2nd unabridged ed. Richard L. Allen et al. (Illus.). 200p. 1998. pap. text 75.00 incl. disk (*1-891502-21-2*, MDT20UPD) Tech Learn Co.

Mechanical Desktop 3.0: Part Modeling. 2nd ed. Laura Martz. Ed. by Richard L. Allen. (Illus.). 419p. 1998. teacher ed., spiral bd. 125.00 (*1-891502-37-9*, MDT30PARI) Tech Learn Co.

Mechanical Desktop 3.0 Update Guide. Daniel T. Banach. LC 98-31478. 144p. (C). 1998. pap. 17.95 (*0-7668-1125-5*) Delmar.

Mechanical Desktop 2.0/3.0: Surface Modeling - Student Manual. 2nd unabridged ed. Richard Allen & Laura Martz. (Illus.). 200p. 1998. pap. text 75.00 incl. disk (*1-891502-27-1*, MDT20SUR) Tech Learn Co.

Mechanical Devices & Systems. Center for Occupational Research & Development Staff. (High Technology Ser.). (Illus.). 200p. (C). 1989. pap. text 25.00 (*1-55502-361-4*) CORD Commns.

Mechanical Devices & Systems Teacher's Guide. Center for Occupational Research & Development Staff. (High Technology Ser.). (Illus.). 37p. 1990. pap. text 10.00 (*1-55502-369-X*) CORD Commns.

Mechanical Devices for Cardiopulmonary Assistance: Proceedings of the Symposium, Boston, 1970. Symposium, Boston Staff. Ed. by R. H. Bartlett et al. (Advances in Cardiology Ser.: Vol. 6). 1971. 59.25 (*3-8055-1163-9*) S Karger.

Mechanical Devices for the Electronics Experimenter. Britt Rorabaugh. LC 94-36306. 1995. 29.95 (*0-07-053546-9*); pap. 19.95 (*0-07-053547-7*) McGraw-Hill Prof.

Mechanical Discipline - Specific Review for the FE/EIT Exam. Michel Saad. LC 97-13363. 80p. 1997. pap. 24.95 (*1-888577-19-3*, DSME) Prof Pubns CA.

Mechanical Disorders of the Low Back. H. F. Farfan. LC 73-3348. 258p. reprint ed. pap. 80.00 (*0-608-30234-1*, 205542400022) Bks Demand.

***Mechanical Drafter.** Jim Dawson. 1999. 19.93 (*0-516-21890-5*) Capstone Pr.

***Mechanical Drafter.** Rosemary Wallner. LC 99-23534. (Career Exploration Ser.). 48p. (YA). 1999. 19.93 (*0-7368-0331-9*) Capstone Pr.

Mechanical Drawing. 9th ed. Jay D. Helsel & Byron Urbanick. Ed. by Hal Lindquist. (Illus.). 1979. text 34.24 (*0-07-022313-0*) McGraw.

Mechanical Drawing. 10th ed. Thomas E. French et al. 576p. 1985. text 33.96 (*0-07-022333-5*) McGraw.

Mechanical Drawing: CAD Communications. 11th ed. Thomas E. French et al. 576p. 1989. pap. text 36.96 (*0-07-022337-8*) McGraw.

Mechanical Drawing: CAD Communications. 11th ed. Thomas E. French et al. 576p. 1990. teacher ed. 18.04 (*0-07-022339-4*) McGraw.

Mechanical Drawing: CAD Communications. 11th ed. Thomas E. French et al. 576p. 1990. student ed. 26.32 (*0-07-022338-6*) McGraw.

Mechanical Drawing: CAD-Communications. 12th ed. Thomas E. French et al. 1999. teacher ed., ring bd. 62.65 incl. disk (*0-02-667959-0*) Glencoe.

Mechanical Drawing: CAD-Communications. 12th ed. Thomas E. French et al. LC 97-114754. (Illus.). 753p. (YA). (gr. 6-12). 1999. student ed. 42.99 (*0-02-667958-2*) Glencoe.

Mechanical Drawing Problem: AutoCAD Release 12. Sigl. (CAD/CAM Ser.). 1993. pap., wbk. ed. 20.95 (*0-8273-4829-0*) Delmar.

Mechanical Drive Systems & Their Service Factors. F. A. Thoma. (Technical Papers: Vol. P159.03). (Illus.). 12p. 1969. pap. text 30.00 (*1-55589-205-1*) AGMA.

Mechanical Effects of Welding: IUTAM Symposium, Lulea, Sweden, 1991. Ed. by I. Karlsson et al. (International Union of Theoretical & Applied Mechanics Symposia Ser.). (Illus.). 296p. 1992. 172.95 (*0-387-55240-5*) Spr-Verlag.

Mechanical End Face Seals: Guidelines for the Pulp & Paper Industry. Technical Association of the Pulp & Paper Industry. Ed. by Gary J. Bosar. LC TJ0246.. 27p. 1981. reprint ed. pap. 30.00 (*0-608-12031-6*, 202281300030) Bks Demand.

Mechanical Engineer. Jack Rudman. (Career Examination Ser.: C-481). 1994. pap. 29.95 (*0-8373-0481-4*) Nat Learn.

Mechanical Engineer in America, 1830-1910: Professional Cultures in Conflict. Monte A. Calvert. LC 66-26683. 317p. reprint ed. pap. 98.30 (*0-608-15004-5*, 202588700046) Bks Demand.

Mechanical Engineering. Seichi Konzo & James W. Bayne. (Opportunities in...Ser.). 160p. 1995. pap. 10.95 (*0-614-95840-7*) NTC Contemp Pub Co.

Mechanical Engineering. 6th ed. Richard Queeney. 154p. (C). 1998. per. 21.95 (*0-7872-4737-5*) Kendall-Hunt.

Mechanical Engineering: Dynamics. 4th ed. Beer. 1987. student ed. 42.81 (*0-07-004583-6*) McGraw.

***Mechanical Engineering: User's Guide to Natural Gas Purchasing & Risk Management.** William F. Payne. (Illus.). 264p. 2000. 87.00 (*0-13-017931-0*) P-H.

Mechanical Engineering No. ME1: Machine Design & Analysis. Hank G. Hoomani. (Professional Engineering Exam Review Ser.). (Illus.). 100p. (Orig.). (C). 1983. pap. text 25.00 (*1-56049-057-8*) NCSU CE IES.

Mechanical Engineering No. ME2: Heat, Power, & Thermodynamics. John K. Whitfield. (Professional Engineering Exam Review Ser.). (Illus.). 246p. (Orig.). (C). 1985. pap. text 25.00 (*1-56049-058-6*) NCSU CE IES.

Mechanical Engineering at Berkeley: The First 125 Years. Werner Goldsmith. LC 97-29115. (Illus.). xii, 154p. 1997. 25.00 (*0-9659929-0-X*) U Ca DME.

Mechanical Engineering Design. 2nd ed. Joseph E. Shigley. LC 74-167497. (Mechanical Engineering Ser.). (Illus.). 768p. (C). 1972. text 19.50 (*0-07-056869-3*) McGraw.

Mechanical Engineering Design. 4th ed. Joseph E. Shigley & Larry D. Mitchell. (C). 1993. pap. text 58.50 (*0-07-056937-1*) McGraw.

Mechanical Engineering Design. 5th ed. Shigley. 1988. teacher ed. 27.50 (*0-07-056900-2*) McGraw.

Mechanical Engineering Design. 5th rev. ed. Joseph E. Shigley & Charles R. Mischke. (Mechanical Engineering Ser.). 779p. (C). 1988. 107.19 (*0-07-056899-5*) McGraw.

Mechanical Engineering Design. 6th ed. Mischke. 2000. 85.00 (*0-07-365939-8*) McGraw.

***Mechanical Engineering Design Education: Issues & Case Studies.** Ed. by Edmund C. Feldy. (DE Ser.: Vol. 102). 103p. 1999. 70.00 (*0-7918-1645-1*) ASME Pr.

***Mechanical Engineering Design with Pro/Engineer Release 2000i.** Mark Archibald. (Illus.). 353p. 2000. pap. 59.95 (*1-58503-019-8*, SDC Pubns) Schroff Dev Corp.

Mechanical Engineering Draftsman. Jack Rudman. (Career Examination Ser.: Vol. C-482). 1994. pap. 27.95 (*0-8373-0482-2*) Nat Learn.

Mechanical Engineering Education in America: It's First Century. 101p. 1982. 6.00 (*0-685-06267-8*, I00146) ASME.

Mechanical Engineering for Public Cleansing. Douglas M. Hamilton & William Robb. (Illus.). 216p. 1969. 21.75 (*0-85334-121-4*) Elsevier.

Mechanical Engineering Handbook. Kreith. 2624p. 1998. 129.00 incl. cd-rom (*0-8493-9751-0*) CRC Pr.

Mechanical Engineering Handbook. Research & Education Association Staff. 1536p. 1999. pap. text 38.95 (*0-87891-980-5*) Res & Educ.

***Mechanical Engineering License Review: For the Professional P. E. Exam.** 5th ed. John D. Constance. (Illus.). 630p. 1999. pap. 59.50 (*1-57645-022-8*, 228) Engineering.

Mechanical Engineering License Review Problems & Solutions see Mechancial Engineering Problems & Solutions

Mechanical Engineering Reference Manual for the PE Exam. 10th ed. Michael R. Lindeburg. LC 97-7741. (Engineering Reference Manual Ser.). 1300p. 1997. 89.95 (*1-888577-13-4*, MERMIO) Prof Pubns CA.

Mechanical Engineering Sample Exam. 3rd ed. Michael R. Lindeburg. LC 97-31464. 52p. 1997. pap. 29.95 (*1-888577-17-7*) Prof Pubns CA.

Mechanical Engineering Solutions. McGraw-Hill Staff. 24p. 1998. 99.95 (*0-07-913724-5*) McGraw.

Mechanical Engineering Technology: Product Design & Drafting Problems. John G. Nee. LC 83-60332. (Illus.). 163p. (C). 1983. pap. 11.95 (*0-911168-52-4*) Prakken.

Mechanical Engineering Technology (MET) (1995 ASME International Mechanical Engineering Congress & Exposition Ser.). 1995. 10.00 (*0-614-16712-4*, 95-WA/MET-1) ASME.

Mechanical Engineering Trainee. Jack Rudman. (Career Examination Ser.: C-519). 1994. pap. 23.95 (*0-8373-0519-5*) Nat Learn.

Mechanical Engineering/Statics. 4th ed. Beer. 1987. 27.50 (*0-07-004581-X*) McGraw.

Mechanical Engineer's Data Handbook. James Carvill. LC 93-12482. 1993. 79.95 (*0-8493-7780-3*, TJ151) CRC Pr.

Mechanical Engineers' Handbook. 2nd ed. Myer Kutz. LC 97-20306. 2376p. 1998. 250.00 (*0-471-13007-9*, Wiley-Interscience) Wiley.

Mechanical Engineers' Handbook Vol. 2: Power. 12th ed. William Kent. LC 50-8435. (Wiley Engineering Handbook Ser.). 1448p. reprint ed. pap. 200.00 (*0-7837-1463-7*, 205683100002) Bks Demand.

Mechanical Engineer's Reference Book. 12th ed. E. H. Smith. (Authored (Royalty) Ser.). 1200p. 1994. 135.00 (*1-56091-450-5*, R-136) Soc Auto Engineers.

Mechanical Engineers Referencebook. 12th ed. Smith. LC 99-166453. 1248p. 2000. pap. text 99.95 (*0-7506-4218-1*) Buttrwrth-Heinemann.

Mechanical Equipment Inspector. Jack Rudman. (Career Examination Ser.: C-2045). 1994. pap. 34.95 (*0-8373-2045-3*) Nat Learn.

Mechanical Equipment Repair Industry (Machine Shops) Guides to Pollution Prevention. (Illus.). 45p. (Orig.). (C). 1996. pap. text 25.00 (*0-7881-2910-4*) DIANE Pub.

Mechanical Estimating Guidebook. 6th ed. Ed. by Kenneth K. Humphreys & John Gladstone. LC 95-19732. 1995. write for info. (*0-07-024227-5*); disk. write for info. (*0-07-852846-1*) McGraw.

Mechanical Estimator. Jack Rudman. (Career Examination Ser.: C-3113). 1994. pap. 27.95 (*0-8373-3113-7*) Nat Learn.

M

***Mechanical Evaluation Strategies for Plastics Materials.** S. Turner & D. R. Moore. 200p. 2000. boxed set 170.00 (*1-85573-379-X*) Am Educ Systs.

Mechanical Face Seal Handbook. John C. Dahlheimer. LC 72-6443. 200p. reprint ed. pap. 62.00 (*0-608-13411-2*, 205574600035) Bks Demand.

Mechanical Factors of Digestion. Walter B. Cannon. LC 86-10161. 1987. 20.00 (*0-88135-082-6*) Watson Pub Intl.

Mechanical Fastening, Joining & Assembly, Vol. 109. James A. Speck. LC 96-52021. (Mechanical Engineering Ser.). (Illus.). 256p. 1997. text 115.00 (*0-8247-9835-X*) Dekker.

Mechanical Fastening of Plastics: An Engineering Handbook. Brayton Lincoln et al. (Mechanical Engineering Ser.: Vol. 26). (Illus.). 240p. 1984. text 99.75 (*0-8247-7078-1*) Dekker.

Mechanical Feature: One Hundred Years of Engineering at Mississippi State University. C. James Haug. LC 91-48006. (Illus.). 224p. 1992. text 49.95 (*0-87805-561-4*) U Pr of Miss.

Mechanical Fitting, No. 1. 1987. 60.00 (*0-7855-2863-6*) St Mut.

Mechanical Fitting, No. 2. 1982. 60.00 (*0-7855-2879-2*) St Mut.

Mechanical Forces: Their Effects on Cells & Tissues. Keith J. Gooch & Chris J. Tennant. LC 96-26773. (Biotechnology Intelligence Unit Ser.). 1997. 114.00 (*1-57059-376-0*) Landes Bioscience.

Mechanical Forces: Their Effects on Cells & Tissues. Keith J. Gooch & Chris J. Tennant. LC 96-26773. (Biotechnology Intelligence Unit Ser.). (Illus.). 210p. 1997. text 114.00 (*3-540-62928-9*) Spr-Verlag.

***Mechanical Forces & the Endothelium.** Ed. by Peter Lelkes. (Endothelial Cell Research Ser.). 392p. 1999. text 115.00 (*90-5702-447-0*, Harwood Acad Pubs) Gordon & Breach.

Mechanical Foundations of Elasticity see Continuum Mechanics

Mechanical Genius. Stewart Crowley. 1997. pap. 6.95 (*0-8167-2787-2*) Troll Communs.

Mechanical Geometry Theorem Proving. Shang-Ching Chou. (C). 1987. text 205.50 (*90-277-2650-7*) Kluwer Academic.

Mechanical God: Machines in Science Fiction, 1. Ed. by Thomas P. Dunn & Richard D. Erlich. LC 81-13429. (Contributions to the Study of Science Fiction & Fantasy Ser.: No. 1). 284p. 1982. 65.00 (*0-313-22274-6*, DME/, Greenwood Pr) Greenwood.

Mechanical Harry. Bob Kerr. LC 98-18765. (Illus.). 28p. (J). (gr. 2 up). 1999. lib. bdg. 21.27 (*0-8368-2248-X*) Gareth Stevens Inc.

***Mechanical Harry & the Flying Bicycle.** Bob Kerr. LC 99-19162. (Illus.). 28p. (J). (gr. 2 up). 1999. lib. bdg. 21.27 (*0-8368-2444-X*) Gareth Stevens Inc.

Mechanical Impedance Approach to the Dynamics (Torsional Vibrations) of Geared Systems. G. V. Tordion. (Technical Papers: Vol. P209.04). (Illus.). 35p. 1963. pap. text 30.00 (*1-55589-379-1*) AGMA.

Mechanical Inspection: Course 30. (Illus.). 428p. (C). 1979. pap. text, ring bd. 95.00 (*0-87683-122-6*) GP Courseware.

Mechanical Investigations of Leonardo da Vinci. Ivor B. Hart. LC 82-2967. (Illus.). 240p. 1982. reprint ed. lib. bdg. 48.50 (*0-313-23489-2*, HAMEC, Greenwood Pr) Greenwood.

Mechanical Loading of Bones & Joints. Hideaki Takahashi. LC 99-19475. 324p. 1999. 169.00 (*4-431-70242-3*) Spr-Verlag.

Mechanical Low Back Pain: Perspectives in Functional Anatomy. 2nd ed. James A. Porterfield & Carl DeRosa. Ed. by Margaret Biblis. LC 97-14398. (Illus.). 304p. 1998. text 45.00 (*0-7216-6837-2*, W B Saunders Co) Harcrt Hlth Sci Grp.

Mechanical Maintainer - Group A. Jack Rudman. (Career Examination Ser.: C-483). 1994. pap. 23.95 (*0-8373-0483-0*) Nat Learn.

Mechanical Maintainer - Group B. Jack Rudman. (Career Examination Ser.: C-484). 1994. pap. 23.95 (*0-8373-0484-9*) Nat Learn.

Mechanical Maintainer - Group C. Jack Rudman. (Career Examination Ser.: C-485). 1994. pap. 23.95 (*0-8373-0485-7*) Nat Learn.

Mechanical Maintenance & Installation, No. 2. 1982. 52.00 (*0-7855-2886-5*) St Mut.

Mechanical Maintenance Supervisor. Jack Rudman. (Career Examination Ser.: C-2793). 1994. pap. 29.95 (*0-8373-2793-8*) Nat Learn.

Mechanical Man: John B. Watson & the Beginnings of Behaviorism. Kerry W. Buckley. LC 88-24081. 233p. 1989. lib. bdg. 26.95 (*0-89862-744-3*) Guilford Pubns.

Mechanical Measurement. 3rd ed. H. C. Drishna & Rajpal S. Sirohi. 284p. 1993. text 59.95 (*0-470-21953-X*) Halsted Pr.

Mechanical Measurement & Instrumentation. Edgar E. Ambrosius. LC 66-21850. (Illus.). 594p. reprint ed. pap. 184.20 (*0-608-11702-1*, 201303700083) Bks Demand.

Mechanical Measurements. 3rd ed. Thomas G. Beckwith et al. 1982. text 39.96 (*0-201-00036-9*) Addison-Wesley.

Mechanical Measurements. 4th ed. Thomas G. Beckwith & Roy D. Marangoni. (Illus.). (C). 1990. text 65.75 (*0-201-17866-4*) Addison-Wesley.

Mechanical Measurements. 5th ed. Thomas G. Beckwith et al. LC 92-23515. (Illus.). 895p. (C). 1993. 100.00 (*0-201-56947-7*) Addison-Wesley.

Mechanical Measurements. 6th ed. Thomas Beckwith. 1999. text. write for info. (*0-201-84765-5*) Addison-Wesley.

Mechanical Measurements: Solutions Manual. 3rd ed. Thomas G. Beckwith et al. 1982. pap. text, teacher ed. 1.25 (*0-201-00037-7*) Addison-Wesley.

Mechanical Measurements: Solutions Manual. 5th ed. Thomas G. Beckwith et al. 1994. pap. text 23.33 (*0-201-90913-8*) Addison-Wesley.

Mechanical Metallurgy. 3rd ed. Dieter. 1986. student ed. 27.50 (*0-07-016894-6*) McGraw.

Mechanical Metallurgy. 3rd ed. George Dieter. (Materials Science & Engineering Ser.). 800p. (C). 1986. 99.38 (*0-07-016893-8*) McGraw.

Mechanical Metamorphosis: Technological Change in Revolutionary America, 78. Neil L. York. LC 84-11845. (Contributions in American Studies: No. 78). (Illus.). 240p. 1985. 62.95 (*0-313-24475-8*, YMM/, Greenwood Pr) Greenwood.

Mechanical Methods of Chaparral Modification. George A. Roby & Lisle R. Green. (Illus.). 60p. 1998. reprint ed. 13.00 (*0-89904-514-6*, Ecosytems Resrch); reprint ed. pap. 7.00 (*0-89904-515-4*, Ecosytems Resrch) Crumb Elbow Pub.

Mechanical Misadventures in Anasthesia. Gordon M. Wyant. LC 78-4864. 1978. text 30.00 (*0-8020-5423-4*) U of Toronto Pr.

Mechanical Muscial Instruments. Alexander Buchner. LC 78-5429. (Illus.). 174p. 1978. reprint ed. lib. bdg. 95.00 (*0-313-20440-3*, BUMM, Greenwood Pr) Greenwood.

Mechanical Music. Keven McElhone. (Album Ser.: No. 333). (Illus.). 32p. 1997. pap. 6.25 (*0-7478-0354-4*, Pub. by Shire Pubns) Parkwest Pubns.

Mechanical Neck Pain: Perspectives in Functional Anatomy. James A. Porterfield & Carl DeRosa. (Illus.). 272p. 1994. text. write for info. (*0-7216-6640-X*, W B Saunders Co) Harcrt Hlth Sci Grp.

***Mechanical Performance of Laminated Composites.** Ed. by D. Lesuer et al. (Illus.). 267p. 1999. 110.00 (*0-87339-414-3*, 4143) Minerals Metals.

Mechanical Philosophy. Ed. by Marie B. Hall & I. Bernard Cohen. LC 80-2108. (Development of Science Ser.). (Illus.). 1981. lib. bdg. 17.95 (*0-405-13873-3*) Ayer.

Mechanical Philosophy & the "Animal Oeconomy" Ed. by Theodore L. Brown & I. Bernard Cohen. LC 80-2085. (Development of Science Ser.). (Illus.). 1981. lib. bdg. 38.95 (*0-405-13851-2*) Ayer.

Mechanical Plant in Construction. Ed. by Leslie Gardener. (Illus.). 138p. 1979. 55.00 (*0-7114-4306-8*) Transatl Arts.

Mechanical Power Transmission. William J. Patton. 1980. text 43.00 (*0-13-569905-3*) P-H.

Mechanical Power Transmission. Terry Wireman. LC 85-702614. 1985. student ed. 7.00 (*0-8064-0329-2*, 820) Bergwall.

Mechanical Power Transmission Components. Ed. by David W. South & Jon R. Mancuso. LC 94-25795. (Mechanical Engineering Ser.: Vol. 92). (Illus.). 920p. 1994. text 185.00 (*0-8247-9036-7*) Dekker.

Mechanical Principles of Engineering & Architecture. Henry Gwyn Jeffreys Moseley. (Industrial Antiquities Ser.). (Illus.). 656p. 1998. reprint ed. pap. 240.00 (*1-85297-017-0*, Pub. by Archival Facs) St Mut.

Mechanical Problems in Measuring Force & Mass: Proceeding of the XIth International Conference on Measurement of Force & Mass Proceedings-Handbook. Ed. by H. Wieringa. 1986. text 205.50 (*90-247-3346-4*) Kluwer Academic.

Mechanical Processes of the Historian. Charles Johnson. 1977. lib. bdg. 59.95 (*0-8490-2217-7*) Gordon Pr.

Mechanical Processes with Repeated Attenuated Impacts. Robert F. Nagaev. Ed. & Tr. by Eugueni B. Kremer. 250p. 1998. 48.00 (*981-02-3504-6*) World Scientific Pub.

Mechanical Properties & Behavior of Solids: Plastic Instabilities. Ed. by V. Balakrishnan & C. E. Bottani. 380p. 1986. text 89.00 (*9971-5-0040-X*) World Scientific Pub.

Mechanical Properties & Deformation Behavior of Materials Having Ultra-Fine Microstructures: Proceedings of the NATO Advanced Study Institute, Porto Novo, Portugal, June 28 - July 10, 1992. NATO Advanced Study Institute on Mechanical Proper. Ed. by Michael A. Nastasi et al. LC 93-12427. (NATO Advanced Study Institutes Series E, Applied Sciences: No. 233). 640p. (C). 1993. text 353.00 (*0-7923-2195-2*) Kluwer Academic.

Mechanical Properties & Phase Transformations of Multi-Phase Intermetallic Alloys. Ed. by Anthony Giamei et al. LC 95-78583. (Illus.). 260p. 1996. 20.00 (*0-87339-303-1*, 3031) Minerals Metals.

Mechanical Properties & Structures of Alpha Keratin Fibers: Wool, Human Hair, & Related Fibers. Max Feughelman. LC 97-204565. 144p. 1996. 69.95 (*0-86840-359-8*, Pub. by New South Wales Univ Pr) Intl Spec Bk.

Mechanical Properties at High Rates of Strain, 1984: Proceedings of the Third Conference on the Mechanical Properties of Materials at High Rates of Strain Held in Oxford, 9-12 April 1984. Conference on the Mechanical Properties of Materia. Ed. by J. Harding. LC 86-102820. (Conference Ser.: No. 70). 568p. reprint ed. pap. 176.10 (*0-7837-3256-2*, 204327500007) Bks Demand.

Mechanical Properties of Bamboo. Jules J. Janssen. 148p. (C). 1991. text 92.50 (*0-7923-1260-0*) Kluwer Academic.

Mechanical Properties of BCC Metals: Proceedings of the U. S. - Japan Seminar. Ed. by M. Meshii. LC 82-81287. (Conference Proceedings Ser.). (Illus.). 253p. reprint ed. pap. 78.50 (*0-608-15985-9*, 205226700084) Bks Demand.

Mechanical Properties of Biomaterials: Proceedings Held at Keele University, September 1978. Ed. by Garth W. Hastings & D. F. Williams. LC 79-41776. (Advances in Biomaterials Ser.: Vol. 2). 590p. reprint ed. pap. 182.90 (*0-608-30882-X*, 202210200024) Bks Demand.

Mechanical Properties of Cement-Based Composites. A. M. Brandt. LC 93-3413. 1993. write for info. (*1-85861-029-X*) Elsevier.

Mechanical Properties of Ceramics. John B. Watchman. LC 95-36612. (Illus.). 472p. 1996. 95.00 (*0-471-13316-7*, Wiley-Interscience) Wiley.

***Mechanical Properties of Ceramics & Composites: Grain & Particle Effects.** R. W. Rice. LC 00-28151. (Materials Engineering Ser.). (Illus.). 2000. write for info. (*0-8247-8874-5*) Dekker.

Mechanical Properties of Coatings. Loren W. Hill. (Illus.). 25p. 1987. pap. 30.00 (*0-934010-31-5*) Fed Soc Coat Tech.

Mechanical Properties of Metallic Composites. Ed. by Shojiro Ochiai. (Materials Engineering Ser.: Vol. 7). (Illus.). 808p. 1993. text 235.00 (*0-8247-9116-9*) Dekker.

Mechanical Properties of Metals. 300p. 1997. 31.00 (*981-02-2622-5*) World Scientific Pub.

Mechanical Properties of Plastics & Composites. E. Miller. (Mechanical Engineering Ser.). Date not set. write for info. (*0-8247-9568-7*) Dekker.

Mechanical Properties of Polymers & Composites. 2nd expanded rev. ed. Ed. by Robert F. Landel & Lawrence E. Nielsen. (Mechanical Engineering Ser.: Vol. 90). (Illus.). 584p. 1993. text 175.00 (*0-8247-8964-4*) Dekker.

***Mechanical Properties of Work Materials.** Edmund Isakov. LC 99-88669. 2000. write for info. (*1-56990-294-1*) Hanser-Gardner.

Mechanical Properties Research, '88. Ed. by D. J. Fisher. 450p. 1989. text 130.00 (*0-87849-596-7*, Pub. by Trans T Pub) Enfield Pubs NH.

Mechanical Properties Research, '89. D. J. Fisher. 374p. 1990. text 130.00 (*0-87849-603-3*, Pub. by Trans T Pub) Enfield Pubs NH.

Mechanical Pulping, Vol. 2. Ed. by Michael J. Kocurek & R. A. Leask. (Pulp & Paper Manufacture Ser.: Vol. 2). 281p. 1987. pap. 60.00 (*0-919893-40-6*, 0202MS02) TAPPI.

Mechanical Relaxation of Interstitials in Irradiated Metals. K. H. Robrock. (Tracts in Modern Physics Ser.: Vol. 118). (Illus.). 112p. 1990. 71.95 (*0-387-51090-7*) Spr-Verlag.

Mechanical Relaxation of Residual Stresses, STP 993. Ed. by Leonard Mordfin. LC 88-15450. (Special Technical Publication (STP) Ser.). (Illus.). 128p. 1988. pap. text 38.00 (*0-8031-1166-5*, STP993) ASTM.

Mechanical Reliability. B. S. Dhillon. (Educ Ser.). 330p. 1988. 57.95 (*0-930403-38-X*, 38-X) AIAA.

Mechanical Reliability & Design. A. D. Carter. LC 97-65. 240p. 1997. text 59.95 (*0-470-23719-8*) Halsted Pr.

***Mechanical Response of Polymers: An Introduction.** Alan S. Wineman & K. R. Rajagopal. (Illus.). 368p. (C). 2000. 90.00 (*0-521-64337-6*); pap. 39.95 (*0-521-64409-7*) Cambridge U Pr.

Mechanical Rights. Ed. by David Lester. 183p. 1992. pap. 102.00 (*90-6215-313-5*, Pub. by Maklu Uitgev) Gaunt.

Mechanical Rubber Goods Catalogue, 1914. New York Belting Company Staff. (Illus.). 215p. 1998. reprint ed. pap. text 25.00 (*0-87556-852-1*) Saifer.

Mechanical Science. William Bolton. LC 93-49. (Illus.). 344p. 1993. pap. 39.95 (*0-632-03579-X*) Blackwell Sci.

Mechanical Seal Design & Technology. J. P. Netzel & B. Gordon. Date not set. write for info. (*0-8247-8950-4*) Dekker.

***Mechanical Seal Handbook.** rev. ed. (Illus.). 45p. 1999. pap. 25.00 (*1-892965-02-X*) Fluid Sealing Assn.

Mechanical Seals: Guidelines for the Pulp & Paper Industry. Ed. by Elton T. Krogel. (Illus.). 48p. (Orig.). 1993. pap. 30.00 (*0-89852-316-8*, 0101R223) TAPPI.

Mechanical Sensors, Vol. 7, Mechanical Sensors. Ed. by W. Gopel et al. 675p. 1993. 415.00 (*3-527-26773-5*, Wiley-VCH) Wiley.

Mechanical Services Bldg. T. D. Eastop. (C). 1992. pap. 51.95 (*0-582-05695-0*, Pub. by Addison-Wesley) Longman.

Mechanical Signature Analysis: Theory & Applications. S. Braun. 1986. text 162.00 (*0-12-127255-9*) Acad Pr.

Mechanical Song: Women, Voice, & the Artificial in Nineteenth-Century French Narrative. Felicia Miller-Frank. LC 94-34279. 223p. 1995. 35.00 (*0-8047-2381-8*) Stanford U Pr.

Mechanical Specifications Writer. Jack Rudman. (Career Examination Ser.: C-3248). 1994. pap. 29.95 (*0-8373-3248-6*) Nat Learn.

Mechanical Spectroscopy of Materials. Magalas. 1000p. 1997. text. write for info. (*0-412-58450-6*, Chap & Hall NY) Chapman & Hall.

Mechanical Springs Markets. Market Intelligence Staff. 360p. 1994. 1895.00 (*0-7889-0090-0*) Frost & Sullivan.

Mechanical Stores Clerk. Jack Rudman. (Career Examination Ser.: C-3080). 1994. pap. 23.95 (*0-8373-3080-7*) Nat Learn.

Mechanical String Model of Adiabatic Chemical Reactions. W. Kliesh. 1998. pap. write for info. (*3-540-64978-6*) Spr-Verlag.

Mechanical System Design for Buildings: Design for Efficiency. Jan F. Kreider & Ari Rabl. LC 93-37693. 832p. (C). 1994. 106.56 (*0-07-834776-9*) McGraw.

Mechanical Systems Design Handbook Modeling Measurement & Control. Osita D. Nwokah. (Electrical Engineering Handbks.). 1999. 110.00 (*0-8493-8596-2*, 8596) CRC Pr.

Mechanical Systems for Health Care Facilities. J. Robin Barrick. (Management & Compliance Ser.: Vol. 8). (Illus.). 308p. 1993. ring bd. 110.00 (*0-87258-654-5*, 055216) Am Hospital.

Mechanical Systems Reference Guide. Harold A. Rothbart. 1989. 34.50 (*0-07-054025-X*) McGraw.

Mechanical Technology. Jack Rudman. (Occupational Competency Examination (OCE) Ser.: Vol. 25). 47.95 (*0-8373-5775-6*) Nat Learn.

Mechanical Technology. Jack Rudman. (Occupational Competency Examination Ser.: OCE-25). 1994. pap. 27.95 (*0-8373-5725-X*) Nat Learn.

Mechanical Technology. 2nd ed. D. H. Bacon & R. C. Stephens. (Illus.). 552p. 1990. 29.95 (*0-8311-3003-2*) Indus Pr.

Mechanical Technology. 3rd ed. D. H. Bacon & R. C. Stephens. LC 98-10453. 544p. 1998. pap. text 44.95 (*0-7506-3886-9*) Buttrwrth-Heinemann.

Mechanical Technology in Agriculture. Donald M. Johnson & David E. Lawver. 640p. 1996. text 66.25 (*0-8134-3017-8*); text, teacher ed. 12.95 (*0-8134-3018-6*) Interstate.

Mechanical Technology of Greek & Roman Antiquity. A. G. Drachmann. (Illus.). 1963. 25.00 (*0-934454-61-2*) Lubrecht & Cramer.

Mechanical Testing for Deformation Model Development - STP 765. Ed. by R.W. Rhode & Swearengen. 478p. 1982. 51.50 (*0-8031-0737-4*, SPT765) ASTM.

Mechanical Testing Methodology for Ceramic Design & Reliability. Ed. by Cranmer & Richerson. (Illus.). 448p. 1998. text. write for info. (*0-8247-9567-9*) Dekker.

***Mechanical Testing of Advanced Fibre Composites.** J. M. Hodgkinson. LC 00-31154. 2000. write for info. (*0-8493-0845-3*) CRC Pr.

Mechanical Testing of Advanced Fibre Composites. John Hodgkinson. 350p. 2000. boxed set 170.00 (*1-85573-312-9*, Pub. by Woodhead Pubng) Am Educ Systs.

***Mechanical Testing of Bone & the Bone-Implant Interface** Yuehuei H. An & Robert A. Draughn. LC 99-36531. 1999. write for info. (*0-8493-0266-8*) CRC Pr.

Mechanical Testing of Ceramics & Ceramic Composites: 1994 International Mechanical Engineering Congress & Exposition, Chicago, Illinois - November 6-11, 1994. (AMD Ser.: Vol. 197). 164p. 1994. 68.00 (*0-7918-1456-4*, G00951) ASME.

Mechanical Tests for Bituminous Materials/Essais Mecaniques pour les Materiaux Bitumineux: Proceedings of the Fifth International RILEM Symposium/Actes du Cinquieme Symposium RILEM, Lyon, 14-16 May 1997. Ed. by H. Di Benedetto & L. Francken. (ENG & FRE., Illus.). 644p. (C). 1997. text 142.00 (*90-5410-876-2*, Pub. by A A Balkema) Ashgate Pub Co.

Mechanical Tests for Bituminous Mixes - Characterization, Design & Quality Control: Proceedings of the Fourth International RILEM Symposium. Ed. by H. W. Fritz & E. Eustacchio. 672p. 1991. 109.95 (*0-442-31374-8*) Chapman & Hall.

Mechanical Theorem Proving in Geometries: Basic Principles. Wen-ts Un Wu. Tr. by Xio Fan Jin & Dongming Wang from CHI. LC 94-1452. (Texts & Monographs in Symbolic Computation). 304p. 1994. 79.95 (*0-387-82506-1*) Spr-Verlag.

Mechanical Theorem Proving in the U. S. S. R. The Leningrad School. Vladimir Lifschitz. Ed. by Rebecca Krafft. (Illus.). 103p. (Orig.). 1986. pap. text 75.00 (*1-55831-026-6*) Delphic Associates.

Mechanical 3.0: Assembly Modeling - Student Manual. 2nd unabridged ed. Richard L. Allen & Laura Martz. (Illus.). 200p. 1998. pap. text 95.00 (*1-891502-32-8*, MDT30ASM) Tech Learn Co.

Mechanical Trades Pocket Manual. 3rd ed. Carl A. Nelson. 364p. 1990. pap. 14.95 (*0-02-588665-7*, Aude IN) IDG Bks.

Mechanical Troubleshooting. Whitman. (Heating, Ventilation/Air Conditioning Ser.). 1992. 108.95 (*0-8273-5107-0*, VNR) Wiley.

Mechanical (Turbines & Auxiliary Equipment) see Modern Power Station Practice

Mechanical Universe: Mechanics & Heat, Advanced Edition. Steven C. Frautschi et al. (Illus.). 608p. 1986. text 49.95 (*0-521-30432-6*) Cambridge U Pr.

***Mechanical Variables Measurement: Solid, Fluid & Thermal.** John G. Webster. LC 99-43783. 664p. 1999. boxed set 79.95 (*0-8493-0047-9*) CRC Pr.

Mechanical Ventilating Systems for Livestock Housing. MWPS Engineers Staff. LC 89-77073. (Illus.). 70p. 1990. pap. 6.00 (*0-89373-075-0*, MWPS-32) MidWest Plan Serv.

***Mechanical Ventilation.** Lonny J. Ashworth. (CPG Mentor - Patient Cases in Respiratory Care Ser.: Unit 6). 1998. write for info. (*0-8151-2290-X*) Mosby Inc.

Mechanical Ventilation. Ed. by F. Lemaire. xii, 198p. 1991. pap. 63.00 (*0-387-53322-2*) Spr-Verlag.

Mechanical Ventilation. Neil R. MacIntyre & Richard D. Branson. LC 99-25457. (Illus.). 700p. 2000. text. write for info. (*0-7216-7361-9*, W B Saunders Co) Harcrt Hlth Sci Grp.

Mechanical Ventilation. 3rd ed. Payne. 1999. pap. text, student ed. 18.95 (*0-8151-4376-1*) Mosby Inc.

Mechanical Ventilation, Vol. 4. Karen Milikowski. (Respiratory Care Workbook Ser.). 24p. (gr. 13). 1995. text, wbk. ed. 8.95 (*0-8151-6307-X*, 26025) Mosby Inc.

Mechanical Ventilation: A Practice Approach. Ed. by Suhail A. Raoof & Faroque Khan. LC 97-3305. 186p. (Orig.). (C). 1998. pap. text 40.00 (*0-943126-57-6*) Amer Coll Phys.

Mechanical Ventilation: Physiological & Clinical Applications. 3rd ed. Pilbeam. LC 97-40495. (Illus.). 460p. (C). (gr. 13). 1998. pap. text 43.00 (*0-8151-2600-X*, 31083) Mosby Inc.

Mechanical Ventilation & Assisted Respiration: Past, Present & Future. Ake Grenvik et al. (Contemporary Management in Critical Care Ser.: Vol. 1, No. 1). (Illus.). 190p. 1991. text 50.00 (*0-443-08828-4*) Church.

An Asterisk (*) at the beginning of an entry indicates that the title is appearing for the first time.

Mechanical Vibration: Analysis, Uncertainties, & Control. Haym Benaroya & Mohammed Ettouney. LC 97-30975. 511p. 1997. 105.00 (*0-13-948373-X*) P-H.

Mechanical Vibration Analysis. R. Srinivasan. 1985. pap. text 9.00 (*0-07-451933-6*) McGraw.

Mechanical Vibration Analysis & Computation. D. E. Newland. (C). 1989. 79.95 (*0-582-02744-6*) Longman.

Mechanical Vibrations. San Diego State University Staff & Singiresu S. Rao. (C). 1986. text. write for info. (*0-201-06550-9*) Addison-Wesley.

Mechanical Vibrations. William W. Seto. 208p. (Orig.). (C). 1968. pap. 12.95 (*0-07-056327-6*) McGraw.

Mechanical Vibrations. Ed. by Den J. Hartog. (Civil, Mechanical & Other Engineering Ser.). 436p. 1985. reprint ed. pap. 12.95 (*0-486-64785-4*) Dover.

Mechanical Vibrations. 2nd ed. Singiresu S. Rao. (C). 1992. pap. text. write for info. (*0-201-55693-6*) Addison-Wesley.

Mechanical Vibrations. 2nd ed. Austin H. Church. LC 63-14755. 452p. reprint ed. 140.20 (*0-8357-9933-6*, 201317900085) Bks Demand.

Mechanical Vibrations. 3rd ed. S. S. Rao. (C). 1995. pap. text, student ed. 42.66 (*0-201-52687-5*) Addison-Wesley.

Mechanical Vibrations. 3rd ed. Singiresu S. Rao. LC 93-3311. 920p. (C). 1995. pap. text 105.00 (*0-201-52686-7*) Addison-Wesley.

Mechanical Vibrations for Engineers. Michel Lalanne et al. Tr. & Adapted by Frederick C. Nelson. LC 83-6908. (Illus.). 274p. reprint ed. pap. 85.00 (*0-8357-3097-2*, 203935400012) Bks Demand.

Mechanical Vibrations Solutions Manual. San Diego State University Staff & Singiresu S. Rao. (C). 1986. teacher ed. 10.25 (*0-201-06551-7*) Addison-Wesley.

Mechanical Vibrations with Applications. A. C. Walshaw. (Mechanical Engineering Ser.). 197p. 1985. text 41.95 (*0-470-20115-0*) P-H.

Mechanical Vibrations with Applications. variorum ed. (C). 1984. text 16.50 (*0-13-567595-2*, Macmillan Coll) P-H.

Mechanical Wear: Being the Proceedings of a Summer Conference on This Subject Held in June 1948. Ed. by John T. Burwell. LC 50-1084. 395p. reprint ed. pap. 122.50 (*0-608-14337-5*, 205196000017) Bks Demand.

Mechanical Wear Prediction & Prevention. Raymond G. Bayer. LC 94-6941. (Mechanical Engineering Ser.: Vol. 91). (Illus.). 672p. 1994. text 199.00 (*0-8247-9027-8*) Dekker.

Mechanical Work. 2nd ed. Harry W. Koch. 1987. 12.00 (*0-910553-08-4*) Ken-Bks.

Mechanical Working & Steel Processing Vol. XIII: Proceedings of the 17th Mechanical Working & Steel Processing Conference, Holiday Inn-Airport, Pittsburgh, PA, January 22-23, 1975. Iron & Steel Society of AIME Staff. LC TS0320.. 382p. reprint ed. pap. 118.50 (*0-608-13728-6*, 202064300018) Bks Demand.

Mechanical Working & Steel Processing Vol. XVIII: Proceedings of the 21st Mechanical Working & Steel Processing Conference, Marriott Inn, Cleveland, Ohio, October 24-25, 1979. Iron & Steel Society of AIME Staff. LC TS0320.. 392p. reprint ed. pap. 121.60 (*0-608-13824-X*, 202064200018) Bks Demand.

Mechanical Working & Steel Processing Vol. XVIII: Proceedings of the 22nd Mechanical Working & Steel Processing Conference, Harbour Castle Inn, Toronto, Ontario, October 29-30, 1980. Iron & Steel Society of AIME Staff. LC 75-17963. (Illus.). 568p. reprint ed. pap. 176.10 (*0-7837-6125-2*, 204566000018) Bks Demand.

Mechanical Working & Steel Processing Vol. XIX: Proceedings of the 23rd Mechanical Working & Steel Processing Conference, Pittsburgh Hilton, Pittsburgh, PA, October 28-29, 1981. Iron & Steel Society of AIME Staff. LC 75-17963. (Illus.). 676p. reprint ed. pap. 200.00 (*0-7837-6123-6*, 204565800019) Bks Demand.

Mechanical Working & Steel Processing Vol. XX: Proceedings of the 24th Mechanical Working & Steel Processing Conference, Sheraton-Houston, Houston, TX, October 27-29, 1982. Iron & Steel Society of AIME Staff. LC 75-17963. (Illus.). 576p. reprint ed. pap. 178.60 (*0-7837-6124-4*, 204565900020) Bks Demand.

Mechanical Working & Steel Processing Vol. XXI: Proceedings of the 25th Mechanical Working & Steel Processing Conference, Franklin Plaza Hotel, Philadelphia, PA. Iron & Steel Society of AIME Staff. LC 75-17963. 631p. reprint ed. pap. 195.70 (*0-608-18700-3*, 202772800056) Bks Demand.

Mechanical Working & Steel Processing Vol. XXII: Proceedings of the 26th Mechanical Working & Steel Processing Conference, McCormick Center Hotel, Chicago, IL. Iron & Steel Society of AIME Staff. LC 75-17963. 307p. reprint ed. pap. 95.20 (*0-608-16978-1*, 202772900056) Bks Demand.

Mechanical Working & Steel Processing Vol. XXIII: Proceedings of the 27th Mechanical Working & Steel Processing Conference, Stouffer Inn on the Square, Cleveland, OH. Iron & Steel Society of AIME Staff. LC 75-17963. (Illus.). 289p. reprint ed. pap. 89.60 (*0-7837-6127-9*, 204566200023) Bks Demand.

Mechanical Working & Steel Processing Vol. XXV: Proceedings of the 29th Mechanical Working & Steel Processing Conference, Royal York Hotel, Toronto, Ontario, Canada, October 21-23, 1987. Iron & Steel Society of AIME Staff. LC 75-17963. (Conference Proceedings Ser.: No. 25). (Illus.). 422p. reprint ed. pap. 130.90 (*0-608-18479-9*, 203299500082) Bks Demand.

Mechanical Working & Steel Processing Vol. XXVII: Proceedings of the 31st Mechanical Working & Steel Processing Conference, Chicago, IL, October 22-25, 1989, Vol. 25. Iron & Steel Society of AIME Staff. LC 75-17963. (Conference Proceedings Ser.: No. 27). (Illus.). 630p. reprint ed. pap. 195.30 (*0-7837-1807-1*, 204200700027) Bks Demand.

Mechanical Working & Steel Processing Vol. XXIX: Proceedings of the 33rd Mechanical Working & Steel Processing Conference, St. Louis, MO, Held October 20-22, 1991. Iron & Steel Society of AIME Staff. LC 75-17963. 480p. 1992. pap. 148.80 (*0-608-01271-8*, 206202100001) Bks Demand.

Mechanical Working & Steel Processing Conference: Proceedings of the Annual ISS Mechanical Working & Steel Processing Conferences, Vol. XXXI. LC 75-17963. 552p. 1994. 110.00 (*0-932897-87-8*) Iron & Steel.

Mechanical Working & Steel Processing Conference: Proceedings of the Annual ISS Mechanical Working & Steel Processing Conferences, Vol. XXXII. LC 75-17963. 596p. 1995. 110.00 (*0-932897-96-7*) Iron & Steel.

Mechanical Working & Steel Processing Conference: Proceedings of the Annual ISS Mechanical Working & Steel Processing Conferences, Vol. XXXIII. 1036p. 1995. 110.00 (*1-886362-05-X*) Iron & Steel.

Mechanical Working & Steel Processing Conference: Proceedings, 30th, Dearborn, MI, October 23-26, 1988. Iron & Steel Society of AIME Staff. LC 75-17963. (Illus.). 472p. reprint ed. pap. 146.40 (*0-7837-6126-0*, 204566100026) Bks Demand.

Mechanical Working & Steel Processing Conference: Proceedings, 32nd, Cincinnati, OH, October 21-24, 1990. Iron & Steel Society of AIME Staff. LC 75-17963. 552p. 1991. reprint ed. pap. 171.20 (*0-608-00372-7*, 206108500007) Bks Demand.

Mechanical Working & Steel Processing Conference & Related Papers Index (1959-1994) LC 95-78137. 336p. 1995. 45.00 (*1-886362-03-3*) Iron & Steel.

Mechanical Working & Steel Processing Conference Proceedings, 1999, Vol. 37. (Illus.). 950p. 1999. pap. text 110.00 (*1-886362-37-8*) Iron & Steel.

Mechanical Working & Steel Processing Conference Proceedings, 34th: Montreal, Quebec, Canada, October 25-28, 1992 - Sponsored by the Mechanical Working & Steel Processing Division of the Iron & Steel Society. Iron & Steel Society of AIME Staff. LC 75-17963. (Illus.). 538p. reprint ed. pap. 166.80 (*0-7837-6850-8*, 204667900030) Bks Demand.

Mechanical Working & Steel Processing Conference, 38th Proceedings Vol. 34: Cleveland, Ohio, October 13-16, 1996. Iron & Steel Society of AIME Staff. LC 75-17963. (Illus.). 671p. 1997. reprint ed. pap. 200.00 (*0-608-07964-2*, 206793600012) Bks Demand.

Mechanical Working of Metals: Theory & Practice. J. N. Harris. (International Series of Monographs on Materials Science & Technology: Vol. 36). (Illus.). 275p. 1983. 109.00 (*0-08-025464-0*, Pub. by Pergamon Repr) Franklin.

Mechanically Alloyed & Nonocrystalline Materials: ISMANAM-94. A. Reza Yavari. (Materials Science Forum Ser.: Vols. 179-181). (Illus.). 902p. (C). 1995. text 266.00 (*0-87849-688-2*, Pub. by Trans T Pub) Enfield Pubs NH.

Mechanically Alloyed, Metastable & Nanocrystalline Materials: ISMANAM-97. Ed. by M. D. Baro & S. Surinach. (Materials Science Forum Ser.: Vols. 269-272). (Illus.). 1148p. (C). 1998. text 295.00 (*0-87849-799-4*, Pub. by Trans T Pub) Enfield Pubs NH.

Mechanically & Electrically Operated Fuel Pumps for Marine Use, UL 1130. 2nd ed. (C). 1999. pap. text 95.00 (*1-55989-131-9*) Underwrtrs Labs.

Mechanically Stabilized Backfill: Proceedings of an International Symposium, Denver, 6-8 February 1997. Ed. by Jonathan T. Wu. (Illus.). 480p. (C). 1997. text 136.00 (*90-5410-902-5*, Pub. by A A Balkema) Ashgate Pub Co.

Mechanics. W. Chester. (Illus.). 1980. text 50.00 (*0-04-510058-6*) Routledge.

Mechanics. C. G. Cleveland & S. Harold Collins. (Straight Forward Advanced English Ser.). 80p. 1993. pap., student ed. 7.95 (*0-931993-56-3*, GP-056) Garlic Pr OR.

Mechanics. Jacob P. Den Hartog. 462p. 1961. pap. 11.95 (*0-486-60754-2*) Dover.

Mechanics. Fenner. 125p. (C). 1991. teacher ed., per. write for info. (*0-8493-8625-X*) CRC Pr.

Mechanics. School Mathematics Project Staff. (School Mathematics Project 16-19 Ser.). 544p. (C). 1998. pap. text 29.95 (*0-521-56615-0*) Cambridge U Pr.

Mechanics. Arnold Sommerfeld. (Lectures on Theoretical Physics Ser.: Vol. 1). 1964. 27.00 (*0-12-654668-1*) Acad Pr.

Mechanics. N. C. Barford. LC 72-2639. (Illus.). 407p. reprint ed. pap. 126.20 (*0-608-18411-X*, 203042600069) Bks Demand.

Mechanics. John C. Slater & Nathaniel H. Frank. LC 83-6694. 297p. 1983. reprint ed. lib. bdg. 69.50 (*0-313-24064-7*, SLME, Greenwood Pr) Greenwood.

Mechanics. 2nd ed. (C). 1973. 88.44 (*0-07-004880-0*) McGraw.

Mechanics. 2nd ed. P. Smith & R. C. Smith. LC 90-31722. 342p. 1990. pap. 94.95 (*0-471-92737-6*) Wiley.

Mechanics. 3rd ed. Keith R. Symon. LC 75-128910. (Physics & Physical Science Ser.). 639p. (C). 1971. 101.00 (*0-201-07392-7*) Addison-Wesley.

Mechanics see Fundamental University Physics

Mechanics, Vol. 1. 2nd ed. 1973. student ed. 40.31 (*0-07-004889-4*) McGraw.

Mechanics: Complete Advanced Level Mathematics. Martin Adams et al. (Illus.). 616p. (YA). (gr. 11 up). 1999. pap. 43.50 (*0-7487-3559-3*, Pub. by S Thornes Pubs) Trans-Atl Phila.

Mechanics: From Newton's Laws to Deterministic Chaos. F. A. Scheck. (Illus.). xiv, 431p. 1990. pap. text 44.00 (*0-387-52715-X*) Spr-Verlag.

Mechanics: From Newton's Laws to Deterministic Chaos. 2nd rev. ed. Florian Schneck. LC 94-21757.Tr. of Mechanik. 1994. 49.00 (*0-387-57475-1*) Spr-Verlag.

Mechanics: From Newton's Laws to Deterministic Chaos. 3rd ed. F. Scheck. LC 99-19386. (Illus.). xiv, 533p. 1999. 59.95 (*3-540-65558-1*) Spr-Verlag.

Mechanics & Biophysics of Hearing: Proceedings of a Conference Held at the University of Wisconsin, Madison, WI June 25-29, 1990. Ed. by C. D. Geisler. (Lecture Notes in Biomathematics Ser.: Vol. 87). vii, 418p. 1991. 60.00 (*0-387-97473-3*) Spr-Verlag.

Mechanics & Chemistry in Lubrication. A. Dorinson & Kenneth C. Ludema. (Tribology Ser.: Vol. 9). xvi, 634p. 1985. 288.50 (*0-444-42492-X*) Elsevier.

Mechanics & Chemistry of Solid Propellants: Proceedings of the 4th Symposium on Naval Structural Mechanics, Lafayette, Apr. 1965. A. Cemal Eringen & H. Liebowitz. LC 65-29256. (Office of Naval Research Structural Mechanics Ser.). 1967. 279.00 (*0-08-011843-7*, Pub. by Pergamon Repr) Franklin.

Mechanics & Combustion of Droplets & Sprays. Ed. by H. H. Chiu & Norman A. Chigier. LC 95-49179. 1995. write for info. (*0-15-670051-4*) Begell Hse.

Mechanics & Combustion of Droplets & Sprays. H. H. Chiu & Norman A. Chigier. 393p. 1996. 97.50 (*1-56700-051-7*) Begell Hse.

Mechanics & Construction Liens in Alaska, Oregon & Washington. Brian A. Blum. 510p. 1993. ring bd. 75.00 (*0-409-20008-5*, MICHIE) LEXIS Pub.

Mechanics & Construction Liens in Alaska, Oregon & Washington. Brian A. Blum. 1994. suppl. ed. 57.50 (*0-685-73841-8*, MICHIE) LEXIS Pub.

Mechanics & Control. R. S. Guttalu. (Illus.). 366p. (C). 1994. 115.00 (*0-306-44669-3*, Plenum Trade) Perseus Pubng.

Mechanics & Control: Proceedings of the 3rd Workshop on Control Mechanics, in Honor of the 65th Birthday of George Leitmann, University of Southern California, January 22-24, 1990. Ed. by J. M. Skoweonski et al. (Lecture Notes in Control & Information Sciences: Vol. 151). (Illus.). 502p. 1991. 102.95 (*0-387-53517-9*) Spr-Verlag.

Mechanics & Control: Proceedings of the 4th Workshop on Control Mechanics, January 21-23, 1991 University of Southern California, U. S. A. Ed. by J. M. Skowronski et al. (Lecture Notes in Control & Information Sciences: Vol. 170). (Illus.). 300p. 1992. 86.95 (*0-387-54954-4*) Spr-Verlag.

Mechanics & Control of Large Flexible Structures. Ed. by John L. Junkins. (PAAS Ser.: Vol. 129). 1990. 99.95 (*0-930403-73-8*, V-129) AIAA.

Mechanics & Control of Robots. K. C. Gupta. LC 96-37619. (Mechanical Engineering Ser.). (Illus.). 192p. 1997. 64.95 (*0-387-94923-2*) Spr-Verlag.

***Mechanics & Design of Tubular Structures.** Ed. by K. Jarmai & J. Farkas. (CISM International Center for Mechanical Sciences Ser.: No. 394). vi, 337p. 1999. pap. 75.00 (*3-211-83145-2*) Spr-Verlag.

Mechanics & Dynamical Systems with Mathematica. Nicola Bellomo et al. LC 99-14394. (Modeling & Simulation in Science, Engineering & Technology Ser.). 400p. (C). 1999. 59.95 (*0-8176-4007-X*) Birkhauser.

Mechanics & Electricity Lab Mnl Physics 158. 3rd ed. 308p. (C). 1996. 29.00 (*0-536-59897-5*) Pearson Custom.

Mechanics & Electrodynamics see Shorter Course of Theoretical Physics

Mechanics & Manufacturers in the Early Industrial Revolution: Lynn, Massachusetts, 1780-1860. Paul G. Faler. LC 80-21619. (SUNY Series in American Social History). 267p. (C). 1981. text 44.50 (*0-87395-504-8*); pap. text 14.95 (*0-87395-505-6*) State U NY Pr.

Mechanics & Materials: Fundamentals & Linkages. Ed. by Marc Andre Meyers et al. LC 98-29974. 648p. 1999. 135.00 (*0-471-24317-5*) Wiley.

Mechanics & Materials for Electronic Packaging Vol. 1: Design & Process Issues in Electronic Packaging: 1994 International Mechanical Engineering Congress & Exposition, Chicago, Illinois - November 6-11, 1994. Ed. by L. C. Brinson & B. Moran. LC 94-79149. (AMD Ser.: Vol. 195). 236p. 1994. 88.00 (*0-7918-1449-1*, G00944) ASME.

Mechanics & Materials for Electronic Packaging Vol. 2: Thermal & Mechanical Behavior & Modeling: 1994 International Mechanical Engineering Congress & Exposition, Chicago, Illinois - November 6-11, 1994. LC 94-79149. (AMD Ser.: Vol. 187). 236p. 1994. 80.00 (*0-7918-1427-0*, G00922) ASME.

Mechanics & Materials for Electronic Packaging Vol. 3: Coupled Field Behavior in Materials: 1994 International Mechanical Engineering Congress & Exposition, Chicago, Illinois - November 6-11, 1994. Ed. by M. L. Dunn. LC 94-79149. (AMD Ser.: Vol. 193). 88p. 1994. 40.00 (*0-7918-1442-4*, G00937) ASME.

Mechanics & Motion. L. MacKinnon. (Oxford Physics Ser.). (Illus.). 1978. 23.50 (*0-19-851825-0*); pap. 10.95 (*0-19-851843-9*) OUP.

Mechanics & Owners Guide to 1941-1959 Harley-Davidson Big Twins, Vol. 1. Kirk Perry. (Illus.). 200p. 1997. spiral bd. write for info. (*0-9672744-0-0*) Vintage Twin.

Mechanics & Physics of Aerating Grain. Navarro. 1995. 284.00 (*0-8493-4542-1*, CRC Reprint) Franklin.

Mechanics & Physics of Energy Density: Characterization of Material-Structure Behaviour with & Without Damage. Ed. by G. C. Sih. 224p. (C). 1992. text 132.00 (*0-7923-0604-X*) Kluwer Academic.

***Mechanics & Physics of Modern Grain Aeration Management.** Shlomo Navarro. 288p. 1999. 139.00 (*0-8493-1355-4*) CRC Pr.

Mechanics & Physiology of Animal Swimming. Ed. by Linda Maddock et al. (Illus.). 260p. (C). 1995. text 59.95 (*0-521-46078-6*) Cambridge U Pr.

Mechanics & Related Processes in Structured Agricultural Soils. Ed. by W. E. Larson et al. (C). 1989. text 160.00 (*0-7923-0342-3*) Kluwer Academic.

Mechanics & Reliability of Flexible Magnetic Media. Bharat Bhushan. (Illus.). 664p. 1992. 174.95 (*0-387-97708-2*) Spr-Verlag.

***Mechanics & Reliability of Flexible Magnetic Media.** 2nd ed. Bharat Bhushan. LC 99-45614. (Illus.). 656p. 2000. 179.00 (*0-387-98936-6*) Spr-Verlag.

Mechanics & Resistance to Plant Diseases. Ed. by R. S. Fraser. (Advances in Agricultural Biotechnology Ser.). 1985. text 233.50 (*90-247-3204-2*) Kluwer Academic.

Mechanics & Sport: Papers of a Symposium Presented During the Winter Annual Meeting of the American Society of the Mechanical Engineers , Detroit , Nov. 11-15, 1973, (Sponsored by the Applied Mechanics Division, ASME) Ed. by Jeffrey L. Bleustein. LC 73-89078. (AMD Ser.: Vol. 4). 320p. reprint ed. pap. 99.20 (*0-608-16199-3*, 205616000052) Bks Demand.

Mechanics & Theory in Organic Chemistry: Answer Book. 4th ed. Ed. by Lowry. (C). 1999. pap. text. write for info. (*0-321-40081-X*) Addison-Wesley.

Mechanics & Thermodynamics of Biomembranes. E. Evans & Richard Skalak. LC 79-57619. 272p. 1980. 151.00 (*0-8493-0127-0*, CRC Reprint) Franklin.

Mechanics & Thermodynamics of Continua: A Collection of Papers Dedicated to B.D. Coleman on His Sixtieth Birthday. Ed. by V. Mizel et al. (Illus.). xii, 578p. 1991. pap. 110.00 (*0-387-52999-3*) Spr-Verlag.

Mechanics & Thermodynamics of Continuous Media. M. Silhavy. LC 96-26659. (Texts & Monographs in Physics). (Illus.). 504p. 1996. 89.50 (*3-540-58378-5*) Spr-Verlag.

Mechanics & Thermodynamics of Propulsion. Philip G. Hill & Carl R. Peterson. 1965. text 67.75 (*0-201-02838-7*) Addison-Wesley.

Mechanics & Thermodynamics of Propulsion. 2nd ed. Philip G. Hill et al. (Illus.). 760p. (C). 1991. 105.00 (*0-201-14659-2*) Addison-Wesley.

Mechanics Applied to the Transport of Bulk Materials: Presented at the Joint ASME-CSME Applied Mechanics, Fluids Engineering, & Bioengineering Conference, Niagara Falls, New York, June 18-20, 1979. ASME Applied Mechanics Summer Conference Staff. Ed. by Stephen C. Cowin. LC 79-50119. (AMD Ser.: Vol. 31). (Illus.). 135p. reprint ed. pap. 41.90 (*0-8357-2852-8*, 203908700010) Bks Demand.

Mechanics, Boundary Layers & Function Spaces. Diarmuid O'Mathuna. 240p. 1989. 68.50 (*0-8176-3464-9*) Birkhauser.

Mechanics Computing in 1990's & Beyond. Ed. by Hojjat Adeli & Robert L. Sierakowski. LC 91-12840. 1352p. 1991. pap. text 15.00 (*0-87262-804-3*) Am Soc Civil Eng.

Mechanics Day. Ed. by William F. Shadwick et al. LC 93-11354. (Fields Institute Communications Ser.: Vol. 7). 260p. 1995. text 89.00 (*0-8218-0261-5*, FIC/7) Am Math.

***Mechanics, Equipment Installer & Repairers.** Government Printing Office Staff. 37p. 1998. pap. 3.25 (*0-16-049366-8*) USGPO.

Mechanics: Essays in Honor of Juan-Carlos Simo: Papers Invited by Journal of Nonlinear Science Editors: Essays in Honor of Juan-Carlos Simo. Journal of Nonlinear Science Editors. LC 98-46020. (Illus.). 515p. 1999. 89.95 (*0-387-98663-4*) Spr-Verlag.

Mechanics for Electrical & Electronic Engineers. J. Roger Calvert. LC 92-18185. (Ellis Horwood Series in Mechanical Engineering). 150p. 1993. pap. 40.00 (*0-13-569922-3*, Pub. by Tavistock-E Horwood) Routldge.

Mechanics for Engineers: Combined, Vol. 99. 4th ed. Ferdinand Pierre Beer & E. Russell Johnston, Jr. 944p. (C). 1987. text 90.25 (*0-07-004584-4*) McGraw.

Mechanics for Engineers: Dynamics, Vol. 2. 4th ed. Ferdinand Pierre Beer & E. Russell Johnston. (C). 1987. text 71.00 (*0-07-004582-8*) McGraw.

Mechanics for Engineers: Statics. 4th ed. Ferdinand Pierre Beer & E. Russell Johnston, Jr. 496p. (C). 1986. text 72.50 (*0-07-004580-1*) McGraw.

Mechanics Fundamentals. Robert W. Wood. LC 97-24173. (Funtastic Science Activities for Kids Ser.). (Illus.). 160p. (YA). (gr. 3 up). 1999. lib. bdg. 22.95 (*0-7910-4844-6*) Chelsea Hse.

Mechanics Fundamentals. Robert W. Wood. (Learning Triangle Press FUNdamentals Ser.). (Illus.). 192p. (J). (gr. 3 up). 1996. 22.95 (*0-07-071806-7*) McGraw.

Mechanics Fundamentals. Robert W. Wood. (Learning Triangle Press FUNdamentals Ser.). (Illus.). 148p. (J). (gr. 3 up). 1997. pap. 14.95 (*0-07-071807-5*) McGraw.

Mechanic's Guide to Precision Measurement Tools - Power Pro: Power Pro. Forbes Aird. LC 99-17761. (Illus.). 128p. 1999. pap. 19.95 (*0-7603-0545-5*) MBI Pubg.

***Mechanics in Material Space: With Applications in Defect & Fracture Mechanics.** R. Kienzler & G. Herrmann. 300p. 2000. 54.00 (*3-540-66965-5*) Spr-Verlag.

Mechanics in Materials Processing & Manufacturing: 1994 International Mechanical Engineering Congress & Exposition, Chicago, Illinois - November 6-11, 1994. (AMD Ser.: Vol. 194). 412p. 1994. 100.00 (*0-7918-1446-7*, G00941) ASME.

Mechanics in Sixteenth-Century Italy: Selections from Tartaglia, Benedetti, Guido Ubaldo, & Galileo. Tr. by Stillman Drake & I. E. Drabkin. LC 68-9015. (University of Wisconsin Publications in Medieval Science: No. 13). (Illus.). 442p. reprint ed. pap. 137.10 (*0-7837-1657-5*, 204195400024) Bks Demand.

Mechanics in Structural Geology. M. Brian Bayly. (Illus.). 224p. 1991. 87.95 (*0-387-97615-9*); 52.95 (*0-387-97652-3*) Spr-Verlag.

M

An Asterisk (*) at the beginning of an entry indicates that the title is appearing for the first time.

Mechanics in the Earth & Environmental Sciences. Gerard V. Middleton & Peter R. Wilcock. (Illus.). 475p. (C). 1994. pap. text 42.95 (*0-521-44669-4*) Cambridge U Pr.

Mechanics Laboratory Manual. Jean-Claude Ba & David E. Wilson. Ed. by Laurence Mayer. (Illus.). 52p. 1996. pap. text, lab manual ed. 16.25 (*1-889766-02-X*) Columbus State Bks.

Mechanics Laboratry Manual for Physics 151. 2nd ed. Francisco Gasparini & Petrou Athos. 190p. (C). 1991. text 32.00 (*0-536-57947-4*) Pearson Custom.

Mechanic's Lien in New York. Robert H. Bowman. LC 93-73624. 1992. 110.00 (*0-317-05376-0*) West Group.

Mechanics Materials. 2nd ed. Beer. 1992. teacher ed. 12.95 (*0-07-004341-8*) McGraw.

Mechanics of Active Salt Diapirism. D. D. Schultz-Ela et al. (Reports of Investigations: No. RI 224). (Illus.). 56p. 1994. pap. 11.50 (*0-614-06199-7*) Bur Econ Geology.

Mechanics of Aerosols. N. A. Fuchs. 408p. 1989. pap. 11.95 (*0-486-66055-9*) Dover.

Mechanics of Aerosols. rev. ed. N. Fuchs & R. Daisley. 1964. 191.00 (*0-08-010066-X*, Pub. by Pergamon Repr) Franklin.

Mechanics of Agricultural Materials. G. Sitkei. (Developments in Agricultural Engineering Ser.: No. 8). 488p. 1987. 295.25 (*0-444-99523-4*) Elsevier.

***Mechanics of Aircraft Structures.** T. C. Sun. LC 97-29337. 255p. 1998. 80.00 (*0-471-17877-2*) Wiley.

Mechanics of Alluvial Channels. Ed. by K. Mahmood et al. LC 87-51101. 536p. 1988. 60.00 (*0-918334-63-2*) WRP.

Mechanics of Ancient Egyptian Magical Practice. Robert K. Ritner. LC 92-61830. (Studies in Ancient Oriental Civilization: No. 54). (Illus.). xviii, 322p. 1992. pap. 50.00 (*0-918986-75-3*) Orient Inst.

Mechanics of Athletics. 7th rev. ed. Geoffrey H. Dyson. LC 77-3430. (Illus.). 264p. 1978. 37.95 (*0-8419-0309-3*) Holmes & Meier.

Mechanics of Baltimore: Workers & Politics in the Age of Revolution, 1763-1812. Charles G. Steffen. LC 83-6891. (Working Class in American History Ser.). 312p. 1984. text 29.95 (*0-252-01088-4*) U of Ill Pr.

Mechanics of Bimodulus Materials: Presented at the ASME Winter Annual Meeting, New York, New York, December 2-7, 1979. American Society of Mechanical Engineers Staff. Ed. by Charles W. Bert. LC 79-54427. (AMD Ser.: Vol. 33). (Illus.). 93p. reprint ed. pap. 30.00 (*0-8357-2853-6*, 203908800010) Bks Demand.

Mechanics of Cellulosic Materials. Ed. by R. W. Perkins. (AMD Series, Vol. 145: MD: Vol. 36). 84p. 1992. 30.00 (*0-7918-1094-1*, G00738) ASME.

Mechanics of Cellulosic Materials Vol. 209-60: Mechanics of Cellulosic Materials. Ed. by Richard Perkins. LC 92-56549. (1995 Joint ASME Applied Mechanics & Materials Summer Meeting Ser.: Vol. 209). 224p. 1995. 108.00 (*0-7918-1324-X*, H00956) ASME.

Mechanics of Cellulosic Materials, 1997: Proceedings. Ed. by Richard Perkins. LC 97-73334. 139p. 56.00 (*0-7918-1564-1*) ASME.

Mechanics of Coastal Sediment Transport. J. Fredsoe & R. Deigaard. (Advanced Series in Ocean Engineering). 392p. 1992. text 67.00 (*981-02-0840-5*); pap. text 32.00 (*981-02-0841-3*) World Scientific Pub.

Mechanics of Coatings: Proceedings of the 16th Leeds-Lyon Symposium on Tribology, Lyon, France, 5-8 September, 1989. Ed. by Duncan Dowson et al. (Tribology Ser.: Vol. 17). xii, 498p. 1990. 250.50 (*0-444-88676-1*) Elsevier.

Mechanics of Components with Treated or Coated Surfaces, Vol. 42. Jaroslav Mencik. LC 95-31283. (Solid Mechanics & Its Applications Ser.). 384p. (C). 1996. text 191.50 (*0-7923-3700-X*) Kluwer Academic.

Mechanics of Composite Materials. Ed. by G. J. Dvorak. 184p. 1983. pap. text 40.00 (*0-317-02631-3*, H00273) ASME.

Mechanics of Composite Materials. Robert M. Jones. 355p. 1975. 66.95 (*0-89116-490-1*) Hemisp Pub.

Mechanics of Composite Materials. Aular K. Kaw. LC 96-41736. (Mechanical Engineering Ser.). 352p. (C). 1997. boxed set 99.95 (*0-8493-9656-5*, No. 9656) CRC Pr.

Mechanics of Composite Materials. R. M. Christensen. 364p. (C). 1991. reprint ed. 65.95 (*0-89464-501-3*) Krieger.

Mechanics of Composite Materials. 2nd ed. Robert M. Jones. LC 98-18290. 1998. 69.95 (*1-56032-712-X*, Pub. by Tay Francis Ltd) Taylor & Francis.

Mechanics of Composite Materials: A Unified Micromechanical Approach. J. Aboudi. (Studies in Applied Mechanics: Vol. 29). 328p. 1991. 161.50 (*0-444-88452-1*, SAM 29) Elsevier.

Mechanics of Composite Materials: Nonlinear Effects. Ed. by M. W. Hyer. LC 93-71573. (AMD Ser.: Vol. 159). 375p. 1993. pap. 65.00 (*0-7918-1138-7*, G00782) ASME.

Mechanics of Composite Materials: Selected Works of Nicholas J. Pagano. Ed. by J. N. Reddy. LC 94-30334. (Solid Mechanics & Its Applications Ser.). 1994. text 272.50 (*0-7923-3041-2*) Kluwer Academic.

***Mechanics of Composite Materials & Structures** Carlos A. Soares et al. LC 99-37367. (NATO Science Ser.). 1999. write for info. (*0-7923-5870-8*) Kluwer Academic.

Mechanics of Composite Metals: Solutions Manual. 1997. lib. bdg. write for info. (*0-8493-1106-3*) CRC Pr.

Mechanics of Composite Structures. V. V. Vasiliev. 500p. 1993. 108.00 (*1-56032-034-6*) Hemisp Pub.

Mechanics of Continua. 2nd ed. A. Cemal Eringen. LC 78-2334. 608p. 1980. lib. bdg. 59.50 (*0-88275-663-X*) Krieger.

Mechanics of Continua & Wave Dynamics. L. M. Brekhovskikh & V. N. Goncharov. (Wave Phenomena Ser.: Vol. 1). (Illus.). 360p. 1985. 93.00 (*0-387-13765-3*) Spr-Verlag.

Mechanics of Continua & Wave Dynamics. 2nd ed. L. Brekhovskikh & V. N. Goncharov. LC 93-39737. (Wave Phenomena Ser.: No. 1). 1994. 59.95 (*0-387-57336-4*) Spr-Verlag.

Mechanics of Continuous Media, 2 vols. L. I. Sedov. (Series in Theoretical & Applied Mechanics: Vol. 4). 1000p. (C). 1997. text 109.00 (*9971-5-0728-5*) World Scientific Pub.

Mechanics of Continuous Media. 2nd ed. Stephen C. Hunter. LC 82-21328. (Mathematics & Its Applications Ser.). 640p. 1983. text 115.00 (*0-470-27398-4*) P-H.

Mechanics of Crack Growth - STP 590. 502p. 1976. 45.25 (*0-8031-0509-6*, STP590) ASTM.

Mechanics of Creep Brittle Materials: Proceedings of the European Mechanics Colloquium 239 Held at Leicester University, UK, 15-17 Aug., 1988, Vol. 1. Ed. by A. C. Cocks. 312p. 1989. 72.00 (*1-85166-354-1*) Elsevier.

Mechanics of Cutting Plant Material. Sverker Persson. LC 87-70989. 280p. (C). 1987. 58.25 (*0-916150-86-0*, M0487) Am Soc Ag Eng.

Mechanics of Damage & Fracture: Proceedings of the IUTAM Symposium, Haifa, Israel, 1-4 June 1985. Ed. by S. R. Bodner & H. Liebowitz. (JEFM Ser.: No. 25). (Illus.). 300p. 1988. 115.00 (*0-08-034931-5*, Pergamon Pr) Elsevier.

Mechanics of Deformable Bodies. C. Aukema. (Chapbook Ser.). 20p. (Orig.). 1996. pap. 2.50 (*0-9636959-2-4*) Coe Review Pr.

Mechanics of Deformable Bodies. Roy C. Craig. LC 95-34726. 752p. 1996. text 109.95 (*0-471-50284-7*) Wiley.

Mechanics of Deformable Bodies. Arnold Sommerfeld. (Lectures on Theoretical Physics Ser.: Vol. 2). 1950. text 78.00 (*0-12-654650-9*) Acad Pr.

Mechanics of Deformable Media. A. B. Bhatia & R. N. Singh. (Graduate Student Series in Physics). (Illus.). 204p. (C). 1986. pap. 49.00 (*0-85274-500-1*) IOP Pub.

Mechanics of Deformable Solids. Ed. by A. Yu Ishlinskii. (Illus.). x, 213p. 1988. 60.00 (*0-89864-043-1*) Allerton Pr.

Mechanics of Deformable Solids. Irving H. Shames. LC 79-17373. 544p. 1979. reprint ed. lib. bdg. 46.50 (*0-89874-013-4*) Krieger.

***Mechanics of Deformable Solids: Linear & Nonlinear, Analytical & Computational Aspects.** I. Doghri. 580p. 2000. 84.95 (*3-540-66960-4*) Spr-Verlag.

Mechanics of Deformation & Flow of Particulate Materials: Proceedings of a Symposium. Ed. by Ching S. Chang et al. LC 97-13759. 472p. 1997. 44.00 (*0-7844-0251-5*) Am Soc Civil Eng.

Mechanics of Design: A Comprehensive Guide to Professional Floral Design. Karey L. Bassett. 64p. 1994. pap. text 12.50 (*0-9648962-1-4*) FTD Assn.

Mechanics of Disease. 2nd ed. David O. Slauson & Cooper. (Illus.). 560p. 1990. text 59.95 (*0-683-07743-0*) Lppncott W & W.

Mechanics of Dislocations: Proceedings of an International Symposium Featuring a Reference to Eshelby & a Workshop on Applications, 28-31 August, 1983, Houghton, MI. International Symposium on Mechanics of Dislocatio. LC 85-71204. (Illus.). 262p. reprint ed. pap. 81.30 (*0-8357-4097-8*, 203686300005) Bks Demand.

Mechanics of Earthquakes & Faulting. Christopher H. Scholz. (Illus.). 461p. (C). 1991. pap. text 44.95 (*0-521-40760-5*) Cambridge U Pr.

Mechanics of Editing: How to Keep a Manuscript Focused with Substantive Editing & Improve Details Through Copy Editing. Cook Communications Ministries International Staff. (Interlit Imprint Ser.: Vol. 17). (Illus.). 40p. (Orig.). 1996. pap. 6.00 (*1-884752-26-8*, 44354) Cook Min Intl.

Mechanics of Electromagnetic Materials & Structures. Ed. by J. S. Lee et al. LC 93-71575. (AMD Series, Vol. 161; MD: Vol. 42). 209p. 1993. pap. 50.00 (*0-7918-1140-9*, G00784) ASME.

Mechanics of Engineering Materials. William H. Bowes et al. LC 83-12341. 1456p. (C). 1984. pap. text 65.00 (*0-471-87374-8*) Wiley.

Mechanics of Engineering Materials. Ed. by C. S. Desai & R. H. Gallagher. LC 83-12556. (Wiley Series in Numerical Methods in Engineering). 705p. reprint ed. pap. 200.00 (*0-7837-6370-0*, 204608200010) Bks Demand.

Mechanics of Engineering Materials. 2nd ed. P. P. Benham. 704p. (C). 1996. pap. text 54.95 (*0-582-25164-8*) Addison-Wesley.

Mechanics of Environmental Carcinogenesis, Vol. I. Barrett. 160p. 1987. 182.00 (*0-8493-4671-1*) CRC Pr.

Mechanics of Failure: Proceedings of the Fracture-Mechanism Program & Related Papers. International Conference & Exposition on Fatigue,. Ed. by V. S. Goel. LC 86-71196. (Illus.). 624p. reprint ed. pap. 193.50 (*0-608-15996-4*, 203306800083) Bks Demand.

Mechanics of Fatigue. Vladimir V. Bolotin. LC 98-29151. (Mechanical Engineering Ser.). 480p. 1999. boxed set 89.95 (*0-8493-9663-8*) CRC Pr.

Mechanics of Fatigue Crack Closure, STP 982. Ed. by J. C. Newman, Jr. & Wolf Elber. LC 88-6303. (Special Technical Publication (STP) Ser.). (Illus.). 650p. 1988. text 105.00 (*0-8031-0996-2*, STP982) ASTM.

Mechanics of Fibrous Composites. Carl T. Herakovich. LC 97-28361. 480p. 1997. text 102.95 (*0-471-10636-4*) Wiley.

Mechanics of Flight. K. Kemode. 474p. (C). 1989. 175.00 (*81-7002-030-1*, Pub. by Himalayan Bks) St Mut.

Mechanics of Flight. 10th ed. Alfred C. Kermode. 528p. (C). 1996. pap. text 44.95 (*0-582-23740-8*) Addison-Wesley.

Mechanics of Fluids. Roger A. Duckworth. LC 76-10368. (Introductory Engineering Ser.). (Illus.). 285p. reprint ed. pap. 88.40 (*0-608-30727-0*, 201960200013) Bks Demand.

Mechanics of Fluids. 3rd ed. Shames. 1992. text, student ed. 72.18 (*0-07-056388-8*) McGraw.

Mechanics of Fluids. 3rd ed. Irving H. Shames. 800p. (C). 1992. 97.50 (*0-07-056387-X*) McGraw.

Mechanics of Fluids. 6th ed. B. Massey. 704p. 1989. 39.95 (*0-278-00047-9*) Chapman & Hall.

Mechanics of Fluids. 7th rev. ed. Bernard Massey. (Illus.). 734p. (C). 1998. pap. text 42.50 (*0-7487-4043-0*) St Mut.

Mechanics of Fracture Initiation & Propagation. G. C. Sih. (C). 1991. text 234.00 (*0-7923-0877-8*) Kluwer Academic.

Mechanics of Free Will: The Astrology of Perception, Reality & Will. Martha Lang-Wescott. LC 87-51613. (Illus.). 226p. (Orig.). 1987. pap. 22.95 (*0-9619852-5-9*) Treehouse Mtn.

Mechanics of Fretting Fatigue. D. A. Hills & D. Nowell. LC 94-15440. (Solid Mechanics & Its Applications Ser.: Vol. 30). 248p. (C). 1994. text 148.50 (*0-7923-2866-3*) Kluwer Academic.

Mechanics of Geomaterial Interfaces. Ed. by A. P. Selvadurai & M. J. Boulon. LC 94-46460. (Studies in Applied Mechanics: No. 42). 568p. 1995. 227.25 (*0-444-81583-X*) Elsevier.

Mechanics of Geomaterials: Rocks, Concretes & Soils. Ed. by Zdenek P. Bazant. LC 84-10448. (Wiley Series in Numerical Methods in Engineering). 631p. reprint ed. pap. 195.70 (*0-8357-8948-9*, 203360900086) Bks Demand.

Mechanics of Global Equity Offerings: Structuring the Offering & Negotiating the Underwriting Agreement. Ed. by Meredith M. Brown. LC 95-32860. 1995. write for info. (*90-411-0855-6*) Kluwer Law Intl.

Mechanics of God: A Theory on the Transition of Species & Events. Thomas Easley. (C). 1990. 26.00 (*81-7023-293-7*, Pub. by Allied Pubs) S Asia.

Mechanics of Granular Materials: An Introduction. M. Oda & K. Iwashita. (Illus.). 383p. (C). 1999. pap. 51.00 (*90-5410-462-7*, Pub. by A A Balkema); text 104.00 (*90-5410-461-9*, Pub. by A A Balkema) Ashgate Pub Co.

Mechanics of Granular Materials & Powder Systems. Ed. by M. M. Mehrabadi. (MD Ser.: Vol. 37). 152p. 1992. 45.00 (*0-7918-1098-4*, G00742) ASME.

Mechanics of Granular Media & Its Application in Civil Engineering: Selected Translation of Russian Geotechnical Literature. I. I. Kandaurov. Ed. & Tr. by Ryszard B. Zeidler from RUS. (Geotechnika Ser.: No. 6). (Illus.). 340p. (C). 1991. text 155.00 (*90-5410-114-8*, Pub. by A A Balkema) Ashgate Pub Co.

Mechanics of Hearing. Ed. by E. De Boer & Max A. Viergever. 1983. text 126.50 (*90-247-2878-9*) Kluwer Academic.

Mechanics of Human Joints: Physiology, Pathophysiology, & Treatment. Verna Wright. Ed. by Eric L. Radin. (Illus.). 480p. 1993. text 225.00 (*0-8247-8763-3*) Dekker.

Mechanics of Hydraulic Fracturing. Ching H. Yew. LC 97-1978. 1997. 95.00 (*0-88415-474-2*, 5474) Gulf Pub.

Mechanics of Immersible Fluids in Porous Media. Arthur T. Corey. LC 86-50589. 1994. 38.00 (*0-918334-83-7*) WRP.

Mechanics of Jointed & Faulted Rock: Proceedings of an International Conference, Vienna, 18-20 April 1990. Ed. by Hans P. Rossmanith. (Illus.). 1008p. (C). 1990. text 181.00 (*90-6191-155-9*, Pub. by A A Balkema) Ashgate Pub Co.

Mechanics of Jointed & Faulted Rock: Proceedings of the 2nd International Conference on the Mechanics of Jointed & Faulted Rock, MJFR-2, Vienna, Austria, 10-14 April 1995. Ed. by Hans P. Rossmanith. (Illus.). 1068p. (C). 1995. text 188.00 (*90-5410-541-0*, Pub. by A A Balkema) Ashgate Pub Co.

Mechanics of Jointed & Faulted Rock: Proceedings of the 3rd International Conference, Vienna, 6-9 April, 1998. Ed. by J. P. Rossmanith. LC 99-496416. (Illus.). 674p. (C). 1998. text 132.00 (*90-5410-955-6*, Pub. by A A Balkema) Ashgate Pub Co.

Mechanics of Laminated Composite Plates: Theory & Analysis. J. N. Reddy. LC 96-38476. 800p. 1996. boxed set 104.95 (*0-8493-3101-3*, 3101) CRC Pr.

***Mechanics of Law Making, 1914.** fac. ed. Courtenay Ilbert. LC 99-47156. 2000. write for info. (*1-58477-044-9*) Lawbk Exchange.

Mechanics of Liquids & Gases. 6th ed. L. G. Loitsyanskii. 984p. 1996. 130.00 (*1-56700-042-8*) Begell Hse.

Mechanics of Liquids & Solids. L. G. Loitsyanskii. 1993. write for info. (*0-8493-9912-2*) CRC Pr.

Mechanics of Machines. Han. 256p. 1998. pap. text, student ed. write for info. (*0-02-349841-2*) P-H.

Mechanics of Machines. 2nd ed. G. H. Ryder & M. D. Bennett. (Illus.). 350p. 1990. 42.95 (*0-8311-3030-X*) Indus Pr.

Mechanics of Machining: An Analytical Approach to Assessing Machinability. P. L. Oxley. 1989. text 72.95 (*0-470-21382-5*) P-H.

Mechanics of Mail Order. 4th rev. ed. Michael F. Rounds & Nancy Miller. (Illus.). 80p. (Orig.). 1996. pap. 19.95 (*0-9629944-2-1*) CPM Systems.

Mechanics of Marine Vehicles. B. R. Clayton. LC 82-81291. 612p. 1982. pap. text 189.80 (*0-608-04972-7*, 206555200004) Bks Demand.

***Mechanics of Materials.** Anthony M. Bedford & Kenneth M Liechti. 855p. 2000. pap. 101.33 (*0-201-89552-8*) P-H.

Mechanics of Materials. David Roylance. LC 95-43057. 336p. 1995. text 102.95 (*0-471-59399-0*, Wiley-Interscience) Wiley.

Mechanics of Materials. Ugural. 1991. student ed. 34.68 (*0-07-065738-6*) McGraw.

Mechanics of Materials. Ansel C. Ugural. 640p. (C). 1991. 97.50 (*0-07-065737-8*) McGraw.

Mechanics of Materials. 2nd ed. Ferdinand P. Beer & E. Russell Johnston. 1995. 88.44 incl. disk (*0-07-911388-5*, WCB McGr Hill) McGrw-H Hghr Educ.

***Mechanics of Materials.** 2nd ed. Roy R. Craig. LC 99-43425. 804p. (C). 1999. text 113.95 incl. cd-rom (*0-471-33176-7*) Wiley.

***Mechanics of Materials.** 4th ed. (C). 2000. (*0-13-016615-4*) S&S Trade.

Mechanics of Materials. 4th ed. James M. Gere & S. P. Timoshenko. LC 96-23310. (General Engineering Ser.). 832p. (C). 1996. mass mkt. 107.95 (*0-534-93429-3*) PWS Pubs.

Mechanics of Materials. 4th ed. James M. Gere & Stephen P. Timoshenko. LC 96-23310. 1996. write for info. (*0-534-95102-3*) PWS Pubs.

***Mechanics of Materials.** 4th ed. Russell C. Hibbeler. 848p. (C). 2000. 101.33 (*0-13-016467-4*) P-H.

Mechanics of Materials 5th ed. Gere. 2000. pap. text 70.00 (*0-534-37133-7*) Brooks-Cole.

Mechanics of Materials. 5th ed. William F. Riley et al. LC 98-16173. 720p. 1998. text 111.95 (*0-471-58644-7*) Wiley.

Mechanics of Materials, No. 1. 3rd ed. E. J. Hearn. LC 96-49967. (Illus.). 450p. 1997. pap. text 39.95 (*0-7506-3265-8*) Buttrwrth-Heinemann.

Mechanics of Materials, No. 2. 3rd ed. E. J. Hearn. LC 96-49967. (Illus.). 512p. 1997. pap. text 39.95 (*0-7506-3266-6*) Buttrwrth-Heinemann.

Mechanics of Materials, Vol. 2. 2nd ed. E. J. Hearn. (Illus.). 450p. 1985. pap. text 42.95 (*0-7506-2541-4*) Buttrwrth-Heinemann.

Mechanics of Materials & Structures. Ed. by George Z. Voyiadjis et al. LC 93-44629. (Studies in Applied Mechanics: Vol. 35). 446p. 1994. 210.50 (*0-444-89918-9*) Elsevier.

Mechanics of Materials Exam File. Ed. by Clarence A. Calder. LC 84-24702. (Exam File Ser.). 378p. (C). 1985. pap. 20.50 (*0-910554-46-3*) Engineering.

Mechanics of Materils with Discontinuities & Heterogeneities Vol. 201: Mechanics of Materials with Discontinuities & Heterogeneities. Ed. by Anil Misra & Ching S. Chang. LC 95-77286. (1995 Joint ASME Applied Mechanics & Materials Summer Meeting Ser.: Vol. 201). 188p. 1995. 100.00 (*0-7918-1316-9*, H00948) ASME.

Mechanics of Micropolar Media. Ed. by O. Brulin & R. K. Hsieh. 484p. 1982. text 66.00 (*9971-950-02-2*) World Scientific Pub.

Mechanics of Mixtures. K. P. Rajagopal. 250p. 1995. text 53.00 (*981-02-1585-1*) World Scientific Pub.

Mechanics of Muscle. Daniel J. Schneck. (Monographs in Biomedical Engineering). (Illus.). 350p. (C). 1991. text 80.00 (*0-8147-7935-2*) NYU Pr.

Mechanics of Musical Instrumentation. Ed. by A. Hirschberg et al. (CISM International Centre for Mechanical Sciences Ser.: No. 355). (Illus.). vii, 369p. 1996. pap. 92.00 (*3-211-82801-X*) Spr-Verlag.

Mechanics of Oil Shale. Ed. by K. P. Chong & J. Ward-Smith. 603p. 1984. 194.50 (*0-85334-273-3*) Elsevier.

Mechanics of Phase Transformations & Shape Memory Alloys: 1994 International Mechanical Engineering Congress & Exposition, Chicago, Illinois - November 6-11, 1994. Ed. by L. C. Brinson & B. Moran. (AMD - PVP Ser.: Vol. 189, Vol. 292). 224p. 1994. 80.00 (*0-7918-1437-8*, G00932) ASME.

Mechanics of Plastic Structures. Antoni Sawczuk. 224p. 1989. text 61.95 (*0-470-21102-4*) P-H.

Mechanics of Plastics & Plastic Composites - 1995 Vol. 68-215: Proceedings of the ASME International Mechanical Engineering Congress & Exposition, 1995, San Francisco, CA. Ed. by M. Boyce. LC 95-81264. (1995 ASME International Mechanical Engineering Congress & Exposition Ser.: MD-Vol. 68/AMD-Vol. 215). 444p. 1995. 110.00 (*0-7918-1750-4*, H01031) ASME.

Mechanics of Poetry: A Glossary of Basic Poetic Terms. Su F. Soref. LC 95-92783. 80p. (Orig.). 1996. pap. text 12.95 (*0-9627090-0-X*) Precision Wordage.

Mechanics of Poroelastic Media. Ed. by A. P. Selvadurai. (Solid & Mechanics & Its Applications Ser.: Vol. 41). 394p. 1996. text 202.50 (*0-7923-3329-2*) Kluwer Academic.

Mechanics of Poroelastic Media, Vol. 41. Ed. by A. P. Selvadurai. LC 95-24707. (Solid Mechanics & Its Applications Ser.). 404p. (C). 1995. lib. bdg. 185.00 (*0-7923-3691-7*) Kluwer Academic.

Mechanics of Porous & Fractured Media. V. N. Nikolaevskij. (Series in Theoretical & Applied Mechanics: Vol. 8). 492p. 1990. text 108.00 (*9971-5-0383-2*) World Scientific Pub.

Mechanics of Porous Continua. Olivier Coussy. LC 96-110649. 472p. 1995. 160.00 (*0-471-95267-2*) Wiley.

Mechanics of Porous Media: Lecture Notes of the Mechanics of Porous Media Summer School June 1995. Ed. by Philippe Charlez. Tr. by Deborah Keramsi from FRE. LC 99-227327. (Illus.). 320p. (C). 1995. text 126.00 (*90-5410-628-X*, Pub. by A A Balkema) Ashgate Pub Co.

Mechanics of Pre-Industrial Technology: An Introduction to the Mechanics of Ancient & Traditional Material Culture. Brian Cotterell & Johan Kamminga. (Illus.). 341p. (C). 1991. text 59.95 (*0-521-34194-9*) Cambridge U Pr.

Mechanics of Protection. 143p. 1998. 59.00 (*0-7680-0175-7*) Soc Auto Engineers.

An Asterisk (*) at the beginning of an entry indicates that the title is appearing for the first time.

Mechanics of Reality: The Teachings of Uywamus. unabridged ed. Ann E. Hastings. 72p. 1998. pap. 10.00 (*0-9665354-0-5*, MR001) BMHC Pr.

Mechanics of Residual Soils: A Guide to the Formation, Classification & Geotechnical Properties of Residual Soils, with Advice for Geotechnical Design. Ed. by G. E. Blight. LC 99-496405. (Illus.). 248p. (C). 1997. text 110.00 (*90-5410-696-4*, Pub. by A A Balkema) Ashgate Pub Co.

Mechanics of Rollers. David R. Roisum. LC 95-52109. 1996. 90.00 (*0-89852-313-3*, 0101R255) TAPPI.

Mechanics of Sandwich Structures: Proceedings of the Euromech 360 Colloquium Held in Saint-Etienne, France, 13-15 May, 1997. A. Vautrin. LC 98-16094. 1998. 189.00 (*0-7923-5050-2*) Kluwer Academic.

Mechanics of Secondary Oil Recovery. Charles R. Smith. LC 74-32220. 512p. 1977. reprint ed. 52.50 (*0-88275-270-7*) Krieger.

Mechanics of Sediment Movement: Lecture Notes for Short Course No. 3, Sponsored by the Eastern Section of the Society of Economic Paleontologists & Mineralogists, & Given in Providence, Rhode Island, March 13-14, 1984. 2nd ed. Gerard V. Middleton & John B. Southard. LC TC0175.2.M54. (SEPM Short Course Ser.: No. 3, 1984). 411p. reprint ed. pap. 127.50 (*0-7837-2417-9*, 204255400005) Bks Demand.

Mechanics of Sediment Transport. Ning Chien & Zhaohui Wan. LC 98-44496. 936p. 1998. 149.00 (*0-7844-0400-3*) Am Soc Civil Eng.

Mechanics of Sediment Transport. 2nd ed. Mehmet S. Yalin. 1977. 143.00 (*0-08-021162-3*, Pub. by Pergamon Repr) Franklin.

Mechanics of Sediment Transport: Proceedings of Euromech 156, Mechanics of Sediment Transport, Istanbul, 12-14th July 1982. Ed. by B. Mutlu Sumer & A. Muller. 296p. (C). 1983. text 136.00 (*90-6191-221-0*, Pub. by A A Balkema) Ashgate Pub Co.

Mechanics of Small Engines. Henry Atkinson. 192p. (C). 1989. text 23.96 (*0-07-002537-1*) McGraw.

Mechanics of Solder Alloy Interconnects. (Illus.). 500p. 1994. text 74.95 (*0-442-01505-4*, VNR) Wiley.

Mechanics of Solid Materials. Jean P. Lemaitre & Jean-Louis Chaboche. (Illus.). 582p. (C). 1994. pap. text 39.95 (*0-521-47758-1*) Cambridge U Pr.

Mechanics of Solids. 512p. 1996. pap. 83.00 (*0-13-237778-0*) P-H.

Mechanics of Solids. Roger T. Fenner. (Illus.). 632p. (C). 1991. boxed set 79.95 (*0-632-02018-0*) CRC Pr.

Mechanics of Solids. Lardner. 1993. text, student ed. 31.25 (*0-07-036404-4*) McGraw.

Mechanics of Solids. Lardner. 1994. text 27.50 (*0-07-036403-6*) McGraw.

*__Mechanics of Solids.__ C. T. F. Ross. 480p. 2000. pap. 49.95 (*1-898563-67-5*, Pub. by Horwood Pub) Paul & Co Pubs.

Mechanics of Solids. Gerald Wempner. LC 94-25417. (C). 1994. mass mkt. 81.95 (*0-534-92739-4*) PWS Pubs.

Mechanics of Solids. Walter D. Pilkey & Orrin H. Pilkey. LC 85-46011. 464p. (C). 1986. reprint ed. text 48.50 (*0-89874-917-4*) Krieger.

Mechanics of Solids see Encyclopedia of Physics

Mechanics of Solids: An Introduction. Thomas J. Lardner & R. R. Archer. LC 93-2372. 992p. (C). 1994. 100.31 (*0-07-833358-X*) McGraw.

Mechanics of Solids: Concepts & Applications. Bill Bickford. 848p. (C). 1992. text 72.75 (*0-256-11425-0*, Irwn McGrw-H) McGrw-H Hghr Educ.

Mechanics of Solids: Concepts & Applications. 2nd ed. William B. Bickford. LC 96-2837. 864p. (C). 1997. 72.75 (*0-256-19271-5*, Irwn McGrw-H) McGrw-H Hghr Educ.

Mechanics of Solids Vol. 4: Waves in Elastic & Viscoelastic Solids (Theory & Experiment) Ed. by Clifford A. Truesdell. (Illus.). 350p. 1984. 72.95 (*0-387-13163-9*) Spr-Verlag.

Mechanics of Solids & Fluids. 2nd ed. Franz Ziegler.Tr. of Technische Mechanik der Festen und Flussigen Korper. (Illus.). xxii, 845p. 1995. 89.95 (*0-387-94399-4*) Spr-Verlag.

Mechanics of Solids & Shells. Gerald Wempner & Demosthenes Talaslidis. (Mechanical Engineering Ser.). Date not set. 79.95 (*0-8493-9654-9*) CRC Pr.

*__Mechanics of Solids & Structures.__ David W. Rees. (Illus.). 2000. pap. 58.00 (*1-86094-218-0*) Imperial College.

Mechanics of Solids & Structures: Proceedings of the International Conference, Singapore, 11-13 September 1991. Ed. by F. Travis et al. 700p. (C). 1991. pap. 42.00 (*981-02-0739-5*); text 130.00 (*981-02-0738-7*) World Scientific Pub.

Mechanics of Solids with Applications to Thin Bodies. G. Wemper. 1982. text 255.50 (*90-286-0880-X*) Kluwer Academic.

Mechanics of Solids with Phase Changes. Ed. by M. Berveiller. (CISM International Center for Mechanical Sciences Ser.: No. 368). (Illus.). vii, 317p. 1997. pap. 80.00 (*3-211-82904-0*) Spr-Verlag.

Mechanics of Sport: A Practitioner's Guide. Gerry Carr. LC 95-52859. (Illus.). 224p. (Orig.). 1996. pap. text 24.00 (*0-87322-974-6*, PCAR0974) Human Kinetics.

Mechanics of Structures: Variational & Computational Methods. Walter D. Pilkey & Walter Wunderlich. 880p. 1993. boxed set 104.95 (*0-8493-4435-2*, 4435) CRC Pr.

Mechanics of Structures & Materials: Proceedings of the Fifteenth Australasian Conference, Melbourne, Victoria, Australia, 8-10 December 1997. Ed. by R. H. Grzebieta et al. (Illus.). 734p. (C). 1997. text 149.00 (*90-5410-900-9*, Pub. by A A Balkema) Ashgate Pub Co.

*__Mechanics of Structures & Materials: Proceedings of the 16th Australiasian Conference, Sydney, NSW, Australia, 8-10 December 1999.__ Ed. by M. A. Bradford et al. (Illus.). 760p. (C). 1999. text 110.00 (*90-5809-107-4*, Pub. by A A Balkema) Ashgate Pub Co.

Mechanics of Success for Families: Evaluation Report, No. 2. Suzanne Knell & Barbara Geissler. (Illinois Family Literacy Reports). 109p. 1992. reprint ed. pap. text 15.00 (*1-885095-51-1*) IL Lit Res Dev.

Mechanics of Success for Families Report No. 1: Family Literacy Programs. Suzanne Knell & Barbara Geissler. (Illinois Family Literacy Reports). 135p. 1992. reprint ed. pap. text 25.00 (*1-885095-50-3*) IL Lit Res Dev.

Mechanics of Success for Families Report No. 4: Policy. Suzanne Knell & Barbara Geissler. (Illinois Family Literacy Reports). 63p. 1992. pap. text 15.00 (*1-885095-53-8*) IL Lit Res Dev.

Mechanics of Superconducting Structures: Presented at the Winter Annual Meeting of the American Society of Mechanical Engineers, Chicago, IL, November 16-21, 1980. American Society of Mechanical Engineers Staff. Ed. by Francis C. Moon. LC 80-69184. (AMD Ser.: Vol. 41). (Illus.). 143p. reprint ed. pap. 44.40 (*0-8357-2910-9*, 203914700011) Bks Demand.

Mechanics of Surgery. Charles Truax. LC 87-31483. (Illus.). 1024p. 1988. reprint ed. 155.00 (*0-930405-01-3*) Norman SF.

Mechanics of Swelling: From Clays to Living Cells & Tissues. Ed. by Theodoros K. Karalis. LC 92-12454. (NATO ASI Series H: Cell Biology: Vol. 64). (Illus.). 808p. 1992. 318.95 (*0-387-54607-3*) Spr-Verlag.

Mechanics of Tectonic Faulting: Models & Basic Concepts. G. Mandl. (Developments in Structural Geology Ser.: No. 1). 408p. 1988. 171.00 (*0-444-42946-8*) Elsevier.

Mechanics of Television: The Story of Mechanical Television. Peter F. Yanczer. (Illus.). 182p. (Orig.). 1987. pap. 20.00 (*0-317-56054-9*) P F Yanczer.

Mechanics of the Coronary Circulation. Ed. by R. E. Mates et al. 94p. 1983. pap. text 24.00 (*0-317-02632-1*, G00221) ASME.

Mechanics of the Feeding of the Mallard (Anas Platryrhynchos L.) the Lingual Apparatus & the Suctio-Pressure Pump Mechanism of Straining. G. A. Zweers et al. (Contributions to Vertebrate Evolution Ser.: Vol. 3). (Illus.). 1977. 44.50 (*3-8055-2424-2*) S Karger.

Mechanics of the Future: Asteroids. rev. ed. Martha Lang-Wescott. (Illus.). 244p. 22.95 (*0-9619852-1-6*) Treehouse Mtn.

Mechanics of the Solid State. Ed. by Friedrich P. Rimrott & J. Schwaighofer. LC 68-110059. 292p. reprint ed. pap. 90.60 (*0-608-30992-3*, 201438300090) Bks Demand.

Mechanics of the Spine. Robert Allen & Peter McCarthy. 1999. pap. 55.00 (*0-7506-2455-8*) Buttrwrth-Heinemann.

Mechanics of Thick Composites. Ed. by Y. D. Rajapakse. LC 93-71576. (AMD Ser.: Vol. 162). 267p. 1993. pap. 55.00 (*0-7918-1141-7*, G00785) ASME.

Mechanics of Thin Film Coatings: Proceedings of the First Biennial European Coating Symposium Held in Leads, 19th-22nd September 1995. Ed. by P. H. Gaskell et al. LC 96-13076. 424p. 1996. write for info. (*981-02-2543-1*) World Scientific Pub.

Mechanics of Transformation Toughening & Related Topics. Bhushan L. Karihaloo & J. H. Andreasen. LC 96-1174. (North-Holland Series in Applied Mathematics & Mechanics: No. 40). 540p. 1996. text 181.00 (*0-444-81930-4*, North Holland) Elsevier.

Mechanics of Transportation Suspension Systems: Presented at the Winter Annual Meeting of the American Society of Mechanical Engineers, Houston, Texas, November 30-December 5, 1975. Symposium on Mechanics of Transportation Suspensio. Ed. by B. Paul et al. LC 75-152. (AMD Ser.: Vol. 15). (Illus.). 116p. reprint ed. pap. 36.00 (*0-8357-2886-2*, 203912200011) Bks Demand.

Mechanics of True Worship. Charles Dixon. 155p. (Orig.). 1996. pap. 11.99 (*0-9634306-7-X*) End-Time Wave.

Mechanics of True Worship: A Practical Workbook. Charles Dixon. 146p. (Orig.). 1996. pap. 14.99 (*1-889389-00-5*) End-Time Wave.

Mechanics of Underwater Noise. D. Ross. LC 76-18731. 1976. 179.00 (*0-08-021182-8*, Pub. by Pergamon Repr) Franklin.

Mechanics of Underwater Noise. Donald Ross. LC 87-61466. 315p. 1987. reprint ed. 55.95 (*0-932146-16-3*) Peninsula CA.

Mechanics of Underwriting, 1996. (Commercial Law & Practice Course Handbook Ser.). Date not set. pap. 99.00 (*0-614-17169-5*, A4-4504) PLI.

Mechanics of Underwriting, 1995. (Corporate Law & Practice Course Handbook, 1985-86 Ser.). 600p. 1995. pap. 99.00 (*0-685-65507-5*, B4-7088) PLI.

Mechanics of Underwriting, 1992. (Corporate Law & Practice Course Handbook, 1985-86 Ser.). 473p. 1992. pap. 70.00 (*0-685-69466-6*) PLI.

Mechanics of Vehicle Collisions. Haim Reizes. (Illus.). 152p. 1973. 35.95 (*0-398-02639-4*); pap. 23.95 (*0-398-06345-1*) C C Thomas.

Mechanics of Vibrations. K. Marguerre. Ed. by H. Wolfel. (Mechanics of Structural Systems Ser.: No. 2). 282p. 1979. text 154.00 (*90-286-0086-8*) Kluwer Academic.

Mechanics of Visco-Elastic Media & Bodies: Proceedings of the International Union of Theoretical & Applied Mechanics Symposium, Gothenburg, Sept. 2-6, 1974. International Union of Theoretical & Applied Mecha. Ed. by J. Hult. LC 75-5667. (International Union of Theoretical & Applied Mechanics Symposia Ser.). (Illus.). xii, 391p. 1975. text 66.00 (*0-387-07228-4*) Spr-Verlag.

Mechanics of Viscoelastic Solids. Aleksey D. Drozdov. LC 97-46065. 484p. 1998. 149.95 (*0-471-97512-5*) Wiley.

Mechanics of Web Handling. David R. Roisum. LC 98-7173. 1998. 90.00 (*0-89852-346-X*) TAPPI.

Mechanics of Winding. David R. Rosium. LC 94-26503. 256p. 1994. 81.00 (*0-89852-281-1*, 0101R236) TAPPI.

Mechanics of Wonder: The Creation of the Idea of Science Fiction. Gary Westfahl. LC 99-214875. 256p. 1998. 44.95 (*0-85323-563-5*, Pub. by Liverpool Univ Pr); pap. 23.95 (*0-85323-573-2*, Pub. by Liverpool Univ Pr) Intl Spec Bk.

Mechanics of Wood & Wood Composites. Jozsef Bodig & Benjamin A. Jayne. 736p. (C). 1993. reprint ed. lib. bdg. 89.50 (*0-89464-777-6*) Krieger.

Mechanics of Wool Structures. Ron Postle et al. (Applied Science & Industrial Technology Ser.). 462p. 1988. text 94.95 (*0-470-21000-1*) P-H.

Mechanics Problem Solver. rev. ed. Research & Education Association Staff. LC 79-92403. (Illus.). 1088p. 1997. pap. text 29.95 (*0-87891-519-2*) Res & Educ.

Mechanics Problems in Geodynamics. R. Wang & K. Aki. 344p. 1996. pap. 34.50 (*3-7643-5412-7*) Spr-Verlag.

Mechanics Problems in Geodynamics. Ed. by Ren Wang & Keiiti Aki. LC 95-49379. 1995. pap. 34.95 (*0-8176-5104-7*) Birkhauser.

Mechanics Problems in Geodynamics. Ed. by Ren Wang & Keiiti Aki. (Topical Volumes in Pure & Applied Geophysics Ser.). 396p. 1996. 34.50 (*3-7643-5104-7*) Spr-Verlag.

Mechanics Sheet Metal Forming. Marciniak. 1993. text 69.50 (*0-340-56405-9*, VNR) Wiley.

Mechanic's Tale: Life in the Pit Lanes of Formula One. Steve Matchett. LC 99-28946. (Illus.). 208p. 1999. 24.95 (*0-7603-0754-7*, Pub. by MBI Pubg) Motorbooks Intl.

Mechanics Today, Set. Ed. by S. Nemat-Nasser. Incl. Vol. 6. 1981. pap. text 40.00 (*0-08-027318-1*); 1978. 121.00 (*0-08-022682-5*, Pub. by Pergamon Repr) Franklin.

Mechanics U. S. A., 1994: Proceedings, U. S. National Congress of Applied Mechanics (12th: 1994: Seattle, WA) Ed. by Albert S. Kobayashi. (Applied Mechanics Reviews Ser.: No. 47, No. 6, Pt. 2). 332p. 1995. reprint ed. pap. 88.00 (*0-614-08386-9*) ASME.

Mechanics, Waves & Heat: Physics 1570. Jerry O'Connor & Mark Davenport. (C). 1995. pap. 15.45 (*1-56870-188-8*) RonJon Pub.

*__Mechanicsburg Reflections, 1900-2000.__ Josephine F. Collitt. (Illus.). 1999. pap. 10.00 (*0-9648441-6-8*) J F Collitt.

Mechanik see Mechanics: From Newton's Laws to Deterministic Chaos

Mechanika. Jan Riley & Michael Burnham. (Illus.). 58p. (Orig.). 1991. pap. 20.00 (*0-917562-57-7*) Contemp Arts.

Mechanisation in Building. 2nd ed. H. G. Vallings. (Illus.). 175p. 1976. 52.25 (*0-85334-651-8*) Elsevier.

Mechanischen Elemente und das Mechanische System. Friedrich Tobler. (Handbuch der Pflanzenanatomie Encyclopedia of Plant Anatomy - Traite d' Anatomie Vegetale Ser.: Band IV, Teil 6). (Illus.). iv, 60p. 1957. 15.00 (*3-443-39006-4*, Pub. by Gebruder Borntraeger) Balogh.

Mechanised Infantry. Bryan Perrett. (Vanguard Ser.: No. 38). (Illus.). 48p. pap. 10.95 (*0-85045-526-X*, 9327, Pub. by Ospry) Stackpole.

Mechanisims of Interferon Actions, 2 vols., Set. Ed. by Lawrence M. Pfeffer. 224p. 1987. 269.90 (*0-8493-6145-1*, QR187) CRC Pr.

Mechanisims of Interferon Actions, 2 vols., Vol. II: Cellular Effects of Interferons. Ed. by Lawrence M. Pfeffer. 224p. 1987. write for info. (*0-318-62189-4*) CRC Pr.

Mechanism - Prevention - Treatment of Aspiration Pneumonia: Theodor Billroth's M.D. Thesis in 1852 on Cervical Vagotomy. fac. ed. Theodor Billroth. (LAT.). 50p. (C). 1994. pap. text 19.50 (*0-930329-67-8*) Kabel Pubs.

Mechanism - Treatment - Prevention of Aspiration Pneumonia (Theodor Billroth) Karel B. Absolon & J. Lee Sedwitz. (Illus.). 102p. (C). 1999. text 29.50 (*0-930329-70-8*) Kabel Pubs.

Mechanism Analysis: Simplified Graphical & Analytical Techniques. 2nd rev. ed. Lyndon O. Barton. LC 92-37563. (Mechanical Engineering Ser.: Vol. 81). (Illus.). 752p. 1993. text 189.00 (*0-8247-8794-3*) Dekker.

Mechanism & Extent of Dietary Adaptation among Certain Groups of California & Nevada Indians. fac. ed. S. F. Cook. (Ibero-Americana Ser.: Vol. 18). 68p. (C). 1941. reprint ed. pap. text 8.13 (*1-55567-805-X*) Coyote Press.

Mechanism & Freedom of Logic. Granville C. Henry. LC 92-35172. 242p. (Orig.). (C). 1993. pap. 28.50 (*0-8191-8964-2*); lib. bdg. 53.00 (*0-8191-8963-4*) U Pr of Amer.

Mechanism & Kinetics of Addition Polymerizations. M. Kucera. (Comprehensive Chemical Kinetics Ser.: Vol. 31). 570p. 1992. 460.00 (*0-444-98795-9*) Elsevier.

Mechanism & Management of Corneal Graft Rejection. John C. Hill. LC 96-1852. 1996. 48.50 (*90-6299-127-0*) Kugler Pubns.

Mechanism & Management of Headache. 6th ed. James W. Lance & Peter J. Goadsby. LC 98-15127. 336p. 1998. text 95.00 (*0-7506-3728-5*) Buttrwrth-Heinemann.

Mechanism & Mysticism: The Influence of Science on the Thought & Work of Theodore Dreiser. Louis J. Zanine. LC 93-16138. 264p. (C). 1993. text 34.95 (*0-8122-3171-6*) U of Pa Pr.

Mechanism & New Approach on Drug Resistance of Cancer Cells: Proceedings of the International Symposium on the Mechanism & New Approach on Drug Resistance of Cancer Cells, Sapporo, 15-17 October 1992. Ed. by Tamotsu Miyazaki et al. LC 93-15706. (International Congress Ser.: No. 1026). 348p. 1993. 166.75 (*0-444-81480-9*, Excerpta Medica) Elsevier.

Mechanism & the Novel: Science in the Narrative Process. Martha A. Turner. LC 92-39414. 211p. (C). 1993. text 59.95 (*0-521-44339-3*) Cambridge U Pr.

Mechanism & Theory in Organic Chemistry. 3rd ed. Thomas H. Lowry & Kathleen S. Richardson. 1090p. (C). 1997. 115.00 (*0-06-044084-8*) Addson-Wesley Educ.

Mechanism-Based Enzyme Inactivation: Chemistry & Enzymology. Richard B. Silverman. LC 87-13825. 1988. write for info. (*0-318-62931-3*, QP601, CRC Reprint) Franklin.

Mechanism-Based Enzyme Inactivation: Chemistry & Enzymology, Vol. 1. Richard B. Silverman. LC 87-13825. 208p. 1988. 128.00 (*0-8493-4543-X*, QP601, CRC Reprint) Franklin.

Mechanism-Based Enzyme Inactivation: Chemistry & Enzymology, Vol. 2. Richard B. Silverman. LC 87-13825. 240p. 1988. 157.00 (*0-8493-4544-8*, QP601, CRC Reprint) Franklin.

Mechanism Demands a Mysticism: An Exploration of Spirit, Matter & Physics. Thomas G. Brophy. LC 99-17722. 360p. 1999. pap. 19.95 (*1-891850-12-1*) Med Bear.

Mechanism Design: Analysis & Synthesis, Vol. 1. 3rd ed. Arthur G. Erdman et al. LC 96-47297. Vol. 1. 645p. (C). 1996. 105.00 (*0-13-267782-2*) P-H.

Mechanism Design: The Practical Kinematics & Dynamics of Machinery. 2nd ed. S. Molian. LC 97-17649. 248p. 1997. 89.00 (*0-08-042264-0*, Pergamon Pr) Elsevier.

Mechanism in Organic Chemistry. Roger W. Alder et al. LC 72-147196. (Illus.). 388p. reprint ed. pap. 120.30 (*0-8357-6433-8*, 203580400097) Bks Demand.

Mechanism in Protein Chemistry. Jack Kyte. LC 95-18614. (Illus.). 552p. 1995. text 73.00 (*0-8153-1700-X*) Garland.

Mechanism, Mentalism, & Metamathematics. Judson C. Webb. (Synthese Library: No. 137). 291p. 1980. text 169.50 (*90-277-1046-5*, D Reidel) Kluwer Academic.

Mechanism of Action of Dehydrogenases: A Symposium in Honor of Hugo Theorell. Ed. by George W. Schwert & Alfred D. Winer. LC 73-80094. 270p. reprint ed. pap. 83.70 (*0-608-14974-8*, 202596400047) Bks Demand.

Mechanism of Action, Safety & Efficacy of Intrauterine Devices. (Technical Reports: No. 753). 91p. 1987. pap. text 12.00 (*92-4-120753-1*, 1100753) World Health.

Mechanism of Cisplatin Resistance & Its Circumvention. Yoshihiro Kikuchi. LC 98-218183. 289p. 1998. 145.00 (*1-56072-548-6*) Nova Sci Pubs.

Mechanism of Denial: The Manifest Content of the Dream. Ed. by Bernard D. Fine et al. LC 79-75242. (Kris Study Group Monographs: No. 3). 113p. 1969. text 27.50 (*0-8236-3210-5*) Intl Univs Pr.

Mechanism of Economic Development: Growth in the Japanese & East Asian Economies. Ken-Ichi Inada et al. (Illus.). 344p. 1993. 75.00 (*0-19-828628-7*) OUP.

Mechanism of Epoxidation of Olefins by Pelacids. V. G. Dryuk. 1977. pap. 32.00 (*0-08-021586-6*, Pergamon Pr) Elsevier.

Mechanism of Evolution: A New Look at Old Ideas. M. I. Wolsky & A. Wolsky. (Contributions to Human Development Ser.: Vol. 4). (Illus.). 160p. 1976. 38.50 (*3-8055-2347-5*) S Karger.

Mechanism of Failure with & Without Titanium Nitride Coating in Roller Tests. Joze Vizintin. (Nineteen Ninety Fall Technical Meeting Ser.: Vol. 90FTM10). (Illus.). 9p. 1990. pap. text 30.00 (*1-55589-562-X*) AGMA.

Mechanism of Fracto Emission. M. K. Park. (Illus.). 100p. (Orig.). 1989. pap. write for info. (*1-877974-04-8*) Prompter Pubns.

Mechanism of Human Facial Expression. Duchenne De Boulogne. Tr. by R. Andrew Cuthbertson. (Studies in Emotion & Social Interaction). (Illus.). 304p. (C). 1990. text 64.95 (*0-521-36392-6*) Cambridge U Pr.

Mechanism of Myofilament Sliding in Muscle Contraction. H. Sugi & G. H. Pollack. (Advances in Experimental Medicine & Biology Ser.: Vol. 332). (Illus.). 882p. (C). 1993. text 175.00 (*0-306-44525-5*, Kluwer Plenum) Kluwer Academic.

Mechanism of Pesticide Action. Ed. by G. K. Kohn. LC 74-22484. (ACS Symposium Ser.: Vol. 2). 192p. 1974. reprint ed. pap. 59.60 (*0-608-03550-5*, 206426900008) Bks Demand.

Mechanism of Protein Synthesis. Cold Spring Harbor Symposia on Quantitative Biolog. LC 34-8174. (Cold Spring Harbor Symposia on Quantitative Biology Ser.: No. 34). 879p. 1969. reprint ed. pap. 200.00 (*0-7837-2029-7*, 204229100002) Bks Demand.

Mechanism of the Linotype. John S. Thompson. Ed. by John Bidwell. LC 78-74413. (Nineteenth-Century Book Arts & Printing History Ser.: Vol. 23). (Illus.). 1980. lib. bdg. 46.00 (*0-8240-3897-5*) Garland.

Mechanism of Tumor Promotion: Cellular Responses to Tumor Promoters, Vol. IV. Ed. by Thomas J. Slaga. 168p. 1984. 98.00 (*0-8493-6524-4*, RC268, CRC Reprint) Franklin.

Mechanism of Tumor Promotion: Tumor Promotion in Internal Organs, I. Ed. by Thomas J. Slaga. 208p. 1983. 111.00 (*0-8493-6521-X*, RC268, CRC Reprint) Franklin.

Mechanism of Tumor Promotion: Tumor Promotion in Internal Organs, II. Ed. by Thomas J. Slaga. 208p. 1984. 125.00 (*0-8493-6522-8*, RC268, CRC Reprint) Franklin.

Mechanism of Tumor Promotion: Tumor Promotion in Internal Organs, III. Ed. by Thomas J. Slaga. 208p. 1984. 118.00 (*0-8493-6523-6*, RC268, CRC Reprint) Franklin.

Mechanism of Weaving. T. W. Fox. (Illus.). 465p. 1988. reprint ed. pap. 15.00 (*0-87556-364-3*) Saifer.

Mechanism Synthesis & Analysis. LC 91-25710. 215p. reprint ed. pap. 66.70 (*0-608-30295-3*, 2054090) Bks Demand.

M

Mechanism Synthesis & Analysis. Atmaram H. Soni. LC 73-22000. 512p. reprint ed. pap. 158.80 (*0-608-10672-0*, 205532800016); reprint ed. pap. 146.00 (*0-608-30571-5*, 2055328) Bks Demand.

Mechanism Synthesis & Analysis. Atmaram H. Soni. LC 73-22000. 512p. reprint ed. pap. 146.00 (*0-608-31021-2*) Bks Demand.

Mechanism Synthesis & Analysis. Atmaram H. Soni. LC 81-11723. 512p. 1981. reprint ed. 49.50 (*0-89874-380-X*) Krieger.

Mechanism Synthesis & Analysis: Proceedings of the 23rd Biennial Mechanisms Conference, Minneapolis, MN, 1994. 542p. 1994. pap. 90.00 (*0-7918-1284-7*) ASME.

*__Mechanism Theory Organic Chem.__ 4th ed. (C). 2001. pap. text 0.00 (*0-321-03769-3*, Celebration) Addson-Wesley Educ.

Mechanisms & Applications of Gene Silencing. Ed. by D. Grierson et al. LC 96-215849. 205p. 1999. 200.00 (*1-897676-25-5*, Pub. by Nottingham Univ Pr) St Mut.

*__Mechanisms & Clinical Management of Chronic Renal Diseases.__ 2nd ed. Ed. by Meguid El Nahas et al. (Oxford Clinical Nephrology Ser.). (Illus.). 480p. 2000. text 139.50 (*0-19-262933-6*) OUP.

Mechanisms & Concepts in Toxicology. Norman Aldrige. 288p. 1996. 99.95 (*0-7484-0413-9*); 44.95 (*0-7484-0414-7*) Taylor & Francis.

Mechanisms & Dynamics of Machinery. 4th ed. Hamilton H. Mabie & Charles F. Reinholtz. LC 86-11115. 656p. 1987. text 106.95 (*0-471-80237-9*) Wiley.

Mechanisms & Effects of Pollutant-Transfer into Forests: Proceedings of the Meeting on Mechanisms & Effects of Pollutant-Transfer into Forests Held in Oberursel-Taunus, F.R.G. November 24-25, 1988. Ed. by H. W. Georgii. (C). 1989. text 196.50 (*0-7923-0430-6*) Kluwer Academic.

*__Mechanisms & Management of COPD Exacerbations.__ L. Allegra & F. Blasi. 100p. 1999. pap. 42.00 (*88-470-0066-1*, Pub. by Spr-Verlag) Spr-Verlag.

Mechanisms & Management of Headache. 5th ed. James W. Lance. 288p. 1993. text 85.00 (*0-7506-0575-8*) Buttrwrth-Heinemann.

Mechanisms & Management of Nausea & Emesis Associated with Cancer Therapy. Ed. by M. Dicato. (Journal Ser.: Vol. 53, Suppl. 1, 1996). (Illus.). iv, 110p. 1996. 49.75 (*3-8055-6335-3*) S Karger.

Mechanisms & Mechanical Devices Sourcebook. 2nd rev. ed. Ed. by Nicholas P. Chironis & Neil J. Sclater. LC 96-5438. (Illus.). 463p. 1996. 84.95 (*0-07-011356-4*) McGraw.

Mechanisms & Mechanics of Composites Fracture: Proceedings of ASM 1993 Materials Congress Materials Week '93 Held October 17-21, 1993, Pittsburgh, PA. Ed. by Ram B. Bhagat et al. LC 93-73754. (Illus.). 264p. 1993. reprint ed. pap. 81.90 (*0-608-02642-5*, 206330000004) Bks Demand.

Mechanisms & Models in Rheumatoid Arthritis. John A. Edwards. (Illus.). 548p. 1995. text 105.00 (*0-12-340440-1*) Acad Pr.

Mechanisms & Models in Toxicology. Ed. by P. L. Chambers et al. (Archives of Toxicology Ser.: Supp. 11). (Illus.). viii, 365p. 1987. pap. 134.60 (*0-387-17614-4*) Spr-Verlag.

Mechanisms & Pathogenesis see **Handbook of Teratology**

Mechanisms & Phylogeny of Mineralization in Biological Systems: Biomineralization '90. Ed. by H. Nakahara & Shoichi Suga. (Illus.). 528p. 1991. 141.95 (*0-387-70068-4*) Spr-Verlag.

Mechanisms & Principles of Epitaxial Growth in Metallic Systems Vol. 528: Proceedings Materials Research Society Symposium. Ed. by L. T. Wille et al. LC 98-34275. 278p. 1998. text 79.00 (*1-55899-434-3*) Materials Res.

Mechanisms & Recent Advances in Therapy of Hypertension. Ed. by H. Liebau. (Contributions to Nephrology Ser.: Vol. 8). (Illus.). 1977. 29.75 (*3-8055-2671-7*) S Karger.

Mechanisms & Reversal of Multidrug Resistance in Cancer: The Other Alternatives. Ed. by John A. Kellen. LC 95-1582. 278p. 1995. 93.50 (*0-8176-3775-3*) Birkhauser.

Mechanisms & Specificity of HIV Entry into Host Cells. Ed. by N. Duzgunes. (Advances in Experimental Medicine & Biology Ser.: Vol. 300). (Illus.). 222p. (C). 1991. text 102.00 (*0-306-44008-3*, Kluwer Plenum) Kluwer Academic.

Mechanisms & Toxicity of Chemical Carcinogens & Mutagens. Ed. by W. G. Flamm & R. J. Lorentzen. LC 85-62106. (Advances in Modern Environmental Toxicology Ser.: Vol. 12). (Illus.). 264p. 1985. 65.00 (*0-911131-12-4*) Specialist Journals.

Mechanisms & Trends in the Decline of the Costanoan Indian Population of Central California No. 4: Health & Nutrition in . . . Ann L. Stodder. Ed. by Gary S. Breschini & Trudy Haversat. (Archives of California Prehistory Ser.: No. 4). (Illus.). 84p. (Orig.). (C). 1986. pap. 9.69 (*1-55567-024-5*) Coyote Press.

Mechanisms for Engineering Design. Stanley B. Tuttle. LC 67-19946. 188p. reprint ed. pap. 58.30 (*0-608-11649-1*, 200740400062) Bks Demand.

Mechanisms for Library Cooperation: Getting Our Act Together. Ed. by Verina Horsnell. 158p. 1988. text 38.95 (*0-566-05757-3*, Pub. by Gower) Ashgate Pub Co.

Mechanisms for the Award of Competitive Tenders for Works & Supply Contracts. Asia Law & Practice Staff. 50p. 1996. pap. 70.00 (*962-7708-91-7*) Am Educ Systs.

Mechanisms in Allergy: Reagin-Mediated Hypersensitivity. International Symposium on Control Mechanisms in R. Ed. by Lawrence Goodfriend et al. LC 73-82704. (Immunology Ser.: No.1). (Illus.). 602p. reprint ed. pap. 186.70 (*0-7837-0725-8*, 204104900019) Bks Demand.

Mechanisms in B-Cell Neoplasia. Ed. by F. Melchers & M. Potter. (Current Topics in Microbiology & Immunology Ser.: Vol. 132). (Illus.). 390p. 1986. 106.00 (*0-387-17048-0*) Spr-Verlag.

Mechanisms in B-Cell Neoplasia, 1994. Ed. by M. Potter & F. Melchers. (Currents Topics in Microbiology & Immunology Ser.: Vol. 194). 480p. 1994. 174.95 (*3-540-58447-1*) Spr-Verlag.

Mechanisms in B-Cell Neoplasia, 1988. Ed. by M. Potter & F. Melchers. (Current Topics in Microbiology & Immunology Ser.: Vol. 141). (Illus.). 340p. 1988. 123.00 (*0-387-50212-2*) Spr-Verlag.

Mechanisms in B-Cell Neoplasia, 1992: Workshop at the National Cancer Institute, National Institutes of Health, Bethesda, MD, U. S. A., April 21-23, 1992. Ed. by Michael B. Oldstone et al. (Current Topics in Microbiology & Immunology Ser.: Vol. 182). (Illus.). 528p. 1992. 188.95 (*0-387-55658-3*) Spr-Verlag.

Mechanisms in Blood Coagulation, Fibrinolysis & the Complement System. Torben Halkier. Tr. by Paul Woolley. (Illus.). 483p. (C). 1992. text 110.00 (*0-521-38187-8*) Cambridge U Pr.

Mechanisms in Fibre Carcinogenesis. Ed. by R. C. Brown et al. (NATO ASI Ser.: Vol. 223). (Illus.). 608p. (C). 1991. text 198.00 (*0-306-44091-1*, Kluwer Plenum) Kluwer Academic.

Mechanisms in Gonadal Differentiation in Vertebrates: Proceedings, Freiburg, FRG, 1982. Ed. by W. W. Franke & U. Mueller. (Illus.). 121p. 1983. 79.95 (*0-387-12480-2*) Spr-Verlag.

Mechanisms in Pigmentation: Proceedings of the International Pigment Cell Conference, 8th, Sydney, March, 1972. International Pigment Cell Conference Staff. Ed. by V. J. McGovern & P. Russel. (Pigment Cell Ser.: Vol. 1). (Illus.). 1973. 115.00 (*3-8055-1480-8*) S Karger.

Mechanisms in Productive Chromosones of Aberrat & Eukary, Vol. 10, No. 3. Akifyev. 54p. 1997. pap. text 27.00 (*3-7186-5829-1*, Harwood Acad Pubs) Gordon & Breach.

Mechanisms in Respiratory Toxicology, 2 vols., Vol. I. Paul Nettesheim & Hanspeter R. Witschi. 288p. 1982. 168.00 (*0-8493-5689-X*, RC732, CRC Reprint) Franklin.

Mechanisms in Respiratory Toxicology, 2 vols., Vol. II. Paul Nettesheim & Hanspeter R. Witschi. 240p. 1982. 138.00 (*0-8493-5690-3*, CRC Reprint) Franklin.

Mechanisms in Symptom Formation: Proceedings. Congress of International College of Psychosomatic. Ed. by H. Musaph. (Psychotherapy & Psychosomatics Ser.: Vol. 23, No. 1-6). 300p. 1974. 83.50 (*3-8055-1689-4*) S Karger.

Mechanisms in the Pathogenesis of Enteric Diseases: Proceedings of the First International Rushmore Conference Held in Rapid City, South Dakota, September 28-30, 1995. Ed. by Prem S. Paul et al. LC 97-5561. (Advances in Experimental Medicine & Biology Ser.: No. 412). (Illus.). 452p. 1997. 125.00 (*0-306-45519-6*, Kluwer Plenum) Kluwer Academic.

Mechanisms in Tobacco Carcinogenesis. Ed. by D. Hoffmann & C. C. Harris. LC 86-12956. (Banbury Reports: No. 23). 428p. 1986. 80.00 (*0-87969-223-5*) Cold Spring Harbor.

Mechanisms of Action of Chemical Biocides. S. Denyer & W. B. Hugo. 1990. 95.00 (*0-632-02928-5*) Blackwell Sci.

Mechanisms of Actions of Neurotoxic Substances. Ed. by Kedar N. Prasad & Antonia Vernadakis. LC 79-5319. (Illus.). 235p. 1982. reprint ed. pap. 72.90 (*0-608-00589-4*, 206117600007) Bks Demand.

Mechanisms of Adaptive Behavior: Clark L. Hull's Theoretical Papers with Commentary. Abram Amsel & Michael E. Rashotte. LC 84-7608. 560p. 1984. text 104.00 (*0-231-05792-X*) Col U Pr.

Mechanisms of Age Cognition Relations in Adulthood. Timothy A. Salthouse. (John M. Memorial Lecture). 152p. 1992. text 29.95 (*0-8058-1129-X*) L Erlbaum Assocs.

Mechanisms of Anesthetic Action in Skeletal, Cardiac & Smooth Muscle. Ed. by T. J. Blanck & D. M. Wheeler. (Advances in Experimental Medicine & Biology Ser.: Vol. 301). (Illus.). 320p. (C). 1991. text 132.00 (*0-306-44011-3*, Kluwer Plenum) Kluwer Academic.

Mechanisms of Apoptotic Cell Death. Ed. by Martin Kroenke. (Journal Ser.: Vol. 6, No. 6, 1996). (Illus.). iv, 78p. 1996. pap. 28.00 (*3-8055-6453-8*) S Karger.

Mechanisms of Arrhythmias. Michiel J. Janse. Ed. by A. John Camm. LC 93-11901. (Clinical Approaches to Tachyarrhythmias Ser.: Vol. 1). (Illus.). 72p. 1993. pap. 15.00 (*0-87993-569-3*) Futura Pub.

Mechanisms of Atmospheric Oxidation of the Alkenes. Jack G. Calvert et al. LC 98-50026. (Illus.). 560p. 2000. text 105.00 (*0-19-513177-0*) OUP.

Mechanisms of B Cell Neoplasia 1998 15th Workshop: Proceedings of the Workshop Held at the Basel Institute for Immunology 4th - 6th October 1998, No. 246. Ed. by F. Melchers et al. (Current Topics in Microbiology & Immunology Ser.). (Illus.). xxvix, 415p. 1999. 250.00 (*3-540-65759-2*) Spr-Verlag.

Mechanisms of Biohalogenation & Dehalogenation. Ed. by D. B. Janssen et al. LC 98-132794. (Verhandelingen der Koninklijke Nederlandse Akademie van Wetenschappen, Afd. Letterkunde, Nieuwe Reeks Ser.: Vol. 98). 224p. 1997. pap. 49.00 (*0-444-85816-4*, North Holland) Elsevier.

Mechanisms of Brain Laterilization. V. L. Bianki. (Monographs in Neuroscience: Vol. 4). 296p. 1993. text 94.00 (*2-88124-460-2*) Gordon & Breach.

Mechanisms of Cancer Metastasis: Potential Therapeutic Implications. Ed. by Kenneth V. Honn et al. (Developments in Oncology Ser.). 1985. text 160.50 (*0-89838-765-5*) Kluwer Academic.

Mechanisms of Carcinogenesis. Ed. by Elisabeth K. Weisburger. (Cancer Growth & Progression Ser.). (C). 1988. text 213.50 (*0-89838-991-7*) Kluwer Academic.

Mechanisms of Carcinogenesis by Dichloroacetate (DCA) & Trichloroacetate (TCA) Richard J. Bull & Anja J. Stauber. LC 98-8262. 1998. write for info. (*0-89867-962-1*) Am Water Wks Assn.

Mechanisms of Carcinogenesis in Risk Identification. Ed. by Harri Vainio et al. (IARC Scientific Publications: No. 116). (Illus.). 630p. 1992. pap. text 145.00 (*92-832-2116-8*) OUP.

Mechanisms of Cardiac Morphogenesis & Teratogenesis. Ed. by Tomas Pexieder. LC 79-65503. (Perspectives in Cardiovascular Research Ser.: No. 5). (Illus.). 528p. 1981. reprint ed. pap. 163.70 (*0-608-00593-2*, 206118000007) Bks Demand.

*__Mechanisms of Cell Death: The 2nd Annual Conference of the Cell Death Society.__ Zahra Zakeri et al. LC 99-42519. (Annals of the New York Academy of Science Ser.). 1999. write for info. (*1-57331-241-X*) NY Acad Sci.

Mechanisms of Cell Injury & Cell Death. B. A. Fowler. 86p. 1990. text 96.00 (*2-88124-411-4*) Gordon & Breach.

Mechanisms of Cell Stability: Subcellular & Molecular Aspects. I. N. Todorov. (Illus.). 242p. 1994. lib. bdg. 145.00 (*1-56072-116-2*) Nova Sci Pubs.

Mechanisms of Cellular Transformation by Carcinogenic Agents. Ed. by D. Grunberger & S. Goff. (International Encyclopedia of Pharmacology & Therapeutics Ser.: No. 126). (Illus.). 442p. 1987. 385.00 (*0-08-034204-3*, Pergamon Pr) Elsevier.

Mechanisms of Cerebral Hypoxia & Stroke. Ed. by G. Somjen. LC 88-25293. (Advances in Behavioral Biology Ser.: Vol. 35). (Illus.). 486p. 1988. 110.00 (*0-306-43015-0*, Plenum Trade) Perseus Pubng.

Mechanisms of Chemical Degradation of Cement-Based Systems. Ed. by K. L. Scrivener & J. F. Young. LC 97-171051. (Illus.). 472p. (C). 1997. 145.00 (*0-419-21570-0*, E & FN Spon) Routledge.

Mechanisms of Chromospheric & Coronal Heating: Proceedings of the International Conference Heidelberg, 5-8 June, 1990. Ed. by P. Ulmschneider et al. (Illus.). xv, 649p. 1991. 107.95 (*0-387-53436-9*) Spr-Verlag.

Mechanisms of Cocaine Abuse & Toxicity. 1991. lib. bdg. 79.95 (*0-8490-4343-3*) Gordon Pr.

Mechanisms of Cocaine Abuse & Toxicity. 1993. lib. bdg. 262.75 (*0-8490-8912-3*) Gordon Pr.

*__Mechanisms of Cognitive Development: Behavioral & Neural Perspectives.__ James L. McClelland & Robert S. Siegler. LC 00-33163. (Carnegie Mellon Symposia on Cognition Ser.). 2000. pap. write for info. (*0-8058-3276-9*) L Erlbaum Assocs.

*__Mechanisms of Cognitive Development: Behavioral & Neural Perspectives.__ Ed. by James L. McClelland & Robert S. Siegler. (A Volume in the Carnegie mellon Symposia on Cognition Series). 510p. 2000. write for info. (*0-8058-3275-0*) L Erlbaum Assocs.

Mechanisms of Conventional & High TC Superconductivity. Vladimir Z. Kresin et al. LC 92-40048. (International Series of Monographs on Physics: Vol. 84). (Illus.). 200p. (C). 1993. text 60.00 (*0-19-505613-2*) OUP.

*__Mechanisms of Cortical Development.__ David Price & David Willshaw. LC 99-39684. (Monographs of the Physiological Society: No. 48). (Illus.). 336p. 2000. text 59.95 (*0-19-262427-X*) OUP.

Mechanisms of Cortical Inhibition. V. M. Okujava. 147p. (C). 1997. lib. bdg. 95.00 (*1-56072-375-0*) Nova Sci Pubs.

Mechanisms of Creep Fracture. H. E. Evans. 328p. 1984. 97.25 (*0-85334-193-1*) Elsevier.

Mechanisms of Deformation & Fracture: Proceedings of the Interdisciplinary Conference, Held at the University of Lulea-Sweden, 20-22, September 1978. Ed. by K. E. Easterling. (Strength & Fracture of Materials & Structures Ser.). 1979. 188.00 (*0-08-024258-8*, Pub. by Pergamon Repr) Franklin.

Mechanisms of Differentiation, 2 vols., I. Ed. by Paul B. Fisher. 176p. 1990. lib. bdg. 153.00 (*0-8493-4947-8*, QH607) CRC Pr.

Mechanisms of Differentiation, 2 vols., II. Ed. by Paul B. Fisher. 216p. 1990. lib. bdg. 166.00 (*0-8493-4948-6*, QH607) CRC Pr.

*__Mechanisms of Disease: A Textbook of Comparative General Pathology.__ 3rd ed. David O. Slauson. 2000. text. write for info. (*0-323-00228-5*) Mosby Inc.

Mechanisms of Disease: An Introduction to Clinical Science. Ed. by S. Tomlinson et al. LC 96-39361. (Illus.). 532p. (C). 1997. text 120.00 (*0-521-46180-4*); pap. text 49.95 (*0-521-46738-1*) Cambridge U Pr.

Mechanisms of Disease: An Introduction to Pathology. 2nd ed. Ruy Perez-Tamayo. LC 84-25728. (Illus.). 668p. reprint ed. pap. 200.00 (*0-8357-6315-3*, 203558800096) Bks Demand.

Mechanisms of DNA Damage & Repair: Implications for Carcinogenesis & Risk Assessment. Ed. by Michael G. Simic et al. LC 86-9363. (Basic Life Sciences Ser.: Vol. 38). 594p. 1986. 110.00 (*0-306-42288-3*, Plenum Trade) Perseus Pubng.

Mechanisms of DNA Damage Recognition in Mammalian Cells. Hanspeter Naegeli. LC 97-6442. (Molecular Biology Intelligence Unit Ser.). 1997. 99.00 (*1-57059-438-4*) Landes Bioscience.

Mechanisms of Drug Action on the Nervous System. 2nd ed. R. W. Ryall. (Illus.). 256p. (C). 1989. text 64.95 (*0-521-25424-8*); pap. text 22.95 (*0-521-27437-0*) Cambridge U Pr.

Mechanisms of Drug Interactions. Ed. by P. F. D'Arcy et al. (Handbook of Experimental Pharmacology Ser.: Vol. 122). 400p. 1996. 349.00 (*3-540-60204-6*) Spr-Verlag.

Mechanisms of Drugs in Anaesthesia. 2nd ed. text. write for info. (*0-340-55157-7*, Pub. by E A) Routldge.

Mechanisms of Egg Activation. Ed. by R. Nuccitelli et al. (Bodega Marine Laboratory Marine Science Ser.). (Illus.). 322p. 1989. 95.00 (*0-306-43245-5*, Plenum Trade) Perseus Pubng.

Mechanisms of Environmental Carcinogenesis, vol. 2. Ed. by A. Kappas. LC 90-14296. (Illus.). 300p. 1987. 86.00 (*0-8493-4672-X*, CRC Reprint) Franklin.

Mechanisms of Environmental Carcinogenesis, 2 vols., Set. Ed. by J. Carl Barrett. 352p. 1987. 274.00 (*0-8493-4670-3*, RC268) CRC Pr.

Mechanisms of Environmental Stress Resistance in Plants. Ed. by Amarjit S. Basra & Ranjit K. Basra. 432p. 1997. text 81.00 (*90-5702-036-X*, ECU121, Harwood Acad Pubs) Gordon & Breach.

Mechanisms of Epileptogenesis: The Transition to Seizure. Ed. by M. A. Dichter. LC 88-25274. (Illus.). 298p. 1988. 79.50 (*0-306-43010-X*, Plenum Trade) Perseus Pubng.

Mechanisms of Everyday Cognition. Ed. by James M. Puckett & Hayne W. Reese. (West Virginia Series on Lifespan Developmental Psychology). 256p. 1993. text 59.95 (*0-8058-0976-7*) L Erlbaum Assocs.

Mechanisms of Fertilization: Plants to Humans. Ed. by B. Dale. (NATO ASI Series H: Cell Biology: Vol. 45). (Illus.). xvi, 708p. 1990. 225.00 (*0-387-51766-9*) Spr-Verlag.

Mechanisms of Fibre Carcinogenesis. Ed. by A. B. Kane et al. LC 97-162025. (IARC Scientific Publications: No. 140). (Illus.). 170p. 1997. pap. text 89.50 (*92-832-2140-0*) OUP.

Mechanisms of Forest Response to Acidic Deposition. Ed. by A. A. Lucier & S. G. Haines. 232p. 1990. 102.95 (*0-387-97205-6*) Spr-Verlag.

Mechanisms of Frost Heave & Salt Expansion of Soils. Zhenzhong Gao & Kenneth A. Eriksson. 200p. 1999. 79.95 (*7-03-006922-6*, Pub. by Sci Pr) Lubrecht & Cramer.

Mechanisms of Gene Expression: Structure, Function & Evolution of the Basal Transcriptional. Robert O. Weinzierl. 1998. 38.00 (*1-86094-126-5*) World Scientific Pub.

*__Mechanisms of Global Climate Change at Millennial Time Scales.__ Lloyd D. Keigwin. Ed. by Peter U. Clark & Robert S. Webber. LC 99-40787. (Geophysical Monograph Ser.: Vol. 112). 394p. 1999. 65.00 (*0-87590-095-X*) Am Geophysical.

Mechanisms of Governance. Oliver E. Williamson. (Illus.). 448p. 1996. text 60.00 (*0-19-507824-1*) OUP.

*__Mechanisms of Governance.__ Oliver E. Williamson. (Illus.). 439p. 1999. pap. 19.95 (*0-19-513260-2*) OUP.

Mechanisms of Heart Failure. Ed. by Pawan K. Singal et al. LC 95-14335. (Developments in Cardiovascular Medicine Ser.: Vol. 167). 480p. (C). 1996. text 236.00 (*0-7923-3490-6*) Kluwer Academic.

Mechanisms of Hepatocyte Injury & Death. Ed. by D. Keppler. 1984. text 225.00 (*0-85200-853-8*) Kluwer Academic.

Mechanisms of Heteroepitaxial Growth. Ed. by M. F. Chisholm et al. (Materials Research Society Symposium Proceedings Ser.: Vol. 263). 513p. 1992. text 17.50 (*1-55899-158-1*) Materials Res.

Mechanisms of High Temperature Superconductivity. Ed. by Hiroshi Kamimura & O. Oshiyama. (Materials Science Ser.: Vol. 11). (Illus.). x, 344p. 1989. 69.95 (*0-387-50726-4*) Spr-Verlag.

Mechanisms of Homogeneous Catalysis from Protons to Proteins. Myron L. Bender. LC 73-153080. 698p. reprint ed. pap. 200.00 (*0-608-10084-6*, 200649000059) Bks Demand.

Mechanisms of Host Resistance to Infectious Agents, Tumors, & Allografts. Ed. by Ralph Steinman & Robert J. North. LC 86-60123. (Illus.). 480p. 1986. pap. 25.00 (*0-87470-042-6*) Rockefeller.

Mechanisms of Immigration Control: A Comparative Analysis of European Regulation Policies. Ed. by Grete Brochmann & Tomas Hammar. 316p. 1999. 65.00 (*1-85973-267-4*, Pub. by Berg Pubs); pap. 19.50 (*1-85973-272-0*, Pub. by Berg Pubs) NYU Pr.

Mechanisms of Immue Regulation. Ed. by R. D. Granstein. (Chemical Immunology Ser.: Vol. 58). (Illus.). xiv, 338p. 1994. 248.75 (*3-8055-5786-8*) S Karger.

Mechanisms of Immunity to Virus-Induced Tumors. Ed. by John W. Blasecki. LC 81-163. (Immunology Series: No. 12). 368p. reprint ed. pap. 114.10 (*0-7837-0942-0*, 204124700019) Bks Demand.

Mechanisms of Implicit Learning: A Connectionist Model of Sequence Processing. Axel Cleeremans. LC 92-35739. (Neural Network Modeling & Connectionism Ser.). (Illus.). 230p. 1993. 36.00 (*0-262-03205-8*, Bradford Bks) MIT Pr.

Mechanisms of Injury in Renal Disease & Toxicity. Ed. by Robin S. Goldstein. 320p. 1994. lib. bdg. 259.00 (*0-8493-8873-2*, TP8873) CRC Pr.

Mechanisms of Inorganic & Organometallic Reactions, Vol. 1. Ed. by M. V. Twigg. LC 83-2140. 390p. 1983. 115.00 (*0-306-41142-3*, Plenum Trade) Perseus Pubng.

Mechanisms of Inorganic & Organometallic Reactions, Vol. 2. Ed. by M. V. Twigg. LC 83-2140. 470p. 1984. 125.00 (*0-306-41404-X*, Plenum Trade) Perseus Pubng.

Mechanisms of Inorganic & Organometallic Reactions, Vol. 3. Ed. by M. V. Twigg. LC 83-2140. 538p. 1985. 125.00 (*0-306-41960-2*, Plenum Trade) Perseus Pubng.

Mechanisms of Inorganic & Organometallic Reactions, Vol. 4. Ed. by M. V. Twigg. (Illus.). 556p. (C). 1986. text 162.00 (*0-306-42332-4*, Kluwer Plenum) Kluwer Academic.

Mechanisms of Inorganic & Organometallic Reactions, Vol. 5. M. V. Twigg. LC 87-648073. (Illus.). 484p. (C). 1988. text 135.00 (*0-306-42841-5*, Kluwer Plenum) Kluwer Academic.

An Asterisk (*) at the beginning of an entry indicates that the title is appearing for the first time.

Mechanisms of Inorganic & Organometallic Reactions, Vol. 6. M. V. Twigg. (Illus.). 552p. (C). 1989. text 135.00 (*0-306-43260-9*, Kluwer Plenum) Kluwer Academic.

Mechanisms of Inorganic & Organometallic Reactions, Vol. 7. M. V. Twigg. (Illus.). 480p. (C). 1991. text 135.00 (*0-306-43787-2*, Kluwer Plenum) Kluwer Academic.

Mechanisms of Inorganic & Organometallic Reactions, Vol. 8. M. V. Twigg. (Illus.). 528p. (C). 1994. text 135.00 (*0-306-44437-2*, Kluwer Plenum) Kluwer Academic.

Mechanisms of Inorganic Reactions. Katakis. 416p. 1987. 130.00 (*0-471-84258-3*) Wiley.

Mechanisms of Inorganic Reactions: A Study of Metal Complexes in Solution. 2nd ed. Fred Basolo & Ralph G. Pearson. LC 66-28755. (Illus.). 715p. reprint ed. pap. 200.00 (*0-608-18195-1*, 205659700078) Bks Demand.

Mechanisms of Inorganic Reactions: Summer Symposium of the Division of Inorganic Chemistry of the American Chemical Society at the University of Kansas, Lawrence, KS, June 21-24, 1964. Summer Symposium on Mechanisms of Inorganic Reacti. LC 65-26226. (Advances in Chemistry Ser.: Vol. 49). (Illus.). 274p. 1965. reprint ed. pap. 85.00 (*0-608-06926-4*, 206713400009) Bks Demand.

Mechanisms of Intelligence: Ashby's Writings on Cybernetics. W. Ross Ashby. Ed. by Roger Conant. (Systems Inquiry Ser.). 394p. (Orig.). (C). 1981. pap. text 17.95 (*0-914105-04-3*) Intersystems Pubns.

Mechanisms of Intracellular Trafficking & Processing of Proteins. Ed. by Y. Peng Loh. 320p. 1992. lib. bdg. 155.00 (*0-8493-6870-7*, QH450) CRC Pr.

Mechanisms of Invasion & Metastasis. Marc M. Mareel et al. (Illus.). 608p. 1991. lib. bdg. 251.00 (*0-8493-6254-7*, RC269) CRC Pr.

Mechanisms of Ionic Polymerization: Current Problems. B. L. Erusalimskii. LC 86-24368. (Macromolecular Compounds Ser.). (Illus.). 316p. (C). 1987. text 132.00 (*0-306-10991-3*, Kluwer Plenum) Kluwer Academic.

Mechanisms of Job Stress & Strain. fac. ed. John R. French et al. LC 81-21871. (Wiley Series on Studies in Occupational Stress). 170p. 1982. reprint ed. pap. 52.70 (*0-7837-8269-1*, 204905000009) Bks Demand.

Mechanisms of Language Acquisition. Brian MacWhinney. (Carnegie-Mellon Symposium Ser.). 480p. (C). 1987. pap. 55.00 (*0-89859-973-3*) L Erlbaum Assocs.

Mechanisms of Learning & Motivation: A Memorial Volume to Jerzy Konorski. Ed. by A. Dickinson & R. A. Boakes. 460p. 1979. 79.95 (*0-89859-460-X*) L Erlbaum Assocs.

Mechanisms of Lung Injury. H. M. Mehendale. 90p. 1989. text 84.00 (*2-88124-410-6*) Gordon & Breach.

Mechanisms of Lymphocyte Activation & Immune Regulation. Ed. by Sudhir Gupta et al. LC 87-7005. (Illus.). 348p. 1987. 85.00 (*0-306-42568-8*, Plenum Trade) Perseus Pubng.

Mechanisms of Lymphocyte Activation & Immune Regulation Vol. 4: Cellular Communications. S. Gupta & T. A. Waldmann. LC 92-26881. (Advances in Experimental Medicine & Biology Ser.: Vol. 323). (Illus.). 214p. (C). 1992. text 85.00 (*0-306-44312-0*, Kluwer Plenum) Kluwer Academic.

Mechanisms of Lymphocyte Activation & Immune Regulation Vol. 5: Molecular Basis of Signal Transduction. S. Gupta et al. (Advances in Experimental Medicine & Biology Ser.: 365). (Illus.). 274p. (C). 1994. text 95.00 (*0-306-44897-1*, Kluwer Plenum) Kluwer Academic.

Mechanisms of Lymphocyte Activation & Immune Regulation II. Ed. by S. Gupta et al. (Illus.). 150p. 1989. 65.00 (*0-306-43250-1*, Plenum Trade) Perseus Pubng.

Mechanisms of Lymphocyte Activation & Immune Regulation VI: Cell Cycle & Programmed Cell Death in the Immune System. Ed. by Sudhir Gupta & John Cohen. LC 96-29392. (Advances in Experimental Medicine & Biology Ser.: Vol. 406). (Illus.). 279p. 1996. 102.00 (*0-306-45483-1*, Kluwer Plenum) Kluwer Academic.

Mechanisms of Lymphocyte Activation & Immune Regulation 3. Ed. by S. Gupta et al. (Advances in Experimental Medicine & Biology Ser.). (Illus.). 268p. (C). 1991. text 114.00 (*0-306-43922-0*, Kluwer Plenum) Kluwer Academic.

Mechanisms of Lymphocyte Activation & Immune Regulation 7: Molecular Determinants of Microbial Immunity: Proceedings of the 7th International Conference Held in Newport Beach, California, February 6-8, 1998. Ed. by Sudhir Gupta et al. LC 98-40455. (Advances in Experimental Medicine & Biology Ser.: No. 452). 223p. (C). 1998. text 85.00 (*0-306-46033-5*, Kluwer Plenum) Kluwer Academic.

Mechanisms of Lymphocyte Extravasation. Ed. by S. Ratner. (Journal: Invasion & Metastasis: Vol. 12, No. 2, 1992). (Illus.). 92p. 1992. pap. 52.25 (*3-8055-5657-8*) S Karger.

Mechanisms of Metallocenter Assembly. Ed. by Gunther L. Eichhorn et al. 267p. 1995. 165.00 (*0-471-18632-5*) Wiley.

Mechanisms of Metallocenter Assembly. Ed. by Robert P. Hausinger et al. LC 95-18371. (Advances in Inorganic Biochemistry Ser.: Vol. 10). (Illus.). 267p. 1995. 110.00 (*1-56081-920-0*, Wiley-VCH) Wiley.

Mechanisms of Microbial Disease. 2nd ed. Moselio Schaechter et al. (Illus.). 996p. 1993. pap. 42.00 (*0-683-07606-X*) Lppncott W & W.

Mechanisms of Microbial Disease. 3rd ed. Moselio Schaechter. LC 98-3835. 733p. 1998. pap. 45.00 (*0-683-07605-1*) Lppncott W & W.

Mechanisms of Morphological Evolution: A Combined Genetic, Developmental & Ecological Approach. Wallace Arthur. LC 83-16993. (Illus.). 291p. reprint ed. pap. 90.30 (*0-7837-1882-9*, 204208300001) Bks Demand.

Mechanisms of Motion-Induced Vomiting. Ed. by N. G. Daunton et al. (Journal: Brains, Behavior & Evolution: Vol. 23, No. 1-2). (Illus.). 80p. 1983. pap. 45.25 (*3-8055-3790-5*) S Karger.

Mechanisms of Mucosal Protection in the Upper Gastrointestinal Tract. Ed. by Adrian Allen et al. LC 83-19257. (Illus.). 416p. 1984. reprint ed. pap. 129.00 (*0-608-00654-8*, 206124200007) Bks Demand.

Mechanisms of Neoplastic Transformation at the Cellular Level. Ed. by George Klein. LC 83-26930. (Advances in Viral Oncology Ser.: No. 4). (Illus.). 349p. 1984. reprint ed. pap. 108.20 (*0-608-00662-9*, 206125000007) Bks Demand.

Mechanisms of Organic Reactions. Howard Maskill. (Oxford Chemistry Primers Ser.: No. 45). (Illus.). 104p. (C). 1996. pap. text 12.95 (*0-19-855822-8*) OUP.

Mechanisms of Osmoregulation in Animals: Maintenance of Cell Volume. Ed. by R. Gilles. LC 78-4608. (Illus.). 679p. reprint ed. pap. 180.00 (*0-685-20689-0*, 2030479) Bks Demand.

Mechanisms of Pain & Analgesic Compounds. fac. ed. Ed. by Roland F. Beers, Jr. & Edward G. Bassett. LC 78-52524. (Miles International Symposium Ser.: No. 11). (Illus.). 510p. pap. 158.10 (*0-7837-7500-8*, 204700600005) Bks Demand.

Mechanisms of Peptic Ulcer Healing. Ed. by F. Halter et al. (C). 1991. text 225.50 (*0-7923-8955-7*) Kluwer Academic.

Mechanisms of Phase Transitions. Ed. by Stanley B. Block. (Transactions of the American Crystallographic Association Ser.: Vol. 7). 154p. 1971. pap. 25.00 (*0-686-60378-8*) Polycrystal Bk Serv.

Mechanisms of Photophysical Processes & Photochemical Reactions in Polymers: Theory & Applications. J. F. Rabek. LC 86-15693. (Illus.). 776p. reprint ed. pap. 200.00 (*0-8357-4627-5*, 203755600008) Bks Demand.

Mechanisms of Physical & Emotional Stress. Ed. by George P. Chrousos et al. LC 88-28384. (Illus.). 542p. 1988. 125.00 (*0-306-43017-7*, Plenum Trade) Perseus Pubng.

Mechanisms of Plant Defense Responses. Ed. by Bernard Fritig. (Developments in Plant Pathology Ser.). 500p. (C). 1993. text 262.50 (*0-7923-2154-5*) Kluwer Academic.

Mechanisms of Plant Growth & Improved Productivity: Modern Approaches. Ed. by Amarjit S. Basra. LC 94-12080. (Books in Soils, Plants & the Environment: Vol. 33). (Illus.). 496p. 1994. text 195.00 (*0-8247-9192-4*) Dekker.

Mechanisms of Platelet Activation & Control. K. S. Authi et al. LC 93-32065. (Advances in Experimental Medicine & Biology Ser.: Vol. 334). (Illus.). 286p. (C). 1994. text 89.50 (*0-306-44631-6*, Kluwer Plenum) Kluwer Academic.

***Mechanisms of Power in the Soviet Union.** Niels E. Rosenfeldt et al. LC 99-53109. 2000. text 69.95 (*0-312-23089-3*) St Martin.

Mechanisms of Progression in Renal Disease. Ed. by J. Floege. (Kidney & Blood Pressure Research Ser.: Vol. 22, No. 1 (1999)). (Illus.). 90p. 1999. pap. 34.00 (*3-8055-6876-2*) S Karger.

Mechanisms of Protease Action. Laszlo Polgar. 288p. 1989. lib. bdg. 225.00 (*0-8493-6901-0*, QP609) CRC Pr.

Mechanisms of Protein Folding. Ed. by Roger H. Pain. LC 93-47574. (Illus.). 284p. (C). 1994. pap. text 55.00 (*0-19-963397-5*) OUP.

Mechanisms of Psychological Influence on Physical Health: With Special Attention to the Elderly. Ed. by John M. Neale & L. L. Carstensen. (Illus.). 196p. 1989. 69.50 (*0-306-43116-5*, Plenum Trade) Perseus Pubng.

Mechanisms of Quality in Long-Term Care: Education. Ed. by Ethel L. Mitty. LC 93-30194. 1993. 13.00 (*0-88737-602-9*) Natl League Nurse.

Mechanisms of Quality in Long-Term Care: Service & Clinical Outcomes. (NLN-Ross Laboratories Long-Term Care Conferences Ser.). (Illus.). 128p. (C). 1991. pap. text 5.95 (*0-88737-506-5*, 41-2382) Natl League Nurse.

Mechanisms of Radiation Effects in Electronic Materials. V. A. Van Lint et al. LC 79-9083. (Wiley-Interscience Publications). 373p. reprint ed. pap. 115.70 (*0-608-12429-X*, 202518100042) Bks Demand.

Mechanisms of Reactions at Transition Metal Sites. Richard A. Henderson. (Oxford Chemistry Primers Ser.: No. 10). (Illus.). 96p. (C). 1994. pap. text 12.95 (*0-19-855746-9*) OUP.

Mechanisms of Reactions of Organometallic Compounds with Surfaces. Ed. by D. J. Cole-Hamilton & J. O. Williams. (Illus.). 312p. 1989. 89.50 (*0-306-43205-6*, Plenum Trade) Perseus Pubng.

Mechanisms of Recent Vertical Crustal Movements in Campi Flegrei Caldera, Southern Italy. J. J. Dvorak & G. Mastrolorenzo. (Special Papers: No. 263). (Illus.). 66p. 1991. pap. 12.00 (*0-8137-2263-2*) Geol Soc.

Mechanisms of Receptor Regulation. Ed. by Stanley T. Crooke & George H. Poste. LC 85-28339. (New Horizons in Therapeutics Ser.). (Illus.). 458p. (C). 1985. text 150.00 (*0-306-42125-9*, Kluwer Plenum) Kluwer Academic.

Mechanisms of Renal Injury & Repair Vol. 21, No. 4-5: Mineral & Electrolyte Metabolism, 1995. Ed. by Manuel Martinez-Maldonado. (Journal Ser.: Vol. 21, No. 4-5, 1995). (Illus.). 122p. 1995. pap. 86.25 (*3-8055-6209-8*) S Karger.

***Mechanisms of Resistance to Plant Diseases.** A. J. Slusarenko et al. LC 00-42407. 2000. write for info. (*0-7923-6418-X*) Kluwer Academic.

Mechanisms of Secondary Brain Damage. Ed. by A. Baethmann et al. LC 86-22671. (NATO ASI Series A, Life Sciences: Vol. 115). 416p. 1986. 95.00 (*0-306-42397-9*, Plenum Trade) Perseus Pubng.

Mechanisms of Secondary Brain Damage: Current State. Ed. by A. Baethmann et al. LC 92-49078. (Acta Neurochirugica - Supplementum Ser.: No. 57). 1993. write for info. (*3-211-82421-9*); 140.00 (*0-387-82421-9*) Spr-Verlag.

Mechanisms of Secondary Brain Damage in Cerebral Ischemia & Trauma, Vol. 66. Ed. by A. Baethmann et al. LC 96-3928. (Acta Neurochirugica - Supplementum Ser.: No. 66). (Illus.). 150p. 1996. suppl. ed. 139.50 (*3-211-82817-6*) Spr-Verlag.

Mechanisms of Speech. N. I. Zinkin. LC 68-15534. (Janua Linguarum, Ser. Major: No. 13). (Illus.). (C). 1968. text 132.35 (*90-279-0607-6*) Mouton.

Mechanisms of Stimulus-Response Coupling in Platelets. Ed. by J. Westwick et al. LC 85-12135. (Advances in Experimental Medicine & Biology Ser.: Vol. 192). 456p. 1986. 110.00 (*0-306-42073-2*, Plenum Trade) Perseus Pubng.

***Mechanisms of Stress & Emotion: Neuroendocrine Based Studies: Proceedings of the 18th University of Occupational & Environmental Health International Symposium, Kitakyushu, 8-10 October, 1998.** UOEH International Symposium Staff et al. LC 99-15861. 359p. 1999. 160.00 (*0-444-50118-5*, Excerpta Medica) Elsevier.

Mechanisms of Systemic Regulation: Acid-Base Regulation, Ion Transfer & Metabolism. Ed. by Norbert Heisler. (Advances in Comparative & Environmental Physiology Ser.: Vol. 22). (Illus.). 257p. 1995. 262.95 (*3-540-59142-7*) Spr-Verlag.

Mechanisms of Systemic Regulation: Respiration & Circulation, Vol.21. Ed. by R. E. Weber et al. (Advances in Comparative & Environmental Physiology Ser.: Vol. 21). (Illus.). 140p. 1995. 217.95 (*3-540-59122-2*) Spr-Verlag.

Mechanisms of Taste Transduction. Ed. by Sidney A. Simon & Stephen D. Roper. 528p. 1993. lib. bdg. 225.00 (*0-8493-5341-6*, QP456) CRC Pr.

Mechanisms of the Mind: An Evolutionary Perspective. Malcolm I. Hale. LC 98-92639. (Illus.). 400p. 1999. pap. 9.95 (*0-9623691-1-X*) Hale-Van Ruth.

Mechanisms of Thin Film Evolution Vol. 317: Materials Research Society Symposium Proceedings. Ed. by S. M. Yalisove et al. LC 94-9652. 631p. 1994. text 73.00 (*1-55899-216-2*) Materials Res.

Mechanisms of Tinnitus. Ed. by Jack A. Vernon & Aage R. Moller. LC 94-27956. 272p. (C). 1994. 68.00 (*0-205-14083-1*, Longwood Div) Allyn.

Mechanisms of Transcription. Contrib. by Cold Spring Harbor Staff. (Cold Spring Harbor Symposia on Quantitative Biology Ser.: Vol. LXIII). (Illus.). 600p. (C). 1999. text 258.00 (*0-87969-550-1*); pap. text 110.00 (*0-87969-552-8*) Cold Spring Harbor.

Mechanisms of Transcription. Ed. by Fritz Eckstein & David M. Lilley. LC 97-6583. (Nucleic Acids & Molecular Biology Ser.: Vol. 11). (Illus.). x, 327p. 1997. 160.00 (*3-540-62397-3*) Spr-Verlag.

Mechanisms of Transdermeal Drug Delivery. Ed. by Russell O. Potts & Richard A. Guy. LC 97-20470. (Drugs & the Pharmaceutical Sciences Ser.: Vol. 82). (Illus.). 376p. 1997. text 165.00 (*0-8247-9863-5*) Dekker.

Mechanisms of Tumor Immunity. Ed. by Ira Green & Stanley Cohen. LC 76-48047. (Basic & Clinical Immunology Ser.). 332p. reprint ed. pap. 103.00 (*0-608-30876-5*, 201519300092) Bks Demand.

Mechanisms of Vasodilatation: Proceeding of the International Congress of Physiological Sciences, Official Satellite Symposium, 27th, Wilrijk, July 1977. International Congress of Physiological Sciences,. Ed. by P. M. Vanhoutte & Isadore Leusen. (Illus.). 1978. 85.25 (*3-8055-2841-8*) S Karger.

Mechanisms of Vasodilatation Abstracts: Journal: Blood Vessels, Vol. 23, No. 2, 1986. Ed. by P. M. Vanhoutte. 60p. 1986. pap. 27.00 (*3-8055-4361-1*) S Karger.

Mechanisms of Vasodilation Symposium, Abstracts. Mechanisms of Vasodilatation Symposium Staff. Ed. by P. M. Vanhoutte. (Journal: Blood Vessels: Vol. 17, No. 3). 56p. 1980. pap. 32.25 (*3-8055-1252-X*) S Karger.

Mechanisms of Viral Carcinogenesis: From Hypercarcinogenic State to Normo- or Hypocarcinogenic States. Ed. by O. Hino. (Journal Ser.: Vol. 38, Nos. 3 & 4, 1995). (Illus.). 128p. 1995. pap. 80.00 (*3-8055-6275-6*) S Karger.

Mechanisms of Viral Pathogenesis: From Gene to Pathogen. Ed. by A. Kohn & P. Fuchs. (Developments in Molecular Virology Ser.). 1983. text 132.00 (*0-89838-605-5*) Kluwer Academic.

Mechanisms of Viral Toxicity in Animal Cells. Luis Carrasco. 208p. 1987. 120.00 (*0-8493-6742-5*, CRC Reprint) Franklin.

Mechanisms of Visual Attention: A Cognitive Neuroscience Perspective. Werner X. Schneider. LC 98-186386. 1998. 59.95 (*0-86377-981-6*, Pub. by Psychol Pr) Taylor & Francis.

Mechanisms of Woody Plant Defenses Against Insects. Ed. by W. J. Mattson et al. (Illus.). 435p. 1987. 141.00 (*0-387-96673-0*) Spr-Verlag.

Mechanisms of Work Production & Work Absorption in Muscle. Ed. by H. Sugi & G. H. Pollack. LC 98-31319. (Advances in Experimental Medicine & Biology Ser.: Vol. 453). (Illus.). 663p. (C). 1998. text 175.00 (*0-306-46037-8*, Kluwer Plenum) Kluwer Academic.

Mechanisms of Yeast Recombination. Ed. by Amar Klar & Jeffrey N. Strathern. LC 86-213265. (Current Communications in Molecular Biology Ser.). (Illus.). 203p. 1986. reprint ed. pap. 63.00 (*0-608-04086-X*, 206481800011) Bks Demand.

Mechanisms Regulating Lactation & Infant Nutrient Utilization. Mary F. Picciano & Bo Lonnerdal. (Contemporary Issues in Clinical Nutrition Ser.). 480p. 1992. 395.00 (*0-471-56134-7*) Wiley.

Mechanisms/Interferon Actions, Vol. I. Pfeffer. 152p. 1987. 89.00 (*0-8493-6146-X*, CRC Reprint) Franklin.

Mechanisms/Interferon Actions, Vol. II. Pfeffer. 200p. 1987. 113.00 (*0-8493-6147-8*, CRC Reprint) Franklin.

Mechanistic & Nonmechanistic Science. Richard L. Thompson. (Illus.). 254p. (Orig.). 1982. pap. 8.00 (*0-89647-014-8*, MNS) Bhaktivedanta.

Mechanistic & Nonmechanistic Science: An Investigation into the Nature of Consciousness & Form. Richard L. Thompson. 254p. (C). 1990. pap. 12.95 (*0-89213-148-9*) Bhaktivedanta.

Mechanistic Approaches to Interactions of Electric & Electromagnetic Fields with Living Systems. Ed. by Martin Blank & E. Findl. LC 87-7170. (Illus.). 454p. (C). 1987. text 156.00 (*0-306-42684-6*, Kluwer Plenum) Kluwer Academic.

Mechanistic Aspects of Inorganic Reactions. Ed. by David B. Rorabacher & John F. Endicott. LC 82-13817. (ACS Symposium Ser.: No. 198). 480p. 1982. 60.95 (*0-8412-0734-8*) Am Chemical.

Mechanistic Aspects of Inorganic Reactions. David B. Rorabacher & John F. Endicott. LC 82-13817. (ACS Symposium Ser.: Vol. 198). 496p. 1982. reprint ed. pap. 153.80 (*0-608-03121-6*, 206357400007) Bks Demand.

Mechanistic Aspects of the Thermal Formation of Halogenated Organic Compounds Including Polychlorinated Dibenzo-p-Dioxins. Ghulam G. Choudhry & O. Hutzinger. LC 83-1640. (Current Topics In Environmental & Toxicological Chemistry Ser.: Vol. 4). (Illus.). x, 194p. 1983. text 173.00 (*0-677-06130-7*) Gordon & Breach.

Mechanistic Basis & Relevance of Kidney Tumors in Male Rats for Use in Risk Assessment. (Illus.). 84p. 1994. pap. 54.00 (*0-89867-741-6*, 90655) Am Water Wks Assn.

Mechanistic Bioinorganic Chemistry. American Chemical Society, Division of Inorganic C. Ed. by H. Holden Thorp & Vincent L. Pecoraro. LC 95-15128. (Advances in Chemistry Ser.: Vol. 246). (Illus.). 400p. 1995. text 120.00 (*0-8412-3062-5*, Pub. by Am Chemical) OUP.

Mechanistic Relationships Between Development & Learning: Report of the Dahlem Workshop on Mechanistic Relationships Between Development & Learning, Berlin, January 19-25, 1997. Thomas J. Carew et al. LC 98-17869. (Dahlem Workshop Reports). 336p. 1998. 165.00 (*0-471-97702-0*) Wiley.

***Mechanization & Automation in Dairy Technology.** A. Y. Tamime & Barry A. Law. LC 00-29730. (Illus.). 2000. write for info. (*0-8493-0509-8*) CRC Pr.

Mechanization & Maize: Agriculture & the Politics of Technology Transfer in East Africa. Constance G. Anthony. (Political Economy of International Change Ser.). 192p. 1988. text 44.00 (*0-231-06596-5*) Col U Pr.

Mechanization & Mexican Labor in California Agriculture. David Runsten & Phillip LeVeen. (Monographs: No. 6). 135p. (Orig.). (C). 1981. ring bd. 7.50 (*0-935391-44-4*, MN-06) UCSD Ctr US-Mex.

Mechanization in Industry. Harry Jerome. (General Ser.: No. 27). 518p. 1934. reprint ed. 134.70 (*0-87014-026-4*) Natl Bur Econ Res.

Mechanization, Land Use, & Ownership: Oklahoma in the Early Twentieth Century. Bonnie Lynn-Sherow. (LTC Paper Ser.: Vol. 155). (Illus.). iii, 16p. (C). 1996. pap. 4.00 (*0-934519-73-0*, LTC155) U of Wis Land.

Mechanization of Agriculture in Brazil: A Sociological Study of Minas Gerais. Harold M. Clements. LC 76-93194. (Latin American Monographs: Ser. 2, No. 7). (Illus.). 104p. reprint ed. pap. 32.30 (*0-7837-4961-9*, 204462700004) Bks Demand.

Mechanization of Small Fishing Craft. Ed. by Jan-Olof Traung. 1978. 60.00 (*0-7855-6938-3*) St Mut.

***Mechanization of the Mind: On the Origins of Cognitive Science.** Jean-Pierre Dupuy. Tr. by M. B. DeBevoise. (New French Thought Ser.). (Illus.). 240p. 2000. 29.95 (*0-691-02574-6*) Princeton U Pr.

Mechanized Archaeology. David Van Horn. (Illus.). 130p. (C). 1988. pap. text 12.95 (*0-937523-02-X*) Wormwood Pr.

Mechanized Combat. Chris Bishop. 1998. 19.99 (*0-7858-0842-6*) Bk Sales Inc.

Mechanized Infantry. Brigadier R. Simpkin. (Illus.). 144p. 1980. 47.00 (*0-08-027030-1*, Pergamon Pr) Elsevier.

Mechanized Juggernaut or Military Anachronism? Horses & the German Army of World War II, 113. R. L. DiNardo. LC 91-9270. (Contributions in Military Studies Ser.: No. 113). 160p. 1991. 49.95 (*0-313-27810-5*, DMH/, Greenwood Pr) Greenwood.

***Mechanobiology: Cartilage & Condrocyte.** Ed. by J. F. Stoltz. (Biomedical & Health Research Ser.: Vol. 42). 198p. 2000. 102.00 (*1-58603-051-5*) IOS Press.

Mechanochemistry of Materials. E. M. Gutman. 200p. 1996. pap. text 55.00 (*1-898326-32-0*, Pub. by CISP) Balogh.

Mechanochemistry of Solid Surfaces. E. M. Gutman. 320p. 1994. text 61.00 (*981-02-1781-1*) World Scientific Pub.

Mechanoids. Kevin Siembieda. Ed. by Alex Marciniszyn et al. (Rifts Sourcebook Ser.: No. 2). (Illus.). 120p. (Orig.). (YA). (gr. 8 up). 1992. pap. 12.95 (*0-916211-55-X*, 805) Palladium Bks.

Mechanoreceptors: Development, Structure, & Function. Ed. by Parvel Hnik et al. LC 88-5796. (Illus.). 458p. 1988. 110.00 (*0-306-42832-6*, Plenum Trade) Perseus Pubng.

Mechanosensory Lateral Line. Ed. by S. Coombs et al. (Illus.). 655p. 1989. 262.00 (*0-387-96837-7*) Spr-Verlag.

Mechant Petit Lapin. Beatrix Potter. (FRE., Illus.). 58p. (J). 1990. 9.95 (*0-7859-3627-0*, 2070560732) Fr & Eur.

Mechant Petit Lapin. Beatrix Potter. (Gallimard Ser.). (FRE.). (J). (gr. 5-10). 1990. 10.95 (*2-07-056073-2*) Schoenhof.

Mechatronic Measurement Systems. Histand. 1998. student ed. 32.81 (*0-07-029104-7*) McGraw.

Mechatronic Systems. Shetty. (Miscellaneous/Catalogs Ser.). 1997. text, teacher ed. 16.00 (*0-534-95132-5*) Wadsworth Pub.

Mechatronic Systems. Devdas Shetty & Richard Kolk. LC 97-13889. (Miscellaneous/Catalogs Ser.). 432p. (C). 1997. mass mkt. 94.95 (*0-534-95285-2*) Wadsworth Pub.

Mechatronics. Ed. by J. R. Hewit. (CISM International Centre for Mechanical Sciences Ser.: Vol. 338). vii, 300p. 1994. 76.95 (*0-387-82518-5*) Spr-Verlag.

***Mechatronics: And the Development of Intelligent Machines & Systems.** D. A. Bradley et al. (Illus.). 400p. 2000. 27.50 (*0-7487-5443-1*, Pub. by S Thornes Pubs) Intl Spec Bk.

Mechatronics: Developments in Japan & Europe. Ed. by Mick McLean. LC 83-22925. 129p. 1983. 55.00 (*0-89930-087-1*, MMT/, Quorum Bks) Greenwood.

Mechatronics: Electromechanics & Contromechanics. Denny K. Miu. Ed. by Frederick F. Ling. LC 92-1604. (Mechanical Engineering Ser.). (Illus.). 264p. 1993. 69.95 (*0-387-97893-3*) Spr-Verlag.

Mechatronics: Electronic Control Systems in Mechanical Engineering. 2nd ed. W. Bolton. 390p. 1998. pap. 97.00 (*0-582-35705-5*, Prentice Hall) P-H.

Mechatronics: Mechanical System Interfacing. David M. Auslander & Carl J. Kempf. LC 95-21844. 243p. (C). 1995. 97.00 (*0-13-120338-X*) P-H.

Mechatronics: The Basis for New Industrial Development. Ed. by M. Acar et al. 848p. 1994. 318.00 (*1-85312-367-6*) Computational Mech MA.

Mechatronics: The Policy Ramifications. Kansai Productivity Center Staff. 200p. 1985. text 30.50 (*92-833-1075-6*); pap. text 25.00 (*92-833-1076-4*) Productivity Inc.

***Mechatronics & Machine Tools.** Machine Tools Limited Hidustan Press. LC 98-51794. 1998. 69.95 (*0-07-134634-1*) McGraw.

***Mechatronics & Machine Vision.** J. Billingsley. LC 00-32338. (Robotics & Mechatronics Ser.). 2000. write for info. (*0-86380-261-3*, Pub. by Research Studies Pr Ltd) Taylor & Francis.

Mechatronics & Machine Vision in Practice, 4th Annual Conference. Contrib. by Institution of Electrical Engineers Staff. LC 97-74200. 300p. 1997. pap. 115.00 (*0-8186-8025-3*) IEEE Comp Soc.

Mechatronics & Robotics. Ed. by P. A. MacConaill et al. (Advances in Design & Manufacturing Ser.: No. 1). 346p. 1991. 90.00 (*90-5199-057-X*, Pub. by IOS Pr) IOS Press.

Mechatronics Design in Textile Engineering: Proceedings of the NATO Advanced Study Institute on Advancements & Applications of Mechatronics Design in Textile Engineering, Side, Antalya, Turkey, April 5-16, 1992. Ed. by Memis Acar. (NATO Advanced Science Institutes Ser.: Series E). 328p. (C). 1994. text 213.00 (*0-7923-3204-0*) Kluwer Academic.

***Mechatronics for Motion.** 2000. write for info. (*0-13-018310-5*) P-H.

Mechatronics in Engineering Design & Product Development. Ed. by Dobrivojie Popovic & Ljubo Vlacic. LC 98-38127. (Illus.). 632p. 1998. text 195.00 (*0-8247-0226-3*) Dekker.

Mechatronics '98: Proceedings of the 6th U. K. Mechatronics Forum International Conference, Skovde, Sweden, 9-11 September 1998. Josef Orum Adolfsson International Conference et al. LC 98-29168. xxi, 918p. 1998. 318.50 (*0-08-043339-1*) Elsevier.

Mechcommander: Desperate Measure. Joe Grant Bell. 1999. pap. 19.99 (*0-7615-2227-1*) Prima Pub.

Mechcommander: The Official Strategy Guide. Bell J. Grant. LC 96-70603. 240p. 1998. pap. text 19.99 (*0-7615-0556-3*) Prima Pub.

Mechene Amoureux. Karen Rose Smith. (Horizon Ser.: No. 517). (FRE.). 1999. mass mkt. 3.99 (*0-373-39517-5*, 1-39517-7) Harlequin Bks.

Mechitza. Karen Alkalay-Gut. Ed. by Stanley H. Barkan. Tr. by Eyal Megged et al. (Review Woman Writers Chapbook Ser.: No. 5).Tr. of Hebrew & Eng.. 48p. 1986. 15.00 (*0-89304-420-2*, CCC164); pap. 5.00 (*0-89304-421-0*) Cross-Cultrl NY.

Mechitza: Mini. Karen Alkalay-Gut. Ed. by Stanley H. Barkan. Tr. by Eyal Megged et al. (Review Woman Writers Chapbook Ser.: No. 5).Tr. of Hebrew & Eng.. 48p. 1986. 15.00 (*0-89304-422-9*); pap. 5.00 (*0-89304-423-7*) Cross-Cultrl NY.

***Mechnical & Quartz Watch Repair.** Mick Watters. 1999. 40.00 (*1-86126-233-7*, Pub. by Crolwood) Trafalgar.

Mechthild of Magdeburg. Tr. by Frank Tobin. LC 97-44826. (Classics of Western Spirituality Ser.: Vol. 91). 1997. pap. 24.95 (*0-8091-3776-3*) Paulist Pr.

Mechthild of Magdeburg: The Flowing Light of the Godhead. Mechthild of Magdeburg. Tr. & Intro. by Frank Tobin. LC 97-44826. (Classics of Western Spirituality Ser.: No. 91). 560p. 1998. 34.95 (*0-8091-0495-4*) Paulist Pr.

Mechthild von Magdeburg: A Medieval Mystic in Modern Eyes. Frank Tobin. (LCGERM Ser.). xi, 152p. 1995. 55.00 (*1-57113-001-2*) Camden Hse.

Mechty i Dumy. Ivan Konevoskoi. (RUS.). 240p. (C). 1989. reprint ed. pap. 16.00 (*0-933884-73-7*) Berkeley Slavic.

MechWarrior. Richard K. Meyer et al. (BattleTech Ser.). (Illus.). 144p. (Orig.). 1991. pap. 15.00 (*0-931787-58-0*) FASA Corp.

MechWarrior Companion: A Mech Warrior Sourcebook. FASA Corp. Staff. (BattleTech Ser.). (Illus.). 128p. 1995. pap. 15.00 (*1-55560-189-8*, 1671) FASA Corp.

***Mechwarrior 3: For Battle Tech.** FASA Corp. Staff. 160p. 1999. pap. 25.00 (*1-55560-386-6*, 03866F, Pub. by FASA Corp) NTC Contemp Pub Co.

***MechWarrior 3: Priate's Moon.** Joe Grant Bell. (Official Strategy Guides Ser.). (Illus.). 288p. (YA). 2000. pap. 14.99 (*0-7615-2731-1*) Prima Pub.

MechWarrior III: Prima's Official Strategy Guide. Joe Grant Bell. LC 96-67260. 288p. 1999. pap. 19.99 (*0-7615-0390-0*) Prima Pub.

MechWarrior 2: Expansion Pack Secrets & Solutions. Joe G. Bell. 1996. pap. text 12.95 (*0-7615-0578-4*) Prima Pub.

MechWarrior II: Mercenaries: The Official Strategy Guide, Vol. 2. Joe Grant Bell. LC 96-70240. 216p. 1996. pap., per. 19.99 (*0-7615-0906-2*) Prima Pub.

Mecklenburg & Cabarrus Counties, North Carolina Decedents for Whom Loose Estates Papers Are Extant Herman W. Ferguson. LC 98-71549. vi, 68 p. 1998. write for info. (*0-9620770-6-2*) H W Ferguson.

***Mecklenburg Co., N. C., a 1792 Petition & Tax Lists, 1792, 1798, 1799, 1806, 1807, 1808, 1810, 1811, 1815, 1823 & 1824.** Herman W. Ferguson & Ralph B. Ferguson. (Illus.). vi, 180p. 1999. pap. 25.00 (*0-9620770-7-0*) H W Ferguson.

Mecklenburg Collection Pt. I: Data on Iron Age Horses of Central & Eastern Europe & Human Skeletal Materials from Slovenia. Sandor Bokonyi. LC 68-22588. (American School of Prehistoric Research Bulletins Ser.: No. 25). (Illus.). 116p. 1968. pap. 8.00 (*0-87365-526-5*) Peabody Harvard.

Mecklenburg Collection Pt. II: The Iron Age Cemetery of Magdalenska gora in Slovenia. Hugh Hencken. LC 78-52401. (American School of Prehistoric Research Bulletins Ser.: No. 32). (Illus.). 328p. 1978. pap. 17.00 (*0-87365-535-4*) Peabody Harvard.

Mecklenburg County, North Carolina Deed Abstracts, 1763-1779, Bks. 1-9. Brent Holcomb. (Orig.). 1981. reprint ed. 30.00 (*0-89308-108-6*) Southern Hist Pr.

Mecklenburg County, North Carolina, Minutes of the Court of Common Pleas & Quarter Sessions, 1780-1800. Herman W. Ferguson. LC 94-62190. (Illus.). 276p. 1995. pap. text 27.50 (*0-9620770-3-8*) H W Ferguson.

Mecklenburg County, North Carolina, Minutes of the Court of Common Pleas & Quarter Sessions, 1780-1800. Herman W. Ferguson & North Carolina Museum of Art Staff. LC 94-62190. 1995. write for info. (*0-9620770-5-4*) H W Ferguson.

Mecklenburg County, North Carolina, Minutes of the Court of Common Pleas & Quarter Sessions, 1801-1820, Vol. II. Herman W. Ferguson. (Illus.). x, 342p. 1997. pap. 30.00 (*0-9620770-4-6*) H W Ferguson.

Mecklenburg County, North Carolina, Will Abstracts, 1791-1968, Bks. A-J. Herman W. Ferguson & Ralph B. Ferguson. (Illus.). xi, 366p. (Orig.). 1993. pap. 30.00 (*0-9620770-2-X*) H W Ferguson.

Mecklenburg County, Virginia Deeds, 1765-1771. T.L.C. Genealogy Staff. LC 90-71201. 157p. (Orig.). 1990. pap., spiral bd. 12.00 (*1-886633-91-6*) TLC Genealogy.

Mecklenburg County, Virginia Deeds, 1771-1776. T.L.C. Genealogy Staff. LC 91-712501. 171p. (Orig.). 1991. pap., spiral bd. 14.00 (*1-886633-92-4*) TLC Genealogy.

Mecklenburg County, Virginia Deeds, 1777-1779. T.L.C. Genealogy Staff. 117p. (Orig.). 1994. pap., spiral bd. 15.00 (*1-886633-93-2*) TLC Genealogy.

Mecklenburg County, Virginia Deeds, 1779-1786. T.L.C. Genealogy Staff. LC 90-71201. 165p. (Orig.). 1991. pap., spiral bd. 14.00 (*1-886633-94-0*) TLC Genealogy.

Mecklenburg County, Virginia Marriages, 1765-1853. John Vogt & T. William Kethley, Jr. 332p. 1989. pap. 17.95 (*0-935931-46-5*) Iberian Pub.

Mecklenburg Declaration of Independence. Francis L. Hawks. (Notable American Authors Ser.). 1992. reprint ed. lib. bdg. 75.00 (*0-7812-3030-6*) Rprt Serv.

Mecklenburg Declaration of Independence. William Henry Hoyt. LC 76-166330. (Era of the American Revolution Ser.). 284p. 1972. reprint ed. lib. bdg. 39.50 (*0-306-70248-7*) Da Capo.

Mecklermedia's Official Internet World Internet Security Handbook. William Stallings. (Illus.). 288p. 1999. reprint ed. pap. text 20.00 (*0-7881-6508-9*) DIANE Pub.

Meckseper's Etchings, 1956-1990: Catalogue Raisonne. Patrick Cramer. (GER., Illus.). 292p. 1993. 195.00 (*1-55660-156-5*) A Wofsy Fine Arts.

Mecox Road. Marc Cohen. LC 96-78066. 88p. (Orig.). 1997. pap. 12.00 (*1-877593-02-8*) GP Hudson NY.

***Med Armageddon.** Epstein. 2000. pap. 26.00 (*0-7382-0347-5*, Pub. by Perseus Pubng) HarpC.

Med Bagaget I Strupen see Jussi Bjorling 1945 Autobiography

Med Center, No. 4. Diane Hoh. 1996. pap. 3.99 (*0-590-67317-3*) Scholastic Inc.

Med Chek. Robert A. Lytle. LC 92-63337. 140p. 1993. pap. 12.95 (*1-882792-01-7*) Proctor Pubns.

Med Cruise. E. L. Digirolamo. 1978. pap. 1.50 (*0-931138-02-7*) Maiden Bks.

Med. for the Millennium: Set. Mark Link. 1998. pap. 27.95 (*0-88347-420-4*, 661-025 7420) T More.

Med-Heavy Truck Set: Med-Heavy Truck, Nos. T1-T8. Delmar Staff. (ASE Test Prep Ser.). 1998. 90.00 (*0-7668-0574-3*) Delmar.

Med Hela Ditt Hjarta see Ethos of the Bible

MED Inc. How Consolidation Is Shaping Tomorrow's Health Care System. Sandy Lutz. LC 97-40890. 192p. 1998. 26.95 (*0-7879-4040-2*) Jossey-Bass.

Med-Math: Dosage Calculation, Preparation & Administration. 3rd ed. Grace Henke. LC 98-8269. 20p. 1998. pap. text. write for info. (*0-7817-1028-6*) Lppncott W & W.

Med-Math: Dosage, Calculation, Preparation & Medication. 2nd ed. Grace Henke. 320p. 1995. pap. text 23.95 (*0-397-55143-6*) Lppncott W & W.

Med Oppna Dorrar: Kvinna Pd Cuba. Inger Holt-Seeland. (Kvinna i U-Land Ser.). 135p. 1981. write for info. (*91-7106-195-9*, Pub. by Nordic Africa) Transaction Pubs.

Med School Mayhem. David J. Fletcher. LC 80-65389. (Illus.). 345p. 1980. pap. 10.95 (*0-935510-01-X*) F Fergeson.

***Med School Survival Guide: How to Make the Challenges of Medical School Seem Like Small Stuff.** Jennifer Danek. 176p. 2000. pap. 12.00 (*0-609-80595-9*, STU014000, Three Riv Pr) Crown Pub Group.

Med Study: The Internal Medicine Board Review, 13 vols. 7th rev. ed. Robert A. Hannaman. 400p. 1997. ring bd. 395.00 (*0-9640788-3-X*) MedStudy.

***Med Terminology: Student-Centered Appr/Flashcards.** Elmer W. Moisio & Marie A. Moisio. (C). 2001. 8.00 (*0-7668-1527-7*) Thomson Learn.

Medaillon Perdu. Megan Stine. (Goosebumps Presents Ser.: No. 1). (Illus.). 64p. (J). (gr. 2-5). 1996. pap. 3.99 (*0-590-74586-7*) Scholastic Inc.

Medal. Ishbel Moore. 126p. (J). (gr. 5-9). 1994. pap. 5.95 (*1-896184-02-2*) Roussan Pubs.

Medal Brigadier: Penguin Reader Level 1. Arthur Conan Doyle. 1998. pap. 7.00 (*0-14-081557-0*) Viking Penguin.

Medal Collectors' Companion: Collecting & Identifying Orders, Medals & Decorations. Sydney B. Vernon. (Illus.). 224p. (Orig.). 1995. pap. 22.95 (*0-9623575-2-9*) S B Vernon.

Medal for Life: A Biography of Capt. Leefe Robinson VC (WWI) Leslie W. Bills. 144p. (C). 1991. 110.00 (*0-946771-56-1*, Pub. by Spellmnt Pubs) St Mut.

Medal in America. Intro. by Alan M. Stahl. (Coinage of the Americas Conference at the American Numismatic Society, New York Ser.: No. 4). 200p. 1988. 15.00 (*0-89722-226-1*) Am Numismatic.

Medal of Honor: A Vietnam Warrior's Story. John R. Craig & Roy P. Benavidez. LC 94-27283. (Illus.). 240p. 1995. 26.95 (*0-02-881098-8*) Brasseys.

Medal of Honor: History & Recipients. John M. Carroll. 1976. 22.00 (*0-8488-1268-9*, J M C & Co) Amereon Ltd.

Medal of Honor: History & Recipients for the Indian Wars. John M. Carroll. 1985. pap. 19.00 (*0-317-28081-3*, J M C & Co) Amereon Ltd.

***Medal of Honor: Official Strategy Guide.** Brady Games Staff. (Strategy Guides Ser.). 1999. pap. 12.99 (*1-56686-926-9*) Brady Pub.

Medal of Honor: One Man's Journey from Poverty & Prejudice. Roy Benavidez. 1999. pap. text 16.95 (*1-57488-203-1*) Brasseys.

Medal of Honor Vol. 1: Aviators of World War One. Alan E. Durkota. (Illus.). 112p. 1998. pap. 24.95 (*1-891268-03-1*) Flying Machines.

Medal of Honor & Two Dollars Will Buy You a Beer: Conflicts in the World of Black Men. Herbert W. Denmark. 72p. 1997. mass mkt. 5.00 (*1-891511-01-7*) H W Denmark.

Medal of Honor at Gettysburg. B. T. Arrington. (Illus.). 60p. (Orig.). 1996. pap. 9.95 (*0-939631-92-X*) Thomas Publications.

Medal of Honor in Vietnam. E. E. Kerrigan. (Illus.). 114p. 1971. 16.00 (*0-9624663-1-X*) Medallic Pub.

***Medal of Honor Recipients, 1863-1978.** Virgil D. White. 401p. 2000. lib. bdg. 37.00 (*0-945099-35-5*) Natl Hist Pub.

Medal of Honor Recipients, 1863-1994, 2 vols. Compiled by George Lang et al. (Illus.). 928p. 1995. 99.00 (*0-8160-3259-9*) Facts on File.

Medal of Magnanimity. Said Salah. (Arabian Story Masterpiece Ser.). 61p. 1990. 8.00 (*1-887584-27-7*) Intl Prom Art.

Medal: The Story of Saint Catherine Laboure see Miraculous Medal: The Story of Our Lady's Appearances to Saint Catherine of Laboure

Medaljerol. Roberts Staff. (C). 1989. 125.00 (*1-873058-01-2*, Pub. by Roberts) St Mut.

Medallic Art of the United States, 1800-1972. Norton, R. W., Art Gallery Staff. LC 72-187912. (Illus.). 1972. pap. 3.00 (*0-9600182-9-8*) Norton Art.

Medallic Illustrations of the History of Great Britain & Ireland. British Museum Staff. (Illus.). 1980. 150.00 (*0-88000-001-5*) Quarterman.

Medallic Portraits of the Duke of Wellington. C. Eimer. (Illus.). 1994. pap. 60.00 (*0-907605-52-4*) S J Durst.

Medallic Portraits of Washington. 2nd ed. Russell Rulau & George Fuld. LC 98-87365. (Illus.). 432p. 1999. 34.95 (*0-87341-681-3*) Krause Pubns.

Medallic Record of the Jacobite Movement. N. Woolf. (Illus.). 1990. pap. 60.00 (*0-907605-26-5*) S J Durst.

Medallion. Dawn L. Watkins. (Illus.). 213p. (J). (gr. 4-6). 1985. pap. 6.49 (*0-89084-282-5*, 023523) Bob Jones Univ.

Medallion Mystery. Ty Heintze et al. (Illus.). 160p. (J). (gr. 5-6). 1995. pap. 6.95 (*1-57168-013-6*) Sunbelt Media.

Medallion Mystery: Rock of the Line of Defense on the Rio Grande. Ty Heintze & Richard Thompson. (Illus.). 160p. (J). (gr. 5-6). 1995. 14.95 (*0-89015-926-2*) Sunbelt Media.

Medallion of the Black Hound. Shirley R. Murphy & Welch Suggs. LC 88-35825. 192p. (J). (gr. 3-7). 1989. 11.95 (*0-06-024368-6*) HarpC Child Bks.

***Medallions.** Zofia Nalkowska. Tr. by Diana Kuprel from POL. LC 99-48758. 80p. 1999. 39.95 (*0-8101-1742-8*); pap. 12.95 (*0-8101-1743-6*) Northwestern U Pr.

Medals & Decorations of the Third Reich. Heinrich Doehle. Tr. by William Hammelman. (Illus.). 160p. 1995. 35.00 (*0-9624883-4-8*) Reddick Enterp.

Medals for Gallantry & Distinguished Conduct Award to Natal, Cape Colony & Union Defence Forces 1877-1961. Roberts Staff. (C). 1989. 110.00 (*1-873058-95-0*, Pub. by Roberts) St Mut.

Medals of Creation: Or, First Lessons in Geology & the Study of Organic Remains, 2 vols., Set. 2nd rev. ed. Gideon A. Mantell. Ed. by Stephen Jay Gould. LC 79-8334. (History of Paleontology Ser.). (Illus.). 1980. reprint ed. lib. bdg. 88.95 (*0-405-12716-2*) Ayer.

Medals of Creation: Or, First Lessons in Geology & the Study of Organic Remains, 2 vols., Vol. 1. 2nd rev. ed. Gideon A. Mantell. Ed. by Stephen Jay Gould. LC 79-8334. (History of Paleontology Ser.). (Illus.). 1980. reprint ed. lib. bdg. 44.95 (*0-405-12717-0*) Ayer.

Medals of Creation: Or, First Lessons in Geology & the Study of Organic Remains, 2 vols., Vol. 2. 2nd rev. ed. Gideon A. Mantell. Ed. by Stephen Jay Gould. LC 79-8334. (History of Paleontology Ser.). (Illus.). 1980. reprint ed. lib. bdg. 44.95 (*0-405-12718-9*) Ayer.

Medals of Giovanni Cavino, the Paduan. Richard H. Laurence. 1981. reprint ed. pap. 6.00 (*0-915262-56-8*) S J Durst.

Medals of Karl Goetz. Gunter W. Kienast. LC 67-21457. (Illus.). 284p. 1980. reprint ed. 38.00 (*0-9606684-0-3*) Artus Co.

Medals of the Republic of Ireland. Eamonn O'Toole. (Illus.). 86p. 1990. pap. 14.00 (*0-9624663-5-2*) Medallic Pub.

Medals Yerar Book. 29.95 (*0-85052-573-X*) Leo Cooper.

Medardo Rosso. Margaret S. Barr. LC 73-169298. (Museum of Modern Art Publications in Reprint). (Illus.). 94p. 1972. reprint ed. 19.95 (*0-405-01558-5*) Ayer.

Medardo Rosso: Impressions in Wax & Bronze: 1882-1906. Luciano Caramel. Tr. by Jeanne M. Wasilik et al. (Illus.). 112p. 1988. 30.00 (*1-878607-03-0*); pap. 25.00 (*1-878607-02-2*) Kent Gallery.

***MedART: Anatomy & Physiology Images.** (Illus.). 1998. cd-rom 230.00 (*0-8385-6366-X*) P-H.

Medcin: A New Nomenclature for Clinical Medicine. Ed. by Peter S. Goltra. LC 96-52993. 717p. 1997. 79.00 (*0-387-94953-4*) Spr-Verlag.

Meddive. Kathy Work & Jon Kushner. Ed. by Michael K. Bielmaier & Michael S. Klush. (Illus.). 123p. (C). 1991. pap. text 22.00 (*0-929905-05-9*) Dive Rescue.

Meddler & Her Murder. Joyce Porter. 176p. 1992. pap. 5.95 (*0-89733-322-5*) Academy Chi Pubs.

Meddler & the Correspondent. John Trumbull. LC 85-1861. 176p. 1985. 50.00 (*0-8201-1402-2*) Schol Facsimiles.

Meddlesome Ghost. Sheila R. Allen. 285p. 1989. 18.95 (*0-8027-1083-2*) Walker & Co.

Meddlesome Ghost. large type ed. Sheila R. Allen. 348p. 1991. reprint ed. lib. bdg. 18.95 (*1-56054-116-4*) Thorndike Pr.

Meddling Gods: Four Essays on Classical Themes. Hazel E. Barnes. LC 73-92003. 149p. 1974. reprint ed. pap. 46.20 (*0-608-02687-5*, 206334000004) Bks Demand.

Meddling with Mythology: AIDS & the Social Construction of Knowledge. Rosaline S. Barbour & Guro Huby. LC 97-49216. 304p. (C). 1998. 85.00 (*0-415-16389-7*); pap. 25.99 (*0-415-16390-0*) Routledge.

Meddling with the Past: An Historical & Archaeological Analysis of Metal Artifacts from San Leandro Reservoir. Jason Coleman. (MA in Anthropology, UC Hayward Ser.). (Illus.). 142p. (C). 1996. pap. text 15.63 (*1-55567-796-7*) Coyote Press.

Medea see Anthology of Roman Drama

Medea see Best American Plays: Third Series, 1945-51

Medea see Ten Plays of Euripides

Medea. Ed. by Alan F. Elliot. 176p. 1970. pap. text 16.95 (*0-19-912006-4*) OUP.

Medea. Tr. by Alistair Elliot. (Oberon Bks.). (Illus.). 64p. 1997. 16.95 (*1-870259-88-2*) Theatre Comm.

Medea. Euripides. Ed. by B. Gredley. (Classical Texts Ser.). 1991. write for info. (*0-85668-242-X*, Pub. by Aris & Phillips); pap. write for info. (*0-85668-243-8*, Pub. by Aris & Phillips) David Brown.

***Medea.** Euripides. Ed. by John Harrison. (Cambridge Translations from Greek Drama). 128p. 2000. pap. 9.95 (*0-521-64479-8*) Cambridge U Pr.

***Medea.** Euripides. Tr. by Nicholas Rudall. (Plays for Performance Ser.). 64p. 2000. 15.95 (*1-56663-320-6*, Pub. by I R Dee); pap. 7.95 (*1-56663-321-4*, Pub. by I R Dee) Natl Bk Netwk.

Medea. Euripides. Tr. by Kenneth McLeish & Frederic Raphael. 128p. 1996. pap. 6.95 (*1-85459-164-9*, Pub. by N Hern Bks) Theatre Comm.

Medea. Euripides. Tr. by Michael Wodhull from GRE. LC 92-53877. 70p. 1992. pap. 7.00 (*0-88734-253-1*) Players Pr.

Medea. Euripides. Ed. by Whitney J. Oates & Eugene O'Neill, Jr. 1955. pap. write for info. (*0-318-55463-1*) Random.

Medea. Euripides. Tr. by Alistair Elliot. 44p. 1998. 12.95 (*1-870259-36-X*) Theatre Comm.

Medea. Franz Grillparzer. Tr. by Arthur Burkhard from GER. 1956. pap. text 9.95 (*0-917324-15-3*) German Bk Ctr.

***Medea.** Photos by Jane Kim. 50p. 2000. 7.99 (*0-9676282-3-7*) Elixir Prods.

Medea. Ed. by Denys Page. 258p. 1976. pap. text 24.00 (*0-19-872092-0*) OUP.

Medea. Lucius Annaeus Seneca. Tr. & Intro. by Frederick Ahl. (Masters of Latin Literature Ser.). 128p. 1986. pap. text 8.95 (*0-8014-9432-X*) Cornell U Pr.

Medea. Lucius Annaeus Seneca. Tr. by Moses Hadas. LC 56-1501. 1956. pap. 1.45 (*0-672-60228-8*, LLA55, Bobbs) Macmillan.

Medea. Lucius Annaeus Seneca. 184p. 1990. pap. 21.00 (*0-19-872135-8*) OUP.

Medea. Tr. by Rex Warner. LC 55-5787. write for info. U Ch Pr.

Medea. Euripides. (GER.). xii, 428p. 1967. reprint ed. write for info. (*0-318-70531-1*); reprint ed. write for info. (*0-318-70918-X*) Lubrecht & Cramer.

Medea. Euripides. Tr. by Rex Warner. LC 92-31819. (Thrift Editions Ser.). 64p. 1993. reprint ed. pap. 1.00 (*0-486-27548-5*) Dover.

Medea: Chamber Orchestra Score. S. Barber. 144p. 1991. pap. 40.00 (*0-7935-0913-0*) H Leonard.

Medea: Essays on Medea in Myth, Literature, Philosophy & Art. James J. Clauss & Sarah I. Johnston. LC 96-8537. 376p. 1997. text 55.00 (*0-691-04377-9*, Pub. by Princeton U Pr) Cal Prin Full Svc.

Medea: Essays on Medea in Myth, Literature, Philosophy& Art. James J. Clauss & Sarah I. Johnston. LC 96-8537. 376p. 1997. pap. text 17.95 (*0-691-04376-0*, Pub. by Princeton U Pr) Cal Prin Full Svc.

Medea: Reproducible Teaching Unit. rev. ed. James Scott. 27p. (YA). (gr. 7-12). 1995. teacher ed., ring bd. 29.50 (*1-58049-064-6*, TU64/U) Prestwick Hse.

Medea: The Classic Steam Yacht. Craig Arnold. LC 94-18961. (Illus.). 228p. (Orig.). 1994. pap. 22.00 (*0-944580-08-4*) Maritime Mus Assn.

Medea & Hippolytus. Euripides. Tr. by Sydney Waterlow. (Temple Greek & Latin Classics: No. 5). reprint ed. 32.50 (*0-404-07905-9*) AMS Pr.

Medea & Other Plays. Euripides. 1963. 14.05 (*0-606-02748-3*, Pub. by Turtleback) Demco.

Medea & Other Plays. Euripides. Tr. by Philip Vellacott. (Classics Ser.). 208p. 1963. pap. 8.95 (*0-14-044129-8*, Penguin Classics) Viking Penguin.

Medea & Other Plays. Euripides. Tr. by James Morwood. LC 98-12866. (Oxford World's Classics Ser.). (Illus.). 266p. 1998. pap. 7.95 (*0-19-282442-2*) OUP.

Medea by Euripides: A New Version. Brendan Kennelly. 80p. 1991. 30.00 (*1-85224-188-8*, Pub. by Bloodaxe Bks) Dufour.

Medea by Euripides: A New Version. Brendan Kennelly & Euripides. 80p. 1991. pap. 14.95 (*1-85224-189-6*, Pub. by Bloodaxe Bks) Dufour.

Medea, Hippolytus, Electra, Helen. Euripides. Ed. & Tr. by James Morwood. LC 97-18775. 272p. (C). 1998. 68.00 (*0-19-814966-2*) OUP.

Medea in der Bildenden Kunst Vom Mittelalter zur Neuzeit: So Im Herzen Bedrangt Ergluhte Verderbliche Liebe. Ekaterini Kepetzis. (Europaische Hochschulschriften Ser.: Reihe 28, Bd. 305). (GER., Illus.). 280p. 1997. 54.95 (*3-631-31758-1*) P Lang Pubng.

***Medea in Performance, 1500-2000.** Ed. by Edith Hall & Oliver Taplin. (Legenda Ser.). 200p. (C). 2000. pap. 49.50 (*1-900755-35-1*, Pub. by E H R C) David Brown.

***Medea in Taos.** James Hoggard. 1999. pap. write for info. (*1-877603-66-X*) Pecan Grove.

Medea the Sorceress. Diane Wakoski. LC 90-22954. (Archaeology of Movies & Bks.: Vol. 1). 202p. 1995. reprint ed. 25.00 (*0-87685-810-8*); reprint ed. pap. 13.00 (*0-87685-809-X*) Black Sparrow.

Medea's Folly: Women, Relationships & the Search for Intimacy. Tanya Wilkinson. LC 98-9821. 240p. 1998. pap. 16.95 (*1-879290-14-6*) PageMill Pr.

Medea's Meditation & Dance: CB Score. 35.00 (*0-7935-4554-4*, 50482401) H Leonard.

Medea/The Lion in Winger: Curriculum Unit. Center for Learning Network Staff. (Drama Ser.). 115p. (YA). (gr. 9-12). 1996. spiral bd. 18.95 (*1-56077-329-4*) Ctr Learning.

Medecin de Campagne. Honore de Balzac. Ed. by Maurice Allem. (Coll. Prestige). 49.95 (*0-685-34089-9*) Fr & Eur.

Medecin de Campagne. Honore de Balzac. Ed. by Pierre Citron. (Coll. GF). pap. 9.95 (*0-685-34090-2*) Fr & Eur.

Medecin de Campagne. Honore de Balzac. (Class. Garnier Ser.). (FRE.). 1974. pap. 12.95 (*0-7859-3470-7*) Fr & Eur.

Medecin de Campagne. Honore de Balzac. (Folio Ser.: No. 636). (FRE.). pap. 10.95 (*2-07-036636-7*) Schoenhof.

Medecin Malgre Lui. Moliere. (Univers des Lettres Bordas Ser.). (FRE.). 1964. pap. 7.95 (*0-8288-9942-8*, F10008) Fr & Eur.

Medecine, Vol. 2. Pierre de Graciansky. (FRE.). 1979. lib. bdg. 155.00 (*0-7859-3843-5*) Fr & Eur.

Medecine: Histoire & Doctrines. 2nd ed. Charles Daremberg. LC 75-13257. (History of Ideas in Ancient Greece Ser.). (FRE.). 1976. reprint ed. 35.95 (*0-405-07300-3*) Ayer.

Medecine de la Reproduction Tome 1: Gynecologie Endocrinienne. P. Mauvais-Jarvis & Fernand Labrie. (Illus.). 520p. 1982. 58.00 (*0-318-04526-5*) S M P F Inc.

Medecine de la Reproduction Tome 2: Medecine de la Reproduction Masculine. P. Mauvais-Jarvis & Fernand Labrie. (Illus.). 1984. 65.00 (*0-318-04527-3*) S M P F Inc.

Medecine et Soins Medicaux en Francais. Conrad J. Schmitt & Katia B. Lutz. (Schaum's Foreign Language Ser.). (FRE.). 160p. (C). 1992. pap. 11.95 (*0-07-056809-X*) McGraw.

Medecine, Maladie et Societe: Recueli de Textes Presentes et Commentes. Claudine Herzlich. (Textes de Sciences Sociales Ser.: No. 4). 1970. pap. 24.60 (*90-279-6757-1*) Mouton.

Medecins de L'Esperance. Bobby Hutchinson. (FRE.). 1998. mass mkt. 4.99 (*0-373-38302-9*) Harlequin Bks.

Medecins de Sont pas des Plombiers. Jacques Audiberti. (FRE.). 200p. 1949. pap. 16.95 (*0-7859-0364-X*, F83810) Fr & Eur.

Medee see Nouvelles Pieces Noires: Jezabel, Antigone, Romeo et Jeanette, Medee

Medee. Jean Anouilh. 1967. pap. 6.95 (*0-7859-0353-4*, F81879) Fr & Eur.

Medee. La Peruse. Ed. by Coleman. (Exeter French Texts Ser.: Vol. 56). (FRE.). 136p. Date not set. pap. text 19.95 (*0-85989-216-6*, Pub. by Univ Exeter Pr) Northwestern U Pr.

Medee et Jason, Tragedie en Musique. Ed. by Leslie Brown. LC 89-755086. (French Opera in the 17th & 18th Centuries Ser.: No. 6, Vol. XXVIII). (Illus.). 1991. lib. bdg. 86.00 (*0-945193-15-7*) Pendragon NY.

MedEMT - Basic Coursebook: Emergency Medical Training-Basic Coursebook. Victory Technologies, Inc. Staff et al. (Illus.). 896p. 1999. pap. 67.33 incl. cd-rom, disk (*0-8385-6369-4*, Medical Exam) Appleton & Lange.

***Medemt Learning System for Prehospital Care.** 400p. 2000. teacher ed. 63.00 (*0-8385-6384-8*) Allyn.

Medemt Multiple User Insert. (C). 1998. write for info. (*0-8385-6381-3*, Medical Exam) Appleton & Lange.

***Medevac.** Hugh M. McClure. 288p. 2000. pap. 16.95 (*1-893162-14-1*) Erica Hse.

Medford. Anthony Mitchell Sammarco. (Images of America Ser.). (Illus.). 1999. pap. 18.99 (*0-7524-1389-9*) Arcadia Publng.

Medgar Evers: Civil Rights Activist. Jennie Brown. (Black American Ser.). (Illus.). 208p. (Orig.). (YA). 1994. mass mkt. 3.95 (*0-87067-594-X*, Melrose Sq) Holloway.

Medgar Evers College - In Relentless Pursuit of Excellence: Policy Statements by Edison O. Jackson. Ed. by J. A. Irish. 147p. (Orig.). Date not set. pap. text 10.00 (*1-878433-13-X*) Caribbean Diaspora Pr.

***Medi-Cal Advantage (How to Save the Family Home from the Cost of Nursing Home Care)** large type ed. F. Douglas Lofton & Mellanese S. Lofton. Ed. by Robin M. Lofton-Koponen. (Illus.). 116p. 1998. pap. 49.95 (*0-9667737-0-5*) Lailabela Pr.

***Medi-Cal County Data Book.** unabridged ed. (Illus.). 138p. 1999. spiral bd. write for info. (*1-929008-19-8*) CA HlthCare Fnd.

***Medi-Cal Outstationing in California: Findings from a Statewide Survey.** unabridged ed. Jennifer Blackburn & Ingrid Aguirre-Happordt. (Illus.). 38p. 1999. pap. write for info. (*1-929008-15-5*) CA HlthCare Fnd.

Medi-Phoria. Paul Dilsaver. (Illus.). 68p. 1998. pap. 9.00 (*0-9637000-3-0*) Acad & Arts.

Medi-Record: Female. Ruben Trottman. (Illus.). 208p. 1996. per. 39.95 (*0-9632430-1-2*) Medi-Record.

Medi-Record: Male. Ruben Trottman. (Illus.). 208p. 1996. per. 39.95 (*0-9632430-0-4*) Medi-Record.

Media. Ed. by Kenneth W. Thompson. LC 84-29086. (Credibility of Institutions, Policies & Leadership Ser.: Vol. 5). 250p. (Orig.). 1985. pap. text 22.50 (*0-8191-4443-6*) U Pr of Amer.

Media. Ed. by Kenneth W. Thompson. LC 84-29086. (Credibility of Institutions, Policies & Leadership Ser.: Vol. 5). 250p. (Orig.). 1985. lib. bdg. 48.00 (*0-8191-4442-8*, Pub. by White Miller Center) U Pr of Amer.

***Media.** 5th ed. Campbell. 1999. student ed. 20.00 (*0-8053-6571-0*) Benjamin-Cummings.

Media: And How to Use It. Martin Tierney. 141p. 1989. pap. 22.00 (*1-85390-067-2*, Pub. by Veritas Pubns) St Mut.

Media: Communication & Production GNVQ, Advanced Level. Ed. by Tricia Jenkins. 1997. 31.95 (*0-240-51425-4*, Focal) Buttrwrth-Heinemann.

Media: Communication & Production GNVQ, Intermediate Level. Ed. by Tricia Jenkins. 1997. 24.95 (*0-240-51424-6*, Focal) Buttrwrth-Heinemann.

Media: Principles of Economy. Gordon Staff. (C). pap. text 29.75 (*0-03-002444-7*) Harcourt Coll Pubs.

Media - Art - History: Media Museum ZKM: Center for Art & Media Karlsruhe. Ed. by Hans-Peter Schwarz. LC 98-108643. (Illus.), 192p. 1997. 65.00 incl. cd-rom (*3-7913-1878-0*, Pub. by Prestel) te Neues.

***Media - Multimedia - Omnimedia.** Ed. by Gabrielle Hogan-Brun & Udo O. Jung. x, 220p. 1999. pap. 40.95 (*3-631-33765-5*) P Lang Pubng.

Media about Media: An Annotated Listing of Media Software. James E. Duane. LC 80-21339. (Instructional Media Library: Vol. 6). 232p. 1981. 34.95 (*0-87778-166-4*) Educ Tech Pubns.

Media Access & the Military: The Case of the Gulf War. Judith R. Baroody. LC 97-50220. 248p. (C). 1998. 59.00 (*0-7618-1025-0*); pap. 36.50 (*0-7618-1026-9*) U Pr of Amer.

Media Advocacy & Public Health: Power for Prevention. Lawrence Wallack et al. (Illus.). 224p. (C). 1993. text 48.00 (*0-8039-4288-5*) Sage.

Media Agenda Setting in a Presidential Election: Issues, Images & Interest. Ed. by David H. Weaver et al. LC 80-39685. 227p. 1981. 38.95 (*0-275-90738-4*, C0738, Praeger Pubs) Greenwood.

Media Alert! 200 Activities to Create Media-Savvy Kids. Sue L. Summers. 75p. 1997. pap. 15.00 (*0-931510-68-6*) Hi Willow.

Media Am Pol. Ed. by Paletz. (C). 1999. text 25.50 (*0-06-501031-0*) Addison-Wesley.

Media an English Approach. Monahan. 1989. pap. text. write for info. (*0-582-87426-2*, Pub. by Addison-Wesley) Longman.

Media an Introduction. Briggs & Cobley. (C). 1997. pap. text 23.44 (*0-582-27798-1*, Pub. by Addison-Wesley) Longman.

Media Analysis Techniques. Arthur A. Berger. (CommText Ser.: Vol. 10). 180p. (C). 1991. text 42.00 (*0-8039-4361-X*); pap. text 18.95 (*0-8039-4362-8*) Sage.

Media Analysis Techniques. 2nd ed. Arthur A. Berger. LC 98-8876. 220p. 1998. 46.00 (*0-7619-1453-6*); pap. 21.95 (*0-7619-1454-4*) Sage.

Media Analysis Tools. R. L. Ehler. LC 90-63639. (Print Media Advertising Ser.: Bk. 3). (Illus.). 63p. 1997. pap. text 34.95 (*1-879299-13-5*) Richler.

Media & Apocalypse: News Coverage of the Yellowstone Forest Fires, Exxon Valdez Oil Spill, & Loma Prieta Earthquake, 36. Conrad Smith. LC 92-9316. (Contributions to the Study of Mass Media & Communications Ser.: No. 36). 228p. 1992. 47.95 (*0-313-27725-7*, SJQ, Greenwood Pr) Greenwood.

Media & Communication for Beginners. Peter Lewis. (Writers & Readers Documentary Comic Bks.). (Illus.). 176p. (Orig.). 1991. pap. 7.95 (*0-86316-115-4*) Writers & Readers.

***Media & Communications.** Clive Gifford. (Eyewitness Books). (Illus.). (J). (gr. 4-7). 2000. 19.99 (*0-7894-6629-5*) DK Pub Inc.

***Media & Communications.** Clive Gifford. (Eyewitness Books). (J). (gr. 4-7). 2000. 15.95 (*0-7894-6294-X*) DK Pub Inc.

Media & Communications. Clive Gifford. LC 99-22723. 1999. 19.00 (*0-375-80223-1*) Random.

Media & Communications, No. 80. Clive Gifford. LC 99-22723. 1999. lib. bdg. 20.99 (*0-375-90223-6*) Random.

Media & Criminal Justice Policy: Recent Research & Social Effects. Ed. by Raymond Surette. (Illus.). 332p. 1990. pap. 41.95 (*0-398-06448-2*) C C Thomas.

Media & Criminal Justice Policy: Recent Research & Social Effects. Ed. by Raymond Surette. (Illus.). 332p. (C). 1990. text 62.95 (*0-398-05687-0*) C C Thomas.

Media & Cultural Careers. Seguin. LC 97-80133. 1997. pap. text 9.95 (*0-312-17962-6*) St Martin.

Media & Cultural Regulation. Ed. by Kenneth Thompson. LC 97-65517. (Culture, Media & Identities Ser.). 256p. 1997. 75.00 (*0-7619-5439-2*); pap. 26.95 (*0-7619-5440-6*) Sage.

***Media & Cultural Studies.** Ed. by Meenakshi Gigi Durham & Douglas Kellner. 2000. 79.95 (*0-631-22095-X*); pap. 34.95 (*0-631-22096-8*) Blackwell Pubs.

Media & Culture. Campbell. 1998. pap. text 10.00 (*0-312-19061-1*) St Martin.

***Media & Culture in Singapore: A Theory of Controlled Commodification.** Kokkeong Wong. LC 00-39562. (Communication Ser.). 2000. write for info. (*1-57273-312-8*) Hampton Pr NJ.

Media & Culture Introduction. Campbell. 1997. pap. text, teacher ed. 10.00 (*0-312-11959-3*) St Martin.

Media & Democracy. Everette E. Dennis & Robert W. Snyder. LC 97-23126. (Media Studies). 202p. 1997. pap. write for info. (*0-7658-0408-5*) Transaction Pubs.

Media & Democracy. John Keane. 150p. (C). 1991. pap. text 28.95 (*0-7456-0804-3*) Blackwell Pubs.

Media & Dependency in South Africa: A Case Study of the Press & the Ciskei "Homeland" Les Switzer. LC 82-91999. (Monographs in International Studies, Africa: No. 47). 97p. 1985. pap. text 10.00 (*0-89680-130-6*) Ohio U Pr.

Media & Disaster: Pam Am 103. Joan Deppa et al. 224p. 1993. pap. 34.00 (*1-85346-225-X*) St Martin.

Media & Disasters: Pan Am 103. Joan Deppa et al. LC 93-34893. (Disasters in the Press Ser.). (C). 1994. text 45.00 (*0-8147-1857-4*); pap. text 19.50 (*0-8147-1856-6*) NYU Pr.

***Media & Entertainment Industries: The Reading in Mass Communications.** Albert N. Greco. LC 99-22845. 279p. (C). 1999. pap. 30.67 (*0-205-30010-3*) Allyn.

***Media & Everyday Life in Modern Society.** Shaun Moores. 208p. 2000. pap. text 24.00 (*0-7486-1179-7*) Col U Pr.

Media & Family Planning with Supplement. Richard J. Udry. LC 74-5075. 1974. 9.75 (*0-89055-123-5*) Carolina Pop Ctr.

Media & Foreign Policy. Ed. by Simon Serfaty. 272p. 1991. pap. 15.95 (*0-312-06498-5*) St Martin.

Media & Government Leaks. American Bar Association, Standing Commission on L. 32p. 1984. pap. 3.00 (*0-89707-157-3*, 355-0007) Amer Bar Assn.

***Media & International Security.** Ed. by Stephen Badsey. LC 99-49658. 296p. 2000. 64.50 (*0-7146-4848-5*, Pub. by F Cass Pubs); pap. 26.50 (*0-7146-4406-4*, Pub. by F Cass Pubs) Intl Spec Bk.

***Media & Literacy: Learning in an Electronic Age-Issues, Ideas & Teaching Strategies.** 2nd ed. Dennis M. Adams & Mary Hamm. LC 99-48808. (Illus.). 244p. 2000. 31.95 (*0-398-07032-6*) C C Thomas.

***Media & Literacy: Learning in an Electronic Age-Issues, Ideas & Teaching Strategies.** 2nd ed. Dennis M. Adams & Mary Hamm. LC 99-48808. 244p. 2000. 43.95 (*0-398-07031-8*) C C Thomas.

Media & Market Forces: Challanges & Opportunities: Proceedings of the Regional Seminars & National Colloquium. V. S. Gupta et al. LC 97-913984. 266 p. 1997. write for info. (*81-7022-698-8*) Concept.

Media & Media Policy in Germany: The Press & Broadcasting since 1945. 2nd ed. Peter J. Humphreys. LC 94-189872. (German Historical Perspectives Ser.). 368p. 1994. pap. 22.50 (*0-85496-853-9*, Pub. by Berg Pubs) NYU Pr.

Media & Military. Young. LC 97-24399. 1997. pap. 19.95 (*0-312-21012-4*) St Martin.

Media & Modernity: A Social Theory of the Media. John B Thompson. LC 95-74796. 336p. 1996. 49.50 (*0-8047-2678-7*) Stanford U Pr.

Media & Modernity: A Social Theory of the Media. John B. Thompson. 336p. 1996. pap. 16.95 (*0-8047-2679-5*) Stanford U Pr.

***Media & Monarchy.** Mallory Wober. LC 99-87798. 189p. 2000. lib. bdg. 34.00 (*1-56072-777-2*) Nova Sci Pubs.

***Media & Morality.** Ed. by Robert M. Baird et al. LC 98-50669. (Contemporary Issues Ser.). (Illus.). 360p. 1999. pap. 18.95 (*1-57392-681-7*) Prometheus Bks.

***Media & Performance: Along the Border.** Johannes H. Birringer. LC 98-12702. (Paj Bks.). (Illus.). 288p. 1998. pap. 19.95 (*0-8018-5852-6*) Johns Hopkins.

Media & Performance: Along the Border. Johannes H. Birringer. LC 98-12702. (Paj Bks.). 1998. 48.00 (*0-8018-5851-8*) Johns Hopkins.

Media & Political Conflict: News from the Middle East. Gadi Wolfsfeld. LC 96-8611. 269p. 1997. text 59.95 (*0-521-58045-5*); pap. text 19.95 (*0-521-58967-3*) Cambridge U Pr.

Media & Politics. Paletz. 416p. (C). 1998. text. write for info. (*0-321-04496-7*) Addison-Wesley.

Media & Politics. Purvis. (C). 1999. pap. text 34.50 (*0-15-503643-2*, Pub. by Harcourt Coll Pubs) Harcourt.

Media & Politics. Ed. by Paul A. Winters. (At Issue Ser.). 80p. (J). (gr. 5-12). 1996. pap. 11.20 (*1-56510-382-3*) Greenhaven.

Media & Politics. Ed. by Paul A. Winters. (At Issue Ser.). 80p. (J). (gr. 5-12). 1996. lib. bdg. 18.70 (*1-56510-383-1*) Greenhaven.

Media & Politics. 2nd ed. Dean E. Alger. LC 95-20843. 532p. (C). 1995. pap. text 44.50 (*0-534-23694-4*) Harcourt.

Media & Politics in Japan. Ed. by Susan J. Pharr & Ellis S. Krauss. LC 95-8730. 1996. text 50.00 (*0-8248-1698-6*); pap. text 19.95 (*0-8248-1761-3*) UH Pr.

Media & Politics in Latin America: The Struggle for Democracy. Ed. by Elizabeth Fox. (Communication & Human Values Ser.). 224p. (C). 1988. text 52.00 (*0-8039-8164-3*); pap. text 24.95 (*0-8039-8165-1*) Sage.

Media & Print Resources. 8th ed. Ed. by Prentice-Hall Staff. (C). 2000. text, teacher ed. write for info. (*0-13-084102-1*) P-H.

Media & Public Life. Ed. by Robert W. Snyder & Everette E. Dennis. LC 96-17934. 200p. (Orig.). 1997. pap. text 21.95 (*1-56000-874-1*) Transaction Pubs.

Media & Public Policy. Ed. by Robert J. Spitzer. LC 92-17810. (Praeger Series in Political Communication). 256p. 1992. 59.95 (*0-275-94303-8*, C4303, Praeger Pubs) Greenwood.

***Media & Religion in American History.** Ed. by Wm. David Sloan. LC 99-45313. 304p. (C). 1999. pap. text 24.95 (*1-885219-14-8*) Vision AL.

Media & Revolution. Ed. by Jeremy D. Popkin. LC 94-31808. (Illus.). 256p. 1995. text 32.50 (*0-8131-1899-9*) U Pr of Ky.

Media & Society. Cambell. 2002. pap. text. write for info. (*0-312-17986-3*) St Martin.

Media & Society. Ryan et al. LC 98-25986. 255p. 1998. pap. text 40.00 (*0-205-17400-0*, Longwood Div) Allyn.

Media & Society: An Introduction. Michael O'Shaughnessy. (Illus.). 328p. 2000. pap. text 24.95 (*0-19-550788-6*) OUP.

***Media & Sports: Watchdog or Lapdog?** Robert Mertzman. (C). 1999. pap. text 89.95 (*0-7872-6122-X*) Kendall-Hunt.

Media & Symbols: The Forms of Expression, Communication, & Education. Ed. by David R. Olson. LC 06-16938. (National Society for the Study of Education Publication Ser.: No. 73, Pt. 1). 560p. 1974. 10.00 (*0-226-60114-5*) U Ch Pr.

Media & Technology in the Classroom. 5th ed. Franklin R. Koontz. 236p. (C). 1996. spiral bd. 39.95 (*0-7872-2832-X*, 41283201) Kendall-Hunt.

Media & the American Mind: From Morse to McLuhan. Daniel J. Czitrom. LC 81-14810. xiv, 254p. 1982. pap. 17.95 (*0-8078-4107-2*) U of NC Pr.

Media & the Chinese Public. Ed. by Brantley Womack. 200p. (C). (gr. 13). 1986. pap. text 34.95 (*0-87332-375-0*) M E Sharpe.

Media & the Gulf War: The Press & Democracy in Wartime. Ed. by Hedrick Smith. LC 92-18303. 438p. 1992. 24.95 (*0-932020-99-2*) Seven Locks Pr.

Media & the Mayor's Race: The Decline of Urban Political Reporting. Phyllis Kaniss. LC 94-13043. (Illus.). 410p. 1995. pap. 16.95 (*0-253-20932-3*); text 39.95 (*0-253-33114-5*) Ind U Pr.

***Media & the Message: Lessons Learned from Past Public Service Campaigns.** 100p. 1998. pap. 15.00 (*1-58671-015-X*) Natl Cpgn Teen Preg.

Media & the Persian Gulf War. Ed. by Robert E. Denton, Jr. LC 92-36554. (Series in Political Communication). 344p. 1993. 65.00 (*0-275-94232-5*, C4232, Praeger Pubs) Greenwood.

***Media & the Presidentialization of Parliamentary Elections.** Anthony Mughan. LC 00-33291. 2000. write for info. (*0-312-23786-3*) St Martin.

Media & the Russian Public. Ellen P. Mickiewicz. LC 80-21544. 156p. 1981. 42.95 (*0-275-90682-5*, C0682, Praeger Pubs) Greenwood.

Media & the Transformation of Religion in South Asia. Ed. by Lawrence A. Babb & Susan S. Wadley. LC 95-13168. (Illus.). 352p. 1995. text 39.95 (*0-8122-3304-2*); pap. text 17.50 (*0-8122-1547-8*) U of Pa Pr.

Media & Voters: The Audience, Content, & Influence of Press & the Television at the 1987 General Election. William L. Miller. (Illus.). 256p. 1991. 58.00 (*0-19-827377-0*) OUP.

Media & You: An Elementary Media Literacy Curriculum. Donna Lloyd-Kolkin & Kathleen R. Tyner. LC 90-42205. (Illus.). 170p. 1991. pap. 34.95 (*0-87778-226-1*) Educ Tech Pubns.

Media Anthropology: Informing Global Citizens. Ed. by Susan L. Allen. LC 93-17649. 208p. 1993. 55.00 (*0-89789-342-5*, Bergin & Garvey) Greenwood.

Media Arabic. Julia Ashtiany. (Illus.). 160p. 1994. pap. text 25.00 (*0-7486-0367-0*, Pub. by Edinburgh U Pr) Col U Pr.

Media Archive. ADILKNO, Foundation for Advancement of Illegal Knowledge Staff. (New Autonomy Ser.). Orig. Title: Bilwet Media-Archief. 224p. 1998. pap. 14.00 (*1-57027-079-1*) Autonomedia.

***Media Art Interaction: The '80s & '90s In Germany.** Rudolf Frieling. (Illus.). 293p. 2000. 65.00 (*3-211-83422-2*) Princeton Arch.

M

An Asterisk (*) at the beginning of an entry indicates that the title is appearing for the first time.

Media As Politics: Theory, Behavior & Change in America. Kahan. LC 98-22653. 267p. (C). 1998. pap. text 27.80 (*0-13-876053-5*) P-H.

*__Media at War.__ Susan L. Carruthers. LC 99-37492. 321p. 2000. text 55.00 (*0-312-22800-7*) St Martin.

*__Media at War: Communication & Conflict in the Twentieth Century.__ Susan L. Carruthers. LC 99-37492. 2000. pap. 21.95 (*0-312-22801-5*) St Martin.

Media at War: Radio's Challenge to the Newspapers, 1924-1937. Gwenyth L. Jackaway. LC 95-13919. 184p. 1995. 57.95 (*0-275-95257-6*, Praeger Pubs) Greenwood.

Media, Audience & Social Structure. Ed. by Sandra J. Ball-Rokeach & Muriel G. Cantor. LC 85-27871. 448p. (Orig.). (C). 1986. text 49.95 (*0-8039-2581-6*); pap. text 24.00 (*0-8039-2582-4*) Sage.

Media, Audience & Social Structure. Ed. by Sandra J. Ball-Rokeach & Muriel G. Cantor. LC 85-27871. 400p. (Orig.). 1986. reprint ed. pap. 124.00 (*0-608-04298-6*, 206507700012) Bks Demand.

Media Audiences in Ireland: Power & Cultural Identity. Mary J. Kelly & Barbara O'Connor. LC 97-212621. 280p. 1998. pap. 29.95 (*1-900621-09-6*, Pub. by Univ Coll Dublin Pr) Dufour.

Media BankT/A Management. 4th ed. Richard L. Daft. (C). 1997. audio compact disk 246.00 (*0-03-018008-2*) Harcourt Coll Pubs.

Media Beyond Socialism: Theory & Practice in East-Central Europe. Slavko Splichal. Ed. by John A. Lent. (International Communication & Popular Culture Ser.). 192p. (C). 1995. pap. 24.00 (*0-8133-1818-1*, Pub. by Westview) HarpC.

*__Media Blasting.__ Jim Richardson. 128p. 2000. pap. 18.95 (*1-884089-48-8*, Pub. by CarTech) Voyageur Pr.

Media Blight & the Dehumanizing of America. William K. Shrader. LC 91-28653. 208p. 1992. 55.00 (*0-275-94119-1*, C4119, Praeger Pubs) Greenwood.

Media Canada: Introductory Analysis. Romanow & Soderlund. 1992. 240p. pap. text. write for info. (*0-7730-5187-2*) Addison-Wes.

*__Media Career.__ 2nd ed. Seguin. 1999. pap. text 9.95 (*0-312-25016-9*) St Martin.

Media Center Facilities Design. fac. ed. Ed. by Jane A. Hannigan & Glenn E. Estes. LC 78-9336. 127p. 1994. pap. 39.40 (*0-7837-7310-2*, 204723700007) Bks Demand.

Media, Children, & the Family: Social Scientific, Psychodynamic, & Clinical Perspective. Ed. by Dolf Zillmann et al. (Communication Ser.). 360p. 1994. pap. 39.95 (*0-8058-1415-9*); text 79.95 (*0-8058-1210-5*) L Erlbaum Assocs.

Media Circus. Howard Kurtz. 1994. pap. 16.00 (*0-8129-6356-3*) Random.

Media Communication: An Introduction to Theory & Process. Watson. LC 97-41486. 320p. 1998. text 55.00 (*0-312-21200-3*) St Martin.

Media, Communication, Culture: A Global Approach. James Lull. 200p. 1995. 46.00 (*0-231-10264-X*) Col U Pr.

Media, Communication, Culture: A Global Approach. James Lull. (Illus.). 200p. 1995. pap. 18.00 (*0-231-10265-8*) Col U Pr.

*__Media, Communication, Culture: A Global Approach.__ 2nd ed. James Lull. LC 99-54090. 288p. 2000. 18.50 (*0-231-12073-7*) Col U Pr.

Media Companies: 2000 Edition. Peterson's Guides Staff. 324p. 1999. pap. 27.95 (*0-7689-0215-0*) Petersons.

Media, Consciousness & Culture: Explorations of Walter Ong's Thought. Ed. by Bruce E. Gronbeck et al. LC 90-27759. (Communication & Human Values Ser.). 290p. reprint ed. pap. 89.90 (*0-608-09205-3*, 205270900003) Bks Demand.

Media, Consciousness, & Culture: Explorations on Walter Ong's Thoughts. Bruce E. Gronbeck et al. (Communication & Human Values Ser.). (Illus.). 320p. 1991. text 52.00 (*0-8039-4025-4*) Sage.

Media Contemporary Marketing. 9th ed. Boone. (C). 1997. pap. text, teacher ed. 28.00 (*0-03-019038-X*) Harcourt.

Media Control: The Spectacular Achievements of Propaganda. Noam Chomsky. (Open Magazine Pamphlet Ser.: No. 10). 21p. (Orig.). 1994. 4.00 (*1-884519-03-2*) Open Media.

Media Control: The Spectacular Achievements of Propaganda. Noam Chomsky. LC 96-53580. (Open Media Pamphlet Ser.: Vol. 2). 64p. (Orig.). 1997. pap. 5.95 (*1-888363-49-5*) Seven Stories.

Media Controversies. Ed. by Lester A. Sobel. LC 80-22880. 185p. reprint ed. pap. 57.40 (*0-608-18328-8*, 203160900075) Bks Demand.

*__Media Courses U. K, 2000 Edition.__ Lavinia Orton. 1999. pap. 24.95 (*0-85170-740-8*) British Film Inst.

Media Courses U. K., 1998. Ed. by Lavinia Orton. 230p. 1998. 15.95 (*0-85170-649-5*, Pub. by British Film Inst) Ind U Pr.

Media Courses U. K., 1997. Ed. by Lavinia Orton. (Distributed for the British Film Institute Ser.). 230p. 1996. pap. 14.95 (*0-85170-587-1*, Pub. by British Film Inst) Ind U Pr.

Media Courses U. K., 1996. Ed. by Lavinia Ortin. 1995. pap. 14.95 (*0-85170-521-9*, Pub. by British Film Inst) Ind U Pr.

Media Courses UK, 1999. Ed. by Lavinia Orton. (Distributed for the British Film Institute Ser.). 288p. Date not set. pap. 15.95 (*0-85170-683-5*, Pub. by British Film Inst) Ind U Pr.

Media Coverage & Political Terrorists: A Quantitative Analysis. Richard W. Schaffert. LC 91-43443. 296p. 1992. 59.95 (*0-275-94243-0*, C4243, Praeger Pubs) Greenwood.

Media Coverage of Terrorism: Methods of Diffusion. A. Odasuo Alali & Kenoye K. Eke. (Focus Editions Ser.: Vol. 130). (Illus.). 272p. 1991. text 59.95 (*0-8039-4190-0*); pap. text 26.00 (*0-8039-4191-9*) Sage.

Media Coverage of Terrorism: Methods of Diffusion. Ed. by A. Odasuo Alali & Kenoye K. Eke. LC 90-28310. (Sage Focus Editions Ser.: Vol. 130). 160p. reprint ed. pap. 49.60 (*0-608-09788-8*, 206996200007) Bks Demand.

Media-Coverage on Taiwan in the People's Republic of China. Jorg M. Rudolph. (Occasional Papers-Reprints Series in Contemporary Asian Studies: No. 3-1983 (56)). 77p. (Orig.). 1983. pap. text 3.50 (*0-942182-55-3*) U MD Law.

Media Credibility S. K. Aggarwal. LC 89-905747. xii, 246 p. 1989. write for info. (*81-7099-157-9*) S Asia.

Media, Crime & Criminal Justice: Images & Realities. Raymond Surette. LC 91-17613. 299p. (C). 1991. mass mkt. 28.95 (*0-534-16440-4*) Wadsworth Pub.

Media, Crime & Criminal Justice: Images & Realities. 2nd ed. Raymond Surette. LC 97-18989. (Criminal Justice Ser.). (C). 1997. pap. 38.95 (*0-534-50863-4*) Wadsworth Pub.

Media, Criminal Justice & Mass Culture. 2nd rev. ed. Ed. & Pref. by Gregg Barak. LC KF224.S485R46 1996. 240p. 2000. pap. text 26.50 (*0-911577-37-8*, Pub. by Willow Tree NY) Lib Res.

Media, Crisis & Democracy: Mass Communication & the Disruption of Social Order. Marc Raboy & Bernard Dagenais. (Media, Culture & Society Ser.). 224p. (C). 1992. text 55.00 (*0-8039-8639-4*); pap. text 25.95 (*0-8039-8640-8*) Sage.

Media Criticism: Journeys in Interpretation. Contrib. by Christine Scodari & Judith M. Thorpe. 224p. 1993. per. 27.95 (*0-8403-8793-8*) Kendall-Hunt.

Media Culture: Cultural Studies, Identity & Politics Between the Modern & the Postmodern. Douglas M. Kellner. LC 94-7262. (Illus.). 320p. (C). 1995. pap. 22.99 (*0-415-10570-6*, B7076) Routledge.

Media, Culture & Catholicism. Paul A. Soukup. LC 96-26535. (Communication, Culture & Theology Ser.). 240p. 1996. pap. 24.95 (*1-55612-769-3*) Sheed & Ward WI.

Media Culture & Modern Conscience. 3rd ed. (C). 1993. write for info. (*0-8087-9455-8*) Pearson Custom.

*__Media, Culture & Politics in Indonesia.__ 288p. 2000. 29.95 (*0-19-553703-3*) OUP.

Media, Culture, & the Environment. Alison Anderson. LC 96-39287. (Communications, Media, & Culture Ser.). (Illus.). 236p. (C). 1997. text 50.00 (*0-8135-2394-X*); pap. text 17.95 (*0-8135-2395-8*) Rutgers U Pr.

Media, Culture & the Environment, 1. Alison Anderson. 1997. 65.00 (*1-85728-383-X*); pap. text 23.95 (*1-85728-384-8*) Taylor & Francis.

Media, Culture & the Religious Right. Linda Kintz & Julia Lesage. LC 97-46351. 1998. 49.95 (*0-8166-3084-4*); pap. 19.95 (*0-8166-3085-2*) U of Minn Pr.

*__Media Debates: Issues in Mass Communication.__ 3rd ed. Everette E. Dennis & John C. Merrill. (Mass Communication Ser.). 2001. pap. 28.00 (*0-534-57933-7*) Wadsworth Pub.

Media Decentralization: The Case of Israel's Local Newspapers. Dan Caspi. (Illus.). 150p. (C). 1985. 44.95 (*0-88738-055-7*) Transaction Pubs.

Media Diplomacy: The Foreign Office in the Mass Communications Age. Yoel Cohen. 224p. 1986. 37.50 (*0-7146-3269-4*, Pub. by F Cass Pubs) Intl Spec Bk.

Media Directory for Metropolitan North Jersey. Ed. by Laura Boss & Maria M. Gillan. 1996. pap. text 5.00 (*0-9621495-3-5*) Poetry Ctr PCCC.

Media Discourse. Norman Fairclough. LC 95-17679. 1995. text. write for info. (*0-340-63222-4*, Pub. by E A); pap. text 18.95 (*0-340-58889-6*, Pub. by E A) OUP.

Media Economics: Concepts & Issues. Robert G. Picard. (CommText Ser.: Vol. 22). 160p. (C). 1989. text 42.00 (*0-8039-3501-3*); pap. text 18.95 (*0-8039-3502-1*) Sage.

Media Economics: Theory & Practice. Ed. by Alison Alexander et al. LC 92-26358. 416p. 1993. 89.95 (*0-8058-0434-X*); pap. 39.95 (*0-8058-1307-1*) L Erlbaum Assocs.

Media Economics: Theory & Practice. 2nd ed. Ed. by Alison Alexander et al. (LEA's Communication Ser.). 425p. 1997. write for info. (*0-8058-1841-3*); pap. write for info. (*0-8058-1842-1*) L Erlbaum Assocs.

Media Economics: Understanding Markets, Industries, & Concepts. Alan B. Albarran. LC 96-513. (Illus.). 238p. 1996. pap. text 36.95 (*0-8138-2128-2*) Iowa St U Pr.

Media Education. Ed. by Scholastic, Inc. Staff. 1990. pap. 14.95 (*0-590-76296-6*, Scholastic Hardcover) Scholastic Inc.

Media Education: An Introduction. Manuel Alvarado & Oliver Boyd-Barrett. (Illus.). 464p. 1992. pap. 35.00 (*0-85170-295-3*, Pub. by British Film Inst) Ind U Pr.

Media Education: Teaching English in the National Curriculum. Cary Bazalgette. (Illus.). 61p. (C). 1991. pap. text 15.00 (*0-340-53695-0*, Pub. by Hodder & Stought Ltd) Lubrecht & Cramer.

*__Media, Education & America's Counter-Culture Revolution: Lost & Found Opportunities for Media Impact on Education, Gender, Race & the Arts.__ Robert L. Hilliard. LC 00-21980. 2000. pap. write for info. (*1-56750-513-9*) Ablx Pub.

*__Media, Education, & America's Counter-Culture Revolution: Lost & Found Opportunities for Media Impact on Education, Gender, Race & the Arts.__ Robert L. Hilliard. 2000. write for info. (*1-56750-512-0*) Greenwood.

Media Education & the Liberal Arts: A Blueprint for the New Professionism. Robert Blanchard & William G. Christ. (Communication Ser.). 200p. (C). 1993. text 39.95 (*0-8058-0488-9*) L Erlbaum Assocs.

Media Education & the Re-Production of Culture. David Sholle & Stan Freire. LC 93-40159. (Critical Studies in Education & Culture). 200p. 1994. pap. 18.95 (*0-89789-255-0*, Bergin & Garvey) Greenwood.

Media Education & the (Re) Production of Culture: Critical Studies in Education & Culture Ser. David Scholle & Stan Denski. LC 93-40159. 200p. 1994. 57.95 (*0-89789-254-2*, Bergin & Garvey) Greenwood.

Media Education Assessment Handbook & Assessing Communication. Christ. 1996. 42.00 (*0-8058-2714-5*) L Erlbaum Assocs.

Media Education in 1990's Europe. 1994. 18.00 (*92-871-2374-8*, Pub. by Council of Europe) Manhattan Pub Co.

Media Effects: Advances in Theory & Research. Ed. by Jennings Bryant & Dolf Zillmann. (LEA's Communication Ser.). 504p. 1994. pap. 39.95 (*0-8058-0918-X*); text 99.95 (*0-8058-0917-1*) L Erlbaum Assocs.

*__Media Effects & Society.__ Elizabeth Perse. (A Volume in LEA's Communication Series). 320p. 2000. write for info. (*0-8058-2505-3*); pap. write for info. (*0-8058-2506-1*) L Erlbaum Assocs.

Media Effects on Voters: A Panel Study of the 1992 Presidential Election. John W. Cavanaugh. 194p. (C). 1995. lib. bdg. 39.00 (*0-8191-9942-7*) U Pr of Amer.

Media Effects Research: A Basic Approach. Sparks. (Mass Communication Ser.). 2001. pap. text 36.50 (*0-534-54586-6*) Thomson Learn.

*__Media Entertainment: The Psychology of Its Appeal.__ Dolf Zillmann & Peter Vorderer. LC 99-59306. 2000. pap. write for info. (*0-8058-3325-0*) L Erlbaum Assocs.

Media Enthralled: Singapore Revisited. Francis T. Seow. LC 96-41596. 254p. 1998. 48.00 (*1-55587-779-6*) L Rienner.

Media Entrepreneurs & the Media Enterprise in the U. S. Congress. Karen M. Kedrowski. Ed. by David L. Paletz. (Communication Ser.). 256p. (Orig.). (C). 1996. text 59.50 (*1-57273-012-9*); pap. text 24.95 (*1-57273-013-7*) Hampton Pr NJ.

Media Equation: How People Treat Computers, Television, & New Media Like Real People & Places. Byron Reeves & Clifford Nass. 317p. (C). 1998. reprint ed. pap. 15.95 (*1-57586-053-8*) CSLI.

Media Equation: How People Treat Computers, Televisions, & New Media Like Real People & Places. Byron Reeves & Clifford Nass. (CSLI Lecture Notes Ser.). 350p. 1996. 28.95 (*1-57586-052-X*) CSLI.

Media Equities: Evaluation & Trading. Christopher Gasson. (International Equities Ser.). 224p. 1995. 180.00 (*1-85573-194-0*, Pub. by Woodhead Pubng) Am Educ Systs.

Media Error Monitoring & Reporting Techniques for Verification of Stored Data on Optical Digital Data Disks: ANSI/AIIM MS59-1996. Association for Information & Image Management Staff. 37p. 1996. 52.00 (*0-89258-307-X*, MS59) Assn Inform & Image Mgmt.

Media Ethics. Conrad C. Fink. LC 94-7522. 336p. (C). 1994. pap. text 44.00 (*0-02-337753-4*, Macmillan Coll) P-H.

Media Ethics. Matthew Kieran. LC 97-39544. (Illus.). 216p. (C). 1998. 75.00 (*0-415-16837-6*); pap. 20.99 (*0-415-16838-4*) Routledge.

*__Media Ethics.__ 6th ed. 352p. (C). 2000. pap. text 46.00 (*0-8013-3338-5*) Longman.

Media Ethics: A Philosophical Approach. Matthew Kieran. LC 97-1916. 184p. 1997. 55.00 (*0-275-95634-2*, Praeger Pubs) Greenwood.

Media Ethics: A Philosophical Approach. Matthew Kieran. LC 97-1916. 184p. 1999. pap. 22.95 (*0-275-96694-1*, Praeger Pubs) Greenwood.

Media Ethics: Issues & Cases. 2nd ed. Philip Patterson & Lee C. Wilkins. 304p. (C). 1994. text. write for info. (*0-697-17099-3*) Brown & Benchmark.

Media Ethics: Issues & Cases. 3rd ed. Phillip Patterson. Ed. by Lee Wilkins. LC 97-8386. 384p. 1997. pap. 24.69 (*0-697-32717-5*) McGraw.

*__Media Ethics: Practices & Representations.__ David Berry. 320p. 1999. pap. 32.95 (*0-7506-4162-2*, Focal) Buttrwrth-Heinemann.

*__Media Ethics & Accountability Systems.__ Claude-Jean Bertrand. LC 99-56519. 158p. 2000. 29.95 (*1-56000-420-7*) Transaction Pubs.

Media Events: The Live Broadcasting of History. Daniel Dayan. (Illus.). 320p. 1994. pap. 19.50 (*0-674-55956-8*) HUP.

Media Events: The Live Broadcasting of History. Daniel Dayan & Elihu Katz. (Illus.). 320p. (C). 1992. 43.00 (*0-674-55955-X*) HUP.

Media Flight Plan III. 3rd ed. Dennis G. Martin & Robert D. Coons. 155p. (C). 1996. pap., student ed. 36.00 incl. 3.5 hd (*0-9632515-1-1*); pap., student ed. 36.00 incl. mac hd (*0-9632515-2-X*) Deer Creek UT.

Media for Business. Robert H. Amend & Michael A. Schrader. (Illus.). 258p. 1991. 44.95 (*0-86729-264-4*, Focal) Buttrwrth-Heinemann.

Media for Interactive Communication. Rudy Bretz & Michael Schmidbauer. LC 83-3085. 264p. reprint ed. pap. 81.90 (*0-8357-8479-7*, 203474600091) Bks Demand.

Media for Managers. Frank M. Corrado. (Illus.). 224p. (C). 1984. pap. text 23.00 (*0-13-572446-5*) P-H.

Media Freedom: The Contradictions of Communication in the Age of Modernity. Barbrook. LC 95-1908. (C). 54.95 (*0-7453-0944-5*, Pub. by Pluto GBR); pap. 19.95 (*0-7453-0943-7*) Pluto GBR.

Media Freedom & Accountability, 14. Ed. by Everette E. Dennis et al. LC 89-2148. (Contributions to the Study of Mass Media & Communications Ser.: No. 14). 220p. 1989. 45.00 (*0-313-26727-8*, DMF/, Greenwood Pr) Greenwood.

Media French: A Guide to Contemporary French Idiom. Adrian Ritchie. 268p. 1997. 39.95 (*0-7083-1399-X*, Pub. by Univ Wales Pr) Paul & Co Pubs.

Media Game: American Politics in the Television Age. Stephen Ansolabehere et al. LC 92-21876. (New Topics in Politics Ser.). 248p. (C). 1992. pap. text 30.13 (*0-02-359965-0*, Macmillan Coll) P-H.

Media Gratifications Research: Current Perspectives. Ed. by Karl E. Rosengren et al. LC 85-2308. (Illus.). 311p. 1985. reprint ed. pap. 96.50 (*0-608-01176-2*, 205947400001) Bks Demand.

Media Guide. McDaniel. Date not set. write for info. (*0-314-08703-6*) West Pub.

Media Guide. Cecily A. Raiborn. Date not set. write for info. (*0-314-08704-4*) West Pub.

Media Guide for Academics. 2nd ed. Joann E. Rodgers & William C. Adams. Ed. by Mike Ferring. LC 94-61228. (Illus.). 72p. 1994. pap. 10.00 (*0-910755-02-7*) Foun Am Comm.

Media Guide, 1998. Steve Peak & Paul Fisher. 384p. 1997. 24.95 (*1-85702-639-X*, Pub. by Fourth Estate) Trafalgar.

*__Media Guide, 1999.__ S. Peak. 1998. pap. 29.95 (*1-85702-872-4*, Pub. by Fourth Estate) Trafalgar.

*__Media Guide 1997.__ Steve Peak. 2000. pap. 27.50 (*1-85702-491-5*, Pub. by Fourth Estate) Trafalgar.

Media Guide, 1992: A Critical Review of the Media. Ed. by Jude Wanniski. 680p. (Orig.). (C). 1992. 39.95 (*0-938081-08-X*); pap. 29.95 (*0-938081-10-1*) Polyconomics.

Media Guide to Cost Accounting 9th ed. 384p. 1997. text, teacher ed. write for info. (*0-13-567314-3*, Macmillan Coll) P-H.

Media Guide to Introductory Management. 11th ed. Horngren. 1998. pap. text, teacher ed. write for info. (*0-13-274168-7*) P-H.

Media Hates Conservatives: How It Controls the Flow of Information. Dale A. Berryhill. LC 94-75121. 224p. 1994. pap. 10.99 (*1-56384-060-X*) Huntington Hse.

Media Impact. Michael Kronenwetter. 128p. (YA). (gr. 7 up). 1998. 22.40 (*0-7613-3018-6*) TFC Bks NY.

Media Impact. 2nd ed. Biagi. (Mass Communication Ser.). 1992. text, teacher ed. write for info. (*0-534-16244-4*) Wadsworth Pub.

Media-Impact: An Introduction to Mass Media. Shirley Biagi. 411p. (C). 1988. pap. write for info. (*0-534-08946-1*) Wadsworth Pub.

Media-Impact: An Introduction to Mass Media. Shirley Biagi. 411p. (C). 1989. pap. write for info. (*0-534-12660-X*) Wadsworth Pub.

Media-Impact: An Introduction to Mass Media. 2nd ed. Shirley Biagi. 564p. (C). 1992. pap. 35.95 (*0-534-16242-8*) Wadsworth Pub.

Media-Impact: An Introduction to Mass Media. 2nd ed. Shirley Biagi. 564p. 1993. mass mkt. 33.75 (*0-534-20184-9*) Wadsworth Pub.

Media-Impact: An Introduction to Mass Media. 3rd ed. Shirley Biagi. LC 95-2932. 1996. pap. 46.95 (*0-534-21744-3*) Wadsworth Pub.

Media Impact: An Introduction to Mass Media. 4th ed. Shirley Biagi. LC 98-22567. 1998. pap. 60.95 (*0-534-54810-5*) Wadsworth Pub.

*__Media Impact: An Introduction to Mass Media.__ 5th ed. Shirley Biagi. LC 00-27152. 2000. pap. write for info. (*0-534-57511-0*) Wadsworth Pub.

*__Media Impact: An Introduction to Mass Medial.__ 5th ed. Biagi. (Mass Communication Ser.). 2000. 43.75 (*0-534-57510-2*) Wadsworth Pub.

Media Impact: Intro to Mass Media. 3rd ed. Biagi. (Mass Communication Ser.). 1995. teacher ed. 48.00 (*0-534-21745-1*) Wadsworth Pub.

Media Imperialism Reconsidered: The Homogenizing of Television Culture. Chin-Chuan Li. LC 80-16763. (People & Communication Ser.: No. 10). 277p. 1980. reprint ed. pap. 85.90 (*0-608-01177-0*, 205947500001) Bks Demand.

Media in Africa & Africa in the Media. Gretchen Walsh. LC 96-3461. 1996. 100.00 (*1-873836-81-3*) Bowker-Saur.

Media in America: A History. 4th ed. Ed. by W. David Sloan & James D. Startt. (Illus.). 498p. 1999. pap. text 39.95 (*1-885219-13-X*) Vision AL.

Media in America: The Wilson Quarterly Reader. rev. ed. Ed. by Douglas Gomery. LC 98-13340. (Woodrow Wilson Center Press Ser.). 304p. 1998. pap. 17.95 (*0-943875-87-0*) Johns Hopkins.

Media in America: The Wilson Quarterly Reader. rev. ed. Ed. by Douglas Gomery. LC 98-13340. (Woodrow Wilson Center Press Ser.). 304p. 1998. text 40.00 (*0-943875-86-2*) Johns Hopkins.

*__Media in American Politics.__ David L. Paletz. LC 98-35082. 352p. (C). 1998. pap. 45.00 (*0-321-02991-7*) Addson-Wesley Educ.

Media in Australia: Industries, Texts, Audiences. Stuart Cunningham & Graeme Turner. LC 97-189485. 512p. 1997. pap. 35.00 (*1-86448-273-7*, Pub. by Allen & Unwin Pty) Paul & Co Pubs.

Media in Black & White. Ed. by Everette Dennis. 182p. 1996. pap. text 21.95 (*1-56000-873-3*) Transaction Pubs.

Media in Britain. Jeremy Tunstall. LC 83-14482. 350p. 1983. text 51.50 (*0-231-05816-0*) Col U Pr.

*__Media in Britain: Current Debates & Developments.__ Jane C. Stokes & Anna Reading. LC 99-21894. 1999. text 59.95 (*0-312-22528-8*) St Martin.

Media in British Politics. Seaton Pimlott. 288p. 1987. 75.95 (*1-85521-060-6*) Ashgate Pub Co.

Media in Church & Mission: Communicating the Gospel. Viggo Sgaard. LC 93-24029. 287p. 1993. pap. text 7.95 (*0-87808-242-5*) William Carey Lib.

Media in Drama Therapy: An Exercise Handbook. Pam B. Dunne. 64p. 1988. pap. 18.00 (*1-888657-03-0*) Drama Thrpy Inst.

Media in France. Raymond Kuhn. LC 94-9595. 304p. (C). 1994. 22.99 (*0-415-01458-1*) Routledge.

Media in Global Context: A Reader. Ed. by Annabelle Serberny-Mohammadi et al. LC 97-209. (Foundations in Media Ser.). (Illus.). 384p. 1997. pap. text 19.95 (0-340-67687-6) OUP.

Media in Global Context: A Reader. Ed. by Annabelle Sreberny-Mohammadi et al. LC 97-209. (Foundations in Media Ser.). (Illus.). 384p. 1997. text 65.00 (0-340-67686-8) OUP.

Media in Ireland: The Search for Diversity. Ed. by Damien Kiberd. 96p. 1997. pap. 20.00 (1-85182-315-8, Pub. by Four Cts Pr) Intl Spec Bk.

***Media in Ireland: The Search for Ethical Journalism.** Ed. by Damien Kiberd. 128p. 1999. pap. 20.00 (1-85182-509-6, Pub. by Four Cts Pr) Intl Spec Bk.

Media in Question: Popular Cultures & Public Interests. Kees Brants et al. LC 97-61883. vi, 184p. 1998. write for info. (0-7619-5723-5) Sage.

Media in the Movies: An Illustrated Catalog of American Journalism, 1900-1996. Larry Langman. LC 97-46949. 341p. 1998. lib. bdg. 65.00 (0-7864-0433-7) McFarland & Co.

Media in the 1984 & 1988 Presidential Campaigns, 21. Ed. by Guido H. Stempel, III & John W. Windhauser. LC 90-2920. (Contributions to the Study of Mass Media & Communications Ser.: No. 21). 232p. 1991. 55.00 (0-313-26527-5, SLD, Greenwood Pr) Greenwood.

Media in the 20th Century. Oscar W. Alexander. (In the 20th Century Ser.). (Illus.). 192p. 1997. pap. 9.95 (0-912517-24-7) Bluewood Bks.

Media in the 20th Century. Dana Graves. (Twentieth Century Ser.). (YA). (gr. 7 up). Date not set. pap. 9.95 (0-614-19179-3) Bluewood Bks.

Media in Western Europe: The Euromedia Handbook. Euromedia Research Group Staff. (Communications in Society Ser.). 288p. (C). 1992. 59.95 (0-8039-8575-4); pap. 24.00 (0-8039-8576-2) Sage.

Media in Western Europe: The Euromedia Handbook. 2nd ed. Euromedia Research Group Staff. Ed. by Bernt S. Ostergaard. 272p. 1997. 79.95 (0-7619-5405-8); pap. 32.00 (0-7619-5406-6) Sage.

Media in Your Life: An Introduction to Mass Communication. Jean Folkerts et al. LC 97-31498. 558p. 1997. pap. text 60.00 (0-205-15414-X) Allyn.

***Media in Your Life: An Introduction to Mass Communication, with Interactive Companion Website.** 2nd ed. Jean Folkerts & Stephen Lacy. 576p. 2000. pap. 57.33 (0-205-31782-0) Allyn.

Media in Your Life: Intro to Mass Communication. (C). 1999. text. write for info. (0-205-29477-4, Longwood Div) Allyn.

Media in Your Life: Introduction to Mass Communication. Folkerts. (C). 1997. write for info. (0-205-28390-X, Macmillan Coll) P-H.

***Media in Your Life & Pin Code.** 2nd ed. 544p. (C). 2000. write for info. (0-205-32172-0) Allyn.

Media Inc.'s Hawaii: Production Index. 5th ed. Richard K. Woltjer. (Illus.). 310p. 1998. pap. 20.00 (0-940317-36-2) Media Index Pub.

Media Inc.'s Hawaii Film, Video Multimedia & Audio Production Index. 3rd ed. Richard K. Woltjer. (Illus.). 272p. 1997. pap. 20.00 (0-940317-29-X) Media Index Pub.

Media Inc.'s Hawaii Production Index. 4th ed. Richard K. Woltjer. 336p. 1997. pap. 20.00 (0-940317-32-X) Media Index Pub.

Media Inc.'s Hawaii Production Index. 6th ed. Richard K. Woltjer. (Illus.). 314p. Date not set. pap. text 20.00 (0-940317-39-7) Media Index Pub.

Media Inc.'s Hawaii Production Index. 7th ed. Richard K. Woltjer. (Illus.). 314p. Date not set. pap. 20.00 (0-940317-43-5) Media Index Pub.

Media Inc.'s Master Lists. Richard K. Woltjer. (Illus.). 176p. Date not set. pap. 15.00 (0-940317-37-0) Media Index Pub.

Media Inc's Master Lists. Richard K. Woltjer. (Illus.). 164p. Date not set. pap. 20.00 (0-940317-44-3) Media Index Pub.

Media Inc.'s Master Lists. 8th ed. Richard K. Woltjer. (Illus.). 176p. 1997. pap. 15.00 (0-940317-33-8) Media Index Pub.

Media Inc.'s Master Lists, 1996. Richard K. Woltjer & Daniel P. Whalen. (Illus.). 176p. 1996. pap. 15.00 (0-940317-30-3) Media Index Pub.

Media Inc.'s Northwest Film, Video Multimedia & Audio Production Index. 14th ed. Ed. by Richard K. Woltjer. (Illus.). 432p. 1996. pap. 25.00 (0-940317-31-1) Media Index Pub.

***Media Inc.'s Northwest Production Index.** Contrib. by Richard K. Woltjer. (Illus.). 448p. 1998. pap. 25.00 (0-940317-38-9) Media Index Pub.

Media Inc.'s Northwest Production Index. 15th ed. Richard K. Woltjer. (Illus.). 432p. 1997. pap. 25.00 (0-940317-34-6) Media Index Pub.

Media Inc.'s Northwest Production Index. 17th ed. Richard K. Woltjer. (Illus.). 424p. Date not set. pap. 25.00 (0-940317-42-7) Media Index Pub.

Media Inc.'s Northwest Production Index. 18th ed. Jim Baker. (Illus.). 400p. Date not set. pap. 25.00 (0-940317-45-1) Media Index Pub.

Media Inc's Northwest Talent Index. 3rd ed. Richard K. Woltjer. (Illus.). 122p. 1997. pap. 20.00 (0-940317-35-4) Media Index Pub.

Media Inc's. Vancouver & Western Canada Production Index. Richard K. Woltjer. (Illus.). 310p. Date not set. pap. 25.00 (0-940317-41-9) Media Index Pub.

Media Inc.'s Western Canada Production Index. 2nd ed. Jim Baker. (Illus.). 320p. Date not set. pap. 25.00 (0-940317-46-X) Media Index Pub.

Media Influence on Presidential Candidates. William C. Adams. (C). 1996. pap. text 13.95 (0-8133-0172-6) Westview.

Media Instructor's Manual to Accompany Understanding Management. Richard L. Daft. 176p. (C). 1995. pap. text, teacher ed. 32.00 (0-03-098908-6) Dryden Pr.

Media Interview: Conversation, Confession & Confrontation. Theo Van Leewing & Phillip Bell. LC 94-134217. 240p. pap. 24.95 (0-86840-389-X, Pub. by New South Wales Univ Pr) Intl Spec Bk.

Media Isn't a Four Letter Word: A Guide to Effective Encounters with the Members of the Fourth Estate. David J. Shea & John F. Gulick. 70p. 1994. 10.00 (0-7908-0059-4) Elec Ind Assn.

Media Issues & Trends: A Mass Communication Reader. Hoyt Purvis. 148p. (C). 1998. per. 38.95 (0-7872-5468-1, 41546801) Kendall-Hunt.

Media Journal. 2nd ed. Harris & Rosen. LC 98-27417. 525p. (C). 1998. pap. text 35.00 (0-205-27483-8) P-H.

***Media, Journalism & Democracy.** Ed. by Margaret Scammell & Holli A. Semetko. LC 99-43340. (International Library of Politics & Comparative Government). 440p. 2000. text 127.95 (1-85521-541-1, Pub. by Ashgate Pub) Ashgate Pub Co.

Media Jungle: A Survival Guide. Carrie Van Dyke. (Illus.). 92p. 1996. 15.00 (0-9665274-0-2) Media Mast.

Media Knowledge: Readings in Popular Culture, Pedagogy, & Critical Citizenship. James Schwoch et al. LC 91-93565. (SUNY Series, Teacher Empowerment & School Reform). 170p. (C). 1992. pap., pap. text 21.95 (0-7914-0826-4) State U NY Pr.

Media Law. Ed. by Eric Barendt. LC 93-25714. (International Library of Essays in Law & Legal Theory: Vol. 21). (C). 1994. lib. bdg. 150.00 (0-8147-1215-0) NYU Pr.

Media Law. Y. M. Burns. 420p. 1990. pap. 98.00 (0-409-01342-0, SA, MICHIE) LEXIS Pub.

Media Law. Rex S. Heinke. LC 94-25572. 800p. 1994. trans. 215.00 (0-87179-800-X) BNA Books.

Media Law. Robert Martin. LC 97-175663. (Essentials of Canadian Law Ser.). xiv, 194p. 1996. pap. 30.95 (1-55221-004-9, Pub. by Irwin Law) Gaunt.

***Media Law.** Geoffrey Robertson & Nicol Andrew. 1998. pap. 50.00 (0-14-013866-8, Pub. by Pnguin Bks Ltd) Trafalgar.

Media Law. 3rd ed. LC 93-26318. (McGraw-Hill Series in Mass Communication). (C). 1994. text 51.25 (0-07-029673-1) McGraw.

Media Law: A User's Guide for Film & Programme Makers Rhonda Baker. LC 99-168078. 292p. 1997. write for info. (0-415-13670-9) Routledge.

Media Law: Cases & Material. Mike Jordan. LC 98-208658. 536p. (C). 1998. per. 51.95 (0-7872-5174-7, 41517401) Kendall-Hunt.

***Media Law: Cases & Materials.** E. M. Barendt & Lesley Hitchens. LC 00-27283. (Law Ser.). 2000. write for info. (0-582-31719-3) Longman.

Media Law: 1997 Supplement. Rex S. Heinke. 1997. pap. 75.00 (1-57018-070-9, 1070) BNA Books.

Media Law & Regulation in the European Union: National Transnational, & U. S. Perspectives. Manny E. Paraschos. LC 97-30366. 288p. 1997. 44.95 (0-8138-2807-4) Iowa St U Pr.

Media Law Dictionary. John Murray. LC 78-63257. 1978. pap. text 18.50 (0-8191-0616-X) U Pr of Amer.

Media Law for Producers. 3rd ed. Philip Miller. LC 98-13926. 379p. 1998. pap. text 36.95 (0-240-80303-5, Focal) Buttrwrth-Heinemann.

Media Law in Illinois. James Tidwell. 112p. (C). 1992. pap. text 10.95 (0-913507-38-5) New Forums.

Media Law in Nevada. Tom Murphy & Barbara Cloud. (State Law Ser.). 74p. (C). 1992. pap. text 10.95 (0-913507-28-8) New Forums.

***Media Law in Tennessee.** 2nd rev. ed. Dorothy A. Bowles. 214p. (C). 1999. pap. text 18.95 (1-58107-022-5, Pub. by New Forums) Booksource.

Media Law in the PRC. Asia Law & Practice Staff. 250p. 1996. pap. 195.00 (962-7708-88-7) Am Educ Systs.

Media Literacy. W. James Potter. LC 97-33726. 1998. 61.50 (0-7619-0925-7); lib. bdg. write for info. (0-7619-0926-5) Sage.

Media Literacy: An Instructor's Manual. Art Silverblatt. 92p. 1995. pap. 4.95 (0-275-95220-7, Praeger Pubs) Greenwood.

Media Literacy: Keys to Interpreting Media Messages. Art Silverblatt. LC 94-22004. 352p. 1995. 69.50 (0-275-94830-7, Praeger Pubs); pap. 22.95 (0-275-94831-5, Praeger Pubs) Greenwood.

Media Literacy Handbook: An Educator's Guide to Bringing New Media into the Classroom. Cornelia Brunner & William Talley. LC 99-11339. 240p. 1999. pap. 14.00 (0-385-49614-1, Anchor NY) Doubleday.

Media Literacy in the Information Age: Current Perspectives. Ed. by Robert Kubey & Brent D. Ruben. (Information & Behavior Ser.: Vol. 6). 496p. (C). 1996. text 54.95 (1-56000-238-7) Transaction Pubs.

Media Literacy Through TV & Multimedia Production: A Mediated Course Book: Student Edition. Robert Kenny. 150p. 1999. pap., student ed. 18.00 (1-56308-726-X) Libs Unl.

Media Literacy Through TV & Multimedia Production: A Mediated Course Book: Teacher Edition. Robert Kenny. 150p. 1999. pap., teacher ed. 28.00 (1-56308-727-8) Libs Unl.

Media Log: A Guide to Film, Television & Radio Programs Supported by the National Endowment for the Humanities. 1995. lib. bdg. 255.95 (0-8490-6853-3) Gordon Pr.

Media-Made Dixie: The South in the American Imagination. rev. ed. Jack T. Kirby. LC 86-11236. (Illus.). 240p. 1986. reprint ed. pap. 14.95 (0-8203-0885-4) U of Ga Pr.

Media Madness: Public Images of Mental Illness. Otto F. Wahl. LC 95-6402. (Illus.). 220p. 1995. 25.95 (0-8135-2212-9) Rutgers U Pr.

Media Madness: Public Images of Mental Illness. Otto F. Wahl. (Illus.). 260p. 1997. pap. 17.00 (0-8135-2213-7) Rutgers U Pr.

Media Management: A Casebook Approach. Stephen Lacy et al. (Communication Textbook Journalism Subseries). 408p. 1993. pap. 32.50 (0-8058-1308-X); text 79.95 (0-8058-0659-8) L Erlbaum Assocs.

Media Management: A Casebook Approach. N. J. Rifon et al. (Communication Textbook Journalism Subseries). 28p. 1993. pap., teacher ed. write for info. (0-8058-1452-3) L Erlbaum Assocs.

Media Management: A Casebook Approach. 2nd ed. Ardyth B. Sohn et al. LC 98-23331. (Communication Ser.). 400p. 1998. pap. write for info. (0-8058-3026-X) L Erlbaum Assocs.

Media Management Library. Michael P. Smith et al. (Illus.). 292p. 1998. pap. 50.00 (0-9656018-5-4) NMC.

Media Management Review. Ed. by Charles Warner. 300p. (C). 1996. text 39.95 (0-8058-1787-5); pap. text 22.50 (0-8058-1788-3) L Erlbaum Assocs.

Media Mania! The Fundamentals & Futures of Removable Mass Storage Media. 2nd ed. Linda S. Kempster. (Illus.). 198p. 1995. pap. text 57.00 (1-879391-02-3) Avedon Assocs.

Media Manifestos: On the Technological Transmission of Cultural Forms. Regis Debray. LC 95-51442. 192p. (C). 1996. pap. 19.00 (1-85984-087-6, Pub. by Verso) Norton.

Media Maps & Myths. Gregg Hoffman. (Illus.). 141p. (Orig.). (C). 1993. pap. 15.00 (0-9637643-0-6) M & T Communs.

Media Marathon: A Twentieth-Century Memoir. Erik Barnouw. LC 95-35529. (Illus.). 280p. 1996. text 22.95 (0-8223-1728-1) Duke.

Media, Market & Democracy in China: Between the Party Line & the Bottom Line. Yuezhi Zhao. LC 97-21144. (The History of Communication Ser.). 272p. 1998. text 44.95 (0-252-02375-7); text 19.95 (0-252-06678-2) U of Ill Pr.

Media Mart: A Computer Activities Flow of Work Simulation. John Steffee et al. LC 96-37148. 1997. mass mkt. 23.95 (0-538-71813-7) S-W Pub.

Media Math. Robert W. Hall. (Illus.). 138p. 1988. pap. 14.95 (0-8442-3142-8, NTC Business Bks) NTC Contemp Pub Co.

Media Math. 2nd ed. Robert W. Hall. (Illus.). 192p. 1994. pap. 19.95 (0-8442-3128-2, NTC Business Bks) NTC Contemp Pub Co.

Media Matrix: Deepening the Context of Communication Studies. Scott T. Eastham. 136p. (Orig.). (C). 1990. lib. bdg. 32.00 (0-8191-7714-8) U Pr of Amer.

Media Matter: TV Use in Childhood & Adolescence. Karl E. Rosengren & Sven Windahl. Ed. by Brenda Dervin. LC 88-38458. (Communication & Information Science Ser.). 304p. (C). 1989. pap. 39.50 (0-89391-570-X); text 73.25 (0-89391-499-1) Ablx Pub.

Media Matters: Race & Gender in U. S. Politics. rev. ed. John Fiske. LC 94-8991. (Illus.). 320p. 1996. pap. 19.95 (0-8166-2463-1) U of Minn Pr.

Media-Mediated AIDS. Ed. by Linda K. Fuller. (Health Communication Ser.). 1999. text 59.50 (1-57273-263-6); pap. text 26.50 (1-57273-264-4) Hampton Pr NJ.

Media-Mediated Relationships: Straight & Gay, Mainstream & Alternative Perspectives. Linda K. Fuller. LC 95-14117. 324p. 1995. pap. 14.95 (1-56023-854-2) Haworth Pr.

Media-Mediated Relationships: Straight & Gay, Mainstream & Alternative Perspectives. Linda K. Fuller. LC 95-14117. (Illus.). 324p. 1995. 39.95 (1-56024-876-9) Haworth Pr.

Media Mental Distress. Ed. by Greg Philo. LC 96-9069. (Illus.). 135p. (C). 1997. pap. 21.20 (0-582-29219-0) Longman.

Media Mergers. Ed. by Nancy J. Woodhull & Robert W. Snyder. LC 97-23197. (Media Studies). 1997. pap. 21.95 (0-7658-0409-3) Transaction Pubs.

***Media Messages: What Film, Television & Popular Music Teach Us about Race, Class, Gender & Sexual Orientation.** Linda Holtzman. (Illus.). 384p. 2000. text 74.95 (0-7656-0336-5) M E Sharpe.

***Media Messages: What Film, Television, & Popular Music Teach Us about Race, Class, Gender, & Sexual Orientation.** Linda Holtzman. 2000. reprint ed. pap. 29.95 (0-7656-0337-3) M E Sharpe.

Media Messages in American Presidential Elections, 25. Diana Owen. LC 90-43384. (Contributions to the Study of Mass Media & Communications Ser.: No. 25). 216p. 1991. 55.00 (0-313-26362-0, OMD/, Greenwood Pr) Greenwood.

Media Meteorology. Aguado. 168p. 1999. pap., wbk. ed. 31.40 (0-13-210858-5) P-H.

Media, Minds & Men: A History of Media in Sweden. Bo Peterson. (Illus.). 366p. 1988. 71.00 (91-22-01206-0) Coronet Bks.

Media Mixes for Container Grown Plants. A. C. Bunt. (Illus.). 332p. 1988. pap. 129.95 (0-04-635016-0) Thomson Learn.

***Media Monopoly.** 6th ed. Ben H. Bagdikian. LC 00-21035. 2000. pap. 17.50 (0-8070-6179-4) Beacon Pr.

Media Mouse Collection of Awards & Incentives: For Media Centers & Libraries. Jan Grubb. (Illus.). 80p. (Orig.). (J). (gr. k-8). 1988. pap. text 9.95 (0-86530-043-7, IP 130-2) Incentive Pubns.

***Media-Multimedia-Omnimedia: Selected Papers from the CETaLL Symposium of the 11th AILA World Congress in Jyvaskla(Finland) & the Vth Man & the Media Symposium in Nancy (France)** Ed. by Udo O. H. Jung & Gabrielle Hogan-Brun. LC 99-12811. (Illus.). X, 220p. 1999. pap. text. write for info. (0-8204-3625-9) P Lang Pubng.

Media Mythologies. Barry Lowe. LC 95-142112. 196p. 1995. pap. 19.95 (0-86840-006-8, Pub. by New South Wales Univ Pr) Intl Spec Bk.

Media Myths & Narratives: Television & the Press. Ed. by James W. Carey. (Annual Reviews of Communication Research Ser.: Vol. 15). 270p. (C). 1987. text 58.00 (0-8039-3048-8); pap. text 26.00 (0-8039-3049-6) Sage.

Media, Myths, & Narratives: Television & the Press. Ed. by James W. Carey. LC 87-36962. (Sage Annual Reviews of Communication Research Ser.: No. 15). 264p. 1988. reprint ed. pap. 81.90 (0-608-01532-6, 205957600002) Bks Demand.

Media Myths, Children's Nightmares: Understanding Children's Emotional Responses to Television. David Buckingham. LC 95-30874. 320p. 1996. text 29.95 (0-7190-4596-7, Pub. by Manchester Univ Pr) St Martin.

Media Now: Communication in the Information Age. 2nd ed. Straubhaar. LC 99-26908. (Mass Communication). 512p. 1999. pap. 63.95 (0-534-54828-8) Wadsworth Pub.

Media of Conflict: War Reporting & Representations of Ethnic Violence. Allen & Seaton. 256p. 1999. pap. 25.00 (1-85649-570-1); text 65.00 (1-85649-569-8) Zed Books.

***Media of Mass Communication.** John Vivian. LC 00-26136. 496p. 2000. pap. text 40.00 (0-205-32261-1) Allyn.

Media of Mass Communication. 5th ed. (C). 1998. text. write for info. (0-205-29344-1, Longwood Div) Allyn.

***Media of Mass Communication.** 5th ed. 1999. cd-rom. write for info. (0-205-30897-X) Allyn.

***Media of Mass Communication.** 5th ed. John Vivian. LC 98-28087. 524p. 1998. pap. text 60.00 (0-205-28739-5) Allyn.

***Media of Mass Communication: A Media Literacy Guide.** 5th ed. 2000. write for info. (0-205-33310-9) Allyn.

***Media of Mass Communication Interactive Edition.** 2000. teacher ed. write for info. (0-205-33096-7) Allyn.

***Media Organisations in Society.** Ed. by James Curran. (An Arnold Publication). 256p. 2000. text 75.00 (0-340-72014-X); pap. text 19.95 (0-340-72015-8) OUP.

Media Performance: Mass Communication & the Public Interest. Denis McQuail. 352p. (C). 1992. text 65.00 (0-8039-8294-1); pap. text 21.95 (0-8039-8295-X) Sage.

Media Planning: A Practical Guide. 3rd ed. Jim Surmanek. LC 95-18554. 224p. 1995. pap. 17.95 (0-8442-3512-1, NTC Business Bks) NTC Contemp Pub Co.

Media Planning Workbook. 3rd ed. William Goodrich & Jack Z. Sissors. 272p. 1992. pap. text 14.95 (0-8442-3161-4, Natl Textbk Co) NTC Contemp Pub Co.

Media Planning Workbook: With Discussions & Problems. 5th ed. William B. Goodrich & Jack Z. Sissors. LC 95-39649. (Illus.). 206p. 1995. 19.95 (0-8442-3502-4, NTC Business Bks) NTC Contemp Pub Co.

Media Policy: An Introduction. David Hutchison. LC 98-8093. 256p. 1999. 62.95 (0-631-20433-4); pap. 32.95 (0-631-20434-2) Blackwell Pubs.

Media, Politics & Identity. Ed. by Brian Shoesmith. (Studies in Western Australian History: Vol. XV). pap. 20.00 (0-86422-397-8, Pub. by Univ of West Aust Pr) Intl Spec Bk.

Media Polls in American Politics. Ed. by Thomas E. Mann & Gary R. Orren. 172p. (C). 1992. 34.95 (0-8157-5456-6); pap. 14.95 (0-8157-5455-8) Brookings.

Media Post Media: Twenty Women Artists. Tricia Collins & Richard Milazzo. 54p. (Orig.). (C). 1988. pap. text. write for info. (0-945295-00-6) T Collins.

Media Power? Alison Cooper. LC 96-53429. (Viewpoints Ser.). (Illus.). 32p. (J). 1997. 20.00 (0-531-14452-6) Watts.

Media Power in Politics. 3rd ed. Ed. by Doris A. Graber. LC 93-30565. 439p. (YA). 1993. 31.95 (0-87187-785-6) Congr Quarterly.

***Media Power in Politics.** 4th ed. Doris A. Graber. LC 99-88687. 420p. 2000. pap. 33.95 (1-56802-416-9) CQ Pr.

Media Power Politics. David L. Paletz & Robert M. Entman. 304p. 1981. pap. 13.95 (0-685-03271-X) Macmillan.

***Media Power Professionals & Policies.** Howard Tumber. LC 99-54955. 304p. 2000. pap. 24.99 (0-415-19669-8) Routledge.

***Media Power Professionals & Policies.** Ed. by Howard Tumber. LC 99-54955. 352p. (C). 2000. text 75.00 (0-415-19668-X) Routledge.

Media, Process, & the Social Construction of Crime: Issues in Criminal Justice. Ed. by Gregg Barak. LC 93-39423. (Current Issues in Criminal Justice Ser.: Vol. 10). (Illus.). 344p. 1995. pap. text 24.95 (0-8153-1855-3, H1690) Garland.

Media Production Agreements. Philip Alberstat. LC 96-6431. 336p. (C). 1996. 85.00 (0-415-13668-7) Routledge.

Media Production for Business or Education. Valentine DelVecchio. (Illus.). 96p. 1994. 28.50 (0-9625749-3-7) Ref Desk Bks.

Media Productions & Computer Activities. Montgomery Walker. 225p. 1990. pap. text 24.95 (0-87436-568-6) ABC-CLIO.

Media Programs: District & School. American Association of School Librarians Staff. LC 74-32316. 136p. reprint ed. pap. 42.20 (0-7837-5918-5, 204571700007) Bks Demand.

Media Rants: Postpolitics in the Digital Nation. Jon Katz. LC 97-10195. 160p. 1997. pap. 13.95 (1-888869-12-7) Wired Bks.

Media Rare: Adventures of a Grass-Roots Newsman. Nat Boynton. (Illus.). 384p. (Orig.). 1988. pap. 12.95 (0-944593-20-8) Chandler Pr.

M

An Asterisk (*) at the beginning of an entry indicates that the title is appearing for the first time.

Media Ratings: Design, Use, & Consequences. Joel Federman. 120p. (Orig.). 1996. pap. write for info. (*1-889162-00-0*) Mediascope.

Media Reader. Ed. by Manuel Alvarado & John O. Thompson. (Illus.). 376p. 1990. 45.00 (*0-85170-258-9*, Pub. by British Film Inst); pap. 22.95 (*0-85170-259-7*, Pub. by British Film Inst) Ind U Pr.

Media-Reader: Perspectives on Mass Media Industries, Effects, & Issues. Shirley Biagi. 366p. (C). 1989. pap. write for info. (*0-534-08955-0*) Wadsworth Pub.

Media-Reader: Perspectives on Mass Media Industries, Effects, & Issues. 2nd ed. Shirley Biagi. 340p. (C). 1993. mass mkt. 25.75 (*0-534-19086-3*) Wadsworth Pub.

***Media Regulation, Public Interest & the Law.** Mike Feintuck. LC 99-488260. 240p. 1999. pap. text 29.00 (*0-7486-0997-0*, Pub. by Edinburgh U Pr) Col U Pr.

Media Relations: Publicizing Your Efforts: Understanding & Getting Exposure in the Media see Communications Series

***Media Relations: The Good, the Blah & the Ugly.** International Festivals & Events Assoc. Staff. 72p. 1999. pap. 44.95 (*1-891202-10-3*) Intl Festivals.

Media Relations for Local Governments: Communicating for Results. Lydia Bjornlund. LC 97-138025. 106p. (Orig.). 1996. pap. text 60.00 (*0-87326-117-8*, 42093) Intl City-Cnty Mgt.

Media Relations in Your Spare Time: A Step-by-Step Guide for Anyone in Business. Laura Brown. 65p. 1995. 37.50 (*0-9630335-2-2*) Natl Assoc Mfrs.

Media Relations Strategies During Emergencies: A Crisis Communication Management Guide. 3rd rev. ed. James E. Lukaszewski. (Crisis Communication Management Ser.: No. 4). 100p. 2000. ring bd. write for info. (*1-883291-27-5*) Lukaszewski.

***Media, Religion & Politics in Pakistan.** Shakil Akhtar. 300p. 2000. text 24.95 (*0-19-579174-6*) OUP.

Media Research: Technology, Art, Communication. Ed. & Comment by Michel A. Moos. (Critical Voices Ser.). 160p. 1997. text 23.00 (*90-5701-091-7*); pap. text 18.00 (*90-5701-081-X*) Gordon & Breach.

Media Research Techniques. Arthur A. Berger. (Illus.). 160p. 1991. 42.00 (*0-8039-4179-X*); pap. 18.95 (*0-8039-4180-3*) Sage.

Media Research Techniques. 2nd ed. Arthur A. Berger. LC 97-45406. 175p. 1998. write for info. (*0-7619-1536-2*); pap. write for info. (*0-7619-1537-0*) Sage.

Media Resource Directory. 90p. 8.75 (*0-318-13282-6*); pap. 10.95 (*0-318-13281-8*, MDMRP) Am Soc Train & Devel.

Media Resource Guide. 5th ed. Ed. by David A. McElwee et al. (Illus.). 108p. 1987. pap. 10.00 (*0-910755-05-1*) Foun Am Comm.

Media Review Digest Vol. 24: The Only Complete Guide to Reviews of Non-Print Media, 1994. 942p. 1994. 245.00 (*0-87650-337-7*) Pierian.

Media Review Digest Vol. 25: The Only Complete Guide to Reviews of Non-Print Media, 1995. 1995. 245.00 (*0-87650-317-2*) Pierian.

Media Review Digest, 1980, Vol. 10, 1980. Ed. by C. Edward Wall et al. LC 73-173772. 1981. 245.00 (*0-87650-129-3*) Pierian.

Media Review Digest, 1988: The Only Complete Guide to Reviews of Non-Print Media, Vol. 18. Ed. by C. Edward Wall et al. LC 73-173772. 1989. 145.00 (*0-87650-232-X*) Pierian.

Media Review Digest, 1985: The Only Complete Guide to Reviews of Non-Print Media, Vol 15. Ed. by C. Edward Wall et al. LC 73-173772. 1986. 245.00 (*0-87650-222-2*) Pierian.

Media Review Digest, 1984: The Only Complete Guide to Reviews of Non-Print Media, Vol. 14. Ed. by C. Edward Wall et al. LC 73-173772. 1985. 145.00 (*0-87650-198-6*) Pierian.

Media Review Digest, 1989: The Only Complete Guide to Reviews of Non-Print Media, Vol. 19. Ed. by C. Edward Wall et al. LC 73-173772. 1990. 245.00 (*0-87650-233-8*) Pierian.

Media Review Digest, 1981: The Only Complete Guide to Reviews of Non-Print Media, Vol. 11. Ed. by C. Edward Wall et al. LC 73-173772. 1981. 145.00 (*0-87650-135-8*) Pierian.

Media Review Digest, 1987: The Only Complete Guide to Reviews of Non-Print Media, Vol. 17. Ed. by C. Edward Wall et al. LC 73-173772. 1988. 145.00 (*0-87650-231-1*) Pierian.

Media Review Digest, 1986: The Only Complete Guide to Reviews of Non-Print Media, Vol. 16. Ed. by C. Edward Wall et al. LC 73-173772. 1987. 145.00 (*0-87650-230-3*) Pierian.

Media Review Digest, 1983: The Only Complete Guide to Reviews of Non-Print Media, Vol. 13. Ed. by C. Edward Wall et al. LC 73-173772. 1984. 145.00 (*0-87650-178-1*) Pierian.

Media Review Digest, 1982: The Only Complete Guide to Reviews of Non-Print Media, Vol. 12. Ed. by C. Edward Wall et al. LC 73-173772. 1982. 145.00 (*0-87650-148-X*) Pierian.

Media Review Digest, 1990: The Only Complete Guide to Reviews of Non-Print Media, Vol. 20. Ed. by C. Edward Wall et al. LC 73-173772. 1991. 245.00 (*0-87650-208-7*) Pierian.

Media Review Digest, 1998 Vol. 28: The Only Complete Guide to Reviews of Non-Print Media. Ed. by C. Edward Wall et al. 1998. 255.00 (*0-87650-353-9*) Pierian.

***Media Review Digest, 1999 Vol. 29: The Only Complete Guide to Reviews of Non-Print Media.** Ed. by C. Edward Wall. 1999. 255.00 (*0-87650-380-6*) Pierian.

Media Review Digest, 1991: The Only Complete Guide to Reviews of Non-Print Media, Vol. 21. Ed. by C. Edward Wall et al. LC 73-173772. 1992. 245.00 (*0-87650-207-9*) Pierian.

Media Review Digest, 1997 Vol. 27: The Only Complete Guide to Reviews of Non-Print Media. Ed. by C. Edward Wall et al. 1997. 245.00 (*0-87650-350-4*) Pierian.

Media Review Digest, 1996: The Only Complete Guide to Reviews of Non-Print Media, Vol. 26. C. Edward Wall. LC 73-173772. 1996. 245.00 (*0-87650-324-5*) Pierian.

Media Review Digest, 1993: The Only Complete Guide to Reviews of Non-Print Media, Vol. 23. Ed. by C. Edward Wall et al. LC 73-173772. 1993. 245.00 (*0-87650-310-5*) Pierian.

Media Review Digest, 1992: The Only Complete Guide to Reviews of Non-Print Media, Vol. 22. Ed. by C. Edward Wall et al. LC 73-173772. 1992. 245.00 (*0-87650-306-7*) Pierian.

Media Review Digest, 1978: The Only Complete Guide to Reviews of Non-Print Media, Vol. 8. Ed. by C. Edward Wall et al. LC 73-173772. 1978. 145.00 (*0-87650-095-5*) Pierian.

Media Review Digest, 1975-76, 2. C. Edward Wall. LC 73-173772. 1976. write for info. (*0-87650-079-3*) Pierian.

Media Review Digest, 1975-76: The Only Complete Guide to Reviews of Non-Book Media, 1. C. Edward Wall. LC 73-173772. 1976. 145.00 (*0-87650-076-9*) Pierian.

Media Review Digest, 1974-75, 2. Ed. by C. Edward Wall et al. LC 73-173772. 1975. write for info. (*0-87650-066-1*) Pierian.

Media Review Digest, 1974-75: The Only Complete Guide to Reviews of Non-Print Media, 1. Ed. by C. Edward Wall et al. LC 73-173772. 1995. write for info. (*0-87650-065-3*) Pierian.

Media Review Digest, 1979, Vol. 9. 1979. Ed. by C. Edward Wall et al. LC 73-173772. 1979. 245.00 (*0-87650-101-3*) Pierian.

Media Review Digest, 1977, Vol. 7. Ed. by C. Edward Wall et al. LC 73-173772. 1977. 245.00 (*0-87650-085-8*) Pierian.

Media Review Digest, 1973-74, Vol. 4. Ed. by C. Edward Wall et al. LC 73-173772. 1974. text 85.00 (*0-87650-059-9*) Pierian.

***Media Review Digest 2000 Vol. 30: The Only Complete Guide to Reviews of Non-Print Media.** Ed. by C. Edward Wall. 900p. 2000. 255.00 (*0-87650-384-9*) Pierian.

Media Revolution in America & Western Europe. Ed. by Everett Rogers et al. LC 84-21680. (Communication & Information Science Ser.). 352p. 1985. text 78.50 (*0-89391-258-1*) Ablx Pub.

Media Revolution of Early Christianity: An Essay on Eusebius's "Ecclesiastical History" Doron Mendels. 269p. 1999. pap. 24.00 (*0-8028-4610-6*) Eerdmans.

Media Ritual & Identity. Tamar Liebes & James Curran. LC 97-45502. (Communication & Society Ser.). (Illus.). 280p. (C). 1998. 75.00 (*0-415-15991-1*) Routledge.

Media, Ritual, & Identity. Tamar Liebes et al. LC 97-45502. (Communication & Society Ser.). 296p. (C). 1998. pap. 24.99 (*0-415-15992-X*) Routledge.

Media Scandals: Morality & Desire in the Popular Culture Marketplace. James Lull. LC 97-22261. 270p. 1997. pap. 18.50 (*0-231-11165-7*) Col U Pr.

Media Scandals: Morality & Desire in the Popular Culture Marketplace. James Lull. LC 97-22261. 270p. 1998. 47.50 (*0-231-11164-9*) Col U Pr.

Media Science Before the Great War. Brooks. LC 96-7159. 220p. 1996. text 55.00 (*0-312-16019-4*) St Martin.

Media Semiotics. Bignell. LC 96-34390. 1997. pap. 19.95 (*0-7190-4501-0*); text 69.95 (*0-7190-4500-2*) St Martin.

Media Sense: The Folklore-Popular Culture Continuum. Ed. by Peter Narvaez & Martin Laba. LC 86-70527. 168p. 1986. 18.95 (*0-87972-343-2*) Bowling Green Univ Popular Press.

Media Services Technician. Jack Rudman. (Career Examination Ser.: C-3181). 1994. pap. 29.95 (*0-8373-3181-1*) Nat Learn.

Media, Sex & the Adolescent. Bradley S. Greenberg et al. Ed. by Lee Becker. LC 92-24164. (Communication Series: Mass Communications & Journalism). 376p. (C). 1993. text 75.00 (*1-881303-36-5*); pap. text 29.50 (*1-881303-37-3*) Hampton Pr NJ.

Media Show: The Changing Face of the News, 1985-1990. Edwin Diamond. (Illus.). 244p. 1991. 27.50 (*0-262-04125-1*) MIT Pr.

Media Skills for Middle Schools: Strategies for Library Media Specialists & Teachers. 2nd ed. Lucille W. Van Vliet. LC 98-33898. (Library & Information Problem-Solving Skills Ser.). 260p. 1998. pap. 28.00 (*1-56308-551-8*) Teacher Ideas Pr.

Media Skills Puzzlers. Ruth Toor & Hilda K. Weisburg. 126p. 1984. 20.00 (*0-931315-00-X*) Lib Learn Res.

Media, Social Science, & Social Policy for Children. Ed. by Eli A. Rubenstein et al. LC 83-1393. (Child & Family Policy Ser.: Vol. 5). 256p. 1985. text 73.25 (*0-89391-229-8*) Ablx Pub.

Media Society: Industries, Images & Audiences. David Croteau & William Hoynes. LC 96-45372. 1997. 29.95 (*0-8039-9065-0*) Pine Forge.

Media Sociology: A Reader. Jeremy Tunstall. LC 77-125598. (Sociology & Social Welfare Ser.). (Illus.). 584p. reprint ed. pap. 181.10 (*0-8357-6205-X*, 203446500090) Bks Demand.

Media Specialist. Jack Rudman. (Career Examination Ser.: C-2894). 1994. pap. 29.95 (*0-8373-2894-2*) Nat Learn.

Media Specialist - Library & Audio-Visual Services (Library Media Specialist) Jack Rudman. (National Teacher Examination Ser.: NT-29). 1994. pap. 23.95 (*0-8373-8439-7*) Nat Learn.

Media Spectacles. Ed. by Marjorie Garber et al. LC 93-3460. 288p. (C). (gr. 13). 1993. pap. 21.99 (*0-415-90751-9*, B0282) Routledge.

Media, Sports, & Society: Foundations for the Communication of Sport. Lawrence A. Wenner. 320p. (C). 1989. text 44.00 (*0-8039-3243-X*) Sage.

Media, State & Nation: Political Violence & Collective Identities. Philip Schlesinger. (Media, Culture & Society Ser.). 240p. (C). 1991. 55.00 (*0-8039-8503-7*); pap. 25.95 (*0-8039-8504-5*) Sage.

Media Student's Book. 2nd ed. Gill Branston. LC 98-42027. 1999. 85.00 (*0-415-17307-8*) Routledge.

***Media Student's Book** 2nd ed. Gill Branston & Roy Stafford. LC 98-42027. 1999. pap. write for info. (*0-415-17308-6*) Routledge.

Media Studies. Brenda Downes & Steve Miller. (Illus.). 192p. 1998. pap. 14.95 (*0-8442-0036-0*, 00360, Teach Yrslf) NTC Contemp Pub Co.

***Media Studies.** 2nd ed. Paul Marris & Sue Thornham. LC 99-55968. 2000. pap. text 29.50 (*0-8147-5647-6*) NYU Pr.

Media Studies: A Reader. Ed. by Paul Marris & Sue Thornham. 544p. Date not set. pap. 24.50 (*0-7486-0778-1*, Pub. by Edinburgh U Pr) Col U Pr.

Media Studies: Ethnomethodological Approaches. Ed. by Paul L. Jalbert. LC 98-45628. (Studies in Ethnomethodology & Conversation Analysis). 304p. 1999. 54.00 (*0-7618-1286-5*) U Pr of Amer.

***Media Studies: Ethnomethodological Approaches.** Ed. by Paul L. Jalbert. LC 98-45628. (Studies in Ethnomethodology & Conversation Analysis). 304p. 1999. pap. 34.50 (*0-7618-1287-3*) U Pr of Amer.

Media Studies: Texts, Institutions & Audiences. Lisa Taylor & Andrew Willis. LC 98-30067. 368p. 1999. 59.95 (*0-631-20026-6*); pap. 29.95 (*0-631-20027-4*) Blackwell Pubs.

Media Studies Book: A Guide for Teachers. Ed. by David Lusted. (Comedia Bk.). 242p. (C). 1991. pap. 22.99 (*0-415-01461-1*) Routledge.

Media Studies Reader. Ed. by Tim O'Sullivan & Yvonne Jewkes. LC 97-208. (An Arnold Publication). 480p. 1997. text 65.00 (*0-340-64526-1*); pap. text 19.95 (*0-340-64547-4*) OUP.

Media Teaching. Dan Fleming. (Illus.). 304p. 1993. pap. 26.95 (*0-631-18706-5*) Blackwell Pubs.

Media Technology & Society: A History from the Telegraph to the Internet. Brian Winston. LC 97-34781. 424p. (C). 1998. pap. 24.99 (*0-415-14230-X*) Routledge.

Media Technology & Society: A History from the Telegraph to the Internet. Brian Winston. LC 97-34781. (Illus.). 392p. (C). 1998. 85.00 (*0-415-14229-6*) Routledge.

Media Technology Road to Democracy & Equality. Donna Allen. (Toward a Radical Restructuring of the Communication Media Ser.: Vol. 5). (Illus.). 28p. (Orig.). 1995. pap. 5.00 (*0-930470-17-6*) Womens Inst Free Press.

Media Texts: Authors & Readers. Ed. by David Graddol & Oliver Boyd-Barrett. 208p. 1993. 74.95 (*1-85359-220-X*, Pub. by Multilingual Matters); pap. 29.95 (*1-85359-219-6*, Pub. by Multilingual Matters) Taylor & Francis.

Media, the Learner & Intellectual Freedom: A Handbook. AECT Intellectual Freedom Commitee. (Orig.). 1979. pap. 8.95 (*0-89240-034-X*) Assn Ed Comm Tech.

Media, the President, & Public Opinion: A Longitudinal Analysis of the Drug Issue, 1984-1991. William J. Gonzenbach. (LEA's Communication Ser.). 136p. 1995. pap. 17.50 (*0-8058-1690-9*); text 34.50 (*0-8058-1689-5*) L Erlbaum Assocs.

Media Therapy - The Good, the Bad, & the Ugly: Television Talk Shows in the Age of Advice. unabridged ed. Clinton Weyand. Ed. by George Morrera & Arthur Lerner. 190p. (Orig.). 1996. pap. 18.00 (*0-938292-16-1*) Being Bks.

Media-tions: Forays into the Culture & Gender Wars. Elayne Rapping. 286p. (C). 1994. pap. 15.00 (*0-89608-478-7*) South End Pr.

Media-tions: Forays into the Culture & Gender Wars. Elayne Rapping. 286p. (C). 1994. lib. bdg. 30.00 (*0-89608-479-5*) South End Pr.

***Media Today: An Introduction to Mass Communication.** Joseph Turow. LC 98-72089. xviii, 490 p. 1999. write for info. (*0-395-87077-1*) HM.

Media Use As Social Action. Lutton Staff. 1997. pap. 49.95 (*0-86196-485-3*, Pub. by J Libbey Med) Bks Intl VA.

Media Use in the Information Age: Emerging Patterns of Adoption & Consumer Use. Ed. by J. L. Salvaggio & Jennings Bryant. 344p. 1989. 69.95 (*0-89859-968-7*) L Erlbaum Assocs.

Media Utilization for the Development of Women & Children. Ed. by S. P. Agrawal. (C). 1989. 23.00 (*81-7022-249-4*, Pub. by Concept) S Asia.

Media Violence. Laurie Beckelman. LC 98-23178. (You Decide! Ser.). (J). 1999. lib. bdg. 13.95 (*0-382-39351-1*, Crstwood Hse) Silver Burdett Pr.

Media Violence. William Dudley. LC 98-22828. (Opposing Viewpoints Ser.). 186p. 1999. lib. bdg. 167.68 (*1-56510-945-7*) Greenhaven.

***Media Violence: Opposing Viewpoints.** William Dudley. LC 98-22828. (Opposing Viewpoints Ser.). 186p. 1999. pap. 103.68 (*1-56510-944-9*) Greenhaven.

Media Virus! Douglas Rushkoff. 368p. 1996. pap. 12.00 (*0-345-39774-6*) Ballantine Pub Grp.

Media-Wise Family. Ted Baehr. LC 97-29005. 350p. 1998. 10.99 (*0-7814-0301-4*, Victor Bks) Chariot Victor.

Media with Microstructures & Wave Propagation: Proceedings of the Conference, Houghton, MI, January 1983. Ed. by E. C. Aifantis & L. W. Davison. 260p. 1985. pap. 130.00 (*0-08-031661-1*, Pergamon Pr) Elsevier.

Media Without Democracy & What to Do about It. Donna Allen. 1991. 5.00 (*0-930470-15-X*) Womens Inst Free Press.

Media Wizards: A Behind-the-Scenes Look at Media Manipulation. Catherine Gourley. LC 99-17741. 128p. (YA). (gr. 5 up). 1999. lib. bdg. 24.90 (*0-7613-0967-5*) TFC Bks NY.

Media Worlds. Schwartz. 1997. pap. 19.50 (*0-85315-837-1*, Pub. by Lawrence & Wishart) NYU Pr.

Media Worlds in the Postjournalism Era. David L. Altheide & Robert P. Snow. (Communication & Social Order Ser.). 287p. 1991. pap. text 26.95 (*0-202-30377-2*); lib. bdg. 51.95 (*0-202-30376-4*) Aldine de Gruyter.

Media Writer. Arnold. 1995. teacher ed., wbk. ed. 13.43 (*0-697-29406-4*, WCB McGr Hill) McGrw-H Hghr Educ.

Media Writer: Computer Lessons Newswriter. Fred Fedler. (C). 1993. 36.50 (*0-15-501269-X*, Pub. by Harcourt Coll Pubs) Harcourt.

Media Writer's Guide: Writing for Business & Educational Programming. William J. Van Nostran. LC 99-26484. 352p. 1999. pap. 34.95 (*0-240-80316-7*) Buttrwrth-Heinemann.

Media Writer's Handbook. George T. Arnold. 100p. (C). 1996. text 12.50 (*0-697-29405-6*) Brown & Benchmark.

Media Writer's Handbook: A Guide to Common Writing & Editing Problems. 2nd ed. George T. Arnold. LC 99-25514. 288p. 1999. pap. 30.00 (*0-697-35501-2*) McGraw.

Media Writing. Doug Newsom. Ed. by James A. Wollert. LC 99-21130. 373p. (C). 1999. pap. text 51.00 (*0-321-01137-6*) Addson-Wesley Educ.

Media Writing: News for the Mass Media. Doug Newsom & James A. Wollert. 437p. (C). 1984. pap. write for info. (*0-534-03969-3*) Wadsworth Pub.

***Media Writing Handbook: Guidelines for Radio, Tv & Film Scripts & Academic Papers.** Califonia St. University Staff. 42p. (C). 1999. spiral bd. 13.95 (*0-7872-6375-3*, 41637501) Kendall-Hunt.

Mediacion para la Ninez, Grade 4-7. Fran Schmidt et al. Tr. by Yvonne W. Sepulveda. (SPA., Illus.). 68p. (Orig.). 1995. pap. text, teacher ed. 23.95 (*1-878227-35-1*) Peace Educ.

Medical Imaging, 1997 Vol. 3037: Ultrasonic Transducer Engineering. Ed. by K. Kirk Shung. LC 97-175332. 220p. 1997. 59.00 (*0-8194-2448-X*) SPIE.

Mediae Latinitatis Lexicon Minus. J. F. Niermeyer. LC 92-42558. (ENG, FRE & LAT.). xvi, 1138p. 1993. reprint ed. 209.00 (*90-04-07108-3*) Brill Academic Pubs.

***Mediaeval Scandinavia 13.** Ed. by Tore Nyberg & Hans Bekker-Nielsen. 300p. 2000. 35.75 (*87-7838-453-2*, Pub. by Odense Universitets Forlag) Intl Spec Bk.

Mediaeval & Modern Coins in the Athenian Agora. Fred S. Kleiner. (Excavations of the Athenian Agora Picture Bks.: No. 18). (Illus.). 32p. 1978. pap. 3.00 (*87661-618-X*) Am Sch Athens.

Mediaeval Antiquity. Ed. by Andries Welkenhuysen et al. (Mediaevalia Lovaniensia, Series I: Vol. XXIV). (ENG, FRE & ITA.). 389p. (Orig.). 1995. pap. 99.50 (*90-6186-693-6*, Pub. by Leuven Univ) Coronet Bks.

Mediaeval Art: From the Peace of the Church to the Eve of the Renaissance, 312-1350. William R. Lethaby. LC 70-157345. (Select Bibliographies Reprint Ser.). 1977. reprint ed. 30.95 (*0-8369-5806-3*) Ayer.

Mediaeval Artist at Work. Virginia W. Egbert. LC 67-12344. (Illus.). 94p. reprint ed. pap. 30.00 (*0-608-11172-4*, 205101000071) Bks Demand.

Mediaeval Cambridgeshire. Henry C. Darby. (Cambridge Town, Gown & County Ser.: Vol. 15). (Illus.). 1977. pap. 5.95 (*0-900891-11-4*) Oleander Pr.

Mediaeval Church Architecture of England. Charles H. Moore. LC 74-37900. (Select Bibliographies Reprint Ser.). 1977. reprint ed. 21.95 (*0-8369-6738-0*) Ayer.

Mediaeval Church Vaulting. Clarence Ward. LC 72-177847. reprint ed. 42.50 (*0-404-06836-7*) AMS Pr.

Mediaeval Deccan History. Ed. by A. R. Kulkarni et al. (C). 1996. 48.00 (*81-7154-579-3*, Pub. by Popular Prakashan) S Asia.

Mediaeval Dimension in Shakespeare's Plays. Ed. by Peter S. Milward. LC 90-31081. (Studies in Renaissance Literature: Vol. 7). 156p. 1990. lib. bdg. 69.95 (*0-88946-116-3*) E Mellen.

Mediaeval England, 1066-1350. Mary Bateson. LC 70-152973. (Select Bibliographies Reprint Ser.). 1977. reprint ed. 35.95 (*0-8369-5725-3*) Ayer.

Mediaeval Feudalism. Carl Stephenson. (Illus.). 127p. 1956. pap. text 7.95 (*0-8014-9013-8*) Cornell U Pr.

Mediaeval French Literature. Gaston B. Paris. LC 78-154160. (Select Bibliographies Reprint Ser.). 1977. reprint ed. 19.95 (*0-8369-5776-8*) Ayer.

Mediaeval Gardens. Frank Crisp. LC 67-4273. (Illus.). 1979. lib. bdg. 90.00 (*0-87817-007-3*) Hacker.

Mediaeval Germany, 911-1250: Essays by German Historians, 2 vols., Set. Tr. by Geoffrey Barraclough. LC 75-41019. (BCL Ser. II). reprint ed. 49.50 (*0-404-14800-X*) AMS Pr.

Mediaeval Greece. Nicolas Cheetham. LC 80-13559. 351p. reprint ed. pap. 108.90 (*0-7837-2500-0*, 208021000003) Bks Demand.

Mediaeval Greek Bookhands: Examples Selected from Greek Manuscripts in Oxford Libraries, 2 vols. in 1. Nigel Wilson. LC 95-77237. (Medieval Academy Bks.: No. 81). (Illus.). 38p. 1995. reprint ed. pap. 40.00 (*0-910956-55-3*, MAB 81) Medieval Acad.

Mediaeval Humanism in the Life & Writings of John of Salisbury, with an Epilogue: John of Salisbury & the School of Chartres. Hans Liebeshutz. (Warburg Institute Studies: Vol. 17). 1969. reprint ed. pap. 50.00 (*0-8115-1392-0*) Periodicals Srv.

Mediaeval India: Under Mohammed Rule. Stanley Lane-Poole. 1990. reprint ed. 12.50 (*0-8364-2517-0*, Pub. by Low Price) S Asia.

An Asterisk (*) at the beginning of an entry indicates that the title is appearing for the first time.

Mediaeval India from the Mohammedan Conquest to the Reign of Akbar the Great. Stanley Lane-Poole. LC 72-14391. (History of India Ser.: No. 3). reprint ed. 110.00 (*0-404-09003-6*) AMS Pr.

*__Mediaeval Inscriptions of Vanstan, Armenia, Vol. 2.__ Ashkharbek Kalantar. (Civilisations du Proche-Orient Ser.). xxii, 94p. 1999. pap. text 94.00 (*2-940032-11-4*, Pub. by Recherches et Pubns) Eisenbrauns.

Mediaeval Italy from Charlemagne to Henry Seventh. Pasquale Villari. Tr. by C. Hulton. LC 73-153608. (Illus.). reprint ed. 47.50 (*0-404-09279-9*) AMS Pr.

Mediaeval Latin Versions of the Aristotelian Scientific Corpus: With Special Reference to the Biological Works. S. D. Wingate. (Medieval Studies). reprint ed. lib. bdg. 40.00 (*0-697-00023-0*) Irvington.

Mediaeval Liar: A Catalogue of the Insolubilia - Literature. Paul V. Spade. 137p. pap. text 18.29 (*0-88844-354-4*) Brill Academic Pubs.

Mediaeval Mind: A History of the Development of Thought & Emotion in the Middle Ages, 2 vols., 1. 4th ed. Henry O. Taylor. LC CB0351.T3. 623p. 1925. reprint ed. pap. 193.20 (*0-7837-4892-2*, 205905900001) Bks Demand.

Mediaeval Mind: A History of the Development of Thought & Emotion in the Middle Ages, 2 vols., 2. Henry O. Taylor. LC CB0351.T3. 628p. 1925. reprint ed. pap. 194.70 (*0-7837-4893-0*, 205905900002) Bks Demand.

Mediaeval Musical Relics of Denmark. Angul Hammerich. LC 74-24104. reprint ed. 45.00 (*0-404-12952-8*) AMS Pr.

*__Mediaeval Nativity.__ Der Meer Ron Van. 1999. 15.95 (*90-76048-20-7*) Abbeville Pr.

Mediaeval Philosophical Texts in Translation, 34 vols., Set. pap. write for info. (*0-87462-200-X*) Marquette.

Mediaeval Reactions to the Encounter Between Faith . . . John F. Wippel. LC 94-74397. (Aquinas Lectures: No. 59). 110p. (C). 1995. 15.00 (*0-87462-162-3*) Marquette.

Mediaeval Rhodesia. David Randall-McIver. 106p. 1971. reprint ed. 45.00 (*0-7146-1885-3*, Pub. by F Cass Pubs) Intl Spec Bk.

Mediaeval Russian Churches. Samuel H. Cross. (Medieval Academy Bks.: No. 53). 1949. 25.00 (*0-910956-27-8*) Medieval Acad.

Mediaeval Slavic Manuscripts: A Bibliography of Printed Catalogues. Ed. by David Djaparidze. LC 57-9659. (Medieval Academy Bks.: No. 64). 1957. 20.00 (*0-910956-38-3*) Medieval Acad.

Mediaeval Society. Sidney Painter. 107p. 1951. pap. text 8.95 (*0-8014-9850-3*) Cornell U Pr.

Mediaeval Spanish Allegory. Chandler R. Post. (Harvard Studies in Comparative Literature: No. 4). xii, 351p. 1971. reprint ed. 50.70 (*3-487-04058-1*) G Olms Pubs.

Mediaeval Stage. unabridged ed. Edmund K. Chambers. LC 96-14913. (Illus.). 960p. 1996. reprint ed. pap. text 19.95 (*0-486-29229-0*) Dover.

Mediaeval Tales (1884) Henry Morley. 260p. 1998. reprint ed. pap. 17.95 (*0-7661-0162-2*) Kessinger Pub.

Mediaeval Tournament. R. Coltman Clephan. LC 94-47975. (Illus.). 240p. 1995. pap. text 11.95 (*0-486-28620-7*) Dover.

Mediaevelism to Modernism: Socio Economic & Cultural History of Hyderabad, 1869-1911. Sheela Raj. (C). 1987. 36.00 (*0-86132-143-X*, Pub. by Popular Prakashan) S Asia.

MediaGuide, 1988: A Critical Review of the Print Media. 3rd ed. Ed. by Jude Wanniski. LC 87-92220. 432p. (Orig.). 1988. pap. 17.95 (*0-938081-01-2*) Polyconomics.

Mediaguide, 1990: A Critical Guide of the Media. Jude Wanniski. 34.95 (*0-938081-06-3*); pap. 19.95 (*0-938081-07-1*) Polyconomics.

MediaGuide, 1992: A Critical Review of the Media. 7th ed. Ed. by Jude Wanniski. 672p. 1992. 39.95 (*0-938081-09-8*); pap. 29.95 (*0-938081-11-X*) Polyconomics.

Media/Impact: An Introduction to Mass Media. 3rd rev. ed. Shirley Biagi. LC 97-14636. (Mass Communication Ser.). (C). 1997. pap. 40.50 (*0-534-50482-5*) Wadsworth Pub.

Medial Geniculate Body of the Cat. J. A. Winer. (Advances in Anatomy, Embryology & Cell Biology Ser.: Vol. 86). (Illus.). 110p. 1985. 42.50 (*0-387-13254-6*) Spr-Verlag.

*__Mediale Textvielfalt und Handlungskompetenz im Fremdsprachenunterricht: Zu Ehren Wilfried Gienows.__ Gabriele Blell & Brigitte Kruck. 238p. 1999. 39.95 (*3-631-34458-9*) P Lang Pubng.

Mediamaker Handbook: The Ultimate Guide for the Independent Producer. Ed. by Karen Weiner & Tamara Gould. (Illus.). 255p. 1997. spiral bd. 35.00 (*0-9662317-0-8*) Bay Area Video.

Mediamaking: Mass Media in a Popular Culture. Lawrence Grossber et al. LC 98-8875. 442p. 1998. 65.00 (*0-7619-1176-6*); pap. 29.95 (*0-7619-1177-4*) Sage.

Mediamerica: Form, Content & Consequence of Mass Communication. 3rd ed. Edward J. Whetmore. 374p. (C). 1984. pap. write for info. (*0-534-03390-3*) Wadsworth Pub.

Mediamerica: Form, Content, & Consequence of Mass Communication. 3rd ed. Edward J. Whetmore. 374p. (C). 1986. pap. write for info. (*0-534-06804-9*) Wadsworth Pub.

Mediamerica: Form, Content, & Consequence of Mass Communication. 4th ed. Edward J. Whetmore. 411p. (C). 1988. pap. write for info. (*0-534-09522-4*) Wadsworth Pub.

Mediamerica: Form, Content, & Consequence of Mass Communication. 4th ed. Edward J. Whetmore. 411p. (C). 1990. pap. write for info. (*0-534-15282-1*) Wadsworth Pub.

Mediamerica: Updated Edition. 4th ed. Whetmore. (Mass Communication Ser.). 1992. pap., teacher ed. write for info. (*0-534-15283-X*) Wadsworth Pub.

Mediamerica, Mediaworld: Form, Content, & Consequence of Mass Communication. 5th rev. ed. Edward J. Whetmore. LC 94-45388. 492p. 1995. pap. 60.95 (*0-534-25818-2*) Wadsworth Pub.

Mediamobiles: Views from the Road. fac. ed. Ed. by Don Roberts & Dierdre Boyle. LC 79-18488. (Public Library Reporter: No. 19). 126p. 1994. pap. 39.10 (*0-7837-7321-8*, 204724800007) Bks Demand.

Mediamorphosis: Understanding New Media. Roger F. Fidler. LC 96-52540. (Journalism & Communication for a New Century Ser.). 1997. 25.95 (*0-8039-9086-3*) Pine Forge.

Median Line. William Haggard. (Orig.). 19.95 (*0-88411-678-6*) Amereon Ltd.

Median Longitudinal Cervical Somatotomy. A. Pansini. (Illus.). 158p. 1986. text 71.00 (*88-299-0382-5*, Pub. by Piccin Nuova) Gordon & Breach.

Median Longitudinal Cervical Somatotomy. A. Pansini & P. Conti. 158p. 1986. text 64.00 (*1-57235-044-X*) Piccin Nuova.

Median Village & Fremont Culture Regional Variation. John P. Marwitt. (Utah Anthropological Papers: No. 95). reprint ed. 24.00 (*0-404-60695-4*) AMS Pr.

Median Village & Fremont Culture Regional Variation. John P. Marwitt. LC 73-623166. (University of Utah, Anthropological Papers: No. 95). (Illus.). 207p. reprint ed. pap. 64.20 (*0-8357-6852-X*, 203554800095) Bks Demand.

*__Mediapolis: Aspects of Texts, Hypertexts, & Multimedial Communication.__ Sam Inkinen. LC 98-33275. x, 388p. 1999. 147.10 (*3-11-016141-9*) De Gruyter.

*__Mediapolitik: How the Mass Media Have Transformed World Politics.__ Lee Edwards. LC 00-26076. 2001. pap. write for info. (*0-8132-0992-7*) Cath U Pr.

Mediapractice: A Media Skills Book. McCubbin. 1991. pap. text. write for info. (*0-582-87133-6*, Pub. by Addison-Wesley) Longman.

*__Media's Dark Age: The Rise & Fall of Western Journalism.__ Jean-Bertrand Aristide et al. LC 99-52468. 1999. write for info. (*0-9656916-5-9*) Intl Action Ctr.

Media's Social Responsibility. John Looney & Danene M. Bender. (Illus.). 92p. (Orig.). 1986. pap. 4.00 (*0-9619819-0-3*) Peace Grows.

Mediascape. Heinrich Klotz et al. (Illus.). 64p. 1997. 19.95 (*0-8109-6900-9*, Pub. by Abrams) Time Warner.

Mediasmart: How to Handle a Reporter, by a Reporter. Dennis Stauffer. 288p. 1994. 19.95 (*0-9640429-0-8*) MinneApplePress.

*__MediaSpeak: Three American Voices.__ Roy F. Fox. LC 00-32372. 256p. 2000. 40.00 (*0-275-96193-1*, Praeger Pubs) Greenwood.

Mediasport. Lawrence A. Wenner. LC 98-2658. (Illus.). 352p. (C). 1998. 85.00 (*0-415-14040-4*); pap. 25.99 (*0-415-14041-2*) Routledge.

Mediastinal Surgery. Thomas W. Shields. LC 90-13346. (Illus.). 400p. 1991. text 99.00 (*0-8121-1362-4*) Lppncott W & W.

Mediastinal Tumors. Ed. by D. E. Wood & C. R. Thomas, Jr. 144p. 1995. 98.00 (*3-540-58750-0*) Spr-Verlag.

Mediastinum. E. R. Heitzman. (Illus.). 380p. 1988. 231.00 (*0-387-18727-8*) Spr-Verlag.

*__Mediatation Kit: Everything You Need to Relax & Rejuvenate.__ Charla Devereux & Fran Stockel. (Illus.). 120p. 2000. reprint ed. pap. text 28.00 (*0-7881-6448-1*) DIANE Pub.

Mediate, Don't Litigate. Peter Lovenheim. 290p. 1990. 19.95 (*0-07-038832-6*) McGraw.

Mediate Your Divorce & Save Attorneys' Fees. Paula Latimer. 52p. (Orig.). 1993. pap. write for info. (*0-9636555-0-7*) P Latimer.

Mediated Communication: A Social Action Perspective. James A. Anderson & Timothy P. Meyer. (Current Communication An Advanced Text Ser.: Vol. 1). 320p. (C). 1988. text 45.00 (*0-8039-3050-X*) Sage.

Mediated Communication: A Social Action Perspective. James A. Anderson & Timothy P. Meyer. LC 88-23903. (Current Communication Ser.: Vol. 1). 368p. 1988. reprint ed. pap. 114.10 (*0-608-02770-7*, 206383600007) Bks Demand.

Mediated Discourse As Social Interaction: A Study of News Discourse. Ronald Scollon. LC 97-34576. 1998. write for info. (*0-582-32726-1*) Longman.

Mediated Discourse as Social Interaction: A Study of News Discourse. Ronald Scollon. LC 97-34576. 1998. pap. text 24.56 (*0-582-32725-3*) Longman.

Mediated Learning in & Out of the Classroom, Vol. 1. Manual Work Team of the Cognitive Research Program. LC 96-77677. (Illus.). 186p. (Orig.). 1996. pap. 32.95 (*1-57517-059-0*, 1446) SkyLght.

Mediated Minds, Mediated Lives. Rubenstein. (Speech & Theater Ser.). Date not set. pap. 28.00 (*0-534-52416-8*) Course Tech.

Mediated Muse: English Translations of Ovid, 1560-1700. Lee T. Pearcy. LC 84-16895. xviii, 179p. (C). 1984. lib. bdg. 30.00 (*0-208-02056-X*, Archon Bks) Shoe String.

Mediated Political Realities. 2nd ed. Dan Nimmo & James E. Combs. 256p. (C). 1990. pap. text 42.00 (*0-8013-0220-X*, 75878) Longman.

*__Mediated Politics: Communication in the Future of Democracy.__ Ed. by W. Lance Bennett & Robert M. Entman. (Communication, Society & Politics Ser.). (Illus.). 472p. 2000. write for info. (*0-521-78356-9*); pap. write for info. (*0-521-78976-1*) Cambridge U Pr.

Mediated Politics in Two Cultures: Presidential Campaigning in the United States & France. Ed. by Lynda L. Kaid et al. LC 90-24143. (Praeger Series in Political Communication). 320p. 1991. 65.00 (*0-275-93595-7*, C3595, Praeger Pubs) Greenwood.

Mediated Sex: Pornography & Postmodern Culture. Brian McNair. LC 96-543. 208p. 1996. pap. text 19.95 (*0-340-61428-5*, Pub. by E A) OUP.

Mediated Sex: Pornography & Postmodern Culture. Brian McNair. LC 96-543. 208p. 1996. text 55.00 (*0-340-66293-X*, Pub. by E A) Routldge.

Mediated Transcendence: A Postmodern Reflection. Jerry H. Gill. LC 88-29667. 120p. (C). 1989. 26.50 (*0-86554-318-6*, MUP/H271); pap. 17.50 (*0-86554-348-8*, MUP/P077) Mercer Univ Pr.

*__Mediated Women: Representations in Popular Culture.__ Ed. by Marian Meyers. LC 99-29090. (Communication Ser.). 400p. (C). 1999. 85.00 (*1-57273-239-3*); pap. 34.50 (*1-57273-240-7*) Hampton Pr NJ.

*__Mediathink.__ James Winter. 222p. 2001. pap. 19.99 (*1-55164-054-6*) Black Rose.

Mediating & Negotiating Marital Conflicts: The Impact of Mediation & Lawyer Negotiations. Desmond Ellis. LC 96-10128. xi, 164p. 1996. write for info. (*0-7619-0502-2*); pap. write for info. (*0-7619-0503-0*) Sage.

Mediating Bioethical Disputes: Community Health Outreach Worker Programs. Nancy N. Dubler & Leonard J. Mareus. LC 94-14572. (Practical Guide Ser.). 40p. 1994. 20.00 (*1-881277-19-4*) United Hosp Fund.

Mediating Child Custody Disputes: A Strategic Approach. rev. ed. Donald T. Saposnek. LC 97-45299. 1998. pap. 32.95 (*0-7879-4051-8*) Jossey-Bass.

Mediating Culture: The Politics of Representation - Essays. William Anselmi. 217p. 1994. pap. 15.00 (*0-920717-85-3*) Guernica Editions.

Mediating Divorce. Marilyn McKnight & Stephen Erickson. (Health & Psychology Ser.). 96p. 1998. pap., wbk. ed. 19.95 (*0-7879-4485-8*) Jossey-Bass.

Mediating Divorce: A Step by Step Manual, Incl. client's wkbk. & chldn's bk. Marilyn McKnight & Stephen Erickson. (Health & Psychology Ser.). 148p. 1998. ring bd., wbk. ed. 295.00 (*0-7879-4304-5*) Jossey-Bass.

Mediating Divorce: Casebook of Strategies for Successful Family Negotiations. John M. Haynes & Gretchen L. Haynes. LC 89-45600. (Social & Behavioral Science Ser.). 352p. text 38.95 (*1-55542-181-4*) Jossey-Bass.

Mediating Divorce: Children's Book. Marilyn S. McKnight & Stephen K. Erickson. 128p. (Orig.). 1998. pap. 9.95 (*1-881111-02-4*) Jossey-Bass.

Mediating Environmental Conflicts: Theory & Practice. J. Walton Blackburn & Willa M. Bruce. LC 94-34271. 320p. 1995. 69.50 (*0-89930-846-5*, Quorum Bks) Greenwood.

*__Mediating Fictions: Literature, Women Healers & the Go-Between in Medieval & Early Modern Iberia.__ Jean Dangler. LC 00-40383. 2001. write for info. (*0-8387-5452-X*) Bucknell U Pr.

Mediating History: The MAP Guide to Independent Video by & about African Americans, Asian Americans, Latino, & Native American People. Ed. by Barbara Abrash & Catherine Egan. 200p. (C). 1992. pap. text 16.50 (*0-8147-0620-7*) NYU Pr.

Mediating in Cyprus: The Cypriot Communities & the United Nations. Oliver P. Richmond. LC 98-11818. (Peacekeeping Ser.: No. 3). 320p. 1998. 54.50 (*0-7146-4877-9*, Pub. by F Cass Pubs) Intl Spec Bk.

Mediating in Cyprus: The Cypriot Communities & the United Nations. Oliver P. Richmond. LC 98-11818. (Peacekeeping Ser.: No. 3). xxxi, 282p. 1998. pap. 24.50 (*0-7146-4431-5*) Intl Spec Bk.

Mediating Languages & Cultures. Ed. by Dieter Buttjes & Michael Byram. (Multilingual Matters Ser.: No. 60). 302p. 1990. 99.00 (*1-85359-071-1*); pap. 39.95 (*1-85359-070-3*) Taylor & Francis.

Mediating Legal Disputes: Effective Strategies for Lawyers & Mediators. Dwight Golann. LC 96-76727. 545p. 1996. pap. text 105.00 (*0-316-31989-9*, Aspen Law & Bus) Aspen Pub.

Mediating Permanency Outcomes: Parent Empowerment Workbooks, 4 vols. Jeanne Etter. 1997. pap. text, wbk. ed. 16.95 (*0-87868-610-X*) Child Welfare.

Mediating Permanency Outcomes: Practice Manual & Parent Empowerment Workbooks. Jeanne Etter. LC 97-20982. (Orig.). 1997. pap. 24.95 (*0-87868-600-2*) Child Welfare.

Mediating Person: Bridges Between Cultures. Ed. by Stephen Bochner. 323p. 1982. pap. text 13.25 (*0-87073-893-3*) Schenkman Bks Inc.

Mediating Self: Mead, Sartre, & Self-Determination. Mitchell Aboulafia. LC 85-20378. 156p. 1986. 22.50 (*0-300-03523-3*) Yale U Pr.

Mediating Sustainability: Growing Policy from the Grassroots. Ed. by Jutta Blauert & Simon Zadek. LC 98-3325. 304p. 1998. 55.00 (*1-56549-082-7*); pap. 25.95 (*1-56549-081-9*) Kumarian Pr.

Mediating the Message. Pamela Shoemaker & Stephen D. Reese. 233p. (Orig.). (C). 1991. pap. text 31.33 (*0-8013-0307-9*, 78012) Longman.

Mediating the Message: Theories of Influences on Mass Media Content. 2nd ed. Pamela J. Shoemaker & Stephen D. Reese. LC 94-3796. 336p. (C). 1995. pap. text 52.00 (*0-8013-1251-5*, 79882) Longman.

Mediating the National. Marsha Butzel. 136p. 1994. pap. text 6.00 (*3-7186-0570-8*, Harwood Acad Pubs) Gordon & Breach.

Mediating the Transition: Labour Markets in Central & Eastern Europe. Tito Boeri et al. (EPI Forum Report: No. 4). 135p. 1998. pap. 14.95 (*1-898128-32-4*, Pub. by Ctr Econ Policy Res) Brookings.

Mediating Two Worlds: Cinematic Encounters in the Americas. Ed. by John King, III et al. (Illus.). 328p. (C). 1993. 45.00 (*0-85170-333-X*, Pub. by British Film Inst); pap. 21.95 (*0-85170-334-8*, Pub. by British Film Inst) Ind U Pr.

Mediation. Michael Noone. Ed. by Julie MacFarland. LC 97-101313. (Essential Legal Skills Ser.). 150p. 1996. pap. 22.00 (*1-85941-202-5*, Pub. by Cavendish Pubng) Gaunt.

Mediation: A Comprehensive Guide to Resolving Conflicts Without Litigation. Jay Folberg & Alison Taylor. LC 83-49259. (Management Ser.). 407p. 1984. text 40.95 (*0-87589-594-8*) Jossey-Bass.

Mediation: A Consumer's Guide. LC 95-210298. 16p. 1995. pap. 2.50 (*1-57073-118-7*, 468-0051) Amer Bar Assn.

Mediation: A Texas Practice Guide Eric Galton. LC 99-208355. 213 p. 1993. write for info. (*1-879590-42-5*) Amer Law Media.

Mediation: Empowerment in Conflict Management. Kathy Domenici. 137p. 1996. pap. text 11.95 (*0-88133-894-X*) Waveland Pr.

Mediation: Law, Policy & Practice. 2nd ed. Nancy H. Rogers & Craig A. McEwen. LC 94-39341. 1994. 120.00 (*0-614-32213-8*) West Group.

Mediation: Principles & Practice. Kimberlee K. Kovach. (American Casebook Ser.). 145p. (C). 1994. pap. text, teacher ed. write for info. (*0-314-04788-3*) West Pub.

Mediation: Principles, Process, Practice. L. Boulle. 275p. 1996. pap. write for info. (*0-409-30975-3*, MICHIE) LEXIS Pub.

Mediation: Simulation of a Construction Dispute. 1988. 15.00 (*1-55917-455-2*, 8214) Natl Prac Inst.

Mediation: Simulation of a Personal Injury Case. 1988. 15.00 (*1-55917-452-8*, 8212) Natl Prac Inst.

Mediation: The Action of the Media in Our Society. Gaston Roberge. 1980. 24.00 (*0-8364-0604-4*, Pub. by Manohar) S Asia.

Mediation: The Book: A Step-by-Step Guide for Dispute Resolvers. Sam Leonard. LC 94-199240. (Illus.). 208p. (Orig.). 1994. pap. 19.95 (*1-879260-25-5*) Evanston Pub.

Mediation - Arbitration: A Reader. Lynn R. Buzzard & Ronald Kraybill. 140p. (Orig.). (C). 1982. pap. text 7.50 (*0-944561-08-X*) Chr Legal.

Mediation - The Coming of Age: A Mediator's Guide to Serving the Elderly. 37p. 1989. pap. 10.00 (*0-89707-528-5*, 474-0040) Amer Bar Assn.

Mediation Advocacy. John W. Cooley. 320p. 1996. 37.95 (*1-55681-503-4*) Natl Inst Trial Ad.

Mediation & Arbitration. Peter D'Ambrumenil. (Medico-Legal Practitioner Ser.). 154p. 1997. 72.00 (*1-85941-155-X*, 15671, Pub. by Cavendish Pubng) Gaunt.

*__Mediation & Arbitration by Patrol Police Officers.__ Christopher Cooper. LC 99-18895. 88p. 1999. pap. 14.50 (*0-7618-1368-3*) U Pr of Amer.

Mediation & Arbitration of Employment Disputes. John T. Dunlop & Arnold M. Zack. LC 97-16797. 223p. 1997. 36.95 (*0-7879-0847-9*) Jossey-Bass.

Mediation & Conference Programs in the Federal Courts of Appeals: A Sourcebook for Judges & Lawyers. Robert J. Niemic. 107p. (C). 1999. pap. text 25.00 (*0-7881-4365-4*) DIANE Pub.

Mediation & Conflict: Resolution in Social Work & Human Sercive. Ed. by Edward Kruk. LC 97-2283. (Social Work). (C). 1997. pap. text 42.95 (*0-8304-1468-1*) Thomson Learn.

Mediation & Criminal Justice: Victims, Offenders, & Community. Ed. by Martin Wright & Burt Galaway. 304p. (C). 1989. text 47.50 (*0-8039-8063-9*); pap. text 19.95 (*0-8039-8064-7*) Sage.

Mediation & Love: A Study of the Medieval Go-Between in Key Romance & Near Eastern Texts. Leyla Rouhi. LC 98-53963. (Studies in Intellectual History). 320p. 1999. 112.50 (*90-04-11268-5*) Brill Academic Pubs.

Mediation & Negotiation: Reaching Agreement in Law & Business. E. Wendy Trachte-Huber & Stephen K. Huber. 865p. (C). 1998. pap. 41.95 (*0-87084-541-1*) Anderson Pub Co.

Mediation & Private Contacts in the Iran Hostage Crisis, April 1980-January 1981. Russell L. Moses. (Pew Case Studies in International Affairs). 94p. (C). 1989. pap. text 3.50 (*1-56927-316-2*) Geo U Inst Dplmcy.

Mediation & the Dynamics of Collective Bargaining. 2nd ed. William E. Simkin & Nicholas A. Fidandis. 320p. 1986. trans. 35.00 (*0-87179-519-1*, 0519) BNA Books.

Mediation Book, Childhood Sexual Abuse, Repressed Memory. William B. Craig. 238p. 1994. student ed. 125.00 (*1-885689-05-5*) Spread the Wrd.

Mediation, Citizen Empowerment & Transformational Politics. Edward W. Schwerin. LC 94-42840. (Transformational Politics & Political Science Ser.). 224p. 1995. 57.95 (*0-275-94552-9*, Praeger Pubs) Greenwood.

Mediation for Kids. 2nd ed. Fran Schmidt et al. (Illus.). 68p. (J). (gr. 4-7). 1992. 21.95 (*1-878227-13-0*) Peace Educ.

Mediation for Kids (La Mediation pour les Jeunes) Fran Schmidt et al. Tr. by Tanya Dugre. (FRE., Illus.). 60p. 1997. teacher ed., ring bd. 23.95 (*1-878227-36-X*) Peace Educ.

Mediation for Kids, Student Handbook. 3rd ed. Fran Schmidt et al. (Illus.). 28p. (J). (gr. 4-7). 1997. student ed. 11.95 (*1-878227-50-5*) Peace Educ.

Mediation for Little Peacemakers. Max Nass & Marcia Nass. 77p. (J). (gr. 3-6). 1995. pap. 20.50 (*1-882732-42-1*) Childswork.

Mediation Getting to Win Win: Student Activity Book. Fran Schmidt et al. Ed. by James A. Burke, II. (Illus.). 48p. (Orig.). (YA). (gr. 8-12). 1994. pap. text 2.79 (*1-878227-21-1*) Peace Educ.

Mediation Getting to Win Win, Grade 8-12. Fran Schmidt et al. Ed. by James A. Burke, II. (Illus.). 96p. (Orig.). 1994. pap. text, teacher ed. 29.95 (*1-878227-22-X*) Peace Educ.

M

An Asterisk (*) at the beginning of an entry indicates that the title is appearing for the first time.

Mediation in Contemporary Native American Fiction. James Ruppert. LC 94-47465. (American Indian Literature & Critical Studies: Vol. 15). 192p. 1995. 29.95 (0-8061-2749-X) U of Okla Pr.

Mediation in Contemporary Native American Fiction. James Ruppert. LC 97-47465. (American Indian Literature & Critical Studies Ser.: Vol. 15). xiii, 174p. 1997. pap. 11.95 (0-8061-2993-X) U of Okla Pr.

Mediation in Family Disputes: A Guide to Practice. Marion Roberts. (Community Care Practice Handbook Ser.). 120p. 1988. pap. text 15.95 (0-7045-0585-1, Pub. by Gower) Ashgate Pub Co.

Mediation in Family Disputes: Principles in Practice. 2nd ed. Marian Roberts. LC 97-70319. 249p. 1997. pap. 31.95 (1-85742-315-1, Pub. by Arena) Ashgate Pub Co.

Mediation in Family Disputes: Principles in Practice. 2nd ed. Marion Roberts. 249p. 1997. text 64.95 (1-85742-318-6, Pub. by Arena) Ashgate Pub Co.

Mediation in PUC Practice. 1997. 99.00 incl. audio PA Bar Inst.

Mediation in Special Education Disputes. Claire B. Gallant. LC 82-60764. (Illus.). 104p. (Orig.). reprint ed. pap. 32.30 (0-7837-6537-1, 204567400007) Bks Demand.

Mediation in the Campus Community: Designing & Managing Effective Programs. William Warters. LC 99-6619. (Jossey-Bass Education Ser.). 1999. pap. text 22.00 (0-7879-4789-X) Jossey-Bass.

***Mediation in the Millennium.** 1998. 99.00 incl. audio PA Bar Inst.

***Mediation in the Workplace: A Guide for Training, Practice & Administration.** Rebecca Jane Weinstein. LC 00-32820. 2000. write for info. (1-56720-336-1, Quorum Bks) Greenwood.

Mediation in Workers' Compensation Cases: An Evaluation of Its Effects. Stevens H. Clarke & Kelly McCormick. LC 97-151586. (Special Ser.: Vol. 16). 15p. (Orig.). 1997. pap. text 14.00 (1-56011-308-1, SS#16) Institute Government.

Mediation, Information, & Communication. Ed. by Brent D. Ruben & Leah A. Lievrouw. (Information & Behavior Ser.: Vol. 3). 496p. 1989. 49.95 (0-88738-278-9) Transaction Pubs.

Mediation, Investigation & Arbitration in Industrial Disputes. George E. Barnett & David A. McCabe. LC 75-156403. (American Labor Ser., No. 2). 1977. reprint ed. 21.95 (0-405-02913-6) Ayer.

Mediation of Cellular Immunity in Cancer by Immune Modifiers. Ed. by Michael A. Chirigos et al. LC 80-5877. (Progress in Cancer Research & Therapy Ser.: No. 19). 287p. 1981. reprint ed. pap. 89.00 (0-608-00606-8, 206119300007) Bks Demand.

Mediation of Christ. Thomas F. Torrance. LC 91-41856. 140p. 1992. pap. 17.95 (0-939443-50-3) Helmers Howard Pub.

Mediation of Christ. Thomas F. Torrance. LC 83-25330. 108p. reprint ed. 33.50 (0-608-16765-7, 202755100055) Bks Demand.

Mediation of Environmental Disputes: A Sourcebook. Scott Mernitz. LC 80-7503. 202p. 1980. 57.95 (0-275-90523-3, C0523, Praeger Pubs) Greenwood.

Mediation of Interpersonal Disputes in North Carolina: An Evaluation. Stevens H. Clarke et al. 84p. (Orig.). (C). 1993. pap. text 16.00 (1-56011-208-5, 92-05) Institute Government.

Mediation of Ornament. Oleg Grabar. LC 92-5725. (A. W. Mellon Lectures in the Fine Arts, 1989: Vol. XXXV, No. 38). (Illus.). 320p. 1992. text 70.00 (0-691-04099-0, Pub. by Princeton U Pr); pap. text 29.95 (0-691-00156-1, Pub. by Princeton U Pr) Cal Prin Full Svc.

Mediation, Principles & Practice. Kimberlee K. Kovach. LC 94-21618. (Miscellaneous Ser.). 287p. 1994. pap. 27.50 (0-314-04053-6) West Pub.

Mediation Process: Practical Strategies for Resolving Conflict. 2nd rev. ed. Christopher W. Moore. (Conflict Resolution Ser.). 400p. 1996. 36.95 (0-7879-0248-9) Jossey-Bass.

Mediation Research: The Process & Effectiveness of Third-Party Intervention. Kressel, Kenneth, & Pruitt, Dean G., & Associates. LC 89-8211. (Social & Behavioral Science-Management Ser.). 490p. 1989. text 47.95 (1-55542-162-8) Jossey-Bass.

Mediation Text. (C). 1996. 15.00 (0-8087-7284-8) Pearson Custom.

Mediation Through the Year: Nature's Cycle of the Seasons in Guilded Visualisation. Dorothea Breitzter-Kings. (Illus.). 96p. 1992. pap. text 13.95 (1-85398-029-3, Pub. by Ashgrove Pr) Words Distrib.

Mediation under Crisis Management Conditions: The U. N. Secretary General & the Falkland - Malvinas Islands Crisis. Gunnar P. Nielsson. (Pew Case Studies in International Affairs). 50p. (C). 1994. pap. text 3.50 (1-56927-127-5) Geo U Inst Dplmcy.

Mediation, 1996. John S. Murray et al. (Paralegal). 351p. 1996. pap. text 15.00 (1-56662-429-0) Foundation Pr.

Mediations. pap. text. write for info. (0-7131-6479-4, Pub. by E A) Routldge.

Mediations for Choir Members. Nancy L. Roth. LC 98-55964. (Faithful Servants Ser.). 96p. 1999. pap. 6.95 (0-8192-1779-4) Morehouse Pub.

Mediator. Richard Swartzbaugh. LC 72-94968. 133p. 1973. 13.00 (0-914576-03-8) Howard Allen.

Mediator Book, Childhood Sexual Abuse, Repressed Memory. William B. Craig. 61p. 1994. student ed. 125.00 (1-885689-04-7) Spread the Wrd.

Mediator Communication Competencies. 4th ed. McKinney et al. 1995. pap. write for info. (0-8087-7699-1) Pearson Custom.

Mediator (Labor Relations) Jack Rudman. (Career Examination Ser.: C-520). 1994. pap. 39.95 (0-8373-0520-9) Nat Learn.

Mediator Revisited: Profile of a Profession, 1960s & 1985. Ruth F. Necheles-Jansyn. LC 90-42215. (Institute of Management & Labor Relations Ser.: No. 3). 209p. 1990. 30.00 (0-8108-2351-9) Scarecrow.

Mediatorial Life of Jesus. Orestes A. Brownson. (Works of Orestes Augustus Brownson). 1989. reprint ed. lib. bdg. 79.00 (0-7812-2107-2) Rprt Serv.

Mediators & Drugs in Gastrointestinal Motility II: Endogenous & Exogenous Agents. Ed. by G. Bertaccini. (Handbook of Experimental Pharmacology Ser.: Vol. 59, II). (Illus.). 460p. 1982. 272.00 (0-387-11333-9) Spr-Verlag.

Mediators Between Human & Divine: From Moses to Muhammad. John Macquarrie. LC 79-5052. 180p. 1999. pap. 15.95 (0-8264-1170-3) Continuum.

***Mediators Between Human & Divine: From Moses to Muhammad.** John MacQuarrie. 171p. 2000. reprint ed. 20.00 (0-7881-9343-0) DIANE Pub.

Mediators Between This World & the Other: Essays on Demonic Beings from the Middle Ages to the Present. Ed. by Ruth Petzoldt et al. LC 98-12436. (Beitrage zur Europaischen Ethnologie und Folklore: Reihe B, Band 8). (GER., Illus.). 176p. (C). 1998. pap. 39.95 (0-8204-3574-0) P Lang Pubng.

***Mediator's Guidebook: A Guide to Successful Mediations.** Marva E. Craig & William L. Carruthers. 24p. (YA). (gr. 6-10). 1999. pap. 5.95 (0-932796-97-4) Ed Media Corp.

Mediator's Handbook. Ruth Charlton & Micheline Dewdney. 200p. 1996. pap. 50.00 (0-455-21361-5, Pub. by LawBk Co) Gaunt.

Mediator's Handbook. 3rd rev. ed. Jennifer E. Beer & Eileen Stief. (Illus.). 176p. 1997. pap. 19.95 (0-86571-359-6) New Soc Pubs.

***Mediator's Handbook: Advanced Practice Guide for Civil Litigation.** John W. Cooley & National Institute for Trial Advocacy Staff. LC 99-88515. 2000. pap. write for info. (1-55681-681-2) Natl Inst Trial Ad.

Mediator's Handbook (Neighborhoods) 4th rev. ed. Jennifer E. Beer. Ed. by Sandi Adams et al. (Illus.). 80p. 1995. reprint ed. pap. 12.00 (0-941308-12-X) Frnds Conflict Res Prog.

Mediators in Airway Hyperreactivity. Ed. by E. P. Nijkamp et al. (Agents & Actions Supplements Ser.: Vol. 31). 296p. 1990. 79.50 (0-8176-2513-5) Birkhauser.

Mediators in Cell Growth & Differentiation. Symposium on Fundamental Cancer Research Staff. Ed. by Richard J. Ford & Abby L. Maizel. LC 84-24875. (UT M. D. Anderson Symposium on Fundamental Cancer Research Ser.: No. 37). (Illus.). 388p. 1985. reprint ed. pap. 120.30 (0-7837-9544-0, 206029300005) Bks Demand.

Mediators in the Cardiovascular System: Regional Ischemia. Ed. by K. Schror & Cecil R. Pace-Asciak. LC 94-43433. (Agents & Actions Supplements Ser.: Vol. 45). 1995. write for info. (3-7643-5130-6) Birkhauser.

Mediators in the Cardiovascular System: Regional Ischemia. Ed. by K. Schror & Cecil R. Pace-Asciak. (Agents & Actions Supplements Ser.: Vol. 45). (Illus.). 340p. 1995. 104.00 (0-8176-5130-6) Birkhauser.

Mediators of Pulmonary Inflammation. Ed. by Michael A. Bray & Wayne Anderson. (Lung Biology in Health & Disease Ser.: Vol. 54). (Illus.). 688p. 1991. text 255.00 (0-8247-8442-1) Dekker.

Mediators of Sepsis. Ed. by L. G. Thijs & M. Lamy. LC 92-32047. (Update in Intensive Care & Emergency Medicine Ser.: Vol. 16). 1992. 142.00 (0-387-55841-1) Spr-Verlag.

Mediators of the Immediate Type Inflammatory Reaction: Proceedings of the Collegium Internationale Allergologicum Symposium, 11th, Heidelberg, May 1976. Collegium Internationale Allergologicum Symposium. Ed. by K. O. Rother. (Monographs in Allergy: Vol. 12). (Illus.). 1977. 85.25 (3-8055-2660-1) S Karger.

Mediators of the Immune Response. N. V. Medunitsyn et al. xiv, 326p. 1987. text 216.00 (3-7186-0310-1) Gordon & Breach.

Mediavisions: The Art & Industry of Mass Communication. Robert H. Stanley. LC 87-6975. 272p. 1987. 59.95 (0-275-92736-9, C2736, Praeger Pubs); pap. 18.95 (0-275-92737-7, B2737, Praeger Pubs) Greenwood.

Mediawriting: Print, Broadcast & Public Relations. Wayne R. Whitaker et al. LC 99-21130. 400p. 1999. write for info. (0-321-01844-3) Addson-Wesley Educ.

Medibears Guide to the Doctor's Exam: For Children & Parents. John A. Ogden. (Illus.). (J). (gr. k-5). 1991. 12.95 (0-8130-1082-9) U Press Fla.

***Medic!** Robert L. Smith. LC 99-66711. (Illus.). 288p. 2000. pap. 17.25 (0-88739-316-0) Creat Arts Bk.

Medic: The Mission of an American Military Doctor in Occupied Japan & Wartorn Korea. Crawford F. Sams. Ed. by Zabelle Zakarian. LC 97-35989. (Illus.). 344p. (C). (gr. 13). 1998. 33.95 (0-7656-0030-7, East Gate Bk) M E Sharpe.

Medic & the Mama-san. Michael H. Hall. LC 93-61126. (Illus.). 283p. 1994. 21.00 (0-9639091-1-8); pap. 12.00 (0-9639091-0-X) Hawkeye Pubng.

***Medic First Aid AED, Facilitator Visual Akill Guide: Featuring the Medtronic Physio-Control LifePak 500.** EMP International Inc., Staff. (Illus.). 70p. 2000. 17.50 (0-940430-94-0, 4318) EMP Intl.

***Medic First Aid AED, Student Visual Skill Guide: Featuring the Medtronic Physio-Control LifePak 500.** EMP International Inc., Staff. (Illus.). 32p. 2000. pap. 7.00 (0-940430-93-2, 3064) EMP Intl.

***Medic First Aid Mark IV, Facilitator Visual Skill Guide: Infant/Child Supplement.** EMP International Inc., Staff. (Illus.). 58p. 1999. 7.50 (0-940430-96-7, 4316) EMP Intl.

***Medic First Aid mark IV, Student Visual Skill Guide: Infant/Child Supplement.** EMP International Inc., Staff. (Illus.). 20p. 1999. pap. text 3.00 (0-940430-95-9, 20973.00) EMP Intl.

Medic Life: Creating Success in EMS. John Becknell. LC 95-872. 1995. pap. text 9.95 (0-8151-3046-5) Jems Comm.

Medicaid. Brenda Willett. 26p. pap. 2.75 (0-685-23167-4, 41,575M) NCLS Inc.

Medicaid: Demographics of Nonenrolled Children Suggest State Outreach Strategies. Ed. by William J. Scanlon. (Illus.). 44p. (C). 1999. pap. text 20.00 (0-7881-8139-4) DIANE Pub.

Medicaid: Oregon's Managed Care Program & Implications for Expansion. 71p. (Orig.). (C). 1992. pap. text 25.00 (1-56806-008-4) DIANE Pub.

Medicaid: Oversight of Institutions for the Mentally Retarded Should Be Strengthened. 32p. pap. text 30.00 (0-7881-4063-9) DIANE Pub.

Medicaid: Restructuring Approaches Leave Many Questions. (Illus.). 25p. (Orig.). (C). 1995. pap. text 25.00 (0-7881-1805-6) DIANE Pub.

Medicaid: States[0012] Efforts to Educate & Enroll Beneficiaries in Managed Care (MC) 32p. pap. text 30.00 (0-7881-4059-0) DIANE Pub.

Medicaid: States Turn to Managed Care to Improve Access & Control Costs. (Illus.). 102p. (Orig.). (C). 1993. pap. text 35.00 (1-56806-588-4) DIANE Pub.

Medicaid: Tennessee's Program Broadens Coverage but Faces Uncertain Future. (Illus.). 54p. (Orig.). (C). 1996. pap. text 20.00 (0-7881-2754-3) DIANE Pub.

Medicaid: Waiver Program for Developmentally Disabled Is Promising, but Poses Some Risks. (Illus.). 48p. (Orig.). (C). 1996. pap. text 25.00 (0-7881-3460-4) DIANE Pub.

Medicaid & Managed Care: Lessons from the Literature. Diane Rowland et al. 88p. 1995. write for info. (0-944525-21-0) H J Kaiser.

Medicaid & Pediatric Primary Care. Janet D. Perloff et al. LC 87-3164. (Johns Hopkins Series in Contemporary Medicine & Public Health). 208p. reprint ed. pap. 64.50 (0-608-06185-9, 206651700008) Bks Demand.

Medicaid & Supplemental Security Income: Options & Strategies for Child Welfare Agencies. Madelyn DeWoody. 64p. 1991. pap. 9.95 (0-87868-450-6) Child Welfare.

Medicaid & the Costs of Federalism, 1984-1992. Jean Donovan Gilman. LC 98-47361. (Health Care Policy in the United States Ser.). 240p. 1998. 56.00 (0-8153-3278-5) Garland.

Medicaid & the Limits of State Health Reform. Michael S. Sparer. LC 95-47190. 235p. (C). 1996. pap. 22.95 (1-56639-434-1); lib. bdg. 69.95 (1-56639-433-3) Temple U Pr.

Medicaid & the States. Paul Offner. LC 98-35591. (Devolution Revolution Ser.). 72p. 1998. pap. 9.95 (0-87078-426-9) Century Foundation.

Medicaid at the Crossroads: A Report of the Kaiser Commission on the Future of Medicaid. Diane Rowland et al. 90p. (Orig.). 1992. pap. 5.00 (0-944525-10-5) H J Kaiser.

Medicaid Claims Examiner. Jack Rudman. (Career Examination Ser.: C-2691). 1994. pap. 27.95 (0-8373-2691-5) Nat Learn.

Medicaid Cost-Based Reimbursement for State & Local Health Department Clinic Services. Tracy M. Orloff et al. Ed. by Karen Glass. 97p. (Orig.). 1993. pap. text 15.00 (1-55877-222-7) Natl Governor.

Medicaid Cost Containment: Long-Term Care Reimbursement. Robert J. Buchanan. LC 85-45028. 200p. 1987. 36.50 (0-8386-3271-8) Fairleigh Dickinson.

Medicaid Cost Explosion: Causes & Consequences: Report of the Kaiser Commission on the Future of Medicaid. Judith Feder et al. (Orig.). 1993. pap. text 10.00 (0-944525-12-1) H J Kaiser.

Medicaid Drug Fraud: Drug Diversion Schemes & "Pill Mills" (Illus.). 53p. (Orig.). (C). 1994. pap. text 30.00 (0-7881-0200-1) DIANE Pub.

Medicaid Drug Fraud, Medical Malpractice, & Reliability of Claims Processing for Medicare, Pt. B. (Illus.). 98p. (Orig.). (C). 1994. pap. text 30.00 (0-7881-1034-9) DIANE Pub.

Medicaid Eligibility for the Elderly in Need of Long Term Care. 159p. 1987. 19.00 (0-685-30147-8, 40,906) NCLS Inc.

Medicaid Expansions for Prenatal Care: State & Local Implementation. 80p. (Orig.). (C). 1994. pap. text 25.00 (0-7881-0628-7) DIANE Pub.

Medicaid Financing Crisis: Balancing Responsibilities, Priorities, & Dollars. Diane Rowland et al. 222p. (C). 1994. pap. 21.95 (0-87168-514-0, 93-04S) Transaction Pubs.

Medicaid Financing for Mental Health & Substance Abuse Services for Children & Adolescents. 1995. lib. bdg. 251.95 (0-8490-6827-4) Gordon Pr.

Medicaid Financing for Mental Health & Substance Abuse Services for Children & Adolescents. Harriette B. Fox et al. (Illus.). 69p. (C). 1997. reprint ed. pap. text 20.00 (0-7881-4596-7) DIANE Pub.

***Medicaid for Long-Term Nursing Home Care.** Richard Moran Enders. 13p. 2000. pap. 15.00 (0-9627964-9-2) SOS Clinton.

Medicaid Home Care Options for Disabled Children. Linda A. Hall. Ed. by Karen Glass. 60p. (Orig.). 1990. pap. text 20.00 (1-55877-062-3) Natl Governor.

Medicaid Long-Term Care: Successful State Efforts to Expand Home Services While Limiting Costs. (Illus.). 68p. (Orig.). (C). 1995. pap. text 20.00 (0-7881-1861-7) DIANE Pub.

Medicaid, Managed Behavioral Health, & Implications for Public Policy: Report of the Hawaii Medicaid Project & Other Readings. N. A. Cummings et al. (Readings in Behavioral Health Ser.: No. 2). 60p. 1993. pap. text. write for info. (0-9637577-0-9) Fnd Behav Hlth.

Medicaid Managed Care: Defining the Issues for Women with HIV/AIDS. Leslie R. Wolfe et al. 16p. (Orig.). 1996. pap. 5.00 (1-877966-29-0) Ctr Women Policy.

Medicaid Managed Care: Serving the Disabled Challenges State Programs. (Illus.). 66p. (Orig.). (C). 1996. pap. text 25.00 (0-7881-3490-6) DIANE Pub.

Medicaid Manual: How to Qualify for Medicaid. Richard T. Taps. 120p. 1994. pap. 12.95 (0-9640442-2-6) Silver Press.

Medicaid Planning Handbook: A Guide to Protecting Your Family's Assets from Nursing Home Costs. 2nd rev. ed. Alexander A. Bove. LC 95-30835. 208p. 1996. pap. 13.95 (0-316-10374-8) Little.

Medicaid Policy in California, 1980-1987, with Special Reference to Pregnant Women & Infants. Eve L. Schenker et al. LC 93-25929. 1993. pap. 13.00 (0-8330-1421-8, MR-146-AHCPR) Rand Corp.

Medicaid Prenatal Care: States Improve Access & Enhance Services, but Face New Challenges. (Illus.). 44p. (Orig.). (C). 1995. pap. text 20.00 (0-7881-1859-5) DIANE Pub.

Medicaid Reform: Four Studies of Case Management. Deborah A. Freund et al. LC 84-11058. (AEI Studies: No. 408). 96p. reprint ed. pap. 30.00 (0-8357-4504-X, 203736000008) Bks Demand.

Medicaid Reform: The Governors' View: Hearing Before the Committee on Commerce, U. S. House of Representatives. Ed. by Michael Bilirakis. 89p. (C). 1998. pap. text 20.00 (0-7881-4970-9) DIANE Pub.

Medicaid Reform & the American States: Case Studies on the Politics of Managed Care. Ed. by Mark R. Daniels. LC 97-23657. 320p. 1998. 59.95 (0-86569-263-7, Auburn Hse) Greenwood.

Medicaid Research & Demonstration Programs. Laura Tobler. 9p. 1995. 15.00 (1-55516-344-0, 7302-2007) Natl Conf State Legis.

Medicaid Review Analyst. Jack Rudman. (Career Examination Ser.: C-3207). 1994. pap. 27.95 (0-8373-3207-9) Nat Learn.

Medicaid Section 1115 Waivers: Flexible Approach to Approving Demonstrations Could Increase Federal Costs. (Illus.). 87p. (Orig.). (C). 1996. pap. text 20.00 (0-7881-3115-X) DIANE Pub.

Medicaid since 1980: Cost, Coverage, & the Shifting Alliance Between the Federal Government & the States. Teresa A. Coughlin et al. 200p. 1994. pap. text 23.00 (0-87766-618-0); lib. bdg. 49.00 (0-87766-617-2) Urban Inst.

Medicaid Source Book: Background Data & Analysis. (Illus.). 510p. 1993. pap. 44.00 (0-16-006301-9, 052-070-06848-5) USGPO.

Medicaid Statistics: Program & Financial Statistics, Fiscal Year 1994. 194p. 1996. pap. 14.00 (0-16-061588-7) USGPO.

***Medicaid Statistics: Program & Financial Statistics, Fiscal Year 1997.** 161p. 1999. per. 16.00 (0-16-050146-6) USGPO.

Medicaid Survival Kit. NCSL Health Program Staff. LC 99-162571. 322p. 1996. 75.00 (1-55516-655-5, 6654) Natl Conf State Legis.

Medicaid Transplant Coverage Manual. 295p. 1988. 30.00 (0-685-30148-6, 42,700) NCLS Inc.

***Medicaid Waivers: California's Use of a Federal Option.** Valerie Lewis. (Illus.). 27p. 2000. pap. write for info. (1-929008-28-7) CA HlthCare Fnd.

Medical. (Professional Education Ser.). 192p. 1966. 14.95 (0-318-15861-2, 106) Natl Ct Report.

Medical - Surgical Care Planning. 2nd ed. Nancy M. Holloway. LC 92-20351. 768p. 1992. 36.95 (0-87434-489-1) Springhouse Corp.

Medical - Surgical Market, '94. Market Intelligence Staff. 346p. 1994. 595.00 (1-56753-934-3) Frost & Sullivan.

Medical - Surgical Nursing: An Integrated Approach. Lois White & Gena Duncan. LC 97-17371. (LPN/LVN Nursing Ser.). 1008p. (C). 1997. text 65.95 (0-8273-6371-0) Delmar.

Medical - Surgical Nursing: An Integrated Approach - Study Guide. Duncan White. (LPN/LVN Nursing Ser.). 272p. (C). 1997. mass mkt., student ed. 13.75 (0-8273-7681-2) Delmar.

Medical - Surgical Sourcebook, '95: Diagnostic Imaging Highlights Medical Technology Trends. Frost & Sullivan Staff. 322p. 1995. spiral bd. 795.00 (0-7889-0274-1, 2725-57) Frost & Sullivan.

Medical- Related Biotechnology in Taiwan: A Strategic Entry Report, 1997. Compiled by Icon Group International Staff. (Illus.). 122p. 1999. ring bd. 1220.00 incl. audio compact disk (0-7418-0972-9) Icon Grp.

Medical Abacus: The Formulas of Clinical Practice & How to Use Them. D. Rifkind. LC 98-44811. (Illus.). 130p. 2000. pap. 21.95 (1-85070-023-0) Prthnon Pub.

Medical (ABBE) Publisher's Tribulations - Sabotage, Surveillance, Watchdog Poisoning, Cat Fright, Attempted Murder of Authors, Disappearance of Shipments, Loss in Important Book Buyers & Damaged Good Will. Alberto M. Zukko. (Illus.). 210p. 1996. 55.50 (0-7883-0228-0); pap. 49.50 (0-7883-0229-9) ABBE Pubs Assn.

Medical Abbreviations: Abkurzungen in der Medizin. 3rd ed. Albrecht Schertel. (ENG, FRE & GER.). 200p. 1984. pap. 39.95 (0-8288-0587-3, M 7292) Fr & Eur.

***Medical Abbreviations: 14,000 Conveniences at the Expense of Communications & Safety.** 9th rev. ed. Neil M. Davis. LC 98-93615. (Illus.). 11p. 1999. pap. 17.95 (0-931431-09-3) N M Davis.

An Asterisk (*) at the beginning of an entry indicates that the title is appearing for the first time.

Medical Abbreviations & Eponyms. 2nd ed. Sheila B. Sloane. Ed. by Margaret Biblis. LC 96-28595. 880p. 1997. pap. text 39.00 (*0-7216-7088-1*, W B Saunders Co) Harcrt Hlth Sci Grp.

Medical Accelerator Safety Considerations: Report of AAPM Radiation Therapy Committee Task Group, No. 35. J. Purdy et al. (AAPM Report Ser.: No. 56). 16p. 1996. reprint ed. write for info. (*1-888340-01-0*) AAPM.

Medical Accidents. Ed. by Charles Vincent et al. (Illus.). 260p. 1993. 59.95 (*0-19-262289-7*) OUP.

Medical Accidents & the Law: A Practical Guide to the Legal Rights of the Patient. AVMA Staff. 448p. 1999. pap. 51.95 (*0-471-96642-8*) Wiley.

Medical Acronyms, Eponyms, & Abbreviations. 3rd ed. Marilyn F. Delong. Ed. by Kathryn Swanson. LC 94-40393. 400p. (C). 1995. pap. 15.95 (*1-57066-007-7*, ME063) Practice Mgmt Info.

Medical Acronyms, Eponyms, & Abbreviations. 3rd rev. ed. Marilyn F. DeLong. LC 96-78925. 332p. 1997. pap. 12.95 (*1-885987-05-6*, ME077, Health Info Pr) Practice Mgmt Info.

***Medical Acronyms, Eponyms & Mnemonics.** Ed. by Kimberly N. Jones. 70p. 1999. pap. text 9.95 (*0-9651162-5-5*) Wysteria Ltd.

Medical Acupuncture. Filshie. 1998. text 72.00 (*0-443-04976-9*, W B Saunders Co) Harcrt Hlth Sci Grp.

Medical Administration: Management Techniques. A. Everette James. 158p. 1994. pap. 24.95 (*0-87527-511-7*) Green.

Medical ADP Systems: Defense's Tools & Methodology for Managing CHCs Performance Needs Strengthening. Helen Lew. (Illus.). 44p. 1998. pap. text 30.00 (*0-7881-4507-X*) DIANE Pub.

Medical Advances. Steve Parker. LC 97-17985. (20th Century Inventions Ser.). 1998. lib. bdg. 24.26 (*0-8172-4896-X*) Raintree Steck-V.

Medical Advances: A User Friendly Guide to the Latest Technology. Dan Burrus & Patti Thomsen. 131p. (Orig.). 1991. pap. 12.95 (*1-880136-52-X*) Intl Mgmt Pubns.

Medical Advisor: The Complete Guide. Time-Life Books Editors. LC 95-45803. (Illus.). 1152p. 1996. 39.95 (*0-8094-6737-2*) Time-Life.

***Medical Advisor: The Complete Guide To Alternative & Conventional Treaments.** 2nd ed. Ed. by Time-Life Books Editors. 1152p. 2000. 39.95 (*0-7370-1622-1*) Time-Life Educ.

Medical Advisor Home Edition: The Complete Guide to Alternative & Conventional Treatments. Time-Life Books Editors. LC 97-10717. (Illus.). 960p. (gr. 11). 1997. pap. 19.95 (*0-7835-5250-5*) Time-Life.

***Medical Advisor Home Edn H/c.** Time-Life Books Editors. (gr. 11). 1999. 29.95 (*0-7835-5301-3*) Time-Life Educ.

Medical Aide. Jack Rudman. (Career Examination Ser.: C-1364). 1994. pap. 23.95 (*0-8373-1364-3*) Nat Learn.

Medical Almanac. Ed. by Pasquale Accardo. LC 91-20882. (Illus.). 254p. 1992. 39.50 (*0-89603-181-0*) Humana.

Medical America in the Nineteenth Century: Readings from the Literature. Ed. by Gert H. Brieger. LC 76-165053. 348p. reprint ed. pap. 107.90 (*0-8357-8217-4*, 203413400088) Bks Demand.

Medical Analysis & Reviews of Human Immunodeficiency Virus: Index of Syntheses of New Information by Research Scientists. Glenn H. Parks. 150p. 1996. pap. 44.50 (*0-7883-0817-3*) ABBE Pubs Assn.

Medical Analysis & Reviews of Human Immunodeficiency Virus: Index of Syntheses of New Information by Research Scientists. Glenn H. Parks. 150p. 1996. 47.50 (*0-7883-0816-5*) ABBE Pubs Assn.

Medical Analysis & Reviews of Human Immunodeficiency Virus (HIV) Index of Synthesis of New Information by Research Scientists. Gleen H. Parks. 161p. 1998. 47.50 (*0-7883-1892-6*); pap. 44.50 (*0-7883-1893-4*) ABBE Pubs Assn.

Medical Analysis of the Neck: The "Choke-Hold" As Practiced by Cops Is Attempted Murder & Pre-Mediated Homicide: Citizens Beware! (Neck Anatomy Made Simple for Consumers & Lawyers) John C. Bartone. (Illus.). 149p. 1997. 47.50 (*0-7883-1394-0*); pap. 44.50 (*0-7883-1395-9*) ABBE Pubs Assn.

Medical Anatomy & Clinical Research: Index of Modern Authors & Subjects with Guide for Rapid Research. John C. Bartone. LC 90-56294. 160p. 1991. 47.50 (*1-55914-372-X*); pap. 44.50 (*1-55914-373-8*) ABBE Pubs Assn.

Medical & Applied Virology. Ed. by Murray Sanders et al. LC 67-26005. (Illus.). 428p. 1968. 22.50 (*0-87527-069-7*) Green.

Medical & Aromatic Plants VII. Y. P. S. Bajaj. (Biotechnology in Agriculture & Forestry Ser.: Vol. 28). 528p. 1994. 350.95 (*0-387-57446-8*) Spr-Verlag.

Medical & Biological Applications, Vol. 6. Ed. by Rinaldo Cubeddu. 1996. pap. 55.00 (*1-55752-464-5*) Optical Soc.

Medical & Biological Applications of Electrochemical Devices. Ed. by Jiri Koryta. LC 79-41212. (Illus.). 341p. reprint ed. pap. 105.80 (*0-608-17680-X*, 203039800069) Bks Demand.

Medical & Biological Dictionary Italian-English - English-Italian. G. Delfino. (ENG & ITA.). 2144p. 1996. 125.00 (*88-08-08854-5*, Pub. by Zanichelli) IBD Ltd.

Medical & Biological Engineering in the Future of Health Care. Ed. by Joseph D. Andrade. LC 94-8413. (Illus.). 176p. (Orig.). (C). 1994. pap. 24.95 (*0-87480-454-X*) U of Utah Pr.

Medical & Biological Progress & the European Convention on Human Rights. 1994. 15.00 (*92-871-2287-3*, Pub. by Council of Europe) Manhattan Pub Co.

Medical & Biological Terminologies: Classical Origins. John Scarborough. LC 92-54139. 320p. (Orig.). 1998. pap. 19.95 (*0-8061-3029-6*) U of Okla Pr.

Medical & Dental Associates. 3rd ed. Chapman. 304p. (C). 1997. mass mkt. 40.95 (*0-8273-7560-3*) Delmar.

Medical & Dental Associates, P. C. Insurance Forms Preparation. 2nd ed. Carol Gense & Lucinda Joy. (Medical Assisting Ser.). 352p. 1990. pap. 21.95 (*0-538-70056-4*) S-W Pub.

***Medical & Dental Equipment in Japan: A Strategic Entry Report, 1996.** Compiled by Icon Group International Staff. (Illus.). 158p. 1999. ring bd. 1580.00 incl. audio compact disk (*0-7418-1305-X*) Icon Grp.

Medical & Dental Equipment, UL 544. 4th ed. (C). 1998. pap. text 215.00 (*1-55989-469-5*) Underwrtrs Labs.

Medical & Dental Negligence. Robert H. Dickson. LC 98-143898. xvii, 125p. 1997. write for info. (*0-567-00521-6*, Pub. by T & T Clark) Bks Intl VA.

Medical & Dental Space Planning for the 1990s. 2nd ed. Jain Malkin. 512p. 1989. 125.00 (*0-471-28944-2*, VNR) Wiley.

Medical & Dental Space Planning for the 1990s. 2nd ed. Jain Malkin. (Illus.). 144p. 1989. text 92.95 (*0-442-26485-2*, VNR) Wiley.

Medical & Dental Suction & Irrigation Equipment Markets: Environment & Infection Control Issues Encourage Innovations. Market Intelligence Staff. 279p. 1993. 1695.00 (*1-56753-451-1*) Frost & Sullivan.

Medical & Economical Botany. John Lindley. (C). 1988. 50.00 (*0-7855-2294-8*, Pub. by Scientific) St Mut.

Medical & Environmental Aspects of Anaerobes. Ed. by Brian I. Duerden et al. 280p. 1992. 89.00 (*1-871816-13-0*, Pub. by Wrightson Biomed) Taylor & Francis.

Medical & Genetic Aspects of Purebred Dogs. Ed. by Ross D. Clark & Joan R. Stainer. LC 83-80248. (Illus.). 584p. 29.50 (*0-935078-24-X*) Veterinary Med.

Medical & Genetic Aspects of Purebred Dogs II. 2nd ed. Ross D. Clark & Joan R. Stainer. LC 94-1762. 687p. (C). 1994. 103.50 (*0-9641609-0-0*) Cortlandt Grp.

Medical & Health Business Including Economic Competition: Index of New Information. Mary R. Klingenhagen & Jay Klingenhagen. LC 95-15404. 1995. 47.50 (*0-7883-0736-3*); pap. 44.50 (*0-7883-0737-1*) ABBE Pubs Assn.

Medical & Health Care Books & Serials in Print 1998, Set, 2 vols., Vols. 1 & 2. Bowker Staff. 1998. 249.95 (*0-8352-3992-6*) Bowker.

Medical & Health Costs of Care, Illness & Disability: Index of New Information with References. rev. ed. Allen Z. Buckner. 182p. 1997. 47.50 (*0-7883-1582-X*) ABBE Pubs Assn.

Medical & Health Costs of Care, Illness & Disability: Index of New Information with References. rev. ed. Allen Z. Buckner & Vincent Z. De Leo. 182p. 1997. pap. 44.50 (*0-7883-1583-8*) ABBE Pubs Assn.

***Medical & Health Information Directory, 3 vols.** 11th ed. 4200p. 1999. 610.00 (*0-7876-3477-8*) Gale.

Medical & Health Practices & Defensive Medicine: New Research Bible of Current Trends. Herbert H. Newson. 160p. 1994. 47.50 (*0-7883-0200-0*); pap. 44.50 (*0-7883-0201-9*) ABBE Pubs Assn.

Medical & Health Sciences Word Book. 3rd ed. Ann Roe-Hafer. 448p. 1992. 12.00 (*0-395-60664-0*) HM.

***Medical & Healthcare Books & Serials in Print, 1999: An Index to Literature in the Health Sciences, 2 vols., Set.** Ed. by Bowker Staff. 1999. 265.95 (*0-8352-4068-1*) Bowker.

Medical & Healthcare Marketplace Guide. 7th ed. 1991. write for info. (*0-926700-04-9*) MLR Pub.

***Medical & Healthcare Marketplace Guide.** 15th ed. Ed. by Robert Smith. 2680p. 1999. pap. 690.00 (*1-880874-58-X*) Dorland Hlthcare.

Medical & Hospital Negligence, 4 Vols. Ed. by Miles J. Zaremski & Louis S. Goldstein. 350.00 (*0-327-12387-7*) LEXIS Pub.

Medical & Hospital Negligence, 1988-1990, 4 vols. Ed. by Miles J. Zaremski & Louis S. Goldstein. LC 88-26231. 1995. ring bd. 350.00 (*0-685-24499-7*, 69555, MICHIE) LEXIS Pub.

Medical & Hospital Negligence 1998 Cumulative Supplement. Louis S. Goldstein & Miles J. Zaremski. 75p. 1998. ring bd. write for info. (*0-327-00838-5*, 6956012) LEXIS Pub.

Medical & Hospital Plastic Products: A Special Report on New Applications & Research. James M. Margolis. LC 83-15199. (Series of Special Reports: No. 10). 180p. reprint ed. pap. 55.80 (*0-7837-0695-2*, 204102800019) Bks Demand.

Medical & Hygiene Textile Production: A Handbook. Allison Mathews & Martin Hardingham. 56p. (Orig.). 1994. pap. 14.00 (*1-85339-211-1*, Pub. by Intermed Tech) Stylus Pub VA.

Medical & Institutional Waste Incineration: Regulations, Management, Technology, Emissions, & Operations. (Illus.). 41p. (Orig.). (C). 1992. pap. text 20.00 (*1-56806-116-1*) DIANE Pub.

Medical & International Cooperation of Local & World Health Problems: Index of New Information. Tom Y. Appler. 1998. 47.50 (*0-7883-1806-3*); pap. 44.50 (*0-7883-1807-1*) ABBE Pubs Assn.

Medical & Legal Liability in Health Sciences: Index of New Information. Roy R. Zimmerman. 150p. 1994. 47.50 (*0-7883-0078-4*); pap. 44.50 (*0-7883-0079-2*) ABBE Pubs Assn.

Medical & Life-Style Risk Factors Affecting Fetal Mortality, 1989-1990. Donna L. Hoyert. LC 96-30479. (Vital & Health Statistics Ser.: Series 20, No. 31). 1996. write for info. (*0-8406-0517-X*) Natl Ctr Health Stats.

***Medical & Musical Byways of Mozartiana.** Benjamin Simkin. 242p. 2001. pap. 14.95 (*1-56474-349-7*) Fithian Pr.

Medical & Nutritional Complications of Alcoholism: Mechanisms & Management. Charles S. Lieber. (Illus.). 598p. (C). 1992. 132.00 (*0-306-43558-6*, Kluwer Plenum) Kluwer Academic.

Medical & Orthopedic Issues of Active & Athletic Women. Ed. by Rosemary Agostini. LC 94-75825. (Illus.). 300p. (Orig.). 1994. pap. text 50.95 (*1-56053-019-7*) Hanley & Belfus.

Medical & Paramedical Dictionary English-French. W. J. Gladstone. Orig. Title: Dictionnaire Anglais-Francais des Sciences Medicales & Paramedicales. 1282p. 1996. 135.00 (*2-224-02446-0*, Pub. by Maloine) IBD Ltd.

***Medical & Pharmaceutical Sales: How to Land the Job of Your Dreams.** Nikki K. Kerzic. viii, 130p. 1999. pap. 29.95 (*0-9673315-3-6*) Executive Connection.

Medical & Psychiatric Issues for Counselors. Brian Daines et al. (Professional Skills for Counselors Ser.). 160p. 1997. 39.95 (*0-8039-7506-6*); pap. 18.95 (*0-8039-7507-4*) Sage.

Medical & Psychological Effects of Concentration Camps on Holocaust Survivors. Institute on the Holocaust & Genocide (Jerusalem) et al. Ed. by Robert Krell & Marc I. Sherman. LC 97-3110. (Genocide Ser.). 290p. 1997. text 49.95 (*1-56000-290-5*) Transaction Pubs.

Medical & Psychological Hypnosis: How It Benefits Patients. Corydon Hammond. 23p. 1994. pap. text 5.00 (*1-886610-00-2*) Am Soc Clin Hyp Pr.

Medical & Psychosocial Aspects of Chronic Illness & Disability. Donna R. Falvo. LC 91-13953. 448p. 1991. 60.00 (*0-8342-0238-7*) Aspen Pub.

***Medical & Psychosocial Aspects of Chronic Illness & Disability.** 2nd ed. Donna R. Falvo. 480p. 1999. 52.00 (*0-8342-1198-X*) Aspen Pub.

Medical & Scientific Aspects of Cycling. Ed. by Edmund R. Burke & Mary M. Newsom. LC 87-3321. (Illus.). 272p. 1988. reprint ed. pap. 84.40 (*0-608-07072-6*, 206728600008) Bks Demand.

Medical & Scientific Reports & Research on Efficiency & Performance in the Health Sciences. American Health Research Institute Staff. 180p. 1993. 47.50 (*1-55914-870-5*); pap. 44.50 (*1-55914-871-3*) ABBE Pubs Assn.

Medical & Service Delivery Guidelines for Family Planning: Russian Edition. 2nd ed. AVSC International Staff. Ed. by Inna Sacci & Vera Grigorieva. (RUS.). 250p. 1999. pap. write for info. (*1-885063-21-0*) AVSC Int.

Medical & Social Aspects of Alcohol Abuse. Ed. by Boris Tabakoff et al. LC 83-4786. 420p. 1983. 80.00 (*0-306-41221-7*, Plenum Trade) Perseus Pubng.

Medical & Social Problems of the Disabled. V. Kallio. (Euro Reports & Studies Ser.: No. 73). 35p. 1982. pap. text 4.00 (*92-890-1239-0*) World Health.

Medical & Surgical Aspects of Renovascular Hypertension. Ed. by J. Rosenthal & H. E. Franz. (Contributions to Nephrology Ser.: Vol. 3). (Illus.). 200p. 1976. 29.75 (*3-8055-2341-6*) S Karger.

Medical & Surgical Care for Children with Down Syndrome: A Guide for Parents. Ed. by D. C. Van Dyke et al. LC 95-1177. (Illus.). 320p. 1995. pap. 14.95 (*0-933149-54-9*) Woodbine House.

Medical & Surgical History of the Civil War, 15 vols., Set. Ed. by James I. Robertson, Jr. Orig. Title: The Medical & Surgical History of the War of the Rebellion. (Illus.). 1992. reprint ed. 1400.00 (*0-916107-86-8*) Broadfoot.

Medical & Surgical History of the Civil War Index, 3 vols., Set. Ed. by James I. Robertson, Jr. 1400p. 1992. 400.00 (*0-916107-95-7*) Broadfoot.

Medical & Surgical History of the War of the Rebellion see Medical & Surgical History of the Civil War

Medical & Surgical Management of Adrenal Disease. Joseph C. Cerny. LC 96-54024. 1999. 99.00 (*0-683-30344-9*) Lppncott W & W.

Medical & Surgical Management of Adrenal Diseases. Joseph C. Cerny. LC 96-54024. 1997. write for info. (*4-260-14339-5*) Igaku-Shoin.

Medical & Surgical Management of Adrenal Diseases. Ed. by Joseph C. Cerny. LC 96-54024. (Illus.). 224p. 1997. text. write for info. (*0-89640-339-4*) Igaku-Shoin.

Medical & Surgical Management of Prostate Cancer. Ed. by Richard G. Middleton, Jr. LC 95-52984. (Topics in Clinical Urology Ser.). (Illus.). 184p. 1996. 58.00 (*0-89640-293-2*) Igaku-Shoin.

***Medical & Surgical Nursing: Study Guide.** 2nd ed. Priscilla Lemone. 448p. (C). 1999. pap. text, student ed. 19.93 (*0-8053-8127-9*) Benjamin-Cummings.

Medical & Surgical Therapeutics of the Foot & Ankle. David E. Marcinko. (Illus.). 968p. 1992. 125.00 (*0-683-05549-6*) Lppncott W & W.

Medical & Veterinary Chemicals, 2 vols., Set. A. Nineham & R. Slack. LC 66-28423. 1968. reprint ed. 225.00 (*0-08-011967-0*, Pub. by Pergamon Repr) Franklin.

Medical & Veterinary Entomology. 2nd ed. D. S. Kettle. LC 96-182455. 750p. 1995. text 140.00 (*0-85198-968-3*) OUP.

Medical & Veterinary Entomology. 2nd ed. D. S. Kettle. LC 96-182455. (CAB International Publication). (Illus.). 736p. 1995. pap. text 70.00 (*0-85198-969-1*) OUP.

Medical Anthropology. Ed. by Francis X. Grollig & Harold B. Haley. (World Anthropology Ser.). (Illus.). xviii, 486p. 1976. 58.50 (*90-279-7799-2*) Mouton.

Medical Anthropology: Contemporary Theory & Method. Ed. by Thomas R. Johnson. LC 95-40052. 584p. 1996. pap. 35.00 (*0-275-95265-7*, Greenwood Pr) Greenwood.

Medical Anthropology & African American Health. Eric J. Bailey. LC 99-21244. 272p. 2000. 65.00 (*0-89789-592-4*, Bergin & Garvey) Greenwood.

Medical Anthropology & the World System: A Critical Perspective. Hans A. Baer et al. LC 97-16134. 288p. 1997. 72.95 (*0-89789-424-3*, Bergin & Garvey); pap. 24.95 (*0-89789-539-8*, Bergin & Garvey) Greenwood.

Medical Anthropology in Ecological Perspective. 3rd ed. Ann McElroy & Patricia K. Townsend. (C). 1996. pap. 36.00 (*0-8133-8610-1*, Pub. by Westview) HarpC.

Medical Anthropology of the Jaunsaris. S. N. Rizvi. (C). 1991. text 16.00 (*81-7211-012-X*, Pub. by Northern Bk Ctr) S Asia.

***Medical Aphorishms, Bks. 1-5.** Moses Maimonides. Ed. by Gerrit Bos. (Graeco-Arabic Sciences Ser.). (ARA & ENG.). 320p. 2000. 29.95 (*0-8425-2474-6*) Brigham.

Medical Application of Liposomes. Ed. by K. Yagi. (Illus.). viii, 204p. 1986. 124.50 (*3-8055-4404-9*) S Karger.

Medical Applications see Autogenic Therapy

***Medical Applications for Shape-Memory Alloys, 1999.** (IMechE Seminar Publication Ser.: Vol. 1999-11). 65p. 1999. 93.00 (*1-86058-241-9*) Prof Eng Pubng.

Medical Applications of Computer Modelling Vol. 1: Cardiovascular & Ocular Systems. Ed. by T. B. Martonen. (Advances in Computational Bioengineering Ser.: Vol. 3). 297p. 2000. 139.00 (*1-85312-613-6*, Pub. by WIT Pr) Computational Mech MA.

***Medical Applications of Computer Modelling Vol. 2: Respiratory System.** Ed. by T. B. Martonen. (Advances in Computational Bioengineering Ser.). 337p. 2000. 157.00 (*1-85312-808-2*, Pub. by WIT Pr) Computational Mech MA.

Medical Applications of Controlled Release, 2 vols., Vol. I: Classes of Systems. Ed. by Robert S. Langer & Donald L. Wise. 272p. 1985. 155.00 (*0-8493-5405-6*, RS201, CRC Reprint) Franklin.

Medical Applications of Controlled Release, 2 vols., Vol. II: Applications & Evaluation. Ed. by Robert S. Langer & Donald L. Wise. 248p. 1985. 137.00 (*0-8493-5406-4*, RS201, CRC Reprint) Franklin.

Medical Applications of Fluorescent Excitation Analysis. Leon Kaufman. 176p. 1979. 104.00 (*0-8493-5507-9*, QP519, CRC Reprint) Franklin.

Medical Applications of Lasers in Dermatology, Cardiology, Gynecology, Ophthalmology & Dentistry II, Ed. by Gregory B. Altshuler et al. LC 98-145664. (Europto Ser.: Vol. 3192). 306p. 1997. 99.00 (*0-8194-2624-5*) SPIE.

Medical Applications of Lasers in Dermatology, Cardiology, Gynecology, Ophthalmology & Dentistry II. Ed. by Peter Bjerring et al. (Europto Ser.: Vol. 3564). 1998. 89.00 (*0-8194-3026-9*) SPIE.

Medical Applications of Liposomes. D. D. Lasic & Demetrios Papahadjopoulos. LC 98-22644. 779p. 1998. 273.00 (*0-444-82917-2*) Elsevier.

Medical Applications of Natural Family Planning: A Contemporary Approach to Women's Health Care. Thomas W. Hilgers. LC 01-62339. (Illus.). 183p. (Orig.). 1991. pap. text 29.95 (*0-9626485-1-5*) Pope Paul Sixth.

Medical Applications of Piezoelectric Polymers. P. M Galletti et al. 352p. 1988. 89.00 (*0-677-21730-7*) Gordon & Breach.

Medical Applications of Piezoelectric Polymers, Vol. 5. Ed. by P. M. Galletti et al. (Ferroelectricity & Related Phenomena Ser.: Vol. No. 5). xii, 306p. 1988. text 249.00 (*2-88124-277-4*) Gordon & Breach.

Medical Applications of Reflexology: Findings in Research about Safety, Efficacy, Mechanism of Action. Kevin Kunz & Barbara Kunz. 36p. (C). 1999. pap. 29.95 (*0-9606070-3-X*) Reflex Res Proj.

Medical Applications of Synchrotron Radiation. Ed. by M. Ando et al. (Illus.). xii, 200p. 1998. 99.00 (*4-431-70229-6*) Spr-Verlag.

Medical Applications of the Behavioral Sciences. Ed. by Jonathan J. Braunstein & Richard P. Toister. LC 81-3435. (Illus.). 544p. reprint ed. pap. 168.70 (*0-608-18136-6*, 203279000081) Bks Demand.

Medical Applications of Titanium No. 1272: The Material & Biological Issues, Vol. 1272. Ed. by Stanley A. Brown & Jack E. Lemons. LC 96-13656. (Special Technical Publication Ser.). (Illus.). 425p. 1996. text 79.00 (*0-8031-2010-9*, STP1272) ASTM.

Medical Armageddon, 4 vols. in 2 bks. Michael L. Culbert. Incl. Bk. 1, Vols. I & II. (Illus.). 1997. pap. (*0-9636487-1-3*); Bk. 2, Vols. III & IV. (Illus.). 1997. pap. (*0-9636487-2-1*); write for info. (*0-9636487-3-X*) C&C Communs.

M

An Asterisk (*) at the beginning of an entry indicates that the title is appearing for the first time.

Medical Armageddon. rev. ed. Michael L. Culbert. LC 97-69817. (Illus.). 830p. 1997. pap. 29.95 (*0-9636487-5-6*) C&C Communs.

Medical Aromatherapy: Healing with Essential Oils. Kurt Schnaubelt. LC 97-46512. (Illus.). 300p. 1999. pap. 16.95 (*1-883319-69-2*) Frog Ltd CA.

Medical Art & Science of Relaxation in Sickness & Health: Index of New Information with Authors & Subjects. Sally M. Frost. 180p. 1993. 47.50 (*1-55914-906-X*); pap. 44.50 (*1-55914-907-8*) ABBE Pubs Assn.

*__Medical Art Therapy with Adults.__ Ed. by Cathy Malchiodi. 240p. 1999. text 69.95 (*1-85302-678-6*, Pub. by Jessica Kingsley) Taylor & Francis.

*__Medical Art Therapy With Adults.__ Cathy A. Malchiodi. 1999. pap. text 29.95 (*1-85302-679-4*) ITCP.

*__Medical Art Therapy with Children.__ Cathy A. Malchiodi. (Illus.). 1998. pap. 25.95 (*1-85302-677-8*) Jessica Kingsley.

Medical Art Therapy with Children. Cathy A. Malchiodi. 1998. 69.95 (*1-85302-676-X*) Taylor & Francis.

Medical Aspects of Balance of Diabetes in Juveniles: Part I: Medical Aspects. Proceedings of the 3rd Beilinson, Symposium, Tel Aviv, April-May 1975. International Beilinson Symposium Staff. Ed. by Z. Laron. (Pediatric & Adolescent Endocrinology Ser.: Vol. 2). (Illus.). 1977. 85.25 (*3-8055-2388-2*) S Karger.

M

Medical Aspects of Biochemistry. William E. Schreiber. 304p. 1984. 22.50 (*0-316-77473-1*, Little Brwn Med Div) Lppncott W & W.

Medical Aspects of Boxing. Jordan. 352p. 1992. lib. bdg. 119.00 (*0-8493-4281-3*, RC1220) CRC Pr.

Medical Aspects of Crime. William N. East. 1980. lib. bdg. 79.95 (*0-8490-3160-5*) Gordon Pr.

Medical Aspects of Developmental Disabilities in Children Birth to Three. 3rd ed. Blackman. LC 96-44579. 320p. 1997. 40.00 (*0-8342-0759-1*) Aspen Pub.

Medical Aspects of Disability: A Handbook for the Rehabilitation Professional. 2nd ed. Ed. by Myron G. Eisenberg et al. LC 98-50679. 744p. 1999. text 62.95 (*0-8261-7971-1*) Springer Pub.

Medical Aspects of Early Intervention. James A. Blackman. 240p. 1995. 33.00 (*0-8342-0648-X*) Aspen Pub.

Medical Aspects of Food Handling: Medical Subject Research Analysis with Bibliography. Tomas J. Punjaba. LC 84-45737. 150p. 1986. pap. 44.50 (*0-88164-253-3*) ABBE Pubs Assn.

Medical Aspects of Mortality Statistics. Ed. by H. Bostrom & N. Ljungstedt. (Illus.). 388p. (Orig.). 1981. pap. text 58.00 (*91-22-00440-8*) Coronet Bks.

Medical Aspects of Nuclear - Biological - Chemical Defensive Operations. 1991. lib. bdg. 75.00 (*0-8490-4198-8*) Gordon Pr.

Medical Aspects of Personal Injury Litigation. Michael Barnes et al. LC 97-23811. 1997. 125.00 (*0-632-04176-5*) Blackwell Sci.

Medical Aspects of Proteases & Protease Inhibitors. Ed. by H. Kido et al. LC 96-78120. 300p. (gr. 12). 1997. 106.00 (*90-5199-292-0*, 292-0) IOS Press.

Medical Aspects of Radiation Accidents. Eugene L. Saenger & AEC Technical Information Center Staff. 369p. 1963. 44.50 (*0-87079-268-7*, TID-18867); fiche 9.00 (*0-87079-388-8*, TID-18867) DOE.

Medical Aspects of Underwriting: Assorted Selection. D. W. Sutherland. (C). 1989. 50.00 (*0-7855-4079-2*) St Mut.

Medical Assessment of Fitness to Dive. David Elliott. (Illus.). 302p. 1994. 78.75 (*0-9525162-0-9*, D746) Best Pub Co.

Medical Assistant. Julie B. Hosley. LC 96-34495. 768p. 1997. text 50.00 (*0-397-55096-0*) Lppncott W & W.

Medical Assistant. Primm. LC 97-35234. (Careers Without College Ser.). 48p. (J). (gr. 3-4). 1998. 19.00 (*1-56065-705-7*) Capstone Pr.

Medical Assistant. E. Russell Primm. (Careers Without College Ser.). (Illus.). 48p. (J). (gr. 3-7). 1998. 19.00 (*0-516-21284-2*) Childrens.

Medical Assistant. Jack Rudman. (Career Examination Ser.: C-1365). 1994. pap. 23.95 (*0-8373-1365-1*) Nat Learn.

Medical Assistant. 6th ed. Marian G. Cooper et al. LC 92-48690. 1992. text 36.95 (*0-8016-1012-5*) Mosby Inc.

Medical Assistant. 6th ed. Marian G. Cooper et al. 1993. teacher ed. write for info. (*0-8151-2663-8*) Mosby Inc.

Medical Assistant. 6th ed. Marian G. Cooper et al. (Illus.). 624p. (C). (gr. 13). 1993. text 43.00 (*0-8016-7445-X*, 01012) Mosby Inc.

Medical Assistant: Administrative & Clinical. 7th ed. Mary E. Kinn et al. (Illus.). 1993. teacher ed. write for info. (*0-7216-6718-X*, W B Saunders Co) Harcrt Hlth Sci Grp.

Medical Assistant: Administrative & Clinical. 7th ed. Mary E. Kinn et al. LC 93-6719. (Illus.). 864p. 1993. text 39.95 (*0-7216-4691-3*, W B Saunders Co); pap. text, student ed. 17.95 (*0-7216-6719-8*, W B Saunders Co) Harcrt Hlth Sci Grp.

Medical Assistant: Administrative & Clinical. 8th ed. Kinn. LC 98-36106. (Illus.). 735p. (C). 1999. text. write for info. (*0-7216-7299-X*, W B Saunders Co) Harcrt Hlth Sci Grp.

Medical Assistant: An Intermediate Level of Health Care Personnel. Ed. by D. M. Pitcairn & D. M. Flahault. (Public Health Papers: No. 60). 1974. pap. text 10.00 (*92-4-130060-4*, 1110060) World Health.

Medical Assistant: Clinical Calculations. 2nd ed. Watts. (Medical Assisting Ser.). 1989. pap., teacher ed. 12.00 (*0-8273-3079-0*) Delmar.

Medical Assistant: Clinical Calculations. 2nd ed. Edith A. Watts. (Medical Assisting Ser.). 1989. pap. 28.95 (*0-8273-3078-2*) Delmar.

Medical Assistant Clinical Comp, Section 1. 2nd ed. Keir. (Medical Assisting Ser.). 1989. 10.95 (*0-8273-5257-3*) Delmar.

Medical Assistant Clinical Comp, Section 3. 3rd ed. Keir. (Medical Assisting Ser.). 1989. 10.95 (*0-8273-5260-3*) Delmar.

Medical Assistant Clinical Comp, Section 4. 2nd ed. Keir. (Medical Assisting Ser.). 1989. 10.95 (*0-8273-5261-1*) Delmar.

Medical Assistant Examination Review. 4th ed. Laverne Dreizen. 267p. (C). 1989. pap. text 24.95 (*0-8385-5772-4*, A5772-7) Appleton & Lange.

Medical Assisting. Keir. (Medical Assisting Ser.). 1986. teacher ed. 22.00 (*0-8273-2388-3*) Delmar.

Medical Assisting. Jack Rudman. (Occupational Competency Examination (OCE) Ser.: Vol. 26). 47.95 (*0-8373-5776-4*) Nat Learn.

Medical Assisting. Jack Rudman. (Occupational Competency Examination Ser.: OCE-26). 1994. pap. 27.95 (*0-8373-5726-8*) Nat Learn.

Medical Assisting. 4th ed. Keir. (Medical Assisting Ser.). (C). 1998. pap. text, suppl. ed. 49.95 (*0-8273-7716-9*) Delmar.

Medical Assisting. 4th ed. Keir et al. (Medical Assisting Ser.). 320p. (C). 1998. teacher ed., spiral bd. 79.95 (*0-8273-7714-2*) Delmar.

Medical Assisting: A Patient-Centered Approach to Administrative & Clinical Competencies. Barbara Prickett-Ramutkowski. (Illus.). (gr. 6-12). 1999. student ed., wbk. ed. 19.75 (*0-02-802429-X*) Glencoe.

Medical Assisting: Administration & Clinical Compensation. 4th ed. Keir et al. (Medical Assisting Ser.). 480p. (C). 1997. pap. text, teacher ed. 24.00 (*0-8273-7715-0*); pap. text, wbk. ed. 24.00 (*0-8273-7713-4*) Delmar.

Medical Assisting: Administration & Clinical Comprehension. 4th ed. Lucille Keir et al. LC 97-16219. (Medical Assisting Ser.). 832p. (C). 1997. mass mkt. 63.95 incl. disk (*0-8273-7712-6*) Delmar.

Medical Assisting: Administrative & Clinical Competencies. 3rd ed. Lucille Keir et al. LC 92-49820. 778p. 1992. text 46.95 (*0-8273-5311-1*) Delmar.

Medical Assisting: Administrative & Clinical Competencies. 3rd ed. Lucille Keir et al. 1993. pap., teacher ed. 25.00 (*0-8273-5313-8*); text, student ed. 22.95 (*0-8273-5314-6*) Delmar.

Medical Assisting: Administrative & Clinical Competencies. 3rd ed. Lucille Keir et al. LC 92-49820. 778p. 1993. pap. 62.95 (*0-8273-5919-5*) Delmar.

Medical Assisting: Administrative & Clinical Competencies: Teacher's Resource Kit. 3rd ed. Lucille Keir et al. 251p. 1993. 74.95 (*0-8273-5694-3*) Delmar.

Medical Assisting: Advanced Clinical Skills Manual. Shea. (Medical Assisting Ser.). 96p. 1996. pap., teacher ed. 14.00 (*0-8273-5642-0*) Delmar.

Medical Assisting: Clinical & Administrative Competencies. 2nd ed. Lucille Keir et al. 495p. 1989. pap., teacher ed. 22.00 (*0-8273-3508-3*) Delmar.

Medical Assisting: Clinical Competencies. Connie Krebs & Barbara A. Wise. LC 93-43603. 612p. (C). 1994. pap. 36.00 (*0-8273-4986-6*) Delmar.

Medical Assisting: Clinical Competencies: Instructor's Guide. Connie Krebs & Barbara A. Wise. 137p. 1993. pap. 18.00 (*0-8273-4987-4*) Delmar.

Medical Assisting: Clinical Skills Manual. Donna Shea & Adrienne L. Carter-Ward. LC 94-30041. 576p. (C). 1995. mass mkt. 43.95 (*0-8273-5641-2*) Delmar.

Medical Assisting - Clinical Competencies: Workbook. Connie Krebs & Barbara A. Wise. 325p. (C). 1994. pap. 18.95 (*0-8273-4988-2*) Delmar.

Medical Assisting Administration: Engine Repair. 3rd ed. Keir. (Medical Assisting Ser.). 1993. 112.50 (*0-8273-6191-2*) Delmar.

Medical Assisting Examination Guide: A Comprehensive Review for Certification. 2nd ed. Karen Lane. (Illus.). 267p. (C). 1995. pap. text 29.95 (*0-8036-0039-9*) Davis Co.

*__Medical Assisting Program.__ Pat Moeck. 1999. pap. text 15.77 (*1-56870-366-X*) RonJon Pub.

Medical Assisting Review Manual. Marsha P. Hemby. LC 94-32087. (Illus.). 192p. 1994. pap. 39.20 (*0-8359-4928-1*) P-H.

Medical Astrology. Heinrich Daath. 108p. 1992. pap. 10.00 (*0-89540-195-9*, SB-195, Sun Bks) Sun Pub.

Medical Astrology. Heinrich Daath. 108p. 1996. reprint ed. spiral bd. 10.00 (*0-7873-0237-6*) Hlth Research.

Medical Astrology. Heinrich Daath. 115p. 1996. reprint ed. pap. 7.95 (*1-56459-758-X*) Kessinger Pub.

Medical Astrology. 3rd rev. ed. Eileen Nauman. 357p. (Orig.). 1996. pap. 29.95 (*0-9634662-4-0*) Blue Turtle.

*__Medical Audiology.__ Wynne. 2000. pap. 52.75 (*0-7693-0004-9*) Thomson Learn.

Medical Audit: Rationale & Practicalities. Ed. by Simon P. Frostick et al. (Illus.). 457p. 1993. pap. text 57.95 (*0-521-44604-X*) Cambridge U Pr.

Medical Audit & General Practice. 2nd ed. Ed. by Marshall Marinker. 250p. 1995. pap. text 12.00 (*0-7279-0908-8*, Pub. by BMJ Pub) Login Brothers Bk Co.

Medical Audit in Primary Health Care. Ed. by Martin S. Lawrence & Theo Schofield. LC 92-48416. (Oxford Medical Pubns.). (Illus.). 270p. 1993. pap. text 34.50 (*0-19-262267-6*) OUP.

Medical Bacteriology. 3rd ed. J. Douglas Sleigh & Morag C. Timbury. (Student Notes Ser.). (Illus.). 438p. 1990. pap. text 34.00 (*0-443-04147-4*) Church.

Medical Bacteriology. 14th ed. Ed. by N. C. Dey. (C). 1988. 155.00 (*0-7210-0123-8*, Pub. by Current Dist) St Mut.

Medical Bacteriology: A Practical Approach. P. M. Hawkey & D. A. Lewis. (Practical Approach Ser.: 52). (Illus.). 344p. 1990. pap. text 49.95 (*0-19-963009-7*) OUP.

Medical Basics: A Self-Instructional Text. Linda Gifford-Meuleveld. 170p. 1996. pap. text, per. 35.00 (*0-7872-2063-9*) Kendall-Hunt.

Medical Basis for Radiation Accident Preparedness. Ed. by Robert C. Ricks & S. A. Fry. 548p. 1991. 175.00 (*0-444-01585-X*) P-H.

Medical Basis of Psychiatry. 2nd ed. Paula Clayton. Ed. by George Winokur. LC 93-22601. (Illus.). 624p. 1994. text 72.00 (*0-7216-6484-9*, W B Saunders Co) Harcrt Hlth Sci Grp.

Medical Bibliography in an Age of Discontinuity. Scott Adams. 244p. 1981. 14.00 (*0-8108-2433-7*) Scarecrow.

*__Medical Bill Survival Guide: What You Need to Know Before You Pay a Dime.__ Pat Palmer et al. 2000. mass mkt. 6.99 (*0-446-60862-9*) Warner Bks.

Medical Biller/Health Claims Examiner Curriculum Package: Including Software. 4th rev. ed. Insurance Career Development Center Staff & Caitlind L. Alexander. Ed. by Sharon E. Brown. (Illus.). 950p. (C). 1998. 1399.00 incl. cd-rom (*1-881159-26-4*, CCP) Ins Career Dev.

Medical Billing: The Bottom Line: An Entrepreneur's Guide. Claudia A. Yalden. (Orig.). Date not set. pap. 24.95 (*1-880325-39-X*) Borderlnds NH.

Medical Billing & Claims Examining, 3 vols. rev. ed. Insurance Career Development Center Staff et al. (Illus.). 1165p. (C). 1999. pap. text 91.95 (*1-881159-09-4*, 24404) Ins Career Dev.

Medical Billing Home-Based Business: Success in Marketing & Consulting, Vol. II. Merlin B. Coslick. 64p. 1998. pap. 4.95 (*1-893978-03-6*) Electron Med Bill.

Medical Billing Home-Based Business Vol. I: Success in Management & Business Strategies. Merlin B. Coslick. 66p. 1998. pap. 4.95 (*1-893978-02-8*) Electron Med Bill.

Medical Billing Home-Based Business Vol. III: More Success in Marketing & Consulting. Merlin B. Coslick. 85p. 1999. pap. 7.95 (*1-893978-04-4*) Electron Med Bill.

Medical Billing Service: A Survival Guide for the 21st Century. Thomas Banks. (Illus.). 300p. (Orig.). 1997. pap. 49.95 (*0-9659278-0-6*) Sounding Bd.

*__Medical Billing the Bottom Line Revised: Entrepreneur's Guide to Understanding Medical Billing.__ Claudia Yalden. (Illus.). 270p. 1999. pap. 29.99 (*0-7392-0361-4*, PO3555) Morris Pubng.

Medical Biochemistry. N. V. Bhagavan. 992p. (C). 1992. 70.00 (*0-86720-030-8*) Jones & Bartlett.

*__Medical Biochemistry.__ 2nd ed. Nadhipuram V. Bhagavan. 960p. 2000. 79.95 (*0-12-095440-0*) Acad Pr.

Medical Biochemistry at a Glance. Ben D. Greenstein et al. LC 95-36168. (Illus.). 112p. 1996. 22.95 (*0-86542-980-4*) Blackwell Sci.

Medical Biochemistry for the Tropics. J. K. Candlish. 1977. text 30.00 (*0-7020-0619-X*) Bailliere Tindall.

Medical Biology of Bees: Index of New Information for Reference & Research. James G. Jinno. 150p. 1997. 47.50 (*0-7883-1332-0*); pap. 44.50 (*0-7883-1333-9*) ABBE Pubs Assn.

Medical Biology of Grief-Reactions & Management: Index of New Information. Jennifer W. Quinn. 150p. 1997. 47.50 (*0-7883-1384-3*); pap. 44.50 (*0-7883-1385-1*) ABBE Pubs Assn.

Medical Biology of Yohimbine & Its Easy Use in Male Sex Erectile Dysfunction: Index of New Information with Authors, Subjects, Research Categories & References. Henry Z. Poche. 167p. 1997. 47.50 (*0-7883-1590-0*); pap. 44.50 (*0-7883-1591-9*) ABBE Pubs Assn.

Medical Biostatistics & Epidemiology: Examination & Board Review. Diane Essex-Sorl. 359p. (C). 1995. pap. text 32.95 (*0-8385-6219-1*, A6219-8, Apple Lange Med) McGraw.

Medical Blemishes: Untrue Stories about Real Problems. Loren Humphrey. 133p. 1997. pap. 9.95 (*1-890622-24-9*) Leathers Pub.

Medical Block Buchenwald. Walter Poller. 1987. pap. 7.95 (*0-8184-0448-5*) Carol Pub Group.

Medical Bloopers!! Amusing & Amazing Stories of Health Care Workers. Melody T. McCloud. (Illus.). 72p. (Orig.). 1994. pap. 6.95 (*0-9643554-0-X*) New Life GA.

Medical Blunders: Amazing True Stories of Mad, Bad, & Dangerous Doctors. Robert M. Youngson & Ian Schott. 416p. (C). 1996. text 55.00 (*0-8147-9678-8*) NYU Pr.

*__Medical Blunders: Amazing True Stories of Mad, Bad & Dangerous Doctors.__ Robert M. Youngson & Ian Schott. 405p. 1999. pap. 17.95 (*0-8147-9689-3*) NYU Pr.

*__Medical Boards - Step 1 Made Ridiculously Simple.__ 2nd ed. Andreas Carl. (Illus.). 367p. (Orig.). (C). 1999. pap. text 24.95 (*0-940780-39-9*) MedMaster.

Medical Boards - Step 2 Made Ridiculously Simple. Andreas Carl. LC 97-122209. 356p. 1999. pap. text 24.95 (*0-940780-28-3*) MedMaster.

Medical Boards Step 3 Made Ridiculously Simple. Andreas Carl. (Illus.). 285p. 1999. pap. text 22.95 (*0-940780-37-2*) MedMaster.

Medical Book Illustration: A Short History. John L. Thornton & Carole Reeves. (Medical Bks.: Vol. 2). (Illus.). 1984. 35.00 (*0-906672-07-4*) Oleander Pr.

Medical Book of Remedies: 50 Ways to Ease Back Pain. Billy Glisan. (Illus.). 80p. 1998. text 20.00 (*0-7881-5391-9*) DIANE Pub.

Medical Book of Remedies: 50 Ways to Manage Diabetes. Anne Betschart & American Association of Diabetes Educators Staff. LC 96-105879. 80p. 1995. write for info. (*0-7853-1233-1*) Pubns Intl Ltd.

Medical Botany: A Herbal Guide to Health. William J. Simmonite. 1992. lib. bdg. 88.00 (*0-8490-8705-8*) Gordon Pr.

Medical Botany: A Herbal Guide to Health. William J. Simmonite. 191p. 1996. reprint ed. spiral bd. 13.00 (*0-7873-0794-7*) Hlth Research.

Medical Botany: Plants Affecting Man's Health. Walter H. Lewis & Memory P. Elvin-Lewis. LC 76-44376. 544p. 1982. pap. 59.95 (*0-471-86134-0*) Wiley.

Medical Brain Teasers, Puzzles & Games. Deena Silverman. 117p. (C). 1993. pap. 24.50 (*0-8273-5635-8*) Delmar.

Medical Briefs: A Dictionary of Realtime Briefs for Court Reporters, 2 vols. Laurie Boucke. LC 98-8417. 1380p. 1998. pap. 75.00 (*1-888580-02-X*) White-Boucke.

Medical Care & Risks of Dysfunctional Chronic Pain: Abstract, Executive Summary, Final Report & Appendices A-C. Michael Van Korff. (Illus.). 99p. (C). 1998. reprint ed. pap. text 25.00 (*0-7881-4505-3*) DIANE Pub.

Medical Care & the General Practitioner, 1750-1850. Irvine Loudon. LC 86-14172. (Illus.). 368p. (C). 1987. text 75.00 (*0-19-822793-0*) OUP.

Medical Care Appraisal *see* **Guide to Medical Care Administration**

Medical Care for the Aged: From Social Problem to Federal Program. Ed. by Henry P. Brehm. LC 85-16753. 264p. 1985. 59.95 (*0-275-90021-5*, C0021, Praeger Pubs) Greenwood.

Medical Care for the American People: Proceedings of the Committee on the Costs of Medical Care, October, 1932. Medical Care Costs Committee. LC 75-180569. (Medicine & Society in America Ser.). 242p. 1977. reprint ed. 19.95 (*0-405-03944-1*) Ayer.

Medical Care for the Elderly: Acute & Chronic Care. Ed. by I. M. Smith et al. LC 80-26495. 276p. 1982. text 35.00 (*0-88331-158-5*) R B Luce.

Medical Care for the Poor & Indigent: Index of Modern Information. Nellie M. Jacobs. LC 88-47987. 150p. 1989. 47.50 (*1-55914-062-3*); pap. 44.50 (*1-55914-063-1*) ABBE Pubs Assn.

Medical Care in Down Syndrome: A Preventive Medicine Approach, No. 8. Paul T. Rogers & Harry Coleman. (Pediatric Habilitation Ser.: Vol. 8). (Illus.). 360p. 1992. text 75.00 (*0-8247-8684-X*) Dekker.

Medical Care in Pioneer Illinois. John K. Crellin. LC 82-81512. (Illus.). 128p. 1982. 15.95 (*0-931369-19-3*) Southern IL Univ Sch.

Medical Care in the Nursing Home. Joseph G. Ouslander et al. 461p. 1991. text 58.00 (*0-07-047949-6*) McGraw-Hill HPD.

Medical Care in the Nursing Home. 2nd ed. Joseph G. Ouslander et al. LC 96-43576. (Illus.). 480p. 1996. text 60.00 (*0-07-048209-8*) McGraw-Hill HPD.

Medical Care in the United States: The Debate Before 1940, 14 vol. Ed. by Charles E. Rosenberg. 433.00 (*0-8153-0321-1*) Garland.

Medical Care, Medical Costs: The Search for a Health Insurance Policy. Rashi Fein. 256p. 1986. 29.00 (*0-674-56052-3*) HUP.

Medical Care, Medical Costs: The Search for a Health Insurance Policy. Rashi Fein. 256p. 1989. pap. 17.50 (*0-674-56053-1*) HUP.

*__Medical Care, Medical Costs: The Search for a Health Insurance Policy.__ Rashi Fein. 256p. 1999. 26.95 (*0-7351-0186-8*) Replica Bks.

Medical Care of Prisoners & Detainees. CIBA Foundation Staff. LC 73-82148. (CIBA Foundation Symposium: New Ser.: No. 16). 246p. reprint ed. pap. 76.30 (*0-608-13499-6*, 202214700024) Bks Demand.

Medical Care of Refugees. Ed. by Richard H. Sandler & Thomas C. Jones. (Illus.). 432p. 1987. text 42.50 (*0-19-504181-X*) OUP.

Medical Care of Terminally Ill Patients. Robert E. Enck. LC 93-20529. (Series in Hematology-Oncology). 224p. (C). 1993. text 65.00 (*0-8018-4675-7*); pap. text 28.95 (*0-8018-4763-X*) Johns Hopkins.

Medical Care of the Adolescent Athlete. Eugene F. Luckstead & Donald E. Greydanus. (Illus.). 325p. 1993. pap. 45.95 (*1-878487-18-3*, 5847M) Practice Mgmt Info.

Medical Care of the Dying Patient. Ed. by Robert DeBellis et al. 1982. 33.95 (*0-405-13947-0*) Ayer.

Medical Care of the Liver Transplant Patient. Paul G. Killenberg & Pierre A. Clavien. LC 96-6592. (Illus.). 200p. (Orig.). 1997. text 95.00 (*0-86542-524-8*) Blackwell Sci.

Medical Care of the Nursing Home Resident: What Physicians Need to Know. Ed. by Richard W. Besdine et al. LC 96-12363. 175p. 1996. pap. 29.00 (*0-943126-48-7*) Amer Coll Phys.

Medical Care of the Pregnant Patient. Richard S. Abrams & Paul Wexler. 404p. 1983. 49.95 (*0-316-00470-7*, Little Brwn Med Div) Lppncott W & W.

Medical Care of the Pregnant Patient. Richard V. Lee et al. LC 99-12514. (Women's Health Ser.). 2000. pap. 55.00 (*0-943126-81-9*, 330301190) Amer Coll Phys.

*__Medical Care of the Soul: A Practical & Healing Guide to End-of-Life Issues for Families, Patients, & Healthcare Providers.__ Bruce G. Bartlow. 304p. 2000. 32.50 (*1-55566-253-6*); pap. 18.00 (*1-55566-254-4*) Johnson Bks.

Medical Care of Women. Phyllis L. Carr et al. LC 94-34774. (Illus.). 874p. 1995. text 105.00 (*0-7216-3779-5*, W B Saunders Co) Harcrt Hlth Sci Grp.

Medical Care Reform: A Guide to Issues & Choices. Henry A. Shenkin. 168p. 1993. pap. 14.95 (*0-9638888-4-6*) Oakvale Pr.

Medical Care Representative. Jack Rudman. (Career Examination Ser.: C-3147). 1994. pap. 29.95 (*0-8373-3147-1*) Nat Learn.

Medical Care System: A Conceptual Model. Michael Long. LC 94-34492. (Illus.). 176p. 1994. pap. 17.50 (*1-56793-016-6*, 0946) Health Admin Pr.

Medical Case Management: Forms, Checklists, & Guidelines. annuals Aspen Reference Group Staff. Ed. by Rufus Howe. 506p. ring bd., suppl. ed. 175.00 (*0-8342-0624-2*, S173) Aspen Pub.

An Asterisk (*) at the beginning of an entry indicates that the title is appearing for the first time.

Medical Casebook of Adolf Hitler see **Adolf Hitler - A Medical Descent That Changed History: His Drug Abuse, Doctors & Illnesses**
***Medical Casebook of Adolf Hitler: His Illnesses, Doctors & Drugs.** Leonard L. Heston. 2000. pap. write for info. (0-8154-1066-2, Pub. by Cooper Sq) Natl Bk Netwk.
Medical Casebook of Adolf Hitler: His Illnesses, Doctors, & Drugs. 2nd rev. ed. Leonard L. Heston & Renate Heston. (Illus.). 204p. Date not set. pap. 14.95 (0-9665852-9-1) Baypoint Pr.
Medical Casebook of Doctor Arthur Conan Doyle: From Practitioner to Sherlock Holmes & Beyond. A. E. Rodin & Jack D. Key. LC 83-16232. 506p. 1984. 53.50 (0-89874-592-6) Krieger.
Medical Catheter Markets: New Applications, Technologies, & Safety Issues Overcome Cost Containment. Market Intelligence Staff. 245p. (Orig.). 1992. 1895.00 (1-56753-057-5) Frost & Sullivan.
Medical Catheters & Catheterizations - Harmful Reactions, Errors, Punctures, Migrations, Displacements & Complications: Index of New Information. rev. ed. Roy R. Zimmerman. 145p. 1997. 47.50 (0-7883-1574-9); pap. 44.50 (0-7883-1575-7) ABBE Pubs Assn.
Medical Causes. Tanya L. Stone. LC 97-25244. (Celebrity Activists Ser.). 64p. (YA). (gr. 5 up). 1997. 20.40 (0-8050-5233-X) TFC Bks NY.
Medical Causes of Deaths in Hospitals: Index of New Information & Medical Research Bible. rev. ed. Joel P. Travis. 145p. 1998. 47.50 (0-7883-2088-2); pap. 44.50 (0-7883-2089-0) ABBE Pubs Assn.
Medical Cell Biology. 2nd ed. Steven R. Goodman. LC 97-26571. 300p. 1997. pap. text 32.95 (0-397-58427-X) Lppncott W & W.
Medical Cell Biology Made Memorable. Robert I. Norman & David Lodwick. LC 98-46714. 1999. write for info. (0-443-06135-1, W B Saunders Co) Harcrt Hlth Sci Grp.
Medical Center Lab. Melvin Berger. LC 76-12964. (Scientists at Work Ser.). (Illus.). (J). (gr. 3 up). 1936. lib. bdg. 11.89 (0-381-99602-6) HarpC Child Bks.
***Medical Center Occupational Health & Safety.** Robert J. McCunney. LC 99-14496. 429p. 1999. text. write for info. (0-7817-2198-9) Lppncott W & W.
Medical Charities, Medical Politics: The Irish Dispensary System & the Poor Law, 1836-1872. Ronald D. Cassell. LC 97-3751. (Royal Historical Society Studies in History). 192p. 1997. 60.00 (0-86193-228-5, Royal Historical Soc) Boydell & Brewer.
Medical Chemistry. Thomas. 2000. text. write for info. (0-471-98807-3) Wiley.
Medical Choice in a Mexican Village. James C. Young & Linda C. Garro. (Illus.). 233p. (C). 1994. reprint ed. pap. text 12.50 (0-88133-785-4) Waveland Pr.
Medical Claim Game - & How to Win It. G. J. Watkins. LC 91-66284. (Illus.). 125p. 1995. pap. 14.95 (0-9639152-1-5) Shadow Pubns.
Medical Claims - & Claims Made about Them: Business Report - Medical Claims Processing. 5th rev. ed. Gary Knox. 64p. 1996. pap. 29.95 (1-887212-08-6) AQC Resource.
Medical Clerk. Jack Rudman. (Career Examination Ser.: C-1796). 1994. pap. 23.95 (0-8373-1796-7) Nat Learn.
Medical-Clinical Bioelectronics. Richard K. Miller & Terri C. Walker. LC 88-80906. (Survey on Technology & Markets Ser.: No. 22). 50p. 1989. pap. text 200.00 (1-55865-021-0) Future Tech Surveys.
Medical, Clinical, Pharmacological & Therapeutic Dictionary: Dictionnaire Medical, Clinique, Pharmacologique et Therapeutique. 3rd ed. Alain Blacque-Belair. 1938p. 1981. 150.00 (0-8288-1789-8, M6036) Fr & Eur.
Medical College Admission Test (MCAT) Jack Rudman. (Admission Test Ser.: Vol. 11). 43.95 (0-8373-5111-1) Nat Learn.
Medical College Admission Test (MCAT) Jack Rudman. (Admission Test Ser.: ATS-11). 1994. pap. 23.95 (0-8373-5011-5) Nat Learn.
Medical College Admission Test Student Guide. rev. ed. David M. Tarlow. LC 78-53092. (Illus.). 1993. pap. 15.95 (0-931572-00-2) Datar Pub.
Medical College Admissions Test (MCAT) - Core Content. David M. Tarlow. (Medical Examinations Ser.). (Illus.). 575p. (Orig.). (C). 1996. pap. 49.95 (1-57774-000-9) Educ Tsting Cnslts.
Medical Complications During Pregnancy. 4th ed. Ed. by Gerard N. Burrow & Thomas F. Ferris. LC 94-25450. (Illus.). 633p. 1994. text 87.00 (0-7216-5150-X, W B Saunders Co) Harcrt Hlth Sci Grp.
Medical Complications During Pregnancy. 5th ed. Gerard N. Burrow & Thomas P. Duffy. Ed. by Ray Kersey. LC 98-38029. (Illus.). viii, 532p. (C). 1999. text. write for info. (0-7216-7508-5, W B Saunders Co) Harcrt Hlth Sci Grp.
Medical Complications in Cancer Patients. Maurice J. Staquet. Ed. by Jean Klastersky. LC 80-20951. (Monograph Series of the European Organization for Research on Treatment of Cancer: Vol. 7). 329p. 1981. reprint ed. pap. 102.00 (0-608-00427-8, 206114200007) Bks Demand.
Medical Complications in Labor & Delivery. Bernard Gonick et al. LC 95-21120. 240p. 1995. pap. 29.95 (0-86542-475-6) Blackwell Sci.
Medical Computing & Applications. David Ellis. LC 86-21333. (Computers & Their Applications Ser.). 325p. 1987. text 44.95 (0-470-20766-3) P-H.
Medical Concepts & Penal Policy. Gerry Johnstone. 204p. 1996. pap. 40.00 (1-85941-021-9, Pub. by Cavendish Pubng) Gaunt.
Medical Conduct Investigator. Jack Rudman. (Career Examination Ser.: C-2287). 1994. reprint ed. pap. 27.95 (0-8373-2287-1) Nat Learn.
Medical Consequences of Natural Disasters. L. Beinin. (Illus.). 195p. 1985. pap. 78.00 (0-387-15506-6) Spr-Verlag.
Medical Consequences of the Chernobyl Nuclear Accident. Ed. by P. V. Ramzaev. 237p. 1994. lib. bdg. 145.00 (1-56072-111-1) Nova Sci Pubs.
Medical Consultation: The Internist on Surgical, Obstetric & Psychiatric Services. 2nd ed. William S. Kammerer & Richard J. Gross. (Illus.). 696p. 1990. 75.00 (0-683-04506-7) Lppncott W & W.
Medical Consultations - Practice, Methods, Preferences, Importance & Necessity: Index of New Information with Authors & Subjects. Eric S. Anderson. 180p. 1993. 47.50 (1-55914-910-8); pap. 44.50 (1-55914-911-6) ABBE Pubs Assn.
Medical Control of Populations: Index of New Information with Authors, Subjects & References. Webster K. Harmonsen. 150p. 1996. 47.50 (0-7883-1340-1); pap. 44.50 (0-7883-1341-X) ABBE Pubs Assn.
Medical Cornea: Corneal & Refractive Surgery. Ed. by Richard E. Selser, Jr. LC 94-2839. (Illus.). xii, 192p. 1994. text 54.50 (90-6299-106-8) Kugler Pubns.
Medical Cost Containment in Workers' Compensation: A National Inventory, 1992-93. Ed. by Carol A. Telles. LC 93-24885. 1993. 95.00 (0-935149-41-4, WC-93-2) Workers Comp Res Inst.
Medical Cost Containment in Workers' Compensation: Innovative Approaches. Ed. by Richard B. Victor. LC 87-27900. 1987. 35.00 (0-935149-06-6, WC-87-1) Workers Comp Res Inst.
Medical Cost Crisis! A Common-Sense Solution. Don W. Larson. 240p. 1993. 24.00 (0-9635576-0-2) Bond Pub MN.
Medical Costs in Workers' Compensation: Interstate Comparisons, Minnesota, & Other Selected States. Greg Gifford. (Illus.). 127p. (C). 1998. reprint ed. pap. text 25.00 (0-7881-7473-8) DIANE Pub.
Medical Costs in Workers' Compensation: Trends & Interstate Comparisons. Leslie I. Boden & Charles A. Fleischman. LC 89-24975. 70p. 1989. 35.00 (0-935149-22-8, WC-89-5) Workers Comp Res Inst.
Medical Curiosities. Robert Youngson. LC 97-19502. 352p. 1997. pap. 10.95 (0-7867-0432-2) Carroll & Graf.
Medical Cyclotrons in Nuclear Medicine: Proceedings of the Medical Cyclotron Users Conference, 4th, Miami, 1976. Medical Cyclotron Users Conference Staff. Ed. by H. Roesler et al. (Progress in Nuclear Medicine Ser.: Vol. 4). 1977. 86.25 (3-8055-2670-9) S Karger.
Medical Cytogenetics & Cell Culture. 2nd ed. Jean H. Priest. LC 76-7402. 364p. reprint ed. pap. 112.90 (0-608-15343-5, 205221300061) Bks Demand.
Medical Dangers to Health & Energy in Our Drinking Water in the United States: Index of New Information. American Health Research Institute Staff. 150p. 1994. 47.50 (0-7883-0070-9); pap. 44.50 (0-7883-0071-7) ABBE Pubs Assn.
Medical Dark Ages Circa 1984: Cancer Alternative Therapies' Cure Rates. 2nd ed. Ralph R. Hovnanian. LC 81-90082. 288p. 1985. pap. 1.00 (0-9607774-0-7) Hovnanian.
Medical Data Portfolio. Burgus C. Garrison. 96p. 1992. pap., student ed. 12.00 (0-9633245-0-0, TXU438774) B C Garrison.
Medical Decision Making. Harold C. Sox et al. 406p. (C). 1988. pap. text 49.50 (0-7506-9288-X) Buttrwrth-Heinemann.
Medical Decision-Making among Chinese-Born & Euro-American Elderly: A Comparative Study of Values. Madeleine Crain. LC 97-33211. (Studies on the Elderly in America). 123p. 1997. text 41.00 (0-8153-3003-0) Garland.
Medical Decisions & "Advance Directives" Index of New Information Including "Do-Not-Resuscitate" Orders, Accuracy of Judgments & Legal Aspects. rev. ed. American Health Research Institute Staff. (Illus.). 189p. 1997. 47.50 (0-7883-0674-X); pap. 44.50 (0-7883-0673-1) ABBE Pubs Assn.
Medical Defense Against Mustard Gas: Toxic Mechanisms & Pharmacological Implications. Bruno Papirmeister et al. (Illus.). 360p. 1991. lib. bdg. 139.00 (0-8493-4257-0, RA1247) CRC Pr.
Medical, Dental & Pharmaceutical Auxiliaries: A Survey of Existing Legislation. (International Digest of Health Legislation Ser: Vol. 19, No. 1). (ENG & FRE.). 143p. 1968. pap. text 9.00 (92-4-169191-3, 1956801) World Health.
Medical-Dental Terminology: Syllabus. 2nd ed. LeGrand H. Woolley. 1974. pap. text 9.95 (0-89420-003-8, 217705); audio 179.15 (0-89420-162-X, 196700) Natl Book.
***Medical Department: Medical Service in the War Against Japan.** Mary Ellen Condon-Rall & Albert L. Cowdrey. (CMH Publication Ser.: Vol. 10-24). (Illus.). 505p. 1998. boxed set 37.00 (0-16-049265-3) USGPO.
Medical Department of the U. S. Army in the Civil War. L. C. Duncan. Date not set. lib. bdg. 27.95 (0-8488-0996-3) Amereon Ltd.
Medical Department of the United States Army from 1775 to 1873. U. S. Surgeon General's Office Staff. Ed. by Harvey E. Brown. LC 75-23763. reprint ed. 45.00 (0-404-13369-X) AMS Pr.
Medical Department of the United States Army in the World War. U. S. Surgeon General's Office Staff. Ed. by Gerald N. Grob. LC 78-22593. (Historical Issues in Mental Health Ser.). 1980. reprint ed. lib. bdg. 42.95 (0-405-11943-7) Ayer.
Medical Department of the United States in the Civil War. Louis C. Duncan. 400p. 1987. reprint ed. 28.50 (0-942211-30-8) Olde Soldier Bks.
Medical Department, United States Army, Surgery in Vietnam, Orthopedic Surgery. William E. Burkhalter. 238p. 1995. boxed set 24.00 (0-16-061320-5) USGPO.
Medical Detectives. Berton Roueche. 448p. 1991. pap. 14.95 (0-452-26588-6, Truman Talley) St Martin.
***Medical Device Register, 2001.** 2001. 325.00 (1-56363-383-3, PDR) Med Econ.
Medical Device Accidents: With Illustrative Cases. L. A. Geddes. LC 97-44271. (Illus.). 1998. boxed set 74.95 (0-8493-9236-5) CRC Pr.
Medical Device & Equipment Design: Usability Engineering & Ergonomics. Ed. by Michael E. Wiklund. 382p. 1995. 139.00 (0-935184-69-4) Interpharm.
***Medical Device Executive Portfolio.** Ed. by Steve Halasey. (Illus.). 136p. 1999. pap. 50.00 (1-884551-06-8) Canon Comns.
Medical Device Industry: Science Technology & Regulation in a Competitive Environment. Estrin. (Illus.). 976p. 1990. text 295.00 (0-8247-8268-2) Dekker.
Medical Device Industry: Business Strategies for Success. 1998. 1195.00 (0-85058-957-6) Economist Intell.
Medical Device Industry Factbook. 3rd rev. ed. Ed. by Amy Allen. (Illus.). 190p. 1996. pap. 45.00 (1-884551-02-5) Canon Comns.
***Medical Device Market in Japan: A Strategic Entry Report, 1999.** Compiled by Icon Group International. (Illus.). 157p. 1999. ring bd. 1570.00 incl. audio compact disk (0-7418-1847-7) Icon Grp.
Medical Device Marketing Opportunities: Turkey. ECRI Staff. 85p. pap. text 17.95 (0-941417-29-8) ECRI.
Medical Device Markets: A Detailed Database on a 41 Billion Dollar Market. Market Intelligence Staff. 240p. 1992. 995.00 (1-56753-085-0) Frost & Sullivan.
Medical Device Packaging Handbook. 2nd ed. Ed. by Sherman. LC 98-36296. (Illus.). 416p. 1998. text 175.00 (0-8247-0199-2) Dekker.
Medical Device Provisions of the Federal Food, Drug & Cosmetic Act. Mark A. Heller & Stephanie Philbin. 78p. (C). 1998. pap. write for info. (1-885259-54-9) Food & Drug Law.
***Medical Device Quality Assurance & Regulatory Compliance.** Richard C. Fries. LC 98-27991. (Illus.). 504p. 1998. text 165.00 (0-8247-0177-1) Dekker.
Medical Device Quality Systems Manual - For GMP & ISO 9001-9002 Compliance: (Includes PC-Word 7.0 Diskettes) Gunther Gumpp. Ed. by Brisitte Gumpp. (C). 1998. text, lab manual ed. 500.00 incl. disk (1-881006-55-7) Qual Cont Systs Srvs.
Medical Device Regulation: Assessment of European System's Value As a Model for the EDA. 48p. (Orig.). (C). 1996. pap. text 20.00 (0-7881-2868-X) DIANE Pub.
***Medical Device Reliability & Associated Areas.** Balbir S. Dhillon. 264p. 2000. 99.95 (0-8493-0312-5) CRC Pr.
Medical Device Reporting under the Safe Medical Devices Act: Final Report. ECRI Staff. 1996. pap. text 195.00 (0-685-55227-6) ECRI.
Medical Device Tracking System, 1993. Ed. by Ronni P. Solomon. 300p. 1993. ring bd. 295.00 (0-941417-26-3) ECRI.
Medical Device Vigilance/Monitoring: European Device Directives Compliance. Robin N. Stephens. LC 96-51891. 225p. 1997. 194.00 (1-57491-030-2) Interpharm.
Medical Devices: FDA Review Time. (Illus.). 87p. (Orig.). (C). 1996. pap. text 30.00 (0-7881-2766-7) DIANE Pub.
Medical Devices: International Perspectives on Health & Safety. Ed. by C. W. Van Gruting. LC 94-24486. 678p. 1994. 357.00 (0-444-89242-7) Elsevier.
Medical Devices: Obtaining FDA Market Clearance. Jonathan S. Kahan. 289p. (Orig.). 1995. pap. 195.00 (1-882615-24-7) Parexel Intl.
Medical Devices: Technological Innovation & Patient-Provider Perspectives. Ed. by Michael Bilirakis. (Illus.). 86p. (C). 1999. reprint ed. pap. text 20.00 (0-7881-8099-1) DIANE Pub.
Medical Devices: Validdtion & Routine Control. (Illus.). 20p. (Orig.). 1994. pap. text 86.00 (1-57020-015-7, ST1135-209) Assn Adv Med Instrn.
Medical Devices & Equipment - Design, Supplies, Failures, Control, Contaminations & Alarms: Index & Research Bible. American Health Research Institute Staff. 160p. 1995. 47.50 (0-7883-0220-5); pap. 44.50 (0-7883-0221-3) ABBE Pubs Assn.
Medical Devices & the Year 2000 Problem: ECRI's Step-by-Step Guide for Addressing the Year 2000 Problem in Healthcare Facilities. ECRI Staff. (Illus.). 12p. 1998. reprint ed. pap. 75.00 (0-941417-65-4) ECRI.
***Medical Devices in China: A Strategic Entry Report, 1999.** Compiled by Icon Group International. (Illus.). 172p. 1999. ring bd. 1720.00 incl. audio compact disk (0-7418-1714-4) Icon Grp.
***Medical Devices in United Kingdom: A Strategic Entry Report, 1996.** Compiled by Icon Group International Staff. (Illus.). 103p. 1999. ring bd. 1030.00 incl. audio compact disk (0-7418-1306-8) Icon Grp.
Medical Devices Measurements, Quality Assurance, & Standards - STP 800. Ed. by C. A. Caceres et al. LC 82-72890. 298p. 1983. text 38.00 (0-8031-0235-6, STP800) ASTM.
Medical Devices Used in Home Health Care. 48p. (Orig.). (C). 1994. pap. text 25.00 (0-7881-0829-8) DIANE Pub.
Medical Diagnosis & Therapy. M. Gabriel Khan. (Illus.). 736p. 1994. 26.50 (0-8121-1602-X) Lppncott W & W.
Medical Diagnosis & Treatment of Alcoholism. Ed. by Nancy K. Mello & Jack H. Mendelson. (Illus.). 656p. 1992. text 65.00 (0-07-041491-2) McGraw-Hill HPD.
Medical Diagnosis Asia, No. 4. Friedman. 1987. 9.95 (0-316-29381-4, Little Brwn Med Div) Lppncott W & W.
Medical Diagnosis Asia, No. 5. Friedman. 1991. 10.95 (0-316-29388-1, Little Brwn Med Div) Lppncott W & W.
Medical Diagnosis Codes: A Consumer's Guide to the Classification of Diseases. Ed. by James Davis. LC 96-78923. 1375p. 1999. pap. 29.95 (1-885987-06-4, ME076, Health Info Pr) Practice Mgmt Info.
Medical Diagnosis of Child Maltreatment: A Guide for Medical Providers. Jean Smith et al. (Illus.). 288p. 1999. pap. text 35.00 (0-07-069765-5) McGraw-Hill HPD.
Medical Diagnostic Electronics Products: Market Share Analysis, 1991. Market Intelligence Staff. 246p. (Orig.). 1992. 1495.00 (1-56753-064-8) Frost & Sullivan.
***Medical Diagnostic Equipment in Argentina: A Strategic Entry Report, 1995.** Compiled by Icon Group International Staff. (Illus.). 143p. 1999. ring bd. 1430.00 incl. audio compact disk (0-7418-1605-9) Icon Grp.
***Medical Diagnostic Imaging Equipment in Italy: A Strategic Entry Report, 1996.** Compiled by Icon Group International Staff. (Illus.). 130p. 1999. ring bd. 1300.00 incl. audio compact disk (0-7418-1307-6) Icon Grp.
Medical Diagnostic Kits & Products. 124p. 1992. 2450.00 (0-89336-868-7, C-045N) BCC.
Medical Diagnostic Kits & Products. Barbara Breindel. LC 98-100567. (Report Ser.: No. C-045U). 138p. 1997. 3150.00 (1-56965-386-0) BCC.
Medical Diagnostics: Pocket Companion. Dugdale. 1992. pap. text 41.00 (0-7216-3499-0, W B Saunders Co) Harcrt Hlth Sci Grp.
***Medical Diary: A Personal Lifeline Link.** vii, 224p. 1999. 19.95 (0-9672518-0-X) Dogwood Pubng.
Medical Diary: My Personal Medical History. Linda L. Jones. (Illus.). 108p. Date not set. 19.95 (0-9662057-0-7) Linda L Jones.
Medical Dictionary see **Diccionario Medico**
Medical Dictionary. Stedman. 20308p. 1995. 52.00 (0-395-73855-5) HM.
Medical Dictionary. D. W. Unseld. (ENG & GER.). 1982. 88.00 (3-8047-0992-3) Adlers Foreign Bks.
Medical Dictionary. 2nd ed. S. Jedraszko. (ENG & POL.). 431p. 1980. write for info. (0-8288-0574-1, M 7983) Fr & Eur.
Medical Dictionary. 2nd ed. Glenn T. Rogers. (ENG & SPA.). 1997. pap. text. write for info. (0-07-053580-9); pap. text. write for info. (0-07-055680-6) McGraw.
***Medical Dictionary.** 3rd rev. ed. Ed. by Editors of Market House Bks. Staff. 544p. 2000. mass mkt. 6.99 (0-553-58189-9) Bantam.
Medical Dictionary, 2 vols., Set. E. Veillon & Albert Nobel. (ENG, FRE, GER & ITA.). 1344p. 1983. 295.00 (0-8288-1892-4) Fr & Eur.
Medical Dictionary: Spanish/English/Spanish. 9th ed. Ruiz Torres. (ENG & SPA.). 956p. 1999. 295.00 (0-320-00699-9) Fr & Eur.
Medical Dictionary Danish-English - English-Danish. M. Pilegaard. (DAN & ENG.). 913p. 1994. 140.00 (87-12-02240-3, Pub. by GAD) IBD Ltd.
Medical Dictionary, English-German, German-English. C. Eichhorst. (ENG & GER.). 1998. 150.00 incl. cd-rom (0-7859-9627-3) Fr & Eur.
Medical Dictionary, English-Spanish/Spanish-English. Mosby. (ENG & SPA.). 370p. 1996. 95.00 (0-7859-9644-3) Fr & Eur.
***Medical Dictionary for Health Related Professionals.** Hearl. (C). 2000. pap. 26.50 (0-7668-0221-3) Thomson Learn.
Medical Dictionary for Stenotypists. George P. Andrews. (Realtime Machine Shorthand Ser.). 526p. (C). 1994. pap. text 46.75 (0-938643-32-0) Stenotype Educ.
Medical Dictionary for Tropical Regions: Dictionnaire Medical pour les Regions. 2nd ed. Bernard Pierre & Genevieve Pierre. (FRE.). 850p. 1988. pap. 75.00 (0-8288-1823-1) Fr & Eur.
Medical Dictionary in Six Languages. Bert Spilker. LC 94-30921. 688p. 1994. text 108.00 (0-7817-0182-1) Lppncott W & W.
Medical Dictionary of Symptoms & Syndromes: Dictionnaire Medical des Symptomes et Syndromes. 2nd ed. Raymond Villey. (FRE.). 312p. 1982. 95.00 (0-8288-1831-2, M15604) Fr & Eur.
Medical Dictionary of the English & German Languages. 8th ed. Dieter W. Unseld. (ENG & GER.). 593p. 1982. 125.00 (0-8288-0573-3, M8016) Fr & Eur.
Medical Dictionary of Women: Dictionnaire Medical de la Femme. Lucien Bouccara. 500p. 1981. 29.95 (0-8288-1792-8, M15419) Fr & Eur.
Medical Dimensions of Mental Retardation. Frank J. Menolascino & Michael L. Egger. LC 76-16503. 501p. 1978. reprint ed. pap. 155.40 (0-608-01842-2, 206249200003) Bks Demand.
Medical Direction in Long-Term Care: A Guidebook for the Future. 2nd ed. Ed. by Steven A. Levenson. LC 93-72380. 694p. 1993. 65.00 (0-89089-547-3) Carolina Acad Pr.
Medical Direction in the Nursing Home: Principles & Concepts for Physician-Administrators. James J. Pattee & Orlo J. Otteson. 405p. 1991. 49.50 (0-9629614-0-X) North Ridge Pr.
Medical Directors: What, Why, How. George E. Linney, Jr. & Barbara J. Linney. LC 92-74400. 44p. (Orig.). (C). 1993. pap. text 20.00 (0-924674-19-9) Am Coll Phys Execs.
Medical Directory, 1989, 2 vols. 89th ed. 4000p. 1989. 150.00 (1-55862-027-3) St James Pr.
Medical Directory, 1990, 2 Vols., Set. 90th ed. 4000p. 1990. 150.00 (0-582-06163-6) St James Pr.
Medical Directory, 1994. Churchill Livingstone. (Illus.). 4672p. 1994. text 295.00 (0-582-23418-2) Church.
Medical Disability Advisor: Workplace Guidelines for Disability Duration. Presley Reed. LC 91-14155. 1994. 275.00 (0-934753-52-0) LRP Pubns.

M

Medical Disability Advisor: Workplace Guidelines for Disability Duration. 3rd rev. ed. Presley Reed. (Illus.). 1935p. 1995. 345.00 (*1-889010-01-4*) Reed Grp Ltd.

Medical Discipline: The Professional Conduct Jurisdiction of the General Medical Council, 1858-1990. Russell G. Smith. LC 93-5959. (Oxford Socio-Legal Studies). (Illus.). 444p. 1994. text 79.00 (*0-19-825795-3*, Clarendon Pr) OUP.

Medical Discoveries: Medical Breakthroughs & the People Who Developed Them. F. Freiman. LC 96-42696. 1996. write for info. (*0-7876-0892-0*, UXL) Gale.

Medical Discoveries: Medical Breakthroughs & the People Who Developed Them. Fran L. Freiman. LC 96-42696. 1996. write for info. (*0-7876-0891-2*, UXL) Gale.

Medical Discoveries: Medical Breakthroughs & the People Who Discover Them, 3 vols. Fran L. Freiman. 442p. 1997. text 84.00 (*0-7876-0890-4*, UXL) Gale.

Medical Discoveries of Edward Bach, Physician. Weeks. write for info. (*0-85207-001-2*, Pub. by C W Daniel) Natl Bk Netwk.

Medical Discoveries of Edward Bach, Physician. 16th ed. Nora Weeks. 144p. pap. 11.95 (*0-8464-4250-7*) Beekman Pubs.

Medical Disorders During Pregnancy. 3rd ed. Barron. 2000. 89.95 (*0-323-00772-4*) Mosby Inc.

Medical Disorders During Pregnancy, No. 2. 2nd ed. John M. Barron & Marshall D. Lindheimer. (Illus.). 576p. (C). (gr. 13). 1994. text 92.00 (*0-8016-8002-6*, 08002) Mosby Inc.

Medical Disorders in Obstetric Practice. 3rd ed. Michael De Swiet. 720p. 1995. 149.95 (*0-632-03671-0*, Pub. by Blckwll Scitfc UK) Blackwell Sci.

Medical Disorders of Alcoholism: Pathogenesis & Treatment. Charles S. Lieber. (Major Problems in Internal Medicine Ser.: Vol. 22). (Illus.). 608p. 1982. text 120.00 (*0-7216-5774-5*, W B Saunders Co) Harcrt Hlth Sci Grp.

Medical Disposable Products in Chile: A Strategic Entry Report, 1997. Compiled by Icon Group International Staff. (Country Industry Report). (Illus.). 119p. 1999. ring bd. 1190.00 incl. audio compact disk (*0-7418-0251-1*) Icon Grp.

***Medical Disposable Supplies in Singapore: A Strategic Entry Report, 1995.** Compiled by Icon Group International Staff. (Illus.). 116p. 1999. ring bd. 1160.00 incl. audio compact disk (*0-7418-1606-7*) Icon Grp.

***Medical Disposables in Indonesia: A Strategic Entry Report, 1998.** Compiled by Icon Group International Staff. (Country Industry Report). (Illus.). 163p. 1999. ring bd. 1630.00 incl. audio compact disk (*0-7418-0507-3*) Icon Grp.

***Medical Disposables in Mexico: A Strategic Entry Report, 1999.** Compiled by Icon Group International. (Illus.). 159p. 1999. ring bd. 1590.00 incl. audio compact disk (*0-7418-1848-5*) Icon Grp.

Medical Disposables in Singapore: A Strategic Entry Report, 1997. Compiled by Icon Group International Staff. (Illus.). 115p. 1999. ring bd. 1150.00 incl. audio compact disk (*0-7418-0866-8*) Icon Grp.

Medical Disposables Markets: A Detailed Database on a 45 Billion Dollar Market. Market Intelligence Staff. 340p. 1992. 995.00 (*1-56753-084-2*) Frost & Sullivan.

Medical Dissertations of Psychiatric Interest. Oskar Diethelm. 1971. 36.75 (*3-8055-1201-5*) S Karger.

Medical Doctors of Maryland in the C. S. A. Daniel D. Hartzler. 98p. 1979. pap. 20.00 (*0-942211-72-3*) Olde Soldier Bks.

Medical Domain. Michelle Burmeister. 365p. mass mkt. 4.99 (*1-896329-14-4*) Picasso Publ.

Medical Dosage Calculations. 4th ed. June L. Olsen. 1987. pap. text 14.36 (*0-201-19185-7*) Addison-Wesley.

Medical Dosage Calculations. 5th ed. June L. Olsen. 246p. (C). 1991. pap. text 25.95 (*0-8053-5603-7*) Addison-Wesley.

Medical Dosage Calculations. 7th ed. June L. Olsen. LC 99-34128. (Illus.). 358p. (C). 1999. pap. text 36.40 incl. cd-rom (*0-8053-9162-2*) Addison-Wesley.

Medical Drugs on Trial: An Expose of the Disease Industrialists. 1992. lib. bdg. 79.95 (*0-8490-8795-3*) Gordon Pr.

Medical Economics & Health Finance. Steven R. Eastaugh. LC 81-3450. 352p. (C). 1981. 35.00 (*0-86569-065-0*, Auburn Hse); pap. 15.00 (*0-86569-066-9*, Auburn Hse) Greenwood.

Medical Edge of Improv: Students & Apprentices at Edinburgh University. Lisa Rosner. 1991. text 68.00 (*0-7486-0245-3*, Pub. by Edinburgh U Pr) Col U Pr.

Medical Education: Annotated Bibliography, 1946-1955. (ENG & FRE.). 391p. 1958. pap. text 12.00 (*92-4-152003-5*, 1150101) World Health.

Medical Education: Curriculum & Financing Strategies Needed to Encourage Primary Care Training. (Illus.). 50p. (Orig.). (C). 1995. pap. text 40.00 (*0-7881-1710-6*) DIANE Pub.

Medical Education, Accreditation, & the Nation's Health: Reflections of an Atypical Dean. Andrew D. Hunt. LC 90-50845. 200p. (C). 1991. text 22.00 (*0-87013-288-1*) Mich St U Pr.

Medical Education & Health Care: A Pluridimensional Paradigm. Jasbir S. Bajaj & Indian Institute of Advanced Study Staff. LC 98-903260. xiv, 218p. 1998. write for info. (*81-85952-51-5*) Indian Inst.

Medical Education & Medical Care: A Scottish American Symposium. Ed. by Gordon McLachlan. (Nuffield Publications). 230p. 1977. text 13.25 (*0-19-721394-4*) OUP.

Medical Education in the Millennium. Ed. by Brian Jolly & Lesley Rees. (Illus.). 278p. 1998. text 98.50 (*0-19-262399-0*) OUP.

Medical Education in the U. S. Before the Civil War. William F. Norwood. LC 72-165726. (American Education, Ser, No. 2). 1975. reprint ed. 30.95 (*0-405-03714-7*) Ayer.

Medical Education in the United States & Canada. Abraham Flexner. LC 78-180575. (Medicine & Society in America Ser.). 368p. 1979. reprint ed. 24.95 (*0-405-03952-2*) Ayer.

Medical Education in Transition. Commission on Medical Education, Sciences of Medic. Ed. by Roseann M. Jones. LC 92-64117. 146p. (Orig.). 1992. pap. write for info. (*0-942054-05-9*) R W Johnson Found.

Medical Effectiveness & Outcomes Management: Issues, Methods, & Case Studies. Ed. by Patrice L. Spath. LC 95-46552. 327p. 1996. pap. 75.00 (*1-55648-150-0*, 169110) AHPI.

Medical Effectiveness Directory, 1995. 1995. 45.00 (*1-56925-028-6*, MED2) Capitol Publns.

Medical Effects of Free Radicals: Index of New Information with Authors & Subjects. American Health Research Institute Staff. LC 95-16341. 1995. 47.50 (*0-7883-0775-4*); pap. write for info. (*0-7883-0776-2*) ABBE Pubs Assn.

Medical Effects of Ionizing Radiation. 2nd ed. Fred A. Mettler & Arthur C. Upton. 464p. 1995. text 140.00 (*0-7216-6646-9*, W B Saunders Co) Harcrt Hlth Sci Grp.

Medical Electrical Equipment, General Requirements for Safety UL 2601-1. 2nd ed. Underwriters Laboratories, Inc. Staff. (C). 1997. pap. text 175.00 (*0-7629-0227-2*) Underwrtrs Labs.

Medical Electron Accelerators. Clarence J. Karzmark et al. LC 92-49307. 336p. 1992. text 125.00 (*0-07-105410-3*) McGraw-Hill HPD.

Medical Emergencies. 6th ed. R. Robinson & R. Stott. 320p. 1993. pap. text 45.00 (*0-7506-0897-8*) Buttrwrth-Heinemann.

Medical Emergencies in the Dental Office. 4th rev. ed. Stanley F. Malamed. LC 92-49542. (Illus.). 480p. (C). (gr. 13). 1992. pap. text 52.00 (*0-8016-6386-5*, 06386) Mosby Inc.

***Medical Emergencies in the Dental Office.** 5th ed. Stanley F. Malamed. LC 99-40660. 1999. write for info. (*1-55664-420-5*) Mosby Inc.

Medical Emergency! The St. Luke's-Roosevelt Hospital Center Book of Emergency Medicine. Stephan G. Lynn & Pamela Weintraub. 1996. pap. 19.95 (*0-614-97846-7*, Wm Morrow) Morrow Avon.

***Medical Emergency! The St. Luke's-Roosevelt Hospital Center Book of Emergency Medicine.** Stephen G. Lynn & Pamela Weintraub. (Illus.). 385p. 1999. pap. text 20.00 (*0-7881-6067-2*) DIANE Pub.

Medical Emergency Dispatcher. Jack Rudman. (Career Examination Ser.: C-2331). 1994. pap. 27.95 (*0-8373-2331-2*) Nat Learn.

***Medical Employer's Guide: A Handbook of Employment Laws & Regulations.** 7th rev. ed. Amy L. Greenspan. LC 93-5412. 758p. 1999. pap. 119.50 (*1-56759-045-4*); ring bd. 119.50 (*1-56759-042-X*) Summers Pr.

Medical EMT: Paramedic Coursebook. (Medical Examination Review Bks.). (C). 1999. 61.00 (*0-8385-6374-0*, Medical Exam) Appleton & Lange.

Medical Encyclopedia *see* **Mawsouat Al Toubiya**

***Medical Encyclopedia: World Book Rush-Presbyterian-St. Luke's Medical Center.** 8th ed. Ed. by World Book Staff. (YA). (gr. 4 up). 1999. write for info. (*0-7166-4206-9*) World Bk.

Medical Encyclopedia of Moses Maimonides. Fred Rosner. LC 97-41034. 288p. 1998. 50.00 (*0-7657-5997-7*) Aronson.

Medical Engineering Dictionary: English, French, German, Russian. (ENG, FRE, GER & RUS.). 592p. 1994. 185.00 (*0-7859-7059-2*, M15740) Fr & Eur.

Medical Engineering Dictionary in Four Languages. Roald Albert. (ENG, FRE, GER & RUS.). 550p. 1994. 150.00 (*3-86117-051-5*) IBD Ltd.

Medical Engineering in Japan: Research & Development. Ed. by K. Atsumi & F. Kajiya. (C). 1987. pap. text 278.50 (*0-89838-973-9*) Kluwer Academic.

Medical English for German Doctors. H. Kleinsorge. (ENG & GER.). 1990. lib. bdg. 115.00 (*0-8288-3590-X*, F106950) Fr & Eur.

Medical English Usage & Abusage. Edith Schwager. LC 90-7644. 232p. 1990. pap. 19.95 (*0-89774-590-6*) Oryx Pr.

***Medical Entomology: A Textbook on Public Health & Veterinary Problems Caused by Arthropods.** Bruce F. Eldridge & John D. Edman. LC 00-37544. 2000. write for info. (*0-7923-6320-5*) Kluwer Academic.

Medical Entomology for Students. Michael W. Service. 1996. write for info. (*0-412-71230-X*) Kluwer Academic.

***Medical Entomology for Students.** 2nd ed. M. W. Service. (Illus.). 300p. (C). 2000. pap. 37.95 (*0-521-66659-7*) Cambridge U Pr.

Medical Epidemiology. 2nd ed. Raymond S. Greenberg. 196p. (C). 1996. pap. text 32.95 (*0-8385-6206-X*, Apple Lange Med) McGraw.

Medical Epidemiology. 3rd ed. Raymond S. Greenberg et al. (Illus.). 220p. 1999. pap. text 31.95 (*0-8385-6295-7*) McGraw.

Medical Eponyms from A to Z. Yvonne T. Sesi. LC 96-61223. 212p. 1997. pap. 18.95 (*0-9642134-0-0*) Univ Scripts.

***Medical Equipment & Pharmaceuticals in Russia: A Strategic Entry Report, 1995.** Compiled by Icon Group International Staff. (Illus.). 152p. 1999. ring bd. 1520.00 incl. audio compact disk (*0-7418-1607-5*) Icon Grp.

***Medical Equipment & Services in Argentina: A Strategic Entry Report, 1995.** Compiled by Icon Group International Staff. (Illus.). 143p. 1999. ring bd. 1430.00 incl. audio compact disk (*0-7418-1608-3*) Icon Grp.

***Medical Equipment & Services in Vietnam: A Strategic Entry Report, 1995.** Compiled by Icon Group International Staff. (Illus.). 154p. 1999. ring bd. 1540.00 incl. audio compact disk (*0-7418-1609-1*) Icon Grp.

***Medical Equipment & Services in Vietnam: A Strategic Entry Report, 1996.** Compiled by Icon Group International Staff. (Illus.). 152p. 1999. ring bd. 1520.00 incl. audio compact disk (*0-7418-1308-4*) Icon Grp.

***Medical Equipment & Supplies in Guatemala: A Strategic Entry Report, 1996.** Compiled by Icon Group International Staff. (Illus.). 114p. 1999. ring bd. 1140.00 incl. audio compact disk (*0-7418-1309-2*) Icon Grp.

***Medical Equipment & Supplies in Kuwait: A Strategic Entry Report, 1999.** Compiled by Icon Group International. (Illus.). 122p. 1999. ring bd. 1220.00 incl. audio compact disk (*0-7418-1849-3*) Icon Grp.

***Medical Equipment & Supplies in Pakistan: A Strategic Entry Report, 1998.** Compiled by Icon Group International Staff. (Country Industry Report). (Illus.). 183p. 1999. ring bd. 1830.00 incl. audio compact disk (*0-7418-0508-1*) Icon Grp.

***Medical Equipment & Supplies in Portugal: A Strategic Entry Report, 1996.** Compiled by Icon Group International Staff. (Illus.). 109p. 1999. ring bd. 1090.00 incl. audio compact disk (*0-7418-1310-6*) Icon Grp.

Medical Equipment & Supplies in Portugal: A Strategic Entry Report, 1997. Compiled by Icon Group International Staff. (Illus.). 111p. 1999. ring bd. 1110.00 incl. audio compact disk (*0-7418-1050-6*) Icon Grp.

***Medical Equipment & Supplies Market in Brazil: A Strategic Entry Report, 1996.** Compiled by Icon Group International Staff. (Illus.). 157p. 1999. ring bd. 1570.00 incl. audio compact disk (*0-7418-1311-4*) Icon Grp.

***Medical Equipment Devices in China: A Strategic Entry Report, 1998.** Compiled by Icon Group International Staff. (Country Industry Report). (Illus.). 179p. 1999. ring bd. 1790.00 incl. audio compact disk (*0-7418-0252-X*) Icon Grp.

***Medical Equipment in Australia: A Strategic Entry Report, 1997.** Compiled by Icon Group International Staff. (Country Industry Report). (Illus.). 134p. 1999. ring bd. 1340.00 incl. audio compact disk (*0-7418-0253-8*) Icon Grp.

***Medical Equipment in Australia: A Strategic Entry Report, 1998.** Compiled by Icon Group International Staff. (Country Industry Report). (Illus.). 126p. 1999. ring bd. 1260.00 incl. audio compact disk (*0-7418-0254-6*) Icon Grp.

***Medical Equipment in Chile: A Strategic Entry Report, 1996.** Compiled by Icon Group International Staff. (Illus.). 127p. 1999. ring bd. 1270.00 incl. audio compact disk (*0-7418-1312-2*) Icon Grp.

***Medical Equipment in Chile: A Strategic Entry Report, 1999.** Compiled by Icon Group International. (Illus.). 119p. 1999. ring bd. 1190.00 incl. audio compact disk (*0-7418-1738-1*) Icon Grp.

***Medical Equipment in Colombia: A Strategic Entry Report, 1998.** Compiled by Icon Group International Staff. (Illus.). 211p. 1999. ring bd. 2110.00 incl. audio compact disk (*0-7418-1530-3*) Icon Grp.

***Medical Equipment in Costa Rica: A Strategic Entry Report, 1998.** Compiled by Icon Group International Staff. (Country Industry Report). (Illus.). 151p. 1999. ring bd. 1510.00 incl. audio compact disk (*0-7418-0509-X*) Icon Grp.

***Medical Equipment in Denmark: A Strategic Entry Report, 1996.** Compiled by Icon Group International Staff. (Illus.). 109p. 1999. ring bd. 1090.00 incl. audio compact disk (*0-7418-1313-0*) Icon Grp.

***Medical Equipment in Egypt: A Strategic Entry Report, 1995.** Compiled by Icon Group International Staff. (Illus.). 155p. 1999. ring bd. 1550.00 incl. audio compact disk (*0-7418-1610-5*) Icon Grp.

Medical Equipment in Finland: A Strategic Entry Report, 1997. Compiled by Icon Group International Staff. (Illus.). 103p. 1999. ring bd. 1030.00 incl. audio compact disk (*0-7418-0867-6*) Icon Grp.

Medical Equipment in Guatemala: A Strategic Entry Report, 1997. Compiled by Icon Group International Staff. (Illus.). 124p. 1999. ring bd. 1240.00 incl. audio compact disk (*0-7418-0868-4*) Icon Grp.

***Medical Equipment in Hungary: A Strategic Entry Report, 1996.** Compiled by Icon Group International Staff. (Illus.). 109p. 1999. ring bd. 1090.00 incl. audio compact disk (*0-7418-1314-9*) Icon Grp.

***Medical Equipment in India: A Strategic Entry Report, 1995.** Compiled by Icon Group International Staff. (Illus.). 210p. 1999. ring bd. 2100.00 incl. audio compact disk (*0-7418-1611-3*) Icon Grp.

***Medical Equipment in Mexico: A Strategic Entry Report, 1998.** Compiled by Icon Group International Staff. (Country Industry Report). (Illus.). 144p. 1999. ring bd. 1440.00 incl. audio compact disk (*0-7418-0255-4*) Icon Grp.

Medical Equipment in Peru: A Strategic Entry Report, 1997. Compiled by Icon Group International Staff. (Illus.). 145p. 1999. ring bd. 1450.00 incl. audio compact disk (*0-7418-1051-4*) Icon Grp.

***Medical Equipment in Poland: A Strategic Entry Report, 1996.** Compiled by Icon Group International Staff. (Illus.). 200p. 1999. ring bd. 2000.00 incl. audio compact disk (*0-7418-1315-7*) Icon Grp.

***Medical Equipment in Slovakia: A Strategic Entry Report, 1998.** Compiled by Icon Group International Staff. (Country Industry Report). (Illus.). 94p. 1999. ring bd. 940.00 incl. audio compact disk (*0-7418-0510-3*) Icon Grp.

***Medical Equipment in Ukraine: A Strategic Entry Report, 1998.** Compiled by Icon Group International Staff. (Country Industry Report). (Illus.). 197p. 1999. ring bd. 1970.00 incl. audio compact disk (*0-7418-0256-2*) Icon Grp.

Medical Equipment Leasing Services Industry. rev. ed. Marketdata Enterprises Inc. Staff. 26p. 1999. 59.00 (*1-891084-33-X*) Mktdata Ent.

***Medical Equipment Market in Argentina: A Strategic Entry Report, 1996.** Compiled by Icon Group International Staff. (Illus.). 131p. 1999. ring bd. 1310.00 incl. audio compact disk (*0-7418-1316-5*) Icon Grp.

***Medical Equipment Sector in Brazil: A Strategic Entry Report, 1996.** Compiled by Icon Group International Staff. (Illus.). 162p. 1999. ring bd. 1620.00 incl. audio compact disk (*0-7418-1319-X*) Icon Grp.

Medical Equipment Technician. Jack Rudman. (Career Examination Ser.: C-2654). 1994. pap. 29.95 (*0-8373-2654-0*) Nat Learn.

Medical Ethics. Ed. by Robert S. Downie. LC 96-608. (International Research Library of Philosophy). (Illus.). 520p. 1996. 163.95 (*1-85521-631-0*, Pub. by Dartmth Pub) Ashgate Pub Co.

Medical Ethics. Bernard Haring. (C). 1988. 39.00 (*0-85439-093-6*, Pub. by St Paul Pubns) St Mut.

Medical Ethics. Bernard Haring. 254p. (C). 1990. 60.00 (*0-85439-391-9*, Pub. by St Paul Pubns) St Mut.

***Medical Ethics.** Robert Snedden. LC 99-26790. (20th Century Issues Ser.). 64p. 1999. 27.12 (*0-8172-5893-0*) Raintree Steck-V.

***Medical Ethics.** James D. Torr. LC 99-34501. (Current Controversies Ser.). 320p. (gr. 9-12). 2000. pap. 17.45 (*0-7377-0144-7*); lib. bdg. 27.45 (*0-7377-0145-5*) Greenhaven.

Medical Ethics. 2nd ed. Max Charlesworth et al. Ed. by Alastair Campbell. LC 97-163622. 238p. 1997. text 45.00 (*0-19-558350-7*) OUP.

Medical Ethics. 2nd ed. Robert M. Veatch. LC 96-24292. (Medical Ser.). 480p. (C). 1996. 57.50 (*0-86720-974-7*) Jones & Bartlett.

Medical Ethics: A Patient-Centered Approach. James E. Giles. 224p. 1983. 18.95 (*0-87073-314-1*); pap. 13.95 (*0-87073-315-X*) Schenkman Bks Inc.

Medical Ethics: A Reader. Arthur Zucker et al. 448p. (C). 1991. pap. text 26.60 (*0-13-572496-1*) P-H.

Medical Ethics: A Reference Handbook. Lawrence H. Berlow. (Contemporary Ethical Issues Ser.). (Illus.). 256p. 1997. 39.50 (*0-87436-930-4*, FN-1718) ABC-CLIO.

Medical Ethics: An Introduction. Kenneth Kearon. 128p. 1995. pap. 10.95 (*0-89622-653-0*) Twenty-Third.

***Medical Ethics: Applying Theories & Principles to the Patient Encounter.** Ed. by Matt Weinberg. 2000. pap. 60.00 (*1-57392-652-3*) Prometheus Bks.

Medical Ethics: Basic Moral Issues. Thomas F. Wall. LC 80-5592. 180p. 1980. lib. bdg. 48.00 (*0-8191-1142-2*) U Pr of Amer.

Medical Ethics: Codes, Opinions & Statements. Ed. by Mark A. Rothstein et al. LC 99-55490. 1600p. 2000. 255.00 (*1-57018-100-4*, 1100) BNA Books.

Medical Ethics: Essays on Abortion & Euthanasia. Robert L. Barry. (American University Studies: Theology & Religion: Ser. VII, Vol. 45). XI, 308p. (C). 1989. text 41.95 (*0-8204-0925-1*) P Lang Pubng.

Medical Ethics: Evolution, Rights & the Physician. Henry A. Shenkin. (Episteme Ser.). 500p. (C). 1990. lib. bdg. 195.50 (*0-7923-1031-4*, Pub. by Kluwer Academic) Kluwer Academic.

Medical Ethics: Policies, Protocols, Guidelines & Programs. Ed. by John F. Monagle & David C. Thomasma. LC 92-21893. ring bd. 230.00 (*0-8342-0349-9*) Aspen Pub.

Medical Ethics: Principles, Persons, & Problems. John M. Frame. 160p. (Orig.). 1988. pap. 7.99 (*0-87552-261-0*) P & R Pubng.

Medical Ethics: Sources of Catholic Teaching. 2nd ed. Ed. by Kevin D. O'Rourke & Philip Boyle. LC 93-4895. 368p. (Orig.). 1993. pap. text 35.00 (*0-87840-540-2*) Georgetown U Pr.

Medical Ethics: Sources of Catholic Teaching. 3rd rev. ed. Kevin D. O'Rourke & Philip Boyle. LC 98-44647. 442p. (Orig.). 1999. pap. 37.50 (*0-87840-722-7*) Georgetown U Pr.

Medical Ethics & Health Sciences: Research Subject Analysis with Reference Bibliography. American Health Research Institute Staff. LC 85-48094. 150p. 1987. 47.50 (*0-88164-460-9*); pap. 44.50 (*0-88164-461-7*) ABBE Pubs Assn.

Medical Ethics & Human Life: Doctor, Patient & Family in the New Technology. John E. Thomas. 1983. 39.95 (*0-88866-624-1*); pap. text 19.95 (*0-88866-625-X*) Edgar Kent.

Medical Ethics & Medical Education: XIVth CIOMS Round Table Conference Bilingual English/Spanish. Z. Bankowski & J. Bernardelli. (CIOMS Round Table Proceedings Ser.: No. 14). 1981. pap. text 20.00 (*92-9036-006-2*) World Health.

***Medical Ethics & the Elderly: Practical Guide.** Ed. by Gurcharan S. Rai. 132p. 1999. text 54.00 (*90-5702-402-0*, Harwood Acad Pubs); pap. text 22.00 (*90-5702-403-9*, Harwood Acad Pubs) Gordon & Breach.

***Medical Ethics at the Dawn of the 21st Century.** Raphael Cohen-Almagor. LC 00-40186. (Annals of the New York Academy of Sciences Ser.). 2000. pap. write for info. (*1-57331-300-9*) NY Acad Sci.

Medical Ethics for Physicians & Health Providers. Jay E. Kantor. 224p. 1999. 74.95 (*1-57309-368-8*); pap. 54.95 (*1-57309-367-X*) Intl Scholars.

Medical Ethics for Physicians-in-Training. J. E. Kantor. (Illus.). 242p. (C). 1989. text 44.50 (*0-306-43194-7*, Kluwer Plenum) Kluwer Academic.

Medical Ethics, Human Choices: A Christian Perspective. Ed. by John Rogers. LC 87-29747. 176p. (Orig.). 1988. pap. 12.99 (*0-8361-3460-5*) Herald Pr.

An Asterisk (*) at the beginning of an entry indicates that the title is appearing for the first time.

Medical Ethics in Antiquity: Philosophical Perspectives on Abortion & Euthanasia. Paul Carrick. (Philosophy & Medicine Ser.: No. 18). 264p. 1985. pap. text 64.50 (90-277-1915-2); lib. bdg. 112.00 (90-277-1825-3) Kluwer Academic.

Medical Ethics In Multicultural & Feminist Perspectives. Teays. (Philosophy). 2000. pap. 37.00 (0-534-50828-6) Wadsworth Pub.

Medical Ethics in Practice: The Ethics Advisory Group at Boston's Beth Israel Hospital: A Case Study. Terry R. Bard. (Death Education, Aging & Health Care Ser.). 128p. 1990. 53.95 (1-56032-056-7) Hemisp Pub.

Medical Ethics in the Renaissance. Winfried Schleiner. LC 95-7359. (Illus.). 256p. 1997. pap. 19.95 (0-87840-601-8) Georgetown U Pr.

Medical Ethnobiology of the Highland Maya of Chiapas, Mexico: The Gastrointestinal Diseases. Elois A. Berlin & Brent Berlin. 352p. 1996. text 85.00 (0-691-03741-8, Pub. by Princeton U Pr) Cal Prin Full Svc.

Medical Evaluation of Physically & Sexually Abused Children. Carole Jenny. LC 96-4507. (APSAC Study Guides Ser.: Vol. 3). 128p. 1996. pap. 95.00 (0-7619-0397-6) Sage.

Medical Evaluation of Psychiatric Patients. R. B. Schiffer et al. LC 88-25380. (Illus.). 268p. (C). 1988. text 49.50 (0-306-42957-8, Kluwer Plenum) Kluwer Academic.

Medical Evaluation of the Surgical Patient. Alan G. Adler et al. (Blue Bk.). (Illus.). 304p. 1985. pap. text 36.95 (0-7216-1146-X, W B Saunders Co) Harcrt Hlth Sci Grp.

Medical Examination Review: Microbiology (MEPC) 11th ed. Charles Kim. 275p. (C). 1996. pap. text 21.95 (0-8385-6308-2, A6308-9, Apple Lange Med) McGraw.

Medical Examination Review: Surgery (MEPC) 11th ed. Michael Metzler. 317p. (C). 1996. pap. text 21.95 (0-8385-6195-0, A6195-0, Apple Lange Med) McGraw.

Medical Examinations: A Preparation Guide. V. Bhushan Bhardwaj. (Illus.). 1979. pap. 9.00 (0-668-03944-2, Arco) Macmillan Gen Ref.

***Medical Examinations: Dissecting the Doctor in French Narrative Prose, 1857-1894.** Mary Donaldson-Evans. LC 00-37427. (Illus.). 256p. 2000. pap. text 49.95 (0-8032-6628-6, Bison Books) U of Nebr Pr.

Medical Examiner. Jack Rudman. (Career Examination Ser.: C-486). 1994. pap. 49.95 (0-8373-0486-5) Nat Learn.

Medical Examiner under Fire: The Malice Green Police Brutality Case. Kalil Jiraki. Ed. by Abdussalam Ahmad. LC 94-62147. 212p. (Orig.). 1995. pap. 17.99 (0-9644884-0-X) Rainbow Flowers.

***Medical Executive Committee Handbook.** Hugh P. Greeley et al. Ed. by Meaghan Dwyer. (Illus.). 216p. 1999. pap. text 87.00 (1-57839-033-8) Opus Communs.

Medical Expenditures for People with Disabilities in the United States. 1997. lib. bdg. 250.95 (0-8490-8214-5) Gordon Pr.

Medical Expense Insurance. Ed. by Jane Stein. LC 98-206181. 309p. 1997. pap. text 30.00 (1-879143-40-2) Health Ins Assn Am.

Medical Expense Insurance Study Manual. HIAA Staff. 80p. 1997. pap., student ed. 10.00 (1-879143-41-0) Health Ins Assn Am.

Medical Experimentation & the Protection of Human Rights: Proceedings of the XIIth CIOMS Round Table Conference. N. Howard-Jones & Z. Bankowski. (CIOMS Round Table Proceedings Ser.: No. 12). 1979. pap. text 25.00 (92-9036-002-X) World Health.

Medical Facilities. Meisei Publications Editorial Staff. (New Concept in Architecture & Design Ser.). (Illus.). 224p. 1994. 85.00 (4-87246-294-7, Pub. by Tenpo Syst Study) Bks Nippan.

Medical Facilities Auditor. Jack Rudman. (Career Examination Ser.: C-2058). 1994. reprint ed. pap. 39.95 (0-8373-2058-5) Nat Learn.

Medical Factors & Psychological Disorders: A Handbook for Psychologists. R. L. Morrison & A. S. Bellack. LC 87-7903. (Illus.). 392p. (C). 1987. 90.00 (0-306-42425-8, Plenum Trade) Perseus Pubng.

Medical Family Therapy: Psychosocial Treatment of Families with Health Problems. Susan H. McDaniel et al. LC 92-11151. 352p. 1992. 38.00 (0-465-04437-9, Pub. by Basic) HarpC.

***Medical Fees in the United States 2000.** Ed. by ADP Context Software staff & James B. Davis. 2000. pap. text 119.95 (1-57066-167-7, 20035) Practice Mgmt Info.

Medical Fees in the United States, 1999. Ed. by ADP Context Software staff & James B. Davis. 380p. 1999. pap. 119.95 (1-57066-129-4, 9935) Practice Mgmt Info.

Medical Fictionary. H. C. Wolford. 80p. 1998. pap. 7.95 (0-9654563-4-X, Big Tree Bks) Easy Money Pr.

Medical Filing. Claeys. (Medical Assisting Ser.). 1993. pap. 14.95 (0-538-70675-9) S-W Pub.

Medical Filing. 2nd ed. Terese Claeys. 112p. 1996. pap., teacher ed. write for info. (0-8273-8178-6) Delmar.

Medical Filing. 2nd ed. Terese Claeys. LC 96-9526. (Illus.). 128p. 1996. mass mkt. 29.95 (0-8273-8177-8) Delmar.

***Medical First: Comprehensive First Repsonder.** Ed. by Appleton & Lange Staff. (C). 1999. text 25.00 (0-8385-6430-5) Appleton & Lange.

***Medical First: Comprehensive First Responder.** Ed. by Appleton & Lange Staff. (C). 1999. text 29.95 (0-8385-6433-X); text 40.00 (0-8385-6431-3); spiral bd. 25.00 (0-8385-6432-1) Appleton & Lange.

Medical First Aid Guide for Use in Accidents Involving Dangerous Goods (MFAG) International Maritime Organization Staff. 1991. text 110.00 (0-89771-875-5, Pub. by Intl Maritime Org) St Mut.

Medical First Aid Guide for Use in Accidents Involving Dangerous Goods MFAG 1994. International Maritime Organization Staff. 1994. pap. 45.00 (0-7855-0500-8, Pub. by Intl Maritime Org) St Mut.

Medical Flora: or Manual of the Medical Botany of the United States of North America, 2 vols., Set. Constantine S. Rafinesque. LC 75-23755. (Illus.). reprint ed. 60.00 (0-404-13191-3) AMS Pr.

***Medical Follow-Up Agency: The First Fifty Years, 1946-1996.** Institute of Medicine Staff. Ed. by Edward D. Berkowitz & Mark J. Santangelo. 148p. 1999. pap. 33.50 (0-309-06440-6) Natl Acad Pr.

Medical Formulary: or Aqrabadhin of Al-Kindi. Al-Kindi. Tr. by Martin Levy. LC 65-12105. (Publications in Medieval Science). 424p. reprint ed. pap. 131.50 (0-608-20448-X, 207170100002) Bks Demand.

Medical Fringe & Medical Orthodoxy, 1750-1850: A Volume in the Wellcome Institute. William F. Bynum & R. S. Porter. (History of Medicine Ser.). 288p. 1986. 57.50 (0-7099-3959-0, Pub. by C Helm) Routldge.

Medical Futility: And the Evaluation of Life-Sustaining Interventions. Ed. by Marjorie B. Zucker & Howard D. Zucker. 217p. (C). 1997. text 69.95 (0-521-56020-9); pap. text 24.95 (0-521-56877-3) Cambridge U Pr.

Medical Gas & Vacuum Systems. Gary D. Slack. (Management & Compliance Ser.: Vol. 3). (Illus.). 108p. 1993. ring bd. 110.00 (0-87258-480-1, 055215) Am Hospital.

Medical Genetic & Behavioral Aspects of Purebred Cats. Ross D. Clark. 253p. 1992. 64.95 (0-9634124-0-X) Cortlandt Grp.

Medical Genetic Studies of the Amish: Selected Papers. Ed. by Victor A. McKusick. LC 76-47386. (Illus.). 528p. 1978. 65.00 (0-8018-1934-2) Johns Hopkins.

Medical Genetics. Sack. LC 99-175561. 1998. 45.00 (0-07-134203-6) McGraw.

Medical Genetics. George Sack. LC 99-175561. (Illus.). 550p. 1999. pap. text 38.00 incl. cd-rom (0-07-057998-9) McGraw-Hill HPD.

Medical Genetics. George H. Sack. LC 99-175561. xvii, 286 p. 1999. write for info. incl. cd-rom (0-07-134204-4) McGraw-Hill HPD.

Medical Genetics. 2nd ed. Lynn B. Jorde et al. LC 98-7537. (Illus.). 384p. (C). (gr. 13). 1998. pap. text 41.95 (0-8151-4608-6, 31253) Mosby Inc.

Medical Genetics: A Self-Instruction Guide & Workbook Based on Mendelian Inheritance in Man (MIM) Victor A. McKusick. LC 93-31306. 128p. 1994. pap., wbk. ed. 30.00 (0-8018-4796-6) Johns Hopkins.

Medical Genetics: Principles & Practice. 4th ed. James J. Nora et al. LC 93-19984. (Illus.). 420p. 1994. 42.50 (0-8121-1663-1) Lppncott W & W.

Medical Genetics & Society. Ed. by N. Fujiki et al. LC 91-7099. (Illus.). 106p. 1991. pap. text 40.00 (90-6299-077-0, Pub. by Kugler) Kugler Pubns.

Medical Genetics Casebook: A Clinical Introduction to Medical Ethics Systems Theory. Colleen D. Clements. LC 81-8220. (Contemporary Issues in Biomedicine, Ethics, & Society Ser.). 250p. 1982. 49.50 (0-89603-033-4) Humana.

Medical Genetics Handbook. Harold Chen. (Illus.). 396p. 1988. pap. 52.50 (0-87527-371-8) Green.

Medical Genetics Today: Papers Presented at the Johns Hopkins Hospital, Baltimore, Maryland, June 15 & 16, 1972. Ed. by Daniel Bergsma. LC 78-78434. (Birth Defects, Original Article Ser.: Vol. 10, no. 10). 314p. reprint ed. pap. 97.40 (0-608-13625-5, 202073600018) Bks Demand.

Medical Gentleman: James J. Waring, M. D. Patricia Paton. LC 93-23589. 1993. write for info. (0-942576-02-0); pap. write for info. (0-942576-33-0) CO Hist Soc.

Medical Geographic Research in Latin America. Ed. by C. Weil. 100p. 1982. pap. 18.00 (0-08-028895-2, Pergamon Pr) Elsevier.

***Medical Geography.** 2nd ed. Melinda S. Meade & Robert J. Earickson. 480p. 2000. lib. bdg. 49.95 (1-57230-558-4) Guilford Pubns.

Medical Geography South & Southeast Asia. Ed. by Ashok K. Dutt. (Illus.). 78p. 1981. pap. 24.00 (0-08-026762-9, Pergamon Pr) Elsevier.

Medical Gloves Markets. (Market Research Reports: No. 243). (Illus.). 76p. 1992. 295.00 (0-317-04998-4) Theta Corp.

Medical Graduates of Foreign Nations: Index of New Information Including Social & Professional Discrimination, Selection, Performance & Problems. Darrell R. Rhodes. 135p. 1997. 47.50 (0-7883-1636-2); pap. 44.50 (0-7883-1637-0) ABBE Pubs Assn.

Medical Greek & Latin Workbook. 2nd ed. James A. McCulloch. 212p. 1984. pap., spiral bd. 33.95 (0-398-04905-X) C C Thomas.

Medical Group Practice Legal & Administrative Guide. Aspen Health Law Center Staff & Aspen Reference Group (Aspen Publishers) Staff. LC 98-12742. 1998. write for info. (0-8342-1100-9) Aspen Pub.

Medical Group Practice Legal & Administrative Guide. Aspen Reference Group Staff. 1998. 189.00 (0-8342-1068-1, S470) Aspen Pub.

Medical Group Practices Face the Uncertain Future: Challenges, Opportunities & Strategies. John D. Blair et al. 63p. (Orig.). 1995. pap. text 27.00 (1-56829-009-8) Med Group Mgmt.

Medical Group Practices in the U. S., 1999 Edition. American Medical Association. 1999. 99.95 (0-89970-958-3) AMA.

Medical Group Treatment in Turbulent Times: How Physicial Leadership Can Optimize Health Plan, Hospital, & Medical Group Performance. Paul A. Sommers. LC 97-50421. (Illus.). 484p. 1998. lib. bdg. 79.95 (0-7890-0487-9) Haworth Pr.

Medical Guide to Hazardous Marine Life. 3rd rev. ed. Paul S. Auerbach. LC 96-79063. (Illus.). 72p. 1997. pap. 19.95 (0-941332-55-1, D267) Best Pub Co.

Medical Guidelines & Outcomes at Work. 1993. 52.00 (1-56925-012-X, MGOW) Capitol Publns.

Medical Guidelines for Airline Travel. Task Force of Aerospace Staff. 52p. 1997. pap. 18.00 (1-890397-00-8) Aerospace Med Assn.

Medical Guidelines for Determining Prognosis in Selected Non-Cancer Diseases. 2nd ed. National Hospice Organization Standards & Accredit & National Hospice Organization Medical Guidelines T. 58p. (Orig.). 1996. pap. 11.85 (0-931207-50-9, 713008) Natl Hospice.

Medical Halacha for Everyone see Comprehensive Guide to Medical Halachah

Medical Handbook for Medical. K. Majumdar. (C). 1989. 65.00 (0-89771-355-9, Pub. by Current Dist) St Mut.

Medical Handbook for Pilots. (Illus.). 74p. 1997. reprint ed. pap. text 25.00 (0-7881-4618-1) DIANE Pub.

Medical Handbook for Pilots: FAA-AC-67-2. rev. ed. FAA Staff. (FAA Reprints Ser.). (Illus.). 1988. reprint ed. pap. 7.00 (1-56027-008-X, ASA-AC67-2) ASA Inc.

Medical Handbook for Senior Citizens & Their Families. Howard A. Thornton. LC 87-30821. 383p. 1989. 59.95 (0-86569-171-1, Auburn Hse) Greenwood.

Medical Handbook for the Layman. J. Tyrone Alfred & C. Cannon-Alfred. 1969. 5.95 (0-686-00411-6) Alfred.

Medical Handbook for the Medical Representative. 7th ed. M. Majumder. (C). 1989. 40.00 (0-7855-4666-9, Pub. by Current Dist) St Mut.

Medical Harm: Historical, Conceptual & Ethical Dimensions of Iatrogenic Illness. Virginia A. Sharpe & Alan I. Faden. LC 97-11814. (Illus.). 292p. (C). 1998. pap. text 27.95 (0-521-63490-3) Cambridge U Pr.

***Medical Health Care Career Prep Path.** Zephyr Tate-Mann. 2000. pap. 10.00 (0-8059-4895-3) Dorrance.

Medical Health of the World: Index of New Information with Authors & Subjects. rev. ed. Science & Life Consultants Association Staff. LC 94-34919. 157p. 1994. 47.50 (0-7883-0356-2); pap. 44.50 (0-7883-0357-0) ABBE Pubs Assn.

Medical Herpetology: Amphibians & Reptiles - Their Influence on, & Relationship to, Human Medicine. Steve Grenard. LC 94-66658. 160p. 1994. pap. 19.95 (0-9641032-0-6) Reptile & Amphibian.

Medical Hieroglyphs. Avice H. Kerr. LC 75-131216. 1970. 14.75 (0-918558-01-8) Enterprise Calif.

Medical Histories of Confederate Generals. Jack D. Welsh. LC 94-8673. 297p. 1994. 35.00 (0-87338-505-5) Kent St U Pr.

***Medical Histories of Confederate Generals.** Jack D. Welsh. 316p. 1999. 16.00 (0-87338-649-3) Kent St U Pr.

Medical Histories of Union Generals. Jack D. Welsh. LC 96-13353. 442p. (C). 1997. 35.00 (0-87338-552-7) Kent St U Pr.

Medical History: Index of Modern Authors & Subjects with Guide for Rapid Research. rev. ed. Arthur Schlefman. LC 94-34373. 129p. 1994. 47.50 (0-7883-0372-4); pap. 44.50 (0-7883-0373-2) ABBE Pubs Assn.

Medical History & Physical Examination in Companion Animals. Ed. by Adam Rijnberk & H. W. De Vries. Tr. by B. E. Belshaw from DUT. LC 94-29947. Orig. Title: Anamnese en Lichamelijk Onderzoek bij Gezelschapsdieren. 1995. lib. bdg. 169.00 (0-7923-3037-4) Kluwer Academic.

Medical History of Current & Old Wars: Index of New Information. Gregg V. Goldin. LC 95-19211. 1995. 47.50 (0-7883-0660-X); pap. 44.50 (0-7883-0661-8) ABBE Pubs Assn.

Medical History of Ishi. fac. ed. Saxton T. Pope. (University of California Publications in American Archaeology & Ethnology: Vol. 13: 5). (Illus.). 38p. (C). 1920. reprint ed. pap. text 4.38 (1-55567-214-0) Coyote Press.

Medical History Through Postage Stamps. A. Furukawa. 480p. 1994. 39.95 (1-56386-020-1, Ishiyaku EuroAmerica) Med Dent Media.

Medical Hypnosis, 2 vols. Lewis R. Wolberg. Incl. Vol. I. Principles of Hypnotherapy. LC 48-2929. 460p. 1948. text 71.00 (0-8089-0536-8, 794871, W B Saunders Co); Vol. II. Practice of Hypnotherapy. LC 48-2929. 520p. 1948. text 71.00 (0-8089-0537-6, 794872, W B Saunders Co); LC 48-2929. 1948. write for info. (0-318-52857-6, Grune & Strat) Harcrt Hlth Sci Grp.

Medical Hypnosis. L. W. De Laurence. 292p. 1999. reprint ed. pap. 17.95 (0-7661-0746-9) Kessinger Pub.

Medical Hypnosis: An Introduction & Clinical Guide. Roberta Temes. Ed. by Marc Staruss. LC 98-25700. (Illus.). 140p. (C). 1998. text 39.50 (0-443-06010-X) Church.

Medical Hypnotism & Suggestion. Alexander Verner & Swami Brahma. reprint ed. pap. 2.00 (0-911662-14-6) Yoga.

Medical I Ching: Oracle of the Healer Within. Miki Shima. Ed. by Robert Flaws. LC 92-73393. (Illus.). 265p. (Orig.). 1992. pap. 21.95 (0-936185-38-4) Blue Poppy Pr.

Medical Illustration Source Book. 7th ed. (Illus.). 192p. 1994. 50.00 (1-883486-01-7) Assn Med Illus.

Medical Illustration Source Book. 8th ed. (Illus.). 252p. 1995. 50.00 (1-883486-02-5) Assn Med Illus.

Medical Illustration Source Book. 9th ed. (Illus.). 232p. 1996. 50.00 (1-883486-04-1) Assn Med Illus.

Medical Illustration Source Book. 10th ed. (Illus.). 230p. 1997. 50.00 (1-883486-05-X) Assn Med Illus.

Medical Illustration Source Book. 11th ed. (Illus.). 184p. 1998. 50.00 (1-883486-06-8) Assn Med Illus.

***Medical Image Computing & Computer-Assisted Intervention - MICCAI'99: 2nd International Conference, Cambridge, UK, September 19-22, 1999, Proceedings.** Ed. by C. Taylor et al. (Lecture Notes in Computer Science Ser.: Vol. 1679). xxi, 1240p. 1999. pap. 116.00 (3-540-66503-X) Spr-Verlag.

Medical Image Computing & Computer-Assisted Intervention-MICCAI'98: First International Conference, Cambridge, MA, U. S. A., October 11-13, 1998, Proceedings. Ed. by S. Delp et al. LC 98-45053. (Lecture Notes in Computer Science Ser.: Vol. 1496). xxii, 1256p. 1998. pap. 120.00 (3-540-65136-5) Spr-Verlag.

Medical Image Databases. Stephen T. Wong. LC 98-33987. (International Series in Engineering & Computer Science). 398p. 1998. 140.00 (0-7923-8289-7) Kluwer Academic.

Medical Image Management Markets: Telemedicine Is Here: PACS & Teleradiology Lead the Way. Market Intelligence Staff. 215p. (Orig.). 1992. 1895.00 (1-56753-079-6) Frost & Sullivan.

Medical Image Processing: The Mathematics of Medical Imaging. James A. Green. LC 94-77688. (Engineering Ser.: Vol. 2). (Illus.). 250p. 1999. 49.20 (1-890121-18-5, 03/02/01) Grnwd Resch.

Medical Images: Formation, Handling, & Evaluation. Ed. by Andrew E. Todd-Pokropek & Max A. Viergever. LC 92-48909. (NATO ASI Series F: Computer & Systems Sciences, Special Programme AET: No. 98). 1993. 234.00 (0-387-56131-5) Spr-Verlag.

Medical Imaging. L. Beolchi & M. H. Kuhn. LC 94-73420. (Studies in Health Technology & Informatics: Vol. 19). 225p. (gr. 12). 1995. 103.00 (90-5199-210-6) IOS Press.

Medical Imaging. Ed. by Stephen J. Riederer. (Illus.). 144p. 1995. pap. 26.00 (0-917853-57-1, RB-65) Am Assn Physics.

Medical Imaging. Peter Scally. LC RC78.7.D53S32 1999. (Oxford Core Texts Ser.). (Illus.). 304p. 2000. pap. text 39.95 (0-19-263056-3) OUP.

Medical Imaging, No. 1. Ed. by H. J. Kaufmann. (Karger Highlights, Medical Imaging Ser.). (Illus.). vi, 142p. 1980. pap. 13.25 (3-8055-3056-0) S Karger.

Medical Imaging: A Concise Textbook. Ed. by Eugene R. Jacobs. LC 87-2644. (Illus.). 570p. 1987. 49.50 (0-89640-126-X) Igaku-Shoin.

Medical Imaging - The Assessment of Image Quality. ICRU Staff. Ed. by W. Roger Ney. (ICRU Reports: No. 54). 100p. (Orig.). 1995. pap. text 60.00 (0-913394-53-X) Intl Comm Rad Meas.

***Medical Imaging Equipment in Argentina: A Strategic Entry Report, 1996.** Compiled by Icon Group International Staff. (Illus.). 147p. 1999. ring bd. 1470.00 incl. audio compact disk (0-7418-1317-3) Icon Grp.

***Medical Imaging Equipment in Saudi Arabia: A Strategic Entry Report, 1999.** Compiled by Icon Group International. (Illus.). 133p. 1999. ring bd. 1330.00 incl. audio compact disk (0-7418-1722-5) Icon Grp.

Medical Imaging, 1998: Image Display. Ed. by Yongmin Kim & Seong K. Mun. LC 98-227269. (Proceedings of SPIE Ser.: Vol. 3335). 710p. 1998. 124.00 (0-8194-2780-2) SPIE.

Medical Imaging, 1998: Image Processing. Ed. by Kenneth M. Hanson. LC 99-182755. (Proceedings of SPIE Ser.: Vol. 3338). 1614p. 1998. 166.00 (0-8194-2783-7) SPIE.

Medical Imaging 1998: PACS Design & Evaluation: Engineering & Clinical Issues. Ed. by Steven C. Horii & G. James Blaine. LC 98-226770. (Proceedings of SPIE Ser.: Vol. 3339). 616p. 1998. 116.00 (0-8194-2784-5) SPIE.

Medical Imaging, 1998: Physics of Medical Imaging. Ed. by James T. Dobbins & John M. Boone. LC 98-227297. (Proceedings of SPIE Ser.: Vol. 3336). 856p. 1998. 132.00 (0-8194-2781-0) SPIE.

Medical Imaging, 1998: Physiology & Function from Multidimensional Images. Ed. by Eric A. Hoffman. LC 98-227288. (Proceedings of SPIE Ser.: Vol. 3337). 396p. 1998. 80.00 (0-8194-2782-9) SPIE.

***Medical Imaging, 1998 Vol. 3340: Image Perception.** Ed. by Harold L. Kundel. 148p. 1998. 48.00 (0-8194-2785-3) SPIE.

***Medical Imaging, 1998 Vol. 3341: Ultrasonic Transducer Engineering.** Ed. by K. Kirk Shung. 292p. 1998. 69.00 (0-8194-2786-1) SPIE.

Medical Imaging, 1997: Image Perception. Ed. by Harold L. Kundel. 346p. 1997. 69.00 (0-8194-2447-1) SPIE.

Medical Imaging, 1997 Vol. 3031: Image Display. Ed. by Yongmin Kim. LC 97-200314. 876p. 1997. 132.00 (0-8194-2442-0) SPIE.

Medical Imaging, 1997 Vol. 3032: Physics of Medical Imaging. Ed. by Richard L. Van Metter & Jacob Beutel. LC 97-193057. 556p. 1997. 107.00 (0-8194-2443-9) SPIE.

Medical Imaging, 1997 Vol. 3033: Physiology & Function from Multidimensional Images. Ed. by Eric A. Hoffman. LC 97-193071. 472p. 1997. 80.00 (0-8194-2444-7) SPIE.

Medical Imaging, 1997 Vol. 3034: Image Processing. Ed. by Kenneth M. Hanson. LC 97-200957. 1182p. 1997. 158.00 (0-8194-2445-5) SPIE.

Medical Imaging, 1997 Vol. 3035: PACS Design & Evaluation: Engineering & Clinical Issues. Ed. by Steven C. Horii & G. James Blaine. LC 97-200313. 652p. 1997. 124.00 (0-8194-2446-3) SPIE.

Medical Imaging 1996: 11-13 February, 1996, Newport Beach, California. Eric A. Hoffman et al. LC 95-72069. xi, 526p. 1996. write for info. (0-8194-2084-0) SPIE.

Medical Imaging of Focal Liver Lesions: Clinico-Radiologic Approach. Kohkan Shamsi & A. M. DeSchepper. LC 94-22473. 144p. 1994. 178.50 (0-444-81919-3) Elsevier.

***Medical Imaging of the Spleen.** Ed. by A. M. de Schepper & F. Vanhoenacker. LC 99-40699. (Medical Radiology Ser.). (Illus.). 160p. 2000. 119.00 (3-540-65535-2) Spr-Verlag.

Medical Imaging VI: Image Capture, Formatting, & Display. 1992. 20.00 (0-8194-0805-0, 1653) SPIE.

Medical Imaging VI: Image Processing. 1992. 20.00 (0-8194-0804-2, 1652) SPIE.

Medical Imaging VI: Instrumentation. 1992. 20.00 (0-8194-0803-4, 1651) SPIE.

M

Medical Imaging VI: PACS Design & Evaluation. 1992. 20.00 (*0-8194-0806-9*, 1654) SPIE.

Medical Imaging Systems. Albert Macovski. (Illus.). 256p. (C). 1983. text 65.20 (*0-13-572685-9*) P-H.

Medical Imaging Systems Techniques & Applications: Brain & Skeletal Systems. Ed. by Cornelius T. Leondes. (International Series in Engineering, Technology & Applied Science: Vol. 2). 258p. 1997. text 52.00 (*90-5699-541-3*) Gordon & Breach.

Medical Imaging Systems Techniques & Applications: Cardiovascular Systems. Ed. by Cornelius T. Leondes. (Gordon & Breach International Ser. I). 226p. 1997. text 49.00 (*90-5699-509-X*) Gordon & Breach.

Medical Imaging Systems Techniques & Applications: Computational Techniques. Ed. by Cornelius T. Leondes. (International Series in Engineering, Technology & Applied Science: Vol. 6). 264p. 1998. text 89.00 (*90-5699-620-7*) Gordon & Breach.

Medical Imaging Systems Techniques & Applications: Diagnosis Optimization Techniques. Ed. by Cornelius T. Leondes. (International Series in Engineering, Technology & Applied Science: Vol. 3). 336p. 1997. text 52.00 (*90-5699-595-2*) Gordon & Breach.

Medical Imaging Systems Techniques & Applications: General Anatomy, Vol. 4. Ed. by Cornelius T. Leondes. (International Series in Engineering, Technology & Applied Science). 334p. 1997. text 58.00 (*90-5699-597-9*) Gordon & Breach.

Medical Imaging Systems Techniques & Applications: Modalities. Ed. by Cornelius T. Leondes. (Gordon & Breach International Ser. I). 340p. 1997. text 58.00 (*90-5699-610-X*) Gordon & Breach.

Medical Imitations of Illness with Pretense & Shams Including Munchausen's Syndrome. rev. ed. Shirley L. Sinclair. 171p. 1997. 47.50 (*0-7883-1554-4*); pap. 44.50 (*0-7883-1555-2*) ABBE Pubs Assn.

Medical Immunology. Stites. 1999. pap. text 44.95 (*0-8385-6300-7*, Medical Exam) Appleton & Lange.

Medical Immunology. 9th ed. Ed. by Daniel P. Stites & Abba I. Terr. 900p. (C). 1997. pap. 43.95 (*0-8385-0586-4*, Apple Lange Med) McGraw.

Medical Immunology for Students. Playfair. 1995. pap. text 26.95 (*0-443-05000-7*, W B Saunders Co) Harcrt Hlth Sci Grp.

Medical Implications of Nuclear War. Institute of Medicine Staff. Ed. by Fredric Solomon & Robert Q. Marston. LC 86-18134. (Illus.). 639p. reprint ed. pap. 198.10 (*0-7837-3569-3*, 204342700009) Bks Demand.

***Medical Importance of the Normal Microflora.** Contrib. by G. W. Tannock. LC 99-27093. (Illus.). 492p. 1999. write for info. (*0-412-79390-3*) Kluwer Academic.

Medical Index of Severity of Illness & Sick Roles: Judgemental Signs, Symptoms, Rules & Controversy. Science & Life Consultants Staff. 151p. 1997. 47.50 (*0-7883-1656-7*); pap. 44.50 (*0-7883-1657-5*) ABBE Pubs Assn.

Medical Informatics. Benson. 1994. pap. text. write for info. (*0-582-08271-4*, Pub. by Addison-Wesley) Longman.

Medical Informatics. Goble. (ITCP-UK Computer Science Ser.). 1996. pap. 39.95 (*1-85032-238-4*) ITCP.

***Medical Informatics: Computer Applications in Health Care.** 2nd ed. Edward H. Shortliffe. Ed. by K. J. Hannah et al. LC 99-89476. (Health Informatics Ser.). 768p. 2000. 69.95 (*0-387-98472-0*) Spr-Verlag.

Medical Informatics: The Essentials. F. T. De Dombal. LC 96-205533. 144p. 1996. pap. text 37.50 (*0-7506-2162-1*, Focal) Buttrwrth-Heinemann.

Medical Informatics Europe, 1984: Proceedings. Ed. by F. H. Roger et al. (Lecture Notes in Medical Informatics Ser.: Vol. 24). xxvii, 778p. 1984. 81.95 (*0-387-13374-7*) Spr-Verlag.

Medical Informatics Europe, 1988: Proceedings Oslo, Norway, August 17-20, 1988. Ed. by Bjarte G. Solheim et al. (Lecture Notes in Medical Informatics Ser.: Vol. 35). xv, 764p. 1988. 135.00 (*0-387-50138-X*) Spr-Verlag.

Medical Informatics Europe, 1999. Ed. by P. Kokol. (Studies in Health Technology & Informatics: Vol. 68). 1999. 142.00 (*0-9673355-1-5*) IOS Press.

Medical Informatics Europe, 1990 Vol. 40: Proceedings Glasgow, Scotland, August 20-23, 1990. R. R. O'Moore et al. Ed. by O. Rienhoff & D. A. Lindberg. (Lecture Notes Ser.). xxv, 820p. 1990. 146.00 (*0-387-52936-5*) Spr-Verlag.

Medical Informatics, '97. LC 97-72897. (Studies in Health Technology & Informatics: No. 43). 950p. (gr. 12). Date not set. 119.00 (*90-5199-343-9*) IOS Press.

Medical Informatics, '96. Ed. by J. Brender et al. LC 96-77454. (Studies in Health Technology & Informatics: Vol. 34). 1100p. (gr. 12). 1996. 143.00 (*90-5199-278-5*, 278-5) IOS Press.

Medical Information: A Profile. Barry S. Hodge & Barbara C. Allan. LC 85-19726. (Professional Librarian Ser.). 145p. 1986. 40.00 (*0-86729-163-X*, Hall Reference) Macmillan.

Medical Information on the Internet. Robert Kiley. 1996. pap. 28.00 (*0-443-05699-4*, K1162) Church.

Medical Information on the Internet: A Guide for Health Professionals. 2nd ed. Robert Kiley. LC 98-48320. 1999. write for info. (*0-443-06194-7*) Church.

Medical Information Systems for Lawyers, 2 vols. 2nd ed. Stanley McQuade. LC 93-73676. 1993. ring bd. 225.00 (*0-685-59889-6*) West Group.

Medical Injuries in the Martial Arts. Richard B. Birrer & Christina D. Birrer. (Illus.). 240p. 1981. pap. 29.95 (*0-398-04134-2*) C C Thomas.

Medical Inquiries & Observations. Benjamin Rush. (Notable American Authors Ser.). 1999. reprint ed. lib. bdg. 125.00 (*0-7812-8851-7*) Rprt Serv.

Medical Inquiries & Observations, 4 vols., Set. 4th ed. Benjamin Rush. LC 76-180588. (Medicine & Society in America Ser.). 1070p. 1972. reprint ed. 65.95 (*0-405-03968-9*) Ayer.

Medical Inquiries & Observations, 4 vols., Vol. 1. 4th ed. Benjamin Rush. LC 76-180588. (Medicine & Society in America Ser.). 1070p. 1972. reprint ed. 33.95 (*0-405-03969-7*) Ayer.

Medical Inquiries & Observations, 4 vols., Vol. 2. 4th ed. Benjamin Rush. LC 76-180588. (Medicine & Society in America Ser.). 1070p. 1972. reprint ed. 33.95 (*0-405-03970-0*) Ayer.

Medical Inquiries & Observations upon the Diseases of the Mind. Benjamin Rush. (Notable American Authors Ser.). 1999. reprint ed. lib. bdg. 125.00 (*0-7812-8853-3*) Rprt Serv.

Medical Insects & Arachnids. Ed. by Richard P. Lane & Roger W. Crosske. LC 92-49000. 1993. write for info. (*0-04-124000-6*) Chapman & Hall.

Medical Inspector. Jack Rudman. (Career Examination Ser.: C-487). 1994. pap. 44.95 (*0-8373-0487-3*) Nat Learn.

Medical Instrument Nurses - Allied Health. 2nd ed. Richard Aston & Katherine K. Brown. (Nursing-Health Science Ser.). 336p. (C). 1994. pap. 40.00 (*0-86720-688-8*) Jones & Bartlett.

Medical Instrumentation: Application & Design. 3rd ed. Ed. by John G. Webster. LC 97-4385. 720p. 1997. text 103.95 (*0-471-15368-0*) Wiley.

***Medical Insurance in Saudi Arabia: A Strategic Entry Report, 1995.** Compiled by Icon Group International Staff. (Illus.). 156p. 1999. ring bd. 1560.00 incl. audio compact disk (*0-7418-1598-2*) Icon Grp.

***Medical Insurance in Saudi Arabia: A Strategic Entry Report, 1998.** Compiled by Icon Group International Staff. (Country Industry Report). (Illus.). 131p. 1999. ring bd. 1310.00 incl. audio compact disk (*0-7418-0502-2*) Icon Grp.

***Medical Insurance Made Easy.** Brown, 2001. pap. text. write for info. (*0-7216-9187-0*) Harcourt.

Medical Insurance Manual for Dentists: Maximizing Reimbursements. Rose Nierman. LC 95-25462. (Pennwell Bks.). 1995. 89.95 (*0-87814-459-5*) PennWell Bks.

Medical Insurance Paperwork: Conquering the Chaos. Connie Clark. (Illus.). 192p. (Orig.). 1992. pap. 18.95 (*0-9643510-0-5*) Med Ins Servs.

Medical Internet Toolkit, 1998. Ed. by Jennifer Wayne-Doppke. (Illus.). 210p. 1998. pap. 97.00 (*0-9645360-6-4*) Cor Hlthcare.

Medical Interview. Mack Lipkin, Jr. et al. LC 94-6511. 1994. 138.00 (*3-540-94257-2*) Spr-Verlag.

Medical Interview. Mack Lipkin, Jr. et al. LC 94-6511. 1996. 99.00 (*0-387-94257-2*) Spr-Verlag.

Medical Interview: A Functional & Operational Approach. Steven A. Cohen & Cole. (Illus.). 224p. (C). (gr. 13). 1990. pap. text 32.95 (*0-8016-0345-5*, 00345) Mosby Inc.

Medical Interview: Gateway to the Doctor Patient Relationship. C. Knight Aldrich. LC 93-18395. (Illus.). 126p. 1993. 17.95 (*1-85070-487-2*) Prthnon Pub.

Medical Interview: Gateway to the Doctor-Patient Relationship. 2nd enl. rev. ed. C. K. Aldrich. (Illus.). 164p. 1999. pap. 24.95 (*1-85070-014-1*) Prthnon Pub.

Medical Interview: Mastering Skills for Clinical Practice. 3rd ed. John L. Coulehan & Marian R. Block. LC 97-6737. (Illus.). 287p. (C). 1997. pap. text 29.95 (*0-8036-0267-7*) Davis Co.

Medical Interview: The Three-Function Approach. 2nd ed. Cole. (Illus.). 225p. (C). 1999. pap. text 25.95 (*0-8151-1992-5*, 30377) Mosby Inc.

Medical Intuition: How to Combine Inner Resources with Modern Medicine. Ruth Berger. LC 95-19107. (Illus.). 160p. (Orig.). 1995. pap. 9.95 (*0-87728-851-8*) Weiser.

***Medical Issues & Health Care Reform in Russia.** Vicki L. Hesli & Margaret H. Mills. LC 99-41404. (Studies in Health & Human Services : Vol. 35). 340p. 1999. text 99.95 (*0-7734-7933-3*) E Mellen.

Medical Issues & the Eating Disorders: The Interface. Ed. by Allan S. Kaplan & Paul E. Garfinkel. LC 92-48961. (Eating Disorders Monographs: No. 7). (Illus.). 224p. 1993. text 35.95 (*0-87630-681-4*) Brunner-Mazel.

Medical Issues for Adults with Mental Retardation/ Developmental Disabilities. Carl V. Tyler. (High Tide Disability Ser.: Vol. 7). 50p. 1999. spiral bd. 10.95 (*1-892696-05-3*) High Tide Pr.

Medical Itch. Claude Benjamin. (Illus.). 1964. 11.95 (*0-8392-1067-1*) Astor-Honor.

***Medical Job Interview.** (Illus.). 56p. 2000. pap. 14.95 (*0-632-05527-8*) Blackwell Sci.

Medical Journalism: A Writers Guide. Tim Albert. 1995. write for info. (*1-85775-088-8*, Radcliffe Med Pr) Scovill Paterson.

Medical Journalism: The Writer's Guide. 2nd ed. Tim Albert. 1995. pap. 24.95 (*1-870905-28-8*, Radcliffe Med Pr) Scovill Paterson.

Medical Jurisprudence. J. Jhala & R. Raju. (C). 1990. text 135.00 (*0-89771-481-4*) St Mut.

Medical Jurisprudence & Criminal Law II: Subject Analysis Index with Research Bibliography. Roy R. Zimmerman. LC 83-70081. 150p. 1987. 47.50 (*0-88164-330-0*); pap. 44.50 (*0-88164-331-9*) ABBE Pubs Assn.

Medical Keyboarding, Typing & Transcribing: Techniques & Procedures. 4th ed. Marcy O. Diehl & Marilyn T. Fordney. Ed. by Margaret Biblis. LC 96-41729. (Illus.). 544p. 1997. pap. text 43.00 (*0-7216-6858-5*, W B Saunders Co) Harcrt Hlth Sci Grp.

Medical Keyboarding, Typing & Transcribing: Techniques & Procedures. 4th ed. Mary O. Diehl & Marilyn T. Fordney. (Illus.). 1997. pap., teacher ed. write for info. (*0-7216-6859-3*, W B Saunders Co) Harcrt Hlth Sci Grp.

Medical Kits on Commercial Airlines: Hearing Before the Subcommittee on Aviation of the Committee on Transportation & Infrastructure, House of Representatives, 105th Fifth Congress, 1st Session, May 21, 1997. USGPO Staff. LC 98-134026. iv, 201p. 1997. pap. write for info. (*0-16-055788-7*) USGPO.

Medical Knots & Suture Technique: A Handbook for Students of Surgery. F. D. Giddings. LC 97-93710. Orig. Title: The Handbook of Surgical Knot Tying. (Illus.). 48p. (C). 1997. spiral bd. 15.00 (*1-889326-00-3*) Giddings Studio Pub.

Medical Knowledge: Doubt & Certainty. Ed. by Clive Seale & Stephen Pattison. LC 93-23599. 1994. pap. 31.95 (*0-335-19251-3*) OpUniv Pr.

Medical Knowledge for Fun. Richard Worcester. LC 95-34795. 108p. 1995. text 18.00 (*1-85070-685-9*) Prthnon Pub.

Medical Knowledge of Shakespeare. John C. Bucknill. LC 72-155634. reprint ed. 29.50 (*0-404-01146-2*) AMS Pr.

Medical Lab Testing Industry. Marketdata Enterprises, Inc. Staff. 25p. 1999. 59.00 (*1-891084-35-6*) Mktdata Ent.

Medical Laboratory Assistant. Jacquelyn Marshall. 224p. 1990. pap. 37.60 (*0-89303-693-5*) P-H.

Medical Laboratory Assistant. Jaquelyn Marshall. 1990. pap., teacher ed. 14.00 (*0-89303-737-0*) P-H.

***Medical Laboratory Equipment in Canada: A Strategic Entry Report, 1997.** Compiled by Icon Group International Staff. (Country Industry Report). (Illus.). 131p. 1999. ring bd. 1310.00 incl. audio compact disk (*0-7418-0257-0*) Icon Grp.

***Medical Laboratory Equipment in India: A Strategic Entry Report, 1999.** Compiled by Icon Group International. (Illus.). 194p. 1999. ring bd. 1940.00 incl. audio compact disk (*0-7418-1697-0*) Icon Grp.

Medical Laboratory Management: Forms, Checklists & Guidelines. Ed. by Sara N. Di Lima & Suzanne Niemeyer. LC 94-34047. ring bd. 190.00 (*0-8342-0667-6*) Aspen Pub.

Medical Laboratory Management & Supervision: Operations, Review, & Study Guide. Lionel A. Varnadoe. LC 95-42716. (Illus.). 321p. (C). 1996. 31.95 (*0-8036-8861-X*) Davis Co.

***Medical Laboratory Management Report 2000 Yearbook.** Sherrye Henry. Ed. by Jan Christian Bernabe. (Illus.). 200p. 1999. pap. 199.00 (*1-58673-014-2*) IOMA.

Medical Laboratory Procedures. 2nd ed. Mary E. Wedding. LC 97-984. 427p. 1997. pap. 39.95 (*0-8036-0052-6*) Davis Co.

Medical Laboratory Technician. Jack Rudman. (Career Examination Ser.: C-2323). 1994. pap. 27.95 (*0-8373-2323-1*) Nat Learn.

Medical Laboratory Technician (Substance Abuse) Jack Rudman. (Career Examination Ser.: C-3119). 1994. pap. 29.95 (*0-8373-3119-6*) Nat Learn.

Medical Landmarks, U. S. A. A Travel Guide to Historical Sites, Architectural Gems, Remarkable. Martin Lipp. 384p. 1990. pap. text 45.00 (*0-07-037974-2*) McGraw-Hill HPD.

***Medical Language.** Chabner. 2000. pap. text. write for info. (*0-7216-8582-X*, W B Saunders Co) Harcrt Hlth Sci Grp.

Medical Language. Collins1. Date not set. teacher ed. write for info. (*0-314-06959-3*) West Pub.

Medical Language. Layman. 1994. audio 107.25 (*0-8273-6923-9*) Delmar.

Medical Language. Dale P. Layman. (Medical Terminology Ser.). 1995. 62.95 (*0-8273-6924-7*) Delmar.

Medical Language: A Programmed Body-System Approach. Peggy M. Krueger. 221p. 1995. teacher ed. 20.00 (*0-8273-5639-0*) Delmar.

Medical Language: A Programmed Body-System Approach. Dale P. Layman. LC 93-37629. 513p. (C). 1994. pap. 52.95 (*0-8273-5612-9*) Delmar.

Medical Language: A Programmed Body-System Approach. Dale P. Layman. 544p. (C). 1994. text 46.00 incl. digital audio (*0-8273-6922-0*) Delmar.

Medical Language: A Programmed Body-System Approach. Dale P. Layman. 544p. 1995. text 42.95 incl. digital audio (*0-8273-6925-5*) Delmar.

Medical Language Processing: Computer Management of Narrative Data. Naomi Sager et al. 320p. (C). 1987. text 51.75 (*0-201-16810-3*) Addison-Wesley.

Medical Language Specialist. Lindsey. (Medical Assisting Ser.). 1995. pap., teacher ed. 12.00 (*0-8273-6053-3*) Delmar.

Medical Language Specialist. Lindsey. (Medical Assisting Ser.). 1997. pap. 21.95 (*0-8273-6052-5*) Delmar.

Medical Larousse (Italian Edition) R. Valenti & M. G. Malesani. (ITA.). 1040p. 1987. 295.00 (*0-8288-7346-1*) Fr & Eur.

Medical Laser Device Markets. (Market Research Reports: No. 523). 195p. 1996. 995.00 (*0-317-05008-7*) Theta Corp.

Medical Laser Endoscopy. Ed. by Dennis M. Jensen & Jean M. Brunetaud. (Developments in Gastroenterology Ser.). (C). 1990. text 299.50 (*0-7923-0579-5*) Kluwer Academic.

Medical Laser Equipment in Mexico: A Strategic Entry Report, 1997. Compiled by Icon Group International Staff. (Illus.). 150p. 1999. ring bd. 1500.00 incl. audio compact disk (*0-7418-0869-2*) Icon Grp.

Medical Laser Safety Reference Guide. 192p. (Orig.). 1992. pap. text 60.00 (*0-912035-47-1*, 121) Laser Inst.

Medical Lasers: Science & Clinical Practice. J. A. Carruth & A. McKenzie. (Illus.). 280p. 1986. 116.00 (*0-85274-560-5*) IOP Pub.

Medical Lasers & Their Safe Use. David H. Sliney & Stephen L. Trokel. LC 92-2299. (Illus.). 264p. 1992. write for info. (*3-540-97856-9*) Spr-Verlag.

Medical Lasers & Their Safe Use. David H. Sliney & Stephen L. Trokel. LC 92-2299. (Illus.). 264p. 1994. 79.00 (*0-387-97856-9*) Spr-Verlag.

***Medical Latin in the Roman Empire.** D. R. Langslow. LC 99-33260. 500p. 2000. text 110.00 (*0-19-815279-5*) OUP.

Medical Law. Michael Davies. 374p. 1996. pap. 48.00 (*1-85431-504-8*, Pub. by Blackstone Pr) Gaunt.

Medical Law. McLean. 67.95 (*1-85521-092-4*) Ashgate Pub Co.

Medical Law. Ed. by Herman Nys. (International Encyclopedia of Laws Ser.). 1993. ring bd. 115.00 (*0-685-58994-3*) Kluwer Law Intl.

Medical Law, 2 vols. Ed. by Herman Nys. (International Encyclopedia of Laws Ser.). 1994. ring bd. 351.00 (*90-6544-943-4*) Kluwer Law Intl.

Medical Law & Ethics. Fremgen. (C). Date not set. 28.87 (*0-8359-5138-3*) P-H.

Medical Law & Ethics. Michel Lipman. LC 93-1344. 139p. (C). 1993. pap. 19.60 (*0-13-064585-0*) P-H.

Medical Law & Ethics. McLean. 185.95 (*0-7546-2003-4*) Ashgate Pub Co.

Medical Law, Ethics, & Bioethics for Ambulatory Health Care. 4th ed. Marcia A. Lewis & Carol A. Tamparo. LC 97-50565. (Illus.). 295p. (C). 1998. pap. text 22.95 (*0-8036-0348-7*) Davis Co.

Medical Law for the Attending Physician: A Case-Oriented Analysis. Salvatore F. Fiscina. LC 82-5559. (Medical Humanities Ser.). 495p. 1982. 44.95 (*0-8093-1045-7*) S Ill U Pr.

***Medical Law in Greece.** Ed. by Theodore B. Koniaris & Anna Karlovassitou-Koniari. 188p. 1999. pap. text 57.00 (*90-411-1286-3*) Kluwer Law Intl.

Medical Law Reports, Vol. 1. Ed. by Geoffrey M. Hall. (C). 1992. 250.00 (*0-9514449-2-1*, Pub. by Busn & Med) St Mut.

Medical Law Reports, Vol. 2. Ed. by Geoffrey M. Hall. (C). 1990. 250.00 (*0-9514449-7-2*, Pub. by Busn & Med) St Mut.

Medical Law Reports, Vol. 3. Ed. by Geoffrey M. Hall. (C). 1990. 250.00 (*0-9514449-3-X*, Pub. by Busn & Med) St Mut.

Medical Law Text, Cases & Materials. John Devereux. LC 98-111617. xxv, 440p. 1997. pap. 62.00 (*1-876213-11-6*, Pub. by Cavendish Pubng) Gaunt.

Medical Legacy of Moses Maimonides. Fred Rosner. LC 97-16874. xii, 308p. 1997. 29.50 (*0-88125-573-4*) Ktav.

Medical Legal Advisor. Salvatore F. Fiscina & Janet B. Seifert. LC 96-10386. 320p. (C). (gr. 13). 1996. pap. text 37.95 (*0-8151-3302-2*, 26930) Mosby Inc.

Medical, Legal & Workplace Issues for the Transsexual: A Guide for Successful Transformation. Sheila Kirk & Martine Rothblatt. 110p. (Orig.). 1995. pap. 18.95 (*1-887796-00-2*) Together Lifeworks.

Medical-Legal Correspondence Course. RiskCare Staff. 111p. 1980. reprint ed. pap. text 199.00 (*1-893929-02-7*) RiskCare.

Medical-Legal Evaluation of Hearing Loss. Robert A. Dobie. LC 93-5118. 400p. 1993. text 81.95 (*0-442-01266-7*, VNR) Wiley.

Medical-Legal Evaluation of Hearing Loss. Robert A. Dobie. (Illus.). 398p. 1998. reprint ed. pap. 69.95 (*0-7693-0023-5*, 2024) Thomson Learn.

Medical-Legal Evaluation of Hearing Loss. 2nd ed. Dobie. 2001. pap. 61.50 (*0-7693-0052-9*) Singular Publishing.

Medical Legal Issues in Long-Term Care: Regulations & Risk Management Safeguards Pennsylvania Physicians Need to Know. RiskCare Staff. 75p. 1999. pap. text 79.00 (*1-893929-03-5*) RiskCare.

Medical Letter Handbook of Adverse Drug Interactions (IC-162) 1995. 99.95 (*1-56712-263-9*, F0682) Franklin Elect.

Medical Letter Handbook of Adverse Drug Interactions, 1997. rev. ed. Martin A. Rizack. 347p. 1997. pap. 18.00 (*0-9660510-0-9*) Med Letter.

Medical Letter Handbook of Adverse Drug Interactions, 1998. rev. ed. Martin A. Rizack. 377p. 1998. 18.00 (*0-9660510-1-7*) Med Letter.

Medical Letter Handbook of Adverse Drug Interactions 1999. rev. ed. Ed. by Martin A. Rizack. 404p. 1999. 18.00 (*0-9660510-4-1*) Med Letter.

***Medical Letter Handbook of Adverse Interactions, 2000.** rev. ed. 455p. 2000. 23.00 (*0-9660510-5-X*) Med Letter.

***Medical Letter Handbook of Antimicrobial Therapy: 2000 Edition.** Ed. by Mark Abramowicz. 214p. 2000. 12.00 (*0-9660510-6-8*) Med Letter.

Medical Lexicon: Lexikon der Medizin. 2nd ed. Dagobert Tutsch. (GER.). 714p. 1982. 49.95 (*0-8288-1841-X*, M7250) Fr & Eur.

Medical Liability: Cases & Materials. Salvatore F. Fiscina et al. (American Casebook Ser.). 487p. (C). 1990. 50.50 (*0-314-75264-1*) West Pub.

Medical Liability: Teacher's Manual to Accompany. Salvatore F. Fiscina et al. (American Casebook Ser.). 146p. 1990. pap. text. write for info. (*0-314-81774-3*) West Pub.

Medical Liability for Pediatricians. 5th ed. American Academy of Pediatrics Staff. 176p. 1995. pap. 49.95 (*0-910761-72-8*) Am Acad Pediat.

Medical Librarianship. David A. Matthews & Fiona M. Picken. LC 79-40833. (Outlines of Modern Librarianship Ser.: No. 12). 173p. reprint ed. pap. 53.70 (*0-7837-5317-9*, 204505600005) Bks Demand.

Medical Libraries - Roles, Services & Challenges: Index of Modern Authors & Subjects with Guide for Rapid Research. American Health Research Institute Staff. LC 90-56303. 160p. 1991. 47.50 (*1-55914-402-5*); pap. 44.50 (*1-55914-403-3*) ABBE Pubs Assn.

***Medical Library Association Guide to Managing Health Care Libraries.** 450p. 2000. pap. 75.00 (*1-55570-397-6*) Neal-Schuman.

Medical Library Budget & Expenditure Report. Primary Research Staff. 110p. 1994. 82.50 (*0-9626749-6-6*) Primary Research.

An Asterisk (*) at the beginning of an entry indicates that the title is appearing for the first time.

Medical Licensing in America, 1650-1965. Richard H. Shryock. LC 67-16045. 136p. reprint ed. pap. 42.20 (*0-608-12103-7*, 202414400035) Bks Demand.
Medical Licensure & Discipline in the United States. Robert C. Derbyshire. LC 78-17712. 183p. 1978. reprint ed. lib. bdg. 59.50 (*0-313-20528-0*, DEML, Greenwood Pr) Greenwood.
Medical Litigation Alert. Ed. by James B. Rosenblum & Ira Zarin. 1990. ring bd. 250.00 (*0-9626905-0-3*) Med Litigation.
Medical Lives & Scientific Medicine at Michigan, 1891-1969. Ed. by Joel D. Howell. 208p. (C). 1993. text 49.50 (*0-472-10465-9*, 10465) U of Mich Pr.
Medical Mafia. Lanctot. 1995. pap. 14.95 (*0-9644126-0-8*) Heres The Key.
Medical Malpractice, 4 vols. David W. Louisell & Williams H. Louisell. 1960. ring bd. 900.00 (*0-8205-1370-9*) Bender.
Medical Malpractice. Edward J. Smith. 308p. 1987. pap. 19.95 (*0-318-22778-9*) Fairfax Pr Ltd.
Medical Malpractice. Ed. by Duncan Yaggy & Patricia Hodgson. LC 86-32981. x, 128p. (C). 1987. text 39.95 (*0-8223-0722-7*) Duke.
Medical Malpractice. 3rd ed. David M. Harney. 849p. 1993. 95.00 (*1-55834-108-0*, MICHIE) LEXIS Pub.
Medical Malpractice. 6th ed. Daniel C. Kramer & Thomas A. Moore. 583p. 1990. pap. text 25.00 (*0-685-45801-6*, Q1-3006) PLI.
Medical Malpractice: A Preventive Approach. William O. Robertson. LC 84-40322. 212p. 1985. text 20.00 (*0-295-96162-7*) U of Wash Pr.
Medical Malpractice: A Primer for Orthopaedic Residents & Fellows. AAOS Committee on Professional Liability Staff. 73p. 1994. 25.00 (*0-89203-093-3*) Amer Acad Ortho Surg.
Medical Malpractice: Bases of Liability. Michael D. McCafferty & Steven M. Meyer. LC 84-23580. 494p. 1985. text 125.00 (*0-07-044837-X*) Shepards.
Medical Malpractice: Checklists & Discoveries. 3rd ed. Douglas Danner. LC 85-81408. 1994. ring bd. 350.00 (*0-685-59893-4*) West Group.
Medical Malpractice: Guide to Medical Issues, 7 vols. Lee S. Goldsmith. 1986. ring bd. 1110.00 (*0-8205-1432-2*) Bender.
Medical Malpractice: Handling Obstetric & Neonatal Cases. Michael D. Volk & Melvin D. Morgan. LC 86-10230. (Medical Malpractice Ser.). 1212p. 1986. text 125.00 (*0-07-043122-1*) Shepards.
Medical Malpractice: Law, Tactics, & Ethics. Frank M. McClellan. 296p. (C). 1993. text 69.95 (*1-56639-065-6*) Temple U Pr.
Medical Malpractice: Maine's Use of Practice Guidelines to Reduce Costs. (Illus.). 100p. (Orig.). (C). 1994. pap. text 40.00 (*0-7881-0395-4*) DIANE Pub.
Medical Malpractice: Pharmacy Law. David B. Brushwood. 1986. text 125.00 (*0-07-008576-5*) Shepards.
Medical Malpractice: Theory, Evidence, & Public Policy. Patricia M. Danzon. (Illus.). 312p. 1985. 44.00 (*0-674-56115-5*) HUP.
Medical Malpractice: 1989 Supplement. 2nd ed. David Harney. 1989. write for info. (*0-87473-528-9*, 62716-10, MICHIE) LEXIS Pub.
Medical Malpractice & the American Jury. Neil Vidmar. 336p. (C). 1997. reprint ed. pap. text 20.95 (*0-472-08479-8*, 08479) U of Mich Pr.
***Medical Malpractice Case.** Anthony Macri. LC 99-91027. 1999. 25.00 (*0-7388-0596-3*); pap. 18.00 (*0-7388-0597-1*) Xlibris Corp.
Medical Malpractice Citations. Shepard's Citations, Inc. Staff. 950p. 1987. 120.00 (*0-685-23121-6*) Shepards.
Medical Malpractice Claims Investigation: A Step-by-Step Approach. Nancy Acerbo-Avalone & Katherine Kremer. LC 96-28261. 288p. 1997. pap. 59.00 (*0-8342-0860-1*, 20860) Aspen Pub.
Medical Malpractice Digest. Dean E. Snyder. LC 90-53851. 1991. 160.00 (*0-685-59887-X*) West Group.
Medical Malpractice Handbook: The Plaintiff. Bruce Livingston & Stephen Morewitz. 113p. 1996. 64.95 (*1-880921-66-9*); pap. 44.95 (*1-880921-65-0*) Austin & Winfield.
Medical Malpractice in New York. New York State Bar Association Staff. Ed. & Pref. by Robert Devine. LC 92-63000. 570p. 1993. 90.00 (*0-942954-54-8*) NYS Bar.
Medical Malpractice in Nineteenth Century America. Kenneth De Ville. (American Social Experience Ser.: No. 19). (C). 1990. text 50.00 (*0-8147-1832-9*) NYU Pr.
Medical Malpractice in Nineteenth Century America. Kenneth De Ville. (American Social Experience Ser.: No. 19). (C). 1992. pap. text 19.50 (*0-8147-1848-5*) NYU Pr.
Medical Malpractice Insurance: A Legislator's View. Tarky Lombardi & Gerald N. Hoffman. LC 78-6409. 232p. reprint ed. pap. 72.00 (*0-8357-3985-6*, 203668300005) Bks Demand.
Medical Malpractice Lawsuit: A Case Study. George Parker. 198p. 2000. lib. bdg. 45.00 (*1-56072-470-6*) Nova Sci Pubs.
Medical Malpractice Lawsuit: A Case Study. George Parker. (Illus.). 198p. 2000. pap. 17.95 (*1-56072-340-8*, Nova Kroshka Bks) Nova Sci Pubs.
Medical Malpractice Liability: An Agenda for Reform. David M. McIntosh & David C. Murray. 1994. 12.95 (*0-614-17718-9*) Hudson Instit IN.
Medical Malpractice Litigation: A New Era. 1997. 58.00 incl. audio PA Bar Inst.
Medical Malpractice, 1998 Cumulative Supplement. David M. Harney. 235p. 1998. suppl. ed. write for info. (*0-327-00490-8*, 6272114) LEXIS Pub.
Medical Malpractice on Trial. Paul C. Weiler. LC 90-15600. 256p. 1991. 37.95 (*0-674-56120-1*, WEIMED) HUP.
Medical Malpractice Panels in Four States. 52p. 1977. 3.65 (*0-318-14440-9*) IJA NYU.
Medical Malpractice Reports. text 255.00 (*0-8205-2082-9*) Bender.
Medical Management of AIDS. 5th ed. Merle A. Sande & Paul A. Volberding. Ed. by Richard Zorab. 608p. 1996. text 62.00 (*0-7216-6908-5*, W B Saunders Co) Harcrt Hlth Sci Grp.
Medical Management of AIDS. 6th ed. Merle A. Sande. LC 98-43930. (Illus.). 670p. (C). 1999. text. write for info. (*0-7216-8102-6*, W B Saunders Co) Harcrt Hlth Sci Grp.
Medical Management of AIDS in Women. Ed. by Deborah Cotton & D. H. Watts. LC 95-48022. 488p. 1996. 119.95 (*0-471-07674-0*) Wiley.
Medical Management of Atherosclerosis. Ed. by John C. Larosa. LC 97-50182. (Illus.). 344p. 1998. text 135.00 (*0-8247-0149-6*) Dekker.
Medical Management of Breast Cancer. Christopher J. Williams & Roger B. Buchanan. LC 87-21529. (Johns Hopkins Series in Contemporary Medicine & Public Health). (Illus.). 254p. reprint ed. pap. 78.80 (*0-608-06093-3*, 206642500008) Bks Demand.
Medical Management of Cerebral Ischemia Vol. 17, Suppl. 1, 1978: Journal: European Neurology. Ed. by H. E. Kaeser. (Illus.). 1979. pap. 50.50 (*3-8055-3077-3*) S Karger.
Medical Management of Chronic Myelogenous Lukemia. Ed. by Kantarjian & Talpaz. LC 98-38123. (Illus.). 464p. 1998. text 185.00 (*0-8247-9901-1*) Dekker.
***Medical Management of Diabetes Mellitus.** Ed. by Jack L. Leahy. (Clinical Guides to Medical Management Ser.). 738p. 2000. 99.75 (*0-8247-8857-5*) Dekker.
***Medical Management of Erectile Dysfunction: A Primary-Care Manual.** Harin Padma-Nathan. 153p. 1999. pap. text 19.95 (*1-884735-40-1*) Prof Comms.
Medical Management of Heart Disease. Burton E. Sobel. LC 96-4747. (Illus.). 584p. 1996. text 99.75 (*0-8247-9315-3*) Dekker.
Medical Management of Hematological Malignant Diseases. Ed. by Kantarjian & Freireich. LC 98-16879. (Illus.). 592p. 1998. text 195.00 (*0-8247-9886-4*) Dekker.
Medical Management of HIV & AIDS. Ed. by Ann Millar. LC 95-40049. (Illus.). 260p. 1995. 132.00 (*3-540-19958-6*) Spr-Verlag.
Medical Management of HIV Infection: 1995 Edition. John Bartlett. 260p. 1995. 17.95 (*0-924428-09-0*) Phys Sci Pub.
Medical Management of HIV Infection: 1995 Edition. John Bartlett. 1996. spiral bd. write for info. (*0-614-05153-3*) Phys Sci Pub.
***Medical Management of Liver Disease.** Edward L. Krawitt. LC 99-32710. (Clinical Guides to Medical Management Ser.). (Illus.). 664p. 1999. text 185.00 (*0-8247-1968-9*) Dekker.
Medical Management of Long-Term Disability. 2nd ed. Ed. by David Green. LC 96-26646. (Rehabilitation Institute of Chicago Publication Ser.). (Illus.). 351p. 1996. text 60.00 (*0-7506-9604-4*) Buttrwrth-Heinemann.
Medical Management of Pregnancy Complicated by Diabetes. 2nd ed. American Diabetes Association. 136p. 1995. pap. 39.95 (*0-945448-44-9*, 5401-01) Am Diabetes.
Medical Management of Prostate Cancer, No. II. Ed. by I. Denis. (ESO Monographs). (Illus.). 112p. 1991. 64.95 (*0-387-53443-1*) Spr-Verlag.
***Medical Management of Pulmonary Diseases.** Gerald S. Davis & Elizabeth A. Seward. LC 99-37340. (Clinical Guides to Medical Management Ser.). (Illus.). 795p. 1999. text 225.00 (*0-8247-6002-6*) Dekker.
Medical Management of Radiation Accidents. Ed. by Fred A. Mettler, Jr. et al. 416p. 1989. boxed set 208.95 (*0-8493-4865-X*, RA1231) CRC Pr.
Medical Management of Rheumatic Musculoskeletal & Connective Tissue Diseases. Grahame et al. LC 97-22374. (Illus.). 408p. 1997. text 135.00 (*0-8247-9847-3*) Dekker.
Medical Management of Stroke: A Guide for Rehabilitation Specialists. Scott Silliman. 325p. 1997. 49.00 (*0-8342-0890-3*, 20890) Aspen Pub.
Medical Management of the Surgical Patient. 2nd ed. Geno J. Merli & Howard H. Weitz. Ed. by Ray Kersey. LC 97-39759. (Illus.). 496p. (C). 1998. pap. text 39.95 (*0-7216-6976-X*, W B Saunders Co) Harcrt Hlth Sci Grp.
Medical Management of the Surgical Patient. 3rd ed. Robert B. Smith et al. (Illus.). 700p. 1995. text 75.00 (*0-397-51318-6*) Lppncott W & W.
Medical Management of the Violent Patient. K. Tardiff. LC 99-26167. (Medical Psychiatry Ser.). (Illus.). 512p. 1999. text 195.00 (*0-8247-9906-2*) Dekker.
Medical Management of Type 1 Diabetes. 3rd ed. Ed. by Jay S. Skyler. LC 98-4108. (Clinical Education Ser.). (Illus.). 246p. 1998. pap. 39.95 (*0-945448-92-9*, 5403-01) Am Diabetes.
Medical Management of Type 2 Diabetes. 4th ed. Ed. by Bruce R. Zimmerman. LC 98-4107. (Clinical Education Ser.). (Illus.). 139p. 1998. pap. 39.95 (*0-945448-93-7*, 5404-01) Am Diabetes.
Medical Manager. Humphrey. (Medical Assisting Ser.). 1995. student ed. 24.00 (*0-538-71312-7*) S-W Pub.
Medical Manager. Ed. by Anthony Young. (Illus.). 289p. 1999. pap. text 45.00 (*0-7279-1376-X*) BMJ Pub.
Medical Manager: Managed Care System. Gartee. 304p. (C). 1998. pap., student ed. 50.95 (*0-8273-8406-8*) Delmar.
Medical Manager: Managed Care System - Student Edition - IML. Gartee. 120p. 1998. teacher ed. 14.95 (*0-8273-8407-6*) Delmar.
Medical Manager, Student Edition, Computerized Practice Management Version 5.3. 2nd ed. Richard Gartee & Doris Humphrey. 288p. 1995. pap., student ed. write for info. incl. disk (*0-538-71311-9*); pap., student ed. write for info. (*0-8273-8073-9*) S-W Pub.
Medical Manager, Version 8.10. 3rd ed. Gartee. 320p. (C). 1997. mass mkt., student ed. 61.95 (*0-8273-8592-7*) Delmar.
Medical Managment of Emesis. 1997. 85.00 (*1-85317-267-7*) Mosby Inc.
Medical Mandarins: The French Academy of Medicine in the Nineteenth & Early Twentieth Centuries. George Weisz. (Illus.). 328p. 1995. text 57.50 (*0-19-509037-3*) OUP.
Medical Manpower in the European Community. Ed. by H. Viefhues. (Illus.). 250p. 1988. 79.95 (*0-387-18733-2*) Spr-Verlag.
Medical Manual for Chinese Family. Ming Tat Wong. (CHI.). 200p. pap. 18.00 (*0-9635700-0-5*) J Wong.
Medical Marriage: A Couple's Survival Guide. Wayne M. Sotile & Mary O. Sotile. LC 95-19234. 320p. 1995. 22.50 (*1-55972-305-X*, Birch Ln Pr) Carol Pub Group.
***Medical Marriage: Sustaining Healthy Relationships for Physicians & Their Families.** rev. ed. Wayne M. Sotile. 2000. pap. 25.00 (*1-57947-075-0*) AMA.
Medical Marriage: The New Partnership Between Orthodox & Complementary Medicine. Ed. by Cornelia Featherstone & Lori Forsyth. (Illus.). 640p. (Orig.). (C). 1997. pap. 29.95 (*1-899171-16-9*, Pub. by Findhorn Pr) Words Distrib.
Medical Marriages. Ed. by Glen O. Gabbard & Roy W. Menninger. LC 88-14653. 182p. 1988. 34.00 (*0-88048-260-5*, 8260) Am Psychiatric.
***Medical Massage.** Turchaninov Ross & C. A. Cox. (Illus.). 413p. 1998. pap. text 50.00 (*0-9675868-0-1*) Aesculapius Bks.
Medical Materials Industry Review. 317p. 1996. 1500.00 (*1-56965-415-8*, DMU95) BCC.
Medical Materials Industry Review. Ed. by Melvin Schlechter & Dori A. Horn. 251p. 1995. 1500.00 (*1-56965-340-2*) BCC.
Medical Mathematics. Thomas J. Taylor. LC 74-79839. (Allied Health Ser.). 1975. pap. 4.55 (*0-672-61393-X*, Bobbs) Macmillan.
***Medical Mathematics & Dosage Calculations for Veterinary Professionals.** Robert Bill. LC 00-33438. (Illus.). 2000. write for info. (*0-8138-2099-5*) Iowa St U Pr.
Medical Matters: A Handbook for Medical Secretaries. 3rd ed. Rozema. 1997. pap. 0.00 (*0-582-80907-X*) Addison-Wesley.
Medical Mavericks, Vol. 1. Hugh D. Riordan. LC 88-63321. 102p. (Orig.). 1988. pap. 7.95 (*0-942333-07-1*) Bio-Comns Pr.
Medical Mavericks, Vol. 2. Hugh D. Riordan. LC 88-63321. 120p. (Orig.). 1989. pap. 7.95 (*0-942333-09-8*) Bio-Comns Pr.
Medical Meanings: A Glossary of Word Origins. Ed. by William S. Haubrich. LC 96-29494. 253p. (C). 1997. pap. text 29.95 (*0-943126-56-8*) Amer Coll Phys.
Medical Measurements of Pain by Research Scientists: Index of New Information with References. Marcella K. Javorekko. 150p. 1996. 47.50 (*0-7883-0796-7*); pap. 44.50 (*0-7883-0797-5*) ABBE Pubs Assn.
***Medical Medicine: Comprehensive Paramedical Care.** Ed. by Appleton & Lange Staff. (C). 2000. text 25.00 (*0-8385-6413-5*); text 24.95 (*0-8385-6415-1*); text 29.95 (*0-8385-6416-X*) Appleton & Lange.
Medical Meeting. Mildred Walker. LC 96-47113. x, 280p. 1997. pap. 12.00 (*0-8032-9788-2*, Bison Books) U of Nebr Pr.
Medical Messiahs: A Social History of Health Quackery in Twentieth-Century America. expanded ed. James H. Young. LC 91-45700. (Illus.). 512p. 1992. pap. 158.80 (*0-608-07128-5*, 206735400009) Bks Demand.
Medical Messiahs: A Social History of Health Quackery in Twentieth-Century America. James H. Young. LC 67-21031. 488p. 1967. reprint ed. pap. 151.30 (*0-8357-3849-3*, 203658200004) Bks Demand.
Medical Micro Lab: Learning Guide. Smith. (Medical Lab Technician Ser.). 1989. teacher ed. 12.00 (*0-8273-4373-6*) Delmar.
Medical Microbiology. Robert F. Boyd & Joseph J. Marr. (Illus.). 760p. 1980. 35.00 (*0-316-10432-9*, Little Brwn Med Div) Lppncott W & W.
Medical Microbiology. Ed. by Felix Milgrom & Thomas D. Flanagan. LC 82-1261. (Illus.). 762p. reprint ed. pap. 200.00 (*0-7837-2581-7*, 204274000006) Bks Demand.
Medical Microbiology. 2nd ed. Samuel Baron. 1296p. (C). 1986. text 50.36 (*0-201-10146-7*, Health Sci) Addison-Wesley.
Medical Microbiology. 2nd ed. Patrick R. Murray. 768p. 1993. text, teacher ed. 35.00 (*0-7234-2010-6*) Mosby Inc.
Medical Microbiology. 3rd ed. Murray. LC 97-18902. (Illus.). 736p. (C). (gr. 13). 1997. pap. text 49.00 (*0-8151-9035-2*, 29126) Mosby Inc.
Medical Microbiology. 3rd ed. Ed. by Samuel Baron & Paula M. Jennings. LC 91-10750. (Illus.). 1358p. 1991. reprint ed. pap. 200.00 (*0-7837-9742-7*, 206047000005) Bks Demand.
Medical Microbiology. 4th ed. Ed. by Samuel Baron. LC 95-50499. (Illus.). (C). 1996. 55.00 (*0-9631172-1-1*) U TX MB Microb.
***Medical Microbiology.** 4th ed. Patrick R. Murray. 2001. pap. text. write for info. (*0-323-01213-2*) Mosby Inc.
Medical Microbiology. 6th ed. C. G. Thomas. (Illus.). 416p. 1988. text 25.95 (*0-7020-1270-X*) Bailliere Tindall.
Medical Microbiology. 22nd ed. (C). 2001. 40.95 (*0-8385-6298-1*, Medical Exam) Appleton & Lange.
Medical Microbiology: A Laboratory Study. 3rd ed. William G. Wu. (Illus.). 420p. (C). 1995. spiral bd. 32.95 (*0-89863-180-7*) Star Pub CA.
Medical Microbiology: A Review with Questions & Explanations. 2nd ed. Ed. by David J. Hentges. LC 94-29942. (Illus.). 288p. 1995. pap. text 31.95 (*0-316-35784-7*) Lppncott W & W.
Medical Microbiology: A Short Course. Ellen Barron et al. LC 93-16481. (Illus.). 1072p. (Orig.). 1994. pap. 74.50 (*0-471-56728-0*, Wiley-Liss) Wiley.
Medical Microbiology: General Concepts. Ed. by Samuel Baron. LC 96-4860. (Illus.). 1996. pap. 12.00 (*0-9631172-2-X*) U TX MB Microb.
Medical Microbiology: Jawtz, Melnick & Adelberg's Medical Microbiology. 21st ed. Brooks et al. (Illus.). 740p. (C). 1998. pap. 44.95 (*0-8385-6316-3*, A-6316-2, Apple Lange Med) McGraw.
Medical Microbiology: Quality & Clinical Relevance. Raymond C. Bartlett. LC 73-18482. (Wiley Biomedical-Health Publication Ser.). (Illus.). 269p. reprint ed. pap. 83.40 (*0-608-30312-7*, 205516800011) Bks Demand.
Medical Microbiology - A Guide to Microbial Infections: Pathogenesis, Immunity, Laboratory Diagnosis & Control. 15th ed. Ed. by D. Greenwood et al. (Illus.). 690p. 1997. pap. write for info. (*0-443-05454-1*) Church.
Medical Microbiology & Immunology: Examination & Board Review. 4th ed. Warren E. Levinson. (C). 1996. pap. text 31.95 (*0-8385-6225-6*, A6225-5) Appleton & Lange.
Medical Microbiology & Immunology: Examination & Board Review. 5th ed. Warren E. Levinson & Ernest Jawetz. (Illus.). 547p. (C). 1998. pap. 34.95 (*0-8385-6287-6*, Apple Lange Med) McGraw.
***Medical Microbiology & Immunology: Examination & Board Review.** 6th ed. Warren Levinson & Ernest Jawetz. (Illus.). 600p. 2000. write for info. (*0-8385-6410-0*) McGraw.
***Medical Microbiology at a Glance.** S. H. Gillespie & Kathleen Bamford. LC 99-26884. (At a Glance Ser.). 117p. 2000. pap. 19.95 (*0-632-05026-8*) Blackwell Sci.
Medical Microbiology Synopsis. Donald M. McLean & John A. Smith. LC 90-5597. (Illus.). 305p. 1991. pap. text 34.50 (*0-8121-1304-7*) Lppncott W & W.
Medical Milestones in Cole County, Missouri: A History of the Cole County Medical Society. Joseph S. Summers, Jr. 200p. 1988. text 35.00 (*0-916109-06-2*) Summers Pub.
***Medical Millennium.** Ed. by H. Lee. (Illus.). 100p. 2000. 45.00 (*1-85070-466-X*) Prthnon Pub.
Medical Millennium. William H. Hay. 133p. 1993. reprint ed. spiral bd. 14.00 (*0-7873-0386-0*) Hlth Research.
Medical Ministry. Ellen Gould Harmon White. 1963. reprint ed. 12.99 (*0-8163-0157-3*, 13371-0) Pacific Pr Pub Assn.
***Medical Misadventure Im Neuseelandischen Accident Compensation Scheme: Eine Antwort Auf die Unzulanglichkeiten des Tort Law Oder ein Fehlgeschlagener Versuch?** Petra Butler. (Europaische Hochschulschriften Ser.: Bd. 2628). 190p. 1999. 37.95 (*3-631-33879-1*) P Lang Pubng.
Medical Miscellany for Genealogists. Jeanette L. Jerger. LC 96-116923. 186p. 1996. pap. 19.50 (*0-7884-0375-3*, J162) Heritage Bk.
Medical Mischief, You Say! Degerminating the Germ Theory. Nell Rogers & Guy Rogers. 1996. reprint ed. spiral bd. 8.50 (*0-7873-0735-1*) Hlth Research.
Medical Mishaps: Pieces of the Puzzle. Ed. by Linda Mulcahy et al. LC 98-21881. 224p. 1998. 29.95 (*0-335-20258-6*) OpUniv Pr.
Medical Mishaps: Pieces of the Puzzle. Linda Mulcahy et al. LC 98-21881. 1998. 95.00 (*0-335-20259-4*) OpUniv Pr.
Medical Molecular Genetics. P. Hoffee. (Integrated Medical Sciences Ser.). (C). 1997. pap. 22.95 (*1-889325-28-7*) Fence Crk Pubng.
Medical Money Mess: A Survivor's Guide to Health Care Costs & Health Insurance in the 1980's. rev. ed. Hugh E. Wilson & Robert Valentine. LC 85-117532. 120p. 1986. pap. 9.95 (*0-933811-02-0*) MCS Pubns KY.
Medical Monitoring & Screening in the Workplace: Results of a Survey. 84p. (Orig.). (C). 1992. pap. text 30.00 (*0-941375-59-5*) DIANE Pub.
Medical Monitoring in the Home & Work Environment. Ed. by Laughton E. Miles & Roger J. Broughton. LC 89-24228. 352p. 1990. reprint ed. pap. 109.20 (*0-608-03431-2*, 206413200008) Bks Demand.
Medical Monitoring Markets: A Detailed Database on a 6 Billion Dollar Market. Market Intelligence Staff. 480p. 1992. 995.00 (*1-56753-087-7*) Frost & Sullivan.
Medical Monitoring of Hostile Environments: Index of New Information. Hugh G. Gartzky. 1998. 47.50 (*0-7883-1832-2*); pap. 47.50 (*0-7883-1833-0*) ABBE Pubs Assn.
Medical Monopoly Versus Your Right to Freedom of Choice in Health Care. 1992. lib. bdg. 75.00 (*0-8490-5261-0*) Gordon Pr.
Medical, Moral & Legal Implications of Recent Medical Advances: A Symposium. Ed. by D. W. Dowd et al. LC 71-152124. (Symposia on Law & Society Ser.). 1971. reprint ed. lib. bdg. 19.50 (*0-306-70128-6*) Da Capo.
Medical Motifs. Macagba. 1998. pap. 1.00 (*0-486-28256-2*) Dover.
Medical Murderers: From the Files of True Detective. Rose G. Mandelsberg. 1992. mass mkt. 4.99 (*1-55817-582-2*, Pinncle Kensgtn) Kensgtn Pub Corp.
Medical Murders. Ed. by Jonathan Goodman. 256p. 1992. pap. 9.95 (*0-8184-0567-8*, L Stuart) Carol Pub Group.
Medical Mycology. Dode Grigoriu et al. Tr. by D. Q. Stephenson. LC 87-3153.Tr. of Traite de Mycologie Medicale. (Illus.). 482p. 1987. text 149.00 (*0-920887-18-X*) Hogrefe & Huber Pubs.

M

An Asterisk (*) at the beginning of an entry indicates that the title is appearing for the first time.

Medical Mycology. K. J. Kwon-Chung & J. E. Bennett. (Illus.). 866p. 1992. text 78.00 (*0-8121-1463-9*) Lppncott W & W.

Medical Mycology. S. Nolting & K. Fegler. 210p. 1987. pap. 29.40 (*0-387-17606-3*) Spr-Verlag.

Medical Mycology: A Self-Instructional Text. 2nd ed. Martha E. Kern. LC 96-46605. 242p. 1997. pap. 37.95 (*0-8036-0036-4*) Davis Co.

Medical Mycology & Human Mycoses. Everette S. Beneke & Alvin L. Rogers. LC 95-47079. (Illus.). 239p. (C). 1996. 54.95 (*0-89863-175-0*) Star Pub CA.

Medical Mycology Protocols. Ken A. Haynes & David C. Coleman. (Methods in Molecular Medicine Ser.). (Illus.). 400p. 1999. 74.50 (*0-89603-533-6*) Humana.

Medical Mysteries: Six Deadly Cases. Dian D. Buchman. 112p. (J). (gr. 4-7). 1993. pap. 2.75 (*0-590-43468-3*) Scholastic Inc.

Medical Needles & Syringes Markets. (Market Research Reports: No. 346). 149p. 1994. 795.00 (*0-317-05478-3*) Theta Corp.

Medical Negligence. Malcolm Khan & Michelle Robson. LC 97-127677. (Medico-Legal Ser.). 432p. 1997. pap. 69.90 (*1-85941-022-7*, Pub. by Cavendish Pubng) Gaunt.

Medical Negligence: A Practical Guide. Charles J. Lewis. 567p. 1992. 165.00 (*0-85459-643-7*, Pub. by Tolley Pubng) St Mut.

Medical Negligence: A Practical Guide. Charles J. Lewis. 600p. 1995. 310.00 (*1-86012-073-3*, Pub. by Tolley Pubng) St Mut.

Medical Negligence: Cost-Effective Case Management. Iain S. Goldrein & Margaret R. De Hass. 1997. pap. write for info. (*0-406-99920-1*, MICHIE) LEXIS Pub.

***Medical Negligence: Managing Medical Disputes.** Susan Rodway & Simon Levene. 260p. 2000. 98.60 (*1-902558-05-7*, Pub. by Palladian Law) Gaunt.

Medical Negligence: The Cranium, Spine & Nervous System. John Garfield & Christopher Earl. LC 99-17519. 1999. write for info. (*0-632-05183-3*) Blackwell Sci.

Medical Negligence Case Law. Rodney Nelson-Jones & Frank Burton. 432p. (C). 1990. text 150.00 (*1-85190-087-X*, Pub. by Tolley Pubng) St Mut.

Medical Negligence Law: Seeking a Balance. Andrew F. Phillips. LC 96-32164. (Medico-Legal Issues Ser.). (Illus.). 248p. 1997. text 82.95 (*1-85521-643-4*, Pub. by Dartmth Pub) Ashgate Pub Co.

Medical Negligence Litigation. Denis Carey. 176p. 1998. pap. 40.00 (*1-85811-162-5*, Pub. by CLT Prof) Gaunt.

Medical Neuroanatomy: A Problem Oriented Manual. Willard. (Illus.). 256p. 1993. spiral bd. 27.95 (*0-397-51171-X*) Lppncott W & W.

Medical Neurology. David Chadwick et al. (Illus.). 506p. 1989. pap. text 59.95 (*0-443-03051-0*) Church.

Medical Neuropsychology: The Impact of Disease on Behavior. R. E. Tarter et al. LC 87-36138. (Critical Issues in Neuropsychology Ser.). (Illus.). 366p. (C). 1988. 65.00 (*0-306-42741-9*, Plenum Trade) Perseus Pubng.

Medical Neuroscience. T. Pritchard & K. Alloway. (Integrated Medical Sciences Ser.). (C). 1998. pap. 22.95 (*1-889325-29-5*) Fence Crk Pubng.

Medical Neurosciences: An Approach to Anatomy, Pathology, & Physiology by Systems & Levels. 2nd ed. Jasper R. Daube et al. 1985. pap. text 27.00 (*0-685-03086-5*, Little Brwn Med Div) Lppncott W & W.

Medical Neurosciences: An Approach to Anatomy, Pathology, & Physiology by Systems & Levels. 3rd ed. Barbara F. Westmoreland et al. LC 93-37762. 576p. 1994. pap. text 39.95 (*0-316-17364-9*) Lppncott W & W.

Medical Neurosciences: An Approach to Anatomy, Pathology, & Physiology by Systems & Levels. 4th ed. Eduardo E. Benarroch. LC 98-24218. 19p. 1998. write for info. (*0-7817-1426-5*) Lppncott W & W.

Medical Neurotoxicology: Occupational & Environmental Causes of Neurological Dysfunction. Ed. by Peter G. Blain & John B. Harris. LC 99-16934. (An Arnold Publication). (Illus.). 388p. 1999. text 150.00 (*0-340-59665-1*, Pub. by E A) OUP.

Medical Nirds Quickie. Afshine Emrani. (Nirds Quickie Ser.). 180p. 1997. pap. 9.95 (*0-9654687-0-4*) Emrani Publns.

Medical Nonwoven Disposables. (Market Research Reports: No. 315). 151p. 1994. 795.00 (*0-317-05479-1*) Theta Corp.

Medical Nursing. Bonnie Allbaugh. Ed. by Kathy V. Gettrust. 620p. (C). 1993. pap. 33.50 (*0-8273-5947-0*) Delmar.

Medical Nutrition & Disease. Lisa Hark & Gail Morrison. LC 96-26674. 288p. 1996. pap. 32.95 (*0-86542-491-8*) Blackwell Sci.

***Medical Nutrition & Disease.** 2nd ed. Gail Morrison & Lisa Hark. LC 99-24988. (Illus.). 1999. pap. 34.95 (*0-632-04339-3*) Blackwell Sci.

Medical Nutrition from Marz. 2nd ed. Russell B. Marz. (Illus.). 587p. 1998. text 69.95 (*1-882550-28-5*, Omni Pr) Quiet Lion Pr.

***Medical Nutrition Therapy: A Case Study Approach.** Marcia Nahikian-Nelms & Anderson. 2001. pap. 38.00 (*0-534-52410-9*) Thomson Learn.

Medical Nutrition Therapy: Case Studies for the Dietary Manager. Litchford. 166p. 1997. spiral bd. 21.00 (*0-7872-3605-5*) Kendall-Hunt.

Medical Nutrition Therapy Across the Continuum of Care. American Dietetic Association Staff. 200p. 1997. ring bd. 80.00 incl. VHS, disk (*0-88091-149-2*) Am Dietetic Assn.

Medical Odysseys: The Different & Sometimes Unexpected Pathways to Twentieth-Century Medical Discoveries. Allen B. Weisse. LC 90-8387. 237p. (C). 1991. pap. 15.95 (*0-8135-1617-X*) Rutgers U Pr.

Medical Office Administrative Procedures. 2nd ed. Mary A. Frew & David R. Frew. LC 88-31065. (Illus.). 439p. (C). 1989. pap. 29.95 (*0-8036-3862-0*) Davis Co.

Medical Office Design: Territory & Conflict. Henry F. Doble, Jr. 200p. (C). 1982. pap. 42.50 (*0-87527-243-6*) Green.

***Medical Office Pharmacology.** 2000. teacher ed. 21.00 (*0-13-030721-1*) P-H.

***Medical Office Pharmacology.** Struck. 224p. 2000. pap. text 38.60 (*0-8359-5290-8*) P-H.

Medical Office Policy Manual. 315p. 1998. 128.00 (*1-58383-012-X*, MOPMAN9) Robert D Keene.

Medical Office Policy Manual. Medical Management Institute Staff. LC 95-39519. (Illus.). 199p. (Orig.). 1996. pap. text 44.95 (*0-07-600796-0*, ME109) Practice Mgmt Info.

Medical Office Practice. Martha Foster. LC 75-4051. (Allied Health Ser.). 1975. pap. 6.25 (*0-672-61381-6*, Bobbs) Macmillan.

Medical Office Practice. 6th ed. Atkinson. (Allied Health Ser.). 128p. (C). 1998. text 52.95 (*0-7668-0605-7*) Delmar.

Medical Office Practice - IML. 6th ed. Atkinson. 1998. teacher ed. 25.95 (*0-7668-0855-6*) Delmar.

Medical Office Practice Set. 4th ed. Phillip S. Atkinson & Deborah Begg. (C). 1990. pap. 29.95 (*0-538-70010-6*, RL40DC) S-W Pub.

Medical Office Practice Set. 5th ed. Phillip S. Atkinson. (Medical Assisting Ser.). (C). 1994. 36.00 (*0-538-71204-X*) S-W Pub.

***Medical Office Procedures.** Karonne Becklin & Edith Stunnarborg. 1999. teacher ed. 14.00 (*0-02-804746-X*) Glencoe.

Medical Office Procedures. 3rd ed. Karonne J. Becklin. 1994. pap. 34.50 (*0-02-800120-6*) Glencoe.

Medical Office Procedures. 4th ed. Karonne J. Becklin & Edith M. Sunnarborg. 1995. pap. 42.95 (*0-02-802531-8*) Glencoe.

***Medical Office Procedures.** 4th ed. Karonne Becklin & Edith Stunnarborg. 1999. wbk. ed. 35.00 incl. disk (*0-02-804881-4*) Glencoe.

***Medical Office Procedures: Contents.** 4th ed. Flores. (Medical Assisting Ser.). (C). 1999. text 34.50 (*0-7668-1646-X*) Delmar.

Medical Office Procedures: With Computer Simulation. 4th ed. Karonne Becklin & Edith Sunnarborg. 128p. teacher ed. 14.04 (*0-02-802533-4*) Glencoe.

Medical Office Procedures Manual. 3rd ed. Ann Ehrlich. (Illus.). 1993. 28.95 (*0-940012-35-9*) Colwell Syst.

Medical Office Projects Simulation. Abell. (Legal Office Procedures Ser.). 1999. pap. 15.75 (*0-538-72126-X*) S-W Pub.

Medical Office Transcription: An Introduction to Medical Transcription. Karonne Becklin & Edith Sunnarborg. 128p. 1998. text, wbk. ed. 27.50 incl. disk (*0-02-802240-8*) Glencoe.

***Medical Office Transcription: An Introduction to Medical Transcription.** Karonne Becklin & Edith M. Sunnarborg. 1998. teacher ed. 9.60 incl. disk (*0-02-802242-4*) Glencoe.

Medical Officer. Jack Rudman. (Career Examination Ser.: C-488). 1994. pap. 39.95 (*0-8373-0488-1*) Nat Learn.

Medical Officer (Departmental) Jack Rudman. (Career Examination Ser.: C-489). 1994. pap. 39.95 (*0-8373-0489-X*) Nat Learn.

Medical Offset Effect & Public Health Policy: Mental Health Industry in Transition. John L. Fiedler & Jonathan B. Wight. LC 88-28927. 216p. 1989. 67.95 (*0-275-92859-4*, C2859, Praeger Pubs) Greenwood.

Medical Oncology: A Comprehensive Review. 2nd ed. Ed. by Richard Pazdur. 520p. 1995. 49.95 (*0-9641823-1-9*) PRR.

Medical Oncology: An Advanced Course: A Self-Assessment Guide for Subspecialty Board Examinations & Practice, Vol. 1. 2nd rev. expanded ed. Joseph G. Sinkovics. LC 86-435. 960p. reprint ed. pap. 200.00 (*0-608-20003-4*, 207128000001) Bks Demand.

Medical Oncology: An Advanced Course: A Self-Assessment Guide for Subspecialty Board Examinations & Practice, Vol. 2. 2nd rev. expanded ed. Joseph G. Sinkovics. LC 86-435. 1140p. reprint ed. pap. 200.00 (*0-608-20004-2*, 207128000002) Bks Demand.

Medical Oncology: Basic Principles & Clinical Management of Cancer. 2nd ed. Ed. by Paul Calabresi & Philip S. Schein. (Illus.). 1408p. 1993. text 139.00 (*0-07-105408-1*) McGraw-Hill HPD.

Medical 100: A Ranking of the Most Influential People in Medicine, Past & Present. John Simmons. (Illus.). 384p. 1998. 29.95 (*0-8065-2008-6*, Citadel Pr) Carol Pub Group.

Medical 100: A Ranking of the Most Influential People in Medicine, Past & Present. John Simmons. 1999. 29.95 (*0-8065-2118-X*) Carol Pub Group.

Medical Optical Tomography: Functional Imaging & Monitoring. Ed. by Gerhard J. Muller. LC 93-5546. 1993. pap. 110.00 (*0-8194-1379-8*, IS11) SPIE.

Medical Orthodoxy & the Future of Psychoanalysis. K. R. Eissler. LC 65-18721. 592p. 1965. 87.50 (*0-8236-3240-7*) Intl Univs Pr.

***Medical Outcomes & Guidelines Sourcebook: A Comprehensive Guide to Medical Outcomes Research & Practical Guidelines: Developments, Data & Implementation.** Ed. by Laura Newman. (Illus.). 768p. 1999. pap. 295.00 (*1-57987-118-6*) Faulkner & Gray.

Medical Parasitology. rev. ed. N. C. Dey. (C). 1984. 57.00 (*0-7855-4660-X*, Pub. by Current Dist) St Mut.

Medical Parasitology. 7th ed. Markell. 1991. pap. text 54.00 (*0-7216-3411-7*, W B Saunders Co) Harcrt Hlth Sci Grp.

Medical Parasitology. 8th ed. Edward K. Markell et al. Ed. by Adrianne Williams. LC 98-15802. (Illus.). 544p. (C). 1998. text 49.95 (*0-7216-7634-0*, W B Saunders Co) Harcrt Hlth Sci Grp.

Medical Parasitology: A Practical Approach. Ed. by S. Gillespie & P. M. Hawkey. (Practical Approach Ser.: Vol. 152). (Illus.). 314p. 1995. text 115.00 (*0-19-963301-0*); pap. text 65.00 (*0-19-963300-2*) OUP.

Medical Parasitology: A Self-Instructional Text. 4th ed. Ruth Leventhal & Russell F. Cheadle. LC 95-4649. (Illus.). 178p. (C). 1995. pap. 37.95 (*0-8036-0041-0*) Davis Co.

Medical Parasitology: International Edition. 8th ed. Markell. (C). 1998. text 40.00 (*0-8089-2068-5*, Grune & Strat) Harcrt Hlth Sci Grp.

Medical Partnerships & Practice Disposition: A Guide for Physicians & Dentists. Martin L. Schulman & Steven Schulman. LC 83-16069. 141p. 1983. 55.00 (*0-275-91726-6*, C1726, Praeger Pubs) Greenwood.

Medical Patents in the Health Sciences Including Legislative Actions: Index of New Information. rev. ed. Albert E. Goldring. 135p. 1997. 47.50 (*0-7883-1592-7*); pap. 44.50 (*0-7883-1593-5*) ABBE Pubs Assn.

Medical Pegboard Procedure: Contents Only. 2nd ed. Taylor. (Medical Assisting Ser.). 1992. pap. 32.95 (*0-538-70438-1*) S-W Pub.

Medical Pegboard Procedures. 2nd ed. (Medical Assisting Ser.). 1992. 39.95 (*0-538-70437-3*) Delmar.

Medical Pegboard Procedures. 3rd ed. Dorothy A. Taylor et al. 80p. (C). 1995. text, teacher ed. 14.00 (*0-8273-7551-4*) Delmar.

Medical Pegboard Procedures, Pegboard Only. 3rd ed. Taylor et al. 1996. text, teacher ed. 11.95 (*0-8273-7550-6*) Delmar.

Medical Pegboard Procedures, Set. 3rd ed. Dorothy A. Taylor et al. 1995. teacher ed. 59.95 (*0-8273-7548-4*) Delmar.

Medical Periodicals: Index of Functions, History & Standards. Alphonse R. Abell. LC 88-48002. 150p. 1989. 47.50 (*1-55914-086-0*); pap. 44.50 (*1-55914-087-9*) ABBE Pubs Assn.

Medical Perioperative Management: Clinical Manual. Susan D. Wolfsthal. 449p. (C). 1992. pap. text 32.50 (*0-8385-1298-4*, A1298-7, Apple Lange Med) McGraw.

Medical Pharmacology at a Glance. 3rd ed. M. J. Neal. LC 97-2123. (At a Glance Ser.). (Illus.). 1997. pap. 29.95 (*0-86542-719-4*) Blackwell Sci.

Medical Photographer. Jack Rudman. (Career Examination Ser.: C-1366). 1994. pap. 29.95 (*0-8373-1366-X*) Nat Learn.

Medical Phrase Index: A One-Step Reference to the Terminology of Medicine. 3rd ed. Jean A. Lorenzini & Laura Lorenzini-Ley. Ed. by Gregg Rogers & Kathryn Swanson. LC 93-42123. 1300p. 1994. 49.95 (*1-878487-58-2*, ME052) Practice Mgmt Info.

Medical Physician Impairments: Index of Modern Information. William T. Weekes. LC 88-47865. 180p. 1988. 47.50 (*0-88164-926-0*); pap. 44.50 (*0-88164-927-9*) ABBE Pubs Assn.

Medical Physicists & Malpractice. Robert J. Shalek & David S. Gooden. LC 96-17117. 128p. 1996. text 27.00 (*0-944838-64-2*); pap. text 21.00 (*0-944838-65-0*) Med Physics Pub.

Medical Physics. Roger Muncaster. (Illus.). 140p. 1998. pap. 34.50 (*0-7487-2324-2*) St Mut.

***Medical Physics: Second Mexican Symposium.** Ed. by Maria-Ester Brandan et al. LC 98-86572. (Conference Proceedings Ser.: Vol. 440). (Illus.). x, 232p. 1998. 85.00 (*1-56396-807-X*) Am Inst Physics.

***Medical Physics & Biomedical Engineering.** B. H. Brown. LC 99-23505. 1999. 180.00 (*0-7503-0367-0*) IOP Pub.

***Medical Physics & Biomedical Engineering.** B. H. Brown et al. LC 99-23505. (Illus.). 800p. 1999. pap. text 60.00 (*0-7503-0368-9*) IOP Pub.

Medical Physics for Human Health Care. P. K. Bhatnagar. 1997. pap. 300.00 (*81-7233-154-1*, Pub. by Scientific Pubs) St Mut.

Medical Physics Handbook of Nuclear Medicine. Mark T. Madsen. (Illus.). 114p. (Orig.). (C). 1992. pap. text 16.95 (*0-944838-14-6*) Med Physics Pub.

Medical Physics Handbook of Radiation Therapy. Ed. by Ann E. Wright. (Illus.). 127p. (Orig.). (C). 1992. pap. text 16.95 (*0-944838-17-0*) Med Physics Pub.

Medical Physics Handbook of Units & Measures. John Freim, Jr. & Arnold Feldman. 47p. 1992. pap. text 7.95 (*0-944838-30-8*) Med Physics Pub.

Medical Physics of CT & Ultrasound: Tissue Imaging & Characterization. Ed. by Gary D. Fullerton & James A. Zagzebski. (Medical Physics Monograph Ser.: No. 6). 717p. 1980. text 50.00 (*1-888340-08-8*) AAPM.

Medical Physics of CT & Ultrasound: Tissue Imaging & Characterization: Proceedings of the AAPM 1980 Summer School Held at the University of Wisconsin - La Cross, Wisconsin, July 20-26, 1980. Ed. by Gary D. Fullerton & James A. Zagzebski. (American Association of Physicists in Medicine Symposium Ser.: No. 6). 725p. 1980. 50.00 (*0-88318-279-3*, Pub. by Am Inst Physics) Med Physics Pub.

Medical Physiology. Boulpaep. (C). 1995. text. write for info. (*0-7216-3256-4*, W B Saunders Co) Harcrt Hlth Sci Grp.

Medical Physiology. Ed. by Rodney A. Rhoades & George A. Tanner. LC 94-24639. (Illus.). 839p. 1995. text 59.95 (*0-316-74228-7*, Little Brwn Med Div) Lppncott W & W.

Medical Physiology: Objectives & Multiple Choice Questions. 2nd ed. Graham Mitchell. 153p. (C). 1986. pap. text 35.00 (*0-409-10727-1*) Buttrwrth-Heinemann.

Medical Plastics: Degradation Resistance & Failure Analysis. LC 98-65533. (SPE/ PDL Ser.). 215p. 1998. text 160.00 (*1-884207-60-X*) William Andrew.

Medical Plastics Conference Proceedings: RETEC - Fall 1988, Boston, MA; the Society of the Plastics Industry, Inc., & Society of Plastics Engineers. Society of Plastics Engineers Staff. LC TP1185.M4. 297p. pap. 92.10 (*0-8357-6206-8*, 203418300089) Bks Demand.

Medical Plastics Today & Tomorrow: Proceedings, RETEC Medical Plastics Conference, January 29-30, 1990, Anaheim, CA. Society of Plastics Engineers Staff. LC R 0857.P6. 237p. reprint ed. pap. 73.50 (*0-8357-2994-X*, 203926200011) Bks Demand.

Medical Politics - Actions, Status & Reactions: Index of Modern Progress. rev. ed. Science & Life Consultants Association Staff. LC 94-32481. 151p. 1994. 47.50 (*0-7883-0240-X*); pap. 44.50 (*0-7883-0241-8*) ABBE Pubs Assn.

Medical Portraits, Supplement 10. 1983. suppl. ed. 420.00 (*0-8161-1391-2*, G K Hall & Co) Mac Lib Ref.

Medical Power & Social Knowledge. Bryan S. Turner. 256p. (C). 1987. text 39.95 (*0-8039-8087-6*); pap. text 16.95 (*0-8039-8088-4*) Sage.

Medical Power & Social Knowledge. 2nd ed. Bryan S. Turner. 288p. 1995. 69.95 (*0-8039-7598-8*); pap. 25.95 (*0-8039-7599-6*) Sage.

Medical Power in Prisons: The Prison Medical Service in England, 1774-1988. Joe Sim. (Crime, Justice & Social Policy Ser.). 224p. 1990. 123.00 (*0-335-15183-3*); pap. 35.95 (*0-335-15182-5*) OpUniv Pr.

Medical Practice Accounting & Finance: A Practical Guide for Physicians, Dentists & Other Medical Practitioners. Rose Marie Bukics & Donald R. Chambers. LC 95-223119. 200p. (C). 1995. text 45.00 (*1-55738-617-X*, Irwn Prfssnl) McGraw-Hill Prof.

Medical Practice & Psychiatry: The Impact of Changing Demands. Group for the Advancement of Psychiatry Staff. LC 62-2872. (Group for the Advancement of Psychiatry, Symposium Ser.: Vol. 5, No. 58). 55p. reprint ed. pap. 30.00 (*0-7837-2120-X*, 204240200004) Bks Demand.

Medical Practice Change Management: Strategies & Techniques for the Changing Business of Healthcare. Peter D. Lucash. LC 96-45342. 240p. 1996. text 45.00 (*0-7863-0998-9*, Irwn McGrw-H) McGrw-H Hghr Educ.

Medical Practice Consolidation: Structural & Legal Issues. Peter N. Grant et al. (BNA's Health Law & Business Ser.: No. 1200). 1996. 125.00 (*1-55871-339-5*) BNA.

***Medical Practice, Defensive Medicine & Legal Issues: Index of New Information with Authors, Subjects, Research Categories & References.** rev. ed. Darnella Devitto. 160p. (Orig.). 1998. 47.50 (*0-7883-2086-6*); pap. 44.50 (*0-7883-2087-4*) ABBE Pubs Assn.

***Medical Practice Divorce: Successfully Managing a Medical Business Breakup.** (Illus.). 128p. 1999. 42.95 (*0-89970-990-7*) AMA.

***Medical Practice Forms: Every Form You Need to Succeed.** Keith C. Borglum. 300p. (Orig.). 1998. pap. text 44.95 (*1-57066-083-2*) Practice Mgmt Info.

Medical Practice in Rural Communities. C. F. Mutel & K. J. Donham. (Illus.). 168p. 1983. 58.00 (*0-387-91224-X*) Spr-Verlag.

Medical Practice in the Current Health Care Environment: A Handbook for Residents & Medical Students. Ed. by Janine C. Edwards & Robert M. Donati. 1995. text 40.00 (*0-8018-4965-9*); pap. text 15.00 (*0-8018-4966-7*) Johns Hopkins.

Medical Practice Management. Dean C. Kramer. 288p. 1982. 19.50 (*0-316-50322-3*, Little Brwn Med Div) Lppncott W & W.

Medical Practice Management Desk Book. Charles H. Walsh & Morton Walker. LC 81-19972. 208p. 1982. 49.95 (*0-13-572701-4*) P-H.

Medical Practice Management Handbook: Complete Guide To Managed Care, Accounting, Tax Issues & Daily Operations. 99th ed. Reed Tinsley. 1999. pap. text 109.00 incl. cd-rom (*0-15-606880-X*) Assessment Sys.

Medical Practice Management Skills. Edward E. Bartlett et al. iv, 288p. 1995. pap. 54.00 (*1-930548-17-6*) Tennenhouse Prof Pubns.

Medical Practice Performance Management Manual: How to Evaluate Employees. Courtney Price & Alys Novak. (Employee Performance Management Ser.). 234p. (Orig.). 1993. pap. 85.00 (*1-56829-027-6*) Med Group Mgmt.

Medical Practices in the Civil War. Susan Provost Beller. LC 92-14960. (Illus.). 96p. 1998. reprint ed. pap. 9.99 (*0-9663758-0-7*, 01) OurStory.

Medical Practitioners' Guide to Paediatric Audiology. Ed. by Barry McCormick. (Illus.). 146p. (C). 1995. pap. text 30.95 (*0-521-45988-5*) Cambridge U Pr.

Medical Prescription of Narcotics: Scientific Foundations & Practical Experiences. Ed. by Swiss Federal Office of Public Health Staff. LC 96-931386. (Illus.). 344p. 1997. pap. text 52.00 (*0-88937-171-7*) Hogrefe & Huber Pubs.

Medical Prescriptions--Abuse, Choices, Control, Evaluation, Habits, Generics & Computerization: Index of New Information with Authors, Subjects, & Bibliography. Darlee M. Bentley. LC 96-12514. 1996. 47.50 (*0-7883-0820-3*); pap. 44.50 (*0-7883-0821-1*) ABBE Pubs Assn.

Medical Primatology, 1970: Proceedings. Conference on Experimental Medicine & Surgery in P. Ed. by E. I. Goldsmith & J. Moor-Jankowski. 1971. 243.50 (*3-8055-1227-9*) S Karger.

Medical Primatology, 1972: Selected Papers, Proceedings, 3 pts, Set. Conference on Experimental Medicine & Surgery in P. Ed. by E. I. Goldsmith & J. Moor-Jankowski. Incl. Pt. 1. General Primatology, Reproduction & Perinatal Studies, Genetics, Phylogenetics, & Evolution. 450p. 1973. 121.75

An Asterisk (*) at the beginning of an entry indicates that the title is appearing for the first time.

(*3-8055-1486-7*); Pt. 2. Surgery, Transplantation, Oral Medicine, Neurophysiology & Psychology. 350p. 1973. 104.50 (*3-8055-1487-5*); Pt. 3. Infectious Diseases, Oncology, Pharmacology & Toxicology, Cardiovascular Studies. 400p. 1973. 121.75 (*3-8055-1488-3*); 1972. 304.50 (*3-8055-1489-1*) S Karger.

Medical Problem Solving: An Analysis of Clinical Reasoning. Arthur S. Elstein et al. LC 77-21505. (Illus.). 352p. 1978. 49.95 (*0-674-56125-2*) HUP.

Medical Problems in Athletes. Karl B. Fields & Peter A. Fricker. LC 97-13110. (Illus.). 1997. pap. 99.00 (*0-86542-480-2*) Blackwell Sci.

Medical Problems in Dentistry. 4th ed. Crispian Scully & R. A. Cawson. LC 97-51176. 592p. 2000. text 110.00 (*0-7236-1056-8*) Buttrwrth-Heinemann.

Medical Problems in the Classroom: The Teacher's Role in Diagnosis & Management. 3rd ed. Robert H. Haslam & Peter J. Valletutti. LC 85-3521. (Illus.). 580p. 1996. pap. 39.00 (*0-89079-630-0*, 7316) PRO-ED.

Medical Procedures Manual. Garabed Eknoyan. LC 81-11642. (Illus.). 240p. reprint ed. pap. 74.40 (*0-8357-8576-9*, 203494200091) Bks Demand.

*__Medical Profession & Human Rights: A Handbook for a Changing.__ British Medical Association Staff. 2000. pap. 29.95 (*1-85649-612-0*, Pub. by Zed Books) St Martin.

*__Medical Profession & Human Rights: Handbook for a Changing.__ British Medical Association Staff. 2000. text 69.95 (*1-85649-611-2*, Pub. by Zed Books) St Martin.

Medical Profession in 19th Century Florida: A Biographical Register. Ashby E. Hammond. LC 96-43502. 1996. write for info. (*0-929595-08-4*) Univ Florida Lib.

Medical Professional Liability & the Delivery of Obstetrical Care, Vol. I. Institute of Medicine Staff. 256p. 1989. text 29.95 (*0-309-03982-7*) Natl Acad Pr.

Medical Professional Liability & the Delivery of Obstetrical Care: An Interdisciplinary Review, Vol. II. Ed. by Victoria P. Rostow et al. 256p. 1989. text 35.00 (*0-309-03986-X*) Natl Acad Pr.

Medical Professions Admission Guide: Strategy for Success. 3rd ed. Ed. by Brice W. Corder. 142p. (C). 1994. pap. 15.95 (*0-911899-11-1*) NAAHP Inc.

Medical Professions & Drug Addiction: Six Studies, 1882 to 1932, An Original Anthology. Gerald N. Grob. LC 80-1206. (Addiction in America Ser.). 1981. lib. bdg. 35.95 (*0-405-13560-2*) Ayer.

*__Medical Progress & Social Reality: A Reader in Nineteenth-Century Medicine & Literature.__ Ed. by Lilian R. Furst. LC 00-26534. (C). 2000. pap. text 17.95 (*0-7914-4804-5*) State U NY Pr.

*__Medical Progress & Social Reality: A Reader in Nineteenth-Century Medicine & Literature.__ Ed. by Lilian R. Furst. LC 00-26534. (C). 2001. text 54.50 (*0-7914-4803-7*) State U NY Pr.

Medical Proof of Social Securities Disability. David A. Morton, III. LC 83-16800. 585p. (C). 1983. reprint ed. text. write for info. (*0-314-72082-0*) West Pub.

Medical Proof of Social Securities Disability: 1995-1996 Supplement. David A. Morton, 3rd. (Miscellaneous Treatise Ser.). 400p. (C). 1995. pap. text, suppl. ed. write for info. (*0-314-08334-0*) West Pub.

Medical Prosthetic Devices & Artificial Organs. Ed. by Peter Allen. 279p. 1983. pap. 295.00 (*0-931634-35-0*) FIND-SVP.

Medical Protestants: The Eclectics in American Medicine, 1825-1939. John S. Haller, Jr. LC 93-7389. (Medical Humanities Ser.). (Illus.). 352p. (C). 1993. 51.95 (*0-8093-1894-6*) S Ill U Pr.

Medical-Psychiatric Practice, Vol. 1. Ed. by Alan Stoudemire & Barry S. Fogel. 645p. 1991. text 29.95 (*0-88048-425-X*, 8425) Am Psychiatric.

Medical-Psychiatric Practice, Vol. 2. Ed. by Alan Stoudemire & Barry S. Fogel. 657p. 1993. text 29.95 (*0-88048-426-8*, 8426) Am Psychiatric.

Medical-Psychiatric Practice, Vol. 3. Ed. by Alan Stoudemire & Barry S. Fogel. 512p. 1995. text 29.95 (*0-88048-427-6*, 8427) Am Psychiatric.

Medical Psychiatry: Theory & Practice, 2 vols., Set. Ed. by Enrique S. Garza-Trevino. 1300p. (C). 1989. text 74.00 (*9971-5-0774-9*) World Scientific Pub.

Medical Psychology of Adolescents: Index of New Information. rev. ed. American Health Research Institute Staff. 165p. 1998. 47.50 (*0-7883-1956-6*); pap. 44.50 (*0-7883-1957-4*) ABBE Pubs Assn.

Medical Psychology of Alcohol Drinking & Addiction: Index of New Information with References. Steve Haggert & Helen R. Haggert. 150p. 1996. 47.50 (*0-7883-0802-5*); pap. 44.50 (*0-7883-0803-3*) ABBE Pubs Assn.

Medical Psychology of Alcohol Drinking & Addiction: Index of New Information with References. rev. ed. Helen R. Haggert. 177p. 1997. 47.50 (*0-7883-1568-4*); pap. 44.50 (*0-7883-1569-2*) ABBE Pubs Assn.

Medical Psychology of Breast Cancer: Index of New Information. Ruth K. Leeson. 153p. 1997. 47.50 (*0-7883-1500-5*); pap. 44.50 (*0-7883-1501-3*) ABBE Pubs Assn.

Medical Psychology of Character & Personalities: Index of New Information with References. Steve Haggert & Helen R. Haggert. 150p. 1996. 47.50 (*0-7883-0804-1*); pap. 44.50 (*0-7883-0805-X*) ABBE Pubs Assn.

Medical Psychology of Crime - Including Patients. American Health Research Institute Staff. 150p. 1996. 47.50 (*0-7883-0918-8*); pap. 44.50 (*0-7883-0919-6*) ABBE Pubs Assn.

*__Medical Psychology of Crime & Its Victims: Index of New Information.__ rev. ed. Casper T. Williamson. 135p. 1999. 47.50 (*0-7883-2126-9*); pap. 44.50 (*0-7883-2127-7*) ABBE Pubs Assn.

Medical Psychology of Delusions in Normal & Abnormal Behaviors: Index of New Information & Bibliography. Gladys G. Petronno. 150p. 1996. 47.50 (*0-7883-0984-6*); pap. 44.50 (*0-7883-0985-4*) ABBE Pubs Assn.

Medical Psychology of Homosexuality Male & Female: Index of New Information with References. rev. ed. Charder R. Eksteen. 169p. 1997. 47.50 (*0-7883-1598-6*); pap. 44.50 (*0-7883-1599-4*) ABBE Pubs Assn.

Medical Psychology of Parents & Parenting: Index & Reference Book of New Information. rev. ed. Francis M. Vizzier. 159p. 1997. 47.50 (*0-7883-1556-0*); pap. 44.50 (*0-7883-1557-9*) ABBE Pubs Assn.

Medical Psychology of Physicians: Index of Modern Information. Roy R. Zimmerman. LC 88-47956. 150p. 1988. 47.50 (*0-88164-982-1*); pap. 44.50 (*0-88164-983-X*) ABBE Pubs Assn.

Medical Psychology of Placebo Effects-Myths, Magic & Reality: Index of New Information for the Health Sciences. William W. Wheeler. 147p. 1997. 47.50 (*0-7883-1382-7*); pap. 44.50 (*0-7883-1383-5*) ABBE Pubs Assn.

Medical Psychology of Regression & Factorial Elements of Personality: Index of New Information with Authors & Subjects. Anita M. Wolman. 180p. 1993. 47.50 (*1-55914-904-3*); pap. 44.50 (*1-55914-905-1*) ABBE Pubs Assn.

*__Medical Psychology of Shame, Self-Blame & Guilt: Index of New Information.__ rev. ed. Joyce C. Kirkland. 160p. 1999. 47.50 (*0-7883-2164-1*); pap. 44.50 (*0-7883-2165-X*) ABBE Pubs Assn.

Medical Psychology of Spouse Abuse: Index of New Information with Authors & Subjects. rev. ed. Willard T. Brainard. LC 94-34611. 1994. 47.50 (*0-7883-0424-0*); pap. 44.50 (*0-7883-0425-9*) ABBE Pubs Assn.

Medical Psychology of the Id, Ego & Superego: Index of Modern Authors & Subjects with Guide for Rapid Research. Nita C. Galanakis. LC 90-56275. 160p. 1991. 47.50 (*1-55914-332-0*); pap. 44.50 (*1-55914-333-9*) ABBE Pubs Assn.

Medical Psychology of (Tobacco) Smoking: Index of New Information with Authors, Subjects & References. Roger S. Ingalsbe. 150p. 1997. 47.50 (*0-7883-1390-8*); pap. 44.50 (*0-7883-1391-6*) ABBE Pubs Assn.

Medical Psychosomatics: Index of Modern Authors & Subjects with Guide for Rapid Research. Tony A. Pellicano. LC 90-56289. 160p. 1991. 47.50 (*1-55914-382-7*); pap. 44.50 (*1-55914-383-5*) ABBE Pubs Assn.

Medical Psychotherapy, Vol. 8. ABMP (Anchor) Staff. 240p. 1995. pap. text, per. 6.95 (*0-7872-0963-5*) Kendall-Hunt.

Medical Psychotherapy, Vol. 10. ABMP Staff. 232p. 1999. per. 7.95 (*0-7872-5756-7*, 41575601) Kendall-Hunt.

Medical Publishing in Nineteenth Century America: Lea of Philadelphia, William Wood & Company of New York City & F. E. Boericke of Philadelphia with a Checklist of Wood's Library of Standard Medical Authors & Specimen Catalogues. Francesco Cordasco. (Illus.). 225p. 1990. 47.50 (*0-940198-06-1*) St Aedans Pr & Bk.

Medical Purchasing Specialist. Jack Rudman. (Career Examination Ser.: C-2448). 1994. pap. 27.95 (*0-8373-2448-3*) Nat Learn.

Medical Q & A. Emanual Grodsky. Ed. by Ross McElroy. (Realtime Machine Shorthand Ser.). 175p. (C). 1992. pap., teacher ed. 34.75 (*0-938643-25-8*) Stenotype Educ.

Medical Q & A. Emanual Grodsky. Ed. by Ross McElroy. (Realtime Machine Shorthand Ser.). 142p. (C). 1993. pap. text, student ed. 32.00 (*0-938643-24-X*) Stenotype Educ.

Medical Quality & the Law: Final Report of the 1989 Chief Justice Earl Warren Conference on Advocacy in the United States. Michael E. Carbine. 116p. (Orig.). 1989. pap. 25.00 (*0-941916-60-X*) Roscoe Pound Inst.

*__Medical Quality Management 2000 Edition.__ Ed. by Beth E. Rosenthal. (Illus.). 576p. 1999. pap. 325.00 (*1-57987-119-4*) Faulkner & Gray.

Medical Racket. Martin L. Gross. LC 98-25668. 256p. 1998. pap. 12.50 (*0-380-78785-7*, Avon Bks) Morrow Avon.

Medical Radiation Detectors: Fundamental & Applied Aspects. Ed. by N. F. Kember. (Medical Science Series). (Illus.). 236p. 1994. 110.00 (*0-7503-0319-0*) IOP Pub.

Medical Radiation Exposure of Pregnant & Potentially Pregnant Women. LC 77-80439. (Report Ser.: No. 54). 39p. 1977. pap. text 20.00 (*0-913392-36-7*) NCRP Pubns.

Medical Radiation Physics: Report of a Joint IAEA/WHO Expert Committee, 1968. (Technical Report Ser.: No. 390). 19p. 1968. pap. text 3.00 (*92-4-120390-0*, 1100390) World Health.

Medical Radiesthesia & Radionics: An Introduction. Vernon D. Wethered. 196p. 1957. pap. 17.95 (*0-8464-1032-X*) Beekman Pubs.

Medical Radiesthesia & Radionics: An Introduction. 4th ed. Vernon D. Wethered. (Illus.). 192p. 17.95 (*0-8464-4251-5*) Beekman Pubs.

Medical Radiographic Techniques. Robert Zimmerman. LC 74-18672. (Allied Health Ser.). 1975. pap. 8.35 (*0-672-61392-1*, Bobbs) Macmillan.

Medical Radiography: Self-Assessment & Review. Linda Lefave. (Specialty Level PreTest Ser.). (Illus.). 304p. 1995. pap. text 28.00 (*0-07-052078-X*) McGraw-Hill HPD.

Medical Radioisotope Scintigraphy, Vol. 1. IAEA Staff. 1968. pap. 105.00 (*92-0-010069-4*, ISP193-1, Pub. by IAEA) Bernan Associates.

Medical Radioisotope Scintigraphy, Vol. 2. IAEA Staff. 1968. pap. 110.00 (*92-0-010169-0*, ISP193-2, Pub. by IAEA) Bernan Associates.

Medical Radioisotope Scintigraphy 1972, Vol. 1. IAEA Staff. 1973. pap. 130.00 (*92-0-010173-9*, ISP315-1, Pub. by IAEA) Bernan Associates.

Medical Radioisotope Scintigraphy 1972, Vol. 2. IAEA Staff. 1973. pap. 100.00 (*92-0-010273-5*, ISP315-2, Pub. by IAEA) Bernan Associates.

Medical Radiology Technician. Jack Rudman. (Career Examination Ser.: C-1367). 1994. pap. 27.95 (*0-8373-1367-8*) Nat Learn.

Medical Radiology Technologist. Jack Rudman. (Career Examination Ser.: C-490). 1994. pap. 29.95 (*0-8373-0490-3*) Nat Learn.

Medical Radionuclides: Radiation Dose & Effects, Proceedings. Ed. by Roger J. Cloutier et al. LC 70-606556. (AEC Symposium Ser.). 528p. 1970. pap. 21.25 (*0-87079-269-5*, CONF-691212); fiche 9.00 (*0-87079-270-9*, CONF-691212) DOE.

Medical Reactions, Treatments & Therapy of Patients with 'Overdose' Substances. Jason M. Marvis. 150p. 1996. 47.50 (*0-7883-0766-5*); pap. 44.50 (*0-7883-0767-3*) ABBE Pubs Assn.

Medical Readiness: Efforts Are Underway for DOD Training in Civilian Trauma Centers. Carol R. Schuster. 52p. (C). 1999. pap. text 20.00 (*0-7881-8138-6*) DIANE Pub.

Medical Receptionists & Secretaries Handbook. Mari Robbins. LC 95-48411. 254p. 1996. pap. 23.00 (*1-85775-084-5*, Radcliffe Med Pr) Scovill Paterson.

Medical Recollections of the Army of Potomac with Memoir of Jonathan Letterman. rev. ed. Jonathan Letterman & Bennett A. Clements. Ed. by Edgar G. Archer. (Illus.). 250p. 1991. reprint ed. write for info. (*1-877791-01-6*) Bohemian Brigade.

Medical Record Abstraction & Guidelines for Assessing Quality of Care for Hospitalized Patients with AIDS-Related Pneumocystis Carinii Pneumonia. Charles Bennett. 172p. (Orig.). (C). 1994. pap. text 45.00 (*0-7881-1055-1*) DIANE Pub.

Medical Record Abstraction Form & Guidelines for Assessing the Appropriateness of Hysterectomy. (Illus.). 174p. (Orig.). (C). 1995. pap. text 45.00 (*0-7881-2298-3*) DIANE Pub.

Medical Record Abstraction Form & Guidelines for Assessing the Appropriateness of Hysterectomy. Elizabeth A. McGlynn et al. LC 93-4601. 1993. pap. 9.00 (*0-8330-1394-7*, MR-239-HF) Rand Corp.

Medical Record Abstraction Form & Guidelines for Assessing the Quality of Prenatal Care. Elizabeth A. McGlynn et al. LC 93-4622. 1993. pap. 9.00 (*0-8330-1393-9*, MR-238-HF) Rand Corp.

Medical Record As Evidence. Elliott B. Oppenheim. LC 98-84349. xxxi, 968 p. 1998. 110.00 (*1-55834-889-1*) LEXIS Pub.

*__Medical Record As Evidence, 1999 Supplement: Pocketpart.__ Elliott B. Oppenheim. 50p. 1999. suppl. ed. write for info. (*0-327-01701-5*, 6606210) LEXIS Pub.

Medical Record Examination Review (MEPC) 6th ed. Susan P. Bailey. (Illus.). 288p. (C). 1994. pap. text 25.95 (*0-8385-6192-6*, A6192-7) Appleton & Lange.

Medical Record Librarian. Jack Rudman. (Career Examination Ser.: C-491). 1994. pap. 27.95 (*0-8373-0491-1*) Nat Learn.

Medical Record Management see Health Information Management

Medical Record Management. 9th ed. Edna K. Huffman. 1990. 35.15 (*0-917036-16-6*) Physicians Rec.

*__Medical Record Review.__ Joint Commission on Accreditation of Healthcare Organizations. (Topics in Clinical Care Improvement Ser.). (Illus.). 102p. 1998. pap. 19.95 (*0-86688-569-2*, CC-600) Joint Comm Hlthcare.

Medical Record Technician. Goldberg. LC 98-20891. (Careers Without College Ser.). (Illus.). 48p. (J). (gr. 4-7). 1998. 19.00 (*0-7368-0035-2*) Capstone Pr.

Medical Record Technician. Jan Goldberg. (Careers Without College Ser.). (J). 1998. 19.00 (*0-516-21397-0*) Childrens.

Medical Record Technician. Jack Rudman. (Career Examination Ser.: C-2329). 1994. pap. 27.95 (*0-8373-2329-0*) Nat Learn.

Medical Records. Anne M. Dellinger. (Hospital Law in North Carolina Ser.: Chap. 8). 67p. (C). 1987. ring bd. 10.50 (*1-56011-080-5*, 85.03H) Institute Government.

Medical Records: Getting Yours. rev. ed. Sidney M. Wolfe & Diann Johnson. (Illus.). 72p. (C). 1995. pap. text 10.00 (*0-937188-56-5*) Pub Citizen.

Medical Records: Management in a Changing Environment. Susan M. Murphy-Muth. (Health Care Administration Ser.). 224p. 1987. 65.00 (*0-87189-872-1*) Aspen Pub.

Medical Records: Policies & Guidelines. annuals Liebler. 1991. ring bd. 210.00 (*0-8342-0136-4*) Aspen Pub.

Medical Records & How They Affect Legal Issues. Arleen N. Kaizer. 127p. 1994. pap. 32.80 (*0-89412-232-0*) Aegean Park Pr.

Medical Records Assistant. Jack Rudman. (Career Examination Ser.: C-2952). 1994. pap. 27.95 (*0-8373-2952-3*) Nat Learn.

Medical Records Clerk. Jack Rudman. (Career Examination Ser.: C-2309). 1994. reprint ed. pap. 27.95 (*0-8373-2309-6*) Nat Learn.

*__Medical Records Confidentiality in the Modern Delivery of Health Care: Congressional Hearing.__ Ed. by Michael Bilirakis. 121p. 2000. pap. text 30.00 (*0-7567-0138-4*) DIANE Pub.

*__Medical Records Handbook for the Physician's Office.__ Barbara O. Wesley. Ed. by Kimberly Koschemann & Debra Farris. 84p. 1999. pap. write for info. (*1-893621-01-4*) TX Med Assn.

Medical Records in Health Information. 2nd ed. Kathleen Waters. 700p. 1995. write for info. (*0-8342-0251-4*) Aspen Pub.

Medical Records Policy & Procedure Guideline Manual. Mary J. Zellner. 1991. student ed. 80.00 (*1-879575-11-6*) Acad Med Sys.

Medical Records Review, 1. 3rd ed. Kristyn S. Appleby & Joanne Tarver. LC 98-49309. 656p. 1998. boxed set 98.65 (*0-7355-0337-0*) Panel Pubs.

Medical Records Review & Analysis. Charles C. Sharpe. LC 98-47758. 224p. 1999. 65.00 (*0-86569-283-1*, Auburn Hse) Greenwood.

Medical Records Supervisor. Jack Rudman. (Career Examination Ser.: C-3731). 1994. pap. 34.95 (*0-8373-3731-3*) Nat Learn.

Medical Records Technology. Alice Mosier & Frank J. Pace. LC 74-18676. (Allied Health Ser.). 1975. pap. 9.95 (*0-672-61396-4*, Bobbs) Macmillan.

Medical Reference, 3 vols., Set. Bantam Books Inc. Editors. 1992. mass mkt., boxed set 20.95 (*0-553-62870-4*) Bantam.

Medical Reference Works, 1973-1974. Compiled by Joy S. Richmond. LC 67-30664. 89p. 1975. pap. 3.50 (*0-8108-2441-8*) Scarecrow.

Medical Reference Works, 1969-1972. Compiled by Joy S. Richmond. LC 67-30664. 1973. pap. 5.00 (*0-8108-2440-X*) Scarecrow.

Medical Referrals for Health Science Practices & Business: Index of New Information with Authors & Subjects. Gene J. Whittlesby. 180p. 1993. 47.50 (*1-55914-908-6*); pap. 44.50 (*1-55914-909-4*) ABBE Pubs Assn.

*__Medical Rehabilitation Equipment & Software in Argentina: A Strategic Entry Report, 1997.__ Compiled by Icon Group International Staff. (Country Industry Report). (Illus.). 134p. 1999. ring bd. 1340.00 incl. audio compact disk (*0-7418-0258-9*) Icon Grp.

Medical Rehabilitation of Traumatic Brain Injury. Ed. by Lawrence J. Horn & Nathan D. Zasler. (Illus.). 650p. 1996. text 93.00 (*1-56053-070-7*) Hanley & Belfus.

Medical Rehabilitation Outcomes Research. Marcus J. Fuhrer. LC 96-31051. 1997. 67.00 (*1-55766-274-6*) P H Brookes.

Medical Rehabilitation Services: Forms, Checklists & Guidelines. Aspen Reference Group Staff. Ed. by Sara N. Di Lima & Sandra J. Painter. LC 94-41112. ring bd. 170.00 (*0-8342-0668-4*, S175) Aspen Pub.

Medical Relations Officer. Jack Rudman. (Career Examination Ser.: C-3351). 1994. pap. 34.95 (*0-8373-3351-2*) Nat Learn.

Medical Reports of Disease Prevention: Index of New Information. David B. Hagley. 150p. 1997. 47.50 (*0-7883-0960-9*); pap. 44.50 (*0-7883-0961-7*) ABBE Pubs Assn.

Medical Reports of the U. S. Office of Research Integrity: Index of New Information & Bibliography. Brian L. Longnecker. 150p. 1996. 47.50 (*0-7883-0996-X*); pap. 44.50 (*0-7883-0997-8*) ABBE Pubs Assn.

Medical Research - Priorities & Responsibilities: Proceedings of the Round Table Conference of CIOM-WHO-UNESCO, Geneva, Oct., 1969. CIOM-WHO-UNESCO Conference Staff. 156p. 1970. pap. text 7.20 (*92-4-156031-2*, 1830004) World Health.

Medical Research & the Jungle of Science: A New System for Universal Organization of All Subjects with Permanent Listing of All Publications, Authors & Contributors. rev. ed. John C. Bartone. (Illus.). 170p. 1996. 59.95 (*0-7883-1022-4*); pap. 49.50 (*0-7883-1023-2*) ABBE Pubs Assn.

Medical Research Centres. 1000p. 1990. text 470.00 (*0-582-06123-7*) Longman.

Medical Research Data: Essential Information for Scientists & Engineers in Medical Devices Industry. 2nd ed. George Cristino & Donna M. Cristino. (Illus.). 387p. (C). 1996. text 295.00 (*1-886974-04-7*) Inst Knowledge.

Medical Research in the Health Sciences: Index of New Information with Authors & Subjects. Science & Life Consultants Association Staff. LC 92-54206. 180p. 1992. 47.50 (*1-55914-564-1*); pap. 44.50 (*1-55914-565-X*) ABBE Pubs Assn.

Medical Research Novel in English & German, 1900-1950. Phillip A. Scott. LC 91-78363. (ENG & GER.). 144p. (C). 1992. 24.95 (*0-87972-551-6*); pap. 13.95 (*0-87972-552-4*) Bowling Green Univ Popular Press.

Medical Research of a New Category: Oxidants - Index of New Information with Authors, Subjects & Bibliographical References. Science & Life Consultants Association Staff. 150p. 1996. 47.50 (*0-7883-0784-3*); pap. 44.50 (*0-7883-0785-1*) ABBE Pubs Assn.

Medical Research of a New Category: Oxidative Stress - Index of New Information with Authors, Subjects & Bibliographical References. Science & Life Consultants Association Staff. 150p. 1996. 47.50 (*0-7883-0798-3*); pap. 44.50 (*0-7883-0799-1*) ABBE Pubs Assn.

Medical Research of Combat Disorders - Diagnosis, Psychology & Therapy: Index of New Information with Authors, Subjects & Bibliographical References. John C. Bartone. 150p. 1996. 47.50 (*0-7883-0678-2*); pap. 44.50 (*0-7883-0679-0*) ABBE Pubs Assn.

Medical Research of Current & Past Wars: Index of New Information. Gregg V. Goldin. LC 95-19212. 1995. write for info. (*0-7883-0658-8*); pap. write for info. (*0-7883-0659-6*) ABBE Pubs Assn.

Medical Research of Deception in Health Sciences Vol. I: Directory of Authors & Index of New Information, 2 vols., Vol. 1. Brian Z. Yardela. 170p. 1997. 47.50 (*0-7883-0964-1*); pap. 44.50 (*0-7883-0965-X*) ABBE Pubs Assn.

Medical Research of Deception in Health Sciences Vol. 2: Directory of Authors & Index of New Information. Brian Z. Yardela. 59p. 1997. pap. 44.50 (*0-7883-0967-6*) ABBE Pubs Assn.

M

Medical Research of Deception in Health Sciences Vol. 2: Directory of Authors & Index of New Information, 2 vols., Vol. 2. Brian Z. Yardela. 159p. 1997. 47.50 (*0-7883-0966-8*) ABBE Pubs Assn.

Medical Research of Famous People--Analysis & Re-Diagnosis of Their Health, Behavior, Diseases & Love-Life: Index of New Information. Henry J. Hossmann. 150p. 1996. 47.50 (*0-7883-0958-7*); pap. 44.50 (*0-7883-0959-5*) ABBE Pubs Assn.

Medical Research of Leisure Activities - Active, Passive or Dangerous: Index of New Information. Virginia C. Venezia. 167p. 1997. 47.50 (*0-7883-1606-0*); pap. 44.50 (*0-7883-1607-9*) ABBE Pubs Assn.

Medical Research of Sexual Partners: Index of New Information. American Health Research Institute Staff. 150p. 1996. 47.50 (*0-7883-0914-5*); pap. 44.50 (*0-7883-0915-3*) ABBE Pubs Assn.

Medical Research of Women's Health: Index & Reference Book of New Information. Angel A. Decker. 150p. 1996. 47.50 (*0-7883-0900-5*); pap. 44.50 (*0-7883-0901-3*) ABBE Pubs Assn.

Medical Research on Radon & Cancer: Index of New Information with References. Thomas S. Wheatley. 150p. 1996. pap. 44.50 (*0-7883-0807-6*) ABBE Pubs Assn.

Medical Research on Radon & Cancer: Index of New Information with References. Thomas S. Wheatley. 150p. 1996. 47.50 (*0-7883-0806-8*) ABBE Pubs Assn.

Medical Research on Students: A Subject Analysis with Bibliography. American Health Research Institute Staff. LC 84-45736. 150p. 1987. 47.50 (*0-88164-250-9*); pap. 44.50 (*0-88164-251-7*) ABBE Pubs Assn.

Medical Research Support - What's Going on in the U. S. A. Index of New Information & Research Bible. Science & Life Consultants Association Staff. LC 96-12494. 1996. 47.50 (*0-7883-1066-6*); pap. 44.50 (*0-7883-1067-4*) ABBE Pubs Assn.

Medical Research Systems in Europe: A Joint Welcome Trust-Ciba Foundation Symposium. CIBA Foundation Staff. LC 73-86342. (CIBA Foundation Symposium: New Ser.: No. 21). 343p. reprint ed. pap. 106.40 (*0-608-13986-6*, 202215100024) Bks Demand.

Medical Research Technician. (Career Examination Ser.: C-3352). 1994. pap. 34.95 (*0-8373-3352-0*) Nat Learn.

Medical Response to Effects of Ionizing Radiation: Proceedings of a Conference on Medical Response to Effects of Ionizing Radiation Held at Queen Elizabeth II Conference Center, London, 28-30 June 1989. Ed. by W. A. Crosbie et al. 310p. 1989. 81.00 (*1-85166-385-1*) Elsevier.

Medical Responsibility: Paternalism, Informed Consent & Euthanasia. Ed. by Wade L. Robison & Michael S. Pritchard. LC 79-87656. (Contemporary Issues in Biomedicine, Ethics, & Society Ser.). 230p. 1979. 49.50 (*0-89603-007-5*) Humana.

Medical Review Criteria Guidelines for Managed Care. Margaret D. Bischel. (Illus.). 605p. 1997. ring bd. 495.00 (*1-893826-00-7*) Apollo Managed.

Medical Review Officer Handbook. 7th ed. Theodore F. Shults. Date not set. pap. text 125.00 (*0-9637094-4-5*) Quadrangle Res.

Medical Review Officer Handbook. 7th ed. Theodore F. Shults. Ed. by Jennifer Harrington. 1999. pap. text 125.00 (*0-9637094-7-X*) Quadrangle Res.

Medical Review Officer Manual: A Guide to Evaluating Urine Drug Analysis for Implementation of the Mandatory Guidelines for Federal Workplace Drug Testing Programs. 1991. lib. bdg. 69.75 (*0-8490-4341-7*) Gordon Pr.

Medical Review Officer's Guide to Drug Testing. Ed. by Robert B. Swotinsky. LC 92-19472. 256p. 1992. pap. 65.95 (*0-442-00892-9*, VNR) Wiley.

Medical Review Officer's Guide to Drug Testing. Ed. by Robert B. Swotinsky. 272p. 1992. pap. 79.95 (*0-471-28445-9*, VNR) Wiley.

Medical Review Officer's Manual: MROCC's Guide to Drug Testing. Robert B. Swotinsky & Donna R. Smith. LC 99-12452. 213p. 1999. pap. text 45.00 (*1-883595-24-X*, 23053, OEM Pr) OEM Health.

Medical Revolution in France, 1789-1796. David M. Vess. LC 74-14916. 222p. reprint ed. pap. 68.90 (*0-7837-4955-4*, 204462100004) Bks Demand.

Medical Revolution in Minnesota: A History of the University of Minnesota Medical School. Leonard G. Wilson. LC 88-29563. (Illus.). 612p. 1989. 55.00 (*0-9620884-0-4*) Midewiwin.

Medical Risk & the Right to an Informed Consent in Clinical Care & Clinical Research. Dennis J. Mazur. LC 98-86506. 183p. 1998. pap. 48.00 (*0-924674-64-4*) Am Coll Phys Execs.

Medical Risk Management: Preventive Legal Strategies for Health Care Providers. Edward P. Richards, III & Katharine C. Rathbun. LC 82-16346. 311p. 1983. 73.00 (*0-89443-840-9*) Aspen Pub.

Medical Risks: Trends in Mortality by Age & Time Elapsed, 2 vols., Set. Ed. by Edward A. Lew & Jerzy Gajewski. LC 90-7707. 1512p. 1990. 195.00 (*0-275-93786-0*, C37860, Praeger Pubs) Greenwood.

Medical Risks: Trends in Mortality by Age & Time Elapsed, 2 vols., Vol. 1. Ed. by Edward A. Lew & Jerzy Gajewski. LC 90-7707. 368p. 1990. 195.00 (*0-275-93787-9*, C37861, Praeger Pubs) Greenwood.

Medical Risks: Trends in Mortality by Age & Time Elapsed, 2 vols., Vol. 2. Ed. by Edward A. Lew & Jerzy Gajewski. LC 90-7707. 368p. 1990. 195.00 (*0-275-93788-7*, C37862, Praeger Pubs) Greenwood.

Medical Risks: 1991 Compendium of Mortality & Morbidity. Ed. by Richard B. Singer et al. LC 94-18560. (Illus.). 344p. 1994. 115.00 (*0-275-94553-7*, Praeger Pubs) Greenwood.

Medical Sales. Chad Ellis. LC 96-45333. (Opportunities In . . . Ser.). (Illus.). 160p. 1997. pap. 11.95 (*0-8442-4561-5*, 45615, VGM Career) NTC Contemp Pub Co.

Medical Savings Accounts: The Singapore Experience. Thomas A. Massaro & Yu-Ning Wong. 22p. 1996. pap. 10.00 (*1-56808-071-9*, 203) Natl Ctr Pol.

Medical School. P. G. Hosmer. 256p. 1988. 16.95 (*0-933905-13-0*); pap. 9.95 (*0-933905-14-9*) Claycomb Pr.

Medical School: Getting in, Staying in, Staying Human. 7th rev. ed. Keith Russell Ablow. 1990. pap. 14.95 (*0-312-04349-X*) St Martin.

Medical School Admission Requirements, 1997-98, United States & Canada. 47th ed. Ed. by Cynthia T. Bennett. xiii, 407p. (Orig.). 1996. pap. 20.00 (*1-57754-000-X*) Assn Am Med Coll.

Medical School Admission Requirements, 1998-99, United States & Canada. 48th rev. ed. Ed. by Cynthia T. Bennett. 416p. (C). 1997. pap. 25.00 (*1-57754-003-4*) Assn Am Med Coll.

Medical School Admission Requirements, 1999-2000, United States & Canada: United States & Canada, 1998-1999. 49th ed. Ed. by Kimberly S. Varner. xvi, 416p. 1998. pap. 25.00 (*1-57754-007-7*) Assn Am Med Coll.

Medical School Admission Requirements, United States & Canada, 2000-2001. 50th ed. Ed. by Kimberly S. Varner. (C). 1999. pap. 25.00 (*1-57754-011-5*) Assn Am Med Coll.

Medical School Admission Success. Stanley Zaslau. Ed. by Paul L. McGrath. 182p. 1995. pap. text 26.00 (*1-886468-04-4*) FMSG.

Medical School Admissions: The Insider's Guide. 5th rev. ed. John A. Zebala et al. LC 99-23877. 192p. 1999. pap. 14.95 (*0-914457-94-2*, Pub. by Mustang Pub) Natl Bk Netwk.

Medical School Admissions Advisor. rev. ed. Kaplan. (Illus.). 272p. 1998. pap. 20.00 (*0-684-84979-8*) S&S Trade.

Medical School Companion. Mary M. Ross-Dolen. LC 96-202427. (Princeton Review Ser.). 1996. pap. 15.00 (*0-679-76462-3*) Villard Books.

Medical School Dean: Reflections & Directions. D. Kay Clawson & Emery A. Wilson. LC 99-60111. (Illus.). 256p. 1999. 21.95 (*0-913383-63-5*) McClanahan Pub.

***Medical School Financing & Research: Problems & Policy Options.** R. Glenn Hubbard. LC 99-170950. (Studies in Policy Reform). v, 23 p. 1998. pap. 9.95 (*0-8447-7120-1*, AEI Pr) Am Enterprise.

Medical School Interview. Randall Zielinski. 18p. 1984. pap. 2.00 (*0-911899-00-6*) NAAHP Inc.

Medical School Is Born: A History of the Conception, Gestation & Infancy of the University of Kentucky College of Medicine. Robert Strauss. LC 96-77768. (Illus.). 224p. (C). 1996. 18.95 (*0-913383-48-1*) McClanahan Pub.

Medical School Manual: A Practical Guide to Admission to American Medical Schools. Mike Mager. 100p. (Orig.). (C). 1996. pap. 9.95 (*1-889793-06-X*) Spencer Bks.

Medical Schools - Activities, Trends & Progress: Index of New Information with Authors, Subjects & Bibliography. Norbert G. Alden. 180p. 1993. 47.50 (*1-55914-804-7*); pap. 44.50 (*1-55914-805-5*) ABBE Pubs Assn.

Medical School's Mission & the Population's Health: Medical Education in Canada, the United Kingdom, the United States, & Australia. Ed. by K. L. White & J. E. Connelly. LC 96-. (Illus.). xi, 281p. 1992. 79.00 (*0-387-97733-3*) Spr-Verlag.

Medical Science & Democratic Truth: Doctors & Revolution in Nepal. Vincanne Adams. LC 97-18016. (Studies in Medical Anthropology: No. 6). (Illus.). 264p. (C). 1998. text 64.95 (*0-521-58486-8*); pap. text 24.95 (*0-521-58548-1*) Cambridge U Pr.

Medical Science & Medical Industry: The Formation of the American Pharmaceutical Industry. Jonathan Liebenau. LC 86-27346. 217p. 1987. reprint ed. pap. 67.30 (*0-608-07329-6*, 206755700009) Bks Demand.

Medical Science Applies to Crime Mystery: Index of New Information. rev. ed. Henry H. Hetterman. 163p. 1997. 47.50 (*0-7883-1158-1*); pap. 44.50 (*0-7883-1159-X*) ABBE Pubs Assn.

Medical Science under Dictatorship. Leo Alexander. 32p. (Orig.). 1996. pap. 4.00 (*0-930429-03-6*) Bibliographic Pr.

Medical Sciences Knowledge Profile Examination (MSKP) Jack Rudman. (Admission Test Ser.: Vol. 86). 89.95 (*0-8373-5186-3*) Nat Learn.

Medical Sciences Knowledge Profile Examination (MSKP) Jack Rudman. (Admission Test Ser.: ATS-86). 1994. pap. 69.95 (*0-8373-5086-7*) Nat Learn.

***Medical Sciences 1998.** Ed. by James G. Anderson & Meyer Katzper. 201p. 1998. 40.00 (*1-56555-138-9*) Soc Computer Sim.

Medical Scientists Research on War & Wars in Active, Passive & Historic Military Operations: Index of New Information with Authors, Subjects & References. Zane L. Rimbach. 150p. 1996. 47.50 (*0-7883-0810-6*); pap. 44.50 (*0-7883-0811-4*) ABBE Pubs Assn.

Medical Screening & the Employee Health Cost Crisis. Mark A. Rothstein. LC 89-977. 315p. 1989. reprint ed. pap. 97.70 (*0-608-00698-X*, 206147000009) Bks Demand.

Medical Screening of Workers. Mark A. Rothstein. LC 83-25198. 297p. 1984. reprint ed. pap. 92.10 (*0-608-00699-8*, 206147100009) Bks Demand.

Medical Secretary: Pediatrics Association. 2nd ed. Humphrey. (KM - Office Procedures Ser.). 1988. pap. 19.50 (*0-538-25870-5*) S-W Pub.

Medical Secretary & Receptionists. 6th ed. Michael Drury. 1998. pap. text 21.00 (*0-7020-1643-8*) Harcourt.

Medical Secretary's & Assistant's Encyclopedic Dictionary. Leonard Karlin & Muriel S. Karlin. 241p. 1983. 19.95 (*0-13-572909-2*) P-H.

Medical Secretary's Handbook. Green. (C). 1998. pap. text 25.00 (*0-7020-2103-2*, W B Saunders Co) Harcrt Hlth Sci Grp.

Medical Secretary's Standard Reference Handbook. Helen N. Saputo & Nancy G. Rutherford. 256p. 1980. 18.50 (*0-686-47897-5*) P-H.

Medical Secrets: Questions You Will Be Asked on Rounds, in the Clinic, on Oral Exams. 2nd rev. ed. Ed. by Anthony J. Zollo, Jr. LC 96-47625. (Secrets Ser.). (Illus.). 600p. 1996. pap. text 39.00 (*1-56053-172-X*) Hanley & Belfus.

Medical Secrets: Spanish Edition. Anthony J. Zollo. (SPA.). 1993. 78.75 (*0-8016-7212-0*) Mosby Inc.

***Medical Sector in Brazil: A Strategic Entry Report, 1998.** Compiled by Icon Group International Staff. (Country Industry Report). (Illus.). 163p. 1999. ring bd. 1630.00 incl. audio compact disk (*0-7418-0260-0*) Icon Grp.

Medical Selection of Life Risks. 4th rev. ed. Ed. by R. D. Brackenridge & W. John Elder. 922p. 1998. 195.00 (*1-56159-196-3*) Groves Dictionaries.

Medical Self-Care & Assessment. Brent Q. Hafen et al. (Illus.). 400p. 1983. pap. 11.95 (*0-685-06832-3*, Scribners Ref) Mac Lib Ref.

Medical Semiotics. Eugen Baer. Ed. by John Deely & Brooke Williams. (Sources in Semiotics Ser.: Vol. VII). (Illus.). 434p. (Orig.). (C). 1988. lib. bdg. 62.50 (*0-8191-6705-3*) U Pr of Amer.

Medical Series. C. Richard Harper & H. Stacy Vereen. Ed. by Becky Dean et al. 24p. 1998. reprint ed. pap. 7.95 (*1-891726-15-3*) Aviation Info.

Medical Services: Casualties & Medical Statistics. T. J. Smith. (Great War Ser.: Vol. 58). (Illus.). 402p. 1997. reprint ed. 49.95 (*0-89839-263-2*) Battery Pr.

Medical Services Administration - Puerto Rico Admin Code see Reglamentos del Estado Libre Asociado de Puerto Rico, Vol. 24, Administracion de Servicios Medicos

Medical Services & the Hospital in Britain, 1860-1939. Steven Cherry. (New Studies in Economic & Social History: No. 28). 100p. (C). 1996. text 34.95 (*0-521-57126-X*) Cambridge U Pr.

Medical Services & the Hospital in Britain, 1860-1939. Steven Cherry. (New Studies in Economic & Social History: No. 28). 200p. (C). 1996. pap. text 10.95 (*0-521-57784-5*) Cambridge U Pr.

Medical Services Market: Increasing Cost Constraints Put 20 Billion Dollar Business Up for Grabs. Market Intelligence Staff. 379p. (Orig.). 1992. 1295.00 (*1-56753-036-2*) Frost & Sullivan.

Medical Services Specialist. Jack Rudman. (Career Examination Ser.: C-2746). 1994. pap. 34.95 (*0-8373-2746-6*) Nat Learn.

Medical Side of Benjamin Franklin. William Pepper. (Illus.). 137p. 1970. reprint ed. 15.00 (*0-87266-039-7*) Argosy.

Medical Sign Language: Easily Understood Definitions of Commonly Used Medical, Dental & First Aid Terms. W. Joseph Garcia. (Illus.). 726p. 1983. 102.95 (*0-398-04805-3*); pap. 78.95 (*0-398-04806-1*) C C Thomas.

Medical Simulation for Word Processing. 1988. text 15.40 (*0-13-573015-5*, Macmillan Coll) P-H.

Medical Skills of Ancient Egypt. J. Worth Estes. LC 89-6004. 1989. 16.95 (*0-88135-093-1*); pap. 10.95 (*0-88135-099-0*) Watson Pub Intl.

Medical Skills of Ancient Egypt. rev. ed. J. Worth Estes. LC 93-16127. (Illus.). xv, 198p. 1993. pap. 15.95 (*0-88135-178-4*, Sci Hist) Watson Pub Intl.

Medical Social Work: The Pre-Professional Paradox. Toba S. Kerson. LC 80-23646. 320p. 1981. text 32.50 (*0-8290-0237-5*); pap. text 14.95 (*0-685-05822-0*) Irvington.

Medical Social Work Assistant. Jack Rudman. (Career Examination Ser.: C-3168). 1994. pap. 27.95 (*0-8373-3168-4*) Nat Learn.

Medical Social Work Coordinator. Jack Rudman. (Career Examination Ser.: C-2578). 1994. pap. 34.95 (*0-8373-2578-1*) Nat Learn.

Medical Social Worker. Jack Rudman. (Career Examination Ser.: C-521). 1994. pap. 29.95 (*0-8373-0521-7*) Nat Learn.

Medical Society of Copenhagen, 1772-1972. J. Genner. (Acta Historica Scientarium Ser.: No. 27). 345p. (Orig.). 1972. pap. 30.00 (*87-7492-066-9*, Pub. by Odense Universitets Forlag) Coronet Bks.

Medical Sociologists at Work. Ed. by Ray H. Elling & M. Sokolowska. LC 76-6204. 347p. 1977. text 39.95 (*0-87855-139-5*) Transaction Pubs.

Medical Sociology. 7th ed. William C. Cockerham. LC 97-6934. 395p. 1997. 57.00 (*0-13-269556-1*) P-H.

Medical Sociology: A Comparative Perspective. Duane A. Matcha. LC 99-13142. 420p. (C). 1999. 57.00 (*0-205-26309-7*) Allyn.

Medical Solution to the Health Care Crisis. Julian Lieb. 129p. 1993. pap. 19.50 (*0-87527-512-5*) Green.

Medical Sonography Clinical Manual. 3rd rev. ed. Lynn Ross & Robert J. Parelli. 210p. (C). 1998. 47.00 (*1-880359-17-0*) Par Rad.

Medical Spanish. (Made Easy Ser.). 1997. pap. 9.99 (*0-9657083-0-6*) A B Anup.

Medical Spanish. Teresa Gonzalez-Lee & Harold J. Simon. LC 89-70896. (SPA.). 256p. (C). 1990. pap. text 68.00 (*0-13-572512-7*) P-H.

Medical Spanish. 2nd ed. Gail L. Bongiovanni & Ariel D. Teitel. 1991. pap. 18.95 (*0-07-064489-6*) McGraw.

***Medical Spanish.** 3rd ed. Bongiovanni. (SPA.). 176p. 1999. pap. 24.95 (*0-07-134550-7*) McGraw.

Medical Spanish: A Conversational Approach. 2nd ed. John Kearon. (C). 1999. text Price not set. (*0-03-026029-9*) Harcourt Coll Pubs.

Medical Spanish: An Instant Translator. Isam Nasr & Marco Cordero. (SPA., Illus.). 394p. 1996. pap. text 20.95 (*0-7216-6052-5*, W B Saunders Co) Harcrt Hlth Sci Grp.

Medical Spanish: Conversational Approach. Maria A. Kearon & Thomas P. Kearon. 256p. (C). 1981. pap. text 38.00 (*0-15-557880-4*) Harcourt Coll Pubs.

Medical Spanish: The Instant Survival Guide. 3rd ed. Cynthia J. Wilber & Susan Lister. 403p. 1995. spiral bd. 37.50 (*0-7506-9597-8*, Focal) Buttrwrth-Heinemann.

Medical Spanish in Pediatrics: An Instant Translator. Isam Nasr & Marco Cordero. 380p. Date not set. pap. text. write for info. (*0-7216-8447-5*, W B Saunders Co) Harcrt Hlth Sci Grp.

***Medical Spanish Made Incredibly Easy.** Lisa A. Atchley. LC 00-33880. 2000. write for info. (*1-58255-040-9*) Springhouse Corp.

***Medical Spanish Made Ridiculously Simple.** rev. ed. Trudy Espinoza-Abrams. 106p. 2000. pap. text 12.95 (*0-940780-45-3*) MedMaster.

Medical Specialist. Jack Rudman. (Career Examination Ser.: C-1965). 1994. reprint ed. pap. 39.95 (*0-8373-1965-X*) Nat Learn.

Medical Specialist, 2 vols., Set. 1992. lib. bdg. 2995.95 (*0-8490-8874-7*) Gordon Pr.

Medical Specialist, 6 vols., Set. 1995. lib. bdg. 5005.99 (*0-8490-6652-2*) Gordon Pr.

Medical Speciality Selector: A Medical Speciality Referral Guide. Presley Reed. 200p. (Orig.). 1996. pap. text 65.00 (*1-889010-00-6*) Reed Grp Ltd.

Medical Specialization in Relation to Health Needs. 67p. 1985. pap. 8.00 (*92-890-1035-5*, 1340023) World Health.

Medical Speech Language Pathology. Alex F. Johnson & Barbara Jacobson. LC 97-41324. (Illus.). 672p. 1997. 79.00 (*0-86577-688-1*) Thieme Med Pubs.

Medical Speech-Language Pathology: A Practitioner's Guide. Alex F. Johnson & Barbara H. Jacobson. LC 97-41324. 1997. 75.00 (*3-13-110531-3*) Thieme Med Pubs.

Medical Staff: Legal Issues. Ed. by Michael M. Biehl & Cathleen S. Biehl. 136p. 1990. 30.00 (*0-918945-07-0*) Am Hlth Lawyers.

Medical Staff Credentialing: A Practical Guide. Fay A. Rozovsky et al. LC 93-33354. (Illus.). 132p. 1993. pap. 49.00 (*1-55648-112-8*, 145102) AHPI.

***Medical Staff Handbook: A Guide to Joint Commission Standards.** Joint Commission on Accreditation of Healthcare Organizations. (Illus.). 211p. 1999. pap. 50.00 (*0-86688-536-6*, MS-500) Joint Comm Hlthcare.

Medical Staff Leaders Practical Guide. 3rd rev. ed. Richard E. Thompson. 200p. 1995. pap. text 97.00 (*1-885829-28-0*) Opus Communs.

Medical Staff Management Forms, Policies, & Procedures for Health Care Providers. Ed. by Christine Mobley & Sheryl Deutsch. LC 94-49233. ring bd. 189.00 (*0-8342-0539-4*) Aspen Pub.

Medical Staff Peer Review: A Strategy for Motivation & Performance. Daniel A. Lang. LC 90-14532. 146p. (Orig.). 1991. pap. 42.50 (*1-55648-065-2*, 145157) AHPI.

Medical Staff Peer Review: Motivation & Performance in the Era of Managed Care. rev. ed. Daniel L. Langford. LC 99-16654. 1999. pap. 35.00 (*1-55648-266-3*) AHPI.

Medical Staff Privileges. Lewis M. Levin. Ed. by Melanie C. Karaffa. 220p. (C). 1992. text 49.95 (*1-878487-36-1*, ME046) Practice Mgmt Info.

Medical Staff Privileges & Peer Review: A Legal Guide for Healthcare Professionals. Jonathan P. Tomes. 304p. (C). 1994. text 60.00 (*1-55738-603-X*, Irwn Prfssnl) McGraw-Hill Prof.

***Medical Statistics: A Commonsense Approach.** 3rd ed. Campbell. LC 99-13004. 218p. 1999. pap. 34.95 (*0-471-98721-2*) Wiley.

***Medical Statistics at a Glance.** Avid Petrie & Caroline Sabin. LC 99-47123. (At a Glance Ser.). (Illus.). 136p. (C). 2000. pap. 21.95 (*0-632-05075-6*) Blackwell Sci.

Medical Statistics from Graunt to Farr: Proceedings of the Royal College of Physicians of London, February, 1943. Royal College of Physicians of London Staff & Major Greenwood. Ed. by Barbara G. Rosenkrantz. LC 76-25665. (Public Health in America Ser.). (Illus.). 1977. reprint ed. lib. bdg. 17.95 (*0-405-09820-0*) Ayer.

Medical Statistics on Microcomputers. R. A. Brown & J. Swanson Beck. 103p. 1990. pap. text 26.00 (*0-7279-0290-3*, Pub. by BMJ Pub) Login Brothers Bk Co.

Medical Statistics on Personal Computers. 2nd ed. Ed. by R. A. Brown & J. Swanson Beck. 160p. 1994. pap. text 21.00 (*0-7279-0771-9*, Pub. by BMJ Pub) Login Brothers Bk Co.

Medical Stenographer. Jack Rudman. (Career Examination Ser.: C-1368). 1994. pap. 23.95 (*0-8373-1368-6*) Nat Learn.

Medical Stewardship: Fulfilling the Hippocratic Legacy. Ed. by M. Oliver Kepler. LC 80-25457. 280p. 1981. 69.50 (*0-313-22489-7*, KMS/, Greenwood Pr) Greenwood.

Medical Student USMLE Pts. II & III: Pearls of Wisdom. Plantz et al. 1998. pap. 32.00 (*1-890369-10-1*) Boston Medical.

Medical Student's Desk Reference: 1999 Edition. large type ed. Ken Bookstein. 226p. (C). 1999. pap. 18.95 (*0-9660645-1-8*) Bookstein Pub.

Medical Student's Guide to Successful Residency Matching, 1994-1995. Lee T. Miller. (Illus.). 112p. 1994. 9.95 (*0-683-05996-3*) Lppncott W & W.

An Asterisk (*) at the beginning of an entry indicates that the title is appearing for the first time.

Medical Student's Guide to Top Board Scores. P. Thomas Rogers. (Illus.). 236p. (Orig.). (C). 1994. pap. text 24.95 (*0-9632231-0-0*) Innovat Pub & Graph.

Medical Student's Guide to Top Board Scores. 2nd ed. Peter T. Rogers. LC 95-34056. 146p. 1995. pap. text 15.95 (*0-316-75436-6*, Little Brwn Med Div) Lppncott W & W.

Medical Student's Pocket Reference. Ken Bookstein. vi, 259p. 1996. pap. text 10.95 (*0-9660645-0-X*) Bookstein Pub.

Medical Student's Pocket Reference: 1999 Edition. rev. ed. Ken Bookstein. 322p. 1999. pap. 12.50 (*0-9660645-2-6*) Bookstein Pub.

Medical Studies of Aggression: Index of New Information. American Health Research Institute Staff. 150p. 1996. 47.50 (*0-7883-0922-6*); pap. 44.50 (*0-7883-0923-4*) ABBE Pubs Assn.

Medical Studies of Gunshot Wounds: Index of New Information with Authors, Subjects & References. American Health Research Institute Staff. 150p. 1996. 47.50 (*0-7883-0926-9*); pap. 44.50 (*0-7883-0927-7*) ABBE Pubs Assn.

Medical Studies of Hallucinogens: Index of Modern Authors & Subjects with Guide for Rapid Research. rev. ed. Salvatore A. Velazo. LC 94-24710. 139p. 1994. 47.50 (*0-7883-0452-6*); pap. 44.50 (*0-7883-0453-4*) ABBE Pubs Assn.

Medical Studies of Human Cadavers - Normal & Diseased: Index of New Information. American Health Research Institute Staff. 150p. 1996. 47.50 (*0-7883-0978-1*); pap. 44.50 (*0-7883-0979-X*) ABBE Pubs Assn.

Medical Studies of Polygraphs & Other Lie Detectors: Index of Modern Authors & Subjects with Guide for Rapid Research. rev. ed. Science & Life Consultants Association Staff. 193p. 1997. 47.50 (*0-7883-0944-7*); pap. 44.50 (*0-7883-0945-5*) ABBE Pubs Assn.

Medical Studies of Saliva: Index of Modern Authors & Subjects with Guide for Rapid Research. Larsen K. Lozzi. LC 90-56295. 160p. 1991. 47.50 (*1-55914-366-5*); pap. 44.50 (*1-55914-367-3*) ABBE Pubs Assn.

Medical Studies of Violence: Index of New Information. American Health Research Institute Staff. 150p. 1996. 47.50 (*0-7883-0920-X*); pap. 44.50 (*0-7883-0921-8*) ABBE Pubs Assn.

Medical Style & Format: An International Manual for Authors, Editors, & Publishers. Edward J. Huth. 355p. 1989. 31.95 (*0-683-04273-4*) Lppncott W & W.

Medical Subject Analysis of a Selected Bibliography Concerning General Counseling. rev. ed. American Health Research Institute Staff. Ed. by John C. Bartone. LC 94-34597. 161p. 1994. 47.50 (*0-7883-0238-8*); pap. 44.50 (*0-7883-0239-6*) ABBE Pubs Assn.

Medical Supervision in Radiation Work. (Technical Report Ser.). 31p. 1960. pap. text 3.00 (*92-4-120196-7*) World Health.

Medical Supply Management after Natural Disaster. (Technical Publications: Vol. 443). 1983. 8.00 (*92-75-11438-2*) PAHO.

Medical Supply Supervisor. Jack Rudman. (Career Examination Ser.: C-3106). 1994. pap. 29.95 (*0-8373-3106-4*) Nat Learn.

Medical Supply Technician. Jack Rudman. (Career Examination Ser.: C-3353). 1994. pap. 27.95 (*0-8373-3353-9*) Nat Learn.

Medical Support: Army Air Forces in World War II. Mae M. Link & Hubert A. Coleman. 1027p. 1992. pap. text. write for info. (*0-912799-69-2*) AFH & MP.

Medical Support in Divisions, Separate Brigades, & Armored Cavalry Regiment. 1995. lib. bdg. 258.99 (*0-8490-6651-4*) Gordon Pr.

Medical, Surgical & Anesthetic Nursing for Veterinary Technicians. 2nd ed. Ed. by P. W. Pratt. LC 94-70822. 621p. 1994. 32.00 (*0-939674-49-1*) Am Vet Pubns.

Medical-Surgical Care Planning. 3rd ed. Holloway. LC 98-17557. 928p. 1998. 39.95 (*0-87434-925-7*) Springhouse Corp.

Medical-Surgical Nurse. Jack Rudman. (Certified Nurse Examination Ser.: CN-11). 1994. pap. 23.95 (*0-8373-6111-7*) Nat Learn.

Medical-Surgical Nursing. Keegan. (Nursing Education Ser.). 1998. teacher ed. 51.50 (*0-8273-7204-3*); student ed. 16.00 (*0-8273-7205-1*); text 65.95 (*0-8273-7203-5*) Delmar.

Medical Surgical Nursing. Reeves. 1998. 37.00 (*0-07-134657-0*) McGraw.

Medical-Surgical Nursing. Charlene Reeves et al. LC 98-20549. (Nursing Core Ser.). (Illus.). 750p. 1999. pap. text 37.00 (*0-07-105480-4*) McGraw-Hill HPD.

Medical-Surgical Nursing. Paulette D. Rollant & Deborah A. Ennis. LC 95-24828. (Mosby's Review Ser.). (Illus.). 544p. (C). (gr. 13). 1995. pap. text 24.95 incl. disk, 3.5 hd (*0-8151-7249-4*, 24862) Mosby Inc.

Medical-Surgical Nursing. Jack Rudman. (Regents College Proficiency Examination Ser.: CPEP-24). 1994. pap. 23.95 (*0-8373-5424-2*) Nat Learn.

Medical-Surgical Nursing. Jack Rudman. (College Level Examination Ser.: CLEP-37). 1994. pap. 23.95 (*0-8373-5337-8*) Nat Learn.

Medical-Surgical Nursing. Marilyn S. Sommers. LC 91-4836. (Nursetest: A Review Ser.). 320p. 1991. pap. 21.95 (*0-87434-303-8*) Springhouse Corp.

*__Medical Surgical Nursing.__ Wilson. (C). 2002. pap. 18.00 (*0-7668-1381-9*); pap. 20.25 (*0-7668-1382-7*) Delmar.

Medical-Surgical Nursing. Susan Wilson & Steward Brown. 2002. pap. 58.50 (*0-7668-1378-9*) Delmar.

Medical Surgical Nursing. 2nd ed. Ed. by Ray A. Hargrove-Huttel. (Lippincott's Review Ser.). 816p. 1996. pap. text 23.95 (*0-397-55212-2*) Lppncott W & W.

Medical-Surgical Nursing. 2nd ed. Ignatavici. (C). 1994. pap. text, student ed. 17.95 (*0-7216-4865-7*) Harcourt.

Medical-Surgical Nursing. 2nd ed. Donna D. Ignatavici. 1994. 76.00 (*0-7216-5908-X*, W B Saunders Co) Harcrt Hlth Sci Grp.

Medical-Surgical Nursing. 2nd ed. Frances D. Monahan. (C). 1998. pap. text 75.00 (*0-7216-8137-9*, W B Saunders Co) Harcrt Hlth Sci Grp.

*__Medical-Surgical Nursing.__ 2nd ed. Springhouse Corporation Staff. LC 99-23705. 1999. pap. 24.95 (*1-58255-003-4*) Springhouse Corp.

Medical-Surgical Nursing. 2nd rev. ed. Audree Reynolds. (Outline Ser.). 275p. (C). 1998. per. 23.95 (*1-56930-068-2*) Skidmore Roth Pub.

Medical-Surgical Nursing. 3rd ed. Mildred Boyd & Barbara Tower. LC 96-29017. (Springhouse Notes Ser.). (Illus.). 416p. 1996. 22.95 incl. disk (*0-87434-861-7*) Springhouse Corp.

Medical-Surgical Nursing. 3rd ed. Barbara C. Long. 1992. 78.00 (*0-8016-7416-6*) Mosby Inc.

Medical-Surgical Nursing, 2 vols. 5th ed. Black. 1997. text 82.00 (*0-7216-7484-4*) Harcourt.

*__Medical-Surgical Nursing.__ 6th ed. Carol J. Green & Penny L. Marshall. 1998. student ed. write for info. (*0-323-00311-7*) Mosby Inc.

Medical-Surgical Nursing: A Nursing Process Approach. 2nd ed. Ed. by Donna D. Ignatavicius et al. (Illus.). 1995. write for info. (*0-7216-4866-5*, W B Saunders Co); teacher ed. write for info. (*0-7216-4864-9*, W B Saunders Co) Harcrt Hlth Sci Grp.

Medical-Surgical Nursing: A Nursing Process Approach. 2nd ed. Donna D. Ignatavicius et al. LC 94-14942. (Illus.). 2490p. 1994. text 74.00 (*0-7216-4863-0*, W B Saunders Co) Harcrt Hlth Sci Grp.

Medical-Surgical Nursing: A Nursing Process Approach. 3rd ed. Barbara C. Long et al. (Illus.). 1728p. (C). (gr. 13). 1992. text 72.00 (*0-8016-6672-4*, 06672) Mosby Inc.

Medical-Surgical Nursing: A Nursing Process Approach. 3rd ed. Barbara C. Long et al. (Illus.). 1728p. 1993. teacher ed. write for info. (*0-8151-4282-X*) Mosby Inc.

Medical Surgical Nursing: Assessment & Management of Clinical Problems. 4th ed. Sharon Lewis. 368p. 1996. student ed. write for info. (*0-8151-5524-7*) Mosby Inc.

Medical-Surgical Nursing: Assessment & Management of Clinical Problems. 4th ed. Ed. by Sharon M. Lewis et al. LC 95-30732. (Illus.). 2176p. (C). (gr. 13). 1995. text 75.00 (*0-8151-5301-5*, 24617) Mosby Inc.

Medical-Surgical Nursing: Assessment & Management of Clinical Problems. 4th ed. Sharon M. Lewis et al. student ed. write for info. (*0-8151-5299-X*) Mosby Inc.

Medical-Surgical Nursing: Assessment & Management of Clinical Problems, 2 vols. 4th ed. Sharon M. Lewis et al. (Illus.). 2176p. (C). (gr. 13). 1996. text 81.00 (*0-8151-5373-2*, 28963) Mosby Inc.

*__Medical-Surgical Nursing: Assessment & Management of Clinical Problems.__ 5th ed. Sharon M. Lewis et al. LC 99-23884. (Illus.). 2176p. (C). 1999. text 76.00 (*1-55664-430-2*) Mosby Inc.

*__Medical Surgical Nursing: Assessment & Management of Clinical Problems.__ 5th ed. Sharon M. Lewis et al. (Illus.). (C). 1999. student ed. write for info. (*0-323-00258-7*) Mosby Inc.

Medical-Surgical Nursing: Assessment & Management of Clinical Problems: Skidmore Drug Guide Package, 2 vols. 4th ed. Sharon Lewis et al. 1996. write for info. (*0-323-00496-2*) Mosby Inc.

Medical-Surgical Nursing: Assessment & Management of Clinical Problems: Text & Skidmore Drug Guide Package. 4th ed. Sharon Lewis et al. (Illus.). 1996. write for info. (*0-323-00495-4*) Mosby Inc.

Medical-Surgical Nursing: Clinical Management for Continuity of Care. 5th ed. Joyce M. Black & Esther Matassarin-Jacobs. (Illus.). 1997. teacher ed. write for info. (*0-7216-6400-8*, W B Saunders Co) Harcrt Hlth Sci Grp.

Medical-Surgical Nursing: Clinical Management for Continuity of Care. 5th ed. Joyce M. Black & Esther Matassarin-Jacobs. Ed. by Thomas Eoyang. LC 96-7419. (Illus.). 2395p. 1997. text 75.00 (*0-7216-6399-0*, W B Saunders Co) Harcrt Hlth Sci Grp.

Medical-Surgical Nursing: Clinical Management for Continuity of Care. 5th ed. Joyce M. Black & Esther Matassarin-Jacobs. (Illus.). 1997. pap. text, student ed. 18.95 (*0-7216-6950-6*, W B Saunders Co) Harcrt Hlth Sci Grp.

Medical-Surgical Nursing: Clinical Management for Continuity of Care, Pocket Companion by Sorrentino & Chunka. 5th ed. Joyce M. Black & Esther Matassarin-Jacobs. (Illus.). 800p. 1997. pap. text 23.00 (*0-7216-7287-6*, W B Saunders Co) Harcrt Hlth Sci Grp.

Medical-Surgical Nursing: Clinical Management for Continuity of Care, Test Manual. 5th ed. Joyce M. Black & Esther Matassarin-Jacobs. (Illus.). 2399p. 1997. write for info. (*0-7216-7086-5*, W B Saunders Co) Harcrt Hlth Sci Grp.

Medical-Surgical Nursing: Concepts, & Clinical Practice. 5th ed. Wilma J. Phipps et al. (Illus.). student ed. write for info. (*0-8016-8131-6*) Mosby Inc.

*__Medical-Surgical Nursing: Concepts & Clinical Practice, Includes Testbank.__ 6th ed. Wilma J. Phipps et al. (Illus.). 2336p. 1998. teacher ed. write for info. (*0-323-00527-6*) Mosby Inc.

*__Medical-Surgical Nursing: Concepts & Clinical Practice: Text-Skidmore Drug Guide Package.__ 6th ed. Wilma J. Phipps et al. (Illus.). 2336p. 1998. write for info. (*0-323-00740-6*) Mosby Inc.

Medical Surgical Nursing: Critical Thinking in Client Care. 2nd ed. Ed. by Priscilla LeMone & Karen M. Burke. LC 99-32955. 2170p. (C). 1999. student ed. 80.00 (*0-8053-8121-X*) Benjamin-Cummings.

Medical-Surgical Nursing: Critical Thinking in Medical-Surgical Settings. Lewis & Winningham. 1995. text 93.00 (*0-8151-9672-5*, 29185) Mosby Inc.

Medical-Surgical Nursing: Critical Thinking in Medical-Surgical Settings, 2 vols. Lewis & Winningham. 1996. text 99.00 (*0-8151-4496-2*, 30630) Mosby Inc.

Medical-Surgical Nursing: Diagnoses & Interventions. 2nd ed. Ed. by Pamela L. Swearingen. LC 95-42113. (Pocket Guide Ser.). 544p. (C). (gr. 13). 1995. pap. text 22.95 (*0-8151-8692-4*, 26103) Mosby Inc.

Medical-Surgical Nursing: Foundations for Clinical Practice. 2nd ed. Frances D. Monahan & Marianne Neighbors. Ed. by Barbara N. Cullen. LC 96-51069. (Illus.). 2000p. 1998. text 72.95 (*0-7216-7006-7*, W B Saunders Co) Harcrt Hlth Sci Grp.

Medical-Surgical Nursing: Foundations for Clinical Practice. 2nd ed. Ed. by Frances D. Monahan & Marianne Neighbors. (Illus.). 1998. teacher ed. write for info. (*0-7216-7007-5*, W B Saunders Co); pap. write for info. (*0-7216-7553-0*, W B Saunders Co) Harcrt Hlth Sci Grp.

Medical-Surgical Nursing: Total Patient Care. 9th ed. Gail Harkness & Judith R. Dincher. (Illus.). 1995. pap. text, wbk. ed. 19.95 (*0-8151-4183-1*) Mosby Inc.

Medical-Surgical Nursing: Total Patient Care. 9th ed. Gail Harkness & Judith R. Dincher. (Illus.). 1997. teacher ed. write for info. (*0-8151-4182-3*); student ed., wbk. ed. write for info. (*0-8151-4594-2*) Mosby Inc.

*__Medical Surgical Nursing: Total Patient Care.__ 10th ed. Gail A. Harkness & Judith R. Dincher. (Illus.). 391p. 1998. wbk. ed. write for info. (*0-323-00246-3*) Mosby Inc.

*__Medical Surgical Nursing: Total Patient Care.__ 10th ed. Gail A. Harkness & Judith R. Dincher. LC 98-46228. (Illus.). 1312p. (C). 1998. text 49.00 (*0-323-00247-1*) Mosby Inc.

*__Medical Surgical Nursing: Total Patient Care, Includes Testbank.__ 10th ed. Gail A. Harkness & Judith R. Dincher. (Illus.). 1312p. 1998. teacher ed. write for info. (*0-323-00245-5*) Mosby Inc.

Medical-Surgical Nursing: View Studies. 4th ed. Sharon M. Lewis. (C). (gr. 13). 1997. pap. text 150.00 (*0-8151-9523-0*, 29394) Mosby Inc.

Medical-Surgical Nursing No. 3: Student Learning Guide. 3rd ed. Barbara C. Long. 193p. 1992. pap. text, student ed. 14.95 (*0-8016-7417-4*) Mosby Inc.

Medical-Surgical Nursing Across the Health Care Continuum. 3rd ed. Donna D. Ignatavicius et al. Ed. by Robin Carter. LC 98-38329. (Illus.). 2205p. (C). 1998. text 76.00 (*0-7216-6981-6*, W B Saunders Co) Harcrt Hlth Sci Grp.

Medical-Surgical Nursing Care Planning Guides. 4th ed. Susan P. Ulrich et al. Ed. by Barbara N. Cullen. 880p. 1998. pap. text 39.95 (*0-7216-6031-2*, W B Saunders Co) Harcrt Hlth Sci Grp.

Medical-Surgical Nursing Care Plans. Barbara Engram. LC 92-49864. 814p. (C). 1993. mass mkt. 38.25 (*0-8273-3413-3*) Delmar.

Medical Surgical Nursing Care Plans. 3rd ed. Marie S. Jaffe. LC 95-4744. (Illus.). 456p. (C). 1995. pap. text 34.95 (*0-8385-6263-9*, A6263-6) Appleton & Lange.

Medical Surgical Nursing Clinical Handbook: Critical Thinking in Client Care. Susan Gauthier. 624p. (C). 1996. pap. text 27.19 (*0-8053-3522-6*) Addison-Wesley.

Medical Surgical Nursing CTB. Keegan. (Nursing Education Ser.). 1998. 52.50 (*0-8273-7206-X*) Delmar.

Medical Surgical Nursing Lab Manual. 3rd ed. Gloria Hankins. 336p. (C). 1993. pap. text 49.00 (*0-536-58369-2*) Pearson Custom.

Medical-Surgical Nursing Study Guide. Mary S. Nichols & Barbara W. Engam. (Illus.). 350p. 1987. pap. text 16.95 (*0-8016-3856-9*) Mosby Inc.

Medical-Surgical Policy & Procedure Guideline Manual. Diane I. Howery. 1991. student ed. 90.00 (*1-879575-15-9*) Acad Med Sys.

Medical-Surgical Psychiatry: Treating Psychiatric Aspects of Physical Disorders. Ed. by Troy L. Thompson, II. LC 87-646993. (New Directions for Mental Health Services Ser.: No. MHS 57). 142p. (Orig.). 1993. pap. 25.00 (*1-55542-694-8*) Jossey-Bass.

Medical-Surgical Supplies Market in Freestanding Outpatient Healthcare Delivery Centers. Ed. by Nal-Dutton Staff. (Marketing Research Reports). 1987. 1975.00 (*0-86621-863-7*, A1684) NAL.

Medical Surveillance for Hazardous Waste. Shirley Conibear. 1990. text. write for info. (*0-442-31901-0*, VNR) Wiley.

Medical Surveillance of Populations for Health & Disease with Global Watch for Transmission & Infections: Index of New Information. rev. ed. Lester B. Ramsey. 149p. 1997. 47.50 (*0-7883-1628-1*); pap. 44.50 (*0-7883-1629-X*) ABBE Pubs Assn.

Medical Surveillance Program. Mark M. Moran. (OSHA Written Compliance Programs Ser.: No. 19). (Illus.). 24p. 1992. ring bd. 169.00 (*1-890966-12-6*) Moran Assocs.

Medical Synonyms: Synonyme der Medizin. Martin E. Westarp & Hans P. Ditz. (GER.). 280p. 1983. 39.95 (*0-8288-1843-6*) Fr & Eur.

Medical Systems Analysis & Management: Subject Dictionary & Research Guidebook. Miyo M. Tanakara. LC 84-45742. 150p. 1987. 47.50 (*0-88164-262-2*); pap. 44.50 (*0-88164-263-0*) ABBE Pubs Assn.

Medical Systems 20506. NCCER Staff. 1997. pap. text 20.00 (*0-13-909904-2*, Prentice Hall); pap. text, teacher ed. 20.00 (*0-13-909912-3*, Prentice Hall) P-H.

Medical Talk & Medical Work: The Liturgy of the Clinic. Paul Atkinson. 192p. 1995. 69.95 (*0-8039-7730-1*); pap. 26.95 (*0-8039-7731-X*) Sage.

Medical Teaching in Ambulatory Care: A Practical Guide. Warren Rubenstein & Yves Talbot. LC 91-5183. (Medical Education Ser.: Vol. 15). 144p. 1992. 27.95 (*0-8261-7690-9*) Springer Pub.

Medical Tech see Careers in Focus Ser.

Medical Technical Assistant. Jack Rudman. (Career Examination Ser.: C-492). 1994. pap. 27.95 (*0-8373-0492-X*) Nat Learn.

*__Medical Technical Equipment in Germany: A Strategic Entry Report, 1995.__ Compiled by Icon Group International Staff. (Illus.). 92p. 1999. ring bd. 920.00 incl. audio compact disk (*0-7418-1612-1*) Icon Grp.

Medical Technical Terms. (C). 1982. write for info. (*0-8087-5836-5*) Pearson Custom.

Medical Technician. Jack Rudman. (Career Examination Ser.: C-512). 1994. pap. 29.95 (*0-8373-0512-8*) Nat Learn.

Medical Technician Instructor. Jack Rudman. (Career Examination Ser.: C-1370). 1994. pap. 39.95 (*0-8373-1370-8*) Nat Learn.

Medical Technician Trainee. Jack Rudman. (Career Examination Ser.: C-1371). 1994. pap. 27.95 (*0-8373-1371-6*) Nat Learn.

Medical Technologies & the Science of Progress: Index of New Information with Authors, Subjects, Research Categories & References. Science & Life Consultants Association Staff. 170p. 1997. 47.50 (*0-7883-1446-7*); pap. 44.50 (*0-7883-1447-5*) ABBE Pubs Assn.

Medical Technologist. Jack Rudman. (Career Examination Ser.: C-493). 1994. pap. 29.95 (*0-8373-0493-8*) Nat Learn.

Medical Technology. annot. ed. Lisa Yount. LC 97-17679. (Milestones in Discovery & Invention Ser.). (Illus.). 160p. (gr. 7 up). 1998. 19.95 (*0-8160-3568-7*) Facts on File.

Medical Technology: A Nursing Perspective. D. W. Hill & R. Summers. LC 93-40111. 204p. 1993. pap. 44.75 (*1-56593-229-3*, 0562) Singular Publishing.

Medical Technology: For Some Cardiac Pacemaker Leads, the Public Health Risks Are Still High. 52p. (Orig.). (C). 1993. pap. text 25.00 (*1-56806-907-3*) DIANE Pub.

Medical Technology: Inventing the Instruments. Robert Mulcahy. LC 96-4939. (Innovators Ser.). (Illus.). 144p. (YA). (gr. 5-12). 1997. lib. bdg. 19.95 (*1-881508-34-X*) Oliver Pr MN.

Medical Technology: Quality Assurance Needs Stronger Management Emphasis & Higher Priority. (Illus.). 100p. (Orig.). (C). 1993. pap. text 30.00 (*1-56806-330-X*) DIANE Pub.

Medical Technology & Society: An Interdisciplinary Perspective. Joseph Bronzino & Vincent K. Smith. (Sloan NLA Ser.). (Illus.). 580p. 1990. 50.00 (*0-262-02300-8*) MIT Pr.

Medical Technology & Society: An Interdisciplinary Perspective. Vincent H. Smith & Joseph D. Bronzino. 1990. pap. text 25.00 (*0-262-52154-7*) MIT Pr.

Medical Technology & the Cost of the Medicare Program. 1992. lib. bdg. 288.00 (*0-8490-5478-8*) Gordon Pr.

Medical Technology Assessment: A Model for Informed Decision Making. rev. ed. Kathleen R. Ciccone & Thomas J. Chesnut. 100p. 1992. student ed. 100.00 (*0-915963-09-4*) Bader Assoc Inc.

Medical Technology Assessment Directory. Institute of Medicine Staff. 712p. 1988. text 250.00 (*0-309-03829-4*) Natl Acad Pr.

Medical Technology Board Examination Review Vol. 2: Questions & Answers. 8th rev. ed. Ed. by James I. Mangels et al. (Illus.). 550p. 1996. text 38.00 (*0-910224-19-6*) Berkeley Sci.

Medical Technology, Ethics & Economics. Joseph Bronzino et al. (C). 1990. text 46.00 (*0-07-008002-X*) McGraw.

Medical Technology Examination Review. Ali A. Hossaini et al. LC 78-1743. (Arco Medical Review Ser.). 1978. pap. text 12.00 (*0-668-04365-2*, Arco) Macmillan Gen Ref.

Medical Technology for the Neonate. (Illus.). 119p. 1984. pap. text 30.00 (*0-910275-39-4*, TAR9-209) Assn Adv Med Instrn.

Medical Technology, Health Care, & the Consumer. Ed. by Allen D. Spiegel et al. LC 79-25559. 352p. 1981. 45.95 (*0-87705-498-3*, Kluwer Acad Hman Sci) Kluwer Academic.

Medical Term. Fremgen. 463p. 1997. pap. 51.00 (*0-8359-5274-6*) P-H.

Medical Terminology. Robert C. Anderson. 52p. (C). 1992. 13.95 incl. audio (*0-9634298-3-3*) Cricket Sci.

Medical Terminology. Cohen. 592p. 1993. 27.50 (*0-685-74492-2*) Lppncott W & W.

Medical Terminology. Nancy Scanlon. (C). 1988. pap. 17.80 (*0-13-572785-5*) P-H.

Medical Terminology. Peggy S. Stanfield. 560p. (Orig.). 1990. pap. 36.25 (*0-86720-409-5*) Jones & Bartlett.

*__Medical Terminology.__ 3rd ed. (C). 1998. 44.00 (*0-8087-9627-5*) Pearson Custom.

Medical Terminology. 4th ed. J. Patrick Fisher. 1993. pap. 20.00 (*0-02-800875-8*); teacher ed. write for info. (*0-02-800876-6*); audio. write for info. (*0-02-800877-4*) Macmillan.

Medical Terminology. 6th ed. Genevieve L. Smith et al. 1991. text 35.75 (*0-8273-4563-1*) Delmar.

Medical Terminology: A Programmed Approach. 7th ed. Genevieve L. Smith et al. LC 80-17970. (Illus.). 512p. 1994. mass mkt. 36.75 (*0-8273-6304-4*) Delmar.

Medical Terminology: A Programmed Systems Approach - IML. Smith & Davis. 176p. 1998. teacher ed. 24.95 (*0-7668-0065-2*) Delmar.

Medical Terminology: A Programmed Systems Approach Eight Editon. 8th ed. Genevieve L. Smith & Phyllis E. Davis. LC 98-24810. 560p. (C). 1998. 52.95 (*0-7668-0063-6*) Delmar.

Medical Terminology: A Programmed Systems Approach Text/Tape Package. 8th ed. Genevieve Love Smith et al. 560p. spiral bd. 63.95 (*0-7668-0117-9*, Pub. by Delmar) Thomson Learn.

M

An Asterisk (*) at the beginning of an entry indicates that the title is appearing for the first time.

M

Medical Terminology: A Programmed Text. 7th ed. Smith. (Medical Terminology Ser.). 1995. 64.95 incl. disk (*0-8273-6919-0*) Delmar.

Medical Terminology: A Programmed Text. 7th ed. Smith et al. 480p. (C). 1994. text, mass mkt. 44.75 incl. digital audio (*0-8273-6917-4*) Delmar.

Medical Terminology: A Programmed Text. 7th ed. Smith et al. (RT-Medical Terminolgy Ser.). 256p. (C). 1995. text, teacher ed. 20.00 (*0-8273-6918-2*) Delmar.

Medical Terminology: A Programmed Text, Testbank. 6th ed. Genevieve L. Smith et al. 1991. 64.95 (*0-8273-4567-4*) Delmar.

***Medical Terminology: A Self-Learning Text.** 3rd ed. Jacqueline J. Birmingham. 1999. teacher ed. write for info. (*0-323-00456-3*) Mosby Inc.

Medical Terminology: A Self-Learning Text. 3rd ed. Jacqueline J. Birmingham. LC 98-42213. 1999. pap. text 31.95 (*0-323-00406-7*) Mosby Inc.

Medical Terminology: A Short Course. Bruce A. Chabner. (Illus.). 240p. 1990. text 17.95 (*0-7216-2939-3*, W B Saunders Co) Harcrt Hlth Sci Grp.

Medical Terminology: A Short Course. Davi-Ellen Chabner. (Illus.). 238p. (C). 1991. pap. text, teacher ed. write for info. (*0-7216-3508-3*, W B Saunders Co) Harcrt Hlth Sci Grp.

***Medical Terminology: A Systems Approach.** Barbara A. Gylys & Mary E. Wedding. 416p. 1999. 31.95 incl. audio (*0-8036-0396-7*) Davis Co.

Medical Terminology: A Systems Approach. 4th ed. Barbara A. Gylys & Mary E. Wedding. 416p. 1999. 38.95 incl. cd-rom (*0-8036-0395-9*) Davis Co.

***Medical Terminology: A Systems Approach.** 4th ed. Barbara A. Gylys & Mary E. Wedding. LC 98-48638. 416p. 1999. 29.95 (*0-8036-0394-0*) Davis Co.

Medical Terminology: A Text/Workbook. 4th ed. Alice V. Prendergast et al. LC 96-35083. 416p. (C). 1996. pap., wbk. ed. 39.60 (*0-8053-9368-4*) Addison-Wesley.

Medical Terminology: Activities. Wistreich. 1993. teacher ed. 51.25 (*0-697-14743-6*, WCB McGr Hill) McGrw-H Hghr Educ.

Medical Terminology: An Illustrated Guide. Cohen. (Illus.). 396p. 1989. text 26.00 (*0-397-54716-1*) Lppncott W & W.

Medical Terminology: An Illustrated Guide. 3rd ed. Barbara Janson Cohen. LC 97-4344. 544p. 1997. spiral bd. 32.00 (*0-7817-1411-7*) Lppncott W & W.

Medical Terminology: Building a Vocabulary. Nancy N. Scanlan. (Medical Ser.). 123p. (C). 1988. pap. 12.95 (*0-935920-57-9*, Ntl Pubs Blck) P-H.

Medical Terminology: Building Blocks for Health Careers. Kinn. 1989. pap., teacher ed. 14.00 (*0-8273-3339-0*) Delmar.

Medical Terminology: Exercises in Etymology. 2nd ed. Charles W. Dunmore & Rita M. Fleischer. LC 85-4350. 305p. (C). 1985. pap. 29.95 (*0-8036-2946-X*) Davis Co.

Medical Terminology: Hsie. Smith. 1986. 13.00 (*0-12-650364-8*) Acad Pr.

Medical Terminology: Instructor's Activity & Resource Kit. 2nd ed. Ann Ehrlich. 221p. 1993. text, teacher ed. 32.95 (*0-8273-5563-7*) Delmar.

Medical Terminology: Instructor's Guide. Wistreich. 1993. teacher ed. 51.25 (*0-697-14243-4*, WCB McGr Hill) McGrw-H Hghr Educ.

Medical Terminology: Self-Directed Approach. Dale P. Layman. 1998. pap. 29.95 (*0-8273-5611-0*) Delmar.

Medical Terminology: Short Course. 2nd ed. Davi-Ellen Chabner. Ed. by Andrew Allan. LC 98-48477. (Illus.). 300p. (C). 1998. text 17.95 (*0-7216-8124-7*, W B Saunders Co) Harcrt Hlth Sci Grp.

Medical Terminology: The Language of Health Care. Margorie C. Willis. 533p. 1996. pap. 31.95 (*0-683-09055-0*) Lppncott W & W.

Medical Terminology App. Smith. 1986. bds. 39.00 (*0-12-650362-1*) Harcourt.

Medical Terminology Challenge. Gladys Pucillo. (Medical Terminology Ser.). 1995. 79.95 (*0-8273-7430-5*, VNR) Wiley.

Medical Terminology Coloring Workbook. (Illus.). (C). Date not set. pap. text. write for info. (*0-13-013934-3*) P-H.

Medical Terminology Companion Dictionary. George P. Andrews & Beverly L. Ritter. (Realtime Machine Shorthand Ser.). 69p. (C). 1992. pap. text 8.00 (*0-938643-29-0*) Stenotype Educ.

Medical Terminology Essentials: Instructor's guide. Alice G. Ettinger & Pamala F. Burch. 14.00 (*0-7638-0315-4*) EMC-Paradigm.

Medical Terminology Essentials: Text with CD Rom. Alice G. Ettinger & Pamala F. Burch. 26.95 (*0-7638-0303-0*) EMC-Paradigm.

Medical Terminology Flash Cards. Ann Ehrlich. 1993. text 18.95 (*0-8273-5562-9*) Delmar.

Medical Terminology for Health Careers. Alice G. Ettinger & Pamala F. Burch. LC 98-9864. 1998. write for info. (*0-7638-0093-7*) Paradigm MN.

Medical Terminology for Health Careers: Text with CD Rom & 4 Audiocassettes. Alice G. Etttinger & Pamala F. Burch. 59.95 incl. cd-rom (*0-7638-0201-8*) EMC-Paradigm.

Medical Terminology for Health Professional. Ehrlich. (Medical Terminology Ser.). 1988. 64.95 incl. 3.5 ld (*0-8273-3023-5*) Delmar.

Medical Terminology for Health Professionals. Ehrlich. (Medical Terminology Ser.). 1988. pap. 25.95 (*0-8273-3036-7*) Delmar.

Medical Terminology for Health Professionals. Ehrlich. (Medical Terminology Ser.). 1988. pap., teacher ed. 24.00 (*0-8273-3037-5*) Delmar.

Medical Terminology for Health Professionals. 3rd ed. Ehrlich. (Medical Terminology Ser.). 176p. 1996. pap., teacher ed. 24.95 (*0-8273-7842-4*) Delmar.

Medical Terminology for Health Professionals. 3rd ed. Ehrlich. (Medical Terminology Ser.). 1997. 62.95 (*0-8273-7841-6*) Delmar.

Medical Terminology for Health Professionals. 3rd ed. Ann Ehrlich. (Medical Terminology Ser.). 244p. 1997. teacher ed. 39.95 (*0-8273-7843-2*) Delmar.

Medical Terminology for Health Professionals. 3rd ed. Ann Erlich. (Medical Terminology Ser.). (Illus.). 528p. (C). 1996. mass mkt. 52.95 incl. disk (*0-8273-7839-4*) Delmar.

Medical Terminology for Health Professions. 2nd ed. Ann Ehrlich. LC 92-9897. 427p. 1992. text 35.95 (*0-8273-4975-0*); text 62.95 (*0-8273-4977-7*) Delmar.

Medical Terminology for Health Professions. 2nd ed. Ann Ehrlich. LC 92-9897. 427p. 1993. audio 124.95 (*0-8273-4979-3*) Delmar.

Medical Terminology for Health Professions. 2nd ed. Ann Ehrlich. LC 92-9897. 427p. 1993. text, teacher ed. 24.00 (*0-8273-4976-9*) Delmar.

Medical Terminology for Health Professions. 3rd ed. Ehrlich. (Medical Terminology Ser.). 1997. 99.95 incl. audio (*0-8273-7840-8*) Delmar.

Medical Terminology for Health Professions. 3rd ed. Ann Ehrlich. 512p. (C). 1996. mass mkt. 44.75 incl. audio (*0-8273-8212-X*) Delmar.

Medical Terminology for Health Professions. 4th ed. Ehrlich. 2000. pap. 45.95 (*0-7668-1297-9*) Delmar.

Medical Terminology for Medical Students. 2nd ed. William B. Tyrrell. (Illus.). 202p. (C). 1989. pap. text 40.95 (*0-398-05550-5*) C C Thomas.

Medical Terminology for Stenotypists. Beverly L. Ritter & George P. Andrews. (Realtime Machine Shorthand Ser.). 189p. (C). 1992. pap. text, teacher ed. 30.75 (*0-938643-54-1*) Stenotype Educ.

Medical Terminology for Stenotypists. Beverly L. Ritter & George P. Andrews. (Realtime Machine Shorthand Ser.). (Illus.). 675p. (C). 1994. pap. text 53.25 (*0-938643-27-4*) Stenotype Educ.

Medical Terminology for the Allied Health Professional: An A & P Systems Approach. Bonnie Fremgen. LC 96-21729. 624p. 1996. pap. 42.00 (*0-8359-4991-5*) P-H.

Medical Terminology from Greek & Latin. Sandra R. Patterson & Lawrence S. Thompson. LC 77-93780. (GRE & LAT.). xii, 275p. 1978. reprint ed. pap. 25.00 (*0-87875-484-9*) Whitston Pub.

Medical Terminology in Action. George A. Wistreich. 624p. (C). 1993. text 40.00 (*0-697-10896-1*, WCB McGr Hill) McGrw-H Hghr Educ.

Medical Terminology Instructor's Guide. 6th ed. Genevieve L. Smith. 1991. pap., teacher ed. 18.00 (*0-8273-4565-8*) Delmar.

Medical Terminology Made Comprehensible: Medizinische Fachsprache Verstaendlich Gemacht. Eduard Strauss & E. Ruediger. 94p. 1981. 19.95 (*0-8288-1853-3*) Fr & Eur.

Medical Terminology Made Easy. Dennerll. 64p. 1997. text, teacher ed. 14.00 (*0-8273-8137-9*) Delmar.

Medical Terminology Made Easy. Jean T. Dennerll. LC 92-48740. 296p. 1993. text 24.95 (*0-8273-5278-6*) Delmar.

Medical Terminology Made Easy. 2nd ed. Dennerll. (C). 1997. 28.00 incl. audio (*0-8273-8139-5*) Delmar.

Medical Terminology Made Easy. 2nd ed. Jean T. Dennerll & Genevieve L. Smith. LC 97-21616. 384p. (C). 1997. mass mkt. 37.95 (*0-8273-8136-0*) Delmar.

Medical Terminology Medical Tapes. Cohen. 1993. 24.95 (*0-397-55135-5*) Lppncott W & W.

Medical Terminology Review Challenge. Mary E. Kinn. LC 86-24019. 168p. (C). 1987. pap. 25.95 (*0-8273-2688-2*) Delmar.

Medical Terminology Simplified: A Programmed Learning Approach by Body Systems. Barbara A. Gylys. 1997. 39.95 (*0-8036-0327-4*) Davis Co.

Medical Terminology Simplified: A Programmed Learning Approach by Body Systems. 2nd ed. Barbara A. Gylys. 1998. pap. text 44.95 incl. cd-rom (*0-8036-0345-2*) Davis Co.

Medical Terminology Simplified: A Programmed Learning Approach by Body Systems. 2nd ed. Barbara A. Gylys & Regina M. Masters. LC 97-43006. 1998. pap. 36.95 (*0-8036-0344-4*) Davis Co.

Medical Terminology with Human Anatomy. 3rd ed. Jane Rice. (Illus.). 574p. (C). 1994. pap. text 32.95 (*0-8385-6268-X*, A6268-5) Appleton & Lange.

Medical Terminology with Human Anatomy: Instructor's Guide. 4th ed. Jane Rice. 1998. pap., teacher ed. 25.00 (*0-8385-6291-4*, Medical Exam) Appleton & Lange.

Medical Terms: Their Roots & Origins. A. R. Tindall. LC 97-26853. 230p. 1997. pap. 38.00 (*90-265-1498-0*) Swets.

Medical Terms & Abbreviations. SPC Staff. LC 97-27804. (Health Care Professional Review Ser.: Vol. 1). 320p. 1997. spiral bd. 24.95 (*0-87434-911-7*) Springhouse Corp.

Medical Terms Made Easy. Dennerll. 1993. 25.95 incl. audio (*0-8273-5907-1*); text 36.95 incl. audio (*0-8273-5918-7*) Delmar.

Medical Testimony on Victims of Torture: A Physician's Guide to Political Asylum Cases. Nancy Arnison et al. 46p. 1991. pap. text 7.00 (*1-879707-02-0*) Phy Human Rights.

Medical Testing & Health Insurance. (Orig.). 1991. lib. bdg. 79.95 (*0-8490-4340-9*) Gordon Pr.

Medical Tests Sourcebook: Basic Consumer Health Information. Ed. by Joyce Shannon. LC 99-35456. (Health Reference Ser.). (Illus.). 600p. 1999. lib. bdg. 78.00 (*0-7808-0243-8*) Omnigraphics Inc.

***Medical Textiles ' 99.** S. Anand. 208p. 2000. text 170.00 (*1-85573-494-X*, Pub. by Woodhead Pubng) Am Educ Systs.

Medical Textiles for Implantation: Proceedings of the 3rd International ITV Conference on Biomaterials, Stuttgart, June 14-16, 1989. H. I. Planck et al. (Illus.). 368p. 1991. 118.95 (*0-387-52741-9*) Spr-Verlag.

Medical Textiles 96. Ed. by S. Anand. 208p. 1996. boxed set 164.95 (*1-85573-317-X*) Technomic.

Medical Theories in Hippocrates: Early Texts & the "Epidemics" Volker Langholf. (Untersuchungen zur Antiken Literatur und Geschichte Ser.: No. 34). vi, 285p. (C). 1990. lib. bdg. 127.70 (*3-11-011956-0*) De Gruyter.

Medical Therapeutics: A Pocket Companion. 3rd ed. Eric B. Larson & Paul G. Ramsey. Ed. by Ray Kersey. (Illus.). 720p. 1997. pap. text 29.95 (*0-7216-5126-7*, W B Saunders Co) Harcrt Hlth Sci Grp.

Medical Thinking. S. C. Schwartz & T. Griffin. (Contributions to Psychology & Medicine Ser.). (Illus.). 290p. 1986. 104.00 (*0-387-96315-4*) Spr-Verlag.

Medical Thinking: A Historical Preface. Lester S. King. LC 81-11965. 347p. reprint ed. pap. 107.60 (*0-8357-4197-4*, 203697500006) Bks Demand.

Medical Topography of Upper Canada. John Douglas. LC 85-14626. 1986. 9.95 (*0-88135-078-8*) Watson Pub Intl.

Medical Training in the European Community. Ed. by Commission of the European Communities. viii, 87p. 1987. pap. 52.80 (*0-387-17761-2*) Spr-Verlag.

Medical Transciptionist's Handbook - IML. 2nd ed. Blake. 96p. 1998. teacher ed. 12.95 (*0-8273-8324-X*) Delmar.

Medical Transcribing Machine Operator. Jack Rudman. (Career Examination Ser.: C-3203). 1994. pap. 23.95 (*0-8373-3203-6*) Nat Learn.

Medical Transcription. Blanche Ettinger & Alice Ettinger. Ed. by Sheri Coalson et al. LC 96-33434. 472p. (C). 1996. pap., student ed. 29.95 (*1-56118-654-6*) Paradigm MN.

Medical Transcription. Blanche Ettinger & Alice G. Ettinger. 272p. (C). 1997. pap. text, teacher ed. 14.00 (*1-56118-655-4*); student ed., ring bd. 150.00 incl. audio (*1-56118-656-2*) Paradigm MN.

***Medical Transcription: Fundamentals & Practice.** 2nd ed. (C). 1999. cd-rom 500.00 (*0-13-017965-5*) P-H.

***Medical Transcription: Fundamentals & Practice.** 2nd ed. Sally Pitman et al. LC 99-36720. 494p. 1999. pap. 47.00 (*0-13-013833-9*) P-H.

Medical Transcription at the Lexington Medical Group. J. Patrick Fisher & Dianne K. Frantz. 400p. 1990. text 28.55 (*0-02-685570-4*) Glencoe.

***Medical Transcription Career Handbook.** Keith A. Drake. LC 99-37072. 149p. 1999. pap. text 20.80 (*0-13-011540-1*) P-H.

Medical Transcription Curriculum: MDT 1 Course. S. Turley. 524p. (C). 1993. ring bd. write for info. (*0-933195-47-8*) CA College Health Sci.

Medical Transcription for Health Information Managers. 98p. 1994. pap. text 60.00 incl. audio (*0-934385-59-9*) Hlth Prof Inst.

Medical Transcription Guide: Do's & Dont's. 2nd ed. Marilyn T. Fordney & Marcy O. Diehl. Ed. by Maureen Pfeiffer. LC 98-28552. (Illus.). 635p. 1999. pap. text 42.50 (*0-7216-7650-2*, W B Saunders Co) Harcrt Hlth Sci Grp.

Medical Transcription Power Building: Student Key & Guide. Bruce Tennant. 90p. 1983. pap. text 9.95 (*0-89420-222-7*, 470020); audio 111.95 (*0-89420-224-3*, 470000) Natl Book.

Medical Transcription Self-Assessment, No. 1. 31p. 1995. student ed. 35.00 incl. audio (*0-935229-28-0*) Am Assoc Med.

Medical Transcription Self-Assessment, No. 2. 27p. 1996. student ed. 35.00 incl. audio (*0-935229-30-2*, MTSA-2) Am Assoc Med.

Medical Transcription with Advanced Terminology. Lois R. Tutherly. LC 86-23962. 384p. (C). 1987. pap. 36.95 (*0-8273-2587-8*) Delmar.

Medical Transcription with Advanced Terminology. Lois R. Tutherly. LC 86-23962. 384p. (C). 1987. teacher ed. 16.00 (*0-8273-2588-6*) Delmar.

Medical Transcriptionist's Handbook. Rachelle S. Blake. 352p. 1993. pap., teacher ed. write for info. (*0-538-70678-3*) S-W Pub.

Medical Transcriptionist's Handbook. 2nd ed. Blake. 112p. (C). 1997. mass mkt., wbk. ed. 9.25 (*0-8273-8323-1*) Delmar.

Medical Treason: Nurses on Drugs. Joyce E. Strom-Paikin. LC 89-60104. 311p. 1989. 21.95 (*0-88282-043-5*) New Horizon NJ.

Medical Treatment of Epilepsy. Ed. by Stanley R. Resor, Jr. & Henn Kutt. (Neurological Disease & Therapy Ser.: Vol. 10). (Illus.). 760p. 1991. text 255.00 (*0-8247-8549-5*) Dekker.

Medical Treatment of Self & Hypochondria: Index of Modern Authors & Subjects with Guide for Rapid Research. Samuel M. Morris. LC 90-56315. 160p. 1991. 47.50 (*1-55914-414-9*); pap. 44.50 (*1-55914-415-7*) ABBE Pubs Assn.

Medical Treatments of Foreign Objects: Invasions, Penetrations & Migrations in the Human Body Including Drug Smuggling in Body Cavities. Science & Life Consultants Association Staff. 150p. 1996. pap. 44.50 (*0-7883-1301-0*) ABBE Pubs Assn.

Medical Treatments of Foreign Objects: Invasions, Penetrations & Migrations in the Human Body Including Drug Smuggling in Body Cavities. Science & Life Consultants Staff. 150p. 1996. 47.50 (*0-7883-1300-2*) ABBE Pubs Assn.

Medical Trial Technique Quarterly, 38 vols. Ed. by Fred Lane. LC 72-136152. 1954. 1100.00 (*0-318-42410-X*) West Group.

Medical Triangle: Physicians, Politicians, & the Public. Eli Ginzberg. 360p. 1990. 34.50 (*0-674-56325-5*) HUP.

Medical Triangle: Physicians, Politicians, & the Public. Eli Ginzberg. 328p. (C). 1992. pap. 18.00 (*0-674-56326-3*) HUP.

Medical Trivia. James M. Navratil. LC 86-82986. 200p. 1998. 12.50 (*0-937557-06-4*) Litarvan Lit.

Medical Tubing Markets. (Market Research Reports: No. 313). 188p. 1993. 795.00 (*0-317-05027-3*) Theta Corp.

Medical Typewriting. 2nd ed. Patsy C. Smith. (Illus.). 128p. 1983. text 17.12 (*0-07-058925-9*) McGraw.

Medical Typing & Transcribing: Techniques & Procedures. 2nd ed. Marcy O. Diehl & Marilyn T. Fordney. (Illus.). 450p. 1984. teacher ed. 7.50 (*0-7216-2009-4*, W B Saunders Co) Harcrt Hlth Sci Grp.

Medical Typing & Transcribing: Techniques & Procedures. 3rd ed. Mary O. Diehl & Marilyn T. Fordney. (Illus.). 1991. pap., teacher ed. write for info. (*0-7216-3736-1*, W B Saunders Co) Harcrt Hlth Sci Grp.

Medical Typing & Transcribing Audiotapes. 3rd ed. Marcy O. Diehl & Marilyn Takahashi. 1980. pap. write for info. (*0-7216-9955-3*, W B Saunders Co) Harcrt Hlth Sci Grp.

Medical Typing Practice. 2nd ed. Kathleen B. Root & Edward E. Byers. 1967. text 50.32 (*0-07-053585-X*) McGraw.

Medical Typist. Jack Rudman. (Career Examination Ser.: C-3396). 1994. pap. 23.95 (*0-8373-3396-2*) Nat Learn.

Medical Ultrasound, Vol. 7. Ed. by James T. Barodte. 1983. text 30.00 (*0-471-88975-X*) Wiley.

Medical Ultrasound Markets. (Market Research Reports: No. 470). (Illus.). 88p. 1994. 795.00 (*0-614-01245-7*) Theta Corp.

Medical Ultrasound Safety. 1994. 19.00 (*1-930047-71-1*) Am Inst Ultrasound.

Medical Use of Snake Venom Proteins. Ed. by Kurt F. Stocker. 524p. 1990. lib. bdg. 210.00 (*0-8493-5846-9*, RM666) CRC Pr.

Medical Uses of Anti-Oxidants for Cancer Prevention: Index of New Information with Authors, Subjects & Bibliography. American Health Research Institute Staff. LC 95-16102. 1995. 47.50 (*0-7883-0470-4*); pap. 44.50 (*0-7883-0471-2*) ABBE Pubs Assn.

Medical Uses of Ionizing Radiation & Radioisotopes. Joint EAEA-WHO Expert Committee. (Technical Reports: No. 492). 56p. 1972. pap. text 4.00 (*92-4-120492-3*, 1100492) World Health.

Medical Uses of Statistics. 2nd ed. Ed. by John C. Bailar, III & Frederick Mosteller. (Illus.). 449p. 1992. pap. text 39.95 (*0-910133-36-0*) Mass Med Pub Div.

Medical Uses of Television As a Media for Health, Dangers, News, Advertising & Brain-Washing: Index of New Information for World Review. John C. Bartone. (Illus.). 160p. 1997. 47.50 (*0-7883-1396-7*); pap. 44.50 (*0-7883-1397-5*) ABBE Pubs Assn.

Medical Uses of Television As a Media for Health, Dangers, News, Advertising & Brain-Washington: Index of New Information for World Review. rev. ed. John C. Bartone. 167p. 1998. 47.50 (*0-7883-1858-6*); pap. 44.50 (*0-7883-1859-4*) ABBE Pubs Assn.

Medical Value of Emotional Power. Jonathan Silver. 9p. 1998. pap. 10.00 (*1-892870-04-5*) Best Years Inc.

Medical Value of Psychoanalysis. Franz Alexander. Ed. by Chicago Institute for Psychoanalysis Staff. LC 84-22475. (Classics in Psychoanalysis Monographs: No. 2). vi, 278p. 1985. 42.50 (*0-8236-3285-7*, BN03285) Intl Univs Pr.

Medical Virology. 4th ed. David O. White & Frank Fenner. (Illus.). 603p. 1994. text 67.00 (*0-12-746642-8*) Acad Pr.

Medical Virology. 9th ed. Morag C. Timbury. (Illus.). 196p. 1991. pap. text 22.95 (*0-443-04148-2*) Church.

Medical Virology, No. 8. Ed. by L. M. De La Maza & E. M. Peterson. (Illus.). 342p. 1989. 85.00 (*0-306-43361-3*, Plenum Trade) Perseus Pubng.

Medical Virology, No. 9. Ed. by L. M. De la Meza & E. M. Peterson. LC 89-657524. (Illus.). 270p. 1990. 85.00 (*0-306-43700-7*, Plenum Trade) Perseus Pubng.

Medical Virology, Vol. 10. Ed. by L. M. De la Maza & E. M. Peterson. (Illus.). 312p. (C). 1991. text 114.00 (*0-306-44010-5*, Kluwer Plenum) Kluwer Academic.

Medical Virology: A Practical Approach. Ed. by U. Desselberger. (The Practical Approach Ser.: No. 147). (Illus.). 232p. 1995. pap. text 55.00 (*0-19-963329-0*); spiral bd. 115.00 (*0-19-963330-4*) OUP.

Medical Visits to Medicare Patients: Physician Coding Practice. Sally Trude. LC 92-9017. 1992. pap. 7.50 (*0-8330-1224-X*, R-4055-HCFA) Rand Corp.

Medical Warrior: Fighting Corporate Socialized Medicine. Miguel A. Faria, Jr. LC 97-72144. 207p. (Orig.). 1997. pap. 23.95 (*0-9641077-2-4*) Hacienda Pub.

***Medical Waste Control Equipment in Taiwan: A Strategic Entry Report, 1995.** Compiled by Icon Group International Staff. (Illus.). 119p. 1999. ring bd. 1190.00 incl. audio compact disk (*0-7418-1613-X*) Icon Grp.

***Medical Waste Control in Germany: A Strategic Entry Report, 1996.** Compiled by Icon Group International Staff. (Illus.). 94p. 1999. ring bd. 940.00 incl. audio compact disk (*0-7418-1397-1*) Icon Grp.

Medical Waste Control in Mexico: A Strategic Entry Report, 1997. Compiled by Icon Group International Staff. (Illus.). 144p. 1999. ring bd. 1440.00 incl. audio compact disk (*0-7418-1069-7*) Icon Grp.

Medical Waste Disposal. Calvin R. Brunner. LC 95-95256. (Illus.). 560p. (C). 1996. text 150.00 (*0-9621774-1-5*) Incinerat Consults.

***Medical Waste Disposal Equipment in Indonesia: A Strategic Entry Report, 1998.** Compiled by Icon Group International Staff. (Country Industry Report). (Illus.). 161p. 1999. ring bd. 1610.00 incl. audio compact disk (*0-7418-0539-1*) Icon Grp.

Medical Waste Management. Richard K. Miller & Christy H. Gunter. (Market Research Survey Ser.: No. 285). 50p. 1996. 200.00 (*1-55865-310-4*) Future Tech Surveys.

Medical Waste Management. Richard K. Miller & Marcia E. Rupnow. LC 90-83866. (Survey on Technology & Markets Ser.: No. 161). 50p. 1991. pap. text 200.00 (*1-55865-186-1*) Future Tech Surveys.

An Asterisk (*) at the beginning of an entry indicates that the title is appearing for the first time.

Medical Waste Management & Disposable Markets: Regulations, Regulations & More Regulations Promote Rapid Technological Innovations. Market Intelligence Staff. 315p. 1992. 1895.00 (*1-56753-382-5*) Frost & Sullivan.

Medical Waste Management & Disposal. U. S. EPA Staff et al. LC 90-23201. (Pollution Technology Review Ser.: No. 200). (Illus.). 541p. 1991. 125.00 (*0-8155-1264-3*) Noyes.

Medical Waste Management & Disposal Markets. Ed. by Frost & Sullivan Staff. 343p. 1997. spiral bd. 2450.00 (*0-7889-0694-1*, 5401-15) Frost & Sullivan.

Medical Waste Markets. (Market Research Reports: No. 451). (Illus.). 94p. 1994. 795.00 (*0-614-01242-2*) Theta Corp.

Medical Waste Solutions. James W. LaMoreaux. Date not set. 64.95 (*0-87371-712-0*, L712) Lewis Pubs.

Medical Waste Tracking Act of 1988: A Legislative History of Public Law 100-582, 5 vols., Set. Ed. by Bernard D. Reams, Jr. LC 93-78606. (Federal Health Law Ser.: Part 8). 4068p. 1993. 395.00 (*0-89941-848-1*, 307940) W S Hein.

***Medical Waste Treatment Equipment & Services in Hong Kong: A Strategic Entry Report, 1999.** Compiled by Icon Group International. (Illus.). 108p. 1999. ring bd. 1080.00 incl. audio compact disk (*0-7418-1863-9*) Icon Grp.

Medical Wit & Humor: Index of Modern Writings. Mary R. Bartone. LC 95-16708. 1995. write for info. (*0-7883-0480-1*); pap. 44.50 (*0-7883-0481-X*) ABBE Pubs Assn.

Medical Wit & Wisdom: The Best Medical Quotations from Hippocrates to Groucho Marx. Ed. by Jess M. Brallier. LC 93-83465. (Illus.). 288p. 1993. 15.95 (*1-56138-289-2*) Running Pr.

Medical Word Book. 3rd ed. Sheila Sloane-Dusseau. (Illus.). 1168p. 1990. pap. text 41.00 (*0-7216-3243-2*, W B Saunders Co) Harcrt Hlth Sci Grp.

Medical Word Book. 4th ed. Sheila Sloane-Dusseau. 1999. pap. text 34.95 (*0-7216-7626-X*, W B Saunders Co) Harcrt Hlth Sci Grp.

Medical Word Building. Park-Davis & Company Staff. 125p. 1970. pap. 19.95 (*0-87489-043-8*) Practice Mgmt Info.

Medical Word Processing Simulation. Linda F. Klafehn & Marilyn G. Fowler. (Word Processing Ser.). 117p. 1985. text 19.50 (*0-471-88528-2*) P-H.

Medical Words: Audio/Visual Dictionary. Victory Technology Staff. 1996. pap. 49.95 incl. cd-rom (*0-8385-6376-7*) Appleton & Lange.

Medical Work in America. Eliot Freidson. LC 89-5448. 304p. (C). 1989. pap. 20.00 (*0-300-04158-6*) Yale U Pr.

Medical Work of the Knights Hospitallers of Saint John of Jerusalem. Edgar E. Hume. LC 40-30162. (Illus.). 379p. reprint ed. pap. 117.50 (*0-608-10082-X*, 201040400069) Bks Demand.

Medical Works, 4 vols. Incl. Vol. 1. Ancient Medicine, Airs, Waters, Places, Epidemics 1 & 2. Oath, Precepts, Nutriment. Tr. by W. H. Jones. 432p. 1923. 19.95 (*0-674-99162-1*); Vol. 3. On Wounds in the Head. in the Surgery. on Fractures, on Joints, Mochlikon. Hippocrates. Vol. 3. On Wounds in the Head. in the Surgery. on Fractures, on Joints, Mochlikon. Tr. by E. T. Withington. 484p. 1928. 19.95 (*0-674-99165-6*); Vol. 4. Nature of Man. Regimen in Health. Humours. Amorphisms. Regimen 1-3. Dreams. Tr. by W. H. Jones. 582p. 1931. 19.95 (*0-674-99166-4*); Vol. 2. Hippocrates. Vol. 2. Tr. by W. H. Jones. 402p. 1923. 19.95 (*0-674-99164-8*); (Loeb Classical Library: Nos. 147-150). 19.95 (*0-318-53103-8*) HUP.

Medical Works of Richard Mead. Richard Mead. LC 75-23740. reprint ed. 94.50 (*0-404-13550-1*) AMS Pr.

Medical World of Early Modern France. Laurence Brockliss & Colin Jones. (Illus.). 982p. 1997. text 150.00 (*0-19-822750-7*) OUP.

***Medical World of the Tribals: Explorations in Illness Ideology, Body Symbolism & Ritual Healing.** Robin D. Tribhuwan. LC 98-903444. xvii, 334p. 1998. 34.00 (*81-7141-408-7*, Pub. by Discovery Pub Hse) Nataraj Bks.

Medical Writing: A Prescription for Clarity. 2nd ed. Neville W. Goodman & Martin B. Edwards. (Illus.). 239p. (C). 1997. pap. text 22.95 (*0-521-49876-7*) Cambridge U Pr.

Medical Writing & Communicating. John J. Gartland. 250p. 1992. 39.00 (*1-55572-018-8*) Univ Pub Group.

Medical Writing in Drug Development: A Practical Guide for Pharmaceutical Research. Robert J. Bonk. LC 97-18243. (Illus.). 139p. (C). 1998. 42.00 (*0-7890-0174-8*, Pharmctl Prods); pap. 19.95 (*0-7890-0449-6*, Pharmctl Prods) Haworth Pr.

Medical X-Ray Electron Beam & Gamma-Ray Protection for Energies up to 50 MeV: Equipment Design, Performance & Use. LC 89-2975. (Report Ser.: No. 102). 139p. (Orig.). 1989. pap. text 45.00 (*0-929600-03-7*) NCRP Pubns.

Medical X-Ray Techniques in Diagnostic Radiology. G. J. Van Der Plaats. 1979. lib. bdg. 79.50 (*90-247-2155-5*) Kluwer Academic.

Medicalese: A Humorous Medical Dictionary. Peter K. Meyer. Ed. by Catherine Graves. LC 93-74044. (Illus.). 96p. (Orig.). 1994. pap. 9.95 (*0-9628186-1-5*) Avian Cetacean.

Medicalization of Eating Vol. 7: Social Control in an Eating Disorders Clinic. Robin J. Vogler. Ed. by Jaber F. Gubrium. LC 93-12496. (Contemporary Ethnographic Studies). 178p. 1993. 73.25 (*1-55938-524-3*) Jai Pr.

Medicalization of Obstetrics: Personnel, Practice, & Instruments. Ed. by Philip K. Wilson. LC 96-794. (Childbirth Ser.: Vol. 2). (Illus.). 424p. 1996. reprint ed. text 88.00 (*0-8153-2231-3*) Garland.

***Medicalized Motherhood: Perspectives from the Lives of African American & Jewish Women.** Jacquelyn S. Litt. LC 99-43560. 224p. 2000. text 50.00 (*0-8135-2781-3*) Rutgers U Pr.

***Medicalized Motherhood: Perspectives from the Lives of African American & Jewish Women.** Jacquelyn S. Litt. LC 99-43560. 224p. (C). 2000. pap. 20.00 (*0-8135-2782-1*) Rutgers U Pr.

Medically Assisted Conception: An Agenda for Research. Institute of Medicine Staff. 370p. 1989. pap. text 29.00 (*0-309-04128-7*) Natl Acad Pr.

Medically Complex Child: The Transition to Home Care. N. J. Hochstadt & D. Yost. xix, 323p. 1991. text 69.00 (*3-7186-0520-1*, Harwood Acad Pubs) Gordon & Breach.

Medically Complex Child: The Transition to Home Care. N. Hochstadt & D. Yost. xix, 323p. 1991. pap. text 43.00 (*3-7186-0521-X*) Gordon & Breach.

Medically Important Fungi: A Guide to Identification. 3rd ed. Ed. by Davise H. Larone. LC 94-40202. 1995. 49.95 (*1-55581-091-8*) ASM Pr.

Medically-Oriented Play for Children in Health Care: The Issues. Ed. by Pat Azarnoff. (Issues in Pediatric Mental Health Ser.: No. 3). (Illus.). 100p. 1986. spiral bd. 18.95 (*0-912599-05-7*) Pediatric Projects.

Medically Refractory Rest Angina. Ed. by Douglass Andrew Morrison & Patrick W. Serruys. (Illus.). 480p. 1992. text 190.00 (*0-8247-8630-0*) Dekker.

***Medically Speaking: A Dictionary of Quotations.** C. C. Gaither. LC 99-52005. 481p. 1999. pap. 39.00 (*0-7503-0635-1*) IOP Pub.

Medical/physiological Effects of Alcohol. Stewart C. Clark & Alberta Alcohol and Drug Abuse Commission. LC 96-218598. ii, 47 p. 1995. write for info. (*0-7732-1543-3*) APAB.

Medical/Surgical Nursing: An Integrated Approach. Duncan White. (LPN/LVN Nursing Ser.). 128p. 1997. pap. text, teacher ed. 16.95 (*0-8273-7680-4*) Delmar.

Medicamentos Indigenas. Ed. by Maria E. Alvarez del Real. (SPA., Illus.). 448p. 1988. pap. 4.00 (*0-944499-42-2*) Editorial Amer.

Medicaments Essentiels. Guide Pratique d'Utilisation pour l'Emploi et la Gestion de Medicaments et Materiel Medical Dans les Dispensaires, les Centres Medicaux et les Camps de Refugies. A l'Usage des Medecins, Infirmier(e) s et Auxiliaries de Sante. Ed. by J. Pinel. (Medecins Sans Frontieres - Hatier Ser.). (FRE.). 255p. 1991. pap. 26.95 (*2-218-02650-3*) Schoenhof.

Medicaments et Aliments, Approche Ethnopharmacologique (Medicines & Foods, Ethnopharmacological Approach) E. Schroder et al. (ENG & FRE.). 418p. 1996. pap. 60.00 (*2-7099-1320-8*, Pub. by LInstitut Francais) Balogh.

Medicamina Faciei Femineae see Amores

Medicare: A Handbook in the History & Issues of Health Care Services for the Elderly. Ed. by William A. Pearman & Phillip Starr. LC 88-2423. 166p. 1988. text 10.00 (*0-8240-8391-1*) Garland.

Medicare: A Strategy for Quality Assurance, Vol. 2. Institute of Medicine (U. S.) Staff. Ed. by Kathleen N. Lohr. LC 90-5787. 471p. 1990. reprint ed. pap. 146.10 (*0-608-02234-9*, 204731000002) Bks Demand.

Medicare: Advancing Towards the 21st Century, 1966-1996. Ed. by Linda F. Wolf. (Illus.). 237p. (Orig.). (C). 1997. pap. text 50.00 (*0-7881-4495-2*) DIANE Pub.

Medicare: Changes to HMO Rate Setting Method Are Needed to Reduce Program Costs. (Illus.). 92p. (Orig.). (C). 1995. pap. text 25.00 (*0-7881-1713-0*) DIANE Pub.

Medicare: Cures for Billing Code Complexity: Hearing Before the Subcommittee on Human Resources of the Committee on Government Reform & Oversight, House of Representatives, One Hundred Fifth Congress, Second Session, April 9, 1998. USGPO Staff. LC 98-212412. iv, 241 p. 1998. write for info. (*0-16-057265-7*) USGPO.

Medicare: Excessive Payments for Medical Supplies Continue Despite Improvements. 44p. (Orig.). (C). 1996. pap. text 20.00 (*0-7881-2758-6*) DIANE Pub.

***Medicare: HCFA Can Improve Methods for Revising Physician Practice Expense Payments.** Ed. by William J. Scanlon. (Illus.). 55p. (C). 1999. pap. text 20.00 (*0-7881-8249-8*) DIANE Pub.

Medicare: HCFA Should Release Data to Aid Consumers, Prompt Better HMO Performance. (Illus.). 60p. (Orig.). (C). 1997. pap. text 30.00 (*0-7881-3778-6*) DIANE Pub.

Medicare: Increased HMO Oversight Could Improve Quality & Access to Care. (Illus.). 44p. 1996. reprint ed. pap. text 20.00 (*0-7881-3211-3*) DIANE Pub.

***Medicare: Issues & Options.** S. N. Colamery. LC 99-29242. 1999. 49.00 (*1-56072-694-6*) Nova Sci Pubs.

***Medicare: Issues in Political Economy.** Ronald J. Vogel. LC 99-6103. 272p. 1999. text 49.50 (*0-472-11060-8*, 11060) U of Mich Pr.

Medicare: Millions in End-Stage Renal Disease Expenditures Shifted to Employer Health Plans. (Illus.). 49p. (Orig.). (C). 1995. reprint ed. pap. text 25.00 (*0-7881-1189-2*) DIANE Pub.

Medicare: Most Beneficiaries with Diabetes Do Not Receive Recommended Monitoring Services. 42p. pap. text 10.00 (*0-9999007-9-X*) DIANE Pub.

Medicare: New Directions in Quality Assurance: Proceedings of an Invitational Conference. Ed. by Molla S. Donaldson et al. LC 90-63821. 217p. 1991. reprint ed. pap. 67.30 (*0-608-02345-0*, 206298600004) Bks Demand.

Medicare: Preparing for the Challenges of the 21st Century. Ed. by Robert D. Reischauer et al. LC 97-33931. 329p. 1998. pap. 19.95 (*0-8157-7399-4*) Brookings.

Medicare: Referrals to Physician-Owned Imaging Facilities Warrant HCFA's Scrutiny. (Illus.). 61p. (Orig.). (C). 1995. pap. text 25.00 (*0-7881-1314-3*) DIANE Pub.

Medicare: The Next 30 Years. Ed. by Bob Packwood. 50p. (C). 1999. reprint ed. pap. text 20.00 (*0-7881-8143-2*) DIANE Pub.

Medicare: 85 Commonly Asked Questions. rev. ed. 28p. (C). 1996. pap. text 15.00 (*0-7881-2691-1*) DIANE Pub.

Medicare Vol. 1: A Strategy for Quality Assurance. fac. ed. Institute of Medicine (U. S.) Staff. Ed. by Kathleen N. Lohr. LC 90-5787. (Illus.). 460p. 1990. pap. 142.60 (*0-7837-7557-1*, 204731000001) Bks Demand.

Medicare & Choice Interim Final Rule: Regulations Effective July 27, 1998 Including CCH Executive Summary & Medicare & Choice Provisions from the Balanced Budget Act of 1997. CCH Editorial Staff. (Health Law Professional Ser.). 320p. 1998. pap. 49.95 (*0-8080-0283-X*) CCH INC.

***Medicare & Choice Program after One Year: Congressional Hearing.** Ed. by Michael Bilirakis. (Illus.). 128p. (C). 2000. reprint ed. pap. text 25.00 (*0-7881-8957-3*) DIANE Pub.

***Medicare & Coding for Ophthalmology.** Robert D. Keene. 245p. 2000. pap. 145.00 (*1-58383-084-7*) Robert D Keene.

***Medicare & Coding for Optimal Reimbursement.** 250p. 1999. pap. 75.00 (*1-58383-051-0*) Robert D Keene.

Medicare & Graduate Medical Education. James Baumgardner. (Illus.). 49p. (Orig.). (C). 1995. pap. text 25.00 (*0-7881-2559-1*) DIANE Pub.

***Medicare & Managed Care: A Primer from Health Affairs & the California Health Care Foundation.** Ed. by John K. Iglehart. 150p. 1999. pap. write for info. (*0-930177-05-3*) P-to-P Hlth Fnd.

Medicare & Medicaid: The 1965 & 1967 Social Security Amendments. Margaret Greenfield. LC 82-25157. 143p. 1983. reprint ed. lib. bdg. 59.50 (*0-313-23841-3*, GRME, Greenwood Pr) Greenwood.

Medicare & Medicaid Benefits, 1997. 32p. 1997. pap. 7.00 (*0-685-67155-0*, 4751) CCH INC.

Medicare & Medicaid Claims & Procedures, 2 vols. Harvey L. McCormick. LC 86-9150. 1440p. 1986. text. write for info. (*0-314-97401-6*) West Pub.

Medicare & Medicaid Data Book. 1990. lib. bdg. 600.00 (*0-8490-4047-7*) Gordon Pr.

Medicare & Medicaid Fraud & Abuse. 2nd ed. Saul, Ewing, Remick & Saul Staff. LC 92-25516. (Primer Series for Health Care Professionals). 72p. 1992. pap. 24.95 (*0-934753-74-1*) LRP Pubns.

Medicare & Medicaid Laws & Regulations: Vol. 1: Medicare & Medicaid Laws; Vol. 2: Medicare & Medicaid Regulations, Vol. 2. 2700p. 1997. pap. 145.00 (*0-8080-0196-5*, 5472) CCH INC.

Medicare & Medicaid Laws & Regulations As of August 20, 1998, 2 vols. CCH Staff. (Vol. 1: Laws). 2958p. 1998. pap. 199.00 (*0-8080-0289-9*) CCH INC.

***Medicare & Medicaid Laws & Regulations As of January 1, 2000, 2 vols.** CCH Editors. 2650p. 2000. pap. text 160.00 (*0-8080-0462-X*) CCH INC.

Medicare & Medicaid Managed Care: A Strategic Guide to Serving Dually Eligible Persons Throughout the Continuum. Catholic Health Association of the United States Staff. LC 98-221767. (Mission in Action Ser.). xv, 131 p. 1998. write for info. (*0-87125-244-9*) Cath Health.

Medicare & Medicaid Patient & Program Protection Act of 1987: A Legislative History of Pub. Law No. 98-507, 3 vols., Set. Ed. by Bernard D. Reams, Jr. LC 89-83920. (Federal Health Law Ser.: Part 5). 1932p. 1990. lib. bdg. 185.00 (*0-89941-695-0*, 305960) W S Hein.

Medicare & Medicaid Statistical Supplement, 1997. Ed. by Linda F. Wolf. (Illus.). 226p. (C). 1998. pap. text 45.00 (*0-7881-4992-X*) DIANE Pub.

Medicare & Medicaid Statistical Supplement (1998) Mary O. Waid. Ed. by Linda F. Wolf. (Illus.). 434p. (C). 1999. pap. text 50.00 (*0-7881-7761-3*) DIANE Pub.

Medicare & Medigaps: A Guide to Retirement Health Insurance. Susan Hellman & Leonard H. Hellman. 120p. (C). 1991. pap. 21.95 (*0-8039-4366-0*) Sage.

Medicare & Medigaps: A Guide to Retirement Health Insurance. Susan Hellman & Leonard H. Hellman. LC 91-22012. (Illus.). 88p. 1991. reprint ed. pap. 30.00 (*0-608-01720-5*, 206237500003) Bks Demand.

Medicare & Other Health Benefits: Who Pays First? Government Printing Office Staff. 22p. 1997. pap. 1.50 (*0-16-048887-7*) USGPO.

Medicare & the American Health Care System: Report to the Congress. Donald A. Young et al. (Illus.). 152p. 1997. pap. text 35.00 (*0-7881-4676-9*) DIANE Pub.

***Medicare & the American Social Contract.** Ed. by Rosemary A. Stevens. (Restructuring Medicare for the Long Term Ser.). 125p. 1999. pap. text. write for info. (*1-884902-13-8*) Natl Acad.

Medicare & You 1999: Original Medicare Plan & Other Medicare Health Plan Choices. rev. ed. Ed. by Nancy-Ann M. DeParle. 35p. 1999. pap. text 15.00 (*0-7881-7978-0*) DIANE Pub.

***Medicare & You 2000.** 56p. 1999. pap. 5.50 (*0-16-059067-1*) USGPO.

Medicare Answer Book. 2nd ed. Connacht Cash. LC 98-65682. 304p. 1998. pap. 19.95 (*0-9633145-4-8*) Race Pt Pr.

***Medicare Answer Book.** 3rd ed. Connacht Cash. LC 98-89280. 304p. 1999. pap. 19.95 (*0-9633145-5-6*) Race Pt Pr.

Medicare As a Secondary Payer Guide: Practical Solutions to Administration & Management. Virginia Peabody & Paul Sullivan. Ed. by Barry Newman. LC 96-11272. (Illus.). 200p. (C). 1996. text 50.00 (*0-7863-0533-9*, Irwn Prfssnl) McGraw-Hill Prof.

***Medicare at Risk: Emerging Fraud in Medicare Programs: Congressional Hearing.** Ed. by Susan M. Collins. 326p. (C). 2000. reprint ed. pap. text 40.00 (*0-7881-8773-2*) DIANE Pub.

***Medicare Benefits for Recipients Living in Mexico: Proceedings of a Conference.** Policy Research Project Staff. (U. S. - Mexican Occasional Papers: Vol. 8). 166p. 1999. pap. 20.00 (*0-89940-580-0*) LBJ Sch Pub Aff.

Medicare Billing: Savings Through Implementation of Commercial Software: Hearing Before the Subcommittee on Oversight & Investigations of the Committee on Commerce, House of Representatives, One Hundred Fifth Congress, Second Session, May 19, 1998. USGPO Staff. LC 98-209457. iii, 42 p. 1998. write for info. (*0-16-057310-6*) USGPO.

***Medicare Billing Guide 2000.** Medicode, Med-Index Division Staff. (C). 2000. 80.00 (*1-56337-328-9*) Thomson Learn.

Medicare Claims Management for Home Health Agencies. Andrea L. Dumat. LC 98-32279. 1999. 149.00 (*0-8342-1220-X*, 1220X) Aspen Pub.

Medicare Compliance. Neil B. Caesar. 1997. 60.00 (*0-7863-1242-4*, Irwn Prfssnl) McGraw-Hill Prof.

***Medicare Compliance Manual 2000.** annuals rev. ed. James B. Davis & Maxine Lewis. (Illus.). 956p. 2000. ring bd. 129.95 (*1-57066-168-5*, 20047) Practice Mgmt Info.

M

Medicare Computer Systems: Year 2000 Challenges Put Benefits & Services in Jeopardy. Ed. by Mark E. Heatwole. (Illus.). 49p. (C). 1999. pap. text 20.00 (*0-7881-7644-7*) DIANE Pub.

***Medicare Contractors: Despite Its Efforts, H C F A Cannot Ensure Their Effectiveness or Integrity.** Ed. by Richard L. Hembra. 80p. (C). 1999. pap. text 20.00 (*0-7881-8464-4*) DIANE Pub.

Medicare Coverage Issues Manual. Government Printing Office Staff. 1987. ring bd. 150.00 (*0-16-016958-5*) USGPO.

Medicare Covered & Noncovered Services. (Illus.). 325p. 1998. 128.00 (*1-58383-006-5*, COVER9) Robert D Keene.

***Medicare Fraud & Abuse: Congressional Hearing.** Ed. by Bob Packwood. 108p. (C). 1999. reprint ed. pap. text 25.00 (*0-7881-8090-8*) DIANE Pub.

Medicare Fraud & Abuse: Understanding the Law. National Health Lawyers Association Staff et al. LC 86-61317. 300p. 1986. 36.00 (*0-918945-01-1*) Am Hlth Lawyers.

Medicare Handbook. 1995. lib. bdg. 255.25 (*0-8490-7429-0*) Gordon Pr.

Medicare Handbook: Complete Guide to Medicare Hospital & Medical Insurance Eligibility, Claims & Appeal. 1991. lib. bdg. 300.00 (*0-8490-5156-8*) Gordon Pr.

Medicare Handbook: 1994 Edition. 1994. lib. bdg. 255.95 (*0-8490-9037-7*) Gordon Pr.

Medicare HMO Risk-Contractor Program: Hearing Before the Subcommittee on Health & the Environment of the Committee on Energy & Commerce, House of Representatives, One Hundred Second Congress, First Session, November 15, 1991. United States Congress Staff. LC 92-210384. 189 p. 1992. write for info. (*0-16-037753-6*) USGPO.

Medicare HMO's: HCFA Can Promptly Eliminate Hundreds of Millions in Excess Payments. Jonathan Ratner. (Illus.). 58p. 1998. pap. text 20.00 (*0-7881-4762-5*) DIANE Pub.

***Medicare HMOs: Making Them Work for the Chronically Ill.** Richard Kronick & Joy De Beyer. LC 98-40045. 238p. 1998. 44.00 (*1-56793-091-3*) Health Admin Pr.

Medicare HMOs: Potential Effects of a Limited Enrollment Period Policy. (Illus.). 48p. 1997. pap. text 30.00 (*1-57979-225-1*) DIANE Pub.

Medicare HMOs: Potential Effects of a Limited Enrollment Period Policy. Ed. by James C. Cosgrove. (Illus.). 48p. (C). 1999. pap. text 20.00 (*0-7881-7645-5*) DIANE Pub.

Medicare HMOs: Rapid Enrollment Growth Concentrated in Selected States. (Illus.). 39p. (Orig.). 1996. pap. text 20.00 (*0-7881-3207-5*) DIANE Pub.

Medicare Home Health: Congressional Hearings. Ed. by Joe Barton. 130p. (C). 1999. reprint ed. pap. text 25.00 (*0-7881-8096-7*) DIANE Pub.

Medicare Home Health: Hearing Before the Subcommittee on Oversight & Investigations of the Committee on Commerce, House of Representatives, 105th Congress, 1st Session, October 29, 1997. USGPO Staff. LC 98-152312. iii, 130p. 1998. pap. write for info. (*0-16-056111-6*) USGPO.

***Medicare Home Health Agencies: Certification Process Ineffective in Excluding Problem Agencies.** Ed. by William J. Scanlon. 48p. 1999. pap. text 20.00 (*0-7881-7891-1*) DIANE Pub.

***Medicare Home Health Agencies: Closures Continue, with Little Evidence Beneficiary Access Is Impaired.** Ed. by William J. Scanlon. (Illus.). 54p. (C). 2000. pap. text 20.00 (*0-7881-8893-3*) DIANE Pub.

Medicare Home Health Agency Manual. Government Printing Office Staff. 1986. ring bd. 109.00 (*0-16-016867-8*) USGPO.

Medicare Home Health Agency Manual Service Coverage Provisions. 202p. 1986. 15.00 (*0-685-30149-4*, 41,750) NCLS Inc.

Medicare Home Health Care, Skilled Nursing Facility, & Other Postacute Care Payment Policies: Hearing Before the Subcommittee on Health of the Committee on Ways & Means, House of Representatives, One Hundred Fifth Congress, First Session, March 4, 1997. United States Staff. LC 98-138585. iii, 168 p. 1997. write for info. (*0-16-055959-6*) USGPO.

Medicare Hospital Manual. Government Printing Office Staff. 1983. ring bd. 639.00 (*0-16-016899-6*) USGPO.
***Medicare in the Twenty-First Century: Seeking Fair & Efficient Reform.** Ed. by Robert B. Helms. LC 99-40486. 260p. 1999. 39.95 (*0-8447-4117-5*, Pub. by Am Enterprise); pap. 19.95 (*0-8447-4118-3*, Pub. by Am Enterprise) Pub Resources Inc.
Medicare Intermediary Manual Pt. 3: Claims Process, Transmittal No. 1365. 20p. 1987. pap. 3.50 (*0-685-30150-8*, 40,904) NCLS Inc.
Medicare Made Easy. Charles B. Inlander. LC 97-40740. (Illus.). 339p. 1998. pap. text 18.95 (*1-882606-32-9*) Peoples Med Soc.
Medicare Made Easy. Charles B. Inlander. LC 98-40921. 256p. 1999. pap. 18.95 (*1-882606-47-7*) Peoples Med Soc.
Medicare Made Easy. Charles B. Inlander & Michael A. Donio. 1998. pap. 18.95 (*1-882606-55-8*) Peoples Med Soc.
Medicare Made Easy. 3rd ed. Charles B. Inlander. 1992. pap. 13.41 (*0-201-63219-5*) Addison-Wesley.
Medicare Made Easy: Everything You Need to Know to Make Medicare. Charles B. Inlander. 1989. pap. 10.53 (*0-201-17269-0*) Addison-Wesley.
Medicare Made Easy: Everything You Need to Know to Make Medicare Work for You. Charles B. Inlander. 1991. pap. 11.95 (*0-201-57089-0*) Addison-Wesley.
***Medicare Made Easy 1999.** Charles B. Inlander & Michael A. Donio. 256p. 1999. pap. 9.98 (*1-56731-309-4*, MJF Bks) Fine Comms.
Medicare Made Simple: A Consumer's Guide to the Medicare Program. Denise L. Knaus. Ed. by Kathryn Swanson & Maureen Lynch. 450p. (Orig.). 1996. pap. 12.95 (*1-885987-00-5*, ME070, Health Info Pr) Practice Mgmt Info.
Medicare Managed Care: Growing Enrollment Adds Urgency to Fixing HMO Payment Problem. (Illus.). 28p. 1996. reprint ed. pap. text 15.00 (*0-7881-3216-4*) DIANE Pub.
Medicare Managed Care: Securing Beneficiary Protections. Geraldine Dallek. (Illus.). 66p. 1998. pap. text 25.00 (*0-7881-7079-1*) DIANE Pub.
***Medicare Managed Care Plans: Many Factors Contribute to Recent Withdrawals; Plan Interest Continues.** Ed. by William J. Scanlon. (Illus.). 69p. (C). 1999. pap. text 20.00 (*0-7881-8393-1*) DIANE Pub.
Medicare Managed Care Resource Information Directory. 1996. lib. bdg. 259.95 (*0-8490-6361-2*) Gordon Pr.
Medicare Managed Care Resource Information Directory, 1995. Government Printing Office Staff. 118p. 1995. pap. 8.00 (*0-16-048334-4*) USGPO.
***Medicare Managed Care Sourcebook 2000 Edition.** Ed. by Melissa Glim. 592p. 1999. pap. 275.00 (*1-57987-159-3*) Faulkner & Gray.
Medicare-Medicaid Nursing Home Information for California, 6 vols., Set. 1991. lib. bdg. 600.95 (*0-8490-5076-6*) Gordon Pr.
Medicare-Medicaid Nursing Home Information for Florida, 3 vols., Set. 1991. lib. bdg. 199.75 (*0-8490-5083-9*) Gordon Pr.
Medicare-Medicaid Nursing Home Information for New Jersey, 2 vols., Set. 1991. lib. bdg. 175.99 (*0-8490-5074-X*) Gordon Pr.
Medicare-Medicaid Nursing Home Information for New York, 3 vols., Set. 1991. lib. bdg. 199.95 (*0-8490-5077-4*) Gordon Pr.
Medicare-Medicaid Nursing Home Information for Texas, 2 vols., Set. 1991. lib. bdg. 545.95 (*0-8490-5075-8*) Gordon Pr.
Medicare Now & in the Future. Marilyn Moon. 285p. 1996. 61.00 (*0-87766-652-0*) Urban Inst.
Medicare Now & in the Future. 2nd ed. Marilyn Moon. LC 98-159087. 1996. pap. text 26.50 (*0-87766-653-9*) Urban Inst.
Medicare Part B: Regional Variation in Denial Rates for Medical Necessity. (Illus.). 58p. (C). 1995. pap. text 20.00 (*0-7881-2212-6*) DIANE Pub.
Medicare Policy: New Directions for Health & Long-Term Care. Karen Davis & Diane Rowland. LC 85-45048. (Illus.). 155p. 1986. reprint ed. pap. 48.10 (*0-608-05948-X*, 206628500008) Bks Demand.
Medicare Policy & Procedure Manual. Diane P. Atchinson. (Illus.). 487p. 1996. 225.00 (*1-929162-00-6*) DPA Assocs.
***Medicare Policy & Procedure Manual: For Long Term Care Facilities.** 3rd rev. ed. Diane P. Atchinson. Ed. by Diana Johnson. 495p. 2000. ring bd. 225.00 (*1-929162-05-7*, MedP003) DPA Assocs.
***Medicare Policy & Procedure Manual for Long Term Care Facilities.** 2nd ed. Diane P. Atchinson. Ed. by Diana Johnson. 427p. 1998. ring bd. 225.00 (*1-929162-02-2*) DPA Assocs.
***Medicare Politics: Exploring the Media Coverage, Political Information & Political Participation.** Felicia E. Mebane. LC 00-42232. (Health Care Policy in the United States Ser.). 2000. write for info. (*0-8153-3717-5*) Garland.
Medicare Practice Manual. Legal Counsel for the Elderly Staff. 314p. 1990. pap. 25.00 (*0-933945-05-1*) Legal Coun Elderly.
Medicare Prenatal Care. 48p. 1994. pap. text 30.00 (*1-57979-120-4*) DIANE Pub.
Medicare Preventive Benefits & Quality Standards: Hearing Before the Subcommittee on Health & Environment of the Committee on Commerce, House of Representatives, One Hundred Fifth Congress, First Session, April 11, 1997. United States Government. LC 98-144128. iii, 116 p. 1997. write for info. (*0-16-055865-4*) USGPO.
Medicare Provider Reimbursement Manual. Government Printing Office Staff. 1986. ring bd. 284.00 (*0-16-016933-X*) USGPO.
***Medicare Provider Service Networks: Congressional Hearing.** Ed. by Michael Bilirakis. 112p. 1999. reprint ed. pap. text 25.00 (*0-7881-8553-5*) DIANE Pub.
Medicare Provider-Sponsored Organizations: A Practical Guide to Development & Certification. Peter N. Grant & William R. Hirsch. LC 98-27335. 66p. 1998. 35.00 (*1-55648-243-4*) AHPI.
Medicare Pt. A Intermediary Manual, Claims Process Part 3. Government Printing Office Staff. 1987. ring bd. 662.00 (*0-16-016910-0*) USGPO.
Medicare Pt. B Carrier Manual, Claims Process Part 3. Government Printing Office Staff. 1986. ring bd. 453.00 (*0-16-016805-8*) USGPO.
Medicare RBRVS: The Physicians' Guide, 1997 Edition. rev. ed. American Medical Association. 496p. 1997. pap. 59.95 (*0-89970-860-9*, OP059697WE) AMA.
Medicare RBRVS: The Physician's Guide, 1998 Edition. Date not set. pap. 59.00 (*0-89970-927-3*, 09273) Aspen Pub.
***Medicare RBRVS: The Physician's Guide, 1999 Manual.** Ed. by American Medical Association Staff. 464p. 1999. pap. 64.00 (*0-89970-967-2*) Aspen Pub.
***Medicare RBRVS: The Physicians' Guide 2000.** 2000. 66.95 (*1-57947-028-9*) AMA.
***Medicare Reform: Beyond the Basics: A Century Foundation Report.** Century Foundation Staff. LC 99-88500. 2000. 10.95 (*0-87078-446-3*) Century Foundation.
***Medicare Reform: Issues & Answers.** Ed. by Andrew J. Rettenmaier & Thomas R. Saving. LC 99-23001. (Volume in the Bush School Series in the Economics of Public Policy). 176p. 1999. 25.00 (*0-226-71013-0*) U Ch Pr.
Medicare Reform: The Private-Sector Impact. Employee Benefit Research Institute Staff. LC 85-25266. 156p. (Orig.). 1985. 39.95 (*0-86643-044-X*, 85-25266); pap. 19.95 (*0-86643-045-8*) Empl Benefit Res Inst.
Medicare Reimbursement & the Quality of Hospital Care. Michael J. McGinty. 137p. (Orig.). (C). 1994. pap. text 40.00 (*0-7881-1053-5*) DIANE Pub.
Medicare Risk & Capitation. 1996. write for info. (*1-57372-044-5*) HCIA.
Medicare Rules & Compliance Regulations. 250p. 1998. pap. 75.00 (*1-58383-013-8*, CCR9) Robert D Keene.
Medicare Rules & Regulations 1998: A Survival Guide to Policies, Procedures & Payment Reform. annuals rev. ed. Denise Knaus. (Illus.). 380p. 1998. pap. text 49.95 (*1-57066-124-3*, 9843) Practice Mgmt Info.
***Medicare Rules & Regulations 2000: A Survival Guide to Policies, Procedures & Payment Reform.** annuals rev. ed. Maxine Lewis. (Illus.). 404p. 2000. pap. text Price not set. (*1-57066-148-0*, 20043) Practice Mgmt Info.
Medicare Skilled Nursing Facility Manual. Government Printing Office Staff. 1984. ring bd. 118.00 (*0-16-016939-9*) USGPO.
Medicare Supplement Insurance Loss Ratios in 1993. annuals 65p. (C). 1994. ring bd. 75.00 (*0-89382-309-0*) Nat Assn Insurance.
Medicare Supplement Insurance Model Regulation Compliance Manual. 3rd rev. ed. Ed. by Diana Wright. 98p. (C). 1997. pap. 25.00 (*0-89382-442-9*, MED-LM) Nat Assn Insurance.
Medicare Supplement Insurance Model Regulations Compliance Manual. 98p. (C). 1993. pap. 25.00 (*0-89382-291-4*) Nat Assn Insurance.
Medicare Supplement Loss Ratio Report in 1990. 136p. (C). 1991. per. 75.00 (*0-89382-181-0*) Nat Assn Insurance.
Medicare Supplement Loss Ratios in 1992. 176p. 1993. ring bd. 75.00 (*0-89382-252-3*) Nat Assn Insurance.
Medicare Supplement Loss Ratios in 1998. 7th rev. ed. Ed. by Jim Bugenhagen. 122p. 1998. reprint ed. pap. 100.00i (*0-89382-531-X*, MED-BB97) Nat Assn Insurance.
Medicare Supplement Loss Ratios in 1991: Annual Edition. 142p. (C). 1992. per. 75.00 (*0-89382-214-0*) Nat Assn Insurance.
Medicare Supplement Loss Ratios Report. rev. ed. Ed. by Jim Bugenhagen. 140p. (C). 1995. ring bd. 100.00 (*0-89382-364-3*, MED-BB) Nat Assn Insurance.
Medicare Supplement Loss Ratios Report for 1995. 7th rev. ed. (C). 1996. ring bd. 100.00 (*0-89382-426-7*, MED-BB) Nat Assn Insurance.
Medicare System of Perspective Payment: Implications for Medical Education & Practice. Ed. by Mohan L. Garg & Barbara M. Barzansky. LC 85-30052. 238p. 1986. 62.95 (*0-275-92009-7*, C2009, Praeger Pubs) Greenwood.
Medicare Transaction System: Success Depends upon Correcting Critical Managerial & Technical Weaknesses. Mark E. Heatwole. (Illus.). 83p. (C). 1998. pap. text 25.00 (*0-7881-4042-6*) DIANE Pub.
Medicare Unique Physician Identification Number Directory, 14 vols., Set. 1994. lib. bdg. 6495.95 (*0-8490-5692-6*) Gordon Pr.
***Medicare Unique Physician Identification Number Supplement, 1999.** 375p. 1999. per. 37.00 (*0-16-050185-7*) USGPO.
Medicare Waste, Fraud & Abuse: Hearing Before the Subcommittee on Oversight & Investigations of the Committee on Commerce, House of Representatives, One Hundred Fifth Congress, First Session, September 29, 1997. United States Government. LC 98-133068. iii, 87 p. 1998. 4.50 (*0-16-055969-3*) USGPO.
Medicare Waste, Fraud & Abuse, a Regional Perspective: Hearing Before the Subcommittee on Oversight & Investigations of the Committee on Commerce, House of Representatives, 105th Congress, Second Session, March 2, 1998. LC 98-175808. iii, 63p. 1998. write for info. (*0-16-056545-6*) USGPO.
Medicare's New Hospital Payment System: Is It Working? Louise B. Russell. 120p. 1989. 32.95 (*0-8157-7624-1*); pap. 12.95 (*0-8157-7623-3*) Brookings.
Medicare's Prospective Payment System: Strategies for Evaluating Cost, Quality & Medical Technology. 1992. lib. bdg. 275.00 (*0-8490-5481-8*) Gordon Pr.
Medicate Me Again. Judith G. Marshall. 132p. 1994. pap. text 10.00 (*0-934385-62-9*) Hlth Prof Inst.
Medicated Intrauterine Devices: Physiological & Clinical Aspects. Ed. by E. S. Hafez & W. A. Van Os. (Developments in Obstetrics & Gynecology Ser.: No. 5). (Illus.). 245p. 1980. text 199.50 (*90-247-2371-X*) Kluwer Academic.
Medicating Schizophrenia: A History. Sheldon Gelman. LC 98-47002. 288p. (C). 1999. text 52.00 (*0-8135-2642-6*); pap. text 23.00 (*0-8135-2643-4*) Rutgers U Pr.
Medication Administration for Unlicensed Personnel. Division of Mental Retardation Staff. (Illus.). 1998. pap. 29.95 (*1-928752-06-3*) Mc Gowan Pubns.
Medication Administration for Unlicensed Personnel. Tennessee Department of Mental Health Staff. (Illus.). 352p. 1999. pap. 35.95 (*1-928752-14-4*) Mc Gowan Pubns.
***Medication Administration for Unlicensed Personnel: Training Guide.** Illus. by Bonnie Kline. 164p. 1999. pap. 249.95 (*1-928752-21-7*) Mc Gowan Pubns.
Medication Calculation & Administration. Welborn. 1995. pap. write for info. (*0-7216-5001-5*, W B Saunders Co) Harcrt Hlth Sci Grp.
Medication Development for the Treatment of Cocaine Dependence: Issues in Clinical Efficacy Trials. Betty Tai. 333p. 1997. per. 23.00 (*0-16-061520-8*) USGPO.
Medication Errors. Ed. by Michael R. Cohen. LC 99-31972. (Illus.). 380p. 1999. text 70.00 (*0-917330-89-7*) Am Pharm Assn.
Medication Errors: The Nursing Experience. Zane R. Wolfe. LC 93-5886. (Real Nursing Ser.). 209p. 1993. pap. 23.75 (*0-8273-6262-5*) Delmar.
***Medication "Fact Sheets" 2000 Edition.** 6th rev. ed. Dean E. Konopasek. LC TX4-28-77. 90p. (C). 1999. pap. text 21.95 (*0-9645719-5-1*) Arctic Tern Pub.
Medication of the Mind. Scott Veggeberg. LC 95-34584. (Scientific American Focus Bks.). 1995. 22.50 (*0-8050-3841-8*); pap. 9.95 (*0-8050-3842-6*) H Holt & Co.
Medication Teaching Aids. 2nd rev. ed. Springhouse Publishing Company Staff. LC 98-19030. 432p. 1998. 34.95 (*0-87434-942-7*) Springhouse Corp.
Medication Teaching Manual see Manual de Ensenanza de Medicamentos En Espanol: A Guide to Patient Drug Information in Spanish
Medication Teaching Manual: The Guide to Patient Counseling. 6th rev. ed. LC 95-123096. 608p. 1994. pap. text 66.00 (*1-879907-51-8*) Am Soc Hlth-Syst.
Medication Teaching Manual: The Guide to Patient Drug Information. 7th rev. ed. LC 98-187236. 1253p. 1998. spiral bd. 81.00 (*1-879907-81-X*) Am Soc Hlth-Syst.
***Medication Use: A Systems Approach to Reducing Errors.** Joint Commission on Accreditation of Healthcare Organizations. (Illus.). 143p. 1998. pap. 60.00 (*0-86688-522-6*) Joint Comm Hlthcare.
Medications. Government Printing Office Staff. 28p. 1995. pap. 27.00 (*0-16-048310-7*) USGPO.
Medications: A Guide for the Health Professions. 2nd rev. ed. Karen Lane & Linda Reed. LC 98-27995. (Illus.). 350p. 1998. pap. 34.95 (*0-8036-0378-9*) Davis Co.
Medications & Math for Allied Health Professions. Rice. (ALLIED HEALTH). (C). 2000. pap. 26.50 (*0-7668-1090-9*) Delmar.
Medications & Math for the Nurse. 6th ed. Jane Rice. (LPN/LVN Nursing Ser.). 1988. pap. 33.95 (*0-8273-2841-9*) Delmar.
Medications & Math for the Nurse - IML. 8th ed. Rice. 96p. 1998. teacher ed. 15.95 (*0-8273-8329-0*) Delmar.
Medications & Mathematics for Nursing. 7th ed. Jane Rice & Esther G. Skelley. LC 92-18283. 620p. 1993. text 33.95 (*0-8273-5119-4*) Delmar.
Medications & Mathematics for the Nurse. 8th ed. Jane Rice. LC 97-13780. 652p. (C). 1997. mass mkt. 45.95 (*0-8273-8328-2*) Delmar.
Medications & Mathematics for the Nurse: Instructor's Guide. 7th ed. Jane Rice & Esther G. Skelley. 87p. 1993. pap. 12.95 (*0-8273-5120-8*) Delmar.
***Medications & Mothers' Milk.** 8th ed. Thomas W. Hale. LC RJ216.H25 1995. 792p. 1999. pap. text 24.95 (*0-9636219-1-2*) Pharmasft Pub.
Medications & Mothers' Milk, Vol. 7. Thomas W. Hale. LC 96-143153. 750p. 1998. pap. 19.95 (*0-9636219-0-4*) Pharmasft Pub.
Medications Development: Drug Discovery, Databases, & Computer-Aided Drig Design. 1995. lib. bdg. 256.99 (*0-8490-7423-1*) Gordon Pr.
Medications Development: Drug Discovery, Databases, & Computer-Aided Drug Design. (Illus.). 288p. (C). 1994. pap. text 65.00 (*0-7881-1137-X*) DIANE Pub.
Medications Development: Drug Discovery, Databases, & Computer-Aided Drug Design. 1997. lib. bdg. 250.99 (*0-8490-7734-6*) Gordon Pr.
Medications Development: Drug Discovery, Databases & Computer-Aided Drug Design. 1994. lib. bdg. 295.00 (*0-8490-8400-8*) Gordon Pr.
Medications for Attention Disorders & Related Medical Problems. 2nd rev. ed. Edna D. Copeland & Stephen C. Copps. (Illus.). 406p. 1995. 37.00 (*1-886941-00-9*) Spec Pr FL.
Medications for School-Age Children: Effects on Learning & Behavior. Ronald T. Brown & Michael G. Sawyer. LC 97-50080. (School Practitioner Ser.). 228p. 1998. lib. bdg. 30.00 (*1-57230-316-6*, C0316) Guilford Pubns.
Medications Guide: Basic Guide to Physical & Psychiatric Medications for Recreational Therapy. Thomas K. Skalko et al. 58p. (Orig.). 1994. pap. text 14.00 (*1-889435-03-1*) Am Therapeutic.
Medications Used in Oral Surgery: A Self-Instructional Guide, Bk. 3. 3rd rev. ed. James R. Hooley & Robert J. Whitacre. 112p. 1984. pap. 19.95 (*0-89939-032-3*) Stoma Pr.
***Medications without Prescriptions.** Ephim Berkin. Ed. by leonora Chernayakhovskaya. (RUS., Illus.). 224p. 2000. pap. 12.00 (*1-893552-07-1*) Mir Collection.
Medici Codex of 1518, Vol. 1: Historical Introduction & Commentary. Ed. by Edward E. Lowinsky. LC 67-13810. (Monuments of Renaissance Music Ser.: Vols. 1, 2 & 3). 259p. 1968. lib. bdg. 120.00 (*0-226-49480-2*) U Ch Pr.
Medici Codex of 1518, Vol. 2: Transcription. Ed. by Edward E. Lowinsky. LC 67-13810. (Monuments of Renaissance Music Ser.: Vols. 1, 2 & 3). 415p. 1968. lib. bdg. 120.00 (*0-226-49481-0*) U Ch Pr.
Medici Codex of 1518, Vol. 3: Facsimile Edition. Ed. by Edward E. Lowinsky. LC 67-13810. (Monuments of Renaissance Music Ser.: Vols. 1, 2 & 3). 318p. 1968. lib. bdg. 120.00 (*0-226-49482-9*) U Ch Pr.
Medici Ring. large type ed. Nicole St. John. 1978. 27.99 (*0-7089-0160-3*) Ulverscroft.
Medici Ring. Nicole St. John. LC 98-89778. 286p. 1999. reprint ed. pap. 16.00 (*1-892323-25-7*) Vivisphere.
Medici Wedding of 1589: Florentine Festival As Theatrum Mundi. James M. Saslow. LC 95-32245. (Illus.). 323p. (C). 1996. 50.00 (*0-300-06447-0*) Yale U Pr.
Medicina Antiqua: Codex Vindobonesis, 1993. fac. ed. (Glanzlichter der Buchkunst (Splendor of Book Craft) Ser.: Band 6). (Illus.). 322p. 1996. 97.47 (*3-201-01659-4*, Pub. by Akademische Druck-und) Balogh.
Medicina Antiqua: Vienna, Cod. Vind. 93. (Manuscripts in Miniature Ser.). (Illus.). 380p. 1999. text 95.00 (*1-872501-20-6*) Gordon & Breach.
Medicina Cientifica en el Siglo XIX Mexico. Fernando M. Cortes. (Ciencia para Todos Ser.). (SPA.). pap. 6.99 (*968-16-2709-1*, Pub. by Fondo) Continental Bk.
Medicina de Dios. Kenneth E. Hagin.Tr. of God's Medicine. (SPA.). 1982. pap. 1.00 (*0-89276-153-9*) Faith Lib Pubns.
Medicina Entre los Purepecha Prehispanicos. Maria T. Sepulveda. 186p. 1989. pap. 9.14 (*968-837-419-9*, UN030) UPLAAP.
Medicina Gerocomica. John Floyer. Ed. by Robert J. Kastenbaum. LC 78-22199. (Aging & Old Age Ser.). 1979. reprint ed. lib. bdg. 17.95 (*0-405-11838-4*) Ayer.
Medicina Natural: Retorno a Nuestra Esencia. Efraibn Rodriquez Malavbe. LC 98-50215. 1999. write for info. (*0-8477-0365-7*) U of PR Pr.
Medicina Plinii - Concordantiae in Medicinam Plinii. Ed. by Anna R. Corsini & Maria P. Segoloni. (Alpha-Omega, Reihe A Ser.: Bd. CI). vi, 351p. 1989. 160.00 (*3-487-09182-8*) G Olms Pubs.
Medicina Popular en Cuba: Medicos de Antano, Curanderos, Santeros y Paleros de Hogano. Lydia Cabrera. LC 84-81080. (Coleccion del Chichereku). (SPA.). 272p. 1984. reprint ed. pap. 19.95 (*0-89729-762-8*) Ediciones.
Medicina Prehispanica de Mexico. Viesca Trevino. 1997. pap. text 10.98 (*968-38-0314-8*) Panorama Edit.
Medicina y Salud: Nueva Enciclopedia Completa. Richard J. Wagman. Tr. by Maria T. Sanz & Pedro Larios A. (SPA., Illus.). 1390p. 1992. 59.95 (*0-915741-33-4*) C D Stampley Ent.
Medicina y Sentido Comun. Amiris Alcover. LC 87-83264. (Coleccion Textos). (SPA.). 205p. (Orig.). 1988. pap. 9.95 (*0-89729-470-X*) Ediciones.
Medicinal & Aromatic Plants, No. 1, Vol. 4. Ed. by Y. P. S. Bajaj. (Illus.). 600p. 1988. 316.95 (*0-387-18414-7*) Spr-Verlag.
Medicinal & Aromatic Plants, Vol. 33. Contrib. by Y. P. S. Bajaj. 1995. 369.00 (*0-387-58298-3*) Spr-Verlag.
Medicinal & Aromatic Plants VIII. Ed. by Y. P. S. Bajaj. (Biotechnology in Agriculture & Forestry Ser.: Vol. 33). (Illus.). 504p. 1995. 369.00 (*3-540-58298-3*) Spr-Verlag.
Medicinal & Aromatic Plants V. Y. P. S. Bajaj. (Biotechnology in Agriculture & Forestry Ser.: Vol. 24). (Illus.). 350p. 1993. 343.95 (*0-387-56008-4*) Spr-Verlag.
Medicinal & Aromatic Plants IV. Ed. by Y. P. S. Bajaj. (Biotechnology in Agriculture & Forestry Ser.: Vol. 21). (Illus.). 464p. 1993. 401.95 (*0-387-54644-8*) Spr-Verlag.
Medicinal & Aromatic Plants in Asia. F. A. O. Staff. (Illus.). 203p. (C). 1995. 35.00 (*1-886106-52-5*) Science Pubs.
Medicinal & Aromatic Plants IX, Vol. 37. Ed. by Y. P. S. Bajaj. 432p. 1996. 339.00 (*3-540-60597-5*) Spr-Verlag.
Medicinal & Aromatic Plants VI. Ed. by Y. P. S. Bajaj. (Biotechnology in Agriculture & Forestry Ser.: Vol. 26). (Illus.). 415p. 1994. 318.95 (*0-387-56391-1*) Spr-Verlag.
Medicinal & Aromatic Plants III. Ed. by Y. P. S. Bajaj. (Biotechnology in Agriculture & Forestry Ser.: Vol. 15). (Illus.). 544p. 1991. 315.00 (*0-387-52098-8*) Spr-Verlag.
Medicinal & Aromatic Plants II. Ed. by Y. P. S. Bajaj. (Biotechnology in Agriculture & Forestry Ser.: Vol. 7). (Illus.). 585p. 1989. 328.95 (*0-387-19196-8*) Spr-Verlag.
Medicinal & Aromatic Plants X. Ed. by Y. P. S. Bajaj. (Biotechnology in Agriculture & Forestry Ser.: Vol. 41). (Illus.). 410p. 1998. 249.00 (*3-540-62727-8*) Spr-Verlag.
Medicinal & Aromatic Plants XI. Ed. by Y. P. S. Bajaj. (Illus.). 400p. 1999. 275.00 (*3-540-63911-X*) Spr-Verlag.
Medicinal & Economical Botany. John Lindley. 274p. (C). 1984. 65.00 (*0-7855-3299-4*, Pub. by Scientific) St Mut.
Medicinal & Other Uses of North American Plants. Charlotte Erichsen-Brown. 1989. pap. 12.95 (*0-486-25951-X*) Dover.

M

An Asterisk (*) at the beginning of an entry indicates that the title is appearing for the first time.

Medicinal & Pharmaceutical Chemistry. J. B. Stenlake. (Foundations of Molecular Pharmacology Ser.: Vol. 1). (Illus.). 936p. (C). 1979. text 105.00 (*0-485-11171-3*, Pub. by Athlone Pr) Humanities.

Medicinal & Poisonous Legumes of India. J. F. Cauis. (C). 1988. 200.00 (*0-7855-3340-0*, Pub. by Scientific) St Mut.

Medicinal & Poisonous Legumes of India. J. F. Cauisi. 187p. (C). 1989. 140.00 (*81-85046-74-3*, Pub. by Scientific) St Mut.

Medicinal & Poisonous Plants of India. Jean F. Caius. 493p. 1986. 500.00 (*81-85046-30-1*, Pub. by Scientific) St Mut.

Medicinal & Poisonous Plants of India. Jean F. Caius. 528p. (C). 1986. 160.00 (*0-7855-2273-5*, Pub. by Scientific) St Mut.

Medicinal & Poisonous Plants of Southern & Eastern Africa: Being an Account of Their Medicinal & Other Uses, Chemical Composition, Pharmacological Effects & Toxicology in Man & Animal. 2nd ed. John M. Watt & Maria G. Breyer-Brandwijk. LC QK0099.W3. 1469p. reprint ed. pap. 200.00 (*0-608-14294-8*, 201733000007) Bks Demand.

Medicinal & Poisonous Plants of the Tropics. A. J. M. Leeuwenberg. 152p. 1988. pap. 250.00 (*81-7089-098-5*, Pub. by Intl Bk Distr) St Mut.

Medicinal Chemistry. Heras. 1981. 25.00 (*0-08-026198-1*, Pergamon Pr) Elsevier.

Medicinal Chemistry. Thomas. pap. text. write for info. (*0-471-48935-2*) Wiley.

Medicinal Chemistry: A Biochemical Approach. 2nd ed. Thomas Nogrady. (Illus.). 542p. 1988. pap. text 49.95 (*0-19-505369-9*) OUP.

Medicinal Chemistry: Investigations in Biological & Pharmaceutical Chemistry. Charles Dickson. LC 98-24742. 224p. 1998. spiral bd., lab manual ed. 44.95 (*0-8493-1888-2*, 1888) CRC Pr.

Medicinal Chemistry: Principles & Practice. Ed. by Frank D. King. 340p. 1994. 73.00 (*0-85186-494-5*, R6494) CRC Pr.

Medicinal Chemistry: The Role of Organic Chemistry in Drug Research. 2nd ed. Ed. by C. R. Ganellin & S. M. Roberts. (Illus.). 324p. 1993. text 76.00 (*0-12-274120-X*) Acad Pr.

Medicinal Chemistry: Today & Tomorrow: Proceedings of the AFMC International Medicinal Chemistry Symposium Held in Tokyo, Japan, 3-8 September 1995. M. Yamazaki et al. LC 96-38942. 292p. (Orig.). 1997. text 99.95 (*0-632-04272-9*) Blackwell Sci.

Medicinal Chemistry No. 6: Proceedings of the 6th International Symposium on Medicinal Chemistry, Brighton, U. K., September 4-7, 1978: Main Lectures. International Symposium on Medicinal Chemistry Staff. Ed. by M. A. Simkins. LC 81-122062. (Illus.). 489p. reprint ed. pap. 151.60 (*0-8357-6207-6*, 203423900089) Bks Demand.

Medicinal Chemistry Case Study Workbook. Bruce L. Currie et al. 377p. 1996. pap. 34.00 (*0-683-02260-1*) Lppncott W & W.

Medicinal Chemistry for the Twenty-First Century. 1992. 120.00 (*0-632-03408-4*) Blackwell Sci.

Medicinal Chemistry of the Renin-Angiotensin System. Ed. by P. B. Timmermans & R. R. Wexler. LC 95-116971. (Pharmacochemistry Library: Vol. 21). 438p. 1994. 321.00 (*0-444-82053-1*) Elsevier.

Medicinal Fatty Acids in Inflammation. J. M. Kremer. LC 98-35853. (Progress in Inflammation Research Ser.). 180p. 1998. 109.00 (*3-7643-5854-8*, Pub. by Birkhauser) Princeton Arch.

Medicinal Fatty Acids in Inflammation. Joel Kremer. LC 98-35853. (PIR, Progress in Inflammation Research Ser.). 1998. 109.00 (*0-8176-5854-8*) Birkhauser.

***Medicinal Flora of the Alaska Natives.** Ann Garibaldi. (ENG.). 199p. (C). 1999. per. 25.00 (*1-57833-118-8*) Todd Commns.

Medicinal Floral Ecology in Central India: A Case Study of the Narmada Basin. Rajendra Kumar Deoll. 238p. 1994. pap. 80.00 (*81-7054-186-7*, Pub. by Print Hse) St Mut.

Medicinal Flowers: Puspayurveda Medicinal Flowers of India & Adjacent Regions. Gyanendra Pandey. (Indian Medical Science Ser.: No. 14). (C). 1992. 18.00 (*81-7030-351-6*) S Asia.

Medicinal Garden. Anne McIntyre. LC 96-41112. 1995. pap. 17.95 (*0-8050-4838-3*) H Holt & Co.

***Medicinal Herb Handbook: An Herbal Application Guide for Novice & Clinician Through Simplified Herbal Remedy Descriptions.** Feather Jones. 36p. 1999. pap. 4.95 (*0-914955-87-X*) Lotus Pr.

Medicinal Herbal Therapy: A Pharmacist's View Point. Steven G. Ottariano. LC 98-22339. (Illus.). 192p. 1999. pap. 14.95 (*0-9637077-6-0*) Nicolin Flds.

Medicinal Herbs. Harper. pap. 14.95 (*0-8464-4501-8*) Beekman Pubs.

Medicinal Herbs & Essential Oils. Anthony Gardiner. 64p. 1997. 7.98 (*0-7858-0713-6*) Bk Sales Inc.

Medicinal Herbs in the Garden, Field & Marketplace: The First Guide to Medicinal Herb Growing & Marketing in the U. S. & Canada. Lee Sturdivant & Tim Blakley. LC 98-60624. (Bootstrap Guide Ser.). (Illus.). 350p. 1998. pap. 24.95 (*0-9621635-7-0*) San Juan Naturals.

Medicinal Mushrooms. Woodland Publishing Staff. 1999. pap. 3.95 (*1-885670-54-0*) Woodland UT.

Medicinal Mushrooms: An Exploration of Tradition, Healing & Culture. 2nd ed. Christopher Hobbs. 240p. 1999. 29.95 (*1-883010-70-5*, Pub. by Interweave) IPG Chicago.

Medicinal Natural Products: A Biosynthetic Approach. Paul M. Dewick. LC 97-12100. 476p. 1997. pap. 72.95 (*0-471-97478-1*) Wiley.

Medicinal Natural Products: A Biosynthetic Approach. Paul M. Dewick. LC 97-12100. 476p. 1997. 200.00 (*0-471-97477-3*) Wiley.

Medicinal Plant Industry. R. O. Wijesekera. 280p. 1991. per. 314.95 (*0-8493-6669-0*, SB293) CRC Pr.

Medicinal Plants, Set, Vols. 1-4. R. Bentley & H. Triman. 1400p. (C). 1981. 700.00 (*0-7855-7512-X*) St Mut.

Medicinal Plants, Set, Vols. 1-4. Ed. by G. Bentley. 1982. reprint ed. 1000.00 (*81-7089-002-0*, Pub. by Intl Bk Distr) St Mut.

Medicinal Plants, Vol. 1. Vimala Ramalingam et al. Ed. by N. Singh & H. C. Mital. 161p. 1974. text 25.50 (*0-8422-7240-2*) Irvington.

Medicinal Plants, Vols. 1-4. R. Bentley. 1999. reprint ed. pap. 1400.00 (*81-7089-167-1*, Pub. by Intl Bk Distr) St Mut.

Medicinal Plants: A Source Guide. 1991. lib. bdg. 76.00 (*0-8490-4907-5*) Gordon Pr.

Medicinal Plants: An Expanding Role in Development. John Lambert et al. LC 96-13421. (World Bank Technical Papers: No. 320). 32p. 1996. pap. 22.00 (*0-8213-3613-4*, 13613) World Bank.

Medicinal Plants: An Illustrated & Descriptive Guide to Plants Indigenous to & Naturalized in the United States Which Are Used in Medicine, 2 vols., Set. Charles F. Millspaugh. 1132p. 1980. lib. bdg. 200.00 (*0-8490-3103-6*) Gordon Pr.

Medicinal Plants: Can Utilization & Conservation Coexist? Jennie W. Sheldon et al. LC 97-16472. (Advances in Economic Botany Ser.: Vol. 12). 104p. 1997. pap. 14.50 (*0-89327-406-2*) NY Botanical.

***Medicinal Plants: Culture, Utilization & Phytopharmacology.** Thomas S. C. Li. LC 00-104016. 544p. 2000. text 134.95 (*1-56676-903-5*) Technomic.

Medicinal Plants: New Vistas of Research, Pt. 1. Ed. by J. N. Govil et al. (Glimpses in Plant Research Ser.: Vol. X). (Illus.). 286p. 1992. 59.00 (*1-55528-272-5*, Pub. by Today Tomorrow) Scholarly Pubns.

Medicinal Plants: New Vistas of Research, Pt. 2. Ed. by J. N. Govil et al. (Glimpses in Plant Research Ser.: Vol. XI). (Illus.). 300p. 1992. 59.00 (*1-55528-273-3*, Pub. by Today Tomorrow) Scholarly Pubns.

Medicinal Plants: Rescuing a Global Heritage. John Lambert et al. LC 96-52234. (Technical Paper Ser.: No. 355). 80p. 1997. pap. 22.00 (*0-8213-3856-0*, 13856) World Bank.

Medicinal Plants: Their Role in Health & Biodiversity. Timothy R. Tomlinson. LC 98-10113. (Illus.). 208p. (C). 1998. text 39.95 (*0-8122-3431-6*) U of Pa Pr.

Medicinal Plants & Folklores: A Strategy Towards Conquest of Human Ailments. V. K. Singh. 230p. 1989. 59.00 (*1-55528-212-1*, Pub. by Today Tomorrow) Scholarly Pubns.

Medicinal Plants & Herbs of Eastern & Central North America. 2nd rev. ed. Steven Foster & James A. Duke. LC 99-33189. (Peterson Field Guides Ser.). (Illus.). 512p. 1999. pap. 19.00 (*0-395-98814-4*) HM.

***Medicinal Plants & Herbs of Eastern & Central North America.** 2nd rev. ed. Steven Foster & James A. Duke. LC 99-33189. (Peterson Field Guides Ser.). (Illus.). 512p. 2000. 30.00 (*0-395-98815-2*) HM.

Medicinal Plants & Their History. Edith G. Wheelwright. LC 74-78815. (Illus.). 288p. 1974. reprint ed. pap. 7.95 (*0-486-23103-8*) Dover.

Medicinal Plants & Traditional Medicine in Africa. Abayomi Sofowora. LC 82-2785. (Illus.). 274p. reprint ed. pap. 85.00 (*0-608-17998-1*, 202789100057) Bks Demand.

Medicinal Plants Col. Book. Arbel. 1998. pap. 2.95 (*0-486-27462-4*) Dover.

Medicinal Plants for Forest Conservation & Health Care. (Non-Wood Forest Products Ser.: No. 11). 164p. 1998. pap. 19.00 (*92-5-104063-X*, F4063X, Pub. by FAO) Bernan Associates.

Medicinal Plants in China. (WHO Regional Publications: No. 2). 327p. 1989. pap. text 50.00 (*92-9061-102-2*, 1510002) World Health.

Medicinal Plants in the Biblical World. Ed. by Walter Jacob & Irene Jacob. (Horticulture & Technology in the Biblical World Ser.: No. I). 160p. (Orig.). 1990. reprint ed. pap. 12.00 (*0-929699-02-5*) Rodef Shalom Pr.

Medicinal Plants in Viet Nam. (WHO Regional Publications: No. 3). 410p. 1992. pap. text 45.00 (*92-9061-101-4*, 1510003) World Health.

Medicinal Plants of Bombay Presidency. S. P. Agharkar. (C). 1991. text 185.00 (*81-7233-017-0*, Pub. by Scientific Pubs) St Mut.

Medicinal Plants of Brazil. Walter B. Mors et al. Ed. by Robert A. DeFilipps. (Medicinal Plants of the World Ser.: No. 6). (Illus.). Date not set. write for info. (*0-917256-42-5*) Ref Pubns.

Medicinal Plants of China, 2 vols., Set. James A. Duke & Edward S. Ayensu. LC 84-4867. (Medicinal Plants of the World Ser.: No. 4). (Illus.). 1985. 99.00 (*0-917256-20-4*) Ref Pubns.

Medicinal Plants of Gwalior. V. M. Pathak. (C). 1987. 130.00 (*0-7855-3123-8*, Pub. by Intl Bk Distr) St Mut.

Medicinal Plants of Himalaya. Gyanendra Pandey. (C). 1995. 44.00 (*81-7030-464-4*, Pub. by Sri Satguru Pubns) S Asia.

Medicinal Plants of India, 2 vols., Set. S. K. Jain & Robert A. DeFilipps. LC 90-8051. (Medicinal Plants of the World Ser.: No. 5). 1991. 99.00 (*0-917256-39-5*) Ref Pubns.

Medicinal Plants of India & Pakistan. J. F. Dastur. 212p. 1988. 11.95 (*0-318-36365-8*) Asia Bk Corp.

Medicinal Plants of India & Pakistan. J. F. Dastur. (C). 1988. 35.00 (*0-7855-2269-7*, Pub. by Scientific) St Mut.

Medicinal Plants of Nepal. HMG Staff. 1997. 40.00 (*0-7855-7608-8*); pap., suppl. ed. 23.00 (*0-7855-7609-6*) St Mut.

Medicinal Plants of Nepal Himalaya. Ed. by N. P. Manandhar. 87p. (C). 1980. 75.00 (*0-89771-096-7*, Pub. by Ratna Pustak Bhandar) St Mut.

Medicinal Plants of North Africa. Loutfy Boulos. Ed. by Edward S. Ayensu. LC 82-20412. (Medicinal Plants of the World Ser.: No. 3). (Illus.). 300p. 1983. 45.00 (*0-917256-16-6*) Ref Pubns.

Medicinal Plants of Papua New Guinea Pt. 1: Morobe Province. Ed. by E. Woodley. (Illus.). 158p. 1991. pap. 33.00 (*3-8236-1185-2*, Pub. by Backhuys Pubs) Balogh.

Medicinal Plants of the Arid Zones. L. C. Chopra & B. K. Abrol. 96p. 1983. 11.00 (*1-55528-035-8*, Pub. by Today Tomorrow) Scholarly Pubns.

Medicinal Plants of the Cumberland Plateau & Appalachian Mountains. 2nd ed. John E. Warner. (Illus.). 109p. 1993. pap. 12.95 (*0-9657937-0-2*) Warner Herb.

Medicinal Plants of the Desert & Canyon West. Michael Moore. (Illus.). 200p. 1989. pap. text 13.95 (*0-89013-182-1*) Museum NM Pr.

Medicinal Plants of the Guianas. Robert A. DeFilipps. (Medicinal Plants of the World Ser.: No. 7). (Illus.). Date not set. write for info. (*0-917256-47-6*) Ref Pubns.

Medicinal Plants of the Heartland. Connie Kaye & Neil Billington. LC 96-86526. (Illus.). 352p. (Orig.). 1997. pap. 18.95 (*0-9627422-8-7*) Cache River Pr.

Medicinal Plants of the Mountain West. Michael Moore. 216p. 1979. pap. 13.95 (*0-89013-104-X*) Museum NM Pr.

***Medicinal Plants of the Pacific Northwest: A Digest of Anthropological Writings about Native American Uses.** Illus. by Rachel Hallett & Julie Gomez. 210p. 1999. 35.00 (*0-9624868-3-3*) Longevity Herb Pr.

Medicinal Plants of the Pacific West. Michael Moore. (Illus.). 360p. 1993. pap. 22.50 (*1-878610-31-7*) Red Crane Bks.

Medicinal Plants of the World: Chemical Constituents, Traditional & Modern Medicinal Uses. Ivan A. Ross. LC 98-34758. (Illus.). 432p. 1998. 99.50 (*0-89603-542-5*) Humana.

Medicinal Plants of Vietnam, Cambodia & Laos. Nguyen Van Duong. LC 93-92625. 528p. (Orig.). (C). 1993. pap. 31.00 (*0-9637303-1-2*) N Van Duong.

Medicinal Plants of West Africa. Edward S. Ayensu. Ed. by Keith Irvine. LC 78-3110. (Medicinal Plants of the World Ser.: No. 1). (Illus.). 1978. 45.00 (*0-917256-07-7*) Ref Pubns.

Medicinal Resources of the Tropical Forest: Biodiversity & Its Importance to Human Health. Ed. by Michael J. Balick et al. LC 95-13809. (Biology & Resource Management in the Tropics Ser.). (Illus.). 464p. 1996. 79.00 (*0-231-10170-8*) Col U Pr.

Medicinal Resources of the Tropical Forest: Biodiversity & Its Importance to Human Health. Ed. by Michael J. Balick et al. (Biology & Resource Management in the Tropics Ser.). (Illus.). 440p. 1996. pap. 37.00 (*0-231-10171-6*) Col U Pr.

Medicinal Value of French Brandy. George H. Jackson. 1977. lib. bdg. 59.95 (*0-8490-2218-5*) Gordon Pr.

Medicinal Wild Plants of the Prairie: An Ethnobotanical Guide. Kelly Kindscher. LC 91-38471. (Illus.). xii, 324p. 1992. 25.00 (*0-7006-0526-6*); pap. 14.95 (*0-7006-0527-4*) U Pr of KS.

Medicine. (How Things Work Ser.). (Illus.). 144p. 1991. lib. bdg. 25.93 (*0-8094-7871-4*) Time-Life.

Medicine. (How Things Work Ser.). (Illus.). 144p. (gr. 3). 1999. 19.95 (*0-8094-7870-6*) Time-Life.

***Medicine.** Nick Arnold. (Future Tech Ser.). (Illus.). 32p. (J). 1999. lib. bdg. 15.95 (*1-929298-39-0*, Pub. by Thameside Pr) Smart Apple.

Medicine. Ed. by John S. Axford. (Essentials Ser.). (Illus.). 800p. 1996. 69.95 (*0-632-02707-X*) Blackwell Sci.

Medicine. Boy Scouts of America Staff. (Illus.). 70p. (YA). (gr. 6-12). 1991. pap. 2.90 (*0-8395-3244-X*, 33244) BSA.

***Medicine.** Deborah Cannarella & Jane Fournier. LC 99-25472. (Into the Next Millennium Ser.). 32p. 1999. lib. bdg. write for info. (*1-57103-271-1*) Rourke Pr.

Medicine, 3 vols. English Language Services Staff. 1967. pap. write for info. (*0-318-54240-4*); audio. write for info. (*0-318-54241-2*) Macmillan.

Medicine. Ed. by Philip Gates. LC 97-14668. (History News Ser.). (Illus.). 32p. (J). (gr. 4-9). 1997. 15.99 (*0-7636-0316-3*) Candlewick Pr.

***Medicine.** Amy Gerstler. LC 99-54554. (Poets Ser.). 96p. 2000. pap. 15.95 (*0-14-058924-4*) Viking Penguin.

Medicine. O'Neill. 1997. pap. text 24.95 (*0-443-05078-3*, W B Saunders Co) Harcrt Hlth Sci Grp.

Medicine. Steve Parker. LC 94-34860. (Eyewitness Books). (Illus.). 64p. (J). (gr. 4-7). 1995. 15.95 (*1-56458-882-3*) DK Pub Inc.

***Medicine.** Steve Parker. (Eyewitness Books). 64p. (J). (gr. 4-7). 2000. 15.95 (*0-7894-5580-3*, D K Ink) DK Pub Inc.

Medicine. 2nd ed. (National Medical Ser.). 1993. 27.00 (*0-685-75176-7*) Lppncott W & W.

Medicine. 3rd ed. Ed. by Allen R. Myers. LC 96-13091. (National Medical Ser.). 752p. 1997. pap. 30.00 (*0-683-18105-X*) Lppncott W & W.

Medicine. 4th ed. Mark C. Fishman et al. LC 96-6181. 672p. 1996. spiral bd. 32.95 (*0-397-51464-6*) Lppncott W & W.

Medicine: A Guide for Prospective Students. Patrick Mackerras. 137p. 1996. 17.95 (*0-644-36056-9*, Pub. by Aust Gov Pub) Accents Pubns.

Medicine: A Guide for Study & Practice. 2nd ed. Ellis H. Friedman & Roger E. Moshy. LC 91-30652. 630p. 1992. pap. 176.95 (*0-471-93166-7*, Wiley-Interscience) Wiley.

Medicine: A Primary Care Approach. Richard H. Rubin et al. LC 95-21763. (Saunders Text & Review Ser.). (Illus.). 517p. 1996. pap. text 33.95 (*0-7216-5200-X*, W B Saunders Co) Harcrt Hlth Sci Grp.

Medicine: An Illustrated History. Albert S. Lyons & R. Joseph Petrucelli. (Illus.). 1978. text 42.95 (*0-8109-1054-3*) Abrams.

Medicine: Diagnosis & Treatment. Robert W. Schier. (Illus.). 600p. 1988. 39.95 (*0-316-77484-7*, Little Brwn Med Div) Lppncott W & W.

Medicine: Essentials of Clinical Practice. 3rd ed. Richard Wilkins & Norman Levinsky. 1013p. 1983. 38.00 (*0-316-94092-5*, Little Brwn Med Div) Lppncott W & W.

Medicine: Pre-Test Self-Assessment & Review. 8th ed. Ed. by Steven Berk. LC 97-18093. (Pretest Clinical Science Ser.). (Illus.). 200p. 1997. pap. text 18.95 (*0-07-052527-7*) McGraw-Hill HPD.

Medicine: Preserving the Passion. Ed. by P. R. Manning & L. DeBakey. (Illus.). 315p. 1988. 62.00 (*0-387-96361-8*) Spr-Verlag.

***Medicine: Pretest Self-Assessment & Review.** 9th ed. S. L. Berk & William R. Davis. LC 00-30562. (Illus.). 190p. 2000. write for info. (*0-07-135960-5*) McGraw.

Medicine: The Year in Review, 1992. Medical Tribune, Inc. Staff. 320p. 1992. 49.95 (*0-931861-81-0*) Med Tribune.

***Medicine: Through the Ages with Dr. Baldassare.** Robert Richardson. 256p. 1999. 18.95 (*1-899163-47-6*) Cimino Pub Grp.

***Medicine: 2001 Edition.** rev. ed. Paul D. Chan et al. (Current Clinical Strategies Ser.). 100p. 1999. pap. 28.95 incl. cd-rom (*1-881528-84-7*) Current Clin Strat.

Medicine - Alternative & Complementary Systems, Methods & Treatments: Index of New Information. Louis D. Volente. 160p. 1997. 47.50 (*0-7883-1594-3*); pap. 44.50 (*0-7883-1595-1*) ABBE Pubs Assn.

Medicine - An Art or a Science. Arnold Galambos. 1984. reprint ed. 6.00 (*0-88078-001-0*) Univ Sci Publns.

Medicine: A History of Healing: Ancient Traditions to Modern Practices. Roy Porter. (Illus.). 224p. 1998. pap. text 24.95 (*1-56924-708-0*) Marlowe & Co.

Medicine among the American Indians. Eric P. Stone. LC 75-23657. (Clio Medica Ser.: 7). (Illus.). reprint ed. 32.50 (*0-404-58907-3*) AMS Pr.

Medicine & American Growth, 1800-1860. James H. Cassedy. LC 86-40047. (Publications in the History of Science & Medicine: Vol. 5). (Illus.). 317p. reprint ed. pap. 98.30 (*0-608-20417-X*, 207167000002) Bks Demand.

Medicine & Anthropology. New York Academy of Medicine Staff. Ed. by Iago Galdston. LC 71-142678. (Essay Index Reprint Ser.). 1977. 19.95 (*0-8369-2118-6*) Ayer.

***Medicine & Charity in Georgian Bath: A Social History of the General Infirmary, 1739-1830.** Anne Borsay. LC 99-63692. (History of Medicine in Context Ser.). (Illus.). 496p. 1999. text 96.95 (*0-7546-0060-2*, Pub. by Ashgate Pub) Ashgate Pub Co.

Medicine & Christian Morality. 3rd rev. ed. Thomas J. O'Donnell. LC 96-20352. 336p. (Orig.). 1996. pap. 19.95 (*0-8189-0765-7*) Alba.

Medicine & Culture. Lynn Payer. 208p. 1995. pap. 11.95 (*0-8050-4803-0*) H Holt & Co.

Medicine & Ethnology: Selected Essays of Erwin H. Ackerknecht. Erwin H. Ackerknecht. Ed. by H. Koelbing & H. Walser. LC 70-165334. 195p. reprint ed. 60.50 (*0-8357-9276-5*, 201402200088) Bks Demand.

Medicine & Health Care. Ed. by Saul Jarcho. LC 76-29724. (Great Contemporary Issues Ser.). 1977. lib. bdg. 27.95 (*0-405-09850-2*) Ayer.

Medicine & Health Care in the U. S. S. R. Ed. by Sergei Burenkov. LC 85-14460. 315p. 1985. 47.50 (*0-8236-3310-1*, 03310) Intl Univs Pr.

Medicine & Health Care into the Twenty-First Century. Shyamal K. Majumdar & David B. Nash. LC 95-67144. (Illus.). xii, 613p. 1995. 50.00 (*0-945809-11-5*) Penn Science.

Medicine & Human Welfare. Henry E. Sigerist. LC 71-119214. 1941. 17.95 (*0-8434-0094-3*, Pub. by McGrath NH) Ayer.

Medicine & Hygiene in the Works of Flavius Josephus. Samuel S. Kottek. LC 94-905. (Studies in Ancient Medicine: Vol. 9). 1994. 84.50 (*90-04-09941-7*) Brill Academic Pubs.

Medicine & Its Technology: An Introduction to the History of Medical Instruments, 7. Audrey B. Davis. LC 80-25202. (Contributions in Medical History Ser.: No. 7). (Illus.). 285p. 1981. 69.50 (*0-313-22807-8*, DMT/, Greenwood Pr) Greenwood.

Medicine & Jewish Law, Vol. I. Ed. by Fred Rosner. LC 89-49410. 216p. 1993. pap. 25.00 (*1-56821-028-0*) Aronson.

Medicine & Jewish Law, Vol. II. Ed. by Fred Rosner. LC 89-49410. 184p. 1993. pap. 25.00 (*0-87668-574-2*) Aronson.

Medicine & Labour: The Politics of a Profession. Watkins. (C). 1987. pap. 19.50 (*0-85315-639-5*, Pub. by Lawrence & Wishart) NYU Pr.

Medicine & Literature. Ed. by Enid R. Peschel. 1980. 17.95 (*0-685-03475-5*) Watson Pub Intl.

Medicine & Madness: A Social History of Insanity in New South Wales 1880-1940. Stephen Garton. 212p. 29.95 (*0-86840-306-7*, Pub. by New South Wales Univ Pr) Intl Spec Bk.

Medicine & Mankind. Ed. by Iago Galdston. LC 70-142632. (Essay Index Reprint Ser.). 1977. 19.95 (*0-8369-2108-9*) Ayer.

Medicine & Mental Illness. Marvin E. Lickey & Barbara Gordon. Orig. Title: Drugs for Mental Illness. (C). 1991. text 24.00 (*0-7167-2195-3*); pap. text 22.95 (*0-7167-2196-1*) W H Freeman.

Medicine & Modernity: Public Health & Medical Care in Nineteenth-& Twentieth-Century Germany. Ed. by Manfred Berg & Geoffrey Cocks. LC 96-15487. (Publications of the German Historical Institute, Washington, D.C.). 249p. 1997. text 64.95 (*0-521-56411-5*) Cambridge U Pr.

M

An Asterisk (*) at the beginning of an entry indicates that the title is appearing for the first time.

Medicine & Money: A Study of the Role of Beneficence in Health Care Cost Containment, 30. Frank H. Marsh & Mark Yarborough. LC 90-2718. (Contributions in Medical Studies: No. 30). 184p. 1990. 52.95 (*0-313-26357-4*, MMM/, Greenwood Pr) Greenwood.

Medicine & Money: Why Some Treatments Are Insured & Others Aren't... How Some Drugs Get to Market & Others Don't... What Insiders Know but the Rest of Us Don't. Christina Blackett Schlank. 300p. 1999. pap. 17.95 (*1-56343-173-4*, Pub. by Silver Lake) Natl Bk Netwk.

Medicine & Moral Philosophy. Ed. by Marshall Cohen et al. LC 81-47986. 320p. reprint ed. pap. 99.20 (*0-7837-0100-4*, 204037800016) Bks Demand.

Medicine & Morality in Haiti: The Contest for Healing Power. Paul Brodwin. (Cambridge Studies in Medical Anthropology: No. 3). (Illus.). 256p. (C). 1996. text 64.95 (*0-521-57029-8*); pap. text 23.95 (*0-521-57543-5*) Cambridge U Pr.

Medicine & Nursing: Professions in a Changing Health Service. Sylvia Walby et al. 224p. 1994. 69.95 (*0-8039-8741-2*); pap. 24.95 (*0-8039-8742-0*) Sage.

Medicine & Peace: IPPNW Model Medical Curriculum. ring bd. 5.00 (*0-614-29346-4*) Intl Phys PONW.

Medicine & Pharmacy in American Political Prints, 1765-1870. William Helfand. (Illus.). 84p. 1978. 11.00 (*0-931292-07-7*) Am Inst Hist Pharm.

Medicine & Public Health. Leonard. 1995. pap. text. write for info. (*0-582-22670-8*, Pub. by Addison-Wesley) Longman.

Medicine & Public Health: The Power of Collaboration. Roz D. Lasker. LC 97-42385. 176p. (C). 1997. pap. text. write for info. (*0-924143-05-3*) NY Acad Med.

Medicine & Public Health: The Power of Collaboration. Roz D. Lasker et al. LC 98-51607. 178p. 1998. 26.00 (*1-56793-100-6*) Health Admin Pr.

Medicine & Public Health in the Arctic & Antarctic: Selected Papers from a Conference. K. Andersen et al. (Public Health Papers: No. 18). 169p. 1963. pap. text 6.00 (*92-4-130018-3*, 1110018) World Health.

Medicine & Religion: Strategies of Care. Ed. by Donald W. Shriver, Jr. LC 79-23420. (Contemporary Community Health - Institute on Human Values in Medicine, Report Ser.: No. 13). 197p. reprint ed. pap. 61.10 (*0-7837-2139-0*, 204242500004) Bks Demand.

***Medicine & Religion c.1300: The Case of Arnau de Vailanova.** Joseph Ziegler. (Oxford Historical Monographs). 352p. 1998. text 80.00 (*0-19-820726-3*) OUP.

Medicine & Science. New York Academy of Medicine Staff. Ed. by Iago Galdston. LC 75-142679. (Essay Index Reprint Ser.). 1977. 18.95 (*0-8369-2122-4*) Ayer.

Medicine & Science in Aquatic Sports. Ed. by Y. Mutoh et al. (Medicine & Sport Science Ser.: Vol. 39). (Illus.). xii, 236p. 1994. 215.75 incl. 5.25 hd (*3-8055-5981-X*) S Karger.

Medicine & Shakespeare in the English Renaissance. F. David Hoeniger. LC 90-50400. 408p. 1992. 60.00 (*0-87413-425-0*) U Delaware Pr.

Medicine & Slavery: The Diseases & Health Care of Blacks in Antebellum Virginia. fac. rev. ed. Todd L. Savitt. LC 78-8520. (Blacks in the New World Ser.). (Illus.). 348p. 1978. pap. 107.90 (*0-7837-8086-9*, 204783900008) Bks Demand.

Medicine & Society in America. Ed. by Jennifer Hanson. LC 97-77588. (Perspectives on History Ser.: Pt. III). (Illus.). 60p. 1997. pap. 6.95 (*1-57960-019-0*) Disc Enter Ltd.

Medicine & Society in America, 47 bks., Set. Ed. by Charles E. Rosenberg. 1972. 1073.00 (*0-405-03930-1*) Ayer.

Medicine & Society in America, 1660-1860. Richard H. Shryock. LC 60-6417. 190p. 1962. pap. text 12.95 (*0-8014-9093-6*) Cornell U Pr.

***Medicine & Society in Early Modern Europe.** Mary Lindemann. LC 99-17819. (New Approaches to European History Ser.: No. 16). (Illus.). 249p. (C). 1999. 49.95 (*0-521-41254-4*); pap. 18.95 (*0-521-42354-6*) Cambridge U Pr.

Medicine & Society in France Vol. 6: Selections from the Annales, Economies, Societies, Civilisations. Ed. by Robert Forster & Orest Ranum. Tr. by Elborg Forster & Patricia M. Ranum. LC 79-16851. (Illus.). 189p. reprint ed. pap. 58.60 (*0-608-06278-2*, 206660700006) Bks Demand.

Medicine & Society in Later Medieval England. Carole Rawcliffe. (History Paperbacks Ser.). (Illus.). 256p. 1998. pap. 22.95 (*0-7509-1497-1*, Pub. by Sutton Pub Ltd) Intl Pubs Mktg.

***Medicine & Sports: Peak Performance Vs. Optimum Health?** Robert Mertzman. (C). 1999. pap. text 89.95 (*0-7872-6120-3*) Kendall-Hunt.

Medicine & Surgery for Dentistry. 2nd ed. Stephen R. Porter. LC 99-10540. (Colour Guide Ser.). 1999. write for info. (*0-443-06169-6*) Harcrt Hlth Sci Grp.

Medicine & Surgery for Lawyers. A. J. Buzzard et al. xxi, 675p. 1986. 121.00 (*0-455-20675-9*, Pub. by LawBk Co) Gaunt.

Medicine & Surgery of South American Camelids: Llama, Alpaca, Vicuna, Guanaco. Murray E. Fowler. LC 89-1870. (Illus.). 399p. reprint ed. pap. 123.70 (*0-608-09063-8*, 206969700005) Bks Demand.

Medicine & Surgery of South American Camelids: Llama, Alpaca, Vicuna, Guanaco. 2nd ed. Murray E. Fowler. LC 97-53127. (Illus.). 558p. 1998. 99.95 (*0-8138-0397-7*) Iowa St U Pr.

Medicine & TAO. 1992. lib. bdg. 88.00 (*0-8490-5379-X*) Gordon Pr.

Medicine & the Allied Sciences: A Medical Course, 3 vols., Set. 1992. lib. bdg. 1500.95 (*0-8490-8703-1*) Gordon Pr.

Medicine & the American Revolution: How Diseases & Their Treatments Affected the Colonial Army. Oscar Reiss. LC 98-20088. 286p. 1998. lib. bdg. 48.50 (*0-7864-0338-1*) McFarland & Co.

Medicine & the Bible. Ed. by Bernard Palmer. 272p. 1992. reprint ed. pap. 17.95 (*0-85364-423-3*, Pub. by Paternoster Pub) OM Literature.

Medicine & the Family: A Feminist Perspective. Lucy M. Candib. LC 95-7114. 1995. 38.00 (*0-465-02374-6*, Pub. by Basic) HarpC.

Medicine & the Five Senses. Ed. by William F. Bynum & Roy Porter. 349p. (C). 1993. text 69.95 (*0-521-36114-1*) Cambridge U Pr.

***Medicine & the History of the Body: Proceedings of the 20th, 21st & 22nd International Symposia on the Comparative History of Medicine - East & West.** Ed. by Yoshio Kawakita. (International Symposium on the Comparative History of Medicine - East & West Ser.: Vol. 20). (JPN., Illus.). 410p. 1999. pap. 70.00 (*4-900978-08-6*, Ishiyaku EuroAmerica) Med Dent Media.

Medicine & the Information Age. Jeffrey S. Rose. LC 97-77013. (Illus.). xx, 278p. 1998. 50.00 (*0-924674-57-1*) Am Coll Phys Execs.

Medicine & the Internet. Luis G. Pareras. 704p. 1996. pap. text 39.95 (*0-316-69059-7*) Lppncott W & W.

Medicine & the Internet: Introducing Online Resources & Terminology. 2nd ed. Bruce McKenzie. LC 97-219195. (Illus.). 372p. 1997. pap. text 29.50 (*0-19-262852-6*) OUP.

Medicine & the Law. Ed. by Bernard M. Dickens. LC 93-16964. (C). 1993. lib. bdg. 150.00 (*0-8147-1846-9*) NYU Pr.

Medicine & the Law. Neil Grauer. (Encyclopedia of Health Ser.). (Illus.). 120p. (YA). (gr. 7 up). 1990. lib. bdg. 19.95 (*0-7910-0088-5*) Chelsea Hse.

Medicine & the Law Vol. 19: Proceedings of the 19th International Symposium on the Comparative History of Medicine - East & West. Ed. by Yoshio Kawakita. 256p. 1998. 28.00 (*4-900978-03-5*, Ishiyaku EuroAmerica) Med Dent Media.

***Medicine & the Making of Roman Women: Gender, Nature, & Authority from Celsus to Galen.** Rebecca Flemming. 380p. 2000. text 87.00 (*0-19-924002-7*) OUP.

Medicine & the Management of Living: Taming the Last Great Beast. William R. Arney & Bernard J. Bergen. LC 83-24380. (Illus.). x, 216p. 1984. 23.95 (*0-226-02792-9*) U Ch Pr.

Medicine & the Marketplace: The Moral Dimensions of Managed Care. Kenman L. Wong. LC 98-30622. 219p. 1999. 32.00 (*0-268-01440-X*) U of Notre Dame Pr.

***Medicine & the Marketplace: The Moral Dimensions of Managed Care.** Kenman L. Wong. LC 98-30622. 256p. (C). 1999. reprint ed. pap. text 17.00 (*0-268-03455-9*, Pub. by U of Notre Dame Pr) Chicago Distribution Ctr.

Medicine & the Raj: British Medical Policy in India, 1835-1911. Anil Kumar. LC 97-43728. 248p. (C). 1998. 39.95 (*0-7619-9233-2*) Sage.

Medicine & the Reign of Technology. Stanley J. Reiser. LC 77-87389. (Illus.). 328p. (Orig.). 1981. pap. text 24.95 (*0-521-28223-3*) Cambridge U Pr.

Medicine & the War. Ed. by William H. Taliaferro. LC 70-37923. (Essay Index Reprint Ser. Charles R. Walgren Foundation Lectures). 1977. reprint ed. 25.95 (*0-8369-2629-3*) Ayer.

Medicine & Western Civilization. Ed. by David J Rothman et al. (Illus.). 450p. (C). 1995. text 50.00 (*0-8135-2189-0*) Rutgers U Pr.

Medicine & Western Civilization. Ed. by David J Rothman et al. (Illus.). 450p. (C). 1996. pap. text 22.95 (*0-8135-2190-4*) Rutgers U Pr.

Medicine As a Human Experience. David H. Rosen & Stanley J. Reiser. 192p. 1984. 55.00 (*0-8391-2037-0*, 12037) Aspen Pub.

Medicine As Culture: Illness, Disease & the Body in Western Societies. Deborah Lupton. 256p. (C). 1994. text 69.95 (*0-8039-8924-5*); pap. text 24.95 (*0-8039-8925-3*) Sage.

Medicine As Ministry: Reflections on Ethics, Suffering & Hope. Margaret E. Mohrman. LC 95-18069. 120p. (Orig.). 1995. pap. 12.95 (*0-8298-1073-0*) Pilgrim OH.

Medicine at Harvard: The First Three Hundred Years. Henry K. Beecher & Mark D. Altschule. LC 75-40869. 603p. reprint ed. pap. 187.00 (*0-608-14819-9*, 202563300045) Bks Demand.

Medicine at the Crossroads: A Global View from Agriculture to Complementary Medicine. Cordell E. Logan. (Illus.). 444p. (Orig.). (C). 1993. pap. 19.95 (*0-9636519-0-0*) C E Logan.

Medicine at the Paris Hospital, 1794-1848. Erwin H. Ackerknecht. LC 66-23003. 256p. reprint ed. pap. 79.40 (*0-7837-4487-0*, 204426400001) Bks Demand.

Medicine at the Threshold of a New Consciousness. Michaela Glocker. 1998. pap. text 14.95 (*0-904693-92-9*, Pub. by Temple Lodge) Anthroposophic.

Medicine at War. Brendan O'Keefe. (Official History of Australia's Involvement in Southeast Asian Conflicts Ser.: Vol. III). (Illus.). 536p. 1994. 59.95 (*1-86373-301-9*, Pub. by Allen & Unwin Pty) Paul & Co Pubs.

Medicine Avenue: The Story of Medical Advertising in America. William Castagnoli et al. (Illus.). 128p. 1998. 60.00 (*0-9667793-0-4*) Med Ad Hall Fame.

Medicine Bag: The Ancient Mystery of the Mind. Don Miguel Ruiz. Date not set. Price not set. (*1-878424-45-9*) Amber-Allen Pub.

Medicine Ball Exercise Cycles. Lineaus H. Lorette. (Illus.). 99p. 1984. 16.95 (*0-93225-00-4*) Comm Pr.

Medicine Bear. Menunqua. 72p. 1997. pap. 10.95 (*1-882376-50-1*) Thunder Bay Pr.

Medicine Betrayed: The Participation of Doctors in Human Rights Abuses. British Medical Association Staff. LC 92-28909. 288p. (C). 1992. pap. 19.95 (*1-85649-104-8*, Pub. by Zed Books); text 55.00 (*1-85649-103-X*, Pub. by Zed Books) St Martin.

Medicine Bow. Beth R. Kotarski. Ed. by Anita Bush. LC 95-62362. 164p. (YA). 1996. pap. 14.95 (*1-880254-34-4*) Vista.

Medicine Burns. Adam Klein. LC 96-146758. (High Risk Ser.). 200p. 1995. pap. 11.99 (*1-85242-403-6*, High Risk Bks) Serpents Tail.

Medicine Cabinet Medicines: Over-the-Counter Drugs. Richard P. Donjon. LC 99-174414. (Illus.). 134p. (C). (gr. 13). 1997. spiral bd. 12.95 (*0-8151-8053-5*, 27217) Mosby Inc.

Medicine Cards. Jamie Sams et al. 240p. 1999. 29.95 (*0-312-20491-4*) St Martin.

Medicine Ceremony of the Manomini, Iowa & Wahpeton Dakota: With Notes on the Ceremony among the Ponca, Bungi, Ojibwa & Potawtomi. Alanson B. Skinner. LC 76-43826. (Indian Notes & Monographs: Vol. 4). (Illus.). 416p. 1984. reprint ed. 59.50 (*0-404-15678-9*) AMS Pr.

Medicine Circle. George S. Bascom. 118p. 1993. pap. 15.95 (*0-89745-169-4*) Sunflower U Pr.

Medicine Civilization. David J. Rothman. (C). 1992. pap. text 12.95 (*0-691-02439-1*, Pub. by Princeton U Pr) Cal Prin Full Svc.

***Medicine Creek.** Charles G. West. 2000. mass mkt. 5.99 (*0-451-19955-3*, Sig) NAL.

Medicine Creek Treaty of 1854. Lynn Kickingbird & Curtis Berkey. (Treaty Manuscripts Ser.: No. 4). 31p. 10.00 (*0-944253-26-1*) Inst Dev Indian Law.

Medicine, Disease & the State in Ireland, 1650-1940. Ed. by Greta Jones & Elizabeth Malcolm. LC 99-176031. 240p. 1998. 60.00 (*1-85918-110-4*, Pub. by Cork Univ); pap. 20.00 (*1-85918-230-5*, Pub. by Cork Univ) Intl Spec Bk.

Medicine Dream: A Nagual Woman's Energetic Healing. Merilyn Tunneshende. 232p. 1996. 16.95 (*1-57174-046-5*) Hampton Roads Pub Co.

Medicine et les Medecins en France a l'Epoque de la Renaissance. Charles A. Wickersheimer. LC 75-23770. (FRE.). reprint ed. 55.50 (*0-404-13396-7*) AMS Pr.

Medicine, Ethics & the Law. Ed. by M. D. Freeman. (Current Legal Problems Ser.). xiv, 166p. 1988. pap. 45.00 (*0-420-48020-X*) W S Hein.

Medicine, Ethics & the Third Reich: Historical & Contemporary Issues. Ed. by John J. Michalczyk. LC 94-25916. (Illus.). 240p. (Orig.). 1994. pap. 19.95 (*1-55612-752-9*, LL1752) Sheed & Ward WI.

Medicine Family Vision: Deep-Heart Sharing in the Wisdom & Guidance of the Earth. Jai J. Daemion. LC 96-76583. (Illus.). 400p. (Orig.). 1997. pap. 16.95 (*0-9651534-3-6*, 1010) Ajna Media.

Medicine for Anaesthetists. 4th ed. Michael D. Vickers & Ian Power. LC 98-34371. (Illus.). 1999. 119.00 (*0-86542-637-6*) Blackwell Sci.

Medicine for Beginners. Richard Clark & Tony Pinchuck. 1984. 4.95 (*0-86316-006-9*); pap. 4.95 (*0-86316-007-7*) Writers & Readers.

***Medicine for Dentists.** Simon Dimmitt. (Illus.). 156p. 1999. pap. 14.95 (*1-876268-12-3*, Pub. by Univ of West Aust Pr) Intl Spec Bk.

Medicine for Depression. Donald A. Miller. (Christian Living Ser.). 33p. 1994. pap. 1.59 (*0-87509-571-2*) Chr Pubns.

Medicine for Disasters. Peter J. Baskett & R. O. Weller. (Illus.). 494p. 1988. text 185.00 (*0-7236-0949-7*, Pub. by John Wright) Buttrwrth-Heinemann.

Medicine for Examinations. 3rd ed. R. J. Epstein. LC 96-6832. 192p. 1996. pap. text 30.00 (*0-443-05377-4*) Church.

Medicine for Examinations: A Streamlined Approach to Revision. 2nd ed. R. J. Epstein. (Illus.). 384p. 1990. pap. text 31.95 (*0-443-04149-0*) Church.

Medicine for Melancholy. Ray Bradbury. LC 97-94680. 320p. 1998. pap. 10.00 (*0-380-73086-3*, Avon Bks) Morrow Avon.

Medicine for Melancholy: And Other Stories. Ray Bradbury. 1998. 15.10 (*0-606-13602-9*, Pub. by Turtleback) Demco.

Medicine for Mountaineering & Other Wilderness Activities. 4th ed. Ed. by James A. Wilkerson. (Illus.). 384p. 1992. pap. 18.95 (*0-89886-331-7*) Mountaineers.

Medicine for Nurses. 13th ed. write for info. (*0-7131-4344-4*, Pub. by E A) Routldge.

Medicine for Student. 14th ed. G. Golwalla. (C). 1989. 105.00 (*0-7855-4673-1*, Pub. by Current Dist) St Mut.

Medicine for the Backcountry. 3rd ed. Buck Tilton & Frank Hubbell. LC 99-35622. (Illus.). 224p. 1999. pap. 14.95 (*0-7627-0527-2*) Globe Pequot.

***Medicine for the Coming Age.** Lisa Sand. (Illus.). 1999. pap. 21.95 (*1-86163-068-9*, Pub. by Capall Bann Pubng) Holmes Pub.

Medicine for the Mind: Coping Skills for People Who Are Surviving Cancer. Jacqueline Grekin. Date not set. pap. write for info. (*0-9659685-2-9*) J Grekin.

Medicine for the Mind: Healing Words to Help You Soar. Christopher Neck. 212p. 1995. pap. 10.00 (*0-07-046292-5*) McGraw.

Medicine for the Outdoors: A Guide to Emergency Medical Procedures & First Aid for Wilderness Travelers. Paul S. Auerbach. (Illus.). 1986. 24.95 (*0-316-05928-5*, Little Brwn Med Div); pap. 12.95 (*0-316-05929-3*, Little Brwn Med Div) Lppncott W & W.

***Medicine for the Outdoors: The Essential Guide to Emergency Medical Procedures & First Aid.** 3rd rev. ed. Paul S. Auerbach. LC 98-12402. (Illus.). 512p. 1999. pap. 22.50 (*1-55821-723-1*) Lyons Pr.

Medicine for the Practicing Physician. 2nd ed. J. Willis Hurst. (Illus.). 1857p. 1988. pap. text 110.00 (*0-409-95176-5*) Buttrwrth-Heinemann.

Medicine for the Practicing Physician. 4th ed. J. Willis Hurst. 2241p. (C). 1996. pap. text 155.00 (*0-8385-6317-1*, A6317-0, Apple Lange Med) McGraw.

Medicine for the Soul. Janice Holman et al. 1999. pap. 8.95 (*0-9640801-3-3*, 8013-3) Jireh Pubns.

Medicine for the Soul: The Life & Work of An English Medieval Hospital. Carole Rawcliffe. 2000. 55.00 (*0-7509-2009-2*) Sutton Pub Ltd.

Medicine for the Twenty-First Century. Keith Mason. 1993. pap. 14.95 (*1-85230-329-8*, Pub. by Element MA) Penguin Putnam.

Medicine for the Whole Person: A Critique of Scientific Medicine. Erich K. Ledermann. LC 97-16364. 192p. 1997. pap. 16.95 (*1-86204-056-7*, Pub. by Element MA) Penguin Putnam.

Medicine from Art to Science: The Role of Complexity & Evolution. Giovanni Felice Azzone. (Veneto Institute of Sciences, Letters & Arts Ser.: Vol. 1). 197p. 1998. 60.00 (*90-5199-390-0*, Pub. by IOS Pr) IOS Press.

Medicine from the Black Death to the French Disease. Ed. by Roger K. French et al. LC 98-2502. (History of Medicine in Context Ser.). (Illus.). 280p. 1998. text 86.95 (*1-85928-382-9*, Pub. by Scolar Pr) Ashgate Pub Co.

Medicine from the Mountains: Medicinal Plants of the Sierra Nevada. Kimball Chatfield. LC 97-92169. (Illus.). 219p. 1997. pap. 17.95 (*0-9658001-0-5*) Range Light.

Medicine Grove: A Shamanic Herbal. Loren Cruden. LC 97-18606. (Illus.). 176p. 1997. pap. 14.95 (*0-89281-647-3*) Inner Tradit.

Medicine Hands: Massage Therapy for People with Cancer. Gayle MacDonald. (Illus.). 192p. 1999. pap. 23.95 (*1-899171-77-0*) Words Distrib.

Medicine Hat. Don Coldsmith. (Spanish Bit Ser.: No. 25). 272p. 1998. mass mkt. 4.99 (*0-553-29475-X*) Bantam.

Medicine Hat: A Novel. Don Coldsmith. LC 97-15335. vi, 266p. 1997. 21.95 (*0-8061-2959-X*) U of Okla Pr.

Medicine, Health, & Risk: Sociological Approaches. Ed. by Jonathan Gabe. LC 95-14115. (Sociology of Health & Illness Monograph Ser.: Vol. 1). 1996. pap. 24.95 (*0-631-19484-3*) Blackwell Pubs.

Medicine Horn. Jory Sherman. 288p. 1992. mass mkt. 3.99 (*0-8125-8875-4*, Pub. by Tor Bks) St Martin.

Medicine in a Changing Society. New York Academy of Medicine Staff. Ed. by Iago Galdston. LC 70-142680. (Essay Index Reprint Ser.). 1977. 19.95 (*0-8369-2123-2*) Ayer.

Medicine in America: A Short History. James H. Cassedy. LC 91-7058. (American Moment Ser.). 204p. 1991. pap. text 14.95 (*0-8018-4208-5*) Johns Hopkins.

Medicine in Canada. William B. Howell. LC 75-23659. (Clio Medica Ser.: 9). (Illus.). reprint ed. 34.50 (*0-404-58909-X*) AMS Pr.

Medicine in Canadian Society: Historical Perspectives. Ed. by Samuel E. Shortt. LC 80-90100. 506p. 1981. pap. 24.95 (*0-7735-0369-2*, Pub. by McG-Queens Univ Pr) CUP Services.

Medicine in Canadian Society: Historical Perspectives. Ed. by Samuel E. Shortt. LC 81-164924. 520p. reprint ed. pap. 161.20 (*0-7837-1022-4*, 204133300020) Bks Demand.

Medicine in Chicago: A Chapter in the Social & Scientific Development of a City, 1850- 1950. 2nd ed. Thomas N. Bonner. 352p. 1991. text 42.50 (*0-252-01760-9*) U of Ill Pr.

Medicine in China: A History of Ideas. Paul U. Unschuld. LC 84-2415. (Comparative Studies of Health Systems & Medical Care: Vol. 13). 1985. pap. 19.95 (*0-520-06216-7*, Pub. by U CA Pr) Cal Prin Full Svc.

Medicine in China: A History of Pharmaceutics. Paul U. Unschuld. LC 83-4937. (Comparative Studies of Health Systems & Medical Care: Vol. 14). 1985. 95.00 (*0-520-05025-8*, Pub. by U CA Pr) Cal Prin Full Svc.

Medicine in China: Historical Artefacts & Images. Paul Huschald. (Illus.). 220p. 1999. 65.00 (*3-7913-2149-8*, Pub. by Prestel) te Neues.

***Medicine in Colonial America.** Oscar Reiss. 536p. 2000. 64.50 (*0-7618-1576-7*) U Pr of Amer.

Medicine in Colonial Massachusetts, 1620-1820. Ed. by Philip Cash et al. LC 80-68589. (Illus.). xxiv, 425p. 1980. text 35.00 (*0-8139-0908-2*) U Pr of Va.

Medicine in England During the Reign of George III. Arnold Chaplin. LC 75-23695. reprint ed. 38.00 (*0-404-13244-8*) AMS Pr.

Medicine in Europe. Ed. by Tessa Richards. 164p. 1992. pap. text 8.00 (*0-7279-0319-5*, Pub. by BMJ Pub) Login Brothers Bk Co.

Medicine in Great Britain from the Restoration to the Nineteenth Century, 1660-1800: An Annotated Bibliography, 8. Compiled by Samuel J. Rogal. LC 91-39004. (Bibliographies & Indexes in Medical Studies: No. 8). 272p. 1992. lib. bdg. 75.00 (*0-313-28115-7*, RMH, Greenwood Pr) Greenwood.

***Medicine in History: A World History Companion.** Janet Ann Harbour. 2001. lib. bdg. 60.00 (*1-57607-088-3*) ABC-CLIO.

Medicine in Maryland: The Practice & the Profession, 1799-1999. Jane Eliot Sewell. LC 98-43609. (Illus.). 238p. 1999. 39.95 (*0-8018-6127-6*) Johns Hopkins.

Medicine in Old Age. 4th ed. S. J. C. Brocklehurst. LC 97-37958. (C). 1998. pap. text 29.95 (*0-443-05778-8*) Church.

Medicine in Persia. Cyril Elgood. LC 75-23665. (Clio Medica Ser.: No. 14). (Illus.). reprint ed. 34.50 (*0-404-58914-6*) AMS Pr.

An Asterisk (*) at the beginning of an entry indicates that the title is appearing for the first time.

***Medicine in Quotations: Views of Health & Disease Through the Ages.** Ed. by Edward J. Huth & T. J. Murray. LC 99-57212. 524p. 2000. 49.00 (*0-943126-83-5*) Amer Coll Phys.

***Medicine in Search of Meaning: A Spiritual Journey for Physicians.** Bill J. Bazan. 176p. 1999. pap. 15.95 (*0-9668228-2-X*) Caritas Commns.

Medicine in Society: Historical Essays. Ed. by Andrew Wear. 407p. (C). 1992. text 74.95 (*0-521-33351-2*); pap. text 25.95 (*0-521-33639-2*) Cambridge U Pr.

Medicine in Sports Training & Coaching. Ed. by J. Karvonen et al. (Medicine & Sport Science Ser.: Vol. 35). (Illus.). x, 244p. 1992. 214.00 (*3-8055-5517-2*) S Karger.

Medicine in the Age of Information. Siann. 272p. pap. 45.00 (*0-471-98661-5*) Wiley.

***Medicine in the Athens of the West: The History & Influence of the Lexington-Fayette County Medical Society.** Porter Mayo. LC 99-65231. (Illus.). 352p. 1999. 24.95 (*0-913383-64-3*) McClanahan Pub.

Medicine in the British Isles. D'Arcy Power. LC 75-23651. (Clio Medica Ser.: No. 2). reprint ed. 32.50 (*0-404-58902-2*) AMS Pr.

Medicine in the English Middle Ages. Faye M. Getz. LC 98-3534. 192p. 1998. text 32.50 (*0-691-08522-6*, Pub. by Princeton U Pr) Cal Prin Full Svc.

Medicine in the Frail Elderly: A Problem-Oriented Approach. Roy A. Fox & John Puxty. (Illus.). 272p. 1993. text 69.50 (*0-7131-4564-1*, Pub. by E A) OUP.

Medicine in the Life Sciences 1450 Through 1700. James Bono. 1999. 22.95 (*0-8057-9513-8*, Twyne) Mac Lib Ref.

Medicine in the Making of Modern Britain, 1700-1920. Christopher J. Lawrence. LC 93-33387. (Historical Connections Ser.). 112p. (Orig.). (C). 1994. pap. 16.99 (*0-415-09168-3*, B3713) Routledge.

Medicine in the Mishneh Torah of Maimonides. Fred Rosner. LC 96-29569. 344p. 1997. pap. 35.00 (*0-7657-5979-9*) Aronson.

Medicine in the Postwar World: The March of Medicine, 1947, Laity Lectures, No. 12. New York Academy of Medicine Staff. LC 78-167392. (Essay Index Reprint Ser.). 1977. reprint ed. 17.95 (*0-8369-2468-1*) Ayer.

Medicine in the West. Ed. by James O. Breeden. (Illus.). 86p. (Orig.). 1982. pap. text 15.00 (*0-89745-025-6*) Sunflower U Pr.

Medicine in Virginia in the Eighteenth Century. Wyndham B. Blanton. LC 80-12669. reprint ed. 78.00 (*0-404-13238-3*) AMS Pr.

Medicine in Virginia in the Seventeenth Century. Wyndham B. Blanton. LC 77-180556. (Medicine & Society in America Ser.). (Illus.). 430p. 1977. reprint ed. 28.95 (*0-405-03936-0*) Ayer.

Medicine Is the Best Laughter. Ed. & Compiled by Gideon Bosker. LC 94-44178. (Illus.). 208p. (C). (gr. 13). 1994. text 35.95 (*0-8016-8113-8*, 08113) Mosby Inc.

Medicine Is the Best Laughter, Vol. II. Gideon Bosker. LC 99-182200. (Illus.). 208p. (C). (gr. 13). 1998. text 29.95 (*0-8151-9640-7*, 31797) Mosby Inc.

Medicine Journeys: Ten Stories. Carl Ginsburg. LC 91-90402. 72p. (Orig.). 1991. pap. 10.00 (*0-916185-00-1*) Ctr Pr NM.

Medicine Keepers. J. B. Allen. 93p. 1997. pap. 20.00 (*1-888609-04-4*) Grey Hrse Pr.

Medicine, Law & Public Policy. Ed. by Nicholas N. Kittrie et al. LC 75-793. (Studies in Modern Society: Political & Social Issues: No. 8). 37.50 (*0-404-10426-6*) AMS Pr.

Medicine, Law & Social Change: How Bioethics, Feminism & Rights Movements Are Affecting Decision Making. Leanna Darvall. (Medico-Legal Issues Ser.). 153p. 1993. 87.95 (*1-85521-077-0*, Pub. by Dartmth Pub) Ashgate Pub Co.

***Medicine Line: Life & Death in an American Borderland.** Beth Ladow. 2001. pap. 25.00 (*0-415-92764-1*) Routledge.

Medicine, Literature & Eponyms: Encyclopedia of Medical Eponymns Derived from Literary Characters. A. E. Rodin & Jack Key. LC 88-542. 370p. 1989. pap. 32.50 (*0-89464-960-4*) Krieger.

Medicine, Literature & Eponyms: Encyclopedia of Medical Eponymns Derived from Literary Characters. A. E. Rodin & Jack Key. LC 88-542. 370p. (C). 1989. lib. bdg. 44.50 (*0-89464-277-4*) Krieger.

Medicine Lodge: The Story of a Kansas Frontier Town. Nellie S. Yost. (Illus.). 237p. 1970. pap. 17.95 (*0-913507-93-8*) New Forums.

Medicine Looks at the Humanities. Ed. by J. D. Newell & Ira W. Gabrielson. LC 87-17925. 206p. (Orig.). (C). 1987. lib. bdg. 44.00 (*0-8191-6607-3*) U Pr of Amer.

Medicine Mad. Mad Magazine Editors. (Mad Ser.: No. 44). (Illus.). (Orig.). 1987. mass mkt. 3.99 (*0-446-34853-8*, Pub. by Warner Bks) Little.

Medicine Made Clear: House Calls from a Maine Country Doctor. Michael A. LaCombe. Ed. by Edward L. Francis. (Illus.). 400p. 1989. 21.95 (*0-9623199-0-2*) Dirigo Bks.

Medicine Made Memorable. McDermott. (C). 1998. pap. text 28.00 (*0-443-05195-X*) Church.

Medicine, Magic & Religion. William H. Rivers. LC 76-44784. reprint ed. 32.50 (*0-404-15967-2*) AMS Pr.

***Medicine Man.** Jesse Voyd Bottoms, Jr. 138p. 1999. pap. 12.00 (*0-9669962-0-8*, Pub. by Jubi Christ) Spring Arbor Dist.

***Medicine Man.** Francisco Rojas Gonzalez. Tr. by Robert S. Rudder & Gloria Ajona from SPA. LC 99-58259. 115p. 2000. pap. 13.95 (*1-891270-07-9*) Lat Am Lit Rev Pr.

Medicine Man. Calvin Hernton. LC 76-11434. 1976. pap. 4.95 (*0-918408-05-9*) Ishmael Reed.

***Medicine Man.** Joan B. Pierce. 124p. (YA). (gr. 5-8). 2000. pap. 9.99 (*0-88092-069-6*, 0696, Kav Bks) Royal Fireworks.

Medicine Man. Owen T. Stratton. Ed. by Owen S. Stratton. LC 89-40224. (Western Frontier Library: Vol. 56). (Illus.). 272p. 1989. 24.95 (*0-8061-2241-2*) U of Okla Pr.

Medicine Man: A Comedy in 2-Acts Based on Moliera's "The Doctor in Spite of Himself" David Grote. 44p. 1980. pap. 4.00 (*0-88680-129-X*) I E Clark.

Medicine Man: A Sociological Study of the Character & Evolution of Shamanism. John L. Maddox. LC 75-23737. reprint ed. 45.00 (*0-404-13294-4*) AMS Pr.

Medicine Man among the Zaramo of Dar Es Salaam. Lloyd Swantz. 159p. 1990. pap. text 19.95 (*91-7106-299-8*) Transaction Pubs.

Medicine-Man of the American Indian & His Cultural Background. William T. Corlett. LC 75-23699. reprint ed. 47.50 (*0-404-13249-9*) AMS Pr.

Medicine Marriage & the Marketplace. 2nd ed. P. D. Cummins. LC 87-81723. 1988. reprint ed. write for info. (*0-9618819-2-5*) Foghrn Pr.

Medicine, Media & Morality: Pulitzer Prize Winning Articles on Health-Related Problems. Ed. by Heinz-Dietrich Fischer. 264p. (C). 1992. lib. bdg. 31.50 (*0-89464-692-3*) Krieger.

***Medicine Meets Business.** Rovin. 2000. boxed set 55.00 (*0-8342-1612-4*) Aspen Pub.

Medicine Meets Virtual Reality: Art, Science, Technology. Ed. by J. Westwood & K. Morgan. LC 97-78103. (Studies in Health Technology & Informatics: Vol. 50). 500p. 1998. 98.00 (*90-5199-386-2*, Pub. by IOS Pr) IOS Press.

Medicine Meets Virtual Reality: Health Care in the Information Age. Ed. by Suzanne J. Weghorst et al. LC 95-8174. (Studies in Health Technology & Informatics: Vol. 29). (Illus.). 734p. (YA). (gr. 12). 1996. 98.00 (*90-5199-250-5*, 250-5) IOS Press.

***Medicine Men.** large type ed. Alice Adams. LC 99-57691. 304p. 2000. lib. bdg. 28.95 (*1-58547-022-8*) Ctr Point Pubg.

Medicine Men: A Novel. Alice Adams. LC 96-42001. 1997. 23.00 (*0-679-45440-3*) Knopf.

Medicine Men: A Novel. Alice Adams. 256p. 1998. mass mkt. 14.00 (*0-671-02067-6*, Pocket Books) PB.

Medicine Men: George Ohsawa's Encounter with Dr. Schweitzer in Africa. Jack Harris-Bonham. 96p. 1993. pap. 7.95 (*1-882984-02-1*) One Peaceful World.

Medicine Men: Oglala Sioux Ceremony & Healing. Thomas H. Lewis. LC 89-22508. (Studies in the Anthropology of North American Indians). (Illus.). viii, 219p. 1990. reprint ed. pap. 10.95 (*0-8032-7939-6*, Bison Books) U of Nebr Pr.

Medicine Men of the Apache: A Paper from the Ninth Annual Report of the Bureau of American Ethnology 1887-1888. John G. Bourke. LC 77-135517. (Beautiful Rio Grande Classics Ser.). (Illus.). 187p. 1983. reprint ed. lib. bdg. 22.50 (*0-87380-050-8*) Popular E Commerce.

Medicine, Money & Morals: Physicians' Conflicts of Interest. Marc A. Rodwin. (Illus.). 432p. 1995. pap. 13.95 (*0-19-509647-9*) OUP.

***Medicine, Monopolies & Malice: How the Medical Establishment Tried to Destroy Chiropractic in the U. S.** 2nd ed. Chester A. Wilk. 245p. 2000. reprint ed. pap. 12.95 (*0-9701625-0-2*) C Wilks.

Medicine, Morals, & the Law. Sheila A. McLean & Gerry Maher. 113p. 1983. text 87.95 (*0-566-00533-6*) Ashgate Pub Co.

Medicine, Mortality & the Book Trade. Ed. by Robin Myers & Michael Harris. LC 99-47430. (Publishing Pathways Ser.). 170p. 1998. 39.95 (*1-884718-81-7*, No. 53864RB) Oak Knoll.

***Medicine News.** Philip Gates. (History News Ser.). (Illus.). 32p. (YA). (gr. 4-9). 2000. pap. 6.99 (*0-7636-0986-2*, Pub. by Candlewick Pr) Penguin Putnam.

Medicine, Nutrition, Demography, & Slavery. Ed. by Paul Finkelman. LC 89-23625. (Articles on American Slavery Ser.: Vol. 15). 384p. 1990. reprint ed. text 20.00 (*0-8240-6795-9*) Garland.

Medicine of ER: An Insider's Guide to the Medical Science Behind America's #1 TV Drama. Harlan Gibbs & Alan D. Ross. 240p. 1997. pap. 11.00 (*0-06-097732-9*, Perennial) HarperTrade.

***Medicine of ER: Or, How We Almost Die.** Harlan Gibbs & Alan Duncan Ross. 232p. 2000. reprint ed. 22.00 (*0-7881-9379-1*) DIANE Pub.

Medicine of the Cherokee: The Way of Right Relationship. J. T. Garrett & Michael T. Garrett. LC 96-16156. 352p. 1996. pap. 14.00 (*1-879181-37-1*) Bear & Co.

Medicine of the Fetus & Mother. E. Albert Reece. 1992. text 155.00 (*0-397-51339-9*) Lppncott W & W.

Medicine of the Fetus & Mother. E. Albert Reece et al. (Illus.). 1488p. 1992. text 145.00 (*0-397-51013-6*) Lppncott W & W.

Medicine of the Fetus & Mother. 2nd ed. E. Albert Reece & John C. Hobbins. LC 98-29286. 1804p. 1998. text 149.00 (*0-397-51862-5*) Lppncott W & W.

Medicine of the Prophet. Ibn Qayyim al-Jawziyya. Tr. by Penelope Johnstone from ARA. (ARA & ENG.). 304p. 1996. text 67.95 (*0-946621-19-5*, Pub. by Islamic Texts); pap. text 32.00 (*0-946621-22-5*, Pub. by Islamic Texts) Intl Spec Bk.

Medicine of the Sun & Moon. Manly P. Hall. pap. 4.95 (*0-89314-332-4*) Philos Res.

Medicine on Ancient Greek & Roman Coins. Raymond G. Penn. (Illus.). 192p. 1994. pap. 50.00 (*0-7134-7670-2*) S J Durst.

Medicine, Patients & the Law. Margaret Brazier. pap. 29.95 (*0-14-012749-6*, Pub. by Pnguin Bks Ltd) Trafalgar.

Medicine, Philosophy & Religion in Ancient China: Researches & Reflections. Nathan Sivin. LC 95-19571. 296p. 1995. 101.95 (*0-86078-493-2*, Pub. by Variorum) Ashgate Pub Co.

Medicine Prices & Innovations: An International Survey. W. Duncan Reekie. (Choice in Welfare Ser.: No. 30). 65p. 1996. pap. 34.50 (*0-255-36369-9*, Pub. by Inst Economic Affairs) Coronet Bks.

Medicine Quest: In Search of Nature's Healing Secrets. Mark J. Plotkin. LC 99-42822. 214p. 2000. 22.95 (*0-670-86937-6*) Viking Penguin.

Medicine, Rationality, & Experience: An Anthropological Perspective. Byron J. Good. LC 92-45254. (Lewis Henry Morgan Lectures: No. 1990). 260p. (C). 1994. pap. text 19.95 (*0-521-42576-X*) Cambridge U Pr.

Medicine Recall. James D. Bergin. LC 97-11939. (Recall Ser.). 901p. 1997. pap. 28.00 (*0-683-18098-3*) Lppncott W & W.

Medicine River. Thomas King. 272p. 1991. pap. 10.95 (*0-14-025474-9*) Viking Penguin.

***Medicine Rotation Value Pak.** John Stobo. 1999. 60.00 (*0-8385-6391-0*, Apple Lange Med) McGraw.

Medicine, Science & Art. Alfred E. Cohn. LC 72-86742. (Essay Index Reprint Ser.). 1977. 18.95 (*0-8369-1126-1*) Ayer.

Medicine, Science & Art. Alfred E. Cohn. (Essay Index Reprint Ser.). 1982. reprint ed. lib. bdg. 15.50 (*0-8290-0840-3*) Irvington.

Medicine Show. Virginia G. Koste. (J). (gr. 4-12). 1983. 6.00 (*0-87602-258-1*) Anchorage.

Medicine Show. Jody L. Nye. 272p. (Orig.). 1994. mass mkt. 4.99 (*0-441-00085-1*) Ace Bks.

Medicine Show. large type ed. Bill Crider. 311p. 1991. reprint ed. lib. bdg. 16.95 (*1-56054-142-3*) Thorndike Pr.

Medicine Society. Paul Scriven. LC 92-53724. 230p. 1992. pap. 18.95 (*0-87013-315-2*) Mich St U Pr.

Medicine, Society, & Faith in the Ancient & Medieval Worlds. Darrel W. Amundsen. LC 95-11759. 368p. 1995. text 42.50 (*0-8018-5109-2*) Johns Hopkins.

Medicine Stories: History, Culture, & the Politics of Integrity. Aurora L. Morales. LC 98-31479. 135p. 1998. 40.00 (*0-89608-582-1*) South End Pr.

Medicine Stories: History, Culture, & the Politics of Integrity. Aurora L. Morales. 135p. 1998. pap. 14.00 (*0-89608-581-3*) South End Pr.

Medicine Story: The Return to Native American Consciousness. Karen Degenhart. (Illus.). 284p. (Orig.). 1996. reprint ed. pap. 15.95 (*0-916337-03-0*) Thndbird Pubns.

Medicine Through the Ages. 2nd ed. Peter Mantin & Richard Pulley. (Key History for GCSE Ser.). (Illus.). 112p. 1996. pap. 19.95 (*0-7487-3026-5*, Pub. by S Thornes Pubs) Trans-Atl Phila.

Medicine Today. Greenhalgh. 1993. pap. text. write for info. (*0-582-09906-4*, Pub. by Addison-Wesley) Longman.

Medicine Today: The March of Medicine, 1946 (Laity Lectures, No. 11) New York Academy of Medicine Staff. LC 71-167393. (Essay Index Reprint Ser.). 1977. reprint ed. 19.95 (*0-8369-2469-X*) Ayer.

Medicine, Tradition, & Development in Kenya & Tanzania, 1920-1970. Ann Beck. 114p. 1981. 12.00 (*0-918456-44-4*) African Studies Assn.

Medicine Trail. G. Clifton Wisler. 320p. 1991. mass mkt. 4.95 (*0-8217-3418-0*, Zebra Kensgtn) Kensgtn Pub Corp.

Medicine Trail: Dreaming Wolf. G. Clifton Wisler. 352p. 1992. mass mkt. 4.99 (*0-8217-3905-0*, Zebra Kensgtn) Kensgtn Pub Corp.

Medicine Trail: The Buffalo Shield. G. Clifton Wisler. 320p. 1992. mass mkt. 4.99 (*0-8217-3748-1*, Zebra Kensgtn) Kensgtn Pub Corp.

***Medicine Trail: The Life & Lessons of Gladys Tantaquidgeon.** Melissa Jayne Fawcett. LC 00-8195. (Illus.). 2000. pap. 16.95 (*0-8165-2069-0*) U of Ariz Pr.

***Medicine Trail: The Life & Lessons of Gladys Tantaquidgeon.** Melissa Jayne Fawcett. LC 00-8195. (Illus.). 170p. 2000. 35.00 (*0-8165-2068-2*) U of Ariz Pr.

Medicine Trail No. 2: Stone Wolf's Vision. G. Clifton Wisler. 1991. mass mkt. 4.99 (*0-8217-3575-6*, Zebra Kensgtn) Kensgtn Pub Corp.

Medicine, 2001 Edition: Current Clinical Strategies. rev. ed. Paul D. Chan. (Current Clinical Strategies Ser.). 100p. 1999. pap. 12.95 (*1-881528-83-9*) Current Clin Strat.

Medicine Unbound: The Human Body & the Limits of Medical Intervention. Ed. by Robert H. Blank & Andrea L. Bonnicksen. LC 94-41829. 287p. 1994. 57.50 (*0-231-08148-0*) Col U Pr.

Medicine Walk. Houghton Mifflin Company Staff. (Literature Experience 1993 Ser.). (J). (gr. 6). 1992. pap. 11.04 (*0-395-61825-8*) HM.

Medicine Way: How to Live the Teachings of the Native American Medicine Wheel: A Shamanic Path to Self-Mastery. Kenneth Meadows. 256p. 1997. pap. 17.95 (*1-86204-022-2*, Pub. by Element MA) Penguin Putnam.

***Medicine Ways: Disease, Health & Survival among Native Americans.** Ed. by Clifford E. Trafzer & Diane Weiner. (Contemporary Native American Communities Ser.: Vol. 5). 324p. 2001. 69.00 (*0-7425-0254-6*) AltaMira Pr.

***Medicine Ways: Disease, Health, & Survival Among Native Americans.** Ed. by Clifford E. Trafzer & Diane Weiner. (Contemporary Native American Communities Ser.: Vol. 5). 324p. 2001. pap. 24.95 (*0-7425-0255-4*) AltaMira Pr.

Medicine Wheel. Les Savage, Jr. 224p. 1998. mass mkt. 4.50 (*0-8439-4444-7*, Leisure Bks) Dorchester Pub Co.

Medicine Wheel. large type ed. Les Savage, Jr. 1999. 20.00 (*0-7838-1668-5*, G K Hall Lrg Type) Mac Lib Ref.

Medicine Wheel: A Western Story. Les Savage, Jr. LC 96-6301. 230p. 1996. 16.95 (*0-7862-0657-8*) Five Star.

Medicine Wheel: Earth Astrology. Peter Nufer & Shelia Mulligan. LC 96-231979. 204p. 1980. per. 11.00 (*0-671-76420-9*) P-H.

Medicine Wheel Ceremonies: Ancient Philosophies for Use in Modern Day Life. Vicki May & C. V. Rodberg. LC 95-50749. (Illus.). 48p. (Orig.). (C). 1996. pap. 8.95 (*0-87961-242-8*) Naturegraph.

Medicine Wheels: Native American Vehicles of Healing. Roy I. Wilson. LC 94-2388. 154p. 1994. pap. 14.95 (*0-8245-1416-5*, Pub. by Crossroad NY) Natl Bk Netwk.

Medicine Woman. Lynn V. Andrews. LC 81-47546. 224p. 1983. pap. 14.00 (*0-06-250026-0*, CN 4062, Pub. by Harper SF) HarpC.

Medicine Woman Deck-Book Set. Carol Bridges. (Illus.). 256p. 1992. pap. 29.00 (*0-88079-537-9*, MWS99) US Games Syst.

Medicine Woman Inner Guidebook. Carol Bridges. LC 91-75047. (Illus.). 256p. 1992. pap. 12.95 (*0-88079-512-3*, BK114) US Games Syst.

Medicine Woman Inner Guidebook: A Woman's Guide to Her Unique Powers. rev. ed. Carol Bridges. (Illus.). 279p. (Orig.). 1987. pap., student ed. 21.00 (*0-945111-00-2*) Earth Nation.

Medicine Woman Tarot. Carol Bridges. 1989. pap. 15.00 (*0-88079-419-4*, MW78) US Games Syst.

Medicine Woman's Guide to Being in Business for Yourself: How to Live by Your Spiritual Vision in a Money-Based World. 3rd ed. Carol Bridges. (Illus.). 160p. (Orig.). 1996. reprint ed. pap. 14.95 (*0-945111-08-8*) Earth Nation.

Medicine Women. Susan Freilicher. LC 93-84776. (Illus.). 96p. 1993. 30.00 (*1-56640-598-X*) Pomegranate Calif.

Medicine Women: A Pictorial History of Women Healers. Elisabeth Brooke. LC 96-44733. (Illus.). 128p. 1997. pap. 20.00 (*0-8356-0751-8*, Quest) Theos Pub Hse.

Medicine Women, Curanderas, & Women Doctors. Bobette Perrone et al. LC 89-4901. (Illus.). 272p. 1993. pap. 14.95 (*0-8061-2512-8*) U of Okla Pr.

Medicine Worth Paying For: Assessing Medical Innovations. Ed. by Howard S. Frazier & Frederick Mosteller. LC 94-48899. (Illus.). 336p. (C). 1995. text 44.50 (*0-674-56362-X*) HUP.

Medicinemaker: Mystic Encounters on the Shaman's Path. Hank Wesselman. 336p. 1999. pap. 13.95 (*0-553-37932-1*) Bantam.

Medicines & Risk-Benefit Decisions. Ed. by S. R. Walker & A. W. Asscher. (CMR Workshop Ser.). 1987. text 154.50 (*0-85200-978-X*) Kluwer Academic.

Medicine's Deadly Dust: A Surgeons Wake-Up Call to Society. Richard F. Edlich & Julia A. Woods. 224p. 1997. 24.95 (*0-918339-45-6*) Vandamere.

Medicine's Dilemmas: Infinite Needs vs. Finite Resources. William L. Kissick. LC 94-1137. (Illus.). 240p. 1994. 32.50 (*0-300-05964-7*); pap. 13.00 (*0-300-05965-5*) Yale U Pr.

***Medicines for the Union Army: The United States Army Laboratories During the Civil War.** George Winston Smith. 2000. 69.95 (*0-7890-0946-3*); pap. 24.95 (*0-7890-0947-1*) Haworth Pr.

Medicines from Nature see Single Titles Series

Medicines from the Bible. M. DeWaal. 1994. pap. 8.95 (*0-942272-37-4*) Original Pubns.

Medicine's Lighter Moments. Ted L. Grisell. LC 94-14863. 184p. 1994. pap. 19.95 (*1-877633-19-4*) Luthers.

Medicines Management. Ed. by Rhona Penton & Stephen Chapman. (Illus.). 196p. 1998. pap. 29.00 (*0-7279-1274-7*, Pub. by BMJ Pub) Login Brothers Bk Co.

Medicines Management for Clinical Nurses. Ed. by Karen A. Luker & David J. Wolfson. LC 98-35983. 348p. 1998. pap. 39.95 (*0-632-04247-8*) Blackwell Sci.

***Medicines of the Soul: Female Bodies & Sacred Geographies in a Transnational Islam.** Fedwa Malti-Douglas. LC 00-21550. (Illus.). 2001. write for info. (*0-520-22284-9*) U CA Pr.

Medicine's 10 Greatest Discoveries. Meyer Friedman & Gerald W. Friedland. LC 98-19921. (Illus.). 296p. 1998. 35.00 (*0-300-07598-7*) Yale U Pr.

***Medicine's 10 Greatest Discoveries.** Meyer Friedman & Gerald W. Friedland. (Illus.). 296p. 2000. pap. 14.95 (*0-300-08278-9*) Yale U Pr.

Medicinisches Gelehrten-Lexicon. Christoph W. Kestner. xvi, 944p. 1971. reprint ed. write for info. (*0-318-71922-3*) G Olms Pubs.

Medicinisches Woerterbuch: English-German, German-English. 2nd ed. C. Eichorst. 703p. 1989. 95.00 (*0-7859-7093-2*) Fr & Eur.

Medicion de la Pobreza en Areas Urbana y Rural del Ecuador. 1994. write for info. (*92-806-3024-5*) U N I C E.

Medicion y Evaluacion. Dalila Rodriguez Irlanda. (SPA.). 282p. 1991. pap. write for info. (*0-929441-11-7*) Pubns Puertorriquenas.

Medico - Legal Aspects of Sexual Offences. K. Kumar. (C). 1991. 170.00 (*0-89771-691-4*) St Mut.

Medico de su Honra see Physician of His Honour

Medico-Legal Aspects of Reproduction & Parenthood. 2nd ed. J. K. Mason. LC 97-38226. (Medico-Legal Ser.). 300p. 1998. pap. 48.95 (*1-85521-816-X*, Pub. by Ashgate Pub); text 115.95 (*1-84014-065-8*, Pub. by Ashgate Pub) Ashgate Pub Co.

Medico-Legal Aspects of Sexual Offences. 3rd ed. R. L. Gupta. (C). 1991. text 150.00 (*0-89771-476-8*) St Mut.

Medico-Legal Directory. Ed. by Geoffrey M. Hall. 1992. 200.00 (*0-9514449-1-3*, Pub. by Busn & Med) St Mut.

Medico Legal Guide with Ewell's Medical Jurisprudence & Mental Health Act, 1987. Ed. by J. Field. (C). 1988. 85.00 (*0-7855-3542-X*) St Mut.

Medico-Legal Reporting in Orthopaedic Trauma. M. A. Foy & P. S. Fagg. (Illus.). 496p. 1995. ring bd. write for info. (*0-443-04834-7*) Church.

Medico-Legal Society (London) Transactions, 1902-1932, Set, Vols. 1-26. 1902. 450.00 (*0-686-89946-6*) W S Hein.

M

M

Medico-Legal Treatise on Malpractice & Medical Evidence: Comprising the Elements of Medical Jurisprudence. John J. Elwell. vi, 588p. 1996. reprint ed. 85.00 (*0-8377-2107-5*, Rothman) W S Hein.

Medico Mnemonica: A Collection of Fun, Fibald, Irreverent & Quite Witty Mnemonics for Medical Students. Evan Marlowe. LC 96-49033. (Illus.). 186p. (Orig.). (C). 1997. pap. text 12.95 (*1-57066-056-5*, ME075) Practice Mgmt Info.

Medico-Social Aspects of Child Abuse (Recommendation & Explanatory Memorandum), No. R(93)2. 1995. 12.00 (*92-871-2616-X*, Pub. by Council of Europe) Manhattan Pub Co.

Medicolegal Aspects of Alcohol. 3rd ed. Ed. by James C. Garriott. LC 96-20278. 526p. 1996. 99.00 (*0-913875-26-0*, 0888-N) Lawyers & Judges.

Medicolegal Aspects of Moral Offences. L. Thoinot. Tr. by Arthur W. Weysse from FRE. xv, 487p. 1997. reprint ed. 152.00 (*1-56169-333-2*) Gaunt.

Medicolegal Consequences of Trauma. William H. Simon & George E. Ehrlich. (Illus.). 536p. 1992. text 97.50 (*0-8247-8745-5*) Dekker.

Medicolegal Essentials in Health. Payne. 1996. pap. text 32.00 (*0-443-05240-9*, W B Saunders Co) Harcrt Hlth Sci Grp.

Medicolegal Examination, Evaluation, & Report, 2 vols., Set, Vols. I & II. Bernard J. Ficarra. 1986. 95.00 (*0-8493-6956-8*, RA1055, CRC Reprint) Franklin.

Medicolegal Examination, Evaluation, & Report, 2 vols., Vol. I. Bernard J. Ficarra. 304p. 1986. 129.00 (*0-8493-6957-6*, RA1055, CRC Reprint) Franklin.

Medicolegal Examination, Evaluation, & Report, 2 vols., Vol. II. Bernard J. Ficarra. 368p. 1986. 152.00 (*0-8493-6958-4*, RA1055, CRC Reprint) Franklin.

Medicolegal Fees in California: An Assessment. Leslie I. Boden. LC 93-50720. 1994. 50.00 (*0-935149-45-7*, WC-94-1) Workers Comp Res Inst.

***Medicolegal Forms with Legal Analysis: Documenting Issues in the Patient-Physician Relationship.** 2nd ed. AMA Staff. 224p. 1999. pap. text 44.95 (*0-89970-905-2*) AMA.

Medicolegal Handbook: A Guide to Winning Verdicts. Bernard J. Ficarra. LC 83-7336. 235p. reprint ed. pap. 72.90 (*0-7837-0837-8*, 204115100019) Bks Demand.

Medicolegal Issues for Radiographers. Robert J. Parelli. 115p. (C). 1991. pap. text 23.95 (*0-9628440-2-0*) Bellwether-Cross.

Medicolegal Issues for Radiographers. 3rd ed. Robert J. Parelli. 200p. 1996. lib. bdg. 39.95 (*1-57444-081-0*) St Lucie Pr.

Medicolegal Issues for Radiographers. 4th ed. Robert J. Parelli. 184p. 1998. spiral bd. 80.00 (*1-880359-15-4*) Par Rad.

Medicolegal Reporting in Orthopaedic Trauma. Ed. by Michael A. Foy & Phillip S. Fagg. (Illus.). 528p. 1990. text 64.95 (*0-443-03918-6*) Church.

Medicolegal Reporting in Surgery. B. J. Jones. (Illus.). 314p. 1996. write for info. (*0-443-05160-7*) Church.

Medicos. Robert James. (Las Personas Que Cuidan Nuestra Salud Ser.).Tr. of Doctors. 24p. (J). (gr. k-4). 1995. lib. bdg. 17.27 (*1-55916-173-6*) Rourke Bk Co.

Medicosocial Work & Nursing: The Changing Needs. (Euro Reports & Studies Ser.: No. 79). 70p. 1983. pap. text 7.00 (*92-890-1245-5*) World Health.

Medics: A Documentation of Paramedics Working in the Harlem Community. Richard Falco. (Illus.). 88p. 1986. 26.95 (*0-941062-21-X*) Begos & Rosenberg.

Medics & Nurses. William B. Sinclair. (Confusion Beyond Imagination Ser.: Bk. 5). (Illus.). 243p. 1989. 25.00 (*0-937577-08-1*); pap. 17.00 (*0-937577-09-X*) J F Whitley.

Medic's Pocket Reference. Ed. by William F. Minikiewicz. (Illus.). iv, 120p. (Orig.). 1997. pap. 12.95 (*0-9656879-0-2*) Medic Pub SC.

Medidas Principales en la Planificacion de la Iglesia Local: Key Steps in Local Church Planning. Richard E. Rusbuldt et al. Tr. by Oscar E. Rodriguez. (SPA.). 134p. 1981. pap. 6.00 (*0-8170-0933-7*) Judson.

Medien Kunst Aktion (Media Art Action) Die 60er und 70er in Deutschland (The '60s & '70s in Germany) Ed. by Goethe-Institut Munchen Staff. (Illus.). 240p. 1998. text 59.00 incl. cd-rom (*3-211-82996-2*) Spr-Verlag.

***Mediendiskurse: Verbal-Workshop Graz 1996.** Bernhard kettemann et al. (Illus.). 167p. 1998. 31.95 (*3-631-33235-1*) P Lang Pubng.

***Medienfiktionen: Illusion - Inszenierung - Simulation Festschrift Fur Helmut Schanze Zum 60. Geburtstag.** Sibylle Bolik et al. 472p. 1999. 63.95 (*3-631-34613-1*) P Lang Pubng.

Medienrecht, Wirtschaftsrecht und Auslanderrecht Im Deutsch-Brasilianischen Dialog. Jurgen Samtleben & Ralf Schmitt. 250p. 1997. 51.95 (*3-631-31556-2*) P Lang Pubng.

Medieval. Steven Farmer. 128p. 1999. pap. 9.00 (*1-928650-00-7*, Pub. by Krupskaya) SPD-Small Pr Dist.

Medieval Abbey of Farfa: Target of Papal & Imperial Ambitions. Mary Stroll. LC 96-49112. (Studies in Intellectual History: Vol. 74). (Illus.). xiv, 298p. 1997. 102.50 (*90-04-10704-5*) Brill Academic Pubs.

Medieval Accessus Ad Auctores. Edwin A. Quain. LC 86-80646. 60p. reprint ed. pap. 30.00 (*0-7837-5616-X*, 204552500005) Bks Demand.

Medieval Aesthetics see History of Aesthetics

Medieval Agriculture & Islamic Science: The Almanac of a Yemeni Sultan. Daniel M. Varisco. LC 94-13486. (Publications on the Near East: Vol. 6). 384p. 1994. text 40.00 (*0-295-97378-1*) U of Wash Pr.

Medieval Agriculture, the Southern French Countryside & the Early Cistercians: A Study of Forty-Three Monasteries. Constance H. Berman. LC 84-71079. (Transactions Ser.: Vol. 76, Pt. 5). 179p. 1986. pap. 15.00 (*0-87169-765-3*, T765-BEC) Am Philos.

Medieval Agriculture, the Southern French Countryside & the Early Cistercians: A Study of Forty-Three Monasteries. Constance H. Berman. LC 84-71079. (American Philosophical Society, Transactions Ser.: Vol. 76). (Illus.). 193p. reprint ed. pap. 59.90 (*0-7837-4331-9*, 204404200012) Bks Demand.

Medieval Alphabet. Bellerophon Books Staff. (J). (gr. 1-9). 1992. pap. 4.95 (*0-88388-001-6*) Bellerophon Bks.

Medieval Alphabets & Decorative Devices. Ed. by Henry Shaw. LC 99-10030. (Design Library). (Illus.). 48p. 1999. pap. text 5.95 (*0-486-40466-8*) Dover.

***Medieval American Art, a Survey in Two Volumes, 2 vols.** Pal Kelemen. (LC History-America-E). 1999. reprint ed. lib. bdg. 180.00 (*0-7812-4282-7*) Rprt Serv.

Medieval & Early Renaissance Medicine: An Introduction to Knowledge & Practice. Nancy G. Siraisi. LC 89-20368. (Illus.). 264p. 1990. lib. bdg. 37.50 (*0-226-76129-0*) U Ch Pr.

Medieval & Early Renaissance Medicine: An Introduction to Knowledge & Practice. Nancy G. Siraisi. LC 89-20368. (Illus.). 264p. 1990. pap. text 17.00 (*0-226-76130-4*) U Ch Pr.

Medieval & Later USK: Report on the Excavations at USK, 1965-1976. Paul Courtney. 165p. 1994. 60.00 (*0-7083-1245-4*, Pub. by Univ Wales Pr) Paul & Co Pubs.

Medieval & Modern Ireland. Ed. by Richard Wall. (Irish Literary Studies: No. 32). 1988. 56.50 (*0-389-20793-4*, N8351) B&N Imports.

Medieval & Modern Perspectives on Muslim-Jewish Relations. Ed. by Ronald L. Nettler. (Studies in Muslim-Jewish Relations). 205p. 1995. text 64.00 (*3-7186-5727-9*, Harwood Acad Pubs) Gordon & Breach.

Medieval & Post-Medieval Finds from Exeter, 1971-1980. J. P. Allan. (Illus.). 400p. 1993. text 80.00 (*0-85989-220-4*, Pub. by Univ Exeter Pr) Northwestern U Pr.

***Medieval & Renaissance Dance Music for Acoustic Guitar.** Jamey Bellizzi. 96p. 1998. pap. 19.95 incl. audio compact disk (*0-7866-4036-7*, 94847BCD) Mel Bay.

Medieval & Renaissance Drama in England, Vol. 7. Ed. by J. Leeds Barroll. (Illus.). 448p. 1995. 72.50 (*0-8386-3570-9*) Fairleigh Dickinson.

Medieval & Renaissance Drama in England, Vol. 8. Ed. by J. Leeds Barroll & Susan P. Cerasano. (Illus.). 288p. 1996. write for info. (*0-8386-3641-1*) Fairleigh Dickinson.

Medieval & Renaissance Drama in England, Vol. 9. Ed. by John Pitcher & Susan Cerasano. 280p. 1997. 72.50 (*0-8386-3703-5*) Fairleigh Dickinson.

Medieval & Renaissance Drama in England, Vol. 10. Ed. by John Pitcher & Susan Cerasano. (Illus.). 400p. 1998. 72.50 (*0-8386-3770-1*) Fairleigh Dickinson.

Medieval & Renaissance Drama in England, Vol. 11. Ed. by John Pitcher. 400p. 1999. 72.50 (*0-8386-3805-8*) Fairleigh Dickinson.

***Medieval & Renaissance Drama in England, Vol. 12.** Ed. by John Pitcher et al. (Illus.). 392p. 1999. 72.50 (*0-8386-3836-8*) Fairleigh Dickinson.

Medieval & Renaissance Drama in England: An Annual Gathering of Research, Criticism, & Reviews, 6 vols. Ed. by J. Leeds Barroll. LC 83-45280. (Illus.). 1991. write for info. (*0-404-62300-X*) AMS Pr.

Medieval & Renaissance Drama in England: An Annual Gathering of Research, Criticism, & Reviews, 6 vols., Vol. 1. Ed. by J. Leeds Barroll. (Illus.). 1984. 57.50 (*0-404-62305-0*) AMS Pr.

Medieval & Renaissance Drama in England: An Annual Gathering of Research, Criticism & Reviews, 6 vols., Vol. 2. Ed. by J. Leeds Barroll. 1985. 57.50 (*0-404-62301-8*) AMS Pr.

Medieval & Renaissance Drama in England: An Annual Gathering of Research, Criticism, & Reviews, 6 vols., Vol. 3. Ed. by J. Leeds Barroll. (Illus.). 1986. 57.50 (*0-404-62302-6*) AMS Pr.

Medieval & Renaissance Drama in England: An Annual Gathering of Research, Criticism, & Reviews, 6 vols., Vol. 4. Ed. by J. Leeds Barroll. (Illus.). 1989. 57.50 (*0-404-62303-4*) AMS Pr.

Medieval & Renaissance Drama in England: An Annual Gathering of Research, Criticism & Reviews, 6 vols., Vol. 5. Ed. by J. Leeds Barroll. (Illus.). 1991. 57.50 (*0-404-62304-2*) AMS Pr.

Medieval & Renaissance Letter Treatises & Form Letters: A Census of Manuscripts Found in Eastern Europe & the Former U. S. S. R. Emil J. Polak. LC 92-36557. (Davis Medieval Texts & Studies: Vol. 8). xxii, 324p. 1992. 126.50 (*90-04-09667-1*) Brill Academic Pubs.

Medieval & Renaissance Manuscript Books in the Library of Congress: A Descriptive Catalog; Bibles, Liturgy, Books of Hours, Vol. 1. Svato Schutzner. LC 85-600260. 421p. 1989. 62.00 (*0-8444-0516-7*, 030-001-00112-1) Lib Congress.

***Medieval & Renaissance Manuscript Books in the Library of Congress, Descriptive Catalog: Theology & Canon Law, Vol. 2.** Svato Schutzner. 676p. 1999. boxed set 96.00 (*0-16-061817-7*, Library of Cong) USGPO.

Medieval & Renaissance Manuscripts at Columbia University. Beatrice Terrien-Somerville. 1991. pap. text 34.50 (*0-231-07648-7*) Col U Pr.

Medieval & Renaissance Manuscripts at the University of California, Los Angeles. Mirella Ferrari. Ed. by Richard H. Rouse. LC 90-40510. (UC Publications in Catalogs & Bibliographies: Vol. 7). (Illus.). 416p. 1991. 65.00 (*0-520-09687-8*, Pub. by U CA Pr) Cal Prin Full Svc.

Medieval & Renaissance Manuscripts in New Zealand. Margaret M. Manion et al. LC 88-51139. (Illus.). 1989. 45.00 (*0-500-23544-9*, Pub. by Thames Hudson) Norton.

Medieval & Renaissance Manuscripts in the Claremont Libraries. Ed. by C. W. Dutschke et al. (UC Publications in Catalogs & Bibliographies: Vol. III). 1987. 55.00 (*0-520-09644-4*, Pub. by U CA Pr) Cal Prin Full Svc.

Medieval & Renaissance Manuscripts in the Walters Art Gallery Vol. 1: France, 875-1420. Lillian M. Randall. LC 88-45410. (Illus.). 432p. 1989. text 85.00 (*0-8018-2869-4*) Johns Hopkins.

Medieval & Renaissance Manuscripts in the Walters Art Gallery Vol. 3: Belgium, 1250-1530. Lilian M. Randall et al. (Illus.). 704p. 1997. text 149.95 (*0-8018-5317-6*) Johns Hopkins.

Medieval & Renaissance Manuscripts in the Walters Art Gallery, Vol. II: France, 1420-1540, 2 vols. Lillian M. Randall. LC 88-45410. (Illus.). 832p. 1993. text 135.95 (*0-8018-2870-8*) Johns Hopkins.

Medieval & Renaissance Miniature Paintings, Catalogue 3. (Illus.). 26p. (Orig.). (C). 1995. pap. write for info. (*0-9645271-0-3*) B Ferrini.

Medieval & Renaissance Music: A Performer's Guide. Timothy J. McGee. LC 86-149637. (Illus.). 303p. reprint ed. pap. 94.00 (*0-8357-6363-3*, 203571700069) Bks Demand.

Medieval & Renaissance Music: A Performer's Guide. Timothy J. McGee. (Illus.). 304p. 1988. reprint ed. pap. 18.95 (*0-8020-6729-8*) U of Toronto Pr.

Medieval & Renaissance Scholarship: Proceedings of the Second European Science Foundation Workshop on the Classical Tradition in the Middle Ages & the Renaissance (London, Warburg Institute, 27-28 November 1992) Nicholas E. Mann & Birger M. Olsen. LC 96-9830. (Mittellateinische Studien und Texte). 1996. 101.50 (*90-04-10508-5*) Brill Academic Pubs.

Medieval & Renaissance Spanish Literature: Selected Essays of Keith Whinnom. Ed. by Deyermond et al. (Illus.). 320p. 1994. text 50.00 (*0-85989-219-0*, Pub. by Univ Exeter Pr) Northwestern U Pr.

Medieval & Renaissance Splendor: The Romance of Arts, Armor & Works of Art from the John Woodman Higgins Armary. Cynthia Duval & Walter J. Karcheski. LC 83-83306. (Illus.). 160p. (Orig.). 1984. pap. 9.95 (*0-916758-15-X*) Ringling Mus Art.

Medieval & Renaissance Studies. Theodor Mommsen & Eugene F. Rice, Jr. LC 82-2855. (Illus.). 353p. 1982. reprint ed. lib. bdg. 59.75 (*0-313-23482-5*, MOMM, Greenwood Pr) Greenwood.

Medieval & Renaissance Studies: Proceedings of the Southeastern Institute of Medieval & Renaissance Studies, Summer 1975. Ed. by Siegfried Wenzel. LC 66-25361. (Medieval & Renaissance Monograph Ser.: No. 7). 141p. reprint ed. pap. 43.80 (*0-8357-4417-5*, 203723700007) Bks Demand.

Medieval & Renaissance Studies: Proceedings of the Southeastern Institute of Medieval & Renaissance Studies, Summer 1979. Ed. by George M. Masters. LC 68-54949. (Medieval & Renaissance Monograph: No. 10). (Illus.). 132p. reprint ed. pap. 41.00 (*0-7837-2467-5*, 204262000005) Bks Demand.

Medieval & Renaissance Studies No. 4: Proceedings of the Southeastern Institute of Medieval & Renaissance Studies. Southeastern Institute of Medieval & Renaissance S. LC 66-25361. 195p. reprint ed. pap. 60.50 (*0-608-15068-1*, 202620700048) Bks Demand.

***Medieval & Renaissance Treatises on the Arts of Painting.** Mary Merrifield. LC 98-48799. 918p. 1999. pap. text 34.95 (*0-486-40440-4*) Dover.

Medieval & Renaissance Venice. Ellen E. Kittell. LC 98-58020. 368p. 1999. 45.00 (*0-252-02461-3*) U of Ill Pr.

Medieval & Tudor Drama: Twenty-Four Plays. Ed. & Intro. by John Gassner. LC 87-18836. 457p. 1995. pap. 12.95 (*0-936839-84-8*) Applause Theatre Bk Pubs.

Medieval Antecedents of Constitutionalism. R. W. Carstens. LC 91-16403. (American University Studies: History: Ser. IX, Vols. 115). 114p. (C). 1992. text 40.95 (*0-8204-1657-6*) P Lang Pubng.

Medieval Archeology. Ed. by Charles L. Redman. (Medieval & Renaissance Texts & Studies: Vol. 60). 320p. 1989. 24.00 (*0-86698-044-X*, MR60) MRTS.

Medieval Archer. Jim Bradbury. (Illus.). 208p. (Orig.). 1999. reprint ed. pap. 29.95 (*0-85115-675-4*) Boydell & Brewer.

Medieval Architecture, 2 vols. A. Kingsley Porter. LC 67-4391. (Illus.). 1969. 150.00 (*0-87817-019-7*) Hacker.

Medieval Architecture & Its Medieval Context: Studies in Honour of Peter Kidson. Ed. by E. Fernie & P. Crossley. 320p. 1990. 65.00 (*1-85285-034-5*) Hambledon Press.

Medieval Architecture in Western Europe: From A. D. 300 to 1500. Robert G. Calkins. LC 97-8135. (Illus.). 352p. (C). 1998. 49.95 incl. cd-rom (*0-19-511241-5*) OUP.

Medieval Architecture, Medieval Learning: Builders & Masters in the Age of Romanesque & Gothic. Charles M. Radding & William W. Clark. (Illus.). 184p. 1994. pap. 20.00 (*0-300-06130-7*) Yale U Pr.

Medieval Architecture of Eastern Europe. Heinrich L. Nickel. LC 82-6254. (Illus.). 210p. 1983. 65.00 (*0-8419-0811-7*) Holmes & Meier.

Medieval Aristotelianism & Its Limits: Classical Traditions in Moral & Political Philosophy, 12-15th Centuries. Cary J. Nederman. LC 96-48557. (Collected Studies: No. 565). 352p. 1997. 106.95 (*0-86078-622-6*, Pub. by Variorum) Ashgate Pub Co.

Medieval Armchair Travels. Bridget A. Henisch. (Illus.). 154p. 1967. 15.00 (*0-87601-000-1*) Carnation.

Medieval Armenian Manuscripts At the University Of California, Los Angeles. Avedis K. Sanjian & University of California, Los Angeles Staff. LC 99-10660. (University Of California Publications.: Vol. 14). 406p. 1999. pap. 80.00 (*0-520-09792-0*, Pub. by U CA Pr) Cal Prin Full Svc.

Medieval Art. W. R. Lethaby. 20.00 (*0-8196-2015-7*) Biblo.

Medieval Art. Marilyn Stokstad. LC 84-48522. (Illus.). 448p. 1986. pap. 40.00 (*0-06-430132-X*, IN-132, Icon Edns) HarpC.

Medieval Art. Marilyn Stokstad. write for info. (*0-8133-3681-3*) Westview.

Medieval Art: A Topical Dictionary. Leslie Ross. LC 96-160. 320p. 1996. lib. bdg. 79.50 (*0-313-29329-5*, Greenwood Pr) Greenwood.

Medieval Art: Painting, Sculpture, Architecture, 4th Thru 14th Century. James C. Snyder. 512p. (C). 1988. text 73.33 (*0-13-573494-0*) P-H.

Medieval Art: Painting, Sculpture, Architecture, 4th-14th Century. James C. Snyder. (Illus.). 512p. 1989. 60.00 (*0-8109-1532-4*, Pub. by Abrams) Time Warner.

Medieval Art in America: Patterns of Collecting, 1800-1940. Elizabeth B. Smith. 248p. (Orig.). 1996. pap. text 25.00 (*0-911209-45-X*) Palmer Mus Art.

Medieval Art of Love: Objects & Subjects of Desire. Michael Camille. LC 98-17485. (Illus.). 182p. 1998. 35.00 (*0-8109-1544-8*, Pub. by Abrams) Time Warner.

Medieval Art-Recent Perspectives: A Memorial Tribute to C. R. Dodwell. Owen-Crocker. LC 98-17826. (Illus.). 304p. 1998. text 79.95 (*0-7190-4992-X*, Pub. by Manchester Univ Pr) St Martin.

Medieval Artistry & Exchange: Economic Institutions, Society, & Literary Form in Old French Narrative. Judith L. Kellogg. LC 89-12359. (American University Studies: Romance Languages & Literature: Ser. II, Vol. 123). 208p. 1989. text 36.50 (*0-8204-0971-5*) P Lang Pubng.

***Medieval Arts Doctrines on Ambiguity & Their Place in Langland's Poetics.** John Chamberlain. 176p. 2000. 55.00 (*0-7735-2073-2*, Pub. by McG-Queens Univ Pr) CUP Services.

***Medieval Ashkenazic History: Studies on German Jewry in the Middle Ages.** Shlomo Eidelberg. LC 99-35251. (Illus.). 224p. 1999. 25.00 (*0-87203-155-1*) Hermon.

Medieval Aspects of Renaissance Learning. Paul O. Kristeller. 185p. 1993. text 52.50 (*0-231-07950-8*) Col U Pr.

Medieval Baker's Daughter: A Bilingual Adventure in Medieval Life with Costumes, Banners, Music, Food, & a Mystery Play. Madeleine P. Cosman. LC 84-71590.Tr. of La/Hija de la Panadera Medieval. (ENG & SPA., Illus.). 112p. (J). (gr. 3-12). 1984. pap. 7.95 (*0-916491-18-8*) Bard Hall Pr.

Medieval Balladry & the Courtly Tradition: Literature of Revolt & Assimilation. Gwendolyn A. Morgan. LC 92-28130. (American University Studies: English Language & Literature: Ser. IV, Vol. 160). 148p. 1993. 36.95 (*0-8204-2042-5*) P Lang Pubng.

Medieval Ballads: Chivalry, Romance, & Everyday Life: A Critical Anthology. Ed. by Gwendolyn A. Morgan. 226p. (C). 1996. pap. text 29.95 (*0-8204-3139-7*) P Lang Pubng.

***Medieval Banquet in the Alhambra Palace.** Audrey Shabbas. (Illus.). 100p. 2000. spiral bd., suppl. ed. 19.95 (*1-889993-04-2*) AWAIR.

Medieval Banquet in the Alhambra Palace. rev. ed. Audrey Shabbas. (Illus.). 181p. 1993. spiral bd. 29.95 (*1-889993-00-X*) AWAIR.

Medieval Beasts. Ann Payne. (Illus.). 96p. (C). 1990. 36.00 (*1-56131-018-2*, NAB) I R Dee.

Medieval Bhakti Movements in India. N. N. Bhattacharya. (C). 1989. 44.00 (*0-685-30850-2*, Pub. by M Manoharial) S Asia.

Medieval Bishops' Houses in England & Wales. Michael W. Thompson. LC 98-9974. (Illus.). 207p. 1998. text 61.95 (*1-84014-277-4*, Pub. by Ashgate Pub) Ashgate Pub Co.

Medieval Boethius: Studies in the Vernacular Translation of De Consolatione Philosophiae. Ed. by Alastair J. Minnis. 207p. 1988. 75.00 (*0-85991-234-5*) Boydell & Brewer.

Medieval Book. Barbara A. Shailor. 1994. reprint ed. text 65.00 (*0-8020-5910-4*); reprint ed. pap. text 24.95 (*0-8020-6853-7*) U of Toronto Pr.

Medieval Book of Beasts: Pierre de Beauvais' Bestiary Followed by a Diplomatic Transcription of the Malines (Mechelen) Manuscript of Pierre de Beauvais, Short Version, & with in Appendix, an English Translation of the Cambrai Bestiary. Tr. by Guy R. Mermier from FRE. LC 91-37833. (Illus.). 364p. 1991. lib. bdg. 99.95 (*0-7734-9629-7*) E Mellen.

Medieval Book of Birds: Hugh of Fouilloy's "Aviarium" Ed. & Tr. by Willene B. Clark. (Medieval & Renaissance Texts & Studies: Vol. 80). (Illus.). 464p. 1996. reprint ed. 38.00 (*0-86698-091-1*, MR80) MRTS.

***Medieval Bridges.** Martin Cook. (Archaeology Ser.: Vol. 77). (Illus.). 1999. pap. text 10.50 (*0-7478-0384-6*, Pub. by Shire Pubns) Parkwest Pubns.

Medieval Britain. Country Miniature Staff. (Weidenfeld Country Miniature Ser.). (Illus.). 64p. 1995. 9.95 (*0-297-83489-4*, Pub. by Orion Pubng Grp) Trafalgar.

Medieval Britain: Conquest, Power & People. Tony McAleavy. (Cambridge History Programme Ser.). (Illus.). 80p. (C). 1993. pap. 14.95 (*0-521-40708-7*) Cambridge U Pr.

An Asterisk (*) at the beginning of an entry indicates that the title is appearing for the first time.

Medieval Britain: The Age of Chivalry. Laing. (Illus.). 224p. 1998. pap. 16.95 (*0-312-21793-5*) St Martin.

Medieval BritainTowns. Swanson. LC 99-12187. 161p. 1999. text 65.00 (*0-312-22326-9*) St Martin.

Medieval Buda. Martyn C. Rady. 1985. text 68.50 (*0-88033-074-0*, Pub. by East Eur Monographs) Col U Pr.

***Medieval Builder & His Methods.** Francis B. Andrews. LC 98-48800. 1999. pap. text 6.95 (*0-486-40672-5*) Dover.

***Medieval Calendar Year.** Bridget Ann Henisch. LC 99-20706. (Illus.). 232p. 1999. 55.00 (*0-271-01903-4*) Pa St U Pr.

Medieval Calendar Year. Bridget Ann Henisch. LC 99-20706. (Illus.). 472p. 1999. pap. 20.00 (*0-271-01904-2*) Pa St U Pr.

Medieval Calligraphy. Marc Drogin. (Illus.). 224p. 1989. pap. 12.95 (*0-486-26142-5*) Dover.

Medieval Callings. Ed. by Jacques Le Goff. Tr. by Lydia G. Cochrane. x, 400p. 1990. 47.50 (*0-226-47086-5*) U Ch Pr.

Medieval Callings. Jacques Le Goff. Tr. by Lydia G. Cochrane from FRE. xiii, 400p. 1995. pap. text 18.00 (*0-226-47087-3*) U Ch Pr.

Medieval Cambridge: Essays on the Pre-Reformation University. Ed. by Patrick Zutshi. LC 93-5915. (History of the University of Cambridge: Texts & Studies: Vol. 2). (Illus.). 206p. (C). 1993. 75.00 (*0-85115-344-5*, Boydell Pr) Boydell & Brewer.

Medieval Canon Law. James A. Brundage. LC 94-33506. (Medieval World Ser.). 264p. (C). 1996. text 51.95 (*0-582-09357-0*) Addison-Wesley.

Medieval Canon Law. James A. Brundage. LC 94-33506. (Medieval World Ser.). 272p. (C). 1995. pap. 40.06 (*0-582-09356-2*) Longman.

Medieval Carpathian Rus' The Oldest Documentation about the Carpatho-Rusyn Church & Eparchy. Aleksei Petrov. LC 97-61166. 250p. 1998. 35.00 (*0-88033-388-X*, 491, Pub. by East Eur Monographs) Col U Pr.

Medieval Castle. Fiona MacDonald. (Inside Story Ser.). (Illus.). 48p. (YA). (gr. 5 up). 1990. lib. bdg. 18.95 (*0-87226-340-1*, 63401B, P Bedrick Books) NTC Contemp Pub Co.

Medieval Castle. Don Nardo. LC 97-34638. (Building History Ser.). (Illus.). 96p. (YA). (gr. 4-12). 1997. lib. bdg. 22.45 (*1-56006-430-7*) Lucent Bks.

Medieval Castle. Jim Pipe. LC 96-12638. (Mystery History Ser.). (Illus.). 32p. (J). (gr. 4-6). 1996. 9.95 (*0-7613-0501-7*, Copper Beech Bks); lib. bdg. 23.90 (*0-7613-0495-9*, Copper Beech Bks) Millbrook Pr.

Medieval Castle. Marjorie Reeves. (Then & There Ser.). 105p. (gr. 7-12). 1963. pap. text 8.60 (*0-582-00381-4*, 78062) Longman.

Medieval Castle in England & Wales: A Political & Social History. Norman J. Pounds. (Illus.). 375p. (C). 1991. text 80.00 (*0-521-38349-8*) Cambridge U Pr.

Medieval Castle in England & Wales: A Political & Social History. Norman J. Pounds. (Illus.). 375p. (C). 1993. pap. text 29.95 (*0-521-45828-5*) Cambridge U Pr.

Medieval Castle in Scotland. W. Mackay MacKenzie. LC 75-174843. (Illus.). 260p. 1972. reprint ed. 24.95 (*0-405-08769-1*, Pub. by Blom Pubns) Ayer.

***Medieval Castle Sticker Picture.** A. G. Smith. (Illus.). (J). 1999. pap. 4.50 (*0-486-40588-5*) Dover.

Medieval Castles. Conrad Cairns. (Cambridge Introduction to World History Topic Bks.). (Illus.). 48p. 1987. pap. 12.95 (*0-521-31589-1*) Cambridge U Pr.

***Medieval Castles of Ireland.** David Sweetman. LC 99-490192. (Illus.). 240p. 2000. 49.95 (*1-898256-75-6*, Pub. by Collins Press) Irish Bks Media.

***Medieval Castles of Ireland.** David Sweetman. LC 99-89487. (Illus.). 224p. 2000. 45.00 (*0-85115-788-2*) Boydell & Brewer.

Medieval Cathedral. Fiona MacDonald. LC 91-16415. (Inside Story Ser.). (Illus.). 48p. (YA). (gr. 4-7). 1994. 18.95 (*0-87226-350-9*, 63509B, P Bedrick Books) NTC Contemp Pub Co.

Medieval Cats. Susan Herbert. (Illus.). 64p. 1995. 16.95 (*0-8212-2179-5*, Pub. by Bulfinch Pr) Little.

Medieval Cats. Susan Herbert. (Illus.). 62p. 1997. reprint ed. text 15.00 (*0-7881-5080-4*) DIANE Pub.

Medieval Celtic Literature: A Select Bibliography. Rachel Bromwich. LC 74-82287. (Toronto Medieval Bibliographies Ser.: No. 5). 128p. reprint ed. pap. 39.70 (*0-608-16924-2*, 202641800049) Bks Demand.

***Medieval Central Europe.** 2000. write for info. (*0-582-07060-0*) Pearson Educ.

Medieval Charlemagne Legend: An Annotated Bibliography. Susan E. Farrier. LC 92-24797. (Medieval Bibliographies Ser.: Vol. 15). 672p. 1992. text 20.00 (*0-8240-0949-5*, H984) Garland.

Medieval Chinese Armies, 1260-1520. Chris J. Peers. (Men-at-Arms Ser.: No. 251). (Illus.). 48p. 1992. pap. 11.95 (*1-85532-254-4*, 9222, Pub. by Ospry) Stackpole.

Medieval Chinese Society & the Local Community. Michio Tanigawa. Ed. & Tr. by Joshua A. Fogel. LC 84-23960. 1985. 50.00 (*0-520-05370-2*, Pub. by U CA Pr) Cal Prin Full Svc.

Medieval Christian Literary Imagery: A Guide to Interpretation. R. E. Kaske et al. 272p. (C). 1988. pap. text 20.95 (*0-8020-6663-1*) U of Toronto Pr.

Medieval Christian Perceptions of Islam: A Book of Essays. John V. Tolan. LC 94-5298. (Medieval Casebooks Ser.: Vol. 10). 442p. 1995. text 77.00 (*0-8153-1426-4*, H1768) Garland.

***Medieval Christmas.** (Illus.). 32p. 2000. 19.95 (*0-7112-1057-8*, Pub. by F Lincoln) Antique Collect.

Medieval Chronicles & the Rotation of the Earth. Robert R. Newton. LC 78-39780. 848p. reprint ed. pap. 200.00 (*0-608-30526-X*, 201229100081) Bks Demand.

Medieval Church. John M. O'Brien. (Quality Paperback Ser.: No. 227). 120p. (Orig.). 1968. pap. 11.00 (*0-8226-0227-X*) Littlefield.

Medieval Church. Roland H. Bainton. LC 78-11433. (Anvil Ser.). 192p. 1979. reprint ed. pap. 12.50 (*0-88275-786-5*) Krieger.

Medieval Church: A Brief History. Joseph H. Lynch. LC 91-45261. 385p. (C). 1995. pap. 50.00 (*0-582-49467-2*, 79361) Longman.

Medieval Church: From the Dawn of the Middle Ages to the Eve of the Reformation. Carl A. Volz. LC 97-26621. 296p. 1997. pap. 18.95 (*0-687-00604-X*) Abingdon.

Medieval Church: Universities, Heresy & the Religious Life. Ed. by Peter Biller & Barrie Dobson. LC 99-18328. (Ecclesiastical History Society Ser.). 352p. 1999. 75.00 (*0-9529733-3-2*) Boydell & Brewer.

Medieval Church Hist. Joseph H. Lynch. (C). 1992. text 66.50 (*0-582-49466-4*) Addison-Wesley.

Medieval Church Music-Dramas: A Repertory of Complete Plays. Ed. by Fletcher Collins, Jr. LC 75-33896. 514p. reprint ed. 159.40 (*0-8357-9809-7*, 201318000085) Bks Demand.

Medieval Churches in the Vale of Glamorgan. Geoffrey R. Orrin. 550p. (C). 1989. 175.00 (*0-905928-80-6*, Pub. by D Brown & Sons Ltd) St Mut.

Medieval Churches in the Vale of Glamorgan. deluxe limited ed. Geoffrey R. Orrin. 550p. (C). 1989. 350.00 (*0-905928-92-X*, Pub. by D Brown & Sons Ltd) St Mut.

Medieval Cities. Howard Saalman. (Orig.). 1968. 7.95 (*0-8076-0467-4*, Pub. by Braziller) Norton.

Medieval Cities: Their Origins & the Revival of Trade. Henri Pirenne. Tr. by Frank D. Halsey. 272p. (C). 1952. pap. text 14.95 (*0-691-00760-8*, Pub. by Princeton U Pr) Cal Prin Full Svc.

Medieval City. Ed. by Harry A. Miskimin et al. LC 77-76302. 355p. reprint ed. pap. 110.10 (*0-8357-8218-2*, 203382800087) Bks Demand.

Medieval City under Siege. Ed. by Ivy A. Corfis & Michael Wolfe. (Medieval Archaeology Ser.). (Illus.). 302p. 1999. pap. 35.00 (*0-85115-756-4*, Suffolk Records Soc) Boydell & Brewer.

Medieval Civilization, 400-1500. Jacques Le Goff. Tr. by Julia Barrow. 1991. pap. 31.95 (*0-631-17566-0*) Blackwell Pubs.

Medieval Codicology, Iconography, Literature, & Translation: Studies for Deith Val Sinclair. Ed. by Peter R. Monks & D. D. Owen. LC 94-2818. (Litterae Textuales Ser.). 1994. 155.50 (*90-04-09958-1*) Brill Academic Pubs.

Medieval Coins in the Christian J. Thomsen Collection, Vol. 1. Kristian Erslev. (Illus.). 408p. 1992. 69.50 (*0-915018-33-0*) Attic Bks.

***Medieval Combat: A Fifteenth-Century Illustrated Manual of Swordfighting & Close-Quarter Combat.** Hans Talhoffer & Mark Rector. LC 00-37194. (Illus.). 2000. pap. write for info. (*1-85367-418-4*) Stackpole.

Medieval Comic Tales. Ed. by Derek S. Brewer. 224p. 1996. pap. 29.95 (*0-85991-485-2*, DS Brewer) Boydell & Brewer.

Medieval Comic Tales. rev. ed. Ed. by Derek S. Brewer. 224p. 1996. 60.00 (*0-85991-430-5*, DS Brewer) Boydell & Brewer.

***Medieval Concepts of the Past: Ritual, Memory, Historiography.** Ed. by Gerd Althoff et al. (Publications of the German Historical Institute, Washington, D. C.). (Illus.). 328p. 2000. write for info. (*0-521-78066-7*) Cambridge U Pr.

Medieval Consolation of Philosophy: An Annotated Bibliography. Noel H. Kaylor, Jr. LC 92-459. (Medieval Bibliographies Ser.: Vol. 7). 272p. 1992. text 15.00 (*0-8240-5548-9*, H1215) Garland.

Medieval Cookbook. Maggie Black. LC 92-81536. (Illus.). 144p. 1992. 24.95 (*0-500-01548-1*, Pub. by Thames Hudson) Norton.

Medieval Coroner. R. F. Hunisett. LC 85-48162. (Cambridge Studies in English Legal History). 230p. 1986. reprint ed. 60.00 (*0-912004-31-2*) Gaunt.

Medieval Cosmology: Theories of Infinity, Place, Time, Void, & the Plurality of Worlds. Pierre M. Duhem. Ed. by Roger Ariew. LC 85-8115. xxxii, 634p. (C). 1987. pap. text 27.00 (*0-226-16923-5*) U Ch Pr.

***Medieval Costume & Fashion.** Herbert Norris. LC 98-49856. 528p. 1999. pap. text 17.95 (*0-486-40486-2*) Dover.

***Medieval Costume, Armour & Weapons.** Eduard Wagner et al. LC 00-38419. 2000. pap. write for info. (*0-486-41240-7*) Dover.

Medieval Costume in England & France: The 13th, 14th, & 15th Centuries. unabridged ed. Houston. LC 95-40171. (Illus.). 240p. reprint ed. pap. 8.95 (*0-486-29060-3*) Dover.

Medieval Costumes Paper Dolls. Tom Tierney. (Illus.). 1998. pap. 3.95 (*0-486-28925-7*) Dover.

Medieval Councils Decretals & Collections of Canon. Kuttner. 1992. 124.95 (*0-86078-336-7*) Ashgate Pub Co.

Medieval Craftsmen, Set, Vols. 1-8. 1992. pap. text 100.00 (*0-8020-3991-X*) U of Toronto Pr.

Medieval Crime & Social Control. Ed. by Barbara A. Hanawalt & David Wallace. LC 98-29192. (Medieval Cultures Ser.: Vol. 16). 268p. 1999. 49.95 (*0-8166-3168-9*); pap. 19.95 (*0-8166-3169-7*) U of Minn Pr.

Medieval Cross Stitch Samplers. Angela Wainwright. (Illus.). 96p. (Orig.). 1996. pap. 14.95 (*0-304-34583-0*, Pub. by Cassell) Sterling.

Medieval Crown of Aragon: A Short History. Thomas N. Bisson. (Illus.). 250p. 1991. reprint ed. pap. 26.00 (*0-19-820236-9*, 11916) OUP.

***Medieval Cult of St. Petroc.** Karen Jankulak. LC 99-56576. (Studies in Celtic History: Vol. 0261-9865). 192p. 2000. 75.00 (*0-85115-777-7*) Boydell & Brewer.

Medieval Cult of Saints: Formations & Transformations. Barbara Abou-El-Haj. (Illus.). 476p. 1997. pap. text 25.95 (*0-521-58716-6*) Cambridge U Pr.

Medieval Culture & Society. Ed. by David Herlihy. 410p. (C). 1993. reprint ed. pap. text 15.95 (*0-88133-747-1*) Waveland Pr.

Medieval Dalmatian Cities: Development & Transformation. Joan Dusa. LC 90-6145. (American University Studies: History: Ser. IX, Vol. 94). 157p. (C). 1992. text 35.95 (*0-8204-1286-4*) P Lang Pubng.

Medieval Death: Ritual & Representation. Paul Binski. LC 96-6007. (Illus.). 232p. (C). 1996. text 39.95 (*0-8014-3315-0*) Cornell U Pr.

Medieval Debate on Jean de Meung's Roman de la Rose: Morality Versus Art. Jillian M. Hill. LC 91-45811. (Studies in Medieval Literature: Vol. 4). 284p. 1992. lib. bdg. 89.95 (*0-88946-318-2*) E Mellen.

Medieval Deccan: Peasants, Social Systems & States Sixteenth to Eighteenth Centuries. Hiroshi A. Fukazawa. (Oxford India Paperbacks Ser.). 272p. 1999. pap. text 13.95 (*0-19-564704-1*) OUP.

***Medieval Decorative Ironwork in England.** Jane Geddes. (Reports of the Research Committee of the Society of Antiquaries Ser.: Vol. 59). (Illus.). 411p. 1999. 135.00 (*0-85431-273-0*, Pub. by Soc Antiquaries) David Brown.

Medieval Decorative Ornament. James K. Colling. 160p. 1995. pap. 9.95 (*0-486-28740-8*) Dover.

Medieval Demography: Essays by Josiah Cox Russell. Josiah C. Russell. LC 86-47837. (Studies in the Middle Ages: No. 12). 37.50 (*0-404-61442-6*) AMS Pr.

Medieval Designs. Gregory Mirow. LC 97-23626. (Dover Design Library). 1997. pap. 5.95 (*0-486-29791-8*) Dover.

Medieval Destinations. Charlene Beeler. (Simulation Ser.). 44p. 1991. pap. 14.95 (*1-882664-02-7*) Prufrock Pr.

Medieval Dialectology. Ed. by Jacek Fisiak. LC 94-24163. (Trends in Linguistics, Studies & Monographs: No. 79). xiii, 331p. (C). 1995. lib. bdg. 144.60 (*3-11-013951-0*) Mouton.

Medieval Dragon: The Nature of the Beast in Germanic Literature. Joyce T. Lionarons. LC 98-215530. 256p. 1998. 59.95 (*1-874312-33-8*, Pub. by Hisarlik Pr) Intl Spec Bk.

Medieval Drama, 001. David M. Bevington. (C). 1975. text 60.36 (*0-395-13915-5*) HM.

Medieval Drama. Jackie Johnston & Christine Richardson. LC 89-77989. (English Dramatists Ser.). 150p. 1991. text 39.95 (*0-312-04612-X*) St Martin.

Medieval Drama. Sandro Sticca. LC 78-152517. (Illus.). 154p. (C). 1972. text 24.50 (*0-87395-085-2*) State U NY Pr.

***Medieval Drama.** Greg Walker. (Anthologies Ser.). 704p. 2000. 79.95 (*0-631-21726-6*); pap. 39.95 (*0-631-21727-4*) Blackwell Pubs.

Medieval Drama & Its Claudelian Revival: Papers. Symposium in Comparative Literature (3rd: 1968, Ca. Ed. by Catherine E. Dunn et al. LC 79-121385. 84p. reprint ed. pap. 30.00 (*0-608-17242-1*, 202949800061) Bks Demand.

Medieval Drama on the Continent of Europe. Ed. by Clifford Davidson & John H. Stroupe. (C). 1993. pap. 12.00 (*1-879288-37-0*) Medieval Inst.

Medieval Dramatic Continuity in Shakespeare's Plays. Ed. by Wayne Narey. 288p. 2001. pap. 28.95 (*0-8143-2602-1*) Wayne St U Pr.

Medieval Dublin: The Living City. Ed. by Howard Clarke. (Illus.). 240p. 1990. 16.95 (*0-7165-2460-0*, Pub. by Irish Acad Pr) Intl Spec Bk.

Medieval Dublin: The Making of a Metropolis. Ed. by Howard Clarke. (Illus.). 320p. 1990. 16.95 (*0-7165-2459-7*, Pub. by Irish Acad Pr) Intl Spec Bk.

***Medieval Dublin Vol. I: Proceedings of the Friends of Medieval Dublin Symposium 1999.** Ed. by Sean Duffy. 224p. 2000. 55.00 (*1-85182-537-1*, Pub. by Four Cts Pr); pap. 19.95 (*1-85182-580-0*, Pub. by Four Cts Pr) Intl Spec Bk.

Medieval Dutch Drama: Four Scholar Plays & Four Forces. Ed. by Martin Stevens & Stephen Wright. Tr. by Johanna C. Prins. LC 99-45763. (Early European Drama in Translation Ser.). 200p. 1998. pap. text 12.95 (*1-889818-07-0*) Pegasus Pr.

Medieval Dutch Literature in Its European Context. Ed. by Erik Kooper. (Cambridge Studies in Medieval Literature: No. 21). (Illus.). 343p. (C). 1994. text 74.95 (*0-521-40222-0*) Cambridge U Pr.

Medieval Ecclesiastical Studies in Honour of Dorothy M. Owen. Ed. by M. J. Franklin & Christopher Harper-Bill. (Studies in the History of Medieval Religion: Vol. VII). (Illus.). 332p. 1995. 90.00 (*0-85115-384-4*) Boydell & Brewer.

Medieval Empire, 2 Vols. Herbert A. Fisher. LC 72-95147. reprint ed. 84.50 (*0-404-02398-3*) AMS Pr.

Medieval England. 2nd ed. Platt. (Illus.). 312p. (C). 1995. pap. 29.99 (*0-415-12913-3*) Routledge.

Medieval England: A Social History & Archaeology from the Conquest to 1600 A. D. Colin Platt. LC 94-42748. 256p. 1989. pap. text 17.95 (*0-415-00278-8*) Routledge.

Medieval England: An Encyclopedia. Ed. by Paul E. Szarmach et al. LC 97-35523. (Encyclopedias of the Middle Ages Ser.: Vol. 3). (Illus.). 952p. 1998. text 135.00 (*0-8240-5786-4*, H0907) Garland.

Medieval England: From Alfred the Great to Richard III. Moira Hook & Arthur MacGregor. LC 97-186663. (Illus.). 64p. 1997. pap. 13.95 (*1-85444-061-6*, 0616, Pub. by Ashmolean Mus) A Schwartz & Co.

Medieval England: Towns, Commerce, & Crafts, 1086-1348. Edward Miller & John Hatcher. LC 94-31297. (Social & Economic History of England Ser.). 488p. (C). 1995. 85.00 (*0-582-48548-7*, 77006) Longman.

Medieval England: Towns, Commerce & Crafts, 1086-1348. Edward Miller & John Hatcher. LC 94-31297. (Sociey & Economic History of England Ser.). 488p. (C). 1995. pap. 48.00 (*0-582-48549-5*, 77005) Longman.

Medieval English Benedictine Liturgy: Studies in the Formation, Structure, & Content of the Monastic Votive Office, c. 950-1540. Sally E. Harper. LC 93-15812. (Outstanding Dissertations in Music from British Universities Ser.). 424p. 1993. text 105.00 (*0-8153-0953-8*) Garland.

Medieval English Drama: Essays Critical & Contextual. Ed. by Jerome Taylor & Alan H. Nelson. LC 72-77479. (Patterns of Literary Criticism Ser.). 368p. (C). 1972. lib. bdg. 22.00 (*0-226-79146-7*) U Ch Pr.

Medieval English Drama: Essays Critical & Contextual. Ed. by Jerome Taylor & Alan H. Nelson. LC 72-77479. (Patterns of Literary Criticism Ser.). 368p. (C). 1993. pap. text 3.95 (*0-226-79147-5*) U Ch Pr.

Medieval English Jetons. G. Berry. 1974. 15.00 (*0-685-51549-4*) S J Durst.

Medieval English Literature. Ed. by J. B. Trapp. (Illus.). 544p. 1973. pap. text 33.95 (*0-19-501624-6*) OUP.

Medieval English Literature. Ed. by Thomas J. Garbaty. 974p. (C). 1997. reprint ed. pap. text 51.95 (*0-88133-950-4*) Waveland Pr.

Medieval English Lyrics. Ed. by R. T. Davies. 384p. 1988. pap. 16.95 (*0-8101-0075-4*) Northwestern U Pr.

Medieval English Lyrics. Ed. by R. Trevor Davies. LC 72-8279. (Granger Index Reprint Ser.). 1977. reprint ed. 23.95 (*0-8369-6386-5*) Ayer.

Medieval English Nunneries. Eileen Power. 1988. pap. 25.00 (*0-8196-0140-3*) Biblo.

Medieval English Poetry. Intro. by Stephanie Trigg. LC 93-10072. (Critical Readers Ser.). (C). 1994. text 68.95 (*0-582-08260-9*, 79870); pap. text 33.25 (*0-582-08261-7*, 79869) Longman.

Medieval English Political Writings. James M. Dean. LC 96-5082. (Middle English Texts Ser.). (Illus.). 1996. pap. 14.00 (*1-879288-64-8*) Medieval Inst.

Medieval English Prose for Women: Selections from the Katherine Group & Ancrene Wisse. 264p. 1992. pap. text 24.00 (*0-19-811997-6*) OUP.

Medieval English Religious & Ethical Literature. Ed. by Gregory C. Kratzmann & James Simpson. 256p. 1986. 75.00 (*0-85991-220-5*) Boydell & Brewer.

Medieval English Romances, 2 vols., Vol. 1. A. V. Schmidt & Nicholas Jacobs. LC 79-48002. (London Medieval & Renaissance Ser.). 210p. 1981. 35.00 (*0-8419-0604-1*) Holmes & Meier.

Medieval English Romances, 2 vols., Vol. 2. A. V. Schmidt & Nicholas Jacobs. LC 79-48002. (London Medieval & Renaissance Ser.). 285p. 1981. 39.00 (*0-8419-0605-X*) Holmes & Meier.

Medieval English Stage: Corpus Christi Pageants & Plays. Alan H. Nelson. LC 73-85247. (Patterns of Literary Criticism Ser.). 288p. 1992. lib. bdg. 21.00 (*0-226-57173-4*) U Ch Pr.

Medieval English Verse. Brian Stone. (Classics Ser.). 256p. (Orig.). 1964. pap. 13.95 (*0-14-044144-1*, Penguin Classics) Viking Penguin.

Medieval Epics. Tr. by William Alfred et al. LC 98-4488. 1998. 24.95 (*0-679-60301-8*) Modern Lib NY.

Medieval Essays. Christopher H. Dawson. LC 68-58785. (Essay Index Reprint Ser.). 1977. 20.95 (*0-8369-0070-7*) Ayer.

Medieval et Humanistica, Vol. 21. Ed. by Paul M. Clogan. LC 75-32451. (Studies in Medieval & Renaissance Culture). 218p. 1994. lib. bdg. 72.00 (*0-8476-7960-8*) Rowman.

Medieval Europe. 9th ed. Bennett. 2001. 25.50 (*0-07-234657-4*) McGraw.

Medieval Europe: A Short History. 7th ed. C. Warren Hollister. LC 93-28531. (C). 1994. pap. text 23.00 (*0-07-029637-5*) McGraw.

Medieval Europe: A Short History. 8th ed. C. Warren Hollister. LC 97-25685. 432p. 1997. pap. 34.06 (*0-07-029729-0*) McGraw.

Medieval Europe: A Short Sourcebook. 3rd ed. Warren C. Hollister. LC 96-34843. 336p. (C). 1996. pap. 34.06 (*0-07-029724-X*) McGraw.

Medieval Europe, 814-1350, Vol. 4. (World Eras Ser.). (Illus.). 400p. 1999. 95.00 (*0-7876-1709-1*, GML00198-111110) Gale.

Medieval Europe, 400-1500. H. G. Koenigsberger. LC 87-6459. (History of Europe Ser.: No. VI). (Illus.). 401p. (C). 1989. pap. 31.20 (*0-582-49403-6*, 73607) Longman.

Medieval European Armies. Terence Wise. (Men-at-Arms Ser.: No. 50). (Illus.). 48p. pap. 11.95 (*0-85045-245-7*, 9006, Pub. by Ospry) Stackpole.

Medieval European Coinage: With a Catalogue of Coins in the Fitzwilliam Museum, Cambridge, Vol. 1: The Early Middle Ages (5th-10th Centuries) Philip Grierson & Mark Blackburn. (Medieval European Coinage Ser.: 1). (Illus.). 700p. 1987. text 200.00 (*0-521-26009-4*) Cambridge U Pr.

Medieval Europeans: Studies in Ethnic Identity & National Perspectives in Medieval Europe. Smyth. LC 97-38829. 240p. 1998. text 59.95 (*0-312-21301-8*) St Martin.

Medieval Exegesis, Vol. 1. Henri De Lubac. Tr. by Mark Sebanc from FRE. LC 97-32802. (Ressourcement Ser.). 467p. 1998. pap. 45.00 (*0-8028-4145-7*) Eerdmans.

Medieval Exegesis in Translation: Commentaries on the Book of Ruth. Lesley Smith. LC 96-29069. (Commentary Ser.). 1996. pap. 7.00 (*1-879288-68-0*) Medieval Inst.

Medieval Expansion of Europe. 2nd ed. J. R. Phillips. LC 99-179710. (Illus.). 342p. 1998. pap. text 24.95 (*0-19-820740-9*) OUP.

M

An Asterisk (*) at the beginning of an entry indicates that the title is appearing for the first time.

Medieval Experience. Francis Oakley. (Medieval Academy Reprints for Teaching Ser.). 240p. 1988. reprint ed. pap. text 12.95 (*0-8020-6707-7*) U of Toronto Pr.
Medieval Experience, 300-1400. Jill N. Claster. (Illus.). 352p. (C). 1982. pap. text 22.50 (*0-8147-1381-5*) NYU Pr.
Medieval Faith & Fable. John A. MacCulloch. 1977. 17.95 (*0-8369-7118-3*, 7952) Ayer.
Medieval Family: The Pastons of Fifteenth-Century England. Frances Gies. (Illus.). 416p. 1999. pap. 14.00 (*0-06-093055-1*) HarpC.
Medieval Family Roles: A Book of Essays. Ed. by Cathy J. Itnyre. LC 95-25381. (Medieval Casebooks Ser.: Vol. 15). 264p. 1996. text 52.00 (*0-8153-1329-2*, H1727) Garland.
***Medieval Family Roles: A Book of Essays.** Cathy J. Itnyre. (Medieval Casebooks Ser.: Vol. 15). 264p. 1999. pap. 24.95 (*0-8153-3663-2*) Garland.
Medieval Farming & Technology: The Impact of Agricultural Change in Northwest Europe. Ed. by Grenville Astill & John Langdon. LC 97-7623. (Technology & Change in History Ser.: No. 1). (Illus.). xii, 321p. 1997. 101.00 (*90-04-10582-4*, NLG 172) Brill Academic Pubs.
Medieval Fashions Coloring Book. Tom Tierney. (Illus.). (J). pap. 2.95 (*0-486-40144-8*) Dover.
Medieval Feast. Aliki. LC 82-45923. (Illus.). 32p. (J). (gr. 2 up). 1983. lib. bdg. 15.89 (*0-690-04246-9*) HarpC Child Bks.
Medieval Feast. Aliki. LC 82-45923. (Illus.). 32p. (J). (gr. 2-6). 1983. 14.95 (*0-690-04245-0*) HarpC Child Bks.
Medieval Feast. Aliki. (J). 1986. 11.15 (*0-606-03251-7*, Pub. by Turtleback) Demco.
Medieval Feast. Aliki. LC 82-45923. (Trophy Nonfiction Bk.). (Illus.). 32p. (J). (gr. 2 up). 1986. reprint ed. pap. 6.95 (*0-06-446050-9*, HarpTrophy) HarpC Child Bks.
Medieval Feudal French Coinage. 2nd ed. John F. Lhotka. (Illus.). 1997. pap. 15.00 (*0-685-36401-1*) S J Durst.
Medieval Fields. David Hall. 1989. pap. 25.00 (*0-85263-599-0*, Pub. by Shire Pubns) St Mut.
Medieval Finance: A Comparison of Financial Institutions in Northwestern Europe. Bryce D. Lyon. LC 67-19657. 100p. reprint ed. 31.00 (*0-608-16575-1*, 202751600055) Bks Demand.
Medieval Flanders. David Nicholas. (C). 1992. pap. text 60.95 (*0-582-01679-7*) Addison-Wesley.
Medieval Flanders. David Nicholas. LC 91-45256. 463p. (C). 1995. pap. 52.00 (*0-582-01678-9*, 79365) Longman.
Medieval Floral Designs. Phoebe Ann Erb. LC 99-13018. (Illus.). 48p. 1999. pap. 9.95 (*0-88045-148-3*, Intl Design) Stemmer Hse.
Medieval Flowers. Miranda Innes & Clay Perry. LC 98-178167. (Illus.). 160p. 1998. 35.00 (*1-85626-259-6*, Pub. by Cathie Kyle) Trafalgar.
Medieval Folk Astronomy & Agriculture in Arabia & the Yemen. Daniel M. Varisco. LC 97-21319. (Collected Studies: Vol. 585). (Illus.). 352p. 1997. text 109.95 (*0-86078-651-X*, GN635.Y4V37, Pub. by Variorum) Ashgate Pub Co.
***Medieval Folklore: An Encyclopedia of Myths, Legends, Tales, Beliefs & Customs, 2 vols.** Carl Lindahl. (Illus.). 800p. 2000. lib. bdg. 150.00 (*1-57607-121-9*) ABC-CLIO.
***Medieval Forest.** Claire Murray. 2000. 10.95 (*0-7407-0591-1*) Andrews & McMeel.
Medieval Fortifications. John R. Kenyon. LC 90-8371. (Illus.). 256p. 1990. text 49.95 (*0-312-04842-4*) St Martin.
Medieval Fortifications. Ed. by John R. Kenyon. (Illus.). 256p. 1992. text 24.50 (*0-7185-1392-4*) St Martin.
Medieval Foundations of the Western Intellectual Tradition, 400-1400. Marcia Colish. LC 97-24370. (Illus.). 448p. 1997. 40.00 (*0-300-07142-6*) Yale U Pr.
Medieval Foundations of the Western Intellectual Tradition, 400-1400. Marcia Colish. (Illus.). 400p. 1999. pap. text 18.00 (*0-300-07852-8*) Yale U Pr.
Medieval Foundations of Western Civilization. A. C. Krey & George C. Sellery. LC 68-24116. (World History Ser.: No. 48). (Illus.). 1968. reprint ed. lib. bdg. 74.95 (*0-8383-0926-7*) M S G Haskell Hse.
Medieval Framlingham: Select Documents, 1270-1524. John Rigard. 176p. (C). 1985. 45.00 (*0-85115-432-8*) Boydell & Brewer.
Medieval France: An Encyclopedia. Ed. by William W. Kibler et al. LC 95-2617. (Encyclopedias of the Middle Ages Ser.: Vol. 2). (Illus.). 1080p. 1995. text 135.00 (*0-8240-4444-4*, H932) Garland.
Medieval France & Her Pyrenean Neighbours. Thomas N. Bisson. (Studies in Early Institutional History). 464p. 1989. 65.00 (*0-907628-69-9*) Hambledon Press.
Medieval Franciscan Houses. John R. Moorman. (History Ser.). xxxii, 710p. 1983. pap. 40.00 (*1-57659-079-8*) Franciscan Inst.
Medieval French Bridges: A History. Marjorie N. Boyer. LC 75-36478. (Medieval Academy Bks.: No. 84). 1976. 25.00 (*0-910956-58-8*) Medieval Acad.
Medieval French Literature: An Introduction. Michel Zink. Tr. by Jeff Rider. 184p. 1995. pap. 12.95 (*0-86698-161-6*, P19) Pegasus Pr.
Medieval French Romance. Douglas Kelly. LC 93-6760. (World Authors Ser.: No. 838). 221p. 1993. 24.95 (*0-8057-8282-6*, Twyne) Mac Lib Ref.
***Medieval French Romance.** Douglas Kelly. 221p. 1999. reprint ed. text 25.00 (*0-7881-6591-7*) DIANE Pub.
Medieval Frontier History in New Catalonia. Lawrence J. McCrank. LC 96-1437. (Collected Studies: CS528). (Illus.). 1996. text 101.95 (*0-86078-582-3*, Pub. by Variorum) Ashgate Pub Co.
Medieval Frontier Societies. Ed. by Robert Bartlett & Angus MacKay. (Illus.). 400p. 1990. text 89.00 (*0-19-822881-3*) OUP.
Medieval Furniture: Plans & Instructions for Historical Reproductions. Daniel Diehl & Mark Donnelly. LC 99-17160. (Illus.). 192p. 1999. pap. 19.95 (*0-8117-2854-4*) Stackpole.
***Medieval Futures.** Ed. by John Burrow & Ian P. Wei. LC 00-20945. 224p. 2000. 90.00 (*0-85115-779-3*) Boydell & Brewer.
Medieval Galician-Portuguese Poetry: An Anthology. Ed. & Tr. by Frede Jensen. LC 91-37480. (Library of Medieval Literature: Vol. 87A). 762p. 1992. text 20.00 (*0-8240-7109-3*) Garland.
Medieval Games: Sports & Recreations in Feudal Society, 30. John M. Carter. LC 91-785. (Contributions to the Study of World History Ser.: No. 30). 172p. 1992. 49.95 (*0-313-26743-X*, CRH, Greenwood Pr) Greenwood.
Medieval Garden. Sylvia Landsberg. LC 95-61563. (Illus.). 144p. 1996. 24.95 (*0-500-01691-7*, Pub. by Thames Hudson) Norton.
Medieval Garden Design Book. Ramona Jablonski. (International Design Library). (Illus.). 48p. 1982. pap. 6.95 (*0-88045-011-8*) Stemmer Hse.
Medieval Gardens. Ed. by Elisabeth B. MacDougall. LC 85-29343. (Colloquium on the History of Landscape Architecture Ser.: No. 9). (Illus.). 352p. 1986. 35.00 (*0-88402-146-7*) Dumbarton Oaks.
Medieval Gentlewoman: Life in A Gentry Househol in the Later Middle Ages. Fiona Swabey. (Illus.). 224p. 1999. 34.95 (*0-7509-1644-3*) A Sutton.
***Medieval Gentlewoman: Life in a Gentry Household in the Later Middle Ages.** Ffiona Swabey. (Illus.). 240p. 1999. 35.00 (*0-415-92511-8*) Routledge.
Medieval German Arthuriad: Some Contemporary Revaluations of the Canon. Neil Thomas. (European University Studies: German Language & Literature: Ser. 1, Vol. 1153). 183p. 1989. 30.00 (*3-261-04109-9*) P Lang Pubng.
Medieval German Literature. Albrecht Classen. 323p. (C). 1994. write for info. (*1-57074-144-1*) Greyden Pr.
Medieval German Literature: A Companion. Marion E. Gibbs & Sidney M. Johnson. LC 97-14299. (Garland Medieval Bibliograhies Ser.). 472p. 1997. text 80.00 (*0-8153-1450-7*) Garland.
Medieval German Lyric, 1150-1300: The Development of Its Themes & Forms in Their European Context. Olive Sayce. 511p. 1982. 83.00 (*0-19-815772-X*) OUP.
Medieval German Lyric Verse in English Translation. John W. Thomas. LC 78-27834. (North Carolina. University. Studies in the Germanic Languages & Literatures: No. 60). reprint ed. 35.00 (*0-404-50953-3*) AMS Pr.
Medieval Germany & Its Neighbours, 900-1250. Karl J. Leyser. 300p. (C). 1982. 55.00 (*0-907628-08-7*); pap. 18.00 (*0-907628-09-5*) Hambledon Press.
Medieval Germany, 500-1300: A Political Interpretation. Benjamin Arnold. LC 97-184168. 224p. 1997. pap. text 19.95 (*0-8020-8053-7*) U of Toronto Pr.
Medieval Germany, 500-1300: A Political Interpretation. Benjamin Arnold. LC 97-184168. 247p. 1997. text 55.00 (*0-8020-4191-4*, DD114) U of Toronto Pr.
Medieval Gospel of Nicodemus: Texts, Intertexts, & Contexts in Western Europe. Ed. by Zbigniew Izydorczyk. LC 96-40460. (Medieval & Renaissance Texts & Studies: Vol. 158). 550p. 1997. 45.00 (*0-86698-198-5*, MR158) MRTS.
Medieval Grange of Abingdon Abbey at Dean Court Farm, Cumnor, Oxford. T. G. Allen. (Illus.). 218p. 1995. pap. 23.50 (*0-946897-91-3*, Pub. by Oxbow Bks) David Brown.
Medieval Greek Romance. 2nd rev. ed. Roderick Beaton. LC 95-23528. 328p. (C). 1996. 85.00 (*0-415-12032-2*); pap. 27.99 (*0-415-12033-0*) Routledge.
Medieval Hagiography: An Anthology. Thomas Head. 500p. Date not set. pap. text 32.00 (*0-8153-2124-4*) Garland.
Medieval Hagiography: An Anthology. Thomas Head. LC 99-45450. (Reference Library of the Humanities: Vol. 26). 888p. 1999. text 75.00 (*0-8153-2123-6*, H1942) Garland.
Medieval Hagiography & Romance. Ed. by Paul M. Clogan. LC 75-16872. (Medievalia et Humanistica: New Ser.: No. 6). 237p. reprint ed. pap. 67.60 (*0-608-17269-3*, 2029216) Bks Demand.
Medieval Hall: The Basis of Secular Domestic Life, 600-1600 A. D. Michael W. Thompson. (Illus.). 224p. 1995. 61.95 (*1-85928-081-1*, Pub. by Scolar Pr) Ashgate Pub Co.
Medieval Handbooks of Penance: A Translation of the Principal Libri Poenitentiales. John T. McNeill & Helena M. Garner. 476p. 1990. pap. text 20.00 (*0-231-09629-1*) Col U Pr.
Medieval Health Handbook: Tacuinum Sanitatis. Luisa C. Arano. Tr. by Oscar Ratti & Adele Westbrook from ITA. LC 75-21725. (Illus.). 156p. 1992. reprint ed. pap. 20.00 (*0-8076-1277-4*, Pub. by Braziller) Norton.
***Medieval Hebrew Encyclopedias of Science & Philosophy.** Steven Harvey. LC 00-28399. (Amsterdam Studies in Jewish Thought). (Illus.). 2000. write for info. (*0-7923-6242-X*) Kluwer Academic.
Medieval Heraldry. Terence Wise. (Men-at-Arms Ser.: No. 99). (Illus.). 48p. pap. 11.95 (*0-85045-348-8*, 9033, Pub. by Osprey) Stackpole.
Medieval Heraldry. Ed. by Evan J. Jones. LC 78-63502. 360p. 1983. reprint ed. 47.50 (*0-404-17149-4*) AMS Pr.
***Medieval Herbals: The Illustrative Traditions.** Minta Collins. (Illus.). 256p. 1999. pap. text 34.95 (*0-8020-8313-7*) U of Toronto Pr.
Medieval Heresies: A Bibliography, 1960-1979. Carl T. Berkhout & Jeffrey B. Russell. xvi, 201p. pap. 22.86 (*0-88844-360-9*) Brill Academic Pubs.
Medieval Heresy: Popular Movements from the Gregorian Reform to the Reformation. rev. ed. Malcolm Lambert. 400p. 1992. reprint ed. pap. 30.95 (*0-631-17432-X*) Blackwell Pubs.
Medieval Heritage of Mexico & New Spain. Luis Weckmann. Tr. by Frances M. Lopez-Morillas. LC 91-55040. xi, 692p. 1992. 85.00 (*0-8232-1324-2*) Fordham.
Medieval Hispanic Studies Presented to Rita Hamilton. Ed. by A. D. Deyermond. (Monagrafias A Ser.: Vol. XLII). (ENG & SPA., Illus.). 281p. (Orig.). (C). 1976. pap. 46.00 (*0-900411-98-8*, Pub. by Tamesis Bks Ltd) Boydell & Brewer.
Medieval History: Selected Course Outlines & Reading Lists from Leading American Colleges & Universities in History. 3rd enl. ed. Ed. by Penelope D. Johnson. (History Syllabi Ser.). 320p. (Orig.). (C). 1988. pap. 16.95 (*0-910129-92-4*) Wiener Pubs Inc.
Medieval History & Discourse: Toward a Topography of Textuality. M. Buda. LC 89-13309. (American University Studies: Comparative Literature: Ser. III, Vol. 28). 123p. (C). 1991. text 27.95 (*0-8204-1130-2*) P Lang Pubng.
Medieval History of India. Meera Singh. 1993. 26.00 (*0-7069-9146-X*, Pub. by Vikas); pap. 10.00 (*0-7069-9145-1*, Pub. by Vikas) S Asia.
Medieval Housebook. num. limited fac. ed. Ed. by Ristoph Graf Zu Waldburg. (Illus.). 1998. 1980.00 (*3-7913-1838-1*) te Neues.
Medieval Household. Geoff Egan. (Medieval Finds from Excavations in London Ser.: No. 6). (Illus.). 355p. 1998. 100.00 (*0-11-290490-4*, Pub. by Statnry Office) Balogh.
Medieval Households. David Herlihy. (Studies in Cultural History: No. 2). (Illus.). 272p. 1985. 39.95 (*0-674-56375-1*); pap. 17.95 (*0-674-56376-X*) HUP.
Medieval Housing. write for info. (*0-8386-3616-0*) Fairleigh Dickinson.
Medieval Housing. Jane Grenville. LC 97-9901. (Studies in the Early History of Britain). 256p. 1998. 95.00 (*0-7185-1478-5*) Bks Intl VA.
Medieval Housing. Jane Grenville. (Illus.). 256p. 1999. pap. 35.00 (*0-7185-0211-6*) Continuum.
Medieval Hungarian Historians: A Critical & Analytical Guide. Carlile A. Macartney. LC 53-7690. 206p. reprint ed. pap. 58.80 (*0-608-30151-5*, 2050792) Bks Demand.
Medieval Iberia: Essays on the History & Literature of Medieval Spain. Ed. by Donald Kagay & Joseph T. Snow. (Iberica Ser.: Vol. 25). XX, 268p. (C). 1997. text 47.95 (*0-8204-3651-8*) P Lang Pubng.
Medieval Iberia: Readings from Christian, Muslim, & Jewish Sources. Ed. by Olivia R. Constable. (Middle Ages Ser.). 448p. 1997. text 49.95 (*0-8122-3333-6*) U of Pa Pr.
Medieval Iberia: Readings from Christian, Muslim, & Jewish Sources. Ed. by Olivia R. Constable. LC 97-4097. (Middle Ages Ser.). 448p. 1997. pap. text 26.50 (*0-8122-1569-9*) U of Pa Pr.
Medieval Iberian Tradition & the Development of the Mexican Hacienda. William Schell, Jr. (Foreign & Comparative Studies Program, Latin American Ser.: No. 8). (Orig.). (C). 1986. pap. 10.00 (*0-915984-99-7*) Syracuse U Foreign Comp.
Medieval Iceland: Society, Sagas, & Power. Jesse L. Byock. (C). 1988. pap. 17.95 (*0-520-06954-4*, Pub. by U CA Pr) Cal Prin Full Svc.
Medieval Iconography: A Research Guide. John B. Friedman & Jessica M. Wegmann. LC 97-42974. (Medieval Bibliographies Ser.: Vol. 20). 464p. 1998. text 95.00 (*0-8153-1753-0*) Garland.
Medieval Iconography & Narrative. Ed. by Flemming G. Andersen et al. 215p. (Orig.). 1980. pap. 26.00 (*87-7492-307-2*, Pub. by Odense Universitets Forlag) Coronet Bks.
Medieval Idea of Law As Represented by Lucas De Penna: A Study in Fourteenth-Century Legal Scholarship. Walter Ulmann. xxxix, 219p. 1999. reprint ed. 78.00 (*1-56169-441-X*) Gaunt.
Medieval Illuminated Address Book. British Library Staff. (Illus.). 96p. 1997. pap. 9.95 (*0-7123-4549-3*) U of Toronto Pr.
Medieval Illuminated Book of Days. British Library Staff. (Illus.). 96p. 1997. pap. 9.95 (*0-7123-4548-5*) U of Toronto Pr.
Medieval Illuminators & Their Methods of Work. Jonathan J. Alexander. LC 92-5576. (Illus.). 221p. 1994. pap. 30.00 (*0-300-06073-4*) Yale U Pr.
Medieval Imagination. Jacques Le Goff. Tr. by Arthur Goldhammer. LC 88-4787. 302p. 1992. pap. text 14.95 (*0-226-47085-7*) U Ch Pr.
Medieval Imagination. Jacques Le Goff. Tr. by Arthur Goldhammer. 302p. 1998. 35.95 (*0-226-47084-9*) U Ch Pr.
Medieval Imagination: Rhetoric & the Poetry of Courtly Love. Douglas Kelly. LC 78-3522. 346p. 1978. 35.00 (*0-299-07610-5*) U of Wis Pr.
Medieval in L. A. A Delightful Romp Through Los Angeles as Seen Through the Mind of a Medieval Man. Jim Paul. LC 97-25494. 1997. pap. 12.00 (*0-15-600537-9*) Harcourt.
Medieval India Vol. 1: Researches in the History of India, 1200-1750. Ed. by Irfan Habib. (Illus.). 234p. (C). 1993. 17.95 (*0-19-562330-4*) OUP.
Medieval India & Hindi Bhakti Poetry: A Socio-Cultural Study. Savitri C. Shobha. 1996. 24.00 (*81-241-0367-4*, Pub. by Har-Anand Pubns) S Asia.
Medieval India from Sultanat to the Mughals: Delhi Sultanat, 1206-1526. Satish Chandra. (C). 1997. 40.00 (*81-241-0522-7*, Pub. by Har-Anand Pubns) S Asia.
Medieval India under Mohammedan Rule. Stanley Lane-Poole. LC 70-132442. (World History Ser.: No. 48). 1970. reprint ed. lib. bdg. 75.00 (*0-8383-1196-2*) M S G Haskell Hse.
Medieval Indian History & Architecture. R. Nath. LC 95-906159. (Illus.). xvi, 331p. 1995. 64.00 (*81-7024-697-0*, Pub. by Ashish Pub Hse) Nataraj Bks.
***Medieval Indian Literature.** Ed. by K. Avyappa Paniker. 1999. 38.00 (*81-260-0648-X*, Pub. by Rabindra Bhawn) S Asia.
Medieval Indian Literature: An Anthology K. Ayyappapanicker & Sahitya Akademi Staff. LC 98-901293. 1997. write for info. (*81-260-0365-0*, Pub. by Rabindra Bhawn) S Asia.
Medieval Inquisition. Bernard Hamilton. 1981. pap. text 15.95 (*0-8419-0695-5*) Holmes & Meier.
Medieval Inquisition. Albert C. Shannon. 168p. 1983. 15.00 (*0-9612336-0-5*, 83-72869); pap. 10.00 (*0-9612336-1-3*) Augustinian Coll Pr.
Medieval Inquisition. Jean Guiraud. Tr. by E. C. Messenger. LC 78-63181. (Heresies of the Early Christian & Medieval Era Ser.: Second Ser.). reprint ed. 31.00 (*0-404-16222-3*) AMS Pr.
Medieval Institutions: Study-Lecture Notes, Vol. 1. John M. Carter. 205p. 1983. pap. text 35.95 (*0-89126-125-7*) MA-AH Pub.
Medieval Instrumental Dances. Timothy J. McGee. LC 88-45498. (Music: Scholarship & Performance Ser.). (Illus.). 192p. 1990. spiral bd. 29.95 (*0-253-33353-9*) Ind U Pr.
***Medieval Insular Romance: Translation & Innovation.** Judith Elizabeth Weiss et al. LC 00-31254. 2001. write for info. (*0-85991-597-2*, DS Brewer) Boydell & Brewer.
Medieval Interpretation: Models of Reading in Literary Narrative, 1100-1500. Robert S. Sturges. LC 89-26357. 336p. (C). 1990. text 41.95 (*0-8093-1556-4*) S Ill U Pr.
***Medieval Ireland.** Tallig O'Keefe. (Illus.). 1999. 32.50 (*0-7524-1464-X*, Pub. by Tempus Pubng) Arcadia Publng.
Medieval Ireland: The Enduring Tradition. Michael Richter. Tr. by Brian Stone & Adrian Keogh from GAE. 224p. 1996. pap. 19.95 (*0-312-15812-2*) St Martin.
Medieval Ireland, Saints & Martyologies. John Hennig. Ed. by Michael Richter. (Collected Studies: No. CS298). 342p. (C). 1989. reprint ed. text 117.95 (*0-86078-246-8*, Pub. by Variorum) Ashgate Pub Co.
***Medieval Irish Lyrics.** Ed. by Barbara Hughes Fowler. 136p. 2000. pap. 12.95 (*0-268-03457-5*, Pub. by U of Notre Dame Pr); lib. bdg. 27.50 (*0-268-03456-7*, Pub. by U of Notre Dame Pr) Chicago Distribution Ctr.
Medieval Irish Lyrics with the Irish Bardic Poet. James Carney. 176p. 1985. pap. 13.95 (*0-85105-360-2*, Pub. by Smyth) Dufour.
Medieval Irish Saints' Lives: An Introduction to Vitae Santorum Hiberniae. Richard Sharpe. (Illus.). 438p. 1991. text 130.00 (*0-19-821582-7*) OUP.
Medieval Islam. Dominique Sourdel. 224p. 1986. pap. 13.95 (*0-7102-0883-9*, Routledge Thoemms) Routledge.
Medieval Islamic City Reconsidered: An interdisciplinary Approach to Samarra. Ed. by Chase Robinsn. (Oxford Studies in Islamic Art: No. 14). (Illus.). 250p. 2000. text 70.00 (*0-19-728024-2*) OUP.
Medieval Islamic Controversy Between Philosophy & Orthodoxy. I. A. Bello. 187p. 1996. 40.00 (*0-614-21183-2*, 771) Kazi Pubns.
Medieval Islamic Medicine. Ibn Ridwan. Tr. by Michael W. Dois. 200p. 1996. 39.95 (*0-614-21553-6*, 772) Kazi Pubns.
Medieval Islamic Pragmatics: Sunni Legal Theorists' Models of Texual Communication. Mohammad M. Ali. 288p. 1998. 75.00 (*0-7007-1102-3*, Pub. by Curzon Pr Ltd) Paul & Co Pubs.
Medieval Islamic Symbolism & the Paintings in the Cefalu Cathedral. Mirjam Gelfer-Jorgensen. (Illus.). 233p. 1986. lib. bdg. 99.50 (*90-04-07927-0*) Brill Academic Pubs.
Medieval Islamic Technology: From Philo to Al-Jazari - From Alexandria to Diyar Bakr. Donald R. Hill. LC 98-46411. (Variorum Collected Studies Ser.: Vol. 555). 350p. 1998. text 110.95 (*0-86078-606-4*, T27.3.175H55, Pub. by Ashgate Pub) Ashgate Pub Co.
Medieval Isma'ili History & Thought. Ed. by Farhad Daftary. 349p. (C). 1996. text 69.95 (*0-521-45140-X*) Cambridge U Pr.
Medieval Ivories in the Walters Art Gallery: A Picture Book. (Illus.). 1969. pap. 1.25 (*0-911886-13-3*) Walters Art.
Medieval Jainism: Culture & Environment. R. M. Lodha & P. S. Jain. 1990. 22.50 (*81-7024-272-X*, Pub. by Ashish Pub Hse) S Asia.
Medieval Japan: Essays in Institutional History. Ed. by John W. Hall & Jeffrey P. Mass. LC 73-86897. 285p. reprint ed. pap. 88.40 (*0-8357-8219-0*, 203374100087) Bks Demand.
Medieval Japan: Essays in Institutional History. Ed. by John W. Hall & Jeffrey P. Mass. LC 88-60489. 288p. 1974. reprint ed. 49.50 (*0-8047-1510-6*); reprint ed. pap. 16.95 (*0-8047-1511-4*) Stanford U Pr.
Medieval Japanese Daimyo: The Ouchi Family's Rule of Suo & Nagato. Peter J. Arnesen. LC 79-10337. (Yale Historical Publications: Miscellany: No. 122). 256p. reprint ed. pap. 79.40 (*0-7837-2781-X*, 204317300006) Bks Demand.
***Medieval Japanese Writers.** Steven D. Carter. LC 98-51750. (Dictionary of Literary Biography Ser.: Vol. 203). 400p. 1998. text 155.00 (*0-7876-3097-7*) Gale.
Medieval Jerusalem & Islamic Worship: Holy Places, Ceremonies, Pilgrimages. Amikam Elad. LC 94-13753. (Islamic History & Civilization, Studies & Texts Ser.: Vol. 8). xxiii, 196p. 1994. 85.50 (*90-04-10010-5*) Brill Academic Pubs.
Medieval Jerusalem & Islamic Worship: Holy Places, Ceremonies, Pilgrimages. Amikam Elad. 193p. 1996. 65.75 (*0-614-21585-4*, 1363) Kazi Pubns.

An Asterisk (*) at the beginning of an entry indicates that the title is appearing for the first time.

Medieval Jewish Philosophy: An Introduction. Dan Cohn-Sherbok. (Jewish Philosophy Ser.). 220p. pap. 14.95 (*0-7007-0453-1*, Pub. by Curzon Pr Ltd) Paul & Co Pubs.

Medieval Jewish Philosophy: Original Anthology. Ed. by Steven Katz. LC 79-7177. (Jewish Philosophy, Mysticism & History of Ideas Ser.). (ENG, FRE, GER, ITA & SPA.). 1980. lib. bdg. 50.95 (*0-405-12235-7*) Ayer.

Medieval Jewish Seals from Europe. Daniel M. Friedenberg. LC 86-26657. (Illus.). 400p. 1987. 65.00 (*0-8143-1769-3*) Wayne St U Pr.

Medieval Jewry in Northern France: A Political & Social History. Robert Chazan. LC 73-8129. (Johns Hopkins University Studies in Historical & Political Science: 91st; 2). 252p. reprint ed. pap. 78.20 (*0-608-12096-0*, 202413200035) Bks Demand.

Medieval Jousts & Tournaments Coloring Book. Green. (Illus.). (J). pap. 2.95 (*0-486-40135-9*) Dover.

***Medieval Kitchen.** Odile Redon. (Illus.). 2000. pap. 18.00 (*0-226-70685-0*) U Ch Pr.

Medieval Kitchen: Recipes from France & Italy. Odile Redon et al. Tr. by Edward Schneider from ENG. LC 97-31785. (Illus.). 348p. (ps). 1998. 32.50 (*0-226-70684-2*) U Ch Pr.

Medieval Knight--Read Me a Book! Adrienne Wigdortz Anderson. LC 98-29284. 256p. 1998. pap. 27.50 (*0-8108-3517-7*) Scarecrow.

Medieval Knighthood Vol. IV: Papers from the Fifth Strawberry Hill Conference, 1990. Ed. by Christopher Harper-Bill & Ruth Harvey. (Illus.). 270p. (C). 1992. 75.00 (*0-85115-319-4*) Boydell & Brewer.

Medieval Knighthood Vol. V: Papers from the Sixth Strawberry Hill Conference, 1994. Ed. by Stephen Church & Ruth Harvey. (Medieval Knighthood Ser.). (Illus.). 282p. (C). 1995. 75.00 (*0-85115-628-2*) Boydell & Brewer.

Medieval Knights. Trevor Cairns. (Cambridge Introduction to World History Topic Bks.). (Illus.). 64p. (YA). (gr. 7 up). 1992. pap. 13.95 (*0-521-38953-4*) Cambridge U Pr.

Medieval Knights. David Nicolle. LC 96-61599. 48p. (gr. 3-7). 1997. 19.99 (*0-670-87463-9*) Viking Penguin.

Medieval Knights Paper Dolls. A. G. Smith. (Illus.). (J). 1996. pap. 4.95 (*0-486-29292-4*) Dover.

***Medieval Knights Stained Glass Coloring Book.** John Green. (Illus.). 1998. pap. 4.50 (*0-486-40365-3*) Dover.

Medieval Landscape of Wessex. Ed. by Michael Aston & Carenza Lewis. (Oxbow Monographs in Archaeology: No. 46). (Illus.). 284p. 1995. 50.00 (*0-946897-78-6*, Pub. by Oxbow Bks) David Brown.

Medieval Latin. Karl P. Harrington. LC 62-18114. 1995. pap. text 25.00 (*0-226-31711-0*) U Ch Pr.

Medieval Latin. 2nd ed. Karl P. Harrington & Joseph M. Pucci. LC 96-50254. 680p. 1997. pap. text 26.00 (*0-226-31713-7*) U Ch Pr.

Medieval Latin. 2nd ed. Karl P. Harrington & Joseph M. Pucci. LC 96-50254. 1997. lib. bdg. 70.00 (*0-226-31712-9*) U Ch Pr.

Medieval Latin: An Introduction & Bibliographical Guide. Ed. by F. A. Mantello & A. G. Rigg. LC 95-11339. 774p. 1996. pap. 44.95 (*0-8132-0842-4*) Cath U Pr.

Medieval Latin Death Ritual: The Monastic Customaries of Bernard & Ulrich of Cluny. Tr. & Comment by Frederick S. Paxton. (Chalice of Repose Project: Studies in Music-Thanatology: Vol. 1). 115p. (C). 1993. pap. text 23.95 (*1-882878-88-4*) Saint Dunstans.

Medieval Latin Liturgy: A Select Bibliography. Richard W. Pfaff. LC 82-178542. (Toronto Medieval Bibliographies Ser.: No. 9). 151p. reprint ed. pap. 46.90 (*0-608-17999-X*, 202649600049) Bks Demand.

Medieval Latin Lyric, No. 2. Penelope Rainey. (Latin Commentaries Ser.). 67p. (Orig.). (C). 1993. pap. text 6.00 (*0-929524-78-0*) Bryn Mawr Commentaries.

Medieval Latin Lyric, No. 3. Penelope Rainey. (Latin Commentaries Ser.). 75p. (Orig.). (C). 1993. pap. text 6.00 (*0-929524-79-9*) Bryn Mawr Commentaries.

Medieval Latin Lyric, Vol. 1. Penelope Rainey. (Latin Commentaries Ser.). 75p. (Orig.). (C). 1993. pap. text 6.00 (*0-929524-76-4*) Bryn Mawr Commentaries.

Medieval Latin Palaeography: A Bibliographical Introduction. Leonard E. Boyle. 416p. 1984. pap. text 19.95 (*0-8020-6558-9*) U of Toronto Pr.

Medieval Latin Palaeography: A Bibliographical Introduction. Leonard E. Boyle. LC 85-157656. (Toronto Medieval Bibliographies Ser.: No. 8). 416p. reprint ed. pap. 129.00 (*0-8357-3657-1*, 203638400003) Bks Demand.

Medieval Latin Poetics. Edgar Lobel. (Studies in Comparative Literature: No. 35). 1972. reprint ed. pap. 39.95 (*0-8383-0051-0*) M S G Haskell Hse.

Medieval Latin Scientific Writings in the Barberini Collection: A Provisional Catalogue. Ed. by Theodore Silverstein. LC 58-5492. 155p. reprint ed. 48.10 (*0-8357-9648-5*, 201698100006) Bks Demand.

Medieval Latin Texts on the Eternity of the World. Richard C. Dales & Omar Argerami. LC 90-28369. (Studies in Intellectual History: No. 23). (ENG & LAT.). 229p. 1991. 87.00 (*90-04-09376-1*) Brill Academic Pubs.

Medieval Latin Translation of the Data of Euclid. Shuntaro Ito. (Illus.). 246p. 1980. 103.00 (*0-8176-3005-8*) Birkhauser.

***Medieval Leper & His Northern Heirs.** Peter Richards. (Illus.). 192p. 2000. pap. 24.95 (*0-85991-582-4*) Boydell & Brewer.

Medieval Libraries of Great Britain. Neil R. Ker. 14.98 (*0-901050-13-X*) David Brown.

***Medieval Life.** Andrew Langley. (Eyewitness Books). (Illus.). (J). (gr. 4-7). 2000. 19.99 (*0-7894-6614-7*) DK Pub Inc.

***Medieval Life.** Andrew Langley. (Eyewitness Books). (J). (gr. 4-7). 2000. 15.95 (*0-7894-6038-6*) DK Pub Inc.

Medieval Life. Andrew E. Langley. LC 95-25064. (Eyewitness Books). (Illus.). (J). (gr. 5-8). 1996. 19.00 (*0-679-88077-1*); lib. bdg. 20.99 (*0-679-98077-6*) Knopf.

Medieval Life: Cecilia Penifader of Brigstock c. 1297-1344. Judith M. Bennett. LC 98-20580. 192p. 1999. pap. 12.25 (*0-07-290331-7*, McGrw-H College) McGrw-H Hghr Educ.

Medieval Life Illustrations: Selected & Arranged. Ed. by Carol B. Grafton. (Pictorial Archive Ser.). (Illus.). 136p. 1995. pap. 9.95 (*0-486-28862-5*) Dover.

Medieval Lindsey Marsh: Select Documents. A. E. Owen. LC 97-137111. (Publications of the Lincoln Record Society: No. 85). (Illus.). 208p. 1997. 75.00 (*0-901503-58-4*) Boydell & Brewer.

Medieval Listening & Reading: The Primary Reception of German Literature 800-1300. D. H. Green. LC 93-33626. 499p. (C). 1994. text 85.00 (*0-521-44493-4*) Cambridge U Pr.

Medieval Literary Theory & Criticism, 1100-1375: The Commentary-Tradition. 2nd ed. Alastair J. Minnis. Ed. by A. B. Scott. 560p. 1992. reprint ed. pap. text 35.00 (*0-19-811274-2*, 8526) OUP.

Medieval Literature: Texts & Interpretation. Ed. by Tim W. Machan. (Medieval & Renaissance Texts & Studies: Vol. 79). 208p. 1991. 24.00 (*0-86698-090-3*, MR79) MRTS.

***Medieval Literature & Historical Inquiry: Essays in Honour of Derek Pearsall.** Ed. by David Aers. LC 99-45485. 240p. 2000. 75.00 (*0-85991-555-7*, DS Brewer) Boydell & Brewer.

Medieval Literature of Poland: An Anthology. Tr. by Michael J. Mikos from POL. LC 91-24676. (Library of Medieval Literature: Vol. 82B). (Illus.). 286p. 1992. text 19.00 (*0-8153-0408-0*, GLML82B) Garland.

Medieval Literature, Style, & Culture. Charles Muscatine. LC 97-45297. 288p. 1999. lib. bdg. 39.95 (*1-57003-249-1*) U of SC Pr.

Medieval Liturgical Music of Zamora. Kathleen E. Nelson. LC 96-148301. (Wissenschaftliche Abhandlungen-Musicological Studies: No. 67). (ENG & LAT., Illus.). 330p. 1996. lib. bdg. 86.00 (*0-931902-40-1*) Inst Mediaeval Mus.

Medieval Liturgy: A Book of Essays. Joyce E. Salisbury. Ed. by Lizette Larson-Miller. LC 97-6824. (Garland Medieval Casebooks Ser.: Vol. 18). 336p. 1997. text 69.00 (*0-8153-1919-3*, H1884) Garland.

Medieval Liturgy: An Introduction to the Sources. Cyril Vogel. 1987. 25.95 (*0-912405-10-4*, Pastoral Press) OR Catholic.

Medieval Lives: Eight Charismatic Men & Women of the Middle Ages. Norman F. Cantor. 224p. 1995. pap. 12.00 (*0-06-092579-5*, Perennial) HarperTrade.

Medieval Lives & the Historian: Studies in Medieval Prosopography. Ed. by Neithard Bulst & Jean Genet. 1986. pap. 19.95 (*0-918720-70-2*); boxed set 39.95 (*0-918720-69-9*) Medieval Inst.

Medieval London Houses. John Schofield. LC 94-36805. (Illus.). 288p. 1995. 65.00 (*0-300-05578-1*) Yale U Pr.

Medieval London Widows, 1300-1500. Ed. by Caroline M. Barron & Anne F. Sutton. LC 94-19301. 1994. 60.00 (*1-85285-085-X*) Hambledon Press.

Medieval Lunar Astrology: A Collection of Representative Middle English Texts. Ed. by Laurel Means. LC 93-22743. 372p. 1993. text 99.95 (*0-7734-9299-2*) E Mellen.

Medieval Lyric. rev. ed. Peter Dronke. 302p. 1996. pap. 29.95 (*0-85991-484-4*) Boydell & Brewer.

***Medieval Lyric: Genres in Historical Context.** William D. Paden. LC 99-50897. (Medieval Studies). 2000. 39.95 (*0-252-02536-9*) U of Ill Pr.

Medieval Machine: The Industrial Revolution of the Middle Ages. Jean Gimpel. 288p. 1977. pap. 13.95 (*0-14-004514-7*, Penguin Bks) Viking Penguin.

Medieval Manichee: A Study of the Christian Dualist Heresy. Steven Runciman. LC 82-4123. 224p. 1982. pap. text 22.95 (*0-521-28926-2*) Cambridge U Pr.

Medieval Manuscript Bookmaking: A Bibliographic Guide. Doris H. Banks. LC 89-27935. (Illus.). 290p. 1989. 36.00 (*0-8108-2274-1*) Scarecrow.

Medieval Manuscripts in British Libraries Vol. 2: Abbotsford-Keele. Ed. by Neil R. Ker. (Illus.). 1977. 155.00 (*0-19-818162-0*) OUP.

Medieval Manuscripts in British Libraries Vol. 3: Lampeter-Oxford. Ed. by Neil R. Ker. (Illus.). 1983. 115.00 (*0-19-818195-7*) OUP.

Medieval Manuscripts in British Libraries Vol. 4: Paisley-York. Neil R. Ker & A. J. Piper. 866p. 1992. text 185.00 (*0-19-818196-5*) OUP.

Medieval Manuscripts in the Library of the Hispanic Society of America Pt. 1: Documents & Letters, 2 vols., Set. Charles B. Faulhaber. 1983. 75.00 (*0-87535-133-6*) Hispanic Soc.

Medieval Manuscripts in the Library of the Hispanic Society of America, Pt. Two: Documents & Letters, 2 vols. Charles B. Faulhaber. (Illus.). 1132p. 1993. 95.00 (*0-87535-147-6*) Hispanic Soc.

Medieval Manuscripts of Kebel College, Oxford. Ed. by M. B. Parkes. 1979. 175.95 (*0-85967-504-1*, Pub. by Scolar Pr) Ashgate Pub Co.

Medieval Manuscripts of the Latin Classics: Production & Use. Ed. by Claudine A. Chavannes-Mazel & Margaret M. Smith. (Proceedings of the Seminar in the History of the Book to 1500 Ser.: Vol. 3). (Illus.). 256p. 1996. 105.00 (*0-9626372-4-6*) Anderson-Lovelace Pubs.

Medieval Marriage: Two Models from Twelfth-Century France. Georges Duby. Tr. by Elborg Forster from FRE. LC 77-17255. (Johns Hopkins Symposia in Comparative History Ser.). 160p. 1991. reprint ed. pap. text 12.95 (*0-8018-4319-7*) Johns Hopkins.

Medieval Masculinities: Regarding Men in the Middle Ages. Ed. by Clare A. Lees. LC 93-37311. 1994. pap. 17.95 (*0-8166-2426-7*); text 44.95 (*0-8166-2425-9*) U of Minn Pr.

***Medieval Masters: Essays in Memory of Msgr. E. A. Synan.** Ed. by R. E. Houser. (Thomistic Papers: Vol. 7). 2000. 35.00 (*0-268-04213-6*); pap. 15.00 (*0-268-04214-4*, Pub. by U of Notre Dame Pr) Chicago Distribution Ctr.

Medieval Media: Mass Communication in the Making of Europe: An Inaugural Lecture Delivered At the University, 14th March 1972. Colin Morris. LC 73-166842. 16 p. 1972. write for info. (*0-85432-084-9*) Univ of Southampton.

Medieval Medicine. James J. Walsh. LC 75-23766. reprint ed. 37.50 (*0-404-13393-2*) AMS Pr.

Medieval Medicine in Illuminated Manuscripts. rev. ed. Peter M. Jones. LC 98-169988. (Illus.). 112p. 1998. reprint ed. text 40.00 (*0-7123-0657-9*) U of Toronto Pr.

Medieval Medicus: A Social History of Anglo-Norman Medicine. Edward J. Kealey. LC 80-21870. (Illus.). 224p. reprint ed. pap. 69.50 (*0-608-17568-4*, 203057300069) Bks Demand.

Medieval Mediterranean: Cross-Cultural Contacts Marilyn Segal Chiat & Kathryn Reyerson. LC 88-28150. (Medieval Studies at Minnesota). xvii, 133 p. 1988. 22.95 (*0-87839-049-9*) North Star.

Medieval Menagerie: Animals in the Art of the Middle Ages. Janetta R. Benton. LC 92-15412. (Illus.). 192p. 1992. 14.98 (*1-55859-133-8*) Abbeville Pr.

Medieval Mercantile Community: The Grocers' Company & the Politics & Trade of London. Pamela Nightingale. LC 95-12262. 1996. 70.00 (*0-300-06325-3*) Yale U Pr.

Medieval Mercantile Community: The Grocers' Company & the Politics & Trade of London, 1000-1485. Pamela Nightingale. LC 95-12262. (Illus.). 650p. 1995. reprint ed. pap. 200.00 (*0-608-07840-9*, 205401600010) Bks Demand.

Medieval Merchants: York, Beverley & Hull in the Later Middle Ages. Jenny Kermode. LC 97-52953. (Cambridge Studies in Medieval Life & Thought: No. 38). (Illus.). 320p. (C). 1998. 64.95 (*0-521-49737-X*) Cambridge U Pr.

Medieval Mereology. Desmond P. Henry. LC 91-26920. (Bochumer Studien zur Philosophie Ser.: Vol. 16). xxvi, 609p. 1991. 130.00 (*90-6032-318-1*, Pub. by B R Gruner) Humanities.

Medieval Messenger. Paul Dowswell. (Newspaper Histories Ser.). (Illus.). 32p. (J). (gr. 5-9). 1997. pap. 6.95 (*0-7460-2749-4*, Usborne) EDC.

Medieval Messenger. Paul Dowswell. (Newspaper Histories Ser.). (Illus.). 32p. (J). (gr. 5 up). 1997. lib. bdg. 14.95 (*0-88110-904-5*, Usborne) EDC.

Medieval Military Revolution, Vol. 1. Andrew Ayton. 1995. text 65.00 (*1-85043-830-7*, Pub. by I B T) St Martin.

Medieval Military Revolution: State, Society & Military Change in Medieval & Early Modern Europe. Ed. by Andrew Ayton & Leslie Price. 216p. 1998. pap. 24.50 (*1-86064-353-1*, Pub. by I B T) St Martin.

Medieval Military Technology. Kelly DeVries. 240p. 1991. pap. 22.95 (*0-921149-74-3*) Broadview Pr.

Medieval Millennium: An Introduction. Frankforter. LC 98-33906. 345p. 1998. pap. text 32.00 (*0-13-842246-X*) P-H.

Medieval Mind see History of Western Philosophy

Medieval Mirror: Speculum Humanae Salvationis, 1324-1500. Adrian Wilson & Joyce L. Wilson. LC 83-24273. (Illus.). 240p. 1985. 250.00 (*0-520-05194-7*, Pub. by U CA Pr) Cal Prin Full Svc.

***Medieval Miscellany.** Selected by Judith Herrin. (Illus.). 208p. 2000. 37.50 (*0-670-89377-3*, Viking) Viking Penguin.

Medieval Miscellany: Romanesque & Early Gothic Metalwork. Larry M. Ayres. (Illus.). 39p. 1974. pap. 5.00 (*0-942006-49-6*) U of CA Art.

Medieval Misogyny & the Invention of Western Romantic Love. R. Howard Bloch. LC 91-12699. 308p. 1992. pap. text 19.95 (*0-226-05993-1*) U Ch Pr.

Medieval Misogyny & the Invention of Western Romantic Love. R. Howard Bloch. LC 91-12699. 304p. 1993. lib. bdg. 45.00 (*0-226-05972-3*) U Ch Pr.

Medieval Moated Sites, Vol. 17. F. A. Aberg. LC 79-306838. (CBA Research Report Ser.). 93p. 1978. 6.00 (*0-900312-58-0*) Council for British Archeology.

Medieval Modal Logic & Science: Augustine on Scientific Truth & Thomas on Its Impossibility Without a First Cause. Robert C. Trundle. LC 99-21904. 208p. 1999. pap. 25.50 (*0-7618-1398-5*) U Pr of Amer.

Medieval Monasteries. J. Patrick Greene. 270p. 1995. pap. 35.00 (*0-7185-2229-X*) Bks Intl VA.

Medieval Monasteries. Patrick Greene. LC 92-15056. (Archaeology of Medieval Britain Ser.). 1992. 79.00 (*0-7185-1296-0*) St Martin.

Medieval Monastery. Marjorie Reeves. (Then & There Ser.). (Illus.). 90p. (Orig.). (gr. 7-12). 1980. reprint ed. pap. text 8.60 (*0-582-00380-6*, 78064) Longman.

Medieval Monastic Preaching. Ed. by Carolyn A. Muessig. LC 98-36284. (Studies in Intellectual History: Vol. 90). (Illus.). xvi, 368p. 1998. 126.50 (*90-04-10883-1*) Brill Academic Pubs.

***Medieval Monasticism.** Marilyn Faherty Dunn. (Illus.). 320p. 2000. 64.95 (*0-631-13463-8*) Blackwell Pubs.

Medieval Monasticism: A Select Bibliography. Giles Constable. LC 75-42284. (Toronto Medieval Bibliographies Ser.: No. 6). 196p. reprint ed. pap. 60.80 (*0-8357-4019-6*, 203670900005) Bks Demand.

Medieval Mothering. Ed. by John C. Parsons & Bonnie Wheeler. (New Middle Ages Ser.: Vol. 3). (Illus.). 400p. 1996. text 72.00 (*0-8153-2341-7*) Garland.

Medieval Muck. Mary Dobson. LC 99-209828. (Smelly Old History Ser.). (Illus.). 32p. (J). (gr. 2 up). 1999. pap. 7.95 (*0-19-910528-6*) OUP.

Medieval Music. John Arnold. (Topics in Music Ser.). (Illus.). 48p. 1985. pap. text 11.95 (*0-19-321332-X*) OUP.

Medieval Music. Richard H. Hoppin. (Introduction to Music History Ser.). (Illus.). 566p. (C). 1978. text 48.75 (*0-393-09090-6*) Norton.

***Medieval Music.** Richard H. Hoppin. (C). 1999. text 52.00 (*0-393-98189-4*) Norton.

Medieval Music: The Sixth Liberal Art. Andrew S. Hughes. LC 73-85087. (Toronto Medieval Bibliographies Ser.: No. 4). (Illus.). 340p. reprint ed. pap. 105.40 (*0-8357-4143-5*, 203691600006) Bks Demand.

Medieval Music: The Sixth Liberal Art. 2nd ed. Andrew S. Hughes. (Medieval Bibliographies Ser.). 1980. text 45.00 (*0-8020-2358-4*) U of Toronto Pr.

***Medieval Music As Medieval Exegesis.** William T. Flynn. LC 99-15108. (Studies in Liturgical Musicology: No. 8). 288p. 1999. 55.00 (*0-8108-3656-4*) Scarecrow.

Medieval Muslim Horsemanship: A Fourteenth-Century Arabic Cavalry Manual G. Rex Smith. LC 81-478645. (British Library Booklets). 36 p. 1979. write for info. (*0-904654-12-5*) Br Library Bd.

Medieval Muslim Scholar at Work: The Life, Sources & Method of Ibn Tawus & His Library. Etan Kohlberg. LC 91-40126. (Islamic Philosophy, Theology & Science, Studies & Texts Ser.: Vol. 12). x, 472p. 1992. 166.00 (*90-04-09549-7*) Brill Academic Pubs.

Medieval Muslim Thinkers & Scientists. Hakim M. Said. (C). 1991. 14.00 (*81-85199-43-4*, Pub. by Renaiss Publng Hse) S Asia.

Medieval Mystical Tradition Vol. 4: Exeter Symposium: Dartington, 1987. Ed. by Marion Glasscoe. 203p. 1987. 75.00 (*0-85991-236-1*) Boydell & Brewer.

Medieval Mystical Tradition in England: Exeter Symposium V: Papers Read at Dartington Hall, July 1992. Ed. by Marion Glasscoe. 229p. (C). 1992. 75.00 (*0-85991-346-5*, DS Brewer) Boydell & Brewer.

Medieval Mystical Tradition in England: Papers Read at Darlington, 1982. 268p. 1982. pap. text 25.95 (*0-85989-183-6*, Pub. by Univ Exeter Pr) Northwestern U Pr.

***Medieval Mystical Tradition in England, Ireland & Wales.** Ed. by Marion Glasscoe. LC 99-38625. (Medieval Mystical Tradition Ser.). 256p. 1999. 75.00 (*0-85991-558-1*, DS Brewer) Boydell & Brewer.

Medieval Mysticism. Raitt. 1996. 24.95 (*0-8057-8614-7*, Twyne) Mac Lib Ref.

Medieval Mythography: From Roman North Africa to the School of Chartres, 433-1177 A.D. Jane Chance. (Illus.). 720p. (C). 1994. 85.00 (*0-8130-1256-2*) U Press Fla.

Medieval Myths. Norma L. Goodrich. 304p. 1994. pap. 13.95 (*0-452-01128-0*, Mer) NAL.

Medieval Naples: A Documentary History: c.500-1400. Ed. by Eileen Gardiner et al. (Documentary History of Naples Ser.: Vol. 2). (Illus.). 300p. pap. 25.00 (*0-934977-50-X*) Italica Pr.

Medieval Narrative: A Book of Translations. Margaret Schlauch. LC 75-93254. 463p. 1970. reprint ed. 75.00 (*0-87752-098-4*) Gordian.

Medieval Narratives & Modern Narratology: Subjects & Objects of Desire. Evelyn B. Vitz. (Studies in French Culture & Civilization). 256p. (C). 1992. pap. text 20.00 (*0-8147-8766-5*) NYU Pr.

Medieval Numerology: A Book of Essays. Ed. by Robert L. Surles. LC 93-16470. (Medieval Casebooks Ser.: Vol. 7). (Illus.). 192p. 1993. text 15.00 (*0-8153-0940-6*, H1640) Garland.

Medieval Objects in the Museum of Fine Arts, Boston: Metalwork. Nancy Netzer. LC 90-63004. (Illus.). 200p. 1991. pap. 11.95 (*0-87846-327-5*) Mus Fine Arts Boston.

***Medieval Optics & Theories of Light in the Works of Dante.** Simon A. Gilson. LC 99-89195. (Studies in Italian Literature: Vol. 8). 316p. 2000. text 99.95 (*0-7734-7808-6*) E Mellen.

Medieval or Renaissance Origins? Historiographical Debates & Deconstructions. A. London Fell. LC 81-22332. (Origins of Legislative Sovereignty & the Legislative State Ser.: Vol. 4). 528p. 1991. 65.00 (*0-275-93974-X*, C3974, Praeger Pubs) Greenwood.

Medieval Orissa & Cult of Jagannatha. Baba Mishra. LC 95-902322. (C). 1995. 29.00 (*81-7013-128-6*, Pub. by Navarang) S Asia.

Medieval Ornament. Karl A. Von Heideloff. LC 95-21220. (Pictorial Archive Ser.). (Illus.). 208p. 1995. pap. 14.95 (*0-486-28578-2*) Dover.

Medieval Outlaws: Ten Tales in Modern English. Thomas H. Ohlgren. LC 99-188144. (Illus.). 352p. 1998. 35.00 (*0-7509-1862-4*) Intl Pubs Mktg.

Medieval Pageant. Tr. by John R. Reinhard. LC 75-129969. (Studies in European Literature: No. 56). 1970. reprint ed. lib. bdg. 75.00 (*0-8383-1166-0*) M S G Haskell Hse.

Medieval Papacy. Geoffrey Barraclough. (Library of World Civilization Ser.). (Illus.). (C). 1979. pap. text 13.25 (*0-393-95100-6*) Norton.

Medieval People. Eileen Power. 1993. 24.75 (*0-8446-6685-8*) Peter Smith.

***Medieval People.** Eileen Edna Power. LC 00-29514. 2000. pap. 8.95 (*0-486-41435-3*) Dover.

Medieval People. Eileen E. Power. LC 91-58523. 240p. 1992. reprint ed. pap. 12.50 (*0-06-092275-3*, Perennial) HarperTrade.

Medieval Persia 1040-1797. David Morgan. (History of the Near East Ser.). (Illus.). 197p. (C). 1989. pap. 47.00 (*0-582-49324-2*, 73578) Longman.

M

An Asterisk (*) at the beginning of an entry indicates that the title is appearing for the first time.

Medieval Persian Court Poetry. Julie S. Meisami. LC 87-1743. (Illus.). 360p. 1987. reprint ed. pap. 111.60 (*0-608-06482-3*, 206677900009) Bks Demand.

Medieval Philosophers. Ed. by Jeremiah Hackett. LC 91-46592. (Dictionary of Literary Biography Ser.: Vol. 115). 465p. 1992. text 155.00 (*0-8103-7592-3*, B721) Gale.

Medieval Philosophy. Frederick C. Copleston. LC 53-2190. (Methuen's Home Study Bks.). 200p. reprint ed. pap. 62.00 (*0-608-30089-6*, 201315300086) Bks Demand.

Medieval Philosophy. 2nd ed. Armand A. Maurer. xxii, 455p. pap. text 26.29 (*0-88844-704-3*) Brill Academic Pubs.

Medieval Philosophy: From St. Augustine to Nicholas of Cusa. Ed. by John F. Wippel & Allen B. Wolter. LC 69-10043. (C). 1969. pap. 16.95 (*0-02-935650-4*) Free Pr.

Medieval Philosophy Vol. 2: From Augustine to Duns Scotus. Frederick J. Copleston. LC 92-34997. 624p. 1993. pap. 17.95 (*0-385-46844-X*, Image Bks) Doubleday.

Medieval Philosophy Vol. 3. Ed. by John Marenbon. LC 97-7483. (Routledge History of Philosophy: Vol. 3). 544p. (C). 1998. 90.00 (*0-415-05377-3*, C0278) Routledge.

Medieval Philosophy & the Transcendentals: The Case of Thomas Aquinas. Jan A. Aertsen. LC 96-5485. (Studien und Texte zur Geistesgeschichte des Mittelalters Ser.: No. 52). x, 468p. 1996. 161.00 (*90-04-10585-9*) Brill Academic Pubs.

Medieval Philosophy & Theology, Vol. 1. LC 90-50965. (C). 1991. text 34.50 (*0-268-01386-1*); pap. text 17.50 (*0-268-01387-X*) U of Notre Dame Pr.

Medieval Philosophy & Theology, Vol. 2. LC 90-50965. (C). 1992. text 34.50 (*0-268-01400-0*); pap. text 17.50 (*0-268-01401-9*) U of Notre Dame Pr.

Medieval Philosophy & Theology, Vol. 3. LC 90-50965. (C). 1994. text 37.00 (*0-268-01404-3*); pap. text 19.50 (*0-268-01405-1*) U of Notre Dame Pr.

Medieval Philosophy & Theology, Vol. 4. LC 90-50965. (C). 1995. text 37.00 (*0-268-01412-4*); pap. text 19.50 (*0-268-01413-2*) U of Notre Dame Pr.

Medieval Piety from Relics to the Eucharist: A Process of Mutual Interaction. G. J. Snoek. LC 94-44924. (Studies in the History of Christian Thought: Vol. 63).Tr. of Eucharistie- en Reliekverering in de Middeleeuwen. 1995. 142.00 (*90-04-10263-9*) Brill Academic Pubs.

Medieval Pilgrim's Companion: Reassessing El Libro de los Huespedes (Escorial MS.h.I.13) Thomas D. Spaccarelli. LC 98-35344. (North Carolina Studies in the Romance Languages & Literatures). 144p. (C). 1999. pap. text 22.50 (*0-8078-9265-3*) U of NC Pr.

Medieval Plays in Scotland. Anna J. Mill. LC 68-56497. 353p. 1972. reprint ed. 26.95 (*0-405-08789-6*, Pub. by Blom Pubns) Ayer.

Medieval Poetics. Paul M. Clogan. LC 75-32451. (Medievalia et Humanistica: New Ser.: No. 7). 221p. reprint ed. pap. 63.00 (*0-608-12238-6*, 2024433) Bks Demand.

Medieval Poetry in Britain, A. D. 900-1600. Michael R. McCarthy. 1995. pap. 31.90 (*0-7185-1271-5*) Bks Intl VA.

Medieval Political Philosophy: A Sourcebook. Ed. by Ralph Lerner & Muhsin Mahdi. (Agora Paperback Editions Ser.). 544p. 1972. pap. text 18.95 (*0-8014-9139-8*) Cornell U Pr.

Medieval Polyphonic Sequences: An Anthology. Bryan Gillingham. (Wissenschaftliche Abhandlungen-Musicological Studies: Vol. 45). (ENG.). 129p. 1985. 40.00 (*0-931902-51-7*) Inst Mediaeval Mus.

Medieval Popular Culture: Problems of Belief & Perception. Aron I. Gurevich. Tr. by Janos M. Bak & Paul A. Hollingsworth. (Cambridge Studies in Oral & Literate Culture: No. 14). 295p. (C). 1990. pap. text 22.95 (*0-521-38658-6*) Cambridge U Pr.

Medieval Popular Religion, 1000-1500: A Reader. Ed. by John Shinners. (Readings in Medieval Civilizations & Cultures Ser.: Vol. 2). 520p. (C). 1997. pap. 26.95 (*1-55111-133-0*) Broadview Pr.

Medieval Pottery in Britain, A. D. 900-1600. Michael McCarthy & Catherine M. Brooks. (Illus.). 520p. 1992. 49.00 (*0-7185-1254-5*) St Martin.

Medieval Prostitution. Jacques Rossiaud. Tr. by Lydia G. Cochrane from FRE. (Family, Sexuality & Social Relations in Past Times). 272p. 1995. pap. text 28.95 (*0-631-19992-6*) Blackwell Pubs.

Medieval Psychology, 14. Simon Kemp. LC 89-29782. (Contributions in Psychology Ser.: No. 14). 192p. 1990. 55.00 (*0-313-26734-0*, KMP/, Greenwood Pr) Greenwood.

Medieval Purity & Piety: Essays on Medieval Clerical Celibacy & Religious Reform. Ed. by Michael Frassetto. LC 97-32004. (Medieval Casebks.: Vol. 19). (Illus.). 424p. 1998. text 75.00 (*0-8153-2430-8*, H2006) Garland.

Medieval Queenship. Ed. by John C. Parsons. LC 93-10879. 272p. 1993. text 55.00 (*0-312-05217-0*) St Martin.

Medieval Queenship. John C. Parsons. 272p. 1997. pap. 17.95 (*0-312-17298-2*) St Martin.

Medieval Reader. Norman R. Cantor. 384p. 1995. pap. 19.50 (*0-06-272055-4*, Harper Ref) HarpC.

Medieval Reading: Grammar, Rhetoric & the Classical Text. Suzanne Reynolds. (Studies in Medieval Literature: No. 27). (Illus.). 251p. (C). 1996. text 59.95 (*0-521-47257-1*) Cambridge U Pr.

Medieval Realms. James Mason. 1991. pap. text 13.32 (*0-582-20735-5*) Longman.

Medieval Realms, 1066-1500. J. F. Aylett. (Illus.). 64p. 1992. pap. 15.75 (*0-340-54823-1*, Pub. by Hodder & Stought Ltd) Lubrecht & Cramer.

Medieval Reckonings of Time. Reginald L. Poole. 1977. lib. bdg. 59.95 (*0-8490-2220-7*) Gordon Pr.

Medieval Record. Alfred J. Andrea. 416p. (C). 1997. pap. text 25.16 (*0-395-71862-7*) HM.

Medieval Religious Houses in England & Wales. David Knowles & R. Neville Hadcock. LC 72-181783. reprint ed. pap. 147.00 (*0-608-30371-2*, 2016312) Bks Demand.

Medieval Religious Houses in England & Wales. 2nd ed. David Knowles & R. Neville Hadcock. 584p. (C). 1995. 134.00 (*0-582-11230-3*, 76996) Longman.

Medieval Religious Houses, Scotland: With an Appendix on the Houses in the Isle of Man. 2nd ed. Ian B. Cowan & David E. Easson. LC 75-42083. 288p. reprint ed. pap. 89.30 (*0-7837-1596-X*, 204188800024) Bks Demand.

Medieval Religious Stage: Shapes & Phantoms. Alois M. Nagler. Tr. by George C. Schoolfield. LC 75-43328. (Illus.). 120p. reprint ed. pap. 37.20 (*0-8357-8220-4*, 203384000087) Bks Demand.

Medieval Religious Women I: Distant Echoes. Ed. by John A. Nichols & M. Thomas Shank. (Cistercian Studies: No. 71). 299p. (C). 1984. pap. 13.95 (*0-87907-971-1*) Cistercian Pubns.

***Medieval Researches from Western Asiatic Sources.** E. Bretschneider. (Illus.). 716p. 2000. 295.00 (*0-7007-1262-3*, Pub. by Curzon Pr Ltd) Paul & Co Pubs.

Medieval Revival & Its Influences on the Romantic Movement. R. R. Agrawal. 1990. 44.00 (*81-7017-262-4*, Pub. by Abhinav) S Asia.

Medieval Rhetoric: A Select Bibliography. 2nd ed. James J. Murphy. (Medieval Bibliographies Ser.). 80p. 1989. pap. 18.95 (*0-8020-6659-3*); text 37.50 (*0-8020-5750-0*) U of Toronto Pr.

Medieval Roads. Brian P. Hindle. 1989. pap. 25.00 (*0-85263-997-X*, Pub. by Shire Pubns) St Mut.

Medieval Roads & Tracks. Brian P. Hindle. (Archaeology Ser.: Vol. 26). (Illus.). 64p. 1999. pap. text 10.50 (*0-7478-0390-0*, Pub. by Shire Pubns) Parkwest Pubns.

Medieval Romance: Critical Heritage, 6 vols. 2577p. (C). 1996. 700.00 (*0-415-13396-3*) Routledge.

Medieval Romances. Ed. by Laura H. Loomis & Roger S. Loomis. LC 57-11169. (Modern Library College Editions). 426p. (C). 1965. pap. 8.44 (*0-07-553650-1*, 30970) McGraw.

Medieval Rome: A Portrait of the City & Its Life. Paul Hetherington. LC 94-25907. 1994. pap. 19.95 (*0-312-12349-3*); text 45.00 (*0-312-12348-5*) St Martin.

Medieval Russia: A Source Book, 850-1700. 3rd ed. Basil Dmytryshyn. 550p. (C). 1991. pap. text 46.00 (*0-03-033422-5*, Pub. by Harcourt Coll Pubs) Harcourt.

Medieval Russian Armies 838-1252, 333. David Nicolle. 1999. pap. text 12.95 (*1-85532-848-8*) Ospry.

Medieval Russian Culture. H. Bormbai & Michael S. Flien. 395p. 1985. 140.00 (*0-7855-0890-2*) St Mut.

Medieval Russian Culture, Vol. II. Ed. by Michael S. Flier. 240p. 1994. 48.00 (*0-520-08638-4*, Pub. by U CA Pr) Cal Prin Full Svc.

Medieval Russian Epics. Serge A. Zenkovsky. 1974. pap. 18.95 (*0-452-01086-1*, Mer) NAL.

Medieval Russian Ornament in Full Color: From Illuminated Manuscripts. Moscow Museum of Art & Industry Staff. LC 94-32632. (Pictorial Archive Ser.). (Illus.). 112p. 1994. pap. 21.95 (*0-486-28258-9*) Dover.

Medieval Saga. Carol J. Clover. LC 81-17432. 224p. 1982. text 42.50 (*0-8014-1447-4*) Cornell U Pr.

Medieval Saints: A Reader. Ed. by Mary-Ann Stouck & Paul Dutton. LC 99-208786. (Readings in Medieval Civilizations & Cultures Ser.: Vol. IV). 545p. 1998. pap. 26.95 (*1-55111-101-2*) Broadview Pr.

Medieval Saints' Lives: Spiritual Renewal & Old French Literature. Duncan Robertson. (Edward C. Armstrong Monographs on Medieval Literature: No. 8). 267p. (Orig.). 1995. pap. 24.95 (*0-917058-90-9*) French Forum.

Medieval Scandinavia: From Conversion to Reformation, Circa 800-1500. Birgit Sawyer & Peter Sawyer. LC 93-3511. (Nordic Ser.: Vol. 16). 284p. (C). 1993. pap. 19.95 (*0-8166-1739-2*) U of Minn Pr.

Medieval Scapini Tarot. Luigi Scapini. 1985. pap. 20.00 (*0-88079-031-8*, SM78) US Games Syst.

***Medieval Scene: An Informal Introduction to the Middle Ages.** G. Coulton. 2000. pap. 7.95 (*0-486-40963-5*) Dover.

Medieval Scholarship: Biographical Studies on the Formation of a Discipline. Ed. by Helen Damico & Joseph B. Zavadil. Incl. Medieval Scholarship Vol. I: History: Biographical Studies on the Formation of a Discipline: History. LC 95-6189. (Illus.). 347p. 1995. text 66.00 (*0-8240-6894-7*); LC 95-6189. write for info. (*0-614-32276-6*) Garland.

Medieval Scholarship, Vol. I: History, Biographical Studies on the Formation of a Discipline: History see Medieval Scholarship: Biographical Studies on the Formation of a Discipline

Medieval Scholarship Vol. 2: Biographical Studies of the Formation of a Discipline. Helen Damico. LC 95-6189. 480p. 1998. text 95.00 (*0-8153-2890-7*, H2071) Garland.

***Medieval Scholarship Vol. 3: Biographical Studies on the Foundation of a Discipline: Philosophy & the Arts.** Ed. by Helen Damico. (Reference Library of the Humanities). 368p. 1999. 90.00 (*0-8153-3339-0*, H2110) Garland.

Medieval Sciences in the Works of John Gower. George G. Fox. LC 65-21089. (Studies in Poetry: No. 38). 1969. reprint ed. lib. bdg. 75.00 (*0-8383-0553-9*) M S G Haskell Hse.

***Medieval Scotland.** A. D. M. Barrell. LC 99-86098. (Cambridge Medieval Textbooks Ser.). (Illus.). 280p. 2000. write for info. (*0-521-58443-4*); pap. write for info. (*0-521-58602-X*) Cambridge U Pr.

***Medieval Scotland: Crown, Lordship & Community.** Alexander Grant & Keith Stringer. 336p. 1998. pap. 30.00 (*0-7486-1110-X*, Pub. by Edinburgh U Pr) Col U Pr.

Medieval Sculpture & Works of Art. Paul Williamson. LC 87-60456. (Illus.). 180p. 1989. 95.00 (*0-85667-335-8*, Pub. by P Wilson) Hoovers TX.

Medieval Sculpture from Eastern India: Selections from the Nalin Collection. David R. Nalin. Ed. by Jane A. Casey. (Illus.). 108p. (Orig.). 1985. pap. 45.00 (*0-9614416-0-7*) Nalini Intl Pubs.

Medieval Semiotic: Reference & Representation in John of St. Thomas' Theory of Signs. Edward J. Furton. LC 94-28485. (History & Language Ser.: Vol. 4). 202p. (C). 1995. text 45.95 (*0-8204-2154-5*) P Lang Pubng.

Medieval Settlement: Continuity & Change. P. H. Sawyer. LC 77-365310. ix, 357p. 1976. write for info. (*0-7131-5864-6*) OUP.

Medieval Ships & Shipping. Gillian Hutchinson. LC 96-38200. (Archaeology of Medieval Britain Ser.). (Illus.). 224p. 1997. pap. 35.00 (*0-7185-0117-9*) Bks Intl VA.

Medieval Ships & Shipping. Gillian Hutchinson. (Illus.). 256p. 1994. 45.00 (*0-8386-3628-4*) Fairleigh Dickinson.

Medieval Sicily: The First Absolute State. Henry Bazbera. Ed. by Gaetano Cipolla. LC 94-27273. (Sicilian Studies: Vol. II). (Illus.). 152p. (C). 1994. pap. text 12.00 (*1-881901-05-X*) LEGAS.

Medieval Siege. Jim Bradbury. (Illus.). 378p. (C). 1997. reprint ed. pap. 29.95 (*0-85115-357-7*) Boydell & Brewer.

Medieval Siege. Jim Bradbury. (Illus.). 378p. (C). 1998. reprint ed. 55.00 (*0-85115-312-7*) Boydell & Brewer.

Medieval Siege: Theme & Image in Middle English Romance. Malcolm Hebron. LC 97-2024. (Oxford English Monographs). 200p. (C). 1997. text 58.00 (*0-19-818620-7*) OUP.

Medieval Siege Warfare. Christopher Gravett. (Elite Ser.: No. 28). (Illus.). 64p. 1990. pap. 12.95 (*0-85045-947-8*, 9428, Pub. by Ospry) Stackpole.

Medieval Siege Warfare, 28. Osprey Staff. 1999. pap. text 14.95 (*1-85532-947-6*) Ospry.

***Medieval Simulations: Challenging.** Max W. Fisher. 96p. 2000. pap. 11.95 (*1-57690-583-7*) Tchr Create Mat.

Medieval Sinner: Confession & Characterization in the Literature of the English Middle Ages. Mary F. Braswell. LC 81-69040. 220p. 1983. 29.50 (*0-8386-3117-7*) Fairleigh Dickinson.

Medieval Skepticism & Chaucer. Mary E. Thomas. LC 73-147314. 184p. 1971. reprint ed. lib. bdg. 53.00 (*0-8154-0379-8*) Cooper Sq.

Medieval Slavery & Liberation. Pierre Dockes. Tr. by Arthur Goldhammer from FRE. LC 81-11594. 304p. 1997. 32.50 (*0-226-15482-3*) U Ch Pr.

Medieval Slavery & Liberation. Pierre Dockes. Tr. by Arthur Goldhammer. LC 81-11594. 299p. reprint ed. pap. 92.70 (*0-608-09450-1*, 205425000005) Bks Demand.

Medieval Slavic Lives of Saints & Princes. Tr. by Marvin Kantor. (Michigan Slavic Translations Ser.: No. 5). 1983. 15.00 (*0-930042-44-1*) Mich Slavic Pubns.

Medieval Society: Everyday Life in the Middle Ages. rev. ed. Sidney Painter. (Illus.). 64p. (C). 1991. pap. text 2.25 (*1-877891-06-1*) Paperbook Pr Inc.

Medieval Society & the Manor Court. Zvi Razi & Richard Smith. LC 96-2644. (Illus.). 726p. 1996. text 140.00 (*0-19-820190-7*, Clarendon Pr) OUP.

Medieval Society in Southern France & Catalonia. Archibald Ross Lewis. (Collected Studies: No. CS197). 280p. (C). 1984. reprint ed. lib. bdg. 89.95 (*0-86078-145-3*, Pub. by Variorum) Ashgate Pub Co.

Medieval Soldier. Gerry A. Embleton & John Houe. (Illus.). 144p. 1995. 39.95 (*1-85915-036-5*, Pub. by Windrow & Green) Motorbooks Intl.

Medieval Soldier. A. Vesey Norman. LC 72-175833. (Medieval Life Ser.). x, 278p. 1971. write for info. (*0-213-76447-4*) Art Barker.

Medieval Soldier: The Men Who Fought the Wars of the Roses. Andrew W. Boardman. LC 99-159663. (Fifteenth Century Ser.). (Illus.). 224p. 1998. 36.95 (*0-7509-1465-3*, Pub. by Sutton Pub Ltd) Intl Pubs Mktg.

Medieval Song & Story, Vol. 4. Intro. by Harry M. Ayres. Date not set. 30.95 (*0-8369-4795-9*) Ayer.

Medieval Songs & Dances of 11th-14th c. Europe. (Illus.). 162p. (C). 1997. 35.00 (*0-615-11404-0*) Catsprey Music.

Medieval Southwark. Martha Carlin. LC 95-47679. 351p. 1996. 60.00 (*1-85285-116-3*) Hambledon Press.

Medieval Spains. Bernard F. Reilly. LC 92-23379. (Cambridge Medieval Textbooks Ser.). 240p. (C). 1993. text 59.95 (*0-521-39436-8*); pap. text 19.95 (*0-521-39741-3*) Cambridge U Pr.

Medieval Spanish Allegory. Chandler R. Post. 1977. lib. bdg. 59.95 (*0-8490-2221-5*) Gordon Pr.

Medieval Spanish Allegory. Chandler R. Post. 1984. lib. bdg. 90.00 (*0-8490-3235-0*) Gordon Pr.

Medieval Spanish Ejempla: A Study of Selected Tales from Calila y Dimna, El Libro de los Enganos de las Mujeres & the Libro de los Exemplos por ABC. Richard A. Picerno. LC 88-81376. (Coleccion Textos). (ENG & SPA.). 55p. (Orig.). 1988. pap. 10.00 (*0-89729-492-0*) Ediciones.

Medieval Spanish Epic: Mythic Roots & Ritual Language. Thomas Montgomery. LC 97-13077. (Penn State Studies in Romance Literatures). 1998. 42.50 (*0-271-01738-4*) Pa St U Pr.

Medieval Spawn Witchblade. Garth Ennis. (Illus.). 96p. (Orig.). (YA). 1997. pap. 9.95 (*1-887279-44-X*) Image Comics.

Medieval Stained Glass of Northhamptonshire. Richard Marke. LC 99-203412. (Great Britain Summary Catalogue Ser.: No. 4). (Illus.). 432p. 1999. text 175.00 (*0-19-726177-9*) OUP.

Medieval Stained Glass of the County of Lincolnshire. Ed. by Penny Hebgin-Barnes. LC 97-161828. (Corpus Vitrearum Medii Aevi; Great Britain British Academy). (Illus.). 448p. 1997. text 225.00 (*0-19-726156-6*) OUP.

***Medieval State: Essays Presented to James Campbell.** John Robert Maddicott et al. LC 99-43948. 2001. write for info. (*1-85285-195-3*) Hambledon Press.

Medieval Stereotypes & Modern Antisemitism. Robert Chazan. LC 96-29259. 196p. 1997. 40.00 (*0-520-20394-1*, Pub. by U CA Pr) Cal Prin Full Svc.

Medieval Structure: The Gothic Vault. James H. Acland. LC 72-76769. (Illus.). 264p. reprint ed. pap. 81.90 (*0-608-11390-5*, 201608500097) Bks Demand.

Medieval Studies, 63 titles in 80 vols., Set. reprint ed. write for info. (*0-404-56500-X*) AMS Pr.

Medieval Studies: An Introduction. 2nd rev. ed. Ed. by James M. Powell. LC 91-31160. (Illus.). 500p. (C). 1992. text 45.00 (*0-8156-2555-3*); pap. text 19.95 (*0-8156-2556-1*) Syracuse U Pr.

Medieval Studies for J. A. W. Bennett: Aetatis suae LXX. Ed. by Peter L. Heyworth. (Illus.). 438p. 1981. text 95.00 (*0-19-812628-X*) OUP.

Medieval Studies in Memory of A. Kingsley Porter, 2 Vols., Set. Ed. by Wilhelm R. Koehler. LC 77-80391. (Essay Index Reprint Ser.). 1977. 69.95 (*0-8369-1044-3*) Ayer.

Medieval Studies in Memory of A. Kingsley Porter, 2 vols., Set. fac. ed. Ed. by Wilhelm R. Koehler. (Essay Index Reprint Ser.). 750p. 1982. lib. bdg. 79.00 (*0-8290-0795-4*) Irvington.

Medieval Super-Companies: A Study of the Peruzzi Company of Florence. Edwin S. Hunt. LC 93-40289. (Illus.). 272p. (C). 1994. text 69.95 (*0-521-46156-1*) Cambridge U Pr.

***Medieval Surgery.** Tony Hunt. (Illus.). 120p. 2000. pap. 23.95 (*0-85115-754-8*, Suffolk Records Soc) Boydell & Brewer.

Medieval Swordsmanship: Illustrated Methods & Techniques. John Clements. LC 99-188076. (Illus.). 334p. 1998. pap. 40.00 (*1-58160-004-6*) Paladin Pr.

***Medieval Tales: That Kids Can Read & Tell.** Lorna MacDonald Czarnota. 96p. 2000. 21.95 (*0-87483-589-5*) August Hse.

***Medieval Tales: That Kids Can Read & Tell.** Lorna MacDonald Czarnota. 96p. (gr. 4-7). 2000. pap. 12.95 (*0-87483-588-7*) August Hse.

***Medieval Tales & Stories.** Tr. & Selected by Stanley Appelbaum. 2000. pap. 9.95 (*0-486-41407-8*) Dover.

Medieval Tapestry: Personalities of Mythic Europe. Ed. by Jeff Tidball. (Ars Magica Ser.). (Illus.). 160p. 1997. pap. 21.95 (*1-887801-60-X*, Atlas Games) Trident MN.

Medieval Tapestry Design. Dolores M. Andrew. (International Design Library). (Illus.). 48p. 1992. pap. 5.95 (*0-88045-121-1*) Stemmer Hse.

Medieval Technology & Social Change. Lynn White, Jr. (Illus.). 216p. 1966. reprint ed. pap. text 12.95 (*0-19-500266-0*) OUP.

Medieval Texts & Contemporary Readers. Ed. by Laurie A. Finke & Martin B. Shichtman. LC 87-47545. 272p. (C). 1987. pap. text 17.95 (*0-8014-9463-X*) Cornell U Pr.

Medieval Texts & Images. Ed. by Margaret M. Manion & Bernard J. Muir. LC 91-8868. xx, 224p. 1991. text 55.00 (*3-7186-5133-5*, Z6) Gordon & Breach.

Medieval Texts & Images: Studies of Manuscripts from the Middle Ages. Ed. by Margaret M. Manion & Bernard J. Muir. (Illus.). 224p. 50.00 (*976-8097-17-5*, Pub. by Craftsman House) Gordon & Breach.

Medieval Texts & Their First Appearance in Print. E. P. Goldschmidt. LC 68-54232. 1969. reprint ed. 25.00 (*0-8196-0226-4*) Biblo.

Medieval Theater in Castile. Charlotte Stern. LC 96-28632. (Medieval & Renaissance Texts & Studies: Vol. 156). 336p. 1996. 26.00 (*0-86698-196-9*, MR156) MRTS.

Medieval Theater of Cruelty: Rhetoric, Memory, Violence. Jody Enders. LC 98-26024. (Illus.). 328p. 1999. 45.00 (*0-8014-3334-7*) Cornell U Pr.

Medieval Theatre. Glynne W. Wickham. 276p. 1987. pap. text 25.95 (*0-521-31248-5*) Cambridge U Pr.

Medieval Theatre in the Round. enl. ed. Richard W. Southern. (Illus.). 1975. 25.00 (*0-87830-085-6*, Thtre Arts Bks) Routledge.

***Medieval Theologians.** G. R. Evans. 650p. 2000. 72.95 (*0-631-21202-7*); pap. 39.95 (*0-631-21203-5*) Blackwell Pubs.

Medieval Theology & the Natural Body. Ed. by Alastair J. Minnis & Peter Biller. LC 97-1032. (York Studies in Medieval Theology: No. 1). (Illus.). 256p. 1997. 75.00 (*0-9529734-0-5*) Boydell & Brewer.

Medieval Thought: An Introduction. B. B. Price. 256p. (C). 1991. pap. text 28.95 (*0-631-17509-1*) Blackwell Pubs.

Medieval Thought: The Western Intellectual Tradition from Antiquity to the Thirteenth Century. 2nd ed. Michael Haren. LC 92-94449. 315p. 1992. text 60.00 (*0-8020-2868-3*); pap. text 19.95 (*0-8020-7758-7*) U of Toronto Pr.

Medieval Thought No. 2: History of Western Philosophy. David Luscombe. LC 96-29604. (A History of Western Philosophy Ser.: No. 2). 256p. 1997. pap. 14.95 (*0-19-289179-0*) OUP.

Medieval Tile Designs. Ed. by John G. Nichols. LC 97-44799. (Illus.). 64p. 1998. pap. 6.95 (*0-486-29947-3*) Dover.

Medieval Times: A Thematic Unit. Cynthia Ross. (Thematic Units Ser.). (Illus.). 80p. (J). (gr. 5-8). 1992. student ed. 9.95 (*1-55734-291-1*) Tchr Create Mat.

An Asterisk (*) at the beginning of an entry indicates that the title is appearing for the first time.

Medieval Times: 325-1453. Frank Edgar & George Lee. (Illus.). 160p. (YA). (gr. 5). 1994. pap. text 13.95 (*1-58037-055-1*, Pub. by M Twain Media) Carson-Dellos.

Medieval Times Activity Book. Linda Milliken. Ed. by Deneen Celecia. (Illus.). 48p. 1995. pap., student ed. 6.95 (*1-56472-049-7*) Edupress Inc.

Medieval Times Photo Fun Activities. Linda Milliken. Ed. by Deneen Celecia. (Illus.). 8p. (J). (gr. 3-6). 1995. pap. 6.95 (*1-56472-050-0*) Edupress Inc.

Medieval Tomb Towers of Iran. Abbas Daneshvari. (Islamic Art & Architecture Ser.: Vol. 2). (Illus.). 112p. (C). 1986. lib. bdg. 17.95 (*0-939214-34-2*) Mazda Pubs.

Medieval Tournament. J. Petruccio. 1995. pap. text 4.50 (*0-486-28721-1*) Dover.

Medieval Town. David Birt. (Resource Units: Middle Ages, 1066-1485 Ser.). (Illus.). 24p. (Orig.). 1974. pap. text, teacher ed. 12.95 (*0-582-39389-2*) Longman.

Medieval Town. Daisy Kerr. LC 96-7755. (Worldwise Ser.: Vol. 16). (Illus.). (J). (gr. 2). 1997. pap. 7.00 (*0-531-15313-4*) Watts.

Medieval Town. Marjorie Reeves. (Then & There Ser.). (Illus.). 90p. (gr. 7-12). 1954. pap. text 8.60 (*0-582-00385-7*, 78065) Longman.

Medieval Town. John H. Mundy & Peter Riesenberg. LC 79-9718. (Anvil Ser.). 192p. 1979. reprint ed. pap. 11.50 (*0-88275-906-X*) Krieger.

Medieval Town: A Reader in English Urban History, 1200-1540. Richard Holt. 1990. text 50.50 (*0-582-05129-0*, Pub. by Addison-Wesley) Longman.

Medieval Town: A Reader in English Urban History, 1200-1540. Ed. by Richard Holt & Gervase Rosser. (Readers in Urban History Ser.). 352p. (C). 1990. pap. text 28.50 (*0-582-05128-2*, 78604) Longman.

Medieval Town Plans. Brian P. Hindle. 1989. pap. 35.00 (*0-7478-0065-0*, Pub. by Shire Pubns) St Mut.

Medieval Towns. John Schofield & Alan Vince. (Illus.). 256p. 1994. 45.00 (*0-8386-3622-5*) Fairleigh Dickinson.

Medieval Trade in the Mediterranean World: Illustrative Documents. Tr. by Irving W. Raymond. 458p. 1990. text 75.00 (*0-231-01865-7*) Col U Pr.

Medieval Tradition of Natural Law. Ed. by Harold J. Johnson. LC 86-31126. (Studies in Medieval Culture: No. 22). 1987. pap. 15.95 (*0-918720-82-6*); boxed set 32.95 (*0-918720-81-8*) Medieval Inst.

Medieval Translator IV. Ed. by Roger Ellis & Ruth Evans. (Medieval & Renaissance Texts & Studies: Vol. 123). 272p. 1994. 24.00 (*0-86698-128-4*, MR123) MRTS.

Medieval Translator 4. Roger Ellis & Ruth Evans. LC 94-213080. x, 256 p. 1994. write for info. (*0-85989-412-6*) Univ Exeter Pr.

Medieval Translators & Their Craft. Ed. by Jeanette M. Beer. (Studies in Medieval Culture: No. 25). 1988. boxed set 37.95 (*0-918720-95-8*) Medieval Inst.

Medieval Translators & Their Craft. Ed. by Jeanette M. Beer. (Studies in Medieval Culture: No. 25). 1988. pap. 17.95 (*0-918720-96-6*) Medieval Inst.

Medieval Treasury: The Art of the Middle Ages in the Victoria & Albert Museum. Paul Williamson. (Illus.). 247p. 1996. pap. 29.50 (*0-948107-38-3*, Pub. by V&A Ent) Antique Collect.

Medieval Triptych: Panels from the Cloister, City, & Castle. Thomas E. Vesce. (ENG & FRE.). 247p. 1987. pap. write for info. (*0-7734-9213-5*) E Mellen.

Medieval Triptych: Panels from the Clorster, City & Castle. Thomas E. Vesce. (MRMS (Medieval & Renaissance Monograph): No. X). (Orig.). (C). 1989. pap. text 15.00 (*0-941107-03-5*) MARC Pub Co.

Medieval Underworld. Andrew McCall. 1979. 22.00 (*0-241-10018-6*, H Hamilton) Viking Penguin.

Medieval Venuses & Cupids: Sexuality, Hermeneutics, & English Poetry. Theresa L. Tinkle. LC 95-21795. 364p. 1996. 39.50 (*0-8047-2515-2*) Stanford U Pr.

Medieval Village. G. G. Coulton. 1989. pap. 13.95 (*0-486-26002-X*) Dover.

Medieval Village. 2nd ed. Marjorie Reeves. (Then & There Ser.). (Illus.). 90p. (Orig.). (gr. 7-12). 1954. pap. text 8.60 (*0-582-00386-5*, 78066) Longman.

Medieval Village Economy: A Study of the Pareto Mapping in General Equilibrium Models. Robert M. Townsend. LC 92-24766. (Illus.). 180p. (C). 1993. text 39.50 (*0-691-04270-5*, Pub. by Princeton U Pr) Cal Prin Full Svc.

Medieval Vision: Essays in History & Perception. Carolly Erickson. LC 75-10179. (Illus.). 256p. (C). 1976. pap. text 19.95 (*0-19-501963-6*) OUP.

Medieval Visions of Heaven & Hell: A Sourcebook. Eileen Gardiner. LC 92-45794. (Medieval Bibliographies Ser.: Vol. 11). 296p. 1993. text 20.00 (*0-8240-3348-5*, H1256) Garland.

***Medieval Voyage.** Lawhead. 2000. pap. 15.00 (*0-534-56157-8*) Thomson Learn.

Medieval Wales. R. Ian Jack. Ed. by Geoffrey R. Elton. LC 79-37005. (Sources of History Ser.). 257p. 1973. pap. text 16.95 (*0-8014-9136-3*) Cornell U Pr.

Medieval Wales. David Walker. (Cambridge Medieval Textbooks Ser.). (Illus.). 245p. (C). 1990. pap. text 19.95 (*0-521-31153-5*) Cambridge U Pr.

Medieval Wall Paintings. Ed. by E. Clive Rouse. (Illus.). 80p. 1989. pap. 12.50 (*0-7478-0144-4*, Pub. by Shire Pubns) Parkwest Pubns.

***Medieval Warfare: A History.** Maurice Keen. (Illus.). 352p. 1999. 40.00 (*0-19-820639-9*) OUP.

Medieval Warfare: History of the Art of War, Vol. III. Hans Delbruck. Tr. by Walter J. Renfroe, Jr. LC 89-24980. (Illus.). 712p. 1990. reprint ed. pap. 25.00 (*0-8032-6585-9*, Bison Books) U of Nebr Pr.

***Medieval Warfare Source Book: Warfare in Western Christendom.** David Nicole. (Illus.). 320p. 2000. reprint ed. 40.00 (*0-7881-9224-8*) DIANE Pub.

Medieval Warfare Source Book Vol. 2: Christian Europe & Its Neighbor. David Nicolle. (Medieval Warfare Source Book: Vol. II). (Illus.). 320p. 1997. 34.95 (*1-85409-307-X*, Pub. by Arms & Armour) Sterling.

Medieval Warrior, 1. Paul Lecroix. 1999. 19.95 (*1-885440-48-0*) First Glance.

Medieval Welsh Erotic Poetry. Dafydd Johnston. 1999. pap. text 19.95 (*1-85411-234-1*) Seren Bks.

Medieval Welsh Literature. Andrew Breeze. 264p. 1996. boxed set 55.00 (*1-85182-229-1*, Pub. by Four Cts Pr) Intl Spec Bk.

***Medieval Welsh Manuscripts.** Daniel Huws. 320p. 2000. 90.00 (*0-7083-1602-6*, Pub. by U Wales Pr) Paul & Co Pubs.

Medieval Welsh Poems: An Anthology. Tr. by Richard M. Loomis & Dafydd Johnston. 240p. 1992. pap. 9.95 (*0-86698-102-0*, P8) Pegasus Pr.

Medieval Welsh Religious Lyric: Poems of the Gogynfeirdd, 1137-1282. Catherine A. McKenna. 241p. 1991. 37.50 (*0-926689-02-9*) Ford & Bailie Pubs.

Medieval West Africa Before 1400: Ghana, Takrur, Gao (Songhay) & Mali as Described by Arab Scholars & Merchants. rev. ed. Ed. & Tr. by Nehemia Levtzion from ARA. Tr. by J. F. Hopkins from ARA. Orig. Title: Corpus of Early Arab Sources for West African History. (Illus.). 320p. (C). Date not set. text 44.95 (*1-55876-164-0*); pap. text 22.95 (*1-55876-165-9*) Wiener Pubs Inc.

Medieval West Meets the Rest of the World. Ed. by Nancy Van Deusen. LC 95-153289. (Wissenschaftliche Abhandlungen-Musicological Studies: Vol. 62/2). vi, 138p. 1995. lib. bdg. 50.00 (*0-931902-94-0*) Inst Mediaeval Mus.

Medieval Western Philosophy: The European Emergence. Patrick J. Aspell. LC 97-20069. (Cultural Heritage & Contemporary Change Ser.: Vol. 9). 340p. Date not set. pap. text 17.50 (*1-56518-094-1*) Coun Res Values.

Medieval Westminster, 1200-1540. Gervase Rosser. (Illus.). 442p. 1989. text 89.00 (*0-19-820156-7*) OUP.

Medieval Woman: An Illuminated Book of Days. Sally Fox. (Illus.). 1985. 13.95 (*0-8212-1587-6*, Pub. by Bulfinch Pr) Little.

Medieval Woman Monastics: Wisdom's Wellsprings. Ed. by Miriam Schmidt & Linda Kulzer. (Illus.). 312p. (Orig.). 1996. pap. 19.95 (*0-8146-2292-5*, Liturg Pr Bks) Liturgical Pr.

Medieval Woman's Mirror of Honor: The Treasury of the City of Ladies. Christine De Pizan. Ed. by Madeleine P. Cosman. Tr. & Intro. by Charity C. Willard. (Illus.). 265p. 1989. 24.95 (*0-89255-144-5*); pap. 11.95 (*0-89255-135-6*) Persea Bks.

Medieval Women. Eileen Power. Ed. by M. M. Postan. (Canto Book Ser.). (Illus.). 132p. (C). 1997. pap. 10.95 (*0-521-59556-8*) Cambridge U Pr.

Medieval Women: An Illuminated Address Book. Sally Fox. (Illus.). 1988. 14.95 (*0-8212-1700-3*, Pub. by Bulfinch Pr) Little.

***Medieval Women & the Law.** Noel James Menuge. LC 00-28941. 192p. 2000. 75.00 (*0-85115-775-0*) Boydell & Brewer.

Medieval Women in Their Communities. Diane Watt. LC 97-229185. 240p. 1997. pap. text 19.95 (*0-8020-8122-3*) U of Toronto Pr.

Medieval Women in Their Communities. Ed. by Diane Watt. 240p. 1997. text 50.00 (*0-8020-4289-9*) U of Toronto Pr.

Medieval Women in Their Communities. Ed. by Diane Watt. 250p. 1997. write for info. (*0-7083-1361-2*, Pub. by Univ Wales Pr); pap. write for info. (*0-7083-1369-8*, Pub. by Univ Wales Pr) Paul & Co Pubs.

Medieval Women Writers. Ed. by Katharina M. Wilson. LC 82-13380. 384p. 1984. pap. text 20.00 (*0-8203-0641-X*) U of Ga Pr.

Medieval Women's Visionary Literature. Ed. by Elizabeth A. Petroff. 416p. (Orig.). 1986. pap. text 26.95 (*0-19-503712-X*) OUP.

Medieval Woodcut Illustrations: City Views & Decorations from the Nuremberg Chronicle. Ed. by Carol Belanger Grafton. LC 99-26476. (Illus.). 96p. 1999. pap. 8.95 (*0-486-40458-7*) Dover.

Medieval Wooden Sculpture in Sweden, 5 vols., Set. Royal Academy of Letters, History, & Antiquities S. Ed. by A. Anderson & B. Thordeman. (Illus.). 1168p. (Orig.). 1966. pap. text 195.00 (*0-685-13807-0*) Coronet Bks.

Medieval Wordbook. Madeleine P. Cosman. LC 95-15335. 304p. 1996. 35.00 (*0-8160-3021-9*) Facts on File.

***Medieval World.** Jane Bingham. (World History Ser.). (Illus.). 96p. 1999. 29.95 (*0-7460-2762-1*, Usborne) EDC.

Medieval World. Jane Bingham. (World History Ser.). (Illus.). 96p. (gr. 3-7). 1999. 29.95 (*1-58086-200-4*) EDC.

Medieval World. Mike Corbishley. LC 92-31445. (Timelink Ser.). (Illus.). 60p. (YA). (gr. 5 up). 1993. lib. bdg. 18.95 (*0-87226-362-2*, P Bedrick Books) NTC Contemp Pub Co.

***Medieval World.** Reg Cox. (Wonders of the World Ser.). (Illus.). (J). 2000. 16.95 (*0-7910-6047-0*) Chelsea Hse.

Medieval World. Helen Howe. 1993. pap. 22.61 (*0-8013-1100-4*) Longman.

Medieval World. P. J. Larkin. (Illus.). 64p. 1974. pap. 11.95 (*0-7175-0663-0*) Dufour.

***Medieval World.** Philip Steele. (Illus.). 96p. (YA). 2000. pap. 12.95 (*0-7534-5303-7*, Kingfisher) LKC.

Medieval World: The History of European Society. Ed. by Jacques Le Goff. Tr. by Lydia G. Cochrane from ITA. 392p. (C). 1998. pap. text 15.00 (*0-7881-5535-0*) DIANE Pub.

Medieval World of Nature: A Book of Essays. Ed. by Joyce E. Salisbury. LC 92-27492. (Medieval Casebooks Ser.: Vol. 5). 288p. 1993. text 20.00 (*0-8153-0752-7*) Garland.

Medieval World View: An Introduction. William R. Cook & Ronald B. Herzman. (Illus.). 394p. 1983. pap. text 23.95 (*0-19-503090-7*) OUP.

Medieval Worlds: Barbarians, Heretics, & Artists in the Middle Ages. Arno Borst. Tr. by Eric Hansen. LC 91-36241. 288p. 1992. 45.00 (*0-226-06656-8*) U Ch Pr.

Medieval Worlds: Barbarians, Heretics, & Artists in the Middle Ages. Arno Borst. (Illus.). 274p. (C). 1996. reprint ed. pap. text 17.95 (*0-226-06657-6*) U Ch Pr.

Medieval Writers & Their Work: Middle English Literature, 1100-1500. J. A. Burrow. 158p. (C). 1982. pap. text 20.95 (*0-19-289122-7*) OUP.

Medieval York. Ed. by R. M. Butler. 1999. pap. 21.00 (*0-900657-69-3*, Pub. by W Sessions) St Mut.

Medievalia et Humanistica. Ed. by Paul M. Clogan. LC 47-36424. (Studies in Medieval & Renaissance Culture: No. 16). 232p. 1989. lib. bdg. 68.00 (*0-8476-7608-0*) Rowman.

Medievalia et Humanistica, No. 15. Ed. by Maurice Clogan. 244p. 1988. 75.50 (*0-8476-7582-3*) Rowman.

Medievalia et Humanistica, Vol. 11. Ed. by Paul M. Clogan. (New Studies in Medieval & Renaissance Culture: No. 11). 318p. (C). 1982. text 57.00 (*0-8476-7105-4*) Rowman.

Medievalia et Humanistica, Vol. 22. Ed. by Paul M. Clogan. (Studies in Renaissance Culture: No. 22). 352p. (C). 1995. lib. bdg. 65.00 (*0-8476-8099-1*) Rowman.

Medievalia et Humanistica: Studies in Medieval & Renaissance Culture. Ed. by Paul M. Clogan. (New Ser.: No. 10). 264p. 1981. 61.00 (*0-8476-6944-0*) Rowman.

Medievalia et Humanistica: Studies in Medieval & Renaissance Culture, Vol. 17. Ed. by Paul M. Clogan. 240p. 1991. 72.00 (*0-8476-7658-7*) Rowman.

Medievalia et Humanistica: Studies in Medieval & Renaissance Culture, Vol. 23. Ed. by Paul M. Clogan. 210p. 1996. lib. bdg. 71.50 (*0-8476-8272-2*) Rowman.

Medievalia et Humanistica: Studies in Medieval & Renaissance Culture, the Columbian Quincentenary. Ed. by Paul M. Clogan. (Medievalia et Humanistica Ser.: No. 19). 210p. (C). 1992. text 66.00 (*0-8476-7777-X*) Rowman.

Medievalia et Humanistica No. 18: Studies in Medieval & Renaissance Culture, No. 18. Ed. by Paul M. Clogan. 240p. (C). 1992. text 72.00 (*0-8476-7705-2*) Rowman.

Medievalia et Humanistica Vol. 24: Studies in Medieval & Renaissance Culture. Ed. by Paul M. Clogan. 304p. 1997. 71.50 (*0-8476-8674-4*) Rowman.

Medievalia et Humanistica (Studies in Medieval & Renaissance Culture) Ed. by Paul M. Clogan. (Medievalia et Humanistica Ser.: No. 42, Vo). 304p. 1998. 68.00 (*0-8476-9213-2*) Rowman.

Medievalism. George Tyrrell. 176p. 1994. pap. 24.00 (*0-86012-229-8*, Pub. by Srch Pr) St Mut.

Medievalism & the Ideologies of the Enlightenment: The World & Work of LaCurne de Sainte-Palaye. Lionel Gossman. LC 68-16274. 397p. reprint ed. pap. 123.10 (*0-8357-6612-8*, 203525700094) Bks Demand.

Medievalism & the Modernist Temper. Ed. by R. Howard Bloch & Stephen G. Nichols. (Parallax). (Illus.). 496p. 1996. text 60.00 (*0-8018-5086-X*); pap. text 19.95 (*0-8018-5087-8*) Johns Hopkins.

Medievalism of Lawrence of Arabia. M. D. Allen. LC 88-43433. 224p. 1991. lib. bdg. 32.50 (*0-271-00673-0*) Pa St U Pr.

Medievalist Impulse in American Literature: Twain, Adams, Fitzgerald, & Hemingway. Kim Moreland. 320p. (C). 1996. text 42.50 (*0-8139-1658-5*) U Pr of Va.

Medievalist in the Eighteenth Century. Wilson. (International Archives of the History of Ideas Ser.: No. 83). 1976. lib. bdg. 176.50 (*90-247-1782-5*) Kluwer Academic.

***MediEvil II: Prima's Official Strategy Guide.** Dimension Publishing Staff. 2000. pap. 14.99 (*0-7615-3006-1*) Prima Pub.

Medigap Insurance: A License to Steal. Frank W. Pandozzi. 61p. (Orig.). 1990. pap. 9.95 (*0-9628734-0-3*) Aa Zz Pub.

Medigap Insurance: Insurers' Compliance with Federal Minimum Loss Ratio Standards, 1988-1991. (Illus.). 45p. (Orig.). (C). 1994. pap. text 20.00 (*0-7881-1465-4*) DIANE Pub.

Medigap Insurance: Insurers' Compliance with Federal Minimum Loss Ratio Standards, 1988-93. (Illus.). 102p. (Orig.). (C). 1996. pap. text 35.00 (*0-7881-2885-X*) DIANE Pub.

Medii Aevi Kalendarium or Dates, Charters & Customs of the Middle Ages, 2 vols., Set. Robert T. Hampson. LC 76-29824. reprint ed. 74.50 (*0-404-16970-8*) AMS Pr.

Medikamentoese Therapie des Genital- Und Mammakarzinoms. 4th enl. rev. ed. M. Kaufmann et al. (Illus.). 106p. 1989. pap. 28.00 (*3-8055-5069-3*) S Karger.

Medina County Gazette Happenings, 1899. Sharon L. Kraynek. 54p. 1996. per. 5.00 (*1-55856-218-4*, 428) Closson Pr.

Medina County Gazette Happenings, 1878-1898. Sharon L. Kraynek. 113p. 1996. per. 8.00 (*1-55856-217-6*, 427) Closson Pr.

Medina County, Ohio Civil War Veterans. Sharon L. Kraynek. 64p. 1995. per. 6.00 (*1-55856-190-0*, 423) Closson Pr.

Medina County (Ohio) Gazette Newspaper Abstracts, 1854-1898. Sharon L. Kraynek. LC 97-65480. 288p. 1997. per. 21.00 (*1-55856-257-5*, 426) Closson Pr.

Medina County, Ohio Gleanings. Sharon L. Kraynek. LC 94-213088. 34p. 1994. per. 5.00 (*1-55856-171-4*, 425) Closson Pr.

Medina, Saudi Arabia: A Geographic Analysis of the City & Region. M. S. Makki. 242p. 1982. text 46.25 (*0-86127-301-X*) Ashgate Pub Co.

Medina vor dem Islam, Muhammeds Gemeindeordnung Von Medina: Seine Schriften und die Gesandtschaften an Ihn. Julius Wellhausen. (Skizzen und Vorarbeiten Ser.: 4 Heft). (ARA & GER.). 272p. 1985. 96.15 (*3-11-009764-8*) De Gruyter.

Medinas: Morocco's Hidden Cities. Tahar Ben Jelloun. 1998. 65.00 (*2-84323-051-9*, Pub. by Assouline) Rizzoli Intl.

Medina's Bostwick Practice Manual, 6 vols. Bender's Editors. 1949. ring bd. 1030.00 (*0-8205-1380-6*) Bender.

Medinet Habu - Epigraphic Survey: The Calendar, the Slaughterhouse, & Minor Records of Ramses III, Vol. 3. Harold H. Nelson. LC 30-6904. (Oriental Institute Publications: No. 23). 1934. lib. bdg. 70.00 (*0-226-62119-7*, OIP23) U Ch Pr.

Medinet Habu, 1924-28. Harold H. Nelson & Uvo Holscher. LC 29-13423. (Illus.). 50p. 1998. pap. text 6.00 (*0-226-62320-3*, OIC5) U Ch Pr.

Medinet Habu Studies, 1924-28. Uvo Holscher & John A. Wilson. LC 29-13423. (Illus.). 33p. 1998. pap. text 7.50 (*0-226-62323-8*, OIC7) U Ch Pr.

Medinfo, 1977: Proceedings of the World Conference, 2nd. Ed. by David B. Shires & H. K. Wolf. (IFIP Ser.). 1090p. 1977. 179.50 (*0-7204-0754-0*, North Holland) Elsevier.

***Mediocracy: French Philosophy since the Mid-1970's.** Dominique Lecourt. Tr. by Gregory Elliott. 240p. 2001. 27.00 (*1-85984-793-5*, Pub. by Verso) Norton.

Mediopollito. Allma F. Ada. (J). 1995. 21.95 (*0-385-44637-3*) BDD Bks Young Read.

Mediopollito. Carmen R. Izcoa & Nivea O. Montanez. 46p. (J). (gr. 1-3). 1996. 10.50 (*0-929157-43-5*) Ediciones Huracan.

Mediopollito, a Folktale in Spanish & English. Alma Flor Ada. (Dell Picture Yearling Ser.). 1997. 11.19 (*0-606-11612-5*, Pub. by Turtleback) Demco.

***Medios de Comunicacion y Violencia.** Sarah S. Garcia & Luciana L. Ramos. 520p. 1999. pap. 8.99 (*968-16-5653-9*) Fondo CA.

Medios de Transporte: Transportation - Spanish. Blanca Sagarna. (SPA., Illus.). 50p. (YA). (gr. 7 up). 1989. pap. text 25.00 incl. audio (*0-939990-75-X*) Intl Linguistics.

MediQuik Cards. 11th ed. SPC Staff. 1997. 28.95 incl. disk (*0-87434-879-X*) Springhouse Corp.

Mediquiz, Vol. 2. Ed. by Alfred J. Bollet & Allan H. Bruckheim. (Illus.). 344p. 50.00 (*0-935466-04-5*) Pierson Pubs.

***Medir y Ensamblar.** Two Can Publishing Ltd. Staff. 2000. mass mkt. 4.95 (*1-58728-967-9*) Two Can Pub.

Meditacion de la Noche. Angel Gaztelu. Ed. by Rosario Hiriart. (SPA.). 100p. (Orig.). 1997. pap. 15.00 (*1-887175-04-0*) ECV NY.

Meditacion en el Umbral (Meditation on the Threshold) Rosario Castellanos. (SPA.). 232p. 1985. pap. 8.99 (*968-16-1888-2*, Pub. by Fondo) Continental Bk.

Meditacion Segun la Mas Antigua Tradicion Budista. Luis Mojica-Sandoz. (UPREX, Manuales Ser.: No. 54). (SPA., Illus.). 92p. 1979. pap. text 1.50 (*0-8477-0054-2*) U of PR Pr.

Meditaciones Acres see Antologia Nueva De Nemesio Canales

Meditaciones Metafisicas: Oraciones, Afirmaciones y Visualizaciones Universales. rev. ed. Paramahansa Yogananda.Tr. of Metaphysical Meditations: Universal Prayers, Affirmations, & Visualizations. (SPA.). 170p. 1998. pap. 8.00 (*0-87612-048-6*, 1355) Self Realization.

Meditaciones para Ninos. Kenneth N. Taylor. Orig. Title: Devotions for the Children's Hour. (SPA., Illus.). 256p. 1981. pap. 5.99 (*0-8254-1707-4*, Edit Portavoz) Kregel.

Meditaciones para Sanar Tu Vida (Meditations to Heal Your Life) Louise L. Hay. 1995. 15.00 (*1-56170-319-2*) Hay House.

Meditaciones Vida Mas Profundo. Oswald Chambers. (SPA.). 1998. pap. 10.99 (*0-8297-0487-6*) Vida Pubs.

Meditacoes de Um Leigo. Tr. by Phillip W. Keller. (Portuguese Bks.).Tr. of Layman Looks at the Lord's Prayer. (POR.). 1979. 1.60 (*0-8297-0788-3*) Vida Pubs.

Meditacyuns on the Soper of Our Lord. Ed. by J. M. Cowper. (EETS, OS Ser.: No. 60). 1969. reprint ed. 30.00 (*0-527-00054-X*) Periodicals Srv.

Meditate: Happiness Lies Within You. Swami Muktananda. LC 98-32235. 80p. (Orig.). 1999. pap. 9.95 (*0-911307-62-1*) SYDA Found.

Meditating on the Mysteries: The Rosary As Biblical Prayer. Michel De Verteuil. 64p. 1998. pap. 7.95 (*1-85390-392-2*, 771, Pub. by Veritas Pubns) Irish Bks Media.

Meditating on the Word. large type ed. Dietrich Bonhoeffer. (Orig.). 1988. pap. 9.95 (*0-8027-2591-0*) Walker & Co.

Meditating with Children: A Practical Guide to the Use & Benefits of Basic Meditation Techniques. David Fontana & Ingrid Slack. LC 97-26610. 160p. 1998. pap. 10.95 (*1-86204-018-4*, Pub. by Element MA) Penguin Putnam.

Meditating with Children: The Art of Concentration & Centering. rev. ed. Deborah A. Rozman. LC 93-44420. (Illus.). 154p. 1994. pap. 16.95 (*1-879052-24-5*) Planetary Pubns.

Meditating with the Angels. Sonia Cafe & Neide Innecco. LC 94-17190. (Illus.). 96p. (Orig.). 1994. pap. 7.00 (*0-87728-812-7*) Weiser.

Meditation. Sri Aurobindo & Mother. Ed. by Vijay. 27p. 1996. pap. 1.00 (*81-7060-026-X*, Pub. by SAA) E-W Cultural Ctr.

Meditation. Dawn Goodrich. (Illus.). iv, 22p. 1997. pap. 7.00 (*0-9657367-0-9*) Less Pr.

Meditation. Monks of the Ramakrishna Order Staff. Ed. by Swami Bhavyananda. 161p. 1977. pap. 16.00 (*0-7025-0073-9*) Vedanta Pr.

Meditation. Sogyal Rinpoche. LC 94-13757. (Little Book of Wisdom Ser.). 96p. 1994. pap. 10.00 (*0-06-251114-9*, Pub. by Harper SF) HarpC.

M

Meditation. Walter Russell & Lao Russell. Ed. by Laara Lindo. 44p. 1997. pap. text 6.00 (*1-879605-49-X*) U Sci & Philos.

Meditation. Mouni Sadhu. 364p. 1977. pap. 10.00 (*0-87980-096-8*) Wilshire.

Meditation. Pam Smith. 187p. 1989. pap. 17.95 (*0-85207-214-7*, Pub. by C W Daniel) Natl Bk Netwk.

Meditation. Compiled by Ferdinand Wulliemier. (Sahaj Marg Educational Ser.). 254p. 1997. 20.00 (*0-945242-34-4*) Shri Ram Chandra.

Meditation. Juan Benet. Tr. by Gregory Rabassa from SPA.Tr. of Una Meditacion. 366p. (C). 1983. reprint ed. pap. 8.95 (*0-89255-065-1*) Persea Bks.

Meditation: A Handbook. Bill Howden. LC 94-69162. 53p. (Orig.). 1994. pap. 9.95 (*0-9643277-5-9*) DragonWagon.

Meditation: A Path To Consciousness. Der Merwe Merwede Van. 1998. pap. 14.95 (*0-7981-3702-9*) Human & Rousseau.

Meditation: A Practical Introduction to the Techniques, the Traditions & the Benefits. Erica Smith & Nicholas Wilks. (Illus.). 120p. 1997. pap. 13.95 (*0-09-181517-7*) Trafalgar.

Meditation: A Practical Study. Adelaide Gardner. LC 68-5856. 1968. pap. 5.95 (*0-8356-0105-6*, Quest) Theos Pub Hse.

Meditation: A Simple Eight-Point Program for Translating Spiritual Ideals into Daily Life. 2nd ed. Eknath Easwaran. LC 91-19426. Orig. Title: Meditation: Commonsense Directions for an Uncommon Life. 252p. 1991. pap. 12.95 (*0-915132-66-4*); text 22.00 (*0-915132-67-2*) Nilgiri Pr.

Meditation: A Three-Minute Guide for Self-Renewal. Gerhard Gschwandtner. LC 92-81659. (Illus.). 54p. (Orig.). 1992. pap. 5.00 (*0-939613-03-4*) Personal Selling.

Meditation: A Treasury of Technique. Pam Smith & Gordon Smith. (Illus.). (Orig.). pap. 26.95 (*0-8464-4252-3*) Beekman Pubs.

Meditation: A Way to Peace & Happiness. 2nd rev. ed. Daniel J. Thottakara. (Illus.). 108p. (Orig.). 1996. pap. text 10.00 (*0-9651395-1-4*) Cmisphna Ctr.

Meditation: Advice to Beginners. Bokar Rinpoche. Ed. by Jennifer Pessereau. LC 92-75390. (Illus.). 160p. (Orig.). 1993. pap. 14.95 (*0-9630371-1-0*) ClearPoint.

Meditation: Bringing Change into Your Life. 2nd rev. ed. Jorgen Smit. 48p. 1996. pap. 9.95 (*1-85584-090-1*, Pub. by R Steiner Pr) Anthroposophic.

Meditation: Cybernetics of Consciousness. Benito F. Reyes. Ed. by Fred J. Volz. 152p. 1978. pap. 10.00 (*0-939375-04-4*) World Univ Amer.

Meditation: Gateway to Light. rev. ed. Elsie Sechrist. 53p. 1972. pap. 4.95 (*0-87604-062-8*, 228) ARE Pr.

***Meditation: Geschichte, Systematik, Forschung, Theorie Stark Erweiterte und Uberarbeitete Zweite Auflage Unter Mitarbeit von Dorothea U. Joachim Galuska; Horst Kaemmerling; Eugenia U. Wilfried Kuhn; Matthias Steurich; Swami Ramateertha.** Klaus Engel. 479p. 1999. 63.95 (*3-631-34546-1*) P Lang Pubng.

Meditation: Guidance of the Inner Life. Friedrich Rittelmeyer. pap. 14.95 (*0-86315-065-9*, 359, Pub. by Floris Bks) Anthroposophic.

***Meditation: Introductory Guide to Relaxation for Mind & Body.** David Fontana. (New Perspectives Ser.). 2000. pap. 9.95 (*1-86204-627-1*, Pub. by Element MA) Penguin Putnam.

Meditation: Its Process, Practice, & Culmination. Swami Satprakashananda. LC 76-15722. 264p. 1976. 10.00 (*0-916356-55-8*) Vedanta Soc St Louis.

Meditation: Key to Spiritual Awakening. Mary Ellen Flora. LC 91-78135. (Key Ser.). (Illus.). 96p. 1992. pap. 7.95 (*0-9631993-0-7*) CDM Pubns.

***Meditation: Key to Spiritual Awakening.** 2nd rev. ed. Mary Ellen Flora. LC 00-25848. 128p. (C). 2000. pap. (*1-886983-11-9*) CDM Pubns.

Meditation: Man-Perfection in God-Satisfaction. Sri Chinmoy. (Illus.). 261p. (C). 1979. pap. 9.95 (*0-88497-444-8*) Aum Pubns.

Meditation: Meditation. Naomi Ozaniec. (Teach Yourself Ser.). (Illus.). 192p. 1998. pap. 9.95 (*0-8442-0018-2*, 00182) NTC Contemp Pub Co.

Meditation: On the Iron Testament. Panayotis Carageorgos. LC 99-187126. 60p. 1998. pap. 9.95 (*1-85756-385-9*, Pub. by Janus Pubng) Paul & Co Pubs.

Meditation: Payam-e-del. Moulana S. Maghsoud. Tr. by Nahid Angha from PER. (Illus.). 65p. (Orig.). 1994. pap. 10.00 (*0-918437-05-9*) Intl Sufism.

Meditation: Quieting the Conscious Mind. Dana Britton. 23p. 1989. ring bd. 2.00 (*0-944478-08-5*) Dock Pub Co.

Meditation: The Ancient Egyptian Path to Enlightenment. Muata A. Ashby. (Illus.). 260p. 1997. pap. 14.99 (*1-884564-26-7*) Cruzian Mystic.

Meditation: The Art of Ecstasy. Osho. Ed. by Ma Prem Mangla. 302p. 1992. 11.95 (*81-7261-000-9*, Pub. by Rebel Hse) Oshos.

Meditation: The Buddhist Way of Tranquility & Insight. Kamalashila. (Illus.). 284p. (Orig.). 1996. pap. 22.99 (*0-904766-56-X*) Windhorse Pubns.

Meditation: The Buddhist Way of Tranquility & Insight. Kamalashila. (Illus.). 304p. (Orig.). 1997. pap. 25.95 (*1-899579-05-2*) Windhorse Pubns.

Meditation: The Complete Guide. Patricia Monaghan & Eleanor G. Viereck. LC 99-34298. 384p. 1999. pap. 16.95 (*1-57731-088-8*) New Wrld Lib.

Meditation: The First & Last Freedom. Osho. LC 96-9227. 304p. 1996. text 22.95 (*0-312-14820-8*) St Martin.

Meditation: The Inner Way. Naomi Humphrey. (Illus.). 160p. (Orig.). 1988. pap. 5.95 (*0-85030-508-X*, Pub. by Aqrn Pr) HarpC.

Meditation: The Journey to Your Inner World. Eidan Or. (Astrolog Complete Guide Ser.). (Illus.). 128p. 1998. mass mkt. 6.95 (*965-494-008-6*, Pub. by Astrolog Pub) Assoc Pubs Grp.

Meditation: White Eagle's Method of Creative Meditation. Grace Cooke. 176p. 1955. pap. (*0-85487-059-8*) White Eagle.

Meditation Pt. 2: Meditation, Endocrine Glands, Prayer, & Affirmations. Ed. by Association for Research & Enlightenment, Readings. (Library: Vol. 3). 274p. 1995. lib. bdg. 22.95 (*0-87604-082-2*, 1103) ARE Pr.

Meditation Vol. I: History & Present Time. Klaus Engel. 243p. 1997. 48.95 (*3-631-31600-3*) P Lang Pubng.

Meditation Vol. I: History & Present Time. expanded ed. Klaus Engel. Tr. by A. H. Davies from GER. LC 97-30758. (Illus.). 243p. 1997. 48.95 (*0-8204-3273-3*) P Lang Pubng.

Meditation Vol. 1: Key to New Horizons in God. 2nd ed. E. Bernard Jordan. Ed. by Deborah Jones. (Illus.). 80p. (Orig.). 1991. reprint ed. pap. 10.00 (*0-939241-11-0*) Faith Print.

Meditation Vol. II: Empirical Research & Theory. Klaus Engel. 178p. 1997. 39.95 (*3-631-31690-9*) P Lang Pubng.

Meditation Vol. II: Empirical Research & Theory. Klaus Engel. 178p. (C). 1997. text 39.95 (*0-8204-3275-X*) P Lang Pubng.

Meditation, a Foundation Course: A Book of Ten Lessons. 2nd rev. ed. Barry Long. LC 96-96014. 160p. 1995. pap. 10.95 (*1-899324-00-3*) B Long Bks.

Meditation According to Rudolf Steiner. Ernst Katz. LC 93-31318. (Illus.). 64p. 1993. pap. 8.00 (*0-9613745-1-9*) R Steiner Inst GL.

Meditation & Human Growth: A Practical Manual for Higher Consciousness. Genevieve L. Paulson. LC 93-42899. (New Age Ser.). (Illus.). 224p. 1999. pap. 12.95 (*0-87542-599-2*) Llewellyn Pubns.

Meditation & Its Methods. Swami Vivekananda. Ed. by Swami Chetanananda. LC 75-36392. 128p. (Orig.). 1976. pap. 6.95 (*0-87481-030-2*) Vedanta Pr.

Meditation & Its Practice. rev. ed. Swami Rama. (Illus.). 110p. 1998. pap. 12.95 (*0-89389-153-3*) Himalayan Inst.

***Meditation & Its Preparation.** Swami Prabhavananda et al. 209p. 2000. pap. 4.95 (*81-7505-195-7*) Vedanta Pr.

Meditation & Kabbalah. Aryeh Kaplan. LC 94-34570. 368p. 1995. text 50.00 (*1-56821-381-6*) Aronson.

Meditation & Kabbalah. Aryeh Kaplan. LC 81-70150. (Illus.). 364p. 1982. reprint ed. pap. 15.95 (*0-87728-616-7*) Weiser.

Meditation & Life. rev. ed. Swami Chinmayananda. (Self-Discovery Ser.). (Illus.). 208p. (C). 1992. pap. 12.00 (*1-880687-00-3*) Chinmaya Pubns.

***Meditation & Mantras: An Authoritative Text by Vishnu Devananda.** Vishnu Devananda. 267p. 1999. pap. 75.00 (*81-208-1615-3*, Pub. by Motilal Bnarsidass) St Mut.

Meditation & Other Spiritual Disciplines. Swami Swahananda. 171p. pap. 4.95 (*81-85301-85-9*, Pub. by Advaita Ashrama) Vedanta Pr.

Meditation & Protection: A Guide to Development of Individual Spirituality. Hermit Staff. Ed. & Intro. by Marc Taubman. (Illus.). 204p. 1994. pap. 19.95 (*0-9643827-0-9*) AUM Pubns NM.

Meditation & Spiritual Life. Swami Yatiswarananda. 735p. 1980. 22.95 (*0-87481-403-0*) Vedanta Pr.

Meditation & the Art of Dying. Pandit Usharbudh Arya. LC 78-78252. 179p. 1979. pap. 12.95 (*0-89389-056-1*) Himalayan Inst.

Meditation & the Bible. Aryeh Kaplan. LC 94-34572. 192p. 1995. text 30.00 (*1-56821-382-4*) Aronson.

Meditation & the Bible. Aryeh Kaplan. LC 84-50350. (Illus.). 192p. 1979. pap. 14.95 (*0-87728-617-5*) Weiser.

Meditation & the Fullness of Life. Jim Wilson. 76p. 1974. pap. 5.00 (*0-227-67810-9*) Attic Pr.

Meditation & the Transformation of Mind. Kamalshila et al. 36p. (Orig.). 1995. pap. 3.95 (*0-904766-25-X*) Windhorse Pubns.

Meditation & Yoga Retreats: An International Directory. Compiled by Frieda Carrol. 200p. 1983. ring bd. 23.95 (*0-913597-06-6*) Prosperity & Profits.

Meditation As an Intervention in Stress Reactivity. Amarjit S. Sethi. LC 86-82027. (Stress in Modern Society Ser.: No. 12). 1987. 32.50 (*0-404-63260-2*) AMS Pr.

Meditation Book. John R. Price. LC 98-3340. 112p. 1998. pap. 7.00 (*1-56170-502-0*, 866) Hay House.

Meditation Breakthrough for the Western World: Bridge to Eternity. Ralph White. LC 95-91012. xvi, 192p. (Orig.). 1996. pap. 13.95 (*0-9651085-0-3*) White Lght NC.

Meditation: Commonsense Directions for an Uncommon Life see Meditation: A Simple Eight-Point Program for Translating Spiritual Ideals into Daily Life

Meditation, Compassion & Lovingkindness: An Approach to Vipassana Practice. Steve Weissman & Rosemary Weissman. LC 96-581. 224p. (Orig.). 1996. pap. 12.95 (*0-87728-852-6*) Weiser.

Meditation Differently. Herbert V. Guenther. (C). 1992. text 16.00 (*81-208-0870-3*, Pub. by Motilal Bnarsidass) S Asia.

Meditation Disciplines & Personal Integration. Manly P. Hall. LC 79-3691. 76p. 1979. reprint ed. pap. 4.95 (*0-89314-800-8*) Philos Res.

Meditation, Ecstasy & Illumination. Swami Ashokananda. 261p. (Orig.). 1991. pap. 6.95 (*0-87481-238-0*, Pub. by Advaita Ashrama) Vedanta Pr.

Meditation for Absolutely Everyone: A Complete Guide. Subagh S. Khalsa. LC 94-6862. 96p. 1994. pap. 16.95 incl. audio (*0-8048-3011-8*) Tuttle Pubng.

Meditation for Beginners. Naomi Ozaniec. (Headway Guide for Beginners Ser.). (Illus.). 88p. 1996. mass mkt. 11.95 (*0-340-64835-X*, Pub. by Headway) Trafalgar.

Meditation for Busy People: Sixty Seconds to Serenity. Dawn Groves. LC 92-12734. 160p. 1993. pap. 10.95 (*1-880032-02-3*) New Wrld Lib.

***Meditation for Dummies: A Reference for the Rest of Us.** Stephan Bodian. LC 99-60185. 384p. 1999. pap. 19.99 (*0-7645-5116-7*) IDG Bks.

Meditation for Every Day. Bill Anderton. 1999. pap. 6.95 (*0-7499-1871-3*, Pub. by Piatkus Bks) London Brdge.

Meditation for Everyday. Bill Anderton. LC 97-109285. 250p. (Orig.). 1996. pap. text 14.95 (*0-7499-1485-8*, Pub. by Piatkus Bks) London Brdge.

Meditation for Extremely Busy People, 3 cass., Vol. 1. Mike George. (Illus.). 1997. wbk. ed. write for info. incl. audio (*1-886872-11-2*) Brahma Kumaris.

Meditation for Healing: Particular Meditations for Particular Results. Justin F. Stone. 182p. 1995. pap. 14.95 (*1-882290-00-3*) Good Karma.

Meditation for Inner Peace: Your Guide to Relaxation & True Happiness see Peace Within the Stillness: Relaxation & Meditation for True Happiness

Meditation for Kids: And Other Beings. Laurie F. Huck. (Illus.). 72p. (Orig.). (YA). (gr. 7 up). 1996. pap. 5.95 (*0-8348-0355-0*) Weatherhill.

Meditation for Little People. Anne Langford. LC 75-46191. (Illus.). 40p. (J). (gr. k-4). 1976. reprint ed. pap. 7.95 (*0-87516-211-8*) DeVorss.

Meditation for Peace & Happiness. Rajinder Singh. 120p. (Orig.). 1993. 15.00 incl. audio (*0-918224-35-7*) S K Pubns.

Meditation for Spiritual Growth. Terry L. Bear. 56p. 1999. pap. 10.00 (*0-9655514-9-0*) Inspiring Word.

Meditation for Starters. J. Donald Walters. 136p. 1996. pap. 9.95 (*1-56589-079-5*) Crystal Clarity.

Meditation for Starters. unabridged ed. J. Donald Walters. 1996. pap. 19.95 incl. audio compact disk (*1-56589-080-9*); pap. 17.95 incl. audio (*1-56589-736-6*); audio compact disk 15.95 (*1-56589-077-9*) Crystal Clarity.

Meditation for Transformation. Samuel A. Holland. 96p. 1989. pap. 9.95 (*0-9625402-0-X*) Altan Pub.

Meditation from the Heart of Judaism: Today's Teachers Share Their Practices, Techniques & Faith. Ed. by Avram Davis. LC 97-35827. 256p. 1997. 21.95 (*1-879045-77-X*) Jewish Lights.

Meditation from the Heart of Judaism: Today's Teachers Share Their Practices, Techniques & Faith. Ed. by Avram Davis. 256p. 1999. pap. 16.95 (*1-58023-049-0*) Jewish Lights.

Meditation from Thought to Action. C. Alexander Simpkins & Annellen M. Simpkins. LC 98-27437. (Illus.). 128p. 1998. pap. 16.95 (*0-8048-3115-7*) Tuttle Pubng.

Meditation Game: Strategy. Layman E. Allen. 1976. pap. 2.00 (*0-911624-41-4*) Wffn Proof.

Meditation Handbook: A Practical Guide to Buddhist Meditation. 3rd ed. Geshe K. Gyatso. (Illus.). 160p. 13.95 (*0-948006-44-7*, Pub. by Tharpa Pubns) ACCESS Pubs Network.

***Meditation Handbook: A Step by Step Manual, Providing a Clear & Practical Guide to Buddhist Meditation.** Geshe K. Gyatso. 144p. 1999. pap. 50.00 (*81-208-1677-3*, Pub. by Motilal Bnarsidass) St Mut.

***Meditation in Action.** Shambhala Publications Staff. 1999. pap. write for info. (*1-56957-115-5*, Pub. by Shambhala Pubns) Random.

Meditation in Action. Chogyam Trungpa. LC 90-53385. (Pocket Classics Ser.). 168p. 1991. reprint ed. pap. 6.95 (*0-87773-550-6*, Pub. by Shambhala Pubns) Random.

Meditation in Christianity. rev. ed. Swami Rama et al. LC 79-92042. 130p. 1983. pap. 12.95 (*0-89389-085-5*) Himalayan Inst.

Meditation in Sankaras Vedanta. Jonathan Bader. (C). 1990. 22.50 (*81-85179-51-4*, Pub. by Aditya Prakashan) S Asia.

***Meditation Is Boring? Putting Life in Your Spiritual Practice.** Linda Johnsen. LC 99-88453. 144p. 2000. pap. 13.95 (*0-89389-179-7*) Himalayan Inst.

Meditation Journal. Amber Lotus. 112p. 1998. spiral bd. 8.95 (*0-945798-27-X*) Amber Lotus.

Meditation Kit, Boxed Set: The Complete Pack for Meditation & Visualization. Charla Devereux & Fran Stockel. LC 97-16729. 128p. 1997. 27.95 incl. audio (*1-885203-48-9*) Jrny Editions.

Meditation Made Easy. Lorin Roche. LC 98-22600. (Illus.). 208p. 1998. pap. 16.00 (*0-06-251542-X*, Pub. by Harper SF) HarpC.

***Meditation Made Easy: An Introduction to the Basics of the Ancient Art of Meditation.** Richard Craze. LC 99-20346. 64p. 1999. pap. text 7.95 (*0-8069-9909-8*) Sterling.

***Meditation Made Easy: Roche,&Lorin.** abr. ed. Lorin Roche. 1998. audio 12.00 (*0-694-52069-1*, CPN10168) HarperAudio.

Meditation Magic: A Course in Freedom & Dreaming. Anami. LC 96-910553. (Illus.). 240p. (Orig.). pap. 15.00 (*0-9635756-0-0*) Beyond Bks.

Meditation of Fire: The Art of James C. Watkins. Kippra D. Hopper. LC 99-10124. 144p. 1999. write for info. (*0-89672-419-0*) Tex Tech Univ Pr.

Meditation of the Sad Soul. Geoffrey Wigoder. 15.00 (*0-8386-3052-9*) Fairleigh Dickinson.

Meditation on a Skull Carved in Crystal. John Haimes. (Illus.). 20p. 1989. 25.00 (*0-918116-56-2*) Brooding Heron Pr.

Meditation on Emptiness. 2nd rev. ed. Jeffrey Hopkins. Ed. by Elizabeth S. Napper. LC 95-25827. (Illus.). 992p. (C). 1996. pap. 29.95 (*0-86171-110-6*) Wisdom MA.

Meditation on God. John T. Ferrier. 24p. 1973. pap. text 5.00 (*0-900235-59-4*) Order Of The Cross.

Meditation on Swami Vivekananda. Swami Tathagatananda. LC 94-60790. 322p. 1994. write for info. (*0-9603104-0-1*) Vedanta NY.

Meditation on the Threshold: A Bilingual Anthology of Poetry. Rosario Castellanos. Tr. by Julian Palley. LC 87-73552. (ENG & SPA.). 176p. 1988. pap. 15.00 (*0-916950-80-8*) Biling Rev-Pr.

***Meditation Pack.** Eddie Shapiro. 2000. 19.95 (*0-8069-3629-0*) Sterling.

Meditation Practice & Yoga Techniques: An Authoritative Guide by Sankara, India's Greatest Religious & Philosophical Genius. Njali Pata & Acarya Sankar. Ed. & Tr. by Trevor Leggett. LC 97-51367. 275p. 1998. 31.00 (*0-7103-0614-8*, Pub. by Kegan Paul Intl) Col U Pr.

Meditation Prayer on Mary Immaculate. Padre Pio. (Illus.). 28p. 1992. pap. 1.50 (*0-89555-099-7*) TAN Bks Pubs.

Meditation Revolution: A History & Theology of the Siddha Yoga Lineage. Douglas R. Brooks. LC 97-73501. (Illus.). 711 p. 1997. 24.95 (*0-9654096-0-0*) Agama Pr.

***Meditation Sourcebook: Meditation for Mortals.** Holly Sumner. 320p. 2000. pap. 15.95 (*0-7373-0396-4*, 03964W, Pub. by Lowell Hse) NTC Contemp Pub Co.

Meditation Sourcebook: Meditation for Mortals. Holly Sumner. LC 98-75385. 320p. 1999. 26.95 (*0-7373-0038-8*, 00388W) NTC Contemp Pub Co.

Meditation Symbols in Eastern & Western Mysticism: Mysteries of the Mandala. Manly P. Hall. 1988. 49.95 (*0-89314-543-2*); pap. 29.95 (*0-89314-829-6*) Philos Res.

Meditation (T. M.) & Yoga: Index of New Information. James J. Wigley. 160p. 1998. 47.50 (*0-7883-1724-5*); pap. 44.50 (*0-7883-1725-3*) ABBE Pubs Assn.

Meditation Temples of Thailand: A Guide. Joe Cummings. (Illus.). 100p. (Orig.). 1990. pap. 10.95 (*1-879220-15-6*) Wayfarer Bks.

Meditation the Answer to Your Prayers. Jerry L. Rothermel. 99p. (C). 1987. reprint ed. pap. 4.95 (*0-944386-01-6*) SOM Pub.

Meditation, the Highway to Happiness. 3rd ed. Richard J. Green. 40p. 1980. reprint ed. pap. 3.00 (*0-87516-407-2*) DeVorss.

Meditation, the Theory & Practice. Douglas M. Baker. 1975. pap. 32.00 (*0-906006-74-0*, Pub. by Baker Pubns) New Leaf Dist.

Meditation Theme for Each Day. 2nd ed. Inayat Khan. 108p. 1999. reprint ed. pap. 10.00 (*0-930872-45-2*) Omega Pubns NY.

Meditation Therapy: Short-Term Decision-Making for Couples & Families in Crisis. Janet M. Wiseman. 216p. 1990. 34.95 (*0-669-20421-8*) Lxngtn Bks.

Meditation Throughout the Day. Vasanthi Bhat. 1999. pap. text 12.95 (*0-9655499-1-7*) Vasantha Yoga.

Meditation Tools Made Simple. write for info. (*0-9649990-4-8*) Transform WA.

Meditation Workbook. Greer Allica. 116p. 1994. pap. 22.00 (*0-86012-193-3*, Pub. by Srch Pr) St Mut.

Meditationes de Prima Philosophia see Meditations on First Philosophy: In Which the Existence of God & the Distinction of the Soul from the Body Are Demonstrated

Meditationes de Prima Philosophia: Meditations Metaphysiques. Rene Descartes & G. Lewis. (FRE & LAT.). 178p. 1967. 24.95 (*0-8288-9578-3*, 2711601854) Fr & Eur.

Meditationes Philosophiae. Gottlieb Canz. (GER.). 1016p. 1996. reprint ed. 198.00 (*3-487-10221-8*) G Olms Pubs.

Meditations see Rationalists: 5 Basic Works on Rationalism

Meditations see Pensamientos

Meditations. (Illus.). 345p. 1996. 45.00 (*1-885206-40-2*, Iliad Pr) Cader Pubng.

Meditations. Marcus Aurelius. Tr. by George Long from LAT. LC 97-18832. (Dover Thrift Editions Ser.). (Illus.). 128p. 1997. pap. 1.50 (*0-486-29823-X*) Dover.

Meditations. Marcus Aurelius. Ed. by G. P. Goold. (Loeb Classical Library: No. 58). 448p. 1930. 19.95 (*0-674-99064-1*) HUP.

Meditations. Marcus Aurelius. Tr. & Intro. by Maxwell Staniforth. (Classics Ser.). 192p. (YA). (gr. 9 up). 1964. pap. 13.99 (*0-14-044140-9*, Penguin Classics) Viking Penguin.

Meditations. Marcus Aurelius. Tr. by George Long. LC 91-61906. (Great Books in Philosophy). 122p. 1991. pap. 5.95 (*0-87975-702-7*) Prometheus Bks.

Meditations. Anthony Bloom. 1970. pap. 11.95 (*0-87193-010-2*) Dimension Bks.

Meditations. Ladislaus Boros. 110p. 1990. pap. 24.00 (*0-85532-316-7*, Pub. by Srch Pr) St Mut.

***Meditations.** Gaydell Bradley. 1999. pap. write for info. (*1-58235-181-3*) Watermrk Pr.

***Meditations.** Sylvia Browne. LC 99-87364. (Illus.). 128p. 2001. 9.95 (*1-56170-719-8*, 5026) Hay House.

Meditations. Alphonse De Lamartine. pap. 9.95 (*0-685-23882-2*) Fr & Eur.

Meditations. Alphonse De Lamartine. Ed. by Fernand Letessier. (Coll. Prestige). 49.95 (*0-685-34927-6*); pap. 28.50 (*0-685-34926-8*) Fr & Eur.

Meditations. J. Krishnamurti. 1999. pap. 6.00 (*1-57062-431-3*, Pub. by Shambhala Pubns) Random.

Meditations. Jiddu Krishnamurti. LC 91-52605. (Pocket Classics Ser.). 96p. 1991. pap. 6.00 (*0-87773-640-5*, Pub. by Shambhala Pubns) Random.

Meditations. Thomas Moore. 1996. pap. 13.50 (*0-614-17409-0*) HarpC.

Meditations. Erwin K. Rohr. (Illus.). 260p. 1989. 13.95 (*0-931660-07-6*) R Oman Pub.

Meditations. Pepper Worthington. LC 93-80104. (Illus.). 202p. (Orig.). 1996. pap. 25.00 (*1-880994-23-2*) Mt Olive Coll Pr.

An Asterisk (*) at the beginning of an entry indicates that the title is appearing for the first time.

Meditations. Marcus Aurelius. Ed. & Tr. by G. M. A. Grube from GRE. LC 83-22722. (HPC Classics Ser.). 170p. (C). 1984. reprint ed. pap. text 6.95 (*0-915145-79-0*); reprint ed. lib. bdg. 24.95 (*0-915145-78-2*) Hackett Pub.

Meditations . . . A Collection of Poems for & about Children. Emory H. Jennings. (Collection of Poems for & about Children). 76p. (J). (gr. k-6). 1992. pap. 7.95 (*1-885754-01-9*) E H Jennings.

***Meditations: A New Guide Book to Simple Wisdom, with Book & Meditation Cards.** Running Press Staff. 128p. 2000. 9.98 (*0-7624-0771-9*) Running Pr.

Meditations: A Woman's Personal Journal, with Quotations. Running Press Staff. 144p. 1997. 14.95 (*0-7624-0052-8*) Running Pr.

Meditations: Creative Visualization & Meditation Exercises to Enrich Your Life. Shakti Gawain. LC 91-41411. 104p. 1991. pap. 9.95 (*0-931432-68-5*) New Wrld Lib.

Meditations: On the Monk Who Dwells in Daily Life. Thomas Moore. 128p. 1995. pap. 10.00 (*0-06-092700-3*, Harp PBks) HarpC.

Meditations: Text & Discourse in Media Studies. Andrew Tolson. LC 95-35893. (Illus.). 256p. 1996. pap. text 18.95 (*0-340-57489-5*) OUP.

Meditations: 365 Days with Shai Sathya Baba. Dominga L. Reyes. 1987. 6.00 (*0-939375-01-X*) World Univ Amer.

Meditations - A Year Book. James Allen. 366p. 1992. pap. 30.00 (*0-89540-192-4*, SB-192) Sun Pub.

Meditations Algebraicae, an English Translation of the Work of Edward Waring. Ed. by D. Weeks. LC 91-17347. 459p. 1991. text 94.00 (*0-8218-0169-4*, WARINGC) Am Math.

Meditations & Disquisitions. Richard Baker. 1995. 23.99 (*0-87377-997-5*) GAM Pubns.

Meditations & Inspirations. Virginia M. Satir. LC 85-13302. 96p. (Orig.). 1995. pap. 6.95 (*0-89087-421-2*) Celestial Arts.

Meditations & Mandalas: Simple Songs for the Spiritual Life. Nan C. Merrill. LC 73-163479. (Illus.). 208p. 1999. 19.95 (*0-8264-1151-7*) Continuum.

***Meditations & Other Metaphysical Writings.** Rene Descartes. (Penguin Classics Ser.). 256p. 1999. pap. 9.95 (*0-14-044701-6*, Penguin Classics) Viking Penguin.

Meditations & Positive Thoughts for Pregnancy & Birth. Gilli Moorhawk. 128p. 1995. text 14.95 (*0-7499-1395-9*, Pub. by Piatkus Bks) London Brdge.

Meditations Before Mass see Preparing Yourself for Mass

Meditations Boxed Set, 3 bks. Incl. Word Embodied Cycle A: Meditations on the Sunday Scriptures. John Kavanaugh. LC 98-20947. 140p. 1998. pap. 13.00 (*1-57075-198-6*); Word Encountered: Meditations on the Sunday Scriptures. John F. Kavanaugh. LC 96-13794. 140p. (Orig.). 1996. pap. 12.00 (*1-57075-093-9*); Word Engaged: Meditations on the Sunday Readings C-Cycle. John F. Kavanaugh. LC 97-6701. 144p. (Orig.). 1997. pap. 12.00 (*1-57075-137-4*); 33.00 (*1-57075-222-2*) Orbis Bks.

Meditations by John Baptist de La Salle. John B. De La Salle. Ed. by Augustine Loes et al. Tr. by Richard Arnandez from FRE. LC 94-70440. (Lasallian Sources, the Complete Works of John Baptist de La Salle: Vol. 4). (Illus.). xviii, 506p. 1994. 25.00 (*0-944808-11-5*) Lasallian Pubns.

Meditations by John Baptist de la Salle. John B. De La Salle. Ed. by Augustine Loes et al. Tr. by Richard Arnandez from FRE. LC 94-70440. (Lasallian Sources, the Complete Works of John Baptist de La Salle: Vol. 4). (Illus.). xviii, 506p. 1994. pap. 20.00 (*0-944808-12-3*) Lasallian Pubns.

Meditations by the Sea. Delia Halverson. 256p. 1999. pap. 9.95 (*1-896836-30-5*) NStone Publ.

Meditations Day by Day. Ali k. Maksad. 1998. pap. write for info. (*1-57553-776-1*) Watermrk Pr.

Meditations, 1596-98. Gaspar de Loarte et al. LC 77-379708. (English Recusant Literature Ser.). 102 p. 1977. write for info. (*0-85967-397-9*) Ashgate Pub Co.

Meditations for a Miserable Christmas. Dan Goodman. 1997. mass mkt. 8.99 (*0-312-96462-5*) St Martin.

Meditations for a Miserable Millennium. Dan Goodman. 112p. 1996. mass mkt. 7.99 (*0-312-95921-4*, St Martins Paperbacks) St Martin.

***Meditations for Actors: For the Actor Within Us All.** Carra Robertson. LC 00-90361. (Illus.). vi, 82p. 2000. pap. 10.00 (*0-9679837-0-3*) Dablond.

Meditations for Adoptive Parents. Vernell K. Miller. LC 92-18480. (Illus.). 88p. (Orig.). 1992. pap. 8.99 (*0-8361-3606-3*) Herald Pr.

Meditations for Alcoholics & Their Families. Ed. by Judy Osgood. LC 92-41267. (Gilgal Meditations Ser.). 72p. 1993. pap. 6.95 (*0-916895-04-1*) Gilgal Pubns.

***Meditations for Altar Guild Members.** Caroline Conklin. Ed. by Christopher L. Webber. 96p. 2000. pap. 6.95 (*0-8192-1845-6*, 6293) Morehouse Pub.

Meditations for Awakening. 2nd rev. ed. Larry Moen. LC 93-37569. 247p. 1994. pap. 11.95 (*1-880698-77-3*, Pub. by US Pub FL) ACCESS Pubs Network.

Meditations for Bereaved Parents. Ed. by Judy Osgood. LC 86-15003. (Gilgal Meditations Ser.). 72p. (Orig.). 1984. pap. 6.95 (*0-916895-00-9*) Gilgal Pubns.

Meditations for Cats Who Do Too Much: Learning to Take Things One Life at a Time. Michael Cader. LC 92-38347. (Illus.). 96p. (Orig.). 1993. pap. 5.95 (*0-14-017799-X*, Penguin Bks) Viking Penguin.

***Meditations for Church School Teachers.** Nell Noonan. 96p. 2001. pap. 6.95 (*0-8192-1861-8*) Morehouse Pub.

Meditations for Compulsive People: Creating Healthy Spirituality. rev. ed. Leo Booth. (Illus.). 136p. 1995. pap. 10.00 (*0-9623282-2-7*) SCP Ltd.

Meditations for Daily Devotionals see Selecciones de Aliento Cotidiano

Meditations for Deepening Love. Christopher A. Anderson. LC 93-74325. (Illus.). 206p. 1994. 15.50 (*0-931353-36-X*) Andersons Pubns.

Meditations for Healing. rev. ed. Larry Moen & Patty Smith. LC 93-34926. (Illus.). 264p. 1994. reprint ed. pap. 11.95 (*1-880698-69-2*) US Pub FL.

Meditations for Healing. 2nd ed. Larry Moen. 247p. 1999. reprint ed. pap. 13.95 (*0-9627209-2-5*) New Leaf Dist.

Meditations for Healing the Earth. Salle M. Redfield. 1997. write for info. (*0-446-52044-6*) Warner Bks.

Meditations for Incest Survivors. 1992. per. 9.95 (*0-13-567413-1*) P-H.

Meditations for Korean American Families. Hea-Sue Kim. 11.00 (*0-687-01818-8*) Abingdon.

Meditations for Lay Eucharistic Ministers. Beth Maynard. LC 98-55966. (Faithful Servants Ser.). 96p. 1999. pap. 6.95 (*0-8192-1770-0*) Morehouse Pub.

Meditations for Lay Readers. Suzanne E. Hunger. LC 98-55385. (Faithful Servants Ser.). 96p. 1999. pap. 6.95 (*0-8192-1771-9*) Morehouse Pub.

Meditations for Lent. Aquinas, Thomas, Saint. Tr. by Philip Hughes. 141p. 1999. reprint ed. 16.95 (*0-912141-68-9*) Roman Cath Bks.

Meditations for Life: Meditations for Personal Prayer. James R. Dolan. (Illus.). 180p. 1992. pap. text. write for info. (*0-9632750-4-6*) McQuaid Jesuit.

Meditations for Life! - The Wisdom of Women: Empowering Meditations Based on the Quotes from Women of the Past & Present. Terry D. Karanen. LC 99-167831. 160p. 1998. pap. 10.95 (*1-893268-23-3*) LoneWolf Pubg.

***Meditations for Living In Balance: Daily Solutions for People Who Do Too Much.** Anne Wilson Schaef. 384p. 2000. pap. 14.00 (*0-06-251643-4*) Harper SF.

Meditations for Meetings: Thoughtful Meditations for Board Meetings & for Leaders. Edgar Stoesz. LC 98-53690. 120p. 1998. pap. 9.95 (*1-56148-244-7*) Good Bks PA.

Meditations for Men Who Do Too Much. Jonathon Lazear. LC 92-20030. (Fireside - Parkside Recovery Bk.). 400p. 1992. pap. 9.00 (*0-671-75908-6*, Fireside) S&S Trade Pap.

Meditations for Messies: A Guide to Order & Serenity. Sandra Felton. LC 92-5474. (Illus.). 122p. (Orig.). (gr. 10). 1992. pap. 7.99 (*0-8007-5447-6*) Revell.

***Meditations for Ministers.** Mark G. Boyer. LC 00-101209. 160p. 2000. pap. 9.95 (*0-87946-213-2*) ACTA Pubns.

Meditations for Moms-to-Be. Sandra D. Lehman. LC 95-36210. 284p. 1995. pap. 7.95 (*1-56148-182-3*) Good Bks PA.

Meditations for Mother. rev. ed. Michael C. Pratt. Ed. by Boyce Mouton. 50p. 1975. pap. 1.99 (*0-89900-651-5*) College Pr Pub.

Meditations for Mothers: Moments with God amidst a Busy Nest. Elisa Morgan. LC 98-32032. 2000. 14.99 (*0-310-22654-6*) Zondervan.

Meditations for Mothers of Toddlers. Beth W. Saavedra. LC 94-21500. (Illus.). 320p. (Orig.). 1994. pap. 7.95 (*1-56305-566-X*, 3566) Workman Pub.

Meditations for New Members: Faithful Servants. June J. McInerney. Ed. by Christopher L. Webber. LC 99-37583. 96p. 1999. pap. 6.95 (*0-8192-1821-9*) Morehouse Pub.

Meditations for New Moms. Sandra Drescher-Lehman. LC 94-32940. (Illus.). 302p. 1994. pap. 7.95 (*1-56148-132-7*) Good Bks PA.

Meditations for New Mothers. Beth W. Saavedra. LC 91-50961. (Illus.). 352p. 1992. pap. 6.95 (*1-56305-181-8*, 3181) Workman Pub.

Meditations for New Parents. Sara W. Shenk & N. Gerald Shenk. LC 95-48808. 80p. (Orig.). 1996. pap. 8.99 (*0-8361-9038-6*) Herald Pr.

Meditations for Parents Who Do Too Much. Jonathon Lazear & Wendy Lazear. LC 93-12432. (Meditation Bk.). 400p. (Orig.). 1993. pap. 10.00 (*0-671-79635-6*, Fireside) S&S Trade Pap.

Meditations for People in Charge: A Handbook for Men & Women Whose Decisions Affect the World. Paul Brunton et al. Ed. & Pref. by Paul Cash. 112p. (Orig.). 1995. pap. 10.95 (*0-943914-72-8*) Larson Pubns.

Meditations for People in Crisis. Paul Brunton. Ed. & Selected by Sam Cohen. 112p. (Orig.). 1996. pap. 10.95 (*0-943914-77-9*) Larson Pubns.

Meditations for People Who May Worry Too Much. Anne W. Schaef. 384p. (Orig.). 1999. pap. 12.00 (*0-345-39406-2*) Ballantine Pub Grp.

***Meditations for People who Worry.** Anne W. Schaef. 1999. pap. 12.00 (*0-345-91514-3*) Ballantine Pub Grp.

Meditations for Piano. 96p. 1997. pap. 12.95 (*1-57623-863-6*, BP3367A) Wrner Bros.

Meditations for Pregnancy. Duncan Lavery. 1999. text. write for info. (*0-312-24558-0*) St Martin.

Meditations for Revival: Revival Principles from the Parables of Jesus. 90p. (Orig.). (YA). (gr. 10 up). 1997. pap. 10.00 (*0-614-29709-5*) Prayer Resources.

Meditations for Self-Discovery: Guided Journeys for Communicating with Your Inner Self. Shepherd Hoodwin. LC 94-92316. 96p. 1995. pap. 8.95 (*1-885469-01-2*) Summerjoy.

Meditations for Single Moms. Susanne C. Donoghue. LC 96-51876. 112p. (Orig.). 1997. pap. 8.99 (*0-8361-9061-0*) Herald Pr.

Meditations for Spiritual Misfits. Robert Badra. (Illus.). 93p. (Orig.). 1982. pap. 7.95 (*0-9610274-0-1*) JCL Hse.

Meditations for Success. Jennifer O'Dell. Ed. by Francis Ramsden. 112p. (Orig.). 1994. pap. 7.95 (*0-9637428-0-9*) Visions Unltd.

Meditations for Surviving Without Cigarettes. Esther Wanning. 368p. 1994. pap. 10.00 (*0-380-76916-6*, Avon Bks) Morrow Avon.

***Meditations for the Days of Awe: Reflections, Guided Imagery & Other Creative Exercises.** Dov P. Elkins. LC 99-62687. 150p. 1999. pap. 20.00 (*0-918834-19-8*) Growth Assoc.

Meditations for the Divorced. Ed. by Judy Osgood. LC 87-17687. (Gilgal Meditations Ser.). 72p. (Orig.). 1987. pap. 5.95 (*0-916895-02-5*) Gilgal Pubns.

Meditations for the Expectant Mother. Helen G. Brenneman. LC 68-12025. (Illus.). 78p. 1968. pap. 8.99 (*0-8361-1567-8*) Herald Pr.

Meditations for the New Mother. rev. ed. Helen G. Brenneman. LC 53-7585. (Illus.). 78p. 1985. pap. 8.99 (*0-8361-3399-4*) Herald Pr.

Meditations for the Newly Married. 3rd rev. ed. John M. Drescher. LC 69-10835. 142p. 1995. pap. 10.99 (*0-8361-9017-3*) Herald Pr.

Meditations for the Newly Married. 4th rev. ed. John M. Drescher. LC 96-52252. 144p. 1997. 19.99 (*0-8361-9069-6*) Herald Pr.

Meditations for the Road Warrior. Ed. by Mark Sanborn & Terry Paulson. LC 98-17859. 128p. 1998. 14.99 (*0-8010-1172-8*) Baker Bks.

Meditations for the Six Days of Holy Week. C. Alton Robertson. 28p. (Orig.). 1997. pap. 5.75 (*0-7880-0731-9*) CSS OH.

Meditations for the Soul. Phillip W. Keller. 1996. 14.98 (*0-88486-139-2*) Arrowood Pr.

Meditations for the Terminally Ill & Their Families. Ed. by Judy Osgood. LC 88-36326. (Gilgal Meditations Ser.). 72p. 1989. pap. 5.95 (*0-916895-05-X*) Gilgal Pubns.

Meditations for the Twelve Steps - A Spiritual Journey. Friends in Recovery. LC 92-42896. (Illus.). 166p. (Orig.). 1993. pap. 8.95 (*0-941405-21-4*) RPI Pubng.

Meditations for the 21st Century: 28 Exercises for Emotional Well-Being & Spiritual Understanding. Mary Sheldon & Christopher Stone. 240p. 1998. 12.00 (*0-7871-8014-9*, Dove Audio) NewStar Media.

Meditations for the Widowed. Ed. by Judy Osgood. LC 86-15002. (Gilgal Meditations Ser.). 72p. (Orig.). 1985. pap. 6.95 (*0-916895-01-7*) Gilgal Pubns.

Meditations for Today's Married Christians: Profiles of Married Saints for Troubled Times. Margaret A. Malsam. LC 94-70558. 64p. (Orig.). 1994. pap. 5.99 (*0-9616108-8-3*) Beaumont Bks.

Meditations for Transformation. 2nd rev. ed. Larry Moen. LC 93-34925. 247p. 1994. pap. 11.95 (*1-880698-33-1*, Pub. by US Pub FL) ACCESS Pubs Network.

Meditations for Vestry Members: Faithful Servants. Colleen McMahon. Ed. by Christopher L. Webber. LC 98-55384. (Faithful Servants Ser.). 96p. 1999. pap. 6.95 (*0-8192-1789-1*) Morehouse Pub.

Meditations for Walking. Lynne Hinton. LC 98-50823. 128p. 1999. pap. 12.00 (*1-57312-264-5*) Smyth & Helwys.

***Meditations for Weary Parents.** Sandra Drescher-Lehman. 204p. 2000. pap. 7.95 (*1-56148-302-8*) Good Bks PA.

Meditations for Women Who Do Too Much. Anne W. Schaef. 400p. 1996. pap. 6.99 (*0-06-251437-7*, Pub. by Harper SF) HarpC.

***Meditations for Women Who Do Too Much: Walker,&Kathryn.** abr. ed. Anne W. Schaef. 2000. audio 12.00 (*1-55994-486-2*, CPN 1883) HarperAudio.

***Meditations for Women Who Do Too Much - 10th Anniversary.** Anne W. Schaef. LC 89-45960. 400p. 2000. reprint ed. pap. 14.00 (*0-06-254866-2*) Harper SF.

Meditations for Working Men. Mary E. Robertson. (Illus.). 72p. (Orig.). 1988. pap. 5.00 (*0-9620614-2-5*) Spirit Connect.

Meditations for Working Women. rev. ed. Mary E. Robertson. (Illus.). 64p. 1988. reprint ed. pap., spiral bd. 5.00 (*0-9620614-5-X*) Spirit Connect.

Meditations for Your Pregnancy. Duncan Lavery. LC 99-27620. 112p. 1999. pap. 17.95 (*1-58238-055-4*, Whitman Coin) St Martin.

***Meditations from a Mother's Heart: Daily Grace for Mothers.** Pamela J. Kennedy. LC 99-55737. 224p. 1999. 12.99 (*0-570-05230-0*, 12-4037) Concordia.

Meditations from a Movable Chair. large type ed. Andre Dubus. 234p. Date not set. 30.00 (*0-7862-1723-5*) Thorndike Pr.

***Meditations from a Movable Chair: Essays.** Andre Dubus. (Vintage Contemporaries Ser.). 210p. 1999. pap. 12.00 (*0-679-75115-7*) Knopf.

***Meditations from a Movable Chair: Essays.** Andre Dubus. LC 97-50551. 209p. 1998. 3.99 (*0-679-43108-X*) Random.

Meditations from a Simple Path: Mother Teresa. Mother Teresa of Calcutta. 96p. 1996. 10.00 (*0-345-40699-0*) Ballantine Pub Grp.

Meditations from Conversations with God Bk. 1: An Uncommon Dialogue. Neale Donald Walsch. LC 97-204039. 384p. 1997. pap. 12.00 (*0-425-16169-2*) Berkley Pub.

Meditations from Conversations with God Bk. 2: A Personal Journal. Neale Donald Walsch. 256p. (Orig.). 1997. pap. 10.95 (*1-57174-072-4*) Hampton Roads Pub Co.

Meditations from Downtown: A Counselor's Reflections on Life. Ralph F. Ranieri. LC 90-61149. 64p. (Orig.). 1990. pap. 1.95 (*0-89243-326-4*) Liguori Pubns.

***Meditations from Mechthild of Magdeburg.** Mechthild of Magdeburg. Ed. by Henry L. Carrigan, Jr. LC 99-11222. (Living Library). Orig. Title: Selections from the Flowing Light of the Godhead. 126p. 1999. pap. 11.95 (*1-55725-217-3*, 930-020, Pub. by Paraclete MA) BookWorld.

Meditations from My Garden. Judith D. Parr. Ed. by Marie Gay. (Illus.). 126p. 1987. spiral bd. 9.00 (*0-941971-00-7*) Peacock CO.

Meditations from Solitude: A Mystical Theology from the Christian East. John M. Talbot. 334p. 1994. pap. 14.95 (*1-883803-05-5*) Troubadour Lord.

Meditations from Steerage: Two Whaling Journal Fragments. Ed. & Compiled by Stuart M. Frank. (Kendall Whaling Museum Monograph: No. 7). (Illus.). 1991. pap. 8.50 (*0-937854-31-X*) Kendall Whaling.

Meditations from the Road. M. Scott Peck. 1993. audio 12.00 (*0-671-87477-2*) S&S Audio.

Meditations from the Road: Daily Reflections from The Road Less Traveled & The Different Drum. M. Scott Peck. 384p. 1993. pap. 9.00 (*0-671-79799-9*, Touchstone) S&S Trade Pap.

Meditations from the Road Less Traveled. M. Scott Peck. 1998. per. 10.00 (*0-684-84729-9*) S&S Trade.

Meditations in an Emergency. Frank O'Hara. 64p. 1996. reprint ed. pap. 10.00 (*0-8021-3452-1*, Grove) Grove-Atltic.

Meditations in John. August Van Ryn. (Orig.). 1997. reprint ed. pap. 8.95 (*1-884838-16-2*) Walterick Pubs.

Meditations in Luke. August Van Ryn. 278p. 1997. reprint ed. pap. 8.95 (*1-884838-11-1*) Walterick Pubs.

Meditations in Mark. August Van Ryn. 247p. (Orig.). 1996. reprint ed. pap. 8.95 (*1-884838-07-3*) Walterick Pubs.

Meditations in Matthew. August Van Ryn. 1997. reprint ed. pap. 8.95 (*1-884838-12-X*) Walterick Pubs.

Meditations Metaphysiques. 7th ed. Rene Descartes. (FRE.). 320p. 1974. 13.95 (*0-8288-9576-7*, 2080703285) Fr & Eur.

Meditations Miserable People. Dan Goodman. 1995. mass mkt. 7.99 (*0-312-95514-6*, Pub. by Tor Bks) St Martin.

Meditations of a Bulldog. Michelle McPherson. (Illus.). 250p. (Orig.). 1995. pap. 13.95 (*1-883893-26-7*) WinePress Pub.

***Meditations of a Great Lakes Sailor.** Photos by U. S. Army Corps of Engineers, Detroit District Staff & Eric Hirsimaki. LC 99-95671. (Illus.). 298p. 2000. pap. 15.95 (*0-9674852-0-7*) Belding Pub.

Meditations of a Holocaust Traveler. Gerald E. Markle. LC 94-42915. 185p. (C). 1995. text 39.50 (*0-7914-2643-2*); pap. text 16.95 (*0-7914-2644-0*) State U NY Pr.

Meditations of Dorothy Day. Dorothy Day. LC 97-60413. (Illus.). 128p. 1997. pap. 9.95 (*0-87243-227-0*) Templegate.

Meditations of Guigo. John J. Jolin. (Medieval Philosophical Texts in Translation Ser.: No. 6). 1951. pap. 10.00 (*0-87462-206-9*) Marquette.

Meditations of Guigo I, Prior of the Charterhouse. Intro. & Text by Gordon Mursell. LC 94-21178. (Cistercian Studies: No. 155). 1994. 25.95 (*0-87907-555-4*); pap. 12.95 (*0-87907-655-0*) Cistercian Pubns.

Meditations of Marcus Aurelius. Marcus Aurelius. 1992. 17.00 (*0-679-41271-9*) Everymns Lib.

Meditations of Marcus Aurelius: A Study. R. B. Rutherford. (Oxford Classical Monographs). 300p. 1991. reprint ed. pap. text 35.00 (*0-19-814755-4*) OUP.

Meditations of Marcus Aurelius Antoninus: And a Selection from the Letters of Marcus & Fronto. Marcus Aurelius Antonius. Tr. by A. S. L. Farquharson. (Oxford's World Classics Ser.). 224p. 1998. pap. 8.95 (*0-19-283907-1*) OUP.

Meditations of Marcus Aurelius Antoninus & a Selection from the Letters of Marcus & Fronto. Marcus Aurelius. Tr. by R. B. Rutherford & A. S. Farquharson. 224p. 1990. 55.00 (*0-19-814761-9*) OUP.

Meditations of Saint Augustine. Augustine, Saint. Ed. by John E. Rotelle. Tr. by Matthew J. O'Connell. 1995. 14.95 (*0-941491-80-3*); pap. 9.95 (*0-941491-79-X*) Augustinian Pr.

Meditations of the Blessed Beauty. Baha'u'llah. 90p. 1992. 29.95 (*1-870989-17-1*); pap. 18.95 (*1-870989-18-X*) Bahai.

Meditations of the Heart. Howard Thurman. LC 99-14815. 216p. 1999. pap. 16.00 (*0-8070-1023-5*) Beacon Pr.

Meditations of the Heart. Howard Thurman. LC 76-18287. 216p. 1976. reprint ed. pap. 12.00 (*0-913408-25-5*) Friends United.

***Meditations of the Heart: A Prayer Devotional.** Joanne L. Gunning. Ed. by Leslie Santamaria. LC 00-191049. 254p. 2000. pap. 8.99 (*0-9701457-0-5*) J L Gunning.

Meditations of the Masters. Ellen K. Hua. LC 76-47649. (Illus.). (Orig.). 1977. pap. 8.00 (*0-87407-203-4*, FP-3) Thor.

Meditations on a D Major Scale. Bertha M. Nicholson. LC 87-63035. 1987. pap. 4.00 (*0-87574-276-9*) Pendle Hill.

Meditations on a Hobby Horse: And Other Essays on the Theory of Art. Ernst H. Gombrich. LC 84-28112. (Illus.). x, 135p. 1985. pap. 14.95 (*0-226-30215-6*) U Ch Pr.

Meditations on a Hobby Horse: And Other Essays on the Theory of Art. Ernst H. Gombrich. 256p. (C). 1994. reprint ed. pap. 22.95 (*0-7148-3245-6*, Pub. by Phaidon Press) Phaidon Pr.

***Meditations on African Literature, 201.** Ed. by Dubem Okafor. LC 99-462059. (Contributions in Afro-American & African Studies: Vol. 201). 296p. 2000. 59.00 (*0-313-29866-1*, GM9866, Greenwood Pr) Greenwood.

Meditations on Aging for the Christian Woman: Revised Selections from "Meditations for the Aged - Adapted to the Progress of Human Life" abr. rev. ed. John Brewster. Ed. by Anne Rutherford. LC 98-67305. iii, 58p. 1998. reprint ed. pap. 5.95 (*1-889298-50-6*) Rhwymbooks.

Meditations on America: John D. MacDonald's Travis McGee Series & Other Fiction. Lewis D. Moore & John D. MacDonald. 200p. (C). 1994. 39.95 (*0-87972-663-6*); pap. text 17.95 (*0-87972-664-4*) Bowling Green Univ Popular Press.

***Meditations on Design: Reinventing Your Home with Style & Simplicity.** John Wheatman. LC 99-42091. (Illus.). 128p. 1999. 24.95 (*1-57324-192-X*, Pub. by Conari Press) Publishers Group.

Meditations on Diabetes: Strengthening Your Spirit for Every Season. Catherine Feste. 384p. 1999. pap. 13.95 (*1-58040-001-9*, 00019Q, Pub. by Am Diabetes) NTC Contemp Pub Co.

Meditations on Ecclesiastes. F. C. Jennings. 143p. 5.95 (*0-88172-090-9*) Believers Bkshelf.

Meditations on 1st Chronicles. Henri L. Rossier.Tr. of First Chronicles. 131p. 1991. 7.95 (*0-88172-195-6*) Believers Bkshelf.

Meditations on First Kings. H. L. Rossier. 210p. 8.95 (*0-88172-165-4*) Believers Bkshelf.

Meditations on First Philosophy. Rene Descartes. Tr. by George Heffernan from LAT. LC 91-50569. (C). 1992. pap. text 5.00 (*0-268-01397-7*) U of Notre Dame Pr.

Meditations on First Philosophy. 2nd ed. Rene Descartes. Tr. by Ronald Rubin from LAT. 53p. (C). 1986. pap. text 4.95 (*0-941736-11-3*) Arete Pr.

Meditations on First Philosophy: In Which the Existence of God & the Distinction of the Soul from the Body Are Demonstrated. 3rd ed. Rene Descartes. Tr. by Donald A. Cress from LAT. LC 93-21653. (Hackett Classics Ser.).Tr. of Meditationes de Prima Philosophia. 72p. (C). 1993. pap. text 4.95 (*0-87220-192-9*) Hackett Pub.

Meditations on First Philosophy-Meditationes de Prima Philosophia: A Bilingual Edition. Rene Descartes. Ed. & Tr. by George Heffernan. LC 89-40751. (ENG & LAT.). 208p. (C). 1990. pap. text 9.50 (*0-268-01381-0*) U of Notre Dame Pr.

Meditations on Freedom & the Spirit. Karl Rahner. 118p. 1994. pap. 21.00 (*0-86012-047-3*, Pub. by Srch Pr) St Mut.

Meditations on Hunting. Jose Ortega & Jose O. Gassett. LC 95-61397. (Illus.). 1995. 60.00 (*1-885106-18-1*) Wild Adven Pr.

Meditations on Joshua. H. Rossier. 7.25 (*0-88172-119-0*) Believers Bkshelf.

Meditations on Joy. Wendy Beckett. LC 95-11886. (Sr. Wendy's Meditations Ser.). (Illus.). 48p. 1995. 8.95 (*0-7894-0179-7*, 6-70486) DK Pub Inc.

Meditations on Love. Wendy Beckett. LC 95-11885. (Sr. Wendy's Meditations Ser.). (Illus.). 48p. 1995. 8.95 (*0-7894-0178-9*, 6-70485) DK Pub Inc.

Meditations on Marriage: Translated from Hermann Oeser's Original. Ed. by Elsa Noak. (C). 1989. pap. 21.00 (*0-900657-98-7*, Pub. by W Sessions) St Mut.

Meditations on Mary. Kathleen Norris. (Illus.). 112p. 1999. 19.95 (*0-670-88820-6*) Viking Penguin.

Meditations on Mary: Conferences. Terence C. Cooke. LC 93-26373. 152p. (Orig.). 1993. pap. 7.95 (*0-8189-0683-9*) Alba.

Meditations on Modern Political Thought: Masculine - Feminine Themes from Luther to Arendt. Jean B. Elshtain. LC 85-28259. (Women & Politics Ser.). 141p. 1986. 49.95 (*0-275-92054-2*, C2054, Praeger Pubs) Greenwood.

Meditations on Modern Political Thought: Masculine - Feminine Themes from Luther to Arendt. Jean B. Elshtain. 144p. 1992. reprint ed. pap. 15.95 (*0-271-00864-4*) Pa St U Pr.

Meditations on Nature: The Drawings of David Johnson. John I. Baur & Margaret C. Conrads. LC 87-32370. (Illus.). 92p. (Orig.). 1988. pap. 6.25 (*0-943651-04-2*) Hudson Riv.

Meditations on Peace. Wendy Beckett. LC 95-11884. (Sr. Wendy's Meditations Ser.). (Illus.). 48p. 1995. 8.95 (*0-7894-0177-0*, 6-70484) DK Pub Inc.

***Meditations on Proverbs for Couples.** Les Parrott. 2000. 12.99 (*0-310-23446-8*) Zondervan.

Meditations on Relationships: 29 Meditations to Deepen & Enhance Your Most Important Connections. Mary Sheldon & Christopher Stone. 240p. 1999. 12.00 (*0-7871-1839-7*, NewStar Pr) NewStar Media.

Meditations on Ruth & First Samuel, 2. Henri L. Rossier. 114p. 1994. 8.95 (*0-88172-209-X*) Believers Bkshelf.

Meditations on St. John. Burns K. Seeley. Ed. by Jerome F. Coniker & Dale Francis. LC 81-65808. (Living Meditation & Prayerbook Ser.). (Illus.). 245p. (Orig.). 1981. pap. text 5.00 (*0-932406-03-3*) AFC.

Meditations on Saint Luke. Arturo Paoli. Tr. by Bernard F. McWilliams. LC 76-58539. 204p. reprint ed. pap. 63.30 (*0-8357-8949-7*, 203351400086) Bks Demand.

Meditations on St. Matthew. Burns K. Seeley. Ed. by Jerome F. Coniker. LC 82-71700. (Living Meditation & Prayerbook Ser.). (Illus.). 250p. (Orig.). 1982. pap. text 5.00 (*0-932406-05-X*) AFC.

Meditations on St. Paul. Burns K. Seeley. Ed. by Jerome F. Coniker. LC 82-72201. (Living Meditation & Prayerbook Ser.). (Illus.). 270p. (Orig.). 1982. pap. text 5.00 (*0-932406-06-8*) AFC.

Meditations on 2nd Chronicles, 2. Henri L. Rossier. 176p. 1993. 8.95 (*0-88172-203-0*) Believers Bkshelf.

Meditations on 2nd Samuel, 2, 2. Henri L. Rossier. 145p. 1994. 8.95 (*0-88172-210-3*) Believers Bkshelf.

Meditations on Shiva: The Shivastotravali of Utpaladeva. Constantina R. Bailly. 133p. (C). 1995. pap. text 9.95 (*0-7914-2530-4*) State U NY Pr.

Meditations on Silence. Wendy Beckett. LC 95-11883. (Sr. Wendy's Meditations Ser.). (Illus.). 48p. 1995. 8.95 (*0-7894-0180-0*, 6-70487) DK Pub Inc.

Meditations on Suffering. JoAnn F. Watson. 1993. pap. 8.50 (*0-533-10477-7*) Vantage.

Meditations on the Book of Psalms: A Guide to the Care & Feeding of the Spirit. Barbara C. Crafton. 448p. 1996. pap. 10.00 (*0-345-39738-X*) Ballantine Pub Grp.

Meditations on the Cross. Dietrich Bonhoeffer & Manfred Weber. Tr. by Douglas W. Stott from GER. LC 97-29636. 128p. 1998. pap. 12.00 (*0-664-25755-0*) Westminster John Knox.

Meditations on the Divine Liturgy. Nikolai Vasilevich Gogol. 58p. (Orig.). 1985. pap. 3.00 (*0-317-30300-7*) Holy Trinity.

Meditations on the Gift of Sexuality. Ted McIlvenna. 77p. 1977. 12.95 (*0-317-34148-0*) Specific Pr.

Meditations on the Gospel According to St. Matthew: A Devotional Commentary. Ed. by Leo Zanchettin. LC 98-104684. 320p. 1997. pap. 22.95 (*0-932085-12-1*) Word Among Us.

Meditations on the Gospel of Matthew: Guidelines for Daily Living. W. Richard Kettering. LC 95-81021. (Illus.). 134p. 1996. pap. write for info. (*0-9649180-0-5*) TRI-MOR Ent.

Meditations on the Gospels. George H. Morrison. LC 96-84208. (Walk in the Word Ser.). 714p. 1996. reprint ed. 24.99 (*0-89957-214-6*) AMG Pubs.

Meditations on the Hero: A Study of the Romantic Hero in Nineteenth-Century Fiction. Walter L. Reed. LC 74-77068. 217p. reprint ed. 67.30 (*0-8357-9384-2*, 201676000005) Bks Demand.

***Meditations on the Holy Sacrament of the Lord's Last Supper: Volume 3 of the Works.** Edward Reynolds. 2000. 29.95 (*1-57358-100-3*) Soli Deo Gloria.

Meditations on the Holy Spirit of God. Sheldon B. Stephenson. LC 98-39730. 128p. 1998. pap. 8.95 (*0-8091-3833-6*) Paulist Pr.

Meditations on the Icons. Thomas Kala. 78p. (C). 1996. pap. 39.95 (*0-85439-426-5*, Pub. by St Paul Pubns) St Mut.

Meditations on the Life & Passion of Christ. (EETS, OS Ser.: No. 158). 1969. reprint ed. 35.00 (*0-527-00155-4*) Periodicals Srv.

Meditations on the Lord's Prayer. Elaine Konstantopolous. Ed. by Patra M. Seuastiades. (Illus.). 30p. 1999. 8.95 (*1-58438-000-4*, Pub. by Greek Orth) BookWorld.

Meditations on the Mystery of Christmas. Charles A. Ramm. Ed. by Catherine M. Lilly. LC 59-15709. (Illus.). 76p. 1959. 12.95 (*0-87015-092-8*) Pacific Bks.

Meditations on the Occult Life. 3rd ed. Geoffrey Hodson. 1986. 8.50 (*81-7059-000-0*, 7225, Quest) Theos Pub Hse.

Meditations on the Path & Its Qualifications. A. Besant. 1985. 9.50 (*0-8356-7575-0*, Quest) Theos Pub Hse.

Meditations on the Peaks: Mountain Climbing As Metaphor for the Spiritual Quest. Julius Evola. Tr. by Guido Stucco from ITA. LC 97-38961. 128p. 1997. pap. 12.95 (*0-89281-657-0*) Inner Tradit.

Meditations on the Return of Christ & the End of the Age: With an Overview of Future Events. Samuel Hardman. 90p. (Orig.). 1997. pap. 6.95 (*1-57502-386-5*, PO1222) Morris Pubng.

Meditations on the Rosary. Lawrence G. Lovasik. LC 82-72204. (Living Meditation & Prayerbook Ser.). (Illus.). 270p. (Orig.). 1985. pap. text 5.00 (*0-932406-09-2*) AFC.

Meditations on the Sand. Allessandro Pronzato. (C). 1988. 60.00 (*0-85439-218-1*, Pub. by St Paul Pubns) St Mut.

Meditations on the Six Days of the Creation: (From a Collection of Meditations & Devotions, in Three Parts) Thomas Traherne. LC 92-23889. (Augustan Reprints Ser.: No. 119). reprint ed. 14.50 (*0-404-70119-1*, BS1235) AMS Pr.

Meditations on the Soul: Selected Letters of Marsilio Ficino. Marsilio Ficino. Ed. by Clement Salaman. 304p. 1996. 24.95 (*0-89281-567-1*) Inner Tradit.

Meditations on the Soul: Selected Letters of Marsilio Ficino. Marsilio Ficino. 304p. 1997. pap. 16.95 (*0-89281-658-9*) Inner Tradit.

Meditations on the Sunday Gospels, Year A. Ed. & Pref. by John E. Rotelle. (Scriptural Commentaries Ser.). 168p. 1995. pap. 9.95 (*1-56548-032-5*) New City.

Meditations on the Sunday Gospels, Year B. Ed. by John E. Rotelle. (Scriptural Commentaries Ser.). 168p. 1996. pap. 9.95 (*1-56548-082-1*) New City.

Meditations on the Sunday Gospels, Year C. John E. Rotelle. 168p. 1997. pap. 9.95 (*1-56548-086-4*) New City.

Meditations on the Tarot. 1987. pap. 19.95 (*0-916349-10-1*) Element MA.

Meditations on the Unknown God. Jay Ramsay. 143p. 1997. pap. 14.95 (*3-7052-0052-6*, Pub. by Poetry Salzburg) Intl Spec Bk.

Meditations on the Way of the Cross. Mother Teresa of Calcutta & Roger of Taize. LC 86-9313. (Illus.). 64p. (Orig.). 1998. reprint ed. pap. 7.95 (*0-8298-0585-0*) Pilgrim OH.

Meditations on Various Grounds. Theodore Enslin. 24p. (Orig.). 1982. pap. 5.50 (*0-937013-13-7*) Potes Poets.

Meditations Poetiques: Nouvelles Meditations Poetiques. Poesies Diverses. Alphonse De Lamartine. (Poesie Ser.). (FRE.). 480p. 1981. pap. 15.25 (*2-07-032200-9*) Schoenhof.

Meditations Poetiques: Poesies Diverse. Alphonse De Lamartine. (FRE.). 1981. pap. 17.95 (*0-7859-2782-4*) Fr & Eur.

Meditations Raciniennes: Seize Ouvertures en Forme d'Oratorio Interieur. Jean-Claude Joye. (FRE.). 320p. 1996. 39.95 (*3-906754-31-6*, Pub. by P Lang) P Lang Pubng.

Meditations Sacrae & Human Philosophy. Francis Bacon. 50p. 1996. reprint ed. pap. 9.95 (*1-56459-641-9*) Kessinger Pub.

Meditations That Lighten the Spirit & Feed the Soul. Samuel A. Holland. 224p. 1994. pap. 9.95 (*0-9625402-4-2*) Altan Pub.

Meditations Through the Rg Veda: Four-Dimensional Man. Antonio T. de Nicolas. LC 76-39692. 284p. 1976. pap. 12.95 (*0-89254-039-7*) Nicolas-Hays.

Meditations to Heal Your Life see Pensees pour Transformer Votre Vie

Meditations to Heal Your Life. Louise L. Hay. Ed. by Jill Kramer. LC 94-26019. 272p. 1994. 12.95 (*1-56170-106-8*, 163) Hay House.

***Meditations to Heal Your Life.** Louise L. Hay. 272p. 2000. pap. 10.95 (*1-56170-689-2*, 163T) Hay House.

Meditations to Make You Smile. Martha J. Beckman. LC 94-30674. (Illus.). 128p. 1995. pap. 8.00 (*0-687-00781-X*) Dimen for Liv.

Meditations to Transform the Mind. Dalai Lama, VII. Ed. & Tr. by Glenn H. Mullin. LC 99-16633. 285p. 1999. pap. 16.95 (*1-55939-125-1*, Pub. by Snow Lion Pubns) Natl Bk Netwk.

Meditations with Animals: A Native American Bestiary. Gerald Hausman. LC 86-70259. (Meditations with Ser.). (Illus.). 144p. (Orig.). 1986. pap. 9.95 (*0-939680-26-2*) Bear & Co.

Meditations with Hildegard of Bingen. Gabriele Uhlein. LC 82-74151. (Meditations with Ser.). (Illus.). 132p. (Orig.). 1983. pap. 9.95 (*0-939680-12-2*) Bear & Co.

Meditations with Julian of Norwich. Brendan Doyle. LC 82-73955. (Meditations with Ser.). (Illus.). 156p. 1997. reprint ed. pap. 9.95 (*0-939680-11-4*) Bear & Co.

Meditations with Meister Eckhart. Matthew Fox. LC 82-71451. (Meditations with Ser.). (Illus.). 132p. 1983. pap. 12.00 (*0-939680-04-1*) Bear & Co.

Meditations with Merton: A Collage of Scripture Quotes, Original Prayers & Merton's Own Words. Nicki V. Vandergrift. LC 95-76475. (Illus.). 128p. (Orig.). 1995. reprint ed. pap. 9.95 (*0-89243-822-3*) Liguori Pubns.

Meditations with Native American Elders, 4 bks., Set. Don Coyhis. 1995. pap. 31.00 (*1-887874-04-6*) Moh-He-Con-Nuck.

Meditations with Teilhard de Chardin. Blanche M. Gallagher. LC 88-10536. (Meditations with Ser.). (Illus.). 156p. (Orig.). 1997. reprint ed. pap. 9.95 (*0-939680-47-5*) Bear & Co.

Meditations with the Hopi. Robert Boissiere. LC 86-70257. (Meditations with Ser.). (Illus.). 144p. (Orig.). 1986. pap. 9.95 (*0-939680-27-0*) Bear & Co.

Meditative Magic, the Pleiadean Glyphs: A Workbook of Mandalas for Spiritual Self Reliance. Judith D. Winston. (Illus.). 72p. (Orig.). 1995. pap. 29.95 (*0-9643282-0-8*) Chewut Pr.

Meditative Medley: Ourselves & One Other: Images Tied Together by a View-of-Faithful-Response-to-Jesus Theme. G. K. Dreher. LC 91-77731. (Illus.). 64p. (Orig.). 1992. pap. 4.95 (*0-9601000-3-2*) Longshanks Bk.

Meditative Mind. Daniel Goleman. 240p. 1996. pap. 12.95 (*0-87477-833-6*, Tarcher Putnam) Putnam Pub Group.

Meditative Mind. rev. ed. Jiddu Krishnamurti. Ed. by William D. Quinn. 88p. 1994. per. 10.00 (*1-888004-00-2*) Krishnamurti.

***Meditative Moments: Imageries & Journeys for Your Inner Self & Your Soul.** Cynthia Amberson. Ed. by Gloria Chadwick. LC 00-130513. 110p. 2000. pap. 11.95 (*1-883717-18-3*) Myst Mndscapes.

Meditative Prayer see IVP Booklets

Meditative Prayer: Entering God's Presence. Richard Peace. (Spiritual Formation Ser.). 1999. pap. 7.00 (*0-89109-901-8*) NavPress.

Meditative Prayers for Today. Adam Bittleston. 56p. 1990. 8.95 (*0-903540-54-1*, 631, Pub. by Floris Bks) Anthroposophic.

Meditative Reason: Toward a Universal Grammar. Ashok K. Gangadean. LC 92-26731. (Revisioning Philosophy Ser.: Vol. 14). (Illus.). XXIX, 386p. (Orig.). (C). 1993. pap. text 33.95 (*0-8204-1991-5*) P Lang Pubng.

Meditative States in Tibetan Buddhism. Lati Rinbochay & Denma L. Rinbochay. Tr. by Leah Zahler & Jeffrey Hopkins. LC 96-24298. (Illus.). 208p. 1996. pap. 15.95 (*0-86171-119-X*) Wisdom MA.

Meditative Therapy: Facilitating Inner-Directed Healing. Michael L. Emmons & Janet Emmons. LC 98-7501. (Practical Therapist Ser.: Vol. 3). 230p. 1999. pap. 27.95 (*1-886230-11-0*) Impact Pubs CA.

Meditative Way: Readings in the Theory & Practice of Buddhist Meditation. Roderick S. Bucknell & Chris Kang. LC 97-186644. 288p. (C). 1997. text 48.00 (*0-7007-0677-1*, Pub. by Curzon Pr Ltd); pap. text 24.95 (*0-7007-0678-X*, Pub. by Curzon Pr Ltd) UH Pr.

Meditators & Drugs in Gastrointestinal Motility I: Morphological Basis & Neurophysiological Control. Ed. by G. Bertaccini. (Handbook of Experimental Pharmacology Ser.: Vol. 59, I). (Illus.). 468p. 1982. 312.00 (*0-387-11296-0*) Spr-Verlag.

Meditator's Guidebook: Pathways to Greater Awareness & Creativity. Lucy Oliver. 160p. (Orig.). 1991. pap. 9.95 (*0-89281-360-1*) Inner Tradit.

Meditator's Handbook: A Comprehensive Guide to Eastern & Western Meditation Techniques. David Fontana. 1993. pap. 14.95 (*1-85230-320-4*, Pub. by Element MA) Penguin Putnam.

Mediteach: Your Complete Electronic Library of Medication Teaching AIDS. Springhouse Publishing Company Staff. 1999. 39.95 (*0-87434-976-1*) Springhouse Corp.

Mediterranean. Leslie Gardiner. (Family Library of World Travel). (Illus.). 62p. 1985. pap. 4.95 (*0-933521-17-0*) AGT Pub.

Mediterranean. Photos by Mimmo Jodice. LC 95-76133. (Illus.). 120p. 1995. 50.00 (*0-89381-612-4*) Aperture.

Mediterranean. Philip Wilkinson. (Mysterious Places Ser.). (Illus.). 96p. (YA). (gr. 5 up). 1994. lib. bdg. 19.95 (*0-7910-2751-1*) Chelsea Hse.

Mediterranean. rev. ed. Frank Hill. (TravelCard Pac Ser.). 1992. 4.00 (*0-88699-020-3*) Travel Sci.

***Mediterranean: A Cultural Landscape.** Predrag Matvejevic. LC 98-47186. 210p. 1999. 29.95 (*0-520-20738-6*, Pub. by U CA Pr) Cal Prin Full Svc.

Mediterranean: Environment & Society. Ed. by Russell King et al. LC 97-213889. (Arnold Publications). (Illus.). 336p. 1997. text 65.00 (*0-340-65280-2*); pap. text 35.00 (*0-340-65281-0*) OUP.

Mediterranean: Imray Mediterranean Almanac, 1997-98. rev. ed. Ed. by Rod Heikell. (Illus.). 530p. 1996. pap. 125.00 (*0-85288-360-9*, Pub. by Laurie Norie & Wilson Ltd) St Mut.

Mediterranean Adventure. Pat Phillips. LC 98-31302. 200p. 1999. write for info. (*0-7540-3628-6*) Chivers N Amer.

Mediterranean Adventure. large type ed. Pat Phillips. LC 98-31302. 1999. 30.00 (*0-7838-0414-8*, G K Hall Lrg Type) Mac Lib Ref.

Mediterranean Africa. Monir Girgis. (Illus.). 346p. (Orig.). 1987. pap. text 30.00 (*0-8191-5955-7*) U Pr of Amer.

Mediterranean & Its People. David Flint. LC 93-39847. (People & Places Ser.). (Illus.). 48p. (J). (gr. 5-8). 1994. lib. bdg. 24.26 (*1-56847-166-1*) Raintree Steck-V.

Mediterranean & the Mediterranean World in the Age of Philip II, Vol. I. Fernand Braudel. Tr. by Sian Reynolds. LC 95-37581. (Illus.). 642p. 1995. pap. 27.50 (*0-520-20308-9*, Pub. by U CA Pr) Cal Prin Full Svc.

Mediterranean & the Mediterranean World in the Age of Philip II, Vol. II. Fernand Braudel. (Illus.). 725p. 1995. pap. 27.50 (*0-520-20330-5*, Pub. by U CA Pr) Cal Prin Full Svc.

Mediterranean Appetizers. Koenemann Inc. Staff. (Mini Cook Bks.). (Illus.). 64p. 1999. pap. 1.95 (*3-8290-3013-4*) Konemann.

Mediterranean Basin see World Architecture 1900-2000: A Critical Mosaic

Mediterranean Basin in the World Petroleum Market. Paul Horsnell et al. 250p. 2000. text 70.00 (*0-19-730021-9*) OUP.

Mediterranean Basins: Tertiary Extension Within the Alpine Orogen. Ed. by B. Durand et al. (Geological Society Special Publication Ser.: No. 156). 584p. 1999. 148.00 (*1-86239-033-9*, Pub. by Geol Soc Pub Hse) AAPG.

***Mediterranean Blue.** large type ed. Paula Forest. 304p. 1999. pap. 18.99 (*0-7089-5581-9*, Linford) Ulverscroft.

Mediterranean by Cruise Ship: The Complete Guide to Mediterranean Cruising. Anne Vipond. Ed. by Stephen York. (Illus.). 400p. 1998. pap. 18.95 (*0-9697991-4-4*) Ocean Cruise.

Mediterranean Caper. Clive Cussler. 1984. mass mkt. 3.95 (*0-553-23328-9*) Bantam.

Mediterranean Caper. Clive Cussler. 256p. 1996. 24.00 (*0-684-82690-9*) Simon & Schuster.

***Mediterranean Caper.** large type ed. Clive Cussler. LC 99-52923. 328p. 2000. lib. bdg. 27.95 (*1-58547-014-7*) Ctr Point Pubg.

Mediterranean Caper. Clive Cussler. 1994. reprint ed. lib. bdg. 32.95 (*1-56849-271-5*) Buccaneer Bks.

Mediterranean Caper. rev. ed. Clive Cussler. Ed. by Paul McCarthy. 256p. 2000. mass mkt. 7.99 (*0-671-73778-3*) PB.

Mediterranean Cat. Hans Silvester. 144p. 1996. 29.95 (*0-8118-1228-6*) Chronicle Bks.

Mediterranean Cat. Hans Silvester. 1998. pap. 19.95 (*0-8118-2096-3*) Chronicle Bks.

Mediterranean City in Transition: Social Change & Urban Development. Lila Leontidou. (Cambridge Human Geography Ser.). (Illus.). 314p. (C). 1990. text 80.00 (*0-521-34467-0*) Cambridge U Pr.

Mediterranean Coasts of Israel & Sinai: Holocene Tectonism from Geology, Geophysics, & Archaeology. K. O. Emery et al. 144p. 1987. 52.95 (*0-8448-1495-4*, Crane Russak) Taylor & Francis.

Mediterranean Colonies, Middle East, Indian Empire, Far East see Subject Catalogue of the Library of the Royal Empire Society, 1930-1937

Mediterranean Color. Jeffrey Becom. (Illus.). 192p. 1990. 45.00 (*0-89659-925-6*) Abbeville Pr.

Mediterranean Color - Postcards. 1992. pap. 7.95 (*1-55859-425-6*) Abbeville Pr.

Mediterranean Cooking. Joyce Goldstein. Ed. by Chuck Williams. LC 96-29832. (Williams-Sonoma Kitchen Library). (Illus.). 108p. (J). (gr. 11). 1999. 18.95 (*0-7835-0323-7*) Time-Life.

***Mediterranean Cooking.** Frederic Lebain. (Illus.). 143p. 1999. 12.99 (*1-84100-126-0*) Quadrillion Media.

Mediterranean Cooking. Hilaire Walden. 128p. 1995. write for info. (*1-57215-107-2*) World Pubns.

Mediterranean Cooking. Paula Wolfert. LC 94-8088. 336p. 1994. pap. 20.00 (*0-06-097464-8*) HarpC.

Mediterranean Cooking Rev Edition. 2nd ed. Paula Wolfert. 320p. 1999. 23.00 (*0-88001-402-4*) HarpC.

Mediterranean Cooking the Healthful Way. Marlena Spieler. (Illus.). 384p. 1997. pap. 18.00 (*0-7615-0387-0*) Prima Pub.

***Mediterranean Cooking II.** Anna M. O'Brien Klironomou. (Illus.). 1999. 12.00 (*0-9672011-1-X*) A Klironomou-OBrien.

***Mediterranean Country Kitchen.** Jacqueline Clark & Joanna Farrow. 96p. 2000. pap. 12.95 (*0-7548-0305-8*) Anness Pub.

Mediterranean Crossroads: Migration Literature in Italy. Graziella Parati. LC 99-19418. 224p. 1999. 37.50 (*0-8386-3813-9*) Fairleigh Dickinson.

Mediterranean Cruising Handbook. Rod Heikell. 180p. 1986. 100.00 (*0-85288-097-9*, Pub. by Laurie Norie & Wilson Ltd) St Mut.

Mediterranean Cruising Handbook. Rod Heikell. 200p. (C). 1987. 150.00 (*0-85288-112-6*, Pub. by Laurie Norie & Wilson Ltd) St Mut.

Mediterranean Cruising Handbook. Rod Heikell. (Illus.). 200p. (C). 1990. 125.00 (*0-85288-148-7*, Pub. by Laurie Norie & Wilson Ltd) St Mut.

Mediterranean Culture & Troubadour Music. Zoltan Falvy. Tr. by Maria Steiner from HUN. (Studies in Central & Eastern European Music: No. 1). 1987. lib. bdg. 47.00 (*963-05-4062-2*) Pendragon NY.

An Asterisk (*) at the beginning of an entry indicates that the title is appearing for the first time.

Mediterranean Debt Crescent: Money & Power in Algeria, Egypt, Morocco, Tunisia, & Turkey. Clement M. Henry. LC 95-23644. (Illus.). 424p. (C). 1996. 49.95 (*0-8130-1380-1*) U Press Fla.

Mediterranean Desertification. Brandt. text. write for info. (*0-471-49113-6*) Wiley.

Mediterranean Desertification. C. Jane Brandt. text 149.00 (*0-471-98555-4*) Wiley.

Mediterranean Desertification & Land Use. Ed. by C. Jane Brandt & John B. Thornes. LC 95-26001. 572p. 1996. 200.00 (*0-471-94250-2*) Wiley.

Mediterranean Diet Cookbook: A Delicious Alternative for Lifelong Health. Nancy H. Jenkins. LC 94-5946. 528p. 1994. 29.95 (*0-553-09608-7*) Bantam.

***Mediterranean Diets.** Ed. by Artemis P. Simopoulos & Francesco Visioli. (World Review of Nutrition & Dietetics Ser.: Vol. 87). (Illus.). xvi, 184p. 2000. 198.25 (*3-8055-7066-X*) S Karger.

***Mediterranean Domestic Architecture for the United States.** Rexford Newcomb. LC 99-40220. (20th Century Ser.). (Illus.). 1999. write for info. (*0-926494-13-9*) Acanthus Pr.

Mediterranean Electrotechnical Conference - Melecon. IEEE, Region 8 - Turnkey Section. Ed. by IEEE, Institute of Electrical & Electronics Engine. LC 93-80825. 1250p. 1994. pap. text. write for info. (*0-7803-1772-6*); lib. bdg. write for info. (*0-7803-1773-4*, 94CH3388-6); fiche. write for info. (*0-7803-1774-2*) Inst Electrical.

Mediterranean Emporium: The Catalan Kingdom of Majorca. David Abulafia. 288p. (C). 1994. text 64.95 (*0-521-32244-8*) Cambridge U Pr.

Mediterranean Europe: Phrasebook. Ed. by Sally Steward. (Illus.). 360p. (Orig.). 1992. pap. 6.95 (*0-86442-153-2*) Lonely Planet.

Mediterranean Feast. Clifford A. Wright. 1997. per. 25.00 (*0-02-631581-5*) Macmillan.

Mediterranean Feast: Celebrated Cuisine from the Merchants of Venice to the Barbary Corsairs. Clifford A. Wright. LC 98-49155. (Illus.). 840p. 1999. 35.00 (*0-688-15305-4*, Wm Morrow) Morrow Avon.

Mediterranean Feud. Andrew Borowiec. LC 82-16624. 190p. 1983. 55.00 (*0-275-90950-6*, C0950, Praeger Pubs) Greenwood.

Mediterranean Flavours: Savouring the Sun. Maria J. Sevilla. (Illus.). 160p. 1997. pap. text 19.95 (*1-85793-861-5*, Pub. by Pavilion Bks Ltd) Trafalgar.

Mediterranean France & Corsica: A Sea Guide. Rod Heikell. (Illus.). 328p. (C). 1990. 64.95 (*0-85288-141-X*) Bluewater Bks.

Mediterranean France & Corsica Pilot. Rod Heikell. (Illus.). 300p. (C). 1996. 175.00 (*0-85288-254-8*, Pub. by Laurie Norie & Wilson Ltd) St Mut.

Mediterranean Gardener. Hugo Latymer. (Illus.). 160p. 2000. 35.00 (*0-7112-0631-7*, Pub. by F Lincoln) Antique Collect.

Mediterranean Gold. Virginia A. Church. (Illus.). 1986. 5.95 (*0-89407-127-0*) Strawberry Hill.

Mediterranean Grains & Greens: A Book of Savory, Sun-Drenched Recipes. Paula Wolfert. LC 98-10228. 400p. 1998. 27.50 (*0-06-017251-7*) HarpC.

***Mediterranean Herb Cookbook: Fresh & Savory Recipes from the Mediterranean Garden.** Georgeanne Brennan. LC 99-40462. (Illus.). 156p. 2000. pap. 22.95 (*0-8118-1990-6*) Chronicle Bks.

***Mediterranean Hot: Spicy Dishes from Southern Italy, Greece, Turkey & North Africa.** Aglaia Kremezi. (Illus.). 112p. 2000. reprint ed. text 20.00 (*0-7881-9114-4*) DIANE Pub.

Mediterranean Hot: Spicy Recipes from Southern Italy, Greece, Turkey & North Africa. Aglaia Kremezi. LC 95-46569. (Illus.). 112p. 1996. text 19.95 (*1-885183-26-7*) Artisan.

Mediterranean in the Ancient World. John H. Rose. 1970. reprint ed. lib. bdg. 59.50 (*0-8371-1933-2*, ROME, Greenwood Pr) Greenwood.

Mediterranean Kitchen. Joyce Goldstein. Ed. by Ann Bramson. LC 89-34476. (Illus.). 332p. 1989. 25.00 (*0-688-07283-6*, Wm Morrow) Morrow Avon.

Mediterranean Kitchen. Joyce Goldstein. 416p. 1998. pap. 16.00 (*0-688-16376-9*, Hearst) Hearst Commns.

Mediterranean Landscape Change: The Archaeology & History of the Biferno Valley. Graeme Barker. LC 94-32222. 1995. 59.95 (*0-7185-1906-X*) St Martin.

Mediterranean Landscapes in Australia: Mallee Ecosystems & Their Management. Ed. by J. C. Noble & R. A. Bradstock. 1989. 70.00 (*0-643-04985-1*, Pub. by CSIRO) Accents Pubns.

***Mediterranean Lifestyle.** Photos by Pere Planells. (Illus.). 192p. 2000. pap. 29.95 (*0-8230-3042-3*) Watsn-Guptill.

***Mediterranean Light: Delicious Recipes from the World's Healthiest Cuisine.** Martha Rose Schulman. LC 99-53830. (Illus.). 432p. 2000. reprint ed. pap. 18.00 (*0-688-17467-1*, Wm Morrow) Morrow Avon.

Mediterranean Living. Lisa Lovatt-Smith. LC 98-2702. 1998. 35.00 (*0-8230-2837-2*) Watsn-Guptill.

Mediterranean Maelstrom: The Story of HMS Jarvis. C. Connel. (C). 1986. text 130.00 (*0-7855-5304-5*, Pub. by Maritime Bks) St Mut.

Mediterranean Menus. (Great Meals in Minutes Ser.). (Illus.). 104p. 1985. 15.93 (*0-86706-293-2*); lib. bdg. 21.93 (*0-86706-294-0*) Time-Life.

Mediterranean Monk Seal. K. Ronald. (UNEP Technical Ser.). 1979. pap. 10.00 (*0-08-025684-8*, Pergamon Pr) Elsevier.

Mediterranean Monk Seal: Proceedings of the International Conference, 1st, Rhodes, Greece, 1978. International Conference on the Mediterranean Monk. Ed. by K. Ronald & R. Duguy. LC 79-41227. (UNEP Technical Ser.: Vol. 1). (Illus.). 250p. 1979. pap. 17.25 (*0-08-025655-4*, Pub. by Pergamon Repr) Franklin.

Mediterranean Mosaic Designs. Anita Benarde. (International Design Library). (Illus.). 48p. (Orig.). 1984. pap. 5.95 (*0-88045-049-5*) Stemmer Hse.

Mediterranean MTBS at War: U.S. Naval Aviation in Camera, 1946-1999. Martin W. Bowman. 224p. 2000. 36.00 (*0-7509-2274-5*) Sutton Publng.

Mediterranean Naval Situation, 1908-1914. Paul G. Halpern. LC 79-131469. (Historical Studies: No. 86). 429p. 1971. 27.50 (*0-674-56462-6*) HUP.

***Mediterranean Opthalmological Society Congress - Michaelson Symposium on Ocular Circulation & Neovascularization: VIth Congress, VIth Symposium, Jerusalem, May 2000: Abstracts.** Ed. by D. BenEzra. (Opthalmologica Ser.: Vol. 214, No. 3 (2000)). (Illus.). 72p. 2000. pap. 25.25 (*3-8055-7105-4*) S Karger.

Mediterranean Orchids. J. D. Lepper. 86p. (C). 1990. pap. 35.00 (*0-7223-2450-2*, Pub. by A H S Ltd) St Mut.

Mediterranean Pantry: Creating & Using Condiments & Seasonings. Aglaia Kremezi. LC 94-11419. (Illus.). 144p. 1994. 25.00 (*1-885183-02-X*) Artisan.

Mediterranean Paradoxes: The Politics & Social Structures of Southern Europe. James Kurth & James Petras. LC 92-28544. (International Perspectives on Europe Ser.). 272p. 1993. 49.50 (*0-85496-968-3*); pap. 19.50 (*0-85496-336-7*) Berg Pubs.

Mediterranean Passion: Victorians & Edwardians in the South. John Pemble. LC 86-33183. (Illus.). 326p. 1987. reprint ed. text 65.00 (*0-19-820100-1*) OUP.

Mediterranean Perspectives: Literature, Social Studies & Philosophy. Ed. by James E. Caraway. (Mediterranean Perspectives Ser.). 176p. 1996. pap. 17.00 (*1-883058-20-1*, Dowling College) Global Pubns.

Mediterranean Perspectives: Philosophy, Literature, History, & Art. Ed. by James E. Caraway. (Mediterranean Perspectives Ser.). 217p. 1997. pap. 17.00 (*1-883058-38-4*, Dowling College) Global Pubns.

Mediterranean Plants & Gardens. Roy Lancaster. (Illus.). 144p. 1990. pap. 17.95 (*0-903001-64-0*, Pub. by Burall Floraprint) J Markham Assocs.

Mediterranean Politics, Vol. 1. Richard Gillespie. 256p. 1995. 42.50 (*0-8386-3609-8*) Fairleigh Dickinson.

Mediterranean Politics, Vol. 2. Ed. by Richard Gillespie. 256p. 1995. 130.00 (*1-85567-191-3*) Bks Intl VA.

Mediterranean Quaternary River Environments: Refereed Proceedings of an International Conference, University of Cambridge, UK, 28-29 September 1992. Ed. by John Lewin et al. (Illus.). 300p. (C). 1995. text 97.00 (*90-5410-191-1*, Pub. by A A Balkema) Ashgate Pub Co.

***Mediterranean Response to Globalization Before 1950.** Sevket Pamuk & Jeffrey G. Williamson. LC 99-53473. 376p. 2000. 115.00 (*0-415-22425-X*) Routledge.

Mediterranean Runs Through Brooklyn. Anthony Valerio. LC 81-70753. 116p. 1982. 9.95 (*0-942016-00-9*) H B Davis.

Mediterranean Scenes. Arnold Bennett. LC 74-1702. (Collected Works of Arnold Bennett: Vol. 54). 1977. reprint ed. 19.95 (*0-518-19135-4*) Ayer.

Mediterranean Sea. David Lambert. LC 96-31163. (Seas & Oceans Ser.). (Illus.). 48p. (J). (gr. 5-9). 1997. lib. bdg. 24.26 (*0-8172-4512-X*) Raintree Steck-V.

Mediterranean Sea. John F. Prevost. LC 98-29320. (Oceans & Seas Ser.). 2002. lib. bdg. 19.92 (*1-57765-097-2*) ABDO Pub Co.

Mediterranean Security: New Issues & Challenges: Conference Proceedings. F. Stephen Larrabee & Carla Thorson. 50p. 1996. pap. text 9.00 (*0-8330-2384-5*, CF-122-NATO) Rand Corp.

Mediterranean Security at the Crossroads: A Reader. Nikolaos A. Stavrou. 1999. 21.95 (*0-8223-2459-8*) Duke.

Mediterranean Security at the Crossroads: Special Issue of Mediterranean Quarterly. Ed. by Nikolas A. Stavrou & Raymond C. Ewing. 240p. 1997. pap. text 6.00 (*0-8223-6449-2*) Duke.

***Mediterranean Security into the Coming Millennium.** Ed. by Stephen J. Blank. 521p. 1999. pap. write for info. (*1-58487-003-6*) SSI US Army.

Mediterranean Shipping Directory, 1993. 1993. pap. 130.00 (*1-85044-519-2*) LLP.

Mediterranean Shipping Directory, 1993. Lloyd's of London Press, Inc. Staff. 1993. pap. 130.00 (*1-85044-332-7*) LLP.

Mediterranean Society. Jacques Santer. 1998. pap. text 25.00 (*0-7494-2709-4*) Kogan Page Ltd.

Mediterranean Society: A Challenge for Islam, Judaism & Christianity. European Communities Publication Staff. LC 98-17319. (Forward Studies Ser.). 87p. 1998. text 39.95 (*0-312-21600-9*) St Martin.

Mediterranean Society: An Abridgement in One Volume. S. D. Goitein & Jacob Lassner. LC 98-54216. 553p. 1999. text 45.00 (*0-520-21734-9*, Pub. by U CA Pr) Cal Prin Full Svc.

Mediterranean Society: The Jewish Communities of the Arab World As Portrayed in the Documents of the Cairo Geniza: Cumulative Indices, Vol. 6. S. D. Goiten & Paula Saunders. (Near Eastern Center Series, UCLA). 55.00 (*0-520-08136-6*, Pub. by U CA Pr) Cal Prin Full Svc.

Mediterranean Society: The Jewish Communities of the Arab World As Portrayed in the Documents of the Cairo Geniza: Daily Life, Vol. 4. S. D. Goitein & Paula Sanders. LC 67-22430. (Near Eastern Center Series, UCLA). 600p. 1983. 75.00 (*0-520-04869-5*, Pub. by U CA Pr) Cal Prin Full Svc.

Mediterranean Society: The Jewish Communities of the Arab World As Portrayed in the Documents of the Cairo Geniza: Economic Foundations, Vol. 1. S. D. Goitein & Paula Sanders. LC 67-22430. (Near Eastern Center Series, UCLA). 550p. 1967. 75.00 (*0-520-00484-1*, Pub. by U CA Pr) Cal Prin Full Svc.

Mediterranean Society: The Jewish Communities of the Arab World As Portrayed in the Documents of the Cairo Geniza: The Community, Vol. 2. S. D. Goitein & Paula Sanders. LC 67-22430. (Near Eastern Center Series, UCLA). 649p. 1972. 75.00 (*0-520-01867-2*, Pub. by U CA Pr) Cal Prin Full Svc.

Mediterranean Society: The Jewish Communities of the Arab World As Portrayed in the Documents of the Cairo Geniza: The Family, Vol. 3. S. D. Goitein & Paula Sanders. LC 67-22430. (Near Eastern Center Series, UCLA). 546p. 1978. 75.00 (*0-520-03265-9*, Pub. by U CA Pr) Cal Prin Full Svc.

Mediterranean Society: The Jewish Communities of the Arab World As Portrayed in the Documents of the Cairo Geniza: The Individual, Vol. 5. S. D. Goitein & Paula Sanders. LC 67-22430. (Near Eastern Center Series, UCLA). 687p. 1988. 75.00 (*0-520-05647-7*, Pub. by U CA Pr) Cal Prin Full Svc.

Mediterranean Society: The Jewish Communities of the Arab Worlds as Portrayed in the Documents of the Cairo Geniza, Cumulative Indices, Vol. Vi: S. D. Goitein. 320p. 2000. pap. 19.95 (*0-520-22164-8*, Pub. by U CA Pr) Cal Prin Full Svc.

Mediterranean Society: The Jewish Communities of the Arab Worlds as Portrayed in the Documents of the Cairo Geniza : Economic Foundations, Vol. 1. S. D. Goitein. LC 99-36039. 550p. 2000. pap. 24.95 (*0-520-22158-3*, Pub. by U CA Pr) Cal Prin Full Svc.

Mediterranean Society: The Jewish Communities of the Arab Worlds as Portrayed in the Documents of the Cairo Geniza, : The Community, Vol. Ii. S. D. Goitein. 649p. 2000. pap. 24.95 (*0-520-22159-1*, Pub. by U CA Pr) Cal Prin Full Svc.

Mediterranean Society: The Jewish Communities of the Arab Worlds as Portrayed in the Documents of the Cairo Geniza, Daily Life, Vol. Iv: S. D. Goitein. LC 99-36039. Vol. IV. (Illus.). 600p. 2000. pap. 24.95 (*0-520-22161-3*, Pub. by U CA Pr) Cal Prin Full Svc.

Mediterranean Society: The Jewish Communities of the Arab Worlds as Portrayed in the Documents of the Cairo Geniza, The Individual, Vol. V: S. D. Goitein. LC 99-36039. Vol. V. 687p. 2000. pap. 24.95 (*0-520-22162-1*, Pub. by U CA Pr) Cal Prin Full Svc.

Mediterranean Society: The Jewish Communities of the Arab Worlds As Portrayed In The Documents Of The Cairo Geniza, Vol. Iii: The Family. S. D. Goitein. 546p. 2000. pap. 24.95 (*0-520-22160-5*, Pub. by U CA Pr) Cal Prin Full Svc.

Mediterranean Sonnets. Frank Cebulski. 152p. 1988. 20.00 (*1-55643-022-1*); pap. 8.95 (*1-55643-020-5*) North Atlantic.

***Mediterranean Stories: Innocent & Profane.** LC 99-66298. (Illus.). 224p. 2000. pap. 17.95 (*1-891519-02-6*) Premiere Edits.

Mediterranean Strategies. 1995. 15.00 (*92-871-2667-4*, Pub. by Council of Europe) Manhattan Pub Co.

Mediterranean Strategy in the Second World War. Michael C. Howard. 112p. 1993. 25.00 (*1-85367-140-1*, 5548) Stackpole.

Mediterranean Studies, 3 pts. in 1 vol. George Hempl. Ed. by Frederick Anderson. Incl. Pt. 1, Vol. 1. Genesis of European Alphabetic Writing. LC 31-33039. Pt. 1, Vol. 2. Minoan Seals. LC 31-33039. Pt. 2, Vol. 3. Three Papers on the History & Language of the Hittites. LC 31-33039. Pt. 3, Vol. 4. Etruscan. LC 31-33039. Pt. 3, Vol. 5. Venetic. LC 31-33039. LC 31-33039. reprint ed. (*0-404-51809-5*) AMS Pr.

Mediterranean Studies, Vol. 1. Benjamin F. Taggie. 1989. pap. 70.95 (*0-7546-0052-1*) Ashgate Pub Co.

Mediterranean Studies, Vol. 4. Benjamin F. Taggie. 1994. 70.95 (*0-7546-0055-6*) Ashgate Pub Co.

Mediterranean Studies, Vol. 5. Benjamin F. Taggie. 1995. 70.95 (*0-7546-0056-4*) Ashgate Pub Co.

Mediterranean Studies, Vol. 6. Benjamin F. Taggie. 1996. 70.95 (*0-7546-0057-2*) Ashgate Pub Co.

***Mediterranean Studies Journal, Vol. 7.** Benjamin F. Taggie. 256p. 1999. 70.95 (*0-7546-0020-3*) Ashgate Pub Co.

Mediterranean Style. Robert Fitzgerald. LC 99-19991. (Architecture & Design Library Ser.). 1999. 17.95 (*1-56799-765-1*, Friedman-Fairfax) M Friedman Pub Grp Inc.

Mediterranean Style. Catherine Haig. LC 98-155281. (Illus.). 144p. 1998. 35.00 (*0-7892-0430-4*) Abbeville Pr.

Mediterranean Table. Lewis Esson. LC 93-37459. (Creative Cook Ser.). 64p. 1993. 16.95 (*1-56426-650-8*) Cole Group.

Mediterranean Theatre see World War II German Military Studies

Mediterranean Tortoises. B. Pursall. (Illus.). 64p. 1995. pap. 9.95 (*0-7938-0284-9*, RE135) TFH Pubns.

***Mediterranean Tourism: Facets of Socioeconomic Development & Cultural Change.** Yiorgos Apostolopoulos et al. LC 00-32822. 2000. write for info. (*0-415-18023-6*) Routledge.

Mediterranean Tradition in Economic Thought. Louis Baeck. LC 94-16498. 272p. (C). (gr. 13). 1994. 85.00 (*0-415-09301-5*, B4238) Routledge.

Mediterranean-Type Ecosystems: A Data Source Book. Ed. by R. L. Specht. (Tasks for Vegetation Science Ser.). (C). 1988. text 245.00 (*90-6193-652-7*) Kluwer Academic.

Mediterranean-Type Ecosystems: The Function of Biodiversity. Ed. by G. W. Davis. LC 94-34429. (Ecological Studies: 109). 1994. write for info. (*3-540-57809-9*) Spr-Verlag.

Mediterranean-Type Ecosystems: The Function of Biodiversity. Ed. by G. W. Davis & D. M. Richardson. LC 94-34429. (Ecological Studies: Vol. 109). xix, 352p. 1995. 140.95 (*0-387-57809-9*) Spr-Verlag.

Mediterranean Urban Culture 1400-1700. Ed. by Alexander Cowan. (Illus.). 240p. 1999. text 60.00 (*0-85989-578-5*, Pub. by Univ Exeter Pr) Northwestern U Pr.

Mediterranean Vegetables. Clifford A. Wright. 2001. write for info. (*0-688-15827-7*, Wm Morrow) Morrow Avon.

Mediterranean Was a Desert: A Voyage of the Glomar Challenger. Kenneth J. Hsu. LC 83-2269. (Illus.). 214p. reprint ed. pap. 66.40 (*0-608-06375-4*, 206673600008) Bks Demand.

Mediterranean World in Late Antiquity, AD 395-600. Averil Cameron. LC 92-34600. (History of the Ancient World Ser.). (Illus.). 264p. (C). (gr. 13). 1993. pap. 24.99 (*0-415-01421-2*) Routledge.

Mediterraneans: A Serenade. Prentiss Moore. (Orig.). 1986. pap. text 2.95 (*0-941169-03-0*) Black Chin Pr.

***Mediterranenan Slow & Easy.** Paula Wolfert. (Cookbook Library). 2002. write for info. (*0-688-17681-X*, Wm Morrow) Morrow Avon.

Mediterraneo. Fernand Bravdel. Tr. by J. Ignacio San Martin. (Nueva Austral Ser.: No. 5). (SPA.). 1991. pap. text 24.95 (*84-239-1805-X*) Elliots Bks.

Mediterranes Gaertnern. Mit Wenig Wasser ein Bluehendes Paradies (Mediterranean Gardens. A Flora Paradise with Little Water) Heide Gildemeister. Tr. by Anette Pause & Vera Bauer. (Illus.). 208p. 1997. 58.00 (*3-8263-3151-6*, Pub. by Blckwell Wissenschafts) Balogh.

M

MediTrends, 1995-1996. 3rd ed. American Hospital Association Staff. 100p. 1995. pap. 75.00 (*0-87258-708-8*, 012010) Am Hospital.

Medium: The Vocal Score Tragedy in Two Acts. Gian-Carlo Menotti. (ENG & FRE.). 128p. 1986. pap. 25.00 (*0-7935-1546-7*, 50337670) H Leonard.

Medium - Term Prospects for Agricultural Commodities: Projections to 2000. FAO Staff. LC 94-233149. (Economic & Social Development Papers: 120). 195p. 1994. pap. 21.00 (*92-5-103482-6*, F34826, Pub. by FAO) Bernan Associates.

Medium Aevum & the Middle Age see Metaphor

Medium & High-Energy Nuclear Physics. Ed. by Keh-Fei Liu et al. 816p. (C). 1989. text 141.00 (*9971-5-0658-0*) World Scientific Pub.

Medium & High Energy Nuclear Physics: Proceedings of the Conference. M. K. Pal et al. 240p. 1992. text 95.00 (*981-02-1095-7*) World Scientific Pub.

Medium & High Voltage Electrical Insulators, 1991-1996 Analysis: North American Markets, Technologies & Opportunities. Tim Archdeacon. (Illus.). 125p. (Orig.). 1991. pap. 1800.00 (*1-878218-16-6*) World Info Tech.

Medium & High Voltage Power Cables - North American Markets, Technologies & Opportunities: 1990-1995 Analysis. Amadee Bender. (Illus.). 200p. 1990. pap. text 1800.00 (*1-878218-13-1*) World Info Tech.

Medium & the Muse: Culture, Telecommunications & the Information Highway. Charles Sirois & Claude E. Forget. (Illus.). 112p. 1995. pap. 13.95 (*0-88645-175-2*, Pub. by Inst Res Pub) Ashgate Pub Co.

Medium & the Scientist: The Story of Florence Cook & William Crookes. Trevor H. Hall. LC 84-43102. (Science & the Paranormal Ser.). (Illus.). 212p. 1984. 29.95 (*0-87975-276-9*) Prometheus Bks.

Medium Density Fibreboard: Basic Properties & Performance. 1980. 70.00 (*0-7855-1065-6*) St Mut.

Medium-Energy Antiprotons & the Quark-Gluon Structure of Hadrons. Ed. by R. Landua et al. (Ettore Majorana International Science Ser., Life Sciences: Vol. 58). (Illus.). 256p. (C). 1992. text 114.00 (*0-306-44087-3*, Kluwer Plenum) Kluwer Academic.

Medium Energy Physics: Proceedings of the International Symposium. Ed. by H. C. Chiang & L. S. Zheng. 684p. (C). 1988. text 125.00 (*9971-5-0403-0*) World Scientific Pub.

Medium for Murder. large type ed. Evelyn Harris. 1994. 27.99 (*0-7089-3166-9*) Ulverscroft.

Medium Format Advantage. Ernst Wildi. (Illus.). 272p. 1995. pap. 29.95 (*0-240-80221-7*, Focal) Buttrwrth-Heinemann.

***Medium Format Cameras: User's Guide to Buying & Shooting.** Peter Williams. (Illus.). 112p. 2000. pap. 19.95 (*1-58428-042-5*, Pub. by Amherst Media) IPG Chicago.

Medium Format Photography. Lief Ericksenn. (Illus.). 144p. 1991. pap. 24.95 (*0-8174-4556-0*, Amphoto) Watsn-Guptill.

Medium Heat Appliances Factory Built Chimneys, UL 959. 7th ed. (C). 1995. pap. text 250.00 (*1-55989-941-7*) Underwrtrs Labs.

Medium Heavy Duty Truck Engines, Fuels & Computerized Systems. Bennett. LC 98-25968. 768p. 1999. text 77.95 (*0-8273-8574-9*) Delmar.

Medium-Heavy Duty Truck Engines, Fuels, Comp Systems IG. Bennett. 128p. 1999. text, teacher ed. 33.95 (*0-8273-8575-7*) Delmar.

Medium-Heavy Duty Truck Service Manual, 1989-92. Chilton Automotive Editorial Staff. 1216p. 1992. 77.00 (*0-8019-8282-0*) Nichols Pub.

Medium is the Message see Medium ist die Botschaft

Medium Is the Message: An Inventory of Effects. Marshall McLuhan & Quentin Fiore. (Illus.). 160p. 1996. reprint ed. pap. 9.95 (*1-888869-02-X*) Wired Bks.

Medium Is the Rear View Mirror, Understanding McLuhan. Donald F. Theall. LC 79-135417. 277p. reprint ed. pap. 85.90 (*0-7837-1145-X*, 204167400022) Bks Demand.

***Medium ist die Botschaft.** M. McLuhan.Tr. of Medium is the Message. (GER., Illus.). 250p. 1998. text 16.00 (*90-5705-095-1*, Verlag Kunst) Gordon & Breach.

Medium of Public Speaking: Classroom Reader. Neil Smith. 268p. (C). 1994. text 45.00 (*0-536-58620-9*) Pearson Custom.

***Medium Passenger Vans in Saudi Arabia: A Strategic Entry Report, 1997.** Compiled by Icon Group International Staff. (Illus.). 133p. 1999. ring bd. 1330.00 incl. audio compact disk (*0-7418-0963-X*) Icon Grp.

Medium PKW of the German Wehrmacht, 1937-1945. Hans-Georg Mayer-St. LC 98-182541. 48p. 1998. pap. 9.95 (*0-7643-0570-0*) Schiffer.

***Medium Rare: Reminiscences of a Clairvoyant.** Muriel Renard. 1998. pap. 22.95 (*1-86163-027-1*, Pub. by Capall Bann Pubng) Holmes Pub.

Medium-Scale Synchrotron Radiation Facilities in Asia - Approaches to Effective & Versatile Use. T. Kasuga & K. Kohra. 216p. 1991. text 101.00 (*981-02-0423-X*) World Scientific Pub.

Medium Secure Psychiatric Provision in the Private Sector. Katrina R. Moss. LC 98-73023. 168p. 1998. text 59.95 (*1-84014-310-X*, Pub. by Ashgate Pub) Ashgate Pub Co.

Medium-Size Photovoltaic Power Plants. Ed. by Wolfgang Palz et al. 1981. text 124.00 (*90-277-1279-4*) Kluwer Academic.

Medium Size Transformers: Practical Methods for Designing, Reconnecting & Testing. Samuel Heller. (Illus.). 220p. (Orig.). 1957. 74.00 (*0-911740-01-5*) Datarule.

Medium-Term Dynamic Forecasting: The 1975 London Conference. Ed. by W. F. Gossling. (Illus.). xxii, 285p. 1977. lib. bdg. 150.00 (*0-678-08075-5*) Kelley.

Medium Voltage 20508. NCCER Staff. 1997. pap. text 20.00 (*0-13-909862-3*, Prentice Hall) P-H.

Medium-Voltage Power Cables, UL 1072. 2nd ed. (C). 1995. pap. text 135.00 (*1-55989-869-0*) Underwrtrs Labs.

Medium Voltage 20508. NCCER Staff. 1997. pap. text, teacher ed. 20.00 (*0-13-909870-4*, Prentice Hall) P-H.

***Medium/Heavy Duty Truck (T8) Preventative Maintenance.** Delmar Publishers Staff. (ASE Test Prep Ser.). 1999. pap. 18.95 (*0-7668-0566-2*) Delmar.

***Medium/Heavy Duty Truck (T4) Brakes.** Delmar Publishers Staff. (ASE Test Prep Ser.). 1999. pap. 18.95 (*0-7668-0562-X*) Delmar.

***Medium/Heavy Duty Truck (T7) Heating, Ventilation & Air Conditioning.** Delmar Publishers Staff. (ASE Test Prep Ser.). 1999. pap. 18.95 (*0-7668-0565-4*) Delmar.

***Medium/Heavy Duty Truck (T6) Electrical & Electronic Systems.** Delmar Publishers Staff. (ASE Test Prep Ser.). 1999. pap. 18.95 (*0-7668-0564-6*) Delmar.

Mediums: Speakers with the Dead. Ronni Radner & Andrew Bates. (Illus.). (Orig.). 1997. pap. 15.00 (*1-56504-619-6*, 6102) White Wolf.

Mediums, & Spirit Rappers, & Roaring Radicals: Spiritualism in American Literature, 1850-1900. Howard Kerr. LC 78-170964. 271p. reprint ed. pap. 84.10 (*0-608-14878-4*, 202591900047) Bks Demand.

Mediums & the Conjurors. Ed. by James H. Webb, Jr. LC 75-36909. (Occult Ser.). 1976. 26.95 (*0-405-07967-2*) Ayer.

Mediums & the Development of Mediumship. Robert G. Chaney. 215p. 1977. 19.95 (*0-8369-2761-3*) Ayer.

Mediums of Language: Vernon Fisher, Myrel Chernick, Paul Sharits. Notes by Kathy Halbreich. (Illus.). 60p. (Orig.). 1982. pap. 5.00 (*0-938437-05-4*) MIT List Visual Arts.

Mediums Rare. Stuart Gray. 110p. (C). 1988. pap. 35.00 (*0-7212-0706-5*, Pub. by Regency Pr GBR) St Mut.

Mediumship: A Beginner's Guide. Leo Gough. 96p. 1997. pap. 11.95 (*0-340-68009-1*, Pub. by Headway) Trafalgar.

Mediumship & Its Laws. Hudson Tuttle. 186p. 1996. reprint ed. spiral bd. 14.50 (*0-7873-0903-6*) Hlth Research.

Mediumship & Survival: A Century of Investigations. Alan Gauld. 287p. 1984. pap. 8.00 (*0-586-08429-0*) Academy Chi Pubs.

Medizin. G. Alexander. 1983. 95.00 (*0-8288-1856-8*, M15409) Fr & Eur.

Medizin-Pharmazie, Zoologie-Tierheilkunde Bis ca. 430 H. Fuat Sezgin. (Geschichte des Arabischen Schrifttums Ser.: Vol. 3). (GER.). xxi, 498p. 1996. 181.00 (*90-04-03131-6*) Brill Academic Pubs.

Medizin Von A Boz Z. (GER.). 464p. 1973. pap. 48.00 (*0-7859-0701-7*, M7553) Fr & Eur.

Medizingeschichte Japans. Erhard Rosner. LC 89-30046. (Handbuch der Orientalistik Ser.: Vol. 5/3/5). (GER.). vi, 135p. (Orig.). 1989. pap. 128.00 (*90-04-08815-6*) Brill Academic Pubs.

Medizinische Erklaerung der Maennlichen Homosexualitaet aus der Antike. P. H. Schrijvers. (Caelius Aurelianus de Morbis Chronicis Ser.: Vol. 9). (GER.). vi, 75p. (Orig.). 1985. pap. 21.00 (*90-6032-266-5*, Pub. by B R Gruner) Humanities.

Medizinische Informatik, Biometrie und Epidemiologie. Ed. by Hans-Juergen Seelos. (GER.). xvi, 299p. (Orig.). (C). 1997. pap. text 42.95 (*3-11-014317-8*) De Gruyter.

Medizinische Schriften see Saemtliche Schriften

Medizinische Universitaets Poliklinik Basel, 100 Jahre. Ed. by J. B. Obrecht & U. C. Dubach. (Illus.). 100p. 1975. 26.00 (*3-8055-2280-0*) S Karger.

Medizinisches Sachwoererbuch: German-English-French-Latin. Albert Nobel. (ENG, FRE & GER.). 846p. 1987. 150.00 (*0-7859-6961-6*) Fr & Eur.

Medizinisches Woerterbuch. Urban Kaps. 17.95 (*0-8288-7823-4*, M7555); pap. 17.95 (*0-686-56632-7*, M-7555) Fr & Eur.

Medizinisches Woerterbuch. Margaret Minker. (GER.). 320p. 1992. 29.95 (*0-7859-8496-8*, 3809400580) Fr & Eur.

Medizinisches Woerterbuch. 36th ed. Boss. (GER.). 864p. 1994. 49.95 (*0-7859-7443-1*, 3541159464) Fr & Eur.

Medizinisches Woerterbuch: Medical Dictionary. 6th rev. ed. E. Veillon & Albert Nobel. (ENG, FRE & GER.). 1329p. 1989. 350.00 (*0-8288-6606-6*, M4673) Fr & Eur.

Medjugore: What the Church Says. 3rd ed. Emmanuel. LC 99-217080. 30p. 1998. pap. 3.00 (*1-57918-054-X*, 3652) Queenship Pub.

Medjugore Rosary Meditations. Rosalie Turton. 20p. 1996. pap. 4.00 (*1-890137-33-2*) One Hund-One Fnd.

Medjugorje: A Time for Truth & a Time for Action. Denis Nolan. 1993. pap. text 2.00 (*1-882972-05-8*, 3061) Queenship Pub.

Medjugorje: After Fifteen Years. 2nd rev. ed. Michael Davies. 95p. 1998. pap. 9.00 (*1-890740-01-2*) Remnant Pr.

Medjugorje: Facts, Documents, Theology. 4th ed. Michael O'Carroll. 224p. (Orig.). 1989. pap. 13.95 (*1-85390-073-7*, Pub. by Veritas Pubns) St Mut.

Medjugorje: Religion, Politics, & Violence in Rural Bosnia. Mart Bax. 180p. 1995. pap. 25.00 (*90-5383-384-6*) Paul & Co Pubs.

Medjugorje: Story of a Picture. Charles R. Toye. (Orig.). 1995. pap. 8.95 (*0-9619732-4-2*) Send Your Spirit Pub.

Medjugorje: The Untold Story. E. Michael Jones. 150p. (Orig.). 1988. pap. 9.95 (*0-929891-00-7*) Fidelity Pr.

Medjugorje: The 90's. Emmanuel Sister. 1999. pap. text 11.95 (*1-57918-104-X*) Queenship Pub.

Medjugorje, a Pilgrims Journey. Armando Minutoli. 224p. (Orig.). 1991. pap. 9.95 (*0-9630544-0-6*) Mrng Star NY.

Medjugorje & the Family: Helping Families to Live the Message. Mark I. Miravalle. 174p. 1990. pap. 6.95 (*0-940535-33-5*, UP133) Franciscan U Pr.

Medjugorje Apocalypse. Ilija Poplasen. (Illus.). 430p. 1991. 20.00 (*0-935352-27-9*) MIR PA.

Medjugorje Apocalypse. 2nd ed. Ilija Poplasen. (Illus.). 430p. 1992. reprint ed. 20.00 (*0-935352-34-1*) MIR PA.

Medjugorje Day by Day: A Daily Meditation Book Based on the Messages of Our Lady of Medjugorje. Richard J. Beyer. LC 92-74779. (Illus.). 544p. (Orig.). 1993. pap. 12.95 (*0-87793-494-0*) Ave Maria.

Medjugorje Deception: Queen of Peace, Ethnic Cleansing, Ruined Lives. E. Michael Jones. LC 98-92846. 1998. pap. 19.95 (*0-929891-05-8*) Fidelity Pr.

Medjugorje Facts Documents Theology. Michael O'Carroll. 265p. 1989. 24.00 (*1-85390-141-5*, Pub. by Veritas Pubns) St Mut.

Medjugorje Journal: Mary Speaks to the World. Robert S. Faricy & Lucy Rooney. 152p. (C). 1988. 39.00 (*0-85597-398-6*, Pub. by McCrimmon Pub) St Mut.

Medjugorje Journal: Mary Speaks to the World. Lucy Rooney & Robert S. Faricy. (Illus.). 200p. (Orig.). 1988. reprint ed. pap. 9.50 (*0-8199-0916-5*, Frncscn Herld) Franciscan Pr.

Medjugorje Retreat. RobertS. Faricy & Lucy Rooney. LC 89-32159. 127p. (Orig.). 1989. pap. 5.95 (*0-8189-0558-1*) Alba.

Medjugorje the Message. Wayne Weible. LC 89-62243. 355p. 1989. pap. 12.95 (*1-55725-009-X*, 930-002, Pub. by Paraclete MA) BookWorld.

Medjugorje the Mission. Wayne Weible. 416p. 1995. pap. 16.95 (*1-55725-127-4*, 930-007, Pub. by Paraclete MA) BookWorld.

Medjugorje under Siege. David Manuel. LC 92-80352. 182p. 1992. pap. 8.95 (*1-55725-052-9*) Paraclete MA.

Medjugorje Up-Close: Mary Speaks to the World. Lucy Rooney & Robert S. Faricy. 105p. 1986. pap. 5.95 (*0-8199-0902-5*, Frncscn Herld) Franciscan Pr.

Medlar Tree. Glenda Beagan. 148p. (Orig.). 1992. pap. 18.95 (*1-85411-068-3*, Pub. by Seren Bks) Dufour.

MedLearn's CPT Coding Workbook. 485350p. 1997. pap. text 49.00 (*1-889115-20-7*) Med Learn.

MedLearn's CPT Coding Workbook: Instructor's Edition. 350p. 1997. 89.00 (*1-889115-21-5*) Med Learn.

Medley: Four Plays & Four Adaptations. Martha Keltz. 171p. (Orig.). 1996. pap. 27.00 (*1-893592-07-3*) Studio Eds.

***Medley: Four Plays & Four Adaptations.** Martha Keltz. 171p. (Orig.). (YA). 2000. pap. write for info. (*1-893592-17-0*, TC Pubs) Studio Eds.

Medley: Poems from Hollywood. Mark Dunster. 11p. 1998. pap. 5.00 (*0-89642-585-1*) Linden Pubs.

Medley for J. Dale Drakeford. 160p. 1997. pap. write for info. (*1-57502-506-X*, P01506) Morris Pubng.

Medley of Myths. Dorothy B. Pollack. (Illus.). 149p. (YA). (gr. 7-12). spiral bd. 4.75 (*0-939507-46-3*, B206) Amer Classical.

Medley of Precast & Prestressed Concrete Systems. (PCI Journal Reprints Ser.). 12p. 1973. pap. 12.00 (*0-686-40050-X*, JR125) P-PCI.

Medley of Short Stories. Alice Sonnier. (J). (gr. 4-6). 1997. 12.00 (*0-9660963-0-4*) A Sonnier.

Medleys. John C. Moon et al. LC 75-19259. (Musick of the Fifes & Drums Ser.: Vol. 3). 23p. 1980. pap. 2.99 (*0-87935-050-4*) Colonial Williamsburg.

Medleys: Poems from Hollywood. Mark Dunster. 12p. (Orig.). (gr. 9-12). 1997. pap. 5.00 (*0-89642-379-4*) Linden Pubs.

Medline: A Basic Guide to Searching. Susan J. Feinglos. 138p. (Orig.). 1985. pap. text 27.00 (*0-8108-2427-2*) Scarecrow.

***Medline: A Guide to Effective Searching.** Brian S. Katcher. LC 99-64479. (Illus.). 160p. (C). 1999. pap. text 29.00 (*0-9673445-0-6*) Ashbury Pr.

Medline for Health Professionals: How to Search Pubmed on the Internet. David Hutchinson. (Illus.). 176p. (Orig.). 1998. pap. 29.95 (*0-9651412-6-8*) New Wind.

Medoere Domain Sourcebook. TSR Inc. Staff. (Advanced Dungeons & Dragons, 2nd Edition: Birthright Campaign World Ser.). 1995. 6.95 (*0-7869-0287-6*, Pub. by TSR Inc) Random.

Medora Deadwood Stageline. Lewis Crawford. (Shorey Historical Ser.). 26p. reprint ed. pap. 10.00 (*0-8466-0036-6*, S36) Shoreys Bkstore.

Medora Leigh: A History & an Autobiography. Ed. by Charles Mackay. LC 78-37700. reprint ed. 39.50 (*0-404-56759-2*) AMS Pr.

MedStudy - A Condensed. 8th ed. Robert A. Hannaman. 450p. 1999. ring bd. 395.00 (*0-9640788-4-8*) MedStudy.

Med/Surg Policy & Procedure Guideline Manual. Diane Johnson. 195p. 1998. spiral bd. 125.00 (*1-879575-89-2*) Acad Med Sys.

Med'Toons. Stephen Goldberg. (Illus.). 145p. 1999. pap. text 8.95 (*0-940780-40-2*) MedMaster.

Medu Nasim Narodom U Americi. Ivo F. Lupis. LC 71-155327. 1971. reprint ed. 10.00 (*0-88247-053-1*) Ragusan Pr.

Medullary Thyroid Carcinoma. L. J. Deftos. (Beitraege Zur Onkologie, Contributions to Oncology Ser.: Vol. 17). (Illus.). x, 114p. 1983. pap. 72.25 (*3-8055-3703-4*) S Karger.

Medullary Thyroid Carcinoma. Ed. by F. Raue et al. LC 92-2297. (Recent Results in Cancer Research Ser.: Vol. 125). (Illus.). 232p. 1992. 104.00 (*0-387-55372-X*) Spr-Verlag.

Medulloblastomas in Children: New Concepts in Tumor Biology, Diagnosis & Treatment. Ed. by Paul M. Zeltzer & Carl Pochedly. LC 86-15105. 274p. 1986. 69.50 (*0-275-92164-6*, C2164, Praeger Pubs) Greenwood.

Medusa. Bernard Evslin. (Monsters of Mythology Ser.). (Illus.). 104p. 1987. lib. bdg. 19.95 (*1-55546-238-3*) Chelsea Hse.

Medusa. Deborah Nourse Lattimore. LC 99-29244. (Illus.). 32p. (J). (gr. 2-5). 2000. 15.95 (*0-06-027904-4*); lib. bdg. 15.89 (*0-06-027905-2*) HarpC Child Bks.

Medusa: A Tiger by the Tail. Jack L. Chalker. (Four Lords of the Diamond Ser.: Bk. 4). 304p. (Orig.). 1983. mass mkt. 4.95 (*0-345-29372-X*, Del Rey) Ballantine Pub Grp.

***Medusa: Solving the Mystery of the Gorgon.** Stephen R. Wilk. LC 99-10739. (Illus.). 352p. 2000. 35.00 (*0-19-512431-6*) OUP.

***Medusa: The Fourth Kingdom.** Marina Minghelli. Tr. by Beverly Allen from ITA. LC 99-17610. 190p. 1999. pap. 10.95 (*0-87286-353-0*) City Lights.

Medusa & the Snail: More Notes of a Biology Watcher. Lewis Thomas. 192p. 1995. pap. 12.95 (*0-14-024319-4*, Penguin Bks) Viking Penguin.

Medusa Child. Sylvie Germain. Tr. by Liz Nash from FRE. (Europe 1992-97 Ser.).Tr. of D'Enfant Meduse. 247p. 1997. pap. 13.99 (*1-873982-31-3*, Pub. by Dedalus) Hippocrene Bks.

Medusa Effect. Justin Richards. (New Adventures Ser.). 1998. mass mkt. 5.95 (*0-426-20524-3*, Pub. by Virgin Bks) London Brdge.

Medusa File: Crimes & Coverups of the U. S. Government. Craig Roberts. 507p. 1997. reprint ed. pap. text 24.95 (*0-9639062-4-0*, Pub. by Consol Pr Intl) ACCESS Pubs Network.

Medusa Head. Mary Meigs. LC 83-91368. 160p. 1983. pap. 12.95 (*0-88922-210-X*, Pub. by Talonbks) Genl Dist Srvs.

Medusa Meets Holofernes: Poetologische, Semiologische und Intertextuelle Diskursivierung von Enthauptung. Volker Mergenthaler. LC 97-206185. (GER., Illus.). 153p. 1997. 28.95 (*3-906757-47-1*, Pub. by P Lang) P Lang Pubng.

Medusa Plague. Mary Kirchoff. (DragonLance Defenders of Magic Ser.). 320p. (Orig.). 1994. pap. 5.99 (*1-56076-905-X*, Pub. by TSR Inc) Random.

***Medusa Reader.** GARBER. 2000. pap. 20.00 (*0-415-90099-9*) Routledge.

Medusa Reader. Marjorie Garber. 256p. (C). (gr. 13). 1999. 55.00 (*0-415-90098-0*) Routledge.

Medusa Snare. (Illus.). 260p. write for info. (*1-885351-21-6*) Cheval Intl.

***Medusa Stone.** Jack Du Brul. 464p. 2000. mass mkt. 6.99 (*0-451-40922-1*, Onyx) NAL.

Medusa Tree. Mylene Dressler. LC 96-45547. 176p. 1997. 18.50 (*1-878448-75-7*) MacMurray & Beck.

Medusario: Muestra de Poesia Latinoamericana (A Sampling of Latin American Poetry) Roberto Echaverren et al. (SPA.). 496p. 1996. pap. 23.99 (*968-16-4857-9*, Pub. by Fondo) Continental Bk.

Medusa's Child. John J. Nance. 1997. mass mkt. 6.99 (*0-312-96245-2*, St Martins Paperbacks) St Martin.

Medusa's Gaze: Casuistry & Conscience in the Renaissance. Lowell Gallagher. LC 90-39914. (Illus.). 344p. 1991. 37.50 (*0-8047-1859-8*) Stanford U Pr.

Medusa's Hair: An Essay on Personal Symbols & Religious Experiences. Gananath Obeyesekere. LC 80-27372. (Illus.). 232p. 1984. pap. text 11.00 (*0-226-61601-0*) U Ch Pr.

Medusa's Mirrors: Spenser, Shakespeare, Milton, & the Metamorphosis of the Female Self. Julia M. Walker. LC 97-35455. 240p. 1998. 39.50 (*0-87413-625-3*) U Delaware Pr.

***Medusa's Overbite.** Peter V. Dugan. 95p. 1999. pap. 9.95 (*0-9651162-4-7*) Wysteria Ltd.

Medusenhaupt der Kritik: Die Kontroverse Zwischen Immanuel Kant und Johann August Eberhard. Manfred Gawlina. (Kantstudien Ergaenzungsheft Ser.: Band 128). (GER.). ix, 345p. (C). 1995. lib. bdg. 123.10 (*3-11-015047-6*) De Gruyter.

Medvedb's Journal. Kendall Merriam. 32p. 1991. pap. 5.00 (*0-942396-64-2*) Blackberry ME.

Medway. Virginia C. Beach. LC 99-10585. (Illus.). 136p. 1999. 35.00 (*0-941711-38-2*) Wyrick & Co.

Medway, Massachusetts, Births, Marriages, & Deaths. Francis D. Donovan. 190p. (Orig.). 1995. pap. text 29.50 (*0-7884-0230-7*) Heritage Bk.

Medytacons of Saynt Bernarde. Saint Bernard. LC 77-6855. (English Experience Ser.: No. 847). 1977. reprint ed. lib. bdg. 20.00 (*90-221-0847-3*) Walter J Johnson.

Mearmeear Traditions. Charles C. Trowbridge. Ed. by Vernon Kinietz. LC 38-1044. (University of Michigan, Museum of Occasional Contributions Ser.: No. 7). (Illus.). 105p. reprint ed. pap. 32.60 (*0-608-17571-4*, 203057600069) Bks Demand.

Meech Lake: The Inside Story. Patrick J. Monahan. 336p. 1991. text 50.00 (*0-8020-5969-4*); pap. text 19.95 (*0-8020-6896-0*) U of Toronto Pr.

Meech Lake Post-Mortem: Is Quebec Sovereignty Inevitable? Pierre Fournier. 168p. (C). 1991. pap. text 24.95 (*0-7735-0867-8*, Pub. by McG-Queens Univ Pr) CUP Services.

Meek & Lowly. Neal A. Maxwell. LC 86-32784. xii, 127p. 1994. pap. 6.95 (*0-87579-945-0*) Deseret Bk.

Meek Shall Inherit the Earth - But Who Wants It? Terry Crist. Ed. by Jimmy Peacock. 64p. (Orig.). 1990. pap. 4.95 (*0-9623768-9-2*) SpiritBuilder.

Meeker: The Story of the Meeker Massacre & Thornburgh Battle. Fred H. Werner. LC 84-52706. (Western Americana Ser.). (Illus.). 150p. (Orig.). 1985. pap. 8.95 (*0-933147-07-4*) Werner Pubn.

Meeker County Cemeteries Vol. 2: Acton, Darwin, Dassel, Forest City, Forest Prairie, Kingston, Manannah, North Kingston, Swede Grove & Union Grove Townships. Illus. & Compiled by Diane Rosenow. LC 93-31365. 140p. (Orig.). 1993. pap. 15.00 (*0-915709-11-2*) Pk Geneal Bk.

Meeker County Minnesota Cemeteries Vol. 1: Cedar Mills, Collinwood, Cosmos, Danielson, Ellsworth, Greenleaf & Litchfield Townships. Illus. & Compiled by Diane Rosenow. LC 93-31365. 132p. (Orig.). 1993. pap. 15.00 (*0-915709-10-4*) Pk Geneal Bk.

Meeker Mansion Mysteries: A Fiction Anthology. Ed. by Penny Lent. LC 94-76615. (Illus.). 84p. (Orig.). 1994. pap. 5.95 (*1-885371-03-9*) Kldoscope Pr.

Meekness: Claiming Your Inheritance. Jim Plueddemann & Carol Plueddemann. (Beatitudes Ser.). 48p. 1993. 5.99 (*0-310-59623-8*) Zondervan.

Meekness & Majesty. R. T. Kendall. Date not set. 8.99 (*1-871676-87-8*, Pub. by Christian Focus) Spring Arbor Dist.

Meeko's Busy Day. LC 96-217848. (Pop Up Ser.). (Illus.). 12p. (J). (ps-1). 1995. 6.98 (*1-57082-120-8*, Pub. by Mouse Works) Little.

Meeko's New Friend Little Play. boxed set 6.98 (*0-7853-1336-2*) Pubns Intl Ltd.

Meeks Bay Memories. Carol Van Etten. (Illus.). 272p. 1994. pap. 24.95 (*0-913814-29-6*) Nevada Pubns.

***Meely LaBauve: A Novel.** Ken Wells. LC 99-36281. 240p. 2000. 19.95 (*0-375-50311-0*) Random.

Meema's Memory Quilt: Treasured Stories of Watauga County History. Jane Wilson & Michaele Haas. LC 99-23795. (Illus.). 32p. 1999. 16.95 (*1-887905-18-9*) Pkway Pubs.

Meena of Nepal. Linda Cloud. (Illus.). 37p. (J). (gr. 1-6). 1982. spiral bd. 5.00 (*1-58318-039-7*, WOL018B) Way of Life.

Meenakshi Hindi-English Dictionary. (ENG & HIN.). 1981. 15.00 (*0-8364-0790-3*, Pub. by Meenakshi) S Asia.

Meere Scholler: Cross-Cultural Perspectives on Our Educational Heritage. Ed. by Lucy F. Townsend et al. LC 95-11577. 1996. 20.00 (*1-879528-13-4*) Ed Studies Pr.

Meeresbiologie: Eine Einfuehrung in die Probleme und Ergebnisse. Hermann Friedrich. (GER.). viii, 436p. 1965. 52.00 (*3-443-39032-3*, Pub. by Gebruder Borntraeger) Balogh.

Meeresprodukte: Ein Handwoerterbuch der Marinen Rohstoffe Unter Mitwirkung. Caesar Boettger. Ed. by Ferdinand Pax. (GER.). xii, 459p. 1962. 46.00 (*3-443-39033-1*, Pub. by Gebruder Borntraeger) Balogh.

Meerkat in Trouble. Allan Frewin Jones. (Illus.). 32p. (J). (ps). 1998. 13.95 (*1-887734-55-4*); pap. 5.95 (*1-887734-61-9*) Star Brght Bks.

Meerkats. Robyn Weaver. LC 98-17332. (Animals Ser.). (J). 1998. 14.00 (*0-7368-0066-2*, Bridgestone Bks) Capstone Pr.

Meerkats. Robyn Weaver. (Bridgestone Animals Ser.). (J). 1998. 14.00 (*0-516-21344-X*) Childrens.

Meespierson International Commodities Handbook, 1997. 170.00 (*1-85564-410-X*, Pub. by Euromoney) Am Educ Systs.

***Meet A. A. Milne.** Stasia Ward Kehoe. LC 99-59755. (About the Author Ser.). 2000. write for info. (*0-8239-5708-X*) Rosen Group.

Meet... a Fish! see Neqem Ayuqucia Nallunritellruan-qaa... Nega!

***Meet Abraham Lincoln.** Barbara Cary. (J). 2001. pap. 5.99 (*0-375-80396-3*) Random Bks Yng Read.

Meet Abraham Lincoln. Barbara Cary. LC 88-19066. (Step-up Biographies Ser.). (Illus.). 72p. (J). (gr. 2-4). 1989. reprint ed. pap. 3.99 (*0-394-81966-7*, Pub. by Random Bks Yng Read) Random.

Meet Addy: An American Girl. Connie Rose Porter. LC 98-6724. (American Girls Collection : Bk. 1). (Illus.). 69p. (YA). (gr. 2 up). 1993. pap. 5.95 (*1-56247-075-2*); lib. bdg. 12.95 (*1-56247-076-0*) Pleasant Co.

Meet Addy: An American Girl. Connie Rose Porter. (American Girls Collection: Bk. 1). (Illus.). (YA). (gr. 2 up). 1993. 11.15 (*0-606-05459-6*, Pub. by Turtleback) Demco.

***Meet African Americans in Minnesota.** Contrib. by Nora Murphy & Mary Murphy-Gnatz. LC 99-54539. 88p. (J). 2000. 11.95 (*0-87351-380-0*, Borealis Book) Minn Hist.

Meet at the Falls: The Story of the Pioneers. Ruth E. Reuther. Ed. by Jody McCall. (Series 2). (Illus.). (J). 1989. pap. text. write for info. (*0-9622632-1-4*) Wee-Chee-Taw.

Meet Babar & His Family see Santa's Take-Along Library: Five Favorite Read-to-Me Books

An Asterisk (*) at the beginning of an entry indicates that the title is appearing for the first time.

Meet Babar & His Family. Laurent de Brunhoff. LC 73-2445. (Illus.). 32p. (J). (ps-1). 1973. pap. 3.25 (*0-394-82682-5*, Pub. by Random Bks Yng Read) Random.

***Meet Bathsheba: Dramatic Portraits of Biblical Women.** Rosanne Gartner. LC 99-58737. 160p. 2000. pap. 16.00 (*0-8170-1355-5*) Judson.

Meet Benjamin Franklin. Maggie Scarf. LC 88-17657. (Step-up Biographies Ser.). (Illus.). 64p. (J). (gr. 2-4). 1989. reprint ed. pap. 3.99 (*0-394-81961-6*, Pub. by Random Bks Yng Read) Random.

***Meet Beverly Cleary.** S. Ward. LC 00-24211. (About the Author Ser.). (Illus.). 2001. write for info. (*0-8239-5710-1*, PowerKids) Rosen Group.

Meet Calliope Day. Charles Haddad. 1999. pap. 3.99 (*0-440-41409-1*) BDD Bks Young Read.

***Meet Chadwick & His Chesapeake Bay Friends.** Priscilla Cummings. (Illus.). 30p. (J). (ps). 1999. 11.95 (*0-87033-516-2*, Tidewtr Pubs) Cornell Maritime.

Meet Charles Barkley. Consumer Guide Editors. 1999. pap. 3.99 (*0-451-18228-6*, Sig) NAL.

Meet Christopher Columbus. James T. de Kay. LC 88-19068. (Step-up Biographies Ser.). (Illus.). 72p. (J). (gr. 2-4). 1989. reprint ed. pap. 3.99 (*0-394-81963-2*, Pub. by Random Bks Yng Read) Random.

Meet Colleen Marie. Kathleen McFarland & Judy Larkin. (Illus.). 22p. (Orig.). (J). (ps). 1985. pap. write for info. (*0-9621691-0-2*, TX 1-650-724) B Bumpers Inc.

Meet Corn Island: The History of Corn Island in Relation to the Ebenezer Baptist Church. Rodwell Morgan. LC 97-104194. 214p. (Orig.). 1996. pap. 14.95 (*1-57502-314-8*, P01063) Morris Pubng.

Meet Danitra Brown. Nikki Grimes. LC 92-43707. (Illus.). (J). (gr. k up). 1994. 16.00 (*0-688-12073-3*); lib. bdg. 15.93 (*0-688-12074-1*) Lothrop.

Meet Danitra Brown. Nikki Grimes. LC 92-43707. (Illus.). 32p. (J). 1997. mass mkt. 4.95 (*0-688-15471-9*, Wm Morrow) Morrow Avon.

Meet Danitra Brown. Nikki Grimes. 1997. 10.15 (*0-606-11613-3*, Pub. by Turtleback) Demco.

Meet Dinah Dinosaur see Boxed Set of 4 Brand New Readers

***Meet Dinah Dinosaur.** B. G. Hennessy. LC 00-20927. (Illus.). (J). 2000. 10.99 (*0-7636-1133-6*) Candlewick Pr.

***Meet Divine Mother: An Intimate Introduction to the Other Half of Heaven.** Wendy Scott. LC 99-71504. (Illus.). 256p. 1999. pap. 16.95 (*1-893724-00-X*) Gold Fire.

***Meet E. B. White.** S. Ward. LC 00-25376. (About the Author Ser.). 2001. write for info. (*0-8239-5713-6*) Rosen Group.

Meet Edgar Degas. Anne Newlands & National Gallery of Canada Staff. LC 88-32035. (Illus.). 32p. (J). (gr. 1 up). 1989. 13.95 (*0-397-32369-7*) HarpC Child Bks.

Meet Emmitt Smith. Consumer Guide Editors. 1999. pap. 3.99 (*0-451-18350-9*, Sig) NAL.

Meet Felicity: An American Girl. Valerie Tripp. (American Girls Collection : Bk. 1). (Illus.). 80p. (YA). (gr. 2 up). 1991. pap. 5.95 (*1-56247-004-3*); lib. bdg. 12.95 (*1-56247-005-1*) Pleasant Co.

Meet Felicity: An American Girl. Valerie Tripp. (American Girls Collection: Bk. 1). (Illus.). (YA). (gr. 2 up). 1991. 11.15 (*0-606-05053-1*, Pub. by Turtleback) Demco.

Meet General Grant. William E. Woodward. (History - United States Ser.). 524p. 1993. reprint ed. lib. bdg. 99.00 (*0-7812-4913-9*) Rprt Serv.

***Meet George Washington.** Joan Hellbroner. (YA). 2001. pap. 5.99 (*0-375-80397-1*) Random Bks Yng Read.

Meet George Washington. Joan Hellbroner. LC 88-19067. (Step-up Biographies Ser.). (Illus.). 72p. (J). (gr. 2-4). 1989. reprint ed. pap. 3.99 (*0-394-81965-9*, Pub. by Random Bks Yng Read) Random.

Meet God! A Young Christian's Handbook for Knowing God. John R. Higgins. LC 88-80294. (Illus.). 128p. (J). (gr. 4-6). 1988. pap. 6.50 (*0-88243-488-8*, 02-0488) Gospel Pub.

Meet God & Live. Vera Stantan. (C). 1988. 39.00 (*0-85439-018-9*, Pub. by St Paul Pubns) St Mut.

Meet Hattie. Marie Frost. LC 94-10280. (Treasures of Childhood: The Hattie Collection: No. 1). (J). (gr. 1). 1994. pap. 4.99 (*1-56179-214-4*) Focus Family.

Meet Him at the Manger: Discovering the Heart of Christmas. Stuart Briscoe & Jill Briscoe. 160p. 1996. 15.99 (*0-87788-557-5*, H Shaw Pubs) Waterbrook Pr.

Meet in the Middle: The Parents Test - The Kids Test. Carole Marsh. (Quantum Leap Ser.). (Illus.). (J). (gr. 4 up). 1994. 29.95 (*0-935326-24-3*) Gallopade Intl.

Meet Initial Guidance Needs of Older Adults Module, Competency-Based Career Guidance (CBCG) - Category C: Implementing. National Center for Research in Vocational Educati. 1985. 7.95 (*0-317-03902-4*, CG100C16) Ctr Educ Trng Employ.

***Meet it, Greet it & Defeat It.** Anna Christian. 196p. 1999. pap. 13.95 (*1-881524-47-7*) Milligan Bks.

Meet It with Faith. Martha Smock. 162p. 1994. pap. 9.95 (*0-87159-074-3*) Unity Bks.

***Meet J. K. Rowling.** S. Ward. LC 00-25375. (Illus.). (J). 2000. write for info. (*0-8239-5711-X*, PowerKids) Rosen Group.

Meet Jemima Puddle Duck. Illus. by Beatrix Potter. (Board Bks. Ser.). 12p. 1996. bds. 3.50 (*0-7232-4324-7*) Warner Juvenile Bks.

Meet Jeremiah: A Devotional Commentary. Burton L. Goddard. LC 91-21205. 144p. 1992. pap. 9.99 (*0-8254-2728-2*) Kregel.

Meet Jesus in the Sunday Gospels: Sermons. Anthony M. Coniaris. 1986. pap. 15.95 (*0-937032-41-7*) Light&Life Pub Co MN.

Meet Jesus in the Sunday Gospels: Sermons, Vol. 2. Anthony M. Coniaris. 1987. pap. 15.95 (*0-937032-45-X*) Light&Life Pub Co MN.

Meet Jim Henson. Susan Canizares & Samantha Berger. LC 99-14914. (Social Studies Emergent Readers Ser.). (J). 1999. 4.35 (*0-439-04575-4*) Scholastic Inc.

Meet John Dark. Simon Gane. 1999. pap. text 9.95 (*1-899866-16-7*) Slab-O-Concrete Pubns.

Meet John Doe. Ed. by Charles K. Wolfe. (Films in Print Ser.). (Illus.). 220p. 1989. pap. text 17.00 (*0-8135-1387-1*) Rutgers U Pr.

Meet Josefina: An American Girl. Valerie Tripp. LC 96-45281. (American Girls Collection : Bk. 1). (Illus.). 96p. (YA). (gr. 2 up). 1997. pap. 5.95 (*1-56247-515-0*); lib. bdg. 12.95 (*1-56247-516-9*) Pleasant Co.

Meet Josefina: An American Girl. Valerie Tripp. LC 96-45281. (American Girls Collection: Bk. 1). (Illus.). (YA). (gr. 2 up). 1997. 11.15 (*0-606-11614-1*, Pub. by Turtleback) Demco.

Meet Josefina: An American Girl see Asi es Josefina: Una Nina Americana

Asi es Josefina: Una Nina Americana. Valerie Tripp. Tr. by Jose Moreno. LC 97-19934. (American Girls Collection : Bk. 1).Tr. of Meet Josefina: An American Girl. (SPA., Illus.). 85p. (YA). (gr. 3-7). 1997. text 5.95 (*1-56247-496-0*, Amer Girl Library) Pleasant Co.

Asi es Josefina: Una Nina Americana. Valerie Tripp. (American Girls Collection).Tr. of Meet Josefina: An American Girl. (Illus.). (YA). (gr. 2 up). 1997. 11.15 (*0-606-11060-7*, Pub. by Turtleback) Demco.

Meet Kirsten: An American Girl. Janet B. Shaw. Ed. by Jeanne Thieme. (American Girls Collection : Bk. 1). (Illus.). 72p. (YA). (gr. 2 up). 1986. pap. 5.95 (*0-937295-01-9*); lib. bdg. 12.95 (*0-937295-79-5*) Pleasant Co.

Meet Kirsten: An American Girl. Janet B. Shaw. (American Girls Collection: Bk. 1). (Illus.). (YA). (gr. 2 up). 1986. 11.15 (*0-606-02754-8*, Pub. by Turtleback) Demco.

***Meet Kit: An American Girl.** Valerie Tripp. LC 99-88029. (American Girls Collection : Bk. 1). (Illus.). (YA). (gr. 4-7). 2000. pap. 12.95 (*1-58485-017-5*); pap. write for info. (*1-58485-016-7*) Pleasant Co.

Meet Kofi, Maria & Sunita: Family Life in Ghana, Peru & India. Lesley A. Simmons. (Stories from the World Bank Ser.: Vol. 1). 80p. (J). (gr. 2-4). 1996. 14.95 (*0-942389-12-3*) Cobblestone Pub Co.

Meet Kropotkin, the Master. Herbert E. Read. 1973. 59.95 (*0-8490-0602-3*) Gordon Pr.

***Meet Laura Ingalls Wilder.** S. Ward. LC 00-25374. (Illus.). (J). 2000. write for info. (*0-8239-5712-8*, PowerKids) Rosen Group.

Meet M & M. Pat Ross. (Puffin Chapters Ser.). (Illus.). 64p. (J). (gr. 2-5). 1997. pap. 3.99 (*0-14-038731-5*, PuffinBks) Peng Put Young Read.

Meet M & M. Pat Ross. (Puffin Chapters Ser.). 1997. 9.19 (*0-606-12766-6*, Pub. by Turtleback) Demco.

Meet Marshall Parks, Founder of Virginia Beach: Portion of Marshall Parks Scrapbook. 2nd ed. Ed. by Calvert W. Tazewell. LC 90-80466. (Tazewell & Allied Families Scrapbooks Ser.: Vol. 5). (Illus.). 54p. 1990. pap. 7.00 (*1-878515-16-0*); 2.00 (*1-878515-59-4*); disk 4.00 (*1-878515-70-5*) W S Dawson.

***Meet Martin Luther King, Jr.** James T. de Kay. (Illus.). (J). 2001. pap. 5.99 (*0-375-80395-5*) Random Bks Yng Read.

***Meet Martin Luther King Jr.** James T. de Kay. 1999. pap. text 11.10 (*0-8335-3924-8*) Econo-Clad Bks.

Meet Martin Luther King, Jr. rev. ed. James T. DeKay. (Bullseye Biographies Ser.). (Illus.). 112p. (J). (gr. 3-5). 1993. pap. 3.99 (*0-679-85411-8*, Pub. by Random Bks Yng Read) Random.

Meet Matt & Roxy. Karen Huszar. (Illus.). 24p. (J). (ps-3). 1996. 12.95 (*1-55143-053-3*) Orca Bk Pubs.

Meet Maya Angelou. Valerie Spain. LC 94-1294. (Bullseye Biography Ser.). (Illus.). 96p. (J). 1995. pap. 3.99 (*0-679-86542-X*, Pub. by Random Bks Yng Read) Random.

Meet Maya Angelou. Valerie Spain. 1994. 9.09 (*0-606-07034-6*, Pub. by Turtleback) Demco.

Meet Me at Carnegie Hall. Gwen Woodruff. Ed. by Dick Woodruff. LC 92-93256. (Illus.). 280p. 1992. 16.95 (*0-9616165-3-9*) Woodruff Pub.

Meet Me at Infinity. Tiptree Staff. LC 99-58425. 384p. 2000. text 25.95 (*0-312-85874-4*) St Martin.

Meet Me at Jim & Andy's: Jazz Musicians & Their World. Gene Lees. 288p. 1990. reprint ed. pap. 10.95 (*0-19-506580-8*) OUP.

Meet Me at Luigi's: An Interactive Dinner Theatre Event in Six Scenes. Celesta Letchworth & Tom Letchworth. 1998. pap. 8.99 (*0-8341-9105-9*) Lillenas.

Meet Me at Midnight. Created by Francine Pascal. (Sweet Valley High Ser.: No. 124). 208p. (YA). (gr. 7 up). 1996. mass mkt. 3.99 (*0-553-56761-6*, Sweet Valley) BDD Bks Young Read.

Meet Me at Midnight. Kate William. (Sweet Valley High Ser.: No. 124). (YA). (gr. 7 up). 1996. 9.09 (*0-606-09923-9*, Pub. by Turtleback) Demco.

***Meet Me at Midnight: With This Ring.** Suzanne Enoch. 384p. 2000. mass mkt. 5.99 (*0-380-80917-6*) Morrow Avon.

Meet Me at the Fair: A "Choose Your Own Adventure" That Lets You Explore the Exciting Treasures of the 1904 St. Louis World's Fair. Barbara McDonough. (Illus.). 64p. (Orig.). (J). (gr. 4-6). 1988. pap. 4.50 (*0-931821-43-6*) Info Res Cons.

Meet Me at the Fair! Country, State, & World's Fairs & Expositions. Judy Alter. LC 97-5700. (First Book Ser.). 64p. (J). 1997. lib. bdg. 22.00 (*0-531-20307-7*) Watts.

Meet Me at the Falls: Activities Book. Ruth E. Reuther & A. G. Richardson. (Series 1). (Illus.). (Orig.). 1989. pap. text 5.98 (*0-9622601-0-6*) Wee-Chee-Taw.

Meet Me at the Loveless: A Southern Cafe's Cookbook. Donna McCabe & Mamie Stroud. LC 98-43872. (Illus.). 208p. 1998. pap. 19.95 (*1-888608-37-4*) Cool Springs Pr.

Meet Me at the Morgue. Ross MacDonald, pseud. 1984. mass mkt. 2.95 (*0-553-24033-1*) Bantam.

Meet Me at the Orange Blossom. Henry M. Schliff & Michael Schliff. (Illus.). 160p. 1997. 18.95 (*0-9658965-0-1*) Orange Blssm.

Meet Me at the Wall. Wynne McCormick. LC 93-9364. 189p. (Orig.). 1995. pap. 7.95 (*1-886825-00-9*) Stetson Pub.

Meet Me for Coffee: Cup of Fast & Furious Energizing Espresso. Frankie Buckley. LC 97-8312. (Illus.). 48p. (Orig.). 1998. 10.99 (*1-56507-661-3*) Harvest Hse.

Meet Me in a Taxi. Earl Diemel. 88p. 1998. pap. 10.00 (*0-8059-4152-5*) Dorrance.

Meet Me in Juneau. Olive Barber. LC 60-53461. (Illus.). 258p. 1960. 12.95 (*0-8323-0079-9*); pap. 9.95 (*0-8323-0256-2*) Binford Mort.

Meet Me in Juneau. Olive Barber. 175p. pap. text 13.00 (*1-57833-024-6*) Todd Commns.

Meet Me in St. Louis. Sally Benson. 1978. pap. 5.50 (*0-87129-246-7*, M24) Dramatic Pub.

Meet Me in St. Louis. Gerald Kaufman. (BFI Film Classics Ser.). (Illus.). 72p. 1995. pap. 10.95 (*0-85170-501-4*) Ind U Pr.

***Meet Me in the Garden.** Pauline E. Cramer. 2000. 15.99 (*1-56292-816-3*) Honor Bks OK.

Meet Me in the Kitchen: A Timeless Collection of Kitchen Tested Recipes! Bevelyn W. Blair. (Illus.). 320p. (Orig.). 1990. pap. 15.95 (*0-9613709-1-2*) Blair Columbus.

Meet Me in Time. Charlotte Vale Allen. 400p. 1998. reprint ed. pap. 22.00 (*0-9657437-9-9*) Isld Nation.

Meet Me in Time. Charlotte Vale Allen. 434p. 1998. reprint ed. 24.95 (*1-892738-14-7*, Pub. by Isld Nation) Brodart.

Meet Me on the Mayflower. Nanette Felloney. (Illus.). 21p. (J). (gr. 3 up). 1992. pap. 3.95 (*1-882684-00-1*) True Tales.

***Meet Me Online: The #1 Practical Guide to Internet Dating.** Lauren Conley. LC 99-67327. 130p. 1999. pap. 8.95 (*1-884778-78-X*, Pub. by Old Mountain) ACCESS Pubs Network.

Meet Me the Magic Kingdom. Kathy Jakobsen. LC 94-74961. (Illus.). 32p. (J). (ps-3). 1995. 13.95 (*0-7868-3038-7*, Pub. by Disney Pr) Little.

***Meet Mew!** Akihito Toda. (Pokemon Tales Ser.: No. 9). (Illus.). 18p. 2000. bds. 4.95 (*1-56931-440-3*, Pub. by Viz Commns Inc) Publishers Group.

Meet Mit. Alan M. Hofmeister et al. (Reading for All Learners Ser.). (Illus.). (J). pap. write for info. (*1-56861-079-3*) Swift Lrn Res.

Meet Molly: An American Girl. Valerie Tripp. Ed. by Jeanne Thieme. (American Girls Collection : Bk. 1). (Illus.). 59p. (YA). (gr. 2 up). 1986. pap. 5.95 (*0-937295-07-8*); lib. bdg. 12.95 (*0-937295-81-7*) Pleasant Co.

Meet Molly: An American Girl. Valerie Tripp. (American Girls Collection: Bk. 1). (Illus.). (YA). (gr. 2 up). 1986. 11.15 (*0-606-02769-6*, Pub. by Turtleback) Demco.

Meet Monica. Jan L. Fausnaugh. (Little Monkey Tales Ser.). (Illus.). 24p. (Orig.). (J). (gr. k-7). 1996. pap. 4.95 (*1-889645-00-1*) Cabin Fev Pubg.

Meet Moses. Mary N. Keithahn. 238p. 1996. pap. 29.95 (*1-877871-96-6*, 5268) Ed Ministries.

Meet Mr. CPU: An Introduction to the Components of a Personal Computer. Barbara Holliday. (Mr. CPU Ser.: No. 1). (Illus.). 31p. (J). (gr. k-5). 1997. pap. text 9.95 (*1-891727-00-1*) Fun Books.

Meet Mr. Jinnah. A. A. Ravoofs. 1983. pap. 9.50 (*1-56744-135-1*) Kazi Pubns.

Meet Mr. Rarebit. Ruth H. Wolf. 32p. (J). 1995. text 9.95 (*1-886094-12-8*) Chicago Spectrum.

***Meet Mudflat Joe Math.** McGraw-Hill Book Company Staff. 1999. 19.95 (*1-57768-315-3*) MG-Hill OH.

Meet My Friend David. Jane McWhorter. 1982. 7.15 (*0-89137-420-5*) Quality Pubns.

Meet My Friends: Children of the World, Vol. 15. Shirley A. Barone. (Illus.). 44p. (Orig.). (J). (ps-2). 1989. pap. write for info. (*0-318-66625-1*) Toad Hse Bks.

***Meet My Grandmother: She's a Deep Sea Explorer.** Lisa Tucker McElroy. LC 00-23091. (Grandmothers at Work Ser.). (Illus.). 2000. lib. bdg. write for info. (*0-7613-1720-1*) Millbrook Pr.

***Meet My Grandmother: She's A Supreme Court Justice.** Lisa Tucker McElroy. LC 99-31130. (J). (gr. 3-5). 1999. 22.90 (*0-7613-1566-7*) Millbrook Pr.

***Meet My Grandmother: She's a United States Senator.** Lisa Tucker McElroy. (Grandmothers at Work Ser.). 32p. (J). (gr. 2-4). 2000. 22.90 (*0-7613-1721-X*) Millbrook Pr.

***Meet My Grandmother: She's a United States Senator.** Lisa Tucker McElroy. (Grandmothers at Work Ser.). (Illus.). (J). 2000. pap. 7.95 (*0-7613-1432-6*) Millbrook Pr.

Meet My Husbands: A Comedy in Two Acts. Fred Carmichael. LC 98-232326. 94 p. 1997. write for info. (*0-573-60230-1*) French.

Meet My Monster, Level 2. Paul Z. Mann. LC 99-19688. (Fisher-Price All-Star Readers Ser.). (Illus.). 32p. (J). (gr. k-3). 1999. pap. 3.99 (*1-57584-308-0*) Rdrs Digest.

Meet My Mouse. Fay Robinson. (Let Me Read Ser.). (J). 1996. 2.95 (*0-673-36344-9*, GoodYrBooks) Addson-Wesley Educ.

Meet My Staff. Patricia Marx. LC 96-37678. (Illus.). 40p. (J). (ps-3). 1998. 14.95 (*0-06-027484-0*) HarpC.

***Meet 98 Degrees.** Lisa Degnen & Deborah Law. LC 99-54033. 2000. 9.98 (*1-56799-975-1*, Friedman-Fairfax) M Friedman Pub Grp Inc.

Meet Our Sages. Jacob Neusner. LC 80-12771. (Illus.). 128p. (J). (gr. 5-8). 1980. pap. text 6.95 (*0-87441-327-3*) Behrman.

***Meet Patrick.** Mandy Stanley. (Illus.). 8p. (J). 1999. 6.99 (*1-58048-057-8*) Sandvik Pub.

Meet Penelope P'Nutt: Conoza Penelope P'Nutt. Nancy Palumbo. (Illus.). 32p. (J). (gr. k-6). 1989. student ed. 0.45 (*0-927024-04-7*) Crayons Pubns.

Meet Penelope P'Nutt: Viens Recontrer Penelope P'Nutt. Nancy Palumbo. (Illus.). 32p. (J). (gr. k-6). 1989. student ed. 0.45 (*0-927024-05-5*) Crayons Pubns.

***Meet Peter Cottontail.** Burgess & Stewart. (Illus.). (J). 2000. pap. 1.00 (*0-486-41030-7*) Dover.

Meet Peter Rabbit. Illus. by Beatrix Potter. 12p. (J). (ps-k). 1996. pap. 3.99 (*0-7232-4322-0*, F Warne) Peng Put Young Read.

Meet Ramona Quimby. Beverly Cleary. Incl. Ramona & Her Father. (J). (gr. 3-5). 1983. pap. Ramona Quimby, Age 8. (J). (gr. 3-5). 1983. pap. Ramona the Pest. (J). (gr. 3-5). 1983. pap. (J). 1983. Set boxed set 11.20 (*0-440-45548-0*) Dell.

Meet Ramona Quimby, 5 bks., Set. Beverly Cleary. Incl. Ramona & Her Family. (J). Ramona Quimby, Age 8. (J). (gr. 3-5). Ramona the Pest. (J). (gr. 3-5). (J). (gr. k-7). Set boxed set 15.50 (*0-685-19114-1*) Dell.

Meet Rory Hohenstein, a Professional Dancer. Jill D. Duvall. LC 96-34906. (Our Neighborhood Ser.). (Illus.). (J). (gr. k-2). 1997. lib. bdg. 19.50 (*0-516-20312-6*) Childrens.

Meet Rory Hohenstein, a Professional Dancer. Jill D. Duvall. (Our Neighborhood Ser.). (J). (gr. k-2). 1997. pap. 6.95 (*0-516-26149-5*) Childrens.

Meet Rosie Posie. Joan Haines. (Illus.). 16p. (Orig.). (J). (ps-1). 1985. pap. 2.65 (*0-936652-00-4*) Two Ems.

***Meet Sailor Jupiter- Thunder.** Mixx Entertainment Inc., Staff. (Sailor Moon Scout Guides Ser.). (Illus.). 96p. (J). (gr. 4-7). 2000. pap. 12.95 (*1-892213-30-3*) Mixx Enter Inc.

***Meet Sailor Mars - Fire.** Mixx Entertainment Inc., Staff. (Sailor Moon Scout Guides Ser.). 2000. pap. 12.95 (*1-892213-28-1*) Mixx Enter Inc.

***Meet Sailor Mercury - Ice.** Mixx Entertainment Inc., Staff. (Sailor Moon Scout Guides Ser.). (Illus.). (J). 2000. pap. 12.95 (*1-892213-31-1*) Mixx Enter Inc.

***Meet Sailor Moon - Crystal.** Mixx Entertainment Inc., Staff. (Sailor Moon Scout Guides Ser.). (Illus.). (J). 2000. pap. 12.95 (*1-892213-32-X*) Mixx Enter Inc.

***Meet Sailor Venus - Love.** Mixx Entertainment Inc., Staff. (Sailor Moon Scout Guides Ser.). (Illus.). (J). 2000. pap. 12.95 (*1-892213-29-X*) Mixx Enter Inc.

Meet Samantha: An American Girl. Susan S. Adler. Ed. by Jeanne Thieme. LC 98-16815. (American Girls Collection : Bk. 1). (Illus.). 61p. (YA). (gr. 2 up). 1986. pap. 5.95 (*0-937295-04-3*); lib. bdg. 12.95 (*0-937295-80-9*) Pleasant Co.

Meet Samantha: An American Girl. Susan S. Adler. (American Girls Collection: Bk. 1). (YA). (gr. 2 up). 1986. 11.15 (*0-606-02770-X*, Pub. by Turtleback) Demco.

Meet Shaquille O'Neal: An Unauthorized Biography. Castello Bob. (J). 1993. 9.09 (*0-606-05923-7*, Pub. by Turtleback) Demco.

Meet Shieldsville: The Story of St. Patrick's Parish, Shieldsville. Mary L. Hagerty. (Illus.). 174p. 1997. reprint ed. lib. bdg. 25.00 (*0-8328-6815-9*) Higginson Bk Co.

Meet Simeon & Anna see Word & Picture Books, Set 3: For Year A/B

***Meet Sister Faustina Kowalska: Saint of Divine Mercy.** Geroge Kosicki. 2001. pap. write for info. (*1-56955-236-3*) Servant.

Meet St. Paul. R. E. White. LC 89-12340. 144p. (Orig.). 1990. pap. 8.95 (*0-8192-1504-X*) Morehouse Pub.

***Meet Stinky Magee.** Edward Sokol. LC 99-50289. 32p. (J). (ps-3). 2000. 14.95 (*0-688-17416-7*, Wm Morrow); lib. bdg. 14.89 (*0-688-17417-5*, Wm Morrow) Morrow Avon.

***Meet the Allens in Whaling Days.** John J. Loeper. LC 97-27963. (Early American Family Ser.). (Illus.). 64p. (J). (gr. 2-4). 1998. lib. bdg. 25.64 (*0-7614-0842-8*, Benchmark NY) Marshall Cavendish.

Meet the Alpha-Soruses. Don Klein et al. (Alpha-Soruses Bks.: No. 1). (Illus.). 15p. (J). (ps-1). 1994. pap. 6.95 (*0-685-71457-8*) Outside Wrld.

Meet the American Girls, 6 bks., Set. Pleasant Company Staff. (American Girls Collection). (J). 1997. pap. text, boxed set 34.95 (*1-56247-542-8*) Pleasant Co.

Meet the American Girls, 5 bks., Set. Pleasant Company Staff et al. (American Girls Collection). (Illus.). (J). (gr. 2-5). 1993. pap., boxed set 28.95 (*1-56247-096-5*) Pleasant Co.

Meet the Animals of the Adirondacks. Fran Betters. Ed. by Nadine Balzer. (Illus.). 64p. 1993. pap. 9.95 (*0-9616439-9-4*) Adirondack S P.

Meet the Apostle Paul & Friends. Paul Sandberg. 28p. 1988. ring bd. 8.00 (*1-58302-048-9*, BPS-18) One Way St.

Meet the Arthropods. Ellen Doris. LC 95-61699. (Real Kids/Real Science Bks.). (Illus.). 64p. (J). (gr. 4-10). 1996. 16.95 (*0-500-19010-0*, Pub. by Thames Hudson) Norton.

Meet the Austins. Madeleine L'Engle. 192p. (YA). (gr. 5-9). 1981. mass mkt. 4.99 (*0-440-95777-X*, LE) Dell.

Meet the Austins. Madeleine L'Engle. LC 96-27655. (Illus.). 224p. (J). (gr. 5-9). 1997. 16.00 (*0-374-34929-0*) FS&G.

Meet the Austins. Madeleine L'Engle. (J). 1960. 9.60 (*0-606-02172-8*, Pub. by Turtleback) Demco.

Meet the Author: Grades K-8. Troll Books Staff. 96p. 1999. pap. text 12.95 (*0-8167-2582-9*) Troll Communs.

Meet the Authors. Deborah Kovaks. (J). 1995. pap. 16.95 (*0-590-49476-7*) Scholastic Inc.

Meet the Authors, Vol.2. Deborah Kovaks & James Preller. 144p. (J). (gr. k-7). 1993. pap. 21.95 (*0-590-49237-3*) Scholastic Inc.

Meet the Authors & Illustrators. Deborah Kovacs & James Preller. pap. 13.95 (*0-590-24111-7*) Scholastic Inc.

M

Meet the Authors & Illustrators, Vol. 1. Scholastic, Inc. Staff. LC 94-231017. 144p. (J). (gr. k-7). 1991. pap. 21.95 (*0-590-49097-4*) Scholastic Inc.

Meet the Beatles . . . Again! Denny Somacht & Ken Sharp. (Illus.). Date not set. reprint ed. pap. 19.95 (*0-9640672-0-X*) Musicom.

Meet the Boxcar Children. Illus. by Daniel M. Duffy. LC 98-6196. (Adventures of Benny & Watch: No. 1). 46p. (J). (gr. 1-3). 1998. pap. 3.95 (*0-8075-5034-5*) A Whitman.

Meet the Boxcar Children. Created by Gertrude Chandler Warner. (Adventures of Benny & Watch: No. 1). (J). (gr. 1-3). 1998. 9.40 (*0-606-13215-5*) Turtleback.

Meet the Brethren. Ed. by Donald F. Durnbaugh. (Illus.). 120p. 1995. reprint ed. pap. 8.00 (*0-936693-11-8*) Brethren Encyclopedia.

Meet the Chicago Bulls. Brendan Hanrahan. LC 49-251060. (Sports Bks.). (J). (gr. 5-7). 1996. pap. 4.99 (*0-590-97327-4*) Scholastic Inc.

Meet the Chicago Bulls. Brendan Hanrahan. 1996. 10.19 (*0-606-11615-X*, Pub. by Turtleback) Demco.

Meet the Cookie Man: The Lattice Inn Bed & Breakfast. Michael Pierce. 138p. 1996. pap. 10.00 (*1-56383-070-1*) G & R Pub.

Meet the Donnellys - Enjoy Their History. limited ed. Mary L. Donnelly. LC 98-174545. (Illus.). 127p. 1997. pap. 36.00 (*0-939142-19-8*) M L Donnelly.

Meet the Dooples. Lynn Hunter et al. LC 97-91899. (Illus.). 32p. (J). (ps-2). 1997. 19.95 (*0-9656279-1-8*); 24.95 incl. audio (*0-9656279-2-6*) Doo Prod.

Meet the Drakes on the Kentucky Frontier. John J. Loeper. LC 97-42198. (Early American Family Ser.). (Illus.). (J). (gr. 2-4). 1998. lib. bdg. 25.64 (*0-7614-0845-2*, Benchmark NY) Marshall Cavendish.

Meet the Dudleys in Colonial Times. John J. Loeper. LC 97-27962. (Early American Family Ser.). (J). 1998. lib. bdg. 25.64 (*0-7614-0841-X*, Benchmark NY) Marshall Cavendish.

Meet the Essay. Elsa Baiz de Gelpi. 180p. (C). 1987. reprint ed. pap. 5.50 (*0-8477-3110-3*) U of PR Pr.

Meet the First Ladies. Cindy Barden. Ed. by Judy Mitchell. (Illus.). 144p. (Orig.). (J). (gr. 3-6). 1996. pap., teacher ed. 13.95 (*1-57310-042-0*) Teachng & Lrning Co.

Meet the Friends. Sharla S. Whalen. LC 96-32660. (Faithful Friends Ser.). (J). 1997. pap. 5.95 (*1-56239-900-4*) ABDO Pub Co.

Meet the Fusco Brothers! J. C. Duffy. (Illus.). 128p. (Orig.). 1990. pap. 8.95 (*0-8362-1849-3*) Andrews & McMeel.

Meet the God Who Loves You. Camille Nehmsmann. 100p. 1998. pap. 6.95 (*0-9657682-2-8*) Moriah Pr.

Meet the Great Composers, Bk. 1. June Montgomery & Maurice Hison. 1995. pap. 19.90 incl. audio compact disk (*0-88284-855-0*) Alfred Pub.

Meet the Great Composers Repertoire Book, Bk. 2. June Montgomery & Maurice Hinson. 44p. 1998. pap. 7.50 (*0-88284-944-1*, 18117) Alfred Pub.

*__Meet the Group of Seven.__ David Wistow. (Illus.). 48p. (J). 1999. 16.95 (*1-55074-494-1*) Kids Can Pr.

Meet the Jungle Cubs: Paint with Water. Golden Books Staff. (Illus.). (J). 1997. pap. text 1.79 (*0-307-08247-4*, 08247, Goldn Books) Gldn Bks Pub Co.

Meet the Lincoln Lion's Band. Patricia Reilly Giff. (Lincoln Lion's Band Ser.). (J). 1992. 8.45 (*0-606-02740-8*, Pub. by Turtleback) Demco.

Meet the Lord & His Church. Richard H. Stadler. Ed. by William E. Fischer. (Bible Class Course for Young Adults Ser.). (Illus.). 64p. 1987. teacher ed. 7.50 (*0-938272-27-6*, 22-2184); pap. text, student ed. 4.00 (*0-938272-26-8*, 22-2183) WELS Board.

Meet the Los Angeles Lakers. Joe Layden. LC 98-137436. 32p. (J). (gr. 2-5). 1997. pap. text 4.99 (*0-590-38382-5*) Scholastic Inc.

Meet the Los Angeles Lakers. Joe Layden. (J). 1997. 10.19 (*0-606-12992-8*, Pub. by Turtleback) Demco.

Meet the Malones. Lenora M. Weber. LC 43-12453. (J). (gr. 5 up). 1944. 10.95 (*0-690-52999-6*) HarpC Child Bks.

*__Meet the Malones.__ Lenora Mattingly Weber. (Beany Malone Ser.). (Illus.). 277p. (J). 1999. reprint ed. pap. 12.95 (*0-9639607-3-3*) Image Cascade.

Meet the Marching Smithereens. Ann Hayes. LC 94-11896. (Gulliver Bks.). (Illus.). 32p. (J). (ps-3). 1995. 15.00 (*0-15-253158-0*) Harcourt.

Meet the Masterpieces. Scholastic, Inc. Staff. 1992. pap. 18.95 (*0-590-49212-8*) Scholastic Inc.

Meet the Masterpieces: Learning about Ancient Civilizations Through Art. Bobbi Chertok et al. 1994. pap. 18.95 (*0-590-49505-4*) Scholastic Inc.

Meet the Masters. Machgielis Euwe. LC 78-90636. (Essay Index Reprint Ser.). 1977. 23.95 (*0-8369-1258-6*) Ayer.

Meet the Masters: Art Education Program, 6 vols., Set. Judy Groman & Bonnie Steele. (Illus.). 1990. ring bd. write for info. (*0-9621702-9-1*) Crtv Arts Enterprises.

Meet the Masters Vol. 1: Year One Teacher's Manual. Judy Groman & Bonnie Steele. (Illus.). 1990. ring bd. write for info. (*0-9621702-6-7*) Crtv Arts Enterprises.

Meet the Masters Vol. 2: Year Two Teacher's Manual. Judy Groman & Bonnie Steele. (Illus.). 1990. ring bd. write for info. (*0-9621702-7-5*) Crtv Arts Enterprises.

Meet the Masters Vol. 3: Year Three Teacher's Manual. Judy Groman & Bonnie Steele. (Illus.). 1990. ring bd. write for info. (*0-9621702-8-3*) Crtv Arts Enterprises.

Meet the Mennonites. (Pennsylvania Dutch Bks.). (Illus.). 1961. 3.00 (*0-911410-05-8*) Applied Arts.

Meet the Mertzes: The Life Stories of I Love Lucy's Other Couple. Rob Edelman & Audrey Kupferberg. LC 99-37037. 272p. 1999. pap. 16.95 (*1-58063-095-2*) Renaissance.

Meet the Methodists: An Introduction to the United Methodist Church. Charles Livingstone Allen. LC 85-28794. 93p. 1986. pap. 4.95 (*0-687-24650-4*) Abingdon.

Meet the Methodists: An Introduction to the United Methodist Church. Charles Livingstone Allen. 1998. pap. text 4.95 (*0-687-08232-3*) Abingdon.

Meet the Missionary. Mark Weinrich. (Illus.). 24p. (Orig.). (J). (gr. k-3). 1993. pap. 4.99 (*0-87509-517-8*) Chr Pubns.

Meet the Molesons. Burny Bos. Tr. by J. Alison James. LC 93-49587. (Illus.). 48p. (J). (ps-3). 1995. pap. 4.95 (*1-55858-409-9*, Pub. by North-South Bks NYC) Chronicle Bks.

Meet the Molesons. Burny Bos. 1995. 10.15 (*0-606-08820-2*, Pub. by Turtleback) Demco.

Meet the Monsters. Jane Yolen & Heidi E. Stemple. LC 96-15126. (Illus.). (J). 1996. 15.95 (*0-8027-8441-0*); lib. bdg. 16.85 (*0-8027-8442-9*) Walker & Co.

Meet the Natives: The Amateur's Field Guide to Rocky Mountain Wildflowers, Trees, & Shrubs. 9th ed. M. Walter Pesman. (Illus.). 244p. 1992. pap. 12.95 (*1-879373-31-9*) Roberts Rinehart.

Meet the New Dawn. Rosanne Bittner. 480p. 1996. mass mkt. 5.99 (*0-8217-5471-8*, Zebra Kensgtn) Kensgtn Pub Corp.

Meet the Orchestra see **Te Presento a la Orquesta**

Meet the Orchestra. Ann Hayes. Ed. by Diane D'Andrade. LC 89-32959. (Illus.). 32p. (J). (ps-3). 1991. 15.00 (*0-15-200526-9*, Gulliver Bks) Harcourt.

Meet the Orchestra. Ann Hayes. LC 89-32959. (Illus.). 32p. (J). (ps-3). 1995. pap. 6.00 (*0-15-200222-7*, Gulliver Bks) Harcourt.

Meet the Orchestra. Ann Hayes. (J). 1991. 10.20 (*0-606-08425-8*, Pub. by Turtleback) Demco.

Meet the Poet Juan Ramon Jimenez: A Guide for High School Spanish Teachers in the U. S. Carmela Marolda. LC 95-78816. 77p. 1995. pap., teacher ed. 9.95 (*1-882573-07-2*) Serena Bay.

Meet the Presidents. Cindy Barden. Ed. by Judy Mitchell. (Illus.). 144p. (Orig.). (J). (gr. 3-6). 1996. pap., teacher ed. 13.95 (*1-57310-041-2*) Teachng & Lrning Co.

Meet the Press: 50 Years of History in the Making. Rick Ball & NBC News Staff. LC 97-73866. (Illus.). 240p. 1997. 39.95 (*0-07-006614-9*) McGraw.

Meet the Prophets: A Beginner's Guide to the Books of the Biblical Prophets. John W. Miller. 288p. 1987. pap. 14.95 (*0-8091-2899-3*) Paulist Pr.

Meet the Real Me. Illus. by Janice Kinnealy. LC 92-21644. 32p. (J). (gr. 2-8). 1992. pap. text 2.50 (*0-8167-2939-5*) Troll Communs.

Meet the Registrar: Firsthand Accounts of ISO 9000 Success from the Registration Source. C. Michael Taylor. LC 96-50961. 183p. 1997. 30.00 (*0-87389-424-3*, H0967) ASQ Qual Pr.

Meet the Residents: America's Most Eccentric Band! Ian Shirley. 1998. pap. 16.95 (*0-946719-12-8*, Pub. by Helter Skelter) Interlink Pub.

Meet the Risen Lord: Scriptures for the Church Seasons, Lent 1999. Kurt Schuermann. 32p. (Orig.). 1999. pap., teacher ed. 3.95 (*0-687-07418-5*) Abingdon.

Meet the Sesame Street Babies. Anna Ross. LC 92-60973. (Board Bks.). 7p. (J). (ps). 1993. 4.99 (*0-679-83486-9*, Pub. by Random Bks Yng Read) Random.

Meet the Seven Dwarfs: Interlocking Board Books. Walt Disney Staff. (J). (ps). 1993. 5.98 (*0-453-03106-4*) NAL.

Meet the Short Story. Elsa Baiz de Gelpi. 230p. (C). 1992. reprint ed. pap. 9.25 (*0-8477-3111-1*) U of PR Pr.

Meet the Son of God: Scriptures for the Church Seasons: Advent, 1998. James A. Harnish. 48p. 1998. pap., student ed. 3.95 (*0-687-06929-7*) Abingdon.

Meet the Son of God: Scriptures for the Church Seasons, Advent 1998 Leaders Guide Edition. James A. Harnish. 1998. pap. text 3.95 (*0-687-02283-5*) Abingdon.

Meet the Stars of Animorphs. Randi Reisfeld. (Animorphs Ser.). (J). (gr. 3-7). 1999. pap. text 59.88 (*0-439-07272-7*); mass mkt. 4.99 (*0-439-06165-2*) Scholastic Inc.

Meet the Stars of Buffy the Vampire Slayer. Stefanie Scott. (Illus.). 128p. (J). (gr. 6-8). 1998. pap. 3.99 (*0-590-51477-6*) Scholastic Inc.

Meet the Stars of Dawson's Creek. Louise Barile. (Illus.). (J). (gr. 5-9). 1998. pap. 4.99 (*0-590-64269-3*) Scholastic Inc.

*__Meet the Stars of Roswell.__ Monica Rizzo. (Illus.). 144p. (J). (gr. 7-12). 2000. mass mkt. 4.99 (*0-439-20758-4*) Scholastic Inc.

*__Meet the Stars of 7th Heaven: The Unofficial Scrapbook.__ Matt Netter. LC 99-230478. (Illus.). 48p. (J). (gr. 3-10). 1999. pap. text 5.99 (*0-439-04299-2*) Scholastic Inc.

Meet the Sweet-Hearts: A Sticker Stories Book. Paige Billin-Frye. (Sticker Stories Ser.). (Illus.). 16p. (J). 1997. pap. text 4.95 (*0-448-41715-4*, G & D) Peng Put Young Read.

Meet the Tazewells: Too Much Birthday Wine. 2nd ed. Ed. by Calvert W. Tazewell, Jr. LC 90-80465. 60p. 1990. 3.00 (*1-878515-92-6*); pap. 8.00 (*1-878515-30-6*); disk 4.00 (*1-878515-72-1*) W S Dawson.

Meet the Teletubbies. (Teletubbies Super Coloring Activity Book Ser.: Vol. 1). (Illus.). 96p. (J). 1998. pap. write for info. (*0-7666-0265-6*, Honey Bear Bks) Modern Pub NYC.

Meet the Teletubbies. Scholastic, Inc. Staff. LC 99-199282. (Illus.). 32p. (J). (ps-3). 1998. 9.99 (*0-590-38623-9*, Pub. by Scholastic Inc) Penguin Putnam.

Meet the Twelve Disciples. 2nd rev. ed. Dale VonSeggen & Liz VonSeggen. (Illus.). 28p. 1996. ring bd. 6.00 (*1-58302-049-7*, BPS-17) One Way St.

Meet the U. S. People & Places in the United States. Leslie J. Kagan & Kay J. Westerfield. (Illus.). 208p. (C). 1983. pap. text 28.20 (*0-13-573808-3*) P-H.

Meet the United Pentecostal Church International. Ed. by R. M. Davis & P. D. Buford. 160p. 1995. pap. 5.99 (*1-56722-056-8*) Word Aflame.

Meet the Villarreals: Big Book. Lada J. Kratky. (Wonders! Ser.). (Illus.). 24p. (Orig.). (J). (gr. 1-3). 1991. pap. text 29.95 (*1-56334-050-X*) Hampton-Brown.

Meet the Villarreals: Small Book. Lada J. Kratky. (Wonders! Ser.). (Illus.). 24p. (Orig.). (J). (gr. 1-3). 1991. pap. text 6.00 (*1-56334-056-9*) Hampton-Brown.

Meet the Wards on the Oregon Trail. John J. Loeper. LC 97-42199. (American Family Ser.). (J). (gr. 2-4). 1998. lib. bdg. 25.64 (*0-7614-0844-4*, Benchmark NY) Marshall Cavendish.

*__Meet the Webbers of Philadelphia.__ John J. Loeper. LC 97-42200. (Early American Family Ser.). (Illus.). 64p. (J). (gr. 2-4). 1998. lib. bdg. 25.64 (*0-7614-0843-6*, Benchmark NY) Marshall Cavendish.

Meet the Werewolf. Georgess McHargue. LC 75-34046. (Illus.). 80p. (J). (gr. 2-5). 1976. 11.95 (*0-397-31662-3*) HarpC Child Bks.

Meet the Wild Southwest: Land of Hoodoos & Gila Monsters. Susan J. Tweit. LC 95-432. (Illus.). 128p. (Orig.). (YA). (gr. 5 up). 1995. pap. 14.95 (*0-88240-468-7*, Alaska NW Bks) Gr Arts Ctr Pub.

Meet the Witches. Georgess McHargue. LC 83-48446. (Eerie Ser.). (Illus.). 128p. (J). (gr. 4-7). 1984. 11.95 (*0-397-32071-X*); lib. bdg. 11.89 (*0-397-32072-8*) HarpC Child Bks.

Meet the Witnesses. John M. Haffert. (Illus.). 160p. 1988. pap. 1.75 (*0-911988-39-4*, 37549) AMI Pr.

*__Meet the Women of American Soccer: An Inside Look at America's Team.__ Wayne Coffey. LC 99-232061. (Illus.). 48p. (gr. 2-7). 1999. pap. text 5.99 (*0-439-08654-X*) Scholastic Inc.

Meet Thomas & His Friends. Reverend Wilbert V. Awdry. (J). 1998. 4.99 (*0-679-89003-3*, Pub. by Random Bks Yng Read) Random.

*__Meet Thomas Jefferson.__ Marvin Barrett. (Illus.). 1999. pap. text 11.10 (*0-8335-3937-X*) Econo-Clad Bks.

Meet Thomas Jefferson. Marvin Barrett. LC 88-19069. (Set-up Biographies Ser.). (Illus.). 72p. (J). (gr. 2-4). 1989. reprint ed. pap. 3.99 (*0-394-81964-0*, Pub. by Random Bks Yng Read) Random.

Meet Tricky Coyote! Gretchen W. Mayo. LC 92-12424. (Native American Trickster Tales Ser.). (Illus.). 35p. (J). (gr. 6-10). 1993. 12.95 (*0-8027-8198-5*); lib. bdg. 13.85 (*0-8027-8199-3*) Walker & Co.

Meet William Shakespeare. large type ed. Joseph Ajlouny. 46p. 1999. pap. 7.95 (*0-929957-15-6*, Push-Pull Pr) JSA Pubns.

*__Meet Your Backyard Friends.__ Magner Publishing Staff. (Illus.). 16p. (J). (ps-7). 1999. pap. 4.95 (*1-929416-04-0*) Magner Pubg.

Meet Your King see **Be Loyal**

Meet Your Neighbors: New England Portraits, Painters & Society, 1790-1850. Ed. by Caroline F. Sloat. LC 91-31274. (Illus.). 160p. (C). 1992. pap. 24.95 (*0-87023-769-1*); lib. bdg. 40.00 (*0-87023-771-3*) U of Mass Pr.

Meet Your Planets: Fun with Astrology. Roy Alexander. LC 97-3512. (Illus.). 240p. (Orig.). 1997. pap. 12.95 (*1-56718-017-5*) Llewellyn Pubns.

Meet Your Teeth: A Fun Creative Dental Unit for Kids in Grades 1-4. Linda Schwartz. Ed. by Barbara Dever & Kimberly Clark. (Illus.). 56p. (Orig.). (J). (gr. 1-4). 1996. pap. 7.95 (*0-88160-274-4*, LW155) Learning Wks.

Meet Your Zoning Hearing Board: A Zoning Handbook & Guide. Charles P. Mills. LC 75-9523. 1975. spiral bd. 4.00 (*0-686-05762-7*) C P Mills.

Meet Yourself in the Bible see **Designed for Conquest: Biblical Models for Overcoming Life's Struggles**

Meet Yourself in the Psalms. Warren W. Wiersbe. 192p. 1983. pap. 9.99 (*0-88207-740-6*, 6-2740, Victor Bks) Chariot Victor.

*__Meet Zippyr the Zebra-Key.__ 2nd ed. Mary Kay Milam. (Illus.). 24p. (J). (ps-k). 1999. reprint ed. pap. 15.95 (*1-58597-008-5*) Leathers Pub.

Meeth Pocket Atlas of Ophthalmology. Suresh Mandava et al. LC 98-25048. 1998. 9.00 (*3-13-107941-X*) Thieme Med Pubs.

Meeting. Jeff Stetson. 1990. pap. 3.25 (*0-8222-0745-1*) Dramatists Play.

*__Meeting.__ Nee Watchman. 1998. pap. 2.00 (*0-7363-0131-3*) Living Stream Ministry.

Meeting. Keith B. Whitney. 160p. 1998. 19.95 (*0-9665028-0-9*); pap. 14.95 (*0-9665028-1-7*) Shoestring Publ.

*__Meeting: An Auschwitz Survivor Confronts an SS Physician.__ Ed. by Bernhard Frankfurter. Tr. by Susan E. Cernyak-Spatz from GER. LC 99-36798. 272p. 1999. 29.95 (*0-8156-0604-4*) Syracuse U Pr.

Meeting: Gatherings in Organizations & Communities. H. B. Schwartzman. (Illus.). 360p. (C). 1989. 65.00 (*0-306-43133-5*, Plenum Trade) Perseus Pubng.

Meeting about Laughter: Sketches, Interludes & Theatrical Parodies by Nikolai Erdman with Vladimir Mass & Others. Ed. & Tr. by John Freedman. (Russian Theatre Archive Ser.: Vol. 2). 256p. 1995. text 42.00 (*3-7186-5580-2*, ECU43, Harwood Acad Pubs); pap. text 15.00 (*3-7186-5581-0*, ECU22, Harwood Acad Pubs) Gordon & Breach.

Meeting & Mastering Your Internal Saboteur. 2nd rev. ed. Martha B. Beveridge. Ed. by Terrisa Bruce-Phipps. 44p. 1989. pap. 3.50 (*1-889237-02-7*) Options Now.

*__Meeting Anthropology Phase to Phase: Growing up, Spreading Out, Crowding in, Switching On.__ Robert B. Graber et al. LC 99-69249. 468p. 2000. pap. 30.00 (*0-89089-774-3*) Carolina Acad Pr.

Meeting at Potsdam. Charles L. Mee. 1995. pap. text 14.95 (*1-879957-50-7*, Franklin Sq Pr) Harpers Mag Found.

Meeting at Telgte. Gunter Grass. Tr. by Ralph Manheim from GER. LC 90-36801.Tr. of Treffen in Telgte. 156p. 1990. pap. 11.00 (*0-15-658575-8*, Harvest Bks) Harcourt.

*__Meeting at the Crossroads.__ Lyn M. Brown & Carol Gilligan. 1999. pap. 12.50 (*0-345-91550-X*) Ballantine Pub Grp.

Meeting at the Crossroads: Women's Psychology & Girls' Development. Lyn M. Brown & Carol Gilligan. 258p. (C). 1998. text 20.00 (*0-7881-5290-4*) DIANE Pub.

Meeting at the Crossroads: Women's Psychology & Girls' Development. Lyn M. Brown & Carol Gilligan. LC 92-14312. 240p. 1992. text 19.95 (*0-674-56464-2*) HUP.

Meeting at the Crossways: Woman's Psychology & Girls' Development. Lyn M. Brown & Carol Gilligan. 272p. 1999. pap. 12.50 (*0-345-38295-1*) Ballantine Pub Grp.

*__Meeting at the Milestone.__ Sigurd Hoel. 400p. 2000. pap. 15.95 (*1-892295-31-8*) Green Integer.

Meeting Aviation's Safety Challenges: Proceedings of the International Air Safety Seminar, 36th Annual Meeting, Rio de Janeiro, 1983. International Air Safety Seminar Staff. LC TL0553.5.I. 316p. reprint ed. pap. 98.00 (*0-608-12010-3*, 202287400031) Bks Demand.

Meeting Basic Competencies in Communications. Eileen L. Corcoran. 68p. 1979. teacher ed. 0.50 (*0-88323-156-5*, 246); pap. 2.50 (*0-88323-152-2*, 242) Pendergrass Pub.

Meeting Basic Competencies in Math. Eileen L. Corcoran. 72p. 1984. teacher ed. 0.50 (*0-88323-141-7*, 230); pap. text 2.50 (*0-88323-203-0*, 227) Pendergrass Pub.

Meeting Basic Competencies in Practical Science & Health: A Workstudy Book to Improve Daily Living Skills. Eileen L. Corcoran. (Illus.). 72p. 1985. 2.50 (*0-88323-210-3*, 237); teacher ed. 0.50 (*0-88323-154-9*, 245) Pendergrass Pub.

Meeting by the River. Christopher Isherwood. LC 99-28809. 160p. 1999. pap. 14.95 (*0-8166-3368-1*, Pub. by U of Minn Pr) Chicago Distribution Ctr.

Meeting Challenges: Scripture References. Greetings Etc. by Alfreda Staff. 1984. pap. text 7.95 (*0-318-04372-6*) Prosperity & Profits.

Meeting Christ in the Sacraments. Colman E. O'Neill. LC 90-25917. 328p. 1991. pap. 16.95 (*0-8189-0598-0*) Alba.

Meeting College Costs: A Workbook for Families 2000. College Board Staff. 1999. pap. text, wbk. ed. 13.95 (*0-87447-636-4*) College Bd.

*__Meeting College Costs: What You Need to Know Before Your Child & Your Money Leave Home; A Work.__ The College Board Staff. 120p. 2000. pap. 13.95 (*0-87447-652-6*) College Bd.

Meeting Community Needs with Job & Career Services: A How-to-Do-It Manual. Joan Durrance. LC 94-16462. (How-to-Do-It Manuals for Libraries Ser.: No. 42). 252p. 1994. 49.95 (*1-55570-177-9*) Neal-Schuman.

Meeting Customer Needs. Ian Smith. 185p. 1994. pap. 34.95 (*0-7506-0668-1*) Buttrwrth-Heinemann.

Meeting Deadlines In Real-Time Systems: A Practical Introduction to Design with Rate Monotonic Analysis. Lo C. Briand & Daniel Roy. LC 99-33707. 250p. 1997. pap. 59.00 (*0-8186-7406-7*) IEEE Comp Soc.

Meeting Death. Margaret O. Hyde & Lawrence E. Hyde. 129p. (J). (gr. 5 up). 1989. 14.95 (*0-8027-6873-3*); lib. bdg. 15.85 (*0-8027-6874-1*) Walker & Co.

Meeting Disability: A European Response. Patrick Daunt. 224p. 1992. pap. text 24.95 (*0-304-32386-1*) Continuum.

*__Meeting Dolphins.__ Kathleen Dudzinski. LC 99-39069. 64p. (J). (gr. 4-6). 2000. per. 17.95 (*0-7922-7129-7*, Pub. by Natl Geog) S&S Trade.

Meeting Each Other in Church Doctrine, Liturgy, & Government: The Bicentennial of the Celebration of the Constitution of the Reformed Church in America. Daniel J. Meeter. LC 93-5093. (Historical Series of the Reformed Church in America: No. 24). 240p. (Orig.). 1993. pap. text 13.00 (*0-8028-0717-8*) Eerdmans.

Meeting Early Intervention Challenges: Issues from Birth to Three. 2nd ed. Ed. by Lawrence J. Johnson et al. 336p. 1994. pap. text 32.95 (*1-55766-131-6*, 1316) P H Brookes.

Meeting Education & Training Needs, Vol. 4. Ed. by Sue Wood. 150p. (C). 1982. 135.00 (*0-85292-292-2*, Pub. by IPM Hse) St Mut.

Meeting Family Needs: The Corporate Response. Shiela B. Kamerman. (Studies in Productivity: No. 33). 45p. 1984. pap. 55.00 (*0-08-030965-8*) Work in Amer.

Meeting Famous Christians. Brian G. Cooper. (Illus.). 111p. 1977. pap. 6.50 (*0-85597-205-X*) Attic Pr.

*__Meeting Frankenstein & Other Stories.__ Lisa-Marie Calderone-Stewart & Ed Kunzman. (Stories for Teens Ser.: Vol. 5). 72p. (YA). 1999. pap. 4.95 (*0-88489-593-9*) St Marys.

Meeting Freud's Family. Paul Roazen. LC 93-22734. (Illus.). 256p. 1993. 30.00 (*0-87023-873-6*) U of Mass Pr.

Meeting Future Financing Needs of Water Utilities. 224p. 1993. pap. 95.00 (*0-89867-718-1*, 90635) Am Water Wks Assn.

Meeting GMP & ISO Expectations for Product Development. Carol DeSain & Charmaine V. Sutton. LC 98-148363. 183p. (Orig.). 1996. pap. 145.00 (*1-882615-31-X*) Parexel Intl.

Meeting God. J. I. Packer. (LifeGuide Bible Studies). 64p. (Orig.). 1986. pap., wbk. ed. 4.99 (*0-8308-1057-9*, 1057) InterVarsity.

Meeting God: Elements of Hindu Devotion. Stephen P. Huyler. LC 99-11035. 1999. write for info. (*0-300-07984-2*) Yale U Pr.

*__Meeting God: Elements of Hindu Devotion.__ Stephen P. Huyler. LC 99-11035. (Illus.). 272p. 1999. 35.00 (*0-300-07983-4*) Yale U Pr.

Meeting God Again. Mark Yurs. 65p. Date not set. pap. 6.95 (*0-7880-1608-3*, Fairway Pr) CSS OH.

Meeting God at a Deadend: Discovering Heaven's Best When Life Closes In. Ron Mehl. 240p. 1998. pap. 12.99 (*1-57673-339-4*) Multnomah Pubs.

Meeting God at Every Turn: A Spiritual Autobiography. Catherine Marshall. (Catherine Marshall Library). (Illus.). 256p. (gr. 10). 1995. pap. 9.99 (*0-8007-9231-9*) Chosen Bks.

Meeting God Behind Enemy Lines: My Christian Testimony As a U. S. Navy SEAL. Steve Watkins. (Illus.). 220p. 2000. pap. 7.99 (*0-9671057-0-6*) Extending Grace.

Meeting God Bible Studies, 8 bks. Incl. Meeting God in Busyness. Juanita Ryan. 64p. 1999. pap. 4.99 (*0-8308-2051-5*, 2051); Meeting God in Change. Stephen D. Eyre. 64p. 1999. pap. 4.99 (*0-8308-2052-3*, 2052); Meeting God in Forgiveness. Stephen D. Eyre. 64p. 1999. pap. 4.99 (*0-8308-2053-1*, 2053); Meeting God in Joy. Juanita Ryan. 64p. 1999. pap. 4.99 (*0-8308-2054-X*, 2054); Meeting God in Praise. Juanita Ryan. 64p. 1999. pap. 4.99 (*0-8308-2055-8*, 2055); Meeting God in Quiet. Ruth Goring. 64p. 1999. pap. 4.99 (*0-8308-2056-6*, 2056); Meeting God in Relationships. Ruth Goring. 64p. 1999. pap. 4.99 (*0-8308-2057-4*, 2057); Meeting God in Waiting. Juanita Ryan. 64p. 1999. pap. 4.99 (*0-8308-2058-2*, 2058); 1999. Set pap. 39.92 (*0-8308-2050-7*, 2050) InterVarsity.

Meeting God in Busyness see Meeting God Bible Studies

Meeting God in Change see Meeting God Bible Studies

Meeting God in Forgiveness see Meeting God Bible Studies

Meeting God in Joy see Meeting God Bible Studies

Meeting God in Praise see Meeting God Bible Studies

Meeting God in Quiet see Meeting God Bible Studies

Meeting God in Quiet Places. F. LaGard Smith. 1992. 17.99 (*1-56507-006-2*) Harvest Hse.

Meeting God in Relationships see Meeting God Bible Studies

Meeting God in the Bible: Sixty Devotions for Groups. Donald L. Griggs. 130p. 1992. pap. 19.95 (*1-882236-01-7*) Kerygma Prog.

Meeting God in the Breakdown Lane: Stories from the Journey. Al Anderson. 192p. 1995. 20.00 (*0-9649789-1-1*) Mtntop Graphics.

Meeting God in Waiting see Meeting God Bible Studies

Meeting God on the Mountain: Devotions for Lent. Mary A. Vidakovich. 112p. 1996. pap. 10.00 (*0-8358-0785-1*) Upper Room Bks.

Meeting God Through Worship. Anne Broyles. (Vital Signs Ser.). 96p. (Orig.). 1992. pap. 1.49 (*0-687-24655-5*) Abingdon.

***Meeting Grandmother: She's a Supreme Court Justice.** Lisa Tucker McElroy. (Grandmother at Work Ser.). (Illus.). (J). 2000. pap. text 7.95 (*0-7613-1386-9*) Millbrook Pr.

Meeting Halfway in American Sign Language: A Common Ground for Effective Communication among Deaf & Hearing People. Bernard Bragg & Jack Olson. 192p. 1994. lib. bdg. 39.95 (*0-9634016-7-X*) MSM Prods.

Meeting House see Casa de Reunion

Meeting House & Farm House. Howard H. Brinton. LC 72-80096. (Orig.). 1972. pap. 4.00 (*0-87574-185-1*) Pendle Hill.

Meeting House on the Green: Three Hundred & Fiftieth Anniversary History, 1635-1985. (Illus.). 360p. 1985. 20.00 (*0-318-19497-X*) First Parish.

Meeting House to Camp Meeting: Toward a History of American Free Church Worship from 1620-1835. Doug Adams. 160p. (Orig.). 1981. pap. text 6.95 (*0-941500-26-8*) Sharing Co.

Meeting Human Needs No. 2: Additional Perspectives from Thirteen Countries. Ed. by Daniel Thursz & Joseph L. Vigilante. LC 76-6314. (Social Service Delivery Systems Ser.: No. 2). 286p. reprint ed. pap. 88.70 (*0-8357-8399-5*, 203467300091) Bks Demand.

Meeting in Infinity. John Kessel. LC 91-45949. (Illus.). 328p. 1992. 22.95 (*0-87054-164-1*) Arkham.

Meeting Individual Differences in Reading. H. Alan Robinson. LC 64-24978. (Supplementary Education Monographs). 1992. lib. bdg. 6.50 (*0-226-72176-0*, SEM94) U Ch Pr.

Meeting Individual Needs: A Sourcebook of Teaching, Study & Learning Strategies. John J. Hoover. LC 89-84851. 102p. (C). 1989. pap. text 10.00 (*0-940059-07-X*) Hamilton Pubns.

Meeting ISO 9000 in a TQM World. 2nd rev. ed. Allan J. Sayle. 458p. 1994. 45.00 (*0-9511739-3-6*, P550) A Sayle Assocs.

Meeting JCAHO Restraint & Seclusion Standards. Eric D. Joseph. Ed. by Nancy Webster. 73p. 1997. pap. 25.00 (*0-916499-69-3*) Care Educ Grp.

Meeting Jesus. Leighton Ford. (LifeGuide Bible Studies). (Orig.). 1988. pap., wbk. ed. 4.99 (*0-8308-1060-9*, 1060) InterVarsity.

Meeting Jesus. Dolores Ready. Ed. by Thomas Zanzig. (Discovering Program Ser.). (Illus.). 42p. 1989. teacher ed. 6.00 (*0-88489-191-7*); text 3.00 (*0-88489-190-9*) St Marys.

***Meeting Jesus.** 2nd rev. ed. Leighton Ford. (LifeGuide Bible Studies). 64p. (Orig.). 2000. pap. 4.99 (*0-8308-3060-X*) InterVarsity.

Meeting Jesus Again for the First Time: The Historical Jesus & the Heart of Contemporary Faith. Marcus J. Borg. LC 93-25390. 160p. 1995. pap. 12.00 (*0-06-060917-6*, Pub. by Harper SF) HarpC.

Meeting Legal Challenges. Joseph C. Beckham. LC 96-60048. (School Leader's Library). 203p. 1996. pap. 39.95 (*1-56676-407-6*) Scarecrow.

Meeting Life: Writings & Talks on Finding Your Path Without Retreating from Society. Jiddu Krishnamurti. LC 90-55785. 240p. (gr. 8). 1991. pap. 14.00 (*0-06-250526-2*, Pub. by Harper SF) HarpC.

Meeting Life Head On: Moving into Life with Courage - Not Backing Away in Fear. Illus. by Dale R. Olen. 212p. (Orig.). 1992. pap. 5.95 (*1-56583-006-7*) JODA.

Meeting Lily. large type ed. Sarah Woodhouse. 1996. 27.99 (*0-7089-3475-7*) Ulverscroft.

Meeting Lily, Vol. 1. Sarah Woodhouse. 1998. 5.99 (*0-312-96583-4*, Pub. by Tor Bks) St Martin.

Meeting Luciano. Anna Esaki-Smith. LC 98-46878. 252p. 1999. 18.95 (*1-56512-215-1*, 72215) Algonquin Bks.

***Meeting Luciano.** Anna Esaki-Smith. 256p. 2000. pap. 12.00 (*0-345-43682-2*, Ballantine) Ballantine Pub Grp.

Meeting Magic: The Facilitator's Guide to Leading Productive, Interactive Meetings. C. Harry Eggleton. 200p. 1996. per. 32.50 (*1-57444-134-5*, SL1345) St Lucie Pr.

***Meeting Management.** (C). 2001. write for info. (*0-13-017391-6*) P-H.

***Meeting Mathematics: Educational Studies with Young Children.** Ann Ahlberg. (Goteborg Studies in Educational Sciences: No. 123). (Illus.). 236p. 1998. pap. 52.50 (*91-7346-332-9*, Pub. by Almqvist Wiksell) Coronet Bks.

Meeting Megacity Challenges: A Role for Innovation & Technology. National Research Council Staff. 150p. (Orig.). (C). 1998. pap. 30.00 (*0-309-05538-5*) Natl Acad Pr.

Meeting Mr. Lincoln. Ed. & Intro. by Victoria Radford. LC 98-24074. (Illus.). 128p. 1998. 18.95 (*1-56663-199-8*, Pub. by I R Dee) Natl Bk Netwk.

Meeting Moral Re-Armament. Kenneth Belden. 1979. 2.00 (*0-901269-46-8*) Grosvenor USA.

Meeting Myself: Beyond Spirit of the Empty Hand. Stan Schmidt. Ed. by Randall G. Hassell. LC 97-26008. (Illus.). 252p. (Orig.). 1997. pap. 17.95 (*0-911921-25-7*) Damashi.

***Meeting National Standards with Handbells & Handchimes.** Michael B. McBride & Marva Baldwin. (Illus.). 80p. 1999. pap. 24.95 (*0-8108-3740-4*) Scarecrow.

Meeting Needs. Jon Bennett. 1995. pap. 30.00 (*1-85383-235-9*, Pub. by Escan Pubns) Island Pr.

Meeting Needs. David Braybrooke. LC 86-43130. (Studies in Moral, Political, & Legal Philosophy). 354p. 1987. reprint ed. pap. 109.80 (*0-608-02531-3*, 206317500004) Bks Demand.

Meeting Needs, Sharing Christ: Ministry Evangelism in Today's New Testament Church. Donald A. Atkinson & Charles L. Roesel. 176p. 1995. pap. text 12.95 (*0-8054-9842-7*, LifeWay Press) LifeWay Christian.

Meeting Needs Through Support Groups. Sara H. Martin. Ed. by Cindy McClain. (Illus.). 96p. (Orig.). 1992. pap. text 7.95 (*1-56309-053-8*, N923112, New Hope) Womans Mission Union.

Meeting New Challenges in the Foreign Language Classroom. Ed. by Robert DiDonato. (Central States Ser.). pap. 14.21 (*0-8442-9345-8*, VF93458) NTC Contemp Pub Co.

Meeting New Friends. Florence M. Lindstrom. 150p. (J). (gr. 1-2). 1992. pap. text 6.00 (*1-930092-26-1*, clp29610) Christian Liberty.

Meeting New Friends from Meg Mel Planet. Constance Hewes. (Illus.). 16p. (Orig.). (J). (ps-2). 1996. mass mkt. write for info. (*1-889969-00-1*) Zuka Pub.

Meeting Number 1941 - July 12, 1976 see United Nations Security Council Official Records, 31st Year

Meeting Number 1942 - July 13, 1976 see United Nations Security Council Official Records, 31st Year

Meeting Number 1954 - August 31, 1976 see United Nations Security Council Official Records, 31st Year

Meeting Number 1957 - September 30, 1976 see United Nations Security Council Official Records, 31st Year

Meeting Objectives. 1994. VHS 114.95 (*0-19-458543-3*) OUP.

Meeting Objectives. (Illus.). 80p. 1994. pap. text 9.95 (*0-19-458563-8*) OUP.

Meeting Objectives: Video Guide. Vicki Hollett & Barnaby Newbolt. (Illus.). 32p. 1994. pap. text 4.95 (*0-19-458564-6*) OUP.

Meeting of a Fantasy. Marian Gates. 40p. 1998. pap. 8.00 (*0-8059-4474-5*) Dorrance.

Meeting of East & West: An Inquiry Concerning World Understanding. F. S. Northrop. LC 79-89839. (Illus.). xxii, 531p. 1979. reprint ed. pap. 22.00 (*0-918024-11-0*) Ox Bow.

Meeting of East & West in Sri Aurobindo's Philosophy. 2nd ed. Sri Aurobindo. 470p. 1988. pap. 0.50 (*81-7058-488-4*, Pub. by SAA) E-W Cultural Ctr.

Meeting of Eastern & Western Art. expanded rev. ed. Michael Sullivan. 1997. pap. 30.00 (*0-520-21236-3*, Pub. by U CA Pr) Cal Prin Full Svc.

***Meeting of Minds.** Nodelman Matas et al. LC 99-12239. 199p. (YA). (gr. 5-8). 1999. per. 17.00 (*0-689-81947-1*) S&S Bks Yung.

Meeting of Minds, 4 vols., Vol. 1. Steve Allen. LC 89-62786. 191p. 1989. pap. 17.95 (*0-87975-550-4*) Prometheus Bks.

Meeting of Minds, 4 vols., Vol. 2. Steve Allen. LC 89-62786. 255p. 1989. pap. 17.95 (*0-87975-565-2*) Prometheus Bks.

Meeting of Minds, 4 vols., Vol. 3. Steve Allen. LC 89-62786. 185p. 1989. pap. 17.95 (*0-87975-566-0*) Prometheus Bks.

Meeting of Minds, 4 vols., Vol. 4. Steve Allen. LC 89-62786. 174p. 1989. pap. 17.95 (*0-87975-567-9*) Prometheus Bks.

Meeting of Minds: Intellectual & Religious Interaction in East Asian Traditions of Thought. Ed. by Irene Bloom & Joshua A. Fogel. 384p. 1996. 52.00 (*0-231-10352-2*) Col U Pr.

Meeting of Minds: Mutuality in Psychoanalysis. Lewis Aron. (RPBS Ser.: Vol. 4). 320p. 1996. 42.50 (*0-88163-159-0*) Analytic Pr.

Meeting of Minds: The Television Scripts, 4 vols., Set. Steve Allen. 805p. 1989. pap. 59.95 (*0-87975-561-X*) Prometheus Bks.

Meeting of Mystic Paths: Christianity & Yoga. Justin O'Brien. LC 96-14872. 180p. 1996. 16.95 (*0-936663-14-6*) Yes Intl.

Meeting of Parliament: A Study of the Law & Practice Relating to the Frequency & Duration of the United Kingdom Parliament. Robert Blackburn. 128p. 1990. text 72.95 (*1-85521-080-0*, Pub. by Dartmth Pub) Ashgate Pub Co.

*** Meeting of Religions & the Trinity.** Gavin D'Costa. (Faith Meets Faith Ser.). 192p. 2000. pap. 20.00 (*1-57075-303-2*) Orbis Bks.

Meeting of Science & Spirit: Guidelines for a New Age. John White. 288p. 1990. 18.95 (*1-55778-302-0*) Paragon Hse.

Meeting of Streams: South Asian Canadian Literature. M. G. Vassanji. 1985. pap. 9.00 (*0-920661-00-9*) S Asia.

Meeting of the Minds. Vincent P. Barabba. 1995. 27.95 (*0-07-103629-6*) McGraw.

Meeting of the Minds: Creating the Market-Based Enterprise. Vincent P. Barabba. LC 95-13342. 224p. 1995. 27.95 (*0-87584-577-0*) Harvard Busn.

Meeting of the Minds 2: ITEC Virtual Conference '97 Proceedings see Net Effect: School Library Media Centers & the Internet

Meeting of the Mountebanks. Niels Werner. LC 98-65844. (Niels Werner Collector Ser.: No. 2). 64p. (J). (gr. k-8). 1999. pap. 9.95 (*0-9663019-2-7*) Pocket Sanity.

Meeting of the OAU-Secretariat & Voluntary Agencies in African Refugees, Arusha, March 1983. Ed. by Peter Nobel. 36p. 1983. write for info. (*91-7106-215-7*, Pub. by Nordic Africa) Transaction Pubs.

Meeting of the Souls. Eric L. Brantley. LC 97-140098. 176p. (Orig.). 1996. pap. 12.00 (*0-9653518-0-7*) Sho U Write.

Meeting of Two Worlds: Cultural Exchange Between East & West During the Period of the Crusades. Ed. by Vladimir P. Goss & Christine V. Bornstein. 1986. boxed set 39.95 (*0-918720-58-3*) Medieval Inst.

Meeting of Two Worlds: The Crusades & the Mediterranean Context. Christine Bornstein et al. (Illus.). 103p. 1981. pap. 15.00 (*0-912303-24-7*) Michigan Mus.

Meeting Organization & Human Resource Challenges: Perspectives, Issues & Strategies. Ed. by Douglas B. Gutknecht. LC 84-7289. 476p. (Orig.). 1984. pap. text 34.00 (*0-8191-3982-3*); lib. bdg. 62.00 (*0-8191-3981-5*) U Pr of Amer.

Meeting Other Believers: The Risks & Rewards of Interreligious Dialogue. Francis Arinze. LC 98-65358. 112p. 1998. pap. 7.95 (*0-87973-949-5*) Our Sunday Visitor.

***Meeting Papaji.** Roslyn Moore. 256p. 1999. pap. 16.50 (*0-9646999-1-5*) DO Publng.

Meeting Patient's Needs: Quality Care in a Changing Environment. Lynn Rogut & Avery Hudson. (Papers). 1995. pap. 12.00 (*1-881277-27-5*) United Hosp Fund.

Meeting Peace Operations' Requirements While Maintaining MTW Readiness. Jennifer M. Taw et al. LC 97-44797. (Illus.). 75p. 1998. pap. 15.00 (*0-8330-2568-6*, MR-921-A) Rand Corp.

***Meeting Physical & Health Needs of Children with Disabilities: Teaching Student Participation & Management.** Kathryn W. Heller. LC 00-22004. 428p. 2000. 84.95 (*0-534-34837-8*) Wadsworth Pub.

***Meeting Place.** E. B. Herman. 128p. 1999. mass mkt. 8.00 (*0-927936-23-2*) Vincom Pubng Co.

Meeting Place. Janette Oke & T. Davis Bunn. LC 99-6376. 256p. 1999. 15.99 (*0-7642-2177-9*); pap. 10.99 (*0-7642-2176-0*) Bethany Hse.

***Meeting Place.** Janette Oke & T. Davis Bunn. LC 99-6376. 1999. audio 14.99 (*0-7642-2179-5*) Bethany Hse.

Meeting Place. Janette Oke & T. Davis Bunn. LC 99-23487. 1999. 26.95 (*0-7838-8658-6*) Thorndike Pr.

Meeting Place. large type ed. Janette Oke & T. Davis Bunn. LC 99-6376. 432p. 1999. pap. 15.99 (*0-7642-2178-7*) Bethany Hse.

Meeting Places with Jesus. Stephen G. Long. (Illus.). 60p. (Orig.). 1992. pap. 4.95 (*0-9629550-1-9*) Word in Action.

Meeting Planners' Complete Guide to Negotiating: You Can Get What You Want. 2nd ed. Stanley M. Wolfson. 316p. (Orig.). 1995. pap. text 49.95 (*0-931273-03-X*) Inst Meeting Con Mgmt.

Meeting Planners' Workbook: Write Your Own Hotel Contract. Stanley M. Wolfson. 244p. (Orig.). 1991. pap. 79.95 (*0-931273-02-1*) Inst Meeting Con Mgmt.

Meeting Procedure for Condominium & Homeowners Associations. Joyce Stephens. 91p. 1993. pap. 15.00 (*1-884048-00-5*) Natl Assn Parliamentarians.

Meeting Quality Standards. Haldane. 1989. pap. text 110.00 (*0-08-040478-2*, Pergamon Pr) Elsevier.

***Meeting Research & Education Needs in Coastal Engineering.** National Research Council Staff. 74p. 1999. pap. 18.00 (*0-309-06381-7*) Natl Acad Pr.

***Meeting Rights & Education Standards for Behavioral Health Care: Examples of Compliance.** Joint Commission on Accreditation of Healthcare Organizations. (Illus.). 140p. 1998. pap. 40.00 (*0-86688-548-X*, BH-400) Joint Comm Hlthcare.

Meeting Room Games: Getting Things Done in Committees. Nan Booth. LC 95-44837. (Illus.). 128p. (Orig.). 1996. pap. 14.95 (*0-918420-25-3*) Brighton Pubns.

Meeting Singles: Where French Is Spoken. J. Frank Carroll. LC 85-50429. (Illus.). 60p. (Orig.). 1985. pap. 6.95 (*0-933571-00-3*) Ure Pr.

Meeting Singles Where Spanish Is Spoken. J. Frank Carroll. LC 85-52049. (Illus.). 78p. (Orig.). pap. 6.95 (*0-933571-01-1*) Ure Pr.

Meeting-Space Ideas for Youth Ministry: 80 Fun Options to Create a Faith-Building Place Kids Want to Be. Todd Outcalt. Ed. by Amy Simpson. LC 97-39561. 176p. 1998. per. 15.99 (*0-7644-2026-7*) Group Pub.

Meeting Special Needs in Mainstream Schools: A Practical Guide for Teachers. Richard Stakes & Garry Hornby. LC 96-217328. 112p. 1996. pap. 24.95 (*1-85346-448-1*, Pub. by David Fulton) Taylor & Francis.

Meeting Special Needs in Ordinary Schools. 2nd ed. Seamus Hegarty. 224p. 1993. pap. 35.00 (*0-304-32673-9*) Weidner & Sons.

***Meeting Standards with Inspiration: Core Curriculum Lesson Plans.** (Illus.). 83p. 1999. 19.95 (*0-928539-35-0*) Inspir Sftware.

***Meeting Standards with Inspiration: Core Curriculum Lesson Plans, School Wide Edition.** (Illus.). 83p. 1999. 195.00 (*0-928539-36-9*) Inspir Sftware.

Meeting Statuary Deadlines: Contractual & Financial Injury Litigation Action Guide - Winter 1997. Katherine S. Clark et al. Ed. by Robert Waxman. 100p. 1997. pap. 58.00 (*0-7626-0051-9*) Cont Ed Bar-CA.

Meeting Statutory Deadlines: Business Entities' Filing Requirements & Deadlines, Winter 1993, Action Guide, Pt. 7. Jacob C. Reinbolt. Ed. by Ellen C. Lester. (Meeting Statutory Deadlines Ser.). 90p. 1993. pap. text 47.00 (*0-88124-603-4*, BU-11422) Cont Ed Bar-CA.

***Meeting Statutory Deadlines: During & after Litigation Action Guide - Fall 1998.** Gail F. Flatt. Ed. by Linda A. Compton. 96p. 1998. pap. text 58.00 (*0-7626-0260-0*, CP-11395) Cont Ed Bar-CA.

***Meeting Statutory Deadlines: Personal Injury & Injury to Personal Property Action Guide - Spring 1998.** Gail F. Flatt et al. Ed. by Linda A. Compton. 64p. 1998. pap. text 58.00 (*0-7626-0258-9*, CP-11334) Cont Ed Bar-CA.

Meeting Statutory Deadlines: Workers' Compensation - Action Guide - Summer 1996. Barry M. Lesch & James P. Pettibone. Ed. by Kay E. Tindel. 96p. 1996. pap. 58.00 (*0-7626-0024-1*, WC-11403) Cont Ed Bar-CA.

Meeting Statutory Deadlines Action Guide Series, 8 pts. 1991. pap. text 47.00 (*0-88124-317-5*) Cont Ed Bar-CA.

Meeting Strangers. Marsha Learner. LC 91-91842. 185p. 1991. pap. 12.95 (*0-9628968-0-2*) M Brandsdorfer.

Meeting Teachers' Management Needs. Alan Bullock. 184p. 1990. 85.00 (*1-870167-05-8*, Pub. by P Francis) St Mut.

Meeting Technology's Advance: Social Change in China & Zimbabwe in the Railway Age, 34. James Z. Gao. LC 97-6412. (Contributions in Comparative Colonial Studies: Vol. 34). 240p. 1997. 67.95 (*0-313-30095-X*, Greenwood Pr) Greenwood.

Meeting Tessie. Julia Blumenreich. 40p. (Orig.). 1994. pap. 6.00 (*0-935162-14-3*) Singing Horse.

Meeting the ADD Challenge: A Practical Guide for Teachers. Steven B. Gordon & Michael J. Asher. LC 94-64445. 196p. (Orig.). 1994. pap. text 15.95 (*0-87822-345-2*, 4760) Res Press.

Meeting the Blues. Alan Govenar. (Illus.). 248p. 1995. reprint ed. pap. 17.95 (*0-306-80641-X*) Da Capo.

Meeting the British. Paul Muldoon. LC 87-50181. 64p. (Orig.). 1987. pap. 6.95 (*0-916390-26-8*) Wake Forest.

Meeting the Buddhas: A Guide to Buddhas, Bodhisattavas, & Tantric Deities. Vessantara. (Illus.). 368p. (Orig.). 1996. pap. 24.00 (*0-904766-53-5*) Windhorse Pubns.

Meeting the Call for Excellence in the Foreign Language Classroom. Ed. by Robert DiDonato. (Central States Ser.). pap. 14.21 (*0-8442-9317-2*, VF9317-2) NTC Contemp Pub Co.

Meeting the Challenge? Ed. by John Pinkerton & Ross McCrea. LC 98-46652. 150p. (C). 1999. text 56.95 (*1-84014-328-2*, HV751.N67P55, Pub. by Ashgate Pub) Ashgate Pub Co.

Meeting the Challenge: A Research Agenda for America's Health, Safety, & Food. (Illus.). 56p. (Orig.). 1996. pap. text 25.00 (*0-7881-3294-6*) DIANE Pub.

Meeting the Challenge: A Research Agenda for America's Health, Safety & Food. Government Printing Office Staff. 62p. 1996. pap. 8.50 (*0-16-048521-5*) USGPO.

Meeting the Challenge: Hearing-Impaired Professionals in the Workplace. fac. ed. Alan B. Crammatte. LC 87-118. 258p. 1994. pap. 80.00 (*0-7837-7690-X*, 204744600007) Bks Demand.

Meeting the Challenge: Innovative Feminist Pedagogies in Action. Maralee Mayberry. LC 98-37302. 1999. 80.00 (*0-415-92248-8*) Routledge.

Meeting the Challenge: Innovative Feminist Pedagogies in Action. Maralee Mayberry & Ellen C. Rose. LC 98-37302. 1999. pap. 22.99 (*0-415-92249-6*) Routledge.

Meeting the Challenge: Living with Chronic Illness. Audrey Kron & Lawrence Kron. Ed. by Edith Brioda. (Illus.). 200p. (Orig.). 1998. pap. 14.00 (*0-9633877-1-5*) A Kron.

Meeting the Challenge: Proceedings of 1982 National Waste Processing Conference: Tenth Biennial Conference: Papers Presented at 1982 National Waste Processing Conference, New York, New York, May 2-5, 1982. National Waste Processing Conference Staff. LC 70-124402. (Illus.). 503p. reprint ed. pap. 156.00 (*0-8357-2862-5*, 203909800011) Bks Demand.

Meeting the Challenge: Rebuilding Inner City Airports: Proceedings of the 24th International Air Transportation Conference. Ed. by Prianka N. Seneviratne. LC 96-19474. 320p. 1996. 38.00 (*0-7844-0179-9*) Am Soc Civil Eng.

Meeting the Challenge: U. S. Industry Faces the 21st Century: The U. S. Biotechnology Industry. Jon Paugh. Ed. by John C. Lafrance. (Illus.). 108p. (C). 1998. pap. text 35.00 (*0-7881-7195-X*) DIANE Pub.

***Meeting the Challenge: Using Love & Logic to Help Children Develop Attention & Behavior Skills.** Jim Fay et al. Ed. by Linda Carlson. 216p. 2000. pap. write for info. (*1-930429-02-9*, Pub. by Cline-Fay Inst) Midpt Trade.

M

Meeting the Challenge of a Nation at Risk. National Commission on Excellence in Education. LC 84-50559. (Illus.). 128p. (Orig.). 1984. pap. 9.95 (*0-917191-04-8*) USA Res.

Meeting the Challenge of Change: Basic Skills for a Competitive Workforce. Jerome M. Rosow & Robert Zager. (Job-Linked Literacy: Innovative Strategies at Work Ser.: Pt. II). 99p. 1992. pap. 95.00 (*0-89361-048-8*) Work in Amer.

Meeting the Challenge of Change at Work ESF Project Examples. European Commission Staff. LC 98-125539. 1997. 20.00 (*92-828-1389-4*, CE-07-97-628ENC, Pub. by Comm Europ Commun) Bernan Associates.

Meeting the Challenge of Charter Reform. Kevin F. McCarthy et al. (Illus.). 133p. 1998. pap. 13.00 (*0-8330-2592-9*, MR-961-LABA) Rand Corp.

Meeting the Challenge of Chinese Enterprise Reform. Harry G. Broadman. LC 95-10466. (Discussion Paper Ser.: Vol. 283). 60p. 1995. pap. 22.00 (*0-8213-3223-6*, 13223) World Bank.

Meeting the Challenge of Community-Acquired Respiratory Tract Infections: The Role of Cephalosporins. Ed. by G. L. Petrikkos & W. Koenig. (Journal: Respiration: Vol. 60, Suppl. 1, 1993). (Illus.). vi, 58p. 1993. pap. 28.00 (*3-8055-5754-X*) S Karger.

Meeting the Challenge of HIV Infection in Family Foster Care. Constance M. Ryan & L. Jean Emery. 96p. 1991. pap. 10.95 (*0-87868-440-9*) Child Welfare.

Meeting the Challenge of Increased Competition. Geothermal Resources Council Staff. LC 98-116294. (Transactions Ser.: Vol. 21). (Illus.). 654p. 1997. 65.00 (*0-934412-81-2*) Geothermal.

Meeting the Challenge of Linguistic & Cultural Diversity in Early Childhood Education. Garcia et al. (Yearbook in ECE Ser.). 224p. (C). 1995. text 54.00 (*0-8077-3467-5*); pap. text 25.95 (*0-8077-3466-7*) Tchrs Coll.

Meeting the Challenge of Parenting in the West: An Islamic Perspective. Ekram Beshir & Mohamed R. Beshir. LC 98-35846. 160p. 1998. pap. 11.75 (*0-915957-87-6*) amana pubns.

Meeting the Challenge of Pro Se Litigation: A Report & Guidebook for Judges & Court Managers. Jona Goldschmidt et al. LC 97-75224. 146p. 1998. pap. 25.00 (*0-938870-81-5*, 815) Am Judicature.

Meeting the Challenge of Sustainable Mobility: The Role of Technological Innovations. H. Geerlings. LC 99-10781. (Illus.). xv, 262p. 1999. 89.95 (*3-540-65488-7*) Spr-Verlag.

Meeting the Challenge of Tomorrow: Johnson C. Smith University. Haris et al. 126p. (C). 1998. per. 28.95 (*0-7872-5452-5*, 41545201) Kendall-Hunt.

Meeting the Challenges in Today's Classroom. Maureen Barbieri & Carol Tateishi. LC 96-20397. 1996. pap. text 24.00 (*0-435-07225-0*) Heinemann.

Meeting the Challenges of a Post-cold War World: Nato Enlargement & U.s.-Russia Relations : A Report to the Committee on Foreign Relations, United States Senate. Joseph R. Biden & United States. LC 98-110367. vii, 59 p. 1997. write for info. (*0-16-055004-1*) USGPO.

Meeting the Challenges of Alzheimer's Disease: The Biomedical Research That Will Carry Us into the 21st Century: Hearing Before the Subcommittee on Aging of the Committee on Labor & Human Resources, United States Senate, 105th Congress, 1st Session ... June 5, 1997. USGPO Staff. LC 98-106707. (S. Hrg. Ser.). iii, 76 p. 1997. write for info. (*0-16-055350-4*) USGPO.

***Meeting the Challenges of Animal Traction: A Resource Book of the Animal Traction Network for Eastern & Southern Africa.** Ed. by Paul Starkey & Pascal Kaumbotho. 326p. 2000. pap. 25.00 (*1-85339-483-1*, Pub. by Intermed Tech) Stylus Pub VA.

Meeting the Challenges of Change. Neva Coyle. 176p. (Orig.). 1993. pap. 8.99 (*1-55661-278-8*) Bethany Hse.

***Meeting the Challenges of Learning Disabilities in Adulthood.** Arlyn J. Roffman. LC 99-86790. 2000. 25.95 (*1-55766-430-7*) P H Brookes.

Meeting the Challenges of Population, Environment, & Resources: The Costs of Inaction. Henry W. Kendall et al. LC 96-9106. (Environmentally Sustainable Development Proceedings Ser.: No. 14). 54p. 1996. pap. 22.00 (*0-8213-3635-5*, 13635) World Bank.

Meeting the Challenges of Primary Schooling. Lloyd Logan & Judyth Sachs. LC 96-51866. (Educational Management Ser.). 280p. (C). 1997. pap. 27.99 (*0-415-14655-0*) Routledge.

Meeting the Challenges of Project Management: A Primer. Frank Greenwood. 1998. pap., wbk. ed. 15.00 (*1-890367-08-7*) ESI Int.

Meeting the Challenges of the European Union: Prospects of Indian Exports. Atul Sarma et al. LC 97-14476. (Indo-Dutch Studies on Development Alternatives: Vol. 20). 300p. 1997. 38.00 (*0-8039-9390-0*) Sage.

Meeting the Challenges of Welfare Reform: Programs with Promise. Jack Tweedie et al. LC 98-162122. 97p. 1998. 20.00 (*1-55516-758-6*) Natl Conf State Legis.

***Meeting the Childcare Challenge: A Childcare Strategy for Scotland: A Framework & Consultation Document.** Great Britain Staff. LC 98-168682. xii, 36 p. 1998. write for info. (*0-10-139582-5*) Seven Hills Bk.

Meeting the Childcare Challenge: A Framework & Consultation Document. LC 98-168734. (CM Ser.). 50 p. 1998. 18.00 (*0-10-139592-2*, Pub. by Statnry Office) Bernan Associates.

Meeting the Coconut Family. unabridged ed. Clodomiro Giraud. (Illus.). 57p. (J). (gr. 2-6). 1991. 12.95 (*0-9630389-0-7*) Coconut.

Meeting the Comet. Fleur Adcock. 24p. (Orig.). 1988. pap. 6.95 (*1-85224-054-7*, Pub. by Bloodaxe Bks) Dufour.

Meeting the Communist Threat: Truman to Reagan. Thomas G. Paterson. 336p. 1989. pap. text 10.95 (*0-19-504532-7*) OUP.

***Meeting the Competency Challenge in Behavioral Health Care.** Ed. by Cathy Cecere. 240p. 2000. 117.00 (*0-9679474-0-5*) C & R Pubns.

Meeting the Costs of Health Care: The Bay Area Experience & the National Issues. Margaret Greenfield. LC 72-5657. 194p. reprint ed. pap. 60.20 (*0-7837-2133-1*, 204241500004) Bks Demand.

Meeting the Educational Needs of Homeless Children & Youth: A Resource for Schools & Communities. 1998. lib. bdg. 251.95 (*0-8490-9091-1*) Gordon Pr.

Meeting the Educational Needs of Homeless Children & Youth: A Resource for Schools & Communities. Amy M. Hightower. LC 97-218485. 67p. 1997. pap. 8.50 (*0-16-049242-4*) USGPO.

Meeting the Educational Needs of the New Californians. Kevin G. Woolfork & Diane Fuentes-Michel. (Illus.). 60p. (C). 1999. reprint ed. pap. text 20.00 (*0-7881-7395-2*) DIANE Pub.

Meeting the Energy Challenges of the 1990's: Experts Define the Key Policy Issues. (Illus.). 194p. (Orig.). (C). 1993. pap. text 45.00 (*1-56806-672-4*) DIANE Pub.

Meeting the Espionage Challenge: A Review of U. S. Counterintelligence & Secret Programs. 156p. (Orig.). (C). 1993. pap. text 25.00 (*1-56806-866-2*) DIANE Pub.

Meeting the Four O'Clock Train & Other Stories: Boyhood Recollections of Prescott, Arizona, 1909-1927. Dixon Fagerberg, Jr. (Illus.). 127p. 1983. pap. 6.95 (*0-927579-15-4*) Sharlot Hall Mus Pr.

Meeting the Goal of a Literate America: The State Response. Ed. by Robert A. Silvanik. 75p. (Orig.). 1990. pap. text 15.00 (*1-55877-076-3*) Natl Governor.

Meeting the Great Bliss Queen: Buddhists, Feminists, & the Art of the Self. Anne C. Klein. 336p. 1996. pap. 14.00 (*0-8070-7307-5*) Beacon Pr.

Meeting the Guidance & Counseling Needs of Boys. Lawrence Beymer. LC 94-31000. 108p. 1995. pap. text 23.95 (*1-55620-136-2*, 72562) Am Coun Assn.

Meeting the Health Needs of Women: Survivors of the Balkan Conflict. unabridged ed. Julie A. Mertus. Ed. by Rachel N. Pine. 116p. 1993. pap. text 8.00 (*1-890671-14-2*) Center Reprod.

***Meeting the Housing Needs of Women Living with HIV-AIDS.** 1998. pap. 5.00 (*1-877966-46-0*) Ctr Women Policy.

Meeting the Information Needs of Education Policymakers. Government Printing Office Staff. 27p. 1997. pap. 4.25 (*0-16-049159-2*) USGPO.

Meeting the IS: Memories & Cogitations. Miriam Hope. LC 92-71976. 256p. 1992. pap. 12.95 (*0-923687-21-1*) Celo Valley Bks.

Meeting the Japanese Challenge, 1969-1971: Balance of Payments Problems Force the Nixon Administration to Act. Robert C. Angel. (Pew Case Studies in International Affairs). 60p. (C). 1988. pap. text 3.50 (*1-56927-135-6*) Geo U Inst Dplmcy.

Meeting the Living God. 3rd rev. ed. William J. O'Malley. LC 98-5532. 336p. (YA). (gr. 9-12). 1998. pap. 14.95 (*0-8091-9576-3*, 9576-3) Paulist Pr.

Meeting the Lovefriend. Royal Satterlee. 330p. 1991. 14.95 (*1-879227-03-7*) Royal Ideas.

Meeting the Make-Out King. Lynn Cullen. LC 93-38850. 144p. (J). 1995. pap. 3.99 (*0-380-72576-2*, Avon Bks) Morrow Avon.

Meeting the Make-Out King. Lynn Cullen. 1995. 9.09 (*0-606-09606-X*, Pub. by Turtleback) Demco.

Meeting the Management, Organizational, & Staffing Challenges of the 1990s. 107p. 1993. pap. 53.00 (*0-89867-706-8*, 90638) Am Water Wks Assn.

Meeting the Mandate: Renewing the College & Departmental Curriculum. William Toombs & William G. Tierney. Ed. by Jonathan D. Fife. LC 92-80932. (ASHE-ERIC Higher Education Reports: No. 91-6). 114p. (Orig.). 1992. pap. text 24.00 (*1-878380-11-7*) GWU Grad Schl E&HD.

Meeting the Master: Stories about Mastery, Slavery, & the Darker Side of Desire. Elissa Wald. 224p. 1998. reprint ed. pap. 12.00 (*0-8021-3550-1*, Grove) Grove-Atltic.

Meeting the Master (1917) Ozora S. Davis. 160p. 1998. reprint ed. pap. 17.95 (*0-7661-0535-0*) Kessinger Pub.

Meeting the Messiah. Donald J. Shelby. 7.95 (*0-687-60737-X*) Abingdon.

Meeting the Millennium: 30 Activities for the Turn of the Century. Elena D. Wright & Alyssa M. Pusey. 48p. (YA). (ps up). 1999. pap. 9.95 (*1-57091-175-4*) Charlesbridge Pub.

Meeting the Minotaur. Carol Dawson. LC 97-4032. 444p. 1997. 22.95 (*1-56512-126-0*, 72126) Algonquin Bks.

Meeting the Moment: Leadership & Well-Being in Ministry. G. Douglass Lewis. 124p. 1997. pap. 12.95 (*0-687-07286-7*) Abingdon.

***Meeting the Monkey Halfway.** Ajahn Sumano Bhikkhu. LC 99-58179. 128p. 2000. pap. 9.95 (*1-57863-146-7*) Weiser.

Meeting the Mountains. Harish Kapadia. LC 98-908468. 1998. 36.00 (*81-7387-085-3*, Pub. by Indus Pub) S Asia.

Meeting the Nation's Needs for Biomedical & Behavioral Scientists. National Research Council Staff. 174p. (Orig.). (C). 1994. pap. text 27.00 (*0-309-05086-3*) Natl Acad Pr.

Meeting the Need for Long-Term Care. Denise Iona. 126p. (Orig.). 1998. pap. write for info. (*1-893360-00-8*) Inkslingers Res.

Meeting the Needs of Children: Creating Trust & Security. Louis E. Raths. LC 98-70460. 166p. (C). 1998. pap. text 21.95 (*0-9658339-7-6*) Educ Intl Pr.

***Meeting The Needs of Children With Autistic Spectrum Disorders.** Rita Jordan. 1999. pap. text 17.95 (*1-85346-582-8*) David Fulton.

***Meeting the Needs of Employees with Disabilities.** 3rd ed. Resources for Rehabilitation Organization Staff. LC 99-33733. 1999. pap. 44.95 (*0-929718-25-9*) Resc Rehab.

Meeting the Needs of Ethnic Minority Children. Ed. by Kedar N. Dwivedi & Ved P. Varma. 200p. 1995. pap. 24.95 (*1-85302-294-2*, Pub. by Jessica Kingsley) Taylor & Francis.

Meeting the Needs of Our Clients Creatively: The Impact of Art & Culture on Caregiving. Ed. by John D. Morgan. LC 99-12799. (Death, Value & Meaning Ser.). 320p. (C). 1999. text 48.95 (*0-89503-193-0*) Baywood Pub.

Meeting the Needs of Out-of-School Youth. David E. Brown. 32p. 1997. pap. 15.00 (*1-55877-276-6*) Natl Governor.

Meeting the Needs of People with Disabilities: A Guide for Librarians, Educators & Other Serv. Ruth A. Velleman. 1990. reprint ed. pap. text 37.95 (*1-57356-157-6*) Oryx Pr.

Meeting the Needs of People with Disabilities Through Federal Technology Transfer: Hearing Before the Committee on Science, Subcommittee on Technology, U.S. House of Representatives, One Hundred Fifth Congress, First Session, July 15, 1997. United States Government. LC 98-144181. iii, 94 p. 1997. write for info. (*0-16-056046-2*) USGPO.

Meeting the Needs of People with Vision Loss: A Multidisciplinary Perspective. Ed. by Susan L. Greenblatt. 1991. pap. 24.95 (*0-929718-07-0*) Resc Rehab.

Meeting the Needs of Small & Medium Sized Manufacturers in California, Vol. 4. Gus Koehler. 18p. 1997. pap. write for info. (*1-58703-068-3*, CRB Note 4) CA St Libry.

Meeting the Needs of Special Students: Legal, Ethical, & Practical Ramifications. Lawrence J. Johnson & Anne M. Bauer. LC 92-4572. 96p. 1992. pap. 17.00 (*0-8039-6021-2*) Corwin Pr.

***Meeting the Needs of Students of All Abilities: How Leaders Go Beyond Inclusion.** Colleen A. Capper et al. (Illus.). 168p. 2000. pap., wbk. ed. 32.95 (*0-7619-7501-2*); lib. bdg., wbk. ed. 69.95 (*0-7619-7500-4*) Corwin Pr.

Meeting the Needs of Students with Special Physical & Health Care Needs. Jennifer Leigh Hill. LC 98-26893. 632p. 1998. 74.00 (*0-13-262601-2*) P-H.

Meeting the Neighbors: Sketches of Life on the Northern Prairie. W. Scott Olsen. LC 93-12827. 1993. pap. 9.95 (*0-87839-080-4*) North Star.

Meeting the Night: Bedtime Prayers & Meditations from Around the World. Brian Wright. LC 98-31839. 160p. 1999. 12.95 (*1-58062-120-1*) Adams Media.

Meeting the Outreach Challenge. 368p. reprint ed. 25.00 (*0-8266-0496-X*, Neshei Chabad) Kehot Pubn Soc.

Meeting the Patients' Needs in the Climacteric: The Proceedings of a Symposium Held at the 15th World Congress on Fertility & Sterility, Montpellier, France, September 1995. Ed. by J. C. Colau. LC 96-33684. (Illus.). 84p. 1996. pap. 25.00 (*1-85070-761-8*) Prthnon Pub.

Meeting the Physical Therapy Needs of Children. Ed. by Susan K. Effgen. (Illus.). 450p. Date not set. pap. 39.00 (*0-8036-0250-2*) Davis Co.

***Meeting the Pieman.** Victor Wartofsky. LC 99-63265. 320p. 2000. reprint ed. pap. 12.95 (*0-88739-282-2*) Creat Arts Bk.

Meeting the Preservation Challenge. Association of Research Libraries Staff. 70p. 1988. pap. 28.00 (*0-918006-15-5*) ARL.

Meeting the Press: A Media Survival Guide. 1995. lib. bdg. 251.95 (*0-8490-7553-X*) Gordon Pr.

Meeting the Press: A Media Survival Guide for the Defense Manager. (Orig.). 1994. lib. bdg. 250.00 (*0-8490-8423-7*) Gordon Pr.

***Meeting the Sensei: The Role of the Master in Shirakaba Writers.** Maya Mortimer. LC 99-56875. (Japanese Studies Library). 308p. 2000. 78.00 (*90-04-11655-9*) Brill Academic Pubs.

Meeting the Shadow: The Hidden Power of the Dark Side of Human Nature. Ed. by Connie Zweig & Jeremiah Abrams. (New Consciousness Reader Ser.). 368p. (Orig.). 1991. pap. 15.95 (*0-87477-618-X*, Tarcher Putnam) Putnam Pub Group.

Meeting the Spirit. Douglas Connelly. (LifeGuide Bible Studies). 64p. (Orig.). 1993. pap., wbk. ed. 4.99 (*0-8308-1068-4*, 1068) InterVarsity.

Meeting the Standards: Improving Middle Level Teacher Education. John H. Swaim & Greg P. Stefanich. 1996. write for info. (*0-614-96376-1*) Natl Middle Schl.

Meeting the Standards: Social Studies Readings for K-6 Educators. Ed. by Mary E. Haas & Margaret A. Laughlin. 353p. 1997. pap. 19.50 (*0-87986-072-3*) Nat Coun Soc Studies.

***Meeting the Technology Challenge: Building New Learning Communities.** Shirley A. Steele. 32p. 1998. pap. 3.25 (*0-16-063664-7*) USGPO.

Meeting the Tree of Life: A Teacher's Path. John Tallmadge. LC 96-42234. 220p. 1997. 44.95 (*0-87480-530-9*); pap. 18.95 (*0-87480-531-7*) U of Utah Pr.

Meeting the Whales: The Equinox Guide to Giants of the Deep. Erich Hoyt. (Illus.). 72p. (YA). (gr. 5 up). 1991. pap. 9.95 (*0-921820-23-2*, Pub. by Camden Hse) Firefly Bks Ltd.

Meeting to Speak the Word of God. Witness Lee. 60p. 1987. per. 4.50 (*0-87083-291-3*, 12-011-001) Living Stream Ministry.

Meeting Tree: Black America's Modern Southern Crisis. Jesse Goodwin. LC 95-70047. (Illus.). 160p. 1996. pap. 9.95 (*0-9628828-7-9*) Prospector Pr.

Meeting Trees. Scott R. Sanders. LC 95-47339. (Illus.). 32p. (J). (gr. k-3). 1997. 16.00 (*0-7922-4140-1*, Pub. by Natl Geog) S&S Trade.

Meeting vs. Energy Resource Needs: The Energy Resources Program of the U. S. Geological Survey. National Research Council Staff. 85p. (C). 1998. pap. text 15.00 (*0-309-06283-7*) Natl Acad Pr.

Meeting with David B. Axelrod & Gnazino Russo. David B. Axelrod. Ed. & Tr. by Nat Scammacca. LC 79-90012. (Sicilian Antigruppo Ser.: No. 3). (Illus.). 1979. 15.00 (*0-89304-505-5*); pap. 5.00 (*0-89304-507-1*) Cross-Cultrl NY.

Meeting with David B. Axelrod & Gnazino Russo. deluxe limited ed. David B. Axelrod. Ed. & Tr. by Nat Scammacca. LC 79-90012. (Sicilian Antigruppo Ser.: No. 3). (Illus.). 1979. 20.00 (*0-89304-506-3*) Cross-Cultrl NY.

Meeting with Disma Tumminello & William Stafford. William Stafford. Ed. by Nat Scammacca. (Sicilian Antigruppo Ser.: No. 2). (ENG & ITA., Illus.). 1978. 15.00 (*0-89304-558-6*); pap. 5.00 (*0-89304-559-4*) Cross-Cultrl NY.

Meeting with EU Social Policy: The Experience of a New Member State. M. Kari. LC 98-223282. 272p. 1998. 118.00 (*90-6215-614-2*) Gaunt.

Meeting with Medusa. Arthur C. Clarke. 192p. 1988. 2.95 (*0-8125-3362-3*) Tor Bks.

Meeting with Nicolo D'Alessandro & Nat Scammacca. Ed. by Nat Scammacca. (Sicilian Antigruppo Ser.: No. 1). (ENG & ITA., Illus.). 15.00 (*0-89304-502-0*); pap. 5.00 (*0-89304-500-4*) Cross-Cultrl NY.

Meeting with the Past see Encuentro con el Pasado: (Meeting with the Past)

Meeting with the Presidents of Constitutional Courts & Other Equivalent Bodies. (Science & Technique of Democracy Ser.: No. 1). (ENG & FRE.). 1993. 12.00 (*92-871-2419-1*, Pub. by Council of Europe) Manhattan Pub Co.

Meeting with the Universe: Science Discoveries from the Space Program. 1994. lib. bdg. 263.95 (*0-8490-6414-7*) Gordon Pr.

Meeting Women's Needs for Post-Abortion Family Planning: Framing the Questions. Janie Benson et al. (Issues in Abortion Care Ser.).Tr. of Cubriendo las Necesidades de las Mujeres en Cuanto a la Planificacion Familiar Post-Aborto. 69p. 1992. pap. 6.00 (*1-882220-01-3*) IPAS.

***Meeting Writing Standards: Descriptive Writing Intermediate.** Contrib. by Austin & Company Inc. Staff. 144p. 2000. pap. 14.95 (*1-57690-991-3*) Tchr Create Mat.

***Meeting Writing Standards: Enhancing Writing with Visuals.** Contrib. by Austin & Company Inc. Staff. 144p. 2000. pap. 14.95 (*1-57690-993-X*) Tchr Create Mat.

***Meeting Writing Standards: Narrative Writing.** Andrea Trischitta. 144p. 2000. pap. 14.95 (*1-57690-994-8*) Tchr Create Mat.

***Meeting Writing Standards: Poetry Writing.** Kimberly A. Williams. 144p. 2000. pap. 14.95 (*1-57690-992-1*); pap. 14.95 (*1-57690-998-0*) Tchr Create Mat.

***Meeting Writing Standards: Pursuasive Writing.** Rebecca J. Rozmiarek. 144p. 2000. pap. 14.95 (*1-57690-990-5*) Tchr Create Mat.

Meeting Your Match: A Practical Guide for Finding Your Perfect Mate. rev. ed. Karen A. Bowen. 180p. 1995. pap. 13.00 (*0-9649343-0-2*) Ariadne Pubs.

Meeting Yourself Halfway: Thirty-One Clarification Strategies for Daily Living. Sidney B. Simon. 102p. 1991. reprint ed. pap. text 7.95 (*1-880424-05-3*) Values.

Meetinghouse Tragedy: An Episode in the Life of a New England Town. Charles E. Clark. LC 98-23577. (Illus.). 170p. 1998. pap. 14.95 (*0-87451-872-5*); text 30.00 (*0-87451-887-3*) U Pr of New Eng.

Meetingplace: A History of the Mennonite Church of Normal 1912-1987. Rachel W. Goossen. Ed. by Terry Stutzman. LC 86-63769. (Illus.). 179p. 1987. text 25.00 (*0-9617978-0-0*); pap. text 18.00 (*0-9617978-1-9*) Mennonite Church.

Meetings. (Open Learning for Supervisory Management Ser.). 1989. pap. text 19.50 (*0-08-070135-3*, Pergamon Pr) Elsevier.

Meetings. 2nd ed. (Open Learning Super Ser.). 1991. pap. text 26.00 (*0-08-041605-5*, Pergamon Pr) Elsevier.

Meetings: A Gower Audio Manual. Greville Janner. 1988. text 49.95 (*0-566-02720-8*, Pub. by Gower) Ashgate Pub Co.

Meetings: A Reporter's Notebook. Jess Stearn. LC 97-7988. 1997. 12.95 (*1-55874-539-4*) Palasades Pub.

Meetings: A Reporter's Notebook - Provocative Interviews That Capture the Spirit of Our Times. Jess Stearn. LC 97-7988. 310p. 1997. pap. 12.95 (*1-55874-500-9*) Health Comm.

Meetings: Do's, Don'ts & Donuts: The Complete Handbook for Successful Meetings. 2nd rev. ed. Sharon M. Lippincott. LC 98-83112. 224p. 1999. pap. 16.95 (*0-9637966-6-6*) Lghthse Pt Pr.

Meetings: How & Why. Red Point Publishing Staff. 1997. pap. text 3.95 (*0-9658795-2-6*) Red Pt Publ.

Meetings: Minutes & Agendas. Michigan Municipal League Staff. 1995. 15.00 (*0-317-05704-9*) MI Municipal.

Meetings & Conventions. S. Strick. 1995. text 55.95 (*0-442-00838-4*, VNR) Wiley.

Meetings & Conventions Management. Marguerite L. Weirich. 1992. pap. 31.95 (*0-8273-4514-3*) Delmar.

Meetings & Conventions Management: Instructor's Guide. Marguerite L. Weirich. 1992. pap. 9.00 (*0-8273-4515-1*) Delmar.

Meetings & Partings. Longman Imprint Bks Staff. Date not set. pap. text. write for info. (*0-582-22311-3*, Pub. by Addison-Wesley) Longman.

An Asterisk (*) at the beginning of an entry indicates that the title is appearing for the first time.

Meetings at the Edge: Dialogues with the Grieving & the Dying, the Healing & the Healed. Stephen Levine. 264p. 1989. pap. 11.95 (*0-385-26220-5*, Anchor NY) Doubleday.

Meetings Between Experts: An Approach to Sharing Ideas in Medical Consultations. David Tuckett et al. 300p. (C). 1986. pap. text 16.95 (*0-422-79660-3*, 9745, Pub. by Tavistock) Routldge.

Meetings, Conventions, & Expositions: An Introduction to the Industry. Rhonda J. Montgomery & Sandra K. Strick. (Hospitality, Travel & Tourism Ser.). 336p. 1994. 59.95 (*0-471-28439-4*, VNR) Wiley.

Meetings for School-Based Decision Making. Keen J. Babbage. LC 96-60908. 123p. 1996. pap. text 24.95 (*1-56676-450-5*) Scarecrow.

Meetings in an Hour or Less. Steve Kaye. 176p. (Orig.). 1995. pap. 19.95 (*1-884110-51-7*) Persnl Quality.

Meetings Management: A Manual of Effective Training Material. Leslie Rae. LC 92-46124. (McGraw-Hill Training Ser.). 1993. 75.00 (*0-07-707782-2*) McGraw.

Meetings, Manners & Civilization. Wilbert van Vree. Tr. by Kathleen Bell from DUT. LC 99-18363. 370p. 1999. 75.00 (*0-7185-0123-3*) Continuum.

Meetings Manual. Francis Walsh. 94p. 1995. 32.95 (*0-644-33248-4*, Pub. by Aust Gov Pub) Accents Pubns.

Meetings, Meetings, Meetings: Accomplishing More with Better & Fewer. Robert Maidment & William Bullock. Ed. by Patricia L. George. 48p. (Orig.). 1984. pap. 6.00 (*0-88210-162-5*) Natl Assn Principals.

Meetings of Shareholders. 2nd ed. R. Franklin Balotti et al. 568p. 1991. ring bd. 110.00 (*0-13-109349-5*) Aspen Law.

Meetings of Stockholders. write for info. (*0-318-66844-0*) P-H.

Meetings of Stockholders. 3rd ed. R. Franklin Balotti et al. 591p. 1996. ring bd. 160.00 (*1-56706-276-8*, 62768) Panel Pubs.

***Meetings of the Mind.** David Damrosch. LC 99-87371. 224p. 2000. 19.95 (*0-691-05055-4*) Princeton U Pr.

***Meetings of the Mind: Life, Literature & the Pursuit of Agreement.** David Damrosch. LC 99-87371. 2000. pap. write for info. (*0-691-05056-2*) Princeton U Pr.

Meetings of the Spheres or Letters from Dr. Coulter (1919) Ed. by Charlotte G. Herbine. 330p. 1998. reprint ed. pap. 24.95 (*0-7661-0551-2*) Kessinger Pub.

Meetings That Work. Richard Y. Chang. 1994. pap. 12.95 (*0-7879-5079-3*) Jossey-Bass.

Meetings That Work. Karen E. Silva. LC 93-18109. (Business Skills Express Ser.). 80p. 1993. pap. 10.95 (*1-55623-866-5*, Irwn Prfssnl) McGraw-Hill Prof.

Meetings That Work. rev. ed. Marlene Caroselli. 123p. 1995. 12.95 (*1-878542-24-9*, 12-0006) SkillPath Pubns.

Meetings That Work! A Practical Guide to Shorter & More Productive Meetings. Chang, Richard, Associates, Inc. Staff. LC 93-77939. (Quality Improvement Ser.). 100p. 1993. pap. 12.95 (*1-883553-18-0*) R Chang Assocs.

Meetings with a Yogi. Paramhansa Syami Mahesvarananda. (C). 1994. 16.00 (*81-7018-795-8*, Pub. by BR Pub) S Asia.

Meetings with Angels. H. C. Moolenburgh. 256p. (Orig.). pap. 19.95 (*0-8464-4253-1*) Beekman Pubs.

Meetings with Angels: A Hundred & One Real-Life Encounters. H. C. Moolenburgh. 187p. 1993. pap. 19.95 (*0-85207-260-0*, Pub. by C W Daniel) Natl Bk Netwk.

Meetings with Improbable Danglers: The Poets Meet John M. Bennett. Al Ackerman. (Illus.). 28p. 1998. pap. 5.00 (*0-935350-99-3*) Luna Bisonte.

Meetings with Jung: Conversations Recorded During the Years 1946-1961. E. A. Bennet. LC 81-40459. 214p. 1995. pap. 12.95 (*3-85630-501-7*) Continuum.

Meetings with Kontoglou: Enlightening, Lively Discussions on Byzantine Iconography & Music, Diverse Writers, Philosophers & Theologians, & Contemporary Events & Trends, Between the Author & the Great Icon Painter, Writer, & Philosopher Photios Kontoglou. Constantine Cavarnos. LC 92-74877. (Illus.). 216p. 1993. pap. 12.00 (*0-914744-95-X*) Inst Byzantine.

Meetings with Mallarme. Ed. by Michael Temple. 256p. 1998. text 70.00 (*0-85989-561-0*, Pub. by Univ Exeter Pr); pap. text 27.95 (*0-85989-562-9*, Pub. by Univ Exeter Pr) Northwestern U Pr.

Meetings with Mary: Visions of the Blessed Mother. Janice T. Connell. 416p. 1996. pap. 10.00 (*0-345-39705-3*) Ballantine Pub Grp.

Meetings with Mentors: A Young Adult Interviews Leading Visionaries. Soren Gordhamer. (Illus.). 288p. (Orig.). 1995. pap. 17.95 (*0-9643158-3-1*) Hanford Mead.

Meetings with Remarkable Men. G. I. Gurdjieff. 320p. 1991. pap. 14.95 (*0-14-019037-6*, Arkana) Viking Penguin.

Meetings with Remarkable Souls: Legends of the Baal Shem Tov. Eliahu Klein. LC 94-27783. 288p. 1995. pap. 30.00 (*0-87668-588-2*) Aronson.

Meetings with Remarkable Trees. Thomas Pakenham. 192p. 1998. pap. 24.95 (*0-375-75268-4*) Random.

***Meetings with Remarkable Women: Buddhist Teachers in America.** Lenore Friedman. LC 00-21722. 320p. (Orig.). 2000. pap. 16.95 (*1-57062-474-7*, Pub. by Shambhala Pubns) Random.

Meetings with the Archangel: A Comedy of the Spirit. Stephen Mitchell. LC 98-18018. 256p. 1999. pap. 13.00 (*0-06-093248-1*) HarpC.

Meetings with the Archangel: A Comedy of the Spirit. Stephen Mitchell. LC 98-18018. 256p. 1998. 24.00 (*0-06-018245-8*, Pub. by Harper SF) HarpC.

***Meetings with the Archangel: A Comedy of the Spirit, Set.** Stephen Mitchell. 1998. audio 18.00 (*0-694-52021-7*) HarperAudio.

***Meets the Eye.** Christopher Golden. (Body of Evidence Ser.: No. 4). 256p. (YA). 2000. per. 4.99 (*0-671-03495-2*, Pocket Pulse) PB.

Meets the Jigsaw Kids, 1, 7. Dandi Daley Mackall. Vol. 7. 80p. (J). (gr. 1-5). 1999. pap. text 4.99 (*0-570-05475-3*) Concordia.

Mefiez-Vous des Monstres Marins. Sylvie Desrosiers. (Novels in the Roman Jeunesse Ser.). (FRE.). 96p. (J). (gr. 4-7). 1991. pap. 8.95 (*2-89021-146-0*, Pub. by La Courte Ech) Firefly Bks Ltd.

Mefisto. John Banville. 240p. 1999. pap. 13.95 (*1-56792-097-7*) Godine.

Mefisto. John Banville. 1991. mass mkt. 8.99 (*0-446-39282-0*, Pub. by Warner Bks) Little.

MEFTA: A Key to Business Peace in the Middle East - Nonthreatening Palestine Gaza State to Block a May 1999 Mideast Disaster, Safe-Passage Bridge Connecting a Middle East Free Trade Area in Gaza to the West Bank & Jordan & a Nuclear-Weapon-Free Iran. S. C. Yuter. 100p. 1999. per. 18.00 incl. 5.25 hd (*0-9603122-9-3*) Expedited.

MEFTA: A Key to Jewish & Israel - Arab Peace, Nuclear Peace & Prosperity: A Middle East Free Trade Area (Mefta) for Jewish & Israel-Arab Peace, a Universally-Binding Test Ban to Deter Iran & North Korea Bombs & Cheap Oil to Spur Economy. 3rd ed. S. C. Yuter. LC 96-83314. 404p. 1996. pap. 35.00 (*0-9603122-5-0*) Expedited.

MEFTA: A Key to Middle East Peace & Prosperity: Middle East Free Trade Area for Israel-Arab Peace, Test Ban to Block Iran's Bomb & Cheap Oil to Spur Economy. S. C. Yuter. LC 97-60344. 60p. (C). 1997. pap. 15.00 (*0-9603122-7-7*) Expedited.

Meg: A Novel of Deep Terror. Steve Alten. 352p. 1997. mass mkt. 6.99 (*0-553-84016-9*) Bantam.

Meg: A Novel of Deep Terror. Steve Alten. 352p. 1998. reprint ed. mass mkt. 6.50 (*0-553-57910-X*) Bantam.

Meg - Poetic Justice. Reg Wright. 1994. 12.95 (*0-533-10796-2*) Vantage.

Meg & Dad Discover Treasure in the Air. Lisa W. Peters. (Illus.). 88p. (J). (gr. k-3). 1995. 15.95 (*0-8050-2418-2*) H Holt & Co.

Meg & Her Circus Tricks. Graham Percy. (Meg & Max Bks.). (Illus.). 32p. (J). (ps-3). 1991. lib. bdg. 22.79 (*0-89565-785-6*) Childs World.

Meg & Jim's Sled Trip. Laura Appleton-Smith. LC 98-96631. (Illus.). (J). (ps-3). 17.95 (*0-9658246-0-8*, Bks To Remember) Flyleaf Pubg.

Meg & the Great Race. Graham Percy. LC 92-44851. (Meg & Max Bks.). (Illus.). 32p. (J). (ps-3). 1994. lib. bdg. 22.79 (*1-56766-077-0*) Childs World.

Meg & the Mystery Man. Elise Title. LC 97-10633. 299p. 1994. per. 3.50 (*0-373-70618-9*, 1-70618-3) Harlequin Bks.

Meg & the Secret Scrapbook. Susan Meyers. (Always Friends Club Ser.). (J). 1995. 8.05 (*0-606-07857-6*, Pub. by Turtleback) Demco.

Meg Mackintosh & the Case of the Curious Whale Watch: A Solve-It-Yourself Mystery. Lucinda Landon. LC 87-2748. (Meg Mackintosh Mysteries Ser.: Vol. 2). (Illus.). 48p. (J). (gr. 2-5). 1996. reprint ed. pap. 4.95 (*1-888695-01-3*) Secret Passage.

Meg Mackintosh & the Case of the Missing Babe Ruth Baseball: A Solve-It-Yourself Mystery. Lucinda Landon. LC 85-20055. (Meg Mackintosh Mysteries Ser.: Vol. 1). (Illus.). 48p. (J). (gr. 2-5). 1996. reprint ed. pap. 4.95 (*1-888695-00-5*) Secret Passage.

Meg Mackintosh & the Mystery at Camp Creepy: A Solve-It-Yourself Mystery. Lucinda Landon. LC 89-38466. (Meg Mackintosh Mysteries Ser.: Vol. 4). (Illus.). 64p. (J). (gr. 2-5). 1996. reprint ed. pap. 4.95 (*1-888695-03-X*) Secret Passage.

Meg Mackintosh & the Mystery at the Medieval Castle. Lucinda Landon. (J). (ps-3). 1993. mass mkt. 4.95 (*0-316-51376-8*) Little.

Meg Mackintosh & the Mystery at the Medieval Castle: A Solve-It-Yourself Mystery. Lucinda Landon. LC 88-28586. (Meg Mackintosh Mysteries Ser.: Vol. 3). (Illus.). (J). (gr. 2-5). 1996. reprint ed. pap. 4.95 (*1-888695-02-1*) Secret Passage.

Meg Mackintosh & the Mystery at the Soccer Match: A Solve-It-Yourself Mystery. Lucinda Landon. (Meg Mackintosh Mysteries Ser.: Vol. 6). (Illus.). 48p. (Orig.). (J). (gr. k up). 1997. pap. 4.95 (*1-888695-05-6*) Secret Passage.

Meg Mackintosh & the Mystery in the Locked Library: A Solve-It-Yourself Mystery. Lucinda Landon. LC 92-19948. (Meg Mackintosh Mysteries Ser.: Vol. 5). (Illus.). 48p. (J). (gr. 2-5). 1996. reprint ed. pap. 4.95 (*1-888695-04-8*) Secret Passage.

Meg Parker, 5 in each set, Set 1 & 2. Eleanor Robins. (Illus.). (J). (gr. 2-7). 1984. pap. 17.00 (*0-87879-439-5*) High Noon Bks.

Meg Parker, 5 in each set, Set 2. Eleanor Robins. (Illus.). (J). (gr. 2-7). 1985. pap. write for info. (*0-87879-472-7*) High Noon Bks.

Meg Play Fair. Constance Savery. (J). 1979. pap. 2.95 (*0-87508-722-1*) Chr Lit.

Meg Swansen's Knitting: 30 Designs for Hand Knitting. Meg Swansen. LC 99-29404. (Illus.). 144p. 1999. 39.95 (*1-883010-58-6*, Pub. by Interweave) IPG Chicago.

Mega. B. L. Holmes. LC 90-63949. 240p. 1991. pap. text 8.95 (*0-941300-19-6*) Mother Courage.

Mega-Bit Memory Technology: From Mega-Bit to Giga-Bit. Ed. by Hiroyuki Tango. 293p. 1998. pap. text 90.00 (*90-5699-098-5*, ECU83) Gordon & Breach.

Mega Brain Power: Transform Your Life with Mind Machines & Brain Nutrients. Michael Hutchinson. LC 93-35576. (Illus.). 496p. 1994. pap. 15.95 (*1-56282-770-7*, Pub. by Hyperion) Time Warner.

Mega Change: Reforming the Corporation. William F. Joyce. 1995. 25.00 (*0-7863-0214-3*, Irwn Prfssnl) McGraw-Hill Prof.

Mega-Choices. rev. ed. Tom Nelson. (Inter Acta Ser.). (Illus.). 6p. (C). 1996. teacher ed., ring bd. 1.25 (*1-57334-024-3*, 741-053t, Inter Acta); student ed., ring bd. 3.25 (*1-885702-86-8*, 741-053s, Inter Acta) WSN Pr.

Mega-City Growth & the Future. LC 96-130702. 136p. 35.00 (*92-808-0820-6*) UN.

Mega-City in Latin America. Ed. by Alan Gilbert. 300p. 30.00 (*92-808-0935-0*) UN.

***Mega Cooking: A Revolutionary New Plan for Quantity Cooking.** Jill Bond. (Illus.). 512p. 2000. pap. 24.95 (*1-58182-096-8*, Cumberland Hearthside) Cumberland Hse.

Mega Forces: Signs & Wonders of the Coming Chaos. Texe Marrs. 266p. 1989. pap. 8.95 (*0-9620086-0-5*) Living Truth Pubs.

Mega-Fun Map Skills. Catherine Tamblyn. 1999. pap. text 14.95 (*0-590-18798-8*) Scholastic Inc.

***Mega-Fun Map Skills: Great Skill-Building Activities, Games & Reproducibles, 1 vol.** Catherine Tamblyn. 64p. 1999. pap. text 14.95 (*0-590-18799-6*) Scholastic Inc.

Mega-Fun Math Games: 70 Quick-&-Easy Games to Build Math Skills. Michael Schiro. (Illus.). (J). 1994. pap. text 14.95 (*0-590-48176-2*) Scholastic Inc.

Mega-Fun Math Skill Builders. Richard Porteus. 48p. (J). (gr. 2-3). 1999. pap. 7.95 (*0-439-04493-6*) Scholastic Inc.

Mega Fun-Math Skill Builders. Richard Porteus. 48p. (J). (gr. 5-6). 1999. pap. 7.95 (*0-439-04494-4*) Scholastic Inc.

***Mega Fun Math Skill Builders.** Richard Porteus. (Illus.). 48p. 1999. pap. 7.95 (*0-439-04495-2*) Scholastic Inc.

Mega-Fun Multiplication Facts Activity Book: Easy Games, Poems, Mini-Books, Reproducibles. Martin Lee. 72p. (J). 1998. pap. text 9.95 (*0-590-37350-1*) Scholastic Inc.

***Mega-Funny Math Poems & Problems, 1 vol.** Dan Greenberg. 56p. 1999. pap. text 9.95 (*0-590-18735-X*) Scholastic Inc.

***Mega Furby Fun.** (Furby Coloring & Activity Pad Ser.). (Illus.). 48p. 1999. pap. write for info. (*0-7666-0408-X*, Honey Bear Bks) Modern Pub NYC.

Mega-Geomorphology. Ed. by Rita Gardner & Helen Scoging. (Illus.). 264p. 1984. 45.00 (*0-19-823244-6*) OUP.

Mega Gifts: Who Gives Them, Who Gets Them. Jerold Panas. LC 83-62498. 231p. 1984. 40.00 (*0-931028-39-6*) Precept Pr.

Mega Learning. Betty L. Randolph. Ed. by Success Education Institute International Staff. (Educational Ser.). 1989. 14.98 incl. audio (*1-55909-242-4*, 310P); Price not set. incl. audio Randolph Tapes.

Mega Man Legends: Prima's Official Strategy Guide. Christine Cain. (Games Ser.). 96p. 1998. per. 12.99 (*0-7615-1871-1*) Prima Pub.

Mega Man X: Official Game Secrets. Rusel Demaria. 1994. pap. 14.95 (*1-55958-787-3*) Prima Pub.

Mega-Marketing for the Private Investigator: How to Drastically Increase Your Agency Business with Effective Mega-Marketing Techniques. Ralph D. Thomas. (Illus.). 66p. (Orig.). (C). 1997. pap. 38.00 (*0-918487-87-0*) Thomas Investigative.

Mega Mazes. Harold Gale. (MENSA Ser.). 160p. 1994. pap. 7.98 (*0-7858-0131-6*) Bk Sales Inc.

Mega Memory. abr. ed. Roger W. Breternitz. 1985. pap. 9.95 incl. audio (*1-893417-22-0*) Vector Studios.

Mega Millennium Series: Third, Fourth & Beyond. Paul D. Meier. 1998. 15.99 (*0-7852-6971-1*) Nelson.

***Mega Mind: Path to Success & Freedom.** Hement Thakur. LC 00-100933. 64p. 2000. 16.95 (*1-58244-075-1*) Rutledge Bks.

Mega Mind-Twisters. Rolf Heimann. (J). (gr. 4-7). 1997. pap. 3.95 (*0-8167-3393-7*) Troll Communs.

Mega Mind-Twisters. Rolf Heinmann. 32p. 1994. pap. 7.95 (*0-385-25468-7*) Doubleday.

***Mega Planning: Practical Tools for Organizational Success** Roger A. Kaufman. LC 99-6731. 1999. write for info. (*0-7619-1325-4*) Sage.

Mega-Safety: For Everyone, with an Emphasis on Laboratory Safety. Albert F. Stang. LC 97-90939. 103p. 1998. 16.95 (*0-533-12519-7*) Vantage.

***Mega-Selling: Secrets of a Master Salesman.** David S. Cowper & Andrew Haynes. 256p. 2000. pap. 24.95 (*0-471-64529-X*) Wiley.

Mega Sex: Achieving Unlimited Sexual Potency Forever. Francine Beck. LC 96-26763. 352p. 1997. pap. text 14.95 (*0-935016-08-2*, Dunhill Pub Co) Zinn Pub Grp.

Mega-Slank from Titanium. Richard Merwin. LC 92-12842. (Widgets Ser.). (J). (gr. 2). 1992. lib. bdg. 13.99 (*1-56239-151-8*) ABDO Pub Co.

Mega Synaxaristes see Lives of the Hierarchs: Basil the Great, Gregory the Theologian, & John Chrysostom

Mega-Trade Method. Michael Chisholm. 1987. pap. 75.00 (*0-930233-18-2*) Windsor.

Mega Traveller: Imperial Encyclopedia. Marc W. Miller. Ed. by Joe Fugate, Sr. & Gary L. Thomas. (Illus.). 96p. (Orig.). 1987. pap. 15.00 (*0-943580-48-X*) Game Designers.

Mega Traveller: Player's Manual. Marc W. Miller. Ed. by Joe Fugate, Sr. & Gary L. Thomas. (Illus.). 104p. (Orig.). 1987. pap. 10.00 (*0-943580-38-2*) Game Designers.

Mega Traveller: Referee's Manual. Marc W. Miller. Ed. by Joe Fugate, Sr. & Gary L. Thomas. (Illus.). 104p. (Orig.). 1987. pap. 10.00 (*0-943580-47-1*) Game Designers.

Mega-Universities & Knowledge Media. John Daniel. (Illus.). 212p. 1998. pap. 24.95 (*0-7494-2634-9*, Kogan Pg Educ) Stylus Pub VA.

Mega Vitamin E: Is It Safe? H. J. Roberts. LC 93-85653. (Illus.). 130p. 1994. pap. 17.95 (*0-9633260-8-2*) Sunshine Sentinel.

MegaBlast. Todd Hester & Curtis A. Taylor. (Adventures of Mark Heroic Ser.: Vol. 2). (Illus.). 184p. (J). 1996. pap. 3.99 (*1-882723-51-1*, Pub. by Gold Leaf Pr) Origin Bk Sales.

Megabrain. Michael Hutchinson. 1996. pap. 12.00 (*0-345-41032-7*) Ballantine Pub Grp.

Megabrain: New Tools & Techniques for Brain Growth & Mind Expansion. Michael Hutchinson. 384p. 1987. mass mkt. 5.99 (*0-345-34175-9*) Ballantine Pub Grp.

Megabrands: How to Build Them; How to Beat Them. D. John Loden. 200p. 1991. 32.50 (*1-55623-469-4*, Irwn Prfssnl) McGraw-Hill Prof.

Megabucking: DBA in America. Grace Adams. LC 89-84485. (Illus.). 189p. (Orig.). 1989. pap. 24.95 (*1-877807-03-6*) Grace Pub MI.

Megabyte of Computer Jokes. Bill Stott. Ed. by Helen Exley & Samantha Armstrong. (Joke Bks.). (Illus.). 60p. 1995. 8.50 (*1-85015-623-9*) Exley Giftbooks.

Megabyting My Mind: 59 Plug-Ins to Add Power. Waldron M. McLellon. LC 97-93033. (Illus.). 224p. (Orig.). Date not set. pap. 14.95 (*1-884489-01-X*) Butternut.

Megaceros. Robert Oliver. (Ice-Age Monsters Ser.). 24p. (J). 1986. lib. bdg. 18.60 (*0-86592-846-0*) Rourke Enter.

Megachange: How General Electric, Nordstrom, Pricewaterhouse Coopers, Citicorp, Lucent Technologies, & Lockheed Martin Have Transformed Their Workforce. William F. Joyce. LC 99-27981. 256p. 1999. 27.50 (*0-684-85625-5*) Free Pr.

***Megacity Saga: Democracy & Citezenship in This Global Age.** Julie-Anne Boudreau. 252p. 2000. 19.99 (*1-55164-164-X*) Black Rose.

***Megacity Saga: Democracy & Citizenship in This Global Age.** Julie-Anne Boudreau. 2000. 48.99 (*1-55164-165-8*) Black Rose.

Megacorp & Macrodynamics: Essays in Memory of Alfred Eichner. Ed. by William Milberg. LC 90-26733. 230p. (C). (gr. 13). 1992. text 75.95 (*0-87332-782-9*) M E Sharpe.

Megacorp & Macrodynamics: Essays in Memory of Alfred Eichner. Ed. by William Milberg. LC 90-26733. 230p. (C). (gr. 13). 1992. pap. text 40.95 (*0-87332-783-7*) M E Sharpe.

Megacorp & Oligopoly: Micro Foundations of Macro Dynamics. Alfred S. Eichner. LC 79-92295. 379p. 1980. reprint ed. pap. 117.50 (*0-7837-9944-6*, 206067100006) Bks Demand.

Megadeth: Peace Sells . . . but Who's Buying & So Far So Good . . . So What, with Notes & Tablature. 160p. 1994. per. 22.95 (*0-7935-3667-7*, 00694953) H Leonard.

***Megadeth: Rust in Peace.** 184p. 1999. per. 24.95 (*0-7935-9253-4*) H Leonard.

Megadeth: Youthanasia. 80p. 1995. otabind 19.95 (*0-7935-4737-7*, 00690011) H Leonard.

Megadeth/Rust in Peace Tab Exper. Guitar Personality Book. 138p. (Orig.). 1991. pap. 24.95 (*0-7692-0574-7*, GF0457) Wrner Bros.

Megaflora from the Quantico Locality (Upper Albian), Lower Cretaceous Potomac Group of Virginia. unabridged ed. Garland R. Upchurch, Jr. et al. LC 95-620112. (Memoir Ser.: No. 4). (Illus.). 64p. (Orig.). 1994. pap. text 18.00 (*0-9625801-9-8*) VA Mus Natl Hist.

Megagauss Fields & Pulsed Power Systems. Ed. by V. M. Titov & G. A. Shvetsov. 859p. (C). 1990. text 345.00 (*0-941743-86-1*) Nova Sci Pubs.

Megagauss Magnetic Field Generation & Pulsed Power Applications. Ed. by M. Cowan & R. B. Spielman. (Illus.). 1097p. (C). 1994. lib. bdg. 295.00 (*1-56072-160-X*) Nova Sci Pubs.

Megagauss Physics & Technology. International Conference on Megagauss Magnetic Fie. Ed. by Peter J. Turchi. LC 80-16385. (Illus.). 697p. 1980. reprint ed. pap. 200.00 (*0-608-05443-7*, 206591200006) Bks Demand.

Megagauss Technology & Pulsed Power Applications. Ed. by C. M. Fowler et al. LC 87-17320. (Illus.). 878p. 1987. 155.00 (*0-306-42574-2*, Plenum Trade) Perseus Pubng.

Megahealth. Marc Sorenson. LC 94-49436. 496p. 1995. 24.95 (*0-87131-779-6*) M Evans.

Megahealth. 2nd ed. Marc Sorenson. 496p. 1997. reprint ed. pap. 14.95 (*0-87131-839-3*) M Evans.

Megaherbivores: The Influence of Very Large Body Size on Ecology. R. Norman Owen-Smith. (Studies in Ecology). (Illus.). 384p. (C). 1992. pap. text 39.95 (*0-521-42637-5*) Cambridge U Pr.

Megali Idea & the Greek Turkish War of 1897. Theodore Tatsios. 302p. 1984. text 63.00 (*0-88033-053-8*, Pub. by East Eur Monographs) Col U Pr.

Megalight Connection. William M. Griggs. 221p. (Orig.). 1990. pap. 9.95 (*0-9622869-5-8*) E & L Pr.

Megalithes et Traditions Populaires Dictionnaire Illustre. Francoise Massa. (FRE.). 191p. 1991. pap. 38.95 (*0-7859-8177-2*, 2876240289) Fr & Eur.

Megalithic Art in Ireland. Muiris O'Sullivan. (Treasures of the National Museum of Ireland Ser.). (Illus.). 48p. (Orig.). 1995. pap. 7.95 (*0-946172-36-6*, Pub. by Town Hse) Roberts Rinehart.

Megalithic Culture of Indonesia. William J. Perry. LC 77-86999. (Manchester, University. Publications. Ethnological Ser.: No. 3). reprint ed. 32.50 (*0-404-16773-X*) AMS Pr.

Megalithic Remains in South Sumatra. Abraham N. Van Der Hoop. Tr. by William Shirlaw. LC 77-87515. reprint ed. 45.00 (*0-404-16783-7*) AMS Pr.

Megalithic Tombs & Long Barrows in Britain. Frances Lynch. (Illus.). 64p. pap. 10.50 (*0-7478-0341-2*, Pub. by Shire Pubns) Parkwest Pubns.

M

An Asterisk (*) at the beginning of an entry indicates that the title is appearing for the first time.

Megalithomania: Artists, Antiquarians & Archaeologists at the Old Stone Monuments. John Michell. LC 81-69643. (Illus.). 168p. 1982. 37.50 (*0-8014-1479-2*) Cornell U Pr.

Megaliths. Paul Caponigro. 1986. 75.00 (*0-685-17622-3*) Little.

Megaliths: Stones of Memory. Jean-Pierre Mohen. LC 98-50716. (Discoveries Ser.). (Illus.). 176p. 1999. 12.95 (*0-8109-2861-2*, Pub. by Abrams) Time Warner.

***Megaliths, Myths & Men: An Introduction to Astro-Archaeology.** Peter Lancaster-Brown. LC 99-52590. 2000. pap. 12.95 (*0-486-41145-1*) Dover.

***Megalodon: Giant Shark of the Prehistoric World.** Caroline Arnold. LC 99-86991. (Illus.). 32p. (J). (gr. 4-7). 2000. 15.00 (*0-395-91419-1*, Clarion Bks) HM.

Megalodon: The Prehistoric Shark. Stephen Cumbaa & Susan Hughes. (Dig & Discover Ser.). (Illus.). 48p. (J). (gr. 1 up). 1998. pap. 14.99 (*1-58184-004-7*, Pub. by S1omerville Hse) Penguin Putnam.

Megalodon: The Prehistoric Shark. Stephen Cumbaa & Susan Hughes. (Dig & Discover Ser.). (Illus.). 48p. (YA). (gr. 1 up). 1998. pap. 14.99 (*1-894042-21-2*) Somerville Hse.

***MegaLog.** Margaret P. Green. 132p. 2000. 59.95 (*0-9677345-0-9*) M P Green.

Megalopolis: Contemporary Cultural Sensibilities. Celeste Olalquiaga. LC 91-12383. (Illus.). 136p. (C). 1992. pap. 13.95 (*0-8166-1999-9*) U of Minn Pr.

Megalopolis: The Giant City in History. Ed. by Theo Barker & Anthony Sutcliffe. LC 92-33445. 200p. 1993. text 65.00 (*0-312-09147-8*) St Martin.

Megalopolis: Washington D. C. to Boston. John R. Borchert. LC 92-9986. (Touring North America Ser.). (Illus.). 188p. 1992. 25.00 (*0-8135-1876-8*); pap. 9.95 (*0-8135-1877-6*) Rutgers U Pr.

Megalopolis Revisited: Twenty-Five Years Later. Jean Gottmann. (Urban Studies: No. 6). 71p. (C). 1987. pap. text 8.00 (*0-913749-04-4*) U MD Urban Stud.

Megalosaurio (Megalosaurus) Laura Alden. (Libros Sobre Dinosaurios! Ser.). (SPA., Illus.). 32p. (J). (gr. k-4). 1994. lib. bdg. 21.36 (*1-56766-142-4*) Childs World.

Megamachines. Ed. by World Book Staff. LC 94-43521. (Info-Adventure Ser.). (Illus.). 32p. (J). (gr. 3-7). 1998. pap. 6.00 (*1-56847-318-4*) World Bk.

Megamedia: How Giant Corporations Dominate Mass Media, Distort Competition & Endanger Democracy. Dean Alger. LC 98-21270. (Illus.). 256p. 1998. 27.95 (*0-8476-8389-3*) Rowman.

Megamedia Shakeout: The Inside Story of the Leaders & the Losers in the Exploding Communications Industry. Kevin Maney. LC 94-43311. 358p. 1995. 24.95 (*0-471-10719-0*) Wiley.

Megamergers: Corporate America's Billion-Dollar Takeovers. Kenneth M. Davidson. LC 85-4025. 432p. 1985. 35.00 (*0-88730-058-8*, HarpBusn) HarpInfo.

Megamistakes: Forecasting & the Myth of Rapid Technological Change. Steven P. Schnaars. LC 88-21196. 224p. 1989. 29.95 (*0-02-927952-6*) Free Pr.

Megamogs. Peter Haswell. (Illus.). 32p. (J). (gr. k-3). 1996. 19.95 (*0-370-31874-9*, Pub. by Bodley Head) Trafalgar.

Megamogs & the Dangerous Doughnut. Peter Haswell. (Illus.). 32p. (J). (gr. k-2). 1996. 19.95 (*0-370-32480-3*, Pub. by Bodley Head) Trafalgar.

Megan. Marisa Carroll. (Superromance Ser.: No. 742). 1997. per. 3.99 (*0-373-70742-8*, 1-70742-1) Harlequin Bks.

Megan. Kathleen Magill. LC 99-24656. 1999. 26.95 (*0-7838-8629-2*) Mac Lib Ref.

***Megan.** Linda Lael Miller. (Women of Primrose Creek Ser.: No. 4). 320p. 2000. mass mkt. 5.99 (*0-671-04247-5*, Sonnet Bks) PB.

Megan & the Borealis Butterfly. Nina Alexander. LC 98-50505. (Magic Attic Club Ser.). 80p. (J). (gr. 2-6). 1999. 5.95 (*1-57513-152-8*); 12.95 (*1-57513-153-6*) Magic Attic.

***Megan & the Borealis Butterfly.** Nina Alexander. (Magic Attic Club Ser.). 80p. (J). (gr. 2-6). 1999. lib. bdg. 16.40 (*1-57513-154-4*) Magic Attic.

***Megan in Ancient Greece.** Susan Korman. (Magic Attic Club Ser.). (Illus.). 71p. (J). (gr. 2-6). 1998. lib. bdg. 16.40 (*1-57513-143-9*) Magic Attic.

Megan in Ancient Greece. Susan Korman. Ed. by Judit Bodnar. LC 98-27013. (Magic Attic Club Ser.). (Illus.). 80p. (J). (gr. 2-6). 1998. 12.95 (*1-57513-128-5*); pap. 5.95 (*1-57513-127-7*) Magic Attic.

Meganet: How the Global Communications Network Will Connect Everyone on Earth. Wilson Dizard, Jr. LC 97-13218. 272p. 1997. text 29.00 (*0-8133-3017-3*, Pub. by Westview) HarpC.

Meganet: How the Global Communications Network Will Connect Everyone on Earth. Wilson Dizard, Jr. 272p. (C). 1998. pap. text 22.00 (*0-8133-3018-1*, Pub. by Westview) HarpC.

Megan's Balancing Act. Susan Korman. (Magic Attic Club Ser.). (Illus.). (J). (gr. 2-5). 1997. pap. 5.95 (*1-57513-092-0*) Magic Attic.

Megan's Balancing Act. Susan Korman. (Magic Attic Club Ser.). (Illus.). (J). (gr. 2-6). 1997. 12.95 (*1-57513-093-9*) Magic Attic.

Megan's Island. Willo D. Roberts. LC 89-18457. 192p. (J). (gr. 4-7). 1990. mass mkt. 4.50 (*0-689-71387-8*) Aladdin.

Megan's Island. Willo D. Roberts. LC 87-17505. 192p. (J). (gr. 3-7). 1988. lib. bdg. 14.95 (*0-689-31397-7*) Atheneum Yung Read.

Megan's Island. Willo Davis Roberts. 1990. 9.60 (*0-606-12600-7*, Pub. by Turtleback) Demco.

***Megan's Island.** Willo Davis Roberts. (2000 Kids Picks Ser.). 192p. (J). (gr. 4-7). 2000. mass mkt. 2.99 (*0-689-83867-0*) Aladdin.

Megan's Marriage. Annette Broadrick. (Desire Ser.). 1996. per. 3.50 (*0-373-05979-5*, 1-05979-9) Silhouette.

Megan's Marriage. large type ed. Annette Broadrick. (Large Print Ser.). 1998. 20.95 (*0-373-59855-6*) Harlequin Bks.

Megan's Masquerade. Trisha Magraw. (Magic Attic Club Ser.). (Illus.). 80p. (J). (gr. 2-6). 1996. 12.95 (*1-57513-071-8*); pap. 5.95 (*1-57513-072-6*) Magic Attic.

Megan's Mate. Nora Roberts. 1996. per. 3.99 (*0-373-07745-9*, 1-07745-2) Silhouette.

***Megan's Mate, Vol. 1.** Nora Roberts. (Silhouette Ser.). 1999. pap. 21.95 (*0-373-59990-0*) Harlequin Bks.

Megan's Miracle. Karen Leabo. (Desire Ser.). 1994. per. 2.99 (*0-373-05880-2*, 1-05880-9) Silhouette.

Megan's World. Marie V. Frantzen. LC 97-65899. 176p. (Orig.). 1997. pap. 14.95 (*1-883122-10-4*) Pearce Pub.

Megaomnibus, Vol. 1. Tony Geiss. 1997. pap. 13.50 (*0-8129-2763-X*, Times Bks) Crown Pub Group.

Megapodes: An Action Plan for Their Conservation 1995-1999. Compiled by Rene W. Dekker & Phillip McGowan. (Illus.). 41p. (Orig.). (C). 1995. pap. text 16.00 (*2-8317-0223-2*, Pub. by IUCN) Island Pr.

Megapodes: MegaPodiidae - Bird Families of the World. Darryl N. Jones et al. (Bird Families of the World Ser.: No. 3). (Illus.). 282p. 1995. text 65.00 (*0-19-854651-3*) OUP.

Megapowers: Science Fact vs. Science Fiction. unabridged ed. Jack Weyland. (Illus.). 80p. (J). (gr. 5-9). 1992. pap. 9.95 (*1-55074-051-2*, Pub. by Kids Can Pr) Genl Dist Srvs.

Megaprofit Commodity Methods: Ten New Technical Trading Methods. Robert M. Barnes. (Illus.). 151p. 1983. 69.95 (*0-930233-14-X*) Windsor.

Megaproject: A Case Study of China's Three Gorges Project. Ed. by Shiu-Hung Luk & Joseph Whitney. LC 91-22964. (Studies in Chinese Environment & Development). 248p. (C). (gr. 13). 1992. text 79.95 (*0-87332-733-0*) M E Sharpe.

Megargee's Guide to Obtaining a Psychological Internship. 3rd ed. Edwin I. Megargee. LC 97-27628. 255p. 1997. pap. 21.95 (*1-56032-750-2*) Hemisp Pub.

Megaron During the Aegean & Anatolian Bronze Age: A Study of Occurence, Shape, Architectural Adaptation, & Function. Kjell Werner. (Studies in Mediterranean Archaeology: Vol. CVIII). (Illus.). 175p. 1993. 78.00 (*91-7081-092-3*, Pub. by P Astroms) Coronet Bks.

***Megasino.** Frederick Schofield. LC 99-65924. 348p. (Orig.). 1999. pap. 13.95 (*1-929625-11-1*) New Hope Bks.

***Megasino: The 13th Casino.** Frederick Schofield. 368p. 2000. mass mkt. 7.99 (*1-929625-13-8*) New Hope Bks.

MegaSkills. expanded rev. ed. Dorothy Rich. LC 97-44833. 384p. 1998. pap. 14.00 (*0-395-87757-1*, Mariner Bks) HM.

Megaskills Moments for Teachers: How-To's for Building Personal & Professional Effectiveness For The Classroom & Beyond. Dorothy Rich. LC 98-24154. 1998. pap. 11.95 (*0-8106-2006-5*) NEA.

Megasthenes & Indian Religion. Allan Dahlquist. 1977. 11.50 (*0-89684-277-0*, Pub. by Motilal Bnarsidass) S Asia.

***Megatooth.** Patrick O'Brien. 2000. pap. text 15.95 (*0-8050-6214-9*) St Martin.

Megatrends. 1985. mass mkt. 4.95 (*0-446-73312-1*, Pub. by Warner Bks) Little.

Megatrends & Volunteerism: Mapping the Future of Volunteer Programs. Sue Vineyard. 1993. pap. 15.95 (*0-911029-43-5*) Heritage Arts.

***Megatrends Asia.** Naisbett. 1999. pap. 9.98 (*0-671-04442-7*) PB.

Megatrends Asia: Eight Asian Megatrends That Are Reshaping Our World. John Naisbitt. 1997. per. 12.00 (*0-684-82706-9*, Touchstone) S&S Trade Pap.

Megatrends Asia: Eight Asian Megatrends That Are Reshaping Our World. John Neisbitt. 320p. 1996. 24.00 (*0-684-81542-7*) S&S Trade.

Megatrends for Women: From Liberation to Leadership. Patricia Aburdene & John Naisbitt. 416p. 1993. pap. 12.50 (*0-449-90825-9*, Columbine) Fawcett.

Megatrends in Industrial-Organizational Psychology: A Special Issue of Journal of Business & Psychology. Hannah R. Hirsh. 93p. 1987. pap. 16.95 (*0-89885-374-5*, Kluwer Acad Hman Sci) Kluwer Academic.

Megatrends in Retail Real Estate. Ed. by John D. Benjamin. LC 95-37846. (Research Issues in Real Estate Ser.: Vol. 3). 392p. (C). 1996. lib. bdg. 144.00 (*0-7923-9640-5*) Kluwer Academic.

Megatrends 2000. John Naisbitt & Patricia Aburdene. 448p. 1991. mass mkt. 6.99 (*0-380-70437-4*, Avon Bks) Morrow Avon.

Megda. Emma D. Kelley. (Schomburg Library of Nineteenth-Century Black Women Writers). 433p. 1988. text 42.00 (*0-19-505245-5*) OUP.

Meggie's Baby. Cheryl Reavis. (Special Edition Ser.: No. 1039). 1996. per. 3.99 (*0-373-24039-2*, 1-24039-9) Silhouette.

Meggie's Journeys. Margaret D'Ambrosio. LC 88-61446. 175p. (Orig.). 1988. pap. 10.95 (*0-685-31954-7*) Dufour.

Meghaduta of Kalidasa. M. R. Kale & Kalidasa. (C). 1997. reprint ed. pap. 8.50 (*81-208-0420-1*, Pub. by Motilal Bnarsidass) S Asia.

Megiddo. Derek Kartun. LC 88-158. 1988. 18.95 (*0-8027-1039-5*) Walker & Co.

Megiddo. Graham I. Davies. LC 86-213062. (Cities of the Biblical World Ser.). (Illus.). 128p. (Orig.). reprint ed. pap. 39.70 (*0-8357-4360-8*, 203718800007) Bks Demand.

Megiddo: Text F, Vol. 2. Gordon Loud. 1997. lib. bdg. 10.00 (*0-226-49386-5*) U Ch Pr.

Megiddo Modern Dictionary: English-Hebrew, Hebrew-English, 2 vols., Set. (ENG & HEB.). 2000p. 1982. lib. bdg. 150.00 (*0-8288-4423-2*, M9904) Fr & Eur.

Megiddo 1918: The Last Great Cavalry Victory. Brian Perret. (Campaign Ser.: Vol. 61). (Illus.). 96p. 1999. pap. 16.95 (*1-85532-827-5*, Pub. by Ospry) Stackpole.

Megiddo Plate F, Vol. 2. Gordon Loud. 1994. lib. bdg. 12.00 (*0-226-49385-7*) U Ch Pr.

***Megiddo III: The 1992-1996 Season, 2 vols.** Ed. by Israel Finkelstein et al. (Monograph Series of the Sonia & Marco Nadler Institute of Archaeology: Vol. 18). xiv, 348p. 2000. text 95.00 (*965-266-013-2*, Pub. by Inst Archaeology) Eisenbrauns.

MEGIDDO Twenty-Five Twenty-Five. Clint Edwards. LC 98-93881. 104p. 1999. 14.95 (*0-9655184-2-6*) Igloo Pub.

Megiddo Water System F. Robert S Lamon. 1994. lib. bdg. 2.00 (*0-226-46798-8*) U Ch Pr.

Megillah: Book of Esther. Arthur Szyk. 1974. 100.00 (*0-685-84454-4*) Bloch.

Megillah: Esther. Meir Zlotowitz. 18.99 (*0-89906-368-3*, ESTH); pap. 15.99 (*0-89906-369-1*, ESTP) Mesorah Pubns.

Megillah: The Book of Esther. Meir Zlotowitz. (Art Scroll Tanach Ser.). 160p. 1976. 17.99 (*0-89906-000-5*); pap. 14.99 (*0-89906-001-3*) Mesorah Pubns.

Megillah & Shekalim. (ENG & HEB.). 15.00 (*0-910218-59-5*) Bennet Pub.

Megillat Esther: The Story of Esther. Ed. & Tr. by Meir H. Letteris. 1979. pap. 1.95 (*0-88482-583-3*) Hebrew Pub.

Megillat Shushan. Itshak Yallouz & N. Alshag. 64p. 1993. pap. 4.95 (*1-58330-104-6*) Feldheim.

Megillath Esther. Tr. by Dovid Landesman. (Illus.). 1993. 9.95 (*1-58330-164-X*) Feldheim.

Megilloth. Ed. by T. H. Robinson et al. (Biblia Hebraica Stuttgartensia Ser.). x, 62p. 1975. pap. 9.99 (*3-438-05213-X*, 104092) Untd Bible Soc.

Mego Action Figure Toys. John Bonavita. (Illus.). 192p. 1996. pap. 19.95 (*0-7643-0025-3*) Schiffer.

Mego Toys: An Illustrated Value Guide. Wallace M. Chrouch. 1995. pap. 15.95 (*0-89145-592-2*, 3823) Collector Bks.

Meg's Car. Helen Nicoll & Jan Pienkowski. (Picture Puffin Ser.). 32p. (J). (ps). 1984. pap. 3.50 (*0-14-050259-9*, Penguin Bks) Viking Penguin.

Meg's Dearest Wish. Charlotte Emerson & Louisa May Alcott. LC 97-7274. (Little Women Journals). 144p. (J). 1998. mass mkt. 10.00 (*0-380-97633-1*, Avon Bks) Morrow Avon.

Meg's Dearest Wish. Charlotte Emerson & Louisa May Alcott. LC 97-7274. (Little Women Journals). (Illus.). 128p. (J). (gr. 3-7). 1999. mass mkt. 3.99 (*0-380-79705-4*, Avon Bks) Morrow Avon.

Meg's Garden. Teresa Warfield. 288p. 1997. mass mkt. 5.99 (*0-515-12004-9*, Jove) Berkley Pub.

Meg's Story: Straight Talk about Drugs. Gilda Berger. (YA). 1992. pap. 4.80 (*0-395-63557-8*) HM.

Meg's Story: Straight Talk about Drugs. Gilda Berger. LC 91-21515. (Get Real! Ser.). (Illus.). 64p. (YA). (gr. 7 up). 1992. pap. 4.95 (*1-56294-804-0*) Millbrook Pr.

Meg's Story: Straight Talk about Drugs. Gilda Berger. (Get Real! Ser.). (J). 1992. 10.15 (*0-606-02741-6*, Pub. by Turtleback) Demco.

Meg's Veg. Helen Nicoll & Jan Pienkowski. 32p. (J). (ps). 1985. pap. 3.50 (*0-14-050356-0*, PuffinBks) Peng Put Young Read.

Meg's Wish. Friedrich Recknagel. LC 99-17370. (Illus.). 32p. (J). (ps-2). 1999. lib. bdg. 15.88 (*0-7358-1117-2*, Pub. by North-South Bks NYC) Chronicle Bks.

***Meg's Wish.** Friedrich Recknagel. LC 99-17370. (Illus.). 32p. (J). (ps-2). 1999. 15.95 (*0-7358-1116-4*, Pub. by North-South Bks NYC) Chronicle Bks.

Meg's World. 6th ed. John Kollock. (Illus.). 64p. 1996. reprint ed. pap. 6.95 (*0-9613242-1-X*) Saturday Shop.

Mehaat Ha-dor Ha-sheni see Urban Social Movements in Jerusalem: The Protest of the Second Generation

Mehalah, a Story of the Salt Marshes, 2 vols., 1 bk. Sabine Baring-Gould. LC 79-8231. reprint ed. 44.50 (*0-404-61769-7*) AMS Pr.

Meharry Medical College. Charles V. Roman. LC 71-38019. (Black Heritage Library Collection). 1977. reprint ed. 26.95 (*0-8369-8986-4*) Ayer.

Meher Baba, an Iranian Liberal. Kevin Shepherd. 303p. (C). 1989. 75.00 (*0-9508680-5-1*, Pub. by Anthropographia) St Mut.

Meher Baba, the Awakener. Charles Haynes. 132p. (Orig.). 1989. pap. 7.95 (*0-685-29361-0*) Avatar Found.

Meher Baba, the Awakener. 2nd ed. Charles Haynes. Ed. by Ken Coleman. (Illus.). 132p. (Orig.). pap. 9.95 (*0-9624472-1-8*) Avatar Found.

Mehilta Shemot: Scanning Exodus. George W. Everett. (ENG & HEB.). 270p. (Orig.). 1997. pap. write for info. (*1-57502-461-6*, PO1380) Morris Pubng.

Mehinaku: The Drama of Daily Life in a Brazilian Indian Village. Thomas Gregor. LC 76-54659. 400p. 1980. pap. text 20.00 (*0-226-30746-8*) U Ch Pr.

Mehinaku: The Drama of Daily Life in a Brazilian Indian Village. Thomas Gregor. LC 76-54659. 1994. lib. bdg. 24.00 (*0-226-30744-1*) U Ch Pr.

Mehmed the Conqueror & His Time. Franz Babinger. Ed. by William C. Hickman. (Bollingen Ser.: No. XCVI). (Illus.). 569p. 1978. pap. text 21.95 (*0-691-01078-1*, Pub. by Princeton U Pr) Cal Prin Full Svc.

Mehmed the Conqueror & His Time. Franz Babinger. Tr. by Ralph Manheim from GER. LC 77-71972. (Bollingen Ser.: No. 96). (Illus.). 604p. reprint ed. pap. 187.30 (*0-8357-3696-2*, 203642000003) Bks Demand.

Mehndi. Roome. LC 98-3362. 128p. 1998. pap. 16.95 (*0-312-18743-2*) St Martin.

***Mehndi: Rediscovering Henna Body Art.** Marie Anakee Miczah. (Miczak Exotic Treasures Ser.). (Illus.). 199p. 1999. pap. 14.95 (*0-7414-0280-7*) Buy Books.

Mehndi: The Art of Henna Body Painting. Carine Fabius & Michele M. Garcia. LC 97-44146. 112p. (YA). 1998. pap. 11.00 (*0-609-80319-0*) C Potter.

Mehndi Kit. Zaynab Mirza. (Illus.). 80p. 1998. pap. 24.95 (*0-8092-2801-7*, 280170, Contemporary Bks) NTC Contemp Pub Co.

Mehr Beschaftigung Durch eine Negative Einkommensteuer Vol. XII: Zur Beschaftigungspolitischen Effektivitat und Effizienz eines Integrierten Steuer- und Transfersystems. Werner Sesselmeier et al. (Sozialokonomische Schriften Ser.: Bd. 10). (GER.). 199p. 1996. pap. 42.95 (*3-631-49613-3*) P Lang Pubng.

Mehr Marchen. Adapted by Douglas Hall & Herbert Lederer. (GER.). 54p. 1997. ring bd. 11.00 (*0-942017-46-3*, 04-64347) Amer Assn Teach German.

Mehr Markt am Arbeitsmarkt: Ein Pladoyer fur weniger Arbeitsmarktpolitik. Rudiger Soltwedel. (International Carl Menger Library). 207p. 1984. pap. 32.00 (*3-88405-054-0*) Philosophia Pr.

Mehrjaehrige Beobachtungen Kleiner Vegetationsflaechen Im Raume Von Karpathos (Nomos Dhodhekanisou, Griechenland) Ein Beitrag Zur Klarung des "Kleininselphaenomens" Dieter Honer. (Dissertationes Botanicae Ser.: Band 173). (GER., Illus.). x, 266p. 1991. pap. 65.00 (*3-443-64085-0*, Pub. by Gebruder Borntraeger) Balogh.

Mehrstimmigkeit und Desintegration: Studien Zu Narration und Geschichte in Morikes Maler Nolten. Achim Nuber. (GER.). 278p. 1997. 54.95 (*3-631-31346-2*) P Lang Pubng.

Mei Cherng's Seven Stimuli & Wang Bor's Pavilion of King Terng. Mei Cherng & Wang Bor. Tr. by Victor H. Mair from CHI. LC 87-23959. (Illus.). 154p. 1987. lib. bdg. 89.95 (*0-88946-020-5*) E Mellen.

Mei Lan-Fang: The Life & Times of a Peking Actor; with Illustrations by the Author. Adolphe C. Scott. LC PN2878.M4. 164p. 1971. reprint ed. pap. 50.90 (*0-608-01385-4*, 206214600002) Bks Demand.

Mei Ling's Tiger. Marcia Tullman & Deborah DeRoo. (Illus.). (J). (gr. k-2). 1993. pap. 8.95 incl. audio (*0-7608-0495-8*); pap. 4.95 (*1-56801-053-2*) Sundance Pub.

Mei Ling's Tiger, Big Book. Marcia Tullman & Deborah DeRoo. (Illus.). (J). (gr. k-2). 1993. pap. 17.95 (*1-56801-052-4*) Sundance Pub.

Mei-Mei Loves the Morning. Margaret H. Tsubakiyama. LC 97-26675. (Illus.). 32p. (J). (ps-3). 1999. lib. bdg. 15.95 (*0-8075-5039-6*) A Whitman.

Meidcal Terminology with Human Anatomy & Student Disk. 4th ed. Jane Rice. LC 98-15836. 574p. 1998. pap. 39.95 incl. audio (*0-8385-6274-4*, Medical Exam) Appleton & Lange.

Meidias Painter. Lucilla Burn. (Oxford Monographs on Classical Archaeology). (Illus.). 160p. 1988. 84.00 (*0-19-813221-2*) OUP.

Meidosems: Poems & Lithographs. Henri Michaux. Tr. & Intro. by Elizabeth R. Jackson. LC 92-27205. (Illus.). 184p. (Orig.). 1993. pap. 24.95 (*0-939952-13-0*) Moving Parts.

Meigs County, Tennessee: A Documented Account of Its European Settlement & Growth. rev. ed. Stewart Lillard. (Illus.). 202p. 1983. reprint ed. 20.00 (*0-317-39990-X*) Southern Hist Pr.

Meigs Field, Hyde Park Civil War Use MDC. rev. ed. Ed. by Nancy Hannan. (Illus.). 257p. 1991. reprint ed. pap. 35.00 (*0-913553-11-5*) Albert Hse Pub.

Meiji: Japanese Art in Transition. Society for Japanese Art & Crafts Staff. 167p. 1987. pap. 165.00 (*0-7855-2024-4*) St Mut.

Meiji Japan, 4 vols. Peter F. Kornicki. LC 97-37916. 1336p. (C). 1998. reprint ed. 700.00 (*0-415-15618-1*) Routledge.

Meiji Japan: The Dynamics of National Change. Sara Thompson et al. (Humanities Approach to Japanese History Ser.). (Illus.). 175p. (Orig.). (YA). (gr. 9-12). 1995. pap. 42.95 (*0-89994-381-0*) Soc Sci Ed.

Meiji Japan Through Woodblock Prints. Yoichi Harashima. (Illus.). 112p. 1990. boxed set 250.00 (*0-86008-450-7*, Pub. by U of Tokyo) Col U Pr.

***Meiji No Takara: Treasures of Imperial Japan, 8 vols., Set.** Ed. by Oliver Impey & Malcolm Fairley. (The Nasser D. Khalili Collection of Japanese Art). (Illus.). 2114p. 1999. text 4200.00 (*1-874780-00-5*) OUP.

Meiji No Takara: Treasures of Imperial Japan: Ceramics (Part II: Earthenware), Vol. V. Oliver Impey et al. Ed. by Malcolm Fairley. (The Nasser D. Khalili Collection of Japanese Art). (Illus.). 300p. 1999. text 715.00 (*1-874780-06-4*) OUP.

Meiji No Takara: Treasures of Imperial Japan: Ceramics (Part 1: Porcelain), Vol. V. Oliver Impey et al. Ed. by Malcolm Fairley. (The Nasser D. Khalili Collection of Japanese Art). (Illus.). 248p. 1999. text 715.00 (*1-874780-05-6*) OUP.

Meiji No Takara: Treasures of Imperial Japan: Enamels, Vol. III. Oliver Impey et al. Ed. by Malcolm Fairley. (The Nasser D. Khalili Collection of Japanese Art). (Illus.). 320p. 1999. text 715.00 (*1-874780-03-X*) OUP.

Meiji No Takara: Treasures of Imperial Japan: Lacquer, 2 vols., Vol. IV. Gole Tadaomi et al. Ed. by Oliver Impey et al. (The Nasser D. Khalili Collection of Japanese Art). (Illus.). 534p. 1999. text 1250.00 (*1-874780-04-8*) OUP.

Meiji No Takara: Treasures of Imperial Japan: Selected Essays, Vol. I. Oliver Impey et al. Ed. by Malcolm Fairley. (The Nasser D. Khalili Collection of Japanese Art). (Illus.). 208p. 1999. text 270.00 (*1-874780-01-3*) OUP.

Meiji No Takara: Treasures of Japan: Metalwork, 2 vols., Vol. II. Oliver Impey et al. Ed. by Malcolm Fairley. (The Nasser D. Khalili Collection of Japanese Art). (Illus.). 504p. 1999. text 1250.00 (*1-874780-02-1*) OUP.

M

Meiji Protestantism in History & Historiography. Aasulv Lande. (Studia Missionalia Upsaliensia: No. 46). 176p. (Orig.). 1988. pap. 38.50 (*91-85424-13-7*, Pub. by Almqvist Wiksell) Coronet Bks.

Meiji Restoration. William G. Beasley. LC 72-78868. xiv, 514p. 1972. 65.00 (*0-8047-0815-0*) Stanford U Pr.

Meiji Restoration & the Rise of Modern Japan. Monique Auakian. (Turning Points in World History Ser.). (Illus.). 64p. (YA). (gr. 7 up). 1991. pap. 7.95 (*0-382-24139-8*); lib. bdg. 14.95 (*0-382-24132-0*) Silver Burdett Pr.

Meiji Revisited: The Sites of Victorian Japan. Dallas Finn. (Illus.). 288p. 1994. 45.00 (*0-8348-0288-0*) Weatherhill.

Meiji Unification Through the Lens of Ishikawa Prefecture. James C. Baxter. LC 94-38297. (Harvard East Asian Monographs: No. 165). 353p. 1995. 38.00 (*0-674-56466-9*, BAXMEI) HUP.

Meiji Yonjusannen Kyoto see Makiko's Diary: A Merchant Wife in 1910 Kyoto

Meijin see Master of Go

Me'ilah, Kimmin, Tamid & Middoth. (ENG & HEB.). 15.00 (*0-910218-86-2*) Bennet Pub.

Meilensteine Auf Dem Wege zur Hohen Schule. Kurt Albrecht. (Documenta Hippologica Ser.). (GER., Illus.). 147p. 1996. write for info. (*3-487-08253-5*) G Olms Pubs.

Meilland: A Life in Roses. Alain Meilland. Tr. by Richard C. Keating & Louis Clark Keating. LC 83-14996. (Illus.). 176p. 1984. 26.95 (*0-8093-1111-9*) S Ill U Pr.

Meilleur des Ours. A. A. Milne, pseud. (FRE.). (J). (gr. 3-8). 9.95 (*0-685-23403-7*) Fr & Eur.

Meilleur des Peres. Gayle Kaye. (Horizon Ser.). (FRE.). 1997. pap. 3.50 (*0-373-39434-9*, 1-39434-5) Harlequin Bks.

Meilleure de la Louisiane: The Best of Louisiana. Jude W. Theriot. LC 82-24680. (Illus.). 368p. 1983. reprint ed. spiral bd. 16.95 (*0-88289-407-2*) Pelican.

Mein Allerschonstes Worterbuch: Deutsch-Englisch-Franzosisch. Richard Scarry. (GER., Illus.). 1971. 19.95 (*3-7735-4902-4*) Intl Lang.

Mein Erster Brockhaus. 142p. 1990. 26.95 (*3-7653-1544-3*, Pub. by Bibliogr Inst Brockhaus) Langenscheidt.

Mein Erster Langenscheidt Englisch. Angela Wilkes & Nina Schindler. (GER., Illus.). 64p. (J). 1996. 23.50 (*3-468-20390-X*) Langenscheidt.

Mein Erstes Zahlenbuch. (Duden Ser.). (GER.). 48p. 1997. pap. write for info. (*3-411-05211-2*, Pub. by Bibliogr Inst Brockhaus) Langenscheidt.

Mein Gespraech, Meine Lieder, Set. Lif Du Pool. 128p. text 38.95 incl. audio (*3-468-49847-0*) Langenscheidt.

Mein Jahrhundert see My Century

***Mein Kampf.** Adolf Hitler. Tr. by James Murphy. 384p. 1999. pap. 12.00 (*0-944379-04-4*) CPA Bk Pub.

***Mein Kampf.** Adolf Hitler. Tr. by James Murphy. 384p. 2000. 20.00 (*0-944379-05-2*) CPA Bk Pub.

Mein Kampf. Adolf Hitler. Tr. by Ralph Manheim. 720p. 1999. pap. 18.00 (*0-395-92503-7*, Mariner Bks) HM.

Mein Kampf. Adolf Hitler. 1927. 23.10 (*0-606-02399-2*, Pub. by Turtleback) Demco.

***Mein Kampf.** Adolf Hitler. 1998. 30.00 (*0-395-95105-4*) HM.

Mein Kampf. Adolf Hitler. 384p. 1986. reprint ed. 20.00 (*0-913022-10-1*) CPA Bk Pub.

Mein Kampf. Adolf Hitler. 384p. 1996. reprint ed. pap. 12.00 (*0-614-25988-6*) CPA Bk Pub.

***Mein Kampf: Original German Language.** Adolf Hitler. 2000. 20.00 (*0-944379-09-5*) CPA Bk Pub.

Mein Kampf: Photographs by David Levinthal. James Young et al. (Illus.). 88p. 1996. 60.00 (*0-944092-40-3*) Twin Palms Pub.

Mein Kampf: Volume I: A Retrospect. Volume II: The National Socialist Movement, 2 vols. in 1. unabridged ed. Adolf Hitler. (GER.). 781p. 1943. reprint ed. 20.00 (*0-945001-61-4*) GSG & Assocs.

Mein Kampf: Volume I: A Retrospect. Volume II: The National Socialist Movement, 2 vols. in 1. unabridged ed. Adolf Hitler. 379p. 1939. reprint ed. pap. 15.00 (*0-945001-18-5*) GSG & Assocs.

Mein Kampf: Volume I: A Retrospect. Volume II: The National Socialist Movement, 2 vols. in 1. unabridged ed. Adolf Hitler. 384p. 1942. reprint ed. 20.00 (*0-945001-19-3*) GSG & Assocs.

Mein Leben Mit Boxern see My Life with Boxers: The Classic Memoirs of the Most Important Boxer Breeder

Mein Leben und Streben. Karl May. xiii, 570p. 1975. reprint ed. write for info. (*3-487-08084-2*) G Olms Pubs.

Mein Lebensweg. L. Von Toscana. (GER., Illus.). 254p. 1992. pap. text 7.00 (*3-364-00225-8*) Gordon & Breach.

Mein Messier-Buch see Atlas of Deep Sky Splendors

Mein Onkel Franz: Level A. text 7.95 (*0-88436-037-7*) EMC-Paradigm.

Mein Schwiegervater see My Father-in-Law: Memories of Karl Barth

Mein Wustenbuch. Gertrud Ashe-Jacobs. (GER., Illus.). 36p. 1997. ring bd. 9.00 (*0-942017-58-7*, 04-64653) Amer Assn Teach German.

Meine Wallfahrt Nach Mekka, 2 vols., Vol. I. Heinrich F. Von Maltzan. vi, 377p. reprint ed. write for info. (*0-318-71528-7*) G Olms Pubs.

Meine Wallfahrt Nach Mekka, 2 vols., Vol. II. Heinrich F. Von Maltzan. vi, 373p. reprint ed. write for info. (*0-318-71529-5*) G Olms Pubs.

Meinertzhagen's Diary Ruse: False Entries on T. E. Lawrence. J. N. Lockman. 114p. 1995. 12.00 (*0-9648897-0-6*) Falcon Books.

Meini, The Blasket Nurse: The Blasket Nurse. Leslie Matson. LC 96-133756. 176p. 1997. pap. 12.95 (*1-85635-131-5*, Pub. by Mercier Pr) Irish Amer Bk.

Meiningen Court Theatre, 1866-1890. John Osborne. (Illus.). 232p. 1988. text 69.95 (*0-521-30394-X*) Cambridge U Pr.

Meininger Theater. Steven DeHart. Ed. by Bernard Beckerman. LC 81-11453. (Theater & Dramatic Studies: No. 4). (Illus.). 249p. 1981. reprint ed. pap. 77.20 (*0-8357-1227-3*, 207005100063) Bks Demand.

Meinong. Reinhardt Grossman. (Arguments of the Philosophers Ser.). 272p. 1974. 25.00 (*0-7100-7831-5*, Routledge Thoemms) Routledge.

Meinongian Logic: The Semantics of Existence & Nonexistence. Dale Jacquette. LC 96-27845. (Perspektiven der Analytischen Philosophie - Perspectives in Analytical Philosophy Ser.: Vol. II). (ENG & GER.). xiii, 297p. (C). 1996. lib. bdg. 146.70 (*3-11-014865-X*) De Gruyter.

Meinong's Theory of Knowledge. Marie-Luise S. Kalsi. (Martinus Nijhoff Philosophy Library: No. 29). 142p. (C). 1987. lib. bdg. 100.50 (*90-247-3552-1*, Pub. by M Nijhoff) Kluwer Academic.

Meinongs Theory of Objects & Values. Findlay. 408p. 1995. 87.95 (*0-7512-0170-7*) Ashgate Pub Co.

Meinung und Wissen in der Philosophie Platons: 'Untersuchungen Zum Charmides', 'Menon' und 'Staat' Theodor Ebert. (GER.). x, 234p. (C). 1974. 79.25 (*3-11-004787-X*) De Gruyter.

Meiobenthology: The Microscopic Fauna in Aquatic Sediments. Olav Giere. (Illus.). 340p. 1993. write for info. (*3-540-56696-1*) Spr-Verlag.

Meiobenthology: The Microscopic Fauna in Aquatic Sediments. Ed. by Olav Giere. LC 93-14010. 1994. 117.95 (*0-387-56696-1*) Spr-Verlag.

Meiosis. Evert. 1998. 1.50 (*0-7167-9356-3*) W H Freeman.

Meiosis. Bernard John. (Developmental & Cell Biology Monographs). (Illus.). 408p. (C). 1990. text 105.00 (*0-521-35053-0*) Cambridge U Pr.

Meir Kahane, Ideologue, Hero, Thinker. S. Daniel Breslauer. LC 86-21703. (Jewish Studies: Vol. 1). 168p. 1986. lib. bdg. 79.95 (*0-88946-252-6*) E Mellen.

Meiroku Zasshi: Journal of the Japanese Enlightenment. William R. Braisted. 579p. 1976. 55.50 (*0-674-56467-7*) HUP.

Meisselbach & Meisselbach-Catucci Fishing Reels: A Collector's Guide. Phil White. 160p. 1995. 28.95 (*1-882418-20-4*) Centenn Pubns.

Meister der Schoenen Madonnen: Herkunft, Entfaltung und Umkreis. Karl H. Clasen. 474p. (C). 1973. 242.35 (*3-11-003944-3*) De Gruyter.

Meister Eckhart, 2 vols. Franz Pfeiffer. 1977. lib. bdg. 400.00 (*0-8490-2222-3*) Gordon Pr.

Meister Eckhart: A Modern Translation. Meister Eckhart. 368p. 1957. 15.00 (*0-06-130008-X*, TB8, Torch) HarpC.

Meister Eckhart: Teacher & Preacher. Bernard McGinn et al. (Classics of Western Spirituality Ser.: Vol. 52). 448p. 1986. pap. 22.95 (*0-8091-2827-6*) Paulist Pr.

Meister Eckhart: The Essential Sermons, Commentaries, Treatises & Defense. Tr. by Edmund Colledge & Bernard McGinn. (Classics of Western Spirituality Ser.). 1987. pap. 22.95 (*0-8091-2370-3*) Paulist Pr.

Meister Eckhart Vol. 1: Sermons & Treatises, 3 vols., 2. Ed. & Tr. by M. O. Walshe. 1993. pap. 24.95 (*1-85230-006-X*, Pub. by Element MA) Penguin Putnam.

Meister Eckhart Vol. 1: Sermons & Treatises, 3 vols., Vol. 1. Ed. & Tr. by M. O. Walshe. 1993. pap. 19.95 (*1-85230-005-1*, Pub. by Element MA) Penguin Putnam.

Meister Eckhart Vol. 3: Sermons & Treatises, Vol. 3. Ed. & Tr. by M. O. Walshe. 1993. pap. 19.95 (*1-85230-182-1*, Pub. by Element MA) Penguin Putnam.

Meister Eckhart & the Beguine Mystics: Hadewijch of Brabant, Mechthild of Magdeburg, & Marguerite Porete. Ed. by Bernard L. Mcginn. LC 77-18605. (Illus.). 160p. 1996. pap. 15.95 (*0-8264-0929-6*) Continuum.

Meister Eckhart, from Whom God Hid Nothing: Sermons, Writings, & Sayings. Ed. by David O'Neal. LC 95-22647. (Illus.). 160p. (Orig.). 1996. pap. 13.95 (*1-57062-139-X*, Pub. by Shambhala Pubns) Random.

Meister Eckhart, German Sermons & Treatises. Eckhart. LC 82-141302. 1987. pap. 15.95 (*0-7224-0176-0*) Element MA.

Meister Eckhart und seine Juenger: Ungedruckte Texte zur Geschichte der deutschen Mystik. Ed. by Franz Jostes. (Deutsche Neudrucke Texte des Mittelalters Ser.). (GER.). 216p. (C). 1972. 46.15 (*3-11-004356-4*) De Gruyter.

Meister Karl's Sketch-Book. Charles G. Leland. LC 75-104510. reprint ed. lib. bdg. 22.50 (*0-8398-1154-3*) Irvington.

Meisterbuch der Schrift see Treasury of Alphabets & Lettering: A Source Book of the Best Letter Forms of Past & Present for Sign Painters, Graphic Artists, Commercial Artists, Typographers, Printers, Sculptors, Architects, & Schools of Art & Design

***Meistersaenger von Nuernberg.** Composed by Richard Wagner. 1998. pap. 7.95 (*963-8303-13-1*) Konemann.

Meisterschule. Marco Meneguzzo & Angela Vettese. (Illus.). 48p. 1998. pap. 16.95 (*88-8158-169-8*, Pub. by Charta) Dist Art Pubs.

Meistersinger von Nurnberg: Complete Vocal & Orchestral Score. Richard Wagner. 823p. 1976. reprint ed. pap. 31.95 (*0-486-23276-X*) Dover.

***Meisterwalzer: Texte und Bilder von Monika Fink, Hans-Dieter Klein und Evelin Klein Analasslich der Ausstellung Evelin Klein, Olbilder, 1998-1999/ Theater-galerie Trier 19. Mai - 30. Juni 1999.** Monika Fink et al. (Persephone Ser.). 55p. 1999. 15.95 (*3-631-35189-5*) P Lang Pubng.

Meisterwerke der Romanischen Sprachwissenschaft, 2 vols. Ed. by Leo Spitzer. vi, 720p. 1929. write for info. (*0-318-71472-8*) G Olms Pubs.

Meisterwerke des Klavierbaus see Stringed Keyboard Instruments

Meisterwerke im J. Paul Getty Museum: Bildhauerei. (GER., Illus.). 128p. 1998. pap. 22.50 (*0-89236-515-3*, Pub. by J P Getty Trust) OUP.

Meisterwerke im J. Paul Getty Museum: Illuminierte Handschriften. (GER., Illus.). 128p. 1997. 34.95 (*0-89236-451-3*, Pub. by J P Getty Trust); pap. 22.50 (*0-89236-452-1*, J P Getty Museum) J P Getty Trust.

Meisterwerke im J. Paul Getty Museum: Kunst der Antike. (GER., Illus.). 128p. 1997. pap. 22.50 (*0-89236-425-4*, Pub. by J P Getty Trust) OUP.

Meisterwerke im J. Paul Getty Museum: Kunstgewerbe. (GER., Illus.). 128p. 1997. pap. 22.50 (*0-89236-461-0*, Pub. by J P Getty Trust) OUP.

Meisterwerke im J. Paul Getty Museum: Kunstgewerbe: German Language Edition. (GER., Illus.). 128p. 1997. 34.95 (*0-89236-460-2*, Pub. by J P Getty Trust) OUP.

Meisterwerke im J. Paul Getty Museum: Zeichnungen: German-Language Edition. (GER., Illus.). 128p. 1997. pap. 22.50 (*0-89236-442-4*, Pub. by J P Getty Trust) OUP.

Meisterwerke Im J. Paul Getty Museum - Fotografien. Ed. by J. Paul Getty Museum Staff. (GER., Illus.). 128p. 1999. 34.95 (*0-89236-522-6*, Pub. by J P Getty Trust); pap. 22.50 (*0-89236-523-4*, Pub. by J P Getty Trust) OUP.

Meisterwerke im J. Paul Getty Museum - Gemalde. (GER., Illus.). 128p. 1997. 34.95 (*0-89236-433-5*, Pub. by J P Getty Trust); pap. 22.50 (*0-89236-434-3*, Pub. by J P Getty Trust) OUP.

Meitheis. 2nd ed. T. C. Hodson. Ed. & Intro. by M. Horam. LC 75-903067. 1975. 10.00 (*0-88386-582-3*) S Asia.

Mejda: The Family & the Early Life of Paramahansa Yogananda. Sananda L. Ghosh. LC 80-54206. (Illus.). 330p. 1980. 12.50 (*0-87612-265-9*) Self Realization.

Mejor: And Other Stories. Mon Roes. 151p. (Orig.). (C). 1988. pap. 1.95 (*0-9618960-1-9*) M M Fain.

Mejor Alcalde, el Rey. Lope de Vega. Ed. by Juan M. Marin Martinez. (Nueva Austral Ser.: No. 118). (SPA.). 1991. pap. text 11.95 (*84-239-1918-8*) Elliots Bks.

Mejor Alcalde, el Rey. 16th ed. Lope de Vega. 144p. 1990. pap. 12.95 (*0-7859-5160-1*) Fr & Eur.

Mejor Cuidado Infantil: Un Libro Para Proveedoras de Cuidado Para Ninos En el Hogar. M. Nash et al. (SPA.). 184p. 1993. pap. text 19.95 (*1-884093-04-3*) Chldrns Fnd.

Mejor de Somos Cubanos. Thoma Benno. 1998. pap. text 7.95 (*3-86187-102-5*) Bookazine Co Inc.

***Mejor Dia.** Susan F. Tierno. Tr. by Ana M. Alvarado. (Think-Kids Book Collection).Tr. of Best-Ever Day. (SPA., Illus.). 16p. (J). (gr. 1). 2000. pap. 2.95 (*1-58237-045-1*) Creat Think.

Mejor Dicho. Carmen Garcia & Emily Spinelli. LC 94-76259. (SPA.). 416p. (C). 1995. pap. text. write for info. (*0-669-28906-X*) HM Trade Div.

Mejor Dicho. Carmen Garcia & Emily Spinelli. (SPA.). (C). 1996. text, teacher ed. 2.66 (*0-669-41833-1*) HM Trade Div.

Mejor Etapa de la Vida - Hacia una Vejez Feliz: The Best Years of Your Life - Growing Old Happily. Eufrasio Deiros. (SPA.). 144p. (Orig.). 1991. pap. 7.50 (*0-311-46127-1*) Casa Bautista.

Mejor Forma de Planear Su Dia. Ed Dayton & Ted W. Engstrom. (Serie Guia de Bolsillo - Pocket Guides Ser.).Tr. of Best Way to Plan Your Day. (SPA.). 1991. 2.79 (*1-56063-032-9*, 498059) Editorial Unilit.

Mejor Forma de Resolver, Conflictos. McDowell. (Serie Enfoque a la Familia - Focus on the Family Ser.).Tr. of Resolving Conflicts. (SPA.). 27p. 1995. pap. write for info. (*0-614-27079-0*) Editorial Unilit.

Mejor Forma de Resolver, Conflictos. J. McDowell. (Serie Enfoque a la Familia - Focus on the Family Ser.).Tr. of Resolving Conflicts. (SPA.). 87p. 1991. pap. 1.99 (*1-56063-131-7*, 497408) Editorial Unilit.

Mejor Manera de Vivir. Mandino Og. (SPA.). 1997. pap. 16.98 (*968-13-2016-6*, Pub. by Edit Diana) Libros Fronteras.

Mejor Marido. Lass Small. (Deseo Ser.).Tr. of Best Husband. (SPA.). 1999. per. 3.50 (*0-373-35309-X*, 1-35309-3) Harlequin Bks.

Mejor Pacto. T. S. Nee.Tr. of Better Covenant. (SPA.). 208p. 1984. pap. 5.99 (*0-8297-0958-4*) Vida Pubs.

***Mejor Postor.** Susanne McCarthy. (Harlequin Bianca Ser.: Vol.158).Tr. of Highest Bidder. (SPA.). 156p. 1999. per. 3.50 (*0-373-33508-3*, 1-33508-2) Harlequin Bks.

***Mejor que Nunca.** Caridad Scordato. (Encanto Ser.). 2000. mass mkt. 3.50 (*0-7860-1141-6*) Kensgtn Pub Corp.

Mejor Regalo: A Cowboy Christmas. Ann Major. (Deseo Ser.). (SPA.). 1996. per. 3.50 (*0-373-35164-X*, 1-35164-2) Harlequin Bks.

Mejor Regalo para un Soltero. Jorge A. Ovando.Tr. of Best Gift for a Single Person. (SPA.). 122p. 1992. pap. 3.99 (*1-56063-107-4*, 498539) Editorial Unilit.

Mejor Sola Que Mal Acompanada: Para la Mujer Golpeada - For the Latina in an Abusive Relationship. Myrna M. Zambrano. LC 85-18255. (New Leaf Ser.). (ENG & SPA.). 243p. (Orig.). 1985. pap. 12.95 (*0-931188-26-1*) Seal Pr WA.

Mejor Tarde Que Temprano: Un Nuevo Enfoque a la Educacion de Su Hijo. Ryamond S. Moore & Dorothy N. Moore. Tr. by Alicia Mejias.Tr. of Better Late Than Early. (SPA., Illus.). 300p. 1997. pap. 7.99 (*1-56063-900-8*, 498389) Editorial Unilit.

Mejor Truco Del Abuelo (Gran Gran's Best Trick) Dwight L. Holden. Tr. by Laureana Ramirez. (SPA., Illus.). 52p. (J). (gr. 1-3). 1993. 12.99 (*968-16-4032-2*, Pub. by Fondo) Continental Bk.

Mejoramiento Del Proceso De Compras. 192p. (C). 1994. pap. 14.33 (*0-201-62184-3*) HEPC Inc.

Mejorando Su Relacion Personal. Silvia Fernandez. (Serie Creciendo - Growing Ser.).Tr. of Improving Your Personal Relationship. (SPA.). 67p. 1993. pap. 2.50 (*1-56063-562-2*, 493033) Editorial Unilit.

Mejores Amigas. Jamie Suzanne. Tr. by Hortensia Martinez Utrilla. (Sweet Valley Twins Ser.: No. 1).Tr. of Best Friends. (SPA.). (J). (gr. 3-7). 1991. 9.70 (*0-606-05411-1*, Pub. by Turtleback) Demco.

Mejores Cuentos de O. Henry see Serie Illustrada, "Now Age"

Mejores Curas Naturales. Ed. by Lao T. Quing. (SPA., Illus.). 202p. 1996. pap. 7.95 (*0-939193-43-4*) Edit Concepts.

Mejores Curas y Remedios Naturales. deluxe ed. Ed. by Atenedor Rojas. (SPA., Illus.). 322p. 1996. pap. 5.95 (*0-939193-42-6*) Edit Concepts.

Mejores Estampas de Eladio Secades. 3rd ed. Eladio Secades. LC 82-84440. (Coleccion Clasicos Cubanos). (SPA., Illus.). 240p. (Orig.). 1998. reprint ed. pap. 13.00 (*0-89729-324-X*) Ediciones.

Mejores Tecnicas de Estudio. Bernabe Tierno. 1998. pap. 9.95 (*84-7880-772-1*) Planeta.

Mejores Trucos de Cartas del Mundo, 1. Bob Longe. 1997. pap. text 10.98 (*968-855-229-1*) Suromex.

Mejores Trucos de Magia del Mundo. Bob Longe. (SPA., Illus.). 147p. 1997. pap. 12.98 (*968-855-230-5*) J H Surovek.

Mejozes Recetas de la Cocina Cubana. Raquel R. Roque. (SPA.). 176p. 1987. pap. 4.95 (*0-941010-02-3*) Downtown Bk.

***Mekanika.** Oscar Chichoni. 80p. 2000. pap. 18.95 (*1-56163-256-2*) NBM.

Mekong. Paul Adirex. 246p. 1995. pap. 17.95 (*974-89245-0-5*, Pub. by Aries Bks) Weatherhill.

Mekong. Paul Adirex. 246p. 1995. 24.95 (*974-89244-9-1*, Pub. by Aries Bks) Weatherhill.

Mekong. Contrib. by Micah Baird et al. (Illus.). 120p. 1999. pap. 22.95 (*0-9671943-1-8*) Majestic Pubg.

***Mekong: Turbulent Past, Uncertain Future.** Milton Osborne. LC 99-86337. 320p. 2000. 30.00 (*0-87113-806-9*, Pub. by Grove-Atltic) Publishers Group.

Mekong Basin Development: Laos & Thailand: Selected Bibliographies. Joel M. Halpern et al. 234p. 1990. reprint ed. pap. 24.50 (*0-923135-17-0*) Dalley Bk Service.

Mekong Delta: Ecology, Economy, & Revolution, 1860-1960. Pierre Brocheux. LC 94-69001. 269p. Date not set. 45.00 (*1-881261-12-3*); pap. 19.95 (*1-881261-13-1*) U Wisc Ctr SE Asian.

Mekong Drillship. Russ Long. LC 98-90805. 1999. 25.00 (*0-533-12920-6*) Vantage.

Mekong River & the Struggle for Indochina. Nguyen T. Dieu. LC 97-49488. 280p. 1999. 59.95 (*0-275-96137-0*, Praeger Pubs) Greenwood.

Mekong/Lancang River Tourism Planning: Economic & Social Commission for Asia & the Pacific. 56p. 1998. pap. 15.00 (*92-1-119824-0*) UN.

Mekons United. Greil Marcus et al. (Illus.). 200p. 1996. pap. 47.98 (*0-9649621-1-X*, QS36) Qrterstick Records.

Mekorot II: Israeli Folk Dance Catalog Hebrew Edition. David Edery. 70p. 1990. reprint ed. 10.00 (*0-9610756-2-7*) D Edery.

Mekorot II: Israeli Folk Dance Catalogue English Edition 1990. rev. ed. David Edery. 100p. 1990. reprint ed. 10.00 (*0-317-99627-4*) D Edery.

Mekranoti: Living among the Painted People of the Amazon. Gustaaf Verswijver et al. (Illus.). 164p. 1996. 45.00 (*3-7913-1431-9*, Pub. by Prestel) te Neues.

Mekton Empire. Guy MacLimore. Ed. by Derek Quintanar. (Mekton Ser.). (Illus.). 120p. (C). 1990. pap. 14.00 (*0-937279-15-3*, MK1301) Talsorian.

Mekton Mecha Manual, Vol. 1. Benjamin Wright et al. (Mekton Ser.). (Illus.). 48p. (Orig.). 1994. pap. 8.00 (*0-937279-53-6*, MK1601) Talsorian.

Mekton Z. Mike MacDonald et al. (Mekton Ser.). (Illus.). 160p. (Orig.). 1995. pap. 20.00 (*0-937279-54-4*, MK1003) Talsorian.

Mel see Phonics Is My Way Series

Mel: The Inside Story. Wensley Clarkson. 1996. 24.95 (*1-85782-045-2*, Pub. by Blake Publng) Seven Hills Bk.

Mel Bay Presents Latin American Songs for Guitar. Jerry Silverman. LC 97-700568. 1996. pap. 17.95 (*0-7866-1418-8*) Mel Bay.

Mel Bay Presents Spanish Chris. Mel Bay. 40p. 1997. pap. 9.95 (*0-7866-3258-5*) Mel Bay.

Mel Bay Story. Ray Dankenbring. LC 97-214629. (Illus.). 208p. 1997. pap. 9.95 (*0-7866-2608-9*, 96470) Mel Bay.

Mel Bay's Chord Diagram Pad. William Bay. 80p. 1997. pap. 4.95 (*0-7866-3101-5*, 96875) Mel Bay.

Mel Bay's Complete Modern Drum Set. Frank Briggs. 158p. 1994. spiral bd. 17.95 (*0-7866-0259-7*) Mel Bay.

Mel Bay's Deluxe Guitar Praise Book. Bill Bay. 64p. (Orig.). 1973. pap. 4.95 (*0-89228-007-7*) Impact Christian.

***Mel Bay's Guide to Guitar Chord Progression.** Mike Christiansen. 56p. 1998. pap. 8.95 (*0-7866-3528-2*, 97169) Mel Bay.

***Mel Bays Guitar Chord Solo Manuscript Book.** William Bay. 32p. 2000. pap. 3.95 (*0-7866-5769-3*, 99242) Mel Bay.

Mel Bay's Guitar Hymnal. Bill Bay. 80p. (Orig.). 1972. pap. 4.95 (*0-89228-009-3*) Impact Christian.

Mel Bay's Guitar Tab Pad. William Bay. 80p. 1997. pap. 4.95 (*0-7866-3100-7*, 96874) Mel Bay.

Mel Bay's Mandolin Chord Chart. William Bay. LC 99-168487. 4p. 1998. pap. 3.95 (*0-7866-2554-6*) Mel Bay.

Mel Bochner: Thought Made Visible, 1966-1973. Richard S. Field. LC 95-40669. (Illus.). 318p. 1996. pap. 50.00 (*0-89467-073-5*, 620812) Yale Art Gallery.

Mel Bochner Drawings, 1966-1973. Barry Schwabsky & Mel Bochner. (Illus.). 80p. 1998. pap. 20.00 (*1-883597-01-3*) L Markey.

M

Mel Foster Story. Connie Heckert. (Illus.). 174p. 1997. 29.95 (*0-938185-08-X*) Wms & Assocs IA.

Mel Gibson. Peter Carrick. (Illus.). 208p. 1999. 24.95 (*0-7090-6088-2*, Pub. by R Hale Ltd) Seven Hills Bk.

Mel Gibson. Wensley Clarkson. 400p. 1998. pap. 13.95 (*1-56025-225-1*, Thunders Mouth) Avalon NY.

Mel Gibson. Sandy Noble. LC 97-26960. (Superstars of Film Ser.). (Illus.). 48p. (YA). (gr. 5 up). 1999. lib. bdg. 15.95 (*0-7910-4643-5*) Chelsea Hse.

***Mel Hashiloach: A Commentary on the Torah by Mordechai Yosef of Isbitza.** Betsalel Philips Edwards. 2001. write for info. (*0-7657-6147-5*) Aronson.

Mel Is Back see Phonics Is My Way Series

Mel Katz Drawings, 1973-1981. Paul Sutinen. (Illus.). 1981. pap. 1.00 (*0-685-67894-6*) Marylhurst Art.

Mel Katz Works, 1971-1978. (Illus.). 1979. pap. 10.00 (*0-87422-045-9*) Wash St U Pr.

Mel Ott: The Little Giant of Baseball. Fred Stein. LC 98-53750. (Illus.). 239p. 1999. pap. 26.95 (*0-7864-0658-5*) McFarland & Co.

Mel-Practice in New Hampshire: A Cartoonist's View of Gov. Meldrim Thomson. D. B. Johnson. 1978. 9.95 (*0-932400-00-0*) Intervale Pub Co.

***Mel Ramos.** (Illus.). 94p. 1999. pap. 19.95 (*1-58423-011-8*) Gingko Press.

Mel Says to Give You His Best. James L. Rosenberg. 1975. pap. 3.25 (*0-8222-0746-X*) Dramatists Play.

***Mel Torme: A Complete Discography & Career Record.** George Hulme. 192p. 2000. lib. bdg. 49.95 (*0-7864-0837-5*) McFarland & Co.

Mel White's Readers Theatre Anthology: Twenty-Eight All Occasion Readings for Storytellers. Melvin R. White. Ed. by Arthur L. Zapel. LC 92-40058. 352p. (YA). (gr. 9-12). 1993. pap. 15.95 (*0-916260-86-0*, B110) Meriwether Pub.

Melagbe "A Life Affirming African Theology" N. K. Dzobo. LC 94-69482. 131p. (Orig.). (C). 1995. pap. text 15.00 (*0-943324-38-6*) Omenana.

Melainie Klein & Critical Social Theory: An Account of Politics, Art, & Reason Based on Her Psychoanalytic Theory. Fred Alford. 256p. (C). 1989. 40.00 (*0-300-04506-9*) Yale U Pr.

Melaka: The Transformation of a Malay Capital c. 1400-1978, 2 vols. Ed. by K. S. Sandhu & Paul Wheatley. (Illus.). 1,660p. 1983. text 195.00 (*0-19-580491-0*) OUP.

Melancholia: A Disorder of Movement & Mood: A Phenomenological & Neurobiological Review. Ed. by Gordon Parker & Dusan Hadzi-Pavlovic. (Illus.). 350p. (C). 1996. text 80.00 (*0-521-47275-X*) Cambridge U Pr.

Melancholia & Depression: From Hippocratic Times to Modern Times. Stanley W. Jackson. 451p. (C). 1990. reprint ed. pap. 25.00 (*0-300-04614-6*) Yale U Pr.

***Melancholics in Love: Representing Women's Depression & Domestic Abuse.** Frances L. Restuccia. LC 99-45718. 160p. 2000. pap. 22.95 (*0-8476-9829-7*); text 65.00 (*0-8476-9828-9*) Rowman.

Melancholie und Bestandigkeit: Humanistische Gelehrsamkeit und Individuelle Weltsicht Im Poetischen Werk Jean de Spondes. Werner Bloch. (Franzosische Sprache und Literatur Ser.: Bd. 220). (GER.). 239p. 1998. 39.95 (*3-631-47755-4*) P Lang Pubng.

Melancholies of Knowledge: Literature in the Age of Science. Ed. by Margery A. Safir. LC 98-6224. (SUNY Ser.). 160p. (C). 1999. text 57.50 (*0-7914-3973-9*); pap. text 18.95 (*0-7914-3974-7*) State U NY Pr.

Melancholy. Ed. by Wolfgang Hageney. (ENG, FRE, GER, ITA & SPA., Illus.). 112p. 1986. pap. 21.95 (*88-7070-054-2*) Belvedere USA.

Melancholy Accidents: The Meaning of Violence in Post-Famine Ireland. Carolyn Conley. LC 98-31624. 272p. 1999. 40.00 (*0-7391-0007-6*) Lxngtn Bks.

Melancholy & Society. Wolf Lepenies. Tr. by Jeremy Gaines & Doris L. Jones from GER. 272p. (C). 1992. 51.95 (*0-674-56468-5*) HUP.

Melancholy & the Critique of Modernity: Soren Kierkegaard's Religious Philosophy. Harvie Ferguson. LC 94-4958. 256p. (C). 1994. pap. 24.99 (*0-415-11723-2*, B4744) Routledge.

Melancholy & the Secular Mind in Spanish Golden Age Literature. Teresa S. Soufas. LC 89-4852. 208p. 1990. text 29.95 (*0-8262-0714-6*) U of Mo Pr.

***Melancholy Baby: The Unplanned Consequences of the G.I.'s Arrival in Europe for World War II.** Pamela Winfield. LC 99-46151. 184p. 2000. write for info. (*0-89789-639-4*, Bergin & Garvey) Greenwood.

Melancholy Death of Oyster Boy: And Other Stories. Tim Burton. LC 97-18468. (Illus.). 128p. 1997. 20.00 (*0-688-15681-9*, Wm Morrow); 20.00 (*0-688-15682-7*, Wm Morrow) Morrow Avon.

Melancholy Dialectics: Walter Benjamin & the Play of Mourning. Max Pensky. LC 92-42229. 296p. 1993. lib. bdg. 32.50 (*0-87023-853-1*) U of Mass Pr.

Melancholy Duty: The Hume-Gibbon Attack on Christianity. Foster. LC 97-37660. 372p. 1997. lib. bdg. 167.00 (*0-7923-4785-4*) Kluwer Academic.

Melancholy Marriage: Depression in Marriage & Psychosocial Approaches to Therapy. Mary K. Hinchliffe. LC 78-4526. 160p. reprint ed. pap. 49.60 (*0-608-14533-5*, 202479900038) Bks Demand.

Melancholy Moments. (In Classical Mood Ser.: Vol. 24). (Illus.). 1998. write for info. incl. cd-rom (*1-886614-37-7*) Intl Masters Pub.

Melancholy Muse: Chaucer, Shakespeare & Early Medicine. Carol F. Heffernan. LC 95-4368. (Language & Literature Ser.: Vol. 19). 200p. (C). 1995. text 48.00 (*0-8207-0262-5*) Duquesne.

Melancholy of Departure: Stories by Alfred DePew. Alfred DePew. LC 91-24281. (Flannery O'Connor Award for Short Fiction Ser.). 144p. 1992. 19.95 (*0-8203-1405-6*) U of Ga Pr.

***Melancholy of Race: Psychoanalysis, Assimilation & Hidden Grief.** Anne Anlin Cheng. (Race & American Culture Ser.). (Illus.). 320p. 2001. 29.95 (*0-19-513403-6*) OUP.

Melancholy of Rebirth: Essays from Post-Communist Central Eruope. George Konrad. 176p. 1995. pap. 12.00 (*0-15-600252-3*) Harcourt.

***Melancholy of Resistance.** Laszlo Krasznahorkai. Tr. by George Szirtes from HUN. 2000. 25.95 (*0-8112-1450-8*, Pub. by New Directions) Norton.

***Melancholy of Resistance.** Laszlo Krasznahorkai. Tr. by George Szirtes. 2000. pap. 13.95 (*0-7043-8009-9*, Pub. by Quartet) Interlink Pub.

Melancholy of Yorick. Joel Chace. (Illus.). 64p. 1998. pap. 12.50 (*0-913559-44-X*) Birch Brook Pr.

Melancholy Scene of Devastation: The Public Response to the 1793 Yellow Fever Epidemic. J. Worth Estes & Billy G. Smith. LC 96-54741. 1997. 35.95 (*0-88135-192-X*) Watson Pub Intl.

Melancholy Science: An Introduction to the Thought of Theodor W. Adorno. Gillian Rose. 212p. 1979. text 60.50 (*0-231-04584-0*) Col U Pr.

Melanchthon: The Quiet Reformer. Clyde L. Manschreck. LC 73-21263. (Illus.). 350p. 1975. reprint ed. lib. bdg. 38.50 (*0-8371-6131-2*, MAMQ, Greenwood Pr) Greenwood.

***Melanchthon in Europe: His Work & Influence Beyond Wittenberg.** Ed. by Karin Maag. LC 99-31488. (Texts & Studies in Reformation & Post-Reformation Thought). 192p. (YA). 1999. pap. 17.99 (*0-8010-2223-1*) Baker Bks.

Melancolia de los Pinguinos. (Arte & Arquitectura Ser.). (Illus.). 82p. 1999. 19.95 (*3-8290-1411-2*, 540873) Konemann.

Melanesian Design: A Study of Style in Wood & Tortoiseshell Carving. Gladys A. Reichard. LC 70-82256. (Illus.). reprint ed. 95.00 (*0-404-50568-6*) AMS Pr.

Melanesian Land Tenure in a Contemporary & Philosophical Context. Ed. by David Lea. LC 96-28822. 204p. 1996. lib. bdg. 34.50 (*0-7618-0456-0*) U Pr of Amer.

Melanesian Languages. Robert H. Codrington. LC 75-32811. reprint ed. 46.50 (*0-404-14115-3*) AMS Pr.

Melanesian Pidgin & the Oceanic Substrate. Roger M. Keesing. LC 87-37604. 280p. 1988. 42.50 (*0-8047-1450-9*) Stanford U Pr.

Melanesian Pidgin & Tok Pisin: Proceedings of the First International Conference of Pidgins & Creoles in Melanesia. Ed. by John W. M. Verhaar. LC 89-18411. (Studies in Language Companion: Vol. 20). xiv, 409p. 1990. 106.00 (*90-272-3023-4*) J Benjamins Pubng Co.

Melanesian Pidgin English: Grammar, Texts, Vocabulary. Robert A. Hall. LC 75-35114. reprint ed. 34.50 (*0-404-14131-5*) AMS Pr.

Melanesian Religion. Garry W. Trompf. (Illus.). 295p. (C). 1991. text 59.95 (*0-521-38306-4*) Cambridge U Pr.

***Melanesians & Australians & the Peopling of America.** Ales Hrdlicka. (LC History-America-E). 58p. 1999. reprint ed. lib. bdg. 69.00 (*0-7812-4337-8*) Rprt Serv.

Melanesians & Polynesians. George Brown. LC 71-174440. (Illus.). 465p. 1972. reprint ed. 19.95 (*0-405-08308-4*, Pub. by Blom Pubns) Ayer.

Melanesians of British New Guinea. Charles G. Seligman. LC 75-35160. reprint ed. 97.50 (*0-404-14174-9*) AMS Pr.

Melanesians of the South-East Solomon Islands. Walter. G. Ivens. LC 74-174430. (Illus.). 1972. reprint ed. 30.95 (*0-405-08662-8*) Ayer.

Melange. Paul Valery. pap. 5.25 (*0-685-36619-7*) Fr & Eur.

***Melange Baby.** Greg Wilkovich. 2000. pap. write for info. (*1-58235-366-2*) Watermrk Pr.

Melange of Treasures from the Lavender Chameleon. Keri Keriotis. Ed. by Judy Goldstein. (Illus.). (Orig.). 1995. pap. 12.95 (*0-9644816-0-X*) K Keriotis.

Melanges. Incl. Correspondance. Henri Bergson. Ed. by Andre Robinet. Documents. Duree et Simultaneite. Henri Bergson. Ed. by Andre Robinet. Idee de Lieu chez Aristote. Henri Bergson. Ed. by Andre Robinet. Pieces Diverses. Henri Bergson. Ed. by Andre Robinet. 125.00 (*0-685-37209-X*) Fr & Eur.

Melanges, 5 vols. Stendhal, pseud. Ed. by Ernest Abravanel & Victor Del Litto. (Illus.). 1972. 9.95 (*0-685-73301-7*) Fr & Eur.

Melanges. Voltaire. Ed. by Jacques Van Den Heuvel. (FRE.). 1961. lib. bdg. 120.00 (*0-7859-3805-2*) Fr & Eur.

Melanges: French-Arabic Text, Vol. I. Institute Dominicain d'Etudes Orientales du Cairo. 1983. 8.00 (*0-86685-323-5*) Intl Bk Ctr.

Melanges: French-Arabic Text, Vol. 15. Institut Dominicain d'Etudes Orientales du Cairo S. 1983. 20.00 (*0-86685-324-3*) Intl Bk Ctr.

Melanges: Their Nature, Origin, & Significance. Ed. by Loren A. Raymond. LC 85-761. (Geological Society of America Ser.: Vol. 198). (Illus.). 182p. 1984. reprint ed. pap. 56.50 (*0-608-07727-5*, 206781500010) Bks Demand.

Melanges & Olistostromes of the U. S. Appalachians. Ed. by J. Wright Horton, Jr. & Nicholas Rast. LC 88-38751. (Geological Society of America Ser.: Vol. 228). (Illus.). 282p. 1989. reprint ed. pap. 87.50 (*0-608-07753-4*, 2067841) Bks Demand.

Melanges Bibliques et Orientaux en l'Honneur de M. Mathias Delcor. Ed. by A. Caquot et al. (Alter Orient und Altes Testament Ser.: Vol. 215). (FRE, SPA & GER.). x, 448p. 1985. text 107.50 (*3-7887-0799-2*, Pub. by NeukirchenerV) Eisenbrauns.

Melanges de Litterature Grecque. E. Miller. 491p. 1968. reprint ed. lib. bdg. 125.00 (*0-685-13371-0*, Pub. by AM Hakkert) Coronet Bks.

Melanges de Musicologie Critique, 4 vols. Incl. Lais et Descorts Francais du XIIIe Siecle, Texte et Musique. A. Jeanroy & E. Brandin. Ed. by Pierre Aubry. (Illus.). 1969. reprint ed. pap. 75.00 (*0-8450-2513-9*); Musicologie Medievale, Histoire et Methodes. Pierre Aubry. (Illus.). 1969. reprint ed. pap. 47.50 (*0-8450-2511-2*); Plus Anciens Monuments de la Musique Francaise. Pierre Aubry. (Illus.). 1969. reprint ed. pap. 47.50 (*0-8450-2514-7*); Proses Texte et Musique, Precedees d'une Etude. Adam De Saint-Victor. Ed. by Pierre Aubry & E. Misset. (Illus.). 1969. reprint ed. pap. 75.00 (*0-8450-2512-0*); (Illus.). 1969. reprint ed. Set pap. 200.00 (*0-8450-2510-4*) Broude.

Melanges Dominique Barthelemy. Ed. by Pierre Casetti et al. (Orbis Biblicus et Orientalis Ser.: Vol. 38). 1981. text 93.75 (*2-8271-0197-1*, Pub. by Ed Univ Fri) Eisenbrauns.

Melanges Marcel Cohen: Etudes de Linguistique, Ethnographie et Sciences Connexes Offertes par Ses Amis et Ses Eleves a IL'Occasion dDe Son 80eme Anniversaire. Ed. by David Cohen. (Janua Linguarum, Series Major: No. 27). 1970. 173.10 (*90-279-0720-X*) Mouton.

Melanges Offerts a Juraj Andrassy: Essays in International Law in Honour of Juraj Andrassy (Festschrift fur Juraj Andrassy) Ed. by V. Ibler. 378p. 1981. pap. text 176.50 (*90-247-0295-X*, Pub. by M Nijhoff) Kluwer Academic.

Melanges Offerts en Hommage au Reverend Pere Etienne Gareau. Etienne Gareau. LC 83-177377. (ENG & FRE.). 264p. 1982. reprint ed. pap. 81.90 (*0-608-02182-2*, 206285100004) Bks Demand.

Melanges Philosophie Juive et Arabe. Salomon Munk. Ed. by Steven Katz. LC 79-7148. (Jewish Philosophy, Mysticism & History of Ideas Ser.). viii, 536p. 1980. reprint ed. lib. bdg. 56.95 (*0-405-12278-0*) Ayer.

Melanges Politiques et Philosophiques Extraits des Memoires et de la Correspondance de Thomas Jefferson, 2 vols. Thomas Jefferson. Ed. by J. P. Mayer. LC 78-67360. (European Political Thought Ser.). 1979. reprint ed. lib. bdg. 68.95 (*0-405-11709-4*) Ayer.

Melanges Premier Fascicule see Maitres Musiciens de la Renaissance Francaise

Melanges, Premier Fascicule see Maitres Musiciens de la Renaissance Francaise

Melanie. Carol Carrick. LC 94-15592. (Illus.). 32p. (J). (gr. k-3). 1996. 14.95 (*0-395-66555-8*, Clarion Bks) HM.

Melanie. Susin Nielsen. (Degrassi Book Ser.). 188p. (J). (gr. 6-9). 1995. mass mkt. 4.95 (*1-55028-256-5*); bds. 16.95 (*1-55028-254-9*) Formac Dist Ltd.

Melanie: They Say I Say. unabridged ed. Teodoro L. Tiangco. LC 98-90931. (Illus.). 73p. 1998. pap. 27.00 (*0-9669222-0-4*) T L Tiangco.

Melanie - And the Story of La Salette. Mary A. Dennis. (Illus.). 136p. 1995. pap. 9.00 (*0-89555-522-0*) TAN Bks Pubs.

Melanie & the Cruise Caper. Elaine L. Schulte. (Twelve Candles Club Ser.: No. 10). 128p. (J). (gr. 3-8). 1996. pap. 5.99 (*1-55661-538-8*) Bethany Hse.

Melanie & the Modeling Mess. Elaine L. Schulte. LC 93-45377. (Twelve Candles Club Ser.: No. 5). 128p. (J). (gr. 3-8). 1994. pap. 5.99 (*1-55661-254-0*) Bethany Hse.

Melanie & the Trash Can Troll: A Modern-Day Fairy Tale. Cheryl M. Thurston. 67p. (Orig.). (J). (gr. 6-9). 1991. pap. text 5.95 (*1-877673-11-0*, MEL) Cottonwood Pr.

Melanie Bluelake's Dream. Betty F. Dorion. LC 95-216575. 156p. (J). (gr. 4-7). 1995. pap. 4.95 (*1-55050-081-3*, Pub. by Coteau) Genl Dist Srvs.

Melanie Jane. Susan A. Couture. LC 94-18699. (Illus.). 32p. (J). (ps-1). 1996. lib. bdg. 14.89 (*0-06-023392-3*) HarpC Child Bks.

Melanie Klein. Julia Segal. (Key Figures in Counselling & Psychotherapy Ser.). (Illus.). 160p. (C). 1992. 44.00 (*0-8039-8476-6*); pap. 18.95 (*0-8039-8477-4*) Sage.

Melanie Klein, Vol. 1. J. M. Petot. Tr. by Christine Trollope from FRE. 324p. 1991. 50.00 (*0-8236-3328-4*) Intl Univs Pr.

Melanie Klein, Vol. 2. J. M. Petot. Tr. by Christine Trollope from FRE. 300p. 1991. 50.00 (*0-8236-3329-2*) Intl Univs Pr.

Melanie Klein: From Theory to Reality. Otto Weininger. 237p. 1992. pap. text 30.00 (*1-85575-011-2*, Pub. by H Karnac Bks Ltd) Other Pr LLC.

Melanie Klein: Her World & Her Work. Phyllis Grosskurth. LC 94-42683. 544p. 1995. 50.00 (*1-56821-445-6*) Aronson.

Melanie Klein: Her World & Her Work. Phyllis Grosskurth. LC 86-27963. (Illus.). 544p. 1987. pap. text 18.50 (*0-674-56470-7*) HUP.

Melanie Klein Today. Ed. by Elizabeth B. Spillius. 350p. 1988. text 47.50 (*0-415-00675-9*) Routledge.

Melanie Klein Today. Ed. by Elizabeth B. Spillius. 365p. (C). 1988. pap. 29.99 (*0-415-00676-7*) Routledge.

Melanie Klein Today Vol. 2: Developments in Theory & Practice: Mainly Practice. Ed. by Elizabeth B. Spillius. 322p. (C). 1989. pap. 29.99 (*0-415-01045-4*) Routledge.

Melanie Klein Today Vol. 2: Developments in Theory & Practice: Mainly Practice. Ed. by Elizabeth B. Spillius. 272p. 1989. 49.95 (*0-415-01044-6*) Routledge.

Melanie Mouse's Moving Day. Cyndy Szekeres. LC 85-82017. (Naptime Tales Bks.). (Illus.). 18p. (J). (ps-3). 1986. 3.99 (*0-307-12290-5*, 12290, Goldn Books) Gldn Bks Pub Co.

Melanin: Conscious Attunement & the God in I. H. Khalif Khalifah. (Orig.). reprint ed. pap. 10.00 (*1-56411-133-4*) Untd Bros & Sis.

Melanin: Its Role in Human Photoprotection. Ed. by Lisa Zeise et al. LC 94-61229. (Illus.). 320p. 1995. 65.00 (*0-9632105-2-1*); pap. 50.00 (*0-9632105-3-X*) Valdenmar.

Melanin 'n Me. Beverly Crespo. Ed. by Maxwell Taylor. LC 96-3487. (Illus.). 32p. (J). (gr. 1-3). 1996. pap. 6.95 (*1-881316-46-7*) A&B Bks.

Melanin 'n Me. Beverly Grespo. Ed. by Maxwell Taylor. (Illus.). 32p. (J). (gr. 1-3). 1996. 14.95 (*1-881316-22-X*) A&B Bks.

Melanins & Melanogenesis. Guiseppe Prota. (Illus.). 290p. 1992. text 69.00 (*0-12-565970-9*) Acad Pr.

Melanism: Evolution in Action. Michael E. N. Majerus. LC 97-28434. (Illus.). 352p. 1998. text 105.00 (*0-19-854983-0*); pap. text 45.00 (*0-19-854982-2*) OUP.

Melanocortin Receptors. Roger D. Cone. (Receptors Ser.). 568p. 2000. 145.00 (*0-89603-579-4*) Humana.

Melanocyte Stimulating Hormone-Control, Chemistry & Effects: Proceedings of the International Symposium of MSH, Amsterdam, 1976. International Symposium of MSH Staff. Ed. by F. J. Tilders et al. (Frontiers of Hormone Research Ser.: Vol. 4). 1977. 86.25 (*3-8055-2635-0*) S Karger.

Melanocytic Tumors: A Guide to Diagnosis. Alistair Cochran et al. LC 96-4715. (Biopsy Interpretation Ser.). 448p. 1996. text 112.00 (*0-397-51633-9*) Lppncott W & W.

Melanogenesis & the Malignant Melanoma: Biochemistry, Cell Biology, Molecular Biology, Pathophysiology, Diagnosis & Treatment: Proceedings of the International Symposium Held in Fukuoka, Japan on 5-6 December 1995. Ed. by Y. Hori et al. (International Congress Ser.: Vol. 1096). 324p. 1996. text 182.25 (*0-444-82209-7*, Excerpta Medica) Elsevier.

Melanoma, Vol. 51. Mackie. 1996. text 99.00 (*0-443-05335-9*, W B Saunders Co) Harcrt Hlth Sci Grp.

Melanoma: Prevention, Detection & Treatment. Catherine M. Poole & Dupont Guerry. LC 97-39658. (Illus.). 176p. 1998. 27.50 (*0-300-07361-5*); pap. 14.00 (*0-300-07362-3*) Yale U Pr.

Melanoma & Naevi. Ed. by J. M. Elwood. (Pigment Cell Ser.: Vol. 9). (Illus.). viii, 156p. 1988. 100.00 (*3-8055-4639-4*) S Karger.

Melanoma Antigens & Antibodies. Ed. by Ralph A. Reisfeld & Soldano Ferrone. LC 82-5288. 462p. 1982. 95.00 (*0-306-40852-X*, Plenum Trade) Perseus Pubng.

***Melanoma Methods & Protocols.** Ed. by Brian J. Nickoloff. 375p. 2000. 99.50 (*0-89603-684-7*) Humana.

Melanoma Research: Genetics, Growth Factors, Metastases & Antigens. Ed. by Larry Nathanson. (Cancer Treatment & Research Ser.). (C). 1991. text 172.50 (*0-7923-0895-6*) Kluwer Academic.

Melanomas: Basic Properties & Clinical Behavior: Proceedings of the International Pigment Cell Conference, 9th, Houston, Texas, Jan., 1975, Pt. 1. International Pigment Cell Conference Staff. Ed. by V. Riley. (Pigment Cell Ser.: Vol. 2). (Illus.). 476p. 1977. 133.25 (*3-8055-2369-6*) S Karger.

Melanommatales: Loculoascomycetes. Margaret E. Barr. LC 90-47767. (North American Flora Ser.: No. 2, Pt. 13). (Illus.). 130p. 1990. pap. 20.50 (*0-89327-360-0*) NY Botanical.

Melanotropic Peptides, 3 vols., Vol. I. Mac E. Hadley. 240p. 1988. 134.00 (*0-8493-5277-0*, QP572) CRC Pr.

Melanotropic Peptides, 3 vols., Vol. II. Mac E. Hadley. 208p. 1988. 121.00 (*0-8493-5278-9*, QP572, CRC Reprint) Franklin.

Melanotropic Peptides, 3 vols., Vol. III. Mac E. Hadley. 176p. 1988. 101.00 (*0-8493-5279-7*, CRC Reprint) Franklin.

Melanotropins. Alex N. Eberle. (Illus.). xx, 556p. 1988. 277.50 (*3-8055-4678-5*) S Karger.

Melaracconti see Of Cannons & Caterpillars

Melatonin. Reiter & Russel. 1996. mass mkt. 8.99 (*0-553-85114-4*) Bantam.

Melatonin. Woodland Publishing Staff. 1999. pap. text 3.95 (*1-885670-22-2*) Woodland UT.

Melatonin: A Universal Photoperiodic Signal with Diverse Actions: International Symposium, Hong Kong, September 1995. Ed. by Russell J. Reiter et al. LC 96-44662. (Frontiers of Hormone Research Ser.: Vol. 21, 1996). (Illus.). viii, 208p. 1996. 198.25 (*3-8055-6344-2*) S Karger.

Melatonin: Binding Sites in Endocrine & Immune Systems. Ed. by G. M. Brown et al. (Journal: Biological Signals: Vol. 3, No. 2, 1994). (Illus.). 60p. 1994. pap. 30.50 (*3-8055-6007-9*) S Karger.

Melatonin: Biosynthesis, Physical Effects & Clinical Applications. Hing-Sing Yu. 560p. 1992. lib. bdg. 249.00 (*0-8493-6900-2*, QP572) CRC Pr.

Melatonin: Clinical Perspectives. Ed. by Andrew Miles et al. (Illus.). 304p. 1988. 80.00 (*0-19-261652-8*) OUP.

Melatonin: From Contraception to Breast Cancer Prevention. Michael Cohen. (Illus.). 180p. (Orig.). (C). 1995. pap. 75.00 (*1-880613-10-7*) Sheba Pr.

Melatonin: Nature's Sleeping Pill. 2nd ed. Ray Sahelian. 160p. 1997. pap. text 9.95 (*0-89529-775-2*, Avery) Penguin Putnam.

***Melatonin: The Anti-Aging Hormone.** Suzanne LeVert. 272p. (Orig.). 1998. mass mkt. 5.99 (*0-380-78304-5*, Avon Bks) Morrow Avon.

Melatonin: Your Body's Natural Wonder Drug. Russel J. Reiter & Jo Robinson. 416p. 1996. mass mkt. 6.99 (*0-553-57484-1*) Bantam.

Melatonin - Current Status & Perspectives: Proceedings of an International Symposium on Melatonin, Held in Bremen, F. R. Germany, September 18-30, 1980. Ed. by N. Birau & W. Schlott. (Advances in the Biosciences Ser.: Vol. 29). 420p. 1981. 72.50 (*0-08-026400-X*, Pergamon Pr) Elsevier.

***Melatonin after Four Decades: An Assessment of Its Potential** James Olcese. LC 99-31757. (Advances in Experimental Medicine & Biology Ser.). 1999. write for info. (*0-306-46134-X*, Kluwer Plenum) Kluwer Academic.

An Asterisk (*) at the beginning of an entry indicates that the title is appearing for the first time.

Melatonin & Aging Sourcebook. Roman Rozencwaig & Hasnain Walji. LC 96-39113. (Illus.). 220p. 1997. text 79.95 (0-934252-76-9, Pub. by Hohm Pr) SCB Distributors.

Melatonin & Its Analogs: From Molecular Biology to Clinical Applications: Erice (Italy), June 1998: Selected Proceedings. Ed. by F. Fraschini et al. (Biological Signals & Receptors Ser.: Vol. 8, No. 1-2). (Illus.). 146p. 1999. pap. 39.25 (3-8055-6840-1) S Karger.

Melatonin & the Biological Clock. Dallas Clouatre & Alan E. Lewis. (Good Health Guides Ser.). 48p. 1996. pap. 3.95 (0-87983-734-9, 37349K, Keats Publng) NTC Contemp Pub Co.

Melatonin & the Pineal: Symposium No. 117. CIBA Foundation Staff. 320p. 1985. 128.00 (0-471-91086-4) Wiley.

Melatonin & the Pineal Gland, from Basic Science to Clinical Application: Proceedings of the International Symposium on Melatonin & the Pineal Gland,from Basic Science to Clinical Application, Paris, 6-9 September 1992. Ed. by Yvan Touitou et al. LC 92-48538. (International Congress Ser.: Vol. 1017). 394p. 1993. 177.25 (0-444-89583-3, Excerpta Medica) Elsevier.

Melatonin Hypothesis: Breast Cancer & Use of Electric Power. Ed. by Richard G. Stevens et al. LC 96-27522. 776p. 1997. 87.50 (1-57477-020-9) Battelle.

Melatonin in Humans. Ed. by Richard J. Wurtman & F. Waldhauser. (Journal of Neural Transmission: Suppl. 2). (Illus.). 330p. 1986. 133.00 (0-387-81927-4) Spr-Verlag.

Melatonin in Psychiatric & Neoplastic Disorders. Ed. by Mohammad Shafii & Sharon L. Shafii. LC 97-3183. (Progress in Psychiatry Ser.). 344p. 1998. text 44.00 (0-88048-919-7, 8919) Am Psychiatric.

Melatonin in the Promotion of Health. Ronald R. Watson. LC 98-45986. (Modern Nutrition Ser.). 240p. 1998. boxed set 94.95 (0-8493-8564-4) CRC Pr.

Melatonin Miracle: Nature's Age-Reversing, Disease-Fighting, Sex-Enhancing Hormone. Walter Pierpaoli. 1996. mass mkt. 6.99 (0-671-53435-1) PB.

Melatonin, Panic Attacks, Anti-Aging & Insomnia. 1996. lib. bdg. 250.95 (0-8490-5896-1) Gordon Pr.

Melatonin Report. 5th ed. Billie J. Sahley. (Illus.). 20p. 1996. pap. text 3.95 (0-9625914-6-7) Pain & Stress.

Melatonin Rhythm Generating System: Developmental Aspects. Ed. by D. C. Klein. (Illus.). 250p. 1983. 137.50 (3-8055-3460-4) S Karger.

Melba: A Biography. Agnes G. Murphy. LC 74-24162. (Illus.). reprint ed. 37.50 (0-404-13057-7) AMS Pr.

Melba: A Biography. Agnes G. Murphy. LC 77-8029. (Music Reprint Ser.). (Illus.). 1977. reprint ed. lib. bdg. 45.00 (0-306-77428-3) Da Capo.

Melba, the Voice of Australia. Therese Radic. 214p. 1986. 14.95 (0-918812-45-3, SB 0005) MMB Music.

Melba Toast, Bowie's Knife & Caesar's Wife: A Dictionary of Eponyms. Martin H. Manser. 256p. 1990. pap. 7.95 (0-380-70877-9, Avon Bks) Morrow Avon.

Melbourne. David Cecil. LC 54-9486. (Illus.). 450p. 1974. 8.95 (0-672-52038-9, Bobbs) Macmillan.

Melbourne. 3rd ed. Insight Guides Staff. (Insight Guides). 1998. pap. text 21.95 (0-88729-710-2) Langenscheidt.

Melbourne: Australia Regional. Periplus Editions Staff. (Periplus Travel Maps Ser.). 1997. 7.95 (962-593-050-7) Periplus.

Melbourne & Victoria's Splendor. Jiri Lochman. (Panoramic Ser.). (Illus.). 128p. 1999. 24.95 (1-86436-371-1, Pub. by New Holland) BHB Intl.

Melbourne Art Director's Annual, 1996. Melbourne Art Directors Club Staff. (Illus.). 200p. 1997. pap. 29.95 (1-56970-549-6) Bks Nippan.

*__Melbourne Beach & Indialantic.__ Frank J. Thomas. (Images of America Ser.). (Illus.). 128p. 1999. pap. 18.99 (0-7385-0121-2) Arcadia Publng.

Melbourne Episode: Case Study of a Missing Pilot. Richard F. Haines. (Illus.). 275p. (Orig.). 1987. pap. 12.95 (0-9618082-0-9) LDA Pr CA.

Melbourne Pocket Guidebook. Little Hills Press Editors. (Illus.). 64p. pap. 3.95 (1-86315-033-1) Pelican.

Melbourne Pocket Guidebook. Little Hills Press Staff. 1994. pap. 3.95 (1-86315-090-0) Pelican.

Melbourne Village: The First 25 Years (1946-1971) Richard C. Crepeau. LC 87-16205. (Illus.). 215p. 1988. 34.95 (0-8130-0867-0) U Press Fla.

Melbourne's Marvellous Trams. Dale Budd & Randall Wilson. (Illus.). 96p. 1997. pap. 29.95 (0-86840-504-3, Pub. by New South Wales Univ Pr) Intl Spec Bk.

Melchior Franck: Dulces Mundani Exilij Deliciae. Melchior Franck. Ed. by Randall C. Sheets. (Recent Researches in Music of the Baroque Era Ser.: Vol. RRB80). (Illus.). xvi, 172p. 1996. pap. 60.00 (0-89579-374-1) A-R Eds.

Melchior Franck: Geistliche Gesang und Melodeyen. Melchior Franck. Ed. by William Weinert. (Recent Researches in Music of the Baroque Era Ser.: Vol. RRB70). (Illus.). xviii, 239p. 1993. pap. 80.00 (0-89579-283-4) A-R Eds.

Melchior Goldast von Heiminsfeld: Collector, Commentator, & Editor. Anne A. Baade. LC 91-43013. (Studies in Old Germanic Languages & Literatures: Vol. 2). X, 206p. (C). 1993. text 39.95 (0-8204-1835-8) P Lang Pubng.

Melchior Hoffman: Social Unrest & Apocalyptic Visions in the Age of Reformation. Klaus Deppermann. Tr. by Malcolm Wren. 440p. 69.95 (0-567-09338-7, Pub. by T & T Clark) Bks Intl VA.

Melchior Hoffman: Social Unrest & Apocalyptic Visions in the Age of Reformation. Klaus Deppermann. 448p. pap. 44.95 (0-567-08654-2) T&T Clark Pubs.

Melchizedek. large type ed. Ellen G. Traylor. LC 97-16230. 308p. 1997. 21.95 (0-7862-1140-7) Thorndike Pr.

Melchizedek: The Secret Doctrine of the Bible. J. C. Grumbine. 1992. lib. bdg. 79.95 (0-8490-8745-7) Gordon Pr.

Melchizedek: The Secret Doctrine of the Bible. J. C. Grumbine. 93p. 1996. reprint ed. pap. 11.00 (0-7873-0360-7) Hlth Research.

Melchizedek & Melchiresa. Paul J. Kobelski. Ed. by Bruce Vawter. LC 80-28379. (Catholic Biblical Quarterly Monographs: No. 10). ix, 166p. 1981. pap. 4.50 (0-915170-09-4) Catholic Bibl Assn.

Melchizedek & the Mystery of Fire. Manly P. Hall. 1996. pap. 4.95 (0-89314-842-3) Philos Res.

Melchizedek Bible. Ed. by Students of Ontology of the Order of Melchizedek S. 1400p. 1989. 100.00 (0-685-26067-4) Embsy Domin.

*__Melchizedek Bible.__ unabridged ed. David E. Pedley & Mark L. Pedley. 589p. 1999. reprint ed. pap. 24.95 (1-893107-29-9, Pub. by Healing Unltd) Assoc Pubs Grp.

Melchizedek Bible: Melchizedek Bible Study, Vol. 1. Branch Vinedresser & Evan David Pedley. 587p. 1993. pap. 24.00 (0-9623237-0-5) Embsy Domin.

Melchizedek: or The Secret Doctrine of the Bible (1919) J. C. Grumbine. 96p. 1996. reprint ed. pap. 9.95 (1-56459-910-8) Kessinger Pub.

Melchizedek Truth Principles: From the Ancient Mystical White Brotherhood. 9th ed. Frater Achad. 210p. (Orig.). 1963. pap. text 11.95 (0-926872-01-X) Great Seal Pr.

Melchoir Neusidler Intabolatura di Liuto. Ed. by Charles Jacobs. (Gesamtausgaben Collected Works: Vol. XV). xxii, 79p. 1994. lib. bdg. 92.00 (0-931902-86-X) Inst Mediaeval Mus.

*__Melcor Computer Code Manuals Version 1.8.4: July 1997.__ R. O. Gauntt. 764p. 1998. ring bd. 64.00 (0-16-062926-8); ring bd. 67.00 (0-16-062927-6) USGPO.

Melding. 2nd ed. Sharmai Amber. 272p. 1999. pap. 14.95 (0-9668036-0-4) Sambershar.

Meleagen - The Poems. Ed. by Jerry Clack. (GRE.). vii, 160p. (Orig.). (C). 1992. pap. text 18.00 (0-86516-254-9) Bolchazy-Carducci.

Melee Symboliste, 3 vols. in 1. Ernest Raynaud. LC 77-11474. reprint ed. 37.50 (0-404-16336-X) AMS Pr.

Melehi: Recent Paintings. (Illus.). 110p. (Orig.). 1984. pap. 14.50 (0-917535-02-2) Bronx Mus.

Meletij Smotryc'kyj. David A. Frick. (Harvard Series in Ukrainian Studies). 419p. 1994. text 32.00 (0-916458-55-5) Harvard Ukrainian.

Meletij Smotryc'kyj. David A. Frick. (Harvard Series in Ukrainian Studies). (Illus.). 419p. 1994. pap. text 18.00 (0-916458-60-1) Harvard Ukrainian.

Melhor Relacionamento com. James Hilt. Orig. Title: How to Have a Better Relationship with Anybody. (POR.). 160p. 1986. pap. 4.95 (0-8297-0542-2) Vida Pubs.

*__Melhoramentos Minidicionario De Sinonimos E Antonimos.__ Distribooks Inc. Staff. 1999. pap. 18.95 (85-06-01988-5) Midwest European Pubns.

Melidore et Phrosine: Drame Lyrique. Etienne N. Mehul. Ed. by Elizabeth Bartlet. LC 85-75346. (French Opera in the 17th & 18th Centuries Ser.: No. 4,vol. LXXIII). (Illus.). 300p. 1990. lib. bdg. 82.00 (0-918728-81-9) Pendragon NY.

Melier-Dialog. G. Deininger & A. Grosskinsky. Ed. by Leonardo Taran. (Ancient Greek Literature Ser.). 263p. 1987. lib. bdg. 15.00 (0-8240-7754-7) Garland.

Melik und Rhythmik des Classischen Hellenentums, 2 vols. Aristoxenus Von Tarent. ccxiv, 649p. 1965. reprint ed. write for info. (0-318-70867-1); reprint ed. write for info. (0-318-70868-X) G Olms Pubs.

Melik und Rhythmik des Classischen Hellenentums, 2 vols., Set. Aristoxenus Von Tarent. ccxiv, 649p. 1965. reprint ed. write for info. (0-318-70866-3) G Olms Pubs.

Melinda & Nock & the Magic Spell. Ingrid Uebe. LC 95-52218. (Illus.). 64p. (J). (gr. 1-4). 1998. pap. 5.95 (1-55858-992-9, Pub. by North-South Bks NYC) Chronicle Bks.

Melinda's Folk Art, Vol. 1. Melinda Neist. (Illus.). 1993. pap. 9.95 (1-883675-00-6, 100) J Shaw Studio.

Melinda's Folk Art, Vol. 2. Melinda Neist. (Illus.). 1994. pap. 9.95 (1-883675-02-2, 102) J Shaw Studio.

Melinda's Folk Art, Vol. 3. Melinda Neist. (Illus.). 1997. pap. 10.95 (1-883675-19-7, 119) J Shaw Studio.

Melindres de Belisa - El Villano en Su Rincon. 5th ed. Lope de Vega. 1980. pap. 12.95 (0-7859-5169-5) Fr & Eur.

Meline Tariff: French Agriculture & Nationalist Economic Policy. Eugene O. Golob. LC 68-58582. (Columbia University. Studies in the Social Sciences: No. 506). reprint ed. 27.50 (0-404-51506-1) AMS Pr.

Meliora: or Better Times to Come: Being the Contributions of Many Men Touching the Present State & Prospects of Society, 2 vols., Set. Viscount Ingestre. 1971. reprint ed. 55.00 (0-7146-1420-3, Pub. by F Cass Pubs) Intl Spec Bk.

Melisande. E. Nesbit. LC 98-33875. (Illus.). 48p. (J). (gr. k-3). 1999. pap. 7.99 (0-7636-0717-7, Pub. by Candlewick Pr) Penguin Putnam.

Melisande. Edith Nesbit. 41p. (J). (gr. k-3). 1989. 13.95 (0-15-253164-5) Harcourt.

Melisar. Mark Dunster. 25p. (Orig.). 1994. pap. 5.00 (0-89642-240-2) Linden Pubs.

Melissa see Three Plays

Melissa. Eva Gibson. (Springsong Bks.). 176p. (Orig.). (J). (gr. 7-10). 1995. mass mkt. 4.99 (1-55661-623-6) Bethany Hse.

*__Melissa.__ Rosie Rushton. (Fab 5 Ser.). 224p. (YA). (gr. 5-9). 2000. pap. 4.99 (0-7868-1502-7) Hyprn Ppbks.

Melissa. large type ed. Sara Hylton. 493p. write for info. (0-7505-1019-6, Pub. by Mgna Lrg Print) Ulverscroft.

Melissa. Taylor Caldwell. 1974. reprint ed. lib. bdg. 27.95 (0-88411-159-8) Amereon Ltd.

Melissa & Joan Rivers. Skip Press. LC 95-13087. (Star Families Ser.). 48p. (J). (gr. 5-6). 1995. pap. 4.95 (0-382-39178-0, Crstwood Hse); lib. bdg. 15.95 (0-89686-883-4, Crstwood Hse) Silver Burdett Pr.

Melissa & the Little Red Book. Agnes Sanford. (Illus.). (J). (gr. 1-6). pap. 3.95 (0-910924-81-3) Macalester.

Melissa Etheridge. Ed. by Carol Cuellar. 56p. (Orig.). (C). 1989. pap. text 14.95 (0-7692-0716-2, P0839SMX) Wrner Bros.

Melissa Etheridge. Ed. by Jeannette DeLisa. (Guitar Anthology Ser.). 128p. (YA). 1995. pap. text 22.95 (0-89724-855-4, PG9532) Wrner Bros.

Melissa Etheridge. Chris Nickson. LC 96-30621. (Illus.). 160p. 1997. pap. 11.95 (0-312-15171-3) St Martin.

Melissa Etheridge: Our Little Secret. Joyce Luck. LC 97-146279. (Illus.). 225p. 1997. pap. text 16.95 (1-55022-298-8) LPC InBook.

Melissa Etheridge: Your Little Secret. Ed. by Jeannette DeLisa. (Illus.). 80p. (Orig.). 1996. pap. text 19.95 (0-89724-667-5, PG9552) Wrner Bros.

Melissa Etheridge - Brave & Crazy. Ed. by Carol Cuellar. 80p. (Orig.). (C). 1990. pap. text 14.95 (0-7692-0715-4, P0866SMG) Wrner Bros.

Melissa Etheridge/Never Enough: Guitar Personality Book. 76p. (Orig.). 1992. pap. 17.95 (0-7692-0575-5, P0950GTX) Wrner Bros.

Melissa Etheridge/Yes I am Guitar: Guitar Personality Book. 64p. (Orig.). 1993. pap. 15.95 (0-7692-0577-1, P1031GTX) Wrner Bros.

Melissa Extract: The Natural Remedy for Herpes. Jan De Vries. (Good Health Guides Ser.). 48p. 1996. pap. 3.95 (0-87983-719-5, 37195K, Keats Publng) NTC Contemp Pub Co.

*__Melissa Joan Hart.__ Ann Gaines. (Real-Life Reader Biography Ser.). (Illus.). 32p. (J). (gr. 3-8). 2000. lib. bdg. 15.95 (1-58415-036-X) M Lane Pubs.

Melissa Meyer. Stephen Westfall. (Illus.). 11p. (Orig.). 1984. pap. 10.00 (0-913263-08-7) Exit Art.

Melissa Miller: A Survey, 1978-1986. Ed. by Douglas G. Schultz. (Illus.). 96p. 1986. pap. 14.95 (0-936080-17-5) Cont Arts Museum.

Melite Ou les Fausses Lettres. Pierre Corneille. 147p. 1950. 5.95 (0-686-54619-9) Fr & Eur.

Melitte. Fatima Shaik. LC 96-29533. 160p. (J). (gr. 5-9). 1997. 15.99 (0-8037-2106-4, Dial Yng Read) Peng Put Young Read.

*__Melitte.__ Fatima Shaik. (Illus.). 160p. (J). (gr. 5-9). 1999. pap. 4.99 (0-14-130420-0, PuffinBks) Peng Put Young Read.

Melkii Bes: Drama vs. Piati Deistviiakh. Fedor Sologub, pseud. (Modern Russian Literature & Culture, Studies & Texts: Vol. 26). (RUS.). 156p. (Orig.). (C). 1988. pap. 10.00 (0-933884-61-3) Berkeley Slavic.

Mellah Society: Jewish Community Life in Sherifian Morocco. rev. ed. Shlomo Deshen. LC 88-27818. (Illus.). 184p. 1989. pap. text 14.95 (0-226-14340-6) U Ch Pr.

Mellah Society: Jewish Community Life in Sherifian Morocco. rev. ed. Shlomo Deshen. LC 88-27818. (Illus.). 184p. 1996. lib. bdg. 36.00 (0-226-14339-2) U Ch Pr.

*__Mellen Biblical Commentary: Intertextual.__ Ed. by George Wesley Buchanan. LC 99-27735. 544p. 1999. text 119.95 (0-7734-2470-9) E Mellen.

Mellen Contemporary Poets. LC 93-7117. 64p. 1993. pap. 14.95 (0-7734-2786-4, Mellen Poetry Pr) E Mellen.

Mellen History of Medicine, 8 vols. Plinio Prioreschi. Incl. Vol. 1. Primitive & Ancient Medicine. LC 91-29934. 672p. 1991. lib. bdg. 129.95 (0-7734-9661-0); write for info. (0-7734-9715-3) E Mellen.

Mellen Intertextual Bible Commentary, Vol. 1, Bk. 1. Ed. by George W. Buchanan. LC 96-31591. (New Testament Ser.). (Illus.). 600p. 1997. text 119.95 (0-7734-2373-7) E Mellen.

Mellen Intertextual Bible Commentary, Vol. 1, Bk. 2. Ed. by George W. Buchanan. LC 96-31591. (New Testament Ser.). (Illus.). 536p. 1997. text 119.95 (0-7734-2421-0) E Mellen.

Mellencamp. John Mellencamp. LC 98-27556. (Illus.). 160p. 1998. 40.00 (0-06-055372-3, Perennial) HarperTrade.

Mellencamp: Paintings & Reflections. John Mellencamp. LC 98-27556. (Illus.). 160p. 1998. pap. 25.00 (0-06-095295-4, Perennial) HarperTrade.

Mellichampe: A Legend of the Santee. rev. ed. William Gilmore Simms. LC 78-116010. reprint ed. 10.00 (0-404-06039-0) AMS Pr.

Mellin de Saint-Gelais & Literary History. Donald Stone, Jr. LC 83-81183. (French Forum Monographs: No. 47). 127p. (Orig.). 1983. pap. 10.95 (0-917058-47-X) French Forum.

Mellis & Eye Railway. Peter Paye. (C). 1985. 45.00 (0-85361-256-0) St Mut.

Mellone's Specialized Cachet Catalogue of First Day Covers of the 1940's, 2 vols. 2nd ed. Michael A. Mellone. (Illus.). 1979. pap. 8.95 (0-89794-019-9) FDC Pub.

Melloni's Illustrated Dictionary of Medical Abbreviations. B. John Melloni & Ida G. Dox. LC 98-11886. (Illus.). 492p. 1998. pap. 26.95 (1-85070-708-1) Prthnon Pub.

Melloni's Illustrated Dictionary of Obstetrics & Gynecology. I. G. Dox & J. L. Melloni. LC 99-56573. (Illus.). 402p. 2000. pap. 39.95 (1-85070-710-3) Prthnon Pub.

Melloni's Illustrated Dictionary of the Musculoskeletal System. B. John Melloni et al. LC 98-2796. (Illus.). 314p. 1998. pap. 29.95 (1-85070-667-0) Prthnon Pub.

*__Melloni's Illustrated Medical Dictionary.__ 4th ed. Ida G. Dox & B. John Melloni. (Illus.). 550p. 2001. 39.95 (1-85070-094-X) Prthnon Pub.

Melloni's Illustrated Review of Human Anatomy: By Structures-Arteries, Bones, Muscles, Nerves, Veins. June L. Melloni et al. LC 88-722. (Illus.). 278p. 1988. reprint ed. pap. 86.20 (0-608-04701-5, 206542200004) Bks Demand.

Melloni's Student Atlas of Human Anatomy. June L. Melloni et al. LC 96-53894. 286p. 1997. pap. 34.95 (1-85070-770-7) Prthnon Pub.

Mellon's Specialized Cachet Catalog of First Day Covers of the 1950's, 2 vols. Michael A. Mellone. 1984. pap. 8.95 (0-685-73681-4); pap. 8.95 (0-685-73682-2) FDC Pub.

Mellops Go Diving for Treasure. Tomi Ungerer. LC 98-56451. (Illus.). 32p. (J). (ps-4). 1999. reprint ed. pap. 5.95 (1-57098-285-6, Pub. by Roberts Rinehart) Publishers Group.

Mellops Go Spelunking. Tomi Ungerer. LC 98-24024. (Illus.). 32p. (J). (ps-5). 1998. pap. 5.95 (1-57098-228-7, TomiCo) Roberts Rinehart.

Mellops Strike Oil. Tomi Ungerer. LC 98-56461. (Illus.). 32p. (J). (ps-4). 1999. reprint ed. pap. 5.95 (1-57098-284-8, Pub. by Roberts Rinehart) Publishers Group.

Mellor Meigs & Howe: A Monograph of the Work of Mellor Meigs & Howe. Alfred Mellor et al. LC 90-47377. (American Architectural Classics Ser.). (Illus.). 228p. 1992. reprint ed. 85.00 (1-878650-01-7) Archit CT.

Mellow Manana: The Public & Private Letters of Franklin Jones, Sr., 1975-1980, Vol. II. Franklin Jones, Sr. Ed. by Ann Adams. 228p. 1985. 29.95 (0-915433-11-7) Packrat WA.

Mellowed by Time. 3rd ed. Elizabeth O. Verner. LC 70-127297. 1978. 15.00 (0-937684-03-1) Tradd St Pr.

Mellows: A Chronicle of Unknown Singers. R. Emmet Kennedy. LC 78-32125. (Illus.). 183p. 1979. reprint ed. lib. bdg. 65.00 (0-8371-5831-1, KME&) Greenwood.

Mellows: Taxation for Executors & Trustees. Contrib. by Julie Anderson & Kevin Prosser. 1991. ring bd. write for info. (0-406-99833-7, MWTESSET, MICHIE) LEXIS Pub.

Mellows: The Law of Succession. 5th ed. Clive V. Margrave-Jones. 680p. 1993. pap. text 66.00 (0-406-02438-3, UK, MICHIE) LEXIS Pub.

Melly's Magic Dreidel. Amye Rosenberg. (Stickers & Shapes Ser.). (Illus.). 24p. (J). (ps-1). 1998. pap. 4.99 (0-689-81810-6) Litle Simon.

Melly's Menorah. Amye Rosenberg. (Illus.). 24p. (J). (ps-1). 1991. per. 3.99 (0-671-74495-X) Litle Simon.

Melmac Dinnerware. Gregory R. Zimmer & Alan Daigle. LC 97-131682. (Illus.). 1997. write for info. (0-89538-085-4) L-W Inc.

Melmon & Morrelli's Clinical Pharmacology: Basic Principles in Therapeutics. 3rd ed. Kenneth L. Melmon et al. (Illus.). 1141p. 1992. pap. text 65.00 (0-07-105385-9) McGraw-Hill HPD.

*__Melmon & Morrelli's the Essentials Clinical Pharmacology: Principles & Practical Applications of Therapeutics.__ 4th ed. Kenneth L. Melmon et al. (Illus.). 1200p. 1999. pap. text 64.00 (0-07-105406-5) McGraw-Hill HPD.

Melmoth. Mark Dunster. 13p. (Orig.). 1995. pap. 4.00 (0-89642-285-2) Linden Pubs.

Melmoth the Wanderer. Charles R. Maturin. LC 88-37955. (Oxford World's Classics Ser.). 584p. 1998. pap. 11.95 (0-19-283592-0) OUP.

Melmoth the Wanderer: A Tale. Charles R. Maturin. LC 61-5561. 434p. reprint ed. pap. 134.60 (0-608-16019-9, 203311400083) Bks Demand.

Melnikhov House, Moscow, 1927 - 1929. Juhani Pallasama. 81p. 1996. pap. 25.00 (1-85490-413-2, Pub. by Wiley) Wiley.

Melnikov: Solo Architect in a Mass Society. S. Starr. (C). 1990. pap. 170.00 (0-7855-4459-3, Pub. by Collets) St Mut.

Melnikov: Solo Architect in a Mass Society. S. Frederick Starr. LC 77-85566. (Illus.). 295p. 1978. reprint ed. pap. 91.50 (0-608-07503-5, 206772600009) Bks Demand.

Melocoton en Almibar - Ninette y un Senor de Murcia. 7th ed. Miguel Mihura. (SPA.). 204p. 1989. pap. 11.95 (0-7859-5136-9) Fr & Eur.

Melodeon. Swarthout. 1986. per. 2.95 (0-671-62573-X) PB.

Melodic & Polyrhythmic Development of John Coltrane's Spontaneous Composition in a Racist Society. Karlton E. Hester. LC 97-27571. (Studies in the History & Interpretation of Music). 1997. write for info. (0-7734-8574-0) E Mellen.

Melodic & Progressive Etudes. Matteo Carcassi. Ed. by Aaron Stang. 36p. (Orig.). (C). 1985. pap. text 8.00 (0-7692-1304-9, K04253) Wrner Bros.

Melodic Banjo. Tony Trischka. LC 75-16970. 96p. (Orig.). 1976. pap. 15.95 (0-8256-0171-1, OK63149, Oak) Music Sales.

Melodic Clawhammer. Ken Perlman. 1979. pap. 15.95 (0-8256-0226-2, OK63644, Oak) Music Sales.

Melodic Etudes for Beginning Clarinet, Level 1. Norman Heim. (Building Excellence Ser.). 24p. 1991. pap. 5.95 (1-56222-167-1, 94546) Mel Bay.

Melodic Etudes for Beginning Saxophone, Level 1. Mike Buerk. (Building Excellence Ser.). 24p. 1991. pap. 5.95 (1-56222-215-5, 94589) Mel Bay.

Melodic Index to the Works of Johann Sebastian Bach. Compiled by May D. Payne. LC 74-24035. reprint ed. 37.50 (0-404-12858-0) AMS Pr.

Melodic Organ Pedal Studies. Albert De Vito. 1969. pap. 4.95 (0-934286-42-6) Kenyon.

Melodic Perception: A Program for Self-Instruction. James C. Carlsen. 1965. text 23.95 (0-07-009975-8) McGraw.

Melodic Similarity: Concepts, Procedures & Applications. Walter B. Hewlett. 1998. pap. text 28.00 (0-262-58175-2) MIT Pr.

M

An Asterisk (*) at the beginning of an entry indicates that the title is appearing for the first time.

Melodic Technic for Bass Clef Trombone & Euphonium. Anton Slama. Ed. by Reginald H. Fink. 48p. (C). 1991. student ed. 11.00 (*0-918194-24-5*) Accura.

Melodic Tradition of Ireland. James Cowdery. LC 89-24436. (World Music Ser.). 215p. 1990. 24.00 (*0-87338-407-5*) Kent St U Pr.

Melodic Tradition of the Ambrosian Office - Antiphons. Terence Bailey & Paul Merkley. (Wissenschaftliche Abhandlungen-Musicological Studies: Vol. 50, Pt. 2). (ENG.). 656p. 1990. 160.00 (*0-931902-64-9*) Inst Mediaeval Mus.

Melodic Whistles in the Columbia River Gorge. Keith McCoy. Ed. by Charles T. Duncan. (Illus.). 136p. 1995. pap. 12.95 (*0-9618402-3-4*) Pahto Pubns.

Melodie Fatale. Laura Pender. (Amours d'Aujourd'Hui Ser.: Bk. 313). 1999. mass mkt. 4.99 (*0-373-38313-4*, 1-38313-2) Harlequin Bks.

Melodie Secrete. Trink X. Thuan. (FRE.). 390p. 1991. pap. 18.95 (*0-7859-3975-X*, 2070326233) Fr & Eur.

Melodien der Deutschen Evangelischen Kirchenlieder Aus Den Quellen Geschopft und Mitgeteilt, 6 vols. Johannes Zahn. (GER.). xxvi, 3688p. 1997. reprint ed. 1200.00 (*3-487-09318-9*) G Olms Pubs.

Melodien der Troubadours. Johann B. Beck. LC 70-39420. reprint ed. 49.50 (*0-404-08347-1*) AMS Pr.

Melodies & Memories. Nellie Melba. LC 73-107821. (Select Bibliographies Reprint Ser.). 1977. 26.95 (*0-8369-5192-1*) Ayer.

Melodies & Memories. Nellie Melba. LC 71-126694. reprint ed. 34.00 (*0-404-04287-2*) AMS Pr.

Melodies & Memories. Nellie Melba. 339p. 1990. reprint ed. lib. bdg. 79.00 (*0-7812-9103-8*, 10103) Rprt Serv.

Melodies from My Father's House: Hasidic Wisdom for the Heart & Soul. Simcha Raz. Ed. & Tr. by Dov Peretz Elkins from HEB. LC 95-82346. (Illus.). 176p. (Orig.). 1996. pap. 12.00 (*0-918834-15-5*) Growth Assoc.

Melodies from the Heart. Meldra Johnson & Fay Moore-Sines. (Illus.). 24p. (Orig.). 1987. pap. 5.95 (*0-941284-43-3*) J Shaw Studio.

Melodies Gregoriennes d'Apres la Tradition. Dom J. Pothier. vii, 306p. 1982. reprint ed. write for info. (*3-487-07199-1*) G Olms Pubs.

Melodies of Spain Acoustic. E. James Kalal. 92p. 1997. pap. 22.95 incl. audio compact disk (*0-7866-2775-1*, 95055BCD) Mel Bay.

Melodies of the Soul. Ed. by Alyssa Stokes. 1998. 69.95 (*1-57553-612-9*) Watermrk Pr.

Melodies of the Wind & Other Poems. Lee T. Rector. 89p. 1984. write for info. (*0-318-58392-5*) Rector Pub.

Melodies Orientales & Other Piano Works. Felicien David. (Music Reprint Ser.). 100p. 1982. 13.95 (*0-306-76214-5*) Da Capo.

Melodious Accord: Good Singing in Church. Alice Parker. (Illus.). 100p. (Orig.). 1991. pap. 5.95 (*0-929650-43-3*, ACCORD) Liturgy Tr Pubns.

Melodious Double-Stops (Melodies en Doubles-Cordes) Bk. 1: For Violin. J. Trott. (ITA.). 24p. 1986. pap. 6.95 (*0-7935-2599-3*, 50327290) H Leonard.

Melodious Double-Stops (Melodies en Doubles-Cordes) Bk. 2: Violin First Position. J. Trott. 24p. 1986. pap. 7.95 (*0-7935-5451-9*, 50327630) H Leonard.

Melodious Etudes for Trombone, Bk. 1. Ed. by Joannes Rochut. (Illus.). 88p. 1928. pap. 11.95 (*0-8258-0149-4*, 0-1594) Fischer Inc NY.

Melodious Guile: Fictive Pattern in Poetic Language. John Hollander. LC 88-10080. 262p. 1988. 42.50 (*0-300-04293-0*) Yale U Pr.

Melodious Guile: Fictive Pattern in Poetic Language. John Hollander. 272p. (C). 1990. reprint ed. pap. 18.00 (*0-300-04904-8*) Yale U Pr.

Melodious Women: A Poetic Celebration of Extraordinary Women. Marjorie Agosin. Tr. by Monica Bruno Galmozzi from SPA. LC 97-42693. (Discoveries Ser.). 112p. 1997. pap. text 13.95 (*0-935480-91-9*) Lat Am Lit Rev Pr.

Melodius Tears: The English Funeral Elegy from Spenser to Milton. Dennis Kay. (Oxford English Monographs). 302p. 1990. text 85.00 (*0-19-811789-2*) OUP.

Melodiya: A Soviet Russian L. P. Discography, 6. Compiled by John R. Bennett. LC 81-4247. (Discographies Ser.: No. 6). (Illus.). 832p. 1981. lib. bdg. 135.00 (*0-313-22596-6*, BME/, Greenwood Pr) Greenwood.

Melodrama: Stage Picture Screen. Ed. by Jacky Bratton et al. (Illus.). 224p. 1994. text 49.95 (*0-85170-437-9*) Ind U Pr.

Melodrama: Stage Picture Screen. Jacky Bratton & Jim Cook. Ed. by Christine Gledhill. (Illus.). 224p. 1994. pap. 23.95 (*0-85170-438-7*) Ind U Pr.

Melodrama: The Cultural Emergence of a Genre. Hays. 288p. 1999. pap. 17.95 (*0-312-22127-4*) St Martin.

Melodrama: The Cultural Emergence of a Literary Genre. Ed. by Michael Hays & Anastasia Nikolopoulou. LC 96-3321. 288p. 1996. text 45.00 (*0-312-12692-1*) St Martin.

Melodrama & Asian Cinema. Ed. by Wimal Dissanayake. LC 92-23862. (Cambridge Studies in Film). 293p. (C). 1993. text 64.95 (*0-521-41465-2*) Cambridge U Pr.

Melodrama & Meaning: History, Culture, & the Films of Douglas Sirk. Barbara Klinger. LC 93-27574. (Illus.). 224p. 1994. pap. 14.95 (*0-253-20875-0*); text 35.00 (*0-253-33199-4*) Ind U Pr.

***Melodrama & Modernity: Early Pulp Cinema & the Social Contexts of Sensationalism.** Ben Singer. 2001. pap. 19.50 (*0-231-11329-3*); text 49.50 (*0-231-11328-5*) Col U Pr.

Melodrama & the Myth of America. Jeffrey D. Mason. LC 92-46375. (Drama & Performance Studies). 268p. 1993. 31.95 (*0-253-33686-4*) Ind U Pr.

Melodrama Heute: Die Adaption melodramatischer Elemente und Strukturen im Werk von John Arden und Arden-D'Arcy. Michael Goring. (Munich Studies in English Literature: Vol. 2). (GER.). 439p. (Orig.). 1986. 50.00 (*90-6032-286-X*, Pub. by B R Gruner) Humanities.

Melodrama Theatres of the French Boulevard. John McCormick. (Theatre in Focus Ser.). (Illus.). 120p. 1982. pap. write for info. incl. sl. (*0-85964-117-1*) Chadwyck-Healey.

Melodrama Unveiled: American Theater & Culture, 1800-1850. David Grimsted. (Approaches to American Culture Ser.: No. 1). 285p. 1987. pap. 15.95 (*0-520-05996-4*, Pub. by U CA Pr) Cal Prin Full Svc.

Melodramatic Formations: American Theatre & Society, 1820-1870. Bruce A. McConachie. LC 91-44085. (Studies in Theatre History & Culture). (Illus.). 334p. 1992. text 42.95 (*0-87745-359-4*); pap. text 16.95 (*0-87745-360-8*) U of Iowa Pr.

Melodramatic Imagination. Peter Brooks. (C). 1976. pap. 17.00 (*0-300-06553-1*) Yale U Pr.

Melodramatic Tactics: Theatricalized Dissent in the English Marketplace, 1800-1885. Elaine Hadley. LC 94-42454. 318p. 1995. 45.00 (*0-8047-2403-2*) Stanford U Pr.

Melodramatic Tactics: Theatricalized Dissent in the English Marketplace, 1800-1885. Elaine Hadley. (Illus.). 318p. 1997. pap. 16.95 (*0-8047-3160-8*) Stanford U Pr.

Melodramatists. Howard Nemerov. LC 91-40801. 352p. (C). 1992. reprint ed. pap. 18.95 (*0-8262-0846-0*) U of Mo Pr.

Melody. V. C. Andrews. LC 97-160353. 384p. 1996. 23.00 (*0-671-53470-X*); per. 7.99 (*0-671-53471-8*) PB.

Melody. V. C. Andrews. 1996. 12.60 (*0-606-13603-7*, Pub. by Turtleback) Demco.

Melody. Judith Gould. 1998. 26.95 (*84-08-02230-X*) Planeta.

Melody. large type ed. V. C. Andrews. LC 96-27669. 1996. 25.95 (*0-7838-1906-4*, G K Hall Lrg Type) Mac Lib Ref.

Melody. Elswyth Thane. 1974. reprint ed. lib. bdg. 22.95 (*0-88411-953-X*) Amereon Ltd.

Melody Bk. 1: The Orgies of Abitibi. Sylvie Rancourt. Ed. by Dave Schreiner. Tr. & Illus. by Jacques Boivin. (Melody; the True Stories of a Nude Dancer Ser.). 128p. 1991. 29.95 (*0-87816-140-6*); pap. 14.95 (*0-87816-141-4*) Kitchen Sink.

Melody & Harmony in Contemporary Songwriting. Ricigliano. 1978. 30.00 (*0-935058-01-X*); student ed. 20.00 (*0-935058-02-8*) Donato Music.

Melody & the Lyric: From Chaucer to Cavaliers. John M. Gibbon. LC 65-15882. (Studies in Poetry: No. 38). 1969. reprint ed. lib. bdg. 75.00 (*0-8383-0555-5*) M S G Haskell Hse.

Melody Bingo Game. 1990. pap. text 24.95 incl. audio (*0-7935-2908-5*) H Leonard.

Melody Chords for Guitar. Allen Holdsworth. 108p. (Orig.). 1997. pap. 19.95 (*1-57424-051-X*) Centerstream Pub.

Melody Dicer. Wolfgang Amadeus Mozart. 32p. 1984. pap. 9.95 (*0-935474-09-9*) Carousel Pubns Ltd.

Melody Dicer Manuscript Book. Wolfgang Amadeus Mozart. Ed. by Carmela Mercuri. 32p. 1984. pap. text 4.95 (*0-935474-10-2*) Carousel Pubns Ltd.

Melody For Nora: One Girl's Story in The Civil War. Mark O'Sullivan. LC 94-204224. 192p. (J). (gr. 4-7). 1997. pap. 6.95 (*0-86327-425-0*, Pub. by Wolfhound Press) Irish Amer Bk.

Melody Harmonization at the Keyboard. 2nd ed. Gene J. Cho. 96p. 1996. spiral bd. 15.95 (*0-8403-7562-X*) Kendall-Hunt.

***Melody in Songwriting.** Jack Perricone. 2000. pap. 19.95 (*0-634-00638-X*, Berklee Pr) H Leonard.

Melody Lingers On: Scenes from the Golden Years of West Coast Jazz. Jo B. Fox & Jules L. Fox. LC 95-35933. (Illus.). 128p. 1996. 14.95 (*1-56474-151-6*) Fithian Pr.

Melody Lingers On: The Great Songwriters & Their Movie Musicals. Roy Hemming. LC 85-61812. (Illus.). 388p. 1999. pap. 24.95 (*1-55704-380-9*) Newmarket.

***Melody Maker History of 20th-Century Popular Music.** Nick Johnstone. (Illus.). 400p. 2000. 35.00 (*0-7475-4190-6*, Pub. by Blmsbury Pub) Trafalgar.

Melody Mooner Stayed up All Night see Lupe Luna Se Quedo Despierta Toda la Noche

Melody Mooner Stayed up All Night. Frank B. Edwards. (Illus.). 24p. (J). (ps-3). 1991. pap. 5.95 (*0-921285-01-9*, Pub. by Bungalo Books); lib. bdg. 16.95 (*0-921285-03-5*, Pub. by Bungalo Books) Firefly Bks Ltd.

Melody Mooner Takes Lessons. Frank B. Edwards. (Illus.). 24p. (J). (ps-3). 1996. pap. 4.95 (*0-921285-46-9*, Pub. by Bungalo Books); lib. bdg. 15.95 (*0-921285-47-7*, Pub. by Bungalo Books) Firefly Bks Ltd.

Melody Never Stops. Kofi Natambu. 72p. (Orig.). 1991. pap. 10.00 (*0-9622474-3-X*) Past Tents Pr.

Melody, 1987. Robert Mapplethorpe. 1993. 25.00 (*0-8212-2007-1*, Pub. by Bulfinch Pr) Little.

Melody of India Cuisine: Tasteful New Vegetarian Recipes Celebrating Soy & Tofu. Laxmi Jain & Manoj Jain. LC 92-7573. (Illus.). 221p. (Orig.). 1991. pap. 14.95 (*0-88007-195-8*) Woodbridge Pr.

Melody of Prayer: How to Personally Experience the Divine Liturgy. Stanley S. Harakas. 1979. pap. 4.95 (*0-686-27068-1*) Light&Life Pub Co MN.

***Melody of the Eagle.** Paul James. Ed. by P. E. Collins. 224p. 2000. 24.95 (*0-9678895-0-2*); pap. 14.95 (*0-9678895-1-0*) Gardenia.

Melody of Theology: A Philosophical Dictionary. Jaroslav J. Pelikan. 320p. 1988. pap. text 10.95 (*0-674-56473-1*) HUP.

Melody of Theology: A Philosophical Dictionary. Jaroslav J. Pelikan. LC 88-690. 320p. 1988. 29.95 (*0-674-56472-3*) HUP.

Melody, Rhythm, Songs & Games: A Multi-Developmental Approach. Coleen Pinar. (Illus.). 1996. teacher ed., spiral bd. 20.95 (*1-881641-54-6*) Pencil Point.

Melody III, Bk. II. Jon Gibson. 1975. pap. 10.00 (*0-89439-003-1*) Printed Matter.

Melody Unheard. Marian Niven. 296p. 1980. 10.00 (*0-8164-9217-4*) Univ South Pr.

Melody Within. Mary J. Clendenin. 152p. (Orig.). 1991. pap. 9.95 (*0-925854-04-2*) Defiant Pr.

Melody Wren's Tea Rooms of Southern Ontario. Melody Wren. LC 98-232968. 1997. pap. text 11.95 (*1-55046-201-6*, Pub. by Boston Mills) Genl Dist Srvs.

Melody Writing & Analysis. Annie O. Warburton. LC 78-5698. 188p. 1978. reprint ed. lib. bdg. 45.00 (*0-313-20426-8*, WAMW, Greenwood Pr) Greenwood.

Melomaniacs. James G. Huneker. reprint ed. 29.50 (*0-404-03388-1*) AMS Pr.

Melomaniacs. James G. Huneker. LC 69-13941. 350p. 1969. reprint ed. lib. bdg. 69.50 (*0-8371-1858-1*, HUME, Greenwood Pr) Greenwood.

Melomaniacs. James G. Huneker. (BCL1-PS American Literature Ser.). 350p. 1992. reprint ed. lib. bdg. 89.00 (*0-7812-6748-X*) Rprt Serv.

Melon: A Play. Simon Gray. (Methuen Modern Plays Ser.). 84p. (C). 1988. pap. 9.95 (*0-413-16550-7*, A0172) Heinemann.

Melon Garnishing. rev. ed. (Illus.). 96p. 2000. 24.99 (*0-939763-11-7*) Int Culinary.

Melon Garnishing: Packaged with Tools. Harvey Rosen. (Illus.). 192p. 1985. boxed set 29.99 (*0-939763-12-5*, 4435) Int Culinary.

***Melonpool Vol. II: The Voyage Home.** Steve Troop. (Ultimate Melonpool Ser.). (Illus.). viii, 202p. 2000. pap. 19.95 (*0-9672306-1-6*) Para-Troop.

Melov's Legacy. Sam Ross. Orig. Title: The Sidewalks Are Free. 308p. 1984. reprint ed. 22.00 (*0-933256-56-6*) Second Chance.

Melov's Legacy. Sam Ross. LC 84-50877. Orig. Title: The Sidewalks Are Free. 308p. 1985. reprint ed. pap. 16.00 (*0-933256-57-4*) Second Chance.

Melozzo Da Forli. Nicholas Clark. (Illus.). 160p. 1990. 95.00 (*0-85667-371-4*, Pub. by P Wilson) Hoovers TX.

Melpome: Translations of Selected Greek Lyrics with Notes. Paul Murgatroyd. 92p. (Orig.). 1989. pap. 15.00 (*90-256-0986-4*, Pub. by AM Hakkert) BookLink Distributors.

Melrose. Anthony Pagano. (Images of America Ser.). (Illus.). 128p. 1998. pap. 16.99 (*0-7524-0485-7*) Arcadia Publng.

Melrose Area. Ann S. Sherry. (Illus.). 332p. 1990. write for info. (*0-9625710-0-8*) A Sherry.

Melrose Confidential: An Unauthorized Guide to Hollywood's Hottest Address. Roberta Caploe & Jamie Caploe. LC 95-26389. (Illus.). 160p. 1996. pap. 14.95 (*0-8065-1743-3*, Citadel Pr) Carol Pub Group.

Melrose Larry Green, Everybody! Melrose L. Green. (Illus.). 252p. (Orig.). 1996. pap. 8.00 (*0-9653324-0-3*) MLG Prods.

Melrose Place: Meet the Stars of Today's Hottest New Show. Randi Reisfeld. Ed. by Lisa Clancey. 192p. (YA). (gr. 5 up). 1992. mass mkt. 4.50 (*0-671-79781-6*) PB.

Melrose Place: Sister Dearest: The Sydney & Jane Story. C. E. Moore. 304p. (Orig.). (YA). (gr. 7 up). 1996. mass mkt. 5.99 (*1-57297-087-1*) Blvd Books.

Melrose II. Anthony Pagano. LC 98-87779. (Images of America Ser.). 1998. write for info. (*0-7524-1393-7*) Arcadia Publng.

Mel's Diner. Marissa Moss. LC 93-38683. (Illus.). 32p. (J). (gr. k-3). 1996. 13.95 (*0-8167-3460-7*) BrdgeWater.

Mel's Diner. Marissa Moss. LC 93-38683. (Illus.). 32p. (J). (gr. k-3). 1996. pap. 4.95 (*0-8167-3461-5*) Troll Communs.

Mel's Diner. Marissa Moss. 1994. 10.05 (*0-606-09607-8*, Pub. by Turtleback) Demco.

Mels Reminders. Mel Krieger. 1996. pap. 4.95 (*0-944169-04-X*) Club Pacific.

Mel's Store see Phonics Is My Way Series

Melsetter House: Orkney, 1898 William Lethaby. Trevor Garnham. (Architecture in Detail Ser.). (Illus.). 60p. (C). 1993. pap. 29.95 (*0-7148-2776-2*, Pub. by Phaidon Press) Phaidon Pr.

***Melt & Mold Soap Crafting.** C. Kaila Westerman. (Illus.). 144p. 2000. pap. 18.95 (*1-58017-293-8*, 67293) Storey Bks.

Melt Bibliography. Compiled by Shirley Brod. 285p. 1987. teacher ed. 20.00 (*0-940723-03-4*) SIIS.

Melt Crystallization Technology. Gerard J. Arkenbout. LC 94-60013. 400p. 1995. pap. text 99.95 (*1-56676-181-6*) Technomic.

Melt Processed High Temperature Superconductors. M. Murakami. 380p. 1993. text 121.00 (*981-02-1244-5*) World Scientific Pub.

Melt-Spinning, Strip Casting, & Slab Casting: A Collection of Papers from the 1996 TMS Annual Meeting & Exhibition in Anaheim, California, February 4-8, 1996. Ed. by E. F. Matthys & W. G. Truckner. (Illus.). 247p. 1996. 20.00 (*0-87339-314-7*, 3147) Minerals Metals.

Melt the Icebergs! A Fresh Look at Prayer. James Handyside. 219p. 1997. pap. 8.99 (*1-56632-101-8*) Revival Lit.

***Meltdown.** 1999. 28.00 (*0-13-030408-5*) P-H.

Meltdown. Chris Archer. (Mindwarp Ser.: No. 10). (YA). (gr. 6-8). 1999. pap. 3.99 (*0-671-02810-7*, Minstrel Bks) PB.

***Meltdown.** Cliff Garnett. (T.A.L.O.N. Force Ser.: Vol. 2). 2000. mass mkt. 5.99 (*0-451-19980-4*, Sig) NAL.

Meltdown. Max Marlow. 320p. 1992. 24.95 (*0-450-53785-4*, Pub. by Hodder & Stought Ltd) Trafalgar.

***Meltdown.** John Peel. (2099 Ser.: Vol. 5). 160p. (J). (gr. 4-7). 2000. pap. 4.99 (*0-439-06034-6*) Scholastic Inc.

Meltdown. Peter Tonkin. 448p. 1996. pap. 11.95 (*0-7472-5265-3*, Pub. by Headline Bk Pub) Trafalgar.

Meltdown: Collapse of the Nuclear Dream. Aubrey. pap. 15.95 (*1-85585-017-6*, Pub. by Jonathan Cape) Trafalgar.

Meltdown: Inside the Soviet Economy. Paul C. Roberts & Karen LaFollette. 152p. 1990. pap. 19.95 (*0-932790-80-1*) Cato Inst.

Meltdown: Poems from the Core. Ed. by Betty Shipley & Nina Langley. LC 80-66372. (Illus.). 64p. 1980. pap. 3.95 (*0-936908-00-9*) Broncho Pr.

***Meltdown: Three Mile Island & the Power of Nuclear Energy: A Reporter's Story.** Wilborn Hampton. LC 00-37959. 2001. write for info. (*0-7636-0715-0*) Candlewick Pr.

Meltdown: With Notes & Tablature. 104p. 1993. per. 19.95 (*0-7935-2125-4*, 00694872) H Leonard.

Meltdown! Diet & Cookbook: Burn Fat 24 Hours a Day, Even While You Sleep. Beth E. Rosenthal. Ed. by Margaret Bradley. LC 94-90295. (Illus.). 134p. (Orig.). 1994. pap. text 15.00 (*1-885676-01-8*) Meltdown Intl.

Meltdown Man, Vol. 1. S. F. Black. (Cyber Zone Ser.). (J). 1997. pap. 3.95 (*0-8167-4279-0*) Troll Communs.

Meltdown '96: And Beyond. Doug Horton. Ed. by David Sweat. (Illus.). 65p. Date not set. 15.00 (*0-9649267-4-1*) Up on the Hill.

***Meltdown of the Russian State: The Deformation & Collapse of the State in Russia.** Piroska Mohacsi Nagy. 160p. 2000. 65.00 (*1-85898-820-9*) E Elgar.

Meltdown on Main Street. Ed. by Eric R. Bates. (Illus.). 64p. (Orig.). 1989. pap. 5.00 (*0-943810-40-X*) Southern Exposure.

Meltdown: or The Bologna Merchants. William Keisling. LC 89-24833. 224p. 1990. 14.95 (*0-9620251-2-7*); pap. 8.95 (*0-9620251-3-5*) Yardbird Bks.

Melted Coins. Franklin W. Dixon. LC 78-86722. (Hardy Boys Mystery Stories Ser.: No. 23). (Illus.). 180p. (J). (gr. 4-7). 1944. 5.95 (*0-448-08923-8*, G & D) Peng Put Young Read.

***Melted Star Journey.** Nanct Hundal. 1999. 13.50 (*0-00-224406-3*) HarpC.

***Melted Star Journey.** Nancy Hundal. 32p. 2000. pap. 6.75 (*0-00-638658-X*) HarpC.

Melting: Poems of a Frozen Man. Jerry Steinberg. 112p. (C). 1992. pap. 12.00 (*1-55022-174-4*, Pub. by ECW) Genl Dist Srvs.

Melting & Casting Aluminum. 1996. lib. bdg. 250.99 (*0-8490-8296-X*) Gordon Pr.

Melting & Casting Aluminum. American Aluminum Company Staff. (Illus.). 180p. 1993. reprint ed. pap. 14.95 (*1-57002-078-7*) Univ Publng Hse.

Melting & Casting Aluminum. Anderson. 1987. reprint ed. pap. 9.95 (*0-917914-59-7*) Lindsay Pubns.

Melting Clock. Stuart M. Kaminsky. (Toby Peters Mystery Ser.). 208p. 1993. mass mkt. 4.99 (*0-446-40304-0*, Mysterious Paperbk) Warner Bks.

Melting Furnace Design in the Glass Industry. Alexis G. Pincus. LC 78-55352. (Processing in the Glass Industry Ser.). 269p. 1980. 24.95 (*0-911993-08-8*) Ashlee Pub Co.

Melting Furnace Operation in the Glass Industry. Alexis G. Pincus. LC 77-55374. (Processing in the Glass Industry Ser.). 250p. 1980. 24.95 (*0-911993-10-X*) Ashlee Pub Co.

Melting Point. Pat Califia. 224p. 1996. pap. 11.95 (*1-55583-380-2*) Alyson Pubns.

Melting Pot: A Drama in Four Acts. Israel Zangwill. LC 74-29532. (Modern Jewish Experience Ser.). 1975. reprint ed. 21.95 (*0-405-06756-9*) Ayer.

Melting Pot: An Adventure in New York. Kenneth Roseman. (Do-It-Yourself Jewish Adventure Ser.). (Illus.). 144p. (Orig.). (J). (gr. 4-6). 1984. pap. 7.95 (*0-8074-0269-9*, 146065) UAHC.

Melting Pot: Balkan Food & Cookery. Maria Kaneva-Johnson. (Illus.). 384p. 1995. 35.00 (*0-907325-57-2*, Pub. by Prospect) Food Words.

Melting Pot: Ethnic Cuisine in Texas. Institute of Texan Cultures, Research Staff. (Illus.). 244p. 1984. 27.95 (*0-86701-050-9*) U of Tex Inst Tex Culture.

Melting Pot: Ethnic Cuisine in Texas. 2nd ed. Institute of Texan Cultures, Research Staff. (Illus.). 244p. 1989. spiral bd. 21.95 (*0-86701-006-1*) U of Tex Inst Tex Culture.

Melting Pot: The Collection. Kevin Eastman & Eric Talbot. (Illus.). 146p. (Orig.). 1995. pap. 19.95 (*0-87816-362-X*) Kitchen Sink.

Melting Pot & Beyond: Italian Americans in the Year 2000. Ed. by Jerome Krase & William Egelman. (Italian American Life Ser.: Vol. XVII). 1985. 9.95 (*0-934675-18-X*); 19.95 (*0-685-20043-4*) Am Italian.

Melting Pot & the Altar: Marital Assimilation in Early Twentieth-Century Wisconsin. Richard M. Bernard. LC 80-16287. 190p. reprint ed. pap. 58.90 (*0-7837-2977-4*, 205747700006) Bks Demand.

Melting Pot Book of Baby Names. 3rd ed. Connie L. Ellefson. (Illus.). 240p. (Orig.). 1995. pap. 12.99 (*1-55870-362-4*, Betrwy Bks) F & W Pubns Inc.

Melting Pot Cookbook. Auxiliary of Women & Infants Hospital of Rhode Isl. LC 92-31743. 1992. 11.95 (*0-87197-353-7*) Favorite Recipes.

Melting Pot Memories: The Rabinowitz Family Cookbook & Nostalgic History. Illus. by Danielle Solomonic & Eva Seligman. LC 99-94263. viii, 342p. 1999. 18.95 (*0-9671633-0-7*) Jan Bart Pubns.

Melting-Pot Mistake. Henry P. Fairchild. Ed. by Gerald N. Grob. LC 76-46076. (Anti-Movements in America Ser.). 1977. reprint ed. lib. bdg. 23.95 (*0-405-09949-5*) Ayer.

Melting Pot Pattern Features. Neila Bredehoft et al. (Illus.). 34p. (Orig.). 1996. pap. 12.00 (*1-885503-09-1*) Cherry H Pubns.

An Asterisk (*) at the beginning of an entry indicates that the title is appearing for the first time.

Melting Pot Soldiers: The Union's Ethnic Regiments. William L. Burton. LC 97-50163. (North's Civil War Ser.: No. 4). xvi, 283p. 1998. 32.50 (*0-8232-1827-9*); pap. 19.95 (*0-8232-1828-7*) Fordham.

Melting Pot Soldiers: The Union's Ethnic Regiments. William L. Burton. LC 87-3299. 292p. reprint ed. pap. 90.60 (*0-7837-2175-7*, 204251300004) Bks Demand.

Melting Pots: Family Stories & Recipes. Judith E. Weber. LC 93-42507. (Family Ties Ser.). (Illus.). 64p. (J). (ps-4). 1994. lib. bdg. 14.95 (*1-881889-53-X*) Silver Moon.

Melting the Darkness: The Dyad & Principles of Clinical Practice. Warren S. Poland. 1996. 45.00 (*1-56821-816-8*) Aronson.

Melting the Earth: The Evolution of Ideas About Volcanic Eruptions. Haraldur Sigurdsson. LC 98-20299. (Illus.). 272p. 1999. 30.00 (*0-19-510665-2*) OUP.

Melting the Stone: A Journey Around My Father. Richard Olivier. 232p. 1995. pap. 18.50 (*0-88214-370-0*) Spring Pubns.

Melton & Pawl's Guide to Civil War Artillery Projectiles. Jack W. Melton, Jr. & Lawrence E. Pawl. 96p. 1996. pap., per. 9.95 (*0-614-30270-6*) Kennesaw Mtn.

Melton & Pawl's Guide to Civil War Artillery Projectiles. Jack W. Melton, Jr. & Lawrence E. Pawl. LC 94-80240. (Illus.). 96p. 1996. 19.95 (*0-9635861-1-4*) Kennesaw Mtn.

Melton Art Reference Library, 2 vols., Set, Vols. 1 & 2. Howard E. Melton. 390p. 1993. spiral bd., ring bd. 195.00 (*0-9640163-0-3*) Melton Art Ref.

Meltwater. Etta R. Weigl. LC 82-60191. (Illus.). 80p. 1982. 10.95 (*0-9608824-0-5*); pap. 5.95 (*0-9608824-1-3*) Stereopticon Pr.

Meltzer's Intensive Coronary Care. 5th ed. Kathleen Dracup. (C). 1995. pap. text 39.95 (*0-8385-4276-X*, A4276-0) Appleton & Lange.

Meluk (Roe) large type ed. Alice Andrew et al. (ESK., Illus.). 8p. (J). (gr. k-3). 1999. pap. text 6.00 (*1-58084-104-X*) Lower Kuskokwim.

Melungeons. Bonnie Ball. Ed. by James W. Mintz. (Illus.). 114p. 1992. pap. 8.95 (*0-932807-74-7*) Overmountain Pr.

Melungeons: An Annotated Bibliography: References in Both Fiction & Nonfiction. large type ed. Barbara T. Langdon. 70p. 1998. pap. 8.00 (*1-887745-10-6*) Dogwood TX.

***Melungeons: Examining an Appalachian Legend.** Pat Spurlock Elder. LC 99-65222. (Illus.). vii, 390p. 1999. pap. 19.95 (*1-929483-02-3*, MI) Contnuity Pr.

Melungeons: The Resurrection of a Proud People. An Untold Story of Ethnic Cleansing in America. rev. ed. N. Brent Kennedy. (Illus.). 208p. 1996. pap. 17.95 (*0-86554-516-2*, MUP/P143) Mercer Univ Pr.

Melusine see Historia de la Linda Melosina

Melusine. Lynne Reid Banks. 256p. (YA). (gr. 5 up). 1997. mass mkt. 4.99 (*0-380-79135-8*, Avon Bks) Morrow Avon.

Melusine, Pt. 1. Jean D'Arras. Ed. by Alexander K. Donald. (EETS, ES Ser.: No. 68). 1969. reprint ed. 63.00 (*0-527-00272-0*) Periodicals Srv.

Melusine: A Ballad & a Diary, Vol. 1. Antonio Porta. Tr. by Anthony Molino from ITA. (Essential Poets Ser.: No. 49). 88p. 1993. pap. 10.00 (*0-920717-58-6*) Guernica Editions.

Melusine: A Mystery. Lynne Reid Banks. LC 88-32798. (Charlotte Zolotow Bk.). 256p. (YA). (gr. 7 up). 1989. 12.95 (*0-06-020394-3*) HarpC Child Bks.

Melusine: A Mystery. Lynne Reid Banks. LC 88-32798. (Charlotte Zolotow Bk.). 224p. (YA). (gr. 7 up). 1991. mass mkt. 3.95 (*0-06-447054-7*, HarpTrophy) HarpC Child Bks.

Melusine: A Mystery. Lynne Reid Banks. 1997. 9.60 (*0-606-13604-5*, Pub. by Turtleback) Demco.

Melusine of Lusignan: Founding Fiction in Late Medieval France. Ed. by Donald Maddox & Sara Sturm-Maddox. LC 95-52471. (C). 1996. 50.00 (*0-8203-1823-X*) U of Ga Pr.

Melusine or Devil Take Her! A Romantic Novel. Charlotte Haldane. Ed. by R. Reginald & Douglas Melville. LC 77-84231. (Lost Race & Adult Fantasy Ser.). 1978. reprint ed. lib. bdg. 29.95 (*0-405-10984-9*) Ayer.

Melutovna: A Novel. Hannah Berman. LC 74-27963. (Modern Jewish Experience Ser.). 1975. reprint ed. 33.95 (*0-405-06694-5*) Ayer.

Melvil Dewey: The Man & the Classification. Ed. by Gordon Stevenson & Judith Kramer-Greene. LC 83-1607. 210p. 1983. 20.00 (*0-910608-34-2*) OCLC Forest Pr.

Melville. Geoffrey Stone. (BCL1-PS American Literature Ser.). 336p. 1993. reprint ed. lib. bdg. 89.00 (*0-7812-6993-8*) Rprt Serv.

Melville: A Biography. Laurie Robertson-Lorant. LC 98-4899. (Illus.). 736p. 1998. reprint ed. pap. 22.95 (*1-55849-145-7*) U of Mass Pr.

Melville & His Circle, 1877-1891. William B. Dillingham. LC 96-767. 1996. 29.95 (*0-8203-1856-6*) U of Ga Pr.

Melville & Male Identity. Charles J. Haberstroh. LC 78-75178. 152p. 1970. 26.50 (*0-8386-2321-2*) Fairleigh Dickinson.

Melville & Melville Studies in Japan, 103. Ed. by Kenzaburo Ohashi. LC 92-36613. (Contributions in American Studies: No. 103). 272p. 1993. 67.95 (*0-313-28622-1*, OMS, Greenwood Pr) Greenwood.

Melville & Repose: The Rhetoric of Humor in the American Renaissance. John Bryant. LC 92-46150. 336p. (C). 1993. text 65.00 (*0-19-507782-2*) OUP.

Melville & the Politics of Identity: From King Lear to Moby Dick. Julian Markels. LC 92-21497. 176p. 1993. text 29.95 (*0-252-01995-4*); pap. text 13.95 (*0-252-06302-3*) U of Ill Pr.

Melville & the Visual Arts: Ionian Form, Venetian Tint. Douglas Robillard. LC 97-6780. (Illus.). 1997. 32.00 (*0-87338-575-6*) Kent St U Pr.

Melville Boys. Norm Foster. LC 86-186795. 114p. (Orig.). 1997. pap. 10.95 (*0-88754-452-5*) Theatre Comm.

Melville Dissertations, 1924-1980: An Annotated Bibliography & Subject Index. John Bryant. LC 83-5683. 166p. 1983. lib. bdg. 59.95 (*0-313-23811-1*, BMD/, Greenwood Pr) Greenwood.

Melville Encyclopedia: The Novels. 2nd ed. Compiled by Kathleen E. Kier. LC 90-70385. xxii, 1220p. 1994. 99.00 (*0-87875-453-9*) Whitston Pub.

Melville Log, Vol. 1. Jay Leyda. 492p. Date not set. 30.95 (*0-8488-2355-9*) Amereon Ltd.

Melville Log, Vol. 2. Jay Leyda. 528p. Date not set. 31.95 (*0-8488-2356-7*) Amereon Ltd.

Melville Sea Dictionary: A Glossed Concordance & Analysis of the Sea Language in Melville's Nautical Novels. Jill B. Gidmark. LC 82-6122. 534p. 1982. lib. bdg. 99.50 (*0-313-23330-6*, GMD/, Greenwood Pr) Greenwood.

Melville, Shame, & the Evil Eye: A Psychoanalytic Reading. Joseph Adamson. LC 96-8837. (SUNY Series in Psychoanalysis & Culture). 457p. (C). 1996. text 65.50 (*0-7914-3279-3*); pap. text 21.95 (*0-7914-3280-7*) State U NY Pr.

Melville Weston Fuller: Chief Justice of the United States, 1888-1910. Willard L. King. LC 67-12152. 1993. pap. text 3.95 (*0-226-43579-2*, P258) U Ch Pr.

Melville y el Mundo Hispanico. Jose De Onis. (UPREX, Estudios Literarios Ser.: No. 38). 143p. (C). 1974. pap. 1.50 (*0-8477-0038-0*) U of PR Pr.

Melville's Anatomies. Samuel Otter. LC 97-50369. 418p. 1998. 48.00 (*0-520-20581-2*, Pub. by U CA Pr) Cal Prin Full Svc.

Melville's Anatomies. Samuel Otter. LC 97-50369. 418p. 1999. pap. 22.50 (*0-520-20582-0*, Pub. by U CA Pr) Cal Prin Full Svc.

Melville's Angles of Vision. Axel C. Bredahl. LC 73-185795. (University of Florida Humanities Monographs: No. 37). 84p. reprint ed. pap. 30.00 (*0-7837-0595-6*, 204094300019) Bks Demand.

Melville's Art of Democracy. Nancy Fredricks. LC 94-15272. 155p. 1995. 35.00 (*0-8203-1682-2*) U of Ga Pr.

Melville's "Benito Cereno" An Interpretation, with an Annotated Text & a Concordance. William D. Richardson. LC 86-70369. 246p. (C). 1987. lib. bdg. 35.00 (*0-89089-274-1*) Carolina Acad Pr.

Melville's City: Literary & Urban Form in Nineteenth-Century New York. Wyn Kelley. (Studies in American Literature & Culture: No. 100). (Illus.). 326p. (C). 1996. text 64.95 (*0-521-56054-3*) Cambridge U Pr.

Melville's Classical Allusions: A Comprehensive Index & Glossary, 2. Gail H. Coffler. LC 84-22513. 153p. 1985. lib. bdg. 55.00 (*0-313-24626-2*, CMV/, Greenwood Pr) Greenwood.

Melville's Confidence Men & American Politics in the 1850s. Helen P. Trimpi. LC 86-32158. (Transactions Ser.: Vol. 49). (Illus.). 339p. 1987. 49.50 (*0-208-02130-2*) CT Acad Arts & Sciences.

Melville's Evermoving Dawn: Centennial Essays. Ed. by John Bryant & Robert Milder. LC 96-42483. 1997. 45.00 (*0-87338-562-4*) Kent St U Pr.

***Melville's Folk Roots.** Kevin J. Hayes. LC 98-45710. 152p. 1999. 28.00 (*0-87338-625-6*) Kent St U Pr.

Melville's Israel Potter: Reflections on the American Dream. Alexander Keyssar. LC 76-99522. (LeBaron Russell Briggs Prize Honors Essays in English Ser.). 72p. 1969. pap. 2.70 (*0-674-56475-8*) HUP.

Melville's Later Novels. William B. Dillingham. LC 85-1192. 448p. 1986. 40.00 (*0-8203-0799-8*) U of Ga Pr.

Melville's Major Fiction: Politics, Theology, & Imagination. James Duban. LC 83-2432. (Illus.). 284p. (C). 1983. 30.00 (*0-87580-086-6*) N Ill U Pr.

Melville's Moby Dick: An American Nekyia. rev. ed. Edward F. Edinger. LC 96-22610. (Illus.). 160p. 1995. pap. 16.00 (*0-919123-70-8*, Pub. by Inner City Bks) BookWorld.

Melville's Muse: Literary Creation & the Forms of Philosophical Fiction. John Wenke. LC 95-3560. 272p. 1996. 35.00 (*0-87338-527-6*) Kent St U Pr.

Melville's Poetry: Toward the Enlarged Heart. Aaron Kramer. LC 79-160457. 146p. 1972. 26.50 (*0-8386-1002-1*) Fairleigh Dickinson.

Melville's Protest Theism: The Hidden & Silent God in "Clarel" Stan Goldman. LC 92-19791. 240p. 1993. lib. bdg. 30.00 (*0-87580-174-9*) N Ill U Pr.

Melville's Science: Devilish Tantalization of the Gods! Richard D. Smith. LC 93-17405. (Studies in 19th Century American Literature: No. 3). 384p. 1993. text 67.00 (*0-8153-1308-X*, H1710) Garland.

Melville's Sources. Mary K. Bercaw. 213p. 1987. 44.95 (*0-8101-0734-1*) Northwestern U Pr.

Melville's Thematics of Form: The Great Art of Telling the Truth. Edgar A. Dryden. LC 68-55612. (Illus.). 240p. 1968. reprint ed. pap. 74.40 (*0-608-04061-4*, 206479700011) Bks Demand.

Melville's Use of Spenser. Carole Moses. (American University Studies: American Literature: Ser. XXIV, Vol. 6). 235p. (C). 1989. text 39.95 (*0-8204-0832-8*) P Lang Pubng.

Melville's Vision of America: A New Interpretation of Moby Dick. John Fentress Gardner. LC 77-80051. (Illus.). 47p. 1977. pap. 1.50 (*0-913098-07-8*) Orion Society.

Melvin B. Tolson, 1898-1966: Plain Talk & Poetic Prophecy. Robert M. Farnsworth. (Illus.). 336p. 1984. text 38.00 (*0-8262-0433-3*) U of Mo Pr.

Melvin B. Tolson's Harlem Gallery: A Literary Analysis. Mariann Russell. LC 80-50306. 153p. reprint ed. pap. 47.50 (*0-7837-2359-8*, AU0042400006) Bks Demand.

Melvin Calvin: Following the Trail of Light, a Scientific Odyssey. Melvin Calvin. LC 92-3989. (Profiles, Pathways, & Dreams Ser.). 175p. 1992. text 36.00 (*0-8412-1828-5*, Pub. by Am Chemical) OUP.

Melvin Gorham's Interpretation of Richard Wagner's The Rhinegold. Melvin Gorham. LC 89-92364. (Illus.). 128p. (Orig.). 1990. pap. 7.00 (*0-914752-28-6*) Sovereign Pr.

Melvin Gorham's Interpretation of Richard Wagner's The Valkyrie: A Play in Three Acts. Melvin Gorham & John Harland. LC 86-63393. 96p. (Orig.). 1987. pap. 6.00 (*0-914752-24-3*) Sovereign Pr.

Melvin Gutman Collection of Antique Jewelry. Frwd. by Henry B. Caldwell. (Illus.). 48p. 1966. 5.00 (*0-940744-07-4*) Chrysler Museum.

***Melvin Sokolsky: Seeing Fashion.** Photos by Melvin Sokolsky. (Illus.). 192p. 2000. 65.00 (*1-892041-36-7*) Arena Editions.

Melvin the Pelican - Musical. Sarah Froeber & Mike Hamer. 40p. Date not set. pap. 5.95 (*0-87129-994-1*, MC4) Dramatic Pub.

Melvin's Adventure. Mary J. Mason. (Illus.). 16p. (J). (ps-6). 1997. pap. 12.00 (*1-890864-01-3*) Breath of Life.

Melvin's Melons. Sherry T. Vaughn. (Illus.). 64p. (Orig.). (J). (gr. 3-5). 1996. pap. 5.95 (*1-57072-022-3*) Overmountain Pr.

MELVYL Online Catalog Reference Manual. 1988. 30.00 (*0-913248-02-9*) UCDLA.

Memar Marqah: The Teaching of Marqah, 2 vols., Set. John MacDonald. (C). 1963. 89.25 (*3-11-005567-8*) De Gruyter.

Mema's House, Mexico City: On Transvestites, Queens & Machos. Annick Prieur. LC 97-25986. 1997. pap. 16.95 (*0-226-68257-9*); lib. bdg. 50.00 (*0-226-68256-0*) U Ch Pr.

Member: An Autobiography. John Galt. 176p. 1989. pap. 40.00 (*0-7073-0464-4*, Pub. by Mercat Pr Bks) St Mut.

Member: The Radical, 2 bks. in 1. John Galt. 280p. 1997. pap. 12.95 (*0-86241-642-6*, Pub. by Canongate Books) Interlink Pub.

***Member Acceptance of Electronic Access Systems: Innovators vs. Laggards.** Nicolette Lemmon et al. 74p. 1999. pap. 100.00 (*1-880572-36-2*, 1752-43) Filene Res.

Member Assistance Programs in the Workplace: The Role of Labor in the Prevention & Treatment of Substance Abuse. Samuel B. Bacharach et al. LC 94-31790. (Bulletin Ser.: 69). 104p. 1994. pap. text 12.95 (*0-87546-336-3*, ILR Press) Cornell U Pr.

Member in Particular. Girault M. Jones. 160p. 1987. pap. 10.95 (*0-918769-10-8*) Univ South Pr.

Member of the Club: Fighting for My Place in a Racially Polarized World. Lawrence O. Graham. 1995. 22.95 (*0-15-158838-4*) Harcourt.

Member of the Club: Reflections on Life in a Racially Polarized World. Lawrence O. Graham. 320p. 1996. pap. 13.50 (*0-06-098430-9*) HarpC.

Member of the Family. Nick Vasile et al. 384p. 1995. 5.99 (*0-8125-2046-7*) Forge NYC.

***Member of the Family: A Novel.** Susan S. Merrell. LC 99-34923. 368p. 2000. 25.00 (*0-06-019280-1*, Pub. by Harper SF) HarpC.

Member of the Third House see Collected Works of Hamlin Garland

Member of the Third House. Hamlin Garland. LC 68-57526. (Muckrakers Ser.). reprint ed. lib. bdg. 16.00 (*0-8398-0656-6*) Irvington.

Member of the Third House. Hamlin Garland. (Collected Works of Hamlin Garland). 1988. reprint ed. lib. bdg. 59.00 (*0-7812-1216-2*) Rprt Serv.

Member of the Wedding see Best American Plays: Third Series, 1945-51

Member of the Wedding. Carson McCullers. 160p. (YA). (gr. 9-12). 1979. mass mkt. 5.99 (*0-553-25051-5*) Bantam.

Member of the Wedding. Carson McCullers. LC 51-10532. 1963. pap. 7.95 (*0-8112-0093-0*, NDP153, Pub. by New Directions) Norton.

Member of the Wedding. Carson McCullers. 1950. 9.60 (*0-606-01060-2*, Pub. by Turtleback) Demco.

***Member Segmentation & Profitability: Current Practice & Future Possibilities.** Ella Mae Matsumura et al. 58p. 1999. pap. 100.00 (*1-880572-38-9*, 1752-45) Filene Res.

Members: How to Get Them, How to Keep Them. Helen Little. (Illus.). 96p. 1999. pap. 24.95 (*1-928892-02-7*, 9902) Panacea Press.

Members for Life: Proven Service & Retention Strategies for Health Clubs. Richard Gerson. LC 98-49538. (Illus.). 240p. 1999. 29.00 (*0-7360-0003-8*, BGER0003, YMCA USA) Human Kinetics.

Members of Congress: A Bibliography. Robert U. Goehlert et al. LC 95-26756. 507p. (YA). (gr. 11). 1995. text 117.00 (*0-87187-865-8*) Congr Quarterly.

Members of One Body: Prophets, Priests & Kings: An Ecclesiology of Mission. Paula J. Miller. LC 98-30621. 300p. 1999. pap. text 14.95 (*0-8189-0854-8*) Alba.

Members of Parliament in Western Europe: Roles & Behaviour. Ed. by Wolfgang C. Muller & Thomas Saalfeld. LC 97-764. 296p. 1997. 45.00 (*0-7146-4821-3*, Pub. by Irish Acad Pr); pap. 19.50 (*0-7146-4369-6*, Pub. by Irish Acad Pr) Intl Spec Bk.

Members of the Club: A Look at One Hundred ALA Presidents. Wayne A. Wiegand & Dorothy Steffens. (Occasional Papers: No. 182). 1988. pap. 2.50 (*0-685-34545-9*) U of Ill Grad Sch.

Members of the Club: The Coming of Age of Executive Women. Dawn-Marie Driscoll & Carol R. Goldberg. 250p. 1993. 24.95 (*0-02-908065-7*) Free Pr.

***Members of the Regiment: Army Officers' Wives on the Western Frontier, 1865-1890, 187.** Michele J. Nacy. LC 99-45564. (Contributions in American History Ser.). 144p. 2000. write for info. (*0-313-30998-1*) Greenwood.

Members Only. David Berreby. 2000. write for info. (*0-316-09030-1*) Little.

Members' Rights: A Blueprint for Transforming the Conservative Party into a Mass Membership Organisation Capable of Winning the Next Election. Philip G. Gott et al. LC 98-169092. 51 p. 1997. write for info. (*0-86129-145-X*) Bow Pubns.

Member's Word from God, \. Joan Waters. 1998. pap. text 5.95 (*1-881524-20-5*) Milligan Bks.

Membership & Morals: The Personal Uses of Pluralism in America. Nancy L. Rosenblum. LC 97-27937. 425p. 1998. text 29.95 (*0-691-01689-5*, Pub. by Princeton U Pr) Cal Prin Full Svc.

***Membership & Morals: The Personal Uses of Pluralism in America.** Nancy L. Rosenblum. 2000. pap. text 18.95 (*0-691-05023-6*, Pub. by Princeton U Pr) Cal Prin Full Svc.

Membership Applications for Clubs, Associations & Organizations: Samples to Duplicate & Use. Carrol, Frieda, Research Division Staff. 40p. 1984. ring bd. 23.95 (*0-318-04334-3*) Prosperity & Profits.

Membership Development: 101 Ways to Get & Keep Your Members. 5th ed. Mark Levin. 176p. 1995. reprint ed. pap. 29.95 (*0-9660080-0-6*) BAI Inc.

Membership Directory. rev. ed. Ed. by Eleanor Brownridge. 224p. 5.00 (*0-614-05244-0*, MEM0694) ASFE.

Membership Directory, 1999-2001. Ed. by Donald W. Smith. 138p. 1999. pap. 25.00 (*0-935991-33-6*) Am Topical Assn.

Membership Directory, 1996-97. 1995. pap. 25.00 (*1-880407-13-2*) Edit Freelancers.

Membership Directory, 1996. 1996. 40.00 (*0-318-01511-0*, 12040) Indus Fabrics.

Membership Directory of the American Crystallographic Association, 1992. 104p. (C). 1992. pap. text. write for info. (*0-937140-35-X*) Am Crystallographic.

Membership in the Reformed Church. Herman Ridder. 1980. pap. 1.95 (*0-686-23484-7*) Rose Pub MI.

***Membership Marketing.** Susan Nicholais. LC 00-26163. (Core Competencies in Membership Management Ser.). 2000. write for info. (*0-88034-164-5*) Am Soc Assn Execs.

Membership Mystique: How to Create Income & Influence With Membership Programs. Richard P. Trenbeth. LC 85-70785. (Illus.). 280p. 1993. 39.00 (*0-930807-01-4*, 600171) Fund Raising.

Membership of the Massachusetts General Court. Robert E. Wall. LC 90-23080. (Early American History Ser.). 624p. 1991. reprint ed. 25.00 (*0-8240-6294-9*) Garland.

Membership Organization: Achieving Top Performance Through the New Workplace Community. Jane G. Seiling. LC 97-26478. 232p. 1997. 27.95 (*0-89106-110-X*, 7763, Davies-Black Pub) Consulting Psychol.

***Membership Plus 6, 8 vols.** Parsons Technology Staff. 1999. 269.99 (*1-57264-322-6*) Parsons Tech.

Membership Promotion. World Council of Credit Unions, Inc. Staff. 144p. (C). 1988. per. 10.00 (*0-8403-4929-7*) Kendall-Hunt.

Membership Records of Seventh Day Baptist Churches in Western New York & Northwestern Pennsylvania, 1800-1900. Ilou M. Sanford. 107p. (Orig.). 1996. pap. 22.50 (*0-7884-0462-8*, S052) Heritage Bk.

Membership Records of Seventh Day Baptists of Central New York State, 1797-1948s. Ilou M. Sanford. 127p. (Orig.). 1994. pap. text 24.00 (*0-7884-0015-0*) Heritage Bk.

Membership Roles in Field Research. Patricia A. Adler & Peter Adler. (Qualitative Research Methods Ser.: Vol. 6). 96p. (C). 1987. text 24.00 (*0-8039-2760-6*); pap. text 10.50 (*0-8039-2578-6*) Sage.

***Membership Tools.** Contrib. by Concordia Publishing Company Staff. 1998. cd-rom 129.95 (*0-570-09619-7*) Concordia.

Membracidae of Ohio. Herbert Osborn. (Bulletin Ser.: No. 37). 1940. pap. text 3.00 (*0-86727-036-5*) Ohio Bio Survey.

Membranas de las Celulas. Antonio Pena. (Ciencia para Todos Ser.). (SPA.). pap. 6.99 (*968-16-2463-7*, Pub. by Fondo) Continental Bk.

Membrane - Membrane Interactions. Ed. by Norton B. Gilula. LC 78-62215. (Society of General Physiologists Ser.: No. 34). (Illus.). 230p. 1980. reprint ed. pap. 71.30 (*0-7837-9526-2*, 206027500005) Bks Demand.

Membrane Abnormalities & Disease, 2 vols., Vol. 1. Ed. by Mariano Tao. 160p. 1982. 94.00 (*0-8493-6160-5*, RB152, CRC Reprint) Franklin.

Membrane Abnormalities & Disease, 2 vols., Vol. 2. Ed. by Mariano Tao. 192p. 1982. 101.00 (*0-8493-6161-3*, CRC Reprint) Franklin.

Membrane Abnormalities in Hypertension, 2 Vols., Vol. 1. C. Kwan. Ed. by Chiu-Yin Kwan. LC 88-26305. 208p. 1989. 116.00 (*0-8493-4527-8*, RC685, CRC Reprint) Franklin.

Membrane Abnormalities in Hypertension, 2 Vols., Vol. 2. Ed. by Chiu-Yin Kwan. LC 88-23605. 224p. 1989. 123.00 (*0-8493-4528-6*, RC685, CRC Reprint) Franklin.

Membrane Activation in Immunologically Relevant Cells. Ed. by E. Lovell Becker. (Progress in Allergy Ser.: Vol. 42). (Illus.). xiv, 312p. 1988. 191.50 (*3-8055-4699-8*) S Karger.

Membrane Alterations in Cancer. Ed. by Akira Makita et al. (GANN Monographs on Cancer Research: No. 29). 312p. 1983. 85.00 (*0-306-41565-8*, Plenum Trade) Perseus Pubng.

Membrane Alternative: Energy Implications for Industry. Ed. by J. A. Howell. (Watt Committee Reports: No. 21). 172p. 1990. mass mkt. 159.95 (*1-85166-476-9*) Elsevier.

M

An Asterisk (*) at the beginning of an entry indicates that the title is appearing for the first time.

Membrane Analysis. J. A. Higgins & J. M. Graham. LC 97-26419. (Introduction to Biotechniques Ser.). (Illus.). 176p. 1997. pap. 34.95 (0-387-91507-9) Spr-Verlag.

Membrane & Separation Conference: Proceedings. 1990. pap. 350.00 (0-89336-708-7, DMC90) BCC.

Membrane & Separations Technology Industry Review. Anna Crull. 306p. 1998. 1500.00 (1-56965-510-3, DMS97) BCC.

Membrane & Separations Technology Industry Reviews. Ed. by Anna Crull & Sandi Grant. 316p. 1995. 1500.00 (1-56965-331-3) BCC.

Membrane Anomalies of Tumor Cells. Ed. by F. Homburger & Donald F. Wallach. (Progress in Experimental Tumor Research Ser.: Vol. 22). (Illus.). 1978. 129.75 (3-8055-2775-6) S Karger.

Membrane Associated Abnormalities - Sickle Cell Diseases - Membrane Linked Diseases, Vol. II. S. Tsuyoshi Ohnishi. 304p. 1993. lib. bdg. 115.00 (0-8493-8092-8, RC641) CRC Pr.

Membrane Biochemistry. Edith Sim. (Outline Studies in Biology). 80p. 1982. pap. 9.95 (0-412-23810-1, NO. 6691) Chapman & Hall.

Membrane Bioenergetics. V. P. Skulachev. (Illus.). 500p. 1988. 319.00 (0-387-18335-3) Spr-Verlag.

Membrane Biogenesis. Ed. by J. A. Op Den Kamp. (NATO ASI Series H: Vol. 16). (Illus.). viii, 477p. 1988. 206.95 (0-387-18566-6) Spr-Verlag.

M

Membrane Biogenesis & Protein Targeting. Ed. by Walter Neupert & Roland Lill. LC 92-24428. (New Comprehensive Biochemistry Ser.: Vol. 22). 344p. 1992. 197.75 (0-444-89638-4) Elsevier.

Membrane Biophysics. H. Ti Tien & A. Ottova. (Membrane Science & Technology Ser.). 648p. 1999. write for info. (0-444-82930-X) Elsevier.

Membrane Concentrate Disposal. (Illus.). 414p. 1993. pap. 115.00 (0-89867-710-6, 90637) Am Water Wks Assn.

Membrane Digestion: Physiology & Pathology. Ed. by A. M. Ugolve. 1990. 68.00 (0-8493-7126-0, QP) CRC Pr.

Membrane Dynamics & Transport of Normal & Tumor Cells: International Symposium, Debrecen, Hungary, July 6-10, 1983. J. C. Somogyi. (Symposia Biologica Hungarica Ser.: No. 26). 388p. (C). 1984. 114.00 (963-05-3889-X, Pub. by Akade Kiado) St Mut.

Membrane Filtration: Applications, Techniques, & Problems. Ed. by Bernard J. Dutka. LC 81-4103. (Pollution Engineering & Technology Ser.: Vol. 17). (Illus.). 628p. reprint ed. pap. 194.70 (0-608-08931-1, 206956600005) Bks Demand.

Membrane Filtration for Microbial Removal. Joseph G. Vacangelo et al. LC 97-154544. (Illus.). 185p. 1997. pap. 195.00 (0-89867-894-3, 90715) Am Water Wks Assn.

Membrane Fluidity: Biophysical Techniques & Cellular Regulation. Ed. by Morris Kates & Arnisa Kuksis. LC 79-93347. (Experimental Biology & Medicine Ser.: Vol. 1). (Illus.). 464p. 1980. 99.50 (0-89603-020-2) Humana.

Membrane Formation & Modification. Ingo Pinnau & Benny D. Freeman. LC 99-39049. (ACS Symposium Ser.: No. 744). (Illus.). 288p. 1999. text 130.00 (0-8412-3604-6, Pub. by Am Chemical) OUP.

Membrane Fusion. Jan Wilshut & Dick Hoekstra. (Illus.). 938p. 1990. text 295.00 (0-8247-8301-8) Dekker.

Membrane Fusion Techniques, Pt. A. Ed. by Nejat Duzgunes et al. (Methods in Enzymology Ser.: Vol. 220). (Illus.). 433p. 1993. text 94.00 (0-12-182121-8) Acad Pr.

Membrane Fusion Techniques, Vol. 221, Pt. B. Ed. by Nejat Duzgunes et al. (Methods in Enzymology Ser.). (Illus.). 462p. 1993. text 89.00 (0-12-182122-6) Acad Pr.

Membrane Hypothesis of Aging. Roberta W. Imre. 220p. 1994. lib. bdg. 210.00 (0-8493-6738-7) CRC Pr.

Membrane Lipid Oxidation, Vol. I. Ed. by Carmen Vigo-Pelfrey. 224p. 1989. boxed set 217.00 (0-8493-4070-5, RB170) CRC Pr.

Membrane Lipid Oxidation, Vol. 2. Ed. by Carmen Vigo-Pelfrey. 240p. 1990. boxed set 218.00 (0-8493-4071-3, RB170) CRC Pr.

Membrane Lipid Oxidation, Vol. 3. Ed. by Carmen Vigo-Pelfrey. 312p. 1990. boxed set 202.00 (0-8493-4072-1, RB170) CRC Pr.

Membrane Microfilters in Biotechnology - Pharmaceutical Separations. 128p. 1993. 1500.00 (0-89336-962-4, C-167) BCC.

Membrane Microfilters in Environmental Management, No. C-168. 126p. 1993. 1500.00 (0-89336-995-0) BCC.

Membrane-Mimetic Approach to Advanced Materials. Janos H. Fendler. LC 94-192355. (Advances in Polymer Science Ser.: Vol. 113). 1994. 135.95 (0-387-57237-6) Spr-Verlag.

Membrane Mimetic Chemistry: Characterizations & Applications of Micelles, Microemulsions, Monolayers, Bilayers, Vesicles, Host-Guest Systems & Polyions. Janos H. Fendler. LC 82-2583. (Wiley-Interscience Publications). 536p. reprint ed. pap. 166.20 (0-7837-2373-3, 204005900006) Bks Demand.

Membrane Organization & Phospholipid Interaction of Cytochrome P-450. Ed. by Klaus Ruckpaul & Horst Rein. (Frontiers in Biotransformation Ser.: Vol. 5). 210p. 1991. lib. bdg. 155.00 (3-05-500461-2, Pub. by Akademie Verlag) Wiley.

Membrane Physiology: Physiology of Membrane Disorders, Chapters 1-23 2nd ed. T. E. Andreoli et al. (Illus.). 384p. (C). 1987. reprint ed. text 59.50 (0-306-42697-8, Kluwer Plenum) Kluwer Academic.

Membrane Physiology of Invertebrates. Ed. by Ronald B. Podesta et al. LC 81-17534. (Illus.). 678p. reprint ed. pap. 200.00 (0-7837-0914-5, 204121900019) Bks Demand.

Membrane Physiopathology. Ed. by Ghassan Bkaily. (Developments in Cardiovascular Medicine Ser.). 432p. (C). 1994. text 198.00 (0-7923-3062-5) Kluwer Academic.

Membrane Potential-Dependent Ion Channels in Cell Membrane: Phylogenetic & Developmental Approaches. Susumu Hagiwara. LC 83-9578. (Distinguished Lecture Series of the Society of General Physiologists: Vol. 3). 127p. 1983. reprint ed. pap. 39.40 (0-608-03415-0, 206411400008) Bks Demand.

Membrane Processes. R. Rautenbach & R. Albrecht. LC 87-23211. 470p. 1989. 785.00 (0-471-91110-0) Wiley.

Membrane Processes: A Technology Guide. Ed. by P. T. Cardew & M. S. Level. (Special Publication Ser.: Vol. 238). viii, 326p. 1999. pap. 100.00 (0-85404-454-X) Spr-Verlag.

Membrane Processes Conference Proceedings. (Illus.). 900p. 1993. pap. 65.50 (0-89867-697-5, 20308) Am Water Wks Assn.

Membrane Processes in Separation & Purification. Ed. by Joao G. Crespo & Karl W. Boddekker. LC 94-17901. (NATO ASI Series E, Applied Sciences: Vol. 272). 1994. text 326.50 (0-7923-2929-5) Kluwer Academic.

Membrane Protein Expression Systems: A User's Guide. Ed. by G. W. Gould. (First Practical Handbook Ser.). (Illus.). 310p. (Orig.). (C). 1993. pap. text 54.40 (1-85578-031-3, Pub. by Portland Pr Ltd) Ashgate Pub Co.

Membrane Protein Models. Ed. by J. B. Findlay. 240p. 1996. 150.00 (1-85996-080-4, Pub. by Bios Sci) Bks Intl VA.

Membrane Protein Structure: Experimental Approaches. Stephen H. White. (APS Methods in Physiology Series Society: No. 1). (Illus.). 416p. 1994. text 69.50 (0-19-507112-3) OUP.

Membrane Protein Transport Vol. 1: A Multi-Volume Treatise, Vol. 1. Ed. by Stephen S. Rothman. 304p. 1995. 128.50 (1-55938-907-9) Jai Pr.

Membrane Protein Transport Vol. 1: A Multi-Volume Treatise, Vol. 2. Ed. by Stephen S. Rothman. 280p. 1996. 128.50 (1-55938-983-4) Jai Pr.

Membrane Protein Transport Vol. 1: A Multi-Volume Treatise, Vol. 3. Ed. by Stephen S. Rothman. 312p. 1996. 128.50 (1-55938-989-3) Jai Pr.

Membrane Proteins: Proceedings of the Membrane Protein Symposium. Ed. by Steven C. Goheen. (Illus.). 782p. (C). 1987. 85.00 (0-9618315-0-2) Bio Rad Labs.

Membrane Proteins: Structure, Function & Expression Control International Symposium on Membrane Proteins, Fukuoka, February 1996. Ed. by Naotaka Hamasaki & Katsuyoshi Mihara. LC 97-143660. (Illus.). x, 414p. 1997. 248.00 (3-8055-6465-1) S Karger.

Membrane Proteins - Structures, Interactions & Models: Proceedings of the Twenty-Fifth Jerusalem Symposium on Quantum Chemistry & Biochemistry Held in Jerusalem, Israel, May 18-21, 1992. Ed. by Alberte Pullman & Joshua Dordrecht. LC 92-26604. (Jerusalem Symposia on Quantum Chemistry & Biochemistry Ser.: Vol. 25). 516p. (C). 1992. text 302.00 (0-7923-1951-6) Kluwer Academic.

Membrane Proteins & Their Interactions with Lipids. Ed. by Roderick A. Capaldi. LC 76-58609. (Membrane Proteins Ser.: No. 1). (Illus.). 272p. reprint ed. pap. 84.40 (0-7837-0607-3, 204095500019) Bks Demand.

Membrane Proteins in Energy Transduction. Ed. by Roderick A. Capaldi. LC 79-17584. (Membrane Proteins Ser.: No. 2). (Illus.). 542p. reprint ed. pap. 168.10 (0-7837-0821-1, 204113500019) Bks Demand.

Membrane Receptors & Enzymes As Targets of Insecticidal Action. Ed. by J. Marshall Clark & Fumio Matsumura. LC 86-4908. 266p. 1986. 65.00 (0-306-42239-5, Plenum Trade) Perseus Pubng.

Membrane Receptors, Dynamics, & Energetics. Ed. by K. W. Wirtz. LC 87-10150. (NATO ASI Series A, Life Sciences: Vol. 133). (Illus.). 406p. 1987. 110.00 (0-306-42596-3, Plenum Trade) Perseus Pubng.

Membrane Science & Technology. Ed. by Yoshihito Osada & Hidemi Nakagawa. (Illus.). 488p. 1992. text 215.00 (0-8247-8694-7) Dekker.

***Membrane Separation.** Savage. 108p. 1998. pap. 1800.00 (0-471-33147-3) Wiley.

Membrane Separation Equipment. Richard K. Miller et al. (Market Research Survey Ser.: No. 282). 50p. 1996. 200.00 (1-55865-308-2) Future Tech Surveys.

Membrane Separation in Biotechnology. McGregor. (Bioprocess Technology Ser.: Vol. 1). (Illus.). 408p. 1986. text 180.00 (0-8247-7465-5) Dekker.

Membrane Separation Systems: Recent Developments & Future Directions. R. W. Baker et al. LC 90-23675. (Illus.). 451p. 1991. 129.00 (0-8155-1270-8) Noyes.

Membrane Separation Systems Market (Europe) Market Intelligence Staff. 387p. 1992. 3600.00 (1-56753-860-6, E1594) Frost & Sullivan.

Membrane Separations Technology: Principles & Applications. Ed. by Richard D. Noble & S. A. Stern. (Membrane Science & Technology Ser.: Vol. 2). 738p. 1995. 389.50 (0-444-81633-X) Elsevier.

Membrane Spectroscopy. Ed. by E. Grell. (Molecular Biology, Biochemistry & Biophysics Ser.: Vol. 31). (Illus.). 512p. 1981. 145.00 (0-387-10332-5) Spr-Verlag.

Membrane Structure & Function: In Focus. W. H. Evans & J. M. Graham. (In Focus Ser.). (Illus.). 98p. (C). 1989. pap. text 19.95 (0-19-963004-6) OUP.

***Membrane Structure in Disease & Drug Therapy.** G. Zimmer. LC 00-29049. 2000. write for info. (0-8247-0361-8) Dekker.

Membrane Systems: Analysis & Design: Applications in Biotechnology, Biomedicine, & Polymer Science. Wolf R. Vieth. 360p. 1993. 98.95 (0-471-03719-2) Wiley.

Membrane Technology: Applications to Industrial Wastewater Treatment. Ed. by Ana Caetano. 208p. (C). 1994. text 119.00 (0-7923-3209-1) Kluwer Academic.

***Membrane Technology & Applications.** Richard W. Baker. 528p. 1999. 99.95 (0-07-135440-9) McGraw.

Membrane Technology Conference Proceedings: February 23-26, 1997, New Orleans, LA. LC 97-146652. (Illus.). 1997. write for info. (0-89867-891-9) Am Water Wks Assn.

Membrane Technology in the Chemical Industry. 91p. 1989. 23.00 (92-1-116465-6, 89.II.E.28) UN.

Membrane Technology in Wastewater Management. O. O. Hart & C. A. Buckley. (Water Science & Technology Ser.: Vol. 25). 402p. 1992. 165.00 (0-08-042189-X, Pergamon Pr) Elsevier.

***Membrane Technology in Water & Wastewater Treatment.** Ed. by P. Hillis. 280p. 2000. 139.00 (0-85404-800-6, Pub. by Royal Soc Chem) Spr-Verlag.

Membrane Transduction Mechanisms. fac. ed. Ed. by Richard A. Cone & John E. Dowling. LC 78-65280. (Society of General Physiologists Ser.: No. 33). (Illus.). 248p. pap. 76.90 (0-7837-7257-2, 204704800005) Bks Demand.

***Membrane Transport: A Practical Approach.** Ed. by Stephen A. Baldwin. (The Practical Approach Ser.: Vol. 230). (Illus.). 352p. 2000. text 110.00 (0-19-963705-9); pap. text 55.00 (0-19-963704-0) OUP.

Membrane Transport: People & Ideas. Ed. by Daniel C. Tosteson. (American Physiological Society Book). (Illus.). 420p. 1989. text 65.00 (0-19-520773-4) OUP.

Membrane Transport in Biology 5. Ed. by Gerhard H. Giebisch et al. (Illus.). 430p. 1992. 147.00 (0-387-54621-9) Spr-Verlag.

Membrane Transport of Antineoplastic Agents. Ed. by I. D. Goldman. (International Encyclopedia of Pharmacology & Therapeutics Ser.: Section 118). (Illus.). 421p. 1986. 235.00 (0-08-032007-4, Pergamon Pr) Elsevier.

Membrane Transport Processes in Organized Systems: Physiology of Membrane Disorders, Chapters 24-41. 2nd ed. T. E. Andreoli et al. LC 87-18655. (Illus.). 408p. (C). 1987. reprint ed. text 59.50 (0-306-42698-6, Kluwer Plenum) Kluwer Academic.

Membrane Transporters. Michael Kavanaugh. (Handbooks of Receptors & Channels Ser.). 2000. 94.95 (0-8493-8323-4) CRC Pr.

Membrane Transporters as Drug Targets. Ed. by G. L. Amidon & W. Sadee. LC 99-37278. (Pharmaceutical Biotechnology Ser.: Vol. 12). (Illus.). 445p. (C). 1999. write for info. (0-306-46094-7, Plenum Trade) Perseus Pubng.

Membranes, 2 vols., Vol. 2. Ed. by George Eisenman. LC 75-163920. (Illus.). 576p. reprint ed. pap. 178.60 (0-7837-0736-3, 204106000002) Bks Demand.

Membranes, 2 vols., Vol. 3. Ed. by George Eisenman. LC 75-163920. (Illus.). 556p. reprint ed. pap. 172.40 (0-7837-0737-1, 204106000003) Bks Demand.

Membranes: Macroscopic Systems & Models, Vol. 1. Ed. by George Eisenman. LC 80-1618. 357p. reprint ed. pap. 110.70 (0-608-13697-2, 205508500001) Bks Demand.

Membranes: Metaphors of Invasion in Nineteenth-Century Literature, Science, & Politics. Laura Otis. LC 98-29763. (Medicine & Culture Ser.). 248p. 1999. 45.00 (0-8018-5996-4) Johns Hopkins.

***Membranes: Metaphors of Invasion in Nineteenth-Century Literature, Science & Politics.** Laura Otis. (Medicine & Culture Ser.). 224p. 2000. pap. 17.95 (0-8018-6527-1) Johns Hopkins.

Membranes: Specialized Functions in Plants. Ed. by M. Smallwood et al. (Illus.). 650p. 1996. 215.00 (1-85996-200-9, Pub. by Bios Sci) Coronet Bks.

Membranes & Circadian Rhythms. Ed. by T. Vanden Driessche et al. (Illus.). 238p. 1995. pap. 104.00 (3-540-60101-5) Spr-Verlag.

Membranes & Disease. International Conference on Biological Membranes S. Ed. by Liana Bolis et al. LC 75-30235. (Illus.). 422p. reprint ed. pap. 130.90 (0-7837-7113-4, 204694200004) Bks Demand.

Membranes & Ion Transport, Vol. 1. Ed. by E. Edward Bittar. LC QH0601.M45. 494p. reprint ed. pap. 153.20 (0-608-14367-7, 201617600001) Bks Demand.

Membranes & Membrane Processes. Ed. by E. Drioli & M. Nakagaki. LC 86-5076. 676p. 1986. 130.00 (0-306-42270-0, Plenum Trade) Perseus Pubng.

Membranes & Molecular Assemblies: The Synkinetic Approach. Jurgen-Hinrich Fuhrhop & Jurgen Koning. Ed. by J. Fraser Stoddart. (Monographs in Supramolecular Chemistry). 230p. 1994. 131.00 (0-85186-732-4, R6732) CRC Pr.

Membranes & Other Extendons. Yuval Ne'Eman & E. Eizenberg. 250p. (C). 1995. text 68.00 (981-02-0630-5); pap. text 36.00 (981-02-0631-3) World Scientific Pub.

Membranes & Sensory Transduction. Ed. by Giuliano Colombetti & Francesco Lenci. LC 84-3373. 396p. 1984. 95.00 (0-306-41439-2, Plenum Trade) Perseus Pubng.

Membranes & Transport, Vol. 1. Ed. by Anthony N. Martonosi. LC 82-3690. 722p. 1982. 110.00 (0-306-40853-8, Plenum Trade) Perseus Pubng.

Membranes & Transport, Vol. 2. Ed. by Anthony N. Martonosi. LC 82-3690. 712p. 1982. 110.00 (0-306-40854-6, Plenum Trade) Perseus Pubng.

Membranes for the Nineties: Surface Modification. BCC Staff. LC 97-120759. 174p. 1990. 2850.00 (0-89336-739-7, C112) BCC.

Membranes in Bioprocessing: Theory & Applications. Ed. by J. A. Howell et al. LC 92-20213. (Applied Biotechnology Ser.). 1993. write for info. (1-85166-890-X) Elsevier.

Membranes in Gas Separation & Enrichment, No. 62. Ed. by Boc Limited Research University. (Illus.). 414p. (Orig.). (C). 1987. pap. text 72.00 (0-85186-676-X, Pub. by Royal Soc Chem) Spr-Verlag.

Membranes in Ground Engineering. Peter R. Rankilor. LC 80-40504. (Illus.). 387p. reprint ed. pap. 120.00 (0-8357-3827-2, 203655100004) Bks Demand.

Membranes, Metabolism & Dry Organisms. Ed. by A. Carl Leopold. LC 86-47646. (Comstock Bk.). (Illus.). 352p. 1986. 55.00 (0-8014-1979-4) Cornell U Pr.

Membranes, Mitochondria, & Connective Tissue see Submicroscopic Cytochemistry

Membranes of Cells. 2nd ed. Philip L. Yeagle. LC 93-17184. 349p. 1993. text 83.00 (0-12-769041-7) Acad Pr.

Membranes of Cells. 2nd ed. Philip L. Yeagle. LC 93-17184. (Illus.). 349p. 1993. text 75.00 (0-12-769001-8) Acad Pr.

Meme et l'Autre: Espace et Rapports de Pouvoir dans le Roman Francais (1871-1914), Vol. 62. Cosmas K. Badasu. (Currents in Comparative Romance Languages & Literatures Ser.). XIV, 207p. (C). 1998. text 45.95 (0-8204-3836-7) P Lang Pubng.

***Meme Machine.** Susan Blackmore. LC 98-49180. 288p. 1999. 25.00 (0-19-850365-2) OUP.

***Meme Machine.** Susan Blackmore. 288p. 2000. pap. 14.95 (0-19-286212-X) OUP.

Meme Mes Critiques Ratent la Cible. Charles M. Schulz. (Peanuts Ser.). (FRE.). (J). 1985. 9.95 (0-8288-4533-6) Fr & Eur.

Meme un Enfant see Even a Child: Poems

Memecyleae. Thomas Morley. LC 76-13371. (Flora Neotropica Monographs: No. 15). (Illus.). 295p. 1976. pap. 22.00 (0-89327-000-8) NY Botanical.

Memed le Faucon. Yachar Kemal. (FRE.). 1981. pap. 12.95 (0-7859-2442-6, 2070372766) Fr & Eur.

Memed le Mince. Yachar Kemal. (FRE.). 1979. pap. 12.95 (0-7859-2418-3, 2070371174) Fr & Eur.

Memed, My Hawk. Yashar Kemal. Tr. by Edouard Roditi from TUR. 1993. pap. 12.00 (0-00-217112-0, Pub. by HarpC) HarpC.

Memed, My Hawk. Yashar Kemal. 352p. 1998. mass mkt. 11.00 (1-86046-391-6) Harvill Press.

Memento. Eleanora Brownleigh. 512p. 1987. mass mkt. 3.95 (0-8217-2037-6, Zebra Kensgtn) Kensgtn Pub Corp.

Memento. Alexandra Roceric. 1982. 5.00 (0-917944-06-2) Am Inst Writing Res.

***Memento de l'Investigateur Promoteur.** T. Dupin-Spriet & A. Spriet. 70p. 1999. 52.25 (3-8055-6844-4) S Karger.

Memento de l'Investigateur Promoteur. 2nd rev. ed. Alain Spriet & Therese Dupin-Spriet. 70p. 1997. pap. 41.75 (3-8055-6459-7) S Karger.

Memento Mori. Richard Flood. Ed. by Elsa Longhauser. (Illus.). 12p. 1985. pap. 20.00 (1-58442-033-2) Galleries at Moore.

Memento Mori. Lewitt. 1996. mass mkt. 5.99 (0-8125-3481-6) Tor Bks.

Memento Mori. Shariann Lewitt. 288p. 1995. 21.95 (0-312-85625-3) Tor Bks.

Memento Mori. Shariann Lewitt. 1997. pap. 14.95 (0-312-86294-6, Pub. by Tor Bks) St Martin.

***Memento Mori.** Muriel Spark. LC 99-58767. 2000. pap. 11.95 (0-8112-1438-9, Pub. by New Directions) Norton.

Memento Mori, the Gravestones of Early Long Island, 1680-1810. Richard F. Welch. LC 83-9027. (Illus.). 104p. 1983. pap. 14.00 (0-911357-01-7) Friends Long Island.

Memento of Finland: A Musical Legacy. Joyce E. Hakala. LC 96-92975. (Illus.). xviii, 440p. (Orig.). 1997. pap. 28.00 (0-9656820-1-3) Pikebone.

Mementoes: Poems from Hollywood. Mark Dunster. 11p. 1999. pap. 5.00 (0-89642-790-0) Linden Pubs.

Memento's The "Wonder" Years Scrapbook. Victoria J. Malyurek. i, 33p. (Orig.). (J). (gr. k-12). 1995. pap. 5.95 (1-889294-05-5) Victorias Pub.

Memere in the Mirror: A Collection of Verses. Rita D. Wilbert. 78p. 1995. pap., per. 7.95 (0-9648375-0-1) Frollies Pub.

Memes of Translation: The Spread of Ideas in Translation Theory. Andrew Chesterman. LC 97-16461. (Benjamins Translation Library: Vol. 22). vii, 219p. 1997. lib. bdg. 69.00 (1-55619-706-3) J Benjamins Pubng Co.

Memewars. Adeena Karasick. LC 94-195141. (Illus.). 112p. 1994. pap. 11.95 (0-88922-344-0, Pub. by Talonbks) Genl Dist Srvs.

Memily. Stephen Cosgrove. LC 99-158475. (Illus.). 1994. write for info. (0-8431-3792-4) Price Stern.

Memily. rev. ed. Stephen Cosgrove. LC 94-25728. (Serendipity Bks.). (Illus.). 32p. (J). (ps-3). 1995. pap. 4.99 (0-8431-3822-X, Price Stern) Peng Put Young Read.

Memling Studies. E. Peters. LC 98-209367. 1998. 87.95 (90-6831-950-7, Pub. by Peeters Pub) Bks Intl VA.

Memmler's Structure & Function of the Human Body. 7th ed. Barbara Janson Cohen & Dena Lin Wood. 416p. pap. text 34.95 (0-7817-2438-4) Lppncott W & W.

***Memmler's Structure of Function of the Human Body.** 8th ed. Barbara Janson Cohen & Dena Lin Wood. LC 99-37062. 384p. 2000. text. write for info. (0-7817-2113-X) Lppncott W & W.

Memmler's Study Guide for Structure & Function of the Human Body. 7th ed. Barbara Janson Cohen & Dena Lin Wood. 320p. pap. text 18.95 (0-7817-2115-6) Lppncott W & W.

Memmler's Study Guide for the Human Body in Health & Disease. 9th ed. Barbara Janson Cohen & Dena Lin Wood. 320p. pap. text 18.95 (0-7817-2111-3) Lppncott W & W.

Memmler's the Human Body in Health & Disease. 9th ed. Barbara Janson Cohen & Dena Lin Wood. 544p. text 39.95 (0-7817-2439-2) Lppncott W & W.

Memnoch the Devil. Anne Rice. (Vampire Chronicles: Bk. 5). 480p. 1996. pap. 14.00 (0-345-38940-9) Ballantine Pub Grp.

Memnoch the Devil. Anne Rice. (Vampire Chronicles: Bk. 5). 368p. 1995. 25.00 (0-679-44101-8) Knopf.

An Asterisk (*) at the beginning of an entry indicates that the title is appearing for the first time.

Memnoch the Devil. limited ed. Anne Rice. (Vampire Chronicles: Bk. 5). 354p. 1995. boxed set 150.00 (*0-9631925-4-X*) B E Trice.

Memo: Learner's Vocabulary German (English) Gernot Haublein et al. 128p. 1995. 14.95 (*3-468-49793-8*); 14.95 (*3-468-49794-6*) Langenscheidt.

Memo: New Soviet Voices on Foreign & Economic Policy. Ed. by Steve Hirsch. LC 89-15907. 655p. 1989. reprint ed. pap. 200.00 (*0-608-00700-5*, 206147200009) Bks Demand.

Memo: Vocabulary Building Text. Gernot Haublein et al. 200p. 1995. 22.95 (*3-468-49791-1*) Langenscheidt.

Memo Book Cards: New York City. 2000. 5.95 (*0-930137-18-3*) Looseleaf Law.

Memo from Darryl F. Zanuck: The Golden Years at 20th Century-Fox. Ed. by Rudy Behlmer. LC 92-32865. (Illus.). 288p. 1995. pap. 14.00 (*0-8021-3332-0*, Grove) Grove-Atltic.

Memo from David O. Selznick. Selected by Rudy Behlmer. LC 89-36530. (Illus.). 518p. 1989. pap. 18.95 (*0-573-60601-3*) S French Trade.

***Memo from David O. Selznick: The Creation of Gone with the Wind & Other Motion-Picture Classics--as Revealed in the Producer's Private Letters, Telegrams, Memorandums & Autobiographical Remarks.** David O. Selznick. Ed. by Rudy Behlmer & Martin Scorsese. LC 99-43161. (Modern Library Movies Ser.). (Illus.). 416p. 2000. pap. 15.95 (*0-375-75531-4*) Modern Lib NY.

Memo 3: In Search of Answers in the Post-Soviet Era. Ed. by Steve Hirsch. LC 92-20574. 275p. 1992. reprint ed. pap. 85.30 (*0-608-00702-1*, 206147400009) Bks Demand.

Memo to a Heart. large type ed. Norma Newcomb. (Linford Romance Library). 240p. 1996. pap. 16.99 (*0-7089-7833-9*, Linford) Ulverscroft.

Memo to All Employees: Poetry by Daniel X. O'Neil. Daniel X. O'Neil. (Illus.). 48p. 1995. 12.00 (*0-9646137-2-7*) Juggernaut.

Memo to Self: Songs of Jewish Living. Ruth Lewis. 1996. 14.95 (*1-56871-104-2*) Feldheim.

Memo to the Boss from Mack: A Contemporary Rendering of the Prince by Niccolo Machiavelli. W. T. Brahmstedt. (Illus.). 104p. 1986. pap. 12.95 (*0-88280-111-2*) ETC Pubns.

Memo 2: Soviets Examine Foreign Policy for a New Decade. Ed. by Steve Hirsch. LC 90-45432. 334p. 1991. reprint ed. pap. 103.60 (*0-608-00701-3*, 206147300009) Bks Demand.

Memo Y Leo, 1. Tomie De Paola. (SPA., Illus.). 32p. (ps-1). 1999. pap. text 6.95 (*980-257-223-3*, Pub. by Ediciones Ekare) Kane-Miller Bk.

Memoir. Edward Crankshaw. 1999. pap. write for info. (*0-670-80405-3*) Viking Penguin.

Memoir. John A. Hannah. (Illus.). 140p. 1980. 12.00 (*0-87013-214-8*) Mich St U Pr.

Memoir. Honor Moore. LC 88-25647. 79p. (Orig.). 1988. pap. 11.95 (*0-9619111-1-5*) Chicory Blue.

Memoir. John Murrell. 124p. 1990. 10.00 (*0-317-91357-3*) Playsmith.

***Memoir.** Dick Schaap. 2001. write for info. (*0-380-97512-2*) Morrow Avon.

***Memoir.** Russell E. Train. LC 00-190622. (Illus.). 416p. 2000. write for info. (*0-9700616-2-5*) R E Train.

Memoir: My Life & Themes Conor C. O'Brien. LC 98-233933. 460 p. 1998. write for info. (*1-85371-877-7*) Poolbeg Pr.

***Memoir: My Life & Themes.** Conor C. O'Brien. 2000. 30.00 (*0-8154-1064-6*) Cooper Sq.

Memoir & Genealogy of John Poore: Ten Generations, 1615-1880. Alfred Poore. 333p. 1989. reprint ed. pap. 50.00 (*0-8328-0975-6*); reprint ed. lib. bdg. 58.00 (*0-8328-0974-8*) Higginson Bk Co.

Memoir & Letters. Thomas Seddon. Ed. by John P. Seddon. LC 72-148300. reprint ed. 39.50 (*0-404-05668-7*) AMS Pr.

Memoir & Letters of Captain W. Glanville Evelyn of the 4th Regiment, King's Own, from North America, 1774-1776. Ed. by G. D. Scoll. LC 71-140882. (Eyewitness Accounts of the American Revolution Ser.). (Illus.). 1971. reprint ed. 13.95 (*0-405-01209-8*) Ayer.

Memoir & Letters of Charles Sumner, 4 vols., Set. Edward L. Pierce. LC 78-82211. (Anti-Slavery Crusade in America Ser.). 1970. reprint ed. 88.95 (*0-405-00650-0*) Ayer.

Memoir & Letters of Charles Sumner, 4 Vols., Set. Edward L. Pierce. (Black Heritage Library Collection). 1977. reprint ed. 96.95 (*0-8369-8641-5*) Ayer.

Memoir & Letters of Charles Sumner, 4 vols., Vol. 1. Edward L. Pierce. LC 78-82211. (Anti-Slavery Crusade in America Ser.). 1970. reprint ed. 23.95 (*0-405-00675-6*) Ayer.

Memoir & Letters of Charles Sumner, 4 vols., Vol. 2. Edward L. Pierce. LC 78-82211. (Anti-Slavery Crusade in America Ser.). 1970. reprint ed. 23.95 (*0-405-00676-4*) Ayer.

Memoir & Letters of Charles Sumner, 4 vols., Vol. 3. Edward L. Pierce. LC 78-82211. (Anti-Slavery Crusade in America Ser.). 1970. reprint ed. 23.95 (*0-405-00677-2*) Ayer.

Memoir & Letters of Charles Sumner, 4 vols., Vol. 4. Edward L. Pierce. LC 78-82211. (Anti-Slavery Crusade in America Ser.). 1970. reprint ed. 23.95 (*0-405-00678-0*) Ayer.

Memoir & Letters of Sara Coleridge. Sara Coleridge. LC 76-37677. reprint ed. 55.00 (*0-404-56736-3*) AMS Pr.

Memoir & Official Correspondence of General John Stark: Also a Biography of Captain Phinebas Stevens & of Col. Robert Rogers. Caleb Stark. 528p. 1999. reprint ed. pap. 32.00 (*0-7884-1088-1*, S705) Heritage Bk.

Memoir & Official Correspondence of General John Stark, with Notices of Several Other Officers of the Revolution. Caleb Stark. LC 72-8760. (American Revolutionary Ser.). 512p. reprint ed. lib. bdg. 62.50 (*0-8398-1884-X*) Irvington.

Memoir & Poems of Phillis Wheatley, a Native African & a Slave. Phillis Wheatley. LC 76-83898. (Black Heritage Library Collection). 1977. 20.95 (*0-8369-8686-5*) Ayer.

Memoir & Remains of R. M. M'Cheyne. Andrew A. Bonar. 1978. 35.99 (*0-85151-084-1*) Banner of Truth.

Memoir Concerning the French Settlements & French Settlers in the Colony of Rhode Island. Elisha R. Potter. (Illus.). 138p. 1996. reprint ed. pap. 14.00 (*0-8063-0280-1*, 4690) Clearfield Co.

Memoir from Antproof Case. Mark Helprin. 1995. 24.00 (*0-15-100097-2*) Harcourt.

Memoir from Antproof Case. Mark Helprin. LC 94-43626. 528p. 1996. pap. 14.00 (*0-380-72733-1*, Avon Bks) Morrow Avon.

Memoir from Antproof Case. large type ed. Mark Helprin. 1995. 25.95 (*1-56895-256-2*, Compass) Wheeler Pub.

Memoir in Two Voices. Francois Mitterrand & Elie Wiesel. Tr. by Richard Seaver & TImothy Bent. 192p. 1996. 21.45 (*1-55970-338-5*, Pub. by Arcade Pub Inc) Time Warner.

Memoir in Two Voices. Francois Mitterrand & Elie Wiesel. Tr. by Richard Seaver & Timothy Bent. LC 95-53369. 1997. pap. 11.45 (*1-55970-379-2*, Pub. by Arcade Pub Inc) Time Warner.

***Memoir of a Cold War Soldier.** Richard E. Mack. LC 00-36878. 2001. write for info. (*0-87338-675-2*) Kent St U Pr.

Memoir of a French & Indian War Soldier: "Jolicoeur" Charles Bonin. Andrew Gallup. (Illus.). 254p. (Orig.). 1993. pap. text 21.00 (*1-55613-872-5*) Heritage Bk.

Memoir of a Friend: Louis Massignon. Herbert Mason. LC 87-40349. 160p. 1988. text 22.00 (*0-268-01365-9*) U of Notre Dame Pr.

Memoir of a Pastoral Counseling Practice. Robert L. Menz. LC 97-10894. 95p. 1997. 29.95 (*0-7890-0268-X*, Haworth Pastrl); pap. 14.95 (*0-7890-0269-8*, Haworth Pastrl) Haworth Pr.

Memoir of a Race Traitor. Mab Segrest. 274p. 1994. 30.00 (*0-89608-475-2*); pap. 15.00 (*0-89608-474-4*) South End Pr.

Memoir of a Thinking Radish. large type ed. Peter Brian Medawar. 16p. 1989. reprint ed. 19.95 (*1-85089-301-2*, Pub. by ISIS Lrg Prnt) Transaction Pubs.

Memoir of a Tour to Northern Mexico: Connected with Col. Doniphan's Expedition in 1846 & 1847. Frederick A. Wislizenus. (American Biography Ser.). 141p. 1991. reprint ed. lib. bdg. 59.00 (*0-7812-8423-6*) Rprt Serv.

Memoir of Benjamin Robbins Curtis, 2 vols. Benjamin R. Curtis. LC 77-75298. (American Scene Ser.). 1970. reprint ed. 115.00 (*0-306-71267-9*) Da Capo.

Memoir of Bookie's Son. Sidney Offit. 176p. 1996. pap. 10.95 (*0-312-14368-0*) St Martin.

Memoir of Captain C. Seton Fleming. F. P. Fleming. 1976. 27.00 (*0-934085-01-3*, J M C & Co) Amereon Ltd.

Memoir of Colonel Benjamin Tallmadge. Benjamin Tallmadge. LC 67-29041. (Eyewitness Accounts of the American Revolution Ser.). 1975. reprint ed. 17.95 (*0-405-01123-7*) Ayer.

Memoir of Colonel Benjamin Tallmadge. Benjamin Tallmadge. (American Biography Ser.). 70p. 1991. reprint ed. lib. bdg. 59.00 (*0-7812-8377-9*) Rprt Serv.

***Memoir of Colonel Seth Warner.** large type enl. ed. Daniel Chipman. 84p. 2000. 12.95 (*1-928837-30-1*) Essence of Vermont.

Memoir of David Scott, R. S. A. William B. Scott. LC 70-144685. (Illus.). 449p. reprint ed. 57.50 (*0-404-05646-6*) AMS Pr.

Memoir of Dr. Samuel Gridley Howe. Julia W. Howe. (Notable American Authors Ser.). 1992. reprint ed. lib. bdg. 75.00 (*0-7812-3219-8*) Rprt Serv.

Memoir of Eli Whitney, Esq. Denison Olmsted. LC 72-5065. (Technology & Society Ser.). 90p. 1977. reprint ed. 19.95 (*0-405-04716-9*) Ayer.

Memoir of George Edmund Street, R. A., 1824-1881. Arthur E. Street. LC 70-173141. 441p. 1972. reprint ed. 21.95 (*0-405-09007-2*, Pub. by Blom Pubns) Ayer.

Memoir of George Fred Cooke. William Dunlap. (Notable American Authors Ser.). 1992. reprint ed. lib. bdg. 75.00 (*0-7812-2717-8*) Rprt Serv.

Memoir of Hungary, 1944-48. Sandor Marai. Tr. by Albert Tuzla. LC 97-119594. 426p. (C). 1996. pap. text 26.95 (*1-85866-064-5*) Ctrl Europ Univ.

Memoir of Indian Wars & Other Occurrences by the Late Colonel Stuart of Greenbrier. John Stuart. Ed. by Charles A. Stuart. LC 75-140883. (Eyewitness Accounts of the American Revolution Ser.). 1971. reprint ed. 21.00 (*0-405-01211-X*) Ayer.

Memoir of Italo Svevo. Livia V. Svevo. Tr. by Isabel Quigly from ITA. LC 89-63597. xiv, 178p. 1990. 28.95 (*0-910395-57-8*) Marlboro Pr.

Memoir of Italo Svevo. Livia V. Svevo. Tr. by Isabel Quigly. 1991. pap. 10.95 (*0-910395-58-6*) Marlboro Pr.

***Memoir of James Jackson: The Attentive & Obedient Scholar, Who Died in Boston, October 31, 1833, Aged Six Years & Eleven Months, by His Teacher Miss Susan Paul.** Susan Paul. Ed. by Lois Brown. LC 99-51781. 160p. 2000. pap. 14.00 (*0-674-00237-7*) HUP.

Memoir of James Jackson, Jr., M. D., with Extracts from His Letters to His Father & Medical Cases Collected by Him. James Jackson. LC 72-180579. (Medicine & Society in America Ser.). 452p. 1972. reprint ed. 28.95 (*0-405-03956-5*) Ayer.

Memoir of James Jackson, Jr., M. D., with Extracts from His Letters to His Father, & Medical Cases, Collected by Him. James Jackson. (American Biography Ser.). 444p. 1991. reprint ed. lib. bdg. 89.00 (*0-7812-8208-X*) Rprt Serv.

Memoir of Jane Austen, by Her Nephew. James E. Austen-Leigh. (BCL1-PR English Literature Ser.). 235p. 1992. reprint ed. lib. bdg. 79.00 (*0-7812-7428-1*) Rprt Serv.

Memoir of Jemima Wilkinson, a Preacheress of the 18th Century. David Hudson. LC 78-134417. reprint ed. 37.50 (*0-404-08475-3*) AMS Pr.

Memoir of John Codman D. D. William Allen. (Works of William Allen). 1989. reprint ed. lib. bdg. 79.00 (*0-7812-1771-7*) Rprt Serv.

Memoir of Lieutenant Colonel Tench Tilghman, Secretary & Aide to Washington. Tench Tilghman. (American Biography Ser.). 176p. 1991. reprint ed. lib. bdg. 59.00 (*0-7812-8391-4*) Rprt Serv.

Memoir of Lieutenant Colonel Tench Tilghman, Secretary & Aide to Washington, Together with an Appendix Containing Revolutionary Journals & Letters Hitherto Unpublished. Tench Tilghman. LC 79-140884. (Eyewitness Accounts of the American Revolution Ser.). 1971. reprint ed. 21.95 (*0-405-01210-1*) Ayer.

Memoir of Marco Parenti: A Life in Medici Florence. Mark Phillips. LC 87-45533. 298p. 1987. reprint ed. pap. 92.40 (*0-608-07138-2*, 206736400009) Bks Demand.

Memoir of Mary Ann. Dominican Nuns Staff. LC 88-43574. 112p. 1991. 16.95 (*0-913720-69-0*) Beil.

Memoir of Maurice Magnus. D. H. Lawrence. Ed. by Keith Cushman. LC 87-22671. (Illus.). 158p. 1987. 30.00 (*0-87685-716-0*) Black Sparrow.

Memoir of Mrs. Barbauld, Including Letters & Notices of Her Family & Friends. Anna L. Le Breton. LC 73-172311. reprint ed. 39.50 (*0-404-07397-2*) AMS Pr.

Memoir of My Sister St. Therese (Counseils et Souvenirs) see My Sister Saint Therese: By Sister Genevieve of the Holy Face

***Memoir of No. 1 in Particular.** Harris. 2000. 26.00 (*0-465-02844-6*, Pub. by Basic); pap. 16.00 (*0-465-02845-4*, Pub. by Basic) HarpC.

Memoir of Pierre Toussaint: Born a Slave in St. Domingo. Hannah S. Lee. LC 91-68114. (Illus.). 93p. (Orig.). 1992. reprint ed. pap. 9.95 (*1-881008-02-9*) Am Soc Defense TFP.

Memoir of Ralph Waldo Emerson, 2 vols. James E. Cabot. LC 78-97164. reprint ed. 75.00 (*0-404-01357-0*) AMS Pr.

Memoir of Rev. Levi Parsons: Late Missionary to Palestine. Daniel O. Morton. Ed. by Moshe Davis. (America & the Holy Land Ser.). 1977. reprint ed. lib. bdg. 36.95 (*0-405-10271-2*) Ayer.

Memoir of Samuel Slater, the Father of American Manufactures: Connected with a History of the Rise & Progress of the Cotton Manufacture in England & America. George S. White. LC 66-18322. (Library of Early American Business & Industry: No. 4). (Illus.). 448p. 1967. reprint ed. 49.50 (*0-678-00218-5*) Kelley.

Memoir of Sebastian Cabot, with a Review of the History of Maritime Discovery, Illustrated by Documents from the Rolls. Richard Biddle. LC 73-107793. (Select Bibliographies Reprint Ser.). 1977. 26.95 (*0-8369-5211-1*) Ayer.

Memoir of Shelley. William M. Rossetti. LC 71-144680. (Shelley Society, Fourth Ser.: No. 2). reprint ed. 39.50 (*0-404-05427-7*) AMS Pr.

Memoir of Sir Benjamin Thompson, Count Rumford, with Notices of His Daughter. George C. Ellis. LC 72-8777. (American Revolutionary Ser.). (Illus.). 708p. 1979. reprint ed. lib. bdg. 75.00 (*0-8398-0457-1*) Irvington.

Memoir of Sukey Harley. unabridged ed. Sukey Harley. (Children's Heritage Ser.). 127p. (J). (gr. 4-6). 1996. pap. 6.95 (*1-58339-131-2*, D31) Triangle Press.

Memoir of the Celebrated Admiral Adam John de Krusenstern, First Russian Circumnavigator. Adam J. Von Krusenstern. Ed. by Charlotte Bernhardi. 75p. 1986. reprint ed. pap. 10.00 (*0-8466-0053-6*, S-53, Shorey Pubns) Shoreys Bkstore.

Memoir of the Comparative Grammar of Egyptian-Coptic & Ude. Hyde Clarke. 1987. reprint ed. pap. 7.95 (*0-89979-045-3*) British Am Bks.

Memoir of the Future. Wilfred R. Bion. 678p. 1991. pap. 50.00 (*0-946439-79-6*, Pub. by H Karnac Bks Ltd) Other Pr LLC.

Memoir of the Life & Character of the Rev. Samuel Bacon. Samuel Bacon. Ed. by Jehudi Ashmun. (Black Heritage Library Collection). 1977. 22.95 (*0-8369-8781-0*) Ayer.

Memoir of the Life & Labors of Francis Wayland, D. D., LL. D. Francis Wayland & H. Lincoln Wayland. LC 76-38465. (Religion in America, Ser. 2). 818p. 1972. reprint ed. 57.95 (*0-405-04092-X*) Ayer.

Memoir of the Life & Labours of the Late Charles Babbage Esq., F. R. S. H. W. Buxton. (Charles Babbage Institute Reprint Series for the History of Computing). (Illus.). 425p. 1987. 65.00 (*0-262-02269-9*) MIT Pr.

Memoir of the Life & Public Services of Sir Thomas Stamford Raffles. Sophia Raffles. LC 77-87000. reprint ed. 89.00 (*0-404-16774-8*) AMS Pr.

Memoir of the Life & Writings of Rev. John Gill, D. D. John Rippon. 1993. 15.99 (*0-87377-920-7*) GAM Pubns.

Memoir of the Life of Elizabeth Fry: With Extracts from Her Journals & Letters, 2 vols. in one. 2nd enl. rev. ed. Elizabeth Fry & Rachel L. Cresswell. LC 70-172597. (Criminology, Law Enforcement, & Social Problems Ser.: No. 187). 1120p. 1974. reprint ed. 45.00 (*0-87585-187-8*) Patterson Smith.

Memoir of the Life of Josiah Quincy, Jr. Josiah Quincy, Jr. (American Biography Ser.). 498p. 1991. reprint ed. lib. bdg. 89.00 (*0-7812-8319-1*) Rprt Serv.

Memoir of the Life of Laurence Oliphant & of Alice Oliphant, His Wife. Margaret O. Oliphant. LC 75-36915. (Occult Ser.). 1976. reprint ed. 35.95 (*0-405-07970-2*) Ayer.

Memoir of the Life, Writings & Mechanical Inventions of Edmund Cartwright. Mary Strickland. LC 70-149329. (Documents of Social History Ser.). 372p. 1971. reprint ed. lib. bdg. 49.50 (*0-678-07769-X*) Kelley.

Memoir of the Mosquito Territory As Respecting the Voluntary Cession of It to the Crown of Great Britain. John Wright. 432p. 1987. reprint ed. pap. 5.00 (*0-913129-18-6*) La Tienda.

Memoir of the Most Eminent American Mechanics. Henry Howe. (Notable American Authors Ser.). 1992. reprint ed. lib. bdg. 75.00 (*0-7812-3199-X*) Rprt Serv.

Memoir of the Nature of the Church of Christ. Apostolos Makrakis. Ed. by Orthodox Christian Educational Society Staff. Tr. by Denver Cummings. 175p. 1947. 8.95 (*0-938366-21-1*); 12.00 (*0-614-23215-5*) Orthodox Chr.

Memoir of the Physical Review: A History of the First Hundred Years. Paul Hartman. LC 94-5660. 1994. pap. 19.95 (*1-56396-282-9*) Spr-Verlag.

Memoir of the Professional Life of Thomas Abthorpe Cooper. Joseph N. Ireland. (Notable American Authors Ser.). 1992. reprint ed. lib. bdg. 75.00 (*0-7812-3341-0*) Rprt Serv.

Memoir of the Public Services of William Henry Harrison, of Ohio. James N. Hall. LC 70-117879. (Select Bibliographies Reprint Ser.). 1977. 24.95 (*0-8369-5332-0*) Ayer.

Memoir of the Rev. David Abeel, D. D. Late Missionary to China. David Abeel. (American Biography Ser.). 315p. 1991. reprint ed. lib. bdg. 79.00 (*0-7812-8000-1*) Rprt Serv.

Memoir of the Rev. David Abeel, D. D. Late Missionary to China. G. R. Williamson. LC 72-79842. (China Library). 1972. reprint ed. lib. bdg. 29.00 (*0-8420-1353-9*) Scholarly Res Inc.

Memoir of the Rev. Elijah P. Lovejoy. Joseph C. Lovejoy & Owen Lovejoy. LC 72-117882. (Select Bibliographies Reprint Ser.). 1977. reprint ed. 34.95 (*0-8369-5335-5*) Ayer.

Memoir of the Rev. John Keble, 2 vols. in 1. 2nd rev. ed. John T. Coleridge. LC 75-30019. reprint ed. 67.50 (*0-404-14024-6*) AMS Pr.

Memoir of the Rev. Pliny Fisk: Late Missionary to Palestine. Bond Alvan. Ed. by Moshe Davis. LC 77-70683. (America & the Holy Land Ser.). 1977. reprint ed. lib. bdg. 36.95 (*0-405-10230-5*) Ayer.

Memoir of the Rev. William Robinson. Edward Robinson. (Notable American Authors Ser.). 1999. reprint ed. lib. bdg. 125.00 (*0-7812-8794-4*) Rprt Serv.

Memoir of the Reverend Elijah P. Lovejoy. Joseph C. Lovejoy & Owen Lovejoy. LC 72-90183. (Mass Violence in America Ser.). 1969. reprint ed. 32.95 (*0-405-01323-X*) Ayer.

Memoir of the Reverend Jesse Lee, with Extracts from His Journals. Jesse Lee & Minton Thrift. LC 72-83428. (Religion in America, Ser. 1). 1977. reprint ed. 21.95 (*0-405-00253-X*) Ayer.

Memoir of the Warsaw Uprising. Miron Bialoszewski. Tr. & Intro. by Madeline Levine. 234p. 1991. reprint ed. pap. 12.95 (*0-8101-1026-1*) Northwestern U Pr.

Memoir of the Wilkinson Family in America: Genealogical Sketches of Lawrence of Providence, R. I., Edward of New Milford, Connecticut, John of Attleborough, Massachusetts, Daniel of Columbia County, N. Y., Etc., & Their Descendants 1645-1868. I. Wilkinson. 589p. 1989. reprint ed. pap. 88.00 (*0-8328-1271-4*); reprint ed. lib. bdg. 97.00 (*0-8328-1270-6*) Higginson Bk Co.

Memoir of Theophilus Parsons. Theophilus Parsons. LC 71-118032. (American Constitutional & Legal History Ser). 1970. reprint ed. lib. bdg. 55.00 (*0-306-71939-8*) Da Capo.

Memoir of Thomas Bewick: Written by Himself, 1822-1828. Thomas Bewick. LC NE1212.B5A3. (Centaur Classics Ser.). (Illus.). 294p. reprint ed. pap. 91.20 (*0-8357-6654-3*, 203532300094) Bks Demand.

Memoir of Thomas McGrath. Jack Beeching. 30p. (Orig.). 1993. pap. 4.00 (*1-882191-02-1*) Spirit Horse Pr.

Memoir of Thomas Thomson, Advocate. Cosmo N. Innes. LC 72-170803. (Bannatyne Club, Edinburgh. Publications: No. 99). reprint ed. 32.50 (*0-404-52847-3*) AMS Pr.

Memoir of Thurlow Weed see Life of Thurlow Weed

Memoir of Toni Wolff. Irene Champernowne. 1980. pap. 7.00 (*0-317-13545-7*) C G Jung Frisco.

Memoir of Washington Irving. Charles F. Adams, Jr. LC 70-148869. (Select Bibliographies Reprint Ser.). 1977. reprint ed. 19.95 (*0-8369-5641-9*) Ayer.

Memoir of William Henry Channing. Octavius B. Frothingham. (Notable American Authors Ser.). 1992. reprint ed. lib. bdg. 75.00 (*0-7812-2909-X*) Rprt Serv.

***Memoir of William Tyndale.** George Offor. 1999. pap. 20.00 (*1-58329-010-9*) Lazarus Minist.

Memoir on Heat. A. L. Lavoisier & P. S. Laplace. Ed. by Henry Guerlac.Tr. of Memoire sur la Chaleur. 1981. 14.95 (*0-88202-195-8*) Watson Pub Intl.

Memoir on Integrable Systems. Y. N. Fedorov, (Springer Monographs in Mathematics). (Illus.). 280p. 1999. 98.95 (*3-540-59000-5*) Spr-Verlag.

Memoir on Nixon. Pat Buchanan. 14.00 (*0-06-098823-1*) HarpC.

Memoir on Pauperism. Alexis De Tocqueville. Tr. by Seymour Drescher from FRE. LC 97-11895. 84p. 1997. pap. 6.95 (*1-56663-168-8*, Elephant Paperbacks); text 15.00 (*1-56663-167-X*) I R Dee.

M

An Asterisk (*) at the beginning of an entry indicates that the title is appearing for the first time.

Memoir on Pauperism. Alexis De Tocqueville. Tr. by Seymour Drescher from FRE. (Rediscovered Riches Ser.: No. 2). 40p. 1997. pap. 13.95 (*0-255-36394-X*, Pub. by Inst Economic Affairs) Coronet Bks.

Memoir on Steamboats of the United States of America, Printed by the Royal Press, Paris, 1824. Jean-Baptiste Marestier. Tr. by Sidney Withington. LC 57-59433. (Marine Historical Association Publication: No. 31). 100p. reprint ed. pap. 31.00 (*0-8357-2794-7*, 203992000014) Bks Demand.

Memoir on the History of the Tooth-Relic of Ceylon: With Preliminary Essay on the Life & System of Gautama Buddha. J. Gerson Da Cunha. (C). 1996. pap. 12.00 (*81-206-1173-X*, Pub. by Asian Educ Servs) S Asia.

Memoir on the Immediate Cause of Blunt or Smut of Wheat & of Several Other Diseases of Plants & on the Preventatives of Bunt. Benedict Prevost. Tr. by G. W. Keitt. (Phytopathological Classics Ser.). 95p. 1939. 22.00 (*0-89054-007-1*) Am Phytopathol Soc.

Memoir on the Pearly Nautilus. Richard Owen. LC 72-1700. (Illus.). reprint ed. 27.50 (*0-404-07978-4*) AMS Pr.

Memoir on the Sawunt Waree State. W. Courtney & J. W. Auld. (C). 1995. reprint ed. 64.00 (*81-206-1016-4*, Pub. by Asian Educ Servs) S Asia.

***Memoire Endormie.** Daphne Clair. 1999. mass mkt. 3.99 (*0-373-34804-5*) Silhouette.

Memoire Ennemie. Catherine Judd. (Amours d'Aujourd'Hui Ser.). (FRE.). 1997. pap. 4.99 (*0-373-38269-3*, 1-38269-6) Harlequin Bks.

Memoire Ensanglantee. Stanley Pean. (Novels in the Roman Plus Ser.). (FRE.). 160p. (YA). (gr. 8 up). 1994. pap. 8.95 (*2-89021-217-3*, Pub. by La Courte Ech) Firefly Bks Ltd.

Memoire et Vie. Henri Bergson. (FRE.). 1975. pap. 24.95 (*0-8288-9078-1*) Fr & Eur.

Memoire sur la Chaleur see Memoir on Heat

Memoire sur la Commerce de la France et de ses Colonies. De Tolosan. (Economistes Francais du XVIIIe Siecle Ser.). 1990. reprint ed. pap. 30.00 (*3-601-00159-4*) Periodicals Srv.

Memoire sur la Musique des Anciens. fac. ed. Pierre J. Roussier. (Monuments of Music & Music Literature in Facsimile, II Ser.: Vol. 41). (Illus.). 1966. lib. bdg. 42.50 (*0-8450-2241-5*) Broude.

Memoire sur le Systeme Primitif des Voyelles dans les Langues Indo-Europeennes. Ferdinand De Saussure. (FRE.). 302p. 1987. reprint ed. lib. bdg. 65.95 (*3-487-01833-0*) G Olms Pubs.

Memoire sur les Foraminiferes de la Craie Blanche du Bassin de Paris. A. D' Orbigny. 1964. reprint ed. pap. 5.00 (*0-934454-63-9*) Lubrecht & Cramer.

Memoire sur les Hypotheses Astronomiques des Plus Anciens Philosophes de la Grece. Thomas H. Martin. Ed. by Gregory Vlastos. (History of Ideas in Ancient Times Ser.). 1976. reprint ed. 39.95 (*0-405-07320-8*) Ayer.

Memoiren Einer Arabischen Prinzessin see Arabian Princess Between Two Worlds: Memoirs, Letters Home, Sequels to My Memoirs: Syrian Customs & Usages

Memoiren eines Dinar. Dahesh. (ARA, ENG & GER., Illus.). 383p. 1990. 35.00 (*0-935359-20-6*) Daheshist.

Memoires. Francois-Rene de Chateaubriand & Claude Roy. 576p. 1964. 8.95 (*0-686-54370-X*) Fr & Eur.

Memoires. Claude H. De Saint-Simon. (Folio Ser.: No. 2165). (FRE.). 1990. pap. 16.95 (*2-07-038234-6*) Schoenhof.

Memoires, 8 Tomes. Saint-Simon. Ed. by Truc. (Pleiade Ser.). (FRE.). 83.95 (*2-07-010958-5*); 80.95 (*2-07-011001-X*); 79.95 (*2-07-011010-9*); 79.95 (*2-07-011011-7*); 89.95 (*2-07-011012-5*); 88.95 (*2-07-011013-3*); 93.95 (*2-07-011014-1*) Schoenhof.

Memoires, 8 Tomes, Tome VIII. Saint-Simon. Ed. by Truc. (Pleiade Ser.). (FRE.). 1961. 108.95 (*2-07-011015-X*) Schoenhof.

Memoires: Ou, Essais sur la Musique, 3 vols. Andre Gretry. LC 73-160852. (Music Ser.). (FRE.). 1971. reprint ed. lib. bdg. 150.00 (*0-306-70194-4*) Da Capo.

Memoires: Publies par les Membres de la Mission Archeologique Francaise au Caire, 2 Vols., Set. M. U. Bouriant. (ARA & FRE.). 1979. 40.00 (*0-86685-333-2*) Intl Bk Ctr.

Memoires Completes et Authentiques, 22 tomes, Set. Saint-Simon. Ed. by Chervel. pap. 350.00 (*0-685-01988-8*) Fr & Eur.

Memoires de Deux Jeunes Mariees. Honore de Balzac. (FRE.). 352p. 1981. pap. 11.95 (*0-7859-1932-5*, 2070372685) Fr & Eur.

Memoires de Deux Jeunes Mariees. Honore de Balzac. (Folio Ser.: No. 1268). (FRE.). 380p. 1969. 9.95 (*2-07-037268-5*) Schoenhof.

Memoires de Dirk Raspe. Pierre Drieu La Rochelle. (FRE.). 338p. 1978. pap. 11.95 (*0-7859-1876-0*, 2070370429) Fr & Eur.

Memoires de Guerre, 3 tomes. Charles De Gaulle. Incl. Tome I. Appel (1940-1942) 1961. 39.95 Tome II. Unite (1942-1944) 1961. 39.95 Tome III. Salut (1944-1946) 1961. 39.95 (FRE.). 897p. 1961. Set pap. 69.95 (*0-318-52050-8*) Fr & Eur.

Memoires de Guerre, 1954-61 Tome I: L'Appel (1940-1942) Charles De Gaulle. 320p. 1970. 39.95 (*0-7859-5248-9*) Fr & Eur.

Memoires de Guerre, 1954-61 Tome II: L'Unite (1942-1944) Charles De Gaulle. (FRE.). 497p. 1979. pap. 15.95 (*0-8288-9375-6*, F101791) Fr & Eur.

Memoires de Guerre, 1954-61 Tome III: Le Salut (1944-1946) Charles De Gaulle. 1959. 59.95 (*0-7859-5249-7*) Fr & Eur.

***Memoires de Lafayette.** Charles Larroque. (FRE., Illus.). 32p. 1999. pap. 7.95 (*1-56554-644-X*) Pelican.

Memoires de Ma Vie. Rene De Chateaubriand. (FRE.). 141p. 1976. 15.95 (*0-8288-9093-5*, M2225) Fr & Eur.

Memoires de Madame Chauverel, 2 vols. Jules Romains, pseud. (FRE.). 304p. 1959. pap. 10.95 (*0-7859-1640-7*, 2080505955) Fr & Eur.

Memoires de Madame Chauverel, 2 vols., Set. Jules Romains, pseud. (FRE.). 304p. 1959. pap. 10.95 (*0-7859-1642-3*, 2080505963) Fr & Eur.

Memoires de Maigret. Georges Simenon. (FRE.). pap. 3.95 (*0-685-11357-4*) Fr & Eur.

Memoires de Marchand see In Napoleon's Shadow, Vol. 1, The First English Edition of the Complete Memoirs of Louis Joseph Marchand, Valet & Friend of the Emperor, 1811-1821

Memoires de Nubar Pacha. (FRE.). 1983. 20.00 (*0-86685-346-4*) Intl Bk Ctr.

Memoires de Robert Guillemard, Sergent en Retraite, Suivis de Documents Historiques, 2 vols. Charles O. Barbaroux. reprint ed. 30.00 (*0-404-07537-1*) AMS Pr.

Memoires de St Martinville. Charles Larroque. (FRE., Illus.). 32p. 1999. pap. 6.95 (*1-56554-398-X*) Pelican.

Memoires D'Espoir, 2 tomes. Charles De Gaulle. Incl. Tome I. Renouveau, 1958-1962. 39.95 Tome II. Effort (1962) 39.95 write for info. (*0-318-52053-2*) Fr & Eur.

Memoires d'Hadrien. Marguerite Yourcenar. (FRE.). 1977. pap. 11.95 (*0-8288-3806-2*, F132621) Fr & Eur.

Memoires d'Hadrien. Marguerite Yourcenar. (Folio Ser.: No. 921). (FRE.). 364p. 1974. pap. 9.95 (*2-07-036921-8*) Schoenhof.

Memoires d'Outre-Tombe. deluxe ed. Francois-Rene De Chateaubriand. Ed. by Maurice Levaillant & Moulnier. (Bibliotheque de la Pleiade Ser.). (FRE.). 1280p. 1989. 150.00 (*0-7859-1096-4*, 2070101274) Fr & Eur.

Memoires d'Outre-Tombe, 3 vols., Set. Francois-Rene de Chateaubriand. (FRE.). 256p. 1980. 13.95 (*0-7859-1182-0*, 2259005403) Fr & Eur.

Memoires D'Outre-Tombe, Tombe 2. Francois-Rene de Chateaubriand. (Pleiade Ser.). (FRE.). 1496p. 1951. pap. 73.95 (*2-07-010128-2*) Schoenhof.

Memoires D'Outre-Tombe, Tome 1. Francois-Rene de Chateaubriand. (Pleiade Ser.). (FRE.). 1232p. 1951. pap. 74.95 (*2-07-010127-4*) Schoenhof.

Memoires d'un Dinar. Dahesh. (ARA, ENG & FRE., Illus.). 399p. 1988. 35.00 (*0-935359-02-8*) Daheshist.

Memoires d'un Fou: Nouvembre et Autres Textes de Jeunesse. Gustave Flaubert. (FRE.). 1991. pap. 20.95 (*0-7859-2999-1*) Fr & Eur.

Memoires d'un Touriste, 3 vols. Stendhal, pseud. Ed. by Ernest Abravanel & Victor Del Litto. (Illus.). 9.95 (*0-685-73307-6*) Fr & Eur.

Memoires d'un Touriste, 3 vols., Set. Stendhal, pseud. (FRE.). 224p. 1981. pap. 10.95 (*0-7859-1501-X*, 2707111988) Fr & Eur.

Memoires d'une Jeune Fille Rangee. Simone de Beauvoir. (FRE.). 1972. pap. 13.95 (*0-8288-3658-2*, F85771) Fr & Eur.

Memoires d'une Jeune Fille Rangee. Simone de Beauvoir. (Folio Ser.: No. 786). (FRE.). 1972. pap. 11.95 (*2-07-036786-X*) Schoenhof.

Memoires Ecrits par Lui-Meme pour Servir a l'Histoire de Sa Vie: Avec: Lettres de Voltaire a Frederic II. rev. ed. Voltaire. Ed. by Jacques Brenner. (FRE.). 306p. 1988. pap. 24.95 (*0-7859-1273-8*, 2040174141) Fr & Eur.

Memoires for Paul de Man. Jacques Derrida. Tr. by Cecile Lindsay et al. LC 85-27999. 1986. text 44.00 (*0-231-06232-X*) Col U Pr.

Memoires for Paul de Man. rev. ed. Jacques Derrida. Tr. by Cecile Lindsay et al. LC 85-27999. 153p. 1989. pap. text 20.00 (*0-231-06233-8*) Col U Pr.

Memoires Improvises. Paul Claudel. (FRE.). 384p. 1969. 10.95 (*0-7859-1149-9*, 2070351904) Fr & Eur.

Memoires Inedits. Alfred De Vigny. (FRE.). 480p. 1958. pap. 16.95 (*0-7859-1332-7*, 2070265307) Fr & Eur.

Memoires Interieurs. Francois Mauriac. 9.95 (*0-686-55468-X*) Fr & Eur.

Memoires Interieurs. Francois Mauriac. (FRE.). 384p. 1959. 24.95 (*0-8288-7444-1*) Fr & Eur.

Memoires Interieurs. Francois Mauriac. (FRE.). 520p. 1985. pap. 29.95 (*0-7859-4611-X*) Fr & Eur.

Memoires Interieurs: Nouveaux Memoires Interieurs. 218p. 1988. 12.95 (*0-7859-4616-0*) Fr & Eur.

Memoires, 1995. Seiichi Furuya. (Illus.). 160p. 1995. 35.00 (*1-881616-54-1*) Dist Art Pubs.

***Memories of World War II.** Martin F. Loughlin. LC 99-98158. 2000. pap. 8.95 (*0-533-13455-2*) Vantage.

Memoires I: Les Annees d'Apprentissage. Andre Maurois. 19.95 (*0-685-36946-3*) Fr & Eur.

Memoires (Ottawa, 1866) Philippe A. Gaspe. (Canadiana Avant 1867 Ser.: No. 1). 1966. 63.85 (*90-279-6322-3*) Mouton.

Memoires Politiques. Francois Mauriac. (FRE.). 1967. 12.95 (*0-8288-9864-2*, F112800); 24.95 (*0-8288-7442-5*) Fr & Eur.

Memoires pour Catherine II. Denis Diderot & Paul Verniere. (FRE., Illus.). 420p. 1966. 29.95 (*0-8288-9957-6*, F46890) Fr & Eur.

Memoires pour Servir a l'Histoire des Spectacles de la Foire, 2 vols., 1 bk. Francois Parfaict & Claude Parfaict. LC 76-43933. (Music & Theatre in France in the 17th & 18th Centuries Ser.). reprint ed. 72.50 (*0-404-60179-0*) AMS Pr.

Memoires, 1756-1763 Vol. 2. Jacques C. De Seingault. (FRE.). 1959. 95.00 (*0-8288-3453-9*, M4975) Fr & Eur.

Memoires, 1725-1756 Vol. 1. Jacques C. De Seingault. (FRE.). 1958. 95.00 (*0-8288-3452-0*, M4974) Fr & Eur.

Memoires, Souvenires de Jeunesse, Complements, Fragments du Journal. Romain Rolland. (FRE.). 336p. 1956. pap. 18.95 (*0-686-55260-1*) Fr & Eur.

Memoires sur la Famille des Fougeres, 1844-66, 11 pts. in 2 vols. A. L. Fee. (Illus.). 1966. 560.00 (*3-7682-0447-2*) Lubrecht & Cramer.

Memoires sur la Famille des Legumineuses. A. De Candolle. (Illus.). 1966. reprint ed. 220.00 (*3-7682-0299-2*) Lubrecht & Cramer.

Memoires sur l'Ancienne Chevalerie, 2 vols., Set. Jean-Baptiste Sainte-Pelaye. LC 79-8371. reprint ed. 59.50 (*0-404-18306-9*) AMS Pr.

Memoires Sur Louis the Eleventh. Phillippe De Commynes. (FRE.). 598p. 1979. pap. 12.95 (*0-7859-2216-4*, 207037078X) Fr & Eur.

Memoirs. 450p. (C). 1994. 39.95 (*0-19-577447-7*) OUP.

Memoirs. Hector Berlioz. (Illus.). 547p. 1966. pap. 13.95 (*0-486-21563-6*) Dover.

Memoirs. Richard Cumberland. Ed. by Henry Flanders. LC 72-91487. 1972. 30.95 (*0-405-08413-7*, Pub. by Blom Pubns) Ayer.

***Memoirs.** Lorenzo Da Ponte. Tr. by Elisabeth Abbott from ITA. LC 99-46014. 512p. 2000. pap. 14.95 (*0-940322-35-8*) NY Rev Bks.

Memoirs. Nicolas De Basily. LC 70-175450. (Publication Ser.: No. 125). 201p. 1973. 8.95 (*0-8179-6251-4*) Hoover Inst Pr.

Memoirs. M. El-Gamasy et al. Tr. by Gillian Potter et al. (Illus.). 464p. 1994. 40.00 (*977-424-316-1*, Pub. by Am Univ Cairo Pr) Col U Pr.

Memoirs. Mikhail S. Gorbachev. 35.00 (*0-614-25659-3*) Doubleday.

Memoirs. Ulysses S. Grant. 642p. 1994. 30.00 (*1-56515-017-1*) Collect Reprints.

Memoirs. Richard Helms. 1999. write for info. (*0-375-50012-X*) Random.

Memoirs. Yevhen Hrycyak. (UKR.). 112p. 1980. pap. 4.75 (*0-914834-30-4*) Smoloskyp.

Memoirs. Joni Mitchell. 2004. 27.50 (*0-609-60006-0*) Crown Pub Group.

***Memoirs.** Pablo Neruda. Tr. by Hardie St. Martin from SPA. 384p. 2001. pap. 15.00 (*0-374-52753-9*) FS&G.

Memoirs. Pablo Neruda. 1992. pap. 13.95 (*0-14-018628-X*, Penguin Bks) Viking Penguin.

Memoirs. Richard M. Nixon. 1994. lib. bdg. 39.95 (*1-56849-498-X*) Buccaneer Bks.

Memoirs. Andrei D. Sakharov. Tr. by Richard Lourie. (Illus.). 773p. 1990. 29.95 (*0-394-53740-8*) Knopf.

Memoirs. William T. Sherman. Ed. by Charles Royster. 1136p. 1990. 35.00 (*0-940450-65-8*, Pub. by Library of America) Penguin Putnam.

Memoirs. Georg Solti. LC 98-30685. (Illus.). 288p. 1998. pap. 15.95 (*1-55652-337-8*, Lawrence Hill) Chicago Review.

Memoirs. Georg Solti. LC 97-74745. (Illus.). 258p. 1997. 25.95 (*0-679-44596-X*) Knopf.

Memoirs. Pierre Trudeau. (Illus.). 360p. 1995. pap. 19.99 (*0-7710-8587-7*) McCland & Stewart.

Memoirs. Pierre E. Trudeau. (Illus.). 384p. 1994. 29.95 (*0-7710-0036-7*) McCland & Stewart.

Memoirs. Mem. of Pierre E. Trudeau. 1996. 35.00 (*0-7710-8588-5*) McCland & Stewart.

Memoirs. B. Wrangel. LC 76-154043. (World History Ser.: No. 48). 1971. lib. bdg. 75.00 (*0-8383-1262-4*) M S G Haskell Hse.

Memoirs. Benjamin Franklin. (History - United States Ser.). 422p. 1993. reprint ed. lib. bdg. 99.00 (*0-7812-4831-0*) Rprt Serv.

Memoirs. John C. Fremont. (Notable American Authors Ser.). 1992. reprint ed. lib. bdg. 75.00 (*0-7812-2901-4*) Rprt Serv.

Memoirs. Charles G. Leland. (American Biography Ser.). 439p. 1991. reprint ed. lib. bdg. 89.00 (*0-7812-8243-8*) Rprt Serv.

Memoirs. Mary A. Maverick. 1993. reprint ed. lib. bdg. 75.00 (*0-7812-5944-4*) Rprt Serv.

Memoirs. William T. Sherman. (American Biography Ser.). 1991. reprint ed. lib. bdg. 99.00 (*0-7812-8353-1*) Rprt Serv.

Memoirs. James Turner. Ed. by Thomas Thomson. LC 77-177579. (Bannatyne Club, Edinburgh. Publications: No.28). reprint ed. 42.50 (*0-404-52734-5*) AMS Pr.

Memoirs. Franz Von Papen. Tr. by Brian Connell. LC 78-63703. (Studies in Fascism: Ideology & Practice). reprint ed. 45.00 (*0-404-16975-9*) AMS Pr.

***Memoirs: Duc de Saint-Simon.** Ed. by Lucy Norton. (Lost Treasures Ser.: Vol. 1). 560p. 2000. pap. 19.95 (*1-85375-352-1*, Pub. by Prion) Trafalgar.

***Memoirs: Duc de Saint-Simon.** Ed. by Lucy Norton. (Lost Treasures Ser.: Vol. 2). 560p. 2000. pap. 19.95 (*1-85375-353-X*, Pub. by Prion) Trafalgar.

***Memoirs: Duc de Saint-Simon.** Ed. by Lucy Norton. (Lost Treasures Ser.: Vol. 3). 560p. 2000. pap. 19.95 (*1-85375-354-8*, Pub. by Prion) Trafalgar.

Memoirs: Fifty Years of Political Reflection. Raymond Aron. Tr. by George Holoch from FRE. LC 89-7621. 509p. 1989. 49.95 (*0-8419-1113-4*) Holmes & Meier.

Memoirs: Fifty Years of Political Reflection. Raymond Aron. Tr. by George Holoch from FRE. LC 89-7621. 510p. 1997. pap. 24.00 (*0-8419-1114-2*) Holmes & Meier.

Memoirs: From Munich to New War & New Victory. Edvard Benes. Tr. by Godfrey Lias. LC 72-4265. (World Affairs Ser.: National & International Viewpoints). 360p. 1972. reprint ed. 23.95 (*0-405-04561-1*) Ayer.

***Memoirs: Laughing & Dancing Our Way to the Precipice.** Madame De La Tour Du Pin. Tr. by Felice Harcourt from FRE. 472p. 1999. pap. 16.00 (*1-86046-548-X*, Pub. by Harvill Press) FS&G.

Memoirs: Selections from Casanova's "Story of My Life" Casanova. 400p. 1999. 30.00 (*1-56886-063-3*, Pub. by Marsilio Pubs) Consort Bk Sales.

Memoirs: Ten Years & Twenty Days. Karl Doenitz. Tr. by R. H. Stevens & David Woodward from GER. LC 96-37395. (Illus.). 554p. 1997. reprint ed. pap. 16.95 (*0-306-80764-5*) Da Capo.

Memoirs about Max Heindel & the Rosicrucian Fellowship. Augusta F. Heindel. (Illus.). 216p. (Orig.). 1997. pap. 15.50 (*0-88112-069-3*) Rosicrucian.

Memoirs & Art of William Terry Badham: A World War I Ace, Flying with the Ninety-First Squadron U. S. Army. William T. Badham. (FRE & SPA., Illus.). 91p. (Orig.). 1987. 39.95 (*0-9618093-0-2*); pap. 25.00 (*0-9618093-1-0*) Menton Repro.

Memoirs & Artistic Studies. Adelaide Ristori. LC 74-81977. (Illus.). 279p. 1972. 24.95 (*0-405-08892-2*, Pub. by Blom Pubns) Ayer.

Memoirs & Correspondence of Francis Horner, 2 vols. Francis Horner. Ed. by Leonard Horner. LC 73-170053. reprint ed. 45.00 (*0-404-07377-8*) AMS Pr.

Memoirs & Correspondence of Madame Recamier. Jeanne F. Recamier. LC 73-37715. (Illus.). reprint ed. 55.00 (*0-404-56808-4*) AMS Pr.

Memoirs & Diaries of Muhammad Farid, an Egyptian Nationalist Leader (1868-1919) Tr. by Arthur Goldschmidt, Jr. from EGY. 556p. 1992. lib. bdg. 119.95 (*0-7734-9454-5*) E Mellen.

Memoirs & Genealogy of Representative Citizens of Northern California: Including Biographies of Many of Those Who Have Passed Away. 831p. 1997. reprint ed. lib. bdg. 85.00 (*0-8328-6603-2*) Higginson Bk Co.

Memoirs & Letters & Journals of Major-General Riedesel, During His Residence in America, 2 vols., Set. Friedrich A. Riedesel. Tr. by William L. Stone. LC 79-77109. (Eyewitness Accounts of the American Revolution Ser.). (Illus.). 1969. reprint ed. 34.95 (*0-405-01172-5*) Ayer.

Memoirs & Letters & Journals of Major-General Riedesel, During His Residence in America, 2 vols., Vol. 1. Friedrich A. Riedesel. Tr. by William L. Stone. LC 79-77109. (Eyewitness Accounts of the American Revolution Ser.). (Illus.). 1969. reprint ed. 15.95 (*0-405-01173-3*) Ayer.

Memoirs & Letters & Journals of Major-General Riedesel, During His Residence in America, 2 vols., Vol. 2. Friedrich A. Riedesel. Tr. by William L. Stone. LC 79-77109. (Eyewitness Accounts of the American Revolution Ser.). (Illus.). 1969. reprint ed. 15.95 (*0-405-01174-1*) Ayer.

***Memoirs & Letters of James Kent, LL.D: Late Chancellor of the State of New York: Author of "Commentaries on American Law," Etc.** William Kent & James Kent. LC 00-26688. 2000. write for info. (*1-58477-100-3*) Lawbk Exchange.

Memoirs & Letters of Oscar W. Firkins. Oscar W. Firkins. LC 34-27148. 320p. reprint ed. pap. 99.20 (*0-608-14650-1*, 205586500039) Bks Demand.

***Memoirs & Memorials of Sir Hugh Cholmley of Whitby, 1600-1657.** Ed. by Jack Binns. (Illus.). 352p. 2000. 60.00 (*0-902122-83-5*, Pub. by Yorkshire) Boydell & Brewer.

Memoirs & Memories. Delores J. Maloy. LC 98-72114. 48p. 1998. pap. 8.95 (*1-56167-435-4*) Am Literary Pr.

Memoirs & Murder: A Louisiana Reconstruction Mystery. Herb R. Graf. 176p. 1995. pap. 8.00 (*1-884725-06-6*) Blue Heron LA.

Memoirs & Recollections of Count Louis Philippe de Segur. Louis De Segur. LC 73-115584. (Russia Observed, Series I). 1970. reprint ed. 66.95 (*0-405-03061-4*) Ayer.

Memoirs & Selected Letters. Ulysses S. Grant. Ed. by Mary D. McFeely & William S. McFeely. 1199p. 1990. 35.00 (*0-940450-58-5*, Pub. by Library of America) Penguin Putnam.

Memoirs by Harry S. Truman: Year of Decisions. Harry S. Truman. 608p. 1999. reprint ed. 14.95 (*1-56852-062-X*, Konecky & Konecky) W S Konecky Assocs.

Memoirs for the History of the War in Texas, Vol. 1. Vicente Filisola. Tr. by Wallace Woolsey. 1997. pap. 16.95 (*1-57168-034-9*, Eakin Pr) Sunbelt Media.

Memoirs for the History of the War in Texas, Vol. II. Vicente Filisola. 314p. 1988. 18.95 (*0-89015-585-2*) Sunbelt Media.

Memoirs from Away: A New Found Land Girlhood. Helen M. Buss & Margaret Clarke. 169p. 1999. pap. write for info. (*0-88920-314-8*) W Laurier U Pr.

***Memoirs from Away: A New Found Land Girlhood.** Helen M. Buss & Margaret Clarke. (Life Writing Ser.). 169p. 1999. pap. 21.95 (*0-88920-350-4*) Wilfrid Laurier.

***Memoirs from Elsinore.** Franz Hellens. Tr. by Howard Curtis from FRE. LC 99-46878. (Belgian Francophone Library: Vol. 12). 320p. 2000. text 58.95 (*0-8204-4469-3*) P Lang Pubng.

Memoirs from John S. Mosby. John S. Mosby. (Great Commanders Ser.). 432p. 1998. reprint ed. 30.00 (*1-56515-015-5*) Collect Reprints.

Memoirs from Occupied Warsaw, 1940-1945: The Memoirs of Helena Szereszewska. Helena Szereszewska. Tr. by Anna Marianska. LC 96-44956. (Library of Holocaust Testimonies: Vol. 11). 512p. 1997. pap. 27.50 (*0-85303-313-7*, Pub. by M Valentine & Co) Intl Spec Bk.

Memoirs from the Baths of Diocletian. Moses J. Ezekiel. Ed. by Joseph Gutmann & Stanley F. Chyet. LC 74-28009. (Illus.). 509p. reprint ed. pap. 157.80 (*0-7837-3591-X*, 204345500009) Bks Demand.

Memoirs from the House of the Dead. Fyodor Dostoyevsky. Ed. by Ronald Hingley. Tr. by Jessie Coulson. (World's Classics Paperback Ser.). 384p. (C). 1983. pap. 7.95 (*0-19-281613-6*) OUP.

***Memoirs from the House of the Dead.** Fyodor Dostoyevsky. Ed. by Ronald Hingley. Tr. by Jessie Coulson. (Oxford World's Classics Ser.). 384p. 2000. pap. 8.95 (*0-19-283868-7*) OUP.

An Asterisk (*) at the beginning of an entry indicates that the title is appearing for the first time.

Memoirs from the Women's Prison. Nawal El-Saadawi. Tr. by Marilyn Booth from ARA. LC 94-11172.Tr. of Mudhakkirati Fi Sijn al-Nisa. 1994. reprint ed. 40.00 (0-520-08887-5, Pub. by U CA Pr); reprint ed. pap. 14.95 (0-520-08888-3, Pub. by U CA Pr) Cal Prin Full Svc.

Memoirs in a Country Churchyard: A Tobaccoman's Plea: Clean up Tobacco Row. Floyd H. Nuttall. LC 96-34852. 288p. 1996. 24.95 (1-55618-159-0) Brunswick Pub.

Memoirs, Incidents, Reminiscences of the Early History of the New Church in Michigan, Indiana, Illinois, & Adjacent States, & Canada. G. Field. LC 70-134423. 1972. reprint ed. 54.00 (0-404-08463-X) AMS Pr.

Memoirs, Journal, & Correspondence of Thomas Moore, 8 vols., Set. Thomas Moore. (BCL1-PR English Literature Ser.). 1992. reprint ed. lib. bdg. 600.00 (0-7812-7606-3) Rprt Serv.

Memoirs, 1945 Vol. 1: Year of Decisions. Harry S. Truman. (Quality Paperbacks Ser.). 608p. 1986. pap. 14.95 (0-306-80266-X) Da Capo.

Memoirs of a Bangkok Warrior: Thailand Only Yesterday. Dean Barrett. LC 98-87832. 320p. 1999. pap. 11.95 (0-9661899-2-2) Village East.

Memoirs of a Barbed Wire Surgeon. Elmer Shabart. LC 96-31856. (Illus.). 179p. 1996. pap. 10.00 (1-889059-02-1) Regent Pr.

Memoirs of a Beatnik. Diane Di Prima. LC 99-158607. 194p. 1998. pap. 12.95 (0-14-023539-6) Viking Penguin.

Memoirs of a Bengal Civilian: Lively Narrative of a Victorian District Officer. John Beames. (Eland Travel Classics Ser.). 250p. (Orig.). 1991. pap. 14.95 (0-907871-75-5) Hippocrene Bks.

Memoirs of a Biafran General. Alexander Madiebo. LC 75-18600. 350p. 1976. 20.00 (0-89388-206-2) Okpaku Communications.

Memoirs of a Bingo Addict. Beverly Garges. (Illus.). 78p. (Orig.). 1994. pap. 5.50 (0-614-12676-2) Lamb Pubns FL.

Memoirs of a Bookbat. Kathryn Lasky. LC 93-36402. 192p. (YA). (gr. 7 up). 1994. 10.95 (0-15-215727-1) Harcourt.

Memoirs of a Bookbat. Kathryn Lasky. 224p. (YA). (gr. 5 up). 1996. pap. 6.00 (0-15-201259-1) Harcourt.

Memoirs of a Bookman. Jack Matthews. LC 89-37615. 178p. 1989. 15.95 (0-8214-0937-9) Ohio U Pr.

Memoirs of a Bookman. Jack Matthews. LC 89-37615. 178p. 1991. pap. 14.95 (0-8214-0974-3) Ohio U Pr.

Memoirs of a Buccaneer. Robert Williams. 320p. 1990. pap. 12.00 (0-87380-174-1) Popular E Commerce.

Memoirs of a Buddhist Woman Missionary in Hawaii. Shigeo Kikuchi. Tr. by Florence Okada from JPN. LC 91-2906. 73p. 1991. pap. 8.95 (0-938474-13-8) Buddhist Study.

Memoirs of a Bystander: A Life in Diplomacy. Igbal Akhund. LC 97-172304. (Illus.). 528p. 1997. pap. text 42.00 (0-19-577736-0) OUP.

Memoirs of a Cajun Bishop. Warren L. Boudreaux. Ed. by Louis G. Aguirre & Irene C. Michel. 400p. 1995. 14.95 (0-9649183-0-7) H-T Pubng.

Memoirs of a Captivity among the Indians of North America. John D. Hunter. (American Biography Ser.). 252p. 1991. reprint ed. lib. bdg. 69.00 (0-7812-8205-5) Rprt Serv.

Memoirs of a Cavalier see Shakespeare Head Edition of the Novels & Selected Writings of Daniel Defoe

Memoirs of a Cavalier. Daniel Defoe. LC 74-13443. (Illus.). reprint ed. write for info. (0-404-07915-6) AMS Pr.

Memoirs of a Century in St. Louis. Karen V. Bewig. 125p. 1993. pap. 14.95 (0-9638054-0-1) K Bewig.

Memoirs of a Certain Nisei. Thomas T. Higa & Elsie Taniguchi. LC 87-90291. (Illus.). 176p. 1988. 17.95 (0-944985-00-9) Higa Pubns.

Memoirs of a Chessnut. Victor A. Keats. LC 96-48605. 208p. 1996. text 89.95 (0-7734-8777-8) E Mellen.

Memoirs of a Chinese Revolutionary. Wang Fan-Hsi. 1991. text 57.50 (0-231-07452-2); pap. text 20.00 (0-231-07453-0) Col U Pr.

Memoirs of a Chinese Revolutionary. Sun Yat-Sen. LC 73-111786. reprint ed. 38.50 (0-404-06305-5) AMS Pr.

***Memoirs of a Cold War Son.** Gaines Post, Jr. LC 99-57732. (Singular Lives Ser.). (Illus.). 246p. 2000. 24.95 (0-87745-701-8) U of Iowa Pr.

Memoirs of a Compassionate Terrorist. Doris Dixon. LC 97-75370. 120p. 1998. pap. 9.95 (1-882792-56-4) Proctor Pubns.

Memoirs of a Computer Pioneer. Maurice Wilkes. (History of Computing Ser.). (Illus.). 200p. 1985. 27.50 (0-262-23122-0) MIT Pr.

Memoirs of a Confederate Staff Officer: From Bethel to Bentonville. James W. Ratchford & Evelyn Sieburg. LC 98-20933. (Civil War Heritage Ser.). 1999. 9.95 (1-57249-092-6) White Mane Pub.

Memoirs of a Confederate Staff Officer: From Bethel to Bentonville. Evelyn Sieburg & James E. Hansen, II. LC 98-20933. 112p. 1998. pap. 9.95 (1-57279-192-6, Burd St Pr) White Mane Pub.

Memoirs of a Dada Drummer. Richard Huelsenbeck. Ed. by Hans J. Kleinschmidt. (Illus.). 252p. 1991. pap. 15.95 (0-520-07370-3, Pub. by U CA Pr) Cal Prin Full Svc.

Memoirs of a Dance Hall Romeo. Jack Higgins. Ed. by Julie Rubenstein. 192p. 1990. reprint ed. mass mkt. 6.50 (0-671-67844-2) PB.

Memoirs of a Dissident Publisher. Henry Regnery. LC 78-22269. 260p. 1979. pap. 9.95 (0-89526-802-7) Regnery Pub.

Memoirs of a Doctor's Wife. Betty Wright. 1982. mass mkt. 2.95 (0-8217-1005-2, Zebra Kensgtn) Kensgtn Pub Corp.

Memoirs of a Dutiful Daughter. Simone de Beauvoir. Tr. by James Kirkup from FRE. 368p. 1974. reprint ed. pap. 13.00 (0-06-090351-1, CN351, Perennial) HarperTrade.

Memoirs of a Fortunate Jew: An Italian Story. Dan V. Segre. LC 94-39308.Tr. of Storia di un Ebreo Fortunato. 284p. 1995. pap. 30.00 (1-56821-437-5) Aronson.

Memoirs of a Fox-Hunting Man. Siegfried Sassoon. 320p. 1960. pap. 13.95 (0-571-06454-X) Faber & Faber.

Memoirs of a Geisha. Arthur Golden. LC 97-74747. 1997. 26.95 (0-375-40011-7) Knopf.

Memoirs of a Geisha. Arthur Golden. LC 98-26449. 448p. 1999. pap. 14.00 (0-679-78158-7) Vin Bks.

Memoirs of a Geisha. large type ed. Arthur Golden. LC 98-13744. 1998. 28.95 (0-7838-0145-9, G K Hall Lrg Type) Mac Lib Ref.

Memoirs of a Geisha. large type ed. Arthur Golden. LC 98-13744. 1999. pap. 20.00 (0-7838-0146-7, G K Hall Lrg Type) Mac Lib Ref.

Memoirs of a Gigolo. Marcos Rey. 224p. 1987. pap. 7.95 (0-380-75000-7, Avon Bks) Morrow Avon.

***Memoirs of a Great Detective.** John Wilson Murray. (Other Literature Ser.). 2000. text 36.00 (1-55246-176-9) Battered Silicon.

Memoirs of a Hidden Child During the Holocaust: My Life During the War. Bronislawa Alland. Tr. by George Alland from POL. LC 92-21427. (Illus.). 108p. 1992. text 59.95 (0-7734-9155-4) E Mellen.

Memoirs of a Highland Lady: Complete Edition, Set, Vols. I & II. Elizabeth Grant. (Classics Ser.). 720p. 1996. pap. 15.95 (0-86241-396-6, Pub. by Canongate Books) Interlink Pub.

Memoirs of a Hunter. Charles Myers. (American Autobiography Ser.). 309p. 1995. reprint ed. lib. bdg. 89.00 (0-7812-8599-2) Rprt Serv.

Memoirs of a Korean Queen. Lady Hong of Hyegyong Palace. Ed. by Yang-hi Choe-Wall. (Illus.). 200p. 1985. text 32.50 (0-7103-0052-2) Routledge.

Memoirs of a Liberian Ambassador, George Arthur Padmore. George A. Padmore. LC 96-21538. (Illus.). 212p. 1996. 89.95 (0-7734-8744-1) E Mellen.

Memoirs of a Lincoln Conspirator. (Illus.). xviii, 205p. (Orig.). 1996. pap. 21.00 (0-7884-0367-2, K082) Heritage Bk.

Memoirs of a Loghborough Man: A. E. Shepherd, 1872-1962. Joy Cross. 1994. pap. 21.00 (1-85041-076-3, Pub. by U of Nottingham) St Mut.

Memoirs of a Lost World. Lascelle De Basily. LC 75-29793. (Special Projects Ser.: No. 15). 308p. 1975. 9.95 (0-8179-9287-1) Hoover Inst Pr.

Memoirs of a Mangy Lover. Groucho Marx. LC 96-46945. (Illus.). 224p. 1997. reprint ed. pap. 13.95 (0-306-80769-6) Da Capo.

Memoirs of a Married Woman. Betty Wright. 1982. mass mkt. 2.95 (0-89083-983-2, Zebra Kensgtn) Kensgtn Pub Corp.

Memoirs of a Maverick Lawyer. Webster Macdonald. (Illus.). 237p. (Orig.). 1993. pap. 19.95 (1-55059-068-5) Temeron Bks.

Memoirs of a Maverick Mathematician. Zoltan P. Dienes. LC 99-492151. 569p. 1998. write for info. (0-7541-0350-1, Pub. by Minerva Pr) Unity Dist.

Memoirs of a Medieval Woman. Louise Collis. LC 82-48226. (Illus.). 288p. 1991. pap. 13.50 (0-06-090992-7, CN 992, Perennial) HarperTrade.

Memoirs of a Mexican Politician. Roderic A. Camp. LC 87-30244. (Illus.). 248p. 1988. reprint ed. pap. 76.90 (0-608-04128-9, 206486100011) Bks Demand.

Memoirs of a Midget. large type ed. Walter De La Mare. 579p. 1997. reprint ed. lib. bdg. 24.00 (0-939495-11-2) North Bks.

Memoirs of a Midget. Walter De La Mare. 454p. 1998. reprint ed. lib. bdg. 24.00 (1-58287-003-9) North Bks.

***Memoirs of a Militia Sergeant.** Miguel V. De Almeida. Ed. by Thomas H. Holloway & Flora Sussekind. Tr. by Ronald W. Sousa from POR. LC 98-48751. 208p. 2000. 30.00 (0-19-511549-X); pap. 14.95 (0-19-511550-3) OUP.

Memoirs of a Millman, 1947-1986, Vol. 2. Norman Weiss. LC 93-94092. 194p. 1993. pap. 19.50 (0-9638124-0-8) WEICO Pubng.

Memoirs of a Minotaur: From Charles Merrill to Patty Hearst to Poetry by Robin Magowan. Robin Magowan. 273p. 1999. pap. 16.95 (1-885266-79-0, Pub. by Story Line) Consort Bk Sales.

Memoirs of a Mountain Man. Andy Russell. 305p. 1984. mass mkt. 5.95 (0-88780-156-0, Pub. by Formac Publ Co) Formac Dist Ltd.

Memoirs of a Navy Major. Richard J. Nowatzki. (Illus.). 256p. (Orig.). 1995. pap. 10.95 (0-9645284-0-1) R J Nowatzki.

Memoirs of a New American. Nathan Kushin. (American Autobiography Ser.). 157p. 1995. reprint ed. lib. bdg. 69.00 (0-7812-8572-0) Rprt Serv.

Memoirs of a News Editor: Thirty Years with the Hindu. Rangaswami Parthasarathy. 1983. 17.50 (0-8364-0930-2, Pub. by Naya Prokash) S Asia.

Memoirs of a Nobody: The Missouri Years of an Austrian Radical, 1849-1866. Henry Boernstein. Ed. & Tr. by Steve Rowan from GER. LC 97-20637. (GER., Illus.). 412p. (Orig.). 1997. 27.95 (1-883982-20-0) MO Hist Soc.

Memoirs of a Nobody: The Missouri Years of an Austrian Radical, 1849-1866. Henry Boernstein. Tr. by Steven Rowan from GER. LC 97-20637. (GER., Illus.). 412p. (Orig.). 1997. pap. 19.95 (1-883982-21-9) MO Hist Soc.

Memoirs of a Nobody: The Missouri Years of an Austrian Radical, 1849-1866. Henry Boernstein. 432p. (Orig.). 1997. 34.95 (0-8143-2725-7) Wayne St U Pr.

Memoirs of a Nun. Denis Diderot. Tr. by Francis Birrell. 1992. 15.00 (0-679-41324-3) Everymns Lib.

***Memoirs of a Papillon: The Canine Guide to Living with Humans without Going Mad.** Dennis Fried & Genevieve. LC 00-132251. (Illus.). 160p. (YA). 2000. pap. 13.95 (0-9679335-0-1, 418) Eiffel Pr.

Memoirs of a Pet Therapist. Warren Eckstein & Denise Madden. LC 97-53125. 272p. 1998. 23.95 (0-449-91123-3) Fawcett.

Memoirs of a Pet Therapist. Warren Eckstein & Denise Madden. 1999. mass mkt. 6.99 (0-449-00534-8) Fawcett.

Memoirs of a Philosopher. Frederick C. Copleston. LC 93-7810. 240p. (Orig.). 1993. 19.95 (1-55612-570-4); pap. 14.95 (1-55612-621-2) Sheed & Ward WI.

***Memoirs of a Physician.** Alexandre Dumas. 252p. 2000. pap. 9.95 (0-594-02976-7) Eightn Hundrd.

***Memoirs of a Physician, Vol. II.** Alexandre Dumas. 252p. 2000. pap. 9.95 (0-594-02981-3) Eightn Hundrd.

***Memoirs of a Physician, Vol. III.** Alexandre Dumas. 252p. 2000. pap. 9.95 (0-594-03016-1) Eightn Hundrd.

Memoirs of a Polish Lancer. Dezydery Chlapowski. Tr. by Tim Simmons. (Illus.). 160p. 1992. 27.00 (0-9626655-2-5, Pub. by Emperors Pr) Combined Pub.

Memoirs of a Political Officer's Wife in Tibet, Sikkim & Bhutan. Margaret D. Williamson. (Tibet Book - Yellow Ser.). (Illus.). 240p. (Orig.). 1987. pap. 18.95 (0-86171-056-8) Wisdom MA.

Memoirs of a Professional Cad. George Sanders. LC 92-24442. (Filmmakers Ser.: No. 32). (Illus.). 298p. 1992. 38.00 (0-8108-2579-1) Scarecrow.

Memoirs of a Provincial Priest: A Novel. Igoumen I. Ekonomtsev. LC 99-15512. (Russian Studies in Art, Literature, Theatre: Vol. 3). (RUS.). 228p. 1999. text 89.95 (0-7734-3249-3) E Mellen.

Memoirs of a Recovering Autocrat: Revealing Insights for Managing the Autocrat in All of Us. Richard W. Hallstein. LC 93-8187. (Illus.). 160p. 1993. 17.95 (1-881052-35-4) Berrett-Koehler.

Memoirs of a Redruth Childhood. Winifred Hawkey. (C). 1989. 45.00 (1-85022-024-7, Pub. by Dyllansow Truran) St Mut.

Memoirs of a Reggae Foundation Legend: The Upside down of Inside Out - Selah! Ricardo Scott. (Reggae Legend Ras Cardo Speaks Unknown Truths Ser.). (Illus.). 115p. 1999. pap. write for info. (1-58470-032-7, RAS9949) Crnerstone GA.

Memoirs of a Revolutionary. Victor Serge. (Illus.). 404p. 1984. 22.95 (0-86316-071-9); pap. 10.95 (0-86316-070-0) Writers & Readers.

Memoirs of a Revolutionist. Peter Kropotkin. 504p. 1989. 48.99 (0-921689-19-5, Pub. by Black Rose); pap. 19.99 (0-921689-18-7, Pub. by Black Rose) Consort Bk Sales.

Memoirs of a Revolutionist. Vera Figner. LC 90-28720. 328p. (C). 1991. reprint ed. pap. text 16.00 (0-87580-552-3) N Ill U Pr.

Memoirs of a Russian Diplomat: Outpost of the Empire, 1893-1917. Ed. by Andrew D. Kalmykow. LC 67-13440. (Yale Russian & East European Studies: No. 10). 306p. reprint ed. pap. 94.90 (0-608-30061-6, 202200700024) Bks Demand.

Memoirs of a Russian Princess. (Red Stripe Ser.). 1989. pap. 4.50 (0-8216-5066-1, Univ Books) Carol Pub Group.

Memoirs of a Semidetached Australian. John Passmore. LC 98-109991. (Illus.). 288p. 1998. 39.95 (0-522-84766-8, Pub. by Melbourne Univ Pr) Paul & Co Pubs.

Memoirs of a Shy Pornographer. rev. ed. Kenneth Patchen. LC 98-37235. (New Directions Classic Ser.). 242p. 1999. pap. 14.00 (0-8112-1411-7, NDP879, Pub. by New Directions) Norton.

Memoirs of a Social Atom, 2 Vols. in 1. William E. Adams. LC 67-29700. xix, 688p. 1968. reprint ed. 75.00 (0-678-00349-1) Kelley.

Memoirs of a Soldier, Nurse & Spy: A Woman's Adventures in the Union Army. Sarah E. Edmonds. LC 99-16625. 250p. 1999. pap. 18.00 (0-87580-584-1, 584-1) N Ill U Pr.

***Memoirs of a Soldier, Nurse & Spy: A Woman's Adventures in the Union Army.** Sarah E. Edmonds. LC 99-16625. (Illus.). 250p. 1999. 38.00 (0-87580-259-1, 259-1) N Ill U Pr.

Memoirs of a Speleologist: The Adventurous Life of a Famous French Cave Explorer. Robert De Joly. Tr. by Peter Kurz. LC 75-31836. (Illus.). 185p. (Orig.). 1975. 10.95 (0-914264-08-7); pap. 5.95 (0-914264-09-5) Cave Bks MO.

***Memoirs of a Spiritual Outsider: Young Women on the Backroads of Religious Tradition.** Suzanne Clores. 250p. 2000. 23.95 (1-57324-172-5) Conari Press.

Memoirs of a Sportsman. Ivan Sergeevich Turgenev. Tr. by Isabel F. Hapgood. LC 75-101823. (Short Story Index Reprint Ser.). 347p. 1977. 31.95 (0-8369-3211-0) Ayer.

Memoirs of a Steelworker. David Kuchta. LC 96-71775. (Illus.). 117p. 1997. pap. 12.95 (0-930973-17-8) H M Historical.

Memoirs of a Superfluous Man. Albert J. Nock. 326p. 1994. pap. 16.95 (0-87319-038-6) Hallberg Pub Corp.

Memoirs of a Superfluous Man. Albert J. Nock. LC 83-45827. reprint ed. 30.00 (0-404-20192-X) AMS Pr.

Memoirs of a Survivor. Doris Lessing. Ed. by Anne Freedgood. LC 87-45951. 224p. 1988. reprint ed. pap. 12.00 (0-394-75759-9) Vin Bks.

Memoirs of a Sword Swallower: Formerly Step Right Up. Daniel P. Mannix. Orig. Title: Step Right Up. (Illus.). 128p. (Orig.). 1996. pap. 15.99 (0-9650469-5-8) RE Search.

Memoirs of a Terrorist. Sally P. Tubach. LC 95-39821. (SUNY Series, The Margins of Literature). 174p. (C). 1996. text 29.50 (0-7914-3005-7) State U NY Pr.

Memoirs of a Terrorist. Sally P. Tubach. LC 95-39821. (SUNY Series, The Margins of Literature). 174p. (C). 1996. pap. text 19.95 (0-7914-3006-5) State U NY Pr.

Memoirs of a Tibetan Lama. Lobsang Gyatso. Ed. & Tr. by Gareth Sparham from TIB. LC 98-25832. (Illus.). 373p. 1998. pap. 16.95 (1-55939-097-2) Snow Lion Pubns.

Memoirs of a Translator of Poetry. Kendall Lappin. 72p. 1999. pap. 10.00 (1-878580-32-9) Asylum Arts.

Memoirs of a Turkish Statesman, 1913-1919. Cemal Pasha. LC 73-6295. (Middle East Ser.). 1973. reprint ed. 25.95 (0-405-05328-2) Ayer.

***Memoirs of a Whenwe: Colonial Life in Tanzania.** Babu. (Illus.). 128p. 2000. 23.50 (1-85776-483-8, Pub. by Book Guild Ltd) Trans-Atl Phila.

Memoirs of a White Crow Indian. Thomas H. Leforge & Thomas B. Marquis. LC 74-6222. xxiv, 356p. 1974. reprint ed. pap. 10.95 (0-8032-5800-3, Bison Books) U of Nebr Pr.

Memoirs of a Widow. Lula Fulson. (Illus.). 89p. 1996. mass mkt. 10.00 (0-9653784-0-3) L Fulson.

Memoirs of a Wobbly. Henry E. McGuckin. LC 87-80042. (First Person Ser.: No. 2). (Illus.). 96p. (Orig.). 1987. pap. 8.00 (0-88286-157-3) C H Kerr.

Memoirs of a Woman Doctor. Nawal Al-Sa'Dawi. Tr. by Catherine Cobham. 1989. pap. 8.95 (0-87286-223-2) City Lights.

Memoirs of a Woman of Pleasure. John Cleland. LC 99-228456. (Oxford World Classics Ser.). 238p. 1999. pap. 7.95 (0-19-283565-3) OUP.

Memoirs of a Woman of Pleasure (Fanny Hill) John Cleland. 270p. 1998. pap. text 15.00 (0-7881-5871-6) DIANE Pub.

Memoirs of a World War Two Pilot. Marvin L. Skelton. 372p. (Orig.). 1978. pap. text 50.00 (0-89126-064-1) MA-AH Pub.

Memoirs of a Yukon Priest. Segundo Llorente. LC 89-27434. (Illus.). 236p. 1990. pap. 17.95 (0-87840-494-5) Georgetown U Pr.

Memoirs of Aaron Burr, 2 vols., Set. Aaron Burr. (American Biography Ser.). 1991. reprint ed. lib. bdg. 148.00 (0-7812-8053-2) Rprt Serv.

Memoirs of Aaron Burr, with Miscellaneous Selections from His Correspondence, 2 Vols, Set. Matthew L. Davis. (Select Bibliographies Reprint Ser.). 1977. 55.95 (0-8369-5213-8) Ayer.

Memoirs of Abdolmadjin Madjidi. Ed. by Habib Ladjevardi. LC 98-70949. (Harvard Iranian Oral History Ser.: Vol. 5). (PER.). 270p. (Orig.). 1998. pap. 15.00 (0-932885-18-7) Harvard CMES.

Memoirs of Alan Dale Parker. Dale Parker. (Wisdom of the Ages Ser.: Vol. 3). 52p. (Orig.). 1996. pap. 20.00 (0-936390-10-7) Dialog Pr.

Memoirs of Alexander Herzen, Parts I & II. Aleksandr Herzen. Tr. by J. D. Duff from RUS. LC 76-48971. 384p. 1977. reprint ed. lib. bdg. 69.50 (0-8371-9319-2, HEMH, Greenwood Pr) Greenwood.

Memoirs of Alexander Iswolsky. Alexander Iswolsky. LC 72-97048. (Russian Ser.: No. 56). 1974. reprint ed. 30.00 (0-87569-057-2) Academic Intl.

Memoirs of Alexander Spitmuller, Freherr Von Harmersbach. Ed. by Carvel De Bussy. 327p. 1987. text 64.50 (0-88033-124-0, Pub. by East Eur Monographs) Col U Pr.

Memoirs of Alfred Horatio Belo: Reminiscences of a North Carolina Volunteer. Ed. by Stuart Wright. 56p. (Orig.). 1992. pap. 8.50 (1-56013-003-2) Olde Soldier Bks.

Memoirs of Ali Amini: Prime Minister of Iran. Ed. by Habib Ladjevardi. LC 95-81862. 244p. (C). 1995. pap. 15.00 (0-932885-11-X) Harvard CMES.

Memoirs of Alice Guy Blache. Ed. by Anthony Slide. Tr. by Roberta Blache & Simone Blache. LC 95-26819. (Filmmakers Ser.: No. 12). 208p. 1996. reprint ed. pap. 29.50 (0-8108-3104-X) Scarecrow.

***Memoirs of Allegheny County Pennsylvania: Personal & Genealogical Portraits, 2 vols.** Northwest Historical Association Staff. (Illus.). 1096p. 1999. reprint ed. pap. 67.50 (0-7884-1105-5, N567) Heritage Bk.

Memoirs of Allegheny County, Personal & Genealogical, 2 vols. (Illus.). 1090p. 1997. reprint ed. lib. bdg. 113.00 (0-8328-6385-8) Higginson Bk Co.

Memoirs of an African Hunter: A Narrative of a Professional Hunter's Experiences in Africa. limited ed. Terry Irwin. (Illus.). 411p. 1998. 125.00 (1-57157-076-4) Safari Pr.

Memoirs of an Air Observation Post Officer. Ed. by Andrew Lyell. 162p. (C). 1990. pap. 36.00 (0-948251-06-9, Pub. by Picton) St Mut.

Memoirs of an American Citizen. Robert Herrick. Ed. by Daniel Aaron. LC 63-10864. (John Harvard Library). 302p. 1963. pap. 13.95 (0-674-56501-0) HUP.

Memoirs of an American Citizen see Collected Works of Robert Herrick

Memoirs of an American Citizen. Robert Herrick. (Collected Works of Robert Herrick). 1988. reprint ed. lib. bdg. 59.00 (0-7812-1268-5) Rprt Serv.

Memoirs of an American Gold Seeker. John E. Brown. 34p. 1986. pap. 5.95 (0-87770-368-X) Ye Galleon.

Memoirs of an American Lady. Anne Grant. 397p. 1993. reprint ed. lib. bdg. 89.00 (0-7812-5122-2) Rprt Serv.

Memoirs of an American Lady: With Sketches of Manners & Scenes in America As They Existed Previous to the Revolution; With Unpublished Letters & a Memoir of Mrs. Grant, by James Grant Wilson. Anne Grant. LC 77-38354. (Select Bibliographies Reprint Ser.). 1977. reprint ed. 35.95 (0-8369-6771-2) Ayer.

Memoirs of an American Prima Donna. Clara L. Kellogg. LC 77-16534. (Music Reprint Ser.: 1978). (Illus.). 1978. reprint ed. lib. bdg. 45.00 (0-306-77527-1) Da Capo.

Memoirs of an American Prima Donna. Clara L. Kellogg. (American Biography Ser.). 382p. 1991. reprint ed. lib. bdg. 79.00 (0-7812-8231-4) Rprt Serv.

Memoirs of an Amnesiac. Oscar Levant. LC 89-36545. 320p. 1989. pap. 12.95 (0-573-60698-6) S French Trade.

Memoirs of an Anti-Semite. Gregor Von Rezzori. LC 90-50157. (Vintage International Ser.). 304p. 1991. pap. 16.00 (0-679-73182-2) Vin Bks.

An Asterisk (*) at the beginning of an entry indicates that the title is appearing for the first time.

Memoirs of an Arabian Princess from Zanzibar. rev. ed. Emily Ruete. Tr. by Markus W. Wiener from GER. LC 89-9064. (Topics in World History Ser.). (Illus.). 326p. (C). 1989. reprint ed. text 39.95 (*1-55876-011-3*) Wiener Pubs Inc.

Memoirs of an Arabian Princess from Zanzibar. rev. ed. Emily Ruete. Tr. by Markus W. Wiener from GER. LC 89-9064. (Topics in World History Ser.). (Illus.). 326p. (C). 1990. reprint ed. pap. text 18.95 (*1-55876-007-5*) Wiener Pubs Inc.

Memoirs of an Around-the-World Mechanic (1924) & Pilot (1941) Alva L. Harvey. 43p. (Orig.). 1978. pap. text 21.95 (*0-89126-065-X*) MA-AH Pub.

***Memoirs of an Artillery Forward Observer, 1944-1945.** J. Russell Major. (Illus.). 184p. 1999. pap. 18.95 (*0-89745-229-1*) Sunflower U Pr.

Memoirs of an Ex-Prom Queen. Alix K. Shulman. LC 97-202764. 288p. 1997. pap. 12.95 (*0-14-026571-6*) Viking Penguin.

Memoirs of an Ex-Prom Queen. Alix K. Shulman. (Cassandra Edition Ser.). 274p. 1985. reprint ed. pap. 10.00 (*0-89733-173-7*) Academy Chi Pubs.

***Memoirs of an Idaho Elk Hunter.** Jens Andersen. 1998. pap. 19.95 (*0-912299-78-9*) Stoneydale Pr Pub.

Memoirs of an Indian Woman. Shudha Mazumdar. Ed. & Intro. by Geraldine H. Forbes. LC 89-10272. (Foremother Legacies). 248p. (C). (gr. 13). 1989. 69.95 (*0-87332-520-6*, East Gate Bk) M E Sharpe.

Memoirs of an Indian Woman. Shudha Mazumdar. Ed. & Intro. by Geraldine Forbes. LC 89-10272. (Foremother Legacies Ser.). 248p. (gr. 13). 1995. pap. 19.95 (*1-56324-552-3*, East Gate Bk) M E Sharpe.

Memoirs of an Indo Woman: Twentieth-Century Life in the East Indies & Abroad. Marguerite Schenkhuizen. Tr. by Lizelot S. Van Balgooy. LC 93-30346. (Monographs in International Studies, Southeast Asia Ser.: No. 92). (Illus.). 248p. (Orig.). 1993. pap. text 25.00 (*0-89680-178-0*) Ohio U Pr.

Memoirs of an Infantry Officer. Siegfried Sassoon. 236p. 1965. pap. 11.95 (*0-571-06410-8*) Faber & Faber.

Memoirs of an Infantry Officer. large type ed. Siegfried Sassoon. 307p. 1990. 19.95 (*1-85089-361-6*, Pub. by ISIS Lrg Prnt) Transaction Pubs.

Memoirs of an Infantryman in World War II. limited ed. Salvatore Galioto. Ed. by Nancy Galioto & Joyce Carbone. (Illus.). 60p. (Orig.). 1997. pap. 6.95 (*1-878116-67-3*) JVC Bks.

Memoirs of an Obscure Professor. Paul F. Boller. LC 91-30356. (Illus.). 258p. 1992. 24.95 (*0-87565-097-X*) Tex Christian.

Memoirs of an Old Actor. Walter M. Leman. LC 78-91905. 1972. 26.95 (*0-405-08741-1*) Ayer.

Memoirs of an Unconventional Soldier. J. F. Fuller. 1976. lib. bdg. 59.95 (*0-8490-2223-1*) Gordon Pr.

Memoirs of an Unrepentant Field Geologist: A Candid Profile of Some Geologists & Their Science, 1921-1981. F. J. Pettijohn. LC 83-12347. (Illus.). 288p. 1993. pap. 10.95 (*0-226-66405-8*) U Ch Pr.

Memoirs of an Unrepetant Leftist. Victor Rabinowitz. LC 95-50239. (C). 1996. text. write for info. (*0-614-95870-9*) U of Ill Pr.

Memoirs of Anastas Mikoyan Vol. I: The Path of Struggle. Tr. by Anatol Kagan from RUS. 583p. 1988. 40.00 (*0-943071-04-6*) Sphinx Pr.

Memoirs of Andrew Sherburne: A Pensioner of the Navy of the Revolution. Andrew Sherburne. LC 71-133532. (Select Bibliographies Reprint Ser.). 1977. 20.95 (*0-8369-5564-1*) Ayer.

Memoirs of Andrew Sherburne: A Pensioner of the Navy of the Revolution, Written by Himself. Andrew Sherburne. Ed. by Karen Zeinert. LC 92-20542. (Illus.). 96p. (YA). (gr. 7-12). 1993. lib. bdg. 17.50 (*0-208-02354-2*, Linnet Bks) Shoe String.

Memoirs of Anne C. L. Botta, Written by Her Friends. Anne C. Botta. (American Biography Ser.). 459p. 1991. reprint ed. lib. bdg. 89.00 (*0-7812-8030-3*) Rprt Serv.

Memoirs of Anne, Lady Halkett, & Ann, Lady Fanshawe. Anne Halkett & Ann Fanshawe. Ed. by John Loftis. 1979. 69.00 (*0-19-812087-7*) OUP.

Memoirs of Baghdad, Kurdistan & Turkish Arabia, 1857. James F. Jones. (Illus.). 544p. 1998. reprint ed. lib. bdg. 495.00 (*1-85207-099-4*, Pub. by Archive Editions) N Ross.

Memoirs of Baron de Tott, 2 vols. Baron De Tott. LC 73-6303. (Middle East Ser.). 1973. reprint ed. 51.95 (*0-405-05363-0*) Ayer.

Memoirs of Baron Von Muffling: A Prussian Officer in the Napoleonic Wars. Friedrich K. Muffling. LC 96-49843. (Napoleonic Library). 1997. write for info. (*1-85367-273-4*) Stackpole.

Memoirs of Barry Lyndon Esq. large type ed. William Makepeace Thackeray. LC 98-19077. 1998. pap. 25.95 (*0-7838-0272-2*, G K Hall Lrg Type) Mac Lib Ref.

Memoirs of Beniamino Gigli. Beniamino Gigli. Ed. by Andrew Farkas. Tr. by Darina Silone. LC 76-29937. (Opera Biographies Ser.). (Illus.). 1979. reprint ed. lib. bdg. 36.00 (*0-405-09679-8*) Ayer.

Memoirs of Ber of Bolechow (1723-1805) Ber of Bolechow. LC 73-2186. (Jewish People; History, Religion, Literature Ser.). 1973. reprint ed. 21.95 (*0-405-05252-9*) Ayer.

Memoirs of Bernardo Vega: A Contribution to the History of the Puerto Rican Community in New York. Bernardo Vega. Ed. by Cesar A. Iglesias. Tr. by Juan Flores from SPA.Tr. of Memorias de Bernardo Vega. (Illus.). 288p. 1984. pap. 16.00 (*0-85345-656-9*, Pub. by Monthly Rev) NYU Pr.

Memoirs of Brigadier General William Passmore Carlin, U.S.A. William P. Carlin. Ed. by Robert I. Girardi & Nathaniel C. Hughes. LC 99-12594. (Illus.). 352p. (Orig.). 1999. text 50.00 (*0-8032-1494-4*) U of Nebr Pr.

Memoirs of Capitalism, Communism, & Nazism. Calvin B. Hoover. LC 65-24926. 312p. reprint ed. pap. 96.80 (*0-608-12746-9*, 202340300033) Bks Demand.

Memoirs of Captain Lemuel Roberts. Lemuel Roberts. Ed. by Peter Decker. LC 70-79945. (Eyewitness Accounts of the American Revolution Ser.). 1969. reprint ed. 15.95 (*0-405-01175-X*) Ayer.

Memoirs of Captain Rock (pseud.) the Celebrated Irish Chieftain: With Some Account of His Ancestors. Thomas Moore. LC 75-28831. reprint ed. 67.50 (*0-404-13821-7*) AMS Pr.

Memoirs of Chancellor Pasquier, 1767-1815. Tr. by Douglas Garmen. LC 68-9353. (Illus.). 292p. 1975. 29.50 (*0-8386-6981-6*) Fairleigh Dickinson.

Memoirs of Chaplain Life: Three Years with the Irish Brigade in the Army of the Potomac William Corby C. S. C. Ed. by Lawrence F. Kohl. LC 89-84565. (Irish in the Civil War Ser.: Vol. 2). (Illus.). xxv, 412p. 1992. 30.00 (*0-8232-1251-3*) Fordham.

Memoirs of Charles G. Finney: The Complete Restored Text. Ed. by Garth M. Rosell & Richard A. Dupuis. 736p. 1997. pap. 22.99 (*0-310-21925-6*) Zondervan.

Memoirs of Charles Henry Veil: A Soldier's Recollections of the Civil War & the Arizona Territory. large type ed. Intro. by Herman J. Viola. LC 94-1085. 326p. 1994. lib. bdg. 19.95 (*0-7862-0194-0*) Thorndike Pr.

Memoirs of Charles Macklin. William Cooke. LC 72-82822. 444p. 1972. 30.95 (*0-405-08378-5*, Pub. by Blom Pubns) Ayer.

Memoirs of Childhood: An Approach to Jewish Philosophy. Nima H. Adlerblum. Ed. by Els Benheim. LC 98-5658. 327p. 1999. pap. 25.00 (*0-7657-6012-6*) Aronson.

Memoirs of Childhood & Youth. Albert Schweitzer et al. Ed. & Tr. by Kurt Bergel & Alice R. Bergel. LC 96-49619. 96p. 1997. 19.95 (*0-8156-0446-7*) Syracuse U Pr.

Memoirs of Cleopatra: A Novel. Margaret George. LC 96-51071. 1997. text 27.95 (*0-312-15430-5*) St Martin.

Memoirs of Cleopatra: A Novel. Margaret George. 1999. pap. 307.00 (*0-312-24601-3*) St Martin.

Memoirs of Cleopatra: A Novel. 4th ed. Margaret George. 964p. 1998. pap. 15.95 (*0-312-18745-9*) St Martin.

Memoirs of Colonel John S. Mosby. Charles W. Russell. 414p. 1987. reprint ed. 35.00 (*0-942211-27-8*) Olde Soldier Bks.

Memoirs of Cordell Hull, 2 vols., Set. Cordell Hull. (History - United States Ser.). 1993. reprint ed. lib. bdg. 150.00 (*0-7812-4811-6*) Rprt Serv.

Memoirs of Count Lavallette. Antoine M. Lavalette. 1977. 41.95 (*0-8369-7145-0*, 7978) Ayer.

Memoirs of Count Witte. Ed. & Tr. by Sidney Harcave from RUS. LC 89-43534. 1120p. (C). (gr. 13). 1990. text 106.95 (*0-87332-571-0*) M E Sharpe.

Memoirs of Cyril Jones: People, Society & Railways in Hyderabad. Ed. by Omar Khalidi. (C). 1991. 15.00 (*81-85425-54-X*, Pub. by Manohar) S Asia.

Memoirs of David Blaustein: Educator & Communal Worker. David Blaustein. LC 74-27966. (Modern Jewish Experience Ser.). (Illus.). 1975. reprint ed. 31.95 (*0-405-06696-1*) Ayer.

Memoirs of Desmond Fitzgerald, 1913-1916. Desmond Fitzgerald. LC 72-366210. xiii, 201p. 1968. write for info. (*0-7100-2878-4*, Routledge Thoemms) Routledge.

Memoirs of Dr. Burney, Arranged from His Own Manuscripts, from Family Papers, & from Personal Recollections, 3 vols., Set. Frances D'O Arblay. LC 78-37680. reprint ed. 210.00 (*0-404-56704-5*) AMS Pr.

Memoirs of Dr. Charles Burney, 1726-1769. Charles Burney. Ed. by Slava Klima et al. LC 87-6060. xl, 233p. 1988. text 55.00 (*0-8032-1197-X*) U of Nebr Pr.

Memoirs of E. A. Jack, Steam Engineer, CSS Virginia. Eugenius A. Jack. Ed. by Alan B. Flanders. LC 98-6559. (Illus.). 76p. 1998. pap. 12.95 (*1-883911-29-X*) Brandylane.

Memoirs of Edmund Ludlow, Lieutenant-General of the Horse in the Army of the Commonwealth of England, 1625-1672, 2 vols., Set. Edmund Ludlow. Ed. by C. H. Firth. LC 75-31098. (Illus.). reprint ed. 95.00 (*0-404-13520-X*) AMS Pr.

Memoirs of Eighty Years. Thomas G. Hake. LC 73-131509. reprint ed. 45.00 (*0-404-03025-4*) AMS Pr.

Memoirs of Elder John White, One of the First Settlers of Hartford, Connecticut, & of His Descendants. A. S. Kellogg. 340p. 1989. reprint ed. pap. 51.00 (*0-8328-1249-8*); reprint ed. lib. bdg. 59.00 (*0-8328-1248-X*) Higginson Bk Co.

Memoirs of Elias Canetti, 3 bks. in 1. Elias Canetti. LC 98-48752. 840p. 1999. 40.00 (*0-374-19950-7*) FS&G.

***Memoirs of Elias Canetti, 3 bks. in 1.** Elias Canetti. LC 98-48752. 840p. 2000. pap. 20.00 (*0-374-52714-8*) FS&G.

Memoirs of Elizabeth Frankenstein. Theodore Roszak. 448p. 1996. mass mkt. 5.99 (*0-553-57637-2*) Bantam.

Memoirs of Elleanor Eldridge. Elleanor Eldridge. (Black Heritage Library Collection). 1977. 27.95 (*0-8369-8748-9*) Ayer.

Memoirs of Emma Courtney. Mary Hays. Ed. by Marilyn Brooks. (Literary Texts Ser.). 340p. 2000. pap. 12.95 (*1-55111-155-1*) Broadview Pr.

Memoirs of Emma Courtney. Mary Hays. Ed. by Eleanor Ty. (World's Classics Ser.). 272p. (C). 1996. pap. 11.95 (*0-19-282306-X*) OUP.

***Memoirs of Emma Courtney.** Mary Hays. Ed. by Eleanor Ty. 272p. 2000. pap. 12.95 (*0-19-283729-X*) OUP.

Memoirs of Esotericist. Mollie Moncrieff. 250p. 1995. write for info. (*1-888477-00-8*) Saunders & Rakauskas.

Memoirs of Eugenie Schumann. Eugenie Schumann. (Music Ser.). 1985. pap. 19.50 (*0-306-87371-0*) Da Capo.

Memoirs of Eunice Irene Tutor Roberts. Eunice Roberts. (Wisdom of the Ages Ser.). 34p. (Orig.). 1996. pap. 20.00 (*0-936390-27-7*, Wisdom of the Ages) Dialog Pr.

Memoirs of Fatemeh Pakravan. Ed. by Habib Ladjevardi. LC 98-71971. (Harvard Iranian Oral History Ser.: Vol. 6). (Illus.). 155p. (Orig.). 1998. pap. 15.00 (*0-932885-19-5*) Harvard CMES.

Memoirs of Father Ripa. Matteo Ripa. LC 75-36239. reprint ed. 32.50 (*0-404-14487-X*) AMS Pr.

Memoirs of Father Samuel Mazzuchelli, O. P. Samuel Mazzuchelli. (American Biography Ser.). 329p. 1991. reprint ed. lib. bdg. 79.00 (*0-7812-8279-9*) Rprt Serv.

Memoirs of Field-Marshal Kesselring. Robert Kesselring. LC 97-15632. 1997. pap. write for info. (*1-85367-287-4*) Greenhill Bks.

***Memoirs of Field-Marshal Wilhelm Keitel: Chief of the German High Command, 1938-1945.** Walter Gorlitz. 2000. pap. 18.95 (*0-8154-1072-7*) Cooper Sq.

Memoirs of Field-Marshall the Viscount Montgomery of Alamein, K. G. 516p. 1989. 18.95 (*0-8306-4010-X*) McGraw-Hill Prof.

Memoirs of Fourth Missouri Cavalry. William S. Burns. (Illus.). 161p. 1988. 20.00 (*0-89029-315-5*) Morningside Bkshop.

Memoirs of Fray Servando Teresa de Mier. Fray S. De Mier. Ed. by Susana Rotker. Tr. by Helen Lane from SPA. LC 97-40671. (Library of Latin America). 304p. 1998. 30.00 (*0-19-510673-3*) OUP.

Memoirs of Fray Servando Teresa de Mier. De Mier Fray Servando Teresa. LC 97-40671. 304p. 1998. pap. 15.95 (*0-19-510674-1*) OUP.

Memoirs of Frederic Mistral. Frederic Mistral. LC 86-8768.Tr. of Moun Espelido. 352p. 1986. pap. 10.95 (*0-8112-1009-X*, NDP632, Pub. by New Directions) Norton.

Memoirs of Frederic Mistral. Frederic Mistral. LC 86-8768.Tr. of Moun Espelido. 352p. 1986. 22.95 (*0-8112-0992-X*, Pub. by New Directions) Norton.

Memoirs of Frederick A. P. Barnard, Tenth President of Columbia College in the City of New York. John Fulton. 1977. 22.95 (*0-8369-7160-4*, 7992) Ayer.

Memoirs of Friedrich Ferdinand, Count Von Beust, 2 vols., Set. Friedrich F. Von Beust. 1971. reprint ed. 59.00 (*0-403-00812-3*) Scholarly.

Memoirs of General Ali-Akbar Derakhshani. Ali-Akbar Derakhshani. LC 94-94333. (PER., Illus.). 570p. (Orig.). 1994. pap. 19.95 (*0-936347-53-8*) IBEX.

Memoirs of General Lord Ismay. Lord Ismay. LC 73-22504. (Illus.). 488p. 1974. reprint ed. lib. bdg. 79.50 (*0-8371-6280-7*, ISMF, Greenwood Pr) Greenwood.

Memoirs of General Miller, in the Service of the Republic of Peru, 2 vols. 2nd ed. John Miller. reprint ed. 135.00 (*0-404-04339-9*) AMS Pr.

Memoirs of General Thomas Francis Meagher. Michael Cavanaugh. 534p. 35.00 (*1-56013-006-7*) Olde Soldier Bks.

Memoirs of General Turner Ashby & His Campaigns. James B. Avirett. 428p. 1987. reprint ed. 28.50 (*0-942211-31-6*) Olde Soldier Bks.

Memoirs of General Turner Ashby & His Compeers. James B. Avirett. 428p. 1984. reprint ed. 35.50 (*0-913419-04-4*, J M C & Co) Amereon Ltd.

***Memoirs of General William T. Sherman.** William T. Sherman. LC 99-89154. (Penguin Classics Ser.). 2000. pap. 16.95 (*0-14-043798-3*) Viking Penguin.

Memoirs of General William T. Sherman by Himself, 2 vols. in one. William T. Sherman. LC 70-170607. 405p. 1972. reprint ed. lib. bdg. 85.00 (*0-8371-6253-X*, SHME, Greenwood Pr) Greenwood.

Memoirs of George E. Harmon. (Illus.). 56p. 1.50 (*0-686-29129-8*) Faith Pub Hse.

Memoirs of George E. Harmon, 2 vols., Set. (Illus.). 56p. 1.00 (*0-686-29130-1*) Faith Pub Hse.

Memoirs of Giambattista Scala: Consult of His Italian Majesty in Lagos in Guinea (1862) Giambattista Scala. Ed. by Robert Smith. Tr. by Brenda Packman. Vol. 2. (Illus.). 200p. 2000. text 49.95 (*0-19-726204-X*) OUP.

Memoirs of Giorgio de Chirico. Giorgio De Chirico. Tr. & Intro. by Margaret Crosland. (Illus.). 262p. 1994. reprint ed. pap. 13.95 (*0-306-80568-5*) Da Capo.

Memoirs of Gluckel of Hamelin. Gluckel of Hameln. Tr. by Marvin Lowenthal from GER. LC 77-75290. (Illus.). 1987. pap. 15.00 (*0-8052-0572-1*) Schocken.

Memoirs of Grassy Creek: Growing up in the Mountains on the Virginia-North Carolina Line. Zetta B. Hamby. LC 97-38307. 264p. 1997. pap. 25.00 (*0-7864-0416-7*) McFarland & Co.

Memoirs of Hadrian. Marguerite Yourcenar. LC 62-18317. (Illus.). 347p. 1963. pap. 14.00 (*0-374-50348-6*) FS&G.

Memoirs of Halide Edib. Halide Edib. LC 72-4272. (World Affairs Ser.: National & International Viewpoints). (Illus.). 528p. 1972. reprint ed. 35.95 (*0-405-04568-9*) Ayer.

Memoirs of Hamid Kadjar. Ed. by Habib Ladjevardi. LC 96-77487. (Iranian Oral History Ser.: Vol. 3). 120p. (Orig.). 1996. pap. 15.00 (*0-932885-15-2*) Harvard CMES.

Memoirs of Harry S. Truman: Years of Trial & Hope. Harry S. Truman. (Quality Paperbacks Ser.). 640p. 1987. reprint ed. pap. 14.95 (*0-306-80297-X*) Da Capo.

Memoirs of Hecate County. large type ed. Edmund Wilson. 196p. 1990. 22.95 (*1-85290-020-2*, Pub. by ISIS Lrg Prnt) Transaction Pubs.

Memoirs of Hector Berlioz from 1803 to 1865. Hector Berlioz. (Music Book Index Ser.). 533p. 1992. reprint ed. lib. bdg. 99.00 (*0-7812-9478-9*) Rprt Serv.

Memoirs of Helene Kottanner, 1439-1440. Helene Kottannerin. Tr. by Maya B. Williamson from HUN. LC 97-37483. (Library of Medieval Women). 96p. 1998. pap. 17.95 (*0-85991-462-3*, DS Brewer) Boydell & Brewer.

Memoirs of Henry Heth, 6. James L. Morrison, Jr. LC 72-820. (Contributions in Military History Ser.: No. 6). 303p. 1974. 42.95 (*0-8371-6389-7*, MHH/, Greenwood Pr) Greenwood.

Memoirs of Hippolyte Clairon, 2 vols., 1 bk. Hippolyte Clairon. LC 79-82821. 1972. 27.95 (*0-405-08359-9*, Pub. by Blom Pubns) Ayer.

Memoirs of His Own Life. Tate Wilkinson. Ed. & Intro. by Lyle Larsen. LC 98-13210. (Illus.). 248p. 1998. 41.50 (*0-8386-3767-1*) Fairleigh Dickinson.

Memoirs of His Own Life. James Melville. LC 74-172724. (Maitland Club, Glasgow. Publications: No. 21). reprint ed. 64.50 (*0-404-52718-3*) AMS Pr.

Memoirs of His Own Time with Reminiscences of the Men & Events of the Revolution. Alexander Graydon. Ed. by John S. Littell & Peter Decker. LC 71-76560. (Eyewitness Accounts of the American Revolution Ser.). 1969. reprint ed. 28.95 (*0-405-01159-8*) Ayer.

Memoirs of Howard, Compiled from His Diary. James B. Brown. LC 73-156007. reprint ed. 39.50 (*0-404-09107-5*) AMS Pr.

Memoirs of J. A. Sibley, Jr. Autobiography. J. A. Sibley, Jr. 224p. 1999. pap. 19.95 (*0-910653-19-4*) Archival Servs.

***Memoirs of Jafar Sharif-Emami.** Ed. by Habib Ladjevardi. (Iranian Oral History Ser.: Vol. 7). (PER.). 328p. 1999. pap. 15.00 (*0-932885-22-5*) Harvard CMES.

Memoirs of James Gordon Bennett & His Times. Isaac C. Pray. LC 73-125712. (American Journalists Ser.). 1977. reprint ed. 35.95 (*0-405-01693-X*) Ayer.

***Memoirs of Jean Lafitte: From le Journal de Jean Laffite.** Gene Marshall. LC 99-91770. 2000. 25.00 (*0-7388-1252-8*); pap. 18.00 (*0-7388-1253-6*) Xlibris Corp.

Memoirs of Jeremiah Mason: Reproduction of Privately Printed Edition of 1873 Illustrated & Annotated, with Enlarged Index. G. J. Clark. (Illus.). xv, 491p. 1997. reprint ed. 152.00 (*1-56169-350-2*) Gaunt.

Memoirs of Jesus of Nazareth, Vol. 1. Dahesh.Tr. of Mudhakkirat Yasu' Al-Nasiry Al-Juz' Al-Awwal. (ARA & ENG., Illus.). 159p. 1993. 40.00 (*0-935359-40-0*) Daheshist.

Memoirs of Jimmie Lavender. Vincent Starrett. (Vincent Starrett Memorial Library: Vol. 8). vii, 248p. 1996. text 25.00 (*1-896032-74-5*) Battered Silicon.

Memoirs of John Addington Symonds: The Secret Homosexual Life of a Leading Nineteenth-Century Man of Letters. John A. Symonds. Ed. by Phyllis Grosskurth. LC 85-27094. (Illus.). 320p. 1986. pap. 11.95 (*0-226-78783-4*) U Ch Pr.

Memoirs of John Quincy Adams, 12 vols. John Q. Adams. Ed. by Charles F. Adams. LC 71-134915. reprint ed. lib. bdg. 894.00 (*0-404-00330-3*) AMS Pr.

Memoirs of John Quincy Adams, Comprising Portions of His Diary from 1795 to 1848, 12 Vols, Set. John Q. Adams, Jr. Ed. by Charles F. Adams. LC 71-85454. (Select Bibliographies Reprint Ser.). 470.00 (*0-8369-5021-6*) Ayer.

Memoirs of John T. McBurney. John T. McBurney. (Wisdom of the Ages Ser.: Vol. 6). 50p. (Orig.). 1996. pap. 20.00 (*0-936390-12-3*) Dialog Pr.

Memoirs of Joseph Gurney "Uncle Joe" Cannon. Joseph G. Cannon. (Illus.). viii, 171p. 1996. pap. 10.75 (*0-9654976-0-7*) Vermil.

Memoirs of Joseph Prost C. SS. R: A Redemptorist Missionary in Ireland, 1851-1854. Ed. by Emmet Larkin & David Fitzpatrick. (Irish Narrative Ser.). 96p. 1998. pap. 12.95 (*1-85918-160-0*, Pub. by Cork Univ) Intl Spec Bk.

Memoirs of Juan Mardre Horne: Mrs. Mack H. Smith. Kearney Smith. LC 91-92953. (Illus.). 232p. 1992. 14.95 (*0-923687-13-0*) Celo Valley Bks.

Memoirs of Keikhosrow Shahrokh. Kikhusraw Shadrukh. Ed. & Tr. by Rashna Writer & Sharokh Sharokh from PER. LC 94-40602.Tr. of Yaddashtha-yi Kikhusraw Shahrukh. (Illus.). 556p. 1994. text 119.95 (*0-7734-9135-X*) E Mellen.

Memoirs of Kelly Field, 1917-1918. John M. Loeblein. 61p. 1974. pap. text 23.95 (*0-89126-010-2*) MA-AH Pub.

Memoirs of King George I: The Yale Edition of Horace Walpole's Memoirs. Horace Walpole. Ed. by John Brooke. LC 84-20963. 840p. 1985. 130.00 (*0-300-03197-1*) Yale U Pr.

Memoirs of Lady Hyegyong: The Autobiographical Writings of a Crown Princess of Eighteenth-Century Korea. Ed. & Tr. by Jahyun Kim Haboush from KOR. (Illus.). 329p. (C). 1996. 55.00 (*0-520-20054-3*, Pub. by U CA Pr) Cal Prin Full Svc.

Memoirs of Lady Hyegyong: The Autobiographical Writings of a Crown Princess of Eighteenth-Century Korea. Ed. & Tr. by JaHyun Kim Haboush from KOR. (Illus.). 329p. 1996. pap. 18.95 (*0-520-20055-1*, Pub. by U CA Pr) Cal Prin Full Svc.

Memoirs of Laetitia Pilkington. Laetitia V. Pilkington. Ed. by A. C. Elias, Jr. LC 94-40317. 1997. 95.00 (*0-8203-1719-5*) U of Ga Pr.

Memoirs of Leticia Valle. Rosa Chacel. Tr. & Afterword by Carol Maier. LC 93-25205. (European Women Writers Ser.). v, 201p. 1994. pap. 12.95 (*0-8032-6360-0*, Bison Books) U of Nebr Pr.

Memoirs of Libraries. G. Edwards. 1976. lib. bdg. 59.95 (*0-8490-2224-X*) Gordon Pr.

Memoirs of Lieutenant General Scott, 2 Vols, Set. Winfield Townley Scott. LC 70-117892. (Select Bibliographies Reprint Ser.). 1977. 48.95 (*0-8369-5345-2*) Ayer.

Memoirs of Lieutenant General Scott, LL. D., 2 vols. Winfield Townley Scott. (American Biography Ser.). 1991. reprint ed. lib. bdg. write for info. (*0-7812-8348-5*) Rprt Serv.

Memoirs of Lieutenant Henry Timberlake. Henry Timberlake. LC 74-146423. (First American Frontier Ser.). 1979. reprint ed. 28.95 (*0-405-02903-9*) Ayer.

An Asterisk (*) at the beginning of an entry indicates that the title is appearing for the first time.

Memoirs of Life in & Out of the Army in Virginia During the War Between the States, 2 vols. 2nd rev. ed. Charles M. Blackford & Susan L. Blackford. Ed. by Peter W. Houck. Incl. Vol. 1. 2nd rev. ed. LC 96-61733. 288p. 1996. reprint ed. bond lthr. (*0-9638455-7-8*); Vol. 2. 2nd rev. ed. LC 96-61733. 264p. 1996. reprint ed. bond lthr. (*0-9638455-8-6*); LC 96-61733. 1996. reprint ed. 95.00 (*0-9638455-9-4*) Warwick Hse.

Memoirs of Lizzie Campbell Doss Barnett. Lizzie Barnett. (Wisdom of the Ages Ser.: Vol. 2). 51p. (Orig.). 1996. pap. 20.00 (*0-936390-09-3*) Dialog Pr.

Memoirs of Lorenzo da Ponte. Lorenzo Da Ponte. Tr. by Elizabeth Abbott from ITA. (Music Reprint Ser.). (Illus.). 512p. 1987. reprint ed. lib. bdg. 49.50 (*0-306-76290-0*) Da Capo.

Memoirs of Lt. Henry Timberlake, 1756-1765. Henry Timberlake. (American Biography Ser.). 197p. 1991. reprint ed. lib. bdg. 59.00 (*0-7812-8392-2*) Rprt Serv.

Memoirs of Lucas County & the City of Toledo: From the Earliest Historical Times down to the Present, Including a Genealogical & Biographical Record of Representative Families, 2 vols. Ed. by Harvey Scribner. (Illus.). 1321p. 1997. reprint ed. lib. bdg. 135.00 (*0-8328-6340-8*) Higginson Bk Co.

Memoirs of Lucky Ken. unabridged ed. Kenneth W. Stevenson. Ed. by Robert E. Forbess. LC 96-85217. (Illus.). xiii, 273p. 1996. 24.95 (*0-9653224-0-8*) R E Forbess.

Memoirs of Ludwik Zychlinski: Reminiscences of the American Civil War, Siberia & Poland. Eugene Podraza. LC 93-73796. 111p. 1994. 20.00 (*0-88033-289-1*, 392, Pub. by East Eur Monographs) Col U Pr.

Memoirs of M. E. Amirteymour Kalali: Tribal Leader, Majles Deputy, Cabinet Minister. Ed. by Habib Ladjevardi. LC 97-73990. (Iranian Oral History Ser.: Vol. 4). 330p. (Orig.). 1997. pap. 19.95 (*0-932885-17-9*) Harvard CMES.

Memoirs of Madame Desbordes-Valmore: With a Selection from Her Poems. Charles-Augustin Sainte-Beuve. Tr. by Harriet W. Preston from FRE. LC 77-11483. (Symbolists Ser.). reprint ed. 49.50 (*0-404-16344-0*) AMS Pr.

Memoirs of Madame Malibran De Beriot. Isaac Nathan. LC 80-2291. reprint ed. 32.50 (*0-404-18860-5*) AMS Pr.

Memoirs of Madame Roland: A Heroine of French Revolution. Marie-Jeanne P. Roland. Tr. by E. S. Shuckburgh from FRE. (Illus.). 264p. 1992. pap. 12.95 (*1-55921-015-X*) Moyer Bell.

Memoirs of Major General William Heath by Himself. William Heath. LC 67-29034. (Eyewitness Accounts of the American Revolution Ser.). 1968. reprint ed. 19.95 (*0-405-01112-1*) Ayer.

Memoirs of Margaret S. Mahler. Ed. by Paul E. Stepansky. 224p. 1988. 29.95 (*0-88163-168-X*) Analytic Pr.

Memoirs of Margaret S. Mahler. Ed. by Paul E. Stepansky. (Illus.). 179p. (C). 1998. text 18.00 (*0-7881-5334-X*) DIANE Pub.

Memoirs of Mary A. Maverick. Mary A. Maverick. Ed. by Rena M. Green. LC 88-31141. (Illus.). 152p. 1989. pap. 47.20 (*0-608-05116-0*, 206567500005) Bks Demand.

Memoirs of Mary Baker Eddy. Adam H. Dickey & Tom Girtin. 54p. 1986. 49.00 (*1-869832-00-0*) St Mut.

Memoirs of Mary Wollstonecraft. William Godwin. 1973. lib. bdg. 250.00 (*0-87968-022-9*) Gordon Pr.

Memoirs of Mary Wollstonecraft. William Godwin. LC 72-92965. (English Biography Ser.: No. 31). 1969. reprint ed. lib. bdg. 75.00 (*0-8383-0975-5*) M S G Haskell Hse.

Memoirs of Mary Wollstonecraft. William Godwin. (BCL1-PR English Literature Ser.). 351p. 1992. reprint ed. lib. bdg. 89.00 (*0-7812-7634-9*) Rprt Serv.

Memoirs of Merle Miller Hill Vaughan. Merle Vaughan. (Wisdom of the Ages Ser.: No. 7). 50p. 1997. pap. 15.00 (*0-936390-15-8*, Wisdom of the Ages) Dialog Pr.

*__Memoirs of Modern Philosophers.__ Elizabeth Hamilton. Ed. by Claire Grogan. (Literary Texts Ser.). 260p. 2000. pap. 12.95 (*1-55111-148-9*) Broadview Pr.

Memoirs of Montparnasse. John Glassco. Ed. & Intro. by Michael Gnarowski. (Illus.). 224p. (C). Date not set. write for info. (*0-19-541098-X*) OUP.

Memoirs of Montparnasse. John Glassco. 1981. pap. text 10.95 (*0-19-540202-2*) OUP.

Memoirs of Mr. Charles J. Yellowplush. William Makepeace Thackeray. LC 97-222496. (Pocket Classics Ser.). 128p. 1997. pap. 10.95 (*0-7509-1558-7*, Pub. by Sutton Pub Ltd) Intl Pubs Mktg.

Memoirs of Mr. Laurence Sterne, the Life & Opinions of Tristram Shandy, a Sentimental Journey, Selected Sermons & Letters. Laurence Sterne. Ed. by Douglas Grant. LC 52-4996. (Reynard Library). (Illus.). 1950. 20.00 (*0-674-56525-8*) HUP.

Memoirs of Mrs. Abigail Bailey Who Had Been the Wife of Major Asa Bailey Formerly of Landoff, N. H. Abigail Bailey. Ed. by Annette K. Baxter. LC 79-5487. (Signal Lives Ser.). 1980. reprint ed. lib. bdg. 31.95 (*0-405-12821-5*) Ayer.

Memoirs of Mrs. Coghlan. Margaret M. Coghlan. (American Biography Ser.). 158p. 1991. reprint ed. lib. bdg. 59.00 (*0-7812-8085-0*) Rprt Serv.

Memoirs of Mrs. Coghlan, Daughter of the Late Major Moncrieffe. Margaret Coghlan. LC 75-140859. (Eyewitness Accounts of the American Revolution Ser.). 1978. reprint ed. 18.95 (*0-405-01213-6*) Ayer.

Memoirs of Mrs. Leeson, Madam, 1727-1797. Mary Lyons. LC 95-235679. 280p. 1995. pap. 19.95 (*1-874675-52-X*, Pub. by Lilliput Pr) Irish Bks Media.

Memoirs of Musick. Roger North. Ed. by Edward F. Rimbault. LC 74-24169. reprint ed. 25.00 (*0-404-13073-9*) AMS Pr.

Memoirs of My Life. Edward Gibbon. Ed. & Intro. by Betty Radice. (English Library). 224p. 1984. pap. 11.95 (*0-14-043217-5*, Penguin Classics) Viking Penguin.

Memoirs of My Nervous Illness. Daniel Paul Screber. LC 99-35601. 500p. 2000. reprint ed. pap. 14.95 (*0-940322-20-X*, Pub. by NY Rev Bks) Midpt Trade.

Memoirs of My Own Times, 4 vols., Set. James Wilkinson. LC 78-177843. reprint ed. lib. bdg. 285.00 (*0-404-06980-0*) AMS Pr.

Memoirs of My Own Times, 4 vols., Set. James Wilkinson. (American Biography Ser.). 1991. reprint ed. lib. bdg. 298.00 (*0-7812-8418-X*) Rprt Serv.

Memoirs of Nahum N. Glatzer. Nahum N. Glatzer et al. LC 97-25622. (Jewish Perspectives Ser.). 175p. 1997. 29.95 (*0-87820-506-3*) Hebrew Union Coll Pr.

Memoirs of 1984. Yuri Tarnopolsky. LC 93-17960. 252p. (Orig.). (C). 1993. pap. text 18.95 (*0-8191-9198-1*); lib. bdg. 49.50 (*0-8191-9197-3*) U Pr of Amer.

Memoirs of Nisqually. Joseph Heath. (Illus.). 1979. 19.95 (*0-87770-222-5*) Ye Galleon.

Memoirs of Peasant Tolstoyans in Soviet Russia. Tr. & Intro. by William Edgerton. LC 92-28608. (Indiana-Michigan Series in Russian & East European Studies). (Illus.). 308p. 1993. 14.95 (*0-253-31911-0*) Ind U Pr.

Memoirs of Peter. Arthur Pitcher. 1981. 4.95 (*0-86544-015-8*) Salv Army Suppl South.

Memoirs of Pliny Earle, M. D. with Extracts from His Diary & Letters (1830-1892) & Selections from His Professional Writings (1839-1891) Pliny Earle. Ed. by F. B. Sanborn. LC 73-2396. (Mental Illness & Social Policy; the American Experience Ser.). 1973. reprint ed. 31.95 (*0-405-05204-9*) Ayer.

*__Memoirs of Pontius Pilate: A Novel.__ James R. Mills. 176p. (gr. 13 up). 2000. pap. 9.99 (*0-8007-5722-X*) Revell.

*__Memoirs of Pontius Pilate: A Novel.__ James R. Mills. LC PS3563.I42315M46. (Illus.). 224p. 2000. 16.99 (*0-8007-1773-2*) Revell.

Memoirs of Prince Adam Czartoryski & His Correspondence with Alexander I. Ed. by Adam Gielgud. LC 78-135808. (Eastern Europe Collection). 1971. reprint ed. 44.95 (*0-405-02750-8*) Ayer.

Memoirs of Prince Chlodwig of Hohenlohe-Schillingsfuerst, 2 vols. Chlodwig K. Hohenlohe-Schillingsfuerst. LC 75-111765. reprint ed. 115.00 (*0-404-03305-9*) AMS Pr.

Memoirs of Prince Metternich, 1773-1835, 5 Vols, Set. Clemens V. Metternich. LC 68-9611. 1970. reprint ed. 225.00 (*0-86527-128-3*) Fertig.

Memoirs of Prince Von Buelow, 4 vols. Bernhard H. Von Buelow. LC 77-127900. reprint ed. 315.00 (*0-404-01230-2*) AMS Pr.

Memoirs of Prince Von Bulow: Royalties Use Only. Bulow Von. 1999. write for info. (*0-316-90438-4*) Little.

Memoirs of Princess Dashkova. Tr. by Kiril Fitzlyon. LC 94-39804. (Illus.). 344p. 1995. pap. text 18.95 (*0-8223-1621-8*) Duke.

Memoirs of Raymond Poincare, 4 vols., Set. Raymond Poincare. Tr. by George Arthur. LC 70-160452. reprint ed. 140.00 (*0-404-09090-7*) AMS Pr.

Memoirs of Richard Cumberland Richard Cumberland & Richard J. Dircks. LC 99-24623. (Studies in the Eighteenth Century). 1999. write for info. (*0-404-63532-6*) AMS Pr.

Memoirs of Robert E. Lee. A. L. Lang. (Illus.). 707p. 1992. 10.98 (*0-89009-694-5*) Bk Sales Inc.

Memoirs of Robert William Elliston, 2 vols., 1 bk. George L. Raymond. LC 77-81218. 1048p. 1972. 48.95 (*0-405-08875-2*, Pub. by Blom Pubns) Ayer.

Memoirs of Roger Clap: Collections of the Dorchester Antiquarian & Historical Society, No. 1. Roger Clap. LC 73-150176. (Select Bibliographies Reprint Ser.). 1977. reprint ed. 15.95 (*0-8369-5689-3*) Ayer.

Memoirs of Samuel Insull. Samuel Insull. Ed. by Larry Plachno. LC 92-22586. (Illus.). 320p. 1992. 39.00 (*0-933449-16-X*); pap. 33.00 (*0-933449-17-8*) Transport Trails.

Memoirs of Sarkis Narzakian. Sarkis Narzakian. Tr. by Garine Narzakian from ARM. LC 95-77088. (Gomidas Institute Memoir Ser.: Vol. 2). (Illus.). x, 247p. 1995. pap. 25.00 (*1-884630-00-6*, Pub. by Gomidas Inst) Whitehurst & Clark.

Memoirs of Senator James G. Douglas: Concerned Citizen. J. Anthony Gaughan. LC 98-235720. 1999. 49.95 (*1-900621-19-3*) Univ Coll Dublin Pr.

Memoirs of Senator Joseph Connolly. Gaughan. 1998. pap. 27.50 (*0-7165-2649-2*, Pub. by Irish Acad Pr) Intl Spec Bk.

Memoirs of Senator Joseph Connolly. J. Anthony Gaughan. 320p. 1996. 57.50 (*0-7165-2611-5*, Pub. by Irish Acad Pr) Intl Spec Bk.

Memoirs of Sergeant Bourgogne, 1812-1813. Paul Cottin & Maurice Henault. 356p. 1998. pap. 19.95 (*0-09-477230-4*, Pub. by Constable & Co) Trafalgar.

Memoirs of Service Afloat During the War Between the States. Raphael Semmes. LC 96-16636. (Illus.). 888p. (C). 1996. pap. 19.95 (*0-8071-2086-3*) La State U Pr.

Memoirs of Several Ladies of Great Britain: Who Have Been Celebrated for Their Writings or Skill in the Learned Languages, Arts & Sciences. George Ballard. Ed. by Ruth Perry. LC 84-10385. 487p. reprint ed. pap. 151.00 (*0-608-10589-9*, 207121000009) Bks Demand.

Memoirs of Several Ladies of Great Britain Who Have Been Celebrated for Their Writings or Skill in the Learned Languages, Arts & Sciences. George Ballard. Ed. by Ruth Perry. LC 84-10385. 488p. 1985. 49.95 (*0-8143-1747-2*) Wayne St U Pr.

Memoirs of Shapour Bakhtiar, Vol. 2. Ed. by Habib Ladjevardi. (Iranian Oral History Ser.). (PER.). 140p. (Orig.). 1996. pap. 15.00 (*0-932885-14-4*) Harvard CMES.

Memoirs of Sherlock Holmes. Arthur Conan Doyle. Ed. by Christopher Roden. (Oxford Sherlock Holmes Ser.). 384p. (C). 1993. 13.95 (*0-19-212309-2*) OUP.

*__Memoirs of Sherlock Holmes.__ Arthur Conan Doyle. Ed. by Christopher Roden. (Oxford World's Classics Ser.). 384p. 2000. pap. 7.95 (*0-19-283811-3*) OUP.

Memoirs of Sherlock Holmes. Arthur Conan Doyle. (Sherlock Holmes Ser.). (Illus.). 160p. 1996. 9.98 (*1-879582-14-7*) Platinum Pr.

Memoirs of Sherlock Holmes. large type ed. Arthur Conan Doyle. (Large Print Ser.). 421p. 1986. reprint ed. lib. bdg. 24.00 (*0-939495-31-7*) North Bks.

Memoirs of Sherlock Holmes. Arthur Conan Doyle. 270p. 1998. reprint ed. lib. bdg. 24.00 (*1-58287-049-7*) North Bks.

Memoirs of Sherlock Holmes. Arthur Conan Doyle. Ed. & Intro. by Christopher Roden. (World's Classics Ser.). 378p. 1995. reprint ed. pap. 6.95 (*0-19-282375-2*) OUP.

Memoirs of Shirley Mae Larsen. Shirley McBurney. (Wisdom of the Ages Ser.: Vol. 5). 50p. (Orig.). 1996. pap. 20.00 (*0-936390-11-5*) Dialog Pr.

Memoirs of Sidney Cotton. Ed. by Omar Khalidi. (Monograph Ser.: No. 4). 63p. (Orig.). 1993. pap. 10.00 (*0-930811-03-8*) Haydarabad Hist Soc.

Memoirs of Sidney Cotton. Omar Khalidi. (Hyderabad Historical Society Monograph Ser.). (Illus.). 63p. (Orig.). (C). 1994. 10.00 (*0-9624595-2-6*) South Asia MA.

Memoirs of Sir Edward Blount. Edward Blount. Ed. by Mira Wilkins & Stuart J. Reid. LC 76-29985. (European Business Ser.). (Illus.). 1977. reprint ed. lib. bdg. 28.95 (*0-405-09717-4*) Ayer.

Memoirs of Sir Ewen Cameron. John Drummond. Ed. by James Macknight. LC 72-983. (Maitland Club, Glasgow. Publications: No. 59). reprint ed. 65.00 (*0-404-53049-4*) AMS Pr.

Memoirs of Sir John Reresby: The Complete Text & a Selection from His Letters. 2nd ed. Ed. by Andrew Browning et al. (Camden Fourth Ser.). 669p. (C). reprint ed. 53.00 (*0-86193-128-9*) David Brown.

Memoirs of Sir Richard Steele, 2 vols., Set. H. R. Montgomery. LC 76-128570. (English Biography Ser.: No. 31). 1970. reprint ed. lib. bdg. 150.00 (*0-8383-0903-8*) M S G Haskell Hse.

Memoirs of Sir Ronald Storrs. Ronald Storrs. LC 77-180678. (Illus.). reprint ed. 49.50 (*0-404-56337-6*) AMS Pr.

Memoirs of Sir Ronald Storrs. Ronald Storrs. LC 72-4302. (World Affairs Ser.: National & International Viewpoints). (Illus.). 612p. 1972. reprint ed. 41.95 (*0-405-04593-X*) Ayer.

Memoirs of Tan Kah-Kee. Ed. by A. H. Ward et al. LC 94-944255. 1994. reprint ed. pap. 48.00 (*9971-69-178-7*) Intl Spec Bk.

Memoirs of Teachers, Educators, & Promoters & Benefactors of Education, Literature, & Science. Ed. by Henry Barnard. LC 74-89147. (American Education: Its Men, Institutions, & Ideas. Series 1). 1977. reprint ed. 35.95 (*0-405-01384-1*) Ayer.

Memoirs of Terrell Davis. Terrell Davis. (Illus.). 320p. (YA). 1999. mass mkt. 6.50 (*0-06-109882-5*) HarpC Child Bks.

Memoirs of the Administration of the Right Honourable Henry Pelham, 2 vols. William Coxe. LC 74-130626. reprint ed. 135.00 (*0-404-01794-0*) AMS Pr.

Memoirs of the Affairs of Scotland. David Moysie. LC 75-193018. (Bannatyne Club, Edinburgh. Publications: No. 39). reprint ed. 37.50 (*0-404-52925-9*) AMS Pr.

Memoirs of the American Academy in Rome. Ed. by Joseph Connors. 248p. (C). 1996. text 59.50 (*0-472-10720-8*, 10720) U of Mich Pr.

Memoirs of the American Academy in Rome, Vols. 3-22, & 26. American Academy in Rome Staff. LC DG0065.. 241p. reprint ed. pap. 74.80 (*0-608-16090-3*, 202673300002) Bks Demand.

*__Memoirs of the American Academy in Rome 1997, Vol. 42.__ American Academy in Rome Staff. Ed. by Malcolm Bell, Jr. (Illus.). 254p. (C). 1999. text 55.00 (*1-879549-06-9*) Am Acad Rome.

Memoirs of the American Academy in Rome (1998), Vol. 43. American Academy in Rome Staff. Ed. by Malcolm Bell, Jr. (Illus.). 254p. (C). text 55.00 (*1-879549-07-7*) Am Acad Rome.

Memoirs of the American Revolution, 2 vols., 1. John Drayton. Ed. by Peter Decker. LC 77-76244. (Eyewitness Accounts of the American Revolution Ser.). 1977. reprint ed. 19.95 (*0-405-01150-4*) Ayer.

Memoirs of the American Revolution, 2 vols., Set. John Drayton. Ed. by Peter Decker. LC 77-76244. (Eyewitness Accounts of the American Revolution Ser.). 1969. reprint ed. 50.95 (*0-405-01149-0*) Ayer.

Memoirs of the American Revolution, 2 vols., Vol. 2. John Drayton. Ed. by Peter Decker. LC 77-76244. (Eyewitness Accounts of the American Revolution Ser.). 1969. reprint ed. 19.95 (*0-405-01151-2*) Ayer.

Memoirs of the American Revolution, So Far As It Related to the States of North & South Carolina & Georgia. William Moultrie. LC 67-29045. (Eyewitness Accounts of the American Revolution Ser.). 1979. reprint ed. 36.95 (*0-405-01139-3*) Ayer.

Memoirs of the Blind: The Self-Portrait & Other Ruins. Jacques Derrida. Tr. by Pascale-Anne Brault & Michael Naas. LC 92-27027. (Illus.). 152p. (C). 1993. pap. 32.50 (*0-226-14308-2*); lib. bdg. 71.50 (*0-226-14307-4*) U Ch Pr.

Memoirs of the Bloomsgrove Family, 2 vols. in 1. Enos Hitchcock. LC 72-104484. 605p. reprint ed. lib. bdg. 50.00 (*0-8398-0783-X*) Irvington.

Memoirs of the Bloomsgrove Family, 2 vols. in 1. Enos Hitchcock. 605p. (C). 1986. reprint ed. pap. text 9.95 (*0-8290-1899-9*) Irvington.

Memoirs of the Celebrated & Beautiful Mrs. Ann Carson, Daughter of an Officer of the U. S. Navy & Wife of Another, Whose Life Terminated in the Philadelphia Prison, 2 vols. rev. ed. Ann Carson. Ed. by Annette K. Baxter. LC 79-8780. (Signal Lives Ser.). 1980. reprint ed. lib. bdg. 47.95 (*0-405-12829-0*) Ayer.

Memoirs of the Colman Family, 2 vols., Set. Richard B. Peake. LC 68-20242. 906p. 1972. reprint ed. 60.95 (*0-405-08842-6*, Pub. by Blom Pubns) Ayer.

Memoirs of the Colman Family, 2 vols., Vol. 1. Richard B. Peake. LC 68-20242. 906p. 1972. reprint ed. 30.95 (*0-405-08843-4*, Pub. by Blom Pubns) Ayer.

Memoirs of the Colman Family, 2 vols., Vol. 2. Richard B. Peake. LC 68-20242. 906p. 1972. reprint ed. 30.95 (*0-405-08844-2*, Pub. by Blom Pubns) Ayer.

Memoirs of the Confederate War for Independence, Vol. 2. Heros Von Borcke. 1985. 14.50 (*0-8446-1462-9*) Peter Smith.

Memoirs of the Confederate War for Independence. Heros Von Borcke. LC 99-17640. (Southern Classics Ser.). xi, 448p. 1999. reprint ed. pap. 15.95 (*1-879941-31-7*) J S Sanders.

Memoirs of the Connecticut Academy of Arts & Sciences, Vol. 1, Pt. 1 see On the Supposed Change in the Temperature of Winter

Memoirs of the Crusades, 333. Geoffroi De Villehardouin et al. LC 83-1515. (Everyman's Library: History: No. 333). 340p. 1983. reprint ed. lib. bdg. 69.50 (*0-313-23856-1*, VIME, Greenwood Pr) Greenwood.

Memoirs of the Different Rebellions in Ireland, from the Arrival of the English: Also, a Particular Detail of That Which Broke Out the 23rd of May 1798. Richard Musgrave. (1798 Collection: Vol. 1). 982p. 1995. 49.95 (*0-9643925-0-X*) Round Tower.

Memoirs of the Duc de Lauzun. Armand L. Biron. 1969. 18.95 (*0-405-01158-X*, 13254) Ayer.

Memoirs of the Four-Foot Colonel. Dun Smith. (Data Papers: Vol. 113). 126p. (C). 1980. pap. 6.00 (*0-87727-113-5*) Cornell SE Asia.

Memoirs of the Four-Foot Colonel. Dun Smith. LC 80-127358. (Cornell University, Southeast Asia Program, Data Paper Ser.: No. 113). 145p. reprint ed. pap. 45.00 (*0-8357-3682-2*, 203640600003) Bks Demand.

Memoirs of the Great Gorgeous. Jack B. Carmichael. 50p. (Orig.). 1992. pap. 7.95 (*0-9626948-3-5*) Dynamics MI.

Memoirs of the Heart. Susanna M. Flavius. 1998. pap. write for info. (*1-57553-779-6*) Watermrk Pr.

Memoirs of the House of Brandenburg, 3 Vols. Leopold Von Ranke. LC 68-25278. (World History Ser.: No. 48). 1969. reprint ed. lib. bdg. 199.00 (*0-8383-0168-1*) M S G Haskell Hse.

Memoirs of the House of Brandenburg, & History of Prussia, During the Seventeenth & Eighteenth Centuries, 3 Vols, Set. Leopold Von Ranke. LC 68-31002. (Illus.). 1970. reprint ed. lib. bdg. 145.00 (*0-8371-0631-1*, RAHB) Greenwood.

Memoirs of the House of Brandenburg, & History of Prussia, During the Seventeenth & Eighteenth Centuries, 3 Vols, Vol. 2. Leopold Von Ranke. LC 68-31002. (Illus.). 3p. 1970. reprint ed. lib. bdg. 65.00 (*0-8371-0836-5*, RAHD) Greenwood.

Memoirs of the House of Brandenburg, & History of Prussia, During the Seventeenth & Eighteenth Centuries, 3 Vols, Vol. 3. Leopold Von Ranke. LC 68-31002. (Illus.). 3p. 1970. reprint ed. lib. bdg. 65.00 (*0-8371-0837-3*, RAHE) Greenwood.

Memoirs of the Late Captain Hugh Crow of Liverpool. Hugh C. Crow. (Illus.). 316p. 1970. reprint ed. 49.50 (*0-7146-1801-2*, Pub. by F Cass Pubs) Intl Spec Bk.

Memoirs of the Late General Le Marchant, 1766-1812. Denis Le Marchant. 1997. 37.95 (*1-885119-47-X*) Sarpedon.

Memoirs of the Late Major-General Le Marchant. Denis Le Marchant. 336p. 1997. 100.00 (*1-873376-94-4*, Pub. by Spellmnt Pubs) St Mut.

Memoirs of the Late Mr. Ashley: An American Comedy. Marianne Hauser. (New American Fiction Ser.: No. 8). 368p. 1986. 16.95 (*0-940650-66-5*); pap. 11.95 (*0-940650-67-3*) Sun & Moon CA.

Memoirs of the Late Mr. Ashley: An American Comedy. deluxe limited ed. Marianne Hauser. (New American Fiction Ser.: No. 8). 368p. 1986. 30.00 (*0-940650-72-X*) Sun & Moon CA.

Memoirs of the Life & Character of Philip Syng Physick. Jacob Randolph. 1993. reprint ed. lib. bdg. 89.00 (*0-7812-5821-9*) Rprt Serv.

Memoirs of the Life & Services of Daniel Drake, M. D. Edward D. Mansfield. 1993. reprint ed. lib. bdg. 89.00 (*0-7812-5386-1*) Rprt Serv.

Memoirs of the Life & Services of Daniel Drake, M. D., Physician, Professor, & Author. Edward D. Mansfield. LC 75-108. (Mid-American Frontier Ser.). 1975. reprint ed. 34.95 (*0-405-06875-1*) Ayer.

Memoirs of the Life & Times of Daniel DeFoe, 3 vols. Walter Wilson. LC 71-153602. reprint ed. 185.00 (*0-404-09790-1*) AMS Pr.

Memoirs of the Life & Travels of the Late Charles Macpherson, Esq. in Asia, Africa & America. Charles Macpherson. 1977. 19.95 (*0-8369-9229-6*, 9083) Ayer.

Memoirs of the Life & Writings of Henry Home of Kames: 1807 Edition, 2 vols., Set. Alexander F. Tytler. 950p. 1996. reprint ed. 195.00 (*1-85506-423-5*) Bks Intl VA.

Memoirs of the Life & Writings of William Hayley, Esq., the Friend & Biographer of Cowper, 2 vols. William Hayley & John Johnson. LC 74-181777. 1971. write for info. (*0-576-02288-8*) Gregg Intl.

Memoirs of the Life of Colonel Hutchinson. Lucy Hutchinson. Ed. by Neil Keeble. 432p. (Orig.). 1995. pap. 8.50 (*0-460-87491-8*, Everyman's Classic Lib) Tuttle Pubng.

M

An Asterisk (*) at the beginning of an entry indicates that the title is appearing for the first time.

Memoirs of the Life of Daniel Mendoza. Daniel Mendoza. Ed. by Paul Magriel. LC 74-29507. (Modern Jewish Experience Ser.). (Illus.). 1975. reprint ed. 20.95 (*0-405-06734-8*) Ayer.

Memoirs of the Life of David Garrick, 2 vols., Set. Thomas Davies. Ed. by Stephen Jones. LC 73-82825. 1972. 60.95 (*0-405-08438-2*) Ayer.

Memoirs of the Life of David Garrick, 2 vols., Vol. 1. Thomas Davies. Ed. by Stephen Jones. LC 73-82825. 1972. 30.95 (*0-405-08439-0*) Ayer.

Memoirs of the Life of David Garrick, 2 vols., Vol. 2. Thomas Davies. Ed. by Stephen Jones. LC 73-82825. 1972. 30.95 (*0-405-08440-4*) Ayer.

Memoirs of the Life of David Garrick: Interspersed with Characters & Anecdotes of His Theatrical Contemporaries, 2 vols., Set. Thomas Davies. (Anglistica & Americana Ser.: No. 132). 1972. reprint ed. 128.70 (*3-487-04224-X*) G Olms Pubs.

Memoirs of the Life of John Adlum in the Revolutionary War. Ed. by Howard H. Peckham. 1968. 12.00 (*0-940550-03-2*) Caxton Club.

Memoirs of the Life of John Constable. rev. ed. C. R. Leslie. Ed. by Jonathan Mayne. LC 96-138171. (Arts & Letters Ser.). (Illus.). 464p. (C). 1995. pap. 14.95 (*0-7148-3360-6*, Pub. by Phaidon Press) Phaidon Pr.

Memoirs of the Life of John Philip Kemble, 2 vols. James Boaden. LC 77-89713. 1972. 60.95 (*0-405-08276-2*, Pub. by Blom Pubns) Ayer.

Memoirs of the Life of John Philip Kemble, Vol. 1. James Boaden. 1972. 30.95 (*0-405-18119-1*) Ayer.

Memoirs of the Life of John Philip Kemble, Vol. 2. James Boaden. 1972. 30.95 (*0-405-18120-5*) Ayer.

Memoirs of the Life of Martha Laurens Ramsay. David Ramsay. (Notable American Authors Ser.). 1999. reprint ed. lib. bdg. 125.00 (*0-7812-8777-4*) Rprt Serv.

Memoirs of the Life of Mrs. Elizabeth Carter, 2 vols., Set. 4th ed. Elizabeth Carter. Ed. by M. Pennington. LC 75-37674. reprint ed. 145.00 (*0-404-56727-4*) AMS Pr.

Memoirs of the Life of Mrs. Manley, Author of the Atalantis. 3rd ed. Mary Manley. LC 71-37701. reprint ed. 29.00 (*0-404-56765-7*) AMS Pr.

Memoirs of the Life of the Right Honorable Richard Brinsley Sheridan, 2 Vols. Thomas Moore. LC 79-152997. (Select Bibliographies Reprint Ser.). 1977. reprint ed. 44.95 (*0-8369-5749-0*) Ayer.

Memoirs of the Life of the Right Honorable Richard Brinsley Sheridan, 2 vols. Thomas Moore. LC 69-14001. 1969. reprint ed. lib. bdg. 75.00 (*0-8371-9944-1*, Greenwood Pr) Greenwood.

Memoirs of the Life of the Right Honorable Richard Brinsley Sheridan, 2 vols., Set. Thomas Moore. (BCL1-PR English Literature Ser.). 1992. reprint ed. lib. bdg. 150.00 (*0-7812-7401-X*) Rprt Serv.

Memoirs of the Life of the Right Honorable Richard Brinsley Sheridan, 2 vols., Vol. 1. Thomas Moore. LC 69-14001. 1969. reprint ed. lib. bdg. 75.00 (*0-8371-0573-0*, MORA, Greenwood Pr) Greenwood.

Memoirs of the Life of the Right Honorable Richard Brinsley Sheridan, 2 vols., Vol. 2. Thomas Moore. LC 69-14001. 1969. reprint ed. lib. bdg. 75.00 (*0-8371-0826-8*, MORB, Greenwood Pr) Greenwood.

Memoirs of the Life of the Right Honorable Sir James Mackintosh, 2 vols. James Mackintosh. LC 76-172711. reprint ed. 40.00 (*0-404-07433-2*) AMS Pr.

Memoirs of the Life of William Wirt. John P. Kennedy. (Notable American Authors Ser.). 1999. reprint ed. lib. bdg. 125.00 (*0-7812-3669-X*) Rprt Serv.

Memoirs of the Life of William Wirt, 2 vols. John P. Kennedy. Ed. by Roy M. Mersky & J. Myron Jacobstein. LC 73-85773. (Classics in Legal History Reprint Ser.: Vols. 19,20). 1973. reprint ed. lib. bdg. 86.00 (*0-89941-260-2*) W S Hein.

Memoirs of the Life, Writings & Correspondence of William Smellie, 2 vols., Set. Ed. by Robert Kerr. (Contemporary Memoirs Ser.: Ser. 7 & 8). 504p. 1996. 160.00 (*1-85506-401-4*) Bks Intl VA.

Memoirs of the Literary Ladies of England from the Commencement of the Last Century, 2 vols., Set. Annel K. Elwood. LC 72-37692. reprint ed. 110.00 (*0-404-56749-5*) AMS Pr.

Memoirs of the Loves of the Poets: Biographical Sketches of Women Celebrated in Ancient & Modern Poetry. Anna Brownell Jameson. LC 72-4605. (Essay Index Reprint Ser.). 1977. reprint ed. 23.95 (*0-8369-2953-5*) Ayer.

Memoirs of the Lower Ohio Valley: Personal & Genealogical, 2 vols. (Illus.). 822p. 1997. reprint ed. lib. bdg. 86.00 (*0-8328-6287-8*) Higginson Bk Co.

Memoirs of the Maelstrom: A Senegalese Oral History of the First World War. Joe Lun. LC 99-29405. 280p. 1999. lib. bdg. 25.95 (*0-325-00138-3*); lib. bdg. 65.00 (*0-325-00139-1*) Greenwood.

Memoirs of the Marshall Count De Rochambeau. Jean B. De Rochambeau. LC 74-140880. (Eyewitness Accounts of the American Revolution Ser.). 1976. reprint ed. 14.95 (*0-405-01212-8*) Ayer.

Memoirs of the Miami Valley, Vol. 3. Ed. by John C. Hover et al. (Illus.). 537p. 1993. reprint ed. lib. bdg. 55.00 (*0-8328-3469-6*) Higginson Bk Co.

Memoirs of the Miami Valley (Ohio), Vols. 1 & 2. Ed. by John C. Hover et al. (Illus.). 1306p. 1993. reprint ed. lib. bdg. 125.00 (*0-8328-3467-X*) Higginson Bk Co.

Memoirs of the New York Botanical Garden: No. 15. 1966. pap. 12.50 (*0-89327-057-1*) NY Botanical.

Memoirs of the New York Botanical Garden: No. 17(2) 1968. pap. 12.50 (*0-89327-060-1*) NY Botanical.

Memoirs of the New York Botanical Garden: No. 21(2) 1971. pap. 12.00 (*0-89327-071-7*) NY Botanical.

Memoirs of the New York Botanical Garden: No. 26(1) 1976. pap. 18.00 (*0-89327-007-5*) NY Botanical.

Memoirs of the New York Botanical Garden: No. 9(2) 1955. pap. 10.00 (*0-89327-034-2*) NY Botanical.

Memoirs of the 149th Regiment New York Infantry: 3rd Brigade, 2nd Division, 12th & 20th A. C. George K. Collins. LC 95-3707. (Illus.). 443p. 1995. reprint ed. 35.95 (*0-9622393-7-2*) Edmonston Publ.

Memoirs of the Opera in Italy, France, Germany & England, 2 vols., Set. G. Hogarth. LC 71-166101. (Music Ser.). 1972. reprint ed. lib. bdg. 85.00 (*0-306-70256-8*) Da Capo.

Memoirs of the Oratory of Saint Francis de Sales from 1815 to 1855: The Autobiography of Saint John Bosco. John Bosco. Tr. by Daniel Lyons from ITA. LC 89-36115. (Illus.). lxvi, 478p. 1990. 29.95 (*0-89944-139-4*); per. 24.95 (*0-89944-135-1*, 135-1) Salesiana Pubs.

Memoirs of the Polish Baroque: The Writings of Jan Chryzostom Pasek, a Squire of the Commonwealth of Poland & Lithuania. Jan Chryzostom Pasek. Ed. by Catherine S. Leach. LC 74-77731. 415p. reprint ed. pap. 128.70 (*0-608-17277-4*, 202959000061) Bks Demand.

Memoirs of the Prince De Talleyrand, 5 vols., Set. Charles M. Talleyrand-Perigord. LC 78-176452. reprint ed. 382.50 (*0-404-07510-X*) AMS Pr.

Memoirs of the Principal Actors in the Plays of Shakespeare. J. Payne Collier. LC 77-113580. reprint ed. 55.00 (*0-404-01599-9*) AMS Pr.

Memoirs of the Rebellion on the Border, 1863. Wiley Britton. LC 86-82410. 463p. 1986. reprint ed. 26.00 (*0-940435-01-2*) Inland Print Ltd.

Memoirs of the Rebellion on the Border, 1863. Wiley Britton. LC 93-1330. 458p. 1993. reprint ed. text 50.00 (*0-8032-1231-3*) U of Nebr Pr.

Memoirs of the Rebellion on the Border, 1863. Wiley Britton. LC 93-1330. (Illus.). 458p. 1993. reprint ed. pap. 14.95 (*0-8032-6109-8*, Bison Books) U of Nebr Pr.

Memoirs of the Reign of Bossa Ahadee King of Dahomey: An Inland Country of Guiney. Robert Norris. (Illus.). 186p. 1968. 45.00 (*0-7146-1840-3*, Pub. by F Cass Pubs) Intl Spec Bk.

Memoirs of the Reign of King George II, 3 vols. Horace Walpole. LC 70-121022. reprint ed. 195.00 (*0-404-06830-8*) AMS Pr.

***Memoirs of the Reign of King George III, 4 vols.** Horace Walpole. LC 99-34228. 1136p. 1999. 250.00 (*0-300-07014-4*) Yale U Pr.

Memoirs of the Reign of King George III, 4 vols. Horace Walpole. Ed. by G. Russell Barker. LC 78-144698. (Illus.). reprint ed. 235.00 (*0-404-06840-5*) AMS Pr.

Memoirs of the Reign of King George III, 4 Vols, Set. Horace Walpole. LC 70-126262. (Select Bibliographies Reprint Ser.). 1977. 108.95 (*0-8369-5489-0*) Ayer.

Memoirs of the Reign of Queen Elizabeth, 2 vols. Thomas W. Birch. LC 79-131513. reprint ed. lib. bdg. 135.00 (*0-404-00909-3*) AMS Pr.

Memoirs of the Rev. Eleazar Wheelock, D. D. David M'Clure & Elijah Parish. LC 75-38454. (Religion in America, Ser. 2). 338p. 1972. reprint ed. 24.95 (*0-405-04074-1*) Ayer.

Memoirs of the Rev. Francis Hodgson, 2 vols. James T. Hodgson. LC 76-169470. reprint ed. 115.00 (*0-404-07374-3*) AMS Pr.

Memoirs of the Reverend David Brainerd: Missionary to the Indians on the Border of New York, New Jersey & Pennsylvania. Ed. by David Brainerd. LC 70-108477. (American Indian History Ser.). 1970. reprint ed. 69.00 (*0-403-00233-8*) Scholarly.

Memoirs of the Reverend Noah Worcester, D. D. Henry Ware. LC 78-137557. (Peace Movement in America Ser.). xii, 155p. 1972. reprint ed. lib. bdg. 25.95 (*0-89198-088-1*) Ozer.

Memoirs of the Right Honorable Sir John Alexander Macdonald, 2 vols. Joseph Pope. LC 76-137271. reprint ed. 115.00 (*0-404-05085-9*) AMS Pr.

Memoirs of the Right Honourable Sir John Alexander Macdonald, 2 vols., Set. Joseph Pope. (BCL1 - History - Canada Ser.). 1991. reprint ed. lib. bdg. 150.00 (*0-7812-6364-6*) Rprt Serv.

Memoirs of the Russian Revolution. Loukomsky. 1976. lib. bdg. 59.95 (*0-8490-2225-8*) Gordon Pr.

Memoirs of the Second World War. Winston L. S. Churchill. 1088p. 1991. pap. 29.95 (*0-395-59968-7*) HM.

Memoirs of the Spirit. Ed. by Edwin S. Gaustad. (Illus.). 382p. 1999. 26.00 (*0-8028-3867-7*) Eerdmans.

***Memoirs of the Spirit** Edwin S. Gaustad. LC 99-32614. 1999. pap. write for info. (*0-8028-4631-9*) Eerdmans.

Memoirs of the Tower of London: Comprising Historical & Descriptive Accounts of That National Fortress & Palace. John Britton & E. W. Brayley. xvi, 374p. 1994. reprint ed. 52.50 (*0-8377-1977-1*, Rothman) W S Hein.

Memoirs of the Vallejos. M. G. Vallejo. (Illus.). 85p. 1994. 14.95 (*1-885852-02-9*) J D Stevenson.

Memoirs of the War Carried on in Scotland & Ireland. Hugh MacKay. LC 70-172707. (Maitland Club, Glasgow. Publications: No. 22). reprint ed. 37.50 (*0-404-52755-8*) AMS Pr.

Memoirs of the War in the Southern Department of the U. S. Henry Lee. Ed. by Peter Decker. LC 75-76561. (Eyewitness Accounts of the American Revolution Ser.). 1969. reprint ed. 36.95 (*0-405-01161-X*) Ayer.

Memoirs of the War in the Southern Department of the United States see Revolutionary War Memoirs of General Henry Lee

Memoirs of the Warrior Kumagai. Donald Richie. 247p. 1999. 18.95 (*0-8048-2126-7*) Tuttle Pubng.

Memoirs of the Year 2500. Louis-Sebastien Mercier. LC 77-6804. 360p. 1977. 35.00 (*0-8398-2380-0*) Ultramarine Pub.

Memoirs of the Year 2500. Louis-Sebastien Mercier. Tr. by W. Hooper from FRE. LC 68-56258. xi, 360p. 1973. reprint ed. 49.50 (*0-678-00915-5*) Kelley.

Memoirs of Theodore Thomas. Rose F. Thomas. LC 73-37356. (Select Bibliographies Reprint Ser.). 1977. reprint ed. 34.95 (*0-8369-6703-8*) Ayer.

Memoirs of Thomas Boston. Thomas Boston. 576p. 1988. reprint ed. 27.99 (*0-85151-528-2*) Banner of Truth.

Memoirs of Thomas H. Gentle. Thomas H. Gentle. (Illus.). vi, 92p. 1993. pap. 22.00 (*0-929558-01-4*) Johnson-Dole.

Memoirs of Thomas Halyburton. Thomas Halyburton. Ed. by Joel R. Beeke. 1996. 19.00 (*1-892777-00-2*) Reform Heritage Bks.

Memoirs of Thomas Hill Green: 1906 Edition. R. L. Nettleship. 272p. 1996. reprint ed. 70.00 (*1-85506-197-X*) Bks Intl VA.

Memoirs of Thomas Woodnutt Miller: A Public Spirited Citizen of Delaware & Nevada. Ed. by Mary E. Glass. 258p. 1966. lib. bdg. 44.50 (*1-56475-027-2*); fiche. write for info. (*1-56475-028-0*) U NV Oral Hist.

Memoirs of Three Railroad Pioneers. Ed. by Stuart Bruchey. LC 80-1293. 1981. lib. bdg. 18.95 (*0-405-13763-X*) Ayer.

Memoirs of Vidocq: Principal Agent of the French Police until 1827, 4 vols. Eugene F. Vidocq. LC 75-32789. (Literature of Mystery & Detection Ser.). 1976. reprint ed. 87.95 (*0-405-07903-6*) Ayer.

Memoirs of Waldo Frank. Waldo Frank. Ed. by Alan Trachtenberg. LC 73-123541. (Illus.). 304p. 1973. 35.00 (*0-87023-081-6*) U of Mass Pr.

Memoirs of William Jennings Bryan. William J. Bryan & M. B. Bryan. LC 72-130261. (American Biography Ser.: No. 32). 1970. reprint ed. lib. bdg. 75.00 (*0-8383-1165-2*) M S G Haskell Hse.

Memoirs of William Jennings Bryan: By Himself & His Wife, 2 vols., Set. William J. Bryan. (American Biography Ser.). 1991. reprint ed. lib. bdg. 148.00 (*0-7812-8048-6*) Rprt Serv.

Memoirs of William Miller. Sylvester Bliss. LC 72-134374. reprint ed. 62.50 (*0-404-08422-2*) AMS Pr.

Memoirs of William Nelson Pendleton. William N. Pendleton. 1992. 30.99 (*0-87377-926-6*) GAM Pubns.

Memoirs of William Smith. John Phillips. Ed. by Claude C. Albritton, Jr. LC 77-6535. (History of Geology Ser.). (Illus.). 1978. reprint ed. lib. bdg. 18.95 (*0-405-10455-3*) Ayer.

Memoirs of William T. Sherman. William T. Sherman & William S. McFeely. (Quality Paperbacks Ser.). 820p. 1984. pap. 17.95 (*0-306-80213-9*) Da Capo.

Memoirs of William Tayler. William Tayler. Ed. by Chaturbhuj. (C). 1990. 36.00 (*81-7099-249-4*, Pub. by Mittal Pubs Dist) S Asia.

Memoirs of William Williams Keen, M. D. William W. Keen. Ed. by W. W. James. LC 90-90402. 345p. (Orig.). 1990. pap. 18.00 (*0-9628197-0-0*) W W Keen James.

Memoirs of William Wordsworth, Poet-Laureate, 2 vols. Christopher Wordsworth. Ed. by Henry Reed. LC 29-24313. reprint ed. 135.00 (*0-404-07040-X*) AMS Pr.

Memoirs of Wollstonecraft. William Godwin. 214p. 1993. reprint ed. pap. 14.95 (*1-85477-125-6*) Continuum.

Memoirs, Official & Personal. Thomas L. McKenney. LC 72-94789. (Bison Bk.: BB565). (Illus.). 368p. reprint ed. pap. 114.10 (*0-7837-6023-X*, 204583500008) Bks Demand.

Memoirs on Fossil Elephants & on Reconstruction of the Genera Palaeotherium & Anoplotherium. Georges Cuvier. Ed. by Stephen Jay Gould. LC 79-8327. (FRE., Illus.). 1980. reprint ed. lib. bdg. 88.95 (*0-405-12709-X*) Ayer.

Memoirs on Paris Hospitals: Resource in Medical History. Jacques Tenon. LC 91-14970. 405p. 1997. 39.95 (*0-88135-074-5*) Watson Pub Intl.

Memoirs on the Late War in North America Between France & England. Pierre Pouchot. Ed. by Brian L. Dunnigan. Tr. by Michael Cardy from FRE. (Illus.). 568p. 1994. 24.95 (*0-941967-14-X*) Old Fort Niagara Assn.

Memoirs sur les Fossiles des Environs de Paris No. 15: Special Publication. Jean Baptiste Lamarck. 380p. 1978. 15.00 (*0-87710-374-7*) Paleo Res.

Memoirs to Illustrate the History of My Time, 8 vols. Ed. by Francois P. Guizot. Tr. by John W. Cole. LC 72-168212. reprint ed. 735.00 (*0-404-08040-5*) AMS Pr.

Memoirs to Serve for the Future Ecclesiastical History of the Diocese of Boston. Benedict J. Fenwick. Ed. by Joseph M. McCarthy. LC 78-64366. (Monographs: No. 35). (Illus.). 270p. 1979. 10.95 (*0-686-65388-2*) US Cath Hist.

Memoirs Touching the Revolution in Scotland. Colin L. Balcarres. LC 73-161754. (Bannatyne Club, Edinburgh. Publications: No. 71). reprint ed. 44.50 (*0-404-52791-4*) AMS Pr.

Memoirs Travel Essays & Theatrical Musings, Vol. 10. Konstantin Stanislavsky. (The Collected Works of Konstantin Stanislavsky). 448p. (C). (gr. 13). 1999. 45.00 (*0-87830-134-8*, Thtre Arts Bks) Routledge.

Memoirs with Anecdotes of Dean Swift, 1748-1754. Laetitia V. Pilkington. LC 75-1027. (Swiftiana Ser.). 1975. write for info. (*0-8240-1278-X*) Garland.

Memoirs with Emphasis on the Immediate Family of Mansul W. & Ida King Blackburn of Johnson County, Arkansas, & upon Arkansas Land: Memoirs with Emphasis upon Family & Arkansas. Dean W. Blackburn. LC 86-90708. vi, 286p. 1990. 24.00 (*0-9618865-0-1*) D W Blackburn.

Memoirs, with Special Reference to Secession & the Civil War. John H. Reagan. Ed. by Walter F. McCaleb. LC 79-174304. reprint ed. 29.50 (*0-404-04620-7*) AMS Pr.

Memoirs, with Special Reference to Secession & the Civil War. John H. Regan. (American Biography Ser.). 351p. 1991. reprint ed. lib. bdg. 79.00 (*0-7812-8322-1*) Rprt Serv.

Memoirs Written on the Island see Dziennik Pisany na Wyspie: Diary Written on an Island

Memor (Latin for "Mindful") Phyllis Keefer. 158p. (Orig.). 1990. pap. 18.95 (*0-9626503-0-7*) Its About Time.

Memorabilia. Xenophon. Tr. & Anno. by Amy L. Bonnette. 208p. 1994. text 29.95 (*0-8014-2963-3*) Cornell U Pr.

Memorabilia. Xenophon. Ed. by W. R. Connor. LC 78-18607. (Greek Texts & Commentaries Ser.). (Illus.). 1979. reprint ed. lib. bdg. 35.10 (*0-405-11447-8*) Ayer.

Memorabilia: The Regional Prints of Jane Dunning Baldwin. Liz Miller. 20p. 1989. pap. 2.95 (*0-910524-14-9*) Eastern Wash.

Memorabilia & Oeconomicus, Symposium, & Apology, Vol. IV. Xenophon. (Loeb Classical Library: No. 168). 704p. 1923. 19.95 (*0-674-99186-9*) HUP.

Memorabilia Mathematica: The Philomath's Quotation Book. Robert E. Moritz. (Spectrum Ser.). 440p. 1993. reprint ed. pap. text 29.95 (*0-88385-321-3*, MEMO) Math Assn.

Memorable & Historic Speeches: A Research Guide. R. J. Gluck. Ed. by D. J. Gluck. 1996. 39.95 (*1-882731-05-0*) Cactus Pub.

Memorable Baby Dedications. Kay Kuzma. LC 97-193951. 176p. (Orig.). 1997. pap. 29.99 (*0-8280-0984-8*) Review & Herald.

Memorable Baseball Moments. Tom Price. (Century of Gamecocks Ser.: Vol. 3). (Illus.). 208p. pap. 5.00 (*1-887714-02-2*) Summerhse Pr.

Memorable Basketball Moments. Tom Price. (Century of Gamecocks Ser.: Vol. 2). (Illus.). 208p. pap. 5.00 (*1-887714-01-4*) Summerhse Pr.

Memorable Ceremonies & Poems: Including Material from "Along the Story Trail" J. L. Alexander. 192p. 1993. pap. 6.50 (*0-88053-302-1*, S-109) Macoy Pub.

Memorable Contacts with the Mother. 2nd ed. Nirodbaran. 190p. 1994. pap. 9.95 (*81-900160-8-3*, Pub. by SAA) E-W Cultural Ctr.

Memorable Days in America. William Faux. LC 71-95144. reprint ed. 62.50 (*0-404-02371-1*) AMS Pr.

Memorable Description of the East Indian Voyage, 1618-1625. W. Y. Bontekoe. Tr. by C. B. Hodgkinson from DUT. (C). 1992. reprint ed. 26.00 (*81-206-0791-0*, Pub. by Asian Educ Servs) S Asia.

Memorable Encounters. Joseph Kaminetsky. 18.99 (*0-89906-617-8*, MEMH); pap. 15.99 (*0-89906-618-6*, MEMP) Mesorah Pubns.

Memorable Film Characters: An Index to Roles & Performers, 1915-1983, 1. Susan Liberman et al. LC 84-10844. (Bibliographies & Indexes in the Performing Arts Ser.: No. 1). 291p. 1984. lib. bdg. 69.50 (*0-313-23977-0*, LMF/, Greenwood Pr) Greenwood.

Memorable Football Moments. Tom Price. (Century of Gamecocks Ser.: Vol. 1). (Illus.). 208p. pap. 5.00 (*1-887714-00-6*) Summerhse Pr.

Memorable Forest Fires: Two Hundred Stories by U. S. Forest Service Retirees. Ed. by Gilbert W. Davies & Florice M. Frank. LC 95-75176. (Illus.). 506p. (C). 1995. pap. 21.95 (*0-9634413-9-6*) HiSt ink Bks.

***Memorable Histories & Historic Memories.** Bowdoin College Staff. LC 99-195086. 64p. 1998. write for info. (*0-916606-29-5*) Bowdoin Coll.

Memorable Japanese Motorcycles, 1959-1996. Doug Mitchel. LC 97-65625. (Schiffer Bks.). (Illus.). 152p. 1997. 34.95 (*0-7643-0235-3*) Schiffer.

Memorable Man. Joan Hohl. (Desire Ser.: No. 1075). 1997. per. 3.50 (*0-373-76075-2*, 1-76075-0) Silhouette.

***Memorable Man.** large type ed. Joan Hohl. (Silhouette Romance Ser.). 2000. 22.95 (*0-373-59735-5*) Harlequin Bks.

Memorable Meals. Vincent Starrett. (Vincent Starrett Memorial Library Ser.: Vol. 2). (Illus.). vi, 217p. 1995. text 24.00 (*1-896032-64-8*) Battered Silicon.

Memorable Meals: A Delicious Blend of Classic & Contemporary Cuisines. Nancy W. Moorman. LC 97-39867. (Illus.). 256p. 1997. 24.95 (*1-57168-210-4*, Eakin Pr) Sunbelt Media.

Memorable Melodies: 50 of the Most Requested Songs. 128p. 1990. otabind 12.95 (*0-7935-0146-6*, 00001245) H Leonard.

Memorable Moments in Purdue Basketball History. Ed. by Lafayette Journal & Courier Staff. (Illus.). 250p. 1998. 29.95 (*1-57167-256-7*) Sports Pub.

Memorable Movie Love Songs. 160p. (YA). 1997. pap. 14.95 (*0-7604-0089-X*, MF9719) Wrner Bros.

Memorable Poetry, 1998: People, Animals, & Events to be Remembered in Our Hearts. Ed. by M. A. Myers. LC 97-75064. 120p. 1998. pap. text 15.95 (*1-879183-37-4*) Bristol Banner.

Memorable Poetry, 1999: People, Animals & Events to be Remembered in Our Hearts. Ed. by M. Myers. LC 99-90109. 85p. 1999. pap. 24.95 (*1-879183-22-6*) Bristol Banner.

Memorable Providences: Relating to Witchcrafts & Possessions. Cotton Mather. (Notable American Authors Ser.). 1999. reprint ed. lib. bdg. 125.00 (*0-7812-3952-4*) Rprt Serv.

Memorable Roasts. (Mini Cook Bks.). 148p. pap. 1.95 (*3-8290-0382-X*, 770249) Konemann.

***Memorable Scenes from Old Testament Homes.** Charles R. Swindoll. 79p. 1998. pap., student ed. 5.95 (*1-57972-191-5*) Insight Living.

Memorable Stories & Parables by Boyd K. Packer. Boyd K. Packer. LC 97-74251. 1997. 14.95 (*1-57008-336-3*) Bookcraft Inc.

Memorable Trial of Bardell Against Pickwick. Charles Dickens. (Extract from Pickwick Papers). (Illus.). 71p. 1989. 75.00 (*0-933861-10-9*) H Berliner.

Memoralia: or Phials of Amber Full of the Tears of Love. Thomas H. Chivers. (Works of Thomas Holley Chivers). 1990. reprint ed. lib. bdg. 79.00 (*0-7812-2287-7*) Rprt Serv.

MemoraMOBILEia: Alabama Gulf Coast Potpourri. Mary S. Palmer & Elizabeth T. Coffman. 195p. pap. 11.95 (*0-9639773-0-X*) Mobile & Bayside.

An Asterisk (*) at the beginning of an entry indicates that the title is appearing for the first time.

Memoranda. Jeffrey Ford. LC 99-30703. 240p. 1999. pap. 12.00 (*0-380-80262-7*, Avon Bks) Morrow Avon.

*__Memoranda.__ Jeffrey Ford. 256p. 2000. mass mkt. 5.99 (*0-380-81368-8*, Avon Bks) Morrow Avon.

Memoranda & Official Correspondence Relating to the Republic of Texas, Its History & Annexation. Anson Jones. LC 72-9455. (Far Western Frontier Ser.). 656p. 1973. reprint ed. 42.95 (*0-405-04983-8*) Ayer.

Memoranda de Parliamento: Records of the Parliament Holden at Westminster, 28th February, in the 33rd Year of the Reign of Edward I (1305) Ed. by Frederic W. Maitland. (Rolls Ser.: No. 98). 1969. reprint ed. 70.00 (*0-8115-1177-4*) Periodicals Srv.

Memoranda During the War. Walt Whitman. LC 93-13029. 68p. 1990. pap. 7.95 (*1-55709-132-3*) Applewood.

Memoranda of Persons, Places, & Events: Embracing Authentic Facts, Visions, Impressions, Discoveries, in Magnetism, Clairvoyance, Spiritualism. Andrew J. Davis. 488p. 1996. reprint ed. spiral bd. 21.00 (*0-7873-0242-2*) Hlth Research.

Memoranda on All's Well That Ends Well, The Two Gentlemen of Verona, Much Ado about Nothing & on Titus Andronicus. James O. Halliwell-Phillipps. LC 77-168224. reprint ed. 29.50 (*0-404-03066-1*) AMS Pr.

Memoranda on Love's Labour's Lost, King John, Othello, & Romeo & Juliet. James O. Halliwell-Phillipps. LC 70-168225. reprint ed. 30.00 (*0-404-03067-X*) AMS Pr.

Memoranda on Shakespeare's Comedy of Measure for Measure. James O. Halliwell-Phillipps. LC 74-168226. 10 p. 1974. reprint ed. 29.50 (*0-404-03068-8*) AMS Pr.

Memoranda on Shakespeare's Tragedy of Troilus & Cressida. James O. Halliwell-Phillipps. LC 78-168227. reprint ed. 29.50 (*0-404-03069-6*) AMS Pr.

Memoranda on the Tragedy of Hamlet. James O. Halliwell-Phillipps. LC 71-168228. reprint ed. 29.50 (*0-404-03081-5*) AMS Pr.

Memorandum De Dios. Mandino Og. (SPA., Illus.). 63p. 1997. pap. text 13.98 (*968-13-2042-5*) Libros Fronteras.

Memorandum of Thoughts, Reflections & Transactions As Transcribed by Basil Nelson Tongsworth on His Journey from Washington Township, Guernsey County, Ohio, to Oregon in the Summer of 1853. Basil N. Longsworth. 44p. 1972. reprint ed. pap. 7.95 (*0-87770-664-6*) Ye Galleon.

Memorandum on Currency & Central Banks, 1913-1924, 2 vols. League of Nations, Secretariat Staff. Ed. by Mira Wilkins. LC 78-3931. (International Finance Ser.). (Illus.). 1979. reprint ed. lib. bdg. 53.95 (*0-405-11234-3*) Ayer.

Memorandum on Currency & Central Banks, 1913-1925, 2 vols. League of Nations, Secretariat Staff. Ed. by Mira Wilkins. LC 78-3930. (International Finance Ser.). (Illus.). 1979. reprint ed. lib. bdg. 34.95 (*0-405-11233-5*) Ayer.

Memorandum on ICAO: The Story of the International Civil Aviation Organization. Ed. by Barry Leonard. (Illus.). 61p. 1998. reprint ed. pap. text 20.00 (*0-7881-2780-2*) DIANE Pub.

Memorandum on Popular Education. James Phillips Kay-Shuttleworth. LC 72-5887. (Social History of Education Series 1: No. 6). 80p. 1969. reprint ed. 27.50 (*0-678-08457-2*) Kelley.

Memorandum on the Postwar International Information Program of the United States. Arthur W. Macmahon. LC 72-4673. (International Propaganda & Communications Ser.). 135p. 1972. reprint ed. 18.95 (*0-405-04757-6*) Ayer.

Memorandum on the Progress of the Madras Presidency During the Last Forty Years of British Administration. S. Srinivasa Raghavaiyangar. (C). 1988. reprint ed. 54.00 (*81-206-0384-2*, Pub. by Asian Educ Servs) S Asia.

Memorandum on Unfair Competition at the Common Law. U. S. Federal Trade Commission Staff. 305p. 1980. reprint ed. 38.00 (*0-8377-1228-9*, Rothman) W S Hein.

Memorandum Re: Application of Section 504 of the Rehabilitation Act to Persons with AIDS. 54p. 1986. pap. 5.25 (*0-685-23178-X*, 41,410) NCLS Inc.

Memoria de Ponce. Rosario Ferre. Date not set. pap. text. write for info. (*1-56758-045-9*) Edit Cultl.

Memoria Extraviada. David Ortiz & Phyllis Chesler. LC 94-21995. 131p. 1995. pap. text. write for info. (*1-56758-038-6*) Edit Cultl.

Memoria Mexicana. Enrique Florescano. (SPA.). 22.99 (*968-16-3999-5*, Pub. by Fondo) Continental Bk.

Memoria Natural y Artificial. Laura V. Catrillon. (Ciencia para Todos Ser.). (SPA.). pap. 6.99 (*968-16-3481-0*, Pub. by Fondo) Continental Bk.

*__Memoria Publica, 1949-1999: Medio Siglo de Recuerdos y Reflexiones.__ Jose Arsenio Torres. LC 00-36414. (Illus.). 2000. pap. write for info. (*0-8477-0103-4*) U of PR Pr.

Memorial. James Amos. 288p. 1990. pap. 3.95 (*0-380-71195-8*, Avon Bks) Morrow Avon.

Memorial. Ferdinando Camon. Tr. by David Calicchio. 122p. 1996. pap. 13.95 (*0-8101-6013-7*, Marlboro) Northwestern U Pr.

Memorial. Francis Stuart. 1996. pap. 10.95 (*0-906897-87-4*) Dufour.

Memorial. Christopher Isherwood. LC 98-54201. 296p. 1999. reprint ed. pap. 15.95 (*0-8166-3369-X*) U of Minn Pr.

Memorial: Portrait of a Family. Christopher Isherwood. LC 87-3540. (Michael di Capua Bks.). 288p. 1988. pap. 8.95 (*0-374-52067-4*) FS&G.

Memorial: Portrait of a Family. Christopher Isherwood. LC 72-106718. 294p. reprint ed. lib. bdg. 32.00 (*0-8371-3544-3*) Irvington.

Memorial Addresses & Tributes in Honor of Thomas P. O'Neill, Late Speaker of the House & a Representative from Massachusetts. 224p. 1996. boxed set 33.00 (*0-16-063267-6*, Congress) USGPO.

Memorial & Biographical History of the Counties of Fresno, Tulare & Kern, California. (Illus.). 822p. 1992. reprint ed. lib. bdg. 82.50 (*0-8328-2580-8*) Higginson Bk Co.

Memorial & Genealogical Record of (East) Texas. Goodspeed Publishing Company Staff. (Illus.). 1982. reprint ed. 42.50 (*0-89308-300-3*) Southern Hist Pr.

Memorial Appreciation: The Sesquicentennial Peirce Congress. Willard Van Orman Quine et al. LC 99-10513. (Peirce Studies: Vol. 6). 48p. 1999. 9.95 (*0-9667695-0-3*) Pr of Arisbe.

Memorial (Biographical) Record of the Counties of Delaware, Union & Morrow. (Illus.). 501p. 1997. reprint ed. lib. bdg. 53.00 (*0-8328-6314-9*) Higginson Bk Co.

Memorial Book: The Gypsies at Auschwitz-Birkenau, 2 vols., Set. Ed. by State Museum of Auschwitz-Birkenau Staff. 1800p. 1993. lib. bdg. 260.00 (*3-598-11162-2*) K G Saur Verlag.

Memorial Candles: Children of the Holocaust. Dina Wardi. LC 91-847. (International Library of Group Psychotherapy & Group Process Ser.). 288p. (Orig.). (C). 1992. pap. 25.99 (*0-415-06099-0*, A7026); text 59.95 (*0-415-06098-2*, A7022) Routledge.

Memorial Cup: Canada's National Junior Hockey Championship. Richard M. Lapp. LC 98-151615. 300p. 1997. pap. 18.95 (*1-55017-170-4*) Harbour Pub Co.

Memorial Day. Mir Tamim Ansary. LC 98-14377. (Holiday Histories Ser.). 32p. (J). 1999. 19.92 (*1-57572-874-5*) Heinemann Lib.

*__Memorial Day.__ Helen Frost. LC 99-52876. (National Holidays Ser.). (Illus.). 24p. (J). (ps-2). 2000. lib. bdg. 13.25 (*0-7368-0544-3*, Pebble Bks) Capstone Pr.

Memorial Day. Lynda Sorensen. LC 94-17722. (Holidays Ser.). (J). 1994. lib. bdg. 14.60 (*1-57103-071-9*) Rourke Pr.

Memorial Day: Its Celebration, Spirit, & Significance as Related in Prose & Verse, with a Non-Sectional Anthology of the Civil War. Ed. by Robert H. Schauffler. LC 90-7446. 339p. 1990. reprint ed. lib. bdg. 40.00 (*1-55888-274-X*) Omnigraphics Inc.

Memorial Day & Always: A Mother Remembers. Ella M. Dobroski. 185p. 1988. pap. 12.00 (*0-9619586-0-X*) Debo Pub Co.

*__Memorial Day & Other Stories.__ Paul Scott Malone. LC 99-48286. 184p. 2000. pap. 15.95 (*0-87565-219-0*, Pub. by Tex Christian) Tex A&M Univ Pr.

Memorial de Isla Negra. 2nd ed. Pablo Neruda. (SPA.). 312p. 1982. pap. 12.95 (*0-7859-5000-1*) Fr & Eur.

Memorial de Saint-Helene, Vol. 1. Las Cases. (FRE.). 1978. lib. bdg. 95.00 (*0-8288-3520-9*, F13311) Fr & Eur.

Memorial de Saint-Helene, Vol. 2. Las Cases. (FRE.). 1978. lib. bdg. 95.00 (*0-8288-3521-7*, F13312) Fr & Eur.

Memorial de Sant-Helene, Chapitres 9-14. Las Casas. 1520p. 41.50 (*0-686-56533-9*) Fr & Eur.

Memorial Essays. Alfred Jules Ayer. Ed. by A. Phillips Griffiths. (Royal Institute of Philosophy Supplements Ser.: No. 30). 239p. (C). 1992. pap. text 22.95 (*0-521-42246-9*) Cambridge U Pr.

Memorial Feast for Kokotoy-Khan: A Kirghiz Epic Poem. Ed. by A. T. Hatto. (London Oriental Ser.). 1977. 89.00 (*0-19-713593-5*) OUP.

Memorial Hall Coloring Book. Illus. by Louise Minks & Leah Minks. 24p. (Orig.). (J). (gr. 1-2). 1989. pap. 2.95 (*0-9612876-7-5*) Pocumtuck Valley Mem.

Memorial Hall Murder. Jane Langton. 1996. pap. write for info. (*0-14-771166-5*) Penguin Putnam.

Memorial Hall Murder. large type ed. Jane Langton. LC 86-2365. 393 p. 1986. write for info. (*0-89621-706-X*) Thorndike Pr.

Memorial History of Augusta, Georgia. Charles C. Jones, Jr. & Salem Dutcher. LC 66-26060. 604p. 1966. reprint ed. 35.00 (*0-87152-030-3*) Reprint.

Memorial History of Boston. Justin Winsor. (Notable American Authors Ser.). 1999. reprint ed. lib. bdg. 125.00 (*0-7812-9991-8*) Rprt Serv.

Memorial History of Daniel Schöttler, Sr. & His Father-in-Law Cristian Schwartzendruker, Sr., & Jacob & Rececca Kauffman, Grandparents of Daniel Shetler, Jr., Comprising a Complete Family Register of Lineal Descendants & Those Related by Intermarriage, 1833-1910. S. D. Guengerich. 119p. 1993. reprint ed. pap. 19.00 (*0-8328-3781-4*); reprint ed. lib. bdg. 29.00 (*0-8328-3780-6*) Higginson Bk Co.

*__Memorial History of Hampstead New Hampshire Vol. 2: Congregation Church 1752-1902.__ Harriette Eliza Noyes. (Illus.). 844p. 1999. reprint ed. pap. 54.50 (*0-7884-1312-0*) Heritage Bk.

Memorial History of Louisville: From Its First Settlement to the Year 1896. With Biographical Sketches, 2 vols. Ed. by J. Stoddard Johnston. (Illus.). 1339p. 1997. reprint ed. lib. bdg. 138.00 (*0-8328-6737-3*) Higginson Bk Co.

Memorial History of Philadelphia from Its First Settlement to the Year 1895, 2 vols. Ed. by John R. Young. (Illus.). 1998. reprint ed. lib. bdg. 105.00 (*0-8328-9621-7*) Higginson Bk Co.

Memorial History of Syracuse, from Its Settlement to the Present Time. With Biographical Sketches. Dwight H. Bruce. (Illus.). 849p. 1997. reprint ed. lib. bdg. 85.00 (*0-8328-6259-2*) Higginson Bk Co.

Memorial History of the Counties of Faribault, Martin, Watonwan & Jackson. (Illus.). 766p. 1997. reprint ed. lib. bdg. 79.00 (*0-8328-6800-0*) Higginson Bk Co.

Memorial History of Utica, from Its Settlement to the Present Time. With Biographical Sketches. Ed. by M. M. Bragg. (Illus.). 736p. 1997. reprint ed. lib. bdg. 75.00 (*0-8328-6266-5*) Higginson Bk Co.

Memorial in Behalf of the Architect of Our Federal Constitution: Pelatiah Webster of Philadelphia, Pennsylvania. Hannis Taylor. 53p. 1992. reprint ed. pap. 27.50 (*0-8377-2723-5*, Rothman) W S Hein.

Memorial of Alexander Anderson M. D. Benson J. Lossing. (Notable American Authors Ser.). 1999. reprint ed. lib. bdg. 125.00 (*0-7812-3862-5*) Rprt Serv.

Memorial of Capt. Thomas Abbey: His Ancestors & Descendants of the Abbey Family Pathfinders, Soldiers, & Pioneer Settlers of Conn., Its Western Reserve in Ohio & the Great West. A. Freeman. (Illus.). 175p. 1993. reprint ed. pap. 26.50 (*0-8328-3006-2*); reprint ed. lib. bdg. 36.50 (*0-8328-3005-4*) Higginson Bk Co.

Memorial of Crispus Attucks, Samuel Maverick, James Caldwell, Samuel Gray & Patrick Carr, from the City of Boston. Boston City Council Staff. LC 71-79022. (Black Heritage Library Collection). 1977. 13.95 (*0-8369-8515-X*) Ayer.

Memorial of Horatio Greenough. Ed. by Henry T. Tuckerman. LC 68-57194. 251p. 1972. reprint ed. 16.95 (*0-405-09033-1*, Pub. by Blom Pubns) Ayer.

Memorial of John Meares. John Meares. 97p. 1985. reprint ed. 14.95 (*0-87770-341-8*) Ye Galleon.

Memorial of Joseph & Lucy Clark Allen. E. W. Allen. (Illus.). 246p. 1988. reprint ed. pap. 37.00 (*0-8328-0109-7*); reprint ed. lib. bdg. 45.00 (*0-8328-0108-9*) Higginson Bk Co.

Memorial of Logan Edwin Bleckley. Georgia Bar Association Staff. LC 82-12459. xviii, 307p. 1982. 29.95 (*0-86554-039-X*, MUP-H049) Mercer Univ Pr.

Memorial of Matthew Clarkson of Philadelphia, (1735-1800), & of His Brother Gerardus (1737-1790) J. Hall & S. Clarkson. (Illus.). 259p. 1993. reprint ed. pap. 39.00 (*0-8328-1357-5*); reprint ed. lib. bdg. 49.00 (*0-8328-1356-7*) Higginson Bk Co.

Memorial of Reverend Samuel Whiting, D. D., & of His Wife Elizabeth St. John; with Reference to Some of Their English Ancestors & American Descendants. 2nd ed. W. Whiting. 334p. 1989. reprint ed. pap. 50.00 (*0-8328-1257-9*); reprint ed. lib. bdg. 58.00 (*0-8328-1256-0*) Higginson Bk Co.

Memorial of Robert Milham Hartley. Isaac S. Hartley. LC 75-17225. (Social Problems & Social Policy Ser.). (Illus.). 1976. reprint ed. 45.95 (*0-405-07495-6*) Ayer.

Memorial of Robert Mills. Robert Mills. Date not set. pap. write for info. (*0-87770-411-2*) Ye Galleon.

Memorial of the Centennial Anniversary of the Settlement of Machias (ME) 55p. 1986. reprint ed. pap. text 6.50 (*0-935207-42-2*) Danbury Hse Bks.

Memorial of the Family of Morse. H. D. Lord. (Illus.). 556p. 1989. reprint ed. pap. 85.00 (*0-8328-0887-3*); reprint ed. lib. bdg. 93.00 (*0-8328-0886-5*) Higginson Bk Co.

Memorial of the Great Rebellion Being a History of the Fourteenth Regiment New Hampshire Volunteers. large type unabridged ed. Francis H. Buffum. LC 96-44052. (Illus.). xii, 443p. (C). 1996. reprint ed. 38.95 (*1-889881-04-X*) Old Bks Pub.

Memorial of the Legislative Assembly of Oregon Territory, August 10, 1848. Joe Meek. (House Misc Doc: No. 98). 26p. 1972. reprint ed. pap. 5.95 (*0-87770-065-6*) Ye Galleon.

*__Memorial of the Town of Hampstead New Hampshire.__ Harriette Eliza Noyes. (Illus.). 658p. 1999. reprint ed. pap. 43.50 (*0-7884-1295-7*, N591) Heritage Bk.

Memorial of the Walkers of the Old Plymouth Colony Embracing Genealogical Sketches of James of Taunton, Philip of Rehoboth, William of Eastham, John of Marshfield, Thomas of Bristol, & Their Descendants. J. Walker. (Illus.). 479p. 1989. reprint ed. pap. 72.00 (*0-8328-1217-X*); reprint ed. lib. bdg. 80.00 (*0-8328-1216-1*) Higginson Bk Co.

Memorial of Thomas Potts, Jr., Who Settled in Pennsylvania, with a Historical & Genealogical Account of His Descendants to the Eighth Generation. T. P. James. (Illus.). 430p. 1989. reprint ed. pap. 66.00 (*0-8328-0981-0*); reprint ed. lib. bdg. 74.00 (*0-8328-0980-2*) Higginson Bk Co.

Memorial of William A. Slacum Praying Compensation for His Services in Obtaining Information in Relation to the Settlements on the Oregon River, December 18, 1837. William A. Slacum. 31p. 1972. reprint ed. pap. 7.95 (*0-87770-101-6*) Ye Galleon.

Memorial of William Cassidy. William Cassidy. LC 73-125684. (American Journalists Ser.). 1978. reprint ed. 19.95 (*0-405-01661-1*) Ayer.

Memorial of William Spooner, 1637, & of His Descendants to the Third Generation, of His Great-Grandson, Elnathan Spooner, & of His Descendants to 1871. T. Spooner. 242p. 1989. reprint ed. pap. 36.00 (*0-8328-1101-7*); reprint ed. lib. bdg. 44.00 (*0-8328-1100-9*) Higginson Bk Co.

Memorial Record of Licking County: Containing Biographical Sketches of Representative Citizens of the County. (Illus.). 526p. 1997. reprint ed. lib. bdg. 55.00 (*0-8328-6337-8*) Higginson Bk Co.

Memorial Record of Southwestern Minnesota: Biographical Sketches of Prominent Residents. (Illus.). 560p. 1997. reprint ed. lib. bdg. 58.50 (*0-8328-6796-9*) Higginson Bk Co.

Memorial Rituals Book for Healing & Hope. Ed. by Ann M. Putter. LC 96-28349. (Death, Value & Meaning Ser.). 88p. 1997. pap. text 23.95 (*0-89503-143-4*) Baywood Pub.

Memorial Service. J. I. Stewart. 1976. 7.95 (*0-393-08751-4*) Norton.

Memorial Service at the Cemetery. Morris Silverman. pap. 1.50 (*0-685-64878-8*) Prayer Bk.

Memorial Services for Women. Meg Bowman. 156p. 1986. pap. 8.95 (*0-940483-01-7*) Hot Flash Pr.

Memorial Services in the Congress of the United States & Tributes in Eulogy of Richard M. Nixon, Late a President of the United States. 93p. 1996. boxed set 22.00 (*0-16-063273-0*, Congress) USGPO.

Memorial to Bishop Cheverus: With a Catalogue of the Books Given by Him to the Boston Athenaeum. Walter M. Whitehill. LC 52-930. (Robert Charles Billings Fund Publication Pamphlet Ser.: No. 3). (Illus.). xxiii, 9p. (Orig.). 1964. reprint ed. pap. 1.50 (*0-934552-19-3*) Boston Athenaeum.

Memorial Tributes: National Academy of Engineering. National Academy of Engineering Staff. 320p. 35.00 (*0-309-05575-X*) Natl Acad Pr.

Memorial Tributes: National Academy of Engineering, Vol. 1. National Academy of Engineering Staff. 303p. 1979. text 24.95 (*0-309-02889-2*) Natl Acad Pr.

Memorial Tributes: National Academy of Engineering, Vol. 2. National Academy of Engineering Staff. 318p. 1984. text 24.95 (*0-309-03482-5*) Natl Acad Pr.

Memorial Tributes: National Academy of Engineering, Vol. 3. National Academy of Engineering Staff. 388p. 1989. text 27.95 (*0-309-03939-8*) Natl Acad Pr.

Memorial Tributes: National Academy of Engineering, Vol. 4. National Academy of Engineering Staff. 356p. (C). 1991. text 42.00 (*0-309-04349-2*) Natl Acad Pr.

Memorial Tributes: National Academy of Engineering, Vol. 5. National Academy of Engineering Staff. 312p. (C). 1992. text 36.00 (*0-309-04689-0*) Natl Acad Pr.

Memorial Tributes: National Academy of Engineering, Vol. 6. National Academy of Engineering Staff. 280p. 1993. text 41.00 (*0-309-04847-8*) Natl Acad Pr.

Memorial Tributes: National Academy of Engineering, Vol. 7. National Academy of Engineering Staff. 256p. 1994. text 46.00 (*0-309-05146-0*) Natl Acad Pr.

Memorial Tributes Delivered in Congress, Ronald H. Brown, 1941-1996, Secretary of Commerce. 261p. 1997. boxed set 43.00 (*0-16-063277-3*) USGPO.

Memorial Volume of Jefferson Davis. J. William Jones. 1995. 38.99 (*0-87377-170-2*) GAM Pubns.

Memorial War Book. George F. Williams et al. 1979. 24.95 (*0-405-12293-4*) Ayer.

Memorial Windows of Church of the Holy Trinity. Timothy D. Ables & Bobbie P. Marascalco. (Illus.). 58p. (Orig.). 1992. pap. 20.00 (*0-9632630-8-0*) Church HT.

Memoriale Fratris Walteri de Coventria (to 1226), 2 vols. Ed. by William Stubbs. (Rolls Ser.: No. 58). 1974. reprint ed. 140.00 (*0-8115-1126-X*) Periodicals Srv.

M

Memorialists. David S. Turk. LC 97-207215. (Illus.). x, 168p. 1997. pap. 17.00 (*0-7884-0687-6*, T866) Heritage Bk.

Memorials Vol. XV: 1983 Decedents. 1985. pap. 5.00 (*0-8137-8083-7*, MML015) Geol Soc.

Memorials Vol. XVI: 1984 Decedents. 1986. pap. 5.00 (*0-8137-8084-5*, MML016) Geol Soc.

Memorials Vol. XVII: 1985 Decedents. 1987. pap. 5.00 (*0-8137-8085-3*, MML017) Geol Soc.

Memorials Vol. XVIII: 1986 Decedents. 1988. pap. 5.00 (*0-8137-8086-1*, MML018) Geol Soc.

Memorials Vol. XIX: 1987 Decedents. 1989. pap. 5.00 (*0-8137-8087-X*, MML019) Geol Soc.

Memorials Vol. XX: 1988 Decedents. 1990. pap. 5.00 (*0-8137-8088-8*, MML020) Geol Soc.

Memorials Vol. XXI: 1989 Decedents. 1991. pap. 10.00 (*0-8137-8089-6*, MML021) Geol Soc.

Memorials Vol. XXII: Decedents. 1992. pap. 7.50 (*0-8137-8090-X*, MML022) Geol Soc.

Memorials Vol. XXIII: Decedents. 1993. pap. 10.00 (*0-8137-8091-8*, MML023) Geol Soc.

Memorials Vol. XXIV: Decedents. 1994. pap. 16.50 (*0-8137-8092-6*, MML024) Geol Soc.

Memorials & Correspondence of Charles James Fox, 4 vols. Charles J. Fox. Ed. by John Russell. LC 75-115362. reprint ed. 345.00 (*0-404-05470-6*) AMS Pr.

Memorials of a Century, Embracing a Record of Individuals & Events, Chiefly in the Early History of Bennington & Its First Church. Isaac Jennings. (Illus.). 408p. 1997. reprint ed. lib. bdg. 43.50 (*0-8328-6501-X*) Higginson Bk Co.

Memorials of Affairs of State in the Reigns of Queen Elizabeth & King James First, 3 vols. Ralph Winwood. Ed. by Edmund J. Sawyer. LC 75-178310. reprint ed. lib. bdg. 245.00 (*0-404-07020-5*) AMS Pr.

Memorials of Alfred Marshall. Alfred Marshall. Ed. by A. C. Pigou. LC 66-24415. (Reprints of Economic Classics Ser.). ix, 518p. 1966. 49.50 (*0-678-00197-9*) Kelley.

*__Memorials of Angus & Mearns: An Account Historical, Antiquarian & Traditionary of the Castles & Towns Visited by Edward I & of the Barons, Clergy & Others Who Swore Fealty to England in 1291-1296.__ Andrew Jervise & James Gammack. (Illus.). 753p. 2000. pap. 38.50 (*0-7884-1438-0*, 1438) Heritage Bk.

Memorials of Edward Burne-Jones, 2 Vols. Georgiana M. Burne-Jones. LC 74-179508. (Select Bibliographies Reprint Ser.). 1977. reprint ed. 47.95 (*0-8369-6637-6*) Ayer.

Memorials of Edward Burne-Jones, 2 vols., 1 bk. Georgiana M. Burne-Jones. LC 71-174396. (Illus.). 704p. 1972. reprint ed. 38.95 (*0-405-08334-3*, Pub. by Blom Pubns) Ayer.

Memorials of Edward Burne-Jones, 2 vols., Vol. I: 1833-1867. Georgiana M. Burne-Jones. 352p. (C). 1993. 50.00 (*0-85331-631-7*) Lund Humphries.

Memorials of Edward Burne-Jones, 2 vols., Vol. II: 1868-1898. Georgiana M. Burne-Jones. 424p. (C). 1993. 50.00 (*0-85331-632-5*, Pub. by Lund Humphries) Antique Collect.

Memorials of George Bannatyne. Ed. by Sir Walter Scott. LC 79-175841. (Bannatyne Club, Edinburgh Publications: No. 35). reprint ed. 54.00 (*0-404-52741-8*) AMS Pr.

Memorials of Great & Good Men Who Were My Friends: Portraits in the Life of Oliver Wolcott, Jr. Ellen G. Miles. (Illus.). 55p. 1998. reprint ed. pap. 8.50 (*0-944026-88-5*) Am Antiquarian.

Memorials of Henry V, King of England. Ed. by Charles A. Cole. (Rolls Ser.: No. 11). 1974. reprint ed. 70.00 (*0-8115-1014-X*) Periodicals Srv.

Memorials of Henry VII: Bernardi Andreae Tholosatis Vita Regis Henrici Septimi; Necnon Alia Quaedam ad Eundem Regem Spectantia. Ed. by James Gairdner. (Rolls Ser.: No. 10). 1974. reprint ed. 70.00 (*0-8115-1013-1*) Periodicals Srv.

Memorials of His Time. Henry Cockburn. 470p. (C). 1989. 32.00 (*0-901824-11-9*, Pub. by Mercat Pr Bks) St Mut.

Memorials of His Time. Henry T. Cockburn. LC 73-148764. reprint ed. 55.00 (*0-404-07228-3*) AMS Pr.

Memorials of Montrose & His Times, 2 vols. Ed. by Mark Napier. LC 73-173012. (Maitland Club, Glasgow. Publications: No. 66). reprint ed. 85.00 (*0-404-53075-3*) AMS Pr.

Memorials of Old Bridgehampton. James T. Adams. (Illus.). 399p. 1997. reprint ed. lib. bdg. 43.00 (*0-8328-6103-0*) Higginson Bk Co.

Memorials of Sarah Childress Polk: Wife of the Eleventh President of the United States. Anson Nelson & Fanny Nelson. LC 73-22435. (Illus.). 298p. 1974. reprint ed. 25.00 (*0-87152-163-6*) Reprint.

Memorials of Shakespeare. Nathan Drake. LC 76-164789. reprint ed. 46.50 (*0-404-02177-8*) AMS Pr.

Memorials of St. Anselm. Ed. by Richard W. Southern & F. S. Schmidt. (Auctores Britannici Medii Aevi Ser.: Vol. I). (Illus.). 380p. 1991. pap. text 29.95 (*0-19-726102-7*) OUP.

Memorials of St. Dunstan, Archbishop of Canterbury. Ed. by William Stubbs. (Rolls Ser.: No. 63). 1974. reprint ed. 70.00 (*0-8115-1131-6*) Periodicals Srv.

Memorials of St. Edmund's Abbey, 3 vols. Ed. by Thomas Arnold. (Rolls Ser.: No. 96). 1974. reprint ed. 210.00 (*0-8115-1175-8*) Periodicals Srv.

Memorials of the Chaunceys, Including President Chauncey, His Ancestors & Descendants. W. C. Fowler. (Illus.). 377p. 1989. reprint ed. pap. 56.00 (*0-8328-0395-2*); reprint ed. lib. bdg. 64.00 (*0-8328-0394-4*) Higginson Bk Co.

Memorials of the Descendants of William Shattuck, the Progenitor of the Family in America That Borne His Name. Lemuel C. Shattuck. 419p. 1989. reprint ed. pap. 63.00 (*0-8328-1065-7*); reprint ed. lib. bdg. 71.00 (*0-8328-1064-9*) Higginson Bk Co.

Memorials of the Faithful. 5th ed. Abdu'l-Baha. Tr. by Marzieh Gail from PER. LC 97-219604. 204p. 1997. pap. 10.95 (*0-87743-242-2*) Bahai.

Memorials of the Great War in Britain: The Symbolism & Politics of Remembrance. Alex King. LC 98-211640. (Legacy of the Great War Ser.). 274p. 1998. 65.00 (*1-85973-983-0*, Pub. by Berg Pubs); pap. 19.50 (*1-85973-988-1*, Pub. by Berg Pubs) NYU Pr.

Memorials of the Justices of the Supreme Court of the United States, 5 vols. Compiled & Intro. by Roger F. Jacobs. (Illus.). 1981. 395.00 (*0-8377-0733-1*, Rothman) W S Hein.

Memorials of the Life of Amelia Opie. Amelia A. Opie. LC 79-37711. reprint ed. 67.50 (*0-404-56774-6*) AMS Pr.

Memorials of the Mauran Family. J. E. Mauran & J. C. Stockbridge. 171p. 1993. reprint ed. pap. 29.50 (*0-8328-3800-4*); reprint ed. lib. bdg. 39.50 (*0-8328-3799-7*) Higginson Bk Co.

Memorials of the Most Noble Order of the Garter from Its Foundation to the Present Time. George F. Beltz. LC 72-178572. reprint ed. 64.50 (*0-404-56527-1*) AMS Pr.

Memorials of the Reign of King Henry VI: Official Correspondence of Thomas Bekynton, Secretary to Henry VI & Bishop of Bath & Wells, 2 vols. Thomas Beckington. Ed. by George Williams. (Rolls Ser.: No. 56). 1974. reprint ed. 140.00 (*0-8115-1118-9*) Periodicals Srv.

Memorials of the Spanish Civil War: The Official Publication of the International Brigade Association. Colin Williams et al. LC 96-203898. (Illus.). 192p. 1996. 31.95 (*0-7509-1186-7*, Pub. by Sutton Pub Ltd) Intl Pubs Mktg.

Memorials of Transactions in Scotland. Richard Bannatyne. Ed. by Robert Pitcairn. LC 73-161738. (Bannatyne Club, Edinburgh. Publications: No. 51). reprint ed. 87.50 (*0-404-52761-2*) AMS Pr.

Memorials of William Cranch Bond: Director of the Harvard College Observatory, 1840-1859, & His Son, George Phillips Bond, Director of the Harvard College Observatory, 1859-1865. Edward S. Holden. Ed. by I. Bernard Cohen. LC 79-8403. (Three Centuries of Science in America Ser.). 1980. reprint ed. lib. bdg. 28.95 (*0-405-12549-6*) Ayer.

Memorias: A West Texas Life. Salvador Guerrero. (Illus.). 112p. 1991. 20.00 (*0-89672-255-4*) Tex Tech Univ Pr.

Memorias: Ocho Anos de Lucha. Machado Gerardo. Ed. by Morales Gerardo et al. LC 82-84134. (Historia y Biografias Ser.). (SPA., Illus.). 224p. (Orig.). 1982. pap. 12.95 (*0-89729-328-2*) Ediciones.

Memorias Cronologicas Sobre el Origen de la Representacion de Comedias en Espana, Ano 1785. Jose A. De Armona. Ed. by Charles Davis et al. (Fuentes Para la Historia del Teatro en Espana, Series C: Vol. XIV). (Illus.). 350p. 1999. 54.00 (*1-85566-045-8*, Pub. by Tamesis Bks Ltd) Boydell & Brewer.

Memorias de Bernardo Vega see Memoirs of Bernardo Vega: A Contribution to the History of the Puerto Rican Community in New York

Memorias de Bernardo Vega. Ed. by Cesar Andreu-Iglesias. LC 80-83696. (Coleccion Norte). 278p. 1977. reprint ed. pap. 8.75 (*0-940238-26-8*) Ediciones Huracan.

Memorias de Cuba: Oscar De San Emilio. LC 77-75161. 1978. pap. 5.95 (*84-399-7886-3*) Ediciones.

Memorias de Jesus de Nazaret. Jose Paulos. LC 96-86649. (Coleccion Felix Varela). (SPA.). 166p. (Orig.). 1996. pap. 16.00 (*0-89729-815-2*) Ediciones.

Memorias de Loisaida. Miguel Algarin. LC 97-2093. 128p. 1997. per. 13.00 (*0-684-82517-1*) S&S Trade.

Memorias de mi Viaje/Recollections of My Trip. LC 94-21543. 142p. 1994. 12.95 (*0-8263-1532-1*) U of NM Pr.

Memorias de Sancho Cota. Sancho Cota. Ed. by Hayward Keniston. LC 64-16064. (Studies in Romance Languages: No. 28). 269p. 1964. 15.00 (*0-674-56600-9*) HUP.

Memorias de un Cubano Sin Importancia. Napoleon S. Padilla. 328p. 1988. pap. 10.00 (*0-9620495-0-6*) N S Padilla.

Memorias de un Desmemoriado: Lena Para el Fuego de la Historia de Cuba. Jose R. Pedrosa. LC 78-67007. (Coleccion Cuba y sus Jueces). 1979. 13.00 (*0-89729-207-3*) Ediciones.

Memorias de un Dinar. Dahesh. (ARA, ENG & SPA., Illus.). 382p. 1990. 35.00 (*0-935359-19-2*) Daheshist.

Memorias de un Pueblito Cubano. Esteban J. Hoyos. LC 84-72857. (Coleccion Caniqui). (SPA.). 110p. (Orig.). 1985. pap. 6.95 (*0-89729-363-0*) Ediciones.

Memorias de un Taquigrafo. Angel V. Fernandez. LC 93-90379. (Coleccion Cuba y sus Jueces). (SPA., Illus.). 224p. (Orig.). 1993. pap. 19.00 (*0-89729-715-6*) Ediciones.

***Memorias de una Geisha.** Arthur S. Golden. (SPA.). 1999. pap. text 19.95 (*968-19-0584-9*) Aguilar.

Memorias del Nuevo Mundo. Aridjis. 1996. 26.95 (*0-15-158872-4*) Harcourt.

Memorias del Primer Congreso del Presidio Politico Cubano. Ed. by Manuel Pozo y Regueiro. (SPA.). 1994. pap. 13.00 (*0-89729-727-X*) Ediciones.

Memorias (Memories), Vol. I. Jose Vasconcelos. (SPA.). 965p. 1982. 31.99 (*968-16-1208-6*, Pub. by Fondo) Continental Bk.

Memorias (Memories), Vol. II. Jose Vasconcelos. (SPA.). 1190p. 1982. 31.99 (*968-16-1209-4*, Pub. by Fondo) Continental Bk.

Memorie Biografiche di Don Giovanni Bosco see Biographical Memoirs of Saint John Bosco

Memorie Dei Compositori Di Musica Del Regno Di Napoli. Carlo A. Villarosa. xv, 250p. reprint ed. write for info. (*0-318-71591-0*) G Olms Pubs.

Memorie della vita e delle peregrinazioni del fiorentino Filippo Mazzei see Philip Mazzei: My Life & Wanderings

Memorie Storico-Critiche Della Vita E Delle Opere Di Giovanni Pierluigi Da Palestrina, 2 vols., Set. Giuseppe Baini. xxxiv, 816p. 1966. reprint ed. 225.00 (*0-318-71580-5*) G Olms Pubs.

Memories. Peggy Darty. LC 97-44218. 256p. 1998. pap. 9.99 (*1-57673-171-5*, Palisades OR) Multnomah Pubs.

Memories. Chrishane Eisel. 154p. (Orig.). 1994. pap. 12.95 (*0-9642840-0-6*) Cee-Gee.

***Memories.** Sandy Gore Evans. 2000. 19.95 (*1-890621-05-6*) Landauer Bks IA.

Memories. Mary I. Fogarty. 101p. (Orig.). 1990. pap. 10.95 (*0-929260-04-X*) Cricklewood Pr.

***Memories.** Leonard M. Grizzle. 1999. pap. write for info. (*1-58235-088-4*) Watermrk Pr.

***Memories.** Barbara Johnson. 1999. pap. write for info. (*1-58235-391-3*) Watermrk Pr.

***Memories.** Warren Kimble. 2000. 19.95 (*1-890621-12-9*) Landauer Bks IA.

Memories. Bonnie Kirin. 1997. pap. write for info. (*1-57553-693-5*) Watermrk Pr.

Memories. Laurie Loveman. LC 98-88466. (Firehouse Family Ser.). 325p. 1998. 25.00 (*0-7388-0155-0*); pap. 15.00 (*0-7388-0156-9*) Xlibris Corp.

Memories. Viola Mercer. 76p. 1998. pap. 9.95 (*1-885206-59-3*) Cader Pubng.

Memories. Teresa O'Brien. LC 90-46155. 5p. (J). 1985. 6.99 (*0-85953-319-0*) Childs Play.

Memories. Edna T. Rush. 1998. pap. write for info. (*1-57553-791-5*) Watermrk Pr.

Memories. Ralph J. Silverman. 1998. pap. write for info. (*1-57553-644-7*) Watermrk Pr.

Memories. Paul L. Smith. LC 98-9210. 1998. pap. 8.95 (*0-533-12737-8*) Vantage.

Memories. Kate William. (Sweet Valley High Ser.: No. 24). (YA). (gr. 7 up). 1986. 9.09 (*0-606-00710-5*, Pub. by Turtleback) Demco.

Memories. Charlotte Vale Allen. 1998. reprint ed. pap. 20.00 (*1-892738-04-X*) Isld Nation.

Memories. Charlotte Vale Allen. 336p. 1998. reprint ed. 23.95 (*1-892738-19-8*, Pub. by Isld Nation) Brodart.

Memories. William J. Linton. LC 69-13753. vi, 236p. 1970. reprint ed. 39.50 (*0-678-00596-6*) Kelley.

***Memories: A Celebration of Life.** Glenn H. Gregg. LC 99-68892. 2000. 18.95 (*1-57736-169-5*, Hillsboro Pr) Providence Hse.

Memories: A Priceless Heirloom. Bobb Biehl. 266p. 1997. 40.00 (*0-9664049-1-2*) Premiere Publng.

Memories: D'Additions au Journal de Dandeau, Vol. 1, 1691-1701. Saint-Simon. Ed. by Yves Coirault. (FRE.). 1983. lib. bdg. 125.00 (*0-7859-3848-6*) Fr & Eur.

Memories: D'Additions au Journal de Dandeau, Vol. 3, 1707-1710. Saint-Simon. Ed. by Yves Coirault. (FRE.). 1984. lib. bdg. 125.00 (*0-7859-3857-5*) Fr & Eur.

Memories: D'Additions au Journal de Dandeau, Vol. 4, 1711-1714. Saint-Simon. Ed. by Yves Coirault. (FRE.). 1985. lib. bdg. 125.00 (*0-7859-3858-3*) Fr & Eur.

Memories: D'Additions au Journal de Dandeau, Vol. 5, 1714-1716. Saint-Simon. Ed. by Yves Coirault. (FRE.). 1985. lib. bdg. 140.00 (*0-7859-3859-1*) Fr & Eur.

Memories: D'Additions au Journal de Dandeau, Vol. 6, 1716-1718. Saint-Simon. Ed. by Yves Coirault. (FRE.). 1986. lib. bdg. 135.00 (*0-7859-3860-5*) Fr & Eur.

Memories: D'Additions au Journal de Dandeau, Vol. 7, 1718-1721. Saint-Simon. Ed. by Yves Coirault. (FRE.). 1987. lib. bdg. 145.00 (*0-7859-3861-3*) Fr & Eur.

Memories: D'Additions au Journal de Dandeau, 1701-1707, Vol. 2. Saint-Simon. Ed. by Yves Coirault. 1983. lib. bdg. 125.00 (*0-7859-3926-1*) Fr & Eur.

Memories: My Life As an International Leader in Health, Suffrage, & Peace. Aletta Jacobs. Ed. by Harriet Feinberg. Tr. by Annie Wright from DUT. LC 95-35736. (Illus.). 272p. 1996. pap. 18.95 (*1-55861-138-X*); lib. bdg. 45.00 (*1-55861-137-1*) Feminist Pr.

Memories: Of Life's Dreams. large type ed. Helen M. Van De Kraats. LC 97-61444. (Illus.). 104p. 1998. spiral bd. 24.95 (*1-883165-54-7*) Fernholm Pub.

Memories: The Autobiography of Ralph Emery. Ralph Emery & Tom Carter. (Illus.). 288p. 1991. text 19.95 (*0-02-535481-7*) Macmillan.

Memories: The Autobiography of Ralph Emery. large type ed. Ralph Emery & Tom Carter. LC 92-22858. (General Ser.). 432p. 1992. 16.95 (*0-8161-5581-X*, G K Hall Lrg Type) Mac Lib Ref.

Memories: The Autobiography of Ralph Emery. Ralph Emery & Tom Carter. Ed. by Denise Silvestro. (Illus.). 296p. 1992. reprint ed. per. 5.50 (*0-671-79157-5*) PB.

Memories: The Story of Dick & Marge Bong (Major Richard Bong America's Ace of Aces) 2nd ed. Marge B. Drucker. (Illus.). 120p. 1995. 25.00 (*0-9647840-0-9*) Drucker Pubns.

Memories Vol. 1: A Memory of Growth - A Growth of Memories. 57p. (Orig.). 1996. write for info. (*0-9656769-0-0*) ExLCor.

Memories Vol. 8: D'Additions au Journal de Dandeau: 1721-1823, Index et Tables. deluxe ed. Saint-Simon. (FRE.). 1904p. 1988. 165.00 (*0-7859-3927-X*, 207011015X) Fr & Eur.

Memories - A Pictorial History of South Louisiana Music, 1912s-1990s Vols. 1 & 2: South Louisiana & East Texas Musicians. Johnnie Allan. LC 95-76557. 330p. 1995. 36.00 (*0-9619335-4-2*); pap. 26.00 (*0-9619335-3-4*) Jadfel Pub.

Memories - Camp Mitre Peak: The First Fifty Years, 1947-1997. Jana Jones. (Illus.). 82p. 1997. pap. 20.00 (*0-9668973-0-7*) Jana Jones.

Memories - JFK, 1961-1963. Cecil Stoughton et al. (Illus.). 208p. 1980. reprint ed. pap. 19.95 (*0-393-00985-8*) Norton.

Memories, a Present from the Past. Kathryn Hillen. 160p. 1987. pap. 9.95 (*0-310-34551-0*, 9950P) Zondervan.

Memories Ago Reminiscings of a Northern Minn. Childhood. Dolores Dahl. (Illus.). 39p. (Orig.). 1985. pap. 9.95 (*0-9608960-4-X*) Single Vision.

Memories, (An Excerpt from the Tarnish on the Golden Years) Nona K. Carver. (Illus.). 32p. (Orig.). 1994. pap. 7.00 (*0-9641195-5-2*) Carver Cntry.

Memories & Adventures. Arthur Conan Doyle. LC 84-73098. (Illus.). 250p. Date not set. 24.95 (*0-934468-23-0*) Gaslight.

Memories & Adventures. Arthur Conan Doyle. (BCL1-PR English Literature Ser.). 410p. 1992. reprint ed. lib. bdg. 99.00 (*0-7812-7522-9*) Rprt Serv.

Memories & Adventures. Louise Heritte-Viardot. LC 77-22220. (Music Reprint Ser.). (Illus.). 1978. reprint ed. lib. bdg. 37.50 (*0-306-77515-8*) Da Capo.

Memories & Commentaries. Igor Stravinsky & Robert Craft. (Orig.). 1981. pap. 12.95 (*0-520-04402-9*, Pub. by U CA Pr) Cal Prin Full Svc.

Memories & Daydreams. Ed. by Jef Sturm. 300p. 1997. 59.95 (*1-888680-12-1*, U912) Poetry Guild.

Memories & Dreams: Reflections on Twentieth Century Australia. Ed. by Richard White & Penny Russell. LC 97-156787. 304p. 1997. pap. 29.95 (*1-86373-536-4*, Pub. by Allen & Unwin Pty) Paul & Co Pubs.

Memories & Hallucinations: A Memoir. D. M. Thomas. LC 89-130288. 195 p. 1988. 11.95 (*0-575-04305-9*) V Gollancz.

Memories & Hopes. Leon-Joseph Suenens. Tr. by Elena French from FRE. 395p. 1992. 19.95 (*1-85390-129-6*) Ignatius Pr.

Memories & Impressions. Ford Madox Ford. (Illus.). xviii, 335p. 1971. reprint ed. 49.00 (*0-403-00966-9*) Scholarly.

Memories & Impressions: An Autobiography. Helena O. Modjeska. (American Biography Ser.). 571p. 1991. reprint ed. lib. bdg. 99.00 (*0-7812-8286-1*) Rprt Serv.

Memories & Impressions of Helena Modjeska: An Autobiography. Helena O. Modjeska. LC 75-81212. (Illus.). 580p. 1972. reprint ed. 24.95 (*0-405-08791-8*, Pub. by Blom Pubns) Ayer.

Memories & Meditations of a Workcamper. David S. Richie. LC 73-84213. 36p. (Orig.). 1973. pap. 4.00 (*0-87574-190-8*) Pendle Hill.

Memories & Memorabilia: More Than 600 Easy Ways to Preserve Them. Lynn Bonsey & Lorna Healey. (Illus.). 203p. (Orig.). 1995. pap. text 15.00 (*0-7884-0208-0*) Heritage Bk.

Memories & Milestones. John J. Chapman. LC 70-152161. (Essay Index Reprint Ser.). 1977. 20.95 (*0-8369-2183-6*) Ayer.

Memories & Milestones: Stepping Forward by Looking Back. Jennifer Pasquale. Tr. by Luis Lopez. 185p. (Orig.). 1997. pap. 10.00 (*0-9658095-4-4*) J Pasquale.

Memories & Musings. K. P. Menon. 361p. 1979. 14.95 (*0-318-36594-4*) Asia Bk Corp.

***Memories & Musings.** James Todd. 1999. pap. write for info. (*1-58235-289-5*) Watermrk Pr.

Memories & Portraits. Ivan A. Bunin. LC 68-8053. (Illus.). 217p. 1968. reprint ed. lib. bdg. 49.75 (*0-8371-0033-X*, BUMP, Greenwood Pr) Greenwood.

Memories & Portraits. Robert Louis Stevenson. LC 06-18298. 1969. reprint ed. 39.00 (*0-403-00055-6*) Scholarly.

Memories & Portraits, Random Memories, Record of a Family of Engineers see Works of Robert Louis Stevenson, Valima Edition

Memories & Reflections: Poems, Prose, Pictures. Lloyd Hamlin. LC 93-40901. (Illus.). 96p. (Orig.). 1994. pap. 10.00 (*1-56474-086-2*) Fithian Pr.

Memories & Studies. William James. LC 68-19276. 411p. 1968. reprint ed. lib. bdg. 75.00 (*0-8371-0496-3*, JAMS, Greenwood Pr) Greenwood.

Memories & Studies. William James. (Notable American Authors Ser.). 1992. reprint ed. lib. bdg. 75.00 (*0-7812-3481-6*) Rprt Serv.

Memories & Studies. William James. Ed. by Henry James. LC 78-115249. 1971. reprint ed. 15.00 (*0-403-00380-6*) Scholarly.

Memories & Visions of Paradise. Richard W. Heinberg. (Illus.). 61p. (Orig.). 1985. pap. 4.95 (*0-932869-00-9*) Emissaries.

***Memories Are Forever.** Clark S. Beardslee. 2000. write for info. (*1-58235-487-1*) Watermrk Pr.

Memories Are Made of This. Edgar C. Alward. (Illus.). 140p. (Orig.). 1995. pap. 22.00 (*1-880836-08-4*) Pine Isl Pr.

Memories Are Made of This. 2nd rev. ed. Edgar C. Alward. (Odyssey of a Teacher Ser.). (Illus.). 258p. (Orig.). 1998. 89.00 (*1-891016-28-8*) Esparto Pr.

Memories Are Made of This: An Anecdotal Autobiography. Charles Ayers. Ed. by Messinger Press Staff. LC 89-91192. (Illus.). 428p. (Orig.). 1989. write for info. (*0-9623170-0-4*) Limelight Celina.

Memories Are Not Subject to Time. rev. unabridged ed. Mabel Conde. (Illus.). 70p. 1997. pap., per. 8.95 (*0-9658473-1-4*) M Conde.

Memories at Midnight: The McCord Family Countdown. Joanna Wayne. (Intrigue Ser.: No. 537). 1999. per. 3.99 (*0-373-22537-7*, 1-22537-4) Harlequin Bks.

Memories, Blessings & Tears. Vivian A. Moore. 1998. pap. write for info. (*1-57553-850-4*) Watermrk Pr.

Memories by Mom. "Mom" Giordano. 12.95 (*1-888125-64-0*) Todd Commns.

***Memories by Mom, Tales of an Alaskan Homesteader.** large type ed. Giordano & Mary Halpin. (Illus.). 75p. 1999. pap. 12.95 (*0-9661665-2-3*) Bear Paw AK.

Memories Can Be Murder. Connie Shelton. Ed. by Lee Ellison. LC 99-16432. (Charlie Parker Mystery Ser.: 5). 224p. 1999. 22.95 (*1-890768-18-9*) Intrigue Press.

Memories Cast in Stone: The Relevance of the Past in Everyday Life. David Sutton. (Mediterranean Ser.). 224p. 1998. 55.00 (*1-85973-943-1*, Pub. by Berg Pubs); pap. 19.50 (*1-85973-948-2*, Pub. by Berg Pubs) NYU Pr.

Memories Come to Us in the Rain & the Wind: Oral Histories & Photographs of Navajo Uranium Miners & Their Families. 2nd ed. Doug Brugge et al. Tr. by Martha Austm-Garrison & Lydia Fasthorse-Begay from NAV. (Illus.). 62p. 1997. reprint ed. pap. 15.00 (*0-9660050-1-5*) Navajo Uranium.

Memories, Dreams, Reflections. C. G. Jung. Ed. by Aniela Jaffe. Tr. by Richard Winston & Clara Winston. LC 88-37040. xiii, 430p. 1989. pap. 13.00 (*0-679-72395-1*) Vin Bks.

Memories, Dreams, Reflections. abr. ed. C. G. Jung. 1991. audio 16.95 (*0-87773-554-9*, Z005, Pub. by Shambhala Pubns) Random.

Memories for Mary Ruth: Mieran, Bergtholdt, Sturtz, & Brasfield Families. Marilyn L. Landreth. (Illus.). (Orig.). 1997. pap. 30.00 (*0-9649896-1-1*) Muddy Water.

***Memories for My Grandchild.** Millie MacKiney. 2000. 19.99 (*1-56245-419-6*) Great Quotations.

Memories Forever. Jody Lebroke. 218p. mass mkt. 4.99 (*1-55197-017-1*) Picasso Publ.

***Memories Forever: A Collection of Poems & Stories from Bereaved Parents Siblings, Friends & Young Cancer Patients.** Jill Lee et al. LC 99-75571. 80p. 1999. pap. 9.95 (*1-58597-002-6*) Leathers Pub.

Memories Form the Heart. Schrena Wilson. 1998. pap. write for info. (*1-57553-745-1*) Watermrk Pr.

***Memories Frames in Glass.** Carla Weaver. (Illus.). 32p. 1999. pap. 14.95 (*0-935133-73-9*) CKE Pubns.

Memories from a Russian Kitchen: From Shteti to Golden Land. Rosalie Sogolow. (Illus.). 272p. 1996. 25.00 (*1-56474-148-6*) Fithian Pr.

***Memories from a Russian Kitchen: From Shteti to Golden Land.** Ed. & Compiled by Rosalie Sogolow. (Illus.). 272p. 1999. pap. 18.95 (*1-56474-310-1*) Fithian Pr.

Memories from Harbor View Pathway. Margret VanOrden Maloney. LC 97-66205. (Illus.). 1997. write for info. (*0-89725-300-0*) Picton Pr.

Memories from Mother. Joan Collins. Ed. by Kimberly J. Wightman & Teresa E. Wightman. 70p. 1998. pap. 9.95 (*1-888911-09-3*) Benson Smythe.

***Memories from My Heart: A Journal.** Linda Coulter. LC 99-75573. 128p. 1999. pap. 9.95 (*1-58597-003-4*) Leathers Pub.

Memories from the Land of Siskiyou: Past Lives & Times in Siskiyou County. Ed. by Gilbert W. Davies & Florice M. Frank. LC 93-78430. (Illus.). 460p. (C). 1993. pap. 24.95 (*0-9634413-1-0*) HiSt ink Bks.

Memories from the Mountains. C. B. Rich. 200p. (Orig.). 1992. pap. 7.95 (*0-9633062-1-9*) Double Arrow.

Memories from the Mountains: A Collection of Short Stories by a Twin Girl Comparing Life in a Small Paper Town to Country Life. Josephine Paxton Green. LC 98-61140. (Illus.). 228p. 1998. pap. 14.95 (*1-56664-137-3*) WorldComm.

***Memories from the Rain.** Michael K. McCracken. 1999. pap. write for info. (*1-58235-386-7*) Watermrk Pr.

M

An Asterisk (*) at the beginning of an entry indicates that the title is appearing for the first time.

Memories from the Trail. Paul Lamb. iii, 122p. (Orig.). 1994. pap. text 10.00 (*0-9639179-0-5*) Lambs Fold Ranch.

Memories Have Tongue: Poetry. Afua Cooper. 128p. 1993. per. write for info. (*0-920813-50-X*) Sister Vis Pr.

Memories Humor of a Second Generation Volga American. Calvin E. Nuss. 1993. pap. 7.50 (*0-614-23856-0*) Am Hist Soc Ger.

***Memories in a Scrapbook: Through the Years Since 1931.** Ethel McNeill. 1999. pap. write for info. (*1-58235-235-6*) Watermrk Pr.

Memories in Minutes. Ellison Craft & Design Staff. (Illus.). 46p. (Orig.). 1997. pap. 16.50 (*0-9656297-0-8*) Ellison Craft.

Memories in Moments: Over 600 Timeless Ideas for Celebrating Life's Special Occasions. Susan Stone. LC 98-91624. (Illus.). 152p. (Orig.). 1998. pap. 14.95 (*0-9664733-0-2*) Marally Pubg.

Memories in My Heart. Diane Richards. 100p. 1988. pap. text 6.50 (*1-56770-189-2*) S Scheewe Pubns.

***Memories in the Making: The History of Garfield Park.** Threefifteen Press Staff. (Illus.). 32p. 1999. pap. write for info. (*1-928880-00-2*) Threefifteen Pr.

Memories in Verse: "Life", Vol. 1. Margaret L. Ingram. (Illus.). 16p. (Orig.). 1989. pap. text. write for info. (*0-318-65940-9*); pap. text 2.00 (*0-9624721-1-5*) Memories Plus.

Memories Linger On. Nellie Beardmore. LC 97-91026. 1998. pap. 8.95 (*0-533-12542-1*) Vantage.

Memories Live Forever: A Memory Book for Grieving Children. 3rd rev. ed. Sharon Rugg et al. (Illus.). 35p. (Orig.). (J). (gr. k-8). 1996. pap. 5.00 (*0-9652410-0-9*) S Rugg.

Memories Live Forever: A Memory Book for Grieving Children see Recuerdos Viven Eternamente: Un Libro de Recuerdos para Ninos Afligidos por una Muerta

Memories, Me & Mountains see Hoofbeats & Heartbeats

Memories of a Berlin Childhood. Marianne Buchwalter. LC 95-67040. (Illus.). 192p. 1995. 17.95 (*0-9633818-4-9*) Premiere Edits.

Memories of a Cat: Lazy Days in the Sun see Lazy Days in the Sun, Pt. 1, A Felonious Feline Memoir

Memories of a Catholic Girlhood. Mary McCarthy. LC 57-8842. (Illus.). 264p. 1972. reprint ed. pap. 12.00 (*0-15-658650-9*, Harvest Bks) Harcourt.

Memories of a Coal Camp Kid. W. C. Stump. 1990. 23.45 (*0-685-45452-5*) W C Stump.

Memories of a Country Childhood. Judith Wallace. 140p. 1988. pap. text 14.95 (*0-7022-1626-7*, Pub. by Univ Queensland Pr) Intl Spec Bk.

Memories of a Cuban Kitchen. Mary U. Randelman. 352p. 1996. 16.95 (*0-02-860998-0*, Pub. by Macmillan) S&S Trade.

Memories of a Farm Boy. Roy Auernheimer. LC 97-62076. (Illus.). viii, 172p. 1997. pap. 14.95 (*0-945530-18-8*) Wordsworth KS.

Memories of a Former Kid. Bob Artley. LC 79-1908. (Illus.). 96p. 1978. pap. 12.95 (*0-8138-1070-1*) Iowa St U Pr.

Memories of a Forty-Eighter: Sketches from the German-American Period of Storm & Stress in the 1850s. Jacob Miller. LC 96-26678. (Werner D. Mueller Reprint Ser.). 244p. 1996. 17.95 (*0-911704-46-9*) Western Res.

Memories of a Half Life. Rikhi Jaipal. 1991. 24.00 (*81-7023-319-4*, Pub. by Allied Pubs) S Asia.

Memories of a Hostess: A Chronicle of Friendships Drawn Chiefly from the Diaries of Mrs. James T. Fields. Mark A. Howe. LC 74-3955. (Women in America Ser.). (Illus.). 376p. 1974. reprint ed. 34.95 (*0-405-06103-X*) Ayer.

Memories of a Hundred Years. Edward E. Hale. (Notable American Authors Ser.). 1992. reprint ed. lib. bdg. 75.00 (*0-7812-2977-4*) Rprt Serv.

Memories of a Kitchen Angel. Mary Hull-Schario. Ed. by Jim Ciano. (Illus.). 1996. 31.95 (*1-888672-07-2*); pap. 21.95 (*1-888672-06-4*) J Ciano Pubng.

Memories of a Lewis Mountain Man. John W. Stoneberger. 80p. 1993. 8.00 (*0-915746-43-3*) Potomac Appalach.

Memories of a Lifetime: Jostens 1897-1997. Jack El-Hai. Ed. by Lory Sutton. (Illus.). 128p. 1998. 20.00 (*0-9615570-0-1*) Jostens Mpls.

Memories of a Lifetime in the Pike's Peak Region. Irving Howbert. (American Biography Ser.). 298p. 1991. reprint ed. lib. bdg. 69.00 (*0-7812-8198-9*) Rprt Serv.

Memories of a Lost Egypt: A Memoir with Recipes. Colette Rossant. LC 98-31942. 160p. 1999. 21.00 (*0-609-60150-4*, Crown) Crown Pub Group.

Memories of a Loving Soul. Tr. by Swami Prabhavananda. (Orig.). 1968. pap. 3.50 (*0-87481-015-9*, Pub. by Advaita Ashrama) Vedanta Pr.

Memories of a Maine Island: Turn-of-the-Century Tales & Photographs. Marie Locke & P. Nancy Montgomery. LC 97-75498. (Northeast Folklore Ser.: Vol. XXXIII). (Illus.). 112p. 1998. pap. 18.00 (*0-943197-25-2*) ME Folklife Ctr.

Memories of a Midwestern Farm. Hutchens. 192p. 1998. mass mkt. 16.00 (*0-671-51071-1*, Pocket Books) PB.

Memories of a Misspent Youth, 1872-1896. Grant Richards. LC 79-8073. reprint ed. 35.00 (*0-404-18383-2*) AMS Pr.

***Memories of a Monarch.** J. Elaine Senack. (Book-a-Day Collection). (Illus.). 32p. (YA). (ps). 2000. pap. 5.95 (*1-58584-362-8*) Huckleberry CT.

Memories of a Musical Life. William Mason. LC 70-133825. 1970. reprint ed. 21.45 (*0-404-07216-X*) AMS Pr.

Memories of a Musical Life. William Mason. (American Biography Ser.). 306p. 1991. reprint ed. lib. bdg. 79.00 (*0-7812-8275-6*) Rprt Serv.

Memories of a Native Son. 2nd rev. ed. Eugene J. McCarthy. Ed. by Ray Howe. LC 99-68850. (Illus.). 196p. 2000. pap. 16.95 (*1-883477-32-8*) Lone Oak MN.

Memories of a Portuguese Immigrant to the San Joaquin Valley. Tony Jerome. (Illus.). 208p. (Orig.). 1991. pap. 17.95 (*0-9629548-0-2*) Sn Joaquin Pub.

***Memories of a Pure Spring.** Duong Tho Huong. Tr. by Nina McPherson & Phan Huy Duong from VIE. LC 99-41340. 356p. 2000. text 23.95 (*0-7868-6581-4*, Pub. by Hyperion) Time Warner.

Memories of a Rancher from the Land of Never Sweats: Milford, Lassen County, California - Neighbors, Family, Horses, Cattle, Dogs, & Reactions, 1899 to 1952. Claude C. Wemple. (Illus.). 370p. (Orig.). 1992. pap. 15.00 (*0-9632366-1-X*) Bornet Bks.

Memories of a Revolution: Egypt, 1952. Khaled M. El Din. (Illus.). 295p. 1996. 29.50 (*977-424-369-2*, Pub. by Am Univ Cairo Pr) Col U Pr.

Memories of a Riverina Childhood. Joan A. Palmer. (Illus.). 183 p. 1993. pap. 22.95 (*0-86840-341-5*, Pub. by New South Wales Univ Pr) Intl Spec Bk.

Memories of a Sailor, His Angel & Me. Irja Wenstrom. (Illus.). 200p. (Orig.). 1994. pap. text 12.95 (*1-886698-00-7*) Sampo Pub.

Memories of a Singer. Minnie Hauk. Ed. by Andrew Farkas & E. B. Hitchcock. LC 76-29938. (Opera Biographies Ser.). (Illus.). 1977. reprint ed. lib. bdg. 29.95 (*0-405-09680-1*) Ayer.

Memories of a Southern Woman of Letters. Grace E. King. LC 76-146863. (Select Bibliographies Reprint Ser.). 1977. reprint ed. 24.95 (*0-8369-5630-3*) Ayer.

Memories of a Southern Woman of Letters. Grace E. King. (American Biography Ser.). 398p. 1991. reprint ed. lib. bdg. 79.00 (*0-7812-8234-9*) Rprt Serv.

Memories of a Tennessee Ridge. (Illus.). 38p. 1998. pap. 5.00 (*0-9642132-1-4*) W Galyon.

Memories of a Village Rectory. Spellmount Ltd. Publishers Staff. (C). 1986. pap. 60.00 (*0-946771-09-X*, Pub. by Spellmnt Pubs) St Mut.

Memories of a Wisconsin Childhood & Winchesters Native Son. Gerald Thorson. 74p. 1998. pap. 4.75 (*1-57502-697-X*, PO1973) Morris Pubng.

Memories of a World War II B-29 Pilot: The Autobiography of Neil W. Wemple. Neil W. Wemple. (Illus.). 379p. (Orig.). 1993. pap. 18.00 (*0-938373-10-2*) Lahontan Images.

Memories of Aberdeen a Hundred Years Ago. Murray, Keith, Publishing Staff. (C). 1990. reprint ed. 50.00 (*0-7855-5984-1*, Pub. by K Murray Pub) St Mut.

Memories of Altagracia. Salvador Garmendia. LC 99-182988. 160p. 1997. 29.95 (*0-7206-1036-2*, Pub. by P Owen Ltd) Dufour.

Memories of an American Impressionist. Abel G. Warshawsky. Ed. & Intro. by Ben L. Bassham. LC 80-82203. (Illus.). 259p. 1980. reprint ed. pap. 80.30 (*0-608-07344-X*, 206757200009) Bks Demand.

Memories of an American Jew. Philip Cowen. LC 74-27974. (Modern Jewish Experience Ser.). (Illus.). 1975. reprint ed. 41.95 (*0-405-06703-8*) Ayer.

Memories of an Iowa Farm Boy. H. E. Wilkinson. LC 94-20662. (Iowa Heritage Collection). (Illus.). 304p. 1994. pap. 14.95 (*0-8138-2813-9*) Iowa St U Pr.

Memories of an Iowa Veterinarian. John W. Sutcliffe. (Illus.). 1990. pap. 7.50 (*0-943164-15-X*) Geronima.

Memories of an Old Actor. Walter M. Leman. (American Biography Ser.). 406p. 1991. reprint ed. lib. bdg. 89.00 (*0-7812-8244-6*) Rprt Serv.

Memories of an Old Actor. Walter M. Leman. LC 70-106905. 1970. reprint ed. 16.00 (*0-403-00199-4*) Scholarly.

Memories of an Old Mission: San Fernando, Rey de Espana. Francis J. Weber. LC 97-10288. 1997. write for info. (*0-87461-917-3*); pap. write for info. (*0-87461-918-1*) McNally & Loftin.

***Memories of an Old Mountain Man.** Charles Pickren. 200p. 2000. pap. 19.95 (*0-938041-76-2*) Arc Pr AR.

Memories of an Ordinary Man. Thomas Larocque. LC 98-86799. 192p. 1999. pap. 11.95 (*1-56167-501-6*) Am Literary Pr.

Memories of Ana Calderon. Graciela Limon. LC 94-8663. 200p. 1994. 9.95 (*1-55885-116-X*) Arte Publico.

Memories of Anne Frank: Reflections of a Childhood Friend. Alison Leslie Gold. LC 96-41185. 176p. (J). (gr. 3-7). 1997. 16.95 (*0-590-90722-0*) Scholastic Inc.

***Memories of Anne Frank: Reflections of a Childhood Friend.** Alison Leslie Gold. 1999. pap. 5.99 (*0-590-90723-9*) Scholastic Inc.

Memories of Another Day. Harold Robbins. 1993. per. 6.99 (*0-671-87491-8*, Pocket Books) PB.

Memories of Beautiful Burke, Virginia. Nan Netherton & Ruth P. Rose. LC 88-71085. (Illus.). 1988. 19.95 (*0-9620619-0-5*) Burke Hist Soc.

Memories of Beethoven: From the House of the Black-Robed Spaniards. Gerhard Von Breuning. Ed. by Maynard Solomon. (Canto Book Ser.). (Illus.). 168p. (C). 1995. pap. 10.95 (*0-521-48489-8*) Cambridge U Pr.

Memories of Birmingham: One Hundred Years of Photographs. (C). 1987. 30.00 (*0-7855-2080-5*, Pub. by Birmingham Midland Soc) St Mut.

Memories of Books & Places. John A. Hammerton. LC 68-57318. (Essay Index Reprint Ser.). 1977. 23.95 (*0-8369-0116-9*) Ayer.

Memories of Boulder City, 1932-1936: An Oral History Interview of Mary Ann Merrill. Ed. & Intro. by R. T. King. (Illus.). 46p. 1987. lib. bdg. 26.50 (*1-56475-319-0*); fiche. write for info. (*1-56475-320-4*) U NV Oral Hist.

Memories of Buddy Holly: In the Words of His Friends, His Fans & Himself. Jim Dawson & Spencer Leigh. 168p. 1996. pap. 19.95 (*0-936433-20-5*) Big Nickel.

Memories of Charles Dickens. Percy H. Fitzgerald. LC 75-148778. reprint ed. 55.00 (*0-404-08779-5*) AMS Pr.

Memories of Che. Guillermo Cabera. Tr. by Jonathan Fried. 224p. 1987. 14.95 (*0-8184-0385-3*) Carol Pub Group.

Memories of Chicano History: The Life & Narrative of Bert Corona. Mario T. Garcia. (Latinos in American Society & Culture Ser.: Vol. 2). (Illus.). 369p. 1995. pap. 17.95 (*0-520-20152-3*, Pub. by U CA Pr) Cal Prin Full Svc.

Memories of Childhood. Margaret Willes. (Country House Estates Ser.). (Illus.). 48p. 1997. pap. 9.95 (*0-7078-0228-8*, Pub. by Natl Trust) Trafalgar.

Memories of Cibola: Stories from New Mexico Villages. Abe M. Pena. LC 96-25288. (Illus.). 240p. 1997. pap. 16.95 (*0-8263-1773-1*) U of NM Pr.

Memories of Coventry: A Pictorial Record. (C). 1987. 50.00 (*0-7855-2085-6*, Pub. by Birmingham Midland Soc) St Mut.

Memories of Cuba. Olivier Beytout. (Illus.). 144p. 1998. pap. text 22.95 (*1-56025-182-4*, Thunders Mouth) Avalon NY.

Memories of Davidson College. Walter Lingle. (American Autobiography Ser.). 157p. 1995. reprint ed. lib. bdg. 69.00 (*0-7812-8580-1*) Rprt Serv.

Memories of Days Gone By: An Oral History of My Elders. Mary E. Huddleston. 100p. (Orig.). 1997. pap. 8.00 (*0-9657453-0-9*) Memo Pr.

***Memories of Days to Come: Das Utopische in Metahistorischen Romanen der Amerikanischen, Kanadischen und Englischen Literatur der 70er und 80er Jahre.** Petra Herz. (Europaische Hochschulschriften Ser.). 258p. 1999. 45.95 (*3-631-34839-8*) P Lang Pubng.

***Memories of Don Meredith & Hometown Mount Vernon.** Jean Pamplin. Ed. by Ray Loyd Johnson. (Illus.). 92p. 1999. pap. 12.95 (*0-9642481-5-8*) NE Texas Pub.

Memories of Dr. Wu Lien-Teh, Plague Fighter. Wu Yu-Lin. 196p. 1995. text 34.00 (*981-02-2287-4*) World Scientific Pub.

Memories of Duke: The Legend Comes to Life. Sandra K. Hall & Greg Ambrose. (Illus.). 160p. 1995. pap. 9.95 (*1-57306-020-8*) Bess Pr.

Memories of Early Michigan City. William Blinks et al. Ed. by Patricia Lewis. (Little Bit of History Ser.: Bk. 4). (Orig.). (J). (gr. 6 up). 1990. pap. 2.00 (*0-935549-14-5*) MI City Hist.

***Memories of Eating.** Tony Medina. LC 99-48825. 1999. write for info. (*0-9654738-3-X*) Lng Shot Prods.

Memories of Eden. Raymond R. Brown. (Illus.). 120p. (Orig.). 1996. pap. 14.95 (*0-9658238-0-6*) R R Brown.

Memories of Edenbrook Farm: Twenty-One Years of Farm Life. Dennie D. McCart. (Illus.). 1984. pap. 7.95 (*0-8323-0432-8*) Binford Mort.

Memories of Eighty Years. James Herrick. (American Autobiography Ser.). 270p. 1995. reprint ed. lib. bdg. 79.00 (*0-7812-8555-0*) Rprt Serv.

Memories of Europe's Future: Farewell to Yesteryear. Simon Serfaty. LC 98-43731. 160p. (C). 1998. pap. text 18.95 (*0-89206-347-5*) CSIS.

Memories of Evil Days. Julien Green. LC 75-44037. (Illus.). 164p. reprint ed. pap. 50.90 (*0-7837-4367-X*, 204407700012) Bks Demand.

Memories of Fifty Years. Lester Wallack. Ed. by Laurence Hutton. LC 71-81979. (Illus.). 246p. 1972. 24.95 (*0-405-09051-X*, Pub. by Blom Pubns) Ayer.

Memories of Fifty Years. John L. Wallack. (American Biography Ser.). 232p. 1991. reprint ed. lib. bdg. 69.00 (*0-7812-8399-X*) Rprt Serv.

Memories of Frederick - Over on the Other Side. Joy Onley. (Illus.). 175p. (Orig.). 1995. pap. 15.95 (*0-9650433-0-4*) J Onley.

Memories of Friedrich Ferdinand Count Von Beust, 2 vols., Set. Friedrich F. Graf Von Beust. 1981. reprint ed. lib. bdg. 59.00 (*0-686-71932-8*) Scholarly.

Memories of Gascony. Pierre Koffman. 1990. text 34.95 (*0-442-30276-2*, VNR) Wiley.

Memories of Gazos Creek & Pigeon Point, 1916-1918. Edward Conant. Ed. by Bessie Conant. LC 98-72358. (Illus.). 112p. 1998. 15.95 (*0-9637265-1-X*) Glenhaven Pr.

Memories of Gliding & Soaring. Theodore Bellak. (Illus.). 214p. (Orig.). 1995. pap. write for info. (*1-57579-004-1*) Pine Hill Pr.

Memories of God: Theological Reflection on a Life. Roberta C. Bondi. LC 94-37755. 224p. (Orig.). 1995. pap. 16.95 (*0-687-03892-8*) Abingdon.

***Memories of God & Creation: Remembering from the Subconscious Mind.** Shakuntala Modi. 2000. pap. 15.95 (*1-57174-196-8*) Hampton Roads Pub Co.

Memories of Golden Sports Years at Cornell University, 1953-1989. John R. West. Ed. by Esther Linke. (Illus.). 141p. (Orig.). 1995. pap. text 8.50 (*0-9644931-0-1*) J R West.

Memories of Gurdjieff. A. L. Staveley. LC 78-56109. 74p. 1999. reprint ed. 12.00 (*0-89756-000-0*) Two Rivers.

Memories of Hawthorne. Rose H. Lathrop. 1972. 59.95 (*0-8490-0606-6*) Gordon Pr.

Memories of Hawthorne. Rose H. Lathrop. (BCL1-PS American Literature Ser.). 482p. 1992. reprint ed. lib. bdg. 99.00 (*0-7812-6729-3*) Rprt Serv.

Memories of Home: The Writings of Alex La Guma. Ed. by Cecil Abrahams. LC 91-70746. 106p. 1992. 29.95 (*0-86543-234-1*); pap. 9.95 (*0-86543-235-X*) Africa World.

Memories of Hoosier Homemakers, 7 vols., Set. Incl. Vol. 1. Feeding Our Families. Ed. by Eleanor Arnold. LC 93-13283. (Illus.). 154p. (C). Date not set. pap. 12.95 (*0-253-20805-X*); Vol. 1. Feeding Our Families: Memories of Hoosier Homemakers. Ed. by Eleanor Arnold. LC 93-13283. (Illus.). 154p. (C). Date not set. 22.50 (*0-253-12992-3*); Vol. 2. Party Lines, Pumps, & Privies. Ed. by Eleanor Arnold. LC 93-13283. (Illus.). 176p. Date not set. pap. 12.95 (*0-253-20800-9*); Vol. 3. Buggies & Bad Times. Ed. by Eleanor Arnold. LC 93-13283. 172p. 1993. 20.00 (*0-253-12991-5*); Vol. 3. Buggies & Bad Times. Ed. by Eleanor Arnold. LC 93-13283. 172p. 1993. pap. 10.95 (*0-253-20804-1*); Vol. 4. Girlhood Days: Indiana Extension Homemakers Association volume. Eleanor Arnold. LC 93-13283. (Illus.). 204p. 1993. 22.50 (*0-253-12989-3*); Vol. 4. Girlhood Days: Indiana Extension Homemakers Association volume. Eleanor Arnold. LC 93-13283. (Illus.). 204p. 1993. pap. 9.95 (*0-253-20802-5*); Vol. 5. Going To Club: Indiana Extension Homemakers Association volume. Eleanor Arnold. LC 93-13283. (Illus.). 176p. (C). 1993. 22.50 (*0-253-12990-7*); Vol. 6. Living Rich Lives: Indiana Extension Homemakers Association volume. Eleanor Arnold. LC 93-13283. (Illus.). 244p. 1993. 21.95 (*0-253-12988-5*); Vol. 6. Living Rich Lives: Indiana Extension Homemakers Association Volume. Eleanor Arnold. LC 93-13283. (Illus.). 244p. pap. 7.95 (*0-253-20801-7*); Vol. 7. Index. Ed. by Eleanor Arnold. LC 93-13283. pap. (*0-253-20806-8*); LC 93-13283. 1994. 40.00 (*0-253-12994-X*); pap. write for info. (*0-253-20807-6*) Ind U Pr.

Memories of Island Thirty-Five. Gladys B. Turner. 148p. (Orig.). 1987. 15.00 (*0-916693-11-2*) Castle Bks.

Memories of Jaime Vick, a Still Young Octogenarian. Jaime Vick. LC 98-90587. 1999. pap. 8.95 (*0-533-12850-1*) Vantage.

Memories of Johann Strauss. J. Strauss, II. 96p. 1984. pap. 8.95 (*0-7935-2773-2*, 00009285) H Leonard.

***Memories of Lafayette.** Charles Larroque. LC 99-34823. (Illus.). 32p. (J). 1999. pap. 7.95 (*1-56554-664-4*) Pelican.

***Memories of Laughter & Garlic: Jewish Wit, Wisdom & Humor to Warm Your Heart.** Leo Lieberman. Ed. by Rob Huberman. 240p. 1999. write for info. (*0-9674074-0-0*) ComteQ Pubg.

Memories of Laura. Marilyn Pappano. (Intimate Moments Ser.). 1993. per. 3.39 (*0-373-07486-7*, 5-07486-9) Silhouette.

Memories of Light: Poetry Chapbook. Robin Greene. 24p. (Orig.). 1991. pap. 5.00 (*0-9624274-6-2*) NC Writers Network.

Memories of Little Traverse Bay. Ed. by Marge May & John Hall. (Illus.). 112p. (Orig.). 1989. pap. 10.00 (*0-685-26072-0*) Little Traverse.

Memories of Louise Coe Runnels: Alias "Bonito Lau" unabridged ed. Louise C. Runnels. LC 97-75329. (Illus.). 162p. 1996. pap. 12.00 (*1-887523-14-6*) Human Systs Res.

Memories of Love: A Treasury of Childhood Keepsakes. Illus. by Maren Scott. 208p. 1997. 16.99 (*0-8499-1497-3*) Word Pub.

Memories of Love & War. Kathleen Cleaver. 1999. write for info. (*0-679-45007-6*) Random.

Memories of Loyang: Yang Hsuan-Chih & the Lost Capital (493-534) William J. Jenner. (Illus.). 314p. 1981. text 74.00 (*0-19-821568-1*) OUP.

Memories of Madame Sun: First Lady of China. Sylvia Wu. (Illus.). 102p. 1982. pap. 8.95 (*0-930422-29-5*) Dennis-Landman.

Memories of Maggie: Martha Raye, a Legend Spanning Three Wars. Noonie Fortin. Ed. by Debra Innocenti & James D. Qualben. LC 95-49178. (Illus.). 360p. (Orig.). 1996. pap. 15.95 (*1-880292-18-1*) LangMarc.

Memories of Majesty. Susan Soong. pap. 12.95 (*0-938851-10-1*) Daughters of HI.

Memories of Mama. Pat Phillips. 50p. 1998. pap. text 12.00 (*1-889745-04-9*) Triangle Publctns.

Memories of Manhattan: In the Sixties & the Seventies. C. T. Harris. 1977. lib. bdg. 59.95 (*0-8490-2226-6*) Gordon Pr.

Memories of Manteo & Roanoke Island, N. C. Suzanne Tate. LC 88-60590. (Illus.). 52p. (Orig.). 1988. pap. 4.95 (*0-9616344-2-1*) Nags Head Art.

Memories of Marbacka. Selma Lagerlof. 200p. 1996. pap. 18.95 (*1-57216-048-9*) Penfield.

Memories of Maryhill. large type ed. Roderick Wilkinson. 1997. 24.95 (*0-7531-5031-X*) T T Beeler.

***Memories of Maud.** Alexandra Heilbrun. (Illus.). 2000. pap. text 14.95 (*1-55041-292-2*) Fitzhenry & W Ltd.

Memories of Me, Baby. Charleen R. Dickman. (Illus.). 86p. (J). (ps). 1994. 29.95 (*1-882237-20-X*) Life Time Pubs.

Memories of Me, Baby. deluxe ed. Charleen R. Dickman. (Illus.). 86p. (J). (ps). 1992. 39.95 (*1-882237-01-3*) Life Time Pubs.

Memories of Men & Women American & British. A. L. Rowse. LC 83-16875. 266p. (Orig.). (C). 1983. reprint ed. pap. text 11.25 (*0-8191-3583-6*); reprint ed. lib. bdg. 20.25 (*0-8191-3582-8*) U Pr of Amer.

Memories of Midnight. Sidney Sheldon. 399p. 1990. 21.95 (*0-688-08488-5*, Wm Morrow) Morrow Avon.

Memories of Midnight. Sidney Sheldon. 416p. 1991. reprint ed. mass mkt. 7.99 (*0-446-35467-8*, Pub. by Warner Bks) Little.

Memories of Migration: Gender, Ethnicity, & Work in the Lives of Jewish & Italian Women in New York, 1870-1924. Kathie Friedman-Kasaba. LC 95-6566. (SUNY Series on Women & Work). 288p. (C). 1996. text 59.50 (*0-7914-2761-7*); pap. text 19.95 (*0-7914-2762-5*) State U NY Pr.

Memories of Mike. Beckett Publications Editors. LC 99-227075. 1999. 19.95 (*1-887432-67-1*) Beckett Pubns.

Memories of Monday (Wash Day Before Advent of Washing Machine) with Added Chapter on Scotland. Joan Pearson. (C). 1989. pap. 21.00 (*1-85072-053-3*, Pub. by W Sessions) St Mut.

Memories of Muldoon. Bob Jones, Jr. LC 98-144026. 224p. 1997. 39.95 (*0-908812-69-8*, Pub. by Canterbury Univ) Accents Pubns.

Memories of My Baptism, Boy. (J). (gr. 3). 1998. 8.95 (*1-57734-271-2*, 01113313) Covenant Comms.

M

Memories of My Baptism, Girl. 8.95 (*1-57734-237-2*, 01113372) Covenant Comms.

Memories of My Father. Henry F. Dickens. LC 72-3169. (Studies in Dickens: No. 52). 1972. reprint ed. lib. bdg. 75.00 (*0-8383-1509-7*) M S G Haskell Hse.

Memories of My Father, Joyce Kilmer. 3rd ed. Kenton Kilmer. (Illus.). 288p. 1993. reprint ed. 20.00 (*0-9637524-0-5*) J K Cent Comm.

Memories of My Father Watching TV. Curtis White. LC 97-51440. 168p. 1998. pap. 12.50 (*1-56478-189-5*) Dalkey Arch.

***Memories of My Garden.** Havoc Publishing Staff. 1999. pap. text 20.00 (*1-57977-157-2*) Havoc Pub.

***Memories of My Garden.** Havoc Publishing Staff. (Illus.). 1999. 8.00 (*0-7416-1705-6*) Havoc Pub.

***Memories of My Garden Address Book.** 2000. spiral bd. 6.00 (*0-7416-2607-1*) Havoc Pub.

Memories of My Ghost. Heinz Fenkl. 1997. pap. 11.95 (*0-452-27717-5*, Plume) Dutton Plume.

Memories of My Grandfather. Jan Kirkman. (Illus.). 60p. 1997. 10.95 (*0-9659653-0-9*) J Kirkman.

Memories of My Life. Auguste Escoffier. Tr. by Laurence Escoffier. LC 96-25141. (Illus.). 252p. 1996. text 31.95 (*0-442-02396-0*, VNR) Wiley.

Memories of My Life. Jess R. Herrera. LC 91-92483. (Illus.). 230p. (Orig.). 1992. pap. write for info. (*1-881156-00-1*) J R Herrera.

Memories of My Life. Sarah Bernhardt. LC 68-56475. (Illus.). 1972. reprint ed. 30.95 (*0-405-08265-7*, Pub. by Blom Pubns) Ayer.

Memories of My Life. Francis Galton. LC 72-1639. reprint ed. 52.50 (*0-404-08128-2*) AMS Pr.

Memories of Nauvoo: Walker County, Alabama. Margaret E. Lee. (Illus.). 272p. 1992. 35.00 (*0-9634326-1-3*); pap. 25.00 (*0-9634326-0-5*) Treasured Mem.

Memories of New Bern: An Oral History. Emily H. Wilson. Ed. by Jane Kelly. (Illus.). xi, 180p. (Orig.). 1995. pap. write for info. (*0-9621194-9-0*) Stratford NC.

Memories of Old Cerro Gordo: First Person & Contemporary Tales, 1850-1890. Ed. by R. Duane Umbarger & Ruth M. Umbarger. LC 90-60817. (Illus.). 340p. (Orig.). 1990. pap. 20.00 (*0-9626167-0-2*) Pioneer Mus Hist Soc of N IA.

Memories of Old Montana. Con Price. (American Autobiography Ser.). 154p. 1995. reprint ed. lib. bdg. 69.00 (*0-7812-8620-4*) Rprt Serv.

Memories of Old Sunrise: Gold Mining on Alaska's Turnagain Arm 1897-1901. Albert W. Morgan. Ed. & Intro. by Rolfe G. Buzzell. LC 94-68464. (Illus.). 125p. (Orig.). 1994. pap. 18.95 (*1-878462-01-6*) Cook Inlet Hist Soc.

Memories of Old Sussex. Lillian Candlin. 96p. 1987. 30.00 (*0-905392-78-7*) St Mut.

Memories of Older Black Peoples, Bk. 2. 450p. 2000. 49.95 (*0-9654700-2-4*) F R Parker.

***Memories of Our Future.** Ammiel Alcalay. LC 99-34696. 330p. 1999. pap. 14.95 (*0-87286-360-3*, Pub. by City Lights) SPD-Small Pr Dist.

Memories of Overdevelopment: Philippine Diaspora in Contemporary Art. Wayne Boerwalst et al. (Illus.). 228p. 1997. pap. 25.00 (*0-921381-16-6*, Pub. by Plug In Editions) RAM Publications.

***Memories of Payne Avenue: Ramsy County, Minnesota.** 1999. reprint ed. pap. 7.00 (*0-915709-70-8*) Pk Geneal Bk.

Memories of Peking: South Side Stories. Lin Hai-yin. Tr. by Nancy C. Ing & Chi Pang-Yuan from CHI. 1994. pap. text 14.95 (*962-201-452-6*, Pub. by Chinese Univ) U of Mich Pr.

Memories of Perfume: Monsen & Baer Perfume Bottle Auction VIII. Randall B. Monsen & Christie M. Lefkowith. Ed. by Rodney L. Baer. (Illus.). 128p. 1998. 45.00 (*0-9636102-8-7*) Monsen & Baer.

Memories of R. D. Laing. Ed. by Bob Mullan. LC 97-185305. (Illus.). 352p. 1997. 99.50 (*0-304-70114-9*); pap. 37.50 (*0-304-70115-7*) Continuum.

Memories of Rain: A Novel. Sunetra Gupta. LC 91-31684. 198p. 1993. pap. 11.00 (*0-8021-3341-X*, Grove) Grove-Atltic.

Memories of Resistance: Women's Voices from the Spanish Civil War. Shirley Mangini-Gonzalez. LC 94-29752. 226p. 1995. 30.00 (*0-300-05816-0*) Yale U Pr.

Memories of Revolt: The 1936-39 Rebellion & the Palestinian National Past. Ted Swedenburg. 288p. 1995. pap. 19.95 (*0-8166-2165-9*); text 49.95 (*0-8166-2164-0*) U of Minn Pr.

Memories of Revolution: Russian Women Remember. Ed. by Anna H. Porter. LC 92-46113. (Illus.). 152p. (C). 1993. pap. 22.99 (*0-415-08807-0*, B2432) Routledge.

Memories of Rudolf Steiner. Ludwig C. Polzer-Hoditz. 1987. pap. 9.95 (*0-916786-93-5*, Saint George Pubns) R Steiner Col.

Memories of Rudolf Steiner. Anna Samweber. 52p. 1991. pap. 9.95 (*1-85584-100-2*, Pub. by R Steiner Pr) Anthroposophic.

Memories of Rufus Choate: With Some Consideration of His Studies, Methods & Opinions & of His Style As a Speaker & Writer. Joseph Neilson. xx, 460p. 1985. reprint ed. 55.00 (*0-8377-0909-1*, Rothman) W S Hein.

***Memories of St. Martinville.** Charles Larroque. LC 99-10417. 32p. 1999. pap. 7.95 (*1-56554-660-1*) Pelican.

Memories of Sandy Point, St. George's Bay, Newfoundland. Phyllis Pieroway. (Illus.). 96p. 1996. pap. 11.25 (*0-921411-33-2*) Genl Dist Srvs.

Memories of Sexual Betrayal: Truth, Fantasy, Repression, & Dissociation. Ed. by Richard B. Gartner. 304p. 1997. 50.00 (*1-56821-704-8*) Aronson.

Memories of Silk & Straw: A Self-Portrait of Small-Town Japan. Junichi Saga. Tr. by Garry O. Evans. (Illus.). 260p. 1990. pap. 17.00 (*0-87011-988-5*) Kodansha.

Memories of Some of Anne's Friends. Intro. by Anne N. Lowenkopf. 125p. (Orig.). 1992. pap. 12.95 (*0-9633753-2-6*) Two Down Pr.

Memories of South Dakota. Ellis Ovesen. Ed. by Janet Leih. LC 93-60173. 60p. (Orig.). 1993. 7.00 (*1-877649-19-8*); pap. 2.50 (*1-877649-18-X*) Tesseract SD.

Memories of Splendor: The Midwestern World of William Inge. Arthur F. McClure. LC 89-62833. (Illus.). 85p. 1989. pap. 10.95 (*0-87726-038-9*) Kansas St Hist.

Memories of Stambourne. Charles H. Spurgeon. 1975. mass mkt. 5.00 (*1-56186-318-1*) Pilgrim Pubns.

***Memories of Summer.** Ruth White. LC 99-54793. 144p. (J). (gr. 5-9). 2000. 16.00 (*0-374-34945-2*) FS&G.

***Memories of Summer: When Baseball Was an Art & Writing about It a Game.** Roger Kahn. LC 96-48711. (Illus.). 304p. (J). 1998. reprint ed. pap. 12.45 (*0-7868-8316-2*, Pub. by Hyperion) Time Warner.

Memories of Sweet Grass. Adelphena Logan. LC 79-65401. (Illus.). 79p. 1979. 6.95 (*0-89488-006-3*) Inst Amer Indian.

Memories of Tennysons. H. Rawnsley. LC 72-675. (Studies in Tennyson: No. 27). 1972. reprint ed. lib. bdg. 75.00 (*0-8383-1417-1*) M S G Haskell Hse.

***Memories of Texas Towns & Cities.** Dave Oliphant. (Illus.). 286p. 2000. 25.00 (*0-924047-18-6*); pap. 12.00 (*0-924047-19-4*) Host Pubns.

Memories of the Alhambra. Nash Candelaria. LC 76-26410. 192p. 1977. 25.00 (*0-9601086-1-0*) Biling Rev-Pr.

Memories of the Alhambra. Nash Candelaria. LC 76-26410. 192p. 1982. reprint ed. pap. 15.00 (*0-916950-32-8*) Biling Rev-Pr.

Memories of the Black Country: One Hundred Years of Photographs. (C). 1987. 30.00 (*0-7855-2081-3*, Pub. by Birmingham Midland Soc) St Mut.

Memories of the Clyde Duchess of Fife, 1903-1953. Hart, Maclagan & Will Publishers Staff. 1990. pap. 35.00 (*0-9516140-0-2*, Pub. by Hart Maclagan & Will) St Mut.

Memories of the Crusade: Account of the Great Uprising of the Women of Ohio in 1873, Against the Liquor Crime. Eliza D. Stewart. LC 72-2627. (American Women Ser.: Images & Realities). (Illus.). 570p. 1974. reprint ed. 35.95 (*0-405-04482-8*) Ayer.

***Memories of the Dance.** Keith Neely. Ed. by Patricia Clutter. LC 98-61857. 368p. 1999. pap. 18.95 (*1-880254-59-X*) Vista.

Memories of the First Years of the Settlement of New Holstein. William G. Thiel. (GER.). 96p. (Orig.). 1995. pap. write for info. (*0-9647495-0-5*) W G Thiel.

Memories of the Ford Administration. John Updike. 371p. 1996. pap. 12.95 (*0-449-91211-6*) Fawcett.

Memories of the Ford Administration: A Novel. John Updike. LC 92-52955. 371p. 1992. 23.00 (*0-679-41681-1*) Knopf.

Memories of the Future: The Daybooks of Tina Modotti. Margaret Gibson. LC 85-23668. 52p. 1986. pap. 12.95 (*0-8071-1309-3*) La State U Pr.

Memories of the Gorbals. Jack Caplan. 123p. (C). 1989. text 50.00 (*1-872795-17-X*, Pub. by Pentland Pr) St Mut.

Memories of the Gorbals: Jewish Life in the Gorbals Section of Glasgow Between the Wars. large type ed. Jack Caplan. (Reminiscence Ser.). 21.95 (*1-85695-151-0*, Pub. by ISIS Lrg Prnt) Transaction Pubs.

Memories of the Great & the Good. Alistair Cooke. 288p. 1999. 24.95 (*1-55970-479-9*, Pub. by Arcade Pub Inc) Time Warner.

***Memories of the Great & the Good.** Alistaire Cooke. (Illus.). 2000. pap. 13.95 (*1-55970-545-0*, Pub. by Arcade Pub Inc) Time Warner.

***Memories of the Great & the Good.** large type ed. Alistaire Cooke. (General Ser.). 2000. pap. 24.95 (*0-7862-2493-2*) Thorndike Pr.

Memories of the Heart: Rural Schools of Illinois. Warren Royer. LC 96-79694. (Illus.). 224p. 2000. pap. 17.95 (*1-878044-17-6*) Mayhaven Pub.

Memories of the Lakes. Dana T. Bowen. 1946. pap. 13.75 (*0-912514-14-0*) Freshwater.

Memories of the Land: Placenames of San Luis Obispo County. Mark P. Hall-Patton. (Illus.). 160p. 1994. pap. 9.95 (*0-945092-36-9*) EZ Nature.

***Memories of the Marshes of Glynn: World War II.** Thora Olsen Kimsey & Sonja Olsen Kinard. (Illus.). 384p. 1999. 36.50 (*1-929619-00-6*) Look Gl Bks.

Memories of the Michigan City Lighthouse & Description of the United States Lighthouse Service. Jean E. Pletcher et al. (Little Bit of History Ser.: Bk. 5). 24p. (Orig.). (YA). (gr. 6 up). 1991. pap. 2.00 (*0-935549-15-3*) MI City Hist.

Memories of the Mick. Maury Allen. LC 96-54060. (Illus.). 208p. 1997. 29.95 (*0-87833-973-6*) Taylor Pub.

Memories of the Moderns. Harry Levin. LC 80-36827. 256p. 1980. 15.95 (*0-8112-0733-1*, Pub. by New Directions) Norton.

Memories of the Moderns. Harry Levin. LC 80-36827. 256p. 1982. pap. 7.95 (*0-8112-0842-7*, NDP539, Pub. by New Directions) Norton.

Memories of the Morning Calm: A Modest Texas Bride's Experiences As She Merged into the Foreign Customs of Korea - the Land of the Morning Calm. Frances K. Lindland. Ed. by Darlene Brown. (Illus.). 228p. 1992. pap. 13.95 (*0-9617572-3-X*) Times Journal Pub.

Memories of the Mount: The Story of Mt. Meigs, Alabama. John B. Scott, Jr. LC 93-3817. 220p. 1993. 32.50 (*1-881320-07-3*, Black Belt) Black Belt Communs.

Memories of the Pasque & Prairie. Mary Ames. (Illus.). 79p. (YA). (gr. 9-12). 1987. 13.95 (*0-9619407-0-0*) Country Messenger Inc.

Memories of the Past. Carole Mortimer. (Presents Ser.: No. 451). 1992. per. 2.89 (*0-373-11451-6*, 1-11451-1) Harlequin Bks.

Memories of the Past. Audrey Smith. Ed. by Julie Al-Sunaidi. (Illus.). 125p. 1993. 12.95 (*1-882935-04-7*) Westphalia.

Memories of the Past. large type ed. Carole Mortimer. 1991. reprint ed. lib. bdg. 18.95 (*0-263-12686-2*) Mac Lib Ref.

Memories of the Sangre de Cristo Mountains. Joseph A. Garduno. LC 82-71884. (Illus.). 272p. 1982. pap. 10.95 (*0-9608806-0-7*) Assoc Pubns.

Memories of the Southern Civil Rights Movement. Danny Lyon. LC 92-5961. (Lyndhurst Series on the South, Published for the Duke University Center for Documentary Studies). (Illus.). vii, 185p. (C). 1992. pap. 27.50 (*0-8078-4386-5*) U of NC Pr.

Memories of the Space Age. J. G. Ballard. LC 88-15075. (Illus.). 224p. 1988. 18.95 (*0-87054-157-9*) Arkham.

Memories of the Theatre-Libre. Andre Antoine. Ed. by H. D. Albright. Tr. by Marvin Carlson. LC 64-8734. (Books of the Theatre: No. 5). (Illus.). 1964. 19.95 (*0-87024-034-X*) U of Miami Pr.

Memories of the Windswept Plains. Eugene Brookings. (Illus.). 300p. 1995. 14.95 (*0-9649583-0-9*) E Brookings.

Memories of This Octogenarian. John Phelps & Ruth Phelps. (Illus.). 210p. Date not set. pap. write for info. (*0-9667166-0-4*) R Phelps.

Memories of This Octogenarian. 2nd ed. John Phelps & Ruth Phelps. (Illus.). 210p. Date not set. write for info. (*0-9667166-1-2*) R Phelps.

Memories of Thomas Wolfe: A Pictoral Companion to Look Homeward Angel. John C. Griffin. (Illus.). 220p. 1996. 19.95 (*1-887714-08-1*) Summerhse Pr.

Memories of Times Past. Ideals Publications Editors. LC 98-12423. 1998. 24.95 (*0-8249-4097-0*) Ideals.

Memories of Tomorrow. Ed. by Chris Tyler. 1996. 69.95 (*1-57553-156-9*) Watermrk Pr.

***Memories of Tomorrow: It's Just a Stage I'm Going Through.** Mark Hertzberg. Ed. by Steve Bedney. (Adventures of Comicman Ser.: Vol. 1). 400p. 1999. pap. 17.00 (*0-9659196-9-2*) Argus Pub.

Memories of Underdevelopment & Inconsolable Memories. Edmundo Desnoes. Ed. by Michael Chanan. (Films in Print Ser.). (Illus.). 220p. (C). 1990. text 37.00 (*0-8135-1536-X*); pap. text 17.00 (*0-8135-1537-8*) Rutgers U Pr.

Memories of War: Beirut Stories. Mai Ghoussoub. LC 98-138955. 140p. 1997. pap. 24.95 (*0-86356-090-3*, Pub. by Saqi) Intl Spec Bk.

***Memories of War Dreams of Peace: Echoes of the Vietnam War.** Stephen T. Banko, III. (Illus.). 36p. 1998. pap. 12.95 (*0-9673458-0-4*, BT-01198-MOW) SHS Pubs.

Memories of World War I: North Carolina Doughboys on the Western Front. R. Jackson Marshall. LC 99-171389. (Illus.). xiii, 208p. 1998. pap. 15.00 (*0-86526-282-9*) NC Archives.

Memories of You. Margot Dalton. (Superromance Ser.: No. 749). 1997. per. 3.99 (*0-373-70749-5*, 1-70749-6) Harlequin Bks.

Memories Originaus Des Createurs de la Photographic. Ed. by Rene Colson et al. LC 76-23043. (Sources of Modern Photography Ser.). (FRE.). 1979. reprint ed. lib. bdg. 15.95 (*0-405-09605-4*) Ayer.

Memories Photograph Album. Bramley. 1998. 14.95 (*1-85833-988-X*, Pub. by CLib Bks) Whitecap Bks.

***Memories Pressed Between the Pages.** Lynn Hoyle. 1999. pap. write for info. (*1-58235-244-5*) Watermrk Pr.

Memories, Reflections & Words of Hope. Charles E. Cravey. 1991. pap. 9.95 (*0-938645-63-3*) In His Steps.

Memories Rekindled: Irish Folk Stories & Historical Narratives. Seamus McMahon. LC 96-92004. (Illus.). 75p. pap. 4.95 (*0-9650556-0-4*) J McMahon.

Memories That Gently Flow. Catherine Tedesco. 72p. 1990. 14.99 (*0-925037-12-5*) Great Lks Poetry.

Memories That Last a Life Time. Calvin White. (Illus.). 100p. 1998. pap. 13.50 (*0-9662455-0-4*) A Boy & A Man.

Memories That Shaped an Industry: Decisions Leading to IBM System 360. Emerson W. Pugh. (History of Computing Ser.). (Illus.). 336p. 1984. 35.00 (*0-262-16094-3*) MIT Pr.

***Memories That Shaped an Industry: Decisions Leading to IBM System-360.** Emerson W. Pugh. (Illus.). 323p. 2000. pap. 30.00 (*0-262-66167-5*) MIT Pr.

Memories That Smell Like Gasoline: Art & Memoirs by David Wojnarowicz. David Wojnarowicz. 64p. 1992. 15.00 (*0-9631095-0-2*) Artspace Bks.

Memories, Thoughts & Convictions. Bernhard Naunyn. LC 94-2999. (Resources in Medical History Ser.).Tr. of Erinnerungen, Gedanken und Meinungen. 1994. 30.00 (*0-88135-059-1*, Sci Hist) Watson Pub Intl.

Memories, Thoughts & Emotions: Essays in Honor of George Mandler. Ed. by William Kessen et al. 376p. 1991. text 75.00 (*0-8058-0869-8*) L Erlbaum Assocs.

Memories, Thoughts & Feelings. Helen K. Hart. 1998. pap. write for info. (*1-57553-967-5*) Watermrk Pr.

Memories, Thoughts & Forget-Me-Nots. Margaret Richards. Ed. by Richard Holst. (Illus.). 80p. (Orig.). 1996. pap. 12.00 (*0-9643280-1-1*) Cape Elizabeth.

Memories Touched by Fancy: Bessie Drennan, Vermont Artist. Jane C. Beck. (Illus.). 40p. (Orig.). 1990. pap. 8.95 (*0-916718-10-7*) VT Folklife Ctr.

Memories with a Christmas Attitude. Bob Olson. LC 96-61542. 96p. 1996. pap. 9.00 (*1-883893-76-3*, Pub. by WinePress Pub) BookWorld.

Memories with Trees. Ilse Tielsch. Tr. & Afterword by David A. Scrase. LC 92-42552. (Studies in Austrian Literature, Culture, & Thought. Translation Ser.). 109p. 1993. pap. 12.50 (*0-929497-65-1*) Ariadne CA.

Memorix Clinical Medicine. Conrad Droste & Martin Von Planta. 384p. 1999. pap. text 19.50 (*0-412-56050-X*, Pub. by E A) OUP.

Memorix Emergency Medicine. S. Muller. Tr. by Andersen Burrows. LC 95-67603. (Illus.). 360p. 1997. pap. text 19.95 (*0-412-56040-2*, Pub. by E A) OUP.

Memorix Gynecology. Thomas Rabe. (Memorix Ser.). 288p. (J). 1996. pap. text 17.95 (*0-412-56060-7*, Pub. by E A) OUP.

Memorix Medical & Biochemical Abbreviations. John Gibson & O. Potparic. LC 96-86060. 232p. 1998. pap. text 14.99 (*0-412-78490-4*, Pub. by E A) OUP.

Memorix Neurology. Peter Berlit. (Memorix Ser.). (Illus.). 304p. 1996. pap. text 16.95 (*0-412-56070-4*, Pub. by E A) OUP.

Memorix Obstetrics. Thomas Rabe. Tr. by A. Davis & R. Davis. LC 94-72653. (Illus.). 304p. (gr. 13). 1996. pap. text 16.50 (*0-412-56080-1*, Pub. by E A) OUP.

Memorix Pediatrics. D. Harms & J. Scharf. (Memorix Ser.). (Illus.). 560p. 1999. pap. text 29.95 (*0-412-73830-9*, Pub. by E A) OUP.

Memorix Physiology. Robert F. Schmidt et al. LC 97-66861. (Memorix Ser.). (Illus.). 296p. 1999. pap. text 22.50 (*0-412-71440-X*, Pub. by E A) OUP.

Memorization in the Transmission of the Middle English Romances. Murray McGillivray. LC 90-3313. (Albert Bates Lord Studies in Oral Tradition: Vol. 5). 152p. 1990. text 10.00 (*0-8240-3423-6*, 1275) Garland.

Memorize God's Word: Advanced, 1. 1998. pap. 9.99 (*0-8024-6792-X*) Moody.

Memorize God's Word: Advanced 2. Moody Press Editors. 1998. pap. text 9.99 (*0-8024-6793-8*) Moody.

Memorize God's Word: Basic. Moody Press Editors. 1998. pap. text 9.99 (*0-8024-6791-1*) Moody.

Memorize in Minutes: The Times Tables. Alan Walker. LC 98-87549. (Illus.). 224p. 1998. pap. text, teacher ed. 24.95 (*0-9651769-5-9*, 695) Krimsten Publng.

***Memorizing Time.** Laura Greenberg. 203p. 2000. pap. 12.00 (*0-9700153-0-5*) Portamento.

Memory. Lois McMaster Bujold. 480p. 1996. 22.00 (*0-671-87743-7*) Baen Bks.

Memory. Lois McMaster Bujold. 480p. 1997. per. 6.99 (*0-671-87845-X*) Baen Bks.

Memory. Hermann Ebbinghaus. 135p. 55.00 (*1-85506-672-6*) Thoemmes Pr.

Memory. Ed. by Patricia Fara et al. LC 98-17394. (Darwin College Lectures). (Illus.). 192p. (C). 1998. 24.95 (*0-521-57210-X*) Cambridge U Pr.

Memory. Ed. by Wolfgang Hageney. (ENG, FRE, GER, ITA & SPA., Illus.). 212p. 1981. pap. 44.95 (*88-7070-010-0*) Belvedere USA.

Memory. Laura Jensen. LC 81-67640. 69p. (C). 1982. 10.00 (*0-937872-02-4*); pap. 5.00 (*0-937872-03-2*) Dragon Gate.

Memory. Elizabeth F. Loftus. (Illus.). 207p. 1980. pap. text 20.95 (*0-912675-28-4*) Ardsley.

Memory. Margaret Mahy. (Illus.). 272p. (gr. 7). 1999. 8.00 (*0-689-82911-6*) Aladdin.

Memory. Bernadette Mayer. 150p. 1975. pap. 4.00 (*0-913028-39-8*) North Atlantic.

Memory. John O'Brien. 1981. pap. 3.50 (*0-87129-232-7*, M52) Dramatic Pub.

Memory. 2nd ed. Ed. by Edward C. Carterette et al. (Handbook of Perception & Cognition Ser.). (Illus.). 586p. 1998. reprint ed. pap. text 39.95 (*0-12-102571-3*) Morgan Kaufmann.

Memory, Vol. 3. Ed. by Susan E. Gathercole & Martin A. Conway. 1995. 64.00 (*0-614-98007-0*) L Erlbaum Assocs.

Memory: A Cognitive Approach. 2nd ed. Gillian Cohen et al. LC 92-40621. (Open Guides to Psychology Ser.). 1993. pap. 25.00 (*0-335-19079-0*) OUP.

Memory: A Fourth Memoir. Wallace Fowlie. LC 89-35872. 160p. (Orig.). (C). 1990. text 39.95 (*0-8223-1003-1*); pap. text 16.95 (*0-8223-1045-7*) Duke.

Memory: Acquiring, Editing, Recalling, Forgetting. Robert Sylwester. (Discover Your Brain Ser.). (Illus.). 56p. 1998. pap. 25.00 incl. digital audio (*1-56976-082-9*, 1818-F3) Zephyr Pr AZ.

Memory: Arthur Bornstein's Memory Training Course. Arthur Bornstein. Orig. Title: Bornstein's Miracle Memory Course. (Illus.). 1979. reprint ed. 22.50 (*0-686-26172-0*) Bornstein Schl Mem.

***Memory: From Mind to Molecules.** Larry R. Squire & Eric R. Kandel. (Illus.). 256p. 2000. pap. text 22.95 (*0-7167-6037-1*) W H Freeman.

Memory: How We Use It, Lose It, & Can Improve It. David Samuel. LC 99-25422. 144p. 1999. 19.95 (*0-8147-8145-4*) NYU Pr.

Memory: Interdisciplinary Approaches. Ed. by P. R. Solomon et al. (Illus.). 310p. 1990. 89.95 (*0-387-96724-9*) Spr-Verlag.

Memory: Luba Art & the Making of History. S. Terry Childs & Pierre De Maret. Ed. by Mary N. Roberts & Allen F. Roberts. LC 93-80699. (Illus.). 256p. 1996. pap. write for info. (*0-945802-14-5*) Museum African.

Memory: Luba Art: The Making of History. Ed. by Mary N. Roberts & Allen F. Roberts. (Illus.). 258p. 1996. 75.00 (*3-7913-1677-X*, Pub. by Prestel) te Neues.

Memory: Neurochemical & Abnormal Perspectives. J. Hunter & John Weinman. v, 235p. 1991. text 125.00 (*3-7186-5083-5*, Harwood Acad Pubs) Gordon & Breach.

Memory: Organization & Locus of Change. Ed. by Larry R. Squire et al. (Illus.). 448p. 1992. text 95.00 (*0-19-506921-8*) OUP.

Memory: Phenomena, Experiment, & Theory. Alan J. Parkin. LC 92-35260. 1993. pap. 29.95 (*0-631-15712-3*) Blackwell Pubs.

Memory: Phenomena, Experiment, & Theory. Alan J. Parkin. 1999. pap. text 27.95 (*0-86377-632-9*) L Erlbaum Assocs.

An Asterisk (*) at the beginning of an entry indicates that the title is appearing for the first time.

*Memory: Systems, Process, or Function? Ed. by Jonathan K. Foster & Marko Jelicic. (Debates in Psychology Ser.). (Illus.). 310p. 1999. pap. text 36.50 (0-19-852406-4) OUP.

Memory: Systems, Processor or Function? Jonathan K. Foster. (Illus.). 310p. 1999. text 110.00 (0-19-852407-2) OUP.

Memory: The Physiological Mechanism of Memory in the Human Center. Hyman Olken. (Illus.). 87p. 1990. 12.00 (0-685-47603-0) Olken Pubns.

Memory - Remembering - Forgetting. Ed. by Wojciech H. Kalaga & Tadeusz Rachwal. LC 99-30528. (Literary & Cultural Theory Ser.: Vol. 2). 198p. 1999. pap. 34.95 (0-8204-3583-X) P Lang Pubng.

Memory - Short Term & Recall Ability: Index of New Information. Rudy R. Ralovich. 160p. 1998. 47.50 (0-7883-1914-0); pap. 44.50 (0-7883-1915-9) ABBE Pubs Assn.

Memory - Theater & Postmodern Drama. Jeanette R. Malkin. LC 99-6220. (Theater: Theory - Text - Performance Ser.). 272p. 1999. text 49.50 (0-472-11037-3, 11037) U of Mich Pr.

Memory Album of a Territorial Lady. Linda K. Rosser. (Illus.). 72p. 1988. 14.95 (0-929546-00-8) Bobwhite Pubns.

*Memory Albums by Design. Cowles Creative Publishing Staff. (Illus.). 80p. 1999. 12.95 (0-86573-183-7) Creat Pub Intl.

Memory, Amnesia, & the Hippocampal System. Neal J. Cohen & Howard Eichenbaum. (Illus.). 344p. 1995. reprint ed. pap. text 27.00 (0-262-53132-1, Bradford Bks) MIT Pr.

Memory & Abuse: Remembering & Healing the Effects of Trauma. Charles L. Whitfield. 375p. (Orig.). 1995. pap. 12.95 (1-55874-320-0, 3200) Health Comm.

Memory & Affect in Development: The Minnesota Symposia on Child Psychology. Ed. by Charles A. Nelson. (Minnesota Symposium on Child Psychology Ser.: Vol. 26). 288p. 1993. text 59.95 (0-8058-1261-X) L Erlbaum Assocs.

Memory & American History. Ed. by David P. Thelen. LC 89-24667. (Illus.). 176p. 1990. 13.95 (0-253-35940-6); pap. 5.95 (0-253-20570-0, MB-570) Ind U Pr.

Memory & Amnesia: An Introduction. 2nd ed. Alan J. Parkin. 1999. pap. 27.95 (0-86377-635-3) L Erlbaum Assocs.

Memory & Amnesia: An Introduction. 2nd rev. ed. Alan J. Parkin. LC 96-36178. (Illus.). 256p. (C). 1997. pap. 29.95 (0-631-19702-8) Blackwell Pubs.

Memory & Awareness in Anaesthesia. Benno Bonke et al. 396p. 1990. 37.25 (90-265-1020-9) Swets.

Memory & Cognition. Walter Kintsch. LC 81-18648. 496p. 1982. reprint ed. 42.50 (0-89874-403-2) Krieger.

Memory & Cognition in Its Social Context. Robert S. Wyer & Thomas K. Srull. 504p. (C). 1989. text 89.95 (0-8058-0599-0) L Erlbaum Assocs.

Memory & Cultural Politics: New Approaches to American Ethnic Literatures. Ed. by Amritjit Singh et al. LC 95-10351. 416p. 1995. text 50.00 (1-55553-234-9) NE U Pr.

Memory & Cultural Politics: New Approaches to American Ethnic Literatures. Ed. by Amritjit Singh et al. LC 95-10351. 357p. 1995. pap. text 20.00 (1-55553-254-3) NE U Pr.

Memory & Dream. Charles De Lint. 448p. 1995. mass mkt. 6.99 (0-8125-3407-7, Pub. by Tor Bks) St Martin.

Memory & Enthusiasm: Essays, 1975-1985. W. S. Di Piero. LC 88-17939. 269p. 1989. reprint ed. pap. 83.40 (0-608-02527-5, 206317100004) Bks Demand.

Memory & Fire: Ten American Jewish Poets. Gary Pacernick. (Twentieth Century American Jewish Writers Ser.). XII, 259p. (C). 1989. text 45.70 (0-8204-0419-5) P Lang Pubng.

Memory & Forgetting John Henderson. LC 98-55199. (Modular Psychology Ser.). 1999. pap. write for info. (0-415-18652-8) Routledge.

*Memory & Forgetting. John Henderson. LC 98-55199. 1999. write for info. (0-415-18651-X) Routledge.

Memory & Heaven: Poems. Christopher Howell. LC 95-42584. 69p. 1997. 24.50 (0-910055-27-0); pap. 14.00 (0-910055-28-9) East Wash Univ.

Memory & History: Essays on Recalling & Interpreting Experience. Ed. by Jaclyn Jeffrey & Glenace Edwall. 340p. 1994. 48.00 (0-8191-9460-3); pap. 23.50 (0-8191-9508-1) U Pr of Amer.

Memory & History As Fiction: An Archetypal Approach to the Historical Novel. Patrick Brady. 168p. 1993. pap. text 16.95 (1-886935-05-X) New Prdigm Pr.

*Memory & History in Christianity & Judaism. Ed. by Michael A. Signer. 272p. 2000. pap. 19.00 (0-268-03460-5, Pub. by U of Notre Dame Pr); lib. bdg. 40.00 (0-268-03454-0, Pub. by U of Notre Dame Pr) Chicago Distribution Ctr.

*Memory & History in George Elliot: Transfiguring the Past. Haoming Liu. LC 99-46744. 2000. text 55.00 (0-312-22834-1) St Martin.

Memory & History in Twentieth Century Australia. Kate Darian-Smith & Paula Hamilton. LC 94-217340. (Illus.). 264p. 1994. pap. text 35.00 (0-19-553569-3) OUP.

Memory & Hope: Strands of Canadian Baptist History. Ed. by David T. Priestley. viii, 211p. 1996. pap. 24.95 (0-88920-267-2) W Laurier U Pr.

Memory & Hypnotic Age Regression: Developmental Aspects of Cognitive Function Explored Through Hypnosis. Robert Reiff & Martin Scheerer. LC 59-13120. 253p. 1970. 40.00 (0-8236-3340-3) Intl Univs Pr.

Memory & Imagination: The Legacy of Maidu Indian Artist Frank Day. Rebecca J. Dobkins et al. LC 96-49341. (Illus.). 120p. 1997. pap. 24.95 (0-295-97612-8) U of Wash Pr.

Memory & Instruction. David Baine. LC 85-16216. (Illus.). 340p. 1986. 44.95 (0-87778-192-3) Educ Tech Pubns.

Memory & Language Impairment in Children & Adults: New Perspectives. Ronald B. Gillam. LC 98-27277. 228p. 1998. pap. 35.00 (0-8342-1213-7) Aspen Pub.

Memory & Learning. Nancy Wartik. (Encyclopedia of Health Ser.). (Illus.). 1162p. (YA). (gr. 7 up). 1992. lib. bdg. 19.95 (0-7910-0022-2) Chelsea Hse.

Memory & Learning: A Practical Guide for Teachers, Vol. 1. Jacqueline Bristow. (Resource Materials for Teachers Ser.). 1999. pap. 27.95 (1-85346-594-1) David Fulton.

Memory & Learning: The Ebbinghaus Centennial Conference. Ed. by David S. Gorfein & Robert R. Hoffman. 458p. 1987. 89.95 (0-89859-653-X) L Erlbaum Assocs.

Memory & Literature: Intertextuality in Russian Modernism. Renate Lachmann. Tr. by Roy Sellars & Anthony Wall. LC 96-50354. (Theory & History of Literature Ser.: Vol. 87). (Illus.). 512p. (C). 1997. pap. 34.95 (0-8166-2907-2); text 49.95 (0-8166-2906-4) U of Minn Pr.

Memory & Manuscript: Oral Tradition & Written Transmission in Rabbinic Judaism & Early Christianity; With, Tradition & Transmission in Early Christianity. Birger Gerhardsson. Tr. by Eric J. Sharpe from UND. LC 97-18990. 426p. 1998. pap. 39.00 (0-8028-4366-2) Eerdmans.

*Memory & Mastery: Primo Levi as a Writer & Witness. Ed. by Roberta S. Kremer. LC 00-34503. (C). 2001. pap. text 19.95 (0-7914-4922-X) State U NY Pr.

*Memory & Mastery: Primo Levi as a Writer & Witness. Ed. by Roberta S. Kremer. LC 00-34503. (C). 2001. text 59.50 (0-7914-4921-1) State U NY Pr.

*Memory & Metaphor: New & Corrected Poems, 1993-1999. Barbara Flaherty. 100p. (YA). 1999. pap. 9.95 (0-7392-0363-0, PO3562) Morris Pubng.

*Memory & Methodology. Ed. by Susannah Radstone. (Illus.). 256p. 2000. 55.00 (1-85973-296-8, Pub. by Berg Pubs); pap. 19.50 (1-85973-202-X, Pub. by Berg Pubs) NYU Pr.

Memory & Modernity: Viollet-Le-Duc at Vezelay. Kevin D. Murphy et al. LC 98-41262. (Illus.). 596p. 1920. 45.00 (0-271-01850-X) Pa St U Pr.

Memory & Mourning: Shared Cultural Experience. Marijo Dougherty et al. LC 97-61742. (Illus.). 1997. write for info. (0-910763-17-8) U Albany Art Mus.

*Memory & Narrative: The Weave of Life-Writing. James Olney. LC 98-17135. (Illus.). 496p. 1999. 35.00 (0-226-62816-7) U Ch Pr.

*Memory & Oblivion. Adriaan W. Reinink & Jeroen Stumpel. LC 99-51941. 1999. write for info. (0-7923-4213-5) Kluwer Academic.

Memory & Postcolony. Werbner. LC 98-8150. 1998. text 65.00 (1-85649-591-4, Pub. by Zed Books) St Martin.

Memory & Re-Creation in Troubadour Lyric. Amelia E. Van Vleck. LC 90-31357. 275p. 1990. 48.00 (0-520-06521-2, Pub. by U CA Pr) Cal Prin Full Svc.

Memory & Remembering: Everyday Memory in Context. John A. Groeger. LC 96-51084. 378p. (C). 1997. pap. text 26.25 (0-582-29220-4, Pub. by Addison-Wesley) Longman.

Memory & Salvation. Charles Elliott. LC 96-147059. pap. write for info. (0-232-52141-7) S Asia.

Memory & Storage. rev. ed. Time-Life Books Editors. (Understanding Computers Ser.). (Illus.). 128p. 1990. lib. bdg. write for info. (0-8094-7599-5) Time-Life.

*Memory & Suggestibility in the Forensic Interview. Ed. by Jodi A. Quas et al. (A Volume in the Personality & Clinical Psychology Series). 400p. 2000. write for info. (0-8058-3080-4) L Erlbaum Assocs.

*Memory & Survival: The French Cinema of Krzysztof Kieslowski. Emma Wilson. (Legenda Ser.: Vol. 7). 100p. (C). 2000. pap. 27.50 (1-900755-27-0, Pub. by E H R C) David Brown.

Memory & Testimony in the Child Witness. Ed. by Maria S. Zaragosa et al. (Applied Psychology: Individual, Social & Community Issues Ser.: Vol. 1). 320p. 1994. 54.00 (0-8039-5554-5) Sage.

Memory & the Brain. Magda B. Arnold. 544p. 1984. text 99.95 (0-89859-290-9) L Erlbaum Assocs.

Memory & the Brain. Larry R. Squire. (Illus.). 336p. 1987. pap. text 29.95 (0-19-504208-5) OUP.

*Memory & the Medieval Tomb. Elizabeth Valdez del Alamo & Carol Stamatis Pendergast. LC 00-25504. 2000. write for info. (0-7546-0076-9, Pub. by Ashgate Pub) Ashgate Pub Co.

Memory & the Middle Ages. Boston College Museum of Art Staff. Ed. by Nancy Netzer & Virginia Reinburg. LC 94-74254. (Illus.). 106p. (Orig.). (C). 1995. pap. text 19.95 (0-9640153-2-3) McMullen Mus Art.

Memory Architecture & Parallel Access. Michael Gossel et al. LC 94-23507. 250p. 1994. 191.50 (0-444-82104-X) Elsevier.

Memory at These Speeds: New & Selected Poems. Jane Miller. 224p. 1996. pap. text 15.00 (1-55659-118-7) Copper Canyon.

Memory, Baa, Moo, Cock-a-doodle-doo. Jennifer Norman. 1995. pap. 12.99 (0-85953-706-4) Childs Play.

Memory Babe: A Critical Biography of Jack Kerouac. Gerald Nicosia. LC 93-33457. 1994. 22.50 (0-520-08569-8, Pub. by U CA Pr) Cal Prin Full Svc.

Memory Bank for Chemotherapy. Fredrica A. Preston. 256p. 1987. spiral bd. 19.95 (0-683-06972-1) Jones & Bartlett.

Memory Bank for Chemotherapy. 3rd ed. Fredrica A. Preston & Cecilia Wilfinger. LC 96-21045. 1996. pap., spiral bd. 31.25 (0-86720-740-X) Jones & Bartlett.

Memory Bank for HIV Drugs. Gail M. Wilkes. (Nursing-Health Science Ser.). (C). 1994. spiral bd. 36.25 (0-86720-685-3) Jones & Bartlett.

Memory Bank for IV's. 2nd ed. Sharon M. Weinstein. (Nursing-Health Science Ser.). 288p. (C). 1992. spiral bd. 27.50 (0-86720-326-9) Jones & Bartlett.

Memory Bank Handbook. Dana Alcock. 257p. 1997. pap. 9.95 (0-9656170-0-9) Danas Gifts.

Memory Bank Hemodynamic Monitoring. Gary W. Ervin & Sylvia Long. (Illus.). 240p. 1993. spiral bd. 24.95 (0-86720-646-2) Jones & Bartlett.

Memory Bank Notebook. Robert D. Joyce. 90p. 1994. pap. 12.95 (1-888292-00-8, Hawthrne Hse) Pygmalion Press.

Memory-Based Text Processing: A Special Issue of "Discourse Processes" Ed. by Edward J. O'Brien et al. 163p. 1998. pap. write for info. (0-8058-9824-7) L Erlbaum Assocs.

Memory Bird: Survivors of Sexual Abuse. Caroline Malone et al. LC 96-35173. 256p. 1997. 59.95 (1-56639-525-9) Temple U Pr.

Memory Bird: Survivors of Sexual Abuse. Caroline Malone et al. LC 96-35173. (Illus.). 256p. 1997. pap. 16.95 (1-56639-526-7) Temple U Pr.

Memory Board. Jane Rule. 336p. 1987. pap. 12.95 (0-941483-02-9) Naiad Pr.

Memory Book. Harry Lorayne. LC 96-96797. 1996. pap. 10.00 (0-345-41002-5) Ballantine Pub Grp.

Memory Book: A Special Way to Remember Someone You Love. Kathleen Knoderer. LC 95-82123. (Illus.). 26p. (J). (gr. 1-6). 1996. 9.95 (1-57543-004-5) Mar Co Prods.

Memory Book: Classic Guide to Improving Your Memory At Work, At School, & At Play. Jerry Lucas & Harry Lorayne. 224p. 1986. mass mkt. 5.99 (0-345-33758-1) Ballantine Pub Grp.

Memory Book of Starr Faithfull. Gloria Vanderbilt. LC 94-271. 336p. 1994. 24.00 (0-394-58775-8) Knopf.

Memory Box. Mary Bahr. Ed. by Kathleen Tucker. LC 91-21628. (Illus.). 32p. (J). (gr. 1-4). 1992. pap. 5.95 (0-8075-5053-1) A Whitman.

Memory Box: Gathering the Keepsakes of the Heart. Mary K. Shanley. Ed. by Carolyn H. Bryant & Alice B. Acheson. (Illus.). 48p. 1995. 14.95 (1-882835-32-8) STA-Kris.

Memory Boy. Will Weaver. Orig. Title: The Boy on Platform One. 144p. (gr. 3-7). mass mkt. 4.95 (0-06-440854-X) HarpC.

*Memory Boy. Will Weaver. Orig. Title: The Boy on Platform One. 144p. (J). (gr. 3-7). 2000. 15.95 (0-06-028811-6) HarpC Child Bks.

*Memory Boy. Will Weaver. Orig. Title: The Boy on Platform One. 144p. (J). (gr. 3-7). 2001. lib. bdg. 15.89 (0-06-028812-4) HarpC Child Bks.

Memory Boy. large type ed. Victor Canning. Orig. Title: The Boy on Platform One. 320p. 1983. 27.99 (0-7089-0926-4) Ulverscroft.

Memory, Brain & Belief. Ed. by Daniel L. Schacter & Elaine Scarry. LC 99-40552. 336p. 2000. 39.95 (0-674-00061-7) HUP.

Memory Can Be Murder. Elizabeth Daniels Squire. 256p. (Orig.). 1995. mass mkt. 5.99 (0-425-14772-X) Berkley Pub.

Memory Cathedral: A Secret History of Leonardo da Vinci. Jack Dann. LC 95-15109. 512p. 1996. reprint ed. pap. 10.95 (0-553-37857-0) Bantam.

Memory Change & Cognitive Function among the Elderly. Janet L. Conant. (Studies on the Elderly in America). 250p. 1995. text 50.00 (0-8153-1894-4) Garland.

Memory Change in the Aged. David F. Hultsch et al. LC 98-16538. (Illus.). 300p. (C). 1998. 59.95 (0-521-47361-6) Cambridge U Pr.

Memory Church. Tim Sebastian. 288p. 1994. mass mkt. 4.99 (0-380-71863-4, Avon Bks) Morrow Avon.

Memory Coat. Elvira Woodruff. LC 95-30048. (Illus.). 32p. (J). (gr. 2-5). 1999. 15.95 (0-590-67717-9) Scholastic Inc.

*Memory-Connections Matter, Art-in-Science, Vol. XIV. Karen S. Mittelman & Patricia Moss-Vreeland. (Illus.). 32p. 2000. 5.00 (0-9678657-0-0) Moss-Vreeland.

Memory Consolidation: Psychobiology of Cognition. Ed. by Herbert Weingartner & Elizabeth S. Parker. 288p. (C). 1984. text 59.95 (0-89859-323-9) L Erlbaum Assocs.

Memory Crafting: Beyond the Scrapbook. Judi Kauffman. LC 99-61441. 126p. 1999. pap. 19.95 (0-87341-795-X) Krause Pubns.

Memory Culture. William W. Atkinson. 92p. 1996. reprint ed. spiral bd. 11.00 (0-7873-0051-9) Hlth Research.

Memory Culture. William W. Atkinson. 92p. 1976. reprint ed. 11.00 (0-911662-61-8) Yoga.

Memory Culture: The Science of Observing, Remembering & Recalling. W. W. Atkinson. 1991. lib. bdg. 75.00 (0-8490-4967-9) Gordon Pr.

Memory Culture: The Science of Observing, Remembering & Recalling (1903) William W. Atkinson. 92p. 1996. reprint ed. pap. 9.95 (1-56459-769-5) Kessinger Pub.

Memory Cure: The Safe, Scientifically Proven Breakthrough That Can Slow, Halt, or Even Reverse Age-Related Memory Loss. Thomas H. Crook, III & Brenda Adderly. LC 98-86288. 320p. 1998. 24.00 (0-671-02642-9, PB Hardcover) PB.

*Memory Cure: The Safe, Scientifically Proven Breakthrough That Can Slow, Halt, or Even Reverse Age-Related Memory Loss. Thomas H. Crook, III & Brenda Adderly. 1999. reprint ed. mass mkt. 6.99 (0-671-02643-7) PB.

Memory Defects in Organic Psychoses. Jonathan Liljencrants. (Psychology Monographs General & Applied: Vol. 32). 1974. reprint ed. 55.00 (0-8115-1431-5) Periodicals Srv.

Memory, Dementia, & Perception of Time, Music, & Faces, Section 11. Ed. by H. Spinnler & F. Boller. (Handbook of Neuropsychology Ser.: Vol. 8). 456p. 1993. 313.00 (0-444-89975-8) Elsevier.

Memory Development: Universal Changes & Individual Differences. Ed. by Franz E. Weinert & Marion Perlmutter. 432p. 1988. text 79.95 (0-8058-0148-0) L Erlbaum Assocs.

Memory Development & Competencies: Issues in Growth & Development. Ed. by Franz E. Weinert & Wolfgang Schneider. 456p. 1995. text 89.95 (0-8058-1645-3) L Erlbaum Assocs.

Memory Development Between 2 & 20. M. Pressley & Wolfgang Schneider. (Cognitive Development Ser.). (Illus.). 255p. 1988. 45.00 (0-387-96742-7) Spr-Verlag.

Memory Development Between 2 & 20. 2nd ed. Wolfgang Schneider & Michael Pressley. LC 96-36766. 416p. 1997. text 99.95 (0-8058-2437-5) L Erlbaum Assocs.

Memory Disorders: Research & Clinical Practice. Ed. by Takehiko Yanagihara & Ronald C. Petersen. (Neurological Disease & Therapy Ser.: Vol. 9). (Illus.). 536p. 1991. text 199.00 (0-8247-8489-8) Dekker.

*Memory Disorders in Psychiatric Practice. Ed. by German E. Berrios & John R. Hodges. (Illus.). 512p. (C). 2000. pap. 64.95 (0-521-57671-7) Cambridge U Pr.

Memory Distortion: How Minds, Brains, & Societies Reconstruct the Past. Ed. by Daniel L. Schacter et al. LC 95-30479. (Illus.). 416p. (C). 1995. 56.00 (0-674-56675-0) HUP.

Memory Distortion: How Minds, Brains, & Societies Reconstruct the Past. Ed. by Daniel L. Schacter. (Illus.). 432p. 1997. reprint ed. pap. 18.50 (0-674-56676-9) HUP.

Memory Distortions & Their Prevention. Ed. by Magaret J. Intons-Peterson & Deborah L. Best. LC 98-21196. (Challenges & Controversies in Applied Cognition Ser.). 200p. 1998. 45.00 (0-8058-3066-9) L Erlbaum Assocs.

Memory Dynamics: A Complete Memory System. William Fauver & Robert L. Birch. 1981. 59.95 (0-939036-01-0); spiral bd. 39.95 (0-939036-00-2) Knowledge Bank.

Memory Dynamics System for Memory & Learning Improvement: Summary of the Theory & Methods. William Fauver. 31p. 1982. pap. 6.95 (0-939036-02-9) Knowledge Bank.

Memory Enhancement in 30 Days. Keith Harary & Pamela Weintraub. 99p. (Orig.). 1997. pap. text 7.00 (0-7881-5066-9) DIANE Pub.

Memory Enhancement Program for Older Adults. Prem S. Fry & May D. Caprio-Prevette. LC 95-32416. 310p. 1996. 85.00 (0-8342-0728-1) Aspen Pub.

Memory-Enhancing Techniques for Investigative Interviewing: The Cognitive Interview. Ronald P. Fisher & R. E. Geiselman. 232p. 1992. pap. 37.95 (0-398-06121-1) C C Thomas.

Memory-Enhancing Techniques for Investigative Interviewing: The Cognitive Interview. Ronald P. Fisher & R. E. Geiselman. 232p. (C). 1992. text 54.95 (0-398-05800-8) C C Thomas.

Memory Eternal: Tlingit Culture & Russian Orthodox Christianity Through Two Centuries. Sergei Kan. LC 98-52344. (Illus.). 696p. 2000. 60.00 (0-295-97806-6) U of Wash Pr.

Memory Exercises: A Handbook of Activities to Stimulate the Mind. Carole Seedman. (Illus.). 146p. 1997. spiral bd., wbk. ed. 25.00 (0-9662006-0-8) Carole Pr.

Memory Factory: Guidelines for Use with Students. Melvin D. Levine. Ed. by Tim Arnold. (Illus.). (YA). (gr. 6-12). 1999. pap., wbk. ed. 9.00 (0-8388-1982-6) Ed Pub Serv.

*Memory Fever. Ray Gonzalez. LC 99-30986. (Camino del Sol - A Latino & Latina Ser.). 240p. 1999. pap. 17.95 (0-8165-2011-9) U of Ariz Pr.

Memory Fitness over Forty. Robin West. 240p. 1985. 18.95 (0-937404-21-7) Triad Pub FL.

*Memory Folding: Tea Bag Paper Folding for Your Scrapbook. Laura Lees & Kris Mason. Ed. by Judith Durant. (Illus.). 36p. 1999. pap. 9.50 (1-892127-06-7) Satellite Publ.

Memory for Actions. Johannes EngelKamp. LC 99-169158. (Essays in Cognitive Psychology Ser.). 1998. 39.95 (0-86377-765-1) Taylor & Francis.

Memory for Everyday & Emotional Events. Ed. by Nancy L. Stein et al. LC 96-35580. 496p. 1996. pap. 39.95 (0-8058-2609-2); text 99.95 (0-8058-1443-4) L Erlbaum Assocs.

Memory for Forgetfulness: August, Beirut, 1982. Mahmoud Darwish. Tr. by Ibrahim Muhawi from ARA. LC 94-26351.Tr. of Dhairah lil-Nisyan. 1995. 40.00 (0-520-08767-4, Pub. by U CA Pr); pap. 14.95 (0-520-08768-2, Pub. by U CA Pr) Cal Prin Full Svc.

Memory for Odors. Ed. by Frank R. Schab & Robert G. Crowder. 200p. 1995. text 39.95 (0-8058-0728-4) L Erlbaum Assocs.

Memory for Tino. Leo F. Buscaglia. (Illus.). 50p. (J). (ps up). 1988. 12.95 (1-55642-020-X) SLACK Inc.

Memory for Wonders: A True Story. Veronica Namoyo. LC 92-74110. 189p. (Orig.). 1993. pap. 9.95 (0-89870-430-8) Ignatius Pr.

Memory Foundations for Reading: Visual Mnemonics for Sound-Symbol Relationships. Regina G. Richards. (Illus.). 65p. (C). 1997. pap. 13.00 (0-9661353-0-X) Richards Educ.

Memory Function & Aging-Related Disorders. Ed. by John E. Morley et al. LC 91-5089. 352p. 1992. 48.95 (0-8261-7710-7) Springer Pub.

Memory Functioning in Dementia. Ed. by Lars B. Ackman. LC 92-11600. xii,300p. 1992. 157.00 (0-444-88920-5, North Holland) Elsevier.

Memory Games: The Emory Center for the Arts. Eisenman Architects Staff. (Illus.). 126p. 1995. 30.00 (0-614-14658-5) Harvard Univ Graduate Schl of.

M

Memory Gardens. Robert Creeley. LC 85-29723. 96p. 1986. pap. 7.95 (*0-8112-0974-1*, NDP613, Pub. by New Directions) Norton.

***Memory Gifts.** Marie Browning. LC 99-54257. 2000. 24.95 (*0-8069-3933-8*) Sterling.

Memory, History & Opposition under State Socialism. Rubie S. Watson. (Advanced Seminar Ser.). 210p. 1994. text 55.00 (*0-933452-86-1*); pap. text 24.95 (*0-933452-87-X*) Schol Am Res.

Memory, History, & the Extermination of the Jews of Europe. Saul Friedlander. LC 92-40377. 164p. 1993. 25.95 (*0-253-32483-1*) Ind U Pr.

***Memory Horse.** Troon Harrison. (Illus.). 32p. (J). (gr. 1-4). 1999. 15.95 (*0-88776-440-1*) Tundra Bks.

Memory, Identity, Community: The Idea of Narrative in the Human Sciences. Ed. by Lewis P. Hinchman & Sandra K. Hinchman. LC 96-8702. (SUNY Series in the Philosophy of the Social Sciences). 393p. (C). 1997. text 59.50 (*0-7914-3323-4*); pap. text 19.95 (*0-7914-3324-2*) State U NY Pr.

Memory, Identity, Power: Poltics in the Jungle Mahals (West Bengal), 1890-1950. Ramabeira Sameaddeara. LC 98-904223. viii, 295 p. 1998. write for info. (*81-250-1025-4*) Orient Longman Ltd.

Memory, Imprinting & the Brain: An Inquiry into Mechanisms. Gabriel Horn. (Oxford Psychology Ser.). (Illus.). 320p. 1986. pap. text 26.00 (*0-19-852156-1*) OUP.

Memory Improved: Reading & Memory Enhancement Across the Life Span Through Strategic Text Structure. Bonnie J. Meyer et al. 264p. 1988. 49.95 (*0-8058-0111-1*) L Erlbaum Assocs.

Memory Improvement: Implications for Memory Theory. Ed. by D. J. Herrmann et al. 296p. 1993. 74.95 (*0-387-97463-6*) Spr-Verlag.

Memory Improvement Programs for Older Adults: A Training Manual. Janet Fogler & Lynn Stern. 58p. (Orig.). 1987. pap. 10.00 (*0-9627777-0-6*) Memory Skills.

Memory Improvement Workbook. Bruce Goldberg. 80p. 1996. 30.00 (*1-885577-85-0*) B Goldberg.

Memory in a Broader Perspective. Alan Searleman & Douglas Herrmann. LC 93-21686. 446p. (C). 1994. 62.81 (*0-07-028387-7*) McGraw.

Memory in Dispute. Valerie Sinason. 232p. 1998. pap. text 31.50 (*1-85575-122-4*, Pub. by H Karnac Bks Ltd) Other Pr LLC.

Memory in Everyday Life. Ed. by Graham M. Davies & Robert H. Logie. LC 93-14511. (Advances in Psychology Ser.: Vol. 100). 568p. 1993. 191.50 (*0-444-88997-3*, North Holland) Elsevier.

Memory in Historical Perspective. Ed. by D. J. Herrmann & R. Chaffin. (Recent Research in Psychology Ser.). (Illus.). 254p. 1988. 72.95 (*0-387-96705-2*) Spr-Verlag.

Memory in Indian Epistemology: Its Nature & Status. Shaila Bhandare. (Sri Garib Dass Oriental Ser.: No. 165). (C). 1993. 17.50 (*81-7030-359-1*) S Asia.

Memory in "La Celestina" Dorothy S. Severin. (Monagrafias A Ser.: No. 19). (C). 1970. pap. 41.00 (*0-900411-13-9*, Pub. by Tamesis Bks Ltd) Boydell & Brewer.

Memory in Mind & Brain: What Dream Imagery Reveals. Morton F. Reiser. 232p. 1994. pap. 17.00 (*0-300-06032-7*) Yale U Pr.

Memory in Neurodegenerative Disease: Biological, Cognitive, & Clinical Perspectives. Ed. by Alexander I. Troster. LC 97-46776. (Illus.). 428p. (C). 1998. text 95.00 (*0-521-57192-8*) Cambridge U Pr.

Memory in Oral Traditions: The Cognitive Psychology of Counting-out Rhymes, Ballads & Epic. David C. Rubin. LC 94-8997. (Illus.). 400p. 1995. text 60.00 (*0-19-508211-7*) OUP.

Memory in Oral Traditions: The Cognitive Psychology of Epic, Ballads & Counting-Out Rhymes. David C. Rubin. (Illus.). 400p. 1997. reprint ed. pap. text 26.00 (*0-19-512032-9*) OUP.

Memory in the Cerebral Cortex: An Empirical Approach to Neural Networks in the Human & NonHuman Primate. Joaquin M. Fuster. LC 94-8307. 372p. 1994. 55.00 (*0-262-06171-6*, Bradford Bks) MIT Pr.

Memory in the Cerebral Cortex: An Empirical Approach to Neural Networks in the Human & Nonhuman Primate. Joaquin M. Fuster. (Illus.). 376p. 1999. reprint ed. pap. 27.00 (*0-262-56124-7*, Bradford Bks) MIT Pr.

Memory, in Your Country. Joseph McLaughlin. 40p. (Orig.). 1995. pap. 4.00 (*0-914720-10-4*) Pale Horse.

Memory is a Fickle Jade: A Collection of Historical Essays about Newfoundland & Her People. Raymond W. Guy. LC 96-950127. (Illus.). 200p. 1996. pap. 10.95 (*1-895387-72-8*) Creative Bk Pub.

Memory Is an Illusive State. Peter Ulisse. LC 95-8702. 72p. 1995. pap. 14.95 (*0-7734-2733-3*, Mellen Poetry Pr) E Mellen.

Memory Issues in Embedded Systems-on-Chip: Optimizations & Exploration. Preeti R. Panda et al. LC 98-44229. xvii, 188 p. 1999. write for info. (*0-7923-8362-1*) Kluwer Academic.

Memory Jogger: A Pocket Guide of Tools for Continuous Improvement. 2nd ed. Ed. by Michael Brassard. (Illus.). 88p. 1988. pap. 4.50 (*1-879364-03-4*) GOAL-QPC.

Memory Jogger Vol. II: A Pocket Guide of Tools for Continuous Improvement & Effective Planning. Michael Brassard & Diane Ritter. Ed. by Francine Oddo. (Illus.). 164p. 1994. spiral bd. 6.95 (*1-879364-44-1*, 1030E) GOAL-QPC.

Memory Jogger for Education: A Pocket Guide for Continuous Improvement in Schools. Ann McManus. 88p. 1994. pap. 4.50 (*1-879364-24-7*) GOAL-QPC.

Memory Jogger 9000: A Pocket Guide to Implementing ISO 9000 Quality Systems Standard & QS-9000 Third EditionRequirements. Robert Peach & Diane Ritter. Ed. by Francine Oddo. (Illus.). 164p. 1996. spiral bd. 6.95 (*1-879364-82-4*, 1060E) GOAL-QPC.

Memory Jogger Plus: Featuring the Seven Management & Planning Tools. rev. ed. Michael Brassard. (Illus.). x, 306p. 1997. pap. 29.95 (*1-879364-83-2*) GOAL-QPC.

***Memory Jug.** Patricia Martin. 236p. (J). (gr. 4-7). 1998. lib. bdg. 16.49 (*0-7868-2368-2*, Pub. by Disney Pr) Little.

***Memory Jug.** Martinpat. 276p. (J). 1998. 15.95 (*0-7868-0357-6*, Pub. by Hyperion) Time Warner.

Memory Keeper. Sara Miller. (Barbie Generation Girl Ser.). (Illus.). 12p. (J). (gr. 4-6). 2000. pap. 12.99 (*1-57584-411-7*, Pub. by Rdrs Digest) S&S Trade.

Memory Keeper. Laura Nadworny. LC 99-90365. xiii, 201p. (YA). (gr. 10 up). 1999. pap. 12.00 (*0-9659078-0-5*) dARCY LIAT.

***Memory Key: Unlock the Secrets to Remembering.** Fiona McPherson. LC 00-23336. 224p. 2000. pap. 12.99 (*1-56414-470-4*) Career Pr Inc.

Memory Kit: Great for School, Work or Just for Fun. Robert Eastaway. 1999. 12.95 (*1-901881-64-4*, Pub. by Element MA) Penguin Putnam.

Memory Lane. Patrick Modiano. 1983. pap. 10.95 (*0-7859-2692-5*) Fr & Eur.

***Memory Lane.** Anna Salter. 2000. write for info. (*0-671-02350-0*) S&S Trade.

Memory Lane: A Pictorial History of Genesee County, Michigan. Ed. by Flint Journal Staff & Alfred P. Sloan Museum Staff. (Illus.). 140p. 1997. text 37.06 (*0-9649832-2-2*, A P Sloan) Booth Newspapers.

Memory Lane: A Willows & Parker Mystery. Laurence Gough. 296p. 1997. mass mkt. 5.95 (*0-7710-3404-0*) McCland & Stewart.

Memory Lane: A Willows & Parker Mystery. Laurence Gough. 289p. 1997. 24.95 (*0-7710-3437-7*) McCland & Stewart.

Memory Lane: The Fun & Easy System for Writing about Your Life. Lifescapes Corporation Staff. 1995. 79.95 incl. reel tape, VHS (*1-886701-02-4*) Lifescapes.

Memory Lapse. Kathleen O'Brien. LC 95-8024. (Temptation Ser.: No. 522). 216p. 1995. per. 3.25 (*0-373-25626-4*, 1-25626-2) Harlequin Bks.

Memory Lapse: An Artist's Book. Clifton K. Meador. (Illus.). 192p. 55.00 (*0-932526-83-7*) Nexus Pr.

Memory, Learning & Higher Function. Charles D. Woody. 483p. 1984. 100.00 (*0-387-90994-X*) Spr-Verlag.

Memory Links. William F. Van Wert. LC 94-48868. 136p. 1995. 24.95 (*0-8203-1750-0*) U of Ga Pr.

Memory Loss. Stephen L. Deflice. 1987. pap. 7.95 (*0-8184-0445-0*) Carol Pub Group.

Memory Loss - Changing Tracks - Growing Older: Don't Act Your Age. Hankins Parker. (Illus.). (Orig.). 1994. pap. 5.00 (*0-85132-200-X*) Park Hurst Pubs.

***Memory Loss & Dementia.** Dorling Kindersley Publishing Co. Staff. (ACP Home Medical Guides). 80p. 2000. pap. 6.95 (*0-7894-5201-4*, D K Ink) DK Pub Inc.

Memory Made Easy. Robert L. Montgomery & Debra Giffen. 32p. 1994. pap. 59.95 incl. audio (*1-55678-048-6*) Learn Inc.

Memory Made Easy: The Complete Book of Memory Training. Robert L. Montgomery. LC 79-10889. 122p. reprint ed. pap. 37.90 (*0-608-10679-8*, 202262300028); reprint ed. pap. 34.80 (*0-608-30647-9*, 2022623) Bks Demand.

Memory Makers: 50 Moments Your Kids Will Never Forget. Doug Fields & Duffy Robbins. LC 96-146110. 112p. (J). 1996. pap. 9.99 (*0-310-21013-5*) Zondervan.

***Memory Makers Baby Scrapbooks: Ideas, Tips & Techniques for Baby Scrapbooks.** Ed. by Mary Jo Regier. (Illus.). 128p. 2000. per. 19.95 (*1-892127-09-1*) Satellite Publ.

***Memory Makers' Great Scrapbooks; Ideas, Tips & Techniques.** Michele Gerbrandt. 2000. 25.00 (*0-88363-927-0*) H L Levin.

Memory Makers Photo Kaleidoscopes: Creating Photo Drama on Scrapbook Pages. Satellite Press Staff. (Illus.). 36p. 1999. pap. text 9.95 (*1-892127-04-0*) Satellite Publ.

***Memory Makers Wedding Idea Book: Scrapbooking Ideas, Tips & Techniques.** Ed. by Mary Jo Regier. (Illus.). 128p. 2000. per. 19.95 (*1-892127-08-3*) Satellite Publ.

Memory Makes Money. Harry Lorayne. 256p. 1988. 16.95 (*0-316-53267-3*) Little.

Memory Makes Music: American Autobiography. Margaret Chanler. 171p. 1995. lib. bdg. 69.00 (*0-7812-8475-9*) Rprt Serv.

Memory Mambo. Achy Obejas. 200p. (Orig.). 1996. pap. 12.95 (*1-57344-017-5*) Cleis Pr.

Memory Management. LC 93-39671. 1993. 22.00 (*0-87051-143-2*) Am Inst CPA.

Memory Management: International Workshop IWMM '92, St. Malo, France, September 17-19, 1992 - Proceedings. Ed. by Y. Bekkers & J. Cohen. LC 92-30705. (Lecture Notes in Computer Science Ser.: Vol. 637). xi, 525p. 1992. 76.95 (*0-387-55940-X*) Spr-Verlag.

Memory Management: Proceedings International Workshop, IWMM '95, Kinross, U. K., September 27-29, 1995. Ed. by Henry G. Baker. (Lecture Notes in Computer Science Ser.: Vol. 986). 417p. 1995. 68.00 (*3-540-60368-9*) Spr-Verlag.

Memory Management for Dummies Quick Reference. 2nd ed. Doug Lowe. LC 96-75758. 384p. 1996. pap. 19.99 (*1-56884-987-7*) IDG Bks.

Memory Manual: 10 Simple Things You Can Do to Improve Your Memory after 50. Betty Fielding. LC 98-36920. 256p. 1998. pap. 14.95 (*1-884956-15-7*) Quill Driver.

***Memory, Matter & Modern Romance.** Bruce Yonemoto & Norman Yonemoto. (Illus.). 104p. 1999. 30.00 (*1-881161-04-8*, Pub. by Japanese Museum) RAM Publications.

Memory, Meaning & Method: Some Psychological Perspectives on Language Learning. 2nd ed. Earl Stevick. (Teaching Methods Ser.). 200p. (J). 1996. mass mkt. 28.95 (*0-8384-5569-7*) Heinle & Heinle.

Memory Mechanisms: A Tribute to G. V. Goddard. Ed. by W. Abraham et al. 400p. (C). 1990. pap. 59.95 (*0-8058-0277-0*); text 120.00 (*0-8058-0276-2*) L Erlbaum Assocs.

Memory, Myth & Time in Mexico. Enrique Florescano. Tr. by Albert G. Bork & Kathryn R. Bork from SPA. (Institute of Latin American Studies). (Illus.). 280p. (Orig.). (C). 1994. pap. 16.95 (*0-292-72486-1*) U of Tex Pr.

Memory, Narrative, & Identity: New Essays in Ethnic American Literatures. Ed. by Amritjit Singh et al. (Illus.). 352p. 1994. text 50.00 (*1-55553-203-9*); pap. text 20.00 (*1-55553-267-5*) NE U Pr.

***Memory, Narrative, Identity: Remembering the Self.** Nicola King. 208p. 2000. text 70.00 (*0-7486-1116-9*) Col U Pr.

Memory New Testament. Stuart Clarke. (Illus.). 700p. (Orig.). 1987. pap. 9.95 (*0-9619291-0-3*) Bibles Intl.

Memory Notebook of Nursing, Vol. I. JoAnn Zerwekh & Jo Carol Claborn. (Illus.). 134p. (C). 1994. pap. text, student ed. 19.95 (*0-9628210-5-5*) Nursing Ed Consultants.

Memory Notebook of Nursing Vol. II: A New & Different Collection of Visual Images. JoAnn Zerwekh & Jo C. Claborn. (Illus.). 158p. 1997. pap., student ed. 24.95 (*0-9628210-8-X*) Nursing Ed Consultants.

Memory Observed. 2nd ed. Neisser. LC 99-49080. 1999. pap. text 27.95 (*0-7167-3319-6*) W H Freeman.

Memory of a Large Christmas. Lillian Smith. LC 95-26348. 1996. 15.95 (*0-8203-1842-6*) U of Ga Pr.

Memory of All That: The Life of George Gershwin. Joan Peyser. LC 97-49642. 320p. 1998. 18.95 (*0-8230-8332-2*, Billboard Bks) Watsn-Guptill.

Memory of Birds in Time of Revolution: Essays. Breyten Breytenbach. LC 95-47982. 169p. 1996. 22.00 (*0-15-100168-5*) Harcourt.

Memory of Certain Persons. John Erskine. (American Autobiography Ser.). 439p. 1995. reprint ed. lib. bdg. 99.00 (*0-7812-8512-7*) Rprt Serv.

Memory of Childhood Trauma: A Clinician's Guide to the Literature. Susan L. Reviere. LC 96-10813. 178p. 1996. pap. text 21.00 (*1-57230-110-4*, 0104); lib. bdg. 36.95 (*1-57230-109-0*) Guilford Pubns.

Memory of Christmas Tea. Tom Hegg. LC 99-12669. (Illus.). 48p. (YA). (gr. 10 up). 1999. 12.95 (*0-931674-39-5*) Waldman Hse Pr.

Memory of Earth. Orson Scott Card. (Homecoming Saga Ser.: No. 1). 336p. 1993. mass mkt. 5.99 (*0-8125-3259-7*, Pub. by Tor Bks) St Martin.

Memory of Earth. Orson Scott Card. (Homecoming Ser.: No. 1). 1993. 11.09 (*0-606-11471-8*, Pub. by Turtleback) Demco.

Memory of Earth. deluxe limited ed. Orson Scott Card. (Homecoming Saga Ser.: No. 1). 336p. 1992. 200.00 (*0-312-85348-3*, Pub. by Tor Bks) St Martin.

***Memory of Fire.** George Foy. LC 99-40439. (Spectra Ser.). 384p. 2000. pap. 13.95 (*0-553-37930-5*, Spectra) Bantam.

Memory of France, Vol. 1. Pierre Nora. 1996. 35.00 (*0-226-59132-8*) U Ch Pr.

Memory of Hands. Reshma Baig. 216p. (YA). (gr. 9-12). 1998. pap. write for info. (*1-889720-27-5*, Pub. by Amirah Pubng) Intl Bks & Tapes.

Memory of Kin: Stories about Family by Black Writers. Intro. by Mary H. Wachington. 432p. 1990. pap. 14.95 (*0-385-24783-4*, Anchor NY) Doubleday.

***Memory of Love.** Bertrice Small. 368p. 2000. pap. 14.00 (*0-345-43434-X*) Ballantine Pub Grp.

***Memory of Old Jack.** Wendell Berry. LC PS3552.E75M4 1999. 176p. 1999. pap. text 13.50 (*1-58243-043-8*, Pub. by Counterpt DC) HarpC.

Memory of Resistance: French Opposition to the Algerian War (1954-1962) Martin Evans. 256p. 1997. 60.00 (*1-85973-922-9*, Pub. by Berg Pubs); pap. 19.50 (*1-85973-927-X*, Pub. by Berg Pubs) NYU Pr.

Memory of Snow. Sandor Csoori. Tr. by Nicholas Kolumban from HUN. (Translation Ser.). (Illus.). 72p. 1983. 22.50 (*0-915778-53-X*); 125.00 (*0-915778-54-8*); pap. 8.50 (*0-915778-52-1*) Penmaen Pr.

Memory of Snow: Poems by A. C. Greene. A. C. Greene. (American Regional Book Ser.: Vol. 5). 130p. 1999. 32.95 (*0-9651359-4-2*, 1305, Pub. by Browder Springs) Herveys Bklink.

Memory of Sound: Observations on the History of Music on Paper. Donald W. Krummel. LC 88-600272. 23p. 1988. 3.95 (*0-8444-0617-1*) Lib Congress.

***Memory of Stones: A Novel.** Mandla Langa. LC 00-22413. 375p. 2000. pap. 16.00 (*0-89410-866-2*, Three Contnts) L Rienner.

Memory of the Body: Essays on Theater & Death. Jan Kott. Tr. by Jadwiga Kosicka et al from POL. 150p. (Orig.). 1992. 39.95 (*0-8101-1019-9*) Northwestern U Pr.

Memory of the Body: Essays on Theater & Death. Jan Kott. Tr. by Jadwiga Kosicka et al from POL. 150p. (Orig.). 1992. pap. 16.95 (*0-8101-1043-1*) Northwestern U Pr.

Memory of the Christian People. Eduardo Hoornaert. 320p. 1994. pap. 30.00 (*0-86012-164-X*, Pub. by Srch Pr) St Mut.

Memory of the Christian People. Eduardo Hoornaert. Tr. by Robert R. Barr from POR. LC 88-38701. (Theology & Liberation Ser.). 318p. reprint ed. pap. 98.60 (*0-608-20197-9*, 207145600012) Bks Demand.

***Memory of the Eyes: Pilgrims to Living Saints in Christian Late Antiquity.** Georgia Frank. LC 99-56845. (Transformation of the Classical Heritage Ser.: Vol. XXX). 216p. 2000. 40.00 (*0-520-22205-9*) U CA Pr.

Memory of the Future. Floyce Alexander. 41p. 1997. 6.00 (*1-890193-04-6*) Red Dragonfly.

Memory of the Modern. Matt K. Matsuda. LC 95-30287. (Illus.). 264p. (C). 1996. pap. 21.00 (*0-19-509365-8*); text 65.00 (*0-19-509364-X*) OUP.

Memory of the World at Risk. LC 98-112384. (Archivum Ser.: Vol. XLII). xi, 239p. 1996. write for info. (*3-598-21243-7*) K G Saur Verlag.

Memory of Tiresias: Intertextuality & Cinema. M. B. Iampolskii. LC 97-25664. 285p. 1998. 48.00 (*0-520-08529-9*, Pub. by U CA Pr); pap. 22.50 (*0-520-08530-2*, Pub. by U CA Pr) Cal Prin Full Svc.

***Memory of Trade.** Patricia Spyer. LC 99-37251. 328p. 2000. pap. 19.95 (*0-8223-2441-5*) Duke.

***Memory of Trains: The Boll Weevil & Others.** Louis Decimus Rubin, Jr. LC 00-9043. (Illus.). 2000. pap. 24.95 (*1-57003-382-X*) U of SC Pr.

Memory of Trees. Perf. by Enya. 48p. 1996. pap. 16.95 (*0-7935-6474-3*) H Leonard.

Memory of Two Mondays. Arthur Miller. 1956. pap. 5.25 (*0-8222-0747-8*) Dramatists Play.

Memory of Vermont: Our Life in the Johnny Appleseed Bookshop. Margaret Hard. 288p. 1995. pap. 14.95 (*1-879923-10-6*) Booksellers Pub.

Memory of Water. Schiff. 1998. pap. 16.00 (*0-7225-3534-1*, 833608Q) Thorsons PA.

Memory of Water. Shelagh Stephenson. 1998. pap. 5.25 (*0-8222-1701-5*) Dramatists Play.

Memory of Water & Five Kinds of Silence. Shelagh Stephenson. LC 98-131207. (Modern Plays Ser.). 1997. pap. 10.95 (*0-413-71470-5*) Methn.

Memory of Whiteness: A Scientific Romance. Kim Stanley Robinson. LC 95-30043. 352p. 1996. pap. 13.95 (*0-312-86143-5*) Orb NYC.

Memory Offended: The Auschwitz Convent Controversy. Ed. by Carol A. Rittner & John K. Roth. LC 90-47333. 312p. 1991. 62.95 (*0-275-93606-6*, C3606, Praeger Pubs); pap. 22.95 (*0-275-93848-4*, B3848, Praeger Pubs) Greenwood.

Memory Pages of My Life. Fannie Andrews. (American Autobiography Ser.). 205p. 1995. reprint ed. lib. bdg. 79.00 (*0-7812-8443-0*) Rprt Serv.

Memory Palace. Colin Hamilton. LC 97-31168. (Wick Poetry Chapbook Ser.). 1998. 4.75 (*0-87338-591-8*) Kent St U Pr.

Memory Palace of Matteo Ricci. Jonathan D. Spence. (Nonfiction Ser.). 368p. 1985. pap. 14.95 (*0-14-008098-8*, Penguin Bks) Viking Penguin.

Memory Performance of Prolong Architectures. Evan Tick. (C). 1987. text 94.00 (*0-89838-254-8*) Kluwer Academic.

Memory Play. Carla Harryman. LC 94-67794. 69p. 1994. 8.50 (*1-882022-22-X*) O Bks.

Memory Power. Jonathan Hancock. (Illus.). 64p. 1997. pap. 19.95 (*0-7641-7058-9*) Barron.

Memory Power for Exams. William G. Browning. (Cliffs Test Preparation Ser.). 1983. pap. 6.95 (*0-8220-2059-9*, Cliff) IDG Bks.

Memory Power for Exams. William G. Browning. (Cliffs Test Preparation Ser.). (Illus.). 113p. (C). 1983. pap. text 5.95 (*0-8220-2020-3*, Cliff) IDG Bks.

Memory Power Plus. Fred B. Chernow. LC 97-23321. 288p. (C). 1997. text 24.95 (*0-13-242074-0*); pap. text 13.95 (*0-13-242066-X*) P-H.

Memory Problems & Alzheimers Disease. 1994. lib. bdg. 250.00 (*0-8490-5672-1*) Gordon Pr.

Memory Quest: Trauma & the Search for Personal History. Elizabeth A. Waites. LC 96-32288. 288p. 1996. 35.00 (*0-393-70234-0*) Norton.

Memory Quilt. Elizabeth M. Hulbert. LC 87-51331. (Illus.). 52p. (Orig.). (J). (ps up). 1996. pap. 6.95 (*0-932433-42-1*) Windswept Hse.

Memory Quilts: Delightful Ways to Capture Today Forever. Nancy Smith & Lynda S. Milligan. Ed. by Sharon Holmes. (Illus.). 104p. 1992. pap. 19.95 (*0-9622477-7-4*) Pssblts Denver.

Memory Quilts in the Making. 160p. 1999. pap. 19.95 (*0-8487-1872-0*) Oxmoor Hse.

Memory Resident Utilities, Interrupts & Disk Management with MS & PC DOS. Michael Hyman. 373p. (Orig.). 1986. pap. 44.95 incl. disk (*1-55851-873-8*, MIS Pr) IDG Bks.

Memory Says Yes. Margaret Randall. LC 87-73442. 80p. 1988. pap. 7.95 (*0-915306-77-8*) Curbstone.

Memory Search by a Memorist. Charles P. Thompson et al. 176p. 1993. text 39.95 (*0-8058-1236-9*) L Erlbaum Assocs.

Memory Skills. S. Reid. (Superskills Ser.). (Illus.). 48p. (YA). (gr. 6-10). 1988. pap. 5.95 (*0-7460-0162-2*); lib. bdg. 13.95 (*0-88110-305-5*) EDC.

Memory Skills in Business. Madelyn Burley-Allen. (Better Management Skills Ser.). 1990. pap. 12.95 (*0-7494-0153-2*) Kogan Page Ltd.

Memory Skills in Business: Basic Techniques for Memory Improvement. Michael G. Crisp & Madelyn Burley-Allen. LC 88-70089. (Fifty-Minute Ser.). (Illus.). 63p. (Orig.). 1988. pap. 10.95 (*0-931961-56-4*) Crisp Pubns.

Memory Slips: A Memoir of Music & Healing. Linda K. Cutting. 256p. 1998. pap. 13.00 (*0-06-092879-4*, Perennial) HarperTrade.

Memory-Soft the Air: Recollections of Life & of Service with Cabinet, Crown & Church. Ronald Harris. 1987. 39.00 (*0-946270-36-8*, Pub. by Pentland Pr) St Mut.

An Asterisk (*) at the beginning of an entry indicates that the title is appearing for the first time.

***Memory Solution: Dr. Julian Whitaker's 10-Step Program to Optimize Your Memory & Brain Function.** Julian M. Whitaker & Peggy Dace. LC 99-35379. 1999. 13.95 (*1-58333-023-2*, Avery) Penguin Putnam.

***Memory Songs.** Lydia Whrilwind Soldier. LC 99-42721. (Illus.). 40p. 1999. pap. 12.95 (*0-931170-70-2*) Ctr Western Studies.

Memory Stones: A History of Welsh-Americans in Central New York & Their Churches. Jay G. Williams, III. LC 93-27303. (Illus.). 239p. 1993. pap. 16.50 (*0-935796-43-6*) Purple Mnt Pr.

Memory Storage Patterns in Parallel Processing. Mary E. Mace. (C). 1987. text 78.00 (*0-89838-239-4*) Kluwer Academic.

Memory Stories. unabridged ed. Edward F. Keller. vi, 158p. 1997. per. 17.50 (*0-9660833-1-8*) E F Keller.

***Memory String.** Eve Bunting. LC 99-42771. (Illus.). 40p. (J). (ps-3). 2000. 15.00 (*0-395-86146-2*, Clarion Bks) HM.

Memory, Superstition & Healing: The History of Domestic Plant Medicine. Gabrielle Hatfield. 2000. 36.00 (*0-7509-1945-0*) Sutton Pub Ltd.

Memory System of the Brain. J. Delacour. LC 93-41418. (Advanced Series in Neuroscience: No. 4). 892p. 1994. text 178.00 (*981-02-1021-3*) World Scientific Pub.

Memory System of the Brain. John Z. Young. LC 85-30577. 136p. 1986. reprint ed. lib. bdg. 59.50 (*0-313-25096-0*, YOME, Greenwood Pr) Greenwood.

Memory System Remember: Everything You Need to, When You Need To. Bob Burg. 1992. pap. 12.95 (*1-55825-063-8*) Worldwide Ch God.

Memory Systems & Pipeline Processors. Harvey Cragon. (Computer Science Ser.). 592p. 1996. 70.00 (*0-86720-474-5*) Jones & Bartlett.

Memory Systems, 1994. Ed. by Daniel L. Schacter & Endel Tulving. LC 93-36582. 415p. (C). 1994. 60.00 (*0-262-19350-7*, Bradford Bks) MIT Pr.

Memory Systems of the Brain: Animal & Human Cognitive Processes. Ed. by Norman M. Weinberger et al. LC 85-24756. (Illus.). 528p. 1985. reprint ed. pap. 163.70 (*0-608-07578-7*, 205989300010) Bks Demand.

***Memory Technology, Design & Testing: Proceedings IEEE International Workshop on Memory Technology, Design & Testing, 7th, San Jose, California, 1999.** Ed. by R. Rajsuman & T. R. Wike. 131p. 1999. 100.00 (*0-7695-0259-8*) IEEE Comp Soc.

Memory Technology, Design & Testing (MTDT '98), 1998 IEEE International Workshop. IEEE Computer Society Members. 1998. pap. 105.00 (*0-8186-8494-1*) IEEE Comp Soc.

Memory Technology, Design & Testing, 1996: IEEE International Workshop On. IEEE Staff. LC 10-874852. 200p. 1996. pap. 50.00 (*0-8186-7466-0*) IEEE Comp Soc.

Memory Technology, Design & Testing, 1997: IEEE International Workshop on (MTDT '97) LC 97-202128. 150p. 1997. pap. 60.00 (*0-8186-8099-7*) IEEE Comp Soc.

***Memory Test.** William Karneges. (Illus.). 48p. 1999. pap. 4.50 (*0-9614914-5-0*) Pax Pub.

Memory Tests & Techniques: A Special Issue of Memory, Vol. 2, No. 2, 1996. Ed. by Gathercole & McCarthy. 1996. reprint ed. pap. 18.50 (*0-86377-947-6*) L Erlbaum Assocs.

Memory, the Holocaust, & French Justice: The Bousquet & Touvier Affairs. Ed. & Tr. by Richard J. Golsan. Tr. by Lucy B. Golsan. LC 95-35728. (Contemporary French Culture & Society Ser.). (Illus.). 253p. 1996. pap. 19.95 (*0-87451-741-9*) U Pr of New Eng.

***Memory Tips for the Forgetful.** Marlene Caroselli. LC 98-70097. (Illus.). 126p. 1999. pap. write for info. (*1-883553-80-6*) R Chang Assocs.

Memory Touches Memory. Weldon. 1995. per. 10.95 (*0-85449-114-7*, Pub. by Gay Mens Pr) LPC InBook.

Memory Trace: Its Formation & Its Fate. Pref. by Erich Goldmeier. (Illus.). 288p. 1982. text 59.95 (*0-89859-172-4*) L Erlbaum Assocs.

Memory Traces in the Brain. Daniel L. Alkon. (Illus.). 204p. 1987. pap. text 21.95 (*0-521-35867-1*) Cambridge U Pr.

Memory Traces in the Brain. Daniel L. Alkon. (Illus.). 208p. 1988. text 59.95 (*0-521-24735-7*) Cambridge U Pr.

Memory Trade: A Prehistory of Cyberculture. Memory Trade: A Prehistory of Cyberculture. (Illus.). 132p. 1998. pap. text 15.00 (*90-5704-181-2*, Pub. by Harvey Miller) Gordon & Breach.

Memory, Trauma Treatment, & the Law. Daniel Brown. LC 97-25902. 960p. 1998. 100.00 (*0-393-70254-5*) Norton.

Memory Tray. Deryn Rees-Jones. 1995. 14.95 (*0-614-07442-8*, Pub. by Seren Bks) Dufour.

Memory Tray. Deryn Rees-Jones et al. 64p. 1995. pap. 14.95 (*1-85411-116-7*) Dufour.

Memory Treasures - New Testament. (J). (gr. 1-2). 1998. pap. text 2.75 (*0-8100-0909-9*) Northwest Pub.

Memory Treasures - New Testament. (J). (gr. 3-4). 1998. pap. text 3.25 (*0-8100-0910-2*) Northwest Pub.

Memory Triggering Book: Using Your Memories to Enhance Your Life & Your Relationships. Robert M. Wendlinger. 208p. (Orig.). 1995. pap. 19.95 (*0-9649910-0-4*) Proust Pr.

Memory Verse Craft Games. Good Apple Staff. Date not set. pap. text 6.95 (*0-86653-764-3*) Good Apple.

Memory Verse Games for Kids: Fun with Bible Verses. Steve Miller & Becky Miller. (Take Me Through the Bible Ser.: Vol. 2). 170p. (Orig.). (J). 1997. pap. 5.99 (*1-56507-621-4*) Harvest Hse.

Memory Wars: Freud's Legacy in Dispute. Frederick C. Crews et al. 300p. 1995. 22.95 (*0-940322-04-8*) NY Rev Bks.

Memory Wars: Freud's Legacy in Dispute. Frederick C. Crews et al. LC 95-37847. 300p. 1997. pap. 12.95 (*0-940322-07-2*) NY Rev Bks.

Memory Wax. Alan Singer. 139p. 1996. 19.95 (*1-57366-014-0*); pap. text 11.95 (*1-57366-013-2*) Fiction Coll.

MemoryMinder: Personal Health Journal. rev. ed. Frances E. Wilkins. (Illus.). 224p. (Orig.). 1999. pap. 12.95 (*0-9637968-0-1*) MemoryMinder Journals.

Memory's Embrace. Linda Lael Miller. Ed. by Linda Marrow. 320p. 1991. per. 6.99 (*0-671-73769-4*) PB.

Memory's Embrace. Linda Lael Miller. 1995. mass mkt. 5.99 (*0-671-53420-3*) PB.

Memory's Fictions: A Personal History. Bienvenido N. Santos. (Illus.). 266p. (Orig.). 1993. pap. 16.50 (*971-10-0536-0*, Pub. by New Day Pub) Cellar.

Memory's Gate. Paul McCusker. LC 96-17155. (Time Twists Ser.: No. 3). 144p. (YA). 1996. pap. text 5.99 (*0-7459-3613-X*) Lion USA.

Memory's Glass. William F. Conner. LC 95-36729. (Appalachian Connection Ser.). (Illus.). 160p. 1995. pap. 12.95 (*0-936015-53-5*) Pocahontas Pr.

Memory's Menu: Poetry. Glenn McKee. LC 99-14762. 78p. 1999. pap. text 14.95 (*0-7734-3089-X*) E Mellen.

Memory's Nation: The Place of Plymouth Rock. John Seelye. LC 97-40784. (Illus.). 720p. 1998. 39.95 (*0-8078-2415-1*) U of NC Pr.

Memory's Tailor. Lawrence Rudner. Ed. by John Kessel & Susan Ketchin. LC 98-15895. 156p. 1998. 25.00 (*1-57806-090-7*) U Pr of Miss.

Memos from the Chairman. Alan C. Greenberg. LC 96-2481. (Illus.). 160p. 1996. 14.95 (*0-7611-0346-5*, 10346) Workman Pub.

Memos from the Desk of the Paper Princess. Hilary T. Kristt. 1997. 15.00 (*0-9658393-0-3*) Light Hse.

Memos in Minutes. Joseph C. Mancuso. 88p. (Orig.). 1995. pap. text 14.95 (*0-9643750-2-8*) Training Edge.

Memos of Betsie Bay: A History of Frankfort. Charles M. Anderson. (Illus.). 128p. (Orig.). (C). 1988. pap. 8.50 (*1-878526-08-1*) Pineapple MI.

Memos to My Almost Fellow-Men. Sue Shay. 100p. 1994. pap. write for info. (*0-9635226-1-2*) Kiva Pr.

Memos to the Governor: An Introduction to State Budgeting. Dall W. Forsythe. LC 96-46214. (Text & Teaching Politics, Policy, Administration Ser.). 112p. 1997. 27.95 (*0-87840-636-0*) Georgetown U Pr.

Memos to the President: A Guide Through Macroeconomics for the Busy Policymaker. Charles L. Schultze. 334p. (C). 1993. 42.95 (*0-8157-7778-7*); pap. 18.95 (*0-8157-7777-9*) Brookings.

***Memos to the President: Management Advice from the Nation's Top CEOs.** PricewaterhouseCoopers Staff. Ed. by James J. Schiro. 256p. 2000. 27.95 (*0-471-39338-X*) Wiley.

Memphis: Metropolis of the American Nile. John E. Harkins. 1982. 24.95 (*0-89781-026-0*, 5039) Am Historical Pr.

Memphis: New Visions, New Horizons. David B. Dawson & Elizabeth Lovejoy. LC 96-51739. (Urban Tapestry Ser.). 464p. 1997. 44.95 (*1-881096-38-6*) Towery Pub.

Memphis: Research, Experiences, Failures, & Successes of New Design. Barbara Radice. LC 94-60789. (Illus.). 208p. 1995. pap. 29.95 (*0-500-27377-4*, Pub. by Thames Hudson) Norton.

Memphis: The City of the White Wall. M. T. Dimick. (Illus.). 29p. 1956. pap. 5.00 (*0-318-01019-4*) U Museum Pubns.

Memphis Vol. 3, Pt. 1: Abu Rawash to Abusir. 2nd ed. Porter. (Topographical Bibliography of Ancient Egyptian Hieroglyphic Texts Ser.: Reliefs & Paintings, Vol. 3, Pt. 1). 1974. 99.00 (*0-900416-19-X*, Pub. by Aris & Phillips) David Brown.

Memphis Vol. 3, Pt. 2, Fasc. 1: Saqqara to Dahshur. Porter. (Topographical Bibliography of Ancient Egyptian Hieroglyphic Texts Ser.: Reliefs & Paintings, Vol. 3, Pt. 2). 1978. 65.00 (*0-900416-13-0*, Pub. by Aris & Phillips) David Brown.

Memphis Vol. 3, Pt. 2, Fasc. 2: Saqqara to Dahshur. Porter. (Topographical Bibliography of Ancient Egyptian Hieroglyphic Texts Ser.: Reliefs & Paintings, Vol. 3, Pt. 2). 1979. 75.00 (*0-900416-14-9*, Pub. by Aris & Phillips) David Brown.

Memphis Vol. 3, Pt. 2, Fasc. 3: Saqqara to Dahshur. B. Porter. (Topographical Bibliography of Ancient Egyptian Hieroglyphic Texts Ser.: Reliefs & Paintings, Vol. 3, Pt. 2). 1981. 85.00 (*0-900416-24-6*, Pub. by Aris & Phillips) David Brown.

Memphis Afternoons. James Conaway. 224p. 1994. reprint ed. pap. 10.00 (*0-380-72298-4*, Avon Bks) Morrow Avon.

Memphis Barbecue, Barbeque, Bar-B-Que, Bar-B-Q, B-B-Q. Carolyn S. Wells. 64p. (Orig.). 1991. pap. 5.95 (*0-925175-16-1*) Pig Out Pubns.

Memphis Beat. Larry Nager. LC 97-47305. 1998. text 23.95 (*0-312-15587-5*) St Martin.

Memphis Blues. Brett Howard. 192p. (Orig.). (J). 1990. mass mkt. 3.50 (*0-87067-356-4*, BH356) Holloway.

Memphis Cookbook. 20th ed. Junior League of Memphis, Inc. Staff. (Illus.). 259p. (Orig.). 1952. reprint ed. pap. 9.95 (*0-9604222-0-X*) Starr-Toof.

Memphis Diary of Ida B. Wells. Ed. by Miriam DeCosta-Willis. 240p. (C). 1996. pap. 15.00 (*0-8070-7065-3*) Beacon Pr.

Memphis During the Progressive Era, 1900-1917. William D. Miller. LC 58-21437. 258p. reprint ed. 80.00 (*0-608-16585-9*, 202751800055) Bks Demand.

Memphis Elvis-Style. Cindy Hazen & Mike Freeman. LC 97-2715. (Illus.). (Orig.). 1997. pap. 11.95 (*0-89587-173-4*) Blair.

***Memphis Entertainment, 2000.** (Illus.). 550p. 1999. pap. 35.00 (*1-58553-038-7*, 004A) Enter Pubns.

Memphis in the Great Depression. Roger Biles. LC 85-22575. (Illus.). 185p. 1986. reprint ed. pap. 57.40 (*0-608-07780-1*, 206786800010) Bks Demand.

***Memphis in Vintage Postcards, Tennessee.** Scott Faragher & Katherine Harrington. (Postcard History Ser.). 128p. (YA). 2000. pap. 18.99 (*0-7385-0560-9*) Arcadia Publng.

Memphis Mazes. Sarah W. Walne. 32p. (J). (gr. k-6). 1992. text 12.95 (*1-881207-00-5*) City Mazes.

Memphis Mazes: Activity Guidebook for Teachers & Parents. Sarah W. Walne. 64p. 1992. teacher ed., spiral bd. 9.95 (*1-881207-02-1*) City Mazes.

Memphis Music of Berl Olswanger. Ed. by Anna Olswanger. 82p. (Orig.). 1985. pap. 14.95 (*0-9614598-3-2*) Anna Olswanger.

Memphis, Nam, Sweden: The Story of a Black Deserter. Terry Whitmore & Richard P. Weber. LC 96-29608. 1997. 45.00 (*0-87805-983-0*) U Pr of Miss.

Memphis, Nam, Sweden: The Story of a Black Deserter. Terry Whitmore & Richard P. Weber. LC 96-29608. 1997. pap. 17.00 (*0-87805-984-9*) U Pr of Miss.

Memphis Ribs. Gerald Duff. LC 98-87928. 209p. 1999. pap. 12.95 (*0-9664520-1-1*) Salvo Pr.

Memphis Riots & Massacres: Report Submitted by E. B. Washburne; Select Committee; 39th Congress 1st Session, Report Number 101. U. S. Congress, House of Representatives Staff. LC 79-89439. (Black Heritage Library Collection). 1977. reprint ed. 32.95 (*0-8369-8673-3*) Ayer.

Memphis Riots & Massacres: Report Submitted by E. B. Washburne, 39th Congress First Session, House Report No. 101. U. S. House of Representatives Staff. LC 79-90202. (Mass Violence in America Ser.). 1973. reprint ed. 32.95 (*0-405-01316-7*) Ayer.

Memphis Since Crump: Bossism, Blacks & Civic Reformers, 1948-1968. David M. Tucker. LC 79-12211. 200p. reprint ed. pap. 62.00 (*0-8357-6916-X*, 203797500009) Bks Demand.

Memphis State Football: The Fighting Tigers. Bill Sorrels & Charles Holmes. LC 81-52630. (College Sports Bks.). (Illus.). 1981. 10.95 (*0-87397-175-2*, Strode Pubs) Circle Bk Service.

Memphis State University Law Review, 1970-1995/96, 26 vols., Set. 1970. 1185.00 (*0-8377-9113-8*, Rothman) W S Hein.

***Memphis Sun.** Jim Murphy. LC PS3563.U738M46 2000. (Wick Poetry Chapbook Ser.). 2000. pap. 4.75 (*0-87338-663-9*) Kent St U Pr.

Memphis, Tennessee. John Dougan. (Images of America Ser.). (Illus.). 128p. 1998. pap. 16.99 (*0-7524-1331-7*) Arcadia Publng.

Memphis, TN. (Streetfinder Ser.). (Illus.). 1995. pap. 14.95 (*0-528-91348-4*) Rand McNally.

Memphis, 1800-1900, 3 vols., set. Carole M. Ornelas-Struve & Fredrick L. Coulter. Ed. by Joan Hassell. LC 81-17920. (Illus.). 384p. 1982. pap., boxed set 24.95 (*0-941684-03-2*) Powers Pub.

A must for scholars & American history buffs, Memphis: 1800 - 1900 is a historical work that captures the indomitable spirit of a freewheeling century. This richly illustrated set of books traces the turbulent birth & growth of Memphis: its roots--its philosophes--its politics--its triumphs & its tragedies. From raw frontier, to the tragic Civil War years, to renewal, Memphis emerges with exciting courage & dignity. Full of information & insight, the city comes alive with an easy fluency of style & delightful glimpses of everyday life. To order your 3-volume set of Memphis: 1800 - 1900, please send a check or money order for $21.95 (plus applicable shipping & handling*) to: Powers Publishing, P O Box 172345, Memphis TN 38187-2345 *Shipping & Handling US=$2.75, Canada=$3.25, International=$4.50. Note: Bookstores, libraries & schools receive 30 discount & purchase orders accepted. www.powerspublishing.com, e-mail: info@powerspublishing.com *Publisher Paid Annotation.*

Memphis, 1800-1900, 3 Bks. in slipcase, Vol. I: Years of Challenge, 1800-1860. Carole M. Ornelas-Struve & Fredrick L. Coulter. Ed. by Joan Hassell. LC 81-17920. (Illus.). 384p. 1982. pap. 9.95 (*0-941684-00-8*) Powers Pub.

Memphis, 1800-1900, 3 Bks. in slipcase, Vol. II: Years of Crisis, 1860-1870. Carole M. Ornelas-Struve & Fredrick L. Coulter. Ed. by Joan Hassell. LC 81-17920. (Illus.). 384p. 1982. pap. 9.95 (*0-941684-01-6*) Powers Pub.

Memphis, 1800-1900, 3 Bks. in slipcase, Vol. III: Years of Courage, 1870-1900. Carole M. Ornelas-Struve & Fredrick L. Coulter. Ed. by Joan Hassell. LC 81-17920. (Illus.). 384p. 1982. pap. 9.95 (*0-941684-02-4*) Powers Pub.

Memphite Tomb: Chapel of Mose. Gaballa. 1978. 75.00 (*0-85668-088-5*, Pub. by Aris & Phillips) David Brown.

***MEMS Manufacturing Challenges.** 1999. 185.00 (*1-892568-36-5*) Smicndctr Equip.

MEMS Manufacturing Challenges: Producers Discuss Future Equipment & Materials Needs. 1998. pap. write for info. (*1-892568-08-X*) Smicndctr Equip.

***MEMS Microelectromechanical.** 120p. 1998. pap. 1995.00 (*0-471-34468-0*) Wiley.

***MEMS Reliability for Critical & Space Applications.** Ed. by Russell A. Lawton et al. 182p. 1999. pap. text 62.00 (*0-8194-3477-9*) SPIE.

Mem's the Word Mem Fox. LC 91-184405. xii, 172p. 1990. write for info. (*0-14-011743-1*) Penguin Books.

Memsahibs Abroad: Writings by Women Travellers in Nineteenth Century India. Ed. by Indira Ghose. LC 98-907627. 316p. 1999. text 29.95 (*0-19-564423-9*) OUP.

Men. Margaret Diehl. LC 88-9691. 282p. 1988. 17.95 (*0-939149-14-1*) Soho Press.

Men. Margaret Diehl. LC 88-9691. 282p. 1997. pap. 13.00 (*1-56947-095-2*) Soho Press.

Men. Alan M. Hofmeister et al. (Reading for All Learners Ser.). (Illus.). (J). pap. write for info. (*1-56861-116-1*) Swift Lrn Res.

Men: A Pictorial Archive from Nineteenth-Century Sources. Jim Harter. (Pictorial Archive Ser.). (Illus.). 128p. (Orig.). 1980. pap. 8.95 (*0-486-23952-7*) Dover.

Men: A Translation for Women. Joan Shapiro & George Hartlaub. 256p. 1993. mass mkt. 4.99 (*0-380-72004-3*, Avon Bks) Morrow Avon.

Men: An Owner's Manual. Stephanie Brush. 1985. pap. 11.00 (*0-671-60413-9*) S&S Trade.

Men! Can't Live with Them, Can't Live "With" Them!, 1. Tania Golightly. 1999. pap. 6.95 (*1-84024-052-0*, Pub. by Summers) Seven Hills Bk.

***MEN! Cry Flustered, Frustrated Females Everywhere.** large type ed. Ed. by Margaret G. Bigger. LC 00-90090. (Illus.). 50p. 2000. pap. 7.50 (*1-893597-01-6*) A Borough Bks.

Men: Move to Paradise: Find Love, Sex & Money in Tropical Getaways. Michael Dallas. LC 95-95030. (Illus.). 265p. (Orig.). 1995. pap. 24.95 (*0-9649039-0-3*) Alex & Watson.

Men: Some Assembly Required: A Woman's Guide to Understanding a Man. Chuck Snyder. 1995. pap. 10.99 (*1-56179-344-2*) Focus Family.

Men: The Sensitive Sex. Derek Bowskill & Anthea Linacre. 1977. 45.00 (*0-584-10252-6*) St Mut.

Men . . . Wake Up! Silvia Martinoli. 1993. pap. 6.95 (*0-9634014-8-3*) S Martinoli.

Men - Women. Herb Ritts. (Illus.). 208p. 1989. 65.00 (*0-944092-11-X*) Twin Palms Pub.

Men--Research on Their Attitudes, Lifestyles & Relations: Index of New Information. Marvin D. De Lore. (Illus.). 160p. Date not set. 44.50 (*0-7883-1922-1*); pap. 44.50 (*0-7883-1923-X*) ABBE Pubs Assn.

***Men Against Fire: The Problem of Battle Command.** S. L. A. Marshall. LC 00-37397. 224p. 2000. write for info. (*0-8061-3280-9*) U of Okla Pr.

Men Against Fire: The Problem of Battle Command in Future War. S. L. Marshall. 1990. 25.00 (*0-8446-4057-3*) Peter Smith.

***Men Against Myths: The Progressive Response.** Fred Greenbaum. LC 99-55225. 240p. 2000. 59.00 (*0-275-96888-X*, C6888, Praeger Pubs) Greenwood.

Men Against the Sea. Charles Nordhoff & J. Norman Hall. 20.95 (*0-89190-564-2*) Amereon Ltd.

Men Against the State: The Expositors of Individualist Anarchism in America, 1827-1908. James J. Martin. (Illus.). 1970. pap. 2.50 (*0-87926-006-8*) R Myles.

Men among the Mammoths: Victorian Science & the Discovery of Human Prehistory. A. Bowdoin Van Riper. LC 93-17006. (Science & Its Conceptual Foundations Ser.). (Illus.). 298p. 1993. pap. text 17.95 (*0-226-84992-9*) U Ch Pr.

Men among the Mammoths: Victorian Science & the Discovery of Human Prehistory. A. Bowdoin Van Riper. LC 93-17006. (Science & Its Conceptual Foundations Ser.). (Illus.). 288p. 1993. lib. bdg. 45.00 (*0-226-84991-0*) U Ch Pr.

Men & Abortion: Losses, Lessons, & Love. Arthur B. Shostak et al. LC 84-4927. 350p. 1984. 57.95 (*0-275-91747-9*, C1747, Praeger Pubs) Greenwood.

Men & Aging: A Selected, Annotated Bibliography, 32. Compiled by Edward H. Thompson, Jr. LC 95-25580. (Bibliographies & Indexes in Gerontology Ser.: Vol. 32). 256p. 1996. lib. bdg. 67.95 (*0-313-29106-3*, Greenwood Pr) Greenwood.

Men & Birds in South America, 1492 to 1900. R. Stowell Rounds. LC 89-43069. (Illus.). 204p. 1989. pap. 14.95 (*0-936609-16-8*) QED Ft Bragg.

Men & Birds of Paradise: Journeys Through Equatorial New Guinea. Alan J. Marshall. LC 75-35141. reprint ed. 37.50 (*0-404-14157-9*) AMS Pr.

Men & Books. Ed. by Earl F. Nation. (Illus.). x, 67p. 1987. reprint ed. 20.00 (*0-937543-01-2*) Sacrum Pr.

Men & Books Famous in the Law, 1921. Frederick C. Hicks. LC 93-78455. 266p. 1993. reprint ed. 75.00 (*1-56169-045-7*) Gaunt.

Men & Books Famous in the Law, 1921. Frederick C. Hicks. LC 92-70809. (Illus.). 259p. 1992. reprint ed. 50.00 (*0-9630106-2-X*) Lawbk Exchange.

Men & Cancer. Neil Priddy. 1999. pap. text 11.95 (*0-85969-793-2*) S C K Pubns.

Men & Centuries. John H. Plumb. LC 78-26300. 294p. 1979. reprint ed. lib. bdg. 52.50 (*0-313-20868-9*, PLMC, Greenwood Pr) Greenwood.

Men & Centuries of European Civilization. Louise F. Brown & George B. Carson. LC 76-134060. (Essay Index Reprint Ser.). 1977. 51.95 (*0-8369-2100-3*) Ayer.

Men & Coal. McAlister Coleman. LC 71-89725. (American Labor, from Conspiracy to Collective Bargaining Ser., No. 1). 350p. 1972. reprint ed. 23.95 (*0-405-02111-9*) Ayer.

Men & Deeds. John Buchan. LC 69-17567. (Essay Index Reprint Ser.). 1977. 20.95 (*0-8369-0065-0*) Ayer.

***Men & Depression.** Sam V. Cochran. (Illus.). 256p. 1999. 44.95 (*0-12-177540-2*) Acad Pr.

Men & Divorce. Michael F. Myers. LC 88-35101. 286p. 1989. lib. bdg. 35.00 (*0-89862-386-3*) Guilford Pubns.

Men & Events of My Time in India. Richard Temple. (C). 1993. 16.00 (*81-85557-06-3*, Pub. by Low Price) S Asia.

M

An Asterisk (*) at the beginning of an entry indicates that the title is appearing for the first time.

Men & Family Planning. Bruce Stokes. 1980. pap. write for info. (0-916468-40-2) Worldwatch Inst.

Men & Forces of Our Time. Valeriu Marcu. LC 68-29231. (Essay Index Reprint Ser.). 1977. reprint ed. 19.95 (0-8369-0678-0) Ayer.

Men & Gardens. Nan Fairbrother. LC 97-3020. (Horticulture Garden Classics Ser.). (Illus.). 288p. 1997. pap. 16.95 (1-55821-583-2, 15832) Lyons Pr.

Men & Gods in Mongolia. Henning Haslund. Tr. by Elizabeth Sprigge & Claude Napier from SWE. (Mystic Traveller Ser.). (Illus.). 358p. (Orig.). reprint ed. pap. 15.95 (0-932813-15-1) Adventures Unltd.

Men & Grief. Carol Staudacher. LC 90-63756. 240p. (Orig.). 1991. pap. 14.95 (0-934986-72-X) New Harbinger.

***Men & Heart Disease: An Atlas of Racial & Ethnic Disparities in Mortality.** Elizabeth Barnett et al. (Illus.). 2000. pap. text. write for info. (0-9665085-2-1) Prevention Ctr.

Men & Horses I Have Known. George Lambton. 320p. 1990. pap. 34.00 (0-85131-031-1, Pub. by J A Allen) St Mut.

Men & Ideas. Graham Wallas. LC 77-134150. (Essay Index Reprint Ser.). 1977. 18.95 (0-8369-2079-1) Ayer.

Men & Ideas in Economics: A Dictionary of World Economists Past & Present. Ludwig H. Mai. (Quality Paperbacks Ser.: No. 284). 270p. (Orig.). 1977. reprint ed. pap. 9.95 (0-8226-0284-9) Rowman.

M

Men & Ideas in the Sixteenth Century. Hans J. Hillerbrand. 130p. (C). 1984. reprint ed. pap. text 11.95 (0-88133-080-9) Waveland Pr.

Men & Idioms of Wall Street. rev. ed. Hickling, John, & Co. Staff. LC 88-82486. 71p. 1988. reprint ed. pap. 10.00 (0-87034-089-1) Fraser Pub Co.

Men & Institutions in American Mathematics. Ed. by J. Dalton Tarwater et al. (Graduate Studies: No. 13). 136p. (Orig.). 1976. pap. 6.00 (0-89672-023-3) Tex Tech Univ Pr.

Men & Iron: History of the New York Central Railroad. Edward Hungerford. 424p. 1993. reprint ed. lib. bdg. 99.00 (0-7812-5213-X) Rprt Serv.

Men & Iron: The History of New York Central Railroad. Edward Hungerford. LC 75-41763. (Companies & Men: Business Enterprises in America Ser.). (Illus.). 1976. reprint ed. 39.95 (0-405-08078-6) Ayer.

Men & Letters. Herbert W. Paul. LC 70-111856. (Essay Index Reprint Ser.). 1977. 21.95 (0-8369-1622-0) Ayer.

Men & Letters. Horace E. Scudder. (Notable American Authors Ser.). 1999. reprint ed. lib. bdg. 125.00 (0-7812-8890-8) Rprt Serv.

Men & Letters: Essays in Characterization & Criticism. Horace E. Scudder. LC 75-37528. (Essay Index Reprint Ser.). 1977. reprint ed. 20.95 (0-8369-2569-6) Ayer.

Men & Marriage. rev. ed. George Gilder. LC 86-9340. 240p. 1992. 19.95 (0-88289-444-7); pap. 14.95 (0-88289-946-5) Pelican.

Men & Masculinity. Ed. by Caroline Sweetman. LC 98-133319. (Focus on Gender Ser.). (Illus.). 72p. 1997. pap. 12.95 (0-85598-377-9, Pub. by Oxfam Pub) Stylus Pub VA.

Men & Masks: A Study of Moliere. Lionel Gossman. LC 63-18695. 324p. reprint ed. pap. 100.50 (0-608-06046-1, 206637800008) Bks Demand.

Men & Matters. Wilfrid P. Ward. LC 68-8503. (Essay Index Reprint Ser.). 1977. 23.95 (0-8369-0131-2) Ayer.

Men & Measures in the Law. Arthur T. Vanderbilt. (William W. Cook Foundation Lectures Ser.). xxii, 156p. 1981. reprint ed. 22.50 (0-8377-1230-0, Rothman) W S Hein.

Men & Measures of Half a Century. Hugh McCulloch. LC 77-87404. (American Scene Ser.). 1969. reprint ed. lib. bdg. 65.00 (0-306-71548-1) Da Capo.

Men & Measures on the Law. Arthur T. Vanderbilt. LC 88-61806. (Michigan Legal Publications). xxii,150,xp. 1988. reprint ed. lib. bdg. 35.00 (0-89941-662-4, 305690) W S Hein.

Men & Memories: Autobiographical Recollections & Reflections. J. R. Jayewardene. xiii, 185p. (C). 1993. text 27.50 (0-7069-6294-X, Pub. by Vikas) S Asia.

Men & Monuments. Janet Flanner. LC 73-121468. (Essay Index Reprint Ser.). 1977. 23.95 (0-8369-1876-2) Ayer.

Men & Monuments. Janet Flanner. (Quality Paperbacks Ser.). (Illus.). 328p. 1990. reprint ed. pap. 12.95 (0-306-80417-4) Da Capo.

***Men & Motors of "The Austin"** Barney Sharratt. (Illus.). 272p. 2000. 59.95 (1-85960-671-7, 130421AE, Pub. by Haynes Manuals) Motorbooks Intl.

Men & Movements in the Primitive Church: Studies in Early Non-Pauline Christianity. F. F. Bruce. (Biblical Classics Library: Vol. 13). 159p. 1995. reprint ed. mass mkt. 5.99 (0-85364-705-4, Pub. by Paternoster Pub) OM Literature.

Men & Nations. Louis J. Halle. LC 62-10889. 240p. reprint ed. pap. 74.40 (0-608-06418-1, 206663100008) Bks Demand.

Men & Not Men. Elio Vittorini. Tr. by Sarah Henry from ITA. LC 85-60665. Orig. Title: Uomini E No. 199p. (Orig.). 1987. pap. 16.95 (0-910395-14-4) Marlboro Pr.

Men & Other Strange Myths: Poems & Art. Hilary Tham. LC 94-4313. 85p. 1994. 20.00 (0-89410-775-5, Three Contnts); pap. 12.95 (0-89410-776-3, Three Contnts) L Rienner.

Men & Policies: Addresses. Elihu Root. Ed. by Robert Bacon & J. B. Scott. LC 68-22942. (Essay Index Reprint Ser.). 1977. reprint ed. 23.95 (0-8369-0832-5) Ayer.

***Men & Popular Music in Algeria: The Social Significance of RAI.** Marc Schade-Poulsen. LC 98-29603. (Modern Middle East Ser.). 264p. 1999. pap. 15.95 (0-292-77740-X) U of Tex Pr.

Men & Popular Music in Algeria: The Social Significance of Rai. Marc Schade-Poulsen. LC 98-29603. (Modern Middle East Ser.). 264p. 1999. 35.00 (0-292-77739-6) U of Tex Pr.

***Men & Power.** Ed. by Joseph A. Kuypers. LC 99-41269. 250p. 1999. 24.95 (1-57392-769-4) Prometheus Bks.

Men & Powers: A Political Retrospective. Helmut D. Schmidt. Tr. by Ruth Hein from GER. (Illus.). 410p. 1990. 24.95 (0-685-31268-2) Random.

Men & Relationships. Steven B. Borst. LC 97-154628. (Godly Man Ser.). 96p. 1996. per. 5.50 (0-570-09671-5, 20-3025) Concordia.

Men & Sex see Hombre y la Sexualidad

Men & Sex: A Case Study in "Sexual Politics" Ed. by S. Wise & L. Stanley. 100p. 1984. pap. 19.25 (0-08-031327-2, Pergamon Pr) Elsevier.

Men & Sex: Discovering Greater Love, Passion & Intimacy with Your Wife. Clifford Penner. 224p. 1997. 17.99 (0-8407-7790-6) Nelson.

Men & Sex: New Psychological Perspectives. Ronald F. Levant & Gary R. Brooks. LC 97-12813. 283p. 1997. 75.00 (0-471-16903-X) Wiley.

Men & Stress. Charmaine Saunders. 1999. pap. 13.95 (0-7322-5823-5, Pub. by HarpC) Consort Bk Sales.

Men & Supermen: The Shavian Portrait Gallery. 2nd ed. Arthur H. Nethercot. LC 65-16245. 1972. 23.95 (0-405-08815-9) Ayer.

Men & Systems. James Allen. 149p. 1997. pap. 15.00 (0-89540-326-9, SB-326) Sun Pub.

Men & Tendencies. Edward I. Watkin. LC 68-16986. (Essay Index Reprint Ser.). 1977. 20.95 (0-8369-0978-X) Ayer.

Men & the Boys. large type ed. Johnny M. Bride. (Linford Western Library). 208p. 1993. pap. 16.99 (0-7089-7314-0, Linford) Ulverscroft.

Men & the Girls. Joanna Trollope. 320p. 1994. pap. 10.95 (0-552-99492-8) Bantam.

Men & the Girls. Joanna Trollope. 1995. pap. 12.00 (0-380-72408-1, Avon Bks) Morrow Avon.

Men & the Girls. large type ed. Joanna Trollope. LC 93-40242. 388p. 1994. lib. bdg. 23.95 (0-8161-5919-X) Thorndike Pr.

Men & the Goddess: Feminine Archetypes in Western Literature. Tom Absher. 192p. (Orig.). 1990. pap. 10.95 (0-89281-268-0) Inner Tradit.

Men & the Mills: A History of the Southern Textile Industry. Mildred G. Andrews. LC 87-29653. (Illus.). 360p. 1988. 35.00 (0-86554-289-9, H259) Mercer Univ Pr.

Men & the Water of Life: Initiation & the Tempering of Men. Michael J. Meade. LC 92-56405. 464p. 1994. reprint ed. pap. 17.00 (0-06-250726-5, Pub. by Harper SF) HarpC.

Men & Their Sex. Robert L. Rowan. LC 80-25539. (Illus.). 168p. 1982. pap. 12.95 (0-8290-0446-7) Irvington.

Men & Their Work. Everett C. Hughes. LC 80-29143. 184p. 1981. reprint ed. lib. bdg. 59.75 (0-313-22791-8, HUMW, Greenwood Pr) Greenwood.

Men & Things. John A. Spender. LC 68-8496. (Essay Index Reprint Ser.). 1977. 20.95 (0-8369-0896-1) Ayer.

Men & Thought in Ancient India. R. K. Mookerji. 1996. reprint ed. 10.00 (81-208-1171-2, Pub. by Motilal Bnarsidass) S Asia.

Men & Violence: Gender, Honor & Rituals in Modern Europe & America. Pieter Spierenburg. LC 97-34278. 1997. text 47.50 (0-8142-0752-9); pap. text 18.95 (0-8142-0753-7) Ohio St U Pr.

Men & Wealth in the United States, 1850-1870. Lee Soltow. LC 74-29738. (Yale Series in Economic History). 226p. reprint ed. pap. 70.10 (0-8357-8221-2, 203389300087) Bks Demand.

Men & Whales. Richard Ellis. LC 99-17164. (Illus.). 560p. 1999. pap. 30.00 (1-55821-696-0) Lyons Pr.

Men & Woman in New Guinea. L. L. Langness. LC 98-36764. (Publications in Anthropology & Related Fields). 224p. (C). 1999. pap. text 16.95 (0-88316-594-5) Chandler & Sharp.

Men & Women. Larry Crabb. 256p. 1991. 15.99 (0-310-33830-1) Zondervan.

Men & Women: A History of Costume, Gender, & Power. Kathy Peiss & Barbara Clark Smith. (Illus.). 80p. (Orig.). 1989. pap. 6.95 (0-929847-02-4) Natl Mus Am.

Men & Women: And Other Poems. Robert Browning. Ed. by J. W. Harper. 256p. 1993. pap. 6.95 (0-460-87328-8, Everyman's Classic Lib) Tuttle Pubng.

Men & Women: Building Communication. Tina Korte & Dennis Korte. (Intersections: Small Group Ser.). 1995. pap. 5.49 (0-8066-0134-5, 15-169) Augsburg Fortress.

Men & Women: Dressing the Part. Ed. by Claudia B. Kidwell & Valerie Steele. LC 88-18259. (Illus.). 226p. (C). 1989. pap. 29.95 (0-87474-559-4) Smithsonian.

Men & Women: Enjoying the Difference. Larry Crabb. 240p. 1993. pap. 12.99 (0-310-33831-X) Zondervan.

Men & Women: How Different Are They? John Nicholson. (Illus.). 193p. 1984. pap. 14.95 (0-19-286034-8) OUP.

Men & Women: How Different Are They? 2nd ed. John Nicholson. LC 92-30066. (Illus.). 240p. 1993. pap. 16.95 (0-19-286157-3) OUP.

Men & Women: Partners at Work. G. Simmons & Deborah Weissman. LC 89-81518. (Fifty-Minute Ser.). (Illus.). 110p. (Orig.). 1990. pap. 10.95 (1-56052-009-4) Crisp Pubns.

Men & Women: Sexual Ethics in Turbulent Times. Ann B. Ulanov et al. LC 88-37002. 226p. (Orig.). 1989. pap. 10.95 (0-936384-72-7) Cowley Pubns.

Men & Women: Talking Together. Deborah Tannen & Robert Bly. 142p. 1995. pap. 16.95 incl. audio (1-879323-09-5, SH10) Sound Horizons AV.

Men & Women: The World Journey of a Sexologist. Magnus Hirschfeld. Tr. by Oliver P. Green. LC 72-9648. reprint ed. 57.50 (0-404-57458-0) AMS Pr.

Men & Women: Together & Alone. Ed. by Morty Sklar & Mary Biggs. LC 88-18333. (Illus.). 176p. 1988. 12.75 (0-930370-29-5); pap. 7.00 (0-930370-30-9) Spirit That Moves.

Men & Women: Together & Alone, Signed A-Z. limited ed. Ed. by Morty Sklar & Mary Biggs. LC 88-18333. (Illus.). 176p. 1988. 25.00 (0-930370-31-7) Spirit That Moves.

Men & Women - Women & Men: A Poetry Chapbook Collection. Ed. by Laura Smith & Larry Smith. (Midwest Writers Ser.). 224p. (Orig.). 1995. 10.95 (0-933087-35-7) Bottom Dog Pr.

Men & Women Adrift: The YMCA & the YWCA in the City. Nina Mjagkij & Margaret Spratt. LC 97-4666. 1997. text 55.00 (0-8147-5541-0); pap. text 19.50 (0-8147-5542-9) NYU Pr.

Men & Women: Enjoying the Difference see Hombres y Mujeres: Disfrutando la Diferencia

***Men & Women Equal Yet Different: A Brief Study of the Biblical Passages on Gender.** Alexander Strauch. 1999. pap. text. write for info. (0-936083-16-6) Lewis-Roth.

***Men & Women, Equal Yet Different: A Brief Study of the Biblical Passages on Gender.** Alexander Strauch. LC 99-32861. 1999. write for info. (0-936083-14-X) Lewis-Roth.

Men & Women in Biological Perspective: A Review of the Literature. Aman U. Khan. LC 84-6802. 240p. 1984. 32.95 (0-275-91438-0, C1438, Praeger Pubs) Greenwood.

Men & Women in Interaction: Reconsidering the Differences. Elizabeth Aires. 304p. 1996. pap. 19.95 (0-19-510358-0) OUP.

Men & Women in Qing China: Gender in the Red Chamber Dreams. Louise P. Edwards. LC 94-28448. (Sinica Leidensia Ser.: 31). x, 181p. 1994. 92.50 (90-04-10123-3) Brill Academic Pubs.

***Men & Women in the Fourth Gospel: Gender & Johannine Characterization.** Colleen M. Conway. LC 99-45667. (Dissertation Studies). 224p. 1999. 35.00 (0-88414-002-4, 062167) Soc Biblical Lit.

Men & Women of Christ. Neal A. Maxwell. 1991. 12.95 (0-88494-785-8) Bookcraft Inc.

Men & Women of the Corporation. 2nd ed. Rosabeth Moss Kanter. LC 93-70244. 384p. 1993. reprint ed. pap. 16.50 (0-465-04454-9, Pub. by Basic) HarpC.

Men & Women of the French Revolution. J. Mills Whitham. LC 68-20346. (Essay Index Reprint Ser.). 1977. 22.95 (0-8369-0990-9) Ayer.

Men & Women of the French Revolution. J. Mills Whitham. (Essay Index Reprint Ser.). 430p. 1982. reprint ed. lib. bdg. 19.50 (0-8290-0803-9) Irvington.

Men & Women of the New Testament. Charles H. Spurgeon. LC 96-80409. (Bible Sermon Ser.: Pulpit Legends Collection). 500p. 1997. 19.99 (0-89957-217-0) AMG Pubs.

Men & Women of the New Testament. Derek Thomas. 1998. pap. 9.99 (1-873796-72-2) Review & Herald.

Men & Women of the Old Testament. Charles H. Spurgeon. (Bible Sermon Ser.: Pulpit Legends Collection). 455p. 1995. 19.99 (0-89957-204-9) AMG Pubs.

Men & Women of the Old Testament. Charles H. Spurgeon. (World Classic Reference Library). 575p. 1995. reprint ed. 19.99 (0-529-10422-9, MWOT) World Publng.

Men & Women of the Renaissance & Reformation, 1300-1600. Thomas R. Rumsey. 487p. (Orig.). (gr. 9-12). 1981. pap. text 15.95 (0-88334-145-X) Longman.

Men & Women of the Word: 45 Meditations on Biblical Heroes of the Faith. Jaroslav J. Vajda. LC 95-8008. (Winners of the Race Ser.). 160p. 1995. pap. 8.99 (0-570-04817-6, 12-3259) Concordia.

Men & Women Together. Semel. 1999. text. write for info. (0-312-15909-9) St Martin.

Men & Women Use . . . Menus. Tina Wold & John Frost. LC 80-68806. 120p. (Orig.). 1980. pap. 5.95 (0-9604802-0-X) Frost Art.

Men & Women Writers of the 1930s: Gender, Agency & History. Janet Montefiore. LC 96-1885. 280p. (C). 1996. 90.00 (0-415-06892-4); pap. 27.99 (0-415-06893-2) Routledge.

Men & Work: An Autobiography. W. M. Citrine. LC 75-36094. (Illus.). 384p. 1976. reprint ed. lib. bdg. 38.50 (0-8371-8613-7, CIMW, Greenwood Pr) Greenwood.

Men Are a Joke. Penelope Snow. LC 97-126902. 96p. 1997. mass mkt. 5.99 (0-7860-0361-8, Pinncle Kensgtn) Kensgtn Pub Corp.

Men Are Clams, Women Are Crowbars: Understanding Your Differences & Make Them Work. David Clarke. LC 99-194420. 256p. 1998. 14.99 (1-57748-450-9) Barbour Pub.

Men Are Cruel, but Women Are Dangerous: Mary & Sinclare. Marvin N. Carr. LC 95-90909. (Illus.). 400p. (Orig.). 1996. pap. 19.95 (0-9641226-8-5) Trom Pubng.

Men Are Dogs, Women Are Cats. B. Peason. LC 98-87198. 365p. 1999. 25.00 (0-7388-0089-9); pap. 15.00 (0-7388-0090-2) Xlibris Corp.

Men Are from Cyberspace: The Single Woman's Guide to Flirting, Dating, & Finding Love. Lisa Skriloff & Jodie Gould. LC 97-4395. 208p. 1997. pap. 11.95 (0-312-17105-6) St Martin.

Men Are from Detroit, Women Are from Paris. 2nd ed. Ed. by Roz Warren. (Illus.). 112p. 1999. pap. 7.95 (1-887166-51-3, Hysteria Pubns) Sourcebks.

Men Are from Earth, Women Are from Earth: A Guide to Winning Cooperation from Your Spouse. Kenneth Wenning. LC 97-18707. (Illus.). 1998. 18.95 (0-7657-0102-2) Aronson.

***Men Are from Israel, Women Are from Moab: Insights about the Sexes from the Book of Ruth.** Norman Wakefield. 180p. 2000. pap. 10.99 (0-8308-2258-5) InterVarsity.

Men Are from Locker Rooms, Women Are from Luxury Boxes: A Woman's Survival Guide to Understanding Spectator Sports. Laurie Selwitz. LC 98-88562. (Illus.). 156p. 1998. pap. 11.95 (0-9667627-9-7) ZuMedia.

Men Are from Mars, but the Peanut Man Is from Mobile: 101 Superlative Ways to Know If You're a Mobilian. David C. Barnette. Ed. by Ashley S. Barnette. (Illus.). 105p. 1996. pap. 8.95 (1-888769-11-4) Pub One Hund One.

Men Are From Mars CD: Gray,&John, Set. John Gray. 1996. audio 18.00 (0-694-51720-8) HarperAudio.

Men Are from Mars, Women Are from Venus see Hommes viennent de Mars, les Femmes viennent de Venus (Men Are from Mars, Women Are from Venus)

Men are from Mars, Women are from Venus see Hommes Viennent de Mars, les Femmes Viennent de Venus

Men are from Mars Women are from Venus. abr. ed. John Gray. 1993. audio 12.00 (1-55994-878-7, CPN 10007, Pub. by HarperAudio) Lndmrk Audiobks.

Men Are from Mars, Women Are from Venus: A Practical Guide for Improving Communication & Getting What You Want in Your Relationships. John Gray. LC 17-3184. 304p. 1992. 25.00 (0-06-016848-X) HarperTrade.

Men Are from Mars, Women Are from Venus: A Practical Guide for Improving Communication & Getting What You Want in Your Relationships. John Gray. LC 91-58370. 256p. 1994. pap. 13.00 (0-06-092416-0, Perennial) HarperTrade.

Men Are From Mars Women Are From Venus International Edition. John Gray. 304p. 1994. pap. 14.00 (0-06-092642-2) HarpC.

***Men are From Mars, Women are From Venus Refle: Inspirations to Enrich Your RelationshipsGray,&Ph.D., John, Set.** John Gray. 1998. audio 18.00 (0-694-52147-7) HarperAudio.

***Men are From Mars, Women are From Venus Unabridged: Gray,&John.** unabridged ed. John Gray. 1998. audio 34.95 (0-694-51992-8, 877126) HarperAudio.

Men Are Just Desserts. Sonya Friedman. 320p. 1984. mass mkt. 5.99 (0-446-30338-0, Pub. by Warner Bks) Little.

Men Are Like Fish: What Every Woman Needs to Know about Catching a Man. Steve Nakamoto. LC 99-60652. (Illus.). 192p. 2000. pap. 14.95 (0-9670893-0-1, Pub. by JAVA Bks) ACCESS Pubs Network.

Men Are Like Street Cars. Graeme Lorimer & Sarah Lorimer. LC 78-122730. (Short Story Index Reprint Ser.). (Illus.). 1977. 18.95 (0-8369-3563-2) Ayer.

Men Are No Damn Good Pending Further Research: Essays on Becoming a Man. Eugene Webb. LC 95-33679. (Illus.). 185p. 1995. pap. 14.95 (0-89390-343-4) Resource Pubns.

Men Are Not Cost-Effective. June Stephenson. 474p. 1991. pap. 18.00 (0-941138-11-9) Diemer-Smith.

Men Are Pigs: Mystery Jigsaw Puzzle Thriller. Larry Zacher. (Bepuzzled Ser.). (Orig.). 1996. pap. 21.00 (1-57561-008-6, 00518MAP) Bepuzzled.

Men Are Pigs - Women Are Bitches. Jan King & Jerry King. Ed. by Cliff Carle. 112p. 1996. mass mkt. 5.95 (0-918259-93-2) CCC Pubns.

Men Are Pigs & Deserve to Die. Sonya Steinem. 136p. (Orig.). 1989. pap. 7.50 (0-929256-00-X) Thundblt Pr NV.

Men Are Pigs & Deserve to Die. Sonya Steinem. (Illus.). 117p. (Orig.). 1991. pap. 9.95 (0-929256-20-4) Thundblt Pr NV.

Men Are Sluts: For the Man Who Wants to Know How, for the Woman Who Wants to Know Why. Spanky. (Illus.). 90p. (Orig.). 1994. pap. 14.95 (1-884973-11-6) SM Pubng.

Men Are Such Babies. Mike Dowdall. (Illus.). 64p. 1997. 16.95 (0-8362-5034-6) Andrews & McMeel.

Men Are Such Fools. Faith Baldwin. 1976. reprint ed. lib. bdg. 23.95 (0-88411-611-5) Amereon Ltd.

***Men Are Visual, Women Are Verbal: A Book about Relationships.** Frank J. Smith. LC 99-56276. 2000. write for info. (1-58141-013-1) Rivercross Pub.

Men Around Churchill. Rene Kraus. LC 79-142653. (Essay Index Reprint Ser.). 1977. 23.95 (0-8369-2056-2) Ayer.

Men Around Hitler: The Nazi Elite & Its Collaborators. Alfred D. Low. 250p. 1996. 45.00 (0-88033-348-0, 451, Pub. by East Eur Monographs) Col U Pr.

Men As Managers, Managers As Men: Critical Perspectives on Men, Masculinities & Management. Ed. by David C. Collinson & Jeff Hearn. 288p. 1996. 75.00 (0-8039-8928-8) Sage.

Men As Managers, Managers As Men: Critical Perspectives on Men, Masculinities & Management. Ed. by David C. Collinson & Jeff Hearn. LC 96-70153. 1996. pap. text 26.95 (0-8039-8929-6) Sage.

***Men As Women, Women As Men: Changing Gender in Native American Cultures.** Sabine Lang. Tr. by John L. Vantine from GER. LC 97-34759. xvii, 398p. (C). 1998. pap. 19.95 (0-292-74701-2, LANMEP) U of Tex Pr.

Men As Women, Women As Men: Changing Gender in Native American Cultures. Sabine Long. Tr. by John L. Vantine from GER. LC 97-34759. 432p. (C). 1998. 50.00 (0-292-74700-4, LANMEN) U of Tex Pr.

Men Astutely Trained: A History of the Jesuits in the American Century. Peter McDonough. 618p. 1991. text 29.95 (0-02-920527-1) Free Pr.

Men at Arms. David Nicolle & Raffaele Ruggeri. (Italian Invasion Ser.: No. 309). (Illus.). 48p. 1997. 12.95 (1-85532-692-2, Pub. by Ospry) Stackpole.

Men at Arms. Terry Pratchett. 1995. mass mkt. 6.99 (0-552-14028-7) Bantam.

Men at Arms. Evelyn Waugh. 1999. audio 16.95 (0-14-086465-2) Viking Penguin.

Men at Arms. large type ed. Evelyn Waugh. 359p. 1998. reprint ed. 19.95 (1-85089-313-6, Pub. by ISIS Lrg Prnt) Transaction Pubs.

***Men at Arms: A Novel.** Evelyn Waugh. (Sword of Honor Ser.). 352p. 2000. pap. 13.95 (0-316-92628-0, Back Bay) Little.

An Asterisk (*) at the beginning of an entry indicates that the title is appearing for the first time.

*Men at Arms: The Play. Terry Pratchett. 2000. pap. 12.95 (0-552-14432-0, Pub. by Transworld Publishers Ltd) Trafalgar.

Men At Arms MM: Men At Arms MM. Terry Pratchett. LC 99-43960. 384p. 1997. mass mkt. 6.50 (0-06-109219-3, HarperPrism) HarpC.

Men at Arnhem. Geoffrey Powell. 1998. 29.95 (0-85052-626-4, Pub. by Leo Cooper) Combined Pub.

Men at Leisure. Bruce Frederickson. (Godly Man Bible Study). 1997. pap. text 4.99 (0-570-09688-X, 20-3028) Concordia.

Men at Mid-Life: Steering Through the Detours. James A. Harnish. LC 92-46043. 144p. 1993. pap. 10.00 (0-687-24774-8) Dimen for Liv.

Men at Mid-Life: Steering Through the Detours. James A. Harnish. 1996. pap. 10.00 (0-687-06155-5) Dimen for Liv.

Men at Midlife. Michael P. Farrell & Stanley Rosenberg. LC 81-3624. 256p. 1981. pap. 21.95 (0-86569-062-6, Auburn Hse) Greenwood.

Men at the Crossroads: Beyond Traditional Roles & Modern Options. Jack Balswick. LC 92-20599. 180p. (Orig.). 1992. pap. 10.99 (0-8308-1385-3, 1385) InterVarsity.

Men at the Office: Working Women Talk about Working with Men. Ed. by Cathy Feldman. (Working Women Ser.). (Illus.). 131p. (Orig.). 1994. pap. 9.95 (1-883423-02-3) Blue Pt Bks.

Men at War. Robert B. Smith. LC 96-37375. 416p. 1997. pap. 14.00 (0-380-78544-7, Avon Bks) Morrow Avon.

Men at War: Politics, Technology & Innovation in the Twentieth Century. Ed. by Timothy Travers & Christon Archer. LC 81-80545. 234p. (C). 1982. 32.95 (0-913750-21-2); pap. text 24.95 (0-913750-46-8) Transaction Pubs.

Men at War, 1914-1918: National Sentiment & Trench Journalism in France During the First World War. Stephane Audoin-Rouzeau. (Reports from the French Trenches). (Illus.). 207p. 1992. pap. 17.00 (0-85496-333-2, Pub. by Berg Pubs) NYU Pr.

Men at Work. LC 97-154629. (Godly Man Ser.). 96p. (Orig.). 1996. per. 5.50 (0-570-09672-3, 20-3027) Concordia.

Men at Work. (Orig.). 1992. mass mkt. 4.95 (1-56333-027-X, Badboy) Masquerade.

Men at Work. Lewis W. Hine. LC 76-50337. (Illus.). 63p. 1977. pap. text 7.95 (0-486-23475-4) Dover.

Men at Work. William Witherup. Ed. by Dale Boyer. LC 89-80857. (Ahsahta Press Modern & Contemporary Poets of the West Ser.). 60p. (Orig.). 1990. pap. 6.95 (0-916272-39-7) Ahsahta Pr.

Men at Work. Charles A. Oakley. Ed. by Leon Stein. LC 77-70522. (Illus.). 1977. reprint ed. lib. bdg. 33.95 (0-405-10190-2) Ayer.

Men at Work: An Action Guide to Masculine Healing. Chris L. Frey. Ed. by Mary J. Graham. LC 97-70958. xvi, 228p. 1997. pap. 15.95 (1-888461-03-9) Islewest Pub.

Men at Work: Costas,&Bob, Set. abr. ed. George F. Will. 1991. audio 15.95 (1-55994-357-2, CPN 2188) HarperAudio.

Men at Work: Labourers & Building Craftsmen in the Towns of Northern England, 1450-1750. Donald Woodward. (Studies in Population, Economy & Society in Past Time: No. 26). (Illus.). 333p. (C). 1995. text 59.95 (0-521-47246-6) Cambridge U Pr.

Men at Work: Life Beyond the Office. James E. Dittes. LC 96-21398. 120p. (Orig.). 1996. pap. 14.95 (0-664-25481-0) Westminster John Knox.

Men at Work: Photographic Modern Men & Machines. Lewis W. Hine. 1990. 23.75 (0-8446-5585-6) Peter Smith.

Men at Work: The Craft of Baseball. George F. Will. 224p. 1990. text 19.95 (0-02-628470-7) Macmillan.

Men at Work: The Craft of Baseball. large type ed. George F. Will. (General Ser.). 534p. 1991. lib. bdg. 23.95 (0-8161-5150-4, G K Hall Lrg Type) Mac Lib Ref.

Men at Work: The Craft of Baseball. George F. Will. LC 90-55518. (Illus.). 384p. 1991. reprint ed. pap. 14.00 (0-06-097372-2, Perennial) HarperTrade.

Men at Work MacKenzie's Lady. Dallas Schulze. (Men at Work Ser.). 1998. per. 4.50 (0-373-81014-8) Harlequin Bks.

Men Before Ten A.M. Pam Houston. LC 96-26207. (Illus.). 144p. 1996. pap. 24.95 (1-885223-19-6) Beyond Words Pub.

Men Behind Bars: Sexual Exploitation in Prison. Wayne S. Wooden & Jay Parker. LC 82-12242. 264p. 1982. 19.95 (0-306-41074-5, Plenum Trade) Perseus Pubng.

Men Behind Bars: Sexual Exploitation in Prison. Wayne S. Wooden & Jay Parker. (Quality Paperbacks Ser.). 275p. 1984. reprint ed. pap. 9.95 (0-306-80230-9) Da Capo.

Men Behind the Medals: The Actions of 21 Aviators During World War Two. Graham Pitchfork. (Illus.). 224p. 1998. 49.95 (0-85052-586-1, Pub. by Leo Cooper) Trans-Atl Phila.

Men Behind the Trident: SEAL Team One in Vietnam. Dennis J. Cummings. LC 96-52042. (Special Warfare Ser.). (Illus.). 288p. 1997. 29.95 (1-55750-139-4) Naval Inst Pr.

Men Behind the Trident: Seal Team One in Vietnam. Dennis J. Cummings. 272p. 1998. reprint ed. mass mkt. 6.50 (0-553-57928-2) Bantam.

Men Beyond the Law: A Western Trio. large type ed. Max Brand. LC 96-53882. 250p. 1997. 17.95 (0-7862-0742-6) Thorndike Pr.

Men Beyond the Law: A Western Trio. large type ed. Max Brand. LC 98-5428. 1998. 22.95 (0-7862-0765-5) Thorndike Pr.

Men, Books, & Mountains. Leslie Stephen. LC 78-1861. 247p. 1978. reprint ed. lib. bdg. 65.00 (0-313-20262-1, STMB, Greenwood Pr) Greenwood.

Men Born Equal. Harry Robinson. LC 74-22806. 384p. 1983. reprint ed. 45.00 (0-404-58462-4) AMS Pr.

Men! By Women. Exley Giftbooks Editors. 1998. 6.00 (1-86187-069-8) Exley Giftbooks.

Men by Women. Ed. by Janet Todd. LC 80-20702. (Women & Literature Ser.: Vol. 2). 270p. 1982. 39.95 (0-8419-0732-3); pap. 21.50 (0-8419-0733-1) Holmes & Meier.

Men Call Me Lucky: Mark Twain & the Pennsylvania. Edgar M. Branch. (Keepsakes Ser.). (Illus.). 87p. (Orig.). 1985. pap. text 20.00 (0-918761-01-8) Miami U Pubns.

Men Called Him Master. Elwyn A. Smith. 1987. pap. 8.99 (0-88019-210-0) Schmul Pub Co.

Men Called Jim: A Collection of Personal Portraits. Lynn Weyand. (Illus.). 48p. 1998. pap. 8.95 (1-888803-08-8) Lenswrk.

*Men Coping with Grief. Ed. by Dale Lund. LC 99-87525. (Death, Value & Meaning Ser.). 300p. 2000. 58.00 (0-89503-211-2) Baywood Pub.

*Men Coping with Grief. Dale A. Lund. LC 99-87525. (Death, Value & Meaning Ser.). 300p. 2000. pap. 34.94 (0-89503-212-0) Baywood Pub.

Men Cry in the Dark. Ed. by Michael Baisden. LC 97-72737. 305p. 1997. 22.95 (0-9643675-0-5) Legacy Publng.

Men Cry in the Dark. Michael Baisden. (Illus.). 305p. 1999. pap. 13.95 (0-9643675-1-3) Legacy Publng.

Men Defined: Nudes. Christopher Schwarz. (Illus.). 144p. 1998. 45.00 (3-908161-44-4) Abbeville Pr.

Men Doing Feminism. Ed. by Tom Digby. LC 97-39468. 359p. (C). 1997. pap. 23.99 (0-415-91626-7) Routledge.

Men Doing Feminism. Ed. by Tom Digby. LC 97-39468. 359p. (C). 1998. 80.00 (0-415-91625-9) Routledge.

Men down West. Kenneth Lincoln. LC 96-34543. 250p. (Orig.). 1997. pap. 15.95 (0-88496-412-4) Capra Pr.

*Men Engaging Feminisms: Pro-Feminism, Backlashes & Schooling. Bob Lingard & Peter Douglas. LC 98-41548. (Feminist Education Thinking Ser.). 192p. 1999. pap. 28.95 (0-335-19817-1) OpUniv Pr.

Men Engaging Feminisms: Pro-Feminism, Backlashes & Schooling. Bob Lingard & Peter Douglas. LC 98-41548. 9p. 1999. 95.00 (0-335-19818-X) Taylor & Francis.

Men Exposed: A Heartless Little Book. Pat Ross. LC 99-10530. 64p. 1999. pap. 8.00 (0-684-85218-7) S&S Trade.

Men First: Last & Always. Langley Kirksite. LC 82-90991. 440p. 1983. 27.95 (0-911821-00-7) Kirk Pub.

*Men for All Seasons: Stories of Sports & Sex. Ed. by Jesse Grant. LC 00-36218. (Illus.). 304p. 2000. pap. 12.95 (1-55583-562-7, Pub. by Alyson Pubns) Consort Bk Sales.

Men for the Mountains. Sid Marty. 270p. 1996. pap. text 18.99 (0-7710-5851-9) McCland & Stewart.

*Men for the Mountains. Sid Marty. 272p. 2001. pap. 18.95 (0-7710-5672-9) McCland & Stewart.

Men Freeing Men: Exploding the Myth of the Traditional Male. Ed. by Francis Baumli. LC 85-21487. 352p. (Orig.). 1985. pap. 16.95 (0-9615480-0-2) New Atlantis.

Men from Ariel. Donald A. Wollheim. LC 81-86242. (Boskone Bks.). (Illus.). 116p. 1982. 13.00 (0-915368-19-6) New Eng SF Assoc.

Men from the Boys. William J. Mann. 448p. 1998. pap. 12.95 (0-452-27856-2, Plume) Dutton Plume.

Men from the Boys. William J. Mann. 1997. 22.95 (0-614-27940-2) NAL.

Men from the Boys: Rites of Passage in Male America. Ray Raphael. LC 88-17369. 246p. 1988. reprint ed. pap. 76.30 (0-608-00483-9, 206130200007) Bks Demand.

Men Ghost Africn Wri Ser. Kofi Aidoo. (Longman African Writers Ser.). (C). 1995. pap. 14.86 (0-582-22871-9) Addison-Wesley.

Men Giving Care: Reflections of Husbands & Sons. Phyllis B. Harris & Joyce Bichler. LC 96-48449. (Issues in Aging Ser.: No. 7). 240p. 1997. text. write for info. (0-8153-1792-1) Garland.

Men Giving Money, Women Yelling: Intersecting Stories. Alice Mattison. LC 96-47658. 244p. 1997. 22.00 (0-688-15109-4, Wm Morrow) Morrow Avon.

Men Giving Money, Women Yelling: Intersecting Stories. Alice Mattison. 256p. 1998. reprint ed. pap. 13.00 (0-688-16106-5, Wm Morrow) Morrow Avon.

Men God Challenged. Dwight Lyman Moody. LC 98-195260. (Moddy Classics Ser.). 1998. mass mkt. 4.99 (0-8024-5433-X) Moody.

Men Have It Maid. Shirley Herring & Gina Holman. 50p. 1991. 7.95 (0-685-52303-9) Men Have It Maid.

Men Have It Maid. Holman. pap. 5.95 (0-9631683-0-4) Men Have It Maid.

Men Healing Shame: An Anthology. Ed. by Roy U. Shenk & John Everingham. (Focus on Men Ser.: vol. 7). (Illus.). 352p. 1995. 44.95 (0-8261-8800-1) Springer Pub.

Men I Have Chosen for Fathers: Literary & Philosophical Passages. Marion Montgomery. LC 90-10854. 264p. 1990. text 32.50 (0-8262-0740-5) U of Mo Pr.

Men I Killed see Three Generals on War

Men I'd Like to Meet. Cliff Schimmels. 170p. 1997. pap. 9.99 (0-87148-603-2) Pathway Pr.

Men, Ideas, & Tanks: British Military Thought & Armoured Forces, 1903-1939. J.P. Harris. 320p. 1996. text 29.95 (0-7190-4814-1, Pub. by Manchester Univ Pr) St Martin.

Men, Ideas & Tanks: British Military Thought & Armoured Forces, 1903-1939. J.P. Harris. 320p. 1996. text 79.95 (0-7190-3762-X, Pub. by Manchester Univ Pr) St Martin.

Men in a Developing Society: Geographic & Social Mobility in Monterrey, Mexico. Jorge Balan et al. LC 72-6282. (Latin American Monographs: No. 30). 406p. reprint ed. pap. 125.90 (0-8357-7747-2, 203610400002) Bks Demand.

Men in America. Leigh Heinneman. (American Scene Ser.). (Illus.). 96p. (C). 1994. pap. 27.50 (1-881616-19-3) Dist Art Pubs.

Men in Arms. 6th ed. Richard A. Preston. (C). Date not set. text. write for info. (0-15-507857-7) Harcourt Coll Pubs.

Men in Arms: A History of Warfare & Its Interrelationships with Western Society. 5th ed. Richard A. Preston et al. (C). 1991. pap. text 37.00 (0-03-033428-4, Pub. by Harcourt Coll Pubs) Harcourt.

Men in Balance: The Mid-Life Male & the Healthy Psyche. John Lee & Lee. 142p. 1995. 16.95 incl. audio (1-879323-13-3) Sound Horizons AV.

Men in Black. John Harvey. LC 95-4585. (Illus.). 280p. 1995. 29.95 (0-226-31879-6) U Ch Pr.

Men in Black. John Harvey. 280p. 1996. pap. 18.95 (0-226-31883-4) U Ch Pr.

Men in Black. Steve Perry. 240p. 1997. mass mkt. 5.99 (0-553-57756-5) Bantam.

Men in Black. Scott Spencer. 352p. 1998. pap. 12.95 (0-425-16606-6) Berkley Pub.

Men in Black. Michael Teitelbaum. (J). (gr. 3-7). 1997. pap. 3.50 (0-8167-4432-7) Troll Communs.

*Men in Black. large type ed. Steve Perry & Ed Solomon. (G. K. Hall Science Fiction Ser.). 2000. 25.95 (0-7838-8986-0, G K Hall Lrg Type) Mac Lib Ref.

Men in Black. Scott Spencer. 352p. 1996. reprint ed. mass mkt. 6.99 (0-425-15379-7) Berkley Pub.

Men in Black: Digest. Scholastic, Inc. Staff. (Illus.). (J). 1997. pap. text 3.99 (0-590-34418-8) Scholastic Inc.

Men in Black: The Green Saliva Blues. Dean Wesley Smith. 288p. 1999. mass mkt. 5.99 (0-553-57768-9) Bantam.

Men in Black: The Script & the Story Behind the Film. Barry Sonnenfeld et al. LC 97-20038. (Illus.). 1997. pap. 16.95 (1-55704-323-X, Pub. by Newmarket) Norton.

Men in Black: The Script & the Story Behind the Film. Barry Sonnenfeld et al. LC 97-20038. (Illus.). 1997. 27.50 (1-55704-312-4, Pub. by Newmarket) Norton.

Men in Black: 8 X 8. Scholastic, Inc. Staff. (J). 1997. pap. text 3.50 (0-590-34416-1) Scholastic Inc.

Men in Blue: Conversations with Umpires. Larry R. Gerlach. LC 93-42576. (Illus.). xvi, 294p. 1994. pap. 14.95 (0-8032-7045-3, Bison Books) U of Nebr Pr.

Men in Business: Essays on the Historical Role of the Entrepreneur. Ed. by William Miller. LC 78-21159. 389p. 1979. reprint ed. lib. bdg. 35.00 (0-313-20867-0, MIME, Greenwood Pr) Greenwood.

Men in Crisis see Mosaic of Despair: Human Breakdowns in Prison

Men in Dark Times. Hannah Arendt. LC 68-24381. 288p. 1970. reprint ed. pap. 15.00 (0-15-658890-0, Harvest Bks) Harcourt.

Men in Darkness. James Hanley. LC 78-121559. (Short Story Index Reprint Ser.). 1977. 21.95 (0-8369-3516-0) Ayer.

Men in Dual-Career Families: Current Realities & Future Prospects. Lucia A. Gilbert et al. 208p. (C). 1985. text 39.95 (0-89859-560-6) L Erlbaum Assocs.

Men in Families. 1994. write for info. (92-806-3166-7) U N I C E.

Men in Families. Thomas Rogers. (Godly Man Bible Study). 96p. 1997. pap. text 5.50 (0-570-09690-1, 20-3029) Concordia.

Men in Families. Ed. by Robert A. Lewis & Robert E. Salt. LC 85-14330. (Sage Focus Editions Ser.: No. 76). 288p. 1986. reprint ed. pap. 89.30 (0-608-01178-9, 205947600001) Bks Demand.

Men in Families: When Do They Get Involved? What Difference Does It Make? Ed. by Alan Booth & Ann C. Crouter. LC 97-12617. 275p. 1998. 89.95 (0-8058-2539-8) L Erlbaum Assocs.

Men in Feminism. Ed. by Alice A. Jardine & Paul Smith. 300p. 1987. 35.00 (0-416-01591-3) Routledge.

Men in Feminism. Ed. by Alice A. Jardine & Paul Smith. 304p. (C). 1987. pap. 17.99 (0-415-90251-7) Routledge.

Men in Groups. 2nd ed. Lionel Tiger. 288p. 1998. reprint ed. pap. 16.95 (0-7145-2899-4) M Boyars Pubs.

Men in Groups: Insights, Interventions & Psychoeducational Work. Michael P. Andronico. LC 95-20968. (Measurement & Instrumentation in Psychology Ser.). 435p. 1995. pap. 29.95 (1-55798-618-5) Am Psychol.

Men in Leadership: One Minute Bible. Bob Briner. LC 99-15732. (One Minute Bible Ser.). 1999. 14.99 (0-8054-9153-8) Broadman.

Men in Love. Nancy Friday. 544p. 1998. pap. 11.95 (0-385-33342-0) Dell.

Men in Love: Masculinity & Sexuality in the Eighteenth Century George E. Haggerty. LC 98-47095. (Between Men - Between Women Ser.). 10p. 1999. 16.50 (0-231-11043-X) Col U Pr.

*Men in Love: Masculinity & Sexuality in the Eighteenth Century George E. Haggerty. (Between Men - Between Women Ser.). 11p. 1999. 49.50 (0-231-11042-1) Col U Pr.

Men in Mid-Life Crisis. Jim Conway. LC 78-67098. 322p. 1976. pap. 9.99 (0-89191-145-6, LifeJourney) Chariot Victor.

Men in Midlife Crisis. rev. ed. Jim Conway. LC 97-29004. 336p. 1997. 11.99 (1-56476-698-5, Victor Bks) Chariot Victor.

Men in My Life. Olga J. Robertson. Ed. by M. B. Steele. (Illus.). 160p. (Orig.). 1992. pap. 6.95 (0-939497-30-1) Promise Pub.

*Men in My Life: A Therapeutic Autobiography. Michael Zonta. LC 99-91452. 2000. 25.00 (0-7388-0804-0); pap. 18.00 (0-7388-0805-9) Xlibris Corp.

Men in My Life, & Other More or Less True Recollections of Kinship: Essays. James D. Houston. LC 93-32683. (Discovery Ser.). 176p. 1994. 12.00 (1-55597-206-3) Graywolf.

Men in Our Time. Audax & Vyvyon Adams. LC 70-99680. (Essay Index Reprint Ser.). 1977. 23.95 (0-8369-1389-2) Ayer.

Men in Petticoats: A Selection of Letters from Victorian Newspapers. Peter Farrer. 1993. pap. 40.00 (0-9512385-0-7, Pub. by Karn Pubns) St Mut.

Men in Prison. Victor Serge. Tr. by Richard Greeman from FRE.Tr. of Les/Hommes Dans la Prison. 260p. 1981. pap. 3.95 (0-904613-50-X) Writers & Readers.

Men in Rebellion: Higher Governmental Leaders & the Coming of the American Revolution. James K. Martin. LC 72-14142. 271p. reprint ed. pap. 84.10 (0-7837-5675-5, 205910200005) Bks Demand.

Men in Sheepskin Coats. Pierre Berton. (Canada Moves West Ser.). (Illus.). 88p. (J). (gr. 6-9). pap. 4.99 (0-7710-1438-4) McCland & Stewart.

Men in the Bible: Examples to Live by. Donald Charles. 1999. pap. text 14.99 (1-56322-067-9) Hensley Pub.

Men in the Middle. Martin Nabhan. (Basketball Heroes Ser.). 48p. (J). (gr. 3-8). 1992. lib. bdg. 15.95 (0-86593-158-5) Rourke Corp.

Men in the Mirror: Men's Fashion, Masculinity & Consumer Fashion. Tim Edwards. LC 97-177128. 150p. 1997. pap. text 17.95 (0-304-33790-0) Continuum.

*Men in the off Hours. Anne Carson. 192p. 2000. 24.00 (0-375-40803-7) Knopf.

Men in the Sun: A Beach Companion. David Leddick. (Illus.). 96p. 1999. pap. 16.95 (0-7893-0266-7, Pub. by Universe) St Martin.

*Men in the Sun & Other Palestinian Stories. Ghassan Kanafani. Tr. by Hilary Kilpatrick. LC 98-46345. (ARA.). 117p. 1998. pap. 12.00 (0-89410-857-3) L Rienner.

Men in the Sunlight of the Word. James Cumming. 1979. pap. 5.99 (0-88019-080-9) Schmul Pub Co.

Men in Their Books. William M. Calder, III. Ed. by John P. Harris & R. Scott Smith. (Studies in the Modern History of Classical Scholarship). (GER.). xii, 324p. 1998. write for info. (3-487-10686-8) G Olms Pubs.

Men in Therapy: The Challenge of Change. Jo Ann Allen et al. (Family Therapy Ser.). 284p. 1991. reprint ed. pap. text 18.95 (0-89862-485-1) Guilford Pubns.

Men in Transition: Theory & Therapy. Ed. by Kenneth Solomon & Norman B. Levy. LC 82-15134. 518p. 1982. 79.50 (0-306-40976-3, Plenum Trade) Perseus Pubng.

Men in War. Adolf A. Latzko. LC 71-116961. (Short Story Index Reprint Ser.). 1977. 20.95 (0-8369-3465-2) Ayer.

Men in White Apparel: Revelations about Death & the Life after Death. Ann R. Colton. LC 68-58. 202p. 1961. 12.95 (0-917187-10-5) A R Colton Fnd.

Men in White Coats. Claude Serre. 1987. pap. 5.95 (0-317-56790-X) PB.

Men I've Loved. Tom Bianchi. 1998. 49.95 (3-925443-81-9) Janvid Pubs.

Men Just Don't Understand: A Womans Dating Dictionary. Nancy Linn-Desmond. LC 95-22289. (Illus.). 160p. 1995. pap. 8.95 (0-8065-1666-6, Citadel Pr) Carol Pub Group.

Men Like Gods & the Dream see Works of H. G. Wells

Men Like Rats. Robert Chilson. 224p. (Orig.). 1989. mass mkt. 3.95 (0-445-20763-9, Pub. by Warner Bks) Little.

Men Like That: A Southern Queer History. John Howard. LC 99-24363. 366p. 1999. 27.50 (0-226-35471-7) U Ch Pr.

Men Like Trees Walking. Robert Di Pasquale. LC 97-68993. 192p. 1998. 23.50 (0-88739-149-4); pap. 13.95 (0-88739-167-2) Creat Arts Bk.

Men Like Us: Ordinary Men, Extraordinary God. Paul H. Heidebrecht & Ted Scheuermann. (Fisherman Bible Studyguide Ser.). 64p. (Orig.). 1990. pap. text 4.99 (0-87788-544-3, H Shaw Pubs) Waterbrook Pr.

*Men Like Us: The GMHC Complete Guide to Gay Men's Sexual, Physical & Emotional Well-Being. Daniel Wolfe. LC 99-28583. 496p. 2000. 39.95 (0-345-41496-9, Ballantine); pap. 24.95 (0-345-41495-0, Ballantine) Ballantine Pub Grp.

Men Like Women Who Like Themselves: And Other Secrets That the Smartest Women Know. Steven Carter. 272p. 1997. pap. 11.95 (0-440-50615-8) Dell.

*Men Love Football/Women Love Foreplay: And Other Crazy Comparisons. Ian Cohen et al. (Illus.). 96p. 2000. pap. text 6.99 (1-57644-114-8) CCC Pubns.

Men Loving Men: A Gay Sex Guide & Consciousness Book. 2nd ed. Mitch Walker. (Illus.). 160p. (Orig.). 1997. pap. 15.95 (0-917342-52-6) Gay Sunshine.

Men, Machines, & Modern Times. Elting E. Morison. 1968. pap. text 14.50 (0-262-63018-4) MIT Pr.

Men Made Easy: How to Get What You Want from Your Man. Kara Oh. Ed. by Duane Unkefer & Martha Whitt. LC 98-96649. 192p. 1999. pap. 15.95 (0-9667875-9-5) Avambre.

Men, Maids & Mustard-Pot: A Collection of Tales. Gilbert Frankau. LC 70-163025. (Short Story Index Reprint Ser.). 1977. reprint ed. 23.95 (0-8369-3939-5) Ayer.

Men, Makeup & Monsters. Anthony Timpone. LC 96-8578. (Illus.). 256p. 1996. pap. 19.95 (0-312-14678-7) St Martin.

Men, Management, & Morality: Toward a New Organizational Ethic. Robert T. Golembiewski. 325p. (Orig.). 1988. pap. 21.95 (0-88738-743-8) Transaction Pubs.

Men, Martians & Machines. Eric Frank Russell. 1993. reprint ed. lib. bdg. 18.95 (0-89968-360-6, Lghtyr Pr) Buccaneer Bks.

Men, Martyrs & Mountebanks. Arthur B. Baxter. LC 73-104992. (Essay Index Reprint Ser.). 1977. 23.95 (0-8369-1446-5) Ayer.

M

An Asterisk (*) at the beginning of an entry indicates that the title is appearing for the first time.

Men, Masculinities & Gender in Welfare. Jennie Popay et al. LC 97-23326. (Illus.). 368p. (C). 1998. 85.00 (*0-415-11970-7*); pap. 25.99 (*0-415-11971-5*) Routledge.

Men, Masculinities & Social Theory. Jeff Hearn & David H. Morgan. (Critical Studies on Men & Masculinities: No. 1). 224p. (C). 1990. pap. text 19.95 (*0-04-445657-3*) Routledge.

Men, Masculinities & Social Welfare. Pringle. LC 95-9566. 1995. 65.00 (*1-85728-401-1*, Pub. by UCL Pr Ltd); pap. write for info. (*1-85728-402-X*, Pub. by UCL Pr Ltd) Taylor & Francis.

Men, Masculinity & the Media. Ed. by Steve Craig. (Research on Men & Masculinities Ser.: Vol. 2). (Illus.). 280p. 1992. 58.00 (*0-8039-4162-5*) Sage.

Men, Masculinity & the Media, No. 2. Ed. by Steve Craig. (Research on Men & Masculinities Ser.: Vol. 2). (Illus.). 280p. 1992. pap. 26.00 (*0-8039-4163-3*) Sage.

Men, Medicine & Water: The Building of the Los Angeles Aqueduct, 1908-1913: A Physicians Recollections. Raymond G. Taylor. Ed. by Doyce B. Nunis, Jr. (Illus.). 202p. 1982. 45.00 (*0-87093-179-2*) Dawsons.

Men Mentoring Men: A Men's Discipleship Course. Daryl Donovan. 222p. 1998. pap. 29.95 (*0-7880-1184-7*) CSS OH.

***Men Mentoring Men - Again: Men's Discipleship Course.** Daryl G. Donovan. 122p. 2000. pap. 19.95 (*0-7880-1594-X*) CSS OH.

Men, Monsters & the Modern Universe. Wil Tirion & Lovi. 1989. 24.95 (*0-943396-24-7*) Willmann-Bell.

***Men My Mother Dated: And Other Mostly True Tales.** Brett Leveridge. LC 99-55381. 192p. 2000. 19.95 (*0-375-50400-1*) Villard Books.

Men near the Top: Filling Key Posts in the Federal Service. John J. Corson & R. S. Paul. LC 66-17010. (Committee for Economic Development, CED Supplementary Papers: No. 20). 208p. reprint ed. pap. 64.50 (*0-608-30045-4*, 202051000018) Bks Demand.

Men Need Space. Judyth Hill. LC 96-30940. 72p. (Orig.). 1996. pap. 12.00 (*0-9644196-3-7*) Sherman Asher Pub.

Men, 1950-1985. Joan Liffring-Zug. Ed. by John Zug & Dorothy Crum. LC 86-63007. (Illus.). 64p. 1986. pap. 20.95 (*0-941016-38-2*) Penfield.

Men of Achievement. 12th ed. (Illus.). 1000p. 1987. 170.00 (*0-900332-91-3*, Pub. by Melrose) Taylor & Francis.

Men of Achievement - Inventors (1893) Philip G. Hubert, Jr. 316p. 1998. reprint ed. pap. 24.95 (*0-7661-0532-6*) Kessinger Pub.

Men of Achievement, 1994-1995. 16th ed. 619p. 1995. 195.00 (*0-948875-46-1*, Pub. by Melrose) Intl Pubns Serv.

Men of Achievement, 1996-1997. 17th ed. 619p. 1996. text 195.00 (*0-948875-27-5*, Pub. by Melrose) Taylor & Francis.

Men of Achievement, 1993-1994. 15th ed. (Illus.). 837p. 1993. 199.00 (*0-948875-75-5*, Pub. by Melrose) Taylor & Francis.

Men of Achievement, 1990. 14th ed. 1990. 175.00 (*0-685-31921-0*, Pub. by Melrose) Taylor & Francis.

Men of Action: A History of the U. S. Life Saving Service on the Pacific Coast. Ernest L. Osborne & Victor West. LC 80-69563. (Illus.). 150p. (Orig.). 1981. pap. 10.00 (*0-932368-05-0*) Bandon Hist.

Men of Albemarle. Inglis Fletcher. 500p. 1976. reprint ed. lib. bdg. 31.95 (*0-89244-004-X*, Queens House) Amereon Ltd.

Men of Albemarle. Inglis Fletcher. 1990. reprint ed. lib. bdg. 27.95 (*0-89968-505-6*) Buccaneer Bks.

Men of Blood: Murder in Everyday Life. Elliott Leyton. 237p. 1998. text 30.00 (*0-7881-5923-2*) DIANE Pub.

Men of Blood: Murder in Everyday Life. Elliott Leyton. (Illus.). 264p. 1996. 29.99 (*0-7710-5310-X*) McCland & Stewart.

Men of Blood: Murder in Everyday Life. Elliott Leyton. 264p. 1997. pap. write for info. (*0-7710-5306-1*) McCland & Stewart.

Men of Brewster Place. Gloria Naylor. 1998. 26.00 (*0-8050-5482-0*) H Holt & Co.

Men of Brewster Place. Gloria Naylor. LC 97-45987. 173p. (J). 1998. 22.45 (*0-7868-6421-4*, Pub. by Hyperion) Time Warner.

***Men of Brewster Place.** Gloria Naylor. LC 99-18709. 1999. 25.95 (*1-56895-712-2*) Wheeler Pub.

Men of Brewster Place: A Novel. Gloria Naylor. 192p. 1999. pap. 11.95 (*0-7868-8405-3*, Pub. by Disney Pr) Time Warner.

Men of Business. William O. Stoddard. LC 72-3490. (Essay Index Reprint Ser.). 1977. reprint ed. 31.95 (*0-8369-2927-6*) Ayer.

Men of Chaos. Hermann Rauschning. LC 71-167405. (Essay Index Reprint Ser.). 1977. reprint ed. 23.95 (*0-8369-2471-1*) Ayer.

Men of Character: Daniel, Samuel. Zondervan Publishing Staff. 1996. pap. write for info. (*0-310-96532-2*) Zondervan.

Men of Color: A Context for Service to Homosexually Active Men. Ed. by John F. Longres. LC 96-35141. (Journal of Gay & Lesbian Social Services: Vol. 5, Nos. 2/3). 174p. (C). 1996. 39.95 (*1-56024-803-3*, Haworth Pastrl) Haworth Pr.

Men of Color: A Context for Service to Homosexually Active Men. Ed. by John F. Longres. LC 96-35141. (Journal of Gay & Lesbian Social Services Ser.: Vol. 5, Nos. 2/3). 174p. (C). 1996. pap. 19.95 (*1-56023-083-5*, Harrington Park) Haworth Pr.

Men of Color: African Americans in the Civil War. (Illus.). 232p. 1996. pap. 17.95 (*1-57747-010-9*) Thomas Publications.

Men of Color: An Essay on the Black Male Couple. Vega Studios Staff. LC 89-50895. 80p. 1989. pap. text 10.00 (*1-880729-00-8*) Vega Pr.

***Men of Color: Fashion, History, & Fundamentals.** Lloyd Boston. (Illus.). 256p. 2000. pap. 25.00 (*1-57965-167-4*, 85167) Artisan.

Men of Color: Fashion, History, Fundamentals. Lloyd Boston. LC 98-22189. (Illus.). 256p. 1998. 35.00 (*1-57965-112-7*, 85112) Artisan.

Men of Color at the Battle of Monmouth, June 28, 1778: The Role of African Americans & Native Americans at Monmouth. Richard Walling. (Illus.). 40p. 1994. pap. text 4.95 (*0-944413-29-3*) Longstreet Hse.

Men of Conviction. Henry B. Washburn. LC 74-134152. (Essay Index Reprint Ser.). 1977. 20.95 (*0-8369-2081-3*) Ayer.

Men of Death. Terry Balcombe. 136p. 1998. pap. 16.00 (*0-8059-4283-1*) Dorrance.

Men of Earth. Bernice Brown. LC 70-122692. (Short Story Index Reprint Ser.). 1977. 20.95 (*0-8369-3525-X*) Ayer.

Men of Earth. Russell Lord. Ed. by Dan C. McCurry & Richard E. Rubenstein. LC 74-30642. (American Farmers & the Rise of Agribusiness Ser.). 1975. reprint ed. 33.95 (*0-405-06812-3*) Ayer.

Men of Europe. Andre Simone. LC 78-156717. (Essay Index Reprint Ser.). 1977. reprint ed. 18.95 (*0-8369-2862-8*) Ayer.

Men of Faith: Francis & Edith Schaeffer. Louis G. Parkhurst. 16p. 1996. mass mkt. 4.99 (*1-55661-843-3*) Bethany Hse.

Men of Fort Foster: Enlisted Uniforms, Equipments & Artifacts of the United States Armed Forces 1835-1842. A. M. DeQuesada, Jr. (Illus.). 96p. (Orig.). 1996. pap. 14.95 (*1-877704-25-3*) Pioneer Pr.

Men of Gambier Bay. Edwin P. Hoyt. 296p. 1981. pap. 3.50 (*0-380-55806-8*, Avon Bks) Morrow Avon.

Men of God: Men for Others: Interview with Fr. Peter H. Kolvenbach, General of the Jesuits. Renzo Giacomelli. 167p. (C). 1990. 49.00 (*0-85439-343-9*, Pub. by St Paul Pubns) St Mut.

Men of God, Men for Others: An Interview with Peter H. Kolvenbach. Renzo Giacomelli. 203p. (Orig.). 1990. pap. 9.95 (*0-8189-0600-6*) Alba.

Men of Good Character: A History of the Sheet Metal Workers Union. Brake. (C). 1985. text 49.50 (*0-85315-580-1*, Pub. by Lawrence & Wishart) NYU Pr.

Men of Habit: The Franciscan Ideal in Action. Bernard Palmer. 198p. 1995. pap. 21.95 (*1-85311-092-2*, 850, Pub. by Canterbury Press Norwich) Morehouse Pub.

***Men of Hellship: World War II Last Untold Story** Joel Millman. 2002. pap. 13.95 (*0-7868-8495-9*, Pub. by Disney Pr) Time Warner.

Men of Honor: Thirty-Eight Highly Decorated Marines of World War II, Korea & Vietnam. Kenneth N. Jordan. LC 96-72152. 320p. 1997. 29.95 (*0-7643-0247-7*) Schiffer.

Men of Honour: A Social & Cultural History of the Duel. Ute Frevert. Tr. by Anthony Williams from GER. 310p. (C). 1995. 70.95 (*0-7456-1197-4*) Blackwell Pubs.

Men of Ideas. Lewis A. Coser. LC 97-19975. 1997. per. 14.00 (*0-684-83328-X*) S&S Trade.

Men of Integrity. Christianity Today Inc., Staff. LC 99-38049. 375p. 1999. pap. 14.99 (*0-8499-3774-4*) Word Pub.

Men of Iron. Earle Hitchner. (Troll Illustrated Classics). 1990. 10.15 (*0-606-01906-5*, Pub. by Turtleback) Demco.

Men of Iron. Howard Pyle. (Airmont Classics Ser.). (Illus.). (J). (gr. 6 up). 1965. mass mkt. 3.95 (*0-8049-0093-0*, CL-93) Airmont.

Men of Iron. Howard Pyle. 25.95 (*0-8488-1131-3*) Amereon Ltd.

Men of Iron. Howard Pyle. 220p. (YA). 1993. pap. 6.49 (*0-89084-694-4*, 070466) Bob Jones Univ.

Men of Iron. Howard Pyle. LC 89-33926. (Illustrated Classics Ser.). (Illus.). 48p. (J). (gr. 3-6). 1990. pap. 5.95 (*0-8167-1872-5*) Troll Communs.

Men of Iron. Howard Pyle. (Illus.). (J). 1965. 9.30 (*0-606-17899-6*) Turtleback.

Men of Kent. Elizabeth Gibson. 256p. 1989. 12.95 (*0-310-32220-0*, 12328) Zondervan.

Men of Kent: A Historical Novel. Elizabeth Gibson. 288p. 1990. pap. 9.99 (*0-310-32221-9*) Zondervan.

Men of Learning in Europe at the End of the Middle Ages. Jacques Verger. Tr. by Lisa Neal. LC 00-26031.Tr. of Gens de Savoir en Europe. (FRE.). 240p. 2000. pap. 22.00 (*0-268-03451-6*, Pub. by U of Notre Dame Pr) Chicago Distribution Ctr.

Men of Letters. Dixon Scott. (BCL1-PR English Literature Ser.). 313p. 1992. reprint ed. lib. bdg. 89.00 (*0-7812-7055-3*) Rprt Serv.

Men of Letters. Dixon Scott. 1971. reprint ed. 19.00 (*0-403-01198-1*) Scholarly.

Men of Letters & the English Public in the 18th Century, 1660-1744. Alexandre Beljame. 1988. reprint ed. lib. bdg. 69.00 (*0-7812-0367-8*) Rprt Serv.

Men of Letters & the English Public in the 18th Century, 1660-1744: Dryden, Addison, Pope. Alexandre Beljame. Ed. by Bonamy Dobree. Tr. by E. O. Lormier. LC 71-159815. 1971. reprint ed. 89.00 (*0-403-03645-3*) Scholarly.

Men of Letters, Writing Lives: Masculinity & Literary Auto Biography in the Late-Victorian Period. Trev L. Broughton. LC 98-30505. 1999. 90.00 (*0-415-08211-0*); pap. 29.99 (*0-415-08212-9*) Routledge.

Men of Maize. Miguel Angel Asturias. Tr. by Gerald Martin. (Latin American Literature Ser.). 504p. (C). 1993. pap. 19.95 (*0-8229-5514-8*) U of Pittsburgh Pr.

Men of Maize. Lam Kam Chuen. 1975. 10.00 (*0-385-28644-9*) Doubleday.

Men of Mammoth Forest. Floyd L. Otter. (Illus.). 169p. 1995. reprint ed. 21.95 (*0-9614459-1-2*) Otter Veterinary.

Men of Mark: Eminent, Progressive & Rising. William J. Simmons. LC 68-29017. (American Negro: His History & Literature. Series 1). 1974. reprint ed. 82.95 (*0-405-01836-3*) Ayer.

Men of Mark: The Washburn Brothers of Maine. Theodore A. Webb. (Illus.). 23p. (Orig.). 1985. pap. 3.00 (*0-317-91174-0*) UUHS.

***Men of Mark & Representative Citizens of Harrisonburg & Rockingham County, Virginia: Portraits & Biographies of Men & Women.** John W. Wayland. 451p. 1999. reprint ed. pap. 36.50 (*0-8063-4834-8*) Clearfield Co.

Men of Mark in Georgia: A Complete & Elaborate History of the State from Its Settlement to the Present Time, Vols. 1-7. Ed. by William J. Northen. Incl. Vol. 1. LC 74-2193. 1974. 30.00 (*0-87152-176-8*); Vol. 3. LC 74-2193. 1974. 30.00 (*0-87152-178-4*); Vol. 4. LC 74-2193. 1974. 30.00 (*0-87152-179-2*); Vol. 5. LC 74-2193. 1974. 30.00 (*0-87152-180-6*); Vol. 6. LC 74-2193. 1974. 30.00 (*0-87152-181-4*); Vol. 7. LC 74-2193. 1974. 30.00 (*0-87152-182-2*); LC 74-2193. (Illus.). 3952p. 1974. reprint ed. 197.75 (*0-87152-331-0*) Reprint.

Men of Maryknoll. James G. Keller & Meyer Berger. LC 78-142650. (Essay Index Reprint Ser.). 1977. reprint ed. 20.95 (*0-8369-2775-3*) Ayer.

Men of Matadequin, Three Hundred Years from New Kent County, Virginia: Sourcebook for Related Lines, Banks, Blackwell, Burnett, Durvin, Gaulding, Goodman, Lipscomb, McGhee, Parsley, Slaughter, Weisiger, Wood, Zall. June B. Evans. LC 84-70618. (Illus.). 198p. 1984. 26.25 (*0-9611114-1-0*) Bryn Ffyliaid.

Men of Mathematics. Eric T. Bell. 608p. 1986. pap. 17.00 (*0-671-62818-6*, Touchstone) S&S Trade Pap.

Men of Men. Wilbur Smith. 569p. Date not set. 33.95 (*0-8488-2395-8*) Amereon Ltd.

Men of Men. Wilbur Smith. 1986. mass mkt. 3.95 (*0-449-44241-1*) Fawcett.

Men of Menlo: Transformation of an American Seminary. James P. Gaffey. (Melville Studies in Church History: Vol. III). 150p. (Orig.). (C). 1992. lib. bdg. 39.00 (*0-8191-8514-0*) U Pr of Amer.

Men of Metals: An Exciting Career Among the Pathfinders of Modern Metallurgy. Samuel L. Hoyt. LC 78-31521. 319p. reprint ed. pap. 98.90 (*0-608-15997-2*, 203306900083) Bks Demand.

Men of Mexico. James A. Magner. LC 68-55849. (Essay Index Reprint Ser.). 1977. 44.95 (*0-8369-0666-7*) Ayer.

Men of Mt. Rushmore. Whitt Brantley. (Illus.). 36p. 1997. pap. text 4.75 (*1-893916-10-3*, 2004) Project Pr.

Men of Ness. Eric Linklater. (C). 1986. 50.00 (*0-907618-03-0*, Pub. by Orkney Pr) St Mut.

Men of 1918. F. J. Hodges. 240p. (C). 1989. pap. 30.00 (*0-7223-2232-1*, Pub. by A H S Ltd) St Mut.

Men of Nineteen Fourteen: T. S. Eliot & Early Modernism. Erik Svarny. 280p. 1989. pap. 34.95 (*0-335-15078-0*) Taylor & Francis.

Men of No Property: Irish Radicals & Popular Politics in the Late Eighteenth Century. Jim Smyth. (Studies in Modern History). 266p. 1998. pap. 19.95 (*0-312-21339-5*) St Martin.

Men of Oflag 64: August 1943-January 1945. Clarence R. Meltesen & Herbert L. Garris. LC 97-216462. 146p. 1997. pap. 20.00 (*0-9627005-2-5*) C R Meltesen.

Men of Our Time: An Anthology of Male Poetry in Contemporary America. Ed. by Fred Moramarco & Al Zolynas. LC 91-31462. 472p. 1992. 45.00 (*0-8203-1404-8*); pap. 19.95 (*0-8203-1430-7*) U of Ga Pr.

Men of Patriotism, Courage & Enterprise: Fort Meigs in the War of 1812. Larry L. Nelson. (Illus.). 174p. 1998. reprint ed. pap. 16.00 (*0-7884-0728-7*, N151) Heritage Bk.

Men of Popular Music. David Ewen. LC 72-6818. (Essay Index Reprint Ser.). 1977. reprint ed. 23.95 (*0-8369-7263-5*) Ayer.

Men of Popular Music. David Ewen. (Essay Index Reprint Ser.). 215p. 1982. reprint ed. lib. bdg. 20.00 (*0-8290-0811-X*) Irvington.

Men of Power: Abraham Lincoln, Leo Tolstoy, John Burroughs, Graham Taylor, Vol. 4. Fred Eastman. LC 74-128236. (Essay Index Reprint Ser.). 1977. 20.95 (*0-8369-1994-7*) Ayer.

Men of Power: Benjamin Franklin, Ralph Waldo Emerson, George Fox, Charles Darwin, Vol. 3. Fred Eastman. LC 74-128236. (Essay Index Reprint Ser.). 1977. 20.95 (*0-8369-1993-9*) Ayer.

Men of Power: Francis of Assisi, Leonardo Da Vinci, Oliver Cromwell, John Milton, Vol. 2. Fred Eastman. LC 74-128236. (Essay Index Reprint Ser.). 1977. 20.95 (*0-8369-1992-0*) Ayer.

Men of Power: Nicolai Lenin, Mahatma Gandhi, Edward Livingston Trudeau, Robert Louis Stevenson, Vol. 5. Fred Eastman. LC 74-128236. (Essay Index Reprint Ser.). 1977. 20.95 (*0-8369-1995-5*) Ayer.

Men of Power: Thomas Jefferson, Charles Dickens, Matthew Arnold, Louis Pasteur, Vol. 1. Fred Eastman. LC 74-128236. (Essay Index Reprint Ser.). 1977. 20.95 (*0-8369-1991-2*) Ayer.

Men of Pride County: The Outsider. Rosalyn West. (Men of Pride County Ser.). 384p. 1998. mass mkt. 5.99 (*0-380-79580-9*, Avon Bks) Morrow Avon.

Men of Pride County: The Pretender. Rosalyn West. (Men of Pride County Ser.). 1999. mass mkt. 5.99 (*0-380-80302-X*, Avon Bks) Morrow Avon.

Men of Pride County: The Rebel. Rosalyn West. 384p. 1998. mass mkt. 5.99 (*0-380-80301-1*, Avon Bks) Morrow Avon.

Men of Property: The Very Wealthy in Britain since the Industrial Revolution. W. D. Rubinstein. LC 80-54836. (Illus.). 261p. reprint ed. pap. 81.00 (*0-8357-7950-5*, 205702500002) Bks Demand.

Men of Property & Intelligence: The Scottish Electoral System Prior to 1884. Ed. by Michael Dyer. 176p. 1990. pap. 33.00 (*1-898218-22-6*) St Mut.

Men of Respect: A Social History of the Sicilian Mafia. Raimondo Catanzaro. 256p. 1992. 24.95 (*0-02-905325-0*) Free Pr.

Men of Science in America: The Story of American Science Told Through the Lives & Achievements of Twenty Outstanding Men from Earliest Colonial Times to the Present Day. rev. ed. Bernard Jaffe. Ed. by I. Bernard Cohen. LC 79-7968. (Three Centuries of Science in America Ser.). (Illus.). 1980. reprint ed. lib. bdg. 68.95 (*0-405-12551-8*) Ayer.

Men of Science, Men of God. rev. ed. Henry M. Morris. LC 82-70271. (Illus.). 107p. (YA). (gr. 7 up). 1988. pap. 7.95 (*0-89051-080-6*) Master Bks.

***Men of Secession & Civil War, 1859-1861.** James L. Abrahamson. LC 99-89807. (American Crisis Ser.: No. 1). (Illus.). 208p. 2000. 55.00 (*0-8420-2818-8*); pap. 17.95 (*0-8420-2819-6*) Scholarly Res Inc.

***Men of Spirit, Men of Sports.** Wally Carew. LC 99-67279. 212p. 2000. pap. 14.95 (*1-929039-00-X*) Ambasdr Bks.

***Men of Star Trek Internet Guide.** Talis Pelucir. 50p. 2000. pap. 10.00 (*1-883573-30-0*, Lightning Rod) Pride & Imprints.

***Men of Steel: SS Panzer Corps in the Ardennes & on the Eastern Front, 1944-45.** Michael Reynolds. (Illus.). 336p. 1999. write for info. (*1-885119-66-6*) Sarpedon.

***Men of Steel: 1st Panzer Corps 1944-45: The Ardennes & Eastern Front.** Ed. by Michael Reynolds. 336p. 1999. 80.00 (*1-86227-051-1*, Pub. by Spellmnt Pubs) St Mut.

Men of Steel Discipline: The Official Oral History of Black Pioneers in the Martial Arts. William Hinton & D'Arcy Rahming. Ed. by Jenifer H. Baarman. LC 94-78600. 154p. (Orig.). 1995. pap. 19.95 (*0-9627898-9-5*) Mdrn Bu-Jutsu.

***Men of Stone.** Gayle Friesen. (Illus.). 216p. (YA). (gr. 6-12). 2000. 16.95 (*1-55074-781-9*, Pub. by Kids Can Press) Genl Dist Srvs.

Men of Subtle Craft. Roy Lewis. 192p. 1988. 13.95 (*0-312-81789-4*) St Martin.

***Men of Sugar Mountain: Two Hearts.** Vivian Leiber. (Zebra Bouquet Ser.: Vol. 49). 256p. 2000. pap. 3.99 (*0-8217-6623-6*, Zebra Kensgtn) Kensgtn Pub Corp.

Men of Summer. Kathleen Eagle et al. 1996. per. 4.99 (*0-373-48319-8*, 1-48319-7) Harlequin Bks.

Men of Summer. Ed. by Harlequin Books Staff. (Romance Digest Ser.: Vol. 82743). 1998. mass mkt. 3.50 (*0-373-82743-1*, 1-82743-5) Harlequin Bks.

***Men of Thailand: Thailand's Culture & Gay Subculture for Travelers.** 7th ed. E. G. Allyn. Ed. by Samorn Chaiyana. (Illus.). 524p. 1999. pap. 23.95 (*0-942777-30-1*) Floating Lotus.

Men of the Battle of Britian. Ken Wynn. (C). 1987. 150.00 (*0-947893-15-6*, Pub. by Gliddon Bks) St Mut.

Men of the Bible: God's Word for the Biblically-Inept. D. Larry Miller. Ed. by Larry Richards. (God's Word for the Biblically-Inept Ser.: Vol. 5). (Illus.). 352p. 2000. pap. 16.95 (*1-892016-07-9*) Starburst.

Men of the Bible: Joshua, Gideon. 1998. pap. 7.99 (*0-88486-214-3*) Arrowood Pr.

Men of the Burma Road. Chiang Yee. (Illus.). (J). (gr. 4-6). 8.50 (*0-685-20604-1*) Transatl Arts.

Men of the California Bear Flag Revolt & Their Heritage. Barbara R. Warner. LC 96-14833. (Illus.). 560p. 1996. 42.50 (*0-87062-259-5*) A H Clark.

Men of the Cloth & the Social-Cultural Fabric of the Norwegian Ethnic Community in North Dakota. Duane R. Lindberg. Ed. by Francesco Cordasco. LC 80-877. (American Ethnic Groups Ser.). 1981. lib. bdg. 42.95 (*0-405-13438-X*) Ayer.

Men of the First French Republic: Political Alignments in the National Convention of 1792. Alison Patrick. LC 72-4018. 425p. reprint ed. pap. 131.80 (*0-8357-4329-2*, 203712900007) Bks Demand.

Men of the Hills. Henry Treece. LC 58-5448. (Illus.). (J). (gr. 6-9). 1958. 26.95 (*0-87599-115-7*) S G Phillips.

Men of the Menkar: United States Coast Guard World War Two Naval Exploits. Niels P. Thomsen. (Journey of an Impatient Heart Ser.: Vol. 2). (Illus.). 500p. 1999. pap. 25.00 (*0-9662745-1-2*) Von Buchholdt.

***Men of the Moss-Hags.** S. R. Crockett. 252p. 2000. pap. 9.95 (*0-594-00030-0*) Eightn Hundrd.

Men of the Mountains. Jesse Stuart. LC 79-11419. 352p. 1979. reprint ed. pap. 18.00 (*0-8131-0143-3*) U Pr of Ky.

Men of the Old Stone Age: Palaeolithic & Mesolithic. Henri Breuil & Raymond Lantier. Tr. by B. B. Rafter. LC 79-16777. (Illus.). 272p. 1980. reprint ed. lib. bdg. 38.50 (*0-313-21289-9*, BRMO, Greenwood Pr) Greenwood.

Men of the Old Stone Age, Their Environment, Life & Art. Henry F. Osborn. LC 78-72705. (Illus.). reprint ed. 47.00 (*0-404-18276-3*) AMS Pr.

Men of the Open Range & Other Poems. Mike Logan. LC 93-72958. (Illus.). 80p. (Orig.). 1993. pap. 9.95 (*1-56044-247-6*) Falcon Pub Inc.

Men of the Outposts: The Romance of the Modern Christian Movement. Herbert Welch. LC 69-17594. (Essay Index Reprint Ser.). 1977. 18.95 (*0-8369-1162-8*) Ayer.

Men of the Pacific Street Social Club Cook Italian: Home-Style Recipes And Unforgettable Stories. Gerard Renny. LC 98-31047. (Illus.). 160p. 1999. 23.00 (*0-688-15617-7*, Wm Morrow) Morrow Avon.

Men of the Sea. Robert A. Carl. (Illus.). 325p. (Orig.). 1993. pap. 10.95 (*0-9637332-0-6*) R Carl.

An Asterisk (*) at the beginning of an entry indicates that the title is appearing for the first time.

Men of the 704: The Illustrated & Pictorial History of the 704th Tank Destroyer Battalion in World War II. Richard R. Buchanan. Ed. by Richard D. Wissocik et al. LC 98-38703. (Joe & Henny Heisel Ser.: Vol. 6). (Illus.). 114p. 1998. 30.00 (*1-885851-12-X*) St Vincent Coll.

Men of the Steel Rails: Workers on the Atchison, Topeka & Santa Fe Railroad, 1869-1900. James H. Ducker. LC 82-17541. 244p. reprint ed. pap. 75.70 (*0-7837-1839-X*, 204204000001) Bks Demand.

Men of the Twentieth: The Story of the 20th Aero Squadron. Cy Martin. 127p. 1974. pap. text 37.95 (*0-89126-006-4*) MA-AH Pub.

Men of Tom of Finland. 1997. pap. 10.00 (*1-879055-01-5*) Tom Finland.

Men of Tomorrow. Ed. by Thomas H. Johnson & Allan V. Heely. LC 70-167371. (Essay Index Reprint Ser.). 1977. reprint ed. 20.95 (*0-8369-2460-6*) Ayer.

***Men of Truth.** Sidney O. Krasnoff. 2000. 23.95 (*0-9672357-3-1*) O Frederick Inc.

Men of Turmoil. LC 71-99711. (Essay Index Reprint Ser.). 1977. 26.95 (*0-8369-1421-X*) Ayer.

***Men of Uncertainty: The Social Organization of Day Laborers in Contemporary Japan.** Tom Gill. LC 00-39478. (C). 2000. pap. text 22.95 (*0-7914-4828-2*) State U NY Pr.

***Men of Uncertainty: The Social Organization of Day Laborers in Contemporary Japan.** Tom Gill. LC 00-39478. (C). 2001. text 68.50 (*0-7914-4827-4*) State U NY Pr.

Men of Viet Nam: A Traveler's Guide to Gay Viet Nam. Douglas Thompson. LC 98-220301. (Illus.). 160p. (Orig.). 1998. pap. 16.95 (*0-942777-24-7*) Floating Lotus.

Men of Vision: Anglo-Jewry's Aid to Victims of the Nazi Regime, 1933-1945. Amy Z. Gottlieb. 224p. 1998. 35.00 (*0-297-84230-7*, Pub. by Weidenfeld & Nicolson) Trafalgar.

Men of War, vol. 8. William R. Forstchen. (Lost Regiment Ser.). 320p. 1999. mass mkt. 6.99 (*0-451-45770-6*, ROC) NAL.

Men-of-War: Life in Nelson's Navy. Patrick O'Brian. 1996. text 23.00 (*0-07-048222-5*) McGraw.

Men-of-War: Life in Nelson's Navy. Patrick O'Brian. LC 95-2297. (Illus.). 96p. 1995. 23.00 (*0-393-03858-0*) Norton.

Men of Wealth. John T. Flynn. LC 79-142629. (Essay Index Reprint Ser.). 1977. 30.95 (*0-8369-2047-3*) Ayer.

Men of Yesterday: A Social History of the Western Districts of Victoria 1834-1890. Margaret Kiddle. 592p. 1996. 39.95 (*0-522-84676-9*, Pub. by Melbourne Univ Pr) Paul & Co Pubs.

Men on a Moor. Paul Van Vlissingen. 70p. 1987. 21.00 (*0-7223-2112-0*, Pub. by A H S Ltd) St Mut.

Men on Divorce. Penny Kaganoff. 1998. pap. 12.00 (*0-15-600547-6*) Harcourt.

Men on Divorce: Conversations with Ex-Husbands. Ellie Wymard. LC 94-17584. 208p. (Orig.). 1994. pap. 12.00 (*1-56170-096-7*, 159) Hay House.

Men on Divorce: The Other Side of the Story. Ed. by Penny Kaganoff & Susan Spano. 1997. 22.00 (*0-15-100115-4*, Harvest Bks) Harcourt.

Men on Men: Best New Gay Fiction. George Stambolian. LC 86-12856. 384p. 1986. pap. 13.95 (*0-452-25882-0*, Plume) Dutton Plume.

Men on Men Five: Best New Gay Fiction. Ed. by David Bergman. 352p. 1994. pap. 13.95 (*0-452-27244-0*, Plume) Dutton Plume.

Men on Men 7: Best New Gay Fiction. David Bergman. LC 98-19321. 368p. 1998. pap. 13.95 (*0-452-27734-5*, Plume) Dutton Plume.

Men on Men 6: Best New Gay Fiction. Ed. by David Bergman. 352p. 1996. pap. 12.95 (*0-452-27708-6*, Plume) Dutton Plume.

Men on Men 3: Best New Gay Fiction. George Stambolian. 1990. pap. 10.95 (*0-525-26514-7*, Dutt) Dutton Plume.

Men on the Moon: Collected Short Stories. Simon J. Ortiz. LC 98-58145. 216p. 1999. pap. 17.95 (*0-8165-1930-7*) U of Ariz Pr.

Men on the Moon: Collected Short Stories. Simon J. Ortiz. LC 98-58145. Vol. 37. 216p. 1999. 35.00 (*0-8165-1929-3*) U of Ariz Pr.

***Men on the Verge of a His-Panic Breakdown.** Guillermo Reyes. 49p. (C). 1998. pap. 5.60 (*0-87129-899-6*, MB5) Dramatic Pub.

Men or Mules. Clyde Crosley. LC 79-50363. (Illus.). 1979. 14.75 (*0-9603268-1-2*) Crosley.

***Men Out of Asia.** Harold S. Gladwin. (LC History-America-E). 390p. 1999. reprint ed. lib. bdg. 89.00 (*0-7812-4324-6*) Rprt Serv.

Men Out There: A Woman's Little Black Book. Susan R. Shapiro & Michelle Kasson. LC 96-71015. 226p. 1997. pap. 12.95 (*1-887750-37-1*) Rutledge Bks.

Men over Industry. Paul Derrick. 1980. lib. bdg. 59.95 (*0-8490-3079-X*) Gordon Pr.

Men Own the Fields, Women Own the Crops: Gender & Power in the Cameroon Grassfields. Miriam Goheen. LC 95-25275. (Illus.). 272p. 1996. 50.00 (*0-299-14670-7*); pap. 24.95 (*0-299-14674-X*) U of Wis Pr.

Men, Power, & Myths: The Quest for Male Identity. Allan Guggenbuhl. Tr. by Gary V. Hartman. LC 97-2431. 252p. 1997. 24.95 (*0-8264-1081-7*) Continuum.

Men Read Newspapers, Not Minds: And Other Things I Wish I'd Known When I First Married. Sandra P. Aldrich. LC 96-9174. 180p. 1996. pap. 10.99 (*0-8423-8175-9*) Tyndale Hse.

Men Released from Prison. Irvin Waller. LC 73-85690. (Canadian Studies in Criminology: No. 2). 299p. reprint ed. pap. 92.70 (*0-608-18000-9*, 202647700049) Bks Demand.

Men, Religion & Melancholia: James, Otto, Jung & Erikson. Donald Capps. LC 96-36548. 240p. 1997. 32.00 (*0-300-06971-5*) Yale U Pr.

Men Seeking Men: Adventures in Gay Personals. Ed. by Michael Lassell. LC 98-27646. 248p. 1998. pap. 15.00 (*1-891305-02-6*) Painted Leaf.

Men Seen: Twenty-Four Modern Authors. Paul Rosenfeld. LC 67-26776. (Essay Index Reprint Ser.). 1977. 24.95 (*0-8369-0836-8*) Ayer.

Men Should Come with Instruction Booklets. Cathy Guisewite. (Illus.). 128p. (Orig.). 1984. pap. 8.95 (*0-8362-2055-2*) Andrews & McMeel.

Men Spake from God: Studies in the Hebrew Prophets. H. L. Ellison. (Biblical Classics Library: Vol. 9). 160p. 1995. reprint ed. mass mkt. 5.99 (*0-85364-650-3*, Pub. by Paternoster Pub) OM Literature.

Men Stood Like Iron: How the Iron Brigade Won Its Name. Lance J. Herdegen. LC 96-31095. 1997. 24.95 (*0-253-33221-4*) Ind U Pr.

Men Surviving Incest. T. Thomas. LC 89-13881. 100p. (Orig.). 1989. pap. 9.95 (*0-9613205-8-3*) Launch Pr.

Men Talk about Going Forward & Other Things: A Guide for Men Returning to School. June F. Esparza. Ed. by Everette K. Wagner. LC 95-90500. (Illus.). 240p. (Orig.). (C). 1997. pap. 16.95 (*0-9647161-3-5*) Thgts in Motion.

Men, the Workers. Henry D. Lloyd. Ed. by Anne Withington & Caroline Stallbohen. LC 79-89751. (American Labor, from Conspiracy to Collective Bargaining Ser., No. 1). 280p. 1974. reprint ed. 21.95 (*0-405-02138-0*) Ayer.

Men They Will Become: The Nature & Nurture of Male Character. Eli H. Newberger. (Merloyd Lawrence Book Ser.). 384p. 1999. 25.00 (*0-7382-0113-8*, Pub. by Perseus Pubng) HarpC.

***Men They Will Become: The Nature & Nurture of Male Character.** Eli H. Newberger. 384p. 2000. reprint ed. pap. text 17.00 (*0-7382-0363-7*, Pub. by Perseus Pubng) HarpC.

Men to Bombay, Women at Home: Urban Influence on Sugao Village, Deccan Maharashtra, India, 1942-1982. Hemalata C. Dandekar. LC 85-48240. (Michigan Papers on South & Southeast Asia: No. 28). (Illus.). 325p. (C). 1986. 31.95 (*0-89148-035-8*); pap. 15.95 (*0-89148-036-6*) Ctr S&SE Asian.

Men to Match My Mountains. Irving Stone. 1987. pap. 17.95 (*0-425-10544-X*) Berkley Pub.

Men to Men: Perspectives of Sixteen African-American Christian Men. Ed. by Lee June & Matthew Parker. 240p. 1996. pap. 12.99 (*0-310-20157-8*) Zondervan.

Men Together. Anderson Jones. LC 96-69231. (Illus.). 128p. 1997. 27.50 (*0-7624-0062-5*) Running Pr.

Men under Construction. rev. ed. Donald Joy. LC 92-42714. (Personal Growth Bookshelf). 204p. 1993. pap. 9.99 (*1-56476-053-7*, 6-3053, Victor Bks) Chariot Victor.

Men under Construction: Rebuilding the Way to Healthy Sexuality, Relationships, & Identity. rev. ed. Donald M. Joy. 190p. 1993. pap. 12.95 (*0-916035-77-8*) Evangel Indiana.

Men under Fire. Ronald Koertge. LC 76-29869. 44p. 1976. pap. 2.00 (*0-916918-02-5*) Duck Down.

Men under Stress. Roy R. Grinker, Sr. & John Speigel. 1985. reprint ed. write for info. (*0-89197-645-0*) Irvington.

Men under Water. Ralph Lombreglia. Ed. by Jane Rosenman. 224p. 1991. reprint ed. pap. 7.95 (*0-671-73260-9*, WSP) PB.

Men Underground. Clinton E. Jencks. 172p. 1969. pap. 13.25 (*0-916304-05-1*) SDSU Press.

Men Versus the Man: A Correspondence Between Robert Rives La Monte, Socialist & H. L. Mencken, Individualist. Robert R. La Monte & H. L. Mencken. LC 79-172220. (Right Wing Individualist Tradition in America Ser.). 1975. reprint ed. 23.95 (*0-405-00429-X*) Ayer.

Men Versus the State: Herbert Spencer & Late Victorian Individualism. Michael Taylor. (Oxford Historical Monographs). 304p. 1992. text 75.00 (*0-19-820239-3*) OUP.

Men Viewing Women As Art Objects: Studies in German Literature. Christoph E. Schweitzer. LC 97-46706. (Studies in German Literature, Linguistics, & Culture). 126p. 1998. 45.00 (*1-57113-259-7*) Camden Hse.

Men Wanted for the U. S. Army: America's Experience with an All-Volunteer Army Between the World Wars, 27. Robert K. Griffith, Jr. LC 81-6686. (Contributions in Military History Ser.: No. 27). (Illus.). 259p. 1982. 59.95 (*0-313-22546-X*, GMU/) Greenwood.

Men We Cherish: African American Women Praise the Men in Their Lives. Ed. by Brooke M. Stephens. LC 97-2830. 432p. 1997. pap. 14.95 (*0-385-48532-8*) Doubleday.

Me We Long to Be: Beyond Lonely Warriors & Desperate Lovers. Stephen B. Boyd. LC 97-29641. 272p. (Orig.). 1997. pap. 17.95 (*0-8298-1201-6*) Pilgrim OH.

Men We Love to Hate: The Book a Man's Garden of Vices. Marnie Winston-Macauley. LC 96-84526. 128p. 1996. pap. text 4.95 (*0-8362-2224-5*) Andrews & McMeel.

Men We Never Knew: How to Deepen Your Relationship with the Man You Love. Daphne R. Kingma. 300p. 1994. reprint ed. pap. 10.95 (*0-943233-66-6*) Conari Press.

Men Were Deceivers Ever. Patricia Veryan. 224p. reprint ed. 19.00 (*0-7278-4541-1*) Severn Hse.

Men Were Different: Five Studies in Late Victorian Biography. Shane Leslie. LC 67-26754. (Essay Index Reprint Ser.). 1977. 20.95 (*0-8369-0615-2*) Ayer.

Men Who Advertise. Rowell, George P. & Staff. Ed. by Henry Asseal. LC 78-299. (Century of Marketing Ser.). 1979. reprint ed. lib. bdg. 72.95 (*0-405-11174-6*) Ayer.

Men Who Are Making the West. Bertie C. Forbes. LC 72-330. (Essay Index Reprint Ser.). 1977. reprint ed. 26.95 (*0-8369-2793-1*) Ayer.

Men Who Batter: An Integrated Approach for Stopping Wife Abuse. Edward W. Gondolf. LC 83-83313. 224p. (C). 1985. pap. 19.95 (*0-918452-79-1*, 791) Learning Pubns.

Men Who Batter Women. Adam Jukes. LC 98-38319. xiv, 192p. 1999. pap. 18.99 (*0-415-04099-X*) Routledge.

Men Who Batter Women. Adam Jukes. LC 98-38319. 224p. (C). 1999. 75.00 (*0-415-12942-7*) Routledge.

Men Who Beat the Men Who Love Them: Battered Gay Men & Domestic Violence. David Island & Patrick Letellier. LC 91-4631. 328p. 1991. pap. 17.95 (*0-918393-97-3*); lib. bdg. 39.95 (*1-56024-112-8*) Haworth Pr.

Men Who Built the West. Arthur A. Gray. LC 73-167348. (Essay Index Reprint Ser.). 1977. reprint ed. 27.95 (*0-8369-2591-2*) Ayer.

Men Who Can't Be Faithful: Build a Better, More Intimate Relationship-Based on New Trust, Honesty, & Love. Carol Botwin. 304p. 1989. mass mkt. 6.50 (*0-446-35623-9*, Pub. by Warner Bks) Little.

Men Who Can't Love. Steven Carter & Julia Sokol. 336p. 1988. mass mkt. 6.99 (*0-425-11170-9*) Berkley Pub.

Men Who Can't Love. Steven Carter & Julia Sokol. 236p. 1994. 6.98 (*1-56731-047-8*, MJF Bks) Fine Comms.

***Men Who Can't Love: How to Recognize a Commitmentphobic Man Before He Breaks Your Heart.** Steven Carter & Julia Sokol. 336p. 2000. reprint ed. pap. 12.95 (*0-425-17445-X*) Berkley Pub.

Men Who Changed the World Vol. I: The Henry Ford Story. Leigh A. Arrathoon. Ed. by John Davio. (Illus.). 56p. (J). (gr. 5-6). pap. text 5.95 (*0-9648564-5-X*) Paint Creek Pr Ltd.

Men Who Changed the World Vol. II: The First Birdmen: Wilbur & Orville Wright. Leigh A. Arrathoon. Ed. by John Davio. (Illus.). 56p. (J). (gr. 5-6). pap. text 5.95 (*0-9648564-6-8*) Paint Creek Pr Ltd.

Men Who Conquered. John T. Faris. LC 68-55846. (Essay Index Reprint Ser.). 1977. 17.95 (*0-8369-0438-9*) Ayer.

Men Who Control Women's Health: The Miseducation of Obstetrician-Gynecologists. Diane H. Scully. LC 93-45686. (Athene Ser.: Vol. 40). 304p. (C). 1994. pap. text 18.95 (*0-8077-6273-3*) Tchrs Coll.

Men Who Flew the Mosquito: Compelling Accounts of the Wooden Wonder's Triumphant WWII Career. Martin W. Bowman. (Illus.). 192p. 1995. 44.95 (*1-85260-488-3*, Pub. by J H Haynes & Co) Motorbooks Intl.

Men Who Fought the Civil War. Linda R. Wade. LC 97-37477. (The Civil War Ser.). (J). 1998. lib. bdg. 14.98 (*1-56239-823-7*) ABDO Pub Co.

Men Who Govern: A Biographical Profile of Federal Political Executives. David T. Stanley et al. LC 67-25422. 183p. pap. 56.80 (*0-608-12490-7*, 202541100043) Bks Demand.

Men Who Hate Women. Susan Forward & Joan Torres. 304p. 1987. mass mkt. 7.99 (*0-553-28037-6*) Bantam.

Men Who Hate Women & the Women Who Hate Them: The Masochistic Art of Dating. Nancy Linn-Desmond. (Illus.). 160p. 1992. pap. 4.50 (*0-8216-2518-7*, Carol Paperbacks) Carol Pub Group.

Men Who Have Walked with God: Being the Story of Mysticism Through the Ages Told in the Biographies of Representative Seers & Saints with Excerpts from Their Writings & Sayings. Sheldon W. Cheney. 415p. 1992. reprint ed. pap. 27.50 (*1-56459-268-5*) Kessinger Pub.

Men Who Lead Labor. Bruce Minton & John Stuart. LC 73-93362. (Essay Index Reprint Ser.). 1977. 21.95 (*0-8369-1309-4*) Ayer.

Men Who Left the Movement. Gertrude Donald. LC 67-23207. (Essay Index Reprint Ser.). 1977. 23.95 (*0-8369-0385-4*) Ayer.

Men Who Love Too Little see Hombres Que Aman Muy Poco

Men Who Love Too Little. Thomas Whiteman & Randy Petersen. LC 94-24637. 1995. pap. 9.99 (*0-8407-9173-9*, Oliver-Nelson) Nelson.

Men Who Loved Me. Felice Picano. 1994. mass mkt. 6.95 (*1-56333-274-4*, Hard Candy) Masquerade.

Men Who Made a New Physics: Physicists & the Quantum Theory. Barbara L. Cline. LC 65-18693. (Illus.). xi, 282p. (C). 1987. pap. text 19.00 (*0-226-11027-3*) U Ch Pr.

Men Who Made History. Frank Schaffer Publications, Inc. Staff. (Middle School Bks.). (Illus.). 1996. wbk. ed. 12.95 (*0-7647-0017-0*, FS-10193) Schaffer Pubns.

Men Who Made Texas Free. Sam H. Dixon. 1993. reprint ed. lib. bdg. 75.00 (*0-7812-5924-X*) Rprt Serv.

Men Who Made the Monsters. Jensen. 1996. 26.95 (*0-8057-9337-2*, Twyne) Mac Lib Ref.

Men Who Made the Monsters. Paul M. Jensen. (Twayne Filmmakers Ser.). (Illus.). 384p. 1996. pap. 23.00 (*0-8057-9338-0*, Twyne) Mac Lib Ref.

Men Who Make Our Novels. rev. ed. Charles C. Baldwin. LC 67-30174. (Essay Index Reprint Ser.). 1977. 22.95 (*0-8369-0171-1*) Ayer.

Men Who Make the Future. Bruce Bliven, Jr. LC 70-111816. (Essay Index Reprint Ser.). 1977. 23.95 (*0-8369-1643-3*) Ayer.

Men Who Met God. A. W. Tozer. LC 86-70773. 128p. (Orig.). 1986. pap. 9.99 (*0-87509-377-9*) Chr Pubns.

Men Who Migrate, Women Who Wait: Population & History in a Portuguese Parish. Caroline Brettell. LC 86-11270. (Illus.). 346p. reprint ed. pap. 107.30 (*0-608-06439-4*, 206665200008) Bks Demand.

Men Who Missed It. Ed. by Clarence E. Macartney. LC 76-128274. (Essay Index Reprint Ser.). 1977. 18.95 (*0-8369-1835-5*) Ayer.

Men Who Never - Male Response to Women, Commitment & Marriage Through the Testimony of 30 Lifelong Bachelors. Marian P. Howard. LC 99-70090. (Illus.). 352p. 1999. pap. 18.95 (*1-57197-169-6*) Pentland Pr.

Men Who Overturned Empires: Fighters, Dreamers, & Schemers. Hugh Tinker. LC 87-6122. 300p. 1987. reprint ed. pap. 93.00 (*0-608-01948-8*, 206260300003) Bks Demand.

Men Who Rape: The Psychology of the Offender. A. N. Groth. LC 79-18624. (Illus.). 246p. (C). 1979. 35.00 (*0-306-40268-8*, Plenum Trade) Perseus Pubng.

Men Who Ruled Kenya: The Kenya Administration, 1892-1963. Charles C. Trench. (Illus.). 224p. (C). 1993. text 39.50 (*1-85043-571-5*, Pub. by I B T) St Martin.

Men Who Sell Sex: International Perspectives on Male Prostitution & AIDS. Ed. by Peter Aggleton. 296p. 1998. text 59.95 (*1-56639-668-9*); pap. text 24.95 (*1-56639-669-7*) Temple U Pr.

Men Who Turn the Age. Witness Lee. 30p. 1991. pap. 3.00 (*0-87083-604-8*, 16-025-001) Living Stream Ministry.

Men Who Wear the Star: The Story of the Texas Rangers. Charles Robinson, III. LC 99-27160. 432p. 2000. 29.95 (*0-679-45649-X*) Random.

Men Will Be Boys: The Modern Woman Explains Football & Other Amusing Male Rituals. Sally Jenkins. 1996. 19.95 (*0-614-20437-2*) Doubleday.

Men Will Be Boys: The Modern Woman Explains Football & Other Amusing Male Rituals. Sally Jenkins. 238p. 1997. pap. 10.95 (*0-385-48389-9*, Main St Bks) Doubleday.

Men with Guns & Lone Star. John Sayles. (Illus.). 224p. 1998. pap. 18.95 (*0-571-19527-X*) Faber & Faber.

Men with Sand: Great Explorers of the American West. John Moring. LC 97-43468. (Illus.). 176p. 1998. pap. 10.95 (*1-56044-620-X*, Two Dot) Falcon Pub Inc.

Men with the Pink Triangle: The True, Life-&-Death Story of Homosexuals in the Nazi Death Camps. 2nd ed. Heinz Heger. LC 94-29646. 120p. 1994. pap. 9.95 (*1-55583-006-4*) Alyson Pubns.

Men with Wooden Feet: The Spanish Exploration of the Pacific Northwest. John Kendrick. 168p. 1986. pap. 9.95 (*0-920053-85-8*, Pub. by NC Ltd) U of Toronto Pr.

Men Withering. Francis MacManus. 1988. pap. 7.95 (*0-85342-115-3*) Dufour.

Men Without Art. Wyndham Lewis. Ed. by Seamus Cooney. LC 87-733. 330p. (Orig.). 1987. pap. 15.00 (*0-87685-686-5*) Black Sparrow.

Men Without Bones. Gerald Kersh. 1993. reprint ed. lib. bdg. 18.95 (*0-89968-434-3*, Lghtyr Pr) Buccaneer Bks.

Men Without Chests. 1994. 19.95 incl. VHS (*1-890553-02-6*, CV 602 VSN) Double Vision.

Men Without Dates & Slam! Two One-Act Plays by Jane Willis. Jane Willis. 1986. pap. 5.25 (*0-8222-0748-6*) Dramatists Play.

Men Without Mercy. Alfred Doblin. Tr. by Trevor Blewitt & Phyllis Blewitt from GER. LC 75-31978. 446p. 1976. reprint ed. 45.00 (*0-86527-277-8*) Fertig.

Men Without Ties. Gianni Versace. 1996. pap. text 7.95 (*0-7892-5217-1*) Abbeville Pr.

Men Without Ties. Gianni Versace. (Illus.). 274p. 1996. 75.00 (*0-7892-0001-5*) Abbeville Pr.

Men Without Ties. Gianni Versace. LC 97-11520. (Tiny Folio Ser.). (Illus.). 288p. 1997. 11.95 (*0-7892-0382-0*) Abbeville Pr.

Men Without Women. Ernest Hemingway. 22.95 (*0-89190-663-0*) Amereon Ltd.

Men Without Women. Ernest Hemingway. LC 96-43940. 160p. 1997. reprint ed. per. 9.00 (*0-684-82586-4*) S&S Trade.

***Men Without Women: Masculinity & Revolution in Russian Fiction, 1917-1929.** Eliot Borenstein. 336p. 2000. lib. bdg. 59.95 (*0-8223-2578-0*) Duke.

***Men Without Women: Masculinity & Revolution in Russian Fiction, 1917-1929.** Eliot Borenstein. LC 00-30309. 336p. 2001. pap. 19.95 (*0-8223-2592-6*) Duke.

Men, Women & Boats. Stephen Crane. LC 70-113652. (Short Story Index Reprint Ser.). 1977. 21.95 (*0-8369-3381-8*) Ayer.

Men, Women & Boats. Stephen Crane. (Works of Stephen Crane). 1990. reprint ed. lib. bdg. 79.00 (*0-7812-2438-1*) Rprt Serv.

Men, Women & Boats. Stephen Crane. 247p. 1998. reprint ed. lib. bdg. 79.00 (*0-7812-4802-7*) Rprt Serv.

Men, Women, & Book. L. Hunt. 1973. 69.95 (*0-8490-0608-2*) Gordon Pr.

Men, Women, & Chain Saws: Gender in the Modern Horror Film. Carol J. Clover. (Illus.). 253p. (C). 1992. pap. text 14.95 (*0-691-00620-2*, Pub. by Princeton U Pr) Cal Prin Full Svc.

Men, Women & Change. 3rd ed. Letha D. Scanzoni & John H. Scanzoni. 691p. (C). 1988. 75.31 (*0-07-055063-8*) McGraw.

Men, Women & Colleges. Russell Briggs. LC 73-167313. (Essay Index Reprint Ser.). 1977. reprint ed. 19.95 (*0-8369-2308-1*) Ayer.

Men, Women & Dogs. James Thurber. reprint ed. lib. bdg. 22.95 (*0-89190-267-8*, Rivercity Pr) Amereon Ltd.

Men, Women & Emotions. Ella W. Wilcox. 306p. 1998. reprint ed. pap. 24.95 (*0-7661-0408-7*) Kessinger Pub.

Men, Women & Ghosts. Amy Lowell. (Collected Works of Amy Lowell). 363p. 1999. lib. bdg. 98.00 (*1-58201-758-1*, c0758) Classic Bks.

Men, Women, & Ghosts. Elizabeth S. Ward. (C). 1972. reprint ed. lib. bdg. 27.00 (*0-8422-8122-3*) Irvington.

Men, Women & Ghosts. Elizabeth S. Ward. (C). 1986. reprint ed. pap. text 7.95 (*0-8290-1875-1*) Irvington.

M

An Asterisk (*) at the beginning of an entry indicates that the title is appearing for the first time.

Men, Women, & God: German Renaissance Prints from St. Louis Collections. Barbara Butts et al. Ed. by Mary A. Steiner. (Illus.). 84p. (Orig.). 1997. pap. 19.95 (*0-89178-046-7*) St Louis Art Mus.

Men, Women, & God(s) Nawal El Saadawi & Arab Feminist Poetics. Fedwa Malti-Douglas. LC 94-44255. (Centennial Bk.). 277p. 1995. 50.00 (*0-520-20071-3*, Pub. by U CA Pr); pap. 18.95 (*0-520-20072-1*, Pub. by U CA Pr) Cal Prin Full Svc.

Men, Women & Household Work. Jacqueline Goodnow & Jennifer Bowes. 232p. 1994. pap. text 23.00 (*0-19-553572-3*) OUP.

Men, Women, & Infertility: Intervention & Treatment Strategies. Aline P. Zoldbrod. LC 92-49301. 256p. 1993. 29.95 (*0-669-27270-1*) Lxngtn Bks.

Men, Women & Madness. Joan Busfield. (C). 1996. pap. text 19.00 (*0-8147-1281-9*) NYU Pr.

Men, Women & Madness: Understanding Gender & Mental Disorder. Joan Busfield. Ed. by Jo Campling. LC 95-42253. 296p. (C). 1996. text 50.00 (*0-8147-1278-9*) NYU Pr.

Men, Women & Manners in Colonial Times. S. G. Fisher. 1972. 59.95 (*0-8490-0609-0*) Gordon Pr.

Men, Women & Manners in Colonial Times, 2 vols. Sydney G. Fisher. LC 99-41319. 2000. reprint ed. 50.00 (*1-55888-188-3*) Omnigraphics Inc.

Men, Women & Margaret Fuller: The Truth That Existed Between Margaret Fuller & Ralph Waldo Emerson, 3 vols. Laurie James. (Margaret Fuller Ser.: Vol. III). (Orig.). 1990. pap. 19.95 (*0-944382-02-9*) Golden Heritage Pr.

Men, Women & Pianos: A Social History. Arthur Loesser. 672p. 1991. pap. 13.95 (*0-486-26543-9*) Dover.

Men, Women & Places. Sigrid Undset. Tr. by A. G. Chater. LC 74-99728. (Essay Index Reprint Ser.). 1977. 23.95 (*0-8369-1431-7*) Ayer.

***Men, Women, & Prostate Cancer: A Medical & Psychological Guide for Women & the Men They Love.** 2nd rev. ed. Barbara Rubin Wainrib et al. LC 99-75278. (Illus.). 287p. 2000. pap. 15.95 (*1-57224-182-9*) New Harbinger.

Men, Women, & Relationships. John Gray. 336p. 1996. mass mkt. 6.99 (*0-06-101070-7*, Harp PBks) HarpC.

Men, Women, & Relationships: Gray,&John. abr. ed. John Gray. 1995. audio 12.00 (*0-694-51534-5*, CPN 10052, Pub. by HarperAudio) Lndmrk Audiobks.

Men, Women & Relationships: Making Peace with the Opposite Sex. John Gray. Ed. by Sara Steinberg. LC 90-80256. 306p. (C). 1990. pap. 12.95 (*0-941831-50-7*) Beyond Words Pub.

Men, Women & Tenors. Frances Alda. LC 72-107790. (Select Bibliographies Reprint Ser.). 1977. 29.95 (*0-8369-5174-3*) Ayer.

Men, Women & Tenors. Frances Alda. LC 75-149653. reprint ed. 32.50 (*0-404-00306-0*) AMS Pr.

Men, Women & Tenors. Frances Alda. (Music Book Index Ser.). 307p. 1992. reprint ed. lib. bdg. 89.00 (*0-7812-9473-8*) Rprt Serv.

Men, Women & Vehicles: Prose Works. David Bromige. LC 90-1061. 176p. 1990. 20.00 (*0-87685-798-5*); pap. 10.00 (*0-87685-797-7*) Black Sparrow.

Men, Women & Vehicles: Prose Works, signed ed. deluxe ed. David Bromige. LC 90-1061. 176p. 1990. 30.00 (*0-87685-799-3*) Black Sparrow.

Men, Women, & Work: Class, Gender, & Protest in the New England Shoe Industry, 1780-1910. Mary H. Blewett. LC 87-19039. (Working Class in American History Ser.). 472p. 1988. text 34.95 (*0-252-01484-7*); pap. text 15.95 (*0-252-06142-X*) U of Ill Pr.

Men, Women, Love, Sex, God & Death: The Collected "Sunday Times" Writings. Chrissey Iley. 390p. 1997. 22.95 (*0-233-99264-2*, Pub. by Andre Deutsch) Trans-Atl Phila.

Men, Work & Family. Ed. by Jane C. Hood. (Research on Men & Masculinities Ser.: Vol. 4). (Illus.). 272p. (C). 1993. text 58.00 (*0-8039-3890-X*) Sage.

Men, Work & Family. 4th ed. Ed. by Jane C. Hood. (Research on Men & Masculinities Ser.: Vol. 4). (Illus.). 272p. (C). 1993. pap. text 26.00 (*0-8039-3891-8*) Sage.

Men Working: A Novel. John Faulkner. LC 95-46728. (Brown Thrasher Bks.). 320p. (C). 1996. pap. 19.95 (*0-8203-1827-2*) U of Ga Pr.

Men Writing the Feminine: Literature, Theory, & the Question of Genders. Ed. by Thais E. Morgan. LC 93-43224. 207p. (C). 1994. text 49.50 (*0-7914-1993-2*); pap. text 16.95 (*0-7914-1994-0*) State U NY Pr.

Mena Centennial History: A Photographic History of Mena, Arkansas. Michael Cate & Harold Coogan. LC 96-77840. (Illus.). 288p. 1996. 45.00 (*1-886130-04-3*) Cate Media.

Mena of Nikiou: The Life of Isaac of Alexandria & the Martyrdom of Saint Marcobius. Tr. by David N. Bell. 1988. 31.95 (*0-317-68104-4*); pap. 12.95 (*0-87907-607-0*) Cistercian Pubns.

Menacante Seduction. Janice Kaiser. (Rouge Passion Ser.). (FRE.). 1997. pap. 3.50 (*0-373-37429-1*, 1-37429-7) Harlequin Bks.

***Menace & Mischief.** large type ed. Sylvia Gunnery. 80p. (J). (gr. 3-7). 1999. mass mkt. 5.95 (*0-7736-7477-2*) Genl Dist Srvs.

***Menace Fantome.** Terry Brooks. 1999. pap. 12.95 (*2-265-06849-7*) Midwest European Pubns.

Menace from Earth. Robert A. Heinlein. 1976. reprint ed. lib. bdg. 22.95 (*0-88411-882-7*) Amereon Ltd.

Menace from Earth. Robert A. Heinlein. 1999. reprint ed. mass mkt. 6.99 (*0-671-57802-2*) Baen Bks.

Menace from Earth. Robert A. Heinlein. 1990. reprint ed. lib. bdg. 19.95 (*0-89968-516-1*) Buccaneer Bks.

Menace from Moresby: A Pictorial History of the Fifth Air Force in World War II. Ed. by Russell L. Sinton. (Aviation Ser.: No. 8). (Illus.). 216p. 1989. reprint ed. 39.95 (*0-89839-133-4*) Battery Pr.

***Menace from the Moon.** Bohun Lynch. 1999. reprint ed. 28.00 (*1-55246-218-8*) Battered Silicon.

Menace in the West: Colorado & the American Experience with Drugs, 1873-1963. Henry O. Whiteside. LC 97-9940. (Illus.). 136p. (Orig.). 1997. pap. 12.95 (*0-942576-38-1*) CO Hist Soc.

Menace in the West: The Rise of French Anti-Americanism in Modern Times, 40. David Strauss. LC 77-94748. (Contributions in American Studies: No. 40). 317p. 1978. 65.00 (*0-313-20316-4*, SMW/, Greenwood Pr) Greenwood.

Menace Multiculturalism: Trojan Horse in America. Alvin J. Schmidt. LC 96-24462. 232p. 1997. 39.95 (*0-275-95598-2*, Praeger Pubs) Greenwood.

Menace of Communism in Germany in 1933. (Studies in Ideology). 1992. lib. bdg. 75.00 (*0-8490-8701-5*) Gordon Pr.

Menace of Inflation: Its Causes & Consequences. Ed. by G. Carl Wiegand. 1976. pap. 8.95 (*0-8159-6215-0*) Devin.

Menace of Narcotics. Robert L. Sumner. 72p. 1971. pap. 1.95 (*0-914012-12-6*) Sword of Lord.

Menace of Overproduction. Ed. by Scoville Hamlin. LC 76-93344. (Essay Index Reprint Ser.). 1977. 20.95 (*0-8369-1295-0*) Ayer.

Menace of the Corporate Newspaper: Fact or Fiction. David P. Demers. LC 95-41462. 350p. 1995. text 41.95 (*0-8138-2269-6*) Iowa St U Pr.

Menace of the Herd. Francis S. Campbell. Ed. by Erik Von Kuehnelt-Leddihn. 1976. lib. bdg. 300.00 (*0-87968-372-4*) Gordon Pr.

Menace of the Nutanator. Jim Davis. (Garfield's Pet Force Ser.: No. 4). (Illus.). (J). (gr. 3-7). 1998. pap. 3.99 (*0-590-05945-9*) Scholastic Inc.

Menace of the Religious Movie. A. W. Tozer. 1974. pap. 1.50 (*0-915374-51-X*, 51-X) Rapids Christian.

Menace of the Sublime to the Individual Self in Kant, Schiller & Coleridge: The Disintegration of Identity in Romanticism. Linda M. Brooks. LC 96-8613. 248p. 1996. text 89.95 (*0-7734-8752-2*) E Mellen.

Menace Sans Visage. Judi Lind. (Rouge Passion Ser.: No. 498). (FRE.). 1999. mass mkt. 3.50 (*0-373-37498-4*, 1-37498-2) Harlequin Bks.

Menaced Assassin. Joe Gores. 384p. 1995. mass mkt. 5.50 (*0-446-40390-3*, Pub. by Warner Bks) Little.

Menaced Assassin. 2nd ed. Ascher-Straus. LC 89-8343. 128p. 1989. pap. 9.00 (*0-929701-03-8*) McPherson & Co.

Menaces, Menaces. large type ed. Michael Underwood. (Linford Mystery Library). 400p. 1997. pap. 16.99 (*0-7089-5069-8*) Ulverscroft.

Menachem's Seed: A Novel. Carl Djerassi. LC 97-12749. 216p. 1997. 21.95 (*0-8203-1925-2*) U of Ga Pr.

Menachem's Seed: A Novel. Carl Djerassi. 224p. 1998. pap. 12.95 (*0-14-027794-3*) Viking Penguin.

Menacing Virgins: Representing Virginity in the Middle Ages. Kathleen C. Kelly & Marina Leslie. LC 98-19983. 1999. write for info. (*0-87413-649-0*) U Delaware Pr.

Menaechmi. Plautus. Ed. by A. S. Gratwick. LC 92-17790. (Greek & Latin Classics Ser.). 286p. (C). 1993. text 65.00 (*0-521-34162-0*); pap. text 24.95 (*0-521-34970-2*) Cambridge U Pr.

Menaechmi. rev. ed. Titus Maccius Plautus. Ed. by Mason Hammond & Nicholas Moseley. 140p. 1961. 22.50 (*0-674-56725-0*) HUP.

Menage. Emma Holly. 1998. mass mkt. 5.95 (*0-352-33231-X*, Pub. by BLA4) London Brdge.

Menage a Trois. Frank Dickerson. (Illus.). 32p. 1996. pap. 6.00 (*0-9657398-0-5*) Pamet River.

Menage a Trois. Paul Groves. 72p. 1996. pap. 14.95 (*1-85411-147-7*, Pub. by Seren Bks) Dufour.

Menagerie. Catherine Cookson. Date not set. lib. bdg. 21.95 (*0-8488-2140-8*) Amereon Ltd.

Menagerie. Catherine Cookson. 1987. pap. 3.95 (*0-552-13163-6*) Bantam.

Menagerie. Catherine Cookson. 224p. 1987. mass mkt. 4.50 (*0-552-08653-3*) Bantam.

Menagerie. Mark Sonnenfeld. 48p. 1992. pap. 3.00 (*0-9632820-0-X*) M Sonnenfeld.

Menagerie Keeper. Jack Rudman. (Career Examination Ser.: C-494). 1994. pap. 23.95 (*0-8373-0494-6*) Nat Learn.

Menageries, Circuses & Theatres. E. H. Bostock. LC 72-80140. (Illus.). 315p. 1972. reprint ed. 24.95 (*0-405-08290-8*, Pub. by Blom Pubns) Ayer.

Menagier de Paris: A Critical Edition. Ed. by Georgine E. Brereton & Janet M. Ferrier. 1981. 95.00 (*0-19-815748-7*) OUP.

Menahem Nahum of Chernobyl: Upright Practices, the Light of the Eyes. Arthur Green. (Classics of Western Spirituality Ser.). 1982. pap. 22.95 (*0-8091-2374-6*) Paulist Pr.

Menahoth, 2 vols. (ENG & HEB.). 30.00 (*0-910218-80-3*) Bennet Pub.

Menaion of the Orthodox Church, No. XI, July. Tr. by Isaac Lambertsen. 448p. 1998. 125.00 (*0-912927-92-5*, D049) St John Kronstadt.

Menaion of the Orthodox Church, Vol. VII. Tr. by Isaac Lambertsen. 224p. 1999. 75.00 (*0-912927-97-6*) St John Kronstadt.

Menaion of the Orthodox Church: Provisional Edition, First Recension. Tr. by Isaac E. Lambertsen from GRE. 1996. write for info. (*0-912927-65-8*) St John Kronstadt.

Menaion of the Orthodox Church: Provisional Edition, First Recension, Vol. I: September. Tr. by Isaac E. Lambertsen from SLA. 432p. 1996. 135.00 (*0-912927-72-0*) St John Kronstadt.

Menaion of the Orthodox Church: Provisional Edition, First Recension, Vol. IV: December. Tr. by Isaac E. Lambertsen from SLO. 432p. 1996. 135.00 (*0-912927-77-1*) St John Kronstadt.

Menaion of the Orthodox Church: Provisional Edition, First Recension, Vol. VI (February) Tr. by Isaac Lambertsen from SLA. 1998. write for info. (*0-912927-91-7*, D047) St John Kronstadt.

Menaion of the Orthodox Church: Provisional Edition, First Recension, Vol. IX: May. Tr. by Isaac E. Lambertsen from SLA. 256p. 1996. 85.00 (*0-912927-71-2*, D037) St John Kronstadt.

Menaion of the Orthodox Church: Provisional Edition, First Recension, Vol. XII (August) Tr. by Isaac Lambertsen from SLA. 351p. 1997. 100.00 (*0-912927-87-9*, D045) St John Kronstadt.

Menaion of the Orthodox Church Vol. VIII: Provisional Edition, First Recension, April. Tr. by Isaac Lambertsen & George Lardas from GRE. 192p. 1997. 75.00 (*0-912927-82-8*, D044) St John Kronstadt.

Menaion of the Orthodox Church, Vol. III, November: Protomartyr of the Lemko People. Tr. by Isaac Lambertsen. 367p. 1998. 100.00 (*0-912927-95-X*, X055) St John Kronstadt.

Menallen Minutes, Marriages & Miscellany: Quaker Records, 1780-1890. Margaret B. Walmer. (Illus.). 273p. (Orig.). 1992. pap. 22.50 (*1-55613-656-0*) Heritage Bk.

***Menander.** W. G. Arnott. (Loeb Classical Library: Vol. 3). 2000. text 19.95 (*0-674-99584-8*) HUP.

Menander. Menander et al. LC 98-9966. (Greek Drama Ser.). 296p. 1998. 40.00 (*0-8122-3444-8*); pap. 17.95 (*0-8122-1652-0*) U of Pa Pr.

Menander, Vol. II. Ed. & Tr. by W. Geoffrey Arnott from GRE. (Loeb Classical Library: No. 459). 528p. 1996. 19.95 (*0-674-99506-6*) HUP.

Menander: A Commentary. A. W. Gomme & F. H. Sandbach. 774p. 1973. text 125.00 (*0-19-814197-1*) OUP.

Menander: Dyskolos. Ed. by E. W. Handley. (Bristol Greek Texts Ser.). (GRE.). 333p. 1992. pap. 33.95 (*1-85399-187-2*, Pub. by Brist Class Pr) Focus Pub-R Pullins.

Menander: Samia. D. M. Bain. (Classical Texts Ser.). 1983. 59.99 (*0-85668-224-1*, Pub. by Aris & Phillips); pap. 22.00 (*0-85668-225-X*, Pub. by Aris & Phillips) David Brown.

Menander: The Bad-Tempered Man. Menander. Ed. & Tr. by Stanley Ireland from GRE. (Classical Texts Ser.). 192p. 1995. pap. 22.00 (*0-85668-611-5*, Pub. by Aris & Phillips); text 59.99 (*0-85668-610-7*, Pub. by Aris & Phillips) David Brown.

Menander - Lexicon Menandreum. Giuseppe Pompella. x, 289p. 1996. write for info. (*3-487-10255-2*) G Olms Pubs.

Menander & the Making of Comedy. J. Michael Walton & Peter D. Arnott. LC 95-38653. 176p. 1996. pap. 17.95 (*0-275-93420-9*, Praeger Pubs) Greenwood.

Menander & the Making of Comedy, 67. J. Michael Walton & Peter D. Arnott. LC 95-38653. (Contributions in Drama & Theatre Studies: No. 67). 192p. 1996. 57.95 (*0-313-27216-6*, Greenwood Pr) Greenwood.

Menander, SAMIA. D. M. Bain. (BC-AP Classical Ser.). (GER.). 200p. 1985. 49.00 (*0-86516-113-5*) Bolchazy-Carducci.

Menander, the Principal Fragments. Menander. Tr. by Frank G. Allinson. LC 70-109789. 539p. 1970. reprint ed. lib. bdg. 75.00 (*0-8371-4279-2*, MEFR, Greenwood Pr) Greenwood.

Menander's Dyskolos. David Konstan. (Greek Commentaries Ser.). 91p. (Orig.). (C). 1983. pap. text 7.00 (*0-929524-20-9*) Bryn Mawr Commentaries.

Menaphon: Camilla's Alarm to Slumbering Euphues in His Melancholy Cell. Robert Greene. Ed. by Brenda Cantar. (Publications of the Barnabe Riche Society : No. 5). 198p. (C). 1996. text 28.00 (*1-895537-23-1*, Pub. by Dovehouse); pap. text 12.00 (*1-895537-32-0*, Pub. by Dovehouse) Sterling.

Menaphon; Camillas Alarum to Slumbering Euphues; Euphues His Censure to Philautus, 1587-1589 see Life & Complete Works in Prose & Verse of Robert Greene

Menasha: A True East Side Story. Mortimer Benisch. (Illus.). 140p. (Orig.). 1990. pap. 8.95 (*0-929256-18-2*) Thundblt Pr NV.

***Menasha Corporation: An Odyssey of Five Generations.** Richard Blodgett. LC 99-60003. (Illus.). 168p. 1999. write for info. (*0-944641-35-0*) Greenwich Pub Group.

***Menashe Kadishman.** Ulrich Schneider. 1999. pap. text 35.00 (*88-8158-217-1*) Charta.

Menasseh Ben Israel & His World. Yosef Kaplan et al. LC 89-7265. (Brill's Studies in Intellectual History: Vol. 15). ix, 278p. 1989. text 119.50 (*90-04-09114-9*) Brill Academic Pubs.

Menches, Komogrammateus of Kerkeosiris: The Doings & Dealings of a Village Scribe in the Late Ptolemaic Period (120-110 B. C.) Arthur Verhoogt. LC 97-35628. (Papyrologica Lugduno-Batava Ser.: No. 29). (Illus.). 330p. 1997. 118.00 (*90-04-10926-9*) Brill Academic Pubs.

Mencius. Mencius. Tr. by David Hinton from CHI. LC 98-30083. 304p. 1999. pap. 13.00 (*1-887178-62-7*, Pub. by Counterpt DC) HarpC.

Mencius. Emile Zola. (Classics Ser.). 288p. (C). 2000. pap. 12.95 (*0-14-044228-6*) Viking Penguin.

Mencius. Mencius. Tr. by David Hinton from CHI. 320p. 1999. reprint ed. pap. text 14.00 (*1-58243-020-9*, Pub. by Counterpt DC) HarpC.

Mencius, Vols. 1 & 2. Mencius. Tr. by D. C. Lau from CHI. (Chinese Classics Ser.: Vol. 2). 206p. (C). 1997. 34.50 (*962-201-313-9*, Pub. by Chinese Univ) U of Mich Pr.

Mencius & Early Chinese Thought. Kwong-Loi Shun. LC 96-12393. 1997. write for info. (*0-8047-2788-0*) Stanford U Pr.

***Mencius & Early Chinese Thought.** Kwong-Loi Shun. 2000. pap. text 18.95 (*0-8047-4017-8*) Stanford U Pr.

Mencius on the Mind: Experiments in Multiple Definition. I. A. Richards. 192p. (C). 1996. text 49.00 (*0-7007-0434-5*, Pub. by Curzon Pr Ltd) UH Pr.

Mencken: A Life. Fred Hobson. LC 95-12735. (Maryland Paperback Bookshelf Ser.). (Illus.). 688p. 1995. reprint ed. pap. 17.95 (*0-8018-5238-2*) Johns Hopkins.

Mencken Chrestomathy. H. L. Mencken. 1982. pap. 19.00 (*0-394-75209-0*) Pantheon.

Mencken Doesn't Live Here Anymore. Dan Rodricks. (Orig.). 1989. 18.95 (*0-913123-27-7*) Galileo.

Mencken Revisited: Author, Editor & Newspaperman. S. L. Harrison. LC 99-28419. (Illus.). 144p. 1999. pap. 26.50 (*0-7618-1450-7*) U Pr of Amer.

Mend the Mind, Mind the Body, Meet the Soul: Exploring the Secrets of Health & Longevity. Raj Kapoor. LC 98-28139. 232p. 1998. pap. 15.95 (*1-882897-27-7*) Lost Coast.

Mend Your English: What You Should Have Been Taught at Primary School. Ian Bruton-Simmonds. 150p. (C). 1990. 80.00 (*0-7855-6630-9*, Pub. by Ivy Pub) St Mut.

Menda-Nkwe: Short History & Folklore. Ndumu L. Taniform. (Illus.). 69p. 1997. pap. 15.00 (*0-9655761-2-4*) Kola Tree Pr.

Mendacity Without Scruples. Frank B. Carter, Jr. Ed. by Sylvia Ashton. LC 77-78384. 1978. 22.95 (*0-87949-093-4*) Ashley Bks.

Mende Government & Politics under Colonial Rule: A Historical Study of Political Change in Sierra Leone 1890-1937. Arthur Abraham. (Illus.). 1979. 29.50 (*0-19-711638-8*) OUP.

***Mended Hearts.** Alix Stokes. viii, 254p. 2000. pap. 14.99 (*1-930928-01-7*, Yellow Rose) Renaissance Alliance.

Mended Hearts, Vol. 1. Linda Shertzer. (Quilting Romance Ser.). 1999. mass mkt. 5.99 (*0-515-12611-X*, Jove) Berkley Pub.

Mendel in 90 Minutes. John Gribbin & Mary Gribbin. (Scientists in 90 Minutes Ser.). 1997. pap. 7.95 (*0-09-477120-0*, Pub. by Constable & Co) Trafalgar.

Mendel Marantz. David Freedman. 301p. 1987. 10.00 (*0-317-62515-2*) Pryor Pettengill.

Mendel Rosenbusch: Tales for Jewish Children. Ilse Weber. Tr. by Hans Fisher & Ruth Fisher from GER. Orig. Title: Mendel Rosenbusch: Geschichen Fur Jud Kinder. (J). (gr. 2-6). 14.00 (*1-928746-19-5*) Herodias.

Mendel Rosenbusch: Geschichen Fur Jud Kinder see Mendel Rosenbusch: Tales for Jewish Children

Mendel the Mouse, Bk. 1. Ruth Finkelstein. (Illus.). 5.00 (*0-914131-43-5*, D350) Torah Umesorah.

Mendelian Genetics: A Problem-Solving Approach. Ruth C. Von Blum et al. (gr. 11-12). 1979. pap. text 6.95 (*0-933694-00-8*, COM 4223A) COMPress.

***Mendelian Inheritance in Cattle.** J. J. Lauvergne. 450p. 2000. 85.00 (*90-74134-75-0*) Wageningen Pers.

Mendelian Inheritance in Man: A Catalog of Human Genes & Genetic Disorders, 2 vols. 11th ed. Victor A. McKusick et al. 1994. text 165.00 (*0-8018-4933-0*) Johns Hopkins.

Mendelian Inheritance in Man: A Catalog of Human Genes & Genetic Disorders. 12th ed. Victor A. McKusick. LC 97-26291. 1997. write for info. (*0-8018-5743-0*) Johns Hopkins.

Mendelian Inheritance in Man: A Catalog of Human Genes & Genetic Disorders, 3 vols. 12th ed. Victor A. McKusick. LC 97-26291. 3972p. 1998. text 195.00 (*0-8018-5742-2*) Johns Hopkins.

Mendelian Inheritance in Man: Catalogs of Autosomal Dominant, Autosomal Recessive, & X-Linked Phenotypes. 2nd ed. Victor A. McKusick. LC 68-19441. 541p. 1968. reprint ed. pap. 167.80 (*0-608-18788-7*, 2029844) Bks Demand.

Mendelian Inheritance in Man: Catalogs of Autosomal Dominant, Autosomal Recessive, & X-Linked Phenotypes. 6th ed. Victor A. McKusick & William Osler. LC 82-47975. 1448p. 1983. reprint ed. pap. 200.00 (*0-608-15525-X*, 2029706) Bks Demand.

Mendelian Inheritance in Man: Catalogs of Autosomal Dominant, Autosomal Recessive, & X-Linked Phenotypes. 8th ed. Victor A. McKusick. LC 88-9328. 1742p. 1988. reprint ed. pap. 200.00 (*0-8357-6907-0*, 203796500009) Bks Demand.

Mendelian Revolution: The Emergence of Hereditarian Concepts in Modern Science & Society. Peter J. Bowler. LC 89-30914. 248p. 1989. text 38.50 (*0-8018-3888-6*) Johns Hopkins.

***Mendelian Threshold.** Robert Humphrey. 2000. pap. write for info. (*0-9640513-5-4*) Tattersall.

Mendell's Principles of Heredity. W. Bateson. 228p. Date not set. 21.95 (*0-8488-2207-2*) Amereon Ltd.

Mendel's Dwarf. Simon Mawer. 1999. pap. 12.95 (*0-14-028155-X*) Viking Penguin.

Mendel's Dwarf. large type ed. Simon Mawer. LC 98-23615. 1998. 26.95 (*0-7862-1519-4*) Thorndike Pr.

Mendel's Principles of Heredity: A Defence. fac. ed. William Bateson. (Illus.). 212p. 1996. 39.50 (*0-9653362-0-4*) Genetics Heritage.

Mendelsohn's Amerika: 82 Photographs. Erich Mendelsohn. LC 93-2259. 96p. 1993. reprint ed. pap. 11.95 (*0-486-27591-4*) Dover.

Mendelssohn. Mozelle Moshansky. (Illustrated Lives of the Great Composers Ser.). (Illus.). 144p. 1996. 17.95 (*0-7119-0252-6*, OP 42381) Omnibus NY.

Mendelssohn: A New Image of the Composer & His Age. Eric Werner. Tr. by Dika Newlin from GER. LC 78-1750. (Illus.). 545p. 1978. reprint ed. lib. bdg. 39.00 (*0-313-20302-4*, WEMN, Greenwood Pr) Greenwood.

Mendelssohn: A Second Elijah. Schima Kaufman. LC 78-110829. (Illus.). 353p. 1971. reprint ed. lib. bdg. 65.00 (*0-8371-3229-0*, KAME, Greenwood Pr) Greenwood.

Mendelssohn - Six Christmas Pieces. Ed. by Willard A. Palmer. (Alfred Masterwork Edition Ser.). 16p. 1980. 4.95 (*0-7390-0590-1*, 1958) Alfred Pub.

An Asterisk (*) at the beginning of an entry indicates that the title is appearing for the first time.

Mendelssohn - Wedding March. Ed. by Allan Small. (Simply Classics Ser.). 4p. 1995. pap. 2.50 (*0-7390-0833-1*, 14314) Alfred Pub.

Mendelssohn & Schumann: Essays on Their Music & Its Context. Jon W. Finson. Ed. by R. Larry Todd. LC 84-10120. vii, 189p. 1985. text 36.95 (*0-8223-0569-0*) Duke.

***Mendelssohn Companion.** Ed. by Douglass R. Seaton. LC 00-33129. 904p. 2001. lib. bdg. 120.00 (*0-313-28445-8*, Greenwood Pr) Greenwood.

Mendelssohn Family, 1729 to 1847, from Letters & Journals, 2 Vols. Sebastian Hensel. LC 68-25290. (Studies in Music: No. 42). 1969. reprint ed. lib. bdg. 150.00 (*0-8383-0304-8*) M S G Haskell Hse.

Mendelssohn Family, 1729 to 1847, from Letters & Journals, 2 vols. Sebastian Hensel. 1990. reprint ed. lib. bdg. 140.00 (*0-7812-9036-8*) Rprt Serv.

Mendelssohn Family Seventeen Twenty-Nine to Eighteen Forty-Seven from Letters & Journals, 2 vols., Set. 2nd ed. Sebastian Hensel. Tr. by Carl Klingemann et al. LC 68-31000. (Illus.). 1969. reprint ed. lib. bdg. 75.00 (*0-8371-0104-2*, HEMF) Greenwood.

Mendelssohn Family Seventeen Twenty-Nine to Eighteen Forty-Seven from Letters & Journals, 2 vols., Vol. 1. 2nd ed. Sebastian Hensel. Tr. by Carl Klingemann et al. LC 68-31000. (Illus.). 1969. reprint ed. lib. bdg. 45.00 (*0-8371-1792-5*, HEMA) Greenwood.

Mendelssohn Family Seventeen Twenty-Nine to Eighteen Forty-Seven from Letters & Journals, 2 vols., Vol. 2. 2nd ed. Sebastian Hensel. Tr. by Carl Klingemann et al. LC 68-31000. (Illus.). 1969. reprint ed. lib. bdg. 45.00 (*0-8371-0876-4*, HEMB) Greenwood.

Mendelssohn Is on the Roof. Jiri Weil. Tr. by Marie Winn. 228p. 1991. 23.95 (*0-374-20810-7*) FS&G.

Mendelssohn Is on the Roof. Jiri Weil. Tr. by Marie Winn. LC 98-31021. 240p. 1998. pap. 15.95 (*0-8101-1686-3*) Northwestern U Pr.

***Mendelssohn Masterpieces for Solo Piano: 25 Works.** Felix Mendelssohn. 2000. pap. 9.95 (*0-486-41161-3*) Dover.

Mendelssohn Studies. Ed. by R. Larry Todd. (Illus.). 275p. (C). 1992. text 80.00 (*0-521-41776-7*) Cambridge U Pr.

Mendelssohn, "The Herbrides" & Other Overtures: A Midsummer Night's Dream, Calm Sea & Prosperous Voyage, the Hebrides (Fingal's Cave) R. Larry Todd. LC 92-36005. (Cambridge Music Handbooks Ser.). (Illus.). 129p. (C). 1993. pap. text 12.95 (*0-521-40764-8*) Cambridge U Pr.

Mendelssohns on Honeymoon: The 1837 Diary of Felix & Cecille Mendelssohn Bartholdy, Together with Letters to Their Families. Felix Mendelssohn & Cecille Mendelssohn. Ed. by Peter W. Jones. LC 97-5419. (Illus.). 256p. 1997. text 65.00 (*0-19-816597-8*) OUP.

Mendelssohn/Songs Without Words: Selected Favorites for the Piano. Ed. by Willard A. Palmer. (Masterwork Edition Ser.). 64p. 1978. pap. 8.95 (*0-7390-0365-8*, 468) Alfred Pub.

***Mendelssohn/Songs Without Words: Selected Favorites for the Piano.** Ed. by Willard A. Palmer. (Exploring Piano Masterworks Ser.). 16p. 1999. 4.95 (*0-7390-0280-5*, 16724) Alfred Pub.

Mendelssohn/Twenty-Four Songs: Medium Voice. Felix Mendelssohn & Fanny Mendelssohn. Ed. by John G. Paton. 96p. (C). 1992. pap. 9.95 (*0-88284-523-3*, 3388) Alfred Pub.

Mendelssohn/Twenty-Four Songs, Medium Voice. Felix Mendelssohn & Fanny Mendelssohn. Ed. by John G. Paton. 96p. (C). 1992. pap. 9.95 (*0-88284-499-7*, 3387) Alfred Pub.

Mendenhall Glacier: A River of Ice. S. Foster. (Illus.). 36p. 1995. pap. 5.95 (*0-614-04304-2*) Alaska Natural.

Mender of My Broken Wings: An Allergy of Thanksgiving & Appreciation. Vanessa W. Polk. (Illus.). 65p. 1997. per. 3.00 (*0-9661134-0-3*) Creat Pub.

Menders of the Mind: A History of the Royal Australian & New Zealand College of Psychiatrists 1946-1996. W. D. Rubinstein & Hilary C. Rubinstein. (Illus.). 288p. 1997. text 49.50 (*0-19-553953-2*) OUP.

Mendes, No. II. Swan-Hall. 1977. 90.00 (*0-85668-007-9*, Pub. by Aris & Phillips) David Brown.

Mendes Da Rocha. Joseph M. Montaner. (Current Architecture Catalogues Ser.). (Illus.). 96p. 1997. pap. text 29.95 (*84-252-1682-6*) Watsn-Guptill.

Mendes I. R. K. Holz et al. (American Research Center in Egypt, Reports: Vol. 2). (Illus.). xxi, 83p. 1980. text 49.50 (*0-936770-02-3*, Pub. by Amer Res Ctr Egypt) Eisenbrauns.

Mendhams. John W. Rae. LC 98-87448. (Images of America Ser.). (Illus.). 128p. 1998. pap. 16.99 (*0-7524-1265-5*) Arcadia Publng.

Mendiant de Jerusalem. Elie Wiesel. (FRE.). 1983. pap. 14.95 (*0-7859-3376-X*, 202006619X) Fr & Eur.

Mendiants et Orgueilleux. Albert Cossery. (FRE.). 1979. pap. 10.95 (*0-7859-1894-9*, 2070371190) Fr & Eur.

Mendicants, Military Orders & Regionalism in Medieval Europe. Ed. by Jurgen Sarnowsky. LC 99-72564. (Illus.). 352p. 1999. text 78.95 (*1-84014-623-0*, Pub. by Ashgate Pub) Ashgate Pub Co.

Mending a Broken Heart. unabridged ed. S. Gianinazzi. 1998. pap. 14.95 (*1-893336-16-6*) B Newton.

Mending & Washing Your Nets: Fishing Lessons from the Disciples. George DeTellis, Jr. 124p. 1998. pap. 9.95 (*0-9653234-1-2*) New Missions.

Mending Bodies, Saving Souls: A History of Hospitals. Guenter B. Risse. (Illus.). 752p. 1999. text 39.95 (*0-19-505523-3*) OUP.

Mending Bridges: Thoughts, Reflections, Lessons Learned, Poetry & Prose. unabridged ed. Marcus Geeter. LC 98-61642. 120p. 1999. mass mkt. 12.95 (*0-9668615-0-7*) Power Summit.

***Mending Broken Hearts: Meditations for Finding Peace & Hope after Heartbreak.** Adele Wilcox. 1999. pap. 12.00 (*0-425-17056-X*) Berkley Pub.

***Mending Broken Promises: Justice for Children at Risk.** Couto-Stutts. 152p. (C). 2000. per. 15.95 (*0-7872-7124-1*) Kendall-Hunt.

Mending Family Relationships. Evelyn Leite. 44p. (Orig.). 1987. pap. 3.95 (*0-9613416-7-X*) Comm Intervention.

Mending Fences. George Lipponer. 350p. (Orig.). 1989. pap. write for info. (*0-9624158-0-4*) Dove Pub NY.

Mending Fences. Livia Reasoner. (Our Town Ser.). 1998. mass mkt. 5.99 (*0-515-12211-4*, Jove) Berkley Pub.

Mending Fences: Renewing Justice between Government & Civil Society. Dan Coats. LC 98-23846. 80p. (C). 1998. pap. 8.99 (*0-8010-5830-9*) Baker Bks.

Mending Lives, Healing Hearts: The Florida Sheriffs' Youth Ranches - The First 40 Years. Prudy T. Board & Esther B. Colcord. LC 97-15320. 1997. write for info. (*0-89865-988-4*) Donning Co.

Mending Minds: A Guide to Today's Psychiatry. Leonard L. Heston. (Illus.). 233p. (C). 1991. pap. 16.95 (*0-7167-2167-8*); text 20.00 (*0-7167-2158-9*) W H Freeman.

Mending Ministry of John. Witness Lee. 154p. 1989. per. 7.00 (*0-87083-455-X*, 04-008-001) Living Stream Ministry.

Mending of the Sky & Other Chinese Myths. Tr. by Xiao M. Li from CHI. (Illus.). 54p. (Orig.). (YA). (gr. 5 up). 1989. pap. 10.00 (*0-9617481-3-3*) Oyster River Pr.

Mending Ourselves: Expressions of Healing & Self-Integration. Ed. by Lynn W. (Illus.). 272p. (Orig.). 1993. pap. 12.95 (*0-9637277-0-2*) Many Voices Pr.

Mending Peter's Heart. Maureen Wittbold. Ed. by David Anderson & Andrea Tronslin. LC 95-200701. (Illus.). 32p. (J). (gr. k-6). 1995. pap. 8.95 (*0-9641330-2-4*) Portunus Pubng.

Mending Rips in the Sky: Options for Somali Communities in the 21st Century. Hussein M. Adam & Richard Ford. LC 97-10801. 1997. 89.95 (*1-56902-073-6*) Red Sea Pr.

Mending Rips in the Sky: Options for Somali Communities in the 21st Century. Ed. by Hussein M. Adam & Richard Ford. 630p. 1997. pap. 29.95 (*1-56902-074-4*) Red Sea Pr.

Mending the Broken Bough: Restoring the Promise of the Mother-Daughter Relationship. Barbara Zax & Stephan Poulter. 288p. 1998. pap. 13.00 (*0-425-16318-0*) Berkley Pub.

Mending the Broken Pieces. Cecilia E. Holloman. 356p. 1999. pap. 20.00 (*0-9670422-0-8*) Eden Legacy Pr.

Mending the Circle - A Native Pepatriation Guide: Understanding & Implementing NAGPRA, the Official Smithsonian & Other Repatriation Policies. J. Trope et al. LC 95-81363. 167p. 1996. ring bd. 25.00 (*0-9648208-0-3*) AIRORF.

Mending the Circle: A Native American Repatriation Guide Supplement 1: Understanding & Implementing NAGPRA & the Official Smithsonian & Other Repatriation Policies. rev. ed. Jack Trope. 57p. 1997. ring bd. 8.00 (*0-9648208-1-1*) AIRORF.

Mending the Cracks in the Ivory Tower: Strategies for Conflict Management in Higher Education. Ed. by Susan A. Holton. 284p. 1998. 35.95 (*1-882982-21-5*) Anker Pub.

Mending the Earth: A World for Our Grandchildren. Ed. by Paul Rothkrug & Robert Olsen. LC 90-23408. 219p. 1990. pap. 9.95 (*1-55643-091-4*) North Atlantic.

Mending the Heart. John Claypool. LC 99-19448. 1999. 8.95 (*1-56101-165-7*) Cowley Pubns.

Mending the Ozone Hole: Science, Technology & Policy. Arjun Makhijani & Kevin R. Gurney. (Illus.). 360p. 1995. 44.00 (*0-262-13308-3*) MIT Pr.

***Mending the Safety Net.** 450p. 2000. 51.75 (*0-309-06497-X*, Joseph Henry Pr) Natl Acad Pr.

***Mending the Skies: Poems.** Celia Brown. LC 99-50657. 96p. 2000. pap. 12.00 (*1-56474-338-1*) Fithian Pr.

Mending the Torn Fabric: For Those Who Grieve & Those Who Want to Help Them. Sarah Brabant. LC 96-14887. (Death, Value, & Meaning Ser.). 168p. 1996. 30.95 (*0-89503-141-8*) Baywood Pub.

Mending the World: Quaker Insights on the Social Order. Kenneth E. Boulding. LC 86-60283. 1986. pap. 4.00 (*0-87574-266-1*) Pendle Hill.

Mending Your Broken Heart: A Survival Kit. Ann McGill & Glynis Wilson. (Life Line Ser.). 128p. (Orig.). 1994. pap. 14.95 (*1-55059-091-X*) Temeron Bks.

Mending Your Soul: 6 Spiritual Laws for Energized Living. Ramesh Richard. LC 99-28735. 160p.1999. pap. 12.99 (*0-8054-1834-2*) Broadman.

Mendocino: The Ultimate Wine & Food Lover's Guide. Heidi H. Cusick. LC 96-30618. 1997. pap. 19.95 (*0-8118-1391-6*) Chronicle Bks.

***Mendocino - Lake Counties.** Jeffrey Caldewey & Mildred Howie. (California Wine Tour Ser.). 128p. 2000. pap. 11.95 (*1-891267-26-4*) Wine Appreciation.

Mendocino & the Movies: Hollywood & Television Motion Pictures Filmed on the Mendocino Coast. Ed. by Bruce Levene. (Illus.). 144p. 1998. pap. 18.95 (*0-933391-14-5*) Pac Transcript.

***Mendocino Artists: An Endangered Species.** Ed. by William P. Brazill. (Illus.). 48p. 2000. pap. 18.95 (*0-9627007-5-4*) Monday Pr CA.

Mendocino City: A Daily Journal, 1852-1938. W. Francis Jackson. Ed. by Bertha Mason & Dorothy Bear. (Illus.). 300p. 1991. pap. 18.87 (*0-9628374-3-1*) FMMC Bks.

Mendocino Coast Bike Rides: Road & Trail Rides from Easy to Advanced. Bob Lorentzen. LC 97-128632. 168p. (Orig.). 1996. pap. 12.00 (*0-939431-11-4*) Bored Feet Pubns.

Mendocino Coast Glove Box Guide: Lodging, Eateries, Sights, History, Activities, & More. 2nd ed. Bob Lorentzen. LC 94-44204. (Glove Box Guides Ser.). (Illus.). 237p. 1997. pap. 13.00 (*0-939431-16-5*) Bored Feet Pubns.

Mendocino Coast Jewish Community Cook Book. Intro. by Margaret Holub. LC 92-80549. (Illus.). 200p. (Orig.). 1993. pap. 12.95 (*0-914046-14-4*) R L Shep.

Mendocino, Humboldt: Lost Coast - The Mystical Coast. 1995. 4.95 (*0-916310-06-X*) North of San Francisco.

Mendocino Malady: On the Eve of My 50th Year. Bobby Markels. (Mendocino Malady Ser.). 34p. Date not set. pap. 6.50 (*1-880991-03-9*) Stone Pub.

Mendocino Menace: (A Kay Roberts Mystery) Beth Howes. 1998. pap. 13.99 (*0-9639147-0-7*) ReGeJe Press.

Mendocino Portfolio. Cynthia Frank & Hannes Krebs. LC 88-61393. (Illus.). 88p. 1988. boxed set 17.95 (*0-936609-12-5*) QED Ft Bragg.

Mendocino Rust. Ed. by Beth Bosk & Gary Thompson. (Illus.). 88p. (Orig.). 1981. pap. 9.99 (*0-9604100-0-7*) Albion Albums.

Mendoza Family in the Spanish Renaissance, 1350-1550. Helen Nader. LC 79-9945. 291p. reprint ed. pap. 90.30 (*0-8357-7949-1*, 205702400002) Bks Demand.

Mendoza in Hollywood: A Novel of the Company. Kage Baker. LC 99-14949. 352p. 2000. 24.00 (*0-15-100448-X*, Harvest Bks) Harcourt.

Mendozas of Mexico. Pavlik. 48p. 1997. spiral bd. 7.81 (*0-07-292787-9*) McGraw.

Menedelian Genetics. Abramoff. Date not set. 1.20 (*0-7167-9090-4*) W H Freeman.

Menehune & the Nene. Susan Yamashita. LC 84-3290. (Treasury of Children's Hawaiian Stories Ser.). (Illus.). (J). (gr. 3-6). 1984. 9.95 (*0-916630-42-0*) Pr Pacifica.

Menehune Mischief. Susan Entz & Sheri Galarza. (Hawaiian Values Ser.: Vol. 5). (Illus.). 24p. (J). (ps-2). 1999. pap. 4.95 (*1-57306-091-7*) Bess Pr.

Menehune Murders. Margot Arnold, pseud. (Penny Spring & Sir Toby Glendower Mystery Ser.). 260p. 1991. pap. 7.95 (*0-88150-196-4*, Foul Play) Norton.

Menehune Scrolls. 2nd ed. William J. Sollner. pap. 5.95 (*0-681-02735-5*) Booklines Hawaii.

Menendez: Pedro Menendez de Aviles: Captain General of the Ocean Sea. Albert Manucy. LC 92-5128. (Illus.). 112p. 1992. 14.95 (*1-56164-015-8*); pap. 7.95 (*1-56164-016-6*) Pineapple Pr.

Menestrel: Le Tout-Puissant. Marc Guiguin. (Serie Rouge). 55p. (C). 1994. pap. 7.50 (*0-521-44980-4*) Cambridge U Pr.

Menfreya in the Morning. Victoria Holt, pseud. 1993. mass mkt. 5.99 (*0-449-45255-7*, Crest) Fawcett.

Menfriends. Odie Hawkins. 192p. (Orig.). 1989. mass mkt. 2.95 (*0-87067-326-2*, BH326-2) Holloway.

Meng Hua Yan Shi De Cang Sang. Zhu Xiao Feng. (Selected Works of Zhu Xiao Feng Ser.: Vol. 1). (CHI.). 228p. 1997. 30.00 (*1-891158-00-7*) Am Int Rare Bks.

***Mengele: The Complete Story.** Gerald Posner & John Ware. (Illus.). 400p. 1999. reprint ed. pap. 18.95 (*0-8154-1006-9*) Cooper Sq.

Meniere's & Its Management. Tom Wilmot. (Illus.). 132p. (C). 1984. 29.95 (*0-398-04965-3*) C C Thomas.

Meniere's Disease. Jeffrey P. Harris. (Illus.). xiii, 419p. 1999. 183.00 (*90-6299-162-9*) Kugler Pubns.

Meniere's Disease. Ed. by M. Kitahara. (Illus.). xv, 220p. 1990. 64.00 (*0-387-70056-0*) Spr-Verlag.

Meniere's Disease. Ed. by Joseph B. Nadol, Jr. LC 89-19868. (Illus.). 568p. 1989. lib. bdg. 163.00 (*90-6299-052-5*, Pub. by Kugler) Kugler Pubns.

Meniere's Disease: A Comprehensive Appraisal. Ed. by Wilhelmus J. Oosterveld. LC 83-5962. (Wiley-Medical Publication). 145p. reprint ed. pap. 45.00 (*0-8357-7878-9*, 203629600002) Bks Demand.

Meniere's Disease: An Information Book for People with Meniere's Disease. V. K. Barton. 136p. 1991. pap. 60.00 (*0-646-05022-2*, Pub. by Menieres Aust) St Mut.

Meniere's Disease: Perspectives in the 90's. Ed. by R. Filipo & Maurizio Barbara. LC 94-23038. (Illus.). 586p. 1994. lib. bdg. 171.50 (*90-6299-112-2*) Kugler Pubns.

Meniere's Disease: What You Need to Know. P. J. Heybach. Ed. by Jerry L. Underwood. LC 98-220287. (Illus.). 300p. 1998. 34.95 (*0-9632611-2-6*); pap. 24.95 (*0-9632611-1-8*) Vestibular.

Meningeal Leukemia. Lawrence E. Broder & Stephen K. Carter. LC 74-190394. 140p. reprint ed. pap. 43.40 (*0-608-30231-7*, 202070600018) Bks Demand.

Meningiomas. Ed. by Ossama Al-Mefty. 656p. 1990. text 176.00 (*0-88167-713-2*, 2188) Lppncott W & W.

Meningiomas & Their Surgical Management. Henry M. Schmidek. (Illus.). 480p. 1991. text 255.00 (*0-7216-3114-2*, W B Saunders Co) Harcrt Hlth Sci Grp.

Meningitis. Yuriy Tarnawsky. LC 77-88231. 1978. 15.95 (*0-914590-48-0*); pap. 5.95 (*0-914590-49-9*) Fiction Coll.

Meningitis. Edward Willett. LC 99-12279. (Diseases & People Ser.). (Illus.). 112p. (YA). (gr. 6 up). 1999. lib. bdg. 20.95 (*0-7660-1187-9*) Enslow Pubs.

Meningitis: 100 Maxims. Karen Roos. (One Hundred Maxims in Neurology Ser.). (Illus.). 224p. 1996. pap. text 35.00 (*0-340-60879-X*) OUP.

Meningococcal Disease. Ed. by Keith Cartwright. LC 94-32088. 324p. 1995. 245.00 (*0-471-95259-1*) Wiley.

Menippean Elements in Paul Scarron's Roman Comique. Barbara L. Merry. LC 91-16266. (American University Studies: Romance Languages & Literature: Ser. II, Vol. 172). 132p. (C). 1992. text 35.95 (*0-8204-1578-2*) P Lang Pubng.

Menippean Satire & the Poetics of Wit: Ideologies of Self-Consciousness in Dunton, D'Urfey, & Sterne. Garry H. Sherbert. (Comparative Cultures & Literatures Ser.: Vol. 8). XVII, 226p. (C). 1996. text 49.95 (*0-8204-2499-4*) P Lang Pubng.

Menitculture or the A-B-C or True Living (1896) Contrib. by Horace Fletcher. 145p. 1998. reprint ed. pap. 16.95 (*0-7661-0489-3*) Kessinger Pub.

Menke Sonnets. Menke Katz. LC 92-80449. (YID.). 64p. 1993. 15.95 (*0-912292-96-2*) Smith.

***Menlo Park, California: Beyond the Gate.** Michael Svanevik & Shirley Burgett. LC 00-31823. 2000. write for info. (*1-881529-64-9*) Custom & Limited.

Menninger: The Family & the Clinic. Lawrence J. Friedman. LC 91-30510. (Illus.). xx, 484p. 1991. reprint ed. pap. 15.95 (*0-7006-0513-4*) U Pr of KS.

***Menno-Lite: A Humorous Look at Mennonite Life.** Merle Good et al. (Illus.). 96p. 1999. pap. 6.95 (*1-56148-295-1*) Good Bks PA.

Menno Simons: His Image & Message. Sjouke Voolstra. LC 97-7550. (Cornelius H. Wedel Historical Ser.: Vol. 10). (Illus.). 110p. (Orig.). 1997. pap. 18.00 (*0-9630160-9-1*) Bethel Coll.

***Mennonite & Nazi? Attitudes among Mennonite Colonists in Latin America, 1933-1945.** John D. Thiesen et al. (Studies in Anabaptist & Mennonite History: Vol. 37). 1999. pap. 25.00 (*0-9683462-5-1*) Pandora Pr.

Mennonite Architecture: Diachronic Evidence for Rapid Diffusion in Rural Communities. Jeffery L. Eighmy. LC 87-45780. (Immigrant Communities & Ethnic Minorities in the U. S. & Canada Ser.: No. 15). 1989. 49.50 (*0-404-19425-7*, HN120) AMS Pr.

M

Mennonite Bibliography, 2 vols. Ed. by Nelson Springer & A. J. Klassen. LC 77-9105. 1977. 147.50 (*0-8361-1208-3*) Herald Pr.

Mennonite Bibliography, Vol. 1. Ed. by Nelson Springer & A. J. Klassen. LC 77-9105. 532p. 1977. 78.00 (*0-8361-1206-7*) Herald Pr.

Mennonite Bibliography, Vol. 2. Ed. by Nelson Springer & A. J. Klassen. LC 77-9105. 634p. 1977. 78.00 (*0-8361-1207-5*) Herald Pr.

Mennonite Brethren Church Gesangbuch. 590p. 1995. 11.95 (*0-919797-17-2*) Kindred Prods.

Mennonite Brotherhood in Russia, 1789-1910. rev. ed. P. M. Friesen. LC 78-52664. 1065p. 1982. 12.95 (*0-919797-19-9*) Kindred Prods.

Mennonite Church in India: Eighteen Ninety-Seven to Nineteen Sixty-Two. John A. Lapp. LC 75-186445. (Studies in Anabaptist & Mennonite History: Vol. 14). 248p. 1972. 12.99 (*0-8361-1122-2*) Herald Pr.

Mennonite Community Cookbook. rev. ed. Mary E. Showalter. LC 57-7627. (Illus.). 494p. 1992. spiral bd. 19.99 (*0-8361-3625-X*) Herald Pr.

Mennonite Confession of Faith. Ed. by Irvin B. Horst. LC 87-80243. (Mennonite Sources & Documents Ser.: No. 2). 88p. 1988. 12.95 (*0-9614479-6-6*) Lancaster Mennonite.

Mennonite Confession of Faith. Mennonite Church Staff. LC 63-22593. 32p. (Orig.). 1963. pap. 1.99 (*0-8361-1314-4*) Herald Pr.

Mennonite Confessions of Faith. 96p. 1965. pap. 3.10 (*0-7399-0223-7*, 2330) Rod & Staff.

***Mennonite Country-Style Recipes.** Esther H. Shank. LC 00-26878. (Illus.). 688p. 2000. 12.99 (*0-517-16210-5*) Gramrcy Bks.

Mennonite Country-Style Recipes & Kitchen Secrets. Esther Shank. LC 87-8518. (Illus.). 680p. 1987. spiral bd. 20.99 (*0-8361-3697-7*) Herald Pr.

Mennonite Encyclopedia, Vol. 1. Ed. by Harold S. Bender & C. Henry Smith. LC 55-4563. 900p. 1955. 90.00 (*0-8361-1118-4*) Herald Pr.

Mennonite Encyclopedia, Vol. 2. Ed. by Harold S. Bender & C. Henry Smith. LC 55-4563. 912p. 1956. 90.00 (*0-8361-1119-2*) Herald Pr.

Mennonite Encyclopedia, Vol. 3. Ed. by Harold S. Bender & C. Henry Smith. LC 55-4563. 952p. 1957. 90.00 (*0-8361-1120-6*) Herald Pr.

Mennonite Encyclopedia, Vol. 4. Ed. by Harold S. Bender & C. Henry Smith. LC 55-4563. 1184p. 1959. 90.00 (*0-8361-1121-4*) Herald Pr.

Mennonite Encyclopedia, Vol. 5. Ed. by Cornelius J. Dyck & Dennis Martin. LC 55-4563. 962p. 1990. text 90.00 (*0-8361-3105-3*) Herald Pr.

Mennonite Encyclopedia Set, Vol. 5. 1990. 400.00 (*0-8361-3107-X*) Herald Pr.

Mennonite Entrepreneurs. Calvin W. Redekop et al. LC 94-46177. (Illus.). 320p. 1995. text 34.95 (*0-8018-5003-7*) Johns Hopkins.

***Mennonite Experience in America, 4 vols.** Prod. by Culmination Mennonite Writ. Proj. Staff. 1999. 79.99 (*0-8361-3120-7*) Herald Pr.

Mennonite Family History Ten-Year Index, 1982-1991. Lois A. Mast. 1992. pap. 23.00 (*1-883294-05-3*) Masthof Pr.

Mennonite Foods & Folkways from South Russia, Vol. I. Norma J. Voth. LC 90-81731. (Illus.). 480p. 1994. pap. 18.95 (*1-56148-136-X*) Good Bks PA.

Mennonite Foods & Folkways from South Russia, Vol. II. Norma J. Voth. LC 90-81731. (Illus.). 288p. 1994. pap. 14.95 (*1-56148-137-8*) Good Bks PA.

Mennonite Furniture: A Migrant Tradition, 1766-1910. Reinhild K. Janzen & John M. Janzen. LC 91-74055. (Illus.). 230p. 1991. 35.00 (*1-56148-047-9*) Good Bks PA.

Mennonite Furniture: The Ontario Tradition in York County. Patricia Musson & Lynda M. Nykor. 95p. 1977. 29.95 (*0-88862-148-5*, Pub. by J Lorimer) Formac Dist Ltd.

Mennonite Furniture: The Ontario Tradition in York County. Patricia Musson & Lynda M. Nykor. 95p. 1977. pap. 2.99 (*0-88862-149-3*, Pub. by J Lorimer) Formac Dist Ltd.

Mennonite Hymnal. LC 69-18131. 640p. 1960. 9.00 (*0-8361-8152-2*) Herald Pr.

Mennonite Hymnal. Ed. by Lester Hostetler & Walter E. Yoder. LC 69-18131. 1969. 8.25 (*0-87303-515-1*) Faith & Life.

Mennonite Hymnal. large type ed. LC 69-18131. 640p. 1982. 11.95 (*0-8361-8158-1*) Herald Pr.

Mennonite Hymnal, Shaped Notes. LC 69-18131. 640p. 1960. 9.00 (*0-8361-8151-4*) Herald Pr.

Mennonite Hymnal Loose-Leaf Edition - Shape Note. LC 69-18131. 640p. 1969. 16.00 (*0-8361-8153-0*) Herald Pr.

Mennonite Idealism & Higher Education: The Story of the Fresno Pacific College Idea. Ed. by Paul Toews. 164p. 1995. pap. 11.95 (*1-877941-05-0*) Ctr Mennonite Brethren Studies.

Mennonite Identity in Conflict. Leo Driedger. LC 87-24733. (Studies in Religion & Society: Vol. 19). 240p. 1988. lib. bdg. 89.95 (*0-88946-855-9*) E Mellen.

Mennonite in Russia: The Diaries of Jacob D. Epp, 1851-1880. Ed. & Tr. by Harvey L. Dyck. (Illus.). 448p. 1991. text 60.00 (*0-8020-2788-1*) U of Toronto Pr.

Mennonite International Study Project: Final Report. Nancy Heisey & Paul Longacre. 88p. (Orig.). 1990. pap. write for info. (*0-318-66838-6*) MB Missions.

Mennonite Journal, 1862-1865: A Father's Account of the Civil War in the Shenandoah Valley. Ed. by John R. Hildebrand. LC 96-10185. 100p. 1996. pap. 9.95 (*1-57249-011-X*, Burd St Pr) White Mane Pub.

***Mennonite Madonna.** Diane Driedger. 80p. 1999. pap. 10.95 (*0-921881-53-3*) gynergy Bks.

Mennonite Martyrs: People Who Suffered for Their Faith from 1920-1940. Aron A. Toews. Tr. by John B. Toews. (Perspectives on Mennonite Life & Thought Ser.: Vol. 6). 225p. (Orig.). 1990. pap. 23.95 (*0-919797-98-9*) Kindred Prods.

Mennonite Mosaic: Identity & Modernization. J. Howard Kauffman & Leo Driedger. LC 91-24568. 336p. (Orig.). 1991. pap. 15.99 (*0-8361-3567-9*) Herald Pr.

Mennonite Peacemaking from Quietism to Activism. Leo Driedger & Donald B. Kraybill. LC 93-36827. 336p. (Orig.). 1994. pap. 16.99 (*0-8361-3648-9*) Herald Pr.

***Mennonite Piety Through the Centuries: Its Genius & Its Literature.** Robert Friedmann. 304p. 1999. pap. 26.00 (*1-57910-214-X*) Wipf & Stock.

Mennonite Polity for Ministerial Leadership: A Statement by the Joint Committee on Ministerial Leadership. Ministerial Leadership Services of the General Con & Mennonite Board of Congregational Ministries Staff. LC 96-84443. 148p. 1996. pap. 8.95 (*0-87303-319-1*) Faith & Life.

Mennonite Quarterly Review: Goshen, Ind., 1927-1976, Set, Vols. 1-50. lib. bdg. 2375.00 (*0-404-19575-X*) AMS Pr.

Mennonite Recipes from the Shenandoah Valley. Phyllis Pellman Good & Kate Good. LC 99-41044. (Illus.). 300p. 1999. pap. 14.95 (*1-56148-233-1*) Good Bks PA.

Mennonite Society. Calvin W. Redekop. LC 88-32013. 456p. (C). 1989. text 55.00 (*0-8018-3729-4*) Johns Hopkins.

Mennonite Statement & Study on Violence. Lois Barrett. 68p. 1998. pap. 8.95 (*0-87303-339-6*) Faith & Life.

Mennonite Statements on Peace. Richard C. Detweiler. 80p. (Orig.). 1968. pap. 2.99 (*0-8361-1581-3*) Herald Pr.

Mennonite Story. Rudy Baergen. 62p. 1981. reprint ed. pap. 4.95 (*0-87303-066-4*) Faith & Life.

Mennonite Theology in Face of Modernity: Essays in Honor of Gordon D. Kaufman. Ed. by Alain E. Weaver. LC 96-20564. (Cornelius H. Wedel Historical Ser.: No. 9). 275p. (Orig.). 1996. pap. write for info. (*0-9630160-7-5*) Bethel Coll.

***Mennonite Tourguide to Western Europe.** Jan Gleysteen. 340p. 2000. pap. 29.00 (*1-57910-343-X*) Wipf & Stock.

Mennonite Witness in the Middle East: A Missiological Introduction. Leroy Friesen. Ed. by Betty Weaver & Ronald Yoder. 161p. (C). 1992. pap. text 31.82 (*1-877736-14-7*) MB Missions.

Mennonite Woman's Life. Photos by Ruth Hershey. LC 93-43577. (Illus.). 96p. 1993. pap. 11.95 (*1-56148-096-7*) Good Bks PA.

Mennonite Women of Lancaster County: A Story in Photographs from 1855-1935. Joanne H. Siegrist. (Illus.). 220p. 1996. pap. 14.95 (*1-56148-205-6*) Good Bks PA.

Mennonites & Baptists: A Continuing Conversation. Ed. by Paul Toews. (Perspectives on Mennonite Life & Thought Ser.: Vol. 7). 270p. 1993. pap. 15.95 (*0-921788-16-9*) Kindred Prods.

Mennonites in American Society, 1930-1970: Modernity & the Persistence of Religious Community. Paul Toews. LC 96-21253. 448p. 1996. 19.99 (*0-8361-3117-7*) Herald Pr.

Mennonites in Canada, 1939-1970 Vol. 3: A People Transformed, Vol. 3. T. D. Regehr. (Illus.). 600p. 1996. text 29.95 (*0-8020-0465-2*) U of Toronto Pr.

Mennonites in China. rev. ed. Robert Ramseyer & Alice R. Ramseyer. Ed. by Herta Funk & Betty Kelsey. (Illus.). 114p. 1989. reprint ed. pap. 6.00 (*1-877736-02-3*) MB Missions.

Mennonites in Europe. John Horsh. 248p. 1995. 13.95 (*0-7399-0665-8*, 2324) Rod & Staff.

Mennonites in the World War: or Nonresistance under Test. Jonas S. Hartzler. LC 76-137543. (Peace Movement in America Ser.). 246p. 1972. reprint ed. lib. bdg. 32.95 (*0-89198-071-7*) Ozer.

Mennyms. Sylvia Waugh. LC 93-15901. 216p. (YA). (gr. 5-7). 1994. 16.00 (*0-688-13070-4*, Greenwillow Bks) HarpC Child Bks.

Mennyms. Sylvia Waugh. (J). 1995. 10.34 (*0-606-07858-4*) Turtleback.

Mennyms. Sylvia Waugh. 240p. (J). (gr. 5-7). 1995. reprint ed. mass mkt. 4.99 (*0-380-72528-2*, Avon Bks) Morrow Avon.

Mennyms Alive. Sylvia Waugh. LC 96-46261. (Mennyms Ser.). 224p. (YA). (gr. 5 up). 1997. 16.00 (*0-688-15201-5*, Greenwillow Bks) HarpC Child Bks.

Mennyms Alive. Sylvia Waugh. 224p. (gr. 3-7). 1999. mass mkt. 4.50 (*0-380-72943-1*, Avon Bks) Morrow Avon.

Mennyms Alone. Sylvia Waugh. LC 95-35740. 196p. (YA). (gr. 5 up). 1996. 16.00 (*0-688-14702-X*, Grenwillow Bks) HarpC Child Bks.

Mennyms Alone. Sylvia Waugh. (J). 1998. mass mkt. 4.50 (*0-380-78867-5*, Avon Bks) Morrow Avon.

Mennyms in the Wilderness. Sylvia Waugh. LC 94-6881. (Illus.). 256p. (YA). (gr. 5 up). 1995. 15.00 (*0-688-13820-9*, Grenwillow Bks) HarpC Child Bks.

Mennyms in the Wilderness. Sylvia Waugh. 272p. (J). (gr. 5-7). 1996. mass mkt. 4.50 (*0-380-72529-0*, Avon Bks) Morrow Avon.

Mennyms in the Wilderness. Sylvia Waugh. (J). 1996. 9.60 (*0-606-08821-0*, Pub. by Turtleback) Demco.

Mennyms Under Seige. Sylvia Waugh. LC 95-1500. 224p. (J). (gr. 5-7). 1997. mass mkt. 4.50 (*0-380-72584-3*, Avon Bks) Morrow Avon.

Mennyms under Siege. Sylvia Waugh. 1997. 9.60 (*0-606-11617-6*, Pub. by Turtleback) Demco.

Meno. Plato. Ed. by R. W. Sharples. 1985. 49.00 (*0-86516-089-9*) Bolchazy-Carducci.

Meno: Text & Critical Essays. Plato. Ed. by Malcolm Brown. Tr. by William K. Guthrie from GRE. LC 78-162302. (Text & Commentary Ser.). (C). 1971. pap. 6.00 (*0-672-61123-6*, TC10, Bobbs) Macmillan.

Menominee. Stephen Dunning. (Illus.). (Orig.). 1987. pap. 10.00 (*0-9608802-3-2*) Years Pr.

***Menominee.** Verna Fowler. (Indian Nations Ser.). (Illus.). 2000. 25.69 (*0-8172-5458-7*) Raintree Steck-V.

Menominee. Joan Kalbacken. LC 93-36671. (New True Books Ser.). (Illus.). 48p. (J). (ps-3). 1994. lib. bdg. 21.00 (*0-516-01054-9*) Childrens.

Menominee. Edward R. Ricciuti. LC 97-560. (Native American People Ser.: Set V). 32p. (J). (gr. 5-8). 1997. lib. bdg. 22.60 (*0-86625-603-2*) Rourke Pubns.

Menominee Music. Frances Densmore. (Bureau of American Ethnology Bulletins Ser.). 230p. 1995. lib. bdg. 89.00 (*0-7812-4102-2*) Rprt Serv.

Menominee Music. Frances Densmore. LC 72-1882. (Music Ser.). (Illus.). 286p. 1972. reprint ed. lib. bdg. 29.50 (*0-306-70510-9*) Da Capo.

Menominee Music. Frances Densmore. 1988. reprint ed. lib. bdg. 75.00 (*0-317-90154-0*) Rprt Serv.

Menomini Texts. Leonard Bloomfield. LC 73-3548. (American Ethnological Society Publications: No. 12). reprint ed. 92.50 (*0-404-58162-5*) AMS Pr.

Menopausal Memoir: Letters from Another Climate. Anne Herrmann. LC 97-31420. (Illus.). 111p. 1997. 39.95 (*0-7890-0296-5*, Harrington Park); pap. 14.95 (*1-56023-919-0*, Harrington Park) Haworth Pr.

Menopausal Woman on the Run: A Wicked Woman's Guide to Growing Old. Jaki Da Costa. 1994. pap. 19.95 (*1-898307-19-9*) Holmes Pub.

***Menopausal Years: The Wise Woman Way, Alternative Approaches for Women 30-90.** rev. ed. Susan S. Weed. 228p. 2000. pap. 11.95 (*1-888123-03-6*) Ash Tree.

Menopausal Years: The Wise Womans Way: Alternative Approaches for Women 30-90. Susun S. Weed. LC 92-70069. (Wise Woman Healing Ser.: No. 3). (Illus.). 228p. (Orig.). (C). 1992. pap. 9.95 (*0-9614620-4-3*) Ash Tree.

Menopause. (Illus.). 36p. (C). 1993. pap. text 20.00 (*1-56806-398-9*) DIANE Pub.

Menopause. Sarah Brewer. 1997. pap. 9.95 (*0-7225-3389-6*) Thorsons PA.

Menopause. Ed. by Herbert J. Buchsbaum. (Clinical Perspectives in Obstetrics & Gynecology Ser.). (Illus.). 225p. 1983. 90.00 (*0-387-90825-0*) Spr-Verlag.

Menopause. Raymond G. Burnett. (Illus.). 144p. 1987. pap. 12.75 (*0-8092-4677-5*, 467750, Contemporary Bks) NTC Contemp Pub Co.

Menopause: A Basic Guide for Women. Alan J. Silverstein & Cynthia S. Cotten. LC 95-14381. (Illus.). 88p. (Orig.). 1996. pap. 9.95 (*0-87573-066-3*) Jain Pub Co.

Menopause: A Gentle, Natural Approach. 2nd ed. Edna C. Ryneveld. LC 98-5984. (Illus.). 240p. 1999. pap. text 12.95 (*1-56718-595-9*) Llewellyn Pubns.

Menopause: A Guide to Health & Happiness. James E. Huston. LC 97-36897. (Illus.). 256p. 1998. 25.95 (*0-8160-3675-6*); pap. 15.95 (*0-8160-3693-4*) Facts on File.

Menopause: A Medical Guide for Women. 2nd rev. ed. Winnifred B. Cutler & Delso-Ramon Garcia. 432p. 1993. pap. 14.95 (*0-393-30995-9*) Norton.

Menopause: A Midlife Passage. Ed. by Joan Callahan. LC 92-41565. 240p. 1993. 31.95 (*0-253-31312-0*); pap. 13.95 (*0-253-20817-3*) Ind U Pr.

Menopause: A Self-Care Manual. rev. ed. Judy Costlow et al. (Illus.). 72p. 1989. 5.00 (*0-9622933-1-8*) Santa Fe Health.

***Menopause: A Woman Doctor's Guide: Essential Facts & Up-to-the-Minute Information for a Woman.** Lois Jovanovic. 2000. mass mkt. 6.99 (*1-57566-601-4*, Knsington) Kensgtn Pub Corp.

Menopause: A Woman's View. large type ed. Anne Dickson & Nikki Henriques. 21.95 (*1-85695-097-2*, Pub. by ISIS Lrg Prnt) Transaction Pubs.

Menopause: Biological & Clinical Consequences of Ovarian Failure: Evaluation & Management. Ed. by Stanley G. Korenman. (Serono Symposia, USA Ser.). (Illus.). 270p. (C). 1990. text 55.00 (*1-878601-00-8*) Serono Symposia USA.

***Menopause: Biology & Pathology.** Ed. by Rogerio A. Lobo et al. 700p. 2000. 159.95 (*0-12-453790-1*) Acad Pr.

***Menopause: Clinical Concepts.** 3rd rev. ed. H. Jane Chihal & Steve London. (Illus.). 235p. 1999. pap. 17.95 (*0-917634-03-9*) EMIS.

Menopause: Comprehensive Management. 3rd ed. Ed. by Bernard A. Eskin. (Illus.). 382p. 1993. text 65.00 (*0-07-019619-2*) McGraw-Hill HPD.

***Menopause: Comprehensive Management.** 4th ed. Bernard A. Eskin. (Illus.). 326p. 2000. 78.00 (*1-85070-090-7*) Prthnon Pub.

Menopause: Endocrinology & Management. Ed. by David B. Seifer & Elizabeth A. Kennard. LC 99-32278. (Contemporary Endocrinology Ser.: Vol. 18). (Illus.). 288p. 1999. 99.50 (*0-89603-677-4*) Humana.

Menopause: Everything You Need to Know about. Joanne Snow. LC 98-38774. (Natural Pharmacist Ser.). (Illus.). 178p. 2000. pap. 6.99 (*0-7615-1560-7*) Prima Pub.

Menopause: How You Can Benefit from Diet, Vitamins. Michael T. Murray. LC 93-41651. 192p. 1996. pap. 8.95 (*1-55958-427-0*) Prima Pub.

Menopause? Nothing to Be Afraid Of. Date not set. pap. write for info. (*1-893637-15-8*) Hlth & Hap.

Menopause: Questions You Have... Answers You Need. Lisa Bonnell Samalonis. LC 98-31192. 1999. pap. 12.95 (*1-882606-45-0*) Peoples Med Soc.

Menopause: Self Help Book. rev. ed. Susan M. Lark. LC 89-25292. 224p. 1995. pap. 16.95 (*0-89087-592-8*) Celestial Arts.

Menopause: The Age of Choice. Susan T. Macfarlan. 110p. (Orig.). 1997. mass mkt. 4.00 (*0-9628604-0-9*) Sumac Pub.

Menopause: The Inner Journey. Susanne F. Fincher. LC 95-8697. (Illus.). 168p. 1995. pap. 18.00 (*1-57062-152-7*, Pub. by Shambhala Pubns) Random.

Menopause: The Most Comprehensive, Up-to-Date Information Available to Help You Understand This Stage of Life, Make the Right Treatment Choices & Cope Effectively. Isaac Shiff & Ann B. Parson. 1996. pap. 15.00 (*0-614-20767-3*, Times Bks) Crown Pub Group.

Menopause - The Common Sense Approach see Pocket Guide to Menopause

Menopause & Beyond: A Fitness Plan for Life. Leora Myers. Ed. by Laura Kath. (Illus.). 208p. (Orig.). 1995. reprint ed. pap. 12.95 (*0-9647666-0-4*) Adelaide Pr.

Menopause & Culture. Gabriella E. Berger. LC 98-46899. 1999. write for info. (*0-7453-1488-0*) Pluto GBR.

Menopause & Emotions: Making Sense of Your Feelings When Your Feelings Make No Sense, Vol. 1. Lafern Page. 256p. 1996. pap. 19.95 (*0-9697874-0-5*) Primavera.

Menopause & Estrogen: Natural Alternatives to Hormone Replacement Therapy. 2nd ed. Ellen Brown & Lynn Walker. LC 96-53863. (Illus.). 197p. (Orig.). 1997. pap. 14.95 (*1-883319-53-6*) Frog Ltd CA.

Menopause & Homeopathy: A Guide for Women in Mid-Life. Ifeoma Ikenze. LC 98-19873. (Illus.). 250p. 1999. pap. 16.95 (*1-55643-291-7*) North Atlantic.

Menopause & Hormonal Replacement Therapy: Facts & Controversies. Ed. by Regine Sitruk-Ware & Wulf H. Utian. 494p. 1991. text 145.00 (*0-8247-8564-9*) Dekker.

Menopause & Hormone Replacement Therapy: A Simple but Complete Guide for Today's Busy Woman. Sharon Lunz. LC 99-94059. 70p. 1999. pap. 11.95 (*0-9669985-0-2*) SL Pubs.

Menopause & Hurt. Kathy Abernethy. 1997. pap. text 25.00 (*0-7020-2023-0*, Pub. by W B Saunders) Saunders.

Menopause & Its Effects on the Family. Daniel J. O'Neill. LC 81-43827. 66p. (Orig.). 1982. pap. text 15.00 (*0-8191-2500-8*) U Pr of Amer.

Menopause & Mid-Life. rev. ed. Robert G. Wells & Mary C. Wells. 240p. 1994. mass mkt. 5.99 (*0-8423-3975-2*) Tyndale Hse.

Menopause & Midlife Health. 3rd ed. Morris Notelovitz & Diana Tonnessen. 528p. 1994. pap. 17.95 (*0-312-11314-5*) St Martin.

Menopause & Osteoporosis: Taking Control of Your Life Change. 6th rev. ed. Linda R. Page. (Dr. Linda Page's Guides: Vol. 2). (Illus.). 64p. 1997. per. 5.95 (*1-884334-90-3*) Hlthy Healing.

Menopause & the Heart. Ed. by M. Neves-e-Castro & M. Birkhauser. LC 98-32248. (Illus.). 138p. 1999. 78.00 (*1-85070-071-0*) Prthnon Pub.

Menopause & the Mind. Claire Warga. LC 99-11244. 416p. 1999. 24.00 (*0-684-85456-2*) S&S Trade.

***Menopause & the Mind: The Complete Guide to Coping with the Cognitive Effects of Perimenopause & Menopause - Including Memory Loss, Foggy Thinking & Verbal Slips.** Simon & Schuster Staff & Claire Warga. 400p. 2000. pap. 14.00 (*0-684-85479-1*) S&S Trade.

Menopause & the Spirit Filled Woman: Something Every Man Needs to Know. Charles M. Washington. 130p. Date not set. write for info. (*0-9638436-3-X*) Indelble Ink.

***Menopause at the Millennium: Proceedings of the 9th World Congress on the Menopause.** Takeshi Aso & T. Yanaihara. (Illus.). 550p. 2000. 115.00 (*1-85070-709-X*) Prthnon Pub.

Menopause Book. Cheryy. 320p. 1993. 20.00 (*0-685-70477-7*) Macmillan.

Menopause Book: A Guide to Health & Well-Being for Women. Sheldon H. Cherry & Carolyn D. Runowicz. LC 95-2054. 272p. 1995. 11.95 (*0-02-860416-4*) Macmillan.

***Menopause Book: A Guide to Health & Well-Being for Women.** Sheldon H. Cherry & Carolyn D. Runowicz. (Illus.). 252p. 2000. reprint ed. pap. text 12.00 (*0-7881-9012-1*) DIANE Pub.

Menopause Book: A Guide to Health & Well-Being for Women After Forty. Sheldon H. Cherry & Carolyn Runowicz. (Illus.). 320p. 1994. 20.00 (*0-02-524758-1*) Macmillan.

Menopause Cookbook: How to Eat Now & for the Rest of Your Life. Hope Ricciotti & Vincent Connelly. LC 99-34029. 256p. 2000. pap. 15.95 (*0-393-31983-0*, Norton Paperbks) Norton.

***Menopause Core Curriculum.** 2000. student ed. 60.00 (*0-9701251-0-0*) N Amer Men.

Menopause Country. Jean Adair & Helen Gregory. (Illus.). 32p. (Orig.). 1996. pap. 5.50 (*0-941973-13-1*) Pinstripe Pub.

Menopause Diet. Woodland Publishing Staff. 1999. pap. 3.95 (*1-58054-048-1*) Woodland UT.

Menopause Diet: Lose Weight & Boost Your Energy. Larrian Gillespie. LC 99-62791. (Illus.). 204p. 1999. pap. 17.95 (*0-9671317-0-7*) Healthy Life Pubns.

***Menopause Diet Daily Journal: Charting Your Personal Course to a Healthy Life.** Larrian Gillespie. LC 99-90560. (Illus.). 96p. 1999. pap. 9.95 (*0-9671317-2-3*, Pub. by Healthy Life Pubns) New Leaf.

***Menopause Diet Mini Meal Cookbook: Good Food for Real Women, Naturally.** Larrian Gillespie. LC 99-90559. (Illus.). 160p. 1999. pap. 14.95 (*0-9671317-1-5*, Pub. by Healthy Life Pubns) New Leaf.

Menopause Handbook. Susan F. Trien. 1991. mass mkt. 5.99 (*0-345-37389-8*) Ballantine Pub Grp.

Menopause, Hormone Therapy, & Women's Health. 126p. (Orig.). (C). 1992. pap. text 30.00 (*1-56806-042-4*) DIANE Pub.

***Menopause, Hormones & Cancer.** M. Neves-e-Castro. (Illus.). 250p. 2001. 65.00 (*1-85070-628-X*) Prthnon Pub.

Menopause Industry: How the Medical Establishment Exploits Women. Sandra Coney. LC 94-11673. (Illus.). 384p. 1994. 24.95 (*0-89793-161-0*); pap. 14.95 (*0-89793-160-2*) Hunter Hse.

Menopause Made Easy: How to Make the Right Decisions for the Rest of Your Life. Carolle Jean-Murat. LC 99-21387. 336p. 1999. pap. 13.95 (*1-56170-606-X*, 578) Hay House.

Menopause Madness. Pat Ross. LC 97-39014. 96p. 1998. per. 8.00 (*0-684-84227-0*, Fireside) S&S Trade Pap.

Menopause Manager: A Safe Path for a Natural Change. Mary Ann Mayo & Joseph L. Mayo. LC 97-20700. 352p. 1998. 19.99 (*0-8007-1740-6*) Revell.

***Menopause Manager: A Safe Path for a Natural Change.** Mary Ann Mayo & Joseph L. Mayo. 352p. 2000. pap. 14.99 (*0-8007-5733-5*) Revell.

Menopause Manager: Mapping Your Choices for Optimal Living. Joseph Mayo & Mary Ann Mayo. 1997. pap. 10.99 (*0-614-27367-6*, Plume) Dutton Plume.

Menopause Matters: A Practical Approach to Midlife Change. Judy Hall & Robert Jacobs. 1994. pap. 13.95 (*1-85230-480-4*, Pub. by Element MA) Penguin Putnam.

Menopause, Me & You: The Sound of Women Pausing. Ann M. Voda. LC 96-52108. 396p. 1997. pap. 24.95 (*1-56023-922-0*, Harrington Park) Haworth Pr.

Menopause, Me & You: The Sound of Women Pausing. Ann M. Voda. LC 96-52108. (Illus.). 396p. (C). 1997. 59.95 (*1-56023-911-5*, Harrington Park) Haworth Pr.

***Menopause Myths & Facts: What Every Woman Should Know about Hormone Replacement Therapy.** Lorraine Rothman & Marcia Wexler. 116p. 1999. pap. 11.00 (*0-9629945-6-1*) Feminist Hlth.

Menopause Naturally. Carolyn Dean. Ed. by Phyllis Herman. (Good Health Guides Ser.). 48p. 1995. pap. 3.95 (*0-87983-681-4*, 36814K, Keats Publng) NTC Contemp Pub Co.

Menopause, Naturally: Preparing for the Second Half of Life. rev. ed. Sadja Greenwood. LC 95-51147. (Illus.). 225p. (Orig.). 1996. pap. 14.95 (*1-884244-05-X*) Volcano Pr.

***Menopause Pink: Mid-Life Reflections of Wisdom & Humor.** Terri Malucci. LC 99-63720. (Illus.). 112p. 1999. pap. 9.95 (*0-9673744-4-8*) Creativa Pr.

***Menopause Relief.** Angela Stengler & Mark Stengler. 32p. 1998. pap. 3.95 (*1-890694-12-6*) IMPAKT Communs.

Menopause Self Help Book: A Woman's Guide to Feeling Wonderful for the Second Half of Her Life. rev. ed. Susan M. Lark. (Illus.). 239p. 1999. pap. text 17.00 (*0-7881-6074-5*) DIANE Pub.

Menopause Sourcebook. Gretchen Henkel. LC 97-51596. 224p. 1998. pap. 16.00 (*1-56565-870-1*) Lowell Hse.

***Menopause Sourcebook.** Gretchen Henkel. (Illus.). 224p. 2000. pap. 15.95 (*0-7373-0378-6*, 03786W, Pub. by Lowell Hse) NTC Contemp Pub Co.

Menopause Sourcebook: Everything You Need to Know. Gretchen Henkel. 204p. 1994. 23.95 (*1-56565-155-3*) Lowell Hse.

Menopause Sourcebook: Everything You Need to Know. Gretchen Henkel. 204p. 1996. pap. 16.00 (*1-56565-435-8*) Lowell Hse.

Menopause, Stress & Amino Acid Therapy. 1996. lib. bdg. 252.75 (*0-8490-5898-8*) Gordon Pr.

Menopause: The Age of Choice see Menopausia: La Edad de las Alternativas

***Menopause the Natural Way.** Deborah Gordon et al. (Women's Natural Health Ser.). 256p. 2001. pap. 14.95 (*0-471-37957-3*) Wiley.

Menopause Time for a Change: The Menopause Handbook for Safe & Effective, Natural Self-Care Approaches. 4th ed. Merri L. Park. LC 97-919107. 304p. 1997. pap. 16.95 (*0-920470-33-5*) Alive Bks.

Menopause Without Medicine. 3rd ed. Linda Ojeda. LC 95-2607. (Illus.). 352p. 1995. 23.95 (*0-89793-178-5*); pap. 14.95 (*0-89793-177-7*) Hunter Hse.

***Menopause Without Medicine.** 4th rev. ed. Linda Ojeda. (Illus.). 352p. 2000. 25.95 (*0-89793-282-X*, Pub. by Hunter Hse) Publishers Group.

***Menopause Without Medicine.** 4th rev. ed. Linda Ojeda. LC 00-38884. (Illus.). 352p. 2000. pap. 15.95 (*0-89793-281-1*, Pub. by Hunter Hse) Publishers Group.

Menopausia: La Edad de las Alternativas. Tr. by Silvia S. Kjolseth. Orig. Title: Menopause: The Age of Choice. (SPA., Illus.). 119p. (Orig.). 1996. mass mkt. 4.50 (*0-9628604-1-7*) Sumac Pub.

Menopaws: The Silent Meow. Martha Sacks. LC 95-17881. (Illus.). 64p. 1995. pap. 9.95 (*0-89815-780-3*) Ten Speed Pr.

An Asterisk (*) at the beginning of an entry indicates that the title is appearing for the first time.

Menora: Gestalt und Funktion des Leuchters Im Tempel Zu Jerusalem. Jens Vos. (Orbis Biblicus et Orientalis Ser.: Vol. 128). (GER.). 112p. 1993. text 24.00 (*3-7278-0877-2*, Pub. by Presses Univ Fribourg) Eisenbrauns.

Menorah. Rappaport. LC 99-33606. 32p. (J). 2000. 14.45 (*0-7868-0400-9*, Pub. by Hyperion); lib. bdg. 15.49 (*0-7868-2352-6*, Pub. by Hyperion) Little.

Menorah. Daniel Sanders. 320p. 1997. mass mkt. 7.95 (*0-9655905-7-7*) Olive Pr NJ.

Menorah Men. Lionel Davidson. 1996. mass mkt. 5.99 (*0-312-95815-3*, Pub. by Tor Bks) St Martin.

Menorah Story. Mark Podwal. LC 97-36300. (Illus.). 24p. (YA). (gr. k-3). 1998. 15.00 (*0-688-15758-0*, Grenwillow Bks) HarpC Child Bks.

***Menorah Story.** Mark Podwal. LC 97-36300. (Illus.). 24p. (YA). (gr. k-3). 1998. 14.93 (*0-688-15759-9*, Grenwillow Bks) HarpC Child Bks.

Menorahs, Mezuzas, & Other Jewish Symbols. Miriam Chaikin. (Illus.). 96p. (J). (gr. 5 up). 1990. 17.00 (*0-89919-856-2*, Clarion Bks) HM.

Menos Bella Historia Jamas Contada. Carlos Salas Ponce. (SPA.). 96p. 1993. pap. write for info. (*0-929441-51-6*) Pubns Puertorriquenas.

***Meno's Gift.** deluxe ed. Patrick M. Gallegos. (Illus.). 64p. (YA). (gr. 1-12). 1999. 19.95 (*0-9675742-0-X*) Wigglys.

Menotti Amahl & the Night Visitors see Classical Connections: Complete Program

***Men's & Boy's Wear Buyers, 2000.** Ed. by Keith Cavedo et al. 731p. 1999. 220.00 (*0-87228-131-0*, Salesmn Gde) Douglas Pubns.

Men's Apparel in Japan: A Strategic Entry Report, 1996. Compiled by Icon Group International Staff. (Country Industry Report). (Illus.). 164p. 1999. ring bd. 1640.00 incl. audio compact disk (*0-7418-0653-3*) Icon Grp.

Men's Bodies, Men's Gods: Male Identities in a (Post-) Christian Culture. Ed. by Bjorn Krondorfer. (Illus.). 320p. (C). 1996. text 55.00 (*0-8147-4668-3*); pap. text 19.00 (*0-8147-4669-1*) NYU Pr.

Men's Bodybuilding Photo Book. (Illus.). 13.95 (*0-02-499330-1*) Anderson World.

Men's Business, Women's Business: The Spiritual Role of Gender in the World's Oldest Culture. Hannah R. Bell. LC 98-30380. (Illus.). 208p. 1998. pap. 14.95 (*0-89281-655-4*) Inner Tradit.

***Men's Cancers: How to Prevent Them, How to Treat Them, How to Beat Them.** Ed. by Pamela J. Haylock. LC 99-59639. (Illus.). 416p. 1999. 29.95 (*0-89793-267-6*, Pub. by Hunter Hse) Publishers Group.

***Men's Cancers: How to Prevent Them, How to Treat Them, How to Beat Them.** Ed. by Pamela J. Haylock. LC 99-59639. (Illus.). 416p. 2000. pap. 19.95 (*0-89793-266-8*, Pub. by Hunter Hse) Publishers Group.

Men's Christmas Collection. Arranged by Tom Fettke. 110p. 1993. pap. 6.99 (*0-8341-9710-3*) Nazarene.

Men's Clothing & Fabrics in the 1890s. Roseann Ettinger. LC 98-85867. 112p. 1998. pap. 24.95 (*0-7643-0616-2*) Schiffer.

Men's Club. Leonard Michaels. LC 92-45612. 200p. 1993. pap. 10.00 (*1-56279-039-0*) Mercury Hse Inc.

***Men's Club: How to Lose Your Prostate Without Losing Your Sense of Humor.** Bert Gottlieb & Thomas Mawn. 200p. 1999. pap. 13.95 (*0-934793-67-0*) Pathfinder CA.

Men's Coats. Vittoria De Buzzaccarini. (Twentieth Century-Histories of Fashion Ser.). (Illus.). 135p. 1996. 29.95 (*0-89676-209-2*, Costume & Fashion Pr) QSMG Ltd.

Men's Cottage: Playscript. Moses Goldberg. (J). (gr. 4 up). 1980. 6.00 (*0-87602-229-8*) Anchorage.

Men's Devotional Prayer Journal. Frwd. by D. James Kennedy. 192p. 1995. 16.99 (*0-8499-5154-2*) Word Pub.

Mens en Recht. E. Peters. 1998. 38.95 (*90-6831-896-9*, Pub. by Peeters Pub) Bks Intl VA.

Men's Encyclopediaclopedia Assort. 1998. 359.40 (*0-02-862713-X*) Macmillan.

***Men's Essential Guide to Prostrate Health.** Doctors' Prescription Staff. 96p. 2000. pap. 4.95 (*1-893910-07-5*, 904-012, Pub. by Freedom Pr Inc) BookWorld.

Men's Family Relations: Report from an International Seminar. Ed. by Ulla Bjornberg & Anna-Karin Kollind. (Goteborg University Department of Sociology Research Reports: Vol. 60). 192p. (Orig.). 1996. pap. 47.50 (*91-972940-0-4*) Coronet Bks.

Men's Fashion: The Complete Sourcebook. John Peacock. LC 96-60141. (Illus.). 216p. 1996. 29.95 (*0-500-01725-5*, Pub. by Thames Hudson) Norton.

Men's Fashion Illustrations from the Turn of the Century. Jno. J. Mitchell Co. Staff. (Illus.). 112p. 1990. pap. text 9.95 (*0-486-26353-3*) Dover.

Men's Fashion in the Twentieth Century: From Frock Coats to Intelligent Fibres. Maria Costantino. (Illus.). 160p. (Orig.). 1997. pap. 29.95 (*0-89676-225-4*, Costume & Fashion Pr) QSMG Ltd.

Men's Fashions, 1850 to 1860. Susan B. Sirkis. (Wish Booklets Ser.: Vol. 21). (Illus.). 52p. 1978. pap. 5.95 (*0-913786-21-7*) Wish Bklets.

Men's Fashions, 1776 to 1850. Susan B. Sirkis. (Wish Booklets Ser.: Vol. 20). (Illus.). 60p. 1977. pap. 5.95 (*0-913786-20-9*) Wish Bklets.

***Men's Feminism: August Bebel & the German Socialist Movement.** Ann Lopes & Gary Roth. 260p. 2000. 49.95 (*1-57392-868-2*) Prometheus Bks.

Men's Fitness Magazine's Complete Guide to Health & Well-Being. Joe Weider. 1996. pap. 20.00 (*0-614-97840-8*, Harper Ref) HarpC.

Men's Fitness Magazine's Complete Guide to Health & Well Being. Joe Weider et al. LC 95-39472. 400p. 1996. pap. 20.00 (*0-06-273354-0*) HarpC.

Men's Frendships. Ed. by Peter M. Nardi. (Research on Men & Masculinities Ser.: Vol. 2). (Illus.). 320p. 1992. 58.00 (*0-8039-3773-3*); pap. 26.00 (*0-8039-3774-1*) Sage.

Men's Garments, 1830-1900: A Guide to Pattern Cutting & Tailoring. R. I. Davis. LC 94-22441. (Illus.). 160p. 1995. pap. 27.00 (*0-88734-648-0*) Players Pr.

***Men's Gift: Steam Engines.** Anness Publishing Staff. 2000. 14.95 (*0-7548-0503-4*) Anness Pub.

***Men's Gift: Tractors.** Anness Publishing Staff. 2000. 14.95 (*0-7548-0444-5*, Pub. by Anness Pub) Random.

Men's Grooming Market. Ed. by Peter Allen. 220p. 1987. pap. 995.00 (*0-941285-08-1*) FIND-SVP.

Men's Guide to Bread Machine Baking: Making Pizza, Bagels, Beer Breads, Pretzels, Sourdough, & over 100 other Great Breads with Your Bread Machine. Jeffrey Gerlach. (Illus.). 208p. 1996. pap. 15.00 (*0-7615-0652-7*) Prima Pub.

Men's Gymnastic Handbook. Gerald A. Carr. (Illus.). 214p. 1981. pap., teacher ed. 14.95 (*0-88839-046-7*) Hancock House.

Men's Gymnastics. Jack Wiley. LC 78-65024. (Illus.). 160p. (Orig.). 1980. pap. 7.95 (*0-89037-165-2*) Anderson World.

Men's Gymnastics Coaching Manual. Lloyd Readhead. (Illus.). 208p. 1997. pap. 29.95 (*1-86126-076-8*, Pub. by Cro1wood) Trafalgar.

Men's Hair Styles. Alex Toth. LC 95-42373. (Cosmetology Ser.). (Illus.). 224p. 1996. pap. 34.95 (*1-56253-265-0*) Milady Pub.

Men's Hats. Giuliano Folledore. (Twentieth Century-Histories of Fashion Ser.). (Illus.). 127p. 1996. 29.95 (*0-89676-210-6*, Costume & Fashion Pr) QSMG Ltd.

Men's Health. (Illus.). 48p. 1998. write for info. (*0-945100-65-5*) Parlay Intl.

Men's Health. Ed. by Tom O'Dowd & David Jewell. (Oxford General Practice Ser.: No. 41). (Illus.). 290p. 1998. pap. text 68.00 (*0-19-262581-0*) OUP.

***Men's Health: Perspectives, Diversity & Paradox** Mike Luckovich et al. LC 99-32983. 1999. write for info. (*0-632-05288-0*) Blackwell Sci.

Men's Health: Your Prostate Sex Gland & Cancer. Anthony Saura. LC 99-202659. 45p. 1998. pap. 8.95 (*0-533-12666-5*) Vantage.

Men's Health - a Guide to Staying Young. Men's Health Magazine Editors. 320p. 1995. reprint ed. 7.98 (*1-56731-069-9*, MJF Bks) Fine Comms.

Men's Health & Illness: Gender, Power & the Body. Ed. by Donald Sabo & David Gordon. LC 95-17398. (Research on Men & Masculinities Ser.: Vol. 8). 320p. 1995. 58.00 (*0-8039-4814-X*); pap. 26.00 (*0-8039-5275-9*) Sage.

***Men's Health & the Hormone Revolution.** Siegfried Meryn et al. 350p. 2000. pap. 18.95 (*1-55321-103-0*, Pub. by NDE Pub) IPG Chicago.

Men's Health Concerns Sourcebook. Ed. by Allan R. Cook. LC 98-33612. (Health Reference Ser.: Vol. 38). (Illus.). 600p. 1998. 78.00 (*0-7808-0212-8*) Omnigraphics Inc.

Mens Health Day Log98. MEN HLTH MAG Mens Health Magazine Editors. 1997. spiral bd. 14.95 (*0-87596-431-1*, Pub. by Rodale Pr Inc) St Martin.

Men's Health for Dummies. Charles B. Inlander & People's Medical Society Staff. LC 99-61113. 408p. 1999. pap. 19.99 (*0-7645-5120-5*) IDG Bks.

Men's Health Guide to Peak Conditioning. Richard Laliberte et al. LC 96-34087. 1997. pap. 29.95 (*0-87596-323-4*) Rodale Pr Inc.

***Men's Health Hard Body Plan: The Ultimate 12-Week Plan for Burning Fat & Building Muscle.** Men's Health Books Editors. Ed. by Larry Keller. (Illus.). 384p. 2000. pap. 19.95 (*1-57954-229-8*) Rodale Pr Inc.

***Men's Health Longevity Program.** Men's Health Books Editors. 2001. pap. 18.95 (*1-57954-366-9*) Rodale Pr Inc.

Men's Health Problems. Loretta H. Kurban. (Orig.). 1991. pap. 8.00 (*0-938863-22-3*) HCI Pr.

Men's Health Sourcebook: Everything You Need to Know. Alfred Dashe. 288p. 1996. 25.00 (*1-56565-465-X*) Lowell Hse.

Men's Health Today. Michael Lafavore. LC 96-48142. (Illus.). 288p. 1997. pap. 12.95 (*0-87596-417-6*) Rodale Pr Inc.

Men's High Jump. Alphonse Juilland. (Evolution of Track & Field Records). (Illus.). 120p. (Orig.). 1996. pap. 10.00 (*1-884868-09-6*) Montparnasse.

Men's House: Masonic Papers & Addresses. Joseph F. Newton. xx, 241p. 1990. text 12.95 (*0-88053-037-5*, M-86) Macoy Pub.

Men's House: Masonic Papers & Addresses. Joseph F. Newton. 262p. 1998. reprint ed. pap. 17.95 (*0-7661-0211-4*) Kessinger Pub.

Men's Ideas, Women's Realities: "Popular Science", Eighteen Seventy to Nineteen Fifteen. Ed. by Louise M. Newman. (Athene Ser.). 384p. 1984. text 55.00 (*0-08-031930-0*, Pergamon Pr); pap. text 19.95 (*0-08-031929-7*, Pergamon Pr) Elsevier.

Men's Ideas, Women's Realities: Popular Science, 1870-1915. Louise M. Newman. LC 84-1072. (Athene Ser.). 367p. 1985. pap. 113.80 (*0-7837-8952-1*, 204966400002) Bks Demand.

Men's Lives. Joe Pintauro & Peter Matthiessen. 1994. pap. 5.25 (*0-8222-1381-8*) Dramatists Play.

Men's Lives. 4th ed. Michael S. Kimmel & Michael Messner. (C). 1998. pap. text, teacher ed. write for info. (*0-205-27273-8*, T7273-0) Allyn.

Men's Lives. 4th ed. Ed. by Michael S. Kimmel & Michael A. Messner. LC 97-22520. 599p. 1997. pap. text 38.00 (*0-205-26649-5*) P-H.

***Mens Lives.** 5th ed. 2000. teacher ed. write for info. (*0-205-32499-1*) Allyn.

***Men's Lives.** 5th ed. Michael S. Kimmel & Michael A. Messner. 576p. 2000. pap. text 40.00 (*0-205-32105-4*) Allyn.

Men's Lives: Surfmen & Baymen of the South Fork. Peter Matthiessen. LC 87-40095. 352p. 1988. pap. 15.00 (*0-394-75560-X*) Vin Bks.

Men's Maintenance Manual. Robin Rout. LC 98-43183. 1999. pap. text 19.95 (*0-7892-0547-5*) Abbeville Pr.

Men's Manual, Vol. I. Bill Gothard. LC 79-88994. (Illus.). 160p. 1979. 25.00 (*0-916888-04-5*) Inst Basic Life.

Men's Manual, Vol. II. Bill Gothard. LC 79-88994. (Illus.). 270p. 1983. 30.00 (*0-916888-09-6*) Inst Basic Life.

Men's Mile. Alphonse Juilland. (Evolution of Track & Field Records). 83p. (Orig.). 1993. pap. 10.00 (*1-884868-08-8*) Montparnasse.

Mens of Manhattan. John Glines. (Illus.). 96p. 1993. mass mkt. 5.95 (*1-58193-079-8*) Brown Bag Prods.

Men's Outer Garments in Japan: A Strategic Entry Report, 1996. Compiled by Icon Group International Staff. (Country Industry Report). (Illus.). 159p. 1999. ring bd. 1590.00 incl. audio compact disk (*0-7418-0654-1*) Icon Grp.

Men's Outerwear Design. Masaaki Kawashima. LC 77-79658. (Illus.). 207p. reprint ed. pap. 64.20 (*0-608-17821-7*, 203248600079) Bks Demand.

Men's Physical Education. Jack Rudman. (National Teacher Examination Ser.: NT-36). 1994. pap. 23.95 (*0-8373-8446-X*) Nat Learn.

***Men's Program: How to Implement a Proven Prevention Workshop.** 2nd ed. John Foubert. LC 99-188638. 128p. 2000. pap. 21.95 (*1-55691-178-5*) Learning Pubns.

Men's Program Rules & Policies, 1993-94: Governing Competitions & Competitors. United States Gymnastics Federation Staff. 80p. 1993. pap. 11.50 (*1-885250-04-5*) USA Gymnastics.

Men's Reproductive Health. Janice Swanson & Katherine Forrest. (Focus on Men Ser.). (Illus.). 416p. 1984. 41.95 (*0-8261-4200-1*) Springer Pub.

Men's Rights: A Handbook for the 80's. Bill Wishard & Laurie Wishard. LC 80-20194. 264p. 1980. 12.95 (*0-89666-011-7*); pap. 6.95 (*0-89666-012-5*) Cragmont Pubns.

***Men's Room.** Michangelo Scruggs. 203p. 1999. pap. 14.00 (*1-892096-32-3*) Ishai Creat.

Men's Secret Wars. Patrick A. Means. LC 96-16252. (Illus.). 256p. (gr. 10). 1996. 15.99 (*0-8007-1721-X*) Revell.

***Men's Secret Wars.** Patrick A. Means. 288p. 1999. pap. 10.99 (*0-8007-5717-3*) Revell.

Men's 17th & 18th Century Costume, Cut & Fashion. R. I. Davis. Ed. by William-Alan Landes. LC 99-56138. (Illus.). 224p. 2000. pap. 60.00 (*0-88734-637-5*) Players Pr.

Men's Share: Masculinities, Male Support & Women's Suffrage in Britain 1890-1920. Ed. by Angela V. John & Claire Eustance. LC 96-41555. (Illus.). 240p. (C). 1997. 80.00 (*0-415-14001-3*) Routledge.

***Men's Show: Photography Patrick McMullan.** Photos by Patrick McMullan. (Illus.). 2000. 65.00 (*3-908163-29-3*, Pub. by Edit Stemmle) Abbeville Pr.

Men's Silences: Predicaments in Masculinity. Jonathan Rutherford. LC 92-2801. (Male Orders Ser.). 224p. (C). (gr. 13). 1992. text 89.95 (*0-415-07543-2*, A7650) Routledge.

Men's Singles. D. B. Gilles. 1986. pap. 5.25 (*0-8222-0749-4*) Dramatists Play.

Men's Studies. (Initiatives Ser.: Vol. 49, No. 4). 1986. 15.00 (*0-614-14213-X*) Natl Assn Women.

Men's Studies Modified: The Impact of Feminism on the Academic Disciplines. Ed. by Dale Spender. (Athene Ser.: Vol. 1). 350p. 1981. text 50.00 (*0-08-026770-X*, Pergamon Pr); pap. text 19.95 (*0-08-026117-5*, Pergamon Pr) Elsevier.

Men's Studies Modified: The Impact of Feminism on the Academic Disciplines. Ed. by Dale Spender. (Athene Ser.). 248p. (C). 1981. pap. text 20.95 (*0-8077-6215-6*) Tchrs Coll.

Men's Transitions to Parenthood: Longitudinal Studies of Early Family Experience. Ed. by Phyllis W. Berman & Frank A. Pedersen. LC 86-29165. 264p. 1987. 49.95 (*0-89859-814-1*) L Erlbaum Assocs.

Men's Travel in Your Pocket: Tours, Accommodations & Nightlife for Gay Men U. S. A. & Worldwide. 16th ed. 784p. 2000. pap. 16.00 (*0-942586-69-7*) Ferrari Intl Pub.

Men's Voices. Ed. by George Y. Gilpatrick. LC 99-176941. 46p. 1997. pap. 4.95 (*1-891232-05-3*, Closet Bks) R Crane Pub.

Men's Ways of Being. Ed. by Christopher McLean et al. (New Directions in Theory & Psychology Ser.). 260p. (C). 1996. pap. 27.00 (*0-8133-2653-2*, Pub. by Westview) HarpC.

Men's Wear: A Guide to Designing Wearable Art for Men. Alexandra Dupre. 160p. 1996. pap. 14.95 (*0-89145-865-4*, 4598, Am Quilters Soc) Collector Bks.

***Men's Wear in Germany: A Strategic Entry Report, 2000.** Compiled by Icon Group International. (Illus.). 92p. 1999. ring bd. 920.00 incl. audio compact disk (*0-7418-2151-6*) Icon Grp.

Men's Work: How to Stop the Violence That Tears Our Lives Apart. Paul Kivel. 1992. mass mkt. 5.99 (*0-345-37939-X*) Ballantine Pub Grp.

Men's Work: How to Stop the Violence That Tears Our Lives Apart. Paul Kivel. 11.00 incl. audio (*0-89486-827-6*, 5658) Hazelden.

Men's Work: How to Stop the Violence That Tears Our Lives Apart. rev. ed. Paul Kivel. 300p. 1998. pap. 13.95 (*1-56838-233-2*, 5279) Hazelden.

Men's Work: The Facilitator's Guide: Taking a Stand Against Violence. Paul Kivel. LC 92-45060. (Workbook Ser.). 96p. 1993. teacher ed. 13.00 (*0-89486-923-X*, 5536) Hazelden.

Men's Work & Male Lives: Men & Work in Britain. John Goodwin. LC 98-74132. (Illus.). 7p. (C). 1999. text 61.95 (*1-84014-577-3*, Pub. by Ashgate Pub) Ashgate Pub Co.

Mensa. Victor Serebriakoff. LC 85-40964. (Illus.). 318p. 1986. 17.95 (*0-8128-3091-1*, Scrbrough Hse) Madison Bks UPA.

Mensa: Know Yourself. Robert Allen. 1995. 7.98 (*0-7858-0426-9*) Bk Sales Inc.

***Mensa: Know Yourself.** Josephine Fulton. 1999. pap. 9.95 (*1-85868-547-8*, Pub. by Carlton Bks Ltd) Natl Bk Netwk.

Mensa: New Number Puzzles. Robert Allen. 128p. 1997. pap. text 7.98 (*0-7858-0810-8*) Bk Sales Inc.

Mensa: New Word Puzzles. Robert Allen. 128p. 1997. pap. text 7.98 (*0-7858-0809-4*) Bk Sales Inc.

***Mensa: Number Puzzles for Kids.** Robert Allen. (Mensa Ser.). (Illus.). 224p. (J). (gr. 4-7). 2000. mass mkt. 4.50 (*0-439-10841-1*) Scholastic Inc.

Mensa: Riddles & Conundrums. Robert Allen. 1995. 7.98 (*0-7858-0425-0*) Bk Sales Inc.

***Mensa All-Color Puzzle Book Vol. 1: Hundreds of Puzzles to Challenge You.** Robert Allen & Carolyn Skitt. (Illus.). (J). 2000. pap. 19.95 (*1-55209-498-7*) Firefly Bks Ltd.

***Mensa All-Color Puzzle Book Vol. 2: Challenge Your Mind with over 400 Full-Color Puzzles.** Robert Allen & Carolyn Skitt. (Illus.). (J). 2000. pap. 19.95 (*1-55209-500-2*) Firefly Bks Ltd.

***Mensa Book of Words, Word Games, Puzzles & Oddities.** Abbie F. Salny. 2000. 6.99 (*1-57866-082-3*) Galahad Bks.

Mensa Book of Words, Word Games, Puzzles, & Oddities. Abbie F. Salny. LC 87-45661. 160p. 1988. pap. 10.00 (*0-06-096208-9*, PL-6208, Perennial) HarperTrade.

Mensa Challenge Your IQ. Robert Allen. (Mensa Word Games for Kids Ser.). 1999. pap. text 9.95 (*1-85868-311-4*, Pub. by Carlton Bks Ltd) Natl Bk Netwk.

***Mensa Covert Puzzles.** David Colton. 1999. pap. 7.99 (*0-7858-1156-7*) Book Sales.

***Mensa Genius.** Josephine Fulton. 1999. pap., wbk. ed. 7.99 (*0-7858-1157-5*) Book Sales.

Mensa Genius A-B-C Quiz Book. Alan Stillson. LC 98-13906. 176p. 1998. pap. 10.00 (*0-201-31135-6*) Addison-Wesley.

Mensa Genius Quiz-a-Day Book. Abbie F. Salny. 1989. pap. 10.00 (*0-201-13549-3*) Addison-Wesley.

Mensa Genius Quiz Almanac. Abbie F. Salny. 1989. pap. 6.95 (*0-318-42569-6*) Addison-Wesley.

Mensa Genius Quiz Book. Marvin Grosswirth & Abbie F. Salny. 1981. pap. 9.00 (*0-201-05959-2*) Addison-Wesley.

Mensa Genius Quiz Book Two, No. 2. Marvin Grosswirth & Abbie F. Salny. LC 83-7244. 160p. 1983. pap. 9.00 (*0-201-05958-4*) Addison-Wesley.

***Mensa Logic Brainteasers.** Philip Carter. 1999. pap. text 9.95 (*1-85868-545-1*, Pub. by Carlton Bks Ltd) Natl Bk Netwk.

Mensa Logic Puzzles. Book Sales, Inc. Staff. 1996. 7.98 (*0-7858-0592-3*) Bk Sales Inc.

Mensa Math Games for Kids. Harold Gale. LC 94-28166. 128p. 1994. pap. text 9.95 (*1-55958-592-7*) Prima Pub.

***Mensa Mind Maze Challenge.** John Bremner. 1999. pap. 7.99 (*0-7858-1158-3*) Book Sales.

Mensa Mind Power. Book Sales, Inc. Staff. 1996. 7.98 (*0-7858-0591-5*) Bk Sales Inc.

***Mensa Mind Workout.** Josephine Fulton. 1999. pap. text 9.95 (*1-85868-546-X*, Pub. by Carlton Bks Ltd) Natl Bk Netwk.

Mensa Number Puzzles. Robert Allen. (Mensa Word Games for Kids Ser.). 1999. pap. text 9.95 (*1-85868-309-2*, Pub. by Carlton Bks Ltd) Natl Bk Netwk.

MENSA Presents Number Puzzles for Math Geniuses. MENSA Publications Staff. 1993. pap. 13.00 (*0-8129-2214-X*, Times Bks) Crown Pub Group.

MENSA Presents Word Puzzles for Language Geniuses. MENSA Publications Staff. 1993. pap. 13.00 (*0-8129-2213-1*, Times Bks) Crown Pub Group.

Mensa Riddles & Conundrums. Robert Allen. (Mensa Word Games for Kids Ser.). 1999. pap. text 9.95 (*1-85868-310-6*, Pub. by Carlton Bks Ltd) Natl Bk Netwk.

Mensa Think-Smart Book. Abbie F. Salny. 1999. 5.99 (*1-57866-054-8*) Galahad Bks.

Mensa Think-Smart Book. Abbie F. Salny & Marvin Grosswirth. LC 84-48619. (Illus.). 128p. 1986. pap. 10.00 (*0-06-091255-3*, PL 1255, Perennial) HarperTrade.

***Mensa Visual Brainteasers.** John Bremner. 1999. pap. text 9.95 (*1-85868-548-6*, Pub. by Carlton Bks Ltd) Natl Bk Netwk.

Mensa Word Games for Kids, Vol. 1. Robert Allen. LC 94-228344. 128p. (J). (gr. 4-7). 1994. pap. 9.95 (*1-55958-593-5*) Prima Pub.

Mensa Word Puzzles. Robert Allen. (Mensa Word Games for Kids Ser.). 1999. pap. text 9.95 (*1-85868-308-4*, Pub. by Carlton Bks Ltd) Natl Bk Netwk.

Mensagem - Poemas Esotericos: Edicao Critica. Fernando Pessoa. (Coleccion Archivos de Ediciones Criticas). (SPA.). 30.99 (*84-88344-04-X*, Pub. by Fondo) Continental Bk.

***Mensaje de Amor.** Cathy Forsythe.Tr. of Love Message. (SPA.). 2000. per. 3.50 (*0-373-33550-4*) Harlequin Bks.

Mensaje de Filipenses. J. Alec Motyer.Tr. of Message of Philippians. (SPA.). 240p. 1993. pap. 7.99 (*0-8254-1486-5*, Edit Portavoz) Kregel.

Mensaje para Ti. (Serie Pensamientos - Thoughts of Life Ser.).Tr. of Message for You. (SPA.). 24p. 1989. pap. write for info. (*0-614-27152-5*) Editorial Unilit.

Mensaje y Vigencia De Jose Enrique Rodo. Orlando Gomez-Gil. LC 91-72582. 203p. (Orig.). 1992. pap. 19.00 (*0-89729-609-5*) Ediciones.

Mensajero de la Paz y la Esperanza: Textos y Documentos de la Visita de Su Santidad Juan Pablo II a Cuba. Juan Pablo, II. (Coleccion Felix Varela Ser.). (Illus.). 183p. 1998. pap. 15.00 (*0-89729-867-5*) Ediciones.

M

An Asterisk (*) at the beginning of an entry indicates that the title is appearing for the first time.

M

Mensajero Especial de Jesus. Tr. of Jesus Special Messenger. (SPA.). 30p. 1995. pap. write for info. (*0-614-27080-4*) Editorial Unilit.

Mensajero Especial de Jesus (Jesus Special Messenger) (SPA.). 30p. (J). 1995. write for info. (*0-614-24378-5*) Editorial Unilit.

Mensajero y Su Mensaji. A. Luce.Tr. of Messenger & His Message. (SPA.). 96p. 1964. pap. 3.99 (*0-8297-0582-1*) Vida Pubs.

Mensajeros al Cerebro. Paul D. Martin. Tr. by Maria T. Sanz & Maia Larios S. (Explora y Aprende Ser.). (SPA., Illus.). 96p. (YA). (gr. 3-8). 1994. 15.00 (*0-915741-54-7*) C D Stampley Ent.

Mensajeros de Esperanza (The Gospel People) Miguel Berg & Pablo Pretiz. (SPA.). 125p. 1994. write for info. (*1-56063-776-5*) Editorial Unilit.

Mensajes al Pueblo Puertorriqueno: Pronunciados ante las Camaras Legislativas, 1949-1964. Luis Munoz-Marin. LC 80-24258. (Illus.). 358p. 1980. 12.50 (*0-913480-47-9*); pap. 6.95 (*0-913480-48-7*); mass mkt. 4.95 (*0-913480-49-5*) Inter Am U Pr.

Mensajes Biblicos. Robert M. McCheyne. (SPA.). 284p. 1988. reprint ed. pap. 6.50 (*0-85151-541-X*) Banner of Truth.

Mensajes de la Princesa Diana Desde la Cuarta Dimension. Juan Caballero. Ed. by Mabel Chia. (SPA., Illus.). 2p. 1997. pap. 20.00 (*0-9662251-0-4*) La Luz del Univ.

Mensajes de Luz Profetica. Manuel C. Lassaletta.Tr. of Messages of Prophetic Light. (SPA.). 1991. pap. 3.99 (*0-945792-71-9*, 498452) Editorial Unilit.

Mensajes para Creyentes Nuevos, 24. Watchman Nee. 1998. pap. text 36.00 (*0-7363-0321-9*) Living Stream Ministry.

Mensch: Eine Moralische Wochenschrift. Ed. by Samuel G. Lange & Georg F. Meier. (GER.). 1992. reprint ed. write for info. (*3-487-09547-5*) G Olms Pubs.

Mensch in der Biosphare: Zur Naturgeschichte der Vernunft Herausgegeben von Wolfgang Hofkirchner. Vladimir I. Vernadskij. (GER.). 249p. 1997. 51.95 (*3-631-49084-4*) P Lang Pubng.

Mensch Karnickel: C Level. Herfurter. text 8.95 (*0-8219-1064-7*) EMC-Paradigm.

Mensch Lebt Nicht Vom Bit Allein: Information in Technik und Gesellschaft 2, Durchgesehene Auflage. 2nd ed. Peter Fleissner et al. (GER., Illus.). XVI, 328p. 1997. 32.95 (*3-631-31702-6*) P Lang Pubng.

Mensch Lebt Nicht Vom Bit Allein... Information In Technik Und Gesellschaft 3., Durchgesehene Auflage. 3rd ed. Peter Fleissner et al. (Illus.). XVI, 328p. 1998. 28.95 (*3-631-33884-8*) P Lang Pubng.

***Mensch: Moral--Religion: Kant-lekturen Aus der Polykontexturalen Gesellschaft.** Martin Carmann. (Beitrage zur Rationalen Theologie Ser.). 373p. 1999. 56.95 (*3-631-34738-3*) P Lang Pubng.

Mensch: Stufen Seiner Religiosen Entwicklung see Religious Judgement: A Developmental Perspective

Mensch-Tier-Verwandlung: Eine Motivgeschichte unter Besonderer Berucksichtigung des Deutschen Marchens in der Ersten Halfte des 19. Jahrhunderts. Gabriela B. Ungricht. (Europaische Hochschulschriften Ser.: Reihe 1, Vol. 1676). (GER.). 337p. 1998. 49.95 (*3-906760-29-4*) P Lang Pubng.

Mensch und Natur Im Mittelalter, Pt. 1. Ed. by Albert Zimmerman & Andreas Speer. (Miscellanea Mediaevalia Ser.: Vol. 21, Pts. 1 & 2). (GER., Illus.). xvi, 534p. (C). 1991. lib. bdg. 212.35 (*3-11-013163-3*) De Gruyter.

Mensch und Natur Im Mittelalter, Pt. 2. Ed. by Albert Zimmerman & Andreas Speer. (Miscellanea Mediaevalia Ser.: Vol. 21, Pts. 1 & 2). (GER., Illus.). 546p. (C). 1992. lib. bdg. 203.10 (*3-11-013164-1*) De Gruyter.

Mensch und Natur in Australien. Gerhard Stilz. (German-Australien Studies). (Illus.). XIII, 248p. 1991. 47.00 (*3-261-04384-9*) P Lang Pubng.

Mensch und Pferd: Zur Kultursoziologie einer Mensch-Tier-Assoziation. Heinz Meyer. (GER., Illus.). vi, 306p. 1975. write for info. (*3-487-08099-0*) G Olms Pubs.

Mensch und Zeit: An Anthology of German Radio Plays. Ed. by Anna Otten. LC 66-19203. (GER., Illus.). 1966. pap. 1.00 (*0-89197-301-X*); pap. text 8.95 (*0-89197-300-1*) Irvington.

Mensch Zwischen Anschauungen und Abstraktion. E. Dreher. (Schriftenreihe des Instituts fuer Konfliktforschung Ser.: Vol. 8). x, 54p. 1982. pap. 10.00 (*3-8055-3489-2*) S Karger.

Menschen in Deutschland. Volker Borbein. (GER., Illus.). 136p. 1995. 17.50 (*3-468-49475-0*) Langenscheidt.

Menschen um Mueller: Textbuch. E. Mueller. (GER., Illus.). 79p. (C). 1972. pap. text 17.25 (*3-12-558500-7*, Pub. by Klett Edition) Intl Bk Import.

Menschen um Mueller: Textbuch. E. Mueller. (GER., Illus.). (C). 1978. audio 33.25 (*3-12-558570-8*, Pub. by Klett Edition) Intl Bk Import.

Menschenbild und Erziehungskonzeption Bei William Godwin. Niels-Peter Ammitzboll. (Philosophische Texte und Studien: Vol. 28). (GER.). 249p. 1991. 40.00 (*3-487-09509-2*) G Olms Pubs.

Menschenbilder. Anna Katharina Reichardt & Eric Kubli. 24.95 (*3-906762-49-1*, Pub. by P Lang) P Lang Pubng.

Menschenbilder - Philosophie Im Krankenhaus. Ed. by Juergen Meier. (GER.). vi, 121p. 1994. write for info. (*3-487-09884-9*) G Olms Pubs.

Menschenbildvorstellungen Im Ijob-Buch: Ein Beitrag zur Alttestamentlichen Anthropologie. Martin Remus. (Beitrage zur Erforschung des Alten Testaments & Antiken Judentums Ser.: Bd. 21). (GER.). 132p. 1993. 28.80 (*3-631-42465-5*) P Lang Pubng.

Menschenrechte in Arabo-Islamischen Staaten: Am Beispiel Agypten Und Sudan. Mark Krieger. 396p. 1998. 56.95 (*3-631-34450-3*) P Lang Pubng.

Menschheitsdammerung: Dawn of Humanity. Ed. by Kurt Pinthus. Tr. by Joanna M. Ratych et al. LC 93-2165. (GERM Ser.). 410p. 1994. 90.00 (*1-879751-48-8*) Camden Hse.

Menschlich: Gesprache Mit Karl Krolow. Vera B. Profit. (Studies in Modern German Literature: Vol. 78). (GER.). 154p. (C). 1996. text 39.95 (*0-8204-2794-2*) P Lang Pubng.

Menschliche Existenz und Moderne Welt: Ein Internationales Symposion Zum Selbstverstaendnis des heutigen Menschen, Teil 1 see Bildung, Kultur, Existenz

Menschliche Existenz und Moderne Welt: Teil 2 see Bildung, Kultur, Existenz

***Menschliche Faktor Als Kern Von Organisationsveranderungen: Eine Diagnose Aus Organisationspsychologischer Sicht.** Gunter W. Weber. 201p. 1999. 39.95 (*3-631-34940-8*) P Lang Pubng.

Menschliche und menschheitliche Entwicklungswanrheiten see Karma of Materialism

Menschlicher Realismus: Erster Versuch in Richtung Einer Rekonstruktion Eines Kantischen Ansatzes Fur die Teilweise Rechtfertigung des Sogenannten "Naiven" Realismus Als Zutreffenden "Evolutionaren" Realismus in der Form Eines Einfuhrenden Lese- und Lehrbuches. Edgar Selzer. (GER.). 321p. 1996. 57.95 (*3-631-30417-X*) P Lang Pubng.

Menschliches, Allzumenschliches. Friedrich Wilhelm Nietzsche. (Cloth Bound Pocket Ser.). (GER.). 238p. 1998. 7.95 (*3-89508-036-5*, 510024) Konemann.

Menschliches, Allzumenschliches: Band 1; Nachgelassene Fragmente, 1876 bis Winter, 1877-78 see Nietzsche Werke

Menschliches, Allzumenschliches: Band 2; Nachgelassene Fragmente, Fruehling, 1878 Bis November, 1879 see Nietzsche Werke

Menschliches Denken: Eine Systematische Studie Am Boden der Kantischen Philosophie. Gernot Reibenschuh. (Kantstudien-Ergaenzungshefte Ser.: Vol. 129). (GER.). x, 306p. (C). 1997. lib. bdg. 102.10 (*3-11-014270-8*) De Gruyter.

Menschwerdung: Eine Untersuchung zur Literarischen und Theologischen Einheit des Funften Buches "Adversus Haereses" des Irenaus von Lyon. Winfried Overbeck. (Basler und Berner Studien zur Historischen und Systematischen Theologie: Bd. 61). (GER.). xvi, 634p. 1995. 76.95 (*3-906755-40-1*, Pub. by P Lang) P Lang Pubng.

Menschwerdung Gottes: Vergottlichung Von Menschen. Dieter Zeller. (Novum Testamentum et Orbis Antiquus Ser.: Vol. 7). (GER.). 236p. 1988. text 45.00 (*3-7278-0604-4*, Pub. by Presses Univ Fribourg) Eisenbrauns.

Menschzeichnung Dreijahriger Kinder: Ein Beitrag zur Anglo-Amerikanischen Kinderzeichnungsforschung. Heidi Schoenmackers. (GER., Illus.). 233p. 1996. 44.95 (*3-631-30200-2*) P Lang Pubng.

Menshevik Leaders in the Russian Revolution: Social Realities & Political Strategies. Ziva G. Garcia. LC 88-32504. (Studies of the Harriman Institute). (Illus.). 470p. reprint ed. pap. 145.70 (*0-608-06313-4*, 206667500008) Bks Demand.

Mensheviks after October: Socialist Opposition & the Rise of the Bolshevik Dictatorship. Vladimir N. Brovkin. LC 87-47952. 352p. 1991. reprint ed. pap. text 18.95 (*0-8014-9976-3*) Cornell U Pr.

Mensheviks in the Revolution of 1917. John D. Basil. 220p. 1984. 24.95 (*0-89357-109-1*) Slavica.

Menshikov Palace. Ed. by N. Kaliazina & L. Dorofeeva. (Illus.). 218p. (C). 1986. text 250.00 (*0-7855-5854-3*, Pub. by Collets) St Mut.

Mensonge du Pacifisme see Voices of French Pacifism

Mensonges. Francoise Mallet-Joris. (FRE.). 1956. 6.95 (*0-8288-9840-5*, F110780) Fr & Eur.

***Mensonges d'Alexandra.** Sally Wentworth. (Azur Ser.: No. 798). (FRE.). 1999. mass mkt. 3.99 (*0-373-34798-7*, 1-34798-8, Harlequin French) Harlequin Bks.

Menstrual & Pre-Menstrual Tension. Jan De Vries. (Well Woman Ser.). 160p. 1992. pap. 11.95 (*1-85158-417-X*, Pub. by Mainstream Pubng) Trafalgar.

Menstrual Cycle. Anne E. Walker. LC 97-213814. (Women & Psychology Ser.). 264p. (C). 1997. 70.00 (*0-415-16330-7*); pap. 22.99 (*0-415-16331-5*) Routledge.

Menstrual Cycle: Physiology, Reproductive Disorders & Infertility. Michael Ferin et al. (Illus.). 264p. 1993. text 63.50 (*0-19-506193-4*) OUP.

Menstrual Cycle & Physical Activity: Proceedings of the Seminar Held February 24-26, 1984, at the Olympic Training Center, Colorado Springs, Colorado, under Sponsorship of the U. S. Olympic Committee Sports Medicine Council in Cooperation with Tampax Incorporated. Ed. by Jacqueline L. Puhl & C. Harmon Brown. LC 85-22427. (Illus.). 174p. reprint ed. pap. 54.00 (*0-608-07036-X*, 206724300009) Bks Demand.

Menstrual Disorders. Annette Scambler & Graham Scambler. LC 92-2319. (Experience of Illness Ser.). (Illus.). 128p. (C). (gr. 13). 1992. pap. 18.99 (*0-415-04646-7*, A9766) Routledge.

Menstrual Disorders & Menopause: Etiology, Maintenance & Treatment. Linda R. Gannon. LC 85-3629. 304p. 1985. 55.00 (*0-275-90103-3*, C0103, Praeger Pubs) Greenwood.

Menstrual Health in Women's Lives. Ed. by Alice J. Dan & Linda L. Lewis. (Illus.). 312p. 1991. pap. text 16.95 (*0-252-06209-4*) U of Ill Pr.

Menstrual Health in Women's Lives. Ed. by Alice J. Dan & Linda L. Lewis. (Illus.). 312p. 1992. text 37.50 (*0-252-01784-6*) U of Ill Pr.

Menstrual Journey: Through the Old & the Dark to the New, the Light, & the Possibility & The Goddess Has Many Faces. Judith Barr. LC TX 2807 677. 51p. (Orig.). 1990. pap. text 9.95 (*1-886264-00-7*) Mysteries of Life.

***Menstrual Purity: Rabbinic & Christian Reconstructions of Biblical Gender.** Charlotte Elisheva Fonrobert. LC 99-462388. (Contraversions Ser.). 2000. 55.00 (*0-8047-3725-8*) Stanford U Pr.

Menstruation & Psychoanalysis. Mary J. Lupton. LC 92-39667. 240p. 1993. text 34.95 (*0-252-02012-X*); pap. text 14.95 (*0-252-06315-5*) U of Ill Pr.

Menstruation, Health, & Illness. Ed. by Diana L. Taylor & Nancy F. Woods. (Health Care for Women International Publication). 410p. 1991. 75.00 (*1-56032-132-6*) Hemisp Pub.

Mensura: Mass, Zahl, Zahlensymbolik im Mittelalter. 260p. 1983. 126.95 (*3-11-009769-9*) De Gruyter.

Mensuration & Proportion Signs: Origins & Evolution. Anna M. Berger. LC 92-12195. (Oxford Monographs on Music). (Illus.). 284p. 1993. text 65.00 (*0-19-816230-8*, Clarendon Pr) OUP.

Menswear: Suiting the Customer. Suzanne Boswell. LC 92-22908. 208p. (C). 1993. pap. text 29.20 (*0-13-571423-0*) P-H.

Menswear in France: A Strategic Entry Report, 1995. Compiled by Icon Group International Staff. (Country Industry Report). (Illus.). 121p. 1999. ring bd. 1210.00 incl. audio compact disk (*0-7418-0655-X*) Icon Grp.

Menswear in United Kingdom: A Strategic Entry Report, 1995. Compiled by Icon Group International Staff. (Country Industry Report). (Illus.). 94p. 1999. ring bd. 940.00 incl. audio compact disk (*0-7418-0656-8*) Icon Grp.

***Mental ABC's of Pitching: A Handbook for Performance Enhancement.** H. A. Dorfman. LC 99-47262. 2000. pap. 19.95 (*1-888698-29-2*) Diamond Communications.

Mental Ability & Higher Educational Attainment in the 20th Century. Paul J. Taubman & Terence Wales. (Occasional Papers: No. 118). 63p. 1972. reprint ed. 20.00 (*0-87014-243-7*) Natl Bur Econ Res.

Mental Acts, 1971. Peter T. Geach. (Key Texts Ser.). 148p. 1996. pap., teacher ed. 18.95 (*1-85506-166-X*) Bks Intl VA.

Mental Aerobics: Exercises for a Stronger, Healthier Mind. Alexis Castorri & Jane Heller. (Illus.). 112p. 1992. pap. 7.95 (*0-8065-1362-4*, Citadel Pr) Carol Pub Group.

Mental Aerobics: Self Power. Tuppacc Amaru, III. Ed. by Sam Chekwas. 160p. (Orig.). 1997. pap. 11.00 (*1-885778-26-0*) Seaburn.

Mental Affections of Childhood & Youth. J. Langdon Down. (Classics in Developmental Medicine Ser.: No. 5). 185p. (C). 1991. text 19.95 (*0-521-41330-3*, Pub. by Mc Keith Pr) Cambridge U Pr.

Mental Alchemy. Ralph M. Lewis. LC 79-66799. 270p. 1978. pap. 17.95 (*0-912057-92-0*, 501830) GLELJ AMORC.

Mental Alchemy: How Thoughts & Feelings Shape Our Lives. C. C. Zain. (Brotherhood of Light Home Study Ser.: Course 9). (Illus.). 1996. pap. 16.95 (*0-87887-349-X*) Church of Light.

Mental Alchemy: The Wonders of Thought Force. O. Hashnu Hara. 121p. 1968. reprint ed. spiral bd. 11.00 (*0-7873-0371-2*) Hlth Research.

Mental Alchemy or the Wonders of Thought-Force, 1909. O. Hashnu Hara. 125p. 1996. reprint ed. pap. 10.50 (*1-56459-748-2*) Kessinger Pub.

Mental & Elemental Nutrients: A Physician's Guide to Nutrition & Health Care. Carl C. Pfeiffer. LC 75-19543. 556p. 1976. 27.95 (*0-87983-114-6*, Keats Publng) NTC Contemp Pub Co.

Mental & Emotional Injuries in Employment Litigation with 1998 Supplement. James J. McDonald, Jr. Ed. by Francine B. Kulick. LC 94-15827. 500p. 1994. text 125.00 (*0-87179-832-8*) BNA Books.

Mental & Emotional Injuries in Employment Litigation, 1998 Supplement. James J. McDonald, Jr. 219p. pap. 55.00 (*1-57018-117-9*, 1117-PR8) BNA Books.

Mental & Intelligence Tests: Medical Subject Analysis with Research Bibliography. American Health Research Institute Staff. LC 84-45652. 150p. 1985. 37.50 (*0-88164-226-6*); pap. 34.50 (*0-88164-227-4*) ABBE Pubs Assn.

Mental & Interest Tests, Their Evaluation & Comparative Effectiveness As Factors of Prognosis in Secondary Education. Leo H. King. LC 77-176957. (Columbia University. Teachers College. Contributions to Education Ser.: No. 444). reprint ed. 37.50 (*0-404-55444-X*) AMS Pr.

Mental & Physical Fitness for Sailing. Alan Beggs et al. 96p. (C). 1993. text 18.95 (*0-906754-94-1*, Pub. by Fernhurst Bks) St Mut.

Mental & Physical Measurements of Working Children. Henry T. Wooley. (Psychology Monographs General & Applied: Vol. 18). 1974. reprint ed. pap. 55.00 (*0-8115-1417-X*) Periodicals Srv.

Mental & Physical Traits of a Thousand Gifted Children. 2nd rev. ed. Lewis M. Terman et al. (Genetic Studies of Genius: Vol. I). xiii, 648p. 1926. 75.00 (*0-8047-0009-5*) Stanford U Pr.

Mental & Social Disorder in Sub-Saharan Africa: The Case of Sierra Leone, 1787-1990, 147. Leland V. Bell. LC 91-14922. (Contributions in Afro-American & African Studies: No. 147). 224p. 1991. 57.95 (*0-313-27942-X*, BLQ, Greenwood Pr) Greenwood.

Mental & Social Life of Babies: How Parents Create Persons. Kenneth Kaye. LC 82-6965. (Illus.). 288p. (C). 1994. pap. text 11.00 (*0-226-42848-6*) U Ch Pr.

Mental & Social Life of Babies: How Parents Create Persons. Kenneth Kaye. LC 82-6965. 299p. reprint ed. pap. 92.70 (*0-608-09421-8*, 205422100004) Bks Demand.

Mental & the Physical: The Essay & a Postscript. LC 67-24556. 189p. reprint ed. pap. 58.60 (*0-608-14649-8*, 205586300039) Bks Demand.

Mental Arithmetic. B. Gillham. (Illus.). (J). mass mkt. 6.95 (*0-340-71066-7*, Pub. by Hodder & Stought Ltd) Trafalgar.

Mental Arithmetic. NCPTA Staff. (Illus.). (YA). (gr. 9-11). 1996. mass mkt. 6.95 (*0-340-65110-5*, Pub. by Hodder & Stought Ltd) Trafalgar.

Mental Arithmetic & Problem Solving 5. Lewis. Date not set. pap. text. write for info. (*0-582-87525-0*, Pub. by Addison-Wesley) Longman.

Mental Arithmetic & Problem Solving 6. Lewis. Date not set. pap. text. write for info. (*0-582-87526-9*, Pub. by Addison-Wesley) Longman.

Mental Art of Putting: Using Your Mind to Putt Your Best. Patrick J. Cohn. LC 95-22030. (Illus.). 140p. 1995. 19.95 (*0-912083-87-5*) Diamond Communications.

Mental Athlete: Inner Training for Peak Performance. Judy Foster & Kay Porter. 1987. mass mkt. 5.99 (*0-345-34174-0*) Ballantine Pub Grp.

***Mental Attitude to Dressage.** Marshall. 2000. pap. 12.95 (*0-85131-739-1*, Pub. by J A Allen) Trafalgar.

Mental Birth Control. Mildred Jackson & Terri Teague. Ed. by Paul Ghelev. (Illus.). 1978. pap. 3.00 (*0-932516-00-9*) Lawton-Teague.

Mental Body. Arthur E. Powell. 1975. pap. 19.95 (*0-8356-5504-0*) Theos Pub Hse.

Mental Capacity: Medical & Legal Aspects of the Aging. J. Brooke Aker et al. (Trial Practice Ser.). 372p. 1977. text 95.00 (*0-07-000756-X*) Shepards.

Mental Case. James N. Harvey. 1997. mass mkt. 6.99 (*0-312-95995-8*) St Martin.

Mental Causation. Ed. by John Heil & Alfred R. Mele. LC 92-22764. (Illus.). 352p. 1993. text 55.00 (*0-19-823929-7*, Clarendon Pr) OUP.

Mental Causation. Ed. by John Heil & Alfred R. Mele. (Illus.). 352p. 1995. pap. text 19.95 (*0-19-823564-X*) OUP.

Mental Chemistry (1922) Charles Haanel. 350p. 1998. reprint ed. pap. 27.95 (*0-7661-0484-2*) Kessinger Pub.

Mental Competency: Index of New Information with Authors, Subjects & References. Larry J. Cantrell. 150p. 1996. 47.50 (*0-7883-1274-X*); pap. 44.50 (*0-7883-1275-8*) ABBE Pubs Assn.

Mental Condition Defences in the Criminal Law. R. D. Mackay. (Oxford Monographs on Criminal Law & Justice). (Illus.). 280p. 1996. text 62.00 (*0-19-825995-6*) OUP.

Mental Conflict. A. W. Price. LC 94-3935. (Issues in Ancient Philosophy Ser.). 208p. (C). 1994. pap. 27.99 (*0-415-11557-4*, B4617) Routledge.

Mental Conflicts & Misconduct. William Healy. LC 69-16237. (Criminology, Law Enforcement, & Social Problems Ser.: No. 88). 1969. reprint ed. 24.00 (*0-87585-088-X*) Patterson Smith.

Mental Defectives: Their History, Treatment & Training. Martin W. Barr. LC 73-2383. (Mental Illness & Social Policy; the American Experience Ser.). 1973. reprint ed. 31.95 (*0-405-05191-3*) Ayer.

Mental Development in the Child. William Preyer. Tr. by H. W. Brown from GER. LC 78-72818. (Brainedness, Handedness, & Mental Abilities Ser.). reprint ed. 42.50 (*0-404-60887-6*) AMS Pr.

Mental Development in the Child & the Race. James Mark Baldwin. 496p. 120.00 (*1-85506-683-1*) Thoemmes Pr.

Mental Development of the Child: Summary of Modern Psychological Theory. Karl Buhler. Tr. by Oscar Oeser from GRE. LC 74-21403. (Classics in Child Development Ser.). 190p. 1978. reprint ed. 28.95 (*0-405-06456-X*) Ayer.

Mental Disabilities & the Americans with Disabilities Act. 2nd ed. Ed. by John W. Parry. LC 97-207758. 144p. 1997. pap. 40.00 (*1-57073-462-3*, 441-0080) Amer Bar Assn.

Mental Disabilities & the Americans with Disabilities Act: A Concise Compliance Manual for Executives. John F. Fielder. LC 93-42762. 216p. 1994. 49.95 (*0-89930-826-0*, Quorum Bks) Greenwood.

Mental Disability: 1990 Supplement. 3rd ed. Michael Perlin. 1990. write for info. (*0-87473-705-2*, 65814-10, MICHIE) LEXIS Pub.

Mental Disability Law: A Primer. 4th ed. Deborah Zuckerman. LC 95-209524. 112p. (C). 1992. pap. 15.00 (*1-57073-215-9*) ABA Prof Educ Pubns.

Mental Disability Law: Cases & Materials. Michael L. Perlin. LC 98-89959. 1080p. 1999. boxed set 85.00 (*0-89089-882-0*) Carolina Acad Pr.

Mental Disability Law: Civil & Criminal, 3 vols. 2nd ed. Michael L. Perlin. LC 98-87895. 1999. write for info. (*0-327-00493-2*) LEXIS Pub.

Mental Disability Law: Civil & Criminal, 3 vols., Set. Michael L. Perlin. 1989. 240.00 (*0-87473-422-3*, 65810-10, MICHIE) LEXIS Pub.

Mental Disability Law Vol. 1: Civil & Criminal, 3 vols. 2nd ed. Michael L. Perlin. LC 98-87895. 500p. 1998. 240.00 (*0-327-00524-6*, 6581111) LEXIS Pub.

***Mental Disability Law Vol. 2: Civil & Criminal.** 2nd ed. Michael L. Perlin. 600p. 1999. write for info. (*0-327-04964-2*, 6581211) LEXIS Pub.

Mental Disability Law Vols. 2 & 3: Civil & Criminal, 1998 Cumulative Supplement. Michael L. Perlin. 900p. 1998. pap. 90.00 (*0-327-00791-5*, 6581616) LEXIS Pub.

Mental Discipline: The Pursuit of Peak Performance. Michael K. Livingston. LC 88-34807. (Illus.). 280p. 1989. reprint ed. pap. 86.80 (*0-608-07067-X*, 206727300009) Bks Demand.

An Asterisk (*) at the beginning of an entry indicates that the title is appearing for the first time.

Mental Disease & Social Welfare. Horatio M. Pollock. LC 75-17237. (Social Problems & Social Policy Ser.). (Illus.). 1976. reprint ed. 20.95 (*0-405-07506-5*) Ayer.

Mental Disease in History: A Selection of Translated Readings. Ed. by J. Thomas Dalby. LC 96-33891. (Reshaping of Psychoanalysis: No. 7). XIX, 264p. (C). 1997. text 51.95 (*0-8204-3056-0*) P Lang Pubng.

Mental Diseases: A Public Health Problem. James V. May. Ed. by Gerald N. Grob. LC 78-22574. (Historical Issues in Mental Health Ser.). 1980. reprint ed. lib. bdg. 40.95 (*0-405-11927-5*) Ayer.

Mental Disorder among Prisoners: Toward an Epidemiologic Inventory. Nathaniel J. Pallone. 186p. (C). 1990. 39.95 (*0-88738-383-1*) Transaction Pubs.

Mental Disorder & Crime. Ed. by Sheilagh Hodgins. (Illus.). 379p. (C). 1993. text 58.00 (*0-8039-5022-5*); pap. text 26.95 (*0-8039-5023-3*) Sage.

Mental Disorder & Criminal Law in Australia & New Zealand. I. G. Campbell. 270p. 1989. 69.00 (*0-409-49482-8*, AT, MICHIE) LEXIS Pub.

Mental Disorder & the Criminal Law: A Study in Medico-Sociological Jurisprudence. S. Sheldon Glueck. LC 93-78309. xxii, 693p. 1993. reprint ed. 75.00 (*0-89941-843-0*, 307840) W S Hein.

Mental Disorder As a Criminal Defense. Henry Weihofen. LC 54-8478. vii, 530p. 1954. lib. bdg. 42.00 (*0-89941-607-1*, 500580) W S Hein.

Mental Disorder in the Criminal Process: Stan Stress & the Vietnam-Sports Conspiracy, 72. Grant H. Morris & Allen C. Snyder. LC 92-21355. (Contributions in Legal Studies: No. 72). 324p. 1993. 65.00 (*0-313-28761-9*, GM8761, Greenwood Pr) Greenwood.

Mental Disorder, Work Disability, & the Law. Ed. by Richard J. Bonnie & John Monahan. LC 96-10971. (John D. & Catherine T. MacArthur Foundation Series on Mental Health & Development). (Illus.). 308p. 1996. 27.50 (*0-226-06450-6*) U Ch Pr.

Mental Disorders see Handbook of Empirical Social Work Practice

Mental Disorders. 2nd ed. Lyttle. 1994. pap. text 55.00 (*0-7020-1416-8*) Harcourt.

Mental Disorders & Cognitive Deficits in MS. K. Jensen et al. (Current Problems in Neurology Ser.: Vol. 10). 224p. 1988. 79.95 (*0-86196-180-3*, Pub. by J Libbey Med) Bks Intl VA.

Mental Disorders & Genetics. 1996. lib. bdg. 251.75 (*0-8490-6042-7*) Gordon Pr.

Mental Disorders & Genetics: Bridging the Gap Between Research & Society. (Illus.). 58p. (Orig.). (C). 1995. pap. text 30.00 (*0-7881-2508-7*) DIANE Pub.

Mental Disorders & the Law. Kok L. Peng et al. LC 94-943831. 360p. (Orig.). 1994. pap. 42.50 (*9971-69-188-4*, Pub. by Sngapore Univ Pr) Coronet Bks.

Mental Disorders in HIV-1 Infection & AIDS. Norman Sartorius et al. (WHO Expert Series on Neuroscience: Vol. 5). (Illus.). 90p. 1993. text 24.00 (*0-88937-096-6*) Hogrefe & Huber Pubs.

Mental Disorders in Later Life. Ed. by Oscar J. Kaplan & Leon Stein. LC 79-8673. (Growing Old Ser.). (Illus.). 1980. reprint ed. lib. bdg. 53.95 (*0-405-12789-8*) Ayer.

Mental Disorders in Older Adults: Fundamentals of Assessment & Treatment. Steven H. Zarit & Judy M. Zarit. LC 98-22968. 418p. 1998. lib. bdg. 40.00 (*1-57230-368-9*) Guilford Pubns.

Mental Disorders in the Community - Progress & Challenge: Proceedings of the 75th Annual Meeting of the American Psychopathological Association, New York City, February 28-March 2, 1985. American Psychopathological Association Staff. Ed. by James E. Barrett & Robert M. Rose. LC 86-14311. 393p. 1986. reprint ed. pap. 121.90 (*0-608-07579-5*, 205989400010) Bks Demand.

Mental Disorders in the Elderly: New Therapeutic Approaches - Rome, April, 1997. Ed. by Nicoletta Brunello et al. LC 97-52828. (International Academy for Biomedical & Drug Research Ser.: Vol. 13, 1997). (Illus.). vi, 192p. 1998. 189.75 (*3-8055-6536-4*) S Karger.

Mental Disorders in Urban Areas: An Ecological Study of Schizophrenia & Other Psychoses. Robert E. Faris & H. Warren Dunham. LC 65-16168. (Phoenix Bks). 304p. reprint ed. pap. 94.30 (*0-608-16542-5*, 202677200052) Bks Demand.

Mental Disorders, Medications, & Clinical Social Work. Sonia G. Austrian. LC 95-14322. 1995. 44.00 (*0-231-08124-3*) Col U Pr.

***Mental Disorders, Medications & Clinical Social Work.** 2nd ed. Sonia G. Austrian. LC 00-24069. (Illus.). 2000. 45.00 (*0-231-11296-3*) Col U Pr.

Mental Disorders, Suicide. Ed. by American Public Health Association Staff et al. LC 74-186673. (Vital & Health Statistics Monographs, American Public Health Association). (Illus.). 331p. 1972. 41.00 (*0-674-56735-8*) HUP.

***Mental Dissability Issues in the Criminal Justice System: What They Are, Who Evaluates Them, How & When.** Harlow M. Huckabee. LC 00-32614. 2000. pap. write for info. (*0-398-07090-3*) C C Thomas.

Mental Dominance: Classics of Personal Magnetism & Hypnotism. Julien Ochorowicz. 300p. 1991. reprint ed. 29.98 (*0-941683-04-4*) Instant Improve.

Mental Dynamics: Power Thinking for Personal Success, 1990. K. Thomas Finley. 184p. (C). 1990. text 26.95 (*0-13-566431-4*) P-H.

Mental Edge: Basketball's Peak Performance Workbook - Second Edition. 2nd ed. Stephen J. Brennan. 300p. (C). 1993. reprint ed. pap. 29.95 (*0-9619230-2-4*) Peak Perf Pub.

Mental Edge: Maximize Your Sports Potential with the Mind-Body Connection. Kenneth Baum & Richard Trubo. LC 98-49937. 182p. 1999. pap. 13.95 (*0-399-52481-9*, Perigee Bks) Berkley Pub.

Mental Edge for Alpine Ski Racing. 4th rev. ed. Jim Taylor. (Mental Edge Ser.). 249p. 1996. pap. 20.00 (*1-884560-10-5*) Alpine Taylor.

Mental Edge for Golf. 4th rev. ed. Jim Taylor. (Mental Edge Ser.). 228p. 1996. pap. 20.00 (*1-884560-07-5*) Alpine Taylor.

Mental Edge for Skiing. 3rd rev. ed. Jim Taylor. (Mental Edge Ser.). 169p. 1996. pap. 20.00 (*1-884560-09-1*) Alpine Taylor.

Mental Edge for Sports. 4th rev. ed. Jim Taylor. (Mental Edge Ser.). 251p. 1996. pap. 20.00 (*1-884560-06-7*) Alpine Taylor.

Mental Edge for Tennis. 4th rev. ed. Jim Taylor. (Mental Edge Ser.). 251p. 1996. pap. 20.00 (*1-884560-08-3*) Alpine Taylor.

Mental Effects of Heroin. Ann Holmes. Ed. by Carol C. Nadelson. LC 98-33640. (Encyclopedia of Psychological Disorders Ser.). 1998. 22.95 (*0-7910-4899-3*) Chelsea Hse.

Mental Efficiency & Other Hints to Men & Women. Arnold Bennett. LC 74-17123. (Collected Works of Arnold Bennett: Vol. 55). 1977. reprint ed. 19.95 (*0-518-19136-2*) Ayer.

Mental Efficiency Program: Positive Self Development for Tennis, Sport, & Life. Nick Bollettieri & Charles A. Maher. (Mental Efficiency & Sport Psychology Ser.). (Orig.). pap. text. write for info. (*1-878843-11-7*) Intl Merc OH.

Mental Equitation: A Guide to Interdisciplinary Horsemanship. James R. Arrigon. LC 98-47580. (Illus.). 144p. 1999. 24.95 (*1-57779-010-3*) Alpine Pubns.

***Mental Essentials: Mental Skills for Becoming a Complete Athlete.** M. Jane Miner. 40p. 1999. pap. 4.95 (*1-887476-03-2*) Perf Publns.

Mental Evolution in Animals: With a Posthumous Essay on Instinct by Charles Darwin. George J. Romanes. LC 71-96472. reprint ed. 55.00 (*0-404-05389-0*) AMS Pr.

Mental Evolution in Man. George J. Romanes. 466p. 100.00 (*1-85506-677-7*) Thoemmes Pr.

Mental Evolution in Man: Origin of Human Faculty. George J. Romanes. LC 74-21426. (Classics in Child Development Ser.). 466p. 1975. reprint ed. lib. bdg. 38.95 (*0-405-06475-6*) Ayer.

Mental Exercises. Torkom Saraydarian. LC 96-60650. 85p. (Orig.). 1996. pap. 6.00 (*0-929874-53-6*) TSG Pub Found.

Mental Fascination No. 1: Side Light Manual. William W. Atkinson. 253p. 1993. reprint ed. spiral bd. 17.00 (*0-7873-0056-X*) Hlth Research.

Mental Fascination, 1907. William W. Atkinson. 253p. 1996. reprint ed. pap. 16.50 (*1-56459-767-9*) Kessinger Pub.

Mental Fatigue: Index of New Information for Reference & Research. Fritz O. Sanders. 150p. 1997. 47.50 (*0-7883-1328-2*) ABBE Pubs Assn.

Mental Fatigue: Index of New information for Reference & Research. Fritz O. Sanders. 150p. 1997. pap. 44.50 (*0-7883-1329-0*) ABBE Pubs Assn.

Mental Fatigue: Index of New Information with Authors, Subjects & References. Larry J. Cantrell. 150p. 1996. 47.50 (*0-7883-1272-3*); pap. 44.50 (*0-7883-1273-1*) ABBE Pubs Assn.

Mental Fatigue - Analysis, Procedures, Tests, Factors, Results & Advice: Index of New Information with Authors, Subjects, Research Categories & References. Carla Dodenhoff. 160p. (Orig.). 1995. 47.50 (*0-7883-0688-X*); pap. 44.50 (*0-7883-0689-8*) ABBE Pubs Assn.

Mental Fitness: Basic Workouts for Mind, Body & Souls. Michiko J. Rolek. 1996. pap. text 14.95 (*0-8348-0373-9*) Weatherhill.

Mental Fitness Puzzles. Kyle Hendrickson & Judy Hendrickson. LC 98-14801. (Illus.). 96p. 1998. 5.95 (*0-8069-0899-8*) Sterling.

Mental Floss. Marilyn Gellis. 1996. 9.95 (*0-9627373-4-8*) Inst Phobic Awareness.

Mental Forms Creating: William Blake Anticipates Freud, Jung, & Rank. Jerry C. Godard. (Illus.). 186p. (Orig.). 1985. pap. text 23.00 (*0-8191-4832-6*) U Pr of Amer.

Mental Game. James E. Loehr. 1990. pap. 11.95 (*0-452-26666-1*, Plume) Dutton Plume.

Mental Game of Baseball: A Guide to Peak Performance. 2nd ed. H. A. Dorfman & Karl Kuehl. LC 89-1407. (Orig.). 1994. pap. 19.95 (*0-912083-78-6*) Diamond Communications.

Mental Game of Golf. Dennis Vardy. 87p. 1999. pap. 50.00 (*1-897676-58-1*, Pub. by Nottingham Univ Pr) St Mut.

Mental Game of Golf: A Guide to Peak Performance. Patrick J. Cohn. LC 93-34172. 1993. 19.95 (*0-912083-65-4*) Diamond Communications.

Mental Game Plan. Stephen J. Bull et al. 216p. 1996. pap. 16.95 (*0-9519543-2-6*, Pub. by Sports Dynamics) Fit Info Tech.

Mental Game (The Inner Game of Bowling) George Allen. LC 83-50980. (Illus.). 192p. 1983. pap. 12.95 (*0-933554-18-4*) Tech-Ed Pub.

Mental Grammar Russian Aspect & Related Issues. Per Durst-Andersen. (Illus.). 268p. (Orig.). 1992. pap. 18.95 (*0-89357-229-2*) Slavica.

Mental Growth: A Study of Changes in Test Ability Between the Ages of Nine & Sixteen Years. Gosta W. Berglund. (Studia Scientiae Paedagogicae Upsaliensia: No. 6). 1965. pap. 79.50 (*0-317-27518-6*) Elliots Bks.

Mental Growth & Personality Development: A Longitudinal Study. Lester W. Sontag et al. (SRCD M Ser.: Vol. 23, No. 2). 1958. 25.00 (*0-527-01574-1*) Periodicals Srv.

Mental Growth of Children from Two to Fourteen Years: Study of the Predictive Value of the Minnesota Pre-School Scales, Vol. 20. Florence L. Goodenough & Katharine Maurer. LC 70-141548. (University of Minnesota Institute of Child Welfare Monographs: No. 20). (Illus.). 130p. 1975. reprint ed. lib. bdg. 45.00 (*0-8371-5895-8*, CWGM) Greenwood.

***Mental Growth of the Pre-School Child.** Arnold Gesell. 2000. reprint ed. lib. bdg. 95.00 (*0-7812-4752-7*) Rprt Serv.

Mental Growth of the Pre-School Child. Arnold L. Gesell. 1968. reprint ed. 59.00 (*0-403-00127-7*) Scholarly.

Mental Handicap. Aelred S. Shanley. 1986. pap. text 43.00 (*0-443-02793-5*, W B Saunders Co) Harcrt Hlth Sci Grp.

Mental Handicap: A Multi-Disciplinary Approach. Michael Craft et al. 1985. text 115.00 (*0-7020-1085-5*) Bailliere Tindall.

Mental Handicap among Rural Indian Children. Anima Sen. LC 92-12461. (Illus.). 308p. (C). 1992. text 36.00 (*0-8039-9430-3*) Sage.

Mental Handicap & the Human Condition: New Approaches from the Tavistock. Valerie Sinason. 366p. (C). 1992. pap. 25.00 (*1-85343-176-1*, Pub. by Free Assoc Bks) NYU Pr.

Mental Healing & Personal Welfare: Index of New Information. Holly K. Young. 160p. 1998. 47.50 (*0-7883-1728-8*); pap. 44.50 (*0-7883-1729-6*) ABBE Pubs Assn.

Mental Health. Ed. by C. S. Aneshensel & J. C. Phelan. LC 99-38201. (Handbooks of Sociology & Social Research Ser.). (Illus.). 600p. (C). 1999. write for info. (*0-306-46069-6*, Plenum Trade) Perseus Pubng.

Mental Health. Dubray. 1993. mass mkt. 16.75 (*0-314-02889-7*) West Pub.

Mental Health. Ed. by Jennifer Hurley. LC 98-33944. (Current Controversies Ser.). (YA). (gr. 9-12). 1998. pap. 17.45 (*1-56510-952-X*); lib. bdg. 27.45 (*1-56510-953-8*) Greenhaven.

Mental Health. Gary W. Stogsdill. LC 93-43479. (LPN - LVN Review Ser.). 227p. (C). 1994. pap. 42.95 (*0-8273-5698-6*) Delmar.

***Mental Health: A Report of the Surgeon General.** Ed. by Howard H. Goldman et al. 487p. (C). 2000. pap. text 40.00 (*0-7881-8976-X*) DIANE Pub.

***Mental Health: Dimensions of Self-Esteem & Emotional Well-Being.** Joseph W. Donnelly et al. LC 00-42093. 2001. write for info. (*0-205-30955-0*) Allyn.

Mental Health: Nursing Edition. 4th ed. Karen L. Fontaine. LC 98-23779. 612p. 1998. 61.00 (*0-8053-1644-2*, Prentice Hall) P-H.

Mental Health: Philosophical Perspectives. Ed. by H. Tristram Engelhardt & Stuart F. Spicker. LC 77-24974. (Philosophy & Medicine Ser.: No. 4). 324p. 1977. text 97.50 (*90-277-0828-2*, D Reidel) Kluwer Academic.

Mental Health: What Every Woman Should Know. Rita Baron-Faust. (Illus.). 416p. 1997. 23.00 (*0-614-19432-6*, Hearst) Hearst Commns.

Mental Health - Psychiatric Nursing: A Holistic Life-Cycle Approach. 3rd ed. Ed. by Ruth P. Rawlins et al. LC 92-49347. (Illus.). 960p. (C). (gr. 13). 1992. text 57.00 (*0-8016-6331-8*, 06331) Mosby Inc.

Mental Health a Report of the Surgeon General. per. 51.00 (*0-16-059001-9*) USGPO.

Mental Health Act, Explained. Bridget Dolan & Debra Powell. (Point of Law Ser.). 250p. 1999. pap. 50.00 (*0-11-702345-0*, Pub. by Statnry Office) Balogh.

***Mental Health Act 1983.** LC 98-205724. viii, 138 p. 1998. write for info. (*0-11-322112-6*) Gale.

***Mental Health, Addiction & Social Services Directory: 1999-2000 Edition.** Ed. by Martha T. Schriver. 284p. 1999. pap. 50.00 (*0-9676583-0-6*) Mntl Hlth.

Mental Health Administration: Principles & Practice, 2 vols., I. Walter E. Barton & Gail M. Barton. LC 81-7064. 845p. 1982. 56.95 (*0-89885-061-4*, Kluwer Acad Hman Sci) Kluwer Academic.

Mental Health Administration: Principles & Practice, 2 vols., II. Walter E. Barton & Gail M. Barton. LC 81-7064. 845p. 1982. 56.95 (*0-89885-062-2*, Kluwer Acad Hman Sci) Kluwer Academic.

Mental Health Aide. Jack Rudman. (Career Examination Ser.: C-1372). 1994. pap. 23.95 (*0-8373-1372-4*) Nat Learn.

Mental Health among Elderly Native Americans. James L. Narduzzi. LC 93-34972. (Studies on the Elderly in America). 248p. 1993. text 30.00 (*0-8153-1568-6*) Garland.

Mental Health & Aging. Ed. by Eugene Aronowitz & Eleanor M. Bromberg. LC 86-22684. 1986. pap. 6.95 (*0-88135-051-6*) Watson Pub Intl.

Mental Health & Aging: Programs & Evaluations. Ed. by Michael A. Smyer & Margaret Gatz. LC 83-13904. (Sage Studies in Community Mental Health: No. 8). 319p. 1983. reprint ed. pap. 98.90 (*0-608-01179-7*, 205947700001) Bks Demand.

Mental Health & Aging: Progress & Prospects. Michael A. Smyer. 192p. 1993. 29.95 (*0-8261-8380-8*) Springer Pub.

Mental Health & Criminal Justice. Ed. by Linda A. Teplin. LC 84-6932. (Sage Criminal Justice System Annuals Ser.: No. 20). 320p. reprint ed. pap. 99.20 (*0-8357-8397-9*, 203467100091) Bks Demand.

Mental Health & Deafness. Peter Hindley. (Orig.). 1998. pap. text 49.95 (*1-897635-39-7*, Pub. by Whurr Pub) Singular Publishing.

Mental Health & Deafness. Ed. by Peter Hindley & Nick Kitson. (Illus.). 256p. (Orig.). 1998. pap. 59.95 (*1-56593-748-1*, 1452) Singular Publishing.

Mental Health & Disability in A Nutshell. Donald H. Hermann. LC 97-10339. (Paralegal). 348p. (C). 1997. pap. text 16.50 (*0-314-06546-6*) West Pub.

Mental Health & Going to School: The Woodlawn Program of Assessment, Early Intervention. Sheppard G. Kellam et al. 1975. 15.00 (*0-226-42968-7*) U Ch Pr.

Mental Health & Going to School: The Woodlawn Program of Assessment, Early Intervention, & Evaluation. Sheppard G. Kellam et al. LC 74-10341. 1979. pap. text 6.50 (*0-226-42969-5*) U Ch Pr.

Mental Health & Industry: Planning for the 1980's. Ed. by Sherman N. Kieffer et al. LC 80-18057. (Problems of Industrial Psychiatric Medicine Ser.: Vol. 6). 210p. 1980. 35.95 (*0-87705-085-6*, Kluwer Acad Hman Sci) Kluwer Academic.

Mental Health & Law. Leo Stone. 1995. pap. write for info. (*1-56821-559-2*) Aronson.

Mental Health & Law: Research, Policy & Services. Ed. by Bruce D. Sales & Saleem A. Shah. LC 96-83448. 384p. 1996. 45.00 (*0-89089-914-2*) Carolina Acad Pr.

Mental Health & Long-Term Physical Illness. Ed. by Eugene Aronowitz & Eleanor M. Bromberg. 96p. 1984. pap. 6.95 (*0-88135-001-X*, N Watson) Watson Pub Intl.

Mental Health & Mental Illness. 6th ed. Patricia D. Barry. LC 97-16220. 464p. 1997. pap. text 28.95 (*0-397-55473-7*) Lppncott W & W.

Mental Health & People of Color: Curriculum Development & Change. Ed. by Jay Chunn, II et al. LC 83-295. (Illus.). 688p. 1982. 34.95 (*0-88258-097-3*) Howard U Pr.

Mental Health & Politics: A History of the Mental Health Services in Northern Ireland. Pauline Prior. 208p. 1993. 66.95 (*1-85628-540-5*, Pub. by Avebry) Ashgate Pub Co.

***Mental Health & Professional Procedure.** Maria Parsons. 256p. 2000. pap. 35.00 (*0-7506-3844-3*) Buttrwrth-Heinemann.

Mental Health & Psychiatric Nursing. O'Connell. 1999. pap. text. write for info. (*0-7216-6853-4*, W B Saunders Co) Harcrt Hlth Sci Grp.

Mental Health & Psychiatric Nursing. Linda E. Reese & Gasparis. LC 91-5211. (Nursetest: A Review Ser.). 288p. 1991. pap. 21.95 (*0-87434-306-2*) Springhouse Corp.

Mental Health & Psychiatric Nursing. 2nd ed. Ann Isaacs. LC 95-41442. (Lippincott's Review Ser.). 288p. 1996. pap. text 21.95 (*0-397-55215-7*) Lppncott W & W.

Mental Health & Psychiatric Nursing. 3rd ed. Margaret Benner. LC 96-29146. (Springhouse Notes Ser.). (Illus.). 208p. 1996. 22.95 incl. disk (*0-87434-862-5*) Springhouse Corp.

Mental Health & Psychiatric Nursing: A Caring Approach. Janet L. Davies & Ellen H. Janosik. 768p. 1991. 62.50 (*0-86720-442-7*) Jones & Bartlett.

Mental Health & Psychiatry in Africa: An Annotated Bibliography. David Westley. LC 93-20491. 224p. 1993. 75.00 (*1-873836-90-2*, Pub. by H Zell Pubs) Seven Hills Bk.

Mental Health & Religion. Loewenthal. 256p. 1994. pap. 41.50 (*1-56593-356-7*, 0680) Singular Publishing.

Mental Health & Rural America, 1980-1993: 1980-1993: An Overview & Annotated Bibliography. Morton O. Wagenfeld et al. 116p. (C). 1996. reprint ed. pap. text 35.00 (*0-7881-3156-7*) DIANE Pub.

Mental Health & Social Change: Fifty Years of Orthopsychiatry, No. 7. Ed. by Fortune V. Mannino. LC 74-26634. (Studies in Modern Society: Political & Social Issues). 34.50 (*0-404-11277-3*) AMS Pr.

Mental Health & Social Policy. 4th ed. Mechanic. LC 97-32789. 289p. 1998. pap. 60.00 (*0-205-26993-1*) P-H.

Mental Health & the Economy. Ed. by Louis A. Ferman & Jeanne P. Gordus. LC 79-25809. 423p. 1979. pap. text 10.00 (*0-911558-68-3*) W E Upjohn.

Mental Health & the Elderly: Social Work Perspective. Ed. by Francis J. Turner. LC 92-14579. 1992. 39.95 (*0-02-932795-4*) Free Pr.

Mental Health & the Environment. Ed. by Hugh L. Freeman. LC 84-9421. (Illus.). 490p. 1985. pap. 132.00 (*0-443-02780-3*) Church.

Mental Health & the Law. Sales. 1994. 39.00 (*0-02-927655-1*) S&S Trade.

Mental Health & the Planned Environment: More than Bricks & Mortar? David Halpern. LC 95-11983. 240p. 1995. text 89.95 (*0-7484-0235-7*); pap. text 29.95 (*0-7484-0236-5*) Taylor & Francis.

Mental Health & Urban Social Policy: A Casebook of Community Action. Ed. by Leonard J. Duhl & Robert L. Leopold. LC 68-54942. (Jossey-Bass Behavioral Science Ser.). 346p. reprint ed. 98.70 (*0-8357-9334-6*, 2013787) Bks Demand.

Mental Health & Violence. LC 85-19098. 129p. 1985. pap. 6.95 (*0-88135-050-8*) Watson Pub Intl.

Mental Health Assessment in Occupational Therapy: An Integrative Approach to the Evaluative Process. Barbara J. Hemphill. LC 86-42925. 281p. 1988. pap. 35.00 (*1-55642-004-8*) SLACK Inc.

Mental Health Assessments, 2. Gwen Howe. LC 99-161854. (Living with Serious Mental Illness Ser.). 1998. pap. text 22.95 (*1-85302-458-9*) Taylor & Francis.

Mental Health Assistant. Jack Rudman. (Career Examination Ser.: C-3397). 1994. pap. 23.95 (*0-8373-3397-0*) Nat Learn.

***Mental Health Association Poetry.** (Special Bks.). (Illus.). 50p. 1999. pap. 9.95 (*1-891030-10-8*) Paragon Agency.

Mental Health Benefits: A Purchaser's Guide. William M. Glazer & Nancy N. Bell. Ed. by Mary Jo Brzezinski. LC 93-77214. 206p. (Orig.). 1993. pap. 40.00 (*0-89154-459-3*) Intl Found Employ.

***Mental Health Care, 2 vols., Vol. 1-2.** Ed. by N. Fernandez. (Illus.). 596p. 1998. text 190.00 (*0-19-963558-7*) OUP.

M

M

***Mental Health Care Administration: A Guide for Practitioners.** Paul Rodenhauser. LC 99-50531. (Illus.). 280p. (C). 2000. text 49.50 (*0-472-11116-7*, 11116) U of Mich Pr.

Mental Health Care & National Health Insurance: A Philosophy of & an Approach to Mental Health Care for the Future. David Upton. LC 83-8049. 334p. 1983. 65.00 (*0-306-41235-7*, Plenum Trade) Perseus Pubng.

Mental Health Care & Social Policy. Ed. by Philip Brown. 428p. 1985. pap. 19.95 (*0-7102-0472-8*, Routledge Thoemms) Routledge.

Mental Health Care & Substance Abuse: A Review of Evidence on Insurance Coverage & Utilization. Jeffrey Robin. (Illus.). 69p. (Orig.). (C). 1992. pap. text 25.00 (*1-56806-131-5*) DIANE Pub.

Mental Health Care Delivery: Innovations, Impediments & Implementation. Ed. by Isaac M. Marks & Robert A. Scott. (Illus.). 280p. (C). 1990. text 74.95 (*0-521-38494-X*) Cambridge U Pr.

Mental Health Care for Allied Health & Nursing Professionals. H. Steven Moffic et al. 240p. 1989. pap. 27.50 (*0-87527-344-0*) Green.

Mental Health Care in Canada. Ed. by Leona L. Bachrach et al. LC 87-646993. (New Directions for Mental Health Services Ser.: No. MHS 61). 105p. (Orig.). 1994. pap. 25.00 (*0-7879-9965-2*) Jossey-Bass.

***Mental Health Care in Prisons: Index of New Information with Authors, Subjects & Bibliography.** rev. ed. Stuart L. Wymer. 155p. 1999. 47.50 (*0-7883-1980-9*); pap. 44.50 (*0-7883-1981-7*) ABBE Pubs Assn.

Mental Health Care of Elderly People. Norman. LC 96-25834. 1996. pap. text 54.00 (*0-443-05173-9*) Church.

Mental Health Computing. Kenric W. Hammond & Mathew G. Hile. Ed. by Marvin J. Miller. LC 95-37689. (Computers & Medicine Ser.). 496p. 1996. 79.00 (*0-387-94580-6*) Spr-Verlag.

Mental Health Concepts. 4th ed. Waughfield. 96p. 1997. pap. text, teacher ed. 12.00 (*0-8273-8219-7*) Delmar.

Mental Health Concepts: Instructor's Guide. 3rd ed. Natalie Kalman et al. 65p. 1993. pap. 15.00 (*0-8273-4981-5*) Delmar.

Mental Health Concepts & Techniques for the Occupational Therapy Assistant. 2nd ed. Mary B. Early. LC 93-16482. 480p. 1993. text 42.00 (*0-7817-0074-4*); pap. text, student ed. 13.00 (*0-7817-0109-0*) Lppncott W & W.

Mental Health Concepts & Techniques for the Occupational Therapy Assistant. 3rd ed. Mary Beth Early. 564p. text 43.95 (*0-7817-1975-5*) Lppncott W & W.

***Mental Health Consultation & Collaboration.** Gerald Caplan & Ruth B. Caplan. 393p. 1999. pap. 27.95 (*1-57766-073-0*) Waveland Pr.

Mental Health Consultation Field. Ed. by Saul Cooper & William F. Hodges. (Community Psychology Ser.: Vol. XI). 247p. (C). 1983. 34.95 (*0-89885-130-0*, Kluwer Acad Hman Sci); pap. 24.95 (*0-89885-286-2*, Kluwer Acad Hman Sci) Kluwer Academic.

Mental Health Consultation in Nursing Homes. Michael A. Smyer et al. Ed. by Steven H. Zarit. (Clinical Gerontology Ser.). 240p. (C). 1990. pap. text 18.50 (*0-8147-7911-5*) NYU Pr.

***Mental Health Consultation in the Early Childhood Years.** Paul J. Donahue et al. LC 99-37494. 2000. pap. 28.95 (*1-55766-449-8*) P H Brookes.

Mental Health Consultation in the Schools: A Comprehensive Guide for Psychologists, Social Workers, Psychiatrists, Counselors, Educators, & Other Human Service Professionals. Joel Meyers et al. LC 79-83567. (Social & Behavioral Science Ser.). 262p. 1979. text 38.95 (*0-87589-400-3*) Jossey-Bass.

***Mental Health Counselors Clinical Practice Companion: A Continuing Education Program.** PTI-AMHCA Staff & AMHCA Staff. 1999. pap. text 195.00 (*0-7872-6384-2*) Kendall-Hunt.

Mental Health Counselor's Handbook. Ed. by G. Seiler. (Illus.). 300p. 1989. 35.00 (*0-89885-476-8*, Kluwer Acad Hman Sci) Kluwer Academic.

Mental Health, Cultural Values & Social Development. Ed. by Richard C. Nann et al. 1983. text 226.00 (*90-277-1622-6*) Kluwer Academic.

***Mental Health Diagnostic Desk Reference: Visual Guides & More for Learning to Use the Diagnostic & Statistical Manual (DSM-IV)** Ed. by Carlton E. Munson. LC 99-20779. 396p. 2000. 59.95 (*0-7890-1075-5*, Hawrth Medical); pap. text 24.95 (*0-7890-1076-3*) Haworth Pr.

Mental Health Directory, 1995. Compiled by Adele S. Fell et al. 559p. 1995. per. 35.00 (*0-16-048255-0*, 017-024-01571-7) USGPO.

Mental Health Disorders Sourcebook. Ed. by Karen Bellenir. (Health Reference Ser.: Vol. 9). 1995. lib. bdg. 78.00 (*0-7808-0040-0*) Omnigraphics Inc.

***Mental Health Disorders Sourcebook.** 2nd ed. Ed. by Karen Bellenir. LC 99-49596. (Health Reference Ser.). (Illus.). 700p. 1999. lib. bdg. 78.00 (*0-7808-0240-3*) Omnigraphics Inc.

Mental Health Field: A Critical Appraisal. Ed. by Morton Levitt & Ben Rubenstein. LC 70-135397. 387p. reprint ed. pap. 120.00 (*0-608-16629-4*, 202768100055) Bks Demand.

Mental Health Financing & Programming a Legislator's Guide. Rebecca T. Craig & Barbara Wright. Ed. by Shirley Michaels. (Illus.). 135p. (Orig.). 1988. pap. 15.00 (*1-55516-679-2*, 6619) Natl Conf State Legis.

Mental Health for Refugees & Other Migrants: Social & Preventive Approaches. Joseph Westermeyer. 236p. 1989. pap. 31.95 (*0-398-06489-X*); text 52.95 (*0-398-05601-3*) C C Thomas.

Mental Health Geriatric Consultant. Jack Rudman. (Career Examination Ser.: C-1582). 1994. pap. 39.95 (*0-8373-1582-4*) Nat Learn.

Mental Health Group Leader. Jack Rudman. (Career Examination Ser.: C-3054). 1994. pap. 34.95 (*0-8373-3054-8*) Nat Learn.

Mental Health in a Multi-Ethnic Society: A Multi-Disciplinary Handbook. Ed. by Suman Fernando. LC 95-8129. 256p. (C). 1995. pap. 25.99 (*0-415-10537-4*) Routledge.

Mental Health in Africa & the Americas Today. Samuel O. Okpaku. 507p. (C). 1993. pap. text 49.95 (*0-916085-01-5*) Chrisolith Bks.

Mental Health in Black America. Ed. by Harold W. Neighbors & James S. Jackson. LC 95-50210. 248p. (C). 1996. 44.00 (*0-8039-3539-0*); pap. 19.95 (*0-8039-3540-4*) Sage.

Mental Health in Children, Vol. 1. Ed. by D. Siva Sankar. LC 74-27252. 1975. 49.95 (*0-9600290-7-9*) PJD Pubns.

Mental Health in Children, Vol. 2. Ed. by D. Siva Sankar. LC 74-27252. 1976. 49.95 (*0-9600290-8-7*) PJD Pubns.

Mental Health in Children, Vol. 3. Ed. by D. Siva Sankar. LC 74-27252. 1976. 49.95 (*0-9600290-9-5*) PJD Pubns.

Mental Health in Children, Vol. 5. write for info. (*0-915340-04-6*) PJD Pubns.

Mental Health in Classroom & Corridor. Alicerose S. Barman. LC 68-25763. 1968. 9.20 (*0-672-75107-0*, Bobbs) Macmillan.

Mental Health in Corrections: An Overview for Correctional Personnel. Wesley Sowers et al. LC 97-12523. 104p. 1998. pap. 21.95 (*1-56991-067-7*) Am Correctional.

Mental Health in Europe: Ends, Beginnings, & Rediscoveries. Shulamit Ramon. 224p. 1996. text 59.95 (*0-312-16066-6*) St Martin.

Mental Health in Indian Schools. M. Kapur. LC 97-31052. 1997. write for info. (*0-7619-9206-5*) Sage.

Mental Health in Late Life: The Adaptive Process. Marguerite D. Kermis. 392p. (Orig.). (C). 1986. pap. text 42.50 (*0-86720-353-6*) Jones & Bartlett.

Mental Health in Our Future Cities. David Goldberg. LC 99-165888. 1998. 59.95 (*0-86377-546-2*) Taylor & Francis.

Mental Health in Primary Care. Linda D. Oakley. LC 97-118473. 480p. (C). (gr. 13). 1996. pap. text 31.95 (*0-8151-7310-5*, 28195) Mosby Inc.

Mental Health in Remote Rural Developing Areas: Concepts & Cases. Committee on Therapeutic Care & Group for the Advancement of Psychiatry Staff. (GAP Report Ser.: No. 139). 230p. 1995. text 12.95 (*0-87318-207-3*, 7207) Am Psychiatric.

Mental Health in the Nursing Home. T. L. Brink. LC 90-4667. (Clinical Gerontologist Ser.: Vol. 9, Nos. 3-4). 226p. 1990. pap. text 19.95 (*1-56024-011-3*) Haworth Pr.

Mental Health in the Nursing Home. T. L. Brink. LC 90-4667. (Clinical Gerontologist Ser.: Vol. 9, Nos. 3-4). 226p. 1990. text 39.95 (*1-56024-010-5*) Haworth Pr.

Mental Health in the Nursing Home: An Educational Approach for Staff. Ed. by David M. Blau & Anne O. Freed. 138p. (Orig.). 1983. pap. 27.50 (*0-8236-3362-4*, 03362) Intl Univs Pr.

Mental Health in the United States: A Fifty-Year History. Nina Ridenour. LC 61-11630. 160p. reprint ed. pap. 49.60 (*0-7837-4707-1*, 205905700002) Bks Demand.

Mental Health in the Workplace. Jeffrey Kahn. 480p. 1992. text 68.95 (*0-442-00632-2*, VNR) Wiley.

Mental Health in the Workplace: A Practical Psychiatric Guide. Ed. by Jeffrey P. Kahn. 462p. 1992. 90.00 (*0-471-28418-1*, VNR) Wiley.

Mental Health in the Workplace: An Employer's & Manager's Guide. Donna R. Kemp. LC 93-27708. 296p. 1994. 67.95 (*0-89930-703-5*, Quorum Bks) Greenwood.

Mental Health in Your School: A Guide for Teachers & Others Working in Schools. Young Minds Staff. LC 97-100824. 64p. 1996. pap. 13.95 (*1-85302-407-4*, Pub. by Jessica Kingsley) Taylor & Francis.

Mental Health Industry: A Cultural Phenomenon. Peter A. Magaro et al. LC 77-14434. (Wiley Series on Personality Processes). 288p. reprint ed. pap. 89.30 (*0-608-13282-9*, 205576100037) Bks Demand.

Mental Health Information Systems: Design & Implementation. David J. Kupfer et al. LC 76-589. (Books in Library & Information Science: No. 19). (Illus.). 167p. reprint ed. pap. 51.80 (*0-7837-0969-2*, 204127500019) Bks Demand.

Mental Health Information Systems: Problems & Prospects. Ed. by E. M. Bennett & Barry Trute. LC 83-23683. (Studies in Health & Human Services: Vol. 1). 318p. 1983. 99.95 (*0-88946-125-2*) E Mellen.

Mental Health Internet Pocket Guide. David Lukoff. 1998. pap. 10.00 (*0-9665126-0-X*) Internet Guides.

Mental Health Interventions for the Aging. Ed. by Arthur M. Horton, Jr. 208p. 1982. 52.95 (*0-275-90821-6*, C0821, Praeger Pubs) Greenwood.

Mental Health Interventions with Preschool Children. R. D. Lyman & T. L. Hembree-Kigin. (Issues in Clinical Child Psychology Ser.: 1). (Illus.). 312p. (C). 1994. 47.50 (*0-306-44860-2*, Plenum Trade) Perseus Pubng.

Mental Health Issues & Aging: Building on the Strengths of Older Persons. Carolyn Tice. (Social Work Ser.). 300p. 1995. 23.87 (*0-534-20754-5*) Brooks-Cole.

***Mental Health Issues & Aging: Building on the Strengths of Older Persons.** Carolyn Tice. (Social Work Ser.). 1999. pap. 26.75 (*0-534-76778-8*) Wadsworth Pub.

Mental Health Issues of the Mexican Origin Population in Texas: Proceedings of the Fifth Robert L. Sutherland Seminar. Ed. by Reymundo Rodriguez & Marion T. Coleman. 240p. (Orig.). 1987. pap. 9.45 (*0-943463-00-9*) Hogg Found.

Mental Health Law: Major Issues. David B. Wexler. LC 80-20523. (Perspectives in Law & Psychology Ser.). 280p. 1981. 49.50 (*0-306-40538-5*, Plenum Trade) Perseus Pubng.

***Mental Health Law: Policy & Practice.** Peter Bartlett & Ralph Sandland. 494p. 2000. pap. 50.00 (*1-85431-941-8*, 18660, Pub. by Blackstone Pr) Gaunt.

Mental Health Law in Context: Doctors Orders. Michael Cavadino. (Medico-Legal Issues Ser.). (Illus.). 192p. 1989. text 78.95 (*1-85521-024-X*, Pub. by Dartmth Pub) Ashgate Pub Co.

Mental Health Matrix: A Pragmatic Guide to Service Improvement. Ed. by Graham Thornicroft & Michele Tansella. LC 98-38431. (Illus.). 300p. (C). 1999. text. write for info. (*0-521-62155-0*) Cambridge U Pr.

***Mental Health Matters in Primary Care.** Elaine Millar & Mark Walsh. (Illus.). 160p. 2000. pap. 34.95 (*0-7487-4528-9*, Pub. by S Thornes Pubs) Intl Spec Bk.

***Mental Health, Mental Retardation & Substance Abuse Laws of Virginia Annotated: 1999 Edition.** 478p. 1999. pap. write for info. (*0-327-09907-0*, 3545814) LEXIS Pub.

Mental Health, Mental Retardation & Substance Abuse Laws of Virginia Annotated 1998. annot. ed. Ed. by Gail D. Haskins. LC 99-180384. 442p. 1998. write for info. (*0-327-06098-0*, 35458-13) LEXIS Pub.

Mental Health Nurse: Views of Practice & Education. Stephen Tilley. LC 97-26992. 1997. pap. 29.95 (*0-632-03999-X*) Blackwell Sci.

Mental Health Nursing. David Arthur et al. (Illus.). 260p. 1992. write for info. (*0-7295-1209-6*) Bailliere Tindall.

Mental Health Nursing. Norma Decastro. 496p. (C). 1994. pap. text; per. 47.95 (*0-8403-9677-5*) Kendall-Hunt.

Mental Health Nursing. Delmar Staff & Nancy Scheutz. (Rapid Nursing Interventions Ser.). 224p. (C). 1995. pap. 31.95 (*0-8273-7096-2*) Delmar.

Mental Health Nursing. Paulette D. Rollant. (Review Ser.). (Illus.). 416p. (C). (gr. 13). 1996. write for info. (*0-8151-7247-8*, 24860) Mosby Inc.

Mental Health Nursing. 2nd ed. Carson. LC 99-35203. (C). 1999. text. write for info. (*0-7216-8053-4*, W B Saunders Co) Harcrt Hlth Sci Grp.

***Mental Health Nursing: An Evidence-Based Approach.** Robert Newell & Kevin Gournay. LC 99-34393. 2000. pap. text. write for info. (*0-443-05873-3*) Church.

Mental Health Nursing: An Introductory Text. 2nd ed. Barbara B. Bauer & Signe S. Hill. LC 99-29020. (Illus.). 430p. (C). 2000. pap. text. write for info. (*0-7216-7753-3*, W B Saunders Co) Harcrt Hlth Sci Grp.

Mental Health Nursing: From First Principles to Professional Practice. Wright. 554p. 1992. pap. 63.75 (*1-56593-022-3*, 0265) Thomson Learn.

***Mental Health Nursing: The Art of Compassionate Care.** Peter Watkins. (Illus.). 224p. 2000. pap. 35.00 (*0-7506-4119-3*) Buttrwrth-Heinemann.

Mental Health Nursing: The Nurse-Patient Journey. Ed. by Verna B. Carson & Elizabeth N. Arnold. (Illus.). 1996. teacher ed. write for info. (*0-7216-6820-8*, W B Saunders Co) Harcrt Hlth Sci Grp.

Mental Health Nursing: The Nurse-Patient Journey: Instructor's Manual. 2nd ed. Robert Carson. 205p. Date not set. pap. text, teacher ed. write for info. (*0-7216-8057-7*, W B Saunders Co) Harcrt Hlth Sci Grp.

Mental Health Nursing & Social Control. Peter Morral. LC 98-153098. v, 164p. 1998. write for info. (*1-86156-050-8*) Whurr Pub.

Mental Health Nursing in the Community. Nancy Worley. (Illus.). 496p. (C). (gr. 13). 1996. pap. text 35.95 (*0-8151-9429-3*, 27462) Mosby Inc.

Mental Health of Adolescents & Young Persons. Proceedings of the WHO Technical Conference, Stockholm, 1969. A. R. May et al. (Public Health Papers: No. 41). 72p. 1971. pap. 5.00 (*92-4-130041-8*, 1110041) World Health.

Mental Health of Asian Americans: Contemporary Issues in Identifying & Treating Mental Problems. Stanley Sue & James K. Morishima. LC 82-48060. (Social & Behavioral Science Ser.). 238p. 1982. 36.95 (*0-87589-535-2*) Jossey-Bass.

Mental Health of Ethnic Minorities. Ed. by Felicisima C. Serafica et al. LC 89-26597. 360p. 1990. 69.50 (*0-275-93111-0*, C3111, Praeger Pubs) Greenwood.

Mental Health of Immigrants & Refugees. Ed. by Wayne H. Holtzman & Thomas H. Bornemann. 348p. (Orig.). 1990. pap. 9.00 (*0-943463-10-6*) Hogg Found.

Mental Health of Indian Children. Malavika Kapur. LC 94-49075. 312p. (C). 1995. 26.95 (*0-8039-9233-5*) Sage.

***Mental Health of Indian Women: A Feminist Agenda.** Bhargavi V. Davar. LC 98-46659. 292p. 1999. 35.00 (*0-7619-9300-2*) Sage.

***Mental Health of Older Populations.** Martin R. Prince & Sube Banerjee. (Illus.). 224p. 2001. pap. 45.00 (*0-7506-4860-0*) Buttrwrth-Heinemann.

Mental Health of Refugees. LC 97-102972. 142p. (Orig.). 1996. pap. text 27.00 (*92-4-154486-4*, 1150433) World Health.

Mental Health of the Child: Program Reports. National Institute of Mental Health Staff. Ed. by Julius Segal. 1973. 19.95 (*0-405-03149-1*) Ayer.

Mental Health on the Community College Campus. 2nd ed. Ed. by Gerald Amada. 152p. (Orig.). (C). 1985. pap. text 20.00 (*0-8191-4915-2*); lib. bdg. 47.50 (*0-8191-4914-4*) U Pr of Amer.

Mental Health Outcome Evaluation. David C. Speer. LC 97-80314. (Illus.). 121p. 1998. text 34.95 (*0-12-656575-9*) Morgan Kaufmann.

Mental Health Outcome Measures. Graham Thornicroft & Michele Tansella. LC 96-15971. 1996. write for info. (*0-387-61073-1*) Spr-Verlag.

Mental Health Outcome Measures. Graham Thornicroft & Michele Tansella. LC 96-15971. 200p. 1996. 99.50 (*3-540-61073-1*) Spr-Verlag.

***Mental Health Outcomes Tracker.** Donald E. Wiger. 250p. 2001. pap. 49.95 (*0-471-38875-0*) Wiley.

Mental Health Parity: What Can It Accomplish in a Market Dominated by Managed Care? Alan L. Otten. (Illus.). 44p. 1998. pap. write for info. (*1-887748-21-0*) Milbank Memorial.

Mental Health Policy & Practice Today. Ed. by Ted R. Watkins & James W. Callicutt. LC 96-51206. 400p. (C). 1997. 58.00 (*0-8039-7138-9*, 71389); pap. 27.95 (*0-8039-7139-7*, 71397) Sage.

Mental Health Practice in Geriatric Health Care Settings. Peter A. Lichtenberg. LC 97-21734. 212p. 1997. 49.95 (*0-7890-0117-9*); pap. 24.95 (*0-7890-0435-6*) Haworth Pr.

Mental Health Practitioner & the Law: A Comprehensive Handbook. Lawrence E. Lifson & Robert I. Simon. LC 97-41510. 416p. 1999. 49.95 (*0-674-69721-9*) HUP.

Mental Health Problems & HIV Infection. Jose Catalan. (Social Aspects of AIDS Ser.). 256p. 1999. pap. 25.95 (*1-85728-171-3*, Pub. by UCL Pr Ltd) Taylor & Francis.

Mental Health Problems & HIV Infection. Ed. by Jose Catalan. (Social Aspects of AIDS Ser.). 256p. 1999. 74.00 (*1-85728-170-5*, Pub. by UCL Pr Ltd) Taylor & Francis.

Mental Health Problems & Older Adults. Greg Hinrichsen. LC 90-40319. (Choices & Challenges Ser.). 300p. 1990. lib. bdg. 45.00 (*0-87436-240-7*) ABC-CLIO.

Mental Health Problems & the Nursing Home Resident. Marylou Hughes. 174p. (C). 1988. 19.50 (*1-877735-21-3*, 2136PP) Prof Prnting & Pub.

Mental Health Procedural Tables. Shaw & Sons Ltd. Staff. (C). 1988. pap. 30.00 (*0-7219-0196-4*, Pub. by Scientific) St Mut.

Mental Health Professional's Guide to Managed Care. Ed. by Rodney L. Lowman & Robert J. Resnick. LC 93-47570. 191p. 1994. pap. text 24.95 (*1-55798-232-5*) Am Psychol.

Mental Health Program Specialist. (Career Examination Ser.: C-3585). 1994. pap. 29.95 (*0-8373-3585-X*) Nat Learn.

Mental Health Promotion: Paradigms & Practice. Keith Tudor. LC 95-4477. 336p. (C). 1996. pap. 27.99 (*0-415-10106-9*) Routledge.

Mental Health Promotion: Paradigms & Practice. Keith Tudor. LC 95-4477. (Illus.). 336p. (C). 1996. 85.00 (*0-415-10105-0*) Routledge.

Mental Health Promotion: Policy, Practice & Partnerships. Gary F. McCulloch & Judy Boxer. (Illus.). 256p. 1997. pap. 31.00 (*0-7020-1981-X*) W B Saunders.

Mental Health Protocols for Occupational Therapy. Catana Brown et al. 32p. (C). 1993. pap. text 6.50 (*0-935273-06-9*) Chess Pub.

Mental Health Psychiatric Nursing. Janosik. 1996. 34.95 (*0-316-45757-4*, Little Brwn Med Div) Lppncott W & W.

Mental Health-Psychiatric Nursing. 3rd ed. Ruth P. Rawlins et al. (Illus.). 960p. 1993. teacher ed. write for info. (*0-8151-3894-6*) Mosby Inc.

Mental Health Psychiatric Nursing: A Continuum of Care. Ed. by Joan Norris et al. 1989. pap. text, teacher ed. 12.95 (*0-8273-4325-6*); 12.95 (*0-8273-4326-4*) Delmar.

Mental Health, Race & Culture. Suman Fernando. 208p. 1991. text 45.00 (*0-312-05807-1*) St Martin.

Mental Health, Racism & Sexism. Ed. by Charles V. Willie et al. 512p. 1995. 85.00 (*0-7484-0391-4*, Pub. by Tay Francis Ltd); pap. 26.95 (*0-7484-0392-2*, Pub. by Tay Francis Ltd) Taylor & Francis.

Mental Health, Racism & Sexism. rev. ed. Charles V. Willie et al. Ed. by Bertram S. Brown. 440p. (C). 1995. pap. 22.95 (*0-8229-5549-0*); text 49.95 (*0-8229-3869-3*) U of Pittsburgh Pr.

Mental Health Rehabilitation: Disputing Irrational Beliefs. Gerald L. Gandy. LC 95-16978. 106p. (C). 1995. text 36.95 (*0-398-06531-4*); pap. text 24.95 (*0-398-06532-2*) C C Thomas.

Mental Health Research in Texas: Retrospect & Prospect. Ed. by Charles M. Bonjean & Donald J. Foss. 400p. (Orig.). 1990. pap. 8.50 (*0-943463-09-2*) Hogg Found.

***Mental Health Resource Guide.** 2000. Price not set. (*0-929718-27-5*) Resc Rehab.

Mental Health Response to Mass Emergencies: Theory & Practice. Ed. by Mary Lystad. LC 88-5025. (Psychosocial Stress Ser.: No. 12). 454p. 1988. text 56.95 (*0-87630-514-1*) Brunner-Mazel.

Mental Health Service Delivery Guidelines. Ed. by AOTA Staff. 176p. (Orig.). 1996. pap. text 25.00 (*1-56900-037-9*, 1135) Am Occup Therapy.

Mental Health Service Evaluation. Ed. by Helle C. Knudsen & Graham Thornicroft. (Studies in Social & Community Psychiatry). (Illus.). 399p. (C). 1996. text 95.00 (*0-521-46088-3*) Cambridge U Pr.

Mental Health Services: A Public Health Perspective. Ed. by Bruce L. Levin & John Petrila. (Illus.). 448p. 1996. text 49.95 (*0-19-508800-X*) OUP.

Mental Health Services: The Cross-Cultural Context. Ed. by Paul B. Pedersen et al. LC 83-26945. (Cross-Cultural Research & Methodology Ser.). 311p. 1984. reprint ed. pap. 96.50 (*0-608-01180-0*, 205947800001) Bks Demand.

Mental Health Services - Law & Practice. Larry Gostin. (C). 1986. ring bd. 850.00 (*0-7219-0197-2*, Pub. by Scientific) St Mut.

Mental Health Services--Status, Trends & Practices: Index of New Information. American Health Research Institute Staff. 160p. 1998. 47.50 (*0-7883-1652-4*); pap. 44.50 (*0-7883-1653-2*) ABBE Pubs Assn.

***Mental Health Services & Sectors of Care** Enola Knisley Proctor et al. LC 99-17012. 1999. write for info. (*0-7890-0760-6*) Haworth Pr.

An Asterisk (*) at the beginning of an entry indicates that the title is appearing for the first time.

Mental Health Services & Vulnerable Populations. Ed. by Linda F. Wolf. (Illus.). 175p. (C). 1998. pap. text 35.00 (*0-7881-7106-2*) DIANE Pub.

Mental Health Services for Older Adults: Implications for Training & Practice in Geropsychology. Ed. by Bob G. Knight et al. LC 95-23757. 158p. 1995. pap. text 19.95 (*1-55798-334-8*) Am Psychol.

Mental Health Services in Criminal Justice System Settings: A Selectively Annotated Bibliography, 1970-1997, 6. Compiled by Rodney Van Whitlock & Bernard Lubin. LC 98-29678. (Research & Bibliographical Guides in Criminal Justice: Vol. 6). 208p. 1999. lib. bdg. 65.00 (*0-313-30186-7*, Greenwood Pr) Greenwood.

Mental Health Services in Developing Countries: Proceedings of the WHO Seminar on the Organization of Mental Health Services, Addis Ababa, 1973. WHO Staff. Ed. by T. A. Baasher et al. (Offset Publications: No. 22). 1975. pap. text 18.00 (*92-4-170022-X*, 1120022) World Health.

Mental Health Services in Europe. A. R. May. (Offset Publications: No. 23). 1976. pap. text 12.00 (*92-4-170023-8*, 1120023) World Health.

Mental Health Services in Europe: Ten Years On. H. L. Freeman et al. (Public Health in Europe Ser.: No. 25). 112p. 1985. pap. text 11.00 (*92-890-1161-0*, 1320025) World Health.

Mental Health Services in Pilot Study Areas: Report on a European Study. 1987. text 70.00 (*92-890-1046-0*) World Health.

Mental Health Services in Southern Countries of the European Region. (Euro Reports & Studies Ser.: No. 107). 46p. 1988. pap. text 6.00 (*92-890-1273-0*) World Health.

Mental Health Services in the United States & England: Struggling for Change: Collected Papers Prepared for the Joint United States-England Conference on Mental Health Services Princeton, New Jersey, February 25-28, 1990. Ed. by Jeffrey C. Merrill. LC 91-61190. (Illus.). 160p. (Orig.). 1991. pap. write for info. (*0-942054-03-2*) R W Johnson Found.

Mental Health Services, Information & Referral Directory, 4 vols., Set. write for info. (*0-318-55486-0*) Ready Ref Pr.

Mental Health Social Work in Ireland: Comparative Issues in Policy & Practice. Ed. by Jim Campbell & Roger Manktelow. LC 98-70982. 200p. 1998. text 59.95 (*1-85972-694-1*, Pub. by Ashgate Pub) Ashgate Pub Co.

Mental Health Social Work Observed. Mike Fisher et al. 1984. 50.00 (*0-7855-0842-2*, Pub. by Natl Inst Soc Work) St Mut.

Mental Health Technology Bible. Larry D. Rosen & Michelle M. Weil. LC 96-42475. 256p. 1997. pap. 55.00 incl. cd-rom (*0-471-17618-4*) Wiley.

Mental Health Through Will-Training: A System of Self Help in Psychotherapy As Practiced by Recovery, Incorporated. 3rd ed. Abraham A. Low. LC 97-60039. 448p. (C). 1997. reprint ed. text 20.00 (*0-915005-06-9*) Willett Pub Co.

Mental Health, United States, 1996. Ronald W. Manderscheid. 261p. 1997. pap. text 22.00 (*0-16-048884-2*) USGPO.

***Mental Health United States, 1998.** Ronald W. Manderscheid. 302p. 1999. pap. text 25.00 (*0-16-049883-X*) USGPO.

Mental Health, United States, 1996, 2 vols. Ed. by Ronald W. Manderscheid & Mary A. Sonnenschein. (Illus.). 260p. 1996. pap. text 45.00 (*1-57979-154-9*) DIANE Pub.

Mental Health, United States, 1996. Ed. by Ronald W. Manderscheid & Mary A. Sonnenschein. (Illus.). 249p. (C). 1998. pap. text 45.00 (*0-7881-4889-3*) DIANE Pub.

Mental Health, United States, 1994. Ed. by Ronald W. Manderscheid & Mary A. Sonnenschein. (Illus.). 192p. (Orig.). (C). 1995. pap. text 45.00 (*0-7881-1833-1*) DIANE Pub.

***Mental Health, United States, 1998.** 8th ed. Ed. by Ronald W. Manderscheid & Marilyn J. Henderson. (Illus.). 292p. 1999. pap. text 45.00 (*0-7881-7999-3*) DIANE Pub.

Mental Health Work in the Community: Theory & Practice in Social Work & Community Psychiatric Nursing. Michael Sheppard. 224p. 1991. 65.00 (*1-85000-978-3*, Falmer Pr); pap. 34.95 (*1-85000-979-1*, Falmer Pr) Taylor & Francis.

***Mental Health Worker: Psychiatric Aide.** Beverly Marshburn. Ed. by Kay Cox-Stevens. LC 97-77991. (Clinical Allied Healthcare Ser.). (Illus.). 540p. 1999. pap. text 44.95 (*0-89262-437-X*) Career Pub.

***Mental Health Worker: Psychiatric Aide: Instructor's Guide.** Beverly Marshburn. Ed. by Kay Cox-Stevens. (Clinical Allied Healthcare Ser.). (Illus.). 464p. 1999. teacher ed., ring bd. 99.95 (*0-89262-445-0*) Career Pub.

Mental Helath Concepts. 4th ed. Waughfield. LC 97-9720. 448p. (C). 1997. mass mkt. 48.95 (*0-8273-8218-9*) Delmar.

Mental Hospitalization: Myths & Facts about a National Crisis. Charles A. Kiesler & Amy E. Sibulkin. LC 86-15571. 312p. 1987. reprint ed. pap. 96.80 (*0-608-01181-9*, 205947900001) Bks Demand.

***Mental Hygiene: Better Living Through Classroom Films, 1945-1970.** Ken Smith. (Illus.). 240p. 1999. pap. text 24.95 (*0-922233-21-7*) Blast Bks.

Mental Hygiene in Twentieth-Century America, Four Studies, 1921-1924: An Original Anthology. Ed. by Gerald N. Grob. LC 78-22586. (Historical Issues in Mental Health Ser.). (Illus.). 1980. lib. bdg. 40.95 (*0-405-11937-2*) Ayer.

Mental Hygiene Nursing Program Coordinator. Jack Rudman. (Career Examination Ser.: C-2665). 1994. pap. 34.95 (*0-8373-2665-6*) Nat Learn.

Mental Hygiene of Childhood. William A. White. Ed. by Gerald N. Grob. LC 78-22595. (Historical Issues in Mental Health Ser.). 1980. reprint ed. lib. bdg. 18.95 (*0-405-11945-3*) Ayer.

Mental Hygiene Staff Development Specialist I. Jack Rudman. (Career Examination Ser.: C-3489). 1994. pap. 29.95 (*0-8373-3489-6*) Nat Learn.

Mental Hygiene Staff Development Specialist II. Jack Rudman. (Career Examination Ser.: C-2490). 1994. pap. 29.95 (*0-8373-2490-4*) Nat Learn.

Mental Hygiene Staff Development Specialist III. Jack Rudman. (Career Examination Ser.: C-2491). 1994. pap. 34.95 (*0-8373-2491-2*) Nat Learn.

Mental Hygiene Staff Development Specialist IV. Jack Rudman. (Career Examination Ser.: C-2492). 1994. pap. 34.95 (*0-8373-2492-0*) Nat Learn.

Mental Hygiene Therapy Aide. Jack Rudman. (Career Examination Ser.: C-3056). 1994. pap. 23.95 (*0-8373-3056-4*) Nat Learn.

Mental Hygiene Therapy Assistant. Jack Rudman. (Career Examination Ser.: C-2188). 1994. pap. 27.95 (*0-8373-2188-3*) Nat Learn.

Mental Hygiene Treatment Team Leader. Jack Rudman. (Career Examination Ser.: C-1885). 1994. pap. 29.95 (*0-8373-1885-8*) Nat Learn.

Mental Illness. Tom Campbell. (Medico-Legal Issues Ser.: Vol. 5). 1991. text 74.95 (*1-85521-028-2*, Pub. by Dartmth Pub) Ashgate Pub Co.

Mental Illness. Vanora Leigh. LC 98-8198. (Talking Points Ser.). 64p. (J). 1999. 27.12 (*0-8172-5311-4*) Raintree Steck-V.

***Mental Illness.** Tamara L. Roleff & Laura K. Egendorf. LC 99-55632. (Opposing Viewpoints Ser.). 360p. (YA). 2000. 17.45 (*0-7377-0348-2*) Greenhaven.

***Mental Illness.** Tamara L. Roleff & Laura K. Egendorf. LC 99-55632. (Opposing Viewpoints Ser.). 360p. (YA). 2000. pap. 13.96 (*0-7377-0347-4*) Greenhaven.

Mental Illness. Victoria Sherrow. LC 95-12284. (Overview Ser.). (Illus.). 128p. (YA). (gr. 7 up). 1996. lib. bdg. 22.45 (*1-56006-168-5*) Lucent Bks.

Mental Illness: A Homecare Guide. Aristide H. Esser & Sylvia Lacey. 274p. 1989. pap. 12.95 (*0-471-61157-3*) Wiley.

Mental Illness: Changes & Trends. Ed. by Philip Bean. LC 82-8603. 498p. reprint ed. pap. 154.40 (*0-608-15626-4*, 203175500076) Bks Demand.

Mental Illness: Cracking The Code to Its Meaning. Melvin P. Firestone. 250p. 1993. 29.95 (*0-9635627-0-3*) Eileen Bks.

Mental Illness: Key Area Handbook. Department of Health Staff. 180p. 1994. pap. 30.00 (*0-11-321829-X*, HM1829X, Pub. by Statnry Office) Bernan Associates.

Mental Illness: Law & Public Policy. Ed. by Baruch A. Brody & H. Tristram Engelhardt. (Philosophy & Medicine Ser.: No. 5). 272p. 1980. text 94.00 (*90-277-1057-0*) Kluwer Academic.

Mental Illness: Survival & Beyond. Virginia S. Wilson. 90p. 1998. pap. 12.03 (*1-55212-213-1*, 98-0031, Pub. by Tra3fford) Trafford Pub.

Mental Illness & American Society, 1875-1940. Gerald N. Grob. LC 83-3047. 443p. reprint ed. pap. 137.40 (*0-608-06394-0*, 206675500008) Bks Demand.

***Mental Illness & Its Effect on School & Work Environments.** Charles J. Shields. LC 99-15632. (Encyclopedia of Psychological Disorders Ser.). 144p. 2000. 24.95 (*0-7910-5318-0*) Chelsea Hse.

Mental Illness & Nutrition. 1996. lib. bdg. 251.95 (*0-8490-5917-8*) Gordon Pr.

Mental Illness & Psychology. Michel Foucault. 1986. pap. 14.95 (*0-520-05919-0*, Pub. by U CA Pr) Cal Prin Full Svc.

Mental Illness & Social Policy: The American Experience, 41 bks., Set. Ed. by Gerald N. Grob et al. 1973. 1390.50 (*0-405-05190-5*) Ayer.

Mental Illness & Substance Abuse. Wyrnn Smith. (Profile of Health & Disease in America Ser.). (Illus.). 192p. 1989. 40.00 (*0-8160-1457-4*) Facts on File.

Mental Illness & the Economy. M. Harvey Brenner. LC 72-85144. 320p. 1973. 34.00 (*0-674-56875-3*) HUP.

Mental Illness & the Naked Truth of Life & Sex. George Brass, Jr. 24p. 1999. pap. 6.00 (*0-8059-4397-8*) Dorrance.

Mental Illness, Delinquency, Addictions, & Neglect. Ed. by Elam W. Nunnally et al. LC 87-13473. (Families in Trouble Ser.: No. 4). 266p. 1988. reprint ed. pap. 82.50 (*0-608-01182-7*, 205948000001) Bks Demand.

Mental Illness, Due Process & the Criminal Defendant: A Second Report & Additional Recommendations. Association of the Bar of the City of New York, Sp. LC 68-19789. 299p. reprint ed. pap. 92.70 (*0-7837-0481-X*, 204080500018) Bks Demand.

Mental Illness for Caregivers. Irving G. Walmann. LC 98-70655. (Illus.). 118p. 1998. pap. 9.95 (*0-9663299-5-3*) ALMA Pub.

Mental Illness Heal Yourself. unabridged ed. Mary M. Harris. LC 93-73310. (Heal Your Self Ser.). (Illus.). 125p. (Orig.). 1993. pap. 14.95 (*0-9636781-9-1*, 560) BBCS.

Mental Illness in General Health Care: An International Study. Ed. by Norman Sartorius & T. B. Usturn. 410p. 1996. 200.00 (*0-471-95491-8*) Wiley.

Mental Illness in Nursing Homes: United States, 1985 PHS 91-1766. (Vital & Health Statistics Ser. 13: Data on Health Resources Utilization: No. 105). 65p. 1991. 3.75 (*0-685-61567-7*, 017-022-01102-0) Natl Ctr Health Stats.

Mental Illness in Perspective. Robert A. Clark. 101p. (Orig.). 1973. 3.75 (*0-910286-34-5*); pap. 2.95 (*0-910286-29-9*) Boxwood.

Mental Illness in the Family: Issues & Trends. Ed. by Beverley Abosh & April Collins. 224p. 1996. text 45.00 (*0-8020-2905-1*) U of Toronto Pr.

Mental Illness in the Family: Issues & Trends. Ed. by Beverley Abosh & April Collins. 224p. 1996. pap. text 15.95 (*0-8020-7412-X*) U of Toronto Pr.

Mental Illness in the United States: Epidemiological Estimates. Bruce P. Dohrenwend. LC 79-18725. 161p. 1980. 45.00 (*0-275-90471-7*, C0471, Praeger Pubs) Greenwood.

Mental Illness, Possession, Exorcism & Life after Death, 1990. Francis Harber. LC 76-57525. 144p. reprint ed. pap. 7.95 (*0-912444-37-1*) DARE Bks.

Mental Illness, Stigma & Self-Help: The Founding of Recovery, Inc. Abraham A. Low. 174p. 1991. reprint ed. 20.00 (*0-915005-04-2*) Willett Pub Co.

Mental Imagery. R. G. Kunzendorf. (Illus.). 288p. (C). 1991. 95.00 (*0-306-43825-9*, Plenum Trade) Perseus Pubng.

Mental Imagery Abstracts: The Journal of Mental Imagery, 1977-1989. Ed. by Akhter Ahsen. LC 89-62538. 302p. 1989. pap. text 29.95 (*0-913412-42-2*) Brandon Hse.

Mental Imagery & Learning. Ed. by Malcolm Fleming & Deane W. Hutton. LC 82-20917. 160p. 1983. 37.95 (*0-87778-185-0*) Educ Tech Pubns.

Mental Imagery in Health Care: An Introduction to Contemporary Therapeutic Practice. H. Graham. 192p. 1995. pap. text 41.50 (*1-56593-333-8*, 0663) Singular Publishing.

Mental Imagery in Health Care: An Introduction to Therapeutic Practice. Helen Graham. 183p. 1995. pap. 34.95 (*0-412-56940-X*) Chapman & Hall.

Mental Imagery in the Child see Jean Piaget

Mental Images in Human Cognition. Robert H. Logie & M. Denis. (Advances in Psychology Ser.: Vol. 80). 434p. 1991. 150.75 (*0-444-88894-2*, AIP 80) Elsevier.

Mental Images, Values, & Reality: Proceedings of the Society for General Systems Research, 1986, Set, Vols. 1 & 2. Ed. by John A. Dillon, Jr. 1100p. 1986. 86.00 (*0-685-14600-6*) Intersystems Pubns.

Mental Immunity Phenomenon: Constructive Difficulties in the Child's World. Jonathan Shatil. Tr. by Sara Kitai from HEB. LC 98-16692. 256p. (C). 1998. 34.00 (*0-7618-1114-1*) U Pr of Amer.

Mental Improvement. Priscilla Wakefield. Ed. by Ann B. Shteir. (Early Women Writers Ser.: 4). 200p. (J). 1995. 29.95 (*0-937191-51-5*) Mich St U Pr.

Mental Influence. William W. Atkinson. reprint ed. pap. 3.00 (*0-911662-42-1*) Yoga.

***Mental Jewelry: Live.** 72p. 1998. otabind 19.95 (*0-7935-8924-X*) H Leonard.

Mental Laxatives for a Constipated Mind. Donald E. Pederson. LC 98-91714. (Illus.). 262p. 1999. pap. 14.95 (*0-9665819-0-3*) Galactic Enterp.

Mental Leaps: Analogy in Creative Thought. Keith J. Holyoak & Paul R. Thagard. LC 94-22734. 320p. 1994. 27.50 (*0-262-08233-0*) MIT Pr.

Mental Leaps: Analogy in Creative Thought. Keith J. Holyoak & Paul R. Thagard. (Illus.). 336p. 1996. reprint ed. pap. text 17.00 (*0-262-58144-2*, Bradford Bks) MIT Pr.

Mental Life of Monkeys & Apes. Robert M. Yerkes. LC 79-22241. (History of Psychology Ser.). 180p. 1979. 50.00 (*0-8201-1341-7*) Schol Facsimiles.

Mental Logic. Ed. by Martin Braine & David P. O'Brien. LC 97-24744. 350p. 1997. write for info. (*0-8058-2388-3*); pap. write for info. (*0-8058-2389-1*) L Erlbaum Assocs.

Mental Machine. Electrifying MoJo. 150p. 1993. 19.95 (*0-9639811-1-0*) C Johnson.

Mental Machinery: The Origins & Consequences of Psychological Ideas, 1600-1850. Graham Richards. LC 92-1552. 416p. (C). 1992. text 55.00 (*0-8018-4544-0*) Johns Hopkins.

Mental Magic. rev. ed. Scorpio. LC 95-68346. (Illus.). 96p. 1997. pap. 9.95 (*0-9645601-2-7*) Scorpio Pub MA.

***Mental Magic: Surefire Tricks to Amaze Your Friends.** Martin Gardner. LC 99-37658. (J). 1999. pap. text 4.95 (*0-8069-2049-1*) Sterling.

Mental Magnetism: A Study of the Seven Realms of Mind & Mastery in the Conflicts of Life. Edmund Shaftesbury. 450p. 1996. reprint ed. pap. 34.95 (*1-56459-570-6*) Kessinger Pub.

Mental Management for Great Golf: How to Control Your Thoughts & Play Out of Your Mind. Bee Epstein-Shepherd. LC 96-84466. 128p. 1996. 24.00 (*0-9616204-4-7*) Becoming Pr.

Mental Management for Great Golf: How to Control Your Thoughts & Play Out of Your Mind. Bee Epstein-Shepherd. LC 96-84466. 128p. 1998. reprint ed. pap. 12.95 (*0-7373-0027-2*, 00272W) NTC Contemp Pub Co.

Mental Management for Great Golf: How to Control Your Thoughts & Play Out of Your Mind. 2nd ed. Bee Epstein-Shepherd. LC 96-84466. 128p. 1998. reprint ed. 24.00 (*1-56565-799-3*, 07993W, Pub. by Lowell Hse) NTC Contemp Pub Co.

Mental Maps. 2nd ed. Peter Gould & Rodney White. LC 92-20206. 184p. (C). 1986. pap. 22.99 (*0-415-08482-2*) Routledge.

Mental Maps. 2nd ed. Peter Gould & Rodney White. (Illus.). 192p. 1985. reprint ed. text 49.95 (*0-04-526001-X*); reprint ed. pap. text 12.95 (*0-04-526002-8*) Routledge.

Mental Math: Computation Activities for Anytime. Richard Picirilli. 1994. pap. text 12.95 (*0-590-49796-0*) Scholastic Inc.

Mental Math: Fifth Grade. large type ed. Kathy J. French. Ed. by Michele Hollister. 150p. (J). (gr. 5). 1998. pap. text 19.95 (*1-893632-04-0*, 300-107) Math Con.

Mental Math: First Grade. large type ed. Kathy J. French. Ed. by Michele Hollister. 150p. (J). (gr. 1). 1998. pap. text 19.95 (*1-893632-00-8*, 300-103) Math Con.

Mental Math: Fourth Grade. large type ed. Kathy J. French. Ed. by Michele Hollister. 150p. (J). (gr. 4). 1998. pap. text 19.95 (*1-893632-03-2*, 300-106) Math Con.

Mental Math: Second Grade. large type ed. Kathy J. French. Ed. by Michele Hollister. 140p. (J). (gr. 2). 1998. pap. text 19.95 (*1-893632-01-6*, 300-104) Math Con.

Mental Math: Third Grade. large type ed. Kathy J. French. Ed. by Michele Hollister. 150p. (J). (gr. 3). 1998. pap. text 19.95 (*1-893632-02-4*, 300-105) Math Con.

Mental Math: Two Complete Games Using Mentalmath Brain Skills, 3 vols. Ellen Hechler. (Addition & Subtraction Ser.). 70p. (Orig.). (J). (gr. 1-4). 1997. pap. text, teacher ed. 8.00 (*0-9638483-1-3*) Midmath.

Mental Math & Estimation. Don Miller. 80p. (J). (gr. 3-8). 1992. pap. text 10.95 (*0-938587-30-7*) Cuisenaire.

Mental Math Brain Skills in French see Mathematiques Mentales en Francais

Mental Math Brain Skills in Spanish see Matematicas Mentales en Espanol

Mental Math Challenges, 1. Michael L. Lobosco. LC 99-18586. 1999. 16.95 (*1-895569-50-8*) Tamos Bks.

***Mental Math Challenges.** Michael L. Lobosco. (Illus.). 2000. pap. 9.95 (*1-895569-60-5*) Tamos Bks.

Mental Math in Junior High. J. Hope et al. 180p. 1997. pap. text 11.95 (*0-86651-433-3*) Seymour Pubns.

Mental Math in the Middle Grades. J. Hope et al. 1997. pap. text 11.95 (*0-86651-312-4*) Seymour Pubns.

Mental Math in the Primary Grades. J. Hope et al. 128p. (Orig.). 1997. pap. text 11.95 (*0-86651-434-1*) Seymour Pubns.

***Mental Math Kids Can't Resist! Tips, Short-Cut Strategies & 60 Fun Practice Pages That Reinforce.** Richard S Piccirilli. (Illus.). (J). 2000. pap. 11.95 (*0-439-18605-6*) Scholastic Inc.

Mental Math, Series I: Two Complete Games Using Mental Math Brain Skills. Ellen Hechler. (Orig.). (J). (gr. 5-8). 1991. pap. 8.00 (*0-9638483-2-1*) Midmath.

Mental Math, Series II: Two Complete Games Using Mental Math Brain Skills. Ellen Hechler. (Orig.). (J). (gr. 6-10). 1992. pap. 8.00 (*0-9638483-7-2*) Midmath.

Mental Math Workout. Michael L. Lobosco. 1999. pap. 9.95 (*1-895569-56-7*) Strlng Pub CA.

Mental Mathematics, Vol. 1. S. P. Nayyar & Francis Fanthome. 76p. 1997. pap. 25.00 (*81-209-0777-9*, Pub. by Pitambar Pub) St Mut.

Mental Mathematics, Vol. 2. S. P. Nayyar & Francis Fanthome. 72p. 1997. pap. 25.00 (*81-209-0778-7*, Pub. by Pitambar Pub) St Mut.

Mental Mathematics, Vol. 3. S. P. Nayyar & Francis Fanthome. 80p. 1997. pap. 25.00 (*81-209-0645-4*, Pub. by Pitambar Pub) St Mut.

Mental Mathematics, Vol. 4. S. P. Nayyar & Francis Fanthome. 80p. 1997. pap. 25.00 (*81-209-0651-9*, Pub. by Pitambar Pub) St Mut.

Mental Mathematics, Vol. 5. S. P. Nayyar & Francis Fanthome. 80p. 1997. pap. 25.00 (*81-209-0726-4*, Pub. by Pitambar Pub) St Mut.

Mental Measurements Vol. 1: The Discovery of Mental Measurements. 8.95 (*1-930343-00-0*) Carson Pubng Co.

Mental Mechanics: A Repair Manual for the Self. Douglas C. McKee. (Orig.). (C). 1997. pap. write for info. (*0-916108-14-7*) Seed Center.

Mental Medicine. Evans. 109p. 1996. reprint ed. spiral bd. 11.50 (*0-7873-1156-1*) Hlth Research.

Mental Models. Dedre Gentner et al. 352p. (C). 1983. text 39.95 (*0-89859-242-9*) L Erlbaum Assocs.

Mental Models. Philip N. Johnson-Laird. (Cognitive Science Ser.: No. 6). (Illus.). 528p. 1983. pap. 20.50 (*0-674-56882-6*) HUP.

Mental Models. Philip N. Johnson-Laird. (Cognitive Science Ser.: No. 6). (Illus.). 528p. 1983. 38.00 (*0-674-56881-8*) HUP.

Mental Models & Human-Computer Interaction, No. 2. Ed. by Michael J. Tauber & D. Ackermann. (Human Factors in Information Technology Ser.: No. 7). 406p. 1991. 181.50 (*0-444-88602-8*, North Holland) Elsevier.

Mental Models & Representations of Discourse & Text. Alan Garnham. (Cognitive Science Ser.). 208p. 1988. text 67.95 (*0-470-21035-4*) P-H.

Mental Models in Cognitive Science: Essays in Honour of Phil Johnson-Laird. Ed. by Jane Oakhill & Alan Garnham. 352p. 1996. 51.00 (*0-86377-448-2*) L Erlbaum Assocs.

Mental Morsels of Simple Wisdom: A Tapestry of Enduring Thoughts. Kamau. LC 98-86022. 208p. 1998. pap. 9.95 (*0-914984-14-4*, Pub. by Starburst) Natl Bk Netwk.

Mental Patients & Social Networks. Robert Perrucci & Dena B. Targ. LC 81-20630. 174p. 1982. 39.95 (*0-86569-095-2*, Auburn Hse) Greenwood.

Mental Poisoning. H. Spencer Lewis. LC 59-55270. 84p. 1937. pap. 6.95 (*0-912057-49-1*, 502010) GLELJ AMORC.

Mental Portraits. Henry T. Tuckerman. (Notable American Authors). 1999. reprint ed. lib. bdg. 125.00 (*0-7812-9843-1*) Rprt Serv.

Mental Practice & Imagery for Musicians: A Practical Guide for Optimizing Practice Time, Enhancing Performance & Preventing Injury. Malva S. Freymuth. LC 99-94063. (Illus.). 114p. 1999. pap. 14.95 (*0-9670027-1-0*) Integrated Musicians Pr.

Mental Processes: Index of Modern Information. Willard W. Welkston. LC 88-47959. 150p. 1990. 47.50 (*1-55914-208-1*); pap. 44.50 (*1-55914-209-X*) ABBE Pubs Assn.

Mental Processes: Studies in Cognitive Science. H. Longuet-Higgins & H. Christopher. (Explorations in Cognitive Science Ser.). 508p. 1987. 55.00 (*0-262-12119-0*) MIT Pr.

Mental Pull-Ups: For Shaping up Your Health. Karen Boscaljon. Ed. by Alice B. Acheson. 160p. (Orig.). 1995. pap. 5.95 (*1-882835-33-6*) STA-Kris.

Mental Radio. Upton Sinclair. Ed. by Rita Mullin. (Collector's Library of the Unknown). (Illus.). 239p. 1991. reprint ed. write for info. (*0-8094-8091-3*); reprint ed. lib. bdg. write for info. (*0-8094-8092-1*) Time-Life.

Mental Reality. Galen Strawson. LC 93-47905. (Representation & Mind Ser.). 350p. 1994. 40.00 (*0-262-19352-3*, Bradford Bks) MIT Pr.

Mental Reality. Galen Strawson. (Representation & Mind Ser.). (Illus.). 355p. 1996. reprint ed. pap. text 20.00 (*0-262-69183-3*, Bradford Bks) MIT Pr.

Mental Representation: A Reader. Ed. by Stephen P. Stich & Ted A. Warfield. LC 93-31974. (Illus.). 448p. 1994. 58.95 (*1-55786-476-4*); pap. 31.95 (*1-55786-477-2*) Blackwell Pubs.

Mental Representation & Consciousness: Towards a Phenomenological Theory of Representation & Reference. Eduard Marbach. LC 92-42687. (Contributions to Phenomenology Ser.: Vol. 14). 208p. (C). 1993. lib. bdg. 147.00 (*0-7923-2101-4*, Pub. by Kluwer Academic) Kluwer Academic.

Mental Representation in Health & Illness. Ed. by J. A. Skelton et al. (Contributions to Psychology & Medicine Ser.). (Illus.). 312p. 1991. 51.95 (*0-387-97401-6*) Spr-Verlag.

Mental Representation of Trait & Autobiographical Knowledge of the Self. Ed. by Robert S. Wyer & Thomas K. Srull. (Advances in Social Cognition Ser.: Vol. 5). 200p. 1993. pap. 24.50 (*0-8058-1312-8*); text 45.00 (*0-8058-1310-1*) L Erlbaum Assocs.

Mental Representation Theory in Old French Allegory from the Twelfth & Thirteenth Centuries. Katharine G. MacCornack. LC 96-17599. (Studies in French Literature: Vol. 26). 184p. 1996. text 79.95 (*0-7734-8815-4*) E Mellen.

Mental Representations: A Dual Coding Approach. Allan Paivio. (Oxford Psychology Ser.: No. 9). (Illus.). 336p. 1990. reprint ed. pap. text 40.00 (*0-19-506666-9*) OUP.

Mental Representations: The Interface Between Language & Reality. Ed. by Ruth M. Kempson. (Illus.). 237p. (C). 1990. pap. text 21.95 (*0-521-39905-X*) Cambridge U Pr.

Mental Retardation. Robert B. Edgerton. LC 78-27199. (Developing Child Ser.). (Illus.). 125p. 1979. 25.95 (*0-674-56885-0*); pap. text 8.50 (*0-674-56886-9*) HUP.

Mental Retardation. Bernard Schlanger. LC 73-9613. (Studies in Communicative Disorders). (C). 1973. pap. write for info. (*0-672-61289-5*, Bobbs) Macmillan.

Mental Retardation. 5th ed. Mary Bierne-Smith et al. LC 97-30617. 647p. (C). 1997. 73.00 (*0-13-894908-5*, Merrill Coll) P-H.

***Mental Retardation: A Life Cycle Approach.** 7th ed. Ed. by Clifford J. Drew. LC 99-18772. (Illus.). 429p. (C). 1999. 73.00 (*0-13-010044-7*) P-H.

Mental Retardation: A Review of Research. Ed. by Harvey A. Stevens & Rick Heber. LC 64-15808. 1994. lib. bdg. 17.50 (*0-226-77388-4*) U Ch Pr.

Mental Retardation: A Review of Research. Ed. by Harvey A. Stevens & Rick Heber. LC 64-15808. (Illus.). 548p. reprint ed. pap. 169.90 (*0-608-09043-3*, 206967800005) Bks Demand.

Mental Retardation: A Source Guide. 1991. lib. bdg. 250.00 (*0-8490-4864-8*) Gordon Pr.

Mental Retardation: Definition, Classification & Systems of Support. 9th ed. Ruth A. Luckasson et al. 189p. 1992. 79.00 (*0-940898-30-6*); pap., student ed. 22.95 (*0-940898-35-7*) Am Assn Mental.

Mental Retardation: Developing Pharmacotherapies. Ed. by John J. Ratey. LC 90-14485. (Progress in Psychiatry Ser.: No. 32). 162p. 1991. text 12.95 (*0-88048-452-7*, 8452) Am Psychiatric.

Mental Retardation: Foundations of Educational Programming. Linda Hickson et al. LC 94-6849. 400p. 1994. 58.00 (*0-205-14016-5*) Allyn.

***Mental Retardation: Life Cycle Approach.** 7th ed. 1999. text, teacher ed. write for info. (*0-13-013587-9*) P-H.

Mental Retardation: Meeting the Challenge. WHO Staff. (WHO Offset Publications: No. 86). 45p. 1985. 7.00 (*92-4-170086-6*) World Health.

Mental Retardation: Nature, Cause & Management. 2nd ed. George S. Baroff. (Illus.). 400p. (C). 1986. 66.95 (*0-89116-263-1*) Hemisp Pub.

***Mental Retardation: Nature, Cause & Management.** 3rd ed. George S. Baroff. (Illus.). 512p. 1999. 69.95 (*1-58391-000-X*) Brunner-Mazel.

***Mental Retardation: Nature, Cause, & Management, 3rd Ed.** 3rd ed. George S. Baroff. LC 99-24045. 1999. pap. text 39.95 (*1-58391-001-8*) Brunner-Mazel.

Mental Retardation: The Developmental-Difference Controversy. D. Balla & Edward F. Zigler. (Illus.). 352p. (C). 1982. text 69.95 (*0-89859-170-8*) L Erlbaum Assocs.

Mental Retardation & Congenital Malformations of the Central Nervous System. Josef Warkany. LC 80-25796. (Illus.). 471p. 1981. reprint ed. pap. 146.10 (*0-8357-7605-0*, 205692700096) Bks Demand.

Mental Retardation & Developmental Disabilities. 2nd ed. Ed. by Phillip J. McLaughlin & Paul Wehman. LC 95-38189. 411p. (C). 1996. text 41.00 (*0-89079-643-2*, 7639) PRO-ED.

Mental Retardation & Developmental Disabilities, Vol. 13. Ed. by Joseph Wortis. LC 73-647002. 226p. 1984. 65.00 (*0-306-41456-2*, Plenum Trade) Perseus Pubng.

***Mental Retardation & Developmental Disability.** Ed. by Arthur E. Jongsma & Kellye Slaggert. (Practice Planners Ser.). 224p. 2000. pap. 39.95 (*0-471-38253-1*) Wiley.

***Mental Retardation & Developmental Disability.** Ed. by Kellye Slaggert & Arthur E. Jongsma. (Practice Planners Ser.). 254p. 2000. pap. 175.00 incl. disk (*0-471-38252-3*) Wiley.

Mental Retardation & Mental Health: Classification, Diagnosis, Treatment, Services. Ed. by Jack A. Stark et al. (Disorders of Human Learning, Behavior, & Communication Ser.). (Illus.). 450p. 1990. 44.00 (*0-387-96577-7*) Spr-Verlag.

Mental Retardation & Other Developmental Disabilities: A Programmed Introduction. 3rd ed. Walter H. Ehlers et al. 520p. (C). 1982. suppl. ed. write for info. (*0-318-54303-6*, Merrill Pub Co) Macmillan.

Mental Retardation & Social Work Education: Proceedings of a Conference Held at Haven Hill Lodge, Milford, MI, June 16-19, 1959. Ed. by Alfred H. Katz. LC HV3006.M5C6. 64p. reprint ed. pap. 30.00 (*0-608-16640-5*, 202768200055) Bks Demand.

Mental Retardation & Sterilization: A Problem of Competency & Paternalism. Ed. by Ruth Macklin & Willard Gaylin. LC 81-7393. (Hastings Center Series in Ethics). 274p. 1981. 39.50 (*0-306-40689-6*, Plenum Trade) Perseus Pubng.

Mental Retardation Handbook. Martin N. Levine. 147p. 1989. pap. text 39.50 (*0-87424-230-4*, W-230) Western Psych.

Mental Retardation in Social Context. Duane F. Stroman. LC 89-5455. 368p. (Orig.). (C). 1989. pap. text 28.00 (*0-8191-7393-2*) U Pr of Amer.

Mental Retardation in the 21st Century Michael L. Wehmeyer & James R. Patton. LC 99-13073. 1999. write for info. (*0-89079-819-2*) PRO-ED.

Mental Retardation in the Year 2000. Ed. by L. Rowitz. (Disorders of Human Learning, Behavior, & Communication Ser.). (Illus.). 344p. 1992. 123.00 (*0-387-97474-1*) Spr-Verlag.

Mental Retardation, Its Nature & Incidence: A Population Survey of the State of Delaware. Joseph F. Jastak et al. LC 62-19658. 184p. 26.50 (*0-87413-103-0*) U Delaware Pr.

Mental Retardation Program Planner. (Career Examination Ser.: C-3464). 1994. pap. 34.95 (*0-8373-3464-0*) Nat Learn.

Mental Retardation Programs: How Does Massachusetts Compare? Edward Moscovitch. (Pioneer Paper Ser.: No. 4). 100p. (Orig.). 1991. pap. 10.00 (*0-929930-06-1*) Pioneer Inst.

***Mental Retardation Sourcebook.** (Health Reference Ser.). 600p. 2000. 78.00 (*0-7808-0377-9*) Omnigraphics Inc.

Mental Retardation:a Community Integration. Crane. (Special Education). 1999. pap. 48.95 (*0-534-33923-9*) Brooks-Cole.

Mental Revolution: Scientific Management since Taylor. Ed. by Daniel Nelson. LC 91-33381. (Historical Perspectives on Business Enterprise Ser.). 259p. reprint ed. pap. 80.30 (*0-608-09860-4*, 206982500006) Bks Demand.

Mental Room of Mirrors: Self-Therapy Technique. Russ Michael. Ed. by G. M. Bennett. (Illus.). 210p. 1997. pap. 15.98 (*1-882786-31-9*) New Dawn NY.

Mental Science: A Compendium of Psychology & the History of Philosophy. Alexander Bain. LC 73-2958. (Classics in Psychology Ser.). 1977. reprint ed. 34.95 (*0-405-05132-8*) Ayer.

Mental Science 101. Gopinathan M. Nair. 1997. pap. 12.95 (*0-7880-0926-5*, Fairway Pr) CSS OH.

Mental Shielding to Brush off Hostility. 2nd unabridged ed. Richard Driscoll. LC 93-74709. 88p. 1994. pap. 18.00 incl. audio (*0-9634126-1-2*) Frontiers Pr.

Mental Simulation: Evaluations & Applications. Ed. by Martin Davies & Tony Stone. (Readings in Mind & Language Ser.). 350p. (C). 1995. 64.95 (*0-631-19872-5*); pap. 30.95 (*0-631-19873-3*) Blackwell Pubs.

Mental Skill Development for Ultimate Performance in Sports. Janet Helfrich. 180p. (C). 1997. per. 19.95 (*0-7872-3948-8*) Kendall-Hunt.

Mental Skills in Martial Arts. Miguel Hernandez. LC 97-93556. 96p. (Orig.). 1997. pap. 12.95 (*1-57502-447-0*, P01344) Morris Pubng.

***Mental Slavery: Psychoanalytic Studies of Caribbean People.** Barbara Fletchman Smith. 161p. 2000. pap. 19.99 (*1-900877-22-8*, Pub. by Rebus Pr Ltd) Intl Spec Bk.

Mental Snacks: Readings for Thinkers on Airplanes. 2nd ed. Michael Phillips. LC 87-72261. (Illus.). 152p. 1988. pap. 10.00 (*0-931425-12-3*) Clear Glass.

Mental Space. Salomon Resnik. 144p. 1995. pap. text 28.00 (*1-85575-058-9*, Pub. by H Karnac Bks Ltd) Other Pr LLC.

Mental Spaces: Aspects of Meaning in Natural Language. Gilles Fauconnier. (Illus.). 238p. (C). 1994. text 59.95 (*0-521-44499-3*); pap. text 17.95 (*0-521-44949-9*) Cambridge U Pr.

Mental State of Hystericals. Pierre Janet. 557p. 120.00 (*1-85506-681-5*) Thoemmes Pr.

Mental State of Hystericals, 2. Pierre Janet. LC 77-72191. (Contributions to the History of Psychology Ser.: Pt. 2, Medical Psychology). 535p. 1977. reprint ed. lib. bdg. 75.00 (*0-313-26941-6*, U6941, Greenwood Pr) Greenwood.

Mental Status Examination in Neurology. 4th ed. Richard L. Strub & F. William Black. LC 99-24985. (Illus.). 208p. 1999. pap. text 26.95 (*0-8036-0427-0*) Davis Co.

Mental Status Schedules & Psychiatric Rating Scales: Index of New Information for Reference & Research. Larry W. Lingeman. 160p. 1997. 47.50 (*0-7883-1326-6*); pap. 44.50 (*0-7883-1327-4*) ABBE Pubs Assn.

Mental Symbols: A Defence of the Classical Theory of Mind. Peter Novak. LC 96-49054. (Studies in Cognitive Systems COGS: Vol. 19). 238p. (C). 1997. text 117.50 (*0-7923-4370-0*) Kluwer Academic.

Mental Territories: Mapping the Inland Empire. Katherine G. Morrissey. LC 97-23223. (Illus.). 240p. 1997. pap. 18.95 (*0-8014-8326-3*); text 45.00 (*0-8014-3250-2*) Cornell U Pr.

Mental Theater: Poetic Drama & Consciousness in the Romantic Age. Alan Richardson. LC 87-10922. 170p. 1988. lib. bdg. 35.00 (*0-271-00612-9*) Pa St U Pr.

Mental Therapeutics. Theron Q. Dumont. 235p. 1972. reprint ed. 15.00 (*0-911662-47-2*) Yoga.

Mental Toughness. Al Gibson. 1998. pap. 8.95 (*0-533-12603-7*) Vantage.

Mental Toughness Training for Softball: A Guide & Workbook for Athletes & Coaches. Jeffrey J. Janssen & J. Mike Candrea. 128p. (Orig.). 1994. pap. 24.95 (*0-9640150-0-5*) SW Camps Pubns.

Mental Training. Bob Hickey. LC 79-67021. (Illus.). (Orig.). 1985. 22.50 (*0-9603432-2-9*) STP.

Mental Training. Jeff Kress. 200p. Date not set. pap. 19.95 (*1-884737-24-2*) NTC Contemp Pub Co.

Mental Training: For the Shotgun Sports. Michael J. Keyes. (Illus.). 160p. Date not set. pap. 24.95 (*0-925012-04-1*) Shotgun Sports.

Mental Training & Performance Enhancement: A Guide for Volleyball Coaches & Players. Brett D. Mills. 107p. (Orig.). (C). 1995. pap. 24.95 (*0-945483-49-X*) E Bowers Pub.

Mental Training for Peak Performance: Top Athletes Reveal the Mind Exercises They Use to Excel. Steven Ungerleider. LC 95-25485. 224p. 1996. pap. 14.95 (*0-87596-282-3*) Rodale Pr Inc.

Mental Training for Tennis. Gary Sailes. 80p. 1995. pap. text, per. 15.95 (*0-7872-1104-4*) Kendall-Hunt.

***Mental Wellness for Women.** Rita Baron-Faust. 384p. 1998. reprint ed. pap. 15.00 (*0-688-16113-8*, Quil) HarperTrade.

Mental Wellness for Women: What Every Woman Should Know. Rita Baron-Faust. 1997. 25.00 (*0-614-20667-7*, Wm Morrow) Morrow Avon.

Mentales Leben & Materielle Welt: Philosophische Studien zum Leib-Seele-Problem. Heinz-Dieter Heckmann. (Foundations of Communication & Cognition Ser.). (GER.). x, 313p. (C). 1994. lib. bdg. 136.95 (*3-11-013963-4*) De Gruyter.

Mentalistic Turn: A Critical Evaluation of Chomsky. Kalyan S. Gupta. (C). 1990. 15.00 (*81-7074-074-6*, Pub. by KP Bagchi) S Asia.

Mentalites, Ideologie et Comportment Politique dans le Chili de Salvador Allende: Etude des cas d'un Quartier de Santiago. Raul Silva-Caceres. (Studia Sociologica Upsaliensia: No. 24). 190p. (Orig.). 1986. pap. text 62.50 (*91-554-1816-3*, Pub. by Uppsala Univ Acta Univ Uppsaliensis) Coronet Bks.

Mentalities of Gorillas & Orangutans: Comparative Perspectives. Ed. by Sue T. Parker et al. (Illus.). 560p. (C). 1999. text 85.00 (*0-521-58027-7*) Cambridge U Pr.

Mentality & Machines. Keith Gunderson. LC 85-973. 285p. reprint ed. pap. 88.40 (*0-8357-2587-1*, 205236700013) Bks Demand.

Mentality of Apes. Wolfgang Kohler. (Illus.). 352p. 1976. reprint ed. pap. 3.95 (*0-87140-108-8*, Pub. by Liveright) Norton.

Mentality of the Arriving Immigrant. E. H. Mullan. LC 77-129408. (American Immigration Collection. Series 2). (Illus.). 1970. reprint ed. 14.95 (*0-405-00562-8*) Ayer.

***Mentallly Ill Offenders in California's Criminal Justice System.** Marcus Nieto. 57p. 1999. pap. write for info. (*1-58703-099-3*, CRB-99-002) CA St Libry.

Mentally Disabled & the Law. 3rd rev. ed. Samuel J. Brakel et al. LC 85-71886. xxii, 845p. 1985. 85.00 (*0-910059-05-5*, 306030) W S Hein.

Mentally Disordered Inmate & the Law. rev. ed. Fred Cohen. LC 98-72903. Orig. Title: Legal Rights of the Mentally Disordered Prison Inmate. 585p. 1998. 98.95 (*1-887554-06-8*) Civic Res Inst.

Mentally Disordered Juvenile Offenders. Donna Hunzeker. (State Legislative Reports: Vol. 18, No. 3). 4p. 1993. 15.00 (*1-55516-333-5*, 7302-1803) Natl Conf State Legis.

Mentally Disordered Offender. Seymour L. Halleck. 214p. 1987. pap. text 12.95 (*0-88048-270-2*, 8270) Am Psychiatric.

Mentally Disordered Offenders: Managing People Nobody Owns. David Webb. LC 98-53740. 1999. write for info. (*0-415-18009-0*) Routledge.

Mentally Disordered Offenders: Managing People Nobody Owns David Webb & Robert Harris. LC 98-53740. 1999. pap. write for info. (*0-415-18010-4*) Routledge.

Mentally Disordered Offenders: Perspectives from Law & Social Science. J. Monahan & H. J. Steadman. LC 83-2329. (Perspectives in Law & Psychology Ser.: Vol. 6). (Illus.). 318p. (C). 1983. 62.50 (*0-306-41151-2*, Plenum Trade) Perseus Pubng.

Mentally, He's a Sick Man. Michael Lally. LC PS3562.A414Z. (Salt Lick Samplers Ser.). 19p. 1975. reprint ed. pap. 30.00 (*0-7837-9160-7*, 204986000003) Bks Demand.

Mentally Ill & Homeless: Special Programs for Special Needs. Ed. by William R. Breakey & James W. Thompson. (Chronic Mental Illness Ser.). 208p. 1998. text 31.00 (*90-5702-557-4*, Harwood Acad Pubs) Gordon & Breach.

Mentally Ill Child Grows Up: Transitions to the World of Work. Bertram J. Black. LC 93-31218. 222p. 1993. text 31.95 (*0-87630-711-X*) Brunner-Mazel.

Mentally Ill in Community-Based Sheltered Care: A Study of Community Care & Social Integration. Steven P. Segal. Ed. by Aviram Uri. LC 77-22474. (Health, Medicine & Society Ser.). 351p. reprint ed. pap. 108.90 (*0-608-12409-5*, 205571600032) Bks Demand.

Mentally Ill in Jail: Planning for Essential Services. Henry J. Steadman et al. LC 88-21557. (Guilford Law & Behavior Ser.). 242p. 1988. lib. bdg. 33.95 (*0-89862-279-4*) Guilford Pubns.

Mentally Ill in Urban America: An Original Anthology. Ed. by Gerald N. Grob. LC 78-22575. (Historical Issues in Mental Health Ser.). (Illus.). 1980. lib. bdg. 48.95 (*0-405-11928-3*) Ayer.

Mentally Ill Mothers & Their Children. 2nd ed. Henry Grunebaum et al. LC 82-10911. xvii, 378p. 1993. lib. bdg. 30.00 (*0-226-31029-9*) U Ch Pr.

Mentally Ill Mothers & Their Children. 2nd ed. Henry Grunebaum et al. LC 82-10911. xvii, 414p. 1996. pap. text 12.00 (*0-226-31022-1*) U Ch Pr.

Mentally Ill Offenders & the Criminal Justice System: Issues in Forensic Services. Ed. by Nancy J. Beran & Beverly G. Toomey. LC 78-19782. 193p. 1979. 57.95 (*0-275-90330-3*, C0330, Praeger Pubs) Greenwood.

Mentally Impaired Elderly: Strategies & Interventions to Maintain Function. Ed. by Ellen D. Taira. LC 91-20816. (Physical & Occupational Therapy in Geriatrics Ser.). (Illus.). 169p. 1991. lib. bdg. 39.95 (*1-56024-168-3*) Haworth Pr.

Mentally Retarded & Normal Children: A Comparative Study of Their Family Conditions. Manju Biswas. 157p. 1980. 19.95 (*0-940500-50-7*, Pub. by Sterling) Asia Bk Corp.

Mentally Retarded Child. enl. rev. ed. Abraham Levinson. LC 77-25884. (Illus.). 187p. 1978. reprint ed. lib. bdg. 48.50 (*0-313-20123-4*, LEMR, Greenwood Pr) Greenwood.

Mentally Retarded Children: What Parents & Others Should Know. Harriet E. Blodgett. LC 72-152301. 175p. reprint ed. pap. 54.30 (*0-608-14092-9*, 205584500039) Bks Demand.

Mentally Sharp Naturally. E. Liva & J. Germain. 1999. pap. 15.00 (*0-7615-1473-2*) Prima Pub.

Mentally Sound Dog: How to Shape, Train & Change Canine Behavior. Gail I. Clark & William N. Boyer. Ed. by Joanne Carriera. LC 95-15516. (Illus.). 280p. 1995. pap. 21.95 (*0-931866-67-7*) Alpine Pubns.

Mentally Subnormal Child. (Technical Report Ser.). 46p. Date not set. pap. text 3.00 (*92-4-120075-8*) World Health.

Mentally Superior & Inferior Children of Junior & Senior High School Age: A Comparative Study of Their Backgrounds, Interests & Ambitions. Glenn M. Blair. LC 71-176567. (Columbia University. Teachers College. Contributions to Education Ser.: No. 766). reprint ed. 37.50 (*0-404-55766-X*) AMS Pr.

Mentally Tough: The Principles of Winning at Sports Applied to Winning in Business. Peter J. McLaughlin et al. LC 86-19654. 240p. 1988. pap. 12.95 (*0-87131-540-8*) M Evans.

***Mentally Tough Online Trader: A Sanity Guide for the Totally Wired Investor.** Robert Koppel. LC 99-87698. 256p. 2000. 35.00 (*0-7931-3809-4*, 56811901) Dearborn.

Mentawai Shaman: Shaman: Keeper of the Rain Forest. Charles Lindsay. (Illus.). 120p. 1992. 60.00 (*0-89381-520-9*) Aperture.

Mentchkins Make Friends. Chaya L. Rothstein. (J). (gr. 4-8). 1988. pap. 7.95 (*0-87306-453-4*) Feldheim.

Mentchkins Make Shabbos. Chaya L. Rothstein. (Sifrei Rimon Ser.). (Illus.). (J). (ps-2). 1986. pap. 2.95 (*0-87306-401-1*) Feldheim.

Menteuse: Roman. Jean Giraudoux. (Coll. Diamant). 13.50 (*0-685-33920-3*) Fr & Eur.

Menteuse par Amour. Daphne Clair. (Azur Ser.: Vol.754). (FRE.). 1999. mass mkt. 3.50 (*0-373-34754-5*, 1-34754-1) Harlequin Bks.

***Mention Your Request Here: The Church's Most Powerful Novenas.** Michael Dubruiel. LC 99-75031. 144p. 2000. pap. 12.95 (*0-87973-341-1*) Our Sunday Visitor.

Mentiras. Catherine O'Connor. (Bianca Ser.: No. 33401).Tr. of Sweet Lies. (SPA.). 1997. per. 3.50 (*0-373-33401-X*, 1-33401-0) Harlequin Bks.

Mentiras Que Creemos. Thurman.Tr. of Lies We Believe. (SPA.). 1994. 9.99 (*0-88113-191-1*, B001-1911) Caribe Betania.

Mentirijillas. Jamie Suzanne. (Sweet Valley Twins Ser.: No. 13).Tr. of Streching the Truth. (J). (gr. 3-7). 1991. 12.05 (*0-606-10451-8*, Pub. by Turtleback) Demco.

Menton City Plan. (Grafocarte Maps Ser.). 1994. 8.95 (*2-7416-0023-6*, 80023) Michelin.

Mentone, Carlo & Corfu. Constance F. Woolson. (Notable American Authors Ser.). 1999. reprint ed. lib. bdg. 125.00 (*0-7812-7796-5*) Rprt Serv.

Mentor. R. A. Forster. 384p. 1998. pap. 5.99 (*0-7860-0488-6*, Pinncle Kensgtn) Kensgtn Pub Corp.

Mentor. Sebastian Stuart. LC 98-51447. 256p. 1999. 22.95 (*0-553-11165-5*) Bantam.

***Mentor.** Sebastian Stuart. 2000. mass mkt. 5.99 (*0-553-58031-0*) Bantam.

Mentor. Don Thornton. (Illus.). 28p. (Orig.). 1993. pap. 5.00 (*1-882913-04-3*) Thornton LA.

***Mentor: A Memoir of Friendship & Gay Identity.** Jay Quinn. LC 99-56495. 200p. (C). 2000. pap. 19.95 (*1-56023-937-9*, Harrington Park); lib. bdg. 49.95 (*0-7890-0496-8*, Harrington Park) Haworth Pr.

***Mentor: Guiding the Journey of Adult Learners.** 2nd ed. Laurent A. Daloz. LC 99-6188. (Higher & Adult Education Ser.). 304p. 1999. pap. text 24.95 (*0-7879-4072-0*) Jossey-Bass.

Mentor: Secrets of the Ages. rev. ed. Art Fettig. (Illus.). 96p. 1997. reprint ed. pap. 9.95 (*0-916927-18-0*) Growth Unltd.

Mentor: 15 Keys to Achieving Success in Sales, Business & Life. Jack Carew. 224p. 1999. pap. 13.95 (*0-452-28021-4*, Plume) Dutton Plume.

Mentor: 15 Keys to Success in Sales, Business, & Life. Jack Carew. LC 97-49231. 160p. 1998. 19.95 (*1-55611-541-5*, Pub. by D I Fine) Penguin Putnam.

Mentor Book of Great Poets. John Hollander. 1999. mass mkt. 5.99 (*0-451-62859-4*, Ment) NAL.

An Asterisk (*) at the beginning of an entry indicates that the title is appearing for the first time.

Mentor Book of Major American Poets from Edward Taylor & Walt Whitman to Hart Crane & W. H. Auden. Oscar Williams. (J). 1962. 13.09 (*0-606-02334-8*, Pub. by Turtleback) Demco.

Mentor Book of Major British Poets. Ed. by Oscar Williams. 576p. (YA). (gr. 9-12). 1985. mass mkt. 7.99 (*0-451-62637-0*, Ment) NAL.

Mentor Connection: Strategic Alliances in Corporate Life. Michael G. Zey. 225p. 1995. pap. 21.95 (*0-88738-865-5*) Transaction Pubs.

Mentor Connection in Nursing. Ed. by Connie Vance & Roberta K. Olson. LC 97-41971. (Illus.). 220p. 1998. 39.95 (*0-8261-1174-2*) Springer Pub.

Mentor Courses: A Resource Book for Trainer-Trainers. Angi Malderez & Caroline Bodoczky. LC 98-44352. (Teacher Training & Development Ser.). (Illus.). 232p. (C). 1999. 59.95 (*0-521-56204-X*); pap. 22.95 (*0-521-56690-8*) Cambridge U Pr.

Mentor Guide: The Training Development Programme. ITD TVU. (Trainer Development Programme Management & Design 7 Ser.). 1994. pap. text 8.00 (*0-08-042171-7*, Pergamon Pr) Elsevier.

Mentor in a Manual: Climbing the Academic Ladder to Tenure. 2nd ed. A. Clay Schoenfeld & Robert Magnan. 498p. 1994. text 39.95 (*1-891859-08-0*); pap. text 31.95 (*1-891859-09-9*) Atwood Pub LLC.

Mentor in a Manual: Climbing the Academic Ladder to Tenure. 2nd ed. A. Clay Schoenfeld & Robert Magnan. LC 94-38177. 498p. 1994. 39.95 (*0-912150-34-3*); pap. 31.95 (*0-912150-35-1*) Atwood Pub LLC.

Mentor Kit: A Step-by-Step Guide to Creating An Effective Mentor Program in Your School. Diane Nash & Donald J. Treffinger. 76p. 1993. pap. 24.95 (*1-882664-06-X*) Prufrock Pr.

Mentor Manual: For Adults Who Work with Pregnant & Parenting Teens. Frederick H. Kanfer et al. LC 95-131150. (Orig.). 1995. pap. 18.95 (*0-87868-580-4*) Child Welfare.

Mentor Relationships: How They Aid Creative Achievement, Endure, Change, & Die. E. Paul Torrance. 72p. (Orig.). (C). 1984. pap. 12.95 (*0-943456-02-9*) Bearly Ltd.

Mentor Teacher Casebook. Ed. by Judith H. Shulman & Joel A. Colbert. LC 87-82636. 104p. (Orig.). 1987. pap. 10.00 (*0-86552-094-1*) U of Oreg ERIC.

Mentor Teacher Programs. Sandra J. Odell. (What Research Says to the Teacher Ser.). 32p. (Orig.). 1990. pap. 4.95 (*0-614-30866-6*, 1086-8) NEA.

Mentor Wisdom: Requisites for Living. Serena G. Mills-Thornton. Ed. by Sharon Allen. (Illus.). 31p. (Orig.). (YA). 1993. write for info. (*0-9614338-0-9*) Ideas.

Mentored in Silence: The Heart of Meditation. Robert Rabbin. LC 99-13330. 1999. pap. 15.95 (*1-889051-46-2*) Acrpls Bks CO.

Mentoring. IPM Staff. (Training Delivery Ser.: No. 6). (C). 1994. pap. 93.00 (*0-08-042162-8*, Pub. by IPM Hse) St Mut.

Mentoring. ITD Staff. (Trainer Development Programme Delivery Ser.). 1994. pap. text 38.00 (*0-08-042446-5*, Pergamon Pr) Elsevier.

Mentoring. Floyd Wickman. 168p. 1996. text 24.95 (*0-7863-1135-5*, Irwn Prfssnl) McGraw-Hill Prof.

Mentoring: A Fifty Minute Book. 2nd rev. ed. Gordon F. Shea. LC 97-66608. (Fifty Minute Ser.). (Illus.). 120p. 1997. pap. 10.95 (*1-56052-426-X*) Crisp Pubns.

Mentoring: A Guide to Corporate Programs & Practices. 65p. 1993. 60.00 (*0-89584-179-7*) Catalyst.

Mentoring: A Resource & Training Guide for Educators. Ken Bergstrom et al. 400p. (C). 1993. 98.00 (*1-878234-06-4*) Reg Lab Educ IOT NE Isls.

Mentoring: An Annotated Bibliography. Ruth B. Noller & Barbara R. Frey. 80p. (Orig.). 1983. pap. 18.95 (*0-943456-01-0*) Bearly Ltd.

Mentoring: An Essential Factor in the Doctoral Process for Minority Students. Contrib. by Howard G. Adams. (C). 1992. 5.00 (*1-887284-05-2*) Natl Consortium.

Mentoring: An Example to Follow. Gary Wilde. (Encouragers for Men Ser.). 64p. 1997. pap. text 3.99 (*1-56476-617-9*, Victor Bks) Chariot Victor.

Mentoring: Confidence in Finding a Mentor & Becoming One. Bobb Biehl. 1997. pap. 11.99 (*0-8054-6347-X*) Broadman.

Mentoring: Contemporary Principles & Issues. Ed. by Theresa M. Bey & C. Thomas Holmes. 1992. pap. 9.95 (*0-685-74810-3*) Assn Tchr Ed.

***Mentoring: Creating Connected, Empowered Relationships.** Valerie L. Schwiebert. LC 99-45898. 182p. 2000. pap. text 29.95 (*1-55620-223-7*, 72668) Am Coun Assn.

Mentoring: Developing Successful New Teachers. Ed. by Theresa M. Bey & C. Thomas Holmes. (Orig.). 9.95 (*0-685-57422-9*) Assn Tchr Ed.

Mentoring: Developing Successful New Teachers. Ed. by Theresa M. Bey & C. Thomas Holmes. 96p. (Orig.). (C). 1990. pap. text. write for info. (*0-9624818-1-5*) U GA Coll Ed.

Mentoring: For Exceptional Performance. Harold E. Johnson. 320p. (Orig.). 1997. pap. 18.95 (*1-882180-83-6*) Griffin CA.

Mentoring: Partnerships for Exceptional Employee Development. Gordon F. Shea. LC 94-36222. (Management Briefing Ser.). 1994. pap. 12.50 (*0-8144-2357-4*) AMACOM.

Mentoring: The Human Touch. Dorothy I. Mitstifer et al. 75p. 1994. ring bd. 35.00 (*1-929083-01-7*) Kappa Omi Nu.

Mentoring: The Right Tool for the Right Job: A Not-So-Quick Fix. David M. Hunt. (International Human Resource Met. & Dev. Ser.). (Illus.). 151p. (Orig.). 1994. pap. 16.95 (*0-9642303-0-5*) Hunt Assocs.

Mentoring: The Tao of Giving & Receiving Wisdom. Chungliang A. Huang & Jerry Lynch. LC 95-2925. 176p. 1995. 18.00 (*0-06-251250-1*, Pub. by Harper SF) HarpC.

Mentoring Adult Learners: A Guide for Educators & Trainers. Norman H. Cohen. LC 94-36430. (Illus.). 224p. (C). 1995. 27.50 (*0-89464-850-0*) Krieger.

Mentoring Advantage: How to Help Your Career Soar to New Heights. Pam Grout. Ed. by Kelly Scanlon & Jane D. Guthrie. (Illus.). 52p. (Orig.). 1995. pap. 12.95 (*1-878542-99-0*) SkillPath Pubns.

Mentoring & Coaching. S. Mathews. (Financial Times Management Briefings Ser.). 1997. pap. 94.50 (*0-273-63252-3*, Pub. by F T P-H) Trans-Atl Phila.

Mentoring & Developing Practice in Primary Schools: Supporting Student Teacher Learning in Schools. Anne Edwards & Jill Collison. LC 96-11910. 160p. 1996. 87.95 (*0-335-19566-0*) OpUniv Pr.

Mentoring & Development Practice: Supporting Student Teacher Learning in Schools. A. Edwards. LC 96-11910. 160p. 1996. pap. 29.95 (*0-335-19565-2*) OpUniv Pr.

***Mentoring & Diversity.** David Clutterbuck. 224p. 2001. 47.95 (*0-7506-4836-8*) Buttrwrth-Heinemann.

Mentoring & Nurturing Communication in Health Contexts: A Special Issue of "Health Communication" Ed. by Jeffery Pittam & Cynthia Gallois. 1998. pap. write for info. (*0-8058-9821-2*) L Erlbaum Assocs.

Mentoring & Preceptorship: A Guide to Support Roles in Clinical Practice. Alison Morton-Cooper & Anne Palmer. LC 93-19829. 192p. 1993. pap. 24.95 (*0-632-03596-X*) Blackwell Sci.

Mentoring & Supervision for Teacher Development. Alan Reiman. LC 97-21568. (Illus.). 384p. (C). 1997. pap. text 70.00 (*0-8013-1539-5*) Addison-Wesley.

Mentoring & the Business Environment: Asset or Liability? Richard Caruso. 170p. 1992. 61.95 (*1-85521-317-6*, Pub. by Dartmth Pub) Ashgate Pub Co.

Mentoring & Tutoring by Students. Sinclair Goodlad. 352p. 1998. pap. 27.50 (*0-7494-2559-8*, Kogan Pg Educ) Stylus Pub VA.

Mentoring at Work: Developmental Relationships in Organizational Life. Kathy E. Kram. 266p. (C). 1988. reprint ed. pap. text 23.00 (*0-8191-6755-X*) U Pr of Amer.

***Mentoring Beginning Teachers: Guiding, Reflecting, Coaching.** Jean Boreen et al. Ed. by Philippa Stratton. LC 99-51645. 144p. 2000. pap. text 17.50 (*1-57110-309-0*) Stenhse Pubs.

Mentoring Dilemmas: Developmental Relationships Within Multicultural Organizations. Ed. by Audrey J. Murrell et al. LC 98-24654. (Applied Social Research Ser.). 280p. 1999. 59.95 (*0-8058-2632-7*); pap. 29.95 (*0-8058-2633-5*) L Erlbaum Assocs.

Mentoring Executives & Directors. David Clutterbuck. 167p. 1999. text 39.95 (*0-7506-3695-5*) Buttrwrth-Heinemann.

Mentoring Experience: Perspectives on School-Based Initial Teacher Education. Val Brooks et al. LC 96-42217. 192p. 1997. 94.00 (*0-335-19759-0*) OpUniv Pr.

Mentoring for Leadership Development see Steps Toward Balancing Life's Demands, Vol. 3, One-to-One Mentoring for Effective Living

***Mentoring for Resiliency: Setting up Programs for Moving Youth from "Stressed to Success"** Ed. by Nan Henderson et al. LC 00-90815. (Illus.). 90p. 2000. pap. 12.95 (*0-9669394-1-7*) Resiliency.

Mentoring for Science Teachers. Terry Allsop. Ed. by Ann Benson. LC 96-23677. 128p. 1996. pap. 27.95 (*0-335-19514-8*) OpUniv Pr.

Mentoring for Science Teachers. Terry Allsop & Ann Benson. LC 96-23677. 128p. 1996. 88.95 (*0-335-19515-6*) OpUniv Pr.

Mentoring for Success. Elizabeth Weinstein & Karen Massetti Miller. LC 98-72663. (How-to Book Ser.). 128p. 1998. pap. 12.95 (*1-884926-94-0*, MENTR) Amer Media.

***Mentoring Heroes: 52 Fabulous Women's Paths to Success & the Mentors Who Empowered Them.** Mary K. Doyle. LC 99-97451. 237p. 2000. 21.95 (*0-9677449-2-X*) ThreeE Press.

Mentoring High-Risk Kids. James Becker. LC 93-46107. 51p. 1994. pap. 6.50 (*1-56246-092-7*, 3209, HazeldenJohnson Inst) Hazelden.

Mentoring in Action: A Practical Guide for Managers. David Clutterbuck & David Megginson. LC 96-144452. 240p. 1995. 49.95 (*0-7494-1390-5*, Pub. by Kogan Pg) Nichols Pub.

***Mentoring in Early Childhood Settings.** Arlene L. Martin & Polly Ashelman. 152p. (C). 1999. per. 20.95 (*0-7872-6014-2*, 41601401) Kendall-Hunt.

Mentoring in General Practice. Rosslynne Freeman. LC 98-27560. 240p. 1998. pap. text 40.00 (*0-7506-3940-7*) Buttrwrth-Heinemann.

Mentoring in Mathematics Teaching. Ed. by Barbara Jaworski & Anne Watson. LC 93-32974. 200p. 1994. 85.00 (*0-7507-0258-3*, Falmer Pr); pap. 27.95 (*0-7507-0259-1*, Falmer Pr) Taylor & Francis.

Mentoring in Physical Education: Issues & Insights. Mick Mawer. LC 96-18405. 224p. 1996. 79.95 (*0-7507-0564-7*, Falmer Pr); pap. 27.95 (*0-7507-0565-5*, Falmer Pr) Taylor & Francis.

Mentoring in Religious Education. Leona M. English. LC 98-20191. 310p. 1998. pap. text 24.95 (*0-89135-107-8*) Religious Educ.

Mentoring Manager: Strategies for Fostering Talent & Spreading Knowledge. Gareth Lewis. (Institute of Management Ser.). (Illus.). 212p. (Orig.). 1996. pap. 47.50 (*0-273-62344-3*, Pub. by Pitman Pub) Trans-Atl Phila.

***Mentoring Manager: Strategies for Fostering Talent & Spreading Knowledge.** 2nd ed. Gareth Lewis. (Smarter Solutions Ser.). 192p. (Orig.). 2000. pap. 22.50 (*0-273-64484-X*, Pub. by F T P-H) Trans-Atl Phila.

***Mentoring Manual.** Mike Whittaker & Ann Cartwright. LC 99-49656. 202p. 2000. 99.95 (*0-566-08147-4*, Pub. by Gower) Ashgate Pub Co.

Mentoring Means Future Scientists: A Guide for Developing Mentoring Programs Based on the AWIS Mentoring Project. Association for Women in Science Staff. LC 93-72802. 150p. (Orig.). 1993. pap. 15.95 (*0-9634590-3-1*); 6.95 (*0-9634590-5-8*) Assn Women Sci.

Mentoring, Methods, & Movements: Colloquium in Honor of Terence K. Hopkins. Ed. by Immanuel Wallerstein. LC 98-74401. 176p. 1998. pap. 30.00 (*1-888024-15-1*) Ahead Desktop.

Mentoring New Teachers. Hal Portner. LC 98-19774. (Illus.). 112p. 1998. 45.95 (*0-8039-6714-4*, 82473); pap. 19.95 (*0-8039-6715-2*, 82474) Corwin Pr.

***Mentoring Pocketbook.** Geof Alred et al. 112p. 2000. pap. 8.95 (*1-57922-006-1*) Stylus Pub VA.

Mentoring Program. NSU (Collins) Staff. 88p. (C). 1995. pap. text 21.95 (*0-8403-8465-3*) Kendall-Hunt.

Mentoring Program Internship Handbook: The Mentoring Experience in Teacher Education. 2nd ed. Northeastern State University Staff. 72p. (C). 1997. per. 25.95 (*0-7872-4564-X*, 41456401) Kendall-Hunt.

Mentoring Programs for New Teachers. Ellen Newcombe. 24p. 1988. pap. 5.95 (*1-56602-021-2*) Research Better.

Mentoring Revisited: Making an Impact on Individuals & Institutions. Ed. by Marie A. Wunsch. LC 85-644763. (New Directions for Teaching & Learning Ser.: No. TL 57). 134p. (Orig.). 1994. pap. 22.00 (*0-7879-9973-3*) Jossey-Bass.

Mentoring Strategic Change in Healthcare: An Action Guide. Chip Caldwell. (Illus.). 262p. 1995. 32.00 (*0-87389-224-0*, H0787) ASQ Qual Pr.

Mentoring Student Teachers: The Growth of Professional Knowledge. John Furlong & Trisha Maynard. LC 94-29165. 224p. (C). 1995. pap. 24.99 (*0-415-11394-6*, C0072) Routledge.

Mentoring Student Teachers: The Growth of Professional Knowledge. John Furlong & Trisha Maynard. LC 94-29165. 224p. (C). (gr. 13). 1995. 80.00 (*0-415-11393-8*, C0071) Routledge.

Mentoring the Mentor: A Critical Dialogue with Paulo Freire. Ed. by Paulo Freire et al. LC 97-1382. (Counterpoints: No. 60). XIX, 334p. (C). 1997. pap. 29.95 (*0-8204-3798-0*) P Lang Pubng.

Mentoring the Stars: A Mentorship Program for New Board Members. Cynthia R. Nowicki. 325p. 1998. spiral bd. write for info. (*0-9655310-2-3*) Jannetti Pubns.

***Mentoring Unrepresented Students in Higher Education.** Ed. by Marilyn J. Haring & Kassie Freeman. 168p. 1999. pap. 20.00 (*0-8058-9781-X*) L Erlbaum Assocs.

Mentoring Works! Facilitator's Guide. Nathan Avani. 70p. 1998. pap. text, teacher ed. 24.95 (*1-56688-439-X*, 3861) Bur For At-Risk.

Mentoring Works! Program: A Peer Helping Program for Middle & High School Students. Nathan Avani. (Illus.). 94p. (YA). (gr. 5-12). 1998. pap. text, teacher ed., wbk. ed. 189.95 (*1-56688-442-X*, 3860A) Bur For At-Risk.

Mentoring Works! Student Workbook. Nathan Avani. (Illus.). 24p. (YA). (gr. 5-12). 1998. pap. text 5.95 (*1-56688-440-3*, 3862) Bur For At-Risk.

***Mentoring Youth for Success, Vol. 8135.** William W. Gray. 22p. 1999. 9.00 (*1-57337-059-2*) WI Dept Pub Instruct.

Mentors. Thomas W. Evans. LC 92-20980. 256p. 1992. 9.95 (*1-56079-152-7*) Petersons.

Mentors & Friends. Moshe Kohl. LC 82-71073. 208p. 1983. 15.00 (*0-8453-4741-1*, Cornwall Bks) Assoc Univ Prs.

Mentors & Mentoring: A Special Issue of the Peabody Journal of Education, Vol. 71, No. 1. Cienkus. 1996. pap. 20.00 (*0-8058-9932-4*) L Erlbaum Assocs.

Mentors & Proteges: How to Select, Manage & Lead Dynamic Relationships. Gary R. Blair. 48p. 1998. pap. 6.95 (*1-889770-12-4*, MNP) GoalsGuy.

Mentors for Mothers. Donna Otto. 1999. pap. text, teacher ed. 34.99 (*0-8474-1331-4*) Back to Bible.

***Mentor's Guide: Facilitating Effective Learning Relationships.** Lois J. Zachary. 208p. 2000. pap. 25.95 (*0-7879-4742-3*, Pfffr & Co) Jossey-Bass.

Mentor's Guide to Biblical Eldership: Twelve Lessons for Mentoring Men to Eldership. Alexander Strauch & Richard Swartley. 192p. (Orig.). 1996. teacher ed., ring bd. 23.99 (*0-936083-12-3*) Lewis-Roth.

Mentors in Schools: Developing the Profession of Teaching. Ed. by Donald McIntyre & Hazel Hagger. 192p. 1995. pap. 25.95 (*1-85346-411-2*, Pub. by David Fulton) Taylor & Francis.

***Mentor's Lair.** Karen Daniels. (Zaddack Trilogy Ser.: Bk. II). 200p. 2000. pap. 16.00 (*1-892323-21-4*, Straw Hse Pr) Vivisphere.

Mentors, Masters & Mrs. MacGregor: Stories of Teachers Making a Difference. Jane Bluestein. 260p. (Orig.). 1995. 22.00 (*1-55874-336-7*, 3367); pap. 11.95 (*1-55874-337-5*, 3375) Health Comm.

Mentors, Models, & Mothers: A Community Writing Project. (Illus.). 240p. 1997. pap. write for info. (*1-57502-638-4*, PO 1812) Morris Pubng.

Mentor's Soiree. Walter A. Coole. 1988. pap. text 7.00 (*0-926725-06-8*) Scaramouche.

Mentor's Spirit. Marsha Sinetar. 176p. 1999. pap. 10.95 (*0-312-20423-X*, St Martins Paperbacks) St Martin.

Mentor's Spirit: Life Lessons on Leadership & the Art of Encouragement. Sinetar. LC 98-5645. 176p. 1998. text 16.95 (*0-312-18630-4*) St Martin.

Mentorship: The Essential Guide for Schools & Business. Jill M. Reilly. LC 91-42116. (Illus.). 274p. 1992. pap. 20.00 (*0-910707-18-9*) Gifted Psych Pr.

Mentorship in the Primary School. Ed. by Robin Yeomans & John Sampson. LC 94-14192. 1994. 85.00 (*0-7507-0262-1*, Falmer Pr); pap. 34.95 (*0-7507-0263-X*, Falmer Pr) Taylor & Francis.

Menu. Jack Bernstein. 96p. (Orig.). 1993. pap. 22.50 (*0-9616226-8-7*) JB & Me.

Menu. Sharon L. Davies-Tight. (My Animal-Free Kitchen Ser.). 187p. 1996. 15.95 (*1-885099-04-5*) Rainbow Sunshine.

Menu. Toby L. Greenberg. 40p. 1995. 30.00 (*1-888636-00-9*) Sara Ranchouse.

Menu. deluxe ed. Toby L. Greenberg. 40p. 1995. 125.00 (*1-888636-01-7*) Sara Ranchouse.

Menu: Phoenix-Scottsdale, the Best Restaurants. Ed. by Donald Downes. (Illus.). 448p. (Orig.). 1995. pap. 12.95 (*0-9628274-9-5*) D Thomas Pub.

Menu: San Diego County - The Best 200 Restaurants. David Nelson. (Illus.). 448p. 1994. pap. 12.95 (*0-9628274-7-9*) D Thomas Pub.

Menu - Connections for Healthy... 5th ed. Mullen et al. 1999. 36.30 (*0-697-29420-X*) McGraw.

Menu! (a.k.a. Menu-Power) CP-M Version. Shari Steiner. (Power User's Manual Ser.). (C). 1983. pap. write for info. (*0-913733-02-4*) Computing.

Menu! (a.k.a. Menu-Power) IBM PC Version. Shari Steiner. (Power User's Manual Ser.). 1983. pap. write for info. (*0-913733-03-2*) Computing.

Menu Analysis, 1995. 68p. 1996. pap. 48.00 (*0-614-31120-9*, CS765) Natl Restaurant Assn.

Menu & the Cycle of Cost Control. McVety et al. 288p. (C). 1997. per. 66.95 (*0-7872-4215-2*, 41421501) Kendall-Hunt.

Menu Book. Lynn E. Robbins. 356p. (C). 1995. pap. 125.00 (*1-888143-10-X*) Robbins Mgmt.

Menu Book: A Comprehensive Guide to Authentic Indian Vegetarian Cuisine. Vasantha Moorthy. 287p. 1992. 23.95 (*0-9634681-0-3*) G Moorthy.

Menu Book: Greater Philadelphia Dining Out Guide. Ed. by Sheldon G. Schorr. (Menu Book Annual Ser.). (Illus.). 108p. (Orig.). 1989. pap. text 4.95 (*0-317-93814-2*) Parkway Pub Corp.

Menu Celebrations: Meal Planning for the Family, Every Day of the Year. Lee Cannon. (Illus.). 416p. 1995. 23.95 (*0-9638568-9-8*) Owl Bay Pubs.

Menu Design: Merchandising & Marketing. 4th ed. Albin G. Seaberg. 224p. 1990. 59.95 (*0-471-28983-3*, VNR) Wiley.

Menu Design: Merchandising & Marketing. 4th ed. Albin G. Seaberg. 212p. 1991. text 55.95 (*0-442-31958-4*, VNR) Wiley.

Menu Design: 25 Keys to Profitable Success. David V. Pavesic. LC 98-39303. (Restaurant Manager's Pocket Handbook Ser.). 96p. 1999. pap. 12.95 (*0-86730-754-4*, Pub. by Lebhar Friedman) Natl Bk Netwk.

Menu Design 5. Judi Radice. (Illus.). 240p. 1993. 60.00 (*0-86636-180-4*) PBC Intl Inc.

***Menu Dictionary: Words & Ways of the International Restaurant World.** deluxe ed. Victoria Luckett et al. 150p. 1999. pap. 14.95 (*0-9673014-0-8*) Sweetwtr Pr.

Menu Engineering: A Practical Guide to Menu Analysis. rev. ed. Michael L. Kasavana & Donald I. Smith. 167p. (Orig.). (C). 1990. pap. text 24.95 (*0-932235-06-9*) Hosp Pubns.

Menu Guide: Physical Fitness. Corbin & Lindsey. 1995. 11.25 (*0-697-31440-5*, WCB McGr Hill) McGrw-H Hghr Educ.

Menu Interpretation Guide: Guide de Redaction des Menus. T. Villa. (ENG & FRE.). 136p. 1984. pap. 9.95 (*0-8288-0841-4*, M8091) Fr & Eur.

***Menu Management: A Profit Approach.** Donald I. Smith et al. LC 99-23636. 2000. 49.95 (*0-86730-764-1*) Lebhar Friedman.

***Menu Math Complete Set, 3 vols., Set.** Janie Haugen. Ed. by Melissa Britt. (Illus.). 300p. 1999. ring bd. 169.95 (*1-884074-74-X*, PCI 906) PCI Educ Pubg.

Menu of Memories: A Jewish Family's Stores & Recepies. Sandy Kreamer. 212p. 1998. pap. 14.95 (*1-890676-32-2*) Beavers Pond.

Menu para Hoy. Sonia Gonzalez. Ed. by Lileana Acosta. (SPA., Illus.). 289p. 1994. 25.00 (*1-56328-054-X*) Edit Plaza Mayor.

Menu Planning & Development Skillbook. Educational Foundation of the National Restaurant. (Management Skills Program Ser.). 48p. (Orig.). 1993. pap. 10.95 (*0-915452-33-2*) Educ Found.

Menu Planning & Foods Merchandising. Restaurant Business Inc. Staff. LC 73-163322. 1971. teacher ed. 6.67 (*0-672-96094-X*, Bobbs); student ed. 7.50 (*0-672-96093-1*, Bobbs) Macmillan.

Menu Planning & Merchandising. 2nd rev. ed. Richard J. Hug & M. C. Warfel. LC 97-74244. (Illus.). 336p. (C). 1997. text, teacher ed. 42.00 (*0-8211-0734-8*) McCutchan.

Menu Pricing: 25 Keys to Profitable Success. David V. Pavesic. LC 98-39304. (Restaurant Manager's Pocket Handbook Ser.). 96p. 1999. pap. 12.95 (*0-86730-752-8*, Pub. by Lebhar Friedman) Natl Bk Netwk.

Menu Pricing & Strategy. 4th ed. Jack E. Miller. LC 96-17742. (Hospitality, Travel & Tourism Ser.). (Illus.). 224p. 1996. text 42.95 (*0-442-02209-3*, VNR) Wiley.

Menu Pricing & Strategy: Why We Can't Keep Up with What Happens in the World & What We Can Do About It. 4th ed. Jack E. Miller & David V. Pavesic. (Hospitality, Travel & Tourism Ser.). 228p. 1996. pap. 49.95 (*0-471-28747-4*, VNR) Wiley.

Menu Reader's Dictionary: A Guide to International Menu Terms. S. M. H. Collin. (FRE, ENG, GER, ITA & SPA.). 260p. 2000. pap. 9.95 (*0-948549-86-6*, Pub. by P Collin) IPG Chicago.

Menu Solutions: Quantity Recipes for Regular & Special Diets. Sandra J. Frank & Robert E. Baker. LC 95-42702. 784p. 1996. 90.00 (*0-471-55458-8*) Wiley.

M

Menu Terminology. H. Clarke. 86p. 1982. pap. 12.95 (*0-8288-1296-9*, M13058) Fr & Eur.

Menu Translator: English/French/German. 17th ed. Pauli & Duchamp. (ENG, FRE & GER.). 85p. 1996. 39.95 (*0-320-00499-6*) Fr & Eur.

Menucha Vesimcha. Mordechai Katz. (Rothman Foundation Ser.). 1982. 15.95 (*0-87306-977-3*); pap. 13.95 (*1-58330-159-3*) Feldheim.

Menuet in BI-Modals. Tibor Serly. 1972. 2.00 (*0-685-51175-8*, CM1016) Consort Music.

Menuez - Menuey Family: Jean Menuez & One Line of His Descendants, & Dominique Prudhon & Some of His Descendants, with Brief Information on the Families of Braun, Frost, Hebrank, Heth, Jardee, Kerns, King, Majors, Miller, Robinson-Evans, Sprague & Sparks, 2 vols., Set. Mary A. Thies. (Illus.). 1516p. 1995. pap. 199.00 (*0-8328-4806-9*); lib. bdg. 219.00 (*0-8328-4805-0*) Higginson Bk Co.

Menuhins: A Family Odyssey. Lionel M. Rolfe. LC 78-13051. 256p. 1978. 15.95 (*0-915572-22-2*) Panjandrum.

Menus. Jane Schulz & Pat Brown. (Illus.). 398p. 1989. reprint ed. write for info. (*0-318-65874-7*) Rainbow OH.

Menus: Graphics & Design. PBC International Editors. (Illus.). 104p. 1999. pap. 16.95 (*0-86636-748-9*) PBC Intl Inc.

Menus & Meals in Minutes! Marty Sprague. (Illus.). 122p. (Orig.). 1989. pap. 9.95 (*0-685-29437-4*); pap. 9.00 (*0-9624803-0-4*) Palmer Pubs.

Menus & Music for Christmas. Willi Elsener. LC 96-31121. 96p. 1996. 25.00 (*0-02-861398-8*) Macmillan.

Menus for Two. Julee Rosso. (Weekend Menus Ser.: No. 16). 1997. write for info. (*0-517-70705-5*, Crown) Crown Pub Group.

Menz Insana. Christopher Fowler. Ed. by Karen Berger. LC 98-101865. (Illus.). 64p. 1997. pap. 7.95 (*1-56389-300-2*) DC Comics.

Menzel Symposium on High Pressure Steam Curing. Menzel Symposium on High Pressure Steam Curing Sta. Ed. by W. H. Kuenning. LC 77-186848. (ACI Publication: No. SP-32). (Illus.). 296p. reprint ed. pap. 91.80 (*0-7837-5216-4*, 204494700005) Bks Demand.

Menzies & Churchill at War. David Day. (Illus.). 288p. 1994. pap. 28.00 (*0-19-553559-6*) OUP.

***Menzies & the 'Great World Struggle' Australia's Cold War, 1948-1954.** David Lowe. 242p. 1999. pap. 35.00 (*0-86840-553-1*, Pub. by NSW U Pr) Intl Spec Bk.

Menzies' Child: The Liberal Party of Australia, 1944-1994. Gerard Henderson. 320p. 1995. pap. 24.95 incl. cd-rom (*1-86373-747-2*, Pub. by Allen & Unwin Pty) Paul & Co Pubs.

Menzies Collection of Shange Dynasty Oracle Bones Vol. I: A Catalogue. Hsu Chin-Hsiung. (Illus.). 300p. 37.14 (*0-88854-022-1*) Brill Academic Pubs.

Menzies Collection of Shange Dynasty Oracle Bones Vol. II: The Text. Hsu Chin-Hsiung. (Illus.). 294p. 37.14 (*0-88854-023-X*) Brill Academic Pubs.

Menzies in War & Peace. Frank Cain. LC 98-142725. 192p. 1998. pap. 24.95 (*1-86448-573-6*, Pub. by Allen & Unwin Pty) Paul & Co Pubs.

Meor Hagolah: Rabbenu Gershom. Marcus Lehman. Tr. by Eva J. Hartheimer from GER. (Illus.). 174p. (YA). reprint ed. 12.00 (*0-8266-0342-4*, Merkos LInyonei Chinuch) Kehot Pubn Soc.

Meow. Bernie Karlin. 32p. (J). (gr. k-3). 1991. pap. 12.95 (*0-671-72639-0*) S&S Bks Yung.

Meow! V. Suteev. LC 97-31646. (Illus.). 32p. (J). (ps). 1998. lib. bdg. 16.95 (*0-8234-1361-6*) Holiday.

Meow! Alabama Cats in History, Mystery, Legend, Lore, Humor & More! Carole Marsh. (Carole Marsh Alabama Bks.). (Illus.). (J). (gr. 3-12). 1994. pap. 19.95 (*0-7933-3315-6*); lib. bdg. 29.95 (*0-7933-3314-8*); disk 29.95 (*0-7933-3316-4*) Gallopade Intl.

Meow! Alaska Cats in History, Mystery, Legend, Lore, Humor & More! Carole Marsh. (Carole Marsh Alaska Bks.). (Illus.). (J). (gr. 3-12). 1994. pap. 19.95 (*0-7933-3318-0*); lib. bdg. 29.95 (*0-7933-3317-2*); disk 29.95 (*0-7933-3319-9*) Gallopade Intl.

Meow! Arizona Cats in History, Mystery, Legend, Lore, Humor & More! Carole Marsh. (Carole Marsh Arizona Bks.). (Illus.). (J). (gr. 3-12). 1994. pap. 19.95 (*0-7933-3321-0*); lib. bdg. 29.95 (*0-7933-3320-2*); disk 29.95 (*0-7933-3322-9*) Gallopade Intl.

Meow! Arkansas Cats in History, Mystery, Legend, Lore, Humor & More! Carole Marsh. (Carole Marsh Arkansas Bks.). (Illus.). (J). (gr. 3-12). 1994. pap. 19.95 (*0-7933-3324-5*); lib. bdg. 29.95 (*0-7933-3323-7*); disk 29.95 (*0-7933-3325-3*) Gallopade Intl.

Meow! California Cats in History, Mystery, Legend, Lore, Humor & More! Carole Marsh. (Carole Marsh California Bks.). (Illus.). (J). (gr. 3-12). 1994. pap. 19.95 (*0-7933-3327-X*); lib. bdg. 29.95 (*0-7933-3326-1*); disk 29.95 (*0-7933-3328-8*) Gallopade Intl.

Meow! Colorado Cats in History, Mystery, Legend, Lore, Humor & More! Carole Marsh. (Carole Marsh Colorado Bks.). (Illus.). (J). (gr. 3-12). 1994. pap. 19.95 (*0-7933-3330-X*); lib. bdg. 29.95 (*0-7933-3329-6*); disk 29.95 (*0-7933-3331-8*) Gallopade Intl.

Meow! Connecticut Cats in History, Mystery, Legend, Lore, Humor & More! Carole Marsh. (Carole Marsh Connecticut Bks.). (Illus.). (J). (gr. 3-12). 1994. pap. 19.95 (*0-7933-3333-4*); lib. bdg. 29.95 (*0-7933-3332-6*); disk 29.95 (*0-7933-3334-2*) Gallopade Intl.

Meow! Delaware Cats in History, Mystery, Legend, Lore, Humor & More! Carole Marsh. (Carole Marsh Delaware Bks.). (Illus.). (J). (gr. 3-12). 1994. pap. 19.95 (*0-7933-3336-9*); lib. bdg. 29.95 (*0-7933-3335-0*); disk 29.95 (*0-7933-3337-7*) Gallopade Intl.

Meow! Florida Cats in History, Mystery, Legend, Lore, Humor & More! Carole Marsh. (Carole Marsh Florida Bks.). (Illus.). (J). (gr. 3-12). 1994. pap. 19.95 (*0-7933-3342-3*); lib. bdg. 29.95 (*0-7933-3341-5*); disk 29.95 (*0-7933-3343-1*) Gallopade Intl.

Meow! Georgia Cats in History, Mystery, Legend, Lore, Humor & More! Carole Marsh. (Carole Marsh Georgia Bks.). (Illus.). (J). (gr. 3-12). 1994. pap. 19.95 (*0-7933-3345-8*); lib. bdg. 29.95 (*0-7933-3344-X*); disk 29.95 (*0-7933-3346-6*) Gallopade Intl.

Meow! Hawaii Cats in History, Mystery, Legend, Lore, Humor & More! Carole Marsh. (Carole Marsh Hawaii Bks.). (Illus.). (J). (gr. 3-12). 1994. pap. 19.95 (*0-7933-3348-2*); lib. bdg. 29.95 (*0-7933-3347-4*); disk 29.95 (*0-7933-3349-0*) Gallopade Intl.

Meow! Idaho Cats in History, Mystery, Legend, Lore, Humor & More! Carole Marsh. (Carole Marsh Idaho Bks.). (Illus.). (J). (gr. 3-12). 1994. pap. 19.95 (*0-7933-3351-2*); lib. bdg. 29.95 (*0-7933-3350-4*); disk 29.95 (*0-7933-3352-0*) Gallopade Intl.

Meow! Illinois Cats in History, Mystery, Legend, Lore, Humor & More! Carole Marsh. (Carole Marsh Illinois Bks.). (Illus.). (J). (gr. 3-12). 1994. pap. 19.95 (*0-7933-3354-7*); lib. bdg. 29.95 (*0-7933-3353-9*); disk 29.95 (*0-7933-3355-5*) Gallopade Intl.

Meow! Indiana Cats in History, Mystery, Legend, Lore, Humor & More! Carole Marsh. (Carole Marsh Indiana Bks.). (Illus.). (J). (gr. 3-12). 1994. pap. 19.95 (*0-7933-3357-1*); lib. bdg. 29.95 (*0-7933-3356-3*); disk 29.95 (*0-7933-3358-X*) Gallopade Intl.

Meow! Iowa Cats in History, Mystery, Legend, Lore, Humor & More! Carole Marsh. (Carole Marsh Iowa Bks.). (Illus.). (J). (gr. 3-12). 1994. pap. 19.95 (*0-7933-3360-1*); lib. bdg. 29.95 (*0-7933-3359-8*); disk 29.95 (*0-7933-3361-X*) Gallopade Intl.

Meow! Kansas Cats in History, Mystery, Legend, Lore, Humor & More! Carole Marsh. (Carole Marsh Kansas Bks.). (Illus.). (J). (gr. 3-12). 1994. pap. 19.95 (*0-7933-3363-6*); lib. bdg. 29.95 (*0-7933-3362-8*); disk 29.95 (*0-7933-3364-4*) Gallopade Intl.

Meow! Kentucky Cats in History, Mystery, Legend, Lore, Humor & More! Carole Marsh. (Carole Marsh Kentucky Bks.). (Illus.). (J). (gr. 3-12). 1994. pap. 19.95 (*0-7933-3366-0*); lib. bdg. 29.95 (*0-7933-3365-2*); disk 29.95 (*0-7933-3367-9*) Gallopade Intl.

Meow! Louisiana Cats in History, Mystery, Legend, Lore, Humor & More! Carole Marsh. (Carole Marsh Louisiana Bks.). (Illus.). (J). (gr. 3-12). 1994. pap. 19.95 (*0-7933-3369-5*); lib. bdg. 29.95 (*0-7933-3368-7*); disk 29.95 (*0-7933-3370-9*) Gallopade Intl.

Meow! Maine Cats in History, Mystery, Legend, Lore, Humor & More! Carole Marsh. (Carole Marsh Maine Bks.). (Illus.). (J). (gr. 3-12). 1994. pap. 19.95 (*0-7933-3372-5*); lib. bdg. 29.95 (*0-7933-3371-7*); disk 29.95 (*0-7933-3373-3*) Gallopade Intl.

Meow! Maryland Cats in History, Mystery, Legend, Lore, Humor & More! Carole Marsh. (Carole Marsh Maryland Bks.). (Illus.). (J). (gr. 3-12). 1994. pap. 19.95 (*0-7933-3375-X*); lib. bdg. 29.95 (*0-7933-3374-1*); disk 29.95 (*0-7933-3376-8*) Gallopade Intl.

Meow! Massachusetts Cats in History, Mystery, Legend, Lore, Humor & More! Carole Marsh. (Massachuseets Bks.). (Illus.). (J). (gr. 3-12). 1994. pap. 19.95 (*0-7933-3378-4*); lib. bdg. 29.95 (*0-7933-3377-6*); disk 29.95 (*0-7933-3379-2*) Gallopade Intl.

Meow! Michigan Cats in History, Mystery, Legend, Lore, Humor & More! Carole Marsh. (Carole Marsh Michigan Bks.). (Illus.). (J). (gr. 3-12). 1994. pap. 19.95 (*0-7933-3381-4*); lib. bdg. 29.95 (*0-7933-3380-6*); disk 29.95 (*0-7933-3382-2*) Gallopade Intl.

Meow! Minnesota Cats in History, Mystery, Legend, Lore, Humor & More! Carole Marsh. (Carole Marsh Minnesota Bks.). (Illus.). (J). (gr. 3-12). 1994. pap. 19.95 (*0-7933-3384-9*); lib. bdg. 29.95 (*0-7933-3383-0*); disk 29.95 (*0-7933-3385-7*) Gallopade Intl.

Meow! Mississippi Cats in History, Mystery, Legend, Lore, Humor & More! Carole Marsh. (Carole Marsh Mississippi Bks.). (Illus.). (J). (gr. 3-12). 1994. pap. 19.95 (*0-7933-3387-3*); lib. bdg. 29.95 (*0-7933-3386-5*); disk 29.95 (*0-7933-3388-1*) Gallopade Intl.

Meow! Missouri Cats in History, Mystery, Legend, Lore, Humor & More! Carole Marsh. (Carole Marsh Missouri Bks.). (Illus.). (J). (gr. 3-12). 1994. pap. 19.95 (*0-7933-3390-3*); lib. bdg. 29.95 (*0-7933-3389-X*); disk 29.95 (*0-7933-3391-1*) Gallopade Intl.

Meow! Montana Cats in History, Mystery, Legend, Lore, Humor & More! Carole Marsh. (Carole Marsh Montana Bks.). (Illus.). (J). (gr. 3-12). 1994. pap. 19.95 (*0-7933-3393-8*); lib. bdg. 29.95 (*0-7933-3392-X*); disk 29.95 (*0-7933-3394-6*) Gallopade Intl.

Meow! Nebraska Cats in History, Mystery, Legend, Lore, Humor & More! Carole Marsh. (Carole Marsh Nebraska Bks.). (Illus.). (J). (gr. 3-12). 1994. pap. 19.95 (*0-7933-3396-2*); lib. bdg. 29.95 (*0-7933-3395-4*); disk 29.95 (*0-7933-3397-0*) Gallopade Intl.

Meow! Nevada Cats in History, Mystery, Legend, Lore, Humor & More! Carole Marsh. (Carole Marsh Nevada Bks.). (Illus.). (J). (gr. 3-12). 1994. pap. 19.95 (*0-7933-3399-7*); lib. bdg. 29.95 (*0-7933-3398-9*) Gallopade Intl.

Meow! New Hampshire Cats in History, Mystery, Legend, Lore, Humor & More! Carole Marsh. (Carole Marsh New Hampshire Bks.). (Illus.). (J). (gr. 3-12). 1994. pap. 19.95 (*0-7933-3401-2*); disk 29.95 (*0-7933-3402-0*) Gallopade Intl.

Meow! New Hampshire Cats in History, Mystery, Legend, Lore, Humor & More! Carole Marsh. (Carole Marsh New Hampshire Bks.). (Illus.). (J). (gr. 3-12). 1997. lib. bdg. 29.95 (*0-7933-3400-4*) Gallopade Intl.

Meow! New Jersey Cats in History, Mystery, Legend, Lore, Humor & More! Carole Marsh. (Carole Marsh New Jersey Bks.). (Illus.). (J). (gr. 3-12). 1994. lib. bdg. 29.95 (*0-7933-3404-7*); disk 29.95 (*0-7933-3406-3*) Gallopade Intl.

Meow! New Jersey Cats in History, Mystery, Legend, Lore, Humor & More! Carole Marsh. (Carole Marsh New Jersey Bks.). (Illus.). (J). (gr. 3-12). 1997. pap. 19.95 (*0-7933-3405-5*) Gallopade Intl.

Meow! New Mexico Cats in History, Mystery, Legend, Lore, Humor & More! Carole Marsh. (Carole Marsh New Mexico Bks.). (Illus.). (J). (gr. 3-12). 1994. pap. 19.95 (*0-7933-3408-X*); lib. bdg. 29.95 (*0-7933-3407-1*); disk 29.95 (*0-7933-3409-8*) Gallopade Intl.

Meow! New York Cats in History, Mystery, Legend, Lore, Humor & More! Carole Marsh. (Carole Marsh New York Bks.). (Illus.). (J). (gr. 3-12). 1994. pap. 19.95 (*0-7933-3411-X*); lib. bdg. 29.95 (*0-7933-3410-1*); disk 29.95 (*0-7933-3412-8*) Gallopade Intl.

Meow! North Carolina Cats in History, Mystery, Legend, Lore, Humor & More! Carole Marsh. (Carole Marsh North Carolina Bks.). (Illus.). (J). (gr. 3-12). 1994. pap. 19.95 (*0-7933-3414-4*); lib. bdg. 29.95 (*0-7933-3413-6*); disk 29.95 (*0-7933-3415-2*) Gallopade Intl.

Meow! North Dakota Cats in History, Mystery, Legend, Lore, Humor & More! Carole Marsh. (Carole Marsh North Dakota Bks.). (Illus.). (J). (gr. 3-12). 1994. pap. 19.95 (*0-7933-3417-9*); lib. bdg. 29.95 (*0-7933-3416-0*); disk 29.95 (*0-7933-3418-7*) Gallopade Intl.

Meow! Ohio Cats in History, Mystery, Legend, Lore, Humor & More! Carole Marsh. (Carole Marsh Ohio Bks.). (Illus.). (J). (gr. 3-12). 1994. pap. 19.95 (*0-7933-3420-9*); lib. bdg. 29.95 (*0-7933-3419-5*); disk 29.95 (*0-7933-3421-7*) Gallopade Intl.

Meow! Oklahoma Cats in History, Mystery, Legend, Lore, Humor & More! Carole Marsh. (Carole Marsh Oklahoma Bks.). (Illus.). (J). (gr. 3-12). 1994. pap. 19.95 (*0-7933-3423-3*); lib. bdg. 29.95 (*0-7933-3422-5*); disk 29.95 (*0-7933-3424-1*) Gallopade Intl.

Meow! Oregon Cats in History, Mystery, Legend, Lore, Humor & More! Carole Marsh. (Oregon Bks.). (Illus.). (J). (gr. 3-12). 1994. pap. 19.95 (*0-7933-3426-8*); lib. bdg. 29.95 (*0-7933-3425-X*); disk 29.95 (*0-7933-3427-6*) Gallopade Intl.

Meow! Pennsylvania Cats in History, Mystery, Legend, Lore, Humor & More! Carole Marsh. (Pennsylvania Bks.). (Illus.). (J). (gr. 3-12). 1994. pap. 19.95 (*0-7933-3429-2*); lib. bdg. 29.95 (*0-7933-3428-4*); disk 29.95 (*0-7933-3430-6*) Gallopade Intl.

Meow! Rhode Island Cats in History, Mystery, Legend, Lore, Humor & More! Carole Marsh. (Rhode Island Bks.). (Illus.). (J). (gr. 3-12). 1994. pap. 19.95 (*0-7933-3432-2*); lib. bdg. 29.95 (*0-7933-3431-4*); disk 29.95 (*0-7933-3433-0*) Gallopade Intl.

Meow! South Carolina Cats in History, Mystery, Legend, Lore, Humor & More! Carole Marsh. (South Carolina Bks.). (Illus.). (J). (gr. 3-12). 1994. pap. 19.95 (*0-7933-3435-7*); lib. bdg. 29.95 (*0-7933-3434-9*); disk 29.95 (*0-7933-3436-5*) Gallopade Intl.

Meow! South Dakota Cats in History, Mystery, Legend, Lore, Humor & More! Carole Marsh. (South Dakota Bks.). (Illus.). (J). (gr. 3-12). 1994. pap. 19.95 (*0-7933-3438-1*); lib. bdg. 29.95 (*0-7933-3437-3*); disk 29.95 (*0-7933-3439-X*) Gallopade Intl.

Meow! Tennessee Cats in History, Mystery, Legend, Lore, Humor & More! Carole Marsh. (Tennessee Bks.). (Illus.). (J). (gr. 3-12). 1994. pap. 19.95 (*0-7933-3441-1*); lib. bdg. 29.95 (*0-7933-3440-3*); disk 29.95 (*0-7933-3442-X*) Gallopade Intl.

Meow! Texas Cats in History, Mystery, Legend, Lore, Humor & More! Carole Marsh. (Texas Bks.). (Illus.). (J). (gr. 3-12). 1994. pap. 19.95 (*0-7933-3444-6*); lib. bdg. 29.95 (*0-7933-3443-8*); disk 29.95 (*0-7933-3445-4*) Gallopade Intl.

Meow! Utah Cats in History, Mystery, Legend, Lore, Humor & More! Carole Marsh. (Utah Bks.). (Illus.). (J). (gr. 3-12). 1994. pap. 19.95 (*0-7933-3447-0*); lib. bdg. 29.95 (*0-7933-3446-2*); disk 29.95 (*0-7933-3448-9*) Gallopade Intl.

Meow! Vermont Cats in History, Mystery, Legend, Lore, Humor & More! Carole Marsh. (Vermont Bks.). (Illus.). (J). (gr. 3-12). 1994. pap. 19.95 (*0-7933-3450-0*); lib. bdg. 29.95 (*0-7933-3449-7*); disk 29.95 (*0-7933-3451-9*) Gallopade Intl.

Meow! Virginia Cats in History, Mystery, Legend, Lore, Humor & More! Carole Marsh. (Virginia Bks.). (Illus.). (J). (gr. 3-12). 1994. pap. 19.95 (*0-7933-3453-5*); lib. bdg. 29.95 (*0-7933-3452-7*); disk 29.95 (*0-7933-3454-3*) Gallopade Intl.

Meow! Washington Cats in History, Mystery, Legend, Lore, Humor & More! Carole Marsh. (Washington Bks.). (Illus.). (J). (gr. 3-12). 1994. pap. 19.95 (*0-7933-3456-X*); lib. bdg. 29.95 (*0-7933-3455-1*); disk 29.95 (*0-7933-3457-8*) Gallopade Intl.

Meow! Washington DC Cats in History, Mystery, Legend, Lore, Humor & More! Carole Marsh. (Washington, D.C. Bks.). (Illus.). (J). (gr. 3-12). 1994. pap. 19.95 (*0-7933-3339-3*); lib. bdg. 29.95 (*0-7933-3338-5*); disk 29.95 (*0-7933-3340-7*) Gallopade Intl.

Meow! West Virginia Cats in History, Mystery, Legend, Lore, Humor & More! Carole Marsh. (West Virginia Bks.). (Illus.). (J). (gr. 3-12). 1994. pap. 19.95 (*0-7933-3459-4*); lib. bdg. 29.95 (*0-7933-3458-6*); disk 29.95 (*0-7933-3460-8*) Gallopade Intl.

Meow! Wisconsin Cats in History, Mystery, Legend, Lore, Humor & More! Carole Marsh. (Wisconsin Bks.). (Illus.). (J). (gr. 3-12). 1994. pap. 19.95 (*0-7933-3462-4*); lib. bdg. 29.95 (*0-7933-3461-6*); disk 29.95 (*0-7933-3463-2*) Gallopade Intl.

Meow! Wyoming Cats in History, Mystery, Legend, Lore, Humor & More! Carole Marsh. (Wyoming Bks.). (Illus.). (J). (gr. 3-12). 1994. pap. 19.95 (*0-7933-3465-9*); lib. bdg. 29.95 (*0-7933-3464-0*); disk 29.95 (*0-7933-3466-7*) Gallopade Intl.

***Meow Monday.** Illus. by Helen Craig. LC 99-47078. 24p. (J). (ps up). 2000. 10.99 (*0-7636-0832-7*) Candlewick Pr.

***Meow Monday.** Phyllis Root. LC 99-47078. (Illus.). 24p. (J). (ps up). 2000. pap. 3.29 (*0-7636-0831-9*) Candlewick Pr.

***Meow Te Ching by Meow Tzu: Mystic, Revolutionary, Romantic.** Meow Tzu. LC 99-56147. 2000. 10.95 (*0-7407-0490-7*) Andrews & McMeel.

Meow, What Now? Melora Romano. (Illus.). 12p. (J). (gr. k-2). 1998. pap. 3.75 (*1-880612-78-X*) Seedling Pubns.

Meows: I Want It & I Shall Have It! Michael K. Witzel & Gyvel Young. LC 90-84515. (Illus.). 120p. (Orig.). 1990. pap. 9.95 (*1-879256-00-2*) Arts Intl.

***Meowth, the Big Mouth.** Bill Michaels. (Pokemon Junior Ser.: Bk. 2). (Illus.). 48p. (J). (gr. k-4). 2000. mass mkt. 3.99 (*0-439-15417-0*) Scholastic Inc.

***MEP Databook.** Sidney M. Levy. (Construction Databook Ser.). 600p. 2000. 79.95 (*0-07-136020-4*) McGraw-Hill Prof.

MEPC: Adult Health Nursing. Sylvia K. Fields. (C). 1984. pap. text 19.95 (*0-8385-0166-4*, A0166-7, Medical Exam) Appleton & Lange.

MEPC: Anatomy. 10th ed. Jack L. Wilson. 251p. (C). 1996. pap. text 21.95 (*0-8385-6218-3*, A6218-0, Apple Lange Med) McGraw.

MEPC: Biochemistry. 11th ed. David Glick. (C). 1996. pap. text 21.95 (*0-8385-5779-1*, A5779-2, Apple Lange Med) McGraw.

MEPC: Biochemistry. 12th ed. Glick. (C). 1998. 17.95 (*0-8385-6346-5*) Appleton & Lange.

MEPC: Child Health Nursing. Sylvia K. Fields. (C). 1984. pap. text 19.95 (*0-8385-1090-6*, A1090-8, Medical Exam) Appleton & Lange.

MEPC: Hand Surgery, Specialty Board Review. Michael Kulick. 340p. (C). 1990. pap. text 49.00 (*0-8385-3558-5*, A3558-2) Appleton & Lange.

MEPC: Obstetrics & Gynecology. R. Douglas Ross. 411p. (C). 1997. pap. 21.95 (*0-8385-6328-7*, Apple Lange Med) McGraw.

MEPC: Pediatrics. 9th ed. L. Clark Hansbarger. 248p. (C). 1996. pap. text 21.95 (*0-8385-6223-X*, A6223-0, Apple Lange Med) McGraw.

MEPC: Pharmacology. 8th ed. J. J. Krzanowski. (Illus.). 267p. (C). 1996. pap. text 21.95 (*0-8385-6227-2*, A6227-1, Apple Lange Med) McGraw.

MEPC: Preventive Medicine & Public Health. 10th ed. Richard Hart. 265p. (Orig.). (C). 1996. pap. text 21.95 (*0-8385-6319-8*, A6319-6, Apple Lange Med) McGraw.

MEPC: Psychiatry. 10th ed. Carlyle Chan et al. 250p. (C). 1997. pap. text 21.95 (*0-8385-5780-5*, A5780-0, Apple Lange Med) McGraw.

MEPC Review for USMLE Step 2. Samuel L. Jacobs. 392p. (C). 1996. pap. 34.95 (*0-8385-6270-1*, A6270-1, Apple Lange Med) McGraw.

MEPC Review of Neurology. 10th ed. Paul S. Slosberg. (Illus.). 267p. (C). 1995. pap. text 24.95 (*0-8385-5778-3*, A5778-4, Apple Lange Med) McGraw.

MEPC Review of Pathology. 10th ed. Olusegun Fayemi. (Illus.). 319p. (C). 1999. pap. text 21.95 (*0-8385-8441-1*, A8441-6, Apple Lange Med) McGraw.

MEPC USMLE Step 1 Review. Olusegun Fayemi. (Illus.). 455p. (C). 1996. pap. text 34.95 (*0-8385-6269-8*, A6269-3, Apple Lange Med) McGraw.

MEPC USMLE Step 3 Review. Carlyle Chan. (C). 1996. pap. text 34.95 (*0-8385-6339-2*, A6339-4, Apple Lange Med) McGraw.

Mephisto. Klaus Mann. Tr. by Robyn Smyth. 272p. 1995. pap. 13.95 (*0-14-018918-1*, Penguin Classics) Viking Penguin.

Mephisto Waltz & Other Works for Solo Piano. Franz Liszt. 192p. 1994. pap. 10.95 (*0-486-28147-7*) Dover.

Mephistopheles: The Devil in the Modern World. Jeffrey B. Russell. LC 86-47648. (Illus.). 352p. 1990. reprint ed. pap. 16.95 (*0-8014-9718-3*) Cornell U Pr.

Mephistopheles' Anvil: Forging a More Human Future. John Alexandra. LC 96-33125. 350p. 1997. 24.95 (*1-889511-50-1*) Rose Harmony.

Mephistophiles in England: Or, the Confessions of a Prime Minister, 3 vols., 1 bk. Robert F. Williams. LC 79-8217. reprint ed. 44.50 (*0-404-62167-8*) AMS Pr.

Mequasset by the Sea & Other Plays. Jolene Goldenthal. LC 96-41538. 1996. pap. 8.95 (*0-916897-24-9*) Andrew Mtn Pr.

Mer. Jules Michelet. (Folio Ser.: No. 1470). (FRE.). 416p. 1983. pap. 13.95 (*2-07-037470-X*) Schoenhof.

Mer. Paul Sebillot. (FRE.). 240p. 1983. pap. 29.95 (*0-7859-1568-0*, 2902702140) Fr & Eur.

Mer see Encyclopedic Poetique: Anthologie Thematique de la Poesie Francaise Contemporaine

***Mer-Baby.** Teresa Bateman & Patience Brewster. LC 00-35097. (Illus.). (J). 2001. write for info. (*0-8234-1531-7*) Holiday.

Mer-Child: A Legend for Children & Other Adults. Robin Morgan. LC 91-3246. (Illus.). 64p. (YA). 1991. 8.95 (*1-55861-054-5*) Feminist Pr.

Mer-Child: A Legend for Children & Other Adults. Robin Morgan. LC 91-3246. (Illus.). 64p. (YA). (gr. 3 up). 1991. 17.95 (*1-55861-053-7*) Feminist Pr.

Mer de Glace. Alison Fell. 256p. (Orig.). 1992. pap. 12.99 (*1-85242-267-X*) Serpents Tail.

Mer Noire et la Romanie Genoise (XIIIE-XVE Siecles) Michel Balard. (Collected Studies: No. CS294). (FRE.). 334p. (C). 1989. lib. bdg. 119.95 (*0-86078-242-5*, Pub. by Variorum) Ashgate Pub Co.

Mer Pleine de Requins see Sea Full of Sharks

An Asterisk (*) at the beginning of an entry indicates that the title is appearing for the first time.

Mer the Sea. Claude Debussy. 1998. 3.95 (*0-486-29848-5*, 741731Q) Dover.

Meran Defense. John Donaldson. 111p. (Orig.). 1987. pap. 6.95 (*0-931462-64-9*) Chess Ent.

***Meran System.** Steffen Pedersen. 192p. 2000. pap. 21.95 (*1-901983-28-5*, Pub. by Gambit) BHB Intl.

Meraviglioso Segreto delle Anime del Purgatorio see Amazing Secret of the Souls in Purgatory

Merc: The Emergence of a Global Financial Powerhouse. Robert A. Tamarkin. LC 92-53335. (Illus.). 304p. 1993. 27.50 (*0-88730-516-4*, HarpBusn) HarpInfo.

***Mercadeo en la Industria del Seguro de Vida y Salud.** Ed. by Ines Vallenilla. (SPA.). 706p. (C). 1999. pap. text 105.00 (*1-57974-075-8*, Pub. by Life Office) PBD Inc.

Mercadeo Social. 65p. 1994. write for info. (*92-806-3152-7*) U N I C E.

Mercader de Venecia: Como Gusteis. William Shakespeare. Ed. & Tr. by Angel-Luis Pujante. (Nueva Austral Ser.: Vol. 219). (SPA.). 1991. pap. text 24.95 (*84-239-7219-4*) Elliots Bks.

***Mercader Venecia.** William Shakespeare. 1998. pap. 8.95 (*84-08-01724-1*) Planeta.

Mercadet. Honore de Balzac. Tr. by Robert Cornthwaite. LC 94-26759. (Great Translations for Actors Ser.). 128p. 1994. pap. 11.95 (*1-880399-63-6*) Smith & Kraus.

Mercadian Masques. Liz Holliday. 341p. 1998. pap. 5.99 (*0-7869-1188-3*, Pub. by TSR Inc) Random.

Mercado. Jock Gunter. Tr. by Carla Clason. (Technical Notes Ser.: No. 4). 13p. 1972. pap. 2.00 (*0-932288-10-3*); pap. 2.00 (*0-932288-11-1*) Ctr Intl Ed U of MA.

Mercado Atlas of Foot Anatomy. O. A. Mercado. Orig. Title: An Atlas of Podiatric Anatomy. (Illus.). 1995. spiral bd. 50.00 (*0-940542-05-6*) Carolando.

Mercantile Dictionary: Norwegian-English-German. B. Hanheide. (ENG, GER & NOR.). 294p. 1979. 49.95 (*0-7859-7499-7*, 8251807549) Fr & Eur.

Mercantile Law. C. Charlesworth. (C). 1984. 70.00 (*0-7855-4078-4*, Pub. by Witherby & Co) St Mut.

Mercantile Law. D. P. Jain. xxvi, 581p. (C). 1991. pap. text 20.00 (*81-220-0246-3*) Advent Bks Div.

Mercantile Law. Dennis Keenan. 628p. (C). 1989. 165.00 (*0-7855-4634-0*, Pub. by Inst Pur & Supply) St Mut.

Mercantile Law. P. W. Redmont. 296p. (C). 1989. 80.00 (*0-7855-4633-2*, Pub. by Inst Pur & Supply) St Mut.

Mercantile Law. Ed. by S. Smith & D. J. Keenan. 628p. (C). 1988. 160.00 (*0-7855-5678-8*, Pub. by Inst Pur & Supply) St Mut.

Mercantile Law. 4th ed. Avtar Singh. 1172p. 1985. 255.00 (*0-7855-1378-7*) St Mut.

***Mercantile Law in Botswana: Cases & Materials** John Kiggundu. LC 98-214175. xxxvii, 383p. 1998. write for info. (*0-7021-4564-5*) Juta & Co.

Mercantile Law, 1985: With Supplement in View of Companies (Amendment) Act, 1988. 4th ed. Avtar Singh. (C). 1989. 85.00 (*0-7855-5484-X*) St Mut.

Mercantile Law of Scotland. D. Ross Macdonald. 1995. pap. text. write for info. (*0-406-10585-5*, UK, MICHIE) LEXIS Pub.

Mercantile States & the World Oil Cartel, 1900-1939. Gregory P. Nowell. LC 93-38020. (Cornell Studies in Political Economy). (Illus.). 344p. (C). 1994. text 47.50 (*0-8014-2878-5*) Cornell U Pr.

Mercantile System & Its Historical Significance: Illustrated Chiefly from Prussian History. Gustav F. Schmoller. LC 87-17247. (Reprints of Economic Classics Ser.). ix, 95p. 1989. reprint ed. 25.00 (*0-678-00252-5*) Kelley.

Mercantilism. (Critical Concepts Ser.). 944p. (C). Date not set. write for info. (*0-415-11357-1*) Routledge.

Mercantilism, 4 vols., Set. Ed. by Lars Magnusson. LC 94-33823. 1384p. (C). (gr. 13). 1996. text, boxed set 660.00 (*0-415-11600-7*) Routledge.

Mercantilism & East India Trade. Parkakunnel J. Thomas. 176p. 1963. reprint ed. 32.00 (*0-7146-1361-4*, BHA-01361, Pub. by F Cass Pubs) Intl Spec Bk.

Mercantilism in a Japanese Domain: The Merchant Origins of Economic Nationalism in 18th-Century Tosa. Luke S. Roberts. LC 97-18070. (Illus.). 280p. (C). 1998. text 59.95 (*0-521-62131-3*) Cambridge U Pr.

Mercantilist Economics. Ed. by Lars Magnusson. LC 93-1423. (Recent Economic Thought Ser.). 288p. (C). 1993. lib. bdg. 127.00 (*0-7923-9359-7*) Kluwer Academic.

Mercantilist Views of Trade & Monopoly: Four Essays, 1645-1720. John Blanch et al. LC 77-38468. (Evolution of Capitalism Ser.). 140p. 1978. reprint ed. 37.95 (*0-405-04127-6*) Ayer.

Mercat Anthology of Earth: Scottish Literature, 1375-1707. R. D. Jack & P. Prozendaal. LC 98-233207. xliii, 528p. 1997. pap. 64.00 (*1-873644-65-5*, Pub. by Mercat Pr Bks) St Mut.

Mercat Cross & Tolbooth: Understanding Scotland's Old Burghs. Craig Mair. 238p. (C). 1996. pap. 23.00 (*0-85976-196-7*, Pub. by J Donald) St Mut.

Mercator Atlas of Europe: Facsimile of the Maps by Gerardus Mercator Contained in the Atlas of Europe, Circa 1570-1572. Marcel Watelet et al. (Illus.). 96p. 1998. 245.00 (*0-9659735-7-3*) Walking Tree.

Mercator Media Guide, Vol. 2. Ed. by Janet Davies. 273p. 1997. pap. 25.00 (*0-7083-1381-7*, Pub. by Univ Wales Pr) Paul & Co Pubs.

Mercator Media Guide, Vol. 3. Ed. by Elin H. Jones. 224p. 1998. pap. write for info. (*0-7083-1465-1*, Pub. by Univ Wales Pr) Paul & Co Pubs.

***Merce Cunningham.** Germano Celant. 317p. 1999. 45.00 (*88-8158-216-3*) Charta.

Merce Cunningham: Creative Elements. Ed. by David Vaughan. (Choreography & Dance Studies: Vol. 4, Pt. 2). 122p. 1996. pap. text 22.00 (*3-7186-5834-8*, ECU17, Harwood Acad Pubs) Gordon & Breach.

Merce Cunningham: Dancing in Space & Time. Ed. by Richard Kostelanetz. LC 98-6776. (Illus.). 280p. 1998. reprint ed. pap. 17.95 (*0-306-80877-3*) Da Capo.

Merce Cunningham: Fifty Years. Merce Cunningham & David Vaughan. LC 97-70518. (Illus.). 320p. 1997. 114.00 (*0-89381-624-8*) Aperture.

Merce Cunningham: Fifty Years David Vaughan & Melissa Harris. LC 97-70518. 315p. 1997. write for info. (*0-89381-767-8*) Aperture.

Merce Cunningham - Fifty Years: Chronicle & Commentary. David Vaughan. 320p. 1999. pap. text 39.95 (*0-89381-863-1*) Aperture.

Mercedes, 2 Vols. Hartmut Lehbrink. 700p. 1998. boxed set 79.95 (*3-89508-899-4*, 520347) Konemann.

Mercedes: Nothing but the Best. Erik Johnson. 1998. 17.99 (*0-7858-0937-6*) Bk Sales Inc.

***Mercedes: Saloons,Coupes & Cabriolets.** Taylor. (Illus.). 80p. 2000. pap. text 15.95 (*1-901432-00-9*, Pub. by MBI Pubg) Motorbooks Intl.

Mercedes: The First & the Best, Harry Haines. (Car Classics Ser.). 32p. (YA). (gr. 5-12). 1991. lib. bdg. 15.95 (*0-86593-142-9*) Rourke Corp.

Mercedes & Later Lyrics. Thomas Bailey Aldrich. (Works of Thomas Bailey Aldrich). 1989. reprint ed. lib. bdg. 79.00 (*0-7812-1667-2*) Rprt Serv.

Mercedes-Benz, 1. Paul W. Cockerham. 1998. pap. text 10.98 (*1-57717-084-9*) Todtri Prods.

Mercedes-Benz. Jay Schleifer. LC 93-17505. (Cool Classics Ser.). (Illus.). 48p. (YA). (gr. 6 up). 1994. pap. 7.95 (*0-382-24809-0*, Crstwood Hse); lib. bdg. 13.95 (*0-89686-815-X*, Crstwood Hse) Silver Burdett Pr.

Mercedes-Benz: 110 Years of Excellence. Dennis Adler. (Enthusiast Color Ser.). (Illus.). 96p. 1995. pap. 13.95 (*0-7603-0046-1*) MBI Pubg.

Mercedes Benz Legends. David Sparrow. (Colour Classics Ser.). (Illus.). 128p. 1997. pap. 10.95 (*1-85532-676-0*, Pub. by Ospry) Motorbooks Intl.

Mercedes-Benz M-Class: The Complete Story Behind the All-New Sport Utility Vehicle. John Lamm. LC 97-25607. 160p. 1997. pap. text 21.95 (*0-7603-0431-9*) MBI Pubg.

Mercedes Benz, 1974-1984: RTUG. Chilton Automotive Editorial Staff. LC 83-45305. 288p. (C). 1984. pap. 17.95 (*0-8019-7463-1*) Thomson Learn.

Mercedes-Benz 190SL, 1955-1963. Walter Zeichner. LC 89-63363. (Illus.). 96p. 1990. 19.95 (*0-88740-209-7*) Schiffer.

Mercedes-Benz Parade & Staff Cars of the Third Reich. Blaine Taylor. LC 99-25574. (Illus.). 1998. 49.95 (*0-938289-93-4*, 289934) Combined Pub.

Mercedes-Benz since 1945: The 1960's, Vol. 2. James Taylor. (Collector's Guide Ser.). (Illus.). 144p. 1985. 27.95 (*0-900549-96-3*) MBI Pubg.

Mercedes-Benz since 1945 Vol. 4: The 1980's. James Taylor. (Collector's Guide Ser.). (Illus.). 128p. 1994. 27.95 (*0-947981-77-2*, Pub. by Motor Racing) Motorbooks Intl.

Mercedes Benz SL. John Heileg. (Illus.). 128p. 1997. pap. 21.95 (*0-7603-0328-2*) MBI Pubg.

Mercedes-Benz SL & SLC, 1952-1986. L. J. Setright. (Illus.). 128p. 1999. pap. 19.95 (*1-85532-880-1*, 128249AE) Motorbooks Intl.

***Mercedes-Benz SL Experience: Five Decades of the Mercedes-Benz SL.** 3rd rev. ed. John R. Olson. Orig. Title: Collecting the Mercedes-Benz SL, 1954-1993. (Illus.). 330p. 2000. 49.95 (*0-9635394-2-6*) SL Mkt Letter.

Mercedes Benz 300, 1951-1962. Walter Zeichner. Tr. by Edward Force from GER. LC 90-60483. (Automotive Ser.). (Illus.). 96p. 1990. 19.95 (*0-88740-249-6*) Schiffer.

Mercedes in Peace & War: German Automobile Workers, 1903-1945. Bernard P. Bellon. (Illus.). 420p. 1992. pap. text 21.00 (*0-231-06857-3*) Col U Pr.

Mercedes since 1945: Early Postwar Years, Vol. 1. J. Taylor. (Collector's Guide .). (Illus.). 120p. 1985. 27.95 (*0-900549-95-5*, Pub. by Motor Racing) Motorbooks Intl.

Mercedes SL Series: The Complete Story. Brian Laban. (Illus.). 192p. 1992. 35.95 (*1-85223-595-0*) MBI Pubg.

Mercedez-Benz, 1974-1984: Coupes, Sedans & Wagons. Chilton Automotive Editorial Staff. (New Total Car Care Ser.). 450p. (C). 1998. pap. text 22.95 (*0-8019-9076-9*) Thomson Learn.

Mercenaries. Guy Arnold. LC 99-18562. 198p. 1999. text 65.00 (*0-312-22203-3*) St Martin.

Mercenaries. Bill Baldwin. 1991. mass mkt. 4.95 (*0-446-36139-9*) Warner Bks.

***Mercenaries: An African Security Dilemma** Abdel-Fatau Musah & Kayode Fayemi. LC 99-34771. 2000. write for info. (*0-7453-1476-7*, Pub. by Pluto GBR) Stylus Pub VA.

***Mercenaries & African Conflicts: An African Security Dilemma.** Kayode Fayemi. Ed. by Abdel Fatau Musah. 304p. 2000. pap. 22.50 (*0-7453-1471-6*) Pluto GBR.

Mercenaries & Lyndon Johnson's "More Flags" The Hiring of Korean, Filipino & Thai Soldiers in the Vietnam War. Richard M. Blackburn. LC 93-42174. 220p. 1994. lib. bdg. 28.50 (*0-89950-931-2*) McFarland & Co.

Mercenaries for the Crimea: The German, Swiss, & Italian Legions in British Service, 1854-1856. Charles C. Bayley. LC 77-357169. 205p. reprint ed. pap. 63.60 (*0-608-12531-8*, 202385900034) Bks Demand.

Mercenaries from Ansbach & Bayreuth, Germany, Who Remained in America after the Revolution. rev. ed. Clifford N. Smith. (German-American Genealogical Research Monographs: No.2). 1979. pap. 20.00 (*0-915162-13-X*) Westland Pubns.

Mercenaries from Hessen-Hanau Who Remained in Canada & the United States after the American Revolution. Clifford N. Smith. (German-American Genealogical Research Monographs: No. 5). Orig. Title: Deserter-Immigrants of the American Revolution from Hessen-Hanau. 75p. (Orig.). 1976. pap. 20.00 (*0-915162-04-0*) Westland Pubns.

***Mercenaries in the Texas Revolution: The New Orleans Greys.** Gary Brown. LC 98-31802. 336 p. 1999. pap. 18.95 (*1-55622-675-6*, Rep of TX Pr) Wordware Pub.

Mercenaries of the Ancient World. Serge Yalichev. (Illus.). 272p. 1999. 24.95 (*0-7818-0674-7*) Hippocrene Bks.

Mercenaries of the Hellenistic World. Guy T. Griffith. x, 340p. 1984. 25.00 (*0-89005-085-6*) Ares.

Mercenaries of the Hellenistic World. Guy T. Griffith. LC 75-41123. reprint ed. 34.50 (*0-404-14667-8*) AMS Pr.

Mercenaries, Pirates & Sovereigns: State-Building & Extraterritorial Violence in Early... Janice E. Thomson. 230p. 1994. pap. text 17.95 (*0-691-02571-1*, Pub. by Princeton U Pr) Cal Prin Full Svc.

Mercenaries, Pirates & Sovereigns: State-Building & Extraterritorial Violence in Early Modern Europe. Janice E. Thomson. LC 93-23880. (Studies in International History & Politics). 236p. 1994. text 49.50 (*0-691-08658-3*, Pub. by Princeton U Pr) Cal Prin Full Svc.

Mercenaries, Spies & Private Eyes. Michael A. Stackpole. (Illus.). 1983. 9.95 (*0-940244-30-6*) Flying Buffalo.

Mercenary. Cherry Adair. 1994. per. 2.99 (*0-373-25592-6*) Harlequin Bks.

Mercenary. Piers Anthony. (Bio of a Space Tyrant Ser.: Vol. II). 384p. 1984. mass mkt. 4.50 (*0-380-87221-8*, Avon Bks) Morrow Avon.

***Mercenary: Bio of a Space Tyrant, Vol. 2.** Piers Anthony. LC 99-91253. 1999. 25.00 (*0-7388-0694-3*); pap. 18.00 (*0-7388-0695-1*) Xlibris Corp.

***Mercenary: Giants.** Vicente Segrelles. Tr. by Robert Legault from SPA. (Illus.). 48p. 1999. pap. 10.95 (*1-56163-235-X*) NBM.

Mercenary: The Lost Civilization, Vol. 7. Vicente Segrelles. Tr. by Robert Legault from SPA. LC 98-181034. (Illus.). 48p. 1998. pap. 10.95 (*1-56163-198-1*) NBM.

Mercenary Vol. 5: The Voyage. Vicente Segrelles. 48p. 1995. pap. 10.95 (*1-56163-122-1*) NBM.

Mercenary Vol. 6: Year 1000. Vicente Segrelles. (Illus.). 48p. 1996. pap. 11.95 (*1-56163-161-2*) NBM.

Mercenary & the Marriage. Doreen Roberts. (Intimate Moments Ser.). 1998. per. 4.25 (*0-373-07861-7*, 1-07861-7) Silhouette.

Mercenary & the New Mom: Follow That Baby. Merline Lovelace. 1999. per. 4.25 (*0-373-07908-7*, Harlequin) Harlequin Bks.

Mercenary Major. Kate Moore. 224p. (Orig.). 1994. mass mkt. 3.99 (*0-380-77541-7*, Avon Bks) Morrow Avon.

Mercenary Raids & the Decline of Siena, Vol. 116. William Caferro. LC 97-38339. (Johns Hopkins University Studies in Historical & Political Science Ser.). (Illus.). 252p. 1998. text 39.95 (*0-8018-5788-0*) Johns Hopkins.

Mercenary Troops from Anhalt-Zerbst, Germany, During the American Revolution, 2 pts., Set. Virginia E. DeMarce. (German-American Genealogical Research Monographs: No. 19). (Orig.). 1984. pap. 40.00 (*0-915162-21-0*) Westland Pubns.

Mercenary's Tactical HBK. Sid Campbell. (Illus.). 120p. (Orig.). 1990. pap. 12.00 (*0-918751-16-0*) Delta Pr.

***Mercenary's Woman: Soldier's of Fortune.** Diana Palmer. Vol. 1444. 2000. per. 3.50 (*0-373-19444-7*) Silhouette.

Mercer: Plays One. David Mercer & Stuart Laing. LC 90-27136. (Methuen World Dramatists Ser.). 362p. (Orig.). (C). 1990. pap. 14.95 (*0-413-63450-7*, A0462, Methuen Drama) Methn.

Mercer: Plays Two. David Mercer. 370p. 1995. pap. 15.95 (*0-413-65200-9*, A0708, Methuen Drama) Methn.

Mercer - Garnett. Genealogy of the Mercer - Garnett Family of Essex County, Va., Supposed to Be Descended from the Garnetts of Lancashire. James M. Garnett. (Illus.). 63p. 1997. reprint ed. pap. 13.00 (*0-8328-9471-0*); reprint ed. lib. bdg. 23.00 (*0-8328-9470-2*) Higginson Bk Co.

Mercer Colonists. Gifford White. Ed. by Carolyn Ericson & Joe E. Ericson. LC 84-80393. 50p. (Orig.). 1984. pap. 9.95 (*0-911317-31-7*) Ericson Bks.

Mercer Commentary on the Bible. Ed. by Watson E. Mills et al. LC 94-23638. 1994. 50.00 (*0-86554-406-9*, MUP-H329) Mercer Univ Pr.

Mercer Commentary on the Bible: The Gospels. 6th ed. Ed. by Watson E. Mills & Richard F. Wilson. 272p. 1996. pap. text 16.95 (*0-86554-511-1*, MUP/P138) Mercer Univ Pr.

Mercer Commentary on the Bible: The Prophets, Vol. 4. Watson E. Mills. 1996. pap. text 18.95 (*0-86554-509-X*, MUP/P136) Mercer Univ Pr.

Mercer Commentary on the Bible Vol. 1: Pentateuch - Torah. Ed. by Watson E. Mills & Richard R. Wilson. LC 98-141144. 324p. 1998. pap. text 19.95 (*0-86554-506-5*, P133) Mercer Univ Pr.

Mercer Commentary on the Bible Vol. 2: The History of Israel Joshua-Esther. Ed. by Watson E. Mills & Richard F. Wilson. 280p. 1998. pap. text 19.95 (*0-86554-507-3*, P134) Mercer Univ Pr.

***Mercer Commentary on the Bible Vol. 3: Wisdom Writings.** Ed. by Watson E. Mills & Richard F. Wilson. (Mercer Commentary on the Bible Ser.). 2000. 19.95 (*0-86554-508-1*) Mercer Univ Pr.

Mercer Commentary on the Bible Vol. 7: Acts & Pauline Writings. Ed. by Watson E. Mills & Richard F. Wilson. LC 97-167955. 280p. (Orig.). 1997. pap. text 18.95 (*0-86554-512-X*) Mercer Univ Pr.

***Mercer Commentary on the Bible Vol. 8: The General Epistles & Revelation.** Ed. by Watson E. Mills & Richard F. Wilson. 240p. 2000. pap. 19.95 (*0-86554-513-8*) Mercer Univ Pr.

Mercer County see Hagstrom Atlases

Mercer County Archives Vol. 1: Deeds. Mark S. Painter. 130p. 1995. per. 12.00 (*1-55856-211-7*, 065) Closson Pr.

Mercer County Archives Vol. 2: Naturalizations. Mark S. Painter. 258p. 1996. per. 19.95 (*1-55856-221-4*, 066) Closson Pr.

Mercer County Centennial Buildings. Ed. by Joyce Alig. (Illus.). 46p. 1995. pap. 10.00 (*1-891095-08-0*, 5362-8) Mercer Cty Hist.

Mercer County, Ohio: The Five Courthouses, 1840-1998. Joyce L. Alig. (Illus.). 64p. 1998. pap. 10.00 (*1-891095-10-2*, 5362-10) Mercer Cty Hist.

Mercer County, Ohio History. Ed. by Joyce L. Alig. (Illus.). 976p. 1980. 88.00 (*1-891095-02-1*, 5362-2) Mercer Cty Hist.

Mercer County, PA Archives, Vol. 4. Mark S. Painter. LC 96-83436. 266p. 1996. per. 24.95 (*1-55856-228-1*, 068) Closson Pr.

Mercer County, PA Archives Vol. 3: First Two Orphans Books, 1804-Mid-1839. Compiled by James K. Sewell. 104p. 1996. per. 12.95 (*1-55856-226-5*, 067) Closson Pr.

Mercer County, PA Soldiers. Paul W. Myers. 78p. 1988. pap. text 8.50 (*0-933227-84-1*, 315) Closson Pr.

Mercer Dictionary of the Bible. Ed. by Watson E. Mills et al. LC 89-13857. (Illus.). 1088p. (C). 1998. pap. 35.00 (*0-86554-373-9*, MUP/P86) Mercer Univ Pr.

Mercer Management Consulting: The WetFeet.com Insider Guide. 4th ed. WetFeet.com Staff. (Insider Guides Ser.). 54p. 1999. spiral bd. 25.00 (*1-58207-035-0*) WetFeet.

M

Mercer Mayer's Little Critter's, 2 vols., Set. Mercer Mayer. (Early Childhood First Bks.). (Illus.). 40p. (J). (gr. k-1). 1999. lib. bdg. 27.90 (*1-56674-943-3*) Forest Hse.

Mercer Mayer's Little Critter's Vol. 1: The Picnic. large type ed. Mercer Mayer. (Early Childhood First Bks.: No. 1). (Illus.). 20p. (J). (gr. k-2). 1999. lib. bdg. 13.95 (*1-56674-219-6*) Forest Hse.

Mercer Mayer's Little Critter's Vol. 2: The Trip. Mercer Mayer. (Early Childhood First Bks.: No. 2). (Illus.). 20p. (J). (gr. k-2). 1999. lib. bdg. 13.95 (*1-56674-254-4*) Forest Hse.

Mercer's Belles: The Journal of a Reporter. Roger Conant. Ed. by Lenna A. Deutsch. LC 92-20225. (Washington State University Press Reprint Ser.). 168p. (Orig.). (C). 1992. reprint ed. 25.00 (*0-87422-089-0*) Wash St U Pr.

Mercer's Belles: The Journal of a Reporter. 2nd ed. Roger Conant. Ed. by Lenna A. Deutsch. LC 92-20225. (Washington State University Press Art Ser.). (Illus.). 168p. (Orig.). (C). 1992. reprint ed. pap. 16.95 (*0-87422-090-4*) Wash St U Pr.

Mercer's Orthopaedic Surgery. 9th ed. Ed. by Robert Duthie & George Bentley. (Arnold Publication). (Illus.). 1376p. 1996. text 145.00 (*0-340-55163-1*) OUP.

***Mercey Blues.** Andrews. 2000. pap. 8.95 (*0-552-14060-0*, Pub. by Transworld Publishers Ltd) Trafalgar.

Merchandise Buying. 3rd ed. Maryanne S. Bohlinger. 550p. 1989. text 46.00 (*0-205-12196-9*, H21967) Allyn.

Merchandise Buying. 3rd ed. Maryanne S. Bohlinger. 550p. 1989. teacher ed. write for info. (*0-318-66368-6*, H21975) P-H.

Merchandise Buying & Management. John Donnellan. 52p. 1998. teacher ed. write for info. (*1-56367-053-4*) Fairchild.

Merchandise Buying & Management. John Donnellan. (Illus.). 473p. 1998. 56.00 (*1-56367-052-6*) Fairchild.

Merchandise Licensing in the Television Industry. Karen Raugust. (Broadcasting & Cable Ser.). 142p. 1995. pap. 34.95 (*0-240-80210-1*, Focal) Buttrwrth-Heinemann.

Merchandising. 2nd ed. Eugene L. Dorr et al. (Occupational Manuals & Projects in Marketing Ser.). 1977. text 12.28 (*0-07-017615-9*) McGraw.

Merchandising: Theory, Principles & Practice. Grace Kunz. LC 97-78088. (Illus.). 405p. 1998. 58.00 (*1-56367-146-8*) Fairchild.

Merchandising & Sponsorship in the Music Business. Ed. by David Peeperkorn. 120p. 1986. pap. 76.00 (*90-6215-167-1*, Pub. by Maklu Uitgev) Gaunt.

Merchandising by Design. Len Fellman. 1981. pap. 26.95 (*0-86730-237-2*) Lebhar Friedman.

Merchandising Challenges & Opportunities. Didactic Systems Staff. (Study Units Ser.). 1977. pap. 9.00 (*0-89401-113-8*) Didactic Syst.

Merchandising Intellect Proper. Joanna R. Jeremiah. LC 96-53328. 446p. 1997. 174.95 (*0-471-96579-0*) Wiley.

Merchandising Intellectual Property. John Adams. 345p. 1987. boxed set 184.00 (*0-406-10340-2*, U.K., MICHIE) LEXIS Pub.

Merchandising Manufacturing Relationship in Men's Clothing. 60p. 1974. 30.00 (*0-318-13703-8*) Clothing Mfrs.

Merchandising Math. Larry Fiber. (General Business & Business Education Ser.). 1996. 12.95 (*0-8273-6247-1*); pap. 14.95 (*0-8273-6246-3*) Delmar.

Merchandising Math for Profit: An Executive Handbook. Murray Krieger. LC 68-17412. 95p. reprint ed. pap. 30.00 (*0-608-16276-0*, 202652700053) Bks Demand.

Merchandising Mathematics. Antigone Kotsiopulos & Jikyeong Kang-Park. 259p. 1994. write for info. incl. 5.25 ld (*1-56367-029-1*); 51.00 incl. 3.5 hd (*1-56367-037-2*) Fairchild.

Merchandising Mathematics. Antigone Kotsiopulos & Jikyeong Kang-Park. 147p. 1998. pap., teacher ed. 3.50 (*1-56367-038-0*) Fairchild.

Merchandising Mathematics. Leslie R. Peltz. LC 79-494. 1979. pap. 9.49 (*0-672-97273-5*) Macmillan.

Merchandising Mathematics. Tuttle. 320p. 2001. pap. 40.00 (*0-13-897430-6*) P-H.

Merchandising Mathematics. 2nd ed. Carlo. (Trade/Tech Math Ser.). 1981. pap., teacher ed. 10.00 (*0-8273-1417-5*) Delmar.

Merchandising Mathematics: High Margin Returns for Retailers & Vendors. Meridith Paidar. LC 93-25984. 405p. (C). 1994. pap. 37.50 (*0-8273-5703-6*) Delmar.

An Asterisk (*) at the beginning of an entry indicates that the title is appearing for the first time.

Merchandising Mathematics: High Margin Returns for Retailers & Vendors. Meridith Paidar. 71p. 1994. teacher ed. 15.75 (0-8273-5704-4) Delmar.

Merchandising Mathematics for Retailing. 2nd ed. Cynthia R. Easterling et al. 368p. (C). 1992. pap. text 48.80 (0-13-569898-7) P-H.

Merchandising New & Used Cars. Phil A. Lancaster. 15.95 (0-87359-030-9, AM 202) Northwood Univ.

Merchandising New & Used Trucks. F. R. Gaylord. 1981. 15.50 (0-685-07172-3) Northwood Univ.

Merchandising Parts & Service. LC 74-83611. 15.95 (0-87359-006-6, AM 203) Northwood Univ.

Merchandising Practice Set in Financial Accounting: Creative Thoughts, Inc. Pitre & Malone. 1994. pap. 15.95 (0-87393-360-5) Dame Pubns.

Merchandising Strategies for the Competitive Nineties: How to Create the Total Shopping Experience. Lauren Daniel-Falk. (Orig.). 1993. pap. 29.95 (0-9638313-3-X) RTW Review.

Merchandising the Anointing: Developing Discernment for These Last Days. Rick Renner. 272p. 1997. pap. 10.99 (1-880089-08-4, AP-908, Pub. by Albury Pub) Appalach Bk Dist.

Merchandising Truck Parts & Service. F. R. Gaylord. 1983. 17.95 (0-685-07171-5) Northwood Univ.

Merchands de Gloire: Piece en Cinq Actes. Marcel Pagnol. (FRE.). 291p. 1976. write for info. (0-7859-4879-1) Fr & Eur.

M

Merchant, Vol. III. Tr. by P. Nixon. (Loeb Classical Library: No. 163). 15.50 (0-674-99181-8) HUP.

Merchant Adventurer: The Story of W. R. Grace. Marquis James. LC 93-7475. (Latin American Silhouettes Ser.). (Illus.). 385p. 1993. 24.95 (0-8420-2444-1, SR Bks) Scholarly Res Inc.

Merchant Adventurers of England: The Company & the Crown, 1474-1564. Douglas R. Bisson. LC 92-50759. 1993. 29.50 (0-87413-465-X) U Delaware Pr.

Merchant & the Genie; The Emperor's New Clothes; The Geesekeeper. (Scheherezade Presents . . . Ser.: No. 10). (J). pap. write for info. (1-85964-100-8, Pub. by Garnet-Ithaca) LPC InBook.

Merchant & the Thief: A Folktale of Godly Wisdom from India. Ravi Zacharias. LC 99-20997. 1999. 14.99 (0-7814-3296-0) Chariot Victor.

Merchant Banking in Australia. Michael T. Skully. (Illus.). 304p. 1987. text 45.00 (0-19-554473-0) OUP.

Merchant Capital & Economic Decolonization: The United Africa Company, 1929-1987. D. K. Fieldhouse. (Illus.). 860p. 1995. text 110.00 (0-19-822625-X) OUP.

Merchant Capital & Islam. Mahmood Ibrahim. LC 89-14635. 256p. reprint ed. pap. 79.40 (0-608-20865-5, 207196400003) Bks Demand.

Merchant Capital & the Roots of State Power in Senegal, 1930-1985. Catherine Boone. (Cambridge Studies in Comparative Politics). (Illus.). 317p. (C). 1992. text 74.95 (0-521-41078-9) Cambridge U Pr.

Merchant Class of Medieval London. Sylvia L. Thrupp. 416p. 1989. pap. text 20.95 (0-472-06072-4, 06072, Ann Arbor Bks) U of Mich Pr.

Belfast Merchant Families in the Seventeenth Century. Jean Agnew. LC 96-219571. (Illus.). 256p. 1996. 49.50 (1-85182-251-8, Pub. by Four Cts Pr) Intl Spec Bk.

Merchant Congressman in the Young Republic: Samuel Smith of Maryland, 1752-1839. Frank A. Cassell. LC 79-157390. (Illus.). 303p. reprint ed. pap. 94.00 (0-8357-6784-1, 203546100095) Bks Demand.

Merchant Countermarks on World Coins. Gregory C. Brunk. (Illus.). 160p. 1989. 39.95 (0-912317-12-4); pap. 29.95 (0-912317-11-6) World Exo.

Merchant Culture in Fourteenth-Century Venice: The Zibaldone da Canal. Tr. by John E. Dotson. (Medieval & Renaissance Texts & Studies: Vol. 98). 240p. 1994. 25.00 (0-86698-112-8, MR98) MRTS.

Merchant from Bethelehem see Miracle of the Sacred Scroll: A Novel of Hope & Inspiration

***Merchant Houses of Stockholm C. 1640-1800: A Comparative Study of Early-Modern Entrepreneurial Behaviour.** Leos Muller. LC 98-171209. (Studia Historica Upsaliensia Ser.: Vol. 188). (Illus.). 304p. 1998. pap. 62.50 (91-554-4233-1, Pub. by Almqvist Wiksell) Coronet Bks.

Merchant in German Literature of the Enlightenment. John W. Van Cleve. LC 85-14142. (University of North Carolina Studies in the Germanic Languages & Literatures: No. 105). (ENG & GER.). 191p. reprint ed. pap. 59.30 (0-608-20060-3, 207133200011) Bks Demand.

Merchant Ivory's English Landscape: Rooms, Views, & Anglo-Saxon Attitudes. John Pym. LC 94-32106. 132p. 1995. 35.00 (0-8109-4275-5, Pub. by Abrams) Time Warner.

Merchant Marine & World Frontiers. Robert E. Anderson. LC 78-5585. (Illus.). xvii, 205p. 1978. reprint ed. lib. bdg. 22.50 (0-313-20437-3, ANMM, Greenwood Pr) Greenwood.

Merchant Marine Days: My Life in World War II. David L. Lee. LC 98-65033. (Illus.). 192p. 1998. 29.95 (1-886391-20-3); pap. 19.95 (1-886391-21-1) Narwhal Pr.

Merchant Marine Deck Examination Reference Material: Reprints from the Tide Tables & Tidal Current Tables. Government Printing Office Staff. 246p. 1996. per. 23.00 (0-16-042688-X) USGPO.

Merchant Marine Engineering Examination Illustration Book, June 1995. (Commandant Publication Ser.: No. P 16721.7). (Illus.). 346p. (Orig.). 1995. pap. 25.00 (0-16-005318-8, 050-012-00370-0) USGPO.

Merchant Marine Examination Questions, 3 vols. 1997. lib. bdg. 1899.99 (0-8490-8100-9) Gordon Pr.

Merchant Marine Examination Questions No. 3: Navigation General. 314p. 1996. per. 24.00 (0-16-036243-1) USGPO.

Merchant Marine Examination Questions Number 1: Rules of the Road. 162p. 1992. per. 14.00 (0-16-062463-0) USGPO.

Merchant Marine Examination Questions Number 5: Navigation Problems. 410p. 1992. per. 34.00 (0-16-062464-9) USGPO.

Merchant Marine Officers' Handbook. 5th ed. Edward A. Turpin & William A. MacEwen. Ed. by William B. Hayler. LC 88-38675. (Illus.). 589p. 1989. text 50.00 (0-87033-379-8) Cornell Maritime.

Merchant-Millers of Humber Valley: A Study of the Early Economy of Canada. Sidney T. Fisher. (Illus.). 192p. 1995. 16.95 (0-920053-78-5, Pub. by NC Ltd) U of Toronto Pr.

Merchant Moscow: Images of Russia's Vanished Borgeoisie. James L. W. West, III & I. U. Petrov. LC 97-9077. 296p. 1998. text 45.00 (0-691-01249-0, Pub. by Princeton U Pr) Cal Prin Full Svc.

Merchant Networks in the Early Modern World, 1450-1800. Ed. by Sanjay Subrahmanyam. (Expanding World Ser.: Vol. 8). 350p. 1996. 138.95 (0-86078-507-6, Pub. by Variorum) Ashgate Pub Co.

Merchant of Groski: And Other Tales My Great Great Grandfather Might Tell About Life in a Ghetto of Russia in the Time of the Czars. Herman I. Kantor. LC 92-24218. 176p. (Orig.). 1993. 18.95 (1-56474-034-X); pap. 9.95 (1-56474-035-8) Fithian Pr.

Merchant of Marvels & the Peddler of Dreams. Frederic Clement. Tr. by Emma Cole. LC 97-13104. (Illus.). 64p. 1997. 17.95 (0-8118-1664-8) Chronicle Bks.

***Merchant of Menace.** Jill Churchill. 256p. 1999. mass mkt. 6.50 (0-380-79449-7, Avon Bks) Morrow Avon.

Merchant of Menace: A Jane Jeffry Mystery. Jill Churchill. LC 98-4493. 224p. 1998. 21.00 (0-380-97569-6, Avon Bks) Morrow Avon.

Merchant of Venice see Merchant of Venice by William Shakespeare: A Modernization

Merchant of Venice. 40p. 1998. 9.95 (1-58130-566-4, NU5664) Novel Units.

Merchant of Venice. 44p. (YA). 1998. 11.95 (1-58130-567-2, NU5672SP) Novel Units.

Merchant of Venice. Ed. by Peggy L. Anderson & Judith D. Anderson. (Streamline Shakespeare Ser.). 72p. (J). (gr. 4-12). 1999. pap. 7.00 (1-57128-123-1, 8123-1) High Noon Bks.

***Merchant of Venice.** Ed. by Cliffs Notes Staff. (Cliffs Complete Ser.). 240p. 2000. pap. 9.99 (0-7645-8575-4) IDG Bks.

Merchant of Venice. Mark Dunster. 21p. 1995. pap. 4.00 (0-89642-255-0) Linden Pubs.

Merchant of Venice. Ed. by Hutchings. 1993. text. write for info. (0-582-24593-1, Pub. by Addison-Wesley) Longman.

Merchant of Venice. Laura Lippman. (C). 3.95 (0-671-00637-1, Arco) Macmillan Gen Ref.

Merchant of Venice. Joyce Milton. (Barron's Book Notes Ser.). (C). 1985. pap. 3.95 (0-8120-3526-7) Barron.

Merchant of Venice. William Shakespeare. (Illustrated Classics Shakespeare Collection). 64p. 1994. pap. 4.95 (0-7854-0808-8, 40606) Am Guidance.

Merchant of Venice. William Shakespeare. LC 97-9573. 170p. 1999. pap. 12.95 (1-55783-292-7) Applause Theatre Bk Pubs.

Merchant of Venice. William Shakespeare. (BBC Television Plays Ser.). 1980. pap. 5.95 (0-563-17856-6, Pub. by BBC) Parkwest Pubns.

Merchant of Venice. William Shakespeare. Ed. by David Bevington et al. (Classics Ser.). 176p. 1988. mass mkt. 3.95 (0-553-21299-0, Bantam Classics) Bantam.

Merchant of Venice. William Shakespeare. Ed. by Alan Durband. (Shakespeare Made Easy Ser.). 1985. 6.95 (0-8120-3570-4) Barron.

***Merchant of Venice.** William Shakespeare. (Literature Made Easy Ser.). 96p. (YA). 1999. pap. 4.95 (0-7641-0826-3) Barron.

Merchant of Venice. William Shakespeare. Ed. by Molly M. Mahood. (New Cambridge Shakespeare Ser.). (Illus.). 206p. 1988. pap. text 11.95 (0-521-29371-5) Cambridge U Pr.

Merchant of Venice. William Shakespeare. Ed. by Jonathan Morris & Robert Smith. (Cambridge School Shakespeare Ser.). (Illus.). 192p. (C). 1993. pap. 9.95 (0-521-42504-2) Cambridge U Pr.

Merchant of Venice. William Shakespeare. Ed. by Roma Gill. (Oxford School Shakespeare Ser.). (C). 1994. text 10.72 (0-669-40355-5) HM Trade Div.

Merchant of Venice. William Shakespeare. Ed. by Ken Roy et al. 1989. pap., student ed. 12.00 (0-7747-1263-5) Harcourt Schl Pubs.

Merchant of Venice. William Shakespeare. Ed. by Bernard Lott. (New Swan Shakespeare Ser.). (Illus.). Date not set. pap. text 2.95 (0-582-52721-X, TG7011) Longman.

Merchant of Venice. William Shakespeare. Ed. by Gamini Salgado & Fenella Salgado. 1988. pap. text 4.29 (0-582-33193-5, 72071) Longman.

Merchant of Venice. William Shakespeare. Ed. by Roy Blatchford. (Literature Ser.). 1993. pap. 5.95 (0-582-08835-6, TG7663) Longman.

Merchant of Venice. William Shakespeare. Ed. & Illus. by Diane Davidson. LC 83-12308. (Shakespeare on Stage Ser.: Vol. 4). 112p. (YA). (gr. 8-12). 1983. pap. 6.95 (0-934048-08-8) Lrn Links.

Merchant of Venice. William Shakespeare. 208p. 1965. mass mkt. 3.95 (0-451-52133-1, Sig Classics) NAL.

Merchant of Venice. William Shakespeare. 264p. 1998. mass mkt. 3.95 (0-451-52680-5, Sig Classics) NAL.

Merchant of Venice. William Shakespeare. (Illus.). 94p. 1993. pap. text 5.95 (0-19-585431-4) OUP.

***Merchant of Venice.** William Shakespeare. (Big Works Collection). (Illus.). 1p. 1999. 29.95 (1-929142-05-6) One Page Bk.

Merchant of Venice. William Shakespeare. Ed. by John Drakakis & Nigel Wood. 224p. 1995. pap. 27.95 (0-335-19237-8) OpUniv Pr.

Merchant of Venice. William Shakespeare. Ed. & Intro. by Annabel Patterson. LC 95-7564. (Shakespearean Originals--First Edition Ser.). 144p. (C). 1995. pap. text 12.95 (0-13-355520-8) P-H.

Merchant of Venice. William Shakespeare. Ed. by Paul Werstine & Barbara A. Mowat. (New Folger Library Ser.). (Illus.). 288p. 1992. per. 3.99 (0-671-72277-8, Folger Shake Ser) PB.

Merchant of Venice. William Shakespeare. Ed. by Martin Coyle. LC 98-21228. 256p. 1998. text 45.00 (0-312-21689-0) St Martin.

Merchant of Venice. William Shakespeare. (Shakespeare Made Easy Ser.). 1985. 12.05 (0-606-01098-X, Pub. by Turtleback) Demco.

Merchant of Venice. William Shakespeare. (New Folger Library Shakespeare Ser.). 1992. 9.09 (0-606-01067-X, Pub. by Turtleback) Demco.

Merchant of Venice. William Shakespeare. Ed. by John F. Andrews. (Everyman Shakespeare Ser.). 228p. 1993. pap. 3.95 (0-460-87180-3, Everyman's Classic Lib) Tuttle Pubng.

Merchant of Venice. William Shakespeare. Ed. by A. L. Rowse. LC 84-5069. (Contemporary Shakespeare Ser.: Vol. I). 120p. (C). 1984. pap. text 3.45 (0-8191-3901-7) U Pr of Amer.

Merchant of Venice. William Shakespeare. Ed. by Brents Stirling. (Pelican Shakespeare Ser.). 132p. (YA). (gr. 9 up). 1960. pap. 3.95 (0-14-071421-9, Pelican Bks) Viking Penguin.

Merchant of Venice. William Shakespeare. Ed. by W. Moelwyn Merchant. (New Penguin Shakespeare Ser.). 216p. 1981. pap. 5.95 (0-14-070706-9, Penguin Classics) Viking Penguin.

***Merchant of Venice.** William Shakespeare. (Pelican Shakespeare Ser.). 144p. 2000. pap. 3.95 (0-14-071462-6, Pelican Bks) Viking Penguin.

Merchant of Venice. William Shakespeare. (English Ser.). (C). 2000. mass mkt. 9.95 (0-17-443527-4) Wadsworth Pub.

Merchant of Venice. William Shakespeare. (Classics Library). 112p. 1997. pap. 3.95 (1-85326-060-6, 0606WW, Pub. by Wrdsworth Edits) NTC Contemp Pub Co.

Merchant of Venice. William Shakespeare. Ed. by John R. Brown. (Shakespeare Library). 192p. 2000. pap. 7.95 (1-55783-388-5) Applause Theatre Bk Pubs.

***Merchant of Venice.** William Shakespeare & Kaplan. 2001. pap. text. write for info. (0-312-25624-8) St Martin.

***Merchant of Venice.** abr. ed. William Shakespeare. Ed. by William-Alan Landes. LC 99-48044. 64p. 1999. pap. 6.00 (0-88734-462-3) Players Pr.

Merchant of Venice. large type ed. William Shakespeare. 1991. pap. 24.95 (0-7089-4501-5, Charnwood) Ulverscroft.

Merchant of Venice see New Variorum Edition of Shakespeare

Merchant of Venice. William Shakespeare. Ed. by Jay L. Halio. (Oxford World's Classics Ser.). (Illus.). 252p. 1998. reprint ed. pap. 7.95 (0-19-283424-X) OUP.

Merchant of Venice. unabridged ed. William Shakespeare. (Thrift Editions Ser.). 88p. 1995. pap. 1.00 (0-486-28492-1) Dover.

Merchant of Venice. 2nd ed. William Shakespeare. (English). (C). 1997. 11.95 (0-17-443475-8) Wadsworth Pub.

Merchant of Venice. 2nd annot. ed. William Shakespeare. Ed. by Roma Gill. (Oxford School Shakespeare Ser.). (Illus.). 140p. (J). (gr. 6). 1992. pap. text 7.95 (0-19-831973-8) OUP.

Merchant of Venice. 3rd ed. William Shakespeare. (English Ser.). (C). 2000. mass mkt. 45.00 (0-17-443560-6) Wadsworth Pub.

Merchant of Venice. 7th ed. William Shakespeare. Ed. by John R. Brown. (Arden Shakespeare Ser.). 1955. reprint ed. pap. 45.00 (0-416-47500-0, NO. 2480); reprint ed. pap. 9.95 (0-415-02751-9, NO. 2481) Thomson Learn.

Merchant of Venice: A Unit Plan. Barbara M. Linde. 160p. 1999. teacher ed., ring bd. 26.95 (1-58337-216-4) Teachers Pet Pubns.

***Merchant of Venice: Arden Playgoers Edition.** William Shakespeare. Ed. by Clifford Leech & John Russell Brown. 320p. 1998. 24.95 (0-17-443617-3) ITP Nelson.

Merchant of Venice: Choice, Hazard & Consequences. Joan O. Holmer. LC 94-33031. 1995. text 45.00 (0-312-12411-2) St Martin.

Merchant of Venice: Curriculum Unit. William Shakespeare & Center for Learning Network Staff. (Shakespeare Ser.). 80p. (YA). (gr. 9-12). 1990. spiral bd. 18.95 (1-56077-107-0) Ctr Learning.

Merchant of Venice: Granville Barker's Prefaces to Shakespeare. William Shakespeare. Ed. by Granville Barker. 70p. 1995. pap. 6.95 (0-435-08653-7, 08653) Heinemann.

Merchant of Venice: Griffith,&Hugh, Set. abr. ed. William Shakespeare. 1991. audio 18.00 (1-55994-096-4, CPN 209) HarperAudio.

Merchant of Venice: Original Text & Modern Verse. William Shakespeare. Ed. by Alan Durband. (Shakespeare Made Easy Ser.). (Orig.). 1995. pap. 17.95 (0-7487-0363-2, Pub. by S Thornes Pubs) Trans-Atl Phila.

Merchant of Venice: Reproducible Teaching Unit. rev. ed. James Scott. 36p. (YA). (gr. 7-12). 1995. teacher ed., ring bd. 29.50 (1-58049-065-4, TU28/U) Prestwick Hse.

***Merchant of Venice by William Shakespeare: A Modernization.** William Shakespeare. Ed. by Rachel Burke. (College Classics: Vol. 10). Orig. Title: The Merchant of Venice. (Illus.). 80p. 2000. pap. text 9.00 (0-942208-10-2) Bandanna Bks.

Merchant of Venice Complete Study Guide. Ed. by Sidney Lamb. 101p. 1965. pap. text, student ed. 6.95 (0-8220-1431-9, Cliff) IDG Bks.

Merchant of Venice Notes. Waldo F. McNeir. (Cliffs Notes Ser.). 72p. 1961. pap. 4.95 (0-8220-0052-0, Cliff) IDG Bks.

Merchant of Venice Readalong. William Shakespeare. (Illustrated Classics Shakespeare Collection). 64p. 1994. pap. 14.95 incl. audio (0-7854-0824-X, 40608) Am Guidance.

Merchant of Venice Study Guide. Bethine Ellie. 36p. (YA). (gr. 8-12). 1993. student ed., ring bd. 14.99 (1-58609-155-7) Progeny Pr WI.

***Merchant Power: A Basic Guide.** Ann Chambers. LC 99-39983. 220p. 1999. 89.95 (0-87814-766-7) PennWell Bks.

***Merchant Prince.** Armin Shimerman & Michael Scott. 304p. 2000. 23.95 (0-671-03592-4, PB Hardcover) PB.

Merchant Prince & Master Builder: Edgar J. Kaufmann & Frank Lloyd Wright. Richard Cleary & Dennis McFadden. LC 98-48686. (Illus.). 200p. 1999. pap. 30.00 (0-88039-036-0) Mus Art Carnegie.

Merchant Prince of Boston, Colonel T. H. Perkins, 1764-1854. Carl Seaburg & Stanley Paterson. LC 71-165419. (Harvard Studies in Business History: No. 26). 506p. reprint ed. pap. 156.90 (0-7837-2330-X, 205741800004) Bks Demand.

Merchant Prince of Dodge City: The Life & Times of Robert M. Wright. C. Robert Haywood. LC 98-2814. (Illus.). 256p. 1998. 27.95 (0-8061-3073-3) U of Okla Pr.

Merchant Prince of Poverty Row: Harry Cohn of Columbia Pictures. Bernard F. Dick. LC 93-3348. 248p. 1993. 29.95 (0-8131-1841-7) U Pr of Ky.

Merchant Prince of the Sandalwood Mountains: Afong & the Chinese in Hawai'i. Bob Dye. LC 96-25678. (Illus.). 336p. 1997. text 35.00 (0-8248-1772-9, Latitude Twenty) UH Pr.

Merchant Princes: An Intimate History of Jewish Families Who Built Great Department Stores. Leon Harris. LC 94-29826. 432p. 1994. reprint ed. pap. 15.00 (1-56836-044-4) Kodansha.

Merchant Princes of Fremantle: The Rise & Decline of a Colonial Elite 1870-1900. Patricia M. Brown. LC 97-114775. (Illus.). 239p. 1996. pap. 24.95 (1-875560-76-9, Pub. by Univ of West Aust Pr) Intl Spec Bk.

Merchant Princes of the East: Cultural Delusions, Economic Success & the Overseas Chinese in Southeast Asia. Rupert A. Hodder. 352p. 1996. text 105.00 (0-471-96230-9) Wiley.

Merchant Sail Vol. 1: Early Days of Exploration & the Influence of Ship Building in the Development of the U. S. William A. Fairburn. 756p. 1992. reprint ed. lib. bdg. 90.00 (0-8328-2452-6) Higginson Bk Co.

Merchant Sail Vol. 2: War of Eighteen Twelve; Pre-Eminence of U. S. Commerce Before Civil War; Fisheries & Whaling. William A. Fairburn. 828p. 1992. reprint ed. lib. bdg. 90.00 (0-8328-2453-4) Higginson Bk Co.

Merchant Sail Vol. 3: U. S. Merchant Sail-Types; Models & Rigs; Clippers & Square-Riggers of the Post-Clipper Period. William A. Fairburn. 574p. 1992. reprint ed. lib. bdg. 90.00 (0-8328-2454-2) Higginson Bk Co.

Merchant Sail Vol. 4: U. S. Merchant Sail in the China, Australia, Manila & India Trade; Development of the Schooner Rig. William A. Fairburn. 560p. 1992. reprint ed. lib. bdg. 90.00 (0-8328-2455-0) Higginson Bk Co.

Merchant Sail Vol. 5: U. S. Woodshipbuilders & Shipbuilding Centers Through the 19th Century, Including Packets, Clippers & Down Easters. William A. Fairburn. Ed. by Ethel M. Ritchie. 862p. 1992. reprint ed. lib. bdg. 90.00 (0-8328-2456-9) Higginson Bk Co.

Merchant Sail Vol. 6: Appendixes; Index of Vessels; General Index. William A. Fairburn. Ed. by Ethel M. Ritchie. 1992. reprint ed. lib. bdg. 90.00 (0-8328-2457-7) Higginson Bk Co.

Merchant Ship Construction. H. J. Pursey. (Illus.). (C). 1987. 120.00 (0-7855-6054-8) St Mut.

Merchant Ship Construction. 7th ed. H. J. Pursey. 217p. 1983. text 48.00 (0-85174-454-0) Sheridan.

Merchant Ship Search & Rescue Manual (Mersar Manual) 4th ed. IMO Staff. (C). 1986. 100.00 (0-7855-0023-5, IMO 963E, Pub. by Intl Maritime Org); 100.00 (0-7855-7115-9, IMO 964F, Pub. by Intl Maritime Org); 100.00 (0-7855-7116-7, IMO 965S, Pub. by Intl Maritime Org) St Mut.

Merchant Ship Stability: Metric Edition. 6th rev. ed. H. J. Pursey. (Illus.). 207p. (C). 1992. text 48.00 (0-85174-442-7) Sheridan.

Merchant Shipping Legislation, 2 vols., Set. Fogartz. 1994. pap. text 785.00 (1-85044-292-4) LLP.

***Merchant Shipping Navigational Equipment: Instructions for the Guidance of Surveyors.** Maritime & Coastguard Agency Staff. 24p. 1999. ring bd. 30.00 (0-11-552198-4, Pub. by Statnry Office) Balogh.

***Merchant Shipping Notices: Consolidated Edition, 3 vols., Set.** 1999. boxed set 165.00 (0-11-551853-3, Pub. by Statnry Office) Balogh.

***Merchant Shipping Notices: Consolidated Edition to January 1999, 3 vols., Set.** 1999. boxed set 190.00 (0-11-552108-9, Pub. by Statnry Office) Balogh.

Merchant Steam Vessels of the United States, 1790-1868: The "Lytle-Holdcamper List" Ed. by C. Bradford Mitchell. LC 75-18930. 322p. 1975. 26.00 (0-913423-02-5) Steamship Hist Soc.

Merchant Tokens of Hard Rubber & Similar Compositions. David E. Schenkman. LC 91-60311. (Illus.). 208p. 1992. text 57.50 (0-942596-04-8) Jade Hse Pubns.

An Asterisk (*) at the beginning of an entry indicates that the title is appearing for the first time.

Merchant Tokens of Washington D. C. David E. Schenkman. LC 81-86671. (Illus.). 80p. 1982. 20.00 (*0-942596-00-5*) Jade Hse Pubns.

Merchant Venturers in Bronze see Corridors of Time: New Haven & London, 1927-1956

Merchant Vessel. Charles Nordhoff. (Notable American Authors Ser.). 1999. reprint ed. lib. bdg. 125.00 (*0-7812-4636-9*) Rprt Serv.

Merchant Vessels of the United States, 2 vols. 1997. lib. bdg. 605.95 (*0-8490-8131-9*) Gordon Pr.

Merchant Vessels of the United States, 1992. Transportation Department, Coast Guard Staff. 1997. write for info. (*0-16-038206-8*) USGPO.

Merchant Vessels of the United States, 1994: Including Recreational Vessels, 2 vols. Transportation Department, Coast Guard Staff. 4372p. 1995. 147.00 (*0-16-048195-3*, 050-012-00369-6) USGPO.

Merchant Writers of the Italian Renissance: From Boccacio to Machiavelli. Vittore Branca. LC 99-39085. 163p. 1999. pap. 16.95 (*1-56886-058-7*, Pub. by Marsilio Pubs) Consort Bk Sales.

Merchanter's Luck. C. J. Cherryh. 208p. 1982. pap. 5.99 (*0-88677-139-0*, Pub. by DAW Bks) Penguin Putnam.

Merchantile Law, 1985: With Supplement in View of Companies (Amendment) Act, 1988. 4th ed. Avtar Singh. (C). 1989. 95.00 (*0-7855-5630-3*) St Mut.

Merchantman? Or Ship of War. Charles D. Gibson. LC 86-80113. (Illus.). 231p. 1986. 18.75 (*0-9608996-1-8*) Ensign Pr.

Merchants see Pregones

Merchants: The Big Business Families of Saudi Arabia & the Gulf States. Michael Field. LC 85-4386. 371p. 1985. pap. 15.95 (*0-87951-226-1*, Pub. by Overlook Pr) Penguin Putnam.

Merchants, Bk. 9, Industrialization & Provincial Politics in Mid-Nineteenth Century France see Florentine Codex, A General History of the Things of New Spain

Merchants Adventurers & the Continental Cloth-Trade, 1560s-1620s. Wolf-Rudiger Baumann. (European University Institute, Series B (History): No. 2). xiv, 425p. (C). 1990. lib. bdg. 135.40 (*3-11-012582-X*) De Gruyter.

Merchant's Almanac of 1622: The Ancient Law-Merchant. Katie F. Hamilton & Gerard Malynes. LC 96-189465. 404p. (Orig.). 1996. pap. 22.50 (*1-889023-02-7*) Metheglin Pr.

Merchants & Capitalists: Industrialization & Provincial Politics in Mid-Nineteenth Century France. David M. Gordon. LC 83-18266. 263p. 1985. pap. 81.60 (*0-7837-8375-2*, 205918500009) Bks Demand.

Merchants & Empire: Trading in Colonial New York. Cathy D. Matson. LC 97-2768. (Early America). (Illus.). 480p. 1997. text 45.00 (*0-8018-5602-7*) Johns Hopkins.

Merchants & Entrepreneurs in Imperial Russia. fac. ed. Alfred J. Rieber. LC 80-28554. (Illus.). 490p. 1982. reprint ed. pap. 151.90 (*0-7837-8058-3*, 204781100008) Bks Demand.

Merchants & Entrepreneurs in Imperial Russia. Alfred J. Rieber. LC 80-28554. (Illus.). xxvi, 464p. (C). 1991. reprint ed. pap. 24.95 (*0-8078-4305-9*) U of NC Pr.

Merchants & Faith: Muslim Commerce & Culture in the Indian Ocean. Patricia Risso. LC 94-42937. (New Perspectives on Asian History Ser.). 168p. (C). 1995. pap. 23.00 (*0-8133-8911-9*, Pub. by Westview) HarpC.

Merchants & Jews: The Struggle for British West Indian Commerce, 1650-1750. Stephen A. Fortune. LC 83-25903. (University of Florida Latin American Monographs: No. 26). 257p. 1984. 29.95 (*0-8130-0735-6*) U Press Fla.

Merchants & Luxury Markets: The Marchands Merciers of Eighteenth-Century Paris. Carolyn Sargentson. (Illus.). 256p. 1996. 60.00 (*0-89236-295-2*, Pub. by J P Getty Trust) OUP.

Merchants & Manufacturers: Studies in the Changing Structure of Nineteenth-Century Marketing. Glenn Porter & Harold C. Livesay. LC 72-156071. 269p. reprint ed. pap. 83.40 (*0-8357-6706-X*, 203526800094) Bks Demand.

Merchants & Manufacturers: Studies in the Changing Structure of 19th-Century Marketing. Glenn Porter & Harold C. Livesay. 276p. 1989. reprint ed. pap. text 8.95 (*0-929587-10-3*, Elephant Paperbacks) I R Dee.

Merchants & Mariners in Medieval Ireland. Timothy O'Neill. LC 87-180747. 164p. 1987. write for info. (*0-7165-2399-X*) Intl Spec Bk.

Merchants & Mariners in Medieval Ireland. Timothy O'Neill. (Illus.). 164p. 1987. 25.00 (*0-7165-2398-1*, Pub. by Irish Acad Pr) Intl Spec Bk.

Merchants & Markets in Revolutionary Russia, 1917-1930. Arup Banerji. LC 96-21858. 304p. 1997. text 69.95 (*0-312-16293-6*) St Martin.

Merchants & Merchandise in Northern India, Ad 600-1000. Anjali Malik. LC 98-909705. 189 p. 1998. write for info. (*81-7304-228-4*) Manohar.

Merchants & Migrants: Ethnicity & Trade among Yunnanese Chinese in Southeast Asia. Ann Maxwell Hill. LC 97-61158. (Monograph Ser.: Vol. 47). (Illus.). 178p. 1998. pap. 20.00 (*0-938692-68-2*); lib. bdg. 32.00 (*0-938692-67-4*) Yale U SE Asia.

Merchants & Migrants in Nineteenth Century Beirut. Leila T. Fawaz. (Middle Eastern Monographs: No. 18). (Illus.). 196p. 1990. 29.00 (*0-674-56925-3*) HUP.

Merchants & Miners in Utah. Jonathan Bliss. 1984. 20.00 (*0-914740-29-6*) Western Epics.

Merchants & Reform in Livorno, 1814-1868. David Lo Romer. 1987. 65.00 (*0-520-05649-3*, Pub. by U CA Pr) Cal Prin Full Svc.

Merchants & Revolution: Commercial Change, Political Conflict, & London's Overseas Traders, 1550-1653. Robert Brenner. LC 90-26252. (Illus.). 754p. reprint ed. pap. 200.00 (*0-608-09106-5*, 206973800005) Bks Demand.

Merchants & Shopkeepers: An Historical Anthropology of an Irish Market Town, 1200-1986. Philip H. Gulliver & Marilyn Silverman. (Anthropological Horizons Ser.). 464p. 1995. text 60.00 (*0-8020-0644-2*); pap. text 29.95 (*0-8020-7597-5*) U of Toronto Pr.

Merchants at War: Survival Tactics for Armed & Unarmed Merchants. Paul Caparatta. LC 98-60175. (Illus.). 269p. 1998. pap. 19.95 (*1-888644-99-0*) Varro Pr.

Merchants Avizo. LC 70-7710. (English Experience Ser.: No. 98). 1969. reprint ed. 20.00 (*90-221-0098-7*) Walter J Johnson.

Merchants, Companies & Commerce on the Coromandel Coast, 1650-1740. Sinnappah Arasaratnam. (Illus.). 400p. 1987. 32.00 (*0-19-561873-4*) OUP.

Merchants, Companies & Trade: Europe & Asia in The Early Modern Era. Ed. by Sushil Chaudhury & Michel Morineau. LC 98-38433. (Studies in Modern Capitalism). (Illus.). 400p. (C). 1999. text 69.95 (*0-521-56367-4*) Cambridge U Pr.

Merchant's Edge: A Guide to Grain Marketing. 2nd ed. Sherry Lorton. 330p. 1994. pap. 22.00 (*0-87563-487-7*) Stipes.

Merchant's Edge: A Guide to Grain Marketing. 3rd ed. Sherry Lorton. 428p. 1998. pap. 29.95 (*0-87563-777-9*) Stipes.

Merchants from Ararat. K. S. Papazian. Ed. by P. M. Manuelian. LC 79-63061. 1979. pap. 3.50 (*0-933706-04-9*) Ararat Pr.

***Merchant's House.** Kate Ellis. LC 99-13680. 256p. 1999. pap. 22.95 (*0-312-20562-7*, Thomas Dunne) St Martin.

Merchants in Crisis: Genoese & Venetian Men of Affairs & the Fourteenth-Century Depression. Benjamin Z. Kedar. LC 75-43320. (Yale Series in Economic History). 272p. reprint ed. pap. 84.40 (*0-8357-8222-0*, 203377700087) Bks Demand.

Merchants, Landlords, Magistrates: The upont Family in Eighteenth-century France. Robert Forster. LC 80-14944. 288p. reprint ed. pap. 89.30 (*0-8357-6610-1*, 203525500094) Bks Demand.

***Merchants, Mamluks & Murder: The Political Economy of Trade in Eighteenth-Century Basra.** Thabit A. J. Abdullah. LC 00-26524. (C). 2000. pap. text 20.95 (*0-7914-4808-8*) State U NY Pr.

***Merchants, Mamluks & Murder: The Political Economy of Trade in Eighteenth-Century Basra.** Thabit A. J. Abdullah. LC 00-26524. (C). 2001. text 62.50 (*0-7914-4807-X*) State U NY Pr.

Merchants, Mandarins, & Modern Enterprise in Late Ch'ing China. Wellington K. Chan. LC 76-30743. (East Asian Monographs: No. 79). 300p. 1977. 24.00 (*0-674-56915-6*) HUP.

Merchants Markets & Manufactor. John Smail. LC 98-55577. 198p. 1999. text 65.00 (*0-312-22162-2*) St Martin.

Merchants, Markets & the State in Early Modern India. Ed. by Sanjay Subrahmanyam. (Illus.). 284p. 1991. text 28.00 (*0-19-562569-2*) OUP.

Merchants, Money & Power: The Portland Establishment, 1843-1913. E. Kimbark MacColl & Harry H. Stein. Ed. by Philippa Brunsman. LC 88-24653. (Illus.). 550p. 1988. 29.95 (*0-9603408-3-1*); pap. 19.95 (*0-9603408-4-X*) Georgian Pr.

Merchants, Monopolists, & Contractors: A Study of Economic Activity & Society in Bourbon Naples 1815-1860. John A. Davis. Ed. by Stuart Bruchey. LC 80-2802. (Dissertations in European Economic History Ser.). (Illus.). 1981. lib. bdg. 39.95 (*0-405-13986-1*) Ayer.

Merchants, National Bank of the City of New York. Philip G. Hubert, Jr. Ed. by Stuart Bruchey. LC 80-1186. (Rise of Commercial Banking Ser.). (Illus.). 1981. reprint ed. lib. bdg. 23.95 (*0-405-13655-2*) Ayer.

Merchants of Hope: British Middlebrow Writers & the First World War, 1919-1939. Maria Bracco. LC 92-12330. (Legacy of the Great War Ser.). 208p. 1993. 37.50 (*0-85496-706-0*) Berg Pubs.

Merchants of Ignorance: An Indictment of Government Education. Douglas Kirk. 302p. (Orig.). 1996. pap. 14.95 (*0-934279-09-8*) Morton Falls Pub.

Merchants of Life: An Account of the American Pharmaceutical Industry. Tom Mahoney. LC 77-167381. (Essay Index Reprint Ser.). 1977. reprint ed. 20.95 (*0-8369-2608-0*) Ayer.

Merchants of Maritime India, 1500-1800. Ashin D. Gupta. 326p. 1994. 109.95 (*0-86078-432-0*, Pub. by Variorum) Ashgate Pub Co.

Merchants of Menace - The Mafia: A Study of Organized Crime. Edward J. Allen. (Illus.). 344p. 1962. pap. 41.95 (*0-398-06004-5*) C C Thomas.

Merchants of Menace - The Mafia: A Study of Organized Crime. fac. ed. Edward J. Allen. (Illus.). 344p. 1962. 55.95 (*0-398-04187-3*) C C Thomas.

Merchants of Misery: How Corporate America Profits from Poverty. Ed. by Michael Hudson. LC 96-496. 275p. (Orig.). 1996. pap. 14.95 (*1-56751-082-5*); lib. bdg. 29.95 (*1-56751-083-3*) Common Courage.

Merchants of Moscow, Fifteen-Eighty to Sixteen-Fifty. Paul Bushkovitch. LC 79-14491. 224p. reprint ed. pap. 63.90 (*0-608-15699-X*, 2031626) Bks Demand.

***Merchants of Souls.** John Barnes. 2000. text 25.95 (*0-312-89076-1*) St Martin.

Merchants of the Jumpweb. Bill Bridges. (Fading Suns: Vol. 231). 1997. pap. 20.00 (*1-888906-09-X*) Holistic Design.

Merchants of Venus: Inside Harlequin & the Empire of Romance. Paul Grescoe. (Illus.). 320p. 1997. 22.95 (*1-55192-010-7*); pap. 14.95 (*1-55192-112-X*) Raincoast Bk.

Merchants of Vision: People Bringing New Purpose & Values to Business. James E. Liebig. LC 93-43269. (Illus.). 256p. 1994. 24.95 (*1-881052-42-7*) Berrett-Koehler.

Merchant's Partner. Michael Jecks. 384p. 1998. pap. 9.95 (*0-7472-5070-7*, Pub. by Headline Bk Pub) Trafalgar.

Merchant's Perspective: Captain Jacobus Boelen's Narrative of His Visit to Hawai'i in 1828. Jacobus Boelan. Ed. & Tr. by Frank J. Broeze. 150p. (C). 1988. text 24.00 (*0-945048-00-9*) HI Hist Soc.

Merchants, Politics & Society in Early Modern India: Bihar, 1733-1820. Kumkum Chatterjee. (Brill's Indological Library: No. 10). (Illus.). 305p. 1996. 94.50 (*90-04-10303-1*) Brill Academic Pubs.

Merchant's Prologue & Tale. Geoffrey Chaucer. Ed. by Maurice Hussey. (Selected Tales from Chaucer Ser.). 116p. 1966. pap. text 10.95 (*0-521-04631-9*) Cambridge U Pr.

Merchant's Tale: The Life & Times of John Cabot. P. Sheaves. (Illus.). 1996. pap. 3.95 (*1-895387-78-7*) Creative Bk Pub.

Merchant's Two Daughters. F. I. Rejab. (Illus.). 40p. (J). 1995. 9.95 (*983-9808-23-0*, Pub. by Delta Edits) Weatherhill.

Merchant's Wife on Knight's Adventure: Permutations of a Medieval Tale in German, Dutch & English Chapbooks Around 1500. Myra J. Heerspink Scholz. LC 94-17827. (German Life & Civilization Ser.: Vol. 17). (Illus.). 266p. (C). 1999. text 53.00 (*0-8204-2573-7*) P Lang Pubng.

Merci Gonaives: A Photgrapher's Account of Haiti & the February Revolution. Danny Lyon. (Illus.). 64p. 1994. pap. 19.95 (*1-881616-28-2*) Dist Art Pubs.

Merci Gonaives: A Photographer's Account of Haiti & the February Revolution. Danny Lyon. LC 87-73298. (Illus.). 64p. (Orig.). (C). 1988. pap. 20.00 (*0-9620992-0-1*) Bleak Beauty.

Mercier & Camier. Samuel Beckett. 24.95 (*0-685-37198-0*, F86050) Fr & Eur.

Mercier & Camier. Samuel Beckett. LC 74-21639. 128p. 1991. pap. 11.00 (*0-8021-3235-9*, Grove) Grove-Atltic.

Mercier Companion to Irish Literature. Sean McMahon. LC 98-230914. 300p. 1998. pap. 15.95 (*1-85635-216-1*, Pub. by Mercier Pr) Irish Amer Bk.

Mercies: Collected Poems. Sheldon Vanauken. 64p. (Orig.). 1988. pap. 6.95 (*0-931888-28-X*) Christendom Pr.

Merciful Disguises: Published & Unpublished Poems. Mona Van Duyn. LC 73-78407. (C). 1982. pap. 9.95 (*0-689-11294-7*) Atheneum Yung Read.

***Merciful Women.** Federico Andahazi. 2000. write for info. (*0-8021-1674-4*, Pub. by Grove-Atltic) Publishers Group.

Merciless. Michael Cross. 352p. 1996. mass mkt. 5.99 (*0-7860-0336-7*, Pinncle Kensgtn) Kensgtn Pub Corp.

Merck Index: An Encyclopedia of Drugs, Chemicals & Biologicals. 12th ed. Ed. by Susan Budavari et al. LC 96-171642. (Illus.). 2500p. 1996. ring bd. 45.00 (*0-911910-12-3*) Merck.

Merck Index: An Encyclopedia of Drugs, Chemicals, & Biologicals, Windows. Susan Budavari et al. 1996. 280.00 incl. cd-rom (*0-412-75990-X*) Chapman & Hall.

Merck Manual: Arabic Language Edition. Ed. by Robert Berkow. (ARA.). Date not set. 150.00 (*0-7859-9677-X*) Fr & Eur.

Merck Manual: Centennial Edition. 17th ed. Ed. by Robert Berkow et al. (Merck Manual of Diagnosis & Therapy Ser.). (Illus.). 1999. 35.00 (*0-911910-10-7*) Merck.

Merck Manual: Chinese Language Edition. Ed. by Robert Berkow. (CHI.). Date not set. 150.00 (*0-7859-9676-1*) Fr & Eur.

Merck Manual: Czech Language Edition. Ed. by Robert Berkow. (CZE.). Date not set. 150.00 (*0-7859-9680-X*) Fr & Eur.

Merck Manual: El Manual Merck. 7th ed. Sharp Merck & Dohme Merck. (SPA.). 1986. 75.00 (*0-8288-1869-X*, S37592) Fr & Eur.

Merck Manual: French Language Edition. Ed. by Robert Berkow. (FRE.). Date not set. 225.00 (*0-7859-9675-3*) Fr & Eur.

Merck Manual: German Language Edition. Ed. by Robert Berkow. (GER.). Date not set. 195.00 (*0-7859-9674-5*) Fr & Eur.

Merck Manual: Hungarian Language Edition. Ed. by Robert Berkow. (HUN.). Date not set. 150.00 (*0-7859-9669-9*) Fr & Eur.

Merck Manual: Italian Language Edition. Ed. by Robert Berkow. (ITA.). Date not set. 150.00 (*0-7859-9672-9*) Fr & Eur.

Merck Manual: Japanese Language Edition. Ed. by Robert Berkow. (JPN.). Date not set. 295.00 (*0-7859-9681-8*) Fr & Eur.

Merck Manual: Polish Language Edition. Ed. by Robert Berkow. (POL.). Date not set. 150.00 (*0-7859-9670-2*) Fr & Eur.

Merck Manual: Portugese Language Edition. Ed. by Merck Editors. (POR.). Date not set. 150.00 (*0-7859-9662-1*) Fr & Eur.

Merck Manual: Russian Language Edition. Ed. by Merck Editors. (RUS.). Date not set. 195.00 (*0-7859-9663-X*) Fr & Eur.

Merck Manual: Turkish Language Edition. Ed. by Merck Editors. (TUR.). Date not set. 150.00 (*0-7859-9664-8*) Fr & Eur.

Merck Manual for Veterinarians: El Manual Merck de Veterinaria. 2nd ed. Sharp Merck & Dohme. (SPA.). 1386p. 1981. 75.00 (*0-8288-2389-8*, S39845) Fr & Eur.

Merck Manual of Geriatrics. 2nd ed. Ed. by Robert Berkow et al. LC 96-168522. 1995. 25.00 (*0-911910-66-2*) Merck.

***Merck Manual of Medical Information.** Robert Berkow. 1536p. 2000. pap. 19.95 (*0-671-02726-3*) PB.

Merck Manual of Medical Information: Home Edition. Robert Berkow. 1648p. 1999. per. 7.99 (*0-671-02727-1*) PB.

Merck Manual of Medical Information: Home Edition. McGraw-Hill Book Company Staff. Ed. by Robert Berkow. 1999. cd-rom 39.95 (*0-07-864285-X*) McGraw.

Merck Manual of Medical Information: Home Edition. Merck & Co., Inc. Staff. Ed. by Robert Berkow et al. LC 96-80494. (Illus.). 1509p. 1997. 29.95 (*0-911910-87-5*) Merck.

Merck Veterinary Manual. 8th rev. ed. Merck Editors. 1998. 32.00 (*0-911910-29-8*) Merck.

Mercosur: Regional Integration, World Markets. Ed. by Riordan Roett. LC 98-37779. 140p. 1998. lib. bdg. 25.00 (*1-55587-837-7*) L Rienner.

***Mercosur: Regional Integration, World Markets.** Ed. by Riordan Roett. LC 98-37779. 140p. 1998. pap. 13.95 (*1-55587-838-5*) L Rienner.

Mercruiser Alpha One, Bravo One & Bravo Two Stern Drives, 1986-1992. Intertec Publishing Staff. LC 95-75411. 648p. 1993. pap. 36.95 (*0-89287-655-7*, B-742) Intertec Pub.

Mercruiser Stern Drive, Alpha Generation II, 1992-96, Vol. II. Joan Coles & Clarence Coles. (Marine Tune-Up & Repair Manuals: Vol. II). (Illus.). 512p. (C). 1998. pap. 34.95 (*0-89330-039-X*, Pub. by Seloc) Natl Bk Netwk.

Mercruiser Stern Drive, Bravo 1, Bravo 2 & Bravo 3, 1992-96, Vol. III. Joan Coles & Clarence Coles. (Marine Tune-Up & Repair Manuals: Vol. III). (Illus.). 360p. (C). 1998. pap. 34.95 (*0-89330-046-2*, Pub. by Seloc) Natl Bk Netwk.

Mercruiser Stern Drive, 1964-1992. Clarence W. Coles & Howard U. Young. LC 99-475069. (Marine Tune-Up & Repair Manuals). (Illus.). 600p. (C). 1998. pap. 34.95 (*0-89330-005-5*, Pub. by Seloc) Natl Bk Netwk.

Mercruiser Stern Drive Shop Manual 1995-1997 Alpha One, Bravo One, Bravo Two & Bravo Three. Clymer Publications Staff. LC 97-78083. (Illus.). 712p. 1997. 36.95 (*0-89287-697-2*) Intertec Pub.

Mercruiser Stern Drive Shop Manual, 1964-1987 (Also Includes 1986-1987 TR & TRS Models) 7th rev. ed. Kalton Lahue. LC 93-79848. (Illus.). 616p. 1993. pap. 36.95 (*0-89287-613-1*, B740) Intertec Pub.

***Mercruiser Stern Drives 1992-2000.** Chilton. (C). 2000. pap. 34.95 (*0-89330-053-5*) NP-Chilton.

Mercs: True Stories of Mercenaries in Action. Bill Fawcett. 304p. 1999. mass mkt. 6.50 (*0-380-79838-7*, Avon Bks) Morrow Avon.

Mercurial Wood: Sites, Tales, Qualities. John Milbank. LC 99-201828. xiv, 69p. 1998. pap. 15.95 (*3-7052-0113-1*, Pub. by Poetry Salzburg) Intl Spec Bk.

Mercurio Volante of Don Carlos de Siguenza y Gongora. Irving A. Leonard. LC 67-24715. (Quivira Society Publications, Vol. 3). 1967. reprint ed. 19.95 (*0-405-00073-1*) Ayer.

Mercurius Nov-Anglicanus. William Douglass. (Notable American Authors Ser.). 1992. reprint ed. lib. bdg. 75.00 (*0-7812-2680-5*) Rprt Serv.

Mercury see Galaxy Series

Mercury. Jonis Agee. LC 81-2998. (Illus.). 12p. (Orig.). 1981. pap. 15.00 (*0-915124-50-5*) Coffee Hse.

Mercury. Larry D. Brimner. LC 97-38648. (True Bks.). (J). 1998. 21.00 (*0-516-20619-2*) Childrens.

Mercury. Larry D. Brimner. (True Bks.). (Illus.). 48p. (J). (gr. 3-5). 1999. pap. text 6.95 (*0-516-26436-2*) Childrens.

Mercury. Michael Daniel & Don Hamm. (J). 1997. pap. 8.95 (*1-878406-15-9*, Paintbrsh) Parker Dstb.

Mercury. Anna Kavan. LC 95-132525. 136p. 1995. 28.00 (*0-7206-0940-2*, Pub. by P Owen Ltd) Dufour.

Mercury. Anna Kavan. 136p. 1996. pap. 19.95 (*0-7206-0984-4*, Pub. by P Owen Ltd) Dufour.

Mercury. Steve Kipp. (Galaxy Ser.). (Illus.). 24p. (J). (gr. k-3). 1997. lib. bdg. 14.00 (*0-516-20893-4*) Childrens.

***Mercury.** Steven L. Kipp. (Galaxy Ser.). (Illus.). 24p. (J). (ps-3). 2000. lib. bdg. 15.93 (*0-7368-0518-4*, Bridgestone Bks) Capstone Pr.

***Mercury.** Amy Margaret. LC 99-40235. (Library of the Planets). 2000. lib. bdg. 15.50 (*0-8239-5642-3*, PowerKids) Rosen Group.

Mercury. Seymour Simon. LC 91-17404. (Illus.). 24p. (J). (ps-3). 1992. 16.00 (*0-688-10544-0*, Wm Morrow) Morrow Avon.

Mercury. Seymour Simon. LC 99-162633. 32p. 1998. mass mkt. 5.95 (*0-688-16382-3*, Wm Morrow) Morrow Avon.

***Mercury.** Ray Spangenburg & Diane Moser. LC 00-38201. (Watts Library). 2001. write for info. (*0-531-11766-9*) Watts.

Mercury. Ed. by Faith Vilas et al. LC 88-29515. 794p. 1988. 56.00 (*0-8165-1085-7*) U of Ariz Pr.

Mercury. Gregory L. Vogt. LC 93-11218. (Gateway Solar System Ser.). (Illus.). 32p. (J). (gr. 2-4). 1994. lib. bdg. 19.90 (*1-56294-390-1*) Millbrook Pr.

Mercury. Gregory L. Vogt. (Gateway Solar System Ser.). (Illus.). 32p. (J). (gr. 2-4). 1996. pap. 6.95 (*0-7613-0157-7*) Millbrook Pr.

Mercury. Robert Daily. (First Bks.). (Illus.). 64p. (J). (gr. 4-6). 1996. reprint ed. pap. 5.95 (*0-531-15769-5*) Watts.

Mercury: An Official Organ of the Societas Rosicruciana in America (1916-1921) Ed. by George W. Plummer. 282p. 1998. reprint ed. pap. 24.95 (*0-7661-0707-8*) Kessinger Pub.

Mercury: Environmental Aspects. WHO Staff. (Environmental Health Criteria Ser.: No. 86). 115p. 1989. 23.00 (*92-4-154286-1*) World Health.

Mercury: The Elusive Planet. Robert G. Strom. LC 86-26030. (Library of the Solar System). (Illus.). 208p. 1987. 34.95 (*0-87474-892-5*) Smithsonian.

M

An Asterisk (*) at the beginning of an entry indicates that the title is appearing for the first time.

Mercury & Arsenic Wastes: Removal, Recovery, Treatment, & Disposal. United State Environmental Protection Agency. LC 92-45154. (Pollution Technology Review Ser.: No. 214). (Illus.). 127p. 1993. 69.00 (0-8155-1326-7) Noyes.

Mercury & Me. Jim Hutton & Tim Wapshott. 256p. (Orig.). 1996. mass mkt. 5.99 (1-57297-080-4) Blvd Books.

Mercury & Other Toxic Metals in Humans: Proceedings of the First International Conference on Biocompatibility of Materials. Ed. by Hal Huggins. (Illus.). 350p. 1989. pap. text 35.00 (0-943685-08-7) Biosocial.

Mercury & Venus. Robin Kerrod. LC 99-18352. (Planet Library). (Illus.). 32p. (J). (gr. 4-7). 2000. 22.60 (0-8225-3904-7, Lerner Publctns) Lerner Pub.

Mercury As a Global Pollutant: Human Health Issues. Brian Wheatley & R. E. Wyzga. LC 97-28626. 1997. text 95.00 (0-7923-4679-3) Kluwer Academic.

Mercury As a Global Pollutant: Proceedings of the Third International Conference Held in Whistler, British Columbia, July 10-14, 1994. Ed. by Donald R. Porcella. 1312p. (C). 1995. text 364.50 (0-7923-3544-9) Kluwer Academic.

Mercury Beach. Tessa Duder. LC 97-161409. 191p. 1997. write for info. (0-14-038575-4, PuffinBks) Peng Put Young Read.

Mercury Bibliography: 12000 Citations. Mats Hanson. 302p. 1993. spiral bd. 39.00 (0-941011-09-7) Bio-Probe.

Mercury Bibliography Update Covering Research Published Between 1991-1993: 1404 Citations, 610 Abstracts. Mats Hanson. 117p. spiral bd. 19.95 (0-941011-12-7) Bio-Probe.

Mercury Cadmium Telluride Imagers: A Patent-Oriented Survey. A. C. Onshage. (Handbook of Sensors & Actuators Ser.: No. 5). 456p. 1997. 215.75 (0-444-82790-0) Elsevier.

Mercury Contaminated Sites: Characterization, Risk Assessment & Remediation. Ed. by W. Salomons et al. LC 98-27745. (Environmental Science Ser.). (Illus.). 552p. 1998. 129.00 (3-540-63731-1) Spr-Verlag.

Mercury Contamination in Man & His Environment. (Technical Reports: No. 137). (Illus.). 181p. (Orig.). 1972. pap. 30.00 (92-0-115172-1, IDC137, Pub. by IAEA) Bernan Associates.

Mercury Free: The Wisdom Behind the Global Consumer Movement to Ban "Silver" Dental Fillings. James E. Hardy. (Illus.). 270p. 1996. 24.95 (0-9649301-1-0); pap. 6.95 (0-9649301-0-2) Gabriel Rose.

Mercury from Gold & Silver Mining: A Chemical Time Bomb? Luiz D. De Lacerda & W. Salomons. Ed. by R. Allan & U. Fsrstner. LC 97-35099. (Environmental Science Ser.). (Illus.). 190p. 1997. 79.95 (3-540-61724-8) Spr-Verlag.

Mercury in Food. 1995. 12.00 (92-871-2880-4, Pub. by Council of Europe) Manhattan Pub Co.

Mercury in Liquids, Compressed Gases, Molten Salts & Other Elements. Ed. by H. L. Celer. (Illus.). 271p. 1987. 120.00 (0-317-66355-0, Pergamon Pr) Elsevier.

Mercury in Liquids, Compressed Gases, Molten Salts & Other Elements. Clever. (IUPAC Solubility Data Ser.: 29). 272p. 1987. 167.00 (0-08-035935-3, Pergamon Pr) Elsevier.

Mercury in the Biogeochemical Cycle: Natural Environment & Hydroelectric Reservoirs of Northern Quebec (Canada. Ed. by M. Lucotte et al. LC 99-24587. (Environmental Science Ser.). (Illus.). xviii, 334p. 1999. 109.00 (3-540-65755-X) Spr-Verlag.

Mercury in the Ecosyptem. S. Mitra. (Illus.). 270p. 1985. 116.00 (0-87849-529-0, Pub. by Trans T Pub) Enfield Pubs NH.

Mercury in Your Mouth Vol. 1: The Truth about Silver Dental Fillings. rev. ed. Quicksilver Associates Staff. LC 95-67129. 208p. (Orig.). 1994. pap. 14.95 (0-9643870-0-X) Quicksilv Pr.

Mercury Labels, 5 vols., 51. Ed. by Ed Novitsky. LC 93-15254. 4240p. 1993. lib. bdg. 395.00 (0-313-27371-5, RMG/, Greenwood Pr) Greenwood.

Mercury Labels Vol. I: The 1945-1956 Era, Vol. 1. Ed. by Ed Novitsky. LC 93-15254. (Discographies Ser.: No. 51). 832p. 1993. lib. bdg. 95.00 (0-313-29031-8, RMG01, Greenwood Pr) Greenwood.

Mercury Labels Vol. II: The 1956-1964 Era, Vol. 2. Ed. by Ed Novitsky. LC 93-15254. (Discographies Ser.: No. 51). 840p. 1993. lib. bdg. 95.00 (0-313-29032-6, RMG02, Greenwood Pr) Greenwood.

Mercury Labels Vol. III: The 1964-1969 Era, Vol. 3. Ed. by Ed Novitsky. LC 93-15254. (Discographies Ser.: No. 51). 768p. 1993. lib. bdg. 95.00 (0-313-29033-4, RMG03, Greenwood Pr) Greenwood.

Mercury Labels Vol. IV: The 1969-1991 Era & Classical Recordings, Vol. 4. Ed. by Ed Novisky. LC 93-15254. (Discographies Ser.: No. 51). 1993. lib. bdg. 95.00 (0-313-29034-2, RMG04, Greenwood Pr) Greenwood.

Mercury Labels Vol. V: Record & Artist Indexes, Vol. 5. Ed. by Ed Novitsky. LC 93-15254. (Discographies Ser.: No. 51). 912p. 1993. lib. bdg. 95.00 (0-313-29035-0, RMG05, Greenwood Pr) Greenwood.

Mercury Larousse French-German, German-French Dictionary: Dictionnaire Mercure Francais-Allemand-Francais. 3rd ed. Larousse Staff & Ernst E. Lange-Kowal. (FRE & GER.). 1206p. 1964. 55.00 (0-7859-4826-0) Fr & Eur.

Mercury-Mariner-Outboard-All Engines 1995-1999. Seloc Publications Staff. (Illus.). 352p. (C). 2000. pap. 34.95 (0-89330-051-9) Thomson Learn.

Mercury Meets Minerva: Business Studies & Higher Education: the Swedish Case. Lars Engwall. LC 92-12052. 240p. 1992. text 92.00 (0-08-041044-8, Pergamon Pr) Elsevier.

Mercury Method of Chart Comparison. Lois M. Rodden. 228p. 1973. 19.00 (0-86690-150-7, R1413-014) Am Fed Astrologers.

***Mercury Mouse Slows down in the House.** Lois Keffer. LC 98-46186. (J). 1999. 9.99 (1-57673-437-4) Zondervan.

Mercury Muscle Cars. David Newhardt. LC 99-32415. (Illus.). 128p. 1999. pap. 21.95 (0-7603-0549-8, 128062AP) MBI Pubg.

Mercury: or The Secret & Swift Messenger: Shewing How a Man with Privacy & Speed May Communicate His Thoughts to a Friend at Any Distance (1707) John Wilkins. LC 84-24279. (Foundations of Semiotics Ser.: No. 6). cix, 124p. 1984. reprint ed. 65.00 (90-272-3276-8) J Benjamins Pubng Co.

Mercury Outboard, 1965-1991 Vol. I: 1 & 2 Cylinder Models. Joan Coles & Clarence W. Coles. LC 86-218766. (Marine Tune-Up & Repair Manuals: Vol. I). (Illus.). 528p. (C). 1998. pap. 34.95 (0-89330-012-8, Pub. by Seloc) Natl Bk Netwk.

Mercury Outboard, 1965-92 Vol. II: 3 & 4 Cylinder Models. Joan Coles & Clarence W. Coles. LC 99-475070. (Marine Tune-Up & Repair Manuals). (Illus.). 575p. (C). 1998. pap. 34.95 (0-89330-013-6, Pub. by Seloc) Natl Bk Netwk.

Mercury Outboard Shop Manual 45-225 HP, 1972-1989. 4th rev. ed. Kalton C. Lahue. (Illus.). 424p. 1989. pap. 34.95 (0-89287-396-5, B726) Clymer Pub.

Mercury Outboard Shop Manual 3.5-40 hp, 1972-1989 (Includes Electric Motors) 5th rev. ed. (Illus.). 368p. 1989. pap. 36.95 (0-89287-395-7, B721) Intertec Pub.

Mercury Outboard Shop Manual 3-275 HP, 1990-1993. Clymer Publications Staff. LC 92-74933. (Illus.). 640p. 1993. pap. 36.95 (0-89287-568-2, B722) Intertec Pub.

Mercury Outboards, 1965-1991 Vol. III: 6-in-Line & V6 Models. Joan Coles & Clarence W. Coles. LC 91-195390. (Marine Tune-Up & Repair Manuals: Vol. III). (Illus.). 640p. (C). 1998. pap. 34.95 (0-89330-014-4, Pub. by Seloc) Natl Bk Netwk.

Mercury Photosensitization. G. R. De Mare. write for info. (0-318-56739-3) Elsevier.

Mercury Poisoning, No. 1. Eusebio Mayz et al. LC 72-13563. (Illus.). 220p. (C). 1972. text 29.50 (0-8422-7072-8) Irvington.

Mercury Poisoning, No. 2. J. W. Daniel et al. LC 72-13563. (Illus.). 220p. (C). 1972. text 32.50 (0-8422-7073-6) Irvington.

Mercury Poisoning from Dental Amalgam - A Hazard to Human Brain. Patrick Stortebecker. 213p. 1986. reprint ed. 20.00 (0-941011-01-1) Bio-Probe.

Mercury Pollution: Integration & Synthesis. Ed. by Carl J. Watras & John W. Huckabee. LC 94-15244. 752p. 1994. lib. bdg. 104.95 (1-56670-066-3, L1066) Lewis Pubs.

Mercury Reader. (The Custom Freshman Composition Series). (C). 1998. text. write for info. (0-13-010862-6) P-H.

***Mercury Reader.** (C). 2000. write for info. (0-536-60931-4); write for info. (0-536-60906-3) Pearson Custom.

***Mercury Reader.** (C). 1998. pap. write for info. (0-536-01706-9) Pearson Custom.

***Mercury Reader.** (C). 1999. write for info. (0-536-60664-1); write for info. (0-536-60660-9) Pearson Custom.

Mercury Reader. (C). 1999. pap. write for info. (0-536-02563-0) S&S Trade.

Mercury Reader. Kathleen Cain. (C). 2000. pap. text. write for info. (0-321-07499-8) Addson-Wesley Educ.

***Mercury Reader Humbolt State University.** (C). 1999. write for info. (0-536-60139-9) Pearson Custom.

***Mercury Reader Illinois State University.** (C). 1999. write for info. (0-536-60127-5) Pearson Custom.

***Mercury Reader: Mississippi State University.** (C). 1999. write for info. (0-536-60655-2) Pearson Custom.

***Mercury Reader: Morningside College.** (C). 1999. write for info. (0-536-60675-7) Pearson Custom.

***Mercury Reader: Northern Illinois University.** (C). 1999. write for info. (0-536-60654-4) Pearson Custom.

***Mercury Reader: Prestonsburg Community College.** (C). 1999. write for info. (0-536-60269-7) Pearson Custom.

***Mercury Reader: Salish Kootenai College.** (C). 1999. write for info. (0-536-60665-X) Pearson Custom.

***Mercury Reader: Solano Community College.** (C). 1999. write for info. (0-536-60673-0) Pearson Custom.

***Mercury Reader: University of Colorado Denver.** (C). 1999. write for info. (0-536-60656-0) Pearson Custom.

***Mercury Reader No. 2: Humbolt State University.** (C). 1999. write for info. (0-536-60140-2) Pearson Custom.

Mercury Reader Arizona State University. (C). 1999. pap. write for info. (0-536-02424-3) Pearson Custom.

Mercury Reader Assumption College. (C). 1999. pap. text. write for info. (0-536-02458-8) Pearson Custom.

Mercury Reader Central Methodist College. (C). 1999. write for info. (0-536-02471-5) Pearson Custom.

Mercury Reader College of the Redwoods. (C). 1999. write for info. (0-536-02414-6) Pearson Custom.

Mercury Reader Delta College. (C). 1999. pap. text. write for info. (0-536-02439-1) Pearson Custom.

***Mercury Reader Illinois State University.** (C). 1999. write for info. (0-536-60110-0) Pearson Custom.

***Mercury Reader Loyola University.** (C). 1999. pap. text 0.00 (0-536-02823-0) Pearson Custom.

Mercury Reader Northampton Community College. (C). 1999. pap. text. write for info. (0-536-02446-4) Pearson Custom.

***Mercury Reader Prestonsburg Cc.** (C). 1999. pap. text 0.00 (0-536-02803-6) Pearson Custom.

***Mercury Reader Saginaw Valley State Univ.** (C). 1999. pap. text 0.00 (0-536-02800-1) Pearson Custom.

Mercury Reader Sample Book 2000. (C). 1999. pap. text. write for info. (0-205-31596-8) Allyn.

***Mercury Reader 3.** (C). 1999. text. write for info. (0-536-60705-2) Pearson Custom.

***Mercury Reader University of Nevada Reno.** (C). 1999. pap. text. write for info. (0-536-02470-7) Pearson Custom.

***Mercury Reader Washington State University Vancouver.** (C). 1999. write for info. (0-536-60642-0) Pearson Custom.

***Mercury Reader Wayne State Univ.** (C). 1999. pap. text 0.00 (0-536-02822-2) Pearson Custom.

***Mercury Reader Yuba College.** (C). 1999. pap. text 0.00 (0-536-02804-4) Pearson Custom.

***Mercury Reader 2.** (C). 1999. text. write for info. (0-536-60706-0) Pearson Custom.

Mercury Rising. Ryne Douglas Pearson. 1998. mass mkt. 6.50 (0-380-80294-5, Avon Bks) Morrow Avon.

***Mercury Rising, Vol. No. 3.** Lianne Sentar. 1999. pap. 4.99 (1-892213-18-4) Mixx Enter Inc.

Mercury Rising: Women, Evil & the Trickster Gods. Deldon A. McNeely. LC 96-50485. 208p. (Orig.). 1997. pap. 18.00 (0-88214-366-2) Spring Pubns.

Mercury Seven. Stuart A. Kallen. (Giant Leaps Ser.). 32p. (J). 1996. lib. bdg. 14.98 (1-56239-565-3) ABDO Pub Co.

Mercury Sport Jet 90-120 hp, 1993-1995. (Illus.). 192p. 1995. pap. 36.95 (0-89287-657-3, W815) Intertec Pub.

Mercury Systems. 2nd ed. B. L. Boyce. 176p. 1986. pap. text 9.96 (0-07-006903-4) McGraw.

Mercury Systems Inc. Practice Set in Word-Information Processing for Conventional & Text-Editing Typewriters. B. L. Boyce. 1981. 12.56 (0-07-006901-8) McGraw.

Mercury, the Open Door, Pt. 1. Bernice P. Grebner. LC 88-70456. 188p. 1988. 19.00 (0-86690-334-8, G2801-014) Am Fed Astrologers.

Mercury, the Open Door, Pt. 2. Bernice P. Grebner. 1990. pap. 19.00 (0-86690-375-5, 3036-014) Am Fed Astrologers.

Mercury 3.9-135 hp Outboards, 1964-1971. Clymer Publications Staff. pap. 34.95 (0-89287-414-7, B719) Clymer Pub.

Mercury 3.9-135 hp Outboards, 1964-1971. (Illus.). 296p. Date not set. reprint ed. pap. 36.95 (0-89287-441-4, B719) Intertec Pub.

***Mercury Universe.** 249p. (C). 1999. pap. 12.00 (0-9677633-0-4) BookBerner Pubng.

Mercury/Mariner, 1990- 1994, Vol. I. Joan Coles & Clarence Coles. (Marine Tune-Up & Repair Manuals: Vol. I). (Illus.). 350p. (C). 1998. pap. 34.95 (0-89330-035-7, Pub. by Seloc) Natl Bk Netwk.

Mercury/Mariner Outboards, 1990-1994 Vol. II: 3 & 4 Cylinder. Joan Coles & Clarence Coles. LC 96-104373. (Marine Tune-Up & Repair Manuals). (Illus.). 430p. (C). 1998. pap. 34.95 (0-89330-036-5, Pub. by Seloc) Natl Bk Netwk.

Mercury/Mariner, 1990-94 Vol. III: V-6 Powerhead Outboard. Joan Coles & Clarence Coles. (Marine Tune-Up & Repair Manuals). (Illus.). 400p. (C). 1998. pap. 34.95 (0-89330-037-3, Pub. by Seloc) Natl Bk Netwk.

Mercury/Mariner Outboard Shop Manual 2.5-60 HP 1994-1997 (Includes Jet Drive Models) Clymer Publications Staff. LC 98-72832. 712p. 1998. pap. 36.95 (0-89287-698-0) Intertec Pub.

Mercury/Mariner 2-Stroke Outboard Shop Manual 75-275 HP 1994-1997 (Includes Jet Drive Models) Clymer Publications Staff. LC 98-72837. (Illus.). 824p. 1998. pap. write for info. (0-89287-707-3) Intertec Pub.

Mercy. Laura Cahill. 5.95 (0-8222-1716-3) Dramatists Play.

Mercy. J. M. DeMatteis. Ed. by Karen Berger. (Illus.). 64p. 1993. pap. 5.95 (1-56389-091-7) DC Comics.

Mercy. Andrea Dworkin. LC 91-18157. 344p. 1991. 22.00 (0-941423-69-7); pap. 13.95 (0-941423-88-3) FWEW.

Mercy. Philip Levine. LC 98-43353. 80p. 1999. 22.00 (0-375-40138-5) Knopf.

Mercy. David L. Lindsey. 608p. 1991. mass mkt. 6.99 (0-553-28972-1) Bantam.

Mercy. Kathleen Peirce. LC 91-50110. (Poetry Ser.). 64p. (C). 1991. pap. 10.95 (0-8229-5457-5); text 19.95 (0-8229-3686-0) U of Pittsburgh Pr.

Mercy. large type ed. Jodi Picoult. LC 96-43978. (Core Ser.). 662p. 1997. lib. bdg. 26.95 (0-7838-2003-8, G K Hall Lrg Type) Mac Lib Ref.

Mercy: Poems. Philip Levine. LC 98-43353. 80p. 2000. pap. 15.00 (0-375-70135-4) Knopf.

Mercy & Eagleflight. Michael R. Phillips. LC 96-9793. 1996. pap. 10.99 (0-8423-3920-5) Tyndale Hse.

Mercy & Grace. Billy J. Daugherty. 32p. (Orig.). 1993. pap. 0.50 (1-56267-083-2) Victory Ctr OK.

Mercy Flights: Stories. Mary Peterson. LC 84-19490. (Breakthrough Ser.: No. 47). 104p. 1985. pap. 10.95 (0-8262-0464-3) U of Mo Pr.

Mercy for the Worlds. Abul Hasan Ali Nadvi. 32p. (Orig.). 1985. pap. 2.00 (1-56744-325-7) Kazi Pubns.

Mercy Hospital: Crisis! Carolyn Carlyle. 128p. (Orig.). (J). (gr. 5). 1993. pap. 3.50 (0-380-76846-1, Avon Bks) Morrow Avon.

Mercy Hospital: Don't Tell Mrs. Harris. Carolyn Carlyle. 128p. (Orig.). (YA). 1993. pap. 3.50 (0-380-76848-8, Avon Bks) Morrow Avon.

Mercy Hospital: Dr. Cute. Carolyn Carlyle. 128p. (Orig.). (YA). 1993. pap. 3.50 (0-380-76849-6, Avon Bks) Morrow Avon.

Mercy Hospital: The Best Medicine. Carolyn Carlyle. 128p. (Orig.). (J). 1993. pap. 3.50 (0-380-76847-X, Avon Bks) Morrow Avon.

Mercy Hospital of Buffalo Parking Ramp. (PCI Journal Reprints Ser.). 5p. 1985. pap. 10.00 (0-318-19784-7, JR267) P-PCI.

Mercy in Moccasins: Playscript. Nellie McCaslin. LC 93-14393. 16p. 1993. pap. 5.00 (0-88734-441-0) Players Pr.

***Mercy Mercy Me: Poems.** Elena Georgiou. LC 99-87728. 2000. pap. 12.00 (1-891305-24-7, Pub. by Painted Leaf) LPC InBook.

***Mercy Mission.** William Christie. 368p. 2000. pap. 5.50 (0-8439-4753-5, Leisure Bks) Dorchester Pub Co.

Mercy Ocean: (Teachings of Abdullah Al Faizi Ad-Daghestani) Shaykh N. Qibrisi. 1991. pap. 9.95 (1-56744-136-X) Kazi Pubns.

Mercy Oceans: Teachings of Maulana Abdullah al-Faiza ad-Daghestani. Shaykh N. Al-Qibrisi. 190p. (Orig.). 1980. pap. 4.75 (0-939830-11-6) New Era Publns MI.

Mercy Oceans I. Shaykh A. Daghistani. 144p. (Orig.). 1995. pap. 9.95 (0-934905-31-2) Kazi Pubns.

Mercy Oceans II. Shaykh A. Daghistani. 144p. (Orig.). 1995. pap. 9.95 (0-934905-32-0) Kazi Pubns.

Mercy of a Rude Stream: A Star Shines over Mt. Morris Park. Henry Roth. LC 94-45086. Vol. 1. 1994. pap. 13.00 (0-312-11929-1) St Martin.

Mercy of Allah. Hilaire Belloc. LC 91-72258. 334p. 1991. reprint ed. pap. 19.00 (0-87034-100-6) Fraser Pub Co.

Mercy of God. Kenneth Copeland. 47p. 1986. pap. 3.95 (0-88114-725-7) K Copeland Pubns.

Mercy of God: Dives in Misericordia. John Paul, II, pseud. 53p. pap. 2.95 (0-8198-4745-3) Pauline Bks.

Mercy of Qur'an & the Advent of Zaman: Commentary on Four Suras. Shaykh F. Haeri. 1990. pap. 12.95 (0-88059-009-2) Zahra Pubns.

Mercy or Murder? Euthanasia, Morality & Public Policy. Ed. by Kenneth R. Overberg. 300p. (Orig.). 1993. pap. 15.95 (1-55612-609-3) Sheed & Ward WI.

Mercy Otis Warren. Jeffrey H. Richards. (Twayne's United States Authors Ser.). 1995. 32.00 (0-8057-4003-1, Twyne) Mac Lib Ref.

Mercy Philbrick's Choice. Helen H. Jackson. (Notable American Authors Ser.). 1992. reprint ed. lib. bdg. 75.00 (0-7812-3350-X) Rprt Serv.

Mercy Philbrick's Choice. Helen Maria Hunt Jackson. LC 70-128925. reprint ed. 34.50 (0-404-03541-8) AMS Pr.

Mercy Road. Dalia Pagani. LC 97-40249. 336p. 1998. 21.95 (0-385-32016-7) Delacorte.

Mercy Road. Dalia Pagani. 352p. 1999. pap. 11.95 (0-385-32356-5, Delta Trade) Dell.

Mercy Road & Other Stories. Benjamin W. Farley. LC 86-14790. (Illus.). 136p. 1986. 13.95 (0-87797-122-6) Cherokee.

Mercy Rule. John T. Lescroart. 640p. 1999. mass mkt. 7.99 (0-440-22282-6) Bantam Dell.

Mercy Rule. large type ed. John T. Lescroart. 684p. 1999. pap. 26.95 (0-7838-0394-X, G K Hall Lrg Type) Mac Lib Ref.

Mercy Rule: A Novel. John T. Lescroart. LC 98-16726. 480p. 1998. 24.95 (0-385-31658-5) Doubleday.

Mercy Seat. Rilla Askew. LC 96-52416. 428p. 1998. pap. 13.95 (0-14-026515-5) Viking Penguin.

Mercy Seat. Bruce Smith. LC 93-38826. 60p. 1994. pap. 8.95 (0-226-76406-0) U Ch Pr.

Mercy Seat. Bruce Smith. LC 93-38826. 64p. 1994. lib. bdg. 20.00 (0-226-76405-2) U Ch Pr.

Mercy to Mankind Vol. 1: Makkah Period. Abidullah Ghazi & Tasneema Ghazi. 60p. (Orig.). (J). (gr. 6-8). 1991. pap. text 6.00 (1-56316-154-0) Iqra Intl Ed Fdtn.

Mercy to Mankind Vol. 2: Madinah Period. 4th ed. Abidullah Ghazi & Tasneema Ghazi. 42p. (J). (gr. 6-8). 1991. reprint ed. text 6.00 (1-56316-156-7) Iqra Intl Ed Fdtn.

Mercy to Mankind I Workbook: Makkah Period. Abidullah Ghazi & Tasneema Ghazi. Ed. by Lynn Uwitzer & Mary Maples. 38p. (YA). (gr. 6-8). 1988. wbk. ed. 4.00 (1-56316-155-9) Iqra Intl Ed Fdtn.

Mercy Trap. James E. Martin. 256p. 1990. pap. 3.95 (0-380-71041-2, Avon Bks) Morrow Avon.

***Mercy Triumphs over Judgement.** Francis Frangipane. 96p. 1999. pap. 7.00 (1-886296-18-9) Arrow Publications.

Mercy Warren. Alice Brown. LC 67-30159. (Illus.). 328p. 1968. reprint ed. 20.00 (0-87152-042-7) Reprint.

MerCycle. Piers Anthony. 352p. 1992. mass mkt. 5.99 (0-441-52562-8) Ace Bks.

Mercy's Birds. Linda Holeman. LC 98-60524. 208p. (YA). (gr. 8 up). 1998. pap. 5.95 (0-88776-463-0) Tundra Bks.

Mercy's Story. large type ed. Dorothy Wakeley. 1991. 27.99 (0-7089-2527-8) Ulverscroft.

Merda! The Real Italian You Were Never Taught at School. Roland Delicio. LC 93-7731. (Illus.). 96p. 1993. pap. 10.95 (0-452-27039-1, Plume) Dutton Plume.

Merde! Genevieve. 1986. pap. 8.00 (0-684-81864-7) Atheneum Yung Read.

Merde: Excursions in Scientific Cultural & Sociological Historical Coprology. Ralph A. Lewin. LC 98-27259. 187p. 1999. 19.95 (0-375-50198-3) Random.

Merde! The Real French You Were Never Taught at School. Genevieve. (Illus.). 112p. 1998. per. 9.00 (0-684-85427-9) S&S Trade Pap.

Merde Encore! Genevieve. 1988. pap. 8.00 (0-684-81865-5) Atheneum Yung Read.

Merde Encore! More of the Real French You Were Never Taught at School. Genevieve. (Illus.). 112p. 1998. per. 9.00 (0-684-85428-7) S&S Trade.

Mere Christianity. Broadman & Holman Staff. LC 99-37906. (Shepherd's Notes Ser.). 1999. pap. 5.95 (0-8054-9347-6) Broadman.

Mere Christianity. C. S. Lewis. 190p. 1986. pap. 3.95 (0-02-086940-1) Macmillan.

Mere Christianity. C. S. Lewis. 1997. 18.00 (0-684-84638-1) S&S Trade.

Mere Christianity. rev. ed. C. S. Lewis. LC 84-20027. 192p. 1996. per. 6.00 (0-684-82378-0, Touchstone) S&S Trade Pap.

Mere Christianity: A Revised & Enlarged Edition, with a new introduction, of the three books, The case for Christianity, Christian behaviour, & Beyond

An Asterisk (*) at the beginning of an entry indicates that the title is appearing for the first time.

Personality. large type enl. rev. ed. C. S. Lewis. LC 86-30451. (Large Print Inspirational Ser.). 384p. 1987. pap. 16.95 (0-8027-2575-9) Walker & Co.

Mere Creation: Science, Faith & Intelligent Design. Ed. by William A. Dembski. LC 98-20999. 475p. 1998. pap. 24.99 (0-8308-1515-5, 1515) InterVarsity.

Mere Creatures: A Study of Modern Fantasy Tales for Children. Elliott Gose. 1988. pap. 15.95 (0-8020-6674-7) U of Toronto Pr.

Mere Creatures: A Study of Modern Fantasy Tales for Children. Elliott B. Gose. LC 88-196128. 214p. reprint ed. pap. 66.40 (0-8357-4139-7, 203691200006) Bks Demand.

Mere Creatures of the State? Education, Religion & the Courts. William B. Bay. (Illus.). 142p. (Orig.). 1994. pap. 13.95 (1-883357-99-3, Crisis Bks) Dumb Ox Bks.

Mere dans la Litterature Francaise, 1678-1831. Maria A. Mann. (American University Studies: Romance Languages & Literature: Ser. II, Vol. 92). 299p. (C). 1989. text 40.10 (0-8204-0878-6) P Lang Pubng.

Mere du Printemps, l'Oum-er-Bia. Driss Chraibi. (FRE.). 1986. pap. 14.95 (0-7859-2707-7) Fr & Eur.

Mere et l'Enfant-Le Pere Perdrix. Charles-Louis Philippe. (FRE.). 1983. pap. 13.95 (0-7859-4194-0) Fr & Eur.

***Mere Interlude.** Thomas Hardy. (Short Stories Ser.). 22p. 2000. pap. 3.95 (1-86092-045-4, Pub. by Travelman Pub) IPG Chicago.

Mere Irish & Fior-Ghael: Studies in the Idea of Irish Nationality, Its Development & Literary Expression Prior to the Nineteenth Century. Joseph T. Leerssen. LC 96-42498. (Critical Conditions Ser.). 1997. pap. text 20.00 (0-268-01427-2) U of Notre Dame Pr.

Mere Irish & Fior-Ghael: Studies in the Idea of Irish Nationality, It's Literary Expression & Development. Joseph Theodoor Leerssen. LC 86-6879. (Utrecht Publications in General & Comparative Literature: Vol. 22). xv, 543p. 1986. 124.00 (90-272-2198-7) J Benjamins Pubng Co.

Mere Literature, & Other Essays. Woodrow Wilson. LC 73-157970. (Essay Index Reprint Ser.). 1977. reprint ed. 20.95 (0-8369-2260-3) Ayer.

Mere Marie of New France see Blessed Marie of New France: The Story of the First Missionary Sisters in Canada

Mere Morality: What God Expects from Ordinary People. Lewis B. Smedes. 292p. 1989. pap. 18.00 (0-8028-0257-5) Eerdmans.

Mere Mortals. Kevin Kiely. 224p. 1989. pap. 15.95 (1-85371-058-X, Pub. by Poolbeg Pr) Dufour.

Mere Mortals: An Evening of Six Short Plays. David Ives. 1998. pap. 5.25 (0-8222-1632-9) Dramatists Play.

Mere Mortals: Poems. Terese Svoboda. LC 94-29146. 152p. 1995. pap. 14.95 (0-8203-1710-1) U of Ga Pr.

Mere ou la Mutation de la Mort see Mother: or The Mutation of Death

Mere ou le Materialisme Divin see Mother: or The Divine Materialism

Mere Ou L'espece Nouvelle see Mother: or The New Species

Mere Parfaite. Sara Grant. (Horizon Ser.: Bk. 494). 1999. mass mkt. 3.50 (0-373-39494-2, 1-39494-9) Harlequin Bks.

Meredith. Bruce D. Heald. LC 96-169617. (Images of America Ser.). 128p. 1996. pap. 16.99 (0-7524-0435-0) Arcadia Publng.

Meredith. Jean Thesman. (Elliott Cousins Ser.: No. 2). 144p. (YA). (gr. 7 up). 1998. mass mkt. 3.99 (0-380-78682-6, Avon Bks) Morrow Avon.

Meredith: A Change of Masks. Gillian Beer. LC 70-546357. (A Study of the Novels). 1970. 23.25 (0-485-11122-5) Athlone Pr.

Meredith: The Critical Heritage. Ed. by Ioan Williams. 549p. 1978. 69.50 (0-7100-6961-8, Routledge Thoemms) Routledge.

Meredith & the Novel. Neil Roberts. LC 96-3208. 224p. 1997. text 55.00 (0-312-16535-8) St Martin.

Meredith Annals & Genealogies. Mary E. Hanaford. 760p. 1997. reprint ed. lib. bdg. 77.50 (0-8328-6013-1) Higginson Bk Co.

Meredith Brooks Blurring the Edges. 88p. 1997. otabind 19.95 (0-7935-8738-7) H Leonard.

Meredith Monk. Ed. by Deborah Jowitt. LC 97-6597. (PAJ Bks.). (Illus.). 208p. 1997. pap. 19.95 (0-8018-5540-3); text 34.95 (0-8018-5539-X) Johns Hopkins.

Meredith Revisited & Other Essays. James Crees. LC 67-30813. (Studies in Fiction: No. 34). 1969. reprint ed. lib. bdg. 75.00 (0-8383-0713-2) M S G Haskell Hse.

Meredith, the Witch Who Wasn't. Dorothea Lachner. Tr. by J. Alison James. LC 97-7545. (Illus.). 32p. (J). (gr. k-3). 1997. 15.95 (1-55858-781-0, Pub. by North-South Bks NYC); lib. bdg. 15.88 (1-55858-782-9, Pub. by North-South Bks NYC) Chronicle Bks.

***Meredith, the Witch Who Wasn't.** Dorothea Lachner. LC 97-7545. (Illus.). 32p. (J). (gr. k-3). 1999. pap. 6.95 (0-7358-1196-2, Pub. by North-South Bks NYC) Chronicle Bks.

***Meredith Willson: The Music & the Man.** M Willson. 104p. 1998. otabind 14.95 (0-7935-8823-5) H Leonard.

Meredith's Big Book of Bible Lists. Joel L. Meredith. 1998. pap. text 9.99 (0-88486-197-X, Inspirational Pr) Arrowood Pr.

Meredith's Book of Bible Lists. Joel L. Meredith. LC 80-14486. 288p. (Orig.). 1980. pap. 9.99 (0-87123-023-2, 210023) Bethany Hse.

***Meredith's Mixed-Up Magic.** Dorothea Lachner. (Illus.). 32p. (gr. k-3). 2000. 15.95 (0-7358-1190-3); pap. 15.88 (0-7358-1191-1) North-South Bks NYC.

Meredith's Second Book of Bible Lists. J. L. Meredith. LC 83-3807. 192p. (Orig.). 1983. pap. 7.99 (0-87123-319-3) Bethany Hse.

Merehurst Cake Book. Merehurst. 1992. 24.95 (1-85391-263-8) Sterling.

***Merely Magic.** Patricia Rice. 2000. mass mkt. 6.99 (0-451-20049-7, Sig) NAL.

Merely Married. Patricia Coughlin. 327p. 1998. mass mkt. 5.99 (0-553-57521-X) BDD Bks Young Read.

***Merely Mortal? Can You Survive Your Own Death?** Antony Flew. 215p. 2000. 26.00 (1-57392-841-0) Prometheus Bks.

Merely Murder. Georgette Heyer. 1976. 26.95 (0-8488-0282-9) Amereon Ltd.

Merely Murder. Georgette Heyer. 369p. 1981. reprint ed. lib. bdg. 21.95 (0-89966-296-X) Buccaneer Bks.

Merely Players. Claude F. Bragdon. LC 72-5692. (Essay Index Reprint Ser.). 1977. reprint ed. 22.95 (0-8369-2983-7) Ayer.

Merely Players: Stories of Stage Life. Virginia Tracy. LC 74-130074. (Short Story Index Reprint Ser.). 1977. 20.95 (0-8369-3655-8) Ayer.

Merely Players (1905) Claude Bragdon. 220p. 1998. reprint ed. pap. 19.95 (0-7661-0159-2) Kessinger Pub.

Mer'em Ayuqucia. Sophie Manutoli.Tr. of Water in All Forms. (ESK., Illus.). 12p. (J). (gr. k-3). 1998. pap. text 6.00 (1-58084-044-2) Lower Kuskokwim.

Mereness Calendar: Federal Documents on the Upper Mississippi Valley, 1780-1890, 13 vols, Set. Ed. by University of Illinois at Urbana, University Libra. 1971. 1755.00 (0-8161-0915-X, G K Hall & Co) Mac Lib Ref.

Merengue. Earl Atkinson. (Ballroom Dance Ser.). 1986. lib. bdg. 250.00 (0-8490-3628-3) Gordon Pr.

Merengue. Earl Atkinson. (Ballroom Dance Ser.). 1983. lib. bdg. 250.00 (0-87700-472-2) Revisionist Pr.

Merengue: Dominican Music & Dominican Identity. Paul Austerlitz. LC 96-24778. (Illus.). 224p. (Orig.). 1997. 69.95 (1-56639-483-X); pap. 22.95 (1-56639-484-8) Temple U Pr.

Meret Oppenheim. Bice Curiger. Tr. by Catherine Schelbert. (Illus.). 54p. 1988. pap. 20.00 (0-685-50295-3) Kent Gallery.

Meret Oppenheim: A Different Retrospective. Bice Curiger. (Illus.). 236p. 1998. 45.00 (3-908161-08-8) Abbeville Pr.

Meret Oppenheim: Beyond the Teacup. Jacqueline Burckhardt & Bice Curiger. LC 96-81295. (Illus.). 176p. 1997. pap. 29.95 (0-916365-46-8) Dist Art Pubs.

Meret Oppenheim: Beyond the Teacup. Meret Oppenheim. 1996. pap. 29.95 (0-614-25261-X) Dist Art Pubs.

Meret Oppenheim: Defiance in the Face of Freedom. Bice Curiger. (Illus.). 290p. 1989. 62.50 (0-262-03165-5) MIT Pr.

Meret Oppenheim, the Book of Ideas: Sketches & Design for Fashion & Jewelry. Christiane Meyer-Thoss. 192p. 1996. 65.00 (3-906127-51-6, Pub. by Gachnang & Springer) Dist Art Pubs.

Merged Evolution: Long-Term Implications of Biotechnology & Information Technology. Susantha Goonatilake. (World Futures General Evolution Studies: Vol. 14). 284p. 1999. text 32.00 (90-5700-521-2, ECU42) Gordon & Breach.

***Merger.** Peter F. Hartz. LC 99-45905. 1999. pap. write for info. (1-893122-33-6) Beard Bks.

Merger: Takeover Conspiracy. David J. Thomsen. 1985. 19.95 (0-8283-1905-7) Branden Bks.

***Merger: The Conglomeration of International Organized Crime.** Jeffrey Robinson. 2000. 27.95 (1-58567-030-8, Pub. by Overlook Pr) Penguin Putnam.

Merger & Acquisitions: Valuations & Structuring: From Cash Flow Derivation to Stock Performance. rev. ed. Alan D. Gasiorek. Ed. by Aloysius R. Gasiorek & Glen R. Gasiorek. LC 97-212183. (Illus.). 378p. 1997. 69.00 (0-9658556-0-0) Corp Dev Inst.

Merger Case Digest, 1982. Antitrust Law Section Members. 756p. 1984. 40.00 (0-685-10016-2, 503-0053) Amer Bar Assn.

Merger Control in the EEC: A Survey of European Competition Laws. 2nd ed. Ed. by Peter Verloop. LC 93-13769. 1993. 84.00 (90-6544-605-2) Kluwer Law Intl.

***Merger Control in the EU: A Survey of European Competition Laws.** 3rd rev. ed. Peter Verloop & Nauta Dutilh. LC 99-38086. 1999. 123.00 (90-411-1232-4) Kluwer Law Intl.

Merger Control in the United Kingdom & European Union. Celli. LC 98-121484. 1997. 125.00 (90-411-0652-9) Kluwer Law Intl.

Merger in Daylight: The Economics & Politics of European Merger Control. Damien Neven et al. 296p. (C). 1994. pap. 29.95 (1-898128-01-4) Brookings.

Merger Law Bibliography, Nineteen Fifty to Nineteen Eighty. Carla A. Hills et al. LC 82-72459. viii, 350p. 1982. pap. 15.00 (0-89707-077-1, 503-0044) Amer Bar Assn.

Merger Movements in American Industry, 1895-1956. Ralph L. Nelson. (General Ser.: No. 66). 198p. 1975. reprint ed. 49.50 (0-87014-065-5) Ayer.

Merger Movements in American Industry, 1895-1956. Ralph L. Nelson. LC 59-11082. (National Bureau of Economic Research. General Ser.: No. 66). 198p. reprint ed. pap. 61.40 (0-608-30171-X, 20517560007) Bks Demand.

Merger of Knowledge with Power: Essays in Critical Science. J. R. Ravetz. 352p. 1990. text 104.00 (0-7201-2021-7) Continuum.

Merger Politics: Local Government Consolidation in Tidewater, Virginia. David G. Temple. LC 72-181718. 241p. reprint ed. pap. 74.80 (0-8357-2716-5, 203983000013) Bks Demand.

Merger Review Process: A Step-by-Step Guide to Federal Merger Review. LC 95-80578. 350p. 1995. pap. 150.00 (1-57073-237-X, 503-0272, ABA Antitrust) Amer Bar Assn.

Merger Standards under U. S. Antitrust Laws. LC 81-67261. 222p. 1981. pap. 20.00 (0-89707-043-7, 503-0039) Amer Bar Assn.

Merger Yearbook. 962p. 1996. 490.00 (0-914470-75-2) Venture Econ.

Merger Yearbook, 1997: U. S./International Edition. 19th ed. Daniel Bokser. (Illus.). 1036p. 1997. 550.00 (0-914470-85-X) SD Pub.

Mergers: Growth in the Fast Lane. Price Pritchett & Robert D. Gilbreath. 27p. 1996. pap. 5.95 (0-944002-17-X) Pritchett Assocs.

Mergers: Growth in the Fast Lane. Price Pritchett & Robert D. Gilbreath. (FRE.). 27p. 1996. pap. 5.95 (0-944002-22-6) Pritchett Assocs.

Mergers, Acquisitions, & Buyouts, 2 vols. annuals Martin D. Ginsburg & Jack S. Levin. 2450p. 1997. pap. 275.00 (0-316-31213-4, 12134) Aspen Law.

Mergers, Acquisitions, & Buyouts, 3 vols. Martin D. Ginsburg & Jack S. Levin. 2450p. pap. 395.00 incl. cd-rom (1-56706-450-7, 64507); pap. 275.00 (1-56706-451-5, 64515) Panel Pubs.

***Mergers, Acquisitions & Buyouts: Combo, October 1999, 3.** Jack S. Levin & Martin D. Ginsburg. 2450p. 2000. pap. text 450.00 (0-7355-1255-8) Panel Pubs.

Mergers, Acquisitions, & Buyouts: Sample Agreements Volume. annuals Martin D. Ginsburg & Jack S. Levin. 650p. 1997. 110.00 (0-316-31212-6, 12126) Aspen Law.

Mergers, Acquisitions, & Buyouts: Transactional Analysis Volume. annuals Martin D. Ginsburg & Jack S. Levin. 1800p. 1997. 190.00 (0-316-31211-8, 12118) Aspen Law.

***Mergers, Acquisitions & Buyouts April 1999, 3.** Jack S. Levin & Martin D. Ginsburg. 3160p. 1999. pap. 295.00 (0-7355-0422-9) Panel Pubs.

***Mergers, Acquisitions & Buyouts, October 1999: A Transactional Analysis of the Governing Tax, Legal & Accounting Considerations, 3 vols.** Jack S. Levin & Martin D. Ginsburg. 3160p. 2000. pap. 325.00 incl. disk (0-7355-1104-7, 11047) Panel Pubs.

Mergers Acquisitions & Divestitures: A Guide to Their Impact for Investors & Directors. Thomas H. Hopkins. 138p. 1983. 24.95 (0-87094-200-X) McTaggart.

***Mergers, Acquisitions & Divestitures: Business, Legal, Finance & Tax Aspects with CD-ROM.** Robert L. Brown. (Illus.). 500p. 2000. pap. 120.00 incl. cd-rom (0-15-607104-5) Harcourt Prof.

Mergers, Acquisitions & Employee Anxiety: A Study of Separation Anxiety in a Corporate Context. Joseph H. Astrachan. LC 90-30002. 176p. 1990. 47.95 (0-275-93568-X, C3568, Praeger Pubs) Greenwood.

Mergers, Acquisitions, & Reorganizations, the Law Of. Dale A. Oesterle. (American Casebook Ser.). 1096p. 1991. 68.50 (0-314-85043-0) West Pub.

Mergers, Acquisitions, & Reorganizations, the Law Of. Dale A. Oesterle. (American Casebook Ser.). 265p. (C). 1992. 20.50 (0-314-01045-9) West Pub.

***Mergers, Acquisitions & Corporate Restructurings.** 2nd ed. Patrick A. Gaughan. LC 99-12056. (Illus.). 576p. 1999. 75.00 (0-471-31670-9) Wiley.

Mergers & Acquisition Handbook for Small & Midsize Companies. Ed. by Thomas L. West & Jeffrey D. Jones. LC 96-34961. 464p. 1997. 155.00 (0-471-13330-2) Wiley.

Mergers & Acquisitions. Ed. by Alan J. Auerbach. (National Bureau of Economic Research Project Report Ser.). (Illus.). 120p. 1988. 17.95 (0-226-03209-4) U Ch Pr.

Mergers & Acquisitions. Ed. by Alan J. Auerbach. (National Bureau of Economic Research Project Report Ser.). (Illus.). 120p. 1991. pap. text 11.95 (0-226-03210-8) U Ch Pr.

***Mergers & Acquisitions.** Glenlake Publishing Company Staff. (The Glenlake Risk Management Ser.). 160p. 2000. 45.00 (1-888998-80-6, 98-80-6) Glenlake Pub.

***Mergers & Acquisitions.** Alastair Graham. (Risk Management Ser.: Vol. 9). 160p. 2000. 45.00 (0-8144-0584-3) AMACOM.

Mergers & Acquisitions. Ed. by Gregory P. Marchildon. (International Library of Critical Writings in Business History: No. 3). 608p. 1991. text 250.00 (1-85278-430-X) E Elgar.

***Mergers & Acquisitions.** J. Fred Weston. 2001. 29.95 (0-07-136432-3) McGraw.

Mergers & Acquisitions. 2nd ed. Ernst & Young Staff & Young. LC 93-7648. 364p. 1994. 49.95 (0-471-57818-5) Wiley.

***Mergers & Acquisitions: A Framework for the Right Executive Decision.** Hazel Johnson. (Corporate Finance Manuals Ser.). (Illus.). 256p. 1999. pap. text 34.95 (0-273-63881-5, Pub. by F T P-H) Natl Bk Netwk.

Mergers & Acquisitions: A Printers Handbook. 106p. 1989. 75.00 (0-317-02014-5, XP116) NAPL.

Mergers & Acquisitions: A Valuation Handbook. Joseph H. Marren. 450p. 1992. text 90.00 (1-55623-676-X, Irwn Prfssnl) McGraw-Hill Prof.

***Mergers & Acquisitions: Business Strategies for Accountants.** 2nd ed. Joseph M. Morris. LC 99-54858. (M & A Library). 432p. 2000. text 125.00 (0-471-38187-X) Wiley.

Mergers & Acquisitions: Managing the Transaction. Joseph C. Krallinger. LC 97-1463. 360p. 1997. 55.00 (0-7863-1166-5) McGraw.

***Mergers & Acquisitions: Business Strategies for Accountants: 1999 Cumulative Supplement.** Morris. 224p. 1999. pap. 69.00 (0-471-29911-1) Wiley.

***Mergers & Acquisitions (Corporate Finance)** 1999. pap. 120.00 (0-85297-460-4, Pub. by Chartered Bank) St Mut.

Mergers & Acquisitions from A to Z: Strategic & Practical Guidance for Buyers & Sellers. Andrew Sherman. LC 97-52037. 300p. 1997. 39.95 (0-8144-0376-X) AMACOM.

Mergers & Acquisitions Handbook. 2nd ed. Milton L. Rock. 608p. 1992. 84.95 (0-07-053353-9) McGraw.

Mergers & Acquisitions Healthcare Sourcebook. 1989. 495.00 (0-926700-01-4) MLR Pub.

Mergers & Acquisitions Healthcare Sourcebook. 2nd ed. Ed. by Robert C. Smith, Jr. 300p. 1990. pap. 495.00 (0-926700-03-0) MLR Pub.

Mergers & Acquisitions in Germany. Gerhard Picot. LC 98-43288. 1998. 90.00 (1-57823-059-4) Juris Pubng.

Mergers & Acquisitions in the Communications Industry. Peter A. Atkins & Stephen A. Sharp. iv, 232p. write for info. (0-318-61624-6) Harcourt.

Mergers & Acquisitions in the 90s: A Step-by-Step Guide. (Corporate Law & Practice Course Handbook, 1985-86 Ser.). 720p. 1994. pap. 99.00 (0-614-17175-X, B4-7081) PLI.

Mergers & Acquisitions in the 90s: A Step-by-Step Guide, 1996. (Corporate Law & Practice Course Handbook, 1985-86 Ser.). Date not set. pap. 99.00 (0-614-17205-5, B4-7124) PLI.

Mergers & Acquisitions of CPA Firms: A Guide to Practice Valuation. Nicholas J. Mastracchio, Jr. LC 98-7430. (Illus.). 156p. 1998. pap. 49.00 (0-87051-205-6, 090411) Am Inst CPA.

Mergers & Acquisitions of Franchise Companies. LC 95-83881. 1996. pap. 69.95 (1-57073-314-7, 562-0046) Amer Bar Assn.

Mergers & Acquisitions of Natural Resources Companies. (Mineral Law Ser.: No. 6). 380p. 1994. student ed., ring bd. 125.00 (0-929047-48-6) Rocky Mtn Mineral Law Found.

Mergers & Acquisitions, 1998. Richard A. Goldberg. LC 98-129427. (Corporate Law & Practice Course Handbook Ser.). 832p. 1998. 129.00 (0-87224-400-8) PLI.

***Mergers & Competition in the Telecommunications Industry: Congressional Hearing.** Ed. by Orrin G. Hatch. (Illus.). 132p. (C). 2000. reprint ed. pap. text 30.00 (0-7881-8859-3) DIANE Pub.

Mergers & Joint Ventures in Europe: The Law & Policy of the EEC. Frank L. Fine. (C). 1989. lib. bdg. 128.00 (1-85333-314-X, Pub. by Graham & Trotman) Kluwer Academic.

Mergers & Joint Ventures in Europe: The Law & Policy of the EEC. Frank L. Fine. LC 93-37473. (European Business Law & Practice Ser.). 800p. (C). 1994. lib. bdg. 254.00 (1-85333-574-6, Pub. by Graham & Trotman) Kluwer Academic.

Mergers & Merger Policy. Ed. by James Fairburn & John A. Kay. (Illus.). 368p. 1989. 74.00 (0-19-877285-8); pap. 29.95 (0-19-877284-X) OUP.

***Mergers & Productivity.** Steven N. Kaplan. LC 99-45131. (A National Bureau of Economic Research Conference Report). (Illus.). 338p. 2000. 40.00 (0-226-42431-6) U Ch Pr.

Mergers & the Federal Antitrust Laws: A Research Guide for Practitioners. Perry Goldberg. LC 92-29891. (Legal Research Guides Ser.: Vol. 14). ix, 36p. 1992. 35.00 (0-89941-818-X, 307700) W S Hein.

Mergers & Ventures: Creative Responses to Shifting Resources. Lu Ann Young. Ed. by Marian M. Pettengill. 150p. (Orig.). 1988. pap. 12.50 (0-942146-15-8) Midwest Alliance Nursing.

Mergers, Efficient Choice & International Competitiveness: Bandwagon Behaviour & Industrial Policy Implications. Hans Schenk. 400p. 1999. 100.00 (1-85898-390-8) E Elgar.

Mergers in Health Care: The Performance of Multi-Institutional Organizations, Vol. 7. Ed. by Richard M. Scheffler et al. (Advances in Health Economics & Health Services Research Ser.). 300p. 1987. 73.25 (0-89232-573-9) Jai Pr.

Mergers in Perspective. Yale Brozen. LC 82-3937. (AEI Studies: No. 353). (Illus.). 96p. reprint ed. pap. 30.00 (0-8357-4505-8, 203736200008) Bks Demand.

Mergers, Markets & Public Policy, Vol. 21. Ed. by Ciuliano Mussati. LC 95-31703. (Studies in Industrial Organization). 232p. (C). 1995. lib. bdg. 125.00 (0-7923-3643-7) Kluwer Academic.

Mergers of Teaching Hospitals in Boston, New York & Northern California. John A. Kastor. (Illus.). 456p. (C). text 54.50 (0-472-11196-5) U of Mich Pr.

Mergers, Sell-Offs, & Economic Efficiency. David J. Ravenscraft & F. M. Scherer. LC 87-14018. 290p. 1987. 36.95 (0-8157-7348-X); pap. 16.95 (0-8157-7347-1) Brookings.

Mergers under EEC Competition Law. Timothy Portwood. (European Community Law Ser.). 240p. (C). 1994. text 90.00 (0-485-70009-3, Pub. by Athlone Pr) Humanities.

Mergerstat Control Premium Study. 395.00 (1-888878-08-8) Mergerstat Rev.

Mergerstat Review. annuals 249.00 (1-888878-05-3) Mergerstat Rev.

Mergerstat Transaction Roster. annuals 150.00 (1-888878-06-1) Mergerstat Rev.

***Merging: A Story of Two Families & Their Child.** Evelyn King Mumaw. 224p. 2000. 13.95 (0-9665021-6-7, DreamSeeker) Pandora PA.

Merging Colleges for Mutual Growth: A New Strategy for Academic Managers. James Martin et al. LC 93-8380. 296p. (C). 1993. text 38.00 (0-8018-4666-8) Johns Hopkins.

Merging Dimensions Vol. 1: The Opening Portals of Sedona. Tom Dongo. (Illus.). 189p. (Orig.). 1995. pap. 14.95 (0-9622748-4-4) T Dongo.

***Merging Ecology & Economy.** Gringras Marks. 2000. pap. 60.00 (0-324-04186-1) Thomson Learn.

Merging Language Intervention with Classroom Practices: A Practical Guide for the Speech Language Pathologist. Eileen Eisner. LC 97-14964. 1998. spiral bd. 34.00 (0-89079-751-X) PRO-ED.

Merging Medical Practices. Keith M. Korenchuk. 147p. 1994. 45.00 (1-56829-041-1, 4619) Med Group Mgmt.

An Asterisk (*) at the beginning of an entry indicates that the title is appearing for the first time.

***Merging Medical Staffs.** Albert L. Fritz et al. Ed. by David Beardsley. (Illus.). 48p. 1999. pap. text 49.00 (1-57839-058-3) Opus Communs.

***Merging Mission & Money: A Board Member's Guide to Social Entrepreneurship.** Jerr Boschee. 22p. 1998. pap. text 16.00 (0-925299-81-2) Natl Ctr Nonprofit.

Merging of Disciplines: New Directions in Pure, Applied & Computational Mathematics. Ed. by R. Ewing et al. (Illus.). 240p. 1986. 58.95 (0-387-96414-2) Spr-Verlag.

Merging of Religious & Secular Rule in Tibet. Dung-Dkar Blo-Bzang 'Phrim-Las. 135p. 1991. pap. 7.15 (7-119-00672-X, 17E-2324P) Cypress Co.

Merging Successfully: A Study & Guide on Congregational Mergers. Carol Greg. 1996. 12.00 (1-56699-171-4) Alban Inst.

Merging Traditions: The Future of Research on School Effectiveness & School Improvement. Ed. by John Gray et al. LC 96-6375. (School Development Ser.). (Illus.). 208p. 1996. pap. 27.95 (0-304-33647-5); text 90.00 (0-304-33653-X) Continuum.

Merging with Siva: Hinduism's Contemporary Metaphysics. Satguru Sivaya Subramuniyaswami. LC 98-73075. (Illus.). 1400p. 1999. pap. text 39.75 (0-945497-74-1) Himalayan Acad.

Meriah of Sorrows. Bonita Porter. LC 94-93949. 188p. (Orig.). 1995. pap. 12.95 (1-55673-974-5, Fairway Pr) CSS OH.

Merica: Images of Italian Greenhorn Experience. Michael A. La Sorte. LC 84-16169. 224p. 1985. 29.95 (0-87722-382-3) Temple U Pr.

Meridan. Alice Walker. Ed. by Julie Rubenstein. 220p. 1990. per. 6.99 (0-671-72701-X) PB.

Meriden: Connecticut's Crossroad: An Illustrated History. Brenda J. Vumbaco. 144p. 1988. 27.95 (0-89781-276-X, 5270) Am Historical Pr.

Meriden, CT. Historical Briefs, Inc. Staff. Ed. by Thomas Antonucci & Michael Antonucci. 176p. 1991. pap. 19.95 (0-89677-008-7) Hist Briefs.

Meridia: The Weight-Loss Breakthrough. Othniel J. Seiden. LC 98-18596. 1998. pap. 14.00 (0-7615-1654-9) Prima Pub.

Meridian. Alice Walker. LC 76-941. 256p. 1976. 18.95 (0-15-159265-9) Harcourt.

Meridian. Norman Zollinger. LC 96-53955. 416p. 1997. text 25.95 (0-312-86131-1) St Martin.

Meridian: A Novel of Kit Carson's West. Norman Zollinger. 1998. mass mkt. 6.99 (0-8125-4287-8, Pub. by Tor Bks) St Martin.

Meridian: The Queen with a Past, Vol. I. Jack Shank. (Meridian Ser.). (Illus.). (Orig.). 1985. pap. 7.95 (0-9616123-1-2) Jack Shank.

Meridian - The Queen with a Past Vol. II: The Golden Years. Jack Shank. (Illus.). 148p. 1986. pap. 8.95 (0-9616123-2-0) Jack Shank.

Meridian Anthology of Restoration & Eighteenth-Century Plays by Women. Ed. by Katharine M. Rogers. 560p. (Orig.). 1998. pap. text 16.00 (0-7881-5784-1) DIANE Pub.

Meridian Exercises: The Oriental Way to Health & Vitality. Shizuto Masunaga. Tr. by Stephen Brown from JPN. Orig. Title: Zen Imagery Exercises. (Illus.). 238p. (Orig.). 1996. pap. 22.00 (0-87040-897-6) Japan Pubns USA.

Meridian Handbook of Classical Literature see Handbook of Classical Literature

Meridian Handbook of Classical Mythology. Edward Tripp. 1974. pap. 18.95 (0-452-00927-8, Mer) NAL.

Meridian Hebrew-English English-Hebrew Dictionary. Dov Ben-Abba. 720p. 1994. pap. 18.95 (0-452-01121-3, Mer) NAL.

Meridian One. Clayton L. Hogg. LC 98-93371. (Illus.). 256p. 1999. pap. 23.95 (0-9665394-0-0) Philo-Math.

Meridian Plus 1. Harmer. Date not set. pap. text, wbk. ed. write for info. (0-582-02748-9, Pub. by Addison-Wesley) Longman.

Meridian Plus 1: Textbook. Harmer. Date not set. pap. text. write for info. (0-582-02745-4, Pub. by Addison-Wesley) Longman.

Meridian Plus 3. Harmer. Date not set. pap. text, wbk. ed. write for info. (0-582-02750-0, Pub. by Addison-Wesley) Longman.

Meridian Plus 3: Textbook. Harmer. Date not set. pap. text. write for info. (0-582-02747-0) Addison-Wesley.

Meridian Plus 2. Harmer. Date not set. pap. text, wbk. ed. write for info. (0-582-02749-7) Addison-Wesley.

Meridian Plus 2: Textbook. Harmer. Date not set. pap. text. write for info. (0-582-02746-2, Pub. by Addison-Wesley) Longman.

Meridian Qigong: Transferring Qi along the Meridian. Li Ding. (Illus.). 261p. 1988. 12.95 (0-8351-2322-7) China Bks.

Meridian 1. J. Harmer. Date not set. pap. text. write for info. (0-582-57947-3, Pub. by Addison-Wesley) Longman.

Meridian 144. Meg Files. LC 91-16335. 264p. 1993. pap. 12.00 (0-939149-87-7) Soho Press.

Meridians. Mark Dunster. 37p. (Orig.). (YA). (gr. 9-12). 1996. pap. 5.00 (0-89642-294-1) Linden Pubs.

Meridians of Acupuncture. Mann. 174p. 1964. text 50.00 (0-433-20303-X) Buttrwrth-Heinemann.

Meridien Dallas Cookbook. Mario Reyes. (Illus.). 106p. (Orig.). 1995. pap., spiral bd. 14.95 (0-9651298-8-8) Le Meridian Dallas.

Meridiens. Pierre Daninos. 8.95 (0-686-55568-6) Fr & Eur.

Meridon. Philippa Gregory. Ed. by Claire Zion. 560p. 1992. mass mkt. 5.99 (0-671-70152-5) PB.

Merie Tales of the Mad Men of Gotam. Ed. by Stanley J. Kahrl. (Renaissance English Text Society Ser.: Vol. 1). (Illus.). xxii, 20p. 1965. 10.00 (0-911028-18-8) Newberry.

Merilainen Paleolimnology. Dihy. 1983. 384.00 (90-6193-766-3, Pub. by Kluwer Academic) Kluwer Academic.

Merina. Rebecca Green. LC 96-22944. (Heritage Library of African Peoples: Set 4). (Illus.). 64p. (YA). (gr. 7-12). 1996. lib. bdg. 16.95 (0-8239-1991-9, D1991-9) Rosen Group.

Merinos, Myths, & MacArthurs. Garran. (Australian National University Press Series). 1985. text 52.00 (0-08-032972-1, Pergamon Pr) Elsevier.

Merion in the Welsh Tract, with Sketches of the Townships of Haverford & Radnor: History & Genealogy Collections Concerning the Welsh Barony in the Province of Pennsylvania. Thomas A. Green. (Illus.). 394p. 1992. reprint ed. lib. bdg. 39.50 (0-8328-2371-6) Higginson Bk Co.

Merise in Practice. Pham T. Quang & C. Chartier-Kastler. Ed. by F. H. Sumner. (Computer Science Ser.). (Illus.). 206p. (Orig.). (C). 1991. pap. text 38.00 (0-333-55020-X, Pub. by Macmillan Ed) Scholium Intl.

Merismos see Releasing the Spirit

Merismos. Randy Shankle. 247p. 1987. pap. write for info. (0-88144-080-9) Christian Pub.

Merit & Blessing in Mainland Southeast Asia in Comparative Perspective. Ed. by Cornelia A. Kammerer & Nicola Tannenbaum. (Monograph Ser.: Vol. 45). 280p. (C). 1997. pap. 20.00 (0-938692-62-3); lib. bdg. 32.00 (0-938692-61-5) Yale U SE Asia.

Merit & Responsibility: A Study in Greek Values. Arthur W. Adkins. (Midway Reprint Ser.). 396p. 1975. reprint ed. pap. text 20.00 (0-226-00728-6) U Ch Pr.

Merit Factor - Rewarding Individual Performance. Incomes Data Services Staff & Institute of Personnel Management Staff. 72p. (C). 1985. 60.00 (0-85292-360-0, Pub. by IPM Hse) St Mut.

Merit in Education. Hans A. Andrews. 120p. (Orig.). 1987. pap. 15.95 (0-913507-05-9) New Forums.

Merit of Our Mothers: A Bilingual Anthology of Jewish Women's Prayers. Tr. by Tracy G. Klirs et al. LC 92-14406. (Jewish Perspectives Ser.: No. 5). (ENG & YID.). 150p. 1992. 16.95 (0-87820-505-5) Hebrew Union Coll Pr.

Merit Pay. Robert Heneman. (Illus.). 298p. (C). 1992. pap. 40.00 (0-201-52504-6) Addison-Wesley.

***Merit Staffing at the NRC.** 12p. 1998. pap. 1.00 (0-16-063010-X) USGPO.

Merit Student Encyclopedia, 1989, Vol. 6. 1989. 35.00 (0-02-945875-7) Mac Lib Ref.

Merit Student Encyclopedia 1991, Vol. 13. Merit. 1991. 45.00 (0-02-943743-1) Mac Lib Ref.

Merit Student Encyclopedia 1991, Vol. 15. 1991. 45.00 (0-02-943745-8) Mac Lib Ref.

Merit Student Encyclopedia 1991, Vol. 20. 1991. 45.00 (0-02-943751-2) Mac Lib Ref.

Merit Students Encyclopedia, 20 vols., Vol. 2. 1987. 32.00 (0-02-943202-2) Mac Lib Ref.

Merit Students Encyclopedia, 1991, 20 vols., Set. Ed. by Macmillan Educational Company Staff. 1991. text 579.00 (0-02-943752-0) Free Pr.

Merit Students Encyclopedia 1987, 20 vols., Vol. 1. 1987. 32.00 (0-02-943201-4) Mac Lib Ref.

Merit Students Encyclopedia 1987, 20 vols., Vol. 3. 1987. 32.00 (0-02-943203-0) Mac Lib Ref.

Merit Students Encyclopedia 1987, 20 vols., Vol. 4. 1987. 32.00 (0-02-943204-9) Mac Lib Ref.

Merit Students Encyclopedia 1987, 20 vols., Vol. 5. 1987. 32.00 (0-02-943205-7) Mac Lib Ref.

Merit Students Encyclopedia 1987, 20 vols., Vol. 6. 1987. 32.00 (0-02-943206-5) Mac Lib Ref.

Merit Students Encyclopedia 1987, 20 vols., Vol. 7. 1987. 32.00 (0-02-943207-3) Mac Lib Ref.

Merit Students Encyclopedia 1987, 20 vols., Vol. 8. 1987. 32.00 (0-02-943208-1) Mac Lib Ref.

Merit Students Encyclopedia 1987, 20 vols., Vol. 9. 1987. 32.00 (0-02-943209-X) Mac Lib Ref.

Merit Students Encyclopedia 1987, Vol. 10. 1987. 32.00 (0-02-943210-3) Mac Lib Ref.

Merit Students Encyclopedia 1987, Vol. 11. 1987. 32.00 (0-02-943211-1) Mac Lib Ref.

Merit Students Encyclopedia 1987, 20 vols., Vol. 12. 1987. 32.00 (0-02-943212-X) Mac Lib Ref.

Merit Students Encyclopedia 1987, Vol. 13. 1987. 32.00 (0-02-943213-8) Mac Lib Ref.

Merit Students Encyclopedia 1987, Vol. 14. 1987. 32.00 (0-02-943214-6) Mac Lib Ref.

Merit Students Encyclopedia 1987, Vol. 15. 1987. 32.00 (0-02-943215-4) Mac Lib Ref.

Merit Students Encyclopedia 1987, Vol. 16. 1987. 32.00 (0-02-943216-2) Mac Lib Ref.

Merit Students Encyclopedia 1987, Vol. 17. 1987. 32.00 (0-02-943217-0) Mac Lib Ref.

Merit Students Encyclopedia 1987, Vol. 18. 1987. 32.00 (0-02-943218-9) Mac Lib Ref.

Merit Students Encyclopedia 1987, Vol. 19. 1987. 32.00 (0-02-943219-7) Mac Lib Ref.

Merit Students Encyclopedia 1987, Vol. 20. 1987. 32.00 (0-02-943220-0) Mac Lib Ref.

Merit Students Encyclopedia 1988, 20 vols., Vol. 1. 1988. 35.00 (0-02-943221-9) Mac Lib Ref.

Merit Students Encyclopedia 1988, 20 vols., Vol. 2. 1988. 35.00 (0-02-943222-7) Mac Lib Ref.

Merit Students Encyclopedia 1988, 20 vols., Vol. 3. 1988. 35.00 (0-02-943223-5) Mac Lib Ref.

Merit Students Encyclopedia 1988, 20 vols., Vol. 4. 1988. 35.00 (0-02-943224-3) Mac Lib Ref.

Merit Students Encyclopedia 1988, Vol. 5. 1988. 35.00 (0-02-943225-1) Mac Lib Ref.

Merit Students Encyclopedia 1988, Vol. 6. 1988. 35.00 (0-02-943226-X) Mac Lib Ref.

Merit Students Encyclopedia 1988, 20 vols., Vol. 7. 1988. 35.00 (0-02-943227-8) Mac Lib Ref.

Merit Students Encyclopedia 1988, 20 vols., Vol. 8. 1988. 35.00 (0-02-943228-6) Mac Lib Ref.

Merit Students Encyclopedia 1988, 20 vols., Vol. 9. 1988. 35.00 (0-02-943229-4) Mac Lib Ref.

Merit Students Encyclopedia 1988, 20 vols., Vol. 10. 1988. 35.00 (0-02-943231-6) Mac Lib Ref.

Merit Students Encyclopedia 1988, Vol. 11. 1988. 35.00 (0-02-943232-4) Mac Lib Ref.

Merit Students Encyclopedia 1988, Vol. 12. 1988. 35.00 (0-02-943233-2) Mac Lib Ref.

Merit Students Encyclopedia 1988, 20 vols., Vol. 13. 1988. 35.00 (0-02-943234-0) Mac Lib Ref.

Merit Students Encyclopedia 1988, 20 vols., Vol. 14. 1988. 35.00 (0-02-943235-9) Mac Lib Ref.

Merit Students Encyclopedia 1988, 20 vols., Vol. 15. 1988. 35.00 (0-02-943236-7) Mac Lib Ref.

Merit Students Encyclopedia 1988, Vol. 16. 1988. 35.00 (0-02-943237-5) Mac Lib Ref.

Merit Students Encyclopedia 1988, 20 vols., Vol. 17. 1988. 35.00 (0-02-943238-3) Mac Lib Ref.

Merit Students Encyclopedia 1988, 20 vols., Vol. 18. 1988. 35.00 (0-02-943239-1) Mac Lib Ref.

Merit Students Encyclopedia 1988, 20 vols., Vol. 19. 1988. 35.00 (0-02-943240-5) Mac Lib Ref.

Merit Students Encyclopedia 1988, 20 vols., Vol. 20. 1988. 35.00 (0-02-943241-3) Mac Lib Ref.

Merit Students Encyclopedia 1989, 20 vols. 1989. 429.00 (0-02-943242-1) Mac Lib Ref.

Merit Students Encyclopedia 1989, Vol. 1. 1989. 35.00 (0-02-945870-6) Mac Lib Ref.

Merit Students Encyclopedia 1989, Vol. 2. 1989. 35.00 (0-02-945871-4) Mac Lib Ref.

Merit Students Encyclopedia 1989, Vol. 3. 1989. 35.00 (0-02-945872-2) Mac Lib Ref.

Merit Students Encyclopedia 1989, Vol. 4. 1989. 35.00 (0-02-945873-0) Mac Lib Ref.

Merit Students Encyclopedia 1989, Vol. 5. 1989. 35.00 (0-02-945874-9) Mac Lib Ref.

Merit Students Encyclopedia 1989, Vol. 7. 1989. 35.00 (0-02-945876-5) Mac Lib Ref.

Merit Students Encyclopedia 1989, Vol. 8. 1989. 35.00 (0-02-945877-3) Mac Lib Ref.

Merit Students Encyclopedia 1989, Vol. 9. 1989. 35.00 (0-02-945878-1) Mac Lib Ref.

Merit Students Encyclopedia 1989, Vol. 10. 1989. 35.00 (0-02-945879-X) Mac Lib Ref.

Merit Students Encyclopedia 1989, Vol. 11. 1989. 35.00 (0-02-945880-3) Mac Lib Ref.

Merit Students Encyclopedia 1989, Vol. 12. 1990. 35.00 (0-02-945881-1) Mac Lib Ref.

Merit Students Encyclopedia 1989, Vol. 13. 1989. 35.00 (0-02-945882-X) Mac Lib Ref.

Merit Students Encyclopedia 1989, Vol. 14. 1989. 35.00 (0-02-945883-8) Mac Lib Ref.

Merit Students Encyclopedia 1989, Vol. 15. 1989. 35.00 (0-02-945884-6) Mac Lib Ref.

Merit Students Encyclopedia 1989, Vol. 16. 1989. 35.00 (0-02-945885-4) Mac Lib Ref.

Merit Students Encyclopedia 1989, Vol. 17. 1989. 35.00 (0-02-945886-2) Mac Lib Ref.

Merit Students Encyclopedia 1989, Vol. 18. 1989. 35.00 (0-02-945887-0) Mac Lib Ref.

Merit Students Encyclopedia 1989, Vol. 19. 1989. 35.00 (0-02-945888-9) Mac Lib Ref.

Merit Students Encyclopedia 1989, Vol. 20. 1989. 35.00 (0-02-945889-7) Mac Lib Ref.

Merit Students Encyclopedia 1990, Vol. 1. 1990. 35.00 (0-02-945900-1) Mac Lib Ref.

Merit Students Encyclopedia 1990, Vol. 2. 1990. 35.00 (0-02-945901-X) Mac Lib Ref.

Merit Students Encyclopedia 1990, Vol. 4. 1990. 35.00 (0-02-945903-6) Mac Lib Ref.

Merit Students Encyclopedia 1990, Vol. 5. 1990. 35.00 (0-02-945902-8); 35.00 (0-02-945904-4) Mac Lib Ref.

Merit Students Encyclopedia 1990, Vol. 6. 1990. 35.00 (0-02-945905-2) Mac Lib Ref.

Merit Students Encyclopedia 1990, Vol. 7. 1990. 35.00 (0-02-945906-0) Mac Lib Ref.

Merit Students Encyclopedia 1990, Vol. 8. 1990. 35.00 (0-02-945907-9) Mac Lib Ref.

Merit Students Encyclopedia 1990, Vol. 9. 1990. 35.00 (0-02-945908-7) Mac Lib Ref.

Merit Students Encyclopedia 1990, Vol. 10. 1990. 35.00 (0-02-945909-5) Mac Lib Ref.

Merit Students Encyclopedia 1990, Vol. 11. 1990. 35.00 (0-02-945910-9) Mac Lib Ref.

Merit Students Encyclopedia 1990, Vol. 12. 1990. 35.00 (0-02-945911-7) Mac Lib Ref.

Merit Students Encyclopedia 1990, Vol. 13. 1990. 35.00 (0-02-945912-5) Mac Lib Ref.

Merit Students Encyclopedia 1990, Vol. 14. 1990. 35.00 (0-02-945913-3) Mac Lib Ref.

Merit Students Encyclopedia 1990, Vol. 15. 1990. 35.00 (0-02-945914-1) Mac Lib Ref.

Merit Students Encyclopedia 1990, Vol. 16. 1990. 35.00 (0-02-945915-X) Mac Lib Ref.

Merit Students Encyclopedia 1990, Vol. 17. 1990. 35.00 (0-02-945916-8) Mac Lib Ref.

Merit Students Encyclopedia 1990, Vol. 18. 1990. 35.00 (0-02-945917-6) Mac Lib Ref.

Merit Students Encyclopedia 1990, Vol. 19. 1990. 35.00 (0-02-945918-4) Mac Lib Ref.

Merit Students Encyclopedia 1990, Vol. 20. 1990. 35.00 (0-02-945919-2) Mac Lib Ref.

Merit Students Encyclopedia 1991, Vol. 1. 1991. 45.00 (0-02-943731-8) Mac Lib Ref.

Merit Students Encyclopedia 1991, Vol. 2. 1991. 45.00 (0-02-943732-6) Mac Lib Ref.

Merit Students Encyclopedia 1991, Vol. 3. 1991. 45.00 (0-02-943733-4) Mac Lib Ref.

Merit Students Encyclopedia 1991, Vol. 4. 1991. 45.00 (0-02-943734-2) Mac Lib Ref.

Merit Students Encyclopedia 1991, Vol. 5. 1991. 45.00 (0-02-943735-0) Mac Lib Ref.

Merit Students Encyclopedia 1991, Vol. 6. 1991. 45.00 (0-02-943736-9) Mac Lib Ref.

Merit Students Encyclopedia 1991, Vol. 7. 1991. 45.00 (0-02-943737-7) Mac Lib Ref.

Merit Students Encyclopedia 1991, Vol. 8. 1991. 45.00 (0-02-943738-5) Mac Lib Ref.

Merit Students Encyclopedia 1991, Vol. 9. 1991. 45.00 (0-02-943739-3) Mac Lib Ref.

Merit Students Encyclopedia 1991, Vol. 10. 1991. 45.00 (0-02-943740-7) Mac Lib Ref.

Merit Students Encyclopedia 1991, Vol. 11. Merit. 1991. 45.00 (0-02-943741-5) Mac Lib Ref.

Merit Students Encyclopedia 1991, Vol. 12. 1991. 45.00 (0-02-943742-3) Mac Lib Ref.

Merit Students Encyclopedia 1991, Vol. 14. 1991. 45.00 (0-02-943744-X) Mac Lib Ref.

Merit Students Encyclopedia 1991, Vol. 16. 1991. 45.00 (0-02-943746-6) Mac Lib Ref.

Merit Students Encyclopedia 1991, Vol. 17. 1991. 45.00 (0-02-943747-4) Mac Lib Ref.

Merit Students Encyclopedia 1991, Vol. 18. 1991. 45.00 (0-02-943748-2) Mac Lib Ref.

Merit Students Encyclopedia 1991, Vol. 19. 1991. 45.00 (0-02-943749-0) Mac Lib Ref.

Merit System & Municipal Civil Service: A Fostering of Social Inequality, 201. Frances Gottfried. LC 87-23759. (Contributions in Political Science Ser.: No. 201). 199p. 1988. 49.95 (0-313-25741-8, GMV/, Greenwood Pr) Greenwood.

***Merit System Protection Act of 1997: Hearing Before the Subcommittee on International Security, Proliferation & Federal Services of the Committee on Governmental Affairs, United States Senate, One Hundred Fifth Congress, Second Session, February 26, 1998.** United States Government. LC 98-213782. iii, 72 p. 1998. write for info. (0-16-057155-3) USGPO.

Merit Systems Protection Board: Mission Performance, Employee Protections, & Working Environment. (Illus.). 72p. (Orig.). (C). 1996. pap. text 20.00 (0-7881-3237-7) DIANE Pub.

Merit Systems Protection Board: Rights & Remedies. Robert G. Vaughn. LC 84-23435. 400p. 1984. 65.00 (0-317-00920-6) NY Law Pub.

Meritorious Price of Our Redemption by William Pynchon (1590-1662) Ed. by Michael W. Vella et al. LC 91-32985. (Worcester Polytechnic Institute Studies in Science, Technology, & Culture: Vol. 10). XLI, 170p. (C). 1993. text 89.95 (0-8204-1760-2) P Lang Pubng.

Meritorious Service Medal to Aerial Forces. Ian McInnes. 63p. (C). 1990. pap. 24.00 (0-902633-92-9, Pub. by Picton) St Mut.

Meritorious Service Medal to Naval Forces. Ian McInnes. 63p. (C). 1987. 50.00 (0-7855-2169-0, Pub. by Picton) St Mut.

Meritorious Service Medal to Naval Forces. Ed. by Ian McInnes. 1990. pap. 40.00 (0-902633-82-1, Pub. by Picton) St Mut.

Merits & Demerits of the EU Policies Towards Associated Developing Countries: An Empirical Analysis of EU-SADC Trade & Overall Economic Relations within the Framework of the Lome Countries. 2nd rev. ed. Francis Matambalya. LC 99-32389. (European University Studies, Series 5: Vol. 2211). (Illus.). 288p. 1999. pap. text 48.95 (0-8204-4333-6) P Lang Pubng.

***Merits & Limits of Markets.** Ed. by Herbert Giersch. LC 98-29925. (Publications of the Egon-Sohmen-Foundation). (Illus.). 265p. 1998. 85.00 (3-540-64446-6) Spr-Verlag.

Merits of Flexible Exchange Rates: An Anthology. Ed. by Leo Melamed. 450p. (Orig.). (C). 1988. pap. text 35.00 (0-913969-15-X); lib. bdg. 68.50 (0-913969-14-1) Univ Pub Assocs.

Meriweather Murder. Malcolm Shuman. (Alan Graham Mystery Ser.: No. 2). 272p. 1998. mass mkt. 5.99 (0-380-79424-1, Avon Bks) Morrow Avon.

Meriwether County, Georgia Cemeteries. Photos & Compiled by Priscilla Turner. LC 93-9988. (Illus.). 1993. 60.00 (0-87152-467-8) Reprint.

Meriwether Lewis. Richard Dillon. LC 65-10888. (Illus.). 363p. 1988. reprint ed. pap. 12.95 (0-934136-39-4) Good Life.

Meriwether Lewis: Boy Explorer. Charlotta M. Bebenroth. 1997. 10.09 (0-606-13605-3, Pub. by Turtleback) Demco.

Merkabah in Rabbinic Literature. David Halperin. (American Oriental Ser.: Vol. 62). xii, 212p. 1980. 14.00 (0-940490-62-5) Am Orient Soc.

***Merkadesh Yibsra.el: Bsirhot U-Temunot Bi-Mesibot Rhatunah.** Menarhem Mendel Schneersohn & Eliezer Zaklikofsky. LC 00-20853. (HEB & ENG.). 2000. write for info. (0-8266-0665-2) Kehot Pubn Soc.

Merkava: Main Battle Tank, 1977-96. Sam Katz. (New Vanguard Ser.: No. 21). 1997. pap. 12.95 (1-85532-643-4, Pub. by Ospry) Stackpole.

Merkava MK2 - MK3. Illus. by Francois Verlinden. (Warmachines Ser.: No. 11). 24p. 1992. 11.95 (1-930607-03-2) Verlinden Prod.

Merklappen Uit de Lage Landen - Dutch Samplers. Joke Visser. (Illus.). 176p. 1994. 35.00 (90-6113-689-X, Pub. by Alboek) Lacis Pubns.

Merkmale, Anbau, und Verwendung Winterharte Hedera-Arten und Sorten. Garry Grueber. (GER., Illus.). 112p. 1983. 65.00 (0-937233-19-6) Am Ivy Soc.

Merkwurdige Erzahlungen und Wundersame Geschichten, Vol. 1. Dahesh. (ARA, ENG & GER., Illus.). 246p. 1988. 20.00 (0-935359-04-4) Daheshist.

Merl & Jasper's Supper Caper. Laura Rankin. (J). 1998. pap. 6.99 (0-679-89311-3, Pub. by Random Bks Yng Read) Random.

An Asterisk (*) at the beginning of an entry indicates that the title is appearing for the first time.

Merl Reagle's Sunday Crosswords, 1. Merl Reagle. Ed. by David Rosen. (Merl Reagle's Sunday Crosswords Ser.). (Illus.). 56p. (Orig.). 1991. pap. 7.95 (*0-9630828-0-9*) PuzzleWorks.

Merl Reagle's Sunday Crosswords, Vol. 2. Merl Reagle. 56p. (Orig.). 1996. pap. 7.95 (*0-9630828-1-7*) PuzzleWorks.

Merl Reagle's Sunday Crosswords, Vol. 3. Merl Reagle. 56p. (Orig.). 1996. pap. 7.95 (*0-9630828-2-5*) PuzzleWorks.

Merl Reagle's Sunday Crosswords, Vol. 4. Merl Reagle. 56p. (Orig.). 1996. pap. 7.95 (*0-9630828-3-3*) PuzzleWorks.

Merl Reagle's Sunday Crosswords, Vol. 5. Merl Reagle. 56p. (Orig.). 1997. pap. 8.95 (*0-9630828-4-1*) PuzzleWorks.

Merl Reagle's Sunday Crosswords, Vol. 6. Merl Reagle. (Illus.). 40p. (Orig.). 1999. pap. 8.95 (*0-9630828-5-X*) PuzzleWorks.

Merlake Towers. large type ed. Mary Williams. (General Ser.). 464p. 1993. 27.99 (*0-7089-2834-X*) Ulverscroft.

Merlan Monopsychism Mysticism. 1970. lib. bdg. 57.00 (*90-247-0178-3*, Pub. by M Nijhoff) Kluwer Academic.

Merle Armitage: Book Designer. Merle Armitage. (Illus.). 32p. 1963. pap. 7.50 (*0-87959-117-X*) U of Tex H Ransom Ctr.

Merle Haggard for the Record: For The RecordHaggard,&Merle. Merle Haggard & Tom Carter. 272p. 1999. 24.00 (*0-06-019308-5*, Cliff Street) HarperTrade.

Merle Haggard's Greatest Hits. 56p. 1983. per. 12.95 (*0-7935-1936-5*, 00306883) H Leonard.

Merle Harmon Stories. Merle Harmon & Sam Blair. LC 98-91300. (Illus.). 144p. 1998. pap. 12.95 (*0-9635844-1-3*) Lilly & Blair.

Merle the High Flying Squirrel, 001. Bill Peet. (Illus.). 30p. (J). (gr. k-3). 1983. reprint ed. pap. 7.95 (*0-395-34923-0*) HM.

***Merle Travis Collection.** 96p. 1998. otabind 19.95 (*0-7935-8663-1*) H Leonard.

Merle Travis Guitar Style. Merle Travis & Tommy Flint. 176p. 1995. pap. 24.95 incl. audio compact disk (*0-7866-0266-X*, 93344BCD) Mel Bay.

Merleau-Ponty. Stephen Priest. LC 97-50003. (Arguments of the Philosophers Ser.). 336p. (C). 1998. 65.00 (*0-415-06263-2*) Routledge.

Merleau-Ponty: Critical Essays. Ed. by Henry Pietersma. LC 89-38160. (Current Continental Research Ser.: No. 553). 300p. (Orig.). (C). 1990. pap. text 25.50 (*0-8191-7589-7*); lib. bdg. 49.00 (*0-8191-7588-9*) U Pr of Amer.

Merleau-Ponty: Difference, Materiality, Painting. Ed. by Veronique M. Foti. LC 95-39917. (Illus.). 304p. (C). 1996. text 55.00 (*0-391-03904-0*) Humanities.

Merleau-Ponty: Language & the Act of Speech. Wayne J. Froman. LC 81-65292. 256p. 1982. 36.50 (*0-8387-5015-X*) Bucknell U Pr.

Merleau-Ponty Aesthetics Reader: Philosophy & Painting. Ed. by Michael B. Smith. (Studies in Phenomenology & Existential Philosophy). (Illus.). 380p. 1993. 69.95 (*0-8101-1073-3*); pap. 24.95 (*0-8101-1074-1*) Northwestern U Pr.

Merleau-Ponty & Marxism: From Terror to Reform. Barry Cooper. LC 78-16829. 239p. reprint ed. pap. 74.10 (*0-8357-3635-0*, 203636300003) Bks Demand.

Merleau-Ponty & Psychology. Ed. by Keith Hoeller. 270p. (Orig.). 1985. pap. 20.00 (*0-914857-02-9*) Rev Exist Psych.

Merleau-Ponty & the Foundation of an Existential Politics. Kerry H. Whiteside. (Studies in Moral, Political, & Legal Philosophy). 352p. 1989. pap. text 19.95 (*0-691-02288-7*, Pub. by Princeton U Pr) Cal Prin Full Svc.

Merleau-Ponty, Hermeneutics, & Postmodernism. Ed. by Thomas W. Busch & Shaun Gallagher. LC 91-33857. 263p. (C). 1992. text 21.50 (*0-7914-1139-7*) State U NY Pr.

Merleau-Ponty in Contemporary Perspective. Ed. by Patrick Burke & Jan Van Der Veken. LC 92-38343. (Phaenomenologica Ser.: Vol. 129). 236p. 1993. text 134.50 (*0-7923-2142-1*) Kluwer Academic.

Merleau-Ponty, Interiority & Exteriority, Psychic Life & the World. Ed. by Dorothea Olkowski & James Morley. LC 98-49628. 288p. (C). 1999. text 65.50 (*0-7914-4277-2*); pap. text 21.95 (*0-7914-4278-0*) State U NY Pr.

Merleau-Ponty Vivant. Ed. by M. C. Dillon. LC 90-42946. (SUNY Series in Contemporary Continental Philosophy). 224p. (C). 1991. text 59.50 (*0-7914-0658-X*); pap. text 19.95 (*0-7914-0659-8*) State U NY Pr.

Merleau-Ponty's Critique of Sartre's Philosophy. Margaret Whitford. LC 81-68140. (French Forum Monographs: No. 33). 180p. (Orig.). 1982. pap. 14.95 (*0-917058-32-1*) French Forum.

***Merleau-Ponty's Later Works & Their Practical Implications: The Dehiscence of Responsibility.** Ed. by Duane Davis. 340p. 2001. 69.95 (*1-57392-862-3*) Prometheus Bks.

Merleau-Ponty's Ontology. 2nd rev. ed. M. C. Dillon. LC 97-35618. (Studies in Phenomenology & Existential Philosophy). 299p. 1997. pap. 19.95 (*0-8101-1528-X*) Northwestern U Pr.

Merle's & Marilyn's Mink Ranch. Randeane Tetu. LC 91-33920. 216p. 1992. 14.00 (*0-918949-17-3*); pap. 9.00 (*0-918949-13-0*) Tetu Randeane.

Merlin. Ed. by Martin H. Greenberg. 320p. 1999. mass mkt. 6.99 (*0-88677-841-7*, Pub. by DAW Bks) Penguin Putnam.

***Merlin.** Marianna Mayer. (J). 1999. 15.99 (*0-8037-2187-0*, Dial Yng Read) Peng Put Young Read.

Merlin. Jane Yolen. (Young Merlin Trilogy Ser.). (J). (gr. 2-5). 1997. 15.00 (*0-614-28815-0*) Harcourt.

Merlin. Jane Yolen. LC 96-11683. 112p. (J). (gr. 4-7). 1997. 15.00 (*0-15-200814-4*) Harcourt.

Merlin. Jane Yolen. (Young Merlin Trilogy Ser.). (J). 1998. pap. 3.50 (*0-590-37119-3*, Apple Paperbacks) Scholastic Inc.

Merlin. Jane Yolen. (Young Merlin Trilogy Ser.). 1998. 8.60 (*0-606-13940-0*, Pub. by Turtleback) Demco.

Merlin. Norma L. Goodrich. LC 88-45303. 400p. 1989. reprint ed. pap. 17.00 (*0-06-097183-5*, PL 7183, Perennial) HarperTrade.

Merlin. Stephen R. Lawhead. (Pendragon Cycle Ser.: Bk. 2). 448p. 1990. reprint ed. mass mkt. 6.99 (*0-380-70889-2*, Avon Bks) Morrow Avon.

Merlin, Pt. 1. Henry Lovelich. Ed. by Ernst A. Kock. (EETS, ES Ser.: Nos. 93, 112). 1974. reprint ed. 45.00 (*0-527-00184-8*) Periodicals Srv.

Merlin, Pt. 2. Henry Lovelich. Ed. by Ernst A. Kock. (EETS, ES Ser.: Nos. 93, 112). 1974. reprint ed. 30.00 (*0-527-00185-6*) Periodicals Srv.

Merlin: A Casebook. Peter Goodrich & Norris J. Lacy. (Arthurian Characters & Themes Ser.). 300p. 1997. 40.00 (*0-8153-0658-X*) Garland.

Merlin: A Thousand Heroes with One Face. Charlotte Spivack. LC 93-48021. 136p. 1994. 69.95 (*0-7734-9116-3*) E Mellen.

Merlin: Priest of Nature. Jean Markale. 230p. 1995. pap. 16.95 (*0-89281-517-5*) Inner Tradit.

Merlin: The Shooting Script. David Stevens & Peter Barnes. LC 98-16124. (Shooting Script Ser.). (Illus.). 272p. 1998. pap. 16.95 (*1-55704-366-3*, Pub. by Newmarket) Norton.

Merlin: The Sorcerer's Guide to Survival in College. Christopher F. Monte. 130p. (C). 1990. 12.00 (*0-534-13482-3*) Wadsworth Pub.

***Merlin Pt. I: The Old Magic.** James Mallory. 273p. 1999. mass mkt. 6.99 (*0-446-60766-5*, Pub. by Warner Bks) Little.

***Merlin Pt. I: The Old Magic.** large type ed. James Mallory. LC 99-40366. 1999. 23.95 (*0-7838-8772-8*, G K Hall Lrg Type) Mac Lib Ref.

Merlin Pt. 2: The King's Wizard. James Mallory. 304p. 1999. mass mkt. 6.99 (*0-446-60791-6*, Pub. by Warner Bks) Little.

***Merlin Pt. 3: The End of Magic.** James Mallory. 304p. 2000. mass mkt. 6.99 (*0-446-60792-4*, Pub. by Warner Bks) Little.

Merlin, a Middle-English Metrical Version of a French Romance, Pt. III. Henry Lovelich. (EETS. OS Ser.: No. 185). 1974. reprint ed. 55.00 (*0-527-00183-X*) Periodicals Srv.

Merlin & Company. Alvaro Cunqueiro. Tr. by Colin Smith. 224p. 1996. pap. 6.95 (*0-460-87731-3*, Everyman's Classic Lib) Tuttle Pubng.

Merlin & the Dragons. Composed by Michel Rubini. (J). (gr. k-6). 1993. pap. 9.95 incl. VHS (*1-879496-49-6*, 54003-3) Lightyear Entrtnmnt.

Merlin & the Dragons. Jane Yolen. 40p. (J). (gr. k up). 1998. pap. 6.99 (*0-14-055891-8*, PuffinBks) Peng Put Young Read.

Merlin & the Dragons. unabridged ed. Jane Yolen. (Stories to Remember Ser.). (J). (gr. 1-5). 1993. pap. 13.98 incl. audio compact disk (*1-56896-035-2*) Lightyear Entrtnmnt.

Merlin & the Dragons. unabridged ed. Jane Yolen. (Stories to Remember Ser.). (J). (gr. 1-5). 1993. pap. 8.98 incl. audio (*1-879496-22-4*) Lightyear Entrtnmnt.

Merlin & the Dragons of Atlantis. Rita Hildebrandt & Tim Hildebrandt. LC 83-15566. (Illus.). 197p. 1984. 16.95 (*0-672-52704-9*) Macmillan.

***Merlin & the Grail Tradition.** Gareth Knight. (Illus.). 136p. 1999. pap. 10.95 (*1-928754-01-5*) Sun Chalice.

Merlin & the Last Trump. Collin Webbere. 269p. 1995. pap. 8.95 (*0-575-05718-1*, Pub. by V Gollancz) Trafalgar.

Merlin Chronicles. Ed. by Mike Ashley. LC 96-154350. 448p. (Orig.). 1995. pap. 12.95 (*0-7867-0275-3*) Carroll & Graf.

Merlin Effect. T. A. Barron. LC 93-36234. 280p. (J). (gr. 5-9). 1994. 19.95 (*0-399-22689-3*, Philomel) Peng Put Young Read.

Merlin Effect. T. A. Barron. (J). 1996. mass mkt. 5.99 (*0-8125-5169-9*, Pub. by Tor Bks) St Martin.

Merlin Effect. T. A. Barron. 1996. 11.09 (*0-606-11618-4*, Pub. by Turtleback) Demco.

Merlin Factor: Keys to the Corporate Kingdom. Charles Smith. 224p. 1997. text 51.95 (*0-566-07942-9*, Pub. by Gower) Ashgate Pub Co.

Merlin Factor: Keys to the Corporate Kingdom. Charles E. Smith. 136p. 1995. pap. text 20.00 (*0-9647687-0-4*) Kairos Prod.

Merlin, 1498. Ed. by Cedric E. Pickford. (French Arthurian Romances Ser.). 1975. 133.95 (*0-85967-196-8*, Pub. by Scolar Pr) Ashgate Pub Co.

Merlin in German Literature. Adelaide M. Weiss. LC 73-140017. (Catholic University Studies in German: No. 3). reprint ed. 37.50 (*0-404-50223-7*) AMS Pr.

Merlin Mystery. Jonathan Gunson & Marten Coombe. LC GV1493.G86 1998. (Illus.). 48p. 1998. 21.00 (*0-446-52432-8*, Pub. by Warner Bks) Little.

***Merlin of St. Gilles' Well.** Ann Chamberlin. 2000. pap. 13.95 (*0-312-87591-6*) St Martin.

***Merlin of St. Gilles' Well.** Ann Chamberlin. 2000. mass mkt. 6.99 (*0-8125-9002-3*) Tor Bks.

***Merlin of St. Gilles' Well.** 2nd ed. Ann Chamberlin. LC 99-22204. 320p. 1999. 23.95 (*0-312-86551-1*, Pub. by Tor Bks) St Martin.

Merlin Through the Ages: A Chronological Anthology & Source Book. Ed. by R. J. Stewart & John Matthews. (Illus.). 352p. 1996. pap. 16.95 (*0-7137-2466-8*, Pub. by Blandford Pr) Sterling.

Merlin Versus Faust: Contending Archetypes in Western Culture. Ed. by Charlotte Spivack. LC 92-20841. 225p. 1992. text 89.95 (*0-7734-9594-0*) E Mellen.

Merlin's Bones. Fred Saberhagen. 1996. mass mkt. 5.99 (*0-8125-3349-6*, Pub. by Tor Bks) St Martin.

***Merlin's Book of Magic & Enchantment.** Nevill Drury. LC 98-75035. (Illus.). 160p. 1999. 8.98 (*0-7651-1026-1*) Smithmark.

Merlin's Castle. Laszlo Gal. (Illus.). 32p. (J). (gr. k-3). 1996. 14.95 (*0-7737-2852-X*) Stoddart Publ.

Merlin's Cave. William Hezlep. LC 96-36078. 55p. (Orig.). (J). (gr. k-12). 1996. pap. 5.00 (*0-88734-420-8*) Players Pr.

Merlins Chronicles. Maia C. Shamayyim. (Illus.). 64p. 1991. spiral bd. 12.95 (*1-888420-11-1*) Johannine Grove.

Merlin's Daughters: Contemporary Women Writers of Fantasy, 23. Charlotte Spivack. LC 86-12088. (Contributions to the Study of Science Fiction & Fantasy Ser.: No. 23). 196p. 1987. 45.00 (*0-313-24194-5*, SEQ/, Greenwood Pr) Greenwood.

Merlin's Destiny. Sigmund Brouwer. LC 96-29181. (Winds of Light Ser.: No. 6). (Illus.). 132p. (Orig.). (J). (gr. 4-8). 1993. pap. 5.99 (*1-56476-049-9*, 6-3049, Victor Bks) Chariot Victor.

Merlin's Disciples: Prophecy, Poetry, & Power in Renaissance England. Howard Dobin. LC 89-26168. 272p. 1990. 37.50 (*0-8047-1783-4*) Stanford U Pr.

Merlin's Gift. Ian McDowell. 256p. (Orig.). 1997. mass mkt. 5.99 (*0-380-78197-2*, Avon Bks) Morrow Avon.

Merlin's Kin: World Tales of the Hero Magicians. Josepha Sherman. LC 98-24524. 192p. 1998. pap. 11.95 (*0-87483-519-4*) August Hse.

Merlin's Kin: World Tales of the Hero Magicians. Josepha Sherman. LC 98-24524. 192p. (J). (gr. 3-9). 1998. 21.95 (*0-87483-523-2*) August Hse.

Merlin's Legacy. Quinn Taylor Evans. LC 99-14360. 1999. 25.95 (*0-7862-1923-8*, Five Star MI) Mac Lib Ref.

Merlin's Legacy: Daughter of Fire. Quinn Taylor Evans. 448p. 1998. pap. 12.00 (*1-57566-306-6*, Knsington) Kensgtn Pub Corp.

Merlin's Legacy: Daughter of the Mist. Quinn Taylor Evans. (Merlin's Legacy Ser.: Bk. 2). 480p. 1996. mass mkt. 5.50 (*0-8217-5347-9*, Zebra Kensgtn) Kensgtn Pub Corp.

Merlin's Legacy: Daughter of the Mist. Quinn Taylor Evans. 384p. 1999. mass mkt. 12.00 (*1-57566-406-2*) Kensgtn Pub Corp.

Merlin's Legacy: Dawn of Camelot. Quinn Taylor Evans. (Merlin's Legacy Ser.: Vol. 5). 320p. 1998. mass mkt. 5.50 (*0-8217-6028-9*, Zebra Kensgtn) Kensgtn Pub Corp.

Merlin's Legacy No. 3: Daughter of Light. Quinn Taylor Evans. Vol. 3. 480p. 1997. mass mkt. 5.50 (*0-8217-5549-8*, Zebra Kensgtn) Kensgtn Pub Corp.

Merlin's Legacy No. 3: Daughter of Light. Quinn Taylor Evans. (Merlin's Legacy Ser.). 320p. 1998. mass mkt. 5.50 (*0-8217-6051-3*, Zebra Kensgtn) Kensgtn Pub Corp.

Merlin's Legacy No. 4: Shadows of Camelot. Quinn Taylor Evans. 320p. 1997. mass mkt. 5.50 (*0-8217-5760-1*, Zebra Kensgtn) Kensgtn Pub Corp.

***Merlin's Message: Reawakening & Remembering, 1.** Marelin the Magician Staff. LC 97-91214. 123p. 1998. pap. 5.00 (*1-891411-00-4*) Serious Comedy.

***Merlin's Message: Reawakening & Remembering.** 2nd rev. ed. Marelin the Magician Staff. 128p. 1998. pap. 7.00 (*1-891411-02-0*) Serious Comedy.

Merlin's Mistake. Robert Newman. (Illus.). (J). (gr. 5-9). 1990. 16.25 (*0-8446-6187-2*) Peter Smith.

Merlin's Premier League Official Annual, 1999. 64p. 1998. write for info. (*1-883313-50-3*) Topps Comics.

Merlin's Puzzle Pastimes. Charles B. Townsend. 64p. 1986. reprint ed. pap. 3.95 (*0-486-25123-3*) Dover.

Merlin's Secret: The African & Near Eastern Presence in the Ancient British Isles. Robert N. List. 432p. 1999. 64.00 (*0-7618-1395-0*); pap. 47.50 (*0-7618-1396-9*) U Pr of Amer.

Merlin's Tale of Arthur's Magic Sword: Playscript. Keith Engar. 1982. 6.50 (*0-87602-228-X*) Anchorage.

Merlin's Tour of the Universe: A Skywatcher's Guide to Everything from Mars & Quasars to Comets, Planets, Blue Moons & Werewolves. Neil D. Tyson. LC 96-37200. 320p. 1997. pap. 13.95 (*0-385-48835-1*) Doubleday.

Merlin's Web. Susan W. Mayse. 368p. 1989. mass mkt. 4.50 (*0-380-70624-5*, Avon Bks) Morrow Avon.

Merlot TasteTour: Generous Noble Red Wines see TasteTour Collection: Fine Wines of the World

Merlusse see Oeuvres Completes

Merlusse-Cigalon. Marcel Pagnol. (FRE.). 1974. 19.95 (*0-7859-0115-9*, M3838) Fr & Eur.

Merlyn: A Guide to Soulmerging. Joshua Ananda. 410p. 1995. pap. 12.95 (*0-9640538-0-2*) Morphos.

***Merlyn's Pen: Fiction, Essays & Poems by America's Teenagers, Vol. IV.** Ed. by R. James Stahl. 100p. (YA). (gr. 6-12). 2000. per. write for info. (*1-886427-50-X*, MP4A) Merlyns Pen.

Merlyn's Pen Vol. I: Fiction, Essays, & Poems by America's Teens. Ed. by R. James Stahl. (Illus.). 100p. (YA). (gr. 6-12). 1997. per. 29.00 (*1-886427-47-X*) Merlyns Pen.

***Merlyn's Pen Vol. II: Fiction, Essays & Poems by America's Teens.** Ed. by R. James Stahl. (Illus.). 100p. (YA). (gr. 6-12). 1998. pap. text 29.00 (*1-886427-48-8*) Merlyns Pen.

***Merlyn's Pen Vol. III: Fiction, Essays & Poems by America's Teens.** Ed. by R. James Stahl. (Illus.). 100p. (YA). (gr. 6-12). 1999. pap. 29.00 (*1-886427-49-6*) Merlyns Pen.

Mermaid. Mark Dunster. 41p. 1982. pap. 4.00 (*0-89642-087-6*) Linden Pubs.

Mermaid. Betina Krahn. 368p. 1997. mass mkt. 5.99 (*0-553-57617-8*, Spectra) Bantam.

Mermaid. Margaret Millar. 216p. 1991. pap. 8.95 (*1-55882-114-7*) Intl Polygonics.

Mermaid Margaret Millar. LC 82-16198. 317p. 1982. write for info. (*0-89340-543-4*) Chivers N Amer.

Mermaid & Other Sea Poems. Illus. & Compiled by Sophie Windham. LC 94-32526. 32p. (J). (gr. 3-6). 1996. 16.95 (*0-590-20898-5*) Scholastic Inc.

***Mermaid & the Minotaur: Sexual Arrangements & Human Malaise.** Dorothy Dinnerstein. LC 99-16337. (Illus.). 288p. 1999. reprint ed. pap. 15.95 (*1-892746-25-5*, 46255) Other Pr LLC.

Mermaid Forest. Rumiko Takahashi. (Illus.). 1995. pap. 16.95 (*1-56931-047-5*, Viz Comics) Viz Commns Inc.

Mermaid in a Tidal Pool. Mimi G. Carpenter. (Illus.). 32p. (Orig.). (J). (ps-6). 1985. pap. 8.95 (*0-9614628-0-9*) Beachcomber Pr.

Mermaid in the Pond: An Erotic Fairy Tale for Adults. Verena Kast. Tr. by Vanessa Agnew. LC 96-8730. 144p. 1999. pap. 17.95 (*0-8264-0926-1*) Continuum.

Mermaid Island. Margaret Frith. LC 97-19380. (Eek! Stories to Make You Shriek Ser.). (Illus.). 48p. (J). (gr. 1-3). 1997. 13.89 (*0-448-41725-1*, G & D); pap. text 3.95 (*0-448-41618-2*, G & D) Peng Put Young Read.

Mermaid Island. Margaret Frith. (Eek! Stories to Make You Shriek Ser.). 1997. 9.15 (*0-606-11619-2*, Pub. by Turtleback) Demco.

Mermaid of Cafur. Evelyn Foster. (Illus.). 32p. (J). (gr. k-3). 1999. 15.95 (*1-902283-40-6*) Barefoot Bks NY.

Mermaid Sticker Paper Doll. Barbara Steadman. (Illus.). (J). 1994. pap. 1.00 (*0-486-28266-X*) Dover.

Mermaid Summer. Mollie Hunter. LC 87-45984. (Charlotte Zolotow Bk.). 128p. (J). (gr. 3-7). 1988. lib. bdg. 15.89 (*0-06-022628-5*) HarpC Child Bks.

Mermaid Summer. Mollie Hunter. LC 87-45984. (Trophy Bk.). (Illus.). 128p. (J). (gr. 4-7). 1990. pap. 4.95 (*0-06-440344-0*, HarpTrophy) HarpC Child Bks.

Mermaid Summer. Mollie Hunter. 1990. 9.60 (*0-606-12601-5*, Pub. by Turtleback) Demco.

Mermaid Tales From Around the World. Illus. by Troy Howell. LC 92-30527. 96p. (J). (gr. 4-6). 1993. 16.95 (*0-590-44377-1*) Scholastic Inc.

Mermaid Tales from Around the World. Mary Pope Osborne. (Illus.). 96p. (J). (gr. 2-6). 1999. pap. 7.99 (*0-439-04781-1*) Scholastic Inc.

Mermaid Tavern. Ed. by Melissa Gish. (Illus.). 60p. (Orig.). 1996. 6.95 (*0-9651215-1-8*) Strait-Jacket.

Mermaid Wife. Rebecca Winters. 1994. per. 2.99 (*0-373-03312-5*) Harlequin Bks.

***Mermaid World: Glow Sticker Stories.** Grosset & Dunlap Staff. (Illus.). 16p. (J). (ps-3). 2000. pap. 4.99 (*0-448-42172-0*, Planet Dexter) Peng Put Young Read.

Mermaids. Patty Dann. 1986. 13.95 (*0-89919-471-0*, Pub. by Ticknor & Fields) HM.

Mermaids. Alexander Nagel. 1996. write for info. (*0-8212-2264-3*) Little.

Mermaids. Elizabeth Ratisseau. 48p. 1998. 16.95 (*1-883211-14-X*) Laughing Elephant.

Mermaids. Barbara J. Zitwer. (Magic of the Ocean Ser.). (Illus.). 60p. 1995. write for info. (*0-446-51880-8*) Warner Bks.

Mermaids & Ikons: A Greek Summer. Gwendolyn MacEwan. 112p. (Orig.). 1978. pap. 6.95 (*0-88784-062-0*, Pub. by Hse of Anansi Pr) Genl Dist Srvs.

Mermaids' Ball. Bea Sloboder. LC 99-192934. (Glitter Tattoos Ser.). (Illus.). 24p. (J). (ps-2). 1998. pap. 3.99 (*0-448-41856-8*, G & D) Peng Put Young Read.

Mermaids Don't Run Track. Debbie Dadey & Marcia Thornton Jones. (Adventures of the Bailey School Kids Ser.: No. 26). (Illus.). 72p. (J). (gr. 4-7). 1997. pap. 3.50 (*0-590-84906-9*, Little Apple) Scholastic Inc.

Mermaids Don't Run Track. Debbie Dadey & Marcia Thornton Jones. (Adventures of the Bailey School Kids Ser.: No. 26). (J). (gr. 2-4). 1997. 8.70 (*0-606-11620-6*, Pub. by Turtleback) Demco.

Mermaid's Dream. Alane Faye. 400p. 1995. mass mkt. 4.99 (*0-8217-0146-0*, Zebra Kensgtn) Kensgtn Pub Corp.

Mermaids for Attila. Jacques Servin. 124p. 1991. 18.95 (*0-932511-50-3*); pap. 8.95 (*0-932511-51-1*) Fiction Coll.

Mermaid's Gaze. Rumiko Takahashi. (Illus.). 184p. 1997. pap. text 15.95 (*1-56931-195-1*, Viz Comics) Viz Commns Inc.

***Mermaid's Ground.** large type ed. Alice Marlow. 480p. 1999. 31.99 (*0-7089-4076-5*) Ulverscroft.

Mermaids in the Basement: Poems for Women. Carolyn Kizer. LC 84-71253. 106p. 1984. 14.00 (*0-914742-80-9*); pap. 10.00 (*0-914742-81-7*) Copper Canyon.

Mermaid's Log. James A. Brennan. Ed. by Lisa Davis & Mary A. Chimera. (Illus.). 224p. (Orig.). 1996. pap. 15.95 (*0-9652907-4-3*) J M Brennan.

Mermaids' Lullaby. Kate Spohn. LC 97-39770. 1998. 16.00 (*0-679-89175-7*, Pub. by Random Bks Yng Read) Random.

Mermaids' Lullaby. Kate Spohn. LC 97-39770. (J). 1998. lib. bdg. 18.99 (*0-679-99175-1*) Vin Bks.

Mermaids, Monasteries, Cherokees & Custer: The Stories Behind Philadelphia Street Names. Robert I. Alotta. (Illus.). 267p. (Orig.). 1990. pap. 14.95 (*0-933893-90-6*) Bonus Books.

Mermaids, Mummies, & Mastodons: The Emergence of the American Museum. LC 92-29830. 1992. 45.00 (*0-931201-15-2*) Am Assn Mus.

***Mermaid's Muse.** David Bouchard. 223p. 2000. 15.95 (*1-55192-248-7*) Raincoast Bk.

Mermaids of Chenonceaux: And 828 Other Stories. Phyllis Meras. 352p. 1982. 16.95 (*0-312-92525-5*) St Martin.

M

An Asterisk (*) at the beginning of an entry indicates that the title is appearing for the first time.

***Mermaids on Parade: America's Love Affair with It's First Olympic Swimmers.** Buck Dawson. (Illus.). 2000. 23.95 (*1-56072-726-8*, Nova Kroshka Bks) Nova Sci Pubs.

Mermaids on the Golf Course. Patricia Highsmith. LC 88-40020. 240p. 1988. 17.45 (*0-89296-352-2*) Mysterious Pr.

Mermaids on the Golf Course. Patricia Highsmith. LC 88-40020. 240p. 1988. 45.00 (*0-89296-358-1*, Pub. by Mysterious Pr) Little.

***Mermaid's Purse.** Ted Hughes. LC 99-46098. 64p. 2000. 15.95 (*0-375-80569-9*, Pub. by Knopf Bks Yng Read) Random.

***Mermaid's Purse.** Ted Hughes. LC 99-46098. 64p. (J). 2000. lib. bdg. 16.99 (*0-375-90569-3*, Pub. by Random Bks Yng Read) Random.

Mermaid's Purse, Vol. 1. Kathleen Estes. LC 96-76390. (Illus.). 40p. (J). (ps-1). 1996. 15.95 (*1-880851-24-5*) Greene Bark Pr.

Mermaid's Scar. Rumiko Takahashi. (Illus.). 304p. 1995. pap. 17.95 (*1-56931-083-1*) Viz Commns Inc.

***Mermaids Singing.** Lisa A. Carey. LC 97-36438. 257p. 1998. mass mkt. 22.00 (*0-380-97674-9*, Avon Bks) Morrow Avon.

Mermaids Singing. Lisa A. Carey. LC 97-36438. 352p. (gr. 8 up). 1999. mass mkt. 6.99 (*0-380-79960-X*, Avon Bks) Morrow Avon.

Mermaids Singing. John Van Druten. 1946. pap. 5.25 (*0-8222-0750-8*) Dramatists Play.

Mermaid's Song, Vol. 1. Marianne Willman. 1997. mass mkt. 5.99 (*0-312-96256-8*) St Martin.

Mermaid's Tales. Ruth Ainsworth. 1997. 14.95 (*0-7188-2460-1*, Lutterworth-Parkwest) Parkwest Pubns.

Mermaids Twin Sister. Lynn Joseph. (Illus.). 64p. 1996. pap. 5.95 (*0-395-81311-5*) HM.

Mermaid's Twin Sister: More Stories from Trinidad. Lynn Joseph. LC 93-28436. (Illus.). 80p. (J). (gr. 3-7). 1994. 13.95 (*0-395-64365-1*, Clarion Bks) HM.

Mermaid's Twin Sister: More Stories from Trinidad. Lynn Joseph. 1994. 11.15 (*0-606-10875-0*, Pub. by Turtleback) Demco.

***Mermaids Underwater Adventure.** Cecile Schoberle & Dana Regan. (Sparkle 'n' Twinkle Bks.). (Illus.). 16p. (J). (ps-2). 1999. pap. 4.99 (*0-689-82702-4*) S&S Childrens.

Mermakk's Behavioral Guide to Success. Louis J. Ronsivalli. LC 96-94141. (Illus.). 165p. 1996. pap. 20.00 (*1-888201-02-9*) Mermakk Publns.

***Merman.** Dick King-Smith. 112p. 2001. pap. 4.99 (*0-440-41718-X*) BDD Bks Young Read.

Merman. Dick King-Smith. LC 98-54302. (Illus.). 102p. (J). (gr. 3-5). 1999. 16.00 (*0-517-80030-6*, Pub. by Crown Bks Yng Read); lib. bdg. 17.99 (*0-517-80031-4*, Pub. by Crown Bks Yng Read) Random.

Mermarkk's Stories for Children at Bedtime. Louis J. Ronsivalli. LC 96-94907. (Illus.). 140p. (Orig.). (J). 1997. pap. 8.95 (*1-888201-04-5*) Mermakk Publns.

Mermoz. Joseph Kessel. (FRE.). 1972. pap. 11.95 (*0-7859-2287-3*, 2070362329) Fr & Eur.

Mermoz. Joseph Kessel. (Folio Ser.: No. 864). (FRE.). 1972. pap. 10.95 (*2-07-036232-9*) Schoenhof.

Meroitic Funerary Inscriptions from Arminna West, Vol. 4. Bruce G. Trigger. LC 72-123644. 1970. 25.00 (*0-686-00127-3*) Penn-Yale Expedit.

Meromorphic Continuation & Functional Equations of Cuspidal Eisenstein Series for Maximal Cuspidal Subgroups. S. Wong. LC 89-28399. (Memoirs Ser.: No. 83/423). ix, 210p. 1990. pap. 27.00 (*0-8218-2486-4*, MEMO/83/423) Am Math.

Meromorphic Functions & Projective Curves. Kichoon Yang. LC 98-49069. (Mathematics & Its Applications Ser.). 12p. 1999. write for info. (*0-7923-5505-9*) Kluwer Academic.

Merope: The Dramatic Impact of a Myth. Marija Petrovska. (American University Studies: Comparative Literature: Ser. III, Vol. 9). 211p. (Orig.). 1984. pap. text 19.00 (*0-8204-0084-X*) P Lang Pubng.

Merosporangiferous Mucorales. Richard K. Benjamin. (Bibliotheca Mycologica Ser.). (Illus.). 1967. reprint ed. 48.00 (*3-7682-0514-2*) Lubrecht & Cramer.

Merovingian Garnet Jewellery. Birgit Arrhenius. (Illus.). 220p. 1985. text 59.00 (*91-7402-160-5*) Coronet Bks.

Merovingian Kingdoms 450-751. Ian Wood. LC 92-46027. 392p. (C). 1994. pap. text 39.38 (*0-582-49372-2*, Pub. by Addison-Wesley) Longman.

Merovingian Kingdoms 450 751. Ian Wood. 392p. (C). 1994. text 72.95 (*0-582-21878-0*, Pub. by Addison-Wesley) Longman.

Merovingian Military Organization, 481-751. Bernard S. Bachrach. LC 70-187164. 169p. reprint ed. pap. 52.40 (*0-608-14648-X*, 205583700039) Bks Demand.

Merovingians. Heimito Von Doderer. (Sun & Moon Classics Ser.: No. 113). 420p. 1996. pap. 15.95 (*1-55713-250-X*) Sun & Moon CA.

Merrang & the Hood Family. Robert Hood. 139p. 1991. pap. 48.00 (*0-949823-20-1*, Pub. by Deakin Univ) St Mut.

Merriam Genealogy in England & America. Charles H. Pope. (Illus.). 515p. 1989. reprint ed. pap. 69.50 (*0-8328-6570-2*); reprint ed. lib. bdg. 85.00 (*0-8328-0866-0*) Higginson Bk Co.

Merriam Genealogy in England & America. rev. ed. Charles H. Pope. LC 86-18882. (Illus.). xxxvi, 522p. 1986. pap. 40.00 (*0-9612610-1-3*) Bullbrier Pr.

Merriam-Webster & Garfield Dictionary. Ed. by Merriam-Webster Editors. LC 99-25351. 816p. 1999. pap. 12.95 (*0-87779-626-2*) Merriam-Webster Inc.

***Merriam-Webster Children's Illustrated Dictionary.** Merriam-Webster Staff. LC 99-43274. (Illus.). 912p. (J). 2000. 17.95 (*0-7894-5238-3*, D K Ink) DK Pub Inc.

Merriam-Webster Concise School & Office Thesaurus. Merriam-Webster Editors. 1991. 15.05 (*0-606-05462-6*, Pub. by Turtleback) Demco.

Merriam-Webster Dictionary. Ed. by Merriam-Webster Editors. 1994. 11.34 (*0-606-07859-2*) Turtleback.

Merriam-Webster Dictionary. Ed. by Merriam-Webster Editors. 1995. 17.30 (*0-606-07860-6*) Turtleback.

***Merriam Webster Dictionary.** Ed. by MERRIAM WEBSTER. 1999. pap. text 8.95 (*0-205-31735-9*) A&B Bks.

Merriam-Webster Dictionary. rev. ed. Merriam-Webster Editors. LC 95-5824. 896p. (C). 1994. mass mkt. 5.99 (*0-87779-911-3*) Merriam-Webster Inc.

Merriam-Webster Dictionary, Home & Office Edition. Merriam-Webster Staff. LC 97-39927. (Illus.). 720p. 1998. pap. 11.95 (*0-87779-606-8*) Merriam-Webster Inc.

Merriam-Webster Dictionary of Quotations. Merriam-Webster Editors. 512p. 1995. mass mkt. 4.99 (*0-87779-904-0*) Merriam-Webster Inc.

Merriam-Webster Dictionary of Quotations. Merriam-Webster Editors. 1992. 10.09 (*0-606-05463-4*, Pub. by Turtleback) Demco.

Merriam-Webster Dictionary of Synonyms & Antonyms. Ed. by Merriam-Webster Editors. 448p. 1995. mass mkt. 4.99 (*0-87779-906-7*) Merriam-Webster Inc.

Merriam-Webster New Book of Word Histories. Merriam-Webster Editors. 544p. 1995. pap. 9.95 (*0-87779-603-3*) Merriam-Webster Inc.

Merriam-Webster Thesaurus. Merriam-Webster Editors. 672p. 1995. mass mkt. 4.99 (*0-87779-902-4*) Merriam-Webster Inc.

Merriam-Webster Thesaurus, Home & Office Edition. Merriam-Webster Staff. LC 95-19061. 704p. 1996. pap. 9.95 (*0-87779-607-6*) Merriam-Webster Inc.

Merriam-Webster's Biographical Dictionary. rev. ed. Merriam-Webster Editors. LC 94-43025. 1184p. 1995. 27.95 (*0-87779-743-9*) Merriam-Webster Inc.

Merriam-Webster's Collegiate Dictionary. 10th deluxe ed. Merriam-Webster Editors. LC 98-13387. (Illus.). 1998. im. lthr. 45.00 (*0-87779-714-5*) Merriam-Webster Inc.

Merriam-Webster's Collegiate Dictionary. 10th deluxe large type ed. Merriam-Webster Editors. LC 93-20206. (Illus.). 1600p. 1993. im. lthr. 34.95 (*0-87779-711-0*) Merriam-Webster Inc.

Merriam Webster's Collegiate Dictionary. 10th rev. ed. Merriam-Webster Editors. Ed. by Frederick C. Mish. LC 93-20206. (Illus.). 1600p. 1995. text 19.95 (*0-87779-707-2*) Merriam-Webster Inc.

Merriam Webster's Collegiate Dictionary. 10th rev. ed. Merriam-Webster Editors. Ed. by FCM Staff. LC 93-20206. (Illus.). 1600p. 1997. im. lthr. 27.95 (*0-87779-710-2*) Merriam-Webster Inc.

Merriam Webster's Collegiate Dictionary. 10th rev. ed. Merriam-Webster Editors. Ed. by Frederick C. Mish. LC 96-42529. (Illus.). 1600p. 1997. kivar 22.95 (*0-87779-708-0*) Merriam-Webster Inc.

Merriam Webster's Collegiate Dictionary: Thumb-Indexed. 10th rev. ed. Merriam-Webster Editors. Ed. by FCM Staff. LC 93-20206. (Illus.). 1600p. (C). 1998. 24.95 (*0-87779-709-9*) Merriam-Webster Inc.

Merriam-Webster's Collegiate Dictionary Tenth Edition & Electronic Edition. 10th ed. Merriam-Webster Editors. 1600p. 1996. 39.95 incl. cd-rom (*0-87779-713-7*) Merriam-Webster Inc.

***Merriam Webster's Collegiate Encyclopedia. (Illus.). 1696p. 2000. 34.95 (*0-87779-017-5*) Merriam-Webster Inc.**

A comprehensive, one-volume desk reference created in cooperation with Encyclopedia Britannica. Features more than 2.5 million words, 25,000 clear & precise articles, over 1,300 illustrations & 350 maps. Includes abundant coverage of pronunciations. ***Publisher Paid Annotation.***

***Merriam-Webster's Collegiate Reference Set with CD-ROM.** Ed. by Merriam-Webster Editors. 1999. boxed set 49.95 incl. cd-rom (*0-87779-715-3*) Merriam-Webster Inc.

Merriam-Webster's Collegiate Thesaurus. Merriam-Webster Staff. LC 93-3177. 894p. 1995. 17.95 (*0-87779-169-4*) Merriam-Webster Inc.

Merriam-Webster's Collegiate Thesaurus. deluxe ed. Ed. by Merriam-Webster Editors. LC 93-3177. 894p. 1993. im. lthr. 21.95 (*0-87779-170-8*) Merriam-Webster Inc.

Merriam-Webster's Concise Dictionary. large type ed. Merriam-Webster Editors. LC 97-50501. 1998. pap. 19.95 (*0-87779-624-6*) Merriam-Webster Inc.

Merriam-Webster's Concise Handbook for Writers. 2nd ed. Merriam-Webster Editors. LC 97-40797. 1998. pap. 9.95 (*0-87779-625-4*) Merriam-Webster Inc.

Merriam-Webster's Crossword Puzzle Dictionary. 2nd ed. Merriam-Webster Editors. 784p. 1997. mass mkt. 5.99 (*0-87779-919-9*) Merriam-Webster Inc.

Merriam-Webster's Crossword Puzzle Dictionary. 2nd rev. ed. Merriam-Webster Editors. LC 96-24796. 784p. 1996. 18.95 (*0-87779-121-X*) Merriam-Webster Inc.

***Merriam-Webster's Crossword Quest, Vol. 2.** Merriam-Webster Editors. 80p. 1999. pap. 8.95 (*0-87779-654-8*) Merriam-Webster Inc.

Merriam-Webster's Crossword Quest, Vol. 3. Ed. by Merriam-Webster Editors. 80p. 1999. pap. 8.95 (*0-87779-655-6*) Merriam-Webster Inc.

Merriam-Webster's Crossword Quest, Vol. 4. Ed. by Merriam-Webster Editors. 1999. pap. 8.95 (*0-87779-656-4*) Merriam-Webster Inc.

***Merriam-Webster's Crossword Quest, Vol. 5.** Ed. by Merriam-Webster Editors. 88p. 2000. pap. 8.95 (*0-87779-657-2*) Merriam-Webster Inc.

***Merriam-Webster's Crossword Quest, Vol. 6.** Ed. by Merriam-Webster Editors. 88p. 2000. pap. 8.95 (*0-87779-658-0*) Merriam-Webster Inc.

Merriam-Webster's Deluxe Dictionary. 10th ed. Merriam-Webster Editors. LC 98-18666. 1998. write for info. (*0-7621-0300-0*) RD Assn.

***Merriam-Webster's Dictionary of Allusions.** Elizabeth Webber et al. LC 99-33125. 608p. 1999. pap. 14.95 (*0-87779-628-9*) Merriam-Webster Inc.

Merriam-Webster's Dictionary of Basic English. Ed. by Merriam-Webster Editors. LC 94-49524. (Illus.). 736p. 1995. pap. 9.95 (*0-87779-605-X*) Merriam-Webster Inc.

Merriam-Webster's Dictionary of Basic English. Ed. by Merriam-Webster Editors. 1995. 15.30 (*0-606-07861-4*) Turtleback.

Merriam-Webster's Dictionary of English Usage. rev. ed. Merriam-Webster Staff. LC 93-19289. Orig. Title: Webster's Dictionary of English Usage. 992p. 1993. 24.95 (*0-87779-132-5*) Merriam-Webster Inc.

Merriam-Webster's Dictionary of Law. Merriam-Webster Editors. 656p. 1996. pap. 15.95 (*0-87779-604-1*) Merriam-Webster Inc.

Merriam-Webster's Dictionary of Synonyms. Merriam-Webster Editors. 944p. 1994. 21.95 (*0-87779-341-7*) Merriam-Webster Inc.

Merriam-Webster's Elementary Dictionary. Ed. by Merriam-Webster Editors. LC 93-41502. (Illus.). 608p. (J). (gr. 2-6). 1994. 15.95 (*0-87779-575-4*) Merriam-Webster Inc.

***Merriam-Webster's Elementary Dictionary. Ed. by Merriam-Webster Staff. (Illus.). 640p. (J). (gr. 2-6). 2000. pap. 11.95 (*0-87779-630-0*) Merriam-Webster Inc.**

Copyright 2000! A new, revised trade paperback version of our popular hardcover at a great price! A first real dictionary for children ages 7-11. Delivers over 32,000 entries, hundreds of illustrations & special sections including U.S. presidents. ***Publisher Paid Annotation.***

Merriam-Webster's Encyclopedia of Literature. Ed. by Encyclopedia Britannica Staff & Merriam-Webster Editors. LC 94-42741. (Illus.). 1248p. 1995. 45.00 (*0-87779-042-6*) Merriam-Webster Inc.

***Merriam-Webster's Encyclopedia of World Religions: An A-Z Guide to the World's Religions.** Merriam-Webster Editors. Ed. by Wendy Doniger. LC 99-33147. (Illus.). 1200p. 1999. 49.95 (*0-87779-044-2*) Merriam-Webster Inc.

Merriam-Webster's English & Spanish Reference Set. Ed. by Merriam-Webster Editors. (SPA & ENG.). 1999. pap., boxed set 16.99 (*0-87779-976-8*) Merriam-Webster Inc.

Merriam-Webster's Everyday Language Reference Set: Dictionary, Thesaurus, Vocabulary Builder. Merriam-Webster Editors. 1994. pap., boxed set 16.99 (*0-87779-970-9*) Merriam-Webster Inc.

Merriam-Webster's French-English Dictionary. Merriam-Webster Editors. (FRE.). 864p. 2000. pap. 5.99 (*0-87779-917-2*) Merriam-Webster Inc.

A bilingual, bidirectional guide to French & North American English, with extensive coverage of Canadian French. Over 80,000 words & phrases. Designed for all skill levels. Abundant examples. Durable hardcover format. ***Publisher Paid Annotation.***

***Merriam-Webster's French-English Dictionary.** Merriam-Webster Staff. (FRE & ENG.). 2000. 19.95 (*0-87779-166-X*) Merriam-Webster Inc.

Merriam Webster's Geographical Dictionary. 3rd rev. ed. Ed. by Merriam-Webster Editors. LC 96-52365. (Illus.). 1392p. 1997. 29.95 (*0-87779-546-0*) Merriam-Webster Inc.

Merriam-Webster's Guide to Business Correspondence. 2nd ed. Ed. by Merriam-Webster Editors. 402p. 1996. reprint ed. 17.95 incl. cd-rom (*0-87779-231-3*) Merriam-Webster Inc.

Merriam-Webster's Guide to Everyday Math, a Home & Business Reference. Brian Burrell. LC 98-18147. 384p. 1998. pap. 14.95 (*0-87779-621-1*) Merriam-Webster Inc.

Merriam-Webster's Guide to Punctuation & Style. Merriam-Webster Editors. 352p. 1995. mass mkt. 4.99 (*0-87779-912-1*) Merriam-Webster Inc.

Merriam-Webster's High School Dictionary. LC 96-103314. (YA). (gr. 9-12). Date not set. 24.00 (*0-03-096484-9*) H Holt & Co.

Merriam-Webster's High School Dictionary Inc., 5 vols. large type ed. 1396p. 349.00 (*0-614-20561-1*, L-36934-00 APHB) Am Printing Hse.

Merriam-Webster's Intermediate Dictionary. Ed. by Merriam-Webster Editors. LC 98-4995. (Illus.). 960p. (YA). (gr. 6-9). 1994. 15.95 (*0-87779-479-0*) Merriam-Webster Inc.

Merriam-Webster's Japanese-English Dictionary. Kenkyusha Ltd. Staff. Ed. by Merriam-Webster Editors. (ENG & JPN.). 512p. 1996. pap. 6.99 (*0-87779-918-0*) Merriam-Webster Inc.

Merriam-Webster's Japanese-English Learner's Dictionary. Kenkyusha Ltd. Staff & Merriam-Webster Editors. Ed. by Shigeru Takebayashi. LC 93-27294. (ENG & JPN.). 1136p. 1993. 27.95 (*0-87779-164-3*) Merriam-Webster Inc.

Merriam-Webster's Legal Secretaries Handbook. 2nd rev. ed. Merriam-Webster Editors. 512p. 1996. 19.95 (*0-87779-134-1*) Merriam-Webster Inc.

Merriam-Webster's Manual for Writers & Editors. Merriam-Webster Editors. LC 97-40798. 448p. 1998. pap. 17.95 (*0-87779-622-X*) Merriam-Webster Inc.

***Merriam Webster's Mass Market Dictionary.** Ed. by MERRIAM WEBSTER. 1999. pap. text 2.40 (*0-205-31733-2*) A&B Bks.

***Merriam Webster's Mass Market Thesaurus.** Ed. by MERRIAM WEBSTER. 1999. pap. text 2.00 (*0-205-31732-4*) A&B Bks.

Merriam Webster's Medical Desk Dictionary. rev. ed. Ed. by Merriam-Webster Editors. LC 96-15564. 928p. 1993. 25.95 (*0-87779-125-2*) Merriam-Webster Inc.

Merriam-Webster's Medical Desk Dictionary with CD-ROM. Ed. by Merriam-Webster Editors. (Illus.). 1998. 49.95 incl. cd-rom (*0-87779-027-2*) Merriam-Webster Inc.

Merriam Webster's Medical Dictionary see Webster's New Explorer Medical Dictionary

Merriam-Webster's Medical Dictionary. Merriam-Webster Editors. 771p. 1995. mass mkt. 6.99 (*0-87779-914-8*) Merriam-Webster Inc.

Merriam-Webster's Medical Office Handbook. 2nd rev. ed. Merriam-Webster Editors. 544p. 1996. 19.95 (*0-87779-235-6*) Merriam-Webster Inc.

Merriam-Webster's Notebook Atlas. Ed. by Merriam-Webster Editors. (Illus.). 68p. 1996. pap., student ed. 3.95 (*0-87779-652-1*) Merriam-Webster Inc.

Merriam-Webster's Notebook Dictionary. Merriam-Webster Editors. 96p. 1996. pap., student ed. 3.95 (*0-87779-650-5*) Merriam-Webster Inc.

Merriam-Webster's Notebook Guide to Punctuation. Merriam-Webster Editors. LC 96-199726. 64p. 1996. pap., student ed. 3.95 (*0-87779-651-3*) Merriam-Webster Inc.

Merriam-Webster's Notebook Value Pack: Dictionary, Atlas, Punctuation Guide. 1996. pap. 9.95 (*0-87779-978-4*) Merriam-Webster Inc.

Merriam-Webster's Pocket Atlas. Ed. by Merriam-Webster Editors. (Illus.). 272p. 1998. pap. 6.95 (*0-87779-515-0*) Merriam-Webster Inc.

Merriam-Webster's Pocket Biographical Dictionary. Merriam-Webster Editors. 384p. 1996. pap. 3.95 (*0-87779-507-X*) Merriam-Webster Inc.

Merriam-Webster's Pocket Dictionary. Merriam-Webster Editors. LC 95-4773. 416p. 1995. pap. 3.95 (*0-87779-500-2*) Merriam-Webster Inc.

Merriam-Webster's Pocket Geographical Dictionary. Merriam-Webster Editors. LC 96-13760. 368p. 1996. pap. 3.95 (*0-87779-506-1*) Merriam-Webster Inc.

Merriam-Webster's Pocket Guide to Business & Everyday Math. Brian Burrell. 368p. 1996. pap. 3.95 (*0-87779-505-3*) Merriam-Webster Inc.

Merriam-Webster's Pocket Guide to English Usage. Merriam-Webster Editors. LC 97-27858. 400p. 1998. pap. 3.95 (*0-87779-514-2*) Merriam-Webster Inc.

Merriam-Webster's Pocket Guide to Punctuation. Merriam-Webster Editors. 320p. 1995. pap. 3.95 (*0-87779-502-9*) Merriam-Webster Inc.

Merriam-Webster's Pocket Guide to Synonyms. Merriam-Webster Editors. 368p. 1995. pap. 3.95 (*0-87779-501-0*) Merriam-Webster Inc.

Merriam-Webster's Premium Gift Set: Merriam-Webster's Collegiate Dictionary & Collegiate Thesaurus. 10th deluxe ed. Merriam-Webster Editors. 1993. boxed set, im. lthr. 49.95 (*0-87779-712-9*) Merriam-Webster Inc.

Merriam-Webster's Reader's Handbook: A Complete Guide to Literary Terms. Merriam-Webster Editors. LC 97-26659. 608p. 1997. pap. 14.95 (*0-87779-620-3*) Merriam-Webster Inc.

Merriam-Webster's Rhyming Dictionary. Merriam-Webster Editors. 369p. 1995. mass mkt. 4.99 (*0-87779-913-X*) Merriam-Webster Inc.

Merriam-Webster's Rules of Order. 336p. pap. 14.95 (*0-87779-615-7*) Merriam-Webster Inc.

Merriam-Webster's School Dictionary. Ed. by Merriam-Webster Editors. LC 98-12888. (Illus.). 1184p. (YA). (gr. 9-12). 1994. 15.95 (*0-87779-380-8*) Merriam-Webster Inc.

Merriam-Webster's School Thesaurus. Merriam-Webster Editors. LC 88-26859. 704p. (YA). (gr. 9-12). 1995. 15.95 (*0-87779-178-3*) Merriam-Webster Inc.

Merriam-Webster's Secretarial Handbook. 3rd ed. Merriam-Webster Editors. LC 96-10632. 608p. 1993. 17.95 (*0-87779-236-4*) Merriam-Webster Inc.

Merriam-Webster's Spanish English Dictionary see Webster's New Explorer Spanish-English Dictionary

Merriam-Webster's Spanish-English Dictionary. Ed. by Merriam-Webster Editors. LC 98-5887. (ENG & SPA.). 848p. 1998. 19.95 (*0-87779-165-1*); pap. 5.99 (*0-87779-916-4*) Merriam-Webster Inc.

***Merriam Webster's Trade Dictionary.** Ed. by MERRIAM WEBSTER. 1999. pap. text 4.45 (*0-205-31734-0*) A&B Bks.

Merriam Webster's Vocabulary Builder. Mary W. Cornog. 576p. 1994. mass mkt. 5.99 (*0-87779-910-5*) Merriam-Webster Inc.

Merriams of Brookfield: Printing in the Economy & Culture of Rural Massachusetts in the Early Nineteenth Century. Jack Larkin. 48p. 1986. pap. 5.00 (*0-912296-84-4*) Am Antiquarian.

Merrick. Anne Rice. LC 99-88556. 320p. 2000. 26.95 (*0-679-45448-9*) Knopf.

***Merrick.** large type ed. Anne Rice. 2000. 26.95 (*0-375-43077-6*) Random.

Merrick & the Neighbouring Hills. J. McBain. 340p. 1985. 30.00 (*0-7855-1040-0*, Pub. by Alloway Pub) St Mut.

Merrick's View. Doris H. Masi. 179p. 1993. per. 12.00 (*0-9628208-7-3*) Canal Side Pubs.

Merridrew Follows the Trail. large type ed. John R. Fearn. (Linford Western Library). 384p. 1992. pap. 16.99 (*0-7089-7252-7*, Linford) Ulverscroft.

An Asterisk (*) at the beginning of an entry indicates that the title is appearing for the first time.

Merrie Melodies. (Looney Tunes Song & Sound Bks.). (Illus.). 24p. (J). (ps-5). 14.98 (0-7853-1249-8, PI4) Pubns Intl Ltd.

Merrie Tales of Jacques Tournebroche & Child life in town & country. Anatole France, pseud. Tr. by Alfred Allinson. LC 77-121548. (Short Story Reprint Ser.). 1977. reprint ed. 19.95 (0-8369-3504-7) Ayer.

Merril Lynch Guide to Retirement. Merrill Lynch Staff. 1999. pap. 15.95 (0-14-017329-3) Viking Penguin.

*__Merrill, Cavafy, Poems & Dreams.__ Rachel Hadas. (Poets on Poetry Ser.). 168p. 2000. pap. 13.95 text 39.50 (0-472-09719-9, 09719) U of Mich Pr.

Merrill Checklist of Edgar Allan Poe. J. Albert Robbins. LC 72-90037. (Charles E. Merrill Program in American Literature Ser.). iv, 44 p. 1969. write for info. (0-675-09463-1) Macmillan.

*__Merrill Chemistry, 1998.__ Smith et al. 1998. teacher ed. 60.59 (0-02-825527-5); teacher ed., student ed. 16.75 (0-02-827227-7); teacher ed., lab manual ed. 18.57 (0-02-827225-0) Glencoe.

Merrill Genealogy. Compiled by Fanie Merrill Carriere. (Illus.). 66p. 1995. pap. 8.95 (0-937242-17-9) Scandia Pubs.

Merrill Lynch: The WetFeet.com Insider Guide. 4th ed. WetFeet.com Staff. (Insider Guides Ser.). 60p. 1999. per. 25.00 (1-58207-026-1) WetFeet.

Merrill Lynch GT Financial Plan. Merrill Lynch Staff. 1985. pap. 17.95 (0-671-25460-X) S&S Trade.

Merrill Markoe's Guide to Love. Merrill Markoe. 192p. 1998. pap. 12.00 (0-87113-706-2, Atlntc Mnthly) Grove-Atltic.

Merrill MW Waves. Arthur A. Merrill. (Illus.). 1979. 20.00 (0-911894-44-6) Analysis.

Merrill Reese: "It's Gooooood!" Merrill Reese & Mark Eckel. (Illus.). 200p. 1998. 22.95 (1-58261-000-2) Sports Pub.

Merrill's Atlas of Radiographic Positions & Radiologic Procedures. 9th ed. Philip W. Ballinger. LC 98-52916. (Illus.). 608p. 1999. text 67.00 (0-8151-2651-4, 31649) Mosby Inc.

Merrill's Atlas of Radiographic Positions & Radiologic Procedures, 3. 9th ed. Philip W. Ballinger. (Illus.). 400p. 1999. text 67.00 (0-8151-2653-0, 31651) Mosby Inc.

Merrill's Atlas of Radiographic Positions & Radiologic Procedures, Set. 9th ed. Philip W. Ballinger. (Illus.). 1696p. 1999. text 169.00 (0-8151-2650-6, 31648) Mosby Inc.

Merrill's Atlas of Radiographic Positions & Radiologic Procedures, Vol.2. 9th ed. Philip W. Ballinger. LC 98-52916. (Illus.). 688p. 1999. text 67.00 (0-8151-2652-2, 31650) Mosby Inc.

Merrill's Atlas-Radiographic Positions & Radiologic Procedures. 8th ed. Philip W. Ballinger. 1995. teacher ed. write for info. (0-8151-6219-7) Mosby Inc.

Merrill's Marauders. Merrill's Marauders Association. LC 87-71198. (Illus.). 112p. 1987. 34.95 (0-938021-14-1) Turner Pub KY.

Merrill's Marauders. U. S. War Dept.-Historical Division Staff. 1980. reprint ed. 15.95 (0-89201-063-0) Zenger Pub.

Merrill's Marauders February-May. 127p. 1999. per. 6.50 (0-16-002004-2) USGPO.

Merrill's Marauders: February to May, 1944. (Illus.). 117p. 1998. reprint ed. pap. text 30.00 (0-7881-3275-X) DIANE Pub.

Merrily Comes Our Harvest In: Poems for Thanksgiving. Lee B. Hopkins. LC 91-70411. (Illus.). 32p. (J). (gr. 2 up). 1993. 9.95 (1-878093-57-6, Wordsong) Boyds Mills Pr.

Merrily, Merrily! Mary Engelbreit. (Illus.). 48p. 1995. 4.95 (0-8362-4641-1) Andrews & McMeel.

Merrily We Roll Along. Stephen Sondheim & George Furth. LC 98-16283. 128p. 1998. pap. 10.95 (1-55936-151-4) Theatre Comm.

Merrily We Roll Along: Vocal Score. Ed. by Sy Feldman. 252p. (Orig.). (C). 1996. pap. text 75.00 (0-7692-0724-3, VAL2016) Wrner Bros.

Merrily We Roll Along: Vocal Selections. Ed. by Sy Feldman. 44p. (Orig.). (C). 1996. pap. text 12.95 (0-7692-0723-5, VAL2015) Wrner Bros.

Merrimack. Merrimack Historical Committee. (Images of America Ser.). 128p. 1996. pap. 16.99 (0-7524-0279-X) Arcadia Publng.

Merrimack River: Its Source & Its Tributaries. J. W. Meader. 320p. 1998. reprint ed. pap. 24.50 (0-7884-0900-X, M105) Heritage Bk.

Merriman: Reunion of Descendants of Nathaniel Merriman at Wallingford, CT, 1913, with a Merriman Genealogy for Five Generations. Donald L. Jacobus. (Illus.). 186p. 1994. reprint ed. pap. 29.50 (0-8328-4346-6); reprint ed. lib. bdg. 39.50 (0-8328-4345-8) Higginson Bk Co.

Merriman on Market Cycles: The Basics. Raymond A. Merriman. 64p. 1994. per. 25.00 (0-930706-20-X) Seek-It Pubns.

Merriam-Webster Thesaurus for Large Print Users. large type ed. Ed. by G & C Merriam Co. 864p. 1991. 44.95 (0-8161-5164-4, G K Hall Lrg Type) Mac Lib Ref.

*__Merrit's Civil Engineers Platinum Edition: The Premier Reference Collection, 1.__ Merrit Frederick's Publishing Staff. 2800p. 1999. pap. text 225.00 (0-07-135536-7) McGraw.

Merritt. rev. ed. D. Merritt. 204p. 1991. reprint ed. pap. 33.50 (0-8328-2077-6); reprint ed. lib. bdg. 43.50 (0-8328-2076-8) Higginson Bk Co.

Merritt Crawford Papers. Eileen Bowser & University Publications of America Inc. LC 88-890243. (Cinema History Microfilm Ser.). 5 p. 1986. write for info. (0-89093-947-0) U Pubns Amer.

Merritt Parkway. Bruce Radde. (Illus.). 176p. 1996. pap. 19.95 (0-300-06877-8) Yale U Pr.

Merritt's Neurology. 10th ed. Lewis P. Rowland. 1,024p. text 89.00 (0-683-30474-7) Lppncott W & W.

Merritt's Neurology: Companion Handbook. 10th ed. Lewis P. Rowland. 500p. pap. text 32.95 (0-683-30496-8) Lppncott W & W.

Merritt's Textbook of Neurology. 9th ed. Ed. by Lewis P. Rowland. (Illus.). 1000p. 1995. 79.50 (0-683-07400-8) Lppncott W & W.

Merritt's Tradition. large type ed. Robert E. Merritt. (Illus.). 200p. 1995. 45.00 (0-9652821-0-4) R Merritt.

Merrivale Holds the Key: Two Classic Locked-Room Mysteries. Carter Dickson, pseud. 628p. 1995. pap. 14.95 (1-55882-027-2) Intl Polygonics.

Merriweather's Reign. Molly A. Mullin. LC 94-2416. 1995. pap. 6.00 (0-88734-239-6) Players Pr.

Merrow: Henry Merrow of Reading, Massachusetts & His Descendants named Marrow, Marrow & Merry. O. E. Merrow. (Illus.). 659p. 1991. reprint ed. pap. 98.00 (0-8328-1934-4); reprint ed. lib. bdg. 108.00 (0-8328-1933-6) Higginson Bk Co.

Merry ABC. Illus. by Bettina Paterson. (Wee Pudgy Board Bks.). 24p. (ps). 1993. bds. 2.95 (0-448-40553-9, G & D) Peng Put Young Read.

Merry Adventures of Robin Hood. Howard Payle. Ed. by Joanne Mattern. LC 92-12702. (Illustrated Classics Ser.). (Illus.). 48p. (J). (gr. 3-6). 1996. pap. 5.95 (0-8167-2859-3) Troll Communs.

Merry Adventures of Robin Hood. Howard Pyle. (YA). 1986. mass mkt. 4.95 (0-451-52284-2, Sig Classics) NAL.

Merry Adventures of Robin Hood. Howard Pyle. (Illus.). (J). (gr. 4-8). 1990. 24.00 (0-8446-2765-8) Peter Smith.

Merry Adventures of Robin Hood. Howard Pyle. Ed. by Malvina Vogel. (Great Illustrated Classics Ser.: Vol. 13). (Illus.). 240p. (J). (gr. 3-6). 1990. 9.95 (0-86611-964-7) Playmore Inc.

Merry Adventures of Robin Hood. Howard Pyle. (Illus.). 288p. (J). (gr. 6-9). 1977. 45.00 (0-684-14838-2) Scribner.

Merry Adventures of Robin Hood. Howard Pyle. Ed. by Joanne Mattern. LC 92-12702. (Illustrated Classics Ser.). (Illus.). 48p. (J). (gr. 3-6). 1992. lib. bdg. 19.95 (0-8167-2858-5, BM210) Troll Communs.

Merry Adventures of Robin Hood. Howard Pyle. 27.95 (0-8488-0858-4) Amereon Ltd.

Merry Adventures of Robin Hood. Howard Pyle. LC 68-55820. (Illus.). 296p. (J). (gr. 3-6). 1968. reprint ed. pap. 7.95 (0-486-22043-5) Dover.

Merry Adventures of Robin Hood: Of Great Renown, in Nottinghamshire. Howard Pyle. (J). 1985. 10.05 (0-606-01909-X, Pub. by Turtleback) Demco.

Merry Bear Book of Dreams: A Book to Read & Color. 2nd ed. Dave Allgood & Stephanie Allgood. (Illus.). 36p. (J). (ps-3). 1985. pap. 2.95 (0-933103-00-X) Merry Bears.

*__Merry Chase.__ Victoria Malvey. 312p. 2000. per. 6.50 (0-671-77525-1, Sonnet Bks) PB.

Merry Christmas. Andrews & McMeel Staff. LC 98-194717. (Tiny Tomes Ser.). (Illus.). 12p. (J). 1997. 3.95 (0-8362-3642-4) Andrews & McMeel.

Merry Christmas. Ariel Books Staff. 128p. 1996. 3.95 (0-8362-0967-2, Arie Bks) Andrews & McMeel.

Merry Christmas. Pam Brown. Ed. by Helen Exley. (To Give & to Keep Ser.). (Illus.). 28p. 1992. 6.00 (1-85015-322-1) Exley Giftbooks.

Merry Christmas! Esther Christensen. Ed. by Janet Leih. 8p. (Orig.). 1990. pap. 1.00 (1-877649-10-4) Tesseract SD.

Merry Christmas. Emma Darcy. (Presents Ser.: No. 1923). 1997. per. 3.50 (0-373-11923-2, 1-11923-9) Harlequin Bks.

Merry Christmas. Charles Dickens. Ed. by Helen Exley. (So-Much-More-Than-a-Card Ser.). (Illus.). 28p. (Orig.). 1995. pap. 2.99 (1-85015-652-2) Exley Giftbooks.

Merry Christmas. Shep Ireland. (Wesley & Wendell Ser.). (Illus.). (J). 1992. 4.75 (0-8378-3799-5) Gibson.

Merry Christmas. Sara Nephew. (Illus.). 36p. (Orig.). 1997. pap. 4.00 (0-9621172-5-0) Clearview Triangle.

*__Merry Christmas.__ Marty Noble. (Little Activity Bks.). (Illus.). (J). 2000. pap. 1.00 (0-486-40986-4) Dover.

*__Merry Christmas.__ Random House Books for Young Readers Staff. (ps-3). 1999. pap. 2.99 (0-375-80376-9, Pub. by Random Bks Yng Read) Random.

*__Merry Christmas, Level 2.__ Dennis Alexander. (Alfred's Basic Adult Piano Library). 32p. 1998. 6.95 (0-7390-0573-1, 18128) Alfred Pub.

Merry Christmas, Level 3. Willard A. Palmer et al. (Alfred's Basic Piano Library). 16p. 1982. 5.50 (0-7390-0568-5, 2213) Alfred Pub.

Merry Christmas, Level 4. Willard A. Palmer et al. (Alfred's Basic Piano Library). 16p. Date not set. 5.50 (0-7390-0574-X, 2233) Alfred Pub.

Merry Christmas: A Pop-Up Book. Mary Engelbreit. LC 95-137710. (Illus.). 16p. (J). (ps-3). 1994. 4.95 (0-8362-3089-2) Andrews & McMeel.

Merry Christmas: A Victorian Verse. Illus. by Mary Teichman. LC 92-29870. 32p. (J). (ps up). 1993. lib. bdg. 9.89 (0-06-022892-X) HarpC Child Bks.

Merry Christmas: Best-Loved Stories & Carols. Ed. & Illus. by Donna Green. 96p. (J). 1997. 14.95 (1-883746-12-4) Vermilion.

*__Merry Christmas! Celebrating America's Greatest Holiday.__ Karal Ann Marling. LC 00-31935. (Illus.). 432p. 2000. 27.00 (0-674-00318-7) HUP.

Merry Christmas: Festive Stories, Songs, Poems, Recipes, & Gift Ideas for the Holidays. Barbara M. Ohrbach. (Illus.). 64p. 1992. 12.00 (0-517-58626-6) C Potter.

*__Merry Christmas: Inspiring Quotes, Poems & Stories to Celebrate the Season.__ Honor Books Staff. 160p. 1999. 6.99 (1-56292-635-7) Honor Bks OK.

Merry Christmas: Level 1A. Amanda Vick Lethco et al. (Alfreds's Basic Piano Library). 16p. 1982. pap. 5.50 (0-7390-0309-7) Alfred Pub.

Merry Christmas: Season of Peace & Goodwill. Compiled by Brownlow Publishing Company, Creative Department S. LC 99-236724. (Little Treasures Ser.). 64p. 1998. 5.99 (1-57051-180-2, 595) Brownlow Pub Co.

Merry Christmas: Treasury of Stories & Songs. LC 97-217772. (Illus.). 384p. 1997. write for info. (0-7853-2454-2) Pubns Intl Ltd.

Merry Christmas ABC. Leisure Arts Staff. LC 93-78286. 96p. 1993. 24.95 (0-942237-27-7) Leisure AR.

*__Merry Christmas, Amelia Bedelia.__ Peggy Parish. (Amelia Bedelia Ser.). (J). (gr. k-2). 1999. write for info. (0-8335-0739-7) Econo-Clad Bks.

Merry Christmas, Amelia Bedelia. Peggy Parish. LC 85-24919. (Amelia Bedelia Ser.: Vol. 1). (Illus.). 64p. (J). (gr. 1-4). 1986. 15.89 (0-688-06102-8, Grenwillow Bks) HarpC Child Bks.

Merry Christmas, Amelia Bedelia. Peggy Parish. LC 85-24919. (Amelia Bedelia Ser.). 64p. (J). (gr. 5-7). 1996. mass mkt. 3.99 (0-380-72797-8, Avon Bks) Morrow Avon.

Merry Christmas, Amelia Bedelia. Peggy Parish. (Amelia Bedelia Ser.). (J). (gr. k-2). 1996. 9.19 (0-606-03615-6, Pub. by Turtleback) Demco.

Merry Christmas, Amelia Bedelia. Peggy Parish. (Amelia Bedelia Ser.). (Illus.). 64p. (J). (gr. k-2). 1987. reprint ed. pap. 3.99 (0-380-70325-4, Avon Bks) Morrow Avon.

Merry Christmas, Baby! (Christmas Board Book Ser.). (Illus.). 28p. (J). (ps). 1994. bds. 2.95 (1-56288-460-3) Checkerboard.

Merry Christmas, Baby. Joan W. Anglund. LC 94-79880. (Sturdy Shape Bks.). (J). 1996. pap. text 3.99 (0-307-12438-X, 12438, Goldn Books) Gldn Bks Pub Co.

Merry Christmas, Baby. Pamela Browning. (American Romance Ser.). 1993. per. 3.50 (0-373-16516-1, 1-16516-6) Harlequin Bks.

Merry Christmas, Baby! Cinderfella, Grady's Kids, It Takes a Miracle. Susan Wiggs et al. 1996. per. 5.99 (0-373-83316-4, 1-83316-9) Harlequin Bks.

Merry Christmas, Bear! Janelle Cherrington. (Bear in the Big Blue House Ser.: No. 2). 16p. (J). 1999. pap. 3.99 (0-689-82808-X, Simon Spot) Litle Simon.

Merry Christmas, Complete, Levels 2 & 3. Willard A. Palmer et al. (Basic Piano Library). 24p. 1995. pap. 5.95 (0-7390-0882-X, 6486) Alfred Pub.

Merry Christmas, Daddy. Susan Meier. 1996. per. 3.25 (0-373-19192-8, 1-19192-3) Silhouette.

Merry Christmas, Davy! Brigitte Weninger. LC 98-6109. (Illus.). 32p. (J). (gr. k-3). 1998. 15.95 (1-55858-980-5, Pub. by North-South Bks NYC); lib. bdg. 15.88 (1-55858-981-3, Pub. by North-South Bks NYC) Chronicle Bks.

Merry Christmas, Dear. 4.95 (0-87895-623-9) Modern Curr.

Merry Christmas, Dear Dragon. Margaret Hillert. (Illus.). (J). (ps). 1981. pap. 5.10 (0-8136-5526-9, TK2345); lib. bdg. 7.95 (0-8136-5026-7, TK2344) Modern Curr.

Merry Christmas Everybody. Constance Allen. (ps-3). 1999. pap. 3.25 (0-375-80370-X, Pub. by Random Bks Yng Read) Random.

Merry Christmas, Everyone: Big Note Piano. 64p. 1995. pap. text 9.95 (0-89524-924-3, Pub. by Cherry Lane) H Leonard.

Merry Christmas, Everyone: Easy Piano. 63p. (YA). 1995. pap. text 9.95 (0-89524-859-X, Pub. by Cherry Lane) H Leonard.

Merry Christmas, Everyone: Piano Solo. 64p. (YA). 1995. pap. text 10.95 (0-89524-925-1, Pub. by Cherry Lane) H Leonard.

*__Merry Christmas from Georgia: Recipes for the Season.__ Michelle Stone. LC 00-104154. 192p. 2000. 19.95 (0-913383-71-6) McClanahan Pub.

Merry Christmas from Kentucky: Recipes for the Season. Michelle Stone. LC 97-74550. (Illus.). 192p. 1997. 19.95 (0-913383-56-2) McClanahan Pub.

*__Merry Christmas from Mandie.__ Lois G. Leppard. (Young Mandie Christmas Special Mysteries Ser.). (Illus.). (J). 2000. pap. 4.50 (0-553-48720-5, Skylark BDD) BDD Bks Young Read.

Merry Christmas from the South: Recipes for the Season. Michelle Stone. 192p. 1998. 19.95 (0-913383-60-0, Commwlth Bk Co) McClanahan Pub.

Merry Christmas, Geraldine. Holly Keller. LC 96-42020. (Geraldine Ser.). (Illus.). 32p. (J). (gr. k-3). 1997. 15.00 (0-688-14500-0, Grenwillow Bks) HarpC Child Bks.

Merry Christmas, Geraldine. Holly Keller. LC 96-42020. (Illus.). 32p. (J). (gr. k-3). 1997. 14.89 (0-688-14501-9, Grenwillow Bks) HarpC Child Bks.

*__Merry Christmas, Grumpy Bunny.__ Justine Korman. LC 99-23497. (Grumpy Bunny Ser.). 32p. (J). (gr. k-3). 1999. 13.95 (0-8167-6270-8) BrdgeWater.

*__Merry Christmas, Grumpy Bunny.__ Justine Korman. LC 99-23497. (Illus.). 32p. (J). (ps-3). 1999. pap. 3.50 (0-8167-6580-4) Troll Communs.

*__Merry Christmas Happy Hanukkah: A Multilingual Songbook & CD, Vol. 1.__ Elizabeth C. Axford. LC 99-93461. (ENG, HEB & SPA.). 112p. 1999. pap. 24.95 incl. audio compact disk (0-9673325-0-8, PP1001) Piano Pr.

Merry Christmas, Harry. Mary Chalmers. LC 90-27516. (Illus.). 32p. (J). (ps-2). 1992. lib. bdg. 12.89 (0-06-022742-7) HarpC Child Bks.

Merry Christmas Jesse Bear. Nancy Carlstrom. LC 99-22599. (J). 2000. per. 15.00 (0-689-81962-5) S&S Bks Yung.

*__Merry Christmas, Jesus.__ Ed. by Jennifer Stewart. (Illus.). 48p. (J). (ps). 1999. pap. 2.49 (0-7847-0996-3, 22066) Standard Pub.

Merry Christmas Jingo. Gary Grimm & Phoebe Wear. 32p. (J). (gr. k-6). 1993. 12.00 (1-56490-004-5) G Grimm Assocs.

Merry Christmas, Laura! Laura Ingalls Wilder. (My First Little House Baby Bks.). (Illus.). 12p. (J). (ps). 1995. 5.95 (0-694-00731-5, HarpFestival) HarpC Child Bks.

Merry Christmas, Little Mouse: A Lift-the-Flap, Scratch-the-Scent Book. Noelle Carter & David A. Carter. (Illus.). 12p. (J). (ps). 1995. 11.95 (0-8050-2712-2, Bks Young Read) H Holt & Co.

*__Merry Christmas, Maisy.__ Lucy Cousins. LC 99-88331. (Maisy Bks.). (Illus.). 24p. (J). (ps). 2000. 12.99 (0-7636-1279-0) Candlewick Pr.

Merry Christmas Maze. Myron M. Morris. (Illus.). 64p. 1997. pap. 2.50 (0-89375-073-5) NAL.

Merry Christmas, Miss McConnell! Colleen O. McKenna. (J). 1990. 8.60 (0-606-01904-9, Pub. by Turtleback) Demco.

Merry Christmas, Mom & Dad. Mercer Mayer. (Look-Look Bks.). (Illus.). 24p. (J). (ps-3). 1982. pap. 3.29 (0-307-11886-X, 11886, Goldn Books) Gldn Bks Pub Co.

Merry Christmas, Mommy. Muriel Jensen. LC 95-22387. 251p. 1995. per. 3.50 (0-373-16610-9, 1-16610-7) Harlequin Bks.

Merry Christmas, My Love. Ed. by Ann LaFarge. 480p. 1996. mass mkt. 4.50 (0-8217-4379-1, Zebra Kensgtn) Kensgtn Pub Corp.

Merry Christmas Old Armadillo. Larry Brimner. LC 94-79155. (Illus.). 32p. (J). (ps-1). 1995. 15.95 (1-56397-354-5) Boyds Mills Pr.

Merry Christmas, Old Armadillo. Larry D. Brimner. LC 94-79155. (Illus.). 32p. (J). (ps-1). 1997. pap. 7.95 (1-56397-678-1) Boyds Mills Pr.

Merry Christmas Piano Solos: Beginner - Five Finger Piano Solos. Ed. by Robert Schultz. 132p. (Orig.). (YA). (gr. 9-12). 1994. pap. text 14.95 (0-910957-75-4, F3427PFX) Wrner Bros.

Merry Christmas Piano Solos: Early Grade - Big Note Piano Solos. Ed. by Robert Schultz. 132p. (Orig.). (YA). (gr. 9-12). 1994. pap. text 14.95 (0-910957-73-8, F3426P3X) Wrner Bros.

Merry Christmas Piano Solos: Intermediate - Easy Piano Solos. Ed. by Robert Schultz. 136p. (Orig.). (YA). (gr. 9-12). 1994. pap. text 14.95 (0-910957-74-6, F3425P2X) Wrner Bros.

Merry Christmas, Rugrats! Kitty Richards. (Rugrats Ser.). (Illus.). (J). (ps-3). 1997. 10.95 (0-689-81807-6) S&S Childrens.

*__Merry Christmas, Rugrats!__ Kitty Richards. (Rugrats Ser.). (Illus.). (J). (ps-3). 1998. 10.95 (0-689-82179-4) S&S Childrens.

*__Merry Christmas, Rugrats!__ Kitty Richards. (Rugrats Ser.). (Illus.). (J). (ps-3). 1999. per. 10.95 (0-671-02941-X) S&S Trade.

Merry Christmas, Santa. Joanne Barkan. (J). 1995. pap. 3.95 (0-8167-3736-3) Troll Communs.

Merry Christmas, Santa! Illus. by Bettina Paterson. 12p. (J). (ps). 1992. bds. 2.95 (0-448-40576-8, G & D) Peng Put Young Read.

*__Merry Christmas, Snowden!__ Sara Miller. (Snowden & Friends Ser.). 12p. (J). (ps-1). 1999. bds. 3.99 (1-57584-418-4, Pub. by Rdrs Digest) S&S Trade.

*__Merry Christmas, Space Ranger.__ Rick Bunsen. (Toy Story 2 Ser.). (Illus.). (J). 2000. pap. 3.29 (0-307-13270-6, Goldn Books) Gldn Bks Pub Co.

Merry Christmas Sticker Book. Nina Barbaresi. (Little Activity Bks.). (Illus.). (J). 1993. pap. 1.00 (0-486-27150-1) Dover.

Merry Christmas, Strega Nona. Tomie De Paola. LC 86-4639. (Illus.). 32p. (J). (ps-3). 1986. 16.00 (0-15-253183-1, Harcourt Child Bks) Harcourt.

Merry Christmas, Strega Nona. Tomie De Paola. LC 86-4639. (Illus.). 32p. (J). (ps-3). 1991. pap. 7.00 (0-15-253184-X, Harcourt Child Bks) Harcourt.

Merry Christmas, Strega Nona. Tomie De Paola. (Voyager Bks.). (J). 1986. 12.20 (0-606-00595-1, Pub. by Turtleback) Demco.

Merry Christmas, Teletubbies! Andrew Davenport. (Teletubbies Ser.). (Illus.). 32p. (J). (ps-k). 1999. 9.99 (0-439-10596-X, Pub. by Scholastic Inc) Penguin Putnam.

Merry Christmas to All: Favorite Stories, Poems & Songs for the Holiday Season. Ed. by Scholastic, Inc. Staff. (Illus.). 128p. (J). (gr. 1-3). 1994. bds. 12.95 (0-590-48476-1, Cartwheel) Scholastic Inc.

Merry Christmas to You! Mouse Works Staff. (J). 1999. 7.98 (1-57082-940-3, Pub. by Mouse Works) Little.

Merry Christmas to You! Mouseworks Staff. (Pooh Ser.). 5p. (J). 1998. 7.98 (0-7364-0026-5, Pub. by Mouse Works) Time Warner.

Merry Christmas to You: Hunny Pot Book. Disney Staff. LC 97-220260. (Pooh Ser.). 5p. (J). 1997. 4.98 (1-57082-630-7, Pub. by Mouse Works) Time Warner.

Merry Christmas, What's Your Name. Bernice Chardiet & Grace Maccarone. (Illus.). (J). (ps-3). 1990. 11.95 (0-590-44334-8, Scholastic Hardcover) Scholastic Inc.

Merry Christmas, What's Your Name School Friends. Bernice Chardiet & Grace Maccarone. (Illus.). 32p. (J). (ps-2). 1991. pap. text 2.50 (0-590-43306-7) Scholastic Inc.

Merry Christmas with Love. (Cherished Moments Ser.). (Illus.). 60p. 1994. 9.99 (1-57051-022-9) Brownlow Pub Co.

Merry Christmas, World! Gibbs Davis. (Full House Michelle Ser.: Vol. 23). 96p. (J). (gr. 4-7). 1998. pap. 3.99 (0-671-02098-6, Minstrel Bks) PB.

Merry Devil of Edmonton. Ed. by Tudor Facsimile Texts Editing Staff. LC 76-133710. (Tudor Facsimile Texts. Old English Plays Ser.: No. 124). reprint ed. 49.50 (0-404-53424-4) AMS Pr.

M

An Asterisk (*) at the beginning of an entry indicates that the title is appearing for the first time.

***Merry Gentleman.** Meg Alexander. 1999. per. 4.99 (*0-373-30340-8*) Harlequin Bks.

Merry-Go-Day. Sheree Fitch. 48p. 1991. 10.00 (*0-385-25244-7*) Doubleday.

Merry Go Round. 1994. pap. 6.95 (*0-8431-6415-8*) Peng Put Young Read.

Merry-Go-Round: A Book about Nouns. Ruth Heller. (Illus.). 48p. (J). (ps-3). 1990. 17.95 (*0-448-40085-5*, G & D) Peng Put Young Read.

Merry-Go-Round: A Book about Nouns. Ruth Heller. (World of Language Ser.). (Illus.). 48p. (J). (gr. k-3). 1998. pap. 6.99 (*0-698-11642-9*, PapStar) Peng Put Young Read.

Merry-Go-Round: A Book about Nouns. Ruth Heller. (J). 1992. 13.15 (*0-606-05464-2*, Pub. by Turtleback) Demco.

Merry Go-Round: A Book about Nouns. Ruth Heller. (Sandcastle Ser.). (Illus.). 48p. (J). (ps-3). 1992. pap. 7.95 (*0-448-40315-3*, Philomel) Peng Put Young Read.

Merry Go Round in Oz. Eloise Jarvis McGraw et al. (Illus.). 313p. (J). (gr. 3 up). 1989. 24.95 (*0-929605-06-3*) Books of Wonder.

Merry Go Round in Oz. Eloise Jarvis McGraw et al. (Illus.). 313p. (J). (gr. 3-10). 1996. reprint ed. pap. 12.95 (*0-929605-60-8*) Books of Wonder.

Merry-Go-Round of Sexual Abuse: Identifying & Treating Survivors. William E. Prendergast. LC 93-17364. (Illus.). 282p. 1993. pap. 19.95 (*1-56024-388-0*); lib. bdg. 49.95 (*1-56024-387-2*) Haworth Pr.

Merry Hall. Beverley Nichols. LC 97-47253. (Illus.). 342p. 1998. reprint ed. 24.95 (*0-88192-417-2*) Timber.

***Merry Heart.** Donna Dean. LC 99-60757. 80p. 1999. pap. 7.99 (*1-57921-216-6*, Pub. by WinePress Pub) BookWorld.

Merry Heart: Reflections on Reading, Writing & the World of Books. Robertson Davies. 1998. pap. 14.95 (*0-14-026391-8*); pap. 14.95 (*0-14-027586-X*) Viking Penguin.

Merry Heart & Happy Alchemy. Robertson Davies. 1997. write for info. (*0-7710-2588-2*) McCland & Stewart.

Merry Hearts Make Light Days: The War of 1812 Journal of Lieutenant John Le Courteur, 104th Foot. Ed. by Donald E. Graves. 308p. 1997. 40.00 (*1-873376-48-0*, Pub. by Spellmnt Pubs) St Mut.

***Merry Hearts Make Light Days: The War of 1812 Journal of Lieutenant John Le Couteur, 104th Foot.** Ed. by Donald E. Graves. (Illus.). 431p. 2000. pap. 17.95 (*0-88629-225-5*, Pub. by McG-Queens Univ Pr) Midpt Trade.

Merry Little Christmas, Bk. 1. Kenon D. Renfrow. 16p. 1996. pap. 5.50 (*0-7390-0851-X*, 16883) Alfred Pub.

Merry Little Christmas: Winning Stories from Covenant's Short Fiction Contest, with a Bonus Story by Anita Stansfield. Anita Stansfield. Ed. by Covenant Communications Staff. LC 96-44060. 1996. pap. 6.95 (*1-57734-027-2*, 01112511) Covenant Comms.

Merry Little Christmas Iron-On Transfers Book. 919th ed. Ed. by Brenda R. Wendling. LC 98-93411. (Illus.). 224p. 1998. pap. 19.96 (*1-882138-38-4*) Hse White Birches.

Merry Maid. Joyce H. James. 115p. 1991. pap. 9.75 (*0-9629287-0-4*) Ladan Res Pr.

Merry-Making in Old Russia & Other Stories. Evgeni I. Popov. Tr. by Robert Porter from RUS. LC 97-12449. (Writings from an Unbound Europe Ser.). 1997. 49.95 (*0-8101-1326-0*) Northwestern U Pr.

Merry-Making in Old Russia & Other Stories. Evgeny Popov. Tr. by Robert Porter from RUS. LC 97-12449. 1997. pap. text 17.95 (*0-8101-1327-9*) Northwestern U Pr.

Merry Mariner: A Travelogue. Keith M. Brown. LC 98-61994. (Illus.). 148p. 1997. mass mkt. 5.95 (*1-56550-078-4*) Vis Bks Intl.

Merry Matchmakers. Helen R. Myers. 1995. per. 2.99 (*0-373-19121-9*, 1-19121-2) Silhouette.

Merry Medieval Christmas! Thomas A. Erhard & Evelyn M. Erhard. 61p. 1984. pap. 3.95 (*0-87129-606-3*, M29) Dramatic Pub.

Merry Meet Again: Poems for Small Children to Recite. Ed. by Elizabeth H. Sechrist. LC 77-160908. (Granger Index Reprint Ser.). 1977. reprint ed. 19.95 (*0-8369-6272-9*) Ayer.

Merry Men. Carolyn Chute. LC 93-11028. 712p. 1995. pap. 16.00 (*0-15-600191-8*) Harcourt.

Merry Men & Other Tales, Memoir of Flemming Jenkin see Works of Robert Louis Stevenson, Valima Edition

Merry, Merry Christmases. Elaine Cannon. 1988. 8.95 (*0-88494-673-8*) Bookcraft Inc.

Merry Month of May. Elvi Rhodes. 224p. 1997. 24.00 (*0-7278-5163-2*) Severn Hse.

Merry Mood: Poe's Uses of Humor. Donald B. Stauffer. Ed. by Averil J. Kadis. 1982. pap. text 3.95 (*0-910556-18-0*) Enoch Pratt.

Merry Moor Winnett. Ed. by Adele Wayman & Deborah Brody. 32p. 1995. text. write for info. (*0-9645490-0-X*) Sawtooth Ctr.

Merry-Mount: A Romance of the Massachusetts Colony, 2 vols., Set. John L. Motley. LC 78-64081. reprint ed. 75.00 (*0-404-17290-3*) AMS Pr.

Merry Muses of Caledonia: A Collection of Favourite Scots Songs, Ancient & Modern, Selected for Use of the Crochallan Fencibles (1799) limited ed. Compiled & Contrib. by Robert Burns. 128p. 1999. 90.00 (*1-57003-324-2*) U of SC Pr.

Merry Order of Saint Bridget. 1992. mass mkt. 5.95 (*1-56201-021-2*, 120) Blue Moon Bks.

Merry Pilgrimage: How Charlemagne Went on a Pilgrimage to Jerusalem in Order to See Whether Hugo of Constantinople Was a Handsomer Man Than He. Charlemagne. Tr. by Merriam Sherwood. LC 78-63455. (Illus.). reprint ed. 29.50 (*0-404-16377-7*) AMS Pr.

***Merry Pranks of Till Eulenspiegel.** Tr. by Anthea Bell. (Illus.). 32p. (gr. 1-4). 2000. 15.95 (*1-55858-806-X*) North-South Bks NYC.

Merry Pranks of Tyll. Daniel J. Fleischhacker. 46p. (J). 1961. 6.00 (*0-87602-157-7*) Anchorage.

Merry Scary Halloween. Illus. by Ellen Appleby. (Chubby Board Bks.). 16p. (J). (ps up). 1990. bds. 3.95 (*0-671-70721-3*) Litle Simon.

Merry Tales. Mark Twain, pseud. Ed. by Shelley F. Fishkin. (Oxford Mark Twain). (Illus.). 288p. 1997. text 30.00 (*0-19-511411-6*) OUP.

Merry Tales. Mark Twain, pseud. (Works of Samuel Clemens). 1989. reprint ed. lib. bdg. 79.00 (*0-685-28365-8*) Rprt Serv.

Merry Tales (1892) Ed. by Shelly F. Fishkin. LC 96-16577. (Oxford Mark Twain Stories Ser.). (Illus.). 288p. 1996. 25.00 (*0-19-510142-1*) OUP.

Merry Tales of the Three Wise Men of Gotham. James K. Paulding. (Notable American Authors Ser.). 1999. reprint ed. lib. bdg. 125.00 (*0-7812-4746-2*) Rprt Serv.

Merry the Lamb Sails with Noah. Thorpe & Hunt Staff. 1998. 6.99 (*1-85608-286-5*) Hunt GBR.

Merry Things to Make: Christmas Fun & Crafts. Boyds Mills Press Staff. (Illus.). 64p. (J). (gr. k-7). 1999. pap. 7.95 (*1-56397-838-5*) Boyds Mills Pr.

Merry-Thought: or The Glass-Window & Bog House Miscellany, Pt. I. 3rd ed. Intro. by George R. Guffey. LC 92-22024. (Augustan Reprints Ser.: No. 216). 1982. reprint ed. 14.50 (*0-404-70216-3*) AMS Pr.

Merry-Thought: or The Glass-Window & Bog House Miscellany, Pts. II, III, & IV. 2nd ed. Intro. by Maximillian E. Novak. LC 92-24240. (Augustan Reprints Ser.: Nos. 221-222). 1983. reprint ed. 21.50 (*0-404-70221-X*) AMS Pr.

Merry Wheels & Spokes of Steel: A Social History of the Bicycle. Robert A. Smith. LC 95-9980. (Stovkis Studies in Historical Chronology & Thought: No. 16). xii, 269p. 1995. pap. 27.00 (*0-8095-1104-5*) Millefleurs.

***Merry Widow.** Meagan McKinney. 1999. 23.00 (*1-57566-487-9*, Knsington) Kensgtn Pub Corp.

***Merry Widow.** large type ed. Meagan McKinney. 2000. 25.95 (*1-56895-863-3*) Wheeler Pub.

Merry Widow: Complete Score for Piano & Voice. Franz Lehar. (Music Ser.). 224p. 1983. reprint ed. pap. 10.95 (*0-486-24514-4*) Dover.

Merry Widower & Other Characters. J. J. Hermans. 192p. 1991. pap. write for info. (*1-880849-00-3*) Chapel Hill NC.

Merry Widows - Catherine. Theresa Michaels. (Historical Ser.: No. 400). 1998. per. 4.99 (*0-373-29000-4*, 1-29000-6) Harlequin Bks.

Merry Widows - Mary. Theresa Michaels. (Historical Ser.: No. 372). 1997. per. 4.99 (*0-373-28972-3*, 1-28972-7) Harlequin Bks.

Merry Widows--Sarah: The Merry Widows. Theresa Michaels. (Historical Ser.: Bk. 469). 1999. per. 4.99 (*0-373-29069-1*, 1-29069-1) Harlequin Bks.

Merry Wives. Mark Dunster. 25p. (Orig.). (YA). 1995. pap. 5.00 (*0-89642-289-5*) Linden Pubs.

Merry Wives of Windsor. Adapted by Charles Jeffries & Jerry Knight. 24p. 1998. pap. 3.25 (*0-87440-076-7*) Bakers Plays.

Merry Wives of Windsor. William Shakespeare. Ed. by David Crane. (New Cambridge Shakespeare Ser.). (Illus.). 174p. (C). 1997. text 44.95 (*0-521-22155-2*); pap. text 11.95 (*0-521-29370-7*) Cambridge U Pr.

***Merry Wives of Windsor.** William Shakespeare. 2000. pap. 1.50 (*0-486-41422-1*) Dover.

Merry Wives of Windsor. William Shakespeare. 1988. pap. 2.95 (*0-671-66913-3*) Folger.

Merry Wives of Windsor. William Shakespeare. Ed. by R. S. White. (Twayne's New Critical Introduction to Shakespeare Ser.: No. 11). 100p. (C). 1991. 24.95 (*0-8057-8722-4*, Twyne); pap. 13.95 (*0-8057-8723-2*, Twyne) Mac Lib Ref.

Merry Wives of Windsor. William Shakespeare. Ed. by T. W. Craik. (Oxford World's Classics Ser.). (Illus.). 252p. 1998. pap. 7.95 (*0-19-283608-0*) OUP.

Merry Wives of Windsor. William Shakespeare. 1990. mass mkt. 3.50 (*0-671-73143-2*) PB.

Merry Wives of Windsor. William Shakespeare. Ed. by H. J. Oliver. (Arden Shakespeare Ser.). 1971. pap. 8.95 (*0-416-17780-8*, NO. 2483) Routledge.

Merry Wives of Windsor. William Shakespeare. Ed. by H. J. Oliver. (Arden Shakespeare Ser.). 1971. pap. 45.00 (*0-416-47690-2*, NO. 2482) Thomson Learn.

Merry Wives of Windsor. William Shakespeare. Ed. by G. R. Hibbard. (New Penguin Shakespeare Ser.). 224p. 1981. pap. 5.95 (*0-14-070726-3*, Penguin Classics) Viking Penguin.

Merry Wives of Windsor. William Shakespeare. (Classics Library). 1998. pap. 3.95 (*1-85326-267-6*, 2676WW, Pub. by Wrdsworth Edits) NTC Contemp Pub Co.

Merry Wives of Windsor. unabridged ed. William Shakespeare. LC 57-1445. 1988. audio 30.00 (*0-694-50651-6*, SWC 203, Caedmon) HarperAudio.

Merry Wives of Windsor. 3rd ed. William Shakespeare. (English). (C). 2000. mass mkt. 11.95 (*0-17-443528-2*); mass mkt. 45.00 (*0-17-443561-4*) Wadsworth Pub.

Merry Wives of Windsor, Set. unabridged ed. William Shakespeare. 1995. audio 18.00 (*0-694-51452-7*, CPN 203) HarperAudio.

Merry Wives of Windsor: An Annotated Bibliography. Ed. by D'Orsay W. Pearson. (Garland Shakespeare Bibliographies Ser.). 500p. Date not set. text 75.00 (*0-8240-4434-7*) Garland.

Merry Wives of Windsor & the Life of King Henry V see Shakespeare Yesterday - Today, 1989-1998

***Merryman's Crossing.** Ellen G. Massey. LC 99-90717. 192p. 1999. 18.95 (*0-8034-9374-6*, Avalon Bks) Bouregy.

***Merrymeeting.** Julie Bigg Veazey. 32p. 1999. pap. 7.95 (*0-9675700-1-8*) Moon Pr.

Merrymeeting Merry Eating. Mid. 1988. pap. 15.95 (*0-9620094-0-7*) Mid Coast Hosp.

Merrymount Press: An Exhibition on the Occasion of the 100th Anniversary of the Founding of the Press. Martin Hutner. (Illus.). 77p. (Orig.). 1993. pap. 30.00 (*0-914630-11-3*) Houghton Lib.

Merrymount Press & Its Work with a Bibliographical List of the Books Printed at the Press: 1893-1933, & a Supplementary Bibliography 1934-1949. J. P. Smith et al. LC 75-28553. 400p. 1975. 30.00 (*0-915346-10-9*) A Wofsy Fine Arts.

Merry's Christmas. Pamela Bauer. LC 95-22605. 299p. 1995. per. 3.75 (*0-373-70670-7*, 1-70670-4) Harlequin Bks.

Merry's Christmas. Mona Gedney. 256p. 1998. mass mkt. 4.99 (*0-8217-6072-6*) Kensgtn Pub Corp.

Merrywinkle: The Adventures of Santa's Big Brother. Anne Fewell. (Illus.). 32p. (J). 1996. 11.95 (*1-888045-02-7*) Action Publng.

Mers Detroublees: Poisies et Textes, 1963-1969. Claude Peloquin. (FRE.). 364p. 1993. pap. write for info. (*2-89135-045-6*) Guernica Editions.

Mersenne & the Learning of the Schools. Peter Dear. LC 87-23935. (History of Science Ser.). (Illus.). 288p. 1988. 39.95 (*0-8014-1875-5*) Cornell U Pr.

Mersenne & the Learning of the Schools. Peter R. Dear. LC 87-23935. (Cornell History of Science Ser.). 281p. reprint ed. pap. 87.20 (*0-608-20880-9*, 207197900003) Bks Demand.

Mersey Estuary - A Report on Environmental Quality. 52p. 1995. pap. 25.00 (*0-11-885844-0*, HM58440, Pub. by Statnry Office) Bernan Associates.

Mersey Flats & Flatmen. Ed. by Mike Stammers. 228p. 1990. 60.00 (*0-86138-099-1*, Pub. by T Dalton) St Mut.

Mersey Goldfish. Ian Duhig. 64p. 1996. pap. 16.95 (*1-85224-325-2*, Pub. by Bloodaxe Bks) Dufour.

Mersey Sound. Adrian Henri & Roger McGough. 160p. (J). pap. 13.95 (*0-14-058534-6*, Pub. by Pnguin Bks Ltd) Trafalgar.

Mersyside Town in the Industrial Revolution: St. Helens, 1750-1900. T. C. Barker & J. R. Harris. LC 93-30817. 1993. 35.00 (*0-7146-4555-9*, Pub. by F Cass Pubs) Intl Spec Bk.

Mert the Blurt. Robert Krauss. LC 80-14508. (Illus.). (J). (ps). 10.95 (*0-671-66537-5*) S&S Bks Yung.

Mertens Code Commentary, 1954-1990, 3 vols., Set. annuals Ed. by Martin M. Weinstein. 218.00 (*0-317-11932-X*) West Group.

Mertens Current Tax Highlights. Mary A. Foran. 1994. 195.00 (*0-614-06136-9*) West Group.

Mertens Rulings, 1954-1990, 19 vols. 475.00 (*0-685-47432-1*) West Group.

Mertens Treatise, 19 vols. 1150.00 (*0-685-43688-8*) West Group.

Merthyr Trilogy: Three Plays. Alan Osborne. 174p. 1998. pap. 14.95 (*0-9521558-6-9*) Parthian Bks.

Mertins: Benchmarking. 1995. 61.95 (*3-540-58685-7*) Spr-Verlag.

Merton: A Biography. Monica Furlong. LC 95-79697. 342p. 1995. pap. 16.95 (*0-89243-829-0*) Liguori Pubns.

***Merton & Ecology: A Double Issue.** Dennis Patrick O'Hara & Donald P. St. John. (Teilhard Studies Ser.: Vol. 37). 1999. pap. 3.50 (*0-89012-080-3*) Am Teilhard.

***Merton & Sufism: The Untold Story, a Complete Compendium.** Gray Henry. 2000. pap. 25.95 (*1-887752-07-2*) Fons Vitae.

Merton Annual: Studies in Culture, Spirituality, & Social Concerns, Vol. 6. Ed. by George Kilcourse et al. 256p. (Orig.). 1994. pap. 24.95 (*0-8146-2250-X*, M Glazier) Liturgical Pr.

Merton Annual: Studies in Culture, Spirituality, & Social Concerns, Vol. 7. George Kilcourse et al. 256p. 1995. pap. 24.95 (*0-8146-2251-8*, Litug Pr Bks) Liturgical Pr.

Merton Annual: Studies in Culture, Spirituality, & Social Concerns, Vol. 10. Victor A. Kramer. 384p. 1998. pap. 24.95 (*0-8146-2254-2*) Liturgical Pr.

Merton Annual: Studies in Thomas Merton, Religion, Culture, Literature, & Social Concerns, 1988-1993, 5 vols., Set. Ed. by Robert E. Daggy et al. LC 87-47815. 1993. write for info. (*0-404-63800-7*) AMS Pr.

Merton Annual Vol. 8: Studies in Culture, Spirituality & Social Concerns. George Kilcourse. Ed. by Victor A. Kramer et al. 296p. 1996. pap. 24.95 (*0-8146-2252-6*, Litug Pr Bks) Liturgical Pr.

Merton Annual Vol. 9: Studies in Culture, Spirituality & Social Concerns, Vol. 9. Victor A. Kramer. Ed. by George Kilcourse & Michael Downey. 140p. 1997. pap. 24.95 (*0-8146-2253-4*) Liturgical Pr.

Merton Miller on Derivatives. Merton H. Miller. LC 97-210562. 240p. 1997. 34.95 (*0-471-18340-7*) Wiley.

Merton of the Movies. Harry Leon Wilson. (Collected Works of Harry Leon Wilson). 335p. 1999. reprint ed. lib. bdg. 98.00 (*1-58201-880-4*) Classic Bks.

Merton's Palace of Nowhere: A Search for God Through Awareness of the True Self. James Finley. LC 78-58738. 160p. 1978. pap. 8.95 (*0-87793-159-3*) Ave Maria.

Merton's Role Types & Paradigm of Deviance. Robert B. Hill. Ed. by Harriet Zuckerman & Robert K. Merton. LC 79-9004. (Dissertations on Sociology Ser.). 1980. lib. bdg. 26.95 (*0-405-12973-4*) Ayer.

Mertz's Wife. Thomas Glynn Thomas. 1997. 20.00 (*0-679-42589-6*) Knopf.

***Meru Temples of Angkor: A New Historical Perspective.** Jain. 1999. 16.00 (*0-8364-5686-6*, Pub. by Abhinav Pubns) S Asia.

Merula, Tomaso: Opere Completi, Pt. 1a. Ed. by Adam Sutkowski. (Gesamtausgaben - Collected Works: Vol. VII). (ENG, FRE, GER, ITA & POL.). 1981. lib. bdg. 7.00 (*0-912024-36-4*) Inst Mediaeval Mus.

Merula, Tomaso: Opere Completi, Pt. 1b. Ed. by Adam Sutkowski. (Gesamtausgaben - Collected Works: Vol. VII). (ENG, FRE, GER, ITA & POL.). 1981. lib. bdg. 7.00 (*0-912024-44-5*) Inst Mediaeval Mus.

Merula, Tomaso: Opere Completi, Pt. 2a. Ed. by Adam Sutkowski. (Gesamtausgaben - Collected Works: Vol. VII). (ENG, FRE, GER, ITA & POL.). 1981. lib. bdg. 7.00 (*0-912024-38-0*) Inst Mediaeval Mus.

Merula, Tomaso: Opere Completi, Pt. 2b-4b. Ed. by Adam Sutkowski. (Gesamtausgaben - Collected Works: Vol. VII). (ENG, FRE, GER, ITA & POL.). 1981. lib. bdg. 7.00 (*0-912024-20-8*) Inst Mediaeval Mus.

Merula, Tomaso: Opere Completi, Pt. 3a. Ed. by Adam Stutowski. (Gesamtausgaben - Collected Works: Vol. VII). (ENG, FRE, GER, ITA & POL.). 1981. lib. bdg. 7.00 (*0-912024-39-9*) Inst Mediaeval Mus.

Merula, Tomaso: Opere Completi, Pt. 4a. Ed. by Adam Stkowski. (Gesamtausgaben - Collected Works: Vol. VII). (ENG, FRE, GER, ITA & POL.). 1981. lib. bdg. 7.00 (*0-912024-40-2*) Inst Mediaeval Mus.

Merv Oasis: Travels & Adventures East of the Caspian During the Years 1879-80-81. Edmond O'Donovan. LC 71-115570. (Russia Observed Ser., No. 1). 1970. reprint ed. 56.95 (*0-405-03053-3*) Ayer.

Merveilles de la Terre D'Outremer. De Vignay. Ed. by Trotter. (FRE.). 196p. Date not set. pap. text 19.95 (*0-85989-348-0*, Pub. by Univ Exeter Pr) Northwestern U Pr.

Merveilleux Nuages. Francoise Sagan. (FRE.). 1983. pap. 10.95 (*0-7859-1481-1*, 2266012525) Fr & Eur.

Mervelous Signals: Poetics & Sign Theory in the Middle Ages. Eugene Vance. LC 85-21013. (Regents Studies in Medieval Culture). xviii, 365p. 1986. reprint ed. pap. text 20.00 (*0-8032-9608-8*, Bison Books) U of Nebr Pr.

***Mervin the Purple Three-Toed Schmoo.** Keith C. Odom. (Illus.). (J). 1999. pap. text. write for info. (*1-886021-32-5*) J W Wood.

Mervyn Peake: The Evolution of a Dark Romantic. Tanya J. Gardiner-Scott. (American University Studies: English Language & Literature: Ser. IV, Vol. 105). 336p. (C). 1989. text 44.95 (*0-8204-0943-X*) P Lang Pubng.

Mervyn Wall. Robert T. Hogan. 75p. 1972. 8.50 (*0-8387-1065-4*); pap. 1.95 (*0-8387-1064-6*) Bucknell U Pr.

Meryl Nelson's Cooking Coast to Coast. Meryl Nelson & Frances Thoman. Ed. by Shirley Sing. LC 83-51697. (Illus.). 120p. (Orig.). 1984. pap. 3.95 (*0-941900-08-8*) This N That.

Meryl Nelson's When You're Out Of . . . Cookbook. rev. ed. Meryl Nelson. Ed. by Shirley Sing. LC 83-51044. (Illus.). 104p. 1983. pap. 4.95 (*0-941900-06-1*) This N That.

Meryon's Etchings: A Catalogue Raisonne. rev. ed. Loys Delteil & Harold J. Wright. 224p. 1989. 95.00 (*1-55660-021-6*) A Wofsy Fine Arts.

Merz. Marisa Merz. (Illus.). 126p. 1999. pap. 32.95 (*88-7757-084-9*, Pub. by Hopefulmonster Editore) Dist Art Pubs.

Merzbook: Kurt Schwitters Poems. Colin Morton. 80p. 1987. pap. 12.95 (*0-919627-46-3*, Pub. by Quarry Pr) LPC InBook.

Mes Arches de Noe. (FRE.). 320p. 1980. pap. 11.95 (*0-7859-1920-1*, 2070372111) Fr & Eur.

***Mes Despacio.** Richard Carlson. 1998. pap. text 19.95 (*84-253-3152-8*) Distribks Inc.

Mes Haines see My Hatreds

Mes Memoires, 5 vols., 4. Alexandre Dumas. 16.50 (*0-686-55825-1*) Fr & Eur.

Mes Memoires, 5 vols., 5. Alexandre Dumas. 1968. 16.50 (*0-685-57721-X*) Fr & Eur.

Mes Memoires, 5 vols., Set. Alexandre Dumas. 95.00 (*0-8288-9977-0*, F60460) Fr & Eur.

Mes Parents. Herve Guibert. (Gallimard Ser.). (FRE.). 1986. pap. 29.95 (*2-07-070657-5*) Schoenhof.

Mes Prisons et Autres Textes Autobiographiques. Paul M. Verlaine. (FRE.). 81p. 1973. pap. 34.95 (*0-7859-1584-2*, 3807400125) Fr & Eur.

Mes Songes Que Voici. Andre Maurois. pap. 17.50 (*0-685-36948-X*) Fr & Eur.

Mes Yeux de l'Interieur (Mes Yeux D'Enfant) see Miguel

Mesa. Charles A. Selzer. 1976. reprint ed. lib. bdg. 23.95 (*0-88411-113-X*) Amereon Ltd.

Mesa: In the Shadow of the Superstitions. Tray C. Mead & Robert C. Price. 144p. 1988. 29.95 (*0-89781-254-9*, 5274) Am Historical Pr.

Mesa: More Than a Spiritual Adventure. Pam Cameron. LC 99-162957. 320p. 1999. pap. 14.95 (*0-9657104-0-8*) Luminaria Pr.

MESA & Trading Market Cycles. John F. Ehlers. LC 91-40274. (Traders' Advantage Ser.). 160p. 1992. 37.95 (*0-471-54943-6*) Wiley.

Mesa China. Ellen Chen. (SPA., Illus.). 138p. 1988. write for info. (*0-9650407-9-8*) Chanyii.

Mesa Grill Guide to Tequila: The Quintessence of the Blue Agave & the Finest Brands of Tequila. Laurence Kretchmer. LC 98-9453. 192p. 1998. 10.98 (*1-57912-010-5*) Blck Dog & Leventhal.

Mesa Mexicana. Mary S. Milliken et al. LC 93-43099. 262p. 1994. 17.95 (*0-688-10649-8*, Wm Morrow) Morrow Avon.

Mesa Verde. Gary McCarthy. 384p. 1997. mass mkt. 5.99 (*0-7860-0390-1*, Pinncle Kensgtn) Kensgtn Pub Corp.

Mesa Verde. Jane Shuter. LC 99-17395. 1999. lib. bdg. write for info. (*1-57572-858-3*) Heinemann Lib.

Mesa Verde: A Complete Guide. Gian Mercurio & Maxymilian L. Peschel. (Illus.). 50p. (Orig.). 1992. pap. 4.95 (*0-9627377-1-2*) Lonewolf Pub.

Mesa Verde: Ancient Architecture. Jesse W. Fewkes. LC 99-14433. (Illus.). 240p. 1999. pap. 16.95 (*0-936755-23-7*) Avanyu Pub.

An Asterisk (*) at the beginning of an entry indicates that the title is appearing for the first time.

Mesa Verde: Fuerher Durch Den Nationalpark. Gian Mercurio & Max Peschel. Tr. by Margie Glosser. (Illus.). (Orig.). 1991. pap. 4.95 (*0-9627377-0-4*) Lonewolf Pub.

Mesa Verde: The Story Behind the Scenery. Linda Martin. LC 93-77024. (Illus.). 48p. (Orig.). 1993. pap. 7.95 (*0-88714-075-0*) KC Pubns.

Mesa Verde: The Story Behind the Scenery. Linda Martin. Tr. by Brigitte Morales. (GER., Illus.). 48p. (Orig.). 1993. pap. 8.95 (*0-88714-735-6*) KC Pubns.

Mesa Verde: The Story Behind the Scenery. Linda Martin. Tr. by Yvon Le Bras. (FRE., Illus.). 48p. (Orig.). 1993. pap. 8.95 (*0-88714-736-4*) KC Pubns.

Mesa Verde & the Four Corners. William H. Jackson & William H. Holmes. Ed. & Intro. by Jack L. Benham. (Illus.). 72p. 1981. reprint ed. pap. 3.95 (*0-941026-07-8*) Bear Creek Pub.

***Mesa Verde National Park.** Susan Lamb. Ed. by Jeff Nicholas. (Pocket Portfolio Ser.: Vol. 14). (Illus.). 32p. 1999. pap. 5.95 (*1-58071-001-8*, Pub. by Panorama Intl) Falcon Pub Inc.

Mesa Verde National Park. Ed. by Jeff Nicholas. (Wish You Were Here Postcard Book Ser.). (Illus.). 32p. 1997. pap. 4.95 (*0-939365-81-2*) Panorama Intl.

***Mesa Verde National Park.** Ed. by Jeff Nicholas. (Wish You Were Here Postcard Book Ser.). (Illus.). 32p. 1999. pap. 4.95 (*1-58071-006-9*, Pub. by Panorama Intl) Falcon Pub Inc.

Mesa Verde National Park. David Petersen. LC 91-35275. (New True Books Ser.). (Illus.). 48p. (J). (gr. k-4). 1992. pap. 5.50 (*0-516-41136-5*) Childrens.

Mesa Verde National Park: Preserving the Past. Robert H. Lister & Florence C. Lister. (Illus.). 80p. 1989. 15.95 (*0-917859-13-8*) Sunrise SBCA.

Mesa Verde National Park: Shadows of the Centuries. Duane A. Smith. LC 88-14773. (Illus.). xii, 256p. 1988. 25.00 (*0-7006-0371-9*); pap. 14.95 (*0-7006-0372-7*) U Pr of KS.

MESA Way: A Success Story of Nuturing Minorities for Math-Science Based Careers. Wilbur H. Somerton et al. LC 94-4775. 214p. (Orig.). (C). 1994. pap. text 17.95 (*1-880192-10-1*) Caddo Gap Pr.

***Mesagerul Sperantei.** Silvia Circa. 1999. 14.99 (*0-9623183-9-6*) Moonfall Pr VA.

Mesair Ussuara: Tezkere of Asik Celebi. Meredith-Owens. (Gibb Memorial New Ser.: Vol. 24). 1971. 72.00 (*0-7189-0200-9*, Pub. by Aris & Phillips) David Brown.

Mesas Redondas de Palenque Vol. 1: Antologia. Silvia Trejo. (SPA., Illus.). 550p. 1996. pap. 29.00 (*968-29-5238-7*, IN91, Pub. by Dir Gen Pubicaiones) UPLAAP.

Mesas to Mountains. Sybil Downing & Jane V. Barker. (Colorado Heritage Ser.). (Illus.). 47p. (J). (ps-8). reprint ed. pap. 7.95 (*1-878611-04-6*) Silver Rim Pr.

Mesca Ulad. Intro. by William Hennessy. LC 78-72681. (Royal Irish Academy. Todd Lecture Ser.: Vol. 1). reprint ed. 27.50 (*0-404-60561-3*) AMS Pr.

Mescalero Apaches. Charles L. Sonnichsen. LC 58-11610. (Civilization of the American Indian Ser.: Vol. 51). (Illus.). 300p. 1979. reprint ed. pap. 16.95 (*0-8061-1615-3*) U of Okla Pr.

***Mesencephalic Trigeminal Nucleus in the Cat.** N. E. Lazarov. LC QL801.E67 vol. 153. (Advances in Anatomy, Embryology & Cell Biology Ser.: Vol. 153). (Illus.). 85p. 2000. pap. 72.00 (*3-540-66524-2*) Spr-Verlag.

Meserve Civil War Record: With the Intriguing War Story by Major William N. Meserve. William N. Meserve. Ed. by Richard A. Huebner. LC 87-23557. (Illus.). xxii, 290p. (C). 1988. 55.00 (*0-9619037-7-5*) RAH Pubns.

Meserve Civil War Record: With the Intriguing War Story by Major William N. Meserve. deluxe limited ed. William N. Meserve. Ed. by Richard A. Huebner. LC 87-23557. (Illus.). xxii, 290p. (C). 1988. 85.00 (*0-9619037-6-7*) RAH Pubns.

Meseta & Campina Landforms in Central Spain: A Geomorphology of the Alto Henares Basin. Bruce G. Gladfelter. LC 75-133028. (University of Chicago, Department of Geography, Research Paper Ser.: No. 130). 219p. 1971. reprint ed. pap. 67.90 (*0-608-02252-7*, 206289300004) Bks Demand.

Mesh. Clark Coolidge. 48p. 1988. pap. 4.95 (*0-932597-05-X*) In Camera.

Mesh & Net: Speculations on Armed Conflict in a Time of Free Silicon. 1997. lib. bdg. 250.95 (*0-8490-7738-9*) Gordon Pr.

Mesh & the Net: Speculations on Armed Conflict in a Time of Free Silicon. Martin C. Libicki. 133p. 1994. per. 7.50 (*0-16-061161-X*) USGPO.

Mesh & the Net: Speculations on Armed Conflict in a Time of Free Silicon. Martin C. Libicki. 127p. (C). 1996. reprint ed. pap. text 30.00 (*0-7881-3504-X*) DIANE Pub.

Mesh & the Net: Speculations on Armed Conflict in a Time of Free Silicon, Analyzing the Relationship of the Revolution in Information Technology to Warfare. 1996. lib. bdg. 253.75 (*0-8490-5924-0*) Gordon Pr.

***Mesh Friction in Gearing.** C. M. Denny. (Technical Papers: Vol. 98FTM2). 11p. 1998. pap. 30.00 (*1-55589-720-7*) AGMA.

Mesh Generation, Finite Elements, Computers in Structural Optimization, Computers in the Engineering Workplace, Computers in Energy Systems, Personal Computing see Computers in Engineering, 1982

***Meshal Haqadmoni Fables from the Distant Past.** Isaac I. Sahula & Raphael Loewe. (Illus.). 512p. 2000. (*1-874774-56-0*) Intl Spec Bk.

Meshes. George. 1969. text. write for info. (*0-471-89915-1*) Wiley.

***Meshivas Nefesh Yitzchok: Matamim.** Y. A. Korff. (HEB & ARA.). 224p. 2000. 18.00 (*0-9645367-1-4*) Jewish Adv.

Meshivat Nefesh see Courage!

Meshivat Nefesh see Restore My Soul

Meshugah. Isaac Bashevis Singer. Tr. by Nili Wachtel. 240p. 1995. pap. 12.95 (*0-452-27384-6*, Plume) Dutton Plume.

Meshugah. Isaac Bashevis Singer. Tr. by Nili Wachtel. LC 93-42785. (ENG & YID.). 240p. 1994. 22.00 (*0-374-20847-6*) FS&G.

Meshugah & Other Stories. Emanuel Fried. 40p. (Orig.). 1982. pap. 2.95 (*0-9603888-2-6*) Labor Arts.

Meshullam! or, Tidings from Jerusalem: Journal of a Believer Recently Returned from the Holy Land. Clorinda Minor. Ed. by Moshe Davis. LC 77-70755. (America & the Holy Land Ser.). 1977. reprint ed. lib. bdg. 19.95 (*0-405-10302-6*) Ayer.

Mesianismo y la Rebelion Indigena: La Rebelion de Oruro en 1781. Nicholas A. Robins. (SPA.). 218p. (Orig.). 1997. pap. 6.00 (*0-9659015-0-5*) N Robins.

Mesmer & Animal Magnetism: A Chapter in the History of Medicine. Frank A. Pattie. LC 93-41168. (Illus.). 303p. 1994. 39.95 (*0-9622393-5-6*) Edmonston Publ.

Mesmerism: The Discovery of Animal Magnetism (1779); A New Translation. Franz A. Mesmer. Ed. & Tr. by Joseph Bouleur from FRE. (Orig.). 1997. pap. 7.95 (*1-55818-382-5*) Holmes Pub.

Mesmerism & Hawthorne: Mediums of American Romance. Samuel Coale. LC 97-10044. 224p. 1998. text 34.95 (*0-8173-0896-2*) U of Ala Pr.

***Mesmerism & Hawthorne: Mediums of American Romance.** Samuel Coale. 216p. 2000. pap. text 19.95 (*0-8173-1038-X*) U of Ala Pr.

Mesmerism & the End of the Enlightenment in France. Robert Darnton. (Illus.). 226p. 1968. pap. 15.95 (*0-674-56951-2*) HUP.

Mesmerism in India, 10. James Esdaile. LC 77-72191. (Contributions to the History of Psychology Ser.: Vol. X, Pt. A, Orientations). 654p. 1977. reprint ed. lib. bdg. 95.00 (*0-313-26934-3*, U6934, Greenwood Pr) Greenwood.

Mesmerism in India & Its Practical Application in Surgery & Medicine. James Esdaile. (C). 1989. 12.00 (*81-206-0456-3*, Pub. by Asian Educ Servs) S Asia.

Mesmerism in India & Its Practical Application in Surgery & Medicine. James Esdaile. LC 75-16702. (Classics in Psychiatry Ser.). 1976. reprint ed. 26.95 (*0-405-07429-8*) Ayer.

Mesmerist's Manual of Phenomena & Practice. George Barth. 104p. 1998. reprint ed. pap. 17.50 (*0-7873-0075-6*) Hlth Research.

***Mesmerized.** Gayle Lynds. 2000. write for info. (*0-671-02407-8*) PB.

***Mesmerized.** Simona Taylor. (Arabesque Ser.). 2000. mass mkt. 5.99 (*1-58314-070-0*) BET Bks.

Mesmerized: Powers of Mind in Victorian Britain. Alison Winter. LC 98-21833. 450p. 1998. 30.00 (*0-226-90219-6*) U Ch Pr.

***Mesmerized: Powers of Mind in Victorian Britain.** Alison Winter. 2000. pap. 17.00 (*0-226-90223-4*) U Ch Pr.

Meso-Optics, Foundations & Applications. 450p. 1996. lib. bdg. 48.00 (*981-02-2700-0*) World Scientific Pub.

Mesoamerica see Pre-Columbian America

Mesoamerica after the Decline of Teotihuacan, A. D. 700-900. Ed. by Richard A. Diehl & Janet Catherine Berlo. LC 88-30596. (Illus.). 500p. 1989. 60.00 (*0-88402-175-0*) Dumbarton Oaks.

Mesoamerica Tolteca: Sus Ceramicas de Comercio Principales. Bernd Fahmel. 178p. 1988. pap. 7.00 (*968-36-0502-8*, UN006) UPLAAP.

***Mesoamerica 250 B.C.** Paperblank Book Company Staff. 128p. 2000. 19.95 (*1-55156-172-7*) Paperblank.

Mesoamerican Architecture As a Cultural Symbol. Ed. by Jeff K. Kowalski. (Illus.). 432p. 1999. text 75.00 (*0-19-507961-2*) OUP.

Mesoamerican Ballgame. Ed. by Vernon L. Scarborough & David R. Wilcox. LC 90-21890. (Illus.). 404p. 1993. reprint ed. pap. 20.95 (*0-8165-1360-0*) U of Ariz Pr.

Mesoamerican Elites: An Archaeological Assessment. Ed. by Diane Z. Chase & Arlen F. Chase. LC 91-40064. (Illus.). 375p. 1994. reprint ed. pap. 18.95 (*0-8061-2666-3*) U of Okla Pr.

Mesoamerican Ethnohistory in United States Libraries: Reconstruction of the William E. Gates Collection of Historical & Linguistic Manuscripts. Compiled by John M. Weeks. LC 89-84021. (Illus.). 256p. (Orig.). (C). 1990. pap. 29.00 (*0-911437-37-1*) Labyrinthos.

Mesoamerican Sites & World-Views: Conference at Dumbarton Oaks, October 16 & 17, 1976. Ed. by Elizabeth P. Benson. LC 79-92647. (Illus.). 256p. 1981. 24.00 (*0-88402-097-5*) Dumbarton Oaks.

Mesoamerican Writing Systems: A Conference at Dumbarton Oaks, October 30 & 31, 1971. Ed. by Elizabeth P. Benson. LC 73-93086. (Illus.). 226p. 1973. 24.00 (*0-88402-048-7*) Dumbarton Oaks.

Mesoamerican Writing Systems: Propaganda, Myth, & History in Four Ancient Civilizations. Joyce Marcus. LC 92-9091. (Illus.). 550p. 1992. text 65.00 (*0-691-09474-8*, Pub. by Princeton U Pr) Cal Prin Full Svc.

Mesoamerica's Ancient Cities. William M. Ferguson et al. (Illus.). 272p. 1990. 49.95 (*0-87081-173-8*) Univ Pr Colo.

***Mesoamerica's Ancient Cities.** rev. ed. William M. Ferguson. (Illus.). 272p. 2000. 70.00 (*0-87081-584-9*); pap. 34.95 (*0-87081-585-7*) Univ Pr Colo.

Mesoamerica's Classic Heritage: Teotihuacan to the Aztecs. Ed. by David Carrasco et al. LC 99-11257. (Illus.). 530p. 1999. 65.00 (*0-87081-512-1*) Univ Pr Colo.

Mesococsm: Hinduism & the Organization of a Traditional Newar City in Nepal. R. I. Levy. (C). 1992. 108.00 (*0-7855-0192-4*, Pub. by Ratna Pustak Bhandar) St Mut.

Mesocosm: Hinduism & the Organization of a Traditional Newar City in Nepal. Robert I. Levy. 1992. 180.00 (*0-7855-0260-2*, Pub. by Ratna Pustak Bhandar) St Mut.

Mesocosm: Hinduism & the Organization of a Traditional Newar City in Nepal. Robert I. Levy. (Illus.). 800p. 1990. 85.00 (*0-520-06911-0*, Pub. by U CA Pr) Cal Prin Full Svc.

Mesolabium Architectionicum That Is a Most Rare Instrument of Measuring. William Bedwell. LC 72-172. (English Experience Ser.: No. 224). 24p. 1970. reprint ed. 25.00 (*90-221-0224-6*) Walter J Johnson.

Mesolimbic Dopamine System: From Motivation to Action. Ed. by Paul Willner & Jrgen Scheel-Kruger. LC 90-12986. 674p. 1991. 575.00 (*0-471-92886-0*) Wiley.

Mesolithic Age in Britain. John G. Clark. LC 76-44704. reprint ed. 40.00 (*0-404-15914-1*) AMS Pr.

Mesolithic Britain. John J. Wymer. (Archaeology Ser.: No. 65). (Illus.). 64p. 1989. pap. 10.50 (*0-7478-0121-5*, Pub. by Shire Pubns) Parkwest Pubns.

Mesolithic in Europe: The Third International Symposium. Clive Bonsall. (Illus.). 500p. (C). 1996. 165.00 (*0-85976-205-X*, Pub. by J Donald) St Mut.

Mesomorphic Order in Polymers & Polymerization in Liquid Crystalline Media. Ed. by Alexandre Blumstein. LC 78-9470. (ACS Symposium Ser.: No. 74). 1978. 34.95 (*0-8412-0419-5*) Am Chemical.

Mesomorphic Order in Polymers & Polymerization in Liquid Crystalline Media. Ed. by Alexandre Blumstein. LC 78-9470. (ACS Symposium Ser.: Vol. 74). 272p. 1978. reprint ed. pap. 84.40 (*0-608-03932-2*, 206437900009) Bks Demand.

Meson Factories. Torlief Ericson et al. LC 90-27281. (Los Alamos Series in Basic & Applied Sciences: No. 11). 600p. 1991. 85.00 (*0-520-07549-8*, Pub. by U CA Pr) Cal Prin Full Svc.

Meson-Nuclear Physics, 1976: Carnegie-Mellon Conference. Ed. by P. D. Barnes et al. LC 76-26811. (AIP Conference Proceedings Ser.: No. 33). 1976. 24.75 (*0-88318-132-0*) Am Inst Physics.

Meson-Nuclear Physics-1979. Ed. by E. V. Hungerford, III. LC 79-53978. (AIP Conference Proceedings Ser.: No. 54). (Illus.). 1979. lib. bdg. 27.75 (*0-88318-153-3*, CP-54) Am Inst Physics.

Meson Production, Interaction & Decay. Ed. by E. Grosse et al. 400p. (C). 1991. text 104.00 (*981-02-0783-2*) World Scientific Pub.

Mesons & Light Nuclei: Proceedings of the Fifth International Symposium on Mesons & Light Nuclei, Prague, September 1-6, 1991. Ed. by E. Truhlik & R. Mach. (Few-Body Systems Ser.: Suppl. 5). (Illus.). 530p. 1992. 144.95 (*0-387-82342-5*) Spr-Verlag.

Mesons & Light Nuclei: Proceedings of the 5th International Symposium, Prague, September 1-6, 1991. Ed. by E. Truhlik & R. Mach. Vol. 5. 1992. write for info. (*0-318-69248-1*) Spr-Verlag.

***Mesons & Light Nuclei; Proceedings of the 7th Conference Prague-pruhonice, Czech Republic, 1998.** J. Adam. 1999. 120.00 (*981-02-3885-1*) WSC Inst MA Studies.

Mesons & Light Nuclei '95: Proceedings of the 6th International Conference, Straz pod Ralskem, Held July 3-7, 1995. Ed. by J. Adam et al. LC 95-51699. (Few-Body Systems Ser.: Vol. 9). 527p. 1996. 159.00 (*3-211-82786-2*) Spr-Verlag.

Mesons & Nuclei at Intermediate Energies: Proceedings of the International Conference. M. K. Khankhasayev et al. 880p. 1995. text 109.00 (*981-02-1787-0*) World Scientific Pub.

Mesoplasticity & Its Applications. Wei Yang. LC 92-41808. 1993. 211.95 (*0-387-55542-0*) Spr-Verlag.

Mesoporous Molecular Sieves 1998: Proceedings of the First International Symposium, Baltimore, Md, U.S.A., July 10-12, 1998, Vol. 117. Laurent Bonneviot. LC 98-22444. (Studies in Surface Science & Catalysis). 1998. write for info. (*0-444-82826-5*) Elsevier.

Mesopotamia. (Illus.). 48p. (J). (gr. 4-8). 1991. 9.95 (*0-86685-486-X*) Intl Bk Ctr.

Mesopotamia. Librairie du Liban Staff. (J). 1991. 9.95 (*0-86685-489-4*) Intl Bk Ctr.

Mesopotamia. Julian Reade. (British Museum Paperbacks Ser.). (Illus.). 72p. (C). 1991. pap. 14.00 (*0-674-56958-X*) HUP.

Mesopotamia: The Mighty Kings see Lost Civilizations Series

Mesopotamia: The Mighty Kings. Ed. by Dale Brown. LC 94-24305. (Lost Civilizations Ser.). (Illus.). 168p. 1995. lib. bdg. write for info. (*0-8094-9042-0*) Time-Life.

Mesopotamia: Writing, Reasoning, & the Gods. Jean Bottero. Tr. by Zainab Bahrani & Marc Van de Mieroop. (Illus.). 312p. 1995. pap. text 17.00 (*0-226-06727-0*) U Ch Pr.

Mesopotamia: Writing, Reasoning, & the Gods. Jean Bottero. Tr. by Zainab Bahrani & Marc Van de Mieroop. LC 91-25917. (Illus.). 326p. 1997. 43.95 (*0-226-06726-2*) U Ch Pr.

Mesopotamia & the East: An Archaeological & Historical Study of Foreign Relations 3400-2000 BC. Timothy Potts. (Oxford University Committee for Archaeology Monograph Ser.: No. 37). (Illus.). 340p. 1995. 48.00 (*0-947816-37-2*, Pub. by Oxford Univ Comm Arch) David Brown.

Mesopotamian Archaeology: With Slides. Marie-Henriette Gates. Ed. by Hershel Shanks. 53p. (Orig.). 1993. pap. text 119.50 (*1-880317-37-0*, 5095) Biblical Arch Soc.

Mesopotamian Astrology: An Introduction to Babylonian & Assyrian Celestial Divination, CNI 19. Ulla Koch-Westenholz. 250p. 1995. 75.00 (*87-7289-287-0*, Pub. by Mus Tusculanum) Paul & Co Pubs.

Mesopotamian Civilization: The Material Foundations. D. T. Potts. LC 96-34832. (Illus.). 340p. 1996. text 67.50 (*0-8014-3339-8*) Cornell U Pr.

Mesopotamian Cosmic Geography. Wayne Horowitz. LC 98-17770. (Mesopotamian Civilizations Ser.: Vol. 8). 1998. text 52.50 (*0-931464-99-4*) Eisenbrauns.

Mesopotamian Epic Literature: Oral or Aural? Ed. by Marianna E. Vogelzang & Herman L. Vanstiphout. LC 92-10198. 328p. 1992. lib. bdg. 99.95 (*0-7734-9538-X*) E Mellen.

Mesopotamian Lexicography. Miguel Civil. (Handbook of Oriental Studies: Pt. 1A, 37). 300p. 1999. 104.00 (*90-04-11007-0*) Brill Academic Pubs.

***Mesopotamian Mathematics, 2100-1600 B. C. Technical Constants in Bureaucracy & Education, Vol. XIV.** Eleanor Robson. LC 98-38018. (Oxford Editions of Cuneiform Texts Ser.). (Illus.). 352p. 1999. pap. text 105.00 (*0-19-815246-9*) OUP.

Mesopotamian Myths. Henrietta McCall. (Legendary Past Ser.). (Illus.). 80p. 1991. pap. 12.95 (*0-292-75130-3*) U of Tex Pr.

Mesopotamian Religious Architecture: Alexander Through the Parthians. Susan B. Downey. LC 87-3336. (Illus.). 216p. reprint ed. pap. 67.00 (*0-7837-6762-5*, 204659200003) Bks Demand.

Mesopotamica - Ugaritica - Biblica: Festchrift fur Kurt Bergerhof zur Vollendung Seines 70, Lebensjahres am 7. Mai 1992. Manfried Dietrich & Oswald Loretz. (Alter Orient und Altes Testament Ser.: Vol. 232). (FRE & GER.). x, 515p. 1993. text 105.00 (*3-7887-1453-0*) NeukirchenerV.

M

***Mesopotamien: Akkade-Zeit und Ur III-Zeit.** Walther Sallaberger & Aage Westenholz. Ed. by Pascal Attinger & Markus Attinger. (Orbis Biblicus et Orientalis Ser.: Vol. 160/3). (GER.). 414p. 1999. text 82.75 (*3-7278-1210-9*, Pub. by Ed Univ Fri) Eisenbrauns.

Mesoscale Atmospheric Dispersion. Ed. by Z. Boybeyi. (Advances in Air Pollution Ser.). 500p. 2000. 262.00 (*1-85312-732-9*, 7329, Pub. by WIT Pr) Computational Mech MA.

Mesoscale Forecasting & Its Applications: Lectures Presented at the Fortieth Session of the WMO Executive Council. World Meteorological Organization Staff. (WMO Ser.: No. 712). (Illus.). 126p. 1989. pap. 27.00 (*92-63-10942-7*, Pub. by Wrld Meteorological) St Mut.

Mesoscale Meteorology & Forecasting. Ed. by Peter S. Ray. (Illus.). 793p. (C). 1987. reprint ed. text 66.25 (*0-933876-66-1*) Am Meteorological.

Mesoscale Modeling of the Atmosphere. Roger A. Pielke & Robert P. Pearce. LC 95-191502. (Meteorological Monograph: Vol. 25, No. 47). 1994. 65.00 (*1-878220-15-2*) Am Meteorological.

***Mesoscopic Charge Density Wave Wires.** O. C. Mantel. (Illus.). 118p. 1999. pap. 39.50 (*90-407-1888-1*, Pub. by Delft U Pr) Coronet Bks.

Mesoscopic Dynamics of Fracture: Computational Materials Design. Ed. by H. Kitagawa et al. LC 98-3587. (Advances in Materials Research Ser.: Vol. 1). (Illus.). 260p. 1998. 59.95 (*3-540-64291-9*) Spr-Verlag.

Mesoscopic Electron Transport: Proceedings of the NATO Advanced Study Institute, 25 June-5 July 1996, Curacao, Netherlands Antilles. Ed. by Lydia L. Sohn et al. LC 97-33974. (NATO Advanced Science Institutes Ser.: No. 345). 692p. 1997. text 331.50 (*0-7923-4737-4*) Kluwer Academic.

Mesoscopic Materials & Clusters: Their Physical & Chemical Properties. Toshihiro Arai et al. LC 99-17748. (Series in Cluster Physics). 470p. 1999. 129.00 (*3-540-64884-4*) Spr-Verlag.

Mesoscopic Phenomena in Solids. Ed. by B. L. Altshuler et al. (Modern Problems in Condensed Matter Sciences Ser.: Vol. 30). xx, 556p. 1991. 311.50 (*0-444-88454-8*, North Holland) Elsevier.

Mesoscopic Physics & Electronics. Ed. by Tsuneya Ando et al. LC 97-43404. (Nanoscience & Technology Ser.). (Illus.). xii, 270p. 1997. 69.95 (*3-540-63587-4*) Spr-Verlag.

***Mesoscopic Physics of Complex Materials.** T. S. Chow. (Graduate Texts in Contemporary Physics Ser.). (Illus.). 252p. 2000. 49.95 (*0-387-95032-X*) Spr-Verlag.

Mesoscopic Quantum Optics. Yoshihisa Yamamoto & Atac Imamoglu. LC 99-14000. 301p. 1999. 79.95 (*0-471-14874-1*) Wiley.

Mesoscopic Quantum Physics: Proceedings of the Les Houches Summer School, Session LXI, 28 June-29 July, 1994. Ed. by E. Akkermans et al. (Houches Summer School Proceedings Ser.: Vol. 61). (FRE.). 836p. 1995. 273.00 (*0-444-82293-3*) Elsevier.

Mesoscopic Systems. Yoshimasa Murayama. 338p. 1999. pap. 99.95 (*3-527-29376-0*, Wiley-VCH) Wiley.

Mesosphere & Thermosphere. G. Schmidtke & K. S. Champion. 1981. pap. 36.00 (*0-08-028393-4*, Pergamon Pr) Elsevier.

Mesospheric Models & Related Experiments: Proceedings of the ESRIN-ESLAB Symposium, 4th, Frascati, Italy, July 6-10, 1970. ESRIN-ESLAB Symposium Staff. Ed. by G. Fiocco. LC 70-154737. (Astrophysics & Space Science Library: No.25). 298p. 1971. text 169.50 (*90-277-0200-4*) Kluwer Academic.

Mesothelial Cell & Mesothelioma. Ed. by Marie-Claude Jaurand & Jean Bignon. LC 94-16595. (Lung Biology in Health & Disease Ser.: Vol. 78). (Illus.). 368p. 1994. text 175.00 (*0-8247-9232-7*) Dekker.

Mesothelioma: The Story of an Illness. Brenda McKessock. LC 95-233331. 240p. 1994. pap. write for info. (*1-874640-21-1*, Pub. by Argyll Pubng) St Mut.

Mesotheliomas of Animals: A Comprehensive, Tabular Compendium of the World's Literature. E. B. Ilgren. 384p. 1993. lib. bdg. 179.00 (*0-8493-4308-9*, RC280) CRC Pr.

An Asterisk (*) at the beginning of an entry indicates that the title is appearing for the first time.

Mesozoic - Cenozoic Vertebrate Paleontology: Classic Localities, Contemporary Approaches, No. T322. Ed. by John J. Flynn. (IGC Field Trip Guidebooks Ser.). 88p. 1989. 21.00 (*0-87590-608-7*) Am Geophysical.

Mesozoic & Cenozoic Oceans. Ed. by K. J. Hsu. (Geodynamics Ser.: Vol. 15). (Illus.). 176p. 1986. 22.00 (*0-87590-515-3*) Am Geophysical.

***Mesozoic & Cenozoic Sequence Stratigraphy of European Basins.** Ed. by Pierre-Charles de Graciansky et al. (Special Publications: Vol. 60). (Illus.). 800p. 1999. 175.00 (*1-56576-043-3*) SEPM.

Mesozoic & Cenozoic Siliceous Sediments of California, No. T109. Ed. by Blueford. (IGC Field Trip Guidebooks Ser.). 56p. 1989. 21.00 (*0-87590-605-2*) Am Geophysical.

Mesozoic & Tertiary Geology of Southern Africa. R. V. Dingle et al. 385p. (C). 1983. text 188.00 (*90-6191-099-4*, Pub. by A A Balkema) Ashgate Pub Co.

Mesozoic Carpentaria Basin & the Cainozoic Karumba Basin, North Queensland. J. Smart. LC 90-134692. (Bulletin Ser.). vi, 73 p. 1980. write for info. (*0-642-04618-2*, Pub. by Aust Inst Criminology) Advent Bks Div.

Mesozoic Coleoptera. L. V. Arnol'di et al. (Illus.). 297p. 1991. 72.00 (*90-73348-05-6*, Pub. by Backhuys Pubs) Balogh.

Mesozoic Geology & Paleontology of the Four Corners Area. Ed. by O. Anderson et al. (Guidebook Ser.: No. 48). (Illus.). 288p. 1997. pap. 60.00 (*1-58546-083-4*) NMex Geol Soc.

Mesozoic of the Western Interior: Abstracts SEPM 1992 Theme Meeting, Ft. Collins, CO, August 17-19, 1992. fac. ed. Society for Sedimentary Geology Staff. LC QE0675.S466. 68p. 1994. pap. 30.00 (*0-7837-7682-9*, 204743500007) Bks Demand.

Mesozoic Pacific: Geology, Tectonics, & Volcanism. Ed. by Malcolm S. Pringle et al. LC 93-33017. (Geophysical Monograph Ser.: No. 77). 435p. 1993. 54.00 (*0-87590-036-4*) Am Geophysical.

Mesozoic Paleogeography of the Western United States No. 2: Symposium. Ed. by David G. Howell & Kristin A. McDougall. (Illus.). 573p. (Orig.). 1978. pap. 10.00 (*1-878861-58-1*) Pac Section SEPM.

Mesozoic Paleogeography of the Western United States-II. George C. Dunne & Kristin A. McDougall. 500p. (Orig.). 1993. pap. 33.00 (*1-878861-64-6*) Pac Section SEPM.

***Mesozoic Sedimentary & Tectonic History of North-Central Mexico.** Claudio Bartolini et al. LC 99-38981. (Special Paper Ser.). 1999. write for info. (*0-8137-2340-X*) Geol Soc.

Mesozoic Volcanic-Intrusive Complexes & Their Metallogenic Relations in East China. Ed. by Wang Dezi et al. (Illus.). 174p. 1996. 95.00 (*90-6764-227-4*, Pub. by VSP) Coronet Bks.

Mesozoic Volcanism & Volcanogenic Iron-Ore Deposits in Eastern China. Xu Zhigang. (Special Papers: No. 237). (Illus.). 56p. 1990. pap. 4.00 (*0-8137-2237-3*) Geol Soc.

Mesozoisch-Tertiaere Verwitterungsdecke (MTV) im Rheinischen Schiefergebirge. Peter Felix-Henningsen. (Relief, Boden, Palaeoklima Ser.: Band 6). (GER., Illus.). ix, 192p. 1990. pap. 67.00 (*3-443-09006-0*, Pub. by Gebruder Borntraeger) Balogh.

Mesozoische Plutone in der Nordchilenischen Kuestenkordillere: Petrogenese, Geochronologie, Geochemie und Geodynamik Mantelbetonten Magmatite. Karsten Berg & Christoph Breitkreuz. (Geotektonische Forschungen Ser.: Vol. 66). (GER.). 107p. 1983. 57.00 (*3-510-50032-6*, Pub. by E Schweizerbartsche) Balogh.

***Mesquite.** Elena Zamora O'Shea. (Rio Grande/Rio Bravo Ser.: Vol. 4). 160p. 2000. 27.95 (*0-89096-966-3*); pap. 15.95 (*1-58544-108-2*) Tex A&M Univ Pr.

Mesquite & Willow. Ed. by Mody C. Boatright et al. LC 56-12566. (Texas Folklore Society Publications: No. 27). 203p. 1957. 12.95 (*0-87074-018-0*) UNTX Pr.

Mesquite Country: Tastes & Traditions from the Tip of Texas. Hidalgo County Museum Staff. 288p. 1996. spiral bd. 19.95 (*1-888594-00-4*) Hidalgo Cty Hist Mus.

Mesquite Jenkins. large type ed. Clarence E. Mulford. 1976. 24.95 (*0-88411-236-5*) Amereon Ltd.

Mesquite Jenkins see Hopalong Cassidy Series

Mesquite Jenkins, Tumbleweed. Clarence E. Mulford. 1976. 24.95 (*0-88411-224-1*) Amereon Ltd.

Mesquite Sighs: A Collection of Short Stories. E. D. Santos. (Illus.). 112p. (Orig.). 1992. pap. 11.50 (*0-9621831-1-3*) La Sombra Pub.

Mesrob Mashtotz: A Fifth Century Life. Elise A. Bayizian. (Armenian Church Classics Ser.). (Illus.). 39p. (Orig.). 1984. pap. 4.00 (*0-934728-14-3*) D O A C.

Mess in Washington: Manpower Mobilization in World War II, 76. George Q. Flynn. LC 78-4027. (Contributions in American History Ser.: No. 76). 294p. 1979. 59.95 (*0-313-20418-7*, FMW/, Greenwood Pr) Greenwood.

Messa da Requiem, 2 vols. Giuseppe Verdi. Ed. by David Rosen. (Works of Giuseppe Verdi: No. 3, Vol. 1). ixiv, 594p. 1990. lib. bdg. 250.00 (*0-226-85309-8*) U Ch Pr.

Message see Message

Message see Poslanie

Message. K. A. Applegate. (Animorphs Ser.: No. 4). 151p. (J). (gr. 4-7). 1996. pap. text 4.99 (*0-590-62980-8*) Scholastic Inc.

***Message.** K. A. Applegate. (Animorphs Ser.: No. 4). (J). (gr. 3-7). 1999. pap. text 4.99 (*0-439-08783-X*) Scholastic Inc.

Message. K. A. Applegate. (Animorphs Ser.: No. 4).Tr. of Message. (FRE.). (J). (gr. 3-7). 1996. 9.09 (*0-606-10126-8*, Pub. by Turtleback) Demco.

***Message.** K. A. Applegate. (Animorphs Ser.: Vol. 39). (Illus.). (J). 2000. 10.34 (*0-606-18510-0*) Turtleback.

Message. Paula Bonnell. 64p. 1999. 20.00 (*1-928668-04-6*) MillCreek Pr.

Message: Furoogh-i-Abadiyat. rev. ed. Jafar Subhani. Tr. by Islamic Seminary Staff & M. Fazal Haq from PER. 783p. 1991. reprint ed. text 22.00 (*0-941724-38-7*) Islamic Seminary.

Message: New Testament Psalms & Proverbs. Eugene H. Peterson. LC 98-35685. 1998. 22.99 (*1-57683-119-1*); pap. 16.99 (*1-57683-120-5*) NavPress.

Message: New Testament with Psalms & Proverbs in Contemporary Language. Eugene H. Peterson. LC 97-194187. 528p. 1997. lthr. 22.00 (*1-57683-022-5*) NavPress.

Message: Old Testament Wisdom Books. 1998. pap. text 14.99 (*1-57683-126-4*) NavPress.

Message: The New Testament in Contemporary Language. Ed. by Eugene H. Peterson. LC 98-10518. 544p. 1998. pap. 5.00 (*1-57683-102-7*) NavPress.

Message & Existence: An Introduction to Christian Theology. Langdon Gilkey. 272p. 1984. 20.00 (*0-8164-0450-X*) Harper SF.

Message & Meaning: An Introduction to Linguistics. Judith I. Schwartz. 1984. pap., teacher ed. 5.00 (*0-89824-090-5*); pap., student ed. 4.00 (*0-89824-091-3*) Trillium Pr.

Message & Ministry of Jesus: An Introductory Textbook. David A. Fiensy. LC 96-34221. 352p. 1996. pap. text 34.00 (*0-7618-0506-0*) U Pr of Amer.

Message & Ministry of Jesus: An Introductory Textbook. David A. Fiensy. LC 96-34221. 352p. 1996. lib. bdg. 57.00 (*0-7618-0505-2*) U Pr of Amer.

Message & Mission of Friends. Seth B. Hinshaw. 19p. (Orig.). 1985. reprint ed. pap. 1.50 (*0-942727-02-9*) NC Yrly Pubns Bd.

Message & Missions: The Communication of the Christian Faith. rev. ed. Eugene A. Nida. LC 60-11785. (Illus.). 315p. 1990. pap. text 10.95 (*0-87808-756-7*, WCL756-7) William Carey Lib.

Message & sa Fiction: La Communication par Messager dans la Litterature Francaise Des XII, Vol. 128. Jacques Merceron. (FRE.). 416p. 1998. pap. 45.00 (*0-520-09822-6*, Pub. by U CA Pr) Cal Prin Full Svc.

Message & the Kingdom: How Jesus & Paul Ignited a Revolution & Transformed the Ancient World. Richard A. Horsley & Neil A. Silberman. LC 97-16218. (Illus.). 304p. 1997. 27.50 (*0-399-14194-4*, Grosset-Putnam) Putnam Pub Group.

Message & the Work. John T. Ferrier. 16p. 1931. pap. text 5.00 (*0-900235-02-0*) Order Of The Cross.

Message Bearer: Poetry-Prose-Photography. Beverly J. Gensamer. (Illus.). 133p. 1998. pap. 12.95 (*1-890050-21-0*) Carlisle Press.

Message Effects in Communication Science. Ed. by James J. Bradac. LC 89-5928. (Sage Annual Reviews of Communication Research Ser.: Vol. 17). 320p. 1989. reprint ed. pap. 99.20 (*0-608-02766-9*, 206383200007) Bks Demand.

Message Effects in Communication Science: Contemporary Approaches. Ed. by James J. Bradac. (Annual Reviews of Communication Research Ser.: Vol. 17). 320p. (C). 1989. text 58.00 (*0-8039-3224-3*); pap. text 26.00 (*0-8039-3225-1*) Sage.

Message Effects Research: Principles of Design & Analysis. Sally Jackson. LC 92-11714. (Communication Ser.). 184p. 1992. lib. bdg. 35.00 (*0-89862-316-2*) Guilford Pubns.

Message for Abby: Patton's Daughters. Janice K. Johnson. (Superromance Ser.: No. 866). 1999. per. 4.25 (*0-373-70866-1*, 1-70866-8) Harlequin Bks.

Message for All in a World So Small. Richard Quisenberry. 42p. 1997. 8.00 (*1-885092-01-6*) Forging Pathways.

Message for General Washington. Vivian Schurfranz. LC 98-15800. (Stories of the States Ser.: Vol. 10). (Illus.). 92p. (J). (gr. 4-7). 1998. lib. bdg. 14.95 (*1-881889-89-0*) Silver Moon.

Message for Michael. Susie Whiting. pap. 6.95 (*1-55517-397-7*) CFI Dist.

Message for the Millennium. Karyn Martin-Kuri. 320p. 1996. 20.00 (*0-345-39522-0*) Ballantine Pub Grp.

Message for the President. rev. ed. Irvin Baxter, Jr. LC 94-66846. 165p. (Orig.). 1994. reprint ed. pap. 12.50 (*0-941559-02-5*) Endtime Pub.

Message for the Sultan - 16th Century Ottoman Turkey: World History Unit for the Middle Grades. rev. ed. Lyn Reese. Ed. by Mary A. Dougherty & Jean B. Wilkinson. (Illus.). 45p. (YA). (gr. 6-9). 1994. spiral bd. 10.00 (*1-890380-03-2*) Wom Wrld Hist.

Message for You see Mensaje para Ti

Message from Absalom. large type ed. Anne A. Thompson. 1977. 27.99 (*0-7089-0016-X*) Ulverscroft.

Message from Avalon. Jenny Wagner. LC 95-119205. 1994. pap. 12.95 (*0-7022-2741-2*, Pub. by Univ Queensland Pr) Intl Spec Bk.

Message from Cupid. Victoria Barrett. 1998. mass mkt. 5.99 (*0-312-96483-8*) St Martin.

Message from Elvis Presley. Harry McKinzie. pap. 16.95 (*0-86626-004-8*) AAIMS Pubs.

Message from Forever: A Novel of Aboriginal Wisdom. Marlo Morgan. LC 98-19903. 288p. 1998. 24.00 (*0-06-019107-4*, Cliff Street) HarperTrade.

***Message from Forever: Rosenblat,&Barbara, Set.** abr. ed. Marlo Morgan. 1998. audio 18.00 (*0-694-51961-8*) HarperAudio.

Message from God & Other Poems. Garry De Young. 1988. pap. 10.00 (*0-936128-21-6*) De Young Pr.

Message from God in the Atomic Age: A Memoir. Irene Vilar. Tr. by Gregory Rabassa from SPA. (Illus.). 336p. 1996. 24.00 (*0-679-42281-1*) Pantheon.

***Message from Heaven: The Life & Crimes of Fr. Sean Fortune.** Allison O'Connor. 224p. 2000. 19.95 (*0-86322-270-6*, Pub. by Brandon Bk Pubs) Irish Bks Media.

Message from Hong Kong. Mignon G. Eberhart. 160p. 1989. mass mkt. 3.95 (*0-88184-505-1*) Carroll & Graf.

Message from Nam. Danielle Steel. 432p. 1991. mass mkt. 6.99 (*0-440-20941-2*) Dell.

Message from Nam. large type ed. Danielle Steel. 408p. 1990. 21.95 (*0-385-29907-9*, Delacorte LT) BDD LT Grp.

Message from Nam. large type ed. Danielle Steel. LC 93-24732. 1993. pap. 19.95 (*0-8161-5794-4*, G K Hall Lrg Type) Mac Lib Ref.

Message from Nam. limited ed. Danielle Steel. 408p. 1990. 125.00 (*0-385-30137-5*) Delacorte.

Message from Outer Space. Penn Mullin. Ed. by Betty Lou Kratoville. (Meridian Bks.). (Illus.). 64p. (J). (gr. 3-9). 1989. lib. bdg. 4.95 (*0-87879-616-9*) High Noon Bks.

Message from Sam: A Story of Love, Loss & Life Beyond Grief. Nancy K. Schriefer. (Illus.). 96p. 1996. pap. 9.95 (*0-9651274-7-8*) Escape Key Pr.

Message from the Blueberries & Other Poems. Margery V. Carlson. (Illus.). 144p. 1999. pap. write for info. (*0-9670922-0-5*) GA Poetry Socy.

Message from the Future. Catherine M. iv, 187p. 1997. pap. 14.99 (*0-9660558-0-2*) Theuism.

Message from the King's Coffer. Ronald Temple. 157p. 1996. reprint ed. spiral bd. 13.50 (*0-7873-0860-9*) Hlth Research.

Message from the King's Coffer, 1920. Ronald Temple. 158p. 1996. reprint ed. pap. 12.50 (*1-56459-961-2*) Kessinger Pub.

Message from the Living God to This Nation. William H. Toel. LC 91-92843. 110p. 1991. write for info. (*0-9623490-3-8*) ICA Pr.

Message from the Masters. Hulda Zusli. 284p. 1996. pap. 15.95 (*0-614-19368-0*) HyperBook.

Message from the Match Girl. Janet T. Lisle. 128p. 1997. pap. 3.99 (*0-380-72518-5*, Avon Bks) Morrow Avon.

Message from the Match Girl. Janet T. Lisle. LC 95-6036. (Investigators of the Unknown Ser.: Bk. 3). (Illus.). 128p. (J). (gr. 4-6). 1996. 15.95 (*0-531-09487-1*); lib. bdg. 16.99 (*0-531-08787-5*) Orchard Bks Watts.

Message from the Match Girl. Janet Taylor Lisle. (Investigators of the Unknown Ser.). 1997. 9.09 (*0-606-11621-4*, Pub. by Turtleback) Demco.

Message from the President of the United States Transmitting a Letter from the Judge of the Juvenile Court of the District of Columbia: A Report Covering the Work of the Juvenile Court During the Period from July 1, 1906 to June 30, 1926. U. S. Senate, Juvenile Court of the District of Co. LC 73-11937. (Metropolitan America Ser.). 174p. 1974. reprint ed. 19.95 (*0-405-05431-9*) Ayer.

Message from the Ruins. Stacey Sollfrey et al. Ed. by Joseph A. Uphoff, Jr. (Illus.). 74p. 1989. pap. text 4.00 (*0-943123-13-5*) Arjuna Lib Pr.

Message from the Stars. Mary M. Wunder. LC 92-75642. 176p. 1993. pap. 11.95 (*1-881852-04-0*) Horus Hse Pr.

Message from the Wind. David Ho. 16p. (Orig.). 1996. pap. write for info. (*1-883331-21-8*) Anderie Poetry.

Message in a Bottle. Jenny Koralek. 1997. 16.95 (*0-7188-2655-8*, Lutterworth-Parkwest) Parkwest Pubns.

Message in a Bottle. Nicholas Sparks. LC 97-39158. 336p. 1998. 20.00 (*0-446-52356-9*, Pub. by Warner Bks) Little.

Message in a Bottle. Nicholas Sparks. 384p. 1999. mass mkt. 6.99 (*0-446-60681-2*, Pub. by Warner Bks) Little.

Message in a Bottle. large type ed. Nicholas Sparks. LC 98-5564. 1998. 28.95 (*0-7862-1422-8*) Thorndike Pr.

Message in a Bottle. large type ed. Nicholas Sparks. LC 98-5564. 464p. 1999. pap. 26.95 (*0-7862-1423-6*) Thorndike Pr.

***Message in a Bottle.** Nicholas Sparks. 352p. 1999. reprint ed. mass mkt. 12.00 (*0-446-67607-1*, Pub. by Warner Bks) Little.

Message in a Bottle: Stories of Men & Addiction. Jefferson A. Singer. LC 97-35601. 256p. 1997. 24.50 (*0-684-82720-4*) Free Pr.

Message in a Bottle: Stories of Men & Addiction. Jefferson A. Singer. 1997. 32.95 (*0-02-874008-4*) Macmillan.

Message in a Box Series, Vol. 1. 96p. 1996. otabind 19.95 (*0-7935-3767-3*, 00694963) H Leonard.

Message in a Box Series, Vol. 2. 80p. 1996. otabind 19.95 (*0-7935-3768-1*, 00694964) H Leonard.

Message in a Box Series, Vol. 3. 72p. 1996. otabind 19.95 (*0-7935-3769-X*, 00694965) H Leonard.

Message in a Box Series, Vol. 4. 72p. 1996. otabind 19.95 (*0-7935-3770-3*, 00694966) H Leonard.

Message in a Minute: Lighthearted Minidramas for Churches. William D. Wolfe & Sheryl J. Anderson. LC 92-5618. 104p. (Orig.). 1992. pap. 12.00 (*0-8170-1181-1*) Judson.

Message in a Minute Vol. 2: More Lighthearted Minidramas for Churches. William D. Wolfe & Sheryl J. Anderson. 1998. pap. 12.00 (*0-8170-1279-6*) Judson.

Message in the Bottle. Walker Percy. LC 75-5846. 262p. 1975. pap. 14.00 (*0-374-51338-4*) FS&G.

***Message in the Bottle: How Queen Man Is, How Queer Language Is, & What One Has to Do with the Other.** Walker Percy. LC 99-89027. 272p. 2000. pap. 14.00 (*0-312-25401-6*, Picador USA) St Martin.

Message in the Hollow Oak. Carolyn Keene. LC 78-181844. (Nancy Drew Mystery Stories Ser.: No. 12). (Illus.). 196p. (J). (gr. 4-7). 1935. 5.95 (*0-448-09512-2*, G & D) Peng Put Young Read.

Message in the Hollow Oak. fac. ed. Carolyn Keene. LC 98-56442. (Nancy Drew Mystery Stories Ser.: No. 12). (Illus.). 210p. (J). (gr. 2-5). 1999. pap. 14.95 (*1-55709-258-3*, Pub. by Applewood) Consort Bk Sales.

Message in the Mirror. Ed. by Mary E. Peterson. (Illus.). 80p. (Orig.). 1983. pap. 4.70 (*0-912701-00-5*) Balance Beam Pr.

Message in the Wind. Ed. & Illus. by Alethea Adams-Wells. LC 95-90233. 304p. 1995. 25.00 (*0-9645787-0-0*) Unole Pub.

Message in Your Emotions: Tracing Emotional Pain to Victorious Living. Wayne McDill. 272p. 1996. pap. 11.99 (*0-8054-6275-9*, 4262-75) Broadman.

Message Is the Medium: Online All the Time for Everyone. Tom Koch. LC 95-53001. 240p. 1996. 45.00 (*0-275-95549-4*, Praeger Pubs) Greenwood.

Message Measurement Inventory: A Profile for Communication Analysis. Raymond G. Smith. LC 77-17677. 235p. reprint ed. pap. 72.90 (*0-608-17057-7*, 205624100056) Bks Demand.

Message of "A Course in Miracles" Vol. I: All Are Called; Vol. II: Few Choose to Listen. Kenneth Wapnick. LC 97-16732. 619p. 1997. pap. 22.00 (*0-933291-25-6*) Foun Miracles.

Message of a Master: A Classic Tale of Wealth, Wisdom, & the Secret of Success. John McDonald. Ed. by Katherine Dieter & Marc Allen. LC 91-38486. 96p. 1993. reprint ed. pap. 8.95 (*0-931432-95-2*) New Wrld Lib.

Message of Acts: The Spirit, the Church & the World see Bible Speaks Today Series

Message of Acts in the History of Redemption. Dennis E. Johnson. LC 96-48100. 256p. (Orig.). 1997. pap. 16.99 (*0-87552-235-1*) P & R Pubng.

Message of Amos see Bible Speaks Today Series

Message of Aquaria. Harriette A. Curtiss & F. Homer Curtiss. 487p. 1981. pap. 38.00 (*0-89540-065-0*, SB-065) Sun Pub.

Message of Astrology. Peter Roberts. 1990. pap. 12.95 (*0-85030-823-2*, Pub. by Aqm Pr) Harper SF.

Message of Chronicles see Bible Speaks Today Series

Message of Colossians & Philemon see Bible Speaks Today Series

Message of Colossians & Philemon. David K. Bernard. LC 90-37051. (Illus.). 186p. (Orig.). 1990. pap. 8.99 (*0-932581-70-6*) Word Aflame.

Message of Daniel see Bible Speaks Today Series

Message of Deuteronomy: Not by Bread Alone see Bible Speaks Today Series

Message of Ecclesiastes see Bible Speaks Today Series

Message of Ecology. Charles J. Krebs. 195p. (C). 1997. pap. 59.00 (*0-06-043773-1*) Addson-Wesley Educ.

Message of Ephesians see Bible Speaks Today Series

Message of Ezekiel. John T. Ferrier. 308p. 1931. text 14.00 (*0-900235-10-1*) Order Of The Cross.

Message of Faith. Jerry R. Flora. 170p. (Orig.). 1996. pap. 9.99 (*0-614-29647-1*) Brethren Church.

Message of Faith & Symbol in European Medieval Bronze Church Doors. Jadwiga I. Daniec. (Illus.). 192p. 1998. pap. 17.95 (*1-887750-95-9*) Rutledge Bks.

Message of Film 5. Michael Scully. (Jesus in the Media Ser.). 165p. 1997. teacher ed., spiral bd. 21.95 (*0-937997-40-4*) Hi-Time Pflaum.

Message of Film 6. Michael Scully. (Jesus in the Media Ser.: No. 6). 174p. 1998. teacher ed., spiral bd. 21.95 (*0-937997-44-7*) Hi-Time Pflaum.

Message of 1 & 2 Thessalonians: The Gospel & the End of Time see Bible Speaks Today Series

Message of 1 Corinthians see Bible Speaks Today Series

Message of 1 Peter: The Way of the Cross see Bible Speaks Today Series

Message of Galatians see Bible Speaks Today Series

Message of Genesis 1-11 see Bible Speaks Today Series

Message of Genesis 12-50: From Abraham to Joseph see Bible Speaks Today Series

Message of Hebrews see Bible Speaks Today Series

Message of Hope: For Surviving the Tragedy of Suicide. Patricia Harness-Overley. 144p. (Orig.). 1992. pap. 12.95 (*0-9634571-0-1*) Bradley Pr.

Message of Hosea see Bible Speaks Today Series

Message of Isaiah see Bible Speaks Today Series

Message of Isaiah. John T. Ferrier. 470p. 1934. text 17.00 (*0-900235-11-X*) Order Of The Cross.

Message of Islam. Abdullah Y. Ali. 127p. 1990. 7.95 (*81-7151-031-0*) Asia Bk Corp.

Message of James see Bible Speaks Today Series

Message of Jeremiah see Bible Speaks Today Series

Message of Jesus Christ. Mohandas Karamchand Gandhi. Ed. by A. T. Hingorani. 64p. (Orig.). 1980. pap. 1.50 (*0-934676-20-8*) Greenlf Bks.

Message of Job: Suffering & Grace see Bible Speaks Today Series

Message of Joel, Micah & Habakkuk. David Prior. LC 98-54078. (Bible Speaks Today Ser.). (Illus.). 279p. 1999. pap. 14.99 (*0-8308-1241-5*, 1241) InterVarsity.

Message of John: Here Is Your King! see Bible Speaks Today Series

Message of John's Letters see Bible Speaks Today Series

***Message of Jonah.** Terence E. Fretheim. 142p. 2000. pap. 16.00 (*1-57910-345-6*) Wipf & Stock.

Message of Judges: Grace Abounding see Bible Speaks Today Series

Message of Life: Studies in the Epistle of St. John (Missionary Message of the New Testament) J. Ireland Hasler. 96p. 1949. 4.50 (*0-87921-013-3*) Attic Pr.

Message of Luke see Bible Speaks Today Series

Message of Mark see Bible Speaks Today Series

Message of Matthew: An Annotated Parallel Aramaic-English Gospel of Matthew. Rocco A. Errico. 288p. 1991. pap. 24.95 (*0-9631292-0-1*) Noohra Found.

Message of Medjugorje: The Marian Message to the Modern World. Mark I. Miravalle. LC 86-1588. 168p. 1986. pap. 19.50 (*0-8191-5289-7*) U Pr of Amer.

Message of Nehemiah. Raymond E. Brown. LC 98-26065. (Bible Speaks Today Ser.). 256p. 1998. pap. 14.99 (*0-8308-1242-3*, 1242) InterVarsity.

Message of Our Master. Ramakrishna's Disciples Staff. 1936. pap. 1.95 (*0-87481-102-3*) Vedanta Pr.

Message of Philippians see Bible Speaks Today Series

Message of Philippians see Mensaje de Filipenses

M

An Asterisk (*) at the beginning of an entry indicates that the title is appearing for the first time.

Message of Philo Judaeus of Alexandria. Kenneth S. Guthrie. 96p. 1992. reprint ed. pap. 14.95 (*1-56459-030-5*) Kessinger Pub.

Message of Proverbs see Bible Speaks Today Series

Message of Revelation see Bible Speaks Today Series

Message of Rock, Vol. 9. Michael Scully. (Jesus in Modern Media Ser.). 136p. 1998. teacher ed., spiral bd. 18.95 (*0-937997-46-3*) Hi-Time Pflaum.

Message of Rock, 1997. Michael Scully. (Jesus in Modern Media Ser.). 129p. 1997. teacher ed., spiral bd. 18.95 (*0-937997-42-0*) Hi-Time Pflaum.

Message of Romans. David K. Bernard. LC 87-14747. (Illus.). 340p. (Orig.). 1987. pap. 9.99 (*0-932581-18-8*) Word Aflame.

Message of Ruth see Bible Speaks Today Series

Message of St. Francis. Sister Nan. 60p. 1999. 16.95 (*0-670-88364-6*, Viking) Viking Penguin.

Message of St. John: The Spiritual Teachings of the Beloved Disciple. Thomas E. Crane. LC 80-11779. 184p. 1980. pap. 5.95 (*0-8189-0402-X*) Alba.

Message of Saint Rita of Cascia. Agostino Trape. Ed. by John E. Rotelle. Tr. by Maria Di Blasi from ITA. LC 88-71356. (Augustinian Ser.). (Illus.). 160p. 1989. pap. 8.50 (*0-941491-16-1*) Augustinian Pr.

Message of 2 Corinthians: Power in Weakness see Bible Speaks Today Series

Message of 2 Peter & Jude see Bible Speaks Today Series

Message of 2 Timothy see Bible Speaks Today Series

Message of Social Psychology: Perspectives on Mind in Society. Ed. by Craig McGarty & S. Alexander Haslan. LC 96-16494. 368p. 1996. 66.95 (*0-631-19779-6*); pap. 28.95 (*0-631-19781-8*) Blackwell Pubs.

Message of Sphinx. Hancock Bauvel. 1997. mass mkt. 18.95 (*0-385-25675-2*) Doubleday.

Message of Sphinx. Hancock & Bauvel. (Illus.). 32p. 1997. mass mkt. write for info. (*0-385-25677-9*) Doubleday.

Message of St. Francis with Frescoes from the Basilica of St. Francis of Assisi. Frances Lincoln. 60p. 1999. 16.95 (*0-7112-1317-8*) F Lincoln.

Message of the Atoms: Wolfgang Pauli & the Unspeakable. Kalervo V. Laurikainen. LC 96-43199. (Illus.). 216p. 1997. 49.00 (*3-540-61754-X*) Spr-Verlag.

Message of the Bible: An Orthodox Christian Perspective. George Cronk. LC 82-7355. 293p. (Orig.). 1982. pap. 11.95 (*0-913836-94-X*) St Vladimirs.

Message of the Book of Revelation. Charles T. Chapman. 152p. (Orig.). 1994. pap. 11.95 (*0-8146-2111-2*) Liturgical Pr.

Message of the Cross. Stephen Wynacht. 48p. (Orig.). 1995. pap. 2.95 (*0-9633111-3-1*) S Wynacht Minist.

Message of the Gita. Ed. by Anilbaran Roy. 311p. 1985. 15.95 (*0-318-37180-4*) Asia Bk Corp.

Message of the Gita. 5th ed. Ed. by Anilbaran Roy. 306p. 1993. pap. 10.95 (*81-7058-305-5*, Pub. by SAA) E-W Cultural Ctr.

Message of the Gita: With Text, Translation & Notes. Sri Aurobindo. Ed. by Anilbaran Roy. (ENG & SAN.). 1979. pap. 12.95 (*0-89744-977-0*, Pub. by Sri Aurob Ashram Trust) Acrpls Bks CO.

***Message of the Hands: Understanding the Principles of Palmistry.** Peter West. 2000. pap. 10.95 (*1-902809-28-9*) Allison & Busby.

Message of the Land: From Egypt to Calvary. Philip Gehlhar & David Manz. LC 95-232867. (Illus.). 244p. 1995. pap. 11.95 (*1-883893-12-7*) WinePress Pub.

Message of the Locust. Richard Marcum & Reyburn W. Myers. 200p. 1988. 17.95 (*0-940375-06-0*) WindRiver Pub.

Message of the Lord's Prayer. Igor I. Sikorsky. 1963. 10.95 (*0-8392-1068-X*) Astor-Honor.

***Message Of The Markets: How Financial Markets Foretell the Future- And How You Can Profit From Their Guidance.** Ron Insana. 288p. 2000. 25.00 (*0-06-662045-7*) HarpC.

Message of the Masters. Robert J. Scrutton. 280p. pap. 19.95 (*0-8464-4254-X*) Beekman Pubs.

Message of the Masters. Robert J. Scrutton. 123p. 1982. 12.95 (*0-85978-091-0*, Pub. by C W Daniel) Natl Bk Netwk.

Message of the Mind in Neo-Confucian Thought. William T. Debary. (Neo-Confucian Studies). (Illus.). 292p. 1988. text 64.50 (*0-231-06808-5*) Col U Pr.

Message of the Minor Prophets. 2nd ed. Ansley F. Rash. 48p. 1989. reprint ed. pap. 4.00 (*0-934666-30-X*) Artisan Pubs.

Message of the New Testament. F. F. Bruce. 120p. 1973. pap. 8.00 (*0-8028-1525-1*) Eerdmans.

Message of the New Testament: Revelations, 2 vols., 176. Frank Pack. (Way of Life Ser.: Nos. 176 & 177). 1984. pap. 6.95 (*0-89112-176-5*) Abilene Christ U.

Message of the New Testament: Revelations, 2 vols., 177. Frank Pack. (Way of Life Ser.: Nos. 176 & 177). 1984. pap. 6.95 (*0-89112-177-3*) Abilene Christ U.

Message of the Old Testament. H. L. Ellison. (Biblical Classics Library: Vol. 3). 94p. 1994. reprint ed. mass mkt. 5.99 (*0-85364-606-6*, Pub. by Paternoster Pub) OM Literature.

Message of the Old Testament, Vol. IV, No. 144. John T. Willis. (Way of Life Ser.). 1977. 6.95 (*0-89112-144-7*) Abilene Christ U.

Message of the Psalms: A Theological Commentary. Walter Brueggemann. LC 84-21734. (Augsburg Old Testament Studies). 208p. (Orig.). 1984. pap. 15.99 (*0-8066-2120-6*, 10-4370, Augsburg) Augsburg Fortress.

Message of the Psalter: An Eschatological Programme in the Book of Psalms. David C. Mitchell. LC 97-206293. (JSOT Supplement Ser.: No. 252). 428p. 1997. 85.00 (*1-85075-689-9*, Pub. by Sheffield Acad) CUP Services.

Message of the Quran. Muhammad Asad. 1000p. (Orig.). 1996. 55.00 (*0-614-21062-3*, 779) Kazi Pubns.

Message of the Quran. Muhammad Asad. 998p. (Orig.). 1980. 49.95 (*0-317-52456-9*) New Era Publns MI.

Message of the Scrolls. Yigael Yadin. 1969. pap. 3.95 (*0-671-20420-3*, Touchstone) S&S Trade Pap.

Message of the Scrolls. Yigael Yadin. (Christian Origins Library). 192p. 1991. pap. 16.95 (*0-8245-1142-5*) Crossroad NY.

Message of the Sermon on the Mount see Bible Speaks Today Series

Message of the Song of Songs see Bible Speaks Today Series

Message of the Sphinx. Hancock. Date not set. 34.95 (*0-385-25592-6*) Doubleday.

Message of the Sphinx. G. Hancock & R. Bauval. LC 97-186931. 1997. pap. 16.00 (*0-517-88852-1*, Crown) Crown Pub Group.

Message of the Sphinx. Graham Hancock & Robert Bauval. 1996. 27.50 (*0-614-96817-8*, Crown) Crown Pub Group.

Message of the Sunday Gospel Readings, Vol. 1. Anthony M. Coniaris. 1982. pap. 15.95 (*0-937032-26-3*) Light&Life Pub Co MN.

Message of the Sunday Gospels, Vol. 2. Anthony M. Coniaris. 1983. pap. 15.95 (*0-937032-29-8*) Light&Life Pub Co MN.

Message of the Wesleys: A Reader of Instruction & Devotion. John Wesley. Ed. by Philip S. Watson. 270p. (C). 1984. reprint ed. pap. 5.95 (*0-310-75031-8*, 17027P) Zondervan.

Message of Thomas Merton. Ed. by Patrick Hart. (Cistercian Studies: No. 42). (Illus.). 1981. pap. 8.95 (*0-87907-942-8*) Cistercian Pubns.

***Message Old Testament Prophets.** Eugene H. Peterson. 2000. 21.00 (*1-57683-195-7*) NavPress.

Message-Passing Concurrent Computers: Their Architecture & Programming. Charles L. Seitz et al. 236p. (C). 1991. text 29.95 (*0-201-06612-2*) Addison-Wesley.

Message Preparation: Analysis & Structure see Putting a Message Together

Message Production: Advances in Communication Theory. Ed. by John O. Greene. LC 97-17200. (Communication Ser.). 330p. 1997. pap. 37.50 (*0-8058-2324-7*); text 69.95 (*0-8058-2323-9*) L Erlbaum Assocs.

Message Promise Book. Eugene H. Peterson. LC 97-194439. 144p. (Orig.). 1997. pap. 5.00 (*1-57683-015-2*) NavPress.

***Message, Sermon Notes & Lord, Speak to Me.** Zondervan Bible Publishers Staff. 48p. (C). 1999. write for info. (*0-9674725-3-9*) Ortriz.

Message That Was Late: Japan's Declaration of War. Ed. by Douglass Hubbard. (Illus.). 12p. 1991. pap. 2.50 (*0-915266-22-9*) Awani Pr.

Message, the Mess, the Mileage. Nolan T. Pitts. LC 94-77544. 96p. (Orig.). 1994. pap. 5.95 (*1-883928-08-7*) Longwood.

Message to a Black Man. Alfredo D. Noble. 52p. (Orig.). (C). 1992. pap. 5.95 (*0-9622849-2-0*) Papito.

***Message to a Black Man.** rev. ed. Ed. by Chris Boolware & Jean E. Noble. (Illus.). 81p. 1999. pap. 9.95 (*1-887653-12-0*) Papito.

Message to a Black Woman. Alfredo D. Noble. Ed. by Victoria Patterson & Chris Boulware. 80p. 1998. pap. 8.95 (*0-9622849-7-1*) Papito.

Message to Adam's Children: The Book of Enoch. Intro. by George S. Lewis. (Orig.). 1990. pap. 12.95 (*0-937771-17-1*); text 18.95 (*0-937771-16-3*) Spencers Intl.

Message to America. Don Pendleton. (Stony Man Ser.). 1998. per. 5.99 (*0-373-61919-7*, 1-61919-6, Wrldwide Lib) Harlequin Bks.

Message to Garcia. Elbert Hubbard. 1976. 20.95 (*0-8488-0697-2*) Amereon Ltd.

Message to Garcia. Elbert Hubbard. 1991. 10.00 (*0-936128-30-5*) De Young Pr.

Message to Garcia. Elbert Hubbard. 32p. 1977. 7.99 (*0-88088-434-7*) Peter Pauper.

Message to Garcia. Elbert Hubbard. 1991. lib. bdg. 250.00 (*0-87700-956-2*) Revisionist Pr.

Message to Garcia. Elbert Hubbard. 24p. 1998. reprint ed. pap. 1.95 (*0-7661-0434-6*) Kessinger Pub.

Message to Garcia: A Message to Garcia . . . Revisited. rev. ed. Elbert Hubbard & Alan Burton. 32p. 1987. reprint ed. pap. text 4.00 (*0-930993-08-X*) Dispatch.

Message to Garcia: Being a Preachment. Elbert Hubbard. LC 92-40294. 22p. 1993. 9.95 (*1-55709-200-1*) Applewood.

Message to Garcia & Other Essays. Elbert Hubbard. 50p. 1996. pap. 3.50 (*0-89540-305-6*, SB-305) Sun Pub.

Message to the Blackman in America. Elijah Muhammad. 356p. 25.00 (*1-56411-005-2*) Untd Bros & Sis.

Message to the Blackman in America. Elijah Muhammad. 392p. 1996. reprint ed. pap. 9.95 (*1-884855-14-8*) Secretarius.

***Message to the Blackman in America.** unabridged ed. 392p. 2000. reprint ed. 21.95 (*1-884855-32-6*) Secretarius.

Message to the Blackwoman: Nature Has Made You Beautiful but Allah Has Perfected It. Antar Shabazz. 70p. (Orig.). 1995. pap. 8.00 (*1-56411-091-5*) Untd Bros & Sis.

Message to the Children. Nicholas J. Cipriani. 78p. (Orig.). 1997. pap. 8.95 (*0-9653570-1-5*) N J Cipriani.

Message to the Incarcerated Blackman & Woman in America. Kevin X. Baker. 72p. (Orig.). 1997. pap. 7.00 (*1-56411-162-8*) Untd Bros & Sis.

Message to the Mother Church for 1900. Mary Baker Eddy. reprint ed. pap. 5.00 (*0-87952-055-8*) Writings of Mary Baker.

Message to the Mother Church for 1901. Mary Baker Eddy. reprint ed. pap. 5.00 (*0-87952-056-6*) Writings of Mary Baker.

Message to the Mother Church for 1902. Mary Baker Eddy. reprint ed. pap. 5.00 (*0-87952-057-4*) Writings of Mary Baker.

Message to the Nurse of Dreams: A Collection of Short Fiction. Lisa Sandlin. LC 97-343. (Hell Yes! Texas Women's Ser.). 192p. (Orig.). 1997. pap. 11.95 (*0-938317-27-X*) Cinco Puntos.

Message to the People: The Course of African Philosophy. Marcus Garvey. Ed. by Tony Martin. (New Marcus Garvey Library: No. 7). (Illus.). xxiv, 215p. 1986. text 22.95 (*0-912469-18-8*); pap. text 9.95 (*0-912469-19-6*) Majority Pr.

Message to the Planet. Iris Murdoch. 640p. 1991. pap. 12.95 (*0-14-012664-3*) Viking Penguin.

Message to the White Man & White Woman in America: Yakub & the Origins of White Supremacy. Dorothy B. Fardan. 182p. (Orig.). 1991. pap. 11.95 (*1-56411-001-X*) Untd Bros & Sis.

Message Understanding: Evaluation & Conference: Proceedings of the 3rd-6th DARPA Workshops. Ed. by ARPA Staff. 413p. (Orig.). (C). 1996. pap. text 40.00 (*1-55860-402-2*) Morgan Kaufmann.

Message Writer. Sara Gogol. LC 97-214659. 122p. (J). (gr. 5-6). 1996. pap. 9.99 (*0-88092-333-4*) Royal Fireworks.

Messages. (C). 1989. text. write for info. (*0-06-500010-2*) Addson-Wesley Educ.

Messages. Linda Curtis. 1998. pap. write for info. (*1-58235-019-1*) Watermrk Pr.

Messages. Lynda Stephenson. LC 97-174734. 112p. (Orig.). 1997. pap. 8.95 (*0-9656689-0-8*) Anna Miriam Pub.

Messages. 4th ed. DeVito. 416p. (C). 1999. 49.00 (*0-321-05562-4*) Addison-Wesley.

***Messages: Buildg Interpersonal Comm Skills.** 4th ed. (C). 1998. write for info. (*0-321-04086-4*) Addison-Wesley.

***Messages: Buildg Interpersonal Comm Skills.** 4th ed. (C). 1999. write for info. (*0-321-04087-2*); write for info. (*0-321-04089-9*); write for info. (*0-321-04090-2*); write for info. (*0-321-04091-0*); write for info. (*0-321-04817-2*) Addison-Wesley.

***Messages: Buildg Interpersonal Comm Skills.** 4th ed. (C). 1999. 67.00 (*0-321-04088-0*) Addison-Wesley.

Messages Building Interpersonal Communication Skills Joseph A. Devito. 416p. 2000. pap. 59.95 (*0-201-61409-X*) Addison-Wesley.

Messages: Building Interpersonal Communication Skills. 3rd ed. Harral. LC 95-6440. (C). 1995. write for info. (*0-673-97042-6*) Addson-Wesley Educ.

***Messages: Building Interpersonal Communication Skills.** 4th ed. (C). 1999. 67.00 (*0-321-04084-8*) Addison-Wesley.

***Messages: Building Interpersonal Communication Skills.** 4th ed. (C). 1999. text 159.33 (*0-321-04787-7*) Addson-Wesley Educ.

***Messages: Building Interpersonal Communication Skills.** 4th ed. (C). 1999. pap. 24.00 (*0-321-04082-1*) S&S Trade.

Messages: Building Interpersonal Communication Skills. 4th ed. Devito. 416p. (C). 1998. pap. text, student ed. 24.00 (*0-321-04083-X*) Addson-Wesley Educ.

***Messages: Building Interpersonal Communication Skills.** 4th ed. Joseph A. Devito. LC 98-29692. 448p. (C). 1998. pap. text 56.00 (*0-321-02509-1*) Addson-Wesley Educ.

Messages: New & Selected Poems. Luke Breit. 136p. 1989. pap. 8.95 (*0-936609-17-6*) QED Ft Bragg.

Messages: Poems from Hollywood. Mark Dunster. 20p. 1998. pap. 5.00 (*0-89642-448-0*) Linden Pubs.

Messages: The Communication Skills Book. 2nd ed. Matthew McKay et al. 320p. 1995. pap. 15.95 (*1-57224-022-9*) New Harbinger.

Messages & Conversations: Readings Composition 1. 1p. (C). 1996. pap. 27.00 (*0-536-59594-1*) Pearson Custom.

Messages & Letters of William Henry Harrison, 2 vols., Set. William H. Harrison. Ed. by Logan Esarey. LC 75-99. (Mid-American Frontier Ser.). 1975. reprint ed. 132.95 (*0-405-06865-4*) Ayer.

Messages & Letters of William Henry Harrison, 2 vols., Vol. 1. William H. Harrison. Ed. by Logan Esarey. LC 75-99. (Mid-American Frontier Ser.). 1975. reprint ed. 65.95 (*0-405-06866-2*) Ayer.

Messages & Letters of William Henry Harrison, 2 vols., Vol. 2. William H. Harrison. Ed. by Logan Esarey. LC 75-99. (Mid-American Frontier Ser.). 1975. reprint ed. 65.95 (*0-405-06867-0*) Ayer.

Messages & Meanings: LAILA - ALILA 12th International Symposium on Latin American Indian Literatures. Ed. by Mary H. Preuss. LC 96-78911. (Illus.). 224p. (Orig.). (C). 1997. pap. 32.00 (*0-911437-78-9*) Labyrinthos.

***Messages & Miracles: Extraordinary Experiences of the Bereaved.** Louis E. LaGrand. LC 99-33212. (Illus.). 336p. 1999. pap. 12.95 (*1-56718-406-5*) Llewellyn Pubns.

Messages & Papers of David Wallace, 1837-1840. Ed. by Dorothy L. Riker. 501p. 1963. 8.25 (*1-885323-20-4*) IN Hist Bureau.

Messages & Papers of Jefferson Davis & the Confederacy, 2 vols., Set. Jefferson Davis. (American Biography Ser.). 1991. reprint ed. lib. bdg. 180.00 (*0-7812-8099-0*) Rprt Serv.

Messages & Papers of Samuel Bigger, 1840-1843. Ed. by Gayle Thornbrough. 669p. 1964. 8.25 (*1-885323-21-2*) IN Hist Bureau.

Messages & Papers Relating to the Administration of James Brown Ray, Governor of Indiana, 1825-1831. Ed. by Dorothy L. Riker. 1954. 8.25 (*1-885323-13-1*) IN Hist Bureau.

Messages & Papers Relating to the Administration of Noah Noble, Governor of Indiana, 1831-1837. Ed. by Dorothy L. Riker. 1958. 6.25 (*1-885323-15-8*) IN Hist Bureau.

Messages & Proclamations of the Governors of Iowa, 7 vols. Compiled by Benjamin F. Shambaugh. LC 74-19616. reprint ed. 475.00 (*0-404-12431-3*) AMS Pr.

Messages for New Believers. (Orthodoxy of the Church Ser.). 952p. 1997. per. 34.75 (*0-87083-813-X*) Living Stream Ministry.

Messages for the Heart: Selected Readings from the Message. Eugene H. Peterson. 1997. pap. 12.00 incl. audio (*1-57683-038-1*) NavPress.

Messages 4: The Washington Post Media Companion. 4th ed. Thomas Beell & Washington Post Writers Staff. 333p. 1996. pap. text 23.00 (*0-205-26559-6*) Allyn.

Messages from a Doctor in the Fourth Dimension. Karl Nowotny. 128p. (C). 1990. 50.00 (*0-7212-0895-9*, Pub. by Regency Pr GBR) St Mut.

Messages from an Owl. Max R. Terman. 230p. 1996. pap. text 14.95 (*0-691-04822-3*, Pub. by Princeton U Pr) Cal Prin Full Svc.

Messages from an Owl. Max R. Terman. LC 95-31091. (Illus.). 208p. 1996. text 24.95 (*0-691-01105-2*, Pub. by Princeton U Pr) Cal Prin Full Svc.

***Messages from Ariel.** Marilyn J. Estenes. 118p. 1999. pap. 12.95 (*0-7392-0409-2*, PO3656) Morris Pubng.

***Messages from Beyond: Spirit-Side Communications after the Passing of the Author's Wife.** James P. R. Mason. Vol. 2. 534p. (Orig.). 1999. pap. 19.95 (*0-9699882-1-4*) Alma Bks.

Messages from Beyond: Spirit-Side Communications after the Passing of the Author's Wife. unabridged ed. James P. R. Mason. 479p. (Orig.). 1995. pap. 19.95 (*0-9699882-0-6*, Pub. by Alma Bks) Koen Bk Distributors.

***Messages from Christ to the People of Prayer.** Lillian F. Clemens. 2001. pap. 14.95 (*1-57733-053-6*) B Dolphin Pub.

Messages from Earth: Nature & the Human Prospect in Alaska. Robert B. Weeden. LC 91-43178. (Illus.). xiv, 189p. 1992. pap. 16.95 (*0-912006-56-0*) U of Alaska Pr.

***Messages from Frank's Landing: A Story of Salmon, Treaties & the Indian Way.** Charles Wilkinson. (Illus.). 128p. 2000. 22.50 (*0-295-98011-7*) U of Wash Pr.

Messages from God: 365 Simple Truths for Success. Lynn S. Marks. (Illus.). 231p. 1999. 14.95 (*1-888783-31-1*) Golden Halo Prodns.

Messages from God to the World: Of the Third Kind. Joe S. (Illus.). 57p. (Orig.). 1991. pap. write for info. (*1-880998-02-5*) State Art OH.

***Messages from Heaven: Amazing Insights on Life After Death, Life's Purpose & Earth's Future.** Patricia Kirmond. 1999. pap. text 12.95 (*0-922729-44-1*) Summit Univ.

Messages from Heaven: Be a Shining Star. Pamela J. Dlugos. (Illus.). 64p. (J). (gr. 4-6). Date not set. pap. 10.95 (*0-9661564-0-4*) Rejoyce Pubns.

Messages from Home . . . Gifts from the Pleiades. Darlana Montague. (Illus.). 107p. 1994. mass mkt. 29.95 (*1-889529-03-6*) Two Feathers.

Messages from Maitreya the Christ. 2nd ed. Intro. by Benjamin Creme. 283p. 1992. pap. 9.00 (*0-936604-11-5*) Tara Ctr.

Messages from Management: A Guide to over 300 Manager-Employee Counseling Situations. Tracey H. DeBruyn. LC 91-62228. 247p. 1991. pap. 12.95 (*0-914607-33-2*) Master Tchr.

Messages from Mathias. Robin James. (Illus.). 77p. (Orig.). 1997. pap. 9.95 (*0-9647066-8-7*) Wellstone Pr.

Messages from Michael. Chelsea Quinn Yarbro. LC 80-82567. 288p. 1987. mass mkt. 5.50 (*0-425-10437-0*) Berkley Pub.

Messages from Michael. Chelsea Quinn Yarbro. 288p. 1995. reprint ed. pap. 12.95 (*0-425-15106-9*) Berkley Pub.

Messages from Mother Earth: Daily Affirmations. Willie C. Hooks. 60p. (Orig.). 1989. pap. 6.95 (*0-685-26323-1*) JTE Assocs.

Messages from My Father. Calvin Trillin. LC 95-47722. 117p. 1996. 18.00 (*0-374-20860-3*) FS&G.

Messages from My Father. Calvin Trillin. 128p. 1997. pap. text 10.00 (*0-374-52508-0*, Noonday) FS&G.

Messages from My Son: Conversations with the Other Side. Betty Hayes. LC 94-96254. 78p. 1995. pap. 12.95 (*0-9639859-1-4*) Hayes Press.

***Messages from the Archangel Gabriel.** 2000. pap. 15.00 (*0-9642344-4-0*) TEA Printers & Pubs.

Messages from the Depths: (Selections from the Writings of Reinhold Schneider) Reinhold Schneider. Ed. by Curt Winterhalter. Tr. by Robert Cunningham from GER. 74p. 1977. pap. 1.00 (*0-8199-0683-2*, Frncscn Herld) Franciscan Pr.

Messages from the Dove. Beverly Hale-Watson. 25p. (Orig.). 1995. pap. 3.75 (*0-9623647-4-6*) B H Watson.

Messages from the Heart. Debra L. Higgason. 129p. 1997. pap. 11.95 (*0-9651546-7-X*) Med Bear.

Messages from the Journey. Sandra Radom. (Illus.). 81p. 1995. text 24.95 (*0-9645441-0-5*) Pr of Journey.

***Messages from the Masters: Tapping into the Power of Love.** Brian Weiss. LC 99-49043. 272p. 2000. 22.95 (*0-446-52596-0*, Pub. by Warner Bks) Little.

Messages from the Masters: The School on Earth Is Hard, However, the Masters of Light on the Other Side of Life Will Enlighten You & Care Your Plight, If Only You Are Willing to Listen & to Learn. Hulda Zirli. 284p. 1996. pap. text. write for info. (*0-9653196-0-1*) HyperBook.

Messages from the Past: Hebrew Bullae from the Time of Isaiah through the Destruction of the First Temple-Shlomo Moussaieff Collection & an Updated Corpus. Robert Deutsch. (HEB.). 172p. 1997. text 80.00 (*965-90240-3-7*, Pub. by Archaeol Ctr) Eisenbrauns.

M

Messages from the Past: Hebrew Bullae from the Time of Isaiah through the Destruction of the First Temple-Shlomo Moussaieff Collection & an Updated Corpus. Robert Deutsch. (HEB.). 172p. 1997. text 60.00 (*965-222-795-1*, Pub. by Archaeol Ctr) Eisenbrauns.

***Messages from the Past: Hebrew Bullae from the Time of Isaiah through the Destruction of the First Temple-Shlomo Moussaieff Collection & an Updated Corpus.** Robert Deutsch. 206p. 1999. text 80.00 (*965-90240-5-3*, Pub. by Archaeol Ctr) Eisenbrauns.

Messages from the People of the Planet Clarion: The True Experiences of Truman Bethurum. Ed. & Intro. by Timothy G. Beckley. 150p. 1997. 14.95 (*0-938294-55-5*) Inner Light.

Messages from the Sky. Rose M. Schulte. (Illus.). 50p. 1995. pap. text 6.00 (*0-9645122-0-3*) R Schulte.

***Messages from the Throne.** Asbury Sellers. 2000. pap. 12.99 (*0-87148-610-5*) Pathway Pr.

Messages from the Underground: Transnational Radio in Resistance & in Solidarity. Nancy L. Street & Marilyn J. Matelski. LC 96-41545. 248p. 1997. 57.95 (*0-275-95602-4*, Praeger Pubs) Greenwood.

Messages from the Universal House of Justice, 1963-1986: The Third Epoch of the Formative Age. Geoffry W. Marks. LC 96-43430. 1996. 24.95 (*0-87743-239-2*) Bahai.

M

Messages from the Zoo. ETR Associates Staff. (Illus.). (J). 1993. write for info. (*0-318-70281-9*) ETR Assocs.

***Messages from Verdante.** Mim Scharlack. 104p. 1998. pap. 10.00 (*1-877603-56-2*, Pub. by Pecan Grove) Herveys Bklink.

Messages from Your Angels, 3 vols., Set. Darlana Montague. (Illus.). (Orig.). (J). (gr. 1-5). 1998. pap. 22.95 (*1-889529-09-5*) Two Feathers.

Messages from Your Angels, Vol. I. Darlana Montague. (Illus.). 24p. (Orig.). (J). (gr. 1-5). 1995. pap. 7.95 (*1-889529-06-0*) Two Feathers.

Messages from Your Angels, Vol. II. Darlana Montague. (Illus.). 18p. (Orig.). (J). (gr. 1-5). 1998. pap. 7.95 (*1-889529-07-9*) Two Feathers.

Messages from Your Angels, Vol. III. Darlana Montague. (Illus.). 20p. (Orig.). (J). (gr. 1-5). 1998. pap. 7.95 (*1-889529-08-7*) Two Feathers.

Messages Given During the Resumption of Watchman Nee's Ministry, 2 vols. Watchman Nee & Witness Lee. 604p. 1991. per. 21.50 (*0-87083-028-7*, 14-006-001) Living Stream Ministry.

Messages Given to the Working Saints. Witness Lee. 92p. 1989. per. 5.50 (*0-87083-480-0*, 13-009-001) Living Stream Ministry.

Messages in Code. Janet Weller. (Hello Out There Ser.). 32p. (J). 1998. lib. bdg. 19.00 (*0-531-14475-5*) Watts.

Messages in Code. Janet Weller. LC 97-32895. (Hello Out There Ser.). (Illus.). 32p. 1998. pap. 6.95 (*0-531-15346-0*) Watts.

Messages in Mosaic: The Royal Programmes of Norman Sicily, 1130-1187. Eve Borsook. 256p. 1998. reprint ed. pap. 55.00 (*0-85115-591-X*, Boydell Pr) Boydell & Brewer.

Messages in Music: Unitarian Universalism for Junior High. Elizabeth Strong et al. 144p. 1994. pap. 30.00 (*1-55896-320-0*) Unitarian Univ.

Messages in Stone: Statues & Sculptures from Tribal Indonesia in the Collection of the Barbier-Mueller Museum. (Illus.). 200p. 1999. 55.00 (*88-8118-391-9*, Pub. by Skira IT) Abbeville Pr.

Messages in the Mailbox: How to Write a Letter. Loreen Leedy. (Illus.). (J). (gr. k-3). 1991. pap. 6.95 (*0-8234-1079-X*) Holiday.

Messages in the Mailbox: How to Write a Letter. Loreen Leedy. LC 91-8718. (Illus.). 32p. (J). (gr. k-3). 1991. lib. bdg. 16.95 (*0-8234-0889-2*) Holiday.

Messages Men Hear: Constructing Masculinities. Ian M. Harris. LC 94-37988. 224p. 1995. 85.00 (*0-7484-0229-2*); pap. 27.95 (*0-7484-0230-6*) Taylor & Francis.

Messages of Despair, Messages of Hope: A Guide to the Recovery from Eating Disorders. Mary Orndorff. 70p. 1990. 8.95 (*0-9636536-0-1*) Garkakee.

***Messages of Friendship & Love.** Virginia Moulton Ruth. 2000. 12.95 (*0-533-13275-4*) Vantage.

Messages of Murder: A Study of the Reports of the Einsatzgruppen of the Security Police & the Security Service, 1941-1943. Ronald Headland. LC 90-56046. 304p. 1992. 45.00 (*0-8386-3418-4*) Fairleigh Dickinson.

Messages of Prophetic Light see Mensajes de Luz Profetica

Messages of Reconciliation & Hope: 75 Years of Birthday Offerings, 1922-1997. Catherine Vaughn. LC 97-68105. (Illus.). 272p. 1997. pap. 16.00 (*1-57736-060-5*) Providence Hse.

Messages of the Governors of the Territory of Washington to the Legislative Assembly, 1854-1889. Ed. by Charles M. Gates. LC 41-52447. (Illus.). 298p. 1940. 20.00 (*0-295-95130-3*, UWPSSXII) U of Wash Pr.

Messages of the Lady of All Nations. Ida Peerdeman & Josef Kunzli. LC 96-70128. 152p. 1996. pap. text 4.95 (*1-882972-87-2*) Queenship Pub.

Messages of Understanding & the Missing Answers. Paul Melanchthon. LC 96-94392. 201p. 1997. pap. 12.00 (*0-9662948-0-7*, M-1) Melanchthon Hse.

Messages Pertaining to Russia & the World. Rosalie Turtan. 35p. 1992. pap. 3.00 (*1-890137-25-1*) One Hund-One Fnd.

Messages Revolutionnaires. Antonin Artaud. (Idees Ser.). (FRE.). 1979. pap. 8.95 (*2-07-035411-3*) Schoenhof.

Messages That Work: A Guide to Communication Design. Patrick O. Marsh. LC 83-1573. 460p. 1983. 49.95 (*0-87778-184-2*) Educ Tech Pubns.

Messages to a Nation in Crisis: An Introduction to the Prophecy of Jeremiah. Steven M. Fettke. LC 82-19997. (Illus.). 72p. (Orig.). (C). 1983. pap. text 14.00 (*0-8191-2839-2*) U Pr of Amer.

Messages to Carver Alan Ames. C. Alan Ames. 237p. 1997. pap. 10.00 (*1-890137-36-7*) One Hund-One Fnd.

Messages to Conventions, Policies of T. S. G. de Purucker. 1993. pap. 10.00 (*0-913004-85-5*) Point Loma Pub.

Messages to Our Family: From the Brotherhood, Mother Mary & Jesus. Annie O. Kirkwood & Byron R. Kirkwood. LC 94-3988. 540p. (Orig.). 1994. pap. 17.95 (*0-931892-81-3*) B Dolphin Pub.

Messages to the Baha'i World, 1950-1957. Shoghi Effendi. 182p. 1995. pap. 5.95 (*0-87743-250-3*) Bahai.

***Messages to You: Short Stories & Essays.** Selena Millman. LC 00-9408. 2000. write for info. (*1-929882-01-7*) Biograph Pub.

Messages We Give Our Kids. Barbara Shaffer. 1998. 3.95 (*0-9642707-1-4*) C C M Pub.

Messaging & Queuing Using the MQI: Concepts, Analysis, Design & Implementation. Burnie Blakeley. 1995. 55.00 (*0-07-005730-3*) McGraw.

Messaging Handbook. F. Huster. 1999. text 55.00 (*0-07-135449-2*) McGraw.

Messaging Technologies for Global Communications. Jerry Cashin. LC 98-2758. (Illus.). 236p. 1998. pap. 290.00 (*1-56607-055-4*) Comput Tech Res.

Messalina of the Suburbs. Edmee E. De La Pasture. LC 75-106286. (Short Story Index Reprint Ser.). 1977. 19.95 (*0-8369-3323-0*) Ayer.

Messe la-Bas. Paul Claudel. (FRE.). 132p. 1919. 10.95 (*0-7859-1105-7*, 2070214796) Fr & Eur.

Messe sur le Monde. Pierre Teilhard De Chardin. pap. 6.25 (*0-685-36598-0*) Fr & Eur.

Messed up Pieces. Jerry Cooper. 24p. (Orig.). 1996. pap. 3.95 (*1-889419-19-2*) J Cooper.

Messed up Ride or a Dressed-Up Walk: A Stirring Autobiography of Hope for the City, Love for God, & a Faith That Stays the Course. Jerald January & Steve Wamberg. LC 94-27606. 176p. 1994. 15.99 (*0-310-48540-1*) Zondervan.

Messel Era. Donald Millar. 1988. pap. text 13.00 (*0-08-034431-3*, Pergamon Pr) Elsevier.

Messel Era: The History of the School of Physics & its Science Foundation with the University of Sydney 1952-1987. Donald Millar. 176p. 1987. 11.75 (*0-317-66359-3*, Pergamon Pr) Elsevier.

Messenger. T. Davis Bunn. 142p. 1995. text 11.99 (*1-55661-669-4*) Bethany Hse.

***Messenger.** Robin V. Heflin. LC 99-71699. 235p. 1999. pap. 11.95 (*1-883697-12-3*) Hara Pub.

Messenger. Joan Kufrin. 63p. 1997. pap. 5.60 (*0-87129-811-2*, MA3) Dramatic Pub.

Messenger. Jack Rudman. (Career Examination Ser.: C-495). 1994. pap. 23.95 (*0-8373-0495-4*) Nat Learn.

***Messenger.** Jason Savas. LC 99-61644. 244p. 1999. pap. 5.95 (*1-56167-522-9*, Five Star Spec Ed) Am Literary Pr.

Messenger. Donald Tyson. LC 93-26249. 272p. 1999. mass mkt. 4.99 (*0-87542-836-3*) Llewellyn Pubns.

***Messenger: A Novel.** Mayra Montero. Tr. by Edith Grossman from SPA. LC 98-41176. 224p. 1999. 23.00 (*0-06-019223-2*, HarperFlamingo) HarpC.

***Messenger: A Novel.** Mayra Montero. Tr. by Edith Grossman. 224p. 2000. pap. 13.00 (*0-06-092961-8*, Perennial) HarperTrade.

Messenger: A Sequel to Lost Horizon. Frank DeMarco. LC 95-136277. 240p. (Orig.). 1994. pap. 9.95 (*1-57174-013-9*) Hampton Roads Pub Co.

Messenger: A Verse Narrative in Fifteen Parts. Riad Nourallah. LC 98-35467. 60p. 1998. pap. 12.00 (*1-883053-34-X*) Univ Pr MD.

Messenger: Edgar Cayce, His Life & Legacy. Sidney D. Kirkpatrick. LC 00-27975. (Illus.). 720p. 1999. 30.00 (*1-57322-139-2*, Riverhead Books) Putnam Pub Group.

Messenger: The Journey of a Spiritual Healer. Geoff Boltwood. 240p. 1995. pap. 14.95 (*0-7499-1458-0*, Pub. by Piatkus Bks) London Brdge.

Messenger: The Life of Mohammed. Ronald V. Bodley. LC 70-92296. 368p. 1970. reprint ed. lib. bdg. 65.00 (*0-8371-2423-9*, BOTM, Greenwood Pr) Greenwood.

Messenger: The Rise & Fall of Elijah Muhammad. Karl Evanzz. LC 99-11826. (Illus.). 704p. 1999. 28.50 (*0-679-44260-X*) Pantheon.

Messenger & His Message see Mensajero y Su Mensaji

Messenger Gods of Battle: The History of Electronic Warfare. Tony Devereux. 348p. 1990. 52.00 (*0-08-035829-2*, Pub. by Brasseys) Brasseys.

Messenger, Messenger. Robert Burleigh. LC 98-20566. (J). 2000. 17.00 (*0-689-82103-4*) Atheneum Yung Read.

Messenger of Allah Vol. 1: Makkah Period. 4th ed. Abidullah Ghazi & Tasneema Ghazi. 70p. (YA). (gr. 9-12). 1988. reprint ed. text 6.00 (*1-56316-160-5*) Iqra Intl Ed Fdtn.

Messenger of Allah Vol. 2: Madinah Period. 4th ed. Abidullah Ghazi & Tasneema Ghazi. 102p. (YA). (gr. 9-12). 1988. reprint ed. pap. text 6.00 (*1-56316-162-1*) Iqra Intl Ed Fdtn.

Messenger of Allah Workbook Vol. 1: Makkah Period. 4th ed. Abidullah Ghazi & Tasneema Ghazi. 37p. (YA). (gr. 9-12). 1988. reprint ed. pap. 4.00 (*1-56316-161-3*) Iqra Intl Ed Fdtn.

Messenger of Allah Workbook Vol. 2: Madinah Period. 4th ed. Abidullah Ghazi & Tasneema Ghazi. 54p. (YA). (gr. 9-12). 1988. reprint ed. pap. 4.00 (*1-56316-163-X*) Iqra Intl Ed Fdtn.

***Messenger of Light Postcard Set.** Thomas Kinkade. 1998. pap. 14.95 (*0-01-202655-7*) Media Arts.

Messenger of Satan. Charles Capps. 64p. 1993. pap. 5.99 (*0-89274-633-5*, HH-633) Harrison Hse.

Messenger of the Cross. Watchman Nee. Tr. by Stephen Kaung. 154p. 1980. pap. text 4.50 (*0-935008-50-0*) Christian Fellow Pubs.

Messenger of the Cross. Watchman Nee. 44p. (J). 1991. pap. 2.50 (*0-87083-605-6*, 07-033-001) Living Stream Ministry.

***Messenger of the Cross.** Watchman Nee. 17p. 1998. pap. 1.00 (*0-7363-0308-1*, 18-074-002) Living Stream Ministry.

Messenger of the Cross. Watchman. 16p. 1998. pap. 1.00 (*1-57593-871-5*, 18-074-001) Living Stream Ministry.

Messenger of the Lord: The Prophetic Ministry of Ellen G. White. Herbert E. Douglass. LC 98-15574. 1998. 24.99 (*0-8163-1622-8*) Pacific Pr Pub Assn.

***Messenger on the Battlefield.** Mel Rice. (Lone Star Heroines Ser.). (Illus.). 128p. (YA). 2000. pap. 8.95 (*1-55622-788-4*, Rep of TX Pr) Wordware Pub.

***Messenger Reader: Stories, Poetry & Essays from The Messenger Magazine, Vol. 1.** Ed. by Sondra Kathryn Wilson. LC 99-39882. (Modern Library Harlem Renaissance Ser.). 420p. 2000. pap. 14.95 (*0-375-75539-X*) Modern Lib NY.

Messenger Texts from the British Museum. M. Sigrist. 160p. 1990. 45.00 (*0-9620013-3-3*) CDL Pr.

Messenger That I Sent. unabridged ed. Joel Brumlik. 580p. 1998. pap. 36.95 (*1-892896-90-7*) Buy Books.

Messenger to the Spirits. Michael Whitaker. LC 96-69724. 384p. 1996. 19.95 (*1-884570-60-7*) Research Triangle.

***Messenger Twelve: Gold Dust, Slaves & a Sing-Song Girl.** James Lynn Bartz. LC 00-90248. 256p. 2000. 24.00 (*0-9678756-0-9*) Westbound.

Messenger Within: Discovering Love & Wholeness Through Meditation. Soraya S. Behbehani. 230p. 1996. pap. 16.90 (*0-614-21311-8*, 1369) Kazi Pubns.

***Messenger Within: Discovering Love & Wholeness Through Meditation.** 3rd ed. Soraya Susan Behbehani. 250p. 1999. pap. 16.95 (*0-910735-68-9*, Pub. by MTO Printing & Pubn Ctr) ACCESS Pubs Network.

Messengers: A True Story of Angelic Presence & the Return to the Age of Miracles. Julea Ingram & G. W. Hardin. 338p. 1998. pap. 6.50 (*0-671-01687-3*, Pocket Star Bks) PB.

Messengers: A True Story of Angelic Presence & the Return to the Age of Miracles. Julia Ingram & G. W. Hardin. Ed. by Scott Penmann. LC 96-78328. 344p. (Orig.). 1996. pap. text 16.00 (*0-9651590-1-9*) Infnty Pub.

Messengers: A True Story of Angelic Presence & the Return to the Age of Miracles. Julia Ingram & G. W. Hardin. LC 97-11906. (Orig.). 1997. 18.00 (*0-671-01686-5*, PB Hardcover) PB.

Messengers: After-Death Appearances of Saints & Mystics. Patricia Treece. LC 95-68834. 336p. 1995. 19.95 (*0-87973-709-3*, 709) Our Sunday Visitor.

Messengers: Among the Stars, Stones & Legends, the Ancient Wisdom Dwells. Julie M. Gillentine. Ed. by Janet Harris. 304p. (Orig.). 1997. pap. 16.99 (*0-9635211-7-9*) Archive Pr CO.

Messengers from Ancient Civilizations. Edmond B. Szekely & Norma N. Bordeaux. (Illus.). 64p. (J). (gr. 5 up). 1974. pap. 3.50 (*0-89564-068-6*) IBS Intl.

Messenger's Memoirs: Sixty-One Southern Baptist Convention Meetings. Robert E. Naylor. LC 95-69284. (Illus.). 304p. (Orig.). 1995. pap. 16.95 (*1-881576-46-9*) Providence Hse.

***Messengers, Morse Code & Modems: The Science of Communication.** Janice Parker. LC 99-40872. (Science at Work Ser.). (gr. 4-7). 2000. lib. bdg. 25.69 (*0-7398-0138-4*) Raintree Steck-V.

Messengers of Day. Anthony Powell. LC 83-124205. (Keep the Ball Rolling : the Memoirs of Anthony Powell Ser.). viii, 209p. 1978. write for info. (*0-434-59923-9*) Buttrwrth-Heinemann.

Messengers of Death: Human Rights in Guatemala, November 1988 to February 1990. Americas Watch Staff. 86p. 1990. pap. 10.00 (*0-929692-43-8*, Am Watch) Hum Rts Watch.

Messengers of Deception. Jacques Vallee. LC 78-73378. 256p. 1979. pap. 14.95 (*0-915904-38-1*) And-Or Bks.

Messengers of God. Catherine Young. 114p. 1984. 40.00 (*0-7212-0685-9*, Pub. by Regency Pr GBR) St Mut.

Messengers of God: A Jewish Prophets' Who's Who. Ronald H. Isaacs. LC 97-33198. 288p. 1998. 35.00 (*0-7657-9998-7*) Aronson.

Messengers of God: Biblical Portraits & Legends. Elie Wiesel. 256p. 1985. per. 11.00 (*0-671-54134-X*) S&S Trade Pap.

Messengers of God: The Sensuous Side of Spirituality. Arthur O. Roberts. 216p. (Orig.). 1996. pap. 14.95 (*0-913342-80-7*) Barclay Pr.

Messengers of Light: The Angels' Guide to Spiritual Growth. Terry L. Taylor. Ed. by Nancy Carleton. LC 89-92333. 240p. 1990. pap. 12.00 (*0-915811-51-0*) H J Kramer Inc.

Messengers of Light by Thomas Kinkade. Illus. by Lucy B. Designs. 44p. 1998. pap. 14.95 (*0-9638635-8-4*) Lightpost Pubng.

Messengers of Love. Robert E. Ward. (Illus.). 450p. 1999. pap. write for info. (*0-7392-0291-X*, PO3398) Morris Pubng.

Messengers of Modernism: American Studio Jewelery, 1940-1960. Toni Greenbaum. LC 96-29415. (Illus.). 168p. 1996. 37.50 (*2-08-013593-7*, Pub. by Flammarion) Abbeville Pr.

Messengers of the New Millennium: "A Walk with the Angels" Judith Roustiau. (Illus.). v, 59p. 1998. 19.95 (*0-9665246-0-8*) Roustiau Ent.

Messengers of the Wind: Native American Women Tell Their Life Stories. Jane Katz. 336p. 1996. pap. 12.00 (*0-345-40285-5*) Ballantine Pub Grp.

Messengers to the Brain: Your Fantastic Five Senses. Paul D. Martin. Ed. by Donald J. Crump. LC 82-45636. (Books for World Explorers Series 5: No. 3). 104p. (J). (gr. 3-8). 1984. 8.95 (*0-87044-499-9*); lib. bdg. 12.50 (*0-87044-504-9*) Natl Geog.

Messengers Unaware. Marion D. Sallani. 160p. 1998. pap. 16.95 (*1-887750-89-4*) Rutledge Bks.

Messenges of the Great Orff. Brian Caswell. LC 98-229292. (Alien Zone Ser.: Bk. 2). (J). 1998. 8.95 (*0-7022-2989-X*, Pub. by Univ Queensland Pr) Intl Spec Bk.

Messer Marco Polo. Donn Byrne. 19.95 (*0-8488-0074-5*) Amereon Ltd.

Messer Marco Polo. Donn Byrne. LC 79-10460. 1979. reprint ed. lib. bdg. 16.00 (*0-8376-0437-0*) Bentley Pubs.

Messerchmitt Gehetmeprojerte see Secret Messerschmitt Projects

Messers Macdermott & Macgough: Paintings, Photographs & Time Experiments, 1950. Robert Rosenblum et al. LC 98-229857. 203 p. 1997. 39.95 (*90-74377-64-5*) Stichting Kunst.

Messerschmidt ME262. David Baker. (Illus.). 192p. 1997. 44.95 (*1-86126-078-4*, Pub. by Crolwood) Motorbooks Intl.

Messerschmitt Bf 110 Day Fighter Aces. John Weal. (Aircraft of the Aces Ser.). (Illus.). 96p. 1999. pap. 16.95 (*1-85532-728-7*, Pub. by Ospry) Stackpole.

Messerschmitt Bf 109. Heinz J. Nowarra. LC 91-60857. (German Aircraft of WWII Ser.). (Illus.). 48p. 1991. pap. 9.95 (*0-88740-311-5*) Schiffer.

Messerschmitt Bf 109, Vol. 2. Fritz X. Kobel & Jakob M. Mathmann. LC 96-220678. (Illus.). 48p. pap. 9.95 (*0-88740-919-9*) Schiffer.

Messerschmitt BF-109: Luftwaffe Fighter. Photos by Dan Patterson. LC 97-73124. (Living History Ser.: No. 5). (Illus.). 64p. 1997. pap. 15.95 (*1-57427-054-0*) Howell Pr VA.

Messerschmitt Bf 109 F/G/K/ Series: An Illustrated Study. Jochen Prien & Peter Rodeike. LC 92-81713. (Illus.). 208p. 1992. 35.00 (*0-88740-424-3*) Schiffer.

Messerschmitt BF 109 G/K No. 2: The Luftwaffe Profile Series. Manfred Griehl. Tr. by David Johnston from GER. LC 95-67544. (Illus.). 52p. (Orig.). 1995. pap. 14.95 (*0-88740-818-4*) Schiffer.

Messerschmitt BF 109 in Action, Pt. 1. (Aircraft in Action Ser.). (Illus.). 50p. 1984. pap. 9.95 (*0-89747-106-7*, 1044) Squad Sig Pubns.

Messerschmitt BF 109 in Action, Pt. 2. Ed. by John Beaman. (Aircraft in Action Ser.). (Illus.). 50p. 1993. pap. 9.95 (*0-89747-138-5*, 1057) Squad Sig Pubns.

***Messerschmitt BF 109 F-K: Development/Testing/ Production.** Willy Radinger & Wolfgang Otto. (Illus.). 160p. 2000. 35.00 (*0-7643-1023-2*) Schiffer.

Messerschmitt Bf110 - Over All Fronts, 1939-1945. Holger Nauroth & Werner Held. LC 90-62987. (Illus.). 248p. 1991. 29.95 (*0-88740-286-0*) Schiffer.

***Messerschmitt Bf110.** Don MacKay. (Illus.). 192p. 2000. 44.95 (*1-86126-313-9*, 130057AE, Pub. by Crolwood) Motorbooks Intl.

***Messerschmitt BF109.** Edward Shacklady. (Illus.). 160p. 2000. 29.99 (*0-7524-2003-8*, Pub. by Tempus Pubng) Arcadia Publng.

Messerschmitt BF109 A-E: Development/Testing/ Production. Willy Radinger & Walter Schick. (Illus.). 136p. 1999. 35.00 (*0-7643-0951-X*) Schiffer.

Messerschmitt Bf109 in the West, 1937-1940. Michael Payne. LC 97-38291. (Luftwaffe at War Ser.). 72p. 1998. pap. 12.95 (*1-85367-305-6*, Pub. by Greenhill Bks) Stackpole.

Messerschmitt ME 163 "Komet", Vol. I. Mano Ziegler. LC 90-60471. (Illus.). 48p. 1990. pap. 9.95 (*0-88740-232-1*) Schiffer.

Messerschmitt Me 163 "Komet", Vol. II. M. Emmerling. Tr. by Edward Force from GER. (Illus.). 48p. 1992. pap. 9.95 (*0-88740-403-0*) Schiffer.

Messerschmitt Me 321/323: Giants of the Luftwaffe. H. P. Dabrowski. (Illus.). 48p. (YA). (gr. 10-13). 1994. pap. 9.95 (*0-88740-671-8*) Schiffer.

***Messerschmitt Me 209.** David Myhra. (Illus.). 112p. 2000. pap. 14.95 (*0-7643-1107-7*) Schiffer.

Messerschmitt Me 263. David Myhra. (Illus.). 64p. 1999. pap. 9.95 (*0-7643-0909-9*) Schiffer.

Messerschmitt Me 262: Development - Testing - Production. Willy Radinger & Walter Schick. (Illus.). 112p. 1993. 24.95 (*0-88740-516-9*) Schiffer.

Messerschmitt ME 262 No. 1. Manfred Griehl. Tr. by David Johnston from GER. LC 95-67542. (Luftwaffe Profile Ser.). (Illus.). 52p. (Orig.). 1995. pap. 14.95 (*0-88740-820-6*) Schiffer.

Messerschmitt ME-262 Sturmvogel. (Illus.). 66p. 1974. pap. 9.25 (*0-87994-020-4*) Aviat Pub.

Messerschmitt Me 262 Sturmvogel. Carroll V. Glines & Dennis Jenkins. (Warbird Tech Ser.: Vol. 6). (Illus.). 100p. (Orig.). 1996. pap. 16.95 (*0-933424-69-8*) Specialty Pr.

Messerschmitt ME 210-410 in Action. George Punica. LC 95-118258. (Aircraft in Action Ser.). (Illus.). 50p. 1994. pap. 9.95 (*0-89747-320-5*) Squad Sig Pubns.

Messerschmitt ME 262: Arrow to the Future. Walter J. Boyne. (Illus.). 192p. (Orig.). 1993. pap. 19.95 (*0-88740-665-3*) Schiffer.

***Messerschmitt 109.** David Lande. (Illus.). 128p. 2000. pap. 21.95 (*0-7603-0803-9*, 129839AP, Pub. by MBI Pubg) Motorbooks Intl.

Messerschmitt P.1101. David Myhra. LC 99-61085. (Illus.). 64p. 1999. pap. 9.95 (*0-7643-0908-0*) Schiffer.

Messerschmitt Routlette: The Western Desert, 1941-42. Geoffrey Morley-Mower. LC 93-85728. (Illus.). 1993. 24.95 (*1-883809-01-0*) Specialty Pr.

Messes. Mark Dunster. 24p. (Orig.). (YA). (gr. 9-12). 1996. pap. 5.00 (*0-89642-313-1*) Linden Pubns.

An Asterisk (*) at the beginning of an entry indicates that the title is appearing for the first time.

Messes a Quatre Voix see Monuments de la Musique Francaise au Temps de la Renaissance

Messes of Dresses. 2nd ed. Faigy Pertzig. Ed. by Dina Rosenfeld. LC 94-80242. (Illus.). 32p. (J). (ps-3). 1999. reprint ed. 9.95 (*0-922613-75-3*) Hachai Pubng.

Messey Bessey & the Birthday Overnight. Patricia McKissack & Frederick McKissack. LC 98-9223. (Rookie Readers Ser.). (Illus.). (J). 1998. 17.00 (*0-516-20828-4*) Childrens.

Messey Bessey's School Desk. Frederick McKissack & Patricia McKissack. Ed. by Dana Rau. (Rookie Readers Ser.). (Illus.). 32p. (J). 1998. pap. 4.95 (*0-516-26361-7*) Childrens.

Messiaen. write for info. (*0-614-10735-0*) Fairleigh Dickinson.

Messiaen. 1996. pap. write for info. (*0-614-10477-7*) Fairleigh Dickinson.

Messiaen. rev. ed. Robert S. Johnson. 1989. pap. 18.95 (*0-520-06734-7*, Pub. by U CA Pr) Cal Prin Full Svc.

Messiaen: Quatuor pour la Fin du Temps. Anthony Pople. LC 98-23937. (Cambridge Music Handbks.). (Illus.). 128p. (C). 1998. 39.95 (*0-521-58497-3*); pap. 12.95 (*0-521-58538-4*) Cambridge U Pr.

Messiaen Companion. Ed. by Peter Hill. (Illus.). 584p. 1995. 49.95 (*0-931340-95-0*, Amadeus Pr); pap. 24.95 (*0-931340-94-2*, Amadeus Pr) Timber.

Messiaen's Language of Mystical Love. Ed. by Siglind Bruhn & Joseph Auner. LC 98-12602. (Twentieth-Century Music Ser.: Vol. 1). 271p. 1998. 45.00 (*0-8153-2747-1*) Garland.

Messiah. Eliyahu Ben Avraham. 32p. 1992. pap. 3.75 (*0-9632485-0-2*) Theiss Pubns.

Messiah. Timothy R. Botts. 112p. 1991. 14.99 (*0-8423-4235-4*) Tyndale Hse.

Messiah. Danes. 1991. pap. 13.95 (*0-7459-1943-X*, Pub. by Lion Pubng) Trafalgar.

Messiah. Milton L. Forbes. LC 89-92056. (Illus.). xvi, 272p. (Orig.). 1989. 29.95 (*0-9623700-0-2*); pap. 19.95 (*0-9623700-1-0*) Mtntop Bks.

*__Messiah.__ George Frideric Handel. 1998. pap. 9.98 (*963-8303-66-2*) Kone Music.

Messiah. Cleyburn L. McCauley. Ed. by Lucy Foley. 198p. (Orig.). 1995. pap. text 9.95 (*0-910531-20-X*) Wolcotts.

Messiah. Navigators Staff. (Life & Ministry of Jesus Christ Ser.). 80p. (Orig.). 1996. pap. 6.00 (*0-89109-967-0*, 99670) NavPress.

*__Messiah.__ Jay E. Simon. LC 00-100659. 300p. 2000. pap. 14.95 (*1-885003-52-8*, Pub. by R D Reed Pubs) Midpt Trade.

Messiah. Boris Starling. 457p. 1999. pap. 6.99 (*0-451-40900-0*, Onyx) NAL.

Messiah. Gore Vidal. 1987. mass mkt. 4.99 (*0-345-33917-7*) Ballantine Pub Grp.

Messiah. Gore Vidal. LC 75-419222. (Illus.). 221p. 1968. write for info. (*0-434-82956-0*) Buttrwrth-Heinemann.

Messiah. Gore Vidal. LC 98-215970. 244p. 1998. pap. 13.95 (*0-14-118039-0*) Viking Penguin.

Messiah. 2nd ed. Sybex, Inc. Staff. (Ultimate Strategy Guide Ser.). 112p. 2000. pap. 14.99 (*0-7821-2480-1*) Sybex.

Messiah: A New Look at the Composer, the Music & the Message. N. A. Woychuk. (Illus.). 235p. 1995. pap. 12.95 (*1-880960-26-5*) Script Memory Fl.

Messiah: A Novel. Andrei Codrescu. LC 98-39032. 368p. 1999. 24.50 (*0-684-80314-3*) S&S Trade.

Messiah: Amazing Prophecies Fulfilled in Jesus. Hal Lindsey. 1996. pap. 9.99 (*1-56507-460-2*) Harvest Hse.

Messiah: An Aramoic Interpretation. Samson H. Levey. 1974. 25.00 (*0-87820-402-4*) Ktav.

Messiah: An Oratorio Complete Vocal Score. George Frideric Handel. 264p. 1986. pap. 6.95 (*0-7935-0507-0*, 50323760) H Leonard.

Messiah: Cello-Bass. George Frideric Handel. 44p. 1986. pap. 4.95 (*0-7935-5376-8*, 50342670) H Leonard.

Messiah: Chorus Parts - Piano. George Frideric Handel. 148p. 1986. per. 5.95 (*0-7935-5501-9*, 50324300) H Leonard.

Messiah: Choruses from Handel's Messiah. deluxe limited ed. Illus. by Joyce Alexander. 24p. 1985. pap. 15.00 (*0-937686-10-7*) Turtles Quill.

Messiah: Commentaries on Kahlil Gibran's the Prophet, Vol. 1. Osho. Ed. by Dhyan Sarito. 520p. (Orig.). 1987. 27.95 (*3-89338-002-7*, Pub. by Rebel Hse) Oshos.

Messiah: Commentaries on Kahlil Gibran's the Prophet, Vol. 1. Osho. Ed. by Dhyan Sarito. (Mystery School Ser.). 520p. (Orig.). 1987. pap. 14.95 (*3-89338-009-4*, Pub. by Rebel Hse) Oshos.

Messiah: Commentaries on Kahlil Gibran's the Prophet, Vol. 2. Osho. Ed. by Ma P. Taranga & Ma P. Melissa. (Mystery School Ser.). 519p. (Orig.). 1987. 27.95 (*3-89338-003-5*, Pub. by Rebel Hse); pap. 14.95 (*3-89338-010-8*, Pub. by Rebel Hse) Oshos.

Messiah: Developments in Earliest Judaism & Christianity. Ed. by James H. Charlesworth. LC 91-36381. 608p. 1992. 53.00 (*0-8006-2563-3*, 1-2563, Fortress Pr) Augsburg Fortress.

Messiah: Official Strategies & Secrets. 4th ed. Sybex, Inc. Staff. 256p. 1999. pap. text 19.99 (*0-7821-2479-8*) Sybex.

Messiah: Selections from Easy Piano. George Frideric Handel. 40p. 1990. pap. 6.95 (*0-7935-5227-3*, 50481092) H Leonard.

Messiah: The Wordbook: A Facsimile of the 1743 Wordbook. fac. ed. Handel & Haydn Society Staff. (Illus.). 32p. 1995. reprint ed. pap. 12.00 (*0-9649823-0-7*) Handel & Haydn.

Messiah: The Wordbook for the Oratorio. limited ed. George Frideric Handel. LC 91-21661. (Willa Perlman Bks.). (Illus.). 48p. (J). (gr. 3 up). 1992. 100.00 (*0-06-021038-9*) HarpC Child Bks.

Messiah: Trumpet. George Frideric Handel. 16p. 1986. pap. 4.95 (*0-7935-5380-6*, 50342600) H Leonard.

Messiah: Viola. George Frideric Handel. 40p. 1986. pap. 4.95 (*0-7935-5381-4*, 50342660) H Leonard.

Messiah: Violin 1 Part. George Frideric Handel. 44p. 1986. pap. 4.95 (*0-7935-5580-9*, 50342640) H Leonard.

Messiah: Violin 2 Part. George Frideric Handel. 44p. 1986. pap. 4.95 (*0-7935-5583-3*, 50342650) H Leonard.

Messiah: War in the Middle East. Jeffrey. pap. 12.95 (*0-921714-02-5*, Pub. by Fon3tier Res) Spring Arbor Dist.

Messiah - Bassoon A. rev. ed. Leonard Van Camp. Ed. by Scott Foss. 32p. (C). 1995. pap. text 10.00 (*0-89328-140-9*, 30-1033A) Lorenz Corp.

Messiah - Bassoon B. rev. ed. Leonard Van Camp. Ed. by Scott Foss. 32p. (C). 1995. pap. text 10.00 (*0-89328-141-7*, 30-1033B) Lorenz Corp.

Messiah - Bassoon Part. rev. ed. Leonard Van Camp. Ed. by Scott Foss. 160p. (Orig.). (C). 1993. pap. text 12.50 (*0-89328-125-5*, 30-1033) Lorenz Corp.

*__Messiah : A Journey Through Time.__ Patty Ann T. Earle. (Illus.). 80p. 2000. pap. 15.00 (*0-943335-19-1*) Marblehead Pub.

Messiah & Christos: Studies in the Jewish Origins of Christianity. Ed. by Ithamar Gruenwald et al. (Texte und Studien zum Antiken Judentum: No. 32). 248p. 1992. 165.00 (*3-16-145996-2*, Pub. by JCB Mohr) Coronet Bks.

Messiah & His Hebrew Alphabet. Dick Mills & David Michael. (Orig.). 1994. pap. 9.95 (*0-9629011-1-3*) D Mills Minis.

Messiah & Temple: The Trial of Jesus in the Gospel of Mark. Donald Juel. LC 76-46397. (Society of Biblical Literature. Dissertation Ser.: No. 31). 229p. reprint ed. 71.00 (*0-8357-9578-0*, 201752700007) Bks Demand.

*__Messiah before Jesus: The Suffering Servant of the Dead Sea Scrolls.__ Israel Knohl. Tr. by David Maisel. LC 00-37404. (Illus.). 171p. 2000. 22.00 (*0-520-21592-3*) U CA Pr.

Messiah Cello - Bass Part. rev. ed. Leonard Van Camp. Ed. by Scott Foss. 112p. (Orig.). (C). 1993. pap. text 15.00 (*0-89328-123-9*, 30-1031) Lorenz Corp.

Messiah Christmas Choruses. rev. ed. Leonard Van Camp & Scott Foss. 56p. (Orig.). (C). 1995. pap. text 5.95 (*0-89328-137-9*, 65-1042P) Lorenz Corp.

Messiah College: A History. E. Morris Sider. LC 84-80542. (Illus.). xi, 314p. 1984. 11.95 (*0-916035-14-X*) Evangel Indiana.

*__Messiah Comes Tomorrow: Tales from the American Shtetl.__ Alan Lupo. 2000. 19.95 (*1-55849-283-6*) U of Mass Pr.

Messiah Conductor Score. rev. ed. Leonard Van Camp. Ed. by Scott Foss. 352p. (Orig.). (C). 1993. pap. text 150.00 (*0-89328-119-0*, 30-1026) Lorenz Corp.

Messiah Continuo Part. rev. ed. Leonard Van Camp. Ed. by Scott Foss. 304p. (Orig.). (C). 1993. pap. text 35.00 (*0-89328-117-4*) Lorenz Corp.

Messiah, History, & the Tribulation Period. Tim Cohen. 2000. write for info. (*0-9662793-1-X*, BK-02, Pub. by Prophecy Hse) Spring Arbor Dist.

Messiah Idea in Jewish History. Julius H. Greenstone. LC 70-97284. 347p. 1973. reprint ed. lib. bdg. 69.50 (*0-8371-2606-1*, GRMI, Greenwood Pr) Greenwood.

Messiah in Context: Israel's History & Destiny in Formative Judaism. Jacob Neusner. (Studies in Judaism). 288p. (C). reprint ed. lib. bdg. 45.00 (*0-8191-6904-8*) U Pr of Amer.

Messiah in Full Score. George Frideric Handel. 240p. 1989. pap. 12.95 (*0-486-26067-4*) Dover.

Messiah in History. Ed. by Wim Beuken et al. (Concilium Ser.). 1993. 15.00 (*0-88344-869-6*) Orbis Bks.

Messiah in Isaiah 53: The Commentaries of Saadia Gaon, Salmon ben Yeruham & Yefet ben Eli on Is 52:13-53:12, No. 2. Ed. by Joseph Alobaidi. (Bible dans l'Historie: Vol. 2). 211p. 1998. 31.95 (*3-906760-54-5*) P Lang Pubng.

Messiah in Isaiah 53: The Commentaries of Saadia Gaon, Salmon Ben Yeruham & Yefet Ben Eli on Is 52:13-53:12 - Edition & Translation. Ed. by Joseph Alobaidi. LC 98-28590. (Bible dans l'Historie Ser.: Vol. 2). 211p. (C). 1998. pap. 31.95 (*0-8204-4201-1*) P Lang Pubng.

Messiah in Stereo: An Overview of Matthew & Mark. Jack Hayford et al. (Bible Book-a-Month Ser.: Vol. 5). (Illus.). 71p. 1997. pap. 3.95 (*0-916847-22-5*) Living Way.

Messiah in the Memorial Gym: And Other Writings, 1973-1998. Sanford Pippen. 445p. 1999. pap. 16.95 (*0-942396-81-2*) Blackberry ME.

Messiah in the Old Testament. Walter C. Kaiser, Jr. (Studies in Old Testament Biblical Theology Ser.). 256p. 1995. pap. 19.99 (*0-310-20030-X*) Zondervan.

Messiah Now! Ten True Stories from Modern-Day Israel of Men & Women Who Met Yeshua. David Zeidan. 159p. 1994. reprint ed. mass mkt. 7.99 (*1-85078-115-X*, Pub. by O M Pubng) OM Literature.

Messiah Oboe 1 & 2 Parts. rev. ed. Leonard Van Camp. Ed. by Scott Foss. 80p. (Orig.). (C). 1993. pap. text 12.50 (*0-89328-124-7*, 30-1032) Lorenz Corp.

Messiah Oboe II. rev. ed. Leonard Van Camp. Ed. by Scott Foss. 32p. (C). 1995. pap. text 10.00 (*0-89328-139-5*, 30-1032A) Lorenz Corp.

Messiah of la Guardia. Elisha Porat. Tr. by Alan Sacks from HEB. 180p. (Orig.). 1996. pap. 14.95 (*0-88962-614-6*) Mosaic.

Messiah of Midtown Park. Rolf Gompertz. LC 83-50871. 136p. 1983. pap., spiral bd. 12.95 (*0-918248-05-1*) Word Doctor.

Messiah of Stockholm: A Novel. Cynthia Ozick. LC 87-45911. 160p. 1988. reprint ed. pap. 11.00 (*0-394-75694-0*) Vin Bks.

Messiah or Antichrist? A Study of the Messianic Myth in the Work of Zola. Anthony J. Evenhuis. LC 97-35062. 288p. 1998. 43.50 (*0-87413-634-2*) U Delaware Pr.

Messiah Selections From: Piano. 36p. 1986. pap. 10.95 (*0-7692-1159-3*, PF0604) Wrner Bros.

Messiah Series, 6 titles, Set. Bruce R. McConkie. 3234p. 1990. pap. 41.95 (*0-87579-401-7*) Deseret Bk.

Messiah Stones. large type ed. Irving Benig. LC 96-11051. 1996. 24.95 (*1-56895-318-6*) Wheeler Pub.

Messiah Texts: Jewish Legends of Three Thousound Years. Raphael Patai. LC 79-5387. 428p. 1988. pap. 21.95 (*0-8143-1850-9*) Wayne St U Pr.

Messiah the Prince: The Mediatorial Dominion of Jesus Christ. William Symington. 268p. 1999. reprint ed. 19.95 (*0-9660044-3-4*) Chrstn Statesman.

Messiah Timpani. rev. ed. Leonard Van Camp. Ed. by Scott Foss. 12p. (C). 1995. pap. text 5.00 (*0-89328-143-3*, 30-1034B) Lorenz Corp.

Messiah Trumpet & Timpani Parts. rev. ed. Leonard Van Camp. Ed. by Scott Foss. (Orig.). (C). 1993. pap. text 10.00 (*0-89328-126-3*, 30-1034) Lorenz Corp.

Messiah Trumpet II. rev. ed. Leonard Van Camp. Ed. by Scott Foss. 16p. (C). 1995. pap. text 5.00 (*0-89328-142-5*, 30-1034A) Lorenz Corp.

Messiah Viola Part. rev. ed. Leonard Van Camp. Ed. by Scott Foss. 80p. (Orig.). (C). 1993. pap. text 15.00 (*0-89328-122-0*, 30-1030) Lorenz Corp.

Messiah Violin I Part. rev. ed. Leonard Van Camp. Ed. by Scott Foss. 112p. (Orig.). (C). 1993. pap. text 15.00 (*0-89328-120-4*, 30-1028) Lorenz Corp.

Messiah Violin II Part. rev. ed. Leonard Van Camp. Ed. by Scott Foss. 112p. (Orig.). (C). 1993. pap. text 15.00 (*0-89328-121-2*, 30-1029) Lorenz Corp.

Messiah Vocal Score. rev. ed. Leonard Van Camp. Ed. by Scott Foss. 304p. (Orig.). (C). 1993. pap. text 7.25 (*0-89328-116-6*, 65-1001) Lorenz Corp.

Messiah Witness - Israel's Destiny & Coming Deliverer. Gordon Lindsay. 1.95 (*0-89985-187-8*) Christ for the Nations.

Messiahs: A Book of Prophecies for the Second Coming. John Hogue. 256p. 1999. pap. 24.95 (*1-86204-549-6*, Pub. by Element MA) Penguin Putnam.

Messiah's Coming Temple: Ezekiel's Prophetic Vision of the Future Temple. John W. Schmitt & J. Carl Laney. LC 96-52012. (Illus.). 192p. 1997. pap. 10.99 (*0-8254-3727-X*) Kregel.

Messiah's Return: Delayed? Fulfilled? or Double-Fulfillment? rev. ed. Timothy A. James. Ed. by Edward E. Stevens. 71p. 1991. reprint ed. pap. 5.95 (*0-9621311-1-3*) Intl Preterist Assn.

Messiah's Second Advent: A Study in Eschatology. 2nd ed. Calvin Goodspeed. 227p. 1997. reprint ed. pap. 12.95 (*0-9625220-3-1*) Millennium Three Pubs.

Messiahship of Shakespeare. Charles Downing. LC 76-57998. (Studies in Shakespeare: No. 24). 1977. lib. bdg. 59.00 (*0-8383-2172-0*) M S G Haskell Hse.

Messianic Character of American Education. Rousas J. Rushdoony. 192p. 1995. reprint ed. text. write for info. (*1-879998-06-8*) Ross Hse Bks.

Messianic Christology. Arnold G. Fruchtenbaum. (Illus.). 166p. 1998. pap. 20.00 (*0-914863-07-X*) Ariel Ministries.

Messianic Ethics: Jesus' Proclamation of the Kingdom of God & the Church in Response. Ben Wiebe. LC 91-58984. 224p. (Orig.). 1992. pap. 16.99 (*0-8361-3585-7*) Herald Pr.

Messianic Exegesis: Christological Interpretation of the Old Testament in Early Christianity. Donald Juel. LC 86-46437. 208p. 1992. pap. 19.00 (*0-8006-2707-5*, 1-2707, Fortress Pr) Augsburg Fortress.

Messianic Expectation in the Old Testament. Joachim Becker. 1996. 35.95 (*0-567-09302-6*) Bks Intl VA.

Messianic Expectation in the Old Testament. Joachim Becker. Tr. by David E. Green. LC 79-8891. 96p. reprint ed. pap. 30.00 (*0-608-17175-1*, 202787500056) Bks Demand.

Messianic Hope: How to Share It with Your Jewish Friends. Albert P. Wellington. LC 83-73555. 68p. (Orig.). 1984. pap. 7.95 (*0-916169-00-6*) Adar Pubns.

Messianic Idea in Judaism: And Other Essays on Jewish Spirituality. Gershom Scholem. 384p. 1995. pap. 16.00 (*0-8052-1043-1*) Schocken.

Messianic Jewish Book of Why. G. Aaron Rogers. LC 97-49086. 110p. (Orig.). 1996. pap. 9.95 (*0-89036-631-4*) Liahona Pub Trust.

Messianic Jewish Book of Why?, Vol. 1. G. Aaron Rogers. 126p. 1997. pap. 9.95 (*1-890828-00-9*, 00-9, Pub. by Camden Ct) Origin Bk Sales.

Messianic Jewish Book of Why?, Vol. 2. G. Aaron Rogers. LC 97-49086. 160p. 1997. pap. 9.95 (*1-890828-05-X*, 05-X, Pub. by Camden Ct) Origin Bk Sales.

*__Messianic Jewish Congregations: Who Sold this Business to the Gentiles?__ Jeffrey S. Wasserman. 208p. 2000. 49.00 (*0-7618-1686-0*); pap. 29.50 (*0-7618-1687-9*) U Pr of Amer.

Messianic Jewish Manifesto. rev. ed. David H. Stern. LC 91-71530. 312p. (Orig.). (C). 1988. pap. 11.99 (*965-359-002-2*) Jewish New Test Pubns.

*__Messianic Judaism.__ Dan Cohn-Sherbok. LC 99-50300. 2000. 29.95 (*0-304-70730-9*) Continuum.

Messianic Judaism: A Rabbi's Journey Through Religious Change in America. Carol Harris-Shapiro. LC 98-54864. 256p. 1999. 26.00 (*0-8070-1040-5*) Beacon Pr.

*__Messianic Judaism: A Rabbi's Journey Through Religious Change in America.__ Carol Harris-Shapiro. 2000. pap. 17.00 (*0-8070-1041-3*) Beacon Pr.

Messianic Judaism: Its History, Theology, Polity. David A. Rausch. LC 82-20382. (Texts & Studies in Religion: Vol. 14). 304p. 1983. lib. bdg. 99.95 (*0-88946-802-8*) E Mellen.

Messianic Kingdom. Jeffrey Seif. 1989. per. 9.95 (*0-89985-276-9*) Christ for the Nations.

Messianic Legacy. Michael Baigent et al. 512p. 1988. pap. 8.99 (*0-552-13182-2*) Bantam.

Messianic Legacy. Michael Baigent et al. 448p. 1989. mass mkt. 7.50 (*0-440-20319-8*) Dell.

Messianic Look at Christmas & Hanukkah. Ed. by Jews for Jesus. (Illus.). 31p. 1995. pap. 3.00 (*1-881022-22-6*, BT031) Purple Pomegranate.

Messianic Mystics. Moshe Idel. LC 98-13905. 464p. 1998. 45.00 (*0-300-06840-9*) Yale U Pr.

*__Messianic Mystics.__ Moshe Idel. 464p. 2000. pap. 18.00 (*0-300-08288-6*) Yale U Pr.

Messianic Passover Curriculum. Lin Johnson. 1998. pap. 7.99 (*1-880226-45-6*) M J Pubs.

*__Messianic Passover Haggadah.__ Barry Rubin & Steffi Rubin. (SPA.). 1998. pap. 4.99 (*1-880226-59-6*) M J Pubs.

Messianic Passover Haggadah. Illus. by Barry Rubin & Steffi K. Rubin. 32p. 1989. pap. 4.99 (*1-880226-07-3*) M J Pubs.

Messianic Passover Seder Preparation Guide: Instructions, Recipes & Music for a Messianic Passover Seder. Barry Rubin & Steffi K. Rubin. 20p. 1989. pap. 2.99 (*1-880226-24-3*) M J Pubs.

Messianic Prophecies in Historic Succession. Franz Delitzsch. 232p. 1997. pap. 20.00 (*1-57910-077-5*) Wipf & Stock.

*__Messianic Prophecy & Fulfillment.__ large type ed. Henry L. Knight. Ed. by Darlene Wooten et al. 2000. pap. 7.50 (*1-887653-15-5*) Papito.

Messianic Psalms: An Inductive Bible Study. Phillip G. Wahlbeck. 64p. 1999. 5.95 (*1-891147-51-X*) Rock Dove.

Messianic Revelation in the Old Testament, 2. Gerard Van Groningen. 1022p. 1997. pap. 60.00 (*1-57910-049-X*) Wipf & Stock.

Messianic Revolution: Radical Religious Politics to the End of the Second Millennium. David S. Katz & Richard H. Popkin. LC 98-46189. 352p. 1999. 22.00 (*0-8090-6885-0*) Hill & Wang.

*__Messianic Revolution: Radical Religious Politics to the End of the Second Millennium.__ David S. Katz & Richard H. Popkin. 352p. 2000. pap. 15.00 (*0-8090-6886-9*) Hill & Wang.

Messianic Secret in Mark's Gospel. Heikki Raisanen. Tr. by Christopher Tuckett from FIN. 320p. 1994. pap. text 31.95 (*0-567-29253-3*, Pub. by T & T Clark) Bks Intl VA.

Messianism, Mysticism, & Magic: A Sociological Analysis of Jewish Religious Movements. Stephen Sharot. LC 81-11668. (Studies in Religion). 316p. 1982. reprint ed. pap. 98.00 (*0-7837-9017-1*, 204976900003) Bks Demand.

Messianism, Zioinism, & Jewish Religious Radicalism. Aviezer Ravitzky. 280p. 1996. pap. text 18.00 (*0-226-70578-1*) U Ch Pr.

Messianism, Zioinism, & Jewish Religious Radicalism. Aviezer Ravitzky. Tr. by Michael Swirsky & Jonathan Chipman. 280p. 1996. lib. bdg. 48.00 (*0-226-70577-3*) U Ch Pr.

Messias: Band 4 Apparat, Section Werke IV, Bd. 4. 1984. 265.50 (*3-11-008898-3*) De Gruyter.

Messie Motivator: New Strategies to Restoring Order in Your Life & Home. Sandra Felton. LC 96-8629. 192p. (gr. 11). 1996. pap. 11.99 (*0-8007-5608-8*) Revell.

Messie No More. Sandra Felton. (Illus.). 188p. 1988. pap. 9.99 (*0-8007-5302-X*) Revell.

*__Messier: Hockey's Dragon Slayer.__ Rick Carpiniello. LC 99-36864. 1999. pap. text 17.95 (*0-9653846-9-1*) MCRHSI.

Messier's Nebulae & Star Clusters. 2nd ed. Kenneth G. Jones. (Practical Astronomy Handbooks Ser.: No. 2). (Illus.). 445p. (C). 1991. text 64.95 (*0-521-37079-5*) Cambridge U Pr.

Messies Manual see Manual del Ama de Casa Desordenada

Messies Manual: The Procrastinator's Guide to Good Housekeeping. Sandra Felton. LC 83-16061. (Illus.). 158p. 1987. pap. 9.99 (*0-8007-5133-7*) Revell.

Messies Superguide: Strategies & Ideas for Conquering Catastrophic Living. Sandra Felton. LC 87-10879. 224p. 1991. pap. 9.99 (*0-8007-5403-4*) Revell.

Messieurs les Ronds-de-Cuir. Georges Courteline. (FRE.). 1990. pap. 10.95 (*0-7859-2960-6*) Fr & Eur.

Messin' Man. Charles V. Kirk. LC 97-75790. 328p. 1998. 24.95 (*1-57197-098-3*) Pentland Pr.

Messines Ridge: Ypres. Peter Oldham. (Illus.). 1998. pap. 16.95 (*0-85052-624-8*, Pub. by Leo Cooper) Combined Pub.

Messing about in Boats: The Nautical Confessions of an Unsinkable Irishman. Will Millar. (Illus.). 192p. 1997. pap. 16.95 (*1-55110-620-5*) Whitecap Bks.

Messing about in Problems: Informal Structured Approach to Identification & Management. C. Eden et al. LC 82-25967. (Frontiers of Operational Research & Applied Systems Analysis Ser.: Vol. 1). (Illus.). 130p. 1983. 67.00 (*0-08-029961-X*, Pub. by Pergamon Repr) Franklin.

Messing Around with Drinking Straw Construction. Bernie Zubrowski. (Illus.). (J). (gr. 3-7). 1981. 10.95 (*0-316-98873-1*, 984785) Little.

Messing Around with Drinking Straw Construction: A Children's Museum Activity Book. Bernie Zubrowski. (Illus.). 64p. (J). (gr. 3-7). 1981. pap. 7.95 (*0-685-57751-1*) Little.

Messkataloge des Sechzehnten Jahrhunderst, Die 1564-1600, 5 vols., 5. Ed. by Bernhard Fabian. reprint ed. write for info. (*0-318-71845-6*) G Olms Pubs.

Messkataloge des Sechzehnten Jahrhunderst, Die 1564-1600, 5 vols., Vol. 1. Ed. by Bernhard Fabian. 1972. reprint ed. write for info. (*3-487-04425-0*) G Olms Pubs.

Messkataloge des Sechzehnten Jahrhunderst, Die 1564-1600, 5 vols., Vol. 2. Ed. by Bernhard Fabian. 1973. reprint ed. write for info. (*3-487-04426-9*) G Olms Pubs.

M

Messkataloge des Sechzehnten Jahrhunderst, Die 1564-1600, 5 vols., Vol. 3. Ed. by Bernhard Fabian. 1980. reprint ed. write for info. (*3-487-04427-7*) G Olms Pubs.

Messkataloge des Sechzehnten Jahrhunderst, Die 1564-1600, 5 vols., Vol. 4. Ed. by Bernhard Fabian. 1978. reprint ed. write for info. (*3-487-05564-3*) G Olms Pubs.

Messkataloge des Sechzehnten Jahrhunderst, 1564-1600, 5 vols. Ed. by Bernhard Fabian. 1980. write for info. (*0-318-71820-0*) G Olms Pubs.

Messy: Very First Picture Book. Nicola Tuxworth. (Illus.). 24p. (J). (ps). 1997. 4.95 (*1-85967-507-7*, Lorenz Bks) Anness Pub.

***Messy, A Very First Picture.** Anness Publishing Staff. (J). (-7). 2000. bds. 4.95 (*0-7548-0708-8*) Anness Pub.

Messy Bessey. Patricia McKissack & Fredrick McKissack. LC 87-15079. (Rookie Readers Ser.). (Illus.). (J). (ps-2). 1987. pap. 4.95 (*0-516-42083-6*) Childrens.

Messy Bessey. rev. ed. Patricia McKissack. LC 99-22472. (Rookie Readers Ser.). 32p. (J). (gr. 1-2). 1999. 17.50 (*0-516-21650-3*) Childrens.

***Messy Bessey.** rev. ed. Patricia McKissack. LC 99-22472. (Rookie Readers Ser.). (Illus.). 32p. (J). (gr. 1-2). 2000. pap. text 4.95 (*0-516-27003-6*) Childrens.

Messy Bessey & the Birthday Overnight. Patricia C. McKissack & Fredrick McKissack. (Rookie Readers Ser.). (Illus.). 32p. (YA). (gr. k-3). 1999. pap. text 4.95 (*0-516-26411-7*) Childrens.

Messy Bessey's Closet. Patricia C. McKissack & Fredrick McKissack. LC 89-34667. (Rookie Readers Ser.). (Illus.). 32p. (J). (ps-3). 1989. lib. bdg. 17.00 (*0-516-02091-9*) Childrens.

***Messy Bessey's Family Reunion.** Patricia McKissack. (Rookie Readers Ser.). (Illus.). 32p. (J). (gr. 1-2). 2000. pap. 4.95 (*0-516-26552-0*) Childrens.

***Messy Bessey's Family Reunion.** Patricia McKissack et al. LC 99-16312. (Rookie Readers Ser.). (J). 2000. 17.50 (*0-516-20830-6*) Childrens.

Messy Bessey's Garden. Patricia McKissack & Fredrick McKissack. LC 91-15333. (Rookie Readers Ser.). (Illus.). 32p. (J). (ps-3). 1991. pap. 4.95 (*0-516-42008-9*); lib. bdg. 17.00 (*0-516-02008-0*) Childrens.

Messy Bessey's Holidays. Pat McKissack & Fredrick McKissack. LC 98-8057. (Rookie Readers Ser.). (Illus.). 32p. (J). (gr. k-3). 1999. 17.00 (*0-516-20829-2*) Childrens.

Messy Bessey's School Desk. Patricia McKissack & Fredrick McKissack. LC 97-13837. (Rookie Readers Ser.). (Illus.). 32p. (J). (gr. k-2). 1998. 17.00 (*0-516-20827-6*) Childrens.

Messy Bessy's Holidays. Patricia C. McKissack. (Rookie Readers Ser.). 1999. lib. bdg. 4.95 (*0-516-26476-1*) Childrens.

Messy Job I Never Did See a Girl Do: Stories. Mary J. Ryals. 144p. 1999. pap. 9.95 (*0-942979-59-1*); lib. bdg. 19.95 (*0-942979-60-5*) Livingston AL.

Messy Mark. Sharon Peters. (Illus.). 32p. (J). (gr. k-2). 1997. pap. 2.50 (*0-89375-281-9*) Troll Communs.

Messy Mark: Big Book Edition. Sharon Peters. 1999. pap. text 16.95 (*0-8167-2664-7*) Troll Communs.

Messy Moose: Big Book. large type ed. Lois Bick. (Little Books & Big Bks.). (Illus.). 8p. (J). (ps-1). 1998. pap. text 19.89 (*0-8215-0842-3*) Sadlier.

Messy Murray Brown. C. West. (Illus.). (J). mass mkt. 7.95 (*0-340-72661-X*, Pub. by Hodder & Stought Ltd) Trafalgar.

Messy on the Inside. Eileen Albrizio. (Illus.). 82p. 1999. pap. 10.00 (*1-889289-32-9*) Ye Olde Font Shoppe.

Messy Tessie Has a Tea Party. Julie Brown. (Illus.). 32p. (J). (gr. 1-3). 1997. 5.95 (*1-885744-10-2*) Otter Creek.

Messy Tessie Takes a Bath. Julie Brown. (Illus.). 32p. (Orig.). (J). (gr. 1-3). 1996. pap. 5.95 (*1-885744-06-4*) Otter Creek.

Messy Zoo. Joyce Vermeer. 16p. (J). (ps). 1994. pap. 6.95 (*1-885964-00-5*) PTwo Educ.

Mestenos: Spanish Ranching in Texas, 1721-1821. Jack Jackson. LC 84-40561. (Centennial Series of the Association of Former Students: Vol. 18). (Illus.). 728p. 1997. reprint ed. 49.95 (*0-89096-230-8*) Tex A&M Univ Pr.

Mesters to Masters: A History of the Company of Cutlers in Hallamshire. Ed. by David Hey & Clyde Binfield. LC 97-2309. (Illus.). 358p. 1997. text 65.00 (*0-19-828997-9*) OUP.

Mesthene: Technology & Social Change. Emmanuel Mesthene. LC 67-23043. (Orig.). (C). 1967. pap. write for info. (*0-672-60900-2*, CR14, Bobbs) Macmillan.

Mestizaje en IberoAmerica see Mestizaje in Ibero-America

Mestizaje in Ibero-America. Claudio Esteva-Fabregat. Tr. by John Wheat from SPA. LC 94-18731.Tr. of Mestizaje en IberoAmerica. 378p. 1995. 56.00 (*0-8165-1219-1*) U of Ariz Pr.

***Mestizo: A Novel.** Ricardo Feierstein. LC 99-6319. (Jewish Latin America Ser.). 352p. 2000. 19.95 (*0-8263-2116-X*); 45.00 (*0-8263-2115-1*) U of NM Pr.

Mestizo: The History, Culture & Politics of the Mexican & the Chicano - The Emerging Mestizol-Americans. Arnolodo C. Vento. LC 97-37402. 336p. (C). 1997. 68.00 (*0-7618-0919-8*); pap. 38.50 (*0-7618-0920-1*) U Pr of Amer.

***Mestizo America: The Country of the Future.** William Ospina. (Illus.). 344p. 2000. 75.00 (*958-9393-87-X*, Pub. by Villegas Ed) Rizzoli Intl.

Mestizo As Crucible: Andean Indian & African Poets of Mixed Origin As Possibility of Comparative Poetics. Christine De Lailhacar. (Studies in Modern Poetry: Vol. 5). X, 318p. (C). 1996. text 54.95 (*0-8204-2891-4*) P Lang Pubng.

Mestizo Christianity: Theology from the Latino Perspective. Ed. by Arturo J. Banuelas. LC 95-23232. 250p. (Orig.). 1995. 17.00 (*1-57075-032-7*) Orbis Bks.

Mestizo Logics: Anthropology of Identity in Africa & Elsewhere. Jean-Loup Amselle. Tr. by Claudia Royal from FRE. LC 97-26993. (Mestizo Spaces Ser.). 240p. 1997. 45.00 (*0-8047-2429-6*); pap. 15.95 (*0-8047-2431-8*) Stanford U Pr.

Mestizo Worship: A Pastorial Approach to Liturgical Ministry. Virgilio P. Elizondo & Timothy M. Matovina. LC 97-52052. 112p. 1998. pap. 9.95 (*0-8146-2490-1*) Liturgical Pr.

Mesure des Gestes: Prolegomenes a la Semiotique Gestuelle. Paul Bouissac. (Approaches to Semiotics Ser.: No. 3). 1973. pap. 55.40 (*90-279-2377-9*) Mouton.

Mesure et Integration dans l'Espace Euclidien see Analyse Fonctionnelle

Met by Moonlight. Rosemary Edghill. 320p. 1998. mass mkt. 5.50 (*0-7860-0482-7*, Pinnacle Kensgtn) Kensgtn Pub Corp.

Met Light der Wereld see Light of the World

MET Publication 516: Port State Control. Richard A. Block. 420p. 1997. pap. 85.00 (*1-879778-65-3*, BK-0722) Marine Educ.

Meta-Analysis: Cumulating Research Findings Across Studies. John E. Hunter et al. LC 82-10741. (Studying Organizations Ser.: No. 4). 176p. 1982. reprint ed. pap. 54.60 (*0-608-01183-5*, 205948100001) Bks Demand.

Meta-Analysis: Quantitative Methods for Research Synthesis. Fredic M. Wolf. (Quantitative Applications in the Social Sciences Ser.: Vol. 59). 80p. (Orig.). (C). 1986. pap. text 10.95 (*0-8039-2756-8*) Sage.

Meta-Analysis by the Confidence Profile Method: The Statistical Synthesis of Evidence. David M. Eddy et al. (Statistical Modeling & Decision Science Ser.). (Illus.). 428p. 1991. text 94.00 (*0-12-230620-1*) Acad Pr.

Meta-Analysis, Decision Analysis & Cost-Effectiveness Analysis: Methods for Quantitative Synthesis in Medicine. 2nd ed. Diana B. Petitti. LC 99-13213. (Monographs in Epidemiology & Biostatistics: No. 31). (Illus.). 320p. 1999. text 49.95 (*0-19-513364-1*) OUP.

Meta-Analysis for Explanation: A Casebook. Thomas Cook et al. LC 91-17999. 1992. 45.00 (*0-87154-220-X*) Russell Sage.

Meta-Analysis for Explanation: A Casebook. Thomas Cook et al. (Illus.). 392p. 1994. reprint ed. pap. 19.95 (*0-87154-228-5*) Russell Sage.

Meta-Analysis in Environmental Economics. LC 97-18875. 1997. lib. bdg. 117.50 (*0-7923-4592-4*) Kluwer Academic.

Meta Analysis in Social Research. Gene V. Glass et al. LC 81-5673. (Illus.). 272p. 1981. 44.00 (*0-8039-1633-7*) Sage.

Meta-Analysis in Social Research. Gene V. Glass et al. LC 81-5673. 279p. 1981. reprint ed. pap. 86.50 (*0-608-01615-2*, 205959400003) Bks Demand.

Meta-Analysis of Drug Abuse Prevention Programs. Ed. by William J. Bukoski. (Illus.). 263p. (C). 1998. pap. text 45.00 (*0-7881-7215-8*) DIANE Pub.

Meta Analysis of Drug Abuse Prevention Programs. William J. Bukoski. 267p. 1997. per. 17.00 (*0-16-061518-6*) USGPO.

Meta-Analysis of Nursing Intervention Research. Mary C. Smith. (Illus.). xvi, 302p. (Orig.). (C). 1988. pap. text 41.95 (*0-9622620-1-3*) M C Smith.

***Meta-Analysis of the Rates of Return to Agricultural R & D: Ex Pede Herculem?** Julian M. Alston. LC 00-40733. 2000. pap. write for info. (*0-89629-116-2*) Intl Pubs Co.

Meta-Analytic Procedures for Social Research. rev. ed. Robert Rosenthal. (Applied Social Research Methods Ser.: Vol. 6). (Illus.). 148p. 1991. text 42.00 (*0-8039-4245-1*); pap. text 18.95 (*0-8039-4246-X*) Sage.

Meta-Emotion: How Families Communicate Emotionally. John M. Gottman et al. 288p. 1996. text 79.95 (*0-8058-1995-9*) L Erlbaum Assocs.

Meta-Emotion: How Families Communicate Emotionally. John M. Gottman et al. 288p. 1996. pap. 39.95 (*0-8058-1996-7*) L Erlbaum Assocs.

Meta Ethics. Ed. by Michael Smith. (International Research Library of Philosophy). 608p. 1995. text 199.95 (*1-85521-502-0*, Pub. by Dartmth Pub) Ashgate Pub Co.

Meta-Ethnography: Synthesizing Qualitative Studies. George W. Noblit & R. Dwight Hare. (Qualitative Research Methods Ser.: Vol. 11). 96p. (C). 1988. text 24.00 (*0-8039-3022-4*); pap. text 10.50 (*0-8039-3023-2*) Sage.

***Meta-Evolution - The Future of Life: A Unified Theory of Evolution.** David Hunter Tow. LC 99-91968. 2000. 25.00 (*0-7388-1462-8*); pap. 18.00 (*0-7388-1463-6*) Xlibris Corp.

Meta-Heuristics: Advances & Trends in Local Search Paradigms for Optimization. Stefan Voss. LC 98-44415. 1998. write for info. (*0-7923-8369-9*) Kluwer Academic.

Meta-Heuristics: Theory & Applications. Ed. by Ibrahim H. Osman. 704p. (C). 1996. lib. bdg. 212.00 (*0-7923-9700-2*) Kluwer Academic.

Meta-Hodos & META Meta-Hodos: A Phenomenology of 20th Century Musical Materials & an Approach to the Study of Form. 2nd rev. ed. James Tenney. Ed. by Lauren Pratt. (Illus.). 116p. (Orig.). (C). 1988. pap. text 15.00 (*0-945996-00-4*) Frog Peak Music.

Meta-Imperialism: A Study in Political Science. Fred Nash. (Avebury Series in Philosophy). 544p. 1994. 104.95 (*1-85628-694-0*, Pub. by Avebry) Ashgate Pub Co.

Meta Incognita. Ruby. Date not set. 30.00 (*0-8050-5215-1*); pap. 18.00 (*0-8050-5214-3*) H Holt & Co.

***Meta Incognita: A Discourse of Discovery: Martin Frobisher's Arctic Expeditions, 1576-1578, 2 vols., Set.** Ed. by Thomas H. Symons. (Mercury Ser.). (Illus.). 636p. 1999. pap. 45.00 (*0-660-17507-X*, Pub. by CN Mus Civilization) U of Wash Pr.

Meta Incognita Project: Contributions to Field Studies. Ed. by Stephen Alsford. (Mercury Ser.: Directorate No. 6). (Illus.). 228p. 1993. pap. 19.95 (*0-660-14010-1*, Pub. by CN Mus Civilization) U of Wash Pr.

***Meta-Level Architectures & Reflection: Proceedings, 2nd International Conference, Reflection '99, Saint Malo, France, July 19-21, 1999.** Ed. by Pierre Cointe. LC 99-39040. (Lecture Notes in Computer Science Ser.: Vol. 1616). xi, 273p. 1999. pap. 52.00 (*3-540-66280-4*) Spr-Verlag.

Meta-Level Control for Deductive Database Systems. H. Schmidt. Ed. by G. Goos & J. Hartmanis. (Lecture Notes in Computer Science Ser.: Vol. 479). vi, 155p. 1991. 27.00 (*0-387-53754-6*) Spr-Verlag.

Meta-Level Inference Systems. Frank Van Harmelen. 1991. pap. text 34.95 (*1-55860-196-1*) Morgan Kaufmann.

Meta-Logics & Logic Programming. Ed. by Krzysztof Apt & Franco Turini. (Logic Programming Ser.). (Illus.). 350p. (C). 1995. 44.00 (*0-262-01152-2*) MIT Pr.

Meta-Modeling: Performance & Information Modeling. Jean-Michel Berge et al. Ed. by Barbara Daniel. LC 96-18914. (Current Issues in Electronic Modeling Ser.). (C). 1996. lib. bdg. 115.00 (*0-7923-9687-1*, D Reidel) Kluwer Academic.

Meta-Modeling: Performance & Information Modeling, 2 vols., Set. Jean-Michel Berge. LC 96-18914. (Current Issues in Electronic Modeling Ser.). 152p. (C). 1996. lib. bdg. 115.00 (*0-614-18916-0*, D Reidel) Kluwer Academic.

Meta-Modeling: Performance & Information Modeling, Set, Issues 5-8. Jean-Michel Berge. LC 96-41149. (Current Issues in Electronic Modeling Ser.). 176p. (C). 1996. text 318.00 (*0-7923-9690-1*) Kluwer Academic.

Meta-Morphing: Visual Transformation & the Culture of Quick-Change. Ed. by Vivian Sobchack. LC 99-44863. 256p. 1999. pap. 18.95 (*0-8166-3319-3*, Pub. by U of Minn Pr); lib. bdg. 47.95 (*0-8166-3318-5*, Pub. by U of Minn Pr) Chicago Distribution Ctr.

Meta-Programming in Logic: Third International Workshop, META-92, Uppsala, Sweden, June 10-12, 1992: Proceedings. Ed. by A. Pettorossi. LC 92-41020. (Lecture Notes in Computer Science Ser.: Vol. 649). 1992. 57.95 (*0-387-56282-6*) Spr-Verlag.

Meta-Psychometry: Key to Power & Abundance. Gavin Frost & Yvonne Frost. 239p. 1993. pap. text 12.95 (*0-9630657-4-2*) Godolphin Hse.

***Meta-State Patterns: Meta-Stating for Excellence.** L. Michael Hall. 230p. 1999. pap. write for info. (*1-890001-12-0*) Empowerment Tech.

Meta-States - A Domain of Logical Levels: Self-Reflexiveness in Human States of Consciousness. L. Michael Hall. 284p. (Orig.). 1996. pap. 20.00 (*1-890001-08-2*) Empowerment Tech.

Meta-Talk. Gerard I. Nierenberg. 1981. pap. 4.95 (*0-685-03973-0*) PB.

Meta-Translators in Advanced Programming Languages: Kiev Institute of Cybernetics R&D. Olga Kholodenko & Gregory Zaytman. (Foreign Technology Assessment Ser.). 120p. (Orig.). 1994. pap. 65.00 (*1-881874-14-1*) Global Cnslts.

Meta-Variations: Studies in the Foundations of Musical Thought - Compose Yourself: A Manual for the Young. Benjamin Boretz & J. K. Randall. LC 91-90388. 500p. 1994. write for info. (*0-9629865-1-8*) Open Space NY.

Metaarchaeology: Reflections by Archeologists & Philosophers. Ed. by Lester Embree. LC 92-33755. (Boston Studies in the Philosophy of Science: Vol. 147). 342p. (C). 1992. lib. bdg. 166.50 (*0-7923-2023-9*, Pub. by Kluwer Academic) Kluwer Academic.

Metabolic Activation & Toxicity of Chemical Agents to Lung Tissue & Cells. Ed. by Theodore E. Gram. LC 92-49048. (International Encyclopedia of Pharmacology & Therapeutics Ser.: Section 138). 324p. 1993. 157.00 (*0-08-041177-0*, Pergamon Pr) Elsevier.

Metabolic Activation of Drugs & Other Xenobiotics in Hapatocellular Carcinoma. Grace S. Lau. 1998. pap. text 44.50 (*962-201-744-4*, Pub. by Chinese Univ) U of Mich Pr.

Metabolic Activities of the Lung. CIBA Foundation Staff. LC 80-20318. (CIBA Foundation Symposium: New Ser.: No. 78). 411p. reprint ed. pap. 127.50 (*0-608-14278-6*, 202219700024) Bks Demand.

Metabolic Adaptation to Climate & Distribution of the Raccoon Procyon Lotor & Other Procyonidae. John N. Mugaas et al. LC 93-3119. (Smithsonian Contributions to Zoology Ser.: No. 542). (Illus.). 38p. reprint ed. pap. 30.00 (*0-7837-5897-9*, 204568800007) Bks Demand.

Metabolic & Degenerative Diseases of the Central Nervous System: Pathology, Biochemistry, & Genetics. Ed. by Jorge Cervos-Navarro & Henry Urich. (Illus.). 873p. 1995. text 129.95 (*0-12-165250-5*) Acad Pr.

Metabolic & Endocrine Disturbances in Renal Diseases. Ed. by Shaul G. Massry et al. (Contributions to Nephrology Ser.: Vol. 49). (Illus.). viii, 224p. 1986. 29.75 (*3-8055-4143-0*) S Karger.

Metabolic & Endocrine Problems in the Elderly. W. J. MacLennan & N. R. Peden. (Illus.). 210p. 1989. 80.95 (*0-387-19541-6*) Spr-Verlag.

Metabolic & Endocrine Problems of the Horse. Ed. by Tim Watson. (Illus.). 260p. (C). 1998. text 80.00 (*0-7020-2241-1*, Pub. by W B Saunders) Saunders.

Metabolic & Molecular Aspects of Cardiomyopathy. Ed. by Lionel H. Opie et al. LC 92-173761. (Cardiomyopathy Update Ser.: No. 4). 259p. 1991. reprint ed. pap. 80.30 (*0-608-01544-X*, 206195100001) Bks Demand.

Metabolic & Molecular Bases of Disease, 2 vols. Cohen. (Illus.). 2248p. 1990. text 375.00 (*0-7020-1493-1*, W B Saunders Co) Harcrt Hlth Sci Grp.

Metabolic & Molecular Bases of Inherited Disease, 1. 7th ed. Charles R. Scriver. write for info. (*0-07-060729-X*) McGraw.

Metabolic & Molecular Bases of Inherited Disease, 2. 7th ed. Charles R. Scriver. write for info. (*0-07-060730-3*) McGraw.

Metabolic & Molecular Bases of Inherited Disease, 3 vols., Set. 7th ed. Ed. by Charles R. Scriver et al. (Illus.). 5024p. 1994. text 325.00 (*0-07-909826-6*) McGraw-Hill HPD.

***Metabolic & Molecular Bases of Inherited Disease: Seventh Edition.** Charles R. Scriver et al. (Illus.). 6000p. 2000. Price not set. (*0-07-913035-6*) McGraw.

Metabolic & Nutritional Abnormalities in Kidney Disease. Ed. by G. Guarnieri et al. (Contributions to Nephrology Ser.: Vol. 98). (Illus.). viii, 196p. 1992. 49.75 (*3-8055-5582-2*) S Karger.

Metabolic & Pediatric Eye Disease: Proceedings of the International Society on Metabolic Eye Disease Symposium, 3rd. International Society on Metabolic Eye Disease Sta. Ed. by Heskel M. Haddad. (Illus.). 240p. 1980. pap. 55.00 (*0-08-024950-7*, Pergamon Pr) Elsevier.

Metabolic Arrest & the Control of Biological Time. Peter W. Hochachka & Michael Guppy. LC 86-14860. (Illus.). 256p. 1987. 43.50 (*0-674-56976-8*) HUP.

Metabolic Aspects of Transport Across Cell Membranes. Ed. by Quillian R. Murphy. LC 57-9808. 406p. reprint ed. pap. 125.90 (*0-608-14475-4*, 202114300021) Bks Demand.

Metabolic Biochemistry. Ed. by Peter W. Hochachka & T. P. Mommsen. (Biochemistry & Molecular Biology of Fishes Ser.: Vol. 4). 530p. 1995. 256.25 (*0-444-82082-5*) Elsevier.

Metabolic Bone & Mineral Disorders. fac. ed. Ed. by Stavros C. Manolagas & Jerrold M. Olefsky. LC 88-22864. (Contemporary Issues in Endocrinology & Metabolism Ser.: No. 5). (Illus.). 266p. 1988. reprint ed. pap. 82.50 (*0-7837-7877-5*, 204763400007) Bks Demand.

Metabolic Bone Disease. 3rd ed. Ed. by Louis V. Avioli & Stephen M. Krane. (Illus.). 811p. 1997. text 179.95 (*0-12-068700-3*) Morgan Kaufmann.

Metabolic Bone Disease: Cellular & Tissue Mechanisms. Ed. by Cherk S. Tam et al. 272p. 1988. 168.00 (*0-8493-6422-1*, RC931, CRC Reprint) Franklin.

Metabolic Bone Disease & Clinically Related Disorders. 2nd ed. Louis V. Avioli & Stephen M. Krane. (Illus.). 912p. 1990. text 270.00 (*0-7216-2766-8*, W B Saunders Co) Harcrt Hlth Sci Grp.

Metabolic Calculations - Simplified. David P. Swain & Brian C. Leutholtz. LC 97-16034. (Illus.). 100p. 1997. pap., spiral bd. 15.00 (*0-683-30137-3*) Lppncott W & W.

Metabolic Consequences of Changing Dietary Patterns. Ed. by A. P. Simopoulos. (World Review of Nutrition & Dietetics Ser.: Vol. 79, 1996). (Illus.). xv, 226p. 1996. 221.00 (*3-8055-6296-9*) S Karger.

Metabolic Control of Disease. 8th ed. Philip K. Bondy & Leon E. Rosenberg. LC 78-52722. (Illus.). 1980. text 225.00 (*0-7216-1844-8*, W B Saunders Co) Harcrt Hlth Sci Grp.

Metabolic Control of Eating, Energy Expenditure & the Bioenergetics of Obesity. Ed. by A. P. Simopoulos. (World Review of Nutrition & Dietetics Ser.: Vol. 70). (Illus.). xii, 176p. 1992. 204.50 (*3-8055-5595-4*) S Karger.

Metabolic, Degenerative, & Inflammatory Diseases of Bones & Joints. Henry L. Jaffe. LC 72-187985. 1112p. reprint ed. pap. 200.00 (*0-608-17779-2*, 205657000074) Bks Demand.

Metabolic Diseases: Foundations of Clinical Management, Genetics & Pathology. Enid Gilbert-Barness & Lewis Barness. (Illus.). 900p. 1999. 249.00 (*1-881299-11-2*) Eaton Pub Co.

Metabolic Diseases in Pediatric Practice. Mary G. Ampola. 1982. text 39.00 (*0-316-03796-6*, Little Brwn Med Div) Lppncott W & W.

Metabolic Disorders & Nutrition Correlated with Skin. Ed. by B. J. Vermeer et al. (Current Problems in Dermatology Ser.: Vol. 20). (Illus.). x, 216p. 1991. 217.50 (*3-8055-5361-7*) S Karger.

Metabolic Disorders & Their Prevention in Farm Animals. Ed. by L. Vrzgula. (Developments in Animal & Veterinary Science Ser.: No. 24). 390p. 1991. 206.25 (*0-444-98734-7*) Elsevier.

Metabolic Disorders, Methods of Examination. Ed. by W. Straub. (Developments in Ophthalmology Ser.: Vol. 4). (Illus.). v, 218p. 1981. 144.50 (*3-8055-2014-X*) S Karger.

Metabolic Disturbances in the Predialytic Phase of Chronic Renal Failure. Ed. by R. Schmicker et al. (Contributions to Nephrology Ser.: Vol. 65). (Illus.). viii, 140p. 1988. 29.75 (*3-8055-4739-0*) S Karger.

Metabolic Drug Interactions. Ren H. Levy et al. 750p. text 159.00 (*0-7817-1441-9*) Lppncott W & W.

Metabolic Effects of Dietary Carbohydrates. Ed. by I Macdonald. (Progress in Biochemical Pharmacology Ser.: Vol. 21). (Illus.). x, 274p. 1986. 186.25 (*3-8055-4229-1*) S Karger.

Metabolic Effects of Dietary Fructose. Ed. by Sheldon Reiser & Judith Hallfrisch. LC 86-31687. 176p. 1987. 105.00 (*0-8493-6457-4*, QP702, CRC Reprint) Franklin.

M

An Asterisk (*) at the beginning of an entry indicates that the title is appearing for the first time.

Metabolic Effects of Utilizable Dietary Carbohydrates. Sheldon Reiser. LC 82-10079. (Illus.). 358p. reprint ed. pap. 111.00 (*0-7837-0669-3*, 204100400019) Bks Demand.

Metabolic Encephalopathies. Di Donato. 216p. 68.00 (*0-86196-489-6*, Pub. by J Libbey Med) Bks Intl VA.

Metabolic-Endocrine Responses to Food Intake in Infancy. Ed. by G. Zoppi. (Monographs in Pediatrics: Vol. 16). (Illus.). viii, 116p. 1982. pap. 56.75 (*3-8055-3477-9*) S Karger.

***Metabolic Engineering.** Sang Yup Lee & E. Terry Papoutsakis. LC 99-38508. (Bioprocess Technology Ser.). (Illus.). 423p. 1999. text 165.00 (*0-8247-7390-X*) Dekker.

Metabolic Engineering. Contrib. by Sahm. xii, 208p. 1996. 149.00 (*3-540-60669-6*) Spr-Verlag.

Metabolic Engineering: Principles & Methodologies. Gregory N. Stephanopoulos et al. LC 98-84372. (Illus.). 725p. (C). 1998. boxed set 99.95 (*0-12-666260-6*) Acad Pr.

***Metabolic Engineering of Plant Secondary Metabolism.** R. Verpoorte & A. W. Alfermann. LC 00-30654. 2000. write for info. (*0-7923-6360-4*) Kluwer Academic.

Metabolic Feedback: Burn Calories Faster. D. M. Foster. 24p. (Orig.). 1987. pap. 3.00 (*0-938451-04-9*) Selena Pr.

Metabolic Functions of the Lung. Ed. by Y. S. Bakhle & John R. Vane. LC 76-41467. (Lung Biology in Health & Disease Ser.: No. 4). (Illus.). 373p. reprint ed. pap. 115.70 (*0-7837-3379-8*, 204333700008) Bks Demand.

Metabolic Homeostasis: A Syllabus for Those Concerned with the Care of Patients. Nathan B. Talbot et al. LC 59-14732. (Commonwealth Fund Publications). 144p. 1959. pap. 18.00 (*0-674-57000-6*) HUP.

Metabolic Modifiers: Effects on the Nutrient Requirements of Food-Producing Animals. National Research Council, Subcommittee on Metabolism Staff. 96p. (Orig.). (C). 1994. pap. text 27.95 (*0-309-04997-0*) Natl Acad Pr.

Metabolic Myopathies. Hilton. 1995. text 72.00 (*0-7020-1607-1*, W B Saunders Co) Harcrt Hlth Sci Grp.

Metabolic, Nutritional, & Endocrine Disorders: International Nomenclature of Diseases. xxiii, 464p. 1991. pap. text 25.00 (*92-4-154432-5*, 1820006) World Health.

Metabolic Pathways of Agrochemicals. Incl. Herbicides & Plant Growth Regulators Pt. 1. Ed. by T. Roberts. 864p. 1998. 450.00 (*0-85404-494-9*, Pub. by Royal Soc Chem); Insecticides & Fungicides Pt. 2. T. Roberts. 1000p. 1999. 450.00 (*0-85404-499-X*, Pub. by Royal Soc Chem); 1864p. 1998. 795.00 (*0-85404-489-2*, Pub. by Royal Soc Chem) Spr-Verlag.

Metabolic Polymorphisms & Susceptibility to Cancer. Ed. by Paolo Vineis et al. (IARC Scientific Publications: No. 148). 528p. 1999. pap. text 90.00 (*92-832-2148-6*) OUP.

Metabolic Problems of the Newborn: Journal: Biology of the Neonate, Vol. 58, Suppl. 1, 1990. Ed. by Firmino F. Rubaltelli. (Illus.). iv, 108p. 1990. pap. 35.00 (*3-8055-5304-8*) S Karger.

Metabolic Regulation: A Human Perspective. K. N. Frayn. Ed. by Keith Snell. (Frontiers in Metabolism Ser.: No. 1). (Illus.). 284p. (Orig.). (C). 1996. pap. text 32.20 (*1-85578-048-8*, Pub. by Portland Pr Ltd) Ashgate Pub Co.

Metabolic Risk Factors in Ischemic Cardiovascular Disease. Ed. by Lars A. Carlson & Bengt Pernow. LC 80-5835. 263p. 1982. reprint ed. pap. 81.60 (*0-608-00308-5*, 206102500007) Bks Demand.

Metabolic Support for the Critically Ill Patient. Ed. by D. W. Wilmore & Y. A. Carpentier. LC 93-28459. (Update in Intensive Care & Emergency Medicine Ser.: Vol. 17). 1993. 125.00 (*0-387-57154-X*) Spr-Verlag.

***Metabolic Syndrome X: Convergence of Insulin Resistance, Hypertension, Obesity & Dyplipidemias-Searching for the Underlying Defects.** Ed. by Barbara C. Hansen et al. 1999. write for info. (*1-57331-207-X*) NY Acad Sci.

Metabolic Treatment of Fibromyalgia. unabridged ed. John C. Lowe. Ed. by Jackie G. Yellin. (Illus.). 850p. 1998. boxed set 99.95 (*0-914609-02-5*) McDowell Pub Co.

***Metabolic Typing Diet: The Ultimate Guide to Permanent Weight Loss & Optimum Health, High Energy & Peak Athletic Performance, Preventing & Reversing Disease, Staying Young at Any Age.** William Linz Wolcott & Trish Fahey. LC 99-55741. 448p. 2000. 23.95 (*0-385-49691-5*) Doubleday.

Metabolicmakeover: A 52 Week Health & Fitness Planner To Guide You In Balancing Blood Sugars, Mo, 1. 2nd ed. Helene Berk. 1998. pap. text. write for info. (*0-9663748-0-0*) Health Commit.

Metabolism. C. Coffee. (Integrated Medical Sciences Ser.). (C). 1997. pap. 22.95 (*1-889325-26-0*) Fence Crk Pubng.

***Metabolism.** Carole J Coffee. 1999. pap. text 18.95 (*1-889325-39-2*) Fence Crk Pubng.

Metabolism see Bilirubin

***Metabolism: A Memoir.** Elaine Shiramizu. (Illus.). 32p. 1999. 12.95 (*0-9674132-1-4*) LightWater.

Metabolism & Action of Anti-Cancer Drugs. Ed. by Garth Powis & R. A. Prough. LC 86-23179. 336p. 1987. 138.00 (*0-85066-369-5*) Taylor & Francis.

***Metabolism & Artificial Nutrition in the Critically Ill** G. Guarnieri & F. Iscra. LC 99-34124. (Topics in Anaesthesia & Critical Care Ser.). 1999. write for info. (*88-470-0042-4*, Pub. by Spr-Verlag) Spr-Verlag.

Metabolism & Behaviour see Current Studies of Hypothalamic Function 1978

Metabolism & Enzymology of Nucleic Acids Including Gene Manipulation. Ed. by J. Zelinka & J. Balan. LC 88-39215. (Illus.). 312p. 1988. 85.00 (*0-306-43089-4*, Plenum Trade) Perseus Pubng.

Metabolism & Molecular Physiology of Saccharomyces Cerevisiae. j Richard Dickonson. LC 99-173817. 1998. 74.95 (*0-7484-0731-6*) Taylor & Francis.

Metabolism & Nutrition in Liver Disease. Ed. by E. Holm & H. Kasper. (Falk Ser.). 1985. text 225.00 (*0-85200-907-0*) Kluwer Academic.

Metabolism & Reaction of Anti Cancer Drugs, 2 vols. Garth Powis. 329.25 (*0-08-042355-8*, Pergamon Pr) Elsevier.

Metabolism & Toxicity of Fluoride. G. M. Whitford. (Monographs in Oral Science: Vol. 13). (Illus.). x, 160p. 1989. 128.00 (*3-8055-4942-3*) S Karger.

Metabolism & Toxicity of Fluoride. 2nd rev. ed. G. M. Whitford. (Monographs in Oral Science: Vol. 16, 1996). (Illus.). xiv, 156p. 1996. 172.25 (*3-8055-6247-0*) S Karger.

Metabolism at a Glance. J. D. Salway. LC 93-45782. (At a Glance Ser.). (Illus.). 96p. 1994. pap. 27.95 (*0-632-03258-8*) Blackwell Sci.

***Metabolism at a Glance.** 2nd ed. Jack G. Salway. LC 98-48798. (At a Glance Ser.). (Illus.). 1999. pap. 29.95 (*0-632-05274-0*) Blackwell Sci.

***Metabolism of Agrochemicals in Plants** T. R. Roberts. LC 99-16222. (Series in Agrochemicals & Plant Protection). 314p. 2000. 175.00 (*0-471-80150-X*) Wiley.

Metabolism of Amino Acids & Amines see Methods in Enzymology

Metabolism of Anabolic-Androgenic Steroids. Victor A. Rogozkin. (Illus.). 168p. 1991. lib. bdg. 225.00 (*0-8493-6415-9*, QP) CRC Pr.

Metabolism of Antiepileptic Drugs. Ed. by Rene H. Levy et al. LC 84-3436. (Illus.). 263p. 1984. reprint ed. pap. 81.60 (*0-608-00624-6*, 206121100007) Bks Demand.

Metabolism of Aromatic Amino Acids & Amines, Vol. 142. Ed. by Seymour Kaufman. (Methods in Enzymology Ser.). 1987. text 149.00 (*0-12-182042-4*) Acad Pr.

Metabolism of Brain Peptides. Ed. by Gerard O'Cuinn. LC 95-14061. 272p. 1995. boxed set 134.95 (*0-8493-7665-3*, 7665) CRC Pr.

Metabolism of Polycyclic Hydrocarbons in the Aquatic Environment. Ed. by Usha Varanasi. 352p. 1989. lib. bdg. 259.00 (*0-8493-6844-8*, QH545) CRC Pr.

Metabolism of the Anthroposphere. P. Baccini & P. H. Brunner. (Illus.). xii, 157p. 1991. 94.95 (*0-387-53778-3*) Spr-Verlag.

Metabolism of the Human Brain Studied with Positron Emission Tomography: Nobel Conference, Karolinska Institute, 7th, Saltsjobaden, Sewden, 1983. Ed. by Torgny Greitz et al. LC 84-24901. 535p. 1985. reprint ed. pap. 165.90 (*0-608-00398-0*, 206111200007) Bks Demand.

Metabolism of Trace Metals in Man, Vol. I. Ed. by Owen M. Rennert & Wayiee Chan. 192p. 1984. 110.00 (*0-8493-5798-5*, QP534, CRC Reprint) Franklin.

Metabolism of Trace Metals in Man, Vol. II. Ed. by Owen M. Rennert & Wayiee Chan. 168p. 1984. 99.00 (*0-8493-5799-3*, QP534, CRC Reprint) Franklin.

Metabolism, Structure & Function of Plant Lipids. Ed. by Paul K. Stumpf et al. LC 87-1749. 742p. 1987. 135.00 (*0-306-42492-4*, Plenum Trade) Perseus Pubng.

Metabolism with Inborn Errors: Medical Subject Analysis with Bibliography. Joel A. Cardoso. LC 87-47681. 150p. 1987. 47.50 (*0-88164-635-0*); pap. 44.50 (*0-88164-636-9*) ABBE Pubs Assn.

Metabolites 3: Lipids, Amino Acids & Related Compounds, Vol. 8, Metabolites 3: Lipids, Amino Acids and Rel. 3rd ed. Hans U. Bergmeyer. LC 84-105641. (Illus.). 629p. 1985. 320.00 (*3-527-26048-X*, Wiley-VCH) Wiley.

Metabolites 2: Tri- & Dicarboxylic Acids, Purines, Pyrimidines & Derivatives, Coenzymes & Inorganic Compounds, Vol. 7, Metabolites 2: Tri- and Dicarboxylic Acids. 3rd ed. Ed. by Hans U. Bergmeyer. 642p. 1985. 325.00 (*3-527-26047-1*, Wiley-VCH) Wiley.

***Metabolize: The Personalized Program for Weight Loss.** Kenneth Baum & Richard Trubo. LC 99-43243. 304p. 2000. 23.95 (*0-399-14590-7*) Putnam Pub Group.

Metabotropic Glutamate Receptors. Ed. by P. Jeffrey Conn & Jitendra Patel. LC 94-18190. (Receptors Ser.). (Illus.). 300p. 1994. text 120.00 (*0-89603-291-4*) Humana.

MetaBusiness: Creating a New Global Culture. Greg Nielsen. LC 90-86068. (Illus.). 136p. 1991. pap. 9.95 (*0-9619917-2-0*) Conscious Bks.

***MetaCapitalism: The E-Business Revolution & the Design of 21st Century Companies & markets.** Grady Means & David Schneider. 160p. 2000. 24.95 (*0-471-39335-5*) Wiley.

Metachlamydeae. Tr. by Israel Program for Scientific Translations Staff from RUS. (Flora of the U. S. S. R. (Flora SSSR) Ser.: Vol. 18). (Illus.). viii, 600p. 1986. reprint ed. 252.00 (*3-87429-238-X*, 003940, Pub. by Koeltz Sci Bks) Lubrecht & Cramer.

Metaclasses & Their Application: Data Model Tailoring & Database Integration. Wolfgang Klas & Michael Schrefl. (Lecture Notes in Computer Science Ser.: Vol. 943). 1995. 43.00 (*3-540-60063-9*) Spr-Verlag.

Metacognition: A Special Issue of the Personality & Social Psychology Review. Ed. by Janet Metcalfe. 73p. 1998. pap. 20.00 (*0-8058-9840-9*) L Erlbaum Assocs.

Metacognition: Knowing about Knowing. Ed. by Janet Metcalfe & Arthur P. Shimamura. (Illus.). 350p. 1994. 42.00 (*0-262-13298-2*, Bradford Bks) MIT Pr.

Metacognition: Knowing about Knowing. Ed. by Janet Metcalfe & Arthur P. Shimamura. (Illus.). 352p. 1996. reprint ed. pap. text 21.00 (*0-262-63169-5*, Bradford Bks) MIT Pr.

Metacognition & Cognitive Neuropsychology: Monitoring & Control Processes. Ed. by Giuliana Mazzoni & Thomas O. Nelson. LC 98-5819. 200p. 1998. write for info. (*0-8058-2662-9*) L Erlbaum Assocs.

Metacognition & Reading Comprehension. Ruth Garner. Ed. by Judith M. Orasanu. LC 86-22261. (Cognition & Literacy Ser.: Vol. 1). 176p. (C). 1987. text 73.25 (*0-89391-398-7*) Ablx Pub.

***Metacognition et Education.** Ed. by Pierre A. Doudin et al. xii, 350p. 1999. 49.95 (*3-906762-48-3*) P Lang Pubng.

Metacognition in Educational Theory & Practice. Ed. by Douglas J. Hacker et al. LC 97-38586. (Educational Psychology Ser.). 304p. 1998. write for info. (*0-8058-2481-2*); pap. 39.95 (*0-8058-2482-0*) L Erlbaum Assocs.

Metacognition, Motivation & Understanding. Ed. by R. H. Kluwe & Franz E. Weinert. (Glazer-Rewnich-Psychology of Education & Instruction Ser.). 344p. (C). 1987. text 59.95 (*0-89859-569-X*) L Erlbaum Assocs.

Metacomet-Monadnock Trail Guide: A Trail Guide with Maps of the 117 Mile Long Distance Foot Path Through the 3 County-Pioneer Valley Region of Western Massachusetts & the Monadnock Region of S. W. New Hampshire. 9th rev. ed. Christopher J. Ryan. (Illus.). 89p. 1999. per. 8.95 (*1-889787-03-5*) NE Cartographics.

***MetaCreation of Personal Realities in Space & Time: Breakthrough Technology on How the Brain & Mind Create Realities for a Prosperous & Meaningful Life.** Victor J. Gibbons. LC 98-92310. 421p. 1999. pap. 24.95 (*0-9669428-0-9*, Pub. by MetaCreations) ACCESS Pubs Network.

***Metacreations Painter Ver. 6: Digital Approach.** 2000. write for info. (*0-13-030512-X*) P-H.

***MetaCreations Painter 5.5: A Digital Approach to Natural Art Media.** Against the Clock, Inc. Staff. LC 98-54897. 1999. 33.33 (*0-13-013537-2*) P-H.

Metacultural Theater of Oh Tae-sok: Five Plays from the Korean Avant-Garde. Tae-Sok Oh. Tr. by Ah-jeong Kim & R. B. Graves from KOR. LC 98-51873. 176p. (C). 1999. 33.00 (*0-8248-2099-1*); pap. 14.95 (*0-8248-2158-0*) UH Pr.

***Metadata for Interchange of Files on Sequential Storage Media Between File Storage Management Systems (FSMSs) ANSI/AIIM MS66-1999.** Association for Information & Image Management Staff. 39p. 1999. 39.00 (*0-89258-365-7*, MS66) Assn Inform & Image Mgmt.

***Metadata Management for Information Control & Business Success.** Guy V. Tozer. LC 99-16539. 1999. 75.00 (*0-89006-280-3*) Artech Hse.

Metadata Management in Statistical Information Processing: A Unified Framework for Metadata-Based Processing of Statistical Data Aggregates. Karl A. Froeschl. LC 97-11133. (Illus.). xii, 537p. 1997. pap. 63.00 (*3-211-82987-3*) Spr-Verlag.

***Metadebates on Science: The Blue Book of 'Einsteen Meets Magritte'** Gustaaf C. Cornelis et al. LC 99-27062. (Einstein Meets Magritte Ser.). 328p. 1999. 156.00 (*0-7923-5762-0*) Kluwer Academic.

MetaDesign: Design from the Word Up. Fay Sweet. (Cutting Edge Ser.). (Illus.). 64p. 1999. 16.95 (*0-8230-1212-3*) Watsn-Guptill.

Metadirectories: From the Instructors at Productivity Point International. 270p. 2000. pap. 24.95 (*1-888232-36-6*) Knwldg Univ.

***Metadirectories for Windows 2000: In the Trenches.** Wes Knight. 368p. 2000. pap. 49.95 (*1-930713-04-5*) Gearhead Pr CA.

Metadiscours et Deceptivite: Julien Torma Vu par le College de 'Pataphysique. Jean Wirtz. (Sciences pour la Communication Ser.: Vol. 48). (FRE.). 176p. 1996. 29.95 (*3-906754-41-3*, Pub. by P Lang) P Lang Pubng.

***Metadiversity: The Call for Community: Proceedings of the Symposium Nov. 9-12, 1988, Natural Bridge, Va.** Ed. by Richard T. Kaser & Victoria C. Kaser. 200p. (C). 1999. pap. 39.00 (*0-942308-51-4*) NFAIS.

Metados Orien Objetos Engineers without Disk. 2nd ed. (SPA.). 640p. (C). 1996. 36.33 (*0-201-65355-9*) P-H Intl.

Metadrama in Shakespeare's Henriad: Richard II to Henry V. James L. Calderwood. LC 77-93467. 235p. reprint ed. pap. 72.90 (*0-7837-4757-8*, 204450400003) Bks Demand.

Metaepistemology & Skepticism. Richard Fumerton. LC 95-32345. (Studies in Epistemology & Cognitive Theory). 320p. (C). 1995. pap. text 22.95 (*0-8476-8107-6*); lib. bdg. 56.00 (*0-8476-8106-8*) Rowman.

Metaficcion Creadora en "Antagonia" de Luis Goytisolo. Antonio Sobejano-Moran. LC 93-7899. (Hispanic Literature Ser.: Vol. 18). (SPA.). 148p. 1993. text 69.95 (*0-7734-9298-4*) E Mellen.

Metafiction. Ed. by Mark Currie. LC 95-13071. (Critical Readers Ser.). 240p. (C). 1995. pap. 38.00 (*0-582-21292-8*) Addison-Wesley.

Metafiction. Ed. by Mark Currie. LC 95-13071. (Critical Readers Ser.). 240p. (C). 1995. text 61.25 (*0-582-21291-X*) Longman.

Metafiction: The Theory & Practice of Self-Conscious. Patricia Waugh. (New Accents Ser.). 192p. (C). 1984. pap. 20.99 (*0-415-03006-4*) Routledge.

Metafiction: The Theory & Practice of Self-Conscious Fiction. Patricia Waugh. 176p. 1984. 35.00 (*0-416-32630-7*, NO. 3845); pap. 13.95 (*0-416-32640-4*, NO. 3844) Routledge.

Metafiction & Myth in the Novels of Peter Ackroyd. Susana Onega. LC 98-52962. (Studies in English & American Literature, Linguistics, & Culture). (Illus.). 190p. 1999. 50.00 (*1-57113-006-3*) Camden Hse.

Metafictional Characters in Modern Drama. June Schlueter. LC 79-4207. 1979. text 57.50 (*0-231-04752-5*) Col U Pr.

Metafictional Muse: The Works of Robert Coover, Donald Barthelme, & William H. Gass. Larry McCaffery. LC 82-1872. 315p. 1982. pap. 97.70 (*0-608-05088-1*, 206564200005) Bks Demand.

Metafisica. Aristotle. Ed. by Miguel Cancel. Tr. by Patricio D. Azcarate. (Nueva Austral Ser.: No. 27). (SPA.). 1991. pap. text 24.95 (*84-239-1827-0*) Elliots Bks.

Metafisica 4 en 1. Connie Mendez.Tr. of Metaphysics Four in One. 1997. pap. text 14.98 (*980-6114-26-4*) Bienes.

Metafisica 4 en 1. Connie Mendez.Tr. of Metaphysics Four in One. (SPA.). 1997. pap. text 14.98 (*980-6329-00-7*) Bienes.

Metafont. Donald E. Knuth. LC 86-1230. (Computers & Typesetting Ser.: Vol. D). 592p. (C). 1986. 51.95 (*0-201-13438-1*) Addison-Wesley.

Metafontbook. Donald E. Knuth. 384p. (C). 1986. pap. text 30.95 (*0-201-13444-6*) Addison-Wesley.

Metafontbook. Donald E. Knuth. (Computers & Typesetting Ser.: Vol. C). 384p. (C). 1986. 51.95 (*0-201-13445-4*) Addison-Wesley.

Metafora Mas (Rustica) Miguel Angel Cornejo. 1997. pap. text 14.98 (*968-6210-08-3*) Edit Diana.

Metaforas y Pergaminos de la Excelencia. Miguel Angel Cornejo. (SPA.). 1997. pap. 14.98 (*968-6210-04-0*) Grijalbo Edit.

Metaform. Alvin Greenberg. LC 75-8448. 72p. 1975. 15.00 (*0-87023-188-X*); pap. 9.95 (*0-87023-189-8*) U of Mass Pr.

Metaformations: Soundplay & Wordplay in Ovid & Other Classical Poets. Frederick Ahl. LC 84-23872. 336p. (C). 1985. 47.50 (*0-8014-1762-7*) Cornell U Pr.

Metaframeworks: Transcending the Models of Family Therapy. Douglas C. Breunlin. LC 97-225287. 1997. pap. 32.95 (*0-7879-1070-8*) Jossey-Bass.

Metahistory: The Historical Imagination in Nineteenth-Century Europe. Hayden V. White. LC 73-8110. 462p. 1974. pap. 17.95 (*0-8018-1761-7*) Johns Hopkins.

Metahorror. Ed. by Dennis Etchison. (Illus.). 1992. 100.00 (*1-880418-02-9*) D M Grant.

Metairie: A Tongue of Land to Pasture. Henry C. Bezou. (Illus.). 248p. 1997. pap. 13.95 (*1-56554-279-7*) Pelican.

Metairie Cemetery - An Historical Memoir: Tales of Its Statesmen, Soldiers & Great Families. Henri A. Gandolfo. LC 81-50815. 115p. 1981. 24.95 (*0-9635640-0-5*); pap. 14.95 (*0-9635640-1-3*) Stewart Ent.

Metaistorie: Ciclu Teatral. Florentin Smarandache. Ed. by Xiquan Publishing House Staff. (RUM.). 220p. (Orig.). 1992. pap. 19.99 (*1-879585-08-1*) Erhus Univ Pr.

Metaji: Collected Works: The Alternative Leadership, Vol. 10. Subhas C. Bose. Ed. by Sisir Kumar & Sugata Bose. LC 99-165331. (Illus.). 262p. 1998. text 19.95 (*0-19-564153-1*) OUP.

Metakritik der Formalen Logik. L. Eley. (Phaenomenologica Ser.: No. 31). 388p. 1969. pap. text 73.00 (*90-247-0268-2*, Pub. by M Nijhoff); lib. bdg. 64.00 (*90-247-0269-0*, Pub. by M Nijhoff) Kluwer Academic.

Metal: Design & Fabrication. David Frisch & Susan Frisch. LC 98-7883. (Illus.). 176p. 1998. 45.00 (*0-8230-3034-2*, Whitney Lib) Watsn-Guptill.

Metal - Metal Bonds & Clusters in Chemistry & Catalysis. Ed. by J. P. Fackler, Jr. LC 90-34855. (Industry-University Cooperative Chemistry Program Symposia Ser.). (Illus.). 352p. (C). 1990. text 126.00 (*0-306-43527-6*, Kluwer Plenum) Kluwer Academic.

Metal Alloys & Patinas for Castings: For Metalsmiths, Jewelers, & Sculptors. William M. Shearman. LC 76-28729. 66p. reprint ed. pap. 30.00 (*0-608-13254-3*, 202545000044) Bks Demand.

Metal & Ceramic Based Composites. S. T. Mileiko. 1996. write for info. (*0-614-17929-7*) Elsevier.

Metal & Ceramic Based Composites. S. T. Mileiko. LC 97-49108. (Composite Materials Ser.: Vol. 12). 704p. 1997. 301.50 (*0-444-82814-1*) Elsevier.

Metal & Ceramic Biomaterials: Strength & Surface, Vol. II. Ed. by Paul Ducheyne & Garth W. Hastings. 184p. 1984. 108.00 (*0-8493-6262-8*, R857, CRC Reprint) Franklin.

Metal & Ceramic Biomaterials: Structure, Vol. I. Ed. by Paul Ducheyne & Garth W. Hastings. 136p. 1984. 83.00 (*0-8493-6261-X*, R857, CRC Reprint) Franklin.

Metal & Ceramic Matrix Composites: Processing, Modeling & Mechanical Behavior: Proceedings of an International Conference Held at the TMS Annual Meeting in Anaheim, California, February 19-22, 1990. Minerals, Metals & Materials Society Staff. Ed. by Ram B. Bhagat et al. LC 89-63253. 682p. reprint ed. pap. 200.00 (*0-7837-6064-7*, 205251000008) Bks Demand.

Metal & Stone: Six Young Sculptors. Frwd. by Marla Price. (Illus.). 76p. (Orig.). 1992. pap. 11.95 (*0-929865-08-1*) Mod Art Mus Ft Worth.

Metal Arc Gas Shielded Welding. 1987. 49.00 (*0-85083-067-2*) St Mut.

Metal-Bearing Waste Streams: Minimizing, Recycling & Treatment. M. Meltzer et al. 406p. 1990. 89.00 (*0-8155-1260-0*) Noyes.

***Metal Boats.** 2nd ed. Ken Scott. LC 98-48731. (Illus.). 216p. 1999. 27.50 (*1-57409-082-8*) Sheridan.

***Metal Boats: Steel, Aluminum, Copper Nickel Building, Maintenance, & Repair.** Bruce Roberts-Goodson. (Illus.). 1998. pap. 44.95 (*1-86163-031-X*, Pub. by Capall Bann Pubng) Holmes Pub.

Metal Bonding & Interactions in High Temperature Systems: With Emphasis on Alkali Metals. Ed. by James L. Gole & William C. Stwalley. LC 81-20555. (ACS Symposium Ser.: No. 179). (Illus.). 640p. 1982. reprint ed. pap. 198.40 (*0-608-03245-X*, 206376400007) Bks Demand.

M

Metal Bonding & Interactions in High Temperature Systems with Emphasis on Alkali Metals. Ed. by James L. Gole & William C. Stwalley. LC 81-20555. (ACS Symposium Ser.: No. 179). 1982. 65.95 (*0-8412-0689-9*) Am Chemical.

Metal Building, Level 1. National Center for Construction Education & Reseach Staff. (Wheels of Learning Ser.). (C). 1996. pap. text, teacher ed. 75.00 (*0-13-245705-9*); pap. text, student ed. 55.00 (*0-13-245697-4*) P-H.

Metal Building, Level 2. National Center for Construction Education & Reseach Staff. (Wheels of Learning Ser.). (C). 1996. pap. text, teacher ed. 75.00 (*0-13-245721-0*); pap. text, student ed. 55.00 (*0-13-245713-X*) P-H.

Metal Building, Level 2. National Center for Construction Education & Reseach Staff. (Wheels of Learning Ser.). (C). 1996. student ed., ring bd. 55.00 (*0-13-265794-5*) P-H.

Metal Building, Level 3. National Center for Construction Education & Reseach Staff. (Wheels of Learning Ser.). (C). 1996. pap. text, teacher ed. 75.00 (*0-13-245748-2*) P-H.

Metal Building: Instructor's Guide, Level 1. National Center for Construction Education & Reseach Staff. (Wheels Ser.). (C). 1996. teacher ed., ring bd. 75.00 (*0-13-265364-8*) P-H.

Metal Building Assembler: Instructor's Guide, Level 2. National Center for Construction Education & Reseach Staff. (Wheels Ser.). (C). 1996. teacher ed., ring bd. 75.00 (*0-13-265372-9*) P-H.

Metal Building Assembler: Instructor's Guide, Level 3. National Center for Construction Education & Reseach Staff. (Wheels Ser.). (C). 1996. teacher ed., ring bd. 75.00 (*0-13-265380-X*) P-H.

Metal Building Assembler: Trainee Guide, Level 1. National Center for Construction Education & Reseach Staff. (Wheels of Learning Ser.). (C). 1996. student ed., ring bd. 55.00 (*0-13-265786-4*) P-H.

Metal Building Assembler Level 3: Trainee Guide, Level 3. National Center for Construction Education & Reseach Staff. (C). 1996. student ed., per. 55.00 (*0-13-245739-3*); student ed., ring bd. 55.00 (*0-13-265802-X*) P-H.

Metal Building Contracting & Construction. William D. Booth. LC 98-43601. (Illus.). 255p. 1999. 64.95 (*0-07-006964-6*, 639785308799) McGraw.

Metal Building Systems. 2nd ed. Building Systems Institute Staff. (Illus.). 230p. (C). 1990. write for info. (*0-9626582-0-0*) Bldg Systs Inst.

Metal Building Systems: Design & Specifications. Alexander Newman. LC 96-49570. (Illus.). 389p. 1997. 74.95 (*0-07-046379-4*) McGraw.

Metal Bulletin Prices & Data Book, 1987. 2nd ed. 370p. 1987. pap. write for info. (*0-947671-07-2*) Taylor & Francis.

Metal Bulletin's Prices & Data, 1992. 6th ed. Ed. by Richard Serjeantson. 423p. 1992. pap. text 94.00 (*0-947671-58-7*) Metal Bulletin.

Metal Candlesticks: History, Styles & Techniques. Veronika Baur. (Illus.). 184p. 1996. 49.95 (*0-7643-0156-X*) Schiffer.

***Metal Canvas: Canadians & World War II Aircraft Nose Art.** Stephen M. Fochuk. 1999. write for info. (*1-55125-013-6*) Vanwell Publ.

Metal Casting: Appropriate Technology in the Small Foundry. Steve Hurst. (Illus.). 192p. (Orig.). 1996. pap. 25.00 (*1-85339-197-2*, Pub. by Intermed Tech) Stylus Pub VA.

Metal Casting & Heat Treating Industry: Guide to Pollution Prevention. (Illus.). 70p. (Orig.). (C). 1996. reprint ed. pap. text 30.00 (*0-7881-2962-7*) DIANE Pub.

Metal-Catalyzed Cross-Coupling Reactions. Ed. by Peter J. Stang & Francois Diederich. 540p. 1998. 260.00 (*3-527-29421-X*, Wiley-VCH) Wiley.

Metal-Ceramic Interfaces: Proceedings of workshop 'Bonding, Structure & Mechanical Properties of Metal-Ceramic Interfaces', University of Metal-Ceramic Interfaces', University of California, USA, 16-18 January 1989. Ed. by Michael F. Ashby et al. (ACTA-Scripta Metallurgica Conference Ser.: No. 4). (Illus.). 448p. 1990. 173.00 (*0-08-040505-3*, Pergamon Pr) Elsevier.

Metal Ceramic Joining: Proceedings of a Symposium Held on Metal-Ceramic Joining Sponsored by the TMS Refactory Metals Committee, Held During the TMS Fall Meeting, Detroit, MI, October 8-9, 1990. Ed. by V. A. Greenhut & P. K. Kumar. LC 91-61798. 279p. 1991. reprint ed. pap. 86.50 (*0-608-00775-7*, 206157300010) Bks Demand.

Metal Church - Blessing in Disguise. (Play-It-Like-It-Is Guitar Ser.). pap. 19.95 (*0-89524-718-6*) Cherry Lane.

Metal Church/Human Factor Tab: Guitar Personality Book. 1p. (Orig.). 1995. pap. 17.95 (*0-7935-0975-0*, HL00694792) Wrner Bros.

Metal-Clad Cables & Cable-Sealing Fittings for Use in Hazardous (Classified) Locations, UL 2225. 1996. write for info. (*0-7629-0068-7*) Underwrtrs Labs.

Metal-Clad Cables, UL 1569. 3rd ed. (C). 1999. pap. text 135.00 (*1-55989-870-4*) Underwrtrs Labs.

Metal Cladding in Hong Kong: A Strategic Entry Report, 1998. Compiled by Icon Group International Staff. (Country Industry Report). (Illus.). 119p. 1999. ring bd. 1190.00 incl. audio compact disk (*0-7418-0436-0*) Icon Grp.

Metal Clusters. Ekardt. LC 98-53083. 300p. (C). 1999. 149.00 (*0-471-98783-2*) Wiley.

***Metal Clusters at Surfaces: Structure, Quantum Properties, Physical Chemistry.** Karl-Heinz Meiwes-Broer. LC 99-56372. (Cluster Physics Ser.). (Illus.). 300p. (C). 2000. 79.95 (*3-540-66562-5*) Spr-Verlag.

***Metal Clusters in Chemistry, 3 Vols.** Ed. by P. Braunstein et al. 1846p. 1999. 850.00 (*3-527-29549-6*) Wiley.

Metal Clusters in Proteins. Ed. by Lawrence Que, Jr. LC 88-14504. (ACS Symposium Ser.: No. 372). (Illus.). ix, 413p. 1988. 84.95 (*0-8412-1487-5*) Am Chemical.

Metal Clusters in Proteins. Lawrence Que, Jr. LC 88-14504. (ACS Symposium Ser.: Vol. 372). 424p. 1988. reprint ed. pap. 131.50 (*0-608-03292-1*, 206381000007) Bks Demand.

Metal Complexes in Aqueous Solutions. A. E. Martell & R. D. Hancock. LC 96-11162. (Modern Inorganic Chemistry Ser.). (Illus.). 264p. (C). 1996. text 71.00 (*0-306-45248-0*, Kluwer Plenum) Kluwer Academic.

Metal Complexes in Biomimetic Chemical Reactions. A. E. Shilov. LC 96-3959. 320p. 1997. boxed set 159.95 (*0-8493-4953-2*) CRC Pr.

Metal Complexes in Cancer ChemoTherapy. Ed. by Bernhard K. Keppler. LC 93-15333. 434p. 1993. 250.00 (*3-527-28425-7*, Wiley-VCH) Wiley.

Metal Complexes in Fossil Fuels: Geochemistry, Characterization, & Processing. Ed. by Royston H. Filby & Jan F. Branthaver. LC 87-14418. (Symposium Ser.: No. 344). (Illus.). 446p. 1987. 98.95 (*0-8412-1404-2*) Am Chemical.

Metal Complexes in Fossil Fuels: Geochemistry, Characterization, & Processing. Ed. by Royston H. Filby & Jan F. Branthaver. LC 87-14418. (ACS Symposium Ser.: Vol. 344). 448p. 1987. reprint ed. pap. 138.90 (*0-608-03537-8*, 206425600008) Bks Demand.

Metal Complexes in Solution. E. A. Jenne et al. 318p. 1986. pap. text 32.00 (*1-57235-053-9*) Piccin Nuova.

Metal Complexes of Chelating Olefin-Group V Ligands see **Coordinative Interactions**

Metal Complexes with Tetrapyrrole Ligands I. J. W. Buchler. (Structure & Bonding Ser.: Vol. 64). (Illus.). 290p. 1987. 158.95 (*0-387-17531-8*) Spr-Verlag.

Metal Compounds in Environment & Life. 526p. 1992. lib. bdg. 139.95 (*0-946682-15-1*) CRC Pr.

Metal-Containing Polymeric Materials. C. U. Pittman, Jr. et al. (Illus.). 528p. (C). 1996. text 135.00 (*0-306-45295-2*, Kluwer Plenum) Kluwer Academic.

Metal Contaminated Aquatic Sediments. Ed. by Herbert E. Allen. 350p. (C). 1996. ring bd. 84.95 (*1-57504-010-7*) CRC Pr.

Metal-Contaminated Soils: In-Situ Inactivation & Phytorestoration. Jaco Vangronsveld & Scott Cunningham. LC 98-14638. 1998. 149.00 (*1-57059-531-3*) Landes Bioscience.

Metal-Contaminated Soils: In Situ Inactivaton & Phytorestoration. Ed. by Jaco Vangronsveld & Scott Cunningham. LC 98-14638. (Environmental Intelligence Unit Ser.). 220p. 1998. 149.00 (*3-540-64208-0*) Spr-Verlag.

Metal Corrosion Damage & Protection Technology. Masamichi Kowaka. (Illus.). x, 539p. 1990. 150.00 (*0-89864-052-0*) Allerton Pr.

Metal Corrosion in Boats. 2nd ed. Nigel Warren. LC 97-51421. (Illus.). 224p. 1998. 27.50 (*1-57409-054-2*) Sheridan.

Metal Cowboy: Tales from the Road Less Pedaled. Joe Kurmaskie. 304p. 1999. 23.00 (*1-891369-10-5*, Pub. by Breakaway Bks) Consort Bk Sales.

***Metal Craft Book: 50 Easy & Beautiful Projects from Copper, Tin, Brass, Aluminum & More.** Deborah Morgenthal & Janice Eaton Kilby. LC 00-37110. (Illus.). 128p. 2000. write for info. (*1-57990-170-0*, Pub. by Lark Books) Sterling.

Metal Craftsmanship in Early Ireland. Michael Ryan. (Treasures of the National Museum of Ireland Ser.). (Illus.). 48p. (Orig.). 1995. pap. 7.95 (*0-946172-37-4*, Pub. by Town Hse) Roberts Rinehart.

Metal Cutting. 2nd ed. E. M. Trent & Paul K. Wright. 224p. 1983. 52.95 (*0-408-05031-4*) Buttrwrth-Heinemann.

***Metal Cutting.** 4th ed. E. M. Trent & Paul K. Wright. LC 99-52104. 356p. 2000. 75.00 (*0-7506-7069-X*) Buttrwrth-Heinemann.

***Metal Cutting & Forming Machinery in Thailand: A Strategic Entry Report, 1995.** Compiled by Icon Group International Staff. (Illus.). 140p. 1999. ring bd. 1400.00 incl. audio compact disk (*0-7418-1619-9*) Icon Grp.

***Metal Cutting Machine Tools in Japan: A Strategic Entry Report, 1996.** Compiled by Icon Group International Staff. (Illus.). 160p. 1999. ring bd. 1600.00 incl. audio compact disk (*0-7418-1336-X*) Icon Grp.

Metal Cutting Mechanics. Viktor Astakhov. LC 98-46338. 320p. 1998. boxed set 84.95 (*0-8493-1895-5*) CRC Pr.

Metal Cutting Principles. Milton C. Shaw. LC 97-206069. (Oxford Series on Advanced Manufacturing: No. 3). (Illus.). 616p. 1997. reprint ed. pap. text 69.95 (*0-19-859020-2*) OUP.

Metal Cutting Theory & Practice. David A. Stephenson & John S. Agapiou. LC 96-41102. (Manufacturing Engineering/Material Process Ser.). (Illus.). 912p. 1996. text 199.00 (*0-8247-9579-2*) Dekker.

Metal Cutting Tool Handbook. 7th ed. U. S. Cutting Tool Institute Staff. (Illus.). 795p. 1989. 45.95 (*0-8311-1177-1*) Indus Pr.

Metal Databook. Alok Nayar. LC 97-218568. (Illus.). 768p. 1997. 89.95 (*0-07-046088-4*) McGraw.

Metal Deformation Processes: Friction & Lubrication. Ed. by John A. Schey. LC 75-107756. (Monographs & Textbooks in Material Science: No. 1). (Illus.). 823p. reprint ed. pap. 200.00 (*0-608-10673-9*, 2055018); reprint ed. pap. 180.00 (*0-608-30307-0*, 2055018) Bks Demand.

Metal Deposits in Relation to Plate Tectonics. Ed. by Frederick J. Sawkins. (Minerals & Rocks Ser.: Vol. 17). (Illus.). 340p. 1983. 65.00 (*0-387-12752-6*) Spr-Verlag.

Metal Deposits in Relation to Plate Tectonics. 2nd ed. Frederick J. Sawkins. (Minerals & Rocks Ser.: Vol. 17). (Illus.). 455p. 1989. 118.95 (*0-387-50920-8*) Spr-Verlag.

Metal Detecting for Treasure: A Guidebook for Beginners. Dorothy B. Francis. (Illus.). 56p. (Orig.). 1992. pap. 8.00 (*0-936335-03-3*) Ballyhoo Bks.

Metal Detecting the Hobby. Dick Stout. 50p. 1993. 6.95 (*1-882279-01-8*) Whites Elect.

Metal Disintegrator: How to Build It. 1996. lib. bdg. 250.75 (*0-8490-8310-9*) Gordon Pr.

Metal-DNA Chemistry. Ed. by Thomas D. Tullius. LC 89-15135. (Symposium Ser.: No. 402). (Illus.). 224p. 1989. text 55.00 (*0-8412-1660-6*, Pub. by Am Chemical) OUP.

Metal Ecotoxicology: Concepts & Applications. Michael C. Newman & A. McIntosh. (Advances in Trace Substances Research Ser.). 424p. 1991. lib. bdg. 110.00 (*0-87371-411-3*, L411) Lewis Pubs.

Metal-Enclosed Low-Voltage Power Circuit Breaker Switchgear, UL 1558. 4th rev. ed. (C). 1999. pap. text 135.00 (*1-55989-493-8*) Underwrtrs Labs.

***Metal Fabrication: A Practical Guide.** 2nd ed. Robert L. O'Con & Richard H. Carr. (Illus.). 334p. (C). 1999. pap. 55.00 (*1-881113-12-4*) Croydon Grp.

Metal Fatigue. N. E. Frost. LC 99-48936. 528p. 1999. pap. text 22.95 (*0-486-40927-9*) Dover.

Metal Fatigue. N. E. Frost. LC TA0460.F75. (Oxford Engineering Science Ser.). 511p. reprint ed. pap. 158.50 (*0-608-30890-0*, 205184500011) Bks Demand.

Metal Fatigue Damage-Mechanism, Detection, Avoidance & Repair-STP 495. 351p. 1971. 21.00 (*0-8031-0722-6*, STP495) ASTM.

Metal Fatigue in Engineering. H. O. Fuchs & Ralph I. Stephens. LC 80-294. 336p. 1980. 160.00 (*0-471-05264-7*) Wiley.

Metal Fatigue in Engineering. 2nd ed. Fuchs. 350p. 80.00 (*0-471-51059-9*) Wiley.

Metal Filled Polymers. Bhattacharya. (Plastics Engineering Ser.: Vol. 11). (Illus.). 376p. 1986. text 175.00 (*0-8247-7555-4*) Dekker.

Metal Finishers. Ed. by ICC Information Group Staff. 1987. 695.00 (*1-85036-938-0*, Pub. by ICC Info Group Ltd) St Mut.

Metal Finishing Industry: Guides to Pollution Prevention. 68p. (Orig.). (C). 1975. pap. text 25.00 (*0-7881-2911-2*) DIANE Pub.

Metal Fire No. 8. Jack McKinney. (Robotech Ser.: No. 8). 224p. 1987. mass mkt. 4.95 (*0-345-34141-4*, Del Rey) Ballantine Pub Grp.

***Metal Foams: A Design Guide.** Tony Evans et al. 256p. 2000. 75.00 (*0-7506-7219-6*) Buttrwrth-Heinemann.

Metal-Forming: An Introduction to Some Theory, Principles & Practice. Edward Lloyd. (C). 1989. 300.00 (*0-7855-4925-0*, Pub. by Fuel Metallurgical Jrnl) St Mut.

Metal Forming: Fundamentals & Applications. Taylan Altan et al. (Illus.). 353p. 1983. 98.00 (*0-87170-167-7*, 6435) ASM.

Metal Forming: Interrelation Between Theory & Practice: Proceedings of a Symposium, Cleveland, Ohio, 1970. Ed. by A. L. Hoffmanner. LC 70-171698. 518p. reprint ed. pap. 160.60 (*0-608-13235-7*, 205579500038) Bks Demand.

Metal Forming: Mechanics & Metallurgy. Robert M. Caddell & William F. Hosford. (Illus.). 352p. (C). 1983. text 66.00 (*0-13-577700-3*) P-H.

Metal Forming: Mechanics & Metallurgy. 2nd ed. William F. Hosford. 384p. (C). 1993. text 58.60 (*0-13-588526-4*) P-H.

Metal Forming: The Application of Limit Analysis. Betzalel Avitzur. LC 79-25348. (Manufacturing Engineering & Materials Processing Ser.: Vol. 4). (Illus.). 220p. reprint ed. pap. 68.20 (*0-608-08910-9*, 206954500005) Bks Demand.

Metal Forming & Impact Mechanics. Ed. by S. R. Reid. (Illus.). 360p. 1985. 163.00 (*0-08-031679-4*, Pub. by PPL) Franklin.

Metal Forming & the Finite Element Method. Shoshichi Kobayashi et al. (Oxford Series on Advanced Manufacturing). (Illus.). 402p. 1989. text 90.00 (*0-19-504402-9*) OUP.

Metal Forming Dictionary. A. M. Abd-El-Wahed. (ARA, ENG, FRE & GER.). 386p. 1978. 75.00 (*0-8288-5251-0*, M9755) Fr & Eur.

Metal Forming Handbook. Ed. by Schuler & H. Hoffman. LC 98-22434. (Illus.). 500p. 1997. 98.00 (*3-540-61185-1*) Spr-Verlag.

***Metal Gear Solid.** Eliabeth J. Hollinger. LC 99-65964. (Illus.). 103p. 1999. pap. 12.99 (*0-7615-2501-7*) Prima Pub.

Metal Gear Solid: Prima's Unauthorized Strategy Guide. Prima Publishing Staff. (Secrets of the Games Ser.). 144p. (gr. 7). 1998. per. 12.99 (*0-7615-1766-9*) Prima Pub.

***Metal Gear Solid: VR Missions.** Steve Honeywell. LC 99-65965. (Official Strategy Guides Ser.). (Illus.). 143p. 1999. pap. 12.99 (*0-7615-2502-5*) Prima Pub.

***Metal Gear Solid Greatest Hits.** Prima Development Staff. (Prima's Official Strategy Guides). (Illus.). 104p. 2000. pap. 9.99 (*0-7615-2889-X*) Prima Pub.

Metal Gear Solid Survival Guide. Ed. by Z. Douglas Arnold. (Illus.). 144p. 1998. pap. 12.95 (*1-884364-31-4*) Sandwich Islands.

Metal Guardian Faust. Tetsuro Ueyama. (Illus.). 264p. 1998. pap. text 16.95 (*1-56931-263-X*, Viz Comics) Viz Commns Inc.

Metal Guitar Jammin' 32p. 1994. pap. 14.95 (*0-7935-2996-4*, 00696524) H Leonard.

Metal Guitar Technique & Style. Ed. by Aaron Stang. (Contemporary Guitar Ser.). 56p. (YA). 1994. pap. text 19.95 incl. audio compact disk (*0-89898-878-0*, F3203GTXCD) Wrner Bros.

Metal Heads: The Case of the Rival Robots. Marianne Meyer. LC 97-209963. (Kinetic City Super Crew Ser.: No. 5). (Illus.). 192p. (J). (gr. 3-5). 1998. pap. 4.25 (*0-07-006386-9*, Lrning Triangle) McGraw.

Metal Hydrides: Fundamentals & Applications. Ed. by M. V. C. Sastri. 200p. 1998. 129.00 (*3-540-64204-8*) Spr-Verlag.

Metal-Hydrogen System: Basic Bulk Properties. Yuh Fukai. LC 92-25415. 1993. 107.95 (*0-387-55637-0*) Spr-Verlag.

Metal Hydrogen Systems. T. Nejat Veziroglu. 1982. 100.00 (*0-08-027609-1*, Pergamon Pr) Elsevier.

Metal-Hydrogen Systems: Proceedings of the International Symposium, Miami Beach, Florida, U. S. A., 13-15 April 1981. Ed. by T. Nejat Veziroglu. (Illus.). 750p. 1982. pap. 100.00 (*0-08-027316-5*, Pub. by Pergamon Repr) Franklin.

Metal Impurities in Silicon Device Fabrication. Klaus Graff. LC 94-24599. (Series in Material Science: 24). 1994. 86.95 (*0-387-58317-3*) Spr-Verlag.

***Metal Impurities in Silicon-Device Fabrication.** 2nd ed. K. Graff. Ed. by H. J. Queisser. LC 99-58100. (Series in Materials Science: Vol. 24). (Illus.). xiv, 234p. 2000. 89.95 (*3-540-64213-7*) Spr-Verlag.

Metal Injection Molding: Preprint of a Seminar Held at the 1988 International Powder Metallurgy Conference, Orlando, Florida, June 7, 1988. Metal Powder Industries Federation Staff. LC TN0695.M44. (Illus.). 103p. reprint ed. pap. 32.00 (*0-7837-1563-3*, 204185500024) Bks Demand.

Metal-Insulator Transitions. 2nd rev. ed. Sir Nevill Francis Mott. 296p. 1990. 121.00 (*0-85066-783-6*) Taylor & Francis.

Metal Interactions with Boron Clusters. Ed. by Russell N. Grimes. LC 82-9068. (Modern Inorganic Chemistry Ser.). (Illus.). 342p. 1982. 85.00 (*0-306-40933-X*, Plenum Trade) Perseus Pubng.

Metal Ion Activation of Dioxygen. Ed. by Thomas G. Spiro. LC 80-125722. (Metal Ions in Biology Ser.: No. 2). (Illus.). 259p. reprint ed. pap. 80.30 (*0-608-18201-X*, 205660500078) Bks Demand.

Metal Ion Separation & Preconcentration: Progress & Opportunities. Andrew H. Bond et al. 716. 12p. 1999. text 130.00 (*0-8412-3594-5*, Pub. by Am Chemical) OUP.

Metal Ions in Biological Systems, Vol. 5. Ed. by Helmut Sigel. LC 72-90966. (Illus.). 415p. reprint ed. pap. 128.70 (*0-8357-4688-7*, 205234300005) Bks Demand.

Metal Ions in Biological Systems, Vol. 7 Iron in Model & Natural Compounds. Ed. by Helmut Sigel. LC 78-17297. 439p. reprint ed. pap. 125.20 (*0-608-16676-6*, 2027817) Bks Demand.

Metal Ions in Biological Systems, Vol. 32. Ed. by Helmut Sigel. (Illus.). 848p. 1996. text 245.00 (*0-8247-9549-0*) Dekker.

Metal Ions in Biological Systems: Amino Acids & Derivatives As Ambivalent Ligands, Vol. 9. Helmut Sigel. (Illus.). 304p. 1979. text 210.00 (*0-8247-6875-2*) Dekker.

Metal Ions in Biological Systems: Calcium & Its Role in Biology. Helmut Sigel. (Metal Ions in Biological Systems Ser.: Vol. 17). (Illus.). 560p. 1984. text 235.00 (*0-8247-7172-9*) Dekker.

Metal Ions in Biological Systems: Carcinogenicity & Metal Ions, Vol. 10. Helmut Sigel. (Illus.). 408p. 1980. text 210.00 (*0-8247-7203-2*) Dekker.

Metal Ions in Biological Systems: Copper Proteins, Vol. 13. fac. ed. Ed. by Helmut Sigel. LC 72-90966. (Illus.). 418p. pap. 129.60 (*0-7837-7389-7*, 202781700013) Bks Demand.

Metal Ions in Biological Systems Vol. 1: Simple Complexes. Ed. by Helmut Sigel. LC 72-90966. 288p. reprint ed. pap. 89.30 (*0-608-13706-5*, 205506200001) Bks Demand.

Metal Ions in Biological Systems Vol. 3: High Molecular Complexes. Ed. by Helmut Sigel. LC 72-90966. 303p. reprint ed. pap. 94.00 (*0-7837-0023-7*, 202781700003) Bks Demand.

Metal Ions in Biological Systems Vol. 11: Metal Complexes As Anticancer Agents. Ed. by Helmut Sigel. LC 72-90966. (Illus.). 447p. 1973. reprint ed. pap. 138.60 (*0-7837-8851-7*, 202781700011) Bks Demand.

Metal Ions in Biological Systems Vol. 16: Methods Involving Metal Ions & Complexes in Clinical Chemistry. Helmut Sigel. (Illus.). 440p. 1983. text 210.00 (*0-8247-7038-2*) Dekker.

Metal Ions in Biological Systems Vol. 19: Antibiotics & Their Complexes. Helmut Sigel. (Illus.). 464p. 1985. text 235.00 (*0-8247-7425-6*) Dekker.

Metal Ions in Biological Systems Vol. 20: Concepts on Metal Ion Toxicity. Helmut Sigel. (Illus.). 416p. 1986. text 235.00 (*0-8247-7540-6*) Dekker.

Metal Ions in Biological Systems Vol. 22: Endor, EPR & Electron Spin Echo for Probing Coordination Spheres. Helmut Sigel. (Illus.). 328p. 1986. text 215.00 (*0-8247-7641-0*) Dekker.

Metal Ions in Biological Systems Vol. 23: Nickel & Its Role in Biology. Helmut Sigel. (Nickel & Its Role & Biology Metal Ions & Biological Systems Ser.). (Illus.). 496p. 1988. text 235.00 (*0-8247-7713-1*) Dekker.

Metal Ions in Biological Systems Vol. 24: Aluminum & Its Role in Biology. Helmut Sigel. (Illus.). 512p. 1988. text 235.00 (*0-8247-7932-0*) Dekker.

Metal Ions in Biological Systems Vol. 26: Compendium on Magnesium & Its Role in Biology, Nutrition, & Physiology. Helmut Sigel. (Self Ser.). (Illus.). 768p. 1990. text 235.00 (*0-8247-8315-8*) Dekker.

Metal Ions in Biological Systems Vol. 27: Electron Transfer Reactions in Metalloproteins. Ed. by Helmut Sigel & Astrid Sigel. (Illus.). 584p. 1991. text 235.00 (*0-8247-8494-4*) Dekker.

Metal Ions in Biological Systems Vol. 28: Degradation of Environmental Pollutants by Microorganisms & Their Metalloenzymes. Helmut Sigel. (Illus.). 592p. 1992. text 235.00 (*0-8247-8639-4*) Dekker.

An Asterisk (*) at the beginning of an entry indicates that the title is appearing for the first time.

Metal Ions in Biological Systems Vol. 29: Biological Properties of Metal Alkyl Derivatives. Helmut Sigel. LC 72-90966. (Illus.). 496p. 1993. text 215.00 (*0-8247-9022-7*) Dekker.

Metal Ions in Biological Systems Vol. 30: Metalloenzymes Involving Amino Acid-Residue & Related Radicals. Helmut Sigel. (Illus.). 536p. 1994. text 245.00 (*0-8247-9093-6*) Dekker.

Metal Ions in Biological Systems Vol. 31: Vanadium & Its Role for Life. Ed. by Helmut Sigel. (Metal Ions in Biological Systems Ser.). (Illus.). 800p. 1995. text 245.00 (*0-8247-9383-8*) Dekker.

Metal Ions in Biological Systems Vol. 33: Probing of Nucleic Acids by Metal Ion Complexes of Small Molecules. Ed. by Helmut Sigel. (Illus.). 728p. 1996. text 215.00 (*0-8247-9688-8*) Dekker.

Metal Ions in Biological Systems Vol. 34: Mercury & Its Effects on Environment & Biology, Vol. 34. Ed. by Helmut Sigel. LC 96-29927. (Illus.). 648p. 1997. text 250.00 (*0-8247-9828-7*) Dekker.

Metal Ions in Biological Systems Vol. 35: Iron Transport & Storage in Microorganisms, Plants, & Animals. Ed. by Sigel. LC 97-46947. (Illus.). 824p. 1998. text 250.00 (*0-8247-9984-4*) Dekker.

Metal Ions in Fungi. Ed. by Gunther Winkelmann & Dennis R. Winge. (Mycology Ser.: Vol. 11). (Illus.). 528p. 1994. text 225.00 (*0-8247-9172-X*) Dekker.

Metal Ions in Gene Regulation. Ed. by Simon Silver & William Walden. LC 97-4469. 488p. (C). (gr. 13). 1997. write for info. (*0-412-05331-4*) Kluwer Academic.

Metal Ions in Solutions. John Burgess. (Chemical Science Ser.). 481p. 1980. pap. text 39.95 (*0-470-26987-1*) P-H.

Metal Lathe. David J. Gingery. LC 80-66142. (Build Your Own Metalworking Shop from Scrap Ser.). (Illus.). 144p. (Orig.). 1980. pap. 9.95 (*1-878087-01-0*) D J Gingery.

Metal Lathes - How to Run Them. Fred H. Colvin. (Illus.). 117p. 1991. reprint ed. pap. 12.00 (*1-877767-20-4*) Univ Publng Hse.

Metal-Ligand Interactions: From Atoms, to Clusters, to Surfaces. Ed. by Dennis R. Salahub & Nino Russo. LC 92-27726. (NATO ASI Series C, Mathematical & Physical Sciences: Vol. 378). 432p. (C). 1992. text 233.00 (*0-7923-1930-3*) Kluwer Academic.

Metal-Ligand Interactions - Structure & Reactivity: Proceedings of the NATO Advanced Study Institute, Cetraro, Italy, September 4-16, 1994. Ed. by Nino Russo. (NATO Advanced Science Institutes Ser.: Series C). 568p. (C). 1995. text 279.50 (*0-7923-3833-2*) Kluwer Academic.

***Metal-ligand Interactions in Chemistry, Physics & Biology.** Nino Russo & Dennis R. Salahub. 468p. 1999. pap. 72.00 (*0-7923-6126-1*) Kluwer Academic.

Metal Ligand Multiple Bonds. William A. Nugent & James M. Mayer. LC 88-233. 334p. 1988. 140.00 (*0-471-85440-9*) Wiley.

Metal Machining & Forming Technology. Joseph P. Vidosic. LC 64-19573. 569p. reprint ed. pap. 176.40 (*0-608-11593-2*, 205162300098) Bks Demand.

Metal Man & Others: The Collected Stories of Jack Williamson. Jack Williamson. 568p. 1999. 32.00 (*1-893887-02-2*) Haffner Pr.

Metal Man & Others: The Collected Stories of Jack Williamson. deluxe limited ed. Jack Williamson. (Illus.). 568p. 1999. boxed set 100.00 (*1-893887-03-0*) Haffner Pr.

Metal Matrix Composites. Ed. by G. Newaz et al. (Key Engineering Materials Ser.: Vols. 104-107). 928p. 1995. 333.00 (*0-87849-697-1*, Pub. by Trans T Pub) Enfield Pubs NH.

Metal Matrix Composites. B. Terry & G. Jones. 150p. 1990. 230.00 (*1-85617-021-7*, Pub. by Elsvr Adv Tech) Elsevier.

Metal Matrix Composites: Testing, Analysis, & Failure Modes. Ed. by W. S. Johnson. LC 89-17661. (Special Technical Publication Ser.: No. 1032). (Illus.). 300p. 1989. text 64.00 (*0-8031-1270-X*, STP1032) ASTM.

Metal Matrix Composites: Thermomechanical Behavior. M. Taya & R. J. Arsenault. (Illus.). 300p. 1989. text 96.00 (*0-08-036984-7*, Pergamon Pr) Elsevier.

Metal Melting Technology Seminar. 175p. 1990. 170.00 (*1-56061-038-7*, ICI-P-22) ICI Dallas.

Metal Metabolism & Disease. Max E. Rafelson. (Journal: Clinical Physiology & Biochemistry: Vol. 4, No. 1, 1986). (Illus.). 112p. 1986. pap. 36.75 (*3-8055-4264-X*) S Karger.

Metal Metabolism in Aquatic Environments. Chapman & Hall Staff. text 140.00 (*0-412-80370-4*) Chapman & Hall.

Metal-Metal Bonded Carbonyl Dimers & Clusters. Catherine E. Housecroft. (Oxford Chemistry Primers Ser.: No. 44). (Illus.). 96p. (C). 1996. pap. text 12.95 (*0-19-855859-7*) OUP.

Metal-Microbe Interactions. Ed. by R. K. Poole & Geoffrey M. Gadd. (Society for General Microbiology Special Publications: Vol. 26). 146p. 1989. pap. 55.00 (*0-19-963025-9*) OUP.

Metal Minds. Anderson. 1986. mass mkt. 2.95 (*0-8125-3070-5*) Tor Bks.

Metal Monster. Abraham Merritt. (Orig.). 1991. reprint ed. lib. bdg. 21.95 (*1-56849-081-X*) Buccaneer Bks.

Metal Neurotoxicity. Ed. by Stephen C. Bondy. 198p. 1987. 117.00 (*0-8493-4941-9*, RC347, CRC Reprint) Franklin.

Metal-Nonmetal Transition Revisited. P. P. Edwards & C. N. Rao. LC 96-133429. 416p. 1995. 125.00 (*0-7484-0385-X*, Pub. by Tay Francis Ltd) Taylor & Francis.

Metal Objects, 1952-1989. Isabelle K. Raubitschek. (Isthmia: Vol. 7). (Illus.). 200p. (C). 1998. text 150.00 (*0-87661-937-5*) Am Sch Athens.

Metal of Dishonor: How Depleted Uranium Penetrates Steel, Radiates People & Contaminates the Environment. unabridged ed. Ramsey Clark et al. LC 97-70773. (Illus.). 200p. (Orig.). 1997. pap. 12.95 (*0-9656916-0-8*) Intl Action Ctr.

Metal on Metal Hip Prostheses: Past Performance & Future Directions. Harlan C. Amstutz & Carl T. Brighton. 314p. 1996. text 72.00 (*0-397-51830-7*) Lppncott W & W.

Metal-Optics & Superconductivity. Ed. by A. I. Golovashkin. (Proceedings of the Lebedev Physics Institute Ser.: Vol. 195). 287p. 1990. 175.00 (*0-941743-80-2*) Nova Sci Pubs.

Metal-Organic Chemical Vapor Deposition of Electronic Ceramics Vol. 335: Materials Research Society Symposium Proceedings. Ed. by S. B. Desu et al. LC 94-5807. 365p. 1994. text 30.00 (*1-55899-234-0*) Materials Res.

Metal-Organic Chemical Vapor Deposition of Electronic Ceramics II: Materials Research Society Symposium Proceedings. Ed. by Seshu B. Desu et al. (MRS Symposium Proceedings Ser.: Vol. 415). 264p. 1996. 75.00 (*1-55899-318-5*) Materials Res.

Metal-Organic Compounds: A Collection of Papers Comprising the Symposium on Metal-Organic Compounds, Presented Before the Division of Industrial & Engineering Chemistry at the 131st National Meeting of the American Chemical Society, Miami, FL, April, 1957. Symposium on Metal-Organic Compounds (1957: Miami,. LC 60-3180. (Advances in Chemistry Ser.: Vol. 23). (Illus.). 377p. 1959. reprint ed. pap. 116.90 (*0-608-06897-7*, 206710500009) Bks Demand.

Metal Oxides. (Illus.). 288p. (C). 1997. text. write for info. (*0-412-72580-0*, Chap & Hall NY) Chapman & Hall.

***Metal-Oxo & Metal-Peroxo Species in Catalytic Oxidations.** Ed. by B. Meunier et al. (Structure & Bonding Ser.: 97). x, 294p. 2000. (*3-540-66943-4*) Spr-Verlag.

Metal Patternmaking. 1996. lib. bdg. 253.95 (*0-8490-8337-0*) Gordon Pr.

Metal-Planet Relationship: A Study of Celestial Influence. Nick Kollerstrom. (Illus.). 174p. (Orig.). 1993. pap. 12.95 (*0-945685-14-9*) Borderland Sciences.

Metal Plate Connected Wood Truss Handbook. Edward E. Callahan. Ed. by Pam Sabean. (Illus.). 318p. (C). 1993. pap. text 39.95 (*0-9638738-0-6*) WoodTruss Coun.

Metal Plating & Patination: Cultural, Technical, & Historical Developments. Ed. by Susan L. Neice & Paul Craddock. LC 93-18065. 327p. Date not set. reprint ed. pap. 101.40 (*0-608-20657-1*, 207209400003) Bks Demand.

Metal Plutonium: Proceedings of the World Metallurgical Congress, 2nd, Chicago, 1957. World Metallurgical Congress Staff. Ed. by A. S. Coffinberry & W. N. Miner. LC 61-17072. 458p. reprint ed. pap. 142.00 (*0-608-13483-X*, 202408800035) Bks Demand.

Metal Poisoning in Fish. Elsa M. Sorensen. (Illus.). 384p. 1991. boxed set 157.95 (*0-8493-4268-6*, SH177) CRC Pr.

Metal Powders: A Global Survey of Production, Applications & Markets. Joseph M. Capus. 200p. 1993. pap. 994.00 (*1-85617-174-4*) Elsevier.

Metal Powders Global Survey. Joseph M. Capus. LC 96-204723. 1996. pap. text 1253.00 (*1-85617-287-2*) Elsevier.

Metal Power: The Soul Life of the Planets. Alison Davidson. Ed. by Tom Brown. LC 91-76081. 112p. (Orig.). 1991. pap. 8.95 (*0-945685-11-4*) Borderland Sciences.

Metal Projects, Bk. 2. Bill Fifer. 96p. 1981. 13.28 (*0-87006-172-0*) Goodheart.

Metal Promoted Selectivity in Organic Synthesis. A. Noels et al. (C). 1900. text 234.00 (*0-7923-1184-1*) Kluwer Academic.

Metal Properties for the Petroleum & Chemical Industries: Presented at International Joint Petroleum Mechanical Engineering & Pressure Vessel & Piping Conference, Mexico City, Mexico, September 14-19, 1976. International Joint Petroleum Mechanical Engineering & Pressure Vessel & Piping Conference Staff. Ed. by Adolph O. Schaefer. LC 76-24332. (Illus.). 208p. reprint ed. pap. 64.50 (*0-608-30398-4*, 201688300005) Bks Demand.

Metal Quality Standards of I/C. (Illus.). 20p. 1987. 5.50 (*1-56061-035-2*, ICI-B-28) ICI Dallas.

Metal Recovery from Industrial Waste. Clyde S. Brooks et al. 288p. 1991. lib. bdg. 84.95 (*0-87371-456-3*, L456) Lewis Pubs.

Metal, Rock, & Jazz: Perception & the Phenomenology of Musical Experience. Harris M. Berger. LC 98-43706. (Music Culture Ser.). (Illus.). 350p. 1999. pap. 22.95 (*0-8195-6376-5*, Wesleyan Univ Pr); text 50.00 (*0-8195-6371-4*, Wesleyan Univ Pr) U Pr of New Eng.

Metal Safety Cans, UL 30. 9th ed. (C). 1995. pap. text 330.00 (*1-55989-187-4*) Underwrtrs Labs.

Metal Science of Joining: Proceeding of a Symposium Sponsored by the TMS Solidification Committee/MDMD & the Physical Metallurgy Committee/SMD, This Symposium Was Held October 20-24, 1991 at the TMS Fall Meeting in Cincinnati, Ohio. Ed. by M. J. Cieslak et al. LC 92-80699. (Illus.). 339p. 1992. pap. 105.10 (*0-608-04985-9*, 206560300004) Bks Demand.

Metal Science of Stainless Steel: Proceedings of a Symposium Held at the 107th AIME Annual Meeting, 1978. Metallurgical Society of AIME Staff. Ed. by E. W. Collings & H. W. King. LC 79-84706. 220p. reprint ed. pap. 68.20 (*0-608-13488-0*, 202544900044) Bks Demand.

***Metal Sculpture & the Mind of Art.** Craig Evans. 60p. 1999. pap. 9.95 (*0-9675996-0-1*) Crag Trail Pubng.

Metal-Semiconductor Contacts. E. H. Rhoderick. (Monographs in Electrical & Electronic Engineering). (Illus.). 1978. text 22.00 (*0-19-859323-6*) OUP.

Metal-Semiconductor Interface. A. Hiraki. LC 94-73403. 1995. 82.00 (*90-5199-205-X*) IOS Press.

Metal-Semiconductor Schottky Barrier Functions & Their Applications. B. L. Sharma. LC 84-1723. (Illus.). 386p. (C). 1984. text 115.00 (*0-306-41521-6*, Kluwer Plenum) Kluwer Academic.

***Metal Separation Technologies Beyond 2000: Integrating Novel Chemistry with Processing: Proceedings.** Ed. by Knona C. Liddell & David J. Chaiko. 375p. 1999. 78.00 (*0-87339-442-9*) Minerals Metals.

Metal Shaper. David J. Gingery. LC 80-66142. (Build Your Own Metalworking Shop from Scrap Ser.). (Illus.). 144p. (Orig.). 1981. pap. 9.95 (*1-878087-02-9*) D J Gingery.

Metal Shop Safety. Gary Hutchinson. LC 80-730754. 1981. student ed. 7.00 (*0-8064-0245-8*, 514) Bergwall.

Metal Sites in Proteins & Models: Iron Centres. Ed. by H. A. Hill et al. LC 99-20161. (Desktop Editions in Chemistry Ser.). 225p. 1999. pap. 54.95 (*3-540-65553-0*) Spr-Verlag.

Metal Sites in Proteins & Models: Phosphatases, Lewis Acids & Vanadium. Ed. by H. A. Hill et al. LC 99-20162. (Desktop Editions in Chemistry Ser.). 225p. 1999. pap. 54.95 (*3-540-65552-2*) Spr-Verlag.

Metal Sites in Proteins & Models: Redox Centres. Ed. by H. O. Hill et al. LC 99-20158. (Desktop Editions in Chemistry Ser.). 210p. 1999. pap. 54.95 (*3-540-65556-5*) Spr-Verlag.

Metal-Slag-Gas Reactions & Processes: Papers. International Symposium on Metal-Slag-Gas Reaction. Ed. by Z. A. Foroulis & W. W. Smeltzer. LC 74-21450. (Illus.). 1046p. 1975. pap. 200.00 (*0-7837-8989-0*, 205925400002) Bks Demand.

Metal Speciation: Theory, Analysis & Application. Ed. by James R. Kramer & Herbert E. Allen. (Illus.). 376p. 1988. lib. bdg. 99.95 (*0-87371-140-8*, L140) Lewis Pubs.

Metal Speciation & Bioavailability in Aquatic Systems. Ed. by Andre Tessier & David R. Turner. (Environmental Analytical & Physical Chemistry Ser.). 696p. 1996. 385.00 (*0-471-95830-1*) Wiley.

Metal Speciation & Contamination of Soil. Ed. by Herbert E. Allen et al. 384p. 1994. lib. bdg. 75.00 (*0-87371-697-3*, L697) Lewis Pubs.

Metal Speciation in the Environment. Ed. by J. A. Broekaert et al. (NATO ASI Series G: Ecological Sciences: Vol. 23). (Illus.). 660p. 1990. 272.95 (*0-387-50423-0*) Spr-Verlag.

Metal Spinning: Metal Spinning for Craftsman, Instructors & Students. James Reagan & Earl Smith. 80p. reprint ed. pap. 9.95 (*0-917914-83-X*) Lindsay Pubns.

Metal Spinning for Craftsmen, Instructors & Students. 1996. lib. bdg. 250.75 (*0-8490-8334-6*) Gordon Pr.

Metal Spinning Projects. Smith & James Reagan. (Illus.). 80p. 1991. reprint ed. pap. 10.00 (*1-877767-55-7*) Univ Publng Hse.

Metal Statistics. (Illus.). 1997. 228.00 (*0-87005-240-3*) AMM.

***Metal Statistics 1999: The Statistical Guide to North American Metals.** 91st ed. Ed. by Gloria T. LaRue & Myra Pinkham. (Illus.). 375p. 1999. 250.00 (*0-910094-00-4*) AMM.

***Metal-Supported Automotive Catalytic Converters.** Ed. by H. Bode. 220p. 1999. 145.00 (*3-527-29925-4*) Wiley.

Metal Surface Characteristics Affecting Organic Coatings. Bruno M. Perfetti. (Illus.). 70p. 1994. pap. 30.00 (*0-934010-32-3*) Fed Soc Coat Tech.

Metal Surface Electron Physics. A. Kiejna & K. F. Wojciechowski. LC 95-45019. 340p. 1996. write for info. (*0-08-042675-1*, Pergamon Pr) Elsevier.

Metal-Surface Reaction: Theory & Applications to Heterogeneous Catalysis, Chemisorption & Surface Diffusion. Ed. by E. Shustorovich. 232p. 1991. 110.00 (*0-471-18745-3*, Wiley-VCH) Wiley.

Metal-Surface Reaction Energetics: Theory & Applications to Heterogeneous Catalysis, Chemisorption & Surface Diffusion. Evgeny Shustorovich. 232p. 1991. text 75.00 (*0-89573-776-0*, Wiley-VCH) Wiley.

Metal Technology. Rex Miller & Thomas J. Morrisey. LC 74-77817. 1976. 22.39 (*0-672-97623-4*, Bobbs); 5.99 (*0-672-97624-2*, Bobbs); teacher ed. 3.67 (*0-672-97625-0*, Bobbs) Macmillan.

Metal Technology & Processes. Feirer & Lindbeck. LC 97-30551. 592p. (C). 1998. text 58.95 (*0-8273-7909-9*) Delmar.

***Metal Technology & Processes: Instructor's Guide.** Feirer & Lindbeck. 96p. 1999. teacher ed. 15.95 (*0-8273-7911-0*) Delmar.

Metal Toxicity in Mammals. B. Venugopal & T. D. Luckey. Incl. Chemical Toxicity of Metals & Metalloids. 420p. 1978. 75.00 (*0-306-37177-4*, Kluwer Plenum); Physiologic & Chemical Basis for Metal Toxicity. 248p. 1977. 55.00 (*0-306-37176-6*, Kluwer Plenum); (Illus.). 1977. write for info. (*0-318-55332-5*, Plenum Trade) Perseus Pubng.

Metal Toys & Automata. Constance King. 1989. 12.98 (*1-55521-412-6*) Bk Sales Inc.

Metal Toys from Nurenberg, 1910-1979. Gerhard Walter. LC 92-60638. (Illus.). 144p. 1992. text 35.00 (*0-88740-435-9*) Schiffer.

Metal Traders of the World. 3rd ed. 733p. 1986. write for info. (*0-947671-00-5*) Taylor & Francis.

Metal Traders of the World. 4th ed. Ed. by Richard Serjeantson. 597p. 1990. text 188.40 (*0-947671-36-6*) Metal Bulletin.

Metal Transfer & Galling in Metallic Systems: Proceedings of a Symposium Sponsored by the Non-Ferrous Metals Committee of the Metallurgical Society & the Erosion & Wear G2 Committee of ASTM, Orlando, Florida, October 8-9, 1986. Metallurgical Society of AIME Staff. Ed. by H. D. Merchant & K. J. Bhansali. LC 87-5740. 307p. reprint ed. pap. 95.20 (*0-7837-4077-8*, 205247400011) Bks Demand.

Metal Treatments Against Wear Corrosion Fretting & Fatigue: Technology - Application - Effects. Ed. by R. B. Waterhouse & Lari A. Niku. LC 88-19588. (Advances in Surface Treatments Ser.: Vol. 6). 225p. 1988. 116.00 (*0-08-035916-7*, Pub. by Pergamon Repr) Franklin.

Metal Vapor & Metal Halide Vapor Lasers. Ed. by G. G. Petrash. (Proceedings of the Lebedev Physics Institute Ser.: Vol. 181). 261p. 1989. text 165.00 (*0-941743-27-6*) Nova Sci Pubs.

Metal Vapour Ion Lasers: Kinetic Processes & Gas Discharges. I. G. Ivanov et al. Ed. by C. E. Little. Tr. by D. N. Astadjov. LC 96-3190. 300p. 1996. 210.00 (*0-471-95563-9*) Wiley.

Metal Vapour Lasers: Physics, Engineering & Applications. Christopher E. Little. LC 98-26739. 620p. 1999. 335.00 (*0-471-97387-4*) Wiley.

Metal Waste Cans, UL 32. 5th ed. (C). 1994. pap. text 175.00 (*1-55989-628-0*) Underwrtrs Labs.

Metal Waste Paper Containers, UL 1315. (C). 1995. pap. text 95.00 (*1-55989-912-3*) Underwrtrs Labs.

Metal Work for Industrial Arts Shops. Dewey F. Barich & Leonard C. Smith. LC 52-8345. 103p. reprint ed. pap. 32.00 (*0-608-10060-9*, 200457000043) Bks Demand.

Metal Workers Benchtop Reference Manual. Joseph W. Serafin. (Illus.). 380p. 1986. 25.95 (*0-8306-0805-2*, NO. 2605); pap. 16.95 (*0-8306-1705-1*) McGraw-Hill Prof.

***Metal Working Machine Tools in Australia: A Strategic Entry Report, 1996.** Compiled by Icon Group International Staff. (Illus.). 131p. 1999. ring bd. 1310.00 incl. audio compact disk (*0-7418-1337-8*) Icon Grp.

Metal y Urnas. Leandro Katz. (SPA.). 1961. 40.00 (*0-931106-06-0*) TVRT.

Metalanguage. Josette Rey-Debove. 326p. 1978. 49.95 (*0-7859-9207-3*) Fr & Eur.

***Metalcaster's Bible.** Ammen. LC 99-33560. 432p. 1999. pap. 34.95 (*0-07-134246-X*) McGraw.

Metalcaster's Bible. C. W. Ammen. 434p. 1980. pap. 27.95 (*0-07-156186-2*) McGraw.

Metalcaster's Bible. Jan P. Norbye. (Illus.). 434p. 1980. 15.95 (*0-8306-9970-8*); pap. 19.95 (*0-8306-1173-8*, 1173) McGraw-Hill Prof.

Metalcaster's Reference & Guide. 2nd ed. 672p. 1989. 120.00 (*0-87433-116-1*, GM8900) Am Foundrymen.

Metalcasting & Molding Processes. 246p. 1981. 40.00 (*0-87433-062-9*, GM8100) Am Foundrymen.

Metalcasting Ergonomics. 80p. 1992. ring bd. 55.00 (*0-87433-159-5*, EC9200) Am Foundrymen.

Metalcrafts of Central Asia. Ken Teague. (Ethnography Ser.: No. 19). (Illus.). 64p. pap. 10.50 (*0-7478-0062-6*, Pub. by Shire Pubns) Parkwest Pubns.

Metalinguistic Activity in Learning to Write. Ed. by Anna Camps & Marta Milian. (International Series on the Research of Learning & Instruction of Writing Ser.). 250p. 1999. pap. 44.50 (*90-5356-341-5*, Pub. by Amsterdam U Pr) U of Mich Pr.

Metalinguistic Awareness & Beginning Literacy: Conceptualizing What It Means to Read & Write. Ed. by David B. Yaden, Jr. & Shane Templeton. LC 85-21967. 345p. (C). 1986. text 45.00 (*0-435-08245-0*) Heinemann.

Metalinguistic Awareness in Children. Ed. by William E. Tunmer et al. (Language & Communication Ser.: Vol. 15). (Illus.). 255p. 1983. 48.00 (*0-387-12432-2*) Spr-Verlag.

Metalinguistic Development. Jean E. Gombert. Tr. by Tim Pownall. 246p. 1992. pap. text 29.95 (*0-226-30209-1*); lib. bdg. 66.00 (*0-226-30208-3*) U Ch Pr.

Metalinguistic Functioning in Children. Judith A. Bowey. 81p. (C). 1988. 51.00 (*0-7300-0551-8*, Pub. by Deakin Univ) St Mut.

Metalinguistic Operators with Reference to French. T. Nyan. 169p. (C). 1998. pap. text 30.95 (*0-8204-3416-7*) P Lang Pubng.

Metalinguistic Performance & Interlinguistic Competence. D. Birdsong. (Language & Communication Ser.: Vol. 25). ix, 246p. 1989. 86.95 (*0-387-50351-X*) Spr-Verlag.

Metalinguistik Im Wandel: Die "Kognitive Wende" in Wissenschaftstheorie und Linguistik. Andras Kertesz. (Metalinguistica Ser.: Bd. 4). (GER., Illus.). 232p. 1996. 44.95 (*3-631-30635-0*) P Lang Pubng.

Metalized Plastics Vol. 2: Fundamental & Applied Aspects. Ed. by K. L. Mittal. (Illus.). 488p. (C). 1992. text 162.00 (*0-306-44107-1*, Kluwer Plenum) Kluwer Academic.

Metallak, His Legacy. Alice D. Noyes. Ed. & Illus. by Jordan Assocs. Staff. 266p. 1988. 18.95 (*0-685-25278-7*) A D Noyes.

Metallic Alloys: Experimental & Theoretical Perspectives. Ed. by J. S. Faulkner & R. G. Jordan. LC 93-50754. (NATO Advanced Study Institutes Series E, Applied Sciences: No. 256). 463p. 1994. text 272.50 (*0-7923-2701-2*) Kluwer Academic.

Metallic & Ceramic Coatings. M. G. Hocking. 1989. pap. text. write for info. (*0-582-03305-5*, Pub. by Addison-Wesley) Longman.

Metallic & Metallopolymeric Composites. Ed. by J. N. Fridlyander & I. H. Marshall. LC 92-42749. (Russian Composite Materials Ser.). 1993. write for info. (*1-85861-000-1*) Elsevier.

An Asterisk (*) at the beginning of an entry indicates that the title is appearing for the first time.

Metallic & Semiconducting Glasses, 3 vols., Set. Ed. by A. K. Bhatnagar. 960p. (C). 1987. text 316.00 (*0-87849-556-8*, Pub. by Trans T Pub) Enfield Pubs NH.

Metallic Bellows & Expansion Joints: Presented at the Joint Conference of the Pressure Vessels & Piping, Materials, Nuclear Engineering, Solar Energy Divisions, Denver, CO, 1. American Society of Mechanical Engineers Staff. Ed. by S. J. Brown et al. LC 81-65236. (PVP Ser.: No. 51). (Illus.). 160p. pap. 49.60 (*0-608-15567-5*, 205639600001) Bks Demand.

Metallic Bond & the Structure of Metals. V. K. Grigorovich. 311p. (C). 1989. text 175.00 (*0-941743-50-0*) Nova Sci Pubs.

Metallic Card Clothing & Its Use in High Production Carding. Ed. by Wira Staff. 1988. 60.00 (*0-7855-1025-7*) St Mut.

Metallic Cartridge Reloading. 3rd ed. M. L. McPherson. LC 81-70996. (Illus.). 352p. 1996. pap. 21.95 (*0-87349-180-7*, MCR3, DBI Bks) Krause Pubns.

Metallic Corrosion. 2nd ed. LC 85-61826. (Illus.). 498p. 1985. 61.00 (*0-915567-12-1*) NACE Intl.

Metallic Corrosion: Tenth International Congress, 4 vols., Set. Ed. by S. Varadarajan. 4700p. 1989. text 766.00 (*0-87849-574-6*, Pub. by Trans T Pub) Enfield Pubs NH.

Metallic Corrosion Vol. V: Supplemental. (Key Engineering Materials Ser.). 380p. 1989. 108.00 (*0-87849-582-7*, Pub. by Trans T Pub) Enfield Pubs NH.

Metallic Finishes Etc. Cy DeCosse Incorporated Staff. LC 96-28583. (Creative Touches Ser.). (Illus.). 64p. 1996. pap. 9.95 (*0-86573-875-0*) Creat Pub Intl.

Metallic Gasket Handbook. 3rd rev. ed. (Illus.). 24p. 1999. pap. 25.00 (*1-892965-01-1*) Fluid Sealing Assn.

Metallic Glasses: Papers Presented at a Seminar of the Materials Science Division of the ASM, September 18 & 19, 1976. Materials Science Seminar, 1976, Metals Park, OH S. LC 77-24014. 360p. reprint ed. pap. 111.60 (*0-608-16822-X*, 202703700053) Bks Demand.

Metallic Glasses: Production, Properties & Applications. Ed. by T. R. Anantharaman. 312p. (C). 1984. text 100.00 (*0-87849-525-8*, Pub. by Trans T Pub) Enfield Pubs NH.

Metallic Magnetism I, Vol. 42. Ed. by H. Capellmann. (Topics in Current Physics Ser.). (Illus.). 280p. 1987. 66.95 (*0-387-16859-1*) Spr-Verlag.

Metallic Materials Specification Handbook. 3rd ed. R. B. Ross. 1980. 120.00 (*0-419-11360-6*, NO. 6339, E & FN Spon) Routledge.

Metallic Mineral Exploration: An Economic Analysis. Roderick G. Eggert. LC 87-42622. 90p. 1987. pap. 14.95 (*0-915707-30-6*) Resources Future.

Metallic Multi-Layers & Epitaxy: Proceedings of a Symposium Co-Sponsored by the TMS Electronic Device Materials Committee (EDMC), & the ASM-MSD Electrical, Magnetic & Optical Phenomena Activity (EMOP), held at the Annual Meeting of the Metallurgical Society in Denver, Colorado, February 24-25, 1987. fac. ed. Metallurgical Society of AIME Staff. Ed. by M. Hong et al. LC 87-42881. 291p. 1988. reprint ed. pap. 90.30 (*0-7837-8303-5*, 204908900010) Bks Demand.

Metallic Multilayers. Ed. by A. Chamberod & J. Hillairet. 648p. (C). 1990. text 183.00 (*0-87849-609-2*, Pub. by Trans T Pub) Enfield Pubs NH.

Metallic Ornaments of the New York Indians. William M. Beauchamp. LC 74-7928. reprint ed. 31.50 (*0-404-11814-3*) AMS Pr.

Metallic Outlet Boxes, UL 514A. 9th ed. (C). 1996. pap. text 330.00 (*1-55989-220-X*) Underwrtrs Labs.

Metallic Parahydrogen - Dark Matter Equivalence & Astronomical Survey. (Scientific Papers). (Illus.). 34p. 1998. mass mkt. 6.00 (*1-881946-10-X*) Gauntlet Bks.

Metallic Pollution. S. G. Misra. (C). 1992. 20.00 (*81-7024-473-0*, Pub. by Ashish Pub Hse) S Asia.

Metallic Textile Designs. Tina Skinner. LC 98-86019. (Illus.). 112p. (Orig.). 1999. pap. 19.95 (*0-7643-0635-9*) Schiffer.

Metallic Wealth of the United States. Josiah D. Whitney. LC 74-125766. (American Environmental Studies). 1975. reprint ed. 34.95 (*0-405-02692-7*) Ayer.

Metallica. (Play-It-Like-It-Is Guitar Ser.). pap. 22.95 (*0-89524-675-9*, Pub. by Cherry Lane); pap. 19.95 (*0-89524-699-6*, Pub. by Cherry Lane); pap. 18.95 (*0-89524-740-2*, Pub. by Cherry Lane); pap. text 12.95 (*0-89524-756-9*, Pub. by Cherry Lane) H Leonard.

***Metallica.** (Garage Inc.). 80p. 1999. otabind 14.95 (*1-57560-201-6*, Pub. by Cherry Lane) H Leonard.

***Metallica.** (Garage Inc.). 112p. 1999. otabind 18.95 (*1-57560-202-4*, Pub. by Cherry Lane) H Leonard.

Metallica. Ross Halfin. 192p. 1996. pap. 40.00 (*1-880985-38-1*) Two Thirteen Sixty-one.

Metallica. Mick Wall. (Making of Ser.). (Illus.). (Orig.). 1996. pap. 7.95 (*1-896522-34-3*) CN06.

Metallica. Mick Wall & Malcolm Dome. (Complete Guides to the Music Of...Ser.). (Illus.). 88p. (Orig.). (C). 1995. pap. 8.95 (*0-7119-4902-6*, OP 47770) Omnibus NY.

Metallica: Easy Recorded Versions. 1995. 12.95 (*0-89524-923-5*, 02506877, Pub. by Cherry Lane) H Leonard.

***Metallica: Fuel & Fire.** Sam Hadland. 1998. pap. 19.95 (*1-896522-09-2*) CN06.

***Metallica: Garage Inc.** 304p. 1999. otabind 24.95 (*1-57560-195-8*, Pub. by Cherry Lane) H Leonard.

***Metallica: Garage Inc.** 208p. 1999. otabind 24.95 (*1-57560-200-8*, Pub. by Cherry Lane) H Leonard.

Metallica: In Their Own Words. Mark Putterford. LC 95-158816. (In Their Own Words Ser.). (Illus.). 96p. pap. 15.95 (*0-7119-3866-0*, OP 47592) Omnibus NY.

***Metallica: Legendary Licks 1983-1988.** Nick Russo. 88p. 2000. pap. 19.95 incl. audio compact disk (*1-57560-281-4*, Pub. by Cherry Lane) H Leonard.

Metallica: Or, the Treatise of New Metallicall Inventions. Simon Sturtevant. LC 74-28887. (English Experience Ser.: No. 764). 1975. reprint ed. 15.00 (*90-221-0764-7*) Walter J Johnson.

Metallica: The Frayed Ends of Metal. Chris Crocker. LC 92-33808. 1992. pap. 12.95 (*0-312-08635-0*) St Martin.

Metallica - ...& Justice for All. (Play-It-Like-It-Is Guitar Ser.). pap. 19.95 (*0-89524-449-7*, Pub. by Cherry Lane); pap. 19.95 (*0-685-75225-9*); pap. 18.95 (*0-89524-576-0*, Pub. by Cherry Lane); pap. text 12.95 (*0-89524-451-9*, Pub. by Cherry Lane) H Leonard.

Metallica - Five of the Best: Play-It-Like-It-Is Guitar, Vol. 1. pap. 12.95 (*0-89524-519-1*, Pub. by Cherry Lane) H Leonard.

Metallica - Five of the Best: Play-It-Like-It-Is Guitar, Vol. 2. 1994. pap. text 12.95 (*0-89524-780-1*, Pub. by Cherry Lane) H Leonard.

Metallica - Kill 'Em All. (Play-It-Like-It-Is Guitar Ser.). pap. 19.95 (*0-89524-496-9*, Pub. by Cherry Lane); pap. 19.95 (*0-89524-514-0*, Pub. by Cherry Lane); pap. 12.95 (*0-89524-515-9*, Pub. by Cherry Lane); pap. 18.95 (*0-89524-657-0*, Pub. by Cherry Lane) H Leonard.

Metallica - Load. Ed. by Jeff Jacobson. 156p. (YA). 1995. pap. 24.95 (*1-57560-014-5*, Pub. by Cherry Lane) H Leonard.

Metallica - Loud Bass/Vocal. Ed. by Steve Gorenberg. 101p. (YA). pap. 19.95 (*1-57560-015-3*, Pub. by Cherry Lane) H Leonard.

Metallica - Master of Puppets. (Easy Guitar Ser.). pap. text 12.95 (*0-89524-488-8*, Pub. by Cherry Lane) H Leonard.

Metallica - Master of Puppets: Drum Edition. Ed. by Jon Chappell. (Illus.). 70p. (Orig.). 1990. pap. text 18.95 (*0-89524-562-0*, Pub. by Cherry Lane) H Leonard.

Metallica - Master of Puppets: Guitar - Vocal. Ed. by Mark Phillips. (Illus.). (Orig.). 1990. pap. text 19.95 (*0-89524-565-5*); pap. text 19.95 (*0-89524-358-X*, Pub. by Cherry Lane) H Leonard.

Metallica - Master of Puppets (Bass Guitar) Ed. by Mark Phillips. (Illus.). 55p. (Orig.). 1990. pap. text 19.95 (*0-89524-408-X*, Pub. by Cherry Lane) H Leonard.

Metallica - Ride the Lightning. (Play-It-Like-It-Is Guitar Ser.). pap. 19.95 (*0-89524-494-2*, Pub. by Cherry Lane); pap. 17.95 (*0-89524-554-X*, Pub. by Cherry Lane); pap. 17.95 (*0-89524-610-4*, Pub. by Cherry Lane); pap. text 12.95 (*0-89524-555-8*, Pub. by Cherry Lane) H Leonard.

Metallica Files. Cimino Publishing Group Staff. 1998. pap. text 24.95 (*1-901674-00-2*) Arrowhead.

Metallica Files. David H. Richter. 1998. pap. text 12.95 (*1-901674-60-6*) Arrowhead.

Metallica Live! With Poster. rev. ed. Martin Power. 96p. 1998. pap. 12.95 (*0-7119-6785-7*, OP48039) Omnibus NY.

Metallica Live - Binge & Purge. 1994. pap. 19.95 (*0-89524-825-5*, Pub. by Cherry Lane) H Leonard.

***Metallica Reload: Play it Like it is Bass.** 124p. 1998. pap. text 21.95 (*1-57560-096-X*, Pub. by Cherry Lane) H Leonard.

Metallica Riff. Riff Bass Riff. 80p. 1997. otabind 17.95 (*1-57560-048-X*, Pub. by Cherry Lane) H Leonard.

Metallica Riff by Riff: Guitar. Ed. by Mark Phillips. 1994. pap. 17.95 (*0-89524-840-9*, Pub. by Cherry Lane) H Leonard.

Metallica Unbound. K. J. Doughton. (Illus.). 176p. (Orig.). 1993. mass mkt. 15.99 (*0-446-39486-6*, Pub. by Warner Bks) Little.

Metallica Visual Documentary. Paul Gambaccini. (Illus.). 96p. pap. 19.95 (*0-7119-3081-3*, OP 47044) Omnibus NY.

Metallica's Lars Ulrich: Drum Transcriptions. Ed. by Dino Fanci. 1994. pap. 14.95 (*0-89524-785-2*); pap. 17.95 (*0-89524-786-0*, Pub. by Cherry Lane) H Leonard.

Metallics & Lustres. Hugh Giese. 36p. 1993. reprint ed. pap. 5.95 (*0-916809-69-2*) Scott Pubns MI.

Metallization: Theory & Practice for VLSI & ULSI. Shyam P. Murarka. 250p. 1992. text 69.95 (*0-7506-9001-1*) Buttrwrth-Heinemann.

Metallization & Metal - Semiconductor Interfaces. Ed. by I. P. Batra. (Illus.). 522p. (C). 1989. text 174.00 (*0-306-43159-9*, Kluwer Plenum) Kluwer Academic.

Metallization of Polymers. Ed. by Edward Sacher et al. LC 90-47471. (ACS Symposium Ser.: No. 440). (Illus.). 530p. 1990. text 110.00 (*0-8412-1868-4*, Pub. by Am Chemical) OUP.

Metallization Overview. TEEX Staff. (Illus.). ix, 57p. 1997. spiral bd. 39.95 (*1-58257-005-1*, 8146B) TX Eng Extsn Servs.

Metallized Plastics: Fundamental & Applied Aspects, Vol. 1. Ed. by K. L. Mittal. LC 89-28395. (Illus.). 292p. (C). 1989. text 114.00 (*0-306-43389-3*, Kluwer Plenum) Kluwer Academic.

Metallized Plastics: Fundamental & Applied Aspects, Vol. 3. K. L. Mittal. (Illus.). 410p. (C). 1993. text 130.00 (*0-306-44341-4*, Kluwer Plenum) Kluwer Academic.

Metallized Plastics: Fundamentals & Applications. K. L. Mittal. LC 97-38708. (Plastics Engineering Ser.). (Illus.). 352p. 1997. text 175.00 (*0-8247-9925-9*) Dekker.

Metallizing of Plastics: A Handbook of Theory & Practice. Ed. by Richard Suchentrunk. LC 93-72311. 348p. 1993. 114.00 (*0-904477-13-4*, 6372U) ASM Intl.

Metallobiochemistry, Pt. A. Ed. by James F. Riordan et al. (Methods in Enzymology Ser.: Vol. 158). 464p. 1988. text 146.00 (*0-12-182059-9*) Acad Pr.

Metallobiochemistry Pt. C: Spectroscopic & Physical Methods for Probing Metal Ion Environments in Metalloenzymes & Metalloproteins. Ed. by John N. Abelson et al. (Methods in Enzymology Ser.: Vol. 226). (Illus.). 674p. 1993. text 115.00 (*0-12-182127-7*) Acad Pr.

Metallobiochemistry Pt. D: Physical & Spectroscopic Methods for Probing Metal Ion Environments in Metalloproteins. Ed. by John N. Abelson et al. (Methods in Enzymology Ser.: Vol. 227). (Illus.). 634p. 1993. text 115.00 (*0-12-182128-5*) Acad Pr.

Metallobiochemistry Pt. B: Metallothionein & Related Molecules. Ed. by John N. Abelson et al. (Methods in Enzymology Ser.: Vol. 205). (Illus.). 681p. 1991. text 125.00 (*0-12-182106-4*) Acad Pr.

***Metallocene-Based Polyolefins, Vol. 1.** John Scheirs. 556p. 2000. 275.00 (*0-471-99911-3*) Wiley.

***Metallocene-Based Polyolefins, Vol. 2.** John Scheirs. 598p. 2000. 275.00 (*0-471-99912-1*) Wiley.

***Metallocene-Based Polyolefins: Preparation, Properties & Technology.** John Scheirs. LC 99-21151. (Series in Polymer Science). (Illus.). 1054p. 2000. 495.00 (*0-471-98086-2*) Wiley.

Metallocene Catalyzed Polymers: Materials, Properties, Processing & Markets. Ed. by George M. Benedikt & Brian L. Goodall. (SPE/ PDL Ser.). 400p. 1998. text 160.00 (*1-884207-59-6*) William Andrew.

Metallocene Elastomers/TPEs. Contrib. by Melvin Schlechter. 173p. 1996. 2850.00 (*1-56965-264-3*, P-159) BCC.

Metallocene Polymers. Eberhard W. Neuse & Harold Rosenberg. LC 77-130360. (Reviews in Macromolecular Chemistry Ser.: Vol. 5, Pt. 1). (Illus.). 170p. 1970. reprint ed. pap. 52.70 (*0-608-00006-X*, 205930800007) Bks Demand.

Metallocene Technology & Modern Catalytic Methods in Commercial Applications. Ed. by George M. Bendikt & Brian L. Goodall. LC 98-89319. 325p. 1999. 160.00 (*1-884207-76-6*) William Andrew.

Metallocenes. Ronald L. Halterman. Ed. by Antonio Togni. LC 98-232708. 832p. 1998. 325.00 (*3-527-29539-9*) Wiley.

Metallocenes: An Introduction to Sandwich Complexes. Nicholas J. Long. LC 97-23272. (Illus.). 288p. 1998. pap. 58.95 (*0-632-04162-5*) Blackwell Sci.

Metallogenesis & Mineral Ore Deposits: Proceedings of the 27th International Geological Congress, Vol. 12. International Geological Congress Staff. 432p. 1984. lib. bdg. 120.00 (*90-6764-021-2*, Pub. by VSP) Coronet Bks.

Metallogenetische Provinzen in Suedamerika. H. Putzer. xii, 316p. 1976. 68.00 (*3-510-65074-3*, Pub. by E Schweizerbartsche) Balogh.

Metallogeny & Plate Tectonics. Ed. by D. F. Strong. LC 77-354111. (Geological Association of Canada. Special Paper: No. 14). 668p. reprint ed. pap. 200.00 (*0-608-17206-5*, 202784300056) Bks Demand.

Metallogeny of the Fairbanks Mining District, Alaska & Adjacent Areas, 2 vols. Paul A. Metz. LC 91-67232. (MIRL Reports: No. 90). (Illus.). 455p. (Orig.). (C). 1991. pap. text 24.00 (*0-911043-13-6*); pap. text 41.00 incl. fiche (*0-685-56388-X*) UAKF Min Ind Res Lab.

Metallogeny of Tin. B. Lehmann. Ed. by S. Bhattacharji et al. (Lecture Notes in Earth Sciences Ser.: Vol. 32). (Illus.). viii, 211p. 1990. 45.95 (*0-387-52806-7*) Spr-Verlag.

Metallograph: History of Metals, Wherein Is Declared the Signs of Ores & Minerals Both Before & after Digging. John Webster. LC 77-6544. (History of Geology Ser.). 1978. reprint ed. lib. bdg. 37.95 (*0-405-10462-6*) Ayer.

***Metallographic Etching** 2nd ed. G. Petzow. LC 99-29323. 1999. write for info. (*0-87170-633-4*) ASM.

Metallographic Etching: Metallographic & Ceramographic Methods for Revealing Microstructure. Gunter Petzow. LC 78-8023. 143p. reprint ed. 44.40 (*0-608-17151-4*, 202698700053) Bks Demand.

Metallographic Specimen Preparation: Optical & Electron Microscopy. Ed. by James L. McCall & William M. Mueller. LC 74-8391. (Illus.). 366p. 1974. reprint ed. pap. 113.50 (*0-608-05493-3*, 206596200006) Bks Demand.

Metallographic Techniques & the Characterization of Composites, Stainless Steels, & Other Engineering Materials. Ed. by M. Shehata et al. LC 95-76678. (Microstructural Science Ser.: Vol. 22). 500p. 1995. 103.00 (*0-87170-537-0*, 6426) ASM.

Metallography: A Practical Tool for Correlating the Structure & Properties of Materials - STP 557. 240p. 1981. 24.25 (*0-8031-0510-X*, STP557) ASTM.

Metallography: Principles & Practice. George F. Vander Voort. LC 99-24360. 752p. 1984. 99.00 (*0-87170-672-5*, 06785G) ASM.

Metallography - Past, Present, & Future: 75th Anniversary Volume. Ed. by George F. Vander Voort et al. LC 93-14998. (STP Ser.: Vol. 1165). (Illus.). 460p. 1993. text 99.00 (*0-8031-1484-2*, STP1165) ASTM.

Metallography & Interpretation of Weld Microstructures: Proceedings of a Symposium Co-Sponsored by the International Metallographic Society, ASM International, & the American Welding Society. Ed. by James L. McCall et al. LC 87-71104. (Illus.). 399p. reprint ed. pap. 123.70 (*0-8357-4091-9*, 203685700005) Bks Demand.

Metallography & Microstructure in Ancient & Historic Metals. David Scott. LC 91-19484. 176p. 1991. pap. 55.00 (*0-89236-195-6*, Pub. by J P Getty Trust) OUP.

Metallography '95: Proceedings of the 9th International Metallographic Symposium. Ed. by I. Hrivnak. 600p. 1995. pap. 167.00 (*1-898326-26-6*, Pub. by CISP) Balogh.

Metallomesogens: Synthesis, Properties, & Applications. Ed. by Jose L. Serrano. LC 95-48227. (Illus.). 498p. 1996. 290.00 (*3-527-29296-9*, Wiley-VCH) Wiley.

Metallopharmaceuticals Vol. 1: DNA Interactions. Ed. by M. J. Clarke et al. LC 99-21036. (Topics in Biological Inorganic Chemistry Ser.). (Illus.). 250p. 1999. 129.00 (*3-540-64889-5*) Spr-Verlag.

***Metallopharmaceuticals II: Diagnosis & Therapy.** Ed. by M. J. Clarke et al. (Topics in Biological Inorganic Chemistry Ser.: Vol. 2). (Illus.). 195p. 1999. 124.00 (*3-540-65308-2*) Spr-Verlag.

Metalloporphyrins Catalyzed Oxidations. Ed. by F. Montanari & L. Casella. LC 93-43396. (Catalysis by Metal Complexes Ser.: Vol. 17). 368p. (C). 1994. text 204.50 (*0-7923-2657-1*) Kluwer Academic.

Metalloporphyrins in Catalytic Oxidations. Ed. by Roger A. Sheldon. (Illus.). 408p. 1994. text 175.00 (*0-8247-9228-9*) Dekker.

***Metalloproteinases as Targets for Anti-Inflammatory Drugs.** Ed. by K. M. Bottomley et al. LC 99-32920. (Progress in Inflammation Research Ser.). 230p. 1999. 139.00 (*3-7643-5856-4*, Pub. by Birkhauser) Spr-Verlag.

***Metalloproteins.** David P. Ballou. (Essays in Biochemistry Ser.: Vol. 34). 180p. 2000. pap. text 29.95 (*0-691-05048-1*) Princeton U Pr.

Metalloproteins see Proteins: Composition, Structure & Function

Metallothionein IV. Curtis D. Klaassen. LC 98-26283. 1998. write for info. (*0-8176-5830-0*) Birkhauser.

Metallothionein IV. C. D. Klassen. LC 98-26283. 600p. 1998. 118.00 (*3-7643-5830-0*, Pub. by Birkhauser) Princeton Arch.

Metallothionein III: Biological Roles & Medical Implications. Ed. by K. T. Suzuki et al. LC 93-41417. 1994. 118.00 (*0-8176-2769-3*) Birkhauser.

Metallothionein in Biology & Medicine. Curtis D. Klaassen & K. T. Suzuki. (Illus.). 432p. 1991. lib. bdg. 189.00 (*0-8493-8832-5*) CRC Pr.

Metallothionein Two. Jeremias Kagi. (BioSeries-EXS: No. 52). 400p. 1987. 156.00 (*0-8176-1804-X*) Birkhauser.

Metallothioneins: Synthesis, Structure & Properties of Metallothioneins, Phytochelatins & Metal-Thiolate Complexes. Ed. by M. J. Stillman & F. C. Shaw. 443p. 1992. 175.00 (*0-471-18776-3*, Wiley-VCH) Wiley.

Metallothioneins: Synthesis, Structure & Properties of Metallothioneins, Phytochelatins & Metal-Thiolate Complexes. Ed. by Martin J. Stillman et al. (Illus.). 443p. 1992. 125.00 (*0-89573-785-X*, Wiley-VCH) Wiley.

Metallurgical Analysis of Gear Failures as Seen Through the Microscope. J. T. Howat. (Technical Papers: Vol. P126). (Illus.). 25p. 1935. pap. text 30.00 (*1-55589-329-5*) AGMA.

Metallurgical & Ceramic Protective Coatings. Ed. by K. H. Stern. 340p. 1996. pap. write for info. (*0-412-54440-7*) Kluwer Academic.

Metallurgical & Materials Applications of Shock-Wave & High-Strain-Rate Phenomena: Proceedings of the 1995 International Conference on Metallurgical & Materials Applications of Shock-Wave & High-Strain-Rate Phenomena, El Paso, Texas. Lawrence E. Murr et al. LC 95-44209. 952p. 1995. 305.75 (*0-444-82010-8*) Elsevier.

Metallurgical Applications of Shock-Wave & High-Strain Rate Phenomena. Marc A. Meyers et al. (Mechanical Engineering Ser.: Vol. 52). (Illus.). 1136p. 1986. text 280.00 (*0-8247-7612-7*) Dekker.

Metallurgical Aspects of Formability of Steels. M. Zidek. 360p. 1995. boxed set 120.00 (*1-898326-15-0*, Pub. by CISP) Balogh.

Metallurgical Changes in Late Bronze Age Cyprus. Sydney Pickles. 40p. 1988. pap. 8.00 (*0-614-21834-9*) David Brown.

Metallurgical Coatings & Thin Films 1998: Proceedings of the 25th International Conference on Metallurgical Coatings & Thin Films, San Diego, CA, U. S. A., April 27-May 1, 1998. Bruce D. Sartwell. LC 98-52928. 1998. write for info. (*0-444-50051-0*) Elsevier.

***Metallurgical Coatings & Thin Films 1999.** Ed. by A. Matthews et al. 1520p. 1999. 353.00 (*0-444-50399-4*, North Holland) Elsevier.

Metallurgical Coatings, 1989: Proc. of the 16th Internat. Conf. San Diego, California, April 1989, 2 vols., Set. Ed. by B. D. Sartwell. 1352p. 1990. 630.00 (*1-85166-805-5*) Elsevier.

Metallurgical Coatings, 1987: Proceedings of the 14th International Conference, San Diego, California, 23-27 March 1987, 4 vols., Set. Ed. by R. C. Krutenat. 1967. 570.75 (*1-85166-182-4*) Elsevier.

Metallurgical Coke: Baseline Analysis of the U. S. Industry & Imports. (Illus.). 110p. (C). 1996. reprint ed. pap. text 35.00 (*0-7881-3618-6*) DIANE Pub.

Metallurgical Engineering Vol. 1: Engineering Principles. R. Schuhmann. 1952. write for info. (*0-201-06770-6*) Addison-Wesley.

Metallurgical Evolution of Stainless Steels: A Discriminative Selection of Outstanding Articles & Papers from the Scientific Literature. American Society for Metals Staff. Ed. by F. B. Pickering. LC 79-12994. 487p. reprint ed. pap. 151.00 (*0-608-13094-X*, 201949500013) Bks Demand.

Metallurgical Failure Analysis. Charles R. Brooks. 409p. 1992. 59.95 (*0-07-008078-X*) McGraw.

Metallurgical Failures in Fossil Fired Boilers. David N. French. LC 90-4536. 288p. (C). 1990. reprint ed. 49.50 (*0-89464-482-3*) Krieger.

Metallurgical Failures in Fossil Fired Boilers. 2nd ed. David N. French. LC 92-8747. 528p. 1993. 150.00 (*0-471-55839-7*) Wiley.

Metallurgical Modelling of Welding. O. Grong. 593p. 1994. 170.00 (*0-901716-37-5*) Ashgate Pub Co.

Metallurgical Modelling of Welding. 2nd ed. Oystein Grong. (Materials Modelling Ser.). (Illus.). 608p. 1997. 170.00 (*1-86125-036-3*, Pub. by Inst Materials) Ashgate Pub Co.

Metallurgical Plantmakers of the World. 3rd ed. Ed. by Milton C. Nurse & Richard M. Serjeantson. 494p. 1989. 167.00 (*0-947671-18-8*) Metal Bulletin.

An Asterisk (*) at the beginning of an entry indicates that the title is appearing for the first time.

Metallurgical Processes for the Early Twenty-First Century: Proceedings of the Second International Symposium on Metallurgical Processes for the Year 2000 & Beyond & the 1994 TMS Extraction & Process Metallurgy Meeting, Held in San Diego, CA, September 20-23, 1994, Vol. 1. International Symposium on Metallurgical Processes. Ed. by Hong Yong Sohn. LC 94-77878. (Illus.). 1052p. 1994. reprint ed. pap. 200.00 (*0-608-05682-0*, 206619800001) Bks Demand.

Metallurgical Processes for the Early Twenty-First Century: Proceedings of the Second International Symposium on Metallurgical Processes for the Year 2000 & Beyond & the 1994 TMS Extraction & Process Metallurgy Meeting, Held in San Diego, CA, September 20-23, 1994, Vol. 2. International Symposium on Metallurgical Processes. Ed. by Hong Yong Sohn. LC 94-77878. (Illus.). 1070p. 1994. reprint ed. pap. 200.00 (*0-608-05683-9*, 206619800002) Bks Demand.

Metallurgical Processes for the Year 2000 & Beyond: Proceedings of the International Symposium on Metallurgical Processes for the Year 2000 & Beyond, Held at the TMS 1989 Annual Meeting, Las Vegas, Nevada, February 27-March 3, 1989 & Sponsored by the TMS Physical Chemistry Committee & the Pyrometallurgy Committee. International Symposium on Metallurgical Processes. Ed. by Hong Y. Sohn & E. S. Geskin. LC 88-63681. 862p. reprint ed. pap. 200.00 (*0-7837-4081-6*, 205247800011) Bks Demand.

Metallurgical Reminiscences & Dialogue: A Collection of Two Works: Metallurgical Reminiscences & Metallurgical Dialogue. Albert Sauveur. LC 81-70044. 254p. reprint ed. pap. 78.80 (*0-8357-6208-4*, 203431300089) Bks Demand.

Metallurgical Slags, Pt. 2. C. R. Masson. 1982. pap. 67.00 (*0-08-028684-4*, Pergamon Pr) Elsevier.

Metallurgical Technologies, Energy Conversion, & Magnetohydrodynamic Flows. Ed. by Herman Branover & Yeshajahu Unger. (PAAS Ser.: Vol. 148). 730p. 1993. 99.95 (*1-56347-019-5*, V-148) AIAA.

Metallurgical Thermochemistry. 5th ed. Ortrud Kubaschewski. 1979. text 160.00 (*0-08-020897-5*, Pergamon Pr); pap. text 46.00 (*0-08-022107-6*, Pergamon Pr) Elsevier.

Metallurgical Treatises: Presentations at the U. S. A. - China Bilateral Conference, Sponsored by the Metallurgical Society of AIME, American Society for Metals, & the Chinese Society of Metals, to Be Held in Beijing, November 13-22, 1981 Will Be in Part Based on the Treatises in This Volume. U. S. A. - China Bilateral Conference (1981: Pekin. LC 81-83754. (Technology of Metallurgy Ser.). 651p. reprint ed. pap. 200.00 (*0-7837-5643-7*, 205249500005) Bks Demand.

Metallurgical Works in Canada: Primary Iron & Steel, 1993. Marian Scollan. (Mineral Bulletin Ser.: No. 234). (FRE., Illus.). 48p. (Orig.). 1993. pap. 32.45 (*0-660-58957-5*, Pub. by Canadian Govt Pub) Accents Pubns.

Metallurgie und Geissereitechnik. Karl Stolzel. (GER & RUS.). 648p. 1986. 125.00 (*0-8288-1922-X*, F44000) Fr & Eur.

Metallurgist. Jack Rudman. (Career Examination Ser.: C-496). 1994. pap. 34.95 (*0-8373-0496-2*) Nat Learn.

Metallurgy. 2nd ed. B. J. Moniz. LC 92-17869. (Illus.). 538p. 1994. 46.96 (*0-8269-3509-5*) Am Technical.

Metallurgy. 2nd ed. B. J. Moniz. (Illus.). 538p. 1996. wbk. ed. 13.96 (*0-8269-3510-9*) Am Technical.

Metallurgy, Vols. 70-71. P. Hatala & I. Lantos. 911p. 1992. 70.00 (*963-05-6242-1*, Pub. by Akade Kiado) St Mut.

Metallurgy & Materials of Tungsten, Titanium, Rare Earths & Antimony: Proceedings of the 1st International Conference, Changsha, China, 5-8 November 1988. Ed. by Nonferrous Metals Society of China Staff. (International Academic Publishers Ser.). (Illus.). 1200p. 1989. 400.00 (*0-08-037202-3*, Pergamon Pr) Elsevier.

Metallurgy & Materials Science: Laboratory Manual. Dell K. Allen & Kay S. Mortensen. LC TN0669.A44. 224p. reprint ed. pap. 69.50 (*0-608-11135-X*, 201157800079) Bks Demand.

Metallurgy & Materials Science of Tungsten, Titanium, Rare Earths & Antimony: Proceedings of the 1st International Conference, Changsha, China, 5-8 November 1988, 2 vols., Set. Ed. by Chongyue Fu. LC 89-8726. (International Academic Publishers Ser.). (Illus.). 1200p. 1989. 276.00 (*0-685-33074-5*, 1603, Pub. by IAP) Elsevier.

Metallurgy & Technology of Practical Titanium Alloys: Proceedings of the First International Symposium on Metallurgy & Technology of Practical Titanium Alloys. International Symposium on Metallurgy & Technology. Ed. by Shiro Fujishiro et al. LC 94-73534. (Illus.). 462p. 1994. reprint ed. pap. 143.30 (*0-608-05689-8*, 206620400007) Bks Demand.

Metallurgy at High Pressures & High Temperatures: Proceedings of a Symposium, Dallas, Texas, February 25-26, 1963. Ed. by K. A. Gechneioner, Jr. et al. LC 64-18801. (Metallurgical Society Conference Ser.: Vol. 22). 423p. reprint ed. pap. 131.20 (*0-608-11193-7*, 200151000079) Bks Demand.

Metallurgy for the Non-Metallurgist. Harry Chandler. LC 98-4664. (Illus.). 284p. 1998. 146.00 (*0-87170-652-0*, 06169G) ASM.

***Metallurgy Fundamentals.** Daniel A. Brandt & J. C. Warner. LC 98-48494. (Illus.). 300p. (YA). (gr. 9-12). 1999. text 32.64 (*1-56637-543-6*) Goodheart.

Metallurgy in Medicine & Industry: Index of New Information & Research Bible of Current Reviews. Donna M. Dolce. 150p. 1994. 47.50 (*0-7883-0006-7*); pap. 44.50 (*0-7883-0007-5*) ABBE Pubs Assn.

Metallurgy of Advanced Electronic Materials: Proceedings of a Technical Conference. Ed. by Geoffrey E. Brock. LC 63-13589. (Metallurgical Society Conference Ser.: Vol. 19). 365p. reprint ed. pap. 113.20 (*0-608-30597-9*, 200150700079) Bks Demand.

Metallurgy of Arc Welding: Arc Processes & Electrode Melting. I. K. Pokhodnaya et al. 250p. 1992. boxed set 100.00 (*1-871313-01-5*, Pub. by CISP) Balogh.

Metallurgy of Basic Weld Metal. G. M. Evans & N. Bailey. 448p. 1997. 225.00 (*1-884207-57-X*) William Andrew.

Metallurgy of Basic Weld Metal. G. M. Evans & N. Bailey. 448p. 1997. 225.00 (*1-85573-243-2*, Pub. by Woodhead Pubng) Am Educ Systs.

Metallurgy of Chromium. N. P. Liakishev & M. I. Gasik. LC 97-8697. 1997. 245.00 (*0-89864-083-0*) Allerton Pr.

Metallurgy of Continuous-Annealed Sheet Steel: Proceedings of a Symposium Sponsored by the Heat Treatment Committee & the Ferrous Metallurgy Committee of the Metallurgical Society of AIME, Held at the AIME Annual Meeting in Dallas, TX, February 15-16, 1982. Metallurgical Society of AIME Staff. Ed. by B. L. Bramfitt & P. L. Mangonon, Jr. LC 82-61947. (Illus.). 407p. reprint ed. pap. 126.20 (*0-8357-7506-2*, 203599800097) Bks Demand.

Metallurgy of Elemental & Compound Semiconductors: Proceedings. Ed. by Ralph O. Grubel. LC 61-9443. (Metallurgical Society Conference Ser.: Vol. 12). 507p. reprint ed. pap. 157.20 (*0-608-30579-0*, 200067500038) Bks Demand.

Metallurgy of Environmental Fracture. C. L. Briant. No. 12. 300p. 1984. write for info. (*0-318-57814-X*) Elsevier.

Metallurgy of Failure Analysis. A. K. Das. LC 97-166769. (Illus.). 354p. 1997. 69.95 (*0-07-015804-5*) McGraw.

Metallurgy of Gold. T. K. Rose & W. A. Newman. 49.95 (*0-931913-05-5*) Met-Chem Rsch.

Metallurgy of Non-Ferrous Metals: Glossary of Technical Terms English-French-German-Spanish. G. Lang. (ENG, FRE, GER & SPA.). 633p. 1994. pap. 154.00 (*3-87017-223-1*) IBD Ltd.

Metallurgy of Non-Ferrous Metals: Glossary of Technical Terms, English/French/German/Spanish. G. Lang. (ENG, FRE, GER & SPA.). 1994. 205.00 (*0-7859-9426-2*) Fr & Eur.

Metallurgy of 17th & 18th Century Music Wire. Martha Goodway & Jay S. Odell. Ed. by Howard Schott. LC 86-30463. (Historical Harpsichord Ser.: No. 2). 200p. 1988. lib. bdg. 42.00 (*0-918728-54-1*) Pendragon NY.

Metallurgy of Soviet High Speed Diesels. Y. Rivkin. Ed. by Steven Jones. 101p. (Orig.). 1984. pap. text 75.00 (*1-55831-041-X*) Delphic Associates.

Metallurgy of Steelmaking. Franz Oeters. (Illus.). 480p. 1994. 216.00 (*3-514-00465-X*, Pub. by Woodhead Pubng) Am Educ Systs.

Metallurgy of Uranium & Its Alloys. AEC Technical Information Center Staff. Ed. by J. C. Warner et al. (National Nuclear Energy Ser.: Div. IV, Vol. 12). 200p. 1953. 24.95 (*0-87079-273-3*, NNES-IV-12A); fiche 9.00 (*0-87079-453-1*, NNES-IV-12A) DOE.

Metallurgy of Vacuum-Degassed Steel Products: Proceedings of an International Symposium - Sponsored by the TMS Ferrous Metallurgy Committee & Held at the 1989 Fall Meeting in Indianapolis, Indiana, October 3-5. Minerals, Metals & Materials Society Staff. Ed. by R. Pradhan. LC 90-70808. (Illus.). 522p. 1990. reprint ed. pap. 161.90 (*0-7837-9138-0*, 204993800004) Bks Demand.

Metallurgy of Welding. 4th ed. J. F. Lancaster. 352p. 1987. text 105.00 (*0-04-669010-7*); pap. text 44.95 (*0-04-669011-5*) Routledge.

Metallurgy of Welding. 6th ed. J. F. Lancaster. 446p. 1999. pap. 89.00 (*1-884207-80-4*) William Andrew.

Metallurgy of Welding. 6th ed. John F. Lancaster. 350p. 1999. pap. 81.00 (*1-85573-428-1*) Am Educ Systs.

Metallurgy, Processing, & Applications of Metal Wires: State of the Art Technology & Challenges for the Future. Ed. by D. K. Kim & Henry G. Paris. (Illus.). 251p. 1996. 72.00 (*0-87339-348-1*, 3481) Minerals Metals.

***Metallurgy/Materials Education Yearbook.** 38th ed. Ed. by Kali Mukherjee. 230p. 1999. pap. 45.00 (*0-87170-645-8*, 41352G) ASM.

Metalogic: An Introduction to the Metatheory of Standard First Order Logic. Geoffrey Hunter. LC 71-131195. 302p. (C). 1996. pap. 17.95 (*0-520-02356-0*, Pub. by U CA Pr) Cal Prin Full Svc.

Metalogical Theory of Reference: Realism & Essentialism in Semantics. Roger Vergauwen. LC 92-23600. 236p. (Orig.). (C). 1993. text 54.50 (*0-8191-8883-2*); pap. text 29.50 (*0-8191-8884-0*) U Pr of Amer.

Metalogicon of John of Salisbury. John of Salisbury. Tr. by Daniel McGarry. 1990. 27.25 (*0-8446-0159-4*) Peter Smith.

Metalogicon of John of Salisbury: A Twelfth-Century Defense of Verbal & Logical Arts of the Trivium. John of Salisbury. Tr. by Daniel D. McGarry from LAT. LC 82-2989. 305p. 1982. reprint ed. lib. bdg. 65.00 (*0-313-23539-2*, JOME) Greenwood.

Metalorganic Catalysts for Synthesis & Polymerization: Recent Results by Ziegler-Natta & Metallocene Investigations. Ed. by W. Kaminsky. LC 99-25652. 665p. 1999. 195.00 (*3-540-65813-0*) Spr-Verlag.

Metals. Robert C. Mebane & Thomas R. Rybolt. (Everyday Material Science Experiments Ser.). (Illus.). 64p. (J). (gr. 5-8). 1995. lib. bdg. 18.90 (*0-8050-2842-0*) TFC Bks NY.

Metals: Born of Earth & Fire. Jean-Pierre Reymond. LC 87-34596. (Illus.). 38p. (J). (gr. k-5). 1988. 5.95 (*0-944589-19-7*, 197) Young Discovery Lib.

Metals: Phonon States of Elements - Electron States & Fermi Surfaces of Alloys see Crystal & Solid State Physics: Group III

Metals: Proceedings. 91p. 1975. 21.00 (*0-911890-14-9*) Indus Health Inc.

Metals, Subvol. A, Electronic Transport Phenomena see Crystal & Solid State Physics: Group III

Metals, Subvol. B, Phonon States, Electron States & Fermi States: Phonon States of Alloys; Electron States & Fermi Surfaces of Strained Elements see Biophysics: Group VII

Metals & Alloys in the Unified Numbering System. 7th ed. LC 96-70039. 1996. 129.00 (*1-56091-897-7*, HS1086/96) Soc Auto Engineers.

Metals & Alloys in the Unified Numbering System. 8th ed. (Handbook Supplements Ser.). 475p. 1998. 139.00 (*0-7680-0407-1*, HS-1086/99) Soc Auto Engineers.

Metals & Alloys in the Unified Numbering System: With A Description of the System & a Cross Index of Chemically Similar Specifications a Joint Activity of the Society of Automotive Engineers, & ASTM. 3rd ed. American Society for Testing & Materials Staff & Society of Automotive Engineers Staff. LC 84-108328. (ASTM Data Ser.: No. 56B). 364p. reprint ed. pap. 112.90 (*0-608-15328-1*, 205633400060) Bks Demand.

Metals & Biomaterials: A Handbook. Ed. by J. Helsen & J. Breme. LC 98-9264. 510p. 1998. 295.00 (*0-471-96935-4*) Wiley.

Metals & Genetics. Ed. by Bibudhendra Sarkar. LC 98-49080. (Illus.). 406p. (C). 1999. text 175.00 (*0-306-46101-3*, Kluwer Plenum) Kluwer Academic.

Metals & Ligard Reactivity: An Introduction to the Organic Chemistry of Metal Complexes. E. C. Constable. 308p. 1996. 150.00 (*3-527-29278-0*); pap. 74.95 (*3-527-29277-2*) Wiley.

Metals & Metabolism, No. 26. D. A. Phipps. (Oxford Chemistry Ser.). (Illus.). 1978. pap. 12.50 (*0-19-855413-3*) OUP.

Metals & Micronutrients: Uptake & Utilization by Plants. D. A. Robb & S. Pierpoint. 1983. text 136.00 (*0-12-589580-1*) Acad Pr.

Metals & Minerals, 2 vols. 1992. lib. bdg. 1799.95 (*0-8490-5484-2*) Gordon Pr.

Metals & Minerals, 5 vols. 1994. lib. bdg. 1495.00 (*0-8490-8574-8*) Gordon Pr.

Metals & Monies in an Emerging Global Economy. Dennis O. Flynn & Arture Giraldez. LC 96-46512. (Expanding World Ser.: No. 14). 416p. 1997. text 134.95 (*0-86078-531-9*, Pub. by Variorum) Ashgate Pub Co.

Metals & Ores, 8 vols., Vol. 3. Intro. by John J. McKetta, Jr. (Illus.). 918p. 1970. 68.50 (*0-06-491104-7*, 06297) B&N Imports.

Metals & Oxidative Damage in Neurological Disorders. Ed. by James R. Connor. LC 97-30552. (Illus.). 396p. (C). 1997. text 114.00 (*0-306-45534-X*, Kluwer Plenum) Kluwer Academic.

Metals & Technology. Ray Stevens. LC 93-36743. (Australian Technology Studies). (C). 1994. pap. 13.95 (*0-521-40415-0*) Cambridge U Pr.

Metals & the Liver. Ed. by Lawrie W. Powell. LC 78-11947. (Liver, Normal Function & Disease Ser.: No. 1). (Illus.). 464p. reprint ed. pap. 143.90 (*0-7837-0822-X*, 204113600019) Bks Demand.

Metals & the Skin: Topical Effects & Systemic Absorption. Richard H. Guy & Jurij J. Hostynek. LC 99-25576. (Illus.). 448p. 1999. text 185.00 (*0-8247-9385-4*) Dekker.

Metals & Their Compounds in the Environment: Occurrence, Analysis, Biological Relevance. Ed. by Ernest Merian. LC 90-12615. 1439p. 1990. 294.00 (*3-527-26521-X*, Wiley-VCH) Wiley.

Metals & Their Weldability see Welding Handbook

Metals & Welding. rev. ed. V. J. Morford. (Illus.). 236p. 1987. spiral bd. 22.35 (*0-913163-19-8*, 170) Hobar Pubns.

Metals at High Temperatures. V. E. Zinovyev. Ed. & Tr. by Victor P. Itkin. 320p. 1990. 181.00 (*0-89116-853-2*) Hemisp Pub.

Metals, Composites & Refractory Materials see Handbook of Materials Science

Metals Databook. Robb. 1988. 90.00 (*0-904357-69-4*) Institute of Management Consultants.

Metals Engineering: A Technical Guide. Leonard E. Samuels. LC 87-73060. (Illus.). 526p. 1988. reprint ed. pap. 163.10 (*0-608-02638-7*, 206329600004) Bks Demand.

Metals from the Cenote of Sacrifice. S. K. Lothrop. (Harvard University Peabody Museum of Archaeology & Ethnology Papers: Vol. 10, No. 2). 1974. reprint ed. 30.00 (*0-527-01177-0*) Periodicals Srv.

Metals Handbook Comprehensive Index. American Society for Metals Staff. LC 85-62432. 557p. reprint ed. pap. 172.70 (*0-8357-6209-2*, 203430700089) Bks Demand.

Metals Handbook Desk Edition. 2nd rev. ed. Ed. by Joseph R. Davis. LC 98-45866. (Illus.). 1521p. 1998. 198.00 (*0-87170-654-7*, 06542G) ASM.

Metals in America's Historic Buildings. Margot Gayle et al. (Illus.). 168p. (C). 1998. reprint ed. pap. text 35.00 (*0-7881-4723-4*) DIANE Pub.

Metals in America's Historic Buildings: Uses & Preservation Treatments, Pt. 1; A Historical Survey of Metals, Pt. 2. LC 92-34883. 1993. pap. 10.00 (*0-16-038073-1*, 024-005-01108-1) USGPO.

Metals in America's Historic Buildings, Uses & Preservation Treatments, a Historical Survey of Metals, Deterioration & Methods of Preserving Metals Pt. 1-2. 176p. 1993. per. 15.00 (*0-16-061655-7*) USGPO.

Metals in Bone. Ed. by Nicholas D. Priest. 1985. text 225.00 (*0-85200-909-7*) Kluwer Academic.

Metals in Coastal Environments of Latin America. Ed. by Ulrich Seeliger et al. (Illus.). xvi, 297p. 1988. 59.00 (*0-387-16945-8*) Spr-Verlag.

Metals in Glassmaking. Ed. by Roland Kirsch. LC 93-31292. (Glass Science & Technology Ser.: Vol. 13). 492p. 1993. 289.00 (*0-444-98706-1*) Elsevier.

Metals in Groundwater. Herbert E. Allen. (Illus.). 464p. 1993. lib. bdg. 75.00 (*0-87371-277-3*, L277) Lewis Pubs.

Metals in Health, Food & Pollution: Index of Modern Progress. Elias J. Holbach. LC 88-47858. 150p. 1988. 47.50 (*0-88164-940-6*); pap. 44.50 (*0-88164-941-4*) ABBE Pubs Assn.

Metals in Mercury. Zbigniew Galus. (Solubility Data Ser.). 1986. 130.00 (*0-08-023959-5*, Pergamon Pr) Elsevier.

Metals in Mercury see Solubility Data Series

Metals in Surface Waters. Ed. by Herbert E. Allen et al. LC 97-33660. (Illus.). 300p. 1997. ring bd. 64.95 (*1-57504-087-5*) CRC Pr.

Metals in the Hydrocycle. W. Salomons & U. Foerstner. (Illus.). 340p. 1984. 160.95 (*0-387-12755-0*) Spr-Verlag.

***Metals in the Service of Man.** Alexander Street. 332p. 1998. pap. 19.95 (*0-14-025776-4*, Pub. by Pnguin Bks Ltd) Trafalgar.

Metals-Physiology & Metabolism: Index of New Information with Authors & Subjects. Bernice R. Schindler. LC 92-54249. 180p. 1992. 47.50 (*1-55914-646-X*); pap. 44.50 (*1-55914-647-8*) ABBE Pubs Assn.

Metals Speciation, Separation & Recovery, Vol. I. Ed. & Intro. by James W. Patterson. (Illus.). 800p. 1987. lib. bdg. 129.00 (*0-87371-034-7*, L034) Lewis Pubs.

Metals Speciation, Separation & Recovery, Vol. II. Ed. by James W. Patterson & Roberto Passino. (Illus.). 654p. 1990. lib. bdg. 119.00 (*0-87371-268-4*, L268) Lewis Pubs.

Metals Technic: A Collection of Techniques for Metalsmiths. Ed. & Illus. by Tim McCreight. 151p. 1997. pap. 17.95 (*0-9615984-7-6*) Brynmorgen.

Metals Trading Handbook. Crabbe. 1998. ring bd. 99.95 (*0-8493-0518-7*) CRC Pr.

Metals Which We Believe Have Application in Wormgearing. B. A. Miller. (Technical Papers: Vol. P216). (Illus.). 18p. 1940. pap. text 30.00 (*1-55589-340-6*) AGMA.

Metalsmith's Book of Boxes & Lockets. Tim McCreight. (Illus.). 1999. 29.99 (*0-9658248-9-6*) GUILDcom.

***Metaluin 2.0 (User's Manual) Statistical Software for Meta-Analysis.** rev. ed. Michael S. Rosenberg et al. (C). 1999. pap. text 25.00 (*0-87893-760-9*) Sinauer Assocs.

Metalwares Price Guide: Including Silver, Brass, Copper, Pewter & More. Ed. & Intro. by Marilyn E. Dragowick. LC 95-76093. (Illus.). 240p. 1995. pap. 14.95 (*0-930625-39-0*, Antique Trader) Krause Pubns.

Metalwork. Boy Scouts of America. (Illus.). 36p. (YA). (gr. 6-12). 1969. pap. 2.90 (*0-8395-3312-8*, 33312) BSA.

Metalwork. Kirkcaldy. Date not set. pap. text. write for info. (*0-582-65129-8*, Pub. by Addison-Wesley) Longman.

Metalwork: Technology & Practice. 9th ed. Victor E. Repp. 1999. teacher ed. 11.29 (*0-02-676485-7*) Glencoe.

Metalwork: Technology & Practice. 9th ed. Victor E. Repp. (Illus.). 192p. (YA). (gr. 6-12). 1999. pap., student ed., wbk. ed. 7.60 (*0-02-676486-5*) Glencoe.

Metalwork: Technology & Practice. 9th ed. Victor E. Repp & Williard J. McCarthy. (Illus.). 702p. (YA). (gr. 6-12). 1994. text, student ed. 40.20 (*0-02-676484-9*) Glencoe.

Metalwork & Enamelling. 4th ed. Herbert Maryon. (Illus.). 335p. 1971. pap. 8.95 (*0-486-22702-2*) Dover.

Metalwork & Machining Hints & Tips. Ian Bradley. (Workshop Practice Ser.: No. 20). (Illus.). 96p. (Orig.). 1988. pap. 18.50 (*0-85242-947-9*, Pub. by Nexus Special Interests) Trans-Atl Phila.

Metalwork, Ceramics, Glass, Glyptics, Painting see Catalogue of the Byzantine & Early Mediaeval Antiquities in the Dumbarton Oaks Collection

Metalwork for Craftsmen: A Step by Step Guide with 55 Projects. Emil F. Kronquist. LC 78-160856. Orig. Title: Art Metalwork. (Illus.). 202p. 1972. reprint ed. pap. 7.95 (*0-486-22789-8*) Dover.

Metalwork from the Hellenized East: The J. Paul Getty Museum. Michael Pfrommer. LC 92-34053. (Illus.). 248p. 1993. 75.00 (*0-89236-218-9*, Pub. by J P Getty Trust) OUP.

Metalwork in Early America: Copper & Its Alloys from the Winterthur Collection. Donald L. Fennimore. LC 96-236. (Illus.). 512p. 1996. 70.00 (*0-912724-37-4*) Winterthur.

Metalwork of Albert Paley. Albert Paley. (Illus.). 60p. 1980. pap. 8.50 (*0-932718-06-X*) Kohler Arts.

Metalwork of the Islamic World. James W. Allan. (Illus.). 128p. 1987. 95.00 (*0-85667-327-7*, Pub. by P Wilson) Scala Books.

Metalwork S.I. Metric Edition. John L. Feirer & John R. Lindbeck. 1979. text 16.60 (*0-02-665150-5*); student ed. 6.64 (*0-02-665160-2*) Glencoe.

Metalworking. Los Angeles Unified School District Staff. LC 77-73297. 96p. (gr. 7-9). 1978. pap. text 7.04 (*0-02-820290-2*) Glencoe.

Metalworking: A Manual of Techniques. Mike George. (Illus.). 160p. 1991. 39.95 (*1-85223-497-0*, Pub. by Crolwood) Trafalgar.

Metalworking: The Best of Projects in Metal 1990-1991, Bk. 2. Contrib. by Joe Rice. (Illus.). 240p. (C). 1994. text 32.00 (*0-941653-17-X*) Village Pr Pubns.

Metalworking Fluids. Jerry P. Byers. (Manufacturing Engineering & Materials Processing Ser.: 41). (Illus.). 504p. 1994. text 150.00 (*0-8247-9201-7*) Dekker.

Metalworking in Africa South of the Sahara: An Annotated Bibliography, 19. Ed. by Ibironke O. Lawal. LC 95-7485. (African Special Bibliographic Ser.: No. 19). 288p. 1995. lib. bdg. 89.50 (*0-313-29324-4*, Greenwood Pr) Greenwood.

Metalworking Lubrication. Ed. by Serope Kalpakjian & S. C. Jain. 259p. 1980. 40.00 (*0-686-69857-6*, H00159) ASME.

***Metalworking Machine Tools in Germany: A Strategic Entry Report, 1999.** Compiled by Icon Group International. (Illus.). 98p. 1999. ring bd. 980.00 incl. audio compact disk (*0-7418-1852-3*) Icon Grp.

***Metalworking, Plastic-Working & Woodworking Occupations.** Government Printing Office Staff. 19p. 1998. pap. 2.00 (*0-16-049368-4*) USGPO.

Metalworking Science & Engineering. Edward M. Mielnik. 848p. (C). 1991. 98.75 (*0-07-041904-3*); pap. text, teacher ed. 18.75 (*0-07-041905-1*) McGraw.

***Metalworking Tech., Mexican Mfg. Sector in Mexico: A Strategic Entry Report, 1996.** Compiled by Icon Group International Staff. (Illus.). 172p. 1999. ring bd. 1720.00 incl. audio compact disk (*0-7418-1338-6*) Icon Grp.

Metalworking Trades in Early America: The Blacksmith, Whitesmith, Farrier, Edgetool Maker, Cutler, Locksmith, Gunsmith, Nailer & Tinsmith. Henry J. Kauffman. (Illus.). 168p. 1995. pap. 22.95 (*1-879335-58-1*) Astragal Pr.

Metamagical Themas: Questing for the Essence of Mind & Pattern. Douglas R. Hofstadter. (Illus.). 896p. 1996. pap. 23.00 (*0-465-04566-9*, Pub. by Basic) HarpC.

Metaman. Gregory Stock. 320p. 1993. 29.95 (*0-385-25380-X*) Doubleday.

Metamanagement Science of Business Survival Vol. I: Basic Concepts, Theory of Decay & Destruction. Alice A. Savitsky. LC 98-90881. (Illus.). xii, 205p. 1999. pap. 24.90 (*0-9668188-7-3*) SPR Consult.

M

Metamathematics of First-Order Arithmetic. P. Hajek & P. Pudlak. (Perspectives in Mathematical Logic Ser.). xiv, 460p. 1998. pap. 49.95 (*3-540-63648-X*) Spr-Verlag.

Metamathematics of First-Order Arithmetic. Petr Hajek & Pavel Pudlak. Ed. by R. O. Gandy et al. LC 92-21885. 350p. 1993. 168.00 (*3-540-50632-2*); 135.95 (*0-387-50632-2*) Spr-Verlag.

Metamathematics of Fuzzy Logic. Petr Hajek. LC 98-30404. (Trends in Logic Ser.). 1998. 130.00 (*0-7923-5238-6*) Kluwer Academic.

Metamedicine: Power & Medicine, the 21st Century Way. Vida C. Baron & Norman Baron. (Illus.). 203p. (Orig.). 1990. pap. 14.95 (*0-9624701-0-4*) Barez Pub.

Metamict State. Roald Hoffmann. LC 87-17621. (University of Central Florida Contemporary Poetry Ser.). 112p. 1987. 16.95 (*0-8130-0869-7*) U Press Fla.

Metamind. Keith Lehrer. 322p. 1990. text 45.00 (*0-19-824850-4*) OUP.

Metamodel & Clinical Social Work. Eleanor R. Tolson. 247p. 1988. text 40.50 (*0-231-05558-7*) Col U Pr.

Metamodelling: Bond Graphs & Dynamic Systems. 350p. 1995. 93.00 (*0-13-489824-9*) P-H.

Metamora: or The Last of the Wampanoags. John A. Stone. Ed. & Intro. by Walter J. Meserve. (On Stage, America! Ser.). 41p. 1996. spiral bd. 4.95 (*0-937657-24-7*) Feedbk Theabks & Prospero.

MetaMorality. Eric Butterworth. LC 87-82241. 137p. 1988. 4.48 (*0-87159-092-1*) Unity Bks.

Metamorfosis y las Heroidas de Ovidio en la General Estoria de Alfonso el Sabio. Ed. by Benito Brancaforte. (Spanish Ser.: No. 62). xl, 418p. 1990. 30.00 (*0-940639-55-6*) Hispanic Seminary.

Metamorfosis y Otros Relatos. Franz Kafka. 1998. pap. 7.95 (*84-320-6981-7*) Planeta.

Metamorphasis of Tobacco. John Beaumont. LC 70-171734. (English Experience Ser.: No. 360). 44p. 1971. reprint ed. 25.00 (*90-221-0360-9*) Walter J Johnson.

Metamorphe- Vulkano- Sedimentaere Abfolge der Insel Tinos (Kykladen, Griechenland) Michael Broecker. (Geotektonische Forschungen Ser.: Vol. 74). (GER.). 108p. 1990. 44.00 (*3-510-50040-7*, Pub. by E Schweizerbartsche) Balogh.

Metamorphic Adventures. Tony Connor. LC 96-143964. 118p. 1997. pap. 15.95 (*0-85646-261-6*, Pub. by Anvil Press) Dufour.

Metamorphic Crystallization. Ralph Kretz. 530p. 1994. pap. 100.00 (*0-471-94214-6*) Wiley.

Metamorphic Petrology. Akiho Miyashiro. (Illus.). 416p. (C). 1994. text 76.95 (*0-19-521026-3*) OUP.

Metamorphic Petrology. B. Bhaskar Rao. 190p. (C). 1986. text 70.00 (*90-6191-483-3*, Pub. by A A Balkema) Ashgate Pub Co.

Metamorphic Petrology. Francis J. Turner. 614p. 1981. 79.95 (*0-89116-510-X*) Hemisp Pub.

Metamorphic Phase Equilibria & Pressure-Temperature-Time Paths. Frank S. Spear. (Mineralogical Society of America Monograph Ser.). (Illus.). 799p. 1995. reprint ed. text 53.00 (*0-939950-34-0*) Mineralogical Soc.

Metamorphic Pressure-Temperature-Time Paths. Ed. by Frank S. Spear & S. M. Peacock. (Short Course Ser.: Vol. 7). 102p. 1989. 18.00 (*0-87590-704-0*) Am Geophysical.

Metamorphic Reactions: Kinetics, Textures & Deformation. Ed. by A. B. Thompson & D. C. Rubie. (Advances in Physical Geochemistry Ser.: Vol. 4), (Illus.). 280p. 1985. 131.00 (*0-387-96077-5*) Spr-Verlag.

Metamorphic Rocks of the Potomac Terrane in the Potomac Valley of Virginia & Maryland. 1989. 13.00 (*0-87590-587-0*) Am Geophysical.

Metamorphic Technique: Principles & Practice. Gaston Saint-Pierre & Debbie Shapiro. (Illus.). 128p. 1993. pap. 13.95 (*1-85230-032-9*, Pub. by Element MA) Penguin Putnam.

Metamorphic Tectonites of the Himalaya. Ed. by P. S. Saklani. (Current Trends in Geology Ser.: Vol. 4). (Illus.). xiii, 370p. 1981. 50.00 (*0-685-24665-5*, Pub. by Today Tomorrow) Scholarly Pubns.

Metamorphic Tradition in Modern Poetry: Essay on the Work of Ezra Pound & Other Poets. Bernetta Quinn. LC 66-19365. 263p. 1966. reprint ed. 50.00 (*0-87752-089-5*) Gordian.

Metamorphic Verse: The Elizabethan Minor Epic. Clark Hulse. LC 81-47135. 311p. reprint ed. pap. 96.50 (*0-7837-0241-8*, 204054900017) Bks Demand.

Metamorphimals. Jay Palefsky. (Illus.). 38p. 1996. 16.00 (*0-9656782-0-2*) Kutzkies Artwrks.

Metamorphisis & Other Stories. Franz Kafka. LC 92-43912. 352p. 2000. pap. 11.00 (*0-684-80070-5*, Touchstone) S&S Trade Pap.

Metamorphism, Ophiolites & Orogenic Belts. Ed. by P. S. Saklani. (Current Trends in Geology Ser.: Vol. 12). 428p. 1989. 65.00 (*1-55528-171-0*) Scholarly Pubns.

Metamorphopsia. Norma Cole. 99p. (Orig.). (C). 1988. pap. 8.50 (*0-937013-23-4*) Potes Poets.

***Metamorphose.** Greg Day. 1998. 44.95 (*3-925443-84-3*) Janssen.

Metamorphose. Franz Kafka. (FRE.). 1996. pap. 7.95 (*2-87714-330-9*, Pub. by Bookking Intl) Distribks Inc.

Metamorphose. Franz Kafka. (FRE.). 1982. pap. 10.95 (*0-7859-2263-6*, 2070360741) Fr & Eur.

Metamorphose des Cloportes. Alphonse Boudard. (FRE.). 246p. 1987. pap. 10.95 (*0-7859-2189-3*, 2253041904) Fr & Eur.

Metamorphose des Dieux: L'Intemporel. Andre Malraux. (FRE., Illus.). 424p. 1976. 125.00 (*0-7859-1282-7*, 2070108619) Fr & Eur.

Metamorphose des Dieux: L'Surnaturel, Vol. 1. Andre Malraux. (FRE., Illus.). 386p. 1977. 125.00 (*0-7859-1283-5*, 2070109070) Fr & Eur.

Metamorphose et Autres Recits. Franz Kafka. (Parus Vivants Kafka Ser.: No. I). (FRE.). 224p. 1989. pap. 10.95 (*0-7859-2564-3*, 2070381056) Fr & Eur.

Metamorphosen, Bd. I, Buch 1-7. Ovid. Ed. by Moritz Haupt et al. viii, 502p. 1966. write for info. (*3-296-14811-6*) G Olms Pubs.

Metamorphosen, Bd. I, Buch 8-15. Ovid. Ed. by Moritz Haupt et al. viii, 559p. 1975. write for info. (*3-296-14812-4*) G Olms Pubs.

Metamorphoseon, Libri XV. Ed. by W. R. Connor & Hugo Magnus. LC 78-67140. (Latin Texts & Commentaries Ser.). (ENG & LAT.). 1979. reprint ed. lib. bdg. 61.95 (*0-405-11609-8*) Ayer.

Metamorphoses. Jorge De Sena. Tr. by Francisco C. Fagundes & James Houlihan from POR. LC 90-25636. (Illus.). 112p. (Orig.). 1991. pap. 9.95 (*0-914278-55-X*) Copper Beech.

Metamorphoses. Tr. by Mary Innes. (Classics Ser.). 368p. 1955. pap. 9.95 (*0-14-044058-5*, Penguin Classics) Viking Penguin.

Metamorphoses. Ovid. Tr. by Rolfe Humphries. LC 55-6269. (Greek & Latin Classics Ser.). 416p. (C). 1955. 31.95 (*0-253-33755-0*); pap. 8.95 (*0-253-20001-6*, MB-1) Ind U Pr.

Metamorphoses. Ovid. Tr. by Horace Gregory. 1960. mass mkt. 6.99 (*0-451-62622-2*, Ment) NAL.

Metamorphoses. A. Ted Schaefer. (Illus.). 112p. 1996. 45.00 (*3-908162-25-4*, Pub. by Edit Stemmle) Dist Art Pubs.

Metamorphoses. Ovid. Tr. by A. D. Melville. (Oxford World's Classics Ser.). 520p. 1998. reprint ed. pap. 8.95 (*0-19-283472-X*) OUP.

Metamorphoses, Bk. VIII. A. S. Hollis. (Illus.). 198p. 1984. reprint ed. text 29.95 (*0-19-814460-1*) OUP.

***Metamorphoses, Bk. XIII.** Ovid. Ed. by Neil Hopkinson. (Cambridge Greek & Latin Classics Ser.). (Illus.). 264p. 2001. write for info. (*0-521-55421-7*); pap. write for info. (*0-521-55620-1*) Cambridge U Pr.

Metamorphoses, Bks. 1-8. Tr. by Frank J. Miller. (Loeb Classical Library: No. 42-43). 484p. 1916. text 18.95 (*0-674-99046-3*) HUP.

Metamorphoses, Bks. 9-15. Tr. by Frank J. Miller. (Loeb Classical Library: No. 42-43). 510p. 1916. text 18.95 (*0-674-99047-1*) HUP.

Metamorphoses, Vol. I. Lucius Apuleius. Tr. by J. Arthur Hanson. (Loeb Classical Library: Nos. 44 & 453). 371p. 1990. text 19.95 (*0-674-99049-8*) HUP.

Metamorphoses, Vol. II. Lucius Apuleius. Tr. by J. Arthur Hanson. (Loeb Classical Library: Nos. 44 & 453). 377p. 1990. text 19.95 (*0-674-99498-1*) HUP.

Metamorphoses, Vols. I & II. Lucius Apuleius. Tr. by J. Arthur Hanson. Nos. 44 & 453. 1989. text. write for info. (*0-318-65540-3*) HUP.

Metamorphoses: Chinese Edition. CRM Staff. (CHI.). 131p. 1984. pap. 4.50 (*1-56582-084-3*) Christ Renew Min.

Metamorphoses de la Reine. Pierrette Fleutiaux. (FRE.). 250p. 1990. pap. 11.95 (*0-7859-2593-7*, 2070382737) Fr & Eur.

Metamorphoses d'Ishtar. 2nd ed. Nadine Ltaif. (FRE.). 62p. 1989. pap. write for info. (*2-89135-025-1*) Guernica Editions.

Metamorphoses du Vingtieme Siecle see Litterature Francaise

Metamorphoses of Apuleius. Judith K. Krabbe. (American University Studies: Classical Languages & Literature: Ser. XVII, Vol. 9). XI, 219p. (C). 1989. text 37.00 (*0-8204-0906-5*) P Lang Pubng.

Metamorphoses of Apuleius: On Making an Ass of Oneself. Carl C. Schlam. LC 91-31412. (Illus.). x, 176p. (C). 1992. 34.95 (*0-8078-2013-X*) U of NC Pr.

Metamorphoses of Don Juan. Leo Weinstein. LC 77-12371. (Stanford University. Stanford Studies in Language & Literature: Vol. 18). 1959. reprint ed. 37.50 (*0-404-51828-1*) AMS Pr.

Metamorphoses of Helen: Authority, Difference, & the Epic. Mihoko Suzuki. LC 89-764. 288p. 1989. 39.95 (*0-8014-2219-1*) Cornell U Pr.

Metamorphoses of Helen: Authority, Difference, & the Epic. Mihoko Suzuki. LC 89-764. 288p. 1992. pap. text 16.95 (*0-8014-8080-9*) Cornell U Pr.

***Metamorphoses of Landscape & Community in Early Quebec.** Colin M. Coates. (Studies on the History of Quebec). 240p. 2000. 45.00 (*0-7735-1896-7*) McG-Queens Univ Pr.

Metamorphoses of Ovid. Tr. by Allen Mandelbaum. LC 93-8118. 1993. 40.00 (*0-15-170529-1*) Harcourt.

Metamorphoses of Ovid. Allen Mandelbaum. 576p. 1995. pap. 17.00 (*0-15-600126-8*) Harcourt.

Metamorphoses of Ovid. Ovid. (Penguin Classics). (J). 1955. 15.05 (*0-606-03857-4*, Pub. by Turtleback) Demco.

Metamorphoses of Ovid. Tr. by David R. Slavitt. LC 93-31580. 1994. 45.00 (*0-8018-4797-4*); pap. 14.95 (*0-8018-4798-2*) Johns Hopkins.

***Metamorphoses of Passion & the Heroic in French Literature - Corneille, Stendhal, Claudel.** Moya Longstaffe. LC 99-29493. (Studies in French Literature: Vol. 35). 500p. 1999. text 109.95 (*0-7734-7989-9*) E Mellen.

Metamorphoses of Shakespearean Comedy. William C. Carroll. LC 84-42877. 303p. 1985. reprint ed. pap. 94.00 (*0-7837-9310-3*, 206005000004) Bks Demand.

Metamorphoses of the Body. Jose Gill. Tr. by Stephen Muecke from ENG. LC 97-37835. (Theory Out of Bounds Ser.). 1998. 57.95 (*0-8166-2682-0*); lib. bdg. 22.95 (*0-8166-2683-9*) U of Minn Pr.

Metamorphoses of the Circle. Georges Poulet. Tr. by Carley Dawson & Elliott Coleman. LC 66-24406. 431p. reprint ed. pap. 133.70 (*0-608-12066-9*, 202414700035) Bks Demand.

Metamorphoses of the Proustian Body Vol. 13: A Study of Bodily Signs in A la Recherche du Temps Perdu. Richard W. Saunders. LC 93-14217. (Reading Plus Ser.). XII, 251p. (C). 1994. text 46.95 (*0-8204-2244-4*) P Lang Pubng.

Metamorphoses of the Self: The Mystic, the Sensualist, & the Artist in the Works of Julien Green. John M. Dunaway. LC 78-88007. (Studies in Romance Languages: No. 19). 125p. reprint ed. pap. 38.80 (*0-7837-5814-6*, 204548100006) Bks Demand.

Metamorphoses of the Soul: Paths of Experience, 2 vols., Vol. 2. 2nd ed. Rudolf Steiner. Tr. by Charles Davy & Christian Von Arnim from GER. 150p. 1983. pap. 15.95 (*0-85440-415-5*, Pub. by R Steiner Pr) Anthroposophic.

Metamorphosis. Claudia G. Ferrari & Manlio Brusatin. (Illus.). 80p. 1997. pap. 19.95 (*88-8158-109-4*) Dist Art Pubs.

Metamorphosis. Franz Kafka.Tr. of Wervandlung. 17.95 (*0-88411-450-3*) Amereon Ltd.

Metamorphosis. Franz Kafka. Tr. & Intro. by Stanley Corngold. (Bantam Classics Ser.).Tr. of Wervandlung. 224p. 1972. mass mkt. 5.95 (*0-553-21369-5*, Bantam Classics) Bantam.

Metamorphosis. Franz Kafka. 1972. 11.05 (*0-606-03979-1*, Pub. by Turtleback) Demco.

Metamorphosis. Lawrence E. Keith. (Illus.). 40p. 1989. 12.00 (*0-932222-03-X*) Sunrise Tortoise.

Metamorphosis. Jean Lorrah. (Star Trek: The Next Generation Ser.). 416p. 1990. per. 5.99 (*0-671-68402-7*) PB.

Metamorphosis. Andres L. Ruiz. LC 96-9200. (Cycles of Life Ser.). (Illus.). 32p. (J). 1996. 12.95 (*0-8069-9325-1*) Sterling.

Metamorphosis. Anthony J. Summers. 1979. 2.75 (*0-918476-06-2*) Cornerstone Pr.

***Metamorphosis.** Jack Whyte. 448p. 2000. mass mkt. 6.99 (*0-8125-4419-6*, Pub. by Tor Bks) St Martin.

Metamorphosis. Mike Wilks. 1997. text. write for info. (*0-7181-0081-6*) Viking Penguin.

Metamorphosis. adapted ed. Franz Kafka.Tr. of Wervandlung. 1977. pap. 5.25 (*0-8222-0751-6*) Dramatists Play.

Metamorphosis. Ernest G. Schachtel. (Psychoanalysis: Examined & Re-Examined Ser.). 344p. 1984. reprint ed. lib. bdg. 39.50 (*0-306-76237-4*) Da Capo.

Metamorphosis: A Guide to the World Wide Web & Electronic Commerce, Version 2.0. 2nd ed. Patrick G. McKeown & Richard T. Watson. LC 96-49204. 192p. 1997. pap. 30.95 (*0-471-18032-7*) Wiley.

Metamorphosis: A Life Journey. Pat J. Schulz. 96p. (Orig.). 1996. pap. 11.95 (*0-9654899-0-6*) ENHEART Pub.

Metamorphosis: A Problem in Developmental Biology. 2nd ed. Ed. by Lawrence I. Gilbert & Earl Frieden. LC 81-17691. 598p. (C). 1981. 85.00 (*0-306-40692-6*, Plenum Trade) Perseus Pubng.

Metamorphosis: A Programmer Looks at the Software Crisis. William Beckett. 362p. 1997. pap. text 15.00 (*0-9660333-9-6*) Numerical Analog.

Metamorphosis: And Other Stories. Franz Kafka. 240p. 2000. pap. 11.95 (*0-14-028336-6*) Viking Penguin.

***Metamorphosis... Becoming Whole from Sexual Abuse.** Shirley Headen-Anthony. Ed. by Deborah Brown. LC 98-92801. xiii, 153p. 1999. pap. 10.00 (*0-9670998-0-3*) Making A Difference.

***Metamorphosis: Change Your Mind, Change Your Body.** J. P. Parikh. LC 99-64521. (Illus.). 248p. 2000. pap. 18.95 (*1-58501-012-X*, Pub. by CeShore Pubg) Natl Bk Netwk.

Metamorphosis: Postembryonic Reprogramming of Gene Expression in Insect & Amphibian Cells. Ed. by Lawrence I. Gilbert et al. (Cell Biology Ser.). (Illus.). 687p. 1996. text 125.00 (*0-12-283245-0*) Acad Pr.

Metamorphosis: Reflections on Recovery. Judith McDaniel. LC 89-80611. 80p. 1989. pap. 7.95 (*0-932379-61-3*); lib. bdg. 16.95 (*0-932379-62-1*) Firebrand Bks.

***Metamorphosis: Reproducible Teaching Unit.** James Scott. 27p. (YA). (gr. 7-12). 1999. ring bd. 29.50 (*1-58049-190-1*, TU60) Prestwick Hse.

***Metamorphosis: Stages in a Life.** D. Suzuki. 1999. 24.99 (*0-7737-2139-8*) Stoddart Publ.

Metamorphosis: The Mind in Exile. Harold Skulsky. LC 80-29526. 244p. 1981. 37.95 (*0-674-57085-5*) HUP.

Metamorphosis: Transformation in Action. Ed. by Ron Tugender. (Illus.). 252p. (Orig.). 1993. pap. 19.95 (*0-9639636-0-0*) Metamorphosis.

Metamorphosis: Transformation in Action. deluxe ed. Ed. by Ron Tugender. (Illus.). 252p. (Orig.). 1993. pap. 45.00 (*0-9639636-1-9*) Metamorphosis.

Metamorphosis: Translations, Backgrounds, & Contexts, Criticism. Franz Kafka. Ed. & Tr. by Stanley Corngold from GER. LC 95-20582. (Critical Editions Ser.).Tr. of Wervandlung. 218p. (C). 1996. pap. text 8.50 (*0-393-96797-2*, Norton Paperbks) Norton.

***Metamorphosis - The Fiber Art of Judith Scott: The Outsider Artist & the Experience of Down's Syndrome.** unabridged ed. John M. MacGregor. (Illus.). 208p. 1999. 45.00 (*0-9673160-0-6*) Creative Growth Art Ctr.

Metamorphosis - The Psychology of Transformation, 10 vols. L. Michael Hall. 100p. 1996. pap. 35.00 (*1-890001-05-8*) Empowerment Tech.

Metamorphosis A-Z. Eura De Freitas. (Illus.). 56p. 1996. pap. 7.50 (*1-885778-15-5*) Seaburn.

Metamorphosis & Other Stories. Franz Kafka. Tr. by Joachim Neugroschel. LC 92-43912. 288p. 1993. text 25.00 (*0-684-19426-0*, Scribners Ref) Mac Lib Ref.

Metamorphosis & Other Stories. unabridged ed. Franz Kafka. Tr. by Stanley Appelbaum from GER. LC 95-20498. (Dover Thrift Editions Ser.). 96p. 1996. pap. 1.50 (*0-486-29030-1*) Dover.

***Metamorphosis & the Emergence of the Feminine: A Motif of "Difference" in Women's Writing.** Paula Smith Allen. LC 98-30528. (Studies on Themes & Motifs in Literature: Vol. 45). 192p. 1999. 46.95 (*0-8204-4122-8*) P Lang Pubng.

Metamorphosis in Greek Myths. P. M. Forbes-Irving. (Oxford Classical Monographs). 342p. 1992. pap. text 36.00 (*0-19-814090-8*) OUP.

***Metamorphosis in Russian Modernism.** Ed. by Peter I. Barta. 300p. (C). 2000. 44.95 (*963-9116-90-4*); pap. 21.95 (*963-9116-91-2*) Ctrl Europ Univ.

Metamorphosis in Shakespeare's Plays: A Pageant of Heroes, Gods, Maids, & Monsters. Elizabeth Truax. LC 91-41705. 300p. 1992. lib. bdg. 89.95 (*0-7734-9434-0*) E Mellen.

Metamorphosis in the Arts. Richard Kostelanetz. LC 80-68968. 328p. 1981. 18.00 (*0-915066-41-6*); pap. 8.00 (*0-915066-43-2*) Assembling Pr.

Metamorphosis, In the Penal Colony, & Other Stories. Franz Kafka. Tr. by Joachim Neugroschel. LC 95-167401. 293p. 1995. per. 10.00 (*0-02-021807-9*) Macmillan.

Metamorphosis, In the Penal Colony & Other Stories. Franz Kafka. Tr. by Edwin Muir & Willa Muir from GER. LC 95-24576. 336p. 1995. pap. 12.00 (*0-8052-1057-1*) Schocken.

Metamorphosis of a Medieval City: Ghent in the Age of the Arteveldes, 1302-1390. David Nicholas. LC 86-27276. 381p. 1987. reprint ed. pap. 118.20 (*0-7837-6491-X*, 204658100003) Bks Demand.

Metamorphosis of a Social Class in Hungary During the Reign of Young Franz Joseph. Peter I. Hidas. (East European Monographs: No. 26). 140p. 1977. text 56.50 (*0-914710-19-2*, Pub. by East Eur Monographs) Col U Pr.

Metamorphosis of Baubo: Myths of Woman's Sexual Energy. Winifred M. Lubell. (Illus.). 219p. (C). 1998. pap. text 16.00 (*0-7881-5588-1*) DIANE Pub.

Metamorphosis of Chinese Foreign Investment Laws & Policies: Implications for Economic Development in the 1990s & Beyond. Wei Jia. LC 94-2990. 216p. 1994. 59.95 (*0-89930-900-3*, Quorum Bks) Greenwood.

Metamorphosis of English: Versions of Other Languages. Richard M. Swiderski. LC 95-38823. 160p. 1996. 52.95 (*0-89789-468-5*, Bergin & Garvey) Greenwood.

Metamorphosis of Flowers. Claude Nuridsany & Marie Perennou. Tr. by Ben Lifson from FRE. LC 97-45862. (Illus.). 136p. 1998. 39.95 (*0-8109-3625-9*, Pub. by Abrams) Time Warner.

Metamorphosis of Greece since World War II. William H. McNeill. LC 77-26105. (Illus.). 272p. 1996. 15.95 (*0-226-56156-9*) U Ch Pr.

Metamorphosis of Greece since World War II. William H. McNeill. LC 77-26105. 272p. reprint ed. pap. 84.40 (*0-608-09023-9*, 206965800005) Bks Demand.

Metamorphosis of Joy. Albert Depas. LC 96-94500. (Illus.). 64p. (Orig.). 1996. pap. 8.95 (*0-9651473-0-4*) Mega Pr.

Metamorphosis of Language in Apuleius: A Study of Allusion in the Novel. Ellen D. Finkelpearl. LC 97-33945. 256p. (C). 1998. text 42.50 (*0-472-10889-1*, 10889) U of Mich Pr.

***Metamorphosis of Ovid.** Sarah A. Brown. LC 99-37998. 2000. text 55.00 (*0-312-22844-9*) St Martin.

Metamorphosis of Peace: Essays & Poems. Sidney Bernard. 25p. 1984. pap. 3.50 (*0-933292-13-9*) Arts End.

Metamorphosis of Persephone: Ovid & the Self-Conscious Muse. Stephen Hinds. LC 86-26923. (Cambridge Classical Studies). (Illus.). 196p. 1987. text 54.95 (*0-521-33506-X*) Cambridge U Pr.

Metamorphosis of Plants. Jochen Bockemuhl. 1997. pap. text 10.95 (*0-9583885-2-0*, Pub. by Novalis Trust) Anthroposophic.

Metamorphosis of Plants. Johann Wolfgang Von Goethe. 1993. pap. 5.95 (*0-938250-36-1*, 364) Bio-Dynamic Farm.

Metamorphosis of the Administrative Welfare State: From Depoliticisation to Political Rationality. Pertti Ahonen & Ari Salminen. LC 98-137309. (Nordeuropaische Beitrage aus den Human- und Gesellschaftswissenschaften Ser.: Bd. 14). 214p. 1997. pap. 42.95 (*3-631-48494-1*) P Lang Pubng.

Metamorphosis of the Administrative Welfare State: From Depoliticisation to Political Rationality. Pertti Ahonen & Ari Salminen. LC 98-137309. (Nordeuropaische Beitrage aus den Human- und Gesellschaftswissenschaften Ser.: Bd. 14). 214p. 1997. pap. 42.95 (*0-8204-3272-5*) P Lang Pubng.

An Asterisk (*) at the beginning of an entry indicates that the title is appearing for the first time.

Metamorphosis of the Cassowaries: Umeda Society, Language & Ritual. Alfred Gell. (London School of Economics Monographs on Social Anthropology: No. 51). (Illus.). 366p. (C). 1975. text 45.00 (*0-485-19551-8*, Pub. by Athlone Pr) Humanities.

Metamorphosis of the Given: Toward an Ecology of Consciousness. Friedemann Schwarzkopf. LC 94-20467. (Revisioning Philosophy Ser.: Vol. 20). XXX, 210p. (C). 1995. text 39.95 (*0-8204-2585-0*) P Lang Pubng.

Metamorphosis of the Given: Toward an Ecology of Consciousness. 2nd ed. Friedemann Schwarzkopf. (Revisioning Philosophy Ser.: Vol. 20). XXX, 210p. (C). 1998. reprint ed. pap. text 24.95 (*0-8204-4082-5*) P Lang Pubng.

***Metamorphosis of the Serpent God.** Robert L. Giron. 96p. (C). 1999. pap. 12.00 (*1-928589-07-3*) Gival Pr.

Metamorphosis or Golden Ass & Philosophical Works of Apuleius & the Habitude of the Doctrines of the Philosophy of Plato. Tr. by Thomas Taylor. 410p. 1992. reprint ed. pap. 20.00 (*1-56459-023-2*) Kessinger Pub.

Metamorphosis: or Why I Love Greece. Bruce Lansdale. LC 78-75129. (Illus.). 128p. 1979. 30.00 (*0-89241-083-3*) Caratzas.

***Metamorphosis to Freedom.** Robert O. Fisch. (Illus.). 64p. 2000. 17.00 (*0-9679746-0-7*) Fisch.

Metamorphosizing the Novel: Kay Boyle's Narrative Innovations. Marilyn Elkins. LC 93-27433. (Writing about Women Ser.: Vol. 7). 216p. 1993. text 42.95 (*0-8204-1947-8*) P Lang Pubng.

Metanoia: A Transformational Journey. Mary O. Davis. LC 84-71551. 154p. 1984. pap. 7.95 (*0-87516-544-3*) DeVorss.

Metapatterns: Across Space, Time & Mind. Tyler Volk. LC 94-40589. (Illus.). 312p. 1995. 39.95 (*0-231-06750-X*) Col U Pr.

Metapatterns: Across Space, Time & Mind. Tyler Volk. (Illus.). 312p. 1996. pap. 15.95 (*0-231-06751-8*) Col U Pr.

Metaperspectives: The Systems Approach & Its Vision. Howard I. Thorsheim & Bruce B. Roberts. (Systems Inquiry Ser.). 250p. 1984. pap. text 13.95 (*0-914105-33-7*) Intersystems Pubns.

Metaphern in Abstrakten Diskurs-Domanen: Eine Kognitiv-Linguistische Untersuchung Anhand der Bereiche Geistestatigkeit, Wirtschaft und Wissenschaft. Olaf Jakel. (Duisburger Arbeiten zur Sprach- und Kulturwissenschaft Ser.: Bd. 30). (GER., Illus.). 346p. 1997. 54.95 (*3-631-31103-6*) P Lang Pubng.

***Metaphern von Musik und Stille Als Erkenntnismittel in Den Filmen Pasolinis.** Gretel Freitag. (Europaische Hochschulschriften, Reihe 36). (GER.). 431p. 1999. 67.95 (*3-631-34243-8*) P Lang Pubng.

Metaphilosophical Inquiries. Nicholas Rescher. LC 93-5179. (System of Pragmatic Idealism Ser.: Vol. 3). 288p. 1994. text 55.00 (*0-691-07394-5*, Pub. by Princeton U Pr) Cal Prin Full Svc.

Metaphilosophy & Free Will. Richard Double. 192p. 1996. text 39.95 (*0-19-510762-4*) OUP.

Metaphor. H. W. Fowler et al. Ed. by Steele Commager. Incl. Briton, British, Britisher. 1979. English Idioms. 1979. English Influence on the French Vocabulary. 1979. Four Words. 1979. Index to Tracts I-XIX. 1979. Logic & Grammar. 1979. Medium Aevum & the Middle Age. 1979. Split Infinitive. 1979. Subjunctives. 1979. (Society for Pure English Ser.: Vol. 2). 1979. Set lib. bdg. 46.00 (*0-8240-3666-2*) Garland.

Metaphor. Terence Hawkes. (Critical Idiom Ser.). 1972. pap. 9.95 (*0-416-09030-3*, NO. 2223) Routledge.

Metaphor: A Bibliography of Post-1970 Publications. Compiled by Jean-Pierre Van Noppen et al. LC 84-28274. (Library & Information Sources in Linguistics: No. 17). x, 497p. 1985. 97.00 (*90-272-3737-9*) J Benjamins Pubng Co.

Metaphor: A Musical Dimension. Ed. by Jamie Kassler. 45.00 (*0-86819-301-1*, Pub. by Currency Pr); 25.00 (*0-86819-277-5*, Pub. by Currency Pr) Accents Pubns.

Metaphor: A Musical Dimension. Ed. by Jamie C. Kassler. (Musicology: A Book Ser.). 256p. 1994. text 18.00 (*2-88449-136-8*) Gordon & Breach.

Metaphor: An Annotated Bibliography & History. Warren Shibles. LC 72-157087. 1971. lib. bdg. 20.00 (*0-912386-00-2*) Language Pr.

Metaphor: Implications & Applications. Ed. by Jeffrey S. Mio & Albert N. Katz. 350p. 1996. 59.95 (*0-8058-1650-X*) L Erlbaum Assocs.

Metaphor: Its Cognitive Force & Linguistic Structure. Eva F. Kittay. (Clarendon Library of Logic & Philosophy). (Illus.). 368p. 1990. reprint ed. pap. text 29.95 (*0-19-824246-8*) OUP.

Metaphor: The Logic of Poetry. rev. ed. John Briggs & Richard Monaco. (Illus.). 304p. (C). 1990. lib. bdg. 46.50 (*0-944473-03-2*) Pace Univ Pr.

Metaphor: The Season Reflected in What You See. Lee Coles. LC 99-34767. (Illus.). 80p. 1999. pap. 12.95 (*1-882897-39-0*) Lost Coast.

Metaphor & Cognition: An Interactionist Approach. Bipin Indurkhya. (Studies in Cognitive Systems). 474p. (C). 1992. lib. bdg. 177.00 (*0-7923-1687-8*, Pub. by Kluwer Academic) Kluwer Academic.

***Metaphor & Emotion: Language, Culture & the Body in Human Feeling.** Zoltan Kovecses. (Studies in Emotion & Social Interaction). (Illus.). 224p. (C). 2000. 49.95 (*0-521-64163-2*) Cambridge U Pr.

***Metaphor & God-Talk.** Ed. by Lieven Boeve & Kurt Feyaerts. (Religions & Discourse Ser.). 291p. 1999. 41.95 (*3-906762-51-3*, Pub. by P Lang) P Lang Pubng.

***Metaphor & God-Talk.** Ed. by Lieven Boeve & Kurt Feyaerts. (Religions & Discourse Ser.: Vol. 2). 291p. (C). 1999. pap. 41.95 (*0-8204-4235-6*) P Lang Pubng.

Metaphor & Material Culture. Christopher Tilley. LC 98-21302. 320p. 1999. 59.95 (*0-631-19202-6*); pap. 29.95 (*0-631-19203-4*) Blackwell Pubs.

***Metaphor & Materiality: German Literature & the World-View of Science, 1780-1955.** Peter D. Smith. (Legenda Ser.: Vol. 4). 378p. (C). 2000. pap. 49.50 (*1-900755-32-7*, Pub. by E H R C) David Brown.

Metaphor & Meaning in D. H. Lawrence's Later Novels. John B. Humma. LC 90-32579. 136p. 1990. text 24.95 (*0-8262-0742-1*) U of Mo Pr.

Metaphor & Meaning in Psychotherapy. Ellen Y. Siegelman. LC 90-2726. 206p. 1993. pap. text 22.00 (*0-89862-014-7*) Guilford Pubns.

Metaphor & Memory: Essays. Cynthia Ozick. LC 92-50093. (Vintage International Ser.). 304p. 1991. pap. 14.00 (*0-679-73425-2*) Vin Bks.

Metaphor & Modernist: The Polarization of Alfred Loisy & His Neo-Thomist Critics. C. J. Talar. 194p. (C). 1988. lib. bdg. 33.00 (*0-8191-6654-5*) U Pr of Amer.

***Metaphor & Moral Experience.** Alison Denham. (Oxford Philosophical Monographs). 376p. 2000. text 65.00 (*0-19-824010-4*) OUP.

Metaphor & Myth in Science & Religion. Earl R. MacCormac. LC 75-23941. 187p. reprint ed. pap. 58.00 (*0-608-15267-6*, 205220700060) Bks Demand.

Metaphor & Organizations. David Grant & Cliff Oswick. 256p. 1996. 75.00 (*0-8039-7629-1*); pap. 25.95 (*0-8039-7630-5*) Sage.

Metaphor & Philosophy, Vol. 10, No. 3. Ed. by Mark Johnson. 90p. 1995. pap. 20.00 (*0-8058-9939-1*) L Erlbaum Assocs.

Metaphor & Reality. Philip E. Wheelwright. LC 62-8971. 192p. reprint ed. pap. 59.60 (*0-608-13239-X*, 205606500044) Bks Demand.

Metaphor & Reason in Judicial Opinions. Haig Bosmajian. LC 91-30037. 208p. (C). 1992. 31.95 (*0-8093-1612-9*) S Ill U Pr.

Metaphor & Religious Language. Janet M. Soskice. 200p. 1987. pap. text 29.95 (*0-19-824982-9*) OUP.

Metaphor & Simile in Minor Elizabethan Drama. Frederick I. Carpenter. LC 77-136372. (Chicago. University. English Studies: No. 4). reprint ed. 37.50 (*0-404-50264-4*) AMS Pr.

Metaphor & the Poetry of Williams, Pound, & Stevens. Suzanne Juhasz. LC 72-13393. 292p. 1974. 38.50 (*0-8387-1243-6*) Bucknell U Pr.

Metaphor & Thought. 2nd ed. Ed. by Andrew Ortony. LC 92-37625. (Illus.). 694p. (C). 1993. pap. text 32.95 (*0-521-40561-0*) Cambridge U Pr.

Metaphor & Thought. 2nd ed. Ed. by Andrew Ortony. LC 92-37625. (Illus.). 694p. (C). 1994. text 80.00 (*0-521-40547-5*) Cambridge U Pr.

Metaphor & Visual, Vol. 8, No. 3. Kennedy. 1993. 20.00 (*0-8058-9979-0*) L Erlbaum Assocs.

***Metaphor as Thought in Elias Canetti's Masse und Macht.** David Scott. LC 99-210317. xiv, 206p. 1999. 35.95 (*3-906759-09-1*, Pub. by P Lang) P Lang Pubng.

Metaphor as Thought in Elias Canetti's Masse und Macht. David Scott. LC 99-210317. (Australian & New Zeland Studies in German Language & Literature: Vol. 18). XIV, 206p. 1999. 35.95 (*0-8204-4222-4*) P Lang Pubng.

***Metaphor, Canon & Community: Jewish, Christian & Islamic Approaches.** Ed. by Ralph Bisschops & James Francis. (Religions & Discourse Ser.). 307p. 1999. 45.95 (*3-906762-40-8*, Pub. by P Lang) P Lang Pubng.

***Metaphor, Canon & Community: Jewish, Christian & Islamic Approaches.** Ed. by Ralph Bisschops & James Francis. LC 99-15409. (Religions & Discourse Ser.: Vol. 1). 307p. (C). 1999. pap. text 45.95 (*0-8204-4234-8*) P Lang Pubng.

Metaphor for the History of American Criticism. M. Van Deusen. (Essays & Studies on American Language & Literature: Vol. 13). (Orig.). 1961. pap. 25.00 (*0-8115-0193-0*) Periodicals Srv.

Metaphor II: A Classified Bibliography of Publications from 1985-1990. Compiled by Jean-Pierre Van Noppen & Edith Hols. LC 90-45405. (Library & Information Sources in Linguistics: Vol. 20). iv, 342p. 1990. 83.00 (*1-55619-250-9*) J Benjamins Pubng Co.

***Metaphor in Cognitive Linguistics: Selected Papers from the 5th International Cognitive Linguistics Conference, Amsterdam, 1997.** Ed. by Raymond W. Gibbs, Jr. & Gerard J. Steen. LC 99-15508. (Current Issues in Linguistic Theory Ser.: Vol. 175). viii, 226p. 1999. 65.00 (*1-55619-892-2*) J Benjamins Pubng Co.

***Metaphor in Context.** Josef Stern. 460p. (C). 2000. 39.95 (*0-262-19439-2*, Bradford Bks) MIT Pr.

Metaphor in Psychotherapy: Clinical Applications of Stories & Allegories. Henry T. Close. LC 98-7500. (Practical Therapist Ser.: Vol. 4). 320p. 1998. 34.95 (*1-886230-10-2*) Impact Pubs CA.

Metaphor, Meaning, & Cognition. Don Ross. LC 93-6956. (American University Studies: Vol. 149). 210p. 1994. 38.95 (*0-8204-2151-0*) P Lang Pubng.

Metaphor of God Incarnate: Christology in a Pluralistic Age. John Hick. LC 93-14538. 192p. (Orig.). 1993. pap. 19.95 (*0-664-25503-5*) Westminster John Knox.

Metaphor of Slavery in the Writings of the Early Church: From the New Testament to the Beginning of the Fifth Century. I. A. Combes. (JSNTS Ser.: Vol. 156). 216p. 1998. 57.50 (*1-85075-846-8*, Pub. by Sheffield Acad) CUP Services.

Metaphor of the Kiss in Renaissance Poetry. Ruth A. Gooley. LC 91-15890. (American University Studies: Romance Languages & Literature: Ser. II, Vol. 175). 208p. (C). 1993. text 39.95 (*0-8204-1620-7*) P Lang Pubng.

Metaphor of Trees. William Bronk. 1999. 35.95 (*1-883689-96-1*) Talisman Hse.

***Metaphor of Trees & Last Poems.** William Bronk. LC 99-47378. 156p. 1999. pap. 14.95 (*1-883689-95-3*, Pub. by Talisman Hse) SPD-Small Pr Dist.

***Metaphor Problem: Again.** John Baldessari. 2000. pap. 35.00 (*3-88375-404-8*) Walther Konig.

Metaphor Reexamined: A Non-Aristotelian Perspective. Liselotte Gumpel. LC 84-47707. (Advances in Semiotics Ser.). (Illus.). 319p. 1984. pap. 98.90 (*0-608-05025-3*, 205968600004) Bks Demand.

Metaphor Stories for Deaf Children. Robert K. Rittenhouse. LC 98-220813. (Illus.). 128p. (YA). (gr. 7-12). 1999. student ed., spiral bd. 14.95 (*1-884362-33-8*) Butte Pubns.

Metaphor Therapy: Using Client-Generated Metaphors in Psychotherapy. Richard R. Kopp. 216p. 1995. text 25.95 (*0-87630-779-9*) Brunner-Mazel.

Metaphoresis: Do We Know What We Are Talking About? Richard Matlick. 224p. 1999. pap. 11.95 (*1-893162-01-X*) Erica Hse.

Metaphoric Analysis of the Debate on Physician Assisted Suicide. Elizabeth S. Spragins. LC 99-26853. (Symposium Series : vol. 54). 144p. 1999. text 69.95 (*0-7734-8041-2*) E Mellen.

Metaphoric Body: Guide to Expressive Therapy Through Images & Archetypes. Nira Ne'eman & Lea Barthal. 200p. 1993. pap. 25.95 (*1-85302-152-0*) Taylor & Francis.

Metaphoric Mind: A Celebration of Creative Consciousness. rev. ed. Bob Samples, pseud. (Creative Teaching Ser.). 272p. 1993. pap. 16.95 (*0-915190-68-0*, JP9068-0) Jalmar Pr.

Metaphoric Narration: The Paranarrative Dimension of a la Recherche du Temps Perdu. Luz A. Pimentel. (Romance Ser.). 168p. 1990. text 45.00 (*0-8020-2735-0*) U of Toronto Pr.

Metaphoric Process: Connections Between Language & Life. Gemma Fiumara. LC 95-5707. 208p. (C). 1995. pap. 24.99 (*0-415-12625-8*) Routledge.

Metaphoric Process: Connections Between Language & Life. Gemma Fiumara. LC 95-5707. 208p. (C). (gr. 13). 1995. 75.00 (*0-415-12624-X*) Routledge.

Metaphoric Process: The Creation of Scientific & Religious Understanding. Mary Gerhart & Allan M. Russell. LC 83-15614. 218p. 1984. 16.95 (*0-912646-82-9*); pap. 10.95 (*0-912646-86-1*) Tex Christian.

Metaphorical Basis of Language: A Study in Cross-Cultural Linguistics of the Left- Handed Hummingbird. E. Morgan Kelley. LC 92-10148. 396p. 1992. lib. bdg. 99.95 (*0-7734-9534-7*) E Mellen.

Metaphorical Brain 2: Neural Networks & Beyond. 2nd ed. Michael A. Arbib. LC 88-27877. 458p. 1989. 145.00 (*0-471-09853-1*) Wiley.

Metaphorical God: An Abecedary of Images for God. Gail Ramshaw. (Illus.). 133p. 1995. 13.00 (*1-56854-128-7*, C/MGOD) Liturgy Tr Pubns.

Metaphorical God: An Abecedary of Images for God. rev. ed. Gail Ramshaw. LC 95-812. (Illus.). 133p. 1995. pap. 8.00 (*1-56854-071-X*, P/MGOD) Liturgy Tr Pubns.

Metaphorical Organism in Herder's Early Works: A Study of the Relation of Herder's Literary Idiom to His World-View. Edgar B. Schick. LC 74-134546. 135p. 1971. pap. text 23.10 (*3-10-800306-2*) Mouton.

Metaphorical Theology: Models of God in Religious Language. Sallie McFague. LC 82-7246. 240p. (C). 1982. pap. 17.00 (*0-8006-1687-1*, 1-1687, Fortress Pr) Augsburg Fortress.

Metaphorical Ways of Knowing: The Imaginative Nature of Thought & Expression. Sharon L. Pugh et al. LC 96-47982. (Illus.). 222p. (Orig.). 1997. pap. 19.95 (*0-8141-3151-4*) NCTE.

Metaphorically Speaking. Patti D. Nogales. LC 98-54375. (Lecture Notes Ser.: Vol. 93). 256p. (C). 1999. text 59.95 (*1-57586-159-3*); pap. text 22.95 (*1-57586-158-5*) CSLI.

Metaphorically Speaking: A Dictionary of 3,800 Picturesque Idiomatic Expressions. N. E. Renton. 1992. reprint ed. mass mkt. 11.99 (*0-446-39353-3*, Pub. by Warner Bks) Little.

Metaphorics of Fiction: Discontinuity & Discourse in the Modern Novel. Alan Singer. LC 83-16860. 183p. 1984. 39.95 (*0-8130-0773-9*) U Press Fla.

Metaphors: Figures of the Mind. Zdravko Radman. LC 96-50080. (Library of Rhetorics). 204p. (C). 1996. text 147.00 (*0-7923-4356-5*) Kluwer Academic.

Metaphors & Action Schemes: Some Themes in Intellectual History. Robert L. Schwarz. LC 96-35861. 288p. 1997. 41.50 (*0-8387-5355-8*) Bucknell U Pr.

Metaphors & Meanings: Essays on English Teaching. Garth Boomer. Ed. by Bill Green. 240p. 1998. pap. text 17.50 (*0-909955-82-4*, 925824) Calendar Islands.

Metaphors & Similes for Yahweh in Hosea 14:2-9(1-8) A Study of Hoseanic Pictorial Language. Bernhard Oestreich. LC 98-36238. (Friedensauer Schriftenreihe. Reihe A Ser.). 278p. 1998. pap. text 48.95 (*0-8204-3615-1*) P Lang Pubng.

***Metaphors & the Dynamics of Knowledge.** Sabine Maasen & Peter Weingart. 256p. 2000. 90.00 (*0-415-20802-5*) Routledge.

Metaphors at Work: The Unseen Influence. Jacques Jimenez & Timothy L. Johnson. LC 98-71311. 268p. 1998. pap. 39.95 (*1-891593-00-5*) Commun Patterns.

***Metaphors Dictionary.** Elyse Sommer & Dorrie Weiss. 612p. 2000. reprint ed. pap. 30.00 (*0-7881-9355-4*) DIANE Pub.

***Metaphors for Living: Stories & Related Experiential Exercises for Individual, Group & Family Growth.** rev. expanded ed. Jackie Gerstein. 2001. pap. 24.95 (*1-885473-37-0*) Wood N Barnes.

Metaphors for Metamorphosis: The Power of Metaphors & Personal Story. 2nd ed. E. Gene Rooney. 94p. reprint ed. student ed. 20.00 (*1-881596-04-4*) L E A D Cnslts.

Metaphors in the History of Psychology. Ed. by David E. Leary. (Studies in the History of Psychology). (Illus.). 397p. (C). 1990. text 69.95 (*0-521-37166-X*) Cambridge U Pr.

Metaphors in the History of Psychology. Ed. by David E. Leary. (Cambridge Studies in the History of Psychology). (Illus.). 397p. (C). 1994. pap. text 19.95 (*0-521-42152-7*) Cambridge U Pr.

Metaphors of Aging in Science & the Humanities. Ed. by James E. Birren et al. LC 91-12798. 272p. (C). 1991. text 33.95 (*0-8261-7440-X*) Springer Pub.

Metaphors of Anger, Pride, & Love: A Lexical Approach to the Structure of Concepts. Zoltan Kovecses. LC 87-15788. (Pragmatics & Beyond Ser.: No. VII:8). vii, 147p. (C). 1987. pap. 50.00 (*1-55619-009-3*) J Benjamins Pubng Co.

Metaphors of Change in the Language of Nineteenth-Century Fiction: Scott, Gaskell & Kingsley. Megan P. Stitt. (Oxford English Monographs). 218p. 1998. text 65.00 (*0-19-818442-5*) OUP.

Metaphors of Consciousness. rev. ed. R. S. Valle & R. Von Eckartsberg. LC 80-24803. (Illus.). 544p. (C). 1981. pap. 37.50 (*0-306-43119-X*, Plenum Trade) Perseus Pubng.

Metaphors of Consciousness. rev. ed. Ed. by Ronald S. Valle & Rolf Von Eckartsberg. LC 80-24803. 544p. 1981. 45.00 (*0-306-40520-2*, Plenum Trade) Perseus Pubng.

Metaphors of Conversion in Seventeenth-Century Spanish Drama, Vol. 174. Leslie Levin. LC 98-29030. (Spanish, Portuguese, Latin American Studies). (SPA.). 160p. 1998. 60.00 (*1-85566-057-1*) Boydell & Brewer.

Metaphors of Dispossession: American Beginnings & the Translation of Empire, 1492-1637. Gesa Mackenthun. LC 96-52787. 370p. 1997. 32.95 (*0-8061-2953-0*) U of Okla Pr.

Metaphors of Family Systems Theory: Toward New Constructions. Paul C. Rosenblatt. LC 93-19476. (Perspectives on Marriage & the Family Ser.). 239p. 1993. lib. bdg. 39.95 (*0-89862-321-9*) Guilford Pubns.

Metaphors of Family Systems Theory: Toward New Constructions. Paul C. Rosenblatt. LC 93-19476. (Perspectives on Marriage & the Family Ser.). 239p. 1997. pap. text 22.00 (*1-57230-172-4*, 0172) Guilford Pubns.

Metaphors of Genre: The Role of Analogies in Genre Theory. David Fishelov. LC 92-12151. 208p. (C). 1993. 32.50 (*0-271-00886-5*) Pa St U Pr.

Metaphors of Identity: A Culture-Communication Dialogue. Thomas K. Fitzgerald. LC 92-27080. (SUNY Series, Human Communication Processes). 264p. (C). 1993. text 64.50 (*0-7914-1595-3*); pap. text 21.95 (*0-7914-1596-1*) State U NY Pr.

Metaphors of Identity: The Treatment of Childhood in Selected Quebecois Novels. Roseanna L. Dufault. LC 90-55832. 88p. 1991. 24.50 (*0-8386-3424-9*) Fairleigh Dickinson.

Metaphors of Interpretation: Essays in Honour of W. E. H. Stanner. D. Barwick et al. LC 84-71361. (Illus.). 318p. 1987. pap. text 38.00 (*0-08-029875-3*, Pergamon Pr) Elsevier.

Metaphors of Interrelatedness: Toward a Systems Theory of Psychology. Linda E. Olds. LC 91-18490. (SUNY Series, Alternatives in Psychology). 217p. (C). 1992. text 49.50 (*0-7914-1011-0*); pap. text 18.95 (*0-7914-1012-9*) State U NY Pr.

Metaphors of Light: Philipp K. Marheineke's Method & the Ongoing Program of Mediating Theology. Luis H. Dreher. 240p. 1998. 86.00 (*3-11-015828-0*) De Gruyter.

Metaphors of Light: Philipp K. Marheineke's Method & the Ongoing Program of Mediation Theology, Vol. 622. Luis H. Dreher. LC 98-33535. (European University Studies: No. 23). 245p. 1998. pap. text 40.95 (*0-8204-3435-3*) P Lang Pubng.

Metaphors of Masculinity: Sex & Status in Andalusian Folklore. Stanley Brandes. LC 79-5258. (Publications of the American Folklore Society, Bibliographical & Special Ser.). 236p. 1980. pap. text 19.95 (*0-8122-1105-7*) U of Pa Pr.

***Metaphors of Memory: A History of Ideas about the Mind.** Douwe Draaisma. LC 99-88502. (Illus.). 270p. 2000. 29.95 (*0-521-65024-0*) Cambridge U Pr.

Metaphors of Mind: Conceptions of the Nature of Intelligence. Robert J. Sternberg. (Illus.). 360p. (C). 1990. text 59.95 (*0-521-35579-6*); pap. text 22.95 (*0-521-38633-0*) Cambridge U Pr.

Metaphors of Mind in Fiction & Psychology. Michael S. Kearns. LC 87-10620. 272p. 1987. text 32.50 (*0-8131-1625-2*) U Pr of Ky.

Metaphors of Self: The Meaning of Autobiography. James Olney. LC 71-173758. 358p. reprint ed. pap. 111.00 (*0-7837-1412-2*, 204176600023) Bks Demand.

Metaphors of Social Control in a Pentecostal Sect. Tom C. Darrand & Anson D. Shupe. LC 83-9006. (Studies in Religion & Society: Vol. 6). 232p. 1984. lib. bdg. 89.95 (*0-88946-870-2*) E Mellen.

Metaphors on Vision. 2nd ed. Stan Brakhage. (Illus.). 1976. pap. 12.00 (*0-317-55956-7*) Anthology Film.

Metaphor's Way of Knowing: The Poetry of D. H. Lawrence & the Church of Mechanism. Patricia L. Hagen. LC 91-29168. (American University Studies, Series IV: Vol. 139). 140p. (C). 1995. text 39.95 (*0-8204-1710-6*) P Lang Pubng.

Metaphors We Live By. George Lakoff & Mark Johnson. LC 80-10783. xiv, 242p. 1980. lib. bdg. 20.00 (*0-226-46800-3*) U Ch Pr.

Metaphors We Live By. George Lakoff & Mark Johnson. LC 80-10783. xiv, 256p. 1981. pap. 13.00 (*0-226-46801-1*) U Ch Pr.

Metaphysica. Ed. by Werner Jaeger. (Oxford Classical Texts Ser.). 334p. 1957. text 45.00 (*0-19-814513-6*) OUP.

M

Metaphysica. 2nd ed. Alexander G. Baumgarten. (GER.). 432p. 1982. reprint ed. write for info. (*3-487-00377-5*) G Olms Pubs.

Metaphysica in Usum Auditorii Sui Ordine Scientifico Bd. 42. Andreas Bohm. 674p. 1998. write for info. (*3-487-10657-4*) G Olms Pubs.

Metaphysical Analysis. John W. Yolton. LC 68-88650. 233p. reprint ed. pap. 72.30 (*0-608-10018-8*, 201446400090) Bks Demand.

Metaphysical & Epistemological Problems of Perception. Richard A. Fumerton. LC 84-11920. 225p. reprint ed. pap. 69.80 (*0-7837-6882-6*, 204671200003) Bks Demand.

Metaphysical & Geometrical Doctrine of Bruno. Ksenija Atanasijevic. Tr. by George V. Tomashevich from FRE. LC 76-155339. 151p. 1972. 12.50 (*0-87527-081-6*) Green.

Metaphysical & Paranormal Hocus Pocus: Why People Embellish Reality with Myths. Ken Albertsen. (Illus.). 142p. 1998. pap. 14.00 (*1-879338-18-1*) Albertsens.

Metaphysical Animal: Divine & Human in Man. Andrew N. Woznicki. LC 95-53026. (Catholic Thought from Lublin Ser.: Vol. 10). XII, 216p. (C). 1997. 48.95 (*0-8204-2883-3*) P Lang Pubng.

Metaphysical Astrology. John Hazelrigg. 71p. 1996. reprint ed. spiral bd. 9.00 (*0-7873-0388-7*) Hlth Research.

Metaphysical Astrology (1900) John Hazelrigg. 72p. 1996. reprint ed. pap. 7.95 (*1-56459-885-3*) Kessinger Pub.

Metaphysical Bible Dictionary. Unity School of Christianity Staff. Ed. by Michael Maday. LC 89-50686. 706p. 2000. 29.95 (*0-87159-067-0*) Unity Bks.

***Metaphysical Club.** Louis Menand. 2000. text (*0-374-19963-9*) FS&G.

Metaphysical Community: The Interplay of the Senses & the Intellect. Greg Urban. (Illus.). (Orig.). (C). 1996. pap. 19.95 (*0-292-78529-1*); text 40.00 (*0-292-78528-3*) U of Tex Pr.

***Metaphysical Confederacy.** James Oscar Farmer. LC 99-56000. 295p. 1999. pap. text 18.95 (*0-86554-673-8*) Mercer Univ Pr.

Metaphysical Counseling of the Astrological Chart. Greenwood. 1992. 14.00 (*0-86690-408-5*) Am Fed Astrologers.

Metaphysical Delusion. Fraser Cowley. LC 91-16767. 200p. (C). 1991. 33.95 (*0-87975-669-1*) Prometheus Bks.

Metaphysical Dictionary: 5000 Definitions. Sunny Tangas. 256p. 1997. pap. write for info. (*0-9681770-0-X*) KT Pubs.

Metaphysical Drift: Love & Judaism. Jerome Eckstein. LC 91-855. (Revisioning Philosophy Ser.: Vol. 10). XX, 241p. (C). 1992. text 44.95 (*0-8204-1733-5*) P Lang Pubng.

Metaphysical Element of Justice: Kant. John Ladd. 192p. (C). 1965. pap. text 7.00 (*0-02-367100-9*, Macmillan Coll) P-H.

Metaphysical Elements of Justice. rev. ed. Immanuel Kant. Tr. by John Ladd from GER. LC 99-34079. (Classics Ser.). 256p. (C). 1998. pap. text 9.95 (*0-87220-418-9*) Hackett Pub.

Metaphysical Elements of Justice. rev. ed. Immanuel Kant. Tr. by John Ladd from GER. LC 99-34079. (Classics Ser.). 194p. (C). 1999. lib. bdg. 34.95 (*0-87220-419-7*) Hackett Pub.

MetaPhysical Fitness: The Complete 30 Day Plan for Your Mental, Emotional & Spiritual Health. David Harp & Nina Feldman. (Illus.). 240p. (Orig.). 1989. pap. 8.95 (*0-918321-50-6*) Musical I Pr.

Metaphysical Foundations: Mereology & Metalogic. Richard M. Martin. (Analytica Ser.). 387p. 1988. 92.00 (*3-88405-053-2*) Philosophia Pr.

Metaphysical Foundations of Logic. Martin Heidegger. Tr. & Intro. by Michael H. Heim. LC 83-48649. (Studies in Phenomenology & Existential Philosophy). (Illus.). 256p. 1984. 31.95 (*0-253-33783-6*) Ind U Pr.

Metaphysical Foundations of Logic. Martin Heidegger. Tr. & Intro. by Michael H. Heim. LC 83-48649. (Studies in Phenomenology & Existential Philosophy). (Illus.). 256p. 1992. pap. 13.95 (*0-253-20764-9*, MB-764) Ind U Pr.

Metaphysical Foundations of Modern Physical Science. 2nd ed. Edwin A. Burtt. LC 89-15426. (C). 1982. reprint ed. pap. 17.50 (*0-391-01742-X*) Humanities.

Metaphysical Handbook. David Pond & Lucy Pond. LC 83-91290. (Illus.). 200p. 1984. pap. 12.95 (*0-915395-18-5*) Reflecting Pond.

Metaphysical Healing, Vols. 1 & 2. A. S. Raleigh. 87p. 1996. reprint ed. spiral bd. 21.00 (*0-7873-1204-5*) Hlth Research.

Metaphysical Imperative: A Critique of the Modern Approach to Science. 2nd ed. Ronald E. Puhek. 135p. 1998. pap. 10.00 (*1-892590-03-4*) Out Your Bk.

Metaphysical Implications of Gandhian Thought. K. C. Chako. 1986. 15.00 (*0-8364-1901-4*, Pub. by Mittal Pubs Dist) S Asia.

Metaphysical Investigations. Ramon M. Lemos. LC 86-46324. 288p. 1988. 38.50 (*0-8386-3307-2*) Fairleigh Dickinson.

***Metaphysical Kipling.** Rudyard Kipling. LC 99-80173. 256p. 2000. write for info. (*1-893766-16-0*) Aeon Pub Co.

Metaphysical Lyrics & Poems of the Seventeenth Century. Herbert J. Grierson. LC 78-12842. 244p. 1979. reprint ed. lib. bdg. 47.50 (*0-313-21163-9*, GRML, Greenwood Pr) Greenwood.

Metaphysical Mediations: Paramhansa Yogananda. LC 84-71201. 1993. pap. 9.95 (*0-937134-17-1*) Amrita Found.

Metaphysical Meditations. 11th ed. Paramahansa Yogananda. LC 40-16548. 126p. 1964. pap. 3.50 (*0-87612-041-9*) Self Realization.

Metaphysical Meditations: Universal Prayers, Affirmations & Visualizations. Paramahansa Yogananda. LC 40-16548. 164p. 1998. reprint ed. 12.00 (*0-87612-047-8*, 1362) Self Realization.

Metaphysical Meditations: Universal Prayers, Affirmations, & Visualizations see Meditaciones Metafisicas: Oraciones, Afirmaciones y Visualizaciones Universales

Metaphysical Mousetraps. 16p. 1986. pap. 5.00 (*0-9607532-1-4*) Squantum Pr.

Metaphysical Myths, Mathematical Practice. Jody Azzouni. 261p. (C). 1994. text 80.00 (*0-521-44223-0*) Cambridge U Pr.

Metaphysical Novel in England: The Romantic Phase. Robert L. Platzner. Ed. by Devendra P. Varma. LC 79-8468. (Gothic Studies & Dissertations). 1980. lib. bdg. 36.95 (*0-405-12656-5*) Ayer.

Metaphysical Passion: Seven Modern American Poets & the Seventeenth Century Tradition. Sonia Raiziss. LC 73-194227. 327p. 1970. reprint ed. lib. bdg. 65.00 (*0-8371-3343-2*, RAMP, Greenwood Pr) Greenwood.

Metaphysical Personalism: An Examination of Austin Farrer's Philosophical Theism. Charles Conti. 326p. 1995. text 65.00 (*0-19-826338-4*) OUP.

Metaphysical Poets. (Poetry Library). 240p. 1998. pap. 7.95 (*1-85326-439-3*, 4393WW, Pub. by Wrdsworth Edits) NTC Contemp Pub Co.

Metaphysical Poets. Helen Gardner. (Poets Ser.). 332p. (Orig.). 1960. pap. 9.95 (*0-14-042038-X*, Penguin Classics) Viking Penguin.

***Metaphysical Poets.** David Reid. LC 99-86025. (Medieval & Renaissance Library). 272p. 2000. pap. 27.00 (*0-582-29835-0*) Longman.

***Metaphysical Poets.** David Reid. LC 99-86025. 272p. 2001. 69.95 (*0-582-29834-2*) Longman.

Metaphysical Poets: A Chronology. Janis Lull. LC 93-8212. (Reference Ser.). 240p. 1994. 50.00 (*0-8161-7251-X*, Hall Reference) Macmillan.

Metaphysical Primer: A Guide to Understanding Metaphysics. 2nd rev. ed. Jane L. Robertson & Deborah L. Hughes. (Illus.). 138p. 1996. pap. 12.95 (*1-879203-02-2*) MetaGnosis.

Metaphysical Principles of Infinitesimal Calculus. Rene Guenon. 2000. pap. 19.95 (*0-614-21604-4*, 780) Kazi Pubns.

Metaphysical Properties & Curative Powers of Plants. Franz Hartmann. 1990. pap. 3.95 (*1-55818-138-5*, Sure Fire) Holmes Pub.

Metaphysical Quality of the Tragic: A Study of Sophocles, Giraudoux, & Sartre. Brenda J. Powell. (American University Studies: Comparative Literature: Ser. III, Vol. 27). 213p. (C). 1989. text 40.50 (*0-8204-1068-3*) P Lang Pubng.

Metaphysical Quest: Historical Sources & Contemporary. 2nd ed. Kevin Kennedy. LC 97-73964. 214p. (C). 1997. per. 30.95 (*0-7872-4391-4*, 41439101) Kendall-Hunt.

Metaphysical Quest: Historical Sources & Contemporary Challenges. Arthur Gianelli. 448p. (C). 1994. pap. text, per. 36.95 (*0-8403-9737-2*) Kendall-Hunt.

Metaphysical Raisin. Virginia Terris. 1996. pap. text 5.00 (*1-878173-45-6*) Birnham Wood.

Metaphysical Rebellion in the Works of Emily Bronte: A Reinterpretation. Jill D. Ghnassia. LC 93-28592. 352p. 1994. text 45.00 (*0-312-10221-6*) St Martin.

Metaphysical Song: An Essay on Opera. Gary Tomlinson. LC 98-25780. (Illus.). 192p. 1999. 49.50 (*0-691-00408-0*, Pub. by Princeton U Pr); pap. 18.95 (*0-691-00409-9*, Pub. by Princeton U Pr) Cal Prin Full Svc.

Metaphysical Spiritual Development Course. Esther R. Berlinquette. Ed. by Arden C. Rizer, Jr. (Illus.). 36p. 1998. 10.25 (*0-939795-48-5*) Amer Spirit.

Metaphysical Study of Reincarnation: Concept or Cosmic Reality? Larry W. Smith. (Illus.). 122p. 1996. pap. 9.95 (*1-57914-001-7*) Campbell-Smith.

Metaphysical Tales: Stories. Eugene K. Garber. LC 80-26057. (Associated Writer's Program Ser.: No. 3). 208p. 1981. text 24.95 (*0-8262-0325-6*) U of Mo Pr.

Metaphysical Techniques That Really Work. Audrey C. Davis. 144p. 1996. pap. text 12.95 (*0-87554-597-1*, B939) Valley Sun.

Metaphysical Themes in Thomas Aquinas. John F. Wippel. LC 82-7296. (Studies in Philosophy & the History of Philosophy: Vol. 10). 293p. 1984. reprint ed. pap. 29.95 (*0-8132-0839-4*) Cath U Pr.

Metaphysical Thought of Godfrey of Fontaines: A Study in Late Thirteenth-Century Philosophy. John F. Wippel. LC 80-16900. 449p. reprint ed. pap. 139.20 (*0-7837-4635-0*, 204435900002) Bks Demand.

***Metaphysical Thought of Thomas Aquinas.** John F. Wippel. LC 99-53039. (Monographs of the Society for Medieval & Renaissance Philosophy: Vol. 1). 704p. (C). 2000. 59.95 (*0-8132-0982-X*); pap. 39.95 (*0-8132-0983-8*) Cath U Pr.

Metaphysical to Augustan: Studies in Tone & Sensibility in the 17th Century. Geoffrey Walton. LC 70-158902. 1971. reprint ed. 59.00 (*0-403-01308-9*) Scholarly.

***Metaphysical Touch.** Sylvia Brownrigg. LC 98-48755. 400p. 1999. text 23.00 (*0-374-19965-5*) FS&G.

***Metaphysical Touch.** Sylvia Brownrigg. LC 00-36721. 400p. 2000. pap. 15.00 (*0-312-26357-0*) St Martin.

Metaphysical Tracts by English Philosophers of the 18th Century. Ed. by Samuel Parr. 351p. reprint ed. lib. bdg. 63.70 (*3-487-05311-X*) G Olms Pubs.

Metaphysical Wit. A. J. Smith. (Illus.). 282p. (C). 1992. text 69.95 (*0-521-34027-6*) Cambridge U Pr.

Metaphysically Yours: A Scrutiny of the "Core Concepts" Housed in Our Awareness. Tom Loizos. Date not set. pap. write for info. (*0-9658557-1-6*) T Loizos.

Metaphysicals & Milton. Eustace M. Tillyard. LC 75-31444. 87p. 1976. reprint ed. lib. bdg. 35.00 (*0-8371-8515-7*, TIMM, Greenwood Pr) Greenwood.

Metaphysics. Aristotle. Tr. & Intro. by Joe Sachs. 366p. (C). 1999. text 45.00 (*1-888009-02-0*); pap. text 24.95 (*1-888009-03-9*) Grn Lion Pr.

Metaphysics. Aristotle. LC 99-461806. 560p. 1999. pap. 11.95 (*0-14-044619-2*, PuffinBks) Peng Put Young Read.

Metaphysics. Aristotle. Tr. by Richard Hope. 416p. 1952. pap. text 15.95 (*0-472-06042-2*, 06042, Ann Arbor Bks) U of Mich Pr.

***Metaphysics.** Ed. by David E. Cooper. LC 99-16130. (Philosophy Ser.: Vol. 4). 304p. 2000. text 59.95 (*0-631-21324-4*); pap. text 24.95 (*0-631-21325-2*) Blackwell Pubs.

Metaphysics. D. V. Hamlyn. 237p. 1984. pap. text 21.95 (*0-521-28690-5*) Cambridge U Pr.

Metaphysics. Josiah Royce. Ed. by William E. Hocking et al. LC 97-47449. (SUNY Series in Philosophy). 352p. (C). 1998. text 73.50 (*0-7914-3865-1*); pap. text 24.95 (*0-7914-3866-X*) State U NY Pr.

Metaphysics. Theophrastos. 109p. 1978. 20.00 (*0-89005-254-9*) Ares.

Metaphysics. Theophrastus of Eresus. Tr. & Comment by Marlein Van Raalte. LC 93-4019. (Mnemosyne, Bibliotheca Classica Batava Ser.: No. 125). xvi, 676p. 1993. 189.00 (*90-04-09786-4*) Brill Academic Pubs.

Metaphysics. Peter Van Inwagen. LC 92-28613. (Dimensions of Philosophy Ser.). 240p. (C). 1993. pap. 25.00 (*0-8133-0635-3*, Pub. by Westview) HarpC.

Metaphysics. W. H. Walsh. (Modern Revivals in Philosophy Ser.). 206p. (Orig.). 1991. 51.95 (*0-7512-0019-0*, Pub. by Gregg Revivals) Ashgate Pub Co.

Metaphysics. Aristotle. Tr. & Comment by Hippocrates G. Apostle. LC 79-88598. (Apostle Translations of Aristotle's Works: Vol. 1). 498p. 1979. reprint ed. 40.00 (*0-9602870-0-0*); reprint ed. pap. 20.00 (*0-9602870-1-9*) Peripatetic.

Metaphysics. Aristotle. Tr. by John H. McMahon. LC 91-60430. (Great Books in Philosophy). 322p. (C). 1991. reprint ed. pap. 9.95 (*0-87975-671-3*) Prometheus Bks.

Metaphysics. John Crosby et al. Tr. by William Marshner from GER. (Aletheia-an International Journal of Philosophy: Vol. 1, Pt. 2). 251p. (Orig.). 1981. reprint ed. pap. 500.00 (*0-86663-784-2*) Ide Hse.

Metaphysics . . . rev. ed. Borden P. Bowne. LC 75-948. (Philosophy in America Ser.). reprint ed. 47.50 (*0-404-59072-1*) AMS Pr.

Metaphysics, 2 vols. rev. ed. Aristotle. Ed. by W. David Ross. 1,064p. 1924. text 170.00 (*0-19-814107-6*) OUP.

Metaphysics. 2nd ed. Peter Van Inwagen. (Dimensions of Philosophy Ser.). 240p. 2000. pap. 22.00 (*0-8133-9055-9*); text 60.00 (*0-8133-9054-0*) Westview.

Metaphysics. 4th ed. Richard Taylor. 168p. (C). 1991. pap. text 24.00 (*0-13-567819-6*) P-H.

Metaphysics, Bks. 1-9. Tr. by H. Tredennick. (Loeb Classical Library: No. 271). 514p. 1933. 18.95 (*0-674-99299-7*) HUP.

Metaphysics, Bks. VII-X. Aristotle. Tr. by Montgomery Furth from GRE. LC 84-19159. (HPC Classics Ser.). 166p. (C). 1985. pap. 10.95 (*0-915145-90-1*); lib. bdg. 29.95 (*0-915145-89-8*) Hackett Pub.

Metaphysics, Bks. 10-14. Tr. by H. Tredennick & G. Cyril Armstrong. (Loeb Classical Library: No. 287). 18.95 (*0-674-99317-9*) HUP.

Metaphysics, Vol. 1. Knud Logstrup. Ed. by Russell Dees. (Studies in Philosophy). (Orig.). 1995. pap. text 40.00 (*0-87462-603-X*) Marquette.

Metaphysics, Vol. 2. Knud Logstrup. Ed. by Russell Dees. (Studies in Philosophy). (Orig.). 1995. pap. text 40.00 (*0-87462-607-2*) Marquette.

Metaphysics: A Contemporary Introduction. Michael J. Loux. LC 97-11036. (Routledge Contemporary Introduction to Philosophy Ser.). 256p. (C). 1997. 65.00 (*0-415-14033-1*); pap. 20.99 (*0-415-14034-X*) Routledge.

Metaphysics: A Contemporary Introduction. John F. Post. (Issues in Philosophy Ser.). 213p. (C). 1991. pap. text 16.95 (*1-55778-204-0*) Paragon Hse.

Metaphysics: A Critical Survey of Its Meaning. 2nd enl. ed. T. Ando. 158p. 1974. pap. text 57.00 (*90-247-0007-8*, Pub. by M Nijhoff) Kluwer Academic.

Metaphysics: An Anthology. Ed. by Jaegwon Kim & Ernest Sosa. LC 98-8538. (Blackwell Philosophy Anthologies Ser.). 672p. 1999. 74.95 (*0-631-20278-1*); pap. 34.95 (*0-631-20279-X*) Blackwell Pubs.

Metaphysics: An Introduction. Archie J. Bahm. LC 73-7469. 266p. 1974. pap. 15.00 (*0-911714-17-0*) World Bks.

Metaphysics: An Outline of the History of Being. Mieczyslaw A. Krapiec. Tr. by Theresa Sandok. LC 91-7737. (Catholic Thought from Lublin Ser.). (POL.). XIII, 540p. (C). 1991. text 69.95 (*0-8204-1448-4*) P Lang Pubng.

Metaphysics: Books M & N. Julia Annas. (Clarendon Aristotle Ser.). 240p. 1988. pap. text 32.00 (*0-19-872133-1*) OUP.

Metaphysics: Constructing a World View. William Hasker. LC 83-10693. (Contours of Christian Philosophy Ser.). 132p. (Orig.). (C). 1983. pap. 11.99 (*0-87784-341-4*, 341) InterVarsity.

Metaphysics: Contemporary Readings. Steven Hales. LC 98-40779. 400p. pap. 43.95 (*0-534-55145-9*) Wadsworth Pub.

Metaphysics: The Big Questions. Peter Van Inwagen & Dean W. Zimmerman. LC 98-11440. (Philosophy Ser.). 500p. 1998. 62.95 (*0-631-20587-X*); pap. 29.95 (*0-631-20588-8*) Blackwell Pubs.

Metaphysics: The Elements. Bruce Aune. LC 85-2540. xiv, 235p. 1985. pap. 18.95 (*0-8166-1414-8*) U of Minn Pr.

Metaphysics Book Beta & Book Kappa. Aristotle. Tr. & Comment by Arthur Madigan. LC 99-26129. (Clarendon Aristotle Ser.). 232p. 2000. text 60.00 (*0-19-875105-2*, Clarendon Pr); pap. text 24.95 (*0-19-875106-0*, Clarendon Pr) OUP.

Metaphysics Books Gamma, Delta & Epsilon. 2nd ed. Aristotle. Tr. & Notes by Christopher Kirwan. LC 93-18390. (Clarendon Aristotle Ser.). 264p. (C). 1993. pap. text 28.00 (*0-19-824087-2*, Clarendon Pr) OUP.

Metaphysics Books Zeta & Eta. Aristotle. Tr. & Comment by David Bostock. (Clarendon Aristotle Ser.). 318p. 1994. 65.00 (*0-19-823946-7*, Clarendon Pr); pap. text 28.00 (*0-19-823947-5*, Clarendon Pr) OUP.

Metaphysics Theta 1-3: On the Essence & Actuality of Force. Martin Heidegger & Aristotle. Tr. by Walter Brogan & Peter Warnek. LC 95-834. (Studies in Continental Thought).Tr. of Aristoteles, Metaphysik, Theta 1-3. (ENG & GER.). 192p. 1995. 35.00 (*0-253-32910-8*) Ind U Pr.

Metaphysics - Metaphysica, Griechisch U. Englisch. Theophrast. Ed. by W. D. Ross & F. H. Fobes. xxxii, 87p. 1983. reprint ed. 19.37 (*3-487-01568-4*) G Olms Pubs.

Metaphysics, a Systematic Survey. Johannes A. Peters. LC 63-8144. (Duquesne Studies, Philosophical Ser.: No. 16). 547p. reprint ed. pap. 169.60 (*0-608-30013-6*, 205134200096) Bks Demand.

Metaphysics & Aesthetics in the Works of Eduardo Barrios. John Walker. (Monografias A Ser.: No. 95). 190p. (C). 1983. 58.00 (*0-7293-0160-5*, Pub. by Tamesis Bks Ltd) Boydell & Brewer.

Metaphysics & Belief. Philip Merlan. 102p. 1966. pap. text 57.00 (*90-247-0289-5*) Kluwer Academic.

Metaphysics & British Empiricism. Robert L. Armstrong. LC 78-109602. 187p. reprint ed. pap. 58.00 (*0-8357-8671-4*, 205682700091) Bks Demand.

Metaphysics & Common Sense. Ayers. (Philosophy Ser.). (C). 1997. mass mkt. 29.50 (*0-534-54243-3*) Wadsworth Pub.

Metaphysics & Culture. Louis Dupre. (Aquinas Lectures). 1994. pap. 15.00 (*0-87462-161-5*) Marquette.

Metaphysics & Historicity. Emil L. Fackenheim. LC 61-10054. (Aquinas Lectures). 1961. 15.00 (*0-87462-126-7*) Marquette.

Metaphysics & Ideology. William O. Martin. LC 59-9870. (Aquinas Lectures). 1959. 15.00 (*0-87462-124-0*) Marquette.

Metaphysics & Its Task: The Search for the Categorical Foundation of Knowledge. Jorge J. Gracia. LC 98-48000. (SUNY Series in Philosophy). 224p. (C). 1999. text 54.50 (*0-7914-4213-6*, Suny Pr); pap. text 17.95 (*0-7914-4214-4*, Suny Pr) State U NY Pr.

Metaphysics & Measurements. Alexandre Koyre. LC 92-26656. (Classics in the History & Philosophy of Science Ser.: Vol. 12). 165p. 1992. reprint ed. pap. text 41.00 (*2-88124-575-7*) Gordon & Breach.

Metaphysics & Moral in Marius Victorinus' Commentary on the Letter to the Ephesians Vol. 155: A Contribution to the History of Neoplatonism & Christianity. Stephen A. Cooper. LC 94-16095. (American University Studies: Series V). XIII, 248p. (C). 1996. text 44.95 (*0-8204-2330-0*) P Lang Pubng.

***Metaphysics & Natural Philosophy of John Buridan.** Ed. by J .M .M. H. Thijssen & Jack Zupko. 290p. 2000. 94.00 (*90-04-11514-5*) Brill Academic Pubs.

Metaphysics & Oppression: Heidegger's Challenge to Western Philosophy. John McCumber. LC 98-45926. (Studies in Continental Thought). (Illus.). 525p. 1999. pap. 24.95 (*0-253-21316-9*); text 49.95 (*0-253-33473-X*) Ind U Pr.

Metaphysics & Philosophy of Science in the Seventeenth & Eighteenth Centuries: Essays in Honour of Gerd Buchdahl. Roger S. Woolhouse. 372p. (C). 1988. text 201.00 (*90-277-2743-0*) Kluwer Academic.

Metaphysics & the Disunity of Scientific Knowledge. Steve Clarke. LC 97-78320. (Avebury Series in Philosophy). 148p. 1998. text 59.95 (*1-85972-538-4*, Pub. by Ashgate Pub) Ashgate Pub Co.

Metaphysics & the Idea of God. Wolfhart Pannenberg. 184p. 1998. 37.95 (*0-567-09570-3*, Pub. by T & T Clark) Bks Intl VA.

Metaphysics & the Origin of Species. Michael T. Ghiselin. LC 96-38957. (SUNY Series in Philosophy & Biology). 377p. (C). 1997. text 75.50 (*0-7914-3467-2*); pap. text 25.95 (*0-7914-3468-0*) State U NY Pr.

Metaphysics As a Guide to Morals: Philosophical Reflections. Iris Murdoch. 784p. 1994. pap. 15.95 (*0-14-017232-7*, Penguin Bks) Viking Penguin.

Metaphysics As Foundation: Essays in Honor of Ivor Leclerc. Ed. by Paul A. Bogaard & Gordon Treash. LC 91-43054. 358p. (C). 1992. pap. text 21.95 (*0-7914-1258-X*) State U NY Pr.

Metaphysics As Rhetoric: Alfarabi's Summary of Plato's "Laws" Joshua Parens. LC 94-49027. (SUNY Series in Middle Eastern Studies). 195p. (C). 1995. text 54.50 (*0-7914-2573-8*); pap. text 17.95 (*0-7914-2574-6*) State U NY Pr.

Metaphysics As Rhetoric: Alfarabi's Summary of Plato's Laws. Joshua Parens. 195p. 1996. pap. 17.95 (*0-614-21233-2*, 1489) Kazi Pubns.

Metaphysics, Epistemology, Natural Philosophy see Classical Philosophy: Collected Papers

Metaphysics for Christians: Towards a Pluralistic Unity of Humankind. Eric W. Robinson. (Illus.). 118p. (Orig.). 1996. pap. 9.95 (*1-57502-118-8*) Morris Pubng.

Metaphysics for Theology: A Study of Some Problems in the Later Philosophy of Alfred North Whitehead & Its Applications to Issues in Contemporary Theology. Sten M. Philipson. (Studia Doctrinae Christianae Upsaliensia: No. 22). 174p. (Orig.). 1982. pap. 31.00 (*91-554-1246-7*, Pub. by Uppsala Univ Acta Univ Uppsaliensis) Coronet Bks.

An Asterisk (*) at the beginning of an entry indicates that the title is appearing for the first time.

Metaphysics Four in One see Metafisica 4 en 1

Metaphysics in Islamic Philosophy. Fadlou Shehadi. LC 81-18069. 168p. 1983. 35.00 (0-88206-049-X) Caravan Bks.

Metaphysics in Islamic Philosophy. Fadlou Shehadi. 168p. 1996. 40.00 (0-614-21312-6, 1368) Kazi Pubns.

Metaphysics in Midwestern America. Melinda B. Wagner. LC 83-2158. 241p. reprint ed. pap. 74.80 (0-608-09893-0, 206985900006) Bks Demand.

Metaphysics in Ordinary Language. Stanley Rosen. LC 98-26477. 304p. 1999. 30.00 (0-300-07478-6) Yale U Pr.

Metaphysics in the Midwest: Stories. deluxe ed. Curtis White. (New American Fiction Ser.: No. 18). 208p. 1988. 30.00 (1-55713-046-9) Sun & Moon CA.

Metaphysics, Materialism, & the Evolution of the Mind: Early Writings of Charles Darwin. Charles Darwin. LC 80-15763. 1994. pap. text 6.95 (0-226-13659-0, P906) U Ch Pr.

Metaphysics of Aquinas: A Summary of Aquinas' Exposition of Aristotle's Metaphysics. Pierre Conway. Ed. by Mary M. Spangler. (C). 1996. pap. text 36.50 (0-7618-0293-2); lib. bdg. 54.00 (0-7618-0292-4) U Pr of Amer.

Metaphysics of Being of St. Thomas Aquinas in a Historical Perspective. Leo J. Elders. LC 92-14864. (Studien und Texte zur Geistesgeschichte des Mittelalters Ser.: Bd. 34). viii, 318p. 1992. 119.00 (90-04-09645-0) Brill Academic Pubs.

Metaphysics of Byron: A Reading of the Plays. John W. Ehrstine. (De Proprietatibus Litterarum, Ser. Practica: No. 120). 145p. (Orig.). 1976. pap. text 40.00 (90-279-3483-5) Mouton.

Metaphysics of Consciousness. William Seager. LC 91-16739. (Philosophical Issues in Science Ser.). 256p. (C). (gr. 13). 1991. 75.00 (0-415-06357-4, A6496) Routledge.

Metaphysics of Creation: Aquinas's Natural Theology in Summa Contra Gentiles Ii. Norman Kretzmann. LC 98-49343. 498p. 1999. text 65.00 (0-19-823787-1) OUP.

Metaphysics of Darkness: A Study in the Unity & Development of Conrad's Fiction. Royal Roussel. LC 74-146458. 208p. reprint ed. pap. 64.50 (0-8357-9277-3, 201100400071) Bks Demand.

Metaphysics of Death. Ed. by John M. Fischer. (Series in Philosophy). xviii, 430p. (C). 1993. 49.50 (0-8047-2046-0); pap. 17.95 (0-8047-2104-1) Stanford U Pr.

Metaphysics of Divorce. Ted Farrell & Lorrie Mackenzie. LC 99-94254. (Illus.). 230p. (Orig.). 1999. pap. 12.95 (0-9667002-2-8) Loridad.

Metaphysics of Edmund Burke. Joseph Pappin, III. LC 92-41383. xx, 188p. 1993. 30.00 (0-8232-1365-X); pap. 19.95 (0-8232-1366-8) Fordham.

Metaphysics of Epistemology: Lectures by Wilfrid Sellars. Wilfrid Sellars. Ed. by P. V. Amaral. xii, 354p. (Orig.). 1989. pap. text 18.00 (0-917930-54-1); lib. bdg. 35.00 (0-917930-94-0) Ridgeview.

Metaphysics of Experience. Leslie Stevenson. 1982. pap. 15.95 (0-19-824699-4) OUP.

Metaphysics of Experience: A Companion to Whitehead's Process & Reality. 2nd rev. ed. Elizabeth Kraus. LC 97-29490. (American Philosophy Ser.: No. 9). xxi, 200p. 1997. 35.00 (0-8232-1795-7) Fordham.

Metaphysics of Experience: A Companion to Whitehead's Process & Reality. 2nd rev. ed. Elizabeth M. Kraus. LC 97-29490. (American Philosophy Ser.: No. 9). xxi, 200p. 1997. pap. 17.00 (0-8232-1796-5) Fordham.

Metaphysics of Free Will: An Essay on Control. John M. Fischer. (Aristotelian Society Ser.). 273p. 1996. pap. 28.95 (1-55786-857-3) Blackwell Pubs.

Metaphysics of G. E. Moore. David O'Connor. (Philosophical Studies: No. 25). 190p. 1982. text 112.50 (90-277-1352-9, D Reidel) Kluwer Academic.

Metaphysics of George Berkeley (1685-1753), Irish Philosopher. F. T. Kingston. LC 92-17533. (Studies in the History of Philosophy: Vol. 28). 220p. 1992. lib. bdg. 89.95 (0-7734-9561-4) E Mellen.

Metaphysics of Good & Evil According to Suarez. Ed. by Jorge J. Gracia & Douglas Davis. (Analytica Ser.). 320p. (C). 1989. 66.00 (3-88405-066-4) Philosophia Pr.

Metaphysics of Haji Mulla Hadi Sabzavari. Tr. by Toshihiko Izutsu. 248p. 1996. 50.00 (0-614-21313-4, 1367) Kazi Pubns.

Metaphysics of Haji Mulla Hadi Sabzavari. Hadi I. Sabzavari. Tr. by Toshihiko Izutsu & Mehdi Mohaghegh from PER. LC 76-18174. 248p. 1977. lib. bdg. 35.00 (0-88206-011-2) Caravan Bks.

Metaphysics of Insect Life & Other Essays. David M. Spooner. 104p. 1995. text 64.95 (1-883255-95-3); pap. text 49.95 (1-883255-94-5) Intl Scholars.

Metaphysics of Iqbal. Ishrat Hasan. 96p. 1985. 14.50 (1-56744-326-5) Kazi Pubns.

Metaphysics of Liberty. Frank Forman. 214p. (C). 1989. text 127.50 (0-7923-0080-7) Kluwer Academic.

Metaphysics of Logical Positivism. Gustav Bergmann. LC 77-28139. 340p. 1978. reprint ed. lib. bdg. 35.00 (0-313-20235-4, BEML, Greenwood Pr) Greenwood.

***Metaphysics of Love: Gender & Transcendence in Levinas.** Stella Sandford. LC 00-31309. 2000. pap. write for info. (0-485-12163-8, Pub. by Athlone Pr) Humanities.

***Metaphysics of Mass Art Vol. 1: Cultural Ontology: Mysticism, Mexico & English Literature.** C. J. Lee. LC 99-13416. (Studies in Art & Religious Interpretation: Vol. 24A). 168p. 1999. lib. bdg. 79.95 (0-7734-8182-6) E Mellen.

***Metaphysics of Mass Art Vol. II: Cultural Ontology:Madness & the Savage Indigenous Peoples of the Americas & the Psychology of the Observer in U. S. Film.** C. J. Lee. LC 99-13416. (Studies in Art & Religious Interpretation: Vol. 24B). 284p. 1999. lib. bdg. 89.95 (0-7734-8184-2) E Mellen.

Metaphysics of Meaning. Jerrold J. Katz. (Illus.). 372p. 1992. reprint ed. pap. text 21.00 (0-262-61082-5, Bradford Bks) MIT Pr.

Metaphysics of Mind. Anthony Kenny. 184p. 1990. 45.00 (0-19-824965-9) OUP.

Metaphysics of Mind. Anthony Kenny. 176p. 1992. reprint ed. pap. 11.95 (0-19-283070-8) OUP.

Metaphysics of Natural Complexes. expanded ed. Justus Buchler. Ed. by Kathleen Wallace et al. LC 89-4416. 308p. (C). 1989. pap. text 21.95 (0-7914-0183-9) State U NY Pr.

Metaphysics of Naturalism. Sterling P. Lamprecht. LC 67-18049. (Century Philosophy Ser.). 1967. 42.50 (0-89197-302-8) Irvington.

Metaphysics of Pragmatism. Sidney Hook. LC 96-8792. 156p. 1996. 39.95 (1-57392-075-4) Prometheus Bks.

Metaphysics of Pragmatism. Sidney Hook. LC 75-3195. reprint ed. 31.50 (0-404-59196-5) AMS Pr.

Metaphysics of Raw Foods. Stella McDermott. 78p. 1996. reprint ed. spiral bd. 11.50 (0-7873-0597-9) Hlth Research.

Metaphysics of Raw Foods (1919) Stella McDermott. 80p. 1996. reprint ed. pap. 9.95 (1-56459-860-8) Kessinger Pub.

Metaphysics of Reading Underlying Dante's "Commedia" The "Ingegno" Paul A. Dumol. LC 97-8501. (Studies in the Humanities: Literature-Politics-Society: No. 35). XVI, 239p. (C). 1999. 49.95 (0-8204-3781-6) P Lang Pubng.

Metaphysics of Religious Belief: An Essay on the Miraculous. A. P. Shooman. (Avebury Series in Philosophy). 175p. 1990. text 82.95 (0-566-07135-5, Pub. by Avebry) Ashgate Pub Co.

Metaphysics of Rumi. Khalifa Abdul Karim. 158p. 1985. 14.50 (1-56744-327-3) Kazi Pubns.

Metaphysics of Science & Freedom: From Descartes to Kant to Hegel. Wayne Cristaudo. (Avebury Series in Philosophy). 187p. 1991. text 82.95 (1-85628-132-9, Pub. by Avebry) Ashgate Pub Co.

Metaphysics of Second Intelligibles in Islamic Philosophy. Muhammad Fana'i. 1999. pap. 17.00 (1-883058-32-5, Nur) Global Pubns.

Metaphysics of Self & World. E. M. Adams. 250p. 1991. 59.95 (0-87722-784-5) Temple U Pr.

Metaphysics of Sound in Wallace Stevens. Anca Rosu. LC 94-43107. 200p. 1995. text 39.95 (0-8173-0797-4) U of Ala Pr.

Metaphysics of Substance: ACPA Proceedings, 1987, Vol. 61. Ed. by Daniel O. Dahlstrom. 250p. (Orig.). 1987. pap. 20.00 (0-918090-21-0) Am Cath Philo.

Metaphysics of the Computer: The Reality Machine & a New Science for the Holistic Age. D. J. Moore. LC 92-10574. 392p. 1992. lib. bdg. 99.95 (0-7734-2302-8) E Mellen.

***Metaphysics of the Moral Law: Kant's Deduction of Freedom.** Carol W. Voeller. (Studies in Ethics). 192p. 1999. 50.00 (0-8153-3772-8) Garland.

Metaphysics of the Social World. David-Hillel Ruben. 189p. (C). 1985. text 24.00 (0-685-46216-1) B&N Imports.

Metaphysics of the Spirit: Facets of Recent Indian Philosophy, No. 1. Ed. by S. P. Dubey. (C). 1994. 19.50 (81-85636-04-4, Pub. by M Manoharial) S Asia.

Metaphysics of Theism: Auinas's Natural Theology in Summa Contra Gentiles I, Vol. 1. Norman Kretzmann. LC 96-26276. 314p. 1997. text 45.00 (0-19-823660-3) OUP.

Metaphysics of Transcedental Subjectivity: Descartes, Kant & W. Sellars. Joseph C. Evans, Jr. (Bochumer Studien zur Philisophie Ser.: Vol. 5). xi, 138p. 1984. 35.00 (90-6032-256-8, Pub. by B R Gruner) Humanities.

Metaphysics of Virtual Reality. Michael Heim. 208p. 1994. reprint ed. pap. 12.95 (0-19-509258-9) OUP.

Metaphysics, Reference, & Language. James W. Cornman. LC 66-21512. 310p. reprint ed. pap. 96.10 (0-8357-8739-7, 203369700087) Bks Demand.

Metaphysics to Metafictions: Hegel, Nietzsche, & the End of Philosophy. Paul S. Miklowitz. LC 97-35112. (Series in Hegelian Studies). 256p. (C). 1998. text 57.50 (0-7914-3877-5); pap. text 18.95 (0-7914-3878-3) State U NY Pr.

Metaphysik, Kunst und Sprache beim Fruhen Nietzsche. Thomas Boning. (Monographien und Texte zur Nietzsche-Forschung Ser.: Vol. 20). (GER.). xiv, 518p. (C). 1988. lib. bdg. 192.35 (3-11-011463-1) De Gruyter.

Metaphysique De Christian Wolff, 2 vols., Set. Jean Ecole. (Christian Wolff, Gesammelte Werke, Materialien und Dokumente Ser.: Vol. III, No. 12.1-12.2). 703p. 1990. write for info. (3-487-09306-5) G Olms Pubs.

Metaphysique De Christian Wolff, 2 vols., Set. Christian Wolff. Ed. by Jean Ecole. (Gesammelte Werke Abteilung: Ergaenzungsreihe: Materialien und Dokumente Ser. Three: Pts. 12.1 & 12.2). 704p. 1990. write for info. (3-487-09207-7) G Olms Pubs.

Metaphysique d'Ibn Gabirol et de la Tradition Platonicienne. Fernand Brunner. Ed. by Daniel Schulthess. LC 97-26921. (Variorum Collected Studies Ser.: Vol. 589). 384p. 1997. text 115.95 (0-86078-654-4, Pub. by Ashgate Pub) Ashgate Pub Co.

Metaphysische Anfangsgrunde der Naturwissenschaft see Kant's Theory of Natural Science: Translation Analytic Introduction & Commentary by Alfred E. & Maria G. Miller

Metaphysische Kritik des Subjekts Bei A. N. Whitehead. Maria-Sibylla Lotter. (Studien und Materialien Zur Geschichte der Philosophie: Band 43). (GER.). viii, 270p. 1996. write for info. (3-487-10155-6) G Olms Pubs.

Metaphysische und transzendentale Dynamik in Kant opus postumum. Burkhard Tuschling. (Quellen und Studien zur Philosophie: Vol. 3). 224p. (C). 1971. 70.00 (3-11-001889-6) De Gruyter.

***Metaplanetary.** Tony Daniel. 2001. write for info. (0-06-105142-X) HarpC.

Metaplectic Groups & Segal Algebra. H. Reiter. (Lecture Notes in Mathematics Ser.: Vol. 1382). xi, 128p. 1989. 29.95 (0-387-51417-1) Spr-Verlag.

Metaplectic Representation, MPC Structures & Geometric Quantization. P. Robinson & J. Rawnsley. LC 89-15191. (Memoirs Ser.: Vol. 81/410). 93p. 1989. pap. 18.00 (0-8218-2473-2, MEMO/81/410) Am Math.

Metapoesis: The Russian Tradition from Pushkin to Chekov. Michael C. Finke. LC 94-38198. (Sound & Meaning: The Roman Jakobson Series in Linguistics & Poetics). 240p. 1995. text 49.95 (0-8223-1556-4); pap. text 18.95 (0-8223-1567-X) Duke.

Metapoetics of the Passage: Architextures in Surrealism & After. Mary A. Caws. LC 80-54468. (Illus.). 218p. reprint ed. pap. 67.60 (0-8357-6511-3, 203588200097) Bks Demand.

Metapop: Self-Referentiality in Contemporary American Popular Culture. Michael Dunne. LC 91-35995. (Studies in Popular Culture). 208p. 1992. text 30.00 (0-87805-548-7) U Pr of Miss.

Metapopulation Biology: Ecology, Genetics, & Evolution. Ed. by Ilkka A. Hanski & Michael E. Gilpin. (Illus.). 512p. 1997. pap. text 50.00 (0-12-323446-8) Morgan Kaufmann.

Metapopulation Ecology. Ilkka A. Hanski. LC 98-31723. (Oxford Series in Ecology & Evolution). (Illus.). 324p. 1999. pap. text 45.00 (0-19-854065-5) OUP.

Metapopulations & Wildlife Conservation. Ed. by Dale R. McCullogh. 432p. (C). 1996. text 58.00 (1-55963-457-X); pap. text 29.95 (1-55963-458-8) Island Pr.

Metaporfosis. deluxe limited ed. Jose Corredor-Matheos. (Ediciones Especiales y de Bibliofilo Ser.). (SPA., Illus.). 120p. 1993. 7500.00 (84-343-0271-3) Elliots Bks.

Metaprograms. Wyatt Woodsmall. (Advanced Neuro Linguistic Programming (NLP) Applications Ser.). 115p. 1998. spiral bd. 35.00 (1-892876-03-5) Next Step Pr.

Metapsychologie. Sigmund Freud. (FRE.). 1985. pap. 12.95 (0-7859-2800-6) Fr & Eur.

Metapsychology in Psychological Practice. Frank A. Gerbode & Gerald D. French. 300p. 1996. lib. bdg. 39.95 (1-57444-050-0, SL0500) St Lucie Pr.

***Metarepresentation: A Relevance-Theory Approach.** Eun-Ju Noh. LC 00-23580. (Pragmatics & Beyond New Ser.: Vol. 69). xii, 236p. 2000. 75.00 (1-55619-947-3) J Benjamins Pubng Co.

***Metarepresentations: A Multidisciplinary Perspective.** Ed. by Dan Sperber. (Vancouver Studies in Cognitive Science: Vol. 10). (Illus.). 480p. 2000. pap. text 29.95 (0-19-514115-6) OUP.

***Metarepresentations: A Multidisciplinary Perspective.** Ed. by Daniel Sperber. (Vancouver Studies in Cognitive Science: Vol. 10). (Illus.). 480p. 2000. text 75.00 (0-19-514114-8) OUP.

Metarules of Paninian Grammar Pts. 1 & 2: Vyadi's Paribhasavrtti. Dominik Wujastyk. (SAN.). 1993. pap. 77.00 (90-6980-034-9, Pub. by Egbert Forsten) Hod1der & Stoughton.

Metary Eleutheron Kai Doulon & Die Lakesdaemonischen Perickon, 2 vols. Detlef Lotze & Franz Hample. Ed. by Gregory Vlastos. LC 78-14616. (Morals & Law in Ancient Greece Ser.). 1979. reprint ed. lib. bdg. 17.95 (0-405-11591-1) Ayer.

Metas Comunicativas para Negocios (Spanish for Business Purposes) Sharon Foerster et al. Ed. by Judy Wetherington. (ENG & SPA.). 226p. 1998. pap. 21.25 (0-07-229552-X) McGraw.

Metas Peligrosas. Joseph Stowell. (SPA.). 208p. 1995. pap. 8.99 (0-8254-1690-6, Edit Portavoz) Kregel.

Metasciences Textbook. Arden C. Rizer, Jr. Ed. by A. S. A. Educations & Research Staff. (Orig.). 1987. pap. 23.50 (0-939795-32-9) Amer Spirit.

Metaskills: The Spiritual Art of Therapy. Amy Mindell. LC 94-68554. 192p. (Orig.). 1995. pap. 12.95 (1-56184-119-6) New Falcon Pubns.

Metasoft Primer. A. Blikle. (Lecture Notes in Computer Science Ser.: Vol. 288). xiii, 140p. 1987. 30.00 (0-387-18657-3) Spr-Verlag.

Metaspaces. Raoul Bunschoten. (Illus.). 32p. pap. 23.00 (1-901033-80-5, Pub. by Black Dog Pubg) RAM Publications.

Metastability & Incompletely Posed Problems. Ed. by Stuart S. Antman et al. (IMA Volumes in Mathematics & Its Applications Ser.: Vol. 3). (Illus.). 367p. 1986. 69.95 (0-387-96462-2) Spr-Verlag.

Metastable Homotopy of S-to-the-N. Mark E. Mahowald. LC 52-42839. (Memoirs Ser.: No. 1/72). 81p. 1967. pap. 16.00 (0-8218-1272-6, MEMO/1/72) Am Math.

Metastable Liquids: Concepts & Principles. Pablo G. Debenedetti. LC 96-18027. (Physical Chemistry: Science & Engineering Ser.). 400p. 1997. text 69.50 (0-691-08595-1, Pub. by Princeton U Pr) Cal Prin Full Svc.

Metastable, Mechanically Alloyed & Nanocrystalline Materials: ISMANAM-95. Ed. by Robert Schulz. (Materials Science Ser.: 225-227). (Illus.). 950p. 1996. text 272.00 (0-87849-738-2, Pub. by Trans T Pub) Enfield Pubs NH.

***Metastable, Mechanically Alloyed & Nanocrystalline Materials: ISMANAM 98: Proceedings of the International Symposium on Metastable, Mechanical Alloyed & Nanocrystalline Materials (ISMANAM 98), Held in Wollongong (Sydney), Australia, December 1998.** Ed. by A. Calka & D. Wexler. (Materials Science Forum Ser.: Vols. 312-314). (Illus.). 688p. (C). 1999. pap. 234.00 (0-87849-838-9, Pub. by Trans T Pub) Enfield Pubs NH.

Metastable Microstructures. Ed. by D. Banerjee & Loren Jacobson. 351p. 1993. text 75.00 (1-881570-06-1) Science Pubs.

Metastable Phases & Microstructures: Materials Research Society Symposium Proceedings. Ed. by Rudiger Bormann et al. (MRS Symposium Proceedings Ser.: Vol. 400). 368p. 1996. 73.00 (1-55899-303-7, 400) Materials Res.

Metastases of Enjoyment: Six Essays on Women & Causality. Slavoj Zizek. LC 94-19936. (Wo Es War Ser.). 288p. (C). 1994. pap. 20.00 (0-86091-688-X, B4625, Pub. by Verso) Norton.

Metastases of Enjoyment: Six Essays on Women & Causality. Slavoj Zizek. LC 94-19936. (Wo Es War Ser.). 288p. (C). (gr. 13). 1994. 60.00 (0-86091-444-5, B4621, Pub. by Verso) Norton.

Metastasis. CIBA Foundation Staff. LC 88-8494. (CIBA Foundation Symposium Ser.: No. 141). 266p. 1989. 128.00 (0-471-91513-0) Wiley.

Metastasis: Basic Research & Its Clinical Application. Ed. by H. Rabes et al. (Beitraege Zur Onkologie, Contributions to Oncology Ser.: Vol. 44). x, 394p. 1992. 68.75 (3-8055-5610-1) S Karger.

Metastasis-Dissemination. Ed. by Elizier Gorelik. (Cancer Growth & Progression Ser.). (C). 1989. text 207.50 (0-89838-997-6) Kluwer Academic.

***Metastasis Methods & Protocols.** Ed. by Susan Brooks & Udo Schumacher. (Methods in Molecular Medicine Ser.). 500p. 2000. 99.50 (0-89603-610-3) Humana.

Metastatic Bone Disease: Fundamental & Clinical Aspects. Ed. by I. J. Diel et al. LC 93-46632. 1993. write for info. (3-540-57356-9); write for info. (0-387-57356-9) Spr-Verlag.

***Metastatic Disease of the Musculoskeletal System.** Ed. by John Heinerman et al. (Illus.). 400p. 2000. text 125.00 (1-57626-088-7) Quality Med Pub.

Metasystems Methodology: New Synthesis & Unification. A. D. Hall, III & G. J. Klir. LC 88-25441. (IFSR International Series on Systems Science & Engineering: Vol. 3). (Illus.). 526p. 1989. 236.00 (0-08-036956-1, Pub. by Pergamon Repr) Franklin.

Metasystox-R, Applied in Mauget Injectors, Ineffective in Protecting Individual Ponderosa Pines from Western Pine Beetles. Michael I. Haverty et al. (Illus.). 12p. 1997. reprint ed. pap. 2.00 (0-89904-648-7, Ecosytems Resrch) Crumb Elbow Pub.

Metataxis. Klaus Schubert. (Distributed Language Translation Ser.). vi, 250p. 1987. 90.75 (90-6765-358-6); pap. 65.40 (90-6765-359-4) Mouton.

Metataxis in Practice: Dependency Syntax for Multilingual Machine Translation. Ed. by Dan Maxwell & Klaus Schubert. (Distributed Language Translation Ser.). 323p. (Orig.). (C). 1989. 98.60 (90-6765-422-1); pap. 80.00 (90-6765-421-3) Mouton.

***Metateaching & the Instructional Map.** William M. Timpson. LC 99-16524. (Teaching Techniques/Strategies Ser.). 1999. write for info. (1-891859-29-3) Atwood Pub LLC.

Metateatro y la Dramatica de Vargas Llosa: Hacia una Poetica del Espectador. Oscar Rivera-Rodas. LC 92-33765. (Purdue University Monographs in Romance Languages: Vol. 41). viii, 213p. 1992. 65.00 (1-55619-310-6); pap. 27.95 (1-55619-311-4) J Benjamins Pubng Co.

Metatheater: The Example of Shakespeare. Judd D. Hubert. LC 90-22718. 171p. 1991. reprint ed. pap. 53.10 (0-608-03480-0, 206419200008) Bks Demand.

Metatheater & Sanskrit Drama. Michael Lockwood & A. Vishnu Bhat. 174p. (C). 1995. 29.50 (81-215-0679-4, Pub. by M Manoharial) Coronet Bks.

Metatheorizing. Ed. by George Ritzer. LC 91-44206. (Key Issues in Sociological Theory Ser.: No. 6). 178p. 1992. reprint ed. pap. 55.20 (0-608-04320-6, 206509900012) Bks Demand.

Metatheorizing: A Coming of Age. Ed. by George Ritzer. (Key Issues in Sociological Theory Ser.: Vol. 6). (Illus.). 200p. (C). 1992. 56.00 (0-8039-3990-6); pap. 26.00 (0-8039-3991-4) Sage.

Metatheory in Social Science: Pluralisms & Subjectivities. Ed. by Donald W. Fiske & Richard A. Shweder. LC 85-16383. (Illus.). 400p. 1986. pap. text 29.00 (0-226-25192-6) U Ch Pr.

Metatheory in Social Science: Pluralisms & Subjectivities. Ed. by Donald W. Fiske & Richard A. Shweder. LC 85-16383. (Illus.). 400p. 1986. lib. bdg. 39.00 (0-226-25191-8) U Ch Pr.

Metathesis Polymerization of Olefins & Polymerization of Alkynes. Yavuz I. Glu. LC 97-48766. (NATO ASI Series, Series C, Mathematical & Physical Sciences). 443p. 1998. 214.00 (0-7923-4941-5) Kluwer Academic.

Metatron: The Recording Angel. Sol Yurick. 169p. Date not set. 7.00 (0-936756-07-1) Autonomedia.

Metatropic Glutamate Receptors & Brain Function. Ed. by F. Moroni et al. (Portland Press Proceedings Ser.: Vol. 12). 318p. 1998. text 110.50 (1-85578-117-4, Pub. by Portland Pr Ltd) Ashgate Pub Co.

***Metcalfe Family Album: Six Generations of Traditions & Memories.** Sallyann J. Murphey. LC 99-89588. (Illus.). 256p. 1999. 29.95 (0-8118-2097-1) Chronicle Bks.

Metcalfe Lineages. 2nd ed. Howard H. Metcalfe. 670p. 1995. reprint ed. pap. 99.50 (0-8328-4882-4); reprint ed. lib. bdg. 109.50 (0-8328-4881-6) Higginson Bk Co.

Metegee: The History & Culture of Guyana. Ovid S. Abrams. LC 98-73091. 320p. 1998. pap. 24.95 (0-9660707-4-7, Ashanti Bks) Eldorado Pubns.

Meteor! Patricia Polacco. (Illus.). 32p. (J). (ps-3). 1996. pap. 6.99 (0-698-11410-8, PapStar) Peng Put Young Read.

Meteor! Patricia Polacco. (ps-3). 1999. 16.99 (0-399-23384-9) Putnam Pub Group.

Meteor! Patricia Polacco. (J). 1996. 11.15 (0-606-05465-0, Pub. by Turtleback) Demco.

***Meteor Book: Construction, Manipulation & Performance.** Rhys Thomas. (Illus.). 66p. 1999. write for info. (0-943292-26-3, 601, Flaming Sparrow) Foreworks.

M

An Asterisk (*) at the beginning of an entry indicates that the title is appearing for the first time.

Meteor Burst Communications: Theory & Practice. Donald L. Schilling. LC 91-42445. (Series in Telecommunications). 480p. 1993. 185.00 (*0-471-52212-0*) Wiley.

Meteor Burst Communications Disk. Jacob Z. Schanker. (Artech House Telecom Engineering Library). 167p. 1990. disk 11.00 (*0-89006-445-8*) Artech Hse.

Meteor in Action. Glenn Ashley. (Aircraft in Action Ser.). (Illus.). 50p. 1995. pap. 9.95 (*0-89747-332-9*) Squad Sig Pubns.

***Meteor in the Madhouse.** Leon Forrest. 2000. 26.95 (*0-8101-5114-6*) Northwestern U Pr.

***Meteor Shining Brightly: Essays on Major General Patrick R. Cleburne.** Mauriel P. Joslyn. 2000. pap. 22.95 (*0-86554-693-2*, P210) Mercer Univ Pr.

Meteor Shining Brightly: Essays on Major General Patrick R. Cleburne. unabridged ed. Mauriel P. Joslyn. LC 97-67004. (Illus.). 328p. 1998. 29.95 (*0-9662903-0-5*) Terrell Hse Pub.

Meteores. Michel Tournier. (FRE.). 1977. pap. 16.95 (*0-8288-3798-8*, M5477) Fr & Eur.

Meteores. Michel Tournier. (Folio Ser.: No. 905). (FRE.). 628p. 1975. pap. 13.95 (*2-07-036905-6*) Schoenhof.

***Meteorite! The Last Days of the Dinosaurs.** Richard Norris. (Turnstone Ocean Explorer Ser.). 64p. (YA). (gr. 5-9). 1999. pap. 8.95 (*0-7398-1241-6*) Raintree Steck-V.

***Meteorite! The Last Days of the Dinosaurs.** Richard Norris. LC 99-27285. (Turnstone Ocean Explorer Bks.). 64p. (YA). (gr. 6-8). 2000. 27.11 (*0-7398-1240-8*) Raintree Steck-V.

Meteorite & Tektite Collectors Handbook. Philip M. Bagnall. 1991. 24.95 (*0-943396-31-X*) Willmann-Bell.

Meteorite Craters. Kathleen Mark. LC 86-19244. 288p. 1995. pap. 19.95 (*0-8165-1568-9*) U of Ariz Pr.

Meteorite Craters & Impact Structures of the Earth. Paul Hodge. LC 93-21350. (Illus.). 132p. (C). 1994. text 49.95 (*0-521-36092-7*) Cambridge U Pr.

Meteorite Research: Proceedings of the Symposium, Vienna, Austria, Aug. 7-13, 1968. Meteorite Research Symposium Staff. Ed. by P. N. Millman. (Astrophysic & Space Science Library: No.12). 941p. 1969. text 239.50 (*90-277-0132-6*) Kluwer Academic.

Meteoritenkunde, Set, Teile I-III. E. Cohen. (Chronostratigraphie und Neostratotypen Ser.). (DUT.). 158.00 (*3-510-99015-3*, Pub. by E Schweizerbartsche) Balogh.

Meteorites. Robert Hutchinson & Andrew Graham. LC 93-15955. (Illus.). 60p. (J). (gr. 7). 1993. pap. 12.95 (*0-8069-0489-5*) Sterling.

Meteorites. Fritz Heide. LC 63-20906. 154p. reprint ed. 47.80 (*0-8357-9649-3*, 201698700005) Bks Demand.

Meteorites: An Introduction. Fritz Heide. (Illus.). 241p. 1995. 24.95 (*0-387-58105-7*) Spr-Verlag.

Meteorites: Messengers from Space. Fritz Heide. LC 94-40204. 1995. pap. text 24.95 (*3-540-58105-7*) Spr-Verlag.

Meteorites: Their Record of Early Solar-System History. John T. Wasson. LC 85-1484. (Illus.). 267p. (C). 1985. text 28.00 (*0-7167-1700-X*) W H Freeman.

Meteorites & Their Parent Planets. Harry Y. McSween, Jr. LC 98-26494. (Illus.). 254p. (C). 1999. pap. text 29.95 (*0-521-58751-4*) Cambridge U Pr.

Meteorites & Their Parent Planets. 2nd ed. Harry Y. McSween, Jr. LC 98-26494. (Illus.). 304p. (C). 1999. text 74.95 (*0-521-58303-9*) Cambridge U Pr.

Meteorologica. Tr. by H. D. Lee. (Loeb Classical Library: No. 337). 468p. 1952. 18.95 (*0-674-99436-1*) HUP.

Meteorological Abstracts & Bibliography: Cumulative Index, Authors-L-Z (1950-1959), 3 vols., Set. Ed. by Malcolm Rigby. 1724p. (Orig.). 1963. pap. write for info. (*0-933876-92-0*) Am Meteorological.

Meteorological Abstracts & Bibliography Vols. 1-10: Cumulative Geographic Index, 1950-1959. Malcolm Rigby. 412p. (Orig.). 1963. pap. 210.00 (*0-933876-93-9*) Am Meteorological.

Meteorological Abstracts & Bibliography Vols. 1-10: Cumulative Index, Authors-A-K, 3 vols., Set. Ed. by Malcolm Rigby. 839p. (Orig.). 1963. pap. write for info. (*0-933876-91-2*) Am Meteorological.

Meteorological & Geoastrophysical Abstracts: Cumulative Author Index, 1970-1975, Vols. 21-26. Malcolm Rigby. 647p. 1978. text 205.00 (*0-933876-94-7*) Am Meteorological.

Meteorological & Geoastrophysical Abstracts: Cumulative Indexes, 1950-1959, Geographic, 1-10, Set. 205.00 (*0-685-73038-7*) Am Meteorological.

Meteorological & Geoastrophysical Abstracts Vols. 21-26: Cumulative Subject Index. 1978. reprint ed. 205.00 (*0-933876-95-5*) Am Meteorological.

Meteorological Aspects of Acid Rain. Ed. by Chandrakant Bhumralkar & John I. Teasley. (Acid Precipitation Ser.: Vol. 1). 200p. 1984. 79.95 (*0-250-40566-0*) Buttrwrth-Heinemann.

Meteorological Aspects of Emergency Response. 1990. 40.00 (*1-878220-00-4*) Am Meteorological.

Meteorological Buoy & Coastal Marine Automated Network for the United States. National Research Council Staff. LC 98-85592. (Compass Ser.). xii, 97 p. 1998. pap. text 15.00 (*0-309-06088-5*) Natl Acad Pr.

Meteorological Fluid Dynamics: Asymptotic Modelling, Stability & Chaotic Atmospheric Motion. R. K. Zeytounian. Ed. by W. Beiglbock et al. (Lecture Notes in Physics Ser.: Vol. M5). xiii, 346p. 1991. 44.95 (*0-387-54446-1*) Spr-Verlag.

Meteorological Instruments. Richard K. Miller & Marcia E. Rupnow. LC 90-83899. (Survey on Technology & Markets Ser.: No. 195). 50p. 1991. pap. text 200.00 (*1-55865-219-1*) Future Tech Surveys.

Meteorological Investigations of the Upper Atmosphere: Proceedings of the AMS Symposium on Meteorological Investigations above 70 Kilometers, Miami, Florida, May 31-June 2, 1967. Ed. by R. S. Quiroz. (Meteorological Monograph: Vol. 9, No. 31). (Illus.). 231p. 1968. 23.00 (*0-933876-29-7*) Am Meteorological.

Meteorological Observations & Instrumentation: Proceedings of the AMS Symposium on Meteorological Observations & Instrumentation, Washington, D. C., 10-14 February 1969. Ed. by S. Teweles & J. Giraylys. (Meteorological Monograph Ser.: Vol. 11, No. 33). (Illus.). 455p. 1970. 30.00 (*0-933876-31-9*) Am Meteorological.

Meteorological Research Reviews: Summaries of Progress from 1951 to 1955. Ed. by Alfred K. Blackadar. (Meteorological Monograph: Vol. 3, No. 12-20). (Illus.). 283p. 1957. pap. 29.00 (*0-933876-07-6*) Am Meteorological.

Meteorological Studies at Plateau Station, Antarctica. Ed. by J. A. Businger. (Antarctic Research Ser.: Vol. 25). (Illus.). 155p. 1977. 38.00 (*0-87590-125-5*, AR2500) Am Geophysical.

Meteorological Studies at Plateau Station, Antarctica: Mini Book, Papers 6-8. Ed. by J. A. Businger. (Antarctic Research Ser.: Vol. 25). (Illus.). 51p. 1977. 38.00 (*0-87590-140-9*) Am Geophysical.

Meteorological Studies at Plateau Station, Antarctica Paper 5: The Radiation Budget. M. Kuhn et al. Ed. by Joost A. Businger. (Antarctic Research Ser.: Vol. 25). (Illus.). 1977. pap. 16.90 (*0-87590-139-5*) Am Geophysical.

Meteorological Tables. T. Beer. 1990. 222.00 (*1-85312-305-6*) Computational Mech MA.

Meteorologicorum Libri Quattuor. Aristotle. (GER.). xlvii, 234p. 1967. reprint ed. 70.00 (*0-318-70449-8*) G Olms Pubs.

Meteorologischen Theorien Des Griechischen Altertums. Otto Gilbert. viii, 746p. 1967. reprint ed. write for info. (*0-318-70924-4*) G Olms Pubs.

Meteorologist. Jack Rudman. (Career Examination Ser.: C-497). 1994. pap. 34.95 (*0-8373-0497-0*) Nat Learn.

Meteorology. (Quick Study Academic Ser.). 4p. pap. 3.95 (*1-57222-319-7*) Barcharts.

***Meteorology.** Aguado. (gr. 12). 1999. pap. text, teacher ed. write for info. (*0-13-236662-2*) P-H.

***Meteorology.** Aguado. (gr. 12). 1999. pap. text, teacher ed. write for info. (*0-13-236621-5*, Prentice Hall) P-H.

Meteorology. Ahrens. (Adaptable Courseware-Hardside Ser.). Date not set. mass mkt. 39.96 (*0-534-16072-7*) Wadsworth Pub.

Meteorology. Eric W. Danielson & James Levin. LC 97-27826. 544p. (C). 1997. per. write for info. (*0-697-21711-6*, WCB McGr Hill) McGrw-H Hghr Educ.

Meteorology. Danielson et al. 272p. 1998. spiral bd., wbk. ed. 29.38 (*0-697-21715-9*) McGraw.

Meteorology. D. J. George. (C). 1992. 30.00 (*0-907649-35-1*, Pub. by Expedit Advisory Ctr) St Mut.

Meteorology. Graham Peacock. (Science Activities Ser.). (Illus.). 32p. (J). (ps-4). 1995. lib. bdg. 21.40 (*1-56847-194-7*) Raintree Steck-V.

Meteorology. Alpay Ulku. (A. Poulin, Jr., New Poets of America Ser.: Vol. 20). 96p. 1999. pap. 12.50 (*1-880238-72-1*, Pub. by BOA Edns) Consort Bk Sales.

Meteorology. Pat Ward & Barb Ward. (Illus.). 64p. (YA). (gr. 5). 1994. pap. text 8.95 (*1-58037-012-8*, Pub. by M Twain Media) Carson-Dellos.

Meteorology. Wise. (C). 2000. text 73.00 (*0-03-097288-4*) Harcourt Coll Pubs.

Meteorology. Wise. (C). 2000. pap. text, student ed. 21.50 (*0-03-097290-6*) Harcourt Coll Pubs.

Meteorology. E. D. Fickett. (Illus.). 10p. 1986. reprint ed. pap. 10.00 (*0-8466-0029-3*, S-29, Shorey Pubns) Shoreys Bkstore.

***Meteorology.** 2nd ed. Eric W. Danielson et al. LC 00-25409. (Illus.). 2000. write for info. (*0-07-365963-0*) McGraw.

Meteorology. 5th ed. Ahrens. Date not set. pap. text, teacher ed. write for info. (*0-314-03305-X*) West Pub.

Meteorology. 5th ed. Ahrens. 1994. student ed. 17.75 (*0-314-03970-8*) West Pub.

Meteorology. 5th ed. Moran. 1997. pap. text, teacher ed. write for info. (*0-13-280793-9*) Allyn.

Meteorology. 7th ed. Richard A. Anthes. LC 96-17574. 214p. (C). 1996. pap. text 43.00 (*0-13-231044-9*) P-H.

Meteorology: Atmosphere in Action. Eagleman. (Physical Science Ser.). 1980. pap., teacher ed. 2.50 (*0-534-25764-X*); pap. text 24.50 (*0-534-21908-X*) Wadsworth Pub.

Meteorology: Observing, Understanding & Predicting Weather. Mary Brown & Rosemary Dickinson. (Learning Packets - Science Ser.). 72p. 1996. ring bd. 18.00 (*1-56976-031-4*, 1429-F3) Zephyr Pr AZ.

Meteorology: The Atmosphere & Science of Weather. 5th ed. Joseph M. Moran & Michael D. Moran. LC 96-43449. (Illus.). 530p. (C). 1996. 74.00 (*0-13-266701-0*) P-H.

Meteorology: The Atmosphere & the Science of Weather. 4th ed. Joseph M. Moran & Michael D. Morgan. LC 93-1035. (Illus.). 550p. (C). 1994. pap. text, student ed. 23.80 (*0-02-383345-9*, Macmillan Coll) P-H.

Meteorology: The Atmosphere in Action. 2nd ed. Joe R. Eagleman. (Illus.). 394p. (C). 1992. reprint ed. text 46.95 (*1-877696-05-6*) Trimedia Pub.

Meteorology & Atomic Energy: 1968. AEC Technical Information Center Staff. Ed. by David H. Slade. LC 68-60097. 450p. 1968. pap. 19.25 (*0-87079-274-1*, TID-24190); fiche 9.00 (*0-87079-275-X*, TID-24190) DOE.

Meteorology & Environmental Sciences. R. Guzzi et al. 820p. 1990. text 151.00 (*981-02-0443-4*) World Scientific Pub.

***Meteorology & Flight: Pilot's Guide to Weather.** 3rd ed. Tom Bradbury. (Illus.). 192p. 2000. pap. 24.95 (*0-7136-4226-2*, Pub. by A & C Blk) Midpt Trade.

Meteorology & Oceanography see Ideas & Investigations in Science: Earth Science

Meteorology & Weather Factors: Index of New Information with Authors, Subjects & Bibliography. rev. ed. Gilbert J. Umanski. LC 95-16706. 137p. 1995. 47.50 (*0-7883-0354-6*); pap. 44.50 (*0-7883-0355-4*) ABBE Pubs Assn.

***Meteorology for Scientist & Engineers.** 2nd ed. Stull. (Earth Science Ser.). 502p. 1999. text 24.95 (*0-534-37214-7*) Brooks-Cole.

Meteorology for Seafarers. R. M. Frampton. 140p. 1988. text 65.00 (*0-85174-530-X*) Sheridan.

Meteorology in America, 1800-1870. James R. Fleming. LC 90-30816. (Illus.). 336p. 1990. text 45.00 (*0-8018-3958-0*) Johns Hopkins.

Meteorology in the Southern Hemisphere. Ed. by Chester W. Newton. (Meteorological Monograph: Vol. 13, No. 35). (Illus.). 263p. 1972. 30.00 (*0-933876-38-6*) Am Meteorological.

Meteorology of the Southern Hemisphere: Meteorological Monographs (MM49) Ed. by David J. Karoly & Dayton G. Vincent. LC 98-74523. (Meteorological Monograph: Vol. 27). (Illus.). 410p. (C). 1999. 65.00 (*1-878220-29-2*) Am Meteorological.

Meteorology Source Book. McGraw-Hill Editors. (Science Reference Ser.). (Illus.). 450p. 1989. 64.95 (*0-07-045511-2*) McGraw.

Meteorology Today. 5th ed. Stuhl. Date not set. teacher ed. write for info. (*0-314-07217-9*) West Pub.

Meteorology Today. 6th ed. Ahrens. 1999. pap. text, student ed. 19.75 (*0-534-37209-0*) Brooks-Cole.

Meteorology Today. 6th ed. Ahrens. (Earth Science Ser.). 1999. pap. 51.75 (*0-534-55773-2*) Wadsworth Pub.

Meteorology Today: An Introduction to Weather, Climate & the Environment. 4th ed. C. Donald Ahrens. Ed. by Clyde Perlee & Simon. 576p. (C). 1991. text 54.75 (*0-314-80905-8*) West Pub.

Meteorology Today: An Introduction to Weather, Climate & the Environment. 5th ed. C. Donald Ahrens. Ed. by Simon Perlee. LC 93-42121. 600p. (C). 1994. pap. 51.75 (*0-314-02779-3*) West Pub.

Meteorology Today: International Version. 6th ed. Ahrens. 1999. pap. text 51.75 (*0-534-37379-8*) Brooks-Cole.

Meteorology Today for Scientists & Engineers: A Technical Companion Book. Roland B. Stull. LC 95-185031. 350p. 1999. 14.75 (*0-314-06471-0*) West Pub.

Meteorology Today w/Infotrac & Blue Skies Cd. 6th ed. Ahrens. LC 99-32123. 1999. pap. text 60.75 incl. cd-rom (*0-534-37201-5*) Brooks-Cole.

Meteors. Billy Aronson. LC 95-48846. (First Bks.). 64p. (J). 1996. lib. bdg. 22.00 (*0-531-20242-9*) Watts.

Meteors. Neil Bone. (Sky & Telescope's Observer's Guides Ser.). (Illus.). 176p. (Orig.). 1993. pap. 18.95 (*0-933346-67-0*) Sky Pub.

***Meteors: Poems from Hollywood.** Mark Dunster. 11p. 1999. pap. 5.00 (*0-89642-853-2*) Linden Pubs.

Meteors: The Truth Behind Shooting Stars. Billy Aronson. (First Bks.). 64p. (J). 1997. pap. 6.95 (*0-531-15813-6*) Watts.

Meteors, Comets, Supernovae: Observing Transient Pehenomena. Neil Bone. LC 98-18112. (Practical Astronomy Ser.). 1998. pap. 29.95 (*1-85233-017-1*) Spr-Verlag.

Meteor's Tale. Michael O'Rourke. Ed. by Sally Smith. 160p. 1999. 20.00 (*1-891437-01-1*) Victorian Essence.

Metepenagiag: New Brunswick's Oldest Village. Patricia Allen. (Illus.). 41p. 1994. pap. 9.95 (*0-86492-139-X*, Pub. by Goose Ln Edits) Genl Dist Srvs.

Meteques Atheniens. Michel Clarc. Ed. by Gregory Vlastos. LC 78-15862. (Morals & Law in Ancient Greece Ser.). 1979. reprint ed. lib. bdg. 37.95 (*0-405-11533-4*) Ayer.

Meter & Case in Latin Elegiac Pentameter. G. J. Siefert. (Language Dissertations Ser.: No. 49). 1952. 25.00 (*0-527-00795-1*) Periodicals Srv.

Meter & Language in the Lyrics of the Suppliants of Aeschtlus. rev. ed. James N. Rash. Ed. by W. R. Connor. LC 80-2665. (Monographs in Classical Studies). 1981. lib. bdg. 34.95 (*0-405-14049-5*) Ayer.

Meter & Melody of Beowulf. Thomas Cable. LC 72-97683. (Studies in Language & Literature: No. 64). 132p. reprint ed. 41.00 (*0-8357-9689-2*, 201493100094) Bks Demand.

Meter As Rhythm. Christopher Hasty. LC 96-24694. (Illus.). 328p. 1997. text 75.00 (*0-19-510066-2*) OUP.

Meter in English: A Critical Engagement. Ed. by David Baker. LC 96-27935. 352p. 1997. pap. 20.00 (*1-55728-444-X*); text 38.00 (*1-55728-422-9*) U of Ark Pr.

Meter in Music, 1600-1800: Performance, Perception & Notation. George Houle. LC 86-45789. (Music: Scholarship & Performance Ser.). (Illus.). 192p. 1987. lib. bdg. 39.95 (*0-253-33792-5*) Ind U Pr.

***Meter in Music, 1600-1800: Performance, Perception & Notation.** George Houle. (Illus.). 192p. 2000. pap. 16.95 (*0-253-21391-6*) Ind U Pr.

Meter Maid. Jack Rudman. (Career Examination Ser.: C-498). 1994. pap. 23.95 (*0-8373-0498-9*) Nat Learn.

Meter Reading Equipment. Ed. by Peter Allen. 200p. 1988. pap. 1795.00 (*0-941285-25-1*) FIND-SVP.

Meter Sockets, UL 414. 7th ed. (C). 1999. pap. text 330.00 (*1-55989-592-6*) Underwrtrs Labs.

Metered Dose Inhaler Technology. Tol S. Purewal. Ed. by David J. Grant. LC 97-41982. (Illus.). 280p. 1998. 194.00 (*1-57491-065-5*) Interpharm.

***Metering of Fluids at High Velocities with Vortex Shedding Flowmeters.** J. D. Siegwarth. 40p. 1998. pap. 3.50 (*0-16-060874-0*) USGPO.

Metering Pump Handbook. Robert McCabe et al. 280p. 1984. 29.95 (*0-8311-1157-7*) Indus Pr.

Metering Pumps: Selection & Application. James P. Poynton. LC 82-23485. (Chemical Industries Ser.: Vol. 9). (Illus.). 212p. reprint ed. pap. 65.80 (*0-608-08977-X*, 206961200005) Bks Demand.

Meterology. Wise. (C). Date not set. pap. text, teacher ed., suppl. ed. 28.00 (*0-03-097289-2*) Harcourt Coll Pubs.

Meters for Flammable & Combustible Liquids & LP-Gas, UL 25. 7th ed. (C). 1996. pap. text 230.00 (*0-7629-0000-8*) Underwrtrs Labs.

Meters of Greek & Latin Poetry. Martin Ostwald et al. LC 93-47104. 152p. (C). 1994. reprint ed. pap. text 9.95 (*0-87220-243-7*); reprint ed. lib. bdg. 29.95 (*0-87220-244-5*) Hackett Pub.

Meters of Greek & Latin Poetry. Thomas G. Rosenmeyer et al. LC 62-21264. (C). 1973. reprint ed. pap. text 9.95 (*0-8290-1666-X*) Irvington.

Meters of John Webster. Betty J. Schlerman. (American University Studies: Linguistics: Ser. XIII, Vol. 12). 253p. (C). 1989. text 37.95 (*0-8204-1096-9*) P Lang Pubng.

Meter's Running. Charles B. Nesbit. 1998. pap. write for info. (*1-57553-907-1*) Watermrk Pr.

***Metes & Bounds Vol. I: Dugal McQueen & Some Descendants.** Donna Hechler. (Illus.). viii, 235p. 1999. 45.00 (*0-944619-53-3*) Gregath Pub Co.

Metes & Bounds Vol. II: David Crews, Ancestors & Descendants. Donna Hechler Porter. (Illus.). x, 269p. 1997. 45.00 (*0-944619-54-1*) Gregath Pub Co.

Methadone, 8 vols. Carolyn Simpson. LC 96-54270. (Drug Abuse Prevention Library). (Illus.). 64p. (YA). (gr. 7-12). 1997. lib. bdg. 17.95 (*0-8239-2286-3*) Rosen Group.

Methadone: Experiences & Issues. Ed. by Carl D. Chambers & Leon Brill. LC 72-6122. 411p. 1973. 52.00 (*0-87705-072-4*, Kluwer Acad Hman Sci) Kluwer Academic.

Methadone Maintenance: Papers. National Methadone Maintenance Conference (2nd: 19. Ed. by Stanley Einstein. LC 79-149717. (Illus.). 263p. reprint ed. pap. 81.60 (*0-608-18001-7*, 202799600058) Bks Demand.

Methadone Maintenance in the Management of Opiod Dependence: An International Review. Ed. by Awni Arif & Joseph Westermeyer. LC 89-78368. 128p. 1990. 47.95 (*0-275-93392-X*, C3392, Praeger Pubs) Greenwood.

Methadone Maintenance Treatment. write for info. (*1-930517-06-8*) Lindesmith Ctr.

Methadone Maintenance Treatment & Other Opioid Replacement Therapies. Richard P. Mattick & Wayne Hall. Ed. by Jeff Ward. LC 99-459989. 480p. 1997. text 34.00 (*90-5702-238-9*, Harwood Acad Pubs); pap. text 15.00 (*90-5702-239-7*, Harwood Acad Pubs) Gordon & Breach.

Methadone Treatment for Opioid Dependence. Eric C. Strain. LC 98-50962. 1999. 58.00 (*0-8018-6136-5*) Johns Hopkins.

***Methadone Treatment for Opioid Dependence.** Eric C. Strain & Maxine L. Stitzer. LC 98-50962. 334p. 1999. 24.95 (*0-8018-6137-3*) Johns Hopkins.

Methamidophos Health & Safety Guide. (Health & Safety Guides Ser.: No. 79). 34p. 1993. pap. text 5.00 (*92-4-151079-X*, 1860079) World Health.

***Methamphetamine: A New Deadly Neighbor: Congressional Hearing.** Ed. by Jon Kly. (Illus.). 71p. (C). 1999. reprint ed. pap. text 20.00 (*0-7881-8434-2*) DIANE Pub.

***Methamphetamine, a New Deadly Neighbor: Hearing Before the Subcommittee on Technology, Terrorism & Government Information of the Committee on the Judiciary, United States Senate, 105th Congress, 2nd Session... Phoeniz, AZ, April 6, 1998.** USGPO Staff. LC 99-170985. iii, 71p. 1998. write for info. (*0-16-057636-9*) USGPO.

Methamphetamines. Jay Schleifer. (Drug Abuse Prevention Library). 64p. (J). (gr. 7-12). 1998. pap. 6.95 (*1-56838-250-2*) Hazelden.

Methamphetamines: Speed Kills see Drug Abuse Prevention Library: Getting Off Dangerous Ground

Methanation of Synthesis Gas: A Symposium Sponsored by the Division of the Fuel Chemistry at the 168th Meeting of the American Chemical Society, Atlantic City, NJ, Sept. 9th,1974. Ed. by Len Seglin. LC 75-33967. (Advances in Chemistry Ser.: 146). 190p. reprint ed. pap. 58.90 (*0-608-15014-2*, 202589600046) Bks Demand.

Methane see Solubility Data Series

Methane. H. L. Clever et al. (IUPAC Solubility Data Ser.: 27). 808p. 1987. 316.50 (*0-08-029200-3*, Pergamon Pr) Elsevier.

Methane: A Critical Assessment of Sources, Technologies, & Economics. American Gas Association Staff. LC 83-15007. (Series of Special Reports: No. 8). 218p. reprint ed. pap. 67.60 (*0-7837-0681-2*, 204101400019) Bks Demand.

Methane Vol. 13: International Thermodynamic Tables of the Fluid State. W. Wagner & K. M. De Reuck. (Illus.). 368p. 1996. 85.00 (*0-632-02381-3*) Blackwell Sci.

Methane Age. Ed. by T. H. Lee et al. (C). 1988. text 153.00 (*90-277-2745-7*) Kluwer Academic.

Methane & Alkane Conversion Chemistry: Proceedings of the American Chemical Society Symposium in San Diego, California, March 13-18, 1994. M. M. Bhasin & D. W. Slocum. (Illus.). 360p. (C). 1996. 125.00 (*0-306-45212-X*, Kluwer Plenum) Kluwer Academic.

Methane & Its Derivatives. Sunggyu Lee. LC 96-41107. (Chemical Industries Ser.: Vol. 70). (Illus.). 424p. 1996. text 180.00 (*0-8247-9754-X*) Dekker.

Methane & Methanol Utilizers. J. C. Murrell & H. Dalton. (Biotechnology Handbooks Ser.: Vol. 5). (Illus.). 304p. (C). 1992. text 79.50 (*0-306-43878-X*, Kluwer Plenum) Kluwer Academic.

Methane Control for High-Production Retreat Faces (Final Report) EUR 17391. 1997. 30.00 (*92-826-9191-8*, CS-NA-17391ENC, Pub. by Comm Europ Commun) Bernan Associates.

Methane Oxidation in Landfill Cover Soils. Gunnar Borjesson. (Acta Uiversitatis Agriculturae Seuciae, Agraia: No. 44). (Illus.). 110p. 1997. pap. 34.00 (*91-576-5298-8*) Coronet Bks.

Methanol & Carbonylation: Rhne-Poulenc Recerches Centre de Recherches de Saint-Fons. Jean Gauthier-Lafaye & Robert Perron. (Illus.). 272p. (C). 1987. pap. 345.00 (*2-7108-0529-4*, Pub. by Edits Technip) Enfield Pubs NH.

Methanol Fuel: A Bibliography. 1991. lib. bdg. 75.00 (*0-8490-5199-1*) Gordon Pr.

Methanol Production & Use. Ed. by Wu-Hsun Cheng & Harold H. Kung. LC 94-14916. (Chemical Industries Ser.: Vol. 57). (Illus.). 344p. 1994. text 160.00 (*0-8247-9223-8*) Dekker.

Methanol Synthesis Technology. Sunggyu Lee & Robert Iredell. 240p. 1989. lib. bdg. 195.00 (*0-8493-4610-X*, TP594) CRC Pr.

Methanol Use in Vehicle Fleet Operations. 110p. 1982. 20.00 (*0-318-17717-X*, DG 82-319) Pub Tech Inc.

Methematical Methods for CAD. J. J. Risler. (Illus.). 198p. 1993. pap. text 42.95 (*0-521-43691-5*) Cambridge U Pr.

Methematics: The Man-Made Universe. 3rd unabridged ed. Sherman K. Stein. LC 98-46319. 592p. 1999. pap. 18.95 (*0-486-40450-1*) Dover.

Methicillin-Resistant Staphylococcus Aureus. Ed. by Mary Cafferkey. (Illus.). 224p. 1992. text 125.00 (*0-8247-8604-1*) Dekker.

Method. Paul R. Walker. LC 89-29284. 256p. (YA). (gr. 7 up). 1990. 14.95 (*0-15-200528-5*, Gulliver Bks) Harcourt.

Method. Paul R. Walker. 240p. (YA). (gr. 7 up). 1996. pap. 6.00 (*0-15-201260-5*) Harcourt.

Method: The Riddell Lectures on Applied Psychology & Vital Christianity (1913) Newton N. Riddell. 320p. 1998. reprint ed. pap. 24.95 (*0-7661-0229-7*) Kessinger Pub.

Method Vol. 1: Towards a Study of Humankind: The Nature of Nature. Edgar Morin. Tr. by J. L. Belanger from FRE. LC 91-45484. (American University Studies: Philosophy: Ser. V, Vol. 111). 435p. (C). 1992. text 63.95 (*0-8204-1878-1*) P Lang Pubng.

***Method Acting Reconsidered: Theory, Practice, Future.** David Krasner. 1999. text. write for info. (*0-312-22305-6*) St Martin.

***Method Acting Reconsidered: Theory, Practice, Future.** David Krasner. LC 00-35269. 288p. 2000. pap. 18.95 (*0-312-22309-9*) St Martin.

Method & Catholic Moral Theology: The Ongoing Reconstruction. Todd Salzman. LC 99-38858. 279p. 1999. pap. 17.00 (*1-881871-31-2*) Creighton U Pr.

***Method & Catholic Moral Theology: The Ongoing Reconstruction.** Todd Salzman. LC 99-38858. 279p. 1999. 25.00 (*1-881871-30-4*) Creighton U Pr.

Method & Context as Problems for Contemporary Theology: Doing Theology in an Alien World. Hans Schwarz. LC 91-29295. (Toronto Studies in Theology: Vol. 58). 248p. 1991. lib. bdg. 89.95 (*0-7734-9677-7*) E Mellen.

Method & Language. Joseph Gruenfeld. viii, 208p. 1982. pap. 35.00 (*90-6032-110-3*, Pub. by B R Gruner) Humanities.

Method & Meaning in Ancient Judaism. Jacob Neusner. LC 79-9881. (Brown Judaic Studies: No. 10). 219p. reprint ed. pap. 67.90 (*0-7837-5398-5*, 204516200005) Bks Demand.

Method & Meaning in Ancient Judaism. Jacob Neusner. LC 80-19449. (Brown Judaic Studies: Third Series). 255p. reprint ed. pap. 79.10 (*0-7837-5425-6*, 204518900005) Bks Demand.

Method & Meaning of the "Mishnah Berurah" Simcha Fishbane. 19.95 (*0-88125-360-X*) Ktav.

Method & Means of Public Speaking. 2nd ed. William S. Smith & Donald J. Canty. (Orig.). (C). 1962. pap. write for info. (*0-672-60859-6*, Bobbs) Macmillan.

Method & Message of Jesus' Teachings. rev. ed. Robert H. Stein. LC 94-3929. 216p. 1994. pap. 19.95 (*0-664-25513-2*) Westminster John Knox.

Method & Message of Matthew. Augustine Stock. 448p. 1994. pap. 26.95 (*0-8146-5022-8*, M Glazier) Liturgical Pr.

Method & Order in Renaissance Philosophy of Nature: The Aristotle Commentary Tradition. Daniel A. Di Liscia et al. LC 97-77049. 450p. 1998. 96.95 (*0-86078-666-8*, Pub. by Ashgate Pub) Ashgate Pub Co.

Method & Politics in Plato's "Statesman" M. S. Lane. LC 97-6077. (Cambridge Classical Studies). 242p. (C). 1998. text 59.95 (*0-521-58229-6*) Cambridge U Pr.

Method & Practice in Aristotle's Biology. Michael Boylan. LC 82-23708. (Illus.). 300p. (Orig.). 1983. lib. bdg. 53.00 (*0-8191-2952-6*) U Pr of Amer.

Method & Theory. Ed. by Amelie Kuhrt & Heleen Sancisi-Weerdenburg. (Achaemenid History Proceedings of the Landon 1985 Achaemeniel History Workshop: Vol. 3). xv, 228p. 1988. pap. text 66.50 (*90-6258-403-9*, Pub. by Netherlands Inst) Eisenbrauns.

Method & Theory see Universals of Human Language

Method & Theory for Activity Area Research: An Ethnoarchaeological Approach. Ed. by Susan Kent. LC 86-6793. 624p. 1987. text 110.50 (*0-231-06080-7*) Col U Pr.

Method & Theory for Investigating the Peopling of the Americas. Ed. by Robson Bonnichsen & D. Gentry Steele. (Illus.). 264p. (Orig.). (C). 1994. pap. text 33.00 (*0-912933-11-9*) Ctr Study First Am.

Method & Theory for Investigating the Peopling of the Americas, Vol. 1. Ed. by Robson Bonnichsen & D. Gentry Steele. (Illus.). 264p. (Orig.). (C). 1994. 42.00 (*0-912933-09-7*) Ctr Study First Am.

Method & Theory in American Archaeology. Gordon R. Willey & Philip Phillips. LC 57-11215. 1962. pap. text 9.00 (*0-226-89888-1*, P88) U Ch Pr.

Method & Theory in Linguistics. Ed. by Paul L. Garvin. LC 75-110950. (Janua Linguarum, Ser. Major: No. 40). 1970. text 69.25 (*90-279-0722-6*) Mouton.

Method & Theory of Ethnology. Paul A. Radin. LC 86-29921. 388p. 1987. pap. 21.95 (*0-89789-118-X*, Bergin & Garvey) Greenwood.

Method Choice & Inquiry Process: Lessons from Programmatic Research into Therapeutic Practice. Lisa Hoshmand & Jack Martin. (Counseling & Development Ser.). 272p. (C). 1995. text 49.00 (*0-8077-3428-4*) Tchrs Coll.

Method Comparison & Bias Estimation Using Patient Samples: Approved Guideline (1995) 1995. 85.00 (*1-56238-283-7*, EP9-A) NCCLS.

Method, Directions, & Examples: Baccalaureate Program see Cost of Nursing Education: A Manual for Analysis of Expenditures

Method, Directions, & Examples: Diploma Program see Cost of Nursing Education: A Manual for Analysis of Expenditures

Method Engineering Principles of Method Construction & Tool Support. Chapman & Hall Staff. text 159.50 (*0-412-79750-X*) Chapman & Hall.

Method for Bassoon. Julius Weissenborn. Ed. by Fred Bettoney. (Illus.). 159p. pap. 16.95 (*0-8258-0169-9*, CU-96) Fischer Inc NY.

Method for Clarinet, 2 pts., Pt. 1. H. Lazarus. Ed. by Simeon Bellison. (Illus.). 140p. 1946. pap. 15.95 (*0-8258-0206-7*, 0-327) Fischer Inc NY.

Method for Clarinet, 2 pts., Pt. 2. H. Lazarus. Ed. by Simeon Bellison. (Illus.). 142p. 1946. pap. 17.95 (*0-8258-0207-5*, 0-328) Fischer Inc NY.

Method for Collecting Dialect. 2nd ed. Frederic G. Cassidy & Audrey R. Duckert. (Publications of the American Dialect Society: No. 20). 96p. 1970. reprint ed. pap. text 9.60 (*0-8173-0620-X*) U of Ala Pr.

***Method for Constructing Complete Annual United States Life Tables.** Robert N. Anderson. 32p. 2000. pap. 3.00 (*0-16-050256-X*) USGPO.

***Method for Constructing Complete Annual United States Life Tables.** Robert N. Anderson & National Center for Health Statistics Staff. LC 99-58350. (Vital & Health Statistics Ser.). 1999. pap. write for info. (*0-8406-0560-9*) Natl Ctr Health Stats.

Method for Cor Alto & Cor Basse. deluxe ed. Louis-Francois Dauprat. Tr. by Viola Roth et al from ENG. LC 93-74474.Tr. of Methode de Cor-Alto et Cor-Basse. (Illus.). 502p. 1994. lthr. 350.00 (*0-929309-03-0*) Birdalone Bks.

Method for Cor Alto & Cor Basse. limited ed. Louis-Francois Dauprat. Tr. by Viola Roth et al from ENG. LC 93-74474.Tr. of Methode de Cor-Alto et Cor-Basse. (Illus.). 502p. 1994. lib. bdg. 150.00 (*0-929309-02-2*) Birdalone Bks.

Method for Creative Design. Adolfo Best-Maugard. (Illus.). 192p. 1990. pap. 5.95 (*0-486-26436-X*) Dover.

Method for Determining Adhesion of Protection Sheet to Aperture Adhesive of Unitized Microfilm Carrier (Aperture Card) ANSI-AIIM MS10-1987 (R1993) Association for Information & Image Management Staff. 8p. 1987. pap. 33.00 (*0-89258-125-5*, MS10) Assn Inform & Image Mgmt.

Method for Estimating the Preharvest Potential for Seedling Height Growth on Cutover Forest Land in Southwestern Oregon. Don Minore. (Illus.). 16p. 1997. reprint ed. pap. 2.30 (*0-89904-768-8*, Ecosytems Resrch) Crumb Elbow Pub.

Method for Flute. A. Brooke. Ed. by James Pappoutsakis. 211p. 1962. pap. 23.50 (*0-8258-0145-1*, CU-20) Fischer Inc NY.

Method for Measuring the Value of Scout/Reconnaissance. Clairice T. Veit & Monti D. Callero. LC 95-8314. (Illus.). 101p. 1995. pap. text 13.00 (*0-8330-1639-3*, MR-476-A) Rand Corp.

Method for Measuring Thickness of Buildup Area on Unitized Microfilm Carriers (Aperture, Camera, Copy & Image Cards) ANSI-AIIM MS9-1987 (A1996) Association for Information & Image Management Staff. 11p. 1987. pap. 33.00 (*0-89258-122-0*, MS09) Assn Inform & Image Mgmt.

Method for Personal Growth & Development. Win Wenger. (Psychegenic Library of Experiential Resources). (Illus.). 135p. (Orig.). (YA). (gr. 7-12). 1986. pap. 24.00 (*0-931865-09-3*) Proj Renaissance.

Method for Prayer. M. Henry. 13.99 (*1-85792-068-6*, Pub. by Christian Focus) Spring Arbor Dist.

Method for Prayer: With Scripture Expressions & Directions for Daily Communion with God: Morning, Noon, Evening. Matthew Henry. Ed. by J. Ligon Duncan, III. 390p. (C). 1995. reprint ed. pap. text 14.95 (*1-884416-08-X*) A Press.

***Method for Predicting the Dynamic Root Stresses of Helical Gear Teeth.** D. R. Houser & J. Harianto. (Technical Papers: Vol. 98FTM1). 10p. 1998. pap. 30.00 (*1-55589-719-3*) AGMA.

***Method for Specifying the Geometry of Spur & Helical Gears.** AGMA Technical Committee. (AGMA Standard Ser.: Vol. 913-A98). 25p. 2000. pap. text 55.00 (*1-55589-714-2*) AGMA.

Method for the Flute. Jean-Louis Tulou. LC 94-14389. (Illus.). 144p. 1995. pap. 19.95 (*0-253-20919-6*) Ind U Pr.

Method for the Harp. S. Lawrence. (ENG & FRE.). 80p. 1986. pap. 13.95 (*0-7935-4531-5*, 50328070) H Leonard.

Method for the Millions. Emily Noble. 38p. 1996. reprint ed. spiral bd. 9.00 (*0-7873-0635-5*) Hlth Research.

Method for the One-Keyed Flute. Janice D. Boland. LC 97-49641. 236p. 1998. pap. 24.95 (*0-520-21447-1*, Pub. by U CA Pr) Cal Prin Full Svc.

Method for the Spanish Guitar. Ferdinand Sor. LC 77-158960. (Music Ser.). 1971. reprint ed. lib. bdg. 25.00 (*0-306-70188-X*) Da Capo.

Method for the Spanish Guitar. Ferdinand Sor. Tr. by A. Merrick. LC 79-27167. (Quality Paperbacks Ser.). (Illus.). 1980. reprint ed. pap. text 5.95 (*0-306-80121-3*) Da Capo.

Method for the Theremin Bk. 1: Basics. Robert B. Sexton. (Thin Air Ser.). (Illus.). 52p. (C). 1996. pap. 20.00 (*1-881428-08-7*) Tactus Pr.

Method for Trombone. David Uber. 1968. pap. 12.00 (*0-318-19427-9*) Peermusic Classical.

Method for Trombone, Bk. 1a. David Uber. 1968. pap. 12.00 (*0-317-01195-2*, 60765-904) Peermusic Classical.

Method for Trombone, Bk. 1b. David Uber. 1968. pap. 12.00 (*0-317-01196-0*, 60766-904) Peermusic Classical.

Method for Trombone, Bk. 2a. David Uber. 1968. pap. 12.00 (*0-317-01197-9*, 60762-904) Peermusic Classical.

Method for Trombone, Bk. 2b. David Uber. 1968. pap. 12.00 (*0-317-03282-8*, 60763-904) Peermusic Classical.

Method for Violin, Pt. 1. C. Deberiot. 80p. 1986. pap. 8.95 (*0-7935-4363-0*, 50326200) H Leonard.

Method for Zither. A. Darr. (GER.). 58p. 1950. pap. 13.95 (*0-8258-0237-7*, 0-630) Fischer Inc NY.

Method in Ancient Philosophy. Ed. by Jyl Gentzler. LC 97-24353. 408p. 1998. text 72.00 (*0-19-823571-2*) OUP.

***Method in Creativity.** Pascale Seurin. 2000. pap. 25.00 (*88-7838-065-2*) L'Arca IT.

Method in Criminology: A Philosophical Primer. Bruce Dicristina. LC 94-23664. (C). 1995. text 30.00 (*0-911577-28-9*, Criminal Justice) Willow Tree NY.

Method in Dealing in Stocks: A Practical Guide & Handbook for Recording & Interpreting the Daily Actions of the Stock Market. Joseph H. Kerr, Jr. LC 87-81870. 1969. reprint ed. pap. 13.00 (*0-87034-052-2*) Fraser Pub Co.

Method in Dealing in Stocks: Reading the Mind of the Market on a Daily Basis. Joseph A. Kerr, Jr. 136p. (Orig.). 1996. pap. 35.00 (*0-9650461-1-7*) M Gordon Pubng.

Method in Ecology: Strategies for Conservation. Kristin S. Shrader-Frechette & Earl D. McCoy. LC 93-9343. (Illus.). 338p. (C). 1993. pap. text 33.95 (*0-521-44693-7*) Cambridge U Pr.

Method in Ecology: Strategies for Conservation. Kristin S. Shrader-Frechette & Earl D. McCoy. LC 93-9343. (Illus.). 340p. (C). 1994. text 90.00 (*0-521-41861-5*) Cambridge U Pr.

Method in Ecumenical Theology: The Lessons So Far. G. R. Evans. 245p. (C). 1996. text 59.95 (*0-521-55304-0*) Cambridge U Pr.

Method in Ethical Theory. Abraham Edel. LC 93-5472. 372p. (C). 1993. pap. text 24.95 (*1-56000-712-5*) Transaction Pubs.

Method in Madness: Case Studies in Cognitive Neuropsychiatry. Peter W. Halligan & John C. Marshall. 320p. 1996. 49.95 (*0-86377-441-5*); pap. 24.95 (*0-86377-442-3*) L Erlbaum Assocs.

Method in Metaphysics. Robert J. Henle. (Aquinas Lectures). 1950. 15.00 (*0-87462-115-1*) Marquette.

Method in Ministry: Theological Reflection & Christian Ministry (revised edition) rev. ed. Evelyn E. Whitehead & James D. Whitehead. LC 95-8755. 170p. (Orig.). 1995. pap. 12.95 (*1-55612-806-1*) Sheed & Ward WI.

Method in Prayer: An Exposition & Exploration. W. Graham Scroggie. 143p. 1997. pap. 8.99 (*1-898787-99-9*) Emerald House Group Inc.

Method in Social Science: Realist Approach. 2nd ed. Andrew Sayer. 336p. (Orig.). (C). 1992. pap. 22.99 (*0-415-07607-2*) Routledge.

Method in Theology. Bernard Lonergan. LC 78-181008. 1984. 14.95 (*0-8164-2204-4*) Harper SF.

Method in Theology. Bernard Lonergan. 403p. 1990. pap. text 19.95 (*0-8020-6809-X*) U of Toronto Pr.

Method in Theology: An Organon for Our Time. Frederick E. Crowe. LC 80-81015. (Pere Marquette Lectures). 68p. 1980. 15.00 (*0-87462-519-X*) Marquette.

Method Integration: Concepts & Case Studies. Ed. by Klaus Kronlof. LC 92-32373. (Wiley Series in Software-Based Systems). (Illus.). 418p. 1993. reprint ed. pap. 129.60 (*0-608-05905-6*, 206624000007) Bks Demand.

Method Is the Message: Marshall McLuhan & Karl Marx. Paul Grosswiler. 250p. 1996. 52.99 (*1-55164-075-9*, Pub. by Black Rose); pap. 24.99 (*1-55164-074-0*, Pub. by Black Rose) Consort Bk Sales.

Method Marketing: How to Make a Fortune by Getting Inside the Heads of Your Customers. Denison Hatch. LC 98-31376. (Illus.). 287p. 1999. pap. 19.95 (*1-56625-115-X*) Bonus Books.

***Method, Meaning & Revelation: The Meaning & Function of Revelation in Bernard Lonergan's Method in Theology.** Neil Ormerod. 320p. 2000. 62.00 (*0-7618-1752-2*); pap. 42.50 (*0-7618-1753-0*) U Pr of Amer.

Method, Model & Matter. Mario Bunge. LC 72-86102. (Synthese Library: No. 44). 204p. 1972. text 140.00 (*90-277-0252-7*, D Reidel) Kluwer Academic.

Method of Averaging in the Theory of Orthogonal Series, & Some Problems in the Theory of Bases. S. V. Bockarev. LC 80-26300. (Proceedings of the Steklov Institute of Mathematics Ser.: No. 146). 92p. 1980. pap. 47.00 (*0-8218-3045-7*, STEKLO/146) Am Math.

Method of Coordinates. I. M. Gelfand et al. x, 73p. 1996. 18.50 (*0-8176-3533-5*) Birkhauser.

Method of Directing Children's Study of Geography. Edwin H. Reeder. LC 73-177184. (Columbia University. Teachers College. Contributions to Education Ser.: No. 193). reprint ed. 37.50 (*0-404-55193-9*) AMS Pr.

Method of Discretization in Time. Karel Rektorys. 1982. text 251.00 (*90-277-1342-1*) Kluwer Academic.

Method of Eliminating Some Ticketing Expense in the Factory. 9p. 1956. 5.00 (*0-318-19663-8*) Clothing Mfrs.

Method of Equivalence & Its Applications. Robert Gardner. LC 89-21972. (CBMS-NSF Regional Conference Series in Applied Mathematics: No. 58). vii, 127p. 1989. pap. 32.50 (*0-89871-240-8*) Soc Indus-Appl Math.

Method of Evaluating the Performance of Positioners with Analog Input Signals & Pneumatic Output: S75.13. ISA Staff. 1989. pap. 40.00 (*1-55617-592-2*, S75.13) ISA.

Method of Freedom. Walter Lippmann. 146p. (C). 1991. pap. text 21.95 (*1-56000-559-9*) Transaction Pubs.

Method of Generalized Characteristics. Marc A. Berger & Alan D. Sloan. LC 82-8741. (Memoirs of the American Mathematical Society Ser.: No. 38/266). 35p. 1982. pap. 16.00 (*0-8218-2266-7*, MEMO/38/266) Am Math.

Method of Grace. J. Flavel. (Illus.). 1997. pap. 14.95 (*0-923309-51-9*) Hartland Pubns.

Method of Henry James. rev. ed. Joseph W. Beach. 1954. 20.00 (*0-87556-020-2*) Saifer.

Method of Jazz Improvisation with Theoretical Explanation for Guitar. Dave Smith. Ed. by Aaron Stang. 116p. 1986. pap. text 20.00 (*0-7692-1501-7*, SB257) Wrner Bros.

Method of Law: An Essay on the Statement & Arrangement of the Legal Standard of Conduct. James H. Monahan. viii, 204p. 1996. reprint ed. 35.00 (*0-8377-2480-5*, Rothman) W S Hein.

Method of Layer Potentials for the Heat Equation in Time-Varying Domains. John L. Lewis & Margaret A. Murray. LC 94-43211. (Memoirs Ser.: Vol. 545). 157p. 1995. pap. 38.00 (*0-8218-0360-3*, MEMO/114/545) Am Math.

Method of Lighting the Stage. 4th ed. Stanley McCandless. LC 56-10331. 1958. 14.95 (*0-87830-082-1*, Thtre Arts Bks) Routledge.

Method of Maximum Entropy. Henryk Gzyl. (Series on Advances in Mathematics: Vol. 29). 160p. 1995. text 48.00 (*981-02-1812-5*) World Scientific Pub.

Method of Newton's Polyhedron in the Theory of Partial Differential Equations. Simon G. Gindikin & L. R. Volevich. LC 92-35072. (Mathematics & Its Applications, Soviet Ser.: Vol. 86). (C). 1992. text 185.00 (*0-7923-2037-9*) Kluwer Academic.

Method of Orbits in Interpolation Theory, Vol. 1. Ed. by V. I. Ovchinnikov. (Mathematical Reports: Vol. 1, Pt. 2). x, 166p. 1984. text 123.00 (*3-7186-0259-8*) Gordon & Breach.

Method of Organ Playing. 8th ed. Harold Gleason. Ed. by Catharine C. Gleason. LC 95-21759. 369p. 1995. 70.00 (*0-13-207531-8*) P-H.

Method of Paired Comparisons. rev. ed. H. A. David. 1963. pap. 17.95 (*0-85264-013-7*) Lubrecht & Cramer.

Method of Paired Comparisons. 2nd ed. write for info. (*0-85264-290-3*) Lubrecht & Cramer.

Method of Philological Study of the English Language. Francis A. March. (Notable American Authors Ser.). 1999. reprint ed. lib. bdg. 125.00 (*0-7812-3940-0*) Rprt Serv.

Method of Prayer. Johannes Kelpius. 54p. (Orig.). 1992. reprint ed. pap. 7.95 (*0-922802-17-3*) Kessinger Pub.

Method of Prayer for Modern Times. Jean Kovalevsky. Ed. by Robin Amis. Tr. by Esther Williams from FRE. 135p. (Orig.). (C). 1993. pap. text 16.95 (*1-872292-18-6*) Praxis Inst.

Method of Reducing the Problems of Soiling in a Clothing Factory & Proper Drycleaning Information. 22p. 1957. 10.00 (*0-318-19665-4*) Clothing Mfrs.

Method of Response Function in Ecology. Ed. by Yuri A. Pykh & I. G. Malkina-Pykh. (Advances in Ecological Sciences Ser.: Vol. 7). 246p. 2000. 125.00 (*1-85312-662-4*, 6624, Pub. by WIT Pr) Computational Mech MA.

Method of Rothe in Evolution Equations. Jozef Kacur. 192p. (C). 1986. 68.00 (*0-7855-4981-1*, Pub. by Collets) St Mut.

Method of Science. Rom Harre & D. G. Eastwood. LC 76-116973. (Wykeham Science Ser.: No. 8). 140p. 1970. 18.00 (*0-8448-1110-6*, Crane Russak) Taylor & Francis.

Method of Selecting Foreign Stories for the American Elementary Schools. Chung I. Shang. LC 73-177795. (Columbia University. Teachers College. Contributions to Education Ser.: No. 398). reprint ed. 37.50 (*0-404-55398-2*) AMS Pr.

Method of Stylistic Analysis Exemplified on C. M. Wieland's "Geschichte des Agathon" Rebecca E. Schrader. (Germanic Studies in America: Vol. 39). 240p. 1980. 44.00 (*3-261-04796-8*) P Lang Pubng.

Method of Summary Representation for Numerical Solution of Problems of Mathematical Physics. G. Polozhii & G. Tee. LC 65-13073. (International Series of Monographs in Pure & Applied Mathematics: Vol. 79). 1965. 134.00 (*0-08-011017-7*, Pub. by Pergamon Repr) Franklin.

Method of the Divine Government Physical & Moral: 1887 Edition. James McCosh. 576p. 1996. reprint ed. 85.00 (*1-85506-196-1*) Bks Intl VA.

Method of the Holy Apostle Paul, in His Epistle to the Romans. David Hollaz. Tr. by Charles Erdmann. 19p. 1998. reprint ed. pap. 2.00 (*1-891469-17-7*) Repristination.

Method of the Siddhas: Talks on the Spiritual Technique of the Saviors of Mankind. Adi Da. (Illus.). 528p. 1996. pap. 7.95 (*1-57097-015-7*) Dawn Horse Pr.

An Asterisk (*) at the beginning of an entry indicates that the title is appearing for the first time.

M

Method of Variation of Parameters for Dynamics Systems. V. Lakshmikantham & S. G. Deo. (Mathematical Analysis & Applications Ser.: Vol. 1). 328p. 1998. text 54.00 (*90-5699-160-4*, ECU71) Gordon & Breach.

Method of Vedanta. Swami Satchidanandendra. 900p. 1989. 99.50 (*0-7103-0120-0*) Routledge.

Method of Volume Averaging. Stephen Whitaker. LC 98-47438. (Theories & Applications of Transport in Porous Media Ser.). 1998. write for info. (*0-7923-5486-9*) Kluwer Academic.

Method of Zen. Eugene Herrigel. Ed. by R. F. C. Hull & Alan W. Watts. LC 74-5120. 1974. pap. 7.00 (*0-394-71244-7*) Vin Bks.

Method or Madness. Robert Lewis. 165p. 1958. 6.50 (*0-573-69033-2*) French.

Method Performance Studies for Speciation Analysis. P. L. Quevauviller. 290p. 1998. 125.00 (*0-85404-467-1*, Pub. by Royal Soc Chem) Spr-Verlag.

Method Study. (Open Learning for Supervisory Management Ser.). 1986. pap. text 19.50 (*0-08-034165-9*, Pergamon Pr) Elsevier.

Method Study. (Open Learning for Supervisory Management Ser.). 1986. pap. text 19.50 (*0-08-070034-9*, Pergamon Pr) Elsevier.

Method, Theory & Policy in Keynes Vol. 3: Essays in Honour of Paul Davidson. Ed. by Philip Arestis. LC 97-25912. 272p. 1998. 85.00 (*1-85898-626-5*) E Elgar.

Method to Evaluate the Likelihood of Grain Shortfalls. David Eaton. (Working Paper Ser.: No. 9). 36p. 1978. pap. 2.50 (*0-89940-559-2*) LBJ Sch Pub Aff.

Method to Learn to Design the Passions, Proposed in a Conference on Their General & Particular Expression. Charles Le Brun. Tr. by John Williams from FRE. LC 92-24907. (Augustan Reprints Ser.: Nos. 200-201). 1980. reprint ed. 21.50 (*0-404-70200-7*, NC825) AMS Pr.

Method to Our Madness. Lloyd Pennbrook. 176p. (Orig.). 1992. pap. 5.95 (*0-9632330-3-3*) Pennywise.

Method to Their Madness: A History of the Actors Studio. Foster Hirsch. (Quality Paperbacks Ser.). (Illus.). 268p. 1986. reprint ed. pap. 14.95 (*0-306-80268-6*) Da Capo.

Methode de Banjo Americain. Ed. by Michael Lefferts. (FRE.). 44p. (Orig.). (C). 1997. pap. text 19.95 (*0-7692-1312-X*, 01010402) Wrner Bros.

Methode de Cor-Alto et Cor-Basse see Method for Cor Alto & Cor Basse

Methode de Flamenco pour la Guitare. Jose De Valencia. Ed. by Michael Lefferts. (FRE.). 32p. (Orig.). (C). 1997. pap. text 11.95 (*0-7692-1317-0*, 01010306) Wrner Bros.

Methode de Guitare Jazz. Jean Bonal. Ed. by Michael Lefferts. (FRE.). 72p. (Orig.). (C). 1997. pap. text 40.95 incl. audio compact disk (*0-7692-1321-9*, 01010314) Wrner Bros.

Methode de Harpe. fac. ed. Jacques G. Cousineau. (Monuments of Music & Music Literature in Facsimile Ser., Series II: Vol. 86). 1968. lib. bdg. 45.00 (*0-8450-2286-5*) Broude.

Methode de Prononciation de Francais. Barret. 29.95 (*0-685-36698-7*) Fr & Eur.

Methode der Reitkunst nach neuen Grundsatzen. Francois Baucher. (Illus.). 124p. 1978. write for info. (*3-487-08160-1*) G Olms Pubs.

Methode des Plans d'Experiences see Methods for Experimental Design: Principles & Applications for Physicists & Chemists

Methode d'Evaluation Rapide pour la Nutrition et les Soins de Sante Primaires. Susan C. Scrimshaw & Elena Hurtado. (Reference Ser.). 74p. 1991. pap. 10.95 (*0-87903-114-X*) UCLA Lat Am Ctr.

Methode et Invention Nouvelle de Dresser les Chevaux. Guillaume de Newcastle. reprint ed. 375.00 (*88-299-1177-1*, Pub. by Piccin Nuova) Gordon & Breach.

Methode et Philosophie en Physique Fondamentale Aujourd'Hui. Ed. by C. Chevalley. 104p. 1984. pap. 19.75 (*0-08-031846-0*, Pergamon Pr) Elsevier.

Methode Matematice in Optimizarea Sistemelor Diferentiale see Mathematical Methods in Optimization of Differential Systems

Methode Orange, Bk 1. Malandain & Verdol. (Methode Orange Ser.). (Illus.). (gr. 7-12). 1979. text 6.25 (*0-88345-407-6*) Prentice ESL.

Methode Orange, Bk 1. Reboullet et al. (Methode Orange Ser.). (FRE., Illus.). (gr. 7-12). 1979. pap. text 5.25 (*0-88345-406-8*) Prentice ESL.

Methode Orange-Workbook 1. Reboullet et al. (Methode Orange Ser.). (FRE., Illus.). (gr. 7-12). 1979. teacher ed. 6.75 (*0-88345-411-4*); pap. text 3.50 (*0-88345-408-4*); audio 85.00 (*0-686-60844-5*) Prentice ESL.

Methode pour Apprendre a Dessiner les Passions. Charles Le Brun. vi, 63p. 1982. reprint ed. write for info. (*3-487-06717-X*) G Olms Pubs.

Methode pour Apprendre Aisement a Jouer de la Flute Traversiere. Michel Corrette. 50p. 1975. reprint ed. 30.00 (*3-487-05714-X*) G Olms Pubs.

Methode Simple pour Apprendre a Preluder. fac. ed. Andre-Ernest Gretry. (Monuments of Music & Music Literature in Facsimile Ser., Series II: Vol. 102). 1968. lib. bdg. 35.00 (*0-8450-2302-0*) Broude.

Methoden der Klinischen Kapillarmikroskopie. Ed. by F. Mahler et al. (Illus.). 168p. 1986. pap. 68.75 (*3-8055-4409-X*) S Karger.

Methoden der Statistik: Statistical Method. W. Wallis & H. Roberts. (GER.). 584p. 1969. 65.00 (*0-8288-6607-4*, M-7557) Fr & Eur.

Methoden des Fremdsprachlichen Deutschunterrichts. Hans Hunfeld & Gerd Neuner. (Fernstudienangebot Ser.). (GER.). 184p. 1996. 11.25 (*3-468-49676-1*) Langenscheidt.

Methoden des Mykologische Laboratoriums. Hanns Kreisel & F. Schauer. (GER., Illus.). 181p. 1987. pap. text 35.00 (*3-437-20382-7*) Lubrecht & Cramer.

Methoden und Ergebnisse der Theoretischen Ozeanographie Band I: Dynamics of the Homogeneous & Quasi-Homogeneous Ocean. Wolfgang Krauss. (GER., Illus.). ix, 302p. 1973. 64.00 (*3-443-01001-6*, Pub. by Gebruder Borntraeger) Balogh.

Methoden und Ergebnisse der Theoretischen Ozeanographie Band II: Intern Wellen. Wolfgang Krauss. (GER.). viii, 248p. 1966. 65.00 (*3-443-39037-4*, Pub. by Gebruder Borntraeger) Balogh.

Methodenentwicklungen Zur Identitaetspruefung Pflanzlicher Drogen Mit Weiterfuehrenden Untersuchungen an Den Infloreszenzen Von Calendula Officinalis L. Mit Weiterfuehrenden Untersuchungen an den Infloreszenzen von Calendula L. Wolfgang Heisig. (Dissertationes Botanicae Ser.: Band 167). (GER., Illus.). vi, 162p. 1991. pap. 42.00 (*3-443-64079-6*, Pub. by Gebruder Borntraeger) Balogh.

Methodenlehre see Transzendentale Dialektik: Ein Kommentar zu Kants Kritik der reinen Vernunft

Methodenlehre der Rechtswissen. 1995. 41.00 (*3-540-59086-2*) Spr-Verlag.

Methodes. Francis Ponge. (FRE.). 248p. 1988. pap. 16.95 (*0-7859-1357-2*, 2070324923) Fr & Eur.

Methodes. Francis Ponge. (Folio Essais Ser.: No. 107). (FRE.). 1988. pap. 14.95 (*2-07-032492-3*) Schoenhof.

Methodic Approach to Writing. Marjorie V. Weber. (Illus.). 28p. 1996. pap. text 5.50 (*1-891150-52-9*) M V Weber.

Methodical Bible Study. Robert A. Traina. 288p. 1985. 22.99 (*0-310-31230-2*, 17031) Zondervan.

Methodical Memory: Invention in Current-Traditional Rhetoric. Sharon Crowley. LC 89-37101. 360p. (C). 1990. 26.95 (*0-8093-1615-3*) S Ill U Pr.

Methodical Notes: The Method & Technique of the First Violin Lessons. Mikhail A. Lobko. (Illus.). 32p. 1998. pap. 8.00 (*0-8059-4502-4*) Dorrance.

Methodical Realism. Etienne Gilson. Tr. by Philip Trower. 146p. 1990. reprint ed. pap. 8.95 (*0-931888-36-0*) Christendom Pr.

***Methodik Und Realisation Von Systemen Zur Effizienten Wissensvermittlung Durch Hypermedia.** Christian Pohl. (Illus.). 272p. 1999. 48.95 (*3-631-33919-4*) P Lang Pubng.

Methodische Dressur des Reitpferdes nach den Letzten Anweisungen von Baucher. F. Faverot De Kerbrech. 122p. 1981. write for info. (*3-487-08226-8*) G Olms Pubs.

Methodische und Standortoekologische Untersuchungen Zum Naehrstoffumsatz Im Gruenland. Walter Beer. (Dissertationes Botanicae Ser.: Band 242). (Illus.). vi, 216p. 1995. pap. 56.00 (*3-443-64154-7*, Pub. by Gebruder Borntraeger) Balogh.

Methodischer Unterricht in der Ueberzeugenden Erkenntniss der Biblischen Religion: Zur Fortgesetzten Ausfuehrung des in der Philalethie Angegebenen Plans. Johann B. Basedow. (GER.). xxxii, 368p. 1985. reprint ed. write for info. (*3-487-07576-8*) G Olms Pubs.

Methodism. 2nd ed. Rupert E. Davies. 1976. pap. text 18.25 (*0-7162-0280-8*) Epworth Pr.

Methodism & Education 1849-1902: J. H. Rigg, Romanism & Wesleyan Schools. John T. Smith. LC 98-20503. (Illus.). 270p. 1998. text 75.00 (*0-19-826964-1*) OUP.

Methodism & the Frontier: Indiana Proving Ground. Elizabeth K. Nottingham. LC 41-19465. reprint ed. 20.00 (*0-404-04798-X*) AMS Pr.

Methodism & the Literature of the 18th Century. Thomas B. Shepherd. LC 68-4718. (Studies in Comparative Literature: No. 35). 1969. reprint ed. lib. bdg. 75.00 (*0-8383-0680-2*) M S G Haskell Hse.

***Methodism & the Southern Mind, 1770-1810.** Cynthia L. Lyerly. (Religion in America Ser.). 264p. 1998. text 45.00 (*0-19-511429-9*) OUP.

Methodism in Mississippi, 2 vols. rev. ed. John G. Jones. 1966. 40.00 (*0-87511-592-6*) Claitors.

Methodism in Russia & the Baltic States: History & Renewal. Ed. by S. T. Kimbrough. 256p. (Orig.). 1995. pap. 19.95 (*0-687-00600-7*) Abingdon.

Methodism in the Town of Boston. William Leary. (C). 1989. text 35.00 (*0-902662-55-4*, Pub. by R K Pubns); pap. text 35.00 (*0-7855-6993-6*, Pub. by R K Pubns) St Mut.

Methodism in Their Madness. Twila J. Roller. Ed. by Bill Roller. (Illus.). 152p. (Orig.). (C). 1993. pap. text 6.95 (*1-880047-04-7*) Creative Des.

***Methodism Spirituality.** Epworth Press Staff. 1998. pap. 18.00 (*0-7162-0525-4*) Epworth Pr.

***Methodism Theology.** Thomas A. Langford. 1998. pap. 18.00 (*0-7162-0521-1*) Epworth Pr.

Methodism's Racial Dilemma: The Story of the Central Jurisdiction. James S. Thomas. 192p. (Orig.). 1992. 17.95 (*0-687-37129-5*) Abingdon.

Methodist: A Poem. Evan Lloyd. LC 92-1718. (Augustan Reprints Ser.: No. 151-152). 1972. reprint ed. 21.50 (*0-404-70151-5*, PR3541) AMS Pr.

Methodist Celebration: A Cornish Contribution. Sarah Foot. (C). 1989. text 40.00 (*1-85022-040-9*, Pub. by Dyllansow Truran) St Mut.

Methodist Church Record Books Milledyeville, Georgia, 1811-1876. Hugh T. Harrington. 307p. 1997. pap. write for info. (*1-890307-04-1*) Boyd Pub Co.

***Methodist Comprehensive Pain Institute's Cancer Pain Sourcebook.** Roger Cicala. 2001. pap. 17.95 (*0-7373-0423-5*, Pub. by Lowell Hse) NTC Contemp Pub Co.

Methodist Conference in America: A History. Russell E. Richey. 320p. 1996. pap. 17.95 (*0-687-02187-1*) Abingdon.

Methodist Doctrine: The Essentials. Ted A. Campbell. LC 98-43793. 144p. 1999. pap. 12.00 (*0-687-03475-2*) Abingdon.

***Methodist Experience in America, Vol. 2.** Russell E. Richey et al. LC 00-42023. 2000. write for info. (*0-687-24673-3*) Abingdon.

Methodist Hospital of Houston. Marilyn M. Sibley. (Illus.). 256p. 1990. 19.95 (*0-87611-088-X*) Tex St Hist Assn.

Methodist Hymnal Concordance. Robert F. Klepper. LC 86-29811. 800p. 1987. 71.00 (*0-8108-1968-6*) Scarecrow.

Methodist Preachers in Georgia, 1783-1900 Supplement. Ed. by Harold A. Lawrence. 224p. 1995. 20.00 (*0-9644858-0-X*) Boyd Pub Co.

Methodist Societies: History, Nature & Design see Works of John Wesley

Methodist Trail Blazer: Philip Gatch. rev. ed. Elizabeth Connor. LC 76-101704. (Illus.). 260p. reprint ed. pap. 12.00 (*0-914960-51-2*) Academy Bks.

Methodist Union Catalog: Pre-1976 Imprints, 20 vols., Vol. I, A[00ad]bj. Ed. by Kenneth E. Rowe. LC 75-33190. 438p. 1975. 35.00 (*0-8108-0880-3*) Scarecrow.

Methodist Union Catalog: Pre-1976 Imprints, Vol. II: Bl[00ad]cha. Ed. by Kenneth E. Rowe. LC 75-33190. 422p. 1976. 35.00 (*0-8108-0920-6*) Scarecrow.

Methodist Union Catalog: Pre-1976 Imprints, Vol. III, Che[00ad]Dix. Ed. by Kenneth E. Rowe. LC 75-33190. 431p. 1978. 35.00 (*0-8108-1067-0*) Scarecrow.

Methodist Union Catalog: Pre-1976 Imprints, Vol. IV, Do[00ad]Fy. Ed. by Kenneth E. Rowe. LC 75-33190. 436p. 1979. 40.00 (*0-8108-1225-8*) Scarecrow.

Methodist Union Catalog: Pre-1976 Imprints, Vol. V. Kenneth E. Rowe. LC 75-33190. 371p. 1981. 35.00 (*0-8108-1454-4*) Scarecrow.

Methodist Union Catalog: Pre-1976 Imprints, Vol. VI. Ed. by Kenneth E. Rowe. LC 75-33190. 360p. 1985. 37.50 (*0-8108-1725-X*) Scarecrow.

Methodist Union Catalog Vol. VII: J-Le: Pre-1976 Imprints. Ed. by Kenneth E. Rowe. 419p. 1994. 52.00 (*0-8108-2669-0*) Scarecrow.

Methodist Way & Responsible Discipleship Leadership. Bishop Caesar & David Coleman. LC 93-80658. 100p. (Orig.). 1993. pap. text 6.00 (*1-883667-06-2*) Christian Meth.

Methodists. James E. Kirby et al. 296p. 1998. pap., student ed. 19.95 (*0-275-96439-6*, Praeger Pubs) Greenwood.

Methodists. D. Wright. xx, 276p. 1993. pap. write for info. (*1-86373-428-7*, Pub. by Allen & Unwin Pty) IPG Chicago.

Methodists, 8. James E. Kirby et al. LC 96-536. (Denominations in America Ser.: No. 8). 424p. 1996. lib. bdg. 85.00 (*0-313-22048-4*, Greenwood Pr) Greenwood.

Methodists & the Making of America. Charles W. Ferguson. 480p. 1983. reprint ed. 17.95 (*0-89015-424-4*) Sunbelt Media.

Methodists & Women's Education in Ontario, 1836-1925. Johanna M. Selles. LC 97-184235. (Studies in the History of Religion: Vol. 25). (Illus.). 320p. 1996. 44.95 (*0-7735-1443-0*, LC1768, Pub. by McG-Queens Univ Pr) CUP Services.

***Methodists at Middletown, 1800-2000: A Bicentennial History of Middletown United Methodist Church.** Jim Cox. Ed. by William H. Strode. LC 99-73603. (Illus.). 214p. 1999. write for info. (*1-56469-063-6*) Harmony Hse Pub.

Methodists in Dialogue. Geoffrey Wainwright. LC 95-6911. (Kingswood Ser.). 320p. (Orig.). 1995. pap. 16.95 (*0-687-01133-7*) Abingdon.

Methodius of Olympus: Divine Sovereignty, Human Freedom, & Life in Christ. L. G. Patterson. LC 96-29371. 270p. (C). 1997. text 59.95 (*0-8132-0875-0*) Cath U Pr.

Methodo Scientifica Pertractatum: Mos geometricus und Kalkuelbegriff in der Philosophischen Theorienbildung des 17. und 18. Hans W. Arndt. (Quellen und Studien zur Philosophie: Vol. 4). 1971. 89.25 (*3-11-003942-7*) De Gruyter.

Methodological & Biostatistical Foundations of Clinical Neuropsychology. Ed. by Byron P. Rourke et al. xii, 556p. 1992. 81.50 (*90-265-1165-5*); pap. 41.00 (*90-265-1245-7*) Swets.

Methodological & Conceptual Issues in Applied Behavior Analysis, Vol. 4. Ed. by Shingo Iwata. 503p. 1989. reprint ed. pap. text 25.00 (*1-882018-01-X*) Jrnl Applied Behavior Analysis.

Methodological & Statistical Advances in the Study of Individual Differences. Ed. by Cecil R. Reynolds & Victor L. Willson. LC 85-17042. (Perspectives on Individual Differences Ser.). (Illus.). 492p. (C). 1985. 114.00 (*0-306-41962-9*, Plenum Trade) Perseus Pubng.

Methodological Approaches in Pharmacoepidemiology: Application to Spontaneous Reporting. Ed. by B. Begaud. 180p. 1993. 149.50 (*0-444-81577-5*) Elsevier.

Methodological Approaches to the Study of Career. Ed. by Richard A. Young & William A. Borgen. LC 89-33969. 286p. 1990. 62.95 (*0-275-93299-0*, C3299, Praeger Pubs) Greenwood.

Methodological Aspects of Construction Price Indices. Eurostat Staff. LC 98-125685. 125p. 1996. pap. 25.00 (*92-827-8921-7*, CA98-96-300-ENC, Pub. by Comm Europ Commun) Bernan Associates.

Methodological Aspects of the Development of Low Temperature Physics 1881-1956: Concepts Out of Context(s) Kostas Gavroglu & Yorgos Goudaroulis. 192p. (C). 1988. lib. bdg. 137.50 (*90-247-3699-4*, Pub. by Kluwer Academic) Kluwer Academic.

Methodological Aspects of Transformational Generative Phonology. Rudolph P. Botha. (Janua Linguarum, Ser. Minor: No. 112). 266p. 1971. pap. text 38.50 (*90-279-1761-2*) Mouton.

Methodological Controversy in Economics Vol. 2: Historical Essays in Honor of T. W. Hutchinson. Ed. by A. W. Coats et al. LC 83-48096. (Political Economy & Public Policy Ser.: Vol. 2). 292p. 1983. 78.50 (*0-89232-395-7*) Jai Pr.

Methodological Dictionary of Marketing: Dictionnaire Methodologique du Marketing. G. Serraf. (FRE.). 272p. 1985. 85.00 (*0-8288-1267-5*, F71270) Fr & Eur.

Methodological Foundations of Macroeconomics: Keynes & Lucas. Allessandro Vercelli. (Illus.). 285p. (C). 1991. text 64.95 (*0-521-39294-2*) Cambridge U Pr.

Methodological Foundations of Standardsetting for Corporate Financial Reporting. James C. Gaa. (Studies in Accounting Research: No. 28). 224p. 1988. 17.00 (*0-86539-065-7*) Am Accounting.

Methodological Introduction to the History of the City of Tokyo. 30p. 1981. pap. write for info. (*92-808-0085-X*, TUNU170, Pub. by UN Univ Pr) Brookings.

Methodological Issues & Strategies in Clinical Research. Ed. by Alan E. Kazdin. (Illus.). 765p. 1992. text 59.95 (*1-55798-154-X*) Am Psychol.

Methodological Issues & Strategies in Clinical Research. 2nd ed. Ed. by Alan E. Kazdin. (Illus.). 825p. 1992. pap. text 39.95 (*1-55798-167-1*) Am Psychol.

Methodological Issues & Strategies in Clinical Research. 2nd ed. Ed. by Alan E. Kazdin. LC 97-42491. 825p. 1998. text 59.95 (*1-55798-481-6*, 431-602A); pap. text 39.95 (*1-55798-482-4*, 431-603A) Am Psychol.

Methodological Issues for Health Care Surveys. Brneda G. Cox & Steven Cohen. (Statistics: Textbooks & Monographs: Vol. 61). (Illus.). 480p. 1985. text 175.00 (*0-8247-7323-3*) Dekker.

Methodological Issues in Aging Research. Ed. by K. Warner Schaie et al. 272p. 1988. 36.95 (*0-8261-5400-X*) Springer Pub.

Methodological Issues in AIDS Behavioral Research. D. G. Ostrow & R. C. Kessler. (AIDS Prevention & Mental Health Ser.). (Illus.). 374p. (C). 1993. text 59.00 (*0-306-44439-9*, Kluwer Plenum) Kluwer Academic.

Methodological Issues in Applied Social Psychology. F. B. Bryant et al. (Social Psychological Applications to Social Issues Ser.: Vol. 2). (Illus.). 328p. (C). 1992. 57.50 (*0-306-44173-X*, Plenum Trade) Perseus Pubng.

Methodological Issues in Chinese Studies. Ed. by Amy A. Wilson et al. LC 83-2131. 136p. 1983. 55.00 (*0-275-91103-9*, C1103, Praeger Pubs) Greenwood.

Methodological Issues in Clinical Child Psychology Research Vol. 24, No. 2, 1995: A Special Issue of the "Journal of Clinical Child Psychology" Ed. by Sheila M. Eyberg. 128p. 1995. pap. 20.00 (*0-8058-9945-6*) L Erlbaum Assocs.

Methodological Issues in Neuropsychological Assessment & Rehabilitation. Ed. by Klaus Willmes. LC 98-149852. (Special Issue of Neuropsychological Rehabilitation). 461p. 1997. 49.95 (*0-86377-977-8*) Taylor & Francis.

Methodological Issues in Religious Studies. Ed. by Robert D. Baird. LC 75-44170. (Orig.). (C). 1976. pap. text 5.95 (*0-914914-07-3*); lib. bdg. 14.95 (*0-914914-08-1*) New Horizons.

Methodological Perception of Imagery Literature. Lillie Pringle. (Orig.). 1990. pap. 12.50 (*0-913412-30-9*) Brandon Hse.

Methodological Problems in Migraine Trails. Ed. by F. Clifford Rose. (Journal: Neuroepidemiology: Vol. 6, No. 4). (Illus.). iv, 80p. 1987. pap. 48.00 (*3-8055-4677-7*) S Karger.

Methodological Problems of Clinical Trials in Dementia. Ed. by Clifford F. Rose. (Journal: Neuroepidemiology: Vol. 9, No. 4, 1990). (Illus.). 60p. 1990. pap. 39.25 (*3-8055-5239-4*) S Karger.

Methodological Status of Grammatical Argumentation. Rudolf B. Botha. LC 79-126050. (Janua Linguarum, Series Major: No. 105). (Orig.). 1970. pap. text 35.40 (*90-279-0714-5*) Mouton.

Methodological Studies in the History of Religions: With Special Reference to Hinduism & Buddhism N. S. Raman & Indian Institute of Advanced Study Staff. LC 99-931770. x, 255p. 1998. write for info. (*81-85952-54-X*) Indian Inst.

Methodological Supplement see Labour Force Estimates & Projections, 1950-2000

Methodological Unity of Science. Ed. by Mario Bunge. LC 73-83554. (Theory & Decision Library: No. 3). 1973. lib. bdg. 112.00 (*90-277-0354-X*) Kluwer Academic.

Methodological Unity of Science. Ed. by Mario Bunge. LC 73-83554. (Theory & Decision Library: No. 3). 1973. pap. text 73.50 (*90-277-0404-X*) Kluwer Academic.

Methodological Variance: Essays in Epistemological Ontology & the Methodology of Science. G. L. Pandit. (Boston Studies in the Philosophy of Science). 440p. (C). 1991. lib. bdg. 215.00 (*0-7923-1263-5*, Pub. by Kluwer Academic) Kluwer Academic.

Methodologie der Wissenschaft und Literaturwissenschaftliche Praxis. Ulrich Charpa. (Philosophische Texte und Studien: Vol. 6). (GER.). 152p. 1983. write for info. (*3-487-07432-X*) G Olms Pubs.

Methodologies for Analyzing Public Policies. Ed. by Frank P. Scioli, Jr. & Thomas J. Cook. 192p. 1975. boxed set 27.95 (*0-669-00596-7*) Transaction Pubs.

Methodologies for Analyzing Public Policies. Frank P. Scioli, Jr. & Thomas J. Cook. 192p. 1985. reprint ed. 42.00 (*0-8191-5158-0*) U Pr of Amer.

***Methodologies for Assessing the Economic Consequences of Nuclear Reactor Accidents.** NEA Staff. (Radiation Protection Ser.). 116p. 2000. pap. 31.00 (*92-64-17658-6*, 66 2000 10 1 P, Pub. by Org for Econ) OECD.

Methodologies for Assessing the Impact of Deep Sea-Bed Minerals on the World Economy. 153p. 1986. pap. 16.50 (*92-1-104188-0*, E.86.II.A.13) UN.

An Asterisk (*) at the beginning of an entry indicates that the title is appearing for the first time.

*__Methodologies for Developing & Managing Emerging Technology-Based Information Systems: Information Systems Metholologies 1998, 6th International Conference on Information Systems Methodologies.__ Ed. by T. Wood-Harper et al. LC 99-13007. xii, 404p. 1999. pap. 109.00 (*1-85233-079-1*, Pub. by Spr-Verlag) Spr-Verlag.

Methodologies for Intelligent Systems: Proceedings of the 7th International Symposium, ISMIS '93, Trondheim, Norway, June 15-18, 1993. Ed. by Zbigniew W. Ras & J. Komorowski. (Lecture Notes in Artificial Intelligence: Vol. 689). xi, 651p. 1993. 93.95 (*0-387-56804-2*) Spr-Verlag.

Methodologies for Intelligent Systems: Proceedings of the 8th International Symposium, ISMIS '94, Charlotte, North Carolina, U. S. A., Oct. 16-19, 1994. International Symposium on Methodologies for Intel. Ed. by Zbigniew W. Ras et al. LC 94-32619. (Lecture Notes in Computer Science, Vol. 869). 1994. write for info. (*0-387-58495-1*) Spr-Verlag.

Methodologies for Intelligent Systems: Proceedings of the 8th International Symposium, ISMIS '94, Charlotte, North Carolina, USA, October 16-19, 1994. Ed. by Zbigniew W. Ras & Maria Zemankova. (Lecture Notes in Computer Science: Lecture Notes in Artificial Intelligence: Vol. 869). x, 610p. 1994. 87.95 (*3-540-58495-1*) Spr-Verlag.

Methodologies for Intelligent Systems: 6th International Symposium, ISMIS '91 Charlotte, NC, U. S. A., October 16-19, 1991 Proceedings. Ed. by Joerg H. Siekmann et al. (Lecture Notes in Artifical Intelligence, Subseries of Lecture Notes in Computer Science: Vol. 542). x, 644p. 1991. 81.00 (*0-387-54563-8*) Spr-Verlag.

Methodologies for Knowledge Discovery & Data Mining: Third Pacific-Asia Conference, PAKDD '99, Beijing, China, April 26-28, 1999, Proceedings. N. Zhong & L. Zhou. Ed. by J. G. Carbonell & J. Siekmann. LC 99-23323. (Lecture Notes in Artificial Intelligence: Vol. 1574). xv, 533p. 1999. pap. 79.00 (*3-540-65866-1*) Spr-Verlag.

Methodologies for Monitoring & Evaluating Vitamin A Deficiency Intervention Programs. Ed. by Guillermo Arrogave et al. LC 89-83358. 66p. 1989. pap. text 3.50 (*0-944398-04-9*) ILSI.

Methodologies for Predicting the Service Lives of Coating Systems. Jonathan W. Martin. (Illus.). 68p. (C). 1998. pap. text 35.00 (*0-7881-7185-2*) DIANE Pub.

Methodologies for Predicting the Service Lives of Coating Systems. Jonathan W. Martin et al. (Illus.). 34p. 1996. pap. 30.00 (*0-934010-33-1*) Fed Soc Coat Tech.

Methodologies for Studying Agricultural Markets in Developing Countries. P. Magrath. 1992. pap. 40.00 (*0-85954-310-2*, Pub. by Nat Res Inst) St Mut.

Methodologies for the Conception, Design & Application of Intelligent Systems: Proceedings of the 4th International Conference on Soft Computing (Iizuka'96): September 30-October 5, 1996, Iizuka, Fukuoka, Japan. Takeshi Yamakawa et al. LC 96-27106. 1996. write for info. (*981-02-2845-7*) World Scientific Pub.

Methodologies for the Conception, Design & Application of Intelligent Systems: Proceedings of the 4th International Conference on Soft Computing (Iizuka'96): September 30-October 5, 1996, Iizuka, Fukuoka, Japan. Takeshi Yamakawa et al. LC 96-27106. 1996. write for info. (*981-02-2930-5*); write for info. (*981-02-2932-1*); write for info. (*981-02-2933-X*); pap. write for info. (*981-02-2846-5*); pap. write for info. (*981-02-2931-3*) World Scientific Pub.

Methodologies for the Conception, Design & Application of Soft Computing: Proceedings of the 5th International Conference on Soft Computing & Information/intelligent Systems Iizuka, Fukuoka, Japan 16 - 20 October 1998, 2 Vol. Ed. by Takeshi Yamakawa & Gen Matsumoto. 1112p. 168.00 (*981-02-3632-8*) World Scientific Pub.

Methodologies for the Determination of Setpoints for Nuclear Safety-Related Instrumentation: RP64.04, Pt. II. ISA Staff. 1994. pap. 120.00 (*1-55617-535-3*, RP67.04) ISA.

Methodologies in Nucleoside Synthesis. Nair. 250p. 1998. 1.00 (*0-12-513810-5*) Acad Pr.

Methodologies of Art. Ed. by Laurie S. Adams. LC 96-10778. 192p. 1996. pap. 25.00 (*0-06-430231-8*) HarpC.

Methodologies of Using Neural Network & Fuzzy Logic Technologies for Motor Incipient Fault Detection. Mo-Yuen Chow. LC 97-34193. 1997. 30.00 (*981-02-3265-9*) World Scientific Pub.

Methodologies, Techniques, & Tools for Design Development. Vol. 5. 248p. 1994. write for info. (*0-318-72841-9*, H0912E) ASME.

Methodologische Aspekte der Semantikforschung: Beitrage der Konferenz Methodologische Aspekte der Semantikforschung an der Universitat Koblenz - Landau/Abteilung Landau (1996) Inge Pohl. (GER., Illus.). 440p. 1997. 63.95 (*3-631-31326-8*) P Lang Pubng.

Methodology: Foundations of Inference & Research in the Behavioral Sciences. Adriaan De Groot. (Psychological Studies: No. 6). 1969. text 43.10 (*90-279-6250-2*) Mouton.

Methodology & African Prehistory see General History of Africa

Methodology & Economics: A Critical Introduction. John Pheby. LC 90-28626. 145p. (C). (gr. 13). 1991. text 64.95 (*0-87332-851-5*) M E Sharpe.

Methodology & Economics: A Critical Introduction. John Pheby. LC 90-28626. 145p. (C). (gr. 13). 1991. pap. text 32.95 (*0-87332-852-3*) M E Sharpe.

Methodology & Epistemology for Social Sciences: Selected Papers. Donald T. Campbell. Ed. by E. Samuel Overman. 630p. 1988. 75.00 (*0-226-09248-8*) U Ch Pr.

Methodology & Software for Interactive Decision Support. Ed. by A. Lewandowski & I. Stanchev. (Lecture Notes in Economics & Mathematical Systems Ser.: Vol. 337). viii, 308p. 1989. 44.95 (*0-387-51572-0*) Spr-Verlag.

*__Methodology & Tacit Knowledge.__ Magnus, pseud. LC 98-47539. 426p. (C). 1999. 121.50 (*0-471-98297-0*) Wiley.

Methodology & Validation (ESC '87) (Simulation Ser.: Vol. 19, No. 1). 90p. 1987. 40.00 (*0-911801-16-2*, SS19-1) Soc Computer Sim.

Methodology, Ecological, Genetic & Nutritional Effects on Growth Vol. 3. 2nd ed. F. Falkner & J. M. Tanner. LC 85-19397. (Human Growth Ser.). (Illus.). 574p. (C). 1986. text 125.00 (*0-306-41953-X*) Kluwer Academic.

Methodology, Epistemology, & Philosophy of Science. Carl G. Hempel et al. 432p. 1983. text 215.00 (*90-277-1646-3*, D Reidel) Kluwer Academic.

Methodology for a New Microeconomics: The Critical Foundations. Lawrence A. Boland. 208p. 1987. pap. text 18.95 (*0-04-330407-9*) Routledge.

Methodology for Analytical Toxicology, Vol. I. Ed. by Irving Sunshine. 478p. 1975. 270.00 (*0-8493-0716-3*, RA1221, CRC Reprint) Franklin.

Methodology for Analytical Toxicology, Vol. II. Irving Sunshine. 272p. 1982. 149.00 (*0-8493-0717-1*, RA1221, CRC Reprint) Franklin.

Methodology for Analytical Toxicology, Vol. 3. rev. ed. Irving Sunshine. LC 74-30747. 312p. 1985. 173.00 (*0-8493-0718-X*, RA1221) Franklin.

*__Methodology for Analyzing Precursors to Earthquake Initiated & Fire Initiated Accident Sequences.__ R. J. Budnitz. 172p. 1998. per. 15.00 (*0-16-062911-X*) USGPO.

Methodology for Assessing the Transportation Energy Impacts of Urban Development: A Project Report. 104p. 1981. 20.00 (*0-318-17723-4*, DG 81-325) Pub Tech Inc.

Methodology for Assessment of Medical It Based Systems. (Studies in Health Technology & Informatics: No. 42). 308p. (gr. 12). 1997. 73.00 (*90-5199-337-4*) IOS Press.

Methodology for Biomass Determinations & Microbial Activities in Sediments-STP 673. Ed. by C. D. Litchfield & P. L. Seyfried. 199p. 1979. 22.50 (*0-8031-0511-8*, STP673) ASTM.

Methodology for Client/Server. Roger Fournier. LC 98-20471. 912p. 1998. pap. 58.00 (*0-13-598426-2*) P-H.

Methodology for Creating Businesss Knowledge. 2nd ed. Ingeman Arbnor & Bjorn Bjerke. LC 96-25244. 1996. 65.00 (*0-7619-0449-2*); pap. 32.00 (*0-7619-0450-6*) Sage.

Methodology for Developing & Deploying Internet & Intranet Solutions. Jeff R. Greenberg. LC 97-41592. 400p. (C). 1997. 45.00 (*0-13-209677-3*) P-H.

Methodology for Editing & Translating a Source Material on History of Science & the Text of the Abhidammatthasangahasarupa, 2 vols. Chandra B. Varma. 1996. 36.00 (*0-614-30754-6*, Pub. by Eastern Bk Linkers) Nataraj Bks.

Methodology for Energy Impact Analysis of Community Development Projects. 100p. 1980. 10.00 (*0-318-16229-6*, PI80314) Pub Tech Inc.

Methodology for Evaluating Highway Air Pollution Dispersion Models. (National Cooperative Highway Research Program Report Ser.: No. 245). 85p. 1981. 8.40 (*0-309-03410-8*, NR245) Transport Res Bd.

Methodology for Family Studies of Genetic Factors: Proceedings of the WHO Scientific Group, Geneva, 1970. WHO Staff. (Technical Reports: No. 466). 1971. pap. text 5.00 (*92-4-120466-4*, 1100466) World Health.

Methodology for Genetic Studies of Twins & Families. Michael C. Neale. 524p. (C). 1992. text 273.50 (*0-7923-1874-9*) Kluwer Academic.

Methodology for Knowledge-Based Systems: A Survey of Training Resources. Sara Hedberg. 1989. 95.00 (*0-471-50884-5*) Wiley.

Methodology for Land & Housing Market Analysis. Ed. by Gareth Jones & Peter M. Ward. 288p. 1994. text 37.95 (*1-55844-123-9*) Lincoln Inst Land.

Methodology for Population Studies & Development. Ed. by Kuttan Mahadevan & Parameswara Krishnan. LC 92-15028. (Illus.). 428p. (C). 1993. text 42.00 (*0-8039-9431-1*, Pub. by Sage India Pvt) Sage.

Methodology for Social Research: With a New Introductory Essay. Gideon Sjoberg & Roger Nett. 416p. (C). 1996. pap. text 20.95 (*0-88133-914-8*) Waveland Pr.

Methodology for Student Drug-Use Surveys. R. Smart & P. Hughes. (WHO Offset Publications: No. 50). 55p. 1980. 7.00 (*92-4-170050-5*) World Health.

Methodology for Teaching the Culturally Particular African American Child: A Guide for Parents & Teachers. E. Curtis Alexander. 1989. 3.95 (*0-938818-21-X*) ECA Assoc.

Methodology for the Human Sciences: Systems of Inquiry. Donald E. Polkinghorn. LC 82-5895. (SUNY Series in Transpersonal & Humanistic Psychology). 349p. (C). 1984. text 49.50 (*0-87395-663-X*) State U NY Pr.

Methodology for the Human Sciences: Systems of Inquiry. Donald E. Polkinghorne. LC 82-5895. (SUNY Series in Transpersonal & Humanistic Psychology). 349p. (C). 1984. pap. text 16.95 (*0-87395-664-8*) State U NY Pr.

Methodology for the Management of Ageing of Nuclear Power Plant Components Important to Safety. (Technical Reports Ser.: No. 338). 50p. 1992. pap. 25.00 (*92-0-102592-0*, STI/DOC/338, Pub. by IAEA) Bernan Associates.

Methodology for the Modeling & Simulation of Microsystems. Bartlomiej F. Romanowicz. LC 98-41309. (Microsystems Ser.). 136p. 1998. 98.00 (*0-7923-8306-0*) Kluwer Academic.

Methodology for the Serum Bactericidal Test: Tentative Guideline (1992), Vol. 7. 1992. 75.00 (*1-56238-142-3*, M21-T) NCCLS.

Methodology for Uncertainty in Knowledge-Based Systems. K. Weichselberger & S. Pohlmann. (Lecture Notes in Artificial Intelligence Ser.). viii, 132p. 1990. 24.50 (*0-387-52336-7*) Spr-Verlag.

Methodology, Implementation & Applications of Decision Support Systems. Ed. by A. Lewandowski et al. (CISM International Centre for Mechanical Sciences Ser.: Vol. 320). (Illus.). vi, 322p. 1991. 52.95 (*0-387-82297-6*) Spr-Verlag.

Methodology in Human Fatigue Assessment: Symposium on Methodology in Human Fatigue Assessment, Kyoto, Japan, 1969. LC 72-304858. 200p. 1971. 42.00 (*0-85066-049-1*) Taylor & Francis.

Methodology in Microcirculation: Proceedings of the European Conference on Microcirculation 7th, Aberdeen, Aug-Sept, 1972. European Conference on Microcirculation Staff. Ed. by D. H. Lewis & J. Ditzel. (Bibliotheca Anatomica Ser.: No. 11). 1974. 248.75 (*3-8055-1571-5*) S Karger.

Methodology in Psychoanalytic Research. Bornstein. (Psychoanalytic Inquiry Ser.: Vol. 9, No. 2). 1989. 20.00 (*0-88163-958-3*) Analytic Pr.

Methodology in TESOL. Michael H. Long & Jack C. Richards. 421p. (J). 1987. mass mkt. 28.95 (*0-8384-2695-6*, Newbury) Heinle & Heinle.

Methodology in the Academic Teaching of Judaism. Ed. by Zev Garber. (Studies in Judaism). 308p. (Orig.). (C). 1987. pap. text 26.00 (*0-8191-5724-4*) U Pr of Amer.

Methodology in the Academic Teaching of the Holocaust. Ed. by Zev Garber et al. LC 88-5591. (Studies in Judaism). 364p. (Orig.). (C). 1988. pap. text 27.00 (*0-8191-6962-5*) U Pr of Amer.

Methodology, Metaphysics & the History of Science: In Memory of Benjamin Nelson. Ed. by Robert S. Cohen & Marx W. Wartofsky. (Boston Studies in the Philosophy of Science: No. 84). 384p. 1984. text 206.50 (*90-277-1711-7*) Kluwer Academic.

Methodology, Money & the Firm: The Collected Essays of D. P. O'Brien, 2 vols., Set. D. P. O'Brien. LC 94-3920. (Economists of the Twentieth Century Ser.). 944p. 1994. 200.00 (*1-85278-966-2*) E Elgar.

Methodology of Anthropological Comparisons: An Analysis of Comparative Methods in Social & Cultural Anthropology. Gopala Sarana. LC 74-16673. (Viking Fund Publications in Anthropology: No. 53). 118p. (C). 1975. pap. 9.95 (*0-8165-0450-4*) U of Ariz Pr.

Methodology of Applying Machine Learning: Papers from the AAAI Workshop. Ed. by Robert Engles. (Technical Reports: Vol. WS-98-16). (Illus.). 58p. 1998. spiral bd. 25.00 (*1-57735-069-3*) AAAI Pr.

Methodology of Clinical Drug Trials. 2nd rev. ed. A. Spriet et al. (Illus.). viii, 270p. 1994. 123.50 (*3-8055-5856-2*) S Karger.

Methodology of Dawah Ilallah. Shamim A. Siddiqi. 1989. write for info. (*0-9625301-0-7*) Forum Islamic.

Methodology of Econometrics, 2 vols., Set. Ed. by Dale J. Poirier. (International Library of Critical Writings in Economics: Vol. 6). 1008p. 1994. 375.00 (*1-85278-844-5*) E Elgar.

Methodology of Economic Model Building: Model Building after Samuelson. Lawrence A. Boland. (New Library of Economics). 208p. (C). 1991. pap. 27.99 (*0-415-06462-7*, A5685) Routledge.

Methodology of Economic Thought. Ed. by Warren J. Samuels. LC 78-62900. 603p. 1980. pap. text 24.95 (*0-87855-645-1*) Transaction Pubs.

Methodology of Economic Thought. 2nd rev. ed. Ed. by Marc R. Tool & Warren J. Samuels. 530p. 1989. 24.95 (*0-88738-757-8*) Transaction Pubs.

Methodology of Economics, 7 vols. Intro. by Roger Backhouse. 1900p. (C). (gr. 13). 1997. 950.00 (*0-415-15380-8*) Routledge.

Methodology of Economics: or How Economists Explain. 2nd ed. Mark Blaug. (Surveys of Economic Literature Ser.). 314p. (C). 1992. pap. text 21.95 (*0-521-43678-8*) Cambridge U Pr.

Methodology of Frontal & Executive Function. Ed. by Patrick Rabbit. LC 98-128198. 264p. 1997. 54.95 (*0-86377-485-7*, Pub. by Psychol Pr) Taylor & Francis.

Methodology of G. E. Moore. Sal Fratantaro. LC 97-77550. 154p. 1998. text 55.95 (*1-85972-084-6*, Pub. by Ashgate Pub) Ashgate Pub Co.

Methodology of Herbert Blumer. Kenneth Baugh, Jr. (American Sociological Assn. Rose Monographs). 118p. (C). 1990. text 42.50 (*0-521-38246-7*) Cambridge U Pr.

Methodology of History. Jerzy Topolski. Ed. by PWN, Polish Scientific Publishers Staff. Tr. by Oligierd Wojtasiewicz from POL. LC 76-25080. (Synthese Library: No. 88). 700p. 1977. text 171.00 (*90-277-0550-X*, D Reidel) Kluwer Academic.

Methodology of Industrial Short-Term Indicators: Rules & Recommendations. 229p. 1996. pap. 40.00 (*92-827-7910-6*, CA97-96-079-ENC, Pub. by Comm Europ Commun) Bernan Associates.

Methodology of Macroeconomic Thought: A Conceptual Analysis of Schools of Thought in Economics. Sheila C. Dow. LC 96-922. Orig. Title: Macroeconomic Thought. 272p. 1996. 90.00 (*1-85278-980-8*) E Elgar.

Methodology of Macroeconomic Thought: A Conceptual Analysis of Schools of Thought in Economics. Sheila C. Dow. LC 96-922. Orig. Title: Macroeconomic Thought. 272p. 1998. pap. 25.00 (*1-85898-909-4*) E Elgar.

Methodology of Measuring the Impact of Family Planning Programmes on Fertility: Addendum Manual IX. (Population Studies: No. 66). 38p. pap. 8.00 (*92-1-151160-7*, E.78.XIII.4) UN.

Methodology of Nutritional Surveillance: 27th Report of a Joint FAO/UNICEF/WHO Expert Committee. (Technical Report Ser.: No. 593). 66p. 1976. pap. text 7.00 (*92-4-120593-8*, 1100593) World Health.

Methodology of Plant Genetic Manipulation: Criteria for Decision Making. Alan C. Cassells. Ed. by Peter W. Jones. (Developments in Plant Breeding Ser.: Vol. 3). 486p. (C). 1995. text 257.50 (*0-7923-3687-9*) Kluwer Academic.

Methodology of Policy Studies. Ed. by Thomas Cook & Frank P. Scioli. (C). 1973. pap. 15.00 (*0-918592-05-4*) Pol Studies.

Methodology of Science & General Philosophy. Jan T. Srzednicki. 84.95 (*1-84014-183-2*) Ashgate Pub Co.

Methodology of Sociological Research, 2 vols, Vol. 1. Stefan Nowak. Tr. by Maria O. Lepa. (Synthese Library: No. 82). 521p. 1977. text 155.50 (*90-277-0486-4*, D Reidel) Kluwer Academic.

Methodology of Systems Integration for Intelligent Automous Systems. 350p. 1997. 55.00 (*981-02-2530-X*) World Scientific Pub.

Methodology of the Evaluation of Psychotropic Drugs. Ed. by D. Benkert et al. (Psychopharmacology Ser.: Vol. 8). (Illus.). 200p. 1990. 103.00 (*0-387-52094-5*) Spr-Verlag.

*__Methodology of the Oppressed.__ Chela Sandoval. (Theory Out of Bounds Ser.: Vol. 18). 2000. 49.95 (*0-8166-2736-3*); pap. 19.95 (*0-8166-2737-1*) U of Minn Pr.

Methodology of the Social Sciences, Ethics, & Economics in the Newer Historical School: From Max Weber & Rickert to Sombart & Rothacker. Ed. by Peter Koslowski. LC 97-41053. (Studies in Economic Ethics & Philosophy). (Illus.). xii, 565p. 1997. text 109.00 (*3-540-63458-4*) Spr-Verlag.

Methodology, Pathology & Immunology, Pt. I. Annual Oholo Biological Conference Staff. Ed. by A. M. Beemer et al. (Contributions to Microbiology & Immunology Ser.: Vol. 3). 1978. pap. 68.00 (*3-8055-2443-9*) S Karger.

*__Methodology, Spectroscopy & Clinical MRI: 16th Annual Scientific Meeting ESMRMB '99.__ Ed. by A. Haase et al. viii, 109p. 1999. pap. 57.00 (*88-470-0083-1*) Spr-Verlag.

Methodology, Theory & Knowledge in the Managerial & Organizational Sciences: Actions & Consequences. Eliezer Geisler. LC 98-51673. 248p. 1999. 59.95 (*1-56720-307-8*, Quorum Bks) Greenwood.

Methods - Nucleic Acids Research. Jim D. Karam et al. 432p. 1990. lib. bdg. 249.00 (*0-8493-5311-4*, QP624) CRC Pr.

Methods Analysis of Musts & Wines. 2nd ed. C. S. Ough & Maynard A. Amerine. LC 87-28004. 400p. 1988. 185.00 (*0-471-62757-7*) Wiley.

Methods Analyst. Jack Rudman. (Career Examination Ser.: C-499). 1994. pap. 34.95 (*0-8373-0499-7*) Nat Learn.

Methods & Aims in Archaeology. William M. Petrie. LC 68-56525. 1972. reprint ed. 18.95 (*0-405-08853-1*, Pub. by Blom Pubns) Ayer.

Methods & Applications in Mental Health Surveys. Ed. by Shosuke Suzuki & Robert Roberts. 1991. text 77.50 (*0-86008-473-6*, Pub. by U of Tokyo) Col U Pr.

Methods & Applications of Economic Dynamics: Proceedings. Ed. by L. Schoonbeek et al. LC 94-44763. (Contributions to Economic Analysis Ser.: No. 228). 340p. 1995. 98.50 (*0-444-81465-5*, North Holland) Elsevier.

Methods & Applications of Error-Free Computation. R. T. Gregory & E. V. Krishnamurthy. (Texts & Monographs in Computer Science). (Illus.). 200p. 1984. 84.95 (*0-387-90967-2*) Spr-Verlag.

Methods & Applications of Intelligent Control. S. G. Tzafestas. LC 97-19894. (International Series on Microprocessor-Based & Intelligent Systems Engineering). 1997. text 301.00 (*0-7923-4624-6*) Kluwer Academic.

Methods & Applications of Interval Analysis. R. E. Moore. LC 79-67191. (Studies in Applied Mathematics: No. 2). xi, 190p. 1979. pap. text 36.00 (*0-89871-161-4*) Soc Indus-Appl Math.

*__Methods & Applications of Inversion: Interdisciplinary Elements of Methodology, Modeling & Computational Algorithms.__ Christian Hansen et al. LC 00-33831. (Lecture Notes in Earth Sciences). 2000. pap. write for info. (*3-540-65916-1*) Spr-Verlag.

Methods & Applications of Linear Models: Regression & the Analysis of Variance. Ronald R. Hocking. LC 95-48052. 731p. 1996. 89.95 (*0-471-59282-X*) Wiley.

Methods & Applications of Mathematical Logic: (Proceedings of the Latin American Symposium on Mathematical Logic, 7th) Carnielli et al. LC 87-33651. (Contemporary Mathematics Ser.: No. 69). 250p. 1988. pap. 36.00 (*0-8218-5076-8*, CONM/69) Am Math.

Methods & Applications of Nonlinear Dynamics. A. W. Saenz. 292p. (C). 1988. text 89.00 (*9971-5-0333-6*) World Scientific Pub.

Methods & Applications of Psychological Research. 5th ed. 148p. (C). 1995. text 28.20 (*0-536-59156-3*) Pearson Custom.

Methods & Applied Fourier Analysis. J. Ramanathan. LC 98-4738. (Applied & Numerical Harmonic Analysis Ser.). 385p. 1998. 65.00 (*0-8176-3963-2*) Spr-Verlag.

*__Methods & Approaches in Forest History.__ Ed. by M. Agnoletti & S. Anderson. LC 99-86187. (IUFRO Research Ser.). 300p. 2000. text 85.00 (*0-85199-420-2*) OUP.

Methods & Associated Tools for the Information Systems Life Cycle: Proceedings of the IFIP WG 8.1 Working Conference on Methods & Associated Tools for the

M

Information Systems Life Cycle, Maastricht, The Netherlands, 26-28 September 1994. Ed. by A. A. Verrijn-Stuart & T. William Olle. LC 94-35677. (IFIP Transactions A: Computer Science & Technology Ser.: Vol. A-55). 284p. 1994. 119.75 (*0-444-82074-4*) Elsevier.

Methods & Data Analysis for Cross-Cultural Research. Fons Van De Vijver & Kwok Leung. LC 96-51274. (Cross-Cultural Psychology Ser.: Vol. 1). 200p. 1997. 28.00 (*0-7619-0106-X*); pap. 12.99 (*0-7619-0107-8*) Sage.

Methods & Equipment for Calibration of Variable Area Meters, Rotameters: ISA Standard RP16.6. 1961. pap. 20.00 (*0-87664-345-4*, RP16.6) ISA.

Methods & Experiences in Impact Assessment. Henk A. Becker & Alan L. Porter. 1986. text 158.50 (*90-277-2264-1*) Kluwer Academic.

Methods & Folklore. Ed. by Philip K. Wilson. LC 96-794. (Childbirth Ser.: Vol. 3). (Illus.). 464p. 1996. reprint ed. text 88.00 (*0-8153-2232-1*) Garland.

Methods & Issues in Social Research. James A. Black & Dean J. Champion. LC 75-26659. 457p. reprint ed. pap. 141.70 (*0-608-13446-5*, 20201870016) Bks Demand.

Methods & Machinery of Practical Banking. Claudius B. Patten. Ed. by Stuart Bruchey. LC 80-1164. (Rise of Commercial Banking Ser.). (Illus.). 1981. reprint ed. lib. bdg. 49.95 (*0-405-13673-0*) Ayer.

M

***Methods & Materials for Teaching the Gifted.** Ed. by Frances A. Karnes & Suzanne M. Bean. 745p. (C). 2000. text 49.95 (*1-882664-58-2*) Prufrock Pr.

Methods & Materials of Construction. William Perkins Spence. LC 97-20499. (Construction/Building Trades Ser.). (C). 1997. mass mkt. 92.95 (*0-314-20537-3*) West Pub.

Methods & Materials of Demography. Henry Shyrock & Jacob Siegel. (Studies in Population). 577p. 1976. text 74.95 (*0-12-641150-6*) Acad Pr.

Methods & Materials of Demography, Condensed Edition. 2nd ed. Siegel. 640p. 1998. write for info. (*0-12-641955-8*) Acad Pr.

Methods & Materials of Dental Hygiene. Parker. pap. write for info. (*0-7216-6014-2*, W B Saunders Co); pap. text, lab manual ed. write for info. (*0-7216-6015-0*, W B Saunders Co) Harcrt Hlth Sci Grp.

Methods & Materials of Residential Construction. Laurence E. Reiner. (Illus.). 336p. 1981. text 48.00 (*0-13-578864-1*) P-H.

Methods & Materials of Residential Construction. James E. Russell. (Illus.). 368p. (C). 1985. text 29.00 (*0-685-09097-3*) P-H.

Methods & Measurements of Periphyton Communities: A Review-STP 690. Ed. by R. L. Weitzel. 183p. 1980. 24.00 (*0-8031-0512-6*, STP690) ASTM.

Methods & Mechanisms for Producing Ions from Large Molecules. Ed. by K. G. Standing & W. Ens. (NATO ASI Ser.: Vol. 269). (Illus.). 344p. (C). 1991. text 138.00 (*0-306-44017-2*, Kluwer Plenum) Kluwer Academic.

Methods & Methodologies for Art Education. Ed. by Sharon D. La Pierre & Enid Zimmerman. 264p. 1997. pap. text 22.00 (*0-937652-97-0*, 234) Natl Art Ed.

Methods & Methodologies of Qualitative Family Research. Ed. by Marvin B. Sussman & Jane F. Gilgun. LC 96-51967. (Marriage & Family Review Monograph Ser.: Vol. 24, Nos. 1-4). 430p. (C). 1997. pap. text 24.95 (*0-7890-0305-8*) Haworth Pr.

Methods & Methodologies of Qualitative Family Research. Ed. by Marvin B. Sussman & Jane F. Gilgun. LC 96-51967. (Marriage & Family Review Monograph Ser.: Vol. 24, Nos. 1-4). 430p. (C). 1997. 69.95 (*0-7890-0015-6*) Haworth Pr.

Methods & Methodology in Composition Research. Ed. by Gesa E. Kirsch & Patricia A. Sullivan. LC 91-20141. 240p. (C). 1992. pap. 21.95 (*0-8093-1727-3*) S Ill U Pr.

Methods & Methodology in Composition Research. Ed. by Gesa E. Kirsch & Patricia A. Sullivan. LC 91-20141. 240p. (C). 1992. 36.95 (*0-8093-1726-5*) S Ill U Pr.

***Methods & Models: A Guide to the Empirical Analysis of Formal Models in Political Science.** Rebecca B. Morton. LC 98-49519. 336p. (C). 1999. 59.95 (*0-521-63300-1*); pap. 22.95 (*0-521-63394-X*) Cambridge U Pr.

Methods & Models for Education in Parapsychology. D. Scott Rogo. LC 73-75209. (Parapsychological Monographs: No. 14). 1973. pap. 5.00 (*0-912328-22-3*) Parapsych Foun.

Methods & Models for Predicting Fatigue Crack Growth under Random Loading - STP 748. Ed. by Chang & Hudson. 140p. 1981. 16.50 (*0-8031-0715-3*, STP748) ASTM.

Methods & Models for Studying the Individual. Robert B. Cairns et al. LC 98-19777. 308p. 1998. 58.00 (*0-7619-1451-X*); pap. 27.95 (*0-7619-1452-8*) Sage.

Methods & Models in Demography. Newell. 224p. 1989. pap. 39.95 (*0-471-94729-6*) Wiley.

Methods & Models in Demography. Colin Newell. LC 88-45079. 217p. 1990. reprint ed. pap. text 22.95 (*0-89862-451-7*, 2451) Guilford Pubns.

Methods & Practice of Elizabethan Swordplay. Craig Turner & Tony Soper. LC 89-6103. (Illus.). 160p. (C). 1990. text 29.95 (*0-8093-1562-9*) S Ill U Pr.

Methods & Principles in Physical Geology: A Laboratory Manual. Christopher Dileonardo. 205p. 1993. pap., lab manual ed. 33.27 (*0-9649253-0-3*) Magellan Press.

Methods & Procedures of Outdoor Photography: How to Make Great Photographs in the Southern Blue Ridge Mountains. John Womack. (Illus.). 125p. (Orig.). 1997. pap., per. 15.95 (*0-9655546-1-9*) Soliloquy Pr.

Methods & Programs for Mathematical Functions. Moshier. 1990. pap. write for info. (*0-318-68280-X*) P-H.

Methods & Programs for Mathematical Functions. Stephen L. Moshier. 1989. text 59.95 (*0-470-21609-3*) P-H.

Methods & Rationale of the New Zealand Soil Classification. A. E. Hewitt. 1993. 25.00 (*0-478-04512-3*, Pub. by Manaaki Whenua) Balogh.

Methods & Skills for Research on Foreign Educational Systems: A Report on the 1994 NAFSA/EAIE Seminars, June 3-5, University of Miami, Coral Gables, Florida, November 22-23, Cambridge, England. Ed. by Caroline Aldrich-Langen. LC 95-34230. 1995. 15.00 (*0-929851-68-4*) Am Assn Coll Registrars.

***Methods & Skills of History: A Practical Guide.** 2nd ed. Michael J. Salevouris & Conal Furay. LC 99-29895. (Illus.). 250p. (C). 2000. pap. text 21.95 (*0-88295-982-4*) Harlan Davidson.

Methods & Strategies for Teaching in Secondary & Middle Schools. Kenneth T. Henson. (Illus.). 405p. (C). 1989. pap. text 27.95 (*0-582-28676-X*, 71690) Addison-Wesley.

Methods & Strategies for Teaching in Secondary & Middle Schools. 2nd ed. Kenneth T. Henson. LC 92-27517. 464p. (C). 1992. pap. text 39.50 (*0-8013-0761-9*, 79791) Longman.

Methods & Strategies for Teaching in Secondary & Middle Schools. 2nd ed. Kenneth T. Henson. LC 92-27517. 464p. (C). 1995. teacher ed. write for info. (*0-8013-1058-X*, 79435) Longman.

Methods & Tactics in Cognitive Science. W. Kintsch et al. 336p. 1984. 49.95 (*0-89859-327-1*) L Erlbaum Assocs.

Methods & Techniques in Business Research. Samuel R. Houston et al. 1973. 34.50 (*0-8422-5099-9*) Irvington.

Methods & Techniques in Virology. Ed. by Payment & Trudel. LC 93-1766. (Illus.). 336p. 1993. text 165.00 (*0-8247-9101-0*) Dekker.

Methods & Techniques of Language Learning: The Secrets of Breaking Through at Any Age & Any Level. Victorien A. Assi. LC 97-91366. (Illus.). 206p. 1998. pap. 18.95 (*0-9662402-0-0*) V A Assi.

Methods & Techniques of Radar Recognition. V. G. Nebabin. LC 94-29878.Tr. of Metody i Tekhnika Radiolokatsionnogo Raspoznavaniia. 1994. 39.00 (*0-89006-719-8*) Artech Hse.

Methods & Tools for Applied Artificial Intelligence. Dobrivoje Popovic & Vijay P. Bhatkar. LC 94-1715. (Computer Aided Engineering Ser.: Vol. 5). (Illus.). 544p. 1994. text 185.00 (*0-8247-9195-9*) Dekker.

Methods & Tools for Compiler Construction: An Advanced Course. Ed. by Bernard Lorho. LC 84-45239. 406p. reprint ed. pap. 115.80 (*0-608-15261-7*, 2029221) Bks Demand.

Methods & Tools for Computer Integrated Manufacturing: Advanced CREST Course on Computer Integrated Manufacturing (CIM 83), Karlsruhe, Germany, Sept. 5-16, 1983. Ed. by R. Dillman & Ulrich Rembold. (Lecture Notes in Computer Science Ser.: Vol. 168). 555p. 1985. pap. 43.00 (*0-387-12926-X*) Spr-Verlag.

Methods & Tools for Software Configuration Management. David Whitgift. LC 91-23191. (Wiley Series in Software Engineering Practice). (Illus.). 252p. 1991. reprint ed. pap. 78.20 (*0-608-07300-8*, 206752800009) Bks Demand.

Methods & Tools in User-Centred Design for Information Technology. M. Galer et al. (Human Factors in Information Technology Ser.: Vol. 9). xviii,438p. 1992. 157.50 (*0-444-89301-6*, North Holland) Elsevier.

Methods & Uses of Anthropological Demography. Ed. by Alaka Basu & Peter Aaby. (International Studies in Demography). (Illus.). 340p. 1998. text 85.00 (*0-19-829337-2*) OUP.

Methods Based on the Wiener-Hopf Technique for the Solution of Partial Differential Equations. 2nd ed. Ben Noble. LC 88-70741. x, 246p. (C). 1988. text 19.95 (*0-8284-0332-5*, 332) Chelsea Pub.

Methods Cardiac Electrophysiology. Ed. by Michael J. Walker & Michael K. Pugsley. LC 97-25186. (CRC Press Methods in Pharmacology Ser.). 224p. 1997. per. 84.95 (*0-8493-3334-2*) CRC Pr.

Methods, Directions, & Examples: Associate Degree Program see Cost of Nursing Education: A Manual for Analysis of Expenditures

Methods, Ethics & Models. Ed. by Jessica Kuper. (Social Science Lexicons Ser.). 176p. 1987. pap. text 9.95 (*0-7102-1172-4*, Routledge Thoemms) Routledge.

Methods for Active Participation: Experiences in Rural Development from East to Central Africa. Terry D. Bergdall. (Illus.). 222p. 1994. pap. text 29.95 (*0-19-572785-1*) OUP.

Methods for Analysis for Soils, Plants & Waters. M. Ali Tabatabai. Date not set. 65.00 (*0-87371-177-7*) Lewis Pubs.

Methods for Analysis of Airborne Particulates Generated by Welding & Allied Processes (F1.4-87) (Illus.). 11p. 1987. pap. 27.00 (*0-87171-269-5*) Am Welding.

Methods for Analysis of Cancer Chemopreventive Agents in Human Serum. Ed. by Jeanice B. Thomas & Katherine E. Sharpless. (Illus.). 110p. 1999. reprint ed. pap. text 25.00 (*0-7881-8024-X*) DIANE Pub.

Methods for Analysis of Nonlinear Elliptical Boundary Value Problems. I. Skrypnik. LC 94-28558. (Translations of Mathematical Monographs: No. 139).Tr. of Metody Issledovaniia Nelineinykh Ellipticheskikh Granichnykh Zadach. (ENG.). 348p. 1994. text 130.00 (*0-8218-4616-7*, MMONO/139) Am Math.

Methods for Analytical Atomic Spectroscopy see Suggested Methods for Analysis of Metals, Ores, & Related Materials

Methods for Analyzing Fuel Supply Limitations on Passenger Travel. (National Cooperative Highway Research Program Report Ser.: No. 229). 132p. 1980. 9.20 (*0-309-03151-6*, NR229) Transport Res Bd.

Methods for Antimicrobial Susceptibility Testing of Anaerobic Bacteria: Approved Standard (1993) 3rd ed. Contrib. by James H. Jorgensen. 1993. 85.00 (*0-614-20211-6*, M11-A3) NCCLS.

Methods for Antimicrobial Susceptibility Testing of Anaerobic Bacteria: Approved Standard (1997) 4th ed. 1997. 110.00 (*1-56238-341-8*, M11-A4) NCCLS.

Methods for Archaeological Site Survey in California. fac. ed. Franklin Fenenga. (Reports of the University of California Archaeological Survey: No. 5). 16p. 1949. reprint ed. pap. 2.19 (*1-55567-331-7*) Coyote Press.

Methods for Assessing & Reducing Injury from Chemical Accidents. Philippe Bourdeau. Ed. by Gareth M. Green. LC 89-30661. 330p. 1989. 450.00 (*0-471-92278-1*) Wiley.

Methods for Assessing Biologal Growth Support Potential of Water Contact Materials. (Illus.). 134p. 1993. pap. 57.00 (*0-89867-660-6*, 90614) Am Water Wks Assn.

Methods for Assessing Children's Syntax. Ed. by Dana McDaniel et al. LC 96-33915. (Language, Speech & Communication Ser.). (Illus.). 408p. 1996. 49.50 (*0-262-13325-3*, Bradford Bks) MIT Pr.

Methods for Assessing Children's Syntax. Ed. by Dana McDaniel et al. (Language, Speech, & Communication Ser.). (Illus.). 408p. 1998. pap. text 20.00 (*0-262-63190-3*, Bradford Bks) MIT Pr.

Methods for Assessing Exposure of Human & Non-Human Biota. Ed. by Robert G. Tardiff & Bernard D. Goldstein. LC 90-24342. (Scientific Committee on Problems of the Environment Ser.: No. 1409). 442p. 1991. 400.00 (*0-471-92954-9*) Wiley.

Methods for Assessing Soil Quality. J. W. Doran & A. J. Jones. (SSSA Special Publications: No. 49). 410p. 1996. 36.00 (*0-89118-826-6*) Soil Sci Soc Am.

Methods for Assessing the Structural Reliability of Brittle Materials-STP 844. Ed. by Freiman & Hudson. 226p. 1984. 39.00 (*0-8031-0265-8*, STP844) ASTM.

Methods for Assessment of Soil Degradation. R. Lal. LC 97-24696. (Advances in Soil Science Ser.). 576p. 1997. boxed set 84.95 (*0-8493-7443-X*) CRC Pr.

Methods for Biological Monitoring: A Manual for Assessing Human Exposure to Hazardous Substances. Ed. by Theodore J. Kneip & John V. Crable. 512p. 1988. 60.00 (*0-87553-148-2*) Am Pub Health.

Methods for Business Analysis & Forecasting: Text & Cases. Peter Tryfos. LC 97-17403. 592p. 1998. text 89.95 (*0-471-12384-6*) Wiley.

Methods for Cloning & Analysis of Eukaryotic Genes. Al Bothwell et al. 336p. (Orig.). 1990. spiral bd. 75.00 (*0-86720-103-7*) Jones & Bartlett.

Methods for Cohort Studies of Chronic Airflow Limitation. C. Florey & S. Leeder. (WHO Regional Publications, European Ser.: No. 12). 134p. 1982. pap. text 19.00 (*92-890-1103-3*) World Health.

Methods for Cutaneous Investigation. Robert L. Rietschel & Thomas S. Spencer. (Cosmetic Science & Technology Ser.: Vol. 9). (Illus.). 248p. 1990. text 145.00 (*0-8247-8264-X*) Dekker.

Methods for Detecting DNA Damaging Agents in Humans: Applications in Cancer Epidemiology & Prevention. Ed. by H. Bartsch et al. (IARC Scientific Publications: No. 89). (Illus.). 544p. 1988. pap. 115.00 (*92-832-1189-8*) OUP.

Methods for Determination of Indoor Air Pollutants: EPA Methods. William T. Winberry et al. LC 92-25246. (Illus.). 836p. 1993. 145.00 (*0-8155-1314-3*) Noyes.

Methods for Determining Bactericidal Activity of Antimicrobial Agents: Tentative Guideline (1992), Vol. 7. 1992. 75.00 (*1-56238-144-X*, M26-T) NCCLS.

Methods for Determining the Location of Abandoned Wells. L. Aller. 130p. 1984. 19.50 (*1-56034-031-2*, T034) Natl Grnd Water.

Methods for Development Work & Research: A Guide for Practioners. Britha Mikkelsen. LC 95-5373. (Illus.). 250p. 1995. 35.00 (*0-8039-9229-7*); pap. 16.95 (*0-8039-9230-0*) Sage.

Methods for Dilution Antimicrobial Susceptibility Tests for Bacteria That Grow Aerobically: Approved Standard (1993) 3rd ed. Contrib. by James H. Jorgensen. 1993. 85.00 (*1-56238-209-8*, M7-A3) NCCLS.

Methods for Direction-Finding of Direct-Sequence Spread-Spectrum Signals. Magnus Finne. (Illus.). 55p. (Orig.). (C). 1996. pap. text 25.00 (*0-7881-3553-8*) DIANE Pub.

Methods for DNA & RNA Sequencing. Ed. by Sherman M. Weissmann. LC 82-22261. 458p. 1983. 65.00 (*0-275-91101-2*, C1101, Praeger Pubs) Greenwood.

Methods for Effective Teaching. 2nd ed. Burden & Byrd. LC 98-34489. 418p. 1998. pap. text 59.00 (*0-205-29193-7*) P-H.

Methods for Electromagnetic Field Analysis. Ismo V. Lindell. 332p. 1996. 69.95 (*0-7803-1154-X*, PC5625) Inst Electrical.

Methods for Electromagnetic Field Analysis. Ismo V. Lindell. (Oxford Engineering Science Ser.: No. 30). (Illus.). 304p. 1992. text 95.00 (*0-19-856239-X*) OUP.

Methods for Evaluating Biological Nitrogen Fixation. Ed. by F. J. Bergersen. LC 79-41785. 712p. reprint ed. pap. 200.00 (*0-8357-2768-8*, 203989300014) Bks Demand.

Methods for Evaluating Highway Improvements. (Transportation Research Record Ser.: No. 1185). 68p. 1988. 10.50 (*0-309-04752-8*) Transport Res Bd.

Methods for Evaluating Nitrogen Fixation by Nodulated Legumes in the Field. Ed. by M. B. Peoples et al. 76p. 1988. pap. 81.00 (*0-949511-90-0*) St Mut.

Methods for Evaluating Pesticides for Control of Plant Pathogens. Ed. by K. D. Hickey. 312p. 1986. 79.00 (*0-89054-071-3*) Am Phytopathol Soc.

Methods for Experimental Design: Principles & Applications for Physicists & Chemists. rev. ed. J. Goupy. LC 93-18963. (Data Handling in Science & Technology Ser.: Vol. 12).Tr. of Methode des Plans d'Experiences. 466p. 1993. pap. 226.00 (*0-444-89529-9*) Elsevier.

Methods for Fish Biology. Ed. by C. B. Schreck & Peter B. Moyle. LC 90-83196. 684p. (C). 1990. text 64.00 (*0-913235-58-X*, 550.16) Am Fisheries Soc.

Methods for General & Molecular Bacteriology. 2nd ed. Ed. by Philipp Gerhardt et al. LC 93-38049. (Illus.). 825p. (C). 1993. 89.95 (*1-55581-048-9*) ASM Pr.

Methods for Genetic Risk Assessment. Ed. by David J. Brunsick. LC 93-5520. 272p. 1994. lib. bdg. 120.00 (*1-56670-039-6*, L1039) Lewis Pubs.

Methods for Identification of Microorganisms in Water. Frank W. Schaefer, III & Jennifer L. Clancy. 300p. 1999. 75.00 (*1-56670-267-4*, L1267) Lewis Pubs.

Methods for Identifying Biased Test Items. Gregory Camilli & Lorrie A. Shepard. (Measurement Methods for the Social Sciences Ser.: Vol. 4). 184p. (C). 1994. text 44.00 (*0-8039-4415-2*); pap. text 19.95 (*0-8039-4416-0*) Sage.

Methods for Improving World Transportation Accounts, Applied to 1950-1953. Herman F. Karreman. (Technical Papers: No. 15). 141p. 1961. reprint ed. 36.70 (*0-87014-421-9*) Natl Bur Econ Res.

Methods for Intercultural Communication Research. Ed. by William B. Gudykunst & Young Y. Kim. LC 83-26970. (International & Intercultural Communication Ser.: No. 8). 248p. 1984. reprint ed. pap. 76.90 (*0-7837-1124-7*, 204165400022) Bks Demand.

Methods for Inverse Heat Conduction Problems. Dinh Nho Hao. Ed. by Bruno Brosowski & Erich Martensen. LC 98-3136. (Methoden und Verfahren der Mathematischen Physik Ser.: Vol. 43). (Illus.). IX, 249p. (C). 1998. pap. 45.95 (*0-8204-3556-2*) P Lang Pubng.

Methods for Inverse Heat Conduction Problems. Dinh Nho Hao. Ed. by Bruno Brosowski & Erich Martensen. (Methoden und Verfahren der Mathematischen Physik Ser.: Vol. 43). (Illus.). ix, 249p. 1998. pap. 45.95 (*3-631-32744-7*) P Lang Pubng.

Methods for Investigating Localized Clustering of Disease. Ed. by F. E. Alexander & P. Boyle. LC 97-183624. (IARC Scientific Publications: No. 135). (Illus.). 264p. 1997. pap. text 89.50 (*92-832-2135-4*) OUP.

Methods for Investigation of Amino Acid & Protein Metabolis. Antoine E. El-Khoury. LC 98-52452. (Methods In Nutritional Research Ser.). 1999. lib. bdg. 99.95 (*0-8493-9612-3*) CRC Pr.

Methods for Land Economics Research. Symposium on Research Methods Staff. Ed. by W. L. Gibson, Jr. et al. LC 66-19269. (Illus.). 260p. reprint ed. pap. 80.60 (*0-8357-2939-7*, 203919500011) Bks Demand.

Methods for Localization of Singularities in the Numerical Solutions of Gas Dynamics Problems. N. N. Yanenko & Evgenii V. Vorozhtsov. (Computational Physics Ser.). (Illus.). 432p. 1989. 141.95 (*0-387-50363-3*) Spr-Verlag.

Methods for Macrosociological Research. Krishnan Namboodiri. (Illus.). 293p. 1994. text 79.95 (*0-12-513345-6*) Acad Pr.

Methods for Measuring Pulse-Echo Ultrasound Imaging Equipment Pt. II: Digital Methods, Stage 1. 38p. 1995. pap. write for info. (*1-930047-55-X*) Am Inst Ultrasound.

Methods for Meta-Analysis in Marketing. Sutton. text. write for info. (*0-471-49066-0*) Wiley.

Methods for Modern Sculptors. Ronald D. Young & Robert A. Fennel. 290p. (Orig.). 16.00 (*0-317-32646-5*, OS8003) Am Foundrymen.

Methods for Modern Sculptors. Ronald D. Young & Robert A. Fennell. Ed. by Shirley Manning. LC 79-92170. (Illus.). 294p. (Orig.). 1994. pap. text 16.95 (*0-9603744-0-X*) Sculpt-Nouveau.

Methods for Monitoring & Diagnosing the Efficiency of Catalytic Converters: A Patent-Oriented Survey, Vol. 115. Marios Sideris. LC 98-23130. (Studies in Surface Science & Catalysis). 448p. 1998. 244.00 (*0-444-82952-0*) Elsevier.

Methods for Monitoring Iron & Manganese Biofouling in Water Wells. (Illus.). 116p. 1992. pap. 62.00 (*0-89867-646-0*, 90617) Am Water Wks Assn.

Methods for Mycological Examination of Food. Ed. by A. D. King, Jr. et al. LC 86-25428. (NATO ASI Series A, Life Sciences: Vol. 122). 328p. 1986. 75.00 (*0-306-42479-7*, Plenum Trade) Perseus Pubng.

Methods for Nutritional Assessment of Fats. Ed. by Joyce Beare-Rogers. 264p. 1985. 40.00 (*0-935315-11-X*) Am Oil Chemists.

Methods for Policy Research. 10th ed. Ann Majchrzak. (Applied Social Research Methods Ser.: Vol. 3). 112p. 1984. 42.00 (*0-8039-2059-8*) Sage.

Methods for Protein Analysis. Ed. by John P. Cherry & Robert A. Barford. 272p. 1989. 75.00 (*0-935315-19-5*) Am Oil Chemists.

Methods for Quality Control in Diagnostic Microbiology. Ed. by J. Michael Miller & Berttina B. Wentworth. LC 85-3991. 368p. 1985. 45.00 (*0-87553-121-0*) Am Pub Health.

Methods for Recovering Viruses from the Environment. Gerald Berg. LC 87-10069. 280p. 1987. 141.00 (*0-8493-6246-6*, QR385, CRC Reprint) Franklin.

Methods for Research on Soilborne Phytopathogenic Fungi. Ed. by L. L. Singleton et al. LC 92-71328. 266p. 1993. pap. 43.00 (*0-89054-127-2*) Am Phytopathol Soc.

Methods for Reticulocyte Counting (Flow Cytometry & Supravital Dyes) Approved Guideline (1997) 1997. 75.00 (*1-56238-302-7*, H44-A) NCCLS.

Methods for Risk Assessment of Transgenic Plants. Ed. by G. Kjellsson et al. LC 97-11971. 1997. write for info. (*3-7643-5696-0*) Birkhauser.

Methods for Risk Assessment of Transgenic Plants. G. Osta Kjellsson et al. LC 97-11971. 1997. write for info. (*0-8176-5696-0*) Birkhauser.

Methods for Risk Assessment of Transgenic Plants: Competition, Establishment & Ecosystems Effect. Gosta Kjellsson & Vibeke Simonsen. LC 94-26893. 224p. 1994. 62.00 (*3-7643-5065-2*); 73.50 (*0-8176-5065-2*) Birkhauser.

***Methods for Risk Assessment of Transgenic Plants Vol. III: Ecological Risks & Prospects of Transgenic Plants, Where Do We Go from Here? A Dialogue Between Biotech Industry & Science.** Ed. by Klaus Ammann et al. LC 99-16245. 350p. 1999. 92.00 (*3-7643-5917-X*, Pub. by Birkhauser) Spr-Verlag.

Methods for Sampling Airborne Particulates Generated by Welding & Allied Processes (F1.1-92) 9p. 1992. 27.00 (*0-87171-386-1*) Am Welding.

Methods for Simultaneous Ensemble Recordings. Miguel Nicolelis. LC 98-38795. 272p. 1998. boxed set 94.95 (*0-8493-3351-2*) CRC Pr.

Methods for Skin Absorption. Kemppainen. 232p. 1990. lib. bdg. 210.00 (*0-8493-4651-7*, SB751) CRC Pr.

Methods for Solution of Nonlinear Operator Equations. Ed. by V. P. Tanana. (Inverse & Ill-Posed Problems Ser.). (Illus.). 248p. 1997. 147.50 (*90-6764-272-X*, Pub. by VSP) Coronet Bks.

Methods for Solving Incorrectly Posed Problems. V. A. Morozov. Ed. by Z. Nashed. Tr. by A. B. Aries from RUS. (Illus.). 270p. 1984. 95.95 (*0-387-96059-7*) Spr-Verlag.

***Methods for Solving Inverse Problems in Mathematical Physics.** A. I. Prilepko et al. LC 99-15462. (Monographs & Textbooks in Pure & Applied Mathematics). (Illus.). 744p. 1999. text 195.00 (*0-8247-1987-5*) Dekker.

Methods for Solving Operator Equations. V. P. Tanana. (Inverse & Ill-Posed Problems Ser.). (Illus.). 230p. 1997. 160.00 (*90-6764-237-1*, Pub. by VSP) Coronet Bks.

Methods for Solving Process Plant Problems. Joel O. Hougen. LC 96-3197. (RMC-Resources for Measurement & Control Ser.). 250p. 1996. 40.00 (*1-55617-539-6*) ISA.

Methods for Solving Systems of Nonlinear Equations. 2nd rev. ed. Werner C. Rheinboldt. LC 98-27321. (CBMS-NSF Regional Conference Series in Applied Mathematics: No. CB70). (Illus.). ix, 148p. 1998. pap. 34.00 (*0-89871-415-X*, BKCB0070) Soc Indus-Appl Math.

Methods for Specifying Acoustic Properties of Tissue Mimicking Phantoms & Objects: Stage I. (Illus.). 13p. 1995. pap. 24.00 (*1-930047-21-5*, TMP) Am Inst Ultrasound.

Methods for Statistical Data Analysis of Multivariate Observations. 2nd ed. Ramanathan Gnanadesikan. LC 76-14994. (Wiley Series in Probability & Mathematical Statistics). 384p. 1997. 84.95 (*0-471-16119-5*) Wiley.

Methods for Structure Elucidation by High-Resolution NMR: Applications to Organic Molecules of Moderate Molecular Weight, Vol. 8. Gy Batta et al. LC 97-40556. (Analytical Spectroscopy Library: 8). 368p. 1997. 244.00 (*0-444-82157-0*) Elsevier.

Methods for Study of the External Gravitational Field & Figure of the Earth. M. S. Molodenskii. LC 62-61244. 254p. reprint ed. pap. 78.80 (*0-608-30227-9*, 200233200012) Bks Demand.

Methods for Studying Language Production. Ed. by Lise Menn & Nan B. Ratner. LC 99-12768. 440p. 1999. 99.95 (*0-8058-3033-2*); pap. 45.00 (*0-8058-3034-0*) L Erlbaum Assocs.

Methods for Teaching. 2nd ed. William K. Esler & Philip Sciortino. (Illus.). 325p. 1991. pap. text 36.95 (*0-89892-095-7*) Contemp Pub Co of Raleigh.

Methods for Teaching: Promoting Student Learning. 5th ed. David Jacobsen et al. LC 98-2887. 340p. 1998. pap. text 60.00 (*0-13-272394-8*, Merrill Coll) P-H.

***Methods for Teaching Children Science.** Joseph Abruscato. 2000. pap. 40.00 (*0-205-33021-5*) Allyn.

***Methods for Teaching Science as Inquiry.** 8th ed. Arthur A. Carin & Joel E. Bass. LC 00-41879. (Illus.). 2000. pap. write for info. (*0-13-021283-0*) P-H.

Methods for Teaching Writing in Secondary Schools, 1. Soven. 312p. 1998. pap. 42.00 (*0-205-18897-4*) Allyn.

Methods for the Analysis of Human Chromosome Aberrations. K. E. Buckton & Harold J. Evans. 1973. pap. text 12.00 (*92-4-154031-1*, 1150105) World Health.

Methods for the Assessment of Exposure to Chemical Agents at the Workplace: EUR 15964. 1997. 35.00 (*92-826-9351-1*, CE-NA-15964-ENC, Pub. by Comm Europ Commun) Bernan Associates.

Methods for the Determination of Metals & Inorganics in Environmental Samples. Environmental Monitoring Systems Laboratory, U. S. 535p. 1996. 64.00 (*0-8155-1398-4*) Noyes.

Methods for the Determination of Metals in Environmental Samples. Environmental Monitoring Systems Laboratory, U. S. 352p. 1992. boxed set 104.95 (*0-87371-831-3*, TD196) Smoley.

Methods for the Economic Evaluation of Health Care Programmes. 2nd ed. Michael F. Drummond et al. LC 97-10273. (Illus.). 316p. 1997. pap. text 42.50 (*0-19-262773-2*) OUP.

Methods for the Estimation & Economic Evaluation of Undiscovered Uranium Endowments. IAEA Staff. (Technical Reports: No. 344). 145p. 1992. pap. 55.00 (*92-0-104092-X*, STI/DOC/344, Pub. by IAEA) Bernan Associates.

Methods for the Evaluation of the Impact of Food & Nutrition Programmes. 291p. 25.00 (*92-808-0473-1*, E 88.III.A.12) UN.

Methods for the Examination of Organismal Diversity in Soils & Sediments. Ed. by G. S. Hall. LC 97-121166. 320p. 1996. pap. text 45.00 (*0-85199-149-1*) OUP.

Methods for the Human Erythrocyte Sedimentation Rate (E. S. R.) Test: Approved Standard. 3rd ed. National Committee for Clinical Laboratory Standar. 1993. 75.00 (*1-56238-034-6*, H2-A3) NCCLS.

Methods for the Microbial Examination of Shellfish. Ed. by B. Austin & D. A. Austin. 1989. text 89.95 (*0-470-21486-4*) P-H.

Methods for the Social Sciences: A Handbook for Students & Non-Specialists, 37. John J. Hartman & Jack H. Hedblom. LC 78-72796. (Contributions in Sociology Ser.: No. 37). (Illus.). 400p. 1980. 79.50 (*0-313-20894-8*, HMS/, Greenwood Pr) Greenwood.

Methods for the Study of Molecules see Comprehensive Biochemistry, Section 1: Physico-Chemical & Organic Aspects of Biochemistry

Methods for the Study of Personality in Young Children. Ed. by E. Lerner. (SRCD M Ser.: Vol. 6, No. 4). 1941. 25.00 (*0-527-01520-2*) Periodicals Srv.

Methods for the Study of Pest Diabrotica. Ed. by J. L. Krysan & T. A. Miller. (Experimental Entomology Ser.). (Illus.). xx, 260p. 1985. 192.00 (*0-387-96210-7*) Spr-Verlag.

Methods for Ultrasensitive Detection, Vol. 3270. Ed. by Bryan L. Fearey. 238p. 1998. 69.00 (*0-8194-2709-8*) SPIE.

Methods Human Geogra. Flowerdew. (C). 1996. pap. text 28.13 (*0-582-28973-4*) Longman.

Methods In Aging Research. 2nd ed. Byung Pal Yu. LC 98-14354. 640p. 1998. lib. bdg. 129.95 (*0-8493-3112-9*) CRC Pr.

Methods in Analytical Psychology: An Introduction. Hans Dieckmann. Tr. by Boris Matthews from GER. 240p. (Orig.). 1991. pap. 24.95 (*0-933029-48-9*) Chiron Pubns.

Methods in Angiology: A Physical-Technical Introduction Written for Clinicians by Physicians. Ed. by Marc Verstraete. (Instrumentation & Techniques in Clinical Medicine Ser.: No. 2). (Illus.). 525p. 1980. text 296.00 (*90-247-2376-0*) Kluwer Academic.

Methods in Animal Physiology. Ed. by Zdenek Deyl & Joseph Zicha. 448p. 1988. lib. bdg. 295.00 (*0-8493-6965-7*, QP43) CRC Pr.

Methods in Applied Soil Microbiology & Biochemistry. Ed. by Kassem Alef & Paolo Nannipieri. (Illus.). 608p. 1995. boxed set 90.00 (*0-12-513840-7*) Acad Pr.

Methods in Approximation. Richard Ernest Bellman & Robert S. Roth. (Mathematics & Its Applications Ser.). 1986. text 137.50 (*90-277-2188-2*) Kluwer Academic.

Methods in Aquatic Microbial Ecology. Paul F. Kemp. 800p. 1993. lib. bdg. 149.00 (*0-87371-564-0*, L564) Lewis Pubs.

Methods in Arabidopsis Research. Jeff Schell et al. 500p. 1993. text 109.00 (*981-02-0904-5*); pap. text 43.00 (*981-02-0905-3*) World Scientific Pub.

Methods in Astmology. Ed. by Luigi Allegra et al. LC 93-14963. 1993. 174.00 (*0-387-56428-4*) Spr-Verlag.

Methods in Behavioral Pharmacology. Ed. by Frans Van Haaren. LC 93-8396. (Techniques in the Behavioral & Neural Sciences Ser.: Vol. 10). 692p. 1993. pap. 129.75 (*0-444-81445-0*) Elsevier.

Methods in Behavioral Research. 6th rev. ed. Paul C. Cozby. LC 96-12005. (Illus.). xii, 335p. (C). 1996. pap. text 39.95 (*1-55934-659-0*, 1659) Mayfield Pub.

***Methods in Behavioral Research.** 7th ed. Paul C. Cozby. LC 00-21365. (Illus.). 2000. write for info. (*0-7674-1063-7*) Mayfield Pub.

Methods in Behavioral Research: Test Bank, Testbank. 6th ed. Paul C. Cozby. (C). 1997. disk. write for info. (*0-318-69287-2*) Mayfield Pub.

Methods in Behavioral Research: Transparencies, Masters. 6th ed. Paul C. Cozby. 1997. trans. write for info. (*0-614-02717-9*) Mayfield Pub.

Methods in Biliary Research. Ed. by Maurizio Muraca. 336p. 1994. lib. bdg. 210.00 (*0-8493-8701-9*, 8701) CRC Pr.

***Methods in Biological Oxidative Stress.** Ed. by Kenneth Hensley & Robert A. Floyd. 350p. 2000. 99.50 (*0-89603-815-7*) Humana.

***Methods in Biomedical Magnetic Resonance Imaging & Spectroscopy.** Ian R. Young. LC 00-42265. (Encyclopedia of Nuclear Magnetic Resonance Ser.). 2000. write for info. (*0-471-98804-9*) Wiley.

Methods in Biotechnology. Ed. by Michael Schweizer. Tr. by Lillian Schweizer. LC 97-198290. 304p. 1997. 89.95 (*0-7484-0429-5*, Pub. by Tay Francis Ltd); pap. 349.95 (*0-7484-0430-9*, Pub. by Tay Francis Ltd) Taylor & Francis.

Methods in Bone Biology. B. Henderson & T. Arnett. 336p. write for info. (*0-412-75770-2*) Kluwer Academic.

Methods in Brain Research. Ed. by Philip B. Bradley. LC 74-404. 567p. reprint ed. pap. 175.80 (*0-608-14531-9*, 202479700038) Bks Demand.

Methods in Bronchial Mucology. Ed. by Pier C. Braga & Luigi Allegra. LC 86-42945. 424p. 1988. reprint ed. pap. 131.50 (*0-608-04725-2*, 206544600004) Bks Demand.

Methods in Calcium Signaling. James W. Putney. LC 99-43588. (Methods in Life Sciences - Signal Transduction Ser.). 400p. 1999. boxed set 129.95 (*0-8493-3386-5*) CRC Pr.

Methods in Cancer Research, Vols. 1-13. Ed. by Harris Busch et al. write for info. (*0-318-50296-8*) Acad Pr.

Methods in Carbohydrate Chemistry: Enzymic Methods, Vol. 10, Enzymic Methods. James N. BeMiller. LC 61-18923. 352p. 1994. 110.00 (*0-471-52940-0*) Wiley.

Methods in Carbohydrate Chemistry: Lipopolysaccharides, Separation & Analysis, Glycosylated Polymers, Vol. 9, Lipopolysaccharides, Separation and Analys. Ed. by James N. BeMiller et al. LC 61-18923. 216p. 1993. 110.00 (*0-471-52941-9*) Wiley.

Methods in Cartilage Research. Ed. by A. Maroudas & K. Kuettner. 392p. 1990. text 188.00 (*0-12-473280-1*) Acad Pr.

Methods in Cell Biology. Rieder. LC 99-172833. (C). 1998. text 99.95 (*0-12-544163-0*) Acad Pr.

Methods in Cell Biology: A Practical Guide to the Study of CA2Plus in Living Cells, Vol. 40. Ed. by Richard Nuccitelli. (Illus.). 368p. 1994. spiral bd. 52.00 (*0-12-522810-4*) Acad Pr.

Methods in Cell Biology: Cell Biological Applications of Confocal Microscopy, Vol. 38. Ed. by Paul T. Matsudaira et al. (Illus.). 380p. 1993. text 104.00 (*0-12-564138-9*) Acad Pr.

Methods in Cell Biology: Cell Biological Applications of Confocal Microscopy, Vol. 38. Ed. by Leslie Wilson et al. (Illus.). 380p. 1993. spiral bd. 53.00 (*0-12-480430-6*) Acad Pr.

Methods in Cell Biology: Drosophila Melanogaster: Practical Uses in Cell & Molecular Biology, Vol. 44. Ed. by Leslie Wilson et al. LC 95-111772. (Illus.). 755p. 1994. text 69.00 (*0-12-564145-1*) Acad Pr.

Methods in Cell Biology: Mitosis & Meiosis, Vol. 61. Ed. by Steven Wilson et al. LC 99-172833. (Illus.). 489p. (C). 1998. 64.95 (*0-12-588540-7*) Acad Pr.

Methods in Cell Biology: Protein Expression in Animals Cells, Vol. 43. Ed. by Leslie Wilson et al. (Illus.). 379p. 1994. text. write for info. (*0-12-564144-3*) Acad Pr.

Methods in Cell Biology: The Zebrafish, Biology, Vol. 59. Ed. by Leslie Wilson et al. (Illus.). 416p. (C). 1999. 64.95 (*0-12-212170-8*) Acad Pr.

Methods in Cell Biology: The Zebrafish, Genetics & Genomics, Vol. 60. Ed. by Leslie Wilson et al. (Illus.). 416p. (C). 1999. 64.95 (*0-12-212172-4*) Acad Pr.

Methods in Cell Biology Vol. 34: Vectorial Transport of Proteins into & Across Membranes. Ed. by Leslie Wilson & Alan M. Tartakoff. (Illus.). 438p. 1991. text 136.00 (*0-12-564134-6*) Acad Pr.

Methods in Cell Biology Vol. 36: Xenopus Laevis: Practical Uses in Cell & Molecular Biology. Ed. by Leslie Wilson et al. (Illus.). 718p. 1991. text 136.00 (*0-12-564136-2*) Acad Pr.

Methods in Cell Biology Vol. 41: Flow Cytometry, Pt. A. 2nd ed. Ed. by J. Paul Robinson et al. (Illus.). 591p. 1994. text 125.00 (*0-12-564142-7*); pap. text 59.95 (*0-12-203051-6*) Acad Pr.

Methods in Cell Biology Vol. 42: Flow Cytometry, Pt. B. 2nd ed. Ed. by Zbigniew Darzynkiewicz et al. (Illus.). 697p. 1994. pap. text 59.95 (*0-12-203052-4*) Acad Pr.

Methods in Cell Biology Vol. 42: Flow Cytometry, Pt. B. 2nd ed. Paul T. Matsudaira & J. Paul Robinson. (Illus.). 697p. 1994. text 125.00 (*0-12-564143-5*) Acad Pr.

Methods in Cell Biology Vol. 45: Microbes As Tools for Cell Biology. Ed. by David G. Russell. (Illus.). 389p. 1995. pap. 48.00 (*0-12-604040-0*); text 84.00 (*0-12-564146-X*) Acad Pr.

Methods in Cell Biology Vol. 46: Cell Death. Ed. by Leslie Wilson et al. (Illus.). 459p. 1995. pap. 58.00 (*0-12-632445-X*) Acad Pr.

Methods in Cell Biology Vol. 46: Cell Death, Vol. 46. Paul T. Matsudaira & Barbara A. Osborne. (Illus.). 459p. 1995. text 100.00 (*0-12-564147-8*) Acad Pr.

Methods in Cell Biology Vol. 47: Cilia & Flagella. Ed. by Leslie Wilson et al. (Illus.). 603p. 1995. text 104.00 (*0-12-564148-6*) Acad Pr.

Methods in Cell Biology Vol. 48: Caenorhibditus Elegans: Modern Biological Analysis of an Organism. Ed. by Henry F. Epstein et al. (Illus.). 659p. 1995. spiral bd. 63.00 (*0-12-240545-5*) Acad Pr.

Methods in Cell Biology Vol. 49, Pt. A: Methods in Plant Cell Biology. Ed. by Leslie Wilson et al. (Illus.). 573p. 1995. boxed set 99.00 (*0-12-564151-6*) Acad Pr.

Methods in Cell Biology Vol. 50, Pt. B: Methods in Plant Cell Biology. Ed. by Leslie Wilson et al. (Illus.). 555p. 1995. boxed set 99.00 (*0-12-564152-4*) Acad Pr.

Methods in Cell Biology Vol. 51: Methods in Avian Embryology, Vol. 51. Ed. by Leslie Wilson et al. (Illus.). 369p. (C). 1996. pap. 55.00 (*0-12-135275-7*) Acad Pr.

Methods in Cell Biology Vol. 51: Methods in Avian Embryology, Vol. 51. Ed. by Leslie Wilson et al. LC 96-157737. Vol. 51. (Illus.). 369p. 1996. text 55.00 (*0-12-564153-2*) Acad Pr.

Methods in Cell Biology Vol. 52: Methods in Muscle Biology. Ed. by Charles P. Emerson, Jr. & H. Lee Sweeney. (Illus.). 496p. 1997. pap. text 64.95 (*0-12-238190-4*) Morgan Kaufmann.

Methods in Cell Biology Vol. 53: Nuclear Structure & Function. Ed. by Miguel Berrios. (Illus.). 625p. 1997. pap. 64.95 (*0-12-093170-2*); text 99.95 (*0-12-564155-9*) Morgan Kaufmann.

Methods in Cell Biology Vol. 54': Cumulative Subject Index, Volumes 31-52, Vol. 54. Ed. by Leslie Wilson & Paul Matsudaira. (Illus.). 287p. 1997. text 99.95 (*0-12-564156-7*) Morgan Kaufmann.

Methods in Cell Biology Vol. 55: Laser Tweezers in Cell Biology. Ed. by Leslie Wilson et al. LC 97-218856. Vol. 55. (Illus.). 228p. 1997. pap. text 64.95 (*0-12-639370-2*) Morgan Kaufmann.

Methods in Cell Biology Vol. 55: Laser Tweezers in Cell Biology. Ed. by Leslie Wilson et al. LC 97-218856. (Illus.). 248p. 1998. text 99.95 (*0-12-564157-5*) Morgan Kaufmann.

Methods in Cell Biology Vol. 56: Video Microscopy. Ed. by Greenfidl Sluder & David E. Wolf. (Illus.). 334p. 1998. pap. 64.95 (*0-12-649160-7*) Morgan Kaufmann.

Methods in Cell Biology Vol. 58: Green Fluorescent Proteins. Ed. by Kevin F. Sullivan et al. (Illus.). 386p. (C). 1998. boxed set 99.95 (*0-12-544160-6*) Acad Pr.

Methods in Cell Biology Vol. 59: The Zebrafish, Biology. Ed. by Leslie Wilson et al. (Illus.). 416p. (C). 1999. boxed set 99.95 (*0-12-544161-4*) Acad Pr.

Methods in Cell Biology Vol. 60: The Zebrafish, Genetics & Genomics. Ed. by Leslie Wilson et al. (Illus.). 416p. (C). 1999. boxed set 99.95 (*0-12-544162-2*) Acad Pr.

***Methods in Cell Biology Vol. 62: Tetrahymena Thermophila.** Ed. by David J. Asai & James D. Forney. 650p. 1999. 125.00 (*0-12-544164-9*) Acad Pr.

***Methods in Cell Biology Vol. 63: Flow Cytometry, Pt. A.** Ed. by Zbigniew Darzynkiewicz. 500p. 1999. 110.00 (*0-12-544166-5*) Acad Pr.

***Methods in Cell Biology Vol. 64: Flow Cytometry, Pt. B.** Ed. by Zbigniew Darzynkiewicz. 500p. 1999. 110.00 (*0-12-544167-3*) Acad Pr.

Methods in Cell Biology, Vol. 35: Functional Organization of the Nucleus - A Laboratory Guide. Ed. by Leslie Wilson et al. (Illus.). 670p. 1991. spiral bd. 73.00 (*0-12-321920-5*) Acad Pr.

Methods in Cell Biology, Vol. 37: Antibodies in Cell Biology. Ed. by David J. Asai et al. (Illus.). 452p. 1993. text 104.00 (*0-12-564137-0*) Acad Pr.

Methods in Cell Biology, Vol. 39: Motility Assays for Motor Proteins. Ed. by Leslie Wilson et al. (Illus.). 304p. 1993. 48.00 (*0-12-628920-4*) Acad Pr.

Methods in Cell Biology, Vol. 40: A Practical Guide to the Study of CA2Plus in Living Cells. Ed. by Richard Nuccitelli. (Illus.). 368p. 1994. text 104.00 (*0-12-564141-9*) Acad Pr.

***Methods in Cell Wall Cytochemistry.** K. V. Krishnamurthy. LC 99-18125. 15p. 1999. lib. bdg. 89.95 (*0-8493-0729-5*) CRC Pr.

Methods in Chemical Ecology: Bioassay Mehods, Vol. 2. Jocelyn G. Millar & Kenneth F. Haynes. LC 97-39820. (Illus.). 416p. 1998. pap. write for info. (*0-412-08041-9*) Kluwer Academic.

Methods in Chemical Ecology: Chemical Methods, Vol. 1. Jocelyn G. Millar & Kenneth F. Haynes. LC 97-39820. 416p. 1998. write for info. (*0-412-08071-0*) Kluwer Academic.

Methods in Chemical Neuroanatomy. Ed. by Anders T. Bjorklund & Tomas B. Hokfelt. (Handbook of Chemical Neuroanatomy Ser.: No. 1). xxvi,548p. 1983. 320.00 (*0-444-90281-3*, Excerpta Medica) Elsevier.

Methods in Chromatography. 250p. 1998. text 33.00 (*981-02-3068-0*) World Scientific Pub.

Methods in Classical & Functional Analysis. Einar Hille. LC 70-137840. (Addison-Wesley Series in Mathematics). 495p. reprint ed. pap. 153.50 (*0-608-16422-4*, 205615000051) Bks Demand.

Methods in Clinical Psychology. Ed. by Robert R. Holt. Incl. Vol. 1, Projective Assessment. LC 77-10429. 360p. 1978. (*0-306-31053-8*, Kluwer Plenum); LC 77-10429. (Illus.). 59.50 (*0-685-04079-8*, Plenum Trade) Perseus Pubng.

Methods in Clinical Toxicology. Orsulak. 420p. 1999. 73.95 (*0-8493-7883-4*) CRC Pr.

Methods in Comparative Psychoacoustics. Ed. by G. M. Klump et al. LC 94-45873. (BioMethods Ser.: Vol. 6). 1995. 74.50 (*0-8176-5079-2*) Birkhauser.

Methods in Computational Chemistry Vol. 1: Electron Correlation in Atoms & Molecules. S. Wilson. LC 87-7249. (Illus.). 382p. (C). 1987. text 105.00 (*0-306-42645-5*, Kluwer Plenum) Kluwer Academic.

Methods in Computational Chemistry Vol. 2: Relativistic Effects in Atoms & Molecules. S. Wilson. LC 87-7249. (Illus.). 306p. (C). 1988. text 95.00 (*0-306-42946-2*, Kluwer Plenum) Kluwer Academic.

Methods in Computational Chemistry Vol. 3: Concurrent Computation in Chemical Calculations. S. Wilson. (Illus.). 262p. (C). 1989. text 85.00 (*0-306-43315-X*, Kluwer Plenum) Kluwer Academic.

Methods in Computational Chemistry Vol. 4: Molecular Vibrations. S. Wilson. (Illus.). 256p. (C). 1992. 89.50 (*0-306-44168-3*, Kluwer Plenum) Kluwer Academic.

Methods in Computational Chemistry Vol. 5: Atomic & Molecular Properties. S. Wilson. (Illus.). 364p. (C). 1992. text 95.00 (*0-306-44263-9*, Kluwer Plenum) Kluwer Academic.

Methods in Computational Molecular Physics. Ed. by G. H. Diercksen & S. Wilson. 1983. text 171.00 (*90-277-1638-2*) Kluwer Academic.

Methods in Computational Molecular Physics. S. Wilson & G. H. Diercksen. (NATO ASI Ser.: Vol. 293). (Illus.). 568p. (C). 1992. text 174.00 (*0-306-44227-2*, Kluwer Plenum) Kluwer Academic.

Methods In Cosmetology: Claim Support for Efficiency. Peter Elsner et al. LC 99-18480. 350p. 1999. write for info. (*3-540-64047-9*) Spr-Verlag.

Methods in Cyclic Nucleotide Research. Ed. by Mark Chasin. LC 72-89528. (Methods in Molecular Biology Ser.: No. 3). 331p. reprint ed. pap. 102.70 (*0-7837-0782-7*, 204109600019) Bks Demand.

Methods in Developmental Toxicology & Biology. Renate Thiel & Stephen Klug. (Illus.). 240p. 1997. 165.00 (*0-632-04187-0*) Blackwell Sci.

Methods in Diabetes Research, Vol. 2. Ed. by William L. Clarke et al. LC 84-3714. (Illus.). 732p. reprint ed. pap. 200.00 (*0-8357-7519-4*, 203601400097) Bks Demand.

Methods in Dialectology. Ed. by Alan R. Thomas. (Multilingual Matters Ser.: No. 48). 700p. 1988. 69.00 (*1-85359-022-3*, Pub. by Multilingual Matters) Taylor & Francis.

Methods in DNA Amplification. Ed. by Arndt Rolfs et al. LC 94-43082. (Illus.). 262p. (C). 1994. text 95.00 (*0-306-44908-0*, Kluwer Plenum) Kluwer Academic.

Methods in Ecological & Agricultural Entomology. Ed. by D. R. Dent & M. P. Walton. LC 96-48888. (A CAB International Publication). 400p. (C). 1997. text 100.00 (*0-85199-131-9*) OUP.

Methods in Ecological & Agricultural Entomology. D. R. Dent & M. P. Walton. LC 96-48888. (A CAB International Publication). (Illus.). 400p. (C). 1997. pap. text 45.00 (*0-85199-132-7*) OUP.

M

An Asterisk (*) at the beginning of an entry indicates that the title is appearing for the first time.

***Methods in Ecosystem Science.** Ed. by Osvaldo E. Sala et al. LC 99-87691. (Illus.). 488p. 2000. 115.00 (*0-387-98734-7*); pap. 69.95 (*0-387-98743-6*) Spr-Verlag.

Methods in Ecotoxicology. L. Maltby & P. Calow. 224p. 1997. pap. 42.95 (*0-632-03549-8*, Pub. by Blckwll Scitfc UK) Blackwell Sci.

Methods in Electromagnetic Wave Propagation. 2nd ed. D. S. Jones. 670p. 1996. 89.95 (*0-7803-1155-8*, PC5626) Inst Electrical.

Methods in Electromagnetic Wave Propagation. 2nd ed. D. S. Jones. (Oxford Engineering Science Ser.: No. 40). (Illus.). 668p. 1994. text 125.00 (*0-19-856262-4*) OUP.

Methods in Environmental Virology. Ed. by Charles P. Gerba & Sagar M. Goyal. LC 82-9005. (Microbiology Ser.: Vol. 7). 392p. reprint ed. pap. 121.60 (*0-7837-5637-2*, 205248900005) Bks Demand.

Methods in Enzymology. Sidney P. Colowick. (C). 1998. text. write for info. (*0-12-182197-8*) Acad Pr.

Methods in Enzymology, Vol. 303. Colowick. 608p. 1999. text 105.00 (*0-12-182204-4*) Acad Pr.

Methods in Enzymology, Vol. 305. Colowick. 640p. 1999. 99.00 (*0-12-182206-0*) Acad Pr.

Methods in Enzymology, Vol. 310. Colowick. 582p. 1999. 99.95 (*0-12-182211-7*) Acad Pr.

Methods in Enzymology, Vol. 311. Colowick. 585p. 1999. 110.00 (*0-12-182212-5*) Acad Pr.

Methods in Enzymology, Vol. 312. Colowick. 540p. 2000. write for info. (*0-12-182213-3*) Acad Pr.

Methods in Enzymology, Vol. 313. Colowick. 279p. 1999. 105.00 (*0-12-182214-1*) Acad Pr.

Methods in Enzymology, Vol. 314. Colowick. 515p. 1999. 105.00 (*0-12-182215-X*) Acad Pr.

Methods in Enzymology, Vol. 315. Colowick. Vol. 315. 774p. 1997. 115.00 (*0-12-182216-8*) Acad Pr.

Methods in Enzymology, Vol. 316. Colowick. Vol. 316. 657p. 1997. 129.95 (*0-12-182217-6*) Acad Pr.

Methods in Enzymology, Vol. 317. Colowick. Vol. 317. 466p. 1997. 90.00 (*0-12-182218-4*) Acad Pr.

Methods in Enzymology, Vol. 318. Colowick. Vol. 318. (Illus.). 431p. 1997. 90.00 (*0-12-182219-2*) Acad Pr.

Methods in Enzymology, Vol. 319. Colowick. Vol. 319. (Illus.). 626p. 2000. 119.95 (*0-12-182220-6*) Acad Pr.

Methods in Enzymology, Vol. 321. Colowick. 1997. write for info. (*0-12-182222-2*) Acad Pr.

Methods in Enzymology, Vol. 322. Colowick. Vol. 322. 650p. 1997. 119.95 (*0-12-182223-0*) Acad Pr.

Methods in Enzymology, Vols. 16-43. Incl. Antibiotics. Ed. by John H. Hash. 1975. text 199.00 (*0-12-181943-4*); Carbohydrate Metabolism. Ed. by W. A. Wood. 1967. text 209.00 (*0-12-181809-8*); Citric Acid Cycle. Ed. by J. M. Lowenstein. 1969. text 209.00 (*0-12-181870-5*); Complex Carbohydrates. Ed. by Elizabeth F. Neufeld. 1966. text 209.00 (*0-12-181808-X*); Cumulative Subject Index: Volumes 1-30. Ed. by Martha G. Dennis & Edward A. Dennis. 1975. text 199.00 (*0-12-181896-9*); Enzyme Purification & Related Techniques. Ed. by William B. Jakoby. 1971. text 209.00 (*0-12-181885-3*); Enzyme Structure. Ed. by C. H. Hirs. 1967. text 209.00 (*0-12-181860-8*); Fast Reactions. Ed. by Kenneth Kustin. 1970. text 209.00 (*0-12-181873-X*); Hormone Action Pt. C: Cyclic Nucleotides. Bert W. O'Malley. 1974. text 199.00 (*0-12-181938-8*); Hormone Action Pt. D: Isolated Cells, Tissues, & Organ Systems. Ed. by J. G. Hardman & Bert W. O'Malley. 1975. text 199.00 (*0-12-181939-6*); Hormone Action Pt. A: Steroid Hormones. Ed. by J. G. Hardman & Bert W. O'Malley. 1975. text 199.00 (*0-12-181936-1*); Hormone Action Pt. B: Peptide Hormones. Ed. by J. G. Hardman & Bert W. O'Mallely. 1975. text 199.00 (*0-12-181937-X*); Hormone Action Pt. E: Nuclear Structure & Function. Ed. by J. G. Hardman & Bert W. O'Malley. 1975. text 199.00 (*0-12-181940-X*); Immobilized Enzymes. Ed. by Klaus Mosbach. 1977. text 199.00 (*0-12-181944-2*); Lipids. J. M. Lowenstein. Ed. by Sidney P. Colowick & Nathan O. Kaplan. 1969. text 209.00 (*0-12-181871-3*); Oxidation & Phosphorylation. Ed. by Ronald W. Estabrook. 1967. text 209.00 (*0-12-181850-0*); Preparation & Assay of Enzymes. Ed. by Sidney P. Colowick & Nathan O. Kaplan. 1955. text 209.00 (*0-12-181801-2*); Preparation & Assay of Enzymes. Ed. by Sidney P. Colowick & Nathan O. Kaplan. 1955. text 209.00 (*0-12-181802-0*); Preparation & Assay of Enzymes. Ed. by Sidney P. Colowick & Nathan O. Kaplan. 1961. text 209.00 (*0-12-181805-5*); Preparation & Assay of Enzymes. Ed. by Sidney P. Colowick & Nathan O. Kaplan. 1963. text 209.00 (*0-12-181806-3*); Preparation & Assay of Substrates. Ed. by Sidney P. Colowick & Nathan O. Kaplan. 1957. text 209.00 (*0-12-181803-9*); Proteolytic Enzymes. Ed. by Gertrude E. Perlmann & Laszlo Lorand. 1970. text 209.00 (*0-12-181881-0*); Special Techniques for the Enzymologist. Ed. by Sidney P. Colowick & Nathan O. Kaplan. 1957. text 209.00 (*0-12-181804-7*); Steroids & Terpenoids. Ed. by R. B. Clayton. 1969. text 209.00 (*0-12-181872-1*); Pt. C. Carbohydrate Metabolism. Ed. by W. A. Wood. 1975. text 199.00 (*0-12-181942-6*); Pt. C. Enzyme Structure. Ed. by C. H. Hirs & Serge N. Timasheff. 1972. text 199.00 (*0-12-181889-6*); Pt. C. Nucleic Acids & Protein Synthesis. Ed. by Kivie Moldave & Lawrence Grossman. 1971. text 209.00 (*0-12-181883-7*); Pt. C. Vitamins & Coenzymes. Ed. by Donald B. McCormick & Lemuel D. Wright. (C). 1971. text 209.00 (*0-12-181882-9*); Pt. D. Enzyme Structure. Ed. by C. H. Hirs & Serge N. Timasheff. 1973. text 209.00 (*0-12-181890-X*); Pt. D. Nucleic Acids. Ed. by Lawrence Grossman & Kivie Moldave. 1971. text 209.00 (*0-12-181884-5*); Pt. A. Biomembranes. Lester Packer. 1974. text 199.00 (*0-12-181894-2*); Pt. A. Metabolism of Amino Acids & Amines. Ed. by H. Tabor & C. W. Tabor. (C). 1971. text 209.00 (*0-12-181874-8*); Pt. A. Photosynthesis. Ed. by Anthony San Pietro. 1971. text 209.00 (*0-12-181886-1*); Pt. A. Vitamins & Coenzymes. Ed. by Donald B. McCormick & Lemuel D. Wright. (C). 1970. text 209.00 (*0-12-181879-9*); Pt. B. Affinity Techniques Enzyme Purification. Ed. by William B. Jacoby & Meir Wilchek. 1974. text 199.00 (*0-12-181897-7*); Pt. B. Biomembranes. Lester Packer. 1974. text 199.00 (*0-12-181895-0*); Pt. B. Carbohydrate Metabolism. Ed. by W. A. Wood. 1975. text 199.00 (*0-12-181941-8*); Pt. B. Complex Carbohydrates. Ed. by Victor Ginsburg. 1972. text 209.00 (*0-12-181891-8*); Pt. B. Enzyme Structure. Ed. by C. H. Hirs & Serge N. Timasheff. 1972. text 199.00 (*0-12-181888-8*); Pt. B. Lipids. Ed. by John M. Lowenstein. 1975. text 199.00 (*0-12-181935-3*); Pt. B. Metabolism of Amino Acids & Amines. Ed. by H. Tabor & C. W. Tabor. (C). 1971. text 209.00 (*0-12-181877-2*); Pt. B. Pholosynthesis & Nitrogen Fixation. Ed. by Anthony San Pietro. 1972. text 199.00 (*0-12-181887-X*); Pt. B. Vitamins & Coenzymes. Ed. by Donald B. McCormick & Lemuel D. Wright. (C). 1971. text 209.00 (*0-12-181880-2*); Pt. E. Nucleic Acids & Protein Synthesis. Ed. by Lawrence Grossman & Kivie Moldave. 1974. text 199.00 (*0-12-181892-6*); Pt. F. Nucleic Acids & Protein Synthesis. Ed. by Lawrence Grossman & Kwie Molve. 1974. text 199.00 (*0-12-181893-4*); Pts. A-B. Nucleic Acids. Ed. by Lawrence Grossman. (C). 1967. text 209.00 (*0-12-181854-3*); Pts. A-B. Nucleic Acids. Ed. by Lawrence Grossman. (C). 1968. text 209.00 (*0-12-181856-X*); write for info. (*0-318-50301-8*) Acad Pr.

Methods in Enzymology, Vols. 47-62. Incl. Bioluminescence & Chemiluminescence. Ed. by Marlene Deluca. 1978. text 199.00 (*0-12-181957-4*); Biomembranes Pt. C: Biological Oxidations: Microsomal, Cytochrome P450, & Other Hemoprotein Systems. Ed. by Sidney P. Colowick & Nathan O. Kaplan. 1978. text 199.00 (*0-12-181952-3*); Biomembranes Pt. D: Biological Oxidations: Mitochondrial & Microbial Systems. Ed. by Sidney Fleischer & Lester Packer. 1978. text 199.00 (*0-12-181953-1*); Biomembranes Pt. E: Biological Oxidations: Specialized Techniques. Ed. by Sidney Fleischer & Lester Packer. 1978. text 199.00 (*0-12-181954-X*); Biomembranes Pt. F: Bioenergetics: Oxidative Phosphorylation. Ed. by Sidney P. Colowick & Sidney Fleischer. 1979. text 199.00 (*0-12-181955-8*); Cell Culture. Ed. by Sidney Colowick & William B. Jacoby. 1979. text 199.00 (*0-12-181958-2*); Purine & Pyrimidine Nucleotide Metabolism. Ed. by Sidney P. Colowick. 1978. text 199.00 (*0-12-181951-5*); Pt. C. Complex Carbohydrates. Ed. by Sidney P. Colowick & Nathan O. Kaplan. 1978. text 199.00 (*0-12-181950-7*); Pt. D. Vitamins & Coenzymes. Ed. by Sidney Colowick. 1979. text 188.00 (*0-12-181962-0*); Pt. E. Enzyme Structure. Ed. by C. H. Hirs & Serge N. Timasheff. 1977. text 199.00 (*0-12-181947-7*); Pt. F. Enzyme Structure. Ed. by C. H. Hirs. 1978. text 199.00 (*0-12-181948-5*); Pt. G. Biomembranes: Bioenergetics, Biogenesis of Mitochondria, Organization, & Transport. Ed. by Sidney P. Colowick. 1979. text 199.00 (*0-12-181956-6*); Pt. G. Enzyme Structure. Ed. by C. H. Hirs & Serge N. Timasheff. 1978. text 199.00 (*0-12-181949-3*); Pt. G. Nucleic Acids & Proteins Synthesis Pt. G: Moldave. Ed. by Sidney Colowick. 1979. text 188.00 (*0-12-181959-0*); Pt. H. Enzyme Structure. Ed. by Sidney Colowick & C. H. Hirs. 1979. text 188.00 (*0-12-181961-2*); Pt. H. Nucleic Acids & Protein Synthesis. Ed. by Sidney Colowick. 1979. text 188.00 (*0-12-181960-4*); write for info. (*0-318-50303-4*) Acad Pr.

Methods in Enzymology: ABC Transporters: Biochemical, Cellular, & Molecular Aspects, Suppl. 292. Colowick. (Illus.). 853p. (C). 1998. text 115.00 (*0-12-182193-5*) Acad Pr.

Methods in Enzymology: Caged Compounds, Vol. 291. Sidney P. Colowick. Ed. by Gerard Marriott. (Illus.). 529p. (C). 1998. text. write for info. (*0-12-182192-7*) Acad Pr.

Methods in Enzymology: Cumulative Subject Index Volumes 290-319. Colowick. Vol. 320. 450p. 2000. 129.95 (*0-12-182221-4*) Acad Pr.

Methods in Enzymology: Ion Channels, Vol. 293. Sidney P. Colowick. (Illus.). 805p. (C). 1998. text 110.00 (*0-12-182194-3*) Acad Pr.

Methods in Enzymology Vol. 285: Cumulative Subject Index Vols. 263, 264, 266-289. Ed. by John N. Abelson & Melvin I. Simon. (Methods in Enzymology Ser.: Vol. 285). (Illus.). 345p. 1998. boxed set 99.95 (*0-12-182186-2*) Morgan Kaufmann.

Methods in Enzymology Vol. 289: Solid-Phase Peptide Synthesis. Ed. by John N. Abelson et al. (Illus.). 780p. 1997. text 110.00 (*0-12-182190-0*) Morgan Kaufmann.

Methods in Enzymology Vol. 290: Molecular Chaperones, Vol. 290. Ed. by George H. Larimer & Thomas O. Baldwin. (Illus.). 500p. 1998. text 99.95 (*0-12-182191-9*) Acad Pr.

Methods in Enzymology Vol. 294, Pt. C: Ion Channels. Ed. by Michael P. Conn et al. (Illus.). 788p. (C). 1998. boxed set 115.00 (*0-12-182195-1*) Acad Pr.

Methods in Enzymology Vol. 295: Energetics of Biological Macromolecules. Ed. by John N. Abelson et al. (Illus.). 548p. (C). 1998. boxed set 99.95 (*0-12-182196-X*) Acad Pr.

Methods in Enzymology Vol. 297: Photosynthesis: Molecular Biology of Energy Capture. Ed. by Lee McIntosh. (Illus.). 395p. (C). 1998. boxed set 99.95 (*0-12-182198-6*) Acad Pr.

Methods in Enzymology Vol. 298: Molecular Motors & the Cytoskeleton. Sidney P. Colowick. Ed. by Richard B. Vallee. (Illus.). 636p. (C). 1998. boxed set 110.00 (*0-12-182199-4*) Acad Pr.

Methods in Enzymology Vol. 299: Oxidants & Antioxidants. Ed. by Lester Packer et al. (Illus.). 506p. (C). 1998. boxed set 99.95 (*0-12-182200-1*) Acad Pr.

Methods in Enzymology Vol. 300: Oxidants & Antioxidants. Colowick. Ed. by John N. Abelson et al. (Illus.). 530p. (C). 1998. boxed set 99.95 (*0-12-182201-X*) Acad Pr.

Methods in Enzymology Vol. 301, Pt. C: Nitric Oxide. Colowick. Ed. by John N. Abelson et al. (Illus.). 589p. (C). 1998. boxed set 99.95 (*0-12-182202-8*) Acad Pr.

Methods in Enzymology Vol. 302: Green Flourescent Proteins. Colowick. Ed. by John N. Abelson & Melvin I. Simon. (Illus.). 528p. 1999. 99.95 (*0-12-182203-6*) Acad Pr.

Methods in Equivariant Bifurcation & Dynamical Systems: With Applications. Pascal Chossat. (Advanced Series in Nonlinear Dynamics). 300p. 1999. 46.00 (*981-02-3828-2*) World Scientific Pub.

Methods in Experimental Embryology of the Mouse. Keen A. Rafferty. LC 70-101642. (Illus.). 109p. reprint ed. pap. 33.80 (*0-608-06188-3*, 206652000008) Bks Demand.

Methods in Experimental Physics Vol. 28: Statistical Methods for Physical Science. Ed. by Robert Celotta et al. (Illus.). 542p. 1994. text. write for info. (*0-12-475973-4*) Acad Pr.

Methods in Field Theory: Les Houches Session XXVIII. Ed. by R. M. Balian & J. Zinn-Justin. 406p. 1981. pap. text 26.00 (*9971-83-015-9*) World Scientific Pub.

Methods in Field Theory: Les Houches Session XXVIII. Ed. by R. M. Balian & J. Zinn-Justin. 406p. 1993. text 33.00 (*9971-83-078-7*) World Scientific Pub.

Methods in Free-Radical Chemistry, Vol. 1. Ed. by Earl S. Huyser. LC 70-85242. (Illus.). 222p. 1969. reprint ed. pap. 68.90 (*0-7837-0754-1*, 204107000001) Bks Demand.

Methods in Free-Radical Chemistry, 3 vols., Vol. 2. Ed. by Earl S. Huyser. LC 70-85242. (Illus.). 256p. 1969. reprint ed. pap. 79.40 (*0-7837-0710-X*, 204104100002); reprint ed. pap. 79.40 (*0-7837-0755-X*, 204107000002) Bks Demand.

Methods in Free-Radical Chemistry, Vol. 3, 1972-184 pgs. Ed. by Earl S. Huyser. LC 70-85242. (Illus.). 184p. reprint ed. pap. 57.10 (*0-7837-0756-8*, 204107000003) Bks Demand.

Methods in Free-Radical Chemistry, 3 vols., Vol. 4. Ed. by Earl S. Huyser. LC 70-85242. (Illus.). 206p. 1973. reprint ed. pap. 63.90 (*0-7837-0711-8*, 204104100004) Bks Demand.

Methods in Free-Radical Chemistry, 3 vols., Vol. 5. Ed. by Earl S. Huyser. LC 70-85242. (Illus.). 222p. 1974. reprint ed. pap. 68.90 (*0-7837-0712-6*, 204104100005) Bks Demand.

Methods in Fruit Breeding. Ed. by James N. Moore & Jules Janick. LC 81-80945. (Illus.). 464p. 1983. 49.95 (*0-911198-63-6*) Purdue U Pr.

Methods in Gene Biotechnology. William Wu. LC 96-49213. 416p. 1997. spiral bd. 99.95 (*0-8493-2659-1*) CRC Pr.

Methods in Gene Technology, Vol. 1. Ed. by Jeremy W. Dale & Peter G. Sanders. 300p. 1991. 128.50 (*1-55938-263-5*) Jai Pr.

Methods in Gene Technology, Vol. 2. Ed. by Jeremy W. Dale & Peter G. Sanders. 354p. 1995. 128.50 (*1-55938-264-3*) Jai Pr.

Methods in Genetic Epidemiology. N. E. Morton et al. (Contributions to Epidemiology & Biostatistics Ser.: Vol. 4). (Illus.). x, 262p. 1983. pap. 131.25 (*3-8055-3668-2*) S Karger.

Methods in Hormone Research: A Multi-Volume Work, 5 vols. Ed. by Ralph Dorfman. Incl. Pt. C. Steroidal Activity in Experimental Animals & Man. 1966. 65.00 (*0-12-221105-7*); Pt. A. Steroidal Activity in Experimental Animals & Man. 1964. 74.50 (*0-12-221103-0*); Pt. B. Steroidal Activity in Experimental Animals & Man. 1965. 65.00 (*0-12-221104-9*); Vol. 1. 2nd ed. 1969. 78.00 (*0-12-221161-8*); Vol. 2a. 2nd ed. 1969. 78.00 (*0-12-221162-6*); write for info. (*0-318-50304-2*) Acad Pr.

Methods in Hypnosis: Guidebook for Medicine, Reference & Research. John C. Bartone. LC 83-46103. 150p. 1985. 47.50 (*0-88164-138-3*); pap. 44.50 (*0-88164-139-1*) ABBE Pubs Assn.

Methods in Immunohematology. 2nd ed. W. John Judd. LC 93-81030. xxii, 476p. 1994. pap. text 30.00 (*0-935643-04-4*) Mont Sci Pubns.

Methods in Immunotoxicology, 2 vols. Ed. by Gary R. Burleson et al. LC 95-979. 1048p. 1995. 350.00 (*0-471-30597-9*, Wiley-Liss) Wiley.

Methods in Immunotoxicology, Vol. 1. Ed. by Gary B. Burleson et al. LC 95-979. 552p. 1995. 339.50 (*0-471-56196-7*, Wiley-Liss) Wiley.

Methods in Immunotoxicology, Vol. 2. Ed. by Gary R. Burleson et al. LC 95-979. 496p. 1995. 339.50 (*0-471-56197-5*, Wiley-Liss) Wiley.

Methods in Inhalation Toxicology. Ed. by Robert F. Phalen. (Methods in Toxicology Ser.). 176p. 1996. spiral bd. 94.95 (*0-8493-3343-1*) CRC Pr.

Methods in Inositide Research. Ed. by Robin F. Irvine. LC 90-8695. 239p. 1990. reprint ed. pap. 74.10 (*0-608-03417-7*, 206411600008) Bks Demand.

Methods in Introductory Oceanography. Bruce Rowell & Wendy Ryan. 184p. (C). 1995. text. write for info. (*0-697-28016-0*, WCB McGr Hill) McGrw-H Hghr Educ.

Methods in Lignin Chemistry. Ed. by C. W. Dence et al. (Wood Science Ser.). (Illus.). 620p. 1992. 368.95 (*0-387-50295-5*) Spr-Verlag.

***Methods in Mammary Gland Biology & Breast Cancer Research.** Margot M. Ip & Bonnie B. Asch. LC 00-25889. 2000. write for info. (*0-306-46397-0*, Kluwer Plenum) Kluwer Academic.

Methods in Marine Zooplankton Ecology. Makoto Omori & Ikeda Tsutomu. LC 91-24425. 348p. (C). 1992. reprint ed. lib. bdg. 59.95 (*0-89464-653-2*) Krieger.

Methods in Mathematical Logic. Ed. by C. A. Di Prisco. (Lecture Notes in Mathematics Ser.: Vol. 1130). vii, 407p. 1985. 54.95 (*0-387-15236-9*) Spr-Verlag.

Methods in Mathematical Physics: Proceedings of the 12th International Hutsulian Workshop. Ed. by Stepan S. Moskaliuk. 469p. (C). 1998. pap. text 80.00 (*1-57485-027-X*) Hadronic Pr Inc.

Methods in Medicine. J. Ridderikhoff. 240p. (C). 1989. lib. bdg. 148.50 (*1-55608-080-8*, Pub. by Kluwer Academic) Kluwer Academic.

Methods in Microbiology, 10. Ed. by John R. Norris & T. Bergen. 1979. 80.00 (*0-12-521510-X*) Acad Pr.

Methods in Microbiology, 14. John R. Norris et al. 1984. text 157.00 (*0-12-521514-2*) Acad Pr.

Methods in Microbiology, 15. John R. Norris et al. 1984. text 157.00 (*0-12-521515-0*) Acad Pr.

Methods in Microbiology, 16. John R. Norris et al. 1985. text 157.00 (*0-12-521516-9*) Acad Pr.

Methods in Microbiology, Vol. 11. Ed. by John R. Norris & T. Bergen. 1979. text 209.00 (*0-12-521511-8*) Acad Pr.

Methods in Microbiology, Vol. 12. Ed. by John R. Norris & D. W. Ribbons. 1979. text 209.00 (*0-12-521512-6*) Acad Pr.

Methods in Microbiology, Vol. 13. John R. Norris & T. Bergan. LC 68-57745. 1980. text 209.00 (*0-12-521513-4*) Acad Pr.

Methods in Microbiology, Vol. 18. Ed. by John R. Norris. (Serial Publication Ser.). 1985. text 157.00 (*0-12-521518-5*) Acad Pr.

Methods in Microbiology, Vol. 19. Ed. by R. R. Colwell & R. Grigorova. 518p. 1988. text 136.00 (*0-12-521519-3*) Acad Pr.

Methods in Microbiology Vol. 20: Electron Microscopy in Microbiology. Ed. by Frank Mayer & John R. Norris. 431p. 1988. text 125.00 (*0-12-521520-7*) Acad Pr.

Methods in Microbiology Vol. 23: Techniques for the Study of Mycorrhiza. Ed. by John R. Norris et al. (Illus.). 480p. 1991. text 125.00 (*0-12-521523-1*) Acad Pr.

Methods in Microbiology Vol. 24: Techniques for the Study of Mycorrhiza. Ed. by John R. Norris et al. (Illus.). 450p. 1992. text 125.00 (*0-12-521524-X*) Acad Pr.

Methods in Microbiology Vol. 25: Immunology of Infection. Ed. by Stefan Kaufmann & Dieter Kabelitz. (Illus.). 720p. (C). 1998. boxed set 99.95 (*0-12-521528-2*) Morgan Kaufmann.

Methods in Microbiology Vol. 26: Yeast Gene Analysis. Ed. by Gordon Dougon et al. (Illus.). 502p. 1998. 59.95 (*0-12-136655-3*); text 99.95 (*0-12-521526-6*) Morgan Kaufmann.

Methods in Microbiology Vol. 27: Bacterial Pathogenesis. Kaufmann. Ed. by Peter Williams et al. (Illus.). 500p. 1998. 59.95 (*0-12-521525-8*) Acad Pr.

Methods in Microbiology Vol. 29: Automation. Norris et al. 500p. (C). 1998. 99.95 (*0-12-521527-4*) Acad Pr.

***Methods in Microbiology Vol. 29: Genetic Methods for Diverse Prokaryotes.** Academic Press Staff et al. (Illus.). 560p. 1999. 59.95 (*0-12-652340-1*) Acad Pr.

Methods in Microbiology Vol. 29: Genetic Methods for Diverse Prokaryotes. Margaret C. Smith & Elizabeth Sockett. (Illus.). 500p. 1999. text 99.95 (*0-12-521529-0*) Acad Pr.

Methods in Module Theory. Ed. by Gene Abrams et al. LC 92-23502. (Lecture Notes in Pure & Applied Mathematics Ser.: Vol. 140). (Illus.). 352p. 1992. pap. text 155.00 (*0-8247-8802-8*) Dekker.

Methods in Molecular Genetics: Gene & Chromosome Analysis, 3 vols., Vols. 1, 2 & 5. Adolph. 1994. 210.00 (*0-12-044355-4*) Acad Pr.

Methods in Molecular Genetics Vol. 3: Molecular Microbiology Techniques, Pt. A. Kenneth W. Adolph. (Illus.). 398p. 1994. text 104.00 (*0-12-044305-8*) Acad Pr.

Methods in Molecular Genetics Vol. 4: Molecular Virology Techniques, Pt. A. Ed. by Kenneth W. Adolph. (Illus.). 410p. 1994. text 104.00 (*0-12-044306-6*) Acad Pr.

Methods in Molecular Genetics Vol. 5: Gene & Chromosome Analysis, Pt. C. Ed. by Kenneth W. Adolph. (Illus.). 402p. 1994. text. write for info. (*0-12-044307-4*) Acad Pr.

Methods in Molecular Genetics Vol. 6: Viral Gene Techniques, Vol. 6. Ed. by Kenneth W. Adolph. (Illus.). 487p. 1995. text 90.00 (*0-12-044308-2*) Acad Pr.

Methods in Molecular Genetics Vol. 8: Human Molecular Genetics, Vol. 8. Ed. by Kenneth W. Adolph. (Illus.). 500p. 1996. text 85.00 (*0-12-044310-4*) Acad Pr.

Methods in Molecular Genetics, Vol. 1: Gene & Chromosome Analysis, Pt. A. Ed. by Kenneth W. Adoplh. (Illus.). 404p. 1993. text 104.00 (*0-12-044301-5*) Acad Pr.

Methods in Molecular Genetics, Vol. 2: Gene & Chromosome Analysis, Pt. B. Kenneth W. Adolph. (Illus.). 369p. 1993. text 104.00 (*0-12-044303-1*) Acad Pr.

Methods in Narcotics Research. Ed. by Seymour Ehrenpreis & Amos Neidle. LC 75-23586. (Modern Pharmacology-Toxicology Ser.: No. 5). (Illus.). 422p. reprint ed. pap. 130.90 (*0-7837-0703-7*, 204103500019) Bks Demand.

Methods in Neurobiology, Vol. 1. Ed. by Robert Lahue. LC 80-15623. 614p. 1981. 110.00 (*0-306-40517-2*, Plenum Trade) Perseus Pubng.

Methods in Neurobiology, Vol. 2. Ed. by Robert Lahue. LC 80-15623. 682p. 1981. 110.00 (*0-306-40518-0*, Plenum Trade) Perseus Pubng.

An Asterisk (*) at the beginning of an entry indicates that the title is appearing for the first time.

Methods in Neuroendocrinology. Louis D. Van de Kar. LC 98-3241. (Methods In Life Science - Cellular & Molecular Neuropharmacology Ser.). 256p. 1998. otabind 94.95 (*0-8493-3363-6*, 3363) CRC Pr.

Methods in Neurology. A. K. Bagchi. (C). 1989. 70.00 (*0-89771-377-X*, Pub. by Current Dist) St Mut.

Methods in Neuronal Modeling: From Ions to Networks. 2nd ed. Ed. by Christof Koch & Idan Segev. LC 97-17166. (Computational Neuroscience Ser.). (Illus.). 687p. 1998. 60.00 (*0-262-11231-0*, Bradford Bks) MIT Pr.

Methods in Neurosciences: Neurobiology of Cytokines, Vol. 17. Ed. by Errol B. De Souza & P. Michael Conn. (Illus.). 327p. 1993. text 104.00 (*0-12-185283-0*) Acad Pr.

Methods in Neurosciences Vol. 18: Lipid Metabolism in Signaling Systems. Ed. by P. Michael Conn & John N. Fain. (Illus.). 357p. 1993. text 104.00 (*0-12-185285-7*) Acad Pr.

Methods in Neurosciences Vol. 19: Ion Channels of Excitable Cells. Ed. by Toshio Narahashi & P. Michael Conn. (Illus.). 387p. 1994. text 104.00 (*0-12-185287-3*) Acad Pr.

Methods in Neurosciences Vol. 20: Pulsatility in Neuroendocrine Systems. Ed. by Jon E. Levine & P. Michael Conn. (Illus.). 510p. 1994. text 104.00 (*0-12-185289-X*) Acad Pr.

Methods in Neurosciences Vol. 21: Providing Pharmacological Access to the Brain, Alternate Approaches. Ed. by Thomas R. Flanagan et al. (Illus.). 508p. 1994. text 104.00 (*0-12-185291-1*) Acad Pr.

Methods in Neurosciences Vol. 22: Neurobiology of Steroids. Ed. by E. Ron De Kloet et al. (Illus.). 552p. 1994. text 104.00 (*0-12-185292-X*) Acad Pr.

Methods in Neurosciences Vol. 23: Peptidases & Neuropeptide Processing. Ed. by A. Ian Smith & P. Michael Conn. (Illus.). 407p. 1995. text 90.00 (*0-12-185293-8*) Acad Pr.

Methods in Neurosciences Vol. 24: Neuroimmunology. Ed. by P. Michael Conn et al. (Illus.). 434p. (C). 1995. text 59.95 (*0-12-185294-6*) Acad Pr.

Methods in Neurosciences Vol. 25: Receptor Molecular Biology. Ed. by P. Michael Conn & Stuart C. Sealfon. (Illus.). 519p. 1995. text 104.00 (*0-12-185295-4*) Acad Pr.

Methods in Neurosciences Vol. 26: PCR in Neuroscience. Ed. by Gobinda Sarkar & P. Michael Conn. (Illus.). 455p. 1995. pap. 58.00 (*0-12-619255-3*) Acad Pr.

Methods in Neurosciences Vol. 26: PCR in Neuroscience. Ed. by Gobinda Sarkar & P. Michael Conn. (Illus.). 455p. 1995. text 100.00 (*0-12-185296-2*) Acad Pr.

Methods in Neurosciences Vol. 27: Measurement & Manipulation of Intracellular Ions. Ed. by Jacob Kraicer et al. LC 97-17438. (Illus.). 400p. 1995. text 100.00 (*0-12-185297-0*) Acad Pr.

Methods in Neurosciences Vol. 28: Quantitative Neuroendocrinology. Ed. by Michael L. Johnson et al. (Illus.). 433p. 1995. text 95.00 (*0-12-185298-9*) Acad Pr.

Methods in Neurosciences Vol. 30: Paradigms of Neural Injury. Ed. by P. Michael Conn & Jose R. Perez-Polo. (Illus.). 335p. 1996. text 85.00 (*0-12-185300-4*) Acad Pr.

Methods in Neurosciences Vol. 31: Nitric Oxide Synthase: Characterization & Functional Analysis. Ed. by P. Michael Conn & Mahin D. Maines. LC 96-200801. (Illus.). 354p. 1996. text 89.00 (*0-12-185301-2*) Acad Pr.

Methods in Neurosciences, Vol. 12: Receptors: Molecular Biology, Receptor Subclasses, Localization, & Ligand Design. Ed. by P. Michael Conn. (Illus.). 419p. 1993. text 104.00 (*0-12-185273-3*) Acad Pr.

Methods in Neurosciences, Vol. 2: Cell Culture. Ed. by P. Michael Conn. 424p. 1990. text 104.00 (*0-12-185253-9*) Acad Pr.

Methods in Neurosciences, Vol. 3: Quantitative & Qualitative Microscopy. Ed. by P. Michael Conn. 494p. 1990. spiral bd. 52.00 (*0-12-185256-3*) Acad Pr.

Methods in Neurosciences, Vol. 4: Electrophysiology & Microinjection. Ed. by P. Michael Conn. (Illus.). 504p. 1991. pap. 73.00 (*0-12-185258-X*) Acad Pr.

Methods in Neurosciences, Vol. 7: Lesions & Transplantation. Ed. by P. Michael Conn. (Illus.). 496p. 1991. spiral bd. 48.00 (*0-12-185264-4*) Acad Pr.

Methods in Neurosciences, Vol. 8: Neurotoxins. Ed. by P. Michael Conn. (Illus.). 423p. 1992. pap. 48.00 (*0-12-185266-0*) Acad Pr.

Methods in Neurosciences, Vol. 9: Gene Expression in Neural Tissues. Ed. by P. Michael Conn. (Illus.). 492p. 1992. pap. 48.00 (*0-12-185268-7*) Acad Pr.

Methods in Neurotransmitter Receptor Analysis. Ed. by Henry I. Yamamura. 288p. 1990. text 65.50 (*0-88167-609-8*) Lppncott W & W.

Methods in Nitric Oxide Research. Ed. by Martin Feelisch & Jonathan Stamler. 732p. 1996. 245.00 (*0-471-95524-8*) Wiley.

***Methods in Non-Aqueous Enzymology.** Ed. by M. N. Gupta. (Methods & Tools in Biosciences & Medicine Ser.). 300p. 2000. (*3-7643-5803-3*); spiral bd. 69.95 (*3-7643-6109-3*) Birkhauser.

***Methods in Non-Aqueous Enzymology.** Munishwar Nath Gupta. LC 00-21710. (Methods & Tools in Biosciences & Medicine Ser.). 2000. write for info. (*0-8176-5803-3*) Birkhauser.

Methods in Nonradioactive Detection. Ed. by Gary C. Howard. LC 92-49351. 1992. write for info. (*0-444-01661-9*) Elsevier.

Methods in Nonradioactive Detection in Biological Systems. Gary C. Howard. (Illus.). 294p. (C). 1994. pap. text 65.00 (*0-8385-6946-3*, A6946-6, Apple Lange Med) McGraw.

Methods in Observational Epidemiology. 2nd ed. Jennifer L. Kelsey et al. (Monographs in Epidemiology & Biostatistics: 26). (Illus.). 448p. (C). 1996. text 52.50 (*0-19-508377-6*) OUP.

***Methods in Personal Care of the Bedridden Patient... Hair, Skin & Nails.** large type ed. Noella Charest-Papagno. LC 97-93160. (Illus.). 48p. 1999. spiral bd. 10.95 (*0-9604610-8-6*, JJPLB) JJ Pub FL.

Methods in Pharmacology Vol. 5: Myocardial Biology. Ed. by Arnold Schwartz. LC 74-34441. 248p. 1984. 69.50 (*0-306-41684-0*, Plenum Trade) Perseus Pubng.

Methods in Pharmacology Vol. 6: Methods Used in Adenosine Research. Ed. by David M. Paton. LC 84-26638. 400p. 1985. 95.00 (*0-306-41872-X*, Plenum Trade) Perseus Pubng.

Methods in Pharmacology Vol. 7: Molecular & Cellular Biology of Pharmacological Targets. H. Glossmann & J. Striessnig. (Illus.). 288p. (C). 1993. text 89.50 (*0-306-44424-0*, Kluwer Plenum) Kluwer Academic.

Methods in Plant Biochemistry Vol. 2: Carbohydrates. Ed. by P. M. Dey. 657p. 1990. text 104.00 (*0-12-461012-9*) Acad Pr.

Methods in Plant Biochemistry Vol. 3: Enzymes of Primary Metabolism. Ed. by Peter J. Lea et al. 414p. 1990. text 104.00 (*0-12-461013-7*) Acad Pr.

Methods in Plant Biochemistry Vol. 4: Lipids, Membranes & Aspects of Photobiology. Ed. by J. L. Harwood & J. R. Bowyer. 353p. 1991. text 104.00 (*0-12-461014-5*) Acad Pr.

Methods in Plant Biochemistry Vol. 5: Amino Acids, Proteins & Nucleic Acids. Ed. by L. E. Rogers. 368p. 1991. text 104.00 (*0-12-461015-3*) Acad Pr.

Methods in Plant Biochemistry Vol. 6: Assays for Bioactivity. Ed. by K. Hostettmann et al. (Illus.). 360p. 1991. text 104.00 (*0-12-461016-1*) Acad Pr.

Methods in Plant Biochemistry Vol. 7: Terpenoids. Ed. by Barry V. Charlwood et al. (Illus.). 565p. 1991. text 104.00 (*0-12-461017-X*) Acad Pr.

Methods in Plant Biochemistry Vol. 8: Tropane Alkaloids. Ed. by P. M. Dey et al. (Illus.). 605p. 1993. text 104.00 (*0-12-461018-8*) Acad Pr.

Methods in Plant Biochemistry Vol. 9: Enzymes of Secondary Metabolism. Ed. by Peter J Lea. (Illus.). 478p. 1993. text 104.00 (*0-12-461019-6*) Acad Pr.

Methods in Plant Biochemistry Vol. 10b: Molecular Biology. Ed. by Jeffrey B. Harborne et al. (Illus.). 136p. 1996. text 52.95 (*0-12-461021-8*) Acad Pr.

Methods in Plant Biochemistry & Molecular Biology. William V. Dashek. LC 96-41196. 480p. 1997. spiral bd., lab manual ed. 99.95 (*0-8493-9480-5*) CRC Pr.

Methods in Plant Cell Biology, Vol. 50. Ed. by Leslie Wilson et al. (Illus.). 573p. 1995. spiral bd. 63.00 (*0-12-273871-3*); spiral bd. 63.00 (*0-12-273872-1*) Acad Pr.

Methods in Plant Molecular Biology. Mary A. Schuler & Raymond E. Zielinski. 150p. 1988. pap., spiral bd. 52.00 (*0-12-632340-2*) Acad Pr.

Methods in Plant Molecular Biology: A Laboratory Course Manual. Ed. by P. Maliga et al. (Illus.). 250p. (C). 1994. pap. text 75.00 (*0-87969-386-X*) Cold Spring Harbor.

Methods in Plant Molecular Biology: A Laboratory Course Manual. P. Maliga et al. LC 94-36570. 1995. write for info. (*0-87969-450-5*) Cold Spring Harbor.

Methods in Plant Molecular Biology & Biotechnology. Bernard R. Glick. Ed. by John E. Thompson. 384p. 1993. per. 104.95 (*0-8493-5164-2*, QK728) CRC Pr.

Methods in Plant Tissue Culture. P. J. Bottino. (Illus.). 74p. 1981. student ed. 13.40 (*1-877960-00-4*, 2-503) Kemtec Educ.

Methods in Practical Laboratory Bacteriology. Ed. by Henrik Chart. LC 94-1321. 176p. 1994. spiral bd. 83.95 (*0-8493-8692-6*, 8692) CRC Pr.

Methods in Protein Sequence Analysis. K. Imahori & F. Sakiyama. LC 93-7788. (Illus.). 326p. (C). 1993. text 89.50 (*0-306-44488-7*, Kluwer Plenum) Kluwer Academic.

Methods in Protein Sequence Analysis, 1986. Ed. by Kenneth A. Walsh. LC 86-27681. (Experimental Biology & Medicine Ser.). (Illus.). 663p. 1987. 99.50 (*0-89603-118-7*) Humana.

Methods in Protein Structure Analysis: Proceedings of the 10th International Conference Held in Snowbird, Utah, September 8-13, 1994. Ed. by M. Zouhair Atassi & Ettore Appella. LC 95-36854. (Illus.). 552p. (C). 1996. text 135.00 (*0-306-45124-7*, Kluwer Plenum) Kluwer Academic.

Methods in Pulmonary Research. S. Uhlig & Aubrey E. Taylor. LC 98-14358. 1998. write for info. (*0-8176-5427-5*) Birkhauser.

Methods in Pulmonary Research. Ed. by S. Uhlig & Aubrey E. Taylor. LC 98-14358. 320p. 1998. 130.00 (*3-7643-5427-5*) Birkhauser.

Methods in Receptor Research, 2 pts., Pt. 1. Ed. by Melvin Blecher. LC 75-40846. (Methods in Molecular Biology Ser.: No. 9). (Illus.). 403p. reprint ed. pap. 125.00 (*0-8357-6210-6*, 203451700001) Bks Demand.

Methods in Receptor Research, 2 pts., Pt. 2. Ed. by Melvin Blecher. LC 75-40846. (Methods in Molecular Biology Ser.: No. 9). (Illus.). 396p. reprint ed. pap. 122.80 (*0-8357-6211-4*, 203451700002) Bks Demand.

Methods in Renal Toxicology. Ed. by Rudolfs K. Zalups & Lawrence H. Lash. (Methods in Toxicology Ser.). 448p. 1996. boxed set 139.95 (*0-8493-3341-5*) CRC Pr.

Methods in Ring Theory. Ed. by Freddy Van Oystaeyen. 1984. text 252.50 (*90-277-1743-5*) Kluwer Academic.

Methods in Ring Theory: Proceedings of the Trento Conference. Vesselin Drensky et al. LC 98-9447. (Lecture Notes in Pure & Applied Mathematics Ser.). (Illus.). 328p. 1998. pap. text 150.00 (*0-8247-0183-6*) Dekker.

Methods in Rock Magnetism & Palaeomagnetism: Techniques & Instrumentation. Ed. by D. W. Collinson. (Illus.). 528p. 1983. text 171.50 (*0-412-22980-3*, NO. 6752) Chapman & Hall.

Methods in Seed Pathology. V. K. Agarwal & James B. Sinclair. 1999. 89.95 (*0-8493-2877-2*) CRC Pr.

Methods in Skin Research. Ed. by D. Skerrow & C. J. Skerrow. LC 84-5245. (Illus.). 685p. 1985. reprint ed. pap. 200.00 (*0-608-06824-1*, 206702100009) Bks Demand.

Methods in Soil Biology. Ed. by Franz F. Schinner et al. (Illus.). 256p. 1996. pap. 79.00 (*3-540-59055-2*) Spr-Verlag.

Methods in Soil Zoology. Ed. by Mieczyslaw Gorny & Leszek Grum. LC 92-8478. 460p. 1993. 307.00 (*0-444-98823-8*) Elsevier.

Methods in Stellar Atmosphere & Interplanetary Plasma Research. Ed. by D. V. Skobel'tsyn. LC 74-26541. (Proceedings of the P. N. Lebedev Physics Institute Ser.: No. 62). (Illus.). 208p. 1974. reprint ed. pap. 64.50 (*0-608-05522-0*, 206599000006) Bks Demand.

Methods in Stream Ecology. F. Richard Hauer. 1998. pap. text 39.95 (*0-12-332906-X*) Acad Pr.

Methods in Stream Ecology. Ed. by F. Richard Hauer & Gary A. Lamberti. (Illus.). 674p. 1996. text 74.95 (*0-12-332905-1*) Acad Pr.

Methods in Studying Cardiac Membranes, Vol. I. Ed. by N. S. Ohalla. 320p. 1984. 181.00 (*0-8493-5995-3*, QP114, CRC Reprint) Franklin.

Methods in Studying Cardiac Membranes, Vol. II. Ed. by N. S. Dhalla. 344p. 1984. 189.00 (*0-8493-5996-1*, QP114, CRC Reprint) Franklin.

Methods in Subnuclear Physics, Vol. 1. M. Nikolic. 516p. 1968. 190.00 (*0-677-11950-X*) Gordon & Breach.

Methods in Subnuclear Physics: Proceedings, 1965-1969, Vols. 1-4. International School of Elementary Particle Physic. Ed. by M. Nikolic. Incl. Vol. 2. 858p. 1968. 286.00 write for info. (*0-318-52705-7*) Gordon & Breach.

Methods in Teaching Consultation-Liaison Psychiatry. Ed. by M. S. Hale. (Advances in Psychosomatic Medicine Ser.: Vol. 20). (Illus.). x, 144p. 1990. 85.25 (*3-8055-5080-4*) S Karger.

Methods in the Determinati0on of Partial Structure Factors. J. B. Suck & B. Maier. 250p. 1993. text 105.00 (*981-02-1463-4*) World Scientific Pub.

Methods in the Mediterranean: Historical & Archaeological Views on Texts & Archaeology. Ed. by David B. Small. LC 94-9844. (Mnemosyne, Bibliotheca Classica Batava Ser.: Vol. 135). v, 294p. 1994. 75.00 (*90-04-09581-0*) Brill Academic Pubs.

Methods in the Neurosciences: Intracellular Perfusions of Excitable Cells, Vol. 5, Intracellular Perfusion of Excitable Cells. 99th ed. Ed. by Platon G. Kostyuk & O. A. Krishtal. (IBRO Handbook Series: Methods in the Neurosciences: No. 1-569). 146p. 1984. 365.00 (*0-471-90379-5*, Wiley-Interscience) Wiley.

Methods in the Qualitative Theory of Dynamical Systems in Astrophysics & Gas Dynamics. O. I. Bogoyavlensky. Tr. by Dimitri Gokhman from RUS. (Soviet Mathematics Ser.). (Illus.). 320p. 1985. 125.95 (*0-387-13614-2*) Spr-Verlag.

Methods in Theoretical Quantum Optics. Stephen M. Barnett & Paul M. Radmore. LC 97-13764. (Oxford Series on Optical & Imaging Sciences: No. 15). (Illus.). 292p. 1997. text 85.00 (*0-19-856362-0*) OUP.

Methods in Toxicology: Male Reproductive Toxicology, Vol. 3, Pt. A. Ed. by Charles A. Tyson et al. (Illus.). 389p. 1993. 58.00 (*0-12-461208-3*) Acad Pr.

Methods in Toxicology, Vol. 1, Pt. B: In Vitro Toxicity Indicators. Ed. by Charles A. Tyson & John M. Frazier. (Illus.). 497p. 1994. text 104.00 (*0-12-461203-2*) Acad Pr.

Methods in Toxicology, Vol. 1, Pt. B: In Vitro Toxicity Indicators. Ed. by Charles A. Tyson & John M. Frazier. (Illus.). 497p. 1994. 58.00 (*0-12-461204-0*) Acad Pr.

Methods in Toxicology, Vol. 2: Mitochondrial Dysfunction. Ed. by Charles A. Tyson et al. (Illus.). 502p. 1993. pap. 58.00 (*0-12-461206-7*) Acad Pr.

Methods in Toxicology, Vol. 3, Pt. B: Female Reproductive Toxicology. Ed. by Jerrold J. Heindel & Robert E. Chapin. (Illus.). 404p. 1993. 58.00 (*0-12-461210-5*) Acad Pr.

Methods in Vitamin Analysis for the Health & Food Sciences. Ronald R. Eitenmiller & W. O. Landen, Jr. LC 98-21970. 544p. 1998. boxed set 94.95 (*0-8493-2668-0*, 2668) CRC Pr.

***Methods in Yeast Genetics: A Cold Spring Harbor Laboratory Course Manual.** Dan Burke et al. LC 00-31721. (Illus.). 2000. pap. write for info. (*0-87969-588-9*) Cold Spring Harbor.

Methods in Yeast Genetics: A Cold Spring Harbor Laboratory Course Manual, 1994. Chris Kaiser et al. LC 94-74966. (Illus.). 242p. 1994. reprint ed. pap. 75.10 (*0-608-04090-8*, 206482200001) Bks Demand.

Methods in Yeast Genetics: A Laboratory Course Manual. Alison Adams et al. LC 97-77211. (Illus.). 200p. (C). 1998. pap. text 61.00 (*0-87969-508-0*) Cold Spring Harbor.

Methods in Yeast Genetics: A Laboratory Course Manual. Mark D. Rose et al. (Illus.). 200p. (C). 1990. text 20.00 (*0-87969-354-1*) Cold Spring Harbor.

Methods Integration: Proceedings of the Methods Integration Workshop, Leeds, 25-26 March 1996. British Computer Society Staff et al. Ed. by Antony Bryant & Lesley Semmens. LC 96-3337. (Electronic Workshops in Computing Ser.). 16p. 1996. 54.50 (*3-540-76065-2*) Spr-Verlag.

Methods, Logic, & Research of Sociology. Robert K. Leik. LC 72-85667. (Studies in Sociology). (C). 1972. pap. write for info. (*0-672-61242-9*, Bobbs) Macmillan.

Methods of Achieving Improved Seismic Performance of Communications Systems. Alex Tang & Anshel J. Schiff. LC 96-47914. (Technical Council on Lifeline Earthquake Engineering Monographs). 184p. 1996. 21.00 (*0-7844-0216-7*) Am Soc Civil Eng.

Methods of Achieving the Paths: Stages of Philosophical & Ethical Development According to the Madhyamika Svatantrika School of Buddhism. Sermey G. Tharchin. Ed. by Barbara D. Taylor.Tr. of Lam-thob-tsul. 59p. (Orig.). 1981. pap. 5.00 (*0-918753-02-3*) Mahayana.

Methods of Algebraic Geometry, Vol. 2. Daniel Pedoe & W. V. Hodge. (Cambridge Mathematical Library). (Illus.). 404p. (C). 1994. pap. text 27.95 (*0-521-46901-5*) Cambridge U Pr.

Methods of Algebraic Geometry, Vol. 3. Daniel Pedoe & W. V. Hodge. (Cambridge Mathematical Library). (Illus.). 346p. (C). 1994. pap. text 27.95 (*0-521-46775-6*) Cambridge U Pr.

Methods of Algebraic Geometry in Control Theory, 2 vols., Vol. 1. P. Faib. Ed. by Christopher I. Byrnes. 350p. 1990. write for info. (*0-318-68539-6*) Spr-Verlag.

Methods of Algebraic Geometry in Control Theory Pt. 1: Scalar Linear Systems & Affine Algebraic Geometry. Peter Falb. (Systems & Control: Foundations & Applications Ser.: Vol. 4). 216p. 1990. 46.50 (*0-8176-3454-1*) Birkhauser.

Methods of Algebraic Geometry in Control Theory Pt. II: Multivariable Linear Systems & Projective Algebraic Geometry. P. Falb. 369p. 1999. 59.95 (*0-8176-4113-0*) Birkhauser.

Methods of Algorithmic Language Implementation. Ed. by A. P. Ershov & C. H. Koster. (Lecture Notes in Computer Science Ser.: Vol. 47). 1977. 22.95 (*0-387-08065-1*) Spr-Verlag.

Methods of Analysis for Nutrition Labeling. Darryl M. Sullivan & Donald Carpenter. LC 93-36961. 624p. 1993. 111.00 (*0-935584-52-8*) AOAC Intl.

Methods of Analysis for Processed Fruits & Vegetables see Codex Alimentarius Commission Reports

Methods of Analysis of the American Society of Brewing Chemists. 8th rev. ed. American Society of Brewing Chemists Society Staff. LC 92-72143. 586p. 1992. ring bd. 460.00 (*1-881696-01-4*) Am Brewing Chems.

Methods of Analytical Dynamics. Leonard Meirovitch. 485p. (C). 1970. 111.25 (*0-07-041455-6*) McGraw.

Methods of Applied Fourier Analysis. Jayakumar Ramanthan. LC 98-4738. (Applied & Numerical Harmonic Analysis Ser.). 1998. write for info. (*3-7643-3963-2*) Birkhauser.

Methods of Applied Mathematics. Francis B. Hildebrand. ix, 362p. 1992. reprint ed. pap. 10.95 (*0-486-67002-3*) Dover.

Methods of Applying Herbicides. Ed. by C. G. McWhorter & M. R. Gebhardt. 358p. 1988. text 35.00 (*0-911733-08-6*) Weed Sci Soc.

Methods of Assessing the Reinforcing Properties of Abused Drugs. Ed. by M. A. Bozarth. (Illus.). 658p. 1987. 65.00 (*0-387-96625-0*) Spr-Verlag.

Methods of Assessment of Avoidable Blindness. WHO Staff. (WHO Offset Publications: No. 54). 42p. 1980. 4.00 (*92-4-170054-8*) World Health.

Methods of Attack, 1997: Scientific Evidence. 3rd ed. Edward A. Imwinkelried. LC 97-75565. 450p. 1997. text 95.00 (*1-55834-777-1*, 63044-11, MICHIE) LEXIS Pub.

Methods of Averaging in Non-Linear Problems of Relativistic Electrodynamics. V. Kulish. LC 98-31186. 1998. write for info. (*1-885978-27-8*) Wrld Fed Pubs.

Methods of Bible Study. Robert Conn & Steve Clapp. (C-Four Youth Bible Materials Ser.). (Illus.). 91p. (Orig.). 1982. pap. 8.00 (*0-914527-14-2*) C-Four Res.

Methods of Bifurcation Theory. Shui-Nee Chow & Jack K. Hale. (Grundlehren der Mathematischen Wissenschaften Ser.: Vol. 251). (Illus.). 512p. 1996. 97.95 (*0-387-90664-9*) Spr-Verlag.

Methods of Biochemical Analysis Protein Structure Determination. Ed. by Clarence H. Suelter. (Methods of Biochemical Analysis Ser.). 310p. 1991. 199.95 (*0-471-51326-1*) Wiley.

Methods of Cell Separation, 3 vols. Ed. by Nicholas Catsimpoolas. LC 77-11018. (Biological Separations Ser.). (Illus.). 1977. 59.50 (*0-306-34604-4*, Plenum Trade) Perseus Pubng.

Methods of Cell Separation, 3 vols. Ed. by Nicholas Catsimpoolas. LC 77-11018. (Biological Separations Ser.). (Illus.). 1979. 59.50 (*0-306-40094-4*, Plenum Trade) Perseus Pubng.

Methods of Cell Separation, 3 vols. Ed. by Nicholas Catsimpoolas. LC 77-11018. (Biological Separations Ser.). (Illus.). 1980. 55.00 (*0-306-40377-3*, Plenum Trade) Perseus Pubng.

Methods of Cell Separation. P. T. Sharpe. Ed. by R. H. Burdon & P. H. Van Knippenberg. (Laboratory Techniques in Biochemistry & Molecular Biology Ser.: Vol. 18). 272p. 1988. pap. 42.00 (*0-444-80927-9*) Elsevier.

Methods of Characterization of Sewage Sludge. Ed. by T. J. Casey et al. 164p. 1984. text 90.50 (*90-277-1782-6*) Kluwer Academic.

Methods of Communicating Biotechnology with the Public: U. S. - EC Task Force on Biotechnology Research Final Report. 20p. (Orig.). (C). 1996. pap. text 20.00 (*0-7881-2617-2*) DIANE Pub.

Methods of Connective Tissue Research. Ed. by L. Robert et al. (Frontiers of Matrix Biology Ser.: Vol. 10). (Illus.). xiv, 250p. 1985. 142.75 (*3-8055-3899-5*) S Karger.

Methods of Construction. Frank R. Dagostino. (Construction & Building Trades Ser.). 1997. teacher ed. 13.95 (*0-8273-7120-9*); text 55.95 (*0-8273-7119-5*) Delmar.

Methods of Criminological Research. Victor Jupp. 160p. 1989. text 55.00 (*0-04-445065-6*); pap. text 19.95 (*0-04-445066-4*) Routledge.

Methods of Decomposition in Inorganic Analysis. Zdenek Sulcek & Pavel Povondra. 368p. 1989. lib. bdg. 295.00 (*0-8493-4963-X*, QD75) CRC Pr.

M

An Asterisk (*) at the beginning of an entry indicates that the title is appearing for the first time.

Methods of Dendrochronology: Applications in the Environmental Sciences. Ed. by E. R. Cook & L. A. Kairiukstis. (C). 1990. text 186.00 (*0-7923-0586-8*) Kluwer Academic.

Methods of Descent for Nondifferentiable Optimization. K. C. Kiwiel. (Lecture Notes in Mathematics Ser.: Vol. 1133). vi, 362p. 1985. 49.95 (*0-387-15642-9*) Spr-Verlag.

Methods of Detection & Identification of Bacteria. B. Mitruka & M. Bonner. LC 76-28809. 1977. 152.00 (*0-8493-5116-2*, CRC Reprint) Franklin.

Methods of Digital Holography. Leonid P. Yaroslavskii & N. S. Merzlyakov. LC 80-16286. 182p. 1980. 79.50 (*0-306-10963-8*, Kluwer Plenum) Kluwer Academic.

Methods of Discrete Vortices. Sergei M. Belotserkovsky & Ivan K. Lifanov. 464p. 1992. boxed set 147.95 (*0-8493-9307-8*, QA925) CRC Pr.

Methods of Display of Ocean Survey Data, Vol. 1. Linton. pap. 24.25 (*0-901875-51-1*, Pergamon Pr) Elsevier.

Methods of Display of Ocean Survey Data, Vol. 2. Linton. pap. 24.25 (*90-70310-10-4*, Pergamon Pr) Elsevier.

Methods of Drug Analysis. James E. Gearien & Bernard F. Grabowski. LC 68-25207. 291p. reprint ed. pap. 90.30 (*0-608-16156-X*, 205599900043) Bks Demand.

Methods of Dynamic & Nonsmooth Optimization. Frank H. Clarke. LC 89-21682. (CBMS-NSF Regional Conference Series in Applied Mathematics: No. 57). v, 90p. 1989. pap. 24.50 (*0-89871-241-6*) Soc Indus-Appl Math.

Methods of Dynamic Economics. John Richard Hicks. (Illus.). 178p. 1986. reprint ed. text 39.95 (*0-19-828530-2*) OUP.

Methods of Dynamic Economics. John Richard Hicks. (Illus.). 180p. 1987. reprint ed. pap. text 19.95 (*0-19-877287-4*) OUP.

Methods of Economic Investigation. Sampat Mukherjee. (C). 1989. 55.00 (*0-89771-424-5*, Pub. by Current Dist) St Mut.

Methods of Education in International Attitudes. Ben M. Cherrington. LC 77-176642. (Columbia University. Teachers College. Contributions to Education Ser.: No. 595). reprint ed. 37.50 (*0-404-55595-0*) AMS Pr.

Methods of Educational & Social Science Research. 2nd ed. David Krathwohl. LC 97-20165. (C). 1997. text. write for info. (*0-8013-2011-9*) Addison-Wesley.

Methods of Educational & Social Science Research. 2nd ed. David Krathwohl. LC 97-20165. (Illus.). 742p. (C). 1997. 80.00 (*0-8013-2029-1*) Addison-Wesley.

Methods of Effective Teaching & Course Management. Siebert et al. LC 97-222333. 300p. (C). 1997. per. 20.95 (*0-7872-3723-X*) Kendall-Hunt.

Methods of Electronic Structure Calculations. O. K. Andersen et al. 396p. 1995. text 116.00 (*981-02-1485-5*) World Scientific Pub.

Methods of Electrophysiology Recordings. Jeffery D. Kocsis. 450p. 1999. 72.95 (*0-8385-6324-4*, Medical Exam) Appleton & Lange.

Methods of Environment Impact Assessment. Ed. by Peter Morris & Riki Therivel. 256p. 1994. 75.00 (*1-85728-214-0*, Pub. by UCL Pr Ltd); pap. 27.50 (*1-85728-215-9*, Pub. by UCL Pr Ltd) Taylor & Francis.

Methods of Enzymatic Analysis: Cumulated Subject Index. 3rd ed. Bergmeyer. (Bergmeyer Methods of Enzymatic Analysis Ser.). 91p. 1987. 105.00 (*3-527-26053-6*) Wiley.

Methods of Enzymatic Analysis: Cumulated Subject Index. 3rd ed. Ed. by Hans U. Bergmeyer. LC 84-105641. 90p. 1987. 80.00 (*0-89573-243-2*, Wiley-VCH) Wiley.

Methods of Enzymatic Analysis: Metabolites 1 - Carbohydrates, Vol. 6, Metabolites 1: Carbohydrates. 3rd ed. Ed. by Hans U. Bergmeyer. 701p. 1984. 320.00 (*3-527-26046-3*, Wiley-VCH) Wiley.

Methods of Estimating Reserves of Crude Oil, Natural Gas, & Natural Gas Liquids. Wallace F. Lovejoy. LC 65-24790. 182p. reprint ed. pap. 56.50 (*0-608-12540-7*, 202380500034) Bks Demand.

Methods of Estimating the Volume of Undiscovered Oil & Gas Resources. Ed. by John D. Haun. LC 75-18993. (Studies in Geology: No. 1). (Illus.). 212p. reprint ed. pap. 65.80 (*0-7837-1653-2*, 204195100024) Bks Demand.

Methods of Ethics. Gerard J. Dalcourt. 254p. (C). 1984. pap. text 22.50 (*0-8191-3550-X*); lib. bdg. 50.00 (*0-8191-3549-6*) U Pr of Amer.

Methods of Ethics. 7th ed. Henry Sidgwick. LC 81-85772. (HPC Classics Ser.). 568p. (C). 1981. reprint ed. 34.95 (*0-915145-29-4*); reprint ed. pap. 16.95 (*0-915145-28-6*) Hackett Pub.

Methods of Ethics. 7th ed. Henry Sidgwick. 528p. 1986. reprint ed. lib. bdg. 64.95 (*0-935005-13-7*) Lincoln-Rembrandt.

Methods of Ethics. 7th ed. Henry Sidgwick. 528p. (C). 1986. reprint ed. pap. 47.95 (*0-935005-12-9*) Lincoln-Rembrandt.

Methods of Evaluating Vertical Ground Water Movement. I. Javandel. 116p. 1984. 25.00 (*1-56034-033-9*, K163) Natl Grnd Water.

Methods of Execution: A Novel. Fredrick Heubner. LC 93-21303. 1994. 22.00 (*0-671-86724-5*) S&S Trade.

Methods of Execution of Orders & Judgements in Europe: Wiley Series in Commercial Law. P. Kaye. 376p. 1996. pap. 144.50 (*0-471-94029-1*) Wiley.

Methods of Experimental Physics see Experimental Methods in the Physical Sciences: Atomic, Molecular & Optical Physics: Charged Particles

Methods of Experimental Physics: Scanning Tunneling Microscopy, Vol. 27. Ed. by Robert Celotta et al. (Illus.). 459p. 1993. text 111.00 (*0-12-475972-6*) Acad Pr.

Methods of External Hyperthermic Heating. J. W. Hand et al. (Clinical Thermology Ser.: Vol. 2). (Illus.). 160p. 1990. 118.00 (*0-387-50976-3*) Spr-Verlag.

Methods of Family Research: Biographies of Research Projects, Set. Irving E. Sigel. 1990. 95.00 (*0-8058-0707-1*) L Erlbaum Assocs.

Methods of Family Research: Biographies of Research Projects, Vol. II. Ed. by G. Brody & Irving E. Sigel. 296p. 1990. 69.95 (*0-89859-827-3*) L Erlbaum Assocs.

Methods of Fertility Regulation-Advances in Research & Clinical Experience: A Report. WHO Staff. (Technical Reports: No. 473). 48p. 1971. pap. text 5.00 (*92-4-120473-7*, 1100473) World Health.

Methods of Fertilizer Application. Ed. by V. E. Bulaev. 1984. 28.00 (*0-8364-2558-8*, Pub. by Oxford IBH) S Asia.

Methods of Finite Mathematics. John W. Brown & Donald R. Sherbert. LC 88-27605. 688p. 1989. text 84.95 (*0-471-63003-9*) Wiley.

Methods of Fracture Mechanics: Solid Matter Physics. Gennadi I. Cherepanov. LC 96-52467. (Solid Mechanics & Its Applications Ser.). 1997. text 164.00 (*0-7923-4408-1*) Kluwer Academic.

Methods of Genome Analysis: A Gene Hunter's Guide. Alan J. Buckler & David E. Houseman. (Illus.). 250p. Date not set. pap. 39.95 (*0-19-509341-0*) OUP.

Methods of Genome Analysis in Plants. Ed. by Prem P. Jauhar. 400p. 1995. boxed set 104.95 (*0-8493-9437-6*, 9437) CRC Pr.

***Methods of Geometry.** James T. Smith. LC 99-10306. 486p. 1999. 79.95 (*0-471-25183-6*) Wiley.

Methods of Golf's Masters. rev. ed. Dick Aultman & Ken Bowden. (Classics of Golf Ser.). (Illus.). 190p. 1985. 28.00 (*0-940889-11-0*) Classics Golf.

***Methods of Golf's Masters: How They Played & What You Can Learn from Them.** Ken Bowden. 2000. pap. 19.95 (*1-58574-048-9*) Lyons Pr.

Methods of Heuristics. Ed. by Rudolf G. Groner et al. 416p. 1983. text 79.95 (*0-89859-251-8*) L Erlbaum Assocs.

Methods of High-Alloy Weldability Evaluation. 1970. 16.00 (*0-318-18632-2*) Welding Res Coun.

Methods of Hilbert Spaces in the Theory of Nonlinear Dynamical Systems. K. Kowalski. 136p. 1994. text 40.00 (*981-02-1753-6*) World Scientific Pub.

Methods of Historical study. Herbert B. Adams. (Principle Works of Herbert Baxter Adams). 1989. reprint ed. lib. bdg. 79.00 (*0-7812-1466-1*) Rprt Serv.

Methods of Homological Algebra. S. J. Gelfand & Y. J. Manin. 395p. 1996. 99.50 (*0-387-54746-0*) Spr-Verlag.

Methods of Homological Algebra. Sergei I. Gelfand & Y. J. Manin. 396p. 1997. 99.50 (*3-540-54746-0*) Spr-Verlag.

Methods of Hormone Analysis. Ed. by Heinz Breuer et al. LC 75-19225. (Illus.). 545p. reprint ed. pap. 169.00 (*0-7837-3432-8*, 205775300008) Bks Demand.

Methods of Hybridoma Formation. Ed. by Arie H. Bartal & Yashar Hirshaut. LC 87-3588. (Contemporary Biomedicine Ser.: Vol. 7). 504p. 1987. 125.00 (*0-89603-100-4*) Humana.

Methods of Hyperthermia Control. T. C. Cetas et al. (Clinical Thermology Ser.: Vol. 3). (Illus.). 120p. 1990. 125.00 (*0-387-50978-X*) Spr-Verlag.

Methods of Immunological Analysis, 3 vols. Incl. Vol. 1, Fundamentals. Methods of Immunological Analysis, Vol. 1, Fundamentals. Ed. by Rene F. Masseyeff. LC 92-49344. 716p. 1992. 425.00 (*3-527-27906-7*, Wiley-VCH); Vol. 2, Samples and Reagents. Methods of Immunological Analysis, Vol. 2, Samples & Reagents. Rene F. Masseyeff & Norman A. Staines. (Illus.). 591p. 1992. 425.00 (*3-527-27907-5*, Wiley-VCH); Vol. 3, Cells and Tissues. Methods of Immunological Analysis, Vol. 3, Cells & Tissues. Rene F. Masseyeff & Norman A. Staines. (Illus.). 604p. 1993. 425.00 (*3-527-27908-3*, Wiley-VCH); 645.00 (*3-527-27905-9*, Wiley-VCH) Wiley.

Methods of Immunological Analysis, Vol. 1, Fundamentals see Methods of Immunological Analysis

Methods of Immunological Analysis, Vol. 2, Samples & Reagents see Methods of Immunological Analysis

Methods of Immunological Analysis, Vol. 3, Cells & Tissues see Methods of Immunological Analysis

***Methods of Inquiry & Measurement: Float & Egg.** Wink. 1999. pap. text 1.95 (*0-7167-9456-X*) W H Freeman.

Methods of Instruction. Leonard C. Silvern. Orig. Title: Textbook in Methods of Instruction. (Illus.). 407p. (C). 1962. text 50.00 (*0-87657-119-4*) Ed & Training.

Methods of Instruction in Social Studies Education, Third Education. James L. Barth. 384p. (Orig.). (C). 1990. pap. text 38.50 (*0-8191-7866-7*) U Pr of Amer.

***Methods of Interregional & Regional Analysis.** Walter Isard et al. LC 98-71955. (Regional Science Studies Ser.). (Illus.). 520p. 1998. pap. 29.95 (*1-85972-410-8*, Pub. by Avebry) Ashgate Pub Co.

Methods of Inverse Problems in Physics. Roy Ghosh. 504p. 1991. lib. bdg. 239.00 (*0-8493-6258-X*, AC20) CRC Pr.

Methods of Investigation of the Dead Sea Scrolls & the Khirbet Qumran Site: Present Realities. Michael Wise. 528p. 1994. 35.00 (*0-8018-6090-3*) Johns Hopkins.

Methods of Joining Fabrics. Shirley Inst. Staff. (C). 1983. 90.00 (*0-7855-4574-3*, Pub. by British Textile Tech) St Mut.

Methods of Knowledge According to Advaita Vendanta. Swami Satprakashananda. 366p. 1975. reprint ed. 7.95 (*81-7505-065-9*, Pub. by Advaita Ashrama) Vedanta Pr.

Methods of Krypton-85 Management, Vol. 10. Ed. by W. Hebel & G. Cottone. (Radioactive Waste Management Ser.). (Illus.). viii, 310p. 1983. text 171.00 (*3-7186-0167-2*) Gordon & Breach.

Methods of Laser Spectroscopy. Ed. by Yehiam Prior et al. LC 86-12304. (Fritz Haber International Symposium Ser.). 510p. 1986. 125.00 (*0-306-42285-9*, Plenum Trade) Perseus Pubng.

Methods of Logic. 4th ed. Willard V. Quine. (Illus.). 344p. 1982. pap. 19.50 (*0-674-57176-2*) HUP.

Methods of Machine Improvement & Contemporary Problems of Machine Science. K. V. Frolov. (Illus.). x, 250p. 1988. 60.00 (*0-89864-042-3*) Allerton Pr.

Methods of Macroeconomic Dynamics. 2nd ed. Stephen J. Turnovsky. LC 99-32865. 715p. 2000. 49.95 (*0-262-20123-2*) MIT Pr.

Methods of Marking Fish & Shellfish. L. A. Nielsen. LC 92-74200. (Special Publication Ser.: No. 23). 208p. 1992. text 48.00 (*0-913235-80-6*, 510.19C) Am Fisheries Soc.

Methods of Materials Selection. Ed. by E. D. Verink. LC 67-29667. (Metallurgical Society Conference Ser.: Vol. 40). 320p. reprint ed. pap. 99.20 (*0-608-11767-6*, 200152900079) Bks Demand.

Methods of Mathematical Finance. I. Karatzas & S. E. Shreve. LC 98-14284. (Applications of Mathematics Ser.: Vol. 39). 375p. 1998. 69.95 (*0-387-94839-2*) Spr-Verlag.

Methods of Mathematical Physics, 2 vols. Richard Courant & D. Hilbert. (Classics Library). 1390p. 1989. pap. 135.00 (*0-471-55760-9*) Wiley.

***Methods of Mathematical Physics.** 3rd ed. Harold Jeffreys & Bertha S. Jeffreys. (Cambridge Mathematical Library). (Illus.). 730p. (C). 2000. pap. 39.95 (*0-521-66402-0*) Cambridge U Pr.

Methods of Mathematical Physics, Vol. 1. Richard Courant & D. Hilbert. (Classics Library). 560p. 1989. pap. 79.95 (*0-471-50447-5*) Wiley.

Methods of Mathematical Physics, Vol. 2. Richard Courant & D. Hilbert. (Classics Library). 856p. 1989. pap. 84.95 (*0-471-50439-4*) Wiley.

Methods of Measuring Women's Economic Activity. 265p. Date not set. pap. 25.00 (*92-1-161353-1*, E.93.XVII.6) UN.

Methods of Measuring Women's Participation in the Informal Sector. 1990. 39.00 (*92-1-161322-1*, 90.XVII.16) UN.

Methods of Meta-Analysis: Correcting Error & Bias in Research Findings. John E. Hunter & Frank L. Schmidt. 460p. (C). 1989. text 69.95 (*0-8039-3222-7*) Sage.

Methods of Meta-Analysis: Correcting Error & Bias in Research Findings. John E. Hunter & Frank L. Schmidt. 592p. 1995. pap. 32.00 (*0-8039-3223-5*) Sage.

Methods of Metaphysics. Alan R. White. 224p. 1988. pap. text 12.95 (*0-7099-5233-3*, Pub. by C Helm); lib. bdg. 49.95 (*0-317-64408-4*, Pub. by C Helm) Routldge.

Methods of Micro-Level Analysis for Agricultural Programmes & Policies. M. Upton & J. M. Dixon. (Farm Systems Management Ser.). 213p. 1995. pap. 25.00 (*92-5-103473-7*, F34737, Pub. by FAO) Bernan Associates.

Methods of Model Based Process Control. Ed. by Rivdan Berber. LC 95-17072. (NATO ASI Ser.; Series E, Applied Sciences: Vol. 293). 1995. text 386.50 (*0-7923-3524-4*) Kluwer Academic.

Methods of Modeling Equations & Analogies in Chemical Engineering. A. D. Polyanin & Victor V. Dilman. 310p. 1991. 125.00 (*0-89116-769-2*) Begell Hse.

Methods of Modeling Equations & Analogies in Chemical Engineering. Andrei D. Polyanin & Victor V. Dilman. Tr. by Mark A. Piterman from RUS. LC 93-2356. 368p. 1994. 212.00 (*0-8493-9914-9*) CRC Pr.

Methods of Modern Mathematical Physics, 4 vols. Michael Reed & Barry Simon. Incl. Vol. 2. Fourier Analysis Self-Adjointness. 1975. text 71.00 (*0-12-585002-6*); Vol. 3. Scattering Theory. 1979. text 84.00 (*0-12-585003-4*); Vol. 4. 1978. text 71.00 (*0-12-585004-2*); write for info. (*0-318-50309-3*) Acad Pr.

Methods of Modern Mathematical Physics: Functional Analysis, Vol. 1. 2nd enl. rev. ed. Ed. by Michael Reed & Barry Simon. 1980. text 71.00 (*0-12-585050-6*) Acad Pr.

Methods of Modifying Habitat to Benefit the Great Lakes Ecosystem. Ed. by J. R. Kelso & J. H. Hartig. (CISTI Occasional Paper Ser.: No. 1). (Illus.). 294p. 1995. pap. 35.00 (*0-660-16047-1*, Pub. by NRC Res Pr) Accents Pubns.

Methods of Molecular Quantum Mechanics. 2nd ed. Ed. by R. McWeeny & B. J. Sutcliffe. (Theoretical Chemistry Ser.). 573p. 1989. text 198.00 (*0-12-486551-8*) Acad Pr.

Methods of Moments & Semiparametric Methods for Limited Dependent & Variable Models. Myoung-Jae Lee. LC 95-44882. 256p. 1996. 54.95 (*0-387-94626-8*) Spr-Verlag.

Methods of Motion: An Introduction to Mechanics, Bk. 1. rev. ed. (Illus.). 168p. 1992. pap. 18.50 (*0-87355-085-4*) Natl Sci Tchrs.

Methods of Multivariate Analysis: Basic Applications, Vol. 1. Alvin C. Rencher. (Series in Probability & Mathematics). 648p. 1995. 99.95 incl. disk (*0-471-57152-0*) Wiley.

Methods of Neurochemistry, 4 vols., Vol. 1. Ed. by Rainer Fried. LC 75-134782. 390p. 1971. reprint ed. pap. 120.90 (*0-7837-0746-0*, 204106600001) Bks Demand.

Methods of Neurochemistry, 4 vols., Vol. 2. Ed. by Rainer Fried. LC 75-134782. 308p. 1972. reprint ed. pap. 95.50 (*0-7837-0747-9*, 204106600002) Bks Demand.

Methods of Neurochemistry, 4 vols., Vol. 4. Ed. by Rainer Fried. LC 75-134782. 346p. 1973. reprint ed. pap. 107.30 (*0-7837-0748-7*, 204106600004) Bks Demand.

Methods of Neurochemistry, 4 vols., Vol. 5. Ed. by Rainer Fried. LC 75-134782. 296p. 1973. reprint ed. pap. 91.80 (*0-7837-0749-5*, 204106600005) Bks Demand.

Methods of Non-Alpha-Amino Acid Synthesis. Michael B. Smith. LC 95-11621. (Illus.). 344p. 1995. text 165.00 (*0-8247-9604-7*) Dekker.

Methods of Noncommutative Analysis: Theory & Applications. Vladimir E. Nazaikinskii et al. LC 95-39641. (Studies in Mathematics: No. 22). x, 374p. (C). 1995. lib. bdg. 98.95 (*3-11-014632-0*) De Gruyter.

Methods of Nonconvex Analysis: Lectures Given at the 1st Session of the Centro Internazionale Estivo Matematico (C. I. M. E.) Held at Varenna, Italy, June 15-23, 1989. Ed. by A. Cellina et al. (Lecture Notes in Mathematics Ser.: Vol. 1446). v, 206p. 1990. 41.95 (*0-387-53120-3*) Spr-Verlag.

Methods of Nonlinear Dynamical Analysis: Lecture Notes. V. M. Matrosov. (Soviet & East European Mathematics Ser.). 1993. text 68.00 (*981-02-1112-0*) World Scientific Pub.

Methods of Normal Form. Ali H. Nayfeh. LC 92-40113. 232p. 1993. 95.95 (*0-471-59354-0*) Wiley.

Methods of Numerical Mathematics. 2nd ed. Gurii I. Marchuk. (Applications of Mathematics Ser.: Vol. 2). (Illus.). 510p. 1982. 79.95 (*0-387-90614-2*) Spr-Verlag.

Methods of Operation & the Credit Accommodations of a Commercial Bank to Small Business in the Pittsburgh Area. Leonard J. Konopa. Ed. by Stuart Bruchey & Vincent P. Carosso. LC 78-18966. (Small Business Enterprise in America Ser.). (Illus.). 1979. lib. bdg. 25.95 (*0-405-11470-2*) Ayer.

***Methods of Operations Research** Philip M. Morse & George E. Kimball. LC 98-85163. vii, 158 p. 1998. write for info. (*0-930473-07-8*) Military Opera Res.

Methods of Operations Research. Philip M. Morse & George E. Kimball. LC 80-83558. (Illus.). 179p. 1980. reprint ed. 25.95 (*0-932146-03-1*) Peninsula CA.

Methods of Optimization. R. F. Gabasov & F. M. Kirillova. Ed. by A. V. Balakrishnan. LC 88-19589. (Translations Series in Mathematics & Engineering).Tr. of Metody Optimizatsii. 394p. 1988. text 80.00 (*0-911575-02-2*) Optimization Soft.

Methods of Optimization. Gordon R. Walsh. LC 74-20714. 208p. 1975. reprint ed. pap. 64.50 (*0-608-10238-5*, 201505700092) Bks Demand.

Methods of Optimization. rev. ed. Gordon R. Walsh. LC 74-20714. (Wiley-Interscience Publications). 230p. 1975. reprint ed. pap. 71.30 (*0-7837-3215-5*, 204323300007) Bks Demand.

Methods of Orbit Determination. Pedro R. Escobal. LC 75-11889. 500p. 1976. reprint ed. 59.50 (*0-88275-319-3*) Krieger.

Methods of Orbit Determination for the Micro Computer. Boulet. 1991. 24.95 (*0-943396-34-4*) Willmann-Bell.

Methods of Perceiving Patterns of Small Group Behavior. Martha Davis. LC 78-322618. (Illus.). 88p. 1977. pap. text 14.95 (*0-932582-11-7*) Dance Notation.

Methods of Pesticide Exposure Assessment: Proceedings of a Workshop Held in Ottawa, Canada, October 5-8, 1993. Ed. by Patricia B. Curry et al. (NATO - Challenges of Modern Society Ser.: Vol. 19). (Illus.). 236p. 1995. 89.50 (*0-306-45130-1*, Kluwer Plenum) Kluwer Academic.

Methods of Petrographic-Microscopic Research. Frederic E. Wright. 1977. lib. bdg. 75.00 (*0-8490-2229-0*) Gordon Pr.

***Methods of Placer Mining.** Garnet Basque. 1999. pap. 9.95 (*1-895811-84-8*) Heritage Hse.

Methods of Placer Mining. rev. ed. Basque. (Illus.). 88p. 1996. pap. 6.95 (*0-919531-40-7*, Pub. by Sunfire Pubns) Gem Guides Bk.

Methods of (Plants) Cultivar Identification with Scanning Electron Microscopy: A Manual. Charles R. Krause. (Illus.). 24p. 1984. pap. text 20.00 (*0-935336-04-4*) Horticult Research.

Methods of Preparation for Electron Microscopy: An Introduction for the Biomedical Sciences. Ed. by D. G. Robinson et al. (Illus.). 200p. 1987. pap. 55.00 (*0-387-17592-X*) Spr-Verlag.

Methods of Privatising Large Enterprises. OECD Staff. 208p. (Orig.). 1993. pap. 36.00 (*92-64-03709-8*) OECD.

Methods of Programming: Selected Papers on the CIP-Project. Ed. by Manfred Broy et al. (Lecture Notes in Computer Science Ser.: Vol. 544). xiv, 268p. 1991. 32.95 (*0-387-54576-X*) Spr-Verlag.

Methods of Projecting Operations & Maintenance Costs for Nuclear Power Plants. LC 96-161355. 90p. (Orig.). 1995. pap. 32.00 (*92-64-14413-7*, Pub. by Org for Econ) OECD.

Methods of Protein & Nucleic Acid Research: Electrophoresis, Isoelectric Focusing, Ultracentrifugation, Vol. 1. L. A. Osterman. (Illus.). 370p. 1985. 219.95 (*0-387-12735-6*) Spr-Verlag.

Methods of Protein & Nucleic Acid Research: Immunoelectrophoresis - Application of Radioisotopes. L. A. Osterman. (Illus.). 220p. 1988. 158.95 (*0-387-13094-2*) Spr-Verlag.

Methods of Protein & Nucleic Acid Research Vol. 3: Chromatography. L. A. Osterman. (Illus.). 520p. 1986. 278.95 (*0-387-16855-9*) Spr-Verlag.

Methods of Protein Microcharacterization: A Practical Handbook. Ed. by John E. Shively. LC 85-30560. (Biological Methods Ser.). 463p. 1986. 125.00 (*0-89603-090-3*) Humana.

Methods of Psychiatric Research. 2nd ed. Ed. by P. Sainsbury & N. Kreitman. (Illus.). 1975. pap. text 36.95 (*0-19-264419-X*) OUP.

Methods of Psychic Development. Irving S. Cooper. 113p. 1996. reprint ed. spiral bd. 12.50 (*0-7873-0198-1*) Hlth Research.

Methods of Psychic Development (1919) Irving S. Cooper. 116p. 1996. reprint ed. pap. 11.00 (*1-56459-868-3*) Kessinger Pub.

Methods of Publishing. Samuel Sprigge. 1977. lib. bdg. 250.00 (*0-8490-2230-4*) Gordon Pr.

An Asterisk (*) at the beginning of an entry indicates that the title is appearing for the first time.

Methods of Qualitative Theory in Nonlinear Dynamics. Leonid Shilnikov et al. (Series on Nonlinear Science: Pt. I). 450p. 1998. 84.00 (*981-02-3382-5*) World Scientific Pub.

***Methods of Qualitative Theory of Differential Equations & Related Topics.** Ed. by L. M. Lerman et al. (TRANS2 Ser.: Vol. 200). 196p. 2000. 89.00 (*0-8218-2663-8*) Am Math.

Methods of Quantum Field Theory in Statistical Physics. A. A. Abrikosov et al. Tr. by Richard A. Silverman from RUS. 352p. (C). 1975. reprint ed. pap. 9.95 (*0-486-63228-8*) Dover.

Methods of Radiochemical Analysis. (Technical Report Ser.: No. 173). 116p. 1959. pap. text 5.00 (*92-4-120173-8*) World Health.

Methods of Radiochemical Analysis. (ENG & FRE., Illus.). 163p. 1966. pap. text 16.00 (*92-4-154019-2*, 1150106) World Health.

Methods of Reading Instruction. James L. Laffey. LC 77-31440. (Reading Research Profiles Ser.). 72p. reprint ed. pap. 30.00 (*0-608-18002-5*, 202625300049) Bks Demand.

Methods of Real Analysis. 2nd ed. Richard R. Goldberg. 416p. (C). 1976. text 100.95 (*0-471-31065-4*) Wiley.

Methods of Recognition, Vol. 20. A. L. Gorelik & V. A. Skripkin. xvi, 228p. 1989. text 220.00 (*2-88124-718-0*) Gordon & Breach.

Methods of Regional Analysis. Walter Isard et al. (Regional Science Reprint Ser.: No. 3). (Illus.). (C). 1982. reprint ed. pap. 5.95 (*0-943019-02-8*) Cornell CRPP.

Methods of Representation Theory: With Applications to Finite Groups & Orders, Vol. 1. Charles W. Curtis & Irving Reiner. 848p. 1990. pap. 104.95 (*0-471-52367-4*) Wiley.

Methods of Representation Theory Vol. 2: With Applications to Finite Groups & Orders, Vol. 2. Charles W. Curtis & Irving Reiner. LC 81-7416. (Pure & Applied Mathematics: A Wiley-Interscience Series of Texts, Monographs & Tracts). 951p. 1994. pap. 99.95 (*0-471-06004-6*) Wiley.

Methods of Research in Criminology & Criminal Justice. Arnold Binder & Gilbert Geis. 288p. (C). 1983. 35.00 (*0-07-005286-7*) McGraw.

Methods of Research in Music Pt. I: Methods. Demar B. Irvine. 69p. 1993. reprint ed. lib. bdg. 69.00 (*0-7812-9682-X*) Rprt Serv.

Methods of Research in Social Psychology. 2nd ed. Elliot Aronson et al. 376p. (C). 1989. 72.19 (*0-07-002466-9*) McGraw.

Methods of Rhetorical Criticism: A Twentieth-Century Perspective. 3rd rev. ed. Ed. by Bernard L. Brock et al. LC 89-35152. 520p. (C). 1990. pap. text 24.95 (*0-8143-2300-6*) Wayne St U Pr.

Methods of Sampling & Analysis. 1986. 32.00 (*0-8176-1773-6*) Birkhauser.

Methods of Sampling & Analyzing Gases from Welding & Allied Processes (F1.5-87) (Illus.). 36p. 1987. pap. 27.00 (*0-87171-270-9*) Am Welding.

Methods of Satellite Oceanography. Robard H. Stewart. LC 83-18017. (Scripps Studies in Earth & Ocean Sciences: No. 1). 1985. 65.00 (*0-520-04226-3*, Pub. by U CA Pr) Cal Prin Full Svc.

Methods of Scale Modeling of Operating Processes of Highway Construction Machines. V. I. Balovnev. 1986. 21.50 (*81-205-0046-6*, Pub. by Oxford IBH) S Asia.

Methods of School Enrollment Projection (UNESCO) E. G. Jacoby. (Education Studies & Documents: No. 32). 1974. reprint ed. pap. 25.00 (*0-8115-1356-4*) Periodicals Srv.

Methods of Seawater Analysis. 3rd ed. Ed. by Klaus Grasshoff et al. LC 99-200191. 632p. 1999. 275.00 (*3-527-29589-5*) Wiley.

Methods of Seismic Hazards Evaluation, Focus '95: Proceedings, Topical Meeting on Methods of Seismic Hazards Evaluation, Las Vegas, NV, 1995. LC 96-139577. 200p. 1997. pap. 75.00 (*0-89448-606-3*, 700228) Am Nuclear Soc.

***Methods of Shape-preserving Spline Approximation.** Boris I Kvasov. 1999. 55.00 (*981-02-4010-4*) WSC Inst MA Studies.

Methods of Singular Integral Equations, Vol. 60. Abduhamid Dzhuraev. (Monographs & Surveys in Pure & Applied Mathematics). 328p. 1992. boxed set 132.00 (*0-582-08373-7*, LM8373, Chap & Hall CRC) CRC Pr.

Methods of Sleep Research. Ed. by S. Kubicki & W. M. Herrmann. (Illus.). 222p. 1985. pap. 40.00 (*0-89574-201-2*, Pub. by Gustav Fischer) Balogh.

Methods of Social Reform: And Other Papers. William S. Jevons. LC 65-20925. viii, 383p. 1965. reprint ed. 45.00 (*0-678-00108-1*) Kelley.

Methods of Social Relating. 6th ed. Judd. (C). 1991. pap. text, teacher ed. 35.00 (*0-03-053684-7*) Harcourt Coll Pubs.

Methods of Social Research. 3rd ed. Kenneth D. Bailey. 608p. (C). 1987. 32.95 (*0-02-901450-6*) Free Pr.

Methods of Social Research. 3rd ed. Kenneth D. Bailey. 533p. 1999. reprint ed. text 20.00 (*0-7881-6239-X*) DIANE Pub.

Methods of Social Research. 4th ed. Kenneth D. Bailey. LC 93-36444. (Illus.). 600p. 1994. 32.95 (*0-02-901279-1*) Free Pr.

Methods of Social Study. Sidney J. Passfield & Beatrice Potter Webb. LC 67-30866. vii, 263p. 1968. reprint ed. 39.50 (*0-678-00351-3*) Kelley.

Methods of Soil Analysis, 2 pts. rev. ed. Ed. by C. A. Black. Incl. Pt. 1. (Illus.). 1965. 17.50 (*0-89118-010-9*); Pt. 2. (Illus.). 1982. 36.00 (*0-89118-072-9*); write for info. (*0-318-59617-2*) Am Soc Agron.

Methods of Soil Analysis, 3 bks., Set. 2nd ed. Ed. by A. Klute et al. (SSSA Book Ser.: No. 5). (Illus.). 1216p. 164.00 (*0-685-33556-9*) Am Soc Agron.

Methods of Soil Analysis Pt. 1: Physical & Mineralogical Methods, 2 pts. 2nd ed. Ed. by Ed A. Klute. (SSSA Book Ser.: No. 5). (Illus.). 1188p. 1986. 60.00 (*0-89118-811-8*) Am Soc Agron.

Methods of Soil Analysis Pt. 2: Microbiological & Biochemical Properties. Ed. by R. W. Weaver et al. LC 94-20752. (Bk.: Vol. 5). 1121p. 1994. 65.00 (*0-89118-810-X*) Soil Sci Soc Am.

Methods of Soil Analysis Pt. 3: Chemical Methods. D. L. Sparks et al. (SSSA Book Ser.: No. 5). 1358p. 1986. 65.00 (*0-89118-825-8*) Soil Sci Soc Am.

Methods of Specifying Precision of Spur Gears. G. W. Michalec. (Technical Papers: Vol. P319.01). (Illus.). 29p. 1956. pap. text 30.00 (*1-55589-386-4*) AGMA.

Methods of Statistical Physics. A. I. Akhiezev & S. V. Peletminskii. Tr. by M. Schukin. (International Series in Natural Philosophy: Vol. 104). (Illus.). 462p. 1981. text 207.00 (*0-08-025040-8*, Pub. by Pergamon Repr) Franklin.

Methods of Statistics of Industrial Injuries see Report Prepared for the 6th International Conference of Labour Statisticians: Montreal, 4 to 12 August, 1948

Methods of Strengthening Existing Highway Bridges. (National Cooperative Highway Research Program Report Ser.: No. 293). 114p. 1987. 12.00 (*0-309-04416-2*, NR293) Transport Res Bd.

Methods of Structural Analysis: Proceedings of the National Structural Engineering Conference, August 22-25, 1976, Madison, Wisconsin, 2 vols., 1. National Structural Engineering Conference Staff. Ed. by William E. Saul & Alain H. Payrot. LC TA0645.N3. 527p. reprint ed. pap. 163.40 (*0-608-11448-0*, 201954100001) Bks Demand.

Methods of Structural Analysis: Proceedings of the National Structural Engineering Conference, August 22-25, 1976, Madison, Wisconsin, 2 vols., 2. National Structural Engineering Conference Staff. Ed. by William E. Saul & Alain H. Payrot. LC TA0645.N3. 555p. reprint ed. pap. 172.10 (*0-608-11449-9*, 201954100002) Bks Demand.

Methods of Structural Analysis of Modulated Structures & Quasicrystals. Ed. by J. M. Perez-Mato et al. 600p. (C). 1991. text 128.00 (*981-02-0692-5*) World Scientific Pub.

Methods of Study in Natural History. Louis Agassiz. LC 72-125728. (American Environmental Studies). 1974. reprint ed. 23.95 (*0-405-02653-6*) Ayer.

Methods of Study of Culture Contact in Africa . . . with an Introductory Essay by B. Malinowski. International African Institute Staff. LC 41-836. (International Institute of African Languages & Cultures Ser.: No. XV). 143p. reprint ed. pap. 44.40 (*0-8357-3019-0*, 205710500010) Bks Demand.

Methods of Studying Root Systems. Wolfgang Boehm. LC 79-9706. (Ecological Studies: Vol. 33). (Illus.). 1987. 94.95 (*0-387-09329-X*) Spr-Verlag.

Methods of Summation. Bertram Ross. ix, 127p. (C). 1987. write for info. (*0-936285-08-7*, JPY7000, Pub. by Descartes); teacher ed. write for info. (*0-318-64056-2*, JPY4000, Pub. by Descartes) NACE Intl.

Methods of Surface Analysis. Ed. by A. W. Czandema. (Methods & Phenomena Ser.: Vol. 1). xiv, 482p. 1989. reprint ed. 198.50 (*0-444-41344-8*) Elsevier.

Methods of Synthesis of Thia Analogues of Gonasteroids: Review of Some Recent Syntheses, Reactions & Bioactivities of Pyridyl Sulfides, Vol. 7. S. R. Ramadas et al. Ed. by Alexander Senning. (Sulfer Reports: Vol. 7, No. 4). 70p. 1987. pap. text 72.00 (*3-7186-0442-6*) Gordon & Breach.

Methods of Teaching see Metodos de Ensenanza

Methods of Teaching Agriculture. 2nd ed. L. H. Newcomb et al. 370p. 1993. 39.95 (*0-8134-2952-8*) Interstate.

Methods of Teaching CAD. R. E. Dennis. 128p. 1986. write for info. (*0-07-018220-5*) McGraw.

Methods of Teaching Elementary School Mathematics. Waldemar Olson. LC 68-56887. 281p. reprint ed. pap. 87.20 (*0-608-30448-4*, 200347400030) Bks Demand.

Methods of Teaching in the Catholic School. Mary L. Welch. 1986. 6.00 (*0-318-20570-X*) Natl Cath Educ.

***Methods of Teaching Secondary Math.** Huetinck. LC 99-31662. 592p. 1999. pap. 72.00 (*0-13-876079-9*) P-H.

Methods of Testing Large Capacity Displacement Meters. (Gas Measurement Committee Reports: No. 6, Pt. 2). 59p. 1974. pap. 2.50 (*0-318-12656-7*, XQ0774) Am Gas Assn.

Methods of Testing Large Capacity Displacement Meters. (Gas Measurement Committee Reports: No. 6, Pt. 4). 78p. 1975. pap. 2.50 (*0-318-12655-9*, XQ0675) Am Gas Assn.

Methods of the Allocation of Limited Resources. K. M. Mjelde. LC 82-16002. 96p. reprint ed. pap. 30.00 (*0-8357-4602-X*, 203753500008) Bks Demand.

Methods of the Classical Theory of Elastodynamics. V. B. Poruchikov. Tr. by V. A. Khokhryakov from RUS. (Illus.). 336p. 1993. 104.95 (*0-387-54817-3*) Spr-Verlag.

Methods of the Way: Early Chinese Ethical Thought. Rune Svarverud & I. Chia. LC 98-15905. (Sinica Leidensia Ser.). 560p. 1998. 179.50 (*90-04-11010-0*) Brill Academic Pubs.

Methods of Theoretical Physics, 2 vols. Philip M. Morse & Herman Feshbach. (International Series in Pure & Applied Physics). (Illus.). (C). 1953. 144.69 (*0-07-043317-8*) McGraw.

Methods of Theoretical Physics, 2 vols., Vol. 1. Philip M. Morse & Herman Feshbach. (International Series in Pure & Applied Physics). (Illus.). (C). 1953. 144.69 (*0-07-043316-X*) McGraw.

Methods of Theoretical Physics, Vol. 2. Morse. 1999. 22.50 (*0-07-043353-4*) McGraw.

Methods of Theoretical Physics & Their Applications to Biopolymer Science. L. V. Yukushevich. 247p. (C). 1995. lib. bdg. 145.00 (*1-56072-246-0*) Nova Sci Pubs.

Methods of Thermodynamics. unabridged ed. Howard R. Reiss. LC 96-35379. (Illus.). 238p. 1997. reprint ed. pap. text 8.95 (*0-486-69445-3*) Dover.

Methods of Truth Which I Use. Brown Landone. 102p. 1996. reprint ed. spiral bd. 10.00 (*0-7873-0528-6*) Hlth Research.

Methods of Urine Drug Testing. Alphonse Poklis. (Methods in Analytical Toxicology Ser.). Date not set. boxed set 50.00 (*0-8493-7882-6*) CRC Pr.

Methods of Vitamin Assay. 4th ed. Ed. by Jorg Augustin et al. LC 84-7335. (Wiley-Interscience Publications). 608p. reprint ed. pap. 188.50 (*0-7837-2382-2*, 204006800006) Bks Demand.

Methods of Wastewater Treatment see Design Handbook of Wastewater Systems

Methods of Wood Chemistry, 2 vols., 1. Bertie L. Browning. LC 66-28537. (Illus.). 406p. reprint ed. pap. 125.90 (*0-608-11506-1*, 200634600058) Bks Demand.

Methods of Wood Chemistry, 2 vols., 2. Bertie L. Browning. LC 66-28537. (Illus.). 521p. reprint ed. pap. 161.60 (*0-608-11507-X*, 200634600059) Bks Demand.

***Methods of Work, 4 vols.** Jim Richey. (Illus.). 2000. pap. 39.95 (*1-56158-468-1*) Taunton.

Methods of Working Coal & Metal Mines: Theory Application Rock Mech. to Roof Control & Support Problems. S. Woodruff. LC 65-28058. 1966. 239.00 (*0-08-010696-X*, Pub. by Pergamon Repr) Franklin.

Methods of X-ray & Neutron Scattering in Polymer Science. Ryong-Joon Roe. LC 99-37446. (Topics in Polymer Science Ser.). (Illus.). 352p. (C). 2000. text 80.00 (*0-19-511321-7*) OUP.

Methods of X-Ray Spectroscopic Research. M. Blokhin & F. Curzon. LC 63-10112. 1965. 203.00 (*0-08-010016-3*, Pub. by Pergamon Repr) Franklin.

Methods on Glycoconjugates. Andrea Verbert. 357p. 1995. text 116.00 (*3-7186-5616-7*, Harwood Acad Pubs) Gordon & Breach.

Methods on Glycoconjugates. Andrea Verbert. 357p. 1995. spiral bd. 50.00 (*3-7186-5617-5*, Harwood Acad Pubs) Gordon & Breach.

Methods I see Handbook of Microscopy: Applications in Materials Science, Solid-State Physics and Chemistry

Methods Political Inquiry: The Discipline, Philosophy, & Analysis of Politics. Stella Z. Theodoulou & Rory O'Brien. LC 98-3319. 222p. (C). (gr. 8). 1998. pap. text 27.40 (*0-13-675562-3*) P-H.

Methods, Sex & Madness. Derek Layder & Julia O. Davidson. LC 94-5596. (Illus.). 240p. (C). 1994. pap. 24.99 (*0-415-09764-9*, B4626) Routledge.

Methods, Standards & Maturity: Developing the Standard for SSADM. Tony Bryant. LC 95-1440. (International Series in Software Engineering). 1995. 29.95 (*0-07-709115-9*) McGraw.

Methods That Matter: Six Structures for Best Practice Classrooms. Harvey Daniels & Marilyn Bizar. LC 97-47516. (Illus.). 272p. 1998. pap. text 19.50 (*1-57110-082-2*) Stenhse Pubs.

Methods-Time Measurement. Harold B. Maynard. LC 48-7173. (McGraw-Hill Industrial Organization & Management Ser.). (Illus.). 302p. reprint ed. pap. 93.70 (*0-608-11457-X*, 205540500019) Bks Demand.

Methods to Assess Adverse Effects of Pesticides on Non-Target Organisms. Robert G. Tardiff. LC 91-27779. (Scientific Committee on Problems of the Environment Ser.: No. 1409), 298p. 1992. 330.00 (*0-471-93156-X*) Wiley.

Methods to Assess DNA Damage & Repair: Interspecies Comparisons, No. 52. Ed. by Robert G. Tardiff et al. LC 93-37549. 284p. 1994. 245.00 (*0-471-94256-1*) Wiley.

Methods to Assess Quality & Stability of Oils & Fat-Containing Foods. Ed. by K. Warner & N. A. Eskin. 1995. 80.00 (*0-935315-58-6*) Am Oil Chemists.

Methods to Assess the Effects of Chemicals on Ecosystems. Ed. by Rick A. Linthurst et al. LC 95-219002. (SCOPE Ser.). 446p. 1995. 275.00 (*0-471-95911-1*) Wiley.

Methods to Defend the Natural Cold & Flu. C. M. Hawkes. 1998. pap. text 7.95 (*1-58054-016-3*) Woodland UT.

Methods to Detect Adulteration of Fruit Juice Beverages, 1 of 3 vols., Vol. 1. Ed. by Steven Nagy & Robert L. Wade. LC 94-40210. (Illus.). 452p. (C). 1995. text 84.00 (*0-9631397-3-8*) AgScience.

Methods to Extend Mechanical Component Life. D. K. Huzel. 117p. 1993. pap. 39.95 (*1-56347-072-1*, 72-1) AIAA.

Methods Toward a Science: Behavior & Experiment. Ray. (Psychology Ser.). 1981. 6.25 (*0-534-01012-1*) Brooks-Cole.

Methods Toward a Science of Behavior & Experience. 2nd ed. William J. Ray & Richard Ravizza. (C). 1984. mass mkt. 32.75 (*0-534-04041-1*) Brooks-Cole.

Methods Toward a Science of Behavior & Experience. 3rd ed. William J. Ray & Richard Ravizza. 373p. (C). 1987. mass mkt. 46.75 (*0-534-08778-7*) Brooks-Cole.

Methods Toward a Science of Behavior & Experience. 4th ed. William J. Ray. 1992. pap., teacher ed. write for info. (*0-534-17839-1*) Brooks-Cole.

Methods Toward a Science of Behavior & Experience. 4th ed. William J. Ray. 480p. (C). 1993. text 45.50 (*0-534-17838-3*) Brooks-Cole.

Methods Toward a Science of Behavior & Experience. 5th ed. William J. Ray. LC 96-12020. (Psychology Ser.). 496p. (C). 1996. pap. 52.25 (*0-534-20346-9*) Brooks-Cole.

Methods Toward a Science of Behavior & Experience. 5th ed. William J. Ray. 1996. mass mkt., teacher ed. write for info. (*0-534-34390-2*) Brooks-Cole.

Methods Toward a Science of Behavior & Experience. 6th ed. William J. Ray. LC 99-34371. (Psychology Ser.). 441p. 1999. pap. text 85.95 (*0-534-35721-0*) Brooks-Cole.

Methods Toward a Science of Behavior & Experience: Methods in Action: Study Guide & Activities Workbook. 4th ed. William J. Ray. Date not set. wbk. ed. 125.20 (*0-534-30725-6*) Brooks-Cole.

Methods Toward a Science of Behavior & Experience: Study Guide & Activities Workbook. 5th ed. William J. Ray. (Psychology Ser.). (C). 1996. mass mkt., student ed., wbk. ed. 20.00 (*0-534-34389-9*) Brooks-Cole.

Methods Toward Scientific Behavior & Explanation. 4th ed. Ray. (Psychology Ser.). 1992. pap., student ed., wbk. ed. 20.00 (*0-534-17840-5*) Brooks-Cole.

Methods II see Handbook of Microscopy: Applications in Materials Science, Solid-State Physics and Chemistry

Methods Used in Compiling the U. N. Price Index II. 142p. 20.00 (*92-1-161332-9*, 91.XVII.8) UN.

Methods Used in Compiling the United Nations Price Indexes for External Trade, Vol. I. 122p. 1987. 20.00 (*92-1-161282-9*) UN.

Methods Used in Establishing Permissible Levels in Occupational Exposure to Harmful Agents: Report of a WHO Expert Committee with the Participation of ILO, 1977. (Technical Report Ser.: No. 601). 68p. 1977. pap. text 8.00 (*92-4-120601-2*, 1100601) World Health.

Methods Used in the U. S. S. R. Proceedings of the WHO Expert Committee, Moscow, Dec. 12-19, 1972. WHO Staff. 1975. pap. text 30.00 (*92-4-156043-6*, 1150114) World Health.

Methodus Ad Facilem Historiarum Cognitionem of Jean Bodin: A Critical Study. John L. Brown. LC 76-94167. (Catholic University of America. Studies in Romance Languages & Literatures: No. 18). reprint ed. 37.50 (*0-404-50318-7*) AMS Pr.

***Metholology in Social Research: Dilemmas & Perspectives: Essays in Honor of Ramkrishna Mukherjee.** Ramkrishna Mukherjee & Partha N. Mukherji. LC 00-28268. 2000. pap. write for info. (*0-7619-9446-7*) Sage.

Methomyl. rev. ed. (Environmental Health Criteria Ser.: Vol. 178). (FRE & SPA.). 150p. (C). 1996. pap. 30.00 (*92-4-157178-0*, 1160178) World Health.

***Methotrexate.** Ed. by B. N. Cronstein. (Milestones in Drug Therapy Ser.). 250p. 2000. 159.00 (*3-7643-5959-5*, Pub. by Birkhauser) Spr-Verlag.

Methotrexate in Cancer Therapy. Ed. by Kiyoji Kimura & Yeu-Ming Wang. LC 85-30049. (Progress in Cancer Research & Therapy Ser.: Vol. 33). 331p. 1986. reprint ed. pap. 102.70 (*0-608-03422-3*, 206412100008) Bks Demand.

Methow River Poems. William Stafford. 20p. (Orig.). 1995. pap. 6.00 (*1-881090-18-3*) Confluence Pr.

***Methuen.** Methuen Historical Society Staff. (Images of America Ser.). 128p. 1999. pap. 18.99 (*0-7524-1264-7*) Arcadia Publng.

Methuen Audition Book for Men. Ed. by Annika Bluhm. 100p. (Orig.). (C). 1990. pap. 11.95 (*0-413-62300-9*, A0404, Methuen Drama) Methn.

Methuen Audition Book for Women. Compiled by Annika Bluhm. 101p. (Orig.). (C). 1990. pap. 11.95 (*0-413-61300-3*, A0405, Methuen Drama) Methn.

Methuen Audition Books for Young Actors. Anne Harvey. 128p. 1993. pap. 13.95 (*0-413-66630-1*, A0684, Methuen Drama) Methn.

Methuen Book of Dialogues for Young Actors. Anne Harvey. LC 96-140996. 192p. 1996. pap. 15.95 (*0-413-68900-X*, Methuen Drama) Methn.

Methuen Book of Shakespeare Anecdotes. Ralph Berry. 224p. 1993. pap. 15.95 (*0-413-68050-9*, A0688, Methuen Drama) Methn.

Methuselah (CA-TUL-1173) A Southern Sierra Bedrock Mortar & Rock Basin Site, Mountain Home Demonstration State Forest, Tulase Cay, CA. William J. Wallace. (California Department of Forestry Archaeological Reports: Vol. 13). (Illus.). 35p. (C). 1988. pap. text 6.25 (*1-55567-650-2*) Coyote Press.

Methuselah Factor. Randolph Hudson. 237p. (YA). 1992. pap. 5.25 (*0-9632097-0-1*) Rattlesnake.

Methuselah Factors: Learning from the World's Longest-Lived Peoples. 2nd rev. ed. Dan Georgakas. LC 95-55. (Illus.). 347p. 1995. reprint ed. pap. 18.95 (*0-89733-416-7*) Academy Chi Pubs.

Methuselah Formula: The Key to Eternal Youth. Johannes Von Buttlar. 1996. 24.95 (*1-85782-142-4*, Pub. by Blake Publng) Seven Hills Bk.

Methuselah Gene: A Science Fiction Adventure Thriller. Sal DeStefano. LC 99-34321. (New Millennium Writers Ser.). 340p. 2000. 24.95 (*1-891696-10-6*) BainBridgeBooks.

Methuselah's Children. Robert A. Heinlein. 21.95 (*0-88411-883-5*) Amereon Ltd.

Methuselah's Father. Terry L. Hamilton. LC 97-74938. (Methuselah Chronicles Ser.: Vol. 1). 254p. 1997. pap. 9.95 (*0-9660753-0-7*) Boot the Mule.

Methyl Bromide. (Environmental Health Criteria Ser.: Vol. 166). (FRE & SPA.). 324p. (C). 1995. pap. 62.00 (*92-4-157166-7*, 1160166) World Health.

Methyl Bromide (Bromomethane) Health & Safety Guide. (Health & Safety Guides Ser.: No. 86). 39p. 1994. pap. text 5.00 (*92-4-151086-2*, 1860086) World Health.

Methyl Bromide Issue. Ed. by N. Price et al. LC 95-42367. (Agrochemicals & Plant Protection Ser.: Vol. 1). 412p. 1997. 235.00 (*0-471-95521-3*) Wiley.

***Methyl Bromide Risk Characterization in California.** National Research Council Staff. 112p. 2000. pap. 26.75 (*0-309-07087-2*) Natl Acad Pr.

Methyl Chloroform & in the Environment. Domingo M. Aviado et al. Ed. by Leon Golberg. (Solvents in the Environment Ser.). 1976. 70.00 (*0-87819-098-8*, RA1242, CRC Reprint) Franklin.

M

Methyl Ethyl Ketone. (Environmental Health Criteria Ser.: No. 143). (ENG, FRE & SPA.). 161p. 1993. pap. text 36.00 (92-4-157143-8, 1160143) World Health.

Methyl Isobutyl Ketone. (Environmental Health Criteria Ser.: No. 117). (ENG, FRE & SPA.). 79p. 1990. pap. text 19.00 (92-4-157117-9, 1160117) World Health.

Methyl Isobutyl Ketone Health & Safety Guide. (Health & Safety Guides Ser.: No. 58). 28p. 1991. pap. text 5.00 (92-4-151058-7, 1860058) World Health.

Methyl Magic: Maximum Health Through Methylation. Craig Cooney & Bill Lawren. LC 98-45810. 1999. 19.95 (0-8362-3585-1) Andrews & McMeel.

Methyl Parathion. (Environmental Health Criteria Ser.: No. 145). (ENG, FRE & SPA.). 244p. 1993. pap. text 45.00 (92-4-157145-4, 1160145) World Health.

Methyl Parathion Health & Safety Guide. (Health & Safety Guides Ser.: No. 75). 41p. 1992. pap. text 5.00 (92-4-151075-7, 1860075) World Health.

***Methylation Miracle: Unleash Your Body's Natural Source of SAMe.** 3rd ed. Paul Frankel. 256p. (Orig.). 1999. pap. text 5.99 (0-312-97124-9, St Martins Paperbacks) St Martin.

Methyldopa in Hypertension. Alberto Zanchetti. LC 78-68086. 1978. 3.00 (0-911910-96-4) Merck-Sharp-Dohme.

Methylene Chloride. (Environmental Health Criteria Ser.: No. 32). 55p. 1984. pap. text 13.00 (92-4-154092-3, 1160032) World Health.

Methylene Chloride Health & Safety Guide. WHO Staff. (Health & Safety Guides: No. 6). 37p. 1987. 5.00 (92-4-154332-9) World Health.

Methylmercury. (Environmental Health Criteria Ser.: No. 101). 144p. 1990. pap. text 26.00 (92-4-157101-2, 1160101) World Health.

Methylnaphthalenes. Ed. by GDCh-Advisory Committee on Existing Chemicals of E. (BUA Report Ser.: No. 47). 122p. 1993. pap. 48.00 (1-56081-176-5, Wiley-VCH) Wiley.

Methylotrophs: Microbiology, Biochemistry & Genetics. Ching T. Hou. 192p. 1984. 112.00 (0-8493-5992-9, QR92, CRC Reprint) Franklin.

Methylphenate HCL (Ritalin) Index of New Information with Authors, Subjects & References. Kevin B. Armstrong. 131p. 1997. 47.50 (0-7883-1252-9); pap. 44.50 (0-7883-1253-7) ABBE Pubs Assn.

Methylxanthines & Phosphodiesterase Inhibitors in the Treatment of Airways Disease: The Proceedings of a Meeting Held by the Royal Society of Medicine's Section of Respiratory Medicine, RSM, London, November 1993. Ed. by John F. Costello & Priscilla J. Piper. LC 94-16137. (Illus.). 200p. (C). 1994. 42.00 (1-85070-597-6) Prthnon Pub.

Metier de Seigneur. Alexandre Dumas. (FRE.). 260p. 1991. 24.95 (0-7859-1185-5, 2268012883) Fr & Eur.

Metier de Sociologue: Prealables Epistemologiques. 4th ed. Ed. by Pierre J. Bourdieu et al. (Textes de Sciences Sociales Ser.: No. 1). 1983. pap. 44.65 (90-279-6964-7) Mouton.

Metier de Vivre, 2 vols., 1. Cesare Pavese. 1977. pap. 10.95 (0-7859-4082-0) Fr & Eur.

Metier de Vivre, 2 vols., 2. Cesare Pavese. 1977. pap. 10.95 (0-685-68142-4) Fr & Eur.

Metier de Zeus see Craft of Zeus: Myths of Weaving & Fabric

Metis: The Octopus & the Olive Tree. Jena Woodhouse. LC 95-119265. (J). 1994. pap. 9.95 (0-7022-2740-4, Pub. by Univ Queensland Pr) Intl Spec Bk.

Metis Families Vol. 1, Letters A-L: A Genealogical Compendium Letters A-L, 2 vols. Gail Morin. 714p. 1996. 125.00 (1-886560-00-5, 096545) Quintin Pub RI.

Metod Linearizatsii see Linearization Method for Constraint Optimization

Metodicka Prirucka K Hudobnej Vychove, Pre. 1. (SLO.). 96p. 1997. write for info. (80-08-02483-6, Pub. by Slov Pegagog Naklad) IBD Ltd.

Metodicka Prirucka K Matematike, Pre. 2. Kittler et al. (SLO.). 72p. 1997. write for info. (80-08-02459-3, Pub. by Slov Pegagog Naklad) IBD Ltd.

Metodicka Prirucka K Matematike, Pre. 4. Koman. (SLO.). 64p. 1997. write for info. (80-08-01149-1, Pub. by Slov Pegagog Naklad) IBD Ltd.

Metodicka Prirucka K Matematike: Metodicka Prirucka K Matematike Pre 1. Roc. ZS, Pre. 1. Kittler. (SLO.). 80p. 1997. write for info. (80-08-01431-8, Pub. by Slov Pegagog Naklad) IBD Ltd.

Metodicka Prirucka K Matematike: Metodicka Prirucka K Matematike Pre 3. Roc. ZS, Pre. 3. Kittler et al. (SLO.). 92p. 1997. write for info. (80-08-02460-7, Pub. by Slov Pegagog Naklad) IBD Ltd.

Metodicka Prirucka K Prirodovede, Pre. 3. Stanko. (SLO.). 176p. 1997. write for info. (80-08-02642-1, Pub. by Slov Pegagog Naklad) IBD Ltd.

Metodicka Prirucka K Prvouke 1. Stanko. (SLO.). 148p. 1997. write for info. (80-08-02584-0, Pub. by Slov Pegagog Naklad) IBD Ltd.

Metodicka Prirucka K Prvouke 2. Stanko. (SLO.). 152p. 1997. write for info. (80-08-02585-9, Pub. by Slov Pegagog Naklad) IBD Ltd.

Metodicka Prirucka K Ucebnici Nemciny Schau Mal! (SLO.). 64p. 1997. write for info. (80-08-02510-7, Pub. by Slov Pegagog Naklad) IBD Ltd.

Metodo Bowdoin Manual. 2nd ed. Ruth Bowdoin. Tr. by Rene Garay from ENG. (SPA., Illus.). 88p. 1978. pap. text. write for info. (1-55997-059-6) Websters Intl.

Metodo Case: Modelo Relacional. Richard Barker. (SPA.). 256p. (C). 1994. pap. text 20.00 (0-201-60111-7) Addison-Wesley.

Metodo de Estenotipia en Espanol Compatible con el Uso de Computadoras. Fernando Altamirano. (SPA.). (Orig.). (C). 1990. pap. write for info. (0-318-66797-5) Stenograph Corp.

Metodo de Guitarra Nivel 1, Bk. 1. Tr. of Guitar Method. (SPA.). 48p. 1993. pap. 5.95 (0-7935-2824-0) H Leonard.

Metodo Perfecto para Bajar de Peso. Runyon Kuntzleman. (Serie Guia de Bolsillo - Pocket Guides Ser.).Tr. of Perfect Way to Lose Weight Pocket Guide. (SPA.). 2.79 (1-56063-010-8, 498082) Editorial Unilit.

Metodo Perfecto para Bajar de Peso. Runyon Kuntzleman.Tr. of Perfect Way to Lose Weight Pocket Guide. (SPA.). 66p. 1990. write for info. (0-614-24379-3) Editorial Unilit.

Metodo Perfecto para Bajar de Peso: Guia de Bolsillo. Runyon Kuntzleman.Tr. of Perfect Way to Lose Weight: Pocket Guide. (SPA.). 66p. 1990. pap. write for info. (0-614-27081-2) Editorial Unilit.

Metodo Practico para Resolver Problemas Personales: Practical Method to Resolve Personal Problems. Carlos Gonzalez. (SPA.). 1993. reprint ed. 15.00 (1-56491-009-1) Imagine Pubs.

Metodo Silva De Control Mental. Jose Silva. (SPA., Illus.). 224p. 1997. pap. text 18.98 (968-13-0089-0) Libros Fronteras.

Metodo Silva del Domino de la Mente. Judith Powell. (SPA.). 1997. pap. 16.98 (968-13-1902-8, Pub. by Edit Diana) Libros Fronteras.

Metodo Silva Para Gerentes. Jose Silva & Robert B. Stone. (SPA.). 1997. pap. text 19.98 (968-13-2200-2) Libros Fronteras.

Metodo Silva Para Obtener Ayuda Del Otro Lado. Silva Jose. (SPA.). 1997. pap. text 15.98 (968-13-2196-0) Libros Fronteras.

Metodologia de Investigacion en Epidemiologia. I. Rebagliato et al. (SPA.). 223p. 1996. pap. 23.00 (84-7978-265-X, Pub. by Ediciones Diaz) IBD Ltd.

Metodologia para el Analisis de la Tecnica Pictorica Mural Prehispanica: El Templo Rojo de Cacaxtla. Diana I. Magaloni. 88p. 1994. pap. 11.00 (968-29-5129-1, IN053) UPLAAP.

Metodologia para la Ensenanza de las Artes Industriales y la Educacion Vocacional Industrial. Efrain Charneco Babilonia & Amalia Llabres De Charneco. LC 76-3715. 191p. (Orig.). 1976. pap. text 5.00 (0-8477-2722-X) U of PR Pr.

Metodologia Pedagogica. Findley B. Edge. Tr. by Celia Mendoza & Sara P. Molina from ENG.Tr. of Helping the Teacher. (SPA.). 155p. 1970. reprint ed. pap., teacher ed. 8.99 (0-311-11026-6) Casa Bautista.

Metodos Cualitativos para La Evaluacion de Programas: Un Manual par Programas de Salud, Planificacion Familiar Y Servicios Sociales. Sally J. Andrade et al. (SPA., Illus.). 146p. (Orig.). 1987. pap. text 3.00 (0-317-59568-7) Pathfinder Fund.

***Metodos Cuantitativos para la Administracion.** 7th ed. Anderson & Pete Sweeney. 1999. pap. 79.95 (968-7529-56-3) Thomson Learn.

Metodos de Ensenanza. rev. ed. L. Walker.Tr. of Methods of Teaching. (SPA.). 1996. pap. 6.99 (0-8297-1842-7) Vida Pubs.

Metodos Infalibles de Relajacion. Paul Wilson. (SPA.). 390p. 1997. mass mkt. 9.99 (0-553-06079-1) Bantam.

Metodos Japoneses de Contabilidad: La Contabilidad en el Entorno de Nuevas Tecnologias. Yasuhiro Monden & Michiharu Sakurai. (SPA., Illus.). 336p. (Orig.). 1992. pap. 60.00 (84-87022-76-6) Productivity Inc.

Metodos Sencillos de Identificacion de Plasticos. 2nd ed. Dietrich Braun. 110p. 1986. 17.50 (1-56990-007-8) Hanser-Gardner.

Metody i Tekhnika Radiolokatsionnogo Raspoznavaniia see Methods & Techniques of Radar Recognition

Metody Issledovaniia Nelineinykh Ellipticheskikh Granichnykh Zadach see Methods for Analysis of Nonlinear Elliptical Boundary Value Problems

Metody Optimizatsii see Methods of Optimization

Metonymy & Drama: Essays on Language & Dramatic Strategy. Jutka Devenyi. LC 96-697. 120p. 1996. 27.50 (0-8387-5313-2) Bucknell U Pr.

Metonymy in Language & Thought. Ed. by Klaus Uwe Panther & Gunter Radden. LC 99-23468. (Human Cognitive Processing Ser.: Vol. 4). vii, 410p. 1999. 95.00 (1-55619-204-5) J Benjamins Pubng Co.

Metre of Macbeth. David L. Chambers. LC 78-113575. reprint ed. 24.50 (0-404-01443-7) AMS Pr.

Metre, Rhythm & Verse Form. Philip Hobsbaum. LC 95-8576. 208p. (C). 1995. pap. 12.99 (0-415-08797-X) Routledge.

Metres to Microwaves. E. B. Callick. (History of Technology Ser.: No. 11). 240p. 1990. 85.00 (0-86341-212-2, HT011) INSPEC Inc.

Metric America: Math & Measures. Paul R. Frey. 1980. teacher ed. 3.33 (0-672-97364-2, Bobbs); pap. 6.95 (0-672-97363-4, Bobbs) Macmillan.

Metric & Standard Measurement. Victoria Sonnenberg. 1997. 4.95 (1-55708-581-1, MCR439) McDonald Pub Co.

Metric Architectural Drawing: A Manual for Designers & Draftsmen. Bernard L. Frishman et al. LC 80-39805. (Illus.). 203p. 1981. reprint ed. pap. 63.00 (0-7837-3441-7, 205776400008) Bks Demand.

Metric Can Be Fun. Munro Leaf. LC 75-29223. (Illus.). (J). (gr. 1-3). 1976. lib. bdg. 12.89 (0-397-31679-8) HarpC Child Bks.

***Metric Characterization of Random Variables & Random Processes.** V. V. Buldygin & Yu. V. Kozachenko. LC 99-87766. (MMONO Ser.: Vol. 188). 264p. 2000. 95.00 (0-8218-0533-9) Am Math.

Metric Constrained Interpolation, Commutant Lifting, & Systems. Ciprian Foias. LC 98-5066. (Operator Theory, Advances & Applications Ser.). 1998. write for info. (0-8176-5889-0) Birkhauser.

Metric Constrained Interpolation, Commutant Lifting, & Systems. Ciprian Foias et al. LC 98-5066. (Operator Theory Ser.: Vol. 100). 600p. 1998. 152.00 (3-7643-5889-0) Birkhauser.

Metric Conversion: A Review of Federal Activities. 72p. (Orig.). (C). 1994. pap. text 25.00 (0-7881-0894-8) DIANE Pub.

Metric Conversion in the Construction Industries: Planning, Coordination & Timing. 62p. 1980. 15.00 (0-686-70963-2) Am Natl.

Metric Conversion Symbols: Pohs Shop. Henry A. Pohs. (Illus.). 24p. 1994. pap. 7.50 (0-9641165-1-0) Flame Pubng.

Metric Converter. Compiled by Barron's Technical Staff. 1977. pap. text 2.50 (0-8120-0707-7) Barron.

Metric Debate. Ed. by David F. Bartlett. LC 79-53270. (Illus.). 150p. reprint ed. pap. 46.50 (0-8357-5501-0, 203511600093) Bks Demand.

Metric Differential Geometry of Curves & Surfaces. Ernest P. Lane. LC 40-12579. 224p. reprint ed. pap. 69.50 (0-608-12124-X, 202412000035) Bks Demand.

***Metric Diophantine Approximation on Manifolds.** V. I. Bernik & M. M. Dodson. (Cambridge Tracts in Mathematics Ser.: No. 137). 192p. (C). 2000. 44.95 (0-521-43275-8) Cambridge U Pr.

Metric Edition of Full Length Roof Framer. (Illus.). 102p. 1992. 12.95 (0-9664629-1-2) Full Length Framer.

Metric Editorial Guide. 4th rev. ed. 1993. pap. text 3.50 (0-916148-13-0) Am Natl.

Metric Engineering Drawing Examples. E. McPherson & D. L. Ashton. LC TA0175.M3. (Illus.). 69p. (Orig.). reprint ed. pap. 30.00 (0-608-18149-8, 203283700081) Bks Demand.

Metric for Me! A Layperson's Guide to the Metric System for Everyday Use with Exercises, Problems, & Estimations. 2nd enl. rev. ed. Robert W. Shoemaker. LC 96-79294. (Illus.). 80p. 1998. pap. 17.00 (0-9627980-3-7) Blackhawk Metric Supply.

Metric for Me! A Layperson's Guide to the Metric System for Everyday Use with Exercises, Problems, & Estimations, Poster. Robert W. Shoemaker. LC 96-79294. 1992. 8.00 (0-9627980-1-0) Blackhawk Metric Supply.

Metric Guide for Educational Materials: A Handbook for Teachers, Writers & Publishers. American National Metric Council, Educational Mate. 1977. pap. text 3.00 (0-916148-09-2) Am Natl.

Metric Guide for Federal Construction & Metric Design Guide. (Illus.). 110p. (Orig.). (C). 1994. pap. text 40.00 (0-7881-0797-6) DIANE Pub.

Metric Guide for Health Professionals on Dosages & Solutions, 3rd Edition. 3rd ed. Deborah L. Duff. (Illus.). 196p. 1994. pap. 22.00 (0-920513-14-X, W B Saunders Co) Harcrt Hlth Sci Grp.

Metric Handbook: Planning & Design Data. 2nd ed. David Adler. LC 99-230878. 1999. pap. text 54.95 (0-7506-0899-4) Buttrwrth-Heinemann.

Metric Handbook CD Rom Version 1.1. David Adler. Date not set. audio compact disk 330.00 (0-7506-4779-5, Architectural Pr) Buttrwrth-Heinemann.

Metric in Minutes: The Comprehensive Resource for Learning the Metric System (SI) Dennis R. Brownridge. (Illus.). 100p. (Orig.). 1994. pap. 19.95 (0-912045-71-X) Prof Pubns CA.

Metric Induced by the Robin Function. N. Levenberg et al. LC 91-13768. (Memoirs Ser.: No. 448). 156p. 1991. pap. 25.00 (0-8218-2520-8, MEMO/92/448) Am Math.

Metric Linear Spaces. Stefan Rolewicz. 1985. text 269.50 (90-277-1480-0) Kluwer Academic.

Metric Madness. J. W. Batchelder. (Illus.). 256p. 1981. 12.95 (0-8159-6220-7); pap. 5.95 (0-8159-6219-3) Devin.

Metric Measure. Ron Marson. (Task Cards Ser.: No. 6). (Illus.). 56p. 1992. teacher ed. 9.50 (0-941008-76-2) Tops Learning.

Metric Measurement in Food Preparation & Service. Lynne N. Ross. LC 78-61488. (Illus.). 73p. 1978. reprint ed. pap. 30.00 (0-608-00084-1, 206084700006) Bks Demand.

Metric Measuring. Ron Marson. LC 81-90446. (Science with Simple Things Ser.: No. 35). (Illus.). 80p. 1984. teacher ed. 15.00 (0-941008-35-5) Tops Learning.

Metric Mechanical Fasteners - STP 587. 122p. 1981. pap. 12.00 (0-8031-0751-X, STP587) ASTM.

Metric Methods for Analyzing Partially Ranked Data. D. E. Critchlow. (Lecture Notes in Statistics Ser.: Vol. 34). x, 216p. 1986. 52.95 (0-387-96288-3) Spr-Verlag.

Metric Number Theory. Glyn Harman. (London Mathematical Society Monographs: No. 18). 316p. 1998. text 125.00 (0-19-850083-1) OUP.

Metric Pattern Cutting for Children's Wear & Babywear: From Birth to 14 Years 3rd ed. Winifred Aldrich. LC 99-19986. 1999. write for info. (0-632-05265-1) Blackwell Sci.

Metric Pattern Cutting for Menswear: Including Unisex Clothes & Computer Aided Design. 3rd ed. Winifred Aldrich. (Illus.). 180p. 1996. pap. 32.95 (0-632-04113-7) Blackwell Sci.

Metric Practice Guide for Surveying & Mapping. ACSM Staff. 11p. 1980. pap. 12.00 (0-614-06119-9, G400) Am Congrs Survey.

Metric Practice Guide for the Welding Industry (A1.1-89) (Illus.). 32p. 1989. pap. 27.00 (0-87171-194-X) Am Welding.

Metric Reference for Consumers. American National Metric Council, Consumer Liaison. 565p. 1990. pap. text 2.50 (3-504-40005-6) Am Natl.

Metric Rigidity Theorems on Hermitian Locally Symmetric Manifolds. Ed. by N. Mok. (Series in Pure Mathematics: Vol. 6). 292p. (C). 1989. text 61.00 (9971-5-0800-1); pap. text 32.00 (9971-5-0802-8) World Scientific Pub.

Metric (SI) in Everyday Science & Engineering. Stan Jakuba. LC 92-30112. 100p. 1992. 19.00 (1-56091-287-1, R-121) Soc Auto Engineers.

Metric Spaces of Fuzzy Sets: Theory & Applications. Phil Diamond. 188p. 1994. text 48.00 (981-02-1731-5) World Scientific Pub.

Metric Spaces of Non-Positive Curvature. M. Bridson & A. Haefliger. Ed. by S. S. Chern et al. LC 99-38163. xv, 575p. 1999. 106.00 (3-540-64324-9) Spr-Verlag.

Metric Standards for Worldwide Manufacturing. 2nd ed. Knut O. Kverneland. 748p. 1996. 115.00 (0-7918-0041-5, 800415) ASME.

Metric Structures for Riemannian & Non-Riemannian Spaces. Mikhael Gromov. Tr. by S. M. Bates. LC 97-24633. (Progress in Mathematics Ser.: Vol. 152). (Illus.). 608p. 1998. 89.50 (0-8176-3898-9, Pub. by Birkhauser) Spr-Verlag.

Metric System. Allan Fowler. LC 94-36352. (New True Books Ser.). (Illus.). 48p. (J). (gr. k-4). 1995. lib. bdg. 21.00 (0-516-01076-X) Childrens.

Metric System: And Its Corresponding Suffixes in Metrology: M,l,g, M2, M3, for Everyday Applications. John Serghi. 65p. (Orig.). 1998. pap. 12.00 (0-9652551-0-7) Cent Twenty-One.

Metric System: Syllabus. Don H. Parker et al. 1974. pap. text 19.95 (0-89420-052-6, 280222); audio 18.15 (0-89420-163-8, 280000) Natl Book.

Metric System: The International System of Units (SI) (Illus.). 56p. (Orig.). (C). 1992. pap. text 25.00 (0-941375-74-9) DIANE Pub.

Metric System Study Aid. Thomas J. Finnegan et al. (J). 1976. pap. 2.50 (0-87738-042-2) Youth Ed.

Metric Transition Plans & Activities of Federal Government Agencies. 110p. (Orig.). (C). 1993. pap. text 30.00 (1-56806-506-X) DIANE Pub.

Metric Units & Conversion Charts: A Metrication Handbook for Engineers, Technologists, & Scientists. 2nd ed. Theodore Wildi. LC 95-3182. 144p. 1995. pap. 19.95 (0-7803-1050-0, PP4044) Inst Electrical.

Metric Units, Guide for Implementation in ICEA Publications. Date not set. 30.00 (0-614-18694-3, P-57-653-1995) Insulated Cable.

Metric Units in Engineering: Going SI: How to Use the International System of Measurement Units (SI) to Solve Standard Engineering Problems. Cornelius Wandmacher. LC 94-48550. 336p. 1995. pap. 30.00 (0-7844-0070-9) Am Soc Civil Eng.

Metric Usage. 3rd rev. ed. AGMA Technical Committee. (AGMA Standard Ser.: Vol. 904-C96). (Illus.). 20p. 1989. pap. text 40.00 (1-55589-681-2) AGMA.

Metric Vendor List. 5th ed. 250p. 1998. 49.00 (0-614-18758-3) US Metric Assn.

Metrical Chronicle of England. (EETS, OS Ser.: No. 196). 1974. reprint ed. 55.00 (0-527-00196-1) Periodicals Srv.

Metrical Chronicle of Robert of Gloucester (to 1270)., 2 vols. Ed. by William A. Wright. (Rolls Ser.: No. 86). 1974. reprint ed. 140.00 (0-8115-1159-6) Periodicals Srv.

Metrical Dindsenchas, 5 vols., bk.2, Set. Dinnseanchus. LC 78-72687. (Royal Irish Academy. Todd Lecture Ser.: Vols. 8-12). reprint ed. 105.00 (0-404-60570-2) AMS Pr.

Metrical Grammar of Beowulf. Calvin B. Kendall. (Cambridge Studies in Anglo-Saxon England: No. 5). 334p. (C). 1991. text 74.95 (0-521-39325-6) Cambridge U Pr.

Metrical Life of St. Robert of Knaresborough: Together with the Other Middle English Pieces in British Museum MS. Egerton 3143. Ed. by Joyce Bazire. (EETS Original Ser.: No. 228). 1968. reprint ed. 30.00 (0-19-722228-5, Pub. by EETS) Boydell & Brewer.

Metrical Organization of Beowulf: Prototype & Isomorphism. Seiichi Suzuki. LC 96-3459. (Trends in Linguistics, Studies & Monographs: Vol. 95). xxiv, 537p. (C). 1996. lib. bdg. 198.60 (3-11-015134-0) Mouton.

Metrical Stress Theory: Principles & Case Studies. Bruce Hayes. LC 93-34063. 472p. (C). 1994. pap. text 29.95 (0-226-32104-5); lib. bdg. 90.00 (0-226-32103-7) U Ch Pr.

Metrical Structure of Arabic. Jean-Pierre Angoujard. (Publications in Language Sciences). iv, 200p. (Orig.). (C). 1990. pap. 106.15 (90-6765-296-2) Mouton.

Metrical Theory of Rhythmic Stress Phenomena. Ellis Visch. (Publications in Language Sciences). iv, 272p. (Orig.). (C). 1990. pap. 57.70 (90-6765-398-5) Mouton.

Metrical Theory of Stress & Destressing in English & Dutch. Rene Kager. (Linguistic Models Ser.). xviii, 344p. (Orig.). (C). 1989. pap. 80.80 (90-6765-436-1) Mouton.

Metrical Version of Mandeville's Travels. Ed. by M. C. Seymour. (EETS Original Ser.: No. 269). 1973. 30.00 (0-19-722271-4, Pub. by EETS) Boydell & Brewer.

Metrically Yours. Helen Hunter & Paul Wallach. LC 78-70040. 72p. reprint ed. pap. 30.00 (0-608-30488-3, 201157600080) Bks Demand.

Metrication: Managing the Industrial Transition - STP 574. 342p. 1975. 30.00 (0-8031-0516-9, STP574) ASTM.

Metrication - U. K. Units for the Measurement of Crude Oil & Petroleum Products. Institute of Petroleum (Great Britain) Staff. LC 74-183161. 11p. reprint ed. pap. 30.00 (0-608-16142-X, 202370000033) Bks Demand.

Metrication for the Manager. John T. Benedict. Ed. by Len Boselovic. LC 77-84932. (Illus.). 1977. pap. text 10.00 (0-916148-12-2) Am Natl.

Metrication of Land Surveying. John E. Keen. 92p. (C). 1995. pap. text 30.00 (1-56569-048-6) Land Survey.

***Metrics.** Steve Davis. (Illus.). 64p. 1999. pap. text 8.95 (1-58037-114-0, Pub. by M Twain Media) Carson-Dellos.

Metrics. Frances F. Loose. (Illus.). 1975. teacher ed. 1.00 (0-87879-802-1, Ann Arbor Div) Acad Therapy.

An Asterisk (*) at the beginning of an entry indicates that the title is appearing for the first time.

Metrics: Reusable Edition. Frances F. Loose. (gr. 9-12). 1975. student ed. 6.50 (*0-87879-801-3*, Ann Arbor Div) Acad Therapy.

Metrics & Models in Software Quality Engineering. Stephen H. Kan. LC 94-26972. 368p. (C). 1994. 49.95 (*0-201-63339-6*) Addison-Wesley.

Metrics at Work. John L. McCabe. (Applied Math Ser.). 89p. (YA). (gr. 8-12). 1995. pap. 7.95 (*0-931993-70-9*, GP-070) Garlic Pr OR.

Metrics, Connections & Gluing Theorems. Clifford H. Taubes. LC 96-5911. (CBMS Regional Conference Series in Mathematics: No. 89). 90p. 1996. pap. 15.00 (*0-8218-0323-9*, CBMS/89) Am Math.

Metrics HandiGuide: Metrics for the Internet Information Systems, Communication & Data Processing. M. Victor Janulaitis. (Illus.). 300p. (Orig.). 1996. pap. 395.00 (*1-881218-25-2*) Pos Support Rev.

***Metrics of Science & Technology.** Eliezer Geisler. LC 00-26. 250p. 2000. 67.00 (*1-56720-213-6*, Q213, Quorum Bks) Greenwood.

Metritocratic Intellect--Studies in the History of Educational Research: Proceedings of the Seminar Held at Aberdeen University, 15-17 September 1979. Ed. by James V. Smith & David Hamilton. 150p. 1980. 25.00 (*0-08-025720-8*, Pergamon Pr) Elsevier.

Metro. Ed. by Ostrom. LC 99-86070. (C). 1999. text. write for info. (*0-321-01132-5*) Addson-Wesley Educ.

***Metro: Sourcebook for Writing Creatively.** (C). 2000. write for info. (*0-321-08095-5*) Addison-Wesley.

Metro - Jonathan Cleaned Up. Robert Munsch. (Droles D'Histories Ser.). (FRE., Illus.). 24p. (J). (ps up). 1991. pap. 6.95 (*2-89021-154-1*, Pub. by La Courte Ech) Firefly Bks Ltd.

Metro Atlanta Street Atlas. Universal Staff. 1996. pap. text 16.95 (*0-7625-0203-7*) Universal Map Enterprises Inc.

***Metro Baltimore Street Guide & Directory: 2000 Edition.** (Illus.). 496p. 2000. pap. 34.95 (*1-58174-212-6*) Thomas Bros Maps.

***Metro Baltimore Street Guide & Thomas Guide Digital Edition: 2000 Edition.** (Illus.). 496p. 2000. pap. 49.95 incl. cd-rom (*1-58174-140-5*) Thomas Bros Maps.

Metro Baltimore Thomas Guide Street Guide & Directory: 1999 Edition. Thomas Bros. Maps Staff. (Illus.). 384p. 1998. pap. 29.95 (*0-88130-976-1*) Thomas Bros Maps.

Metro Bay Area Street Guide & Directory: 1999 Edition. Thomas Bros. Maps Staff. (Illus.). 440p. 1998. pap. 44.95 (*1-58174-026-3*) Thomas Bros Maps.

***Metro Bay Area Street Guide & Directory: 2000 Edition.** (Illus.). 440p. 1999. pap. 44.95 (*1-58174-131-6*) Thomas Bros Maps.

***Metro Bay Area Street Guide & Thomas Guide Digital Edition: 2000 Edition.** (Illus.). 440p. 1999. pap. 59.95 incl. cd-rom (*1-58174-188-X*) Thomas Bros Maps.

***Metro Bay Area Thomas Guide 2000.** 1999. cd-rom 29.95 (*1-58174-120-0*) Thomas Bros Maps.

Metro Chicago Political Atlas, 1994. Chicago Urban League Staff et al. LC 94-24833. (Illus.). 102p. (Orig.). 1994. pap. 20.00 (*0-938943-07-3*) U IL Spgfld Pub Affrs.

Metro Chicago Political Atlas, 97-98. Chicago Urban League Staff et al. (Illus.). 166p. 1997. pap. 19.95 (*0-938943-13-8*) U IL Spgfld Pub Affrs.

Metro Daily News. Bartel. (C). 1994. pap. text, teacher ed. 9.27 (*0-13-043852-9*) P-H.

***Metro DC Collaborative for Women with HIV-AIDS--Telling the Story: An Evaluation & Replication Report.** Leslie R. Wolfe et al. 1999. 15.00 (*1-877966-71-1*) Ctr Women Policy.

Metro Futures: Economic Solutions for Cities & Their Suburbs. Daniel D. Luria & Joel Rogers. LC 99-28328. 80p. 1999. pap. 11.00 (*0-8070-0603-3*) Beacon Pr.

Metro Gangs Attack. (Knockout Ser.). Date not set. pap. text. write for info. (*0-582-25095-1*, Pub. by Addison-Wesley) Longman.

***Metro Ice: A Century of Hockey in Greater New York Starring Rangers, Islanders, Devels, etc.** (Illus.). 272p. 1999. 49.95 (*1-882608-21-6*) H & M Prods.

Metro Inland Empire Street Guide & Directory: 1999 Edition. Thomas Bros. Maps Staff. (Illus.). 376p. 1998. pap. 34.95 (*1-58174-008-5*) Thomas Bros Maps.

***Metro Inland Empire Street Guide & Directory: 2000 Edition.** (Illus.). 400p. 1999. pap. 34.95 (*1-58174-132-4*) Thomas Bros Maps.

***Metro Inland Empire Street Guide & Thomas Guide Digital Edition: 2000 Edition.** (Illus.). 400p. 1999. pap. 49.95 incl. cd-rom (*1-58174-187-1*) Thomas Bros Maps.

Metro Insights. Data Resources Staff. (Illus.). 1137p. 1988. 449.00 (*0-07-607001-8*) McGraw.

Metro Monterey Bay Street Guide & Directory: 1999 Edition. Thomas Bros. Maps Staff. (Illus.). 1998. pap. 29.95 (*1-58174-102-2*) Thomas Bros Maps.

***Metro Monterey Bay Street Guide & Directory: 2000 Edition.** (Illus.). 312p. 1999. pap. 29.95 (*1-58174-133-2*) Thomas Bros Maps.

Metro Museum Journal 5. Metro Museum Staff. 1985. 35.00 (*0-226-52102-8*) U Ch Pr.

Metro Museum Journal 4. Metro Museum Staff. 1985. 35.00 (*0-226-52100-1*) U Ch Pr.

Metro Museum Journal 1. Metro Museum Staff. 1985. 35.00 (*0-226-52097-8*) U Ch Pr.

Metro Museum Journal 3. Metro Museum Staff. 1985. 35.00 (*0-226-52099-4*) U Ch Pr.

Metro Museum Journal 2. Metro Museum Staff. 1985. 35.00 (*0-226-52098-6*) U Ch Pr.

Metro Office Systems: A Payroll Practice Set. 2nd ed. Merle W. Wood. 112p. 1988. pap. text 17.12 (*0-07-071688-9*) McGraw.

Metro Phoenix: The Gold Book, 1987. Ed. by Duffy Busch. (Annual Ser.). 243p. (Orig.). 1988. pap. 15.00 (*0-932053-05-X*) Prime Pubns.

Metro Phoenix: The Gold Book, 1988-89. Ed. by Duffy Busch. (Annual Ser.). (Orig.). 1988. pap. 15.00 (*0-932053-08-4*) Prime Pubns.

***Metro Pudget Sound 2000.** Thomas Brothers Maps Staff. (Thomas Guides Ser.). 1999. 54.95 (*1-58174-194-4*) Thomas Bros Maps.

Metro Tech Vocational Institute of Phoenix Case Study Report. Anne M. Rogers & Susan Hubbard. (Cross Case Report & Case Studies). 50p. 1995. text, teacher ed. 20.00 (*0-614-24546-X*); pap. text, teacher ed. 10.00 (*0-614-24547-8*) Natl Inst Work.

Metro Transportation Finance: Can Denver Avoid a Hollow Core? Rex Reed. 24p. 1989. pap. text 8.00 (*1-57655-085-0*) Independ Inst.

Metro Transportation Menu: Bureaucracy or Markets: Colorado Mobility Issues in a Jeffersonian Light. Brian Erickson. (Issue Papers: No. 1-91). 17p. 1991. pap. text 8.00 (*1-57655-042-7*) Independ Inst.

***Metro Washington, D. C. Street Guide & Directory: 2000 Edition.** (Illus.). 480p. 2000. pap. 29.95 (*1-58174-134-0*) Thomas Bros Maps.

***Metro Washington, D. C. Street Guide & Thomas Guide Digital Edition: 2000 Edition.** (Illus.). 480p. 2000. pap. 44.95 incl. cd-rom (*1-58174-213-4*) Thomas Bros Maps.

Metro Washington, D. C. Thomas Guide Street Guide & Directory: 1999 Edition. Thomas Bros. Maps Staff. (Illus.). 480p. 1998. pap. 29.95 (*1-58174-027-1*) Thomas Bros Maps.

Metro Web Kit. Dolores Pusins. 1998. teacher ed. 22.99 (*1-58076-005-8*) Que Educ & Trng.

***Metro Women's & Children's & Fashion Accessories Buyers.** Ed. by Keith Caredo et al. 184p. 1999. write for info. (*0-87228-134-5*) Douglas Pubns.

***Metro X for Linux & FreeBSD.** 2000. 39.95 (*0-9670172-1-1*) Metro Link.

Metro 1980-1990. Chilton Automotive Editorial Staff. (Porter Manuals Ser.). (Illus.). 128p. (C). 1998. pap. 24.95 (*1-899238-12-3*, Pub. by Porter Pub) Nichols Pub.

***Metrodog: A Guide to Raising Your Dog in the City.** Brian Kilcommons & Sarah Wilson. 256p. 2000. 23.95 (*0-446-52603-7*, Pub. by Warner Bks) Little.

MetroFarm: The Guide to Growing for Big Profit on a Small Parcel of Land. Michael Olson. (Illus.). 576p. 1995. pap. 29.95 (*0-9637876-0-8*) T S Bks.

MetroKey, Acadiana Parishes. 4th ed. (Illus.). 328p. 1998. 28.95 (*1-892964-02-3*); pap. 28.95 (*1-892964-03-1*) Stinson Map Co.

MetroKey, Baton Rouge Area. (Illus.). 284p. 1999. 28.95 (*1-892964-07-4*) Stinson Map Co.

MetroKey, Baton Rouge Area. 7th ed. (Illus.). 312p. 1997. 28.95 (*1-892964-00-7*); pap. 28.95 (*1-892964-01-5*) Stinson Map Co.

MetroKey, Central Louisiana Area. (Illus.). 184p. 1997. 24.95 (*1-892964-06-6*) Stinson Map Co.

MetroKey, Mississippi Coast. (Illus.). 332p. 1996. 28.95 (*1-892964-05-8*) Stinson Map Co.

MetroKey, New Orleans Area. 3rd ed. (Illus.). 342p. 1998. 28.95 (*1-892964-04-X*) Stinson Map Co.

Metroland. Julian Barnes. LC 92-50092. 1992. pap. 11.00 (*0-679-73608-5*) Vin Bks.

Metrological Assurance for Environmental Control. 2nd ed. Ed. by K. Havrilla. (Illus.). 202p. 1989. text 175.00 (*0-941743-60-8*) Nova Sci Pubs.

Metrological Control - Industrial Measurement Management. Hiroshi Yano. 512p. 1991. text 67.50 (*92-833-1107-8*, 311078); pap. text 62.25 (*92-833-1108-6*, 311086) Productivity Inc.

Metrology. Jerome V. Scholle. LC 92-33530. (Six Sigma Research Institute Ser.). 1993. pap. text 25.95 (*0-201-63414-7*) Addison-Wesley.

Metrology: Course 27. (Illus.). 446p. (C). 1979. pap. text, ring bd. 95.00 (*0-87683-079-3*) GP Courseware.

Metrology at the Frontiers of Physics & Technology: Proceedings of the International School of Physics "Enrico Fermi," 27 June-7 July, 1989. Ed. by L. Crovini & T. J. Quinn. LC 92-25710. (Enrico Fermi International School of Physics Ser.: Vol. 110). xxii, 646p. 1992. 304.00 (*0-444-89770-4*, North Holland) Elsevier.

Metrology for Quality Control in Production (IAP) Proceedings of the IMEKO TC 14 International Symposium on Metrology for Quality Control in Production, Beijing, China, 9-12 May 1989, No. 2. Ed. by Zhaoqian Meng. (International Academic Publishers Ser.). 382p. 1989. 110.00 (*0-08-037515-4*, Pergamon Pr) Elsevier.

Metrology, Inspection & Process Control for Microlithography XI. Ed. by Susan K. Jones. LC 98-122097. 648p. 1997. 89.00 (*0-8194-2464-1*) SPIE.

Metrology, Inspection & Process Control for Microlithography XII, Vol. 3332. Ed. by Bhanwar Singh. LC 98-226775. 760p. 1998. 132.00 (*0-8194-2777-2*) SPIE.

***Metrology, Inspection & Process Control for Microlithography XIII.** Ed. by Bhanwar Singh. 1084p. 1999. pap. text 153.00 (*0-8194-3151-6*) SPIE.

Metrology Needs in the Measurement of Environmental Radioactivity: Seminar Sponsored by the International Committee for Radionuclide Metrology. Ed. by J. M. Hutchinson & W. B. Mann. (Illus.). 1980. pap. 43.00 (*0-08-022943-3*, Pergamon Pr) Elsevier.

Metrology, Why Not?!! Proceedings of the 1998 Workshop & Symposium. unabridged ed. NCSL Staff. (Illus.). 1046p. 1998. 40.00 (*1-58464-022-7*) Natl Conf Stds Labs.

Metromex: A Review & Summary. Ed. by Stanley A. Changon. (Meteorological Monograph: Vol. 18, No. 40). (Illus.). 181p. 1981. 40.00 (*0-933876-52-1*) Am Meteorological.

Metronome & Its Precursors. Rosamond E. Harding. 48p. 1983. 45.00 (*0-905418-42-5*, Pub. by Gresham Bks) St Mut.

Metronomic Society: Natural Rhythms & Human Timetables. Michael Young. LC 87-30663. 384p. 1988. text 35.00 (*0-674-57195-9*) HUP.

***Metropolis.** Thomas Elsaesser. 96p. 2000. pap. 10.95 (*0-85170-777-7*, Pub. by British Film Inst) Ind U Pr.

Metropolis. Emrys Jones. (Illus.). 240p. 1990. pap. 17.95 (*0-19-282578-X*) OUP.

***Metropolis.** Upton Sinclair. (Collected Works of Upton Sinclair). 376p. 1999. reprint ed. lib. bdg. 108.00 (*1-58201-827-8*) Classic Bks.

Metropolis, Vol. 184. Antonio Porta. (Sun & Moon Classics Ser.: Vol. 154). 1999. 10.95 (*1-55713-326-3*) Sun & Moon CA.

Metropolis: A Bilingual. Antonio Porta. Tr. by Pasquale Verdicchio. (Green Integer Bks.: No. 25). 102p. 1999. pap. text 10.95 (*1-892295-12-1*, Pub. by Green Integer) Consort Bk Sales.

Metropolis: A Sourcebook for KULT. LC 99-164665. 176p. 1995. write for info. (*1-883716-07-1*) Eidolon Studio.

Metropolis: Center & Symbol of Our Times. Ed. by Philip Kasinitz et al. (Main Trends of the Modern World Ser.). 420p. (C). 1994. text 50.00 (*0-8147-4639-X*); pap. text 18.50 (*0-8147-4640-3*) NYU Pr.

Metropolis: Ein Filmisches Laboratorium der Modernen Architektur / a Cinematic Laboratory for Modern Architecture. Wolfgang Jacobsen & Werner Sudendorf. (GER & ENG., Illus.). 240p. 79.00 (*3-930698-85-4*) Edition A Menges.

Metropolis: From the Division of Labor to Urban Form. Allen J. Scott. 272p. 1988. pap. 16.95 (*0-520-07198-0*, Pub. by U CA Pr) Cal Prin Full Svc.

Metropolis: London Histories & Representations Since 1800. Ed. by David Feldman & Gareth Stedman Jones. (History Workshop Ser.). 288p. 1989. 69.50 (*0-415-02515-X*) Routledge.

Metropolis: New York As Myth, Marketplace, & Magical Land. Jerome Charyn. 304p. 1987. pap. 8.95 (*0-380-70401-3*, Avon Bks) Morrow Avon.

Metropolis: Ten Cities & Ten Centuries. Albert Lorenz & Joy Schleh. LC 96-83709. (Illus.). 42p. 1996. 17.95 (*0-8109-4284-4*, Pub. by Abrams) Time Warner.

Metropolis & Beyond: Selected Essays. Hans Blumenfeld & Paul D. Spreiregen. LC 78-17955. 436p. reprint ed. pap. 135.20 (*0-608-12411-7*, 205571400032) Bks Demand.

Metropolis & Hinterland: The City of Rome & the Italian Economy, 200 BC-AD 200. Neville Morley. LC 95-51652. 222p. (C). 1996. text 54.95 (*0-521-56006-3*) Cambridge U Pr.

***Metropolis & Its Image: Constructing Identities for London, 1750-1950.** Dana Arnold. LC 99-56077. (Art History Special Issues Ser.). 184p. 2000. pap. 22.95 (*0-631-21667-7*) Blackwell Pubs.

Metropolis & Nation in Thailand: The Political Economy of Uneven Development. Bruce London. LC 79-3287. (Replica Edition Ser.). 1979. pap. text 37.50 (*0-89158-592-3*) Westview.

Metropolis & Region. Otis D. Duncan et al. LC 77-86393. (Resources for the Future Ser.). (Illus.). 608p. reprint ed. 64.50 (*0-404-60331-9*) AMS Pr.

Metropolis & Region. Otis D. Duncan et al. LC 60-10656. 607p. reprint ed. pap. 188.20 (*0-7837-3133-7*, 204285400006) Bks Demand.

Metropolis, 1890-1940. Ed. by Anthony Sutcliffe. LC 83-40340. (Illus.). x, 468p. 1984. 48.00 (*0-226-78025-2*) U Ch Pr.

Metropolis Era: A World of Giant Cities, Vol. 1. Ed. by Mattei Dogan & John D. Kasarda. 400p. (C). 1988. 26.00 (*0-8039-3789-X*); text 55.00 (*0-8039-2602-2*) Sage.

Metropolis Era: Mega-Cities, Vol. 2. Ed. by Mattei Dogan & John D. Kasarda. 400p. (C). 1988. 24.00 (*0-8039-3790-3*); text 52.00 (*0-8039-2603-0*) Sage.

Metropolis in Black & White: Place, Power & Polarization. Ed. by George C. Galster & Edward W. Hill. LC 91-45182. 404p. (C). 1992. pap. 15.95 (*0-88285-139-X*); text 29.95 (*0-88285-138-1*) Ctr Urban Pol Res.

Metropolis, 1985: An Interpretation of the Findings of the New York Metropolitan Region Study. Raymond Vernon. LC 60-15243. (New York Metropolitan Region Study). 265p. 1960. 34.95 (*0-674-57200-9*) HUP.

Metropolis of New England: Colonial Boston, 1630-1776. (Picture Bks.). 1976. pap. 4.00 (*0-934909-59-8*) Mass Hist Soc.

Metropolis of Tomorrow. Hugh Ferriss. (Illus.). 200p. 1998. reprint ed. 40.00 (*0-910413-11-8*) Princeton Arch.

Metropolis to Metroplex: The Social & Spatial Planning of Cities. Jack Meltzer. LC 83-49195. 215p. reprint ed. pap. 66.70 (*0-608-08797-1*, 206943600004) Bks Demand.

***Metropolis und Nordische Moderne: Gro** beta;stadtthematik Als Herausforderung Literarischer Innovationen in Skandinavien Seit 1830 Bearbeitet von Annika Krummacher, Klaus Muller-wille, Frithjof Strau & Beta; und Antje Wischmann. Bernhard Glienke. (Beitrage Zur Skandinavistik Ser.). 189p. 1999. 32.95 (*3-631-34279-9*) P Lang Pubng.

Metropolital Area Problems: The Role of the Federal Government. Theodore M. Hutchison. LC 61-63259. (Michigan Legal Publications). v, 65p. 1985. reprint ed. lib. bdg. 32.00 (*0-89941-382-X*, 303520) W S Hein.

Metropolitan: A Portrait of Paris. Fiona Biddulph. (Illus.). 240p. 1994. text 55.00 (*0-7148-3156-5*, Pub. by Phaidon Press) Phaidon Pr.

Metropolitan Museum Journal 6. Metro Museum Staff. 1985. 35.00 (*0-226-52103-6*) U Ch Pr.

Metropolitan America, 55 vols. Ed. by Richard C. Wade. 1974. 1423.50 (*0-405-05380-0*) Ayer.

Metropolitan America: Challenge to Freedom. U. S. Advisory Commission on Intergovernmental Rel. LC 77-74942. (American Federalism-the Urban Dimension Ser.). 1978. reprint ed. lib. bdg. 19.95 (*0-405-10489-8*) Ayer.

Metropolitan America: Urban Life & Urban Policy in the U. S., 1940-1980. Kenneth Fox. 288p. (C). 1990. reprint ed. pap. text 16.00 (*0-8135-1506-8*) Rutgers U Pr.

Metropolitan America: Urban Life & Urban Policy in the United States, 1940-1980. Kenneth Fox. LC 85-15057. 288p. 1986. text 37.50 (*0-87805-283-6*) U Pr of Miss.

Metropolitan Anthony. Metropolitan A. Bloom. Ed. by Hugh Wybrew. (Modern Spirituality Ser.). 96p. 1987. pap. 4.95 (*0-87243-167-3*) Templegate.

Metropolitan Area Exports: An Export Performance Report on over 250 U. S. Cities. William F. Kolarik et al. (Illus.). 127p. (C). 1997. reprint ed. pap. text 30.00 (*0-7881-4736-6*) DIANE Pub.

Metropolitan Area Exports: An Export Performance Report on over 250 United States Cities. 1998. lib. bdg. 255.95 (*0-8490-9092-X*) Gordon Pr.

Metropolitan Area Exports: An Export Performance Report on over 250 United States Cities. 127p. 1996. per. 8.50 (*0-16-048616-5*) USGPO.

***Metropolitan Area Exports: An Export Performance Report on over 250 United States Cities, 1993- 1998.** 100p. 1999. per. 9.00 (*0-16-059083-3*) USGPO.

Metropolitan Area Exports: An Export Performance Report on Over 250 United States Cities, 1996. 103p. 1997. per. 8.50 (*0-16-049284-X*) USGPO.

***Metropolitan Area Exports: An Export Performance Report on over 250 U.S. Cities, 1993-1998.** Ed. by Barry Leonard. (Illus.). 96p. (C). 2000. pap. text 25.00 (*0-7567-0010-8*) DIANE Pub.

Metropolitan Area Exports: An Export Performances Report on over 250 United States Cities. 1997. lib. bdg. 251.95 (*0-8490-6107-5*) Gordon Pr.

Metropolitan Area Networks. M. Conti et al. 440p. 1997. 89.00 (*0-7803-3471-X*, PC5728-QOE) Inst Electrical.

Metropolitan Area Networks. Marco Conti et al. LC 96-46893. (Telecommunications Networks & Computer Systems Ser.). (Illus.). 440p. 1996. 89.95 (*3-540-19883-0*) Spr-Verlag.

Metropolitan Area Networks: The Only Single-Source Reference on MAN! Matthew N. Sadiku. LC 94-34033. 176p. 1994. boxed set 83.95 (*0-8493-2474-2*, 2474) CRC Pr.

Metropolitan Area Problems & Municipal Home Rule. Neil Littlefield. LC 63-62226. (Michigan Legal Publications). vi, 83p. 1985. reprint ed. lib. bdg. 34.00 (*0-89941-383-8*, 303530) W S Hein.

Metropolitan Atlanta Update, 1970-1974, Nos. 765-766. Ed. by James C. Starbuck. 1975. 8.50 (*0-686-20345-3*, Sage Prdcls Pr) Sage.

***Metropolitan Baltimore.** Thomas Brothers Maps Staff. 1999. pap. 29.95 (*1-58174-191-X*) Thomas Bros Maps.

Metropolitan Cats. John P. O'Neill. LC 81-9590. (Illus.). 112p. 1981. 16.95 (*0-87099-276-7*) Metro Mus Art.

Metropolitan Children. Barbara Burn. (Illus.). 112p. 1984. 16.95 (*0-87099-373-9*) Metro Mus Art.

Metropolitan Cities & Their Hinterlands in Early Modern Europe: Proceedings of the 10th International Economic History Congress, Leuven, Belgium, August 1990. Ed. by E. Aerts & P. Clark. (Studies in Social & Economic History: No. 9). 100p. (Orig.). 1990. pap. 32.50 (*90-6186-381-3*, Pub. by Leuven Univ) Coronet Bks.

Metropolitan Communities: Trade Guilds, Identity & Change in Early Modern London. Joseph P. Ward. LC 96-52156. 216p. 1997. 37.50 (*0-8047-2917-4*) Stanford U Pr.

Metropolitan Corridor. Ray DiPalma. 1992. pap. 7.00 (*84-87467-13-X*, Pub. by Zasterle Pr) SPD-Small Pr Dist.

Metropolitan Corridor: Railroads & the American Scene. John R. Stilgoe. LC 83-3585. (Illus.). 416p. 1985. pap. 20.00 (*0-300-03481-4*) Yale U Pr.

Metropolitan Cow. Tim Egan. LC 95-23382. (Illus.). 32p. (J). (ps-3). 1996. 15.00 (*0-395-73096-1*) HM.

Metropolitan Cow. Tim Egan. LC 95-23382. (Illus.). 32p. (J). (ps-3). 1999. pap. 5.95 (*0-395-96059-2*, Sandpiper) HM.

Metropolitan Crime Patterns. Ed. by Robert M. Figlio et al. LC 85-51936. 224p. 1986. pap. text 27.50 (*0-9606960-3-2*, Criminal Justice); lib. bdg. 37.50 (*0-9606960-1-6*, Criminal Justice) Willow Tree NY.

Metropolitan Daily News: Understanding American Newspapers. Joan Bartel. 272p. 1993. pap. text 26.33 (*0-13-043258-X*) P-H.

Metropolitan Decision-Making Further Analysis from the Syracuse Study of Local Community Leadership. Linton C. Freeman. 1962. 2.50 (*0-87060-079-6*, PUC 27) Syracuse U Cont Ed.

Metropolitan Denver (Close up) Atlas - Street Guide. (Illus.). 1994. pap. 15.95 (*0-914449-37-0*) Pierson Graph.

Metropolitan Denver (Close up) Atlas - Street Guide: 1996 Edition. 168p. 1996. 17.95 (*0-914449-67-2*) Pierson Graph.

Metropolitan Desegregation. Ed. by Robert L. Green. LC 85-12032. 250p. 1985. 65.00 (*0-306-41964-5*, Plenum Trade) Perseus Pubng.

***Metropolitan Desk Diary 2001.** (Illus.). 214p. 2000. im. lthr. 35.00 (*1-57499-079-9*) Per Annum.

***Metropolitan Desk Diary 2001: Black.** (Illus.). 214p. 2000. lthr. 60.00 (*1-57499-078-0*) Per Annum.

***Metropolitan Desk Diary 2001: Refill.** (Illus.). 214p. 2000. 18.00 (*1-57499-077-2*) Per Annum.

Metropolitan Diary: The Best of the New York Times Column. Ron Alexander. LC 97-7061. (Illus.). 256p. 1997. 20.00 (*0-688-14889-1*, Wm Morrow) Morrow Avon.

M

An Asterisk (*) at the beginning of an entry indicates that the title is appearing for the first time.

***Metropolitan Diary 2000.** (Illus.). 214p. 1999. 32.50 (*1-57499-071-3*); 17.00 (*1-57499-073-X*) Per Annum.

***Metropolitan Diary 2000, Burgandy Leather.** (Illus.). 214p. 1999. 32.50 (*1-57499-072-1*) Per Annum.

***Metropolitan Diary 2001.** (Illus.). 214p. 2000. im. lthr. 18.00 (*1-57499-075-6*) Per Annum.

***Metropolitan Diary 2001: Black.** (Illus.). 214p. 2000. lthr. 32.50 (*1-57499-124-8*) Per Annum.

***Metropolitan Diary 2001: Burgundy.** (Illus.). 214p. 2000. lthr. 32.50 (*1-57499-076-4*) Per Annum.

Metropolitan Dominance & Integration. Rupert B. Vance & Sara S. Sutker. (Reprint Series in Social Sciences). (C). 1993. reprint ed. pap. text 5.00 (*0-8290-2705-X*, S-535) Irvington.

Metropolitan Enigma: Inquiries into the Nature & Dimensions of America's Urban Crisis. rev. ed. Ed. by James Q. Wilson. LC 68-25620. (Joint Center for Urban Studies). (Illus.). 402p. 1968. reprint ed. 41.50 (*0-674-57250-5*) HUP.

Metropolitan Fashions of the 1880s: From the 1885 Butterick Catalog. Butterick Publishing Co. Staff. LC 97-13138. (Illus.). 144p. 1997. reprint ed. pap. text 8.95 (*0-486-29706-3*) Dover.

Metropolitan Financing: City, State & Federal Government, 2 vols. 1992. lib. bdg. 179.95 (*0-8490-5466-4*) Gordon Pr.

Metropolitan Financing: The Milwaukee Experience, 1920-1970. Donald J. Curran. LC 72-7984. (Illus.). 181p. reprint ed. pap. 56.20 (*0-8357-6788-4*, 203546500095) Bks Demand.

Metropolitan Financing & Growth Management Policies: Principles & Practice, Proceedings of a Symposium. Ed. by George F. Break. LC 77-77444. (Publications of the Committee on Taxation, Resources & Economic Development: Vol. 9). 345p. 1978. reprint ed. pap. 107.00 (*0-608-01983-6*, 206263800003) Bks Demand.

Metropolitan Frontier: Cities in the Modern American West. Carl Abbott. LC 93-11035. (Modern American West Ser.). (Illus.). 244p. 1993. 42.00 (*0-8165-1129-2*) U of Ariz Pr.

Metropolitan Frontier: Cities in the Modern American West. Carl Abbott. LC 93-11035. 244p. 1995. pap. 19.95 (*0-8165-1570-0*) U of Ariz Pr.

Metropolitan Frontiers: A Short History of Atlanta. Andy Ambrose & Darlene Roth. LC 95-82239. (Illus.). 226p. 1996. pap. 14.95 (*1-56352-284-5*) Longstreet.

Metropolitan Governance Revisited: American-Canadian Intergovernmental Perspectives. Ed. by Donald N. Rothblatt & Andrew Sancton. LC 98-24288. 530p. 1998. 29.95 (*0-87772-381-8*) UCB IGS.

Metropolitan Government & Governance: Theoretical Perspective, Empirical Analysis & the Future. G. Ross Stephens & Nelson Wikstrom. LC 98-36766. (Illus.). 256p. 1999. text 49.95 (*0-19-511297-0*); pap. text 22.50 (*0-19-511298-9*) OUP.

Metropolitan Growth & Migration in Peru. Gunnar Malmberg. (University of Umea Geographical Reports: No. 9). (Illus.). 266p. (Orig.). 1988. pap. 87.50 (*91-7174-329-4*, Pub. by Umea U Bibl) Coronet Bks.

Metropolitan Housing Market: A Study of Ahmedabad. Meera Mehta & Dinesh Mehta. 192p. (C). 1990. text 25.00 (*0-8039-9596-2*) Sage.

Metropolitan Icons: Selected Poems of Janos Pilinszky. Ed. & Tr. by Emery George from HUN. LC 94-36506. (Illus.). 312p. 1995. text 99.95 (*0-7734-9058-2*) E Mellen.

Metropolitan Impacts on Rural America. Richard F. Lamb. LC 74-84782. (University of Chicago, Department of Geography, Research Paper Ser.: No. 162). 210p. 1975. reprint ed. pap. 65.10 (*0-608-02288-8*, 206292900004) Bks Demand.

Metropolitan Improvements: or London in the Nineteenth Century. Thomas H. Shepherd & James Elmes. LC 67-13342. (Illus.). 1978. reprint ed. 27.95 (*0-405-08963-5*) Ayer.

***Metropolitan Inland Empire 2000.** Thomas Bros. Maps Staff. (Guides Ser.). 1999. pap. (*1-58174-202-9*) Thomas Bros Maps.

Metropolitan Innocent of Moscow, the Apostle of Alaska. Charles R. Hale. 1984. pap. 1.50 (*0-89981-058-6*) Eastern Orthodox.

Metropolitan Latin America: The Challenge & the Response. Ed. by Wayne A. Cornelius & Robert V. Kemper. LC 77-79867. (Latin American Urban Research Ser.: Vol. 6). 346p. reprint ed. pap. 107.30 (*0-608-14197-6*, 202188100026) Bks Demand.

Metropolitan Libraries: The Challenge & the Promise. Judith Guthman. LC 71-78896. (Public Library Reporter: No. 15). 63p. reprint ed. pap. 30.00 (*0-608-12797-3*, 202421200035) Bks Demand.

Metropolitan Life: A Study in Business Growth. Marquis James. LC 75-41765. (Companies & Men: Business Enterprises in America Ser.). (Illus.). 1976. reprint ed. 47.95 (*0-405-08080-8*) Ayer.

***Metropolitan Life Foundation Awards: Round II Winners in Supportive Housing & Property & Asset Management.** Diana Meyer & David Fromm. (Illus.). 52p. 1998. pap. 15.00 (*0-942901-15-0*) Enterprise Fnd.

Metropolitan Life Foundation Awards for Excellence in Affordable Housing: Case Studies of the Awardees in Supportive Housing & Property & Asset Management. (Illus.). (Orig.). 1997. pap. 10.00 (*0-942901-09-6*) Enterprise Fnd.

***Metropolitan Life Foundation Awards for Excellence in Affordable Housing Case Studies: Award Winners in Supportive Housing & Property & Asset Management.** 3rd ed. 50p. 1999. pap. 15.00 (*0-942901-66-5*, Pub. by Enterprise Fnd) BookMasters.

Metropolitan Lives: The Ashcan Artists & Their New York. Robert Zurier et al. 1995. write for info. (*0-937311-27-8*) Natl Mus Amer Art.

Metropolitan Lives: The Ashcan Artists & Their New York, 1897-1917. Rebecca Zurier et al. (Illus.). 256p. 1996. 50.00 (*0-393-03901-3*) Norton.

Metropolitan London: Politics & Urban Change, 1837-1981. Ken Young & Patricia L. Garside. LC 82-1042. (Studies in Urban History: Vol. 6). 401p. (C). 1982. 59.50 (*0-8419-0798-6*) Holmes & Meier.

Metropolitan Midwest: Policy Problems & Prospects for Change. Ed. by B. Checkoway & C. V. Patton. (Illus.). 320p. 1985. text 29.95 (*0-252-01114-7*) U of Ill Pr.

Metropolitan Mobility & Air Quality. Ralph Craft et al. Ed. by Gerry R. Feinstein & Karen Glass. 60p. (Orig.). 1992. pap. text 15.00 (*1-55877-173-5*) Natl Governor.

Metropolitan Museum Journal. Barbara Burn. (Canadian Museum of Civilization Mercury Ser.: Vol. 29). 350p. 1994. lib. bdg. 66.00 (*0-226-52126-5*) U Ch Pr.

Metropolitan Museum Journal, Vol. 7 Ed. by Barbara Burns. 1985. 35.00 (*0-226-52104-4*) U Ch Pr.

Metropolitan Museum Journal, Vol. 8 Ed. by Barbara Burn. 1985. 35.00 (*0-226-52105-2*) U Ch Pr.

Metropolitan Museum Journal, Vol. 9 Ed. by Barbara Burn. 1985. 35.00 (*0-226-52106-0*) U Ch Pr.

Metropolitan Museum Journal, Vol. 10 Ed. by Barbara Burn. 1985. 35.00 (*0-226-52107-9*) U Ch Pr.

Metropolitan Museum Journal, Vol. 11 Ed. by Barbara Burn. 1985. 35.00 (*0-226-52108-7*) U Ch Pr.

Metropolitan Museum Journal, Vol. 12 Ed. by Barbara Burn. 1985. 35.00 (*0-226-52109-5*) U Ch Pr.

Metropolitan Museum Journal, Vol. 17 Ed. by Barbara Burn. 1985. 35.00 (*0-226-52114-1*) U Ch Pr.

Metropolitan Museum Journal, Vol. 18. Ed. by Barbara Burn. 1985. 35.00 (*0-226-52116-8*) U Ch Pr.

Metropolitan Museum Journal, Vol. 19-20, 1984-1985. M. E. Laing. LC 68-28799. 268p. 1986. 75.00 (*0-226-52117-6*) U Ch Pr.

Metropolitan Museum Journal, Vol. 21. Metropolitan Museum Staff. 1987. 50.00 (*0-226-52118-4*) U Ch Pr.

Metropolitan Museum Journal, Vol. 22. Ed. by Barbara Burn. 1988. lib. bdg. 50.00 (*0-226-52119-2*) U Ch Pr.

Metropolitan Museum Journal, Vol. 23. Metropolitan Museum Staff. 1989. lib. bdg. 60.00 (*0-226-52120-6*) U Ch Pr.

Metropolitan Museum Journal, Vol. 25 Ed. by Barbara Burn. 1990. lib. bdg. 60.00 (*0-226-52122-2*) U Ch Pr.

Metropolitan Museum Journal, Vol. 31. Ed. by Barbara Burn. (Illus.). 1996. lib. bdg. 70.00 (*0-226-52127-3*) U Ch Pr.

Metropolitan Museum Journal, Vol. 33. Ed. by Barbara Burn. 1999. lib. bdg. 77.00 (*0-226-52131-1*) U Ch Pr.

Metropolitan Museum Journal Vol. 30. Ed. by Barbara Burn. 200p. 1995. lib. bdg. 60.00 (*0-226-08116-8*) U Ch Pr.

Metropolitan Museum Journal Vol. 32: Metropolitan Museum of Art. Ed. by Barbara Burn. 200p. 1998. lib. bdg. 70.00 (*0-226-52128-1*) U Ch Pr.

Metropolitan Museum Journal 15. Metropolitan Museum Art Staff. 1985. 35.00 (*0-226-52112-5*) U Ch Pr.

Metropolitan Museum Journal 14. Metropolitan Museum Art Staff. 1985. 35.00 (*0-226-52111-7*) U Ch Pr.

Metropolitan Museum Journal 1989. Metropolitan Museum Staff. 1989. lib. bdg. 75.00 (*0-226-52121-4*) U Ch Pr.

Metropolitan Museum Journal, (1991) Vol. 27: Essays in Memory of Guy C. Bauman. Ed. by Barbara Burn. (Illus.). 192p. 1992. lib. bdg. 60.00 (*0-226-52124-9*) U Ch Pr.

Metropolitan Museum Journal 16. Metropolitan Museum Art Staff. 1986. 35.00 (*0-226-52113-3*) U Ch Pr.

Metropolitan Museum Journal 13. Metropolitan Museum Art Staff. 1985. 35.00 (*0-226-52110-9*) U Ch Pr.

Metropolitan Museum Journal 1991, Vol. 26. (Illus.). 274p. 1991. lib. bdg. 60.00 (*0-226-52123-0*) U Ch Pr.

Metropolitan Museum Journal 1993, Vols. 1-30. Metropolitan Museum of Art Staff. Ed. by Barbara Burn. (Illus.). 1993. lib. bdg. 60.00 (*0-226-52125-7*) U Ch Pr.

Metropolitan Museum of Art. H. Hibbard. 1986. 24.95 (*0-685-43723-X*, 612011) Random Hse Value.

Metropolitan Museum of Art: Hearts & Flowers Stamps with Book. Metropolitan Museum of Art Staff. 1998. text 14.99 (*0-670-87457-4*, PuffinBks) Peng Put Young Read.

Metropolitan Museum of Art: Masterworks from the Collection, 1. Harry & Abrams Inc. Staff. 1998. 39.95 (*0-8109-5154-1*, Pub. by Abrams) Time Warner.

Metropolitan Museum of Art Guide. Ed. by Philippe De Montebello. LC 94-9094. 1994. write for info. (*0-87099-711-4*) Metro Mus Art.

Metropolitan Museum of Art Guide. 2nd ed. Selected by Philippe De Montebello. (Illus.). 470p. 1995. 19.95 (*0-8109-6486-4*, Pub. by Abrams) Time Warner.

Metropolitan Museum of Art Guide. 2nd ed. Ed. by Philippe De Montebello & Curatorial Staff. LC 94-9094. (Illus.). 470p. 1994. pap. 12.95 (*0-87099-710-6*) Metro Mus Art.

Metropolitan Museum of Art Guide. 3rd rev. ed. Ed. by Kathleen Howard. LC 83-13097. 448p. (Orig.). 1983. 19.00 (*0-685-42700-5*) Metro Mus Art.

Metropolitan Opera: Stories of the Great Operas, 002. John Freeman. 512p. 1996. 35.00 (*0-393-04051-8*) Norton.

Metropolitan Opera (1883-1939) Irving Kolodin. 646p. 1993. reprint ed. lib. bdg. 109.00 (*0-7812-5276-8*) Rprt Serv.

Metropolitan Opera Guide to Opera on Video. Ed. by Paul Gruber. LC 97-5009. 500p. 1997. 35.00 (*0-393-04536-6*) Norton.

Metropolitan Opera Guide to Recorded Opera. Ed. by Paul Gruber. 550p. 1993. 35.00 (*0-393-03444-5*) Norton.

Metropolitan Opera Guide to Recorded Opera: The Metropolitan Opera Stories of the Great Operas. Paul Gruber & John Freeman. 1993. 59.95 (*0-393-03611-1*) Norton.

Metropolitan Opera on Record: A Discography of the Commercial Recordings, 9. Compiled by Frederick P. Fellers. LC 83-22587. (Discographies Ser.: No. 9). 101p. 1984. lib. bdg. 49.95 (*0-313-23952-5*, FMO/, Greenwood Pr) Greenwood.

Metropolitan Opera Stories of the Great Operas, 2 vols. John Freeman. 1080p. 1997. 75.00 (*0-393-04548-X*) Norton.

Metropolitan Opera Stories of the Great Operas, Vol. 1. John W. Freeman. LC 84-8030. 565p. 1984. 29.95 (*0-393-01888-1*) Norton.

Metropolitan Operas by Joe Pintauro: 27 Short Plays. Joseph Pintauro. LC 97-162422. 1996. pap. 9.75 (*0-8222-1508-X*) Dramatists Play.

Metropolitan Organising Capacity: Experiences with Organising Major Projects in European Cities. Leo Van Den Berg et al. LC 97-73460. 304p. 1997. text 73.95 (*1-85972-684-4*, Pub. by Ashgate Pub) Ashgate Pub Co.

Metropolitan Plan Making. Boyce et al. (Monographs: No. 4). 1970. 25.00 (*1-55869-075-1*) Regional Sci Res Inst.

Metropolitan Police Manuals, 1871-1913: Rules & Regulations for the Government of the Richmond County Police Force, of the State of New York. New York, 1871. Ed. by Richard C. Wade. Incl. Patrolman's Manual (Philadelphia), 1913. LC 73-11934. 1974. LC 73-11934. (Metropolitan America Ser.). 330p. 1974. reprint ed. 25.95 (*0-405-05403-3*) Ayer.

Metropolitan Political Structure: Intergovernmental Relations & Political Integration in the Quad-Cities. H. Paul Friesema. LC 73-147925. 176p. reprint ed. pap. 54.60 (*0-608-17460-2*, 202994100066) Bks Demand.

***Metropolitan Poor: Semifactual Accounts, 1795-1910, 6 vols.** John Marriott & Masaie Matsumura. LC 99-52651. 2536p. 1999. 795.00 (*1-85196-524-6*, Pub. by Pickering & Chatto) Ashgate Pub Co.

Metropolitan Public Library Users. Mary Lee Bundy. 1968. pap. 3.50 (*0-911808-03-5*) U of Md Lib Serv.

***Metropolitan Puget Sound; Street Guide & Directory, 2000 ed., Vol. 1.** Thomas Brothers Maps Staff. 1999. pap. (*1-58174-209-6*); pap. (*1-58174-210-X*) Thomas Bros Maps.

Metropolitan Reading, Pennsylvania. rev. ed. Gulf Publishing Staff. 3.95 (*0-88719-029-4*) Marshall Penn-York Co Inc.

Metropolitan Reorganization: A Response to Urban Fragmentation. Roger K. Hedrick. LC 93-17561. 45p. 1993. pap. 10.00 (*0-86602-291-0*, Sage Prdcls Pr) Sage.

Metropolitan Slave Anthology II. Jeb. (Illus.). 186p. (Orig.). 1996. pap. 16.95 (*0-9631226-0-6*) Selective Pub.

Metropolitan Story. Patrick R. Foster. LC 96-76688. 208p. 1996. 24.95 (*0-87341-459-4*) Krause Pubns.

Metropolitan Tabernacle: Its History & Work & Spurgeon's Jubilee Services. Charles H. Spurgeon. 168p. 1990. reprint ed. pap. 7.00 (*1-56186-220-7*) Pilgrim Pubns.

Metropolitan Tabernacle Pulpit, Vol. 38. Charles H. Spurgeon. 640p. 1991. text 27.99 (*0-85151-611-4*) Banner of Truth.

Metropolitan Tabernacle Pulpit: Sermons Preached by C. H. Spurgeon, 1890-1917, 57 vols., Set, Vols. 7-63. Charles H. Spurgeon. Incl. Vol. 36, 1890. 708p. 1975. reprint ed. 25.00 (*1-56186-036-0*); Vol. 37. 1891. 660p. 1975. reprint ed. 25.00 (*1-56186-037-9*); Vol. 38, 1892. 624p. 1975. reprint ed. 25.00 (*1-56186-038-7*); Vol. 39, 1893. 636p. 1975. reprint ed. 25.00 (*1-56186-039-5*); Vol. 40, 1894. 624p. 1975. reprint ed. 25.00 (*1-56186-040-9*); Vol. 41, 1895. 624p. 1976. reprint ed. 25.00 (*1-56186-041-7*); Vol. 42, 1896. 624p. 1976. reprint ed. 25.00 (*1-56186-042-5*); Vol. 43, 1897. 624p. 1976. reprint ed. 25.00 (*1-56186-043-3*); Vol. 44, 1898. 624p. 1976. reprint ed. 25.00 (*1-56186-044-1*); Vol. 45, 1899. 636p. 1976. reprint ed. 25.00 (*1-56186-045-X*); Vol. 46, 1900. 624p. 1977. reprint ed. 25.00 (*1-56186-046-8*); Vol. 47, 1901. 624p. 1977. reprint ed. 25.00 (*1-56186-047-6*); Vol. 48, 1902. 660p. 1977. reprint ed. 25.00 (*1-56186-048-4*); Vol. 49, 1903. 660p. 1978. reprint ed. 25.00 (*1-56186-049-2*); Vol. 50, 1904. 624p. 1978. reprint ed. 25.00 (*1-56186-050-6*); Vol. 51, 1905. 624p. 1978. reprint ed. 25.00 (*1-56186-051-4*); Vol. 52, 1906. 636p. 1978. reprint ed. 25.00 (*1-56186-052-2*); Vol. 53, 1907. 624p. 1978. reprint ed. 25.00 (*1-56186-053-0*); Vol. 54, 1908. 624p. 1979. reprint ed. 25.00 (*1-56186-054-9*); Vol. 55, 1909. 636p. 1979. reprint ed. 25.00 (*1-56186-055-7*); Vol. 56, 1910. 636p. 1979. reprint ed. 25.00 (*1-56186-056-5*); Vol. 57, 1911. 624p. 1979. reprint ed. 25.00 (*1-56186-057-3*); Vol. 58, 1912. 624p. 1980. reprint ed. 25.00 (*1-56186-058-1*); Vol. 59, 1913. 624p. 1980. reprint ed. 25.00 (*1-56186-059-X*); Vol. 60, 1914. 636p. 1980. reprint ed. 25.00 (*1-56186-060-3*); Vol. 61, 1915. 624p. 1980. reprint ed. 25.00 (*1-56186-061-1*); Vols. 62-63, 1916-1917. 828p. 1980. reprint ed. 25.00 (*1-56186-062-X*); Vol. 7, 1861. 25.00 (*1-56186-007-7*); Vol. 8, 1862. 25.00 (*1-56186-008-5*); Vol. 9, 1863. 25.00 (*1-56186-009-3*); Vol. 10, 1864. 25.00 (*1-56186-010-7*); Vol. 11, 1865. 25.00 (*1-56186-011-5*); Vol. 12, 1866. 25.00 (*1-56186-012-3*); Vol. 13, 1867. 25.00 (*1-56186-013-1*); Vol. 14, 1868. 25.00 (*1-56186-014-X*); Vol. 15, 1869. 25.00 (*1-56186-015-8*); Vol. 16, 1870. 25.00 (*1-56186-016-6*); Vol. 17, 1871. 25.00 (*1-56186-017-4*); Vol. 18, 1872. 25.00 (*1-56186-018-2*); Vol. 19, 1873. 25.00 (*1-56186-019-0*); Vol. 20, 1874. 25.00 (*1-56186-020-4*); Vol. 21, 1875. 25.00 (*1-56186-021-2*); Vol. 22, 1876. 25.00 (*1-56186-022-0*); Vol. 23, 1877. 25.00 (*1-56186-023-9*); Vol. 24, 1878. 25.00 (*1-56186-024-7*); Vol. 25, 1879. 25.00 (*1-56186-025-5*); Vol. 26, 1880. 25.00 (*1-56186-026-3*); Vol. 27, 1881. 25.00 (*1-56186-027-1*); Vol. 28, 1882. 25.00 (*1-56186-028-X*); Vol. 29, 1883. 25.00 (*1-56186-029-8*); Vol. 31, 1885. 25.00 (*1-56186-031-X*); Vol. 32, 1886. 25.00 (*1-56186-032-8*); Vol. 33, 1887. 25.00 (*1-56186-033-6*); Vol. 34, 1888. 25.00 (*1-56186-034-4*); Vol. 35, 1889. 25.00 (*1-56186-035-2*); Vol. 30, 1884. 25.00 (*1-56186-030-1*); reprint ed. 1400.00 (*1-56186-006-9*) Pilgrim Pubns.

Metropolitan Transportation Planning. 2nd ed. John W. Dickey et al. 607p. 1983. pap. 75.00 (*0-89116-922-9*) Taylor & Francis.

Metropolitan Transportation Problem. rev. ed. Wilfred Owen. LC 66-21151. 280p. reprint ed. pap. 86.80 (*0-608-12463-X*, 202539800043) Bks Demand.

Metropolitan Universities: An Emerging Model in American Higher Education. Ed. by Daniel M. Johnson & David A. Bell. LC 94-47375. 360p. 1995. pap. 18.95 (*0-929398-93-9*) UNTX Pr.

Metropolitan Visitations. Peter Van Oort Keers. LC 96-90507. 1997. 15.95 (*0-533-12079-9*) Vantage.

Metropolitan Washington D.C. Annual Guides for the Arts 1998-1999, 1. Annual Guides for the Arts Staff. 1999. pap. text 9.95 (*0-9668970-0-5*) Annual Guides Arts.

Metropolitan Washington Preschool & Daycare Guidebook: A Descriptive Guide to Preschool & Daycare Programs in Washington, Maryland & Virginia. 5th ed. Merry Cavanaugh. (Illus.). 208p. 1998. pap. text 12.95 (*0-9614212-4-X*) Cavanaugh.

Metropolitan Water Management. J. G. Milliken & G. Taylor. (Water Resources Monograph Ser.: Vol. 6). 180p. 1981. 10.00 (*0-87590-307-X*) Am Geophysical.

Metropolitan Wichita: Past, Present, & Future. Ed. by Glenn W. Miller & Jimmy M. Skaggs. LC 77-16690. x, 194p. 1978. pap. 12.95 (*0-7006-0169-4*) U Pr of KS.

Metropolitan Winnipeg: Politics & Reform of Local Government. Meyer Brownstone & T. J. Plunkett. LC 81-19658. (Publication of the Franklin K. Lane Memorial Fund, Institute of Governmental Studies, University of California, Berkeley). (Illus.). 262p. reprint ed. pap. 81.30 (*0-608-20127-8*, 207139900011) Bks Demand.

***Metropolitan Wolid Waste Management Policy Plan: 1997-2017 (Minnesota)** (Illus.). 120p. 2000. reprint ed. pap. text 30.00 (*0-7881-8652-3*) DIANE Pub.

Metropolitane Transformation Durch Urbane Regime: Berlin-Brandenburg Auf Dem Weg Zu Regionaler Handlungsfahigkeit. Heinz Kleger. (Europaische Urbanitat-Politik der Stadte Ser.). (GER.). 208p. 1996. text 37.00 (*90-5708-021-4*); pap. text 16.00 (*90-5708-022-2*) Gordon & Breach.

Metropolitanization & Public Services: Papers. John G. Wofford et al. LC 74-186472. (Governance of Metropolitan Regions Ser.: No. 3). 77p. reprint ed. pap. 30.00 (*0-7837-3043-8*, 204288200006) Bks Demand.

Metropolitics: A Regional Agenda for Community & Stability. Myron W. Orfield. LC 96-45202. (Illus.). 224p. 1998. pap. 18.95 (*0-8157-6639-4*); text 42.95 (*0-8157-6640-8*) Brookings.

Metroscapes: The Minneapolis Gateway Photographs of Jerome Liebling & Robert Wilcox: Suburban Landscapes of the Twin Cities & Beyond. Robert B. Silberman et al. LC 98-17807. (Illus.). 52p. 1998. pap. 17.00 (*1-885116-06-3*) Weisman Art.

Metrowerks CodeWarrior Programming for the Mac. Dan P. Sydow. LC 95-17269. 400p. 1995. pap. 39.95 incl. cd-rom (*1-55851-435-X*, M&T Bks) IDG Bks.

Metrowerks Codewarrior Programming for Windows. Dan P. Sydow. 1997. pap. text 39.95 (*1-55851-557-7*) Macmillan Tech.

Metrowest, Time, Place & Possibility. Paul Lingard et al. LC 97-16065. 128p. 1997. 39.00 (*1-885352-62-X*) Community Comm.

***Mets.** Matt Silverman. (Total Baseball Companions Ser.). 96p. 2000. mass mkt. 2.50 (*1-892129-68-X*) Total Sprts.

Metsamor (Armenie): La Necropole: Les Tombes Du Bronze Moyen et Recent. E. Khanzadian. (Hors Serie Ser.: Vol. 1). xi, 110p. 1995. 115.00 (*0-614-96339-7*, Pub. by Recherches et Pubns); pap. 90.00 (*0-614-96340-0*, Pub. by Recherches et Pubns) Eisenbrauns.

Metsudah Chumash-Rashi on Bereishis. Avrohom Davis & Avrohom Kleinkaufman. Date not set. 23.95 (*0-88125-389-8*) Ktav.

Metsudah Chumash-Rashi on Devarim Deutoronomy, Vol. 5. Avrohom Davis & Avrohom Kleinkaufman. 1996. 23.95 (*0-88125-529-7*) Ktav.

Metsudah Chumash-Rashi on Exodus, Vol. 2. Avrohom Davis. Date not set. 23.95 (*0-88125-414-2*) Ktav.

Metsudah Chumash-Rashi on Levitcus, Vol. 3. Avrohom Davis. Date not set. 23.95 (*0-88125-493-2*) Ktav.

Metsudah Chumash-Rashi on Numbers, Vol. 4. Avrohom Davis. 1995. 23.95 (*0-88125-514-9*) Ktav.

Metsudah Five Megillahs. Avrohom Davis. Date not set. 14.95 (*0-88125-510-6*) Ktav.

Metsudah Haggadah. Avrohom Davis. Date not set. 10.95 (*0-88125-480-0*) Ktav.

Metsudah Shabbat Siddur. Ed. by A. Davis. 1998. pap. 14.95 (*0-88125-623-4*) Ktav.

Metsudah Siddur. Avrohom Davis. 1995. pap. 10.95 (*0-88125-552-1*) Ktav.

Metsudah Tehillim. Avrohom Davis. 1995. 14.95 (*0-88125-576-9*); pap. 9.95 (*0-88125-513-0*) Ktav.

Metta: Loving Kindness in Buddhism. Sujin Boriharnwanaket. 128p. 1995. pap. 11.95 (*1-897633-14-9*, Pub. by Triple Gem) Assoc Pubs Grp.

Metta: The Philosophy & Practice of Universal Love. Acharya Buddharakkhita. 56p. 1989. 3.00 (*955-24-0036-8*, Pub. by Buddhist Pub Soc) Vipassana Res Pubns.

Metta & R. E. Olds: Love, Labors, & Lives. Patricia E. Heyden. LC 96-92096. (Illus.). 112p. 1997. text 17.95 (*0-9631348-2-5*) Stuart MI.

Metta Morpheus. Casey Cyr. (Illus.). 80p. (Orig.). 1995. pap. 7.00 (*1-885175-05-1*) Hozomeen Pr.

Mettalurgie. Guljanickij. (GER & RUS.). 960p. 1991. lib. bdg. 95.00 (*0-8288-3837-2*, F111930) Fr & Eur.

M

An Asterisk (*) at the beginning of an entry indicates that the title is appearing for the first time.

Metternich. Desmond Seward. 1999. pap. 12.00 (*0-14-011782-2*) Viking Penguin.

Metternich & the German Question: States' Rights & Federal Duties, 1820-1834. Robert D. Billinger. LC 90-50002. 1991. 40.00 (*0-87413-407-2*) U Delaware Pr.

Metternich's German Policy Vol. 2: The Congress of Vienna, 1814-1815. Enno E. Kraehe. LC 63-9994. 458p. 1983. reprint ed. pap. 142.00 (*0-608-04650-7*, 206533600002) Bks Demand.

Mettlach Book. 3rd rev. ed. Gary Kirsner. (Illus.). 1994. 35.00 (*0-9614130-6-9*) Glentiques.

Mettle. Kimberly Lyons. (Illus.). 45p. 1997. 200.00 (*1-887123-10-5*) Granary Bks.

Mettle of the Pasture. James L. Allen. LC 74-94468. reprint ed. 31.50 (*0-404-00328-1*) AMS Pr.

Mettle of the Pasture. James L. Allen. LC 03-15441. 1969. reprint ed. 13.00 (*0-403-00137-4*) Scholarly.

Mettle of the Pasture. James L. Allen. (Principle Works of James Lane Allen). 1989. reprint ed. lib. bdg. 79.00 (*0-7812-1735-0*) Rprt Serv.

Mettlesome & Meddlesome: Selections from the Collection of Robert J. Shiffler. Marcia Tucker et al. (Illus.). 104p. (Orig.). 1993. pap. 35.00 (*0-917562-65-8*) Contemp Arts.

La Mettrie: Machine a Man & Other Writings. Ann Thomson. (Cambridge Texts in the History of Philosophy Ser.). 209p. 1996. pap. text 18.95 (*0-521-47849-9*) Cambridge U Pr.

La Mettrie: Medicine, Philosophy, & Enlightenment. Kathleen Wellman. LC 91-23992. 358p. 1992. text 42.95 (*0-8223-1204-2*) Duke.

Metu Neter Vol. 1: The Great Oracle of Tehuti & the Egyptian System of Spiritual Cultivation. Ra Un Nefer Amen I. 439p. 1990. pap. 16.95 (*1-877662-03-8*) Kamit Pubns.

***Metu Neteru: Divine Words.** (Illus.). 2000. write for info. (*0-9675581-1-5*) Papyrus Pubng Inc.

***Metuchen.** Stacy Spies. LC 00-102560. (Images of America Ser.). (Illus.). 128p. 2000. pap. 18.99 (*0-7385-0433-5*) Arcadia Publng.

Metz City Plan. (Grafocarte Maps Ser.). 1992. 8.95 (*2-7416-0024-4*, 80024) Michelin.

Metz Flash Systems. Bob Shell & Heiner Hennings. Tr. by Phyllis M. Riffler-Bonham from GER. LC 95-114237. (Magic Lantern Guides Ser.). (Illus.). 176p. (Orig.). 1998. pap. 19.95 (*1-883403-04-9*, H 170, Silver Pixel Pr) Saunders Photo.

Metzgeriaceae of the Neotropics. Yukinobu Kuwahara. Ed. by S. R. Gradstein. (Bryophytorum Bibliotheca: Vol. 28). (GER., Illus.). 254p. 1986. pap. 71.00 (*3-443-62002-7*, Pub. by Gebruder Borntraeger) Balogh.

Meu Livro de Historias Biblicas. Hayes & Hook.Tr. of My Book of Bible Stories. (POR.). (J). (gr. k-6). 1979. 3.00 (*0-8297-0758-1*) Vida Pubs.

Meunier d'Angibault. George Sand. (FRE.). 336p. 1990. pap. 29.95 (*0-7859-1581-8*, 2903950393) Fr & Eur.

Meurtre d'un Etudiant. Georges Simenon. Ed. by Ernst. (FRE.). 240p. (C). 1971. pap. text 39.00 (*0-03-084993-4*) Harcourt Coll Pubs.

Meurtres pour Memoire. Didier Daeninckx. (FRE.). 215p. 1988. pap. 10.95 (*0-7859-2094-3*, 2070380491) Fr & Eur.

Meutre au Marche des Forgerons. Yachar Kemal. (Seigneurs de l'Aktchasaz Ser.: No. I). (FRE.). 761p. 1989. pap. 17.95 (*0-7859-2569-4*, 2070381293) Fr & Eur.

Mevlana Celaleddin Rumi. Nevit O. Ergin. 1998. pap. write for info. (*1-887991-05-0*); pap. write for info. (*1-887991-07-7*) Echo Pubns CA.

Mevlana Celaleddin Rumi: Divan-I Kebir. Melvana Rumi. 418p. 1997. pap. text 19.95 (*1-887991-01-8*) Echo Pubns CA.

Mevlana Celaleddin Rumi: Divan-I Kebir, Meter 2. Nevit O. Ergin. 1999. pap. text. write for info. (*1-887991-08-5*); pap. text. write for info. (*1-887991-09-3*) Echo Pubns CA.

Mevlana Celaleddin Rumi: Divan-I Kebir, Meter 2. Melvana Rumi. 418p. 1996. pap. text 19.95 (*1-887991-00-X*) Echo Pubns CA.

***Mevlevi Wird: The Prayers Recited Daily by Mevlevi Dervishes.** Ed. & Tr. by Camille Helminski from ARA. Tr. by Cuneyt Eroglu et al from ARA. LC 99-69022. 160p. 2000. 25.00 (*0-939660-91-1*) Threshold CA.

Mewin Directory of Individuals & Organizations Specializing in Water Resources in the Middle East. Ed. by Middle East Water Information Network Staff. 333p. (Orig.). 1996. pap. 27.00 (*0-9639821-2-5*) Osage.

Mews. Betty L. Wilder. LC 96-90927. 80p. (Orig.). 1997. pap. 9.00 (*1-57502-382-2*, PO1216) Morris Pubng.

***Mewtoo Strikes Back: Movie Storybook.** Golden Books Staff. (J). 1999. pap. text 5.99 (*0-307-30403-5*, Goldn Books) Gldn Bks Pub Co.

***Mewtwo Strikes Back.** Ed. by Golden Books Staff. (Illus.). (J). 1999. 2.29 (*0-307-98916-X*, Goldn Books) Gldn Bks Pub Co.

Mewtwo Strikes Back. Scholastic, Inc. Staff. (Pokemon Ser.). (Illus.). 109p. (gr. 3-7). 1999. mass mkt. 4.99 (*0-439-13741-1*) Scholastic Inc.

Mewu Kansu: A Tibetan Tribe of Kapau. rev. ed. Hans Stuebel. Tr. by Frieda Schutze from GER. LC 58-14790. (Behavior Science Translations Ser.). 90p. reprint ed. pap. 30.00 (*0-608-30341-0*, 200464600045) Bks Demand.

Mexamerica, Dos Paises un Futuro. Lester Langley. (SPA.). pap. 12.99 (*968-16-4288-0*, Pub. by Fondo) Continental Bk.

***Mexican.** Ed. by Lorenz Books Staff. (Illus.). 2000. pap. 9.95 (*0-7548-0107-1*, Lorenz Bks) Anness Pub.

***Mexican.** large type ed. Harold Lamb. 264p. 1999. pap. 18.99 (*0-7089-5619-X*, Linford) Ulverscroft.

Mexican Accounts of the Battle of the Alamo: A Collection & Critical Analysis. Roger Borroel. LC 98-60887. (Illus.). 143p. 1998. pap. 12.99 (*1-928792-00-6*) LaVillita Pubns.

Mexican Adventure. Daniel Dawson. 1976. lib. bdg. 59.95 (*0-8490-2232-0*) Gordon Pr.

Mexican Adventure. Daniel Dawson. (Select Bibliographies Reprint Ser.). 1977. reprint ed. 29.95 (*0-8369-6682-1*) Ayer.

Mexican Adventure, 1861-67. Rene Chartrand. (Men-at-Arms Ser.: No. 272). (Illus.). 48p. 1994. pap. 11.95 (*1-85532-430-X*, 9244, Pub. by Ospry) Stackpole.

Mexican Agrarian Revolution. Frank Tannenbaum. (Brookings Institution Reprint Ser.). (Illus.). 543p. reprint ed. pap. 9.95 (*0-89197-845-3*); reprint ed. lib. bdg. 35.00 (*0-697-00172-5*) Irvington.

Mexican Agriculture, 1521-1630: Transformation of the Mode of Production. Andre G. Frank. LC 78-6201. (Studies in Modern Capitalism). 105p. reprint ed. pap. 30.00 (*0-608-15722-8*, 2031653) Bks Demand.

Mexican American, 21 vols., Set. Ed. by Carlos E. Cortes. 1974. 623.00 (*0-405-05670-2*) Ayer.

Mexican American: A Critical Guide to Research Aids. Barbara J. Robinson & J. Cordell Robinson. Ed. by Robert D. Stueart. LC 76-5643. (Foundations in Library & Information Science: Vol. 1). 287p. 1980. 78.50 (*0-89232-006-0*) Jai Pr.

Mexican American & the Law. Ed. by Carlos E. Cortes. LC 73-14207. 1977. reprint ed. 26.95 (*0-405-05681-8*) Ayer.

Mexican-American Answer Book. Ed. by Reed Ueda & Sandra Stotsky. (Ethnic Answer Bks.). (Illus.). 136p. (YA). (gr. 5 up). 1999. pap. 8.95 (*0-7910-4887-X*); lib. bdg. 17.95 (*0-7910-4886-1*) Chelsea Hse.

Mexican American Art. (Multicultural Art Print Series: No. II). (Illus.). 5p. 1991. teacher ed. 40.00 (*1-56290-061-7*, 6016) Crystal.

Mexican-American Authors. Americo Paredes. Ed. by William Adams. (Multi-Ethnic Literature Ser.). (YA). (gr. 9-12). 1976. teacher ed. 8.24 (*0-685-02295-1*) HM.

Mexican American Bibliographies. Ed. by Carlos E. Cortes. LC 73-14421. (Mexican American Ser.). 1975. reprint ed. 29.95 (*0-405-05682-6*) Ayer.

Mexican American Biographies: A Historical Dictionary, 1836-1987. Matt S. Meier. LC 87-12025. 279p. 1988. lib. bdg. 55.00 (*0-313-24521-5*, MMX/, Greenwood Pr) Greenwood.

Mexican-American Border Region: Issues & Trends. Raul A. Fernandez. LC 89-40018. 147p. (C). 1990. pap. text 11.50 (*0-268-01377-2*) U of Notre Dame Pr.

Mexican American Education Study, 5 vols. U. S. Commission on Civil Rights Staff. Ed. by Francesco Cordasco. LC 77-90561. (Bilingual-Bicultural Education in the U. S. Ser.). 1978. reprint ed. lib. bdg. 41.95 (*0-405-11100-2*) Ayer.

Mexican-American Experience. Elizabeth C. Martinez. (Coming to America Ser.). (Illus.). 64p. (J). (gr. 4-6). 1995. lib. bdg. 22.40 (*1-56294-515-7*) Millbrook Pr.

Mexican American Family: Tradition & Change. Norma Williams. LC 89-82581. 184p. (Orig.). 1990. text 36.95 (*0-930390-26-1*); pap. text 16.95 (*0-930390-25-3*) Gen Hall.

Mexican American Family Album. Dorothy Hoobler & Thomas Hoobler. (American Family Albums Ser.). (Illus.). 128p. (J). (ps-12). 1994. 19.95 (*0-19-509459-X*) OUP.

Mexican American Family Album. Dorothy Hoobler & Thomas Hoobler. (American Family Albums Ser.). (Illus.). 128p. (J). 1998. reprint ed. pap. 12.95 (*0-19-512426-X*) OUP.

Mexican-American Farm Workers: The California Agricultural Industry. Juan L. Gonzales, Jr. LC 84-26401. 240p. 1985. 55.00 (*0-275-90108-4*, C0108, Praeger Pubs) Greenwood.

Mexican American Fertility Patterns. Frank D. Bean & Gray Swicegood. (Mexican American Monographs: No. 10). 192p. 1985. text 20.00 (*0-292-75087-0*) U of Tex Pr.

Mexican-American Folklore. John O. West. (American Folklore Ser.). 314p. (Orig.). 1988. pap. 17.95 (*0-87483-059-1*) August Hse.

Mexican American Food Practices, Customs, & Holidays. Diabetes Care & Education Dietetic Practice Group. (Ethnic & Regional Food Practices Ser.). 1989. ring bd. 10.00 (*0-88091-048-8*, 0865) Am Dietetic Assn.

Mexican-American Food Practices, Customs, & Holidays. 2nd ed. Susan J. Algert et al. LC 98-20449. (Ethnic & Regional Food Practices Ser.). 1998. 10.00 (*0-88091-164-6*) Am Dietetic Assn.

Mexican American Heritage with Writing Exercises. 2nd rev. ed. Carlos M. Jimenez. LC 94-590. (Illus.). 333p. 1997. pap. text 39.95 (*0-89229-036-6*) TQS Pubns.

Mexican American Labor. Juan Gomez-Quinones. LC 93-48898. 462p. 1994. pap. 25.00 (*0-8263-1526-7*) U of NM Pr.

Mexican American Labor: 1790-1990. Juan Gomez-Quinones. LC 93-48898. 462p. 1994. 80.00 (*0-8263-1516-X*) U of NM Pr.

Mexican American Literature. Tatum. 1990. pap., teacher ed. 15.50 (*0-15-347500-5*) Holt R&W.

Mexican American Literature. C. Tatum. 1990. 28.25 (*0-15-347499-8*) Harcourt Schl Pubs.

Mexican American Literature: A Preliminary Bibliography of Literary Criticism. Mike Anzaldua. (Latin American Curriculum Units for Junior & Community Colleges Ser.). vii, 29p. (Orig.). (C). 1980. pap. text 3.95 (*0-86728-004-2*) U TX Inst Lat Am Stud.

Mexican American Orquesta: Music, Culture & the Dialectic of Conflict. Manuel Pena. LC 99-6098. 384p. 1999. pap. 19.95 (*0-292-76587-8*) U of Tex Pr.

***Mexican American Orquesta: Music, Culture & the Dialectic of Conflict.** Manuel Pena. LC 99-6098. 384p. 1999. 45.00 (*0-292-76586-X*) U of Tex Pr.

Mexican-American Schoolchildren: A Neo-Piagetian Analysis. Edward A. DeAvila et al. LC 76-11847. 97p. reprint ed. pap. 30.10 (*0-7837-6314-X*, 204602900010) Bks Demand.

Mexican American Students. Richard Baker. LC 98-75415. 180p. (C). 1999. per. 31.95 (*0-7872-5623-4*, 41562301) Kendall-Hunt.

Mexican American Theatre: Legacy & Reality. Nicolas Kanellos. Ed. by Yvette E. Miller. LC 86-15330. 128p. 1987. pap. 10.00 (*0-935480-22-6*) Lat Am Lit Rev Pr.

Mexican American Theatre: Then & Now. Nicolas Kanellos. LC 83-70675. (Illus.). 120p. (C). 1983. pap. 11.00 (*0-934770-22-0*, Pub. by Arte Publico) Empire Pub Srvs.

***Mexican American Voices.** Ed. by Steven Mintz. 272p. (C). 2000. pap. text 14.50 (*1-881089-44-4*) Brandywine Press.

Mexican-American War. Compiled by Milton Meltzer. 39.00 (*1-56696-091-6*) Jackdaw.

Mexican-American War. Don Nardo. LC 99-14263. (World History Ser.). (Illus.). 128p. (YA). (gr. 4-12). 1999. lib. bdg. 23.70 (*1-56006-495-1*) Lucent Bks.

Mexican-American War: An Annotated Bibliography. Compiled by Norman E. Tutorow. LC 80-1789. (Illus.). 427p. 1981. lib. bdg. 99.50 (*0-313-22181-2*, TMA/, Greenwood Pr) Greenwood.

Mexican-American War, 1846-48. Ron Field. LC 96-40466. (History of Uniforms Ser.). (Illus.). 144p. 1997. 29.95 (*1-85753-210-4*, Pub. by Brasseys) Brasseys.

Mexican-American War of 1846-1848: A Bibliography of the Holdings of the Libraries, the University of Texas at Arlington. Ed. by Katherine R. Goodwin. LC 95-1668. (Special Collections Publication of the University of Texas at Arlington Ser.: No. 2). (Illus.). 720p. 1995. 75.00 (*0-89096-587-0*) Tex A&M Univ Pr.

Mexican-American War of Independence. Philip R. Katcher. (Men-at-Arms Ser.: No. 56). (Illus.). 48p. 1989. pap. 11.95 (*0-85045-253-8*, 9165) Stackpole.

Mexican American Women: Changing Images, Vol. 5. Juan R. Garcia. (Perspectives in Mexican American Studies). 1996. pap. text 15.00 (*0-939363-05-4*) U of Ariz Pr.

Mexican American Women Activists: Identity & Resistance in Two Los Angeles Communities. Mary Pardo. LC 97-13960. 256p. 1998. 59.95 (*1-56639-572-0*) Temple U Pr.

Mexican American Women in Houston: Work, Family, & Community, 1990-1940. Emma Perez. 67p. write for info. (*0-614-06975-0*) Univ Houston Mex Amer.

Mexican-American Workers of San Antonio, Texas. Robert G. Landolt. Ed. by Carlos E. Cortes. LC 76-1291. (Chicano Heritage Ser.). (Illus.). 1977. 33.95 (*0-405-09509-0*) Ayer.

Mexican American Youth Organization: Avant-Garde of the Chicano Movement in Texas. Armando Navarro. (Illus.). (C). 1995. pap. 16.95 (*0-292-75557-0*); text 40.00 (*0-292-75556-2*) U of Tex Pr.

Mexican Americans. Alexandra Bandon. LC 92-41001. (Footsteps to America Ser.). (Illus.). 112p. (YA). (gr. 6 up). 1993. lib. bdg. 14.95 (*0-02-768142-4*, New Dscvry Bks) Silver Burdett Pr.

Mexican Americans. Julie Catalano. LC 95-14181. (Immigrant Experience Ser.). 120p. (YA). (gr. 5 up). 1995. lib. bdg. 19.95 (*0-7910-3359-7*) Chelsea Hse.

Mexican Americans. Julie Catalano. LC 95-14181. (Immigrant Experience Ser.). 120p. (YA). (gr. 5 up). 1995. pap. 9.95 (*0-7910-3381-3*) Chelsea Hse.

Mexican Americans. Del. 1997. pap. 20.00 (*0-8057-4587-4*) Macmillan.

Mexican Americans. Paula Lannert. (American Voices Ser.). 112p. (J). 1991. lib. bdg. 18.95 (*0-86593-139-9*); lib. bdg. 18.60 (*0-685-59187-5*) Rourke Corp.

Mexican Americans: Are They an Ambivalent Minority? Ed. by Lisa Magana. LC 95-117322. 138p. (YA). (gr. 12 up). 1994. pap. text 15.00 (*1-57240-000-5*) T Rivera Ctr.

Mexican Americans: Leadership, Ideology, & Identity, 1930-1960. Mario T. Garcia. (Illus.). 384p. (C). 1991. reprint ed. pap. 20.00 (*0-300-04984-6*) Yale U Pr.

Mexican Americans: Political Power, Influence, or Resource. Ed. by Frank L. Baird. (Graduate Studies: No. 14). (Illus.). 108p. (Orig.). 1977. pap. 7.00 (*0-89672-024-1*) Tex Tech Univ Pr.

Mexican Americans: The Ambivalent Minority. Peter Skerry. (Illus.). 480p. 1995. pap. 15.95 (*0-674-57262-9*, SKEMEX) HUP.

Mexican Americans, American Mexicans: From Conquistadors to Chicanos. rev. ed. Matt S. Meier & Feliciano Ribera. LC 93-3385. (American Century Ser.). 288p. 1994. pap. 13.00 (*0-8090-1559-5*) Hill & Wang.

Mexican Americans & Educational Change. Ed. by Alfredo Castaneda et al. LC 73-14196. (Mexican American Ser.). 424p. 1976. 31.95 (*0-405-05671-0*) Ayer.

Mexican Americans & the Catholic Church, 1900-1965. Ed. by Jay P. Dolan & Gilberto Hinojosa. LC 94-14003. 392p. 1997. pap. 16.00 (*0-268-01428-0*) U of Notre Dame Pr.

Mexican Americans & the Mass Media. Bradley S. Greenberg et al. LC 82-11658. (Communication & Information Science Ser.). 304p. (C). 1983. text 78.50 (*0-89391-126-7*) Ablx Pub.

Mexican Americans in Texas: A Brief History. 2nd ed. Arnoldo De Leon. LC 98-54219. (Illus.). 200p. (C). 1999. pap. text 15.95 (*0-88295-948-4*) Harlan Davidson.

***Mexican Americans in Texas History.** Emilio Zamora. LC 99-50292. 2000. pap. text 15.95 (*0-87611-174-6*) Tex St Hist Assn.

Mexican Americans in the 1900s: Politics, Policies, & Perceptions. Garcia. (Perspectives in Mexican American Studies: No. 6). 228p. 1997. pap. 15.00 (*0-939363-06-2*) U of AZ Mex Am.

Mexican Americans in Urban Society: A Selected Bibliography. Compiled by Albert Camarillo. LC 86-22741. 296p. 1990. pap. 29.95 (*0-915745-12-7*) Floricanto Pr.

Mexican Anarchism after the Revolution. Donald C. Hodges. LC 04-20488. 256p. (C). 1995. pap. 17.95 (*0-292-73097-7*); text 40.00 (*0-292-73093-4*) U of Tex Pr.

Mexican & American Responses to the International Narcotics Threat. Ed. by Jesse Helms. (Illus.). 142p. 1999. pap. text 35.00 (*0-7881-8008-8*) DIANE Pub.

Mexican & Central American Antiquities, Calendar Systems & History. Charles Bowditch. (Bureau of American Ethnology Bulletins Ser.). 682p. 1995. lib. bdg. 149.00 (*0-7812-4028-X*) Rprt Serv.

Mexican & Mexican-American Agricultural Labor in the United States: An International Bibliography. Martin H. Sable. LC 85-27346. (Supplement to Behavioral & Social Sciences Librarian: Supp. No. 1). 429p. 1987. text 13.95 (*0-86656-542-6*) Haworth Pr.

Mexican & Mexican American Experience in the 19th Century. Ed. by Jaime E. Rodriguez. LC 88-64099. 136p. 1989. 20.00 (*0-916950-93-X*); pap. 12.00 (*0-916950-94-8*) Biling Rev-Pr.

Mexican & Native American Dances in Christian Worship & Education. Martha A. Kirk. Ed. by Doug Adams. (Orig.). 1981. pap. 3.00 (*0-941500-22-5*) Sharing Co.

Mexican & Peruvian Communities see Contemporary Change in Traditional Societies

Mexican & South American Poems. Ed. & Tr. by Ernest S. Green. 400p. 1974. lib. bdg. 250.00 (*0-8490-0612-0*) Gordon Pr.

Mexican & Spanish Family Research. J. Konrad. 70p. 1987. pap. 10.00 (*0-685-20963-6*, Heritge House) Ye Olde Genealogie Shoppe.

Mexican & Spanish Family Research. rev. ed. J. Konrad. (Illus.). 70p. 1987. pap. 10.00 (*1-878311-07-7*, Heritge House) Ye Olde Genealogie Shoppe.

***Mexican Apparel Industry Trade Directory.** 11th rev. ed. 168p. 2000. pap. 110.00 (*1-930512-04-X*) Marche Pubng.

Mexican Architecture of the Vice-Regal Period. Walter H. Kilham. 1976. lib. bdg. 59.95 (*0-8490-2233-9*) Gordon Pr.

Mexican Architecture of the Vice-Regal Period. Walter H. Kilham. LC 75-137252. reprint ed. 24.00 (*0-404-03675-9*) AMS Pr.

Mexican Art Masterpieces. Marcus B. Burke. (Illus.). 120p. 1998. 34.50 (*0-88363-598-4*) H L Levin.

Mexican-Aryan Comparative Vocabulary. T. S. Denison. (SPA.). 1976. lib. bdg. 59.95 (*0-8490-0613-9*) Gordon Pr.

Mexican Autobiography (La Autobiografia Mexicana) An Annotated Bibliography (Una Bibliografia Razonada), 13. Tr. by Josefina Cruz-Melendez. LC 88-3129. 245p. 1988. lib. bdg. 75.00 (*0-313-25945-3*, WDX/) Greenwood.

Mexican Aztec Society: A Mexican American Voluntary Association in Diachronic Perspective. Stanley A. West. Ed. by Carlos E. Cortes. LC 76-5230. (Chicano Heritage Ser.). 1977. 24.95 (*0-405-09532-5*) Ayer.

Mexican Ballads, Chicano Poems: History & Influence in Mexican-American Social Poetry. Jose E. Limon. (New Historicism: Studies in Cultural Poetics: No. 17). (C). 1992. pap. 17.95 (*0-520-07633-8*, Pub. by U CA Pr) Cal Prin Full Svc.

Mexican Banking & Investment in Transition. John A. Adams. LC 96-38333. 272p. 1997. 72.95 (*1-56720-054-0*, Quorum Bks) Greenwood.

***Mexican Birds.** Roger Tory Peterson. (Peterson Field Guides Ser.). 1999. pap. 21.00 (*0-395-97514-X*) HM.

Mexican Bone Rattles see Studies in Middle America

Mexican Border Ballads & Other Lore. Ed. by Mody C. Boatright. LC 48-7407. (Texas Folklore Society, Publication Ser.: No. 21). 151p. reprint ed. pap. 46.90 (*0-608-17197-2*, 202700300053) Bks Demand.

Mexican Border Cities: Landscape Anatomy & Place Personality. Daniel D. Arreola & James R. Curtis. LC 92-22777. (Illus.). 258p. 1993. 42.50 (*0-8165-1287-6*) U of Ariz Pr.

Mexican Border Cities: Landscape Anatomy & Place Personality. Daniel D. Arreola & James R. Curtis. LC 92-22777. (Illus.). 258p. 1994. reprint ed. pap. 18.95 (*0-8165-1441-0*) U of Ariz Pr.

Mexican Borderlands. Ed. by Felix D. Almaraz. (Illus.). 116p. 1985. pap. 15.00 (*0-89745-066-3*) Sunflower U Pr.

Mexican Breakfast Cookbook: Spicy & Sweet Morning Meals. Jacqueline H. McMahan. 170p. 1992. pap. 14.95 (*1-881656-00-4*) Olive Pr.

Mexican Brick Culture in the Building of Texas, 1800s-1980s. Scott Cook. (Illus.). 400p. 1998. 44.95 (*0-89096-792-X*) Tex A&M Univ Pr.

Mexican California: An Original Anthology. Smith et al. Ed. & Intro. by Carlos E. Cortes. LC 76-5567. (Chicano Heritage Ser.). (Illus.). 1977. 57.95 (*0-405-09538-4*) Ayer.

Mexican Catholicism in Southern California: The Importance of Popular Religiosity & Sacramental Practice in Faith Experience. Jeffrey S. Thies. LC 92-2425. (American University Studies: Theology & Religion: Ser. VII, Vol. 139). 258p. 1993. 47.95 (*0-8204-2013-1*) P Lang Pubng.

Mexican Celebrations. Maria-Garza Lubeck & Ana M. Salinas. 54p. (J). (gr. k-12). 1987. pap. text 3.95 (*0-86728-019-0*) U TX Inst Lat Am Stud.

Mexican Central & South American Art. John F. Scott. LC 97-143881. (International Encyclopedia of Art Ser.). (Illus.). 64p. 1996. 19.95 (*0-8160-3329-3*) Facts on File.

Mexican Churches. Eliot Porter & Ellen Auerbach. (Illus.). 120p. 1999. pap. 18.95 (*0-8118-2359-8*) Chronicle Bks.

M

An Asterisk (*) at the beginning of an entry indicates that the title is appearing for the first time.

Mexican Cinema. Ed. by Paulo A. Paranagua. Tr. by Ana Lopez. (Illus.). 432p. 1996. 70.00 (0-85170-515-4, Pub. by British Film Inst); pap. 29.95 (0-85170-516-2, Pub. by British Film Inst) Ind U Pr.

Mexican Cinema: Reflections of a Society. Carl J. Mora. LC 81-7507. (Illus.). 392p. 1982. pap. 16.95 (0-520-04304-9, Pub. by U CA Pr) Cal Prin Full Svc.

Mexic Cinema/Mexic Woman. Curtus et al. LC 96-10110. (Illus.). 1996. pap. 16.95 (0-8165-1637-5) U of Ariz Pr.

Mexican Cinema Mexican Woman, 1940-1950. Joanne Hershfield. LC 96-10110. 185p. 1996. 39.95 (0-8165-1636-7) U of Ariz Pr.

***Mexican Coal Mining Labor in Texas & Coahuila, 1880-1930.** Roberto R. Calderon. LC 99-34596. 1999. 39.95 (0-89096-884-5) Tex A&M Univ Pr.

Mexican Collection. Carole Curlee. (Illus.). 196p. 1993. spiral bd. 18.99 (0-9645657-1-4) Casually Catered.

Mexican Collection, 1978. Cottler H. Weathers. 163p. 1978. write for info. (0-940764-23-7) Genealog Inst.

Mexican Colonial Parish Registers, 1981, set only. David J. Robinson. 288p. 1981. 22.50 (0-940764-22-9) Genealog Inst.

Mexican Color. Elena Poniatowska. LC 98-17169. 160p. 1998. 35.00 (1-55670-835-1) Stewart Tabori & Chang.

Mexican Color. Elena Poniatowska. (SPA., Illus.). 160p. 1998. 35.00 (1-55670-856-4) Stewart Tabori & Chang.

Mexican Communism, 1968-1983: Eurocommunism in the Americas? Barry Carr. (Research Reports: No. 42). 36p. (Orig.). (C). 1985. pap. 5.00 (0-935391-41-X, RR-42) UCSD Ctr US-Mex.

Mexican Connection: Crises, Poverty & the New Emperium. 5th ed. Richard Krooth. 280p. 1999. pap. 30.00 (0-939074-18-4) Harvest Pubns.

Mexican Consuls & Labor Organizing: Imperial Politics in the American Southwest. Gilbert G. Gonzalez. LC 99-20648. 320p. 1999. pap. 19.95 (0-292-72824-7) U of Tex Pr.

***Mexican Consuls & Labor Organizing: Imperial Politics in the American Southwest.** Gilbert G. Gonzalez. LC 99-20648. 320p. 1999. 40.00 (0-292-72823-9) U of Tex Pr.

Mexican Contemporary. Herbert Ypma. (World Design Ser.). (Illus.). 160p. 1997. pap. 27.50 (1-55670-557-3) Stewart Tabori & Chang.

Mexican Contract. Allan De Serpa. LC 84-223722. 148p. 1981. pap. 5.95 (0-939460-15-7) Devyn Pr.

Mexican Cookbook. Erna Fergusson. LC 46-214. (Illus.). 120p. 1999. reprint ed. pap. 8.95 (0-8263-0035-9) U of NM Pr.

Mexican Cooking. (Mini Cook Bks.). 148p. pap. 1.95 (3-8290-0391-9, 770138) Konemann.

Mexican Cooking. Better Homes & Gardens & Carolyn B. Mitchell. LC 96-78801. (Illus.). 96p. 1997. 14.95 (0-696-20647-1) Meredith Bks.

Mexican Cooking. BHB International Staff. (Illus.). 72p. 1997. 7.95 (1-85833-676-7, Pub. by CLib Bks) Whitecap Bks.

Mexican Cooking. Judith Ferguson. 64p. 1995. write for info. (1-57215-018-1) World Pubns.

Mexican Cooking. Roger Hicks. 1995. 6.98 (0-7858-0503-6) Bk Sales Inc.

Mexican Cooking. Steven Raichlen. LC 99-12872. (High-Flavor, Low-Fat Cookbook Ser.). 272p. 1999. 29.95 (0-670-88388-3, Viking) Viking Penguin.

Mexican Cooking for Dummies. Mary S. Milliken et al. (For Dummies Ser.). (Illus.). 384p. 1999. pap. 19.99 (0-7645-5169-8, Dummies Trade Pr) IDG Bks.

Mexican Cooking Made Easy. Diane Soliz-Martese. (ENG & SPA., Illus.). 96p. 1992. pap. 15.95 (0-941676-29-3); pap. 15.95 (0-941676-32-3) Wei-Chuan Pub.

Mexican Coordination of National Public Security: A Discussion of Legal & Human Rights Issues. MN. Advocates for Human Rights Staff. 9p. (Orig.). 1994. pap. 3.00 (0-929293-22-3) MN Advocates.

Mexican Corrido: A Feminist Analysis. Maria Herrera-Sobek. LC 89-45568. (Illus.). 174p. 1990. 31.95 (0-253-32739-3) Ind U Pr.

Mexican Corrido: A Feminist Analysis. Maria Herrera-Sobek. LC 89-45568. (Illus.). 174p. 1993. pap. 17.95 (0-253-20795-9) Ind U Pr.

Mexican Country Style. Karen Witynski & Joe P. Carr. LC 97-6920. (Illus.). 160p. 1997. 39.95 (0-87905-814-5) Gibbs Smith Pub.

Mexican Crafts & Craftspeople. Marian Harvey. LC 84-63144. (Illus.). 216p. 1988. 40.00 (0-87982-512-X) Art Alliance.

Mexican Crafts & Craftspeople. Marian Harvey. LC 84-63144. (Illus.). 1988. 40.00 (0-8453-4800-0, Cornwall Bks) Assoc Univ Prs.

Mexican Cuisine see Al Mexiqui

Mexican Debt Crisis, 1982. Adhip Chaudhuri. (Pew Case Studies in International Affairs). 50p. (C). 1993. pap. text 3.50 (1-56927-204-2) Geo U Inst Dplmcy.

Mexican Delights: A Treasury of Favorite Mexican Recipes. Dorothy K. Hilburn. LC 93-72733. 120 p. 1994. 8.95 (1-879924-14-5) Camelback Design.

Mexican Democracy: A Critical View. 3rd ed. Kenneth F. Johnson. LC 84-11614. 279p. 1984. 45.00 (0-275-91197-7, C1197, Praeger Pubs) Greenwood.

Mexican Desserts & Drinks: The Sweet Side of Mexican Cooking. Socorro M. Kimble & Irma S. Noriega. LC 87-21168. (Illus.). 144p. 1987. ring bd. 6.95 (0-914846-31-0) Golden West Pub.

Mexican Devotional Retablos: From the Peters Collection at Saint Joseph's University, Philadelphia. Nancy Hamilton et al. (Illus.). 192p. 1994. 75.00 (0-916101-19-3); pap. 45.00 (0-916101-20-7) St Joseph.

Mexican Documents of the Texan Revolt, 1836. Roger Borroel. (Illus.). 30p. 1998. pap. 5.99 (1-928792-02-2) LaVillita Pubns.

Mexican Dream: or The Interrupted Thought of Amerindian Civilizations. J. M. Le Clezio. Tr. by Teresa L. Fagan. (Illus.). 232p. 1993. 22.50 (0-226-11002-8) U Ch Pr.

Mexican Earth. T. Downing. 1976. lib. bdg. 59.95 (0-8490-2234-7) Gordon Pr.

Mexican Earth. 2nd ed. Todd Downing. LC 95-39840. (American Indian Literature & Critical Studies Ser.: Vol. 20). (Illus.). 384p. (Orig.). 1996. pap. 16.95 (0-8061-2788-0) U of Okla Pr.

Mexican Economy. Ed. by George Philip. 256p. 1988. lib. bdg. 57.50 (0-415-01265-1) Routledge.

Mexican Elite Family, 1820-1980: Kinship, Class, & Culture. Larissa A. Lomnitz & Marisol Perez-Lizaur. (Illus.). 300p. 1988. pap. text 24.95 (0-691-02284-4, Pub. by Princeton U Pr) Cal Prin Full Svc.

Mexican Emigration to the United States, 1897-1931: Socio-Economic Patterns. Lawrence A. Cardoso. LC 79-20029. 215p. reprint ed. pap. 66.70 (0-7837-1904-3, 204210800001) Bks Demand.

Mexican Empire of Iturbide. Timothy E. Anna. LC 89-4944. xii, 286p. 1990. text 60.00 (0-8032-1027-2) U of Nebr Pr.

Mexican Ethnic Leadership in San Antonio, Texas. Frances J. Woods. Ed. by Carlos E. Cortes. LC 76-1623. (Chicano Heritage Ser.). 1977. reprint ed. 15.95 (0-405-09533-3) Ayer.

Mexican Experience in Arizona: An Original Anthology. George Griggs et al. Ed. & Intro. by Carlos E. Cortes. LC 76-5566. (Chicano Heritage Ser.). (Illus.). 1977. 24.95 (0-405-09539-2) Ayer.

Mexican Experience in Texas: An Original Anthology. Claudia J. Jarratt et al. Ed. & Intro. by Carlos E. Cortes. LC 76-7305. (Chicano Heritage Ser.). (Illus.). 1977. lib. bdg. 26.95 (0-405-09540-6) Ayer.

Mexican Expropriations. Joseph L. Kunz. LC 43-3233. 1974. reprint ed. pap. 25.00 (0-527-53600-8) Periodicals Srv.

Mexican Eyeless Characin Fishes, Genus Astyanax: Environment, Distribution, & Evolution. Robert W. Mitchell et al. (Special Publications: No. 12). (Illus.). 89p. (Orig.). 1977. pap. 10.00 (0-89672-038-1) Tex Tech Univ Pr.

Mexican Fairy Tales. J. H. Cornyn. 1972. 59.95 (0-8490-0614-7) Gordon Pr.

Mexican Family Favorites Cook Book. Maria T. Bermudez. LC 83-11692. 144p. 1983. ring bd. 6.95 (0-914846-17-5) Golden West Pub.

Mexican Favorites. Deirdre Fretz. 36p. (Orig.). 1992. pap. 3.25 (0-940844-44-3) Wellspring.

Mexican Favorites. Susanna Palazuelos. Ed. by Laurie Wertz. LC 93-28229. (Williams-Sonoma Kitchen Library). (Illus.). 108p. 1994. lib. bdg. write for info. (0-7835-0271-0) Time-Life.

Mexican Financial Reform & Prospects. Ed. by Robert G. Taylor. 98p. 1990. 145.00 (0-9627235-6-8) Intl Reports.

Mexican Folk Dance, Vol. III, Bk. 11. Vicki Corona. (Celebrate the Cultures Ser.). (Illus.). 22p. 1989. pap. 14.95 (1-58513-040-0) Dance Fantasy.

Mexican Folk Dances. 2nd ed. Ed. by Debbie Cavalier. (World Dance Ser.). (Illus.). 20p. (YA). 1994. pap. text 19.95 incl. cd-rom (0-89898-947-7, BMR05117) Wrner Bros.

Mexican Folk Plays. Josephina Niggli. Ed. by Frederick H. Koch. LC 76-1260. (Chicano Heritage Ser.). (Illus.). 1977. reprint ed. 23.95 (0-405-09517-1) Ayer.

Mexican Folk Pottery Tradition: Cognition & Style in Material Culture in the Valley of Puebla. Flora S. Kaplan. LC 91-46827. (Illus.). 304p. (C). 1994. 51.95 (0-8093-1730-3) S Ill U Pr.

Mexican Folk Retablos. 2nd ed. Gloria F. Giffords. LC 92-10494. (Illus.). 216p. 1992. pap. 29.95 (0-8263-1369-8) U of NM Pr.

Mexican Folk Tales. Anthony J. Campos. (J). 1977. 14.05 (0-606-04382-9, Pub. by Turtleback) Demco.

Mexican Folk Tales. Ed. by Anthony J. Campos. LC 77-10603. 136p. 1977. reprint ed. pap. 10.95 (0-8165-0560-8) U of Ariz Pr.

Mexican Folksongs see Canciones Mexicanas

Mexican Folkways. F. Toor. 1976. lib. bdg. 250.00 (0-8490-2235-5) Gordon Pr.

Mexican Food Crisis: An Analysis of the SAM. Rose J. Spalding. (Research Reports: No. 33). 44p. (Orig.). (C). 1984. ring bd. 5.00 (0-935391-32-0, RR-33) UCSD Ctr US-Mex.

Mexican Food Market. LC 99-171292. 315 p. 1997. write for info. (1-56241-442-9) FIND-SVP.

Mexican Frontier 1821-1846: The American Southwest under Mexico. David J. Weber. LC 82-8200. (Histories of the American Frontier Ser.). (Illus.). 416p. 1982. pap. 17.95 (0-8263-0603-9) U of NM Pr.

Mexican Ghost Tale of the Southwest. Alfred Avila. Ed. by Kat Avila. LC 94-6919. 172p. (YA). (gr. 6-12). 1994. pap. 9.95 (1-55885-107-0, Pinata Bks) Arte Publico.

Mexican Girl & Boy Paper Dolls. Kathy Allert. (Illus.). (J). (gr. k-3). 1992. pap. 3.50 (0-486-27229-X) Dover.

Mexican Government & Industrial Development in the Early Republic: The Banco de Avio. rev. ed. Robert A. Potash. LC 82-15969.Tr. of El/Banco de Avio de Mexico: El Fomento de la Industria 1821-1846. 264p. 1983. lib. bdg. 32.50 (0-87023-382-3) U of Mass Pr.

Mexican Government Publications. Anita M. Ker. 1976. lib. bdg. 59.95 (0-8490-0615-5) Gordon Pr.

Mexican Government Today. William P. Tucker. LC 57-5802. 496p. reprint ed. pap. 153.80 (0-608-18649-X, 205592400039) Bks Demand.

Mexican Handbook. L. Hamilton. 1976. lib. bdg. 59.95 (0-8490-2236-3) Gordon Pr.

Mexican Hat. Michael McGarrity. LC 96-35735. 304p. 1997. 22.95 (0-393-04063-1) Norton.

Mexican Hat. Michael McGarrity. (Kevin Kerney Novels Ser.). 300p. 1998. mass mkt. 6.50 (0-671-00253-8, Pocket Books) PB.

***Mexican History.** Spielvogel. 1998. pap., wbk. ed. 11.75 (0-538-42701-9) Sth-Wstrn College.

Mexican Homes of Today. Warren Shipway & Verna C. Shipway. 15p. 1990. reprint ed. 37.50 (0-8038-0157-2) Archit CT.

Mexican House: Old & New. Warren Shipway & Verna C. Shipway. 15p. 1995. reprint ed. 40.00 (0-8038-0158-0) Archit CT.

Mexican House Old & New. Verna C. Shipway. 2000. 40.00 (0-942655-12-5, Pub. by Archit CT) Natl Bk Netwk.

Mexican Illegal Alien Workers in the United States. Walter Fogel. (Monograph & Research Ser.: No. 20). 204p. 1978. 7.50 (0-89215-091-2) U Cal LA Indus Rel.

Mexican Image in Nineteenth Century Texas. Arnoldo De Leon. (Texas History Ser.). (Illus.). 45p. 1983. pap. text 9.95 (0-89641-106-0) American Pr.

Mexican Immigrant: His Life Story. Manuel Gamio. 1990. 22.95 (0-88143-111-7) Ayer.

Mexican Immigrant: His Life Story. Manuel Gamio. LC 69-18778. (American Immigration Collection. Series 1). (Illus.). 1971. reprint ed. 30.95 (0-405-00526-1) Ayer.

Mexican Immigrant: His Life Story. Manuel Gamio. LC 69-18778. 287p. 1998. reprint ed. pap. 19.95 (0-88143-202-4) Ayer.

Mexican Immigrant Cooking, 1. Gamez Family Staff. 1999. 29.95 (1-885440-50-2) First Glance.

Mexican Immigrant Students in American Schools. Alex M. Saragoza. (New Faces of Liberty Background Essays Ser.). 20p. (Orig.). 1994. pap. 5.00 (0-936434-77-5, Pub. by Zellerbach Fam Fund) Intl Spec Bk.

Mexican Immigrants & Southern California: A Summary of Current Knowledge. Intro. by Wayne A. Cornelius et al. (Research Reports: No. 36). 99p. (Orig.). (C). 1982. ring bd. 5.00 (0-935391-35-5, RR-36) UCSD Ctr US-Mex.

Mexican Immigrants in the San Francisco Bay Area: A Summary of Current Knowledge. Intro. by Wayne A. Cornelius et al. (Research Reports: No. 40). 86p. (Orig.). (C). 1982. ring bd. 5.00 (0-935391-39-8, RR-40) UCSD Ctr US-Mex.

Mexican Immigration: Changing Terms of the Debate in the United States & Mexico. Ann L. Craig. (Research Reports: No. 4). 29p. (Orig.). (C). 1981. pap. 5.00 (0-935391-03-7, RR-04) UCSD Ctr US-Mex.

Mexican Immigration to the United States. Manuel Gamio. LC 69-18777. (American Immigration Collection. Series 1). (Illus.). 1973. reprint ed. 18.95 (0-405-00525-3) Ayer.

Mexican Imperial Coinage: The Medals & Coinage. Benjamin Betts. (Illus.). 1982. reprint ed. pap. 10.00 (0-915262-75-4) S J Durst.

Mexican in the United States. Emory S. Bogardus. LC 70-129389. (American Immigration Collection. Series 2). 1974. reprint ed. 12.95 (0-405-00575-X) Ayer.

Mexican Independence Day & Cinco de Mayo. Dianne M. MacMillan. LC 96-47244. (Best Holiday Bks.). (Illus.). 48p. (J). (gr. 1-4). 1997. lib. bdg. 18.95 (0-89490-816-2) Enslow Pubs.

Mexican Indian Costumes. Donald B. Cordry. LC 68-20363. (Texas Pan American Ser.). (Illus.). 425p. reprint ed. pap. 131.80 (0-7837-0092-X, 204036700016) Bks Demand.

Mexican Indian Folk Designs: Two-Hundred Motifs from Textiles. Irmgard Weitlaner-Johnson. LC 93-48. (Pictorial Archive Ser.). 80p. 1993. pap. 6.95 (0-486-27524-8) Dover.

Mexican Indian Manuscript Painting: A Catalog of the Tulane University Collection. Martha B. Robertson. (Illus.). 20p. (Orig.). 1991. pap. 7.50 (0-87409-100-4) Tulane Univ.

Mexican Industrial Relations Viewed from the Perspective of the Mexican Labor Court. Frederic Meyers. (Monograph & Research Ser.: No. 24). 103p. 1979. 5.00 (0-89215-104-8) U Cal LA Indus Rel.

Mexican Insights: Mexican Civil Society Speaks to the United States. 50p. 1995. pap. 7.00 (0-614-25730-1) WOLA.

Mexican Interiors. Verna C. Shipway & Warren Shipway. 15p. 1991. reprint ed. 37.50 (0-8038-0159-9) Archit CT.

Mexican Jewelry. Mary L. Davis & Greta Pack. (Illus.). 278p. 1963. pap. 19.95 (0-292-75073-0) U of Tex Pr.

Mexican Journeys: Myth, Magic & Mummies. Ed. by Elsa Longhauser et al. LC 90-262265. (Illus.). 32p. 1990. pap. write for info. (1-58442-034-0) Galleries at Moore.

Mexican Kickapoo Indians. Felipe Latorre. (Illus.). 416p. 1991. pap. 11.95 (0-486-26742-3) Dover.

Mexican Kitchen Garden. John Meeker. LC 97-28458. (Illus.). 96p. 1998. pap. 6.95 (0-8362-3257-7) Andrews & McMeel.

Mexican Kitchen with Rod Santana. 288p. pap. 17.95 (0-9636763-0-X) KMBH-TV.

***Mexican Labor & World War II: Braceros in the Pacific Northwest, 1942-1947.** Erasmo Gamboa. LC 99-42805. (Illus.). 208p. 1999. pap. text 16.95 (0-295-97849-X) U of Wash Pr.

Mexican Labor in the United States. Ed. by Carlos E. Cortes. LC 73-14208. (Mexican American Ser.). (Illus.). 480p. 1976. reprint ed. 35.95 (0-405-05683-4) Ayer.

Mexican Labor in the United States, 2 vols., Set. Paul S. Taylor. LC 77-129416. (American Immigration Collection. Series @). 1970. reprint ed. 48.95 (0-405-00570-9) Ayer.

Mexican Labor in the United States, 2 vols., Vol. 1. Paul S. Taylor. LC 77-129416. (American Immigration Collectio. Series 2). 1970. reprint ed. 30.95 (0-405-00578-4) Ayer.

Mexican Labor in the United States, 2 vols., Vol. 2. Paul S. Taylor. LC 77-129416. (American Immigration Collection. Series 2). 1970. reprint ed. 30.95 (0-405-00579-2) Ayer.

Mexican Landscape Architecture - From the Street & from Within. Rosina G. Kirby. LC 72-83818. (Illus.). 167p. 1972. reprint ed. pap. 51.80 (0-608-00928-8, 206172100011) Bks Demand.

Mexican Law of Sales, a Primer. Julio Romanach, Jr. LC 97-209977. 208p. (C). 1997. pap. text 34.50 (0-9633610-3-1) Lawrence LA.

Mexican Laws & Regulations Governing Occupational Safety & Health, 2 vols., Set. 1996. lib. bdg. 646.99 (0-8490-5964-X) Gordon Pr.

Mexican Laws & Regulations Governing Occupational Safety & Health: A Selection of Principal Documents. 1994. lib. bdg. 350.00 (0-8490-5732-9) Gordon Pr.

Mexican Legal System. 2nd ed. Francisco Avalos. 1999. write for info. (1-57588-410-0, 311550) W S Hein.

***Mexican Legal System.** 2nd ed. Francisco Avalos. LC 99-57329. 2000. write for info. (0-8377-0226-7) W S Hein.

Mexican Legal System No. 1: Reference Guides to National Legal Systems, 1. Francisco A. Avalos. LC 91-39512. 272p. 1992. lib. bdg. 59.95 (0-313-27565-3, AMN/, Greenwood Pr) Greenwood.

Mexican Lepidoptera: Eurytelinae I. E. R. De la Maza & D. R. Turrent. (Sociedad Mexicana de Lepidopterologia Special Publication Ser.: No. 4). (Illus.). 44p. (Orig.). 1985. pap. 25.00 (0-911836-16-0) Entomological Repr.

Mexican Liberalism in the Age of Mora, 1821-1853. Charles A. Hale. LC 68-13908. (Caribbean Ser.: No. 11). 359p. reprint ed. pap. 111.30 (0-8357-8223-9, 203374000087) Bks Demand.

***Mexican Light: Exciting, Healthy Dishes from the Border & Beyond.** Martha Rose Schulman. LC 99-39648. 432p. 2000. pap. 16.00 (0-688-17466-3, Wm Morrow) Morrow Avon.

Mexican Literature: A Bibliography of Secondary Sources. 2nd enl. ed. David W. Foster. LC 92-4630. 698p. 1992. 76.00 (0-8108-2548-1) Scarecrow.

Mexican Literature: A History. Ed. by David William Foster. LC 93-40185. (Texas Pan American Ser.). 488p. (C). 1994. text 50.00 (0-292-72482-9) U of Tex Pr.

Mexican Lives. Judith A. Hellman. LC 93-40506. 256p. 1994. 22.95 (1-56584-177-8, Pub. by New Press NY) Norton.

Mexican Lives. Judith A. Hellman. 1995. pap. 12.95 (1-56584-178-6, Pub. by New Press NY) Norton.

Mexican Lobby: Matias Romero in Washington, 1861-1867. Thomas D. Schoonover. LC 86-5530. 204p. 1986. 27.00 (0-8131-1586-8) U Pr of Ky.

Mexican Los Angeles: A Narrative & Pictorial History. Antonio Rios-Bustamante. (Illus.). 250p. 1990. 35.00 (0-915745-19-4) Floricanto Pr.

Mexican Low-Fat Cooking. Cole Group Editors Staff. LC 95-45067. (Cole's Cooking Companion Ser.). (Illus.). 96p. 1996. pap. 7.95 (1-56426-816-0) Cole Group.

Mexican Macaws: Comparative Osteology. Lyndon L. Hargrave. LC 72-125168. (Anthropological Papers: No. 20). 67p. 1970. pap. 7.95 (0-8165-0212-9) U of Ariz Pr.

Mexican Main Dishes. Book Sales, Inc. Staff. 80p. 1996. 10.98 (0-7858-0383-1) Bk Sales Inc.

Mexican Majolica in Northern New Spain. Mark Barnes & Ronald V. May. 1980. reprint ed. pap. 4.95 (0-686-62076-3) Acoma Bks.

Mexican Majolica in Northern New Spain: A Model for Interpreting Ceramic Change. Ronald V. May. (Illus.). 147p. 1975. pap. text 16.25 (1-55567-031-8) Coyote Press.

Mexican Manuscript Painting of the Early Colonial Period: The Metropolitan Schools. Donald Robertson. LC 94-12120. 234p. (Orig.). 1994. pap. 31.95 (0-8061-2675-2) U of Okla Pr.

Mexican Martyrdom: Firsthand Experiences of the Religious Persecution in Mexico, 1926-1935. Wilfrid Parsons. LC 87-51412. 295p. 1994. reprint ed. pap. 10.00 (0-89555-330-9) TAN Bks Pubs.

Mexican Masquerade. Sergio Galindo. Ed. by Yvette E. Miller. Tr. by John S. Brushwood & Carolyn Brushwood from SPA. LC 84-21826. (Discoveries Ser.).Tr. of Comparsa. 92p. 1984. pap. 11.50 (0-935480-17-X) Lat Am Lit Rev Pr.

Mexican Medley, Vol. 32. Susan F. Slack. 64p. (Orig.). 1991. pap., per. 3.95 (0-942320-39-5) Am Cooking.

Mexican Microwave Cookery. Carol M. Maze. Ed. by Virginia Lark & Robert C. Medina. LC 84-72508. 116p. (Orig.). 1984. pap. text 6.00 (0-933196-03-2) Bilingue Pubns.

Mexican Migration to the United States: An Original Anthology. Paul S. Taylor et al. Ed. & Intro. by Carlos E. Cortes. LC 76-7304. (Chicano Heritage Ser.). (Illus.). 1977. 20.95 (0-405-09541-4) Ayer.

Mexican Migration to the United States: Origins, Consequences, & Policy Options. Ed. by Wayne A. Cornelius & Jorge A. Bustamante. (Dimensions of U. S.-Mexican Relations Ser.: Vol. 3). 177p. 1989. pap. 12.50 (0-935391-92-4, BC-03) UCSD Ctr US-Mex.

Mexican Migration to the United States: The Limits of Government Intervention. Wayne A. Cornelius. (Research Reports: No. 5). 11p. (Orig.). (C). 1981. pap. 5.00 (0-935391-04-5, RR-05) UCSD Ctr US-Mex.

Mexican Migration to the United States: The Role of Migration Networks & Human Capital Accumulation. Steven S. Zahniser. LC 98-45164. 1998. 79.00 (0-8153-3199-1) Garland.

Mexican Militarism: The Political Rise & Fall of the Revolutionary Army, 1910-1940. Edwin Lieuwen. LC 80-28937. (Illus.). 194p. 1981. reprint ed. lib. bdg. 59.50 (0-313-22911-2, LIMM, Greenwood Pr) Greenwood.

Mexican Motifs. Grafton. 1998. pap. 1.00 (0-486-28174-4) Dover.

Mexican Motifs. Harriet Tidball. LC 76-23998. (Guild Monographs: No. 6). (Illus.). 22p. 1962. pap. 7.95 (0-916658-06-6) Shuttle Craft.

Mexican Motor Carrier Directory. 1998. ring bd. 145.00 (*1-880701-13-8*) Trans Tech Srvs.

Mexican Mural Renaissance, 1920-1925. Jean Charlot. LC 62-8238. (Illus.). 386p. reprint ed. pap. 119.70 (*0-608-18585-X*, 200538400054) Bks Demand.

Mexican Muralists: Orozco, Rivera, Siqueiros. Desmond Rochfort. LC 97-27544. 239p. 1998. 27.50 (*0-8118-1928-0*) Chronicle Bks.

Mexican Muralists: Orozco, Rivera, Siqueiros. Desmond Rochfort. (Illus.). 240p. 1994. 50.00 (*0-87663-626-1*, Pub. by Universe) St Martin.

Mexican Murals. Cynthia Kraman. 1986. pap. 5.95 (*0-938979-01-9*) EG Bksellers.

Mexican National Army, 1822-1852. William A. DePalo, Jr. LC 96-51447. (Military History Ser.: Vol. 52). (Illus.). 272p. (C). 1997. text 39.95 (*0-89096-744-X*) Tex A&M Univ Pr.

Mexican Notebook. Eugene E. Snyder. LC 98-72370. (Illus.). 208p. 1998. 19.95 (*0-8323-0528-6*); pap. 14.95 (*0-8323-0527-8*) Binford Mort.

Mexican Novel Comes of Age. Walter M. Langford. LC 77-160486. 239p. 1971. text 21.95 (*0-8290-2401-8*) Irvington.

Mexican Oil: Issues Affecting Potential U. S. Trade & Investment. (Illus.). 36p. (Orig.). (C). 1993. pap. text 20.00 (*1-56806-559-0*) DIANE Pub.

Mexican Oil & Natural Gas: Political, Strategic & Economic Implications. Richard B. Mancke. LC 78-27095. 163p. 1979. 49.95 (*0-275-90386-9*, C0386, Praeger Pubs) Greenwood.

Mexican Oil Problem. George W. Stocking. 1976. lib. bdg. 59.95 (*0-8490-0618-X*) Gordon Pr.

Mexican Outsiders: A Community History of Marginalization & Discrimination in California. Martha Menchaca. LC 94-46190. (Illus.). 272p. (C). 1995. 40.00 (*0-292-75173-7*); pap. 18.95 (*0-292-75174-5*) U of Tex Pr.

Mexican Painters: Rivera, Orozco, Siqueiros & Other Artists of the Social Realist School. MacKinley Helm. 1991. 24.50 (*0-8446-6466-9*) Peter Smith.

Mexican Papercutting: Simple Techniques for Creating Colorful Cut-Paper Projects: Banners * Greeting Cards * Masks * Luminaria * Table Runners * & More. Kathleen Trenchard. LC 97-22638. (Illus.). 96p. 1998. pap. 14.95 (*1-57990-011-9*, Pub. by Lark Books) Random.

Mexican People: Their Struggle for Freedom. L. Gutierrez De Lara & Edgcumb Pinchon. 1976. lib. bdg. 59.95 (*0-8490-0619-8*) Gordon Pr.

Mexican People: Their Struggle for Freedom. L. Gutierrez De Lara & Edgcumb Pinchon. LC 75-111730. (American Imperialism: Viewpoints of United States Foreign Policy, 1898-1941 Ser.). 1977. reprint ed. 25.95 (*0-405-02033-3*) Ayer.

Mexican Peso Crisis: Program on U. S.-Mexico Relations, the Paul H. Nitze School of Advanced International Studies, Johns Hopkins University. Riordan Roett. LC 96-8605. 1996. 13.95 (*1-55587-667-6*) L Rienner.

Mexican Pet: More "New" Urban Legends & Some Old Favorites. Jan H. Brunvand. 1988. pap. 11.95 (*0-393-30542-2*) Norton.

Mexican Petroleum Industry in the Twentieth Century. Ed. by Jonathan C. Brown & Alan Knight. LC 92-30049. (Symposia on Latin America Ser.). 331p. 1992. text 35.00 (*0-292-76533-9*) U of Tex Pr.

Mexican Picaresque Narratives: Periquillo & Kin. Timothy G. Compton. LC 97-451. 152p. 1997. 32.50 (*0-8387-5348-5*) Bucknell U Pr.

Mexican Pig Bandit. James Crumley. (Illus.). 48p. 1998. 125.00 (*1-892011-01-8*); pap. 45.00 (*1-892011-00-X*) ASAP Pub.

Mexican Poetry. Ed. by Octavio Paz. Tr. by Samuel Beckett from SPA. LC 85-17684. 224p. (Orig.). 1985. reprint ed. pap. 12.00 (*0-8021-5186-8*, Grove) Grove-Atltic.

Mexican Poetry: An Anthology. Ed. by Isaac Goldberg. 1977. lib. bdg. 59.95 (*0-8490-2238-X*) Gordon Pr.

Mexican Political Biographies, 1884-1934. Roderic A. Camp. 490p. 1991. text 80.00 (*0-292-75119-2*) U of Tex Pr.

Mexican Political Biographies, 1935-1993. Roderic A. Camp. 652p. (C). 1995. text 55.00 (*0-292-71174-3*) U of Tex Pr.

Mexican Political Biographies, 1935-1993. 3rd ed. Roderic A. Camp. 652p. (C). 1995. pap. 24.95 (*0-292-71181-6*) U of Tex Pr.

Mexican Politics. Handelman. LC 95-73203. 304p. 1996. pap. text 30.95 (*0-312-10154-6*) St Martin.

Mexican Politics: The Containment of Conflict. 3rd ed. Martin C. Needler. LC 95-34439. 168p. 1995. 59.95 (*0-275-95251-7*, Praeger Pubs); pap. 18.95 (*0-275-95252-5*, Praeger Pubs) Greenwood.

Mexican Politics in Transition: The Breakdown of a One-Party-Dominant Regime. Wayne A. Cornelius. (Monographs: No. 41). 119p. 1996. pap. 11.95 (*1-878367-29-3*) UCSD Ctr US-Mex.

Mexican Popular Arts. F. Toor. (Mexico Ser.). 1976. lib. bdg. 250.00 (*0-8490-2239-8*) Gordon Pr.

Mexican Postcards. Carlos Monsivais. Tr. by John Kraniaukas. LC 96-52425. (Critical Studies in Latin American Culture). 240p. 1997. pap. 18.00 (*0-86091-604-9*, B4627, Pub. by Verso) Norton.

Mexican Potters of Prado. John M. Foster et al. (Statistical Research Technical Ser.: Vol. 57). (Illus.). 214p. (Orig.). 1995. per. 17.50 (*1-879442-53-1*) Stats Res.

Mexican Product Guide. Ed. by C. DePaula. 350p. 2000. pap. 95.00 (*0-915344-87-4*) Todd Pubns.

Mexican Question. W. E. Walling. 1976. lib. bdg. 250.00 (*0-8490-0620-1*) Gordon Pr.

Mexican Real Estate: Law & Practices Affecting Private U. S. Ownership. John De La Vega. LC 75-27888. 78p. reprint ed. pap. 30.00 (*0-608-15686-8*, 203148800074) Bks Demand.

Mexican Rebel: Pascual Orozco & the Mexican Revolution, 1910-1915. Michael C. Meyer. LC 67-10667. (Illus.). 198p. 1967. reprint ed. pap. 61.40 (*0-7837-6758-7*, 205915700011) Bks Demand.

Mexican Recipe Shortcuts or Casserolization of the Classics. Helen C. Duran. (Wild & Woolly West Ser.). (Illus.). 52p. (Orig.). 1983. pap. 3.50 (*0-86541-013-5*) Filter.

Mexican Recipes. Ed. by G & R Publishing Staff. (Uni-Bks.). 160p. (Orig.). 1994. pap. text 3.00 (*1-56383-034-5*, 7000) G & R Pub.

Mexican Remedies: Homegrown Wisdom. Annette Sandoval. 192p. 1998. mass mkt. 6.99 (*0-425-16155-2*) Berkley Pub.

Mexican Republic: The First Decade, 1823-1832. Stanley C. Green. LC 86-4310. (Pitt Latin American Ser.). 324p. 1987. pap. 100.50 (*0-7837-8547-X*, 204936200011) Bks Demand.

Mexican Rescue. Joseph Kraft. (Report Ser.). 66p. 1984. pap. 10.00 (*1-56708-065-0*) Grp of Thirty.

Mexican Response: A Twentieth Century Fund Paper. Luis F. Rubio & Francisco Gil-Diaz. 72p. (Orig.). 1987. pap. 9.00 (*0-87078-215-0*) Century Foundation.

Mexican Revolution. Mary P. Frost & Susan Keegan. (World History Ser.). (Illus.). (J). (gr. 4-12). 1996. lib. bdg. 22.45 (*1-56006-292-4*) Lucent Bks.

Mexican Revolution: The Constitutionalist Years. Charles C. Cumberland. LC 74-38506. (Illus.). 487p. reprint ed. pap. 151.00 (*0-8357-3616-4*, 203612700004) Bks Demand.

Mexican Revolution Vol. 1: Porfirians, Liberals & Peasants. Alan Knight. LC 89-28488. (Illus.). xxiv, 619p. 1990. reprint ed. pap. text 30.00 (*0-8032-7770-9*) U of Nebr Pr.

Mexican Revolution Vol. 2: Counter-Revolution & Reconstruction. Alan Knight. LC 89-28488. (Illus.). xxvi, 679p. 1990. reprint ed. pap. text 33.00 (*0-8032-7771-7*) U of Nebr Pr.

Mexican Revolution & the Anglo-American Powers: The End of Confrontation & the Beginning of Negotiation. Lorenzo Meyer. (Research Reports: No. 34). 40p. (Orig.). (C). 1985. pap. 5.00 (*0-935391-33-9*, RR-34) UCSD Ctr US-Mex.

Mexican Revolution & the Catholic Church, 1910-1929. Robert E. Quirk. LC 85-30209. 276p. 1986. reprint ed. lib. bdg. 69.50 (*0-313-25121-5*, QUMC, Greenwood Pr) Greenwood.

Mexican Revolution & the Limits of Agrarian Reform, 1915-1946. Dana Markiewicz. LC 93-12003. 216p. 1993. lib. bdg. 45.00 (*1-55587-321-9*) L Rienner.

Mexican Revolution & the United States. C. W. Hackett. 1972. 59.95 (*0-8490-0621-X*) Gordon Pr.

Mexican Revolution, Genesis under Madero. Charles C. Cumberland. LC 71-90495. 298p. 1969. reprint ed. lib. bdg. 65.00 (*0-8371-2126-4*, CUMR, Greenwood Pr) Greenwood.

Mexican Revolution in Puebla, 1908-1913: The Maderista Movement & the Failure of Liberal Reform. David G. LaFrance. LC 88-34923. 272p. 1989. 45.00 (*0-8420-2293-7*) Scholarly Res Inc.

Mexican Revolution, 1910-1920. R. Conrad Stein. LC 93-17259. (Timestop Bks.). (Illus.). 144p. (J). (gr. 4-7). 1994. lib. bdg. 14.95 (*0-02-786950-4*, New Dscvry Bks) Silver Burdett Pr.

Mexican Revolution of Ayutla, 1854-1855. Richard A. Johnson. LC 40-1957. (Augustana College Library Publication: No. 17). 125p. 1939. pap. 5.00 (*0-910182-12-4*) Augustana Coll.

Mexican Right: The End of Revolutionary Reform, 1929-1940. John W. Sherman. LC 96-22015. 176p. 1997. 55.00 (*0-275-95736-5*, Praeger Pubs) Greenwood.

Mexican Rural Development & the Plumed Serpent: Technology & Maya Cosmology in the Tropical Forest of Campeche, Mexico. Betty Bernice Faust. LC 96-28277. 240p. 1998. 59.95 (*0-89789-482-0*, Bergin & Garvey) Greenwood.

Mexican Rural Development & the Plumed Serpent: Technology & Maya Cosmology in the Tropical Forest Of Campeche, Mexico. Betty Bernice Faust. 240p. 1999. pap. 22.95 (*0-89789-699-8*, Bergin & Garvey) Greenwood.

Mexican Saddle: A Western Story. Bennett Foster. Date not set. 19.95 (*0-7862-1328-0*) Thorndike Pr.

***Mexican Saddle: A Western Story.** large type ed. Bennett Foster. 245p. 1999. 20.00 (*0-7838-8397-8*, G K Hall Lrg Type) Mac Lib Ref.

Mexican Sayings: The Treasure of a People. Octavio A. Ballesteros & Maria D. Ballesteros. (ENG & SPA., Illus.). 95p. 1992. 14.95 (*0-89015-810-X*) Sunbelt Media.

Mexican School of Particles & Fields. Ed. by J. L. Lucio et al. LC 86-81187. (AIP Conference Proceedings Ser.: No. 143). 267p. 1986. lib. bdg. 60.00 (*0-88318-342-0*) Am Inst Physics.

Mexican Shock: Its Meaning for the U. S. Jorge Castaneda. 256p. 1995. 23.00 (*1-56584-311-8*, Pub. by New Press NY) Norton.

Mexican Shock: Its Meaning for the U. S. Jorge Castaneda. 288p. 1996. pap. 13.00 (*1-56584-312-6*, Pub. by New Press NY) Norton.

Mexican Showdown. Jory Sherman. (Gunn Ser.: No. 2). 224p. (Orig.). 1980. mass mkt. 1.95 (*0-89083-628-0*, Zebra Kensgtn) Kensgtn Pub Corp.

Mexican Side of the Texan Revolution. Carlos Castaneda. 1993. reprint ed. lib. bdg. 75.00 (*0-7812-5920-7*) Rprt Serv.

Mexican Side of the Texan Revolution, 1836. Antonio L. Santa Anna. (BCL1 - United States Local History Ser.). 391p. 1991. reprint ed. lib. bdg. 89.00 (*0-7812-6310-7*) Rprt Serv.

Mexican Side of the Texan Revolution, 1836: By the Chief Mexican Participants. Ed. by Carlos E. Cortes. Tr. by Carlos E. Castenada. LC 76-1215. (Chicano Heritage Ser.). 1980. reprint ed. 33.95 (*0-405-09487-6*) Ayer.

Mexican Silver. Clara Bargellini et al. (Exhibitions International Ser.). (Illus.). 176p. 1994. pap. 40.00 (*90-6988-059-8*) U of Wash Pr.

Mexican Silver: Twentieth Century Handwrought Jewelry & Metalwork. Penny C. Morrill. LC 94-65616. (Illus.). 272p. 1994. 59.95 (*0-88740-610-6*) Schiffer.

Mexican Silver: 20th Century Handwrought Jewelry & Metalwork. 2nd rev. ed. Penny C. Morrill & Carole A. Berk. (Illus.). 272p. 1999. 59.95 (*0-7643-0663-4*) Schiffer.

Mexican Slang: A Guide. Linton H. Robinson. 156p. (YA). 1998. reprint ed. pap. 6.95 (*0-9627080-7-0*) In One EAR.

Mexican Slang: A Guide see Mexican Slang Plus Graffiti

Mexican Slang Plus Graffiti. rev. ed. Linton H. Robinson et al. Ed. by B. A. Reid. Orig. Title: Mexican Slang: A Guide. (Illus.). 128p. 1999. pap. 9.95 (*1-881791-10-6*, Bueno Bks) In One EAR.

Mexican Snacks & Salsas. Book Sales, Inc. Staff. 80p. 1996. 10.98 (*0-7858-0385-8*) Bk Sales Inc.

Mexican So Fat, Low Fat, No Fat. Betty Rohde. LC 97-29292. 1998. pap. 12.00 (*0-684-83525-8*) S&S Trade.

Mexican Social Policy: Affordability, Conflict & Progress. Bruce Nord. LC 93-42083. 296p. (C). 1994. pap. text 39.00 (*0-8191-9418-2*) U Pr of Amer.

Mexican Songs for Guitar. Jerry Silverman. 88p. 1994. pap. 10.95 (*0-7866-0174-4*, 95066) Mel Bay.

***Mexican Spanish.** 2nd ed. Rough Guides Staff. (Phrasebooks Ser.). (Illus.). 272p. 2000. pap. 5.00 (*1-85828-609-3*, Pub. by Rough Guides) Penguin Putnam.

Mexican Standoff. B. J. Lanagan. (Bushwhackers Ser.: Vol. 5). 1998. mass mkt. 4.99 (*0-515-12263-7*, Jove) Berkley Pub.

Mexican Studies in the History & Philosophy of Science. Ed. by Santiago Ramirez & Robert S. Cohen. LC 95-13783. (Boston Studies in the Philosophy of Science: Vol. 172). 1995. lib. bdg. 144.00 (*0-7923-3462-0*, Pub. by Kluwer Academic) Kluwer Academic.

***Mexican Style Source Book: Creative Ideas for Enhancing Your Space.** Peter Aprahmian. (Illus.). 144p. 2000. 29.95 (*0-7893-0402-3*) Universe.

Mexican Sugarcane Growers: Economic Restructuring & Political Options. Ed. by Peter Singelmann. 85p. 1995. pap. 12.00 (*1-878367-26-9*) UCSD Ctr US-Mex.

***Mexican Suite: A History of Photography in Mexico.** Olivier Debroise. Tr. by Stella De Sa Rego. LC 00-39295. (Illus.). 344p. 2001. 60.00 (*0-292-71611-7*) U of Tex Pr.

***Mexican Sunsets.** Jude Liebermann. 160p. 1999. pap. 10.95 (*0-9660653-1-X*) Lee Bks FL.

Mexican Supplement, 1979. Roger M. Haigh & Shirley A. Weathers. 28p. 1979. write for info. (*0-940764-24-5*) Genealog Inst.

Mexican Tapestry Weaving. deluxe ed. Joanne Hall. LC 77-351132. (Illus.). 1976. spiral bd. 14.95 (*0-9602098-0-8*) J Arvidson.

Mexican Textile Techniques. Chloe Sayer. (Ethnography Ser.: No. 9). (Illus.). 64p. pap. 10.50 (*0-85263-970-8*, Pub. by Shire Pubns) Parkwest Pubns.

***Mexican Tiles: Color, Style, Design.** Masako Takahashi. LC 99-38349. (Illus.). 120p. 2000. pap. 18.95 (*0-8118-2629-5*) Chronicle Bks.

Mexican Time Bomb: A Twentieth Century Fund Paper. Norman A. Bailey & Richard Cohen. 61p. (Orig.). (C). 1987. pap. text 9.00 (*0-87078-209-6*) Century Foundation.

Mexican Tongue Twisters: Trabalenguas Mexicanos. Tr. & Compiled by Robert J. Haddad. LC 89-81489. 74p. 1989. pap. 8.00 (*0-927534-02-9*) Biling Rev-Pr.

Mexican Treasure Hunt. Linda Lowery Keep. (Hannah & the Angels Ser.: No. 3). (J). (gr. 3-6). 1998. pap. 3.99 (*0-679-89160-9*, Pub. by Random Bks Yng Read) Random.

***Mexican Treasury: The Writings of Dr. Francisco Hernandez.** Francisco Hernandez & Simon Varey. LC 00-26519. 2000. write for info. (*0-8047-3963-3*) Stanford U Pr.

Mexican Tree Duck. James Crumley. 256p. 1993. 19.95 (*0-89296-391-3*) Mysterious Pr.

Mexican Tree Duck. James Crumley. 272p. 1994. mass mkt. 5.99 (*0-446-40407-1*, Pub. by Warner Bks) Little.

Mexican Truck Driver see Contemporary Latin American Culture

Mexican-U. S. Border Region & the Free Trade Agreement. Ed. by Paul Ganster & Eugenio O. Valenciano. 118p. (Orig.). (C). 1992. pap. text 10.00 (*0-925613-09-6*) SDSU Inst Reg Studies.

Mexican-U. S. Relations: Conflict & Convergence. Ed. by Carlos Vasquez & Manuel Garcia y Griego. LC 83-1878. (Anthology Ser.: No. 3). 490p. 1983. 21.95 (*0-89551-054-5*) UCLA Chicano Studies.

Mexican Ulysses, an Autobiography. Jose Vasconcelos. Tr. by W. Rex Crawford. LC 72-6215. 288p. 1972. reprint ed. lib. bdg. 87.50 (*0-8371-6477-X*, VAMU, Greenwood Pr) Greenwood.

Mexican University & the State: Student Conflicts, 1910-1971. Donald J. Mabry. LC 81-48377. 344p. 1982. 28.95 (*0-89096-128-X*) Tex A&M Univ Pr.

Mexican Urban Household: Organizing for Self-Defense. Henry A. Selby et al. 250p. 1990. text 30.00 (*0-292-78521-6*) U of Tex Pr.

Mexican Vegetarian Cooking. Edith M. De Plata. (Illus.). 128p. (Orig.). 1989. pap. 10.95 (*0-89281-341-5*) Inner Tradit.

Mexican View of America in the 1860s: A Foreign Diplomat Describes the Civil War & Reconstruction. Ed. by Thomas D. Schoonover. LC 90-55960. 272p. 1991. 39.50 (*0-8386-3432-X*) Fairleigh Dickinson.

Mexican Voices - American Dreams: An Oral History of Mexican Immigration to the United States. Marilyn P. Davis. LC 90-31640. 464p. 1995. 29.95 (*0-8050-1216-8*); pap. 15.95 (*0-8050-1859-X*, Owl) H Holt & Co.

Mexican War. Wim Coleman. (Perspectives on History Ser.: Pt. III). 1998. pap. 6.95 (*1-57960-044-1*) Disc Enter Ltd.

Mexican War. Bronwyn Mills. Ed. by John Bowman. (America at War Ser.). (Illus.). 128p. (YA). (gr. 5-12). 1992. lib. bdg. 19.95 (*0-8160-2393-X*) Facts on File.

Mexican War. Otis A. Singletary. LC 60-7248. (Chicago History of American Civilization Ser.). 193p. 1962. pap. text 12.95 (*0-226-76061-8*, CHAC19) U Ch Pr.

***Mexican War: A Brief History with Documents.** Chavez. 2002. pap. text. write for info. (*0-312-24921-7*) St Martin.

Mexican War Correspondence of Richard Smith Elliott. Richard S. Elliott. Ed. by Mark Gardner & Marc Simmons. LC 97-1027. (American Exploration & Travel Ser.: Vol. 76). (Illus.). 304p. 1997. 29.95 (*0-8061-2951-4*) U of Okla Pr.

Mexican War, 1846-1848. K. Jack Bauer. LC 92-13927. (Illus.). xxviii, 486p. (C). 1992. pap. 22.00 (*0-8032-6107-1*, Bison Books) U of Nebr Pr.

Mexican War of Independence. LC 96-14216. (World History Ser.). (Illus.). 112p. (J). (gr. 4-12). 1996. lib. bdg. 22.45 (*1-56006-297-5*) Lucent Bks.

Mexican Women in Anahuac & New Spain: Three Study Units: Aztec Roles, Spanish Notary Revelations, Creole Genius. Doris M. Ladd. (Latin American Curriculum Units for Junior & Community Colleges Ser.). vii, 87p. (Orig.). (C). 1979. pap. text 4.95 (*0-86728-003-4*) U TX Inst Lat Am Stud.

Mexican Workers & American Dreams: Immigration, Repatriation, & California Farm Labor, 1900-1939. Camille Guerin-Gonzales. LC 93-24223. (Class & Culture Ser.). (Illus.). 190p. 1994. text 42.00 (*0-8135-2047-9*); pap. text 17.00 (*0-8135-2048-7*) Rutgers U Pr.

Mexican Workers & the State: From the Porfiriato to NAFTA. Norman Caulfield. LC 98-16392. (Illus.). 224p. 1998. 24.95 (*0-87565-192-5*) Tex Christian.

Mexican Yearbook. R. Cleland. 1976. lib. bdg. 59.95 (*0-8490-2240-1*) Gordon Pr.

Mexicanas at Work in the United States. Ed. by Margarita B. Melville. (Mexican American Studies: No. V). (Illus.). (Orig.). (C). 1988. pap. text 11.95 (*0-939709-04-X*) Univ Houston Mex Amer.

Mexicano (Mexican Things) 2nd ed. Jose M. Villa. (SPA.). 176p. 1986. 14.99 (*968-16-2234-0*, Pub. by Fondo) Continental Bk.

Mexicano Resistance in the Southwest. Robert J. Rosenbaum. LC 98-3839. (Illus.). 264p. 1998. reprint ed. pap. 14.95 (*0-87074-429-1*) SMU Press.

Mexicano/Chicano Concerns & School Desegregation in Los Angeles. Carlos M. Haro. (Monographs: No. 9). 92p. 1974. pap. 10.00 (*0-89551-012-X*) UCLA Chicano Studies.

***Mexicanos: A History of Mexicans in the United States.** Manuel G. Gonzales. LC 98-50954. (Illus.). 400p. 1999. text 29.95 (*0-253-33520-5*) Ind U Pr.

***Mexicanos: A History of Mexicans in the United States.** Manuel G. Gonzales. 2000. pap. 16.95 (*0-253-21400-9*) Ind U Pr.

Mexicanos Indocumentados en los E. U. David Heer. (SPA.). pap. 13.99 (*968-16-3981-2*, Pub. by Fondo) Continental Bk.

Mexicans: A Personal Portrait of a People. Patrick Oster. LC 89-45843. 336p. 1990. reprint ed. pap. 14.00 (*0-06-097310-2*, Perennial) HarperTrade.

Mexicans at Arms: Puro Federalists & the Politics of War, 1845-1848. Pedro Santoni. LC 95-52183. (Illus.). 324p. 1996. 29.50 (*0-87565-158-5*) Tex Christian.

***Mexicans in California.** Michelle Motoyoshi. (California Cultures Ser.). (Illus.). 64p. (J). (gr. 4-8). 1999. pap. text 14.95 (*1-884925-91-X*) Toucan Valley.

Mexicans in the Midwest, 1900-1932. Juan R. Garcia. 293p. 1996. 39.95 (*0-8165-1560-3*) U of Ariz Pr.

Mexicanville. Lorenzo L. Sandoval. 1994. 5.50 (*0-87129-494-X*, M15) Dramatic Pub.

Mexico see American Nations Past & Present

Mexico see MacDonald Countries

Mexico see Cultures of the World - Group 2

Mexico see Statements of the Laws of the OAS Member States in Matters Affecting Business

Mexico see Let's Investigate Series

Mexico see Countries of the World Series

Mexico see Countries of the World

Mexico. (Panorama Bks.). (FRE., Illus.). 3.95 (*0-685-11369-8*) Fr & Eur.

Mexico. (Insight Guides Ser.). 1998. 22.95 (*0-88729-141-4*) Langenscheidt.

Mexico. pap. 16.95 (*0-528-94979-9*) Rand McNally.

Mexico. (Case Studies in Population Policy). 52p. pap. 7.50 (*92-1-151213-1*, 90.XIII.27) UN.

Mexico. (Your School Reports). 1995. boxed set 19.95 (*1-884618-24-3*) Unique Information.

Mexico. Rob Alcraft. LC 98-37737. (Visit to Ser.). (Illus.). 32p. (J). 1999. lib. bdg. 13.95 (*1-57572-848-6*) Heinemann Lib.

Mexico. Rob Alcraft & Sean Sprague. LC 95-52957. (Worldfocus Ser.). (J). 1998. 18.50 (*1-57572-078-7*) Heinemann Lib.

Mexico. Carole Allen. (Gifted Learning Ser.). 64p. 1995. teacher ed. 8.99 (*0-86653-854-2*, GA1536) Good Apple.

M

An Asterisk (*) at the beginning of an entry indicates that the title is appearing for the first time.

***Mexico.** David Armentrout & Patricia Armentrout. LC 00-29080. (Treasures from the Past Ser.). (Illus.). 2000. write for info. (1-55916-290-2) Rourke Bk Co.

Mexico. Helen Arnold. LC 95-7595. (Postcards from Ser.). (YA). 1995. lib. bdg. 21.40 (0-8172-4012-8) Raintree Steck-V.

Mexico. Helen Arnold. LC 95-7595. (Postcards From Ser.). (Illus.). 32p. (J). (gr. 2-4). 1996. pap. text 4.95 (0-8172-4233-3) Raintree Steck-V.

Mexico. Mary Berendes. LC 96-30665. (Countries Ser.). (Illus.). 32p. (J). (gr. 2-6). 1997. lib. bdg. 22.79 (1-56766-372-9) Childs World.

Mexico. Peggy Bond. (Insider's Guides Ser.). (Illus.). 288p. 1992. pap. 18.95 (1-55650-454-3) Hunter NJ.

Mexico. Susan Canizares & Pamela Chanko. LC 98-53355. (Social Studies Emergent Readers Ser.). 1999. 2.50 (0-439-04570-3) Scholastic Inc.

Mexico. John Collis. (Blue Guide Ser.). Date not set. 27.50 (0-393-01665-X) Norton.

Mexico. John Collis. LC 96-32289. (Blue Guide Ser.). 960p. 1996. pap. 25.00 (0-393-30072-2, Norton Paperbks) Norton.

Mexico. DK Publishing Staff. LC 99-22557. (Eyewitness Travel Guides Ser.). 384p. 1999. pap. 24.95 (0-7894-4623-5) DK Pub Inc.

Mexico. C. Reginald Enock. 1976. lib. bdg. 59.95 (0-8490-2243-6) Gordon Pr.

Mexico. David Flint. LC 93-7529. (On the Map Ser.). (Illus.). 32p. (J). (gr. 2-4). 1993. lib. bdg. 22.83 (0-8114-3419-2) Raintree Steck-V.

***Mexico.** Kate A. Furlong. LC 00-26671. (Countries Ser.). (Illus.). 2000. write for info. (1-57765-390-4) ABDO Pub Co.

Mexico. Anita Ganeri & Rachel Wright. (Country Topics for Craft Projects Ser.). (Illus.). 32p. (J). (gr. 5-8). 1995. pap. 5.95 (0-531-15278-2) Watts.

Mexico. William Goodwin. LC 98-29730. (Overview Ser.). (Illus.). (J). (gr. 4-12). 1998. lib. bdg. 23.70 (1-56006-351-3) Lucent Bks.

***Mexico.** Shirley W. Gray. (First Reports). (Illus.). 48p. (J). (gr. 2-3). 2000. write for info. (0-7565-0031-1) Compass Point.

***Mexico.** Jen Green. LC 99-41920. (Nations of the World Ser.). (Illus.). 128p. (J). (gr. 6-7). 2000. 31.40 (0-8172-5779-9) Raintree Steck-V.

Mexico. Griffin Trade Paperbacks Staff. 688p. 1999. pap. 21.99 (0-312-24476-2, St Martin Griffin) St Martin.

Mexico. Harvey. 1993. text 69.50 (1-85043-514-6, Pub. by I B T) St Martin.

Mexico. Ann Heinrichs. LC 96-28156. (True Bk.). (J). 1997. lib. bdg. 21.00 (0-516-20337-1) Childrens.

Mexico. Paula Heusinkveld. LC 94-32188. 144p. 1994. pap. 15.95 (0-471-08979-6) Wiley.

Mexico. John Howard. (Countries Ser.). (Illus.). 48p. (J). (gr. 5 up). 1992. lib. bdg. 14.95 (0-382-24247-5) Silver Burdett Pr.

***Mexico.** Linda Illsley. LC 98-21844. (Food & Festivals Ser.). (Illus.). 32p. (J). (ps-3). 1999. lib. bdg. 22.83 (0-8172-5553-2) Raintree Steck-V.

Mexico. Mona King. LC 94-67672. (Illustrated Travel Guides from Thomas Cook Ser.). (Illus.). 192p. 1994. pap. 12.95 (0-8442-9074-2, Passprt Bks) NTC Contemp Pub Co.

***Mexico.** Michael Kramme. (Illus.). 96p. (YA). (gr. 5-8). 1999. pap. text 10.95 (1-58037-088-8, Pub. by M Twain Media) Carson-Dellos.

***Mexico.** David F. Marx & Linda Cornwell. LC 99-43654. (Rookie Read-About Geography Ser.). (Illus.). (YA). 2000. 19.00 (0-516-22041-1) Childrens.

Mexico. Cari Meister. LC 98-10131. (Going Places Ser.). (Illus.). 24p. (J). 2000. lib. bdg. 18.60 (1-57765-029-8, Checkerboard Library) ABDO Pub Co.

Mexico. James A. Michener. 1994. mass mkt. 7.99 (0-449-22187-3, Crest) Fawcett.

***Mexico.** New Holland Publishing Staff. (Globetrotter Travel Guides Ser.). 2000. pap. 10.95 (1-85974-327-7); pap. 8.95 (1-85974-328-5) New5 Holland.

***Mexico.** Ed. by New Holland Publishing Staff. (Globetrotter Travel Packs Ser.). (Illus.). 2000. pap. 14.95 (1-85974-330-7) New5 Holland.

Mexico. NTC Publishing Staff. (Passport Essential Guide Ser.). 128p. 1999. pap. text 8.95 (0-8442-0086-7, 00867, Passprt Bks) NTC Contemp Pub Co.

Mexico. Ed. by Pan American Union Staff. 1976. lib. bdg. 34.95 (0-8490-0622-8) Gordon Pr.

***Mexico.** Contrib. by Ted Park. LC 99-58643. (Taking Your Camera to Ser.). 32p. (J). 2000. lib. bdg. 22.83 (0-7398-1804-X) Raintree Steck-V.

Mexico. Edward A. Parker. LC 96-52702. (Country Insights Ser.). (J). 1998. lib. bdg. 25.69 (0-8172-4791-2) Raintree Steck-V.

Mexico. Lewis K. Parker. LC 93-42777. (Dropping in On Ser.). 32p. (J). (gr. 2-5). 1994. lib. bdg. 21.27 (1-55916-001-2) Rourke Bk Co.

Mexico. Axel Rail. Ed. & Illus. by Pat Nobles. 224p. (Orig.). 1986. write for info. (0-938105-00-0) Seabird Pub.

Mexico. Adele Richardson. LC 98-14261. (Let's Investigate Ser.). 32p. (J). (gr. 1-4). 1998. lib. bdg. 19.95 (0-88682-984-4, Creat Educ) Creative Co.

Mexico. R. Conrad Stein. LC 95-2701. (Games People Play Ser.). (Illus.). 64p. (J). (ps-2). 1995. lib. bdg. 23.50 (0-516-04439-7) Childrens.

Mexico. Thomas Streissguth. LC 96-51781. (Globetrotters Club Ser.). 48p. (J). 1997. lib. bdg. 19.93 (1-57505-100-1, Carolrhoda); lib. bdg. 22.60 (1-57505-125-7, Carolrhoda) Lerner Pub.

Mexico. Kitty M. Villa. (World Education Ser.). 288p. 1982. 40.00 (0-614-23465-4, 5334) Am Assn Coll Registrars.

***Mexico.** Victoria Wise. (Vegetarian Table Ser.). 2000. pap. 16.95 (0-8118-3036-5) Chronicle Bks.

***Mexico.** rev. ed. Let's Go Staff. (Let's Go 2001 Ser.). (Illus.). 688p. 2000. pap. 21.99 (0-312-24683-8, St Martin Griffin) St Martin.

Mexico. rev. ed. Compiled by Nelles Verlag. (Nelles Guides Ser.). 256p. 1993. pap. 14.95 (3-88618-384-X, Pub. by Nelles Verlag) Seven Hills Bk.

Mexico. 2nd ed. R. Conrad Stein. LC 97-40708. (Enchantment of the World Ser.). (Illus.). 144p. (J). (gr. 4-7). 1998. lib. bdg. 32.00 (0-516-20650-8) Childrens.

Mexico. 2nd rev. ed. Nelles Verlag Staff. (Nelles Guides Ser.). (Illus.). 256p. 1999. pap. 15.95 (3-88618-119-7) Hunter NJ.

Mexico. 2nd rev. ed. George D. E. Philip. LC 94-182921. (World Bibliographical Ser.). 214p. 1994. lib. bdg. 52.50 (1-85109-198-X) ABC-CLIO.

Mexico. 4th ed. John Fisher. (Rough Guide Ser.). (Illus.). 688p. 1998. pap. text 19.95 (1-85828-342-6) Rough Guides.

***Mexico.** 7th ed. John Noble et al. 2000. reprint ed. pap. 24.99 (1-86450-089-1) Lonely Planet.

Mexico: A Colorful & Concise History. Joe Ajlouny. LC 91-62784. (Tourist Companion Histories Ser.). (Illus.). 120p. (Orig.). 1989. pap. 4.95 (0-929957-03-2, Scrivener Pr) JSA Pubns.

Mexico: A Country Guide. Tom Barry. 401p. (Orig.). (C). 1992. pap. text 14.95 (0-911213-35-X) Interhemisp Res Ctr.

Mexico: A Country Study. Tim L. Merrill. 464p. 1997. boxed set 29.00 (0-16-061205-5) USGPO.

Mexico: A Country Study. Ed. by Tim L. Merrill & Ramon Miro. LC 97-13481. (Area Handbook Ser.). 414p. 1997. 25.00 (0-8444-0855-7, F1208, Pub. by Lib Congress) Bernan Associates.

***Mexico: A Country Study Guide.** Global Investment & Business Center, Inc. Staff. (World Country Study Guides Library: Vol. 112). (Illus.). 350p. 2000. pap. 59.00 (0-7397-2410-X) Intl Business Pubns.

Mexico: A Higher Vision. Michael Calderwood. (Illus.). 192p. 1995. 35.00 (1-883051-06-1) ALTI Pub.

Mexico: A Hiker's Guide to Mexico's Natural History. Jim Conrad. LC 94-45479. (Illus.). 224p. 1995. pap. 16.95 (0-89886-424-0) Mountaineers.

Mexico: A History. Robert R. Miller. LC 84-28105. (Illus.). 384p. 1989. pap. 17.95 (0-8061-2178-5) U of Okla Pr.

Mexico: A History of Its Progress & Development in One Hundred Years. Marie R. Wright. (Mexico Ser.). 1979. lib. bdg. 250.00 (0-8490-2971-6) Gordon Pr.

Mexico: A Landscape in People. Text by Eloise Bethell & Will Inman. (C). 1989. text 39.00 (0-946270-29-5, Pub. by Pentland Pr) St Mut.

Mexico: A Landscape Revisited. LC 94-32301. 1994. write for info. (0-87663-613-X) Universe.

Mexico: A Landscape Revisited. Smithsonian Institute Travel Exhibitions Staff. LC 94-32301. (Illus.). 128p. 1995. 35.00 (0-87663-617-2, Pub. by Universe) St Martin.

***Mexico: A Play.** Gertrude Stein. Vol. 42. 71p. 1999. pap. 5.95 (1-892295-36-9, Pub. by Green Integer) SPD-Small Pr Dist.

Mexico: A Storm & a Prophecy. Marcos. 4.00 (1-884519-08-3) Open Media.

Mexico: A Study of an Economically Developing Country. Anna Lewington. (Illus.). 48p. (J). (gr. 3-5). 1996. lib. bdg. 24.26 (0-8172-4528-6) Raintree Steck-V.

Mexico: All about the Country & Its People. Caesar C. Cantu. (Illus.). 10.95 (0-685-16804-2, 0-910978-3-4) Modern World.

Mexico: An Illustrated History. Ed. by Michael E. Burke. LC 99-25595. (Hippocrene Illustrated Histories Ser.). (Illus.). 150p. 1999. 11.95 (0-7818-0690-9) Hippocrene Bks.

Mexico: Aztec, Spanish & Republican, 2 vols. B. Mayer. 1976. lib. bdg. 250.00 (0-8490-2246-0) Gordon Pr.

Mexico: Biography of Power: A History of Modern Mexico, 1810-1996. Enrique Krauze. (Illus.). 896p. 1998. pap. 20.00 (0-06-092917-0, Perennial) HarperTrade.

Mexico: Casas del Pacifico. Marie-Pierre Colle. Ed. by Gabriel Loera. LC 94-71534. (SPA., Illus.). 224p. 1994. 55.00 (1-883051-02-9) ALTI Pub.

Mexico: Class Formation, Capital Accumulation, & the State. rev. ed. James Cockroft. LC 81-84740. 384p. 1990. reprint ed. pap. 19.00 (0-85345-561-9) Monthly Rev.

Mexico: Eine Landeskunde. Hans G. Gierloff-Emden. (Illus.). 634p. 1970. 123.10 (3-11-002708-9) De Gruyter.

Mexico: Environmental Technologies Export Market Plan. 25p. 1994. pap. 2.50 (0-16-045738-6) USGPO.

Mexico: From Conquest to NAFTA. Philip Russell. Date not set. pap. 24.95 (0-9639223-2-7) Mexico Res Ctr.

Mexico: From Corporatism to Pluralism. George W. Grayson. LC 97-73399. 192p. (C). 1997. pap. text 24.00 (0-15-505365-5, Pub. by Harcourt Coll Pubs) Harcourt.

Mexico: From Montezuma to NAFTA, Chiapas, & Beyond. Jaime Suchlicki. (Illus.). 238p. 1995. 21.95 (1-57488-031-4) Brasseys.

***Mexico: From Montezuma to Nafta, Chiapas & Beyond.** Jaime Suchlicki. 228p. 2000. pap. 24.95 (0-7658-0652-5) Transaction Pubs.

Mexico: From Montezuma to NAFTA, Chiapas, & Beyond. 2nd ed. Jaime Suchlicki. (Illus.). 224p. Date not set. pap. 16.95 (1-57488-026-8) Brasseys.

Mexico: From the Olmecs to the Aztecs. 4th rev. ed. Michael D. Coe. LC 93-60419. (Illus.). 192p. 1994. pap. 16.95 (0-500-27722-2, Pub. by Thames Hudson) Norton.

Mexico: Houses of the Pacific. Marie-Pierre Colle. Ed. by Gabriel Loera. LC 94-71535. (Illus.). 224p. 1994. 55.00 (1-883051-01-0) ALTI Pub.

Mexico: Human Rights in Rural Areas. Amnesty International Staff. 136p. (Orig.). 1986. pap. 5.00 (0-939994-19-4, Pub. by Amnesty Intl Pubns) Science Pubs.

Mexico: In Search of Security. Ed. by Bruce M. Bagley & Sergio A. Quezada. LC 93-527. (University of Miami North-South Center Ser.). 384p. (C). 1993. pap. 24.95 (1-56000-686-2, Pub. by U Miami N-S Ctr) L Rienner.

Mexico: Its Ancient & Modern Civilization. C. Reginald Enock. 1976. lib. bdg. 59.95 (0-8490-0629-5) Gordon Pr.

Mexico: Land & Liberty. Ricardo F. Magon. (Illus.). 156p. 1977. 41.99 (0-919618-29-4, Pub. by Black Rose); pap. 12.99 (0-919618-30-8, Pub. by Black Rose) Consort Bk Sales.

Mexico: Life on the Volcano. Andrew Coe. (SPA., Illus.). 288p. 1993. pap. 15.95 (0-8442-9657-0, Passprt Bks) NTC Contemp Pub Co.

Mexico: Major World Nations. Jack Rummel. (Major World Nations Ser.). (Illus.). 144p. (YA). (gr. 5 up). 1999. lib. bdg. 19.95 (0-7910-4763-6) Chelsea Hse.

Mexico: Mutual Adjustment Planning. Robert J. Shafer. LC 65-25986. (National Planning Ser.: No. 4). 238p. reprint ed. pap. 73.80 (0-608-13895-9, 202039900017) Bks Demand.

Mexico: Neighbor in Transition. Peter H. Smith. LC 84-80974. (Headline Ser.: No. 267). (Illus.). 1984. 5.95 (0-87124-089-0) Foreign Policy.

Mexico: Revolution to Evolution, 1940 to 1960. 3rd ed. Howard F. Cline. LC 81-3819. (Illus.). 375p. 1981. reprint ed. lib. bdg. 65.00 (0-313-22993-7, CLME, Greenwood Pr) Greenwood.

Mexico: Rich in Spirit & Tradition see Exploring Cultures of the World - Group 1

Mexico: Simple Projects & Inspiration for the Home. Karin Hossack. LC 99-14414. (Handmade Style Ser.). (Illus.). 112p. 1999. pap. 18.95 (0-8118-2567-1) Chronicle Bks.

Mexico: Systemic Injustice: Torture, "Disappearance" & Extrajudicial Execution. Human Rights Watch, America, Staff. 136p. 1999. pap. 10.00 (1-56432-198-3) Hum Rts Watch.

Mexico: The Beautiful Cookbook. Susanna Palazuelos et al. (Beautiful Cookbook Ser.). (Illus.). 256p. 1991. 50.00 (0-00-215949-X) Collins SF.

Mexico: The Culture see Lands, Peoples & Cultures Series

Mexico: The Fertilizer Industry. J. H. Allgood et al. (Technical Bulletin Ser.: No. T-16). (Illus.). 60p. (Orig.). 1979. pap. 4.00 (0-88090-015-6) Intl Fertilizer.

Mexico: The Geography. Laura Conlon. LC 94-15000. (South of the Border Discovery Library). 24p. (J). (gr. k-4). 1994. lib. bdg. 15.93 (1-55916-056-X) Rourke Bk Co.

Mexico: The Land see Lands, Peoples & Cultures Series

Mexico: The Next Step. 2nd ed. Paul Hannon. (Illus.). 200p. 1995. 170.00 (1-85564-340-5, Pub. by Euromoney) Am Educ Systs.

Mexico: The People see Lands, Peoples & Cultures Series

Mexico: The People Next Door. G. Creel. 1976. lib. bdg. 59.95 (0-8490-2251-7) Gordon Pr.

Mexico: The Promise of NAFTA. (Industrial Development Review Ser.: No. M302). 1993. 150.00 (0-85058-783-2) Economist Intell.

Mexico: The Remaking of an Economy. Nora Lustig. 186p. (C). 1992. 14.95 (0-8157-5314-4) Brookings.

Mexico: The Remaking of an Economy. Nora Lustig. LC 98-26072. 260p. 1998. pap. 18.95 (0-8157-5319-5); text 44.95 (0-8157-5320-9) Brookings.

Mexico: The Strategy to Achieve Sustained Economic Growth. (Occasional Papers: No. 99). 91p. 1992. pap. 15.00 (1-55775-312-1) Intl Monetary.

Mexico: The Struggle for Peace & Bread. Frank Tannenbaum. LC 84-6034. 293p. 1984. reprint ed. lib. bdg. 65.00 (0-313-24453-7, TAMS, Greenwood Pr) Greenwood.

Mexico: The Uprising In Chiapas & Democratization In Mexico: Hearings Before the Subcommittee on Western Hemisphere of the Committee on Foreign Affairs, House of Representatives, 103rd Congress, 2nd Session, February 2, 1994. LC 94-238322. iii, 149 p. 1994. write for info. (0-16-044760-7) USGPO.

Mexico: Travel with Someone You Trust. 478p. 1999. pap. 15.00 (1-56251-273-0) AAA.

Mexico: Una Vision de Altura: Un Recorrido Aereo de Pasado al Presente. Tr. by Richard Lindley. (SPA., Illus.). 192p. 1996. 35.00 (1-883051-08-8) ALTI Pub.

Mexico: Waiting for Justice in Chiapas. Human Rights Watch Americas Staff & Physicians for Human Rights Staff. LC 94-68655. 100p. (Orig.). 1994. pap. 15.00 (1-879707-17-9) Phy Human Rights.

Mexico! 40 Activities to Experience Mexico Past & Present. Susan Milord. LC 98-34153. (Kaleidoscope Kids Ser.). 96p. (J). (gr. 1-7). 1999. pap. 10.95 (1-885593-22-8) Williamson Pub Co.

Mexico Vol. 1: Around the World. Betsy Franco. (Illus.). 48p. (J). (gr. 1-3). 1993. pap. text 7.95 (1-55799-256-8, EMC 275) Evan-Moor Edu Pubs.

Mexico - A Country Study Guide: Basic Information for Research & Pleasure. Global Investment Center, USA Staff. (World Country Study Guide Library: Vol. 112). (Illus.). 350p. 1999. pap. 59.00 (0-7397-1509-7) Intl Business Pubns.

Mexico - A Golden Past, a Hopeful Future. R. Conrad Stein. LC 95-42578. (Discovering Our Heritage Ser.). (J). 1996. pap. 6.95 (0-382-39291-4, Dillon Silver Burdett) Silver Burdett Pr.

Mexico - Human Rights in Mexico: A Policy of Impunity. Americas Watch Staff. LC 90-82958. 96p. (Orig.). 1990. pap. 7.00 (0-929692-62-4, Am Watch) Hum Rts Watch.

Mexico - Implausible Deniability: State Responsibility for Rural Violence in Mexico. 102p. 1997. pap. 10.00 (1-56432-210-6) Hum Rts Watch.

Mexico - Its Educational Problems: Suggestions for Their Solution. Manuel Barranco. LC 79-176518. (Columbia University, Teachers College, Contributions to Education Ser.: No. 73). reprint ed. 37.50 (0-404-55073-8) AMS Pr.

Mexico - Politica y Practica Laboral: Mexico - Labor Policy & Practice. Ed. by Paul F. Shaw. LC HD8013.M4. (ENG & SPA.). 150p. reprint ed. pap. 46.50 (0-7837-4595-8, 204431400002) Bks Demand.

Mexico - The Culture. Bobbie Kalman. LC 93-34765. (Lands, Peoples & Cultures Ser.). (SPA., Illus.). 32p. (YA). (gr. 4-9). 1993. pap. 7.95 (0-86505-400-2) Crabtree Pub Co.

Mexico - The People. Bobbie Kalman. LC 93-34764. (Lands, Peoples & Cultures Ser.). (SPA., Illus.). 32p. (YA). (gr. 4-9). 1994. pap. 7.95 (0-86505-399-5) Crabtree Pub Co.

Mexico - U. S. Free Trade Agreement. Ed. by Peter M. Garber. LC 93-8946. (Illus.). 329p. 1994. 37.50 (0-262-07152-5) MIT Pr.

Mexico - United States Relations, 34. Ed. by Susan K. Purcell. LC 80-70867. 213p. 1981. 49.95 (0-275-90707-4, C0707, Praeger Pubs) Greenwood.

Mexico - Viaje Al Pais de Los Tarahumaras (Mexico & Voyage to the Land of the Tarahumaras) Antonin Artaud. (SPA.). 381p. 1984. 9.99 (968-16-1572-7, Pub. by Fondo) Continental Bk.

Mexico a Fines de Siglo I, II. Jose Blanco. (SPA.). 20.99 (968-16-4051-9, Pub. by Fondo) Continental Bk.

Mexico Access. 3rd ed. Access Guides Staff. 272p. 1996. pap. 19.00 (0-06-277166-3) HarpC.

Mexico Activity Book: Arts, Crafts, Cooking & Historical Aids. Mary J. Keller. Ed. by Kathy Rogers. (Illus.). 48p. (J). (gr. 2-6). 1996. pap., wbk. ed. 6.95 (1-56472-073-X) Edupress Inc.

Mexico & Central America. Marion Morrison. LC 94-37192. (Places & People Ser.). 32p. (J). (gr. 5-8). 1995. lib. bdg. 20.80 (0-531-14366-X) Watts.

Mexico & Central America. Marion Morrison. (Places & People Ser.). (Illus.). 32p. (J). (gr. 5-8). 1996. reprint ed. pap. 6.95 (0-531-15288-X) Watts.

Mexico & Central America. 5th ed. (Handbooks of the World Ser.). (Illus.). 864p. 1994. 21.95 (0-8442-8977-9, Passprt Bks) NTC Contemp Pub Co.

Mexico & Central America: The All-in-One Travel & Language Guide. BBC Staff. (Get Around in . . . Ser.). (SPA., Illus.). 128p. 1998. pap. 8.95 (0-8442-0150-2, 01502) NTC Contemp Pub Co.

Mexico & Central America: The All-in-One Travel & Language Guide. NTC Publishing Group Staff. (Get Around in . . . Ser.). (SPA., Illus.). 128p. 1998. pap. 17.95 incl. audio (0-8442-0161-8, 01618) NTC Contemp Pub Co.

***Mexico & Central America by Campervan: Travel Adventure Guide.** John Plaxton & Elizabeth Plaxton. (Illus.). 1998. pap. 24.95 (1-895907-87-X) ITMP Pub.

***Mexico & Central America Handbook 2000.** 10th ed. Ben Box. (Footprints Bks.). 1344p. 1999. pap. 25.95 (0-8442-4838-X, 4838X, Natl Textbk Co) NTC Contemp Pub Co.

Mexico & Central American Handbook. Ed. by Ben Box. (Handbooks of the World Ser.). 1995. pap. 21.95 (0-614-15526-6) NTC Contemp Pub Co.

Mexico & Central American Handbook. 6th ed. Ed. by Ben Box. (Illus.). 928p. 1995. 21.95 (0-8442-8882-9, Passprt Bks) NTC Contemp Pub Co.

Mexico & Central American Handbook, 1994. 4th ed. Ben Box. 800p. 1994. pap. 21.95 (0-8442-9977-4, Passprt Bks) NTC Contemp Pub Co.

Mexico & Central American Handbook, 1999. 9th ed. Sarah Cameron. (Footprint Handbooks Ser.). (Illus.). 1344p. 1998. 27.95 (0-8442-4962-9) NTC Contemp Pub Co.

Mexico & Her People Today. N. O. Winter. 1977. lib. bdg. 69.95 (0-8490-2244-4) Gordon Pr.

Mexico & Mexico City in the World Economy. Edgar Butler et al. (Illus.). 400p. 2000. text 65.00 (0-8133-3542-6) Westview.

Mexico & NAFTA: The Real Impact. John L. Manzella. 1994. 35.00 (0-926566-03-2) Manzella Trade.

Mexico & Peru: Myths & Legends. Lewis Spence. (Illus.). 367p. 1998. pap. text 14.00 (0-7881-5340-4) DIANE Pub.

Mexico & Spanish Conquest. Ross Hassig. (C). 1993. text 75.95 (0-582-06828-2) Addison-Wesley.

Mexico & Texas, 1821-1835. Eugene C. Barker. 1993. reprint ed. lib. bdg. 75.00 (0-7812-5913-4) Rprt Serv.

Mexico & the Confederacy, 1860-1867. Harry T. Mahoney & Marjorie L. Mahoney. LC 96-53879. (Illus.). 286p. 1997. pap. 49.95 (1-57292-066-1) Austin & Winfield.

Mexico & the Confederacy, 1860-1867. Harry Thayer Mahoney & Marjorie Locke Mahoney. LC 96-53879. (Illus.). 240p. 1997. 69.95 (1-57292-067-X) Intl Scholars.

Mexico & the Hispanic Southwest in American Literature. Cecil Robinson. LC 76-24082. 391p. 1977. pap. 19.95 (0-8165-0593-4) U of Ariz Pr.

Mexico & the NAFTA Environment Debate: The Transnational Politics of Economic Integration. Barbara Hogenboom. LC 98-204411. 279p. 1998. pap. 29.95 (90-5727-014-5, Pub. by Intl Bks) Paul & Co Pubs.

Mexico & the North American Free Trade Agreement. Ed. by Victor Bulmer-Thomas et al. LC 94-5688. (Who Will Benefit? Ser.). 1994. text 55.00 (0-312-12176-8) St Martin.

***Mexico & the Sexenio Crisis: Presidential Successions & Economic Crises in Modern Mexico.** Jonathan Heath. LC 99-46638. (Significant Issues Ser.). 144p. 1999. pap. 17.95 (0-89206-357-2) CSIS.

An Asterisk (*) at the beginning of an entry indicates that the title is appearing for the first time.

Mexico & the Soviet Block. Zbigniew A. Kruszewski. (WVSS in International Relations Ser.). (C). 1996. pap. text 22.50 (*0-8133-7118-X*) Westview.

Mexico & the Spanish Civil War. Thomas G. Powell. LC 80-52280. 224p. reprint ed. pap. 69.50 (*0-608-15407-5*, 202931700060) Bks Demand.

Mexico & the Spanish Conquest: Wars in Context. Ross Hassig. 216p. (C). 1995. pap. 43.00 (*0-582-06829-0*) Addison-Wesley.

Mexico & the Survey of Public Lands: The Management of Modernization, 1876-1911. Robert H. Holden. LC 93-34379. 251p. (C). 1994. lib. bdg. 32.00 (*0-87580-181-1*) N Ill U Pr.

Mexico & the United States. Lester D. Langley. (Twayne's International History Ser.: No. 8). 160p. 1991. 27.95 (*0-8057-7912-4*, Twyne); pap. 15.95 (*0-8057-9209-0*, Twyne) Mac Lib Ref.

Mexico & the United States. Ed. by Robert E. McBride. LC 81-5171. 312p. 1981. 11.95 (*0-13-579565-6*) Am Assembly.

Mexico & the United States. Frederick Starr. 1976. lib. bdg. 50.00 (*0-8490-0623-6*) Gordon Pr.

Mexico & the United States. American Assembly Staff. LC 81-5171. 208p. reprint ed. pap. 64.50 (*0-608-16983-8*, 205625400056) Bks Demand.

Mexico & the United States: Ambivalent Vistas. 2nd ed. W. Dirk Raat. LC 96-18124. 1996. pap. 20.00 (*0-8203-1812-4*) U of Ga Pr.

Mexico & the United States: Neighbors in Crisis. Daniel G. Aldrich, Jr. & Lorenzo Mayer. LC 93-924. (Great Issues of the Day Ser.: No. 6). (Illus.). x, 390p. 1993. pap. 35.00 (*0-89370-445-8*) Millefleurs.

Mexico & the United States - Cooperation & Conflict see Single Titles Series

Mexico As I Saw It. Alec Tweedie. 1976. lib. bdg. 250.00 (*0-8490-0624-4*) Gordon Pr.

Mexico at the World's Fair: Crafting a Modern Nation. Mauricio Tenorio-Trillo. LC 95-47068. (New Historicism Ser.: Vol. 35). (Illus.). 383p. (C). 1996. 48.00 (*0-520-20267-8*, Pub. by U CA Pr) Cal Prin Full Svc.

Mexico Automotive Outlook - Taking off with NAFTA. Marc N. Scheinman. 1993. 150.00 (*0-614-10587-0*) Wards Comm.

***Mexico Between Hitler & Roosevelt: Mexican Foreign Relations in the Age of Lazaro Cardenas.** Friedrich E. Schuler. 2000. pap. 19.95 (*0-8263-2160-7*) U of NM Pr.

Mexico Blue-Ribbon Fly Fishing Guide. Ken Hanley. LC 99-195319. (Illus.). 80p. 1999. pap. 24.95 (*1-57188-154-9*) F Amato Pubns.

Mexico Business: The Portable Encyclopedia for Doing Business with Mexico. James L. Nolan et al. LC 94-15696. (Country Business Guide Ser.). 488p. 1994. pap. 24.95 (*0-9631864-0-X*) Wrld Trade Pr.

Mexico Business & Legal Briefing, 1998-1999. Ed. by Scott Studebaker. 156p. 1998. pap. 235.00 (*1-893323-12-9*) WorldTrade Exec.

***Mexico Business Intelligence Report, 190 vols.** Global Investment & Business Center, Inc. Staff. (World Business Intelligence Library: Vol. 112). (Illus.). 350p. 2000. pap. 99.95 (*0-7397-2610-2*) Intl Business Pubns.

***Mexico Business Law Handbook, 190 vols.** Global Investment & Business Center, Inc. Staff. (Global Business Law Handbooks Library: Vol. 112). (Illus.). 350p. 2000. pap. 99.95 (*0-7397-2010-4*) Intl Business Pubns.

Mexico Business Law Handbook-98. Russian Information & Business Center, Inc. Staff. (World Business Law Library-98). (Illus.). 350p. 1998. pap. 99.00 (*1-57751-841-1*) Intl Business Pubns.

***Mexico Business Opportunity Yearbook.** Global Investment & Business Center, Inc. Staff. (Global Business Opportunity Yearbooks Library: Vol. 112). (Illus.). 2000. pap. 99.95 (*0-7397-2210-7*) Intl Business Pubns.

***Mexico Business Opportunity Yearbook: Export-Import, Investment & Business Opportunities.** International Business Publications, U. S. A. Staff & Global Investment Center, U. S. A. Staff. (Global Business Opportunity Yearbooks Library: Vol. 112). (Illus.). 350p. 1999. pap. 99.95 (*0-7397-1310-8*) Intl Business Pubns.

Mexico City see Cities of the World

Mexico City. 128p. text 14.95 (*88-8029-632-9*, Pub. by Bonechi) Eiron.

Mexico City. Frommer's Staff. (Frommer's Travel Guides Ser.). (Illus.). 240p. 1995. 12.95 (*0-02-860059-2*, P-H Travel) Prntice Hall Bks.

Mexico City. Insight Guides Staff. (Insight Guides Ser.). 1998. 21.95 (*0-88729-712-9*) Langenscheidt.

Mexico City. Olive Percival. 1976. lib. bdg. 59.95 (*0-8490-0625-2*) Gordon Pr.

***Mexico City.** 2nd ed. Andrew Coe. 1999. pap. 19.95 (*962-217-581-3*) Norton.

***Mexico City.** 2nd ed. Ed. by Fodors Travel Publications, Inc. Staff. 2000. pap. write for info. (*0-679-00576-5*) Fodors Travel.

***Mexico City.** 2nd ed. Fodors Travel Publications, Inc. Staff. (Pocket Guides Ser.). 2000. pap. 10.00 (*0-679-00657-5*, Pub. by Fodors Travel) Random House.

Mexico City. 2nd ed. Insight Guides Staff. (Insight Guides). 1998. pap. text 12.95 (*0-88729-912-1*) Langenscheidt.

Mexico City. 2nd ed. Peter M. Ward. LC 97-22251. (World Cities Ser.). 358p. 1998. 100.00 (*0-471-97529-X*) Wiley.

Mexico City. 3rd ed. Insight Guides Staff. (Insight Guides). 1998. 21.95 (*0-88729-589-4*) Langenscheidt.

Mexico City: A Cultural & Literary Companion. Nick Caistor. LC 99-56320. (Cities of the Imagination Ser.). 256p. 2000. pap. 15.00 (*1-56656-349-6*) Interlink Pub.

Mexico City: The Production & Reproduction of an Urban Environment. Peter Ward. (Illus.). 264p. 1990. 40.00 (*0-8161-7259-5*, Hall Reference) Macmillan.

Mexico City & Acapulco, 1991-92. (Frommer's City Guides Ser.). 240p. 1990. pap. 7.95 (*0-685-54073-1*, P-H Travel) Prntice Hall Bks.

Mexico City Blues: Two Hundred Forty-Two Choruses. Jack Kerouac. LC 90-2748. 256p. (Orig.). 1987. pap. 12.00 (*0-8021-3060-7*, Grove) Grove-Atltic.

Mexico City's Alternative Futures. Bruce Nord. 218p. (C). 1995. lib. bdg. 29.50 (*0-7618-0172-3*) U Pr of Amer.

Mexico City's Water Supply: Improving the Outlook for Sustainability. National Research Council Staff. 256p. 1995. pap. text 30.00 (*0-309-05245-9*) Natl Acad Pr.

Mexico, Civil Code of: With 1958 Supplement. annot. ed. Otto Schoenrich. xxii, 627p. 1950. suppl. ed. 45.00 (*0-89941-610-1*, 500490) W S Hein.

Mexico Cookbook. Alexandra G. Greeley. (Illus.). 64p. 1995. 27.50 incl. disk (*0-02-860387-7*) Macmillan.

***Mexico Country Review 2000.** Robert C. Kelly et al. (Illus.). 60p. 1999. pap. 39.95 (*1-58310-536-0*) CountryWatch.

Mexico Earthquakes, 1985: Factors Involved & Lessons Learned. Ed. by Michael A. Cassaro & Enrique M. Romero. 488p. 1987. 40.00 (*0-87262-579-6*) Am Soc Civil Eng.

Mexico Embraces the "Third Age" Genie Nyer. (Working Paper Ser.: No. 77). 32p. (C). 1994. pap. 5.50 (*0-89940-571-1*) LBJ Sch Pub Aff.

Mexico en la Globalizacion (Mexico in the Globalization) Compiled by Victor L. Urquidi. (SPA.). 223p. 1997. reprint ed. pap. 13.99 (*968-16-5084-0*, Pub. by Fondo) Continental Bk.

Mexico en una Nuez. Alfonso Reyes. (Fondo 2000 Ser.). (SPA.). pap. 2.99 (*968-16-5056-5*, Pub. by Fondo) Continental Bk.

Mexico Environmental Report: A Resource for Business. Paulette S. Wolfson. 254p. 1996. pap. 495.00 (*0-86587-516-2*) Gov Insts.

Mexico Faces the 21st Century. Ed. by Donald E. Schulz & Edward J. Williams. LC 95-4669. (Contributions in Latin American Studies: 5). 232p. 1995. pap. 20.95 (*0-275-95358-0*, Praeger Pubs) Greenwood.

Mexico Faces the 21st Century, Vol. 5. Ed. by Donald E. Schulz & Edward J. Williams. LC 95-4669. (Contributions in Latin American Studies: Vol. 5). 232p. 1995. 59.95 (*0-313-29518-2*, Greenwood Pr) Greenwood.

***Mexico, Facing the Challenges of Human Rights & Crime.** Ed. by William Cartwright. LC 99-57634. 1999. text 125.00 (*1-57105-134-1*) Transnatl Pubs.

***Mexico Foreign Policy & Government Guide.** Contrib. by Global Investment & Business Center, Inc. Staff. (World Foreign Policy & Government Library: Vol. 108). (Illus.). 350p. 1999. pap. 99.00 (*0-7397-3606-X*) Intl Business Pubns.

***Mexico Foreign Policy & Government Guide.** Global Investment & Business Center, Inc. Staff. (World Foreign Policy & Government Library: Vol. 108). (Illus.). 350p. 2000. pap. 99.95 (*0-7397-3810-0*) Intl Business Pubns.

Mexico from A to Z see Alphabasics Series

***Mexico from Within, Vol. 1.** Bernard Bennett. 260p. 1999. text 26.95 (*0-9673681-0-3*) B Bennett.

***Mexico Government & Business Contacts Handbook: Strategic Government & Business Contacts for Conducting succesful Business, Export-Import & Investment Activity.** International Business Publications, USA Staff & Global Investment Center, USA Staff. (World Export-Import & Business Library: 53). (Illus.). 250p. 2000. pap. 99.95 (*0-7397-6092-0*) Intl Business Pubns.

Mexico Green Guide. 2nd ed. Michelin Staff. (SPA.). 1996. pap. 19.95 (*0-7859-9172-7*) Fr & Eur.

Mexico Guatemala Belize Green Guide. Michelin Staff. (SPA.). 1998. per. 20.00 (*2-06-457801-3*, 4578) Michelin.

Mexico Guatemala Belize Green Guide: Amerique du Nord. Ed. by Michelin Staff. (FRE.). 1998. per. 20.00 (*2-06-057801-9*, 578) Michelin.

Mexico Guatemala Belize Green Guide: North America. Michelin Staff. 1998. per. 20.00 (*2-06-157801-2*, 1578) Michelin.

***Mexico High Tech 3000: An Annotated Directory of 3000 of the Most Prominent Users.** Expansion Factor, Inc. Staff. LC 99-76471. vi, 515p. 1999. pap. 95.00 (*0-9676471-1-8*) Expansion Factor.

Mexico in Crisis. 2nd ed. Judith A. Hellman. LC 83-8485. (Illus.). 346p. 1983. pap. 19.95 (*0-8419-0895-8*) Holmes & Meier.

Mexico in Focus. John Ross. (In Focus Ser.). (Illus.). 80p. Date not set. pap. 12.00 (*0-85345-979-7*, Pub. by Lat Am Bur) Monthly Rev.

Mexico in Pictures. Department of Geography, Lerner Publications. (Visual Geography Ser.). (Illus.). 64p. (YA). (gr. 6-9). 1994. lib. bdg. 19.93 (*0-8225-1801-5*, Lerner Publctns) Lerner Pub.

Mexico in the Age of Democratic Revolutions, 1750-1850. Jaime E. Rodriguez O. LC 93-33325. 330p. 1994. lib. bdg. 42.00 (*1-55587-476-2*) L Rienner.

***Mexico in the Age of Proposals, 1821-1853, Vol. 12.** Will Fowler. LC 98-13977. (Contributions in Latin American Studies: Vol. 12). 344p. 1998. 69.50 (*0-313-30427-0*, Greenwood Pr) Greenwood.

Mexico in the Global Economy: High Technology & Work Organization in Export Industries. Harley Shaiken. (Monographs: No. 33). 136p. 1990. pap. 14.95 (*0-935391-99-1*, MN-33) UCSD Ctr US-Mex.

Mexico in the 1990s: Government & Opposition Speak Out. Miguel A. Centeno. (Current Issue Briefs Ser.: No. 1). 37p. 1991. pap. 7.50 (*1-878367-01-3*, CIB01) UCSD Ctr US-Mex.

***Mexico in the 1940s: Modernity, Politics & Corruption.** Stephen R. Niblo. LC 99-28870. (Latin American Silhouettes Ser.). 1999. 55.00 (*0-8420-2794-7*) Scholarly Res Inc.

Mexico in the Theater. Rodolfo Usigli. Tr. by Wilder P. Scott. LC 75-38748. (Romance Monographs: No. 18). 1976. 29.00 (*84-399-4744-5*) Romance.

Mexico in Transition. Phillip L. Russell. (Illus.). 176p. 1977. pap. 7.95 (*0-931302-01-3*) Colo River Pr.

***Mexico Investment & Business Guide.** Global Investment & Business Center, Inc. Staff. (Global Investment & Business Guide Library: Vol. 112). (Illus.). 2000. pap. 99.95 (*0-7397-1810-X*) Intl Business Pubns.

Mexico Investment & Business Guide: Economy, Export-Import, Business & Investment Climate, Business Contacts. Contrib. by Russian Information & Business Center, Inc. Staff. (Russia, NIS & Emerging Markets Investment & Business Library-98). (Illus.). 350p. 1998. pap. 99.00 (*1-57751-898-5*) Intl Business Pubns.

***Mexico Investment & Business Guide: Export-Import, Investment & Business Opportunities.** International Business Publications, USA Staff & Global Investment Center, USA Staff. (World Investment & Business Guide Library-99: Vol. 112). (Illus.). 350p. 1999. pap. 99.95 (*0-7397-0307-2*) Intl Business Pubns.

Mexico Investment & Trade: Progress & Prospects. (Commercial Law & Practice Course Handbook Ser.: Vol. 653). 472p. 1993. 70.00 (*0-685-69710-X*, A4-4422) PLI.

Mexico Is Forever. Benjamin M. Schutz. 1999. pap. 3.95 (*0-14-012891-3*, Viking) Viking Penguin.

Mexico Labor Law. 100p. 1996. pap. 295.00 (*0-7605-4318-6*) Rector Pr.

Mexico Living & Travel. 3rd rev. ed. Jean R. Bryant & John D. Bryant. LC 94-228235. (Illus.). 290p. 1999. pap. text 29.95 (*1-878061-01-1*) M R T A.

***Mexico Megacity.** Pick. 1999. pap. 40.00 (*0-8133-3754-2*, Pub. by Westview) HarpC.

Mexico Megacity. James B. Pick & Edgar W. Butler. LC 96-38152. (C). 1997. text 95.00 (*0-8133-8983-6*, Pub. by Westview) HarpC.

Mexico Mestizo. Basave Benitez. (SPA.). pap. 11.99 (*968-16-3715-1*, Pub. by Fondo) Continental Bk.

Mexico, Mother of Towns: Fragments of Local History. Elizabeth M. Simpson. (Illus.). 551p. 1997. reprint ed. lib. bdg. 58.00 (*0-8328-6174-X*) Higginson Bk Co.

Mexico Mystique: The Coming Sixth World of Consciousness. Frank Waters. LC 74-18579. (Illus.). 336p. 1989. pap. 14.95 (*0-8040-0922-8*) Swallow.

Mexico Nine: Mexico Nueve. Clinton Adams et al. Ed. by Kate Downer. Tr. by Latin American Institute Staff. (ENG & SPA., Illus.). 56p. (Orig.). 1988. pap. 16.00 (*0-9619735-0-1*) Tamarind Inst.

Mexico, 1985. Florence Lemkowitz. Ed. by Robert C. Fisher. (Fisher Annotated Travel Guides Ser.). 448p. 1984. 13.95 (*0-8116-0068-8*) NAL.

Mexico, 1994: Anatomy of an Emerging-Market Crash. Ed. by Sebastian Edwards & Moises Naim. LC 97-51274. 326p. 1997. pap. 22.95 (*0-87003-154-6*) Carnegie Endow.

Mexico of the Mexicans. Lewis Spence. 1972. 250.00 (*0-8490-0630-9*) Gordon Pr.

Mexico of the Twentieth Century, 2 vols. P. Martin. 1976. lib. bdg. 200.00 (*0-8490-2249-5*) Gordon Pr.

Mexico on Fifty Dollars a Day, '94. Arthur Frommer. 1993. pap. 19.00 (*0-671-84908-5*, P-H Travel) Prntice Hall Bks.

Mexico on the Verge. Emile J. Dillon. 1976. lib. bdg. 59.95 (*0-8490-0631-7*) Gordon Pr.

Mexico on the Verge: American Imperialism: Viewpoints of United States Foreign Policy 1898-1941. Emile J. Dillon. LC 78-111712. 1970. reprint ed. 23.95 (*0-405-02013-9*) Ayer.

***Mexico One Plate at a Time.** Rick Bayless. 2000. 30.00 (*0-684-84186-X*) Scribner.

Mexico Photo Fun Activities. Mary Jo Keller. Ed. by Kathy Rogers. (Social Studies Photo Fun Activities Ser.). (Illus.). 8p. 1996. 6.95 (*1-56472-074-8*) Edupress Inc.

***Mexico Pocket Guide.** Berlitz Publishing Staff. (Berlitz Pocket Guide Ser.). 256p. 1999. pap. 10.95 (*2-8315-7221-5*) Berlitz.

***Mexico Pocket Guide.** rev. ed. Berlitz Publishing Staff. (Berlitz Pocket Guide Ser.). (SPA.). 256p. 1999. pap. 8.95 (*2-8315-7275-4*) Berlitz.

Mexico Procedures & Documentation. unabridged ed. Janis F. Seal. 213p. 2000. spiral bd. 65.00 (*1-891249-11-8*) Global Train Ctr.

Mexico Profundo: Reclaiming a Civilization. Guillermo Bonfil Batalla. Tr. by Philip A. Dennis from SPA. (Translations from Latin America Ser.). 216p. (Orig.). 1996. pap. 16.95 (*0-292-70843-2*); text 30.00 (*0-292-70844-0*) U of Tex Pr.

Mexico Reborn. Victor Millan. 1976. 59.95 (*0-8490-2250-9*) Gordon Pr.

Mexico Shining: Versions of Aztec Songs. Nancy P. Arbuthnot. (Illus.). 120p. (Orig.). 1995. 25.00 (*0-89410-785-2*, Three Contnts); pap. 12.00 (*0-89410-786-0*, Three Contnts) L Rienner.

Mexico since Independence. Ed. by Leslie Bethell. (Illus.). 463p. (C). 1991. text 80.00 (*0-521-41306-0*); pap. text 24.95 (*0-521-42372-4*) Cambridge U Pr.

Mexico South: The Isthmus of Tehuantepec. Miguel Covarrubias. (Illus.). 400p. 1986. pap. text 19.95 (*0-7103-0184-7*) Routledge.

Mexico, Su Gente. Bobbie Kalman.Tr. of Mexico, the People. (SPA.). (J). 1994. 13.15 (*0-606-07863-0*) Turtleback.

Mexico, Su Tierra. Bobbie Kalman.Tr. of Mexico, the Land. (SPA.). (J). 1994. 13.15 (*0-606-07864-9*) Turtleback.

Mexico: The Geography see Geografia de Mexico

Mexico, the Land see Mexico, Su Tierra

Mexico, the People see Mexico, Su Gente

Mexico, the Wonderland of the South. W. E. Carson. 1977. lib. bdg. 59.95 (*0-8490-2252-5*) Gordon Pr.

Mexico Through Foreign Eyes: Visto por Ojos Extranjeros, 1850-1990. Carole Naggar & Fred Ritchin. (Illus.). 320p. 1996. pap. 35.00 (*0-393-31491-X*, Norton Paperbks) Norton.

***Mexico Today: An Encyclopedia of Contemporary History & Culture.** Don M. Coerver et al. 2001. lib. bdg. 75.00 (*1-57607-132-4*) ABC-CLIO.

Mexico Today & Tomorrow. E. D. Trowbridge. 1976. lib. bdg. 250.00 (*0-8490-0633-3*) Gordon Pr.

***Mexico Travelbook 2000.** (Illus.). 478p. 2000. per. 15.00 (*1-56251-316-8*) AAA.

Mexico Trilogy. D. N. Steufloten. 310p. (Orig.). 1996. pap. 12.95 (*1-57366-019-1*) Fiction Coll.

Mexico, 2005: The Challenge of the New Millennium. Michael J. Mazarr & Ram Irez De La O., Rogelio. LC 98-41066. (Global Trends 2005 Ser.). 192p. (C). 1998. pap. text 21.95 (*0-89206-338-6*) CSIS.

***Mexico 2001.** Fodor's Staff. 2000. pap. 20.00 (*0-679-00547-1*) Fodors Travel.

Mexico under Fire: Being the Diary of Samuel Ryan Curtis, 3rd Ohio Volunteer Regiment, During... Samual R. Curtis. Ed. by Joseph E. Chance. 308p. (C). 1994. 29.95 (*0-87565-127-5*) Tex Christian.

Mexico under Salinas. Philip Russell. LC 93-81213. (Illus.). x, 486p. (C). 1994. pap. text 14.95 (*0-9639223-0-0*) Mexico Res Ctr.

Mexico under Spain, Fifteen Twenty One-Fifteen Fifty Six: Society & the Origins of Nationality. Peggy K. Liss. LC 74-33507. xvi, 230p. 1994. pap. text 9.95 (*0-226-48496-3*) U Ch Pr.

Mexico under Spain, Fifteen Twenty One-Fifteen Fifty Six: Society & the Origins of Nationality. Peggy K. Liss. LC 74-33507. xvi, 230p. 1994. lib. bdg. 21.00 (*0-226-48495-5*) U Ch Pr.

Mexico under Zedillo. Ed. by Susan K. Purcell & Luis Rubio. LC 97-32753. (Americas Society Ser.). 152p. 1998. pap. 13.50 (*1-55587-315-4*) L Rienner.

Mexico Vivo Learner Partner -users Guide/ Flame. (College Spanish). (SPA.). (C). 1997. mass mkt., suppl. ed. 21.95 (*0-8384-6379-7*) Heinle & Heinle.

Mexico Vivo Teacher Partner -users Guide. Flame. (College Spanish). (SPA.). (C). 1995. mass mkt. 21.95 (*0-8384-6370-3*) Heinle & Heinle.

Mexico West Book. Tom Miller. 1991. pap. 15.95 (*0-914622-09-9*) Baja Source.

Mexicolor: The Spirit of Mexican Design. Masako Takahashi. (Illus.). 176p. 1998. pap. 24.95 (*0-8118-1893-4*) Chronicle Bks.

Mexico's Agricultural Dilemma. Paul Lamartine Yates et al. LC 81-10279. 307p. 1981. reprint ed. pap. 95.20 (*0-7837-9237-9*, 204998800004) Bks Demand.

Mexico's Alternative Political Futures. Ed. by Wayne A. Cornelius et al. 468p. 1989. 19.95 (*0-935391-84-3*, MN30C); pap. 11.95 (*0-935391-83-5*, MN-30) UCSD Ctr US-Mex.

***Mexico's Cinema: A Century of Film & Filmmakers.** Joanne Hershfield. Ed. by David R. Maciel et al. LC 99-24763. (Latin American Silhouettes Ser.). 328p. 1999. pap. 21.95 (*0-8420-2682-7*) Scholarly Res Inc.

***Mexico's Cinema: A Century of Film & Filmmakers.** Ed. by Joanne Hershfield et al. LC 99-24763. (Latin American Silhouettes Ser.). 328p. 1999. 55.00 (*0-8420-2681-9*) Scholarly Res Inc.

Mexico's Colonial Heart. Mexico Mike Nelson. LC 94-90360. (Sanborn's Travelog - Mexico by Land Ser.). (Illus.). 336p. (Orig.). 1995. pap. 5.00 (*1-878166-17-4*) Wanderlust Pubns.

Mexico's Copper Canyon Country: A Hiking & Backpacking Guide. rev. ed. M. John Fayhee. LC 94-17399. (Illus.). 224p. 1994. pap. 16.95 (*1-55566-124-6*) Johnson Bks.

Mexico's Economic Crisis: Challenges & Opportunities. Intro. by Donald L. Wyman. (Monographs: No. 12). 126p. (Orig.). (C). 1983. pap. 9.95 (*0-935391-50-9*, MN-12) UCSD Ctr US-Mex.

Mexico's Economic Crisis: Its Origins & Consequences. Miguel D. Ramirez. LC 88-30738. 164p. 1989. 52.95 (*0-275-92867-5*, C2867, Praeger Pubs) Greenwood.

Mexico's Economic Policy: Past, Present & Future. James H. Street et al. Ed. & Intro. by William E. Cole. (International Socioeconomic Ser.). 96p. (Orig.). (C). 1987. pap. text 9.00 (*0-940191-09-1*) Univ TN Ctr Bus Econ.

Mexico's Financial Crisis: Origins, Awareness, Assistance, & Initial Efforts to Recover. (Illus.). 167p. (Orig.). 1996. pap. text 35.00 (*0-7881-2888-4*) DIANE Pub.

Mexico's Fortress Monasteries. Richard Perry. (Illus.). 224p. (Orig.). 1992. pap. 19.95 (*0-9620811-1-6*) Espadana Pr.

Mexico's General Law of Ecological Balance & Environmental Protection: Secretariat of Urban Development & Ecology (SEDUE), 1988. 1988. 10.00 (*0-614-11100-5*, ID04) Waste-Mgmt Educ.

Mexico's Gulf Coast: And Costa Esmeralda. Mike Nelson. (Sanborn's Travelog Ser.). 90p. 1997. pap. 15.95 (*1-878166-27-1*) Wanderlust Pubns.

Mexico's Hidden Revolution: The Catholic Church in Law & Politics since 1929. Peter L. Reich. LC 95-16516. (From the Helen Kellogg Institute for International Ser.). (C). 1996. text 28.95 (*0-268-01418-3*) U of Notre Dame Pr.

Mexico's Hope: An Encounter with Politics & History. James D. Cockcroft. LC 98-46777. 1998. 18.00 (*0-85345-925-8*, Pub. by Monthly Rev) NYU Pr.

Mexico's Hope: An Encounter with Politics & History. James D. Cockcroft. LC 98-46777. 435p. 1998. 48.00 (*0-85345-926-6*, Pub. by Monthly Rev) NYU Pr.

M

***Mexico's Lake Chapala & Ajijie: The Insider's Guide to the Northshore.** Teresa A. Kendrick. Ed. by Adelle M. Cordero. (Illus.). 120p. 1999. pap. 18.95 (0-9675248-0-6, 00100) Mexico Reality.

Mexico's Leaders, Their Education & Recruitment. Roderic A. Camp. LC 79-19836. 277p. 1980. pap. 85.90 (0-608-05648-0, 206610200006) Bks Demand.

Mexico's Merchant Elite, 1590-1660: Silver, State, & Society. Louisa S. Hoberman. LC 90-20659. (Illus.). 369p. 1991. text 47.95 (0-8223-1134-8) Duke.

Mexico's Miguel Caldera: The Taming of America's First Frontier, 1548-1597. Phillip W. Powell. LC 76-62551. 334p. reprint ed. pap. 95.20 (0-8357-8585-8, 2034956) Bks Demand.

Mexico's Pacific Coast: And Copper Canyon. Mike Nelson. (Sanborn's Travelog Ser.). 150p. 1996. pap. 15.95 (1-878166-26-3) Wanderlust Pubns.

***Mexico's Political Awakening.** Vikram K. Chand. (From the Helen Kellogg Institute for International Ser.). 270p. 2000. pap. 20.00 (0-268-03459-1, Pub. by U of Notre Dame Pr); lib. bdg. 40.00 (0-268-03458-3, Pub. by U of Notre Dame Pr) Chicago Distribution Ctr.

Mexico's Political Economy: Challenges at Home & Abroad. Ed. by Jorge I. Dominguez. LC 81-18472. (Sage Focus Editions Ser.: No. 47). 240p. reprint ed. pap. 74.40 (0-8357-4781-6, 203771800009) Bks Demand.

Mexico's Private Sector: Recent History, Future Challenges. Ed. by Riordan Roett. LC 98-25921. 252p. 1998. lib. bdg. 49.95 (1-55587-713-3) L Rienner.

Mexico's Progress Demands Its Price. L. Warner. 1976. lib. bdg. 250.00 (0-8490-2254-1) Gordon Pr.

Mexico's Regions: Comparative History & Development. Ed. by Eric Van Young. (U. S. - Mexico Contemporary Perspectives Ser.: No. 04). 254p. 1992. pap. 21.95 (1-878367-10-2, CP-04) UCSD Ctr US-Mex.

Mexico's Ruling Party: Stability & Authority. Dale Story. LC 86-22690. 172p. 1986. 37.95 (0-275-92127-1, C2127, Praeger Pubs) Greenwood.

Mexico's Ruta Maya: Yucatan Penisula Cancune & Belize. Mike Nelson. LC 97-60402. (Sanborn's Travelog Ser.). 142p. (Orig.). 1997. pap. 15.95 (1-878166-08-5) Wanderlust Pubns.

Mexico's Second Agrarian Reform: Household & Community Responses, 1990-1994. Alain De Janvry et al. LC 97-8991. (Transformations of Rural Mexico Ser.: No. 1). 1997. pap. 16.00 (1-878367-30-7) UCSD Ctr US-Mex.

Mexico's Sierra Tarahumara: A Photohistory of the People of the Edge. W. Dirk Raat & George R. Janecek. LC 95-50961. (Illus.). 136p. 1996. 49.95 (0-8061-2815-1) U of Okla Pr.

***Mexico's Tehuantepec Canal Controversy: A Lesson in American Diplomacy.** ix, 161p. 1999. pap. 11.95 (0-9678681-0-6) Schade.

Mexico's Trade Policy: The U. S. Blanca Torres. Ed. by Pamela S. Falk. (C). 1996. text 28.00 (0-8133-7666-1) Westview.

Mexico's Treasure House: Guanajuato. Percy F. Martin. 1977. lib. bdg. 59.95 (0-8490-2255-X) Gordon Pr.

Mexico's Volcanoes. 2nd ed. Ed. by R. J. Secor. (Illus.). 120p. 1993. pap. 14.95 (0-89886-329-5) Mountaineers.

Mexico's "War" on Drugs: Causes & Consequences, 3. Celia Toro. LC 94-34472. (Studies on the Impact of the Illegal Drug Trade). 115p. 1995. pap. text 25.00 (1-55587-548-3) L Rienner.

Mexiko, Heterogenitat & Bevolkerungsentwicklung: Der Zusammenhang Zwischen Demographischer & Soziookonomischer Entwicklung unter Besonderer Berucksichtigung der Sozialen & Regionalen Heterogenitat der Fertilitat. Martina Krause. (GER., Illus.). XI, 316p. 1996. 57.95 (3-631-30627-X) P Lang Pubng.

Mexiko Im Werk von Bodo Uhse, das Nie Verlassene Exil. Renata Von Hanffstengel. (Exilstudien - Exile Studies: Vol. 4). (GER.). XIV, 236p. (C). 1996. text 49.95 (0-8204-2683-0) P Lang Pubng.

Mexique: Des Plantes pour les Hommes. Ed. by J. Rammeloo. (FRE., Illus.). 143p. 1993. pap. 45.00 (1-878762-81-8, Pub. by Natl Botanic Grdn Belgium) Balogh.

Mexperimental Cinema: 60 Years of Avant-Garde Media Arts from Mexico. Rita Gonzales & Jesse Lerner. (ENG & SPA., Illus.). 168p. 1998. pap. 10.00 (1-889195-30-8) Smart Art Pr.

MexWX (Weather-Radio for Boaters in Mexico) 2nd ed. John Rains. 1998. 19.95 (0-9638470-1-5) Pt Loma Pubng.

Meyah P'Amim V'Echad - Haveh (One Thousand Times & One - Present Tense) Dikduk L'Talmidim (Grammar for Students) Kalman Bachrach. (HEB.). 32p. (J). (gr. 1-3). 1937. pap. text 1.00 (1-878530-22-4) K Bachrach Co.

Meyah P'Amim V'Echad - Ovar (One Thousand Times & One - Past Tense) Dikduk L'Talmidim (Grammar for Students) Kalman Bachrach. (HEB.). 48p. (J). (gr. 1-3). 1937. pap. text 1.00 (1-878530-20-8) K Bachrach Co.

Meyer - Moyer. Genealogical Record of the Descendants of Christian & Hans Meyer (Moyer) & Other Pioneers. A. J. Fretz. (Illus.). 739p. 1991. reprint ed. pap. 105.00 (0-8328-2010-5); reprint ed. lib. bdg. 115.00 (0-8328-2009-1) Higginson Bk Co.

Meyer & Meyer Form Articulated Locomotives. Donald Binns & Gunther Koch. LC 94-20062. 1994. write for info. (0-87315-005-8) Golden Bell.

Meyer & Meyer Form Articulated Locomotives, Vol. 1. Ed. by Donald Binns & Gunther Koch. 104p. 1994. pap. 25.90 (1-873150-05-9) Taylor & Francis.

***Meyer Schapiro: His Painting, Drawing & Sculpture.** Lillian M. Schapiro & Daniel Esterman. LC 99-38216. 256p. 2000. 49.50 (0-8109-4392-1, Pub. by Abrams) Time Warner.

Meyer Waxman Jubilee Volume. Intro. by Judah M. Rosenthal. (ENG & HEB.). 427p. (C). 1967. 30.00 (0-935982-07-8, JMR-01) Spertus Coll.

Meyerbeer. Arthur Hervey. 63p. 1990. reprint ed. lib. bdg. 59.00 (0-7812-9074-0) Rprt Serv.

Meyerbeer, Giacomo Briefwechsel und Tagebucher, 1849-1851, Vol. 5. 704p. 1998. 181.00 (3-11-014244-9) De Gruyter.

Meyerhold: A Revolution in Theatre. Edward Braun. LC 95-60652. (Studies in Theatre History & Culture). (Illus.). 360p. 1998. reprint ed. pap. text 19.95 (0-87745-633-X) U of Iowa Pr.

Meyerhold at Work. Ed. & Tr. by Paul Schmidt. 272p. 1996. pap. 19.95 (1-55783-246-3) Applause Theatre Bk Pubs.

Meyerhold, Eisenstein & Biomechanics: Actor Training in Revolutionary Russia. Alma Law & Mel Gordon. LC 95-42738. (Illus.). 294p. 1995. lib. bdg. 47.50 (0-7864-0098-6) McFarland & Co.

Meyerhold Speaks/Meyerhold Rehearses. Alma Law. (Russian Theatre Archive Ser.). (Illus.). 288p. 1998. text 53.00 (90-5702-044-0, Harwood Acad Pubs); pap. text 18.00 (90-5702-045-9, Harwood Acad Pubs) Gordon & Breach.

Meyerhold's Theatre of the Grotesque: The Post-Revolutionary Productions, 1920-1932. James M. Symons. LC 74-149007. (Books of the Theatre: No. 8). (Illus.). 1971. 19.95 (0-87024-192-3) U of Miami Pr.

Meyers Enzyklopaedisches Lexikon, 25 vols. Meyers. (GER.). 1973. 3995.00 (0-8288-6321-0, M-7558) Fr & Eur.

Meyers Enzyklopaedisches Lexikon, Vol. 9. Academia Espanola Staff. (SPA.). 1989. pap. 75.00 (0-7859-6350-2, 8478482040) Fr & Eur.

Meyers Enzyklopaedisches Lexikon Vol. 4: Bes-Buc und 1 Nachtrag. Mary L. Apelt. (ENG & GER.). 240p. 1987. 95.00 (0-8288-0774-4, F56700) Fr & Eur.

Meyers Enzyklopaedisches Lexikon Vol. 5: Bud-Con. 9th ed. Wolfgang Bauer et al. (GER.). 872p. 1971. 275.00 (0-7859-6896-2, 3411012552) Fr & Eur.

Meyers Enzyklopaedisches Lexikon Vol. 17: Nau-Os. 9th ed. Dieter Baacke et al. (GER.). 848p. 1976. 275.00 (0-7859-6907-1, 3411012676) Fr & Eur.

Meyers Enzyklopaedisches Lexikon Vol. 22: Sn-Sud & Nachtrag 7. 9th ed. Jurgen Baumann et al. (GER.). 872p. 1978. 275.00 (0-7859-6912-8, 3411012722) Fr & Eur.

Meyers Grosses Handlexikon. 14th ed. Meyers. (GER.). 1072p. 1985. 75.00 (0-8288-1962-9, M15509) Fr & Eur.

Meyers Grosses Personenlexikon. (GER.). 85.00 (3-411-01152-1, M-7559) Fr & Eur.

Meyers Grosses Taschenlexikon, 24 vols. 4th ed. 1992. 395.00 (0-7859-9872-1) Fr & Eur.

Meyers Grosses Taschenlexikon, 24 vols. 5th ed. Meyers. (GER.). 1995. 395.00 (0-320-00102-4) Fr & Eur.

Meyers Kinderlexikon. (Memo Ser.). (GER.). Date not set. 21.95 (3-411-07814-6, Pub. by Bibliogr Inst Brockhaus) Langenscheidt.

Meyers Kinderlexikon. 259p. 1979. 17.50 (3-411-01774-0, Pub. by Bibliogr Inst Brockhaus) Langenscheidt.

Meyers Kleine Kinderbibliothek: Das Pferd. (Memo Ser.). (GER.). Date not set. 13.25 (3-411-09731-0, Pub. by Bibliogr Inst Brockhaus) Langenscheidt.

Meyers Kleine Kinderbibliothek: Der Affe. (Memo Ser.). (GER.). Date not set. 13.25 (3-411-09681-0, Pub. by Bibliogr Inst Brockhaus) Langenscheidt.

Meyers Kleine Kinderbibliothek: Die Erde. (Memo Ser.). (GER.). Date not set. 13.25 (3-411-09771-X, Pub. by Bibliogr Inst Brockhaus) Langenscheidt.

Meyers Kleine Kinderbibliothek: Die Ersten Menschen. (Memo Ser.). (GER.). Date not set. 13.25 (3-411-09741-8, Pub. by Bibliogr Inst Brockhaus) Langenscheidt.

Meyers Kleine Kinderbibliothek: Die Katze. (Memo Ser.). (GER.). Date not set. 13.25 (3-411-09761-2, Pub. by Bibliogr Inst Brockhaus) Langenscheidt.

Meyers Kleine Kinderbibliothek: Die Kuh. (Memo Ser.). (GER.). Date not set. 13.25 (3-411-09721-3, Pub. by Bibliogr Inst Brockhaus) Langenscheidt.

Meyers Kleine Kinderbibliothek: Die Schildkrote. (Memo Ser.). (GER.). Date not set. 13.25 (3-411-09751-5, Pub. by Bibliogr Inst Brockhaus) Langenscheidt.

Meyers Kleine Kinderbibliothek: Landschaften. (Memo Ser.). (GER.). Date not set. 13.25 (3-411-09711-6, Pub. by Bibliogr Inst Brockhaus) Langenscheidt.

Meyers Kleine Kinderbibliothek: Portrats. (Memo Ser.). (GER.). Date not set. 13.25 (3-411-09701-9, Pub. by Bibliogr Inst Brockhaus) Langenscheidt.

Meyers Kleine Kinderbibliothek: Weihnachten. (Memo Ser.). (GER.). Date not set. 13.25 (3-411-09691-8, Pub. by Bibliogr Inst Brockhaus) Langenscheidt.

Meyers Kontinente und Meere-Daten, Karten die Enzyklopadie der Erde, 8 vols. Meyers. (GER.). 1973. 625.00 (0-7859-0118-3, M7560) Fr & Eur.

Meyers Large Pocket Lexicon: Meyers Grosses Taschenlexikon des Gesamten Wissens. 2nd ed. Meyers. (GER.). 8640p. 1987. 350.00 (0-8288-1963-7, M15512) Fr & Eur.

Meyer's Manual on Louisiana Real Estate. M. Meyer. 1991. 90.00 (0-87511-913-1) Claitors.

Meyers Neues Lexikon, 10 vols. 5280p. 1994. 1495.00 (0-7859-9871-3) Fr & Eur.

Meyers Neues Lexikons, 10 vols. (GER.). 5280p. 1994. 1495.00 (0-7859-9290-1) Fr & Eur.

***Meyers Orts und Verkehrs-Lexikon des Deutschen Reichs.** Raymond S. Wright. LC 99-85938. 3464p. 2000. reprint ed. 300.00 (0-8063-1631-4) Genealog Pub.

Meyers Physik-Lexikon: Meyers Physics Lexicon. Meyers. (GER.). 1973. 85.00 (0-8288-6323-7, M-7561) Fr & Eur.

Meyers Standardlexikon des Gesamtes Wissesns. 2nd ed. Meyers. (GER.). 1118p. 1980. 45.00 (0-8288-1964-5, M7562) Fr & Eur.

***Meyerson Symphony Center: Building a Dream.** Laurie C. Shulman. LC 99-54375. (Illus.). 399p. 2000. 39.95 (1-57441-082-2, Pub. by UNTX Pr) Tex A&M Univ Pr.

Meyler's Side Effects of Drugs: An Encyclopedia of Adverse Reactions & Interactions. 12th ed. Ed. by M. N. Dukes. (Side Effects of Drugs Ser.: Vol. 12). xxii,1308p. 1992. 316.00 (0-444-89524-8) Elsevier.

Meyler's Side Effects of Drugs: An Encyclopedia of Adverse Reactions & Interactions. 13th ed. Ed. by M. N. G. Dukes. 1610p. 1996. 316.00 (0-444-82405-7) Elsevier.

***Meze.** Diane Kochilas. 2001. write for info. (0-688-17511-2, Wm Morrow) Morrow Avon.

Mezhdunarodnyi Turnir v Blede see Bled Nineteen Thirty-One International Chess Tournament

Mezogazdasac es Elelmezesugy: Agriculture & Food Dictionary. Vladimir Beck. (ENG, FRE, GER, HUN & RUS.). 513p. 1980. 45.00 (0-8288-0034-0, M169) Fr & Eur.

Mezuzah in the Madonnna's Foot: Marranso & Other Secret Jews--A Woman Discovers Her Spiritual Heritage. Trudi Alexy. LC 94-18549. 320p. 1994. pap. 14.00 (0-06-060340-2, Pub. by Harper SF) HarpC.

Mezza Voce. Anne-Marie Albiach. Tr. by Joseph Simas et al from FRE. (Poetry Ser.). 164p. (Orig.). 1988. pap. 12.95 (0-942996-11-9) Post Apollo Pr.

Mezzaluna Cookbook. Aldo Bozzi & Isabel B. Madden. 176p. 1995. 23.00 (0-517-70181-2) Random Hse Value.

***Mezzamorphis.** 88p. 1999. otabind 19.95 (0-634-00973-7) H Leonard.

***Mezzamorphis.** 1999. pap. 10.98 (7-474-00663-4) Sparrow TN.

Mezzanine. Nicholson Baker. (Vintage Contemporaries Ser.). 1990. pap. 11.00 (0-679-72576-8) Vin Bks.

Mezzanine Finance. Brian Sturgess & Catherine Leen. 141p. 1991. 132.00 (0-946559-86-4, Pub. by IFR Pub) Am Educ Systs.

Mezzo Cookbook: With John Torode. John Torode et al. LC 97-30192. (Illus.). 224p. 1997. 30.00 (1-57959-003-9, SOMA) BB&T Inc.

Mezzo Soprano & Contralto see Singer's Repertoire

Mezzo Soprano or Alto. 240p. 1987. otabind 19.95 (0-88188-545-2, 0361072) H Leonard.

MezzoMessiah. unabridged ed. Anthony M. Tedeschi. 300p. (Orig.). 1996. pap. 10.95 (0-9655375-1-X) Natural Traveler.

Mezzotint: History & Technique. Carol Wax. (Illus.). 296p. 1996. pap. text 35.00 (0-8109-2649-0, Pub. by Abrams) Time Warner.

Mezzotints. Henry Miller. Ed. by Roger Jackson. (Illus.). 40p. (C). 1993. 40.00 (0-9634136-2-7) R Jackson.

Mezzotints in Modern Music: Brahms, Tchaikovsky, Chopin, Richard Straus, Liszt & Wagner. James G. Huneker. LC 79-181181. 318p. 1905. reprint ed. 22.00 (0-403-01586-3) Scholarly.

Mezzotints in Modern Music: Brahms, Tchaikovsky, Chopin, Richard Strauss, Liszt, & Wagner. James G. Huneker. 318p. 1990. reprint ed. lib. bdg. 79.00 (0-7812-9037-6) Rprt Serv.

MF On-Line. Brian Wyant & Eric Wyant. (Illus.). 128p. 1997. pap. 9.95 (1-883788-13-7) Event Horzn.

***MFA: A Guide to the Collections of the Museum of Fine Arts, Boston.** Gilian Shallcross Wohlano. LC 99-60201. (Illus.). 400p. 1999. pap. 19.95 (0-87846-472-7, 00820) Mus Fine Arts Boston.

MFA, 1996. Laura Letinsky. Ed. & Pref. by Courtenay Smith. Pref. by Tom Mapp. (Illus.). 13p. (Orig.). 1996. pap. text 2.95 (0-935573-16-X) D & A Smart Museum.

***Mfana Mischief.** T. D. Motsau. (Illus.). 73p. 1999. pap. 9.00 (0-627-02220-0, Pub. by J L Van Schaik) BHB Intl.

MFAO - International Favorites. Prod. by Zobeida Perez. 112p. (Orig.). 1997. pap. 12.95 (0-7692-0067-2, FB9705) Wrner Bros.

Mfc Application Programming. Parker. 2000. 32.00 (0-13-244971-4) P-H.

MFC Developer's Workshop. 2nd ed. Frank Crockett & Jocelyn Garner. 475p. 39.99 incl. cd-rom (1-57231-859-7) Microsoft.

***MFC from Scratch.** 450p. 1999. 29.99 (0-7897-2205-4) Que.

MFC Interface Solutions. Eugene Kain. LC 98-18901. 704p. (C). 1998. pap. 42.95 (0-201-18537-7) Addison-Wesley.

MFC Internals: Inside the Microsoft Foundation Class Architecture. George Shepherd & Scot Wingo. 736p. (C). 1996. pap., pap. text 44.95 incl. disk (0-201-40721-3) Addison-Wesley.

Mfc Programmg In C++ W/Standard Templte Lib. William H. Murray & Chris H. Pappas. 550p. (C). 2000. pap. 44.99 (0-13-016111-X) P-H.

Mfc Programming. Alan Feuer. 480p. 1997. 39.95 (0-201-63358-2) Addison-Wesley.

MFC Programming from the Ground Up. Herbert Schildt. LC 96-208520. 656p. 1996. pap. text 34.95 (0-07-882222-X) Osborne-McGraw.

MFC Programming from the Ground Up. 2nd ed. Herbert Schildt. LC 98-215636. 663p. 1998. pap. text 34.99 (0-07-882573-3) Osborne-McGraw.

***MFC Programming with Visual C++6 Unleashed.** David White et al. LC 98-88891. (Sams Unleashed Series). (Illus.). 1306p. 1999. pap. 49.99 incl. cd-rom (0-672-31557-2) Sams.

MFC Windows Controls Construction Kit: A Programmer's Resource. Jack Tackett, Jr. & Keith E. Bugg. LC 94-48066. (Illus.). 400p. 1995. pap. text 39.95 (0-9644301-0-X, Tristar Pr) Tristar Systs.

MFDBS 87. Ed. by J. Biskup et al. (Lecture Notes in Computer Science Ser.: Vol. 305). v, 249p. 1988. 36.00 (0-387-19121-6) Spr-Verlag.

MFDBS '91: Third Symposium on Mathematical Fundamentals of Database & Knowledge Base Systems, Rostock, FRG, May 6-9, 1991, Proceedings. Ed. by Bernhard Thalheim et al. (Lecture Notes in Computer Science Ser.: No. 495). vi, 395p. 1991. 39.95 (0-387-54009-1) Spr-Verlag.

***Mfecane: An Annotated Bibliography** David Westley. LC 99-23177. 1999. write for info. (0-942615-41-7) U Wis African Stud.

Mfecane: Scattering of the People. Said K. Dibinga. LC 95-67261. (Illus.). 24p. (Orig.). (J). 1994. pap. 4.95 (0-943324-58-0) Omenana.

Mfecane Aftermath: Credulity & Skepticism in Southern African Historical Debates. Ed. by Carolyn Hamilton. 1996. pap. 35.00 (0-253-32957-4) Ind U Pr.

"Mfecane" Aftermath: Credulity & Skepticism in Southern African Historical Debates. Carolyn Hamilton. LC 96-148032. 1996. pap. text 35.00 (1-86814-252-3, Pub. by British Film Inst) Ind U Pr.

***M15: The First Ten Years, 1909-1919.** 1999. 6.95 (1-873162-52-9, Pub. by PRO Pubns) Midpt Trade.

M'Fingal: A Modern Epic in Four Cantos. John Trumbull. (Notable American Authors). 1999. reprint ed. lib. bdg. 125.00 (0-7812-9827-X) Rprt Serv.

M'Fingal Canto 1. John Trumbull. (Notable American Authors). 1999. reprint ed. lib. bdg. 125.00 (0-7812-9826-1) Rprt Serv.

***MFK Fisher Reader.** M. F. K. Fisher. Ed. by Dominique Gioia. LC 99-55111. 432p. 1999. text 30.00 (1-58243-031-4, Pub. by Counterpt DC) HarpC.

M4 Badenien (Moravien, Wielicien, Kosovien), Band VI. A. Papp et al. (Chronostratigraphie und Neostratotypen Ser.). (DUT.). 594p. 1978. 44.00 (3-510-60006-1, Pub. by E Schweizerbartsche) Balogh.

M14 Type Rifles: A Shooter's & Collector's Guide. Joe Poyer. LC 98-105024. (Illus.). 1997. pap. 14.95 (1-882391-18-7) N Cape Pubns.

MFS - Best of Cole Porter Bk. 5: Piano. 47p. 1983. pap. 9.95 (0-7692-1164-X, PF0168) Wrner Bros.

MFS - Best of George Gershwin Bk. 6: Piano. 49p. 1983. pap. 9.95 (0-7692-1165-8, PF0170) Wrner Bros.

MFS - Big Band Hits Bk. 12: Piano. 48p. 1984. pap. 9.95 (0-7692-1169-0, PF0214) Wrner Bros.

MFS - Broadway Songs Bk. 7: Piano. 49p. 1983. pap. 9.95 (0-7692-1166-6, PF0203) Wrner Bros.

MFS - Country Songs Bk. 2: Piano. 48p. 1985. pap. 9.95 (0-7692-1162-3, PF0327) Wrner Bros.

MFS - Homecoming & 11 Big Hits: Piano. 48p. 1991. pap. 9.95 (0-7692-1167-4, PF0777) Wrner Bros.

MFS - Love Songs Bk. 9: Piano. 48p. 1984. pap. 9.95 (0-7692-1168-2, PF0213) Wrner Bros.

MFS - Nostalgic Songs Bk. 4: Piano. 48p. 1983. pap. 9.95 (0-7692-1163-1, PF0165) Wrner Bros.

MFS - Popular Songs Bk. 1: Piano. rev. ed. 49p. 1982. pap. 9.95 (0-7692-1161-5, PF0433) Wrner Bros.

MFS - Rock & Roll Classics Bk. 20: Piano. 40p. 1989. pap. 9.95 (0-7692-1170-4, PF0618) Wrner Bros.

MFS Best of My Favorite Songs: Piano. 128p. 1989. pap. 10.95 (0-7692-1160-7, PF0584) Wrner Bros.

MFS My Favorite Rock Classics: Piano. 80p. 1992. pap. 10.95 (0-7692-1171-2, PF0789) Wrner Bros.

MG. F. Wilson McComb. (Album Ser.: No. 152). (Illus.). 32p. pap. 6.25 (0-7478-0421-4, Pub. by Shire Pubns) Parkwest Pubns.

MG: A Pictorial History. John Tipler. (Illus.). 128p. 1995. 34.95 (1-85223-923-9, Pub. by Crolwood) Motorbooks Intl.

MG by McComb. 3rd ed. Jonathan Wood. (Illus.). 392p. 1998. 39.95 (1-85532-754-6, Pub. by Ospry) Motorbooks Intl.

MG Collection: The Post War Models. Richard Monk. (Illus.). 192p. 1995. 29.95 (1-85260-516-2, Pub. by J H Haynes & Co) Motorbooks Intl.

MG Collection Vol. 1: Pre-War Models, Vol. 1. Richard Monk. (Illus.). 192p. 1994. 39.95 (1-85260-496-4, Pub. by J H Haynes & Co) Motorbooks Intl.

Mg-Deficiency in Forest Ecosystems. Ed. by Reinhard F. Huttl & Wolfgang Schaaf. LC 96-34056. (Nutrients in Ecosystems Ser.). 1997. text 251.00 (0-7923-4220-8) Kluwer Academic.

***MG from A to Z.** Wood. (Illus.). 192p. 2000. 19.95 (1-899870-29-6, Pub. by Motor Racing) Motorbooks Intl.

MG Haynes Classic Makes Series. Malcolm Green. LC 98-71572. (Illus.). 176p. 1998. 34.95 (1-85960-420-X, Pub. by J H Haynes & Co) Motorbooks Intl.

MG MGA 1500 Parts Catalogue, 1955-1959. British Leyland Motors Staff. (Illus.). 60.00 (0-8376-0570-9) Bentley Pubs.

MG Midget & Austin-Healey Sprite: Guide to Purchase & DIY Restoration. 2nd ed. Lindsay Porter. (Illus.). 288p. 1995. 29.95 (0-85429-969-6, Pub. by J H Haynes & Co) Motorbooks Intl.

***MG Midget & Austin Healey Sprite: Step-by-Step Service Guide.** Chilton Automotive Editorial Staff. (Porter Manuals Ser.). (C). 1998. pap. text 26.25 (1-899238-07-7, Pub. by Porter Pub) Nichols Pub.

***Mg Midget, Austin Healey & Sprite Restoration Manual.** Porter. (Illus.). 296p. 2000. 36.95 (1-85960-614-8, Pub. by Haynes Manuals) Motorbooks Intl.

MG Midget 1500 Driver's Handbook. British Leyland Motors Staff. (Illus.). 64p. 1979. 16.00 (0-8376-0590-3) Bentley Pubs.

MG Midget 1500 Worksh., 1975-79. Bentley, Robert, Inc. Staff. (Illus.). 384p. 1994. 40.00 (0-8376-0596-2) Bentley Pubs.

MG Midget MK3 Driver's Handbook (1974) British Leyland Motors Staff. (Illus.). 1979. pap. 16.00 (0-8376-0549-0) Bentley Pubs.

MG Midget TD Drivers Handbook. Bentley, Robert, Inc. Staff. (Illus.). 74p. 1994. pap. 16.00 (0-8376-0584-9) Bentley Pubs.

MG Midget TF & TF 1500 Driver. Bentley, Robert, Inc. Staff. (Illus.). 64p. 1994. pap. 16.00 (*0-8376-0583-0*) Bentley Pubs.

MG Saloon Cars - From the 1920s to the 1970s. Anders Clausager. (Illus.). 192p. 1998. 39.95 (*1-901432-06-8*, Bay View Bks) MBI Pubg.

MG Sports Cars. (Illus.). 192p. 1997. 34.95 (*1-870979-88-5*, Bay View Bks) MBI Pubg.

MG Sports Cars. John Heilig. (Enthusiast Color Ser.). (Illus.). 96p. 1996. pap. 13.95 (*0-7603-0112-3*) MBI Pubg.

MG Sports Cars: Illustrated History of the World Famous Sporting Marquee. Malcolm Greene. (Illus.). 1997. 29.95 (*1-85833-606-6*, Pub. by CLib Bks) Whitecap Bks.

MG T-Series. Graham Robson. (Illus.). 192p. 1998. 35.95 (*1-86126-179-9*, Pub. by Cro1wood) Motorbooks Intl.

MG T Series Restoration Guide. Malcom Green. (Illus.). 160p. 1993. pap. 29.95 (*1-85520-211-5*) MBI Pubg.

MG the Untold Story: Postwar Concepts, Styling Exercises & Development Cars. David Knowles. LC 97-42101. (Illus.). 256p. 1997. 39.95 (*0-7603-0408-4*) MBI Pubg.

MG Workshop Manual: Complete Turning & Maintenance for All Models from "M" Type to "T. F. 1500": 1929-1955. W. E. Blower. LC 75-33494. (Illus.). 608p. (Orig.). 1975. pap. 60.00 (*0-8376-0117-7*) Bentley Pubs.

MGA. John P. Williams. (Illus.). 160p. 1997. 39.95 (*1-874105-66-9*, Pub. by Vloce Pub) Motorbooks Intl.

MGA: A History & Restoration Guide. Robert P. Vitrikas. (Illus.). 240p. 1989. reprint ed. 49.95 (*0-9621881-0-7*); reprint ed. pap. 30.95 (*0-9621881-1-5*) Scarborough Faire.

***MGA: 1500, Twin Cam, 1600.** F. Wilson McComb. (Expert Histories Ser.). (Illus.). 144p. 2000. pap. 19.95 (*1-84176-012-9*, 130038AE, Pub. by Ospry) Motorbooks Intl.

MGA - The Complete Story. David G. Styles. (Illus.). 192p. 1995. 35.95 (*1-85223-909-3*, Pub. by Cro1wood) Motorbooks Intl.

MGA 1500 Driver's Handbook, 1960. Bentley, Robert, Inc. Staff. (Illus.). 64p. 1994. pap. 16.00 (*0-8376-0589-X*) Bentley Pubs.

MGA 1500, 1600, 1600 (MK II) Workshop Manual, 1955-1962. British Motor Corporation Ltd., MG Car Division. (Illus.). 272p. (Orig.). 55.00 (*0-8376-0510-5*) Bentley Pubs.

Mga Kuwentong Bayan see Folk Stories from the Philippines

***MGA, MGB & MGC: A Collector's Guide.** Graham Robson. 2000. pap. 19.95 (*1-899870-43-1*, 129756AE, Pub. by Motor Racing) Motorbooks Intl.

MGA Restoration Guide. Malcolm Green. (Illus.). 160p. 1995. 29.95 (*1-85520-302-2*, Pub. by Brooklands Bks) Motorbooks Intl.

MGA 1600 Parts Catalogue, 1959-1962. British Leyland Motors Staff. (Illus.). (Orig.). 65.00 (*0-8376-0569-5*) Bentley Pubs.

MGA 1600 Twin Cam Wor., 58-60. BMC Staff. (Illus.). 204p. 1994. 50.00 (*0-8376-0501-6*) Bentley Pubs.

MGB: Landmarques. David Knowles. LC 99-52135. (Illus.). 192p. 2000. text 39.95 (*1-901432-25-4*, 128279AE, Pub. by MBI Pubg) Motorbooks Intl.

***MGB: MGB Roadster & GT, MCG, MGB V8.** F. Wilson McComb. (Expert Histories Ser.). (Illus.). 144p. 2000. pap. 19.95 (*1-84176-013-7*, 130039AE, Pub. by Ospry) Motorbooks Intl.

MGB: The Complete Story. Brian Laban. (Illus.). 192p. 1990. pap. 35.95 (*1-85223-358-3*) MBI Pubg.

MGB: The Illustrated History. 2nd ed. Jonathon Wood & Lional Burrell. (Illus.). 256p. 1993. 38.95 (*0-85429-948-3*, Pub. by J H Haynes & Co) Motorbooks Intl.

MGB Driver's Handbook: 1965 Edition. British Leyland Motors. (Illus.). 68p. 16.00 (*0-8376-0530-X*) Bentley Pubs.

MGB Driver's Handbook U. S., 1975. Bentley, Robert, Inc. Staff. (Illus.). 100p. 1994. pap. 16.00 (*0-8376-0588-1*) Bentley Pubs.

MGB Driver's Handbook U. S., 1972. Bentley, Robert, Inc. Staff. (Illus.). 76p. 1994. pap. 16.00 (*0-8376-0592-X*) Bentley Pubs.

MGB Model Years 1962-1974, the Complete Official: Comprising the Official Driver's Handbook, Workshop Manual, Special Tuning Manual. 4th rev. ed. British Leyland Motors Staff. LC 75-7766. (Illus.). 480p. (Orig.). 1975. pap. 50.00 (*0-8376-0115-0*) Bentley Pubs.

MGB Restoration - Preparation - Maintenance. Jim Tyler. (Illus.). 238p. 1992. pap. 39.95 (*1-85532-190-4*, Pub. by Osprey) Motorbooks Intl.

***MGB Restoration Manual.** 2nd ed. Lindsay Porter. (Illus.). 352p. 2000. 36.95 (*1-85960-607-5*, 128581AE, Pub. by Haynes Manuals) Motorbooks Intl.

MGB Tourer & GT Drive Handbook. Bentley, Robert, Inc. Staff. (Illus.). 62p. 1994. pap. 16.00 (*0-8376-0586-5*); pap. 16.00 (*0-8376-0587-3*) Bentley Pubs.

MGB Tourer & GT Driver's Handbook (1969) Bentley, Robert, Inc. Staff. (Illus.). 76p. 1994. pap. 16.00 (*0-8376-0591-1*) Bentley Pubs.

MGB Tourer & GT Parts Catalogue, 1977-1980. British Leyland Motors. (Illus.). 170p. 40.00 (*0-8376-0500-8*) Bentley Pubs.

MGB Tourer & GT Tuning Handbook, 1975-1980. British Leyland Motors. (Illus.). 50p. (Orig.). 16.00 (*0-8376-0504-0*) Bentley Pubs.

MGB Tourer, GT & V8 Parts Catalogue, 1962-1976. British Leyland Motors. (Illus.). 440p. (Orig.). 60.00 (*0-8376-0505-9*) Bentley Pubs.

MGB Tuning Handbook (1800cc), 1962-1974. British Leyland Motors. (Illus.). 50p. (Orig.). 16.00 (*0-8376-0506-7*) Bentley Pubs.

MGC Driver's Handbook: 1967-1969. British Leyland Motors Staff. (Illus.). 64p. 16.00 (*0-8376-0503-2*) Bentley Pubs.

MGH Board Review of Anesthesiology. 4th rev. ed. Mark Dershwitz. (C). 1994. pap. text 47.95 (*0-8385-8611-2*, A8611-4) Appleton & Lange.

MGH Board Review of Anesthesiology. 5th ed. Mark Dershwitz et al. LC 98-21937. (Illus.). 302p. (C). 1999. pap. 49.95 (*0-8385-6348-1*) McGraw.

***MGI Photosuite III for Dummies.** Gilbert. (For Dummies Ser.). 384p. 2000. pap. 19.99 (*0-7645-0749-4*) IDG Bks.

MGM Grand Hotel, Inc. Hotel-Casino-Theme Park: Grand Opening Commemorative. Ed. by Myrtle D. Malone. (Illus.). 135p. 1993. 20.00 (*1-881547-17-5*) Pioneer Pubns.

MGM Labels: A Discography, 75. Compiled by Michel Ruppli & Ed Novitsky. LC 98-9602. (Discographies Ser.: Vol. 75). 2736p. 1998. lib. bdg. 325.00 (*0-313-30052-6*, Greenwood Pr) Greenwood.

MGM Labels: A Discography, 1946-1960, Vol. 1. Compiled by Michel Ruppli & Ed Novitsky. LC 98-9602. (Discographies Ser.: 75). 1016p. 1998. lib. bdg. 135.00 (*0-313-30778-4*, Greenwood Pr) Greenwood.

MGM Labels Vol. 2: A Discography, 1961-1982, Vol. 2. Compiled by Michel Ruppli & Ed Novitsky. LC 98-9602. (Discographies Ser.: 75). 984p. 1998. lib. bdg. 135.00 (*0-313-30779-2*, Greenwood Pr) Greenwood.

MGM Labels Vol. 3: A Discography: Additional Recordings/Record & Artist Indexes, Vol. 3. Compiled by Michel Ruppli & Ed Novitsky. LC 98-9602. (Discographies Ser.: 75). 864p. 1998. lib. bdg. 135.00 (*0-313-30780-6*, Greenwood Pr) Greenwood.

MGM Posters: The Golden Years. Frank Miller. 192p. 15.99 (*1-57215-269-9*) World Pubns.

MGM's Greatest Musicals: The Arthur Freed Unit. Hugh Fordin. LC 96-18962. Orig. Title: That's Entertainment! Hollywood's Greatest Musicals. (Illus.). 576p. 1996. pap. 22.50 (*0-306-80730-0*) Da Capo.

Mgr & The Legal Environment 2e. 2nd ed. Constance E. Bagley. LC 94-45225. (SWC-Business Law). 974p. (C). 1995. mass mkt. 68.50 (*0-314-04391-8*) West Pub.

***Mgr. Rene Vilatte: Community Organizer of Religion.** Serge A. Theriault. (Old Catholic Studies).Tr. of Mgr. Rene Vilatte, Organisateur Communitarre de Religic. (Illus.). 200p. 2000. pap. 19.95 (*1-883938-75-9*) Dry Bones Pr.

Mgr. Rene Vilatte, Organisateur Communitarre de Religic see Mgr. Rene Vilatte: Community Organizer of Religion

Mgt Compet & Global Case. Michael A. Hitt et al. LC 94-34795. (SWC-Management). 650p. (C). 1994. mass mkt. 38.25 (*0-314-04338-1*) West Pub.

Mg2 & Excitable Membranes. Ed. by P. Strata & E. Carbone. (Illus.). 164p. 1990. 71.95 (*0-387-52479-7*) Spr-Verlag.

MH & XMH: E-Mail for Users & Programmers. 3rd ed. Jerry Peek. Ed. by Tim O'Reilly & Frank Willison. (Illus.). 750p. (Orig.). 1995. pap. 34.95 (*1-56592-093-7*) Thomson Learn.

M'Hashish. Mohammed Mrabet. Tr. by Paul Bowles. LC 70-88228. (Orig.). 1969. pap. 8.95 (*0-87286-034-5*) City Lights.

MHC: A Practical Approach. Ed. by Nelson Fernandez & Geoff Butcher. LC 97-2434. (Practical Approach Ser.: No. 180). (Illus.). 236p. (C). 1997. text 105.00 (*0-19-963554-4*) OUP.

***MHC: A Practical Approach, 2 vols., Vols. 1-2.** Ed. by N. Fernandez. 180. (Illus.). 596p. 1998. pap. text 95.00 (*0-19-963557-9*) OUP.

MHC: A Practical Approach to Genes, Cells & Molecules, Vol. 2. Ed. by N. Fernandez & G. Butcher. LC 97-2434. (The Practical Approach Ser.: No. 181). (Illus.). 254p. 1998. pap. text 55.00 (*0-19-963555-2*) OUP.

MHC: A Practical Approach to Genes, Cells & Molecules, Vol. 2. Ed. by N. Fernandez & G. Butcher. LC 97-2434. (The Practical Approach Ser.: No. 181). (Illus.). 256p. (C). 1998. text 105.00 (*0-19-963556-0*) OUP.

MHC Antigens & NK Cells. Ed. by Rafael Solana & Jose Pena. (Molecular Biology Intelligence Unit Ser.). 125p. 1994. 99.00 (*1-57059-062-1*, LN9062) Landes Bioscience.

MHC Ligands & Peptide Motifs. Hans-Georg Rammensee & Jutta Bachmann. LC 97-18997. (Molecular Biology Intelligence Unit Ser.). 1997. text 99.00 (*1-57059-460-0*) Landes Bioscience.

MHC Molecules & Antigen Processing. Clifford V. Harding. LC 97-578. (Molecular Biology Intelligence Unit Ser.). 162p. 1997. 99.00 (*1-57059-428-7*) Landes Bioscience.

MHC 1 - A Practical Approach: Antigen Processing & Presentation. Ed. by Nelson Fernandez & Geoff Butcher. LC 97-2434. (Practical Approach Ser.: No. 180). (Illus.). 236p. 1997. pap. text 55.00 (*0-19-963553-6*) OUP.

MHC Plus X. Ed. by P. Ivanyi. (Illus.). 290p. 1989. 132.00 (*0-387-50247-5*) Spr-Verlag.

MHC Protocols. Ed. by Stephen H. Powis & Robert Vaughan. (Methods in Molecular Biology Ser.). 350p. 1999. 79.50 (*0-89603-548-4*) Humana.

MHD & Microinstabilities in Confined Plasma. Wallace M. Manheimer & C. N. Lashmore-Davies. (Plasma Physics Ser.). (Illus.). 300p. 1989. 208.00 (*0-85274-282-7*) IOP Pub.

MHD Energy Conversion: Physicotechnical Problems. Ed. by V. A. Kirillin & A. E. Sheyndlin. LC 86-10787. (PAAS Ser.: Vol. 101). 588p. 1986. 75.95 (*0-930403-05-3*) AIAA.

MHD Structures, Waves & Turbulence in the Solar Wind: Observations & Theories. C. Y. Tu & E. Marsch. LC 94-48070. 1995. text 166.00 (*0-7923-3345-4*) Kluwer Academic.

MHEG: International Standard for Multimedia Hypermedia. Casey. 1995. text 69.95 (*0-442-02201-8*, VNR) Wiley.

Mi. Paul Brenner. (Orig.). 1983. pap. 5.00 (*0-914135-00-7*) Rainbow Med Clinic.

Mi Abuela Fumaba Puros. Sabine R. Ulibarri. LC 77-85179. (Illus.). 1977. pap. 10.95 (*0-88412-105-4*) TQS Pubns.

Mi Abuelita Siempre Me Escucha see Homeplay: La Alegria de Aprender Entre Ninos y Adultos, Series I

Mi Abuelito y Yo. Barbara M. Wolff. (SPA., Illus.). 16p. (J). (ps-1). 1992. lib. bdg. 13.95 (*1-879567-12-1*, Valeria Bks) Wonder Well.

Mi Adolescente Me Esta Volviendo Loco. Joyce L. Vedral. (SPA.). 161p. 1997. pap. text 12.98 (*968-13-2710-1*) Edit Diana.

Mi Amado Adversario. W. G. Evans.Tr. of Beloved Adversary. (SPA.). 1985. 4.99 (*0-685-74954-1*, 490230) Editorial Unilit.

Mi Amado Adversario. W. Glyn Evans.Tr. of Beloved Adversary. (SPA.). 143p. 1985. pap. write for info. (*0-614-27084-7*) Editorial Unilit.

***Mi Amigo Gorila (My Friend Gorilla)** Atsuko Morozumi. Tr. by Rita Guibert.Tr. of My Friend Gorila. (Illus.). 32p. (J). (ps-k). 1999. text 5.95 (*0-374-44831-0*, Mirasol) FS&G.

Mi Amigo Jesus - I Learn about Jesus. Mary E. Tebo. Tr. by Dolores Catarroja & Dolores Enriquez. (Illus.). 153p. (Orig.). (J). (ps-3). 1995. pap. 5.95 (*0-8198-4773-9*) Pauline Bks.

Mi Asombroso Cuerpo. Rachel Wright. (Biblioteca de Descubrimientos).Tr. of My Amazing Body. (SPA., Illus.). (J). (gr. 3-6). 1997. 11.95 (*0-915741-85-7*, SY7077) C D Stampley Ent.

Mi Bacinica y Yo (Once upon a Potty: Hers) Alona Frankel. (SPA., Illus.). 36p. (J). (ps). 1986. 5.50 (*0-8120-5751-1*) Barron.

Mi Barrio y Mi Esquina: A la una Mi Mula, a las Dos Mi Reloj. Jose Sanchez-Boudy. LC 88-82469. (Coleccion Espejo de Paciencia). (SPA.). 70p. (Orig.). 1989. pap. 7.95 (*0-89729-318-5*) Ediciones.

Mi Bebe: Un Buen Comienzo. Warren.Tr. of My Infant: Off to a Good Start. (SPA.). 1996. 8.99 (*0-88113-337-X*, B001-337X) Caribe Betania.

Mi Bebe y Yo: Una Guia Esencial para el Embarazo. 3rd rev. ed. Deborah D. Stewart. Tr. by Ricardo Perugorria & Ana C. Matiella.Tr. of Baby & Me: The Essential Guide to Pregnancy. (SPA., Illus.). 160p. 1998. pap. 10.95 (*1-884255-04-3*) Willapa Bay.

***Mi Caja de Insectas.** Pat Blanchard & Joanne Suhr. Tr. by Alberto Romo. (Books for Young Learners).Tr. of My Bug Box. (SPA., Illus.). 12p. (J). (gr. k-2). 1999. pap. text 5.00 (*1-57274-341-7*, A2877) R Owen Pubs.

***Mi Calle (My Street)** Rebecca Treays & Rachell Wells. (Young Geography Ser.). (SPA., Illus.). 24p. (J). (ps up). 1999. pap. 8.95 (*0-7460-3658-2*, Usborne) EDC.

Mi Casa O la Tuya: My House or Yours? Lass Small. (Deseo Ser.). (SPA.). 1997. per. 3.50 (*0-373-35210-7*, 1-35210-3) Harlequin Bks.

Mi Casa Su Casa's Bed & Breakfast Directory, 1991-93: Arizona & the Southwest. Ruth Young. 1991. write for info. (*0-9631014-8-X*) MCSC Bed & Break.

***Mi Ciudad (My Town)** Rebecca Treays. (Young Geography Ser.). (SPA., Illus.). 24p. (J). (ps up). 1999. pap. 8.95 (*0-7460-3657-4*, Usborne) EDC.

Mi Companero el Espiritu Santo. David Y. Cho.Tr. of Holy Spirit, My Senior Partner. (SPA.). 168p. 1992. pap. 8.99 (*0-8297-0334-9*) Vida Pubs.

***Mi Corazon Que Baila Con Espigas.** Carmen Rigalt. (SPA.). 1998. 22.95 (*84-08-02081-1*, Pub. by Planeta Edit) Planeta.

Mi Cruz Llena de Rosas: Cartas a Sandra, mi Hija Enferma. rev. ed. Xiomara J. Pages. LC 95-83639. (Coleccion Felix Varela: 6). (SPA., Illus.). 80p. (Orig.). 1998. pap. 12.00 (*0-89729-885-3*) Ediciones.

Mi Cuerpo Es Mio. Lory Freeman. Tr. by Lois Dunn from ENG. LC 85-62435. (SPA., Illus.). 32p. (Orig.). (J). (ps-3). 1985. pap. 5.95 (*0-943990-19-X*) Parenting Pr.

Mi-Culture of the Mount Hagen People, No. 13. Hermann Strauss. Ed. by A. J. Strathern & Gabriele Sturzenhofecker. Tr. by Brian Shields. LC 90-82889. (Illus.). xxvi, 361p. (Orig.). 1990. pap. text 25.00 (*0-945428-06-5*) Ethnology Monographs.

Mi Declaracion De Amor. Irene Fohri. 1997. pap. text 6.98 (*968-38-0628-7*) Panorama Edit.

Mi Declaracion de Amor 2. Irene Fohri. 1997. pap. text 6.98 (*968-38-0691-0*) Panorama Edit.

Mi Desarrollo Sexual: Growing up with Sex. Paul D. Simmons & Kenneth Crawford. Tr. by Dafne Sabanes De Plou from ENG. (Sexo en la Vida Cristiana Ser.). (SPA.). 96p. (YA). (gr. 10-12). 1979. reprint ed. pap. 5.50 (*0-311-46257-X*, Edit Mundo) Casa Bautista.

Mi Dia: Figuras Que Aparecen. Mills. (Figuras Que Aparecen (A Chunky Pop-up Bk.)).Tr. of My Day: Chunky Pop-Up Book. (SPA.). 5p. (J). 1995. 3.50 (*1-56063-631-9*, 494604) Editorial Unilit.

Mi Diccionario: Primera Coleccion de Palabras-Educacion Primaria, Primer Ciclo. Melitina Rivera Gonzalez. (SPA., Illus.). 223p. 1992. pap. 49.50 (*84-207-4697-5*) Elliots Bks.

Mi Diccionario No. 2: Educacion Primaria, 8-12 Anos. Melitina Rivera Gonzalez. (SPA., Illus.). 479p. 1993. pap. 69.50 (*84-207-5003-4*) Elliots Bks.

Mi Diccionario Ilustrado. 2nd ed. Concepcion Zendrera. (SPA.). 20p. 1974. 17.95 (*0-8288-6072-6*, S-16498) Fr & Eur.

Mi Diccionario Infantil. 3rd ed. Richard Scarry. (SPA.). 96p. (J). 1974. pap. 14.95 (*0-8288-6073-4*, S-27628) Fr & Eur.

Mi Diccionario Spanish. (SPA.). 1972. pap. text 16.07 (*0-673-02780-5*) Addison-Wesley.

Mi Direccion Global (My Global Address), Vol. 4099. Tamara Nunn. Ed. by Rozanne L. Williams. Tr. by Nora Mallernee. (Learn to Read Social Studies). (SPA., Illus.). 16p. (J). (ps-1). 1997. pap. 2.75 (*1-57471-286-1*, 4099) Creat Teach Pr.

Mi Escalera. Sally Derby. Tr. by Eida De la Vega. LC 97-43713. (SPA., Illus.). 32p. (J). (ps-4). 1998. 15.95 (*1-880000-74-1*); pap. 6.95 (*1-880000-75-X*) Lee & Low Bks.

Mi Esposo No Es Cristiano. Jaime Miron. (Serie Cruzada - Crusade Ser.).Tr. of My Husband Is Not a Christian. (SPA.). 1991. pap. 1.99 (*1-56063-044-2*, 498010) Editorial Unilit.

Mi Estilo de Hombre. Barbara McCauley. Orig. Title: Her Kind of Man. (SPA.). 1996. per. 3.50 (*0-373-35133-X*) Harlequin Bks.

Mi Experiencia con Dios. Henry T. Blackaby & Claude V. King.Tr. of Experiencing God. (SPA.). 288p. 1996. pap. text 12.99 (*0-311-11053-3*, Edit Mundo) Casa Bautista.

***Mi Experiencia Con Dios en el Trabajo.** Mike Rogers & Debi Rogers. Orig. Title: The Kingdom Agenda. (SPA.). 160p. 1998. pap. text 9.50 (*0-311-11200-5*, Edit Mundo) Casa Bautista.

Mi Flor Amarilla. 38p. 1994. write for info. (*92-806-3053-9*) U N I C E.

Mi Flor Azul. 38p. 1994. write for info. (*92-806-3054-7*) U N I C E.

Mi Flor Rosada. 44p. 1994. write for info. (*92-806-3055-5*) U N I C E.

Mi Fu: Style & the Art of Calligraphy in Northern Song China. Peter C. Sturman. LC 96-9556. 320p. 1997. 37.00 (*0-300-06569-8*) Yale U Pr.

Mi Gran Libro De Cuentos. 1997. pap. text 14.98 (*84-7773-029-6*) Grafalco.

Mi Gran Libro de Palabras. Playskool Staff.Tr. of My Play-Doh Book of Words. (SPA.). 5p. (J). (ps). 1997. pap. 9.99 (*0-525-45813-1*, Dutton Child) Peng Put Young Read.

Mi Gran Padre. Bruce Farnham.Tr. of My Big Father. (SPA.). 110p. 1990. pap. write for info. (*0-614-27083-9*) Editorial Unilit.

Mi Gran Padre (My Big Father) Bruce Farnham. (SPA.). 110p. 1990. write for info. (*0-614-24380-7*) Editorial Unilit.

Mi Gua de DeFensa Personal. Jo Stowell & Mary Dietzel. Tr. by Esther M. Sobrino.Tr. of My Very Own Book about Me. (SPA., Illus.). 48p. (J). (gr. 3-6). 1985. wbk. ed. write for info. (*1-930489-01-3*) Act For Kids.

***Mi Hermanito Ben.** Karen Cogan. Tr. by Alberto Romo. (Books for Young Learners).Tr. of My Little Brother Ben. (SPA., Illus.). 12p. (J). (gr. k-2). 1999. pap. text 5.00 (*1-57274-343-3*, A2878) R Owen Pubs.

Mi Hermano Carlos (My Brother Carlos) Jorge L. Paez. (SPA.). 224p. 1965. 11.99 (*968-16-4475-1*, Pub. by Fondo) Continental Bk.

***Mi Hermosa Biblia.** Spanish House Inc. Staff. (SPA., Illus.). (J). 1999. 10.99 (*0-7899-0703-8*) Editorial Unilit.

Mi Hija, Con Amor, Sobre las Cosas Importantes de la Vida. Susan Polis Schutz. LC 92-14014.Tr. of To My Daughter, with Love, on the Important Things in Life. (SPA & ENG., Illus.). 64p. 1992. pap. 7.95 (*0-88396-360-4*) Blue Mtn Art.

***Mi Hija, Mi Hijo, el Aguila, la Paloma.** Ana Castillo. (SPA., Illus.). 48p. (J). 2000. 12.99 (*0-525-45867-0*, Dutton Child) Peng Put Young Read.

Mi Historia: Compendio Historico de Vida Tradicional - Non-Denominational. 2nd ed. Lynda Nelson.Tr. of My Story: Life History Outline Non-Denominational. (SPA.). 97p. 1992. reprint ed. ring bd. 12.95 (*0-9652557-3-5*) Hist Happenings.

Mi Historia Compendio Historico de Vida: Para Miembros de la Iglesia de los Santos de los Ultimos Dias. 2nd ed. Lynda Nelson.Tr. of My Story Life History Outline for Latter-Day Saints. (SPA.). 127p. 1992. reprint ed. ring bd. 14.95 (*0-9652557-2-7*, LDSS) Hist Happenings.

Mi i Drugi u Sedmom Stoljecu: Us & Others in the Seventh Century. Ivo Omrcanin. (CRO., Illus.). 160p. 1993. pap. 10.00 (*1-878716-13-1*) Ivor Pr.

Mi Infancia en Cuba: (Lo Visto y Lo Vivido Por una Nina de Doce Anos) Cosette A. Carballosa. LC 96-83524. (Coleccion Cuba y sus Jueces). (SPA.). 122p. (Orig.). 1996. pap. 13.00 (*0-89729-796-2*) Ediciones.

Mi Lado (Close to Me), No. 133. Cathie Linz. (Harlequin Deseo Ser.). (SPA.). 1998. mass mkt. 3.50 (*0-373-35263-8*, 1-35263-2) Harlequin Bks.

Mi Libro de Animales (My Book of Animals) Eyewitness Sticker Book. Santillana Staff. 1995. pap. text 9.95 (*84-372-3792-0*) Santillana.

Mi Libro de Escritura. Ursula O. Ronnholm. (SPA., Illus.). 74p. (J). (gr. k-3). 1986. 4.00 (*0-941911-05-5*) Two Way Bilingual.

Mi Libro de Palabras. Alana Trisler & Patrice Cardiel. Tr. by Dorcas Seisedos. (SPA., Illus.). 72p. (J). (gr. k). 1996. wbk. ed. 2.50 (*1-56762-065-5*) Modern Learn Pr.

Mi Libro de Palabras: Oraciones y Cuentos. rev. ed. Ursula O. Ronnholm. Ed. & Tr. by Edda Rabell. Tr. by Miguel Montero. (SPA., Illus.). 100p. (J). (gr. k-6). 1989. reprint ed. pap. 7.00 (*0-941911-08-X*) Two Way Bilingual.

Mi Libro de Palabras, Oraciones y Cuentos. Ursula O. Ronnholm. Ed. by Osdila O. Deliz. (Illus.). 100p. (J). (gr. k-6). pap. text 7.00 (*0-941911-02-0*) Two Way Bilingual.

Mi-Lou: Poetry & the Labyrinth of Desire. Stephen Owen. LC 88-28393. (Studies in Comparative Literature: No. 39). 240p. 1989. 39.50 (*0-674-57275-0*) HUP.

M

Mi Mama. Debbie Bailey.Tr. of My Mom. (SPA., Illus.). 14p. (J). (ps). 1992. bds. 5.95 (*1-55037-264-5*, Pub. by Annick) Firefly Bks Ltd.

Mi Mama' Me Ama. rev. ed. Ruth Bowdoin. (Bowdoin Method I Ser.). Orig. Title: My Mommy Likes Me. (SPA., Illus.). 23p. (Orig.). 1991. pap. write for info. (*1-55997-069-3*) Websters Intl.

Mi Mascota. Lynn Salem & Josie Stewart. Tr. by Mariana Robles. (SPA., Illus.). 8p. (J). (gr. k-1). 1994. pap. 3.75 (*1-880612-24-0*) Seedling Pubns.

Mi Mascota Secreta see Homeplay: La Alegria de Aprender Entre Ninos y Adultos, Series I

Mi Mayor Legado. Jose L. Navajo-Ayora. (SPA.). 1998. pap. 5.99 (*0-8297-0987-8*) Vida Pubs.

***Mi Moto Fidel: Motorcycling Through Castro's Cuba.** Christopher P. Baker. 2001. 26.00 (*0-7922-7961-1*) Natl Geog.

Mi Mujer Ideal. Jackie Merritt. (Deseo Ser.: No. 217).Tr. of My Ideal Woman. (SPA.). 1997. per. 3.50 (*0-373-35217-4*, 1-35217-8) Harlequin Bks.

Mi Mundo de Palabras see My World of Spanish Words

***Mi Neva Know Sey.** Erica McKoy-Hibbert. LC 99-97828. 167p. 2000. 12.95 (*1-930331-00-2*) Machibb.

Mi Nombre es Lupita y Tengo un Hijo Sordo: Folletos Informativos para Padres Precupados por la Audicion de Sus Hijos, 6 bks., Set. Gina Aguirre-Larson. (SPA., Illus.). (Orig.). 1996. pap. 45.00 (*1-884362-16-8*) Butte Pubns.

Mi Otro Yo. Clarence J. Enzler. 1984. pap. 9.95 (*0-87193-213-X*) Dimension Bks.

Mi Papa. Debbie Bailey.Tr. of My Dad. (SPA., Illus.). 14p. (J). (ps). 1992. bds. 5.95 (*1-55037-265-3*, Pub. by Annick) Firefly Bks Ltd.

Mi Papalote Rojo Vol. 8: Pasitos Spanish Language Development Books. Darlyne F. Schott. (Pasitos Hacia la Lectura Ser.). 11p. (J). (gr. k-1). 1990. pap. text 11.50 (*1-56537-057-0*) D F Schott Educ.

Mi Parvulo: El Comienzo de la Independencia. Warren.Tr. of My Toddler: The Beginning of Independence. (SPA.). 1996. 8.99 (*0-88113-338-8*, B001-3388) Caribe Betania.

Mi Pecado Fue Quererte. Jose A. Ponjoan. LC 88-81863. (Coleccion Caniqui). (SPA.). 280p. (Orig.). 1989. pap. 15.00 (*0-89729-499-8*) Ediciones.

Mi Pequeno Calendario de Navidad. M. Water. (Libros Ventanitas - Windows Bks.).Tr. of Lantern Advent Book. (SPA.). 6p. (J). 1995. 9.99 (*1-56063-835-4*, 497745) Editorial Unilit.

Mi Pequeno Mundo. Charles M. Schulz. (Peanuts Ser.). (SPA.). 64p. (J). 1971. 4.95 (*0-8288-4501-8*) Fr & Eur.

Mi Perrito. 3rd ed. Inez Greene. Tr. by Alma F. Ada. (Dejame Leer Ser.).Tr. of My Puppy. (SPA., Illus.). 8p. (J). (ps-k). 1995. bds. 2.95 (*0-673-36289-2*, GoodYrBooks) Addson-Wesley Educ.

Mi Preescolar: Listo para Nuevas Aventuras. Warren.Tr. of My Preschooler: Ready for New Adventures. (SPA.). 208p. 1996. 9.99 (*0-88113-339-6*, B001-3396) Caribe Betania.

Mi Primer ABC. Illus. by Nadine Piette. (Pequenos Libros Ser.). (SPA.). 60p. (J). (ps). 1993. reprint ed. 3.95 (*970-607-186-5*, Larousse LKC) LKC.

***Mi Primer Atlas.** Two Can Publishing Ltd. Staff. (Illus.). 2000. 7.95 (*1-58728-656-4*) Two Can Pub.

Mi Primer Catecismo, 10 vols. Lawrence G. Lovasik. (San Jose de Libros en Laminas Ser.). (SPA., Illus.). (J). 1989. pap. 1.50 (*0-89942-470-8*, 470/S) Catholic Bk Pub.

Mi Primer Diccionario. Illus. by Gill Guile.Tr. of My First Storybook Dictionary. (ENG & SPA.). 80p. (J). (ps-1). 1995. 7.98 (*1-85854-437-8*) Brimax Bks.

Mi Primer Diccionario Biblico. William N. McElrath. Tr. by Ruth G. McElrath from ENG.Tr. of Bible Dictionary for Young Readers. (SPA., Illus.). 128p. (J). (gr. 4-6). 1975. reprint ed. pap. 7.99 (*0-311-03656-2*) Casa Bautista.

Mi Primer Diccionario Biblico: My First Bible Dictionary. William N. McElrath. (SPA.). 122p. 1978. pap. 7.95 (*0-8288-5252-9*, S37577) Fr & Eur.

Mi Primer Diccionario Escolar. 4th ed. (SPA.). 480p. (J). 1975. pap. 5.95 (*0-7859-0890-0*, S-27087) Fr & Eur.

Mi Primer Gran Diccionario Infantil. 4th ed. Richard Scarry. (SPA.). 90p. (J). 1978. 13.95 (*0-8288-5253-7*, S26637) Fr & Eur.

Mi Primer Libro de Contar. Illus. by Gill Guile.Tr. of My First Counting Book. (ENG & SPA.). 64p. (J). (ps-1). 1995. 7.98 (*1-85854-341-X*) Brimax Bks.

Mi Primer Libro de Costura: Hand Sewing - Level 1. Winky Cherry. Tr. by Rosy A. Alas. (My First Sewing Book Ser.). (SPA., Illus.). 40p. (J). (gr. k-6). 1994. pap. 12.95 (*0-935278-37-0*) Palmer-Pletsch.

Mi Primer Libro de Dichos see My First Book of Proverbs (Mi Primer Libro de Dichos)

Mi Primer Libro de Musica. Karyn Henley. Date not set. pap. text 8.99 (*0-917143-44-2*) Sparrow TN.

Mi Primer Libro de Oraciones. Lawrence G. Lovasik. (San Jose de Libros en Laminas Ser.). (SPA., Illus.). (J). 1989. pap. 1.50 (*0-89942-460-0*, 460/S) Catholic Bk Pub.

Mi Primer Libro de Palabras: Mil Palabras Que Se Debe Saber Cada Nino. Lena Shiffman. (Cartwheel Learning Bookshelf Ser.). (SPA.). (J). 1992. 11.19 (*0-606-01907-3*, Pub. by Turtleback) Demco.

Mi Primer Libro de Palabras: My First Book of Words. Illus. by Lena Shiffman. (ENG & SPA.). 64p. (J). (ps-k). 1992. 5.99 (*0-590-46028-5*, 044, Cartwheel) Scholastic Inc.

Mi Primer Libro de Palabras de Espanol. Angela Wilkes & Rubi Borgia. LC 92-56498. (SPA., Illus.). 64p. (J). (ps-3). 1993. 16.95 (*1-56458-262-0*) DK Pub Inc.

Mi Primer Libro de Pegatinas Con Formas & Colores. Maggie Kate. (SPA., Illus.). (J). 1995. pap. 1.00 (*0-486-28842-0*) Dover.

Mi Primer Libro de Teatro. (SPA.). 9.00 (*84-241-5624-2*) E Torres & Sons.

Mi Primera Bible. Hanon. 5.95 (*0-88271-096-6*) Regina Pr.

Mi Primera Biblia. Ed. by Lion. (Biblias para Ninos Ser.).Tr. of My First Bible. (SPA., Illus.). (J). 1999. 12.99 (*0-7899-0402-0*, 490299) Editorial Unilit.

Mi Primera Biblia. Ed. by K. Taylor. (Biblias para Ninos Ser.).Tr. of My First Bible. (SPA.). (J). 1999. 13.99 (*1-56063-674-2*, 490282) Editorial Unilit.

***Mi Primera Biblia.** Kenneth N. Taylor. (SPA.). 2000. pap. 9.99 (*0-7899-0573-6*); pap. 9.99 (*0-7899-0574-4*) Editorial Unilit.

Mi Primera Biblia Bolsillo. Ed. by K. Taylor. (Biblias para Ninos Ser.).Tr. of My Little First Bible. (SPA.). (J). 1999. 7.99 (*0-7899-0571-X*, 490294); 10.99 (*0-7899-0572-8*, 490295) Editorial Unilit.

Mi Primera Biblia Ilustrada. E. Reeves. (Biblias para Ninos Ser.).Tr. of My First Picture Bible. (SPA., Illus.). (J). 1999. 9.99 (*0-7899-0456-X*, 496625) Editorial Unilit.

Mi Primera Enciclopedia, 10 vols., Set. Ed. by Espasa Staff. (SPA., Illus.). 1993. 239.50 (*84-239-5839-6*) Elliots Bks.

Mi Primera Enciclopedia, 10 vols., Set. Espasa Staff. (SPA.). 1992. 250.00 (*0-7859-0541-3*, 8423958396) Fr & Eur.

Mi Primera Enciclopedia, 2 vols., Set. 7th ed. Nauta Staff. (SPA.). 420p. (J). 1978. 65.00 (*0-8288-5254-5*, S26910) Fr & Eur.

***Mi Primera Enciclopedia del Mundo (First Encyclopedia of Our World.** (ENG & SPA., Illus.). 64p. (J). (ps up). 2000. pap. 9.95 (*0-7460-3883-6*, Usborne) EDC.

Mi Primera Gramatica. 2nd ed. Delfina Huerta & Susana Velazquez Huerta. (SPA., Illus.). 128p. (J). (ps-3). 1997. pap. 17.98 (*968-24-5213-9*) Trillas.

Mi Primera Visita a la Granja. J. M. Parramon. (SPA., Illus.). 32p. (J). 1990. pap. 6.95 (*0-8120-4400-2*) Barron.

Mi Primera Visita al Aviario. J. M. Parramon. (SPA., Illus.). 32p. (J). 1990. pap. 5.95 (*0-8120-4403-7*) Barron.

Mi Primera Visita al Zoo. J. M. Parramon. (SPA., Illus.). 32p. (J). 1990. pap. 6.95 (*0-8120-4402-9*) Barron.

Mi Primeros Colores. J. M. Parramon. (SPA., Illus.). 32p. (J). (ps-3). 1991. pap. 6.95 (*0-8120-4726-5*) Barron.

Mi Primeros Formas. J. M. Parramon. (SPA., Illus.). 32p. (J). (ps-3). 1991. pap. 6.95 (*0-8120-4728-1*) Barron.

Mi Primeros Numeros. J. M. Parramon. (SPA., Illus.). 32p. (J). (ps-3). 1991. pap. 6.95 (*0-8120-4727-3*) Barron.

Mi Querida Sunday. Mary Higgins Clark. 1998. pap. 6.50 (*84-01-49316-1*) Lectorum Pubns.

Mi Rancho: Black & White Nellie Edge I Can Read & Sing Big Book. Tr. by Hector Pichardo. (Illus.). (J). (ps-2). 1996. 20.00 (*0-922053-39-1*) N Edge Res.

Mi Respuesta. Luis Palau.Tr. of My Response. (SPA.). 112p. 1987. pap. 3.79 (*0-8423-6485-4*, 498018) Editorial Unilit.

Mi Rincon en la Montana. Jean Craighead George. Tr. by Carmen Gomez de Aguero. (SPA.). 192p. (J). (gr. 5-9). 1996. pap. 5.99 (*0-14-038181-3*, PuffinBks) Peng Put Young Read.

Mi Rincon En La Montana. Jean Craighead George. (SPA.). 1996. 10.09 (*0-606-09608-6*, Pub. by Turtleback) Demco.

Mi Segundo Libro de Teatro. (SPA.). 9.00 (*84-241-5633-1*) E Torres & Sons.

Mi Sem Voltunk Rosszabbak Masoknal Es Pillanatfelvetel a Mai Magyarorszagrol, 1985. Gyula Dessewffy & Zoltan Kovacs. LC 86-51435. 121p. (Orig.). pap. write for info. (*0-935484-15-9*) Universe Pub Co.

***MI Strategies for Kids: Featuring Brilliant Brain & Magnificent Mind.** Ellen Arnold. (Illus.). 80p. 2000. pap. 21.00 (*1-56976-110-8*, 1146) Zephyr Pr AZ.

MI Strategy Bank. Ellen Arnold. LC 98-43674. (Illus.). 96p. (J). (gr. k-12). 1998. pap. 18.00 (*1-56976-097-7*) Zephyr Pr AZ.

Mi Testimonio-Actor (My Testimony-Actor), No. 3. (SPA., Illus.). 0.39 (*0-685-74958-4*, 490595) Editorial Unilit.

Mi Testimonio-Diputado (My Testimony-Delegate), No. 2. (SPA., Illus.). 0.39 (*0-685-74957-6*, 490594) Editorial Unilit.

Mi Testimonio-Drogadicto (My Testimony-Drug Addict), No. 5. (SPA., Illus.). 0.39 (*0-685-74960-6*, 490597) Editorial Unilit.

Mi Testimonio-Militar (My Testimony-Military Man), No. 4. (SPA., Illus.). 0.39 (*0-685-74959-2*, 490596) Editorial Unilit.

Mi Testimonio-Senador (My Testimony-Senator), No. 1. (SPA., Illus.). 0.39 (*0-685-74956-8*, 490593) Editorial Unilit.

Mi tio Mario: Level D Books. Julio Llamazares. 8.95 (*0-8219-1473-1*) EMC-Paradigm.

Mi-24 Hind in Action. Hans-Heiri Stapfer. (Aircraft in Action Ser.). (Illus.). 50p. 1988. pap. 9.95 (*0-89747-203-9*, 1083) Squad Sig Pubns.

Mi Vida Loca. Eric Overmyer. 1991. pap. 6.95 (*0-88145-100-2*) Broadway Play.

Mi Visita a los Dinosaurios (My Visit to the Dinosaurs) Aliki. (SPA., Illus.). (ps-3). 1996. 9.95 (*84-261-2755-X*) Lectorum Pubns.

MIA. Michael K. Denny. LC 94-76850. 214p. 1994. pap. 8.95 (*0-9641492-9-X*) Buffalo Hse.

MIA: Missing in Action. (Illus.). 200p. 1977. pap. write for info. (*0-614-29620-X*) Phipps Pub.

MIA - World War II. Frank N. Kautzmann, Jr. (Illus.). 197p. (Orig.). (C). 1992. pap. text 14.95 (*0-9634563-0-X*) Austin Press.

***Mia Hamm.** Andrews McMeel Publishing Staff. (Illus.). 2000. 4.95 (*0-7407-0602-0*) Andrews & McMeel.

***Mia Hamm.** Terri Dougherty. LC 99-41950. (Jam Session Ser.). 2000. pap. 6.95 (*1-57765-365-3*) ABDO Pub Co.

***Mia Hamm.** Carl Emerson. LC 00-38339. (Illus.). (J). 2000. lib. bdg. write for info. (*1-56766-829-1*) Childs World.

***Mia Hamm.** Heather Feldman. LC 00-27219. (Illus.). (J). 2001. write for info. (*0-8239-5716-0*, PowerKids) Rosen Group.

***Mia Hamm.** Clay Latimer. (Sports Heroes Ser.). 48p. (YA). (gr. 5 up). 2000. lib. bdg. 21.26 (*0-7368-0579-6*, Capstone Bks) Capstone Pr.

Mia Hamm. Richard Rambeck. LC 97-42443. 24P32p. (J). 1998. lib. bdg. 21.36 (*1-56766-523-3*) Childs World.

***Mia Hamm.** Ed. by Joseph Romain. (Champion Sports Biography Ser.). (Illus.). 96p. 2000. pap. 8.95 (*1-894020-76-6*) Warwick Publ.

***Mia Hamm.** Robert Schnakenberg. (Women Who Win Ser.). (Illus.). 2000. pap. 7.95 (*0-7910-6151-5*) Chelsea Hse.

***Mia Hamm.** Robert Schnakenberg. LC 00-22840. (Women Who Win Ser.). 2001. 17.95 (*0-7910-5791-7*) Chelsea Hse.

Mia Hamm. John Torres. LC 99-19949. (Real-Life Reader Biography Ser.). (Illus.). 32p. (J). (gr. 3-8). 1999. lib. bdg. 15.95 (*1-883845-94-7*) M Lane Pubs.

Mia Hamm: Good as Gold. Mark Stewart. 1999. lib. bdg. 5.95 (*0-516-26487-7*) Childrens.

Mia Hamm: Good As Gold. Mark Stewart. LC 98-45308. (Sports Stars Ser.). 48p. (J). (gr. 3-4). 1999. 18.00 (*0-516-21221-4*) Childrens.

***Mia Hamm: Striking Superstar.** Rachel Rutledge. (Soccer's New Wave Ser.). 48p. (J). 2000. 20.90 (*0-7613-1802-X*) Millbrook Pr.

***Mia Hamm: Striking Superstar.** Rachel Rutledge. (Soccer's New Wave Ser.). (Illus.). 2000. pap. 6.95 (*0-7613-1381-8*) Millbrook Pr.

***Mia Hamm Rocks!, 1.** Chloe Weber. 1999. pap. 12.95 (*1-56649-026-X*) Welcome Rain.

Mia Indiana Knabeco. Luther S. Bear. Tr. by William R. Harmon from ENG. (ESP., Illus.). 88p. 1995. pap. 6.95 (*1-882251-09-1*) Eldonejo Bero.

Mia Parabola, Memorie. Titta Ruffo. Ed. by Andrew Farkas. LC 76-29966. (Opera Biographies Ser.).Tr. of My Parable, Reminiscences. (ITA., Illus.). 1977. reprint ed. lib. bdg. 39.95 (*0-405-09705-0*) Ayer.

Mia Poems. Burton Raffel. 1968. 6.95 (*0-8079-0082-6*); pap. 4.25 (*0-8079-0083-4*) October.

MIA Rescue: LRRP Manhunt in the Jungle. Kregg P. Jorgenson. (Illus.). 296p. 1995. text 29.95 (*0-87364-822-6*) Paladin Pr.

MIA Rescue: LRRPs in Cambodia. Kregg P. Joergenson. 1996. mass mkt. 5.99 (*0-8041-0980-X*) Ivy Books.

Mia the Beach Cat. Wolfram Hanel. Tr. by J. Alison James. LC 94-5064. (Illus.). 48p. (J). (gr. 2-4). 1994. lib. bdg. 12.88 (*1-55858-315-7*, Pub. by North-South Bks NYC) Chronicle Bks.

Mia the Beach Cat. Wolfram Hanel. Tr. by J. Alison James. LC 94-5064. (Illus.). 48p. (J). (gr. 2-4). 1996. 12.95 (*1-55858-314-9*, Pub. by North-South Bks NYC); pap. 5.95 (*1-55858-508-7*, Pub. by North-South Bks NYC) Chronicle Bks.

Mia Westerlund Roosen. Carter Ratcliff. Ed. by Shoshana Blank. (Illus.). 22p. (Orig.). 1989. pap. text 10.00 (*0-317-93161-X*) Shoshana Wayne Gall.

MIAA Football: The Illustrated Gridiron History of the Michigan Intercollegiate Athletic Association. Todd E. Harburn et al. LC 86-91208. (Illus.). 172p. 1986. 12.95 (*0-9617171-0-6*) T & G Harburn.

***Miaiden's Revenge.** Hillary Fields. 352p. 2000. mass mkt. 5.99 (*0-312-97282-2*, St Martins Paperbacks) St Martin.

Miajon de los Castuos (Rapsodias Extremenas) Luis Chamizo. Ed. by Camarasa A. Viudas. (Nueva Austral Ser.: Vol. 244). (SPA.). 1991. pap. text 24.95 (*84-239-7244-5*) Elliots Bks.

Miami. (Frommer's Irreverent Guides Ser.). 1996. pap. 12.95 (*0-614-12832-3*) Macmillan.

***Miami.** Photos by Tony Arruza. LC 00-26018. (Citylife Pictorial Guides Ser.). (Illus.). 96p. 2000. pap. 16.95 (*0-89658-498-4*) Voyageur Pr.

Miami. Balliet & Fitzgerald Staff. (Edge Guide to . . . Ser.). 256p. 1999. pap. 14.00 (*1-56352-519-4*) Longstreet.

***Miami.** Berlitz Publishing Staff. (Pocket Guide Ser.). (SPA., Illus.). 1999. pap. 8.95 (*2-8315-7035-2*) Berlitz.

***Miami.** Joann Biondi. LC 00-26018. (Citylife Pictorial Guides Ser.). (Illus.). 96p. 2000. 24.95 (*0-89658-445-3*) Voyageur Pr.

Miami. Susanne Cummings & Stuart Cummings. (Florida Sights & Scenes Ser.). 64p. 1995. pap. 7.95 (*0-88415-644-3*, 5644) Gulf Pub.

Miami. Joan Didion. LC 98-7127. 238p. 1999. pap. 12.00 (*0-679-78180-3*) Vin Bks.

Miami. Marsha Fischer. LC 89-25694. (Downtown America Ser.). (Illus.). 60p. (J). (gr. 3 up). 1990. lib. bdg. 13.95 (*0-87518-428-6*, Dillon Silver Burdett) Silver Burdett Pr.

Miami. Fodors Travel Publications, Inc. Staff. (Citypacks Ser.). 96p. 1998. pap. 12.00 (*0-679-03427-7*) Fodors Travel.

Miami. Insight Guides Staff. (Insight Guides). 1998. pap. text 12.95 (*0-88729-913-X*) Langenscheidt.

Miami. Santi Visalli. LC 93-83943. (Illus.). 224p. 1993. 55.00 (*0-8478-1716-4*, Pub. by Rizzoli Intl) St Martin.

Miami. Santi Visalli. (Illus.). 192p. 1996. pap. 25.00 (*0-7893-0053-2*) St Martin.

Miami. 2nd ed. Insight Guides Staff. (Insight Guides). 1998. pap. text 21.95 (*0-88729-713-7*) Langenscheidt.

***Miami.** 2nd ed. Nick Selby & Corinna Arnold. (Illus.). 208p. 1999. pap. 15.95 (*0-86442-653-4*) Lonely Planet.

Miami. 4th ed. Access Press Staff. (Illus.). 272p. 1997. pap. 19.00 (*0-06-277226-0*, Access Trvl) HarpInfo.

Miami: A Saga. large type ed. Evelyn W. Mayerson. LC 94-17035. 778p. 1994. lib. bdg. 23.95 (*0-7862-0267-X*) Thorndike Pr.

Miami: American Crossroad. Arva M. P. McCabe & Gregory Bush. 232p. (C). 1996. text 15.60 (*0-536-59693-X*) Pearson Custom.

Miami: Architecture of the Tropics. Ed. by Maurice Culot & Jean-Francois Lejeune. (Illus.). 192p. (Orig.). 1993. pap. 39.95 (*1-878271-75-X*) Princeton Arch.

Miami: City of Dreams. Alan S. Maltz. LC 96-33441. (Illus.). 204p. 1997. 60.00 (*0-9626677-3-0*) Light Key West.

Miami: Gateway to the Americas. Miguel Gonzalez-Pando et al. 1996. 39.95 (*0-9647106-1-7*) Copperfld Pubns.

Miami: Hot & Cool. Laura Cerwinski. 240p. 1998. pap. 25.00 (*0-609-80382-4*) Crown Pub Group.

Miami: In Our Own Words. Miami Herald Staff. Ed. by Nancy Ancrum & Richard Bard. (Illus.). 212p. 1995. pap. 15.95 (*0-8362-0572-3*) Andrews & McMeel.

Miami: Oasis. Kathryn S. Orosz. (Illus.). 80p. 1995. 28.00 (*0-9644807-0-0*) Orosz FL.

Miami: The Magic City. 2nd ed. Arva M. Parks. LC 91-75436. (Illus.). 256p. 1991. 39.95 (*0-9629402-2-4*) Centennial Pr.

Miami: Then & Now. Arva M. Parks. LC 92-85502. (Illus.). 64p. 1992. pap. 4.95 (*0-9629402-1-6*) Centennial Pr.

Miami: Trends & Traditions. Photos by Roberto Schezen. (Illus.). 1996. 60.00 (*0-614-21984-1*) Monacelli Pr.

Miami: Trends & Traditions. Roberto Schezen & Beth Dunlop. (Illus.). 240p. 1996. 60.00 (*1-885254-37-7*, Pub. by Monacelli Pr) Penguin Putnam.

***Miami Airport.** John K. Morton. (Illus.). 112p. 1999. pap. 15.95 (*1-84037-061-0*, Pub. by Airlife Publishing) Motorbooks Intl.

Miami Alive. Ethel Blum. (SPA.). 1981. pap. 5.95 (*0-935572-06-6*) Alive Pubns.

Miami American Crossroad Centennial Teachers Guidbook. 66p. (C). 1997. pap. 1.50 (*0-536-00628-8*) Pearson Custom.

***Miami & South Florida.** 5th ed. Access Press Staff. 272p. 1999. pap. 19.00 (*0-06-277276-7*, HarpRes) HarpInfo.

***Miami & the Florida Keys.** Rough Guides Staff. (Miniguides Ser.). 2000. pap. 9.95 (*1-85828-547-X*, Pub. by Rough Guides) Penguin Putnam.

***Miami & the Keys.** Lisa Simundson. (Alive! Guides Ser.). (Illus.). 300p. 2000. pap. 15.95 (*1-55650-913-8*) Hunter NJ.

***Miami & the Keys 2000: Gold Guides.** Fodors Travel Publications, Inc. Staff. (Illus.). 224p. 1999. pap. 14.00 (*0-679-00337-1*) Fodors Travel.

Miami Beach. Isaac Bashevis Singer & Gary L. Monroe. (Illus.). 60p. 1989. pap. 25.00 (*0-9618986-1-5*) Forest & Trees.

Miami Beach: A History. Howard Kleinberg. Ed. by Donna K. Born & Martha Reiner. (Illus.). 236p. 1994. 34.95 (*0-9629402-3-2*) Centennial Pr.

Miami Beach: Photographs of an American Dream. David Scheinbaum. (Illus.). 96p. (Orig.). 1990. 34.95 (*0-8130-0933-2*); pap. 19.95 (*0-8130-1031-4*) U Press Fla.

Miami Beach: The Paradise in the Sun. (ENG, FRE, GER & SPA., Illus.). 1992. pap. 5.00 (*1-877833-02-9*) Pro Pub Inc.

Miami Beach Deco. Alan Rose. (Illus.). 24p. 1997. pap. 16.95 (*0-312-14679-5*) St Martin.

***Miami Beach Deco: The World at Your Feet.** Alan Rose. (Illus.). 15p. 2000. pap. text 17.00 (*0-7881-6988-2*) DIANE Pub.

Miami Beach Models' Diet. Donald J. Barbas. (Illus.). 202p. 1996. pap. 14.95 (*0-9658346-0-3*) Miami Beach.

***Miami Beach Nineteen Hundred Twenty.** Abraham D. Lavender. (Illus.). 260p. 2000. 24.95 (*0-9677694-1-8*) Miami Beach Hist.

Miami Bibliography. Compiled by Susan Weiss. LC 97-155121. (Illus.). 153p. (Orig.). 1996. pap. 9.95 (*0-935761-08-X*) Hist Assn S Fla.

Miami "Chupacabras" Virgilio Sanchez-Ocejo. (Illus.). 58p. 1997. pap. 9.95 (*0-9660232-0-X*) Pharaoh.

Miami Cochlear Implant, Auditory, & Tactile Skills Curriculum: CHATS. Kathleen C. Vergara & Lynn W. Miskiel. LC 94-74538. 327p. 1994. pap. text 75.00 (*1-886887-00-4*); pap. text 75.00 (*1-886887-01-2*) Intell Hearing.

Miami County History. (Illus.). 403p. 1993. reprint ed. lib. bdg. 43.50 (*0-8328-2792-4*) Higginson Bk Co.

Miami County, Indiana: A Pictorial History. Marilyn Coppernoll. LC 95-33444. (Illus.). 1995. write for info. (*0-89865-951-5*) Donning Co.

Miami Daily Record Herald: November 1917-Sept. 1922 Vital Records Index. Hildred Hughes Ables. 1990. 26.00 (*1-892744-53-8*, A-153) Maloy.

Miami District Daily News: August 1917-March 1922 Vital Records Index. Hildred Hughes Ables. 1990. 26.00 (*1-892744-52-X*, A-152) Maloy.

Miami Dolphins. Bob Italia. LC 96-22380. (Inside the NFL Ser.). (Illus.). 32p. (J). (gr. 3-8). 1996. lib. bdg. 15.98 (*1-56239-460-6*) ABDO Pub Co.

***Miami Dolphins.** Miami Dolphins. Ed. by CWC Sports Inc. (NFL Team Yearbooks Ser.). (J). (gr. 1-12). 1998. pap. 9.99 (*1-891613-13-8*) Everett Sports.

***Miami Dolphins.** 3rd rev. ed. Julie Nelson. (Pro Football Today Ser.). (Illus.). 32p. (YA). (gr. 3-12). 2000. lib. bdg. 22.60 (*1-58341-048-1*, Creat Educ) Creative Co.

Miami Dolphins Football Team. J. J. DiLorenzo. LC 96-26414. (Great Sports Teams Ser.). 48p. (J). (gr. 4-10). 1997. lib. bdg. 18.95 (*0-89490-796-4*) Enslow Pubs.

Miami En Brumas. Nicolas Abreu Felippe. (Coleccion Caniqui). 203p. pap. 16.00 (*0-89729-919-1*) Ediciones.

Miami for Kids: A Family Guide to Greater Miami Including Everglades National Park & the Florida Keys. Elizabeth Livingston & Carol Starbuck. LC 81-65980. (Illus.). 80p. 1981. pap. 4.95 (*0-916224-63-5*) Banyan Bks.

Miami Generation: Nine Cuban Americans. 3.00 (*0-614-14840-5*) Balch Inst Ethnic Studies.

Miami Generation: Nine Cuban Americans. Cuban Museum of Arts & Culture Staff. (Illus.). 1985. 3.00 (*0-614-32311-8*) Balch IES Pr.

***Miami Gets It Straight.** Pat McKissack. LC 99-36116. (Road to Reading Ser.). 80p. 2000. 10.99 (*0-307-46501-2*) Gldn Bks Pub Co.

M

An Asterisk (*) at the beginning of an entry indicates that the title is appearing for the first time.

***Miami Gets It Straight.** Pat McKissack et al. LC 99-36116. (Road to Reading Ser.: 3). 80p. (J). 2000. pap. 3.99 (*0-307-26501-3*, Goldn Books) Gldn Bks Pub Co.
Miami Giant. Arthur Yorinks. (Illus.). 36p. (J). (gr. 5-8). 1999. text 16.00 (*0-7881-6464-3*) DIANE Pub.
Miami Giant. Arthur Yorinks. LC 94-79526. (Michael di Capua Bks.). (Illus.). 40p. (J). (gr. 2 up). 1995. 15.95 (*0-06-205068-0*) HarpC Child Bks.
Miami Heat see Pro Basketball Today
***Miami Heat, Vol. 1.** Berta Platas Fuller. 1999. mass mkt. 5.99 (*0-7860-1022-3*) Pinal County Schl Office.
Miami Heat. D. A. Hodgman. (Stakeout Ser.). 1995. per. 4.99 (*0-373-63411-0*, 1-63411-2) Harlequin Bks.
Miami Heat. Paul Joseph. LC 96-39617. (Inside the NBA Ser.). (Illus.). 32p. (J). (gr. 3-8). 1997. lib. bdg. 16.95 (*1-56239-763-X*) ABDO Pub Co.
Miami Herald Dining Guide. Lucy Cooper & Bob Hosmon. (Illus.). 144p. (Orig.). 1984. pap. text 3.95 (*0-685-09725-0*) S&S Trade.
Miami Herald Guide to South Florida's Best Restaurants. Miami Herald Staff & Felicia Gressette. LC 95-44801. 176p. 1995. pap. 7.95 (*0-8362-0785-8*) Andrews & McMeel.
Miami Herald 1995 South Florida Outdoor Guide. Miami Hearld Staff. Ed. by Ken Millman. (Illus.). 262p. 1994. pap. 12.95 (*0-8362-8080-6*) Andrews & McMeel.
Miami Ice: Winning the NHL Rat Race with the Florida Panthers. David Rosenbaum. LC 96-78068. (Illus.). 252p. (Orig.). 1997. pap. 18.95 (*0-9653846-6-7*) McGregor Pub.
***Miami Indians.** Bert Anson. (Civilization of the American Indian Ser.: Vol. 103). (Illus.). 352p. 1999. pap. 25.95 (*0-8061-3197-7*) U of Okla Pr.
Miami Indians. Bert Anson. LC 74-108793. (Civilization of the American Indian Ser.: Vol. 103). (Illus.). 363p. reprint ed. 112.60 (*0-8357-9735-X*, 201619100002) Bks Demand.
Miami Indians of Indiana: A Persistent People, 1654-1994. Stewart Rafert. (Illus.). xxvii, 358p. 1996. 29.95 (*0-87195-111-8*) Ind Hist Soc.
***Miami Indians of Indiana: A Persistent People, 1654-1994.** Stewart Rafert. (Illus.). xxvii, 358p. 1999. pap. 14.95 (*0-87195-132-0*) Ind Hist Soc.
Miami, It's Murder. large type ed. Edna R. Buchanan. LC 93-28628. 1994. lib. bdg. 24.95 (*0-7862-0033-2*) Thorndike Pr.
Miami, It's Murder. large type ed. Edna R. Buchanan. LC 93-28628. 409p. 1994. pap. 15.95 (*0-7862-0034-0*) Thorndike Pr.
Miami, It's Murder: A Britt Montero Novel. Edna R. Buchanan. 320p. 1995. mass mkt. 6.99 (*0-380-72261-5*, Avon Bks) Morrow Avon.
Miami Job Source: Everything You Need to Know to Land the Internship Entry-Level or Middle Management Job of Your Choice in the Miami Metro Area. Mary McMahon. Ed. by Benjamin S. Psillas & Donna C. Hicks. (Job Source Ser.). (Illus.). 352p. (Orig.). 1996. 15.95 (*0-9635651-6-8*) Benjamin Scott.
Miami Memoirs - John Sewell: A New Pictorial Edition. John W. Sewell. Ed. by Ellen S. Blakey. (Illus.). 267p. 1987. 29.95 (*0-914381-07-5*) Centennial Pr.
Miami Model Agency Directory, Vol. 1. Peter Glenn Staff. 1998. pap. 12.95 (*0-87314-225-X*) Peter Glenn.
Miami Now: Immigration, Ethnicity, & Social Change. Ed. by Guillermo Grenier & Alex Stepick, III. LC 92-10100. (Illus.). 256p. 1992. 24.95 (*0-8130-1154-X*); pap. 19.95 (*0-8130-1155-8*) U Press Fla.
Miami of Ohio: The Cradle of Coaches. Bob Kurz. LC 83-50646. (Illus.). 262p. (Orig.). 1983. pap. 10.95 (*0-942520-00-9*); text 12.95 (*0-942520-01-7*) Distributors.
Miami Oklahoma News-Record No. 2: 1923-1924 Vital Records Index. Ed. by Hildred Hughes Ables & Audrey Topliff. 59p. 1981. 26.00 (*1-892744-08-2*, A-108) Maloy.
Miami Oklahoma News-Record No. 3: 1925-1926 Vital Records Index. Ed. by Hildred Hughes Ables & Audrey Topliff. 67p. 1981. 26.00 (*1-892744-09-0*, A-109) Maloy.
Miami Oklahoma News-Record No. 4: 1927-1928 Vital Records Index. Ed. by Hildred Hughes Ables & Audrey Topliff. 78p. 1982. 26.00 (*1-892744-10-4*, A-110) Maloy.
Miami Oklahoma News-Record No. 5: 1929-1930 Vital Records Index. Ed. by Hildred Hughes Ables & Audrey Topliff. 95p. 1982. 26.00 (*1-892744-11-2*, A-111) Maloy.
Miami Oklahoma News-Record No. 6: 1931-1932 Vital Records Index. Ed. by Hildred Hughes Ables & Audrey Topliff. 83p. 1983. 26.00 (*1-892744-12-0*, A-112) Maloy.
Miami Oklahoma News-Record No. 7: 1933-1934 Vital Records Index. Ed. by Hildred Hughes Ables & Audrey Topliff. 94p. 1983. 26.00 (*1-892744-13-9*, A-113) Maloy.
Miami Oklahoma News-Record No. 8: 1935-1936 Vital Records Index. Ed. by Hildred Hughes Ables & Audrey Topliff. 97p. 1984. 26.00 (*1-892744-14-7*, A-114) Maloy.
Miami Oklahoma News-Record No. 9: 1937-1938 Vital Records Index. Ed. by Hildred Hughes Ables & Audrey Topliff. 108p. 1984. 26.00 (*1-892744-15-5*, A-115) Maloy.
Miami Oklahoma News-Record No. 10: 1939-1940 Vital Records Index. Ed. by Hildred Hughes Ables & Audrey Topliff. 86p. 1985. 26.00 (*1-892744-16-3*, A-116) Maloy.
Miami Oklahoma News-Record No. 11: 1941-1942 Vital Records Index. Ed. by Hildred Hughes Ables & Audrey Topliff. 86p. 1985. 26.00 (*1-892744-17-1*, A-117) Maloy.
Miami Oklahoma News-Record No. 12: 1943-1944 Vital Records Index. Ed. by Hildred Hughes Ables & Audrey Topliff. 80p. 1986. 26.00 (*1-892744-18-X*, A-118) Maloy.
Miami Oklahoma News-Record No. 13: 1945-1946 Vital Records Index. Ed. by Hildred Hughes Ables & Audrey Topliff. 60p. 1986. 26.00 (*1-892744-19-8*, A-119) Maloy.
Miami Oklahoma News-Record No. 14: 1947-1948 Vital Records Index. Ed. by Hildred Hughes Ables & Audrey Topliff. 82p. 1987. 26.00 (*1-892744-20-1*, A-120) Maloy.
Miami Oklahoma News-Record No. 15: 1949-1950 Vital Records Index. Ed. by Hildred Hughes Ables & Audrey Topliff. 71p. 1987. 26.00 (*1-892744-21-X*, A-121) Maloy.
Miami Oklahoma News-Record No. 16: 1951-1952 Vital Records Index. Ed. by Hildred Hughes Ables & Audrey Topliff. 61p. 1988. 26.00 (*1-892744-22-8*, A-122) Maloy.
Miami Oklahoma News-Record No. 17: 1953-1954 Vital Records Index. Ed. by Hildred Hughes Ables & Audrey Topliff. 90p. 1988. 26.00 (*1-892744-23-6*, A-123) Maloy.
Miami Oklahoma News-Record No. 18: 1955-1956 Vital Records Index. Ed. by Hildred Hughes Ables & Audrey Topliff. 88p. 1989. 26.00 (*1-892744-24-4*, A-124) Maloy.
Miami Oklahoma News-Record No. 19: 1957-1958 Vital Records Index. Ed. by Hildred Hughes Ables & Audrey Topliff. 81p. 1989. 26.00 (*1-892744-25-2*, A-125) Maloy.
Miami Oklahoma News-Record No. 20: 1959-1960 Vital Records Index. Ed. by Hildred Hughes Ables. 75p. 1990. 26.00 (*1-892744-26-0*, A-126) Maloy.
Miami Oklahoma News-Record No. 21: 1961-1962 Vital Records Index. Ed. by Hildred Hughes Ables. 75p. 1990. 26.00 (*1-892744-27-9*, A-127) Maloy.
Miami Oklahoma News-Record No. 22: 1963-1964 Vital Records Index. Ed. by Hildred Hughes Ables. 72p. 1990. 26.00 (*1-892744-28-7*, A-128) Maloy.
Miami Oklahoma News-Record No. 23: 1965-1966 Vital Records Index. Ed. by Hildred Hughes Ables. 108p. 1991. 26.00 (*1-892744-29-5*, A-129) Maloy.
Miami Oklahoma News-Record No. 24: 1967-1968 Vital Records Index. Ed. by Hildred Hughes Ables. 84p. 1991. 26.00 (*1-892744-30-9*, A-130) Maloy.
Miami Oklahoma News-Record No. 25: 1969-1970 Vital Records Index. Ed. by Hildred Hughes Ables. 96p. 1991. 26.00 (*1-892744-31-7*, A-131) Maloy.
Miami Oklahoma News-Record No. 26: 1971-1972 Vital Records Index. Ed. by Hildred Hughes Ables. 81p. 1992. 26.00 (*1-892744-32-5*, A-132) Maloy.
Miami Oklahoma News-Record No. 27: 1973-1974 Vital Records Index. Ed. by Hildred Hughes Ables. 80p. 1992. 26.00 (*1-892744-33-3*, A-133) Maloy.
Miami Oklahoma News-Record No. 28: 1975-1976 Vital Records Index. Ed. by Hildred Hughes Ables. 86p. 1992. 26.00 (*1-892744-34-1*, A-134) Maloy.
Miami Oklahoma News-Record No. 29: 1977-1978 Vital Records Index. Ed. by Hildred Hughes Ables. 87p. 1993. 26.00 (*1-892744-35-X*, A-135) Maloy.
Miami Oklahoma News-Record No. 30: 1979-1980 Vital Records Index. Ed. by Hildred Hughes Ables. 84p. 1993. 26.00 (*1-892744-36-8*, A-136) Maloy.
Miami Oklahoma News-Record No. 31: 1981-1982 Vital Records Index. Ed. by Hildred Hughes Ables. 81p. 1993. 26.00 (*1-892744-37-6*, A-137) Maloy.
Miami Oklahoma News-Record No. 32: 1983-1984 Vital Records Index. Ed. by Hildred Hughes Ables. 87p. 1994. 26.00 (*1-892744-38-4*, A-138) Maloy.
Miami Oklahoma News-Record No. 33: 1985-1986 Vital Records Index. Ed. by Hildred Hughes Ables. 85p. 1994. 26.00 (*1-892744-39-2*, A-139) Maloy.
Miami Oklahoma News-Record No. 34: 1987-1988 Vital Records Index. Ed. by Hildred Hughes Ables. 75p. 1994. 26.00 (*1-892744-40-6*, A-140) Maloy.
Miami Oklahoma News-Record No. 35: 1989 Vital Records Index. Ed. by Hildred Hughes Ables. 45p. 1995. 26.00 (*1-892744-41-4*, A-141) Maloy.
Miami Oklahoma News-Record No. 36: 1990-1991 Vital Records Index. Ed. by Hildred Hughes Ables. 104p. 1995. 26.00 (*1-892744-42-2*, A-142) Maloy.
Miami Oklahoma News-Record No. 37: 1992-1993 Vital Records Index. Ed. by Hildred Hughes Ables. 89p. 1995. 26.00 (*1-892744-43-0*, A-143) Maloy.
Miami Oklahoma News-Record No. 38: 1994-1995 Vital Records Index. Ed. by Hildred Hughes Ables. 88p. 1996. write for info. (*1-892744-44-9*, A-144) Maloy.
Miami Oklahoma News-Record No. 39: 1996-1997 Vital Records Index. Ed. by Hildred Hughes Ables. 100p. 1997. 26.00 (*1-892744-45-7*, A-145) Maloy.
***Miami Oklahoma News-Record No. 40: 1998-1999 Vital Records Index.** Ed. by Hildred Hughes Ables. 110p. 2000. 26.00 (*1-892744-46-5*, A-146) Maloy.
Miami, Orlando & South Florida. Ed. by Time Out Magazine Staff. LC 98-107794. (Time Out Ser.). (Illus.). 290p. 1998. pap. 14.95 (*0-14-026685-2*, Penguin Bks) Viking Penguin.
Miami Pocket Guide, 1998. rev. ed. Berlitz Editors. (Pocket Guides Ser.). (Illus.). 144p. 1998. pap. 8.95 (*2-8315-6975-3*) Berlitz.
Miami Poets: Percy MacKaye & Ridgely Torrence. Percy MacKaye & Ridgely Torrence. Ed. by William Pratt. (Keepsakes Ser.). (Illus.). 74p. (Orig.). 1988. pap. text. write for info. (*0-918761-02-6*) Miami U Pubns.
Miami Poppycock: The First 100 Years. Ralph Bodek. LC 93-80955. (Illus.). 1995. pap. 14.95 (*0-9646914-0-X*); pap. 7.95 (*0-9646914-1-8*) Hallmark Pubns.
Miami Production Guide: A South Florida Directory of Film, Video & Print. 8th rev. ed. Ed. by Richard Sears. 350p. 1998. spiral bd. 15.00 (*1-891308-00-9*) Film Fla Pubg.
***Miami Production Guide: A South Florida Directory of Film, Video & Print.** annuals 9th rev. ed. 350p. 1999. spiral bd. 15.00 (*1-891308-01-7*) Film Fla Pubg.
Miami Production Guide: A South Florida Directory of Film, Video & Print. annuals 11th rev. ed. spiral bd. 15.00 (*1-891308-04-1*, Miami Prod Guide) Film Fla Pubg.
Miami Report III: Recommendations for a North American Free Trade Agreement & for Future Hemispheric Trade. 140p. 1992. pap. 16.95 (*0-935501-48-7*) Transaction Pubs.
***Miami Restaurants.** Andre Gayot. (Gayot Restaurants Ser.: Vol. 1). (Illus.). 208p. 2000. pap. 14.00 (*1-881066-63-0*, Pub. by Gault Millau) Publishers Group.
Miami River & Its Tributaries. Donald C. Gaby. (Illus.). xiii, 195p. (Orig.). 1993. pap. text. write for info. (*0-935761-04-7*) Hist Assn S Fla.
Miami Savvy. Barbara Blumin. Ed. by Cookie Miller. (Illus.). 196p. (Orig.). 1989. pap. 7.95 (*0-685-23211-5*) Portobello Bks.
Miami Sourcebook: For Millennium's End. Robin M. Allnutt. (Illus.). 144p. (Orig.). 1995. pap. 15.00 (*0-9628748-8-4*) Chameleon Eclectic.
Miami Spice: The New Florida Cuisine. Steven Raichlen. LC 93-25446. (Illus.). 352p. (Orig.). 1993. pap. 12.95 (*1-56305-346-2*, 3346) Workman Pub.
Miami Street Atlas: Covering Coconut Grove, Coral Gables, Homestead & Miami Beach. (Illus.). 96p. 1996. pap. text 14.95 (*1-877651-81-8*) Trakker Maps.
***Miami: Tempting Tropical Tastes.** Martin & Martin Kotkin. 1999. pap. 15.95 (*0-8050-5674-2*) St Martin.
Miami University: A Personal History. Phillip R. Shriver & William Pratt. LC 98-6081. 1998. write for info. (*1-881163-28-8*) Miami Univ Pr.
Miami University - Then & Now. Photos by Dan Dry. (Illus.). 112p. 1993. 39.95 (*1-56469-007-5*) Harmony Hse Pub.
***Miami, U.S.A. An Expanded Edition.** Helen Muir. 2000. 24.95 (*0-8130-1831-5*) U Press Fla.
Miami Valley Senior Resource Guide. large type ed. Senior Resource Connection Staff. 250p. (Orig.). 1997. pap. 4.95 (*0-9654235-0-6*) Sr Resource Conn.
Miami Valley Senior Resource Guide, 1999-2000 Edition. 2nd ed. Senior Resource Connection Staff. (Illus.). 240p. 1999. pap. 4.95 (*0-9654235-1-4*) Sr Resource Conn.
Miami Vice Scrapbook. Jeanette Friedman. (Illus.). 64p. 1986. pap. 5.95 (*0-317-01182-0*, Sig) NAL.
Miami/Dade/Broward/Palm Beach Counties Florida. Rand McNally Staff. (Rand McNally Streetfinder Ser.). 1999. pap. text 35.00 (*0-528-97889-6*) Rand McNally.
***Miami/Florida Keys Entertainment, 2000.** (Illus.). 806p. 1999. pap. 25.00 (*1-58553-039-5*, 00P9) Enter Pubns.
Miamis! Nancy N. Baxter. 100p. (J). (gr. 4-6). 1987. 16.95 (*0-9617367-3-9*) Guild Pr IN.
***Miami's Parrot Jungle & Gardens.** Cory H. Gittner. 2000. pap. 12.95 (*0-8130-1817-X*) U Press Fla.
***Mian Xiang: The Ancient Chinese Art of Face Reading.** Henning Hai Lee Yang. (Illus.). 256p. 2000. pap. 12.95 (*1-86204-837-1*) Element MA.
Mianping Introduction to Salin. Mobi. LC 97-207860. 1997. text 234.00 (*0-7923-4098-1*) Kluwer Academic.
Miao & Yao Linguistic Studies: Selected Articles in Chinese. Ed. by Herbert C. Purnell. LC 73-155571. (Cornell University, Southeast Asia Program, Data Paper Ser.: No. 88). 306p. reprint ed. pap. 94.90 (*0-8357-3677-6*, 203640100003) Bks Demand.
Miao Textile Design. Fu Jen Catholic University Textiles & Clothing Gra. (CHI & ENG., Illus.). 312p. 1993. 99.95 (*957-9000-02-6*) Oriental Bk Store.
MIAs: A Reference Handbook. Jeanne M. Lesinski. LC 98-42275. (Contemporary World Issues Ser.). 256p. 1998. lib. bdg. 45.00 (*0-87436-954-1*) ABC-CLIO.
***Mia's Sun Hat.** School Zone Publishing Staff. (Start to Read Board Bks.). (Illus.). (J). 2000. bds. 4.99 (*0-88743-811-3*) Sch Zone Pub Co.
Miasma: "Haecceitas' in Scotus, the Esoteric in Plato, & 'Other Related Matters' John W. McGinley. LC 96-28882. 226p. 1996. lib. bdg. 36.50 (*0-7618-0453-6*) U Pr of Amer.
Miasma: Pollution & Purification in Early Greek Religion. Robert Parker. 432p. (C). 1996. reprint ed. pap. text 45.00 (*0-19-814742-2*) OUP.
Miasmas & Disease: Public Health & Environment in the Pre-Industrial Age. Carlo M. Cipolla. Tr. by Elizabeth Potter from ITA. 144p. (C). 1992. 32.00 (*0-300-04806-8*) Yale U Pr.
Miau. Benito Perez Galdos. Ed. by Ricardo Gullon. (Biblioteca De Cultura Basica Ser.). 677p. 1987. pap. 8.75 (*0-8477-0728-8*) U of PR Pr.
Miau Miau. (Libros de Carton Con Sonido Ser.). (SPA.). 1995. bds. 4.98 (*1-85854-296-0*) Brimax Bks.
Miau y Marianela. Benito Perez Galdos. (SPA.). 1989. 7.95 (*0-8288-2573-4*) Fr & Eur.
MIB, Aliens among Us. Timothy G. Beckley. 30p. 1996. reprint ed. spiral bd. 9.50 (*0-7873-0085-3*) Hlth Research.
MiBbrauch und Verfall der Vernunft. Friedrich A. Hayek. (International Carl Menger Library). vi, 360p. 1979. reprint ed. pap. 45.00 (*3-88405-009-5*) Philosophia Pr.
MIC - Marians of the Immaculate Conception: Sources of Marian History & Spirituality. Shaun O'Connor & Kazimierz Chwalek. Ed. by John Bukowicz & Thaddeus Gorski. 300p. 1988. write for info. (*0-318-62733-7*) Marian Pr.
MIC & MMIC Amplifier & Oscillator Circuit Design. Allen A. Sweet. LC 89-49100. (Artech House Microwave Library). (Illus.). 379p. 1990. reprint ed. pap. 117.50 (*0-608-00008-6*, 206077300006) Bks Demand.
Mica. (Metals & Minerals Ser.). 1993. lib. bdg. 243.95 (*0-8490-8980-8*) Gordon Pr.
Mi'Ca: Buffalo Hunter. Jane Bendix. (Illus.). 188p. (J). (gr. 4-12). 1992. 9.95 (*0-89992-131-0*) Coun India Ed.
Mica & Mica Industry. B. B. Madhukar & S. N. Srivastava. LC 99-227034. (Illus.). 212p. (C). 1995. text 104.00 (*90-5410-209-8*, TN953, Pub. by A A Balkema) Ashgate Pub Co.
Mica, Mica Parva, Stella. Ed. by Maureen R. Stover. 53p. (YA). 1996. teacher ed., spiral bd. 7.15 (*0-939507-50-1*, B 310T); spiral bd. 7.15 (*0-939507-49-8*, B 310) Amer Classical.
Micaela's Cookbook of Poetry: For the Connoisseur & the Poem Phobic. M. H. Estrada. (Illus.). 65p. 1998. pap. 14.00 (*0-9661051-4-1*) Intl Language.
Micaela's Daughter Vol. 16: Complete Plays 16. Manuel P. Garcia. 122p. 1998. 4.95 (*1-885901-66-6*, Liberts) Presbyters Peartree.
Micah. Delbert R. Hillers. LC 83-48002. (Hermenaia Ser.). 120p. 1983. 33.00 (*0-8006-6012-9*, 1-6012, Fortress Pr) Augsburg Fortress.
***Micah.** Ehud Ben Zvi. 2000. pap. text 35.00 (*0-8028-4599-1*) Eerdmans.
Micah: A Commentary. James L. Mays. LC 76-2599. (Old Testament Library). 180p. 1976. 21.00 (*0-664-20817-7*) Westminster John Knox.
Micah: A Commentary. Hans W. Wolff. Tr. by Gary Stansell from GER. LC 89-35669. (Continental Commentary Ser.). 208p. 1990. 38.00 (*0-8006-9513-5*, 1-9513) Augsburg Fortress.
Micah: A New Translation with Introduction & Commentary. Francis I. Andersen & David Noel Freedman. LC 99-22814. (Anchor Bible Ser.). 720p. 2000. 42.50 (*0-385-08402-1*) Doubleday.
Micah: Introduction & Commentary. William McKane. 256p. 49.95 (*0-567-08615-1*) T&T Clark Pubs.
Micah - Malachi see Layman's Bible Commentary
Micah-Malachi. Ralph L. Smith. (Biblical Commentary Ser.: Vol. 32). 1984. 29.99 (*0-8499-0231-2*) Word Pub.
Micah-Malachi. Walter C. Walter. (Communicator's Commentary Ser.: Vol. 21). 1992. 22.99 (*0-8499-0427-7*) Word Pub.
Micah Mandate: Balancing the Christian Life. George Grant. LC 99-30190. 256p. 1999. pap. 10.95 (*1-58182-055-0*, Cumberland Hearthside) Cumberland Hse.
Micah, Nahum & Obadiah. R. Mason. (Old Testament Guides Ser.: No. 28). 116p. 1991. pap. 12.50 (*1-85075-702-X*, Pub. by Sheffield Acad) CUP Services.
Micah, Nahum, Habakkuk, Zephaniah, Haggai, Zechariah, Malachi. Walter C. Kaiser. (Mastering the Old & New Testament Ser.: Vol. 21). 1993. pap. 14.99 (*0-8499-3559-8*) Word Pub.
Micah, Zephaniah, Nahum, Habakkuk, Obadiah & Joel: Critical & Exegetical Commentary. John M. Smith et al. Ed. by Samuel R. Driver et al. (International Critical Commentary Ser.). 560p. 1995. 39.95 (*0-567-05019-X*, Pub. by T & T Clark) Bks Intl VA.
***MICAI 2000: Advances in Artificial Intelligence: Mexican International Conference on Artificial Intelligence, Acapulco, Mexico, April 11-14, 2000, Proceedings.** Intelligence Mexican International Conference on Artificial Intelligence Staff. Ed. by Osvaldo Cairo et al. LC 00-37337. (Lecture Notes in Artificial Intelligence Ser.: Vol. 1793). (Illus.). xiv, 750p. 2000. pap. 106.00 (*3-540-67354-7*) Spr-Verlag.
Micajah's White Horse & Red Wagon. Hankins Parker. (Illus.). 189p. (Orig.). 1995. pap. 12.50 (*1-885132-02-6*) Park Hurst Pubs.
Micali Painter & His Followers. Nigel J. Spivey. (Oxford Monographs on Classical Archaeology). (Illus.). 158p. 1987. text 62.00 (*0-19-813225-5*) OUP.
Micas. Ed. by S. W. Bailey. (Reviews in Mineralogy Ser.: Vol. 13). 584p. 1984. per. 28.00 (*0-939950-17-0*) Mineralogical Soc.
Micashards, Mothwings: Poems of Forty Years. Mike Shields. 96p. 1996. pap. 11.95 (*3-7052-0982-5*, Pub. by Poetry Salzburg) Intl Spec Bk.
Mice see Animals Series
Mice. Horst Bielfeld. (Pet Care Ser.). 1985. pap. 6.95 (*0-8120-2921-6*) Barron.
***Mice.** Horst Bliefeld. (Complete Pet Owner's Manual Ser.). (Illus.). 2000. pap. text 6.95 (*0-7641-1450-6*) Barron.
Mice! Julie E. Frankel. LC 86-1008. (Rookie Readers Ser.). (Illus.). 32p. (J). (ps-2). 1986. pap. 3.50 (*0-516-42070-4*) Childrens.
Mice. Beatrix Potter. (Peter Rabbit Peek-Through Board Bks.). (Illus.). (J). 1996. bds. 4.99 (*0-614-15583-5*, F Warne) Peng Put Young Read.
Mice. Mervin F. Roberts. (Mice). 32p. pap. 1.79 (*0-87666-209-2*) TFH Pubns.
Mice. unabridged ed. Earvin McBride, Jr. (Earvin MacBride's Fun Fun Lovable Cartoons Ser.). (Illus.). 123p. (J). (gr. 7-12). 2000. pap. 3.95 (*1-892511-04-5*) E J MacBride.
Mice & Ice. Alan M. Hofmeister et al. (Reading for All Learners Ser.). (Illus.). (J). pap. write for info. (*1-56861-159-5*) Swift Lrn Res.
Mice & Nice. (Young Dragon Readers 2 Ser.). (J). 1995. pap. text. write for info. (*962-359-534-4*) Addison-Wesley.
Mice & Voles. J. F. Flowerdew. (Illus.). 128p. text 19.95 (*1-873580-08-8*, Pub. by Whittet Bks) Diamond Farm Bk.
Mice Are Men: Language & Society among the Murle of Sudan. Jonathan E. Arensen. LC 92-73535. (International Museum of Cultures Ser.: Vol. 27). 384p. 1992. pap. 27.00 (*0-88312-606-0*) S I L Intl.
Mice Are Nice. Charles Ghigna. LC 98-27971. (Step into Reading Ser.: A Step 1 Book). (Illus.). 32p. (J). (gr. k-3). 1999. pap. 3.99 (*0-679-88929-9*) Random.
Mice Are Nice. Charles Ghigna. LC 98-27971. (Step into Reading Ser.: A Step 1 Book). (Illus.). 32p. (J). (gr. k-3). 1999. lib. bdg. 11.99 (*0-679-98929-3*) Random.
Mice As a Hobby. Jack Young. (Illus.). 96p. 1993. 8.95 (*0-86622-949-3*, TT019) TFH Pubns.
Mice As a New Pet. Richard Pfarr. 1991. pap. 6.95 (*0-86622-530-7*, TU022) TFH Pubns.
Mice at Bat. Kelly Oechsli. LC 85-45266. (I Can Read Bks.). (Illus.). 64p. (J). (ps-3). 1986. 11.95 (*0-06-024623-5*) HarpC Child Bks.

M

Mice at Bat. Kelly Oechsli. LC 85-45266. (I Can Read Bks.). (Illus.). 64p. (J). (ps-3). 1990. pap. 3.95 (*0-06-444139-3*, HarpTrophy) HarpC Child Bks.

Mice at Bat. Kelly Oechsli. (I Can Read Bks.). (J). (ps-3). 1986. 8.95 (*0-606-04476-0*, Pub. by Turtleback) Demco.

***Mice Make Trouble.** Becky Bloom. LC 99-37708. (Illus.). 32p. (J). (ps-2). 2000. 15.95 (*0-531-30253-9*); lib. bdg. 16.99 (*0-531-33253-5*) Orchard Bks Watts.

Mice, Myths, & Men. R. J. Fry. LC 95-1235. (L.S. Taylor Lectures in Radiation Protection & Measurements: No. 18). 61p. 1994. pap. text 25.00 (*0-929600-41-X*) NCRP Pubns.

Mice of Mousehold: A Moving Picture Book. Michelle Cartlidge. LC 96-84673. (Illus.). 14p. (J). (ps). 1997. 14.99 (*0-7636-0117-9*) Candlewick Pr.

Mice of the British Isles. Michael Leach. (Natural History Ser.: No. 54). (Illus.). 24p. 1989. pap. 5.25 (*0-7478-0056-1*, Pub. by Shire Pubns) Parkwest Pubns.

Mice of the Herring Bone. Tim Davis. LC 92-11425. (Illus.). 106p. (J). 1992. pap. 6.49 (*0-89084-626-X*, 058537) Bob Jones Univ.

***Mice of the Herring Bone, 2 vols.** Tim Davis. 2000. pap. 14.98 (*0-89084-907-2*) Bob Jones Univ.

Mice of the Nine Lives. Tim Davis. LC 94-26128. (Illus.). 86p. (J). (gr. 1-5). 1994. pap. 6.49 (*0-89084-755-X*, 080556) Bob Jones Univ.

***Mice of the Nine Lives, 2 vols.** Tim Davis. 2000. pap. 14.98 (*1-57924-089-5*) Bob Jones Univ.

Mice of the Seven Seas. Tim Davis. LC 95-36840. 138p. (J). 1995. pap. 6.49 (*0-89084-845-9*, 092312) Bob Jones Univ.

Mice of the Westing Wind, Bk. 2. Tim Davis. LC 98-14559. (Illus.). 120p. (gr. 2-3). 1998. pap. 6.49 (*1-57924-067-4*) Bob Jones Univ.

Mice of the Westing Wind Book One. Tim Davis. LC 98-14559. (Illus.). 120p. (J). 1998. pap. 6.49 (*1-57924-065-8*) Bob Jones Univ.

Mice on Ice: Easy Phonics Reader. Carratello. (Illus.). 16p. (J). (ps-1). 1996. pap. 2.49 (*1-57690-012-6*) Tchr Create Mat.

***Mice Squeak, We Speak.** Arnold L. Shapiro. (Illus.). 32p. (J). (ps-1). 2000. pap. 5.99 (*0-698-11873-1*, PuffinBks) Peng Put Young Read.

Mice to the Rescue! Michelle V. Dionetti. (Illus.). (J). (gr. 1-4). 1995. lib. bdg. 14.00 (*0-8167-3712-6*, Little Rainbow) Troll Communs.

Mice to the Rescue! Michelle V. Dionetti. (J). (ps-3). 1997. pap. 3.95 (*0-8167-3515-8*, Little Rainbow) Troll Communs.

Mice Twice. Joseph Low. 1983. 11.19 (*0-606-00922-1*, Pub. by Turtleback) Demco.

Mice Twice. Joseph Low. LC 85-26768. (Illus.). 32p. (J). (ps-3). 1986. reprint ed. mass mkt. 5.99 (*0-689-71060-7*) Aladdin.

Mice Way to Learn about Government: A Curriculum Guide. Peter W. Barnes et al. (Illus.). 64p. 1999. pap. text 9.95 (*1-893622-00-2*, VSP Bks) Vacation Spot.

***"Mice" Way to Learn about Voting, Campaigns & Elections: A Curriculum Guide to Woodrow for President.** Peter W. Barnes et al. (Illus.). 24p. 1999. pap., teacher ed. 7.95 (*1-893622-02-9*, Pub. by Vacation Spot) Koen Bk Distributors.

Micellar Liquid Chromatography. Alain Berthod. (Chromatographic Science Ser.). (Illus.). 418p. Date not set. text. write for info. (*0-8247-9993-3*) Dekker.

Micellar Solutions & Microemulsions. Ed. by S. H. Chen & R. Rajagopalan. (Illus.). 304p. 1990. 144.00 (*0-387-97106-8*) Spr-Verlag.

Micelles: Theoretical & Applied Aspects. Y. Moroi. (Illus.). 264p. (C). 1992. text 69.50 (*0-306-43996-4*, Kluwer Plenum) Kluwer Academic.

Micelles, Membranes, Microemulsions & Monolayers. Ed. by W. Gelbart et al. LC 94-15496. (Partially Ordered Systems Ser.). 1995. 69.95 (*0-387-94177-0*) Spr-Verlag.

Micelles, Microemulsions, & Monolayers: Science & Technology. D. O. Shah. LC 97-52810. (Illus.). 632p. 1998. text 195.00 (*0-8247-9990-9*) Dekker.

Micelles, Monolayers, & Biomembranes. Dennis Chapman & Malcolm Jones. (Illus.). 264p. 1994. pap. 79.95 (*0-471-30596-0*) Wiley.

Micellization in Surfactant Solutions. Anatolii I. Rusanov. (Chemistry Reviews Ser.: Vol. 22, No. 1). 326p. 1998. pap. text 88.00 (*90-5702-297-4*, Harwood Acad Pubs) Gordon & Breach.

Micest Gift of All. Celeste J. Hutchins. (Illus.). 31p. (J). (gr. k-5). 1997. 16.95 (*0-9658010-0-4*) Topaz Angel.

Mich-Again's Day. Gary W. Barfknecht. (Illus.). 265p. (Orig.). 1984. pap. 7.95 (*0-9608588-2-2*) Friede Pubns.

***Micha Klein.** Micha Klein. (Illus.). 118p. 1998. 60.00 (*90-71691-40-3*, Pub. by Groninger Museum) RAM Publications.

Michael. Tony Bradman. (Illus.). 32p. (J). (ps-1). 1998. pap. 9.95 (*0-86264-759-2*, Pub. by Andersen Pr) Trafalgar.

***Michael.** Henry Flesh. LC 00-101837. (Illus.). 150p. 2000. 12.95 (*1-888451-12-2*, AkB09) Akashic Bks.

Michael. Weeks. 32p. (J). (ps-2). Date not set. 14.95 (*0-06-028231-2*); pap. 4.95 (*0-06-443541-5*) HarpC Child Bks.

Michael: Fun & Facts about a Popular Name & the People Who Made It Great. Alvin Silverstein et al. LC 90-80673. (All about Names Ser.). (Illus.). 64p. (J). (gr. 5 up). 1990. 11.95 (*0-9623653-6-X*); pap. 4.95 (*0-9623653-7-8*) AVSTAR Pub.

***Michael: Historical, Epigraphical & Biblical Studies in Honor of Professor Michael Heltzer.** Ed. by Yitzhak Avishur & Robert Deutsch. 301p. 1999. text 80.00 (*965-222-939-3*, Pub. by Archaeol Ctr) Eisenbrauns.

Michael: The Defender. Joann Ross. 1997. per. 3.50 (*0-373-25754-6*, 1-25754-2) Harlequin Bks.

Michael: Warrior Prince. Lisa Iodice. Date not set. pap. 10.95 (*1-881542-60-2*) Blue Star Prodns.

Michael A. Smith: A Visual Journey: Photographs from Twenty-Five Years. deluxe limited ed. Michael A. Smith & John P. Bratnober. LC 92-71298. (Illus.). 192p. 1992. 250.00 (*0-9605646-5-9*) Lodima.

Michael A. Smith: A Visual Journey: Photographs from Twenty-Five Years. Michael A. Smith & John P. Bratnober. LC 92-71298. (Illus.). 192p. 1992. 85.00 (*0-9605646-4-0*) Lodima.

Michael Aaron Piano Course: Lessons. Michael Aaron. Ed. by Carole Flatau. 64p. (Orig.). 1994. pap. 5.95 (*0-89898-867-5*, 11004A) Wrner Bros.

Michael Aaron Piano Course Vol. 24: Lessons. Michael Aaron. Ed. by Carole Flatau. (Illus.). 64p. (Orig.). (J). (gr. k-1). 1994. pap. 5.95 (*0-89898-855-1*, 11001A) Wrner Bros.

Michael Aaron Piano Course Vol. 24: Lessons. Michael Aaron. Ed. by Carole Flatau. (Illus.). 64p. (Orig.). (J). (gr. 2). 1994. pap. 5.95 (*0-89898-859-4*, 11002A) Wrner Bros.

***Michael & Christ: Michael Traditions & Angel Christology in Early Christianity.** Darrell D. Hannah. (Wissenshaftliche Untersuchungen zum Neuen Testament Ser.: Reihe 109). 305p. 1999. pap. 75.00 (*3-16-147054-0*, Pub. by JCB Mohr) Coronet Bks.

Michael & Dorothy Blankfort Collection. Anne Edgerton & Maurice Tuchman. LC 81-23629. (Illus.). 108p. (Orig.). 1982. pap. 16.00 (*0-87587-106-2*) LA Co Art Mus.

Michael & Kirk Douglas. Skip Press. LC 94-28650. (Star Families Ser.). (Illus.). (YA). (gr. 5 up). 1995. pap. 4.95 (*0-382-24941-0*, Crstwood Hse) Silver Burdett Pr.

Michael & Me & the Sun. Barbara Hanrahan. 166p. (Orig.). 1992. pap. 22.95 (*0-7022-2484-7*, Pub. by Univ Queensland Pr) Intl Spec Bk.

***Michael & Natasha: The Life & Love of Michael II, the Last of the Romanov Tsars.** Donald Crawford. 464p. 2000. pap. 15.00 (*0-380-73191-6*, Avon Bks) Morrow Avon.

Michael & Natasha: The Life & Love of Michael II, the Last of the Romanov Tsars. Rosemary Crawford & Donald Crawford. LC 97-22550. (Illus.). 433p. 1997. 29.50 (*0-684-83430-8*) S&S Trade.

Michael & the Cats. Barbara Abercrombie. LC 92-23950. (Illus.). 32p. (J). (ps-2). 1993. lib. bdg. 13.95 (*0-689-50543-4*) McElderry Bks.

Michael & the Dragon: or Christ Tempted & Satan Foiled. unabridged ed. Daniel Dyke. 275p. 1997. reprint ed. 29.95 (*1-889058-06-8*) Old Paths Pubns.

Michael & the Pied Piper. Michael Lancy. 54p. 1983. pap. 5.00 (*1-890298-21-2*) Centerstage Pr.

***Michael & the Two Horned Beast: Challenge of Evil Today in the Light of Rudolf Steiner's Science of the Spirit.** Bernard Nesfield-Cookson. 384p. 1998. pap. 29.95 (*0-904693-98-8*, Pub. by Temple Lodge) Anthroposophic.

Michael Andretti at Indianapolis. Michael Andretti et al. LC 91-38815. (Illus.). 64p. (J). (gr. 3-7). 1993. pap. 5.95 (*0-671-79674-7*) S&S Bks Yung.

Michael Asher. Michael Asher. (Illus.). 64p. 1991. pap. 15.00 (*0-941548-20-1*) Ren Soc U Chi.

Michael Asher. Birgit Pelzer et al. 96p. Date not set. 32.00 (*3-85780-104-2*) Kunsthalle Bern.

***Michael Asks Why: Ellen G. White's Classic the Great Controversy Adapted for Children.** Sally Pierson Dillon & Ellen Gould Harmon White. LC 99-49058. (YA). 2000. pap. 10.99 (*0-8163-1759-3*) Pacific Pr Pub Assn.

***Michael Asks Why Kids Activity Book.** Sally Dillon. (Illus.). 77p. (J). 2000. pap. 1.99 (*0-8163-1793-3*) Pacific Pr Pub Assn.

Michael Atiyah Vol. 1: Collected Works: Early Papers: General Papers. Michael F. Atiyah. (Illus.). 388p. 1988. 85.00 (*0-19-853275-X*) OUP.

Michael Atiyah Vol. 2: Collected Works: K-Theory. Michael F. Atiyah. 854p. 1988. 125.00 (*0-19-853276-8*) OUP.

Michael Atiyah Vol. 3: Collected Works: Index Theory: 1. Michael F. Atiyah. (Illus.). 618p. 1988. 95.00 (*0-19-853277-6*) OUP.

Michael Atiyah Vol. 4: Collected Works: Index Theory; 2. Michael F. Atiyah. (Illus.). 642p. 1988. 115.00 (*0-19-853278-4*) OUP.

Michael Atiyah Vol. 5: Collected Works: Gauge Theories. Michael F. Atiyah. (Illus.). 720p. 1988. 130.00 (*0-19-853279-2*) OUP.

Michael Augustine Corrigan & the Shaping of Conservative Catholicism in America, 1878-1902. Robert E. Curran. 1978. 51.95 (*0-405-10814-1*) Ayer.

Michael Ayrton: A Biography. Justine Hopkins. (Illus.). 480p. 1994. 55.00 (*0-233-98846-7*, Pub. by Andre Deutsch) Trafalgar.

Michael Ayrton: Exhibition Catalogue. Intro. by David Piper. (Illus.). 16p. 1973. pap. 1.00 (*0-911209-01-8*) Palmer Mus Art.

Michael Bakunin: Roots of Apocalypse. Arthur P. Mendel. LC 81-5168. 517p. 1981. 65.00 (*0-275-91699-5*, C1699, Praeger Pubs) Greenwood.

Michael Balint: Object Relations Pure & Applied. Harold Stewart. 160p. (C). 1996. 75.00 (*0-415-14465-5*); pap. 25.99 (*0-415-14466-3*) Routledge.

Michael Barry's Christmas Recipes the Crafty Way. Michael Barry. 64p. 1998. 8.95 (*0-7117-0963-7*, Pub. by JARR UK) Seven Hills Bk.

Michael Bernhard: Goswin Kempgyn de Nussia, Trivita Studentium. (Munchener Beitrage zur Mediavistik und Renaissance-Forschung Ser.: Band 26). (GER.). xii, 112p. 1976. 24.80 (*3-615-00159-1*, Pub. by Weidmann) Lubrecht & Cramer.

Michael Bird-Boy. Tomie De Paola. LC 74-23563. (Illus.). 32p. (J). (gr. 4 up). 1987. 12.95 (*0-317-63504-2*) P-H.

Michael Bird Boy. Tomie De Paola. LC 74-23563. (Illus.). 32p. (J). (gr. k-4). 1987. 12.95 (*0-671-66468-9*) S&S Bks Yung.

Michael Bird Boy. Tomie De Paola. LC 74-23563. (Illus.). 32p. (J). (ps-3). 1987. pap. 5.95 (*0-671-66469-7*) S&S Bks Yung.

Michael Bishop. Ed. by Charles Desmarais. LC 79-10942. (Illus.). 1979. pap. 5.00 (*0-932026-03-6*) Columbia College Chi.

***Michael Bloomfield: If You Love These Blues.** Jan M. Wolkin & Bill Keenom. 2000. 24.95 incl. audio compact disk (*0-87930-617-3*) Miller Freeman.

Michael Bolton - Soul Provider. Ed. by Carol Cuellar. 68p. (Orig.). (C). 1990. pap. text 16.95 (*0-7692-0223-3*, VF1635) Wrner Bros.

Michael Bolton - Time, Love, & Tenderness. Ed. by Carol Cuellar. 60p. (Orig.). (C). 1991. pap. text 16.95 (*0-7692-0224-1*, VF1739) Wrner Bros.

Michael Bolton - Timeless. Ed. by Carol Cuellar. 52p. (Orig.). (C). 1992. pap. text 16.95 (*0-7692-0228-4*, VF1908) Wrner Bros.

Michael Bolton Best of Guitar Tag. 60p. pap. 12.95 (*0-7692-0437-6*, GF0563) Wrner Bros.

Michael Bolton Greatest Hits, 1985-1995. Michael Bolton. 1997. pap. 22.95 (*1-57623-817-2*) Wrner Bros.

Michael Bond's Book of Bears. Michael Bond. 144p. (J). 1992. write for info. (*1-85479-111-7*, Pub. by M OMara) Assoc Pubs Grp.

Michael Borgolte: Der Gesandtenaustausch der Karolinger Mit Den Abbasiden und Mit Den Patriarchen Von Jerusalem. (Munchener Beitrage zur Mediavistik und Renaissance-Forschung Ser.: Band 25). (GER.). vi, 165p. 1976. 39.80 (*3-615-00158-3*, Pub. by Weidmann) Lubrecht & Cramer.

Michael Brecker: Saxophone. 128p. 1995. per. 16.95 (*0-7935-2959-X*, 00673237) H Leonard.

***Michael Brecker Collection.** 128p. 1999. otabind 17.95 (*0-7935-9755-2*) H Leonard.

Michael Brein's Guide to Amsterdam by the Tram. Michael Brein. (Michael Brein's Guides Ser.). (Orig.). 2000. pap. 5.00 (*1-886590-14-1*) Michael Brein.

Michael Brein's Guide to Barcelona by the Metro. Michael Brein. (Michael Brein's Guides Ser.). (Orig.). 1999. pap. 5.00 (*1-886590-04-4*) Michael Brein.

Michael Brein's Guide to Berlin by the U-Bahn. Michael Brein. (Michael Brein's Guides Ser.). (Orig.). 1999. pap. 5.00 (*1-886590-07-9*) Michael Brein.

Michael Brein's Guide to Honolulu & Oahu by the Bus. rev. ed. Michael Brein. (Michael Brein's Guides Ser.). 1p. 1998. pap. 5.00 (*1-886590-01-X*) Michael Brein.

Michael Brein's Guide to London by the Underground. rev. ed. Michael Brein. (Michael Brein's Guides Ser.). 1p. 1998. pap. 5.00 (*1-886590-02-8*) Michael Brein.

Michael Brein's Guide to Madrid by the Metro. Michael Brein. (Michael Brein's Guides Ser.). (Orig.). 1999. pap. 5.00 (*1-886590-05-2*) Michael Brein.

Michael Brein's Guide to Munich by the U-Bahn. Michael Brein. (Michael Brein's Guides Ser.). (Orig.). 1999. pap. 5.00 (*1-886590-06-0*) Michael Brein.

Michael Brein's Guide to New York by the Subway. Michael Brein & Penelope Franklin. (Michael Brein's Guides Ser.). (Orig.). 2001. pap. 5.00 (*1-886590-08-7*) Michael Brein.

MIchael Brein's Guide to Paris by the Metro. rev. ed. Michael Brein. (Michael Brein's Guides Ser.). 1p. 1999. pap. 5.00 (*1-886590-03-6*) Michael Brein.

Michael Brein's Guide to Prague by the Metro. Michael Brein. (Michael Brein's Guides Ser.). (Orig.). 1999. pap. 5.00 (*1-886590-13-3*) Michael Brein.

***Michael Brein's Guide to Rome by the Metro.** Michael Brein. (Michael Brein's Travel Guides Ser.). 2001. pap. 5.00 (*1-886590-19-2*, Pub. by Michael Brein) Map Link.

Michael Brein's Guide to San Francisco by Public Transit. Michael Brein. (Michael Brein's Guides Ser.). (Orig.). 2002. pap. 5.00 (*1-886590-10-9*) Michael Brein.

Michael Brein's Guide to Sydney by Public Transit. Michael Brein. (Michael Brein's Guides Ser.). (Orig.). 1998. pap. 5.00 (*1-886590-11-7*) Michael Brein.

Michael Brein's Guide to Tokyo by the Subway. Michael Brein & Richard Dickison. (Michael Brein's Guides Ser.). (Orig.). 2001. pap. 5.00 (*1-886590-15-X*) Michael Brein.

Michael Brein's Guide to Vienna by the U-Bahn. Michael Brein. (Michael Brein's Guides Ser.). (Orig.). 2000. pap. 5.00 (*1-886590-12-5*) Michael Brein.

Michael Brein's Guide to Washington by the Metro. Michael Brein & Penelope Franklin. (Michael Brein's Guides Ser.). (Orig.). 2000. pap. 5.00 (*1-886590-09-5*) Michael Brein.

Michael Broadbent's Wine Tasting: How to Approach & Appreciate Wine. Michael Broadbent. 1997. 14.95 (*1-85732-761-6*, Pub. by Mitchell Beazley) Antique Collect.

Michael Broadbent's Wine Vintages. Michael Broadbent. (Mitchell Beazley Pocket Guides Ser.). 208p. 1998. 14.95 (*1-84000-090-2*, Pub. by Mitchell Beazley) Antique Collect.

Michael Broadbent's Winetasting: How to Approach & Appreciate Wine. Michael Broadbent. (Mitchell Beazley Pocket Guides Ser.). (Illus.). 176p. 1998. 14.95 (*1-84000-091-0*, Pub. by Mitchell Beazley) Antique Collect.

***Michael Brother of Jerry.** Jack London. (Collected Works of Jack London). 344p. 1998. reprint ed. lib. bdg. 98.00 (*1-58201-727-1*) Classic Bks.

Michael Byron: Mindfields: 100 Works on Paper. Douglas Blau. (Illus.). 220p. 1995. 65.00 (*91-630-2985-5*) Dist Art Pubs.

***Michael Caine.** large type ed. Michael Freedland. LC 00-44698. 2000. write for info. (*0-7862-2814-8*) Thorndike Pr.

Michael Chekhov: On Theatre & the Art of Acting, 4 vols. Michael Chekhov. Ed. by Mala Powers. (Acting Ser.). 48p. 1992. 39.95 incl. audio (*1-55783-117-3*) Applause Theatre Bk Pubs.

Michael Chernishov - Aggressive Symbols. Timothy Cohrs. (Illus.). 20p. (Orig.). 1987. pap. 10.00 (*0-913263-15-X*) Exit Art.

Michael Coleman: Wilderness Artist. Ed. by Gayle Maxon & Quincie Hopkins. LC 86-60905. (Illus.). 53p. 1986. pap. 12.00 (*0-935037-11-X*) G Peters Gallery.

Michael Collins. 2nd ed. Desmond Ryan. 160p. 1994. reprint ed. pap. 13.95 (*0-947962-83-2*, Pub. by Anvil Books Ltd) Irish Bks Media.

Michael Collins: A Life. James Mackay. (Illus.). 320p. 1997. pap. 19.95 (*1-85158-949-X*, Pub. by Mainstream Pubng) Trafalgar.

Michael Collins: In His Own Words. Ed. by Frank Costello. LC 97-161282. 192p. 1997. pap. 17.95 (*0-7171-2436-3*, Pub. by Gill & MacMill) Irish Bks Media.

Michael Collins: The Lost Leader. Margery Forester. 370p. 1989. reprint ed. pap. 25.95 (*0-7171-1711-1*, Pub. by Gill & MacMill) Irish Bks Media.

Michael Collins: The Man Who Made Ireland. Tim P. Coogan. LC 95-72787. (Illus.). 480p. 1996. pap. text 16.95 (*1-57098-075-6*) Roberts Rinehart.

Michael Collins: The Man Who Won The War. T. Ryle Dwyer. 160p. 1997. pap. 12.95 (*0-85342-931-6*, Pub. by Mercier Pr) Irish Amer Bk.

Michael Collins: The Secret File. A.T. Stewart. LC 97-226238. 192p. 1998. pap. 21.95 (*0-85640-614-7*, Pub. by Blackstaff Pr) Dufour.

Michael Collins & the Making of a New Ireland, 2 vols. P. S. Beaslai. 1985. reprint ed. 130.00 (*0-527-41198-1*) Periodicals Srv.

***Michael Collins & the Making of the Irish State.** Ed. by Gabriel Doherty & Dermot Keogh. (Illus.). 200p. 1998. pap. 15.95 (*1-85635-211-0*, Pub. by Mercier Pr) Irish Amer Bk.

Michael Collins & The Women in His Life. Meda Ryan. LC 97-116359. (Illus.). 208p. 1997. pap. 12.95 (*1-85635-166-1*, Pub. by Mercier Pr) Irish Amer Bk.

Michael Crichton: A Critical Companion. Elizabeth A. Trembley. LC 95-503. (Critical Companions to Popular Contemporary Writers Ser.). 208p. 1996. 29.95 (*0-313-29414-3*, Greenwood Pr) Greenwood.

***Michael Crichton: A Reader's Checklist & Reference Guide.** CheckerBee Publishing Staff. 1999. pap. text 4.95 (*1-58598-015-3*) CheckerBee.

Michael Crichton Companion. Martin Greenberg. 1998. pap. write for info. (*0-345-38880-1*) Ballantine Pub Grp.

Michael Crichton's Jurassic World. Michael Crichton. LC 97-73821. 1997. 14.95 (*0-375-40107-5*) Knopf.

Michel Delacroix at 65: Eternal Paris. Sam Hunter. LC 97-46954. (Illus.). 152p. 1998. 49.95 (*0-7892-0443-6*) Abbeville Pr.

Michael Dorris. Ann Weil. LC 96-44613. (Contemporary Native Americans Ser.). (Illus.). 48p. (J). (gr. 3-7). 1997. lib. bdg. 24.26 (*0-8172-3994-4*) Raintree Steck-V.

Michael Douglas. large type ed. Alan Lawson. 347p. 1994. 27.99 (*0-7505-0596-6*, Pub. by Mgna Lrg Print) Ulverscroft.

Michael Dransfield: Collected Poems. Michael Dransfield. LC 84-21992. 401p. (Orig.). 1988. pap. text 19.95 (*0-7022-1828-6*, Pub. by Univ Queensland Pr) Intl Spec Bk.

Michael Drayton. Joseph A. Berthelot. LC 67-19341. (English Authors Ser.). 1967. lib. bdg. 20.95 (*0-8057-1172-4*) Irvington.

Michael Drayton: A Critical Study. Oliver Elton. (BCL1-PR English Literature Ser.). 216p. 1992. reprint ed. lib. bdg. 79.00 (*0-7812-7205-X*) Rprt Serv.

Michael Drayton, Revisited. Jean R. Brink. (Twayne's English Authors Ser.: No. 476). 168p. (C). 1990. text 25.95 (*0-8057-6989-7*, Twyne) Mac Lib Ref.

Michael Dred, Detective: The Unravelling of a Mystery of Twenty Years. Marie C. Leighton & Robert Leighton. LC 75-32761. (Literature of Mystery & Detection Ser.). (Illus.). 1976. reprint ed. 28.95 (*0-405-07882-X*) Ayer.

Michael Dummett: Contributions to Philosophy. Ed. by B. M. Taylor. (Philosophy Ser.: Vol. 25). 352p. 1987. lib. bdg. 151.50 (*90-247-3463-0*, Pub. by M Nijhoff) Kluwer Academic.

Michael Dummett & the Theory of Meaning. Darryl Gunson. LC 97-77385. (Avebury Series in Philosophy). 178p. 1998. text 59.95 (*1-84014-134-4*, Pub. by Ashgate Pub) Ashgate Pub Co.

Michael E. Arth Introspective Nineteen Seventy-Two to Nineteen Eighty-Two. Michael E. Arth. LC 83-80162. (Illus.). 256p. 1983. 29.95 (*0-912467-00-2*) G Apple Pubg Co.

Michael E. Arth Introspective Nineteen Seventy-Two to Nineteen Eighty-Two. limited ed. Michael E. Arth. LC 83-80162. (Illus.). 256p. 1983. 295.00 (*0-912467-01-0*) G Apple Pubg Co.

Michael E. Porter on Competition & Strategy. Harvard Business School Press Staff. 80p. 1991. pap. 19.95 (*0-07-103332-7*) McGraw.

***Michael E. Tiger's Opening & Closing Arguments from U.S. vs. Terry Lynn Nichols: The Oklahoma City Bombing Case, XXV.** Michael E. Tiger. (Classics of the Courtroom Trial Transcript Series). 1999. pap. 20.00 (*0-943380-31-6*) PEG MN.

Michael Eisner: Fun for Everyone. Sherill Tippins. Ed. by Richard G. Young. LC 91-28544. (Wizards of Business Ser.). (Illus.). 64p. (J). (gr. 4-8). 1992. lib. bdg. 17.26 (*1-56074-014-0*) Garrett Ed Corp.

Michael Fairless. Mary E. Dowson & A. M. Haggard. LC 76-30785. (Studies in Women's Rights: No. 51). 1977. lib. bdg. 57.00 (*0-8383-2158-5*) M S G Haskell Hse.

Michael Faraday see **What Would You Ask?**

An Asterisk (*) at the beginning of an entry indicates that the title is appearing for the first time.

Michael Faraday. Geoffrey Cantor et al. (Illus.). 124p. (C). 1996. pap. 12.50 (*0-391-03982-2*) Humanities.

Michael Faraday. Geoffrey Cantor et al. (Illus.). 124p. (C). 1996. text 39.95 (*0-391-03981-4*) Humanities.

Michael Faraday. Geoffrey Cantor et al. 1996. pap. 18.00 (*1-57392-556-X*, Humanity Bks) Prometheus Bks.

***Michael Faraday.** Ann Fullick. LC 00-24354. (J). 2000. lib. bdg. write for info. (*1-57572-375-1*) Heinemann Lib.

***Michael Faraday.** Colin A. Russell. (Oxford Portraits in Science Ser.). (Illus.). 144p. (YA). 2000. lib. bdg. 22.00 (*0-19-511763-8*) OUP.

Michael Faraday: Un Genio de la Fisica. Gerardo Carmona et al. (Ciencia para Todos Ser.). (SPA.). pap. 6.99 (*968-16-4439-5*, Pub. by Fondo) Continental Bk.

Michael Faraday & the Royal Institution: The Genius of Man & Place. J. M. Thomas. (Illus.). 234p. 1991. pap. 34.00 (*0-7503-0145-7*) IOP Pub.

Michael Faraday, Father of Electronics. Charles Ludwig. LC 78-15028. 224p. (YA). (gr. 7-10). 1988. ring bd. 9.99 (*0-8361-3479-6*) Herald Pr.

Michael Faraday's Chemical Notes, Hints, Suggestions, & Objects of Pursuit of 1822. Ed. by Ryan Tweney & David Gooding. (IEE History of Technology Ser.: No. 17). (Illus.). 152p. 1991. 62.00 (*0-86341-255-6*, Pub. by Peregrinus) Dist Unknown.

Michael Fath: Showcase Solos for the Rock Guitarist. Michael Fath. 1994. pap. 14.95 incl. audio (*0-89524-830-1*) Cherry Lane.

Michael Fath: Showcase Solos for the Rock Guitarist. Michael Fath. 1994. pap. 17.95 (*0-89524-831-X*) Cherry Lane.

Michael Feinstein: Forever. 64p. 1994. per. 12.95 (*0-7935-3058-X*, 00308221) H Leonard.

Michael Feinstein - Isn't It Romantic. (Piano-Vocal-Guitar Music Bk.). 72p. 1989. per. 12.95 (*0-88188-839-7*, HL 00490083) H Leonard.

Michael Field. Mary C. Sturgeon. LC 75-12361. (Homosexuality Ser.). 1975. reprint ed. 15.95 (*0-405-07401-8*) Ayer.

Michael Field's Cooking School: A Selection of Great Recipes Demonstrating the Pleasures & Principles of Fine Cooking. Michael Field. LC 97-35935. (Cook's Classic Library). 369p. 1998. reprint ed. pap. 14.95 (*1-55821-559-X*) Lyons Pr.

Michael Finnegan, Tap Your Chinigin: Developing Music Skills with New Songs from Old Favorites. unabridged ed. Sue Nicholls. (Illus.). (J). (gr. 1-2). 1998. pap. 11.95 (*0-7136-4716-7*, Pub. by A & C Blk) Midpt Trade.

Michael Folden Vol. 1: The Language of Enigma. Jack McLarty. Ed. by Barbara L. McLarty. (Illus.). 15p. 1997. pap. 6.00 (*0-9644916-4-8*) McLartys Choice.

Michael Foot. Mervyn Jones. (Illus.). 576p. 1995. 39.95 (*0-575-05197-3*, Pub. by V Gollancz) Trafalgar.

Michael for the Millenium: The Fourth Book in the Michael Teaching. Chelsea Quinn Yarbro. LC 96-100937. 304p. (Orig.). 1995. pap. 12.95 (*0-425-15074-7*) Berkley Pub.

Michael Fordham: Innovations in Analytical Psychology. James Astor. LC 94-48784. (Makers of Modern Psychotherapy Ser.). 288p. (C). 1995. 75.00 (*0-415-09348-1*); pap. 25.99 (*0-415-09349-X*) Routledge.

Michael Foreman's Christmas Treasury C. Foreman. 1999. Price not set. (*0-15-202162-0*) Harcourt Coll Pubs.

Michael Foreman's Mother Goose. Michael Foreman. LC 90-5343. (Illus.). 160p. (J). (ps up). 1991. 22.00 (*0-15-255820-9*, Harcourt Child Bks) Harcourt.

Michael Foreman's World of Fairy Tales. Ed. & Illus. by Michael Foreman. 144p. (J). (gr. 1 up). 1991. lib. bdg. 18.95 (*1-55970-164-1*) Arcade Pub Inc.

Michael Franks Songbook. Ed. by Carol Cuellar. 132p. (Orig.). (C). 1986. pap. text 16.95 (*0-7692-0456-2*, VF1301) Wrner Bros.

Michael Game: One Hundred & One Questions to Ask a Channel & More. Michael Digest Group Staff. 160p. 1988. pap. 7.95 (*0-941109-01-1*) Warwick Pr CA.

Michael Gibbons of South Carolina & His Descendants: History & Genealogy of the Gibbons Family & Related Families. 840p. 1989. write for info. (*0-318-64613-7*) L G Hersperger.

Michael Gitlin: Sculptures Drawings, 1982-1985. Steven H. Madoff. (Illus.). 23p. (Orig.). 1985. pap. 10.00 (*0-913263-11-7*) Exit Art.

Michael Graves see Architects: Artists Who Build

Michael Graves. Ed. by Alex Buck & Matthias Vogt. (Designer Monographs Ser.: No. 3). (Illus.). 1995. 35.00 (*1-85490-903-7*) Academy Ed UK.

Michael Graves. Collectors Classic Antiques Staff. 1999. 59.95 (*1-875498-73-7*) Images Aust AT.

Michael Graves. Curtis. pap. text 47.00 (*0-471-98592-9*) Wiley.

Michael Graves: Buildings & Projects, 1982-1990. Karen Nichols et al. LC 89-10615. (Illus.). 352p. (Orig.). 1990. pap. 40.00 (*0-910413-17-7*) Princeton Arch.

Michael Graves: Buildings & Projects 1990-1994. Janet Abrams. (Illus.). 304p. 1995. 65.00 (*0-8478-1901-9*, Pub. by Rizzoli Intl); pap. 40.00 (*0-8478-1902-7*, Pub. by Rizzoli Intl) St Martin.

Michael Graves & Riverbend: A Summer Pavillion for the Cincinnati Symphony Orchestra. Jayne S. Merkel. (Illus.). 1987. 15.95 (*0-917562-33-X*) Contemp Arts.

Michael Hague's Family Christmas Treasury. Michael Hague. LC 95-6068. (Illus.). 160p. (J). (ps up). 1995. 19.95 (*0-8050-1011-4*, BYR) H Holt & Co.

Michael Hague's Family Easter Treasury. Michael Hague. LC 95-46916. (Illus.). 144p. (YA). (gr. k up). 1999. 19.95 (*0-8050-3819-1*) H Holt & Co.

Michael Hague's Favourite Hans Christian Andersen Fairy Tales. Hans Christian Andersen. LC 81-47455. (Illus.). 168p. (J). (ps-2). 1995. 19.95 (*0-8050-0659-1*, Bks Young Read) H Holt & Co.

Michael Hague's Little Treasury of Christmas Carols. Illus. by Michael Hague. 96p. (J). 1997. 6.99 (*1-57866-001-7*) Galahad Bks.

Michael Handbook: A Channeled System for Self Understanding. Jose L. Stevens & Simon Warwick-Smith. 352p. 1988. pap. 14.95 (*0-941109-00-3*) Warwick Pr CA.

Michael Harrington. Pizzano. 1999. write for info. (*0-201-62293-9*) Addison-Wesley.

Michael Harrington: Speaking American. Robert A. Gorman. (American Radicals Ser.). (Illus.). 288p. (C). (gr. 13). 1995. pap. 19.99 (*0-415-91118-4*, B4840) Routledge.

Michael Haslam: A Whole Bauble. Michael Haslam. 260p. 1996. pap. 27.95 (*1-85754-187-1*, Pub. by Carcanet Pr) Paul & Co Pubs.

Michael Haydn: Tedeuminc, 1770. Michael Haydn. Ed. by Reinhard G. Pauly. (Collegium Musicum: Vol. YCMI/3). (Illus.). 97p. 1961. pap. 20.00 (*0-89579-364-4*) A-R Eds.

Michael Hedges: Rhythm, Sonority, Silence. Michael Hedges & John Stropes. (Illus.). 136p. (Orig.). 1995. pap., spiral bd. 30.00 (*0-9608512-1-6*) Stropes Editions.

Michael Heizer. (Illus.). 547p. pap. 85.00 (*88-87029-09-1*, Pub. by Fondazione Prada) Dist Art Pubs.

Michael Heizer. Germano Celant. 1997. pap. 85.00 (*88-87029-02-4*, Pub. by Fondazione Prada) Dist Art Pubs.

***Michael Heseltine.** Michael Crick. 496p. 1998. pap. 19.95 (*0-14-025969-4*, Pub. by Pnguin Bks Ltd) Trafalgar.

Michael Hill on Science, Invention & Information. Compiled by Purabi Ward. (History of Science & Technology Ser.). 277p. 1988. pap. 39.95 (*0-7123-0758-3*, Pub. by SRIS) L Erlbaum Assocs.

***Michael Hillegas & His Descendants.** fac. ed. Emma S. Whitney. 118p. 1999. reprint ed. 29.00 (*0-8328-9909-7*) Higginson Bk Co.

***Michael Hillegas & His Descendants.** Michael Hillegas. 118p. 1999. reprint ed. pap. 19.00 (*0-8328-9910-0*) Higginson Bk Co.

Michael Hopkin's Bauten und Projekte. Fawcett. pap. write for info. (*0-471-48954-9*) Wiley.

Michael Innes Omnibus. Michael Innes. Incl. Daffodil Affair. 1983. Death at the President's Lodging. 1983. Hamlet, Revenge! 1983. 672p. 1983. Set pap. 8.95 (*0-14-006059-6*, Penguin Bks) Viking Penguin.

Michael Irvin. Rich Rosenblatt. LC 96-52618. (Football Legends Ser.). (Illus.). 64p. (J). (gr. 3 up). 1997. lib. bdg. 15.95 (*0-7910-4397-5*) Chelsea Hse.

***Michael J. Fox.** Gary Cohn. (Overcoming Adversity Ser.). (Illus.). 128p. 1999. 19.95 (*0-7910-5425-X*) Chelsea Hse.

***Michael J. Fox.** Richard Kozar. LC 99-43943. (Overcoming Adversity Ser.). (Illus.). 128p. 2001. pap. 9.95 (*0-7910-5426-8*) Chelsea Hse.

Michael J. S. Dewar: A Semiempirical Life. Michael J. Dewar. Ed. by Jeffrey I. Seeman. LC 90-911. (Profiles, Pathways, & Dreams Ser.). (Illus.). 216p. 1992. text 36.00 (*0-8412-1771-8*, Pub. by Am Chemical) OUP.

Michael Jackson. Christopher Andersen. 1999. pap. write for info. (*0-451-18262-6*, Sig) NAL.

Michael Jackson. Christopher Andersen. 1995. pap. 6.99 (*0-671-89240-1*) PB.

***Michael Jackson.** Karen M. Graves. LC 00-8929. (People in the News Ser.). (Illus.). (J). 2000. pap. write for info. (*1-56006-707-1*) Lucent Bks.

Michael Jackson. Lois Nicholson. (Black Americans of Achievement Ser.). (J). 1994. 14.05 (*0-606-07865-7*) Turtleback.

Michael Jackson. Rosemary Wallner. LC 91-73036. (Reaching for the Stars Ser.). (Illus.). 32p. (J). 1991. lib. bdg. 13.98 (*1-56239-057-0*) ABDO Pub Co.

Michael Jackson: A Visual Documentary. rev. ed. Adrian Grant. (Illus.). 200p. 1997. 25.95 (*0-7119-6652-4*, OP48022) Omnibus NY.

Michael Jackson: Entertainer. Ed. by Nathan I. Huggins. (Black Americans of Achievement Ser.). (Illus.). 124p. (YA). (gr. 5 up). 1994. pap. 8.95 (*0-7910-1930-6*) Chelsea Hse.

Michael Jackson: Entertainer. Lois P. Nicholson. Ed. by Nathan I. Huggins. (Black Americans of Achievement Ser.). (Illus.). 124p. (YA). (gr. 5 up). 1994. lib. bdg. 19.95 (*0-7910-1929-2*) Chelsea Hse.

Michael Jackson: In His Own Words. Catherine Dineen. (In Their Own Words Ser.). (Illus.). 96p. pap. 15.95 (*0-7119-3216-6*, OP 47188) Omnibus NY.

Michael Jackson: King of Pop. Lisa Campbell. Ed. by A. Caso. (Illus.). 300p. 1993. reprint ed. 24.95 (*0-8283-1957-X*) Branden Bks.

Michael Jackson: Live & Dangerous. Adrian Grant. (Illus.). 32p. 1997. pap. 9.95 (*0-7119-3125-9*, OP 47128) Omnibus NY.

Michael Jackson: Making History. Adrian Grant. (Illus.). 30p. 1998. pap. 9.95 (*0-7119-6723-7*) Omnibus NY.

Michael Jackson: The Magic & the Madness. J. Randy Taraborrelli. 1991. 21.95 (*1-55972-064-6*, Birch Ln Pr) Carol Pub Group.

Michael Jackson: Thrill. Caroline Latham. 1984. mass mkt. 2.95 (*0-8217-1430-9*, Zebra Kensgtn) Kensgtn Pub Corp.

Michael Jackson - Bad. Ed. by Carol Cuellar. 104p. (Orig.). (C). 1987. pap. text 16.95 (*0-7692-0758-8*, VF1423) Wrner Bros.

Michael Jackson - Dangerous. Ed. by Carol Cuellar. 112p. (Orig.). (C). 1994. pap. text 19.95 (*0-7692-0754-5*, VF1799) Wrner Bros.

Michael Jackson - History: Past, Present, & Future. Ed. by Sy Feldman. 204p. (Orig.). (C). 1995. pap. text 24.95 (*1-85909-314-0*, PF9538) Wrner Bros.

Michael Jackson - The King of Pop: His Darkest Hour. Lisa Campbell. Ed. by A. Caso. (Illus.). 250p. 1994. 24.95 (*0-8283-2003-9*) Branden Bks.

Michael Jackson - Who's Bad? Longman Publishing Staff. Date not set. pap. text. write for info. (*0-17-556583-X*) Addison-Wesley.

Michael Jackson American Master. C. Mecca. (Illus.). 272p. 1996. 54.95 (*0-9655174-0-3*) CAM Publng CA.

Michael Jackson American Master. 2nd rev. ed. C. Mecca et al. (Illus.). 280p. 1997. 54.95 (*0-9655174-1-1*) CAM Publng CA.

Michael Jackson Unauthorized. Christopher Andersen. (Illus.). 352p. 1994. 23.00 (*0-671-89239-8*) S&S Trade.

Michael Jackson's Bar & Cocktail Companion: The Connoisseur's Handbook. Michael Jackson. (Illus.). 224p. 1995. 17.95 (*1-56138-603-0*) Running Pr.

***Michael Jackson's Bar & Cocktail Companion: The Connoisseur's Handbook.** Michael Jackson. (Illus.). 224p. 2000. reprint ed. 20.00 (*0-7881-9307-4*) DIANE Pub.

***Michael Jackson's Beer Companion.** 2nd rev. ed. Michael Jackson. (Illus.). 255p. 2000. 35.00 (*0-7624-0772-7*) Running Pr.

***Michael Jackson's Complete Guide to Single Malt Scotch: A Connoisseur's Guide to the Single Malt Whiskies of Scotland.** rev. ed. Michael Jackson. (Illus.). 272p. 2000. 25.00 (*0-7881-9211-6*) DIANE Pub.

***Michael Jackson's Great Beer Guide: The Best 500 Beers of the World.** Michael Jackson. LC 00-24039. 544p. 2000. pap. write for info. (*0-7894-5156-5*, Pub. by DK Pub Inc) Pub Resources Inc.

Michael Jackson's Great Beers of Belgium. 3rd ed. Michael Jackson. LC 98-65549. (Illus.). 348p. 1998. 24.95 (*0-7624-0403-5*) Running Pr.

Michael James: Art & Inspirations. Michael James. Ed. by Barb Kuhn & Joyce Lytle. LC 97-44777. (Illus.). 144p. 1998. pap. 29.95 (*1-57120-040-1*, 10164) C & T Pub.

Michael James Studio Quilts. Patricia Harris et al. LC 95-60086. (Illus.). 120p. 1995. 75.00 (*0-9646133-2-8*) Whetstone Hill Pubns.

***Michael Johnson.** Ed. by GHB Publishers Staff. (Sport Snaps Ser.). (Illus.). (YA). 2000. pap. text 12.95 (*1-892920-32-8*) G H B Pubs.

Michael Johnson. Richard Rambeck. LC 97-5466. (Sports Superstars Ser.). 24p. (J). (gr. 2-6). 1997. lib. bdg. 21.36 (*1-56766-460-1*) Childs World.

Michael Johnson. Richard Rambeck. (Sports Superstars Ser.). (Illus.). 24p. (J). 1997. lib. bdg. 21.36 (*1-56766-413-X*, 6413X) Childs World.

Michael Jones: Solos & Sketches for New Age Piano. (Piano Solos Ser.). 88p. (Orig.). 1992. per. 12.95 (*0-7935-0059-1*, 00490413) H Leonard.

Michael Jordan. Richard Brenner. LC 99-160559. (Illus.). 32p. (J). (ps-3). 1999. pap. 3.95 (*0-688-16587-7*, Wm Morrow) Morrow Avon.

Michael Jordan. Richard Brenner. (J). 2000. 25.01 (*0-688-16586-9*, Wm Morrow) Morrow Avon.

***Michael Jordan.** Jack Clary. 72p. 1998. write for info. (*1-57215-268-0*) World Pubns.

Michael Jordan. Sean Dolan. LC 94-5779. (Basketball Legends Ser.). (Illus.). 64p. (J). (gr. 3 up). 1994. lib. bdg. 15.95 (*0-7910-2432-6*) Chelsea Hse.

Michael Jordan. Sean Dolan. (Black Americans of Achievement Ser.). (J). 1994. 13.15 (*0-606-07867-3*) Turtleback.

Michael Jordan. Denis Dougherty. LC 98-22325. (Jam Sessions Ser.). (J). 1998. write for info. (*1-57765-038-7*) ABDO Pub Co.

Michael Jordan. Terri Dougherty. LC 98-22325. 1999. pap. 6.95 (*1-57765-340-8*) ABDO Pub Co.

Michael Jordan. Bill Gutman. 1995. 9.09 (*0-606-07866-5*, Pub. by Turtleback) Demco.

Michael Jordan. Michael Jordan. (Illus.). (J). (gr. 4-7). 1990. mass mkt. 4.95 (*0-316-09229-0*) Little.

Michael Jordan. Paul Joseph. (Awesome Athletes Ser.). (Illus.). 32p. (J). (gr. 2-3). 1998. lib. bdg. 13.98 (*1-56239-641-2*) ABDO Pub Co.

Michael Jordan. Paul Joseph & Kal Gronvall. LC 96-27215. (Awesome Athletes Ser.). (J). 1997. lib. bdg. 13.95 (*0-15-623961-2*) ABDO Pub Co.

Michael Jordan. Mitchell Krugel. 1991. mass mkt. 4.99 (*0-312-92818-5*, Pub. by Tor Bks) St Martin.

Michael Jordan. Chip Lovitt. (Scholastic Biography Ser.). 1996. 9.09 (*0-606-09610-8*, Pub. by Turtleback) Demco.

Michael Jordan. David Pietrusza. LC 98-22485. (People in the News Ser.). (Illus.). 144p. (YA). (gr. 4-12). 1998. lib. bdg. 23.70 (*1-56006-350-5*) Lucent Bks.

Michael Jordan. Richard Rambeck. LC 97-44096. (Illus.). 24[00d0]32p. (J). 1998. lib. bdg. 21.36 (*1-56766-520-9*) Childs World.

Michael Jordan. 2nd rev. ed. Chip Lovitt. LC 99-160139. (Scholastic Biography Ser.). (Illus.). 213p. (YA). (gr. 4-9). 1998. pap. 4.50 (*0-590-59644-6*) Scholastic Inc.

***Michael Jordan.** 3rd ed. Chip Lovitt. 1999. mass mkt. 4.50 (*0-439-12961-3*) Scholastic Inc.

Michael Jordan: A Biography. Bill Gutman. Ed. by Lisa Clancy. 176p. (YA). (gr. 5 up). 1995. per. 3.99 (*0-671-51972-7*, Minstrel Bks) PB.

Michael Jordan: A Life Above the Rim. Robert Lipsyte. LC 93-50561. (Superstar Lineup Ser.). (Illus.). 96p. (J). (gr. 5-9). 1994. lib. bdg. 14.89 (*0-06-024235-3*) HarpC Child Bks.

Michael Jordan: Airborne. Michael Boughn. (Champion Sports Biography Ser.). (Illus.). 91p. (J). (gr. 7-12). 1999. pap. 8.95 (*1-894020-51-0*) Warwick Publ.

Michael Jordan: An Illustrated Tribute to the World's Greatest Athlete. Beckett Publications Editors. 1998. pap. 24.95 (*1-887432-61-2*) Beckett Pubns.

Michael Jordan: Basketball Champ. Bill Gutman. (J). (gr. 4-7). 1992. pap. 4.80 (*0-395-64545-X*) HM.

Michael Jordan: Basketball Great. Sean Dolan. Ed. by Nathan I. Huggins. LC 93-16714. (Black Americans of Achievement Ser.). (Illus.). 124p. (YA). (gr. 5 up). 1994. lib. bdg. 19.95 (*0-7910-2150-5*) Chelsea Hse.

Michael Jordan: Basketball Great. Sean Dolan. Ed. by Nathan I. Huggins. LC 93-16714. (Black Americans of Achievement Ser.). (Illus.). 124p. (YA). (gr. 5 up). 1994. pap. 8.95 (*0-7910-2151-3*) Chelsea Hse.

Michael Jordan: Basketball Skywalker. 3rd ed. Thomas R. Raber. LC 96-33510. (Sports Achievers Biographies Ser.). 80p. (YA). (gr. 4-9). 1997. lib. bdg. 19.93 (*0-8225-3654-4*, LernerSports) Lerner Pub.

Michael Jordan: Basketball to Baseball & Back. rev. ed. Bill Gutman. (Millbrook Sports World Ser.). (Illus.). 48p. (J). (gr. 3-6). 1995. lib. bdg. 19.90 (*1-56294-924-1*) Millbrook Pr.

Michael Jordan: Beyond Air. Philip Brooks. LC 94-24336. (Sports Stars Ser.). 48p. (J). (gr. 2-8). 1995. lib. bdg. 19.00 (*0-516-04391-9*) Childrens.

Michael Jordan: Beyond Air. Philip Brooks. (Sports Stars Ser.). (J). 1995. pap. 5.95 (*0-516-44391-7*) Childrens.

Michael Jordan: Legendary Guard. Tom Owens. LC 97-3864. (Sports Greats Ser.). (J). 1997. lib. bdg. 17.27 (*0-8239-5090-5*, PowerKids) Rosen Group.

***Michael Jordan: Mini Edition.** Wilson. 1999. 4.95 (*0-8362-1939-2*) Andrews & McMeel.

Michael Jordan: Simply the Best. rev. ed. Bill Gutman. (Sports World Ser.). (Illus.). 48p. (J). (gr. 3-6). 1995. pap. 6.95 (*1-56294-902-0*) Millbrook Pr.

Michael Jordan: Star Guard. Ron Knapp. LC 93-43744. (Sports Reports Ser.). (Illus.). 104p. (J). (gr. 4-10). 1994. lib. bdg. 20.95 (*0-89490-482-5*) Enslow Pubs.

Michael Jordan: The Many Sides of an American Icon. Phil Jackson. LC 98-234795. 1998. 19.95 (*1-887432-48-5*) Beckett Pubns.

Michael Jordan & the New Global Capitalism. Walter LaFeber. LC 98-55910. (Illus.). 160p. 1999. 22.95 (*0-393-04747-4*) Norton.

***Michael Jordan & the New Global Capitalism.** Walter LaFeber. 192p. 2000. pap. text 12.95 (*0-393-32037-5*) Norton.

Michael Jordan, Basketball to Baseball & Back. Bill Gutman. LC 95-19671. (Millbrook Sports World Ser.). 1995. 11.15 (*0-606-10261-2*, Pub. by Turtleback) Demco.

Michael Jordan Memorabilia: Everything You Need to Know about Collecting. Beckett Publications Editors. LC 99-189068. 1998. pap. 24.95 (*1-887432-55-8*) Beckett Pubns.

Michael Jordan Scrapbook. Michael Bradley et al. LC 98-66431. 128 p. 1998. write for info. Pubns Intl Ltd.

Michael Jordan Speaks: Insight from the World's Greatest Champion. Janet Lowe. LC 99-30533. 240p. 1999. 17.95 (*0-471-34564-4*) Wiley.

Michael Jordan Unauthorized: A Collection of Quotes on Competition, Image, Loyalty, & His Legacy. Ed. by David Whitaker. LC 97-77529. 80p. 1997. pap. 7.95 (*1-56625-094-3*) Bonus Books.

***Michael Jordan, 3rd Revised & Expanded ed.** 3rd ed. Thomas R. Raber. (Lerner Sports Achievers Ser.). 80p. 1999. pap. text 5.95 (*0-8225-9846-9*) Lerner Pub.

Michael Jordan's 50 Greatest Games: From His NCAA Championship to Five NBA Titles. Robert Condor. LC 98-30392. (Illus.). 224p. 1998. pap. 15.95 (*0-8065-2030-2*) Carol Pub Group.

Michael Jordon. rev. ed. Chip Lovitt. 128p. (J). (gr. 3-9). 1995. pap. 3.50 (*0-590-65174-9*) Scholastic Inc.

Michael Kalteisen: Ein Deutscher in South Carolina. large type ed. Helene M. Kastinger Riley. (GER., Illus.). 42p. 1995. pap. 15.00 (*1-929751-01-X*) Sagas Pubg.

Michael Kalteisen: Founder of the German Friendly Society. Helene M. Riley. 1995. pap. 15.00 (*1-929751-02-8*) Sagas Pubg.

Michael Kenna: The Rouge. Michael Kenna. (Illus.). 60p. 1995. 45.00 (*0-9630785-1-8*) RAM Publications.

Michael Kenny. Peter Davies & Michael Kenny. LC 97-3962. (Illus.). 96p. 1997. text 56.95 (*1-85928-410-8*, Pub. by Scolar Pr) Ashgate Pub Co.

Michael Kenny. limited ed. Peter Davies & Michael Kenny. LC 97-3962. (Illus.). 96p. 1997. text 250.00 (*1-85928-411-6*, Pub. by Scolar Pr) Ashgate Pub Co.

Michael Landon. Jill Wheeler. Ed. by Rosemary Wallner. LC 92-16571. (Young at Heart Ser.). (Illus.). 32p. (J). (gr. 4). 1992. lib. bdg. 14.98 (*1-56239-113-5*) ABDO Pub Co.

Michael Landon: Life, Love & Laughter. Harry Flynn & Pamela Flynn. (Illus.). 112p. 1991. 18.95 (*0-938817-31-0*); pap. 9.95 (*0-938817-29-9*) Pomegranate Pr.

Michael Landon: The Triumph & the Tragedy. Joyce Aileen. 1991. mass mkt. 4.50 (*0-8217-3651-5*, Zebra Kensgtn) Kensgtn Pub Corp.

Michael Langford's 35mm Handbook. 3rd ed. Michael J. Langford. LC 92-54920. 1993. pap. 22.00 (*0-679-74634-X*) Knopf.

Michael Lucero: Sculpture 1976-1995. Mark Richard Leach et al. LC 95-43867. (Illus.). 160p. 1996. 45.00 (*1-55595-126-0*, Pub. by Hudson Hills) Natl Bk Netwk.

***Michael M. Hickey's the Death of Warren Baxter Earp: A Closer Look.** Michael M. Hickey & Richard Lapidus. LC 00-32519. 2000. write for info. (*0-9631772-5-7*) Talei Pubs.

Michael Manley: The Making of a Leader. Darrell E. Levi. LC 86-30826. (Illus.). 364p. 1990. 35.00 (*0-8203-1221-5*) U of Ga Pr.

***Michael Meets a Special Friend: A Play about Angels.** Alice E. Ross. (Illus.). (J). 1999. write for info. (*1-929486-05-7*) SonRises Bk Pubg.

Michael, Michael, Why Do You Hate Me? Michael Esses. LC 73-85241. v, 167p. 1973. write for info. (*0-88270-046-4*) Bridge-Logos.

Michael Miller & Susanna Bechtol Family Record. Floyd R. Mason & Kathryn G. Mason. 1007p. 1999. 139.00 (*0-8328-9832-5*) Higginson Bk Co.

M

An Asterisk (*) at the beginning of an entry indicates that the title is appearing for the first time.

M

Michael Monkey Pretends. large type ed. Pam Jarrell. (Cuddle Bks.). (Illus.). 7p. (J). (ps-k). 1999. pap. text 10.95 (*1-57332-128-1*) HighReach Lrning.

Michael Moorcock's Multiverse. Michael Moorcock. (Illus.). 288p. 1999. pap. text 19.95 (*1-56389-516-1*, Pub. by DC Comics) Time Warner.

Michael New: Mercenary... Or American Soldier? 2nd rev. ed. Daniel New & Cliff Kincaid. (Illus.). 1999. pap. 19.95 (*0-9666813-2-0*) D New.

Michael Nyman Film Music for Piano Solo. Transcribed by Michael Nyman. 47p. 1998. pap. 19.95 (*0-7119-6722-9*, CH61400) Music Sales.

Michael O'Conner First Catholic Bishop of Pittsburgh. Henry Szarnicki & Marty Wolfson. (Illus.). 1975. pap. 8.95 (*0-916114-06-6*) Wolfson.

Michael O'Halloran. Gene Stratton-Porter. LC 95-14554. (Library of Indiana Classics). 1996. 27.95 (*0-253-33021-1*); pap. 14.95 (*0-253-21045-3*) Ind U Pr.

Michael O'Halloran. Gene Stratton-Porter. reprint ed. lib. bdg. 33.95 (*0-89190-934-6*, Rivercity Pr) Amereon Ltd.

Michael Olaf's Essential Montessori: A Guide & Catalogue for Montessori Education from Birth - at Home & at School. Susan Stephenson. Ed. by Jim Stephenson. (Illus.). 72p. (Orig.). 1990. pap. text 5.00 (*1-879264-00-5*) M Olaf Co.

Michael Olesker's Baltimore: If You Live Here, You're Home. Michael Olesker. 176p. 1995. 22.95 (*0-8018-5203-X*) Johns Hopkins.

Michael Ondaatje. Douglas Barbour. (Twayne's World Authors Ser.). 170p. 1993. pap. 32.00 (*0-8057-8290-7*, Twyne) Mac Lib Ref.

Michael Ondaatje: Express Yourself. Ed Jewinski. LC 94-232090. (Illus.). 144p. 1994. pap. 9.95 (*1-55022-189-2*, Pub. by ECW) LPC InBook.

Michael Ondaatje: Express Yourself Beautifully. large type ed. Ed Jewinski. (Illus.). 190p. 1996. pap. 15.95 (*1-55022-268-6*, Pub. by ECW) Genl Dist Srvs.

Michael Ondaatje: World, Image, Imagination. Leslie Mundwiler. 160p. 1984. pap. 12.95 (*0-88922-216-9*, Pub. by Talonbks) Genl Dist Srvs.

Michael Ondaatje & His Works. Nell Waldman. (Canadian Author Studies). 52p. (C). 1992. pap. 9.95 (*1-55022-061-6*, Pub. by ECW) Genl Dist Srvs.

***Michael Owens Soccer Skills.** Michael Owens. 2000. pap. 17.95 (*0-00-218935-6*) HarpC.

Michael Palin's Hemingway Adventure. Michael Palin. (Illus.). 255p. 2000. 29.95 (*0-312-24399-5*, Thomas Dunne) St Martin.

***Michael Patrick.** Victoria Thompson. Ed. by Kathleen O'Malley. 328p. 2000. pap. 12.95 (*0-9700492-0-X*) Steel Pr Pubng.

Michael Polanyi: A Critical Exposition. Harry Prosch. LC 85-27849. (SUNY Series in Cultural Perspectives). 354p. (C). 1986. text 64.50 (*0-88706-277-6*); pap. text 21.95 (*0-88706-276-8*) State U NY Pr.

Michael Porter's Landmark Trilogy: Competitive Strategy/Competitive Advantage/Competitive Advant. Michael E. Porter. 1998. 115.00 (*0-684-00577-8*) Free Pr.

***Michael Ramsey: A Life.** Owen Chadwick. 1998. pap. 25.00 (*0-334-02736-5*) S C M Pr Ltd.

Michael Ramsey As Theologian. Ed. by Robin Gill & Lorna Kendall. LC 95-13735. 199p. 1995. pap. 12.95 (*1-56101-117-7*) Cowley Pubns.

Michael Ray Charles. Intro. by Spike Lee & Calvin Reid. (Illus.). 80p. 1998. pap. 29.95 (*1-891475-10-X*, 810531) T Shafrazi.

Michael Ray Charles, 1989-1997: An American Artist's Work. Don Bacigalupi & Marilyn Kern-Foxworth. LC 96-78844. (Illus.). 52p. 1997. pap. 24.95 (*0-941193-12-8*) U of Tex Pr.

Michael Redgrave: My Father. Corin Redgrave. (Illus.). 176p. 1996. 29.95 (*1-86066-000-2*, Pub. by R Cohen Bks) Trafalgar.

Michael Ripper Unmasked. Derek Pykett. (Illus.). 192p. 1999. pap. 20.00 (*1-887664-27-0*) Midnght Marquee Pr.

Michael Robartes & the Dancer: Manuscript Materials. William Butler Yeats. Ed. by Thomas Parkinson & Anne Brannen. (Cornell Yeats Ser). (Illus.). 232p. 1994. text 47.50 (*0-8014-2934-X*) Cornell U Pr.

***Michael Rosenfeld Gallery: The First Decade.** Michael Rosenfeld & Halley K. Harrisburg. (Illus.). 96p. 2000. 25.00 (*1-930416-04-0*) M Rosenfeld.

Michael Rosen's ABC. Michael Rosen. (Illus.). 64p. (J). (ps-1). 1996. 16.95 (*0-7613-0127-5*); lib. bdg. 24.90 (*1-56294-138-0*) Millbrook Pr.

***Michael Row Your Boat Ashore: A Novel.** George E. Furnival. LC 00-190298. 269p. 2000. 25.00 (*0-7388-1715-5*); pap. 18.00 (*0-7388-1716-3*) Xlibris Corp.

Michael Rumaker: Eroticizing the Nation. Leverett T. Smith, Jr. Ed. by James Thompson. (Black Mountain College Dossier Ser.: No. 6). 91p. 1999. 20.00 (*0-9649020-6-0*, Pub. by Blck Mtn Coll) SPD-Small Pr Dist.

Michael Ryan, Capitalist. Faxon F. Albery. LC 74-22766. (Labor Movement in Fiction & Non-Fiction Ser.). 1976. reprint ed. 38.50 (*0-404-58402-0*) AMS Pr.

Michael Sadleir, 1888-1957. Roy Stokes. LC 80-11419. (Great Bibliographers Ser.: No. 5). 160p. 1980. 18.50 (*0-8108-1292-4*, 10290, Pub. by Scarecrow) Oak Knoll.

Michael Schmidt: U-ni-ty. Michael Schmidt. 1995. 49.95 (*0-614-96884-4*) DAP Assocs.

Michael Schumacher. Peter Braun. (Illus.). 96p. 1998. pap. 14.95 (*3-89365-732-0*, Pub. by Vloce Pub) Motorbooks Intl.

***Michael Schumacher.** Christopher Hilton. (Illus.). 160p. 2000. 29.95 (*1-85960-652-0*, 130365AE, Pub. by Haynes Manuals) Motorbooks Intl.

Michael Schumacher: Formula for Success. Michael Schumacher. LC 97-126678. (Illus.). 144p. 1996. 19.95 (*0-7603-0318-5*) MBI Pubg.

Michael Schumacher: Living on the Limit. Ken Sparling. (Champion Sports Biography Ser.). (Illus.). 96p. (YA). (gr. 6-10). 1999. pap. 8.95 (*1-894020-52-9*) Warwick Publ.

***Michael Schumacher - Quest For Red.** Allen. 2000. 32.50 (*1-85225-272-3*, Pub. by Transworld Publishers Ltd) Trafalgar.

Michael Scot. Ralph Shirley. 1993. reprint ed. pap. 6.95 (*1-55818-242-X*) Holmes Pub.

Michael Scott's Fitness Centerfolds: Super Bodies of Swimsuit & Fitness. Scott Schisler. (Illus.). 148p. 1996. pap. 29.95 (*1-888981-00-8*) M Scott.

Michael Servetus, His Life & Teachings. Carl T. Odhner. LC 83-45626. reprint ed. 18.50 (*0-404-19844-9*) AMS Pr.

Michael Servetus, Humanist & Martyr. John F. Fulton & Madeline E. Stanton. (Illus.). 99p. 40.00 (*0-8139-1089-7*) H Reichner.

Michael Shapiro's Internet Travel Planner: How to Plan Trips & Save Money Online. Michael Shapiro. (Illus.). 320p. 2000. pap. text 18.95 (*0-7627-0579-5*) Globe Pequot.

Michael Shmith's Australian Musical Anecdotes. Michael Shmith. LC 98-163881. (Illus.). 1997. write for info. (*0-19-553773-4*) OUP.

Michael Singer. Diane Waldman. (Illus.). 80p. (Orig.). 1984. pap. 9.00 (*0-89207-045-5*) S R Guggenheim.

Michael Sivy's Rules of Investing: How to Pick Stocks Like a Pro. Michael Sivy. 288p. 1996. 24.95 (*0-446-51982-0*, Pub. by Warner Bks) Little.

Michael Sivy's Rules of Investing: How to Pick Stocks Like a Pro. rev. ed. Michael Sivy. 288p. 1999. pap. write for info. (*0-446-67443-5*) Warner Bks.

Michael Sorkin Studio: Wiggle. Michael Sorkin. LC 98-18254. (Illus.). 192p. (Orig.). 1996. pap. 35.00 (*1-885254-25-3*, Pub. by Monacelli Pr) Penguin Putnam.

Michael Steiner. Nicholas F. Weber. 36p. 1998. pap. 18.00 (*0-9665644-0-5*) Grnds for Sclpture.

Michael Steiner: Bronze Sculpture. Illus. by Elizabeth Richbourg Rea. LC 90-60996. 113p. 1990. pap. 40.00 (*1-58821-068-5*) Salander OReilly.

Michael Steiner: Bronze Sculpture 1979-89. Intro. by William Agee. (Illus.). 59p. 1990. pap. 25.00 (*1-58821-069-3*) Salander OReilly.

***Michael Steiner: Sculpture 1988-1999.** Text by Karen Wilken. (Illus.). 88p. 1999. 50.00 (*1-58821-070-7*) Salander OReilly.

Michael Stoffa: Artist & Storyteller. Michael Stoffa. (Illus.). 144p. 1999. 29.95 (*1-885435-05-3*) Twin Lights.

Michael Strogoff. deluxe ed. Jules Verne. LC 96-22115. (J). 1997. 75.00 (*0-689-81097-0*) S&S Childrens.

Michael Strogoff: A Courier of Czar. Jules Verne. LC 96-22115. (Illus.). 397p. (J). 1997. 25.00 (*0-689-81096-2*) S&S Childrens.

Michael Strogoff: A Screenplay. Thomas Roberdeau. 248p. (Orig.). 1995. pap. 10.95 (*1-55713-098-1*) Sun & Moon CA.

Michael Strogoff: An Airmont Classic C148. Jules Verne. (Airmont Classics Ser.). (YA). (gr. 8 up). 1964. mass mkt. 1.50 (*0-8049-0048-5*, CL-48) Airmont.

Michael Strogoff: The Couries of the Czar. Jules Verne. 26.95 (*0-88411-920-3*) Amereon Ltd.

Michael Taubenheim: Fotografien. Michael Taubenheim. (Illus.). 1998. pap. text 7.95 (*3-86187-120-3*) B Gmunder.

Michael Thompson: Passion over Reason. Frwd. by Paul Duval. LC 95-189558. (Illus.). 72p. (C). 1994. pap. 15.00 (*0-91423-94-9*) W Laurier U Pr.

Michael Timpson. Huston Paschal. LC 91-60862. (Illus.). 24p. (Orig.). 1991. pap. 7.95 (*0-88259-964-X*) NCMA.

Michael Tippett. Meiron Bowen. (Contemporary Composers Ser.). (Illus.). 318p. 1998. pap. 19.95 (*1-86105-099-2*, Pub. by Robson Bks) Parkwest Pubns.

Michael Tippett, O. M. A Celebration. Geraint Lewis. (Illus.). 255p. 1985. 39.95 (*0-85936-140-3*, Pub. by The Baton Pr) Pro-Am Music.

Michael Todd: Twenty-Five Year Survey. Katherine P. Hough & Michael Zakian. LC 88-63194. (Illus.). 64p. (Orig.). 1991. pap. 14.95 (*0-295-97073-1*) U of Wash Pr.

Michael Upton Paintings, 1977-1987. Mel Gooding. LC 87-50611. (Illus.). 19p. (Orig.). 1987. pap. 3.50 (*0-930606-55-8*) Yale Ctr Brit Art.

Michael V. Pregnoff, John E. Rinne. Michael V. Pregnoff et al. LC 96-3088. (Connections: the EERI Oral History Ser.). 1996. pap. 15.00 (*0-943198-53-4*) Earthquake Eng.

Michael W. Smith: Change Your World. (Piano-Vocal-Guitar Ser.). 72p. 1993. per. 12.95 (*0-7935-1982-9*, 00308172) H Leonard.

Michael W. Smith: Go West Young Man. (Piano-Vocal-Guitar Ser.). 64p. 1991. otabind 12.95 (*0-7935-0956-4*, 00308110) H Leonard.

Michael, Wait for Me. Patricia Calvert. LC 99-19104. (Illus.). 160p. (J). 2000. 16.00 (*0-689-82102-6*) Atheneum Yung Read.

Michael Wilkinson: The Acrylic Sculpture of Michael Wilkinson. Michael Wilkinson. (Art Bks.). 52p. 1994. 20.00 (*0-9644548-0-7*) Meisner Gall.

Michael William Kaluta Treasury. Todd R. Adams. (Illus.). 80p. (Orig.). 1988. pap. 9.95 (*0-9621421-0-7*) Glimmer Graph.

Michael Wm. Kaluta Sketchbook. Michael W. Kaluta. 1998. 34.95 (*0-87816-575-4*) Kitchen Sink.

Michael Wm. Kaluta Sketchbook. Michael Wm. Kaluta. (Illus.). 96p. 1998. reprint ed. pap. 14.95 (*0-87816-236-4*) Kitchen Sink.

Michael Wm. Kaluta Sketchbook. Michael Wm. Kaluta. (Li'l Abner Dailies Ser.: Vol. XIV). (Illus.). 180p. 1998. reprint ed. 39.95 (*0-87816-115-5*) Kitchen Sink.

Michaelangelo's Call. Sy Hakim. LC 98-74543. 80p. 1999. pap. 12.95 (*0-9659417-4-4*) Century Pr ME.

***Michaelangelo's Call.** Sy Hakim. LC 98-74543. 80p. 1999. pap. 12.95 (*0-913054-17-8*, Pub. by Poet Gal Pr) Century Pr ME.

Michaelis Business English - Portuguese Dictionary. 5th ed. Michaelis. 407p. 1992. 125.00 (*0-7859-8713-4*) Fr & Eur.

Michaelis Dicionario Pratico de Informatica, Ingles-Portugues Portugues-Ingles. S. Collin. (ENG & POR.). 452p. 1993. 95.00 (*0-7859-9797-0*) Fr & Eur.

Michaelis Pequeno Dicionario Espanhol-Portugues - Portugues-Espanhol. Helena B. Pereira. (POR & SPA.). 636p. 1992. 24.95 (*0-7859-9316-9*) Fr & Eur.

Michaelis Pequeno Dicionario Frances-Portugues - Portugues-Frances. Helena B. Pereira. (FRE & POR.). 680p. 1992. 24.95 (*0-7859-9315-0*) Fr & Eur.

Michaelis Pselli: Historia Syntomos. Ed. by Willem J. Aerts. (Corpus Fontium Historiae Byzantinae Ser.: Berolinensis Vol. XXX). xxx, 237p. (C). 1990. lib. bdg. 152.35 (*3-11-011219-1*) De Gruyter.

Michaelis S. O. S. Ingles, Guia Pratico de Gramatica. Marisa M. J. De Britto. 386p. 1995. 24.95 (*0-7859-9312-6*) Fr & Eur.

***Michaelis Tech: Dicionario Tecnico Multilingue; English, Portuguese, French, Italian, German & Spanish.** Distribooks Inc. Staff. 1999. 125.00 (*85-06-01990-7*) Midwest European Pubns.

Michaelmas & the Soul-Forces of Man. Rudolf Steiner. Tr. by Samuel Lockwood & Loni Lockwood from GER. 69p. 1982. pap. 7.95 (*0-88010-007-9*) Anthroposophic.

Michaelmas Term. Thomas Middleton. Ed. by Richard Levin. LC 66-17765. (Regents Renaissance Drama Ser.). 165p. reprint ed. pap. 51.20 (*0-7837-0147-0*, 204043600017) Bks Demand.

Michael's Angel. Lyn Ellis. LC 96-2424. (Temptation Ser.). 219p. 1996. per. 3.50 (*0-373-25675-2*, 1-25675-9) Harlequin Bks.

Michael's Baby. Cathie Linz. (Desire Ser.). 1996. per. 3.50 (*0-373-76023-X*, 1-76023-0) Silhouette.

Michael's Brothers. Crystal Forsberg. (Illus.). 16p. (J). (ps-k). 1998. pap. 5.95 (*0-9655442-3-0*) Busn Word.

Michael's Decision. Carol Apacki et al. (Illus.). 24p. (J). (gr. k-2). 1993. pap. text 12.95 (*1-56095-082-X*) Quest Intl.

Michael's Family. Kathryn Shay. (Superromance Ser.). 1997. per. 3.99 (*0-373-70727-4*, 1-70727-2) Harlequin Bks.

Michael's Father. Dallas Schulze. 1994. per. 3.50 (*0-373-07565-0*) Silhouette.

Michael's Father. large type ed. Dallas Schulze. 1996. lib. bdg. 19.95 (*0-373-59743-6*, G K Hall Lrg Type) Mac Lib Ref.

Michael's Fire. Pam Blackwell. 350p. 1999. pap. 15.95 (*0-9653327-5-6*) BF Publng.

Michael's Garden. (PNI Healing Stories for Children Ser.). 24p. (J). (gr. k-6). 1998. 6.95 (*1-893351-02-5*) Asclepian Pr.

Michael's Gift: (American Hero, New Orleans Knights) Marilyn Pappano. (Intimate Moments Ser.). 1994. per. 3.50 (*0-373-07583-9*, 1-07583-7) Harlequin Bks.

Michael's House. Pat Warren. (Intimate Moments Ser.). 1996. per. 3.99 (*0-373-07737-8*, 1-07737-9) Silhouette.

Michael's Magic. Charlotte Maclay. (American Romance Ser.). 1994. per. 3.50 (*0-373-16532-3*, 1-16532-3) Harlequin Bks.

***Michael's Mommy Has Breast Cancer.** Lisa Torrey. LC 98-73169. (Illus.). 40p. (J). (gr. k-5). 1999. pap. write for info. (*0-9647763-6-7*) Hibiscus FL.

Michaels on Gay Life, Vol. 1. Kevin Michaels. 140p. (Orig.). 1986. pap., ring bd. 11.95 (*0-939020-78-5*) MLP Ent.

Michaels on Gay Life, Vol. 2. Kevin Michaels. 140p. (Orig.). 1987. ring bd. 12.95 (*0-939020-81-5*) MLP Ent.

Michael's Silence. Kathleen O'Brien. 1994. per. 2.99 (*0-373-11698-5*, 1-11698-7) Harlequin Bks.

***Michael's Stable: The Best Gift is to Belong.** Jerry Seiden. Ed. by Chelese Guthrie Palmer. (Illus.). 128p. 1999. pap. 9.95 (*1-929753-00-4*) Spirit of Hope.

Michael's Story: The Story of a Burn Victim. Joan Brunette. 105p. (Orig.). (YA). (gr. 7-12). 1995. pap. 6.95 (*1-57515-085-9*) PPI Pubng.

Michael's Suite: Solo Flute. 12p. pap. 6.95 (*0-7935-4712-1*, 50482426) H Leonard.

Michael's Wife. Tracy Morgan. (Temptation Ser.). 1993. per. 2.99 (*0-373-25530-6*, 1-25530-6) Harlequin Bks.

Micah-Zephaniah. Ken Barker. LC 98-40576. (New American Commentary Ser.: Vol. 20). 320p. 1998. 29.99 (*0-8054-0120-2*, 4201-20) Broadman.

Michal Kalecki, 1899-1970. Ed. by Mark Blaug. (Pioneers in Economics Ser.: Vol. 39). 208p. 1992. 100.00 (*1-85278-503-9*) E Elgar.

Michal, Princess. Marilyn K. Stout. LC 97-73559. 214p. 1997. pap. 8.95 (*1-891049-01-1*) Jennkay.

Michalopoulos. Dean Pulley. Ed. & Des. by Jim Cass. Des. by David Foster. (Illus.). 128p. 1997. 60.00 (*0-9659554-0-0*) Cattywompus Pr.

Michaud: A Paleoindian Site in the New England-Maritimes Region. Arthur E. Spiess & Deborah B. Wilson. (Occasional Publications in Maine Archaeology). (Illus.). (Orig.). 1987. pap. 15.00 (*0-935447-04-0*) ME Hist Preserv.

Micheal Macliammoir: Outlines. Dennis Staunton. 96p. 2000. pap. 9.95 (*1-899791-75-2*) Stewart Tabori & Chang.

Michel Angelo. Bull. 1998. pap. 17.95 (*0-312-18746-7*) St Martin.

Michel Anguier's Pluto: The Marble of 1669: New Light on the French Sculptor's Career. Bernard Black & Hugues W. Nadeau. LC 90-37517. (Illus.). 104p. (C). 1990. text 42.00 (*0-485-11400-3*, Pub. by Athlone Pr) Humanities.

***Michel Comte: Aiko T.** Michel Comte. 2000. 195.00 (*3-88243-702-2*) Steidl.

***Michel Comte: People & Places Without Name.** Michel Comte. 400p. 2000. 65.00 (*3-88243-704-9*, Pub. by Steidl) Dist Art Pubs.

Michel Corette & Flute Playing in the 18th Century. Ed. by Carol Ferrar. (Musical Theorists in Translation Ser.: Vol. 9). 1970. lib. bdg. 27.00 (*0-912024-29-1*) Inst Mediaeval Mus.

Michel Corrette: Premier Livre D'Orgue & Nouveua Livre de Noels. Michel Corrette. Ed. by Gwilym Beechey. (Recent Researches in Music of the Baroque Era Ser.: Vol. RRB18). (Illus.). x, 118p. 1974. pap. 45.00 (*0-89579-055-6*, RRB18) A-R Eds.

Michel de Certeau. Jeremy Ahearne. LC 95-70478. 240p. (Orig.). 1996. pap. 16.95 (*0-8047-2672-8*) Stanford U Pr.

Michel de Certeau. John Ahearne. LC 95-70478. (Key Contemporary Thinkers Ser.). 240p. 1996. 45.00 (*0-8047-2670-1*) Stanford U Pr.

***Michel de Certeau in the Plural.** Ian Buchanan. 290p. 2000. pap. 12.00 (*0-8223-6473-5*) Duke.

Michel de Ghelderode. David B. Parsell. (Twayne's World Authors Ser.). 128p. 1993. 24.95 (*0-8057-4303-0*, Twyne) Mac Lib Ref.

Michel de Klerk: Master Builder & Draghtsman of the Amsterdam School. Sigrid Johanisse & Vladimir Stissi. LC 97-217913. (Illus.). 272p. 1997. 80.00 (*90-5662-047-9*) Dist Art Pubs.

Michel de Klerk, 1884-1923: An Architect of the Amsterdam School. Suzanne S. Frank. Ed. by Stephen Foster. LC 84-132. (Architecture & Urban Design Ser.: No. 4). 324p. reprint ed. pap. 100.50 (*0-8357-1546-9*, 207043400089) Bks Demand.

Michel de L'Hospital: The Vision of a Reformist Chancellor During the French Religious Wars. Seong-Hak Kim. LC 97-2252. (Sixteenth Century Essays & Studies: No. 36). 216p. 1997. 40.00 (*0-940474-38-7*, SCJP) Truman St Univ.

Michel de Saint Pierre: A Catholic Novelist at the Crossroads. David O'Connell. LC 89-52103. 189p. 1990. lib. bdg. 27.95 (*0-917786-76-9*) Summa Pubns.

Michel Delacroix. Michel Delacroix. Ed. by Michelle L. Cassanetti. LC 86-83287. (Illus.). 200p. 1987. 150.00 (*0-941393-05-4*) Lublin Graph.

Michel Delacroix's Paris. Richard Howard. Ed. by Marshall Lee. (Illus.). 198p. 1990. 85.00 (*0-940577-01-1*, Balance Hse Ltd) Intl Archive Art.

Michel Erhart: Ein Beitrag zur Schwaebischen Plastik der Spaetgotik. Anja Broschek. LC 72-81548. (Beitraege zur Kunstgeschichte Ser.: Vol. 8). (C). 1973. 192.35 (*3-11-001765-2*) De Gruyter.

Michel Fokine & His Ballets. Cyril W. Beaumont. (Illus.). 170p. 1996. reprint ed. pap. 21.95 (*1-85273-050-1*) Princeton Bk Co.

Michel Foucault see Michel Foucault

Michel Foucault. Didier Eribon. Tr. by Betsy Wing. 448p. (C). 1991. text 39.50 (*0-674-57287-4*) HUP.

Michel Foucault. Didier Eribon. Tr. by Betsy Wing from FRE. (Illus.). 392p. 1992. pap. text 15.95 (*0-674-57286-6*) HUP.

Michel Foucault. David R. Shumway. (World Authors Ser.: No. 814). 227p. 1989. 26.95 (*0-8057-8252-4*, TWAS 814, Twyne) Mac Lib Ref.

Michel Foucault. Barry Smart. 152p. (C). 1985. pap. 17.99 (*0-415-03676-3*) Routledge.

Michel Foucault, 7 vols. Barry Smart. Incl. Michel Foucault., **vols. 1-3** LC 94-28914. (Illus.). 1200p. (C). (gr. 13). 1994. 655.00 (*0-415-08890-9*, B4297); Michel Foucault., **vols. 4-7** (Illus.). 3576p. (C). (gr. 13). 1995. 700.00 (*0-415-11230-3*, C0386); (C). 1998. 1235.00 (*0-415-12680-0*) Routledge.

Michel Foucault. David R. Shumway. LC 92-13504. 192p. (C). 1992. reprint ed. pap. text 14.50 (*0-8139-1415-9*) U Pr of Va.

Michel Foucault: A Bibliography. Ed. by Joan Nordquist. (Social Theory: A Bibliographic Ser.: No. 4). 50p. 1986. pap. 20.00 (*0-937855-06-5*) Ref Rsch Serv.

***Michel Foucault: An Introduction.** Philip Barker. 176p. 2000. pap. text 19.00 (*0-7486-1038-3*) Col U Pr.

Michel Foucault: An Introductory Study of His Thought. Barry Cooper. LC 82-8260. (Studies in Religion & Society: Vol. 2). 170p. (C). 1982. lib. bdg. 79.95 (*0-88946-867-2*) E Mellen.

Michel Foucault: Beyond Structuralism & Hermeneutics. 2nd ed. Hubert L. Dreyfus & Paul Rabinow. LC 83-9316. (Illus.). 280p. 1983. pap. text 14.50 (*0-226-16312-1*) U Ch Pr.

Michel Foucault: Beyond Structuralism & Hermeneutics. 2nd ed. Hubert L. Dreyfus & Paul Rabinow. LC 83-9316. (Illus.). 232p. 1992. lib. bdg. 25.00 (*0-226-16311-3*) U Ch Pr.

Michel Foucault: Critical Assessments. Barry Smart. LC 94-28914. 1994. write for info. (*0-415-08889-5*) Routledge.

Michel Foucault: Critical Assessments, 4 vols. Ed. by Barry Smart. LC 94-28914. 1400p. 1994. write for info. (*0-415-08887-9*, B4297); pap. write for info. (*0-415-08888-7*) Routledge.

Michel Foucault: Genealogy As Critique. Rudi Visker. Tr. by Chris Turner. 288p. (C). 1995. 65.00 (*0-86091-468-2*, B4624, Pub. by Verso) Norton.

Michel Foucault: Genealogy As Critique. Rudi Visker. 288p. (C). 1995. pap. 19.00 (*1-85984-095-7*, Pub. by Verso) Norton.

***Michel Foucault: Materialism & Education.** Mark Olssen. LC 98-49933. (Critical Studies in Education & Culture). 216p. 1999. 59.95 (*0-89789-587-8*, Bergin & Garvey) Greenwood.

Michel Foucault: Personal Automony & Education. James D. Marshall. LC 96-11697. (Philosophy & Education Ser.: Vol. 7). 254p. 1996. text 120.50 (*0-7923-4016-7*) Kluwer Academic.

An Asterisk (*) at the beginning of an entry indicates that the title is appearing for the first time.

Michel Foucault: Social Theory & Transgression. Charles C. Lemert & Garth Gillan. LC 82-4276. 187p. reprint ed. pap. 58.00 (*0-8357-7782-0*, 203614200002) Bks Demand.

Michel Foucault: Subversions of the Subject. Philip Barker. LC 93-23231. 1993. text 45.00 (*0-312-10587-8*) St Martin.

Michel Foucault: The Will to Truth. Alan Sheridan. 1986. 29.50 (*0-422-77350-6*, NO. 3497, Pub. by Tavistock); pap. 13.95 (*0-422-76570-8*, NO. 6357, Pub. by Tavistock) Routldge.

Michel Foucault & the Politics of Freedom. Thomas L. Dumm. (Modernity & Political Thought Ser.: Vol. 9). 167p. 1996. 44.00 (*0-8039-3864-0*); pap. 19.95 (*0-8039-3865-9*) Sage.

Michel Foucault, the Will to Truth. Alan Sheridan. 243p. (C). 1986. pap. 24.99 (*0-415-05117-7*) Routledge.

Michel Foucault Two: A Bibliography. Ed. by Joan Nordquist. (Social Theory: A Bibliographic Ser.: No. 27). 68p. (Orig.). (C). 1992. pap. 20.00 (*0-937855-53-7*) Ref Rsch Serv.

Michel Foucault's Archaeology of Western Culture: Toward a New Science of History. Pamela Major-Poetzl. LC 81-19689. 295p. reprint ed. pap. 91.50 (*0-7837-0308-2*, 204063000018) Bks Demand.

Michel Foucault's Force of Flight: Toward an Ethics for Thought. James W. Bernauer. LC 89-31526. (Contemporary Studies in Philosophy & the Human Sciences). 280p. (C). 1992. reprint ed. pap. 17.50 (*0-391-03740-4*) Humanities.

Michel Kagan. Michel Kagan. Ed. by Oscar R. Ojeda. (Contemporary World Architects Ser.). (Illus.). 132p. (Orig.). 1997. pap. 19.99 (*1-56496-359-4*) Rockport Pubs.

Michel Legrand - Brimhall: Easy Piano. 56p. 1997. pap. 10.95 (*1-57623-668-4*, AF9678) Wrner Bros.

Michel Legrand Songbook. Ed. by Sy Feldman. (Illus.). 184p. (Orig.). 1997. pap. text 22.95 (*1-57623-933-0*, PF9650) Wrner Bros.

Michel Pignolet de Monteclair: Cantatas for One & Two Voices. Michel Pignolet De Monteclair. Ed. by James R. Anthony & Diran Akmajian. (Recent Researches in Music of the Baroque Era Ser.: Vol. RRB29-30). (Illus.). xxvi, 169p. 1978. pap. 60.00 (*0-89579-106-4*, RRB29-30) A-R Eds.

Michel Roux: Sauces. Michel Roux. LC 96-20167. (Illus.). 176p. 1996. 35.00 (*0-8478-1970-1*, Pub. by Rizzoli Intl) St Martin.

Michel Roux's Finest Desserts. Michel Roux. LC 95-35427. (Illus.). 192p. 1995. 45.00 (*0-8478-1857-8*, Pub. by Rizzoli Intl) St Martin.

Michel Salmon Anatomic Studies, 2 vols., Set. G. Ian Taylor et al. LC 93-21903.Tr. of Les Arteres des Muscles des Membres et du Tronc, Les Vois Anastomotiques Arterielles des Membres. (Illus.). 307p. 1993. 90.00 (*0-942219-27-9*) Quality Med Pub.

Michel Salmon Anatomic Studies: Arterial Anastomotic Pathways of the Extremities. G. Ian Taylor & Rosa M. Razaboni. LC 93-21903.Tr. of Les Arteres des Muscles des Membres et du Tronc, Les Vois Anastomotiques Arterielles des Membres. (Illus.). 1994. 90.00 (*0-614-08698-1*) Quality Med Pub.

Michel Sedaine (1719-1797) Charlton. 78.95 (*1-84014-677-X*) Ashgate Pub Co.

Michel Strogoff. Jules Verne. pap. 8.95 (*0-685-37135-2*) Fr & Eur.

Michel Strogoff. Jules Verne. (FRE.). 530p. 1992. pap. 14.95 (*0-7859-1604-0*, 226604317X) Fr & Eur.

Michel Strogoff. Jules Verne & Adolphe D'Ennery. Ed. by Louis Bilodeau. (Exeter French Texts Ser.: No. 91). (FRE., Illus.). 142p. 1995. pap. text 19.95 (*0-85989-463-0*, Pub. by Univ Exeter Pr) Northwestern U Pr.

Michel Strogoff. unabridged ed. Jules Verne. (FRE.). 1996. pap. 7.95 (*2-87714-333-3*, Pub. by Bookking Intl) Distribks Inc.

Michel Tournier. David Gascoigne. Ed. by John Flower. (New Directions in European Writing Ser.). 352p. 1996. 53.00 (*1-85973-024-8*); pap. 22.50 (*1-85973-084-1*) Berg Pubs.

Michel Tournier: "Bricolage" & Cultural Mythology. Martin Roberts. (Stanford French & Italian Studies: No. 79). 192p. 1995. pap. 56.50 (*0-915838-95-8*) Anma Libri.

Michel Tournier: Le Coq de Bruyere. Walter Redfern. LC 95-32323. 144p. (C). 1996. 27.50 (*0-8386-3627-6*) Fairleigh Dickinson.

Michel Tournier: Marginalite et Creation. Pary Pezechkian-Weinberg. (Currents in Comparative Romance Languages & Literatures Ser.: Vol. 48). (ENG & FRE.). XII, 170p. (C). 1998. text 41.95 (*0-8204-3316-0*) P Lang Pubng.

Michel Tournier: Philosophy & Fiction. Colin Davis. (Oxford Modern Languages & Literature Monographs). 232p. 1988. 75.00 (*0-19-815152-7*) OUP.

Michel Tournier & the Metaphor of Fiction. David Platten. LC 98-27468. 256p. 1999. text 49.95 (*0-312-21810-9*) St Martin.

Michel Tournier's Children: Myth, Intertext, Initiation, Vol. 180. Christopher Anderson. LC 91-43009. (American University Studies: No. II). XV, 145p. (C). 1998. text 34.95 (*0-8204-1654-1*) P Lang Pubng.

Michel Tournier's Metaphysical Fictions. Susan Petit. LC 91-40887. (Purdue University Monographs in Romance Languages: No. 37). xvi, 224p. 1991. 71.00 (*1-55619-302-5*); pap. 27.95 (*1-55619-303-3*) J Benjamins Pubng Co.

Michel Verjux: L'Exposition sous la Lumiere. Michel Verjux. (Illus.). 48p. 1991. pap. 30.00 (*90-72191-31-5*, Pub. by Imschoot) Dist Art Pubs.

Michel Zink - Medieval French Literature: An Introduction. Tr. by Jeff Rider. (Medieval & Renaissance Texts & Studies: Vol. 110). 184p. (C). 1995. 25.00 (*0-86698-163-2*, MR110) MRTS.

Michelangelo. Jeffery Daniels. 1990. 6.98 (*1-55521-600-5*) Bk Sales Inc.

Michelangelo. Gabriella Di Cagno. LC 97-118074. (Masters of Art Ser.). (Illus.). 64p. (J). (gr. 5). 1996. lib. bdg. 22.50 (*0-87226-319-3*, 63193B, P Bedrick Books) NTC Contemp Pub Co.

***Michelangelo.** Michelangelo di Lodovico Buonarroti Simoni. (Illus.). 2000. pap. 1.00 (*0-486-41077-3*) Dover.

Michelangelo. Jen Green. (Famous Artists Ser.). (Illus.). 32p. (YA). (gr. 5 up). 1994. 10.95 (*0-8120-6461-5*) Barron.

Michelangelo. Jen Green. (Famous Artists Ser.). 1994. 12.15 (*0-606-07036-2*, Pub. by Turtleback) Demco.

Michelangelo. Tony Hart. LC 93-2384. (Famous Children Ser.). (Illus.). 24p. (J). (ps-3). 1994. pap. 5.95 (*0-8120-1827-3*) Barron.

Michelangelo. Frederick N. Hartt. (Masters of Art Ser.). (Illus.). 128p. 1984. 24.95 (*0-8109-1335-6*, Pub. by Abrams) Time Warner.

Michelangelo. Lutz Heusinger. (Grandes Maestros del Arte Ser.). (SPA., Illus.). 80p. 1992. pap. 12.99 (*1-878351-21-4*) Riverside NY.

Michelangelo. Anthony Hughes. (Illus.). 352p. 1997. pap. 19.95 (*0-7148-3483-1*, Pub. by Phaidon Press) Phaidon Pr.

Michelangelo. Eberhard Konig. (Masters of Italian Art Ser.). (Illus.). 140p. 1998. 19.95 (*3-8290-0253-X*, 520533) Konemann.

Michelangelo. Antony Mason et al. (Famous Artists Ser.). (Illus.). 32p. (YA). (gr. 5 up). 1994. pap. 6.95 (*0-8120-1998-9*) Barron.

Michelangelo. Richard B. McLanathan. LC 92-27688. (First Impressions Ser.). (Illus.). 92p. (J). 1993. 19.95 (*0-8109-3634-8*, Pub. by Abrams) Time Warner.

Michelangelo. Linda Murray. (World of Art Ser.). (Illus.). 216p. 1985. pap. 14.95 (*0-500-20174-9*, Pub. by Thames Hudson) Norton.

Michelangelo. Linda Murray. (World of Art Ser.). (Illus.). 216p. 1985. 19.95 (*0-500-18175-6*, Pub. by Thames Hudson) Norton.

Michelangelo. Gilles Neret. 1998. 9.99 (*3-8228-8272-0*, Pub. by Taschen Amer) Bks Nippan.

***Michelangelo.** Klaus Ottmann. (Essential Ser.). 2000. pap. 12.95 (*0-8109-5817-1*) Abrams.

***Michelangelo.** Klaus Ottmann. (Essential Ser.). (Illus.). 112p. 2000. 12.95 (*0-7407-0728-0*, Abrams Essential) Andrews & McMeel.

Michelangelo. Random House Value Publishing Staff. 80p. 1998. 9.99 (*0-517-16058-7*) Random Hse Value.

Michelangelo. Christopher Ryan. 1998. pap. text 3.50 (*0-460-87963-4*, Everyman's Classic Lib) Tuttle Pubng.

***Michelangelo.** Diane Stanley. LC 99-52380. 48p. (J). (gr. 2 up). 2000. 15.95 (*0-688-15085-3*); lib. bdg. 15.89 (*0-688-15086-1*) Morrow Avon.

Michelangelo. Mike Venezia. LC 91-555. (Getting to Know the World's Greatest Artists Ser.). (Illus.). 32p. (J). (ps-4). 1991. pap. 6.95 (*0-516-42293-6*); lib. bdg. 21.00 (*0-516-02293-8*) Childrens.

Michelangelo. Pieluigi De Vecchi. (Illus.). 160p. 1998. reprint ed. write for info. (*1-56852-202-9*, Konecky & Konecky) W S Konecky Assocs.

Michelangelo. rev. ed. Lutz Heusinger. Tr. by Lisa C. Pelletti from ITA. (Library of Great Masters). (Illus.). 80p. 1989. pap. 14.99 (*1-878351-02-8*) Riverside NY.

***Michelangelo.** 2nd ed. Gabriella Di Cagno et al. LC 00-39747. (Masters of Art Ser.). (Illus.). 2000. write for info. (*0-87226-641-9*, P Bedrick Books) NTC Contemp Pub Co.

Michelangelo. 2nd ed. Howard Hibbard. LC 84-48636. (Illus.). 352p. 1985. pap. 25.00 (*0-06-430148-6*, IN-148, Icon Edns) HarpC.

Michelangelo: A Biography. George A. Bull. LC 96-9923. 1996. text 29.95 (*0-312-15172-1*) St Martin.

Michelangelo: A Self-Portrait. Ed. by Robert J. Clements. LC 68-31495. (Illus.). 237p. reprint ed. pap. 73.50 (*0-608-11187-2*, 200906200072) Bks Demand.

Michelangelo: Genius of the Renaissance. Jayne Pettit. LC 97-26724. (Impact Biography Ser.). 112p. (J). (gr. 4-6). 1998. lib. bdg. 22.00 (*0-531-11490-2*) Watts.

Michelangelo: On & Off the Sistine Ceiling. Creighton E. Gilbert. LC 93-41240. (Illus.). 256p. 1994. 29.95 (*0-8076-1338-X*) Braziller.

Michelangelo: Paintings, Sculpture, Architecture. rev. ed. Ludwig Goldscheider. LC 97-104493. (Illus.). 266p. (C). 1996. reprint ed. pap. 29.95 (*0-7148-3296-0*, Pub. by Phaidon Press) Phaidon Pr.

Michelangelo: Pieta. Robert E. Hupka. (Illus.). 96p. 1975. 8.95 (*0-9635132-0-6*) R E Hupka.

Michelangelo: Sculptor. Rupert Hodson & Antonio Paolucci. (Illus.). 112p. 1999. pap. 20.00 (*0-85667-515-6*, Pub. by P Wilson) Antique Collect.

Michelangelo: Six Lectures by Johannes Wilde. Johannes Wilde. Ed. by John Shearman & Michael Hirst. (Oxford Studies in the History of Art & Architecture). (Illus.). 206p. 1979. pap. text 32.00 (*0-19-817346-6*) OUP.

Michelangelo: Sonnets. Tr. by Elizabeth Jennings. LC 96-177818. 144p. pap. 14.95 (*1-85754-244-4*, Pub. by Carcanet Pr) Paul & Co Pubs.

Michelangelo: Sonnets. Tr. by Elizabeth Jennings. 144p. 1996. pap. 14.95 (*0-85635-777-4*, Pub. by Carcanet Pr) Paul & Co Pubs.

Michelangelo: The Bruges Madonna & the Piccolomini Altar. Harold R. Mancusi-Ungaro, Jr. LC 70-151582. (College Ser.: No. 11). (Illus.). 240p. reprint ed. 74.40 (*0-8357-9387-7*, 201319200085) Bks Demand.

Michelangelo: The Genius of the Sculptor in Michelangelo's Work. Pietro Marani. (Illus.). 527p. 1996. 100.00 (*2-89192-159-3*) McCland & Stewart.

***Michelangelo: The Last Judgment.** (Illus.). 208p. 2000. 29.98 (*0-8109-8190-4*, Pub. by Abrams) Time Warner.

Michelangelo: The Medici Chapel. 2nd ed. Antonio Paolucci et al. LC 94-60290. (Illus.). 216p. 2000. reprint ed. 75.00 (*0-500-23690-9*, Pub. by Thames Hudson) Norton.

Michelangelo: The Pieta. Photos by Aurelio Amendola. (Illus.). 208p. 1999. boxed set 65.00 (*88-8118-108-8*, Pub. by Skira IT) Abbeville Pr.

***Michelangelo: The Pietas.** Antonio Paolucci. 208p. 2000. 65.00 (*88-8118-318-8*, Pub. by Skira IT) Abbeville Pr.

Michelangelo: The Sistine Chapel Ceiling. Ed. by Charles Seymour, Jr. (Critical Studies in Art History: Vol. 1). (Illus.). 272p. 1995. pap. 17.95 (*0-393-31405-7*, Norton Paperbks) Norton.

Michelangelo: The Sistine Chapel Ceiling, Rome. Loren Partridge. LC 96-31543. (Great Fescoes of the Italian Renaissance Ser.). (Illus.). 128p. 1996. 25.00 (*0-8076-1315-0*) Braziller.

Michelangelo: The Vatican Frescoes. Pierluigi De Vecchi. 1997. 85.00 (*0-614-28067-2*) Abbeville Pr.

Michelangelo: The Vatican Frescoes: The Complete Works Restored. Pierluigi De Vecchi & Gianluigi Colalucci. (Illus.). 272p. 1997. 85.00 (*0-7892-0142-9*) Abbeville Pr.

Michelangelo - Bibliographie, 1510-1926. Ernst Steinmann & Rudolf Wittkower. (Rom. Forschungen der Biblioteca Hertziana Ser.: Vol. 1). xxvi, 523p. 1967. reprint ed. write for info. (*3-487-01758-X*) G Olms Pubs.

Michelangelo - Die Sixtinische Decke.Beitraege ueber ihre Quellen und zu ihrer Auslegung. Rudolf Kuhn. LC 73-93163. (Beitraege zur Kunstgeschichte Ser.: Vol. 10). (Illus.). 173p. (C). 1975. text 100.00 (*3-11-004497-8*) De Gruyter.

Michelangelo--The Last Judgment: A Glorious Restoration. Loren W. Partridge et al. LC 97-16157. (Illus.). 208p. 1997. 65.00 (*0-8109-1549-9*, Pub. by Abrams) Time Warner.

Michelangelo & His Drawings. Michael Hirst. 304p. (Orig.). (C). 1990. reprint ed. pap. 30.00 (*0-300-04796-7*) Yale U Pr.

Michelangelo & His Influence. Paul Joannides. 1998. pap. text 50.00 (*0-85331-713-5*) Lund Humphries.

Michelangelo & His Influence: Drawings from Windsor Castle. Paul Joannides. (Illus.). 224p. 1996. 90.00 (*0-85331-722-4*, Pub. by Lund Humphries) Antique Collect.

Michelangelo & His World: Sculpture of the Italian Renaissance. Joachim Poeschke. Tr. by Russell Stockman from GER. LC 95-34373. (Illus.). 272p. 1996. 125.00 (*0-8109-4276-3*) Abrams.

Michelangelo & Me: Six Years in My Carrara Heaven. Hanna M. Eshel. LC 95-77061. (Illus.). 160p. 1996. pap. 14.00 (*1-877675-19-9*) Midmarch Arts.

Michelangelo & Raphael in the Vatican. Francesco Rossi et al. (Illus.). 215p. 1997. 75.00 (*88-86921-05-5*); pap. 55.00 (*88-86921-04-7*) Treasures Inc.

Michelangelo & the Creation of the Sistine Chapel. Robin Richmond. LC 95-14238. (Illus.). 160p. 1995. 14.99 (*0-517-14194-9*) Random Hse Value.

Michelangelo & the Language of Art. David Summers. LC 80-7556. (Illus.), 678p. reprint ed. pap. 200.00 (*0-8357-3697-0*, 203642100003) Bks Demand.

***Michelangelo & the Reform of Art.** Alexander Nagel & Michelangelo Buonarroti. LC 99-55668. 2000. write for info. (*0-521-66292-3*) Cambridge U Pr.

Michelangelo & the Renaissance. David Spence. (Illus.). 32p. 1997. pap. 5.95 (*0-7641-0296-6*) Barron.

Michelangelo Antonioni. Tomasulo. 1998. 22.95 (*0-8057-7840-3*); per. 12.95 (*0-8057-9241-4*) Macmillan.

Michelangelo Antonioni's Neo-Realism: A World View. Robert J. Lyons. LC 75-21433. (Dissertations on Film Ser.). 1976. lib. bdg. 19.95 (*0-405-07618-5*) Ayer.

Michelangelo Architect. Guilio C. Argan & Bruno Contardi. Tr. by Marion L. Grayson from ITA. LC 92-38117. (Illus.). 388p. 1993. 125.00 (*0-8109-3638-0*, Pub. by Abrams) Time Warner.

Michelangelo at San Lorenzo: The Genius As Entrepreneur. William E. Wallace. (Illus.). 284p. (C). 1994. text 80.00 (*0-521-41021-5*) Cambridge U Pr.

***Michelangelo Bramante & Raphael.** Cole. 2000. 35.00 (*0-8133-3787-9*, Pub. by Westview); pap. 25.00 (*0-8133-3788-7*, Pub. by Westview) HarpC.

***Michelangelo Buonarotti.** Richard Tames. LC 00-25785. (Life & Work of... Ser.). 2000. pap. write for info. (*1-57572-343-3*) Heinemann Lib.

Michelangelo Drawings. Ed. by Craig H. Smyth. (Illus.). 1996. 55.00 (*0-300-07514-6*) Yale U Pr.

Michelangelo Painter. Howard Hibbard. 1981. 27.98 (*0-89009-425-X*) Bk Sales Inc.

Michelangelo Pistoletto. Chiara Dafflitto. (Illus.). 200p. 1996. pap. text 39.95 (*88-8158-050-0*, Pub. by Charta) Dist Art Pubs.

***Michelangelo Pistoletto: Anzioni Materiali.** Silvia Eiblmayr. 2000. pap. 30.00 (*3-88375-392-0*) Walther Konig.

Michelangelo Postcard Book. Gilles Neret. 1998. pap. 5.99 (*3-8228-7985-1*) Taschen Amer.

***Michelangelo, the Sistine Chapel.** Stefano Zuffi. (Quadrifolios Ser.). (Illus.). 16p. 2000. 35.00 (*0-8478-2310-5*) Rizzoli Intl.

Michelangelo's Drawings: The Science of Attribution. Alexander Perrig. Tr. by Michael Joyce from GER. (Illus.). 320p. (C). 1991. 65.00 (*0-300-03948-4*) Yale U Pr.

Michelangelo's Last Judgment: The Renaissance Response. Bernadine A. Barnes. LC 97-82. (California Studies in the History of Art Ser.). 160p. 1998. 50.00 (*0-520-20549-9*, Pub. by U CA Pr) Cal Prin Full Svc.

Michelangelo's Medici Chapel: A New Interpretation. Edith Balas. LC 94-78511. (Memoirs Ser.: Vol. 216). (Illus.). 195p. (C). 1995. 40.00 (*0-87169-216-3*, M216-bae) Am Philos.

Michelangelo's Nose: A Myth & Its Maker. Paul Barolsky. LC 90-7506. (Illus.). 190p. 1990. text 35.00 (*0-271-00695-1*) Pa St U Pr.

Michelangelo's Nose: A Myth & Its Maker. Paul Barolsky. (Illus.). 192p. 1997. pap. 19.95 (*0-271-01684-1*) Pa St U Pr.

Michelangelo's Snowman: A Commonplace Collection. Ed. by George Herrick. 150p. 1985. pap. 6.95 (*0-938864-08-4*) Ipswich Pr.

Michelangelo's Surprise. Tony Parillo. LC 97-37244. 32p. (YA). (ps-3). 1998. 16.00 (*0-374-34961-4*) FS&G.

Michele Blondel. Eleanor Heartney. (Illus.). 32p. 1994. pap. 8.00 (*0-929597-06-0*) UMass Univ Gallery.

Michele de Lucchi. Ed. by Alex Buck & Matthias Vogt. (Designer Monographs: No. 1). (Illus.). 160p. 1994. 35.00 (*1-85490-901-0*) Academy Ed UK.

Michele Felice Corne, 1752-1845. Ed. by Philip C. Smith & Nina F. Little. LC 72-83502. 1972. pap. 15.00 (*0-87577-042-8*, PEMP117, Peabody Museum) Peabody Essex Mus.

***Michele Le Doeuff: Operative Philosophy & Imaginary Practice.** Ed. by Max Deutscher. 316p. 2000. 65.95 (*1-57392-863-1*) Prometheus Bks.

Michele Saee: Buildings & Projects. Michele Saee & Frederic Migayrou. LC 97-11861. 1997. pap. 35.00 (*0-8478-2066-1*, Pub. by Rizzoli Intl) St Martin.

Michele, the Nursing Toddler: A Story about Sharing Love. Jane Pinczuk. LC 98-67505. (Illus.). (J). (gr. 1-5). 1998. 14.95 (*0-912500-40-9*, 253) La Leche.

Michelet. Roland Barthes. Tr. by Richard Howard. 1992. pap. 14.95 (*0-520-07826-8*, Pub. by U CA Pr) Cal Prin Full Svc.

Michelet. rev. ed. Roland Barthes. (FRE., Illus.). 187p. 1988. pap. 18.95 (*0-7859-0664-9*, F68560) Fr & Eur.

Michelet, Historia: Rebirth & Romanticism in Nineteenth-Century France. Arthur Mitzman. LC 89-27244. 368p. (C). 1990. 42.50 (*0-300-04551-4*) Yale U Pr.

Michelet, Historian: Rebirth & Romanticism in Nineteenth-Century France. Arthur Mitzman. LC 89-27244. 365p. 1990. reprint ed. pap. 113.20 (*0-608-07838-7*, 205401400010) Bks Demand.

Michelet's Poetic Vision: A Romantic Philosophy of Nature, Man, & Woman. Edward K. Kaplan. LC 76-45050. 256p. 1977. 30.00 (*0-87023-236-3*) U of Mass Pr.

Michelin: The Green Guide to Spain. 3rd ed. 1998. 20.00 (*2-06-152303-X*) Michelin.

***Michelin Alsace, Lorraine, Champagne Green Guide.** Ed. by Michelin Staff. 1999. pap. 19.95 (*0-320-03746-0*) Fr & Eur.

***Michelin Amsterdam Green Guide.** Ed. by Michelin Staff. 1999. pap. 19.95 (*0-320-03760-6*) Fr & Eur.

***Michelin Atlantic Coast Green Guide.** Ed. by Michelin Staff. 1999. pap. 19.95 (*0-320-03765-7*) Fr & Eur.

***Michelin Atlas France.** 8th ed. Michelin Staff. (Illus.). 1999. pap. text 9.00 (*2-06-091528-7*) Michelin.

***Michelin Austria Green Guide.** Ed. by Michelin Staff. 1999. pap. 19.95 (*0-320-03753-3*) Fr & Eur.

***Michelin Auvergne & Rhone Valley Green Guide.** Ed. by Michelin Staff. 1999. pap. 19.95 (*0-320-03764-9*) Fr & Eur.

***Michelin Belgium, Luxembourg Green Guide.** Ed. by Michelin Staff. 1999. pap. 19.95 (*0-320-03758-4*) Fr & Eur.

Michelin Benelux Hotel & Restaurant Guide, 1997. Ed. by Michelin. (ENG, FRE, GER & ITA.). 1997. 26.95 (*0-7859-9386-X*) Fr & Eur.

***Michelin Benelux Hotel & Restaurant Red Guide.** Ed. by Michelin Staff. 2000. 24.95 (*0-320-03725-8*) Fr & Eur.

Michelin Benelux Red Guide, 1995 (Restaurants & Hotels) 1995. pap. 24.00 (*0-7859-9012-7*) Fr & Eur.

***Michelin Brittany Green Guide.** Ed. by Michelin Staff. 1999. pap. 19.95 (*0-320-03762-2*) Fr & Eur.

***Michelin California Green Guide.** Ed. by Michelin Staff. 1999. pap. 19.95 (*0-320-03770-3*) Fr & Eur.

***Michelin Canada Green Guide.** Ed. by Michelin Staff. 1999. pap. 19.95 (*0-320-03771-1*) Fr & Eur.

***Michelin Chateaux de la Loire Green Guide.** Ed. by Michelin Staff. 1999. pap. 19.95 (*0-320-03737-1*) Fr & Eur.

Michelin Deutschland Red Guide, 1995 (Restaurants & Hotels) 1995. pap. 26.00 (*0-7859-9013-5*) Fr & Eur.

***Michelin Dordogne, Berry, Limousin Green Guide.** Ed. by Michelin Staff. 1999. pap. 19.95 (*0-320-03747-9*) Fr & Eur.

***Michelin Espana Green Guide.** Ed. by Michelin Staff. (SPA.). 1999. pap. 19.95 (*0-320-03767-3*) Fr & Eur.

Michelin Espana-Portugal Red Guide, 1995 (Hotels & Restaurants) 1995. 24.00 (*0-7859-9014-3*) Fr & Eur.

Michelin Europe (Main Cities) Red Guide, 1995 (Hotels & Restaurants) 1995. 25.00 (*0-7859-9015-1*) Fr & Eur.

***Michelin Europe Red Guide, Hotels & Restaurants: 2000 Edition.** Illus. by Michelin Staff. 708p. 2000. pap. 25.00 (*0-320-03718-5*) Fr & Eur.

Michelin France. Michelin Staff. (Illus.). 256p. 1995. 40.00 (*0-8212-2219-8*, Pub. by Bulfinch Pr) Little.

Michelin France, Camping Caravaning Guide, 1995. 1995. 15.00 (*0-7859-9017-8*) Fr & Eur.

***Michelin France Green Guide.** Ed. by Michelin Staff. 1999. pap. 19.95 (*0-320-03728-2*) Fr & Eur.

***Michelin France Red Guide, Hotels & Restaurants: 2000 Edition.** Illus. by Michelin Staff. 1488p. 2000. 26.00 (*0-320-03719-3*) Fr & Eur.

Michelin France Red Guide, 1995 (Hotels & Restaurants) 1995. 25.00 (*0-7859-9016-X*) Fr & Eur.

Michelin France Road Atlas. Michelin Staff. 1995. pap., spiral bd. 39.95 (*0-7859-9073-9*) Fr & Eur.

***Michelin French Riviera Green Guide.** Ed. by Michelin Staff. 1999. pap. 19.95 (*0-320-03736-3*) Fr & Eur.

***Michelin Germany Green Guide.** Ed. by Michelin Staff. 1999. pap. 19.95 (*0-320-03740-1*) Fr & Eur.

***Michelin Germany Hotel & Restaurant Red Guide.** Ed. by Michelin Staff. 1248p. 2000. 25.95 (*0-320-03722-3*) Fr & Eur.

***Michelin Great Britain & Ireland Hotel & Restaurant Red Guide.** Ed. by Michelin Staff. 2000. 259.95 (*0-320-03743-6*) Fr & Eur.

Michelin Great Britain & Ireland Red Guide, 1995 (Hotels & Restaurants) 1995. 24.00 (*0-7859-9018-6*) Fr & Eur.

***Michelin Great Britain Green Guide.** Ed. by Michelin Staff. 1999. pap. 19.95 (*0-320-03752-5*) Fr & Eur.

***Michelin Great Britain Hotel & Restaurant Red Guide.** Ed. by Michelin Staff. 2000. 25.95 (*0-320-03726-6*) Fr & Eur.

***Michelin Greece Green Guide.** Ed. by Michelin Staff. 1999. pap. 19.95 (*0-320-03756-8*) Fr & Eur.

Michelin Green - Portugal. 2nd ed. Michelin Travel. 1998. 20.00 (*2-06-156102-0*, 857079Q) Michelin.

Michelin Green Atlantic Coast, France Green Guide. Michelin Staff. 1995. 18.95 (*0-7859-9102-6*) Fr & Eur.

***Michelin Green Bourgogne.** 5th ed. Ed. by Michelin Travel Publication Staff. (Illus.). 2000. pap. 18.00 (*2-06-030705-8*) Michelin.

***Michelin Green Corse.** 4th ed. Ed. by Michelin Travel Publication Staff. (Illus.). 2000. pap. 20.00 (*2-06-319048-8*) Michelin.

Michelin Green-Dordogne: France (Regional Guides) Michelin Staff. (Green Guides for All Ser.). 1998. 20.00 (*2-06-132501-7*) Michelin.

Michelin Green Guide - Alpes du Nord. Michelin Staff. (FRE.). 14.95 (*0-8288-6171-4*) Fr & Eur.

Michelin Green Guide - Alpes du Sud. Michelin Staff. (FRE.). 14.95 (*0-8288-6172-2*) Fr & Eur.

Michelin Green Guide - Alsace et Lorraine (Vosges) Michelin Staff. (FRE.). 14.95 (*0-8288-6173-0*) Fr & Eur.

Michelin Green Guide - Austria. Michelin Staff. 14.95 (*0-8288-6117-X*) Fr & Eur.

Michelin Green Guide - Auvergne. Michelin Staff. (FRE.). 14.95 (*0-8288-6174-9*) Fr & Eur.

Michelin Green Guide - Belgium - Luxemburg. Michelin Staff. (FRE.). 14.95 (*0-8288-6142-0*) Fr & Eur.

Michelin Green Guide - Berry-Limousin. Michelin Staff. (FRE.). 14.95 (*0-8288-6176-5*) Fr & Eur.

Michelin Green Guide - Bourgogne. Michelin Staff. (FRE.). 14.95 (*0-8288-6175-7*) Fr & Eur.

Michelin Green Guide - Bretagne. Michelin Staff. (FRE.). 14.95 (*0-8288-6177-3*) Fr & Eur.

Michelin Green Guide - Brittany. Michelin Staff. 14.95 (*0-8288-6133-1*) Fr & Eur.

Michelin Green Guide - Burgundy. Michelin Staff. 14.95 (*0-8288-6134-X*) Fr & Eur.

Michelin Green Guide - Canada. Michelin Staff. 14.95 (*0-8288-6103-X*); 14.95 (*0-8288-6143-9*) Fr & Eur.

Michelin Green Guide - Champagne-Ardennes. Michelin Staff. (FRE.). 14.95 (*0-8288-6178-1*) Fr & Eur.

Michelin Green Guide - Chateaux de la Loire. Michelin Staff. (FRE.). 14.95 (*0-8288-6179-X*) Fr & Eur.

Michelin Green Guide - Chateaux of the Loire. Michelin Staff. 14.95 (*0-8288-6135-8*) Fr & Eur.

Michelin Green Guide - Corse. Michelin Staff. (FRE.). 14.95 (*0-8288-6180-3*) Fr & Eur.

Michelin Green Guide - Cote d'Azur. Michelin Staff. (FRE.). 14.95 (*0-8288-6181-1*) Fr & Eur.

Michelin Green Guide - Dordogne. Michelin Staff. 14.95 (*0-8288-6136-6*) Fr & Eur.

Michelin Green Guide - England - West Country. Michelin Staff. 14.95 (*0-8288-6118-8*) Fr & Eur.

Michelin Green Guide - Espana. Michelin Staff. (SPA.). 14.95 (*0-8288-6194-3*) Fr & Eur.

Michelin Green Guide - Flandres - Artois - Picardie. Michelin Staff. (FRE.). 14.95 (*0-8288-6182-X*) Fr & Eur.

Michelin Green Guide - France. Michelin Staff. 14.95 (*0-8288-6119-6*); 14.95 (*0-8288-6144-7*) Fr & Eur.

Michelin Green Guide - French Riviera. Michelin Staff. 14.95 (*0-8288-6137-4*) Fr & Eur.

Michelin Green Guide - Germany. Michelin Staff. 14.95 (*0-8288-6120-X*) Fr & Eur.

Michelin Green Guide - Gorges du Tarn. Michelin Staff. (FRE.). 14.95 (*0-8288-6183-8*) Fr & Eur.

Michelin Green Guide - Holland. Michelin Staff. (FRE.). 14.95 (*0-8288-6145-5*) Fr & Eur.

Michelin Green Guide - Ile de France. Michelin Staff. 14.95 (*0-8288-6138-2*); 14.95 (*0-8288-6184-6*) Fr & Eur.

Michelin Green Guide - Jura - Franche Comte. Michelin Staff. (FRE.). 14.95 (*0-8288-6185-4*) Fr & Eur.

Michelin Green Guide - London. Michelin Staff. 14.95 (*0-8288-6130-7*) Fr & Eur.

Michelin Green Guide - Mexico. Michelin Staff. 14.95 (*0-8288-6114-5*); 14.95 (*0-8288-6195-1*) Fr & Eur.

Michelin Green Guide - New England. Michelin Staff. 14.95 (*0-8288-6101-3*); 14.95 (*0-8288-6147-1*) Fr & Eur.

Michelin Green Guide - New York. Michelin Staff. (FRE.). 14.95 (*0-8288-6149-8*) Fr & Eur.

Michelin Green Guide - New York City. Michelin Staff. 14.95 (*0-8288-6113-7*) Fr & Eur.

Michelin Green Guide - Normandie Cotentin. Michelin Staff. (FRE.). 14.95 (*0-8288-6186-2*) Fr & Eur.

Michelin Green Guide - Normandie Vallee Seine. Michelin Staff. (FRE.). 14.95 (*0-8288-6187-0*) Fr & Eur.

Michelin Green Guide - Normandy Cotentin. Michelin Staff. 14.95 (*0-8288-6139-0*) Fr & Eur.

Michelin Green Guide - Normandy Seine Valley. Michelin Staff. 14.95 (*0-8288-6140-4*) Fr & Eur.

Michelin Green Guide - Paris. Michelin Staff. (FRE.). 14.95 (*0-8288-6170-6*) Fr & Eur.

Michelin Green Guide - Perigord-Ouercy. Michelin Staff. (FRE.). 14.95 (*0-8288-6188-9*) Fr & Eur.

Michelin Green Guide - Poitou-Vendee-Charente. Michelin Staff. (FRE.). 14.95 (*0-8288-6189-7*) Fr & Eur.

Michelin Green Guide - Portugal. Michelin Staff. (SPA.). 14.95 (*0-8288-6196-X*) Fr & Eur.

Michelin Green Guide - Provence. Michelin Staff. 14.95 (*0-8288-6141-2*); 14.95 (*0-8288-6190-0*) Fr & Eur.

Michelin Green Guide - Pyrenees-Aquitaine. Michelin Staff. (FRE.). 14.95 (*0-8288-6191-9*) Fr & Eur.

Michelin Green Guide - Pyrenees-Roussillon. Michelin Staff. (FRE.). 14.95 (*0-8288-6192-7*) Fr & Eur.

Michelin Green Guide - Quebec Province. Michelin Staff. 14.95 (*0-8288-6115-3*); 14.95 (*0-8288-6148-X*) Fr & Eur.

Michelin Green Guide - Scotland. Michelin Staff. 14.95 (*0-8288-6127-7*) Fr & Eur.

Michelin Green Guide - Vallee du Rhone. Michelin Staff. (FRE.). 14.95 (*0-8288-6193-5*) Fr & Eur.

Michelin Green Guide - Washington D. C. Michelin Staff. 14.95 (*0-8288-6116-1*) Fr & Eur.

Michelin Green Guide Belgium. Michelin Staff. 1994. pap. 19.95 (*0-7859-9106-9*) Fr & Eur.

Michelin Green Guide Brittany. Michelin Staff. 1995. pap. 18.95 (*0-7859-9074-7*) Fr & Eur.

Michelin Green Guide Canada. 7th ed. Michelin Staff. 1999. pap. text 20.00 (*2-06-151707-2*) Michelin.

Michelin Green Guide Chateaux of the Loire. Michelin Staff. 1994. pap. 18.95 (*0-7859-9107-7*) Fr & Eur.

Michelin Green Guide Dordogne. Michelin Staff. 1994. pap. 18.95 (*0-7859-9111-5*) Fr & Eur.

Michelin Green Guide France. Michelin Staff. 1994. pap. 19.95 (*0-7859-9108-5*); pap. 19.95 (*0-7859-9109-3*) Fr & Eur.

***Michelin Green Guide Languedoc Roussillon Tarn Gorges.** 2nd ed. Ed. by Michelin Travel Publication Staff. (Illus.). 1998. pap. 20.00 (*2-06-136602-3*) Michelin.

***Michelin Green Guide Le Quebec.** 3rd ed. Michelin Travel Publication Staff. 1999. pap. text 20.00 (*2-06-057203-7*) Michelin.

Michelin Green Guide Netherlands. Michelin Staff. 1994. pap. 19.95 (*0-7859-9110-7*) Fr & Eur.

Michelin Green Guide Normandy. Michelin Staff. 1994. pap. 18.95 (*0-7859-9112-3*) Fr & Eur.

Michelin Green Guide Portugal. Michelin Staff. 1995. 19.95 (*0-7859-9093-3*) Fr & Eur.

Michelin Green Guide Pyrenees Roussillon. Michelin Staff. 1994. pap. 18.95 (*0-7859-9113-1*) Fr & Eur.

Michelin Green Guide Quebec. 3rd ed. Travel Publications Michelin Staff. 1999. pap. 20.00 (*2-06-157303-7*) Michelin.

***Michelin Green Guide to Andalucia.** Ed. by Michelin Travel Publication Staff. (Illus.). 2000. 20.00 (*2-06-458301-7*) Michelin.

***Michelin Green Guide to Bruselas.** Ed. by Michelin Travel Publication Staff. (Illus.). 2000. 18.00 (*2-06-451301-9*) Michelin.

***Michelin Green Guide to Budapest et la Hongrie.** Ed. by Michelin Travel Publication Staff. (Illus.). 2000. 20.00 (*2-06-054201-4*) Michelin.

***Michelin Green Guide to Costa Azul.** Michelin Travel Publication Staff. 2000. 20.00 (*2-06-432001-6*) Michelin.

***Michelin Green Guide to Escocia.** Ed. by Michelin Travel Publication Staff. (Illus.). 2000. 20.00 (*2-06-457501-4*) Michelin.

***Michelin Green Guide to Estados Unidos Este.** Ed. by Michelin Travel Publication Staff. (Illus.). 2000. 20.00 (*2-06-455701-6*) Michelin.

***Michelin Green Guide to Estados Unidos Oeste.** Michelin Travel Publication Staff. (Illus.). 2000. 20.00 (*2-06-455901-9*) Michelin.

***Michelin Green Guide to Florencia y la Toscana.** Ed. by Michelin Travel Publication Staff. (Illus.). 2000. 20.00 (*2-06-459701-8*) Michelin.

***Michelin Green Guide to Gran Bretana.** Ed. by Michelin Travel Publication Staff. (Illus.). 2000. 20.00 (*2-06-450501-6*) Michelin.

***Michelin Green Guide to Hungary/Budapest.** Ed. by Michelin Travel Publication Staff. (Illus.). 2000. 20.00 (*2-06-154201-8*) Michelin.

Michelin Green Guide To London. 2nd ed. Michelin Staff. (Illus.). 1997. per. 18.00 (*2-06-159002-0*, 1590) Michelin.

***Michelin Green Guide to Nueva York.** Michelin Travel Publication Staff. (Michelin Green Guide Ser.). (Illus.). 2000. 20.00 (*2-06-000058-0*) Michelin.

***Michelin Green Guide to Pacific Northwest.** Ed. by Michelin Travel Publication Staff. (Illus.). 2000. 20.00 (*2-06-158401-2*) Michelin.

***Michelin Green Guide to Praga.** Ed. by Michelin Travel Publication Staff. (Illus.). 2000. 18.00 (*2-06-456501-9*) Michelin.

***Michelin Green Guide to Prague.** Ed. by Michelin Travel Publication Staff. (Illus.). 2000. 18.00 (*2-06-056501-4*); 18.00 (*2-06-156501-8*) Michelin.

***Michelin Green Guide to U. S. A.** Ed. by Michelin Travel Publication Staff. (Illus.). 2000. 20.00 (*2-06-055701-1*) Michelin.

***Michelin Green Guide to U. S. A. East.** Ed. by Michelin Travel Publication Staff. (Illus.). 2000. 20.00 (*2-06-155701-5*) Michelin.

***Michelin Green Guide to U. S. A. Ouest.** Ed. by Michelin Travel Publication Staff. (Illus.). 2000. 20.00 (*2-06-055901-4*) Michelin.

***Michelin Green Guide to U. S. A. West.** Ed. by Michelin Travel Publication Staff. (Illus.). 2000. 20.00 (*2-06-155901-8*) Michelin.

***Michelin Green Guide to Venicia.** Ed. by Michelin Travel Publication Staff. (Illus.). 2000. 18.00 (*2-06-458701-2*) Michelin.

Michelin Green Guide to Washington D. C., Vol. 1. Michelin Staff. 1999. pap. 18.00 (*2-06-157704-0*) Michelin.

Michelin Green Guide Washington D. C. 2nd ed. Michelin Staff. 1964. pap. 18.95 (*0-7859-9114-X*) Fr & Eur.

Michelin Green Guides - Great Britain. Michelin Staff. 14.95 (*0-8288-6121-8*) Fr & Eur.

Michelin Green Guides - Greece. Michelin Staff. 14.95 (*0-8288-6122-6*) Fr & Eur.

Michelin Green Guides - Ireland. Michelin Staff. 14.95 (*0-8288-6123-4*) Fr & Eur.

Michelin Green Guides - Italy. Michelin Staff. 14.95 (*0-685-66129-6*) Fr & Eur.

Michelin Green Guides - Netherlands. Michelin Staff. 14.95 (*0-8288-6125-0*) Fr & Eur.

Michelin Green Guides - Paris. Michelin Staff. 14.95 (*0-8288-6131-5*) Fr & Eur.

Michelin Green Guides - Portugal. Michelin Staff. 14.95 (*0-8288-6126-9*) Fr & Eur.

Michelin Green Guides - Rome. Michelin Staff. 14.95 (*0-8288-6132-3*) Fr & Eur.

Michelin Green Guides - Spain. Michelin Staff. 14.95 (*0-8288-6128-5*) Fr & Eur.

Michelin Green Guides - Switzerland. Michelin Staff. 14.95 (*0-8288-6129-3*) Fr & Eur.

***Michelin Green-Jura Franche Comte: France (Guides Regionaux)** 4th ed. (FRE.). 1998. pap. text 20.00 (*2-06-034004-7*) Michelin.

***Michelin Green Normandie Vallee de Seine Gg.** 4th ed. Ed. by Michelin Travel Publication Staff. (FRE., Illus.). 2000. pap. 20.00 (*2-06-034704-1*) Michelin.

Michelin Green Paris. 2nd ed. Michelin Staff. (Michelin Green Guides (foreign Language) Ser.). 1998. pap. text 18.00 (*2-06-435902-8*) Michelin.

***Michelin Green Paris.** 5th ed. Ed. by Michelin Travel Publication Staff. (FRE., Illus.). 2000. pap. 18.00 (*2-06-035205-3*) Michelin.

Michelin Green Travel Guide: Chateaux of the Loire. (ENG & FRE.). 14.95 (*0-685-11374-4*) Fr & Eur.

Michelin Green Travel Guide: Environs De Paris. (FRE.). 14.95 (*0-685-11376-0*) Fr & Eur.

Michelin Green Travel Guide: French Riviera. (ENG & FRE.). 14.95 (*0-685-11377-9*) Fr & Eur.

Michelin Green Travel Guide: Germany. (ENG & FRE.). 14.95 (*0-685-11392-2*) Fr & Eur.

Michelin Green Travel Guide: Gorges Du Tarn. (FRE.). 14.95 (*0-685-11378-7*) Fr & Eur.

Michelin Green Travel Guide: Italy. (ENG & FRE., Illus.). 14.95 (*0-685-11379-5*) Fr & Eur.

Michelin Green Travel Guide: Jura. (FRE.). 14.95 (*0-685-11380-9*) Fr & Eur.

Michelin Green Travel Guide: New York City. (ENG & FRE., Illus.). 1992. 18.95 (*0-685-11385-X*) Fr & Eur.

Michelin Green Travel Guide: Normandy. (ENG & FRE.). 14.95 (*0-685-11381-7*) Fr & Eur.

Michelin Green Travel Guide: Paris. (ENG.). 14.95 (*0-685-11382-5*) Fr & Eur.

Michelin Green Travel Guide: Portugal. annuals (ENG & FRE., Illus.). 14.95 (*0-685-11408-2*) Fr & Eur.

Michelin Green Travel Guide: Provence. 14.95 (*0-685-11383-3*) Fr & Eur.

Michelin Green Travel Guide: Switzerland. (ENG & FRE., Illus.). 14.95 (*0-685-11384-1*) Fr & Eur.

Michelin Green Travel Guide: Vosges. 14.95 (*0-685-11386-8*) Fr & Eur.

***Michelin Green Vallee du Rhone.** 4th ed. Ed. by Michelin Travel Publication Staff. (FRE., Illus.). 2000. pap. 20.00 (*2-06-037304-2*) Michelin.

Michelin Guide No. 301: Alpes du Nord. Michelin Staff. (Green Guides Ser.). (FRE.). 1988. pap. 16.95 (*0-7859-0217-1*, 2067003011) Fr & Eur.

Michelin Guide No. 302: Alpes du Sud. Michelin Staff. (Green Guides Ser.). (FRE.). 1988. pap. 16.95 (*0-7859-0218-X*, 2060030218) Fr & Eur.

Michelin Guide No. 304: Auvergne. Michelin Staff. (Green Guides Ser.). (FRE.). 1992. pap. 18.95 (*0-7859-0219-8*, 2067003046) Fr & Eur.

Michelin Guide No. 305: Berry-Limousin. Michelin Staff. (Green Guides Ser.). (FRE.). 1990. pap. 16.95 (*0-7859-0220-1*, 2067003054) Fr & Eur.

Michelin Guide No. 307: Bourgogne. Michelin Staff. (Green Guides Ser.). (FRE.). 1988. pap. 16.95 (*0-7859-0221-X*, 2067003070) Fr & Eur.

Michelin Guide No. 308: Burgundy. Michelin Staff. (Green Guides Ser.). 1992. pap. 19.95 (*0-7859-0222-8*, 2067013084) Fr & Eur.

Michelin Guide No. 309: Bretagne. Michelin Staff. (Green Guides Ser.). (FRE.). 1986. pap. 16.95 (*0-7859-0223-6*, 2060030943) Fr & Eur.

Michelin Guide No. 314: Brittanny. Michelin Staff. (Green Guides Ser.). 1992. pap. 18.95 (*0-7859-0224-4*, 2067013149) Fr & Eur.

Michelin Guide No. 316: Champagne-Ardennes. Michelin Staff. (Green Guides Ser.). (FRE.). 1992. pap. 19.95 (*0-7859-0225-2*, 2060031621) Fr & Eur.

Michelin Guide No. 317: Chateaux de la Loire. Michelin Staff. (Green Guides Ser.). (FRE.). 1990. pap. 16.95 (*0-7859-0226-0*, 2067003178) Fr & Eur.

Michelin Guide No. 319: Corse. Michelin Staff. (Green Guides Ser.). (FRE.). 1989. pap. 16.95 (*0-7859-0227-9*, 2060031915) Fr & Eur.

Michelin Guide No. 320: Cote d'Azur. Michelin Staff. (Green Guides Ser.). (FRE.). 1987. pap. 16.95 (*0-7859-0228-7*, 2060032016) Fr & Eur.

Michelin Guide No. 322: Chateaux of the Loire. Michelin Staff. (Green Guides Ser.). 1989. pap. 14.95 (*0-7859-0229-5*, 206701322X) Fr & Eur.

Michelin Guide No. 323: Dordogne - Description & Travel. Michelin Staff. (Green Guides Ser.). 1992. pap. 18.95 (*0-7859-0230-9*, 2067013238) Fr & Eur.

Michelin Guide No. 326: Ile de France - Descripton & Travel. Michelin Staff. (Green Guides Ser.). (FRE.). 1992. pap. 18.95 (*0-7859-0231-7*, 206003261X) Fr & Eur.

Michelin Guide No. 335: French Riviera. Michelin Staff. (Green Guides Ser.). 1988. pap. 14.95 (*0-7859-0232-5*, 2067013351) Fr & Eur.

Michelin Guide No. 337: Gorges du Tarn. Michelin Staff. (Green Guides Ser.). (FRE.). 1989. pap. 16.95 (*0-7859-0233-3*, 2060033721) Fr & Eur.

Michelin Guide No. 338: Flandres-Artois-Picardie. Michelin Staff. (Green Guides Ser.). (FRE.). 1988. pap. 16.95 (*0-7859-0234-1*, 2067003380) Fr & Eur.

Michelin Guide No. 340: Jura-Franche Comte. Michelin Staff. (Green Guides Ser.). (FRE.). 1992. pap. 18.95 (*0-7859-0235-X*, 2060034019) Fr & Eur.

Michelin Guide No. 341: Ile de France. Michelin Staff. (Green Guides Ser.). 1990. pap. 14.95 (*0-7859-0236-8*, 2060134110) Fr & Eur.

Michelin Guide No. 346: Normandie Cotentin. Michelin Staff. (Green Guides Ser.). (FRE.). 1988. pap. 16.95 (*0-7859-0237-6*, 2060034612) Fr & Eur.

Michelin Guide No. 347: Normandie Vallee de la Seine. Michelin Staff. (Green Guides Ser.). (FRE.). 1988. pap. 16.95 (*0-7859-0238-4*, 206003471X) Fr & Eur.

Michelin Guide No. 349: Normandy Cotentin. Michelin Staff. (Green Guides Ser.). 1989. pap. 14.95 (*0-7859-0239-2*, 2060134919) Fr & Eur.

Michelin Guide No. 350: Normandy Seine Valley. Michelin Staff. (Green Guides Ser.). 1989. pap. 14.95 (*0-7859-0240-6*, 206013501X) Fr & Eur.

Michelin Guide No. 352: Paris. Michelin Staff. (Green Guides Ser.). (FRE.). 1989. pap. 16.95 (*0-7859-0241-4*, 2067003526) Fr & Eur.

Michelin Guide No. 355: Paris. Michelin Staff. (Green Guides Ser.). 1990. pap. 14.95 (*0-7859-0242-2*, 2060135516) Fr & Eur.

Michelin Guide No. 362: Provence. Michelin Staff. (Green Guides Ser.). (FRE.). 1988. pap. 16.95 (*0-7859-0243-0*, 2060036216) Fr & Eur.

Michelin Guide No. 367: Pyrenees-Aquitaine. Michelin Staff. (Green Guides Ser.). (FRE.). 1989. pap. 16.95 (*0-7859-0244-9*, 2060036720) Fr & Eur.

Michelin Guide No. 368: Pyrenees-Roussillon. Michelin Staff. (Green Guides Ser.). (FRE.). 1989. pap. 16.95 (*0-7859-0245-7*, 2067003682) Fr & Eur.

Michelin Guide No. 370: Perigord-Quercy. Michelin Staff. (Green Guides Ser.). (FRE.). 1990. pap. 18.95 (*0-7859-0246-5*, 2067003704) Fr & Eur.

Michelin Guide No. 371: Poitou-Vendee-Charente. Michelin Staff. (Green Guides Ser.). (FRE.). 1990. pap. 16.95 (*0-7859-0247-3*, 2067003712) Fr & Eur.

Michelin Guide No. 372: Alsace et Lorraine, Vosges. Michelin Staff. (Green Guides Ser.). (FRE.). 1989. pap. 16.95 (*0-7859-0248-1*, 2060037247) Fr & Eur.

Michelin Guide No. 373: Vallee du Rhone. Michelin Staff. (Green Guides Ser.). (FRE.). 1989. pap. 16.95 (*0-7859-0249-X*, 2067003739) Fr & Eur.

Michelin Guide No. 375: Provence. Michelin Staff. (Green Guides Ser.). 1989. pap. 14.95 (*0-7859-0250-3*, 2067013750) Fr & Eur.

Michelin Guide No. 390: France. Michelin Staff. (Green Guides Ser.). (FRE.). 1989. pap. 16.95 (*0-7859-0251-1*, 2060039010) Fr & Eur.

Michelin Guide No. 481: Euro-Disney. Michelin Staff. (Green Guides Ser.). 1992. pap. 18.95 (*0-7859-0276-7*, 2067014811) Fr & Eur.

Michelin Guide No. 491: France. Michelin Staff. (Green Guides Ser.). 1992. pap. 19.95 (*0-7859-0277-5*, 2067014919) Fr & Eur.

Michelin Guide No. 503: Germany. Michelin Staff. (Green Guides Ser.). 1987. pap. 16.95 (*0-7859-0278-3*, 2060150337) Fr & Eur.

Michelin Guide No. 507: Austria. Michelin Staff. (Green Guides Ser.). 1992. pap. 19.95 (*0-7859-0279-1*, 2067015079) Fr & Eur.

Michelin Guide No. 510: Belgique-Luxembourg, French Edition. Michelin Staff. (Green Guides Ser.). (FRE.). 1992. pap. 19.95 (*0-7859-0280-5*, 2060051044) Fr & Eur.

Michelin Guide No. 517: Canada. Michelin Staff. (Green Guides Ser.). 1990. pap. 16.95 (*0-7859-0282-1*, 2060151732) Fr & Eur.

Michelin Guide No. 520: Greece. Michelin Staff. (Green Guides Ser.). 1992. pap. 19.95 (*0-7859-0283-X*, 2067015206) Fr & Eur.

Michelin Guide No. 521: Spain. Michelin Staff. (Green Guides Ser.). 1987. pap. 16.95 (*0-7859-0284-8*, 2060152135) Fr & Eur.

Michelin Guide No. 534: Italy. Michelin Staff. (Green Guides Ser.). 1989. pap. 16.95 (*0-7859-0286-4*, 2067015346) Fr & Eur.

Michelin Guide No. 535: Ireland. Michelin Staff. (Green Guides Ser.). 1992. pap. 19.95 (*0-7859-0287-2*, 2067015354) Fr & Eur.

Michelin Guide No. 541: Great Britain. Michelin Staff. (Green Guides Ser.). 1992. pap. 19.95 (*0-7859-0288-0*, 2067015419) Fr & Eur.

Michelin Guide No. 543: London. Michelin Staff. (Green Guides Ser.). 1990. pap. 14.95 (*0-7859-0289-9*, 2060154359) Fr & Eur.

Michelin Guide No. 545: Maroc. Michelin Staff. (Green Guides Ser.). (FRE.). 1988. pap. 16.95 (*0-7859-0290-2*, 2060054532) Fr & Eur.

Michelin Guide No. 548: New York. Michelin Staff. (Green Guides Ser.). (FRE.). 1989. pap. 16.95 (*0-7859-0291-0*, 2067005480) Fr & Eur.

An Asterisk (*) at the beginning of an entry indicates that the title is appearing for the first time.

Michelin Guide No. 551: New York City. Michelin Staff. (Green Guides Ser.). 1992. pap. 19.95 (*0-7859-0292-9*) Fr & Eur.

Michelin Guide No. 553: Hollande. Michelin Staff. (Green Guides Ser.). (FRE.). 1992. pap. 19.95 (*0-7859-0293-7*, 2060055342) Fr & Eur.

Michelin Guide No. 555: Netherlands. Michelin Staff. (Green Guides Ser.). 1990. pap. 19.95 (*0-7859-0294-5*, 2060155517) Fr & Eur.

Michelin Guide No. 557: Portugal. Michelin Staff. (Green Guides Ser.). 1989. pap. 16.95 (*0-7859-0295-3*, 2060155738) Fr & Eur.

Michelin Guide No. 559: Rome. Michelin Staff. (Green Guides Ser.). 1985. pap. 14.95 (*0-7859-0296-1*, 2067015591) Fr & Eur.

Michelin Guide No. 562: England-The West Country. Michelin Staff. (Green Guides Ser.). 1990. pap. 14.95 (*0-7859-0297-X*, 206015622X) Fr & Eur.

Michelin Guide No. 563: Switzerland. Michelin Staff. (Green Guides Ser.). 1988. pap. 16.95 (*0-7859-0298-8*, 206701563X) Fr & Eur.

Michelin Guide No. 565: Portugal. Michelin Staff. (Green Guides Ser.). (SPA.). 1988. pap. 19.95 (*0-7859-0299-6*, 2067045652) Fr & Eur.

Michelin Guide No. 568: Nouvelle Angleterre. Michelin Staff. (Green Guides Ser.). (FRE.). 1988. pap. 16.95 (*0-7859-0300-3*, 2060056829) Fr & Eur.

Michelin Guide No. 569: New England. Michelin Staff. (Green Guides Ser.). 1988. pap. 14.95 (*0-7859-0301-1*, 2067015699) Fr & Eur.

Michelin Guide No. 572: Province de Quebec. Michelin Staff. (Green Guides Ser.). (FRE.). 1992. pap. 19.95 (*0-7859-0302-X*, 2980083348) Fr & Eur.

Michelin Guide No. 573: Quebec Province. Michelin Staff. (Green Guides Ser.). 1992. pap. 19.95 (*0-7859-0303-8*, 2980083356) Fr & Eur.

Michelin Guide No. 575: Scotland. Michelin Staff. (Green Guides Ser.). 1990. pap. 16.95 (*0-7859-0304-6*, 2060157528) Fr & Eur.

Michelin Guide No. 577: Washington, D. C. Michelin Staff. (Green Guides Ser.). 1988. pap. 14.95 (*0-7859-0305-4*, 206701577X) Fr & Eur.

Michelin Guide No. 579: Mexico. Michelin Staff. (Green Guides Ser.). 1990. pap. 19.95 (*0-7859-0306-2*, 2060157919) Fr & Eur.

Michelin Guide No. 580: Mexico. Michelin Staff. (Green Guides Ser.). (SPA.). 1988. pap. 19.95 (*0-7859-0307-0*, 2060458013) Fr & Eur.

Michelin Guide No. 603: Benelux. Michelin Staff. (Red Guides Ser.). 1993. 23.95 (*0-7859-0310-0*, 2060060397) Fr & Eur.

Michelin Guide No. 613: Camping, France. Michelin Staff. (Green Guides Ser.). 1993. pap. 17.95 (*0-7859-0311-9*, 2060061393) Fr & Eur.

Michelin Guide No. 623: Deutschland. Michelin Staff. (Red Guides). 1993. 25.95 (*0-7859-0312-7*, 206006239X) Fr & Eur.

Michelin Guide No. 633: Espana-Portugal. Michelin Staff. (Red Guides). 1993. 23.95 (*0-7859-0313-5*, 2060063396) Fr & Eur.

Michelin Guide No. 643: France. Michelin Staff. (Red Guides). 1993. 24.95 (*0-7859-0314-3*, 2060064392) Fr & Eur.

Michelin Guide No. 653: Great Britain & Ireland. Michelin Staff. (Red Guides). 1993. 23.95 (*0-7859-0315-1*, 5060065399) Fr & Eur.

Michelin Guide No. 663: Greater London. Michelin Staff. (Red Guides). 1993. pap. 12.95 (*0-7859-0316-X*, 2060066395) Fr & Eur.

Michelin Guide No. 673: Italia. Michelin Staff. (Red Guides). 1993. 23.95 (*0-7859-0317-8*, 2060067391) Fr & Eur.

Michelin Guide No. 683: Paris & Environs. Michelin Staff. (Red Guides). 1993. pap. 12.95 (*0-7859-0318-6*, 2060068398) Fr & Eur.

Michelin Guide No. 703: Europe, Main Cities. Michelin Staff. (Red Guides). 1993. 24.95 (*0-685-63826-X*, 2030070392) Fr & Eur.

Michelin Guide No. 713: Ireland. Michelin Staff. (Red Guides). 1993. pap. 12.95 (*0-7859-0320-8*, 2060071399) Fr & Eur.

Michelin Hotel & Restaurant Guide to Benelux, 1997. Ed. by Michelin. 1997. 24.95 (*0-7859-9460-2*) Fr & Eur.

Michelin Hotel & Restaurant Guide to Germany, 1997. Ed. by Michelin. 1997. 25.95 (*0-7859-9461-0*) Fr & Eur.

***Michelin Ireland Green Guide.** Ed. by Michelin Staff. 1999. pap. 19.95 (*0-320-03749-5*) Fr & Eur.

Michelin Ireland Red Guide, 1995 (Hotels & Restaurants) 1995. 10.00 (*0-7859-9019-4*) Fr & Eur.

Michelin Italia Red Guide, 1995 (Hotels & Restaurants) 1995. 24.00 (*0-7859-9020-8*) Fr & Eur.

***Michelin Italy Green Guide.** Ed. by Michelin Staff. 1999. pap. 19.95 (*0-320-03729-0*) Fr & Eur.

***Michelin Italy Red Guide, Hotels & Restaurants: 2000 Edition.** Illus. by Michelin Staff. 924p. 1999. 26.00 (*0-320-03721-5*) Fr & Eur.

***Michelin London.** Michelin Travel Publications Staff. (Illus.). 2000. 12.95 (*2-06-002034-4*) Michelin.

***Michelin London Green Guide.** Ed. by Michelin Staff. 1999. pap. 19.95 (*0-320-03739-8*) Fr & Eur.

***Michelin London Hotel & Restaurant Red Guide.** Ed. by Michelin Staff. 2000. 11.95 (*0-320-03724-X*) Fr & Eur.

Michelin London Red Guide, 1995 (Hotels & Restaurants) 1995. 10.00 (*0-7859-9023-2*) Fr & Eur.

Michelin Map No. 11: Paris Atlas. Michelin Staff. (Main Roads Maps with Useful Addresses Ser.). 1988. pap. 14.95 (*0-7859-0130-2*, 206700011X) Fr & Eur.

Michelin Map No. 14: Paris Atlas with Metro & Regional Connections. Michelin Staff. (Main Roads Maps Ser.). 1992. pap. 14.95 (*0-7859-0132-9*, 2067000144) Fr & Eur.

Michelin Map No. 15: Paris by Arrondissements. Michelin Staff. (Main Roads Maps Ser.). 1992. pap. 19.95 (*0-7859-0133-7*, 2067000152) Fr & Eur.

Michelin Map No. 30: Lyon. Michelin Staff. (Specialized Maps Ser.). 1992. pap. 9.95 (*0-7859-0134-5*, 2067000306) Fr & Eur.

Michelin Map No. 31: Lyon with Index. Michelin Staff. (Specialized Maps Ser.). 1992. pap. 9.95 (*0-7859-0135-3*, 2067000314) Fr & Eur.

Michelin Map No. 40: Barcelona. Michelin Staff. (Main Roads Maps Ser.). 1992. pap. 9.95 (*0-7859-0136-1*, 2067040405) Fr & Eur.

Michelin Map No. 41: Barcelona with Index. Michelin Staff. (Main Roads Maps Ser.). 1992. pap. 9.95 (*0-7859-0137-X*, 2067040413) Fr & Eur.

Michelin Map No. 51: Calais - Lille - Bruxelles. Michelin Staff. (Road Maps with Tourist Index Ser.). 1992. pap. 7.95 (*0-7859-0138-8*, 2067000519) Fr & Eur.

Michelin Map No. 52: Le Havre - Dieppe - Amiens. Michelin Staff. (Road Maps with Tourist Index Ser.). 1992. pap. 7.95 (*0-7859-0139-6*, 2067000527) Fr & Eur.

Michelin Map No. 53: Arras - Char. - Mex. - St. Quentin. Michelin Staff. (Road Maps with Tourist Index Ser.). 1992. pap. 7.95 (*0-7859-0140-X*, 2067000535) Fr & Eur.

Michelin Map No. 54: Cherbourg - Caen - Rouen. Michelin Staff. (Road Maps with Tourist Index Ser.). 1992. pap. 7.95 (*0-7859-0141-8*, 2067000543) Fr & Eur.

Michelin Map No. 55: Caen - Rouen - Paris. Michelin Staff. (Road Maps with Tourist Index Ser.). 1992. pap. 7.95 (*0-7859-0142-6*, 2067000551) Fr & Eur.

Michelin Map No. 56: Paris - Rheims - Chalons-sur-Marne. Michelin Staff. (Road Maps with Tourist Index Ser.). 1992. pap. 7.95 (*0-7859-0143-4*, 206700056X) Fr & Eur.

Michelin Map No. 57: Verdun - Metz - Wissembourg. Michelin Staff. (Road Maps with Tourist Index Ser.). 1992. pap. 7.95 (*0-7859-0144-2*, 2067000578) Fr & Eur.

Michelin Map No. 58: St. Brieuc - St. Malo - Rennes. Michelin Staff. 1992. pap. 7.95 (*0-7859-0145-0*, 2067000586) Fr & Eur.

Michelin Map No. 59: Brest - Quimper - St. Brieuc. Michelin Staff. (Road Maps with Tourist Index Ser.). 1992. pap. 7.95 (*0-7859-0146-9*, 2067000594) Fr & Eur.

Michelin Map No. 60: Le Mans - Chartres - Paris. Michelin Staff. 1992. pap. 7.95 (*0-7859-0147-7*, 2067000608) Fr & Eur.

Michelin Map No. 61: Paris - Troyes - Chaumont. Michelin Staff. (Road Maps with Tourist Index Ser.). 1992. pap. 7.95 (*0-7859-0148-5*, 2067000616) Fr & Eur.

Michelin Map No. 62: Epinal - Nancy - Strasbourg. Michelin Staff. (Road Maps with Tourist Index Ser.). 1992. pap. 7.95 (*0-7859-0149-3*, 2067000624) Fr & Eur.

Michelin Map No. 63: Vannes - Le Baule - Angers. Michelin Staff. (Road Maps with Tourist Index Ser.). 1992. pap. 7.95 (*0-7859-0150-7*, 2067000632) Fr & Eur.

Michelin Map No. 64: Angers - Tours - Orleans. Michelin Staff. (Road Maps with Tourist Index Ser.). 1992. pap. 7.95 (*0-7859-0151-5*, 2067000640) Fr & Eur.

Michelin Map No. 65: Montargis - Auxerre - Dijon. Michelin Staff. (Road Maps with Tourist Index Ser.). 1992. pap. 7.95 (*0-7859-0152-3*, 2067000659) Fr & Eur.

Michelin Map No. 66: Dijon - Besancon - Mulhouse. Michelin Staff. (Road Maps with Tourist Index Ser.). 1992. pap. 7.95 (*0-7859-0153-1*, 2067000667) Fr & Eur.

Michelin Map No. 67: Nantes - Les Sables-de l'O. - Poitiers. Michelin Staff. (Road Maps with Tourist Index Ser.). 1992. pap. 7.95 (*0-7859-0154-X*, 2067000675) Fr & Eur.

Michelin Map No. 68: Niort - Poitiers - Chateauroux. Michelin Staff. (Road Maps with Tourist Index Ser.). 1992. pap. 7.95 (*0-7859-0155-8*, 2067000683) Fr & Eur.

Michelin Map No. 69: Bourges - Nevers - Macon. Michelin Staff. (Road Maps with Tourist Index Ser.). 1992. pap. 7.95 (*0-7859-0156-6*, 2067000691) Fr & Eur.

Michelin Map No. 72: Angouleme - Limoges - Gueret. Michelin Staff. 1992. pap. 7.95 (*0-7859-0157-4*, 2067000721) Fr & Eur.

Michelin Map No. 73: Clermont-FD - Vichy - Lyon. Michelin Staff. (Road Maps with Tourist Index Ser.). 1992. pap. 7.95 (*0-7859-0158-2*, 206700073X) Fr & Eur.

Michelin Map No. 74: Lyon - Chambery - Geneve. Michelin Staff. (Road Maps with Tourist Index Ser.). 1992. pap. 7.95 (*0-7859-0159-0*, 2067000748) Fr & Eur.

Michelin Map No. 75: Bordeaux - Perigueux - Tulle. Michelin Staff. 1992. pap. 7.95 (*0-7859-0160-4*, 2067000756) Fr & Eur.

Michelin Map No. 76: Aurillac - le Puy - St. Etienne. Michelin Staff. (Road Maps with Tourist Index Ser.). 1992. pap. 7.95 (*0-7859-0161-2*, 2067000764) Fr & Eur.

Michelin Map No. 77: Valence - Grenoble - Gap. Michelin Staff. (Road Maps with Tourist Index Ser.). 1992. pap. 7.95 (*0-7859-0162-0*, 2067000772) Fr & Eur.

Michelin Map No. 78: Bordeaux - Dax - Biarritz. Michelin Staff. (Road Maps with Tourist Index Ser.). 1992. pap. 7.95 (*0-7859-0163-9*, 2067000780) Fr & Eur.

Michelin Map No. 79: Bordeaux - Agen - Montauban. Michelin Staff. (Road Maps with Tourist Index Ser.). 1992. pap. 7.95 (*0-7859-0164-7*, 2067000799) Fr & Eur.

Michelin Map No. 80: Albi - Rodez - Nimes. Michelin Staff. (Road Maps with Tourist Index Ser.). 1992. pap. 7.95 (*0-7859-0165-5*, 2067000802) Fr & Eur.

Michelin Map No. 81: Montelimar - Avignon - Digne. Michelin Staff. (Road Maps with Tourist Index Ser.). 1992. pap. 7.95 (*0-7859-0166-3*, 2067000810) Fr & Eur.

Michelin Map No. 82: Mont-de-Marsan - Pau - Toulouse. Michelin Staff. (Road Maps with Tourist Index Ser.). 1992. pap. 7.95 (*0-7859-0167-1*, 2067000829) Fr & Eur.

Michelin Map No. 83: Carcassone - Montpellier - Nimes. Michelin Staff. (Road Maps with Tourist Index Ser.). 1992. pap. 7.95 (*0-7859-0168-X*, 2067000837) Fr & Eur.

Michelin Map No. 84: Marseille - Toulon - Nice. Michelin Staff. (Road Maps with Tourist Index Ser.). 1992. pap. 7.95 (*0-7859-0169-8*, 2067000845) Fr & Eur.

Michelin Map No. 85: Biarritz - Lourdes - Luchon. Michelin Staff. (Road Maps with Tourist Index Ser.). 1992. pap. 7.95 (*0-7859-0170-1*, 2067000853) Fr & Eur.

Michelin Map No. 86: Luchon - Andorre - Perpignan. Michelin Staff. (Road Maps with Tourist Index Ser.). 1992. pap. 7.95 (*0-7859-0171-X*, 2067000861) Fr & Eur.

Michelin Map No. 87: Vosges - Alsace. Michelin Staff. (Road Maps with Tourist Index Ser.). 1992. pap. 7.95 (*0-7859-0172-8*, 206700087X) Fr & Eur.

Michelin Map No. 88: Clermont - Ferrand - Lyon - St. Etienne. Michelin Staff. 1992. pap. 7.95 (*0-7859-0173-6*, 2067000888) Fr & Eur.

Michelin Map No. 90: Corse. Michelin Staff. (Road Maps with Tourist Index Ser.). 1992. pap. 7.95 (*0-7859-0174-4*, 206700090X) Fr & Eur.

Michelin Map No. 92: France. Michelin Staff. (Road Atlases Ser.). 1992. spiral bd. 39.95 (*0-7859-0175-2*, 600569179) Fr & Eur.

Michelin Map No. 96: France. Michelin Staff. (Road Atlases Ser.). 1992. pap. 39.95 (*0-7859-0176-0*, 600571653) Fr & Eur.

Michelin Map No. 98: France. Michelin Staff. (Road Atlases Ser.). 1992. 39.95 (*0-7859-0177-9*, 060057167X) Fr & Eur.

Michelin Map No. 101: Outskirts of Paris. Michelin Staff. (Main Roads Maps: France Ser.). 1992. pap. 9.95 (*0-7859-0178-7*, 2067001019) Fr & Eur.

Michelin Map No. 102: Battle of Normandy. Michelin Staff. (WW Two Battlefields Ser.). 1992. pap. 12.95 (*0-7859-0179-5*, 206700102X) Fr & Eur.

Michelin Map No. 106: Environs of Paris. Michelin Staff. (Main Roads Maps: France Ser.). 1992. pap. 9.95 (*0-7859-0180-9*, 206700102X) Fr & Eur.

Michelin Map No. 115: Cote d'Azur. Michelin Staff. (Main Roads Maps: France Ser.). 1992. pap. 9.95 (*0-7859-0181-7*, 2067001159) Fr & Eur.

Michelin Map No. 121: Great Britain & Ireland. Michelin Staff. (Road Atlases Ser.). pap. 39.95 (*0-7859-0339-9*, 2067011219) Fr & Eur.

Michelin Map No. 122: Great Britain & Ireland. Michelin Staff. (Road Atlases Ser.). spiral bd. 39.95 (*0-7859-0182-5*, 2067011227) Fr & Eur.

Michelin Map No. 129: Europe. Michelin Staff. (Road Atlases Ser.). 1992. spiral bd. 39.95 (*0-7859-0183-3*, 2067001299) Fr & Eur.

Michelin Map No. 133: Europe. Michelin Staff. (Road Atlases Ser.). 1992. 39.95 (*0-7859-0184-1*, 600571637) Fr & Eur.

Michelin Map No. 134: Europe. large type ed. Michelin Staff. (Road Atlases Ser.). 1992. pap. 39.95 (*0-7859-0185-X*, 600572595) Fr & Eur.

Michelin Map No. 135: Europe. Michelin Staff. (Road Atlases Ser.). 1992. pap. 39.95 (*0-7859-0186-8*, 600573214) Fr & Eur.

Michelin Map No. 170: Beaune - Macon - Evian. Michelin Staff. (Road Maps with Tourist Index Ser.). 1992. pap. 7.95 (*0-7859-0187-6*, 2067001701) Fr & Eur.

Michelin Map No. 171: La Rochelle - Royan - Bordeaux. Michelin Staff. 1992. pap. 7.95 (*0-7859-0188-4*, 206700171X) Fr & Eur.

Michelin Map No. 189: Evian - Annecy - Briancon. Michelin Staff. (Road Maps with Tourist Index Ser.). 1992. pap. 7.95 (*0-7859-0189-2*, 2067001892) Fr & Eur.

Michelin Map No. 212: Brugge - Rotterdam - Antwerpen. Michelin Staff. (Road Maps with Tourist Index Ser.). 1990. pap. 7.95 (*0-7859-0190-6*, 2067002120) Fr & Eur.

Michelin Map No. 213: Brussel - Oostende - Liege. Michelin Staff. (Road Maps with Tourist Index Ser.). 1992. pap. 7.95 (*0-7859-0340-2*, 2067002139) Fr & Eur.

Michelin Map No. 214: Mons - Dinant - Luxembourg. Michelin Staff. (Road Maps with Tourist Index Ser.). 1990. pap. 7.95 (*0-7859-0191-4*, 2067002147) Fr & Eur.

Michelin Map No. 215: Luxembourg. Michelin Staff. (Road Maps with Tourist Index Ser.). 1992. pap. 7.95 (*0-7859-0192-2*, 2067002155) Fr & Eur.

Michelin Map No. 216: Neuchatel - Basel - St. Gallen. Michelin Staff. (Road Maps with Tourist Index Ser.). 1992. pap. 7.95 (*0-7859-0193-0*, 2067002163) Fr & Eur.

Michelin Map No. 217: Geneve - Bern - Andermatt. Michelin Staff. (Road Maps with Tourist Index Ser.). 1992. pap. 7.95 (*0-7859-0194-9*, 2067002171) Fr & Eur.

Michelin Map No. 218: Andermatt - St. Moritz - Bolzano-Bozen. Michelin Staff. (Road Maps with Tourist Index Ser.). 1992. pap. 7.95 (*0-7859-0195-7*, 206700218X) Fr & Eur.

Michelin Map No. 219: Aosta - Aoste - Zermatt - Milano. Michelin Staff. (Road Maps with Tourist Index Ser.). 1992. pap. 7.95 (*0-7859-0196-5*, 2067002199) Fr & Eur.

Michelin Map No. 230: Bretagne. Michelin Staff. (Main Roads Maps: France Ser.). 1990. pap. 9.95 (*0-7859-0197-3*, 2067002309) Fr & Eur.

Michelin Map No. 231: Normandie. Michelin Staff. (Main Roads Maps: France Ser.). 1990. pap. 9.95 (*0-7859-0198-1*, 2067002317) Fr & Eur.

Michelin Map No. 232: Loire Region (Pays de Loire) Michelin Staff. (Main Roads Maps: France Ser.). 1990. pap. 9.95 (*0-7859-0199-X*, 2067002325) Fr & Eur.

Michelin Map No. 233: Poitou-Charentes. Michelin Staff. (Main Roads Maps: France Ser.). 1990. pap. 9.95 (*0-7859-0200-7*, 2067002333) Fr & Eur.

Michelin Map No. 234: Aquitaine. Michelin Staff. (Main Roads Maps: France Ser.). 1990. pap. 9.95 (*0-7859-0201-5*, 2067002341) Fr & Eur.

Michelin Map No. 235: Midi Pyrenees. Michelin Staff. (Main Roads Maps: France Ser.). 1990. pap. 9.95 (*0-7859-0202-3*, 206700235X) Fr & Eur.

Michelin Map No. 236: Nord de la France. Michelin Staff. (Main Roads Maps: France Ser.). 1990. pap. 9.95 (*0-7859-0203-1*, 2067002368) Fr & Eur.

Michelin Map No. 237: Ile de France. Michelin Staff. (Main Roads Maps: France Ser.). 1988. pap. 9.95 (*0-7859-0204-X*, 2067002376) Fr & Eur.

Michelin Map No. 238: Centre France. Michelin Staff. (Main Roads Maps: France Ser.). 1990. pap. 9.95 (*0-7859-0205-8*, 2067002374) Fr & Eur.

Michelin Map No. 239: Auvergne-Limousin. Michelin Staff. (Main Roads Maps: France Ser.). 1990. pap. 9.95 (*0-7859-0206-6*, 2067002392) Fr & Eur.

Michelin Map No. 240: Languedoc - Roussillon. Michelin Staff. 1990. pap. 9.95 (*0-7859-0207-4*, 2067002406) Fr & Eur.

Michelin Map No. 241: Champagne-Ardennes. Michelin Staff. (Main Roads Maps: France Ser.). 1990. pap. 9.95 (*0-7859-0208-2*, 2067002414) Fr & Eur.

Michelin Map No. 242: Alsace et Lorraine. Michelin Staff. (Main Roads Maps: France Ser.). 1990. pap. 9.95 (*0-7859-0209-0*, 2067002422) Fr & Eur.

Michelin Map No. 243: Bourgogne-Franche Comte. Michelin Staff. (Main Roads Maps: France Ser.). 1990. pap. 9.95 (*0-7859-0210-4*, 2067002430) Fr & Eur.

Michelin Map No. 244: Rhone - Alpes. Michelin Staff. 1990. pap. 9.95 (*0-7859-0211-2*, 2067002449) Fr & Eur.

Michelin Map No. 245: Provence-Cote d'Azur. Michelin Staff. (Main Roads Maps: France Ser.). 1988. pap. 9.95 (*0-685-64752-8*, 2067002457) Fr & Eur.

Michelin Map No. 246: Vallee du Rhone. Michelin Staff. (Main Roads Maps: France Ser.). 1990. pap. 9.95 (*0-7859-0213-9*, 2067002465) Fr & Eur.

Michelin Map No. 263: Battle of Provence. Michelin Staff. (WW Two Battlefields Ser.). 1992. pap. 12.95 (*0-7859-0214-7*, 2067002635) Fr & Eur.

Michelin Map No. 264: Battle of Alsace. Michelin Staff. (WW Two Battlefields Ser.). 1992. pap. 12.95 (*0-7859-0215-5*, 2067002643) Fr & Eur.

Michelin Map No. 265: Victory Road. Michelin Staff. (WW Two Battlefields Ser.). 1992. pap. 12.95 (*0-7859-0216-3*, 2067002651) Fr & Eur.

Michelin Map No. 401: Scotland. Michelin Staff. (Main Roads Maps, Great Britain & Ireland Ser.). 1988. pap. 9.95 (*0-7859-0252-X*, 2067004018) Fr & Eur.

Michelin Map No. 402: Midlands-The North. Michelin Staff. (Main Roads Maps, Great Britain & Ireland Ser.). 1988. pap. 9.95 (*0-7859-0253-8*, 2067004026) Fr & Eur.

Michelin Map No. 403: Wales-West Country-Midlands. Michelin Staff. (Main Roads Maps, Great Britain & Ireland Ser.). 1988. pap. 9.95 (*0-7859-0254-6*, 2067004034) Fr & Eur.

Michelin Map No. 404: South East-Midlands-East Anglia. Michelin Staff. (Main Roads Maps, Great Britain & Ireland Ser.). 1992. pap. 9.95 (*0-7859-0255-4*, 2067004042) Fr & Eur.

Michelin Map No. 405: Ireland. Michelin Staff. (Main Roads Maps, Great Britain & Ireland Ser.). 1992. pap. 9.95 (*0-7859-0256-2*, 2067004050) Fr & Eur.

Michelin Map No. 407: Benelux. Michelin Staff. (Main Roads Maps Ser.). 1992. pap. 9.95 (*0-7859-0257-0*, 2067004077) Fr & Eur.

Michelin Map No. 408: Netherlands. Michelin Staff. (Main Roads Maps Ser.). 1989. pap. 9.95 (*0-7859-0258-9*, 2067004085) Fr & Eur.

Michelin Map No. 409: Belgium-Luxemburg. Michelin Staff. (Main Roads Maps Ser.). 1992. pap. 9.95 (*0-7859-0259-7*, 2067004093) Fr & Eur.

Michelin Map No. 411: Northern Germany. Michelin Staff. (Main Roads Maps Ser.). 1988. pap. 9.95 (*0-7859-0260-0*, 2067004115) Fr & Eur.

Michelin Map No. 412: Central Germany. Michelin Staff. (Main Roads Maps Ser.). 1990. pap. 9.95 (*0-7859-0261-9*, 2067004123) Fr & Eur.

Michelin Map No. 413: Bavaria, Southern Germany. Michelin Staff. (Main Roads Maps Ser.). 1992. pap. 9.95 (*0-7859-0262-7*, 2067004131) Fr & Eur.

Michelin Map No. 428: North West Italy. Michelin Staff. (Main Roads Maps Ser.). 1990. pap. 9.95 (*0-7859-0263-5*, 206700428X) Fr & Eur.

Michelin Map No. 429: North East Italy. Michelin Staff. (Main Roads Maps Ser.). 1990. pap. 9.95 (*0-7859-0264-3*, 2067004298) Fr & Eur.

Michelin Map No. 430: Central Italy. Michelin Staff. (Main Roads Maps Ser.). 1992. pap. 9.95 (*0-7859-0265-1*, 2067004301) Fr & Eur.

Michelin Map No. 431: South Italy. Michelin Staff. (Main Roads Maps Ser.). 1992. pap. 9.95 (*0-7859-0266-X*, 206700431X) Fr & Eur.

Michelin Map No. 432: Sicily. Michelin Staff. (Main Roads Maps Ser.). 1992. pap. 9.95 (*0-7859-0267-8*, 2067004328) Fr & Eur.

Michelin Map No. 433: Sardinia. Michelin Staff. (Main Roads Maps Ser.). 1992. pap. 9.95 (*0-7859-0268-6*, 2067004336) Fr & Eur.

Michelin Map No. 441: North West Spain. Michelin Staff. (Main Roads Maps Ser.). 1990. pap. 9.95 (*0-7859-0269-4*, 2067004417) Fr & Eur.

Michelin Map No. 442: Northern Spain. Michelin Staff. (Main Roads Maps Ser.). 1990. pap. 9.95 (*0-7859-0270-8*, 2067004425) Fr & Eur.

Michelin Map No. 443: North East Spain. Michelin Staff. (Main Roads Maps Ser.). 1990. pap. 9.95 (*0-7859-0271-6*, 2067004433) Fr & Eur.

Michelin Map No. 444: Central Spain. Michelin Staff. (Main Roads Maps Ser.). 1990. pap. 9.95 (*0-7859-0272-4*, 2067004441) Fr & Eur.

Michelin Map No. 445: Central-Eastern Spain. Michelin Staff. (Main Roads Maps Ser.). 1990. pap. 9.95 (*0-7859-0273-2*, 206700445X) Fr & Eur.

Michelin Map No. 446: Southern Spain. Michelin Staff. (Main Roads Maps Ser.). 1990. pap. 9.95 (*0-7859-0274-0*, 2067004468) Fr & Eur.

Michelin Map No. 450: Canary Islands. Michelin Staff. (Main Roads Maps Ser.). 1990. pap. 9.95 (*0-7859-0275-9*, 2067004501) Fr & Eur.

Michelin Map No. 585: Valley of the Kings. Michelin Staff. (France Historical Ser.). 1992. pap. 9.95 (*0-7859-0308-9*, 2067005855) Fr & Eur.

Michelin Map No. 588: Treasure Houses of the Sun King. Michelin Staff. (France Historical Ser.). 1992. pap. 9.95 (*0-7859-0309-7*, 206700588X) Fr & Eur.

Michelin Map No. 918: Northern France. Michelin Staff. (Specialized Maps Ser.). 1992. pap. 7.95 (*0-7859-0321-6*, 2067009184) Fr & Eur.

Michelin Map No. 919: Southern France. Michelin Staff. (Specialized Maps Ser.). 1992. pap. 7.95 (*0-7859-0322-4*, 2067009192) Fr & Eur.

Michelin Map No. 953: Africa, North & West. Michelin Staff. (Main Roads Maps Ser.). 1988. pap. 9.95 (*0-7859-0323-2*, 2067009532) Fr & Eur.

Michelin Map No. 954: Africa, NE Including Egypt & Arabia. Michelin Staff. (Main Roads Maps Ser.). 1988. pap. 9.95 (*0-7859-0324-0*, 2067009540) Fr & Eur.

Michelin Map No. 955: Africa, Central & South Madagascar. Michelin Staff. (Main Roads Maps Ser.). 1988. pap. 9.95 (*0-7859-0325-9*, 2067009559) Fr & Eur.

Michelin Map No. 969: Morocco. Michelin Staff. (Main Roads Maps Ser.). 1992. pap. 9.95 (*0-7859-0326-7*, 2067009699) Fr & Eur.

Michelin Map No. 970: Europe. Michelin Staff. (Main Roads Maps Ser.). 1990. pap. 9.95 (*0-7859-0327-5*, 2067009702) Fr & Eur.

Michelin Map No. 972: Algeria-Tunisia. Michelin Staff. (Main Roads Maps Ser.). 1990. pap. 9.95 (*0-7859-0328-3*, 2067009729) Fr & Eur.

Michelin Map No. 975: Ivory Coast. Michelin Staff. (Main Roads Maps Ser.). 1990. pap. 9.95 (*0-7859-0329-1*, 2067009753) Fr & Eur.

Michelin Map No. 980: Greece. Michelin Staff. (Main Roads Maps Ser.). 1992. pap. 9.95 (*0-7859-0330-5*, 206700980X) Fr & Eur.

Michelin Map No. 984: Germany. Michelin Staff. (Main Roads Maps Ser.). 1988. pap. 9.95 (*0-7859-0331-3*, 2067009842) Fr & Eur.

Michelin Map No. 985: Scandinavia & Finland. Michelin Staff. (Main Roads Maps Ser.). 1988. pap. 9.95 (*0-7859-0332-1*, 2067009850) Fr & Eur.

Michelin Map No. 986: Great Britain & Ireland. Michelin Staff. (Main Roads Maps Ser.). 1992. pap. 9.95 (*0-7859-0333-X*, 2067009869) Fr & Eur.

Michelin Map No. 987: Germany - Austria - Benelux. Michelin Staff. (Main Roads Maps Ser.). 1992. pap. 9.95 (*0-7859-0334-8*, 2067009877) Fr & Eur.

Michelin Map No. 988: Italy. Michelin Staff. (Main Roads Maps Ser.). 1992. pap. 9.95 (*0-7859-0335-6*, 2067009885) Fr & Eur.

Michelin Map No. 989: France. Michelin Staff. (Main Roads Maps Ser.). 1992. pap. 9.95 (*0-7859-0336-4*, 2067009893) Fr & Eur.

Michelin Map No. 990: Spain & Portugal. Michelin Staff. (Main Roads Maps Ser.). 1992. pap. 9.95 (*0-7859-0337-2*, 2067009907) Fr & Eur.

Michelin Map No. 991: Yugoslavia. Michelin Staff. (Main Roads Maps Ser.). 1988. pap. 9.95 (*0-7859-0338-0*, 2067009915) Fr & Eur.

***Michelin Neos Guide Cuba.** Michelin Travel Publication Staff. 2000. 22.00 (*2-06-855201-9*) Michelin.

***Michelin Neos Guide Guatemala, Belize.** Michelin Travel Publication Staff. 2000. 22.00 (*2-06-855801-7*) Michelin.

***Michelin Neos Guide Indonesia.** Michelin Travel Publication Staff. 2000. 26.00 (*2-06-855701-0*) Michelin.

***Michelin Neos Guide Rajasthan.** Michelin Travel Publication Staff. 2000. 22.00 (*2-06-855901-3*) Michelin.

***Michelin Neos Guide Reunion, Mauritius, Seychelles.** Michelin Travel Publication Staff. 2000. 24.00 (*2-06-855301-5*) Michelin.

***Michelin Neos Guide Sri Lanka, Maldives.** Michelin Travel Publication Staff. 2000. 24.00 (*2-06-856001-1*) Michelin.

***Michelin Neos Guide Syria, Jordan.** Michelin Travel Publication Staff. 2000. 24.00 (*2-06-855401-1*) Michelin.

***Michelin Neos Guide to Rajasthan.** Ed. by Michelin Travel Publication Staff. (Illus.). 2000. 22.00 (*2-06-850901-6*) Michelin.

***Michelin Neos Guide Tunisia.** Michelin Travel Publication Staff. 2000. 22.00 (*2-06-855501-8*) Michelin.

***Michelin Neos Guide Turkey.** Michelin Travel Publication Staff. 2000. 26.00 (*2-06-855601-4*) Michelin.

***Michelin Netherlands Green Guide.** Ed. by Michelin Staff. 1999. pap. 19.95 (*0-320-03761-4*) Fr & Eur.

***Michelin New England Green Guide.** Ed. by Michelin Staff. 1999. pap. 19.95 (*0-320-03759-2*) Fr & Eur.

***Michelin New York City Green Guide.** Ed. by Michelin Staff. 1999. pap. 19.95 (*0-320-03727-4*); pap. 19.95 (*0-320-03734-7*) Fr & Eur.

***Michelin New York Green Guide.** Ed. by Michelin Staff. (FRE.). 1999. pap. 24.95 (*0-320-03772-X*) Fr & Eur.

***Michelin New York, New Jersey & Pennsylvania Green Guide.** Ed. by Michelin Staff. 1999. pap. 19.95 (*0-320-03769-X*) Fr & Eur.

***Michelin Northern France & Paris Region Green Guide.** Illus. by Michelin Staff. 1999. pap. 19.95 (*0-320-03773-8*) Fr & Eur.

Michelin Paris & Environs Red Guide, 1995 (Hotels & Restaurants) 1995. 10.00 (*0-7859-9024-0*) Fr & Eur.

***Michelin Paris Green Guide.** Ed. by Michelin Staff. 2000. pap. 19.95 (*0-320-03733-9*) Fr & Eur.

Michelin Paris Hotel & Restaurant Guide, 1997. Ed. by Michelin Staff. (ENG, FRE & GER.). 1997. pap. 14.95 (*0-7859-9398-3*) Fr & Eur.

***Michelin Paris Red Guide, Hotels & Restaurants: 2000 Edition.** Illus. by Michelin Staff. 384p. 2000. pap. 12.00 (*0-320-03720-7*) Fr & Eur.

***Michelin Portugal Green Guide.** Ed. by Michelin Staff. 1999. pap. 19.95 (*0-320-03755-X*) Fr & Eur.

Michelin Portugal Red Guide (Hotels & Restaurants) 1995. 10.00 (*0-7859-9021-6*) Fr & Eur.

***Michelin Provence Green Guide.** Ed. by Michelin Staff. 1999. pap. 19.95 (*0-320-03732-0*) Fr & Eur.

***Michelin Red France Hotels & Restaurants 2000.** 100th ed. Ed. by Michelin Staff. (Red Guide France Ser.). (Illus.). 2000. pap. 26.00 (*2-06-864091-0*) Michelin.

***Michelin Red Guide Suisse/Schweiz/Svizzera 1998: Hotels & Restaurants.** Ed. by Michelin Travel Publication Staff. (Michelin Red Guide Ser.). (Illus.). 1999. 25.00 (*2-06-969999-4*) Michelin.

Michelin Red Travel Guide: Deutschland (West Germany - West Berlin) (FRE., Illus.). 1992. 19.95 (*0-685-11389-2*) Fr & Eur.

Michelin Red Travel Guide: Italie. annuals (FRE., Illus.). 19.95 (*0-685-11390-6*) Fr & Eur.

Michelin Red Travel Guide - Camping - France. Michelin Staff. (ENG, FRE, GER & ITA.). 1992. 14.95 (*0-685-66128-8*) Fr & Eur.

Michelin Red Travel Guide - Greater London. Michelin Staff. 1992. 8.95 (*0-8288-6110-2*) Fr & Eur.

Michelin Road Atlas - Europe. Michelin Staff. pap. 19.95 (*0-8288-6200-1*) Fr & Eur.

Michelin Road Atlas - Europe. large type ed. Michelin Staff. pap. 19.95 (*0-8288-6201-X*) Fr & Eur.

Michelin Road Atlas - France. Michelin Staff. 29.95 (*0-8288-6199-4*) Fr & Eur.

Michelin Road Atlas - France. large type ed. Michelin Staff. pap. 19.95 (*0-8288-6198-6*) Fr & Eur.

Michelin Road Atlas - Great Britain - Ireland. Michelin Staff. 19.95 (*0-8288-6197-8*) Fr & Eur.

Michelin Road Atlas - Italy. Michelin Staff. 1994. pap., spiral bd. 39.95 (*0-7859-9115-8*) Fr & Eur.

Michelin Rome Green Guide. Ed. by Michelin Staff. pap. 19.95 (*0-320-03744-4*) Fr & Eur.

***Michelin Scandinavia Green Guide.** Ed. by Michelin Staff. 1999. pap. 19.95 (*0-320-03751-7*) Fr & Eur.

***Michelin Scotland Green Guide.** Ed. by Michelin Staff. 1999. pap. 19.95 (*0-320-03748-7*) Fr & Eur.

***Michelin Sicily Green Guide.** Ed. by Michelin Staff. 1999. pap. 19.95 (*0-320-03745-2*) Fr & Eur.

***Michelin Spain Green Guide.** Ed. by Michelin Staff. 1999. pap. 19.95 (*0-320-03730-4*) Fr & Eur.

***Michelin Spain Hotel & Restaurant Red Guide.** Ed. by Michelin Staff. 2000. 25.95 (*0-320-03738-X*) Fr & Eur.

***Michelin Switzerland Green Guide.** Ed. by Michelin Staff. 1999. pap. 19.95 (*0-320-03731-2*) Fr & Eur.

***Michelin Switzerland Hotel & Restaurant Red Guide.** Ed. by Michelin Staff. 468p. 2000. 24.95 (*0-320-03723-1*) Fr & Eur.

Michelin Switzerland Red Guide, 1995 (Hotels & Restaurants) 1995. 24.00 (*0-7859-9022-4*) Fr & Eur.

***Michelin Tourist & Motoring Atlas: Europe.** 3rd ed. Michelin Staff. (Illus.). 2000. pap. 20.00 (*2-06-113503-X*); pap. 20.00 (*2-06-113603-6*) Michelin.

***Michelin Tourist & Motoring Atlas: France.** Michelin Staff. (Illus.). 1999. pap. 20.00 (*2-06-109203-9*) Michelin.

Michelin Tourist & Motoring Atlas Europe. 2nd ed. Michelin Staff. 1999. pap. text 20.00 (*2-06-113602-8*) Michelin.

***Michelin Tourist & Motoring Atlas Europe.** 3rd ed. Michelin Staff. (Illus.). 2000. pap. 20.00 (*2-06-112903-X*) Michelin.

***Michelin Tourist & Motoring Atlas Great Britain & Ireland.** 11th ed. Ed. by Michelin Staff. (Illus.). 1999. pap. 20.00 (*2-06-112211-6*) Michelin.

***Michelin Tourist & Motoring Atlas Italy.** 6th ed. Michelin Staff. (Illus.). 2000. pap. text. write for info. (*2-06-146506-4*) Michelin.

***Michelin Tourist & Motoring Atlas Spain & Portugal.** 7th ed. Michelin Staff. (Illus.). 2000. pap. text. write for info. (*2-06-146007-0*) Michelin.

***Michelin Tuscany Green Guide.** Ed. by Michelin Staff. 1999. pap. 19.95 (*0-320-03741-X*) Fr & Eur.

***Michelin Venice Green Guide.** Ed. by Michelin Staff. 1999. pap. 19.95 (*0-320-03754-1*) Fr & Eur.

***Michelin Vienna Green Guide.** Ed. by Michelin Staff. 1999. pap. 19.95 (*0-320-03763-0*) Fr & Eur.

***Michelin Washington, D. C. Green Guide.** Ed. by Michelin Staff. 1999. pap. 19.95 (*0-320-03757-6*) Fr & Eur.

***Michelin West Country of England Green Guide.** Ed. by Michelin Staff. 1999. pap. 19.95 (*0-320-03766-5*) Fr & Eur.

Michelin's Europe Hotel & Restaurant Guide, 1997. Ed. by Michelin Staff. (ENG, FRE & GER.). 1997. pap. 26.95 (*0-7859-9389-4*) Fr & Eur.

Michelin's France Hotel & Restaurant Guide, 1997. Michelin Staff. (ENG, FRE & GER.). 1997. pap. 26.95 (*0-7859-9390-8*) Fr & Eur.

Michelin's Germany Hotel & Restaurant Guide, 1997. Ed. by Michelin Staff. (ENG, FRE & GER.). 1997. pap. 26.95 (*0-7859-9387-8*) Fr & Eur.

Michelin's Great Britain & Ireland Hotel & Restaurant Guide, 1997. Michelin Staff. (ENG, FRE & GER.). 1997. pap. 26.95 (*0-7859-9391-6*) Fr & Eur.

Michelin's Guide to Scandinavia & Finland. Michelin Staff. 1997. pap. 19.95 (*0-7859-9399-1*) Fr & Eur.

Michelin's Guide to Venice. Ed. by Michelin Staff. 1997. pap. 19.95 (*0-7859-9401-7*) Fr & Eur.

Michelin's Guide to Wales. Ed. by Michelin Staff. 1997. pap. 19.95 (*0-7859-9400-9*) Fr & Eur.

Michelin's Ireland Hotel & Restaurant Guide, 1997. Ed. by Michelin Staff. (ENG, FRE & GER.). 1997. pap. 14.95 (*0-7859-9392-4*) Fr & Eur.

Michelin's Italy Hotel & Restaurant Guide, 1997. Ed. by Michelin Staff. (ENG, FRE & GER.). 1997. pap. 26.95 (*0-7859-9393-2*) Fr & Eur.

Michelin's London Hotel & Restaurant Guide, 1997. Ed. by Michelin Staff. (ENG, FRE & GER.). 1997. pap. 14.95 (*0-7859-9397-5*) Fr & Eur.

Michelin's Portugal Hotel & Restaurant Guide, 1997. Michelin Staff. (ENG, FRE & GER.). 1997. 14.95 (*0-7859-9394-0*) Fr & Eur.

Michelin's Spain-Portugal Hotel & Restaurant Guide, 1997. Ed. by Michelin Staff. (ENG, FRE & GER.). 1997. pap. 26.95 (*0-7859-9388-6*) Fr & Eur.

Michelin's Switzerland Hotel & Restaurant Guide, 1997. Michelin Staff. (ENG, FRE & GER.). 1997. pap. 26.95 (*0-7859-9395-9*) Fr & Eur.

Michelle. Eva Gibson. LC 94-164366. (Springsong Bks.). 176p. (J). (gr. 7-10). 1994. mass mkt. 4.99 (*1-55661-447-0*) Bethany Hse.

Michelle & Debra. Jack Weyland. LC 90-3647. 137p. (YA). (gr. 7-12). 1990. 11.95 (*0-87579-369-X*) Deseret Bk.

Michelle & Debra. Jack Weyland. LC 90-3647. 137p. (YA). (gr. 7-12). 1995. pap. 5.95 (*0-87579-959-0*) Deseret Bk.

***Michelle Cliff's Novels: Piecing the Tapestry of Memory & History.** Noraida Agosto. LC 98-42387. 208p. 1999. 49.95 (*0-8204-4255-0*) P Lang Pubng.

***Michelle Kwan.** Sherry Paprocki. LC 00-29041. 2000. 17.95 (*0-7910-5792-5*) Chelsea Hse.

***Michelle Kwan.** Sherry Beck Paprocki. (Women Who Win Ser.). (Illus.). 2000. pap. 7.95 (*0-7910-6152-3*) Chelsea Hse.

Michelle Kwan. Richard Rambeck. LC 97-12956. (Sports Superstars Ser.). 24p. (J). (gr. 2-6). 1997. lib. bdg. 21.36 (*1-56766-461-X*) Childs World.

Michelle Kwan. Richard Rambeck. (Illus.). 24p. 1997. lib. bdg. 21.36 (*1-56766-412-1*) Childs World.

***Michelle Kwan.** John Torres. LC 99-19933. (Real-Life Reader Biography Ser.). (Illus.). 32p. (J). (gr. 3-8). 1999. lib. bdg. 15.95 (*1-883845-97-1*) M Lane Pubs.

Michelle Kwan. Sam Wellman. LC 97-29627. (Female Sports Stars Ser.). (Illus.). 64p. (YA). (gr. 3 up). 1999. lib. bdg. 15.95 (*0-7910-4875-6*) Chelsea Hse.

Michelle Kwan: Champion on Ice. Kimberly Gatto. LC 98-16846. (Lerner Sports Achievers Ser.). (Illus.). 64p. (J). (gr. 4-9). 1998. pap. 5.95 (*0-8225-9830-2*) Lerner Pub.

***Michelle Kwan: Champion on Ice.** Kimberly Gatto. LC 98-16846. (Lerner Sports Achievers Ser.). (J). 1998. 19.93 (*0-8225-3669-2*) Lerner Pub.

Michelle Kwan: Heart of a Champion. Michelle Kwan. LC 97-30183. (Illus.). 176p. (YA). (gr. 4-7). 1997. 14.95 (*0-590-76340-7*) Scholastic Inc.

Michelle Kwan: My Book of Memories. Michelle Kwan. (Illus.). (J). (gr. 4-7). 1998. pap. 5.99 (*0-590-45890-6*) Scholastic Inc.

Michelle Kwan: Skating Like the Wind. Linda Shaughnessy. LC 96-48350. (Figure Skaters Ser.). 1997. 22.00 (*0-382-39445-3*, Crstwood Hse) Silver Burdett Pr.

Michelle Kwan: Skating Like the Wind. Linda Shaughnessy. LC 96-48350. (Figure Skaters Ser.). (J). (gr. 5). 1997. pap. 6.95 (*0-382-39446-1*, Crstwood Hse) Silver Burdett Pr.

***Michelle Kwan: Star Figure Skater.** Barry Wilner. LC 00-9524. (Sports Reports). (Illus.). (J). 2001. write for info. (*0-7660-1504-1*) Enslow Pubs.

Michelle Kwan Autobiography. Michelle Kwan. 166p. 2001. pap. 15.99 (*0-7868-0530-7*, Pub. by Hyprn Ppbks) Little.

***Michelle Kwan Chapterbook.** Michelle Kwan. 64p. (J). 2000. pap. 4.99 (*0-7868-1383-0*, Pub. by Disney Pr) Time Warner.

Michelle Kwan Coffee Table Book. Michelle Kwan. 96p. 2000. pap. 19.99 (*0-7868-0529-3*, Pub. by Hyprn Ppbks) Little.

Michelle Kwan, Heart of a Champion: An Autobiography. Michelle Kwan & Laura M. James. LC 97-30183. (J). 1997. pap. 4.99 (*0-590-76356-3*) Scholastic Inc.

Michelle Kwan: Heart of a Champion: In Her Own Words. Michelle Kwan. 1998. 10.09 (*0-606-13607-X*, Pub. by Turtleback) Demco.

Michelle Kwan Middle Grade, Vol. 3. Michelle Kwan. (J). pap. 4.50 (*0-7868-1381-4*, Pub. by Disney Pr) Time Warner.

***Michelle Kwan Middle Grade, Vol. 4.** Michelle Kwan. 144p. (J). 2000. pap. 4.50 (*0-7868-1382-2*, Pub. by Disney Pr) Time Warner.

Michelle Kwan Picture Book. Michelle Kwan. (Illus.). 32p. 2001. 15.49 (*0-7868-2461-1*, Pub. by Hyprn Ppbks) Little.

Michelle Remembers. Michelle Smith. 1989. mass mkt. 5.50 (*0-671-69433-2*) PB.

Michelle Stuart: The Elements, 1973-1979. Lucy Lippart. 1992. pap. 15.00 (*0-9634941-0-4*) Fanbush.

Michelles, Monolayers & Biomembranes. Dennis Chapman & Malcolm Jones. 264p. 1994. 169.95 (*0-471-56139-8*) Wiley.

Michelsen Book of Tables: Placidus & Koch Tables of Houses. Neil F. Michelsen et al. 176p. (Orig.). 1997. pap. 15.95 (*0-935127-60-7*) ACS Pubns.

Michelson & the Speed of Light. Bernard Jaffe. LC 78-25969. (Illus.). 197p. 1979. reprint ed. lib. bdg. 35.00 (*0-313-20777-1*, JAMI, Greenwood Pr) Greenwood.

Michelson Era in American Science, 1870-1930. Ed. by Stanley Goldberg & Roger H. Stuewer. LC 88-83369. (AIP Conference Proceedings Ser.: No. 179). 315p. 1989. lib. bdg. 60.00 (*0-88318-379-X*) Am Inst Physics.

Michelson in the Desert: Stories. Tom Alderson. LC 86-16159. 88p. (Orig.). 1987. pap. 12.95 (*0-8262-0621-2*, 83-36299) U of Mo Pr.

Michelson's Book of World Baseball Records. Court Michelson. 184p. (Orig.). 1985. pap. 9.95 (*0-934175-00-4*) Sports Rec.

Michels's Retinal Detachment. 2nd ed. Charles P. Wilkinson & Thomas A. Rice. LC 96-4878. Orig. Title: Retinal Detachment. (Illus.). 1184p. (C). (gr. 13). 1996. text 210.00 (*0-8151-9416-1*, 26954) Mosby Inc.

Michener & Me: A Memoir. HERMAN SILVERMAN. LC 98-68459. 224p. 1999. 17.95 (*0-7624-0620-8*) Running Pr.

Michi y Su Nueva Familia. Barbara Williams. (SPA.). (gr. 6-8). 1998. pap. text 8.95 (*84-239-7127-9*) Espasa Calpe.

Michie on Banks & Banking: 1999 Cumulative Supplement, 14 vols. Ed. by Mary Jane Divine et al. 1810p. 1999. suppl. ed. write for info. (*0-327-00355-3*, 7464816) LEXIS Pub.

Michie on Banks & Banking: 1999 Cumulative Supplement. Ed. by Gary Legner et al. 1999. pap. write for info. (*0-327-01081-9*, 5011216) LEXIS Pub.

Michie on Banks & Banking: 1999 Cumulative Supplement, Vol. 1A. Ed. by Gary Legner et al. 1999. suppl. ed. write for info. (*0-327-01071-1*, 5010016) LEXIS Pub.

Michie on Banks & Banking: 1999 Cumulative Supplement, Vol. 1B. Ed. by Gary Legner et al. 1999. suppl. ed. write for info. (*0-327-01072-X*, 5010116) LEXIS Pub.

Michie on Banks & Banking: 1999 Cumulative Supplement, Vol. 2. Ed. by Gary Legner et al. 1999. suppl. ed. write for info. (*0-327-01073-8*, 5010216) LEXIS Pub.

Michie on Banks & Banking: 1999 Cumulative Supplement, Vol. 3. Ed. by Gary Legner et al. 1999. suppl. ed. write for info. (*0-327-01074-6*, 5010316) LEXIS Pub.

Michie on Banks & Banking: 1999 Cumulative Supplement, Vol. 4. Ed. by Gary Legner et al. 1999. suppl. ed. write for info. (*0-327-01075-4*, 5010416) LEXIS Pub.

Michie on Banks & Banking: 1999 Cumulative Supplement, Vol. 5A. Ed. by Gary Legner et al. 1999. suppl. ed. write for info. (*0-327-01076-2*, 5010516) LEXIS Pub.

Michie on Banks & Banking: 1999 Cumulative Supplement, Vol. 5B. Ed. by Gary Legner et al. 1999. suppl. ed. write for info. (*0-327-01077-0*, 5010616) LEXIS Pub.

Michie on Banks & Banking: 1999 Cumulative Supplement, Vol. 6A. Ed. by Gary Legner et al. 1999. suppl. ed. write for info. (*0-327-01078-9*, 5010716) LEXIS Pub.

Michie on Banks & Banking: 1999 Cumulative Supplement, Vol. 6B. Ed. by Gary Legner et al. 1999. suppl. ed. write for info. (*0-327-01079-7*, 5010816) LEXIS Pub.

Michie on Banks & Banking: 1999 Cumulative Supplement, Vol. 8. Ed. by Gary Legner et al. 1999. suppl. ed. write for info. (*0-327-01080-0*, 5011016) LEXIS Pub.

Michie on Banks & Banking, 1999, 13 vols. rev. ed. Ed. by M. J. Divine & Paul Ernest. 501p. 1999. write for info. (*0-327-00956-X*, 7468310); 440.00 (*0-327-00931-4*) LEXIS Pub.

Michie on Banks & Banking, 1999, 13 vols., Vol. 7A. rev. ed. Ed. by M. J. Divine & Paul Ernest. 507p. 1999. write for info. (*0-327-00955-1*, 7468210) LEXIS Pub.

Michie on Banks & Banking, 1955-1992, 13 vols., Set. Michie Butterworth Editorial Staff. 1994. suppl. ed. 440.00 (*0-87215-034-8*, 74600-10, MICHIE) LEXIS Pub.

***Michie on Banks & Banking, 1999, Vol. 1A.** rev. ed. Ed. by Paul Ernest & Mary Jane Divine. 435p. 1999. write for info. (*0-327-01764-3*, 7464911) LEXIS Pub.

***Michie on Banks & Banking, 1999, Vol. 1C.** rev. ed. Ed. by Paul Ernest & Mary Jane Divine. 495p. 1999. write for info. (*0-327-01765-1*, 7468510) LEXIS Pub.

Michie's Alabama Advance Code Service, No. 3. 65p. 1998. pap. write for info. (*0-327-05159-0*, 40161-11) LEXIS Pub.

Michie's Alabama Code, 34 Vols. The Publisher's Editorial Staff. 375.00 (*0-327-11026-0*) LEXIS Pub.

***Michie's Alabama Code - 1999 Replacement, Vol. 3.** 450p. 1999. Price not set. (*0-327-19707-2*, 4001811) LEXIS Pub.

***Michie's Alabama Code Annotation Citator.** 950p. 1999. Price not set. (*0-327-09767-1*, 4014311) LEXIS Pub.

Michie's Alabama Code, 1998 Interim Supplement: AL 98 Int. Supp. 900p. 1998. pap., suppl. ed. write for info. (*0-327-05367-4*, 50796-17) LEXIS Pub.

Michie's Alabama Code, 1998 Advance Legislative Service Pamphlet No. 3: Acts 98-313 - 98-677. 1998. pap. write for info. (*0-327-05368-2*, 40178-12) LEXIS Pub.

Michie's Alabama Code 1998 Index A-G. 1998. write for info. (*0-327-07093-5*, 40153-13) LEXIS Pub.

Michie's Alabama Code 1998 Index H-Z. 1998. write for info. (*0-327-07094-3*, 40154-13) LEXIS Pub.

***Michie's Alabama Code 1999 Cumulative Supplement.** 4000p. 1999. Price not set. (*0-327-09971-2*, 4000614) LEXIS Pub.

***Michie's Alabama Code 1999, Vol. 7A** 650p. 1999. Price not set. (*0-327-19708-0*, 4002911) LEXIS Pub.

***Michie's Alabama Code 1999, Vol. 17A.** 400p. 1999. Price not set. (*0-327-19709-9*, 4006611) LEXIS Pub.

Michie's Alabama Code, 1975 Vol. 16: Michie's Alabama Code Replacement. 718p. 1998. write for info. (*0-327-06364-5*, 4006411) LEXIS Pub.

Michie's Alabama Code Replacement, 021. Lexis Law Publishing Staff. 1037p. 1998. write for info. (*0-327-06677-6*) LEXIS Pub.

Michie's Alabama Code Replacement, Vol. 16A. 425p. 1998. write for info. (*0-327-06365-3*, 4005410) LEXIS Pub.

Michie's Alabama Code Replacement, Vol. 17. 521p. 1998. write for info. (*0-327-06366-1*, 4006511) LEXIS Pub.

Michie's Alabama Code, 1998 Cumulative Supplement, 31 vols. Incl. Constitution of Ala. 1901 (Amendment 52 to End) Tables. 210p. 1998. suppl. ed. (*0-327-06410-2*, 50762-17); Revenue & Taxation Vol. 21. Ed. by Lexis

An Asterisk (*) at the beginning of an entry indicates that the title is appearing for the first time.

Law Publishing Staff. 20p. 1998. (*0-327-06509-5*, 50786-17); Rules of Alabama Supreme Court (Rules of Civil Procedure to Rules of Evidence) 78p. 1998. suppl. ed. (*0-327-06454-4*, 50789-17); Rules of Alabama Supreme Court (Rules of Criminal Procedure to State Bar Rules of Specialization) 104p. 1998. suppl. ed. (*0-327-06455-2*, 50790-17); Title 8, Commercial Law & Consumer Protection. 107p. 1998. suppl. ed. (*0-327-06415-3*, 50791-17); Title 11, Chapters 46-50A, Counties & Municipal Corporations. 91p. 1998. suppl. ed. (*0-327-06419-6*, 50770-17); Title 9, Conservation & Natural Resources. 194p. 1998. suppl. ed. (*0-327-06416-1*, 50767-17); Title 7, Commercial Code. 1998. suppl. ed. (*0-327-06414-5*, 50766-17); Title 17, Elections. 36p. 1998. suppl. ed. (*0-327-06425-0*, 50794-17); Title 6, Civil Practice. 165p. 1998. suppl. ed. (*0-327-06413-7*, 50765-17); Title 16, Education. 127p. 1998. suppl. ed. (*0-327-06424-2*, 50775-17); Title 10, Corporations, Partnerships & Associations. 275p. 1998. suppl. ed. (*0-327-06417-X*, 50768-17); Title 35, Property. 85p. 1998. suppl. ed. (*0-327-06432-3*, 50783-17); Title 36, Public Officers & Employees. 208p. 1998. suppl. ed. (*0-327-06433-1*, 50784-17); Title 32, Motor Vehicles & Traffic. 211p. 1998. suppl. ed. (*0-327-06430-7*, 50780-17); Title 12, Courts. 134p. 1998. suppl. ed. (*0-327-06421-8*, 50772-17); Title 26, Infants & Incompetents. 92p. 1998. suppl. ed. (*0-327-06429-3*, 50778-17); Title 11, Chap. 51-End, Counties & Municipal Corporations. 77p. 1998. suppl. ed. (*0-327-06420-X*, 50771-17); Title 11, Chapters 1-45, Counties & Municipal Corporations. 116p. 1998. suppl. ed. (*0-327-06418-8*, 50769-17); Titles 18-19, Eminent Domain to Fiduciaries & Trusts. 1998. suppl. ed. (*0-327-06426-9*, 50776-17); Titles 41-42, State Government to United States. 211p. 1998. suppl. ed. (*0-327-06435-8*, 50787-17); Titles 43-44, Wills & Decedents' Estates to Youth Services. 54p. 1998. suppl. ed. (*0-327-06453-6*, 50788-17); Titles 14-15, Criminal Correctional Facilities to Criminal Procedure. 78p. 1998. suppl. ed. (*0-327-06423-4*, 50774-17); Titles 1-2, General Provisions to Agriculture. 214p. 1998. suppl. ed. (*0-327-06411-0*, 50763-17); Titles 13-13A, Criminal Code. 170p. 1998. suppl. ed. (*0-327-06422-6*, 50773-17); Titles 37-39, Public Utilities to Public Works. 112p. 1998. suppl. ed. (*0-327-06434-X*, 50785-17); Titles 33-34, Navigation to Professions & Business. 68p. 1998. suppl. ed. (*0-327-06431-5*, 50782-17); Titles 3-5, Animals to Banks. 27p. 1998. suppl. ed. (*0-327-06412-9*, 50764-17); Titles 23-25, Highways to Industrial Relations. 258p. 1998. suppl. ed. (*0-327-06428-5*, 50777-17); Titles 20-22, Food, Drugs & Cosmetics to Healt & Mental Health. 31p. 1998. suppl. ed. (*0-327-06427-7*, 50792-17); U. S. Constitution; Constitution of Ala. 1875; Constitution of Ala. 1901 (Through Amendment 51) 180p. 1998. suppl. ed. (*0-327-06409-9*, 50761-17); 1998. lib. bdg. write for info. (*0-327-06408-0*, 4000613) LEXIS Pub.

Michie's Alabama Criminal Code Advance Legislative Service, 1998 Edition. 22p. 1998. pap. write for info. (*0-327-06383-1*, 2001410) LEXIS Pub.

Michie's Alabama Criminal Code Advance Legislative Service, 1998 Edition. Ed. by Lexis Law Publishing Staff. 721p. 1998. write for info. (*0-327-06671-7*) LEXIS Pub.

***Michie's Alabama Criminal Code Annotated with Commentaries: 1999 Edition.** 596p. 1999. pap. 39.50 (*0-327-09923-2*, 2000416) LEXIS Pub.

Michie's Alabama Criminal Code Annotated with Commentaries & Michie's Alabama Motor Vehicle Laws, 1999. 63.50 incl. cd-rom (*0-327-11251-4*) LEXIS Pub.

***Michie's Alabama Motor Vehicle Laws Advance Legislative Service.** 30p. 1999. pap. Price not set. (*0-327-09738-8*, 2001611) LEXIS Pub.

Michie's Alabama Motor Vehicle Laws Advance Legislative Service, 1998 Edition. 26p. 1998. pap. write for info. (*0-327-06384-X*, 2001610) LEXIS Pub.

Michie's Alabama Motor Vehicle Laws Annotated with Commentaries: 1998 Replacement. Lexis Law Publishing Staff. LC 99-180271. 389p. 1999. write for info. (*0-327-06649-0*) LEXIS Pub.

***Michie's Alabama Motor Vehicle Laws Annotated with Commentaries: 1999 Edition.** The Publisher's Editorial Staff. 302p. 1999. ring bd. 34.00 (*0-327-09850-3*, 2000616) LEXIS Pub.

Michie's Alabama 1998 Index. 1970p. 1998. write for info. (*0-327-06808-6*) LEXIS Pub.

Michie's Alabama 1999 Advance Code Service, April 1999. 212p. 1999. pap. write for info. (*0-327-08229-1*, 40160-12) LEXIS Pub.

Michie's Alabama 1999 Advance Code Service (December 1998), No. 1. 1998. pap. write for info. (*0-327-06592-3*, 4015812) LEXIS Pub.

***Michie's Alabama 1999 Index, 2 vols.** 2166p. 1999. 32.50 (*0-327-19718-8*, 4000414) LEXIS Pub.

***Michie's Alabama Worker's Compensation Law Annotated 1999 Edition.** 271p. 1999. 25.00 (*0-327-09797-3*, 2016814, MICHIE) LEXIS Pub.

***Michie's Alabama 1999 Advance Code Service #3 (July 1999) Alabama ACS #3.** 224p. 1999. Price not set. (*0-327-08778-1*, 4016112) LEXIS Pub.

Michie's Annotated Code of Maryland, 40 Vols. Compiled by Publisher's Editorial Staff. 725.00 (*0-327-11754-0*) LEXIS Pub.

Michie's Annotated Code of Maryland Annotated Citator, 1998 Edition. 1500p. 1998. write for info. (*0-327-06568-0*, 41340101) LEXIS Pub.

***Michie's Annotated Code of Maryland Annotation Citator.** 1200p. 1999. Price not set. (*0-327-09762-0*, 4134011) LEXIS Pub.

Michie's Annotated Code of Maryland, 1998 Supplement, 33 vols. Incl. Vol. 3. 1957 Code Articles 27A-41. 1998. (*0-327-06264-9*, 52589-15); Vol. 1. 1957 Code Articles 1-26A. annot. ed. 1998. (*0-327-06262-2*, 52587-15); Vol. 2. 1957 Code Article 27. 1998. (*0-327-06263-0*, 52588-15); Vol. CL, Bk. 1. Commercial Law, Sections 1-101 - 10-112 (UCC) annot. ed. Date not set. (*0-327-06268-1*, 52563-15); Vol. CL, Bk. 2. Commercial Law, Sections 11-101 to End. annot. ed. Date not set. (*0-327-06269-X*, 52564-15); Vol. BOP. Business Occupations & Professions. annot. ed. Date not set. (*0-327-06266-5*, 52561-15); Vol. CA. Corporations & Associations. annot. ed. Date not set. (*0-327-06267-3*, 52566-15); Vol. Const. Constitutions Edition. annot. ed. Date not set. (*0-327-06292-4*, 52586-15); Vol. ED. Education Edition. annot. ed. Date not set. (*0-327-06270-3*, 52569-15); Vol. EN, Bk. 1. Environment, Sections 1-101 - 8-601. annot. ed. Date not set. (*0-327-06271-1*, 52570-15); Vol. EN, Bk. 2. Environment, Sections 9-101 to End. annot. ed. Date not set. (*0-327-06272-X*, 52598-15); Vol. ET. Estates & Trusts. annot. ed. Date not set. (*0-327-06273-8*, 52571-15); Vol. FI. Financial Institutions. annot. ed. Date not set. (*0-327-06274-6*, 52573-15); Vol. FL. Family Law. annot. ed. Date not set. (*0-327-06275-4*, 52572-15); Vol. HG, Bk. 1. Health-General, Sections 1-101 - 18-701. annot. ed. Date not set. (*0-327-06276-2*, 52575-15); Vol. HG, Bk. 2. Health-General, Sections 19-101 to End. annot. ed. Date not set. (*0-327-06277-0*, 52576-15); Vol. HO. Health Occupations. annot. ed. Date not set. (*0-327-06278-9*, 52574-15); Vol. IN, Bk. 1. Insurance, Sections 1-101 - 12-306. annot. ed. Date not set. (*0-327-06279-7*, 52599-15); Vol. IN, Bk. 2. Insurance, Sections 13-101 to End. annot. ed. Date not set. (*0-327-06280-0*, 52600-15); Vol. LE. Labor & Employment. annot. ed. Date not set. (*0-327-06281-9*, 52577-15); Vol. NR, Bk. 1. Natural Resources, Sections 1-101 - 7-909. annot. ed. Date not set. (*0-327-06282-7*, 52578-15); Vol. NR, Bk. 2. Natural Resources, Sections 8-101 to End. annot. ed. Date not set. (*0-327-06283-5*, 52579-15); Vol. RP. Real Property. annot. ed. Date not set. (*0-327-06284-3*, 52580-15); Vol. SF. State Finance & Procurement. annot. ed. Date not set. (*0-327-06285-1*, 52581-15); Vol. SG. State Government Edition. annot. ed. Date not set. (*0-327-06286-X*, 52582-15); Vol. SPP. State Personnel & Pensions. annot. ed. Date not set. (*0-327-06287-8*, 52593-15); Vol. TG. Tax - General. annot. ed. Date not set. (*0-327-06288-6*, 52584-15); Vol. TP. Tax - Property. annot. ed. Date not set. (*0-327-06289-4*, 52583-15); Vol. TR, Bk. 1. Transportation, Sections 1-101 - 10-207. annot. ed. Date not set. (*0-327-06290-8*, 52585-15); Vol. TR, Bk. 2. Transportation, Sections 11-101 to End. 1998. (*0-327-06291-6*, 52586-15); write for info. (*0-327-06258-4*) LEXIS Pub.

Michie's Hawaii Revised Statues Annotated 1999 Replacement, Vol. 7. 825p. 1999. write for info. (*0-327-07711-5*, 4211112) LEXIS Pub.

Michie's Hawaii Revised Statues Annotated 1999 Replacement, Vol. 14. 600p. 1999. write for info. (*0-327-07710-7*, 4211812) LEXIS Pub.

***Michie's Hawaii Revised Statutes Annotated Court Rules: June 2000 Supplement.** (Michie's Hawaii Revised Statutes Annotated Ser.). 210p. 2000. write for info. (*0-327-11617-X*, 4219618) LEXIS Pub.

***Michie's Hawaii Revised Statutes Annotated Court Rules June 1999 Supplement.** 250p. 1999. Price not set. (*0-327-08777-3*, 4219616) LEXIS Pub.

***Michie's Hawaii Revised Statutes Annotated 1999 Replacement Volume, No. 11.** annot. rev. ed. 700p. 1999. write for info. (*0-327-10340-X*, 4212211) LEXIS Pub.

***Michie's Hawaii Revised Statutes Annotated 1999 Replacement Volume, No. 12A.** 600p. 1999. write for info. (*0-327-10341-8*, 4212712) LEXIS Pub.

***Michie's Hawaii Revised Statutes Annotated 2000 Replacement Volume 5.** Ed. by LEXIS Law Publishing Editors. 780p. 2000. write for info. (*0-327-13116-0*, 4212312) LEXIS Pub.

***Michie's Hawaii Revised Statutes Annotated 2000 Replacement 6A.** Ed. by LEXIS Law Publishing Editors. 780p. 2000. write for info. (*0-327-13117-9*, 4212112) LEXIS Pub.

Michie's Idaho Code, 1998 General Index Vols. 12 & 13: 1998 Edition. rev. ed. 1781p. 1998. write for info. (*0-327-05167-1*, 42382-15) LEXIS Pub.

Michie's Idaho Code, 1997 General Index Vol. 12: 1998 Edition, A to H. rev. ed. 865p. 1998. write for info. (*0-327-05165-5*, 42393-15) LEXIS Pub.

Michie's Idaho Code, 1997 General Index Vol. 13: 1998 Edition, I to Z. 939p. 1998. write for info. (*0-327-05166-3*, 42394-15) LEXIS Pub.

Michie's Jurisprudence, 49 vols. Ed. by M. J. Divine et al. Date not set. text 1200.00 (*0-327-00332-4*) LEXIS Pub.

Michie's Jurisprudence: 1998 Interim Supplement. 1998. pap. text. write for info. (*0-327-00176-3*, 74878-12) LEXIS Pub.

Michie's Jurisprudence for Virginia & West Virginia Replacement Vol. 21B, Pt. 2: State Court Rules, 53 vols. Ed. by M. J. Divine & G. E. Legner. 850p. 1999. write for info. (*0-327-00964-0*, 7482112) LEXIS Pub.

Michie's Jurisprudence for Virginia & West Virginia, 1999 Interim Supplement: A Complete Treatise Virginia & West Virginia Law. 303p. 1999. pap., suppl. ed. write for info. (*0-327-01267-6*, 7487813) LEXIS Pub.

Michie's Jurisprudence for Virginia & West Virginia, 1999 Replacement: A Complete Treatise of Virginia & West Virginia Law, Vol. 4A. Ed. by G. E. Legner et al. 485p. 1999. write for info. (*0-327-01500-4*, 7472411) LEXIS Pub.

Michie's Jurisprudence for Virginia & West Virginia, 1999 Replacement: A Complete Treatise of Virginia & West Virginia Law, Vol. 4B. Ed. by G. E. Legner et al. 565p. 1999. write for info. (*0-327-01501-2*, 7473411) LEXIS Pub.

Michie's Jurisprudence for Virginia & West Virginia, 1999 Replacement Vol. 4C: A Complete Treatise of Virginia & West Virginia Law, 53 vols. Ed. by M. J. Divine & G. E. Legner. 557p. 1999. write for info. (*0-327-01054-1*, 7475410) LEXIS Pub.

Michie's Jurisprudence for Virginia & West Virginia 1999 Replacement Vol. 21B, Pt. 1: State Court Rules, 53 vols. Ed. by M. J. Divine & G. E. Legner. 550p. 1999. write for info. (*0-327-00944-6*, 7482012) LEXIS Pub.

Michie's Jurisprudence, 1998 Replacement, Vol. 7A. 1998. text. write for info. (*0-327-00177-1*, 74748-11) LEXIS Pub.

Michie's Jurisprudence, 1998 Replacement, Vol. 7B. 1998. text. write for info. (*0-327-00178-X*, 74749-11) LEXIS Pub.

Michie's Jurisprudence 1998 Citator, 2 vols. Ed. by M. J. Divine. Incl. Michie's Jurisprudence 1998 Citator: Vol. A-L. Ed. by G. E. Legner. 1998. (*0-327-00852-0*, 7491010); Michie's Jurisprudence1998 Citator: Vol. M-Z. Ed. by Gary Legner. 1998. (*0-327-00853-9*, 7491210); 1400p. 1998. write for info. (*0-327-00851-2*, 7491010) LEXIS Pub.

Michie's Jurisprudence 1998 Citator: Vol. A-L see Michie's Jurisprudence 1998 Citator

Michie's Jurisprudence1998 Citator: Vol. M-Z see Michie's Jurisprudence 1998 Citator

***Michie's Jurisprudence 99 Table of Statutes: A Complete Treatise of Virginia/West Virginia.** Ed. by M. J. Divine et al. 200p. 1999. pap. write for info. (*0-327-04960-X*, 7484211) LEXIS Pub.

Michie's Jurisprudence of Virginia & West Virginia with 1991 Cumulative Supplement, 50 vols., Set. rev. ed. Michie Butterworth Editorial Staff & J. P. Munger. 1993. 1200.00 (*0-87215-128-X*, 74700-10, MICHIE) LEXIS Pub.

***Michie's Jurisprudence of Virginia & West Virginia 2000 Replacement Vol. 11B: A Complete Treatise of Virginia-West Virginia, 51 vols.** Ed. by G. E. Legner et al. 576p. 2000. write for info. (*0-327-04943-X*, 7476811) LEXIS Pub.

***Michie's Jurisprudence of Virginia & West Virginia 2000 Replacement Vol. 16: A Complete Treatise of Virginia - West Virginia.** Ed. by G. E. Legner et al. 512p. 2000. write for info. (*0-327-04941-3*, 7479211) LEXIS Pub.

Michie's Jurisprudence Table of Statutes: 1998 Cumulative Supplement, 50 vols. Ed. by M. J. Divine & Gary Legner. 125p. 1998. write for info. (*0-327-00175-5*, 7484210) LEXIS Pub.

***Michie's Jurisprudence, 1999 Citator Vols. A-L & M-Z: A Complete Treatise of Virginia/West Virginia.** Ed. by M. J. Divine et al. 1300p. 1999. write for info. (*0-327-04959-6*, 7491011) LEXIS Pub.

***Michie's Nevada Court Rules Annotated: 2000 Edition.** 1280p. 1999. pap. write for info. (*0-327-09909-7*, 4554117) LEXIS Pub.

Michie's Nevada Revised Statutes Annotated, 26. 800.00 (*0-327-11815-6*) LEXIS Pub.

Michie's Nevada Revised Statutes Annotated, Court Rules Annotated, June 1999 Supplement: Pocket Part. annot. ed. 107p. 1999. write for info. (*0-327-08705-6*) LEXIS Pub.

***Michie's Nevada Revised Statutes Annotated, Replacement Volume 16.** Ed. by LEXIS Law Publishing Editors. 851p. 2000. write for info. (*0-327-13122-5*, 4548613) LEXIS Pub.

***Michie's Nevada Revised Statutes Annotated, Replacement Volume 17.** Ed. by LEXIS Law Publishing Editors. 1392p. 2000. write for info. (*0-327-13123-3*, 4549112) LEXIS Pub.

Michie's Nevada Revised Statutes Annotated 1999 Advance Service Pamphlet, No. 2. 600p. 1999. pap. write for info. (*0-327-08001-9*, 45552-15) LEXIS Pub.

Michie's Nevada Revised Statutes Annotated, 1999 Replacement, Vol. 9. annot. ed. 1000p. 1999. write for info. (*0-327-08648-3*, 45450-12) LEXIS Pub.

***Michie's Nevada Revised Statutes Annotated 2000 Replacement, Vol. 11.** 1250p. 2000. write for info. (*0-327-13121-7*, 4546112) LEXIS Pub.

Michie's Research Guide to Nebraska Law. Ann C. Fletcher & Michie (Firm) Staff. LC 95-81039. xiii, 111p. 1995. write for info. (*1-55834-286-9*) LEXIS Pub.

***Michie's Revised Statutes Annotated Court Rules: June 2000 Supplement.** 100p. 2000. pap. write for info. (*0-327-11836-9*, 4554217) LEXIS Pub.

***Michie's West Virginia Code Vol. 14: 1999 Edition Replacement.** 462p. 1999. write for info. (*0-327-09225-4*, 4947914) LEXIS Pub.

***Michie's West Virginia Code Vol. 14A: 1999 Edition Replacement.** 630p. 1999. write for info. (*0-327-09224-6*, 4948210) LEXIS Pub.

***Michie's West Virginia Code Annotated: 2000 Court Rules Supplement, 2.** The Publisher's Editorial Staff. 50p. 2000. pap. write for info. (*0-327-12204-8*, 4965118) LEXIS Pub.

Michie's West Virginia Code Annotated Advance Court Rules Service. 48p. 1999. pap. write for info. (*0-327-07616-X*, 4127110) LEXIS Pub.

***Michie's West Virginia Code Annotated Advance Court Rules Service.** 80p. 1999. pap. write for info. (*0-327-09827-9*, 4128110) LEXIS Pub.

***Michie's West Virginia Code Annotated Advance Court Rules Service.** 80p. 1999. write for info. (*0-327-09837-6*, 4128210) LEXIS Pub.

Michie's West Virginia Code Annotated Annotation Citator. 1600p. 1998. write for info. (*0-327-07112-5*, 43150-10) LEXIS Pub.

***Michie's West Virginia Code Annotated, Annotation Citator.** 1300p. 2000. write for info. (*0-327-11055-4*, 4135012) LEXIS Pub.

Michie's West Virginia Code Annotated, 1999 Court Rules Supplement. 100p. 1999. write for info. (*0-327-08238-0*, 49651-17) LEXIS Pub.

Michie's West Virginia Code Annotated, Replacement, Vol. 1. 749p. 1999. write for info. (*0-327-07471-X*, 4941311) LEXIS Pub.

Michie's West Virginia Code Annotated, Replacement Volume: 1998 Edition, Vol. 8A. annot. ed. Ed. by Ruth Knight. 1000p. 1998. write for info. (*0-327-05789-0*, 49448-12) LEXIS Pub.

Michie's West Virginia Code Annotated, Replacement Volume: 1998 Edition, Vol. 9A. annot. ed. Ed. by Ruth Knight. 570p. 1998. write for info. (*0-327-05790-4*, 49453-11) LEXIS Pub.

Michie's West Virginia Code Annotated, Replacement Volume: 1998 Edition, Vol. 14. annot. ed. Ed. by Ruth Knight. 1000p. 1998. write for info. (*0-327-05788-2*, 49479-13) LEXIS Pub.

Michie's West Virginia Code Annotated, 1999 Cumulative Supplement, 23 vols. annot. ed. Incl. Michie's West Virginia Code Annotated, 1999 Cumulative Supplement: Chapters 12 to 15 Public Moneys/Public Safety. 1999. (*0-327-08908-3*, 50526-16); Michie's West Virginia Code Annotated, 1999 Cumulative Supplement Vol. 1: Constitutions/Tables. 1999. (*0-327-08903-2*, 50521-16); Michie's West Virginia Code Annotated, 1999 Cumulative Supplement Vol. 2A: Chapters 5A-7. 1999. (*0-327-08904-0*, 50523-16); Michie's West Virginia Code Annotated, 1999 Cumulative Supplement Vol. 3: Chapters 8-10 (Municipal Corps./Veterans' Affairs) 1999. (*0-327-08905-9*, 50524-16); Michie's West Virginia Code Annotated, 1999 Cumulative Supplement Vol. 4: Split Volume Chapter 11 Taxation. 1999. (*0-327-08906-7*, 50525-16); Michie's West Virginia Code Annotated, 1999 Cumulative Supplement Vol. 4A: Chapters 11 to 11A Taxation. 1999. (*0-327-08907-5*, 50545-16); Michie's West Virginia Code Annotated, 1999 Cumulative Supplement Vol. 5A: Chapter 16 Public Health. 1999. (*0-327-08909-1*); Michie's West Virginia Code Annotated, 1999 Cumulative Supplement Vol. 6: Chapters 17 to 17E Roads & Highways/Motor. 1999. (*0-327-08910-5*, 50527-16); Michie's West Virginia Code Annotated, 1999 Cumulative Supplement Vol. 7: Chapter 18 Education. 1999. (*0-327-08911-3*, 50528-16); Michie's West Virginia Code Annotated, 1999 Cumulative Supplement Vol. 7A: Chapters 18A to 19 Shool Personnel/Student Loans/Dept. of Agriculture. 1999. (*0-327-08912-1*, 50529-16); Michie's West Virginia Code Annotated, 1999 Cumulative Supplement Vol. 8: Chapters 20 to 21A Natural Resources/Labor/ Unemployment Compensation. 1999. (*0-327-08913-X*, 50530-16); Michie's West Virginia Code Annotated, 1999 Cumulative Supplement Vol. 8A: Chapters 22 to 23 Environmental Resources/Workers' Compensation. 1999. (*0-327-08914-8*, 50531-16); Michie's West Virginia Code Annotated, 1999 Cumulative Supplement Vol. 9: Chapters 24 to 29 Public Service Commission/State Penal Institutions. 1999. (*0-327-08915-6*, 50532-16); Michie's West Virginia Code Annotated, 1999 Cumulative Supplement Vol. 9A: Chapters 29A to 30 Uniform Notary Act/Professions & Occupations. 1999. (*0-327-08916-4*, 50533-16); Michie's West Virginia Code Annotated, 1999 Cumulative Supplement Vol. 10: Chapters 31 to 31C Corporations/Banks & Banking/Credit Unions. 1999. (*0-327-08917-2*, 50534-16); Michie's West Virginia Code Annotated, 1999 Cumulative Supplement Vol. 10A, Chpts. 32 & 33: Uniform Securities Act/Land Sales/Insurance. 1999. (*0-327-08918-0*, 50535-16); Michie's West Virginia Code Annotated, 1999 Cumulative Supplement Vol. 11: Chapters 34 to 38 Real Property/Zoning/Liens. 1999. (*0-327-08919-9*, 50536-16); Michie's West Virginia Code Annotated, 1999 Cumulative Supplement Vol. 12: Chapters 39 to 45 Estates & Trusts/Suretyship/Guardianship. 1999. (*0-327-08920-2*, 50537-16); Michie's West Virginia Code Annotated, 1999 Cumulative Supplement Vol. 13: Chapter 46 Uniform Commercial Code. 1999. (*0-327-08921-0*, 50538-16); Michie's West Virginia Code Annotated, 1999 Cumulative Supplement Vol. 14: Chapters 46A to 49 West Virginia Lending & Credit Rate Board/Child Welfare. 1999. (*0-327-08922-9*, 50539-16); Michie's West Virginia Code Annotated, 1999 Cumulative Supplement Vol. 15: Chapters 50 to 55 Magistrate Courts/Eminent Domain. 2000. (*0-327-08923-7*, 50540-16); Michie's West Virginia Code Annotated, 1999 Cumulative Supplement Vol. 16: Chapters 56 to 59 Pleading & Practice/Fees, Allowances & Costs. 1999. (*0-327-08924-5*, 50541-16); Michie's West Virginia Code Annotated, 1999 Cumulative Supplement Vol. 17: Chapters 60 to 64 State Control of Alcoholic Liquors/Criminal Procedure/Repeal of Statutes/Legislative Rules. 1999. (*0-327-08925-3*, 50542-16); 3500p. 1999. write for info. (*0-327-08518-5*, 4964816) LEXIS Pub.

Michie's West Virginia Code Annotated, 1999 Cumulative Supplement: Chapters 12 to 15 Public Moneys/Public Safety see Michie's West Virginia Code Annotated, 1999 Cumulative Supplement

Michie's West Virginia Code Annotated, 1999 Cumulative Supplement, Vol. 1, Constitutions/Tables see Michie's West Virginia Code Annotated, 1999 Cumulative Supplement

Michie's West Virginia Code Annotated, 1999 Cumulative Supplement, Vol. 2A, Chapters 5A-7 see Michie's West Virginia Code Annotated, 1999 Cumulative Supplement

Michie's West Virginia Code Annotated, 1999 Cumulative Supplement, Vol. 3, Chapters 8-10 (Municipal Corps./Veterans' Affairs) see Michie's West Virginia Code Annotated, 1999 Cumulative Supplement

Michie's West Virginia Code Annotated, 1999 Cumulative Supplement, Vol. 4, Split Volume Chapter 11 Taxation see Michie's West Virginia Code Annotated, 1999 Cumulative Supplement

M

An Asterisk (*) at the beginning of an entry indicates that the title is appearing for the first time.

Michie's West Virginia Code Annotated, 1999 Cumulative Supplement, Vol. 4A, Chapters 11 to 11A Taxation see Michie's West Virginia Code Annotated, 1999 Cumulative Supplement

Michie's West Virginia Code Annotated, 1999 Cumulative Supplement, Vol. 5A, Chapter 16 Public Health see Michie's West Virginia Code Annotated, 1999 Cumulative Supplement

Michie's West Virginia Code Annotated, 1999 Cumulative Supplement, Vol. 6, Chapters 17 to 17E Roads & Highways/Motor see Michie's West Virginia Code Annotated, 1999 Cumulative Supplement

Michie's West Virginia Code Annotated, 1999 Cumulative Supplement, Vol. 7, Chapter 18 Education see Michie's West Virginia Code Annotated, 1999 Cumulative Supplement

Michie's West Virginia Code Annotated, 1999 Cumulative Supplement, Vol. 7A, Chapters 18A to 19 Shool Personnel/Student Loans/Dept. of Agriculture see Michie's West Virginia Code Annotated, 1999 Cumulative Supplement

Michie's West Virginia Code Annotated, 1999 Cumulative Supplement, Vol. 8, Chapters 20 to 21A Natural Resources/Labor/Unemployment Compensation see Michie's West Virginia Code Annotated, 1999 Cumulative Supplement

M

Michie's West Virginia Code Annotated, 1999 Cumulative Supplement, Vol. 8A, Chapters 22 to 23 Environmental Resources/Workers' Compensation see Michie's West Virginia Code Annotated, 1999 Cumulative Supplement

Michie's West Virginia Code Annotated, 1999 Cumulative Supplement, Vol. 9, Chapters 24 to 29 Public Service Commission/State Penal Institutions see Michie's West Virginia Code Annotated, 1999 Cumulative Supplement

Michie's West Virginia Code Annotated, 1999 Cumulative Supplement, Vol. 9A, Chapters 29A to 30 Uniform Notary Act/Professions & Occupations see Michie's West Virginia Code Annotated, 1999 Cumulative Supplement

Michie's West Virginia Code Annotated, 1999 Cumulative Supplement, Vol. 10, Chapters 31 to 31C Corporations/Banks & Banking/Credit Unions see Michie's West Virginia Code Annotated, 1999 Cumulative Supplement

Michie's West Virginia Code Annotated, 1999 Cumulative Supplement, Vol. 10A, Chpts. 32 & 33, Uniform Securities Act/Land Sales/Insurance see Michie's West Virginia Code Annotated, 1999 Cumulative Supplement

Michie's West Virginia Code Annotated, 1999 Cumulative Supplement, Vol. 11, Chapters 34 to 38 Real Property/Zoning/Liens see Michie's West Virginia Code Annotated, 1999 Cumulative Supplement

Michie's West Virginia Code Annotated, 1999 Cumulative Supplement, Vol. 12, Chapters 39 to 45 Estates & Trusts/Suretyship/Guardianship see Michie's West Virginia Code Annotated, 1999 Cumulative Supplement

Michie's West Virginia Code Annotated, 1999 Cumulative Supplement, Vol. 13, Chapter 46 Uniform Commercial Code see Michie's West Virginia Code Annotated, 1999 Cumulative Supplement

Michie's West Virginia Code Annotated, 1999 Cumulative Supplement, Vol. 14, Chapters 46A to 49 West Virginia Lending & Credit Rate Board/Child Welfare see Michie's West Virginia Code Annotated, 1999 Cumulative Supplement

Michie's West Virginia Code Annotated, 1999 Cumulative Supplement, Vol. 15, Chapters 50 to 55 Magistrate Courts/Eminent Domain see Michie's West Virginia Code Annotated, 1999 Cumulative Supplement

Michie's West Virginia Code Annotated, 1999 Cumulative Supplement, Vol. 16, Chapters 56 to 59 Pleading & Practice/Fees, Allowances & Costs see Michie's West Virginia Code Annotated, 1999 Cumulative Supplement

Michie's West Virginia Code Annotated, 1999 Cumulative Supplement, Vol. 17, Chapters 60 to 64 State Control of Alcoholic Liquors/Criminal Procedure/Repeal of Statutes/Legislative Rules see Michie's West Virginia Code Annotated, 1999 Cumulative Supplement

*Michie's West Virginia Code Annotation Citator. 950p. 1999. pap. 59.95 (0-327-09460-5, 4135011) LEXIS Pub.

*Michie's West Virginia Code, 1999 Edition Replacement Volume 4. 740p. 1999. Price not set. (0-327-09631-4, 4942812) LEXIS Pub.

*Michie's West Virginia Code, 1999 Edition Replacement Volume 7. 735p. 1999. Price not set. (0-327-09632-2, 4944412) LEXIS Pub.

Michie's West Virginia Code, 1999 Advance Legislative Service, No. 1. 400p. 1999. pap. write for info. (0-327-07974-6, 49671-13) LEXIS Pub.

Michie's West Virginia Code, 1999 Advance Legislative Service, No. 2. 800p. 1999. pap. write for info. (0-327-07975-4, 49672-13) LEXIS Pub.

Michie's West Virginia Code, 1999 Advance Legislative Service, No. 3. 800p. 1999. pap. write for info. (0-327-07976-2, 49673-13) LEXIS Pub.

Michie's West Virginia Code, Replacement, Vol. 9. 1107p. 1999. write for info. (0-327-07442-6, 4945111) LEXIS Pub.

*Michie's West Virginia Code, 1999 Edition Replacement, No. 2. 930p. 1999. Price not set. (0-327-08789-7, 4941912) LEXIS Pub.

*Michie's West Virginia 2000 Advance Code Service Pamphlet No. 1. 100p. 1999. pap. Price not set. (0-327-09721-3, 4958316) LEXIS Pub.

Michigan see From Sea to Shining Sea

Michigan see Atlas of Historical County Boundaries

Michigan see One Nation Series

Michigan see Celebrate the States - Group 4

*Michigan. (Switched on Schoolhouse Ser.). (Illus.). (J). 2000. pap. 24.95 (0-7403-0274-4) Alpha AZ.

*Michigan. Alliance for Safe Driving Staff. (Career Education - License to Drive Ser.). 2001. 31.50 (0-7668-2372-5) Delmar.

Michigan. Capstone Press Geography Department Staff. (One Nation Ser.). (Illus.). 48p. (J). (gr. 3-7). 1996. 19.00 (0-516-20263-4) Childrens.

*Michigan. Jim Fizzell. (Midwest Fruit & Vegetables Ser.). (Illus.). 2000. pap. 19.95 (1-930604-12-2) Cool Springs Pr.

Michigan. Dennis B. Fradin. (From Sea to Shining Sea Ser.). (Illus.). 64p. (J). (gr. 3-5). 1994. pap. 7.95 (0-516-43822-0) Childrens.

Michigan. Kevin Hillstrom. (Adventure Guide). 356p. 1998. pap. text 16.95 (1-55650-820-4) Hunter NJ.

Michigan. Paul Joseph. LC 97-10497. (United States Ser.). (Illus.). 32p. (J). 1998. lib. bdg. 19.93 (1-56239-860-1, Checkerboard Library) ABDO Pub Co.

Michigan. Photos by David Muench et al. (Illus.). 112p. 1995. pap. 17.95 (1-56313-761-5) BrownTrout Pubs Inc.

*Michigan. Evelyn Pena. (Illus.). 64p. (gr. 1-5). 2000. pap. 5.95 (1-892920-48-4) G H B Pubs.

*Michigan. John Penrod. 32p. 1999. pap. 5.95 (0-942618-90-4) Penrod-Hiawatha.

Michigan. Karen Sirvaitis. LC 92-44847. (Hello U. S. A. Ser.). (Illus.). 72p. (J). 1994. pap. 5.95 (0-8225-9707-1, Lerner Publctns) Lerner Pub.

Michigan. Karen Sirvaitis. LC 92-44847. (Hello U. S. A. Ser.). (Illus.). 72p. (J). (gr. 3-6). 1994. lib. bdg. 19.93 (0-8225-2722-7, Lerner Publctns) Lerner Pub.

Michigan. Kathleen Thompson. LC 87-16373. (Portrait of America Library). 48p. (YA). (gr. 4-8). 1996. pap. 5.95 (0-8114-7447-X) Raintree Steck-V.

Michigan. Kathleen Thompson. LC 87-16373. (Portrait of America Library). (Illus.). 48p. (YA). (gr. 3-6). 1996. lib. bdg. 22.83 (0-8114-7342-2) Raintree Steck-V.

Michigan: A Book of 30 Postcards. Ed. by BrownTrout Publishing Company Staff. (Illus.). 1995. pap. 7.95 (1-56313-775-5) BrownTrout Pubs Inc.

Michigan: A Guide to the Wolverine State. Federal Writers' Project Staff. LC 72-84482. (American Guidebook Ser.). 1981. reprint ed. 89.00 (0-403-02172-3) Somerset Pub.

Michigan: A Guide to the Wolverine State. Federal Writers' Project Staff & Writers Program-WPA Staff. (American Guide Ser.). 1989. reprint ed. pap. 39.00 (0-685-35458-X, 1021); reprint ed. lib. bdg. 89.00 (0-7812-1021-6, 1021) Rprt Serv.

Michigan: A History of the Great Lakes State. 2nd rev. ed. Bruce A. Rubenstein & Lawrence E. Ziewacz. (Illus.). 282p. (C). 1995. pap. text 21.95 (0-88295-919-0) Harlan Davidson.

Michigan: A History of the Wolverine State. 3rd rev. ed. Willis F. Dunbar & George S. May. (Illus.). 784p. 1995. pap. 30.00 (0-8028-7055-4) Eerdmans.

Michigan: A Photographic Portfolio. Photos by David Muench et al. (Illus.). 112p. 1995. 25.95 (1-56313-760-7) BrownTrout Pubs Inc.

Michigan: An Illustrated History for Children. 2nd ed. John C. Mitchell. (Illus.). 52p. (J). (gr. 1-6). 1987. reprint ed. 16.95 (0-9621466-0-9) Suttons Bay Pubns.

Michigan: Champions of the West. Bruce Madej. 274p. 1997. 39.95 (1-57167-115-3) Sports Pub.

Michigan: From the Eyry of the Eagle. Dale Fisher. Ed. by Shannon M. Culver. (Illus.). 148p. 1986. 60.00 (0-9615623-1-5) Eyry Eagle Pub.

Michigan: Its Land & Its People. James Killoran et al. (Illus.). 354p. (YA). (gr. 4 up). 1997. pap. text 14.95 (1-882422-31-7) Jarrett Pub.

*Michigan: Off the Beaten Path: A Guide to Unique Places. 5th ed. Jim Dufresne. LC 99-21342. (Illus.). 225p. 1999. pap. 12.95 (0-7627-0269-9) Globe Pequot.

Michigan: Photos of Dennis Cox. Photos by Dennis Cox. (Illus.). 144p. 1993. 39.95 (1-55868-099-3) Gr Arts Ctr Pub.

Michigan: Savor Its Flavors. Gail Main. 1996. pap. 8.95 (0-9629554-0-X) Mainly Food.

Michigan: The Spirit of the Land. Kathy-Jo Wargin. LC 98-45251. (Illus.). 144p. 1999. 35.00 (0-89658-381-3) Voyageur Pr.

Michigan: The State & It's Educational System. Harold L. Hodgkinson. 10p. 1987. 7.00 (0-937846-85-6) Inst Educ Lead.

Michigan: The Wolverines Championship Season. Ed. by Tom Panzenhagen. (Illus.). 112p. 1998. pap. 12.95 (0-937247-25-1) Detroit Pr.

Michigan: Zoos & Animal Parks. Bill Bailey. (Glovebox Guidebooks Travel Guide Ser.). 160p. 1992. write for info. (1-881139-00-X) Glovebox Guidebks.

Michigan - Collected Works of Federal Writers Project. Federal Writers' Project Staff. 1991. reprint ed. lib. bdg. 98.00 (0-7812-5632-1) Rprt Serv.

Michigan, a History. Bruce Catton. 1984. pap. 13.95 (0-393-30175-3) Norton.

Michigan, a History of Governments. rev. ed. Thomas M. Cooley. LC 72-3764. (American Commonwealths Ser.: No. 5). reprint ed. 42.50 (0-404-57205-7) AMS Pr.

Michigan, Adjutant General Vol. 1: Record First Michigan Infantry, Civil War, 1861-1865. 151p. 1988. reprint ed. 12.95 (0-914905-01-5) Detroit Bk Pr.

Michigan, Adjutant General Vol. 2: Record Second Michigan Infantry, Civil War, 1861-1865. 151p. 1988. reprint ed. 12.95 (0-914905-02-3) Detroit Bk Pr.

Michigan, Adjutant General Vol. 3: Record Third Michigan Infantry, Civil War, 1861-1865. 151p. 1988. reprint ed. 12.95 (0-914905-03-1) Detroit Bk Pr.

Michigan, Adjutant General Vol. 4: Record Fourth Michigan Infantry, Civil War, 1861-1865. 151p. 1988. reprint ed. 12.95 (0-914905-04-X) Detroit Bk Pr.

Michigan, Adjutant General Vol. 5: Record Fifth Michigan Infantry, Civil War, 1861-1865. 151p. 1988. reprint ed. 12.95 (0-914905-05-8) Detroit Bk Pr.

Michigan, Adjutant General Vol. 6: Record Sixth Michigan Infantry, Civil War, 1861-1865. 151p. 1988. reprint ed. 12.95 (0-914905-06-6) Detroit Bk Pr.

Michigan, Adjutant General Vol. 7: Record Seventh Michigan Infantry, Civil War, 1861-1865. 151p. 1988. reprint ed. 12.95 (0-914905-07-4) Detroit Bk Pr.

Michigan, Adjutant General Vol. 8: Record Eighth Michigan Infantry, Civil War, 1861-1865. 151p. 1988. reprint ed. 12.95 (0-914905-08-2) Detroit Bk Pr.

Michigan, Adjutant General Vol. 9: Record Ninth Michigan Infantry, Civil War, 1861-1865. 151p. 1988. reprint ed. 12.95 (0-914905-09-0) Detroit Bk Pr.

Michigan, Adjutant General Vol. 10: Record Tenth Michigan Infantry, Civil War, 1861-1865. 151p. 1988. reprint ed. 12.95 (0-914905-10-4) Detroit Bk Pr.

Michigan Administrative Code, 1979: 1988 Annual Supplement. Intro. by Roger W. Peters. (Illus.). 1050p. 1988. pap. 27.00 (1-878210-01-7) Legis Serv Bur.

Michigan Administrative Code, 1979: 1989 Annual Supplement. Michigan Legislative Council Staff. Ed. by Roger W. Peters. 1071p. 1990. pap. 26.50 (1-878210-02-5) Legis Serv Bur.

Michigan Administrative Code, 1979: 1990 Annual Supplement. Michigan Legislative Council Staff. Ed. by Roger W. Peters. 1991. pap. 30.00 (1-878210-03-3) Legis Serv Bur.

Michigan Administrative Code, 1979: 1992 Annual Supplement. Michigan Legislative Council Staff. Ed. by Roger W. Peters. 1993. pap. 36.00 (1-878210-05-X) Legis Serv Bur.

Michigan Administrative Code, 1979: 1993 Annual Supplement. Michigan Legislative Council Staff. Ed. by Roger Peters. 1994. pap. 33.00 (1-878210-07-6) Legis Serv Bur.

Michigan Administrative Code, 1979: 1994 Annual Supplement. Michigan Legislative Council Staff. Ed. by Roger Peters. 1995. pap. write for info. (1-878210-08-4) Legis Serv Bur.

Michigan Administrative Code 1979 1997 Annual Supplement. Michigan Legislative Council Staff. Ed. by Roger Peters. pap. write for info. (1-878210-11-4) Legis Serv Bur.

Michigan & It's Educational System: Another Look. Harold L. Hodgkinson. 18p. 1989. 7.00 (0-937846-65-1) Inst Educ Lead.

Michigan & Other State Greats (Biographies) Carole Marsh. (Carole Marsh Michigan Bks.). (Illus.). (J). (gr. 3 up). 1994. pap. 19.95 (1-55609-678-X); lib. bdg. 29.95 (1-55609-677-1); disk 29.95 (1-55609-679-8) Gallopade Intl.

Michigan & the Cleveland Era: Sketches of University of Michigan Staff Members & Alumni Who Served the Cleveland Administrations, 1885-89,1893-97. Ed. by Earl D. Babst & Lewis G. Vander Velde. LC 70-179724. (Biography Index Reprint Ser.). 1977. reprint ed. 30.95 (0-8369-8092-1) Ayer.

Michigan Antitrust Digest. Irwin M. Alterman. 190p. 1975. ring bd., suppl. ed. 55.00 (0-685-38200-1, 75-005) U MI Law CLE.

Michigan Antitrust Digest: 1989 Supplement. Irwin M. Alterman. 190p. 1989. suppl. ed. 12.00 (0-685-47523-9) U MI Law CLE.

Michigan Antitrust Digest: 1990 Supplement. Irwin M. Alterman. 190p. 1990. suppl. ed. 15.00 (0-685-58875-0) U MI Law CLE.

Michigan Antitrust Digest: 1992 Supplement. Irwin M. Alterman. 190p. 1992. suppl. ed. 18.00 (0-685-58876-9) U MI Law CLE.

Michigan Appellate Handbook. 2nd ed. Nancy L. Bosh et al. LC 91-78185. 786p. 1992. ring bd. 110.00 (0-685-65988-7, 85-009) U MI Law CLE.

Michigan Approved Court Forms. LC 85-60148. 1594p. 1987. suppl. ed. 55.00 (0-685-44338-8, 87-024) U MI Law CLE.

Michigan at Gettysburg. Luther S. Trowbridge. (Illus.). 230p. 1998. reprint ed. 25.00 (0-944413-56-0, 214) Longstreet Hse.

*Michigan Atlas & Gazetteer. 7th ed. Ed. by DeLorme Mapping Staff. (Illus.). 2000. pap. 19.95 (0-89933-278-1) DeLorme Map.

Michigan Authors. 3rd rev. ed. Compiled & Pref. by Carol Smallwood. LC 93-30097. 439p. 1993. 39.95 (0-910726-28-0) Hillsdale Educ.

Michigan Automotive Directory. Ed. by T. L. Spelman. 1985. 24.95 (1-55527-018-2) Auto Contact Inc.

Michigan Avenue: From Museums to the Magnificent Mile. (Skyline: Pt. III). write for info. (1-880005-04-2) Perspectvs Intl.

Michigan Bandits, Bushwackers, Outlaws, Crooks, Devils, Ghosts, Desperadoes & Other Assorted & Sundry Characters! Carole Marsh. (Carole Marsh Michigan Bks.). (Illus.). (J). (gr. 3 up). 1994. pap. 19.95 (0-7933-0598-5); lib. bdg. 29.95 (0-7933-0599-3); disk 29.95 (0-7933-0600-0) Gallopade Intl.

Michigan Basic Practice Handbook, 2 vols. 3rd ed. LC 89-81571. 1500p. 1989. ring bd., suppl. ed. 135.00 (0-685-45470-3, 89-031) U MI Law CLE.

Michigan Basic Practice Handbook, 2 vols. 3rd ed. LC 89-81571. 1500p. 1990. suppl. ed. 45.00 (0-685-45471-1) U MI Law CLE.

Michigan Basic Practice Handbook, 2 vols. 3rd ed. LC 89-81571. 1500p. 1991. suppl. ed. 50.00 (0-685-58668-5) U MI Law CLE.

Michigan Basic Practice Handbook, 2 vols. 3rd ed. LC 89-81571. 1500p. 1992. suppl. ed. 55.00 (0-685-58669-3) U MI Law CLE.

Michigan Beyond 2000. William Johnston et al. LC 87-10725. (Illus.). 188p. (Orig.). (C). 1988. lib. bdg. 44.00 (0-8191-6462-3, Pub. by Hudson Instit IN) U Pr of Amer.

Michigan "BIO" Bingo! 24 Must Know State People for Kids to Learn about While Having Fun! Carole Marsh. (Bingo! Ser.). (Illus.). (J). (gr. 2-8). 1998. pap. 14.95 (0-7933-8588-1) Gallopade Intl.

*Michigan Biographies, 2 vols. Ed. by Michigan Historical Commission Staff. 966p. 1999. pap. 65.00 (0-8063-4930-1) Clearfield Co.

Michigan Birds. James Kavanagh. (Pocket Naturalist Ser.). (Illus.). 12p. (YA). 1999. pap. 5.95 (1-889903-85-X, Pub. by Waterford WA) Falcon Pub Inc.

*Michigan Blue-Ribbon Fly Fishing Guide. Bob Linsenman. (Illus.). 96p. 2000. pap. 24.95 (1-57188-160-3) F Amato Pubns.

Michigan Book of Bests: An Eclectic Barrage of Great Places to Go & Things to Know. Gary W. Barfknecht. (Illus.). 120p. 1999. pap. 13.95 (0-923756-20-5) Friede Pubns.

Michigan Bookstore Book: A Surprising Guide to Our State's Bookstores & Their Specialties for Students, Teachers, Writers & Publishers. Carole Marsh. (Carole Marsh Michigan Bks.). (Illus.). 1994. pap. 19.95 (0-7933-2922-1); lib. bdg. 29.95 (0-7933-2921-3); disk 29.95 (0-7933-2923-X) Gallopade Intl.

*Michigan Business Directory, 1999-2000. American Business Directories Staff. 3520p. 1999. boxed set 520.00 incl. cd-rom (0-7687-0136-8, 1047-1790) Am Busn Direct.

*Michigan Business Directory (2000-2001) American Business Directories Staff et al. 3,250p. 2000. boxed set 520.00 incl. cd-rom (0-7687-0221-6) Am Busn Direct.

Michigan Business Formbook, 3 Vols. Ed. by Mark A. Kleist et al. LC 89-80299. 1356p. 1989. suppl. ed. 210.00 incl. disk (0-685-44321-3, 89-003) U MI Law CLE.

Michigan Business Formbook, 3 Vols. Ed. by Mark A. Kleist et al. LC 89-80299. 1356p. 1991. suppl. ed. 65.00 (0-685-58357-0, 91-002) U MI Law CLE.

Michigan Business Formbook, 3 Vols. Ed. by Mark A. Kleist et al. LC 89-80299. 1356p. 1992. suppl. ed. 85.00 incl. disk (0-685-58358-9, 92-001) U MI Law CLE.

Michigan Business Formbook, 3 Vols. Ed. by Mark A. Kleist et al. LC 89-80299. 1356p. 1993. suppl. ed. 90.00 incl. disk (0-685-58359-7, 92-033) U MI Law CLE.

Michigan Business Formbook, 3 Vols., Vol. 3: Supplement. Ed. by Mark A. Kleist et al. LC 89-80299. 1356p. 1990. 80.00 (0-685-44322-1, 90-002) U MI Law CLE.

Michigan Business Torts. Edward H. Pappas & Jon R. Steiger. LC 91-73439. 332p. 1991. 115.00 (0-685-51910-4, 91-009) U MI Law CLE.

Michigan Butterflies & Skippers No. E2675: A Field Guide & Reference. Mogens C. Nielsen. Ed. by Leslie Johnson. LC 99-6307. (Illus.). 252p. 1999. pap. 19.95 (1-56525-012-5) MSU Ext.

Michigan Census Index, 1850 Mortality Schedules. (Illus.). 1979. lib. bdg. 53.00 (0-89593-379-9, Accel Indexing) Genealogical Srvcs.

Michigan Census Index, 1890 Union Vets. (Illus.). lib. bdg. 125.00 (0-89593-383-7, Accel Indexing) Genealogical Srvcs.

Michigan Census Index, 1837: Kalamazoo County Edition. Ronald V. Jackson. (Illus.). lib. bdg. 47.00 (0-89593-678-X, Accel Indexing) Genealogical Srvcs.

Michigan Citation Manual. John Doyle. LC 85-82097. 122p. 1986. lib. bdg. 32.00 (0-89941-462-1, 303780) W S Hein.

Michigan City's First Hundred Years. Elizabeth M. Munger. 97p. 1992. pap. 10.00 (0-935549-16-1) MI City Hist.

Michigan Civil Procedure During Trial. Ed. by Robert P. Young, Jr. & Daniel D. Kopka. LC 89-80473. 544p. 1992. suppl. ed. 40.00 (0-685-22719-7, 92-014) U MI Law CLE.

Michigan Civil Procedure During Trial. 2nd ed. Ed. by Robert P. Young, Jr. & Daniel D. Kopka. LC 89-80473. 544p. 1989. ring bd., suppl. ed. 110.00 (0-685-22718-9, 89-021) U MI Law CLE.

Michigan Civil Procedure Forms. Jeffrey N. Shillman et al. 760p. 1991. suppl. ed. 82.00 (0-685-74618-6, MICHIE) LEXIS Pub.

Michigan Civil Procedure Forms. Jeffrey N. Shillman et al. 760p. 1993. disk 50.00 (0-685-74619-4, MICHIE) LEXIS Pub.

Michigan Civil Procedure Forms. Jeffrey N. Shillman et al. 760p. 1994. spiral bd. 159.00 (0-8342-0104-6, 81695-10, MICHIE) LEXIS Pub.

Michigan Civil Procedure Litigation Manual. pap. 57.50 (1-58360-171-6) Anderson Pub Co.

Michigan Civil War History: An Annotated Bibliography. Ed. by George S. May. LC 61-14050. 140p. reprint ed. pap. 43.40 (0-7837-3670-3, 204354400009) Bks Demand.

Michigan Classic Christmas Trivia: Stories, Recipes, Activities, Legends, Lore & More! Carole Marsh. (Carole Marsh Michigan Bks.). (Illus.). (J). (gr. 3 up). 1994. pap. 19.95 (0-7933-0601-9); disk 29.95 (0-7933-0603-5) Gallopade Intl.

Michigan Classic Christmas Trivia: Stories, Recipes, Activities, Legends, Lore & More! Carole Marsh. (Carole Marsh Michigan Bks.). (Illus.). (J). (gr. 3 up). 1997. lib. bdg. 29.95 (0-7933-0602-7) Gallopade Intl.

Michigan Closely Held Corporations. Louis W. Kasischke. LC 86-81441. 944p. 1987. 125.00 (0-685-22686-7, 87-001) U MI Law CLE.

Michigan Closely Held Corporations. Louis W. Kasischke. LC 86-81441. 944p. 1990. suppl. ed. 65.00 (0-685-22687-5, 90-04) U MI Law CLE.

Michigan Coastales. Carole Marsh. (Carole Marsh Michigan Bks.). (Illus.). (J). (gr. 3 up). 1994. pap. 19.95 (*1-55609-672-0*); lib. bdg. 29.95 (*1-55609-671-2*); disk 29.95 (*1-55609-673-9*) Gallopade Intl.

Michigan Coastales! Carole Marsh. (Carole Marsh Michigan Bks.). (J). 1994. lib. bdg. 29.95 (*0-7933-7287-9*) Gallopade Intl.

Michigan Construction Liens. John F. Rohe. 500p. 95.00 (*0-327-12337-0*) LEXIS Pub.

Michigan Construction Liens. John F. Rohe. 500p. 1995. 95.00 (*1-55834-235-4*, 66615, MICHIE) LEXIS Pub.

Michigan Construction Liens: 1998 Cumulative Supplement. John F. Rohe. 1998. suppl. ed. 29.50 (*0-327-00186-0*, 66616-11) LEXIS Pub.

***Michigan Construction Liens, 1999 Cumulative Supplement: Pocketpart.** John F. Rohe. 71p. 1999. write for info. (*0-327-01393-1*, 6661612) LEXIS Pub.

Michigan Cookbook. Golden West Publisher. (Illus.). 94p. 1999. pap. 6.95 (*1-885590-29-6*) Golden West Pub.

Michigan Cookin' B. Carlson. (Illus.). 160p. 1994. spiral bd. 5.95 (*1-878488-99-6*) Hearts N Tummies.

Michigan Cooking . . . And Other Things. Carole Eberly. (Illus.). 112p. (Orig.). 1977. pap. 6.95 (*0-932296-00-9*) Eberly Pr.

Michigan Cooks: Favorite Recipes from Friends of C. S. Mott Childrens' Hospital University of Michigan. C.S. Mott Childrens Hospital Staff. (Illus.). 1997. 16.95 (*0-9652189-0-2*) UMI Hlth System.

Michigan Corporate Forms, 2 vols. Charles W. Borgsdorf. 1989. disk 75.00 (*0-685-74621-6*, MICHIE) LEXIS Pub.

Michigan Corporate Forms, 2 vols. Charles W. Borgsdorf. 1994. suppl. ed. 79.00 (*0-685-74620-8*, MICHIE) LEXIS Pub.

Michigan Corporate Forms, Issue 10. Charles W. Borgsdorf. 160p. 1999. ring bd. write for info. (*0-327-01262-5*, 8170515) LEXIS Pub.

Michigan Corporate Forms, 2 vols., Set. Charles W. Borgsdorf. 1520p. 1994. spiral bd. 259.00 (*0-8342-0074-0*, 81701-10, MICHIE) LEXIS Pub.

Michigan Corporation Law & Practice. Stephen H. Schulman. (National Corporation Law Ser.). 758p. 1998. ring bd. 165.00 (*0-13-109356-8*) Aspen Law.

Michigan Corporation Law with Federal Tax Analysis. Robert M. Schmidt & Zolman Cavitch. 1963. ring bd. 225.00 (*0-8205-1400-4*) Bender.

Michigan County Atlas. 1996. pap. text 19.95 (*0-7625-0108-1*) Universal Map Enterprises Inc.

Michigan County Map Guide. Michigan United Conservation Staff. 2000. pap. text 18.95 (*0-933112-18-1*) Mich United Conserv.

Michigan Court Rules Annotated: 1999 Edition see Michigan Court Rules Annotated, 1999 Edition

Michigan Court Rules Annotated, 1999 Edition, 2 vols. annot. ed. John F. Wagner, Jr. Incl. Vol. 1. Michigan Court Rules Annotated: 1999 Edition. annot. ed. 1300p. 1999. pap. (*0-327-07803-0*, 4438612); Vol. 2. Michigan Court Rules Annotated: 1999 Edition. annot. ed. 1300p. 1999. pap. (*0-327-07804-9*, 4438912); 2400p. 1999. Set pap. 70.00 (*0-327-07802-2*, 37671-12) LEXIS Pub.

Michigan Court Rules Annotated, 1998 Edition: December 1998 Supplement. 200p. 1998. pap. write for info. (*0-327-06813-2*, 57037-11) LEXIS Pub.

Michigan Court Rules Annotated, 1998 Edition: December 1998 Supplement, Vol. 1. 100p. 1998. write for info. (*0-327-06814-0*, 57029-11) LEXIS Pub.

Michigan Court Rules Annotated, 1998 Edition: December 1998 Supplement, Vol. 2. 100p. 1998. write for info. (*0-327-06815-9*, 57030-11) LEXIS Pub.

Michigan Court Rules Annotated, 1999 Edition: December 1999 Supplement, 2 vols. annot. ed. John F. Wagner, Jr. Incl. Vol. 2. Michigan Court Rules Annotated, 1999 Edition: December 1999 Supplement. annot. ed. 100p. 1999. pap. (*0-327-07823-5*, 5703012); Vol. 1. annot. ed. 100p. 1999. pap. (*0-327-07822-7*, 5702912); 200p. 1999. pap. write for info. (*0-327-07821-9*, 5703712) LEXIS Pub.

Michigan Court Rules Annotated, 1999 Edition: December 1999 Supplement see Michigan Court Rules Annotated, 1999 Edition: December 1999 Supplement

***Michigan Court Rules Annotated 2000 Edition Vols. 1 & 2.** 2418p. 2000. write for info. (*0-327-11209-3*, 3767113) LEXIS Pub.

***Michigan Court Rules Annotated 1999 Edition, 2 bks.** annot. ed. 2400p. 1999. pap. write for info. (*0-327-08720-X*, 3767112) LEXIS Pub.

Michigan Court Rules Practice - Text (Rules 6.000-6.999) 1993 Interim Pamphlet. 600p. 1993. pap. text. write for info. (*0-314-01736-4*) West Pub.

Michigan Court Rules Practice - Text (Rules 6.000-6.999) 1994 Interim Pamphlet. 447p. 1994. pap. text. write for info. (*0-314-04072-2*) West Pub.

Michigan Court Rules Practice - Text (Rules 6.000-6.999) 1995 Interim Pamphlet. 460p. (C). 1995. pap. text. write for info. (*0-314-06914-3*) West Pub.

Michigan Court Rules Practice - Text (Rules 6.000-6.999) 1996 Interim Pamphlet. 499p. 1996. pap. text. write for info. (*0-314-20309-5*) West Pub.

Michigan Court Rules Practice - Text (Rules 6.000-6.999) 1997 Interim Pamphlet. 479p. 1997. pap. text. write for info. (*0-314-22681-8*) West Pub.

Michigan Courtroom Evidence. rev. ed. Michael D. Wade & Jennifer J. Strom. Ed. by Lynn M. Collins. 700p. 1989. ring bd., suppl. ed. 110.00 (*0-685-45472-X*, 89-023) U MI Law CLE.

Michigan Courtroom Evidence. rev. ed. Michael D. Wade & Jennifer J. Strom. Ed. by Lynn M. Collins. 700p. 1992. suppl. ed. 45.00 (*0-685-35020-7*, 92-021) U MI Law CLE.

***Michigan Crime in Perspective 2000.** Ed. by Kathleen O'Leary Morgan & Scott E. Morgan. 22p. 2000. spiral bd. 19.00 (*0-7401-0321-0*) Morgan Quitno Corp.

Michigan Crime Perspective, 1998. Ed. by Kathleen O'Leary Morgan & Scott E. Morgan. 20p. 1998. pap. 19.00 (*1-56692-921-0*) Morgan Quitno Corp.

Michigan Crime Perspectives, 1999. Kathleen O'Leary Morgan. 22p. 1999. spiral bd. 19.00 (*0-7401-0121-8*) Morgan Quitno Corp.

***Michigan Criminal Code 2000: Handbook for Law Enforcement Officers.** rev. ed. Anderson Publishing Co. Staff. 576p. 1999. pap. 14.95 (*1-58360-100-7*) Anderson Pub Co.

Michigan Criminal Jury Instructions, 3 vols. 2nd ed. Michigan State Bar Special Committee on Standard C. LC 89-82310. 1500p. 1991. suppl. ed. 75.00 (*0-685-58877-7*, 92-030); disk. write for info. (*0-318-68094-7*) U MI Law CLE.

Michigan Criminal Jury Instructions, 3 vols., Set. 2nd ed. Michigan State Bar Special Committee on Standard C. LC 89-82310. 1500p. 1991. ring bd., suppl. ed. 210.00 (*0-685-38202-8*, 76-010) U MI Law CLE.

Michigan Criminal Law, 2 Vols. Alan Saltzman. 183.50 (*0-327-13434-8*) LEXIS Pub.

Michigan Criminal Procedure Benchbook. Michigan Judicial Institute Staff. LC 92-74196. 276p. 1992. ring bd. 85.00 (*0-685-65664-0*, 92-024) U MI Law CLE.

Michigan "Crinkum-Crankum" A Funny Word Book about Our State. Carole Marsh. (Carole Marsh Michigan Bks.). (Illus.). (J). 1994. pap. 19.95 (*0-7933-4875-7*); lib. bdg. 29.95 (*0-7933-4874-9*); disk 29.95 (*0-7933-4876-5*) Gallopade Intl.

Michigan Critical Care Handbook: Physiology, Pharmacology, Treatment Algorithms, Scoring Systems: 1,000 Indispensable Facts, Figures, & Graphs for the Adult ICU. 13th ed. Robert H. Bartlett. 40p. 1995. spiral bd. 29.00 (*0-316-08268-6*) Lppncott W & W.

***Michigan Curiosities: The Most Outlandish People, Places & Things in the Great State of Michigan.** Neal Rubin. (Illus.). 224p. 2000. pap. text 12.95 (*0-7627-0601-5*) Globe Pequot.

Michigan Damages Awards: 1996 Edition. rev. ed. Ed. by Timothy M. Hall. LC 94-76232. 600p. 1996. pap. text. write for info. (*0-7620-0090-2*) West Group.

Michigan Digest, 43 Vols. 1785.00 (*0-327-12545-4*) LEXIS Pub.

Michigan Digest: Table of Cases P-Z. rev. ed. LC 41-3091. 700p. 1998. write for info. (*0-327-00244-1*, 76441-11) LEXIS Pub.

Michigan Digest Vol. 19: Table of Cases A-F. rev. ed. LC 41-3091. 586p. 1998. write for info. (*0-327-00234-4*, 76539-11) LEXIS Pub.

Michigan Digest Vol. 19A: Table of Cases G-O. rev. ed. LC 41-3091. 540p. 1998. write for info. (*0-327-00243-3*, 76440-11) LEXIS Pub.

Michigan Dingbats! Bk. 1: A Fun Book of Games, Stories, Activities & More about Our State That's All in Code! for You to Decipher. Carole Marsh. (Carole Marsh Michigan Bks.). (Illus.). (J). (gr. 3-12). 1994. pap. 19.95 (*0-7933-3840-9*); lib. bdg. 29.95 (*0-7933-3839-5*); disk 29.95 (*0-7933-3841-7*) Gallopade Intl.

Michigan Directions: Flint Area Artists. LC 94-61869. (Illus.). 50p. 1994. pap. 12.95 (*0-939896-18-4*) Flint Inst Arts.

Michigan Divorce Book: A Guide to Doing an Uncontested Divorce Without an Attorney (with Minor Children) 4th rev. ed. Michael Maran. (Illus.). 288p. 1998. pap. 29.95 (*0-936343-11-7*) Grand River.

Michigan Divorce Book: A Guide to Doing an Uncontested Divorce Without an Attorney (Without Minor Children) 4th rev. ed. Michael Maran. (Illus.). 192p. 1998. pap. 24.95 (*0-936343-10-9*) Grand River.

Michigan Drunk Driving Law & Practice. 2nd ed. Ed. by Michael V. Morgan. LC 91-78184. 624p. 1992. ring bd. 95.00 (*0-685-65989-5*, 92-007) U MI Law CLE.

Michigan Early Census, Vol. 2. Ronald V. Jackson. (Illus.). 1981. lib. bdg. 48.00 (*0-89593-655-0*, Accel Indexing) Genealogical Srvcs.

Michigan Early Census, Vol. 3. Ronald V. Jackson. (Illus.). 1981. lib. bdg. 48.00 (*0-89593-727-1*, Accel Indexing) Genealogical Srvcs.

Michigan Early Census, Vol. 4. Ronald V. Jackson. (Illus.). 1981. lib. bdg. 53.00 (*0-89593-728-X*, Accel Indexing) Genealogical Srvcs.

***Michigan Employer's Guide: A Handbook of Employment Laws & Regulations.** Ed. by Summers Press, Inc. Staff. 658p. 2000. 92.50 (*1-56759-056-X*) Summers Pr.

Michigan Environmental Law, 3 vols., Set. Marc K. Shaye. LC 92-36598. 1992. ring bd. 280.00 (*0-317-05375-2*) West Group.

Michigan Environmental Law Deskbook. Ed. by Jeffrey K. Haynes & Eugene E. Smary. LC 91-78181. 946p. 1992. ring bd. 155.00 (*0-685-65665-9*, 92-018) U MI Law CLE.

Michigan Environmental Law Handbook. Honigman, Miller, Schwartz, & Cohn Staff. 235p. 1994. pap. text 85.00 (*0-86587-310-0*) Gov Insts.

Michigan Estate Planning Book: A Complete Do-It-Yourself Guide to Planning an Estate in Michigan. Michael Maran. (Illus.). 1997. pap. 29.95 (*0-936343-09-5*) Grand River.

Michigan Estate Planning Guide: The Twenty Most Commonly Asked Estate Planning Questions. P. Mark Accettura. LC 99-90087. 200p. 1999. pap. 12.95 (*0-9669278-0-X*) Collinwood Pr.

Michigan Estate Planning, Will Drafting & Estate Administration Forms, 2 vols. Joyce Q. Lower & Henry M. Grix. 1989. disk. write for info. (*0-318-71302-0*, MICHIE) LEXIS Pub.

Michigan Estate Planning, Will Drafting & Estate Administration Forms, 2 vols. Joyce Q. Lower & Henry M. Grix. 1993. suppl. ed. 80.00 (*0-685-74622-4*, MICHIE) LEXIS Pub.

Michigan Estate Planning, Will Drafting & Estate Administration Forms, Issue 8. Henry M. Grix. LC 89-14981. 300p. 1998. ring bd. write for info. (*0-327-00728-1*, 8171714) LEXIS Pub.

Michigan Estate Planning, Will Drafting & Estate Administration Forms, 2 vols., Set. Joyce Q. Lower & Henry M. Grix. 970p. 1994. spiral bd. 294.00 (*0-8342-0087-2*, 81711-10, MICHIE) LEXIS Pub.

Michigan Evidence Courtroom Manual. pap. 60.00 (*1-58360-185-6*) Anderson Pub Co.

Michigan Experience. Sadayoshi Omoto & Eldon N. Van Liere. (Illus.). 176p. (Orig.). 1986. pap. 8.00 (*1-879147-08-4*) Kresge Art Mus.

***Michigan Experience Pocket Guide.** Carole Marsh. (Michigan Experience! Ser.). (Illus.). (J). 2000. pap. 6.95 (*0-7933-9562-3*) Gallopade Intl.

Michigan Facts & Factivities. Carole Marsh. (Carole Marsh State Bks.). (Illus.). (J). (gr. 4-7). 1996. pap., teacher ed. 19.95 (*0-7933-7891-5*, C Marsh) Gallopade Intl.

***Michigan Facts & Symbols.** Emily Mcauliffe. LC 98-15484. (States & Their Symbols Ser.). 24p. (J). 1999. write for info. (*0-7368-0083-2*, Hilltop Bks) Capstone Pr.

Michigan Facts & Symbols. Emily McAuliffe. (J). 1998. 14.00 (*0-531-11607-7*) Childrens.

Michigan Family Law, 2 vols. 4th ed. Ed. by Judith A. Curtis et al. LC 93-77007. 1300p. 1993. ring bd. 165.00 (*0-685-65990-9*, 93-011) U MI Law CLE.

Michigan Family Law Sourcebook. Katharine B. Soper & Joseph W. Cunningham. LC 90-81123. 1310p. 1990. ring bd. 115.00 (*0-685-38203-6*, 90-003) U MI Law CLE.

Michigan Family Law Sourcebook: 1991 Supplement. Katharine B. Soper & Joseph W. Cunningham. LC 90-81123. 1310p. 1991. suppl. ed. 55.00 (*0-685-47524-7*, 91-010) U MI Law CLE.

Michigan Family Law Sourcebook: 1992 Supplement. Katharine B. Soper & Joseph W. Cunningham. LC 90-81123. 1310p. 1992. suppl. ed. 55.00 (*0-685-58878-5*, 92-009) U MI Law CLE.

Michigan Family Law Statutes & Rules Annotated: 1998 Edition, 3. pap. 180.00 (*0-327-12224-2*) LEXIS Pub.

Michigan Family Law Statutes & Rules Annotated - 1999 Supplement. John F. Wagner, Jr. 260p. 1999. pap. write for info. (*0-327-08003-5*, 26701-12) LEXIS Pub.

Michigan Family Law Statutes & Rules Annotated 1999 Supplement. annot. ed. 260p. 1999. pap. write for info. (*0-327-08621-1*, 26705-10) LEXIS Pub.

Michigan Farmhouse. Barbara E. Shisler. LC 94-65917. 80p. (Orig.). 1994. pap. text 9.00 (*0-9634083-7-2*) Ryanna Bks.

Michigan Federal Census Index, 1860. (Illus.). lib. bdg. 350.00 (*0-89593-380-2*, Accel Indexing) Genealogical Srvcs.

Michigan Federal Census Index, 1880. (Illus.). 1981. lib. bdg. 48.00 (*0-89593-382-9*, Accel Indexing) Genealogical Srvcs.

Michigan Federal Census Index, 1830. Ronald V. Jackson. LC 77-85968. (Illus.). 1976. lib. bdg. 54.00 (*0-89593-073-0*, Accel Indexing) Genealogical Srvcs.

Michigan Federal Census Index, 1840. Ronald V. Jackson. LC 77-85969. (Illus.). 1977. lib. bdg. 40.00 (*0-89593-074-9*, Accel Indexing) Genealogical Srvcs.

Michigan Federal Census Index, 1820. Ronald V. Jackson. (Illus.). 1981. lib. bdg. 38.00 (*0-89593-676-3*, Accel Indexing) Genealogical Srvcs.

Michigan Federal Census Index, 1850. Ronald V. Jackson & Gary R. Teeples. LC 77-85970. (Illus.). 1978. lib. bdg. 96.00 (*0-89593-075-7*, Accel Indexing) Genealogical Srvcs.

Michigan Festival Fun for Kids! Carole Marsh. (Carole Marsh Michigan Bks.). (Illus.). (J). (gr. 3-12). 1994. pap. 19.95 (*0-7933-3993-6*); lib. bdg. 29.95 (*0-7933-3992-8*) Gallopade Intl.

Michigan Festival Fun for Kids! Carole Marsh. (Carole Marsh Michigan Bks.). (Illus.). (YA). (gr. 3-12). 1994. disk 29.95 (*0-7933-3994-4*) Gallopade Intl.

Michigan First-Out Cases Digest. Martin J. Hillard. LC 96-78122. xxx, 186p. 1998. pap. text. write for info. (*0-7620-0082-1*) West Group.

Michigan Flora Pt. I: Gymnosperms & Monocots. Edward G. Voss. LC 72-189610. (Bulletin Ser.: No. 55). (Illus.). 488p. 1997. reprint ed. text 12.50 (*0-87737-032-X*) Cranbrook.

Michigan Flora Pt. II: Dicots (Saururaceae-Cornaceae) Edward G. Voss. LC 85-72083. (Cranbrook Institute of Science Bulletin Ser.: No. 59). (Illus.). 724p. 1998. reprint ed. 12.50 (*0-87737-037-0*) Cranbrook.

Michigan Flora Pt. III: Dicots (Pyrolaceae - Compositae) Edward G. Voss. LC 72-189610. (Bulletin Ser.: No. 61). (Illus.). 644p. 1996. 15.00 (*0-87737-040-0*) Cranbrook.

Michigan Folklife Reader. Ed. by C. Kurt Dewhurst & Yvonne R. Lockwood. LC 88-42622. (Illus.). 400p. (C). 1987. 17.00 (*0-87013-259-8*) Mich St U Pr.

Michigan Football: The Wolverines 1999 Calendar. (Illus.). 1998. boxed set 10.99 (*0-8362-6568-8*) Andrews & McMeel.

Michigan Free: A Comprehensive Guide to Free Travel, Recreation, & Entertainment Opportunities. Eric Freedman. (Illus.). 256p. 1993. pap. 18.95 (*0-472-08200-0*, 08200) U of Mich Pr.

Michigan Freedom of Information Act. Kenneth Verburg. LC 92-620000. 55p. (Orig.). 1992. pap. text 4.50 (*0-941872-60-2*) MSU Dept Res Dev.

Michigan Fresh: A Food-Lover's Guide to Growers & Bakeries. Don Hunt & Mary Hunt. (Illus.). 288p. (Orig.). 1992. pap. 9.95 (*0-9623499-4-1*) Midwestern Guides.

Michigan Frogs, Toads & Salamanders: A Fieldguide & Pocket Reference. James J. Harding & J. Alan Holman. (Illus.). 144p. 1999. pap. 13.95 (*1-56525-002-8*, E-2350) MSU Ext.

Michigan Fur Trade. Ida A. Johnson. LC 74-155928. 1981. reprint ed. 17.50 (*0-912382-07-4*) Black Letter.

Michigan Gambler: The Guide to Michigan Casinos. Michael Sutherland. (Illus.). 192p. 1997. pap. 8.95 (*1-890394-12-2*, Sage Creek) Rhodes & Easton.

Michigan Gardener's Guide: The What, Where, When, How & Why of Gardening in Michigan. Laura Coit et al. LC 97-181167. (Illus.). 424p. (Orig.). 1997. pap. 19.95 (*1-888608-29-3*) Cool Springs Pr.

Michigan Gardening Guide. Jerry Minnich. LC 97-45271. (Illus.). 328p. 1998. pap. 19.95 (*0-472-08398-8*, 08398) U of Mich Pr.

Michigan Gazetteer, 1838. John T. Blois. 418p. 1979. 19.75 (*0-686-27820-8*) Bookmark.

Michigan "GEO" Bingo! 38 Must Know State Geography Facts for Kids to Learn While Having Fun! Carole Marsh. (Bingo! Ser.). (Illus.). (J). (gr. 2-8). 1998. pap. 14.95 (*0-7933-8589-X*) Gallopade Intl.

Michigan German in Frankenmuth: Variation & Change in an East Franconian Dialect. Renate Born. LC 93-9927. (GERM Ser.). xvi, 137p. 1994. 60.00 (*1-879751-59-3*) Camden Hse.

Michigan Ghost Towns: Lower Peninsula, 2 vols. in 1. rev. ed. Roy L. Dodge. (Illus.). 311p. (Orig.). 1995. reprint ed. 13.95 (*0-932212-64-6*) Glendon Pub.

Michigan Ghost Towns: Upper Peninsula. Roy L. Dodge. (Illus.). 301p. (Orig.). 1996. reprint ed. 13.95 (*0-934884-02-1*) Glendon Pub.

Michigan Gold: Mining in the Upper Peninsula. Daniel R. Fountain. Ed. by Paul L. Hayden. LC 92-72995. (Illus.). 176p. 1992. pap. 12.95 (*0-942235-15-0*) LSPC Inc.

Michigan Golfers Travel Guide. Ed. by Roy H. Rasmussen. 36p. (Orig.). 1992. pap. 6.95 (*0-940703-01-7*) RSG Pub MI.

Michigan Gourmet Cookbook: Recipes from the Television Series, Vol. 2. 2nd rev. ed. Ed. by Walter Sorg et al. x, 170p. (Orig.). 1997. pap. 14.95 (*0-9657633-0-7*) G W Pepper.

Michigan Government! The Cornerstone of Everyday Life in Our State! Carole Marsh. (Carole Marsh Michigan Bks.). (Illus.). (J). (gr. 3-12). 1996. pap. 19.95 (*0-7933-6248-2*); lib. bdg. 29.95 (*0-7933-6247-4*); disk 29.95 (*0-7933-6249-0*) Gallopade Intl.

Michigan Government & You. David B. McConnell & Steven Thomas. LC 91-32794. (Illus.). 323p. (Orig.). 1991. pap. 26.95 (*0-910726-47-7*) Hillsdale Educ.

Michigan Governments Performance Standards, 1990. Ed. by Greg Michels. (Governments Performance Standards Ser.). (Illus.). 150p. 1990. text 125.00 (*1-55507-489-8*) Municipal Analysis.

Michigan Governors: Their Life Stories. Willah Weddon. LC 93-87563. (Illus.). 192p. (Orig.). (J). (ps-12). 1994. pap. text 14.95 (*0-9638376-2-1*) Weddon Pr.

Michigan Governors Growing Up. Willah Weddon. LC 93-94953. (Illus.). 100p. (Orig.). (J). (gr. 1-8). 1994. pap. text 14.95 (*0-9638376-1-3*) Weddon Pr.

Michigan (Grand Rapids, Saginau, Kent) Federal Census, 1870. 1990. 145.00 (*0-89593-624-0*, Accel Indexing) Genealogical Srvcs.

Michigan Haunts & Hauntings. Marion Kuclo. (Illus.). 128p. (Orig.). 1992. pap. 11.95 (*1-882376-00-5*) Thunder Bay Pr.

***Michigan Health Care in Perspective 2000.** Ed. by Kathleen O'Leary Morgan & Scott E. Morgan. 21p. 2000. spiral bd. 19.00 (*0-7401-0221-4*) Morgan Quitno Corp.

Michigan Health Care Perspective, 1998. Ed. by Kathleen O'Leary Morgan & Scott E. Morgan. 20p. 1998. pap. 19.00 (*1-56692-821-4*) Morgan Quitno Corp.

Michigan Health Care Perspective, 1999. Kathleen O'Leary Morgan. 21p. 1999. spiral bd. 19.00 (*0-7401-0071-8*) Morgan Quitno Corp.

***Michigan Herb Cookbook.** Suzanne Breckenridge & Marjorie Snyder. 300p. 2000. pap. 19.95 (*0-472-08694-4*, 08694) U of Mich Pr.

***Michigan High School Chemistry.** Joseph Krajcik & Brian P. Coppola. 2002. pap. text. write for info. (*0-7167-3689-6*) W H Freeman.

Michigan Highway Handbook. Dennis Staszak & Lynne Staszak. LC 93-73924. (Illus.). 120p. (Orig.). 1994. pap. 10.95 (*1-883169-06-2*) Friar & Friar.

Michigan "HISTO" Bingo! 42 Must Know State History Facts for Kids to Learn While Having Fun! Carole Marsh. (Bingo! Ser.). (Illus.). (J). (gr. 2-8). 1998. pap. 14.95 (*0-7933-8590-3*) Gallopade Intl.

Michigan Historical & Biographical Index, Vol. 1. Ronald V. Jackson. LC 78-53704. (Illus.). 1984. lib. bdg. 30.00 (*0-89593-187-7*, Accel Indexing) Genealogical Srvcs.

Michigan Historical Sights, Vol. 4. 2nd rev. ed. Nicholas P. Georgiady et al. (Illus.). 30p. (J). (gr. 4-8). 1998. pap. 4.50 (*0-917961-10-2*) Argee Pubs.

Michigan History! Surprising Secrets about Our State's Founding Mothers, Fathers & Kids! Carole Marsh. (Carole Marsh Michigan Bks.). (Illus.). (J). (gr. 3-12). 1996. pap. 19.95 (*0-7933-6095-1*); lib. bdg. 29.95 (*0-7933-6094-3*); disk 29.95 (*0-7933-6096-X*) Gallopade Intl.

Michigan History Magazine Subject Index, 1978-1994. LC 97-129883. 72p. 1995. 12.95 (*0-935719-22-9*) MI Hist Mag.

Michigan Hot Air Balloon Mystery. Carole Marsh. (Carole Marsh Michigan Bks.). (Illus.). (J). (gr. 2-9). 1994. 29.95 (*0-7933-2516-1*); pap. 19.95 (*0-7933-2517-X*); disk 29.95 (*0-7933-2518-8*) Gallopade Intl.

Michigan Hot Zones! Viruses, Diseases, & Epidemics in Our State's History. Carole Marsh. (Hot Zones! Ser.). (Illus.). (J). (gr. 3-12). 1998. pap. 19.95 (*0-7933-8895-3*); lib. bdg. 29.95 (*0-7933-8894-5*) Gallopade Intl.

Michigan in Literature. Clarence A. Andrews. LC 91-31020. (Great Lakes Bks.). 334p. reprint ed. pap. 103.60 (*0-608-10590-2*, 207121100009) Bks Demand.

M

M

Michigan in Perspective, 1998. Ed. by Kathleen O'Leary Morgan & Scott E. Morgan. 24p. 1998. pap. 19.00 (*1-56692-871-0*) Morgan Quitno Corp.

Michigan in Perspective, 1999. Ed. by Kathleen O'Leary Morgan. 26p. 1999. spiral bd. 19.00 (*1-56692-971-7*) Morgan Quitno Corp.

***Michigan in Perspective 2000.** Ed. by Kathleen O'Leary Morgan & Scott E. Morgan. 26p. 2000. spiral bd. 19.00 (*0-7401-0271-0*) Morgan Quitno Corp.

Michigan in Quotes. Tom Powers. LC 94-207331. (Illus.). 176p. (Orig.). 1994. pap. 12.95 (*0-923756-08-6*) Friede Pubns.

Michigan in the Novel, 1816-1996: An Annotated Bibliography. annot. ed. Robert Beseacker. LC 97-32194. (Great Lakes Books Publication). (Illus.). 448p. 1998. 54.95 (*0-8143-2712-5*) Wayne St U Pr.

Michigan Indian Dictionary for Kids! Carole Marsh. (Carole Marsh State Bks.). (J). (gr. 2-9). 1996. 29.95 (*0-7933-7710-2*, C Marsh); pap. 19.95 (*0-7933-7711-0*, C Marsh) Gallopade Intl.

Michigan Inheritance Tax. Michael A. Shield & Katherine B. Soper. LC 93-77008. 408p. 1993. ring bd. 85.00 (*0-685-65666-7*, 93-023) U MI Law CLE.

Michigan Interuniversity Community of Mathematical Geographers: Papers. 400p. (Orig.). 1986. reprint ed. pap. 39.95 (*1-877751-25-1*) Inst Math Geo.

***Michigan Investment & Business Guide: Business, Investment, Export-Import Opportunities, 50 vols., Vol. 22.** Global Investment Center, USA Staff. (U. S. Regional Investment & Business Library-99: Vol. 22). (Illus.). 350p. (Orig.). 1999. pap. 59.95 (*0-7397-1121-0*) Intl Business Pubns.

***Michigan Jeopardy.** Carole Marsh. (Michigan Experience! Ser.). (Illus.). (J). (gr. 2-6). 2000. pap. 7.95 (*0-7933-9564-X*) Gallopade Intl.

Michigan Jeopardy! Answers & Questions about Our State! Carole Marsh. (Carole Marsh Michigan Bks.). (Illus.). (J). (gr. 3-12). 1994. pap. 19.95 (*0-7933-4146-9*); lib. bdg. 29.95 (*0-7933-4145-0*); disk 29.95 (*0-7933-4147-7*) Gallopade Intl.

***Michigan Jography.** Carole Marsh. (Michigan Experience! Ser.). (Illus.). (J). (gr. 2-6). 2000. pap. 7.95 (*0-7933-9565-8*) Gallopade Intl.

Michigan "Jography" A Fun Run Thru Our State. Carole Marsh. (Carole Marsh Michigan Bks.). (Illus.). (J). (gr. 3 up). 1994. pap. 19.95 (*1-55609-667-4*); lib. bdg. 29.95 (*1-55609-666-6*); disk 29.95 (*1-55609-668-2*) Gallopade Intl.

Michigan Kid's Cookbook: Recipes, How-To, History, Lore & More! Carole Marsh. (Carole Marsh Michigan Bks.). (Illus.). (J). (gr. 3 up). 1994. pap. 19.95 (*0-7933-0610-8*); lib. bdg. 29.95 (*0-7933-0611-6*); disk 29.95 (*0-7933-0612-4*) Gallopade Intl.

Michigan Labor: A Brief History from 1818 to the Present. Doris B. McLaughlin. LC 73-633304. (Orig.). 1970. 10.00 (*0-87736-312-9*); pap. 5.00 (*0-87736-333-1*) U of Mich Inst Labor.

Michigan Land Surveying Law: Questions & Answers. John E. Keen. 29p. (C). 1995. pap. text 25.00 (*1-56569-029-X*) Land Survey.

Michigan Law & Practice, 31 vols. Publisher's Editorial Staff. Date not set. text 1790.00 (*0-318-57515-9*, 63830, MICHIE) LEXIS Pub.

Michigan Law & Practice, 31 vols. Publisher's Editorial Staff. 1998. text 1790.00 (*0-327-00088-0*, 63830, MICHIE) LEXIS Pub.

***Michigan Law & Practice Encyclopedia: Interim Index.** 2nd ed. Ed. by Kimberly MacAdam. 150p. 1999. pap. write for info. (*0-327-04986-3*, 6387010) LEXIS Pub.

Michigan Law & Practice Encyclopedia: 1998 Cumulative Supplement, 31 vols. Ed. by Lexis Law Publishing Staff. lib. bdg., suppl. ed. 240.00 (*0-327-00193-3*) LEXIS Pub.

***Michigan Law & Practice Encyclopedia Vol. 1: Special Supplement, 32 vols., Set.** 2nd ed. Ed. by Heather Hayes. 323p. 1999. pap. write for info. (*0-327-01591-8*, 6388114) LEXIS Pub.

Michigan Law & Practice Encyclopedia Vol. 1: 1998 Cumulative Supplement. 1998. write for info. (*0-327-00361-8*, 63881-12) LEXIS Pub.

Michigan Law & Practice Encyclopedia Vol. 2: 1998 Cumulative Supplement. 1998. write for info. (*0-327-00362-6*, 63882-12) LEXIS Pub.

Michigan Law & Practice Encyclopedia Vol. 3: 1998 Cumulative Supplement. 1998. write for info. (*0-327-00363-4*, 63883-12) LEXIS Pub.

***Michigan Law & Practice Encyclopedia Vol. 3: 1999 Replacement.** 2nd ed. Kimberly MacAdam. 500p. 1999. write for info. (*0-327-01770-8*, 6383311) LEXIS Pub.

Michigan Law & Practice Encyclopedia Vol. 3A: 1998 Cumulative Supplement. 1998. write for info. (*0-327-00364-2*, 63884-12) LEXIS Pub.

Michigan Law & Practice Encyclopedia Vol. 4: 1998 Cumulative Supplement. 1998. write for info. (*0-327-00365-0*, 63885-12) LEXIS Pub.

***Michigan Law & Practice Encyclopedia Vol. 4: 1999 Replacement.** 2nd ed. Kimberly MacAdam. 500p. 1999. write for info. (*0-327-01771-6*, 6383511) LEXIS Pub.

Michigan Law & Practice Encyclopedia Vol. 5: 1998 Cumulative Supplement. 1998. write for info. (*0-327-00366-9*, 63886-12) LEXIS Pub.

Michigan Law & Practice Encyclopedia Vol. 6: 1998 Cumulative Supplement. 1998. write for info. (*0-327-00367-7*, 63887-12) LEXIS Pub.

Michigan Law & Practice Encyclopedia Vol. 6A: 1998 Cumulative Supplement. 1998. write for info. (*0-327-00368-5*, 63888-12) LEXIS Pub.

Michigan Law & Practice Encyclopedia Vol. 7: 1998 Cumulative Supplement. 1998. write for info. (*0-327-00369-3*, 63889-12) LEXIS Pub.

Michigan Law & Practice Encyclopedia Vol. 7A: 1998 Cumulative Supplement. 1998. write for info. (*0-327-00370-7*, 63890-12) LEXIS Pub.

Michigan Law & Practice Encyclopedia Vol. 8: 1998 Cumulative Supplement. 1998. write for info. (*0-327-00371-5*, 63891-12) LEXIS Pub.

***Michigan Law & Practice Encyclopedia Vol. 8: 1999 Replacement.** 2nd ed. Ed. by Kimberly MacAdam. 500p. 1999. write for info. (*0-327-04966-9*, 6384111) LEXIS Pub.

Michigan Law & Practice Encyclopedia Vol. 8A: 1998 Cumulative Supplement. 1998. write for info. (*0-327-00372-3*, 63892-12) LEXIS Pub.

Michigan Law & Practice Encyclopedia Vol. 9: 1998 Cumulative Supplement. 1998. write for info. (*0-327-00373-1*, 63893-12) LEXIS Pub.

Michigan Law & Practice Encyclopedia Vol. 9A: 1998 Cumulative Supplement. 1998. write for info. (*0-327-00374-X*, 63894-12) LEXIS Pub.

Michigan Law & Practice Encyclopedia Vol. 10: 1998 Cumulative Supplement. 1998. write for info. (*0-327-00375-8*, 63895-12) LEXIS Pub.

Michigan Law & Practice Encyclopedia Vol. 11: 1998 Cumulative Supplement. 1998. write for info. (*0-327-00376-6*, 63896-12) LEXIS Pub.

Michigan Law & Practice Encyclopedia Vol. 12: 1998 Cumulative Supplement. 1998. write for info. (*0-327-00377-4*, 63897-12) LEXIS Pub.

Michigan Law & Practice Encyclopedia Vol. 13: 1998 Cumulative Supplement. 1998. write for info. (*0-327-00378-2*, 63898-12) LEXIS Pub.

Michigan Law & Practice Encyclopedia Vol. 14: 1998 Cumulative Supplement. 1998. write for info. (*0-327-00379-0*, Vol. 14) LEXIS Pub.

Michigan Law & Practice Encyclopedia Vol. 15: 1998 Cumulative Supplement. 1998. write for info. (*0-327-00380-4*, 63900-12) LEXIS Pub.

Michigan Law & Practice Encyclopedia Vol. 16: 1998 Cumulative Supplement. 1998. write for info. (*0-327-00381-2*, 63901-12) LEXIS Pub.

Michigan Law & Practice Encyclopedia Vol. 17: 1998 Cumulative Supplement. 1998. write for info. (*0-327-00382-0*, 63902-12) LEXIS Pub.

Michigan Law & Practice Encyclopedia Vol. 18: 1998 Cumulative Supplement. 1998. write for info. (*0-327-00383-9*, 63903-12) LEXIS Pub.

Michigan Law & Practice Encyclopedia Vol. 19: 1998 Cumulative Supplement. 1998. write for info. (*0-327-00384-7*, 63904-12) LEXIS Pub.

Michigan Law & Practice Encyclopedia Vol. 20: 1998 Cumulative Supplement. 1998. write for info. (*0-327-00385-5*, 63905-12) LEXIS Pub.

Michigan Law & Practice Encyclopedia Vol. 21: 1998 Cumulative Supplement. 1998. write for info. (*0-327-00386-3*, 63906-12) LEXIS Pub.

Michigan Law & Practice Encyclopedia Vol. 22: 1998 Cumulative Supplement. 1998. write for info. (*0-327-00387-1*, 63907-12) LEXIS Pub.

Michigan Law & Practice Encyclopedia Vol. 23: 1998 Cumulative Supplement. 1998. write for info. (*0-327-00388-X*, 63908-12) LEXIS Pub.

Michigan Law & Practice Encyclopedia Vol. 24: 1998 Cumulative Supplement. 1998. write for info. (*0-327-00389-8*, 63909-12) LEXIS Pub.

Michigan Law & Practice Encyclopedia Vol. 25: 1998 Cumulative Supplement. 1998. write for info. (*0-327-00390-1*, 63910-12) LEXIS Pub.

Michigan Law & Practice Encyclopedia Vol. 26: 1998 Cumulative Supplement. 1998. write for info. (*0-327-00391-X*, 63911-12) LEXIS Pub.

***Michigan Law & Practice Encyclopedia Finder's Materials: Table of Cases, 32 vols.** Ed. by Heather Hayes. 700p. 1999. write for info. (*0-327-01589-6*, 6386211) LEXIS Pub.

Michigan Law & Practice Encyclopedia Finder's Materials: Tables of Cases/Statutes, 32 vols. Ed. by Heather Hayes. 400p. 1998. write for info. (*0-327-00641-2*, 6386210) LEXIS Pub.

Michigan Law & Practice Encyclopedia, 1998 Replacement, Vol. 1. 2nd ed. Ed. by John Wagner. 500p. 1998. write for info. (*0-327-00643-9*, 6383111) LEXIS Pub.

Michigan Law & Practice Encyclopedia, 1999 Table of Statutes, Vol. 2. 2nd ed. Ed. by John Wagner. 500p. 1998. write for info. (*0-327-00644-7*, 6383211) LEXIS Pub.

Michigan Law & Practice Encyclopedia Special Supplement, Vol. 1. 2nd ed. Ed. by Heather Hayes. 325p. 1999. suppl. ed. write for info. (*0-327-00921-7*, 6388113) LEXIS Pub.

***Michigan Law & Practice Encyclopedia, Special Supplement, Vol. 2.** 2nd ed. 74p. 1999. write for info. (*0-327-01364-8*, 6388213) LEXIS Pub.

***Michigan Law & Practice Encyclopedia, 1999 Cumulative Supplement: Pocketpart, 31 vols.** Incl. Vol. 1. Michigan Law & Practice Encyclopedia, 1999 Cumulative Supplement: Pocketpart. Ed. by Heather Hayes. 1999. pap. (*0-327-01538-1*, 6388113); Vol. 2. Michigan Law & Practice Encyclopedia, 1999 Cumulative Supplement: Pocketpart. Ed. by Heather Hayes. 1999. pap. (*0-327-01539-X*, 6388213); Vol. 3. Michigan Law & Practice Encyclopedia, 1999 Cumulative Supplement: Pocketpart. Ed. by Heather Hayes. 1999. pap. (*0-327-01540-3*, 6388313); Vol. 3A. Michigan Law & Practice Encyclopedia, 1999 Cumulative Supplement: Pocketpart. Ed. by Heather Hayes. 1999. pap. (*0-327-01541-1*, 6388413); Vol. 4. Michigan Law & Practice Encyclopedia, 1999 Cumulative Supplement: Pocketpart. Ed. by Heather Hayes. 1999. pap. (*0-327-01542-X*, 6388513); Vol. 5. Michigan Law & Practice Encyclopedia, 1999 Cumulative Supplement: Pocketpart. Ed. by Heather Hayes. 1999. pap. (*0-327-01543-8*, 6388613); Vol. 6. Michigan Law & Practice Encyclopedia, 1999 Cumulative Supplement: Pocketpart. Ed. by Heather Hayes. 1999. pap. (*0-327-01544-6*, 6388713); Vol. 6A. Michigan Law & Practice Encyclopedia, 1999 Cumulative Supplement: Pocketpart. Ed. by Heather Hayes. 1999. pap. (*0-327-01545-4*, 6388813); Vol. 7. Michigan Law & Practice Encyclopedia, 1999 Cumulative Supplement: Pocketpart. Ed. by Heather Hayes. 1999. pap. (*0-327-01546-2*, 6388913); Vol. 7A. Michigan Law & Practice Encyclopedia, 1999 Cumulative Supplement: Pocketpart. Ed. by Heather Hayes. 1999. pap. (*0-327-01547-0*, 6389013); Vol. 8. Michigan Law & Practice Encyclopedia, 1999 Cumulative Supplement: Pocketpart. Ed. by Heather Hayes. 1999. pap. (*0-327-01548-9*, 6389113); Vol. 8A. Michigan Law & Practice Encyclopedia, 1999 Cumulative Supplement: Pocketpart. Ed. by Heather Hayes. 1999. pap. (*0-327-01549-7*, 6389213); Vol. 9. Michigan Law & Practice Encyclopedia, 1999 Cumulative Supplement: Pocketpart. Ed. by Heather Hayes. 1999. pap. (*0-327-01550-0*, 6389313); Vol. 9A. Michigan Law & Practice Encyclopedia, 1999 Cumulative Supplement: Pocketpart. Ed. by Heather Hayes. 1999. pap. (*0-327-01551-9*, 6389413); Vol. 10. Michigan Law & Practice Encyclopedia, 1999 Cumulative Supplement: Pocketpart. Ed. by Heather Hayes. 1999. pap. (*0-327-01552-7*, 6389513); Vol. 11. Michigan Law & Practice Encyclopedia, 1999 Cumulative Supplement: Pocketpart. Ed. by Heather Hayes. 1999. pap. (*0-327-01553-5*, 6389613); Vol. 12. Michigan Law & Practice Encyclopedia, 1999 Cumulative Supplement: Pocketpart. Ed. by Heather Hayes. 1999. pap. (*0-327-01554-3*, 6389713); Vol. 13. Michigan Law & Practice Encyclopedia, 1999 Cumulative Supplement: Pocketpart. Ed. by Heather Hayes. 1999. pap. (*0-327-01555-1*, 6389813); Vol. 14. Michigan Law & Practice Encyclopedia, 1999 Cumulative Supplement: Pocketpart. Ed. by Heather Hayes. 1999. pap. (*0-327-01556-X*, 6389913); Vol. 15. Michigan Law & Practice Encyclopedia, 1999 Cumulative Supplement: Pocketpart. Ed. by Heather Hayes. 1999. pap. (*0-327-01557-8*, 6390013); Vol. 16. Michigan Law & Practice Encyclopedia, 1999 Cumulative Supplement: Pocketpart. Heather Hayes. 1999. pap. (*0-327-01558-6*, 6390113); Vol. 17. Michigan Law & Practice Encyclopedia, 1999 Cumulative Supplement: Pocketpart. Ed. by Heather Hayes. 1999. pap. (*0-327-01559-4*, 6390213); Vol. 18. Michigan Law & Practice Encyclopedia, 1999 Cumulative Supplement: Pocketpart. Ed. by Heather Hayes. 1999. pap. (*0-327-01560-8*, 6390313); Vol. 19. Michigan Law & Practice Encyclopedia, 1999 Cumulative Supplement: Pocketpart. Ed. by Heather Hayes. 1999. pap. (*0-327-01561-6*, 6390413); Vol. 20. Michigan Law & Practice Encyclopedia, 1999 Cumulative Supplement: Pocketpart. Ed. by Heather Hayes. 1999. pap. (*0-327-01562-4*, 6390513); Vol. 21. Michigan Law & Practice Encyclopedia, 1999 Cumulative Supplement: Pocketpart. Ed. by Heather Hayes. 1999. pap. (*0-327-01563-2*, 6390613); Vol. 22. Michigan Law & Practice Encyclopedia, 1999 Cumulative Supplement: Pocketpart. Ed. by Heather Hayes. 1999. pap. (*0-327-01564-0*, 6390713); Vol. 23. Michigan Law & Practice Encyclopedia, 1999 Cumulative Supplement: Pocketpart. Ed. by Heather Hayes. 1999. pap. (*0-327-01565-9*, 6390813); Vol. 24. Michigan Law & Practice Encyclopedia, 1999 Cumulative Supplement: Pocketpart. Ed. by Heather Hayes. 1999. pap. (*0-327-01566-7*, 6390913); Vol. 25. Michigan Law & Practice Encyclopedia, 1999 Cumulative Supplement: Pocketpart. Ed. by Heather Hayes. 1999. pap. (*0-327-01567-5*, 6391013); Vol. 26. Michigan Law & Practice Encyclopedia, 1999 Cumulative Supplement: Pocketpart. Ed. by Heather Hayes. 1999. pap. (*0-327-01568-3*, 6391113); 5760p. 1999. pap. write for info. (*0-327-01537-3*) LEXIS Pub.

Michigan Law & Practice Encyclopedia, 1999 Cumulative Supplement: Pocketpart see Michigan Law & Practice Encyclopedia, 1999 Cumulative Supplement: Pocketpart

***Michigan Law & Practice Encyclopedia, 2000, Vol. 2.** 2nd rev. ed. Ed. by Heather Hayes. 500p. 2000. write for info. (*0-327-01284-6*, 6383211) LEXIS Pub.

Michigan Law & Practice, 1999 Interim Supplement, 32 vols. Ed. by M. J. Divine & Heather Hayes. 85p. 1999. pap. write for info. (*0-327-01053-3*, 6391510) LEXIS Pub.

Michigan Law for Everyone: Plus Law Dictionary. 4th ed. Sherry A. Wells. (Illus.). vi, 218p. 1996. pap. 21.95 (*0-934981-07-8*) Lawells Pub.

Michigan Law of Damages, 2 vols. 2nd ed. Ed. by N. O. Stockmeyer, Jr. LC 89-81007. 888p. 1989. ring bd. 125.00 (*0-685-51909-0*, 89-030) U MI Law CLE.

Michigan Law of Damages, 2 vols. 2nd ed. Ed. by N. O. Stockmeyer, Jr. LC 89-81007. 888p. 1992. suppl. ed. 50.00 (*0-685-59115-8*, 92-025) U MI Law CLE.

Michigan Law Quadrangle: Architecture & Origins. Kathryn Horste. 160p. (C). 1997. 32.50 (*0-472-10749-6*, 10749) U of Mich Pr.

Michigan Laws Relating to Economic Development & Housing. Ed. by Nancy Gendell. 680p. (Orig.). 1991. pap. text 17.50 (*0-941872-59-9*) MSU Dept Res Dev.

Michigan Laws Relating to Planning. 4th ed. Kenneth VerBurg. 625p. (Orig.). 1989. pap. text 17.00 (*0-941872-57-2*) MSU Dept Res Dev.

Michigan League Cookbook. Ed. by Alice J. Gottesman & Beverley Burlingame. LC 84-50923. (Illus.). 200p. (Orig.). 1984. pap. 10.50 (*0-9613460-0-0*) U of Mich Alumnae.

Michigan Legal Literature: An Annotated Guide. 2nd ed. Richard L. Beer & Judith J. Field. LC 90-5206. 200p. 1991. pap. 27.50 (*1-57588-330-9*); lib. bdg. 37.50 (*0-89941-740-X*, 306390) W S Hein.

Michigan Legal Publications. Ed. by Hessel E. Yntema. write for info. (*1-57588-331-7*) W S Hein.

Michigan Library Book: A Surprising Guide to the Unusual Special Collections in Libraries Across Our State for Students, Teachers, Writers & Publishers - Includes Reproducible Mailing Labels Plus Activities for Young People! Carole Marsh. (Carole Marsh Michigan Bks.). (Illus.). 1994. pap. 19.95 (*0-7933-3072-6*); lib. bdg. 29.95 (*0-7933-3071-8*); disk 29.95 (*0-7933-3073-4*) Gallopade Intl.

Michigan Lichens. Julie J. Medlin. LC 96-83208. (Bulletin Ser.: No. 60). (Illus.). 100p. (Orig.). 1996. pap. 12.00 (*0-87737-039-7*) Cranbrook.

Michigan Lighthouses: 75 Color Pictures Covering Michigan's Most Scenic Lighthouses. John Penrod. 1992. pap. 5.95 (*0-942618-36-X*) Penrod-Hiawatha.

Michigan Limited Liability Company Forms & Practice Manual. Vicki R. Harding et al. LC 94-36226. 512p. 1995. ring bd. 219.90 (*0-9637468-6-3*) Data Trace Pubng.

Michigan Local Planning Commissioners Handbook. 3rd ed. Robert B. Hotaling. Ed. by Nancy Gendell. LC 88-620442. 106p. 1988. pap. text 6.50 (*0-941872-56-4*) MSU Dept Res Dev.

Michigan Local Property Tax Primer. 8th ed. Kenneth Verburg. Ed. by Nancy Gendell. LC 88-620132. 70p. 1996. pap. text 5.00 (*0-941872-55-6*) MSU Dept Res Dev.

Michigan Long Term Care Companion. 2nd ed. LC 94-223031. (Illus.). 1998. pap. 24.95 (*1-880697-05-X*) Cit Bet Care.

Michigan Magic. Williamston MI Elementary School 4th & 5th Grade C. (Illus.). 128p. (Orig.). 1993. pap. 12.95 (*0-923568-34-4*) Wilderness Adventure Bks.

Michigan Man: The Life & Times of Kalamazoo's Al Connable. Tom Thinnes. (Illus.). 338p. 1998. 22.50 (*1-886167-09-5*) Priscilla Pr.

Michigan Manual: A Guide to Neonatal Intensive Care. 2nd ed. Steven M. Donn. LC 97-20394. (Illus.). 464p. 1997. 37.50 (*0-87993-676-2*) Futura Pub.

Michigan Manual, 1995-1996. Michigan Legislative Council Staff. Ed. by Roger W. Peters. (Illus.). 1176p. 1995. 20.00 (*1-878210-06-8*) Legis Serv Bur.

Michigan Manual, 1991-1992. rev. ed. Michigan Legislative Council Staff. (Illus.). 1135p. 1991. 15.00 (*1-878210-04-1*) Legis Serv Bur.

Michigan Manual of Clinical Diagnosis: The Basis of Cost-Effective Medical Practice. Richard D. Judge et al. LC 97-34667. 300p. 1997. spiral bd. 32.95 (*0-316-47581-5*, Little Brwn Med Div) Lppncott W & W.

Michigan Manufacturers Directory. rev. ed. Ed. by Paul Pickell. Orig. Title: Directory of Michigan Manufacturers. 964p. 1999. 157.00 (*0-936526-37-8*) Pick Pub ML

Michigan Marriages Index, Early to 1850. Heritage Quest Staff. 100p. lib. bdg. 31.50 (*0-945433-46-8*) Herit Quest.

Michigan Math! How It All Adds up in Our State. Carole Marsh. (Carole Marsh Michigan Bks.). (Illus.). (YA). (gr. 3-12). 1996. pap. 19.95 (*0-7933-6554-6*); lib. bdg. 29.95 (*0-7933-6553-8*) Gallopade Intl.

Michigan Media Book: A Surprising Guide to the Amazing Print, Broadcast & Online Media of Our State for Students, Teachers, Writers & Publishers - Includes Reproducible Mailing Labels Plus Activities for Young People! Carole Marsh. (Carole Marsh Michigan Bks.). (Illus.). 1994. pap. 19.95 (*0-7933-3228-1*); lib. bdg. 29.95 (*0-7933-3227-3*); disk 29.95 (*0-7933-3229-X*) Gallopade Intl.

Michigan Memories: Inside Bo Schemblechler's Football Scrap Book. Bo Schembechler & Dan Ewald. LC 98-34925. (Illus.). 224p. 1998. 45.00 (*1-886947-44-9*) Sleepng Bear.

Michigan Memories: True Stories from Two Peninsulas' Past. Larry B. Massie. LC 95-128553. (Illus.). 288p. 1994. pap. 12.50 (*1-886167-00-1*) Priscilla Pr.

Michigan Men, Vol. 2. 2nd ed. Nicholas P. Georgiady et al. (Illus.). 32p. (J). (gr. 4-8). 1998. reprint ed. pap. 4.50 (*0-917961-07-2*) Argee Pubs.

Michigan Military Records: The D. A. R. of Michigan Historical Collections: Records of the Revolutionary Soldiers Buried in Michigan; the Pensioners of Territorial Michigan; & the Soldiers of Michigan Awarded the "Medal of Honor" Sue I. Silliman. 244p. 1996. reprint ed. pap. 23.00 (*0-8063-0312-3*, 5370) Clearfield Co.

Michigan Model of World Production Trade: Theory & Application. Alan Deardorff & Robert Stern. 296p. 1985. 35.00 (*0-262-04081-6*) MIT Pr.

Michigan Motor Vehicle Laws: With Uniform Traffic Code. annuals Gould Editorial Staff. (C). student ed. 6.00 (*0-87526-282-1*); ring bd. 17.95 (*0-87526-253-8*) Gould.

Michigan Murders. Edward Keyes. 1988. mass mkt. 6.50 (*0-671-73480-6*) PB.

Michigan Mystery Van Takes Off! Book 1: Handicapped Michigan Kids Sneak Off on a Big Adventure. Carole Marsh. (Carole Marsh Michigan Bks.). (Illus.). (J). (gr. 3-12). 1994. 29.95 (*0-7933-5027-1*); pap. 19.95 (*0-7933-5028-X*); disk 29.95 (*0-7933-5029-8*) Gallopade Intl.

Michigan Natural Resources 10th Biennial Commemorative Edition, 1977-1995. (Illus.). 64p. 1995. pap. 24.95 (*1-882376-98-6*) Thunder Bay Pr.

An Asterisk (*) at the beginning of an entry indicates that the title is appearing for the first time.

Michigan Nature Association - In Retrospect: Celebrating 28 Years of Preserving Michigan's Wild & Rare Natural Lands, 1960-1988. Edna S. Newnan. Ed. by Bertha A. Daubendiek. LC 88-62060. (Illus.). 99p. 1989. 29.75 (0-318-37923-6) MI Nature Assn.

Michigan Nature Association Nature Sanctuary Guidebook. 7th ed. LC 94-76665. (Illus.). 128p. 1994. pap. 29.00 (0-318-72925-3) MI Nature Assn.

Michigan Nature Centers & Other Environmental Education Facilities. Compiled by Charles T. Black & Diane D. Worden. 64p. 1982. pap. 6.50 (0-939294-06-0, LB 1047-M5) Beech Leaf.

Michigan Negotiable Instruments Law & the Uniform Commercial Code. Roy L. Steinheimer, Jr. (Michigan Legal Publications). ix, 169p. 1985. reprint ed. lib. bdg. 38.50 (0-89941-389-7, 303590) W S Hein.

Michigan No-Fault Automobile Cases: Law & Practice. Robert E. Logeman. LC 88-82096. 540p. 1988. ring bd., suppl. ed. 110.00 (0-685-22735-9, 88-011) U MI Law CLE.

Michigan No-Fault Automobile Cases: Law & Practice. Robert E. Logeman. LC 88-82096. 540p. 1992. 45.00 (0-685-22736-7, 92-015) U MI Law CLE.

Michigan Notary Law Primer. National Notary Association Editors. LC 97-68874. 124p. 1997. pap. 16.00 (0-933134-91-6, 5135) Natl Notary.

Michigan on Fire, Vol. 1. Betty Sodders. (Illus.). 400p. 1997. pap. 19.95 (1-882376-52-8) Thunder Bay Pr.

Michigan on Fire 2, No. 2. Betty Sodders. (Illus.). 1999. pap. 14.95 (1-882376-65-X) Thunder Bay Pr.

Michigan One Hundred Years Ago. Kirke et al. (Historical Ser.). (Illus.). 1977. pap. 3.50 (0-89540-053-7, SB-053) Sun Pub.

Michigan Open Meetings Act. Kenneth VerBurg. LC 93-620001. 44p. (Orig.). 1994. pap. text 5.00 (0-941872-62-9) MSU Dept Res Dev.

Michigan PACE: Program for Athletic Coaches' Education. Ed. by Robert Malina. (Illus.). 490p. (C). 1995. pap. text, spiral bd. 30.00 (1-884125-49-2) Cooper Pubng.

Michigan Papyri (P. Mich. XII) Michigan Papyri Staff. LC 71-649942. (American Studies in Papyrology: No. 14). 142p. reprint ed. pap. 44.10 (0-7837-5486-8, 204525100005) Bks Demand.

Michigan Papyri XIV. Michigan Papyri Staff. Ed. by Vincent P. McCarren. LC 71-649942. (American Studies in Papyrology: No. 22). 110p. reprint ed. pap. 34.10 (0-7837-5491-4, 204525600005) Bks Demand.

Michigan Parks & Forest Guide. Barbara McCaig & Lynn D. Soli. (Illus.). 100p. (Orig.). 1986. pap. 7.95 (0-935201-09-2) Affordable Adven.

Michigan Passport. Ronald J. Reiser. (Illus.). 36p. (Orig.). (YA). (gr. 9-12). 1991. 3.95 (0-9625515-7-0) VJR Passports.

Michigan Penal Code. annuals Gould Editorial Staff. 430p. ring bd. 17.95 (0-87526-254-6); 6.00 (0-87526-286-4) Gould.

Michigan Penal Code & Motor Vehicle Law Handbook. annuals rev. ed. 760p. (C). 29.95 (0-87526-557-X) Gould.

Michigan Place Names. Walter Romig. LC 86-15858. (Great Lakes Bks.). 676p. 1986. reprint ed. pap. 21.95 (0-8143-1838-X) Wayne St U Pr.

Michigan Politics & Government: Facing Change in a Complex State. William P. Browne & Kenneth VerBurg. LC 94-18928. (Politics & Governments of the American States Ser.). (Illus.). xxxiv, 409p. 1995. text 55.00 (0-8032-1209-7) U of Nebr Pr.

Michigan Poor Law: Its Development & Administration with Special Reference to State Provision for Medical Care of the Indigent. Isabel Bruce & Edith Eickhoff. LC 75-17210. (Social Problems & Social Policy Ser.). 1976. reprint ed. 25.95 (0-405-07482-4) Ayer.

Michigan Portraits. Phil Palmer. (Illus.). (C). text. write for info. (0-472-10433-0) U of Mich Pr.

Michigan Power of Attorney Book: A Guide to Making Financial, Health Care & Custodial Powers of Attorney Without a Lawyer. Michael Maran. (Illus.). 140p. (Orig.). 1991. pap. 5.95 (0-936343-05-2) Grand River.

Michigan Practice - Criminal Law, 1998 Combined Cumulative Supplement, Vols. 11 & 12. Alan Saltzman. 150p. 1998. pap. write for info. (0-327-00811-3, 6888212) LEXIS Pub.

Michigan Prescriptive Program in English. rev. ed. William E. Lockhart. Ed. by Nancy Martin. 72p. 1996. pap., wbk. ed. 10.00 (1-57128-031-6, 031-6) Acad Therapy.

Michigan Prescriptive Program in Math. William E. Lockhart. 1996. pap. 8.00 (1-57128-037-5); pap., student ed. 15.00 (1-57128-036-7); 3.00 (1-57128-038-3) Acad Therapy.

Michigan Prescriptive Program in Math. William E. Lockhart. Ed. by Nancy Martin. (Illus.). 200p. 1996. pap., wbk. ed. 14.00 (1-57128-035-9) Acad Therapy.

Michigan Press Women: Today & Yesterday. Willah Weddon. LC 95-90743. (Illus.). 176p. (Orig.). 1996. pap. 14.95 (0-9638376-3-X) Weddon Pr.

Michigan Probate. Leonard Edelman. LC 79-92366. (Practice Systems Library Manual). ring bd. 120.00 (0-317-00437-9) West Group.

Michigan Probate. Leonard Edelman. LC 79-92366. (Practice Systems Library Manual). 1993. suppl. ed. 62.50 (0-317-03172-4) West Group.

Michigan Probate Code: Annual Edition. Ed. by Gould Editorial Staff. 220p. (C). pap. 16.00 (0-87526-306-2) Gould.

Michigan Probate Sourcebook, 3 vols. 2nd ed. Ed. by Lynn P. Chard & Anna Headly. LC 91-71293. 1300p. 1991. ring bd., suppl. ed. 145.00 (0-685-54242-4, 91-004) U MI Law CLE.

Michigan Probate Sourcebook, 3 vols. 2nd ed. Ed. by Lynn P. Chard & Anna Headly. LC 91-71293. 1300p. 1992. suppl. ed. 70.00 (0-685-58917-X, 92-003) U MI Law CLE.

Michigan Probate Sourcebook, 3 vols. 2nd ed. Ed. by Lynn P. Chard & Anna Headly. LC 91-71293. 1300p. 1993. suppl. ed. 75.00 (0-685-58918-8, 93-006) U MI Law CLE.

Michigan Proficiency Practice Tests. 2nd ed. George P. McCallum George P. 1996. pap. text 11.90 (0-17-557000-0) Addison-Wesley.

Michigan Proficiency Pratice. 2nd ed. McCallum. 1996. text 12.53 (0-17-556995-9) S&S Trade.

Michigan Programmed Spelling Series, Basic Word List Level 1: Reusable Edition. Enid L. Huelsberg. (J). (gr. 1). 1974. student ed. 12.00 (0-87879-772-6, Ann Arbor Div) Acad Therapy.

Michigan Programmed Spelling Series, Basic Word List, Level 2: Reusable Edition. Enid L. Huelsberg. (J). (gr. 2). 1974. 12.00 (0-87879-773-4, Ann Arbor Div) Acad Therapy.

Michigan Programmed Spelling Series, Basic Word List, Level 3: Reusable Edition. Enid L. Huelsberg. (J). (gr. 3). 1974. student ed. 12.00 (0-87879-774-2, Ann Arbor Div) Acad Therapy.

Michigan Programmed Spelling Series, Use Frequency Based Words, Level 4: Reusable Edition. Enid L. Huelsberg. (J). (gr. 4). 1975. student ed. 12.00 (0-87879-778-5, Ann Arbor Div) Acad Therapy.

Michigan Programmed Spelling Series, Use Frequency Based Words, Level 5: Reusable Edition. Enid L. Huelsberg. (J). (gr. 5). 1975. student ed. 12.00 (0-87879-779-3, Ann Arbor Div) Acad Therapy.

Michigan Programmed Spelling Series, Use Frequency Based Words, Level 6: Reusable Edition. Enid L. Huelsberg. (J). (gr. 6). 1975. student ed. 12.00 (0-87879-780-7, Ann Arbor Div) Acad Therapy.

Michigan Quakers: Abstracts of 15 Meetings of the Society of Friends 1831-1960. Ann M. Burton & Conrad Burton. LC 89-82300. (Illus.). 601p. 1989. 50.00 (0-937505-05-6) Glyndwr Resc.

Michigan Quilters & Their Designs. Betty Boyink & Milly Splitstone. 52p. (Orig.). 1983. pap. 10.50 (0-9612608-2-3) B Boyink.

Michigan Quilts: One Hundred & Fifty Years of a Textile Tradition. Marsha MacDowell & Ruth D. Fitzgerald. LC 87-62538. (Illus.). 175p. (Orig.). (C). 1987. 34.95 (0-944311-00-8); pap. 24.95 (0-944311-01-6) MSU Museum.

Michigan Quiz Bowl Crash Course! Carole Marsh. (Carole Marsh Michigan Bks.). (Illus.). (J). (gr. 3 up). 1994. pap. 19.95 (1-55609-675-5); lib. bdg. 29.95 (1-55609-674-7); disk 29.95 (1-55609-676-3) Gallopade Intl.

Michigan Railroads & Railroad Companies. Graydon M. Meints. LC 92-32966. (C). 1993. 35.00 (0-87013-318-7) Mich St U Pr.

Michigan Real Estate: Principles & Practices. 2nd ed. Ralph A. Palmer & Marge Fraser. LC 97-31189. 464p. (C). 1997. pap. text 38.00 (0-13-899659-8) P-H.

Michigan Real Estate Forms, 3 vols. John G. Cameron, Jr. 1988. disk 75.00 (0-685-74624-0, MICHIE) LEXIS Pub.

Michigan Real Estate Forms, 3 vols. John G. Cameron, Jr. 1993. suppl. ed. 85.00 (0-685-74623-2, MICHIE) LEXIS Pub.

Michigan Real Estate Forms, Issue 8. John G. Cameron, Jr. LC 93-39800. 300p. 1998. ring bd. write for info. (0-327-00563-7, 8172514) LEXIS Pub.

Michigan Real Estate Forms, 3 vols., Set. John G. Cameron, Jr. 1990p. 1994. spiral bd. 299.00 (0-8342-0032-5, 81720-10, MICHIE) LEXIS Pub.

Michigan Real Estate Practice & Forms, 2 Vols. Nyal D. Deems & James M. Tervo. LC 89-80297. 974p. 1989. ring bd., suppl. ed. 155.00 (0-685-22742-1, 89-001) U MI Law CLE.

Michigan Real Estate Practice & Forms, 2 Vols. Nyal D. Deems & James M. Tervo. LC 89-80297. 974p. 1992. suppl. ed. 75.00 incl. disk (0-685-58360-0, 91-027) U MI Law CLE.

Michigan Real Property Law, 2 vols. 2nd ed. John G. Cameron, Jr. LC 93-77009. 1900p. 1993. 165.00 (0-685-65991-7, 93-020) U MI Law CLE.

***Michigan Related Laws to the Insurance Laws.** Michigan & NILS Publishing Company. LC 98-61115. 1999. write for info. (0-89246-503-4) NILS Pub.

Michigan Reports & Michigan Court of Appeals Reports. write for info. (0-318-57154-4) West Group.

Michigan Reports Court Rules. 1989. ring bd. write for info. (0-318-68087-4) West Group.

Michigan Research Guide, 2 vols. Lawyers Cooperative Publishing Staff. 1991. 87.50 (0-318-43162-9) West Group.

Michigan Research Guide, 2 vols. Lawyers Cooperative Publishing Staff. 1993. suppl. ed. 40.00 (0-317-03347-6) West Group.

Michigan Retirement & Relocation Guide. (Retirement & Relocation Guides Ser.). (Illus.). 350p. 1998. pap. 24.95 (1-56559-123-2) HGI-Over Fifty.

Michigan Revocable Grantor Trusts. Richard C. Lowe & George F. Bearup. LC 90-85064. 1991. ring bd., suppl. ed. 95.00 incl. disk (0-685-47729-0) U MI Law CLE.

Michigan Revocable Grantor Trusts. Richard C. Lowe & George F. Bearup. LC 90-85064. 1992. suppl. ed. 40.00 (0-685-58921-8, 92-010) U MI Law CLE.

Michigan Revocable Grantor Trusts. Richard C. Lowe & George F. Bearup. LC 90-85064. 1993. suppl. ed. 55.00 incl. disk (0-685-58922-6, 93-012) U MI Law CLE.

Michigan Riding & Hiking Trail Vol. 1: True Stories of the First Crossing & Further Adventures. Rhoda Ritter. LC 96-208917. (Illus.). 135p. (Orig.). 1996. pap., mass mkt. 14.95 (0-9651614-0-4) River Outpost.

Michigan Roll. Tom Kakonis. 228p. 2000. reprint ed. pap. 14.95 (1-882376-72-2, Pub. by Thunder Bay Pr) Partners Pubs Grp.

Michigan Rollercoasters! Carole Marsh. (Carole Marsh Michigan Bks.). (Illus.). (J). (gr. 3-12). 1994. pap. 19.95 (0-7933-5291-6); lib. bdg. 29.95 (0-7933-5290-8) Gallopade Intl.

Michigan Rollercoasters! Carole Marsh. (Carole Marsh Michigan Bks.). (Illus.). (YA). (gr. 3-12). 1994. disk 29.95 (0-7933-5292-4) Gallopade Intl.

Michigan Rules of Evidence & Trial Objections at a Glance. rev. ed. Kent Sinclair, Jr. 1991. 20.00 (0-685-51908-2, 91-032) U MI Law CLE.

Michigan Rules of Professional Conduct & Disciplinary Procedure. Lawrence A. Dubin & Michael A. Schwartz. LC 89-80298. 632p. 1989. ring bd., suppl. ed. 85.00 (0-685-38204-4) U MI Law CLE.

Michigan Rules of Professional Conduct & Disciplinary Procedure. Lawrence A. Dubin & Michael A. Schwartz. 632p. 1991. suppl. ed. write for info. (0-318-68095-5, 89-012); suppl. ed. 45.00 (0-685-47525-5) U MI Law CLE.

Michigan Rules of Professional Conduct & Disciplinary Procedure. Lawrence A. Dubin & Michael A. Schwartz. LC 89-80298. 632p. 1992. suppl. ed. 50.00 (0-685-58879-3, 92-002) U MI Law CLE.

Michigan Rules of Professional Conduct & Disciplinary Procedure. Lawrence A. Dubin & Michael A. Schwartz. LC 89-80298. 632p. 1993. suppl. ed. 55.00 (0-685-58880-7, 93-004) U MI Law CLE.

Michigan School Trivia: An Amazing & Fascinating Look at Our State's Teachers, Schools & Students! Carole Marsh. (Carole Marsh Michigan Bks.). (Illus.). (J). (gr. 3 up). 1994. pap. 19.95 (0-7933-0607-8); lib. bdg. 29.95 (0-7933-0608-6); disk 29.95 (0-7933-0609-4) Gallopade Intl.

Michigan Seasons: Classic Tales of Life Outdoors. Ed. by Ted J. Rulseh. LC 97-69590. (Illus.). 246p. 1997. 22.95 (0-9653381-3-4) Cabin Bkshelf.

Michigan, 1799, 1806, 1827 Early Census Index. Ronald V. Jackson. LC 77-85962. (Illus.). lib. bdg. 45.00 (0-89593-072-2, Accel Indexing) Genealogical Srvcs.

Michigan Silly Basketball Sportsmysteries, Vol. I. Carole Marsh. (Carole Marsh Michigan Bks.). (Illus.). (J). (gr. 3 up). 1994. pap. 19.95 (0-7933-0604-3); lib. bdg. 29.95 (0-7933-0605-1); disk 29.95 (0-7933-0606-X) Gallopade Intl.

Michigan Silly Basketball Sportsmysteries, Vol. II. Carole Marsh. (Carole Marsh Michigan Bks.). (Illus.). (J). (gr. 3 up). 1994. pap. 19.95 (0-7933-1712-6); lib. bdg. 29.95 (0-7933-1711-8); disk 29.95 (0-7933-1713-4) Gallopade Intl.

Michigan Silly Football Sportsmysteries, Vol. I. Carole Marsh. (Carole Marsh Michigan Bks.). (Illus.). (J). (gr. 3 up). 1994. pap. 19.95 (1-55609-703-4); lib. bdg. 29.95 (1-55609-702-6); disk 29.95 (1-55609-704-2) Gallopade Intl.

Michigan Silly Football Sportsmysteries, Vol. II. Carole Marsh. (Carole Marsh Michigan Bks.). (Illus.). (J). (gr. 3 up). 1994. pap. 19.95 (1-55609-706-9); lib. bdg. 29.95 (1-55609-705-0); disk 29.95 (1-55609-707-7) Gallopade Intl.

Michigan Silly Trivia! Carole Marsh. (Carole Marsh Michigan Bks.). (Illus.). (J). (gr. 3 up). 1994. pap. 19.95 (1-55609-664-X); lib. bdg. 29.95 (1-55609-663-1); disk 29.95 (1-55609-665-8) Gallopade Intl.

Michigan Soldiers & Sailors Alphabetical Index, Civil War, 1861-1865. 1097p. 1988. reprint ed. 50.00 (0-914905-00-7) Detroit Bk Pr.

Michigan Soldiers in the Civil War. Frederick D. Williams. LC 97-143161. 80p. 1994. 12.95 (0-935719-23-7) MI Hist Mag.

Michigan Spelling Bee! Score Big by Correctly Spelling Our State's Unique Names. Carole Marsh. (Carole Marsh Michigan Bks.). (Illus.). (YA). (gr. 3-12). 1996. pap. 19.95 (0-7933-6707-7); lib. bdg. 29.95 (0-7933-6706-9) Gallopade Intl.

Michigan Standard Jury Instructions - Civil, 2 vols. 2nd ed. Michigan Supreme Court Committee on Standard Jury. LC 81-80665. 1100p. 1981. ring bd., suppl. ed. 140.00 (0-685-39007-1, 81-101) U MI Law CLE.

Michigan Standard Jury Instructions - Civil, 2 vols. 2nd ed. Michigan Supreme Court Committee on Standard Jury. LC 81-80665. 1100p. 1993. pap., suppl. ed. 45.00 (0-685-47731-2, 93-013) U MI Law CLE.

Michigan State & National Parks: A Complete Guide. 3rd rev. ed. Tom Powers. LC 98-139754. (Illus.). 240p. (Orig.). 1997. pap. 14.95 (0-923756-16-7) Friede Pubns.

Michigan State Baseball: A Concerned Look. Robert W Ellis. 160p. 1993. pap. 5.95 (0-9634609-0-0) McGriff & Bell.

Michigan State Census for Oakland County, 1845. Ed. by Joan Pate. 290p. (Orig.). 1985. pap. 15.00 (1-879766-01-9) OCG Society.

Michigan State Census Index, 1845. (Illus.). lib. bdg. 60.00 (0-89593-384-5, Accel Indexing) Genealogical Srvcs.

Michigan State Constitution: A Reference Guide, 24. Susan P. Fino. LC 95-41689. (Reference Guides to the State Constitutions of the United States Ser.: Vol. 24). 304p. 1996. lib. bdg. 89.50 (0-313-26575-5, Greenwood Pr) Greenwood.

***Michigan State Credit Directory, 2000 Edition.** rev. ed. American Business Directories Staff. 880p. 1999. boxed set 175.00 incl. cd-rom (0-7687-0308-5) Am Busn Direct.

Michigan State Parks: A Complete Recreation Guide. Jim DuFresne. LC 97-43534. (State Parks Ser.). (Illus.). 250p. 1998. pap. 16.95 (0-89886-544-1) Mountaineers.

Michigan State Parks: Yesterday Through Tomorrow. Claire V. Korn. LC 89-42811. (Illus.). 200p. (Orig.). 1989. pap. 12.95 (0-87013-275-X) Mich St U Pr.

Michigan State Rules of Evidence with Objections. Anthony J. Bocchino et al. 193p. 1995. pap. 25.95 (1-55681-459-3) Natl Inst Trial Ad.

Michigan State University: East Lansing Michigan. John Penrod. 1997. pap. 5.45 (0-942618-68-8) Penrod-Hiawatha.

Michigan State University Art Collection. Ed. by Paul Love. (Illus.). 45p. (Orig.). 1966. pap. 4.00 (1-879147-00-9) Kresge Art Mus.

Michigan Statistical Abstract: Michigan Employment Security Commission. 21st ed. 664p. 1996. text 52.50 (0-472-08370-8, 08370) U of Mich Pr.

Michigan Statistics Annotated Quarterly, October 1998. annot. ed. 800p. 1998. pap. write for info. (0-327-06325-4, 5704013) LEXIS Pub.

Michigan Statutes: 1999 Advance Legislative Service, No. 1. annot. ed. John F. Wagner, Jr. 200p. 1999. pap. write for info. (0-327-07807-3, 4445113) LEXIS Pub.

Michigan Statutes: 1999 Advance Legislative Service, No. 2. annot. ed. John F. Wagner, Jr. 200p. 1999. pap. write for info. (0-327-07808-1, 4445213) LEXIS Pub.

Michigan Statutes: 1999 Advance Legislative Service, No. 3. annot. ed. John F. Wagner, Jr. 300p. 1999. pap. write for info. (0-327-07809-X, 4445313) LEXIS Pub.

Michigan Statutes: 1999 Advance Legislative Service, No. 4. annot. ed. John F. Wagner, Jr. 300p. 1999. pap. write for info. (0-327-07810-3, 4445413) LEXIS Pub.

Michigan Statutes: 1999 Advance Legislative Service, No. 5. annot. ed. John F. Wagner, Jr. 400p. 1999. pap. write for info. (0-327-07811-1, 4445513) LEXIS Pub.

Michigan Statutes: 1999 Advance Legislative Service, No. 6. annot. ed. John F. Wagner, Jr. 400p. 1999. pap. write for info. (0-327-07812-X, 4445613) LEXIS Pub.

Michigan Statutes: 1999 Cumulative Supplement. annot. ed. Incl. Vol. 1. 21p. 1999. pap. (0-327-07897-9, 56961-12); Vol. 1B. 56p. 1999. pap. (0-327-07898-7, 56963-12); Vol. 2. 256p. 1999. pap. (0-327-07899-5, 56964-12); Vol. 2A. 76p. 1999. pap. (0-327-07900-2, 56965-12); Vol. 2B. 31p. 1999. pap. (0-327-07901-0, 56966-12); Vol. 3. 236p. 1999. pap. (0-327-07902-9, 56967-12); Vol. 4. 116p. 1999. pap. (0-327-07903-7, 56968-12); Vol. 4A. 126p. 1999. pap. (0-327-07904-5, 56969-12); Vol. 4B. 226p. 1999. pap. (0-327-07905-3, 56970-12); Vol. 4C. 256p. 1999. pap. (0-327-07906-1, 56971-12); Vol. 5. 166p. 1999. pap. (0-327-07907-X, 56972-12); Vol. 6. 96p. 1999. pap. (0-327-07908-8, 56973-12); Vol. 6A. 231p. 1999. pap. (0-327-07909-6, 56974-12); Vol. 6B. 96p. 1999. pap. (0-327-07910-X, 56975-12); Vol. 7. 46p. 1999. pap. (0-327-07911-8, 56976-12); Vol. 8. 206p. 1999. pap. (0-327-07912-6, 56977-12); Vol. 8A. 81p. 1999. pap. (0-327-07913-4, 56978-12); Vol. 8B. 66p. 1999. pap. (0-327-07914-2, 56979-12); Vol. 9. 176p. 1999. pap. (0-327-07915-0, 56980-12); Vol. 9A. 66p. 1999. pap. (0-327-07916-9, 56981-12); Vol. 9B-I. 116p. 1999. pap. (0-327-07917-7, 56982-12); Vol. 9B-II. 116p. 1999. pap. (0-327-07918-5, 57045-12); Vol. 9C. 131p. 1999. pap. (0-327-07919-3, 56983-12); Vol. 10. 246p. 1999. pap. (0-327-07920-7, 56984-12); Vol. 10A. 31p. 1999. pap. (0-327-07921-5, 56985-12); Vol. 10B. 16p. 1999. pap. (0-327-07922-3, 57038-12); Vol. 11. 326p. 1999. pap. (0-327-07923-1, 56986-12); Vol. 11A. 56p. 1999. pap. (0-327-07924-X, 56987-12); Vol. 11B. 16p. 1999. pap. (0-327-07942-8, 56988-12); Vol. 12. 106p. 1999. pap. (0-327-07925-8, 56989-12); Vol. 12A. 136p. 1999. pap. (0-327-07926-6, 56990-12); Vol. 12B. 216p. 1999. pap. (0-327-07927-4, 56991-12); Vol. 13. 91p. 1999. pap. (0-327-07928-2, 56992-12); Vol. 13A. 406p. 1999. pap. (0-327-07929-0, 56993-12); Vol. 14. 26p. 1999. pap. (0-327-07930-4, 56994-12); Vol. 14A. 256p. 1999. pap. (0-327-07931-2, 56995-12); Vol. 15. 210p. 1999. pap. (0-327-07932-0, 56996-12); Vol. 16. 56p. 1999. pap. (0-327-07933-9, 56997-12); Vol. 16A. 96p. 1999. pap. (0-327-07934-7, 56998-12); Vol. 17A. 286p. 1999. pap. (0-327-07935-5, 57000-12); Vol. 17B. 96p. 1999. pap. (0-327-07936-3, 57001-12); Vol. 17C. 106p. 1999. pap. (0-327-07937-1, 57002-12); Vol. 18. 256p. 1999. pap. (0-327-07938-X, 57003-12); Vol. 18A. 166p. 1999. pap. (0-327-07939-8, 57004-12); Vol. 19. 196p. 1999. pap. (0-327-07940-1, 57005-12); Vol. 20. 36p. 1999. pap. (0-327-07941-X, 57006-12); Vol. 20A. 506p. 1999. pap. (0-327-07943-6, 57007-12); Vol. 21. 166p. 1999. pap. (0-327-07944-4, 57008-12); Vol. 21A. 96p. 1999. pap. (0-327-07945-2, 57009-12); Vol. 22. 156p. 1999. pap. (0-327-07946-0, 57010-12); Vol. 22A. 86p. 1999. pap. (0-327-07947-9, 57011-12); Vol. 23. 86p. 1999. pap. (0-327-07948-7, 57012-12); Vol. 23A. 166p. 1999. pap. (0-327-07949-5, 57013-12); Vol. 24. 216p. 1999. pap. (0-327-07950-9, 57014-12); Vol. 24A. 166p. 1999. pap. (0-327-07951-7, 57015-12); Vol. 24B. 156p. 1999. pap. (0-327-07952-5, 57016-12); Vol. 25. 40p. 1999. pap. (0-327-07953-3, 57017-12); Vol. 25A. 95p. 1999. pap. (0-327-07954-1, 57018-12); Vol. 25B. 235p. 1999. pap. (0-327-07955-X, 57019-12); Vol. 26B. 65p. 1999. pap. (0-327-07956-8, 57022-12); 8661p. 1999. pap. write for info. (0-327-07749-2, 5696012) LEXIS Pub.

Michigan Statutes 1999 Edition, Vol. 26A. annot. ed. John F. Wagner, Jr. 1000p. 1999. pap. write for info. (0-327-07801-4, 4437211) LEXIS Pub.

Michigan Statutes Annotated, Vol. 11B. rev. ed. 650p. 1998. write for info. (0-327-05821-8, 44338-11) LEXIS Pub.

Michigan Statutes Annotated, Vol. 14. 1000p. 1998. write for info. (0-327-05822-6, 44344-11) LEXIS Pub.

Michigan Statutes Annotated Advance Legislative Service, No. 2. 300p. 1998. pap. 45.00 (0-327-05687-8, 44452-12) LEXIS Pub.

Michigan Statutes Annotated Advance Legislative Service, No. 3. 300p. 1998. pap. 45.00 (0-327-05816-1, 44453-12) LEXIS Pub.

Michigan Statutes Annotated Advance Legislative Service, No. 4. 300p. 1998. pap. 45.00 (0-327-05817-X, 44454-12) LEXIS Pub.

An Asterisk (*) at the beginning of an entry indicates that the title is appearing for the first time.

Michigan Statutes Annotated Advance Legislative Service, No. 5. 400p. 1998. pap. 45.00 (*0-327-05818-8*, 44455-12) LEXIS Pub.

Michigan Statutes Annotated Advance Legislative Service, No. 6. 400p. 1998. pap. 45.00 (*0-327-05819-6*, 44456-12) LEXIS Pub.

Michigan Statutes Annotated Advance Legislative Service, Pamphlet No. 7. 600p. 1999. pap. write for info. (*0-327-07148-6*, 44457-12) LEXIS Pub.

Michigan Statutes Annotated Advance Legislative Service, Pamphlet No. 8. 600p. 1999. pap. write for info. (*0-327-07149-4*, 44458-12) LEXIS Pub.

***Michigan Statutes Annotated, 1999 Advance No. 2: June 1999.** annot. ed. 235p. 1999. pap. write for info. (*0-327-08735-8*, 44452-13) LEXIS Pub.

Michigan Statutes Annotated, 1998. rev. ed. 1200p. 1998. 68.50 (*0-327-05689-4*, 44311-11) LEXIS Pub.

Michigan Statutes Annotated, 1998, Vol. 10A. rev. ed. 550p. 1998. 68.50 (*0-327-05690-8*, 44335-11) LEXIS Pub.

Michigan Statutes Annotated, 1998, Vol. 10B. rev. ed. 650p. 1998. 68.50 (*0-327-05691-6*) LEXIS Pub.

Michigan Statutes Annotated 1998 Supplement to the Rules Volumes. 200p. 1998. write for info. (*0-327-06804-3*, 5703711) LEXIS Pub.

Michigan Statutes Annotated 1999 General Index, 3 vols., Set. Incl. Vol. 27 (A-D). 1999. (*0-327-07986-X*, 44378-12); Vol. 27A (E-M). 1999. (*0-327-07987-8*, 44379-12); Vol. 27B (N-Z). 1999. (*0-327-07988-6*, 44380-12); 1999. write for info. (*0-327-07985-1*, 37670-12) LEXIS Pub.

Michigan Statutes Annotated 1999, Vol. 1A. rev. ed. 900p. 1999. write for info. (*0-327-07140-0*, 44312-11) LEXIS Pub.

Michigan Statutes Annotated 98 Quarterly Update, January 1999. 2000p. 1999. pap. write for info. (*0-327-07393-4*, 5704014) LEXIS Pub.

Michigan Statutes Annotated 98 Advance No. 7. 600p. 1999. pap. write for info. (*0-327-07392-6*, 445712) LEXIS Pub.

Michigan Statutes Annotated 98 Advance No. 8. 600p. 1999. pap. write for info. (*0-327-07397-7*, 4445812) LEXIS Pub.

Michigan Statutes Annotated 99 Supplement to 2 Research Guide Volumes. 1999. write for info. (*0-327-08009-4*, 57033-12) LEXIS Pub.

Michigan Statutes Annotated Quarterly Update, Pt. 1. 1000p. 1999. pap. write for info. (*0-327-07146-X*, 57040-14) LEXIS Pub.

Michigan Statutes Annotated Quarterly Update, Pt. 2. 1000p. 1999. pap. write for info. (*0-327-07147-8*, 57050-14) LEXIS Pub.

Michigan Statutes Annotated Quarterly Update, July 1998. 250p. 1998. pap. write for info. (*0-327-05688-6*, 57040-11) LEXIS Pub.

Michigan Statutes Annotated Quarterly Update, October 1998. 800p. 1998. pap. 35.00 (*0-327-05820-X*, 57040-12) LEXIS Pub.

Michigan Statutes Annotated Research Guide 1999 Supplement, Vol. 1. annot. ed. 140p. 1999. pap. write for info. (*0-327-08529-0*, 57034-12) LEXIS Pub.

Michigan Statutes Annotated Research Guide 1999 Supplement, Vol. 2. annot. ed. 109p. 1999. pap. write for info. (*0-327-08530-4*, 57035-12) LEXIS Pub.

***Michigan Statutes Annotated 2000 General Index.** Ed. by LEXIS Law Publishing Editors. 3833p. 2000. write for info. (*0-327-11208-5*, 3767013) LEXIS Pub.

***Michigan Statutes, 1999, Vol. 4B.** annot. rev. ed. 750p. 1999. write for info. (*0-327-08723-4*, 44320-11) LEXIS Pub.

***Michigan Statutes, 1999, Vol. 4C.** annot. rev. ed. 800p. 1999. write for info. (*0-327-08724-2*, 44321-11) LEXIS Pub.

***Michigan Statutes, 1999, Vol. 10.** annot. rev. ed. 950p. 1999. write for info. (*0-327-08722-6*, 44334-11) LEXIS Pub.

***Michigan Statutes, 1999, Vol. 13A.** annot. rev. ed. 1050p. 1999. write for info. (*0-327-08721-8*, 44343-11) LEXIS Pub.

Michigan Statutes Quarterly Update: July 1999. annot. ed. John F. Wagner, Jr. 500p. 1999. pap. write for info. (*0-327-07805-7*, 5704015) LEXIS Pub.

Michigan Statutes Quarterly Update: October 1999. annot. ed. John F. Wagner, Jr. 1000p. 1999. pap. write for info. (*0-327-07806-5*, 5704016) LEXIS Pub.

Michigan Study Manual for Life & Accident & Sickness Insurance. Dearborn-R & R Newkirk Staff. LC 98-106321. iv, 40 p. 1992. write for info. (*0-7931-0508-0*) Dearborn.

Michigan Summers: Tales & Recipes. Carole Eberly. (Illus.). 136p. (Orig.). 1990. pap. 7.95 (*0-932296-14-9*) Eberly Pr.

Michigan Survival. rev. ed. Betty L. Hall. 160p. (YA). (gr. 10-12). 1986. pap. text 5.84 (*0-936159-02-2*) Westwood Pr.

Michigan Tax Handbook. Mary A. Mead. 328p. 1988. pap. 17.00 (*0-13-580457-4*) P-H.

Michigan Tax Handbook. 1987th ed. Mary A. Mead. 1986. pap. 17.00 (*0-13-579913-9*) P-H.

Michigan Tax Handbook, 1985. Mary A. Mead. write for info. (*0-318-58206-6*) P-H.

Michigan Tax Handbook, 1998. rev. ed. Samuel J. McKim. 194p. 1997. pap. text 45.00 (*0-7811-0182-4*) Res Inst Am.

Michigan Tax Handbook, 1999. rev. ed. Samuel J. McKim et al. Ed. by Richard E. Jenis. 216p. 1999. pap. text 35.75 (*0-7811-0195-6*) Res Inst Am.

Michigan Territorial Census Index, 1827. Ronald V. Jackson. (Illus.). 1984. lib. bdg. 38.00 (*0-89593-677-1*, Accel Indexing) Genealogical Srvcs.

Michigan, the Great Lakes State: Celebrating a Century of Success. Carol Malis. LC 98-71770. (Illus.). 414p. 1999. 39.95 (*1-882933-23-0*) Cherbo Pub Grp.

Michigan 13 Personality Profile. Darrell Franken. (Illus.). 95p. 1990. ring bd. 59.95 incl. disk (*0-934957-58-4*) Wellness Pubns.

Michigan Timeline: A Chronology of Michigan History, Mystery, Trivia, Legend, Lore & More. Carole Marsh. (Carole Marsh Michigan Bks.). (Illus.). (J). (gr. 3-12). 1994. pap. 19.95 (*0-7933-5942-2*); lib. bdg. 29.95 (*0-7933-5941-4*); disk 29.95 (*0-7933-5943-0*) Gallopade Intl.

Michigan Townships Planning & Zoning Handbook. rev. ed. Robert B. Hotaling & Geoffrey Moffat. LC 86-620000. 231p. 1986. 16.00 (*0-941872-51-3*) MSU Dept Res Dev.

Michigan Trade Tokens. Paul A. Cunningham. LC 87-91297. (Illus.). 752p. 1988. 32.50 (*0-945008-00-7*) MI Exonumia Pubs.

Michigan Trailmakers. Henry O. Severance. 1930. reprint ed. 15.00 (*1-884739-06-7*) Wahr.

Michigan Trees: A Guide to the Trees of Michigan & the Great Lakes. Burton V. Barnes & Warren H. Wagner, Jr. (Biological Science Ser.). (Illus.). 392p. 1981. pap. 18.95 (*0-472-08018-0*, 08018) U of Mich Pr.

Michigan Trivia. rev. ed. Ernie Couch. LC 95-5333. 192p. 1995. pap. 6.95 (*1-55853-344-3*) Rutledge Hill Pr.

Michigan Trout Streams: A Fly-Angler's Guide. Bob Linsenman & Steve Nevala. LC 93-6118. (Illus.). 272p. (Orig.). 1993. pap. 17.00 (*0-88150-271-5*, Pub. by Countryman) Norton.

Michigan Turtles & Lizards Vol. E2234: A Field Guide & Pocket Reference. rev. ed. James J. Harding & J. Alan Holman. (Illus.). 100p. 1997. pap. 8.95 (*1-56525-011-7*, E-2234) MSU Ext.

Michigan 2000! Coming Soon to a Calendar Near You - The 21st Century! - Complete Set of AL 2000 Items. Carole Marsh. (Two Thousand! Ser.). (Illus.). (J). (gr. 3-12). 1998. pap. 75.00 (*0-7933-9353-1*); lib. bdg. 85.00 (*0-7933-9354-X*) Gallopade Intl.

Michigan 2000! Coming Soon to a Calendar near You--The 21st Century! Carole Marsh. (Two Thousand! Ser.). (Illus.). (J). (gr. 3-12). 1998. pap. 19.95 (*0-7933-8742-6*); lib. bdg. 29.95 (*0-7933-8741-8*) Gallopade Intl.

Michigan UFO's & Extraterrestrials! A Look at the Sightings & Science in Our State. Carole Marsh. (Carole Marsh Michigan Bks.). (Illus.). (J). (gr. 3-12). 1997. pap. 19.95 (*0-7933-6401-9*); lib. bdg. 29.95 (*0-7933-6400-0*) Gallopade Intl.

***Michigan Upper Peninsula: Scenic North Country.** John Penrod. 1999. pap. 5.95 (*0-942618-87-4*) Penrod-Hiawatha.

Michigan Vacation Guide: Cottages, Chalets, Condos, B&B's. 5th rev. ed. (Illus.). 240p. 1999. pap. 12.95 (*0-9635953-3-4*) TR Desktop.

Michigan Vacation Guide: Cottages, Chalets, Condos, B&Bs (1997-98) 4th rev. ed. Kathleen Tesden & Beverlee Rydel. (Illus.). 216p. 1997. pap. 12.95 (*0-9635953-2-6*) TR Desktop.

Michigan Vets & Widows, 1890. Ronald V. Jackson. 1990. 145.00 (*0-89593-822-7*, Accel Indexing) Genealogical Srvcs.

Michigan Voices. Compiled by Joe Grimm. LC 87-271542. (Great Lakes Bks.). (Illus.). 208p. 1987. pap. 18.95 (*0-8143-1968-8*) Wayne St U Pr.

Michigan Voices: Our State's History in the Words of the People Who Lived It. Ed. by Joe Grimm. LC 87-71542. (Illus.). 207p. reprint ed. pap. 64.20 (*0-608-10591-0*, 2071212) Bks Demand.

Michigan Walleye Hot Spots: Guide to Michigan's Best Walleye Fishing. James D. Wagner. (Illus.). 104p. (Orig.). 1994. pap. 12.95 (*0-9643943-0-8*) J W Design.

Michigan Wayne County Federal Census Index, 1870 Detroit. (Illus.). lib. bdg. 155.00 (*0-89593-381-0*, Accel Indexing) Genealogical Srvcs.

Michigan Wildflowers in Color. Harry C. Lund. Ed. by Eloise E. Lund. (Illus.). 120p. (Orig.). 1985. pap. 10.95 (*0-685-10417-6*) H C Lund.

Michigan Wildflowers in Color: Revised Edition with Wildflower Walks. 3rd rev. ed. Harry C. Lund. (Illus.). 144p. 1998. pap. 18.95 (*1-882376-56-0*) Thunder Bay Pr.

Michigan Wildlife Sketches see Wildlife Sketches

Michigan Wildlife Viewing Guide. Phil T. Seng. (Illus.). 152p. 1994. pap. 9.95 (*0-87013-350-0*) Mich St U Pr.

Michigan Will Drafting. Michael W. Irish & John H. Martin. LC 87-83699. 280p. 1988. ring bd., suppl. ed. 90.00 incl. disk (*0-685-39004-7*, 91-023) U MI Law CLE.

Michigan Will Drafting. Michael W. Irish & John H. Martin. LC 87-83699. 280p. 1990. suppl. ed. 45.00 (*0-685-58923-4*, 90-001) U MI Law CLE.

Michigan Will Drafting. Michael W. Irish & John H. Martin. LC 87-83699. 280p. 1991. ring bd., suppl. ed. 45.00 incl. disk (*0-685-39005-5*, 90-001) U MI Law CLE.

Michigan Wolverines Football Team. David Aretha. LC 98-25727. (Great Sports Teams Ser.). 48p. (J). (gr. 4-10). 1999. lib. bdg. 18.95 (*0-7660-1101-1*) Enslow Pubs.

Michigan Women, Vol. 1. 2nd rev. ed. Nicholas P. Georgiady et al. (Illus.). 32p. (J). (gr. 4-8). 1998. pap. 4.50 (*0-917961-08-0*) Argee Pubs.

Michigan Women Vol. II: Firsts & Founder. Rachel B. Harley & Betty MacDowell. (Illus.). 182p. (Orig.). 1995. pap. 13.95 (*0-9619390-2-8*) MI Womens Studies.

Michigan Wrongful Discharge & Employment Discrimination Law. rev. ed. Ed. by Barbara A. Ruga & Daniel D. Kopka. LC 90-81125. 540p. 1990. ring bd., suppl. ed. 110.00 (*0-685-22730-8*, 90-016) U MI Law CLE.

Michigan Wrongful Discharge & Employment Discrimination Law. rev. ed. Ed. by Barbara A. Ruga & Daniel D. Kopka. LC 90-81125. 540p. 1993. suppl. ed. 40.00 (*0-685-44340-X*, 93-014) U MI Law CLE.

Michigan Zoning & Planning. Clan Crawford, Jr. LC 87-83703. 550p. 1993. suppl. ed. 35.00 (*0-685-22741-3*, 93-007) U MI Law CLE.

Michigan Zoning & Planning. 3rd ed. Clan Crawford, Jr. LC 87-83703. 550p. 1988. 95.00 (*0-685-22740-5*, 88-009) U MI Law CLE.

***Michigan's Best Campgrounds.** 3rd rev. ed. Jim DuFresne. Orig. Title: Camping Michigan: Lower Michigan's 75 Best Campgrounds. (Illus.). 2000. pap. 15.95 (*1-882376-73-0*, Pub. by Thunder Bay Pr) Partners Pubs Grp.

Michigan's Best Outdoor Adventures with Children. Jim Dufresne. LC 90-37450. 240p. 1990. pap. 12.95 (*0-89886-249-3*) Mountaineers.

***Michigan's Big Activity Book.** Carole Marsh. (Michigan Experience! Ser.). (Illus.). (J). (gr. k-5). 2000. pap. 9.95 (*0-7933-9566-6*) Gallopade Intl.

Michigan's Capital Cities. Melissa Stimson. (Illus.). 104p. 1997. pap. 10.95 (*1-882376-42-0*) Thunder Bay Pr.

Michigan's Capitol: Construction & Restoration. William Seale. (Illus.). 104p. 1995. 47.50 (*0-472-09573-0*, 09573); pap. 32.50 (*0-472-06573-4*, 06573) U of Mich Pr.

Michigan's First Settlers: The Indians - Native Americans, Vol. 3. 2nd rev. ed. Nicholas P. Georgiady et al. (Illus.). 31p. (J). (gr. 4-8). 1998. pap. 4.50 (*0-917961-09-9*) Argee Pubs.

Michigan's Heartland. Forrest B. Meek. (Illus.). 449p. 1979. lib. bdg. 24.95 (*0-9602472-0-3*) Edgewood.

Michigan's Heritage Barns: The Photographs of Mary Keithan. Mary Keithan. LC 99-6074. 128p. 1999. 39.95 (*0-87013-520-1*) Mich St U Pr.

Michigan's Indians. Dirk Gringhuis. 48p. 1993. pap. 5.50 (*0-910726-04-3*) Hillsdale Educ.

Michigan's Land & Song of Hiawatha. John S. Penrod. 1986. pap. 5.95 (*0-942618-05-X*) Penrod-Hiawatha.

Michigan's Lumbertowns: Lumbermen & Laborers in Saginaw, Bay City, & Muskegon, 1870-1905. Jeremy W. Kilar. LC 89-38826. (Great Lakes Bks.). 362p. (C). 1990. pap. 22.95 (*0-8143-2073-2*) Wayne St U Pr.

Michigan's Marguerite de Angeli. William Anderson. (Illus.). 70p. 1987. pap. 10.00 (*0-9610088-6-5*) Anderson Publns.

Michigan's Master Carver Oscar W. Peterson, 1887-1951. Ron Fritz. Ed. by Steven Bowyer. LC 87-70425. (Illus.). 104p. 1987. 60.00 (*0-9604906-4-7*) Aardvark WI.

Michigan's (Most Devastating!) Disasters & (Most Calamitous!) Catastrophies! Carole Marsh. (Carole Marsh Michigan Bks.). (Illus.). (J). (gr. 3 up). 1994. pap. 19.95 (*0-7933-0595-0*); lib. bdg. 29.95 (*0-7933-0596-9*); disk 29.95 (*0-7933-0597-7*) Gallopade Intl.

Michigan's Only Antique & Flea Market Guidebook. Bill Bailey & Penny Bailey. (Glovebox Guidebooks Travel Guide Ser.). (Illus.). 207p. 1994. 11.95 (*1-881139-02-6*) Glovebox Guidebks.

Michigan's Only Antique & Flea Market Guidebook. Bill Bailey & Penny Bailey. 208p. 1997. pap. 11.95 (*1-881139-20-4*) Glovebox Guidebks.

Michigan's Porcupine Mountains Wilderness State Park see Porcupine Mountains Wilderness State Park: A Backcountry Guide for Hikers, Backpackers, & Winter Visitors

Michigan's Roadkill Cookbook. B. Carlson. (Illus.). 112p. 1994. pap. 7.95 (*1-878488-75-9*) Quixote Pr IA.

Michigan's Story. David B. McConnell. LC 95-493. (Illus.). 256p. (J). 1995. 29.95 (*0-910726-85-X*); pap. 21.95 (*0-910726-84-1*) Hillsdale Educ.

Michigan's Timber Battleground. 2nd rev. ed. Forrest B. Meek. (Illus.). 483p. 1991. reprint ed. lib. bdg. 34.95 (*0-9602472-1-1*) Edgewood.

Michigan's Town & Country Inns. 4th ed. Susan Newhof & Stephen J. Pyle. LC 97-33944. (Illus.). 280p. 1998. pap. 16.95 (*0-472-08392-9*, 08392) U of Mich Pr.

Michigan's Unsolved Mysteries (& Their "Solutions") Includes Scientific Information & Other Activities for Students. Carole Marsh. (Carole Marsh Michigan Bks.). (Illus.). (J). (gr. 3-12). 1994. pap. 19.95 (*0-7933-5789-6*); lib. bdg. 29.95 (*0-7933-5788-8*); disk 29.95 (*0-7933-5790-X*) Gallopade Intl.

Michigan's Vanishing Outhouse. B. Carlson. (Illus.). 183p. 1994. pap. 9.95 (*1-878488-77-5*) Quixote Pr IA.

Michigan's Victorian Poets. Kit Lane. 52p. 1993. pap. 4.00 (*1-877703-10-9*) Pavilion Pr.

Michiko Itatani. Alternative Museum Staff. LC 85-73084. (Illus.). 1985. pap. 5.00 (*0-932075-04-5*) Alternative Mus.

Michiko Itatani: Paintings since 1984. Intro. by Janet Koplos. (Exhibition Catalog Ser.). (Illus.). 28p. (Orig.). 1992. pap. 12.00 (*0-938903-14-4*) Cty of Chicago.

Michiko Kon: Still Lifes. Michiko Kon. (Illus.). 124p. 1997. 68.00 (*0-89381-729-5*) Aperture.

Michiko Kon: Still Lifes. Michiko Kon. LC 97-70511. 128p. 1999. pap. text 29.95 (*0-89381-768-6*) Aperture.

Michilimackinac: A Tale of the Straits. David A. Turrill. LC 89-40415. (Illus.). 490p. (Orig.). 1989. pap. 12.95 (*0-923568-04-2*) Wilderness Adventure Bks.

Michio Ito: The Dancer & His Dances. Helen Caldwell. LC 76-7756. (Illus.). 200p. reprint ed. pap. 62.00 (*0-7837-4671-7*, 204441700003) Bks Demand.

***Michka.** Marie Colmont. (SPA.). 2000. 12.95 (*84-241-3345-5*) Everest SP.

***Michoacan & Eden: Vasco de Quiroga & the Evangelization of Western Mexico.** Bernardino Verastique. (Illus.). 222p. 2000. 40.00 (*0-292-78737-5*); pap. 19.95 (*0-292-78738-3*) U of Tex Pr.

Michotte's Experimental Phenomenology of Perceptions. George Thines et al. (Resources for Ecological Psychology Ser.). 272p. 1990. 69.95 (*0-89859-606-8*) L Erlbaum Assocs.

Michtams of David. Christian Chen. (CHI.). 128p. 1997. pap. 14.00 (*0-9661121-3-X*) Liv Word.

Michtav M'Eliyahu see Strive for the Truth, Vol. 1, The World of Rav E. E. Dessler

Mick. Chris Lynch. LC 94-18725. (Trophy Bk.: Bk. 1). 160p. (YA). (gr. 7 up). 1996. pap. 4.50 (*0-06-447121-7*, HarpTrophy) HarpC Child Bks.

Mick. Chris Lynch. LC 94-18725. 1996. 9.60 (*0-606-09089-4*, Pub. by Turtleback) Demco.

Mick. Mickey Mantle & Herb Gluck. 288p. 1986. mass mkt. 5.99 (*0-515-08599-5*, Jove) Berkley Pub.

Mick. Teacher Created Materials Staff. (Go Bks.). 8p. (J). (gr. k-1). 1997. pap. 2.49 (*1-57690-826-7*) Tchr Create Mat.

Mick Doohan: Thunder from Down Under. Mat Oxley. LC 98-75398. (Illus.). 160p. 1999. 29.95 (*1-85960-635-0*) J H Haynes & Co.

***Mick Foley: Behind the Mankind Mask.** Terry West. (Illus.). 80p. (J). (gr. 3-7). 2000. pap. 4.99 (*0-439-24383-1*); mass mkt. 4.99 (*0-439-24384-X*) Scholastic Inc.

Mick Harte Was Here. Barbara Park. LC 94-27272. (J). (gr. 3-6). 1995. 15.00 (*0-679-87088-1*) Knopf.

Mick Harte Was Here. Barbara Park. 88p. (J). (gr. 4-6). pap. 4.99 (*0-8072-1502-3*) Listening Lib.

Mick Harte Was Here. Barbara Park. 89p. (J). (gr. 3-6). 1996. pap. 4.99 (*0-679-88203-0*, Pub. by Random Bks Yng Read) Random.

Mick Harte Was Here. Barbara Park. (J). 1996. 9.84 (*0-606-10991-9*, Pub. by Turtleback) Demco.

***Mick Harte Was Here.** unabridged ed. Barbara Park & Dana Lubotsky. (J). 1998. pap. 16.98 incl. audio (*0-8072-7796-7*, 395059, Pub. by Listening Lib) Lndmrk Audiobks.

***Mick Jagger: Primitive Cool.** Christopher Sandford. LC 99-40635. (Illus.). 354p. 1999. pap. 16.95 (*0-8154-1002-6*) Cooper Sq.

Mick Jagger: The Story Behind the Rolling Stone. Davin Seay. (Illus.). 256p. 1993. 19.95 (*1-55972-192-8*, Birch Ln Pr) Carol Pub Group.

Mick Kinane - Big Race King: The Authorised Biography. Michael Clower. (Illus.). 192p. 1996. 35.00 (*1-85158-806-X*, Pub. by Mainstream Pubng) Trafalgar.

Mick Kinane - Big Race King: The Authorised Biography. Michael Clower. (Illus.). 224p. 1997. pap. 19.95 (*1-84018-002-1*, Pub. by Mainstream Pubng) Trafalgar.

Mick Walker on Motorcycles: Cafe Racers of the 1960's, No. 1. Mick Walker. (Illus.). 96p. 1994. pap. 15.95 (*1-872004-19-9*, Pub. by Windrow & Green) Motorbooks Intl.

***Mick Walker's British Racing Motorcycles.** Mick Walker. (Illus.). 208p. 2000. pap. 34.95 (*0-9531311-0-6*, 127989AE, Pub. by Redline Books) Motorbooks Intl.

***Mick Walker's European Racing Motorcycles.** Mick Walker. (Illus.). 240p. 2000. pap. 34.95 (*0-9531311-3-0*, 130090AE, Pub. by Redline Books) Motorbooks Intl.

***Mick Walker's German Racing Motorcycles.** Mick Walker. (Illus.). 256p. 2000. pap. 34.95 (*0-9531311-2-2*, 130091AE, Pub. by Redline Books) Motorbooks Intl.

***Mick Walker's Italian Racing Motorcycles.** Mick Walker. (Illus.). 256p. 2000. pap. 34.95 (*0-9531311-1-4*, 128710AE, Pub. by Redline Books) Motorbooks Intl.

Mickey. (Squeeze Me Bks.). (J). 1996. 6.98 (*1-57082-385-5*, Pub. by Mouse Works) Time Warner.

Mickey. Mary Chase. 1969. pap. 5.25 (*0-8222-0752-4*) Dramatists Play.

Mickey: My Coloring Book. (Mickey & Friends Ser.). (J). 1.09 (*0-307-08673-9*, 08673) Gldn Bks Pub Co.

Mickey & Donald Pillow Book. Sideline. (J). 1990. pap. 19.95 (*1-55923-048-7*) Wicklow Ltd.

Mickey & Friends. (Super Coloring Book Ser.). (J). pap. text 2.29 (*0-307-03156-X*, 03156) Gldn Bks Pub Co.

***Mickey & Friends: Animal Kingdom.** Golden Books Staff. (Disney's Animal Kingdom Ser.). 40p. (J). 1999. pap. text 1.09 (*0-307-21123-1*, 21123) Gldn Bks Pub Co.

Mickey & Friends: The Twisters. (Disney's Look & Find Ser.). (Illus.). 24p. (J). 1993. write for info. (*0-7853-0104-6*) Pubns Intl Ltd.

Mickey & Friends Roly Poly. Mouseworks Staff. 1998. 9.99 (*0-7364-0035-4*, Pub. by Mouse Works) Little.

Mickey & Goofy: My Coloring Book. (Mickey & Friends Ser.). (J). 1.09 (*0-307-08670-4*, 08670) Gldn Bks Pub Co.

Mickey & Honor. Geraldine M. Bennett. LC 95-67420. (Illus.). 54p. (Orig.). (YA). (gr. 5 up). 1995. pap. 10.98 (*1-882786-21-1*) New Dawn NY.

Mickey & Minnie. (Disney Learn to Draw Ser.). (Illus.). 32p. (J). 1991. pap. 6.95 (*1-56010-087-7*, DS01) W Foster Pub.

***Mickey & Minnie: Watch the Birdie/Animal Buddies.** Golden Books Staff. (Mickey & Friends Ser.). (Illus.). (J). 2000. pap. 2.99 (*0-307-25227-2*, Goldn Books) Gldn Bks Pub Co.

Mickey & Minnie Pillow Book. Sideline. (J). 1990. pap. 19.95 (*1-55923-047-9*) Wicklow Ltd.

Mickey Baker's Jazz Guitar. Mickey Baker. (Illus.). 72p. pap. 12.95 (*0-86001-016-3*, CL10158) Music Sales.

***Mickey Big Book.** Diane Muldrow. 48p. (J). 2000. 12.99 (*0-7364-1018-X*, Pub. by Disney Pr) Time Warner.

Mickey Cochrane: The Life of a Baseball Hall of Fame Catcher. Charlie Bevis. LC 98-13679. (Illus.). 214p. 1998. pap. 26.50 (*0-7864-0516-3*) McFarland & Co.

Mickey Esta Feliz: Un Libro Disney de Emociones. Tr. by Daniel M. Santacruz. (Libros Buena Vista Ser.). (SPA., Illus.). 6p. (J). 1993. 5.95 (*1-56282-459-7*, Pub. by Disney Pr) Little.

Mickey Gilley's Favorite Recipes. Anderson Publishing Company Staff. Ed. by Edward Anderson. (Illus.). 106p. 1992. 7.95 (*0-9636666-1-4*) Anderson MO.

Mickey Mantle. Ed. by James Beckett. 1995. pap. 15.00 (*0-614-15517-7*, Harvest Bks) Harcourt.

Mickey Mantle. Phil Berger. LC 98-20175. (Illus.). 192p. 1998. 20.00 (*0-517-20099-6*) Random Hse Value.

Mickey Mantle. Rick Wolff. (Baseball Legends Ser.). (Illus.). 64p. (J). (gr. 3 up). 1991. lib. bdg. 7.95 (*0-7910-1181-X*) Chelsea Hse.

Mickey Mantle: Classic Sports Shots. Bruce Weber. 48p. (J). (gr. 4-6). 1993. pap. 1.25 (*0-590-47024-8*) Scholastic Inc.

Mickey Mantle: My Very Best Friend. Marshall Smith. LC 97-142895. 1996. 49.95 (*1-888170-01-8*) Advent Quest.

Mickey Mantle Day in Amsterdam: Another Novella by Jim LaBate. Jim LaBate. LC 99-70005. (Illus.). 64p. (YA). (gr. 7-12). 1999. pap. 7.95 (*0-9662100-7-7*) Mohawk River Pr.

Mickey Mantle Memorabilia. Ed. by Rick Hines et al. LC 93-77548. (Illus.). 208p. 1993. pap. 14.95 (*0-87341-261-3*, MM01) Krause Pubns.

Mickey Mantle, the American Dream Comes to Life, 1998: 30th Anniversary Commerative Photo Calendar Book, Vol. 1. 30th anniversary ed. Lewis Early & Mickey Mantle. Ed. by Douglas A. Mackey et al. (Illus.). 28p. 1997. pap. 19.95 (*0-9661206-0-4*) Amer Legend.

Mickey Mantle, The Yankee Years: The Classic Photography of Ozzie Sweet. Larry Canale. LC 98-87758. 224p. 1998. 39.95 (*0-930625-21-8*, Antique Trader) Krause Pubns.

Mickey Moose. Bob Reese. (Yellowstone Ser.). (Illus.). (J). (gr. k-6). 1986. 9.95 (*0-89868-171-5*); pap. 3.95 (*0-89868-172-3*) ARO Pub.

Mickey Mouse. Bob Italia. Ed. by Rosemary Wallner. LC 91-73048. (Behind the Creation of Ser.). 202p. (J). 1991. lib. bdg. 13.95 (*1-56239-053-8*) ABDO Pub Co.

Mickey Mouse. Lorraine Santoli. (J). 2001. 19.99 (*0-7868-3184-7*, Pub. by Disney Pr) Time Warner.

Mickey Mouse. deluxe ed. Pierre Lambert. LC 98-26026. (Illus.). 240p. (J). 1998. 150.00 (*0-7868-6453-2*, Pub. by Hyperion) Time Warner.

Mickey Mouse: My Life in Pictures. Russell Schroeder. LC 97-66143. (J). 1997. lib. bdg. 14.89 (*0-7868-5059-0*, Pub. by Disney Pr) Little.

Mickey Mouse: My Life in Pictures. Russell Schroeder. LC 97-66143. (Illus.). 64p. (J). 1997. 14.95 (*0-7868-3150-2*, Pub. by Disney Pr) Time Warner.

Mickey Mouse & Minnie Mouse Pop-Up Boxed Collector's Set. deluxe ed. Disney, Walt, Studios Staff. LC 93-31910. (Illus.). 32p. (J). 1999. reprint ed. 100.00 (*1-55709-215-X*) Applewood.

Mickey Mouse & the Pet Shop. Mary Packard. (Super Shape Bks.). (Illus.). 24p. (J). (ps-3). 1996. pap. text 3.29 (*0-307-10008-1*, 10008) Gldn Bks Pub Co.

Mickey Mouse et Monte Cristo. (FRE.). (J). (gr. 3-8). 6.25 (*0-685-28446-8*) Fr & Eur.

Mickey Mouse History: The Politics of Public Memory. Mike Wallace. LC 96-3555. (Critical Perspectives on the Past Ser.). (Illus.). 336p. (C). 1996. pap. 22.95 (*1-56639-445-7*) Temple U Pr.

Mickey Mouse Telling Time. Tk. (Illus.). 24p. 2000. 12.99 (*0-7868-3248-7*, Pub. by Disney Pr) Time Warner.

Mickey Mouse Watch: From the Beginning of Time. John Heide et al. LC 98-117884. (Illus.). 128p. 1997. 21.45 (*0-7868-6343-9*, Pub. by Hyperion) Time Warner.

Mickey Mouse's Bedtime Stories Picture Book. Liane Onish. (Illus.). (J). 1999. 12.99 (*0-7364-0030-3*, Pub. by Mouse Works) Time Warner.

Mickey Mouse's Christmas. Mouseworks Staff. 64p. 1999. 6.99 (*0-7364-0126-1*, Pub. by Mouse Works) Little.

Mickey Mouse's Telling Time. LC 96-124473. (Clock Book Ser.). (Illus.). 24p. (J). 1994. 8.98 (*1-57082-155-0*, Pub. by Mouse Works) Little.

Mickey Mouse's Xmas Carol. Mousework Staff. (J). 1997. 7.98 (*1-57082-799-0*, Pub. by Mouse Works) Little.

***Mickey Mysteries.** 3rd ed. (Illus.). 96p. (J). 2001. pap. 3.99 (*0-7868-4451-5*, Pub. by Disney Pr) Time Warner.

***Mickey Mysteries.** 4th ed. (Illus.). 96p. (J). 2001. pap. 3.99 (*0-7868-4452-3*, Pub. by Disney Pr) Time Warner.

Mickey No, Do Re, Mi, Fa, Ehon - Mickey Do, Re, Mi, Fa Picture Book. Tr. by Tomy Company Ltd. Staff. (Comes to Life Bks.). (ENG & JPN.). 20p. (J). (ps-2). 1995. write for info. (*1-57234-051-7*) YES Ent.

Mickey No Doubutsu Zukan - Mickey's Animal Illustrated Book. Tr. by Tomy Company Ltd. Staff. (Comes to Life Bks.). (ENG & JPN.). 20p. (J). (ps-2). 1995. write for info. (*1-57234-049-5*) YES Ent.

Mickey No Kazu Asobi 1, 2, 3 - Mickey's Numbering Study. Tr. by Tomy Company Ltd. Staff. (Comes to Life Bks.). (ENG & JPN.). 20p. (J). (ps-2). 1995. write for info. (*1-57234-050-9*) YES Ent.

Mickey Spilane's Mike Danger Collection, Vol. 1. Mickey Spillane, pseud. (Mike Danger Collection). (Illus.). 160p. (Orig.). 1996. reprint ed. pap. 15.95 (*1-57780-001-X*) Big Enter Inc.

Mickey Steals the Show. Diane Harris-Filderman. LC 94-69081. 85p. (Orig.). (J). (gr. 3-5). 1995. 16.95 (*0-943864-75-5*) Davenport.

Mickey Unlimited Ultimate Cross Stitch Collection: 63 Projects! Sandra S. Ritchie et al. LC 98-67367. 96p. 1998. 19.95 (*1-57486-142-5*) Leisure AR.

Mickey's ABC. Ann Braybrooks. 32p. Date not set. write for info. (*0-7868-3088-3*, Pub. by Disney Pr) Little.

Mickey's Alphabet Soup see Walt Disney's Read & Grow Library

Mickey's Big-Note Christmas Treats. 48p. 1986. pap. 6.95 (*0-7935-3881-5*, 00240550) H Leonard.

Mickey's Christmas. Mouse Works Staff. LC 98-226119. (Mickey Mouse Ser.). 5p. (J). 1998. 8.99 (*1-57082-757-5*, Pub. by Mouse Works) Time Warner.

Mickey's Christmas Candy Cane. Mouse Works Staff. LC 98-232698. (Standard Characters Ser.). 8p. (J). 1998. 2.99 (*1-57082-820-2*, Pub. by Mouse Works) Time Warner.

Mickey's Christmas Carol. Golden Books Staff. (Little Golden Bks.). (J). 1996. 2.29 (*0-307-98789-2*, 98789, Goldn Books) Gldn Bks Pub Co.

Mickey's Christmas Carol. Mouse Works Staff. (J). 1995. 7.98 (*1-57082-005-8*, Pub. by Mouse Works) Time Warner.

Mickey's Christmas Carol. Mouseworks Staff et al. LC 99-158608. (Little Library). (J). 1997. 5.98 (*1-57082-720-6*, Pub. by Mouse Works) Little.

Mickey's Christmas Carol Read-Along. (J). 1991. 6.98 incl. audio (*1-55723-250-4*) W Disney Records.

Mickey's Class Play. Judith Caseley. LC 97-33036. (Illus.). 32p. (J). (ps-3). 1998. 15.00 (*0-688-15405-0*, Grenwillow Bks) HarpC Child Bks.

***Mickey's Class Play.** Judith Caseley. LC 97-33036. (Illus.). 32p. (J). (ps-3). 1998. 14.93 (*0-688-15406-9*, Grenwillow Bks) HarpC Child Bks.

Mickey's Day of the Week. Ellen Milnes. (Illus.). (J). 1999. 2.99 (*0-7364-0049-4*, Pub. by Mouse Works) Time Warner.

Mickey's Favorites. (Disney Sing-Alongs Ser.). (J). 11.99 incl. audio (*1-55723-962-2*) W Disney Records.

Mickey's Friendly Tale, Vol. 1. Mouseworks Staff. 10p. 1999. 6.74 (*0-7364-0176-8*, Pub. by Mouse Works) Time Warner.

Mickey's Gourmet Cookbook: The Most Popular Recipes from Walt Disney World & Disneyland. LC 93-38706. (Illus.). 304p. (J). 1994. pap. 9.70 (*0-7868-8016-3*, Pub. by Hyperion) Time Warner.

Mickey's Manuscript Paper. 32p. 1986. pap. 2.50 (*0-88188-504-5*) H Leonard.

Mickey's Mementos, Vol. 1. Mickey Theobald. (Illus.). 48p. 1998. pap. 9.95 (*1-57377-049-3*, 019884-02244) Easl Pubns.

Mickey's Millennium Mystery, Vol. 1. Ellen Weiss. 32p. 1999. 9.99 (*0-7364-1022-8*, Pub. by Mouse Works) Time Warner.

Mickey's Moonbeams. Maxine Theabald. 1997. pap. text 9.95 (*1-57377-002-7*) Easl Pubns.

Mickey's New York Xmas. (J). 2000. 15.45 (*0-7868-3153-7*, Pub. by Hyperion) Little.

Mickey's Safari Park Adventure. Marilyn Bollinger. (Magic Touch Talking Bks.). (Illus.). 22p. (J). (ps-2). 1996. 19.99 (*1-888208-13-9*) Hasbro.

Mickey's Talent. 5p. (J). 1996. 5.98 (*1-57082-346-4*, Pub. by Mouse Works) Time Warner.

Mickey's Teeth & Bindle Stiff. Amlin Gray. 1992. pap. 5.25 (*0-8222-1385-0*) Dramatists Play.

Mickey's Thankgiving. Fun Works Staff. LC 98-233655. (Wacky Farm Ser.). (Illus.). 8p. (J). (ps-1). 1998. bds. 2.99 (*1-57082-859-8*, Pub. by Mouse Works) Time Warner.

Mickey's Things That Go Word. Mouseworks Staff. 48p. (J). 1999. 12.99 (*0-7364-0114-8*, Pub. by Mouse Works) Time Warner.

Mickey's Toon Town. Mouseworks Staff. (Illus.). (J). 1999. bds. write for info. (*0-7364-0063-X*) Mouse Works.

Mickey's Treehouse Treasury. Walter Elias Disney. 1989. 17.50 (*0-88704-251-1*) Sight & Sound.

Mickey's Weather Machine see Walt Disney's Read & Grow Library

Mickey's World of Words see Walt Disney's Read & Grow Library

Mickiewicz: The Great Improvisation. Louise Varese. 1956. 4.00 (*0-940962-51-9*) Polish Inst Art & Sci.

Mickle, Boswell, Garrick, & "The Siege of Marseilles" Frank Brady. LC 86-26593. (Transactions Ser.: Vol. 46, Pt. 5). 62p. 1987. pap. 17.50 (*0-208-02131-0*) CT Acad Arts & Sciences.

Mickle's Directory of Colorado Foundation & Government Grants. Ruth L. Wadsworth. viii, 504p. (Orig.). 1997. pap. 125.00 (*0-9656778-0-X*) Mickle Pubng.

Micklethwaite's Muskoka. John Denison. (Illus.). 192p. 1995. 48.00 (*1-55046-069-2*, Pub. by Boston Mills) Genl Dist Srvs.

Mickley: Genealogy of the Mickley Family of America, with a Brief General Record of the Michelet Family of Metz & Some Interesting & Valuable Correspondence, Biographical Sketches, Obits & History Memorabilia. M. F. Mickley. (Illus.). 182p. 1991. reprint ed. pap. 27.50 (*0-8328-1708-2*); reprint ed. lib. bdg. 37.50 (*0-8328-1707-4*) Higginson Bk Co.

***Mick's Archaeology.** Mick Aston. (Illus.). 2000. pap. 19.99 (*0-7524-1480-1*, Pub. by Tempus Pubng) Arcadia Publng.

Micky Darlin' Victor Kelleher. (YA). 1995. 12.95 (*0-7022-2801-X*, Pub. by Univ Queensland Pr) Intl Spec Bk.

Micky Mouse. Mouseworks Staff. (Friendly Tales Ser.). (Illus.). (J). 1998. 6.99 (*1-57082-929-2*, Pub. by Mouse Works) Time Warner.

Micmac. Harold McGee & Ruth H. Whitehead. (Illus.). 64p. 1991. pap. 7.95 (*0-920852-21-1*) Nimbus Publ.

Micmac by Choice: Elsie Sark - An Island Legend. M. Olga McKenna. 194p. 1990. pap. 16.95 (*0-88780-077-7*) Formac Publ Co.

Micmac Medicines: Remedies & Recollections. Laurie Lacey. (Illus.). 128p. 1993. pap. 10.95 (*1-55109-041-4*) Nimbus Publ.

Micmac Quillwork. Ruth H. Whitehead. (Illus.). 230p. 1991. 29.95 (*0-919680-22-4*, Pub. by Nov2a Scotia Mus) Nimbus Publ.

Micmac Texts. Albert D. Deblois. (Mercury Ser.: CES No. 117). 102p. 1994. pap. 11.95 (*0-660-12907-8*, Pub. by CN Mus Civilization) U of Wash Pr.

***Micmacs.** Glen W. Gonder. Ed. by Sharon J. Gonder. (Adventures of Willy Whacker Ser.). (Illus.). 125p. (YA). (gr. 6-8). 1999. lib. bdg. 8.95 (*1-58389-003-3*) Osage Bend Pub.

***MICO: An Open Source Corba Implementation.** 3rd ed. Arno Puder & Kay Rhomer. LC 99-86924. (Illus.). 180p. 2000. pap. 39.95 (*1-55860-666-1*) Morgan Kaufmann.

Mico Is Corba: A Corba 2.0 Compliant Implementation. Arno Puder. (C). 1998. pap. text 39.95 (*3-932588-11-8*) Morgan Kaufmann.

***MICO is Corba: A Corba 2.2 Compliant Implementation.** Arno Puder. 170p. 1998. pap. 39.95 incl. cd-rom (*3-932588-42-8*) Morgan Kaufmann.

MiCon 86: Optimization of Processing, Properties & Service Performance Through Microstructural Control. Ed. by B. L. Bramfitt et al. LC 87-30731. (Special Technical Publication Ser.: No. 979). (Illus.). 310p. 1988. text 61.00 (*0-8031-0985-7*, STP979) ASTM.

MiCon 90: Advances in Video Technology for Microstructural Control. Ed. by George F. Vander Voort. (Special Technical Publication Ser.: STP 1094). (Illus.). 400p. 1991. text 75.00 (*0-8031-1399-4*, STP1094) ASTM.

MiCon 78: Optimization of Processing, Properties & Service Performance Through Microstructural Control - STP 672. Ed. by H. Abrams et al. 677p. 1979. 59.50 (*0-8031-0517-7*, STP672) ASTM.

Micro: A Relational Database Management System. 444p. 1992. 20.00 (*0-87736-350-1*) U of Mich Inst Labor.

Micro - Macro Scale Phenomena in Solidification. Ed. by Christoph Beckermann et al. (HTD Series, Vol. 218: AMD: Vol. 139). 160p. 1992. 45.00 (*0-7918-1060-7*, G00704) ASME.

Micro- & Macrodata of Firms: Statistical Analysis & International Comparison. Ed. by Silvia Biffignandi. LC 98-55551. (Contibutions to Statistics Ser.). (Illus.). xii, 751p. 1999. pap. 119.00 (*3-7908-1143-2*) Spr-Verlag.

Micro- & Nanofabricated Electro-Optical Mechanical Systems for Biomedical & Environmental Applications, Vol. 2978. Ed. by Paul L. Gourley. LC 97-203565. 246p. 1997. 69.00 (*0-8194-2389-0*) SPIE.

Micro- & Nanofabricated Structures & Devices for Biomedical Environmental Applications, Vol. 3258. Ed. by Paul L. Gourley. LC 98-171717. 236p. 1998. 69.00 (*0-8194-2697-0*) SPIE.

Micro- & Nanopatterning Polymers, \Vol. 706. Ed. by Hiroshi Ito et al. LC 98-25955. (ACS Symposium Ser.: No. 706). (Illus.). 400p. 1998. text 125.00 (*0-8412-3581-3*) OUP.

Micro Action Chemistry. Carmen V. Ciardullo. (Illus.). (Orig.). 1990. pap., teacher ed. write for info. (*1-877991-23-6*, AP2044); pap., student ed. write for info. (*1-877991-22-8*, AP2042) Flinn Scientific.

Micro-Acupuncture Comprehensive Manual & Prescription Index. Ralph A. Dale. LC L11000x08500. (Illus.). 400p. 2001. 125.00 (*1-877589-06-3*) Dialectic Pubng.

Micro Adventure Series. Incl. Jungle Quest. Megan Stine & H. William Stine. 1984. pap. 1.95 Million Dollar Gamble. Chassie West. 1984. pap. 1.95 Time Trap. Jean Favors. 1984. pap. 1.95 128p. (J). (gr. 4 up). 1984. pap. write for info. (*0-318-57933-2*) Scholastic Inc.

Micro Analysis. 2nd ed. Hal R. Varian. (C). 1984. pap., teacher ed. write for info. (*0-393-95343-2*) Norton.

Micro & Macro Mechanics of Crack Growth: Proceedings of a Symposium. Ed. by K. Sadananda et al. LC 82-81289. (Conference Proceedings Ser.). (Illus.). 253p. reprint ed. pap. 78.50 (*0-608-17839-X*, 203260100088) Bks Demand.

***Micro & Nanofabricated Structures & Devices for Biomedical Environmental Applications II.** Ed. by Mauro Ferrari. 178p. 1999. pap. text 62.00 (*0-8194-3076-5*) SPIE.

Micro Applications Web Site. Stephen W. Salant. (C). 1999. pap. text. write for info. (*0-393-97472-3*) Norton.

Micro-Approaches to Demographic Research. John C. Caldwell et al. 400p. 1988. lib. bdg. 75.00 (*0-7103-0297-5*) Routledge.

Micro Budget Hollywood: Budgeting (& Making) Feature Films for $50,000 to $500,000. Philip Gaines. (Illus.). 220p. (Orig.). 1995. pap. 17.95 (*1-879505-22-3*) Silman James Pr.

Micro Bunches Workshop: AIP Conference Proceedings. E. B. Blum et al. (AIP Press Conference Proceedings Ser.: No. 367). (Illus.). 536p. 1996. 145.00 (*1-56396-555-0*, CP 367, AIP Pr) Spr-Verlag.

Micro-Cap II: Student Manual & Software. Martin S. Roden. (C). 1989. pap. text 24.95 (*0-685-18622-9*); 5.25 hd 37.45 (*0-201-50542-8*) Benjamin-Cummings.

Micro Computer: Specialty Care Products. Thomas J. Zarecki. (Illus.). 14p. (Orig.). 1986. 2.00 (*0-685-14594-8*) TJ Enter IL.

Micro-Computers in Personnel. Michael Norman & Tim Edwards. 128p. (C). 1984. 75.00 (*0-85292-337-6*) St Mut.

Micro-Director User Manual. Donald J. Jonovic. 90p. 1985. ring bd. 125.00 incl. disk (*0-915607-03-4*) Jamieson Pr.

***Micro-Economia.** 4th ed. McEachern. 1999. pap. 64.95 (*968-7529-50-4*) Thomson Learn.

Micro-Economic Policy. Keith Hartley & Clement A. Tisdell. LC 80-42311. (Illus.). 424p. reprint ed. pap. 131.50 (*0-608-15571-3*, 202963200062) Bks Demand.

Micro-Economic Theory. 4th enl. rev. ed. M. L. Jhingan. (Illus.). xv, 784p. 1988. text 40.00 (*81-220-0012-6*, Pub. by Konark Pubs Pvt Ltd) Advent Bks Div.

Micro Economics. William A. McEachern. (SWC-Economics). 832p. (C). 1988. pap. 37.75 (*0-538-08840-0*, H84) S-W Pub.

Micro Economy Today. 7th ed. Bradley R. Schiller. LC 96-19068. (C). 1996. pap. text 46.74 (*0-07-057716-1*) McGraw.

***Micro Economy Today** 8th ed. Bradley R. Schiller. LC 99-16176. 544p. 1999. pap. 60.00 (*0-07-366273-9*) McGraw.

Micro Economy-Wide Models for Migration & Policy Analysis: An Application to Rural Mexico. OECD Staff & J. Edward Taylor. (ENG & FRE.). 88p. (Orig.). 1996. pap. 18.00 (*92-64-14687-3*, Pub. by Org for Econ) OECD.

Micro (ed # 6E) 6th ed. Robert Ekelund. LC 99-49580. (C). 1999. pap. text. write for info. (*0-201-68027-0*) Addison-Wesley.

Micro-Electro-Mechanical Systems: Proceedings, International Mechanical Engineering Congress & Exposition, Atlanta, GA, 1996. LC 96-78683. (DSC Ser.: Vol. 59). 460p. 1996. pap. 150.00 (*0-7918-1541-2*, TK153) ASME.

Micro-Electro-Mechanical Systems (MEMS), 1998; Proceedings: ASME International Mechanical Engineering Congress & Exposition (1998: Anaheim, CA) Ed. by Liwei Lin et al. LC 99-192238. 593p. 1998. pap. 180.00 (*0-7918-1596-X*) ASME Pr.

***Micro-Electro-Mechanical Systems, 1999.** Ed. by Y. C. Lee. (MEMS Ser.). 611p. 1999. 170.00 (*0-7918-1638-9*) ASME Pr.

Micro-Electronics & Clothing: The Impact of Technical Change on a Global Industry. Kurt Hoffman & Howard Rush. LC 87-25736. 285p. 1988. 65.00 (*0-275-92798-9*, C2798, Praeger Pubs) Greenwood.

Micro-Electronics & Employment Revisited: A Review. Raphael Kaplinsky. xiv, 181p. (Orig.). 1987. 36.00 (*92-2-105610-4*); pap. text 27.00 (*92-2-105611-2*) Intl Labour Office.

***Micro-endoscopic Surgery of the Paranasal Sinuses & the Skull Base.** Ed. by A. J. Stamm & W. Draf. 610p. 2000. (*3-540-66629-X*) Spr-Verlag.

Micro-ErrorChecker with Micro-Typewriter: User Manual for Macintosh--Version 5. S. E. Warner Software, Inc. Staff. 40p. 1993. pap. text 2.95 (*1-57094-018-5*); 3.5 hd 1090.00 (*1-57094-017-7*) S E Warner Sftware.

Micro-ErrorChecker with Micro-Typewriter: Users Manual for IBM--Version 5. S. E. Warner Software, Inc. Staff. 42p. 1992. pap. text 2.95 (*1-57094-007-X*); 3.5 hd 1090.00 (*1-57094-005-3*); 5.25 hd 1090.00 (*1-57094-006-1*) S E Warner Sftware.

Micro-ErrorChecker with Word Processing Supervisor: User Manual for IBM--Version 2.0. S. E. Warner Software, Inc. Staff. 80p. 1994. pap. text 2.95 (*1-57094-027-4*); 3.5 hd 790.00 (*1-57094-025-8*); 5.25 hd 790.00 (*1-57094-026-6*) S E Warner Sftware.

Micro Essentials: The Library of Software Reference Cards. 8p. 1986. lib. bdg. 49.95 (*0-924256-92-3*) Gray Data.

Micro Fiction. Jerome Stern. 128p. 1996. 22.50 (*0-393-03968-4*); pap. 8.95 (*0-393-31432-4*) Norton.

Micro File Pro 2.1 for the MAC. David Bragg et al. 54p. 1998. pap. 4.50 (*0-07-230632-7*) McGraw.

***Micro-Finance Systems: Designing Quality Financial Services.** Graham Wright. LC 99-52392. 256p. 1999. pap. 25.00 (*1-85649-788-7*); text 69.50 (*1-85649-787-9*) Zed Books.

Micro Focus CICS Option 3.0: Developing CICS Applications on the PC. Clayton L. McNally, Jr. 1993. pap. 59.99 (*0-471-58406-1*, GD4604) Wiley.

Micro Focus COBOL Workbench for the Application Developer. Clayton L. McNally & Peter Molchan. 360p. 1993. pap. 52.00 (*0-471-58420-7*) Wiley.

Micro Focus Workbench: Developing Mainframe COBOL Applications on the PC. Alida M. Jatich & Phil Nowak. LC 92-14038. 448p. 1992. pap. 54.99 (*0-471-55611-4*) Wiley.

Micro Focus Workbench & Toolset Developer's Guide. Ron K. Lamb. 1995. pap. 40.00 (*0-07-036122-3*) McGraw.

Micro-Formatting: User Manual for IBM, Apple DOS 3.3, & Apple ProDOS Version 1.0. S. E. Warner Software, Inc. Staff. 74p. 1990. pap. text 2.95 (*1-57094-033-9*); 3.5 hd 449.00 (*1-57094-031-2*); 5.25 hd 449.00 (*1-57094-032-0*); 5.25 hd 449.00 (*1-57094-030-4*) S E Warner Sftware.

Micro Fouling & Corrosion of Copper Alloys in the Marine Environment: Phase One. 49p. 1981. write for info. (*0-318-60078-1*, 316) Intl Copper.

Micro House Encyclopedia of Hard Drives, Rev. A-3, Vol. 2: Drive Settings. Douglas T. Anderson. (Illus.). 1992. write for info. (*1-880252-07-4*) Micro Hse.

Micro House Encyclopedia of Hard Drives, Rev. A-3, Vol. 3: Controller Cards. Douglas T. Anderson. (Illus.). 1992. write for info. (*1-880252-08-2*) Micro Hse.

Micro House Encyclopedia of Hard Drives, Rev. B, 3 vols., Set, Vols. 1-3. Douglas T. Anderson. (Illus.). 1992. write for info. (*1-880252-12-0*) Micro Hse.

Micro House Encyclopedia of Hard Drives, Rev. B, 3 vols., Vol. 1: Setup Guide. Douglas T. Anderson. (Illus.). 1992. write for info. (*1-880252-09-0*) Micro Hse.

Micro House Encyclopedia of Hard Drives, Rev. B, 3 vols., Vol. 2: Drive Settings. Douglas T. Anderson. (Illus.). 1992. write for info. (*1-880252-10-4*) Micro Hse.

Micro House Encyclopedia of Hard Drives, Rev. B, 3 vols., Vol. 3: Controller Cards. Douglas T. Anderson. (Illus.). 1992. write for info. (*1-880252-11-2*) Micro Hse.

Micro House PC Hardware Library. Scott Mueller & Micro House Staff. LC 98-84620. (Scott Muller Library). 1998. write for info. (*0-7897-1665-8*) Que.

Micro Hydro Electric Power. Ray Holland. (Technical Papers: Vol. 1). 50p. (Orig.). 1983. pap. 12.00 (*1-85339-363-0*, Pub. by Intermed Tech) Stylus Pub VA.

M

Micro Hydroelectric Power Stations. fac. ed. Lucien Monition et al. Tr. by Joan McMullan. LC 84-7454. 187p. pap. 58.00 (*0-7837-7377-3*, 204718700005) Bks Demand.

Micro in Your Library. M. C. Boehmer. 50p. (Orig.). (C). 1984. pap. 5.00 (*0-914677-00-4*) Contemp Issues.

Micro Interactive: Software Visualization for Economics. Paul Estenson. (C). 1995. text 19.95 incl. disk (*0-256-20165-X*, Irwn McGrw-H) McGrw-H Hghr Educ.

Micro-Ledger: Demonstration Guide for IBM--Version 2.2. S. E. Warner Software, Inc. Staff & Galen Research, Inc. Staff. 24p. 1991. pap. text. write for info. (*1-57094-036-3*); 3.5 hd 650.00 (*1-57094-034-7*); 5.25 hd 650.00 (*1-57094-035-5*) S E Warner Sftware.

Micro-Ledger: Financial Accounting Student Workbook Manual & Computer Applications for IBM--Version 2.2. Harry J. Murvin & Richard L. Price. 158p. 1990. pap. text 10.95 (*1-57094-039-8*); pap. text 5.95 (*1-57094-040-1*) S E Warner Sftware.

Micro-Ledger: Instructor's Manual for IBM--Version 2.2. S. E. Warner Software, Inc. Staff & Galen Research, Inc. Staff. 300p. 1991. pap. text 99.00 (*1-57094-037-1*) S E Warner Sftware.

Micro-Ledger: Problem Booklet for IBM--Version 2.2. Darrel W. Davis. 58p. 1991. pap. text 5.95 (*1-57094-038-X*) S E Warner Sftware.

Micro-Ledger: Student Manual for IBM--Version 2.2. S. E. Warner Software, Inc. Staff & Galen Research, Inc. Staff. 104p. 1991. pap. text 5.95 (*1-57094-047-9*); disk. write for info. (*1-57094-048-7*) S E Warner Sftware.

Micro-Level Energy Plannning: A Case Study of Orissa. P. P. Gusain & Manoj Pandey. (Development Alternatives Ser.). 1993. text 35.00 (*0-7069-4936-6*, Pub. by Vikas) S Asia.

Micro-Level School Finance: Issues & Implications for Policy. Ed. by David Monk & Julie Underwood. 344p. 1988. text 35.00 (*0-88730-291-2*, HarpBusn) HarpInfo.

Micro-Logic. Spectrum Software Staff. 1989. student ed. 41.95 incl. 5.25 hd (*0-201-50552-5*) Addison-Wesley.

Micro-Macro Dilemmas in Political Science: Personal Pathways Through Complexity. Heinz Eulau. LC 96-22376. 560p. 1996. 37.95 (*0-8061-2873-9*) U of Okla Pr.

Micro-Macro Dilemmas in Political Science: Personal Pathways Through Complexity. Heinz Eulau. LC 96-22376. 560p. 1998. pap. 21.95 (*0-8061-2899-2*) U of Okla Pr.

Micro-Macro Link. Ed. by Jeffrey C. Alexander et al. 1987. pap. 19.95 (*0-520-06068-7*, Pub. by U CA Pr) Cal Prin Full Svc.

Micro-Macro Relations: Social Organization in Antalya, Southern Turkey. Reidar Gronhaug. (Bergen Studies in Social Anthropology: No. 7). (Illus.). 518p. (Orig.). 1985. pap. text 15.95 (*0-936508-52-3*, Pub. by Bergen Univ Dept Social Anthro) MBIPubg.

Micro Mainframe Connection. Mykytyns. 1985. text. write for info. (*0-442-26419-4*, VNR) Wiley.

Micro Man: What Life Might Be Like If You Were Bill Gates. I.B. McIntosh. 128p. 1998. pap. 9.95 (*1-55152-057-5*, Pub. by Arsenal Pulp) LPC InBook.

Micro-Management Is for Mushrooms' Or The "Wave Maker" T. S. Milne. LC 98-90248. 153p. 2000. pap. 10.95 (*0-533-12746-7*) Vantage.

***Micro Maniacs: Prima's Official Strategy Guide.** Julian Gale. 2000. pap. 8.99 (*0-7615-3033-9*) Prima Pub.

Micro Mechanical Systems: Principles & Technology. T. Fukuda & W. Menz. LC 98-20529. (Handbook of Sensors & Actuators Ser.). 1998. 201.00 (*0-444-82363-8*) Elsevier.

Micro-Nanotribology & Its Applications: Proceedings of the NATO Advanced Study Institutes, held in Sesimbra, Portugal, June 16-28, 1996. Ed. by Bharat Bhushan. LC 96-40248. (NATO Advanced Science Institutes Series C). 692p. (C). 1997. text 331.50 (*0-7923-4386-7*) Kluwer Academic.

Micro 90: Proceedings of the International Symposium Held in Montreal, Canada, May 22-24, 1990. Ed. by Z. Jacyno. 186p. 1990. 68.00 (*0-88986-148-X*, 167) Acta Pr.

Micro-Optical Technologies for Measurement Sensors & Mircosystems II & Optical Fiber Sensor Technologies & Applications. Olivier Pariaux. LC 98-125243. 418p. 1997. pap. 89.00 (*0-8194-2519-2*) SPIE.

Micro-Optics: Elements, Systems & Applications. Ed. by Hans P. Herzig. LC 97-197788. 600p. 1997. 115.00 (*0-7484-0481-3*, Pub. by Tay Francis Ltd) Taylor & Francis.

Micro-Optics & Lithography. Maria Kufner & Stefan Kufner. LC 97-195775. (Illus.). 206p. 1997. pap. 49.90 (*90-5487-167-9*, Pub. by VUB Univ Pr) Paul & Co Pubs.

Micro-Optics Integration & Assemblies. Ed. by Michael R. Feldman & Yung-Cheng Lee. 208p. 1998. 59.00 (*0-8194-2728-4*) SPIE.

Micro Organisms: A Laboratory Manual. University of Idaho Staff. 208p. (C). 1998. spiral bd. 42.95 (*0-7872-5392-8*, 41539201) Kendall-Hunt.

Micro-Organisms in Building Services. L. J. Stewart. (C). 1988. 105.00 (*0-86022-209-8*, Pub. by Build Servs Info Assn) St Mut.

Micro-Organisms in Permafrost, Vol. 9, No. 2. D. Zvyagintsev. 40p. 1997. pap. text 20.00 (*3-7186-5824-0*, Harwood Acad Pubs) Gordon & Breach.

Micro-Organisms in Ruminant Nutrition. Ed. by R. A. Prins & C. S. Stewart. 249p. 1999. pap. 160.00 (*1-897676-54-9*, Pub. by Nottingham Univ Pr) St Mut.

Micro-Personal-Small Business-Home Computing Directory. Richard Gardner. 265p. 1985. pap. 29.95 (*0-933342-05-5*) Resources MA.

Micro-Personal-Small Business-Home Computing Directory. Richard Gardner. 265p. 1987. pap. 29.95 (*0-933342-10-1*) Resources MA.

Micro-Photofabrication: Proceedings of the Winter Symposium, 1975, Palo Alto Cabana Hyatt House, Palo Alto, California, February 6-7, 1975. Society of Photographic Scientists & Engineers Sta. LC Z 0286.M5. 256p. reprint ed. pap. 79.40 (*0-608-15008-8*, 202570400046) Bks Demand.

Micro-Politics: Agency in a Postfeminist Era. Patricia S. Mann. LC 93-28965. 264p. 1994. pap. 18.95 (*0-8166-2049-0*) U of Minn Pr.

Micro-Politics of the School Towards a Theory of School Organization. Stephen J. Ball. 256p. 1988. pap. 15.95 (*0-416-00112-2*) Routledge.

Micro-Practice I Packet. Hepworth & Larsen. (Adaptable Courseware Ser.). 1993. 28.75 (*0-534-31687-5*) Brooks-Cole.

Micro-Preview Book. Stockman. (C). 1995. pap. 4.00 (*0-03-016499-0*) Harcourt.

Micro Problems. 10th ed. Lucile Mansfield. (C). pap. text. write for info. (*0-393-97597-5*) Norton.

Micro Problems: Case Studies & Exercises for Review. 9th ed. Edwin Mansfield. LC 97-120789. 1996. pap. write for info. (*0-393-97036-1*) Norton.

Micro-Programming. Norman E. Sondak. Ed. by Efrem G. Mallach. LC 77-18741. 395p. reprint ed. pap. 122.50 (*0-608-10244-X*, 201532000093) Bks Demand.

Micro-Qualiflex. J. P. Ancot. (C). 1988. lib. bdg. 814.50 (*90-247-3615-3*) Kluwer Academic.

Micro-Real Estate. James R. Webb. 1979. pap. text 12.95 (*0-933012-04-7*) Coker Pub.

Micro-Review in French. Clare J. Tufts. (FRE.). (C). 1990. write for info. (*0-03-051664-1*) Harcourt Coll Pubs.

Micro Revolution Revisited. Peter Large. LC 84-2164. 224p. 1984. 36.00 (*0-8476-7361-8*) Rowman.

Micro Robert. 35.00 (*0-685-36078-4*) Fr & Eur.

Micro-Robert, Dictionnaire du Francais Primordial. Paul Robert. (FRE.). 1988. 49.95 (*0-8288-1949-1*, M6487) Fr & Eur.

Micro Robert en Poche: Dictionnaire du Francais Primordial. Paul Robert et al. (FRE.). 1210p. 1988. pap. 29.95 (*0-8288-1948-3*, M4519) Fr & Eur.

Micro Saint Simulation Software: Users Guide 2.0. Margo Toth & Catherine Drury. (Orig.). 1996. pap. 100.00 (*0-614-29896-2*) Micro Analysis.

Micro SAINT User's Guide. Micro Analysis & Design Staff. (Version 2.0 Ser.). 1986. text 50.00 (*0-937197-01-7*) Micro Analysis.

Micro SAINT User's Guide. rev. ed. Micro Analysis & Design Staff. (Version 2.2 Ser.). 1986. text 50.00 (*0-937197-05-X*) Micro Analysis.

Micro SAINT User's Guide: Version 2.1. Micro Analysis & Design Staff. 1986. 50.00 (*0-937197-03-3*) Micro Analysis.

Micro SAINT User's Guide: Version 3.0. Micro Analysis & Design Staff. 1987. 60.00 (*0-317-64493-9*) Micro Analysis.

Micro Sftwr Win Microeco. 6th ed. Ralph T. Byrns & Gerald W. Stone. (C). 1997. text, student ed. 27.40 incl. disk (*0-673-99363-9*) Addson-Wesley Educ.

Micro Silver Bullet: A Preliminary Scientifically Documented Answer to the Three Largest Epidemics in the World. 5th rev. ed. M. Paul Farber. 700p. Date not set. pap. text 29.95 (*1-887742-01-8*) Prof Phys Pub.

Micro Skills Lab: Beginning WordPerfect Works for DOS. Charlotte Montanus et al. 244p. 1994. pap. 21.95 (*0-534-24108-5*) Course Tech.

Micro Space Craft. Rick Fleeter. 256p. 1992. pap. text 29.95 (*0-9648242-0-5*) Edge City Pr.

Micro Split-Principles of Economic Omics. 2nd ed. Gottheil. LC 98-7444. (Miscellaneous/Catalogs Ser.). 1998. pap. 66.95 (*0-538-86820-1*) S-W Pub.

Micro Station for AUTOCAD Users. Frank Conforti & Ralph Grabowski. LC 98-8797. (CAD/CAM Ser.). 780p. 1998. text 55.95 (*0-7668-0656-1*) Delmar.

Micro Structural Studies of High TC Superconductors & More on Quaternary Borocarbides. Ed. by Anant Narlikar. LC 99-22945. (Studies of High Temperature Superconductors: Vol. 28). 287p. 1999. lib. bdg. 93.00 (*1-56072-685-7*) Nova Sci Pubs.

Micro Surface Damages on Tooth Flanks of Carburized Gears. Louis Faure. (Nineteen Eighty-Eight Fall Technical Meeting Ser.: Vol. 88FTM4). (Illus.). 7p. 1988. pap. text 30.00 (*1-55589-509-3*) AGMA.

Micro Systems Technologies 90: First International Conference on Micro, Electro, Mechanic Systems & Components, Berlin, 10-13 September 1990. Ed. by H. Reichl. (Illus.). xv, 858p. 1990. 238.95 (*0-387-53025-8*) Spr-Verlag.

Micro-Tec: A Merchandising Sole Proprietorship Practice Set, 6 vols. 4th ed. Belverd E. Needles, Jr. (C). 1995. text, teacher ed. 11.96 (*0-395-75952-8*) HM.

Micro-Tech Index, Vol. 1. John F. Graves. 550p. 1986. 236.00 (*0-9617152-0-0*) Micro Tech.

Micro Theory & Applications. 6th ed. Zupan Browning. (C). 1999. pap. text, student ed. 22.50 (*0-321-03345-0*) Addson-Wesley Educ.

MICRO 30 - 1997: MICRO: 30th Annual International Symposium on Microarchitecture. 369p. 1997. pap. 52.00 (*0-89791-980-7*, 520970) Assn Compu Machinery.

Micro-to-Mainframe: Creating an Integrated Environment. Michael Durr & Dwayne Walker. write for info. (*0-318-59577-X*) Addison-Wesley.

Micro-to-Mainframe Connection. Penn Brumm. (Illus.). 210p. 1986. pap. 15.95 (*0-8306-2637-9*, NO. 2637) McGraw-Hill Prof.

Micro-to-Mainframe Data (3.5) 2nd ed. Michael S. Bodner. 1991. 49.95 (*0-8306-6743-1*) McGraw-Hill Prof.

Micro Total Analysis Systems '98: Proceedings of the [mu] Tas '98 Workshop, Held in Banff Canada, 13-16 October 1998. Daniel J. Harrison & A. Vanden Berg. LC 98-37274. xvi, 492 p. 1998. 208.00 (*0-7923-5322-6*) Kluwer Academic.

Micro Total Analysis Systems, '94: Proceedings of the UTAS '94 Workshop, Held at MESA Research Institute, University of Twente, The Netherlands, 22-22 November 1994. Albert J. Van den Berg. LC 94-39666. 324p. (C). 1994. text 166.50 (*0-7923-3217-2*) Kluwer Academic.

***Micro Total Analysis Systems 2000: Proceedings of the [MU] TAS 2000 Symposium, Held in Enschede, the Netherlands, 14-18 May 2000.** A. van den Berg et al. LC 00-31324. 2000. write for info. (*0-7923-6387-6*) Kluwer Academic.

Micro-Trainer Manual. 2nd ed. Christopher E. Strangio. (Illus.). 132p. (C). 1990. pap. text 19.00 (*0-929955-09-9*) CAMI Research.

Micro-Trains: A Color History. Ray Brown. 140p. 1993. pap. 49.95 (*1-881341-04-6*) Two-Ten-Four.

Micro-Trains: A Color History. 2nd ed. Ray Brown. (Illus.). 130p. 1995. 59.95 (*1-881341-06-2*); pap. 49.95 (*1-881341-07-0*) Two-Ten-Four.

Micro-Trains: A Color History, Vol. 1. Ray Brown. (Illus.). 140p. 1993. 59.95 (*1-881341-03-8*) Two-Ten-Four.

Micro Travelling: How to Travel the World with Only Carry-on Luggage. Darhon Rees-Rohrbacher. 75p. (Orig.). Date not set. pap. 8.00 (*1-882712-48-X*) Dragonflower.

Micro-Typewriter: Tutorial Guide. Donna L. Madsen & Lynda B. Nelson. 56p. 1986. pap. text 5.95 (*1-57094-041-X*) S E Warner Sftware.

Micro-Typewriter: Tutorial Guide. 2nd ed. Donna L. Madsen & Lynda B. Nelson. 58p. 1987. pap. text 5.95 (*1-57094-042-8*) S E Warner Sftware.

Micro-Typewriter: Tutorial Guide. 3rd ed. Donna L. Madsen & Lynda B. Nelson. 60p. 1988. pap. text 5.95 (*1-57094-043-6*) S E Warner Sftware.

Micro-Typewriter: Tutorial Guide. 4th ed. Donna L. Madsen & Lynda B. Nelson. 62p. 1989. pap. text 5.95 (*1-57094-044-4*) S E Warner Sftware.

Micro-Typewriter: Tutorial Guide. 5th ed. Donna L. Madsen & Lynda B. Nelson. 64p. 1992. pap. text 5.95 (*1-57094-045-2*) S E Warner Sftware.

Micro-Typewriter: User Manual for Macintosh--Version 5. S. E. Warner Software, Inc. Staff. 40p. 1993. pap. text 2.95 (*1-57094-016-9*); 3.5 hd 795.00 (*1-57094-015-0*) S E Warner Sftware.

Micro-Typewriter: User's Manual for Apple DOS 3.3--for Version 3. S. E. Warner Software, Inc. Staff. 58p. 1989. pap. text 2.95 (*1-57094-009-6*) S E Warner Sftware.

Micro-Typewriter: User's Manual for Apple Pro DOS--Version 4. S. E. Warner Software, Inc. Staff. 30p. 1989. pap. text 2.95 (*1-57094-012-6*); 3.5 hd 795.00 (*1-57094-010-X*); 5.25 hd 795.00 (*1-57094-008-8*) S E Warner Sftware.

Micro-Typewriter: User's Manual for IBM Version 4. S. E. Warner Software, Inc. Staff. 46p. 1991. pap. text 2.95 (*1-57094-002-9*) S E Warner Sftware.

Micro-Typewriter: User's Manual for IBM Version 5. S. E. Warner Software, Inc. Staff. 42p. 1992. pap. text 2.95 (*1-57094-046-0*); 3.5 hd 795.00 (*1-57094-003-7*); 5.25 hd 795.00 (*1-57094-004-5*) S E Warner Sftware.

Micro-Typewriter: User's Manual for Macintosh--Version 4. S. E. Warner Software, Inc. Staff. 56p. 1990. pap. text 2.95 (*1-57094-014-2*); 5.25 hd 795.00 (*1-57094-011-8*); mac hd 795.00 (*1-57094-013-4*) S E Warner Sftware.

***Micro-Vehicle Punch-Outs.** Illus. by Jennifer Foster. (Star Wars). 16p. (J). (ps-3). 1999. pap. 3.99 (*0-375-80014-X*, Pub. by Random Bks Yng Read) Random.

Micro View of Economics Today. 10th ed. Roger Leroy Miller. 320p. (C). 1998. pap. text, student ed. 24.00 (*0-321-03352-3*) Addson-Wesley Educ.

Micro World. Atlas Staff. 1995. teacher ed., lab manual ed. (*0-8151-0329-8*) Mosby Inc.

MICRO 27: International Workshop in Microarchitecture, 1994. 240p. 1994. pap. text 34.00 (*0-89791-707-3*, 520940) Assn Compu Machinery.

Microactuators. Ed. by Richard S. Muller & Albert P. Pisano. 450p. 2000. 89.95 (*0-7803-3441-8*, PC4291-QOE) Inst Electrical.

Microactuators: Electrical, Magnetic, Thermal, Optical, Mechanical, Chemical, & Smart Structures. Massood Tabib-Azar. LC 97-42709. (Kluwer International Series in Electronic Materials, Science & Technology). 304p. 1998. text 129.00 (*0-7923-8089-4*) Kluwer Academic.

MicroAge Way. Jeffrey L. Rodengen. LC 96-60604. 1997. 39.95 (*0-945903-12-X*) Write Stuff Syndicate.

Microalbuminuria: Biochemistry, Epidemiology & Clinical Practice. Peter H. Winocour et al. LC 98-25128. (Illus.). 230p. (C). 1998. pap. 49.95 (*0-521-45703-3*) Cambridge U Pr.

Microalgae: Biotechnology & Microbiology. E. W. Becker. (Studies in Biotechnology: No. 10). (Illus.). 301p. (C). 1994. text 74.95 (*0-521-35020-4*) Cambridge U Pr.

Microalgae for Food & Feed: Proceedings of a German-Israeli Workshop Held 17-18, October 1977 at Neuherberg. Ed. by Carl J. Soeder & Rudolf Binsack. (Advances in Limnology Ser.: Vol. 11). (GER., Illus.). iv, 300p. 1978. pap. text 58.00 (*3-510-47009-5*, Pub. by E Schweizerbartsche) Balogh.

Microaliens: Dazzling Journeys with an Electron Microscope. Howard Tomb. LC 93-1403. 80p. (J). (gr. 4-7). 1993. 16.00 (*0-374-34960-6*) FS&G.

Microalloying in Steels: Proceedings of the International Conference on Microalloying in Steels, Donostia-San Sebastian, Basque Country, Spain, September 1998. Ed. by J. M. Rodriguez-Ibabe et al. (Materials Science Forum Ser.: Vols. 284-286). (Illus.). 604p. (C). 1998. text 230.00 (*0-87849-816-8*, Pub. by Trans T Pub) Enfield Pubs NH.

Microalloying, '95: Proceedings of the International Conference "Microalloying '95" Held under the Auspices of the Iron & Steel Society, Inc. Pittsburgh, PA, U. S. A., June 11-14, 1995. International Conference "Microalloying 95". LC 95-79765. 459p. 1995. reprint ed. pap. 142.30 (*0-608-01270-X*, 206202000001) Bks Demand.

Microanalysis & Quantification. Ed. by Jasmin Gaetan & L. Proschek. (Methods & Achievements in Experimental Pathology Ser.: Vol. 11). (Illus.). vi, 190p. 1984. 142.75 (*3-8055-3717-4*) S Karger.

Microanalysis of Solids. B. G. Yacobi et al. LC 93-40984. (Illus.). 474p. (C). 1994. text 115.00 (*0-306-44433-X*, Kluwer Plenum) Kluwer Academic.

***Microanatomical Aspects for Neurosurgeons & Neuroradiologists.** W. Seeger. (Illus.). 440p. 2000. 298.00 (*3-211-83376-5*) Spr-Verlag.

***Microanatomy & Function of the Spleen.** Birte Steiniger & Peter Barth. LC 99-32588. (Advances in Anatomy, Embryology & Cell Biology Ser.: Vol. 151). (Illus.). vi, 96p. 1999. pap. 78.00 (*3-540-66161-1*) Spr-Verlag.

***Microarchitecture: Proceedings of the Annual ACM/IEEE International Symposium Haifa, Israel 1999.** 300p. 1999. 120.00 (*0-7695-0437-X*) IEEE Comp Soc.

Microarchitecture of Pipelined & Superscalar Computers. Amos R. Omondi. LC 99-13874. 1999. write for info. (*0-7923-8463-6*) Kluwer Academic.

Microarchitecture of VLSI Computers. Ed. by P. Antognetti et al. 1985. text 184.00 (*90-247-3202-6*) Kluwer Academic.

Microarchitecture, 30th Annual International Symposium. LC 10-724451. 360p. 1997. pap. 120.00 (*0-8186-7977-8*) IEEE Comp Soc.

Microarchitecture, 29th Annual International Symposium on (MICRO-29) LC 10-724451. 375p. 1996. pap. 70.00 (*0-8186-7641-8*) IEEE Comp Soc.

Microarchitecture, 29th Annual International Symposium on (Micro-29) (C). 1996. text, boxed set 70.00 incl. cd-rom (*0-8186-7855-0*, SW07855) IEEE Comp Soc.

Microarchitecture, 29th Annual International Symposium on (Micro-29), Set. 1996. text 100.00 (*0-8186-7856-9*) IEEE Comp Soc.

Microarray Biochip Tools & Techniques. Ed. by March Schena. LC 99-88465. (Molecular Laboratory Methods Ser.). (Illus.). 298p. 1999. 49.95 (*1-881299-37-6*) Eaton Pub Co.

Microbe Base - Apple. John Magee. 1986. text 1049.00 incl. disk (*0-12-465014-7*) Acad Pr.

Microbe Hunters. Paul De Kruif. LC 67-34588. 337p. 1966. pap. 7.95 (*0-15-659413-7*, Harvest Bks) Harcourt.

Microbe Hunters. Paul D. Kruif. 372p. 1996. pap. 13.00 (*0-15-600262-0*, Harvest Bks) Harcourt.

Microbe Hunters - Then & Now. Ed. by Hilary Koprowski & Michael B. Oldstone. LC 96-28898. (Illus.). 456p. 1996. 45.00 (*0-936741-11-2*) Medi-Ed Pr.

Microbe Id. - Mac. Fulford. 1994. 83.25 (*0-697-23362-6*) McGraw.

Microbeam Analysis. Ed. by E. S. Etz. 461p. 1995. pap. 169.95 (*0-471-18631-7*) Wiley.

Microbeam Analysis: Proceedings of the 27th Annual MAS Meeting in Los Angeles, CA, July 1993. Ed. by J. T. Armstrong & J. R. Porter. 298p. 1993. pap. 50.00 (*1-56081-659-7*, Wiley-VCH) Wiley.

Microbeam Analysis, 1995: Proceedings of the 29th Annual Conference of the Microbeam Analysis Society. Ed. by E. S. Etz. 430p. 1995. pap. 125.00 (*1-56081-919-7*, Wiley-VCH) Wiley.

Microbeam Analysis Society Proceedings. (Illus.). 1976. 10.00 (*0-685-74225-3*) San Francisco Pr.

Microbeam Analysis Society Proceedings. (Illus.). 1977. 10.00 (*0-614-24716-0*) San Francisco Pr.

Microbeam Analysis Society Proceedings. (Illus.). 1979. 10.00 (*0-614-24717-9*) San Francisco Pr.

Microbeam Analysis Society Proceedings. (Illus.). 1980. 10.00 (*0-614-24718-7*) San Francisco Pr.

Microbeam Analysis Society Proceedings. (Illus.). 1981. 10.00 (*0-614-24719-5*) San Francisco Pr.

Microbeam Analysis Society Proceedings. (Illus.). 1982. 10.00 (*0-614-24720-9*) San Francisco Pr.

Microbeam Analysis Society Proceedings. (Illus.). 1986. 10.00 (*0-685-74226-1*); lib. bdg. 10.00 (*0-614-24721-7*) San Francisco Pr.

Microbeam Analysis Society Proceedings. (Illus.). 1987. lib. bdg. 10.00 (*0-614-11158-7*) San Francisco Pr.

Microbeam Analysis Society Proceedings. (Illus.). 1988. lib. bdg. 10.00 (*0-614-24722-5*) San Francisco Pr.

Microbeam Analysis Society Proceedings. (Illus.). 1989. lib. bdg. 10.00 (*0-614-11159-5*) San Francisco Pr.

Microbeam Analysis Society Proceedings. (Illus.). 1990. lib. bdg. 10.00 (*0-614-11160-9*) San Francisco Pr.

Microbeam Analysis Society Proceedings. (Illus.). 1991. lib. bdg. 10.00 (*0-614-11161-7*) San Francisco Pr.

Microbeam & Nanobeam Analysis. Ed. by D. Benoit et al. (Illus.). 560p. 1996. pap. 219.50 (*3-211-82874-5*) Spr-Verlag.

Microbes. Claus. (C). 1989. pap. text 5.60 (*0-7167-2051-5*) W H Freeman.

Microbes. Snape & Rowlands. (Science at Work Ser.). 1992. pap. text. write for info. (*0-582-07436-3*, Pub. by Addison-Wesley) Longman.

Microbes & Malignancy: Infection as a Cause of Human Cancers. Ed. by Julie Parsonnet. LC 98-22168. (Illus.). 480p. 1999. text 79.95 (*0-19-510401-3*) OUP.

Microbes & Man. 4th ed. John Postgate. LC 99-13564. (Illus.). 352p. (C). 2000. pap. 19.95 (*0-521-66579-5*) Cambridge U Pr.

Microbes & Microbial Products As Herbicides. Ed. by Robert E. Hoagland. LC 90-1284. (Symposium Ser.: No. 439). (Illus.). 352p. 1990. text 85.00 (*0-8412-1865-X*, Pub. by Am Chemical) OUP.

Microbes & Minie Balls: An Annotated Bibliography of Civil War Medicine. Frank R. Freemon. LC 92-23153. (Illus.). 256p. 1993. 39.50 (*0-8386-3484-2*) Fairleigh Dickinson.

An Asterisk (*) at the beginning of an entry indicates that the title is appearing for the first time.

Microbes & People: An A to Z of Microorganisms in Our Lives. Neeraja Sankaran. (Illus.). 272p. 2000. text, boxed set 55.00 (*1-57356-217-3*) Oryx Pr.

Microbes, Bugs & Wonder Drugs. Fran Balkwill. Ed. by Victor Darley-Ujmar. (Making Sense of Science Ser.: Vol. 1). (Illus.). 128p. (YA). (gr. 7-11). 1995. 20.00 (*1-85578-065-8*, Pub. by Portland Pr Ltd) Ashgate Pub Co.

Microbes in Action: A Laboratory Manual of Microbiology. Harry W. Seeley, Jr. (Illus.). 430p. (C). 1990. 12.80 (*0-7167-2137-6*) W H Freeman.

Microbes in Action: A Laboratory Manual of Microbiology. 4th ed. Harry W. Seeley, Jr. (Illus.). 351p. (C). 1990. pap. text 43.95 (*0-7167-2100-7*) W H Freeman.

Microbes in Extreme Environments. Ed. by R. A. Herbert & Geoffrey A. Codd. (Society for General Microbiology Special Publications: Vol. 17). 1986. text 94.00 (*0-12-341460-1*) Acad Pr.

Microbes in the Indoor Environment: A Manual for the Indoor Air Quality Field Investigator. Libero Ajello et al. LC 98-207773. (Illus.). x, 125p. 1998. pap. 150.00 (*0-9664048-0-7*, Pathogen Control) PathCon Lab.

Microbes in the Sea. Sleigh. 241p. 1987. text 68.95 (*0-470-20978-X*) P-H.

Microbes, Man & Animals: The Natural History of Microbial Interactions. Alan H. Linton. LC 81-14719. (Illus.). 358p. reprint ed. pap. 111.00 (*0-608-17651-6*, 203050900069) Bks Demand.

Microbes, Our Unseen Friends. Harold W. Rossmoore. LC 76-17795. 238p. reprint ed. pap. 73.80 (*0-7837-3643-6*, 204351200009) Bks Demand.

Microbes Versus Mankind: The Coming Plague. Laurie Garrett. Ed. by Karen Rohan & Nancy L. Hoepli-Phalon. LC 96-84227. (Headline Ser.: No. 309). (Illus.). 72p. (YA). 1996. pap. text 5.95 (*0-87124-169-2*) Foreign Policy.

Microbiak Composition Amino Acids, Proteins & Nucleic Acids. 2nd ed. A. Laskin & Hubert A. Lechevalier. LC 77-12460. (Handbook of Microbiology Ser.: Vol. 3). 1008p. 1981. 540.00 (*0-8493-7203-8*, CRC Reprint) Franklin.

Microbial Activity on Filter-Adsorbers. (Illus.). 116p. 1992. pap. 75.00 (*0-89867-633-9*, 90606) Am Water Wks Assn.

Microbial Adhesion & Invasion. Ed. by M. Hook & L. Switalski. (Illus.). 194p. 1992. 87.95 (*0-387-97815-1*) Spr-Verlag.

Microbial Aggregation. Gode B. Calleja. 288p. 1984. 163.00 (*0-8493-5708-X*, QR73, CRC Reprint) Franklin.

Microbial & Enzymatic Bioproducts. Ed. by A. Fiechter et al. (Advances in Biochemical Engineering/ Biotechnology Ser.: Vol. 52). (Illus.). 216p. 1995. 161.95 (*3-540-59113-3*) Spr-Verlag.

Microbial & Enzymatic Degradation of Wood & Wood Components. K. E. Eriksson et al. (Wood Science Ser.). (Illus.). 416p. 1990. 225.00 (*0-387-51600-X*) Spr-Verlag.

***Microbial & Phenotypic Definition of Rats & Mice: Proceedings of the 1998 U. S. - Japan Conference.** National Research Council Staff. 110p. 1999. pap. 26.25 (*0-309-06591-7*) Natl Acad Pr.

Microbial & Plant Cytochrome P-450: Biochemical Characteristics, Genetic Engineering & Practical Implications. Ed. by Klaus Ruckpaul & Horst Rein. (Frontiers in Biotransformation Ser.: Vol. 4). 280p. 1991. 90.00 (*0-7484-0029-X*, Pub. by Tay Francis Ltd) Taylor & Francis.

Microbial & Viral Pesticides. fac. ed. Ed. by Edouard Kurstak. LC 82-5054. (Illus.). 736p. 1982. reprint ed. pap. 200.00 (*0-608-00955-5*, 206180100011) Bks Demand.

***Microbial Antibiotic Resistance: Food Safety.** 1999. 16.00 (*0-11-322295-5*, Pub. by Statnry Office) Balogh.

Microbial Antibiotic Resistance: Genetics, Physiology & Epidemiology. A. Tomasz & D. S. Thaler. Date not set. write for info. (*0-8247-9536-9*) Dekker.

Microbial Antigenodiagnosis: General Considerations, 2 vols., I. Ed. by Konrad Wicher. 274p. 1987. 156.00 (*0-8493-6345-4*, CRC Reprint) Franklin.

Microbial Antigenodiagnosis: Practical Application, 2 vols., II. Ed. by Konrad Wicher. 274p. 1987. 104.00 (*0-8493-6346-2*, CRC Reprint) Franklin.

Microbial Antigenodiagnosis: Practical Application, 2 vols., Set. Ed. by Konrad Wicher. 274p. 1987. 349.00 (*0-8493-6344-6*, RC113) CRC Pr.

Microbial Associations & Interactions in Food. Ed. by Istvan Kiss et al. 1984. text 250.00 (*90-277-1802-4*) Kluwer Academic.

Microbial Autoregulators. A. S. Khokhlov. v, 450p. 1991. text 360.00 (*3-7186-4985-3*, Harwood Acad Pubs) Gordon & Breach.

Microbial Biofilms. Ed. by Hilary M. Lappin-Scott & J. William Costerton. (Plant & Microbiotechnology Research Ser.: No. 5). (Illus.). 324p. (C). 1995. text 110.00 (*0-521-45412-3*) Cambridge U Pr.

Microbial Biofilms: Formation & Control. Ed. by S. P. Denyer et al. LC 93-17040. (Society for Applied Bacteriology Technical Ser.: No. 30). 1993. 65.00 (*0-632-03753-9*) Blackwell Sci.

Microbial Biology. Eugene Rosenberg & Irun Cohen. 433p. (C). 1983. text 75.00 (*0-03-085658-2*, Pub. by SCP) Harcourt.

Microbial Bioproducts. Ed. by A. Feichter. (Advances in Biochemical Engineering-Biotechnology Ser.: Vol. 41). (Illus.). vii, 139p. 1990. 103.95 (*0-387-52569-6*) Spr-Verlag.

Microbial Biotechnology. Alexander N. Glazer. LC 94-11367. 640p. (C). 1994. pap. text 76.95 (*0-7167-2608-4*) W H Freeman.

Microbial Biotechnology: Proceedings of National Symposium on Frontiers, UGC & CSIR November 1994, New Delhi. S. M. Reddy. 1997. pap. 180.00 (*81-7233-153-3*, Pub. by Scientific Pubs) St Mut.

***Microbial Calorimetry.** Katsutada Takahashi & Oana-Arina Antoce. 250p. 2000. 38.00 (*1-86094-202-4*, Pub. by Imperial College) World Scientific Pub.

Microbial Cell-Cell Interactions. Ed. by Martin Dworkin. (Illus.). 369p. 1991. text 69.00 (*1-55581-037-3*) ASM Pr.

Microbial Cell Cycle. Ed. by Paul Nurse & Eva Streiblova. 304p. 1984. 164.00 (*0-8493-5574-5*, QR73, CRC Reprint) Franklin.

Microbial Cell Surface Analysis: Structural & Physico-Chemical Methods. Ed. by Nava Mozes et al. 368p. 1991. 95.00 (*0-89573-783-3*, Wiley-VCH) Wiley.

Microbial Cell Surface Hydrophobicity. Ed. by Ronald J. Doyle & Mel Rosenberg. (Illus.). 435p. 1990. text 65.00 (*1-55581-028-4*) ASM Pr.

Microbial Cell Walls. H. R. Perkins et al. 575p. 1980. 85.00 (*0-412-12030-5*, NO. 6415) Chapman & Hall.

Microbial Communities: Functional vs. Structural Approaches. Heribert Insam & Andrea Rangger. LC 97-22416. 1997. write for info. (*3-540-62405-8*) Spr-Verlag.

Microbial Control of Pests & Plant Diseases, 1970 to 1980. Ed. by H. D. Burges. LC 80-41480. 960p. 1981. text 272.00 (*0-12-143360-9*) Acad Pr.

Microbial Corrosion. 136p. (Orig.). 1983. 20.00 (*0-904357-58-9*, Pub. by Inst Materials) Ashgate Pub Co.

Microbial Corrosion: Proceedings of the 3rd International EFC Workshop Portugal, 1994. Ed. by A. K. Tiller & Cesar A. Sequeira. (European Federation of Corrosion Publications Ser.: No. 15). 412p. 1995. 160.00 (*0-901716-62-6*, Pub. by Inst Materials) Ashgate Pub Co.

Microbial Culture. S. Isaac & D. Jennings. (Introduction to Biotechniques Ser.). 160p. (Orig.). 1995. pap. 48.50 (*1-872748-92-9*, Pub. by Bios Sci) Coronet Bks.

Microbial Degradation of Natural Products. Ed. by Gunther Winkelmann. LC 91-46460. (Illus.). 421p. 1992. 231.00 (*3-527-28354-4*, Wiley-VCH) Wiley.

Microbial Degradation of Organic Compounds. David T. Gibson. (Microbiology Ser.: Vol. 13). (Illus.). 552p. 1984. text 245.00 (*0-8247-7102-8*) Dekker.

Microbial Degradation Processes in Radioactive Waste Repository & in Nuclear Fuel Storage Areas: Proceedings of the NATO Advanced Research Workshop, Budapest, Hungary, 9-12 May 1996. Ed. by J. H. Wolfram et al. LC 97-7526. (NATO Advanced Sciences Institutes: No. 11). 302p. 1997. text 160.50 (*0-7923-4488-X*) Kluwer Academic.

Microbial Development. Ed. by Richard Losick & Lucy Shapiro. LC 84-9599. (Monographs: Vol. 16). 303p. 1984. 60.00 (*0-87969-172-7*); pap. 35.00 (*0-87969-173-5*) Cold Spring Harbor.

Microbial Disease see Handbook of Clinical Neurology

Microbial Diseases: A Veterinarian's Guide to Laboratory Diagnosis. G. R. Carter & M. M. Chengappa. LC 92-35999. 318p. (C). 1993. text 49.95 (*0-8138-0671-2*) Iowa St U Pr.

Microbial Diseases in Nephrology. Ed. by A. W. Asscher & William Brumfitt. LC 85-91279. (Wiley-Medical Publication). (Illus.). 384p. reprint ed. pap. 119.10 (*0-8357-3095-6*, 203935200012) Bks Demand.

Microbial Diseases of Occupations, Sports, & Recreations. C. H. Collins et al. LC 96-38862. 192p. 1996. pap. text 52.50 (*0-7506-2183-4*) Buttrwrth-Heinemann.

Microbial Diversity & Ecosystem Function. Ed. by D. Allsopp et al. (Illus.). 400p. 1995. text 120.00 (*0-85198-898-9*) OUP.

Microbial Diversity & Genetics of Biodegradation. Ed. by Koki Horikoshi et al. LC 98-118871. (Illus.). xii, 210p. 1997. 214.00 (*3-8055-6589-5*) S Karger.

Microbial Diversity in Time & Space. Ed. by R. R. Colwell et al. LC 96-13455. (Illus.). 180p. 1996. 75.00 (*0-306-45194-8*, Kluwer Plenum) Kluwer Academic.

Microbial Ecology. Wimpenny & Boddy. 1995. pap. text. write for info. (*0-582-20990-0*, Pub. by Addison-Wesley) Longman.

Microbial Ecology. 4th ed. Ronald M. Atlas. LC 97-31965. (Illus.). 640p. (C). 1997. 94.00 (*0-8053-0655-2*) Addison-Wesley.

Microbial Ecology: Fundamentals & Applications. L. V. Atkinson & Peter J. Harley. (Life Sciences Ser.). 500p. 1981. write for info. (*0-201-00051-2*) Addison-Wesley.

Microbial Ecology: Organisms, Habitats & Activities. Heniz Stolp. (Cambridge Studies in Ecology). (Illus.). 324p. 1988. pap. text 34.95 (*0-521-27636-5*) Cambridge U Pr.

Microbial Ecology & Infectious Disease. Ed. by Eugene Rosenberg. LC 98-30758. 340p. 1998. 79.95 (*1-55581-148-5*) ASM Pr.

***Microbial Ecology of Biofilms.** Ed. by B. E. Rittmann. (Water Science & Technology Ser.). 280p. 1999. pap. 163.00 (*0-08-043654-4*, Pergamon Pr) Elsevier.

Microbial Ecology of Lake Plusssee. Ed. by Jurgen Overbeck & Ryszard J. Chrost. LC 93-5258. (Ecological Studies: Vol. 105). 1993. 118.00 (*0-387-94120-7*) Spr-Verlag.

Microbial Ecology of Leaves. Ed. by J. H. Andrews & S. S. Hirano. (Contemporary Bioscience Ser.). (Illus.). xvii, 499p. 1991. 144.00 (*0-387-97579-9*) Spr-Verlag.

Microbial Ecology of Pelagic Environments: Proceedings of the Fifth International Workshop on the Measurement of Microbial Activities in the Carbon Cycle in Aquatic Environments. Ed. by Peter K. Bjornsen & Bo Rie-mann. (Advances in Limnology Ser.: Vol. 37). (GER., Illus.). vi, 278p. 1992. pap. text 99.00 (*3-510-47038-9*, Pub. by E Schweizerbartsche) Balogh.

***Microbial Ecology of the Oceans.** David L. Kirchman. LC 99-45537. 416p. 2000. pap. 69.95 (*0-471-29992-8*) Wiley.

***Microbial Ecology of the Oceans.** David L. Kirchman. LC 99-45537. 512p. 2000. text 139.00 (*0-471-29993-6*) Wiley.

Microbial Ecosystems of Antarctica. Warwick F. Vincent. (Studies in Polar Research). (Illus.). 320p. 1989. text 100.00 (*0-521-32875-6*) Cambridge U Pr.

***Microbial Endophytes.** Ed. by Charles W.. Bacon & James F. White, Jr. (Books in Soils, Plants & the Environment: Vol. 75). 487p. 2000. 175.00 (*0-8247-8831-1*) Dekker.

Microbial Energetics. E. A. Dawes. (Tertiary Level Biology Ser.). (Illus.). 192p. (C). 1985. text 39.95 (*0-412-01041-0*, 9444, Chap & Hall NY); pap. text 29.50 (*0-412-01051-8*, 9445, Chap & Hall NY) Chapman & Hall.

Microbial Energy Transduction: Genetics, Structure, & Function of Membrane Proteins. Ed. by Douglas C. Youvan & Fevzi Daldal. LC 86-206940. (Current Communications in Molecular Biology Ser.). 191p. (Orig.). 1986. reprint ed. pap. 59.30 (*0-608-01815-5*, 206246400003) Bks Demand.

Microbial Enhanced Oil Recovery. Ed. by Teh Fu Yen. 192p. 1989. lib. bdg. 159.00 (*0-8493-5142-1*, TN871) CRC Pr.

Microbial Enhancement of Oil Recovery: Recent Advances. Ed. by Eugene T. Premuzic & Avril D. Woodhead. LC 93-22897. (Developments in Petroleum Science Ser.: Vol. 39). 446p. 1993. 182.75 (*0-444-89690-2*) Elsevier.

Microbial Enzymes in Aquatic Environments. Ed. by Ryszard J. Chrost. (Contemporary Bioscience Ser.). (Illus.). xviii, 317p. 1991. 128.00 (*0-387-97452-0*) Spr-Verlag.

***Microbial Extracellular Polymeric Substances: Characterization, Structure & Function.** Ed. by Jost Wingender et al. LC 99-38891. (Illus.). viii, 232p. 1999. 120.00 (*3-540-65720-7*) Spr-Verlag.

Microbial Food Poisoning. Adrian R. Eley et al. (Illus.). 240p. (Orig.). (C). (gr. 13). Date not set. pap. text 49.50 (*0-412-37390-4*, Chap & Hall NY) Chapman & Hall.

***Microbial Foodborne Diseases: Mechanisms of Pathogenesis & Toxin Synthesis.** Ed. by Jeffrey W. Cary et al. LC 99-66881. 568p. 1999. text 149.95 (*1-56676-787-3*) Technomic.

Microbial Gas Metabolism. Ed. by Robert K. Poole & Crawford S. Dow. (Society for General Microbiology Special Publications: Vol. 14). 1985. text 157.00 (*0-12-561480-2*) Acad Pr.

Microbial Genetics. 2nd ed. Stanley R. Maloy et al. (Life Science Ser.). 512p. 1994. 66.25 (*0-86720-248-3*) Jones & Bartlett.

***Microbial Genetics.** 3rd ed. Stanley R. Maloy & John Cronan. (Illus.). 544p. (C). 2000. text 67.50 (*0-7637-1059-8*) Jones & Bartlett.

Microbial Genome Methods. Ed. by Kenneth W. Adolph. 304p. 1996. 79.95 (*0-614-29958-6*, 4410H3Y) CRC Pr.

Microbial Growth Dynamics. Ed. by Robert K. Poole et al. (Society for General Microbiology Special Publications: Vol. 28). (Illus.). 184p. 1990. 85.00 (*0-19-963118-2*) OUP.

Microbial Growth on C1 Compounds. Ed. by H. W. Verseveld & J. A. Duine. 1987. text 144.00 (*90-247-3459-2*) Kluwer Academic.

Microbial Growth on C1 Compounds: Proceedings of the 4th International Symposium. International Symposium on Microbial Growth on C1. Ed. by Ronald L. Crawford & R. S. Hanson. LC 84-3073. 353p. reprint ed. pap. 109.50 (*0-7837-4038-7*, 204386800011) Bks Demand.

Microbial Growth on C1 Compounds: Proceedings of the 8th International Symposium on Microbial Growth on C1 Compounds, Held in San Diego, U. S. A., 27 August-1 September, 1995. Ed. by Mary E. Lidstrom & F. Robert Tabita. LC 96-198. 376p. (C). 1996. text 166.00 (*0-7923-3938-X*) Kluwer Academic.

Microbial Hazards of Diving in Polluted Waters. Ed. by Rita R. Colwell et al. 1981. 3.00 (*0-943676-08-8*) MD Sea Grant Col.

Microbial Impact of Biological Filtration. Mark W. Lechevallier & AWWA Research Foundation Staff. LC 97-31912. 1998. write for info. (*0-89867-939-7*) Am Water Wks Assn.

Microbial Infections: Role of Biological Response Modifiers. H. Friedman et al. LC 92-21809. (Advances in Experimental Medicine & Biology Ser.: Vol. 319). (Illus.). 358p. (C). 1992. text 105.00 (*0-306-44237-X*, Kluwer Plenum) Kluwer Academic.

Microbial Interactions in Agriculture & Forestry. Ed. by N. S. Subbarao & Y. R. Dommergues. (Illus.). 278p. 1998. 79.00 (*1-57808-017-7*) Science Pubs.

Microbial Life in the Soil: An Introduction. Tsutomu Hattori. LC 72-90959. (Books in Soils & the Environment). (Illus.). 448p. reprint ed. pap. 138.90 (*0-7837-0907-2*, 204121200019) Bks Demand.

Microbial Limit & Bioburden Tests: Validation Approaches & Global Requirements. Lucia Clontz. LC 97-41282. (Illus.). 240p. 1998. 189.00 (*1-57491-062-0*) Interpharm.

Microbial Lipids, Vol. 1. Ed. by Colin Ratledge & S. G. Wilkinson. 450p. 1988. text 209.00 (*0-12-582304-5*) Acad Pr.

Microbial Lipids, Vol. 2. Ed. by Colin Ratledge & S. G. Wilkinson. 726p. 1989. text 209.00 (*0-12-582305-3*) Acad Pr.

Microbial Mats: Physiological Ecology of Benthic Microbial Communities. Ed. by Yehuda Cohen & Eugene Rosenberg. LC 88-34241. (Illus.), 512p. reprint ed. pap. 158.80 (*0-608-08634-7*, 206915700003) Bks Demand.

Microbial Mats: Structure, Development & Environmental Significance. Ed. by Lucas J. Stal & Pierre Caumette. LC 94-15483. (NATO ASI Series G: Ecological Sciences: No. 35). 1994. 238.95 (*0-387-57975-3*) Spr-Verlag.

Microbial Mediation of Plant-Herbivore Interactions. Pedro Barbosa et al. LC 90-42726. 530p. 1991. 190.00 (*0-471-61324-X*) Wiley.

Microbial Metabolism & the Carbon Cycle. S. R. Hagedorn et al. xi, 521p. 1988. text 299.00 (*3-7186-0472-8*) Gordon & Breach.

Microbial Metabolism in the Digestive Tract. Michael J. Hill. 264p. 1986. 150.00 (*0-8493-5936-8*, QR171, CRC Reprint) Franklin.

Microbial Metabolites: Extended Abstracts from the 3rd International Conference on the Biotechnology of Microbial Products: Novel Pharmacological & Agrobiological Activities. Ed. by Vincent P. Gullo et al. (Developments in Industrial Microbiology Ser.: Vol. 33, 1993). 1993. 50.00 (*0-614-29706-0*) Society Indust Microb.

Microbial Metabolites: Proceedings of the 2nd International Conference on the Biotechnology of Microbial Products: Novel Pharmacological & Agrobiological Activities. Sim. Ed. by Claude Nash, III et al. (Developments in Industrial Microbiology Ser.: Vol. 32, Ed. 1). 240p. (C). 1993. text. write for info. (*0-697-16688-0*, WCB McGr Hill) McGrw-H Hghr Educ.

Microbial Pathogenesis. B. McClane et al. (Integrated Medical Sciences Ser.). (C). 1998. pap. 22.95 (*1-889325-27-9*) Fence Crk Pubng.

Microbial Pathogenesis: Current & Emerging Issues: Proceedings of the 2nd Annual Indiana Conference. Ed. by Donald J. LeBlanc et al. LC 98-73482. (Illus.). 179p. 1998. text. write for info. (*0-9655149-1-9*) IN Univ Schl Dentstry.

***Microbial Pathogenesis: Lecture Supplements.** David Rollinson & Sam Joseph. 166p. (C). 1999. per. 29.95 (*0-7872-6500-4*, 41650001) Kendall-Hunt.

Microbial Pathogenesis & Immune Response II: Proceedings of a New York Academy of Sciences Conference, October 25-28, 1995, Vol. 797. Ed. by Edwin W. Ades et al. 1996. 90.00 (*1-57331-016-6*) NY Acad Sci.

Microbial Pathogens Within Aquifers: Principles & Protocols. Suresh D. Pillai. LC 97-47086. (Environmental Intelligence Unit Ser.). 1998. 129.00 (*1-57059-520-8*) Landes Bioscience.

Microbial Pathogens Within Aquifers: Principles & Protocols. Ed. by Suresh D. Pillai. LC 97-47086. (Environmental Intelligence Unit Ser.). 150p. 1998. 129.00 (*3-540-63891-1*) Spr-Verlag.

Microbial Pentose Utilization: Current Applications in Biotechnology. Ajay Singh & Prashant Mishra. LC 95-39029. (Progress in Industrial Microbiology Ser.: Vol. 33). 414p. 1995. 243.25 (*0-444-82039-6*, QR53) Elsevier.

Microbial Physiology. Albert G. Moat & John W. Foster. LC 95-15648. 608p. 1995. pap. 86.50 (*0-471-01452-4*) Wiley.

Microbial Physiology. 2nd ed. Ian W. Dawes & Ian W. Sutherland. (Basic Microbiology Ser.). (Illus.). 304p. 1991. pap. 44.95 (*0-632-02463-1*) Blackwell Sci.

Microbial Physiology. 3rd ed. Albert G. Moat & John W. Foster. LC 95-15648. 608p. 1995. 219.95 (*0-471-01295-5*) Wiley.

Microbial Physiology & Biochemistry Laboratory: A Quantitative Approach. Ed. by David White & George D. Hegeman. LC 97-82555. (Illus.). 176p. (C). 1997. pap. text 26.95 (*0-19-511313-6*) OUP.

Microbial Physiology & Metabolism. Daniel R. Caldwell. 384p. (C). 1994. text 50.00 (*0-697-17192-2*, WCB McGr Hill) McGrw-H Hghr Educ.

Microbial Physiology & Metabolism. 2nd rev. ed. Daniel R. Caldwell. LC 98-53183. (Illus.). 11p. 1999. 69.95 (*0-89863-208-0*) Star Pub CA.

Microbial-Plant Interactions. Ed. by J. E. Giddens & R. L. Todd. (ASA Special Publications: No. 47). 68p. 1984. 7.00 (*0-89118-078-8*) Am Soc Agron.

Microbial Polyesters. Y. Doi. 156p. 1990. 74.95 (*0-471-18732-1*, Wiley-VCH) Wiley.

Microbial Polyesters. Yoshiharu Doi. LC 90-42419. 156p. 1990. 39.50 (*0-89573-746-9*, Wiley-VCH) Wiley.

Microbial Process Development. H. W. Doelle. 350p. 1994. text 44.00 (*981-02-1515-0*) World Scientific Pub.

Microbial Processes for Bioremediation 3(8) Ed. by Robert E. Hinchee et al. 374p. 1995. 69.95 (*1-57477-009-8*) Battelle.

Microbial Processes in Reservoirs. Ed. by D. Gunnison. (Developments in Hydrobiology Ser.). 1985. text 195.50 (*90-6193-525-3*) Kluwer Academic.

Microbial Production & Consumption of Greenhouse Gases: Methane, Nitrogen Oxides, & Halomethanes. Ed. by John E. Rogers & William B. Whitman. (Illus.). 308p. 1991. text 64.00 (*1-55581-035-7*) ASM Pr.

Microbial Production & Consumption of Greenhouse Gases: Methane, Nitrogen Oxides, & Halomethanes. Ed. by John E. Rogers & William B. Whitman. LC 91-15621. 308p. reprint ed. pap. 95.50 (*0-608-08632-0*, 206915500003) Bks Demand.

Microbial Quality Assurance in Pharmaceuticals: Cosmetics & Toiletries. Bloomfield et al. (Pharmaceutical Technology Ser.). 264p. 1988. text 62.95 (*0-470-21122-9*) P-H.

Microbial Quality Assurance in Pharmaceuticals, Cosmetics, & Toiletries. 2nd ed. R. Baird & S. Bloomfield. LC 96-217818. (Series in Pharmaceutical Sciences). 300p. 1996. 126.00 (*0-7484-0437-6*) Taylor & Francis.

M

An Asterisk (*) at the beginning of an entry indicates that the title is appearing for the first time.

Microbial Quality of Water Supply in Distribution Systems. Edwin E. Geldreich. 512p. 1996. boxed set 94.95 (*1-56670-194-5*, L1194) CRC Pr.

Microbial Reagents in Organic Synthesis. Ed. by Stefano Servi. LC 92-26739. 500p. (C). 1992. text 279.50 (*0-7923-1953-2*) Kluwer Academic.

Microbial Resistance to Drugs. Ed. by L. E. Bryan. (Handbook of Experimental Pharmacology Ser.: Vol. 91). (Illus.). 510p. 1989. 322.00 (*0-387-50318-8*) Spr-Verlag.

Microbial Responses to Light & Time. Ed. by M. X. Caddick et al. LC 98-172807. (Society for General Microbiology Symposium Ser.: No. 56). (Illus.). 330p. (C). 1998. 115.00 (*0-521-62286-7*) Cambridge U Pr.

***Microbial Sediments.** Ed. by Robert B. Ridinger & S. M. Awramik. LC 99-52961. (Illus.). 345p. 2000. 206.00 (*3-540-61828-7*) Spr-Verlag.

Microbial Signalling & Communication. Ed. by Reg England et al. (Society for General Microbiology Symposium Ser.: No. 57). (Illus.). 400p. (C). 1999. text 115.00 (*0-521-65261-8*) Cambridge U Pr.

Microbial Succession in Soil, Vol. 9, No. 1. T. Turpaev. 67p. 1997. pap. text 33.00 (*3-7186-5823-2*, Harwood Acad Pubs) Gordon & Breach.

Microbial Surface Components & Toxins in Relation to Pathogenesis. Ed. by E. Z. Ron & S. Rottem. (FEMS Symposium Ser.: No. 51). (Illus.). 210p. (C). 1991. text 107.00 (*0-306-43908-5*, Kluwer Plenum) Kluwer Academic.

Microbial Technologies to Overcome Environmental Problems of Persistent Pollutants. 132p. 29.00 (*92-807-1110-5*, E.86.III.D.2) UN.

Microbial Technology. Ed. by Henry J. Peppler. LC 67-26866. 464p. reprint ed. pap. 143.90 (*0-608-11278-X*, 200581100054) Bks Demand.

Microbial Technology in the Developing World: An Introduction. Ed. by E. J. DaSilva et al. (Illus.). 456p. 1988. 65.00 (*0-19-854719-6*) OUP.

Microbial Testers: Probing Carcinogenesis. Ed. by I. Cecil Felkner. LC 80-29034. (Microbiology Ser.: No. 5). (Illus.). 284p. reprint ed. pap. 88.10 (*0-7837-0938-2*, 204124300019) Bks Demand.

Microbial Toxins: Tools in Enzymology. Ed. by Sidney Harsman et al. (Methods in Enzymology Ser.: Vol. 165). 440p. 1988. text 146.00 (*0-12-182066-1*) Acad Pr.

Microbial Toxins & Diarrhoeal Disease. CIBA Foundation Staff. LC 85-193279. (CIBA Foundation Symposium: New Ser.: No. 112). (Illus.). 296p. reprint ed. pap. 91.80 (*0-8357-6212-2*, 203421900089) Bks Demand.

Microbial Toxins in Foods & Feeds: Cellular & Molecular Modes of Action. Ed. by A. E. Pohland et al. LC 90-14343. (Illus.). 634p. (C). 1990. text 198.00 (*0-306-43716-3*, Kluwer Plenum) Kluwer Academic.

Microbial Transformation & Degradation of Toxic Organic Chemicals. Ed. by Lily Y. Young & Carl E. Cerniglia. LC 95-15401. 672p. 1995. 185.00 (*0-471-52109-4*) Wiley.

Microbial Transformation of Low Rank Coals. Ed. by Don L. Crawford. 240p. 1992. lib. bdg. 179.00 (*0-8493-4551-0*, QR53) CRC Pr.

Microbial Transformations of Bioactive Compounds, Vol. II. Ed. by John P. Rosazza. 200p. 1982. 114.00 (*0-8493-6066-8*, QR88, CRC Reprint) Franklin.

Microbial Updates for the 90's. Ingraham. (Biology Ser.). 1995. mass mkt. 2.00 (*0-534-16727-6*) Wadsworth Pub.

Microbial Water Stress Physiology: Principles & Perspectives. A. D. Brown. LC 89-70451. 328p. 1990. 270.00 (*0-471-92579-9*) Wiley.

***Microbial World.** 5th ed. 1999. teacher ed. write for info. (*0-13-581182-1*) P-H.

Microbial World. 6th ed. (C). 1989. 52.00 (*0-13-579939-2*, Macmillan Coll) P-H.

Microbially Influenced Corrosion of Materials: Scientific & Engineering Aspects. W. Sand. Ed. by Ewald Heitz & H. C. Flemming. LC 96-34061. 484p. 1996. 129.00 (*3-540-60432-4*) Spr-Verlag.

Microbicides for the Protection of Materials: A Handbook. Wilfried Paulus. LC 92-31479. 1993. write for info. (*1-85166-949-3*) Elsevier.

Microbio Pat Care W/lm-wb&mm P. 6th ed. Morello. 1998. 89.50 (*0-07-228988-0*) McGraw.

***Microbioglia: General.** Garcia. (C). 1999. text 78.20 (*84-8174-170-1*) Mosby Inc.

Microbiol & Parasitic Infection. 7th ed. Brian I. Duerden et al. 256p. 1993. pap. text 36.50 (*0-340-56018-5*, Pub. by E A) OUP.

***Microbiologia Clinica.** Inglis. (C). 1999. text 13.62 (*84-8174-413-1*) Mosby Inc.

***Microbiologia Medica.** 2nd ed. Mims. (C). 1999. text 60.64 (*84-8174-396-8*) Mosby Inc.

Microbiological Analysis of Food & Water: Guidelines for Quality Assurance. N. F. Lightfoot & E. A. Maier. LC 98-13035. 1998. 210.00 (*0-444-82911-3*) Elsevier.

Microbiological Analysis of Food & Water: Guidelines for Quality Assurance. Ed. by N. F. Lightfoot & E. A. Maier. 284p. 1998. 143.50 (*0-444-50203-3*) Elsevier.

Microbiological & Parasitic Diseases of the Dog & Cat. Ed. by P. J. Quinn et al. (Illus.). 500p. 1997. text 90.00 (*0-7020-1985-2*, Pub. by W B Saunders) Saunders.

Microbiological Applications. 7th ed. Harold J. Benson. 480p. (C). 1997. text 41.00 (*0-697-34139-9*, WCB McGr Hill) McGrw-H Hghr Educ.

Microbiological Applications: A Laboratory Manual in General Microbiology. 5th ed. Harold J. Benson. 384p. (C). 1990. text. write for info. (*0-697-05762-3*, WCB McGr Hill) McGrw-H Hghr Educ.

Microbiological Applications: A Laboratory Manual in General Microbiology. 7th ed. Harold J. Benson. 1997. pap. text, lab manual ed. 31.00 (*0-697-34140-2*) McGraw.

Microbiological Applications: Short. 4th ed. Harold J. Benson. 368p. (C). 1985. spiral bd. write for info. (*0-697-00306-X*, WCB McGr Hill) McGrw-H Hghr Educ.

***Microbiological Aspects of Biofilms & Drinking Water: Public Health Effects & Implications.** Steven Lane Percival et al. LC 99-98186. (Microbiology of Unusual & Extreme Environments Ser.). 240p. 2000. boxed set 119.95 (*0-8493-0590-X*, Chap & Hall CRC) CRC Pr.

Microbiological Control for Foods & Agricultural Products see Analysis & Control Methods for Food & Agricultural Products

Microbiological Control for Foods & Agricultural Products. Ed. by C. M. Bouregois et al. LC 95-7026. (Analysis & Control Methods for Foods & Agricultural Products Ser.). Orig. Title: Techniques d'Analyse et de Controle Dans les Industries Agro-Alimentaires. (Illus.). x, 548p. 1995. 145.00 (*1-56081-673-2*, Wiley-VCH) Wiley.

Microbiological Decomposition of Chlorinated Aromatic Compounds. Melissa L. Rochkind-Dubinsky. (Microbiology Ser.: Vol. 18). (Illus.). 336p. 1986. text 150.00 (*0-8247-7527-9*) Dekker.

Microbiological Degradation of Materials & Methods of Protection. (European Federation of Corrosion Publications Ser.: No. 9). 90p. 1992. pap. 50.00 (*0-901716-02-2*, Pub. by Inst Materials) Ashgate Pub Co.

Microbiological Effects on Metallurgical Processes: Proceedings of the Metallurgical Society. Ed. by J. A. Clum & Larry A. Haas. LC 85-28541. (Illus.). 173p. reprint ed. pap. 53.70 (*0-608-17840-3*, 203260200080) Bks Demand.

Microbiological Examination of Water & Wastewater. Maria Csuros. LC 98-48684. 11p. 1999. 55.00 (*1-56670-179-1*) Lewis Pubs.

***Microbiological Laboratory Guidebook: Nineteen Ninety Eight, 2, V. 1&2.** B. P. Dey. 620p. 1998. boxed set 63.00 (*0-16-060823-6*, Agriculture Dept) USGPO.

Microbiological Methods Pt. 1: Estimation of the Population of Microorganisms on Product. (Illus.). 16p. (Orig.). 1995. pap. 74.00 (*1-57020-049-1*, 11737-1-209) Assn Adv Med Instrn.

Microbiological Methods for Biological Control of Pests of Agricultural Crops. Ed. by K. V. Novozhilov. Tr. by Indira Nair from RUS. (Russian Translation Ser.: Vol. 51). (Illus.), 91p. (C). 1987. text 71.00 (*90-6191-493-0*, Pub. by A A Balkema) Ashgate Pub Co.

Microbiological Methods for Gamma Irradiation Sterilization of Medical Devices. 21p. 1991. pap. 82.00 (*0-614-08395-8*, TIR8-113) Assn Adv Med Instrn.

Microbiological Quality Assurance: A Guide Towards Relevance & Reproducibility of Inocula. Ed. by Michael R. Brown & Peter Gilbert. LC 94-43936. 320p. 1995. boxed set 179.95 (*0-8493-4752-1*, 4752) CRC Pr.

Microbiological Risk Assessment: An Interim Report. 1996. 25.00 (*0-11-321990-3*, HM19903, Pub. by Statnry Office) Bernan Associates.

Microbiological Safety & Quality of Food, 2 vols. Barbara M. Lund et al. LC 99-14425. (Illus.). 2752p. 1999. 425.00 (*0-8342-1323-0*, 13230) Aspen Pub.

Microbiological Standardisation of Laboratory Animals. F. J. Roe & A. A. Deeny. 116p. 1983. text 57.95 (*0-470-27401-8*) P-H.

Microbiologically Influenced Corrosion. Brenda J. Little et al. (Corrosion Testing Made Easy Ser.: Vol. 5). 120p. 1997. 127.00 (*1-57590-035-1*) NACE Intl.

Microbiologically Influenced Corrosion: A State-of-the-Art Review. Daniel H. Pope. LC 85-115610. (MTI Publication: No. 13). 88p. reprint ed. pap. 30.00 (*0-7837-0120-9*, 204039700016) Bks Demand.

Microbiologically Influenced Corrosion: A State of the Art Review. 2nd ed. LC 90-60532. (MTI Publication: No. 13). (Illus.). 64p. 1989. 10.00 (*1-877914-09-6*) NACE Intl.

Microbiologically Influenced Corrosion: A State-of-the-Art Review. 2nd ed. Daniel H. Pope et al. LC 90-60532. (MTI Publication Ser.: No. 13). 64p. 1989. reprint ed. pap. 30.00 (*0-608-06736-9*, 206693300009) Bks Demand.

Microbiologically Influenced Corrosion Handbook. Susan W. Borenstein. 310p. 1994. 79.95 (*0-8311-3056-3*) Indus Pr.

Microbiologically Influenced Corrosion Handbook. Susan Watkins Borenstein. 304p. 1994. boxed set 153.00 (*1-85573-127-4*, Pub. by Woodhead Pubng) Am Educ Systs.

Microbiologically Influenced Corrosion in Pipelines. Daniel Pope. 240p. 55.00 (*0-88415-473-4*, 5473) Gulf Pub.

Microbiologically Influenced Corrosion Testing. Ed. by Jeffrey R. Kearns & Brenda J. Little. LC 94-5900. (Special Technical Publication (STP) Ser.: Vol. 1232). (Illus.). 310p. 1994. 92.00 (*0-8031-1892-9*, STP1232) ASTM.

Microbiologist. Jack Rudman. (Career Examination Ser.: C-2477). 1994. pap. 29.95 (*0-8373-2477-7*) Nat Learn.

Microbiology. (Quick Study Academic Ser.). 4p. pap. 3.95 (*1-57222-305-7*) Barcharts.

Microbiology. (C). 1996. wbk. ed., lab manual ed. write for info. (*0-8087-1577-1*) Pearson Custom.

Microbiology. 168p. (C). 1997. text, lab manual ed. 22.95 (*0-536-00360-2*) Pearson Custom.

***Microbiology.** (C). 1998. lab manual ed. 17.60 (*0-8087-9669-0*) Pearson Custom.

Microbiology. Ackerman. 1992. pap. text 49.00 (*0-7295-0352-6*, W B Saunders Co) Harcrt Hlth Sci Grp.

Microbiology. I. Edward Alcamo. (Blond's Medical Guides Ser.). (Illus.). 181p. (Orig.). (C). 1994. pap. text 19.99 (*0-945819-41-2*) Sulzburger & Graham Pub.

Microbiology. Batzing. (Biology Ser.). 2001. text, wbk. ed. 15.00 (*0-534-37566-9*); text, lab manual ed. 28.00 (*0-534-37564-2*); pap. text 48.00 (*0-534-55620-5*) Brooks-Cole.

Microbiology. Pamela Fouche. 122p. (C). 1995. text, lab manual ed. 25.80 (*0-536-58950-X*) Pearson Custom.

Microbiology. Alex F. Huang. (The Licensing Examination Review Pop-up Book Series for Medical Study). 96p. 1995. pap. 44.95 (*1-884142-05-2*) AFH Softech.

***Microbiology.** Lammert. 2002. pap. text. write for info. (*0-7167-2867-2*); pap. text, student ed. write for info. (*0-7167-3942-9*) W H Freeman.

Microbiology. Luftig. LC 97-50434. (Rypins' Intensive Reviews Ser.). 325p. 1998. pap. text 19.95 (*0-397-51547-2*) Lppncott W & W.

Microbiology. Nester. 1994. teacher ed. 50.00 (*0-697-12761-3*) McGraw.

Microbiology. Cynthia F. Norton. LC 80-23350. (Life Sciences Ser.). (Illus.). 850p. (C). 1981. teacher ed. write for info. (*0-201-05308-X*); text. write for info. (*0-201-05304-7*); student ed. write for info. (*0-201-05307-1*) Addison-Wesley.

Microbiology. Perry. (C). 1997. pap. text, teacher ed. 28.00 (*0-03-019452-0*) Harcourt.

Microbiology. Perry. 1996. 246.00 (*0-03-019454-7*) Harcourt Coll Pubs.

Microbiology. Perry. LC 96-69306. (C). 1997. text 99.00 (*0-03-053893-9*, Pub. by Harcourt Coll Pubs) Harcourt.

Microbiology. Lansing Prescott et al. 1016p. (C). 1989. text. write for info. (*0-697-03005-9*, WCB McGr Hill) McGrw-H Hghr Educ.

Microbiology. Jack Rudman. (College Level Examination (CLEP) Ser.: Vol. 35). 43.95 (*0-8373-5385-8*) Nat Learn.

Microbiology. Jack Rudman. (ACT Proficiency Examination Program Ser.: PEP-55). 1994. pap. 23.95 (*0-8373-5905-8*) Nat Learn.

Microbiology. Jack Rudman. (College Level Examination (CLEP) Ser.: Vol. CLEP-35). 1994. pap. 23.95 (*0-8373-5335-1*) Nat Learn.

Microbiology. A. Von Graevenitz. (Clinical Lab Science Ser.: Section E). 1977. 223.00 (*0-8493-7031-0*, CRC Reprint) Franklin.

Microbiology. Stuart Walker. Ed. by William Schmitt. LC 97-9774. (STARS (Saunders Text & Review Ser.)). 576p. 1997. pap. text 29.95 (*0-7216-4641-7*, W B Saunders Co) Harcrt Hlth Sci Grp.

Microbiology. Jay W. Wilborn. (Applied Science Review Ser.). (Illus.). 128p. 1992. 12.95 (*0-87434-457-3*) Springhouse Corp.

Microbiology. 2nd ed. (National Medical Ser.). 1990. 25.00 (*0-685-75177-5*) Lppncott W & W.

Microbiology. 2nd ed. 278p. 1997. spiral bd. 22.19 (*0-697-26188-3*) McGraw.

Microbiology. 2nd ed. (C). 2001. pap., lab manual ed. 40.00 (*0-13-010029-3*) P-H.

Microbiology. 2nd ed. (C). 1991. lab manual ed. write for info. (*0-8087-9278-4*) Pearson Custom.

Microbiology. 2nd ed. T. J. Inglis. LC 96-51002. (Colour Guide Ser.). 1997. write for info. (*0-443-05772-9*) Harcrt Hlth Sci Grp.

Microbiology. 2nd ed. D. W. Kingsbury & G. Wagner. (National Medical Ser.). (Illus.). 436p. 1990. 26.00 (*0-683-06234-0*) Lppncott W & W.

Microbiology. 2nd ed. B. Larsen. LC 97-41309. 1997. pap. 45.00 (*0-915473-37-2*) Am Coll Obstetric.

Microbiology. 2nd ed. Daniel V. Lim. 720p. (C). 1997. text. write for info. (*0-697-26186-7*, WCB McGr Hill) McGrw-H Hghr Educ.

Microbiology. 2nd ed. Jacquelyn R. Marshall. LC 93-38266. (Clinical Laboratory Manual Ser.). 160p. (C). 1994. mass mkt. 28.95 (*0-8273-5363-4*) Delmar.

Microbiology. 2nd ed. Cynthia F. Norton. LC 85-3909. 800p. (C). 1986. student ed. 16.25 (*0-201-11037-7*) Addison-Wesley.

Microbiology. 2nd ed. Prescott. 1993. 229.06 (*0-697-09934-2*) McGraw.

Microbiology. 2nd ed. Lansing Prescott et al. 992p. (C). 1992. text. write for info. (*0-697-01372-3*) Brown & Benchmark.

Microbiology. 2nd ed. Lansing Prescott et al. 992p. (C). 1993. text, student ed. 28.75 (*0-697-09935-0*) Brown & Benchmark.

Microbiology. 2nd ed. Lansing Prescott et al. 992p. (C). 1993. text. write for info. (*0-697-16888-3*) Brown & Benchmark.

Microbiology. 2nd ed. Gerard J. Tortora et al. 820p. (C). 1986. text 44.95 (*0-8053-9315-3*); pap. text, student ed. 13.95 (*0-8053-9318-8*) Benjamin-Cummings.

Microbiology. 3rd ed. (C). 1994. write for info. (*0-8087-9508-2*) Pearson Custom.

***Microbiology.** 3rd ed. 208p. (C). 1999. lab manual ed. 25.50 (*0-536-60358-8*) Pearson Custom.

Microbiology. 3rd ed. Nester. 2000. student ed. 20.00 (*0-07-231884-8*) McGraw.

Microbiology. 3rd ed. Prescott. 1996. teacher ed. 14.37 (*0-697-21864-3*, WCB McGr Hill) McGrw-H Hghr Educ.

Microbiology. 3rd ed. Lansing Prescott et al. 1024p. (C). 1995. text. write for info. (*0-697-21863-5*, WCB McGr Hill) McGrw-H Hghr Educ.

Microbiology. 3rd ed. Gerard J. Tortora. Ed. by Edith B. Brady. 880p. (C). 1992. text 21.95 (*0-685-48066-6*) Benjamin-Cummings.

Microbiology. 3rd ed. Gerard J. Tortora et al. (Illus.). 864p. (C). 1989. text 51.95 (*0-8053-0141-0*); pap. text, student ed. 16.95 (*0-8053-0148-8*) Benjamin-Cummings.

***Microbiology.** 4th ed. (C). 1999. 15.60 (*0-8087-6677-5*) Pearson Custom.

Microbiology. 4th ed. Gerard J. Tortora et al. 880p. (C). 1992. text 61.25 (*0-8053-8480-4*) Benjamin-Cummings.

Microbiology. 4th ed. Bernard D. Davis et al. LC 89-2338. (Illus.). 1237p. 1990. reprint ed. pap. 200.00 (*0-608-07243-5*, 206746800009) Bks Demand.

Microbiology. 5th ed. Prescott. 2001. 74.25 (*0-07-232041-9*) McGraw.

Microbiology. 5th ed. Lansing Prescott. 2001. lab manual ed. 38.50 (*0-07-233345-6*); pap., student ed. 22.50 (*0-07-233336-7*) McGraw.

Microbiology. 8th ed. Benson. 2001. lab manual ed. 42.74 (*0-07-231888-0*); lab manual ed. 37.00 (*0-07-231889-9*) McGraw.

Microbiology. 9th ed. Richard C. Tilton. (Basic Sciences: Pretest Self Assessment & Review Ser.). (Illus.). 1998. pap. text 18.95 (*0-07-052688-5*) McGraw-Hill HPD.

Microbiology, 1. 3rd ed. Lansing Prescott & John P. Harley. 672p. (C). 1997. per. write for info. (*0-07-114628-8*, WCB McGr Hill) McGrw-H Hghr Educ.

Microbiology, 2. 3rd ed. Lansing Prescott & Jonh P. Harley. 392p. (C). 1997. per. write for info. (*0-07-114629-6*, WCB McGr Hill) McGrw-H Hghr Educ.

Microbiology, II. 2nd ed. Lansing Prescott et al. 992p. (C). 1992. text. write for info. (*0-697-16886-7*) Brown & Benchmark.

Microbiology, III. 2nd ed. Lansing Prescott et al. 992p. (C). 1992. text. write for info. (*0-697-16887-5*) Brown & Benchmark.

Microbiology, Vol. 1. 3rd ed. Prescott & Benson. 1996. (*0-697-36542-5*, WCB McGr Hill) McGrw-H Hghr Educ.

Microbiology, Vol. I. 3rd ed. Lansing Prescott et al. 688p. (C). 1995. text. write for info. (*0-697-21865-1*, WCB McGr Hill) McGrw-H Hghr Educ.

Microbiology, Vol 1. 4th ed. Lansing Prescott. 1998. pap. text 51.25 (*0-697-35440-7*) McGraw.

Microbiology, Vol. 1. 4th ed. Lansing Prescott. 512p. 1998. student ed., spiral bd. 50.31 (*0-697-35443-1*) McGraw.

Microbiology, Vol. 1. 4th ed. Lansing Prescott. 408p. 1998. spiral bd. 28.75 (*0-697-35445-8*) McGraw.

Microbiology, Vol. 1. 5th ed. Lansing Prescott. 2001. 47.00 (*0-07-233341-3*) McGraw.

Microbiology, Vol. II. 3rd ed. Lansing Prescott et al. 368p. (C). 1995. text. write for info. (*0-697-21866-X*, WCB McGr Hill) McGrw-H Hghr Educ.

Microbiology: A Centenary Perspective. Ed. by Wolfgang K. Joklik et al. LC 99-20173. 1999. 79.95 (*1-55581-162-0*); pap. 49.95 (*1-55581-169-8*) ASM Pr.

Microbiology: A Human Perspective. Eugene W. Nester et al. 832p. (C). 1994. text, student ed. 23.12 (*0-697-14788-6*, WCB McGr Hill) McGrw-H Hghr Educ.

Microbiology: A Human Perspective. 2nd ed. Eugene W. Nester. 206p. 1998. pap., student ed. 22.19 (*0-697-28605-3*) McGraw.

Microbiology: A Human Perspective. 2nd ed. Eugene W. Nester & Martha T. Nester. LC 97-15264. 864p. (C). 1997. text. write for info. (*0-697-28602-9*, WCB McGr Hill) McGrw-H Hghr Educ.

Microbiology: A Human Perspective. 3rd ed. Nester. 2000. 63.00 (*0-07-231878-3*) McGraw.

Microbiology: A Laboratory Manual. 2nd ed. James G. Cappuccino & Natalie Sherman. (Biology Ser.). (Illus.). 466p. (C). 1987. pap. text 20.76 (*0-201-11636-7*) Addison-Wesley.

Microbiology: A Laboratory Manual. 3rd ed. Gerard J. Tortora et al. (Illus.). 864p. (C). 1989. pap. text, student ed. 22.95 (*0-8053-0149-6*) Benjamin-Cummings.

Microbiology: A Laboratory Textbook. 3rd ed. William C. Matthai. 356p. (C). 1997. pap. text 31.95 (*1-890871-27-3*) Holcomb Hath.

Microbiology: A "Pet" Based Approach Introductory Lab Manual. Hecht & Bounds. 92p. (C). 1998. spiral bd., lab manual ed. 20.95 (*0-7872-5248-4*, 41524801) Kendall-Hunt.

Microbiology: An Introduction. 2nd ed. Gerard J. Tortora. (Illus.). 1986. 9.00 (*0-8053-9317-X*) Benjamin-Cummings.

Microbiology: An Introduction. 2nd ed. Gerard J. Tortora et al. 820p. (C). 1986. student ed. 18.95 (*0-685-43136-3*) Benjamin-Cummings.

Microbiology: An Introduction. 4th ed. Gerard J. Tortora. 1991. 56.95 (*0-8053-9480-X*) Benjamin-Cummings.

Microbiology: An Introduction. 6th ed. Berdell R. Funke. 368p. (C). 1997. pap. text, student ed. 23.00 (*0-8053-8447-2*) Addison-Wesley.

***Microbiology: An Introduction.** 6th ed. Gerard J. Tortora. (C). 1999. text. write for info. (*0-8053-7544-9*) Benjamin-Cummings.

***Microbiology: An Introduction.** 6th ed. Gerard J. Tortora et al. 832p. 1998. pap. 99.47 (*0-8053-2155-1*) Benjamin-Cummings.

Microbiology: An Introduction. 6th ed. Gereard J. Tortora. LC 97-25184. 880p. (C). 1998. text. write for info. (*0-8053-8446-4*) Addison-Wesley.

***Microbiology: An Introduction.** 7th ed. 2000. 95.00 (*0-8053-7543-0*) Benjamin-Cummings.

Microbiology: Applications to Patient Care. 6th ed. Morello et al. 1997. pap., wbk. ed., lab manual ed. 34.00 (*0-697-25766-5*, WCB McGr Hill) McGrw-H Hghr Educ.

Microbiology: Concepts & Applications. Paul A. Ketchum. LC 87-34607. 795p. 1988. text 87.95 (*0-471-88897-4*) Wiley.

Microbiology: Concepts & Applications. Michael J. Pelczar, Jr. et al. (C). 1993. pap. text, student ed. 28.12 (*0-07-049260-3*) McGraw.

Microbiology: Concepts & Applications. Michael J. Pelczar, Jr. et al. (C). 1993. text 72.50 (*0-07-049258-1*) McGraw.

Microbiology: Concepts & Applications. 6th ed. Michael J. Pelczar, Jr. et al. 576p. (C). 1993. pap. 47.19 (*0-07-049264-6*) McGraw.

M

An Asterisk (*) at the beginning of an entry indicates that the title is appearing for the first time.

Microbiology: Concepts & Applications. 99th ed. Paul A. Ketchum. 311p. 1988. pap., suppl. ed. 34.95 (*0-471-88899-0*) Wiley.

Microbiology: Diversity, Disease, & the Environment. Abigail A. Salyers & Dixie B. Whitt. (Illus.). 500p. 2000. pap. text 59.00 (*1-891786-01-6*) Fitzgerald Sci.

Microbiology: Essentials & Applications. Larry K. McKane & J. Kandel. 800p. (C). 1985. text 62.25 (*0-07-045125-7*) McGraw.

Microbiology: Essentials & Applications. 2nd ed. Larry K. McKane & Judy Kandel. LC 94-25301. 880p. (C). 1995. 82.81 (*0-07-045154-0*) McGraw.

Microbiology: Essentials & Applications Study Companion. 2nd ed. Larry K. McKane & Judith Kandel. (C). 1995. pap., student ed. 22.19 (*0-07-035008-6*) McGraw.

***Microbiology: General Topics with Microbes in Motion II CD-ROM.** 4th ed. Lansing Prescott et al. (C). 1998. 65.63 incl. cd-rom (*0-07-232632-8*) McGrw-H Hghr Educ.

Microbiology: High-School Science Fair Experiments. H. Steven Dashefsky. LC 94-23117. (Illus.). 160p. (YA). (gr. 9-12). 1994. 21.95 (*0-07-015663-8*) McGraw-Hill Prof.

Microbiology: Human Perspective. 2nd ed. Nester. 1998. 31.25 (*0-697-28598-7*, WCB McGr Hill) McGrw-H Hghr Educ.

Microbiology: Human Perspective & Student Study Art Notebook. 2nd ed. Nester. 1994. student ed. 66.00 (*0-697-26398-3*, WCB McGr Hill) McGrw-H Hghr Educ.

Microbiology: Infection. Inglis. 1996. pap. text 22.00 (*0-443-05034-1*, W B Saunders Co) Harcrt Hlth Sci Grp.

Microbiology: Introduction. 5th ed. (C). 1995. 142.00 (*0-8053-8515-0*) Addison-Wesley.

Microbiology: Introduction. 5th ed. (C). 1995. 52.00 (*0-8053-8518-5*) Benjamin-Cummings.

***Microbiology: Introduction.** 6th ed. 2000. lab manual ed. write for info. (*0-8053-7586-4*) Addison-Wesley.

***Microbiology: Introduction.** 7th ed. 2000. teacher ed. write for info. (*0-8053-7583-X*) Benjamin-Cummings.

***Microbiology: Introduction Repromote.** 6th ed. (C). 1999. write for info. (*0-8053-7542-2*) Longman.

***Microbiology: Introduction: Study Guide.** 7th ed. 2000. student ed. 23.00 (*0-8053-7585-6*) Benjamin-Cummings.

Microbiology: Lab Experiments. Christine L. Case & Ted R. Johnson. 350p. (C). 1984. pap. text 28.13 (*0-8053-5040-3*) Benjamin-Cummings.

Microbiology: Lab Manual & Instructor Manual. 6th ed. Lois Beishir. 544p. 1997. text, teacher ed. 18.00 (*0-673-55987-4*) Addson-Wesley Educ.

Microbiology: Pretest Self-Assessment & Review John W. Foster & Robert E. Humphreys. LC 76-2398. (Pretest Self-Assessment & Review Ser.). iv, 156p. 1976. pap. write for info. (*0-07-050795-3*, PreTest Series) McGraw-Hill Prof.

Microbiology: Pretest Self-Assessment & Review. 2nd ed. Richard C. Tilton. LC 79-8372. vii, 187p. 1979. write for info. (*0-07-050966-2*) McGraw-Hill HPD.

Microbiology: PreTest Self-Assessment & Review. 5th ed. Richard C. Tilton. 1988. pap. text 15.95 (*0-07-051964-1*) McGraw.

Microbiology: Pretest Self-Assessment & Review. 6th ed. Richard C. Tilton & Kay Buchanan. LC 90-5600. vii, 177p. 1991. write for info. (*0-07-051981-1*) McGraw-Hill HPD.

Microbiology: Principles & Applications. 3rd ed. Jacquelyn G. Black. (Illus.). 880p. (C). 1995. text 90.00 (*0-13-190745-X*) P-H.

***Microbiology: Principles & Applications.** 4th ed. Jacquelyn G. Black. 376p. 1999. pap., student ed. 37.95 (*0-471-36835-0*) Wiley.

***Microbiology: Principles & Explorations.** 4th ed. Jacquelyn G. Black. 912p. 1999. pap. 84.95 (*0-471-38322-8*) Wiley.

Microbiology: Principles & Health Science Applications. Lois M. Bergquist & Barbara Pogosian. LC 99-40813. (Illus.). 590p. 2000. pap. text. write for info. (*0-7216-7663-4*, W B Saunders Co) Harcrt Hlth Sci Grp.

Microbiology: Proceedings of a Conference Held in London, 19-20 September, 1967. Ed. by Peter Hepple. LC 79-353970. 109p. reprint ed. pap. 33.80 (*0-608-13848-7*, 202369300033) Bks Demand.

Microbiology: Research Guide. 3rd ed. Prescott et al. 1996. 8.25 (*0-697-21870-8*, WCB McGr Hill) McGrw-H Hghr Educ.

Microbiology: Review for New National Boards. Gerald V. Stokes. LC 93-77103. (Illus.). 193p. 1993. pap. 25.00 (*0-9632873-2-X*) J & S Pub VA.

***Microbiology: 2000 Multiple-Choice Questions & Answers.** 310p. 1999. spiral bd. 25.95 (*1-893720-03-9*) Biotest.

***Microbiology An Introduction: Student Tutorial Package.** 7th ed. 2000. text. write for info. (*0-8053-7546-5*) P-H.

Microbiology & Biochemistry of Cheese & Fermented Milk. 2nd ed. Ed. by B. A. Law. LC 96-86400. 365p. 1997. 169.00 (*0-7514-0346-6*) Chapman & Hall.

Microbiology & Biochemistry of Strict Anaerobes Involved in Interspecies Hydrogen Transfer. J. P. Belaich et al. LC 90-7023. (FEMS Symposium Ser.: No. 54). (Illus.). 556p. (C). 1990. text 155.00 (*0-306-43517-9*, Kluwer Plenum) Kluwer Academic.

Microbiology & Biogeochemistry of Hypersaline Environments. Aharon Oren. LC 98-18052. (Microbiology of Extreme & Unusual Environments Ser.). 384p. 1998. boxed set 159.95 (*0-8493-8363-3*) CRC Pr.

Microbiology & Biotechnology. 96p. 1994. pap. text 14.95 (*0-521-42204-3*) Cambridge U Pr.

Microbiology & Chemistry for Environmental Scientists & Engineers. J. N. Lester. LC 98-49280. 1999. pap. write for info. (*0-419-22680-X*) Routledge.

Microbiology & Engineering of Sterilization Processes. 8th rev. ed. Irving J. Pflug. Orig. Title: A Textbook for an Introductury Course in the Microbiology & Engineering of Sterilization Processes. 526p. (C). 1995. pap. text 65.00 (*0-929340-01-9*) Environ Sterilization Lab.

Microbiology & Epidemiology of Infection for Health Science Students. J. Sedgwick & Peter Meers. (Illus.). 352p. 1995. pap. text 41.50 (*1-56593-350-8*, 0674) Singular Publishing.

Microbiology & Immunology. R. M. Hyde. (Oklahoma Notes Ser.). (Illus.). x, 228p. (C). 1988. pap. 15.95 (*0-387-96336-7*) Spr-Verlag.

Microbiology & Immunology. 2nd ed. R. M. Hyde. (Oklahoma Notes Ser.). x, 229p. 1991. pap. 17.95 (*0-387-97008-8*) Spr-Verlag.

Microbiology & Immunology. 2nd ed. Arthur G. Johnson et al. LC 92-49680. (Board Review Ser.). (Illus.). 284p. 1992. 19.95 (*0-683-04465-6*) Lppncott W & W.

Microbiology & Immunology. 3rd ed. R. M. Hyde. (Oklahoma Notes Ser.). (Illus.). 272p. Date not set. 17.95 (*0-387-97775-9*) Spr-Verlag.

Microbiology & Immunology. 3rd ed. Arthur G. Johnson et al. LC 96-7007. (Board Review Ser.). (Illus.). 284p. 1996. pap. 21.95 (*0-683-18005-3*) Lppncott W & W.

Microbiology & Immunology. 4th rev. ed. Richard M. Hyde. LC 95-2578. (Oklahoma Notes Ser.). (Illus.). 229p. 1995. 17.95 (*0-387-94392-7*) Spr-Verlag.

Microbiology & Immunology Vol. 2: Digging up the Bones, Vol. 2. 2nd ed. Ed. by Linas M. Linardakis. (Digging Up the Bones Medical Review Ser.). (Illus.). 122p. 1997. pap. text 18.95 (*0-07-038215-8*) McGraw-Hill HPD.

Microbiology & Immunology - An Encyclopedic Approach. M. K. Majundar. (C). 1989. 90.00 (*0-89771-367-2*, Pub. by Current Dist) St Mut.

Microbiology & Immunology Casebook. James T. Barrett. LC 95-13078. 272p. 1995. pap. text 19.95 (*0-316-08132-9*) Lppncott W & W.

Microbiology & Immunology for the Health Team. Peter R. Stewart et al. 1985. pap. text 27.95 (*0-471-33385-9*) Wiley.

Microbiology & Immunology Review. Rosenthal. 2000. text. write for info. (*0-323-00840-2*) Harcrt Hlth Sci Grp.

Microbiology & Infectious Disease. 3rd ed. Gabriel T. Virella. LC 96-5707. (National Medical Series for Independent Study). 575p. 1997. write for info. (*0-683-06235-2*) Lppncott W & W.

Microbiology & Student Study Art Notebook. 3rd ed. Prescott. 1995. student ed. write for info. (*0-697-29390-4*) McGrw-H Hghr Educ.

Microbiology & Study Cards & Student Study Art Notebook: Study Cards, Student Study Art Notebook. Nester. 1996. incl. cd-rom (*0-697-36802-5*, WCB McGr Hill) McGrw-H Hghr Educ.

Microbiology & Treatment of Life-Threatening Infections. A. M. Emmerson. LC 82-13666. (Antimicrobial Chemotherapy Research Studies: No. 3). 199p. reprint ed. pap. 61.70 (*0-8357-8950-0*, 203333400085) Bks Demand.

Microbiology & Virology Testing Markets. (Market Research Reports: No. 333). 138p. 1994. 795.00 (*0-317-05476-7*) Theta Corp.

Microbiology Applications in Food Biotechnology: Proceedings of the 2nd Congress of the Singapore Society for Microbiology, Singapore, 31 Oct.-3 Nov. 1989. Ed. by B. H. Nga & Y. K. Lee. (Illus.). 232p. 1990. mass mkt. 79.95 (*1-85166-530-7*) Elsevier.

Microbiology Apps. Hyperclinic. Delisle. 1997. 40.00 (*0-697-38672-4*, WCB McGr Hill) McGrw-H Hghr Educ.

Microbiology Coloring Book. Lawrence M. Elson & Edward Alcamo. (Illus.). 242p. (Orig.). (C). 1997. pap. text 19.99 (*0-06-041925-3*) Addson-Wesley Educ.

Microbiology Companion. Joel Topf & Sarah Faubel. (Illus.). 212p. (C). pap., student ed. 24.00 (*0-9640124-0-5*) Alert & Oriented.

Microbiology Companion. 2nd ed. Joel Topf & Sarah Faubel. (Illus.). 243p. (C). 1994. pap. text 27.95 (*0-9640124-1-3*) Alert & Oriented.

Microbiology Companion: An Illustrated Guide. Pommervelle. (C). 2001. pap. 21.33 (*0-13-944463-7*) P-H.

Microbiology Computerized SSG. 3rd ed. Prescott et al. 1996. 20.00 (*0-697-21872-4*) McGraw.

Microbiology Experiments. 3rd ed. Kleyn. 2000. 37.00 (*0-07-231903-8*) McGraw.

Microbiology for Health Careers. 4th ed. Elizabeth Fong. LC 86-19720. 256p. (C). 1986. pap. 27.95 (*0-8273-2565-7*) Delmar.

Microbiology for Health Careers. 4th ed. Elizabeth Fong. LC 86-19720. 256p. (C). 1987. teacher ed. 16.00 (*0-8273-2566-5*) Delmar.

Microbiology for Health Careers. 5th ed. Elizabeth Fong et al. LC 93-34553. 440p. (C). 1994. mass mkt. 29.50 (*0-8273-6049-5*) Delmar.

Microbiology for Health Careers. 5th ed. Elizabeth Fong et al. 101p. 1994. teacher ed. 16.00 (*0-8273-6050-9*) Delmar.

Microbiology for Health Careers. 6th ed. Lakomia. LC 98-53502. (Allied Health Ser.). 464p. (C). 1998. text 37.95 (*0-7668-0917-X*) Delmar.

***Microbiology for Health Careers: Instructor's Manual.** 6th ed. Lakomia. 96p. 1999. teacher ed. 14.95 (*0-7668-0918-8*) Delmar.

Microbiology for Health Science. 4th ed. Marcus M. Jensen & Donald N. Wright. LC 96-28137. 530p. 1996. 92.00 (*0-13-251464-8*) P-H.

Microbiology for Majors. Mark Wheelis. Ed. by Anne Scanlan-Rotter. (Electronic Companion Ser.). (Illus.). 300p. (Orig.). (C). 1997. pap. text, wbk. ed. write for info. (*1-888902-58-2*); pap. text, wbk. ed. 34.95 incl. cd-rom (*1-888902-77-9*) Cogito Lrning.

Microbiology for Nurses. 7th ed. Vivien Stucke. (C). 1993. pap. text 22.00 (*0-7020-1417-6*) Harcourt.

Microbiology for Public Health & Environmental Engineers. J. N. Lester & R. M. Sterritt. 284p. 1988. text 65.00 (*0-419-12760-7*, E & FN Spon); pap. text 29.50 (*0-419-12770-4*, E & FN Spon) Routledge.

Microbiology for the Allied Health Professions. 2nd ed. Adrian N. Delaat. LC 78-5731. (Illus.). 470p. reprint ed. pap. 145.70 (*0-8357-7644-1*, 205696900096) Bks Demand.

Microbiology for the Health Sciences. Deborah Simon. 90p. (C). 1996. pap. text, lab manual ed. 15.95 (*0-7872-2342-5*) Kendall-Hunt.

Microbiology for the Health Sciences. 5th ed. Gwendolyn R. W. Burton & Paul G. Engelkirk. 464p. 1995. pap. text 25.95 (*0-397-55187-8*) Lppncott W & W.

Microbiology for the Health Sciences. 6th ed. Gwendolyn R. W. Burton & Paul G. Engelkirk. LC 99-19388. 1999. write for info. (*0-7817-1844-9*) Lppncott W & W.

Microbiology for Veterinary Technicians. M. Ikram & E. Hill. LC 90-83303. (Illus.). 275p. 1994. pap. text 29.00 (*0-939674-30-0*) Am Vet Pubns.

***Microbiology for Water/Wastewater Operators.** rev. ed. Frank R. Spellman. LC 99-68514. 240p. 1999. reprint ed. pap. text 74.95 (*1-56676-908-6*) Technomic.

Microbiology Health Science. 4th ed. Jensen. 1996. pap. text, student ed. 29.33 (*0-13-267493-9*) P-H.

Microbiology, Immunology & Infectious Diseases. Gabriel T. Virella. 148p. pap. text 27.00 (*0-683-30712-6*) Lppncott W & W.

Microbiology in Action. J. Heritage et al. LC 98-44695. (Studies in Biology). (Illus.). 288p. (C). 1999. text 54.95 (*0-521-62111-9*); pap. text 20.95 (*0-521-62912-8*) Cambridge U Pr.

Microbiology in Patient Care. 5th ed. Josephine A. Morello et al. 592p. (C). 1993. text, student ed. write for info. (*0-697-13784-8*, WCB McGr Hill) McGrw-H Hghr Educ.

Microbiology in Patient Care. 6th ed. Josephine A. Morello et al. LC 97-14452. 576p. (C). 1997. text. write for info. (*0-697-25763-0*, WCB McGr Hill) McGrw-H Hghr Educ.

Microbiology in Patient Care: Microbes in Motion. 5th ed. Josephine A. Morello et al. (C). 1995. text, student ed. write for info. (*0-697-34041-4*, WCB McGr Hill) McGrw-H Hghr Educ.

Microbiology in Practice: A Self-Instructional Laboratory Course. 6th ed. Lois Beishir. 522p. (C). 1996. pap. text 52.00 (*0-673-99559-3*) Addson-Wesley Educ.

Microbiology in the Nineties: Proceedings of the Third SSM International Congress Singapore, Dec. 1993. Ed. by T. S. Sim & M. Singh. LC 95-135372. 428p. 1994. pap. 61.00 (*981-3049-03-0*) World Scientific Pub.

Microbiology in the Patient. 5th ed. Morello. 1994. 12.81 (*0-697-25097-0*, WCB McGr Hill) McGrw-H Hghr Educ.

Microbiology in Today's World. Barbara A. Hudson. 160p. (C). 1994. spiral bd. 21.95 (*0-8403-6704-X*) Kendall-Hunt.

Microbiology in Today's World. 2nd ed. Barbara Hudson. 160p. (C). 1998. spiral bd. 25.95 (*0-7872-5142-9*) Kendall-Hunt.

Microbiology Lab Exercises: Complete Version. 2nd ed. Margaret E. Barnett. 576p. (C). 1992. text. write for info. (*0-697-11308-6*, WCB McGr Hill) McGrw-H Hghr Educ.

Microbiology Lab Guide. Dipak Roy. 72p. (C). 1995. pap. text, per. 15.95 (*0-7872-0993-7*) Kendall-Hunt.

Microbiology Lab Manual. Jake Barnes & Randall Brand. 132p. (C). 1995. pap. text, spiral bd. 23.04 (*0-7872-0494-3*) Kendall-Hunt.

Microbiology Lab Manual: Principles & Applications. Karen Messley & Stephen A. Norrell. 331p. (C). 1996. pap. text, lab manual ed. 51.00 (*0-13-255373-2*) P-H.

Microbiology Lab Notebook. Josephine Coursey & Jeanette Stewart. 112p. (C). 1995. ring bd. 13.95 (*0-7872-1889-8*) Kendall-Hunt.

Microbiology Laboratory: Biology 115 Preliminary Edition. (C). 1995. text 15.00 (*0-536-58893-7*) Pearson Custom.

Microbiology Laboratory Exercises. Colome. Date not set. pap. text, teacher ed. write for info. (*0-314-91279-7*) West Pub.

Microbiology Laboratory Exercises. 2nd abr. ed. Margaret E. Barnett. 368p. (C). 1996. text. write for info. (*0-697-16011-4*, WCB McGr Hill) McGrw-H Hghr Educ.

Microbiology Laboratory Exercises: Short Version. Margaret E. Barnett. 368p. (C). 1991. text. write for info. (*0-697-11967-X*, WCB McGr Hill) McGrw-H Hghr Educ.

Microbiology Laboratory Exercises for Allied Health. Jay Sperry. 112p. (C). 1994. pap. text, spiral bd. 26.95 (*0-8403-9622-8*, 40962201) Kendall-Hunt.

Microbiology Laboratory Fundamentals & Applications. George A. Wistreich. 676p. (C). 1996. 48.00 (*0-02-428980-9*, Macmillan Coll) P-H.

***Microbiology Laboratory Manual.** Brenda Wellmeyer. 104p. (C). 1999. spiral bd. 20.95 (*0-7872-6068-1*) Kendall-Hunt.

Microbiology Lm. 2nd ed. Penner. 1999. 31.74 (*0-07-013774-9*) McGraw.

Microbiology Manual. Stukus. (C). 1997. pap. text, teacher ed. 28.00 (*0-03-018554-8*) Harcourt Coll Pubs.

Microbiology, 1971: Proceedings, London, 27-28 January, 1971. Ed. by Peter Hepple. LC 73-168075. 120p. reprint ed. pap. 37.20 (*0-608-13849-5*, 202369400033) Bks Demand.

***Microbiology of Activated Sludge.** C. Seviour. LC 99-14200. 368p. 1999. 240.00 (*0-412-79380-6*) Kluwer Academic.

Microbiology of Animals & Animal Products. Ed. by J. B. Woolcock. (World Animal Science Ser.: Vol. A6). 278p. 1991. 206.25 (*0-444-43010-5*) Elsevier.

Microbiology of Atmospheric Trace Gases: Sources, Sinks & Global Change Processes. Ed. by J. Colin Murrell & Donovan P. Kelly. LC 95-45667. (NATO ASI Series I: Global Environmental Change: Vol. 39). 306p. 1996. 141.00 (*3-540-60612-2*) Spr-Verlag.

Microbiology of Chlamydia, Vol. I. Ed. by Almen L. Barron. 256p. 1988. 149.00 (*0-8493-6877-4*, QR201, CRC Reprint) Franklin.

Microbiology of Deep-Sea Hydrothermal Vents. Ed. by David M. Karl. 336p. 1995. lib. bdg. 189.00 (*0-8493-8860-0*, TP8860) CRC Pr.

Microbiology of Extreme Environments. Clive Edwards. 1990. 42.95 (*0-07-091443-5*) McGraw.

Microbiology of Foods. John C. Ayres et al. LC 79-16335. (Food & Nutrition Ser.). (Illus.). 708p. (C). 1980. text 32.00 (*0-7167-1049-8*) W H Freeman.

Microbiology of Landfill Sites. Ed. by Eric Senior. 224p. 1989. lib. bdg. 190.95 (*0-8493-4996-6*, TD795) CRC Pr.

Microbiology of Landfill Sites. 2nd ed. Eric Senior. LC 94-27855. 224p. 1995. lib. bdg. 85.00 (*0-87371-968-9*, L968) Lewis Pubs.

Microbiology of Marine & Freshwater Environments. Smith. 256p. (Orig.). (C). (gr. 13). 1997. pap. text. write for info. (*0-412-38590-2*, Chap & Hall NY) Chapman & Hall.

Microbiology of Solid Waste. Ed. by Anna C. Palmisano & Morton A. Barlaz. LC 96-18240. (Microbiology of Extreme & Unusual Environments Ser.). 240p. 1996. boxed set 89.95 (*0-8493-8361-7*) CRC Pr.

Microbiology of the Terrestrial Deep Subsurface. Penny S. Amy & Dana L. Haldeman. LC 96-82013. 368p. 1997. boxed set 129.95 (*0-8493-8362-5*) CRC Pr.

Microbiology of Tropical Soils & Plant Productivity. Ed. by Y. R. Dommergues & H. G. Diem. 1982. 69.50 (*90-247-2405-8*) Kluwer Academic.

***Microbiology of Well Biofouling.** Roy Cullimore. LC 99-35336. (Sustainable Well Ser.). 435p. 1999. 79.95 (*1-56670-400-6*) Lewis Pubs.

Microbiology, Packaging, HAACP & Ingredients see Complete Course in Canning & Related Processes

Microbiology Perspectives: A Color Atlas. Wistreich. LC 98-22035. 189p. 1998. pap. text 26.00 (*0-13-856824-3*) P-H.

***Microbiology; Principles & Applications.** 4th ed. Jacquelyn G. Black. 912p. 1999. text 102.95 (*0-471-36819-9*) Wiley.

Microbiology Quick Review. I. Edward Alcamo. (Cliffs Quick Reviews Ser.). (Illus.). 101p. (Orig.). 1996. pap. text 9.95 (*0-8220-5333-0*, Cliff) IDG Bks.

Microbiology Review. T. Stuart Walker. Ed. by William Schmitt. LC 98-34637. (Illus.). 235p. (C). 1998. pap. text. write for info. (*0-7216-4642-5*, W B Saunders Co) Harcrt Hlth Sci Grp.

Microbiology Study Guide Set: Principles & Applications. 3rd ed. Jacquelyn G. Black. (Illus.). 1996. student ed. 137.90 (*0-471-37533-0*) Wiley.

***Microbiology Study Guide Set Principles & Applications.** 4th ed. Jacquelyn G. Black. 1999. text 137.90 (*0-471-37532-2*) Wiley.

Microbiology Techniques. Susan G. Kelley & Frederick J. Post. (Illus.). 400p. (C). 1991. pap., student ed. 32.95 (*0-89863-149-1*) Star Pub CA.

***Microbiology the Lab.** 2nd ed. (C). 1999. write for info. (*0-8087-6545-0*) Pearson Custom.

Microbiology V1 3E V3 2E Lab E. 3rd ed. Prescott. 1995. 97.00 (*0-697-34867-9*, WCB McGr Hill) McGrw-H Hghr Educ.

Microbiology with Health Care Applications: A Laboratory Manual. Isaiah A. Benathen. (Illus.). 416p. (C). 1993. pap. 32.95 (*0-89863-150-5*) Star Pub CA.

***Microbiology with Microbes in Motion II CD-ROM.** 4th ed. Lansing Prescott et al. (C). 1998. 94.06 incl. cd-rom (*0-07-232514-3*) McGrw-H Hghr Educ.

Microbiotic Family Health Care & Shiatsu see Shiatsu Handbook

Microblade Technology & Variability in the Chehalis River Region, Southwest Washington. Marcia K. Kelly. 125p. (Orig.). (C). 1984. pap. text 13.75 (*1-55567-056-3*) Coyote Press.

Microbore Column Chromatography: A Unified Approach to Chromatography. Ed. by Finak J. Yang. (Chromatographic Science Ser.: Vol. 45). (Illus.). 424p. 1988. text 190.00 (*0-8247-7989-4*) Dekker.

***Microcantilevers for Atomic Force Microscope Data Storage.** Benjamin W. Chui. LC 98-40855. (Microsystems Ser.). 11p. 1998. write for info. (*0-7923-8358-3*) Kluwer Academic.

Microcapsule Processing & Technology. Asali Kondo. Ed. by J. Wade Van Valkenburg. LC 79-18821. 191p. reprint ed. pap. 59.30 (*0-608-18696-1*, 202781800054) Bks Demand.

Microcapsules & Nanoparticles in Medicine & Pharmacy. M. Donbrow. 360p. 1991. lib. bdg. 249.00 (*0-8493-6986-X*, RS201) CRC Pr.

MicroCase Analysis System Reference Manual: Version 3. Microcase Corporation Staff. (Illus.). 400p. 1994. pap. 24.95 (*0-922914-14-1*) MicroCase.

Microcase Guide-America At Odds. Sidlow. (Political Science). 1999. pap. 12.50 (*0-534-53627-1*) Wadsworth Pub.

M

Microcavities & Photonic Bandgaps - Physics & Applications: Proceedings of the NATO Advanced Study Institute on 'Quantum Optics in Wavelength Scale Structures', Cargese, Corsica, August 26-September 2, 1995. Claude Weisbuch. Ed. by John Rarity. LC 96-28441. (NATO Advanced Science Institutes Series C). 616p. (C). 1996. text 327.50 (*0-7923-4170-8*) Kluwer Academic.

Microcharacterization of Proteins. 2nd ed. R. Kellner. LC 99-200094. 348p. 1999. pap. 130.00 (*3-527-30084-8*) Wiley.

Microchemistry. Timothy L. Schaap & John Young. (Illus.). 62p. 1995. pap. text, teacher ed. 23.10 (*1-877960-22-5*) Kemtec Educ.

Microchemistry, Vol. I. Timothy Schaap & John Young. (Illus.). 1995. pap. text 20.00 (*1-877960-21-7*) Kemtec Educ.

Microchemistry, Vol. II. Jo Combs et al. (Illus.). 20p. 1995. pap. text 20.00 (*1-877960-19-5*) Kemtec Educ.

Microchemistry: Spectroscopy & Chemistry in Small Domains; Proceedings of the JRDC-KUL Joint International Symposium on "Spectroscopy & Chemistry in Small Domains", Brussels, Belgium, August 11-14, 1993. JRDC-KUL Joint International Symposium on "Spectro et al. Ed. by Hiroshi Masuhara et al. LC 94-12674. (Delta Ser.). 588p. 1994. 175.50 (*0-444-81513-9*, North Holland) Elsevier.

MicroChemistry for Physical Sciences. Tom Russo. (Illus.). 120p. (Orig.). 1996. pap. text, lab manual ed. 40.00 (*1-888167-04-1*) Theta Tech.

Microchemistry 1. Thomas J. Russo. 165p. (YA). (gr. 10 up). 1995. lab manual ed. 39.00 (*1-888167-00-9*) Theta Tech.

Microchemistry 2. Thomas J. Russo. 120p. (YA). (gr. 10 up). 1995. lab manual ed. 39.00 (*1-888167-01-7*) Theta Tech.

***Microchip Fabrication.** 4th ed. Peter Van Zant. (Professional Engineering Ser.). (Illus.). 600p. 2000. 65.00 (*0-07-135636-3*) McGraw-Hill Prof.

Microchip Fabrication: A Practical Guide to Semiconductor Processing. 3rd ed. Peter Van Zant. LC 96-15729. (Illus.). 623p. (Orig.). 1996. 60.00 (*0-07-067250-4*) McGraw.

Microchip Science & Technology. Van Zant. 1999. 60.00 (*0-07-134198-6*) McGraw.

Microchip Technology: The Past & the Future. Charles Kerridge. LC 83-6674. (Illus.). 190p. reprint ed. pap. 58.90 (*0-8357-6213-0*, 203422800089) Bks Demand.

Microchipped: How the Education Establishment Took Us Beyond Big Brother. B. K. Eakman. 285p. 1994. pap. 14.95 (*0-89420-294-4*, 344125, Halcyon) Natl Book.

Microchips with Everything: The Consequences of Information Technology. Ed. by Paul Seighart. (Comedia Bks.). 160p. 1988. pap. 14.95 (*0-906890-32-2*, Pub. by Comedia) Routldge.

Microcircuit Engineering, '80: Proceedings of the International Conference on Microlithography, Amsterdam, 1980. Ed. by R. P. Kramer et al. 568p. 1981. pap. text 57.50 (*90-6275-060-5*, Pub. by Delft U Pr) Coronet Bks.

Microcircuit Production Technology. fac. ed. Douglas F. Horne. LC 86-197761. (Illus.). 160p. 1986. reprint ed. pap. 49.60 (*0-7837-8006-0*, 204776200008) Bks Demand.

Microcirculation & Inflammation: Vessel Wall, Inflammatory Cells, Mediator Interaction. Ed. by K. Messmer & F. Hammersen. (Progress in Applied Microcirculation Ser.: Vol. 12). xvi, 330p. 1987. pap. 130.50 (*3-8055-4552-5*) S Karger.

Microcirculation in Cancer Metastasis. F. William Orr et al. LC 96-6236. (Illus.). 304p. 1991. lib. bdg. 202.00 (*0-8493-6154-0*, RC269) CRC Pr.

Microcirculation in Chronic Venous Insufficiency: 15th Bodensee Symposium on Microcirculation, June 1998. Ed. by K. Messmer. LC 99-30254. (Progress in Applied Microcirculation Ser.: Vol. 23, 1999). (Illus.). x, 216p. 1999. 149.75 (*3-8055-6821-5*) S Karger.

Microcirculation in Diabetes. Ed. by E. Davis. (Advances in Microcirculation Ser.: Vol. 8). (Illus.). 1979. 100.00 (*3-8055-2916-3*) S Karger.

Microcirculation in Inflammation: Proceedings of the European Conference on Microcirculation, 10th, Cagliari, Oct. 24, 1978. European Conference on Microcirculation Staff. Ed. by J. W. Irwin & G. Hauck. (Bibliotheca Anatomica Ser.: No. 17). (Illus.). 1979. pap. 42.75 (*3-8055-3016-1*) S Karger.

Microcirculation in Organ Transplantation. Ed. by K. Messmer et al. (Progress in Applied Microcirculation Ser.: Vol. 21). (Illus.). x, 126p. 1994. 129.75 (*3-8055-5849-X*) S Karger.

Microcirculation in Venous Disease. 2nd ed. P. D. Coleridge Smith. LC 97-49120. (Medical Intelligence Unit Ser.). 1998. 99.00 (*1-57059-476-7*) Landes Bioscience.

Microcirculation of the Alimentary Tract: Physiology & Pathophysiology. Ed. by A. Koo et al. 400p. 1983. 75.00 (*9971-950-75-8*) World Scientific Pub.

Microcirculation of the Brain: A Synoptic View by World Experts. Ed. by M. Tomita et al. 283p. (C). 1992. text 195.00 (*1-56072-014-X*) Nova Sci Pubs.

Microcirculatory Approach to Asian Traditional Medicine: Strategy for the Scientific Evaluation: Selected Proceedings from the Satellite Symposium of the 2nd Asian Congress for Microcirculation, Beijing, China, 17 August 1995. Ed. by Hideyuki Niimi et al. LC 96-17518. (International Congress Ser.: No. 1117). 206p. 1996. text 139.00 (*0-444-82343-3*, Excerpta Medica) Elsevier.

Microcirculatory Approaches to Current Therapeutic Problems: Lung in Shock, Organ Transplantation, Diabetic Microangiopathy. Proceedings. Conference on Microcirculation, 6th European, Aalb. Ed. by J. Ditzel & D. H. Lewis. (Illus.). 1971. 45.25 (*3-8055-1186-8*) S Karger.

Microcirculatory Disorders in the Heart & Brain. Ed. by Hideyuki Nimi. xv, 195p. 1991. text 223.00 (*3-7186-5090-8*, Harwood Acad Pubs) Gordon & Breach.

Microclimate: The Biological Environment. 2nd ed. Norman J. Rosenberg et al. LC 83-7031. 528p. 1983. 140.00 (*0-471-06066-6*) Wiley.

Microclimate & Spray Dispersion. David H. Bache & Donald R. Johnstone. LC 92-30471. (Ellis Horwood Series in Environmental Management, Science & Technology). 1992. 76.95 (*0-13-217910-5*, Pub. by Tavistock-E Horwood) Routldge.

Microclimate for Cultural Heritage. Dario Camuffo. LC 98-9287. (Developments in Atmospheric Science Ser.). 428p. 1998. 227.00 (*0-444-82925-3*) Elsevier.

Microclimate Measurement for Ecologists. D. Unwin. (Biological Techniques Ser.). 1981. text 83.00 (*0-12-709150-5*) Acad Pr.

Microclimates & Macroclimate of Neotoma, a Small Valley in Central Ohio. John N. Wolfe et al. (Bulletin Ser.: No. 41). 1972. reprint ed. pap. text 10.00 (*0-86727-040-3*) Ohio Bio Survey.

Microclimatic Landscape Design: Creating Thermal Comfort & Energy Efficiency. Robert D. Brown & Terry J. Gillespie. LC 95-10902. 208p. 1995. pap. 54.95 (*0-471-05667-7*) Wiley.

Microcluster Physics. S. Sugano. Ed. by J. P. Toennies et al. (Materials Science Ser.: Vol. 20). (Illus.). ix, 158p. 1991. 65.95 (*0-387-53926-3*) Spr-Verlag.

Microcluster Physics. 2nd ed. S. Sugano & H. Koizumi. LC 98-14856. (Springer Series in Materials Science: Vol. 20). (Illus.). x, 231p. 1998. 69.95 (*3-540-63974-8*) Spr-Verlag.

Microclusters. Ed. by S. Surgano et al. (Materials Science Ser.: Vol. 4). 305p. 1987. 71.95 (*0-387-17675-6*) Spr-Verlag.

Microcognition: Philosophy, Cognitive Science, & Parallel Distributed Processing. Andy Clark. 240p. 1989. 35.00 (*0-262-03148-5*) MIT Pr.

Microcognition: Philosophy, Cognitive Science & Parallel Distributed Processing. Andy Clark. 248p. 1991. reprint ed. pap. text 20.00 (*0-262-53095-3*, Bradford Bks) MIT Pr.

Microcompartmentation. Ed. by Dean P. Jones. 272p. 1988. 155.00 (*0-8493-4779-3*, QH604, CRC Reprint) Franklin.

Microcomposites & Nanophase Materials: Proceedings of a Symposium Sponsored by the Physical Metallurgy Committee, Held at the 120th Annual Meeting of the Minerals, Metals & Materials Society in New Orleans, LA, February 17-21, 1991. Ed. by David C. Van Aken et al. LC 91-67427. 163p. 1991. reprint ed. pap. 50.60 (*0-608-00778-1*, 206157600010) Bks Demand.

Microcomputer: Concepts & Software. Larry Long & Nancy Long. 1992. write for info. (*0-318-68776-3*) P-H.

***Microcomputer Accounting: Tutorial & Applications for Peachtree Accounting, Release 7.0.** 3rd ed. Gregory E. Anders et al. LC 99-40025. 1999. write for info. (*0-02-804754-0*) Glencoe.

***Microcomputer Accounting: Tutorial & Applications for Peachtree Accounting, Release 7.0.** 3rd ed. Gregory E. Anders et al. LC 99-40025. 1999. write for info. (*0-02-804752-4*); write for info. (*0-02-804753-2*) Glencoe.

Microcomputer Accounting: Tutorial & Applications with ACCPAC Simply Accounting. Gregory E. Anders et al. LC 94-8323. 1994. 98.00 (*0-02-801068-X*) Glencoe.

Microcomputer Accounting: Tutorial & Applications with DacEasy. Emma J. Spiegelberg & Sally Nelson. LC 93-32461. 1994. 98.00 (*0-02-801062-0*) Glencoe.

Microcomputer Accounting: Tutorial & Applications with Peachtree. Sally Nelson et al. LC 93-44207. 1994. 35.95 (*0-02-801065-5*) Glencoe.

Microcomputer Accounting: Tutorial & Applications with Peachtree for Windows. Gregory E. Anders et al. LC 95-35134. 1995. 72.44 (*0-02-802250-5*) Glencoe.

Microcomputer Accounting Applications. S. S. Hamilton et al. (Microcomputer Software Program Ser.). 128p. 1983. pap. text 8.76 (*0-07-025818-X*) McGraw.

Microcomputer Activities for the Office. 2nd ed. Anthony A. Olinzock. (KM - Office Procedures Ser.). 1988. mass mkt. 10.50 (*0-538-60021-7*) S-W Pub.

Microcomputer Aided Engineering: Basic Soil Mechanics. R. Hussein. (Illus.). 277p. 1990. text 49.95 (*0-925760-10-2*) SciTech Pubs.

Microcomputer Algorithms: Action from Algebra. J. P. Killingbeck. LC 90-22739. (Illus.). 256p. 1991. pap. 48.00 (*0-7503-0097-3*) IOP Pub.

Microcomputer-Analog Converter Software & Hardware Interfacing: Technibook VII. Jonathan A. Titus & Christopher A. Titus. LC 78-2293. (Bugbook Reference Ser.). 1978. pap. text 11.95 (*0-89704-009-0*) E&L Instru.

Microcomputer & Information Processing. 11th ed. Susan K. Baumann. (DF - Computer Applications Ser.). (C). 1997. pap. write for info. (*0-314-20548-9*) West Pub.

Microcomputer & VCR Usage in Schools. Quality Education Data Staff. (School Trend Ser.). 204p. 1988. pap. 49.95 (*0-88747-217-6*, 2176Q) Quality Ed Data.

Microcomputer Application Accounting. Wright. 1991. 26.87 (*0-07-072084-3*) McGraw.

Microcomputer Applications. California College for Health Sciences Staff. 96p. (C). 1990. spiral bd. write for info. (*0-933195-27-3*) CA College Health Sci.

Microcomputer Applications. Wolff. 1985. mass mkt. 29.50 (*0-87835-813-7*) Course Tech.

Microcomputer Applications. Wolff. 1986. pap. write for info. (*0-87835-811-0*) Thomson Learn.

Microcomputer Applications. 3rd ed. Robert T. Grauer & Paul K. Sugrue. (C). 1990. pap. text 24.50 (*0-07-024151-1*) McGraw.

Microcomputer Applications. 3rd ed. Robert T. Grauer & Paul K. Sugrue. (C). 1991. text 54.00 (*0-07-024150-3*) McGraw.

Microcomputer Applications: A Hands-On Approach to Problem Solving. Larry J. Goldstein. 608p. (C). 1988. pap. text 28.95 (*0-201-11898-X*) Addison-Wesley.

Microcomputer Applications: Computer Education Course. Rosemary T. Fruehling et al. 208p. (C). 1992. pap. text, student ed. 16.95 (*1-56118-431-4*) Paradigm MN.

Microcomputer Applications: Goldstein Text & Goldspread Version 1.1. Larry Joel Goldstein. 1987. pap. 41.95 (*0-201-15392-0*) Addison-Wesley.

Microcomputer Applications, '89: Proceedings of the International Symposium Held in Los Angeles, California, U. S. A., December 14-16, 1989, & Sponsored by the International Society for Mini & Microcomputers. International Society for Mini & Microcomputers St. Ed. by M. H. Hamza. 141p. 1989. 64.00 (*0-88986-135-8*, 158) Acta Pr.

Microcomputer Applications for Business: DOS, WordPerfect 5.1, Lotus 1-2-3 Release 2.2, dBASE III Plus. Roy Ageloff et al. (Illus.). 864p. (C). 1992. pap. text 64.95 incl. 5.25 hd (*1-56527-018-5*); pap. text 44.95 incl. 5.25 hd (*1-878748-75-0*); pap. text 69.95 incl. 5.25 hd (*1-878748-77-7*) Course Tech.

Microcomputer Applications for Business: DOS, WordPerfect 5.1, Lotus 1-2-3 Release 2.2, dBASE III Plus. Roy Ageoff et al. (Illus.). 864p. (C). 1992. pap. text 69.95 incl. 3.5 hd (*1-878748-78-5*) Course Tech.

Microcomputer Applications for Business: DOS 6.0, dBase IV. Roy Ageloff et al. (New Perspectives Ser.). pap. write for info. (*1-56527-174-2*) Course Tech.

Microcomputer Applications for Business: DOS 6.0, WordPerfect 6.0, Lotus 1-2-3 Release 2.4, dBASE IV. Roy Ageloff et al. (New Perspectives Ser.). 1072p. pap. write for info. (*1-56527-175-0*) Course Tech.

Microcomputer Applications for Business: DOS/WP/123R2.4/dBIV. Roy Ageloff et al. (New Perspectives Ser.). 952p. pap. write for info. (*1-56527-063-0*) Course Tech.

Microcomputer Applications for Strategic Management in Education: A Case Study Approach. Craig E. Richards. 127p. (C). 1989. pap. text 22.95 (*0-582-28668-9*, 71684) Longman.

Microcomputer Applications for Technicians. Donald D. Voisinet. LC 92-36081. 1993. teacher ed. write for info. (*0-02-800941-X*); 3.5 hd. write for info. (*0-02-800940-1*); 5.25 hd. write for info. (*0-02-800939-8*) Glencoe.

Microcomputer Applications in Banking. Chun H. Lam & George H. Hempel. LC 85-32322. 221p. 1986. 57.95 (*0-89930-117-7*, HMI/, Quorum Bks) Greenwood.

Microcomputer Applications in Business. Bruce J. McLaren. (C). 1997. 62.67 (*0-673-46383-4*) Addson-Wesley Educ.

Microcomputer Applications in City Planning & Management. Steven I. Gordon & Richard F. Anderson. LC 88-30748. 347p. 1989. 75.00 (*0-275-92866-7*, C2866, Praeger Pubs) Greenwood.

Microcomputer Applications in Fisheries: A Manual for a Course in the Use of Microcomputers in Fisheries & Stock Assessment. Karim Erzini & Margarida Castro. ix, 176p. 1991. pap. text 15.00 (*1-882027-05-1*) URI ICMRD.

Microcomputer Applications in Geology. Ed. by J. T. Hanley & Daniel F. Merriam. (Computers & Geology Ser.: Vol. 5). 274p. 1986. text 105.75 (*0-08-031452-X*, Pub. by PPL) Elsevier.

Microcomputer Applications in Geology II. Ed. by J. T. Hanley & Daniel F. Merriam. (Computers & Geology Ser.: No. 6). (Illus.). 322p. 1990. text 86.50 (*0-08-040261-5*, Pergamon Pr) Elsevier.

Microcomputer Applications in Health Education. Robert S. Gold. 304p. (C). 1990. text. write for info. (*0-697-10628-4*) Brown & Benchmark.

Microcomputer Applications in Libraries: A Management Tool for the 1980s & Beyond, 5. Richard M. Kesner & Clifton H. Jones. LC 83-22566. (New Directions in Librarianship Ser.: No. 5). 250p. 1984. 59.95 (*0-313-22939-2*, KMI/) Greenwood.

Microcomputer Applications in Manufacturing. A. Galip Ulsoy & Warren R. DeVries. LC 88-32123. 368p. 1989. pap. 96.95 (*0-471-61189-1*) Wiley.

Microcomputer Applications in Medicine & Bioengineering: Proceedings, ISMM Symposium, New York, U. S. A., October 22-24, 1984. Ed. by M. H. Hamza. 107p. 1984. 60.00 (*0-88986-067-X*, 073) Acta Pr.

Microcomputer Applications in Occupational Health & Safety. Ed. by Denny Dobin. (Illus.). 228p. 1987. lib. bdg. 68.00 (*0-87371-078-9*, L078) Lewis Pubs.

Microcomputer Applications in Qualitative Research. Bryan Pfaffenberger. (Qualitative Research Methods Ser.: Vol. 14). 96p. (C). 1988. text 24.00 (*0-8039-3119-0*); pap. text 10.50 (*0-8039-3120-4*) Sage.

Microcomputer Applications in Transportation II. Ed. by Robert E. Stammer, Jr. & Mark D. Abkowitz. LC 87-19571. 744p. 1987. 8.00 (*0-87262-623-7*) Am Soc Civil Eng.

Microcomputer Applications in Transportation III. Ed. by Kenneth S. Opiela & Robert E. Stammer. LC 90-716. 1320p. 1990. pap. text 105.00 (*0-87262-757-8*) Am Soc Civil Eng.

Microcomputer Applications of, & Modifications to, the Modular Fault Trees. 1996. lib. bdg. 257.75 (*0-8490-5921-6*) Gordon Pr.

Microcomputer Applications Using Shareware. 2nd ed. Fritz H. Grupe. 304p. (C). 1990. spiral bd. write for info. (*0-697-07738-1*) Bus & Educ Tech.

Microcomputer Applications with Microsoft Works 3.0 for Windows. Fritz J. Erickson & John A. Vonk. 528p. (C). 1995. text 35.00 (*0-697-23992-6*) Bus & Educ Tech.

Microcomputer Applications with Wordperfect, Lotus 1-2-3, dBASE III Plus. Fritz H. Grupe. 408p. (C). 1989. spiral bd. write for info. (*0-697-05930-8*) Bus & Educ Tech.

Microcomputer Applications with WordPerfect 5.0, Lotus 1-2-3 & DBase III+ Fritz H. Grupe et al. 416p. (C). 1989. text 59.45 (*0-697-11064-8*, Irwn McGrw-H) McGrw-H Hghr Educ.

Microcomputer Applications Within the Urban Transportation Environment: Proceedings of a Conference Sponsored by the Urban Transportation Division. Ed. by Mark D. Abkowitz & Robert E. Stammer, Jr. 824p. 1985. 9.00 (*0-87262-508-7*) Am Soc Civil Eng.

Microcomputer Architecture & Programming: 68000 Version. John F. Wakerly. LC 88-27849. 784p. 1989. text 99.95 (*0-471-85319-4*) Wiley.

Microcomputer Assisted Quality Assurance. Gary Hill. LC 84-81671. 106p. (Orig.). 1984. pap. text 21.20 (*0-930531-00-0*); pap. text 95.00 incl. disk (*0-685-09412-X*) LOTIC.

Microcomputer-Based Adaptive Control to Thyristor-Driven D-C Motors. Ulrich Keuchel & Richard M. Stephan. LC 93-33452. (Advances in Industrial Control Ser.). 1994. 59.95 (*0-387-19855-5*) Spr-Verlag.

Microcomputer-Based Aid for the Disabled. Julia M. Schofield. LC 81-30458. (Monographs in Informatics). (Illus.). 128p. reprint ed. pap. 39.70 (*0-608-17861-6*, 203268500080) Bks Demand.

Microcomputer-Based Labs: Educational Research & Standards. Ed. by Robert F. Tinker. LC 96-30575. (NATO SAI Ser.: Ser. f, Computer & Systems Sciences). 393p. 1996. 114.50 (*3-540-61558-X*) Spr-Verlag.

Microcomputer Based Primer on Structural Behavior. James Lefter & Thomas J. Bergin. (Illus.). 448p. (C). 1986. disk. write for info. (*0-318-60165-6*) P-H.

Microcomputer Bus Structures & Bus Interface Design. Arthur L. Dexter. (Electrical Engineering & Electronics Ser.: No. 32). (Illus.). 368p. 1986. text 155.00 (*0-8247-7435-3*) Dekker.

Microcomputer Business Applications & Projects. Don Busche. 1987. pap. text 188.95 (*0-471-84451-9*) P-H.

Microcomputer Business Applications & Projects. Don Busche. 1988. pap. text 5.95 (*0-471-50073-9*) P-H.

Microcomputer Coloring Book. Donald D. Spencer. 32p. (J). (gr. 2-4). 1982. pap. 3.25 (*0-89218-052-8*, NO. 1126) Camelot Pub.

Microcomputer Communications. rev. ed. (Illus.). 1110p. 1988. ring bd. 587.00 (*0-942155-03-3*) Faulkner Tech Reports.

Microcomputer Control of Thermal & Mechanical Systems. William F. Stoecker & Paul Stoecker. (Illus.). 470p. (gr. 13). 1988. text 84.95 (*0-442-20648-8*) Chapman & Hall.

Microcomputer Correlation. Flynn. Date not set. pap. text. write for info. (*0-314-75003-7*) West Pub.

Microcomputer Custom Bdr. 93-94. O'Leary. 1993. 6.56 (*0-07-911544-6*) McGraw.

Microcomputer Database Management Using Access. James Pratt & Leidig. (C). 1994. text. write for info. (*0-318-70356-4*, BF3911) S-W Pub.

Microcomputer Database Management Using dBASE IV, Version 2.0. Philip J. Pratt. LC 94-1014. 1994. write for info. (*0-87709-513-2*) Course Tech.

Microcomputer Database Management Using dBASE IV, Version 2.0. Philip J. Pratt. LC 94-1014. 539p. (C). 1994. pap. 44.95 (*0-87709-539-6*) Course Tech.

Microcomputer Database Management Using Microsoft Access, Version 2, Incl. instr. manual. Philip J. Pratt & Paul M. Leidig. (Illus.). 480p. (C). 1994. pap. 33.00 incl. 3.5 ld (*0-87709-560-4*) Course Tech.

Microcomputer Database Management Using Paradox for Windows. Philip J. Pratt & Mary Z. Last. 1994. write for info. (*0-318-72549-5*) Course Tech.

Microcomputer Dictionary: Dicctionnaire de la Microinformatique. A. Fantapie. (ENG & FRE.). 131p. 1984. 59.95 (*0-8288-0893-7*, M14494) Fr & Eur.

Microcomputer Dictionary: Dictionnaire Micro-Informatique. Eric Duceau. (FRE.). 191p. 1986. pap. 39.95 (*0-7859-4743-4*) Fr & Eur.

Microcomputer Displays, Graphics, & Animation. Bruce A. Artwick. LC 84-61429. (Illus.). 384p. (C). 1985. pap. 31.95 (*0-13-580226-1*) P-H.

Microcomputer Engineering. 2nd ed. Gene H. Miller. LC 98-24745. 544p. 1998. pap. 100.00 (*0-13-895368-6*) P-H.

Microcomputer Essentials. Sarah E. Hutchinson & Stacey C. Sawyer. LC 92-46873. 176p. (C). 1993. text 23.95 (*0-256-14294-7*, Irwn McGrw-H) McGrw-H Hghr Educ.

Microcomputer Essentials. Sarah E. Hutchinson et al. (C). 1999. text 33.95 (*0-256-18283-3*, Irwn McGrw-H) McGrw-H Hghr Educ.

Microcomputer Essentials dBase IV. Sarah E. Hutchinson & Stacey C. Sawyer. (C). 1994. text 37.95 (*0-256-18518-2*, Irwn McGrw-H) McGrw-H Hghr Educ.

Microcomputer Essentials DOS 5.0. Sarah E. Hutchinson et al. (C). 1999. text 39.95 (*0-256-18722-3*, Irwn McGrw-H) McGrw-H Hghr Educ.

Microcomputer Experimentation with the IBM PC. Lance A. Leventhal. (Oxford Series in Electrical & Computer Engineering). (Illus.). 464p. (C). 1995. pap. text 44.00 (*0-03-009542-5*) OUP.

Microcomputer Experimentation with the MOS Technology KIM-1. Lance A. Leventhal. (Illus.). 480p. (C). 1982. pap. text 41.00 (*0-13-580779-4*) P-H.

M

An Asterisk (*) at the beginning of an entry indicates that the title is appearing for the first time.

Microcomputer Experimentation with the Motorola MC6800ECB. Lance A. Leventhal. 368p. (C). 1988. write for info. (*0-03-211783-3*) SCP.

Microcomputer Experimentation with the Synertek SYM-1. Lance A. Leventhal. (Illus.). 512p. (C). 1983. text 37.00 (*0-13-580910-X*) P-H.

Microcomputer Facility & the School Library Media Specialist. Ed. by E. Blanche Woolls & David V. Loertscher. LC 85-26827. (Illus.). 212p. 1986. reprint ed. pap. 65.80 (*0-7837-9690-0*, 206042000005) Bks Demand.

Microcomputer Fault-Finding & Design. Robin C. Holland. (Illus.). 212p. (C). 1991. text 72.50 (*0-333-54268-1*); pap. text 32.50 (*0-333-54269-X*) Macmillan.

Microcomputer Fault-Finding & Design. 2nd ed. Robin C. Holland. (Illus.). 232p. (C). 1995. pap. text 35.00 (*0-333-64166-3*, Pub. by Macmillan Ed) Scholium Intl.

Microcomputer Fundamentals. Sarah E. Hutchinson & Stacey C. Sawyer. LC 92-36228. (Irwin Advantage Series for Computer Education). 352p. (C). 1992. text 29.95 (*0-256-13396-4*, Irwn McGrw-H) McGrw-H Hghr Educ.

Microcomputer Graphics. Roy E. Myers. (Illus.). 304p. 1984. pap. text. write for info. (*0-318-56714-8*) Addison-Wesley.

Microcomputer Graphics for the IBM PC. Roy E. Myers. 1438p. 1984. pap. 14.95 (*0-201-05158-3*); Apple II. write for info. (*0-201-05312-8*) Addison-Wesley.

Microcomputer Graphics for the IBM Personal Computer: Techniques & Applications. D. Donald Hearn & M. Pauline Baker. (Illus.). 272p. 1983. pap. 22.50 (*0-13-580662-3*) P-H.

***Microcomputer Hardware, Software & Troubleshooting for Engineering & Technology Students.** James L. Antonakos & Kenneth Mansfield. LC 99-58000. (Illus.). 616p. (C). 2000. pap. text 81.00 incl. audio compact disk (*0-13-011466-9*) P-H.

Microcomputer Industry: Business & Professional Systems, a Competitive International Assessment. 1992. lib. bdg. 88.95 (*0-8490-5503-2*) Gordon Pr.

Microcomputer Industry in Brazil: The Case of a Protected High Technology Industry. Eduardo Luzio. LC 94-36640. 192p. 1996. 62.95 (*0-275-94923-0*, Praeger Pubs) Greenwood.

Microcomputer Information for School Media Centers. Ed. by Nevada W. Thomason. LC 84-23566. 334p. 1985. 34.50 (*0-8108-1769-1*) Scarecrow.

Microcomputer Interfacing. Bruce A. Artwick. 1980. text 45.00 (*0-13-580902-9*) P-H.

Microcomputer Interfacing. H. S. Stone. LC 81-17619. 480p. (C). 1982. text 62.50 (*0-201-07403-6*) Addison-Wesley.

Microcomputer Interfacing & Applications. 2nd rev. ed. M. A. Mustafa. (Illus.). 432p. 1994. pap. text 59.95 (*0-7506-1752-7*) Buttrwrth-Heinemann.

Microcomputer Interpretation of Clinical Lab Results. D. Bloch & Derek Enlander. 90p. 1984. 30.00 (*0-685-08623-2*) Med Software.

Microcomputer Keyboard Application Textbook: Version 1.1 Software. EMC-Paradigm Publishing Staff et al. text 34.75 (*0-8219-1075-2*) EMC-Paradigm.

Microcomputer Keyboarding. 2nd ed. JoAnn Sherron & Ronald H. Sherron. 1994. pap. text 24.95 (*1-56118-600-7*) Paradigm MN.

Microcomputer Keyboarding & Applications: Annotated teacher's edition, Version 1.1 Software. Jo Ann Sherron et al. 44.75 (*0-8219-1076-0*) EMC-Paradigm.

Microcomputer Keyboarding & Document Processing. Johnson & Stanley. 1996. teacher ed. write for info. (*0-02-814097-4*) Glencoe.

Microcomputer Keyboarding & Document Processing: Instructor's Guide. 2nd ed. JoAnn E. Sherron & Ronald H. Sherron. 1993. pap. text, teacher ed. 17.00 (*1-56118-625-2*) Paradigm MN.

Microcomputer Keyboarding & Document Processing: Test, Easelback. Jo Ann E. Sherron & Ronald H. Sherron. 432p. 29.95 (*1-56118-631-7*) EMC-Paradigm.

Microcomputer Keyboarding & Document Processing: Text with Student Disks, 3.5. Jo Ann E. Sherron & Ronald H. Sherron. 32.95 (*1-56118-633-3*) EMC-Paradigm.

Microcomputer Keyboarding & Formatting. 2nd ed. Jo Ann Sherron & Ronald H. Sherron. 1993. pap. text 26.95 (*1-56118-630-9*) Paradigm MN.

Microcomputer Knowledge-Based Expert Systems in Civil Engineering. Ed. by Hojjat Adeli. (Symposium Proceedings Ser.). 220p. 1988. 5.00 (*0-87262-653-9*) Am Soc Civil Eng.

Microcomputer Lexicon: Mikrocomputerlexikon. 2nd ed. Reinhold Falkner. (ENG & GER.). 184p. 1984. 45.00 (*0-8288-0242-4*, M15292) Fr & Eur.

Microcomputer Literacy Program: All about Personal Computers. Continuing Education Center Staff. 89p. 1982. student ed. 99.99 (*0-07-010297-X*) McGraw.

Microcomputer Methods for Social Scientists, 1987. Philip A. Schrodt. (Quantitative Applications in the Social Sciences Ser.: Vol. 40). 96p. (Orig.). (C). 1987. pap. text 10.95 (*0-8039-3043-7*) Sage.

Microcomputer Modules for Management Decision Making. 3rd ed. Terry L. Dennis & Laurie B. Dennis. Ed. by Fenton. 350p. (C). 1993. pap. text 38.25 incl. disk (*0-314-01252-4*) West Pub.

Microcomputer Networks: Troubleshooting. Adamson. (Electronics Technology Ser.). 1996. teacher ed. 18.76 (*0-8273-6955-7*); text 54.95 (*0-8273-6954-9*) Delmar.

Microcomputer Operator. Jack Rudman. (Career Examination Ser.: C-3733). 1994. pap. 27.95 (*0-8373-3733-X*) Nat Learn.

Microcomputer Program to Calculate Spur Gears. Henri Yelle et al. (Nineteen Eighty-Six Fall Technical Meeting Ser.: Vol. 86FTM12). (Illus.). 10p. 1986. pap. 30.00 (*1-55589-476-3*, 86FTM12) AGMA.

Microcomputer Programs in Medicine, Vol. I. Derek Enlander. (Illus.). 116p. 1983. 80.00 (*0-88672-000-1*) Med Software.

Microcomputer Programs in Medicine, Vol. II. Derek Enlander. 105p. 1984. 80.00 (*0-685-08620-8*) Med Software.

Microcomputer Quantum Mechanics. 2nd ed. J. P. Killingbeck. (Illus.). 200p. 1985. 48.00 (*0-85274-803-5*) IOP Pub.

Microcomputer Repair. 3rd ed. James L. Antonakos. LC 98-24766. 693p. 1998. pap. text 90.00 (*0-13-893454-1*) P-H.

Microcomputer Resource Manual: Software & Applications - Apple Edition. Daphne E. Swabey & Dennis P. Curtin. 368p. (C). 1987. pap. text 17.05 (*0-13-580565-1*) P-H.

Microcomputer Resource Manual: Software & Applications - IBM Edition. Dennis P. Curtin. (Illus.). 432p. (C). 1986. 11.95 (*0-317-45978-3*) P-H.

Microcomputer Security. Information Technology Division Staff. LC 94-2017. 1994. 22.00 (*0-87051-148-3*) Am Inst CPA.

Microcomputer Servicing: Practical Systems & Troubleshooting. Stuart A. Asser et al. (C). 1990. pap. text, lab manual ed. 30.60 (*0-675-21109-3*, Merrill Coll) P-H.

Microcomputer Servicing: Practical Systems & Troubleshooting. 3rd ed. Stuart M. Asser et al. LC 96-3063. 662p. 1996. 105.00 (*0-13-263781-2*) P-H.

Microcomputer Simulations in Business. Anthony A. Olinzock. (KM - Office Procedures Ser.). 1986. pap. 13.95 (*0-538-13620-0*) S-W Pub.

Microcomputer 68000 Organization & Programming. Per Stenstrom. LC 92-27338. 1992. 35.00 (*0-13-009960-0*) P-H.

Microcomputer Software Distribution. Ed. by Peter Allen. 180p. 1984. pap. 295.00 (*0-931634-34-2*) FIND-SVP.

Microcomputer Software for Adult Vocational Education: Guidelines for Evaluation. Antonia Stone. 35p. 1983. 3.25 (*0-318-22152-7*, IN261) Ctr Educ Trng Employ.

Microcomputer Software for Information Management. Mel Collier. 150p. 1986. text 54.95 (*0-566-03555-3*) Ashgate Pub Co.

Microcomputer Software for Management Science & Operations Management. 2nd ed. Barry Render et al. 1989. 3.5 hd 26.67 (*0-205-11969-7*) Allyn.

Microcomputer Software for Management Science & Operations Management. 2nd ed. Barry Render et al. 1989. pap. 24.00 (*0-685-44218-7*) P-H.

Microcomputer Software for Performing Statistical Analysis: A Handbook Supporting Library Decision Making. Ed. by Peter Hernon et al. LC 88-6360. (Information Management, Policies & Services Ser.). 352p. 1988. text 73.25 (*0-89391-496-7*) Ablx Pub.

Microcomputer Spreadsheet Models for Libraries: Preparing Documents, Budgets, & Statistical Reports. Philip M. Clark. LC 84-20470. 132p. 1985. reprint ed. pap. 41.00 (*0-7837-9678-1*, 206040600005) Bks Demand.

Microcomputer Survey. S. R. Pasewark. (C). pap. text 14.00 (*0-685-65257-2*) P-H.

Microcomputer System Design: An Advanced Course. Ed. by M. J. Flynn et al. (Lecture Notes in Computer Science Ser.: Vol. 126). 397p. 1981. 34.00 (*0-387-11172-7*) Spr-Verlag.

Microcomputer System Theory Service: MC-3000. rev. ed. Charles J. Brooks. (Illus.). 1991. pap. text, teacher ed. 27.00 (*1-884268-02-1*) Marcraft Intl.

Microcomputer System Theory Service: MC-3000. 3rd ed. Charles J. Brooks. (Illus.). (C). 1991. pap. text, lab manual ed. 25.00 (*1-884268-01-3*) Marcraft Intl.

Microcomputer System Theory Service: MC-3000. 3rd rev. ed. Charles J. Brooks. (Illus.). (C). 1991. pap. text 27.00 (*1-884268-00-5*) Marcraft Intl.

Microcomputer Systems: The 8086-8088 Family Architecture, Programming & Design. 2nd ed. Yu-Cheng Liu & Glenn A. Gibson. (Illus.). 640p. (C). 1986. text 66.80 (*0-13-580499-X*) P-H.

Microcomputer Systems Theory & Service. 7th ed. Charles J. Brooks. Ed. by Anthony Tonda. 1998. teacher ed., ring bd. 35.00 (*1-58122-006-5*) Marcraft Intl.

Microcomputer Systems Theory & Service: MC-6000. Charles J. Brooks & Todd Whittington. (Illus.). (C). 1996. pap. text, lab manual ed. 59.95 (*1-884268-97-8*) Marcraft Intl.

Microcomputer Systems Theory & Service: MC-6000. rev. ed. Charles J. Brooks. (Illus.). (C). 1996. teacher ed., ring bd. 35.00 (*1-884268-98-6*) Marcraft Intl.

Microcomputer Systems Theory & Service: MC-6000. 5th rev. ed. Charles J. Brooks. (Illus.). (C). 1996. pap. text 59.95 (*1-884268-96-X*) Marcraft Intl.

Microcomputer Systems Theory & Service - IC-Level Theory/Lab Guide. 7th ed. Charles J. Brooks. 1998. pap. text 20.00 (*1-58122-005-7*) Marcraft Intl.

Microcomputer Systems Theory & Service - Lab Guide. 7th ed. Charles J. Brooks. Ed. by Whitney G. Freeman. 1998. pap. text 59.95 (*1-58122-009-X*) Marcraft Intl.

Microcomputer Systems Theory & Service - Theory. 7th ed. Charles J. Brooks. Ed. by Whitney G. Freeman. 1998. pap. text 59.95 (*1-58122-008-1*) Marcraft Intl.

Microcomputer Systems Using STE Bus. Ed. by R. J. Mitchell. 1989. 22.00 (*0-8493-7144-9*, TK) CRC Pr.

Microcomputer Technician. Jack Rudman. (Career Examination Ser.: Vol. C-3821). 1997. pap. 29.95 (*0-8373-3821-2*) Nat Learn.

Microcomputer Theory & Application. 2nd ed. Mohamed Rafiquzzaman. (C). 1989. text 61.51 (*0-13-583691-3*) P-H.

Microcomputer Theory & Applications with the Intel SDK-85. 2nd ed. Mohamed Rafiquzzaman. LC 86-15972. 761p. 1987. text 47.95 (*0-471-80040-6*) P-H.

***Microcomputer Theory & Servicing.** 4th ed. Stuart M. Asser et al. 896p. 2000. 102.00 (*0-13-010955-X*, Prentice Hall) P-H.

Microcomputer Tools for Communications Engineering. Shing T. Li et al. LC 83-71834. (Illus.). 279p. reprint ed. pap. 86.50 (*0-608-16024-5*, 203312300083) Bks Demand.

Microcomputer Tools for Transportation & Residential Energy Conservation: Technical Report & Program Listings, 2 vols., Set. 198p. 1982. 40.00 (*0-318-17724-2*, DG 82-317) Pub Tech Inc.

Microcomputer Troubleshooting. James Perozzo. 352p. 1986. pap. 26.95 (*0-8273-2500-2*) Delmar.

Microcomputer Troubleshooting. James Perozzo. (Electronics Technology Ser.). 1987. pap., teacher ed. 15.00 (*0-8273-2501-0*) Delmar.

Microcomputer Troubleshooting & Repair. Bob Cahill & John G. Stephenson. 368p. 1988. 24.95 (*0-672-22629-4*) Sams.

Microcomputer Use Lab Manual. Teresa Alberte-Hallam et al. 1985. write for info. incl. disk (*0-318-67043-7*) Harcourt.

Microcomputer/Audio Visual Repair Supervisor. Jack Rudman. (Career Examination Ser.: No. C-3732). 1994. pap. 34.95 (*0-8373-3732-1*) Nat Learn.

Microcomputers. Flynn. 1991. mass mkt. 43.00 (*0-314-66760-1*) West Pub.

Microcomputers. Meredith Flynn. Date not set. pap. text, teacher ed. 21.95 (*0-314-73483-X*) West Pub.

Microcomputers. 3rd ed. Zimmerman. Date not set. pap. text, teacher ed. write for info. (*0-314-81927-4*) West Pub.

Microcomputers: A Source Guide. 1991. lib. bdg. 79.95 (*0-8490-4905-9*) Gordon Pr.

Microcomputers: Business & Personal Applications. James R. Burns & Darrell Eubanks. 614p. (C). 1988. text 57.00 (*0-314-93159-7*) West Pub.

Microcomputers: Concepts, Skills & Applications. 2nd ed. Flynn. 1997. 54.95 (*0-314-20499-7*, Pub. by West Pub) Thomson Learn.

Microcomputers: Programming & Utilization. K. K. Mohindroo. 200p. 1997. pap. 60.00 (*81-209-0015-4*, Pub. by Pitambar Pub) St Mut.

Microcomputers: Security, Auditability & Controls. Javier F. Kuong et al. 240p. 1985. pap. 50.00 (*0-940706-16-4*) Management Advisory Pubns.

Microcomputers: The Users Perspective. Sarah E. Hutchinson & Stacey C. Sawyer. (C). 1992. 22.46 (*0-256-12377-2*, Irwn McGrw-H) McGrw-H Hghr Educ.

Microcomputers & Applications. Ernest S. Colantonio. LC 88-83917. (Laboratory Ser.). 750p. (C). 1989. student ed. 17.00 incl. disk (*0-318-42521-1*) HM Trade Div.

Microcomputers & Clinical Psychology: Issues, Applications, & Future Developments. Ed. by Alastair Ager & Sue Bendall. LC 91-12241. (Wiley Series in Clinical Psychology). 234p. 1991. reprint ed. pap. 72.60 (*0-608-04597-7*, 206536700003) Bks Demand.

Microcomputers & Economic Analysis: Spreadsheet Templates for Local Government. rev. ed. Patricia L. McKay et al. (Bureau of Economic & Business Research Monographs). 182p. 1987. pap. text 15.00 (*0-930885-03-1*) Bur Econ & Bus Res.

Microcomputers & Education: 85th Yearbook of the National Society for the Study of Education. Ed. by Jack Culbertson & Luvern L. Cunningham. LC 85-62667. xii, 308p. 1986. lib. bdg. 22.00 (*0-226-60141-2*) U Ch Pr.

Microcomputers & Electronic Instrumentation: Making the Right Connections. Howard V. Malmstadt et al. LC 94-1407. 1994. 75.00 (*0-8412-2861-2*) Am Chemical.

Microcomputers & Exceptional Children. Ed. by Randy E. Bennett & Charles A. Maher. LC 84-10784. (Special Services in the Schools Ser.: Vol. 1, No. 1). 113p. (C). 1984. text 39.95 (*0-86656-297-4*); pap. text 19.95 (*0-86656-440-3*) Haworth Pr.

Microcomputers & Information Technology. 10th ed. Susan K. Baumann & Meredith Flynn. 400p. 1996. mass mkt. 41.00 (*0-314-04945-2*); mass mkt. 46.25 (*0-314-04944-4*) West Pub.

Microcomputers & Laboratory Instrumentation. 2nd ed. D. J. Malcolme-Lawes. LC 88-5794. (Illus.). 284p. (C). 1988. text 55.00 (*0-306-42903-9*, Kluwer Plenum) Kluwer Academic.

Microcomputers & Libraries: A Bibliographic Sourcebook. Thomas L. Kilpatrick. LC 86-31341. xii, 726p. 1987. 52.00 (*0-8108-1977-5*) Scarecrow.

Microcomputers & Libraries: A Bibliographic Sourcebook, 1986-1989. Thomas L. Kilpatrick. 1100p. 1990. 94.00 (*0-8108-2392-6*) Scarecrow.

Microcomputers & Libraries: An Annotated Bibliography. Julia J. Bewsey. (CompuBibs Ser.: No. 8). 63p. 1985. pap. 15.00 (*0-914791-07-9*) Vantage Info.

Microcomputers & Local Government: A Handbook (Instructor's Manual) Donald F. Norris. (Illus.). 174p. (Orig.). 1984. pap. 12.50 (*1-55719-012-7*) U NE CPAR.

Microcomputers & Local Government: A Handbook (Participant's Manual) Donald F. Norris. 108p. (Orig.). 1984. pap. 8.00 (*1-55719-028-3*) U NE CPAR.

Microcomputers & Mathematics. J. W. Bruce et al. (Illus.). 441p. (C). 1990. pap. text 44.95 (*0-521-31238-8*) Cambridge U Pr.

Microcomputers & Microprocessors. 3rd ed. John E. Uffenbeck. LC 98-50972. (Illus.). 729p. 1999. 101.00 (*0-13-209198-4*) P-H.

Microcomputers & Music. Gary E. Wittlich et al. 320p. 1986. text 43.00 (*0-13-580515-5*) P-H.

Microcomputers & Physiological Simulation. James E. Randall. 1980. pap. write for info. (*0-201-06128-7*) Addison-Wesley.

Microcomputers & Physiological Simulation. James E. Randall. LC 86-26275. 303p. 1987. reprint ed. pap. 94.00 (*0-608-03438-X*, 206413900008) Bks Demand.

Microcomputers & Their Applications: Proceedings ISMM Symposium, Cairo, Egypt, March 3-5, 1987. Ed. by M. H. Hamza. 111p. 1987. 51.00 (*0-88986-112-9*, 122) Acta Pr.

Microcomputers As Decision Aids in Law Practice. Stuart S. Nagel. LC 86-16873. 394p. 1987. 79.50 (*0-89930-197-5*, NLU/, Quorum Bks) Greenwood.

Microcomputers, Corporate Planning, & Decision Support Systems. Ed. by WEFA Group Staff et al. LC 88-6011. 269p. 1988. 72.95 (*0-89930-164-9*, BMP/, Quorum Bks) Greenwood.

Microcomputers Directory: Applications in Educational Settings. 1983. write for info. (*0-318-57973-1*) HUP.

Microcomputers for Building Surveyors. Stephen Mika. (C). 1986. text 50.00 (*0-85406-309-9*, Pub. by Surveyors Pubns) St Mut.

Microcomputers for Library Decision Making: Issues, Trends & Applications. Ed. by Peter Hernon & Charles R. McClure. LC 86-1043. 320p. 1986. text 73.25 (*0-89391-376-6*) Ablx Pub.

Microcomputers in Adult Education. Ed. by Stephen J. Bostock & Roger V. Seifert. 176p. 1986. 37.50 (*0-7099-3944-2*, Pub. by C Helm) Routldge.

Microcomputers in Art Education. Ed. by Virginia M. Brouch. 48p. (C). 1988. pap. 7.00 (*0-937652-39-3*) Natl Art Ed.

Microcomputers in Biochemical Education: Proceedings of the FEBS Meeting, Brussels, July 1983. Ed. by E. J. Wood. 220p. 1984. pap. 44.95 (*0-85066-289-3*) Taylor & Francis.

Microcomputers in Business. Greenwood. (Management Information Systems Ser.). 1994. pap. 38.95 (*0-534-92264-3*) S-W Pub.

Microcomputers in Business Education. Jeffrey R. Stewart et al. (Rapid Reader Ser.: No. 7). (Illus.). 28p. (C). 1985. pap. text 8.00 (*0-9603064-7-1*) Delta Pi Epsilon.

Microcomputers in Canada: A Strategic Entry Report, 1998. Compiled by Icon Group International Staff. (Country Industry Report). (Illus.). 135p. 1999. ring bd. 1350.00 incl. audio compact disk (*0-7418-0152-3*) Icon Grp.

Microcomputers in Civil Engineering. Trevor Bell & Roger Plank. LC 84-17053. (Illus.). 164p. reprint ed. pap. 50.90 (*0-8357-2988-5*, 203925100011) Bks Demand.

Microcomputers in Education: Papers of the Online Conference, Mersey Micro Shoe, 1980. 55p. 1980. pap. 23.00 (*0-685-42718-8*) Taylor & Francis.

Microcomputers in Emergency Management: Implementation of Computer Technology. Thomas E. Drabek. (Monograph: No. 51). 224p. 1991. pap. 20.00 (*1-877943-06-1*) Natural Hazards.

Microcomputers in Engineering & Science. J. F. Craine & G. R. Martin. (C). 1985. pap. text 34.50 (*0-201-14217-1*) Addison-Wesley.

Microcomputers in Engineering Applications. Ed. by B. A. Schrefler & R. W. B. Lewis. LC 86-5585. (Wiley Series in Numerical Methods in Engineering). (Illus.). 343p. 1987. reprint ed. pap. 106.40 (*0-608-05311-2*, 206584900001) Bks Demand.

Microcomputers in Environmental Biology. J. N. Jeffers. 344p. (C). 1992. 68.00 (*1-85070-293-4*) Prthnon Pub.

Microcomputers in France: A Strategic Entry Report, 1996. Compiled by Icon Group International Staff. (Illus.). 131p. 1999. ring bd. 1310.00 incl. audio compact disk (*0-7418-1125-1*) Icon Grp.

Microcomputers in Geometry. Adrian J. Oldknow. LC 86-27874. (Mathematics & Its Applications Ser.). 21p. 1987. text 78.95 (*0-470-20805-8*) P-H.

Microcomputers in Geometry. Adrian J. Oldknow. LC 86-27874. (Mathematics & Its Applications Ser.). 21p. 1987. pap. text 31.95 (*0-470-20814-7*) P-H.

Microcomputers in Health Care Management: Strategies & Applications for the 1990's. 2nd ed. William W. Christensen & Eugene I. Stearns. LC 90-271. 256p. 1990. 69.00 (*0-8342-0152-6*) Aspen Pub.

Microcomputers in Library & Information Services: An Annotated Bibliography. Paul Burton. 126p. 1986. text 49.95 (*0-566-03540-5*, Pub. by Gower) Ashgate Pub Co.

Microcomputers in Numerical Analysis. G. R. Indfield & J. E. Penny. 1989. text 69.95 (*0-470-21415-5*) P-H.

Microcomputers in Numerical Analysis. G. R. Lindfield & J. E. Penny. LC 93-23169. (Mathematics & Its Applications Ser.: Statistics, Operational Research, & Computational Mathematics Section). 1993. 23.95 (*0-13-336744-4*, Pub. by Tavistock-E Horwood) Routldge.

Microcomputers in Property: A Surveyor's Guide to Lotus 1-2-3 & dBASE IV. T. J. Dixon et al. (Illus.). 319p. (C). 1991. pap. 45.00 (*0-419-15260-1*, E & FN Spon) Routledge.

Microcomputers in Public Works. rev. ed. American Public Works Association Staff. (Special Reports: No. 53). 600p. 1987. ring bd. 75.00 (*0-917084-54-3*) Am Public Works.

Microcomputers in Small Business Management. Betty Heath & William G. Camp. 92p. 1984. 6.50 (*0-318-22153-5*, LT64) Ctr Educ Trng Employ.

Microcomputers in Transportation. 1986. lib. bdg. 79.95 (*0-8490-3767-0*) Gordon Pr.

Microcomputers in Transportation: Proceedings of the Fourth International Conference on Microcomputers in Transportation, Baltimore, MD., July 22-24, 1992. International Conference on Microcomputers in Tran. Ed. by John Chow. LC 93-184. 872p. 1993. 75.00 (*0-87262-875-2*) Am Soc Civil Eng.

Microcomputers in Urban Planning & Management. Richard K. Brail. LC 86-31767. 351p. 1987. 1.00 (*0-88285-121-7*) Ctr Urban Pol Res.

M

Microcomputers in Vocational Education: A Decision Guide. Gale L. Zahniser et al. 70p. 1983. 8.75 (*0-318-22155-1*, RD239A) Ctr Educ Trng Employ.

Microcomputers in Vocational Education: Programs & Practices. Judith Rodenstein. (Illus.). 224p. 1986. pap. text 25.00 (*0-13-580507-4*) P-H.

Microcomputers on the Farm: Getting Started. 2nd ed. Duane E. Erickson et al. LC 90-36492. (Illus.). 107p. (Orig.). 1990. reprint ed. pap. 33.20 (*0-608-06883-7*, 206709100009) Bks Demand.

Microcomputers Today. Steven L. Mandell. LC 95-31207. 260p. (C). 1996. mass mkt. 40.95 (*0-314-04624-0*) West Pub.

Microcomputing. Heath Company Staff. (Illus.). 416p. ring bd. 44.95 incl. audio (*0-87119-082-6*, EC-1000) Heathkit-Zenith Ed.

Microcomputing Accounting: Tutorial & Applications with Peachtree for DOS. Greg Anders et al. 1994. teacher ed. 79.76 incl. disk (*0-02-801067-1*) Glencoe.

Microcomputing Accounting: Tutorial & Applications with Peachtree for Windows. Gregory E. Anders et al. 1996. teacher ed. 75.52 incl. disk (*0-02-802251-3*) Glencoe.

Microcomputing & Qualitative Data Analysis. Anna Weaver & Paul Atkinson. LC 94-26910. (Cardiff Papers in Qualitative Research). 184p. 1994. 61.95 (*1-85628-576-6*, Pub. by Avebry) Ashgate Pub Co.

Microcomputing Dictionary Spanish-English-French. V. Mesters. (ENG, FRE & SPA.). 547p. 1996. pap. 50.00 (*84-283-2328-3*, Pub. by Paraninfo) IBD Ltd.

Microcomputing Dictionary, Spanish-English-French. V. Mesters. (ENG, FRE & SPA.). 1996. 50.00 (*0-7859-9688-5*) Fr & Eur.

Microcomputing Labs: Edition C, DOS 3.3 - 6.0, WordPerfect 6.0 for DOS, Lotus 1-2-3, Release 2.4, dBASE IV, Version 2.0. Timothy J. O'Leary & Linda I. O'Leary. (C). 1994. pap. text 33.00 (*0-07-048982-3*) McGraw.

Microcomputing Today! with DOS 5.0. Fritz J. Erickson & John A. Vonk. LC 92-44586. 1993. write for info. (*0-87709-196-X*) Course Tech.

Microcomputing Today! with Lotus 1-2-3 2.3. Fritz Erickson & John A. Vonk. 1993. spiral bd. write for info. (*0-318-69949-4*) Course Tech.

Microcomputing Today! with Quattro Pro for Windows. Erickson & John A. Vonk. 224p. 1993. pap. 19.00 (*0-87709-240-0*) Course Tech.

Microcomputing Today! with WordPerfect 5.1 for Windows. Erickson & John A. Vonk. 224p. 1993. pap. 19.00 (*0-87709-242-7*) Course Tech.

Microcontamination. TEEX Staff. (Illus.). xiii, 132p. 1998. student ed., spiral bd. 185.00 incl. cd-rom (*1-58257-025-6*); spiral bd. 59.95 (*1-58257-024-8*) TX Eng Extsn Servs.

Microcontinuum Field Theories: Foundations & Solids. A. C. Eringen. LC 98-30560. 360p. 1999. 84.50 (*0-387-98620-0*) Spr-Verlag.

***Microcontinuum Field Theories II: Fluent Media.** A. Cemal Eringen. (Illus.). 320p. 2000. 89.00 (*0-387-98969-2*) Spr-Verlag.

Microcontroller Beginner's Handbook. 2nd ed. Lawrence Duarte. (Illus.). 272p. 1998. pap. 29.95 (*0-7906-1153-8*) Prompt Publns.

Microcontroller Cookbook. Mike James. LC 97-182223. (Illus.). 208p. 1997. pap. text 39.95 (*0-7506-2701-8*) Buttrwrth-Heinemann.

***Microcontroller Cookbook.** Mike James. (Illus.). 288p. 2000. pap. 37.95 (*0-7506-4832-5*, Newnes) Buttrwrth-Heinemann.

Microcontroller 80251. Kenneth J. Ayala. LC 99-20362. (Illus.). 374p. (Orig.). 1999. pap. 97.00 incl. audio compact disk (*0-13-907551-8*) P-H.

Microcontroller Idea Book: Circuits, Programs & Applications Featuring the 8052-Basic Single-Chip Computer. Jan Axelson. (Illus.). 277p. (Orig.). 1997. pap. 31.95 (*0-9650819-0-7*) Lakeview Res.

***Microcontroller Projects in C for the 8051.** Dogan Ibrahim. 192p. 2000. pap. 39.95 (*0-7506-4640-3*, Newnes) Buttrwrth-Heinemann.

Microcontroller Projects with Basic Stamps. Al Williams. 432p. 1999. pap. 44.95 incl. cd-rom (*0-87930-587-8*, Pub. by C M P Books) Publishers Group.

Microcontroller, 68HC11. Joseph D. Greenfield. 420p. (C). 1992. text 82.00 (*0-03-051588-2*, Pub. by SCP) Harcourt.

Microcontroller 68Hc11: Applications in Control, Instrumentation & Communication. Michael R. Kheir. LC 96-36941. 399p. (C). 1996. 72.80 (*0-13-205550-3*, Prentice Hall) P-H.

Microcontroller Technology, the 68HC11. 3rd ed. Peter Spasov. LC 98-5480. 690p. (C). 1998. 106.00 (*0-13-901240-0*) P-H.

Microcontrollers: A Practical Approach to Embedded Control. William H. Rigby & Terry L. Dalby. (C). 2001. 62.00 (*0-13-190232-6*, Macmillan Coll) P-H.

Microcontrollers: Design, Application, & Programming. Kenneth J. Hintz. (Illus.). 483p. 1991. 58.00 (*0-07-028977-8*) McGraw.

Microcontrollers & Microcomputers: Principles of Software & Hardware Engineering. Frederick M. Cady. LC 96-23410. (Illus.). 272p. (C). 1997. text 49.95 (*0-19-511008-0*) OUP.

Microcosm. Nathaniel Tarn. 1977. pap. 3.00 (*0-87924-038-5*) Membrane Pr.

Microcosm. William H. Pyne. LC 68-56512. (Illus.). 1972. reprint ed. 27.95 (*0-405-08872-8*, Pub. by Blom Pubns) Ayer.

Microcosm & Mediator: The Theological Anthropology of Maximus the Confessor. Lars Thunberg. LC 80-2368. 1981. reprint ed. 58.00 (*0-404-18917-2*) AMS Pr.

***Microcosm for Windows, Version 3.0, User's Guide: An Energy Sector Simulation of a Developing Country.** 3rd unabridged ed. David J. Edelman. (Illus.). 100p. (C). 1999. pap. 50.00 incl. cd-rom (*0-9675582-0-4*) Univ of Cin Schl Plan.

Microcosm of Events: Inside California State Bureaucracy. Harold E. Simmons. 1978. pap. 5.00 (*0-87312-009-4*) Gen Welfare Pubns.

Microcosm of the Platte: A Guide to Bader Memorial Park Natural Area. Prairie-Plains Resource Institute Staff & William S. Whitney. Ed. by Jan Whitney & Curt Twedt. (Illus.). 140p. (Orig.). (YA). (gr. 10-12). 1988. pap. text 10.00 (*0-945614-00-4*) Prairie Plains Res Inst.

***Microcosmic God: The Complete Stories of Theodore Sturgeon, Vol. 11.** Theodore Sturgeon. Ed. by Paul Williams. 400p. 1999. pap. text 18.95 (*1-55643-301-8*) North Atlantic.

Microcosmic Tales: One Hundred Wondrous Science Fiction Short-Short Stories. Selected by Isaac Asimov et al. 320p. 1992. 4.99 (*0-88677-532-9*, Pub. by DAW Bks) Penguin Putnam.

Microcosmographia Academica. F. M. Cornford. 32p. 1979. pap. 6.00 (*0-89005-318-9*) Ares.

Microcosmographie, 1628. John Earle. Ed. by Edward Arber. 125p. 1968. reprint ed. pap. 15.00 (*0-87556-083-0*) Saifer.

Microcosmography: Or, a Piece of the World Discovered in Essays & Characters. John Earle. LC 71-16968. 178p. 1933. reprint ed. 29.00 (*0-403-01325-9*) Scholarly.

Microcosmos: A Curriculum Guide to Exploring Microbial Space. Boston University Staff. 480p. 1995. boxed set 36.95 (*0-8403-8386-X*) Kendall-Hunt.

Microcosmos: Four Billion Years of Evolution from Our Microbial Ancestors. Lynn Margulis & Dorion Sagan. LC 96-49685. 304p. 1997. pap. 13.95 (*0-520-21064-6*, Pub. by U CA Pr) Cal Prin Full Svc.

Microcosmos: The Invisible World of Insects. Claude Nurissany et al. (Illus.). 160p. 1997. 35.00 (*1-55670-555-7*) Stewart Tabori & Chang.

***Microcosmos Vol. 1: Sex & Reproduction.** Lynn Margulis. (Illus.). 64p. (C). 2000. pap. text 150.00 (*0-7637-1233-7*) Jones & Bartlett.

***Microcosmos Vol. 2: Evolution & Diversity.** Lynn Margulis. (Illus.). 64p. (C). 2000. pap. text 150.00 (*0-7637-1234-5*) Jones & Bartlett.

Microcosmos Coloring Book. Lynn Margulis & Dorion Sagan. (HBJ-Boston Bk.). 160p. 1988. pap. 14.95 (*0-15-659430-7*) Harcourt.

Microcosmos Curriculum Guide to Exploring Microbial Space. Microcosmos-B. U. Staff. 480p. 1994. boxed set 44.95 (*0-8403-8515-3*) Kendall-Hunt.

***Microcosms.** Claudio Magris. 2000. 25.00 (*1-86046-787-3*) Harvill Press.

Microcosms in Ecological Research: Proceedings. Ed. by John P. Giesy. LC 80-23472. (DOE Symposium Ser.). 1139p. 1980. pap. 36.50 (*0-685-01479-7*, CONF-781101); fiche 9.00 (*0-87079-454-X*, CONF-781101) DOE.

Microcosmus, An Essay Concerning Man & His Relation to the World, 2 vols, Set. Rudolf Hermann Lotze. Tr. by Elizabeth Hamilton & E. E. Jones. LC 76-169769. (Select Bibliographies Reprint Ser.). 1977. reprint ed. 84.95 (*0-8369-5989-2*) Ayer.

Microcosmus: or A Little Description of the Great World. Peter Heylyn. LC 74-28863. (English Experience Ser.: No. 743). 1975. reprint ed. 45.00 (*90-221-0743-4*) Walter J Johnson.

Microcounseling: Innovations in Interviewing, Counseling, Psychotherapy & Psychoeducation. 2nd ed. Allen E. Ivey & Jerry Authier. (Illus.). 624p. 1978. pap. 62.95 (*0-398-06175-0*); text 91.95 (*0-398-03712-4*) C C Thomas.

Microcrystalline & Nanocrystalline Semiconductors. Ed. by Robert W. Collins et al. (MRS Symposium Proceedings Ser.: Vol. 358). 1059p. 1995. 88.00 (*1-55899-259-6*) Materials Res.

Microcrystalline & Nanocrystalline Semiconductors--1998, Vol. 536. Ed. by Leigh T. Canham et al. LC 99-18521. (Symposium Proceedings Ser.). 569p. 1999. 83.00 (*1-55899-442-4*) Materials Res.

Microcrystalline Semiconductors: Materials Science & Devices. Ed. by Y. Aoyagi et al. (Materials Research Society Symposium Proceedings Ser.: Vol. 283). 951p. 1993. text 79.00 (*1-55899-178-6*) Materials Res.

Microcystic Aeruginosa - Removal by Dissolved Air Flotation (DAF) Options for Enhanced Process Operation & Kinetic Modelling. Aleksander Vlaski. (IHE-Thesis Ser.: Vol. 11). (Illus.). 270p. (C). 1998. pap. text 42.00 (*90-5410-410-4*, Pub. by A A Balkema) Ashgate Pub Co.

Microdialysis in the Neurosciences. T. E. Robinson & J. B. Justice, Jr. (Techniques in the Behavioral & Neural Sciences Ser.: Vol. 7). 450p. 1991. 203.25 (*0-444-81194-X*); pap. 89.00 (*0-444-89375-X*) Elsevier.

Microdifferential Systems in the Complex Domain. P. Schapira. (Grundlehren der Mathematischen Wissenschaften Ser.: Band 269). 240p. 1985. 107.95 (*0-387-13672-X*) Spr-Verlag.

Microdisk Drives vs. Flash Memory Cards: World Technology Battle over Form, Function, Power, Capacity, Price & Access. Market Intelligence Staff. 259p. (Orig.). 1992. 1695.00 (*1-56753-056-7*) Frost & Sullivan.

Microdistribution of Foraminifera in a Single Bed of the Monterey Formation, Monterey County, California. Roberta K. Smith & Martin A. Buzas. LC 85-600357. (Smithsonian Contributions to Paleobiology Ser.: No. 60). 37p. reprint ed. pap. 30.00 (*0-608-15308-7*, 202955000061) Bks Demand.

Microdomains in Polymer Solutions. Ed. by Paul Dubin. LC 85-24246. (Polymer Science & Technology Ser.: Vol. 30). 472p. 1986. 105.00 (*0-306-42110-0*, Plenum Trade) Perseus Pubng.

Microdosimetry, No. 36. International Commission on Radiation Units & Meas. LC 83-22817. 117p. 1983. pap. text 60.00 (*0-913394-30-0*) Intl Comm Rad Meas.

Microdosimetry: An Interdisciplinary Approach. Ed. by P. O'Neill et al. 450p. 1997. 180.00 (*0-85404-737-9*) Am Chemical.

Microdosimetry & Its Applications. H. H. Rossi. (Illus.). 352p. 1995. 53.95 (*3-540-58541-9*) Spr-Verlag.

Microdosimetry, 7th Symposium. Ed. by H. G. Ebert & J. Booz. (Commission of the European Communities Ser.). xx, 1588p. 1981. text 932.00 (*3-7186-0049-8*) Gordon & Breach.

Microdot, History & Application. William White. Ed. by Jim Phillips. (Illus.). 156p. 1993. 49.95 (*0-932572-19-7*) Phillips Pubns.

Microecology: Social Situations & Intimate Space. Donald W. Ball. LC 72-10541. (Studies in Sociology). 40p. (C). 1973. pap. text. write for info. (*0-672-61209-7*, Bobbs) Macmillan.

Microecology: Social Situations & Intimate Space. Donald W. Ball. reprint ed. pap. text 7.95 (*0-8290-0328-2*) Irvington.

Microeconomics Interactive SoftWare Supplement. Felder. (C). 1998. pap. text. write for info. (*0-201-83434-0*) Addison-Wesley.

***Microecon: Principles & Policy.** 8th ed. Baumol. (C). 1999. pap. text 47.00 (*0-03-026847-8*, Pub. by Harcourt Coll Pubs) Harcourt.

Microeconmics: Drill & Review. 2nd ed. Colander. 1996. 47.74 (*0-256-22871-X*) McGraw.

Microeconomia. Michael L. Katz. (SPA.). (C). 1994. pap. text. write for info. (*0-201-60128-1*) Addison-Wesley.

Microeconomia. 2nd ed. 704p. (C). 1995. pap. 26.66 (*0-201-62584-9*) HEPC Inc.

Microeconomic Analysis. 3rd ed. Hal R. Varian. (Illus.). (C). 1992. text 59.75 (*0-393-95735-7*) Norton.

Microeconomic Analysis. 3rd ed. Hal R. Varian. (Illus.). (C). 1993. pap. text 23.75 (*0-393-95737-3*) Norton.

Microeconomic Analysis of Southern African Agriculture. William R. Duggan. LC 85-12191. 271p. 1985. 59.95 (*0-275-90203-X*, C0203, Praeger Pubs) Greenwood.

Microeconomic Concepts for Attorneys: A Reference Guide. Wayne C. Curtis. LC 83-23051. 153p. 1984. 45.00 (*0-89930-060-X*, CMC/, Quorum Bks) Greenwood.

Microeconomic Contributions to Strategic Management. J. Thepot & R. A. Thietart. (Advanced Series in Management: Vol. 16). 244p. 1991. 101.25 (*0-444-89082-3*, Pergamon Pr) Elsevier.

Microeconomic, Decisions Optimal dans L'enterprise et dans la Nation see Microeconomics: Optimal Decision Making by Private Firms & Public Authorities

Microeconomic Foundations of Employment & Inflation Theory. Ed. by Edmund S. Phelps. (C). 1973. pap. text 21.00 (*0-393-09326-3*) Norton.

Microeconomic Fundamentals for Managerial Economics. Martin L. Primack et al. 574p. (C). 1994. pap. text 44.89 (*1-56226-182-7*) CAT Pub.

Microeconomic Horizons. Martin L. Primack et al. 452p. 1998. pap. text 48.60 (*1-56226-413-3*) CAT Pub.

Microeconomic Issues of Labor Markets in Developing Countries: Analysis & Policy Implications. Dipak Mazumdar. (EDI Seminar Ser.: No. 40). 128p. 1989. pap. 22.00 (*0-8213-1183-2*, 11183) World Bank.

Microeconomic Issues Today: Alternative Approaches. 5th ed. Robert B. Carson. 207p. (C). 1990. teacher ed. write for info. (*0-318-68119-6*) St Martin.

Microeconomic Issues Today: Alternative Approaches. 6th ed. Robert B. Carson et al. LC 98-29533. 200p. (C). (gr. 13). 1999. pap. text 23.95 (*0-7656-0364-0*) M E Sharpe.

Microeconomic Models of Housing Markets. K. Stahl. (Lecture Notes in Economics & Mathematical Systems Ser.: Vol. 239). vii, 197p. 1985. 36.00 (*0-387-15193-1*) Spr-Verlag.

***Microeconomic Policy.** S. I. Cohen. LC 00-30607. 2000. pap. write for info. (*0-415-23601-0*) Routledge.

Microeconomic Predicates to Law & Economics. Mark Seidenfeld. LC 96-227501. 100p. (C). 1996. pap. 19.95 (*0-87084-804-6*) Anderson Pub Co.

Microeconomic Principles & Policy. 6th ed. Ryan C. Amacher & Holley H. Ulbrich. LC 94-17223. (C). 1994. mass mkt. 72.95 (*0-538-83850-7*) S-W Pub.

Microeconomic Roots of the Farm Crisis. James Lowenberg-DeBoer. LC 86-21202. 185p. 1986. 57.95 (*0-275-92226-X*, C2226, Praeger Pubs) Greenwood.

Microeconomic Theories of Imperfect Competition: Old Problems & New Perspectives. Ed. by Jean J. Gabszewicz & Jacques-Francois Thisse. LC 98-46608. 848p. 1999. 295.00 (*1-85898-146-8*) E Elgar.

Microeconomic Theory. Ed. by Geoffrey Alexander Jehle. LC 97-25251. 497p. (C). 1997. 98.00 (*0-321-01436-7*) Addson-Wesley Educ.

Microeconomic Theory. David G. Luenberger. 496p. (C). 1994. 65.31 (*0-07-049313-8*) McGraw.

Microeconomic Theory. Andrea Mas-Colell. 1008p. 1995. pap., teacher ed. 34.00 (*0-19-510268-1*) OUP.

Microeconomic Theory. Andreu Mas-Colell et al. (Illus.). 1008p. 1995. text 72.95 (*0-19-507340-1*) OUP.

Microeconomic Theory. Y. Otani & M. A. El-Hodiri. (Illus.). 310p. 1987. 47.95 (*0-387-17994-1*) Spr-Verlag.

Microeconomic Theory. Larry A. Samuelson. 1986. lib. bdg. 92.00 (*0-89838-170-3*) Kluwer Academic.

Microeconomic Theory. 7th ed. Nicholson. (C). 1997. pap. text, teacher ed. write for info. (*0-03-024696-2*) Harcourt Coll Pubs.

Microeconomic Theory. 7th ed. Nicholson. (C). 1997. pap. text, student ed. 31.00 (*0-03-024697-0*, Pub. by Harcourt Coll Pubs) Harcourt.

Microeconomic Theory. 7th ed. Walter Nicholson. LC 97-67941. (C). 1997. text 88.50 (*0-03-024474-9*, Pub. by Harcourt Coll Pubs) Harcourt.

Microeconomic Theory, Test bank. 6th ed. Walter Nicholson. 296p. (C). 1995. teacher ed. write for info. (*0-03-007557-2*) Dryden Pr.

Microeconomic Theory: An Introduction. Stefano Zamagni. (Modern Revivals in Economics Ser.). 550p. (C). 1994. text 79.95 (*0-7512-0261-4*, Pub. by Gregg Revivals) Ashgate Pub Co.

Microeconomic Theory: Applied Approach. Mulligan. (C). 1994. pap., student ed. 13.50 (*0-205-12273-6*, Macmillan Coll) P-H.

Microeconomic Theory: Applied Approach. James G. Mulligan. (C). 1999. 52.00 (*0-205-12276-0*, Macmillan Coll) P-H.

Microeconomic Theory: Solution Manual. Chiaka Hara et al. 736p. (C). 1996. pap. text. write for info. (*0-19-510798-5*) OUP.

Microeconomic Theory & Applications. 6th ed. Edgar K. Browning & Mark A. Zupan. LC 97-47610. (C). 1999. text 78.75 (*0-321-00933-9*) Addison-Wesley.

***Microeconomic Theory & Applications Study Guide.** 6th ed. Edgar K. Browning. 384p. 1999. pap. 31.95 (*0-471-36443-6*) Wiley.

Microeconomic Theory & Applications/Microeconomic Cases & Applications. 4th ed. Edgar K. Browning. 1992. 87.00 (*0-673-52264-4*) Addison-Wesley.

Microeconomics. (C). 1992. text. write for info. (*0-201-54427-X*) Addison-Wesley.

***Microeconomics.** (C). 1999. text. write for info. (*0-201-70340-8*) Addison-Wesley.

Microeconomics. (Quick Study Academic Ser.). 4p. pap. 3.95 (*1-57222-088-0*) Barcharts.

Microeconomics. (C). 1985. pap. write for info. (*0-15-601585-4*) Harcourt Coll Pubs.

Microeconomics. 152p. (C). 1996. text, student ed. 12.60 (*0-536-59782-0*) Pearson Custom.

***Microeconomics.** (C). 2002. pap. text 0.00 (*0-201-65877-1*) HEPC Inc.

Microeconomics, 2 vols. Boyes. (C). Date not set. text, teacher ed., suppl. ed. 54.76 (*0-395-69065-X*) HM.

Microeconomics, 2 vols. Boyes. (C). 1993. pap., student ed. 16.76 (*0-395-67545-6*) HM.

Microeconomics, 3 vols. Boyes. (C). 1996. pap., teacher ed., suppl. ed. 54.76 (*0-395-74659-0*) HM.

Microeconomics. Bradley. (C). 1990. text 48.00 (*0-06-040902-9*) HarperTrade.

Microeconomics. Ralph T. Byrns & Gerald W. Stone, Jr. (C). 1997. text 48.33 (*0-673-46561-6*) Addson-Wesley Educ.

Microeconomics. David Colander. 344p. (C). 1993. text, student ed. 21.25 (*0-256-12690-9*, Irwn McGrw-H) McGrw-H Hghr Educ.

Microeconomics. Dillingham. Date not set. pap. text. write for info. (*0-314-61511-3*) West Pub.

***Microeconomics.** Ekelund. 1999. pap. text, student ed. 25.00 (*0-201-68030-0*) Addison-Wesley.

Microeconomics. Ferguson. (C). 1997. pap. text 28.50 (*0-15-504372-2*) Harcourt Coll Pubs.

Microeconomics. Paul R. Gregory & Roy J. Ruffin. (C). 1997. 51.00 (*0-673-99044-3*) Addson-Wesley Educ.

Microeconomics. Grinols. LC 93-78635. (C). 1993. text 84.76 (*0-395-53998-6*) HM.

Microeconomics. Grinols. (C). 1994. pap. text, student ed. 23.56 (*0-395-53999-4*) HM.

Microeconomics. Earl L. Grinols. (C). 1994. text, teacher ed. 7.96 (*0-395-68249-5*) HM.

Microeconomics. Ed. by Jehle. (C). 1998. text. write for info. (*0-321-01075-2*) Addson-Wesley Educ.

Microeconomics. J. Bruce Lindeman. LC 91-35214. (Barron's EZ-101 Study Keys Ser.). 144p. 1992. pap. 6.95 (*0-8120-4601-3*) Barron.

Microeconomics. Richard G. Lipsey. (C). 1993. pap. 51.33 (*0-06-501024-8*); pap., student ed. 26.00 (*0-06-501095-7*) Addson-Wesley Educ.

Microeconomics. Osullivan & Sheffrin. 1997. pap. text, student ed. 21.33 (*0-13-855602-4*) P-H.

Microeconomics. Jack Rudman. (Advanced Placement (AP) Test Ser.: No. AP-5). Date not set. pap. 23.95 (*0-8373-6205-9*) Nat Learn.

Microeconomics. Roy J. Ruffin & Paul R. Gregory. (C). 1997. student ed. 26.00 (*0-673-46585-3*) Addson-Wesley Educ.

Microeconomics. Robert L. Sexton. 656p. 1995. text 90.00 (*0-13-103672-6*) P-H.

Microeconomics. Taylor. (C). Date not set. pap., teacher ed., suppl. ed. 53.16 (*0-395-71686-1*) HM.

Microeconomics. Taylor. (C). 1995. pap. text, student ed. 17.56 (*0-395-72200-4*) HM.

Microeconomics. Thaler. (Case; Hb - Economics Ser.). 1997. mass mkt. 4.95 (*0-538-85802-8*) S-W Pub.

Microeconomics. Tim Tregarthen. 495p. 1995. pap. text 41.80 (*1-57259-094-7*) Worth.

Microeconomics. Tim Tregarthen. 192p. 1996. pap. text, student ed. 13.20 (*1-57259-044-0*) Worth.

Microeconomics. Irwin B. Tucker. LC 96-20561. 1997. 43.00 (*0-314-09243-9*) West Pub.

Microeconomics. Weiler. (C). 1990. pap. 18.00 (*0-06-047003-8*, Perennial) HarperTrade.

Microeconomics, 2 vols. 2nd ed. Boyes. (C). 1993. pap. text 54.76 (*0-395-67543-X*) HM.

Microeconomics. 2nd ed. David C. Colander. LC 94-32399. (Series in Economics). 1994. teacher ed. write for info. (*0-256-16821-0*, Irwn McGrw-H) McGrw-H Hghr Educ.

Microeconomics. 2nd ed. David C. Colander. LC 94-32399. (Series in Economics). 560p. (C). 1994. text 46.75 (*0-256-13825-7*, Irwn McGrw-H) McGrw-H Hghr Educ.

An Asterisk (*) at the beginning of an entry indicates that the title is appearing for the first time.

Microeconomics. 2nd ed. B. C. Eaton. (C). 1991. pap. text 25.60 (*0-7167-2168-6*) W H Freeman.

Microeconomics. 2nd ed. B. C. Eaton. (C). 1991. teacher ed. 16.00 (*0-7167-2183-X*) W H Freeman.

Microeconomics. 2nd ed. Hugh Gravelle & Rees. 1992. pap. text. write for info. (*0-582-02386-6*, Pub. by Addison-Wesley) Longman.

Microeconomics. 2nd ed. Gravelle & Rees. 1994. pap. text, wbk. ed. write for info. (*0-582-09800-9*, Pub. by Addison-Wesley) Longman.

Microeconomics. 2nd ed. David N. Hyman. 512p. (C). 1991. pap. text 39.95 (*0-256-09016-5*, 05-2951-02, Irwn McGrw-H) McGrw-H Hghr Educ.

Microeconomics. 2nd ed. Michael L. Katz & Harvey S. Rosen. LC 93-41425. (Economics Ser.). (C). 1993. text 71.75 (*0-256-11171-5*, Irwn McGrw-H) McGrw-H Hghr Educ.

Microeconomics. 2nd ed. Mcconnell. 1998. 47.00 (*0-07-229580-5*) McGraw.

Microeconomics. 2nd ed. Michael Parkin. (C). 1992. pap. text, student ed. 20.00 (*0-201-54666-3*) Addison-Wesley.

Microeconomics. 2nd ed. Michael Parkin. LC 92-15487. (Illus.). 688p. (C). 1993. pap. text 40.95 (*0-201-54698-1*) Addison-Wesley.

Microeconomics. 2nd ed. Michael Parkin. 1994. student ed. write for info. (*0-201-87626-4*) Addison-Wesley.

Microeconomics. 2nd ed. Michael Parkin. LC 93-45830. 688p. (C). 1994. text 47.00 (*0-201-50032-9*) Addison-Wesley.

Microeconomics. 2nd ed. Michael Parkin. (C). 1995. pap. text 25.33 (*0-201-62877-5*) Addison-Wesley.

Microeconomics. 2nd ed. Paul Anthony Samuelson & William D. Nordhaus. (C). 1995. pap., student ed. 17.50 (*0-07-054999-0*) McGraw.

Microeconomics, 2 vols. 2nd ed. Taylor. (C). 1998. pap. text, student ed. 17.56 (*0-395-87456-4*) HM.

Microeconomics. 2nd ed. Allen R. Thompson. LC 87-910. (C). 1988. pap. text 26.00 (*0-201-09683-8*) Addison-Wesley.

Microeconomics. 2nd ed. Tregarthen. 1999. pap. text, student ed. 22.95 (*1-57259-886-7*) St Martin.

Microeconomics. 2nd ed. Tregarthen. write for info. (*1-57259-884-0*) Worth.

Microeconomics. 2nd ed. Tregarthen. LC 99-43479. 2000. write for info. (*1-57259-420-9*) Worth.

Microeconomics. 3rd ed. 390p. (C). 1996. text 39.00 (*0-536-58999-2*) Pearson Custom.

Microeconomics. 3rd ed. Roger A. Arnold. 570p. (C). 1996. mass mkt. 70.95 (*0-314-06969-0*) West Pub.

Microeconomics, 3 vols. 3rd ed. Boyes. (C). Date not set. pap. write for info. (*0-395-78145-0*) HM.

Microeconomics, 3 vols. 3rd ed. Boyes. (C). 1995. pap. text 29.16 (*0-395-74434-2*) HM.

Microeconomics, 3 vols. 3rd ed. Boyes. (C). 1995. pap. text, student ed. 16.76 (*0-395-74436-9*) HM.

Microeconomics. 3rd ed. Colander. 1997. pap. 20.31 (*0-07-109304-4*) McGraw.

Microeconomics. 3rd ed. David C. Colander. 560p. 1997. pap. 60.94 (*0-256-17273-0*) McGraw.

Microeconomics. 3rd ed. Heyne. 1994. pap. text, student ed. 23.00 (*0-02-354444-9*, Pub. by P-H) S&S Trade.

Microeconomics. 3rd ed. Paul Heyne. 448p. (C). 1994. pap. text 72.00 (*0-02-354441-4*, Macmillan Coll) P-H.

Microeconomics. 3rd ed. Michael Katz & Harvey S. Rosen. LC 96-40004. 672p. (C). 1997. per. 71.75 (*0-256-17176-9*, Irwn McGrw-H) McGrw-H Hghr Educ.

Microeconomics. 3rd ed. Machael Parkin. (C). 1996. pap. text. write for info. (*0-201-87427-X*) Addison-Wesley.

Microeconomics. 3rd ed. Michael Parkin. LC 95-697. 640p. (C). 1995. pap. text 70.00 (*0-201-60981-9*) Addison-Wesley.

Microeconomics. 3rd ed. Michael Parkin. (C). 1996. pap. text. write for info. (*0-201-88057-1*); pap. text, student ed. 66.56 (*0-201-87872-0*) Addison-Wesley.

Microeconomics. 3rd ed. Michael Parkin. (C). 1996. pap. text 43.00 (*0-201-30345-0*) Addison-Wesley.

Microeconomics. 3rd ed. Dominick Salvatore. LC 96-563. 736p. (C). 1997. 98.00 (*0-673-99993-9*) Addson-Wesley Educ.

Microeconomics. 3rd ed. Steven L. Slavin. LC 93-3735. 496p. (C). 1993. text 39.50 (*0-256-14181-9*, Irwn McGrw-H) McGrw-H Hghr Educ.

Microeconomics. 3rd ed. Lewis C. Solmon. LC 79-25515. 528p. 1980. text 16.75 (*0-201-07218-1*); pap. text, student ed. 4.75 (*0-201-07221-1*) Addison-Wesley.

Microeconomics. 3rd ed. Trieff. 1997. pap. 17.19 (*0-256-17274-9*) McGraw.

Microeconomics. 4th ed. (C). 1997. pap. text 67.00 (*0-201-35792-5*) Addison-Wesley.

Microeconomics. 4th ed. (C). 1997. text 67.00 (*0-201-35800-X*) Addison-Wesley.

***Microeconomics.** 4th ed. (C). 1998. text 67.00 (*0-201-35816-6*) Addison-Wesley.

Microeconomics. 4th ed. Roger A. Arnold. LC 97-37701. (HC - Intermediate Microeconomics Ser.). (C). 1997. pap. 67.95 (*0-538-88044-9*) S-W Pub.

Microeconomics. 4th ed. Roger A. Arnold. (HC - Intermediate Microeconomics Ser.). (C). 1997. mass mkt., student ed. 19.95 (*0-538-88050-3*) S-W Pub.

Microeconomics. 4th ed. Jon L. Boyes. LC 98-71996. 1998. pap. text 44.97 (*0-395-90807-8*) HM.

Microeconomics. 4th ed. Ed. by Byrns. (C). 1989. pap. text 17.66 (*0-673-38337-7*) Addson-Wesley Educ.

Microeconomics. 4th ed. Ralph T. Byrns & Gerald W. Stone. (C). 1989. text 40.00 (*0-673-38339-3*, Scott Frsmn) Addson-Wesley Educ.

Microeconomics. 4th ed. Colander. 2001. 47.74 (*0-07-231794-9*) McGraw.

Microeconomics. 4th ed. Robert B. Ekelund & Robert D. Tollison. 862p. (C). 1997. 72.00 (*0-673-52305-5*); pap. text, student ed. 27.00 (*0-673-52306-3*) Addson-Wesley Educ.

Microeconomics. 4th ed. David N. Hyman. LC 96-210615. 592p. (C). 1996. text 46.75 (*0-256-16175-5*, Irwn McGrw-H) McGrw-H Hghr Educ.

Microeconomics. 4th ed. Katz. 2001. 65.25 (*0-07-231858-9*) McGraw.

Microeconomics. 4th ed. Michael Parkin. (C). 1997. text, pap. text 69.00 incl. cd-rom (*0-201-33625-1*) Addison-Wesley.

Microeconomics. 4th ed. Michael Parkin. LC 97-11791. 544p. (C). 1997. pap. text 75.00 (*0-201-31690-0*) Addison-Wesley.

Microeconomics. 4th ed. Michael Parkin. 544p. (C). 1998. pap. text. write for info. (*0-201-32263-3*) Addison-Wesley.

Microeconomics. 4th ed. Pindyck. 1997. pap. text, student ed. 23.00 (*0-13-849472-X*) P-H.

Microeconomics. 4th ed. Robert S. Pindyck & Daniel L. Rubinfield. LC 97-6658. 726p. 1997. 91.33 (*0-13-272923-7*) P-H.

Microeconomics. 4th ed. Stephen L. Slavin. LC 95-39656. (Illus.). 496p. (C). 1995. text 39.50 (*0-256-17172-6*, Irwn McGrw-H) McGrw-H Hghr Educ.

***Microeconomics.** 5th ed. 448p. (C). 1999. pap. text 24.00 (*0-201-65713-9*) Addison-Wesley.

***Microeconomics.** 5th ed. 352p. (C). 1999. text 25.20 (*0-201-65711-2*) S&S Trade.

***Microeconomics.** 5th ed. 1p. (C). 1999. text 27.40 (*0-201-65725-2*) S&S Trade.

***Microeconomics.** 5th ed. Michael Parkin. 416p. (C). 1999. pap. text, student ed. 26.40 (*0-201-63786-3*) Addison-Wesley.

Microeconomics 5th ed. Michael Parkin. LC 98-55283. 576p. 1999. pap. 67.00 (*0-201-47385-2*) Addison-Wesley.

***Microeconomics.** 5th ed. Robert S. Pindyck & Daniel L. Rubinfeld. 704p. 2000. write for info. (*0-13-016583-2*) P-H.

Microeconomics. 5th ed. Stephen L. Slavin. LC 98-16407. 1998. 35.75 (*0-256-26329-9*, Irwn Prfssnl) McGraw-Hill Prof.

Microeconomics. 5th ed. Roger N. Waud. (C). 1997. pap. 55.00 (*0-06-500247-4*) Addson-Wesley Educ.

Microeconomics. 6th ed. Ralph T. Byrns & Gerald W. Stone. (C). 1997. pap. text, student ed. 31.00 (*0-673-99343-4*) Addson-Wesley Educ.

Microeconomics. 6th ed. Ralph T. Byrns & Gerald W. Stone. LC 95-129582. 505p. (C). 1997. pap. text 70.00 (*0-673-99328-0*) Addson-Wesley Educ.

Microeconomics. 6th ed. Slavin. 2001. 26.00 (*0-07-237410-1*) McGraw.

Microeconomics. 6th ed. Craig Swan. 378p. (C). 1994. pap. text, student ed. 32.00 (*0-03-098606-0*) Dryden Pr.

Microeconomics. 7th ed. Baumol. (C). 1997. pap. 66.50 (*0-03-023164-7*) Dryden Pr.

Microeconomics. 7th ed. Baumol. 1997. 256.00 (*0-03-011738-0*) Harcourt Coll Pubs.

Microeconomics. 7th ed. Baumol. (C). 1997. pap. text, student ed. 29.50 (*0-03-011734-8*, Pub. by Harcourt Coll Pubs) Harcourt.

Microeconomics. 7th ed. Byrns & Stone. (C). 1999. pap. text. write for info. (*0-321-03066-4*) Addson-Wesley Educ.

Microeconomics. 7th ed. Edwin G. Dolan & David E. Lindsey. LC 93-71250. 496p. (C). 1994. pap. text 51.00 (*0-03-097569-7*) Dryden Pr.

Microeconomics. 8th ed. Gwartne. 1997. pap. text 33.50 (*0-03-019293-5*, Pub. by Harcourt Coll Pubs) Harcourt.

Microeconomics. 8th ed. Gwartne. (C). 1997. pap. text, student ed. 28.00 (*0-03-019292-7*, Pub. by Harcourt Coll Pubs) Harcourt.

Microeconomics. 9th ed. Richard G. Lipsey et al. 540p. (C). 1990. pap. 38.66 (*0-06-044113-5*) Addson-Wesley Educ.

Microeconomics. 10th ed. Lipsey. 250p. (C). 2000. pap., student ed. 22.95 (*0-201-66470-4*) Addison-Wesley.

Microeconomics. 11th ed. Richard G. Lipsey & Paul N. Courant. LC 95-34895. (Illus.). 528p. (C). 1997. text 63.00 (*0-673-99477-5*) Addson-Wesley Educ.

Microeconomics. 11th ed. Mutti & Fredric C. Menz. LC 95-34895. (C). 1997. pap. text, student ed. 34.80 (*0-673-99926-2*) Addson-Wesley Educ.

***Microeconomics.** 12th ed. Lipsey. 512p. (C). 1998. pap. text 70.00 (*0-201-36011-X*) Addison-Wesley.

Microeconomics. 13th ed. Campbell R. McConnell & Stanley L. Brue. (C). 1995. text 67.50 (*0-07-046820-6*) McGraw.

Microeconomics. 13th ed. William B. Walstad. (C). 1995. pap., student ed. 17.19 (*0-07-046823-0*) McGraw.

Microeconomics. 14th ed. McConnell. 1998. pap., student ed. 17.19 (*0-07-289838-0*) McGraw.

Microeconomics. 15th ed. Campbell R. McConnell. 2001. 47.50 (*0-07-234037-1*) McGraw.

Microeconomics. 15th ed. Paul Anthony Samuelson & William D. Nordhaus. LC 94-31485. (C). 1994. pap. text 46.74 (*0-07-054993-1*) McGraw.

Microeconomics. 16th ed. Samuelson. 1998. pap., student ed. 19.69 (*0-07-057954-7*) McGraw.

Microeconomics. 16th ed. Paul Anthony Samuelson & William D. Nordhaus. LC 97-38898. 512p. (C). 1997. pap. 60.00 (*0-07-057953-9*) McGraw.

Microeconomics. 17th ed. Samuelson. 2000. 46.74 (*0-07-231490-7*) McGraw.

Microeconomics, 3 vols., Set. Ed. by Robert E. Kuenne. (International Library of Critical Writings in Economics: Vol. 11). 1328p. 1990. text 480.00 (*1-85278-307-9*) E Elgar.

***Microeconomics: A Computational Approach.** Gerald E. Thompson. (Illus.). 168p. 2000. text 44.95 incl. cd-rom (*0-7656-0664-X*) M E Sharpe.

Microeconomics: A Contemporary Introduction. 4th ed. McEachern. (HB - Economics Ser.). 1996. mass mkt., student ed. 20.95 (*0-538-85523-1*) S-W Pub.

Microeconomics: A Framework of Theory, Policies & Values. Martin L. Primack et al. 476p. (C). 1993. pap. text 40.39 (*1-56226-149-5*) CAT Pub.

Microeconomics: A Modern Approach. Andrew R. Schotter. (C). 1994. write for info. (*0-318-70215-0*) Addison-Wesley Educ.

Microeconomics: A Modern Approach. Andrew R. Schotter. 672p. (C). 1997. 94.00 (*0-06-045768-6*) Addison-Wesley Educ.

Microeconomics: A Modern Approach. 2nd ed. Ed. by Andrew R. Schotter. (C). 1997. text, teacher ed. 9.00 (*0-673-98580-6*) Addison-Wesley.

Microeconomics: A Modern Approach. 2nd ed. Andrew R. Schotter. LC 96-569. 720p. (C). 1997. 98.00 (*0-673-99944-0*) Addson-Wesley Educ.

Microeconomics: A Synthesis of Modern & Neoclassical Theory. R. Robert Russell & Maurice Wilkinson. LC 78-17175. 476p. reprint ed. pap. 147.60 (*0-7837-3501-4*, 205783400008) Bks Demand.

Microeconomics: Concepts & Applications. Ed. by Day. (C). 1988. pap. text, student ed. 11.00 (*0-673-38117-X*) Addson-Wesley Educ.

Microeconomics: Contemporary Introduction. 4th ed. McEachern. LC 96-18536. (HB - Economics Ser.). 1996. mass mkt. 48.95 (*0-538-85516-9*) S-W Pub.

Microeconomics: Economic Way of Thinking. (C). 1997. 9.80 (*0-536-00236-3*) Pearson Custom.

***Microeconomics: Economic Way of Thinking.** 2nd ed. Heyne. 362p. 1998. pap. text 42.00 (*0-536-01907-X*) Pearson Custom.

***Microeconomics: Economics Way of Thinking.** 5th ed. (C). 1999. text 38.00 (*0-536-02342-5*) Pearson Custom.

Microeconomics: Economy Today. 9th ed. Miller. (C). 1998. 85.80 (*0-321-80186-5*) Addison-Wesley.

Microeconomics: Essays in Theory & Applications. Franklin M. Fisher. LC 98-24905. (Illus.). 584p. (C). 1999. text 84.95 (*0-521-62423-1*) Cambridge U Pr.

Microeconomics: Exams. Grinols. (C). Date not set. text 84.76 (*0-395-69271-7*) HM.

***Microeconomics: Incentives in an Imperfect World.** Jeffrey M. Perloff. LC 98-23043. 800p. (C). 1998. 98.00 (*0-201-59137-5*); pap. text 67.00 (*0-201-38063-3*) Addison-Wesley.

***Microeconomics: Incentives in an Imperfect World.** Jeffrey M. Perloff. (C). 1999. write for info. (*0-201-70254-1*) Addison-Wesley.

***Microeconomics: Incentives in an Imperfect World.** 2nd ed. Jeffrey M. Perloff. LC 00-33190. 2001. write for info. (*0-201-63773-1*) Addison-Wesley.

***Microeconomics: Incentives in Imperfect World.** (C). 1998. pap. text 133.33 (*0-201-38070-6*) Addison-Wesley.

***Microeconomics: Incentives in Imperfect World.** 272p. (C). 1998. pap. text 24.00 (*0-201-38062-5*); pap. text 24.00 (*0-201-38061-7*) Addison-Wesley.

Microeconomics: Individual Choice & Its Consequences. Alan E. Dillingham et al. 576p. (C). 1992. pap. write for info. (*0-205-13528-5*) Allyn.

Microeconomics: Institutions, Equilibrium & Optimality. M. C. Blad & H. Keiding. (Advanced Textbooks in Economics Ser.: No. 30). 424p. 1990. 88.00 (*0-444-88644-3*, North Holland) Elsevier.

***Microeconomics: Microeconomic Theory with Applications.** 6th ed. (C). 1998. text (*0-321-03339-6*) Addison-Wesley.

Microeconomics: Modern Application. (C). 1994. text 118.00 (*0-06-501609-2*) S&S Trade.

Microeconomics: Modern Approach. 2nd ed. (C). 1997. 67.00 (*0-673-97608-4*) Addison-Wesley.

Microeconomics: Modern Approach. 2nd ed. (C). 1997. 67.00 (*0-673-97609-2*, GoodYrBooks) Addson-Wesley Educ.

Microeconomics: Modern Approach. 2nd ed. (C). 1997. text 24.00 (*0-673-97607-6*) S&S Trade.

Microeconomics: Modern Approach & Study Guide. (C). 1995. text, student ed. write for info. (*0-321-01425-1*) Addison-Wesley.

Microeconomics: Optimal Decision Making by Private Firms & Public Authorities. C. Abraham & A. Thomas. Tr. by D. V. Jones from FRE. LC 79-188001. Orig. Title: Microeconomic, Decisions Optimal dans L'enterprise et dans la Nation. (Illus.). 507p. 1972. lib. bdg. 211.50 (*90-277-0237-3*) Kluwer Academic.

Microeconomics: Price Theory Practice. Bell. (C). 1997. text. write for info. (*0-06-501602-5*) Addson-Wesley Educ.

Microeconomics: Principles & Applications. Lieberman. LC 97-17925. (AB - Accounting Principles Ser.). (C). 1997. 67.95 (*0-538-84758-1*) S-W Pub.

***Microeconomics: Principles & Applications.** 2nd ed. Hall & Lieberman. 2000. pap. 47.00 (*0-324-01953-X*) Thomson Learn.

Microeconomics: Principles & Tools. O'Sullivan & Steven M. Sheffrin. LC 97-24097. 448p. (C). 1997. pap. text 63.00 (*0-13-742859-6*) P-H.

***Microeconomics: Principles & Tools.** 2nd ed. 2000. write for info. (*0-13-018983-9*) P-H.

***Microeconomics: Principles & Tools.** 2nd ed. Arthur O'Sullivan & Steven M. Sheffrin. 480p. 2000. pap. 61.33 (*0-13-018982-0*, Prentice Hall) P-H.

Microeconomics: Principles of Micro Economics Workbook. ABC Educational Partnership Co. Staff. (C). 1994. 15.08 (*1-884775-01-2*) It Works.

Microeconomics: Principles of Micro Economics Workbook. ABC Educational Partnership Co. Staff. 210p. (C). 1995. 15.08 (*1-884775-00-4*) It Works.

Microeconomics: Principles of Policy. 7th ed. William J. Baumol & Alan S. Blinder. 624p. (C). 1997. pap. text 73.00 (*0-03-025051-X*) Dryden Pr.

Microeconomics: Principles, Problems, & Policies. 14th ed. Campbell R. McConnell & Stanley L. Brue. LC 98-7747. 1998. 47.50 (*0-07-289840-2*) McGraw.

***Microeconomics: Principles, Problems, & Policies.** 14th ed. Campbell R. McConnell & Stanley L. Brue. LC 98-7747. (Illus.). 1999. write for info. (*0-07-366216-X*) McGrw-H Hghr Educ.

Microeconomics: Private & Public Choice. 8th ed. James D. Gwartney. (C). 1997. pap. text 246.00 (*0-03-019289-7*) Harcourt Coll Pubs.

Microeconomics: Private & Public Choice. 9th ed. James D. Gwartney. (C). 1999. pap. text 44.50 (*0-03-025782-4*) Harcourt Coll Pubs.

Microeconomics: Private Market & Public Choice. 5th ed. Robert B. Ekelund & Robert D. Tollison. LC 96-38800. 576p. (C). 1996. pap. text 60.00 (*0-201-91669-X*) Addison-Wesley.

Microeconomics: Private Markets & Public Choice. 5th ed. Robert B. Ekelund & Robert D. Tollison. LC 96-38800. (C). 1996. pap. text 31.60 (*0-201-85315-9*) Addison-Wesley.

Microeconomics: Problems & Solutions. David M. Winch. (Illus.). 286p. (Orig.). 1984. pap. text 19.95 (*0-19-540454-8*) OUP.

Microeconomics: Study Guide. 5th ed. Roger N. Waud. (C). 1992. pap. 23.66 (*0-06-500539-2*) Addson-Wesley Educ.

Microeconomics: Study Guide. 12th ed. Lipsey. 336p. (C). 1999. pap. text, student ed. 23.20 (*0-201-45842-X*) Addison-Wesley.

Microeconomics: The Economic Way of Thinking. Paul T. Heyne. 384p. (C). 1996. pap. 42.00 (*0-536-59676-X*) Pearson Custom.

***Microeconomics: Theory & Applications.** Anindya Sen. (Illus.). 424p. 2000. text 32.00 (*0-19-564806-4*) OUP.

Microeconomics: Theory & Applications. 5th ed. Edwin Mansfield. (C). 1985. pap. text 18.25 (*0-393-95403-X*) Norton.

***Microeconomics: Theory & Applications.** 10th ed. Edwin Mansfield. LC 99-32766. (Illus.). 646p. (C). 2000. text 65.00 (*0-393-97466-9*) Norton.

Microeconomics: Theory & Practice. 3rd ed. (C). 1997. text 24.00 (*0-673-97602-5*, GoodYrBooks); text 67.00 (*0-673-97603-3*, GoodYrBooks) Addson-Wesley Educ.

Microeconomics: Theory & Practice. 3rd ed. (C). 1997. pap. text 67.00 (*0-673-97605-X*) S&S Trade.

Microeconomics: Theory & Practice. 3rd ed. (C). 1997. text 67.00 (*0-673-97604-1*) S&S Trade.

Microeconomics: Wall Street Journal Edition. 4th ed. David N. Hyman. 592p. (C). 1996. text 51.20 (*0-256-22215-0*, Irwn McGrw-H) McGrw-H Hghr Educ.

Microeconomics: Wall Street Journal Edition. 4th ed. Stephen L. Slavin. 520p. (C). 1995. text 48.00 (*0-256-21700-9*, Irwn McGrw-H) McGrw-H Hghr Educ.

Microeconomics - Economic Times, Vol. 3, No. 1. 2nd ed. Michael Parkin. 1994. pap. 36.00 (*0-201-60707-7*) Addison-Wesley.

***Microeconomics - Professional Copy.** 5th ed. Michael Parkin. 576p. (C). 1999. text. write for info. (*0-201-63783-9*) Addison-Wesley.

Microeconomics & Behavior. Frank. 1991. write for info. (*0-07-021874-9*); write for info. (*0-07-834860-9*) McGraw.

Microeconomics & Behavior. 3rd ed. Robert H. Frank. LC 96-15499. (C). 1996. text 66.25 (*0-07-021892-7*) McGraw.

Microeconomics & Behavior. 3rd ed. James Halteman. (C). 1996. pap., student ed. 20.31 (*0-07-021894-3*) McGraw.

***Microeconomics & Behavior.** 4th ed. 288p. (C). 1999. pap., student ed. 20.94 (*0-07-366088-4*) McGrw-H Hghr Educ.

***Microeconomics & Behavior.** 4th ed. Robert H. Frank & Amy J. Glass. LC 99-31721. 704p. 1999. 84.69 (*0-07-366083-3*) McGraw.

Microeconomics & Economic Times. 3rd ed. Michael Parkin. (C). 1996. pap. text 63.00 (*0-201-85997-1*) Addison-Wesley.

Microeconomics & Macroeconomics. 3rd ed. Michael Parkin. (C). 1996. pap. text, student ed. 37.00 (*0-201-43217-X*) Addison-Wesley.

Microeconomics & Microeconomics Study Guide Bundle. 2nd ed. Michael Parkin. 1993. 57.00 (*0-201-52952-1*) Addison-Wesley.

Microeconomics Applied Price Theory Manual. 2nd ed. Michael Katz & David Boyd. (C). 1996. text 11.25 (*0-256-22795-0*, Irwn McGrw-H) McGrw-H Hghr Educ.

Microeconomics (Canadian) David Colander & Peter Sephton. 480p. (C). 1996. per. 39.95 (*0-256-17575-6*, Irwn McGrw-H) McGrw-H Hghr Educ.

Microeconomics Drill & Review. 2nd ed. David Colander. (C). 1995. text, student ed. 21.25 (*0-256-22262-2*, Irwn McGrw-H) McGrw-H Hghr Educ.

***Microeconomics Fifth Edition Michael.** 5th ed. 384p. (C). 1999. text 25.20 (*0-201-63790-1*) S&S Trade.

Microeconomics for Business & Marketing: Lectures, Cases & Worked Essays. Peter E. Earl. LC 94-45021. 448p. 1995. 100.00 (*1-85278-861-5*); pap. 35.00 (*1-85278-862-3*) E Elgar.

Microeconomics for Business Decisions. Eric J. Solberg. 716p. (C). 1992. text 84.76 (*0-669-16705-3*); pap. text 23.56 (*0-669-16707-X*); teacher ed. 2.66 (*0-669-16706-1*) HM Trade Div.

Microeconomics for Today. Tucker. (Miscellaneous/Catalogs Ser.). (C). 1997. student ed. 17.00 (*0-314-20850-X*) S-W Pub.

Microeconomics for Today. 2nd ed. Tucker. LC 99-30239. (SWC-Economics Ser.). 400p. 1999. pap. 64.95 (*0-324-00623-3*) Thomson Learn.

M

Microeconomics for Today. 2nd ed. Tucker. (SWC-Economics Ser.). 1999. pap., student ed. 18.50 (*0-324-00786-8*) Thomson Learn.

Microeconomics, Growth & Political Economy Vol. 1: The Selected Essays of Richard G. Lipsey, Vol. 1. Richard G. Lipsey. LC 96-35917. (Economists of the Twentieth Century Series). 528p. 1997. 110.00 (*1-85278-126-2*) E Elgar.

Microeconomics of an Indigenous African Credit Institution: Rotating Savings & Credit Associations. CFNPP Staff et al. (Working Papers). (C). 1991. pap. text 7.00 (*1-56401-115-1*) Cornell Food.

Microeconomics of Banking. Xavier Freixas & Jean-Charles Rochet. LC 97-20047. (Illus.). 400p. 1997. 45.00 (*0-262-06193-7*) MIT Pr.

Microeconomics of Consumer Behavior. 2nd ed. Eastwood. (SWC-Economics). 1997. 48.95 (*0-87393-424-5*) Dame Pubns.

***Microeconomics of Market Failures.** Bernard Salanie. LC 00-38670. (Illus.). 300p. (C). 2000. 35.00 (*0-262-19443-0*) MIT Pr.

***Microeconomics of Policy Analysis.** Friedman. 1999. text 18.25 (*0-07-022449-8*) McGraw.

Microeconomics of the Shorter Working Week. Marcus Rubin & Ray Richardson. 192p. 1997. text 59.95 (*1-85972-482-5*, Pub. by Avebry) Ashgate Pub Co.

Microeconomics of the Timber Industry. David H. Jackson. (Replica Edition Ser.). (Illus.). 136p. 1980. text 31.00 (*0-89158-887-6*) Westview.

Microeconomics of Trade. Seymour Patterson. LC 88-29228. (Illus.). 232p. (C). 1989. lib. bdg. 40.00 (*0-943549-02-7*) Truman St Univ.

Microeconomics of Transformation & Growth. Egon Franck. Ed. by Horst D. Brezinski & Michael Fritsch. LC 98-22240. (European Association for Comparative Economic Studies). 288p. 1998. 90.00 (*1-85898-954-X*) E Elgar.

Microeconomics Principles & Applications. 6th rev. ed. Martin L. Primack et al. 656p. (C). 1997. pap. text 45.95 (*1-56226-374-9*) CAT Pub.

Microeconomics Ready Notes. 2nd ed. Paul Estenson. 130p. (C). 1995. text 8.12 (*0-256-13851-6*, Irwn McGrw-H) McGrw-H Hghr Educ.

Microeconomics Split - Economics: Contemporary Introductions. 3rd ed. McEachern. (HB - Economics Ser.). (C). 1994. mass mkt. 40.00 (*0-538-82852-8*) S-W Pub.

Microeconomics Student Workbook. 2nd ed. David Colander & Douglas Copeland. 336p. (C). 1995. text, wbk. ed. 18.12 (*0-256-18631-6*, Irwn McGrw-H) McGrw-H Hghr Educ.

Microeconomics Study Guide. 2nd ed. (C). 1996. text. write for info. (*0-201-44362-7*) Addison-Wesley.

Microeconomics Study Guide. 4th ed. David N. Hyman. 432p. (C). 1996. text, student ed. 21.25 (*0-256-16176-3*, Irwn McGrw-H) McGrw-H Hghr Educ.

Microeconomics the Easy Way. Walter J. Wessels. LC 96-53214. (Barron's Easy Way Ser.). 330p. 1997. pap. 12.95 (*0-8120-9601-0*) Barron.

***Microeconomics Theory & Applications** 6th ed. Edgar K. Browning. (Economics Ser.). 608p. 1999. text 96.95 (*0-471-36442-8*) Wiley.

Microeconomics 2.0. Muraoka. Date not set. pap. text, student ed. write for info. (*0-314-00838-1*) West Pub.

***Microeconomics University of Pennsylvania.** 3rd ed. 480p. (C). 1999. 34.80 (*0-536-02362-X*) Pearson Custom.

Microeconomics Update & Economic Times. 2nd ed. Michael Parkin. (C). 1994. text 44.06 (*0-201-76496-2*) Addison-Wesley.

Microeconomics U.S. 3rd ed. Katz. 1997. pap., student ed. 25.31 (*0-256-17177-7*) McGraw.

Microeconomics with Calculus. 2nd ed. Ed. by Brian Binger. LC 97-25855. (Illus.). 633p. (C). 1997. 98.00 (*0-321-01225-9*) Addson-Wesley Educ.

Microeconomics with Economics in the News. 2nd ed. Michael Parkin. 1993. 62.00 (*0-201-54088-6*) Addison-Wesley.

Microeconomics with EIA 3.0. 4th ed. Michael Parkin. (C). 1997. pap. text. write for info. (*0-201-34737-7*) Addison-Wesley.

Microeconomics with TAG SW Windows. 8th ed. Gwartne. 1997. 66.50 (*0-03-019883-6*, Pub. by Harcourt Coll Pubs) Harcourt.

Microeconomics WSJ Edition. 3rd ed. Colander. 560p. 1997. pap. 76.88 (*0-256-26614-X*) McGraw.

Microeconomics, 2e. 2nd ed. Roger A. Arnold. Ed. by Clyde Perlee. (SWC-Economics). 525p. (C). 1992. pap. 47.25 (*0-314-88423-8*) West Pub.

Microeconomy Today. 7th ed. Bradley R. Schiller. (C). 1996. pap., student ed. 20.31 (*0-07-057806-0*) McGraw.

***Microeconomy Today.** 8th ed. (C). 2000. pap., student ed. 20.31 (*0-07-242956-9*) McGrw-H Hghr Educ.

Microeconomy Today. 8th ed. Schiller. 1999. pap., student ed. 20.31 (*0-07-366276-3*) McGraw.

Microecononmic Theory. Tatsuro Ichiishi. LC 96-32588. (Illus.). 416p. 1997. 66.95 (*1-57718-037-2*) Blackwell Pubs.

Microelectric Circuits. 3rd ed. Adel S. Sedra. 448p. 1995. teacher ed., lab manual ed. 10.00 (*0-03-096600-0*) OUP.

***Microelectric Design of Fuzzy Logic-Based Systems.** I. Baturone. LC 00-29235. 2000. write for info. (*0-8493-0633-7*) CRC Pr.

***Microelectric Device Technology III.** Ed. by David Burnett & Toshiaki Tsuchiya. 314p. 1999. pap. text 72.00 (*0-8194-3478-7*) SPIE.

Microelectric Structures & MEMS for Optical Processing IV. Ed. by Hans P. Herzig & M. Edward Motamedi. LC 98-226767. (Proceedings of SPIE Ser.: Vol. 3513). 248p. 1998. 69.00 (*0-8194-2972-4*) SPIE.

Microelectric Test Structures. A. Walton. 1994. text. write for info. (*0-442-01638-7*, VNR) Wiley.

Microelectro Mechanical Systems in Japan. unabridged ed. Kensall D. Wise. LC 96-105114. (JTEL Panel Report Ser.). (Illus.). 291p. (Orig.). 1994. pap. write for info. (*1-883712-35-1*) Intl Tech Res.

Microelectrode Methods for Intracellular Recording & Ionophoresis. R. D. Purves. (Biological Techniques Ser.). 1981. text 79.00 (*0-12-567950-5*) Acad Pr.

Microelectrodes. Ed. by Joseph Wang. LC 89-70634. 87p. 1990. pap. 40.00 (*1-56081-027-0*, Wiley-VCH) Wiley.

Microelectrodes: Theory & Applications. Ed. by M. Irene Montenegro et al. (C). 1991. text 237.50 (*0-7923-1229-5*) Kluwer Academic.

Microelectromechanical Devices (MEMs) Powerhouse for Growth in Sensors, Actuators & Control Systems. 175p. 1998. spiral bd. 1995.00 (*1-56217-023-6*) Tech Insights.

Microelectromechanical Structures for Materials Research Vol. 518: Proceedings Materials Research Society Symposium. Ed. by S. B. Brown et al. 248p. 1998. text 84.00 (*1-55899-424-6*) Materials Res.

Microelectromechanical Systems: Advanced Materials & Fabrication Methods. National Research Council Staff. 76p. (C). 1997. pap. text 15.00 (*0-309-05980-1*) Natl Acad Pr.

Microelectromechanical Systems, 1997: Proceedings, ASME International Mechanical Engineering Congress & Exposition, Dallas, TX, 1997. Ed. by Chang-Jin Kim et al. LC 98-184993. (DSC - HTD Ser.: Vols. 62 & 354). 284p. 1997. pap. 110.00 (*0-7918-1843-8*, TK153) ASME Pr.

Microelectronic Circuit Design. Richard C. Jaeger. (Illus.). 1152p. (C). 1996. 95.31 (*0-07-032482-4*) McGraw.

Microelectronic Circuit Design. Richard C. Jaeger. (C). 1997. pap., student ed. 41.88 (*0-07-032484-0*) McGraw.

Microelectronic Circuit Design. 2nd ed. Jaeger. 2001. 73.50 (*0-07-232099-0*) McGraw.

Microelectronic Circuitry. 2nd ed. Wasserman. 1995. pap. text, lab manual ed. 30.40 (*0-13-711102-9*) P-H.

Microelectronic Circuits. Muhammadrashid. LC 97-46066. (Electrical Engineering Ser.). (C). 1998. pap. 102.95 (*0-534-95174-0*) Wadsworth Pub.

Microelectronic Circuits. Muhammadrashid. (Electrical Engineering). 1999. pap., lab manual ed. 25.95 (*0-534-95173-2*) Wadsworth Pub.

Microelectronic Circuits, 2 vols. Schwarz. 1987. 520.00 (*0-12-632430-1*) Acad Pr.

Microelectronic Circuits rev. ed. Rashid. 1999. pap. text 67.50 (*0-534-37241-4*) Thomson Learn.

Microelectronic Circuits. 3rd ed. Kenneth C. Smith. (Illus.). 448p. 1995. pap. text, lab manual ed. 18.75 (*0-19-511103-6*) OUP.

Microelectronic Circuits. 4th ed. Adel S. Sedra & Kenneth C. Smith. LC 97-11254. (The Oxford Series in Electrical & Computer Engineering). (Illus.). 1360p. (C). 1997. text 97.00 (*0-19-511663-1*) OUP.

Microelectronic Circuits. 4th ed. Sedra & Smith. (The Oxford Series in Electrical & Computer Engineering). 1360p. 1997. student ed. 36.00 incl. cd-rom (*0-19-511690-9*) OUP.

Microelectronic Circuits: Problem Supplement, 1995. 3rd ed. Kenneth C. Smith. (Illus.). 64p. (C). 1995. pap. text 17.95 (*0-19-510367-X*) OUP.

Microelectronic Circuits & Devices. 2nd ed. Mark N. Horenstein. LC 94-29107. 1126p. (C). 1995. 100.00 (*0-13-701335-3*, Pub. by P-H) S&S Trade.

Microelectronic Device & Multilevel Interconnection Technology II, Vol. 2875. Ed. by Ih-Chin Chen et al. 400p. 1996. 76.00 (*0-8194-2273-8*) SPIE.

Microelectronic Device Technology, Vol. 3212. Ed. by Mark Rodder et al. LC 98-122056. 406p. 1997. 89.00 (*0-8194-2644-X*) SPIE.

Microelectronic Device Technology II. Ed. by David Burnett et al. LC 99-184109. (Proceedings of SPIE Ser.: Vol. 3506). 364p. 1998. 89.00 (*0-8194-2965-1*) SPIE.

Microelectronic Devices. Yang. 1988. student ed. 22.50 (*0-07-072239-0*) McGraw.

Microelectronic Devices. Edward S. Yang. 447p. (C). 1988. 101.56 (*0-07-072238-2*) McGraw.

Microelectronic Devices. 2nd ed. Keith Leaver. 200p. 1997. 36.00 (*1-86094-013-7*); pap. 18.00 (*1-86094-020-X*) World Scientific Pub.

Microelectronic Devices & Circuits. Clifton G. Fonstad. LC 93-32500. (McGraw-Hill Series in Electrical & Computer Engineering). 640p. (C). 1994. 98.13 (*0-07-021496-4*) McGraw.

Microelectronic Fabrication, Vol. V. Richard C. Jaeger. LC 86-22128. (Modular Series on Solid State Devices: Vol. 5). (Illus.). 224p. (C). 1988. pap. text 23.40 (*0-201-14695-9*) Addison-Wesley.

Microelectronic Failure Analysis: Desk Reference. 3rd ed. Ed. by Thomas W. Lee & Seshu V. Pabbisetty. LC 93-7792. 425p. 1993. 163.00 (*0-87170-479-X*, 9103) ASM.

***Microelectronic Failure Analysis Desk Reference.** 4th ed. LC 99-75422. 643p. 1999. 175.00 (*0-87170-638-5*, 09105G) ASM.

Microelectronic Interconnections & Assembly. George G. Harman & Pavel Mach. LC 98-8189. (NATO Science Ser.). 1998. 144.00 (*0-7923-5139-8*) Kluwer Academic.

Microelectronic Manufacturing Yield, Reliability & Failure Analysis II, Vol. 2874. Ed. by Ali Keshavarzi et al. 376p. 1996. 85.00 (*0-8194-2272-X*) SPIE.

Microelectronic Manufacturing Yield, Reliability & Failure Analysis III, Vol. 3216. Ed. by Ali Keshavarzi et al. LC 98-122069. 206p. 1997. 59.00 (*0-8194-2648-2*) SPIE.

Microelectronic Manufacturing Yield, Reliability & Failure Analysis IV. Ed. by Sharad Prasad et al. LC 99-194427. (Proceedings of SPIE Ser.: Vol. 3510). 248p. 1998. 69.00 (*0-8194-2969-4*) SPIE.

Microelectronic Materials. C. Grovenor. (Graduate Student Series in Materials Science & Engineering). (Illus.). 556p. 1989. pap. 66.00 (*0-85274-270-3*) IOP Pub.

Microelectronic Materials. C. Grovenor. LC 88-28415. (Graduate Student Series in Materials Science & Engineering). (Illus.). 554p. reprint ed. pap. 171.80 (*0-7837-3928-1*, 205791800010) Bks Demand.

Microelectronic Materials & Processes. Ed. by R. A. Levy. (C). 1989. pap. text 196.50 (*0-7923-0154-4*); lib. bdg. 348.50 (*0-7923-0147-1*) Kluwer Academic.

Microelectronic Packaging: The Electrical Principles. Eric Bogatin. (C). 2001. 39.00 (*0-13-582370-6*, Macmillan Coll) P-H.

Microelectronic Packaging & Laser Processing. Yong-Khim Swee et al. 1997. pap. 69.00 (*0-8194-2611-3*) SPIE.

Microelectronic Packaging Handbook. Ed. by Rao R. Tummala & Eugene J. Rymaszewski. (Illus.). 1312p. 1989. text 129.95 (*0-442-20578-3*, VNR) Wiley.

Microelectronic Packaging Technology: Materials & Processes, Proceedings of the 2nd ASM International Electronic Materials & Processing Congress, Philadelphia, Pennsylvania, 24-28 April 1989. ASM International Electronic Materials & Processin. Ed. by Wei T. Shieh. LC 89-80612. 489p. reprint ed. pap. 151.60 (*0-7837-2767-4*, 204315800006) Bks Demand.

Microelectronic Polymers. Ed. by Maung S. Htoo. LC 88-30402. 421p. 1989. reprint ed. pap. 130.60 (*0-608-01282-3*, 206202800001) Bks Demand.

Microelectronic Processes: An Introduction to the Manufacture of Integrated Circuits. W. S. Ruska. (McGraw-Hill Series in Computer Engineering). 488p. (C). 1987. text 77.74 (*0-07-054280-5*) McGraw.

Microelectronic Processing. Ruska. 1987. 27.50 (*0-07-054281-3*) McGraw.

Microelectronic Reliability Vol. 1: Reliability, Test & Diagnostics. Ed. by Edward B. Hakim. LC 88-7814. (Artech House Materials Science Library). 392p. 1989. reprint ed. pap. 121.60 (*0-608-02363-9*, 206300500001) Bks Demand.

Microelectronic Structures & MEMS for Optical Processing II, Vol. 2881. Ed. by M. Edward Motamedi & Wayne Bailey. 226p. 1996. 56.00 (*0-8194-2279-7*) SPIE.

Microelectronic Structures & MEMS for Optical Processing III, Vol. 3226. Ed. by M. Edward Motamedi & Hans P. Herzig. LC 98-122103. 220p. 1997. 59.00 (*0-8194-2658-X*) SPIE.

Microelectronic Switched Capacitor Filters with ISICAP: A Computer-Aided-Design Package. H. Baher. LC 95-38186. 384p. 1996. 215.00 (*0-471-95404-7*) Wiley.

Microelectronic System, Level 2. Sinclair. (C). 1982. pap. write for info. (*0-03-910373-0*) Harcourt Coll Pubs.

Microelectronic System Interconnections: Performance & Modeling. Ed. by Stuart K. Tewskbury. LC 93-13467. (Illus.). 528p. 1993. 79.95 (*0-7803-0405-5*, PC0300-4) Inst Electrical.

Microelectronic Systems. write for info. (*0-340-58486-6*, Pub. by E A); write for info. (*0-340-61442-0*, Pub. by E A) Routldge.

Microelectronic Systems. R. E. Vears. (Illus.). 256p. 1996. pap. text 28.95 (*0-7506-2819-7*, Newnes) Buttrwrth-Heinemann.

Microelectronic Systems: Design, Modelling & Testing. W. Buchanan. 314p. 1997. pap. 44.95 (*0-471-19142-6*) Wiley.

***Microelectronics.** Jerry C. Whitaker. LC 99-44874. 403p. 1999. boxed set 89.95 (*0-8493-0050-9*) CRC Pr.

Microelectronics. 2nd ed. Millman. 1987. text, student ed. 27.50 (*0-07-042331-8*) McGraw.

Microelectronics. 2nd ed. Jacob Millman. 992p. (C). 1999. 107.19 (*0-07-042330-X*) McGraw.

Microelectronics: An Integrated Approach. Roger T. Howe & Charles Sodini. LC 96-17867. 912p. (C). 1996. 100.00 (*0-13-588518-3*) P-H.

Microelectronics: Process & Device Design. Roy A. Colclaser. LC 79-29727. 84p. 1980. pap. text 8.50 (*0-471-08709-2*) Wiley.

***Microelectronics: Systems & Devices.** Owen Bishop. 288p. 2000. pap. 29.95 (*0-7506-4723-X*, Newnes) Buttrwrth-Heinemann.

Microelectronics: The Structure & Operation of Microprocessor-Based Systems. Douglas M. Boniface. LC 97-153703. 208p. 1997. pap. text 24.95 (*1-898563-32-2*, Pub. by Horwood Pub) Paul & Co Pubs.

Microelectronics A to Z. M. Plant. Date not set. pap. text 4.95 (*0-582-89285-6*) Addison-Wesley.

Microelectronics & Office Jobs: The Impact of the Chip on Women's Employment. Diane Werneke. 102p. 1986. pap. 15.75 (*92-2-103278-7*) Intl Labour Office.

Microelectronics & Society: For Better or for Worse; A Report to the Club of Rome. Ed. by G. Friedrichs & Adam Schaff. (Club of Rome Publications Ser.). (Illus.). 353p. 1982. pap. text 24.50 (*0-08-028955-X*, Pergamon Pr) Elsevier.

Microelectronics at Work: Productivity & Jobs in the World Economy. Colin Norman. 1980. pap. write for info. (*0-916468-38-0*) Worldwatch Inst.

***Microelectronics Design of Fuzzy Logic-Based Systems.** Angel Barriga. (Illus.). 2000. 89.95 (*0-8493-0091-6*) CRC Pr.

Microelectronics Dictionary. M. Plant. Date not set. pap. text. write for info. (*0-582-89200-7*, Pub. by Addison-Wesley) Longman.

Microelectronics Dictionary in Three Languages. Kovacs Magda. 1990. pap. 28.50 (*0-7859-8964-1*) Fr & Eur.

Microelectronics Education: Proceedings of the European Workshop. LC 96-225066. 320p. 1996. lib. bdg. 51.00 (*981-02-2653-5*) World Scientific Pub.

Microelectronics Education: Proceedings of the 2nd European Workshop Held in Noordwijkerhout, the Netherlands, 14-15 May 1998. Ton J. Mouthaan & Cora Salm. LC 98-21506. 298p. 1998. write for info. (*0-7923-5107-X*) Kluwer Academic.

***Microelectronics Education: Proceedings of the 3rd European Workshop on Microelectronics Workshop Hosted by St. University, France, May 18 & 19, 2000.** B. Courtois. Ed. by European Workshop on Microelectronics Education Staff. LC 00-41592. 2000. write for info. (*0-7923-6456-2*) Kluwer Academic.

Microelectronics for Neural, Fuzzy & Bio-Inspired Systems (Microneuro '99), 1999 International Conference on, 1 vol. LC 98-89357. 450p. 1999. pap. 130.00 (*0-7695-0043-9*) IEEE Comp Soc.

Microelectronics for Neural Networks & Fuzzy Systems, 5th International Conference On. LC 10-861947. 384p. 1996. pap. 80.00 (*0-8186-7373-7*, PRO7373) IEEE Comp Soc.

Microelectronics in Agriculture & Horticulture: Electronics & Computers in Farming. S. W. Cox. 240p. (C). 1982. pap. text 44.00 (*0-86598-087-X*) Rowman.

Microelectronics in the Sport Science. Charles F. Cicciarella. LC 86-287. (Illus.). 111p. 1986. reprint ed. pap. 34.50 (*0-608-07111-0*, 206733800009) Bks Demand.

Microelectronics, International Competiton & Development Strategies: The Unavoidable Issues. Ed. by K. Hoffman. 200p. 1985. pap. 26.00 (*0-08-032687-0*, Pub. by PPL) Elsevier.

***Microelectronics Laboratory Using Electronics Workbench: Self Study Course.** Muhammad Rashid. 100p. 2000. 395.00 (*0-7803-4804-4*) Inst Electrical.

Microelectronics Packaging Handbook. Rao R. Tummala. (Electrical Engineering Ser.). 1997. text 99.95 (*0-442-01993-9*, VNR) Wiley.

Microelectronics Packaging Handbook: Technology, Vol. 1. Roa R. Tummala. (Electrical Engineering Ser.). 1995. 99.95 (*0-442-01963-7*, VNR) Wiley.

Microelectronics Processing: Chemical Engineering Aspects. Ed. by Dennis W. Hess & Klavs F. Jensen. LC 89-6862. (Advances in Chemistry Ser.: No. 221). (Illus.). 523p. 1989. text 55.00 (*0-8412-1475-1*, Pub. by Am Chemical) OUP.

Microelectronics Processing: Chemical Engineering Aspects. Ed. by Dennis W. Hess & Klavs F. Jensen. LC 89-6862. (Advances in Chemistry Ser.: No. 221). (Illus.). 562p. 1989. reprint ed. pap. 174.30 (*0-608-06789-X*, 206698600009) Bks Demand.

Microelectronics Processing: Inorganic Materials Characterization. Ed. by Lawrence A. Casper. LC 85-30648. (ACS Symposium Ser.: No. 295). (Illus.). x, 440p. 1986. 87.95 (*0-8412-0934-0*, Pub. by Am Chemical) OUP.

Microelectronics Processing: Inorganic Materials Characterization. Ed. by Lawrence A. Casper. LC 85-30648. (ACS Symposium Ser.: Vol. 295). 454p. 1986. reprint ed. pap. 140.80 (*0-608-03922-5*, 206436900009) Bks Demand.

Microelectronics Systems Education, 1997 International Conference. LC 97-70930. 250p. 1997. pap. 110.00 (*0-8186-7996-4*) IEEE Comp Soc.

Microelectronics Technology: Polymers in Advanced Imaging & Packaging Developed from a Symposium Sponsored by the ACS Division of Polymeric Materials: Science & Engineering, Inc., & the Polymers for Microelectronics Division of the Society of Polymer Science, Japan, at the 209th National Meeting of the American Chemical Society, Anaheim, California, April 2-6, 1995. Ed. by Elsa Reichmanis et al. LC 95-44669. (Symposium Ser.: Vol. 614). 590p. 1995. text 145.00 (*0-8412-3332-2*, Pub. by Am Chemical) OUP.

Microelonic. Circuit Design CCCA. Jaeger. 1997. 105.50 (*0-07-289822-4*) McGraw.

Microembolism Syndrome. Ed. by Tom Saldeen. (Illus.). 240p. (Orig.). 1979. pap. text 40.00 (*91-22-00295-2*) Coronet Bks.

Microemulsion Systems. Henri L. Rosano. (Surfactant Science Ser.: Vol. 24). (Illus.). 440p. 1987. text 245.00 (*0-8247-7439-6*) Dekker.

Microemulsions. Ed. by I. D. Robb. LC 81-17766. 268p. (C). 1982. 75.00 (*0-306-40834-1*, Plenum Trade) Perseus Pubng.

Microemulsions & Related Systems: Formulation, Solvency, & Physical Properties. Maurice Bourrel & Robert S. Schechter. (Surfactant Science Ser.: Vol. 30). (Illus.). 504p. 1988. text 250.00 (*0-8247-7951-7*) Dekker.

Microemulsions Structure & Dynamics: Structure & Dynamics. Stig E. Friberg & Pierre Bothorel. LC 86-6168. 256p. 1987. 132.00 (*0-8493-6598-8*, TP156, CRC Reprint) Franklin.

Microencapsulation. Simon Benita. (Drugs & the Pharmaceutical Sciences Ser.: Vol. 73). (Illus.). 664p. 1996. text 165.00 (*0-8247-9703-5*) Dekker.

Microencapsulation. International Symposium on Microencapsulation (2nd. Ed. by J. R. Nixon. LC 75-37112. (Drugs & the Pharmaceutical Sciences Ser.: Vol. 3). 229p. reprint ed. pap. 71.00 (*0-608-16750-9*, 202680700052) Bks Demand.

Microencapsulation: Processes & Applications. Ed. by Jan E. Vandegaer. LC 74-6125. 180p. 1974. 59.50 (*0-306-30788-X*, Plenum Trade) Perseus Pubng.

Microencapsulation - Microgels - Iniferters. Ed. by S. DiMari et al. (Advances in Polymer Science Ser.: Vol. 136). (Illus.). 210p. 1997. 179.00 (*3-540-64015-0*) Spr-Verlag.

An Asterisk (*) at the beginning of an entry indicates that the title is appearing for the first time.

Microencapsulation & Related Drug Processes. Patrick B. Deasy. LC 83-26267. (Drugs & the Pharmaceutical Sciences Ser.: Vol. 20). (Illus.). 375p. reprint ed. pap. 116.30 (*0-608-08926-5*, 206956100005) Bks Demand.

Microencapsulation of Drugs. Ed. by Tony L. Whateley. LC 92-49642. (Drug Targeting & Delivery Ser.: Vol. 1). 309p. 1992. text 141.00 (*3-7186-5247-1*) Gordon & Breach.

Microengineering Aerospace Systems. Henry Helvajian. LC 99-18130. 1999. write for info. (*1-884989-03-9*) Aerospace CA.

Microenterprise & the Poor: Findings from the Self-Employment Learning Project 5 Year Survey of Microentrepreneurs. Peggy Clark. (Economic Opportunities Program Ser.). 84p. pap. 15.00 (*0-89843-260-X*) The Aspen Inst.

***Microenterprise Development For Better Health Outcomes.** Rosalia A. Rodriguez-Garcia et al. Vol. 222. 2001. write for info. (*0-313-31633-3*) Greenwood.

Microenterprises Development in the Philippines: Proceedings of a National Conference on Microenterprise Development. 233p. 1992. pap. 6.00 (*0-942717-44-9*) Intl Inst Rural.

Microenvironment & Vision. Ed. by J. B. Sheffield & S. R. Hilfer. (Cell & Developmental Biology of the Eye Ser.). xiii, 247p. 1987. 205.00 (*0-387-96540-8*) Spr-Verlag.

Microenvironment of the Human Thymus: Thymus Update, 4, Vol. 1. Ed. by Marion D. Kendall & M. A. Ritter. xii, 306p. 1988. text 189.00 (*3-7186-4806-7*) Gordon & Breach.

Microevolution of Fishes: Evolutionary Aspects of Phenetic Diversity. M. V. Mina. Ed. by A. V. Yablokov. (Russian Translation Ser.: No. 79). (Illus.). 220p. (C). 1990. text 110.00 (*90-6191-032-3*, Pub. by A A Balkema) Ashgate Pub Co.

Microexam: Applied Business Law. 13th ed. Adamson & Norbert J. Mietus. (LA - Business Law Ser.). 1988. 172.95 (*0-538-12877-1*) S-W Pub.

Microexam II General Tests & Grade Book - DOS, User's Guide. 3rd ed. Eugene Hite. (DC - Introduction to Computing Ser.). 1994. pap. write for info. (*0-538-62742-5*) S-W Pub.

Microexam II Test/Grade Book Mac, User's Guide. 2nd ed. Eugene Hite. (DC - Introduction to Computing Ser.). 1994. pap. write for info. (*0-538-62738-7*) S-W Pub.

Microexam II User's Guide. 2nd ed. Eugene Hite. (DC - Introduction to Computing Ser.). 1991. 17.95 (*0-538-28233-9*) S-W Pub.

Microexam II User's Guide: Macintosh Version. Eugene Hite. (DC - Introduction to Computing Ser.). 1992. pap. 12.25 (*0-538-24072-5*) S-W Pub.

Microexam Users Guide. 2nd ed. Hite & Eerkes. (Thomson Executive Press Ser.). Date not set. write for info. (*0-538-28238-X*) S-W Pub.

Scorpri e Confronta: "Extreme Science Kit from Planet Ex" rev. ed. (Planet Ex Ser.: No. 1). (ITA., Illus.). 240p. (J). (gr. 1-6). 1998. 19.95 (*1-893264-00-9*) Planet Crea Inc.

Microexplorers Series: Physical Science, 4 vols., Set. Patrick A. Baeuerle & Norbert Landa. (Illus.). 168p. 1999. lib. bdg. 75.80 (*1-56674-946-8*) Forest Hse.

***Microfabric Analysis in the Earth Sciences.** Norman K. Tovey. (Series on Environmental Science & Management). (Illus.). 2000. 64.00 (*1-86094-215-6*) World Scientific Pub.

Microfabricated High Aspect Ratio Silicon Flexures: Hexsil, RIE, & KOH Etched Design & Fabrication. Chris G. Keller. LC 98-96861. (Illus.). xii, 356p. 1998. pap. 80.00 (*0-9666376-0-7*) MEMS Precision.

***Microfabrication in Tissue Engineering & Bioartificial Organs.** Sangeeta Bhatia. LC 99-35715. (Microsystems Ser.). 145p. 1999. write for info. (*0-7923-8566-7*) Kluwer Academic.

Microfacies Analysis of Limestones. Erik Fluegel. (Illus.). 550p. 1982. 119.00 (*0-387-11269-3*) Spr-Verlag.

Microfauna Marina, Band 2. Ed. by Peter Ax. (Illus.). 410p. 1985. lib. bdg. 60.00 (*3-437-30490-9*, Pub. by Gustav Fischer) Balogh.

Microfauna Marina, Band 1. Ed. by Peter Ax. (Illus.). 277p. 1984. lib. bdg. 54.00 (*3-437-30460-7*, Pub. by Gustav Fischer) Balogh.

Microfauna Marina, Band 3. Ed. by Peter Ax. (Illus.). 438p. 1987. lib. bdg. 60.00 (*3-437-30558-1*, Pub. by Gustav Fischer) Balogh.

Microfauna Marina, Band 5. Ed. by Peter Ax. (Illus.). 329p. 1989. pap. 57.00 (*3-437-30608-1*, Pub. by Gustav Fischer) Balogh.

Microfauna Marina, Band 8. Matthias Franke. (Illus.). 283p. 1993. 54.00 (*3-437-30744-4*) Gustav Fischer.

Microfauna Marina, Band 9. Ed. by Peter Ax. (ENG & GER.). 350p. 1994. 60.00 (*3-437-30779-7*, Pub. by Gustav Fischer) Balogh.

Microfauna Marina, Band 10. Peter Ax. (Illus.). 332p. 1995. 60.00 (*3-437-30828-9*) Gustav Fischer.

Microfauna Marina, Band 11. (Illus.). 320p. 1998. 57.00 (*3-437-25696-3*) Gustav Fischer.

Microfauna Marina, Vol. 6. Ed. by Peter Ax. 272p. 1991. lib. bdg. 70.00 (*1-56081-318-0*, Pub. by Gustav Fischer) Balogh.

Microfauna Marina: Metahuntemarria, Vol. 7. Peter Ax. (Illus.). 342p. 1992. 59.00 (*1-56081-359-8*) Balogh.

Microfauna Marina Band 4: The Ultrasound of Polychaeta. Ed. by Peter Ax. (Illus.). 494p. 1988. 72.00 (*3-437-30581-6*, Pub. by Gustav Fischer) Balogh.

Microfauna Marina Band 6: Brackish Water, Playhelminthes of Alaska etc. etc. Ed. by Peter Ax. (Illus.). 272p. 1990. lib. bdg. 54.00 (*3-437-30663-4*, Pub. by Gustav Fischer) Balogh.

Microfauna Marina Band 7: Metahuntemannia Smirnov. Hans-Uwe Dahms & Mark Pottek. (Illus.). 342p. 1964. pap. 59.00 (*3-437-30698-7*) Gustav Fischer.

Microfauna Marina Vol. 5: Kalyptorhynchia. Peter Ax. (Illus.). 1989. 57.00 (*0-89574-305-1*) Balogh.

Microfax Gallimimus. Microfax Staff. (J). 1997. pap. text 0.99 (*0-7894-2125-9*) DK Pub Inc.

Microfiche: ANSI-AIIM MS5-1992 (R1998) Association for Information & Image Management Staff. 24p. 1992. pap. 33.00 (*0-89258-251-0*, MS05) Assn Inform & Image Mgmt.

Microfile. Fosegan. (KG - Filing/Records Management Ser.). 1987. mass mkt. 13.50 (*0-538-11231-X*) S-W Pub.

Microfile II Database. 2nd ed. Fosegan. (KG - FIling/Records Management Ser.). 1992. mass mkt. 13.50 (*0-538-61295-9*) S-W Pub.

Microfilm Computer Assisted Retrieval (CAR) Interface Commands: ANSI-AIIM MS40-1987 (R1999) Association for Information & Image Management Staff. 8p. 1987. pap. 33.00 (*0-89258-105-0*, MS40) Assn Inform & Image Mgmt.

Microfilm in Business. Joseph L. Kish & James Morris. LC 66-16217. (Illus.). 171p. reprint ed. pap. 53.10 (*0-608-10859-6*, 205157300089) Bks Demand.

Microfilm Index & Bibliography of the Concordia Historical Institute: Report I. Ed. by August R. Suelflow. 1966. pap. 3.50 (*0-318-04801-9*) Concordia Hist.

Microfilm Index & Bibliography of the Concordia Historical Institute: Report II. Ed. by August R. Suelflow. 1978. pap. 3.50 (*0-318-04800-0*) Concordia Hist.

Microfilm Jacket Formatting & Loading Techniques: AIIM TR11-1987 (A1993) (R1998) Association for Information & Image Management Staff. 19p. 1987. pap. 33.00 (*0-89258-111-5*, TR11) Assn Inform & Image Mgmt.

Microfilm Jackets: ANSI-AIIM MS11-1987 (R1999) Association for Information & Image Management Staff. 9p. 1987. pap. 33.00 (*0-89258-114-X*, MS11) Assn Inform & Image Mgmt.

Microfilm Package Labeling: ANSI/AIIM MS6-1981 (R1999) Association for Information & Image Management Staff. 7p. 1981. 33.00 (*0-89258-275-8*, MS06) Assn Inform & Image Mgmt.

Microfilming Your Church's Records. Ronald A. Tonks. Ed. by Charles W. Deweese. (Resource Kit for Your Church's History Ser.). 8p. 1984. pap. 0.60 (*0-939804-16-6*) Hist Comm S Baptist.

Microfiltration & Ultrafiltration: Principles & Applications. Leos J. Zeman & Andrew L. Zydney. LC 96-18793. (Illus.). 640p. 1996. text 199.00 (*0-8247-9735-3*) Dekker.

Microfinance & Poverty: Questioning the Conventional Wisdom. Hege Gulli. LC 99-197757. 124p. 1998. pap. text 14.95 (*1-886938-45-8*) IADB.

***Microfinance & Poverty Alleviation: Case Studies from Asia & the Pacific.** Joe Remenyi & B. Quidnones. LC 99-44978. (Global Development & the Environment Ser.). 2000. pap. 82.95 (*1-85567-643-5*) P P Pubs.

Microfinance Handbook: An Institutional & Financial Perspective. Joanna Ledgerwood. LC 98-21754. 302p. 1998. 30.00 (*0-8213-4306-8*, 14306) World Bank.

***Microfinance in Indonesia: Between State, Market & Self-Organization.** Detlev Holloh. 280p. 1999. pap. 33.95 (*3-8258-3909-5*, Pub. by CE24) Transaction Pubs.

***Microfinanzas y Pobreza: Son Validas las Ideas Preconcebidas.** Hege Gulli. (SPA.). 125p. 1999. 14.95 (*1-886938-46-6*) IADB.

Microfloral & Faunal Interactions in Natural & Agro-Ecosystems. Ed. by Myron J. Mitchell & James P. Nakas. (Developments in Biogeochemistry Ser.). 1985. text 220.00 (*90-247-3246-8*) Kluwer Academic.

Microfluidic Devices & Systems. Ed. by A. B. Frazier & Chong H. Ahn. LC 98-233146. (Proceedings of SPIE Ser.: Vol. 3515). 300p. 1998. 69.00 (*0-8194-2974-0*) SPIE.

***Microfluidic Devices & Systems II.** Ed. by Chong H. Ahn & A. Bruno Frazier. 322p. 1999. pap. text 84.00 (*0-8194-3474-4*) SPIE.

***Microfluidic Technology & Applications.** Michael Koch et al. LC 99-89448. (Microtechnologies & Microsystems Ser.). (Illus.). 2000. write for info. (*0-86380-244-3*, Pub. by Research Studies Pr Ltd) Taylor & Francis.

Microform Revolution in Libraries. Michael R. Gabriel & William C. Roselle. Ed. by Robert D. Stueart. LC 76-5646. (Foundations in Library & Information Science Ser.: Vol. 3). 176p. 1980. 78.50 (*0-89232-008-7*) Jai Pr.

Microforms. E. Dale Cluff. Ed. by James E. Duane. LC 80-21457. (Instructional Media Library: Vol. 7). (Illus.). 104p. 1981. 27.95 (*0-87778-167-2*) Educ Tech Pubns.

Microforms in Libraries: A Manual for Evaluation & Management. Ed. by Francis F. Spreitzer. LC 85-6036. (Illus.). 74p. 1985. reprint ed. pap. 30.00 (*0-7837-9689-7*, 206041900005) Bks Demand.

Microfoundations. E. Roy Weintraub. LC 78-16551. (Cambridge Surveys of Economic Literature Ser.). 184p. 1979. pap. text 24.95 (*0-521-29445-2*) Cambridge U Pr.

***Microfoundations & Macroeconomics: An Austrian Perspective.** Steven Horwitz. LC 00-36890. (Foundations of the Market Economy Ser.). 2000. write for info. (*0-415-19762-7*) Routledge.

Microfoundations, Methods & Causation on the Philosophy of Social Science. Daniel Little. LC 97-46819. 231p. 1998. text 34.95 (*1-56000-369-3*) Transaction Pubs.

Microfoundations of Economic Growth: A Schumpeterian Perspective. Ed. by Gunnar K. Eliasson & Christopher Green. LC 98-5012. (Illus.). 456p. (C). 1998. text 80.00 (*0-472-10904-9*, 10904) U of Mich Pr.

Microgames & Puzzles. I. Edward Alcamo. (Illus.). 120p. 1996. pap. text 15.95 (*0-89863-184-X*) Star Pub CA.

Microgardening Repla. 1968. 97.80 (*0-07-521090-8*) McGraw.

Microgolf Primer: Raise Golf Acres in Yards. Brian L. McGonegal & David C. Enger. LC 97-222644. 87p. 1997. pap. 24.95 (*0-9658430-0-9*) Microgolf Pr.

Micrographia. Robert Hooke. (History of Microscopy Ser.). 1987. 29.00 (*0-940095-07-6*) Sci Heritage Ltd.

Micrographics - ISO Resolution Test Chart No. 2 Description & Use: ANSI/AIIM MS51-1991. Association for Information & Image Management Staff. (Illus.). 10p. 1991. pap. 33.00 (*0-89258-225-1*, MS51) Assn Inform & Image Mgmt.

Micrographics Handbook. Charles Smith. LC 78-2561. 317p. reprint ed. pap. 98.30 (*0-8357-4185-0*, 203696300006) Bks Demand.

Micrographics Operator. Jack Rudman. (Career Examination Ser.: C-2157). 1994. reprint ed. pap. 23.95 (*0-8373-2157-3*) Nat Learn.

Micrographics, '76 Winter Symposium: Proceedings of the Winter Symposium, New Orleans, Feb. 11-13, 1976. Society of Photographic Scientists & Engineers Sta. Ed. by Philip Anastasio & Raymond A. Eynard. LC 76-450. 72p. reprint ed. pap. 30.00 (*0-608-15015-0*, 202570700046) Bks Demand.

Micrographics Technician. Jack Rudman. (Career Examination Ser.: C-2761). 1994. pap. 23.95 (*0-8373-2761-X*) Nat Learn.

Microgravimetry. Wang Qianshen et al. (Illus.). 158p. 1996. 92.50 (*90-6764-222-3*, Pub. by VSP) Coronet Bks.

Microgravity. Ed. by E. Kaldis & J. C. Legros. (Advances in Space Research Ser.: Vol. 8). 330p. 1989. pap. 78.00 (*0-08-037375-5*, Pergamon Pr) Elsevier.

Microgravity: A Novel. unabridged ed. Beth Partin. LC 98-65281. 124p. 1998. pap. 9.95 (*0-942979-49-4*); lib. bdg. 19.95 (*0-942979-50-8*) Livingston U Pr.

Microgravity Fluid Mechanics: IUTAM Symposium, Bremen, 1991. Ed. by H. J. Rath. (International Union of Theoretical & Applied Mechanics Symposia Ser.). xxii, 611p. 1992. 163.95 (*0-387-55122-0*) Spr-Verlag.

***Microgravity Fluid Physics & Heat Transfer: Proceedings of the International Conference on Microgravity Fluid Physics & Heat Transfer Held at the Tutle Bay Hilton, Oahu, Hawaii, September 19-24, 1999.** International Conference on Microgravity Fluid Physics & Heat Transfer Staff et al. LC 00-31182. 2000. write for info. (*1-56700-147-5*) Begell Hse.

Microgravity Research: Materials & Fluid Sciences: Proceedings of Symposium 11 of the COSPAR 28th Plenary Meeting Held in The Hague, The Netherlands, 25 June-6 July, 1990. Ed. by H. U. Walter et al. (Advances in Space Research Ser.: Vol. 11, No. 7). (Illus.). 394p. 1991. pap. 147.00 (*0-08-041164-9*, Pergamon Pr) Elsevier.

Microgravity Sciences: Results & Analysis of Recent Spaceflights: Proceedings of the G1 Symposium of COSPAR Scientific Commission G, Held During the Thirtieth COSPAR Scientific Assembly, Hamburg, Germany, 11-21 July, 1994. G1 Symposium of COSPAR Scientific Commission. Ed. by H. J. Rath. (Advances in Space Research Ser.: Vol. 16). 244p. 1995. pap. 97.75 (*0-08-042627-1*, Pergamon Pr) Elsevier.

Microgravity Sciences & Processes. Luigi G. Napolitano. 1983. pap. 37.00 (*0-08-029985-7*, Pergamon Pr) Elsevier.

Microguia De Powerpoint 4. (C). 1996. 0.00 (*0-201-87970-0*) HEPC Inc.

Microguia Excel 5. (C). 1996. 0.00 (*0-201-87942-5*) HEPC Inc.

***Microhardness of Polymers.** Francisco Jose Balta Calleja & Stoyko Fakirov. (Illus.). 350p. 2000. write for info. (*0-521-64218-3*) Cambridge U Pr.

Microheterogeneity of Glycoprotein Hormones. Ed. by Brooks A. Keel & H. Edward Grotjan, Jr. 256p. 1988. 145.00 (*0-8493-4959-1*, QP572, CRC Reprint) Franklin.

Microhistories: Demography, Society & Culture in Rural England, 1800-1930. Barry Reay. (Cambridge Studies in Population, Economy & Society in Past Time: No. 30). (Illus.). 313p. (C). 1996. text 59.95 (*0-521-57028-X*) Cambridge U Pr.

Microhistory & the Lost Peoples of Europe. Ed. by Edward Muir & Guido Ruggiero. LC 90-27638. (Selections from Quaderni Storici Ser.). 240p. 1991. text 38.50 (*0-8018-4182-8*); pap. text 15.95 (*0-8018-4183-6*) Johns Hopkins.

Microindentation Techniques in Materials Science & Engineering, STP 889. Ed. by Peter J. Blau & Brian R. Lawn. LC 85-28577. (Illus.). 300p. 1986. text 46.00 (*0-8031-0441-3*, STP889) ASTM.

Microinjection. Ed. by J. Feramisco et al. LC 98-43502. (Methods & Tools in Biosciences & Medicine Ser.). 350p. 1999. 118.00 (*3-7643-5973-0*) Birkhauser.

Microinjection. Juan Carlos Lacal. LC 98-43502. (Methods & Tools in Biosciences & Medicine Ser.). 1999. write for info. (*0-8176-5973-0*); pap. write for info. (*0-8176-6019-4*) Birkhauser.

Microinjection. Ed. by Juan Carlos Lacal et al. LC 98-43502. (Methods & Tools in Biosciences & Medicine Ser.). 350p. 1999. spiral bd. 98.00 (*3-7643-6019-4*) Birkhauser.

Microinjection & Transgenesis: Strategies & Protocols. Ed. by Angel Cid-Arregui & Alejandro Garcia-Carranca. LC 97-27747. (Lab Manual Ser.). (Illus.). 400p. 1997. 104.00 (*3-540-61895-3*) Spr-Verlag.

Microiology Lab Manual. 5th ed. James G. Cappuccino. LC 98-18844. 477p. (C). 1998. pap. text, lab manual ed. 42.00 (*0-8053-7646-1*) Benjamin-Cummings.

Microirrigation: A Compilation of Technical Papers. Compiled by American Society of Agricultural Engineers. (Illus.). 363p. 1995. pap. 39.50 (*0-929355-63-6*, M0395) Am Soc Ag Eng.

Microirrigation for a Changing World: Conserving Resources/Preserving the Environment. LC 95-60363. (Illus.). 1006p. (Orig.). 1995. pap. 66.00 (*0-929355-62-8*, P0495) Am Soc Ag Eng.

Microkinetics of Heterogeneous Catalysis. James A. Dumesic et al. LC 92-36488. (Professional Reference Book Ser.). 316p. 1993. text 69.00 (*0-8412-2214-2*, Pub. by Am Chemical) OUP.

***Microlaparascopy.** Oscar D. Almeida. 119p. 2000. 149.95 (*0-471-34574-1*) Wiley.

Microlaryngoscopy & Endolaryngeal Microsurgery. 3rd ed. Oskar Kleinsasser. Tr. by Philip M. Stell from GER. (Illus.). 131p. 1992. text 132.00 (*1-56053-006-5*) Hanley & Belfus.

Microlenses: Coupling Light to Optical Fibers. Ed. by Huey-Daw Wu & Frank S. Barnes. LC 90-4081. 512p. 1990. 89.95 (*0-87942-259-9*, PC02493) Inst Electrical.

Microlepidoptera. E. Zimmerman & E. Hardy. (Insects of Hawaii Ser.: Vol. 9). (Illus.). 1936p. 1978. 7.50 (*0-614-05657-8*, ESAHI9) Entomol Soc.

Microlife. David Burnie. LC 97-18888. (Inside Guides Ser.). (J). (gr. 3-6). 1997. write for info. (*0-7894-2036-8*) DK Pub Inc.

Microlithographic Techniques in Integrated Circuit Fabrication. Soon-Fatt Yoon et al. LC 98-122037. 1997. pap. 69.00 (*0-8194-2610-5*) SPIE.

Microlithography: High Integration in Microelectronics. Ed. by A. Craievich et al. 192p. (C). 1990. text 81.00 (*981-02-0137-0*) World Scientific Pub.

Microlithography: Science & Technology. James R. Sheats & Bruce W. Smith. LC 98-16713. (Illus.). 800p. 1998. text 175.00 (*0-8247-9953-4*) Dekker.

Microlithography & Metrology in Micromachining II, Vol. 2880. Ed. by Michael T. Postek & Craig R. Friedrich. 306p. 1996. 66.00 (*0-8194-2278-9*) SPIE.

Microlithography & Metrology in Micromachining III, Vol. 3225. Ed. by Craig R. Friedrich & Akira Umeda. LC 98-122576. 142p. 1997. 59.00 (*0-8194-2657-1*) SPIE.

Microlithography Fundamentals in Semiconductor Devices & Fabrication Technology. Saburo Nonogaki & Takumi Ueno. LC 98-4222. (Illus.). 336p. 1998. text 135.00 (*0-8247-9951-8*) Dekker.

Microlivestock: Little-Known Small Animals with a Promising Economic Future. Ed. by Panel on Microlivestock, National Research Council. 472p. 1991. pap. text 29.95 (*0-309-04295-X*) Natl Acad Pr.

Microlocal Analysis. M. Salah Baoudndi et al. Ed. by Richards Beals & Linda Preiss. LC 84-2852. (Contemporary Mathematics Ser.: No. 27). 252p. 1984. pap. 37.00 (*0-8218-5031-8*, CONM/27) Am Math.

Microlocal Analysis. Ed. by M. Salah Baouendi et al. LC 84-2852. (Contemporary Mathematics Ser.: No. 27). (Illus.). 260p. reprint ed. pap. 80.60 (*0-608-09193-6*, 205269700003) Bks Demand.

Microlocal Analysis & Applications. Ed. by L. Cattabriga & J. M. Bony. (Lecture Notes in Mathematics Ser.: Vol. 1495). vii, 349p. 1992. pap. 52.00 (*0-387-54948-X*) Spr-Verlag.

Microlocal Analysis & Nonlinear Waves. Ed. by M. Beals et al. (IMA Volumes in Mathematics & Its Applications Ser.: Vol. 30). (Illus.). xiii, 199p. 1991. 42.95 (*0-387-97591-8*) Spr-Verlag.

Microlocal Analysis & Precise Spectral Asymptotics. V. Ivrii. LC 97-49029. (Springer Monographs in Mathematics). xv, 731p. 1998. 109.00 (*3-540-62780-4*) Spr-Verlag.

Microlocal Analysis & Spectral Theory. LC 97-13929. 1997. text 240.50 (*0-7923-4544-4*) Kluwer Academic.

Microlocal Analysis for Differential Operators: An Introduction. Alain Grigis & Johannes Sjostrand. (London Mathematical Society Lecture Note Ser.: No. 196). 157p. (C). 1994. pap. text 36.95 (*0-521-44986-3*) Cambridge U Pr.

***Micromachined Devices & Components V.** Ed. by Patrick J. French & Eric Peeters. 312p. 1999. pap. text 72.00 (*0-8194-3473-6*) SPIE.

Micromachined Devices & Components II, Vol. 2882. Ed. by Kevin Chau & Ray M. Roop. 350p. 1996. 66.00 (*0-8194-2280-0*) SPIE.

Micromachined Devices & Components III, Vol. 3224. Ed. by Kevin Chau & Patrick J. French. LC 98-122098. 392p. 1997. 80.00 (*0-8194-2656-3*) SPIE.

Micromachined Devices & Components IV. Ed. by Patrick J. French & Kevin Chau. LC 98-226766. (Proceedings of SPIE Ser.: Vol. 3514). 448p. 1998. 99.00 (*0-8194-2973-2*) SPIE.

Micromachined Transducers Sourcebook. Gregory T. Kovacs. LC 98-4846. 944p. 1998. 98.75 (*0-07-290722-3*) McGraw.

***Micromachined Ultrasound-Based Proximity Sensors.** Mark R. Hornung & Oliver Brand. LC 99-20175. (Microsystems Ser.). 1999. 88.00 (*0-7923-8508-X*) Kluwer Academic.

Micromachines: A New Era in Mechanical Engineering. Iwao Fujimasa. (Illus.). 170p. 1996. pap. text 35.00 (*0-19-856528-3*) OUP.

Micromachines & Nantechnology: The Amazing New World of the Ultrasmall. David Darling. (Beyond Two Thousand Ser.). (Illus.). 64p. (J). (gr. 5-9). 1995. pap. 7.95 (*0-382-24953-4*, Dillon Silver Burdett) Silver Burdett Pr.

Micromachining & Imaging, Vol. 3009. Ed. by Terry A. Michalske & Mark A. Wendman. 158p. 1997. 59.00 (*0-8194-2420-X*) SPIE.

Micromachining & Microfabrication Process Technology II. Ed. by James H. Smith. LC 99-200342. (Proceedings of SPIE Ser.: Vol 3511). 414p. 1998. 89.00 (*0-8194-2970-8*) SPIE.

Micromachining & Microfabrication Process Technology II, Vol. 2879. Ed. by Stella W. Pang & Shih-Chia Chang. 376p. 1996. 76.00 (*0-8194-2277-0*) SPIE.

Micromachining & Microfabrication Process Technology III, Vol. 3223. Ed. by Shih-Chia Chang & Stella W. Pang. LC 98-122577. 320p. 1997. 80.00 (*0-8194-2655-5*) SPIE.

***Micromachining & Microfabrication Process Technology V.** Ed. by James H. Smith & Jean M. Karam. 444p. 1999. pap. text 103.00 (*0-8194-3471-X*) SPIE.

***Micromachining Techniques Using Layers Grown in an Epitaxial Reactor.** Paul Gennissen. (Illus.). 164p. 1999. pap. 44.50 (*90-407-1843-1*, Pub. by Delft U Pr) Coronet Bks.

Micromagnetics. William F. Brown, Jr. LC 78-2342. 154p. 1979. reprint ed. lib. bdg. 18.50 (*0-88275-665-6*) Krieger.

Micromanagement: How to Solve the Problems of Growing Companies. William A. Delaney. LC 80-69691. 174p. reprint ed. pap. 54.00 (*0-608-12161-4*, 202391400034) Bks Demand.

Micromanipulation by Light in Biology & Medicine: Laser Microbeam & Optical Tweezers. K. O. Greulich. LC 97-29317. 300p. 1999. 129.00 (*3-7643-3873-3*) Birkhauser.

Micromanipulation by Light in Biology & Medicine: Laser Microbeam & Optical Tweezers. Karl O. Greulich. Ed. by D. L. Farkas. LC 97-29317. (Methods in Bioengineering Ser.). (Illus.). 450p. 1998. 79.95 (*0-8176-3873-3*) Spr-Verlag.

***Micromanipulation in Assisted Conception: A Handbook & Troubleshooting Guide.** Steven D. Fleming & Robert S. King. (Illus.). 240p. 2001. pap. write for info. (*0-521-64847-5*) Cambridge U Pr.

Micromanipulation of Human Gametes & Embryos. Jacques Cohen et al. 336p. 1991. text 98.00 (*0-88167-835-X*) Lppncott W & W.

MicroMash CPA Review Reference, Vol. 1, The MicroMash Way to Pass see MicroMash CPA Review Reference, 1998-1999

MicroMash CPA Review Reference, Vol. 2, Financial Accounting (FARE) see MicroMash CPA Review Reference, 1998-1999

MicroMash CPA Review Reference, Vol. 3, Managerial/Governmental/Taxation (ARE) see MicroMash CPA Review Reference, 1998-1999

MicroMash CPA Review Reference, Vol. 4, Auditing (AUDIT) see MicroMash CPA Review Reference, 1998-1999

MicroMash CPA Review Reference, Vol. 5, Business Law & Professional Responsibilities (LPR) see MicroMash CPA Review Reference, 1998-1999

MicroMash CPA Review Reference, 1998-1999, 5 vols. Incl. MicroMash CPA Review Reference Vol. 1: The MicroMash Way to Pass. rev. ed. (Illus.). 142p. (C). 1998. pap. 7.00 (*0-926709-78-X*); MicroMash CPA Review Reference Vol. 2: Financial Accounting (FARE) rev. ed. M. Herschel Mann. (Illus.). 432p. 1998. pap. 7.00 (*0-926709-81-X*); MicroMash CPA Review Reference Vol. 3: Managerial/Governmental/Taxation (ARE) rev. ed. J. Owen Cherrington. (Illus.). 386p. (C). 1998. pap. 7.00 (*0-926709-82-8*); MicroMash CPA Review Reference Vol. 4: Auditing (AUDIT) rev. ed. Raymond J. Clay. (Illus.). 257p. (C). 1998. pap. 7.00 (*0-926709-79-8*); MicroMash CPA Review Reference Vol. 5: Business Law & Professional Responsibilities (LPR) rev. ed. David G. Jaeger. (Illus.). 319p. (C). 1998. pap. 7.00 (*0-926709-80-1*); write for info. (*0-926709-77-1*) MicroMash.

***MicroMash MBE Review Reference: Constitutional Law/Criminal Law & Procedure/Evidence.** 4th rev. ed. Walter H. McLaughlin, Jr. 487p. 1998. pap. text 75.00 (*0-15-900431-4*) Harcourt.

***MicroMash MBE Review Reference: Contracts/Real Property/Torts.** 4th rev. ed. Walter H. McLaughlin, Jr. 487p. 1999. pap. text 18.95 (*0-15-900432-2*) Harcourt.

***MicroMash MBE Review Reference: The MicroMash Way to the MBE.** 4th rev. ed. 109p. 1998. pap. text 75.00 (*0-15-900430-6*) Harcourt.

MicroMash MBE Review Reference Vol. 1: The MicroMash Way to the MBE. 3rd rev. ed. Walter H. McLaughlin. 105p. 1998. pap. text 75.00 (*0-926709-83-6*) MicroMash.

MicroMash MBE Review Reference Vol. 2: Constitutional Law/Criminal Law & Procedure/Evidence. 3rd rev. ed. Walter H. McLaughlin, Jr. 470p. 1998. pap. 75.00 (*0-926709-84-4*) MicroMash.

MicroMash MBE Review Reference Vol. 3: Contracts/Real Property/Torts. 3rd rev. ed. Walter H. McLaughlin, Jr. 460p. 1998. pap. text 75.00 (*0-926709-85-2*) MicroMash.

Micromatic. 2nd ed. Timothy W. Scott, III & Alonzo J. Strickland, III. 144p. 1989. teacher ed. write for info. (*0-318-63338-8*) HM.

Micromatic, 2 vols. 2nd ed. Timothy W. Scott, III & Alonzo J. Strickland, III. 144p. (C). 1989. pap. 41.16 (*0-395-43365-7*) HM.

Micromatic: A Strategic Management Simulation, 2 vols. 2nd ed. Timothy W. Scott et al. (C). 1991. text, teacher ed. 25.16 incl. 5.25 hd (*0-395-54200-6*); text, teacher ed. 25.16 incl. 3.5 hd (*0-395-54201-4*); spiral bd. 45.56 incl. 5.25 hd (*0-395-58075-7*) HM.

Micromechanical Modelling & Damage Characteriztion of Advanced Materials Vol. 199-55: Micromechanical Modelling & Damage Characterization of Advanced Materials. Ed. by S. A. Meguid. LC 95-76451. (1995 Joint ASME Applied Mechanics Summer Meeting Ser.). 120p. 1995. 80.00 (*0-7918-1313-4*, H00945) ASME.

Micromechanical Modelling of the Transverse Strengths of Unidirectional Glass Fibre Reinforced Polyester. Albert T. Busschen. (Illus.). 246p. (Orig.). 1996. pap. 57.50 (*90-407-1354-5*, Pub. by Delft U Pr) Coronet Bks.

Micromechanical Systems. Ed. by David Y. Cho. (DSC Ser.: Vol. 40). 380p. 1992. 67.50 (*0-7918-1099-2*, G00743) ASME.

Micromechanical Systems, 1993. Ed. by A. P. Pisano et al. LC 93-73713. 107p. 1993. pap. 40.00 (*0-7918-1000-3*) ASME.

Micromechanics: Overall Properties of Heterogeneous Materials. S. Nemat-Nasser & Motoo Hori. LC 93-11093. (Applied Mathematics & Mechanics Ser.). 708p. 1993. 173.00 (*0-444-89881-6*, North Holland) Elsevier.

Micromechanics: Overall Properties of Heterogeneous Materials. 2nd rev. ed. S. Nemat-Nasser. LC 98-48057. 810p. 1999. pap. 94.00 (*0-444-50084-7*, North Holland) Elsevier.

Micromechanics & Constitutive Modelling of Composite Materials Vol. 202-61: Micromechanics & Constitutive Modelling of Composite Materials. Ed. by Hussein M. Zbib et al. LC 95-77180. (1995 Joint ASME Applied Mechanics & Materials Summer Meeting Ser.: Vol. 202). 196p. 1995. 100.00 (*0-7918-1317-7*, H00949) ASME.

Micromechanics & Inhomogeneity: The Toshio Mura Anniversary Volume. Ed. by G. J. Weng et al. (Illus.). xxxv, 622p. 1989. 165.95 (*0-387-97043-6*) Spr-Verlag.

Micromechanics & MEMS: Classic & Seminal Papers to 1990. W. Trimmer & Institute of Electrical & Electronics Engineers, I. LC 96-34081. 720p. 1997. 129.95 (*0-7803-1085-3*, PC4390) Inst Electrical.

Micromechanics of Advanced Materials: A Symposium Dedicated to Professor James C. M. Li's Seventieth Birthday. Ed. by W. W. Gerberich et al. (Illus.). 408p. 1995. 20.00 (*0-87339-294-9*, 2949) Minerals Metals.

Micromechanics of Composites: Composite Properties of Fibre & Matrix Constituents. Kuno Stellbrink. 118p. 1996. pap. 68.00 (*1-56990-206-2*) Hanser-Gardner.

Micromechanics of Defects in Solids. Toshio Mura. 1982. lib. bdg. 263.50 (*90-247-2560-7*) Kluwer Academic.

Micromechanics of Defects in Solids. 2nd rev. ed. Toshio Mura. 1987. pap. text 115.00 (*90-247-3256-5*); lib. bdg. 318.50 (*90-247-3343-X*) Kluwer Academic.

Micromechanics of Failure of Quasi-Brittle Materials: Proceedings of the International Conference, Albuquerque, New Mexico, 6-8 June, 1990. Ed. by Surendra P. Shah et al. 652p. 1990. mass mkt. 166.95 (*1-85166-511-0*) Elsevier.

Micromechanics of Random Media: Selected & Revised Proceedings of the Symposium on Micromechanics of Random Media, MEET'N '93. Ed. by Martin Ostoja-Starzewski & Iwona Jasiuk. 240p. 1994. pap. 170.00 (*0-614-32147-6*) ASME.

Micromegas. 2nd ed. Voltaire. Ed. by Ben Barkow. Tr. by W. Fleming from FRE. (European Classics). 171p. 1999. reprint ed. pap. 8.95 (*0-946626-55-3*, Pub. by Dedalus) Hippocrene Bks.

Micrometeorological Methods in Ecology. J. Grace & J. Moncrieff. 1997. pap. 39.95 (*0-632-02971-4*) Blackwell Sci.

Micrometers Calipers & Gages. Intro. by Thomas A. Hoerner & W. Forrest Bear. (Illus.). 21p. 1969. pap. text 5.20 (*0-913163-03-1*, 169) Hobar Pubns.

***Micromonsters: Life under the Microscope.** Christopher Maynard. LC 99-20401. (Eyewitness Readers). 48p. (J). (gr. 2-4). 1999. 3.95 (*0-7894-4756-8*); 12.95 (*0-7894-4757-6*, D K Ink) DK Pub Inc.

Micromorphology: A Basic & Applied Science: Proceedings of the VIIIth International Working Meeting, San Antonio, Texas, July 1988. Ed. by L. A. Douglas. (Developments in Soil Science Ser.: Vol. 19). xviii,716p. 1990. 221.50 (*0-444-88302-9*) Elsevier.

Micromosaics. Jeanette Hanisee Gabriel. (Gilbert Collection). 288p. 1999. 90.00 (*0-85667-511-3*, Pub. by P Wilson) Antique Collect.

Micromotives & Macrobehavior. Thomas C. Schelling. (Illus.). (C). 1978. pap. text 15.50 (*0-393-09009-4*) Norton.

Micromovement in Orthopaedics. Alan R. Smith. (Illus.). 342p. 1993. text 95.00 (*0-19-262306-0*) OUP.

Micromycetes in Foodstuffs & Feedstuffs. Z. Jesenska. (Progress in Industrial Microbiology Ser.: Vol. 28). 256p. 1993. 201.25 (*0-444-98684-7*) Elsevier.

Micromysteries: Stories of Scientific Detection. Gail K. Haines. LC 89-70166. (Illus.). 196p. 1988. 14.99 (*0-399-61270-X*) Putnam Pub Group.

***Micronesia.** Monique Carriveau Storie & William L. Wuerch. (World Bibliographical Ser.: Vol. 220). 215p. 1999. 82.00 (*1-85109-289-7*) ABC-CLIO.

***Micronesia: A Country Study Guide.** Global Investment & Business Center, Inc. Staff. (World Country Study Guides Library: Vol. 113). (Illus.). 350p. 2000. pap. 59.00 (*0-7397-2411-8*) Intl Business Pubns.

Micronesia - A Country Study Guide: Basic Information for Research & Pleasure. Global Investment Center, USA Staff. (World Country Study Guide Library: Vol. 113). (Illus.). 350p. 1999. pap. 59.00 (*0-7397-1510-0*) Intl Business Pubns.

***Micronesia Business Intelligence Report, 190 vols.** Global Investment & Business Center, Inc. Staff. (World Business Intelligence Library: Vol. 113). (Illus.). 350p. 2000. pap. 99.95 (*0-7397-2611-0*) Intl Business Pubns.

***Micronesia Business Law Handbook, 190 vols.** Global Investment & Business Center, Inc. Staff. (Global Business Law Handbooks Library: Vol. 113). (Illus.). 350p. 2000. pap. 99.95 (*0-7397-2011-2*) Intl Business Pubns.

***Micronesia Business Opportunity Yearbook.** Global Investment & Business Center, Inc. Staff. (Global Business Opportunity Yearbooks Library: Vol. 113). (Illus.). 2000. pap. 99.95 (*0-7397-2211-5*) Intl Business Pubns.

***Micronesia Business Opportunity Yearbook: Export-Import, Investment & Business Opportunities.** International Business Publications, U. S. A. Staff & Global Investment Center, U. S. A. Staff. (Global Business Opportunity Yearbooks Library: Vol. 113). (Illus.). 350p. 1999. pap. 99.95 (*0-7397-1311-6*) Intl Business Pubns.

***Micronesia Country Review 2000.** Robert C. Kelly et al. (Illus.). 60p. 1999. pap. 39.95 (*1-58310-537-9*) CountryWatch.

***Micronesia Foreign Policy & Government Guide.** Contrib. by Global Investment & Business Center, Inc. Staff. (World Foreign Policy & Government Library: Vol. 109). (Illus.). 350p. 1999. pap. 99.00 (*0-7397-3607-8*) Intl Business Pubns.

***Micronesia Foreign Policy & Government Guide.** Global Investment & Business Center, Inc. Staff. (World Foreign Policy & Government Library: Vol. 109). (Illus.). 350p. 2000. pap. 99.95 (*0-7397-3811-9*) Intl Business Pubns.

***Micronesia Investment & Business Guide.** Global Investment & Business Center, Inc. Staff. (Global Investment & Business Guide Library: Vol. 113). (Illus.). 2000. pap. 99.95 (*0-7397-1811-8*) Intl Business Pubns.

***Micronesia Investment & Business Guide: Export-Import, Investment & Business Opportunities.** International Business Publications, USA Staff & Global Investment Center, USA Staff. (World Investment & Business Guide Library-99: Vol. 113). (Illus.). 350p. 1999. pap. 99.95 (*0-7397-0308-0*) Intl Business Pubns.

Micronesia, 1944-1974: A Bibliography of Anthropological & Related Source Materials. Mac Marshall & James D. Nason. LC 75-28587. (Bibliographies Ser.). 348p. 1975. 10.00 (*0-87536-215-X*) HRAFP.

Micronesia, 1975-1987: A Social Science Bibliography, 5. Ed. by William L. Wuerch. LC 89-11979. (Bibliographies & Indexes in Anthropology Ser.: No. 005). 207p. 1989. lib. bdg. 62.95 (*0-313-26852-5*, GIE/, Greenwood Pr) Greenwood.

***Micronesian Reef Fishes: A Comprehensive Guide to the Coral Reef Fishes of Micronesia.** 3rd ed. (Illus.). 522p. 1999. 74.95 (*0-9621564-5-0*) Coral Graphics.

***Micronesian Reef Fishes: A Field Guide for Divers & Aquarists.** 3rd ed. (Illus.). 406p. 1999. pap. 49.95 (*0-9621564-4-2*) Coral Graphics.

Micronesian Reef Fishes: A Practical Guide to the Identification of the Coral Reef Fishes of the Tropical Central & Western Pacific. Robert F. Myers. (Illus.). iv, 288p. 1989. text 49.95 (*0-9621564-1-8*); pap. text 35.95 (*0-9621564-0-X*) Coral Graphics.

Micronesian Reef Fishes: A Practical Guide to the Identification of the Coral Reef Fishes of the Tropical Central & Western Pacific. 2nd ed. Robert F. Myers. (Illus.). 442p. 1991. 46.00 (*0-9621564-3-4*); pap. 33.50 (*0-9621564-2-6*) Coral Graphics.

Micronesian Religion & Lore: A Guide to Sources, 1526-1990, 32. Douglas Haynes & William L. Wuerch. LC 94-38504. (Bibliographies & Indexes in Religious Studies: Vol. 32). 328p. 1995. lib. bdg. 79.50 (*0-313-28955-7*, Greenwood Pr) Greenwood.

***Micronesia's Never-Forgotten Island.** Raymond Refoen. (Illus.). 2000. pap. 17.49 (*0-9679288-0-X*) Virginia Pines.

Microneurosurgery, Vol. 1. M. Gazi Yasargil. (Illus.). 386p. 1984. 199.00 (*0-86577-141-3*) Thieme Med Pubs.

Microneurosurgery, Vol. 2. M. Gazi Yasargil et al. (Illus.). 386p. 1984. text 199.00 (*0-86577-142-1*) Thieme Med Pubs.

Microneurosurgery, Vol. 3A. M. Gazi Yasargil. (Illus.). 432p. 1987. text 210.00 (*0-86577-258-4*) Thieme Med Pubs.

Microneurosurgery, Vol. 3B. M. Gazi Yasargil. (Illus.). 596p. 1987. text 210.00 (*0-86577-259-2*) Thieme Med Pubs.

Microneurosurgery, Vols. 3A & 3B. Yasargil. 379.00 (*0-86577-656-3*) Thieme Med Pubs.

Microneurosurgery, Vols. 4A & 4B. M. G. Yasargil. 1996. 479.00 (*0-86577-657-1*) Thieme Med Pubs.

Microneurosurgery Vol. IVB: Microsurgery of CNS Tumors, Vol. 4B. M. G. Yasargil. LC 97-202615. (Illus.). 552p. 1995. 269.00 (*0-86577-546-X*) Thieme Med Pubs.

Microneurosurgical Atlas. K. Sugita. (Illus.). 275p. 1985. 383.00 (*0-387-15110-9*) Spr-Verlag.

Micronutrients Vol. 53, No. 9, Pt. 2: Their Role in a Modern Lifestyle: The Kellogg Nutrition Symposium (Sydney, Australia) 45p. 1995. pap. 20.00 (*0-614-22652-X*) ILSI.

Micronutrients in Health & in Disease Prevention. Ed. by Adrianne Bendich & C. E. Butterworth. (Illus.). 504p. 1991. text 175.00 (*0-8247-8539-8*) Dekker.

Micronutrients in Tropical Food Crop Production. Ed. by Paul L. Vlek. (Developments in Plant & Soil Sciences Ser.). (Orig.). 1985. text 195.50 (*90-247-3085-6*) Kluwer Academic.

Microoptics. Jurgen Jahns. 428p. 1999. 145.00 (*3-527-29428-7*) Wiley.

Microoptics Technology: Fabrication & Applications of Lens Arrays & Devices. Nicholas F. Borrelli. LC 98-56646. (Optical Engineering Ser.: Vol. 36). (Illus.). 360p. 1999. text 175.00 (*0-8247-1348-6*) Dekker.

Microorganic Matter in Water, STP 448. 129p. 1981. pap. 9.25 (*0-8031-0066-3*, STP448) ASTM.

Microorganism in Foods: Microbial Ecology of Food Commodities. 6th ed. Ed. by ICMSF Staff. 615p. 1997. 165.00 (*0-8342-1825-9*) Aspen Pub.

Microorganismos. (Serie de Biologia: No. 6). (SPA.). 1968. pap. 3.50 (*0-8270-6065-3*) OAS.

Microorganismos. 3rd ed. J. M. Butilerrez-Vasquez. Ed. by OAS General Secretariat Staff. (Serie de Biologia: No. 6). (SPA., Illus.). 79p. (C). 1981. pap. 3.50 (*0-685-03621-9*) OAS.

***Microorganisms.** Pat Ward & Barb Ward. (Illus.). 64p. (YA). (gr. 5). 1998. pap. text 8.95 (*1-58037-080-2*, Pub. by M Twain Media) Carson-Dellos.

***Microorganisms: Applications in Biology & Chemistry.** 2nd ed. Cord. 1998. pap. 7.25 (*1-57837-081-7*) Thomson Learn.

Microorganisms & Autoimmune Diseases. Ed. by H. Friedman et al. LC 96-25100. (Infectious Agents & Pathogenesis Ser.). (Illus.). 275p. (C). 1996. text 95.00 (*0-306-45236-7*, Kluwer Plenum) Kluwer Academic.

Microorganisms & Minerals. Ed. by Eugene D. Weinberg. LC 76-53191. (Microbiology Ser.: No. 3). 510p. 1977. reprint ed. pap. 158.10 (*0-608-01298-X*, 206204400001) Bks Demand.

Microorganisms & Nitrogen Sources: Transport & Utilization of Amino Acids, Peptides, Proteins, & Related Substrates. Ed. by J. W. Payne. LC 79-42900. (Illus.). 884p. reprint ed. pap. 200.00 (*0-608-17685-0*, 203040400069) Bks Demand.

Microorganisms As Model Systems for Studying Evolution. Ed. by Robert P. Mortlock. LC 84-17938. (Monographs in Evolutionary Biology). 344p. 1984. 95.00 (*0-306-41788-X*, Plenum Trade) Perseus Pubng.

Microorganisms in Activated Sludge & Biofilm Processes: Proceedings fo the IAWQ 1st International Specialized Conference on Microorganisms in Activated Sludge & Biofilm Processes, Held in Paris, France, 27-28 September 1993. R. Pujol. (Water Science & Technology Ser.). 392p. pap. 197.75 (*0-08-042538-0*, Pergamon Pr) Elsevier.

***Microorganisms in Activated Sludge & Biofilm Processes II.** Ed. by Conference Program Committee Staff. 630p. 1998. pap. 318.00 (*0-08-043382-0*, Excerpta Medica) Elsevier.

Microorganisms in Foods, Vol. 2. Fred S. Thatcher & D. S. Clark. LC 73-2628. 225p. reprint ed. pap. 69.80 (*0-608-15406-7*, 202933100002) Bks Demand.

Microorganisms in Foods: Their Significance & Methods of Enumeration, Vol. 1. 2nd ed. International Commission on Microbiological Specif. LC 77-17842. 1978. text 60.00 (*0-8020-2293-6*) U of Toronto Pr.

Microorganisms in Foods Bk. 2: Sampling for Microbiological Analysis; Principles & Specific Applications. Internal Commission on Microbiological Specificati. 448p. 1986. text 55.00 (*0-8020-5693-8*) U of Toronto Pr.

Microorganisms in Foods Bk. 4: Application of the Hazard Analysis Critical Control Point (HACCP) System to Ensure Microbiological Safety & Quality. International Commission on Microbiological Specif. (Illus.). 372p. (C). 1989. pap. text 59.95 (*0-632-02651-0*) Blackwell Sci.

Microorganisms in Our World. Ronald M. Atlas & Lawrence C. Parks. 400p. (C). 1995. text, lab manual ed. write for info. (*0-8151-0337-9*, WCB McGr Hill) McGrw-H Hghr Educ.

Microorganisms in Our World. Ronald M. Atlas & William R. Wellnitz. 216p. (C). 1995. text, student ed. 20.62 (*0-8151-0336-0*, WCB McGr Hill) McGrw-H Hghr Educ.

Microorganisms to Combat Pollution. Ed. by Eugene Rosenberg. LC 93-3223. 288p. (C). 1993. text 233.00 (*0-7923-2226-6*) Kluwer Academic.

Micro/OS-II: The Real-Time Kernel. 2nd ed. Jean J. Labrosse. (Illus.). 524p. 1992. 69.95 incl. disk (*0-87930-543-6*) C M P Books.

Micropac - Biological. 2nd ed. Kalat. (Psychology). Date not set. write for info. (*0-534-03545-0*) Wadsworth Pub.

Micropace Handbook for All Software. Warner. (TE - Keyboarding Ser.). 1985. 10.95 (*0-538-20757-4*) S-W Pub.

Micropalaeontology in Petroleum Exploration. R. Wynn Jones. (Illus.). 448p. (C). 1996. text 165.00 (*0-19-854091-4*) OUP.

Micropalaeontology of Carbonate Environments. M. B. Hart. LC 86-27873. 296p. 1987. text 142.00 (*0-470-20762-0*) P-H.

Micropalaeontology of Oceans: Proceedings of the Symposium Held in Cambridge from 10 to 17 September, 1967 under the Title 'Micropalaeontology of Marine Bottom Sediments' Ed. by B. M. Funnell & W. R. Riedel. LC 71-96089. (Illus.). 838p. reprint ed. pap. 180.00 (*0-608-17512-9*, 2030596) Bks Demand.

Micropaleontology & Biostratigraphy of the Coastal Basins of West Africa. C. A. Kogbe. 102p. 1986. pap. 24.00 (*0-08-033926-3*, G115, Pub. by PPL) Elsevier.

Micropanastron: or An Astrological Vade Mecum. large type ed. John Partridge. Ed. by Carol A. Wiggers. Tr. by J. Lee Lehman. (Illus.). 352p. (C). 1995. pap. text 30.00 (*1-878935-12-7*) JustUs & Assocs.

Microparametric Syntax & Dialect Variation. Ed. by James R. Black & Virginia Motapanyane. LC 96-38230. (Current Issues in Linguistic Theory Ser.: No. 139). xviii, 269p. 1996. lib. bdg. 69.00 (*1-55619-594-X*) J Benjamins Pubng Co.

Microparticulate Systems for the Delivery of Proteins & Vaccines. Smadar Cohen & Howard Bernstein. LC 96-25983. (Drugs & the Pharmaceutical Sciences Ser.: Vol. 77). (Illus.). 552p. 1996. text 180.00 (*0-8247-9753-1*) Dekker.

Micropatterns: Tying & Fishing the Small Fly. Darrel Martin. 336p. 1999. pap. text 29.95 (*1-55821-894-7*) Lyons Pr.

Micropatterns: Tying & Fishing the Small Fly. Darrell Martin. LC 94-6300. 352p. 1994. 40.00 (*1-55821-260-4*) Lyons Pr.

***Microphone Book.** John Eargle. (Illus.). 400p. 2001. pap. 39.95 (*0-240-80445-7*, Focal) Buttrwrth-Heinemann.

Microphone Fiends: Youth Music & Youth Culture. Ed. by Andrew Ross & Tricia Rose. LC 93-44005. 288p. (C). (gr. 13). 1994. 80.00 (*0-415-90907-4*); pap. 20.99 (*0-415-90908-2*) Routledge.

Microphone Handbook. John M. Eargle. LC 81-70852. (Illus.). 240p. 1982. lib. bdg. 31.95 (*0-914130-02-1*) Elar Pub Co.

Microphone Wars: A History of Triumph & Betrayal at CBC. Knowlton Nash. (Illus.). 584p. 1996. pap. text 24.99 (*0-7710-6715-1*) McCland & Stewart.

Microphone Wars: A History of Triumph & Betrayal at the CBC. Knowlton Nash. (Illus.). 528p. 1994. 35.00 (*0-7710-6712-7*) McCland & Stewart.

Microphones. A. R. Kazuk. 1987. pap. 9.95 (*0-919626-31-9*, Pub. by Brick Bks) Genl Dist Srvs.

Microphones. 3rd ed. Martin Clifford. (Illus.). 352p. 1986. 22.95 (*0-8306-0475-8*); pap. 17.95 (*0-8306-2675-1*, NO. 2675) McGraw-Hill Prof.

Microphones: Technology & Technique. John Borwick. LC 89-71327. (Illus.). 253p. reprint ed. pap. 78.50 (*0-608-20294-0*, 207155300001) Bks Demand.

Microphones, Acoustics, Soundproofing & Monitoring, Vol. 2. Paul White. (Creative Recording Ser.). 1999. pap. 19.95 (*1-86074-231-9*) Sanctuary Pubng.

Microphysical Processes in Clouds. Kenneth C. Young. (Illus.). 448p. (C). 1993. text 77.00 (*0-19-507563-3*) OUP.

Microphysical Reality & Quantum Formalism, 2 vols., Set, Vols. 1 & 2. Ed. by Alwyn Van Der Merwe et al. 992p. (C). 1988. lib. bdg. 395.50 (*90-277-2686-8*, D Reidel) Kluwer Academic.

Microphysical Reality & Quantum Formalism: Proceedings of the Conference, Held in Urbino, Italy, September 25-October 3, 1985, Vol. 1. Ed. by Gino Tarozzi et al. (Fundamental Theories of Physics Ser.: No. 25-26). 496p. 1900. lib. bdg. 477.00 (*90-277-2683-3*) Kluwer Academic.

Microphysical Reality & Quantum Formalism: Proceedings of the Conference, Held in Urbino, Italy, September 25-October 3, 1985, Vol. 2. Ed. by Gino Tarozzi et al. (Fundamental Theories of Physics Ser.: No. 25-26). 484p. 1900. lib. bdg. write for info. (*90-277-2684-1*) Kluwer Academic.

Microphysics of Atmospheric Clouds & Precipitation. Hans R. Pruppacher & James D. Klett. 1978. lib. bdg. 145.00 (*90-277-0515-1*) Kluwer Academic.

Microphysics of Clouds & Precipitation: An Introduction to Cloud Chemistry & Cloud Electricity. 2nd enl. rev. ed. Hans R. Pruppacher. 976p. (C). 1997. pap. text 99.00 (*0-7923-4409-X*); lib. bdg. 290.00 (*0-7923-4211-9*) Kluwer Academic.

Microphysics of Surfaces: Nanoscale Processing. LC 95-67213. (1995 Technical Digest Ser.: Vol. 5). 105p. 1995. pap. 66.00 (*1-55752-380-0*) Optical Soc.

Microphyte Toxins: A Manual for Toxin Detection, Evironmental Monitoring. Guido Premazzi & Laura Volterra. 338p. 1994. pap. 50.00 (*92-826-2731-4*, CL-NA-14854-ENC, Pub. by Comm Europ Commun) Bernan Associates.

Microplancton des Eaux Marines et Saumatres de la Guyane et des Antilles Francaises (Microplankton in Sea Water & Brackish Water in Guiana & the French West Indies) G. Paulmier.Tr. of Microplankton in Sea Water & Brackish Water in Guiana & the French West Indies. (FRE., Illus.). 438p. 1993. pap. 28.00 (*2-7099-1131-0*, Pub. by LInstitut Francais) Balogh.

Microplanificacion: Un Proceso de Programacion y Desarrollo con Base en la Comunidad. Reinhard Goethert et al. LC 92-26056. (Documento Tecnico del IDE Ser.). 176p. 1992. pap. 22.00 (*0-8213-2214-1*, 12214) World Bank.

Microplankton in Sea Water & Brackish Water in Guiana & the French West Indies see Microplancton des Eaux Marines et Saumatres de la Guyane et des Antilles Francaises (Microplankton in Sea Water & Brackish Water in Guiana & the French West Indies)

Microplasticity, Vol. 2. Ed. by Charles J. McMahon, Jr. LC 68-4384. (Advances in Materials Research Ser.). 439p. reprint ed. pap. 136.10 (*0-608-11667-X*, 200740200062) Bks Demand.

Microplate Markets for Products. (Market Research Reports: No. 531). (Illus.). 129p. 1996. 995.00 (*0-317-05009-5*) Theta Corp.

Micropolar Fluids: Theory & Application. G. Lukaszewicz. LC 98-29998. (Modeling & Simulation in Science, Engineering & Technology Ser.). 256p. 1998. 59.95 (*0-8176-4008-8*) Spr-Verlag.

Micropolar Fluids: Theory & Applications. Grzegorz Lukaszewicz. LC 98-29998. xv, 253p. 1999. write for info. (*3-7643-4008-8*) Birkhauser.

Micropolitics in Contemporary China: A Technical Unit During & after the Cultural Revolution. Marc J. Blechner & Gordon White. LC 79-67176. 149p. 1979. reprint ed. pap. 46.20 (*0-7837-9965-9*, 206069200006) Bks Demand.

Micropolitics of Educational Leadership: From Control to Empowerment. Ed. by Joseph R. Blase & Gary L. Anderson. (Teacher Development Ser.). 176p. (C). 1995. pap. text 22.95 (*0-8077-3501-9*) Tchrs Coll.

Micropolitics of Knowledge: Communication & Indirect Control in Workgroups. Emmanuel Lazega. (Communication & Social Order Ser.). 156p. 1992. lib. bdg. 44.95 (*0-202-30426-4*) Aldine de Gruyter.

Micropolitics of Knowledge: Communication & Indirect Control in Workgroups. Emmanuel Lazega. (Communication & Social Order Ser.). 156p. 1992. pap. text 21.95 (*0-202-30427-2*) Aldine de Gruyter.

Micropollutants in River Sediments: Report on a WHO Working Group. (Euro Reports & Studies Ser.: No. 61). 85p. 1982. pap. text 8.00 (*92-890-1227-7*) World Health.

Micropollutants in the Environment, Vol. 14 No. 12. S. H. Jenkins. 1983. pap. 40.00 (*0-08-029091-4*, Pergamon Pr) Elsevier.

Microporous & Macroporous Materials. Ed. by J. S. Beck et al. (MRS Symposium Proceedings Ser.: Vol. 431). 551p. 1996. 73.00 (*1-55899-334-7*, 431) Materials Res.

Micropower Circuits. James D. Meindl. LC 68-28502. (Illus.). 258p. reprint ed. pap. 80.00 (*0-608-09956-2*, 201017800068) Bks Demand.

Micropractice in Social Work. Hepworth. (Adaptable Courseware Ser.). 1996. 44.25 (*0-534-49753-5*) Brooks-Cole.

Microprocessor: A Biography. Michael S. Malone. (TELOS - the Electronic Library of Science). (Illus.). 333p. 1995. 32.95 incl. cd-rom (*0-387-94342-0*) Spr-Verlag.

Microprocessor & Digital Computer Technology. J. Olesky & George B. Rutkowski. 1981. text 54.00 (*0-13-581116-3*) P-H.

Microprocessor & Microcontroller Fundamentals: 8085 & 8051 Hardware & Software. William Kleitz. LC 97-24124. 262p. (C). 1997. 85.00 (*0-13-262825-2*) P-H.

Microprocessor Applications. Andrew C. Jr. Staugaard & Ron Johnson. (Illus.). 600p. (C). 1984. 99.95 (*0-87119-046-X*, EB-6405); teacher ed. 9.95 (*0-87119-049-4*, EB-6405); student ed. 10.95 (*0-87119-048-6*, EB-6405); pap. text 24.95 (*0-87119-047-8*, EB-6405) Heathkit-Zenith Ed.

Microprocessor Architecture, Programming, & Applications with the 8085. 4th ed. Rameshs Gaonkar. LC 98-45804. 788p. 1998. 101.00 (*0-13-901257-5*) P-H.

Microprocessor Architectures: From VLIW to TTA. Henk Corporaal. LC 97-15958. 428p. 1997. 140.00 (*0-471-97157-X*) Wiley.

Microprocessor Architectures RISC, CISC & DSP. 2nd ed. Steve Heath. (Illus.). 400p. 1995. pap. text 52.95 (*0-7506-2303-9*) Buttrwrth-Heinemann.

Microprocessor; Automotive Development; Systems; Data Base; Finite Elements; Graphics; Education; Manufacturing; Management; Language Standards; Personal Computing see Advances in Computer Technology

Microprocessor Background for Management Personnel. J. Cooper. 208p. 1981. 32.00 (*0-13-580829-4*) P-H.

Microprocessor-Based Control Systems. Ed. by Naresh K. Sinha. 1986. text 186.00 (*90-277-2287-0*) Kluwer Academic.

Microprocessor Based Design. 2nd ed. Slater. 2001. text 50.00 (*0-13-567702-5*) P-H.

Microprocessor-Based Parallel Architecture of Reliable Digital Signal Programs. Alan D. George. 288p. 1992. boxed set 89.95 (*0-8493-7176-7*, QA) CRC Pr.

Microprocessor-Based System Design. David J. Comer. (Oxford Series in Electrical & Computer Engineering). (Illus.). 400p. (C). 1995. text 79.95 (*0-03-063781-3*) OUP.

Microprocessor-Based System Design. David J. Comer. 390p. (C). 1986. student ed. write for info. (*0-03-063782-1*) SCP.

Microprocessor-Based Systems. Richard C. Seals. 224p. (Orig.). (C). 1992. 42.50 (*0-7487-1533-9*, Pub. by S Thornes Pubs) Trans-Atl Phila.

Microprocessor Concepts & Applications. (Illus.). 600p. 1982. pap. text 20.00 (*0-86657-005-5*) Lab-Volt.

Microprocessor Control for Motor Drives & Power Converters. R. W. De Doncker et al. Ed. by V. R. Stefanovic & R. M. Nelms. LC 92-31625. (Tutorial Course Ser.). 1992. 60.00 (*0-7803-9965-X*) Inst Electrical.

Microprocessor Control for Motor Drives & Power Converters: Presented October 3 at the 1993 IEEE Industry Applications Society Annual Meeting, Toronto, Ontario, Canada, 3rd ed. R. W. De Doncker et al. Ed. by V. R. Stefanovic & R. M. Nelms. LC 93-30691. 1993. pap. 60.00 (*0-7803-9969-2*) Inst Electrical.

Microprocessor 8086. Ayala. Date not set. pap. text, student ed. write for info. (*0-314-06387-0*) West Pub.

Microprocessor Interfacing. Graham Dixey. Ed. by Andy Thomas. 112p. (Orig.). (C). 1991. 36.50 (*0-7487-0583-X*, Pub. by S Thornes Pubs) Trans-Atl Phila.

Microprocessor Interfacing. Andrew C. Staugaard, Jr. (Illus.). (C). 1982. teacher ed. 9.95 (*0-87119-079-6*); student ed. 10.95 (*0-87119-078-8*); pap. text 24.95 (*0-87119-077-X*, EB-6402); ring bd. 99.95 (*0-87119-090-7*, EE-3402) Heathkit-Zenith Ed.

Microprocessor-Micro Computer Technology. 2nd ed. Driscoll. (Electronics Technology Ser.). 1990. text 57.95 (*0-8273-4084-2*) Delmar.

Microprocessor Software Project Management. Eli T. Fathi & Cedric V. Armstrong. LC 85-13018. (Electrical Engineering & Electronics Ser.: Vol. 27). 368p. reprint ed. pap. 114.10 (*0-608-08933-8*, 206956800005) Bks Demand.

Microprocessor Support Chips: Theory, Design & Applications. T. J. Byers. 302p. (Orig.). 1982. 38.00 (*0-942412-05-2*) Micro Text Pubns.

Microprocessor System Design Fundamentals. Kenneth J. Breeding. LC 94-8257. 408p. 1994. text 69.00 (*0-13-564279-5*) P-H.

Microprocessor System Development. Alain Amghar. 1991. pap. 38.00 (*0-13-582651-9*) P-H.

Microprocessor System Servicing John D. Ferguson et al. LC 86-21246. 1987. write for info. (*0-13-581132-5*) P-H Intl.

Microprocessor Systems. Michel Aumiaux. LC 81-16251. (Wiley Series in Computing). (Illus.). 228p. reprint ed. pap. 70.70 (*0-8357-4565-1*, 203746700008) Bks Demand.

Microprocessor Systems: Mikroprozessorsysteme. R. Hedtke. (GER.). 203p. 1984. 99.50 (*0-8288-1357-4*, M15287) Fr & Eur.

Microprocessor Systems Design. 3rd ed. Alan Clements. LC 96-44239. (Electrical Engineering Ser.). 992p. (C). 1997. 100.95 (*0-534-94822-7*) PWS Pubs.

Microprocessor Systems Engineering. John Ferguson. (C). 1985. pap. text. write for info. (*0-201-14657-6*) Addison-Wesley.

Microprocessor Systems in Signal Processing. C. K. Yuen et al. (Microelectronics & Signal Processing Ser.). 300p. 1989. text 82.00 (*0-12-774955-1*) Acad Pr.

Microprocessor Technology. Stuart Anderson. LC 94-22233. (Illus.). 240p. 1995. pap. text 34.95 (*0-7506-1839-6*) Buttrwrth-Heinemann.

Microprocessor Technology: Theory & Experimentation. Frederick W. Hughes. 308p. 1988. pap. text 75.00 (*0-13-582180-0*) P-H.

Microprocessor Theory & Operation a Self-Study Guide with Experiments. J. A. Wilson & Ron Walls. (Illus.). 224p. (Orig.). 1987. 21.95 (*0-8306-0191-0*) McGraw-Hill Prof.

Microprocessor 68000. I. Scott MacKenzie. 1995. 74.25 (*0-13-018266-4*) P-H.

Microprocessor/Micro Computer Tech. 2nd ed. Driscoll. (Electronics Technology Ser.). 1990. pap., teacher ed. 16.00 (*0-8273-4085-0*) Delmar.

Microprocessors. Heath Company Staff. (Illus.). 614p. 1979. pap. text 24.95 (*0-87119-039-7*, EB-6401); ring bd. 99.95 (*0-87119-038-9*, EE-3401); 9.95 (*0-87119-041-9*); 11.95 (*0-87119-040-0*) Heathkit-Zenith Ed.

Microprocessors. Kreiger. (C). 1996. pap. text 50.00 (*0-03-005217-3*) Harcourt Coll Pubs.

Microprocessors: Fundamental Concepts & Applications. 3rd ed. Victor E. Gibson. LC 92-21490. 372p. 1994. text 46.95 (*0-8273-4761-8*) Delmar.

Microprocessors: Principles & Applications. Charles M. Gilmore. 416p. (C). 1989. text 37.96 (*0-07-023411-6*); teacher ed. 6.95 (*0-07-023413-2*); 19.96 (*0-07-023412-4*) McGraw.

Microprocessors: Principles & Applications, 3 vols. large type ed. Charles M. Gilmore. 662p. 165.50 (*0-614-20556-5*, L-31636-00 APHB) Am Printing Hse.

Microprocessors: Principles & Applications. 2nd ed. Charles M. Gilmore. LC 94-32670. (Basic Skills in Electricity & Electronics Ser.). 1996. 60.50 (*0-02-801837-0*) Glencoe.

Microprocessors: Principles & Applications. 2nd ed. Charles M. Gilmore. 1996. teacher ed. 17.49 (*0-02-801839-7*) Glencoe.

Microprocessors - Experiments for the Intel 8088. 3rd ed. Kerry Urbaniak. 138p. 1994. 28.50 (*0-8273-5847-4*) Delmar.

Microprocessors - Fundamental Concepts & Applications: Instructor's Guide. Victor E. Gibson. 49p. 1994. pap. 16.00 (*0-8273-4762-6*) Delmar.

Microprocessors & Interfacing: Programming & Hardware. 2nd ed. Douglas V. Hall. 576p. 1991. text 81.48 (*0-07-025742-6*) McGraw.

Microprocessors & Interfacing: Programming & Hardware. 2nd ed. Douglas V. Hall. 576p. 1991. 23.52 (*0-07-025743-4*) McGraw.

Microprocessors & Interfacing: Programming & Hardware, 68000 Family. Douglas V. Hall. 576p. 1992. 23.94 (*0-07-025692-6*) McGraw.

Microprocessors & Microcomputer-Based System Design. Mohamed Rafiquzzaman. (C). 1990. lib. bdg. 53.95 (*0-8493-4275-9*, QA76) CRC Pr.

Microprocessors & Microcomputer-Based Systems Design. 2nd ed. Mohamed Rafiquzzaman. 189p. 1995. per. write for info. (*0-8493-2642-7*) CRC Pr.

Microprocessors & Microcomputers: Hardware & Software. 5th ed. Ronald J. Tocci. LC 98-47317. (Illus.). 591p. 1999. 98.00 (*0-13-010494-9*) P-H.

Microprocessors & Microcomputers: The 6800 Family. Ronald J. Tocci & Lester P. Laskowski. (Illus.). 432p. (C). 1985. text 61.60 (*0-13-581745-5*) P-H.

Microprocessors & Minicomputers in the Textile Industry. Ed. by Perry L. Grady & Gary N. Mock. LC 80-82119. (Illus.). 521p. reprint ed. pap. 161.60 (*0-7837-5153-2*, 204488200004) Bks Demand.

Microprocessors & Peripherals: Hardware, Software, Interfacing & Applications. 2nd ed. Barry B. Brey. 512p. (C). 1990. text 61.60 (*0-675-20884-X*, Merrill Coll) P-H.

Microprocessors & Programmed Logic. 2nd ed. Ken Short. 576p. (C). 1987. text 46.20 (*0-13-580606-2*) P-H.

Microprocessors 8088 & 8086: Programming, Interfacing, Software, Hardware & Applications. 3rd ed. Walter A. Triebel. LC 99-17763. (Illus.). 978p. 1999. 105.00 (*0-13-010560-0*) P-H.

Microprocessors for Engineers. 1987. 45.50 (*0-13-582602-0*) P-H.

Microprocessors for Engineers: Interfacing for Real Time Applications. P. K. Sinha. (Electrical & Electronic Engineering Ser.). 870p. 1988. text 81.95 (*0-470-21011-7*) P-H.

Microprocessors in Analytical Chemistry, Vol. 27, No. 7b. R. A. Chalmers. 64p. 1982. pap. 28.00 (*0-08-026284-8*, Pergamon Pr) Elsevier.

Microprocessors in Industrial Control. Instrument Society of America Staff. Ed. by Robert J. Bibbero. LC 82-48556. (Illus.). 256p. (C). 1983. pap. text 46.00 (*0-13-581165-1*) P-H.

Microprocessors in Operational Hydrology. Ed. by World Meteorological Organization Staff. 1986. text 129.50 (*90-277-2156-4*) Kluwer Academic.

Microprocessors in Robotic & Manufacturing Systems. Spyros G. Tzafestas. 425p. (C). 1991. text 225.00 (*0-7923-0780-1*) Kluwer Academic.

Microprocessors in Signal Processing: Measurement & Control. Ed. by Spyros G. Tzafestas. (Microprocessor Based & Intelligent Systems Engineering Ser.). 1983. text 211.50 (*90-277-1497-5*) Kluwer Academic.

Microprocessors Made Easy: A Practical Approach. Thompson. (Electronics Technology Ser.). 1995. teacher ed. 14.00 (*0-8273-5348-0*) Delmar.

Microprogrammed State Machine Design. Michel A. Lynch. 512p. 1993. boxed set 89.95 (*0-8493-4464-6*, QA76) CRC Pr.

Microprogrammed Systems. D. Mange. (ITCP-UK Computer Science Ser.). (C). 1992. mass mkt. 62.95 (*0-412-40800-7*) Chapman & Hall.

Microprogrammed Systems: An Introduction to Firmware Theory. D. Mange. 400p. 1992. pap. 49.95 (*0-442-31551-1*) Chapman & Hall.

Microprogrammed Systems Design. J. S. Florentin. (Illus.). 287p. 1991. pap. text 35.00 (*0-333-54250-9*) Scholium Intl.

Micropropagation: Technology & Application. Ed. by P. Debergh & R. H. Zimmerman. (C). 1991. pap. text 92.50 (*0-7923-0819-0*); lib. bdg. 213.50 (*0-7923-0818-2*) Kluwer Academic.

***Micropropagation, Genetic Engineering, & Molecular Biology of Populus.** Ed. by Ned B. Klopfenstein. (Illus.). 326p. (C). 2000. reprint ed. pap. text 40.00 (*0-7881-8933-6*) DIANE Pub.

Micropropagation of Forest Trees Through Tissue Culture: 53 Colour Plates. P. W. Evers. (Illus.). 84p. 1988. pap. 325.00 (*81-7089-117-5*, Pub. by Intl Bk Distr) St Mut.

Micropropagation of Orchids. Joseph Arditti & Robert Ernst. LC 91-40768. 696p. 1993. 195.00 (*0-471-54905-3*) Wiley.

Micropropagation of Woody Plants. Ed. by M. R. Ahuja. LC 92-14824. (Forestry Sciences Ser.: Vol. 41). 528p. 1992. text 307.50 (*0-7923-1807-2*) Kluwer Academic.

Micropublishing: A History of Scholarly Micropublishing in America, 1938-1980, 40. Alan M. Meckler. LC 81-6955. (Contributions in Librarianship & Information Science Ser.: No. 40). (Illus.). 179p. 1982. 55.00 (*0-313-23096-X*, MMP/) Greenwood.

Micropuzzles see Math & Logic Puzzles for PC Enthusiasts

Microradio & Democracy: (Low) Power to the People. Greg Ruggiero. LC 99-11326. (Open Media Pamphlet Ser.: Vol. 10). 64p. 1999. pap. text 5.95 (*1-58322-000-3*, Pub. by Seven Stories) Publishers Group.

Microreaction Technology: Proceedings of the First International Conference on Microreaction Technology. Ed. by Wolfgang Ehrfeld. LC 97-46100. (Illus.). xiv, 356p. 1998. 69.95 (*3-540-63883-0*) Spr-Verlag.

***Microreaction Technology: Industrial Prospects: IMRET 3: Proceedings of the Third International Conference on Microreaction Technology.** Ed. by W. Ehrfeld. 700p. 2000. (*3-540-66964-7*) Spr-Verlag.

Microrecording of Engineering Graphics - Computer-Output Microfilm: ANSI-AIIM MS38-1995. Association for Information & Image Management Staff. 16p. 1995. pap. 33.00 (*0-89258-100-X*, MS38) Assn Inform & Image Mgmt.

Microrecording of Engineering Source Documents on 35mm Microfilm: ANSI-AIIM MS32-1996. Association for Information & Image Management Staff. 15p. 1996. pap. 33.00 (*0-89258-085-2*, MS32) Assn Inform & Image Mgmt.

Microref for dBASE III Plus. 1987. pap. 19.95 (*0-913365-11-4*) Microref Educ Systs.

Microref for Displaywrite 4. 1988. pap. 19.95 (*0-913365-15-7*) Microref Educ Systs.

Microref for Framework. write for info. (*0-318-58196-5*) P-H.

Microref for MS & PC-DOS. Micoref Educational Systems Staff. 1986. pap. 19.95 (*0-913365-09-2*) Microref Educ Systs.

Microref for Multimate Advantage, Nos. I & II. 62p. 1988. spiral bd. 19.95 (*0-913365-14-9*) Microref Educ Systs.

Microref for 1-2-3. write for info. (*0-318-58195-7*) P-H.

Microref for Symphony. Educational Systems Staff. write for info. (*0-318-58191-4*) P-H.

Microref for WordPerfect 4.1. 1986. pap. 19.95 (*0-913365-10-6*) Microref Educ Systs.

Microref for Wordstar Release 4. 80p. 1987. spiral bd. 19.95 (*0-913365-12-2*) Microref Educ Systs.

Microref, 1993 Guide Series. Microref Educational Systems Staff. (Illus.). (Orig.). 1993. pap., spiral bd. 99.75 (*1-56351-098-7*) Microref Educ Systs.

Microref Quick Reference Guide for Lotus 1-2-3, Release 2.2. Educational Systems, Inc. Staff. (MICROREF Quick Reference Guide Ser.). (Illus.). 145p. (Orig.). (C). 1984. pap. text 19.95 (*0-913365-71-8*) Microref Educ Systs.

Microregional Fragmentation: Contrasts Between a Welfare State & a Market Economy. 132p. 1995. 54.00 (*3-7908-0855-5*) Spr-Verlag.

Microrobotics Vol. 2906: Components & Applications. Ed. by Armin Sulzmann. 220p. 1996. 56.00 (*0-8194-2308-4*) SPIE.

***Microrobotics & Microassembly.** Ed. by Bradley J. Nelson & Jean M. Breguet. 230p. 1999. pap. text 62.00 (*0-8194-3427-2*) SPIE.

Microrobotics & Micromanipulation, Vol. 3519. Ed. by Armin Sulzmann & Bradley J. Nelson. LC 99-192227. 1998. 69.00 (*0-8194-2980-5*) SPIE.

Microrobotics & Microsystem Fabrication, Vol. 3202. Ed. by Armin Sulzmann. 248p. 1998. 59.00 (*0-8194-2634-2*) SPIE.

Micros for Managers: A Software Guide for School Administrators. rev. ed. Ed. by Joseph R. Little et al. LC 84-62050. xxi, 298p. (Orig.). 1984. pap. 25.00 (*0-912337-05-2*) NJ Schl Bds.

Micros, Minis, & Geoscience Information: Proceedings of the Twentieth Meeting, Orlando, FL, October 27-31, 1985. Geoscience Information Society Staff. LC QE0048.85.G4. (Geoscience Information Society Proceedings Ser.: No. 16). 186p. reprint ed. pap. 57.70 (*0-8357-2796-3*, 203992300014) Bks Demand.

Micros Plus: Educational Peripherals. S. Wills & R. Lewis. 202p. 1988. 79.50 (*0-444-70380-2*, North Holland) Elsevier.

Micros with a Message: Computers in Christian Youth Work. John Fewings. (C). 1989. 25.00 (*0-7855-4422-4*, Pub. by Jay Bks) St Mut.

M

Microsales of Turbulence: Heat & Mass Transfer Correlations. Vedat S. Arpaci. 211p. 1997. text 33.00 (*90-5699-565-0*) Gordon & Breach.

Microsatellites: Evolution & Applications. Ed. by David B. Goldstein & Christian Schlotterer. LC 98-49876. (Illus.). 368p. 1999. text 95.00 (*0-19-850408-X*); pap. text 47.50 (*0-19-850407-1*) OUP.

Microsatellites as Research Tools: Proceedings of Cospar Colloquium on Microsatellites As Research Tools Held in Tainan, Taiwan, 14-17 December 1997. COSPAR Staff & Fei-Bin Hsiao. LC 98-54989. (COSPAR Colloquia Ser.). 398p. 1999. 215.50 (*0-444-50196-7*) Elsevier.

Microscae Experiments in Organic Chemistry. H. Dupont Durst & George W. Gokel. text. write for info. (*0-07-018405-4*) McGraw.

Microscale & Macroscale Experiments for General Chemistry. Jerry L. Mills & Michael D. Hampton. 307p. (C). 1991. lab manual ed. 35.94 (*0-07-042442-X*) McGraw.

***Microscale & Miniscale Lab Investigations in Organic.** Paul G. Johnson. 280p. (C). 2000. spiral bd. 65.00 (*0-7872-7200-0*) Kendall-Hunt.

***Microscale & Miniscale Organic Chemistry Laboratory Experiments.** Allen M. Schoffstall et al. LC 99-50356. 2000. write for info. (*0-07-237549-3*) McGrw-H Hghr Educ.

Microscale & Selected Macroscale Experiments for General & Advanced General Chemistry: An Innovation Approach. Mono M. Singh et al. 768p. 1995. pap. 58.95 (*0-471-58596-3*) Wiley.

Microscale Chemical Experiments. John Little & Kenneth L. Williamson. (C). 1997. pap. text, teacher ed. 11.96 (*0-669-41607-X*) HM Trade Div.

Microscale Chemical Experiments. John Little & Kenneth L. Williamson. (C). 1997. pap. text 43.96 (*0-669-41606-1*) HM Trade Div.

Microscale Chemistry Experiments in Miniature. J. Skinner. 207p. 1998. pap. 34.95 (*1-870343-49-2*) Spr-Verlag.

Microscale Energy Transport. Chan L. Tien et al. LC 97-23695. (Series in Chemical & Mechanical Engineering). 1997. 85.00 (*1-56032-459-7*) Taylor & Francis.

Microscale Experiments for General Chemistry. 2nd ed. Jerry L. Mills & Michael D. Hampton. 208p. (C). 1991. spiral bd. 35.94 (*0-07-042447-0*) McGraw.

Microscale Experiments in Organic Chemistry. George H. Wahl. (C). 1990. 40.00 (*0-205-12381-3*, Macmillan Coll) P-H.

Microscale General Chemistry Laboratory with Selected Macroscale Experiments. Zvi Szafran et al. LC 92-19604. 576p. (C). 1992. pap. 61.95 (*0-471-62114-5*) Wiley.

***Microscale Heat Conduction in Integrated Circuits & Their Constituent Films** Y. Sungtaek Ju & Kenneth E. Goodson. LC 99-37208. (Microsystems Ser.). 1999. write for info. (*0-7923-8591-8*) Kluwer Academic.

Microscale Heat Transfer: 1994 International Mechanical Engineering Congress & Exposition, Chicago, Illinois - November 6-11, 1994. (HTD Ser.: Vol. 291). 100p. 1994. 48.00 (*0-7918-1409-2*, G00904) ASME.

Microscale Inorganic Chemistry: A Comprehensive Laboratory Experience. Zvi Szafran et al. LC 90-46328. 384p. 1991. text 64.95 (*0-471-61996-5*) Wiley.

Microscale Organic Laboratory: With Multistep & Multiscale Syntheses. 4th ed. Dana W. Mayo et al. LC 99-30131. 688p. 2000. text 80.95 (*0-471-32185-0*) Wiley.

Microscale Organic Laboratory with Selected Macroscale Experiments. 3rd ed. Dana W. Mayo et al. 800p. 1994. text 80.95 (*0-471-57505-4*) Wiley.

Microscale Syntheses. Zanger-Mckee & McKee. 1999. pap. text 37.00 (*0-697-33008-7*) McGraw.

Microscale Testing in Aquatic Toxicology: Advances, Techniques, & Practice. P. G. Wells et al. LC 97-18407. 720p. 1997. boxed set 89.95 (*0-8493-2626-5*) CRC Pr.

Microscope. Saville Bradbury. 1968. 129.00 (*0-08-012848-3*, Pub. by Pergamon Repr) Franklin.

Microscope. Evert. 1998. 1.50 (*0-7167-9349-0*) W H Freeman.

Microscope. Maxine Kumin. LC 82-47728. (Illus.). 32p. (J). (ps-3). 1984. 11.95 (*0-06-023523-3*) HarpC Child Bks.

Microscope. Maxine Kumin. LC 82-47728. (Trophy Picture Bk.). (Illus.). 32p. (J). (ps-3). 1987. pap. 2.95 (*0-06-443136-3*, HarpTrophy) HarpC Child Bks.

Microscope. Ed. by Kelly O'Donnell. (Illus.). 10p. (Orig.). (J). (gr. 4-7). 1998. pap. text 8.95 (*1-57532-153-X*) Press-Tige Pub.

Microscope: How to Use It & Enjoy It. Eve Stwertka & Albert Stwertka. LC 88-23127. (Illus.). 80p. (J). (gr. 4-7). 1988. pap. 4.95 (*0-671-67060-3*, Julian Messner); lib. bdg. 9.95 (*0-671-63705-3*, Julian Messner) Silver Burdett Pr.

***Microscope: Technology, Lenses & Light, Student Science Journal.** Peter R. Bergethon. (Illus.). 137p. (YA). (gr. 6-8). 2000. pap. text. write for info. (*1-58447-047-X*) Symmetry Lrng.

***Microscope: Technology, Lenses & Light, Teacher Manual.** Peter R. Bergethon. (Illus.). xxiv, 137p. 2000. pap. text, teacher ed. write for info. (*1-58447-046-1*) Symmetry Lrng.

Microscope & How to Use It. Philip B. Carona. LC 73-131927. (Instruments of Science Ser.). (Illus.). 63p. reprint ed. pap. 30.00 (*0-608-15597-7*, 202967000062) Bks Demand.

Microscope & How to Use It. George Stehli. (Illus.). 160p. 1970. reprint ed. pap. 4.95 (*0-486-22575-5*) Dover.

Microscope Book. Shar Levine & Leslie Johnstone. LC 95-43239. (Illus.). 80p. (J). (gr. 5). 1996. 19.95 (*0-8069-4898-1*) Sterling.

Microscope Book. Shar Levine & Leslie Johnstone. (Illus.). 80p. 1997. pap. 9.95 (*0-8069-4899-X*) Sterling.

Microscope Cabinet. Andrew Pritchard. (History of Microscopy Ser.). 256p. 1987. reprint ed. 62.40 (*0-940095-02-5*) Sci Heritage Ltd.

Microscope in the Dutch Republic: The Shaping of Discovery. E. G. Ruestow. (Illus.). 360p. (C). 1996. text 59.95 (*0-521-47078-1*) Cambridge U Pr.

Microscope Made Easy: The Description & Manner of Using Mr. Wilson's Set of Pocket Microscopes. Henry E. Baker & James Wilson. (History of Microscopy Ser.). 390p. 1987. reprint ed. 29.00 (*0-940095-03-3*) Sci Heritage Ltd.

Microscope on a Budget: A Complete Guide to the Low Cost Light Microscope for the Laboratory, Photographers, & Hobbyists. M. Brian Stevens. 247p. 1993. pap. write for info. (*0-9638839-1-7*) M B Stevens.

MicroScope Savoir Faire see Microwave Know-How

Microscope II. Sharon Levine. LC 97-27609. (Illus.). 80p. (J). 1998. 19.95 (*0-8069-9945-4*) Sterling.

Microscope/Automated Imaging Systems Markets. (Market Research Reports: No. 500). 100p. 1995. 995.00 (*0-614-11268-0*) Theta Corp.

Microscopes. B. K. Hixson. 64p. 1993. pap. text 14.99 (*1-57156-004-1*) Wild Goose UT.

Microscopes & Accessories for the Microscope Catalog of 1914. Carl Zeiss. (Illus.). 1984. reprint ed. pap. text 35.00 (*0-87556-395-3*) Saifer.

Microscopes & Their Uses. Claude Marmasse. xiv, 330p. 1980. text 101.00 (*0-677-05510-2*) Gordon & Breach.

Microscopes, Riflescopes, Binoculars, Telescopes & Optical Elements: Markets, Technologies & Opportunities: 1990-1995 Analysis. Dennis M. Zogbi et al. (Illus.). 250p. 1990. pap. 995.00 (*1-878218-14-X*) World Info Tech.

Microscopic Analysis of the Anastomoses Between the Cranial Nerves. Ernst Bischoff. Ed. by Ernst Sachs, Jr. & Eva W. Valtin. LC 77-72520. 148p. reprint ed. pap. 45.90 (*0-608-11919-9*, 202323100032) Bks Demand.

***Microscopic Anatomy of Invertebrates, 20 Vol.Set.** Ed. by Frederick W. Harrison & Edward E. Ruppert. 1999. 5000.00 (*0-471-33252-6*) Wiley.

Microscopic Anatomy of Invertebrates: Insect, Vol. 11. Frederick W. Harrison & Michael Locke. (Microscopic Anatomy of Invertebrates Ser.). 2517p. 1998. 975.00 (*0-471-15955-7*) Wiley.

Microscopic Anatomy of Invertebrates: Lophophorates & Entoprocta, Vol. 13, Lophophorates, Entoprocta, and Cycliophor. Ed. by Frederick W. Harrison & Robert M. Woollacott. LC 89-12117. (Microscopic Anatomy of Invertebrates Ser.). 500p. 1997. 325.00 (*0-471-56120-7*) Wiley.

Microscopic Anatomy of Invertebrates Vol. 1: Protozoa, 4 vols., Vol. 1, Protozoa. Ed. by Frederick W. Harrison et al. LC 89-12117. 512p. 1990. 325.00 (*0-471-56842-2*, Wiley-Liss) Wiley.

Microscopic Anatomy of Invertebrates Vol. 2: Placozoa, Porifera, Cnidaria, Ctenophora, 4 vols., Vol. 2, Placozoa, Porifera, Cnidaria, and Ctenopho. Ed. by Frederick W. Harrison et al. LC 89-12117. 456p. 1990. 325.00 (*0-471-56224-6*, Wiley-Liss) Wiley.

Microscopic Anatomy of Invertebrates Vol. 3: Platyhelminthes & Nemertinea, 4 vols., Vol. 3, Platyhelminthes and Nemertinea. Ed. by Frederick W. Harrison et al. LC 89-12117. 368p. 1990. 325.00 (*0-471-56843-0*, Wiley-Liss) Wiley.

Microscopic Anatomy of Invertebrates Vol. 4: Aschelminthes, 4 vols., Vol. 4, Aschelminthes. Ed. by Frederick W. Harrison et al. LC 89-12117. 438p. 1991. 325.00 (*0-471-56103-7*, Wiley-Liss) Wiley.

Microscopic Anatomy of Invertebrates Vol. 5: Mollusca I, Vol. 5, Mollusca One. Ed. by Frederick W. Harrison & Alan J. Kohn. (Microscopic Anatomy of Invertebrates Ser.). 404p. 1994. 325.00 (*0-471-56112-6*, Wiley-Liss) Wiley.

Microscopic Anatomy of Invertebrates Vol. 6: Mollusca II, Vol. 6 Set, Mollusca II. Ed. by Frederick W. Harrison & Alan J. Kohn. 828p. 1996. 650.00 (*0-471-56113-4*, Wiley-Liss) Wiley.

Microscopic Anatomy of Invertebrates Vol. 8: Chelicerate Arthropoda. Ed. by Frederick W. Harrison et al. 1432p. 1999. 975.00 (*0-471-15956-5*, Wiley-Liss) Wiley.

Microscopic Anatomy of Invertebrates Vol. 8: Chilicerate Arthropoda, Vol. 8A, Chelicerate Arthropoda. Frederick W. Harrison. 336p. 1998. 325.00 (*0-471-56115-0*, Wiley-Liss) Wiley.

Microscopic Anatomy of Invertebrates Vol. 10: Decapod Crustacea, Vol. 10, Decapod Crustacea. Ed. by Frederick W. Harrison et al. 474p. 1992. 325.00 (*0-471-56117-7*, Wiley-Liss) Wiley.

Microscopic Anatomy of Invertebrates Vol. 11, Pts. A & B: Insecta. Frederick W. Harrison. 496p. 1998. 325.00 (*0-471-56118-5*, Wiley-Liss) Wiley.

Microscopic Anatomy of Invertebrates Vol. 12: Onychophora, Chilopoda, & Lesser Protostomata, Vol. 12, Onychophora, Chilopoda, and Lesser Protos. Ed. by Frederick W. Harrison & Mary E. Rice. 498p. 1993. 325.00 (*0-471-56119-3*, Wiley-Liss) Wiley.

Microscopic Anatomy of Invertebrates Vol. 14: Enchinodermata, Vol. 14, Enchinodermata. Frederick W. Harrison. Ed. by Fu-Shiang Chia. 524p. 1994. 325.00 (*0-471-56121-5*, Wiley-Liss) Wiley.

Microscopic Anatomy of Invertebrates Vol. 15: Hemichordata, Chaetognatha, & the Invertebrate Chordates, Vol. 15, Hemichordata, Chaetognatha, and the Inver. Ed. by Frederick W. Harrison & Edward E. Ruppert. LC 89-12117. 552p. 1997. 325.00 (*0-471-56122-3*) Wiley.

***Microscopic Anatomy of Invertebrates Vols. 8A, 8B, 8C: Acari-Ticks - Taxonomic Index, Vol. 8.** Ed. by Frederick W. Harrison. 320p. 1999. 325.00 (*0-471-18014-9*) Wiley.

***Microscopic Anatomy of Invertebrates C, Vol. 11.** Harrison. 1998. 325.00 (*0-471-18009-2*) Wiley.

Microscopic Anatomy of the Invertebrates, Vol. 6A, Mollusca II. Harrison. 480p. 1996. 325.00 (*0-471-15447-4*) Wiley.

Microscopic Anatomy of the Invertebrates, Vol. 6B, Mollusca II. Harrison. 432p. 1996. 325.00 (*0-471-15441-5*) Wiley.

***Microscopic & Chemical Parts of Plants.** Thomas P. Hanna. 211p. 1999. 49.00 (*1-56072-547-8*) Nova Sci Pubs.

Microscopic & Spectroscopic Imaging of the Chemical State. Michael D. Morris. (Practical Spectroscopy Ser.: Vol. 16). (Illus.). 504p. 1993. text 225.00 (*0-8247-9104-5*) Dekker.

Microscopic & Surface Analysis. Gary McGuire. (C). 2001. pap. text 14.95 (*0-13-123217-7*) P-H.

Microscopic Approaches to the Structure of Light Nuclei. Raymond F. Bishop. (Series on Advances in Quantum Many-Body Theory - Vol. 2: Vol. 2). 400p. 1999. 85.00 (*981-02-3875-4*) World Scientific Pub.

Microscopic Aspects of Adhesion & Lubrication: Proceedings of the 34th International Meeting of the Societe Chimie Physique, Paris, France, 14-18 September, 1981. Ed. by J. M. Georges. (Tribology Ser.: Vol. 7). xx, 812p. 1982. 304.00 (*0-444-42071-1*) Elsevier.

Microscopic Aspects of Nonlinearity in Condensed Matter. A. R. Bishop et al. (NATO ASI Ser.: Vol. 264). (Illus.). 374p. (C). 1991. text 115.00 (*0-306-44001-6*, Kluwer Plenum) Kluwer Academic.

Microscopic Diagnosis in Forensic Pathology. Joshua A. Perper & Cyril H. Wecht. (Illus.). 488p. 1980. 87.95 (*0-398-03969-0*) C C Thomas.

Microscopic Explorations: A GEMS Festival Teacher's Guide. Susan Brady & Carolyn Willard. Ed. by Lincoln Bergman et al. (Great Explorations in Math & Science (GEMS) Ser.). (Illus.). 168p. 1998. pap., teacher ed. 21.00 (*0-924886-00-5*, GEMS) Lawrence Science.

Microscopic Haematology: A Practical Guide for the Laboratory. Gillian Rozenberg. 160p. 1997. pap. text 31.00 (*90-5702-247-8*, Harwood Acad Pubs) Gordon & Breach.

Microscopic Haematology: A Practical Guide to the Haematology Laboratory. Gillian Rozenberg. 160p. 1996. text 78.00 (*90-5702-093-9*, Harwood Acad Pubs) Gordon & Breach.

Microscopic Imaging in Experimental Neurobiology. Ed. by Robert A. Nichols & Patrice Mollard. (Neuromethods Ser.). 1999. 99.50 (*0-89603-707-X*) Humana.

Microscopic Models in Nuclear Structure Physics. Ed. by Michael W. Guidry et al. 444p. (C). 1989. text 125.00 (*9971-5-0824-9*) World Scientific Pub.

Microscopic Photographs of J. B. Dancer. James B. McCormick & Brian Bracegirdle. (Illus.). 288p. 1993. 50.00 (*0-940095-10-6*) Sci Heritage Ltd.

Microscopic Procedures for Primary Care Providers. Shirley Lowe. LC 98-22966. 1998. write for info. (*0-7817-1432-X*) Lppncott W & W.

***Microscopic Properties & Processes in Minerals.** Kate Wright & C. R. A. Catlow. LC 99-45981. (NATO Science Ser.). 1999. write for info. (*0-7923-5981-X*) Kluwer Academic.

Microscopic Quantum Many-Body Theories & Their Applications: Proceedings of a European Summer School, Held at Valencia, Spain, 8-19 September 1997. Ed. by Jesus Navarro et al. LC 98-23302. (Lecture Notes in Physics Ser.: Vol. 510). xiii, 379p. 1998. 86.00 (*3-540-64471-7*) Spr-Verlag.

***Microscopic Simulation of Financial Markets: From Investor Behavior to Market Phenomena.** Haim Levy. 2000. 69.95 (*0-12-445890-4*) Acad Pr.

Microscopic Simulation of Interfacial Phenomena in Solids & Liquids Vol. 492: Materials Research Society Symposium Proceedings. Ed. by S. R. Phillpot et al. LC 98-15404. 410p. 1998. text 77.00 (*1-55899-397-5*) Materials Res.

Microscopic Simulations of Complex Flows. Ed. by M. Mareschal. LC 90-46797. (NATO ASI Ser.: Vol. 229). (Illus.). 374p. (C). 1990. text 144.00 (*0-306-43687-6*, Kluwer Plenum) Kluwer Academic.

Microscopic Simulations of Complex Hydrodynamic Phenomena. M. Mareschal & B. L. Holian. (NATO ASI Ser.: Vol. 292). (Illus.). 436p. (C). 1992. text 125.00 (*0-306-44226-4*, Kluwer Plenum) Kluwer Academic.

Microscopic Theory. Katsnelson. 1997. 79.95 (*5-03-001400-4*) Spr-Verlag.

Microscopic Theory of Condensation in Gases & Plasma. LC 97-3965. 300p. 1997. lib. bdg. 40.00 (*981-02-2907-0*) World Scientific Pub.

Microscopic Theory of Crystal Growth. Hubert Pfeiffer et al. (Physical Research Ser.: Vol. II). 400p. 1989. 60.00 (*3-05-500684-4*, Pub. by Akademie Verlag) Wiley.

Microscopic Theory of Nonhomogenous Structurese. Ed. by A. A. Katsnel'son & Al Olemskoi. (Translation Ser.). 1990. 60.00 (*0-88318-774-4*) Spr-Verlag.

Microscopic Theory of Semiconductors: Quantum Kinetics, Confinement & Laser. Ed. by Stephan W. Koch. LC 95-46570. 428p. 1996. write for info. (*981-02-2511-3*) World Scientific Pub.

Microscopic to Macroscopic: Atomic Environments to Mineral Thermodynamics. Ed. by S. W. Kieffer & Alexandra Navrotsky. (Reviews in Mineralogy Ser.: Vol. 14). (Illus.). 428p. (C). 1985. pap. 20.00 (*0-939950-18-9*) Mineralogical Soc.

Microscopic Venation Patterns of Leaves & Their Importance in the Distinction of Tropical Species. Ingrid Roth. LC 96-185014. (Handbuch der Pflanzenanatomie Encyclopedia of Plant Anatomy - Traite d' Anatomie Vegetale Ser.: Vol. 14, Pt. 4). (Illus.). viii, 196p. 1996. 99.00 (*3-443-14023-8*, Pub. by Gebruder Borntraeger) Balogh.

Microscopical Examination & Interpretation of Portland Cement & Clinker. Donald H. Campbell. LC 85-63563. (Illus.). 48p. 1985. 55.00 (*0-89312-084-7*, SP030T) Portland Cement.

Microscopical Examination & Interpretation of Portland Cement & Clinker. rev. ed. Donald H. Campbell. LC 85-63563. (Illus.). 48p. 1999. pap. 55.00 (*0-89312-179-7*, SPO30.T) Portland Cement.

Microscopio: Los Muertos Tambien Hablan. Ramon R. Baez. (SPA.). 240p. 1997. pap. 14.95 (*0-9658743-0-3*) Edit Sitel.

Microscopy Anatomy of Invertebrates Vol. 8B: Chelicerate Arthropoda. Ed. by Frederick W. Harrison & Rainer F. Foelix. 768p. 1998. 325.00 (*0-471-14743-5*, Wiley-Liss) Wiley.

Microscopy & Microanalysis: Official Journal of the Microscopy Society of America, Microbeam Analysis Society, & The Microscopical Society of Canada, 6 issues, 2 supplements, Vol. 3. Ed. by D. E. Johnson. 1997. 495.00 (*0-614-30191-2*, 10005) Spr-Verlag.

JMSA Proceedings: Microscopy & Microanalysis, 1995. Ed. by G. W. Bailey et al. 1132p. 1995. 225.00 (*1-56700-032-0*) Begell Hse.

Microscopy & Microsurgery of Larynx & the Laryngopharynx. V. S. Pogosov & V. F. Antoniv. 1987. 37.50 (*0-8236-3363-2*, BN#03363) Intl Univs Pr.

Microscopy & Photomicrography: A Practical Guide. Robert F. Smith. (Illus.). 200p. 1989. 45.00 (*0-936923-36-9*); pap. 24.50 (*0-936923-37-7*) Telford Pr.

Microscopy & Photomicrography: A Working Manual. Robert F. Smith. 200p. 1990. 31.95 (*0-8493-8803-1*, QH212) CRC Pr.

Microscopy & Photomicrography: A Working Manual. 2nd ed. Roger F. Smith. LC 93-14269. 176p. 1993. spiral bd. 62.95 (*0-8493-8682-9*, QH211) CRC Pr.

Microscopy & Semiconducting Materials, 1995: Proceedings of the Institute of Physics Conference Held at Oxford University, 20-23 March 1995. Ed. by A. G. Cullis & A. E. Staton-Bevan. (Institute of Physics Conference Ser.: Vol. 146). (Illus.). 795p. 1996. 353.00 (*0-7503-0347-6*) IOP Pub.

Microscopy of Liquid Crystals, Vol. 48. Norman H. Hartshorne. LC 73-91899. 1974. 30.00 (*0-904962-03-2*) Microscope Pubns.

Microscopy of Oxidation: Proceedings of the International Conference Held at the University of Cambridge, UK. Ed. by M. J. Bennett & G. W. Lorimer. 428p. 1991. pap. 130.00 (*0-901462-90-X*, Pub. by Inst Materials) Ashgate Pub Co.

Microscopy of Oxidation 3: Proceedings of the 3rd International Conference on the Microscopy of Oxidation. Ed. by S. B. Newcomb & J. A. Little. (Illus.). 792p. 1997. 300.00 (*1-86125-034-7*, Pub. by Inst Materials) Ashgate Pub Co.

Microscopy of Oxidation 2: Proceedings of the 2nd International Conference Held in Selwyn College, University of Cambridge, March 1993. Ed. by S. B. Newcomb & M. J. Bennett. (Illus.). 600p. 1994. 170.00 (*0-901716-50-2*, Pub. by Inst Materials) Ashgate Pub Co.

***Microscopy of Semiconducting Materials 1999: Proceedings of the Institute of Physics Conference, Vol. 164.** A. G. Cullis. LC 99-58027. (Institute of Physics Conference Ser.). 1999. 275.00 (*0-7503-0650-5*) IOP Pub.

Microscopy of Semiconducting Materials, 1981: Proceedings of the Royal Microscopical Society Conference Held in St. Catherine's College, Oxford, 6-10 April 1981. Oxford Conference on Microscopy of Semiconducting. Ed. by A. G. Cullis & D. C. Joy. LC QC0611.6.M5M. (Conference Ser.: No. 60). 476p. reprint ed. pap. 147.60 (*0-7837-3255-4*, 204327400007) Bks Demand.

Microscopy of Semiconducting Materials, 1997: Proceedings of the Royal Microscopical Society Conference Held at Oxford University, 7-10 April, 1997. Royal Microscopical Society (Great Britain) Staff et al. LC 97-42765. (Institute of Physics Conference Ser.). 1997. 420.00 (*0-7503-0464-2*) IOP Pub.

Microscopy of Textile Fibres. P. H. Greaves & B. P. Saville. (Microscopy Handbooks Ser.: No. 32). 112p. 1995. pap. 44.50 (*1-872748-24-4*, Pub. by Bios Sci) Bks Intl VA.

Microscopy, Optical Spectroscopy & Macroscopic Techniques. Ed. by Christopher Jones et al. LC 93-23977. (Methods in Molecular Biology Ser.: Vol. 22). (Illus.). 274p. 1993. student ed., spiral bd. 69.50 (*0-89603-232-9*) Humana.

Microscopy Society of America Proceedings. (Illus.). 1983. 10.00 (*0-614-11166-8*) San Francisco Pr.

Microscopy Society of America Proceedings. (Illus.). 1984. 10.00 (*0-614-11167-6*) San Francisco Pr.

Microscopy Society of America Proceedings. (Illus.). 1985. 10.00 (*0-614-11168-4*) San Francisco Pr.

Microscopy Society of America Proceedings. (Illus.). 1986. 10.00 (*0-614-11169-2*) San Francisco Pr.

Microscopy Society of America Proceedings. (Illus.). 1987. 10.00 (*0-614-11170-6*) San Francisco Pr.

Microscopy Society of America Proceedings. (Illus.). 1988. 10.00 (*0-614-11171-4*) San Francisco Pr.

Microscopy Society of America Proceedings. (Illus.). 1989. 10.00 (*0-614-11172-2*) San Francisco Pr.

Microscopy Society of America Proceedings. (Illus.). 1991. 10.00 (*0-614-11173-0*) San Francisco Pr.

Microscopy Society of America Proceedings. (Illus.). 1994. 10.00 (*0-614-11176-5*) San Francisco Pr.

Microscopy Society of America Proceedings. (Illus.). 1995. 50.00 (*0-614-24723-3*) San Francisco Pr.

An Asterisk (*) at the beginning of an entry indicates that the title is appearing for the first time.

Microscopy Society of America Proceedings. (Illus.). 1996. 75.00 (*0-614-24724-1*) San Francisco Pr.

Microscopy Society of America Proceedings, 2 vols., Set. (Illus.). 1992. 20.00 (*0-614-11174-9*) San Francisco Pr.

Microscopy Society of America Proceedings, Vol. 1: Imaging Sciences. (Illus.). 1990. 10.00 (*0-614-11162-5*) San Francisco Pr.

Microscopy Society of America Proceedings, Vol. 2: Analytical Science. (Illus.). 1990. 10.00 (*0-614-11163-3*) San Francisco Pr.

Microscopy Society of America Proceedings, Vol. 3: Biological Science. (Illus.). 1990. 10.00 (*0-614-11164-1*) San Francisco Pr.

Microscopy Society of America Proceedings, Vol. 4: Materials Science. (Illus.). 1990. 10.00 (*0-614-11165-X*) San Francisco Pr.

Microseismic & Infrasound Waves. Valentina N. Tabulevich. LC 92-10893. (Research Reports in Physics). (Illus.). ix, 150p. 1992. 70.95 (*0-387-53293-5*) Spr-Verlag.

Microsensors. Ed. by R. S. Muller et al. LC 90-4745. 480p. 1990. 79.95 (*0-87942-245-9*, PC02576) Inst Electrical.

Microsensors: Principles & Applications. J. W. Gardner. LC 94-10066. 344p. 1994. 225.00 (*0-471-94135-2*); pap. 94.95 (*0-471-94136-0*) Wiley.

Microserfs. Douglas Coupland. 384p. 1996. pap. 13.00 (*0-06-098704-9*) HarpC.

Microserfs. Douglas Coupland. 371p. Date not set. 21.00 (*0-614-32429-7*) HarperTrade.

Microserfs. Douglas Coupland. 1996. pap. 12.00 (*0-614-97780-0*, Perennial) HarperTrade.

Microseusors Fabrication & Applications. BCC Staff. 154p. 1990. 1850.00 (*0-89336-734-6*, G124) BCC.

Microsft Windows NT 5.0 Plus. Salkind & Johnson. (Illus.). (C). 2000. pap. 38.95 (*0-7600-5476-2*) Course Tech.

***Microsim Pspice & Circuit Analysis.** 4th ed. 2000. teacher ed. write for info. (*0-13-019378-X*) P-H.

***Microsim Pspice for Win: Dc/Ac Circuits, 1.** 3rd ed. 2000. teacher ed. write for info. (*0-13-019379-8*) P-H.

Microsim PSpice for Windows: A Circuit Simulation Primer, Vol. 1. 2nd ed. Roy Goody. LC 97-7764. 447p. 1997. pap. text 45.00 (*0-13-655796-1*) P-H.

Microsim PSpice for Windows Vol. 2: Operational Amplofoers & Digital Circuits, Vol. 2. 2nd ed. Roy Goody. LC 97-7764. Vol. 2. 316p. 1997. pap. text 43.00 (*0-13-655804-6*) P-H.

MicroSim PSpice with Circuit. 2nd ed. Franz Monssen. LC 96-30084. 548p. (C). 1997. pap. text, student ed. 50.00 (*0-02-382010-1*) P-H.

MICROSIM II: Simulation & Design of Microsystems & Microstructures. Ed. by R. A. Adey & P. Renaud. LC 97-67021. (MICROSIM Ser.: Vol. 2). 296p. 1997. 145.00 (*1-85312-501-6*, 5016) Computational Mech MA.

Microsimulated Transactions Model of the United States Economy. Robert L. Bennett & Barbara R. Bergmann. LC 85-45049. 165p. reprint ed. pap. 51.20 (*0-7837-2193-5*, 204253100004) Bks Demand.

Microsimulation & Public Policy: Selected Papers from the IARIW Special Conference on Microsimulation & Public Policy, Canberra, 5-9 December, 1993. Ed. by Ann Harding. LC 96-5320. (Contributions to Economic Analysis Ser.: Vol. 232). 546p. 1996. text 115.00 (*0-444-81894-4*, North Holland) Elsevier.

***Microsimulation Modelling for Policy Analysis: Challenges & Innovations.** Ed. by Lavinia Mitton et al. (Department of Applied Economics Occasional Papers: Vol. 65). (Illus.). 320p. 2000. write for info. (*0-521-79006-9*) Cambridge U Pr.

Microsimulation Modelling of the Corporate Firm: Exploring Micro-Macro Economic Relations. F. W. Van Tongeren. (Lecture Notes in Economics & Mathematical Systems Ser.: Vol. 427). 1995. 65.00 (*3-540-59443-4*) Spr-Verlag.

Microsimulation Techniques for Tax & Transfer Analysis. Ed. by Gordon H. Lewis & Richard C. Michel. LC 89-24832. (Illus.). 1990. pap. 25.50 (*0-87766-433-1*); lib. bdg. 50.50 (*0-87766-432-3*) Urban Inst.

Microsloth Joke Book. David Pogue. LC 98-183280. 128p. 1997. pap. 9.95 (*0-425-16054-8*) Berkley Pub.

MicroSociety Handbook. George H. Richmond & Carolynn K. Richmond. Ed. by Lynn Schweber & Rachel Kharfen. LC 96-77961. (Illus.). 586p. 1996. ring bd. write for info. (*0-9654262-0-3*) MicroSociety.

Microsociology: Discourse, Emotion & Social Structure. Thomas J. Scheff. 232p. 1994. pap. text 14.95 (*0-226-73667-9*) U Ch Pr.

Microsociology: Discourse, Emotion & Social Structure. Thomas J. Scheff. (Illus.). 230p. 1997. 35.95 (*0-226-73666-0*) U Ch Pr.

Microsoft: Internet Explorer 4.0. Timothy J. O'Leary & Linda I. O'Leary. LC 98-27515. 224p. 1998. pap. 27.50 (*0-07-228534-6*) McGraw.

***Microsoft: Simple Projects (Intermediate) with CD-ROM.** Mindy Pines. 96p. 2000. pap. 18.95 incl. cd-rom (*1-57690-728-7*) Tchr Create Mat.

Microsoft Powerpoint 4 for Windows. Zimmerman. (New Perspectives Ser.). 1995. pap. 6.00 (*0-7600-3558-X*) Course Tech.

Microsoft Works 4.0 for Mac: Computer Skill Resource Guide. 2nd ed. Melnyk. (Computer Applications). 1997. pap. 28.25 (*0-314-13009-8*) West Pub.

Microsoft Access. Maria Reidelbach. 1993. pap. 12.00 (*1-56243-115-3*, MA-18) DDC Pub.

***Microsoft Access - Intermediate: Pratice & Reference Guide.** Juanita B. Tischendorf. vi, 167p. 1999. pap. 25.00 (*1-928613-09-8*) J Tischendorf.

***Microsoft Access - Introduction: Practice & Reference Guide.** Juanita B. Tischendorf. (Illus.). viii, 172p. 1999. pap. text 25.00 (*1-928613-08-X*) J Tischendorf.

Microsoft Access Answers: Certified Tech Support. Mary Campbell. (Certified Tech Support Ser.). 352p. 1994. pap. text 16.95 (*0-07-882069-3*) McGraw.

Microsoft Access Book of Examples. Larry W. Smith. (Illus.). 1020p. 1996. pap. 29.95 (*1-57914-002-5*) Campbell-Smith.

Microsoft Access for Windows 95 Step by Step. Catapult, Inc., Staff. (Step by Step Ser.). 352p. 1995. 29.95 incl. disk (*1-55615-876-9*) Microsoft.

Microsoft Access for Windows 95. Patricia Murphy. (Quicktorial Ser.). (Illus.). 240p. 1996. pap., mass mkt. 21.95 incl. disk (*0-538-71541-3*) S-W Pub.

Microsoft Access for Windows 95: Quick Course. Patricia Murphy. (Quicktorial Ser.). 1996. mass mkt. 22.95 (*0-538-71494-8*) S-W Pub.

Microsoft Access for Windows 97. Sarah E. Hutchinson. (C). 1997. text 25.00 (*0-256-26973-4*) McGraw.

Microsoft Access for Windows 97. Sarah E. Hutchinson & Glen Coulthard. LC 97-188751. 240p. (C). 1997. text 21.00 (*0-256-26000-1*, Irwn McGrw-H) McGrw-H Hghr Educ.

Microsoft Access for Windows 95. Rick Sullivan. (Computer Training Ser.). 1997. pap. 19.95 (*0-538-67482-2*) S-W Pub.

***Microsoft Access 97.** Azimuth Interactive Staff. (Inter@ctiveLearning Ser.). (Illus.). 108p. 2000. pap. 14.95 (*1-930581-00-9*) Azimuth.

Microsoft Access 97. DDC Publishing Staff. LC 97-209730. (Quick Reference Guide Ser.). 230p. spiral bd. 27.00 (*1-56243-470-5*, G-28) DDC Pub.

Microsoft Access 97. Carita Virenius. LC 97-39329. (Visual Ser.). 1997. 18.69 (*0-7638-0085-6*) Paradigm MN.

***Microsoft Access 97.** deluxe ed. Azimuth Interactive Staff. (Inter@ctiveLearning Ser.). 2000. pap. 39.95 incl. cd-rom (*1-930581-01-7*) Azimuth.

Microsoft Access 97: Blue Ribbon Edition. 2nd ed. Duffy. 176p. (C). 1998. pap. text 25.00 (*0-201-44851-3*, Prentice Hall) P-H.

Microsoft Access 97: Complete Concepts & Techniques. 10th ed. Gary B. Shelly et al. (Shelly Cashman Ser.). 392p. (C). 1997. mass mkt. 38.95 (*0-7895-1344-7*) Course Tech.

Microsoft Access 97: Double Diamond Edition. 10th ed. Gary B. Shelly et al. (Shelly Cashman Ser.). 200p. (C). 1997. mass mkt. 22.95 (*0-7895-2756-1*) Course Tech.

Microsoft Access 97: Illustrated Brief Edition. 10th ed. Elizabeth E. Reding & Lisa Friedrichsen. (Illustrated Ser.). (Illus.). 96p. (C). 1997. pap. 12.95 (*0-7600-4703-0*) Course Tech.

Microsoft Access 97: Illustrated PLUS Edition. Elizabeth E. Reding & Lisa Friedrichsen. (Illustrated Ser.). (Illus.). 488p. (C). 1997. pap. 38.95 (*0-7600-5157-7*) Course Tech.

Microsoft Access 97: Illustrated Projects. (Illustrated Ser.). (Illus.). (C). 1997. pap., teacher ed. 18.50 (*0-7600-5132-1*) Course Tech.

Microsoft Access 97: Illustrated Projects. 10th ed. (Illustrated Ser.). (Illus.). 160p. (C). 1997. pap. 19.95 (*0-7600-5131-3*) Course Tech.

Microsoft Access 97: Illustrated Standard Edition, a Second Course. 10th ed. Elizabeth E. Reding & Lisa Friedrichsen. (Illustrated Ser.). (Illus.). 192p. (C). 1997. pap. 21.95 (*0-7600-5154-2*) Course Tech.

Microsoft Access 97 - Illustrated Standard Edition: A First Course. 10th ed. Elizabeth E. Reding & Lisa Friedrichsen. (Illus.). 192p. (C). 1997. pap. 21.95 (*0-7600-4697-2*) Course Tech.

Microsoft Access 97 at a Glance. Perspection, Inc. Staff. LC 96-36628. 1996. pap. text 16.95 (*1-57231-369-2*) Microsoft.

***Microsoft Access 97 Bible: Gold Edition.** Cary N. Prague et al. LC 99-60125. (Bible Ser.). (Illus.). 1552p. 1999. pap. 59.99 (*0-7645-3355-X*) IDG Bks.

Microsoft Access 97 Developer's Handbook: Using the New Microsoft Access Object Model & VBA. Timothy M. O'Brien et al. LC 97-1922. (Solution Developer Ser.). 700p. 1997. pap. 39.99 incl. cd-rom (*1-57231-358-7*) Microsoft.

***Microsoft Access 97 Field Guide.** Stephen L. Nelson. (Field Guide Ser.). (Illus.). 2000. pap. 7.99 (*0-7356-1062-2*) Microsoft.

Microsoft Access 97 for Windows 95. Patricia Murphy. (Quicktorial Ser.). 144p. 1997. pap. text 19.95 (*0-538-68426-7*) S-W Pub.

Microsoft Access 97 for Windows Quickstart. Jim O'Shea. LC 97-159619. 1996. pap. text 29.99 incl. cd-rom (*1-56276-473-X*, Ziff-Davis Pr) Que.

Microsoft Access 97 Introduction. Pamela W. Adams & Kathryn K. Baskett. Ed. by Susan D. Carnes. (Micrsoft Office 97 Ser.). (Illus.). 139p. 1998. pap. text 28.95 (*1-58163-059-X*) CPI Train.

Microsoft Access 97 Introductory & Advanced. (Illus.). 167p. 1997. pap. 32.95 (*1-888323-19-1*) DataPower Intl.

Microsoft Access 97 Quick Reference. Que Development Group, Staff. LC 97-66486. 307p. 1997. 16.99 (*0-7897-1212-1*) Que.

***Microsoft Access 97 Quick Source Guide.** Quick Source Staff. (Illus.). 6p. 1998. pap. 4.95 (*1-930674-20-1*) Quick Source.

Microsoft Access 97 Step by Step. Catapult, Inc., Staff & Microsoft Corporation Staff. (Illus.). 276p. 1997. pap. 29.95 incl. disk (*1-57231-316-1*) Microsoft.

Microsoft Access 97/Visual Basic Step by Step. Evan Callahan. LC 96-37208. 416p. 34.95 incl. cd-rom (*1-57231-319-6*) Microsoft.

Microsoft Access 7. Carita Virenius. LC 97-5754. (Paradigm Visual Ser.). 1997. write for info. (*0-7638-0021-X*) Paradigm MN.

Microsoft Access 7 for Windows - Illustrated, Incl. instr. resource kit, test mgr., Web pg. Gregory Schultz. (Illustrated Ser.). (Illus.). 208p. 1996. text, mass mkt. 20.95 incl. 3.5 ld (*0-7600-3562-8*) Course Tech.

Microsoft Access 7 for Windows 95. Gary B. Shelly & T. Cashman. LC 96-35076. 392p. 1996. pap. 25.00 (*0-7895-0725-0*) Course Tech.

Microsoft Access 7 for Windows 95: Comprehensive, Incl. instr. resource kit, labs, test mgr., files. Joseph J. Adamski. (New Perspectives Ser.). (Illus.). 616p. 1996. pap. 42.95 (*0-7600-3543-1*) Course Tech.

Microsoft Access 7 for Windows 95: Double Diamond. Gary B. Shelly & T. Cashman. 200p. 1996. pap. 22.95 (*0-7895-1154-1*) Course Tech.

Microsoft Access 7 for Windows 95: Illustrated Brief Edition, Incl. instr. resource kit, test mgr., Web pg. Elizabeth E. Reding. (Illustrated Ser.). (Illus.). 96p. 1996. pap. 11.95 (*0-7600-3812-0*) Course Tech.

Microsoft Access 7 for Windows 95: Introductory, Incl. instr. resource kit, labs, test mgr., files. Joseph J. Adamski. (New Perspectives Ser.). (Illus.). 304p. 1996. pap. 30.95 (*0-7600-3542-3*) Course Tech.

Microsoft Access 7.0 Introduction. Pamela W. Adams & Kathryn K. Baskett. Ed. by Susan D. Carnes. (Microsoft Office 95 Ser.). (Illus.). 122p. 1997. pap. text 28.95 (*1-58163-044-1*) CPI Train.

Microsoft Access 7.0. Don Cassel. LC 97-158754. 112p. 1997. pap. text 7.00 (*0-13-236879-X*) P-H.

Microsoft Access 7.0. Timothy J. O'Leary & Linda I. O'Leary. (C). 1996. pap. text 21.50 (*0-07-049106-2*) McGraw.

Microsoft Access 7.0 by Pictorial. Dennis Curtin. LC 96-22054. 235p. 1996. spiral bd. 37.33 (*0-13-238361-6*) P-H.

Microsoft Access 7.0 for Window 95. Sarah E. Hutchinson & Glen Coulthard. (C). 1996. write for info. (*0-256-22961-9*, Irwn McGrw-H) McGrw-H Hghr Educ.

Microsoft Access 7.0 for Windows 95. Sarah E. Hutchinson & Glen J. Coulthard. LC 96-13175. (Advantage Series for Computer Education). 240p. (C). 1996. text 25.00 (*0-256-22050-6*, Irwn McGrw-H) McGrw-H Hghr Educ.

Microsoft Access 7.0 for Windows 95: Introductory Coursebook. (Illus.). 1996. pap. text 29.95 (*1-888323-12-4*) DataPower Intl.

Microsoft Access 2 for Windows - New Perspectives Introductory, Incl. instr. resource kit, test bank, transparency. Joseph J. Adamski. (New Perspectives Ser.). (Illus.). 272p. (C). 1995. pap. 20.25 (*1-56527-148-3*) Course Tech.

Microsoft Access 2 for Windows - New Perspectives Comprehensive, Incl. instr. resource kit, test bank, transparency. Joseph J. Adamski. (New Perspectives Ser.). (Illus.). 600p. (C). 1995. mass mkt. 28.50 (*1-56527-987-5*) Course Tech.

Microsoft Access 2.0 by PicTorial. Dennis P. Curtin. LC 95-13810. (Pictorial Ser.). 240p. (C). 1995. pap. text 37.33 (*0-13-376849-X*) P-H.

***Microsoft Access 2000.** Course Technology Staff. (SAM's License Card for Course CBT Ser.). (C). 2000. text. write for info. (*0-619-00930-6*) Course Tech.

***Microsoft Access 2000.** Tim Duffy. 230p. (C). 1999. pap. text 25.00 (*0-201-45916-7*, Prentice Hall) P-H.

***Microsoft Access 2000.** Sarah E. Hutchinson & Glen J. Coulthard. LC 99-37327. 2000. write for info. (*0-07-234800-3*) McGrw-H Hghr Educ.

***Microsoft Access 2000.** Kenneth C. Laudon & Jason Eiseman. LC 99-62020. 1999. write for info. (*0-07-234075-4*) McGrw-H Hghr Educ.

***Microsoft Access 2000.** Timothy J. O'Leary. LC 99-62021. 2000. write for info. (*0-07-233751-6*) McGrw-H Hghr Educ.

***Microsoft Access 2000.** Nita H. Rutkosky & Meredith Flynn. LC 99-35407. (Benchmark Ser.). 1999. text 64.20 (*0-7638-0240-9*) Paradigm MN.

***Microsoft Access 2000: Advanced.** Stevens-Adamski Fullam. (New Perspectives Ser.). (C). 2000. text 48.95 (*0-619-01915-8*) Course Tech.

Microsoft Access 2000: Complete Tutorial. Pasewark. LC 99-23423. (Computer Applications Ser.). 1999. pap. 36.95 (*0-538-68841-6*); pap., wbk. ed. 12.95 (*0-538-68843-2*) S-W Pub.

Microsoft Access 2000 - Illustrated Brief. Lisa J. Friedrichsen. (Illus.). 112p. per. 12.95 (*0-7600-6069-X*, Pub. by Course Tech) Thomson Learn.

Microsoft Access 2000 - Illustrated Introductory. Lisa J. Friedrichsen. (Illus.). 192p. per. 21.95 (*0-7600-6070-3*, Pub. by Course Tech) Thomson Learn.

Microsoft Access 2000 Bible. Cary N. Prague & Michael Irwin. (Bible Ser.). (Illus.). 1272p. 1999. pap. 49.99 incl. cd-rom (*0-7645-3286-3*) IDG Bks.

Microsoft Access 2000 Certified: Course CBT. 26.95 (*0-619-00122-4*, Pub. by Course Tech) Thomson Learn.

***Microsoft Access 2000 Developer's Guide to Microsoft SQL Server.** Mary Chipman & Andy Baron. 650p. 2000. 39.99 (*0-672-31944-6*) Sams.

***Microsoft Access 2000 Developer's Guide.** Edward Jones. LC 99-18612. (Illus.). 888p. 1999. pap. 49.99 (*0-7645-3321-5*) IDG Bks.

***Microsoft Access 2000 Expert.** Course Technology Staff. (SAM's License Card for Course CBT Ser.). (C). 2000. text. write for info. (*0-619-00931-4*) Course Tech.

***Microsoft Access 2000 in Brief.** Sarah Hutchinson-Clifford & Glen Coulthard. 144p. (C). 1999. spiral bd. 19.06 (*0-07-233798-2*) McGrw-H Hghr Educ.

***Microsoft Access 2000 in Layman's Terms: The Reference Guide for the Rest of Us.** Katie Layman. (Illus.). 60p. 1999. pap. write for info. (*1-893532-11-9*) Compute Made.

Microsoft Access 2000 Introductory Concepts & Techniques. Gary B. Shelly et al. 208p. per. 22.95 (*0-7895-4674-4*, Pub. by Course Tech) Thomson Learn.

***Microsoft Access 2000 Mouse Cheat Sheet.** Joe Habraken. 300p. 1999. 19.99 (*0-7897-2117-1*) Que.

***Microsoft Access 2000 Quick Source Guide.** Quick Source Staff. (Illus.). 6p. 1999. pap. 4.95 (*1-930674-15-5*) Quick Source.

Microsoft Access 2.0: Introduction. M. G. Detienne. 50p. 1994. pap. text 29.00 (*1-887580-02-6*) Tec Trek.

Microsoft Access 2.0: Introductory Coursebook. DataPower AS Staff. 141p. 1995. pap. text 29.95 (*1-888323-04-3*) DataPower Intl.

Microsoft Access 2.0: LTU Windows Applications. Gary B. Shelly & T. Cashman. 336p. (C). 1994. pap. 38.95 (*0-87709-594-9*) S-W Pub.

Microsoft Access 2.0 for Windows. Timothy J. O'Leary & Linda I. O'Leary. LC 93-78724. (C). 1995. pap. text 11.50 (*0-07-048992-0*) McGraw.

Microsoft Access 2.0 for Windows. Sullivan. (C). 1995. 125.00 (*0-538-64131-2*) Thomson Learn.

Microsoft Access 2.0 for Windows. Rick Sullivan. (Computer Training Ser.). 180p. (C). 1995. spiral bd. 21.95 (*0-538-64132-0*) S-W Pub.

Microsoft Access 2.0 for Windows: Acumen Series. Boyd & Fraser Staff & Micheal Reilly. (DF - Computer Applications Ser.). 272p. (C). 1995. mass mkt. 20.95 (*0-87709-983-9*) Course Tech.

Microsoft Access 2.0 for Windows: Comprehensive Edition. Joseph Adamski. (New Perspectives Ser.). 600p. (C). 1996. pap. 42.95 (*0-7600-4582-8*) Course Tech.

Microsoft Access 2.0 for Windows: Double Diamond. Gary B. Shelly et al. 184p. (C). 1994. mass mkt. 22.95 (*0-87709-881-6*) Course Tech.

Microsoft Access 2.0 for Windows: Quick Course. Murphy. (Quick Course Ser.). 192p. 1995. mass mkt. 15.95 (*0-538-64861-9*) S-W Pub.

Microsoft Access 2.0 How-To CD. Ken Getz et al. 500p. 1995. pap. 44.95 (*1-878739-93-X*) Sams.

Microsoft Access 2.0 for Windows. Sarah E. Hutchinson et al. LC 95-153795. 192p. (C). 1994. text 12.50 (*0-256-17606-X*, Irwn McGrw-H) McGrw-H Hghr Educ.

Microsoft Access 2.0 for Windows. 2nd ed. Sarah E. Hutchinson & Glen Coulthard. LC 96-112877. 192p. (C). 1995. text 12.50 (*0-256-20225-7*, Irwn McGrw-H) McGrw-H Hghr Educ.

Microsoft Access 2.0 Windows. O'Leary. 1995. 22.50 (*0-07-049070-8*) McGraw.

***Microsoft Access 2000.** (C). 1999. write for info. (*0-201-69935-4*) HEPC Inc.

***Microsoft Access 2000.** (C). 2000. 0.00 (*0-201-69936-2*); 0.00 (*0-201-69937-0*) HEPC Inc.

***Microsoft Access 2000.** 222p. (C). 2000. text 18.75 (*0-536-60494-0*) Pearson Custom.

***Microsoft Access 2000.** Julia Kelly. LC 99-30668. (One Step at a Time Ser.). 360p. 1999. pap. 29.99 (*0-7645-3290-1*) IDG Bks.

Microsoft Access 2000. Napier. LC 99-235883. 1999. pap. 31.95 (*0-538-42610-1*); pap. 12.95 (*0-538-42623-3*) S-W Pub.

***Microsoft Access 2000.** Nita Hewitt Rutkosky & Denise Seguin. LC 99-57581. (Marquee Ser.). 2000. write for info. (*0-7638-0368-5*) Paradigm MN.

Microsoft Access 2000: Complete Edition. Sarah E. Hutchinson & Glen J. Coulthard. LC 00-33543. (Advantage Series for Computer Education). 2000. pap. 28.50 (*0-07-234801-1*) McGraw.

***Microsoft Access 2000: Complete Tutorial.** Sandra Cable & William Pasewark. LC 99-23423. (Tutorial Ser.). 368p. 1999. pap. 40.95 (*0-538-68842-4*) Sth-Wstrn College.

Microsoft Access 2000: Comprehensive Concepts & Techniques. Gary B. Shelly. (Shelly Cashman Ser.). 1999. pap. text 44.95 (*0-7895-5610-3*) Course Tech.

Microsoft Access 2000: Illustrated Complete Edition. Elizabeth E. Reding. 1999. pap. text 38.95 (*0-7600-6072-X*) Course Tech.

***Microsoft Access 2000: Introduction.** Pamela W. Adams & Elizabeth Carpenter. Ed. by Jenell L. Davis. (Office 2000 Ser.). (Illus.). 150p. 2000. pap. 28.95 (*1-58163-095-6*) CPI Train.

Microsoft Access 2000: Quicktorial. Murphy. LC 98-47591. (Computer Applications Ser.). 180p. 1999. pap. 21.95 (*0-538-68857-2*) S-W Pub.

***Microsoft Access 2000: Simplified.** Ruth Maran. 240p. 1999. pap. 24.99 (*0-7645-6058-1*) IDG Bks.

***Microsoft Access 2000 Bible: Gold Edition.** Cary N. Prague & Michael R. Irwin. LC 99-38068. (Bible Ser.). 1600p. 1999. pap. 64.99 (*0-7645-3404-1*) IDG Bks.

Microsoft Access 2000 Exam Cram. David Mercer. (Exam Cram / Coriolis' Certification Insi Ser.). 1999. pap. text 26.99 (*1-57610-511-3*) Coriolis Grp.

***Microsoft Access 2000 Introduction.** Timothy O'Leary & Linda O'Leary. 440p. (C). 1999. pap. 27.50 (*0-07-233749-4*) McGrw-H Hghr Educ.

***Microsoft Access 2000 Learning Kit.** John Vies. Ed. by Microsoft Corporation Staff. (gr. 8). 2000. boxed set 69.99 (*0-7356-0756-7*) Little.

***Microsoft Access 2000, QuickTutorial.** Patricia Murphy. LC 98-47591. (Quicktorial Ser.). (Illus.). 144p. 1999. pap. 24.95 (*0-538-68858-0*) Sth-Wstrn College.

Microsoft Access 2000 Step by Step. Catapult, Inc., Staff. LC 98-48188. (Step by Step Ser.). 940p. 1999. pap. text 29.99 (*1-57231-976-3*) Microsoft.

Microsoft Access 2000 Unleashed. Stephen Forte et al. LC 98-85915. (Sams Unleashed Series). (Illus.). 878p. 1999. 49.99 incl. cd-rom (*0-672-31291-3*) Sams.

***Microsoft Access 2000 VBA Fundamentals/Mastering Solution Set.** Evan Callahan. 1999. pap., boxed set 99.99 incl. cd-rom (*0-7356-0814-8*) Microsoft Pr.

Microsoft Access 2000 Visual Basic Fundamentals. Evan Callahan. LC 99-13362. 475p. 1999. pap. 39.99 (*0-7356-0592-0*) Microsoft.

Microsoft Access 7.0 Pal. (College Title Ser.). (C). 1996. write for info. (*0-13-255555-7*) P-H.

Microsoft Access 97. Adams. (C). 1998. pap. text 22.50 (*0-03-023721-1*) Harcourt Coll Pubs.

M

Microsoft Access 97. 10th ed. David Mercer. LC 98-29401. (Exam Cram Ser.). 300p. (C). 1998. mass mkt. 26.99 (*1-57610-223-8*) Coriolis Grp.

Microsoft Access 97, Pt. 1. (C). 1997. text 11.50 (*0-03-022539-6*) Harcourt Coll Pubs.

Microsoft Access 97 Intermediate. Elizabeth Carpenter. 1999. pap. text 28.95 (*1-58163-086-7*) CPI Train.

Microsoft Access/Visual Basic Step by Step. Evan Callahan. (Step by Step Ser.). 368p. 1995. 29.95 incl. disk (*1-55615-890-4*) Microsoft.

***Microsoft Active Directory Administration.** 400p. 2000. 29.99 (*0-672-31975-6*) Sams.

***Microsoft Active Directory Developer's Reference Library, 5 vols.** David Iseminger. (Microsoft Windows Programmer's Reference Library). 2000. pap. text 149.99 (*0-7356-0992-6*) Microsoft.

***Microsoft Active Directory for Dummies.** Marcia Loughry. (For Dummies Ser.). 408p. 1999. pap. 24.99 incl. cd-rom (*0-7645-0659-5*) IDG Bks.

***Microsoft Active Platform Developer's Guide.** Cruyningen Ike Van. (Enterprise Computing Ser.). 450p. 1999. pap. 44.99 (*0-07-134930-8*) McGraw.

Microsoft Age of Empires: Inside Moves. expanded rev. ed. Steven L. Kent. LC 98-38728. (Inside Moves Ser.). 304p. 1998. pap. 16.99 (*0-7356-0569-6*) Microsoft.

***Microsoft Age of Empires Ii.** Mark H. Walker. LC 99-42531. 272p. 1999. pap. text 19.99 (*0-7356-0513-0*) Microsoft.

***Microsoft Age of Empires II: The Age of Kings Official Scenario Design Toolkit.** Paul Schuytema & Scott McCabe. (Illus.). 288p. 2000. pap. 24.99 incl. audio compact disk (*0-7821-2771-1*) Sybex.

***Microsoft Age of Empires II: The Conquerors Expansion: Inside Moves.** Mark H. Walker. 320p. 2000. pap. 19.99 (*0-7356-1177-7*) Microsoft.

***Microsoft Application Center Resource Kit.** Microsoft Press Staff. (IT Resource Kits Ser.). (Illus.). 2000. pap. 69.99 (*0-7356-1023-1*) Microsoft.

Microsoft BackOffice Administrator's Survival Guide. Arthur Knowles. LC 95-70080. (Illus.). 1008p. 1996. 59.99 (*0-672-30849-5*) Sams.

Microsoft Backoffice for Small Business Server Bible. William C. Jeansonne. LC 98-70266. 672p. 1998. pap. 39.99 (*0-7645-3210-3*) IDG Bks.

Microsoft BackOffice Resource Kit. 2nd ed. Microsoft Corporation Staff. LC 98-2588. 2706p. 1998. 199.99 incl. cd-rom (*1-57231-632-2*, 868458) S&S Childrens.

Microsoft BackOffice Resource Kit Pt. 2: Microsoft SQL Server, Pt. 2. Microsoft Corporation Staff. LC 97-831. 500p. 1997. pap. text 79.99 incl. cd-rom (*1-57231-534-2*) Microsoft.

***Microsoft Backoffice Server 5.0 Integration & Interoperability Technical.** Microsoft Corporation Staff. 2000. 49.99 (*0-7356-1036-3*) Microsoft.

***Microsoft BackOffice Small Business Server 4.5 Resource Kit.** Microsoft Corporation Staff. LC 99-13774. 1000p. 1999. pap. 69.99 (*0-7356-0577-7*) Microsoft.

Microsoft BackOffice System Management. Kenneth L. Spencer & Techknowquest Inc. Staff. 350p. (C). 1998. pap. text 49.99 (*0-13-848052-4*) P-H.

Microsoft BackOffice 2 Administrator's Survival Guide. 2nd ed. Arthur Knowles. LC 96-69394. 1136p. 1996. 59.99 (*0-672-30977-7*) Sams.

Microsoft BackOffice 2 Unleashed. Joe Greene et al. LC 96-67199. 1200p. 1996. 59.99 (*0-672-30816-9*) Sams.

Microsoft BackOffice 2.5 Unleashed. 2nd ed. Joe Greene. LC 97-65734. 1504p. 1997. 75.00 (*0-672-31085-6*) Sams.

Microsoft BackOffice 4.5 Resource Kit. Microsoft Corporation Staff. LC 99-13771. 2500p. 1999. boxed set 199.99 (*0-7356-0583-1*) Microsoft.

Microsoft Basic Answers. Grimes. Date not set. pap. text. write for info. (*0-314-65514-X*) West Pub.

Microsoft BASIC Decoded & Other Mysteries. James L. Farvour. (TRS-80 Information Ser.: Vol. II). (Illus.). 312p. (Orig.). 1981. pap. 29.95 (*0-936200-01-4*) Blue Cat.

***Microsoft BizTalk Exposed.** LC 99-64930. 266p. 2000. pap. 29.99 (*0-672-31787-7*) Sams.

Microsoft Bookshelf, Single User License. Microsoft Corporation Staff. (NO - Novell/Wordperfect Ser.). 1995. 44.95 (*0-538-65626-3*) S-W Pub.

Microsoft C - C++ 7: The Complete Reference. William H. Murray, III & Chris H. Pappas. 1008p. 1992. pap. 29.95 (*0-07-881664-5*) Osborne-McGraw.

Microsoft Certification Career: Earn 100K+Beyond. William C. Jeansonne. LC 99-16044. 696p. 1999. pap. 24.99 (*0-7645-3305-3*) IDG Bks.

Microsoft Certified Professional + Internet Training Kit. Microsoft Corporation Staff. LC 98-6122. 2224p. 299.99 incl. cd-rom (*1-57231-906-2*) Microsoft.

Microsoft Certified Professional Training Kit for Excel 7. Productivity Point International Staff. 1100p. 1996. pap. text 99.99 incl. cd-rom (*0-7897-0761-6*) Que.

Microsoft Certified System Engineer TCP/IP Exam Guide. James Farhat et al. 900p. 1997. pap. 99.99 incl. cd-rom (*0-7897-1153-2*) Que.

Microsoft Certified Systems Engineer Core Requirements Training Kit. Microsoft Corporation Staff. LC 98-6123. 2280p. 329.99 incl. cd-rom (*1-57231-905-4*) Microsoft.

***Microsoft Chess.** Yasser Seirawan. (Illus.). 1999. pap. text 49.99 (*0-7356-0921-7*) Microsoft.

Microsoft COBOL. Ken Seidel. 200p. 1983. pap. 19.95 (*0-88056-117-3*) Weber Systems.

Microsoft Combat Flight Simulator: Inside Moves. Ben Chlu. LC 98-38263. 224p. 1998. 16.99 (*1-57231-592-X*) Microsoft.

***Microsoft Combat Flight Simulator: WWII Pacific Theater: Inside Moves.** Jeff Van West. 320p. 2000. pap. 19.99 (*0-7356-1176-9*) Microsoft.

***Microsoft Commerce Server 2000 System Administrator's Handbook.** (C). 2000. pap. 49.99 (*0-13-017044-5*) P-H.

Microsoft Corporation: The WetFeet.com Insider Guide. 5th ed. WetFeet.com Staff. (Insider Guides Ser.). 65p. 1999. per. 25.00 (*1-58207-042-3*) WetFeet.

Microsoft Critical Depth: Inside Moves. Phil Powell. 1997. pap. text 16.99 (*1-57231-633-0*) Microsoft.

Microsoft Data Warehousing: Building Distributed Decision Support Systems. Robert S. Craig et al. LC 99-21793. 384p. 1999. pap. 39.99 (*0-471-32761-1*) Wiley.

***Microsoft Devil's Own: Inside Moves.** Doug Brumley & Leslie Mizell. 1998. pap. 16.99 (*1-57231-714-0*) Microsoft.

Microsoft Dictionnaire de l'Informatique. Pierre Brandois. (FRE.). 415p. 1992. 120.00 (*0-7859-7731-7*, 2100013149) Fr & Eur.

Microsoft DirectX 2 Games Programming with Delphi. David Bowden et al. (Illus.). 500p. Date not set. pap. 49.95 (*1-55622-557-1*) Wordware Pub.

***Microsoft Edge: Insider Strategies for Building Sucess.** Julie Bick. 176p. 1999. 20.00 (*0-671-03413-8*, PB Hardcover) PB.

***Microsoft Encyclopedia of Networking.** Mitch Tulloch. LC 00-24947. (Illus.). 1500p. (C). (gr. 8). 2000. pap. 79.99 incl. cd-rom (*0-7356-0573-4*) Microsoft.

***Microsoft Excel: Simple Projects.** Teacher Created Materials Staff. (Illus.). 2000. pap. 18.95 incl. cd-rom (*1-57690-443-1*) Tchr Create Mat.

***Microsoft Excel: Using Graphics.** DK Publishing Staff. (Illus.). 72p. 2000. pap. 6.95 (*0-7894-5536-6*, D K Ink) DK Pub Inc.

Microsoft Excel - Visual Basic Programmer's Guide for Windows 95: The Guide to Increasing Productivity with Microsoft Excel/Visual Basic. Microsoft Corporation Staff. (Professional Editions Ser.). 368p. 1995. 24.95 (*1-55615-819-X*) Microsoft.

Microsoft Excel - Visual Basic Reference: For Microsoft Excel for Windows 95 & for Microsoft Excel for Windows 3.1 & Macintosh Systems. 2nd ed. Microsoft Corporation Staff. (Professional Editions Ser.). 848p. 1995. 29.95 (*1-55615-920-X*) Microsoft.

Microsoft Excel Developer's Kit: For Microsoft Excel for Windows 95, & for Microsoft Excel for Windows 3.1 & Macintosh Systems. 3rd ed. Microsoft Corporation Staff. (Professional Editions Ser.). 450p. 1996. 49.95 incl. cd-rom (*1-55615-879-3*) Microsoft.

Microsoft Excel 5/7 for Windows 95: Illustrated Projects. 10th ed. Carol M. Cram. (Illustrated Ser.). (Illus.). 160p. (C). 1997. pap. 19.95 (*0-7600-4681-6*) Course Tech.

Microsoft Excel 5 for Windows: Double Diamond. Gary B. Shelly & Thomas J. Cashman. 208p. (C). 1994. pap. 22.95 (*0-87709-880-8*) Course Tech.

Microsoft Excel 5 for Windows - Illustrated, Incl. instr. resource kit, test bank, transparency. Elizabeth E. Reding. (Illustrated Ser.). (Illus.). 192p. (C). 1996. pap. 20.95 (*1-56527-264-1*) Course Tech.

Microsoft Excel 5 for Windows - New Perspectives Introductory, Incl. instr. resource kit, test bank, transparency. June J. Parsons & Dan Oja. (New Perspectives Ser.). (Illus.). 304p. (C). 1994. text 20.25 (*1-56527-154-8*) Course Tech.

Microsoft Excel 5 for Windows - New Perspectives Comprehensive, Incl. instr. resource kit, test bank, transparency. June J. Parsons et al. (New Perspectives Ser.). (Illus.). 600p. (C). 1994. pap. 28.50 (*1-56527-324-9*) Course Tech.

Microsoft Excel 5 for Windows Step by Step. 3rd ed. Catapult, Inc., Staff. LC 93-23634. (Step by Step Ser.). 368p. 1994. pap. 29.95 incl. disk (*1-55615-587-5*) Microsoft.

Microsoft Excel 5.0 for Windows. 2nd ed. Sarah E. Hutchinson & Glen Coulthard. 216p. (C). 1995. text 25.00 (*0-256-20240-0*, Irwn McGrw-H) McGrw-H Hghr Educ.

Microsoft Excel 5.0: A Professional Approach. Judith J. Lambrecht & Nina M. Edgmand. LC 93-42004. 1994. write for info. (*0-02-801955-5*) Glencoe.

Microsoft Excel 5.0: Basics & Beyond. M. G. Detienne & J. Marcotte. 116p. 1995. pap. text 29.00 (*1-887580-03-4*) Tec Trek.

Microsoft Excel 5.0: Quick Comprehension Guide. Carole K. Tobias. LC 93-42005. 1994. write for info. (*0-02-801956-3*) Glencoe.

Microsoft Excel 5.0 for Macintosh. Patricia Murphy. (Quicktorial Ser.). (C). 1996. mass mkt. 21.95 (*0-538-71577-4*) S-W Pub.

Microsoft Excel 5.0 for Macintosh: Quick Course. Murphy. (DF - Computer Applications Ser.). 1996. mass mkt., wbk. ed. 22.95 (*0-538-71575-8*) S-W Pub.

Microsoft Excel 5.0 for Windows. Boyd & Fraser Staff. (Acumen Ser.). (C). 1995. mass mkt. 20.95 (*0-87709-980-4*) Course Tech.

Microsoft Excel 5.0 for Windows. Timothy O'Leary & Linda I. O'Leary. LC 94-75716. (C). 1995. pap. text 12.50 (*0-07-048990-4*) McGraw.

Microsoft Excel 5.0 for Windows. Rick Sullivan. (Computer Training Ser.). 144p. (C). pap. text 18.95 (*0-538-63425-1*) S-W Pub.

Microsoft Excel 5.0 for Windows. Rick Sullivan. (Computer Training Ser.). 180p. (C). 1995. spiral bd. 21.95 (*0-538-64092-8*) S-W Pub.

Microsoft Excel 5.0 Windows. Systems Select Staff. 256p. 1995. pap. text 25.00 (*0-8053-2864-5*) Addison-Wesley.

Microsoft Excel 5.0 for Windows: Comprehensive. 10th ed. June J. Parsons et al. (New Perspectives Ser.). 600p. (C). 1997. pap. 42.95 (*0-7600-4578-X*) Course Tech.

Microsoft Excel 5.0 for Windows: Introductory Coursebook. DataPower AS Staff. 126p. 1995. pap. text 29.95 (*1-888323-02-7*) DataPower Intl.

Microsoft Excel 5.0 for Windows: Quick Course. Murphy. (Quick Course Ser.). 192p. 1995. mass mkt. 15.95 (*0-538-64841-4*) S-W Pub.

Microsoft Excel 5.0 for Windows: Standard Course. Sandra Cable. (DF - Computer Applications Ser.). (C). 1995. mass mkt. 34.95 (*0-538-64439-7*) S-W Pub.

***Microsoft Excel for Accounting Principles.** Katherine Smith et al. LC 99-17434. 156p. (C). 1999. pap. text 27.00 incl. disk (*0-13-013567-4*) P-H.

Microsoft Excel for Chemists: A Comprehensive Guide. E. J. Billo. 400p. 1997. pap. 49.95 incl. disk (*1-56081-959-6*) Wiley.

Microsoft Excel for Engineers. Delores M. Etter. 128p. 1995. pap. text 21.33 (*0-8053-6536-2*) Benjamin-Cummings.

***Microsoft Excel for Terrified Teachers.** Jan Rader & Karen Wiburg. (Illus.). 304p. 1999. pap., teacher ed. 24.95 (*1-57690-442-3*, TCM 2442) Tchr Create Mat.

Microsoft Excel for the Macintosh. Danny Goodman. LC 94-8359. 1994. write for info. (*0-02-801053-1*) Glencoe.

Microsoft Excel for Windows 95 Step by Step. Catapult, Inc., Staff. (Step by Step Ser.). 368p. 1995. 29.95 incl. disk (*1-55615-825-4*) Microsoft.

Microsoft Excel for Windows 95 (Version 7.0) by PicTorial. Dennis P. Curtin. LC 96-4038. (Pictorial Ser.). 320p. (C). 1996. spiral bd. 37.33 (*0-13-238379-9*) P-H.

Microsoft Excel for Windows 95. Patricia Murphy. (Quicktorial Ser.). (C). 1996. mass mkt. 21.95 (*0-538-71545-6*) S-W Pub.

Microsoft Excel for Windows 95. James S. Quasney et al. LC 96-35075. 432p. 1996. pap. 38.95 (*0-7895-0734-X*) Course Tech.

Microsoft Excel for Windows 95. Gary B. Shelly & T. Cashman. 232p. 1996. pap. 22.95 (*0-7895-1156-8*) Course Tech.

***Microsoft Excel Intermediate: Practice & Reference Guide.** Juanita B. Tischendorf. (Illus.). viii, 173p. 1999. pap. text 25.00 (*1-928613-07-1*) J Tischendorf.

Microsoft Excel 97. Pamela W. Adams & Kathryn K. Baskett. Ed. by Susan D. Carnes. (Microsoft Office 97 Ser.). 1997. pap. text 44.95 (*1-58163-073-5*) CPI Train.

***Microsoft Excel 97.** Azimuth Interactive Staff. (Inter@ctiveLearning Ser.). (Illus.). 148p. 2000. pap. 19.95 (*1-930581-08-4*) Azimuth.

Microsoft Excel 97. DDC Publishing Staff. LC 97-226283. (Quick Reference Guide Ser.). spiral bd. 27.00 (*1-56243-456-X*, G-27) DDC Pub.

Microsoft Excel 97. Tara O'Keefe. 1997. pap. text 24.99 (*0-7600-5609-9*) Course Tech.

Microsoft Excel 97. Helj A. Pulkkinen. LC 97-41633. (Paradigm Visual Ser.). 1997. 18.68 (*0-7638-0091-0*) Paradigm MN.

Microsoft Excel 97. Nita H. Rutkosky. LC 97-20570. 1997. write for info. (*0-7638-0089-9*); pap. write for info. (*0-7638-0090-2*) Paradigm MN.

***Microsoft Excel 97.** deluxe ed. Azimuth Interactive Staff. (Inter@ctiveLearning Ser.). (Illus.). 148p. 2000. pap. 39.95 incl. cd-rom (*1-930581-09-2*) Azimuth.

Microsoft Excel 97: Advanced Courseware. (Illus.). 125p. 1997. pap. text 32.95 (*1-888323-21-3*) DataPower Intl.

Microsoft Excel 97: Blue Ribbon Edition. 2nd ed. Duffy. 224p. (C). 1998. pap. text 25.00 (*0-201-44850-5*, Prentice Hall) P-H.

Microsoft Excel 97: Complete Concepts & Techniques. 10th ed. Gary B. Shelly et al. (Shelly Cashman Ser.). 432p. (C). 1997. mass mkt. 38.95 (*0-7895-1341-2*) Course Tech.

Microsoft Excel 97: Double Diamond Edition. 10th ed. Gary B. Shelly et al. (Shelly Cashman Ser.). 240p. (C). 1997. mass mkt. 22.95 (*0-7895-2753-7*) Course Tech.

Microsoft Excel 97: Illustrated Brief Edition. Elizabeth E. Reding & Tara O'Keefe. (Illus.). 96p. (C). 1997. pap., teacher ed. 40.00 (*0-7600-5310-3*) Course Tech.

Microsoft Excel 97: Illustrated Brief Edition. 10th ed. Elizabeth E. Reding & Tara O'Keefe. (Illustrated Ser.). (Illus.). 96p. (C). 1997. pap. 12.95 (*0-7600-4701-4*) Course Tech.

Microsoft Excel 97: Illustrated Plus Edition. Elizabeth E. Reding & Tara O'Keefe. (Illustrated Ser.). (Illus.). 488p. (C). 1997. pap. 38.95 (*0-7600-5149-6*) Course Tech.

Microsoft Excel 97: Illustrated Projects. Carol M. Cram. (Illustrated Ser.). (Illus.). (C). 1997. pap., teacher ed. 18.50 (*0-7600-5126-7*) Course Tech.

Microsoft Excel 97: Illustrated Projects. 10th ed. Carol M. Cram. (Illustrated Ser.). (Illus.). 160p. (C). 1997. pap. 19.95 (*0-7600-5125-9*) Course Tech.

Microsoft Excel 97: Illustrated Standard Edition: A First Course. 10th ed. Elizabeth E. Reding & Tara O'Keefe. (Illustrated Ser.). (Illus.). 192p. (C). 1997. pap. 21.95 (*0-7600-4695-6*) Course Tech.

Microsoft Excel 97: Illustrated Standard Edition: A Second Course. Elizabeth E. Reding & Tara O'Keefe. (Illustrated Ser.). (Illus.). 192p. (C). 1997. pap. 16.50 (*0-7600-5146-1*) Course Tech.

Microsoft Excel 97: Introductory Coursebook. (Illus.). 125p. 1997. pap. text 29.95 (*1-888323-17-5*) DataPower Intl.

Microsoft Excel 97 - Illustrated Standard Edition: A First Course. Elizabeth E. Reding & Tara O'Keefe. (Illus.). 192p. (C). 1997. teacher ed. 5.00 incl. 3.5 hd (*0-7600-5151-8*) Course Tech.

Microsoft Excel 97 Advanced. Pamela W. Adams. Ed. by Elizabeth Carpenter & Sara Pressley. (Microsoft Office 97 Ser.). (Illus.). 100p. 1998. pap. text 28.95 (*1-58163-074-3*) CPI Train.

Microsoft Excel 97 at a Glance. Perspection, Inc. Staff. LC 96-36632. 1996. pap. text 16.95 (*1-57231-367-6*) Microsoft.

***Microsoft Excel 97 Field Guide.** Stephen L. Nelson. (Field Guide Ser.). (Illus.). 2000. pap. 7.99 (*0-7356-1060-6*) Microsoft.

Microsoft Excel 97 for Windows. Sandra Cable. (DF - Computer Applications Ser.). 1997. mass mkt. 33.95 (*0-538-71930-3*) S-W Pub.

Microsoft Excel 97 for Windows Quickstart. Logical Operations Staff. LC 97-159615. 392p. 1996. pap. text 29.99 incl. cd-rom (*1-56276-470-5*, Ziff-Davis Pr) Que.

Microsoft Excel 97 for Windows 95. Patricia Murphy. (Quicktorial Ser.). 1997. pap. text 19.95 (*0-538-68420-8*) S-W Pub.

Microsoft Excel 97 for Windows. Sullivan. (IN - Computer Training Ser.). 1998. pap. 20.95 (*0-538-68019-9*) S-W Pub.

Microsoft Excel 97 for Windows: Tutorial & Applications. Sandra Cable. 1997. pap. 32.75 (*0-538-71932-X*) Thomson Learn.

Microsoft Excel 97 Intermediate. Pamela W. Adams & Kathryn K. Baskett. Ed. by Susan D. Carnes. (Micrsoft Office 97 Ser.). (Illus.). 105p. 1997. pap. text 28.95 (*1-58163-058-1*) CPI Train.

***Microsoft Excel 97 Introduction: Practice & Reference Guide.** Juanita B. Tischendorf. (Illus.). ix, 187p. 1999. pap. text 25.00 (*1-928613-02-0*) J Tischendorf.

***Microsoft Excel 97 Quick Source Guide.** Quick Source Staff. (Illus.). 6p. 1998. pap. 4.95 (*1-930674-18-X*) Quick Source.

Microsoft Excel 97 Step by Step, Advanced Topics. Catapult, Inc., Staff. LC 97-10658. 300p. 1997. pap. text 29.99 (*1-57231-564-4*) Microsoft.

Microsoft Excel 97 Step by Step, Complete Course, 2 Vols. Catapult, Inc., Staff. LC 97-221618. 672p. 1997. pap. text 49.99 incl. cd-rom (*1-57231-580-6*) Microsoft.

Microsoft Excel 97 Step by Step. Catapult, Inc. Staff. LC 96-38988. (Step by Step Ser.). (Illus.). 269p. pap. 29.95 (*1-57231-314-5*) Microsoft.

Microsoft Excel 97/Visual Basic Step by Step. Reed Jacobson. LC 97-4203. (Step by Step Ser.). (Illus.). 340p. pap. 34.95 (*1-57231-318-8*) Microsoft.

Microsoft Excel 1.5 Teaching Guide. Pierre-Jean Charra. 106p. 1989. ring bd. 495.00 incl. disk (*0-929533-11-9*) Tutorland.

Paradigm Visual Series: Microsoft Excel 7: Text with disk, 3.5. Helja Pulkkinen & E. Valtanen. 128p. 14.95 incl. cd-rom (*0-7638-0015-5*) EMC-Paradigm.

Microsoft Excel 7 for Windows 95 - Advanced, Incl. instr. resource kit, Online comp., files. Roy Ageloff & Roger Hayen. (New Perspectives Ser.). (Illus.). 696p. 1996. pap. 33.00 (*0-7600-3533-4*) Course Tech.

Microsoft Excel 7 for Windows 95 - Introductory, Incl. instr. resource kit, test mgr., labs, files. June J. Parsons & Dan Oja. (New Perspectives Ser.). (Illus.). 624p. 1995. text, mass mkt. 30.95 incl. 3.5 ld (*0-7600-3541-5*) Course Tech.

Microsoft Excel 7 for Windows 95 - Comprehensive, Incl. instr. resource kit, test mgr., labs, files. June J. Parsons et al. (New Perspectives Ser.). (Illus.). 328p. 1996. text 42.95 (*0-7600-3535-0*) Course Tech.

Microsoft Excel 7 for Windows 95 - Illustrated Plus, Incl. instr. resource kit, test mgr., Web pg. Tara O'Keefe. (Illustrated Ser.). (Illus.). 384p. 1996. text, mass mkt. 38.95 incl. 3.5 ld (*0-7600-3742-6*) Course Tech.

Microsoft Excel 7 for Windows 95 - Illustrated Brief Edition, Incl. instr. resource kit, test mgr., Web pg. Elizabeth E. Reding. (Illustrated Ser.). (Illus.). 96p. 1995. text, mass mkt. 11.95 incl. 3.5 ld (*0-7600-3811-2*) Course Tech.

Microsoft Excel 7 for Windows 95 - Illustrated, Incl. instr. resource kit, test mgr., Web pg. Ann Shafer & Elizabeth E. Reding. (Illustrated Ser.). (Illus.). 208p. 1995. text, mass mkt. 20.95 incl. 3.5 ld (*0-7600-3523-7*) Course Tech.

Microsoft Excel 7.0. Pamela W. Adams & Kathryn K. Baskett. Ed. by Susan D. Carnes. (Microsoft Office 95 Ser.). (Illus.). 166p. 1997. pap. text 44.95 (*1-58163-045-X*) CPI Train.

Microsoft Excel 7.0 for Windows 95. Rick Sullivan. (Computer Training Ser.). 1997. pap. text 19.95 incl. cd-rom (*0-538-67470-9*) S-W Pub.

Microsoft Excel 7.0A for Windows 95. Timothy J. O'Leary & Linda I. O'Leary. LC 95-82267. (C). 1996. pap. text 22.50 (*0-07-049110-0*) McGraw.

Microsoft Excel 7.0 for Windows 95. Sarah E. Hutchinson & Glen Coulthard. 216p. (C). 1996. write for info. (*0-256-22960-0*, Irwn McGrw-H) McGrw-H Hghr Educ.

Microsoft Excel 7.0 for Windows 95. Sarah E. Hutchinson & Glen J. Coulthard. (Irwin Advantage Series for Computer Education). 216p. (C). 1996. text 25.00 (*0-256-22049-2*, Irwn McGrw-H) McGrw-H Hghr Educ.

Microsoft Excel 7.0 for Windows 95: Advanced Coursebook. Datapower A/S Staff. (Illus.). 1996. pap. text 32.95 (*1-888323-09-4*) DataPower Intl.

Microsoft Excel 7.0 for Windows 95: Introductory Coursebook. (Illus.). 165p. (Orig.). 1996. pap. text 29.95 (*1-888323-07-8*) DataPower Intl.

Microsoft Excel 7.0 for Windows 95: Quick Course. Murphy. (DF - Computer Applications Ser.). (C). 1996. mass mkt. 22.95 (*0-538-71481-6*) S-W Pub.

Microsoft Excel 7.0 for Windows 95: Tutorial & Applications Ser. Sandra Cabel. (Tutorial & Applications Ser.). 1996. mass mkt., student ed. 37.95 (*0-538-71518-9*) S-W Pub.

Microsoft Excel 7.0 for Windows 95: Tutorial & Applications Ser. Sandra Cabel. LC 95-49657. (Tutorial & Applications Ser.). 1996. mass mkt. 37.95 (*0-538-71508-1*) S-W Pub.

***Microsoft Excel Simple Projects: Challenging.** Steve Bitz. Ed. by Teacher Created Materials Staff. (Illus.). 96p. 2000. pap., teacher ed. 18.95 (*1-57690-734-1*, TCM 2734) Tchr Create Mat.

Microsoft Excel Supplement. 7th ed. 200p. (C). 1998. text. write for info. (*0-13-080907-1*) P-H.

An Asterisk (*) at the beginning of an entry indicates that the title is appearing for the first time.

*Microsoft Excel 2000. Teresa Adams & Stella Smith. LC 99-61509. 2000. text. write for info. (0-03-026133-3) Harcourt Coll Pubs.
*Microsoft Excel 2000. Course Technology Staff. (SAM's License Card for Course CBT Ser.). (C). 2000. text. write for info. (0-619-00928-4) Course Tech.
*Microsoft Excel 2000 Expert. Course Technology Staff. (SAM's License Card for Course CBT Ser.). (C). 2000. text. write for info. (0-619-00929-2) Course Tech.
*Microsoft Excel 2000. Tim Duffy. 238p. (C). 1999. pap. text 25.00 (0-201-45914-0, Prentice Hall) P-H.
*Microsoft Excel 2000. Sarah E. Hutchinson & Glen J. Coulthard. LC 99-49954. 2000. write for info. (0-07-234808-9); write for info. (0-07-234802-X) McGrw-H Hghr Educ.
*Microsoft Excel 2000. Philip Koneman. 180p. (C). 1999. pap. text 25.00 (0-201-45898-5, Prentice Hall) P-H.
*Microsoft Excel 2000. Kenneth C. Laudon & Kenneth Rosenblatt. LC 99-62388. 1999. write for info. (0-07-234076-2) McGrw-H Hghr Educ.
*Microsoft Excel 2000. Nita Hewitt Rutkosky. LC 99-32175. (Benchmark Ser.). 1999. write for info. (0-7638-0332-4) Paradigm MN.
*Microsoft Excel 2000: Brief Edition. Sarah E. Hutchinson & Glen J. Coulthard. LC 99-12479. (Illus.). 2000. write for info. (0-07-233796-6) McGrw-H Hghr Educ.
Microsoft Excel 2000: Complete Tutorial. Pasewark. (Computer Applications Ser.). 1999. pap. 36.95 (0-538-68836-X); pap., wbk. ed. 12.95 (0-538-68838-6) S-W Pub.
*Microsoft Excel 2000: Illustrated Complete. Elizabeth E. Reding. (Illus.). 488p. 1999. pap. text 38.95 (0-7600-6064-9) Course Tech.
*Microsoft Excel 2000: Introduction. Pamela W. Adams. Ed. by Jenell L. Davis. (Office 2000 Ser.). (Illus.). 122p. 1999. pap. 28.95 (1-58163-092-1) CPI Train.
*Microsoft Excel 2000: Power Programming with VBA. John Walkenbach. LC 99-18447. 912p. 1999. pap. text 49.99 (0-7645-3263-4) IDG Bks.
Microsoft Excel 2000 - Illustrated Brief. Elizabeth Eisner Reding. (Illus.). 112p. per. 12.95 (0-7600-6061-4, Pub. by Course Tech) Thomson Learn.
Microsoft Excel 2000 - Illustrated Introductory. Elizabeth Eisner Reding & Tara Lynn O'Keefe. (Illus.). 208p. per. 21.95 (0-7600-6062-2) Course Tech.
*Microsoft Excel 2000 Bible: Gold Edition. John Walkenbach. LC 99-56016. 1440p. 2000. 59.99 (0-7645-3449-1) IDG Bks.
Microsoft Excel 2000 Certified: Course CBT. Elizabeth Eisner Reding & Tara Lynn O'Keefe. 26.95 (0-619-00118-6, Pub. by Course Tech) Thomson Learn.
*Microsoft Excel 2000 in Brief. Timothy O'Leary & Linda O'Leary. 280p. (J). 1999. pap. 19.06 (0-07-233750-8) McGrw-H Hghr Educ.
*Microsoft Excel 2000 in Layman's Terms: The Reference Guide for the Rest of Us. Katie Layman. (Illus.). 50p. 1999. pap. write for info. (1-893532-10-0) Compute Made.
Microsoft Excel 2000 Introductory Concepts & Techniques. Gary B. Shelly et al. 218p. per. 22.95 (0-7895-4676-0, Pub. by Course Tech) Thomson Learn.
*Microsoft Excel 2000 Introduction. Timothy O'Leary & Linda O'Leary. 480p. (C). 1999. pap. 27.50 (0-07-233739-7) McGrw-H Hghr Educ.
*Microsoft Excel 2000 Mouse Cheat Sheet. Rick Winter. 450p. 1999. 19.99 (0-7897-2116-3) Que.
*Microsoft Excel 2000 Quick Source Guide. Quick Source Staff. (Illus.). 6p. 1999. pap. 4.95 (1-930674-13-9) Quick Source.
Microsoft Excel Worksheet Function Reference. 3rd ed. Microsoft Corporation Staff. LC 96-33464. 312p. 1996. pap. text 24.95 (1-57231-341-2) Microsoft.
Microsoft Excel Worksheet Function Reference: For Microsoft Excel for Windows 95, & for Microsoft Excel for Windows 3.1 & Macintosh Systems. 2nd ed. Microsoft Corporation Staff. (Professional Editions Ser.). 344p. 1995. 22.95 (1-55615-878-5) Microsoft.
Microsoft Excel 2000. DDC Publishing Staff. 1999. pap. text 15.00 (1-56243-783-6) DDC Pub.
Microsoft Excel 2000. Napier. 1999. pap. 39.95 (0-538-42613-6) S-W Pub.
MicroSoft Excel 2000. Napier. (School Transfer from CT). 1999. pap., wbk. ed. 12.95 (0-538-42624-1) S-W Pub.
*Microsoft Excel 2000. Alan Neibauer. LC 99-15718. (One Step at a Time Ser.). 400p. 1999. pap. 29.99 (0-7645-3291-X) IDG Bks.
*Microsoft Excel 2000 Complete Concepts & Techniques. James Quasney. 440p. (C). 1999. 38.95 (0-7895-4675-2) Course Tech.
*Microsoft Excel 2000: Complete Tutorial. William Pasewark & Sandra Cable. LC 99-23439. 432p. 1999. pap. 40.95 (0-538-68837-8) Sth-Wstrn College.
Microsoft Excel 2000: Comprehensive Concepts & Techniques. Gary B. Shelly. (Shelly Cashman Ser.). 1999. pap. text 44.95 (0-7895-5609-X) Course Tech.
Microsoft Excel 2000: Function Reference. Patrick Blattner. 1999. pap. 29.99 (0-7897-2045-0) Que.
Microsoft Excel 2000: Quicktorial. Murphy. LC 98-47588. (Computer Applications Ser.). 1999. pap. 21.95 (0-538-68853-X) S-W Pub.
Microsoft Excel 2000: Visual Basic Fundamentals. Reed Jacobson. LC 99-13030. 450p. 1999. pap. 39.99 (0-7356-0593-9) Microsoft.
Microsoft Excel 2000 Exam Cram. Trudi Reisner. 1999. pap. text 26.99 (1-57610-512-1) Coriolis Grp.
*Microsoft Excel 2000 Formulas. Walkenbach. LC 99-38070. (Out of Ser.). 792p. 1999. pap. 39.99 (0-7645-4609-0) IDG Bks.
Microsoft Excel 2000 Quick Reference. Nancy Warner. LC 99-61235. (Quick Reference Guides Ser.). (Illus.). 164p. 1999. pap. 9.99 (0-7897-2027-2) Que.
*Microsoft Excel 2000, Quick Tutorial. Patricia Murphy. LC 98-47588. (Illus.). 176p. 1999. pap. 24.95 (0-538-68855-6) Sth-Wstrn College.
*Microsoft Excel 2000 Simplified. Ruth Maran. LC 99-62445. (... Simplified Ser.). (Illus.). 240p. 1999. pap. 24.99 (0-7645-6053-0) IDG Bks.
Microsoft Excel 2000 Step by Step. Catapult, Inc., Staff. (Step by Step Ser.). 432p. 1998. pap. text 34.99 (1-57231-974-7) Microsoft.
Microsoft Excel 3.0 Hotline. Thomas Tai. (C). 1991. text. write for info. (0-201-55965-X) Addison-Wesley.
Microsoft Excel 4.0 for the MAC. David Bragg et al. 78p. 1998. pap. 5.25 (0-07-230646-7) McGraw.
Microsoft Excel 5.0 Windows. O'Leary. 232p. 1995. pap. 27.50 (0-07-049076-7) McGraw.
Microsoft Excel 7.0 Pal. (College Titles Ser.). (C). 1997. write for info. (0-13-255571-9) P-H.
Microsoft Excel 95 Pal. Curtin. 1997. pap. write for info. (0-13-237546-X) P-H.
Microsoft Excel 97. Access Publishing Staff. (Beginner's Guide Ser.). 1997. pap. text 19.99 (1-57671-039-4) INST Publishing.
Microsoft Excel 97. Adams. (C). 1998. pap. text 22.50 (0-03-023717-3) Harcourt Coll Pubs.
Microsoft Excel 97. 10th ed. Trudi Reisner. LC 98-11496. (Exam Cram Ser.). xxiv, 384 p. (C). 1999. mass mkt. 26.99 (1-57610-221-1) Coriolis Grp.
*Microsoft Excell, 2000: Expert Certification. Meredith Flynn. LC 99-34553. 328p. 1999. 33.84 incl. cd-rom (0-7638-0334-0) Paradigm MN.
Microsoft Exchange: Messaging Using MAPI & ActiveX. Joseph J. Graf. 480p. 1997. pap. text 44.99 (0-471-18011-4, CS00) Wiley.
Microsoft Exchange 5.0 Connectivity Guide. Rodney Bliss & Rebecca Wynne. LC 96-36636. 400p. 29.95 (1-57231-220-3) Microsoft.
Microsoft Exchange 5.0 Field Guide. Stephen L. Nelson. LC 97-26072. 192p. 1997. 9.99 (1-57231-705-1) Microsoft.
Microsoft Exchange 5.0 Step-by-Step. Catapult, Inc. Staff. LC 97-11549. 336p. 1997. 29.99 incl. cd-rom (1-57231-627-6) Microsoft.
Microsoft Exchange 4.0: Introduction. Ed. by Ron Pronk. (Illus.). 120p. 1996. pap. 20.00 (1-58264-010-6, 85) ActiveEd.
Microsoft Exchange Productivity Guide. Katherine Murray. LC 96-68065. (Essentials Ser.). 408p. 1996. per. 24.99 (0-7615-0689-6) Prima Pub.
Microsoft Exchange Server. Tony Redmond. 1996. pap. 36.95 (0-614-20270-1, Digital DEC) Buttrwrth-Heinemann.
Microsoft Exchange Server: Programmer's Guide. Date not set. pap. text 39.95 (1-55615-919-6) Microsoft.
*Microsoft Exchange Server Connectivity: Bridging the Gap to Lotus Messaging Systems. Olivier D'Hose. 304p. 1999. pap. text 34.95 (1-55558-223-0) Buttrwrth-Heinemann.
Microsoft Exchange Server 5.5: Planning, Design & Implementation. Tony Redmond. LC 98-21457. 685p. 1998. pap. 54.95 (1-55558-213-3) DEC.
*Microsoft Exchange Server for Windows 2000: Planning, Design & Implementation. Tony Redmond. 656p. 2000. pap. 49.95 (1-55558-224-9, Digital DEC) Buttrwrth-Heinemann.
Microsoft Exchange Server 5. Greg Todd et al. LC 96-72004. 1012p. 1997. 59.99 (0-672-31034-1) Sams.
Microsoft Exchange Server Gateway Programmer's Guide. Microsoft Corporation Staff. (gr. 8). 1998. pap. 24.95 (1-55615-859-9) Little.
Microsoft Exchange Server in a Nutshell. Mitch Tulloch. Ed. by Robert Denn. (In a Nutshell Ser.). (Illus.). 404p. 1999. pap. 24.95 (1-56592-601-3) OReilly & Assocs.
Microsoft Exchange Server Internet Mail Connector. Spyros Sakellariadis. LC 96-51201. 234p. (Orig.). 1997. pap. 23.95 (1-882419-60-X) News Four-Hund.
Microsoft Exchange Server Survival Guide. Pete McPhedran. LC 96-67960. 840p. 1996. 49.99 (0-672-30890-8) Sams.
Microsoft Exchange Server Training. Microsoft Corporation Staff. LC 98-3872. 600p. 1997. 99.99 incl. cd-rom (1-57231-709-4) Microsoft.
Microsoft Exchange Server V5.0: Planning, Design & Implementation. Tony Redmond. LC 97-19416. 640p. 1997. pap. text 52.95 (1-55558-189-7, Digital DEC) Buttrwrth-Heinemann.
*Microsoft Exchange Server 5.5: Resource Guide. Microsoft Corporation Staff. (IT Resource Kits Ser.). (Illus.). 1999. pap. 49.99 (0-7356-0896-2) Microsoft.
Microsoft Exchange Server 5.5 Unleashed. Greg Todd. LC 98-84470. (Unleashed Ser.). 1104p. 1998. pap. text 49.99 (0-672-31283-2) Sams.
*Microsoft Exchange Server 6.0 Administrator's Companion. Paul Robichaux & Walter Glenn. (gr. 8). 2000. pap. 59.99 (0-7356-0938-1) Microsoft.
Microsoft Exchange Step by Step: For Windows 95. Catapult, Inc., Staff. (Step by Step Ser.). 336p. 1996. pap. 29.95 incl. disk (1-55615-853-X) Microsoft.
*Microsoft Exchange 2000 Server Administrator's Pocket Consultant. Microsoft Press Staff. (IT-Administrator's Companion Ser.). (Illus.). 2000. pap. text 29.99 (0-7356-0962-4) Microsoft.
*Microsoft Exchange 2000 Server Training Kit. Kay Unkroth. (IT-Training Kits Ser.). (Illus.). 2000. pap. 59.99 (0-7356-1028-2) Microsoft.
Microsoft Exchange User's Handbook. Sue Mosher. LC 96-45905. (Illus.). 692p. (Orig.). 1997. pap. 49.95 incl. cd-rom (1-882419-52-9) News Four-Hund.
Microsoft Exchange 5TM Sourcebook. William Mann & Bruce Backa. LC 97-5930. 612p. 1997. pap. text 49.95 incl. cd-rom (0-471-17841-1) Wiley.
Microsoft Exchange 5.0 in Business: Project Management, Scheduling, E-Mail, Forms, Public Folders. Russell Borland. LC 95-44648. 512p. 24.95 (1-57231-218-1) Microsoft.
Microsoft Exchange 5.5 Administrator's Pocket Consultant. Kathy Ivens. LC 99-13768. (Illus.). 450p. 1999. pap. 29.99 (0-7356-0623-4) Microsoft.
Microsoft File: The Secret Case Against Bill Gates. Wendy Goldman Rohm. LC 98-4450. 1998. 25.95 (0-8129-2716-8, Times Bks) Crown Pub Group.
*Microsoft First Generation: The Success Secrets of the Visionaries Who Launched a Technology Empire. Cheryl D. Tsang. LC 99-27007. 254p. 1999. 24.95 (0-471-33206-2) Wiley.
Microsoft Flight Simulator: The Official Strategy Guide. Nick Dargahi. LC 93-85785. (Secrets of the Games Ser.). (Illus.). 467p. 1994. pap. 19.95 (1-55958-466-1) Prima Pub.
Microsoft Flight Simulator 5.1: The Official Strategy Guide. Nick Dargahi. 1995. pap. text 19.95 (0-7615-0155-X) Prima Pub.
Microsoft Flight Simulator 98: Inside Moves. Ben Chiu. LC 97-29194. 288p. 1997. pap. text 16.99 (1-57231-635-7) Microsoft.
*Microsoft Flight Simulator 98: Prima's Unauthorized Strategy Guide. Douglas King. 2000. pap. 9.99 (0-7615-2895-4) Prima Pub.
Microsoft Flight Simulator 98: Unauthorized Game Secrets. Kiang Douglas. LC 97-69769. 400p. 1997. per. 19.99 (0-7615-1250-0) Prima Pub.
*Microsoft Flight Simulator 2000: Offical Strategies & Secrets. 4th ed. Ben Chiu. 352p. 1999. pap. 19.99 (0-7821-2634-0) Sybex.
*Mircosoft Flight Simulator 2000: Unauthorized Strategy Guide. Prima's Temp Authors Staff. (Illus.). 300p. (J). 2000. pap. 29.99 (0-7615-2657-9) Prima Pub.
Microsoft Flight Simulator Win 95: The Official Strategy Guide, Vol. 6. Bart Farkas. LC 96-67727. 1996. pap. text 19.99 (0-7615-0514-8) Prima Pub.
*Microsoft Flight Simulator 2000. Bart Farkas. LC 99-43751. 352p. 1999. pap. text 19.99 (0-7356-0547-5) Microsoft.
Microsoft FoxPro 2.5 for DOS: The Master Reference. 3rd ed. Robin Stark & John C. Fitzsimmons. 624p. 1994. pap. 24.95 (0-07-060984-5) McGraw.
Microsoft Front Page 98: Illustrated Standard Edition. 10th ed. Ann Barron & Chet Lyskawa. (Illustrated Ser.). 216p. (C). 1998. pap. 21.95 (0-7600-5947-0) Course Tech.
Microsoft Frontpage 98. Ciampa. (Computer Applications Ser.). 1998. pap. 27.95 (0-538-68601-4) S-W Pub.
Microsoft FrontPage 98 - No Experience Required. Gene Weisskopf. LC 97-61958. 560p. 1997. pap. text 29.99 (0-7821-2188-8) Sybex.
Microsoft Frontpage 98 at a Glance. Stephen Nelson. LC 97-33676. 288p. 1997. pap. text 16.99 (1-57231-637-3) Microsoft.
Microsoft Frontpage 98 Step by Step. Stephen Nelson. LC 97-37380. 352p. 1997. pap. text 29.99 incl. cd-rom (1-57231-636-5) Microsoft.
Microsoft Frontpage 97 at a Glance. Stephen L. Nelson. LC 96-29987. (Field Guide Ser.). 288p. 1997. pap. 16.99 (1-57231-573-3) Microsoft.
Microsoft Frontpage 97 Step by Step. Catapult, Inc., Staff. LC 96-38985. 336p. 1996. pap. text 29.99 incl. cd-rom (1-57231-336-6) Microsoft.
Microsoft Frontpage Quickstart. Bob Conway & Robert Kulik. LC 98-16021. 1996. 24.99 (1-56276-465-9, Ziff-Davis Pr) Que.
Microsoft FrontPage 2000. Gene Weisskopf. LC 99-60022. (No Experience Required Ser.). 432p. 1999. pap. 19.99 (0-7821-2482-8) Sybex.
*Microsoft FrontPage 2000: A Hands-On Guide. Ben Rand et al. 192p. 1999. spiral bd. 26.60 (1-57426-139-8) Computer Lit Pr.
*Microsoft Frontpage 2000: An Introduction to Web Design. Against the Clock, Inc. Staff. LC 00-26995. (Illus.). 2001. write for info. (0-13-016697-9) P-H.
Microsoft Frontpage 2000 - Illustrated Essentials. Sasha Vodnik. (Illus.). 64p. per. 10.95 (0-7600-6581-0, Pub. by Course Tech) Thomson Learn.
Microsoft Frontpage 2000 - Illustrated Introductory. Ann Barron & Chet Lyskawa. (Illus.). 216p. per. 21.95 (0-7600-6346-X, Pub. by Course Tech) Thomson Learn.
Microsoft Frontpage 2000 Introductory Concepts & Techniques. Gary B. Shelly et al. 216p. per. 25.95 (0-7895-5612-X, Pub. by Course Tech) Thomson Learn.
*Microsoft Frontpage 2000. Mark D. Ciampa. LC 99-231659. 192p. 1999. pap. 31.95 (0-538-69092-5) Sth-Wstrn College.
Microsoft FrontPage 2000 at a Glance. Stephen L. Nelson. LC 98-43586. (At A Glance Ser.). (Illus.). 211p. 1999. pap. 19.99 (1-57231-951-8) Microsoft.
*Microsoft FrontPage 2000 Bible. David Elderbrock & David Karlins. LC 99-11047. (Bible Ser.). (Illus.). 816p. 1999. pap. 39.99 (0-7645-3313-4) IDG Bks.
Microsoft FrontPage 2000 Step by Step. SES Publishing Staff. LC 98-48189. (Step by Step Ser.). 304p. 1999. pap. text 29.99 (1-57231-980-1) Microsoft.
Microsoft FrontPage 97: Illustrated Standard Edition. (SPA.). 1997. write for info. (0-7600-5306-5) Course Tech.
*Microsoft Frontpages 98: Complete Concepts & Techniques. Cashman Shelly. (C). 1998. text 42.95 (0-7895-4640-X) Course Tech.
Microsoft Getting Started in Windows 95: Upgrader Coursebook. DataPower AS Staff. 46p. 1995. pap. text 14.95 (1-888323-01-9) DataPower Intl.
*Microsoft Help Desk for Microsoft Office 2000: Support Solutions Direct from Microsoft. Stephen L. Nelson. LC 99-56530. (EU-Help Desk Ser.). (Illus.). 2000. pap. 39.99 (0-7356-0850-4) Microsoft.
*Microsoft Help Desk for Microsoft Windows NT Workstation 4.0. Compiled by Stephen L. Nelson. LC 99-21355. (Illus.). 1116p. 2000. pap. 39.99 (0-7356-1097-5) Microsoft.
*Microsoft Help Desk for Microsoft Windows 98. Stephen L. Nelson. (Help Desk Ser.). (Illus.). 2000. pap. 39.99 (0-7356-1096-7) Microsoft.
Microsoft Hypercard 2.1. David Bragg et al. 90p. 1998. pap. 5.74 (0-07-230631-9) McGraw.
Microsoft IBM QuickBASIC. Harvey M. Dietel & Paul J. Dietel. (C). 1989. pap. text 41.25 (0-13-449422-9) P-H.
Microsoft IBM QuickBASIC: A Structured Approach. Harvey M. Deitel & Paul J. Deitel. 288p. 1989. pap. 27.00 (0-13-587064-X) P-H.
Microsoft IIS 4 on Site: The Ultimate On-the-Job Solution Finder. Rick Lehtinen. 1998. pap. 39.99 (1-57610-330-7) Coriolis Grp.
Microsoft Implimentation of TCP-IP for Windows NTu4.0. 373p. 1997. pap. write for info. (1-884486-18-5) Wave Tech.
*Microsoft Internet Explorer. LC 98-48191. 1998. pap. 22.95 (1-57231-968-2) Microsoft.
*Microsoft Internet Explorer. Perspecti. LC 98-31457. 1998. pap. 16.99 (1-57231-964-X) Microsoft.
Microsoft Internet Explorer 5 Introductory Concepts & Techniques. Gary B. Shelly et al. 232p. per. 22.95 (0-7895-4646-9, Pub. by Course Tech) Thomson Learn.
*Microsoft Internet Explorer 5.0. Sarah E. Hutchinson & Glen J. Coulthard. LC 99-40844. 2000. write for info. (0-07-235887-4) McGrw-H Hghr Educ.
*Microsoft Internet Explorer 5.0 Quick Source Guide. Quick Source Staff. (Illus.). 6p. 1999. pap. 4.95 (1-930674-25-2) Quick Source.
Microsoft Internet Explorer 4 - Introduction. Ed. by Ron Pronk. (Illus.). 180p. 1997. pap. 20.00 (1-58264-031-9, 149) ActiveEd.
Microsoft Internet Explorer 4 at a Glance: The Easy Way to Find the Right Answers, Right Now. Perception Staff. LC 97-37610. 288p. pap. 16.99 (1-57231-740-X) Microsoft.
Microsoft Internet Explorer 4 Guru. Bill Hartman. (Computer Guru Ser.). (Illus.). 20p. 1998. spiral bd. 5.99 (1-58187-024-8) Guru Books.
Microsoft Internet Explorer 4.0 Quick Source Guide. Quick Source Staff. (Illus.). 6p. 1997. pap. 4.95 (1-930674-24-4) Quick Source.
Microsoft Internet Explorer 4.0. 2nd ed. Tim Duffy. 80p. (C). 1998. pap. text 19.00 (0-201-43868-2, Prentice Hall) P-H.
Microsoft Internet Explorer 4 Unleashed. 2nd ed. Glenn Fincher et al. 1000p. 1997. 49.99 (1-57521-234-X) Sams.
Microsoft Internet Explorer 3: An Introduction. 10th ed. Gary B. Shelly et al. (Shelly Cashman Ser.). 176p. (C). 1997. pap. 22.95 (0-7895-2836-3) Course Tech.
Microsoft Internet Explorer 3.0 Frontrunner for Macintosh. Mary Millhollon. 1996. pap. 29.99 (1-57610-053-7) Coriolis Grp.
Microsoft Internet Explorer 3.0: Illustrated Brief Edition. Barron et al. (Illustrated Ser.). (Illus.). 96p. (C). 1997. pap. 12.95 (0-7600-4687-5) Course Tech.
Microsoft Internet Explorer Three Point O: A Jumpstart Tutorial. Elizabeth A. Parker. (Illus.). 300p. (Orig.). 1996. pap. 19.95 (1-886801-05-3) Thomson Learn.
Microsoft Internet Explorer 3.0 Wizardry. Patrick Vincent. 500p. 1996. pap. text 39.99 incl. cd-rom (1-57610-049-9) Coriolis Grp.
Microsoft Internet Explorer 4 Field Guide. Stephen L. Nelson. LC 97-42102. 192p. pap. write for info. (1-57231-741-8) Microsoft.
Microsoft Internet Explorer 4.0 Step by Step. Catapult, Inc., Staff. LC 97-31137. 208p. 1996. pap. text 24.99 incl. 3.5 hd (1-57231-514-8) Microsoft.
Microsoft Internet Explorer 5 - Illustrated Essentials. Jessica Evans. (Illus.). 64p. (C). per. 10.95 (0-7600-6147-5, Pub. by Course Tech) Thomson Learn.
*Microsoft Internet Explorer 5.0. ENI Publishing Ltd. Staff. (Straight to the Point Ser.). 1999. pap. 7.95 (2-7460-0134-9) ENI Publng.
Microsoft Internet Gaming Zone: Fighter Ace: Inside Moves. Ben Chiu. LC 97-29195. 256p. 16.99 (1-57231-646-2) Microsoft.
Microsoft Internet Information Server. Microsoft Corporation Staff. 1999. boxed set 55.00 (0-7356-0521-1) Little.
Microsoft Internet Information Server. Microsoft Corporation Staff. LC 97-53095. (Academic Learning Ser.). (Illus.). 379p. 1998. 99.99 incl. cd-rom (1-57231-731-0) Microsoft.
Microsoft Internet Information Server 4.0. Keith Sutherland. 160p. 1999. pap. text 44.95 (0-7506-4466-4) Buttrwrth-Heinemann.
Microsoft Internet Information Server 4 for Dummies. David Angell & Dummies Technical Press Staff. LC 98-84963. 384p. 1998. pap. 24.99 (0-7645-0265-4) IDG Bks.
Microsoft Internet Information Server 4: The Complete Reference. Thomas Sheldon & John Paul Mueller. LC 98-127846. (Complete Reference Ser.). 848p. 1998. pap. text 39.99 (0-07-882457-5) Osborne-McGraw.
Microsoft Internet Information Server Resource Kit. Microsoft Corporation Staff. LC 97-48754. 1200p. 1998. pap. text 99.99 (1-57231-638-1) Microsoft.
Microsoft Internet Information Server 2 Unleashed. Art Knowles et al. LC 96-67957. 863p. 1996. 49.99 (1-57521-109-2) Sams.
*Microsoft Internet Information Server 4.0 Jason Helmick. LC 99-26163. 1999. write for info. (0-538-69203-0) Sth-Wstrn College.
Microsoft Internet Information Server 4.0 Sourcebook. Michele Petrovsky. LC 97-13143. 660p. 1997. pap. 34.99 (0-471-17805-5) Wiley.

M

An Asterisk (*) at the beginning of an entry indicates that the title is appearing for the first time.

*__Microsoft Internet Information Server 5.0 Documentation.__ Microsoft Corporation Staff. LC 99-50192. 1999. pap. text 49.99 (*0-7356-0652-8*) Microsoft.

Microsoft Internet Mail 4 Guru. Bill Hartman. (Computer Guru Ser.). (Illus.). 20p. 1998. spiral bd. 5.99 (*1-58187-025-6*) Guru Books.

*__Microsoft Internet Server Four Point O.__ Jason Hemlock. LC 99-26163. 400p. 1999. pap. 46.95 (*0-538-69201-4*) Thomson Learn.

Microsoft Intranet Solutions. Micro Modeling Associates Staff. LC 97-7687. 500p. 1997. pap. text 39.99 (*1-57231-509-1*) Microsoft.

Microsoft Jet Database Engine Programmer's Guide. 3rd ed. Corporation Microsoft. 1999. pap. text 49.99 (*0-7356-0585-8*) Microsoft.

Microsoft Jet Database Engine Programmer's Guide: The Essential Reference for the Database Engine Used in Microsoft Windows-Based Applications & Programming Environments. 2nd ed. Microsoft Corporation Staff. LC 97-15488. (Professional Editions Ser.). 700p. 1997. pap. 39.95 incl. cd-rom (*1-57231-342-0*) Microsoft.

Microsoft LAN Manager for Windows NT. Microsoft Corporation Staff. LC 92-37697. 1993. pap. 39.95 (*1-55615-543-3*) Microsoft.

Microsoft Liquid Motion by Design. Gavin Schmitz. LC 98-30226. 288p. 1998. pap. 34.99 incl. cd-rom (*0-7356-0526-2*) Microsoft.

Microsoft Macro Assembler 6.0 Programming. Marc J. Neuberger & Len Dorfman. 1993. pap. 34.95 (*0-07-017809-7*) McGraw.

Microsoft Macro 5.1. John Mueller & Wallace Wang. 1991. 24.95 (*0-8306-8691-6*) McGraw-Hill Prof.

Microsoft Mail. 1993. 29.95 (*1-56877-097-9*); teacher ed. 49.95 (*1-56877-098-7*) Catapult WA.

Microsoft Mail: Illustrated Brief Edition. Marie L. Swanson. (Illustrated Ser.). (Illus.). 40p. 1996. pap. 9.95 (*0-7600-4219-5*) Course Tech.

Microsoft Mail Fundamentals. 1993. teacher ed. 49.95 (*1-56877-145-2*); student ed. 29.95 (*1-56877-144-4*) Catapult WA.

*__Microsoft Management Console Design & Development Kit.__ Microsoft Press Staff. LC 00-23796. (DV-MPE Software Development Kits Ser.). (Illus.). 829p. 2000. pap. text 59.99 (*0-7356-1038-X*) Microsoft.

Microsoft Manual of Style for Technical Publications. 3rd ed. Microsoft Corporation Staff. LC 98-14000. 336p. 29.99 incl. cd-rom (*1-57231-890-2*) Microsoft.

*__Microsoft Mastering: E-Commerce Development: Business-to-Business.__ Microsoft Press Staff. (DV-DLT Mastering Ser.). (Illus.). 2000. pap. text. write for info. (*0-7356-1043-6*) Microsoft.

*__Microsoft Mastering MFC Development Using Microsoft Visual C++__ Microsoft Press Interactive Staff. (DV-DLT Mastering Ser.). (Illus.). 2000. pap. 49.99 (*0-7356-0925-X*) Microsoft.

Microsoft MCSE Readiness Review Exam 70-098: Implementing & Supporting Microsoft Windows 98. Dave Perkovich. LC 99-10772. 322p. 1999. pap. 29.99 (*0-7356-0671-4*) Microsoft.

*__Microsoft Mechwarrior 4 Inside Moves.__ D. Ian Hopper. 320p. 2000. pap. 19.99 (*0-7356-1179-3*) Microsoft.

Microsoft Money 98 at a Glance. Stephen Nelson. LC 97-29787. 352p. 1997. pap. 16.99 (*1-57231-639-X*) Microsoft.

Microsoft Money 98 for Dummies. Peter Weverka. LC 97-80749. 384p. 1997. pap. 24.99 incl. cd-rom (*0-7645-0295-6*) IDG Bks.

Microsoft Money 99 at a Glance. Stephen L. Nelson. LC 98-29960. 224p. 1998. pap. 16.99 (*1-57231-993-3*) Microsoft.

*__Microsoft Money 99 at a Glance.__ Stephen L. Nelson. (Illus.). 205p. 1999. pap. write for info. (*0-7356-0696-X*) Microsoft.

Microsoft Money 99 for Dummies. Peter Weverka. LC HG179.W4763 1998. (For Dummies Ser.). 384p. 1998. pap. 19.99 incl. cd-rom (*0-7645-0433-9*) IDG Bks.

*__Microsoft Money 2000 at a Glance.__ Stephen L. Nelson. LC 99-33880. (At a Glance Ser.). 1999. pap. text 19.99 (*0-7356-0811-3*) Microsoft.

Microsoft Money X for Dummies. Peter Weverka. (For Dummies Ser.). 408p. 1999. pap. 19.99 (*0-7645-0579-3*) IDG Bks.

*__Microsoft Money 99 Fast & Easy.__ Paul Marchesseault & Lisa Wagner. LC 98-67609. (Fast & Easy Ser.). 350p. 1998. pap. 16.99 (*0-7615-1799-5*) Prima Pub.

Microsoft MS-DOS & Windows. Mahesh. (DF-Computer Applications Ser.). 1996. mass mkt., wbk. ed. 12.75 (*0-314-09340-0*) S-W Pub.

Microsoft MS-DOS Step by Step, Revised for Version 6.2: Versions 6.0 & 6.2. Catapult, Inc., Staff. LC 93-41595. (Step by Step Ser.). 304p. 1994. 29.95 incl. disk (*1-55615-635-9*) Microsoft.

*__Microsoft Netscape Communicator 4.5.__ ENI Publishing Ltd. Staff. (Straight to the Point Ser.). 1999. pap. 7.95 (*2-7460-0138-1*) ENI Publng.

*__Microsoft Network Services Developer's Reference Library, 5 vols.__ David Iseminger. LC 00-20241. (Illus.). 3000p. 2000. pap. text 149.99 (*0-7356-0993-4*) Microsoft.

Microsoft Networking Made Simple. McBride. 160p. Date not set. pap. text 19.95 (*0-7506-2837-5*) Buttrwrth-Heinemann.

Microsoft NT Server Resource Kit. Microsoft Corporation Staff. 912p. 1996. pap. text, boxed set 149.95 incl. cd-rom (*1-57231-344-7*) Microsoft.

Microsoft NT Server 5.0. Smith. (Computer Applications Ser.). 2000. pap., student ed. write for info. (*0-538-68901-3*) Thomson Learn.

Microsoft Nt Server 5.0. Smith. (Computer Applications Ser.). 2000. pap. 46.95 (*0-538-68900-5*) Thomson Learn.

*__Microsoft NT Workstation 4.0 for End Users: Basic.__ Course Technology Staff. (SAM's License Card for Course CBT Ser.). (C). 2000. text. write for info. (*0-619-00945-4*) Course Tech.

Microsoft NT Workstation 5.0. Miller. (Computer Applications Ser.). 2000. pap., student ed. write for info. (*0-538-68911-0*) Thomson Learn.

Microsoft NTu4.0 Self Study Kit. 1997. write for info. (*1-884486-24-X*) Wave Tech.

Microsoft ODBC 3.0 Software Development Kit & Programmer's Reference, 2 vols. 2nd ed. Microsoft Corporation Staff. LC 96-45660. 1488p. 1997. 99.99 (*1-57231-516-4*) Microsoft.

Microsoft Office. Speers et al. (DF - Computer Applications Ser.). 928p. 1995. mass mkt. 50.95 (*0-7895-0199-6*) Course Tech.

Microsoft Office: Advanced Concepts & Techniques. Gary B. Shelly & T. Cashman. 736p. 1995. mass mkt. 57.35 (*0-7895-0116-3*) S-W Pub.

Microsoft Office: Advanced Concepts & Techniques. Gary B. Shelly & Thomas J. Cashman. 736p. 1995. pap. 63.95 (*0-7895-0106-6*) S-W Pub.

Microsoft Office: Expert Solutions. 1998. 49.99 (*0-7897-0394-7*) Que.

Microsoft Office: Introductory Concepts & Techniques, Incl. instr. ed. Gary B. Shelly et al. (Illus.). 960p. 1995. mass mkt. 46.00 incl. cd-rom, 3.5 ld (*0-87709-861-1*); mass mkt. 48.00 incl. cd-rom, 3.5 ld (*0-87709-885-9*) Course Tech.

Microsoft Office: Training on CD. Quay2 Multimedia Staff. 1995. pap. 99.95 incl. cd-rom (*0-201-88413-5*) Peachpit Pr.

Microsoft Office - Windows X Quick & Easy. Claudia Willen. 1996. pap. text 22.99 (*0-7821-1955-7*) Sybex.

*__Microsoft Office Automation with Visual FoxPro.__ Tamar E. Granor & Della Martin. Ed. by Ted Roche. 436p. 2000. pap. 49.95 (*0-9655093-0-3*) Hentzenwerke.

Microsoft Office Based Solutions: A Manager's Guide. Christine Solomon. Date not set. pap. write for info. (*1-57231-215-7*) Microsoft.

Microsoft Office Bundle with Access. 2nd ed. Que Development Group Staff. 1994. pap. 105.00 (*1-56529-852-7*) Que.

Microsoft Office Developer's Handbook for Windows 95. Mike Gunderlog. 1,072p. 1996. pap. text 44.99 incl. cd-rom (*0-7821-1782-1*) Sybex.

Microsoft Office Essentials. Ronny Richardson. LC 96-15538. 460p. 1996. pap. 24.95 (*1-884777-18-X*) Manning Pubns.

Microsoft Office Essentials. Ronny Richardson. 400p. (C). 1996. pap. text 24.95 (*0-13-262312-9*) P-H.

Microsoft Office for Macintosh: Visual QuickStart Guide. Stephen W. Sagman. 296p. 1995. pap. text. write for info. (*0-201-48599-0*, Pub. by Peachpit Pr) Addison-Wesley.

Microsoft Office for Windows: Complete Course. Murphy. 1995. pap. 42.75 (*0-538-64857-0*) Thomson Learn.

Microsoft Office for Windows: Complete Course. Patricia Murphy. (Quick Course Ser.). 816p. 1995. mass mkt. 53.95 (*0-538-64856-2*) S-W Pub.

*__Microsoft Office for Windows: Skills Resource Guide.__ 2nd ed. Melnyk. (Computer Applications). 1998. pap. 28.25 (*0-314-13005-5*) West Pub.

Microsoft Office for Windows 95 Bible. Edward Jones & Derek Sutton. LC 95-79912. 816p. 1995. pap. 39.99 (*1-56884-490-5*) IDG Bks.

Microsoft Office for Windows 95 for Dummies. Roger C. Parker. 362p. 1995. pap. 19.99 (*1-56884-917-6*) IDG Bks.

Microsoft Office for Windows 95. Ed. by Ron Pronk. (Illus.). 180p. 1996. pap. 20.00 (*1-58264-056-4*, 92) ActiveEd.

Microsoft Office for Windows 95 Essentials. Suzanne Weixel. 1996. pap. text 49.99 (*1-57576-014-2*) Que Educ & Trng.

Microsoft Office for Windows 95 Integrated - Advanced, Incl. instr. resource kit, test mgr., files. Joseph J. Adamski & Judy Adamski. (New Perspectives Ser.). (Illus.). 504p. 1996. text. write for info. incl. 3.5 ld (*0-7600-4191-1*) Course Tech.

Microsoft Office for Windows 95, Professional Edition: A First Course. Reding et al. (Illustrated Ser.). (Illus.). 512p. (C). 1996. pap., per. 38.00 (*0-7600-4797-9*) Course Tech.

Microsoft Office for Windows 95, Professional Edition: A First Course - Illustrated, Incl. instr. resource kit, test mgr., Web pg. Elizabeth E. Reding et al. (Illustrated Ser.). (Illus.). 512p. 1995. text, mass mkt. 50.95 incl. 3.5 ld (*0-7600-3531-8*) Course Tech.

Microsoft Office for Windows 95 Professional Edition: A Second Course - Illustrated, Incl. instr. resource kit, test mgr., Web pg. Elizabeth E. Reding et al. (Illustrated Ser.). (Illus.). 600p. 1996. text 50.95 incl. 3.5 ld (*0-7600-3729-9*) Course Tech.

Microsoft Office for Windows 95: Complete Course. Murphy. (DF - Computer Applications Ser.). (C). 1996. mass mkt. 51.95 (*0-538-71478-6*) S-W Pub.

Microsoft Office for Windows 95: Professional Edition - Illustrated Projects. 10th ed. Carol M. Cram. (Illustrated Ser.). (Illus.). 192p. (C). 1996. pap. 19.95 (*0-7600-4675-1*) Course Tech.

Microsoft Office for Windows 95: Tutorial & Applications. William R. Pasewark. (DF - Computer Applications Ser.). (C). 1996. mass mkt. 43.95 (*0-538-71490-5*) S-W Pub.

Microsoft Office for Windows 95 Reproduction Study Exercise Set: Tutorial & Applications. William R. Pasewark, Sr. (DF - Computer Applications Ser.). 1996. mass mkt. 37.95 (*0-538-71491-3*) S-W Pub.

Microsoft Office for Windows Step by Step. Catapult, Inc., Staff. LC 94-31277. (Step by Step Ser.). 328p. 1994. pap. 39.95 incl. audio compact disk (*1-55615-648-0*) Microsoft.

Microsoft Office for Windows 3.1 Introductory Concepts & Techniques: Course One Enhanced Edition. 10th ed. Gary B. Shelly et al. (Shelly Cashman Ser.). 884p. (C). 1996. pap. 47.00 (*0-7895-2829-0*); pap., mass mkt., per. 60.95 (*0-7895-2828-2*) Course Tech.

Microsoft Office for Windows 3.1: Tutorial & Applications, Vol. 4. Pasewark Pasewark. 1996. 46.50 (*0-538-71718-1*) Sth-Wstrn College.

Microsoft Office 4.3: Running under Windows 95. (Shelly Cashman Ser.). 1996. pap., mass mkt., per. write for info. (*0-7895-1274-2*) Course Tech.

Microsoft Office 4.3 for Windows 3.1: Tutorial & Applications. William R. Pasewark. LC 96-3087. 1996. mass mkt. 41.95 (*0-538-71715-7*) S-W Pub.

Microsoft Office 4.3, Running under Windows 95: Introductory Concepts & Techniques: Windows 95, Word 6, Excel 5, Access 2, PowerPoint 4. Gary B. Shelly et al. LC 96-11312. 1996. mass mkt. 47.00 (*0-7895-1266-1*) Course Tech.

Microsoft Office 4.2 for Windows. Marangraphics Staff. 1995. text 34.95 (*1-896283-04-7*, Pub. by MaGr) IDG Bks.

Microsoft Office 4.2 Simplificado. Maran Graphics Staff. (SPA.). 368p. 1996. pap. 31.99 (*0-7645-6014-X*) IDG Bks.

Microsoft Office in Concert. John Weingarten. 1994. pap. 24.95 (*1-55958-447-5*) Prima Pub.

Microsoft Office in Concert: Professional Edition. John Weingarten. LC 94-66631. (Illus.). 450p. 1994. pap. 27.95 (*1-55958-640-0*) Prima Pub.

Microsoft Office Integration. Timothy J. O'Leary & Linda I. O'Leary. (C). 1995. pap. text 9.00 (*0-07-049095-3*) McGraw.

Microsoft Office Macintosh Bundle. 1994. pap. 75.00 (*1-56529-956-6*) Que.

*__Microsoft Office 98: Macintosh Basics.__ Pat Murphy. 2000. pap. 43.95 (*0-538-72431-5*) Thomson Learn.

Microsoft Office 98 for Macintosh: Visual QuickStart Guide. Dan Henderson. Ed. by Jeanne Woodward. LC 98-224668. 304p. (C). 1998. pap. 18.95 (*0-201-35351-2*, Pub. by Peachpit Pr) Addison-Wesley.

Microsoft Office 98 for Macs for Dummies. Tom Negrino. LC HF5548.4.M525N43. 384p. 1998. pap. 19.99 (*0-7645-0229-8*) IDG Bks.

*__Microsoft Office 98 Macintosh Basics.__ Patricia Murphy. LC 00-26541. (Illus.). 2001. pap. write for info. incl. cd-rom (*0-538-72432-3*) S-W Pub.

Microsoft Office 98 MacIntosh Edition at a Glance. Perception Staff. LC 98-9351. 256p. 16.99 (*1-57231-916-X*) Microsoft.

Microsoft Office 98 Step by Step: Macintosh Edition. Bonita Sebastian. LC 98-20089. (Illus.). 156p. 1998. spiral bd. 26.60 (*1-57426-093-6*) Computer Lit Pr.

*__Glencoe Visual Approach Series for Office 97.__ (Visual Ser.). 1998. teacher ed. 38.15 (*0-02-803946-7*) Glencoe.

Microsoft Office 97. Diana Rain. LC 97-170224. (Quick Reference Guide Ser.). pap., spiral bd. 27.00 (*1-56243-454-3*, G-25) DDC Pub.

Microsoft Office 97 for Windows. Peter Weverka & Dummies Technical Press Staff. LC 96-80225. (Dummies 101 Ser.). (Illus.). 272p. 1997. pap. 24.99 incl. cd-rom (*0-7645-0097-X*) IDG Bks.

Microsoft Office 97: A First Course. Marie Swanson. 1997. pap. text 29.99 (*0-7600-5606-4*) Course Tech.

Microsoft Office 97: Advanced Concepts & Techniques. 10th ed. Gary B. Shelly et al. (Shelly Cashman Ser.). 744p. (C). 1997. mass mkt. 60.95 (*0-7895-1335-8*) Course Tech.

Microsoft Office 97: Developer Edition Resource Library. Microsoft Corporation Staff. 2000p. 99.99 incl. cd-rom (*1-57231-606-3*) Microsoft.

Microsoft Office 97: Illustrated Projects. 10th ed. Carol M. Cram. (Illustrated Ser.). (Illus.). 184p. (C). 1997. pap. 19.95 (*0-7600-5133-X*) Course Tech.

Microsoft Office 97: Introductory Concepts & Techniques. Gary B. Shelly et al. (Shelly Cashman Ser.). 1064p. (C). 1997. pap. 47.00 (*0-7895-1333-1*) Course Tech.

Microsoft Office 97: Introductory Concepts & Techniques. 10th ed. Gary B. Shelly et al. (Shelly Cashman Ser.). 1064p. (C). 1997. pap., mass mkt., per. 57.95 (*0-7895-1332-3*) Course Tech.

Microsoft Office 97: Professional, Blue Ribbon Edition. 2nd ed. Tim Duffy. 992p. (C). 1998. pap. text 62.67 (*0-201-43859-3*, Prentice Hall) P-H.

Microsoft Office 97: The Complete Reference. Stephen L. Nelson & Peter Weverka. LC 97-208953. 967p. 1997. pap., pap. text 39.99 incl. cd-rom (*0-07-882338-2*) Osborne-McGraw.

Microsoft Office 97 at a Glance, Updated Edition. Perception, Inc. Staff. LC 98-9289. (At A Glance Ser.). 352p. 16.99 (*1-57231-891-0*) Microsoft.

Microsoft Office 97 for Developers Unleashed. Sams Development Team Staff. 1000p. 1997. 49.99 (*0-672-31017-1*) Sams.

Microsoft Office '97 for Windows for Dummies. Wallace Wang & Roger Parker. LC 96-79274. (Illus.). 408p. 1997. pap. 19.99 (*0-7645-0050-3*) IDG Bks.

Microsoft Office 97 for Windows. Doug Lowe. LC 96-79261. (For Dummies). (Illus.). 224p. 1997. spiral bd. 12.99 (*0-7645-0062-7*) IDG Bks.

Microsoft Office 97 for Windows. William R. Pasewark. (Tutorial & Applications Ser.). 1997. pap. text 33.95 (*0-538-71958-3*) S-W Pub.

Microsoft Office 97 for Windows for Teachers. Neil J. Salkind. LC 96-80228. (Illus.). 384p. 1997. pap., teacher ed. 24.99 (*0-7645-0082-1*) IDG Bks.

Microsoft Office 97 for Windows: Tutorial & Applications. Pasewark Pasewark. (Computer Applications Ser.). 1997. pap. 28.25 (*0-538-71921-4*) Sth-Wstrn College.

Microsoft Office 97 Integration Step by Step. Catapult, Inc. Staff. LC 96-44274. 336p. 29.95 (*1-57231-317-X*) Microsoft.

Microsoft Office 97 Step by Step: Windows Version. Bonita Sebastian. LC 97-15255. (Illus.). 204p. 1997. spiral bd. 26.60 (*1-57426-035-9*) Computer Lit Pr.

Microsoft, Office 97 Professional: Microsoft Access 97. Tim O'Leary & Linda O'Leary. 216p. (C). 1997. pap. 27.50 (*0-07-012594-5*) McGraw.

Microsoft, Office 97 Professional: Microsoft Excel 97. Tim O'Leary & Linda O'Leary. LC 97-72181. 240p. (C). 1997. pap. 28.75 (*0-07-012576-7*) McGraw.

Microsoft, Office 97 Professional: Microsoft Office without PowerPoint. Tim O'Leary & Linda O'Leary. 832p. (C). 1997. spiral bd. 54.69 (*0-07-561041-8*) McGraw.

Microsoft, Office 97 Professional: Microsoft PowerPoint 97. Tim O'Leary & Linda O'Leary. 128p. (C). 1997. pap. 28.75 (*0-07-012573-2*) McGraw.

Microsoft, Office 97 Professional: Microsoft Word 97. Tim O'Leary & Linda O'Leary. LC 97-72182. 240p. (C). 1997. pap. 27.50 (*0-07-092038-9*) McGraw.

Microsoft Office 97 Professional, 6 in 1 Step by Step. Catapult, Inc. Staff. LC 97-27386. 800p. 1997. pap. text 39.99 incl. cd-rom (*1-57231-703-5*) Microsoft.

Microsoft Office 97 Professional. Sarah E. Hutchinson et al. LC 97-42401. (Irwin Advantage Ser.). 608p. 1997. spiral bd. 45.31 (*0-07-030667-2*); spiral bd. 14.06 (*0-07-289508-X*) McGraw.

Microsoft Office 97 Professional Essentials AIE. Donna Matherly. 1997. 39.99 (*1-57576-788-0*) Que Educ & Trng.

Microsoft Office 97 Professional Quick Reference. Robert Mullen et al. LC 96-72201. 410p. 1997. pap. 19.99 (*0-7897-1061-7*) Que.

Microsoft Office 97 Professional Edition: A First Course. Reding et al. (Illustrated Ser.). (Illus.). 608p. (C). 1997. pap. 38.00 (*0-7600-4693-X*) Course Tech.

Microsoft Office 97 Professional: A Mastery Approach. Patricia L. Sullivan. LC 97-11980. 1997. spiral bd. 48.95 (*1-887902-24-4*) Franklin Beedle.

Microsoft Office 97 Professional Edition: A Second Course. 10th ed. Reading et al. (Illustrated Ser.). (Illus.). 544p. (C). 1997. pap. 50.95 (*0-7600-5135-6*) Course Tech.

Microsoft Office 97 Professional: Instructor's Guide. Nita H. Rutkosky. 24.00 (*0-7638-0066-X*) EMC-Paradigm.

Microsoft Office 97 Quick Reference. Ed. by Ron Pronk. (Illus.). 130p. 1997. pap. 20.00 (*1-58264-009-2*, 126) ActiveEd.

Microsoft Office 97 Quickpack for Dummies. 832p. 1999. pap. 29.99 (*0-7645-0333-2*) IDG Bks.

Microsoft Office 97 Resource Kit. Microsoft Corporation Staff. LC 96-45661. 1997. pap. text 59.99 incl. disk (*1-57231-329-3*) Microsoft.

Microsoft Office Resource Kit. rev. ed. Microsoft Corporation Staff. LC 97-38787. 1360p. 59.99 incl. cd-rom (*1-57231-640-3*) Microsoft.

Microsoft Office 97 Shortcuts, Tips & Tricks. deluxe ed. Kay S. Tatum. (Illus.). 184p. 1998. 21.95 (*0-9963093-0-6*) Perf Dimen.

Microsoft Office 97 Starts Here. Microsoft Press Interactive Staff. 1997. pap. text 29.95 (*1-57231-607-1*) Microsoft.

Microsoft Office 97 User Certification: Study Guide. Gini Courter. LC 97-81080. 864p. 1998. student ed. 39.99 incl. cd-rom (*0-7821-2263-9*) Sybex.

Microsoft Office 97-Visual Basic Step by Step. David Boctor. LC 97-8039. 384p. 1997. pap. text 34.99 (*1-57231-389-7*) Microsoft.

Microsoft Office 97-Visual Basic Language Reference, 5 vols. Microsoft Corporation Staff. LC 97-3521. 4192p. 1997. pap. text 129.99 (*1-57231-339-0*) Microsoft.

Microsoft Office 97-Visual Basic Programmer's Guide. Microsoft Corporation Staff. LC 96-29988. 700p. 1997. pap. text 34.99 (*1-57231-340-4*) Microsoft.

Microsoft Office Plus Pak with Microsoft Mail. Marie L. Swanson et al. (New Perspectives Ser.). 48p. 1996. pap. 20.95 (*0-7600-4255-1*) Course Tech.

Microsoft Office Pro for Windows 95: Introduction. Gary B. Shelly & T. Cashman. LC 96-23754. 1064p. 1996. pap. 60.95 (*0-7895-0742-0*); pap., mass mkt., spiral bd. 48.00 (*0-7895-1229-7*) Course Tech.

Microsoft Office Professional: Simply Windows, Word 6.0, Excel 3.0, Access 2.0, Powerpoint 4.0, & Integrating Microsoft Office 4.2/4.3. Sarah E. Hutchinson & Glen Coulthard. LC 97-139470. 1056p. (C). 1995. text 50.00 (*0-256-20763-1*, Irwn McGrw-H) McGrw-H Hghr Educ.

Microsoft Office Professional: Version 7. Nita H. Rutkosky. LC 96-39680. 1997. write for info. (*0-7638-0001-5*) Paradigm.

Microsoft Office Professional - New Perspectives, Incl. instr. resource kit, test bank, transparency, June J. Parsons et al. (New Perspectives Ser.). (Illus.). 982p. 1995. pap. 41.50 (*0-7600-3465-6*) Course Tech.

Microsoft Office Professional Essentials. Mary Kelly. LC 95-68938. 500p. 1995. 49.99 (*0-7897-0258-4*) Que.

Microsoft Office Professional Essentials. Mary Kelly. 1995. teacher ed. 39.99 (*0-7897-0274-6*) Que.

Microsoft Office Professional for Windows - New Perspectives Intermediate, Incl. instr. resource kit, test mgr., files. S. Scott Zimmerman et al. (New Perspectives Ser.). (Illus.). 784p. 1995. text, mass mkt. write for info. incl. 3.5 ld (*0-7600-3711-6*) Course Tech.

Microsoft Office Professional for Windows 3.1 - Illustrated Enhanced Edition, Incl. instr. resource kit, test mgr., Web pg. Elizabeth E. Reding et al. (Illustrated Ser.). (Illus.). 576p. 1996. text, mass mkt. 50.95 incl. 3.5 ld (*0-7600-4034-6*) Course Tech.

An Asterisk (*) at the beginning of an entry indicates that the title is appearing for the first time.

Microsoft Office Professional for Windows 95. Sarah E. Hutchinson & Glen Coulthard. (C). 1996. text 50.00 (*0-256-22055-7*, Irwn McGrw-H) McGrw-H Hghr Educ.

Microsoft Office Professional for Windows 95 - Intermediate, Incl. instr. resource kit, test mgr., files. Beverly B. Zimmerman et al. (New Perspectives Ser.). (Illus.). 784p. 1996. text. write for info. (*0-7600-3821-X*) Course Tech.

Microsoft Office Professional for Windows 95 Integrated - Introductory, Incl. instr. resource kit, test mgr., files. Joseph J. Adamski & Judy Adamski. (New Perspectives Ser.). (Illus.). 648p. 1996. pap. 56.95 (*0-7600-3579-2*) Course Tech.

Microsoft Office Professional for Windows 95 with Powerpoint. O'Leary. (C). 1996. pap. text 43.00 (*0-07-049112-7*) McGraw.

Microsoft Office Professional 97: Text with disks, 3.5. Nita Hewitt Rutkosky. 834p. 45.00 incl. 3.5 hd (*0-7638-0065-1*) EMC-Paradigm.

Microsoft Office 97 Professional 6-in-1. Faithe Wempen & Que Development Group Staff. LC 96-70772. 800p. 1996. 26.99 (*0-7897-0957-0*) Que.

Microsoft Office 97 Professional 6 in 1. 2nd ed. Faithe Wempen et al. LC 97-80837. (Illus.). 804p. 1998. pap. 29.99 (*0-7897-1515-5*) Que.

Microsoft Office Professional, Version 7: Instructor's Guide. Nita H. Rutkosky. 460p. 24.00 (*0-7638-0002-3*) EMC-Paradigm.

Microsoft Office Professional (Win 3.1) June J. Parsons et al. 988p. 1995. write for info. (*0-7600-3467-2*) Course Tech.

Microsoft Office Professional (Win 3.1) 10th ed. June J. Parsons et al. (New Perspectives Ser.). 988p. (C). 1996. pap. 63.95 (*0-7600-4664-6*) Course Tech.

Microsoft Office Short Cuts, Tips & Tricks. Kay S. Tatum. 98p. 1998. spiral bd. 15.95 (*0-9663093-0-8*) Perf Dimen.

Microsoft Office Starter Kit for Macintosh. Hayden Development Group Staff. (Illus.). 720p. 1995. 35.00 (*1-56830-173-1*, Alpha Ref) Macmillan Gen Ref.

***Microsoft Office 2000 Certified Edition.** Tim Duffy. 1000p. (C). 1999. spiral bd. 62.67 (*0-201-61188-0*, Prentice Hall) P-H.

***Microsoft Office 2000 Development.** Microsoft Corporation Staff. LC 99-33883. (Microsoft Mastering Ser.). 1999. pap. 49.99 (*0-7356-0899-7*) Microsoft.

***Microsoft Office 2000.** Ann Miller. (Marquee Ser.). 2001. 44.00 (*0-7638-0359-6*) EMC-Paradigm.

***Microsoft Office 2000.** Morrison. 2000. pap. 44.95 (*0-538-72412-9*) Thomson Learn.

***Microsoft Office 2000 Basics.** Connie Morrison. LC 00-37415. (Illus.). 2000. write for info. (*0-538-72413-7*) Sth-Wstrn College.

***Microsoft Office 2000.** Timothy O'Leary & Linda O'Leary. 880p. (C). 1999. spiral bd. 43.44 (*0-07-233747-8*) McGrw-H Hghr Educ.

Microsoft Office 2000. Nita H. Rutkosky. LC 99-10805. 2000. text. write for info. (*0-7638-0255-7*) Paradigm MN.

***Microsoft Office 2000: A Hands-On Guide.** Bonita Sebastian. 204p. 1999. spiral bd. 26.60 (*1-57426-105-3*) Computer Lit Pr.

***Microsoft Office 2000: An Introduction.** Pasewark. (Computer Applications Ser.). 1999. 6.90 (*0-538-50904-X*); 20.00 (*0-538-50905-8*); 9.50 (*0-538-50906-6*); 4.50 (*0-538-50907-4*) Sth-Wstrn College.

***Microsoft Office 2000: An Introduction.** Pasewark. (Computer Applications Ser.). (C). 1999. text 4.50 (*0-538-50903-1*); text 18.50 (*0-538-50902-3*) Sth-Wstrn College.

***Microsoft Office 2000: An Introduction.** Reding-Beskeen Swanson. (Illustrated Ser.). 1999. 42.00 (*0-7600-6352-4*) Course Tech.

***Microsoft Office 2000: Certified Edition.** (C). 1999. spiral bd. write for info. (*0-201-69941-9*) Addison-Wesley.

***Microsoft Office 2000: Certified Edition.** (C). 2000. spiral bd. write for info. (*0-201-69938-9*) Addison-Wesley.

Microsoft Office 2000: Instructor's Guide, CD Rom Package. Nita H. Rutkosky. 69.00 incl. cd-rom (*0-7638-0256-5*) EMC-Paradigm.

Microsoft Office 2000: No Experienced Required. 2nd ed. Gini Courter & Annette Marquis. LC 99-60014. (No Experience Required Ser.). (Illus.). 742p. 1999. pap. 24.99 (*0-7821-2293-0*) Sybex.

Microsoft Office 2000 Brief Concepts & Techniques. Gary B. Shelly et al. 672p. per. 50.95 (*0-7895-4651-5*, Pub. by Course Tech) Thomson Learn.

Microsoft Office 2000 Certified with Windows 98 -- Expert: Course CBT. David W. Beskeen et al. 56.95 (*0-619-00134-8*, Pub. by Course Tech) Thomson Learn.

Microsoft Office 2000 Cheat Sheet. Jennifer Fulton. 1999. pap. text 14.99 (*0-7897-1847-2*) Que.

Microsoft Office 2000 Complete. Sybex, Inc. Staff. (Complete Ser.). 1056p. 1999. pap. 19.99 (*0-7821-2411-9*) Sybex.

***Microsoft Office 2000 Expert Companion.** Reed Jacobson. LC 99-27215. 900p. (C). (gr. 8). 1999. pap. 49.99 (*0-7356-0527-0*) Little.

Microsoft Office 2000 for Dummies Value Pack. Wallace Wang et al. (For Dummies Ser.). (Illus.). 1278p. 1999. boxed set 49.99 incl. cd-rom (*0-7645-0518-1*, 215935) IDG Bks.

Microsoft Office 2000 for Windows: Visual QuickStart Guide. Steve Sagman. 320p. 1999. pap. text 19.99 (*0-201-35440-3*) Peachpit Pr.

***Microsoft Office 2000 in Brief.** Kenneth Laudon et al. 528p. (C). 1999. pap. 44.69 (*0-07-234085-1*) McGrw-H Hghr Educ.

Microsoft Office 2000 Post-Advanced Concepts & Techniques. Gary B. Shelly et al. 872p. per. 60.95 (*0-7895-5691-X*, Pub. by Course Tech) Thomson Learn.

***Microsoft Office 2000 Technical Support Training Kit.** Ed. by Microsoft Corporation Staff. LC 99-33882. 800p. (C). (gr. 8). 1999. boxed set 99.99 (*0-7356-0669-2*) Little.

Microsoft Office 2000 User Specialist Study Guide. 3rd ed. Gini Marquis Courter. 1008p. 1999. 39.99 (*0-7821-2574-3*) Sybex.

Microsoft Office 2000 with Windows 98 -- Basic: Course CBT. David W. Beskeen et al. (C). 40.95 (*0-619-00151-8*, Pub. by Course Tech) Thomson Learn.

***Microsoft Office 2000 for Windows.** Peter Weverka. LC 99-61336. (Dummies 101 Ser.). (Illus.). 288p. 1999. pap. 24.99 incl. cd-rom (*0-7645-0454-1*) IDG Bks.

***Microsoft Office 2K Certified with Window 98 Expert.** Course Technology Staff. (SAM's License Card for Course CBT Ser.). (C). 2000. text 25.00 (*0-619-00935-7*) Course Tech.

Microsoft Office User Specialist Microsoft Word 97 Exam Guide. Jane Calabria & Dorothy Burke. LC 97-81449. 352p. 1998. pap. 29.99 (*0-7897-1507-4*) Que.

Microsoft Office User Specialist Microsoft Word 97 Exam Guide. Jane Calabria et al. LC 97-80541. 430p. 1997. pap. 29.99 (*0-7897-1290-3*) Que.

Microsoft Office Virtual Tutor. Que Education & Training Staff. 1996. pap. text 50.00 incl. cd-rom (*1-57576-107-6*) Que Educ & Trng.

Microsoft Office VisiRef Bundle. Que Staff. 1994. pap. 39.00 (*0-7897-0043-3*) Que.

Microsoft Office with Windows 95, Word 7.0, Excel 7.0, Access 7.0. Timothy J. O'Leary & Linda I. O'Leary. (C). 1996. pap. text 37.00 (*0-07-049103-8*) McGraw.

Microsoft Office with Windows 3.1, Word 6.0, Excel 5.0, Access 2.0, Itegration, & Powerpoint. O'Leary. (C). 1995. pap. text 43.00 (*0-07-049102-X*) McGraw.

Microsoft Office with Windows 3.1, Word 6.0, Excel 5.0, Access 2.0, & Integration. O'Leary. (C). 1995. pap. text 37.00 (*0-07-049101-1*) McGraw.

Microsoft Office X for Dummies Quick Reference. Roger C. Parker. 224p. 1996. spiral bd. 12.99 (*1-56884-978-8*) IDG Bks.

***Microsoft Office "X" for Macs for Dummies.** Tom Negrino. (For Dummies Ser.). (Illus.). 384p. 2000. pap. 19.99 (*0-7645-0702-8*) IDG Bks.

***Microsoft Office 2000.** Hutchinson. LC 99-15465. 72p. 1999. spiral bd. 43.44 (*0-07-233793-1*) McGraw.

Microsoft Office 2000. Napier. (School Transfer from CT). 1999. pap., wbk. ed. 12.95 (*0-538-42621-7*) S-W Pub.

***Microsoft Office 2000.** Nancy Stevenson. LC 99-29836. (One Step at a Time Ser.). 480p. 1999. pap. 29.99 (*0-7645-3292-8*) IDG Bks.

Microsoft Office 2000: Advanced Concepts & Techniques. Gary B. Shelly. 1999. pap. text 60.95 (*0-7895-4649-3*) Course Tech.

Microsoft Office 2000: Advanced Course. Sandra Cable et al. LC 99-23145. (Computer Applications Ser.). 1999. pap. 52.95 (*0-538-68828-9*) S-W Pub.

***Microsoft Office 2000: Advanced Course.** Connie Morrison & Sandra Cable. LC 99-23145. 752p. 1999. pap. 54.95 (*0-538-68829-7*) Sth-Wstrn College.

Microsoft Office 2000: Advanced Tutorial. Connie Morrison et al. (Computer Applications Ser.). 1999. pap., wbk. ed. 12.95 (*0-538-68830-0*) S-W Pub.

Microsoft Office 2000 Illustrated Introductory. David W. Beskeen. (Illus.). 1999. pap. text 50.95 (*0-7600-6050-9*) Course Tech.

Microsoft Office 2000: Illustrated Second Course. Marie L. Swanson. (Illus.). 1999. pap. text 50.95 (*0-7600-6118-1*) Course Tech.

Microsoft Office 2000: Introductory Concepts & Techniques. Gary B. Shelly. (Shelly Cashman Ser.). 1999. pap. text 60.95 (*0-7895-4635-3*) Course Tech.

Microsoft Office 2000: Introductory Course. Pasewark. LC 99-23219. (Computer Applications Ser.). 1999. pap. 52.95 (*0-538-68824-6*); pap., wbk. ed. 12.95 (*0-538-68826-2*) S-W Pub.

***Microsoft Office 2000: Introductory Course.** William P. Pasewark. LC 99-23219. (Tutorial Ser.). 688p. 1999. pap. 54.95 (*0-538-68825-4*) Sth-Wstrn College.

***Microsoft Office 2000: Simplified.** Ruth Maran. LC 98-75597. (Illus.). 416p. 1999. pap. 29.99 (*0-7645-6052-2*) IDG Bks.

Microsoft Office 2000 Administrator's Desk Reference. Bill Camarda. 1000p. 2000. 49.99 (*0-7897-1931-2*) Que.

Microsoft Office 2000 at a Glance: Small Business Edition. Perspection, Inc. Staff. LC 98-43584. (At A Glance Ser.). 352p. 1999. pap. 19.99 (*0-7356-0546-7*) Microsoft.

Microsoft Office 2000 at a Glance Library. Jerry Joyce et al. (At A Glance Ser.). 1008p. 1999. pap. 71.99 (*0-7356-0759-1*) Microsoft.

***Microsoft Office 2000 Bible With CDROM.** Edward Willett et al. (Illus.). 1296p. 1999. pap. 39.99 incl. cd-rom (*0-7645-3261-8*) IDG Bks.

Microsoft Office 2000 Developer for Dummies. Jaskolka. 408p. 1999. pap. 29.99 incl. cd-rom (*0-7645-0564-5*) IDG Bks.

***Microsoft Office 2000 Developers Guide.** D. F. Scott. 1008p. 1999. pap. 49.99 (*0-7645-3330-4*) IDG Bks.

***Microsoft Office 2000 for Dummies.** Wallace Wang. 896p. 1999. pap. 34.99 (*0-7645-0519-X*) IDG Bks.

***Microsoft Office 2000 for Windows.** Doug Lowe. LC 98-88795. (Windows for Dummies Ser.). (Illus.). 240p. 1999. spiral bd. 12.99 (*0-7645-0453-3*) IDG Bks.

***Microsoft Office 2000 for Windows for Dummies.** Wallace Wang & Robert C. Parker. LC 99-60744. (Windows for Dummies Ser.). (Illus.). 496p. 1999. pap. 19.99 (*0-7645-0452-5*) IDG Bks.

***Microsoft Office 2000 Programming/mastering Set.** David Boctor. 1999. pap. text 99.99 (*0-7356-0815-6*) Microsoft.

Microsoft Office 2000 Resource Kit With CDROM. Microsoft Corporation Staff. LC 99-19168. (Resource Kit Ser.). (Illus.). 875p. 1999. pap. 59.99 (*0-7356-0555-6*) Microsoft.

Microsoft Office 2000 Starts Here. Microsoft Corporation Staff. 1999. cd-rom 29.99 (*0-7356-0506-8*) Microsoft.

***Microsoft Office 2000 Step-By-Step Interactive.** Learnit Corporation Staff. (SPA.). 2000. pap. 29.99 incl. cd-rom (*0-7356-0659-5*) Microsoft Pr.

***Microsoft Office 2000 Step-By-Step Interactive.** Learnit Corporation Staff. (JPN.). 2000. pap. 41.67 incl. cd-rom (*0-7356-0657-9*) Microsoft Pr.

***Microsoft Office 2000 Step-By-Step Interactive, Brazilian.** Learnit Corporation Staff. 2000. pap. 29.99 incl. cd-rom (*0-7356-0827-X*) Microsoft Pr.

Microsoft Office 2000 User Manual. Que Corporation Staff. (Illus.). 869p. 1999. pap. 19.99 (*0-7897-1930-4*) Que.

Microsoft Office 2000 Visual Basic Fundamentals. David Boctor. LC 99-20167. 1999. pap. text 39.99 (*0-7356-0594-7*) Microsoft.

Microsoft Office 2000 6-In-1: Small Business Edition. Joe Habraken. (6 in 1 / Que Ser.). (Illus.). 813p. 1999. pap. 29.99 (*0-7897-1972-X*) Que.

Microsoft Office 2000 8 in 1. Joe Habraken. (8 in 1 / Que Ser.). (Illus.). 1278p. 1999. pap. 29.99 (*0-7897-1840-5*) Que.

Microsoft Office 2000 8-1 Step by Step. Catapult Inc. Staff. LC 99-13767. 1999. pap. 44.99 (*1-57231-984-4*) Microsoft.

***Microsoft Office 2000/Visual Basic Programmer's Guide.** David A. Shank. LC 98-44826. 1999. pap. text 49.99 (*1-57231-952-6*) Microsoft.

Microsoft Office 9X. Napier. LC 99-218729. 2000. pap. 38.95 (*0-538-42604-7*) S-W Pub.

Microsoft Office 97: Introduction Cocepts & Techniques. Gary B. Shelly et al. (Shelly-Cashman Ser.). 1997. pap. 49.00 (*0-7895-4424-5*) Course Tech.

***Microsoft Office 97: Introductory Concepts & Techniques Enhanced.** Shelly & Cashman. (Shelly Cashman Ser.). (C). 1999. pap. 60.95 (*0-7895-5797-5*); pap. 47.00 (*0-7895-5798-3*) Course Tech.

Microsoft Office 97: Professional, Blue Ribbon Edition. 2nd ed. Duffy. 935p. (C). 1998. spiral bd. 64.00 (*0-201-43860-7*, Prentice Hall) P-H.

Microsoft Office 97 Essentials. Gary B. Shelly et al. (C). 1997. pap. 39.00 (*0-7895-4387-7*) Course Tech.

Microsoft Office 97 For Windows Illustrated. Swanson et al. (C). 1997. pap. 38.50 (*0-7600-5994-2*) Thomson Learn.

***Microsoft Office 97 Pro Illustrated Enchanced.** Marie L. Swanson et al. (C). 1999. pap. 38.00 (*0-7600-5924-1*) Course Tech.

***Microsoft Office 97 Professional Applicatios & Visual Basic.** Duffy & Paul B. Thurrott. 1999. pap. text 71.00 (*0-201-67688-5*) Addison-Wesley.

Microsoft Office 97 Small Business Edition Microsoft Corporation Staff. 1997. cd-rom 29.99 (*1-57231-735-3*) Microsoft.

Microsoft Office 97 User Manual. Rick Winter. LC 98-85049. 608p. 1998. 19.99 (*0-7897-1706-9*) Que.

Microsoft Office 98 for Macintosh: The Comprehensive Guide. Brian Little & Ned Snell. LC 98-3884. 600p. 1998. 39.99 (*1-57610-279-3*) Coriolis Grp.

Microsoft OLAP for SQL Server 7 Unleashed. 900p. 1999. text 49.99 (*0-672-31671-4*) Sams.

***Microsoft OLAP Solutions.** Erik Thomsen et al. LC 99-26922. 528p. 1999. pap. 49.99 incl. cd-rom (*0-471-33258-5*) Wiley.

Microsoft OLE DB Software Development Kit & Programmer's Reference. Microsoft Corporation Staff. LC 97-7697. 784p. 1997. 39.99 incl. cd-rom (*1-57231-612-8*) Microsoft.

Microsoft OLE DB 2.0 Programmer's Reference & Data Access Software Development Kit. Microsoft Corporation Staff. LC 98-39268. 1000p. 1998. pap. 49.99 (*0-7356-0590-4*) Microsoft.

Microsoft Outlook. Diana Rain. LC 97-174137. (New Visual Reference Ser.). spiral bd. 17.00 (*1-56243-438-1*, G-23) DDC Pub.

Microsoft Outlook E-Mail & Fax Guide. Sue Mosher. LC 97-33936. 450p. 1997. pap. 39.95 (*1-882419-82-0*) News Four-Hund.

Microsoft Outlook for Dummies. Bill Dyszel & Dummies Technical Press Staff. LC 96-80190. (Illus.). 384p. 1997. pap. 19.99 (*0-7645-0005-X*) IDG Bks.

***Microsoft Outlook 98: Basic.** TBD. (Illustrated Ser.). 2001. write for info. (*0-619-01764-3*) Course Tech.

Microsoft Outlook 98 at a Glance: The Easy Way to Find the Right Answers, Right Now. Stephen L. Nelson. LC 97-52075. (At A Glance Ser.). 224p. 16.99 (*1-57231-719-1*) Microsoft.

***Microsoft Outlook 98 Field Guide.** Stephen L. Nelson. (Field Guide Ser.). (Illus.). 2000. pap. 7.99 (*0-7356-1065-7*) Microsoft.

Microsoft Outlook 98 for Windows for Dummies. Bill Dyszel. LC 98-85133. 384p. 1998. pap. 19.99 (*0-7645-0393-6*) IDG Bks.

Microsoft Outlook 98 for Dummies Quick Reference. Bill Dyszel. LC 98-85430. (For Dummies). 224p. 1998. spiral bd. 12.99 (*0-7645-0394-4*) IDG Bks.

***Microsoft Outlook 98 Quick Source Guide.** Quick Source Staff. (Illus.). 6p. 1998. pap. 4.95 (*1-930674-16-3*) Quick Source.

Microsoft Outlook 98 Step by Step. Catapult, Inc. Staff. LC 98-11186. (Step by Step Ser.). 320p. 29.99 (*1-57231-717-5*) Microsoft.

Microsoft Outlook 97: Illustrated Brief Edition. 10th ed. (Illus.). (C). 1997. pap. 10.95 (*0-7600-5333-2*) Course Tech.

Microsoft Outlook 97 at a Glance. Stephen L. Nelson. LC 97-7750. (Field Guide Ser.). 208p. 16.99 (*1-57231-390-0*) Microsoft.

***Microsoft Outlook 97 Field Guide.** Stephen L. Nelson. (Field Guide Ser.). (Illus.). 2000. pap. text 7.99 (*0-7356-1063-0*) Microsoft.

Microsoft Outlook 97 for Windows for Dummies Quick Reference. Bill Dyszel & Dummies Technical Press Staff. LC 97-70738. 202p. 1997. spiral bd. 12.99 (*0-7645-0184-4*) IDG Bks.

Microsoft Outlook 97 Introductory. (Illus.). 167p. 1997. pap. 29.95 (*1-888323-22-1*) DataPower Intl.

Microsoft Outlook Quick Reference. Gordon Padwick. 300p. 1997. 19.99 (*0-7897-1267-9*) Que.

***Microsoft Outlook 2000: Basic.** TBD. (Illustrated Ser.). 2001. write for info. (*0-619-01763-5*) Course Tech.

***Microsoft Outlook 2000: Complete Concepts & Techniques.** Shelly et al. (Shelly-Cashman Ser.). (C). 2000. text 38.95 (*0-7895-5965-X*) Course Tech.

***Microsoft Outlook 2000.** Dyszel. LC 98-99798. (Windows for Dummies Ser.). 384p. 1999. pap. 19.99 (*0-7645-0471-1*); spiral bd. 12.99 (*0-7645-0472-X*) IDG Bks.

***Microsoft Outlook 2000 Programming Bible.** Jeffrey A. Kent. (Illus.). 576p. 2000. pap. 39.99 (*0-7645-4650-3*) IDG Bks.

Microsoft Outlook 2000. Gini Marquis. LC 99-60024. (No Experience Required Ser.). 480p. 1999. pap. 19.99 (*0-7821-2483-6*) Sybex.

***Microsoft Outlook 2000: Brief Edition.** Sarah E. Hutchinson & Glen J. Coulthard. LC 00-38295. (Advantage Series for Computer Education). 2001. pap. write for info. (*0-07-235873-4*, McGrw-H College) McGrw-H Hghr Educ.

***Microsoft Outlook 2000: E-Mail & Fax Guide.** Sue Mosher. (Illus.). 1999. pap. text 39.95 (*1-55558-235-4*, Digital DEC) Buttrwrth-Heinemann.

***Microsof Outlook 2000: Essentials.** Goding Swanson. (Illustrated Ser.). (Illus.). (C). 1999. text 10.95 (*0-7600-6075-4*) Course Tech.

***Microsoft Outlook 2000: Introductory Concepts & Techniques.** Shelly et al. (Shelly-Cashman Ser.). (C). 2000. text 22.95 (*0-7895-5964-1*) Course Tech.

Microsoft Outlook 2000 at a Glance. Stephen L. Nelson. LC 98-43579. 208p. 1999. pap. 19.99 (*1-57231-948-8*) Microsoft.

***Microsoft Outlook 2000 Quick Source Guide.** Quick Source Staff. (Illus.). 6p. 1999. pap. 4.95 (*1-930674-11-2*) Quick Source.

Microsoft Outlook 2000. Adams. (C). 1999. text 19.50 (*0-03-026381-6*) Harcourt.

***Microsoft Outlook 2000: One Step at a Time.** Rick Darnell & Trudi Reisner. LC 99-15721. 360p. 1999. pap. 29.99 (*0-7645-3293-6*) IDG Bks.

***Microsoft Outlook 2000 Bible.** Todd A. Klieinke. LC 99-15722. (Bible Ser.). 672p. 1999. pap. 39.99 (*0-7645-3365-7*) IDG Bks.

***Microsoft Outlook 2000 Essential Concepts & Techniques.** Shelly & Cashman. (Shelly Cashman Ser.). (C). 1999. pap. 8.95 (*0-7895-5948-X*) Course Tech.

Microsoft Outlook 2000 Quick Reference. 200p. 1999. pap. text 9.99 (*0-7897-2113-9*) Que.

Microsoft Outlook 2000 Step by Step. Catapult, Inc., Staff. LC 98-48190. (Step by Step Ser.). 304p. 1999. pap. text 29.99 (*1-57231-982-8*) Microsoft.

***Microsoft Outlook 97.** Parkes. (C). 1998. pap. text 13.80 (*0-7600-6010-X*) Thomson Learn.

***Microsoft Outlook 98: Student Text.** Krueger. (Computer Applications Ser.). (C). 1999. text 13.95 (*0-538-72409-9*) Sth-Wstrn College.

Microsoft Photodraw 2000 Essential Concepts & Techniques Premium Add-On. Gary B. Shelly et al. (Illus.). 64p. per. 9.95 (*0-7895-5740-1*, Pub. by Course Tech) Thomson Learn.

***Microsoft Photodraw 2000: Beginning Course.** Mark D. Ciampa. LC 00-23848. (Illus.). 2001. pap. 133.95 (*0-538-72428-5*) S-W Pub.

Microsoft PhotoDraw 2000 at a Glance. Stephen W. Sagman. LC 98-31460. (At A Glance Ser.). 256p. 1999. 19.99 (*1-57231-954-2*) Microsoft.

***Microsoft Photodraw 2000 by Design.** William Tait. LC 99-13773. (Illus.). 450p. 1999. pap. 34.99 incl. cd-rom (*1-57231-938-0*) Microsoft.

***Microsoft Photodraw 2000 for Dummies.** Julie Adair King. 384p. 1999. pap. 19.99 (*0-7645-0601-3*) IDG Bks.

***Microsoft Pocket Guide to Microsoft Access 2000.** Stephen L. Nelson. (Microsoft Pocket Guides Ser.). 2000. pap. 7.99 (*0-7356-1066-5*) Microsoft.

***Microsoft Pocket Guide to Microsoft Excel 2000.** Stephen L. Nelson. (Pocket Guides Ser.). (Illus.). 2000. pap. 7.99 (*0-7356-1067-3*) Microsoft.

***Microsoft Pocket Guide to Microsoft Internet Explorer 5.** Stephen L. Nelson. (Pocket Guides Ser.). (Illus.). 2000. pap. 7.99 (*0-7356-1071-1*) Microsoft.

***Microsoft Pocket Guide to Microsoft Outlook 2000.** Stephen L. Nelson. (Pocket Guides Ser.). (Illus.). 2000. pap. 7.99 (*0-7356-1070-3*) Microsoft.

***Microsoft Pocket Guide to Microsoft PowerPoint 2000.** Stephen L. Nelson. (Pocket Guides Ser.). (Illus.). 2000. pap. 7.99 (*0-7356-1068-1*) Microsoft.

Microsoft Pocket Guide To Microsoft Windows **Canceled 2000 Professional. Stephen L. Nelson. (C). (gr. 8). 1999. pap. 12.99 (*1-57231-844-9*) Little.

***Microsoft Pocket Guide to Microsoft Word 2000.** Stephen L. Nelson. (Pocket Guides Ser.). (Illus.). 2000. pap. 7.99 (*0-7356-1069-X*) Microsoft.

Microsoft PowerPoint. Shelly Cashman. (C). 1994. text. write for info. (*0-318-70360-2*) S-W Pub.

***Microsoft PowerPoint: Creating Presentations.** DK Publishing Staff. (Essential Computers Ser.). (Illus.). 72p. 2000. pap. 6.95 (*0-7894-5537-4*, D K Ink) DK Pub Inc.

***Microsoft PowerPoint - Introduction: Practice & Reference Guide.** Juanita B. Tischendorf. vi, 183p. 1999. pap. text 25.00 (*1-928613-10-1*) J Tischendorf.

M

M

Microsoft Powerpoint for Windows 97. Sarah E. Hutchinson & Glen Coulthard. LC 97-178384. 224p. (C). 1997. text 21.00 (*0-256-26001-X*, Irwn McGrw-H) McGrw-H Hghr Educ.

Microsoft PowerPoint for Windows 95. Patricia Murphy. (Quicktorial Ser.). 1996. mass mkt. 21.95 (*0-538-71543-X*) S-W Pub.

Microsoft PowerPoint for Windows 95 Step by Step. Perspection, Inc. Staff. (Step by Step Ser.). 352p. 1995. 29.95 incl. disk (*1-55615-829-7*) Microsoft.

Microsoft PowerPoint 4 for Windows. Gary B. Shelly et al. LC 94-30618. (Shelly Cashman Ser.). 192p. (C). 1994. pap. 22.95 (*0-87709-572-8*) Course Tech.

Microsoft PowerPoint 4 for Windows - Illustrated, Incl. instr. resource kit, test bank, transparency. David W. Beskeen & Steven M. Johnson. (Illustrated Ser.). (Illus.). 184p. 1995. pap. 20.95 (*1-56527-523-3*) Course Tech.

Microsoft PowerPoint 4 for Windows - New Perspectives Brief, Incl. instr. resource kit, test mgr., Web pg. Beverly B. Zimmerman & S. Scott Zimmerman. (New Perspectives Ser.). (Illus.). 128p. 1995. pap. text, mass mkt. 13.00 incl. 3.5 ld (*0-7600-3277-7*) Course Tech.

Microsoft PowerPoint 4.0: Introductory Coursebook. DataPower AS Staff. 147p. 1995. pap. text 29.95 (*1-888323-03-5*) DataPower Intl.

Microsoft PowerPoint 4.0 for Windows. Sarah E. Hutchinson & Glen Coulthard. 152p. (C). 1994. text 12.50 (*0-256-18922-6*, Irwn McGrw-H) McGrw-H Hghr Educ.

Microsoft PowerPoint 4.0 for Macintosh. Patricia Murphy. (Quicktorial Ser.). (C). 1997. mass mkt. 21.95 (*0-538-71581-2*) S-W Pub.

Microsoft PowerPoint 4.0 for Windows. Timothy J. O'Leary & Linda I. O'Leary. (C). 1995. pap. text 22.50 (*0-07-049043-0*) McGraw.

Microsoft PowerPoint 4.0 for Windows: Illustrated Brief Edition. David W. Beskeen. Ed. by Steven M. Johnson. (Illustrated Ser.). (Illus.). 104p. (C). 1995. pap. 11.95 (*1-56527-593-4*) Course Tech.

Microsoft PowerPoint 4.0 for Macintosh: Quick Course. Murphy. (DF - Computer Applications Ser.). 1996. mass mkt. 22.95 (*0-538-71580-4*) S-W Pub.

Microsoft PowerPoint 4.0 for Windows: Quick Course. Murphy. (Quick Course Ser.). 192p. 1995. mass mkt. 15.95 (*0-538-64851-1*) S-W Pub.

Microsoft PowerPoint 97 Intermediate. Pamela W. Adams. Ed. by Elizabeth Carpenter & Sara Pressley. (Microsoft Office 97 Ser.). (Illus.). 53p. 1998. pap. text 28.95 (*1-58163-075-1*) CPI Train.

***Microsoft PowerPoint 97.** Azimuth Interactive Staff. (Inter@ctiveLearning Ser.). (Illus.). 148p. 2000. pap. 19.95 (*1-930581-02-5*) Azimuth.

Microsoft Powerpoint 97 - Illustrated Standard Edition. David W. Beskeen. (Illus.). 232p. per. 21.95 (*0-7600-6164-5*, Pub. by Course Tech) Thomson Learn.

***Microsoft PowerPoint 97.** deluxe ed. Azimuth Interactive Staff. (Inter@ctiveLearning Ser.). 148p. 2000. pap. 39.95 incl. cd-rom (*1-930581-03-3*) Azimuth.

Microsoft PowerPoint 97: Complete Concepts & Techniques. 10th ed. Gary B. Shelly et al. (Shelly Cashman Ser.). 304p. (C). 1997. mass mkt. 38.95 (*0-7895-1347-1*) Course Tech.

Microsoft PowerPoint 97: Double Diamond Edition. 10th ed. Gary B. Shelly et al. (Shelly Cashman Ser.). 152p. (C). 1997. mass mkt. 22.95 (*0-7895-2759-6*) Course Tech.

Microsoft PowerPoint 97: Illustrated Brief Edition. 10th ed. David W. Beskeen & Steve M. Johnson. (Illustrated Ser.). (Illus.). 96p. (C). 1997. pap. 12.95 (*0-7600-4704-9*) Course Tech.

Microsoft PowerPoint 97: Illustrated Standard Edition: A First Course. 10th ed. David W. Beskeen. (Illustrated Ser.). (Illus.). 192p. (C). 1997. pap. 16.50 (*0-7600-5160-7*) Course Tech.

Microsoft PowerPoint 97: Introductory Coursebook. (Illus.). 147p. 1997. pap. text 29.95 (*1-888323-18-3*) DataPower Intl.

Microsoft PowerPoint 97 at a Glance. Perspection, Inc. Staff. LC 96-36629. 1996. pap. text 16.95 (*1-57231-368-4*) Microsoft.

Microsoft PowerPoint 97 Field Guide. Stephen L. Nelson. LC 96-36634. 192p. pap. 9.95 (*1-57231-327-7*) Microsoft.

***Microsoft PowerPoint 97 Field Guide.** Stephen L. Nelson. (Field Guide Ser.). 2000. pap. 7.99 (*0-7356-1061-4*) Microsoft.

Microsoft PowerPoint 97 for Windows Quickstart. Ann DeVries. LC 97-160194. 1996. pap. text 29.99 incl. cd-rom (*1-56276-472-1*, Ziff-Davis Pr) Que.

Microsoft PowerPoint 97 Introduction. Pamela W. Adams & Kathryn K. Baskett. Ed. by Susan D. Carnes. (Micrsoft Office 97 Ser.). (Illus.). 129p. 1998. pap. text 28.95 (*1-58163-056-5*) CPI Train.

***Microsoft PowerPoint 97 Quick Source Guide.** Quick Source Staff. (Illus.). 6p. 1998. pap. 4.95 (*1-930674-19-8*) Quick Source.

Microsoft PowerPoint 97 Step by Step. Perspection, Inc. Staff. LC 96-38987. 352p. 29.95 (*1-57231-315-3*) Microsoft.

Paradigm Visual Series: Microsoft Powerpoint 7: Text with data disk, 3.5 IBM. O. Lammi. 128p. text 14.95 (*0-7638-0017-1*) EMC-Paradigm.

Microsoft PowerPoint 7 for Windows 95 - Illustrated, Incl. instr. resource kit, test mgr., files. David W. Beskeen. (Illustrated Ser.). (Illus.). 200p. 1996. text, mass mkt. 20.95 incl. 3.5 ld (*0-7600-3525-3*) Course Tech.

Microsoft PowerPoint 7 for Windows 95 - Brief, Incl. instr. resource kit, test mgr., Web pg. Beverly B. Zimmerman & S. Scott Zimmerman. (New Perspectives Ser.). (Illus.). 128p. 1995. text, mass mkt. 17.95 incl. 3.5 ld (*0-7600-3547-4*) Course Tech.

Microsoft PowerPoint 7 for Windows 95: Double Diamond. Gary B. Shelly & T. Cashman. 152p. 1996. pap. 22.95 (*0-7895-1158-4*) Course Tech.

Microsoft PowerPoint 7 for Windows 95: Illustrated Brief Edition. David W. Beskeen. (Illustrated Ser.). (Illus.). 96p. 1995. pap. 11.95 (*0-7600-3526-1*) Course Tech.

Microsoft PowerPoint 7.0 for Windows 95. Sarah E. Hutchinson & Glen Coulthard. 692p. (C). 1996. write for info. (*0-256-22957-0*, Irwn McGrw-H) McGrw-H Hghr Educ.

Microsoft PowerPoint 7.0 for Windows 95. Sarah E. Hutchinson & Glen J. Coulthard. LC 96-6164. (Advantage Series for Computer Education). (Illus.). 192p. (C). 1996. text 25.00 (*0-256-22051-4*, Irwn McGrw-H) McGrw-H Hghr Educ.

Microsoft PowerPoint 7.0 for Windows 95. Timothy J. O'Leary & Linda I. O'Leary. LC 95-82265. (C). 1996. pap. text 21.50 (*0-07-049108-9*) McGraw.

Microsoft PowerPoint 7.0 for Windows 95. Rick Sullivan. (Computer Training Ser.). 1997. pap. text 19.95 (*0-538-67476-8*) S-W Pub.

Microsoft PowerPoint 7.0 for Windows 95: Introductory Coursebook. (Illus.). 1996. pap. text 29.95 (*1-888323-11-6*) DataPower Intl.

Microsoft PowerPoint 7.0 for Windows 95: Quick Course. Murphy. (DF - Computer Applications Ser.). 1996. mass mkt. 22.95 (*0-538-71487-5*) S-W Pub.

***Microsoft Powerpoint 2000: Comprehensive.** TBD. (New Perspectives Ser.). (C). 2000. text 24.50 (*0-619-01977-8*) Course Tech.

***Microsoft PowerPoint 2000.** Teresa Adams & Stella Smith. LC 99-61511. (Illus.). 2000. write for info. (*0-03-026142-2*) Harcourt Coll Pubs.

Microsoft Powerpoint 2000 - Illustrated Brief. David W. Beskeen. (Illus.). 112p. per. 12.95 (*0-7600-6073-8*, Pub. by Course Tech) Thomson Learn.

***Microsoft Powerpoint 2000.** Course Technology Staff. (SAM's License Card for Course CBT Ser.). (C). 2000. text. write for info. (*0-619-00932-2*) Course Tech.

***Microsoft Powerpoint 2000.** Meredith Flynn & Nita H. Rutkosky. LC 99-35135. (Benchmark Ser.). 1999. text. write for info. incl. cd-rom (*0-7638-0270-0*) Paradigm MN.

***Microsoft PowerPoint 2000.** Sarah E. Hutchinson & Glen J. Coulthard. LC 99-34912. 2000. write for info. (*0-07-234810-0*) McGrw-H Hghr Educ.

***Microsoft PowerPoint 2000.** Sarah E. Hutchinson & Glen J. Coulthard. LC 99-14616. (Illus.). 2000. write for info. (*0-07-233800-8*) McGrw-H Hghr Educ.

***Microsoft Powerpoint 2000.** Sarah E. Hutchinson & Glen J. Coulthard. LC 99-54015. 2000. write for info. (*0-07-234809-7*) McGrw-H Hghr Educ.

***Microsoft PowerPoint 2000.** Kenneth C. Laudon & Kenneth Rosenblatt. LC 99-63168. (Illus.). 2000. write for info. (*0-07-234078-9*) McGrw-H Hghr Educ.

***Microsoft Powerpoint 2000 Introduction.** Timothy O'Leary & Linda O'Leary. 368p. (C). 1999. pap. 27.50 (*0-07-233748-6*) McGrw-H Hghr Educ.

***Microsoft Powerpoint 2000 in Brief.** Timothy O'Leary & Linda O'Leary. 216p. (C). 1999. pap. 19.06 (*0-07-233752-4*) McGrw-H Hghr Educ.

***Microsoft PowerPoint 2000.** Nita Hewitt Rutkosky & Denise Seguin. LC 99-57582. (Marquee Ser.). 2000. write for info. (*0-7638-0369-3*) Paradigm MN.

Microsoft Powerpoint 2000 Introductory Concepts & Techniques. Gary B. Shelly et al. 184p. per. 22.95 (*0-7895-4680-9*, Pub. by Course Tech) Thomson Learn.

Microsoft Powerpoint 2000 Comprehensive Concepts & Techniques. Gary B. Shelly et al. 640p. per. 44.95 (*0-7895-5611-1*, Pub. by Course Tech) Thomson Learn.

***Microsoft PowerPoint 2000: Core Certification** Nita H. Rutkosky. LC 99-35151. (Benchmark Ser.). 1999. write for info. (*0-7638-0336-7*) Paradigm MN.

***Microsoft Powerpoint 2000: Expert Certification** Meredith Flynn. LC 99-35141. (Benchmark Ser.). 1999. write for info. (*0-7638-0338-3*) Paradigm MN.

Microsoft PowerPoint 2000: Instructor's guide/CD Rom. Meredith Flynn & Nita H. Rutkosky. 69.00 incl. cd-rom (*0-7638-0271-9*) EMC-Paradigm.

***Microsoft PowerPoint 2000: Introduction.** Pamela W. Adams. Ed. by Jenell L. Davis. (Office 2000 Ser.). (Illus.). 148p. 2000. pap. 28.95 (*1-58163-093-X*) CPI Train.

***Microsoft PowerPoint 2000: Presentation Graphics with Impact.** Against the Clock, Inc. Staff. LC 99-39275. 2000. write for info. (*0-13-012639-X*) P-H.

Microsoft Powerpoint 2000 Certified: Course CBT. David W. Beskeen. 26.95 (*0-619-00126-7*, Pub. by Course Tech) Thomson Learn.

***Microsoft Powerpoint 2000 Complete Tutorial.** William Robert Pasewark & Catherine H. Skintik. LC 00-37416. (Illus.). 2000. ring bd. write for info. (*0-538-72442-0*) S-W Pub.

***Microsoft PowerPoint 2000 in Layman's Terms: The Reference Guide for the Rest of Us.** Katie Layman. 1999. pap. write for info. (*1-893532-12-7*) Compute Made.

***Microsoft PowerPoint 2000 Quick Source Guide.** Quick Source Staff. (Illus.). 6p. 1999. pap. 4.95 (*1-930674-14-7*) Quick Source.

***Microsoft Powerpoint 2000.** (C). 2000. 0.00 (*0-13-016991-9*) HEPC Inc.

***Microsoft PowerPoint 2000.** Tim Duffy. 124p. (C). 1999. pap. text 25.00 (*0-201-45918-3*, Prentice Hall) P-H.

Microsoft Powerpoint 2000. Napier. LC 99-230371. 1999. pap. 37.95 (*0-538-42616-0*); pap., wbk. ed. 12.95 (*0-538-42625-X*) S-W Pub.

Microsoft PowerPoint 2000: Complete Concepts & Techniques. Gary B. Shelly. 1999. pap. text 38.95 (*0-7895-4679-5*) Course Tech.

Microsoft PowerPoint 2000: Illustrated Introductory. David W. Beskeen. 1999. pap. text 21.95 (*0-7600-6074-6*) Course Tech.

Microsoft Powerpoint 2000: Quicktorial. Murphy. LC 98-47590. 174p. 1999. pap. 21.95 (*0-538-68861-0*) S-W Pub.

Microsoft PowerPoint 2000 One Step at a Time. Marilyn G. Kyd. LC 99-15716. 336p. 1999. pap. 29.99 (*0-7645-3294-4*) IDG Bks.

***Microsoft PowerPoint 2000, QuickTutorial.** Patricia Murphy. LC 98-47590. (Illus.). 144p. 1999. pap. 24.95 (*0-538-68862-9*) Sth-Wstrn College.

***Microsoft Powerpoint 2000 Step by Step Courseware Core Skills.** Perspection Staff. 300p. 2000. pap., student ed. 25.00 (*0-7356-1115-7*) Microsoft.

***Microsoft Powerpoint 2000 Step by Step Courseware Core Skills Student Guide.** 300p. 2000. pap. 20.00 (*0-7356-1114-9*) Microsoft.

***Microsoft Powerpoint 2000 Step by Step Courseware Instructor Guide.** 320p. 2000. pap. 30.00 (*0-7356-1113-0*) Microsoft.

Microsoft PowerPoint 2000 Step by Step With CDROM. Perspection, Inc. Staff. LC 98-49818. (Step by Step Ser.). (Illus.). 328p. 1999. pap. 29.99 (*1-57231-972-0*) Microsoft.

Microsoft Powerpoint 97. O'Leary. 1999. pap., student ed. 27.50 (*0-07-231669-1*) McGraw.

Microsoft Powerpoint 97. 10th ed. Carlos Gonzales. LC 98-11197. (Exam Cram Ser.). (C). 1998. mass mkt. 26.99 (*1-57610-224-6*) Coriolis Grp.

Microsoft PowerPoint 97: Fundamentals. (C). 1997. text 11.50 (*0-03-022553-1*, Pub. by Harcourt Coll Pubs) Harcourt.

***Microsoft PowerPoint 97: One Step at a Time.** Marilyn G. Kyd. LC T385.K8647 1999. (One Step at a Time Ser.). (Illus.). 368p. 1999. pap. 29.99 (*0-7645-3277-4*) IDG Bks.

Microsoft Powerpoint 97 Basic. Beskeen. (C). 1997. spiral bd. 20.95 (*0-7600-5825-3*) Thomson Learn.

Microsoft Press Computer Dictionary. 4th ed. Microsoft Corporation Staff. LC 99-20168. 1999. pap. 34.99 (*0-7356-0615-3*) Microsoft.

Microsoft Press Computer User's Dictionary. Microsoft Corporation Staff. LC 98-13998. 416p. 14.99 (*1-57231-862-7*) Microsoft.

Microsoft Press Exchange Server 5.5 Administrator's Companion. Rick Greenwald. LC 99-22855. 1999. pap. text 49.99 (*0-7356-0646-3*) Microsoft.

Microsoft Project for Windows 95 Step by Step. Catapult, Inc., Staff & Stephen W. Sagman. LC 95-35792. (Step by Step Ser.). 400p. 1995. 29.95 incl. disk (*1-55615-866-1*) Microsoft.

Microsoft Project for Windows 3.1 & Windows 95, Quick Reference. Glen Davis & Gosselin. (Orig.). 1996. pap. 12.00 (*1-56243-279-6*, MP-17) DDC Pub.

Microsoft Project 4.0 for Windows & the Macintosh: Setting Project Management Standards. Peggy J. Day. 320p. 1994. pap. 34.95 (*0-471-28610-9*, VNR) Wiley.

Microsoft Project 4.0 for Windows & the Macintosh: Setting Project Management Standards - Version 4. Peggy J. Day. (Illus.). 296p. 1994. pap. 34.95 (*0-442-01767-7*, VNR) Wiley.

Microsoft Project 98 for Dummies. Martin Doucette. LC 97-81230. (For Dummies Ser.). 384p. 1998. pap. 24.99 incl. cd-rom (*0-7645-0321-9*) IDG Bks.

Microsoft Project 98 Step by Step. Catapult, Inc. Staff. LC 97-27389. (Step by Step Ser.). (Illus.). 292p. 1997. pap. 29.99 incl. cd-rom (*1-57231-605-5*) Microsoft.

***Microsoft Project 2000: Advanced.** TBD. (Illustrated Ser.). 2001. write for info. (*0-619-01762-7*) Course Tech.

***Microsoft Project 2000: Intermediate.** TBD. (Illustrated Ser.). 2001. write for info. (*0-619-01761-9*) Course Tech.

***Microsoft Project 2000: Introductory Concetps & Techniques.** Shelly et al. (Shelly-Cashman Ser.). (C). 2000. text 22.95 (*0-7895-5963-3*) Course Tech.

***Microsoft Project 2000 Bible.** Elaine Marmel. LC 99-88435. (Bible Ser.). 696p. 2000. pap. 39.99 (*0-7645-3319-3*) IDG Bks.

***Microsoft Project 2000 for Dummies Quick Reference.** Nancy Stevenson. (For Dummies (Computers) Ser.). (Illus.). 224p. 2000. spiral bd. 12.99 (*0-7645-0717-6*) IDG Bks.

***Microsoft Project 2000 Step by Step.** Carl S. Chatfield & Tim Johnson. 2000. pap. 29.99 incl. cd-rom (*0-7356-0920-9*) Microsoft.

***Microsoft Project 2000 Complete Concepts & Techniques.** Shelly & Cashman. (Shelly Cashman Ser.). (C). 2000. pap. 28.50 (*0-7895-5956-0*) Course Tech.

***Microsoft Project 2000 Step by Step Courseware.** Timothy Johns & Carl S. Chatfield. 416p. 2000. pap., teacher ed. 30.00 (*0-7356-1118-1*) Microsoft.

***Microsoft Project 2000 Step by Step Courseware Core Skills.** Timothy Johns & Carl S. Chatfield. 192p. 2000. pap. 20.00 (*0-7356-1119-X*); pap. 25.00 (*0-7356-1120-3*) Microsoft.

***Microsoft Project 2000 Step by Step Courseware Expert Skills.** Timothy Johns & Carl S. Chatfield. 256p. 2000. pap. 25.00 (*0-7356-1122-X*); pap. 20.00 (*0-7356-1121-1*) Microsoft.

Microsoft Projects for Windows 95. Gary R. Brent. LC 96-207443. (C). 1996. pap. text 6.00 (*0-8053-1613-2*) Benjamin-Cummings.

Microsoft Project/Visual Basic Reference. 2nd ed. Microsoft Corporation Staff. LC 97-31955. 700p. 1997. 39.99 (*1-57231-680-2*) Microsoft.

***Microsoft Proxy Server 2.0 MCSE.** Curt Simmons. LC 99-18441. (MCSE Ser.). (Illus.). 544p. 1999. pap., student ed. 49.99 (*0-7645-3336-3*, CPG Pr) IDG Bks.

***Microsoft Publisher.** Against the Clock, Inc. Staff. LC 99-37113. (Against the Clock Ser.). 292p. 1999. spiral bd. 36.00 (*0-13-012630-6*) P-H.

Microsoft Publisher by Design: An Example-Packed Guide to Desktop Publishing Using Microsoft Publisher. 3rd ed. Luisa Simone. 512p. 1996. 24.95 (*1-55615-896-3*) Microsoft.

Microsoft Publisher for Everyday of the School Year. Kathleen Schrock. (Illus.). 180p. 1998. pap. 44.95 (*0-938865-72-2*) Linworth Pub.

***Microsoft Publisher 98 Quicktorial.** Mary Alice Eisch & Kathy Kruger. 1998. pap. 22.95 (*0-538-68881-5*) Thomson Learn.

Microsoft Publisher 98. Reding. (Illustrated Ser.). (C). 1998. mass mkt. 21.95 (*0-7600-6106-8*) Course Tech.

Microsoft Publisher 98 - Using. Ed. by Ron Pronk. (Illus.). 232p. 1998. pap. 20.00 (*1-58264-071-8*, 168) ActiveEd.

Microsoft Publisher 98 for Dummies. Jim McCarter et al. LC Z253.532.M53M4 1998. 384p. 1998. pap. 19.99 (*0-7645-0395-2*) IDG Bks.

Microsoft Publisher, Single User License. Microsoft Corporation Staff. (NO - Novell/Wordperfect Ser.). 1995. 46.95 (*0-538-65237-3*) S-W Pub.

Microsoft Publisher 3.0 for Windows 95. Mary Alice Eisch & Kathy Kruger. 240p. 1997. mass mkt. 20.95 incl. disk (*0-538-67914-X*) S-W Pub.

Microsoft Publisher 2.0 for Windows: Quick Course. Mary Alice Eisch. (DF - Computer Applications Ser.). (C). 1995. mass mkt., wbk. ed. 15.95 (*0-538-71457-3*) S-W Pub.

Microsoft Publisher 2000 - Illustrated Essentials. Nicole Jones Pinard. (Illus.). 88p. per. 10.95 (*0-7600-6146-7*, Pub. by Course Tech) Thomson Learn.

Microsoft Publisher 2000 - Illustrated Introductory. Elizabeth Eisner Reding. (Illus.). 192p. per. 21.95 (*0-7600-6366-4*, Pub. by Course Tech) Thomson Learn.

***Microsoft Publisher 2000: An Introductory Concepts & Techniques.** Cashman Shelly. (C). 1999. text 22.95 (*0-7895-5597-2*) Course Tech.

Microsoft Publisher 2000 at a Glance. Perspection, Inc. Staff. LC 99-13361. 1998. 16.99 (*1-57231-950-X*) Microsoft.

Microsoft Publisher 2000 Complete Concepts & Techniques. Gary B. Shelly et al. 392p. per. 38.95 (*0-7895-5713-4*, Pub. by Course Tech) Thomson Learn.

***Microsoft Publisher 2000.** (C). 2000. pap. text 0.00 (*0-13-016980-3*); pap. text 0.00 (*0-13-016989-7*) HEPC Inc.

***Microsoft Publisher 2000 Bible.** Sue Plumley. LC 99-30304. (Bible Ser.). (Illus.). 877p. 1999. pap. 34.99 (*0-7645-3343-6*) IDG Bks.

Microsoft Publisher 2000 by Design. Luisa Simone. LC 98-48181. 1999. pap. text 29.99 (*1-57231-953-4*) Microsoft.

***Microsoft Publisher 2000 for Dummies.** McCarter. LC 99-61891. (For Dummies Ser.). 384p. 1999. pap. 19.99 (*0-7645-0525-4*) IDG Bks.

***Microsoft Publisher 2000 Step by Step.** ActiveEducation Staff. LC 98-48192. 1999. pap. text 29.99 (*1-57231-987-9*) Microsoft.

Microsoft Publisher 3.0 for Windows 95: Quicktorial. Kreuger & Eisch. 1997. 22.95 (*0-538-67913-1*) Thomson Learn.

***Microsoft Publisher 97 Illustrated Project.** Carol M. Cram & Hirsch. (C). 1998. pap. 23.95 (*0-7600-5843-1*) Thomson Learn.

Microsoft Publisher 98 by Design. Luisa Simone. LC 97-51966. 560p. 29.99 (*1-57231-641-1*) Microsoft.

Microsoft QuickBASIC see QBASIC with an Introduction to Visual BASIC: For Engineering, Mathematis & Sciences

Microsoft QuickBASIC see Brief Course in QBASIC with an Introduction to Visual Basic

Microsoft Quickbasic: Quick Reference Guide. Ed DeJesus. 1993. pap. 12.00 (*1-56243-089-0*, Y-17) DDC Pub.

Microsoft QuickBASIC for Scientists: Guide to Writing Better Programs. James W. Cooper. LC 88-10140. 281p. 1988. pap. 68.50 (*0-471-61301-0*) Wiley.

***Microsoft Rising: And Other Tales of the Silicon Valley.** Ted Lewis. 350p. 1999. pap. 29.95 (*0-7695-0200-8*) IEEE Comp Soc.

Microsoft Secrets. Michael Cusumano. 1997. pap. 14.00 (*0-684-82552-X*) S&S Trade.

Microsoft Secrets: How the World's Most Powerful Software Company Creates Technology, Shapes Markets, & Manages People. Michael A. Cusumano & Richard W. Selby. (Illus.). 416p. 1995. 29.50 (*0-02-874048-3*) Free Pr.

Microsoft Secrets: How the World's Most Powerful Software Company Creates Technology, Shapes Markets, & Manages People. Michael A. Cusumano & Richard W. Selby. 544p. 1998. pap. 16.00 (*0-684-85531-3*, Touchstone) S&S Trade Pap.

Microsoft Site Server 3.0 Bible. Brad Harris. LC QA76.9.C55H367 1998. (Bible Ser.). (Illus.). 984p. 1998. pap. 49.99 incl. cd-rom (*0-7645-3193-X*) IDG Bks.

Microsoft SMS Administrators Survival Guide. Ahsan Farooqi. LC 96-69393. 678p. 1997. pap. text 59.99 incl. cd-rom (*0-672-30984-X*) Sams.

Microsoft SNA Server Training Kit. Microsoft Corporation Staff. LC 98-40875. 450p. 1998. 217.99 incl. cd-rom (*1-57231-932-1*) Microsoft.

***Microsoft SNA Server 4.0 Resource Guide.** Microsoft Corporation Staff. (IT Resource Kits Ser.). (Illus.). 1999. pap. 69.99 (*0-7356-0927-6*) Microsoft.

Microsoft Solutions Framework Programmers Guide. Microsoft Corporation Staff. pap. write for info. (*1-57231-223-8*) Microsoft.

Microsoft Sourcebook for the Help Desk. 2nd ed. Microsoft Corporation Staff. LC 97-832. 400p. 1997. pap. text 49.99 incl. cd-rom (*1-57231-582-2*) Microsoft.

An Asterisk (*) at the beginning of an entry indicates that the title is appearing for the first time.

Microsoft SQL Server: A Developer's Guide. Vince Kellen. 800p. 1995. pap. 49.95 incl. cd-rom (*1-55851-468-6*, M&T Bks) IDG Bks.

Microsoft SQL Server Black Book. Patrick Dalton. 1997. pap. 39.99 (*0-614-28448-1*) Coriolis Grp.

Microsoft SQL Server Black Book. 10th ed. Patrick Dalton. LC 98-123586. 500p. (C). 1997. pap. text 49.99 incl. cd-rom (*1-57610-149-5*) Coriolis Grp.

Sams Microsoft SQL Server 6.5 in 21 Days. Rick Sawtell et al. 636p. 1998. 39.99 (*0-672-31138-0*) Macmillan.

***Microsoft SQL Server 7 OLAP Developer's Guide.** William C. Amo. 384p. 2000. pap. 39.99 (*0-7645-4643-0*) IDG Bks.

Microsoft SQL Server 7 Administrator's Guide. Ron Talmage. LC 98-65195. (Illus.). 770p. 1999. 50.00 (*0-7615-1389-2*) Prima Pub.

Microsoft SQL Server 7 for Dummies. Anthony Mann. LC QA76.9.D3.M3374 1998. (For Dummies Ser.). 384p. 1998. pap. text 29.99 incl. cd-rom (*0-7645-0416-9*) IDG Bks.

Microsoft SQL Server 7 on Site. Robert C. Scoglund. LC 99-10820. (On Site Ser.). 1999. pap. 39.99 (*1-57610-303-X*) Coriolis Grp.

***Microsoft SQL Server 7.0 Database Implementation Online Training Kit.** Microsoft Corporation Staff. 1999. pap. 99.99 incl. cd-rom (*0-7356-0679-X*) Microsoft.

Microsoft SQL Server 6.5 DBA Survival Guide. 2nd ed. Mark Spenik. 912p. 1996. pap. text 49.99 incl. cd-rom (*0-672-30959-9*) Sams.

Microsoft SQL Server 6.5 Unleashed. 3rd ed. David Solomon. 1998. 59.99 (*0-672-31190-9*) Sams.

Microsoft SQL Server 6 Unleashed. 2nd ed. Jeffrey Garbus et al. LC 95-72916. (Illus.). 1008p. 1996. 59.99 incl. cd-rom (*0-672-30903-3*) Sams.

Microsoft SQL Server Survival Guide. Jim Panttaja. LC 96-14607. 432p. 1996. pap. 44.99 (*0-471-12743-4*) Wiley.

Microsoft SQL Server Training: Hands-on Self-Paced Training Kit for Version 6.5, 2 vols. Microsoft Corporation Staff. LC 96-18665. 1400p. 1996. 199.95 (*1-55615-930-7*) Microsoft.

***Microsoft SQL Server 2000 Administrator's Companion.** Jamie R. Garcia & Marci Frohock. 900p. 2000. pap. 59.99 (*0-7356-1051-7*) Microsoft.

***Microsoft SQL Server 2000 Administrator's Pocket Consultant.** William R. Stanek. 2000. pap. 29.99 (*0-7356-1129-7*) Microsoft.

***Microsoft SQL Server 2000 Optimization Guide.** Jenny L. Fields. 600p. 2000. pap. 49.99 (*0-13-088358-1*, Prentice Hall) P-H.

***Microsoft SQL Server 2000 Programming Step by Step.** Rebecca Riordan. 400p. 2000. pap. 49.99 (*0-7356-1142-4*) Microsoft.

Microsoft SQL Server 6.5 Programming Unleased. Peter Debetta et al. (Unleashed Ser.). 900p. 1998. 49.99 (*0-672-31244-1*) Sams.

***Microsoft SQL Server 7 DBA Survival Guide.** 3rd ed. Mark Spenik. LC 97-69134. (Illus.). 1039p. 1999. 49.99 incl. cd-rom (*0-672-31226-3*) Macmillan.

Microsoft SQL Server 7 Programming Unleashed. 2nd ed. John Papa & Matthew Shepker. (Sams Unleashed Series). (Illus.). 946p. 1999. pap. 49.99 (*0-672-31293-X*) Sams.

Microsoft SQL Server 7.0 Administrator's Companion. John Fronckowiak et al. LC 99-22854. (IT Professional Ser.). (Illus.). 887p. 1999. 49.99 incl. cd-rom (*1-57231-815-5*) Microsoft.

Microsoft SQL Server 7.0 Administrator's Pocket Consultant. William R. Stanek. LC 99-33879. 500p. 1999. 29.99 (*0-7356-0596-3*) Microsoft.

***Microsoft SQL Server 7.0 Data Warehousing Online Training.** Microsoft Corporation Staff. 2000. pap., boxed set 99.99 incl. cd-rom (*0-7356-0782-6*) Microsoft Pr.

Microsoft SQL Server 7.0 Database Implementation Training Kit: Exam #70-029. Microsoft Corporation Staff. LC 99-13770. (Training Kit Ser.). 800p. 1999. pap. 99.99 incl. cd-rom (*1-57231-826-0*) Microsoft.

***Microsoft SQL Server 7.0 Performance Tuning Technical Reference.** Marcilina S. Ga & Steve Deluca. LC 99-52145. (gr. 8). 2000. pap. 49.99 (*0-7356-0909-8*) Microsoft.

Microsoft SQL Server 7.0 System Administration Training Kit. Microsoft Corporation Staff. LC 99-13556. 800p. 1999. 99.99 incl. cd-rom (*1-57231-827-9*) Microsoft.

***Microsoft SQL Server 7.0 Training & Resource Bundle.** 1999. pap. 99.99 incl. cd-rom (*0-7356-0924-1*) Microsoft Pr.

***Microsoft SQL 7.0 Resource Guide.** Microsoft Corporation Staff. (Illus.). 1999. pap. 59.99 (*0-7356-0894-6*) Microsoft.

Microsoft Systems: Management Server Training. Microsoft Corporation Staff. LC 97-36002. 500p. 1997. 99.99 incl. cd-rom (*1-57231-614-4*) Microsoft.

***Microsoft Systems Management Server 2.0 Administrator's Companion.** Steven D. Kaczmarek. (gr. 8). 2000. pap. 59.99 (*0-7356-0834-2*) Microsoft.

***Microsoft Systems Management Server 2.0 Resource Guide.** Microsoft Corporation Staff. (IT Resource Kits Ser.). (Illus.). 1999. pap. 79.99 (*0-7356-0928-4*) Microsoft.

Microsoft Systems Management Server 2.0 Training Kit. Microsoft Corporation Staff. LC 99-13364. 500p. 1998. 99.99 incl. cd-rom (*1-57231-834-1*) Microsoft.

Microsoft TCP/IP Training: Hands-On, Self-Paced Training for Internetworking Microsoft TCP/IP on Microsoft Windows NT 4.0. Microsoft Corporation Staff. LC 97-20760. 500p. 1997. 99.99 incl. cd-rom (*1-57231-623-3*) Microsoft.

Microsoft TCP/IP Unleashed. 2nd ed. Timothy Parker et al. 900p. 1999. 49.99 (*0-672-31112-7*) Sams.

Microsoft Team Manager 97 Step by Step. Catapult, Inc. Staff. LC 96-44281. 336p. 29.95 incl. cd-rom (*1-57231-217-3*) Microsoft.

Microsoft Technology: Networking, Concepts, Tools. Shay Woodard. LC 99-192155. 500p. (C). 1998. pap. text 49.99 (*0-13-080558-0*) P-H.

***Microsoft 2000 Windows Professional Handbook.** Louis Columbus. (Illus.). 400p. 2000. pap. 41.95 (*1-58450-009-3*) Chrles River Media.

Microsoft Urban Assault: Inside Moves. Phill Powell et al. LC 98-28533. (Inside Moves Ser.). 224p. 16.99 (*1-57231-861-9*) Microsoft.

Microsoft Visual Basic. Shelly Cashman. (C). 1994. text. write for info. (*0-318-70361-0*) S-W Pub.

Microsoft Visual Basic Deluxe Learning Edition Version 5.0. Microsoft Corporation Staff. 384p. 1997. pap. text 129.99 incl. cd-rom (*1-57231-551-2*) Microsoft.

Microsoft Visual Basic 5.0: Programmer's Guide. Microsoft Corporation Staff. LC 97-828. 912p. 1997. 29.99 (*1-57231-604-7*) Microsoft.

Microsoft Visual Basic 5.0 Developer's Workshop: With CD-ROM. 4th ed. John Craig & Jeff Webb. LC 97-837. 700p. 1997. pap. text 44.99 (*1-57231-436-2*) Microsoft.

Microsoft Visual Basic 5 Step by Step. Michael Halvorson. LC 97-3522. (C). 1998. pap. text 34.99 (*1-57231-435-4*) Microsoft.

Microsoft Visual Basic for Windows. W. Michael Field. (C). 2001. 53.00 (*0-13-260886-3*, Macmillan Coll) P-H.

Microsoft Visual Basic 4: Introductory Concepts & Techniques. John Repede et al. LC 96-32235. 304p. 1996. pap. 38.95 (*0-7895-0728-5*) Course Tech.

Microsoft Visual Basic 4 for Windows 95: Complete Course. Gary B. Shelly & T. Cashman. LC 96-9888. 192p. 1996. pap. 22.95 (*0-7895-1181-9*) Course Tech.

Microsoft Visual Basic Professional 6.0 Step by Step. Michael Halvorson. LC 98-18208. (Step by Step Ser.). (Illus.). 632p. pap. 39.99 (*1-57231-809-0*) Microsoft.

Microsoft Visual Basic 6 Complete Concepts & Techniques. Gary B. Shelly et al. 448p. per. 46.95 (*0-7895-4654-X*, Pub. by Course Tech) Thomson Learn.

***Microsoft Visual Basic 6.0 Development.** Microsoft Corporation Staff. LC 99-33876. (Microsoft Mastering Ser.). 1999. pap. 49.99 (*0-7356-0900-4*) Microsoft.

***Microsoft Visual Basic Six Point O: Certification Guide.** Phillips Sprague. 2000. pap. 26.95 (*0-538-96689-0*) Thomson Learn.

***Microsoft Visual Basic Six Point O: Introduction to Programming.** Phillips Sprague. 1999. pap. 46.95 (*0-538-68818-1*) Thomson Learn.

Microsoft Visual Basic 6.0 Programmer's Guide: Programmer's Guide. Microsoft Corporation Staff. LC 98-14786. 960p. 39.99 (*1-57231-863-5*) Microsoft.

***Microsoft Visual Basic 6.0 Programming/Mastering Solution Set: Complete Two-in-One Learning Solution.** Microsoft Corporation Staff. (Illus.). 1999. pap. 99.99 incl. audio compact disk (*0-7356-0812-1*) Microsoft.

Microsoft Visual Basic 3.0 for Windows: Double Diamond Edition. Gary B. Shelly & T. Cashman. 192p. (C). 1994. mass mkt. 15.00 (*0-87709-879-4*) Course Tech.

Microsoft Visual Basic 5 Language Reference Volume 2: ActiveX Controls, Vol. 2. Microsoft Corporation Staff. LC 97-3523. 600p. 1997. pap. text 24.99 (*1-57231-508-3*) Microsoft.

Microsoft Visual Basic 6; Exam 70-176. Howard Hawhee. 1999. 49.99 (*0-7357-0031-1*) New Riders Pub.

Microsoft Visual Basic 6.0, Deluxe Learning Edition. Microsoft Corporation Staff. LC 98-15687. 1390p. 139.99 incl. cd-rom (*1-57231-873-2*) Microsoft.

Microsoft Visual Basic 6.0 Developer's Workshop: Developer's Workshop. 5th ed. John C. Craig & Jeff Webb. LC 98-34255. 750p. 49.99 incl. cd-rom (*1-57231-883-X*) Microsoft.

***Microsoft Visual Basic 6.0 Fundamentals.** Microsoft Corporation Staff. LC 99-33884. (Microsoft Mastering Ser.). (Illus.). 1999. pap. 49.99 (*0-7356-0898-9*) Microsoft.

Microsoft Visual Basic 6.0 Reference Library: Reference Library. Microsoft Corporation Staff. LC 98-14787. 3284p. 89.99 (*1-57231-864-3*) Microsoft.

Microsoft Visual C++ 6.0 Reference Library: Reference Library. Microsoft Corporation Staff. LC 98-14785. 4729p. 149.99 (*1-57231-865-1*) Microsoft.

Microsoft Visual C++ Language Reference. Microsoft Corporation Staff. LC 97-2404. 750p. 1997. pap. text 29.99 (*1-57231-521-0*) Microsoft.

Microsoft Visual C++ MFC Library Reference, Pt. 1. Microsoft Corporation Staff. LC 97-2421. 1000p. 1997. pap. text 39.99 (*1-57231-518-0*) Microsoft.

Microsoft Visual C++ MFC Library Reference, Pt. 2. Microsoft Corporation Staff. 1000p. 1997. pap. text 39.99 (*1-57231-519-9*) Microsoft.

Microsoft Visual C++ Programmer's References, 6 vols., Set. 2nd ed. Microsoft Corporation Staff. (Professional Editions Ser.). 1995. pap. 159.95 (*1-55615-901-3*) Microsoft.

Microsoft Visual C++ Run-Time Library Reference. Microsoft Corporation Staff. LC 97-2405. 1000p. 1997. pap. text 29.99 (*1-57231-520-2*) Microsoft.

Microsoft Visual C++ 6.0 Programmer's Guide: Programmer's Guide. Beck Zaratian. LC 98-13997. 640p. 39.99 incl. cd-rom (*1-57231-866-X*) Microsoft.

Microsoft Visual C++ 6.0 Deluxe: Learning Ed., 3. Microsoft Corporation Staff. LC 99-13360. 1440p. 1999. boxed set 139.99 (*0-7356-0636-6*) Microsoft.

Microsoft Visual FoxPro 6.0 Programmer's Guide. Microsoft Corporation Staff. LC 98-15689. 832p. 29.99 (*1-57231-868-6*) Microsoft.

Microsoft Visual FoxPro 6.0 Language Reference. Microsoft Corporation Staff. LC 98-7484. 1166p. 39.99 (*1-57231-870-8*) Microsoft.

Microsoft Visual InterDev 6.0 Web Technologies Reference: Web Reference. Microsoft Corporation Staff. LC 98-7485. 1575p. 39.99 (*1-57231-871-6*) Microsoft.

Microsoft Visual InterDev 6.0 Programmer's Guide. Microsoft Corporation Staff. LC 98-18207. 464p. 24.99 (*1-57231-867-8*) Microsoft.

Microsoft Visual Interdev Wizardry. Paul Lomax. 1997. pap. 39.99 (*1-57610-136-3*) Coriolis Grp.

Microsoft Visual InterDev 6.0 Enterprise Developer's Workshop. G. Andrew Duthie. LC 98-42528. 500p. 1998. pap. 49.99 (*0-7356-0568-8*) Microsoft.

Microsoft Visual J++ 6.0 Reference Library: Reference Library. Microsoft Corporation Staff. LC 98-30054. 1800p. 99.99 (*1-57231-872-4*) Microsoft.

Microsoft Visual J++ 1.1 Sourcebook. Jay Cross & Al. Saganich. LC 96-29888. 539p. 1997. pap. text 39.95 incl. cd-rom (*0-471-17840-3*) Wiley.

Microsoft Visual J++ 6.0 Programmer's Guide: Programmer's Guide. Microsoft Corporation Staff. LC 98-30056. 500p. 27.99 (*1-57231-869-4*) Microsoft.

Microsoft Visual J++ 6.0 Developer's Workshop. Shannon Dunn. LC 98-30227. 560p. 1998. 44.99 incl. cd-rom (*1-57231-925-9*) Microsoft.

Microsoft Visual J++ 6.0 Deluxe Learning Edition. deluxe ed. Microsoft Corporation Staff. LC 98-30055. 992p. 1998. 139.99 incl. cd-rom (*1-57231-930-5*) Microsoft.

Microsoft Visual Studio 6 for Dummies. Dummies Technical Press Staff. LC QA76.76.A65M334 1998. (For Dummies Ser.). 500p. 1998. pap. 29.99 incl. cd-rom (*0-7645-0374-X*) IDG Bks.

Microsoft Visual Studio 6.0 Core Reference Set. Microsoft Corporation Staff. LC 98-6655. 3576p. 129.99 (*1-57231-884-8*) Microsoft.

Microsoft vs. Netscape: The Battle for the Internet Infrastructure. Paul Korzeniowski. LC 97-24156. (Illus.). 200p. 1997. pap. 295.00 (*1-56607-989-6*) Comput Tech Res.

Microsoft Way. Randall E. Stross. 336p. 1997. pap. 13.00 (*0-201-32797-X*) Addison-Wesley.

Microsoft Way: The Real Story of How the Company Outsmarts Its Competition. Randall E. Stross. 318p. 1998. text 25.00 (*0-7881-5735-3*) DIANE Pub.

***Microsoft Web Administrator's Pocket Consultant.** William R. Stanek. 400p. 2000. 29.99 (*0-7356-1024-X*) Microsoft.

Microsoft Web Commerce Solutions. Micro Modeling Associates, Inc. Staff. LC 99-10307. 800p. 1999. pap. 49.99 (*0-7356-0579-3*) Microsoft.

***Microsoft Web Publishing Step by Step.** Actoveedication Staff. 368p. 2000. pap. 29.99 (*0-7356-1156-4*) Microsoft.

***Microsoft Windows.** Rich Levin. 2000. pap. 18.95 (*0-7894-5982-5*) DK Pub Inc.

Microsoft Windows Architecture Training. Microsoft Corporation Staff. LC 97-53090. 500p. 1997. 79.99 incl. cd-rom (*1-57231-708-6*) Microsoft.

***Microsoft Windows at a Glance, Millennium.** Jerry Joyce. 2000. pap. 19.99 (*0-7356-0970-5*) Microsoft.

Microsoft Windows CE Programmers Guide. Microsoft Corporation Staff. LC 97-43824. 848p. 1997. pap. text 49.99 incl. cd-rom (*1-57231-643-8*) Microsoft.

***Microsoft Windows CE Resource Kit.** Microsoft Press Staff. (IT Resource Kits Ser.). (Illus.). 2000. pap. text 59.99 (*0-7356-0969-1*) Microsoft.

***Microsoft Windows DNA Exposed.** Bill Wolff et al. LC 98-89190. (Illus.). 270p. 1999. pap. 29.99 (*0-672-31561-0*) Sams.

Microsoft Windows Environment: Changes & Enhancements to the SAS(R) System, Release 6.11. 128p. (C). 1995. pap. 12.00 (*1-55544-271-4*, BR55276) SAS Publ.

Microsoft Windows Environment, Changes & Enhancements to the SAS System, Release 6.10. LC 95-189020. 96p. (C). 1996. pap. 10.00 (*1-55544-632-9*, BR55107) SAS Publ.

Microsoft Windows for Workgroups Version 3.11: Introductory Course Book. DataPower AS Staff. 116p. 1995. pap. text 29.95 (*1-888323-05-1*) DataPower Intl.

***Microsoft Windows Media Player Handbook.** Seth McEvoy. 336p. 2000. pap. 29.99 (*0-7356-1178-5*) Microsoft.

***Microsoft Windows Movie Maker Handbook.** Bill Birney & John Michalakias. 336p. 2000. 29.99 (*0-7356-1180-7*) Microsoft.

Microsoft Windows 95 with Active Desktop & Windows 98. 2nd rev. ed. Duffy. 144p. (C). 1998. pap. text 19.00 (*0-201-45553-6*, Prentice Hall) P-H.

Microsoft Windows 98. Tim Duffy. 104p. (C). 1999. pap. text 25.00 (*0-201-45910-8*, Prentice Hall) P-H.

Microsoft Windows 98. M. Karhula. LC 98-29147. (Visual Ser.). 1998. write for info. (*0-7638-0192-5*) Paradigm MN.

Microsoft Windows 98. 2nd ed. Ken Laudon. (Interactive Computing Ser.). 200p. 1999. 20.00 incl. cd-rom (*0-07-228448-X*) McGraw.

***Microsoft Windows 98 for End Users: Advance.** Course Technology Staff. (SAM's License Card for Course CBT Ser.). (C). 2000. text. write for info. (*0-619-00943-8*) Course Tech.

Microsoft Windows 98: Complete Course. Don Busche & Marly Bergerud. LC 97-48423. 1998. mass mkt. 53.95 (*0-538-72054-9*) S-W Pub.

Microsoft Windows 98: Text with Data Disk, 3.5. M. Karhula et al. LC 98-29147. (Visual Ser.). 160p. 1998. text. write for info. incl. 3.5 hd (*0-7638-0191-7*) Paradigm MN.

Microsoft Windows 98 - Illustrated Advanced. Joan Carey & Steven M. Johnson. (Illus.). 216p. spiral bd. 20.95 (*0-7600-6084-3*, Pub. by Course Tech) Thomson Learn.

Microsoft Windows 98 at a Glance. Jerry Joyce & Marianne Moon. LC 98-9352. 320p. 1998. pap. 16.99 (*1-57231-631-4*) Microsoft.

Microsoft Windows 98 Companion. Martin Matthews. 704p. 29.99 (*1-57231-931-3*) Microsoft.

Microsoft Windows 98 Essentials: Instructor's Guide. Edward J. Coburn. 19.00 (*0-7638-0286-7*) EMC-Paradigm.

***Microsoft Windows 98 Essentials: Text with CD Rom.** Edward J. Coburn. 480p. 1999. 29.95 (*0-7638-0283-2*) EMC-Paradigm.

***Microsoft Windows 98 Field Guide.** Stephen L. Nelson. (Field Guide Ser.). (Illus.). 2000. pap. text 7.99 (*0-7356-1064-9*) Microsoft.

***Microsoft Windows 98 Quick Source Guide.** Quick Source Staff. (Illus.). 6p. 1999. pap. 4.95 (*1-930674-22-8*) Quick Source.

Microsoft Windows 98 Training Kit. Microsoft Corporation Staff. LC 98-22197. 1350p. 99.99 incl. cd-rom (*1-57231-730-2*) Microsoft.

Microsoft Windows 98 - Illustrated Basic. Patrick Carey et al. (Illus.). 184p. spiral bd. 20.95 (*0-7600-6083-5*, Pub. by Course Tech) Thomson Learn.

***Microsoft Windows 95.** Azimuth Interactive Staff. (Inter@ctiveLearning Ser.). (Illus.). 116p. 2000. pap. 19.95 (*1-930581-06-8*) Azimuth.

Microsoft Windows 95. Marly Begerud & Don Busche. (Quicktorial Ser.). 1996. mass mkt. 21.95 (*0-538-66409-6*) S-W Pub.

Microsoft Windows 95. Edward J. Coburn. LC 96-7210. 1996. 32.95 (*1-56118-871-9*); pap. text. write for info. (*1-56118-872-7*) Paradigm MN.

Microsoft Windows 95. Rick Sullivan. (Computer Training Ser.). 132p. 1996. mass mkt., spiral bd. 19.95 incl. 3.5 hd (*0-538-66013-9*) S-W Pub.

***Microsoft Windows 95.** deluxe ed. Azimuth Interactive Staff. (Inter@ctiveLearning Ser.). (Illus.). 116p. 2000. pap. 39.95 incl. cd-rom (*1-930581-07-6*) Azimuth.

Microsoft Windows 95, Incl. instr. resource kit, online comp., test mgr. Neil J. Salkind. (Illustrated Ser.). (Illus.). 144p. (C). 1995. text, mass mkt. 21.95 incl. 3.5 ld (*1-56527-595-0*) Course Tech.

Microsoft Windows 95: Illustrated Brief Edition, Incl. instr. resource kit, online comp., test mgr. Marie L. Swanson. (Illustrated Ser.). (Illus.). 72p. 1995. pap. 10.95 (*0-7600-3274-2*) Course Tech.

Microsoft Windows 95: Illustrated PLUS Edition. Patrick Carey et al. 296p. 1996. teacher ed. 18.50 (*0-7600-4056-7*) Course Tech.

Microsoft Windows 95: Instructor's guide. Edward J. Coburn. 19.00 (*1-56118-873-5*) EMC-Paradigm.

Microsoft Windows 95: Introductory Coursebook. DataPower AS Staff. 151p. 1995. pap. text 29.95 (*1-888323-00-0*) DataPower Intl.

Paradigm Vision Series for Microsoft Windows 95: Text with disk, 3.5. E. Valtanen & T. Vihijarvi. 128p. text 14.95 (*0-7638-0013-9*) EMC-Paradigm.

Microsoft Windows 95 - Advanced, Incl. instr. resource kit, online comp., files. Harry Phillips. (New Perspectives Ser.). (Illus.). 480p. 1996. pap. 48.95 (*0-7600-3572-5*) Course Tech.

Microsoft Windows 95 - Brief, Incl. instr. resource kit, online comp., test mgr. rev. ed. June J. Parsons & Dan Oja. (New Perspectives Ser.). (Illus.). 64p. 1995. pap. 8.00 (*1-56527-287-0*) Course Tech.

Microsoft Windows 95 - Comprehensive, Incl. instr. resource kit, online comp., test mgr. June J. Parsons & Dan Oja. (New Perspectives Ser.). (Illus.). 504p. 1996. pap. 44.95 (*1-56527-998-0*) Course Tech.

Microsoft Windows 95 - Illustrated Plus, Incl. instr. resource kit, test mgr., Web pg. Neil J. Salkind et al. (Illus.). 296p. 1996. text, mass mkt. 38.95 incl. 3.5 ld (*0-7600-4054-0*) Course Tech.

Microsoft Windows 95 - Introductory, Incl. instr. resource kit, online comp., test mgr. expanded rev. ed. June J. Parsons & Dan Oja. (New Perspectives Ser.). (Illus.). 176p. 1996. pap. 21.95 (*0-7600-3489-3*) Course Tech.

Microsoft Windows 95 & Internet Explorer 4.0 Starts Here. Microsoft Press Interactive Staff. 1997. pap. text 29.99 (*1-57231-523-7*) Microsoft.

Microsoft Windows 95 at a Glance. Jerry Joyce & Marianne Moon. LC 96-29986. 1997. pap. text 16.95 (*1-57231-370-6*) Microsoft.

Microsoft Windows 95 Complete Concepts & Techniques. Gary B. Shelly et al. LC 96-38618. 400p. 1996. mass mkt. 38.95 (*0-7895-0300-X*) Course Tech.

***Microsoft Windows 95 Comprehensive.** Parsons & Oja. (C). 2000. pap. 33.50 (*0-619-01990-5*) Course Tech.

Microsoft Windows 95 Developer's Guide. Stefano Maruzzi. 1040p. 1996. pap. text 49.99 incl. cd-rom (*1-56276-335-0*, Ziff-Davis Pr) Que.

Microsoft Windows 95 Introductory Concepts & Techniques. Gary B. Shelly et al. 96p. (C). 1997. mass mkt., teacher ed. 18.50 incl. cd-rom (*0-7895-1323-4*) Course Tech.

***Microsoft Windows 95 Quick Source Guide.** Quick Source Staff. (Illus.). 6p. 1998. pap. 4.95 (*1-930674-21-X*) Quick Source.

Microsoft Windows 95 Resource Kit. Microsoft Corporation Staff. LC 96-175225. (Resource Kit Ser.). 1376p. 1995. pap. 67.95 incl. cd-rom (*1-55615-678-2*) Microsoft.

Microsoft Windows 95 Starts Here! (C). 1995. write for info. (*0-7600-3438-9*) Course Tech.

Microsoft Windows 95 Starts Here. 1997. 29.99 incl. cd-rom (*1-57231-736-1*) Microsoft.

Microsoft Windows 95 Training Kit, Deluxe Multimedia Edition. deluxe ed. Microsoft Corporation Staff. 1200p. 1998. 199.99 incl. cd-rom (*1-57231-830-9*) Microsoft.

Microsoft Windows 95 Training: Hands-On, Self-Paced Training for Supporting Windows 95, 2 vols. Microsoft Corporation Staff. LC 95-36241. (Training Kit Ser.). 1200p. 1995. pap. 199.95 incl. cd-rom (*1-55615-931-5*) Microsoft.

M

Microsoft Windows 95/96 Simplified: Tutorial & Applications. Knowlton. (C). 1997. pap. 34.95 (*0-538-71628-2*) Thomson Learn.

Microsoft Windows NT. 775p. 1998. boxed set 55.00 (*1-57231-911-9*) Microsoft.

Microsoft Windows NT for Graphics Professionals. New Riders Development Group Staff. (Illus.). 420p. (Orig.). 1996. pap. 35.00 (*1-56205-548-8*) New Riders Pub.

Microsoft Windows NT 4 for Workstation QuickStart. Logical Operations Staff. LC 98-160277. 400p. 1996. 29.99 (*1-56276-430-6*, Ziff-Davis Pr) Que.

Microsoft Windows NT 4.0 Network Administrator's Training. Microsoft Corporation Staff. LC 97-829. 800p. 1997. 99.99 (*1-57231-439-7*) Microsoft.

Microsoft Windows NT 4.0 Upgrade Training. Microsoft Corporation Staff. 49.99 (*1-57231-528-8*) Microsoft.

Microsoft Windows NT 4.0 Workstation: Introductory Course Book. (Illus.). 150p. 1997. pap. text 29.95 (*1-888323-13-2*) DataPower Intl.

Microsoft Windows NT 4.0 Workstation: Standard Edition. 10th ed. Neil Salkind et al. (Illustrated Ser.). 192p. (C). 1996. pap. 21.95 (*0-7600-5192-5*) Course Tech.

***Microsoft Windows NT-4 Quick Source Guide.** Quick Source Staff. (Illus.). 6p. 1998. pap. 4.95 (*1-930674-23-6*) Quick Source.

Microsoft Windows NT Resource Kit Version 3.51 Update with CD-ROM. Microsoft Corporation Staff. (Resource Kit Ser.). 272p. 1995. pap. 39.95 incl. cd-rom (*1-55615-929-3*) Microsoft.

***Microsoft Windows NT Server Administrator's Bible.** Kenneth Gregg et al. LC 99-14113. (Bible (IDG) Ser.). (Illus.). 1232p. 1999. pap. 59.99 incl. cd-rom (*0-7645-3213-8*) IDG Bks.

Microsoft Windows NT Server Enterprise Training. Microsoft Corporation Staff. 1999. boxed set 55.00 (*0-7356-0520-3*) Little.

Microsoft Windows NT Server Enterprise Training. Microsoft Corporation Staff. LC 97-43134. 900p. 1997. 99.99 incl. cd-rom (*1-57231-710-8*) Microsoft.

Microsoft Windows NT Server 4.0 One Step at a Time. Microsoft Corporation Staff. (Independent Ser.). 275p. pap. 22.95 (*1-57231-449-4*) Microsoft.

Microsoft Windows NT Server Resource Kit: Supplement Four. Microsoft Corporation Staff. (Resource Kit Ser.). 1998. pap. text 49.99 (*1-57231-806-6*) Microsoft.

Microsoft Windows NT Technical Support Training. Microsoft Corporation Staff. LC 97-830. (Training Kit Ser.). 800p. 1997. pap. 99.99 incl. cd-rom (*1-57231-373-0*) Microsoft.

Microsoft Windows NT Training: Interactive Self-Paced Training & Preparation for the Microsoft Certified Professional Exams, 2 vols. Microsoft Educational Services Staff. LC 97-178163. (Training Kit Ser.). 1320p. 1996. boxed set 199.95 (*1-55615-864-5*) Microsoft.

Microsoft Windows NT Training, International Version: Interactive Self-Paced Training & Preparation for the Microsoft Certified Professional Exams. Microsoft Corporation Staff. (Training Kit Ser.). boxed set 199.95 (*1-57231-278-5*) Microsoft.

Microsoft Windows NT Workstation. Ed. by Microsoft Corporation Staff. 1998. 29.99 (*1-57231-915-1*) Microsoft.

Microsoft Windows NT Workstation 4.0 Starts Here. Microsoft Corporation Staff. (gr. 8). 1997. cd-rom 29.99 (*1-57231-737-X*) Little.

Microsoft Windows NT Workstation 4.0 at a Glance. Jerry Joyce & Marianne Moon. LC 96-29985. 336p. 1997. 16.99 (*1-57231-574-1*) Microsoft.

Microsoft Windows NT Workstation 4.0 Starts Here. Microsoft Press Interactive Staff. 1997. pap. text 29.99 incl. cd-rom (*1-57231-522-9*) Microsoft.

Microsoft Windows NT Workstation Resource Kit. Microsoft Corporation Staff. 1408p. 1996. pap. text 69.95 incl. cd-rom (*1-57231-343-9*) Microsoft.

Microsoft Windows NT Workstation 6 in 1. Jane Calabria. 600p. 1997. 29.99 (*0-7897-1386-1*) Que.

Microsoft Windows NT Workstation Version 4.0 Step by Step. Catapult, Inc. Staff. LC 96-31376. 288p. 29.95 (*1-57231-225-4*) Microsoft.

Microsoft Windows NT 4.0 Administrator's Pocket Consultant. William Stanek. LC 99-10308. 1999. pap. text 29.99 (*0-7356-0574-2*) Microsoft.

Microsoft Windows NT 4.0 Security Technical Reference: Guidelines for Security, Audit & Control. James G. Jumes et al. LC 98-38727. 400p. 1998. 49.99 (*1-57231-818-X*) Microsoft.

***Microsoft Windows NT 4.0-5.0 Server Testing & Troubleshooting.** Gilbert Held. LC 99-30652. (Illus.). 308p. 1999. pap. 42.95 (*1-55622-662-4*) Wordware Pub.

***Microsoft Windows NT 5 BETA Training Kit.** Corporation Microsoft. LC 99-17058. (Illus.). 800p. 1999. pap. 79.99 (*0-7356-0644-7*) Microsoft.

Microsoft Windows NT 5.0. Salkind & Barron. (C). 2000. pap. 21.95 (*0-7600-5473-8*) Course Tech.

Microsoft Windows NT 5.0. Swanson & Barron. (C). 2000. pap. 10.95 (*0-7600-5470-3*) Course Tech.

Microsoft Windows Sound System Book. Ivan Luk. 1994. pap. 24.95 (*0-07-882015-4*) Osborne-McGraw.

***Microsoft Windows Step by Step, Millennium.** Catapult Inc. Staff. 2000. pap. 19.99 (*0-7356-0990-X*) Microsoft.

Microsoft Windows 3.1: Concepts & Applications. Marly Bergerud. (DF - Computer Applications Ser.). (C). 1993. mass mkt. 41.95 (*0-538-70713-5*) S-W Pub.

Microsoft Windows 3.1: Quick Reference Guide. Karl Schwartz. 1992. spiral bd. 12.00 (*1-56243-083-1*, N317) DDC Pub.

Microsoft Windows 3.1 - Illustrated Brief Edition, Incl. instr. resource kit, test bank, transparency. Michael Halvorson. (Illus.). 56p. 1995. pap. 9.95 (*1-56527-596-9*) Course Tech.

Microsoft Windows 3.0. Taylor R. Taylor. (LogicNotes Ser.). (Illus.). (Orig.). 1990. pap. text 24.95 (*0-929978-45-5*) M-USA Busn Systs.

Microsoft Windows 2000 Administrators Reference. 456p. 29.99 (*0-7897-2471-5*) Que.

***Microsoft Windows 2000 Performance Tuning Technical Reference.** Douglas Frisk. 550p. (C). (gr. 8). 2000. pap. 49.99 (*0-7356-0633-1*) Little.

***Microsoft Windows 2000: Advanced.** Salkind et al. (Illustrated Ser.). 2000. 20.95 (*0-619-01759-7*) Course Tech.

***Microsoft Windows 2000: An Introductory Concepts & Techniques.** Cashman Shelly. (C). 2000. text 27.95 (*0-7895-4468-7*) Course Tech.

***Microsoft Windows 2000: Basic.** Kemper. (Illustrated Ser.). 2000. 20.95 (*0-619-01758-9*) Course Tech.

***Microsoft Windows 2000: Brief.** Oja Parsons. (New Perspectives Ser.). (C). 2000. text 11.95 (*0-7600-6548-9*) Course Tech.

***Microsoft Windows 2000: Complete Concepts & Techniques.** Cashman Shelly. (C). 2000. text 38.95 (*0-7895-4542-X*) Course Tech.

***Microsoft Windows 2000 Beginning Course.** Bergerud & Busche. 2000. pap. 19.95 (*0-538-72417-X*) Thomson Learn.

***Microsoft Windows 2000 Beta Upgrade Training Kit.** Microsoft Corporation Staff. LC 99-33261. 1999. pap. 79.99 (*1-57231-894-5*) Microsoft.

***Microsoft Windows 2000 Comprehensive.** Bergerud & Busche. (Computer Applications Ser.). (C). 2000. pap., wbk. ed. 9.95 (*0-538-72404-8*) Sth-Wstrn College.

***Microsoft Windows 2000 Installation & Configuration Handbook with CD-ROM.** Jim Boyce. LC 99-65437. (Illus.). 598p. 2000. pap. 39.99 (*0-7897-2133-3*) Que.

***Microsoft Windows 2000 MCSE Core Requirements Training Kit.** Microsoft Press Staff. (IT-Training Kits Ser.). (Illus.). 2000. pap. 199.99 (*0-7356-1130-0*) Microsoft.

***Microsoft Windows 2000 Professional Unleashed.** 914p. 2000. pap. 49.99 incl. cd-rom (*0-672-31742-7*) Sams.

***Microsoft Windows 2000 Professional Resource Kit.** Microsoft Corporation Staff. LC 99-88818. (Illus.). 1808p. 2000. pap. text 69.99 incl. cd-rom (*1-57231-808-2*) Microsoft.

***Microsoft Windows 2000 Professional Companion.** Craig Stinson & Carl Siechert. 800p. (gr. 8). 2000. pap. 39.99 (*1-57231-838-4*) Little.

***Microsoft Windows 2000 Professional Expert Companion.** Craig Stinson & Carl Siechert. 2000. pap. 39.99 (*0-7356-0855-5*) Microsoft.

***Microsoft Windows 2000 Professional.** Brian Underdahl. LC 99-49234. (Teach Yourself Ser.). 440p. 1999. pap. 19.99 (*0-7645-4602-3*) IDG Bks.

***Microsoft Windows 2000 Secrets.** Brian Livingston et al. LC 99-48112. (Secrets Ser.). (Illus.). 744p. 2000. pap. 39.99 incl. cd-rom (*0-7645-3413-0*) IDG Bks.

Microsoft Windows 2000 Security Technical Reference. John Hayday. 49.99 (*0-7356-0858-X*) Microsoft.

***Microsoft Windows 2000 Server Administrator's Companion.** Charlie Russell & Sharon Crawford. LC 99-48555. 1520p. 2000. 69.99 incl. cd-rom (*1-57231-819-8*) Microsoft.

***Microsoft Windows 2000 Server Resource Kit.** Microsoft Corporation. LC 99-45616. 2000. 299.99 incl. cd-rom (*1-57231-805-8*) Microsoft.

***Microsoft Windows 2000 Server Unleashed.** Chris Miller et al. (Unleashed Ser.). 800p. 2000. pap. 49.99 (*0-672-31739-7*) Sams.

Microsoft Windows User Experience: Official Guidelines for User Interface Developers & Designers. Microsoft Corporation Staff. LC 99-36326. 864p. 1999. pap. 49.99 (*0-7356-0566-1*) Microsoft.

Microsoft Windows 2000: Configuration & Troubleshooting. 1000p. 1920. 49.99 (*0-672-31878-4*) Sams.

***Microsoft Windows 2000-Essential Concepts & Techniques.** Shelly. (Shelly Cashman Ser.). (C). 2000. pap. 9.95 (*0-7895-5982-X*) Course Tech.

Microsoft Windows 2000 Professional. Miller. LC 99-59927. (Computer Applications Ser.). 2000. pap. 46.95 (*0-538-68910-2*) Thomson Learn.

***Microsoft Windows 2000 TCP/IP Protocols & Services Technical Reference.** Thomas Lee & Joseph E. Davies. LC 99-56120. 800p. (gr. 8). 2000. pap. 49.99 (*0-7356-0556-4*) Microsoft.

Microsoft Windows 3.1: A Quick Study. Margaret Brown. 1992. teacher ed. 5.00 (*1-56243-082-3*, MW-TM); teacher ed. 5.00 (*1-56243-366-0*, MW-TM); spiral bd. 27.00 (*1-56243-081-5*, WQS-1) DDC Pub.

Microsoft Windows 32 Programmer's Reference Vol. 2: Functions A-G. 1995. pap. 34.95 (*1-55615-687-1*) Microsoft.

***Microsoft Windows 95 Corporate Migration Kit.** Microsoft Corporation Staff. 1998. boxed set 99.95 (*1-57231-266-1*) Microsoft.

Microsoft Windows 95 New Perspectives. Dan Oja & June Parsons. (C). 1997. spiral bd. 36.00 (*0-7600-7264-7*) Thomson Learn.

Microsoft Windows 98. 2nd ed. Laudon. 96p. 1999. pap. 15.31 (*0-07-228567-2*) McGraw.

Microsoft Windows 98: Complete Course. Bergerud & Busche. (Computer Applications Ser.). 1998. mass mkt. 35.25 (*0-538-72119-7*) S-W Pub.

***Microsoft Windows 98: Core Concepts & Applications.** Edward J. Coburn. LC 98-51282. 1998. write for info. (*0-7638-0282-4*) Paradigm MN.

***Microsoft Windows 98: Introduction Web.** Gary B. Shelly et al. (C). 1998. pap. 27.95 (*0-7895-5619-7*) Course Tech.

Microsoft Windows 98: Quick Reference. Keith Powell. LC 99-62269. 1999. pap. 9.99 (*0-7897-2030-2*) Que.

***Microsoft Windows 98: Quicktorial.** Bergerud & Busche. 1998. pap. 22.95 (*0-538-72062-X*); pap. 16.75 (*0-538-72064-6*) Thomson Learn.

***Microsoft Windows 98 Complete Concepts & Techniques.** Shelly Cashman & Forsythe. (C). 1998. pap. 44.95 (*0-7895-4746-5*) Course Tech.

***Microsoft Windows 98 Illustrated.** Mary Kemper Barron & Chet Lyskawa. (C). 1998. pap. 10.95 (*0-7600-5959-4*) Thomson Learn.

Microsoft Windows 98 Plus. Carey & Salkind. (Illus.). (C). 1998. pap. 38.95 (*0-7600-5485-1*) Course Tech.

Microsoft Windows 98 Resource Kit. Microsoft Corporation Staff. LC 98-2768. 1766p. 1998. 69.99 incl. cd-rom (*1-57231-644-6*) Microsoft.

Microsoft Windows '98 Simplified: Tutorial. Knowlton. (Computer Applications Ser.). 1998. mass mkt. 25.50 (*0-538-72047-6*) S-W Pub.

Microsoft Windows 98 Step by Step. Catapult, Inc. Staff. LC 98-13999. 320p. 1997. 29.99 incl. 3.5 hd (*1-57231-683-7*) Microsoft.

Microsoft Word: Easy Reference Guides for IBM & Macintosh. Connie Morrison. 1991. text, mass mkt. 7.95 incl. mac hd (*0-538-61758-6*); text, mass mkt. 7.95 incl. disk (*0-538-61757-8*) S-W Pub.

***Microsoft Word: Good-Looking Documents.** DK Publishing Staff. (Essential Computers Ser.). (Illus.). 72p. 2000. pap. 6.95 (*0-7894-5534-X*, D K Ink) DK Pub Inc.

***Microsoft Word: Simple Projects.** Teacher Created Materials Staff. (Illus.). 2000. pap. 18.95 incl. cd-rom (*1-57690-439-3*) Tchr Create Mat.

***Microsoft Word: Tables, Charts & Graphs.** DK Publishing Staff. (Essential Computers Ser.). (Illus.). 72p. 2000. pap. 6.95 (*0-7894-5535-8*, D K Ink) DK Pub Inc.

Microsoft Word: The Useable Portable Guide. Jon Haber & Herbert R. Haber. (Illus.). 32p. (Orig.). (C). 1989. pap. text 4.95 (*0-945765-06-1*) Useable Portable Pubns.

Microsoft Word: Tutorial & Applications. Cluck. (DF - Computer Applications Ser.). 1990. mass mkt. 24.95 (*0-538-60385-2*) S-W Pub.

Microsoft Word: Word 97 text with MOUS Ready CD-ROM. Nita Hewitt Rutkosky. 54.00 (*0-7638-0298-0*) EMC-Paradigm.

Microsoft Word 2000. Hutchinson. LC 99-17736. 208p. 1999. spiral bd. 19.06 (*0-07-233795-8*) McGraw.

Microsoft Word 7.0 PAL. (C). 1997. write for info. (*0-13-266073-3*) P-H.

Microsoft Word a Practical Approach. Cluck. (DF - Computer Applications Ser.). (C). 1990. mass mkt., wbk. ed. 33.95 (*0-538-60389-5*) S-W Pub.

Microsoft Word 5.5 Procedures Manual. Dennis P. Curtin. 287p. 1991. pap. text 19.00 (*0-13-581364-6*, 220302) P-H.

Microsoft Word 5.5 Quick Reference Guide. 1991. pap. 12.00 (*1-56243-040-8*, E-17) DDC Pub.

Microsoft Word 5.5 Quick Reference Guide. 19.95 (*1-56351-009-X*, G149) Microref Educ Systs.

Microsoft Word 5.1 - Macintosh: Easy Reference Guide. Connie Morrison. LC 93-19714. 1994. mass mkt. 7.95 (*0-538-62676-3*) S-W Pub.

Microsoft Word 5.0 Simplified for the IBM PC. David Bolocan & Robert Bixby. (Illus.). 368p. 1993. pap. 19.95 (*0-685-47250-7*, 3318) McGraw-Hill Prof.

***Microsoft Word for Terrified Teachers.** Paula Patton & Karla Neeley Hase. Ed. by Kathy Humrichouse. 304p. 1999. pap., teacher ed. 24.95 (*1-57690-438-5*, TCM2438) Tchr Create Mat.

Microsoft Word for the IBM PC. Leo J. Scanlon. LC 84-18149. (Personal Computing Ser.). 156p. 1986. 27.95 (*0-13-581729-3*) P-H.

Microsoft Word for the Macintosh. Danny Goodman. LC 94-8360. 1994. write for info. (*0-02-801052-3*) Glencoe.

Microsoft Word for Windows. rev. ed. Herbert L. Tyson. 1991. 24.95 (*0-8306-3072-4*); 24.95 (*0-8306-3076-7*) McGraw-Hill Prof.

Microsoft Word for Windows: Tutorial/Applications. Ann Ambrose. (WP - Word Processing Concepts Ser.). (C). 1994. mass mkt. 16.95 (*0-538-70948-0*) S-W Pub.

Microsoft Word for Windows in One Hour for Lawyers. LC 95-83182. 1995. pap. 29.95 (*1-57073-261-2*, 511-0358) Amer Bar Assn.

Microsoft Word for Windows 95 (Version 7.0) by PicTorial. Dennis P. Curtin. (Pictorial Ser.). 352p. (C). 1996. spiral bd. 37.33 (*0-13-238387-X*) P-H.

Microsoft Word for Windows 95. Gary B. Shelly & T. Cashman. LC 96-36476. 400p. 1996. pap. 38.95 (*0-7895-0719-6*) Course Tech.

Microsoft Word for Windows 95. Rick Sullivan. (Computer Training Ser.). 140-180p. 1996. spiral bd. 21.95 incl. 3.5 hd (*0-538-66008-2*) S-W Pub.

Microsoft Word for Windows 95: Double Diamond. Gary B. Shelly & T. Cashman. 208p. 1996. pap. 22.95 (*0-7895-0738-2*) Course Tech.

Microsoft Word for Windows 95: Quick Course. Murphy. (DF - Computer Applications Ser.). 1996. mass mkt. 22.95 (*0-538-71469-7*) S-W Pub.

Microsoft Word for Windows 95: The Complete Reference. Mary Campbell & Gabrielle A. Lawrence. LC 96-135032. (The Complete Reference Ser.). 880p. 1995. pap. text 29.95 (*0-07-882150-9*) McGraw.

Microsoft Word for Windows 95 Made Easy: The Basics & Beyond! Alan Neibauer. (Made Easy Ser.). 480p. 1995. pap. text 24.95 (*0-07-882152-5*) McGraw.

Microsoft Word for Windows 95 Quicktorial. Patricia Murphy. (DF - Computer Applications Ser.). 1996. pap. 21.95 (*0-538-71551-0*) S-W Pub.

Microsoft Word for Windows 97 Made Easy Easy Short Course: Version 7.0. Katie Layman & Lavaugh Hart. LC 97-23744. 429p. (C). 1997. pap. text 51.00 (*0-13-676818-0*) P-H.

Microsoft Word for Windows Revealed. Herbert L. Tyson. 1991. 24.95 (*0-07-065740-8*) McGraw.

Microsoft Word for Windows 2.0: A Professional Approach. Deborah A Hinkle. LC 92-42254. 1993. write for info. (*0-02-800382-9*) Glencoe.

Microsoft Word for Windows 2.0: Easy Reference Guide. Connie Morrison. LC 93-33039. 1995. mass mkt. 9.95 (*0-538-63383-2*) S-W Pub.

Microsoft Word 4.0-5.0 Quick Reference Guide. 1990. pap. 19.95 (*0-913365-59-9*) Microref Educ Systs.

Microsoft Word 4.0 Quick Reference. 1988. pap. 19.95 (*0-913365-16-5*) Microref Educ Systs.

Microsoft Word 4 Procedures Manual. Dennis P. Curtin. LC 88-12106. 1988. pap. 18.00 (*0-13-964305-2*) P-H.

***Microsoft Word Intermediate: Practice & Reference Guide.** Juanita B. Tischendorf. (Illus.). vi, 163p. 1999. pap. text 25.00 (*1-928613-05-5*) J Tischendorf.

***Microsoft Word Introduction: Practice & Reference Guide.** Juanita B. Tischendorf. (Illus.). ix, 194p. 1999. pap. text 25.00 (*1-928613-01-2*) J Tischendorf.

Microsoft Word Macintosh: The Useable Portable Guide. Jon Haber & Herbert R. Haber. (Illus.). 32p. (Orig.). 1989. pap. 4.95 (*0-945765-11-8*) Useable Portable Pubns.

Microsoft Word Macintosh Version 5.1. Smith. (DF - Computer Applications Ser.). 1994. mass mkt., wbk. ed. 30.95 (*0-538-62672-0*) S-W Pub.

Microsoft Word Made Easy. Leo J. Scanlon. (Personal Computing Ser.). (Illus.). 144p. 1985. pap. text 12.95 (*0-317-13087-0*) P-H.

Microsoft Word 97. Pamela W. Adams & Kathryn K. Baskett. Ed. by Susan D. Carnes. (Microsoft Office 97 Ser.). (Illus.). 183p. 1997. pap. text 44.95 (*1-58163-072-7*) CPI Train.

***Microsoft Word 97.** Azimuth Interactive Staff. (Inter@ctiveLearning Ser.). (Illus.). 164p. 2000. pap. 19.95 (*1-930581-04-1*) Azimuth.

Microsoft Word 97. Mayo. LC 98-158672. (Quick Reference Guide Ser.). pap., spiral bd. 27.00 (*1-56243-455-1*, G-26) DDC Pub.

Microsoft Word 97. Nita H. Rutkosky. LC 97-20994. 1997. write for info. (*0-7638-0094-5*); pap. write for info. (*0-7638-0095-3*) Paradigm MN.

Microsoft Word 97. Marie Swanson. 1997. pap. text 24.99 (*0-7600-5608-0*) Course Tech.

***Microsoft Word 97.** deluxe ed. Azimuth Interactive Staff. (Inter@ctiveLearning Ser.). (Illus.). 164p. 2000. pap. 39.95 incl. cd-rom (*1-930581-05-X*) Azimuth.

Microsoft Word 97: Advanced Courseware. (Illus.). 170p. 1997. pap. text 32.95 (*1-888323-20-5*) DataPower Intl.

Microsoft Word 97: Complete Concepts & Techniques. 10th ed. Gary B. Shelly et al. (Shelly Cashman Ser.). 400p. (C). 1997. mass mkt. 38.95 (*0-7895-1338-2*) Course Tech.

Microsoft Word 97: Double Diamond Edition. 10th ed. Gary B. Shelly et al. (Shelly Cashman Ser.). 208p. (C). 1997. mass mkt. 22.95 (*0-7895-2750-2*) Course Tech.

Microsoft Word 97: Economy Pack. Paula Ladd. (Illus.). (C). 1998. pap. text 25.99 (*1-57676-010-3*) Scott Jones Pubng.

Microsoft Word 97: Illustrated Projects. 10th ed. Carol M. Cram. (Illustrated Ser.). (Illus.). 160p. (C). 1997. pap. 19.95 (*0-7600-5123-2*) Course Tech.

Microsoft Word 97: Instructor's Guide. Nita H. Rutkosky. 24.00 (*0-7638-0071-6*) EMC-Paradigm.

Microsoft Word 97: Introductory Coursebook. (Illus.). 170p. 1997. pap. text 29.95 (*1-888323-16-7*) DataPower Intl.

Microsoft Word 97: Text with Data Disk, 3.5. Outi Lammi & Jukka Kolari. LC 97-35439. (Paradigm Visual Ser.). 128p. 1997. pap. write for info. incl. 3.5 hd (*0-7638-0087-2*) Paradigm MN.

Microsoft Word 97 - Visual Basic Step by Step. Michael Halvorson & Chris Kinata. LC 97-8035. 384p. 1997. pap. text 34.99 (*1-57231-388-9*) Microsoft.

Microsoft Word 97 Advanced. Pamela W. Adams. Ed. by Sara R. Pressley. (Microsoft Office 97 Ser.). (Illus.). 116p. 1998. pap. text 28.95 (*1-58163-064-6*) CPI Train.

Microsoft Word 97 at a Glance. Jerry Joyce & Marianne Moon. LC 96-36631. (At a Glance Ser.). (Illus.). 320p. 1997. pap. 16.95 (*1-57231-366-8*) Microsoft.

Microsoft Word 97 Developer's Handbook. Catapult, Inc., Staff. Date not set. 39.99 (*1-57231-453-2*) Microsoft.

***Microsoft Word 97 Field Guide.** Stephen L. Nelson. (Field Guide Ser.). (Illus.). 2000. pap. 7.99 (*0-7356-1059-2*) Microsoft.

Microsoft Word 97 for Windows. Sarah E. Hutchinson & Glen Coulthard. LC 97-178392. 224p. (C). 1997. text 21.00 (*0-256-25996-8*, Irwn McGrw-H) McGrw-H Hghr Educ.

Microsoft Word 97 for Windows 95. Patricia Murphy. (Quicktorial Ser.). 1997. pap. text 19.95 (*0-538-67966-2*) S-W Pub.

Microsoft Word 97 for Windows Quickstart. Jim O'Shea. LC 97-160191. 352p. 1996. pap. text 29.99 incl. cd-rom (*1-56276-471-3*, Ziff-Davis Pr) Que.

Microsoft Word 97 for Windows. Sullivan. (IN - Computer Training Ser.). 1998. pap. 20.95 (*0-538-68014-8*) S-W Pub.

Microsoft Word 97 for Windows. Rick Sullivan. (Computer Training Ser.). 1997. pap. text 19.95 (*0-538-68015-6*) S-W Pub.

Microsoft Word 97 for Windows: Illustrated PLUS Edition. 10th ed. Marie L. Swanson. (Illustrated Ser.). (Illus.). 480p. (C). 1997. pap. 38.95 (*0-7600-4698-0*) Course Tech.

Microsoft Word 97 Intermediate. Pamela W. Adams & Kathryn K. Baskett. Ed. by Susan D. Carnes. (Microsoft Office 97 Ser.). (Illus.). 103p. 1998. pap. text 28.95 (*1-58163-057-3*) CPI Train.

An Asterisk (*) at the beginning of an entry indicates that the title is appearing for the first time.

Microsoft Word 97 Made Easy: Extended Course. Katie Layman & Lavaughn Hart. LC 97-29748. 528p. (C). 1997. pap. text 65.00 (*0-13-676826-1*) P-H.

Microsoft Word 97 Quick Reference. Patty Winter. LC 97-65541. 224p. 1997. 16.99 (*0-7897-1211-3*) Que.

***Microsoft Word 97 Quick Source Guide.** Quick Source Staff. (Illus.). 6p. 1998. pap. 4.95 (*1-930674-17-1*) Quick Source.

Microsoft Word 97 Step by Step, Advanced Topics. Catapult, Inc., Staff. LC 97-10663. 300p. 1997. pap. text 29.99 (*1-57231-563-6*) Microsoft.

Microsoft Word 97 Step by Step, Complete Course, 2 Vols. Catapult, Inc., Staff. 672p. 1997. pap. text 49.99 incl. cd-rom (*1-57231-579-2*) Microsoft.

Microsoft Word 97 Step by Step. Catapult, Inc. Staff. LC 96-44021. 320p. 29.95 (*1-57231-313-7*) Microsoft.

Microsoft Word 97 for Engineers. 2nd ed. Sheryl S. Sorby. 128p. (C). 1997. pap. text 21.33 (*0-201-35092-0*, Prentice Hall) P-H.

Microsoft Word on the Macintosh. Judy R. Smith. 1991. mass mkt. 27.95 (*0-538-60911-7*) S-W Pub.

Microsoft Word 7: Instructor's Guide. Nita H. Rutkosky. 24.00 (*1-56118-890-5*) EMC-Paradigm.

Microsoft Word 7 Essentials: Instructor's Guide. Nita H. Rutkosky. 24.00 (*1-56118-894-8*) EMC-Paradigm.

Microsoft Word 7 for Windows 95 - Introductory, Incl. instr. resource kit, test mgr., labs, files. Beverly B. Zimmerman & S. Scott Zimmerman. (New Perspectives Ser.). (Illus.). 328p. 1996. pap. 30.95 (*0-7600-3544-X*) Course Tech.

Microsoft Word 7 for Windows 95 - Comprehensive, Incl. instr. resource kit, test mgr., labs, files. Beverly B. Zimmerman & S. Scott Zimmerman. (New Perspectives Ser.). (Illus.). 632p. 1996. text, mass mkt. 42.95 incl. 3.5 ld (*0-7600-3545-8*) Course Tech.

Microsoft Word 7 for Windows 95 - Illustrated Plus, Incl. instr. resource kit, test mgr., online. Marie L. Swanson. (Illustrated Ser.). (Illus.). 384p. 1996. text, mass mkt. 38.95 incl. 3.5 ld (*0-7600-3748-5*) Course Tech.

Microsoft Word 7 for Windows 95 - Illustrated Brief Edition, Incl. instr. resource kit, test mgr., Web pg. Marie L. Swanson. (Illus.). 120p. 1995. text, mass mkt. 11.95 incl. 3.5 ld (*0-7600-3810-4*) Course Tech.

Microsoft Word 7 for Windows 95, Incl. instr. resource kit, test mgr., Web pg. Marie L. Swanson & Shari A. Dornquast. (Illustrated Ser.). (Illus.). 216p. 1995. pap. 20.95 incl. 3.5 ld (*0-7600-3524-5*) Course Tech.

Microsoft Word 7 for Windows 95: Essentials. Nita H. Rutkosky. LC 96-10898. 1996. pap. text 31.95 (*1-56118-892-1*) Paradigm MN.

Microsoft Word 7 for Windows 95: Illustrated Projects. 10th ed. Carol M. Cram. (Illustrated Ser.). (Illus.). 160p. (C). 1996. pap. 19.95 (*0-7600-4678-6*) Course Tech.

Microsoft Word 7.0. Pamela W. Adams & Kathryn K. Baskett. Ed. by Susan D. Carnes. (Microsoft Office 95 Ser.). (Illus.). 161p. 1997. pap. text 44.95 (*1-58163-046-8*) CPI Train.

Microsoft Word 7.0: Text with Data Disk, 3.5. E. Valtanen et al. 128p. text 14.95 incl. disk (*0-7638-0011-2*) EMC-Paradigm.

Microsoft Word 7.0 Advanced. Pamela W. Adams & Kathryn K. Baskett. Ed. by Susan D. Carnes. (Microsoft Office 95 Ser.). (Illus.). 118p. 1997. pap. text 28.95 (*1-58163-039-5*) CPI Train.

Microsoft Word 7.0 Intermediate. Pamela W. Adams & Kathryn K. Baskett. Ed. by Susan D. Carnes. (Microsoft Office 95 Ser.). (Illus.). 86p. 1997. pap. text 28.95 (*1-58163-038-7*) CPI Train.

Microsoft Word 7.0 Introduction. Pamela W. Adams & Kathryn K. Baskett. Ed. by Susan D. Carnes. (Microsoft Office 95 Ser.). (Illus.). 82p. 1997. pap. text 28.95 (*1-58163-037-9*) CPI Train.

Microsoft Word 7.0 for Windows 95. Sarah E. Hutchinson & Glen Coulthard. 232p. (C). 1996. write for info. (*0-256-22958-9*, Irwn McGrw-H) McGrw-H Hghr Educ.

Microsoft Word 7.0 for Windows 95. Sarah E. Hutchinson & Glen J. Coulthard. LC 96-11145. (Advantage Series for Computer Education). (Illus.). 232p. (C). 1996. text 25.00 (*0-256-22048-4*, Irwn McGrw-H) McGrw-H Hghr Educ.

Microsoft Word 7.0 for Windows 95: Advanced Coursebook. Datapower A/S Staff. (Illus.). 1996. pap. text 32.95 (*1-888323-10-8*) DataPower Intl.

Microsoft Word 7.0 for Windows 95: Applications for Reinforcement. Wendt & Jaehne. (DF - Computer Applications Ser.). 1996. mass mkt. 31.95 (*0-538-71455-7*) S-W Pub.

Microsoft Word 7.0 for Windows 95: Complete Course. Morrison. LC 96-323. (DF - Computer Applications Ser.). 1996. mass mkt. 51.95 (*0-538-71519-7*) S-W Pub.

Microsoft Word 7.0 for Windows 95: Introductory Coursebook. 150p. (Orig.). 1996. pap. text 29.95 (*1-888323-08-6*) DataPower Intl.

Microsoft Word 7.0 for Windows 95: Tutorial & Applications. Morrison. LC 96-12649. (DF - Computer Applications Ser.). 1996. mass mkt. 39.95 (*0-538-71522-7*) S-W Pub.

Microsoft Word 7.0 for Windows 95: Tutorial & Applications. Morrison. (DF - Computer Applications Ser.). 1996. mass mkt., student ed. 37.95 (*0-538-71524-3*) S-W Pub.

Microsoft Word 7.0 for Windows 95. Timothy J. O'Leary & Linda I. O'Leary. LC 95-82266. (C). 1996. pap. text 21.50 (*0-07-049104-6*) McGraw.

Microsoft Word 6 for the Macintosh Step by Step. Catapult, Inc., Staff. LC 94-15138. (Step by Step Ser.). 336p. 1994. pap. text 29.95 incl. disk (*1-55615-643-X*) Microsoft.

Microsoft Word Six for Windows: Tutorial & Application. Morrison & Lewis. 1995. 46.50 (*0-538-64763-9*) Thomson Learn.

Microsoft Word 6 for Windows - Illustrated Brief Edition, Incl. instr. resource kit, test bank, transparency. Marie L. Swanson. (Illustrated Ser.). (Illus.). 104p. (C). 1995. pap. 11.95 (*1-56527-592-6*) Course Tech.

Microsoft Word 6 for Windows - New Perspectives Introductory, Incl. instr. resource kit, test bank, transparency. Cheryl L. Willis. (New Perspectives Ser.). (Illus.). 304p. (C). 1994. text 20.25 (*1-56527-153-X*) Course Tech.

Microsoft Word 6 for Windows - New Perspectives Comprehensive, Incl. instr. resource kit, test bank, transparency. Cheryl L. Willis. (New Perspectives Ser.). (Illus.). 584p. (C). 1994. pap. 28.50 (*1-56527-160-2*) Course Tech.

Microsoft Word 6.0: Basics & Beyond. M. G. Detienne. (Illus.). 118p. pap. text 29.00 (*1-887580-06-9*) Tec Trek.

Microsoft Word 6.0 & Excel 5.0 for Windows. 2nd ed. Sarah E. Hutchinson et al. (C). 1996. text 19.95 (*0-256-23088-9*, Irwn McGrw-H) McGrw-H Hghr Educ.

Microsoft Word 6.0 for Macintosh. Patricia Murphy. (Quicktorial Ser.). (C). 1996. mass mkt. 21.95 (*0-538-71572-3*) S-W Pub.

Microsoft Word 6.0 for Macintosh: Quick Course. Murphy. (DF - Computer Applications Ser.). 1996. mass mkt. 21.95 (*0-538-71570-7*) S-W Pub.

Microsoft Word 6.0 for Windows. Hinkle. 1995. teacher ed. write for info. incl. disk (*0-02-803086-9*) Glencoe.

Microsoft Word 6.0 for Windows - A Practical Approach. Morrison. (DF - Computer Applications Ser.). (C). 1994. mass mkt. 44.95 (*0-538-71275-9*) S-W Pub.

Microsoft Word 6.0 for Windows. Timothy J. O'Leary & Linda I. O'Leary. LC 94-78092. (C). 1994. pap. text 12.50 (*0-07-049041-4*) McGraw.

Microsoft Word 6.0 for Windows. Nita H. Ruskosky. 1994. pap. text, teacher ed. 19.00 (*1-56118-734-8*) Paradigm MN.

Microsoft Word 6.0 for Windows. Nita H. Rutkosky. LC 94-5236. 1995. pap. text 38.95 (*1-56118-738-0*) Paradigm MN.

Microsoft Word 6.0 for Windows. Rick Sullivan. (Computer Training Ser.). (C). 1994. spiral bd. 20.95 (*0-538-64087-1*) S-W Pub.

Microsoft Word 6.0 for Windows. Rick Sullivan. (Computer Training Ser.). 144p. 1995. text 17.95 (*0-538-63423-5*) S-W Pub.

Microsoft Word 6.0 for Windows. 2nd ed. Sarah E. Hutchinson & Glen Coulthard. 208p. (C). 1995. text 25.00 (*0-256-20228-1*, Irwn McGrw-H) McGrw-H Hghr Educ.

Microsoft Word 6.0 for Windows: Application for Reinforcement. Wendt. (DF - Computer Applications Ser.). 1995. mass mkt. 31.95 (*0-538-64773-6*) S-W Pub.

Microsoft Word 6.0 for Windows: Comprehensive. 10th ed. Cheryl Willis. (New Perspectives Ser.). 584p. (C). 1996. pap. 42.95 (*0-7600-4580-1*) Course Tech.

Microsoft Word 6.0 for Windows: Double Diamond. Gary B. Shelly & T. Cashman. LC 95-106972. 184p. 1994. mass mkt. 15.50 (*0-87709-878-6*) Course Tech.

Microsoft Word 6.0 for Windows: Easy Reference Guide. Rigola. (DF - Computer Applications Ser.). 144-160p. 1996. mass mkt. 9.95 (*0-538-71462-X*) S-W Pub.

Microsoft Word 6.0 for Windows: Introductory Course Book. DataPower AS Staff. 170p. 1995. pap. text 29.95 (*1-888323-06-X*) DataPower Intl.

Microsoft Word 6.0 for Windows: Quick Course. Murphy. (DF - Computer Applications Ser.). 1995. mass mkt. 15.95 (*0-538-64846-5*) S-W Pub.

Microsoft Word 6.0 for Windows: Text with disk, 3.5. Nita H. Rutkosky. LC 94-5236. 1994. pap. text 38.95 (*1-56118-732-1*) Paradigm MN.

Microsoft Word 6.0 for Windows at a Glance: The Fastest & Easiest Way to Learn Microsoft Word 6.0 for Windows. Russell A. Stultz. (At a Glance Ser.). 128p. (Orig.). 1995. pap. 15.95 (*1-55622-437-0*) Wordware Pub.

Microsoft Word 6.0 for Windows & Word 95 Simplified: Tutorial & Applications. Jaehne. (DF - Computer Applications Ser.). 1996. mass mkt. 35.95 (*0-538-65028-1*) S-W Pub.

Microsoft Word 6.0 Mac: Tutorial & Applications. Morrison. (DF - Computer Applications Ser.). 1995. mass mkt. 36.95 (*0-538-64914-3*) S-W Pub.

Microsoft Word 6.0-7.0 College Keyboard - Complete. 14th ed. Duncan et al. LC 98-131509. (TA - Typing/Keyboarding Ser.). (C). 1998. pap. 81.95 (*0-538-71538-3*) S-W Pub.

Microsoft Word 3.0 for the Macintosh. Neil J. Salkind. 224p. 1987. pap. 15.60 (*0-8306-2953-X*, 2953P) McGraw-Hill Prof.

***Microsoft Word 2000 Step-by-Step Courseware Expert Skills.** Ed. by Active Education Film Staff. LC 99-44097. (Illus.). 2000. pap., student ed. write for info. incl. cd-rom (*0-7356-0984-5*) Microsoft.

***Microsoft Word 2000 Step-by-Step Courseware Core Skills.** Ed. by Active Education Firm Staff. LC 99-44098. (Illus.). 2000. pap., student ed. write for info. incl. cd-rom (*0-7356-0978-0*) Microsoft.

***Microsoft Word 2000.** Teresa Adams & Stella Smith. LC 99-61510. 2000. text. write for info. (*0-03-026137-6*) Harcourt Coll Pubs.

***Microsoft Word 2000.** Course Technology Staff. (SAM's License Card for Course CBT Ser.). (C). 2000. text. write for info. (*0-619-00926-8*) Course Tech.

***Microsoft Word 2000.** Tim Duffy. 272p. (C). 1999. pap. text 25.00 (*0-201-45912-4*, Prentice Hall) P-H.

***Microsoft Word 2000.** Kenneth C. Laudon & Kenneth Rosenblatt. LC 99-62006. 1999. write for info. (*0-07-234087-8*) McGrw-H Hghr Educ.

***Microsoft Word 2000.** Judd Napier. LC 99-232324. 2000. ring bd. 37.95 (*0-538-42607-1*) S-W Pub.

***Microsoft Word 2000.** Marie L. Swanson. (Illus.). 2000. pap. 21.95 (*0-7600-6386-9*) Course Tech.

***Microsoft Word 2000: A Hands-On Guide.** Bonita Sebastian. 180p. 2000. spiral bd. 26.20 (*1-57426-127-4*) Computer Lit Pr.

***Microsoft Word 2000: Brief Version.** Timothy J. O'Leary & Linda O'Leary. LC 99-60730. 2000. write for info. (*0-07-233738-9*) McGrw-H Hghr Educ.

Microsoft Word 2000: Certified Course CBT. Carol M. Cram et al. 26.95 (*0-619-00112-7*, Pub. by Course Tech) Thomson Learn.

Microsoft Word 2000: Complete Tutorial. Pasewark. (Computer Applications Ser.). 1999. pap. 12.95 (*0-538-68834-3*) S-W Pub.

Microsoft Word 2000: Complete Tutorial. William Pasewark. LC 99-23416. (Computer Applications Ser.). 1999. pap. 52.95 (*0-538-68832-7*) S-W Pub.

***Microsoft Word 2000: Complete Tutorial.** William Pasewark & Connie Morrison. LC 99-23416. (Tutorial Ser.). 752p. 1999. pap. 54.95 (*0-538-68833-5*) Sth-Wstrn College.

***Microsoft Word 2000: Expert Certification** Nita Hewitt Rutkosky. LC 99-35240. (Benchmark Ser.). 1999. write for info. (*0-7638-0342-1*) Paradigm MN.

Microsoft Word 2000: Instructor's Guide, CD Rom Package. Nita H. Rutkosky. 848p. 78.95 (*0-7638-0251-4*) EMC-Paradigm.

***Microsoft Word 2000: Introduction.** Pamela W. Adams. Ed. by Jenell L. Davis & Sara R. Pressley. (Office 2000 Ser.). (Illus.). 131p. 1999. pap. 28.95 (*1-58163-091-3*) CPI Train.

***Microsoft Word 2000: Introductory Edition** Sarah E. Hutchinson & Glen J. Coulthard. LC 99-34914. (Advantage Series for Computer Education). 2000. write for info. (*0-07-116824-9*) McGraw.

***Microsoft Word 2000: Introductory Edition.** Sarah E. Hutchinson & Glen J. Coulthard. LC 99-34914. 2000. write for info. (*0-07-234812-7*) McGrw-H Hghr Educ.

Microsoft Word 2000 - Illustrated Brief. Marie L. Swanson. (Illus.). 112p. per. 12.95 (*0-7600-6065-7*, Pub. by Course Tech) Thomson Learn.

Microsoft Word 2000 - Illustrated Introductory. Marie L. Swanson. 216p. per. 21.95 (*0-7600-6066-5*, Pub. by Course Tech) Thomson Learn.

***Microsoft Word 2000 Bible.** Brent Heslop & David F. Angell. LC 98-75377. (Bible Ser.). (Illus.). 1176p. 1999. pap. 39.99 incl. cd-rom (*0-7645-3281-2*) IDG Bks.

Microsoft Word 2000 Complete Concepts & Techniques. Gary B. Shelly et al. 432p. per. 38.95 (*0-7895-4683-3*, Pub. by Course Tech) Thomson Learn.

***Microsoft Word 2000 Essentials.** Nita H. Rutkosky. LC 99-37718. (Signature Ser.). 2000. text. write for info. (*0-7638-0278-6*) Paradigm MN.

Microsoft Word 2000 Essentials: Text with CD ROM. Nita H. Rutkosky. 568p. 69.00 (*0-7638-0279-4*) EMC-Paradigm.

***Microsoft Word 2000 in Layman's Terms: The Reference Guide for the Rest of Us.** Katie Layman. (Illus.). 60p. 1999. pap. write for info. (*1-893532-09-7*) Compute Made.

***Microsoft Word 2000 Made Easy: Extended Course.** Katie Layman & LaVaughn Hart. LC 99-16574. (Illus.). 694p. 1999. pap. 59.00 incl. disk (*0-13-012951-8*) P-H.

***Microsoft Word 2000 Mouse Cheat Sheet.** Mary Millhollon. 450p. 1999. 19.99 (*0-7897-2114-7*) Que.

***Microsoft Word 2000 Quick Source Guide.** Quick Source Staff. (Illus.). 6p. 1999. pap. 4.95 (*1-930674-12-0*) Quick Source.

Microsoft Word, Version 5.5. Miguel Pendas. LC 92-17123. (Increasing Your Productivity Ser.). 1992. disk. write for info. (*0-02-800683-6*) Glencoe.

Microsoft Word, Version 5.5. Miguel Pendas. LC 92-17123. (Increasing Your Productivity Ser.). 1993. write for info. (*0-02-800682-8*) Glencoe.

Microsoft Word, Version 5.5. large type ed. Miguel Pendas. 1993. 124.00 (*0-614-09561-1*, L-31415-00) Am Printing Hse.

Microsoft Word 2000. Napier. (School Transfer from CT). 1999. pap., wbk. ed. 12.95 (*0-538-42622-5*) S-W Pub.

***Microsoft Word 2000.** Trudi Reisner. LC 99-15717. (One Step at a Time Ser.). 360p. 1999. pap. 29.99 (*0-7645-3295-2*) IDG Bks.

***Microsoft Word 2000.** Nita Hewitt Rutkosky. LC 99-31328. 2000. text. write for info. incl. cd-rom (*0-7638-0250-6*) Paradigm MN.

Microsoft Word 2000. Nancy Warner. LC 99-61237. (Quick Reference Guides Ser.). (Illus.). 188p. 1999. pap. 9.99 (*0-7897-2031-0*) Que.

Microsoft Word 2000: Comprehensive Concepts & Techniques. Gary B. Shelly. (Shelly Cashman Ser.). 1999. pap. text 44.95 (*0-7895-5608-1*) Course Tech.

Microsoft Word 2000: Illustrated Complete Edition. Marie L. Swanson. (Illus.). 1999. pap. text 38.95 (*0-7600-6068-1*) Course Tech.

Microsoft Word 2000: Quicktorial. Murphy. LC 98-47587. 227p. 1999. pap. 21.95 (*0-538-68849-1*) S-W Pub.

***Microsoft Word 2000 & Excel 2000 Step By Step Interactive.** Learnit Corporation Staff. (gr. 8). 1999. cd-rom 29.99 (*0-7356-0507-6*) Microsoft Pr.

Microsoft Word 2000 at a Glance. Jerry Joyce. LC 98-48187. 288p. 1998. 19.99 (*1-57231-940-2*) Microsoft.

Microsoft Word 2000 Exam Cram. Deborah Alyne Christy. 1999. pap. text 26.99 (*1-57610-513-X*) Coriolis Grp.

***Microsoft Word 2000 Introduction.** Timothy O'Leary & Linda O'Leary. 472p. (C). 1999. pap. 27.50 (*0-07-233640-4*) McGrw-H Hghr Educ.

***Microsoft Word 2000 Learning Kit.** Learnit Corporation Staff. 1999. pap. text 29.99 (*0-7356-0913-6*) Microsoft.

***Microsoft Word 2000, QuickTutorial.** Patricia Murphy. LC 98-47587. (Quicktorial Ser.). (Illus.). 192p. 1999. pap. 24.95 (*0-538-68850-5*) Sth-Wstrn College.

***Microsoft Word 2000 Simplified.** Ruth Maran. LC 99-62446. (... Simplified Ser.). 240p. 1999. pap. 24.99 (*0-7645-6054-9*) IDG Bks.

Microsoft Word 2000 Step by Step. Catapult Inc. Staff. LC 98-48194. 432p. 1999. pap. 34.99 (*1-57231-970-4*) Microsoft.

Microsoft Word 6.0 for Windows, Microcomputer & Information Technology. Baumann. (Data Processing & Information System Ser.). 1996. pap. 26.50 (*0-314-07124-5*) West Pub.

Microsoft Word 7 for Windows 95. Nita H. Rutkosky. LC 96-13304. 1996. pap. text. write for info. (*1-56118-888-3*); pap. text. write for info. (*1-56118-889-1*) Paradigm MN.

Microsoft Word 95 Windows Pal. Curtin. 1997. pap. write for info. (*0-13-237553-2*) P-H.

Microsoft Word 97. Access Publishing Staff. (Beginner's Guide Ser.). 1997. pap. text 19.99 (*1-57671-013-0*) INST Publishing.

Microsoft Word 97. Outi Lammi & Jukka Kolari. LC 97-35439. (Paradigm Visual Ser.). 1997. write for info. (*0-7638-0086-4*) Paradigm MN.

Microsoft Word 97. 10th ed. Michael Banks. LC 98-4560. (Exam Cram Ser.). xxv, 437 p. (C). 1999. mass mkt. 26.99 (*1-57610-222-X*) Coriolis Grp.

Microsoft Word 97 for Windows: Illustrated Standard Edition: A Second Course. Marie L. Swanson. (Illustrated Ser.). (Illus.). 192p. (C). 1997. pap. 16.50 (*0-7600-5141-0*) Course Tech.

Microsoft Word 97 for Windows 95: Quicktorial. Murphy. 1997. 22.95 (*0-538-67965-4*) Thomson Learn.

Microsoft Word 97 Illustrated: First Course. Illus. by Swanson. (C). 1997. pap. 21.95 (*0-7600-5996-9*) Thomson Learn.

Microsoft Word 97 Professional. (C). 1997. 11.50 (*0-03-022537-X*) Harcourt Coll Pubs.

Microsoft Word 98 for the MAC. David Bragg et al. 65p. 1998. pap. 5.25 (*0-07-230628-9*) McGraw.

Microsoft Wordperfect 6.0 for Windows: Double Diamond. Gary B. Shelly & T. Cashman. (C). 1994. mass mkt. 16.50 (*0-87709-883-2*) Course Tech.

***Microsoft Words Simple Projects: Primary.** Debi Hooper. (Illus.). 96p. 2000. pap., teacher ed. 18.75 (*1-57690-459-8*, TCM 2459) Tchr Create Mat.

***Microsoft Works: Simple Projects.** Debi Hooper. (Illus.). 2000. pap. text 18.95 incl. cd-rom (*1-57690-437-7*) Tchr Create Mat.

Microsoft Works: Tutorial & Applications: IBM Version. large type ed. William R. Pasewark, Jr. et al. 1991. 124.00 (*0-614-09876-9*, L-83972-00) Am Printing Hse.

Microsoft Works Applications. rev. ed. Ralph Ruby et al. 1991. pap. text 13.95 (*1-56118-540-X*); pap. text, teacher ed. 8.00 (*1-56118-541-8*) Paradigm MN.

Microsoft Works, DOS Version. Duffy. (Management Information Systems Ser.). 1996. pap. 32.95 (*0-534-23623-5*) S-W Pub.

***Microsoft Works for Terrified Teachers.** Debi Hooper & Stephen Wright. Ed. by Kathy Humrichouse. 304p. 1999. pap., teacher ed. 24.95 (*1-57690-436-9*, TCM2436) Tchr Create Mat.

Microsoft Works for Windows. William R. Pasewark, Sr. (DF - Computer Applications Ser.). (C). 1994. mass mkt., wbk. ed. 43.95 (*0-538-70940-5*) S-W Pub.

Microsoft Works for Windows: Tutorial & Applications. William R. Pasewark, Sr. (DF - Computer Applications Ser.). 1994. mass mkt. 30.95 (*0-538-62281-4*) S-W Pub.

Microsoft Works for Windows 95 for Dummies. David C. Kay. 384p. 1995. pap. 19.99 (*1-56884-944-3*) IDG Bks.

Microsoft Works for Windows 95. Gary B. Shelly & T. Cashman. 216p. 1996. pap. 16.50 (*0-7895-1175-4*) Course Tech.

Microsoft Works for Windows 95. Gary B. Shelly et al. LC 96-38598. 800p. 1996. pap. 45.00 (*0-7895-1167-3*) Course Tech.

Microsoft Works for Windows 95 for Dummies Quick Reference. Barrie Sosinsky. 224p. 1996. spiral bd. 12.99 (*1-56884-984-2*) IDG Bks.

Microsoft Works for Windows 95 - Illustrated, Incl. instr. resource kit, test mgr., Web pg. Michael Halvorson. (Illustrated Ser.). (Illus.). 376p. 1996. text, mass mkt. 24.50 incl. 3.5 ld (*0-7600-3563-6*) Course Tech.

Microsoft Works for Windows 95: Visual Learning Guide. Grace J. Beatty. 1996. pap. 19.95 (*0-7615-0385-4*) Prima Pub.

Microsoft Works 4 for Windows 95 - Illustrated. Michael Halvorson. (Illus.). 376p. 1996. teacher ed. 18.50 (*0-7600-3906-2*) Course Tech.

Microsoft Works 4 for Windows 95 - Introductory, Incl. instr. resource kit, test mgr., labs. Christopher Kelly. (New Perspectives Ser.). (Illus.). 568p. 1996. pap. 31.50 (*0-7600-3540-7*) Course Tech.

Microsoft Works 4.5 for Windows for Dummies: Quick Reference. Bjoern Hartsfvang. LC 98-70177. 224p. 1998. spiral bd. 12.99 (*0-7645-0249-2*) IDG Bks.

***Microsoft Works 4.5 for Windows: Tutorial & Applications.** William Pasewark. (C). 1998. pap. 43.95 (*0-538-72158-8*) Sth-Wstrn College.

Microsoft Works 4.0 for the Macintosh: A Workbook for Educators. rev. ed. Suzanne Painter et al. (Illus.). 274p. 1996. spiral bd., wbk. ed. 26.95 (*1-56484-126-X*) Intl Society Tech Educ.

Microsoft Works 4.0 for Mac: Tutorial & Applications. William R. Pasewark. (DF - Computer Applications Ser.). 1995. mass mkt. 35.95 (*0-538-64727-2*) S-W Pub.

Microsoft Works 4.0 for the Mac. Danny Goodman. 1995. pap. 29.95 (*0-02-801143-0*) Glencoe.

Microsoft Works 4.0 for Windows 95. William R. Pasewark. (Quicktorial Ser.). 1996. mass mkt. 21.95 (*0-538-71547-2*) S-W Pub.

Microsoft Works 4.0 for Windows 95: Quick Course. William R. Pasewark, Sr. (DF - Computer Applications Ser.). 1996. mass mkt. 22.95 (*0-538-71475-1*) S-W Pub.

M

An Asterisk (*) at the beginning of an entry indicates that the title is appearing for the first time.

Microsoft Works 4.0 for Windows 95: Tutorial & Applications. William R. Pasewark, Sr. LC 95-47943. (DF - Computer Applications Ser.). (C). 1996. mass mkt. 40.95 (*0-538-71497-2*) S-W Pub.

Microsoft Works 4.0 for Windows 95: Tutorial & Applications. William R. Pasewark, Sr. (DF - Computer Applications Ser.). 1996. mass mkt., student ed. 37.95 (*0-538-71498-0*) S-W Pub.

Microsoft Works 4.0 MAC Quick Course. William R. Pasewark. (DF - Computer Applications Ser.). 1995. mass mkt., wbk. ed. 18.95 (*0-538-64073-1*) S-W Pub.

***Microsoft Works 4/4.5 Windows 95: Illustrated Standard Edition.** Halvorson. (C). 1998. pap. text 34.95 (*0-7600-6024-X*) Thomson Learn.

Microsoft Works 4.5: 6-in-1. Jane Calabria. LC 97-68088. 648p. 1997. 29.99 (*0-7897-1357-8*) Que.

Microsoft Works Guide: Century 21 Keyboarding, Formatting, & Document Processing. large type ed. Mary S. Stacy. 1994. 22.50 (*0-614-09843-2*, L-83774-00) Am Printing Hse.

***Microsoft Works Simple Projects: Intermediate with CD-ROM.** Debi Hooper. 96p. 2000. pap. 18.95 incl. cd-rom (*1-57690-447-4*) Tchr Create Mat.

Microsoft Works Step-by-Step: Macintosh Version 4.0. George Lynch & Helen Lynch. LC 94-46423. (Illus.). 34p. 1995. pap., teacher ed. 21.25 (*0-941681-81-5*); spiral bd. 26.60 (*0-941681-80-7*) Computer Lit Pr.

Microsoft Works Step-by-Step: Windows 95 Version 4.0/4.5. George Lynch & Helen Lynch. LC 96-38139. (Illus.). 124p. 1996. spiral bd. 26.60 (*1-57426-004-9*) Computer Lit Pr.

Microsoft Works Suite for Dummies. Kay. LC QA76.76.I59K39 1998. (For Dummies Ser.). 432p. 1998. pap. 19.99 (*0-7645-0477-0*) IDG Bks.

***Microsoft Works Suite for Dummies 2000.** David Kay. (Illus.). 432p. 2000. pap. 19.99 (*0-7645-0685-4*) IDG Bks.

Microsoft Works Suite 99 at a Glance. David Busch. LC 98-31459. (At A Glance Ser.). (Illus.). 224p. 1999. pap. 19.99 (*0-7356-0571-8*) Microsoft.

***Microsoft Works Suite 2001 Step by Step.** Microsoft Corporation Staff. 240p. 2000. 19.99 (*0-7356-1035-5*) Microsoft.

Microsoft Works 3 for Windows Student Resource Guide. Arnowitz Productions Inc., Staff. (DA - Computer Education Ser.). (J). (gr. k-8). 1995. text 11.95 (*0-538-64336-6*) S-W Pub.

Microsoft Works 3.0 for the Mac. Taylor. (Step-by-Step Ser.). 1993. teacher ed. write for info. (*0-02-800347-0*) Glencoe.

Microsoft Works 3.0. Shaw et al. (C). 1994. text. write for info. (*0-318-70357-2*, BF4635) S-W Pub.

Microsoft Works 3.0: A Practical Approach. John Weingarten. 288p. (C). 1993. text 23.25 (*0-697-21204-1*) Bus & Educ Tech.

Microsoft Works 3.0: Easy Reference Guide - Macintosh. Myra Whatley & James Whatley. LC 93-34963. 1995. mass mkt. 9.95 (*0-538-63385-9*) S-W Pub.

Microsoft Works 3.0 DOS: Quick Course. Willuiam R. Pasewark. (DF - Computer Applications Ser.). 1995. mass mkt. 18.95 (*0-538-64103-7*) S-W Pub.

Microsoft Works, 3.0 DOS: Tutorial & Applications Text. William R. Pasewark. LC 93-86135. (DT-Fortran Ser.). 1995. mass mkt. 35.95 (*0-538-63435-9*) S-W Pub.

Microsoft Works 3.0 DOS, Easy Reference. Whatley. (DF - Computer Applications Ser.). 1995. mass mkt. 9.95 (*0-538-63386-7*) S-W Pub.

Microsoft Works 3.0 for DOS+ Lewis. (C). 1994. pap. text 27.00 (*0-03-004804-4*) Harcourt Coll Pubs.

Microsoft Works 3.0 for DOS. Timothy J. O'Leary & Linda I. O'Leary. (C). 1994. pap. 35.50 (*0-07-048988-2*) McGraw.

Microsoft Works 3.0 for Windows. Timothy J. O'Leary & Linda I. O'Leary. LC 94-75715. 444p. (C). 1994. pap. text 36.44 (*0-07-049009-0*) McGraw.

Microsoft Works 3.0 for Windows, Quick Course. William R. Pasewark. (DF - Computer Applications Ser.). 1995. mass mkt. 15.95 (*0-538-64389-7*) S-W Pub.

Microsoft Works 3.0 for Windows. Gary B. Shelly. (Double Diamond Ser.). 208p. 1995. mass mkt. 19.95 (*0-7895-0358-1*) S-W Pub.

Microsoft Works 3.0 for Windows, Incl. instr. resource kit, test bank, transparency. Michael Halvorson. (Illustrated Ser.). (Illus.). 288p. (C). 1994. pap., per. 22.50 (*1-56527-255-2*) Course Tech.

Microsoft Works 3.0 for Windows: LTU Windows Applications. Gary B. Shelly & T. Cashman. 800p. (C). 1994. mass mkt. 53.35 (*0-87709-770-4*) S-W Pub.

Microsoft Works 3.0 for Windows: Tutorial & Applications. William R. Pasewark. (DF - Computer Applications Ser.). 1994. mass mkt. 35.95 (*0-538-64068-5*) S-W Pub.

Microsoft Works 3.0 Mac Version: Tutorial & Applications. William R. Pasewark. LC 93-84939. (DF - Computer Appications Ser.). 1994. mass mkt. 30.95 (*0-538-63360-3*) S-W Pub.

Microsoft Works 3.0 - 4.0 Mac: Applications for Reinforcement. William R. Pasewark. (DF - Computer Applications Ser.). 1996. mass mkt. 31.95 (*0-538-65197-0*) S-W Pub.

Microsoft Works 3 Quick Reference Guide. Cathy Vento. 1993. pap. 12.00 (*1-56243-105-6*, M-18) DDC Pub.

Microsoft Works 2.0. Orrell & Elston. 1992. pap. text. write for info. (*0-273-03833-8*) Addison-Wesley.

Microsoft Works 2.0 - 3.0 for Windows: Applications for Reinforcement. William R. Pasewark. LC 95-69606. (DF - Computer Applications Ser.). 1995. mass mkt. 31.95 (*0-538-65194-6*) S-W Pub.

***Microsoft Works 2000.** Penrod. (New Perspectives Ser.). (C). 2000. text 49.95 (*0-619-01945-X*) Course Tech.

***Microsoft Works 2000: A Hands-On Guide.** Arthur Luehrmann & Herbert Peckham. 148p. 2000. spiral bd. 26.60 (*1-57426-062-6*) Computer Lit Pr.

***Microsoft Works 2000: Illustrated Complete.** Halvorson. (C). 2000. 34.95 (*0-619-01742-2*) Course Tech.

***Microsoft Works 2000 Basics.** Pasewark Pasewark. (C). 2000. pap., student ed. 43.95 (*0-538-72340-8*) Thomson Learn.

***Microsoft Works 2000 Basics.** William Robert Pasewark. LC 00-37417. (Illus.). 2000. ring bd. write for info. (*0-538-72411-0*) S-W Pub.

Microsoft Works Version 2.0 IBM PCs & Compatibles: Increasing Your Productivity. Ron Pronk. 1993. pap. 26.33 (*0-02-800326-8*) Glencoe.

Microsoft Works 2.0 & 3.0 DOS Application. Pasewark. 1995. pap. 24.50 (*0-538-64380-3*) Thomson Learn.

***Microsoft Works 2000: Quick Reference.** Bjoern Hartsfvang. 224p. 1999. spiral bd. 12.99 (*0-7645-0664-1*) IDG Bks.

***Microsoft Works 2000: Quick Reference.** Kay. (For Dummies Ser.). 432p. 1999. pap. 19.99 (*0-7645-0666-8*) IDG Bks.

***Microsoft Works 2000 Complete Concepts & Techniques.** Shelly & Cashman. (Shelly Cashman Ser.). (C). 2000. pap. 61.95 (*0-7895-5990-0*) Course Tech.

***Microsoft Works 2000 Introductory Concepts & Techniques.** Shelly & Cashman. (Shelly Cashman Ser.). (C). 2000. pap. 17.00 (*0-7895-5989-7*) Course Tech.

Microsoft Works 2000 Step by Step. Perspection, Inc. Staff. LC 99-40199. (Step by Step Ser.). 1999. pap. text 29.99 (*0-7356-0836-9*) Microsoft.

Microsoft Works 3.0 Windows 3.0: Computer Skills Resource Guide. 2nd ed. Melnyk. (Computer Applications). 1997. pap. 28.25 (*0-314-13007-1*) West Pub.

Microsoft Works 4.5: Introduction to Concepts/ Technology. Shelly & Cashman. (Shelly-Cashman Ser.). 1998. 22.95 (*0-7895-4552-7*) Course Tech.

Microsoft Works 4.5 Complete Concepts & Techniques. Gary B. Shelly et al. (Shelly-Cashman Ser.). (C). 1998. pap. 61.95 (*0-7895-4553-5*) Course Tech.

Microsoft Works 4.5 Essentials. Dwight Graham & Terri Dousias. LC 98-88690. (Illus.). 512p. (C). 1999. pap. text. write for info. (*1-58076-090-2*) Que Educ & Trng.

Microsoft XML 2.0 Programmer's Guide & Software Development Kit. Microsoft Corporation Staff. (Microsoft Programming Series Ser.). 1999. pap. text 49.99 (*0-7356-0639-0*) Microsoft.

***Microsoft's Active Directory: Administration, Security & Migration.** Richard R. Taha. (Professional Ser.). 350p. 2000. pap. 42.50 (*0-7897-2210-0*) Que.

Microsoft's Middle Tier-Technologies for Web Applications. Mitchell I. Kramer. (Illus.). 22p. 1998. pap. 395.00 (*1-892815-02-8*) Patricia Seybold.

***Microsoft's Windows Millennium Edition for Dummies.** Greg Harvey. (Quick Reference Ser.). (Illus.). 224p. 2000. pap. 12.99 (*0-7645-0730-3*) IDG Bks.

***Microsoft's Windows Millennium Edition for Dummies.** Andy Rathbone. (For Dummies Ser.). (Illus.). 384p. 2000. pap. 19.99 (*0-7645-0735-4*) IDG Bks.

***Microsoft's Windows Millennium Edition Simplified.** Ruth Maran. (... Simplified Ser.). 240p. 2000. pap. 24.99 (*0-7645-3494-7*) IDG Bks.

Microspectroscopic Chemistry of Polymers. Jack Koenig. LC 97-41362. (Professional Reference Ser.). (Illus.). 432p. 1998. text 119.95 (*0-8412-3493-0*, Pub. by Am Chemical) OUP.

Microspheres & Drug Therapy: Pharmaceutical, Immunological & Medical Aspects. Ed. by S. S. Davis et al. 448p. 1985. 168.25 (*0-444-80577-X*) Elsevier.

Microspheres & Regional Cancer Therapy. Neville Willmott. 256p. 1993. lib. bdg. 179.00 (*0-8493-6952-5*, RC271) CRC Pr.

Microspheres Medical & Biological Applications. Ed. by Alan Rembaum & Zoltan A. Tokes. LC 88-7343. 272p. 1988. 140.00 (*0-8493-6571-6*, RS201, CRC Reprint) Franklin.

Microsplit - Economics: A Contemporary Introduction. 3rd ed. McEachern. (HB - Economics Ser.). (C). 1994. mass mkt., student ed. 16.00 (*0-538-82855-2*) S-W Pub.

Microspores: Evolution & Ontogeny. Ed. by Stephen Blackmore & R. B. Knox. 347p. 1990. text 104.00 (*0-12-103458-5*) Acad Pr.

Microsporida of Vertebrates. Elizabeth U. Canning & Jiri Lom. 1986. text 136.00 (*0-12-158790-8*) Acad Pr.

Microsporidia & Microsporidiosis. Ed. by Murray Wittner & Louis M. Weiss. LC 98-47495. (Illus.). 570p. 1999. 99.95 (*1-55581-147-7*) ASM Pr.

MICROSTART: A Guide for Planning, Starting & Managing a Microfinance Programme. 30.00 (*92-1-126060-4*) UN.

Microstate Studies. Ed. by Norwell Harrigan. LC 77-641878. 102p. reprint ed. pap. 31.70 (*0-7837-5023-4*, 204469100001) Bks Demand.

Microstates in World Affairs: Policy Problems & Options. Elmer Plischke. LC 77-1351. (AEI Studies: No. 144). 168p. reprint ed. pap. 52.10 (*0-8357-4506-6*, 203736300008) Bks Demand.

Microstation. Assadipour. Date not set. teacher ed. write for info. (*0-314-06624-1*) West Pub.

MicroStation Command Summary Book: Version 5.0. Paul Karius. (Illus.). 153p. (Orig.). 1994. pap. 22.00 (*1-885248-75-X*) K St Systs.

MicroStation 5.X Workbook. Michael Ward. (Illus.). 516p. (Orig.). (C). 1994. pap. text 32.80 (*0-87563-494-X*) Stipes.

***MicroStation J Workbook: A Complete Educational & Training Guide for Mastering 2D Applications of MicroStation J.** Michael J. Ward. (Illus.). 498p. 1999. spiral bd. 39.80 (*0-87563-873-2*) Stipes.

MicroStation Modeler Workbook: An Introduction to Parametric Modeling. Michael K. Ward & Mike A. Arroyo. (Illus.). 650p. 1997. spiral bd. 49.80 (*0-87563-703-5*) Stipes.

MicroStation 95 Exercise Book. 2nd ed. Thomas Synnott & Robert McElligott. 1995. teacher ed., spiral bd. 15.00 (*1-56690-093-X*, 1438, OnWord Pr) High Mtn.

MicroStation 95 Exercise Book. 2nd ed. Thomas Synnott & Robert McElligott. LC 96-19501. (Illus.). 392p. (C). 1996. pap. 39.95 (*1-56690-091-3*) Thomson Learn.

MicroStation 95 Fundamentals. Nancy Olson. 600p. 1996. pap. text 39.99 (*1-56205-607-7*) New Riders Pub.

MicroStation 95 Productivity Book: Using MicroStation's Advanced Tools. Ed. by Kenneth W. Riddle. (Illus.). 416p. (C). 1996. pap. 57.95 (*1-56690-077-8*) Thomson Learn.

MicroStation 95 Workbook for Windows: A Complete Educational & Training Guide for Mastering 2D Applications of Microstation 95. Michael K. Ward. (Illus.). 476p. (C). 1996. spiral bd. 34.80 (*0-87563-649-7*) Stipes.

Microstation 95: Geoengineering Academic Suite. (C). 1997. 261.33 (*0-201-35616-3*) HEPC Inc.

Microstatn 1995 Mechancl Engrg Academc Suit. (C). 1997. 261.33 (*0-201-35615-5*) HEPC Inc.

Microstrip & Microgap Chambers: A New Generation of Gaseous Radiation Detectors. J. Van der Marel. 139p. (Orig.). 1997. pap. 44.50 (*90-407-1426-6*, Pub. by Delft U Pr) Coronet Bks.

Microstrip Antenna Design. Ed. by K. C. Gupta & Abdelaziz Benalla. LC 88-7442. (Artech House Microwave Library). 409p. reprint ed. pap. 126.80 (*0-7837-1334-7*, 204148200020) Bks Demand.

Microstrip Antennas. Prakash Bhartia & Inder J. Bahl. LC 80-70174. (Illus.). 364p. 1980. reprint ed. pap. 112.90 (*0-608-16025-3*, 203312400083) Bks Demand.

Microstrip Antennas: The Analysis & Design of Microstrip Antennas & Arrays. Ed. by David M. Pozar & Daniel H. Schaubert. LC 95-1229. 448p. 1995. reprint ed. 89.95 (*0-7803-1078-0*, PC4325) Inst Electrical.

Microstrip Circuit Analysis. David H. Schrader. LC 95-9926. 304p. (C). 1995. 92.00 (*0-13-588534-5*) P-H.

Microstrip Circuits. Fred Gardiol. LC 93-1946. (Microwave & Optical Engineering Ser.). 320p. 1994. 98.50 (*0-471-52850-1*) Wiley.

Microstrip Lines & Slotlines. K. C. Gupta et al. LC 79-1375. (Illus.). 391p. reprint ed. pap. 121.30 (*0-7837-4619-9*, 204434000002) Bks Demand.

Microstrip Lines & Slotlines. 2nd ed. K. C. Gupta et al. LC 95-51852. 535p. 1996. 105.00 (*0-89006-766-X*) Artech Hse.

Microstructural Analysis of Revelation 4-11. Ekkehardt Muller. (Andrews University Seminary Doctoral Dissertation Ser.: Vol. 21). 788p. (Orig.). 1996. pap. 19.99 (*1-883925-11-8*) Andrews Univ Pr.

Microstructure vs. Machinability of Alloy Gear Steels. N. E. Wolman. (Technical Papers: Vol. P162). (Illus.). 28p. 1937. pap. text 30.00 (*1-55589-333-3*) AGMA.

Microstructural & Electrical Properties of Resolidified Submicron Al Lines. Marc J. Van den Homberg. (Illus.). 126p. 1998. pap. 42.50 (*90-407-1623-4*, Pub. by Delft U Pr) Coronet Bks.

Microstructural Characterisation of Fibre-Reinforced Composites. John Summerscales. 320p. 1998. ring bd. 169.95 (*0-8493-3882-4*) CRC Pr.

Microstructural Characterisation of Fibre-Reinforced Composites. Ed. by John Summerscales. 304p. 1998. boxed set 170.00 (*1-85573-240-8*, Pub. by Woodhead Pubng) Am Educ Systs.

***Microstructural Characterization.** Brandon. LC 98-46589. 424p. 1999. pap. 69.95 (*0-471-98502-3*) Wiley.

Microstructural Characterization of Materials. David Brandon & Wayne D. Kaplan. LC 98-46589. 424p. 1999. 190.00 (*0-471-98501-5*) Wiley.

Microstructural Control in Aluminum Alloys: Deformation, Recovery, & Recrystallization: Proceedings of a Symposium Held at the Annual Meeting of TMS in New York, February 27, 1985. Metallurgical Society of AIME Staff. Ed. by E. Henry Chia & H. J. McQueen. LC 85-29842. 233p. reprint ed. pap. 72.30 (*0-8357-2510-3*, 205239000013) Bks Demand.

Microstructural Design by Solidification Processing: Proceedings of a Symposium Sponsored by the TMS Synthesis, Control & Analysis in Materials Processing Committee Held During Materials Week '92 in Chicago, IL, November 1-5, 1992. Minerals, Metals & Materials Society Staff. Ed. by Enrique J. Lavernia & Mehmet N. Gungor. LC 92-83764. (Illus.). 259p. reprint ed. pap. 80.30 (*0-608-20028-X*, 207130100010) Bks Demand.

Microstructural Development & Stability in High Chromium Ferritic Power Plant Steels. Ed. by A. Strang & D. J. Gooch. (Microstructure of High Temperature Materials Ser.: No. 1). (Illus.). 228p. 1997. 100.00 (*1-86125-021-5*, Pub. by Inst Materials) Ashgate Pub Co.

Microstructural Development During Hydration of Cement. Ed. by P. Brown et al. (MRS Symposium Proceedings Ser.: Vol. 85). 1987. text 17.50 (*0-931837-50-2*) Materials Res.

Microstructural Evolution in Thin Films. Atwater. 450p. 1998. write for info. (*0-12-067010-0*) Acad Pr.

***Microstructural Principles of Food Processing & Engineering.** 2nd ed. J. M. Aguilera & D. W. Stanley. LC 99-31202. 350p. 1999. 125.00 (*0-8342-1256-0*, 12560) Aspen Pub.

Microstructural Processes in Irradiated Materials Vol. 540. Ed. by Steven J. Zinkle et al. LC 99-24110. (Symposium Proceedings Ser.). 735p. 1999. 87.00 (*1-55899-446-7*) Materials Res.

Microstructural Science: Proceedings of the Twelfth Annual Technical Meeting of the International Metallographic Society, Vol. 8. Ed. by Donald W. Stevens et al. LC 73-10895. 414p. reprint ed. pap. 128.40 (*0-608-16350-3*, 202626800049) Bks Demand.

Microstructural Science Vol. 23: Advances & Applications in the Metallography & Characterization. Ed. by D. W. Stevens et al. LC 96-83825. (Microstructural Science Ser.). 316p. 1996. 108.00 (*0-87170-570-2*, 6065) ASM.

Microstructural Science for Thin Film Metallization in Electronic Applications: Proceedings of the Topical Symposium Held at the Annual Meeting of the Minerals, Metals, & Materials Society at Phoenix, AZ, January 26-27, 1988. Minerals, Metals & Materials Society Staff. Ed. by John Sanchez et al. LC 88-62442. (Illus.). 199p. 1988. reprint ed. pap. 61.70 (*0-608-02490-2*, 206313400004) Bks Demand.

Microstructural Stability of Creep Resistant Alloys for High Temperature Plant Applications. Ed. by Andrew Strang et al. (Illus.). 492p. 1998. 100.00 (*1-86125-045-2*, Pub. by Inst Materials) Ashgate Pub Co.

Microstructure: The Organization of Trading & Short Term Price Behavior, 2 Vol. Ed. by Hans R. Stoll. LC 98-46610. 1040p. 1999. 370.00 (*1-85898-749-0*) E Elgar.

Microstructure Analysis of the Execution of Complex Motor Actions: Methods & Results. N. D. Gordeeva et al. 1989. 27.50 (*0-8364-2559-6*, Pub. by Oxford IBH) S Asia.

Microstructure & Function of Cells: Electron Micrographs of Cell Ultrastructure. Andreas Bubel. 280p. 1989. text 69.95 (*0-470-21176-8*) P-H.

Microstructure & Macrostructure of Elastic Waves in One-Dimensional Continuous Nonhomogeneous Media. B. N. Ivakin. LC 60-9253. (Soviet Research in Geophysics in English Translation Ser.: Vol. 3). 121p. reprint ed. pap. 37.60 (*0-608-30356-9*, 202066100018) Bks Demand.

Microstructure & Mechanical Properties of Aging Materials II. Ed. by P. K. Liaw et al. LC 96-80436. (Illus.). 458p. 1995. 100.00 (*0-87339-339-2*, 3392) Minerals Metals.

Microstructure & Mechanical Properties of Material: Proceedings of a Symposium, 1990. Ed. by Erich Tenckhoff & Otmar Vohringer. (Illus.). 284p. 1991. 60.00 (*3-88355-171-6*, Pub. by DGM Metallurgy Info) IR Pubns.

***Microstructure & Microtribology of Polymer Surfaces.** Ed. by Vladimir V. Tsukruk & Kathryn J. Wahl. LC 99-16494. (ACS Symposium Ser.: No. 741). (Illus.). 526p. 2000. 145.00 (*0-8412-3682-8*) OUP.

Microstructure & Phase Transition. Ed. by David S. Kinderlehreer et al. LC 93-5144. (IMA Volumes in Mathematics & Its Applications Ser.: Vol. 54). 1993. 75.95 (*0-387-94112-6*) Spr-Verlag.

Microstructure & Properties of Catalysts. Ed. by J. M. Thomas et al. (Symposium Proceedings Ser.: Vol. 111). 1988. text 17.50 (*0-931837-79-0*) Materials Res.

Microstructure & Properties of Materials, 1. 500p. 1996. 31.00 (*981-02-2503-2*) World Scientific Pub.

Microstructure & Properties of Materials, Vol. 1. J. C. Li. LC 96-225067. 500p. 1996. text 98.00 (*981-02-2403-6*) World Scientific Pub.

***Microstructure & Properties of Materials, Vol. 2.** J. C. M. Li. 2000. 78.00 (*981-02-4180-1*) World Scientific Pub.

Microstructure & Thermal Analysis of Solid Surfaces. Raouf S. Mikhail & Erich Robens. LC 82-17507. (Wiley Heyden Publication). 506p. reprint ed. pap. 156.90 (*0-7837-3237-6*, 204325600007) Bks Demand.

Microstructure & Wear of Materials. K. H. Zum Gahr. (Tribology Ser.: Vol. 10). x, 560p. 1987. 285.25 (*0-444-42754-6*) Elsevier.

Microstructure Evolution During Irradiation. Ed. by Ian M. Robertson et al. LC 97-6963. (Materials Research Society Symposium Proceedings Ser.: No. 439). 733p. 1997. text 75.00 (*1-55899-343-6*) Materials Res.

Microstructure Formation During Solidification of Metal Matrix Composites. Ed. by Pradeep K. Rohatgi. LC 93-79590. (Illus.). 171p. 1993. pap. 53.10 (*0-608-04881-X*, 206557300004) Bks Demand.

Microstructure, Fracture Toughness, & Fatigue Crack Growth Rate in Titanium Alloys: Proceedings of the 1987 TMS-AIME Annual Symposia on Effect of Microstructure on Fracture Toughness & Fatigue Crack Growth Rate in Titanium Alloys, Held at Marriott City Center, Denver, Colorado, 1987, February 24-25. Metallurgical Society of AIME Staff. Ed. by A. K. Chakrabarti & J. C. Chesnutt. LC 87-42879. 281p. reprint ed. pap. 87.20 (*0-7837-4071-9*, 205246800011) Bks Demand.

Microstructure, Materials & Applications see **Fracture Mechanics of Ceramics**

Microstructure of Bronze Sinterings. American Society for Testing & Materials Staff. LC 62-20903. (American Society for Testing & Materials Special Technical Publication Ser.: Special Technical Publication, No. 323). 11p. reprint ed. pap. 30.00 (*0-608-11478-2*, 200013000025) Bks Demand.

Microstructure of Cement-Based Systems - Bonding & Interfaces in Cementitious Materials. Ed. by Sidney Mindess et al. (MRS Symposium Proceedings Ser.: Vol. 370). 575p. 1995. 67.00 (*1-55899-272-3*, 370N) Materials Res.

Microstructure of Fine-Grained Sediments: From Mud to Shale. Ed. by R. H. Bennett et al. (Frontiers of Sedimentary Geology Ser.). (Illus.). 624p. 1990. 190.00 (*0-387-97339-7*) Spr-Verlag.

Microstructure of Foreign Exchange Markets. Jeffrey Frankel. (National Bureau of Economic Research Conference Report Ser.). 368p. 1996. 65.00 (*0-226-26000-3*) U Ch Pr.

Microstructure of Irradiated Materials. Ed. by Ian M. Robertson et al. (MRS Symposium Proceedings Ser.: Vol. 373). 569p. 1995. 76.00 (*1-55899-275-8*) Materials Res.

Microstructure of Materials. Ed. by K. M. Krishnan. (Illus.). 1993. 24.00 (*0-911302-71-9*) San Francisco Pr.

Microstructure of Polymer Cement Concrete. Z. Su. 192p. 1994. pap. 57.50 (*90-407-1083-X*, Pub. by Delft U Pr) Coronet Bks.

Microstructure of Superalloys. Madeleine Durand-Charre. 140p. 1998. text 45.00 (*90-5699-097-7*) Gordon & Breach.

Microstructure of World Trading Markets: A Special Issue of the Journal of Financial Services Research. Ed. by Hans R. Stoll. LC 92-43846. 164p. (C). 1993. lib. bdg. 104.50 (*0-7923-9295-7*) Kluwer Academic.

Microstructure-Property Relationships in Magnetic Materials No. IMAM-11: Materials Research Society International Symposium Proceedings. Ed. by M. Homma & Y. Imaoka. 317p. 1989. text 17.50 (*1-55899-040-2*, Vol. IMAM-11) Materials Res.

Microstructure Property Relationships in Titanium Aluminides & Alloys: Proceedings of the Seven Session Symposium on Microstructure Property Relationships in Titanium Alloys & Titanium Aluminides Held at the 1990 TMS Fall Meeting, Detroit, MI, October 7-11, 1990. Symposium on Microstructure Property Relationships. Ed. by Young-Won Kim & Rodney R. Boyer. LC 91-61991. 686p. 1991. reprint ed. pap. 200.00 (*0-608-00776-5*, 206157400010) Bks Demand.

Microstructure-Property Relationships of Titanium Alloys: Proceedings: Harold Margolin Symposium on Microstructure-Property Relationships of Titanium Alloys (1994: San Francisco, CA) Proceedings. Ed. by S. Ankem et al. LC 94-73570. (Illus.). 327p. 1995. 20.00 (*0-87339-246-9*, 2469) Minerals Metals.

Microstructure Science: Heterostructures & Quantum Devices. Ed. by Norman G. Finspruch & William R. Frensley. (VLSI Electronics Ser.: Vol. 24). (Illus.). 452p. 1994. text 133.00 (*0-12-234124-4*) Acad Pr.

***Microstructures & Mechanical Properties of Metalic High Temperature Material.** Ed. by Hael Mughrabi et al. LC 99-203042. 580p. 1999. pap. 195.00 (*3-527-27142-2*) Wiley.

Microstructures & Microfabricated Systems II. Ed. by P. J. Hesketh et al. LC 95-61600. (Proceedings Ser.: Vol. 95-27). (Illus.). 362p. 1995. 70.00 (*1-56677-123-4*) Electrochem Soc.

Microstructures & Microfabricated Systems III. Ed. by P. J. Hesketh et al. LC 97-190680. (Proceedings Ser.: Vol. 97-5). (Illus.). 226p. 1997. 46.00 (*1-56677-132-3*) Electrochem Soc.

Microstructures & Microfabricated Systems IV. Ed. by P. J. Hesketh et al. (Proceedings Ser.: Vol. 98-14). (Illus.). 270p. 1998. 50.00 (*1-56677-206-0*) Electrochem Soc.

Microstructures & Properties of Refractories. Ed. by J. P. Singh & S. Banerjee. (Key Engineering Materials Ser.: Vol. 88). (Illus.). 221p. 1993. text 100.00 (*0-87849-664-5*, Pub. by Trans T Pub) Enfield Pubs NH.

***Microstructures & Related Studies of High Temperature Superconductors II.** Anant Narlikar. LC 99-56622. (Studies of High Temperature Superconductors: Vol. 30). 187p. 2000. lib. bdg. 97.00 (*1-56072-771-3*) Nova Sci Pubs.

Microstructures & Structural Defects in High-Temperature Superconductors. Zhi-Xiong Cai & Yimei Zhu. 400p. 1998. 68.00 (*981-02-3285-3*) World Scientific Pub.

Microstructures in Elastic Media: Principles & Computational Methods. Phan-Thein Nhan & Sangtae Kim. (Illus.). 256p. 1994. text 85.00 (*0-19-509086-1*) OUP.

Microstructures of Ceramics: Structures & Properties of Grinding Tools. M. Moser. 364p. (C). 1980. 105.00 (*963-05-1576-8*, Pub. by Akade Kiado) St Mut.

Microstudy (3.5)-Fianc Acct. Porter. (C). 1995. 276.50 incl. 3.5 ld (*0-15-501621-7*) Harcourt Coll Pubs.

Microsurgery: Transplantation-Replantation: An Atlas-Text. Harry J. Buncke. LC 90-6142. 832p. 1991. text 275.00 (*0-8121-0981-3*) Lppncott W & W.

Microsurgery Forum. 250p. 1997. 40.00 (*981-02-2616-0*) World Scientific Pub.

Microsurgery in Female Infertility. Victor Gomel. 1983. 132.95 (*0-316-31988-0*, Little Brwn Med Div) Lppncott W & W.

Microsurgery in Orthopaedic Practice. P. C. Leung & Y. D. Gu. LC 94-43237. 360p. 1995. text 61.00 (*9971-5-0860-5*) World Scientific Pub.

Microsurgery of Cataract, Vitreous & Astigmatism: Proceedings of the Ophthalmic Microsurgery Study Group Symposium, 5th, London, June 1974. Ophthalmic Microsurgery Study Group Symposium Staf. Ed. by J. Kersley & D. Pierse. (Advances in Ophthalmology Ser.: Vol.33). 400p. 1976. 155.75 (*3-8055-2323-8*) S Karger.

Microsurgery of Cerebral Aneurysms. Zentaro Ito. (Illus.). 350p. 1985. 520.75 (*90-219-3062-5*, Excerpta Medica) Elsevier.

Microsurgery of Cerebral Veins. Wolfgang Seeger. (Illus.). 420p. 1985. 214.00 (*0-387-81807-3*) Spr-Verlag.

Microsurgery of Intracranial Tumors, 2 vols. Wolfgang Seeger. 1997. 350.00 (*0-387-91500-1*, S2307) Spr-Verlag.

Microsurgery of Intracranial Tumors Vol. 1: Supratentorial Tumors, Vol. 1. Wolfgang Seeger et al. LC 95-12163. 1995. 217.00 (*3-211-82677-7*) Spr-Verlag.

Microsurgery of Intracranial Tumors Vol. 2: Special Lesions of the Midline & Rhombenecephalon, Vol. 2. Wolfgang Seeger et al. LC 95-12163. 1995. 217.00 (*3-211-82678-5*) Spr-Verlag.

Microsurgery of Ocular Injuries. Ed. by R. C. Troutman. (Advances in Ophthalmology Ser.: Vol. 27). 1972. 85.25 (*3-8055-1355-0*) S Karger.

Microsurgery of the Anterior & Posterior Segments for the Eye. Ed. by Michael J. Roper-Hall. (Developments in Ophthalmology Ser.: Vol. 5). (Illus.). vi, 134p. 1982. pap. 78.50 (*3-8055-2711-X*) S Karger.

Microsurgery of the Brain, 2 vols., Set. Wolfgang Seeger. (Illus.). 750p. 1981. 260.00 (*0-387-81573-2*) Spr-Verlag.

Microsurgery of the Cervical Spine. Paul H. Young. 208p. 1991. text 121.50 (*0-88167-799-X*) Lppncott W & W.

Microsurgery of the Cervical Spine. Paul H. Young. LC 91-18632. (Illus.). 208p. reprint ed. pap. 64.50 (*0-608-09715-2*, 206988100007) Bks Demand.

Microsurgery of the Cornea: An Atlas & Textbook. Joaquin Barraquer. 400p. 1984. text 231.00 (*84-85835-03-4*) Gordon & Breach.

Microsurgery of the Cranial Base. Wolfgang Seeger. 416p. 1983. 189.00 (*3-211-81769-7*) Spr-Verlag.

Microsurgery of the Cranial Base. Wolfgang Seeger. (Illus.). 400p. 1984. 207.00 (*0-387-81769-7*) Spr-Verlag.

Microsurgery of the Eye: Main Aspects. Ed. by S. N. Fyodorov. (Illus.). 280p. (C). 1987. text 295.00 (*0-941743-65-9*) Nova Sci Pubs.

Microsurgery of the Lumbar Spine. Ed. by Robert W. Williams et al. LC 89-17604. (Principles & Techniques in Spine Surgery Ser.). (Illus.). 290p. 1990. reprint ed. pap. 89.90 (*0-608-05810-6*, 205977500007) Bks Demand.

Microsurgery of the Skull Base. Ugo Fisch. (Illus.). 500p. 1988. 210.00 (*0-86577-288-6*) Thieme Med Pubs.

Microsurgery of the Spinal Cord & Surrounding Structure: Anatomical & Technical Principles. Wolfgang Seeger. 410p. 1982. 185.00 (*3-211-81648-8*) Spr-Verlag.

Microsurgery of the Spinal Cord & Surrounding Structures: Anatomical & Technical Principles. Wolfgang Seeger. (Illus.). 410p. 1982. 203.00 (*0-387-81648-8*) Spr-Verlag.

Microsurgery of the Spine. John A. McCulloch. 600p. 1998. text 165.00 (*0-397-51861-7*) Lppncott W & W.

Microsurgery of the Temporo-Medical Region. R. R. Renella. (Illus.). 220p. 1989. 126.00 (*0-387-82144-9*) Spr-Verlag.

Microsurgery Retinal Detachment. 2nd ed. Mireille Bonnet. 1989. 120.00 (*0-938607-12-X*) Field & Wood Inc Medical.

Microsurgery Update, 1982-1984. Ed. by F. Bigar. (Developments in Ophthalmology Ser.: Vol. 11). (Illus.). x, 206p. 1985. 110.50 (*3-8055-4004-3*) S Karger.

Microsurgical Anatomy. Zhong Shizhen et al. 1985. text 445.50 (*0-85200-904-6*) Kluwer Academic.

Microsurgical Anatomy of the Brain: A Stereo Atlas. Gary E. Kraus & Gregory J. Bailey. LC 93-5757. (Illus.). 272p. 1994. 225.00 (*0-683-04780-9*) Lppncott W & W.

Microsurgical Anatomy of the Skull Base & Approaches to the Cavernous Sinus. Kalmon D. Post et al. (Illus.). 450p. 1996. 189.00 incl. 5.25 hd (*0-86577-598-2*) Thieme Med Pubs.

Microsurgical Approach to Cerebro-Spinal Lesions. Ed. by H. Krayenbuehl et al. (Progress in Neurological Surgery Ser.: Vol. 9). (Illus.). 1978. 170.50 (*3-8055-2819-1*) S Karger.

Microsurgical Approaches to the Target Areas of the Brain. Wolfgang Seeger. (Illus.). 300p. 1993. 179.00 (*3-211-82406-5*) Spr-Verlag.

Microsurgical Approaches to the Target Areas of the Brain. Wolfgang Seeger et al. LC 92-49017. 1993. 196.00 (*0-387-82406-5*) Spr-Verlag.

Microsurgical Carotid Endarterectomy. Ed. by Julian E. Bailes & Robert F. Spetzler. (Illus.). 208p. 1995. text 155.00 (*0-7817-0149-X*) Lppncott W & W.

Microsurgical Dissection of the Cranial Base. J. Diaz Day et al. 176p. 1996. text 116.00 (*0-443-07550-6*) Church.

Microsurgical Models in Rats for Transplantation Research. Ed. by A. Thiede et al. (Illus.). 420p. 1985. 221.00 (*0-387-13221-X*) Spr-Verlag.

Microsurgical Procedures. Ed. by Viktor E. Meyer & Michael J. Black. (Illus.). 268p. 1991. text 149.00 (*0-443-03463-X*) Church.

Microsurgical Reconstruction of the Cancer Patient. Mark Schusterman. LC 96-29739. 350p. 1997. text 165.00 (*0-397-51391-7*) Lppncott W & W.

Microsurgical Reconstruction of the Extremities. L. Gordon. (Illus.). 200p. 1988. 199.00 (*0-387-96632-3*) Spr-Verlag.

Microsurgical Reconstruction of the Head & Neck. Ed. by Shan R. Baker. (Illus.). 366p. 1989. text 171.00 (*0-443-08587-0*) Church.

***Microsurgical Thrombosis: Development, Standardisation & Application of an Expiremental Model.** Filip Stockmans. (Acta Biomedica Loveniensia Ser.: Vol. 191). (Illus.). 174p. 1999. pap. 39.50 (*90-6186-944-7*, Pub. by Leuven Univ) Coronet Bks.

Microsurveys in Discrete Probability: DIMACS Workshop, June 2-6, 1997. Ed. by David J. Aldous & James Propp. LC 98-4520. (DIMACS Ser.: Vol. 41). (Illus.). 220p. 1998. 39.00 (*0-8218-0827-3*, DIMACS/41) Am Math.

Microsystem Technology. H. P. Saluz. 1998. 88.00 (*3-7643-5774-6*) Birkhauser.

Microsystem Technology: A Powerful Tool for Biomolecular Studies. M. Kohler. (Biomethods Ser.). 1999. write for info. (*0-8176-5774-6*) Birkhauser.

Microsystem Technology & Microrobotics, Vol. XII. S. Fatikow & Ulrich Rembold. LC 96-53992. (Illus.). 400p. 1997. 74.95 (*3-540-60658-0*) Spr-Verlag.

Microsystem Technology in Chemistry & Life Science. Ed. by A. Manz & H. Becker. LC 99-13179. (Desktop Editions in Chemistry Ser.). 265p. 1999. pap. 54.95 (*3-540-65555-7*) Spr-Verlag.

Microsystem Technology in Chemistry & Life Sciences. Ed. by H. Becker & A. Manz. (Topics in Current Chemistry Ser.: Vol. 194). (Illus.). 262p. 1997. text 159.00 (*3-540-63424-X*) Spr-Verlag.

***Microsystem Technology (Menz)** 400p. 2000. text 155.00 (*3-527-29634-4*) Wiley.

***Microsystems Metrology & Inspection.** Ed. by Christophe Gorecki. (Europto Ser.). 192p. 1999. pap. text 62.00 (*0-8194-3311-X*) SPIE.

Microteaching in Teacher Education & Training. Brian McGarvey & Derek Swallow. (New Patterns of Learning Ser.). 320p. 1986. 37.50 (*0-7099-4613-9*, Pub. by C Helm) Routldge.

Microtech 2000 Workshop Report: Semiconductor Technology Roadmaps. (Illus.). 47p. (Orig.). (C). 1993. pap. text 25.00 (*1-56806-888-3*) DIANE Pub.

Microtech U. S. A MCSE Training Guide: Microsoft TCP IP. Dulaney et al. 1998. 53.49 (*1-56205-906-8*, New Riders Sftwre) MCP SW Interactive.

Microtech U. S. A MCSE Training Guide: Networking Essentials. Joe Casad & Dan Newland. 1998. 53.49 (*1-56205-905-X*, New Riders Sftwre) MCP SW Interactive.

Microtech U. S. A. MCSE Training Guide: SQL Server 6.5 Administration. Laferty et al. 1998. 53.49 (*1-56205-907-6*, New Riders Sftwre) MCP SW Interactive.

Microtech U. S. A MCSE Training Guide: Windows NT Server 4. Jose Casad & Wayne Dalton. 1998. 53.49 (*1-56205-903-3*, New Riders Sftwre) MCP SW Interactive.

Microtech U. S. A. MCSE Training Guide: Windows NT Server 4 Enterprise. Sirockman et al. 1998. 53.49 (*1-56205-904-1*) MCP SW Interactive.

Microtech U. S. A. MCSE Training Guide: Windows NT Workstation 4. Erin Dunigan. 1998. 53.49 (*1-56205-902-5*, New Riders Sftwre) MCP SW Interactive.

Microtechniques for the Clinical Laboratory: Concepts & Applications. Ed. by Mario Werner. LC 75-34373. 460p. reprint ed. 142.60 (*0-8357-9935-2*, 201520000092) Bks Demand.

Microtechnology in Special Education. Andrew Rostron & David Sewell. LC 83-22248. (Illus.). 320p. 1983. reprint ed. pap. 99.20 (*0-608-04017-7*, 206475300011) Bks Demand.

Microtectonics, Vol. X. C. W. Passchier & R. A. Trouw. LC 98-41286. (Illus.). 289p. 1995. 44.95 (*3-540-58713-6*) Spr-Verlag.

Microtectonics along the Western Edge of the Blue Ridge, Maryland, & Virginia. Ernst Cloos. LC 77-156828. (Johns Hopkins University Studies in Geology: No. 20). 261p. reprint ed. pap. 81.00 (*0-608-14275-1*, 201568800095) Bks Demand.

Microtexture Determination & Its Application. Valerie Randle. 192p. 1992. 80.00 (*0-901716-35-9*, Pub. by Inst Materials) Ashgate Pub Co.

Microtextures of Igneous & Metamorphic Rocks. J. P. Bard. 1986. pap. text 69.00 (*90-277-2313-3*); lib. bdg. 143.00 (*90-277-2220-X*) Kluwer Academic.

Microtheory: Applications & Origins. William J. Baumol. 336p. 1986. 45.00 (*0-262-02245-1*) MIT Pr.

Microtomists Formulary & Guide. Peter Gray. LC 74-23818. 808p. 1975. reprint ed. 81.50 (*0-88275-247-2*) Krieger.

Microtomist's Vade-Mecum. Arthur B. Lee. (History of Microscopy Ser.). 448p. 1987. reprint ed. 33.00 (*0-940095-04-1*) Sci Heritage Ltd.

Microtools. 3rd ed. Warren W. Allen. (DF - Computer Applications Ser.). 1993. mass mkt. 30.95 (*0-538-61656-3*) S-W Pub.

Microtools: Integrated Software for Word. Warren W. Allen. (DF - Computer Applications Ser.). 1988. mass mkt. 25.95 (*0-538-10160-1*) S-W Pub.

Microtools: Integrated Software for Word Processing, Spreadsheet, & Database. large type ed. Warren W. Allen & Dale H. Klooster. 1991. 80.50 (*0-614-09877-7*, L-85812-00) Am Printing Hse.

Microtools: Integrated Software for WP, Spreadsheet & Data... Allen. (Computer Applications Ser.). 1990. pap. 25.75 (*0-538-61440-4*) Sth-Wstrn College.

Microtools Reference Handbook. Warren W. Allen. (DF - Computer Applications Ser.). 1988. mass mkt. 11.95 (*0-538-10167-9*) S-W Pub.

Microtools 3.0 DOS Student Resource Guide. Arnowitz Productions Inc., Staff. (DA - Computer Education Ser.). (J). (gr. k-8). 1995. text 11.95 (*0-538-64333-1*) S-W Pub.

***Microtrading CDROM Course.** Lawrence Black. 2000. 125.00 (*1-883272-37-8*) Traders Lib.

***Microtrading Manual.** Marcus Bowman et al. (Illus.). 120p. 1999. pap. 80.00 (*0-9662601-1-2*) Microtrade.

Microtransducer CAD: Physical & Computational Aspects. A. Nathan & H. Baltes. Ed. by S. Selberherr. LC 99-23861. (Computational Microelectronics Ser.). (Illus.). 300p. 1998. 189.00 (*3-211-83103-7*) Spr-Verlag.

Microtron. S. P. Kapitza & V. N. Melekhin. Ed. by Ednor Rowe et al. Tr. by I. N. Sviatoslavsky. (Accelerators & Storage Rings Ser.: Vol. 1). xvii, 204p. 1978. text 155.00 (*0-906346-01-0*) Gordon & Breach.

Microtubule Proteins. Ed. by Jesus A. De Grado. 288p. 1989. lib. bdg. 219.00 (*0-8493-5527-3*, QP552) CRC Pr.

Microtubules. Ed. by Jeremy S. Hyams & Clive W. Lloyd. LC 93-30114. 439p. 1993. 175.00 (*0-471-56193-2*, Wiley-Liss) Wiley.

Microtubules in Microorganisms. Ed. by Piero Cappuccinelli & N. Ronald Morris. LC 82-13003. (Microbiology Ser.: No. 8). (Illus.). 428p. reprint ed. pap. 132.70 (*0-7837-0636-7*, 204098000019) Bks Demand.

Microtunnel Construction: Proceedings: International Symposium on Microtunnel Construction (3d: 1995: Munich, Germany) Part of the 3rd Symposium Staff. (Illus.). 166p. (C). 1995. 91.00 (*90-5410-542-9*, Pub. by A A Balkema) Ashgate Pub Co.

Microtunnel Construction: Proceedings of the 4th International Symposium, Muenchen, 1998. (GER.). 94p. 1998. 58.00 (*90-5410-950-5*, Pub. by A A Balkema) Ashgate Pub Co.

Microtunnel Construction: Proceedings of the 4th International Symposium, Munchen, 2-3 April, 1998. LC 99-496399. (Illus.). 86p. (C). 1998. text 61.00 (*90-5410-949-1*, Pub. by A A Balkema) Ashgate Pub Co.

Microtunnelling: Installation & Renewal of Nonman-Size Supply & Sewage Lines by the Trenchless Construction Method. Deitrich Stein et al. (Illus.). 353p. 1989. 140.00 (*3-433-01201-6*, Pub. by Ernst & Sohn) Wiley.

Microtunnelling: Proceedings of the Second International Symposium on Microtunnelling, Munich, 8 April 1992. (Illus.). 99p. (C). 1992. text 71.00 (*90-5410-072-9*, Pub. by A A Balkema) Ashgate Pub Co.

Microtype: The Wonderful World of Paws. 2nd ed. Jackson. (PB - Keyboarding Ser.). 1992. 71.95 (*0-538-62052-8*) S-W Pub.

Microtype: The Wonderful World of Paws. 2nd ed. Jackson. (PB - Keyboarding Ser.). 1992. 71.95 (*0-538-62054-4*) S-W Pub.

Microtype: The Wonderful World of Paws. 2nd ed. Jackson. (PB - Keyboarding Ser.). (J). (gr. k-8). 1992. 101.95 (*0-538-61251-7*); 101.95 (*0-538-61250-9*) S-W Pub.

Microtype Multimedia, User's Guide, Retail Version. Eai. (Keyboarding/Typesetting-1st Yr Ser.). 1999. pap. 10.00 (*0-538-68379-1*) S-W Pub.

MicroUse Directory: Software. Ching-Chih Chen. 440p. (Orig.). 1984. pap. 99.50 (*0-931555-01-9*) MicroUse Info.

Microvascual Surgery & Free Tissue Transfer. text. write for info. (*0-340-54925-4*, Pub. by E A) Routldge.

Microvascular & Neurological Complication of Diabetes. Ed. by G. Crepaldi et al. (FIDIA Research Ser.: Vol. 10). 325p. 1988. 162.00 (*0-387-96619-6*) Spr-Verlag.

Microvascular Bone Reconstruction. Michael B. Wood & Alain Gilbert. 224p. 1998. text. write for info. (*0-948269-71-5*, Pub. by Martin Dunitz) Mosby Inc.

Microvascular Corrosion Casting in Scanning Electron Microscopy: Techniques & Applications. S. H. Aharinejad & A. Lametschwandtner. LC 92-48882. 400p. 1993. 159.00 (*0-387-82377-8*) Spr-Verlag.

Microvascular Free Flaps in Head & Neck Reconstruction. Richard L. Arden & John M. Truelson. LC 97-36821. (Monograph Ser.). (Illus.). 130p. 1998. pap. text 60.00 (*1-56772-057-9*, 5206265) AAO-HNS.

Microvascular Mechanics. Ed. by J. S. Lee & T. C. Skalak. (Illus.). xv, 222p. 1989. 130.00 (*0-387-97038-X*) Spr-Verlag.

Microvascular Motricity & Haemorheology Effects of Buflomedil: Journal: Blood Vessels, Vol. 28, Suppl. 1. Ed. by Marcos Intaglietta. (Illus.). iv, 48p. 1991. pap. 16.75 (*3-8055-5491-5*) S Karger.

Microvascular Networks: Experimental & Theoretical Studies. Ed. by A. S. Popel & P. C. Johnson. (Illus.). x, 226p. 1986. 172.25 (*3-8055-4323-9*) S Karger.

Microvascular Perfusion & Transport in Health & Disease. Ed. by P. F. McDonagh. (Illus.). x, 254p. 1986. 209.75 (*3-8055-4394-8*) S Karger.

Microvascular Reconstruction. R. T. Manktelow. (Illus.). 245p. 1986. 427.00 (*0-387-15271-7*) Spr-Verlag.

Microvascular Surgeory. David S. Soutar. 1993. 145.00 (*0-316-80470-3*, Little Brwn Med Div) Lppncott W & W.

Microvascular Surgery of the Extremities. Zhongjia Yu. Tr. by Bingfang Zeng. LC 92-2302. 1993. 350.00 (*0-387-55273-1*); 298.00 (*3-540-55273-1*) Spr-Verlag.

Microvascular Therapeutic Advances in Venous Disorders Vol. 15, Suppl. 1: Journal: Int. J. Microcirc., 1995. Ed. by C. Allegra & A. Bollinger. (Journal Ser.: Vol. 15, Suppl. 1, 1995). (Illus.). iv, 56p. 1995. pap. 26.25 (*3-8055-6253-5*) S Karger.

Microvascular Tissure Transplant in the Head & Neck. Friedrich Bootz & Gottfried H. Muller. LC 93-8837. Tr. of Mikrovaskul are Gewebetransplantation im Kopt-Hals-Bereich. (GER.). 101p. 1993. 105.00 (*0-86577-503-6*) Thieme Med Pubs.

***Microvias: Low Cost, High Density Interconnects.** John H. Lau. 2000. 89.95 (*0-07-136327-0*) McGraw.

Microview. 7th ed. Linda Pulsinelli. (C). 1991. pap. 22.00 (*0-06-045353-2*) Addson-Wesley Educ.

Microwave. Barbara L. Hanson. 36p. (Orig.). 1994. pap. 3.25 (*0-940844-49-4*) Wellspring.

Microwave: Solves Fast Meal Problems. Ed. by G & R Publishing Staff. (Uni-Bks.). 160p. (Orig.). 1994. pap. text 3.00 (*1-56383-011-6*, 1400) G & R Pub.

Microwave Affair: Single Servings Cookbook. Paula J. Smith. (Illus.). 1983. ring bd. 13.95 (*0-914749-00-5*) RiskTrek.

Microwave & Geometric Optics. S. Cornbleet. (Techniques of Physics Ser.). (Illus.). 640p. 1994. text 143.00 (*0-12-189651-X*) Acad Pr.

Microwave & Millimeter-Wave Diode Frequence Multipliers. Mark T. Faber et al. LC 95-24010. 368p. 1995. 103.00 (*0-89006-611-6*) Artech Hse.

Microwave & Millimeter Wave Phase Shifters Vol. I: Dielectric & Ferrite Phase Shifters. Shiban K. Koul & Barathi Bhat. (Microwave Library). 395p. 1991. text. write for info. (*0-89006-319-2*) Artech Hse.

Microwave & Optical Ray Geometry. S. Cornbleet. LC 83-16737. (Illus.). 162p. reprint ed. pap. 50.30 (*0-8357-4314-4*, 203711300007) Bks Demand.

Microwave & Optical Technology Letters. Kai Chang. 1988. pap. 120.00 (*0-471-60578-6*) Wiley.

M

Microwave & Optical Transmission S. O. L. Olver. 86p. 1992. pap. text 2.00 (*0-471-93767-3*) Wiley.

Microwave & Optical Waveguides. N. J. Cronin. (Illus.). 132p. 1995. 90.00 (*0-7503-0215-1*); pap. 34.00 (*0-7503-0216-X*) IOP Pub.

***Microwave & RF Wireless Systems.** David M. Pozar. 480p. 2000. write for info. (*0-471-32282-2*) Wiley.

Microwave & Wireless Communications Technology. Joseph J. Carr. 435p. 1996. pap. text 49.95 (*0-7506-9707-5*) Buttrwrth-Heinemann.

Microwave Antenna Theory & Design. Ed. by S. Silver. (Electromagnetic Waves Ser.: No. 19). 640p. 1984. 85.00 (*0-86341-017-0*, EW019) INSPEC Inc.

Microwave Approach to Highly-Irregular Fiber Optics. Huang Hung-Chia. LC 97-15393. (Series in Microwave & Optical Engineering). 307p. 1998. 84.95 (*0-471-31023-9*) Wiley.

Microwave Aquametry: Electromagnetic Wave Interaction with Water-Containing Materials. Ed. by Andrezej Kraszewski. LC 95-43232. (TAB-IEEE Press Book Ser.). 504p. 1996. 110.00 (*0-7803-1146-9*, PC5617) Inst Electrical.

Microwave Attenuation Measurement. Frank L. Warner. LC 78-310658. (IEE Monograph Ser.: Vol. 19). (Illus.). 360p. reprint ed. pap. 111.60 (*0-608-17789-X*, 203225400079) Bks Demand.

Microwave Behaviour of Ferrimagnetics & Plasmas: Proceedings of the International Conference, London, 1965. International Conference on the Microwave Behavior. LC 66-36909. (Institution of Electrical Engineers Conference Report Ser.: No. 13). 437p. reprint ed. pap. 135.50 (*0-608-11027-2*, 200738500061) Bks Demand.

Microwave Bible. Norene Gilletz. 1991. pap. 9.99 (*0-446-39297-9*) Warner Bks.

Microwave Cavity Antennas. Akhileshwar Kumar. LC 89-217. (Artech House Antenna Library). (Illus.). 484p. 1989. reprint ed. pap. 150.10 (*0-608-00566-5*, 206144900009) Bks Demand.

Microwave Circuit Design: Using Linear & Nonlinear Techniques. George D. Vendelin et al. 784p. (Orig.). 1992. pap. 89.95 (*0-471-58060-0*) Wiley.

Microwave Circuit Design Using Programmable Calculators. James L. Allen & Max W. Medley. LC 80-17806. (Artech House Microwave Library). (Illus.). 304p. reprint ed. pap. 94.30 (*0-8357-4186-9*, 203696400006) Bks Demand.

Microwave Circuit Theory & Foundations of Microwave Metrology. Glenn F. Engen. (Electrical Measurement Ser.: No. 9). 216p. 1992. boxed set 55.00 (*0-86341-287-4*, EL009) INSPEC Inc.

Microwave Circuits & Passive Devices. M. L. Sisodia & G. S. Raghuvanshi. 1987. write for info. (*0-85226-856-4*, Pub. by Wiley Estrn) Franklin.

Microwave Circulator Design. Douglas K. Linkhart. LC 89-6550. (Artech House Microwave Library). (Illus.). 206p. 1989. reprint ed. pap. 63.90 (*0-608-03159-3*, 206361200007) Bks Demand.

Microwave Communication. George M. Kizer. LC 89-48041. (Illus.). 702p. (C). 1990. text 72.95 (*0-8138-0026-9*) Iowa St U Pr.

Microwave Communications: Devices & Circuits. E. Hund. 384p. 1989. pap. text 77.20 (*0-07-031277-X*) McGraw.

Microwave Conference, 1997 Asia Pacific, 3 vols. IEEE Staff. 1340p. 1998. pap. 230.00 (*0-7803-4288-7*, TH8336) Inst Electrical.

Microwave Cookbook. Annemarie Rosier. 1986. 4.98 (*0-671-07750-3*) S&S Trade.

Microwave Cooking. Deni Bown. (101 Essential Tips Ser.). (Illus.). 72p. 1997. 4.95 (*1-56458-987-0*) DK Pub Inc.

Microwave Cooking Appliances, UL 923. 4th ed. (C). 1995. pap. text 175.00 (*1-55989-099-1*) Underwrtrs Labs.

Microwave Cooking Explained. Thelma Snyder. (Series 923). (Orig.). 1983. pap., student ed. 7.00 (*0-8064-0397-7*) Bergwall.

Microwave Cooking Market. Ed. by Peter Allen. 200p. 1986. pap. 1250.00 (*0-931634-67-9*) FIND-SVP.

***Microwave Cooking Properly Explained: With Recipes.** Annette Yates. 128p. 2000. pap. 7.95 (*0-7160-2014-9*, Pub. by Elliot RW Bks) Midpt Trade.

Microwave Cooking Starts Here. Patricia E. Hutt. reprint ed. 4.95 (*0-9613884-0-4*) A Thomas Pub.

Microwave Cooking Techniques. Thelma Snyder. (Series 924). (Orig.). 1983. pap., student ed. 7.00 (*0-8064-0399-3*) Bergwall.

***Microwave Cooking Times at a Glance.** Annette Yates. 192p. 2000. pap. 6.95 (*0-7160-2067-X*, Pub. by Elliot RW Bks) Midpt Trade.

Microwave Craft Magic. Marjie Lambert. 112p. 1996. write for info. (*1-57215-178-1*) World Pubns.

Microwave Cuisine Adult Education Microwave Cooking Course: Intermediate Techniques. Millie Delahunty. 41p. (Orig.). 1985. pap. text 12.95 (*0-932243-07-X*) Microwave Cuisine.

Microwave Cuisine Cooks Appetizers. Millie Delahunty. (Illus.). 32p. (Orig.). 1984. pap. 2.95 (*0-932243-06-1*) Microwave Cuisine.

Microwave Cuisine Cooks Desserts. Millie Delahunty. (Illus.). 32p. (Orig.). 1989. pap. 2.95 (*0-932243-11-8*) Microwave Cuisine.

Microwave Cuisine Cooks Italian-Style. Millie Delahunty. (Illus.). 32p. (Orig.). 1985. pap. 2.95 (*0-932243-08-8*) Microwave Cuisine.

Microwave Cuisine Cooks Low-Sodium. Millie Delahunty. (Illus.). 32p. (Orig.). 1985. pap. 2.95 (*0-932243-09-6*) Microwave Cuisine.

Microwave Cuisine Cooks New England Style. Millie Delahunty. (Illus.). 32p. (Orig.). 1986. pap. 2.95 (*0-932243-10-X*) Microwave Cuisine.

Microwave Deception. 1989. spiral bd. 29.95 (*0-930165-13-6*) Greensward Pr.

Microwave Delights. 4th rev. ed. Camille Ronzio & Trina Wilkinson. LC 80-65640. (Illus.). 206p. 1980. pap. 7.95 (*0-686-85760-7*) Cam-Tri Prods.

Microwave Devices: Device Circuit Interactions. Ed. by M. J. Howes & D. V. Morgan. LC 75-15887. (Wiley Series in Solid State Devices & Circuits). 414p. reprint ed. pap. 128.40 (*0-608-15788-0*, 203102600073) Bks Demand.

Microwave Devices, Circuits & Their Interaction. Charles A. Lee & G. Conrad Dalman. (Microwave & Optical Engineering Ser.). 384p. 1994. 98.50 (*0-471-55216-X*) Wiley.

Microwave Diabetes Cookbook. Betty Marks. LC 90-24555. 200p. (Orig.). 1991. pap. 10.95 (*0-940625-26-1*) Surrey Bks.

Microwave Dielectric Spectroscopy of Ferroelectrics & Related Materials. Jonas P. Grigas. (Ferroelectricity & Related Phenomena Ser.). 416p. 1996. text 75.00 (*2-88449-190-2*) Gordon & Breach.

Microwave Diet Cookbook. Jane Hunter. (FRE., Illus.). 208p. (Orig.). 1993. pap. write for info. (*1-882330-23-4*) Magni Co.

Microwave Diet Cookbook: 365 Quick & Easy Low Calorie, Delicious Microwave Recipes. Jane Hunter. (Illus.). 208p. 1993. pap. 12.95 (*1-882330-22-6*) Magni Co.

Microwave Diode Control Devices. Robert V. Garver. LC 74-82596. (Modern Frontiers in Applied Science Ser.). (Illus.). 382p. reprint ed. pap. 118.50 (*0-8357-5582-7*, 203521300093) Bks Demand.

Microwave Discharges: Fundamentals & Applications. C. M. Ferreira & M. Moisan. (NATO ASI Ser.: Vol. 302). (Illus.). 574p. (C). 1993. text 145.00 (*0-306-44355-4*, Kluwer Plenum) Kluwer Academic.

Microwave Discrete Solid-State Devices & Interface Considerations. (Tech Edge Ser.). (Illus.). 125p. 1990. 25.00 (*0-944916-17-1*) emf-emi Control.

Microwave Dough Craft. Alison Jenkins. 1996. 12.98 (*0-7858-0631-8*) Bk Sales Inc.

Microwave Electronic Circuit Technology. Ed. by Yoshihiro Konishi. LC 97-33114. (Illus.). 432p. 1997. text 175.00 (*0-8247-0101-1*) Dekker.

Microwave Electronics. Paynter. (Electronics Technology Ser.). 1997. teacher ed. 12.00 (*0-8273-6382-6*) Delmar.

Microwave Electronics. Paynter. (Electronics Technology Ser.). 1997. text 52.95 (*0-8273-6381-8*) Delmar.

Microwave Engineering. Peter A. Rizzi. (Illus.). 640p. (C). 1987. 70.60 (*0-13-586702-9*) P-H.

Microwave Engineering. 2nd ed. T. Koryu Ishii. 576p. (C). 1995. text 61.95 (*0-15-558658-0*) OUP.

Microwave Engineering. 2nd ed. David M. Pozar. LC 97-20878. 736p. 1997. text 114.95 (*0-471-17096-8*) Wiley.

Microwave Engineering: Passive, Active & Non-Reciprocal Circuits. Joseph Helszajn. 392p. 1991. 80.00 (*0-07-707375-4*) McGraw.

Microwave Engineering: With Wireless Applications. S. R. Pennock & P. R. Shepherd. 352p. 1998. 65.00 (*0-07-049722-2*) McGraw.

Microwave Engineering & Systems Applications. Edward A. Wolff & Roger Kaul. LC 87-25223. 672p. 1988. 185.00 (*0-471-63269-4*) Wiley.

Microwave Engineering Handbook. J. Michael Golio. (Electrical Engineering Handbook Ser.). 1999. 125.00 (*0-8493-8592-X*) CRC Pr.

Microwave Engineering Handbook, 3 vols. Ed. by B. L. Smith & M. H. Carpentier. (Microwave Technology & Techniques Ser.). 1522p. 1997. 270.00 (*0-7803-3436-1*) Inst Electrical.

Microwave Engineering Handbook, 1. Ed. by Bradford L. Smith & Michel-Henri Carpentier. LC 92-34490. (Microwave Technology Ser.: Vols. 1-3). 1992. text 125.95 (*0-442-31588-0*) Chapman & Hall.

Microwave Engineering Handbook, 2. Ed. by Bradford L. Smith & Michel-Henri Carpentier. LC 92-34490. (Microwave Technology Ser.: Vols. 1-3). 1992. text 145.95 (*0-442-31628-3*) Chapman & Hall.

Microwave Engineering Handbook, 3. Ed. by Bradford L. Smith & Michel-Henri Carpentier. LC 92-34490. (Microwave Technology Ser.: Vols. 1-3). 1992. text 145.95 (*0-442-31657-7*) Chapman & Hall.

Microwave Engineers' Handbook, 2 vols., Vol. 1. Ed. by Theodore Saad. LC 76-168891. 192p. 1971. 39.00 (*0-89006-002-9*) Artech Hse.

Microwave Engineers' Handbook, 2 vols., Vol. 2. Ed. by Theodore Saad. LC 76-168891. 208p. 1971. 39.00 (*0-89006-003-7*) Artech Hse.

Microwave-Enhanced Chemistry: Fundamentals, Sample Preparation & Applications. Ed. by H. M. Kingston & Stephen J. Haswell. LC 97-5983. (ACS Professional Reference Bks.). 800p. 1997. text 110.00 (*0-8412-3375-6*, Pub. by Am Chemical) OUP.

Microwave Excited Plasmas. Ed. by Michel Moisan & Jacques Pelletier. LC 92-30694. (Plasma Technology Ser.: Vol. 4). 520p. 1992. 214.25 (*0-444-88815-2*) Elsevier.

Microwave Facilities & Regulations. Edward Kurcina. LC 73-85629. (Specialized Ser.). (Illus.). 232p. (Orig.). (C). 1987. pap. text 33.95 (*1-56016-023-3*) ABC TeleTraining.

Microwave Field-Effect Transistors: Theory, Design & Applications. 3rd ed. Raymond S. Pengelly. Ed. by Crawford Hammond. (Illus.). 704p. 1996. reprint ed. 79.00 (*1-884932-50-9*) Noble Pubng.

Microwave Filters for Communications Systems. Chandra M. Kudsia & Valentine O'Donovan. LC 73-81239. (Modern Frontiers in Applied Science Ser.). 144p. reprint ed. pap. 44.70 (*0-608-09951-1*, 201007600068) Bks Demand.

Microwave Filters, Impedance-Matching Networks, & Coupling Structures. G. L. Matthaei et al. LC 80-68976. (Artech Microwave Library). (Illus.). 1096p. 1980. reprint ed. 99.00 (*0-89006-099-1*) Artech Hse.

Microwave Filters Using Parallel Coupled Lines. Leo Young. LC 72-168945. (Illus.). 253p. reprint ed. pap. 78.50 (*0-608-10030-7*, 201210200080) Bks Demand.

Microwave Fixation of Labile Metabolites: Proceedings of an Official Satellite Symposium of the 8th International Congress of Pharmacology Held in Tokyo, Japan, 25 July 1981. Ed. by Yosh Maruyama et al. (Advances in the Biosciences Ser.: 45). (Illus.). 191p. 1983. 60.50 (*0-08-029829-X*, Pergamon Pr) Elsevier.

Microwave Foods: New Product Development. Robert V. Decareau. 213p. 1992. 50.00 (*0-917678-30-3*) Food & Nut Pr.

***Microwave Foregrounds.** Ed. by Angelica de Oliveira-Costa & Max Tegmark. (Conference Series Proceedings: Vol. 181). 377p. 1999. text 52.00 (*1-58381-006-4*) Astron Soc Pacific.

***Microwave Gourmet.** Barbara Kafka. 576p. 1998. pap. 20.00 (*0-688-15792-0*, Wm Morrow) Morrow Avon.

Microwave Gourmet. Barbara Kafka. 656p. 1991. reprint ed. mass mkt. 5.95 (*0-380-71251-2*, Avon Bks) Morrow Avon.

Microwave Homodyne Systems. Ray J. King. LC 78-314375. (IEE Electromagnetic Waves Ser.: No. 3). 378p. reprint ed. pap. 117.20 (*0-8357-8951-9*, 203345000086) Bks Demand.

Microwave Horns & Feeds. A. D. Olver et al. 512p. 1994. 99.95 (*0-7803-1115-9*, PC4689) Inst Electrical.

Microwave Hostess. Marty Klinzman & Shirley Guy. 96p. (C). 1989. 110.00 (*1-85368-068-0*, Pub. by New5 Holland) St Mut.

Microwave Imaging Techniques. Bernard D. Steinberg & Harish Subbaram. LC 90-12941. (Series in Remote Sensing). 361p. 1991. 150.00 (*0-471-50078-X*) Wiley.

Microwave Impedance Measurement. P. I. Somlo & J. D. Hunter. (Electrical Measurement Ser.: No. 2). 224p. 1985. boxed set 92.00 (*0-86341-033-2*, EL002) INSPEC Inc.

Microwave, Infrared, & Laser Transitions of Methanol: Atlas of Assigned Lines from 0 to 1258 CM. Ed. by Giovanni Moruzzi et al. LC 95-23097. 544p. 1995. boxed set 254.95 (*0-8493-2478-5*, 2478) CRC Pr.

Microwave Integrated Circuits. I. Kasa. 298p. 1991. 435.00 (*963-05-5890-4*, Pub. by Akade Kiado) St Mut.

Microwave Integrated Circuits. Ed. by I. Kneppo. (Microwave Technology & Techniques Ser.). 352p. 1997. 110.00 (*0-7803-3437-X*, PC5710-QOE) Inst Electrical.

Microwave Integrated Circuits. Ed. by Yoshihiro Konishi. (Electrical Engineering & Electronics Ser.: Vol. 71). (Illus.). 648p. 1991. text 215.00 (*0-8247-8199-6*) Dekker.

Microwave Integrated Circuits. Ed. by Jeffrey Frey. LC 74-82595. (Modern Frontiers in Applied Science Ser.). (Illus.). 440p. reprint ed. pap. 136.40 (*0-8357-4181-8*, 203695900006) Bks Demand.

Microwave Integrated Circuits. 2nd ed. Ed. by J. Frey & K. B. Bhasin. (Microwave Software Library). 446p. 1985. pap. text. write for info. (*0-89006-160-2*) Artech Hse.

Microwave Integrated Circuits & Interfaces. (Tech Edge Ser.). (Illus.). 125p. 1990. 25.00 (*0-944916-13-9*) emf-emi Control.

***Microwave Kitchen Bible.** Carol Bowen. 256p. 2000. pap. 19.95 (*1-84215-109-6*) Anness Pub.

Microwave Know-How. 224p. 1981. spiral bd. 10.95 (*0-685-45696-X*) Starr-Toof.

Microwave Know-How. CiCi Williamson & Ann Steiner. LC 81-90173. Orig. Title: MicroScope Savoir Faire. (Illus.). 222p. 1985. reprint ed. pap. 10.95 (*0-9607740-2-5*) MicroScope TX.

***Microwave Magic: Step-by-Step from Family Suppers to Gourmet Entertaining.** Carol Bowen. (Illus.). 2000. pap. 14.95 (*0-7548-0511-5*, Lorenz Bks) Anness Pub.

Microwave Magnetics. Ronald F. Soohoo. 272p. (C). 1985. text 64.95 (*0-685-57945-X*) HarperTrade.

Microwave Mastery: Microwave Cooking. Carol Trench. Ed. & Illus. by Robert Trench. 288p. (Orig.). 1988. text 19.95 (*0-317-90862-6*); pap. text 14.95 (*0-317-90863-4*) Mic-it Pub.

Microwave Mastery Cookbook. Carol Trench. 286p. 1991. pap. 12.95 (*0-929573-00-5*) Mic-it Pub.

Microwave Materials. Ed. by V. R. Murthy et al. vii,257p. 1994. 69.00 (*0-387-58075-1*) Spr-Verlag.

Microwave Materials & Fabrication Techniques. Thomas S. Laverghetta. LC 84-71819. (Artech House Microwave Library). (Illus.). 237p. reprint ed. pap. 73.50 (*0-608-16026-1*, 203312500083) Bks Demand.

***Microwave Materials & Fabrication Techniques.** 3rd ed. Thomas S. Laverghetta. (Microwave Library). 2000. 83.00 (*1-58053-064-8*) Artech Hse.

Microwave Meals in Minutes. Mary Norwak. (Getting It Right Ser.). 1995. pap. 3.95 (*0-572-01764-2*, Pub. by Foulsham UK) Assoc Pubs Grp.

Microwave Measurements. 2nd rev. ed. Ed. by A. E. Bailey. (Electrical Measurement Ser.: No. 3). 1989. pap. 119.00 (*0-86341-184-3*, EL003) INSPEC Inc.

Microwave Measurements & Techniques. Thomas S. Laverghetta. LC 75-31383. (Illus.). 411p. reprint ed. pap. 127.50 (*0-8357-4233-4*, 203702000002) Bks Demand.

Microwave MESFETs & HEMTs. Ed. by J. Michael Golio. LC 91-4554. (Artech House Microwave Library). (Illus.). 367p. 1991. reprint ed. pap. 113.80 (*0-608-03155-0*, 206360800007) Bks Demand.

Microwave Mixers. 2nd ed. Stephen A. Maas. (Microwave Library). 375p. 1992. text 93.00 (*0-89006-605-1*) Artech Hse.

Microwave Mobile Communications. William C. Jakes. 656p. 1994. 84.95 (*0-7803-1069-1*, PC4234) Inst Electrical.

Microwave Modified Procedures for the Histotechnician - In an Hour or Less. Patricia A. Jumer. LC 95-94745. (Illus.). 116p. (Orig.). 1995. student ed. 39.50 (*0-9647623-0-7*) I S A C Tech.

Microwave NDT. Nathan Ida. LC 92-33611. (Developments in Electromagnetic Theory & Application Ser.: Vol. 10). 1992. text 260.00 (*0-7923-2007-7*) Kluwer Academic.

Microwave Nondestructive Evaluation: State-of-the-Art Review. R. Zoughi & S. Ganchev. (Illus.). iii, 171p. (Orig.). 1995. pap. 50.00 (*1-890596-02-7*) TX Res Inst.

Microwave Nondestructive Testing Methods. A. J. Bahr. xvi, 86p. 1982. pap. 75.00 (*0-685-47156-X*) Gordon & Breach.

Microwave Oven Repair. 2nd ed. Homer L. Davidson. (Illus.). 368p. 1991. 29.95 (*0-8306-6457-2*, 3457); pap. 19.95 (*0-8306-3457-6*) McGraw-Hill Prof.

Microwave Ovens. (Concise Monographs). (Illus.). 24p. 1996. pap. 12.50 (*0-944398-86-3*, 398862) ILSI.

Microwave Passive Direction Finding. Stephen Lipsky. LC 86-33995. 320p. 1987. 160.00 (*0-471-83454-8*) Wiley.

Microwave Physics & Technique. A. Y. Spasov et al. 768p. (C). 1990. text 123.00 (*981-02-0090-0*) World Scientific Pub.

Microwave Physics & Technique: Fifth International School on Microwave Physics & Engineering. 524p. (C). 1988. text 125.00 (*9971-5-0429-4*) World Scientific Pub.

Microwave Physics & Technique: Proceedings of the 7th International School. A. Y. Spasov. 500p. 1997. text 114.00 (*981-02-0920-7*) World Scientific Pub.

Microwave Physics & Techniques: Proceedings of the NATO Advanced Research Workshop on Microwave Physics & Technique, Sozopol, Bulgaria, 1996. Ed. by Groll. LC 97-14125. 457p. 1997. text 251.00 (*0-7923-4582-7*) Kluwer Academic.

Microwave Planar Passive Circuits & Filters. J. Helszjan. 418p. 1994. 280.00 (*0-471-94056-9*) Wiley.

***Microwave Planner.** Annette Yates. 128p. 2000. pap. 7.95 (*0-7160-2060-2*, Pub. by Elliot RW Bks) Midpt Trade.

Microwave-Plasma Interactions. Ed. by D. V. Skobel'tsyn. Tr. by Dave Parsons from RUS. LC 75-20239. (Proceedings of the P. N. Lebedev Physics Institute Ser.: No. 73). (Illus.). 143p. reprint ed. pap. 44.40 (*0-608-05532-8*, 206600000006) Bks Demand.

Microwave Polarimetric Backscattering from Natural Rough Surfaces. fac. ed. Yisok Oh. LC QC0676.7. (University of Michigan Report: No. RL904). 249p. 1994. pap. 77.20 (*0-7837-7699-3*, 204745600007) Bks Demand.

Microwave Power Coupling & Related Interfacing Devices. (Tech Edge Ser.). (Illus.). 125p. 1990. 25.00 (*0-944916-15-5*) emf-emi Control.

Microwave Power Measurement. J. A. Lane. LC TK6553.L3. (IEE Monograph Ser.: No. 12). (Illus.). 80p. reprint ed. pap. 30.00 (*0-8357-8952-7*, 203345400086) Bks Demand.

Microwave Processing of Materials. National Research Council, Microwave Proccessing o. LC 94-66560. (Publication NMAB Ser.: No. 473). (Illus.). 166p. 1994. reprint ed. pap. 51.50 (*0-608-04259-5*, 206501400012) Bks Demand.

Microwave Processing of Materials V. Ed. by M. F. Iskander et al. (MRS Symposium Proceedings Ser.: Vol. 430). 662p. 1996. 73.00 (*1-55899-333-9*, 430) Materials Res.

Microwave Processing of Materials III. Ed. by Ronald L. Beatty et al. (Symposium Proceedings Ser.: Vol. 269). 623p. 1992. text 30.00 (*1-55899-164-6*) Materials Res.

Microwave Processing of Materials II, Vol. 189/124. Ed. by W. B. Snyder, Jr. et al. 932p. 1993. reprint ed. text 62.00 (*1-55899-214-6*) Materials Res.

Microwave Propagation in Ferrimagnetics. N. C. Srivastava & Mahendra S. Sodha. LC 81-15364. 428p. 1981. 95.00 (*0-306-40716-7*, Plenum Trade) Perseus Pubng.

Microwave Propagation Through Cultural Vegetation Canopies. Ahad Tavakoli et al. LC G 0070.. (Technical Reports: No. 026511-3-T). 166p. reprint ed. pap. 51.50 (*0-7837-1391-6*, 204157200021) Bks Demand.

Microwave Properties of Magnetic Films. Carmine Vittoria. 248p. 1993. text 61.00 (*981-02-1412-X*) World Scientific Pub.

***Microwave Radar: Imaging & Advanced Processing.** Roger J. Sullivan. LC 00-29989. 350p. 2000. 95.00 (*0-89006-341-9*) Artech Hse.

Microwave Radar Signatures of Sea Vessels: Krylov Shipbuilding Institute R&D. Boris Lande & Evgenii Shtager. (Foreign Technology Assessment Ser.). 380p. (Orig.). 1994. pap. 55.00 (*1-881874-16-8*) Global Cnslts.

***Microwave Radio Transmission Design Guide.** Trevor Manning. LC 99-41774. (Microwave Library). 231p. 1999. 79.00 (*1-58053-031-1*) Artech Hse.

Microwave Radiometry & Remote Sensing Applications. P. Pampaloni. (Illus.). 167p. 1989. 135.00 (*90-6764-108-1*, Pub. by VSP) Coronet Bks.

***Microwave Radiometry & Remote Sensing of the Earth's Surface & Atmosphere.** Ed. by P. Pampaloni & S. Paloscia. (Illus.). 566p. 1999. 247.50 (*90-6764-318-1*, Pub. by Uppsala Universitet) Coronet Bks.

Microwave Radiometry & Remote Sensing of the Environment. Ed. by D. Solimini. (Illus.). 562p. 1995. 225.00 (*90-6764-189-8*, Pub. by VSP) Coronet Bks.

Microwave Receivers with Electronic Warfare Applications. James B. Tsui. LC 92-1257. 478p. (C). 1992. reprint ed. lib. bdg. 74.95 (*0-89464-724-5*) Krieger.

Microwave Recipes. Mary Norwalk. (Getting It Right Ser.). 1994. pap. 9.95 (*0-572-01773-1*, Pub. by W Foulsham) Trans-Atl Phila.

***Microwave Recipes for One.** Annette Yates. 128p. 2000. pap. 6.95 (*0-7160-2044-0*, Pub. by Elliot RW Bks) Midpt Trade.

Microwave Remote Sensing: From Theory to Applications, 3 vols., Vol. 3. Fawwaz T. Ulaby et al. 1120p. 1986. text 89.00 (*0-89006-192-0*) Artech Hse.

An Asterisk (*) at the beginning of an entry indicates that the title is appearing for the first time.

Microwave Remote Sensing: Fundamentals & Radiometry, 3 vols., Vol. 1. Fawwaz T. Ulaby et al. 456p. 1986. text 81.00 (*0-89006-190-4*) Artech Hse.

Microwave Remote Sensing for Oceanographic & Marine Weather-Forecast Models. Ed. by Robin A. Vaughan. (C). 1990. text 284.50 (*0-7923-0581-7*) Kluwer Academic.

Microwave Remote Sensing of Sea Ice. Ed. by Frank Carsey. LC 92-41032. (Geophysical Monograph Ser.: Vol. 68). 1993. 68.00 (*0-87590-033-X*) Am Geophysical.

Microwave Remote Sensing of the Atmosphere & Environment. Ed. by Tadahiro Hayasaka et al. LC 99-169806. (Proceedings of SPIE Ser.: Vol. 3503). 464p. 1998. 99.00 (*0-8194-2962-7*) SPIE.

Microwave Remote Sensing of the Earth System. Ed. by Alain Chedin. LC 89-1335. (Illus.). 173p. 1989. 50.00 (*0-937194-17-4*) A Deepak Pub.

***Microwave Resonators & Filters for Wireless Communication: Theory, Design & Application.** M. Makimoto & S. Yamashita. LC 00-41924. (Series in Advanced Microelectronics). (Illus.). 2000. write for info. (*3-540-67535-3*) Spr-Verlag.

Microwave Ring Circuits & Antennas. Kai Chang. LC 95-38581. (Series in Microwave & Optical Engineering). 296p. 1996. 125.00 (*0-471-13109-1*) Wiley.

Microwave Robust: Ssri RF. Loren F. Root. LC 92-26383. (Six Sigma Research Institute Ser.). 1992. pap. 16.95 (*0-201-63428-7*) Addison-Wesley.

Microwave Scattering & Emission Models & Their Applications. Adrian K. Fung. LC 93-41694. 573p. 1994. 49.00 (*0-89006-523-3*) Artech Hse.

Microwave Semiconductor Devices. Sigfrid Yngvesson. (C). 1991. text 88.00 (*0-7923-9156-X*) Kluwer Academic.

Microwave Sensing & Synthetic Aperture Radar. Ed. by Giorgio Franceschetti et al. (Europto Ser.: Vol. 2958). 444p. 1996. 94.00 (*0-8194-2362-9*) SPIE.

Microwave Solid State Circuit design. Inder J. Bahl & Prakash Bhartia. LC 87-31652. 944p. 1988. 240.00 (*0-471-83189-1*) Wiley.

Microwave Solid-State Circuits & Applications. Kai Chang. (Series in Microwave & Optical Engineering). 456p. 1994. 120.00 (*0-471-54044-7*) Wiley.

Microwave Solid State Circuits & Applications Solutions Management. Chang. 107p. 1994. pap. 27.50 (*0-471-07412-8*) Wiley.

Microwave Spectroscopy. Arthur L. Schawlow & C. H. Townes. LC 74-83620. (Illus.). 698p. (C). 1975. reprint ed. pap. text 16.95 (*0-486-61798-X*) Dover.

Microwave Studies of Exciton Condensation in Germanium. Ed. by N. G. Basov. Tr. by David L. Burdick from RUS. LC 78-10160. (Proceedings of the P. N. Lebedev Physics Institute Ser.: No. 100). (Illus.). 97p. 1979. reprint ed. pap. 30.10 (*0-608-05554-9*, 206602200006) Bks Demand.

Microwave Studies of High Temp Superconductors. Ed. by Anant Narlikar. (Studies of High Temperature Superconductors: Vol. 17, Pt. I). 262p. 1996. text 175.00 (*1-56072-380-7*) Nova Sci Pubs.

Microwave Technology. Erich Pehl. LC 85-70815. (Artech House Microwave Library). (Illus.). 230p. reprint ed. pap. 71.30 (*0-608-17721-0*, 203012900067) Bks Demand.

Microwave Theory & Applications. Stephen F. Adam. (Illus.). (C). 1992. reprint ed. text 60.00 (*0-9634284-0-3*) A Microwave Cnslt.

Microwave Touch. Galen N. Hill. 200p. 1985. spiral bd. 9.95 (*0-9614205-0-2*) Microwave Touch.

Microwave Transistor Amplifiers: Analysis & Design. 2nd ed. Guillermo Gonzalez. LC 96-9182. 506p. 1996. 105.00 (*0-13-254335-4*) P-H.

Microwave Transistors. Edward D. Graham, Jr. & Charles W. Gwyn. LC 74-82594. 586p. reprint ed. 181.70 (*0-8357-9037-1*, 201532100094) Bks Demand.

Microwave Transition Design. Jamal S. Izadian & Shahin W. Izadian. LC 88-6342. (Illus.). 162p. 1988. reprint ed. pap. 50.30 (*0-7837-9700-1*, 206043100005) Bks Demand.

Microwave Transmission for Telecommunications. Paul F. Combes. LC 90-38435. (Illus.). 331p. 1991. reprint ed. pap. 102.70 (*0-608-05277-9*, 206581500001) Bks Demand.

Microwave Transmission Line Couplers. J. A. Malherbe. LC 88-19338. (Artech House Microwave Library). 231p. reprint ed. pap. 71.70 (*0-7837-3018-7*, 204292200006) Bks Demand.

Microwave Transmission Line Filters. J. A. Malherber. LC 78-31243. (Illus.). 352p. reprint ed. pap. 109.20 (*0-8357-5589-4*, 203522000093) Bks Demand.

Microwave Transmission-Line Impedance Data. rev. ed. M. A. R. Gunston. Ed. by Crawford Hammond. LC 96-7953. (Illus.). 296p. 1996. 54.00 (*1-884932-57-6*) Noble Pubng.

Microwaveable Foods Market. Ed. by Peter Allen. 188p. 1988. pap. 1295.00 (*0-941285-31-6*) FIND-SVP.

Microwaved Pressed Flowers: New Techniques for Brilliant Pressed Flowers, Vol. 8. Joanna Sheen. LC 98-40662. 112p. 1999. pap. text 19.95 (*0-8230-3058-X*) Watsn-Guptill.

***Microwave/Make It Tonight: Home Library Mini-Menu Cookbooks.** Home Library Editors. 64p. 1999. pap. 3.95 (*1-56426-208-1*, Pub. by Cole Group) ACCESS Pubs Network.

Microwaves. 3rd ed. A. J. Fuller. LC 89-26630. (Illus.). 322p. 1990. pap. 99.90 (*0-608-04993-X*, 206561100004) Bks Demand.

Microwaves: Theory & Application in Materials Processing II. Ed. by David E. Clark et al. (Ceramic Transactions Ser.: Vol. 36). 596p. 1993. 74.00 (*0-944904-66-1*, CT036) Am Ceramic.

Microwaves: Theory & Application in Materials Processing III. Ed. by David E. Clark et al. LC 95-43601. (Ceramic Transactions Ser.: Vol. 59). 592p. 1995. 95.00 (*1-57498-002-5*, CT059) Am Ceramic.

Microwaves & Wireless Simplified. Thomas S. Laverghetta. LC 97-40457. 266p. 1997. 55.00 (*0-89006-908-5*) Artech Hse.

Microwaves in the Food Processing Industry. Robert V. Decareau. (Food Science & Technology Ser.). 1985. text 94.00 (*0-12-208430-6*) Acad Pr.

Microwaves Made Simple: The Workbook. Salvatore J. Algeri et al. LC 86-72681. (Artech House Microwave Library). 117p. reprint ed. pap. 36.30 (*0-7837-5846-4*, 204556500006) Bks Demand.

Microwaves: Theory & Application in Materials Processing IV: First World Congress on Microwave Processing & RF Technology from Science to Application. Ed. by David E. Clark et al. (Ceramic Transactions Ser.: Vol. 80). 731p. 1997. text 95.00 (*1-57498-025-4*, CT080) Am Ceramic.

Microwaving with a Gourmet Flair. Joyce Batcher. Ed. by Arlene Hamernik. (Illus.). 67p. 1983. reprint ed. pap. 2.50 (*0-9602930-1-9*) Microwave Helps.

MicroWays: For Busy Days, Lazy Days, Holidays, Everyday! Norene Gilletz. 399p. 1994. ring bd. 33.95 (*0-9697972-1-4*) GOUR.

Microworld: Addendum: Basic Principles of the Avkoan Theory & New Perceptions in the Microworld. unabridged ed. Yecheskiel Zamir. 75p. (Orig.). 1999. pap. text 9.50 (*0-9614730-2-9*, YZ 207) Y Z Pubns.

***Microworld Simulations for Command & Control Training of Theater Logistics & Support Staffs: A Curriculum Strategy.** J. Bondanella. LC 98-49149. 1998. pap. 13.00 (*0-8330-2671-2*) Rand Corp.

Microworlds: Complete Unit. National Science Resources Center Staff. (Science & Technology for Children Ser.). (Illus.). (J). (gr. 5). 1991. pap. text, student ed. write for info. (*0-89278-664-7*) Carolina Biological.

Microworlds: Writings on Science Fiction & Fantasy. Stanislaw Lem. Ed. by Franz Rottensteiner. 288p. 1986. pap. 11.00 (*0-15-659443-9*, Harvest Bks) Harcourt.

Microworlds Student Activity Book. National Science Resources Center Staff. (Science & Technology for Children Ser.). (Illus.). 61p. (J). (gr. 5). 1991. pap. text, student ed. write for info. (*0-89278-666-3*) Carolina Biological.

Microworlds Teacher's Guide. National Science Resources Center Staff. (Science & Technology for Children Ser.). (Illus.). 123p. (J). (gr. 5). 1991. pap. text, teacher ed. write for info. (*0-89278-665-5*) Carolina Biological.

Microworlds 2.0: Hypermedia Project Development & Logo Scripting. Sharon Yoder. (Illus.). 440p. 1998. spiral bd. 34.95 (*1-56484-128-6*) Intl Society Tech Educ.

Micturition. Ed. by J. O. Drife et al. (Illus.). 372p. 1990. 125.00 (*0-387-19614-5*) Spr-Verlag.

Mid-American Chants (Poems in Prose) Sherwood Anderson. (Collected Works of Sherwood Anderson). 82p. 1998. reprint ed. lib. bdg. 88.00 (*1-58201-504-X*) Classic Bks.

Mid-American Frontier, 47 vols., Set. Ed. by Jerome O. Steffen. (Illus.). 1975. 1835.00 (*0-405-06845-X*) Ayer.

***Mid-Atlantic: Woodall's 2000 Regional Camping Guide.** Woodall's Publishing Staff. 444p. 1999. pap. text 6.99 (*0-7627-0589-2*) Globe Pequot.

Mid-Atlantic & Southeastern States Public Land Forum: Proceedings. 1970. 5.00 (*0-686-20719-X*) SUNY Environ.

Mid-Atlantic Budget Angler. Ann McIntosh. LC 97-28629. (Illus.). 320p. 1998. pap. 21.95 (*0-8117-2851-X*) Stackpole.

***Mid-Atlantic Camping Guide 2001.** Woodalls Publishing Staff. (Regional Camping Guides Ser.). (Illus.). 2000. pap. 6.99 (*0-7627-0864-6*) Globe Pequot.

Mid-Atlantic Guide to Boardsailing. Ed. by Leslie Killeen & Kenneth Pugh. (Illus.). 48p. (Orig.). 1986. pap. 3.95 (*0-937853-01-1*) Pugh Killeen.

Mid-Atlantic Lighthouses: Hudson River to Chesapeake Bay. Bruce Roberts & Ray Jones. LC 99-26342. (Lighthouse Ser.). (Illus.). 112p. 1999. 29.95 (*0-7910-5489-6*) Chelsea Hse.

Mid-Atlantic Lighthouses: Hudson River to Cheseapeake Bay. Ray Jones. (Lighthouses Ser.). (Illus.). 112p. (Orig.). 1996. pap. 19.95 (*1-56440-984-8*) Globe Pequot.

Mid-Atlantic National Parks: Five Tour Guidebook. Michael Frome. (Illus.). 142p. 1987. pap. 4.95 (*0-915992-44-2*) Eastern National.

Mid-Atlantic Piedmont: Tectonic Missing Link of the Appalachians. David W. Valentino & Alexander E. Gates. LC 98-55401. (Special Paper Ser.). 139p. 1999. write for info. (*0-8137-2330-2*) Geol Soc.

***Mid-Atlantic Region.** Tracey Menges. (Annual Directory of American & Canadian Bed & Breakfasts Ser.: Vol. II). 255p. 2000. pap. 9.95 (*1-57748-772-9*) Barbour Pub.

Mid-Atlantic Roadside Delights: Roadside Architecture of Yesterday & Today in New Jersey, New York, & Pennsylvania. Will Anderson. LC 90-85283. (Illus.). 164p. (Orig.). 1991. pap. 19.95 (*0-9601056-4-6*) Anderson & Sons.

Mid-Atlantic Shorebirds. 1995. pap. 8.95 (*0-945582-35-8*) Down the Shore Pub.

Mid-Atlantic States see Mobil Travel Guide

Mid-Atlantic States. Michael S. Durham et al. LC 96-40540. (Smithsonian Guide to Historic America Ser.). 495p. 1998. pap. 19.95 (*1-55670-634-0*) Stewart Tabori & Chang.

Mid-Atlantic States: Pennsylvania, New York, New Jersey. Eugene Walter. (Illus.). 1996. pap. 19.95 (*0-614-20485-2*) Random.

***Mid-Atlantic States: Regional Map & Travel Panner; Including West Virginia, Virginia, Maryland.** National Geographic Society Staff. 1998. pap. 7.95 (*1-57262-425-6*) MapQuest.

Mid-Atlantic States Region: Grades 4-6. Ruth Emmel & Lynn Smith. (Illus.). 64p. 1997. pap., teacher ed. 6.95 (*1-889369-16-0*, TI0046) Teaching Ink.

***Mid-Atlantic States, State of the Environment, 1998: The Challenge Ahead.** Government Printing Office Staff. 64p. 1999. pap. 8.00 (*0-16-049981-X*) USGPO.

Mid-Atlantic Trout Streams & Their Hatches: Overlooked Angling in Pennsylvania, New York, & New Jersey. Charles R. Meck et al. LC 97-10386. (Trout Streams Ser.). (Illus.). 192p. (Orig.). 1997. pap. 17.00 (*0-88150-397-5*, Pub. by Countryman) Norton.

***Mid-Atlantic 2000.** Mobil Travel Guides Staff. (Mobil Travel Guides Ser.). 2000. pap. 16.95 (*0-7853-4156-0*) Pubns Intl Ltd.

Mid-Atlantic Winter Sports & Ski America: Complete Guide to Winter Sports Throughout the Mid-Atlantic Region. John Phillips. (Illus.). 284p. 2000. pap. text 19.95 (*1-882997-08-5*, Pub. by Beachway Pr) Globe Pequot.

Mid-Atlantic's Best Bed & Breakfasts: Mid-Atlantic. 4th ed. Fodors Travel Publications, Inc. Staff. LC 98-143999. 320p. 1998. pap. 16.00 (*0-679-03434-X*) Fodors Travel.

Mid-California Illustrated History. (Illus.). 1995. 20.00 (*0-9607520-6-4*) Diablo Bks.

Mid Cape Cod. Cheryl J. Huban. (Twelve Short Hikes Ser.). (Illus.). 32p. 1997. pap. 4.95 (*1-57540-095-2*) Falcon Pub Inc.

Mid-Career Changes: Strategies for Success. John D. Shingleton & James Anderson. Ed. by Valerie L. Harris. LC 93-71651. (Illus.). 270p. 1993. pap. 16.95 (*0-89262-407-8*) Career Pub.

Mid-Career Job Hunting. 2nd ed. Patricia E. Birsner. 272p. 1991. pap. 14.00 (*0-13-508532-2*, Arco) Macmillan Gen Ref.

Mid-Career Planner: Mid-Career Planning & the Interralated Issues of Work, Family & Finances (Federal Edition) R. N. Garnitz. (Illus.). 1999. pap. 13.95 (*0-927289-46-6*) LifeSpan Services.

Mid-Career Planner: Mid-Career Planning & the Interrelated Issues of Work, Family, & Finances (Regular Edition) R. N. Garnitz. (LifeSystems Ser.). (Illus.). 102p. 1997. pap. 13.95 (*0-927289-39-3*) LifeSpan Services.

***Mid-Career Tune-Up: 10 New Habits for Keeping Your Edge in Today's Fast-Paced Workplace.** William A. Salmon & Rosemary T. Salmon. LC 99-40033. 224p. 1999. pap. 17.95 (*0-8144-0523-1*) AMACOM.

Mid-Century American Novel. large type ed. Linda Wagner-Martin. 1997. 33.00 (*0-8057-7860-8*, Twyne) Mac Lib Ref.

Mid Century Design: Decorative Arts, 1940-1960. Cara Greenberg. LC 85-61867. (Illus.). 61p. (Orig.). 1984. pap. 9.99 (*1-880511-04-5*) Bass Museum.

Mid-Century French Poets see Modern French Poets: Selections with Translations

Mid-Century Modern. Cara Greenberg. 1995. pap. 25.00 (*0-517-88475-5*) Harmony Bks.

Mid-Channel. Ludwig Lewisohn. LC 74-29502. (Modern Jewish Experience Ser.). 1975. reprint ed. 28.95 (*0-405-06729-1*) Ayer.

Mid-Ch'ing Rice Markets & Trade: An Essay in Price History. Han-Sheng Chuan & Richard A. Kraus. LC 74-24937. (East Asian Monographs: No. 54). 185p. (Orig.). (C). 1975. pap. 20.00 (*0-674-57340-4*) HUP.

Mid-Connaught: The Ancient Territory of Sliabh Lugha. Maire McDonnell-Garvey. LC 96-106178. (Illus.). 208p. (Orig.). 1995. pap. 17.95 (*1-873437-12-9*, Pub. by Drumlin Pubns Ltd) Irish Bks Media.

Mid-Continent Area Power Planners: A New Approach to Planning in the Electric Power Industry. William S. Nelson. LC 68-63563. (MSU Public Utilities Studies: Vol. 1968). 141p. reprint ed. pap. 43.80 (*0-608-20507-9*, 207175900002) Bks Demand.

Mid Continent Petroleum Directory. 10th rev. ed. Ed. by Paula Jepperson. 550p. 1995. pap. 79.00 (*0-912553-51-0*) Hart Pubns.

***Mid-Course Correction: Re-Ordering Your Private World for the Next Part of Your Journey.** Gordon MacDonald. LC 99-88448. 224p. 2000. 16.99 (*0-7852-7841-9*) Nelson.

Mid-Course Correction: Toward a Sustainable Enterprise: The Interface Model. Ray Anderson. 1999. pap. 17.95 (*0-9645953-5-4*, Pub. by Peregrinzilla) Chelsea Green Pub.

Mid-Day Gleanings: A Book for Home & Holiday Readings. James T. Franklin. LC 76-168134. reprint ed. 21.50 (*0-404-00052-5*) AMS Pr.

Mid-East Studies, 55 titles in 67 vols., Set. reprint ed. write for info. (*0-404-56200-0*) AMS Pr.

Mid-East-World Center: Yesterday, Today & Tomorrow. Ed. by Ruth N. Anshen. LC 78-20183. (Science & Culture Ser.). xiv, 386p. 1975. reprint ed. lib. bdg. 65.00 (*0-8154-0508-1*) Cooper Sq.

Mid 18th Century Cello Sonatas: Continuo Sonatas for Cello. Ed. by Jane Adas. LC 91-755832. (18th Century Continuo Sonata Ser.: No. 7). 328p. 1992. text 100.00 (*0-8153-0180-4*) Garland.

Mid Eighteenth-Century Masters: Continuo Sonatas for Violin. Ed. by Jane Adas. LC 91-752337. (Eighteenth Century Continuo Sonata Ser.: Vol. 5). 376p. 1991. text 50.00 (*0-8153-0178-2*) Garland.

Mid-Flinx. Alan Dean Foster. 1996. mass mkt. 5.99 (*0-345-40644-3*) Ballantine Pub Grp.

Mid-Hudson Dine-a-Mate Book. 256p. 1996. pap. text 25.00 (*0-614-20360-0*) Dine-A-Mate.

***Mid-Hudson Valley Entertainment, 2000.** (Illus.). 822p. 1999. pap. write for info. (*1-880248-41-7*, 00T8) Enter Pubns.

Mid-Journey: An Unfinished Autobiography. Nicholas Rescher. LC 82-45083. (Illus.). 204p. (Orig.). 1983. pap. 18.75 (*0-8191-2523-7*); lib. bdg. 50.50 (*0-8191-2522-9*) U Pr of Amer.

Mid-Latitude Weather Systems. Toby Carlson. (Illus.). 512p. (C). 1991. pap. text 39.95 (*0-04-551116-0*, A8240) Routledge.

Mid-Latitude Weather Systems. Toby N. Carlson. LC 98-73847. (Illus.). 507p. 1998. pap. 42.00 (*1-878220-30-6*) Am Meteorological.

Mid-Level Practitioners: Their Role in Providing Quality Health Care. Sara R. McGonagle. (Working Paper Ser.: No. 64). 42p. 1992. pap. 5.50 (*0-89940-546-0*) LBJ Sch Pub Aff.

Mid-Life: Coming Home. Sarah Smith. LC 99-28019. (Illus.). 169p. 1999. pap. 9.95 (*1-57249-141-8*, Ragged Edge) White Mane Pub.

Mid-Life Body Signals: The Over-40 Guide to Health Symptoms & What They Mean. Bruce K. Lowell. 464p. 1997. pap. 14.00 (*0-06-273477-6*, Harper Ref) HarpC.

Mid-Life Divorce Counseling. Ed. by Lita L. Schwartz. LC 93-36923. (Family Psychology & Counseling Ser.). 130p. 1994. pap. text 17.95 (*1-55620-131-1*, 72585) Am Coun Assn.

Mid-Life Issues & the Workplace of the 90s: A Guide for Human Resource Specialists. Shirley A. Waskel. LC 90-26217. 192p. 1991. 59.95 (*0-89930-619-5*, WML/, Quorum Bks) Greenwood.

***Mid-Life Planning for Retirement.** Ed. by Wladech Koch. 160p. 1999. pap. 30.00 (*0-86242-249-3*, Pub. by Age Concern Eng) St Mut.

Mid-Life Sexuality: Enrichment & Problem-Solving. James Semmens. 1991. pap. 12.95 (*0-929240-20-0*) EMIS.

Mid-Life Spirituality & Jungian Archetypes. Janice Brewi & Anne Brennan. LC 99-32541. 304p. 1999. pap. 18.95 (*0-89254-046-X*) Nicolas-Hays.

Mid-Michigan First: A Capital Choice for Future Growth. Ed. by Joyce L. Moffett. (Illus.). 184p. 1993. 29.95 (*0-9616743-4-2*) NTC Contemp Pub Co.

Mid-Ocean Ridges: Dynamics of Processes Associated with Creation of New Ocean Crust. Ed. by J. R. Cann et al. LC 98-8322. (Illus.). 288p. (C). 1999. text 69.95 (*0-521-58522-8*) Cambridge U Pr.

Mid-Oceanic Ridges: Mountains below Sea Level. A. Nicolas. (Geology, Tectonics, Structural Geology, Oceanographic Science Geochemistry, Volcanology). (Illus.). 192p. 1995. 43.95 (*0-387-57380-1*) Spr-Verlag.

Mid-Pacific Supply Ship: A Voyage in the Thirties. 1984. pap. 5.75 (*0-9607530-1-X*) Seacoast CA.

Mid-Passage. Wendy Bishop. (Poetry Chapbook Ser.). (Illus.). 36p. 1998. pap. 7.95 (*1-879205-77-7*) Nightshade Pr.

Mid-River. Dale Zieroth. 71p. (Orig.). 1981. pap. 6.95 (*0-88784-084-1*, Pub. by Hse of Anansi Pr) Genl Dist Srvs.

Mid-Sized Firms: Success Strategies & Methodology. Robert L. Kuhn. LC 81-21031. 294p. 1985. 55.00 (*0-275-90842-9*, C0842, Praeger Pubs) Greenwood.

Mid-South Bird Notes of Ben B. Coffey, Jr. Jerome A. Jackson. (Special Publications: No. 1). 127p. (Orig.). 1981. pap. 10.00 (*0-686-37622-6*) Mississippi Orni.

***Mid-Stream.** Arpad Goncz. 240p. 1999. pap. 28.00 (*963-13-4801-6*, Pub. by Corvina Bks) St Mut.

Mid-Suffolk Light Railway. N. A. Comfort. 120p. (C). 1985. 60.00 (*0-85361-338-9*) St Mut.

Mid-Summer Morning. large type ed. Pamela Bennetts. (Large Print Ser.). 352p. 1994. 27.99 (*0-7089-3000-X*) Ulverscroft.

Mid-Term Report. Tim Page. LC 94-60653. (Illus.). 112p. 1995. pap. 29.95 (*0-500-27795-8*, Pub. by Thames Hudson) Norton.

Mid-Term Review of the Implementation of the Programme of Action for the Least Developed Countries for the 1990s: The Asian & Pacific Region. 90p. pap. 15.00 (*92-1-119691-4*, E.95.II.F.25) UN.

Mid-Term Status, 1998. rev. ed. Bill Groves. Ed. by Klaus Shruegraf & Jerry Karls. 500p. 1998. text 1075.00 (*1-877750-69-7*) Integrated Circuit.

Mid-Tertiary Stratigraphy & Paleogeographic Evolution of Hungary. rev. ed. T. Baldi. (Illus.). 201p. (C). 1986. 60.00 (*963-05-3945-4*, Pub. by Akade Kiado) St Mut.

Mid-Twentieth Century Nationalism. Ed. by William J. Bossenbrook. LC 65-11610. (Franklin Memorial Lectures Ser.: No. 13). 125p. reprint ed. pap. 38.80 (*0-7837-3806-4*, 204362600010) Bks Demand.

Mid Twentieth Century Novelists, 6 vols. (Collected Critical Heritage Ser.). 2654p. (C). (gr. 13). 1997. 745.00 (*0-415-15927-X*) Routledge.

Mid Twentieth Century Novelists: D. H. Lawrence. Ed. by R. P. Draper. (Critical Heritage Ser.). 394p. (C). 1997. 125.00 (*0-415-15922-9*) Routledge.

Mid Twentieth Century Novelists: Evelyn Waugh. Ed. by Martin Stannard. (Critical Heritage Ser.). 560p. (C). 1997. 160.00 (*0-415-15924-5*) Routledge.

Mid Twentieth Century Novelists: Ford Maddox Ford. Ed. by Frank McShane. (Critical Heritage Ser.). 288p. (C). 1997. 125.00 (*0-415-15921-0*) Routledge.

Mid Valley Nostalgia - Hollybush, Markham Village, Argoed Blackwood. Ed. by W. W. Tasker. 160p. (C). 1989. 59.00 (*1-872808-07-7*, Pub. by D Brown & Sons Ltd) St Mut.

***Mid-Victorian Generation 1846-1886.** K. Theodore Hoppen. LC 97-18126. (New Oxford History of England Ser.). (Illus.). 808p. 1998. 45.00 (*0-19-822834-1*) OUP.

***Mid-Victorian Generation 1846-1886.** K. Theodore Hoppen. (New Oxford History of England Ser.). (Illus.). 808p. 2000. pap. 24.95 (*0-19-873199-X*) OUP.

***Mid-Victorian Poetry, 1860-1879.** Catherine W. Reilly. LC 99-26552. 2000. 140.00 (*0-7201-2318-6*) Continuum.

M

An Asterisk (*) at the beginning of an entry indicates that the title is appearing for the first time.

Mid-Victorian Wales: The Observers & the Observed. Ieuan G. Jones. 215p. 1992. 50.00 (*0-7083-1148-2*, Pub. by Univ Wales Pr) Paul & Co Pubs.

Mid Wales & the Marshes. (Ordnance Survey Pathfinder Guides Ser.). (Illus.). 80p. (Orig.). 1995. pap. 14.95 (*0-7117-0818-5*, Pub. by JARR UK) Seven Hills Bk.

Mid-West. Eleanor Berman. (52 Weekend & Day Trips Ser.). 1996. pap. 16.00 (*0-614-12770-X*) Crown Pub Group.

Mid-Winter Festivals: Anthology of Stories, Traditions & Poems. Frwd. by Steve Clapp. (Family Reading Ser.). 211p. (Orig.). 1983. pap. 10.00 (*0-914527-01-0*) C-Four Res.

***Mid-Year Book.** Good Housekeeping Editors. 2000. write for info. (*0-688-17806-5*, Hearst) Hearst Commns.

Midaq Alley. Naguib Mahfouz. 304p. 1991. pap. 12.95 (*0-385-26476-3*, Anchor NY) Doubleday.

Midaq Alley. Naguib Mahfouz. 304p. 1992. pap. 7.99 (*0-385-26940-4*) Doubleday.

Midaregami see Tangled Hair: Selected Tanka from Midaregami

***Midas.** Wolfgang Jeschke. 2001. text 23.95 (*0-312-86981-9*) St Martin.

Midas. Peter O'Leary. (Poetry New York Pamphlet Ser.: Vol. 4). 16p. 1998. pap. 5.00 (*0-923389-17-2*) Meet Eyes Bind.

Midas: An English Burletta, in Two Acts. 3rd ed. O'Hara Kane. LC 92-22695. (Augustan Reprints Ser.: No. 167). 1974. reprint ed. 14.50 (*0-404-70167-1*, ML50.Z99M416) AMS Pr.

***Midas Mouse.** David Ellwand. 2000. lib. bdg. 14.89 (*0-06-029225-3*) HarpC.

Midas Mouse. David Ellwand & Ruth Ellwand. LC 98-44728. (Illus.). 32p. (J). (ps-3). 2000. 14.95 (*0-688-16745-4*) Morrow Avon.

Midas Murders. Margot Arnold, pseud. (Penny Spring & Sir Toby Glendower Mystery Ser.). 224p. 1995. 20.00 (*0-88150-340-1*, Foul Play) Norton.

Midas Murders. Margot Arnold, pseud. 224p. 1997. pap. 7.95 (*0-88150-394-0*) Norton.

Midas of the Rockies: The Story of Stratton & Cripple Creek. Frank Waters. LC 73-163716. 347p. 1949. pap. 15.95 (*0-8040-0591-5*) Swallow.

Midas: or The United States & the Future. C. H. Bretherton. LC 73-13123. (Foreign Travelers in America, 1810-1935 Ser.). 100p. 1974. reprint ed. 16.95 (*0-405-05445-9*) Ayer.

Midas Touch. Jess Carr. LC 85-70064. 256p. 1986. 14.95 (*0-89227-112-4*) Commonwealth Pr.

***Midas Touch.** Kenneth E. Hagin. 1999. 19.95 (*0-89276-549-6*) Faith Lib Pubns.

***Midas Touch.** Illus. by Juan Wijngaard. LC 98-21922. 32p. (J). (gr. 2-5). 1999. text 16.99 (*0-7636-0488-7*) Candlewick Pr.

Midas Touch: Understanding the Dynamic New Money Societies Around Us. Anthony Sampson. 1990. 19.95 (*0-317-02691-7*, Truman Talley) St Martin.

Midas World. Frederik Pohl. 320p. 1984. pap. 2.95 (*0-8125-4925-2*, Pub. by Tor Bks) St Martin.

Midas's Daughter. Vuyelwa Carlin. 80p. (Orig.). 1991. pap. 15.95 (*1-85411-054-3*, Pub. by Seren Bks) Dufour.

Midbrain Periaqueductal Gray Matter: Functional, Anatomical & Neurochemical Organization. Ed. by A. Depaulis & Richard Bandler. (NATO ASI Ser.: Vol. 213). (Illus.). 490p. (C). 1991. text 186.00 (*0-306-44033-4*, Kluwer Plenum) Kluwer Academic.

Midcap 400 Guide 1998. Standard & Poor's Staff. 832p. 1997. pap. 24.95 (*0-07-052620-6*) McGraw.

Midcentury. Ben Howard. LC 97-189907. 80p. 1998. pap. 12.95 (*1-897648-74-X*) Salmon Poetry.

Midcentury Journey. William L. Shirer. 1994. lib. bdg. 27.95 (*1-56849-429-7*) Buccaneer Bks.

Midcentury Quartet: Bishop, Lowell, Jarrell, Berryman & the Making of a Postmodern Aesthetic. Thomas Travisano. LC 99-16426. 1999. 35.00 (*0-8139-1887-1*) U Pr of Va.

Midcontinent Petroleum Directory. 11th ed. Ed. by Paula Jepperson. 500p. 1996. pap. text 89.00 (*0-912553-58-8*) Hart Pubns.

Midcontinent Petroleum Directory. 12th rev. ed. Ed. by Kelly Holder. 500p. 1997. pap. text 99.00 (*0-912553-66-9*) Hart Pubns.

Midday in Italian Literature: Variations on an Archetypal Theme. Nicolas J. Perella. LC 78-70313. 347p. reprint ed. pap. 107.60 (*0-8357-7895-9*, 203631400002) Bks Demand.

Midday Muse. Matthew Mead. 64p. 1979. pap. 14.95 (*0-85646-050-8*, Pub. by Anvil Press) Dufour.

Midden. Tom Sharpe. LC 97-9909. 244p. 1997. 23.95 (*0-87951-801-4*, Pub. by Overlook Pr) Penguin Putnam.

Midden. Tom Sharpe. LC 97-9909. 245p. 1999. pap. 13.95 (*0-87951-928-2*, Pub. by Overlook Pr) Penguin Putnam.

Middens of the Tribe. Daniel Hoffman. 80p. 1995. pap. 9.95 (*0-8071-2001-4*); text 17.95 (*0-8071-2000-6*) La State U Pr.

Middle Managers in Europe. Ed. by Yves F. Livian & John G. Burgoyne. LC 96-12600. (Advances in Management & Tourism Ser.). 232p. (C). 1997. 80.00 (*0-415-13902-3*) Routledge.

Middle Age & Aging: A Reader in Social Psychology. Ed. by Bernice L. Neugarten. LC 68-55150. 610p. 1968. pap. text 24.00 (*0-226-57382-6*) U Ch Pr.

Middle Age Is Not a Disease. James R. Sherman. LC 84-63051. 1985. pap. 3.95 (*0-935538-07-0*) Pathway Bks.

Middle Age of Mrs. Eliot. Angus Wilson. LC 97-5834. 1997. pap. 15.95 (*0-312-15588-3*) St Martin.

Middle Age Spread: A For Better or For Worse Collection. Lynn Johnston. LC 98-85337. (For Better or for Worse Collection). (Illus.). 128p. 1998. pap. 9.95 (*0-8362-6822-9*) Andrews & McMeel.

Middle Age Spread, (An Excerpt of the Tarnish on the Golden Years) Nona K. Carver. (Illus.). 24p. (Orig.). 1994. pap. 7.00 (*0-9641195-2-8*) Carver Cntry.

Middle Age Survival Kit. June Taylor. Ed. by Anne Crouse. LC 86-70802. 138p. (Orig.). 1986. pap. 8.95 (*0-9616108-1-6*) Beaumont Bks.

Middle Aged & Dating Again. Tom Blake. LC 97-92964. 188p. (Orig.). 1997. pap. 12.95 (*1-57502-423-3*, PO1300) Tooters Pub.

Middle-Aged Children: Getting Through the Tough Preteens. Janet Tubbs. 111p. 1995. pap. 14.95 (*1-881185-05-2*) Arcadia AZ.

Middle-Aged, Female & Homeless: The Stories of a Forgotten Group. Sandra S. Butler. LC 93-34143. (Children of Poverty Ser.). 184p. 1993. text 20.00 (*0-8153-1544-9*) Garland.

Middle Aged Love Stories. Josephine D. Bacon. LC 74-169538. (Short Story Index Reprint Ser.). 1977. reprint ed. 20.95 (*0-8369-3285-4*) Ayer.

Middle-Aged Man on the Flying Trapeze. James Thurber. reprint ed. lib. bdg. 21.95 (*0-89190-268-6*, Rivercity Pr) Amereon Ltd.

Middle-Aged Man on the Flying Trapeze. James Thurber. 1977. reprint ed. lib. bdg. 26.95 (*0-89244-059-7*) Queens Hse-Focus Serv.

Middle Aged Princess & the Frog. Alison Zier. LC 78-51357. (Illus.). 80p. (Orig.). 1978. pap. text 3.95 (*0-918606-01-2*) Heidelberg Graph.

Middle Aged Rebel: Embracing the Challenge of Midlife, a Dynamic Approach. Peter Lambley. 1995. pap. 10.95 (*1-85230-644-0*, Pub. by Element MA) Penguin Putnam.

Middle Ager - Crabby, Flabby, Gabby. Rick Stromoski. (Illus.). 46p. 1994. write for info. (*1-886386-03-X*) Trisar.

***Middle Ages.** Barron's Educational Editors. 128p. 1999. pap. text 8.95 (*0-7641-0948-0*) Barron.

Middle Ages. Bellerophon Books Staff. (J). (gr. 1-9). 1992. pap. 4.95 (*0-88388-007-5*) Bellerophon Bks.

Middle Ages. Morris Bishop. (American Heritage Library). 352p. 1986. pap. 15.00 (*0-8281-0487-5*) HM.

Middle Ages. K. C. Chowdhury. (C). 1989. 35.00 (*0-89771-441-5*, Pub. by Current Dist) St Mut.

Middle Ages. Peter Chrisp. LC 97-1833. (My World Ser.). (Illus.). 32p. (J). (gr. 2-7). 1997. write for info. (*0-7166-9408-5*) World Bk.

Middle Ages. Mike Corbishley. (Cultural Atlas for Young People Ser.). (Illus.). 96p. (J). (gr. 4-9). 1990. 17.95 (*0-8160-1973-8*) Facts on File.

***Middle Ages.** Ed. by Antonia Fraser. (Royal History of England Ser.). (Illus.). 128p. 2000. pap. 12.95 (*0-520-22799-9*) U CA Pr.

***Middle Ages.** Cathy Freeman et al. (Students' Active Interdisciplinary Learning Ser.). (YA). (gr. 1-12). 2000. pap. 20.00 (*1-893413-07-1*) Univ Schl Tulsa.

Middle Ages. A. R. Gurney. 1978. pap. 5.25 (*0-8222-0753-2*) Dramatists Play.

Middle Ages. Sarah Howarth. (See Through History Ser.). (Illus.). 48p. (J). (gr. 3-7). 1993. 19.99 (*0-670-85098-5*, Viking Child) Peng Put Young Read.

Middle Ages. Ladybird Books Staff. (History of Britain Ser.: No. F895-3). (Illus.). (YA). (gr. 5 up). 1990. pap. 3.95 (*1-85543-008-8*, Ladybrd) Penguin Putnam.

Middle Ages. Fiona MacDonald. (Illustrated History of the World Ser.). (Illus.). 80p. (J). (gr. 4-9). 1993. 19.95 (*0-8160-2788-9*) Facts on File.

Middle Ages. Tara McCarthy. (Illus.). (J). 1996. pap. 12.95 (*0-590-25103-1*) Scholastic Inc.

Middle Ages. Sarah McNeill. (Spotlights Ser.). (Illus.). 46p. (J). (gr. 4-6). 1998. 11.95 (*0-19-521394-7*) OUP.

Middle Ages. Kate Needham. LC 95-39832. (Time Trekkers Visit The--). 1996. 11.15 (*0-606-09976-X*, Pub. by Turtleback) Demco.

Middle Ages. Salem Press Editors. LC 97-51154. (Dictionary of World Biography Ser.: Vol. 2). (Illus.). 1049p. (YA). (gr. 9-12). 1998. lib. bdg. 125.00 (*0-89356-314-5*) Salem Pr.

Middle Ages. Jane Shuter. Date not set. 7.00 (*1-57572-489-8*) Heinemann Lib.

Middle Ages. Jane Shuter. LC 99-11818. (History Opens Windows Ser.). 32p. (J). (gr. 4-6). 1999. lib. bdg. 14.95 (*1-57572-886-9*) Heinemann Lib.

Middle Ages. Gloria Verges & Oriol Verges. (Journey Through History Ser.). (Illus.). 32p. (J). (gr. 2-4). 1988. pap. 6.95 (*0-8120-3386-8*); pap. 6.95 (*0-8120-3387-6*) Barron.

***Middle Ages.** Morris Bishop. (Illus.). 368p. 2001. reprint ed. pap. 16.00 (*0-618-05703-X*, Mariner Bks) HM.

Middle Ages. Frantz Funck-Brentano. LC 70-168075. (National History of France Ser.: No. 2). reprint ed. 45.00 (*0-404-50792-1*) AMS Pr.

***Middle Ages.** rev. ed. Peter Chrisp. (My Word Ser.). (Illus.). (J). 2000. 9.95 (*1-58728-063-9*); pap. 5.95 (*1-58728-069-8*) Two Can Pub.

Middle Ages. 2nd ed. R. J. Cootes. (Longman Secondary Histories Ser.). 208p. (YA). (gr. 6-12). 1989. pap. text 21.52 (*0-582-31783-5*, 78446) Longman.

Middle Ages. 2nd ed. Giovanni Caselli. (History of Everyday Things Ser.). (Illus.). 48p. (YA). (gr. 5 up). 1998. reprint ed. pap. 10.95 (*0-87226-263-4*, 62634B, P Bedrick Books) NTC Contemp Pub Co.

***Middle Ages.** 3rd ed. Brooke Christopher. 464p. 2000. 79.95 (*0-582-36905-3*) Longman.

***Middle Ages: A Watts Guide for Children** William C. Jordan. LC 99-30619. 2000. 32.00 (*0-531-11715-4*) Watts.

***Middle Ages: A Watts Guide for Children.** William Chester Jordan. (Reference Ser.). (Illus.). (YA). 2000. pap. 19.95 (*0-531-16488-8*) Watts.

Middle Ages: An Encyclopedia for Students. William C. Jordan. LC 95-49597. (J). 1996. 375.00 (*0-684-19773-1*) Scribner.

Middle Ages: An Encyclopedia for Students, 4 vols., Vol. 1. Jordan. 1996. 95.00 (*0-684-80483-2*) S&S Trade.

Middle Ages: An Encyclopedia for Students, 4 vols., Vol. 3. Jordan. 1996. 95.00 (*0-684-80485-9*) S&S Trade.

Middle Ages: An Encyclopedia for Students, 4 vols., Vol. 4. Jordan. 1996. 95.00 (*0-684-80486-7*) S&S Trade.

Middle Ages: An Illustrated History. Barbara A. Hanawalt. LC 98-5889. (Illus.). 160p. (J). (gr. 5). 1999. 29.95 (*0-19-510359-9*) OUP.

Middle Ages: Book & Poster. Rebecca Stark. Date not set. teacher ed. 12.95 (*1-56644-971-5*, 971-5APS) Educ Impress.

Middle Ages: Learning Through Literature. Nancy Polette. (Illus.). 48p. 1994. pap. 7.95 (*1-879287-27-7*, BL037) Pieces of Lrning.

Middle Ages: Readings in Medieval History, Vol. II. 5th ed. Brian Tierney. 480p. 1999. pap. 25.93 (*0-07-303290-5*, McGrw-H College) McGrw-H Hghr Educ.

Middle Ages: Sources of Medieval History, Vol. 1. 6th ed. Brian Tierney. LC 98-16808. 456p. 1999. pap. 25.93 (*0-07-303289-1*, McGrw-H College) McGrw-H Hghr Educ.

***Middle Ages: Turbulent Centuries: From the Dark Ages to the New World.** Kate Brookes. 1999. 9.99 (*1-84100-270-4*) Quadrillion Pubng.

Middle Ages: 8 Short Plays for the Classroom with Background Information & Writing Prompts. Jeanette Sanderson. 1998. pap. text 12.95 (*0-590-76993-6*) Scholastic Inc.

Middle Ages Vol. I: Sources of Medieval History. 5th ed. Brian Tierney. 415p. (C). 1992. pap. 29.69 (*0-07-064611-2*) McGraw.

Middle Ages Vol. 2: An Encyclopedia for Students, 4 vols. Jordan. 1996. 95.00 (*0-684-80484-0*) S&S Trade.

Middle Ages after the Middle Ages in the English-Speaking World. Ed. by Marie-Francoise Alamichel & Derek S. Brewer. LC 96-54703. 176p. 1997. 75.00 (*0-85991-508-5*) Boydell & Brewer.

Middle Ages Coloring Book. Edmund V. Gillon. (Illus.). (J). (gr. k-3). 1976. pap. 2.95 (*0-486-22743-X*) Dover.

***Middle Ages Early Modern Restoration &18th Century.** (C). 1999. 49.00 (*0-201-66126-8*) Addison-Wesley.

Middle Ages in the Athenian Agora. Alison Frantz. LC 69-68253. (Excavations of the Athenian Agora Picture Bks.: No. 7). (Illus.). 32p. 1961. pap. 3.00 (*0-87661-607-4*) Am Sch Athens.

Middle Ages in the North-West. Tom Scott & Pat Starkey. 270p. 1995. pap. 25.00 (*0-904920-31-3*, Pub. by Leopards Head Pr) David Brown.

Middle Ages of the Internal-Combustion Engine, 1794-1886. Horst O. Hardenberg. LC 99-12325. 504p. 1999. 29.00 (*0-7680-0391-1*, R-262) Soc Auto Engineers.

Middle Ages Reconsidered: Attitudes in France from the Eighteenth Century Through the Romantic Movement. Barbara G. Keller. LC 92-41534. (Studies in the Humanities: Vol. 11). 282p. (C). 1994. text 47.95 (*0-8204-1415-8*) P Lang Pubng.

***Middle Ages Reference Library.** 200p. 2000. text 42.00 (*0-7876-4856-6*, UXL); text 79.00 (*0-7876-4857-4*, UXL); text 42.00 (*0-7876-4860-4*, UXL) Gale.

Middle Ages, Reformation, Volkskunde. John G. Kunstmann. LC 68-24470. (North Carolina. University. Studies in the Germanic Languages & Literatures: No. 26). reprint ed. 32.50 (*0-404-50926-6*) AMS Pr.

Middle Ages Through the Eighteenth Century see Oxford Anthology of English Literature

Middle America. Charles M. Wilson. LC 75-128334. (Essay Index Reprint Ser.). 1977. 25.95 (*0-8369-2092-9*) Ayer.

Middle American Research Records, Set. (Publication Ser.: No. 28). 1967. write for info. (*0-939238-31-4*) Tulane MARI.

Middle American Research Records, Vol. III. (Publications: No. 28). 185p. 1967. 20.00 (*0-939238-30-6*) Tulane MARI.

Middle & Junior High School Library Catalog. 7th ed. Ed. by Anne Price & Juliette Yaakov. LC 95-38272. (Standard Catalog Ser.). 1008p. 1995. 175.00 (*0-8242-0880-3*) Wilson.

Middle & Late Life Transitions. Ed. by Felix F. Berardo. LC 82-61685. (Annals of the American Academy of Political & Social Science Ser.: Vol. 464). 1982. 26.00 (*0-8039-1932-8*); pap. 17.00 (*0-8039-1933-6*) Sage.

Middle & Late Woodland Research in Virginia, a Synthesis, Vol. 29. Ed. by Theodore R. Reinhart & Mary E. Hodges. 311p. 1992. pap. 28.00 (*1-884626-12-2*) Archeolog Soc.

Middle & Late Woodland Subsistence & Ceramic Technology in the Central Mississippi River Valley: Selected Studies from the Burkemper Site, Lincoln County, Missouri. Michael J. O'Brien et al. (Illinois State Museum Reports of Investigations: Vol. 52). (Orig.). 1996. pap. write for info. (*0-89792-151-8*) Ill St Museum.

Middle & Upper Atmosphere Results: Proceedings of the Topical Meeting of the COSPAR Interdisciplinary Scientific Commission C (Meetings C2 & C3) & A (Meeting A5) of the COSPAR 28th Plenary Meeting Held in The Hague, The Netherlands, 25 June-6 July, 1990. Ed. by G. M. Keating et al. (Advances in Space Research Ser.: Vol. 13). 342p. 1992. pap. 165.00 (*0-08-042047-8*, Pergamon Pr) Elsevier.

Middle & Upper Atmospheres: Small Scale Structures & Remote Sensing, Vol. 19. Ed. by K. U. Grossman et al. (Advances in Space Research Ser.: No. 4). 148p. 1997. 108.00 (*0-08-043104-6*, Pergamon Pr) Elsevier.

Middle Assyrian Laws. Claudio Saporetti. (Cybernetica Mesopotamica, Graphemic Categorization Ser.: Vol. 2). (Illus.). xii, 117p. 1984. pap. text 12.00 (*0-89003-120-7*) Undena Pubns.

Middle Atlantic Projectile Point Typology & Nomenclature. 3rd ed. W. Jack Hranicky. LC 95-198211. (Special Publications: No. 33). 110p. 1994. pap. 19.00 (*1-884626-22-X*) Archeolog Soc.

Middle Atlantic States. Miriam Sagan. LC 93-49007. (American Food Library). 48p. (J). (gr. 3-6). Date not set. lib. bdg. 22.60 (*0-86625-508-7*) Rourke Pubns.

Middle Atlantic/Allegheny Highlands Map (U. S. A.) 1997. 4.95 (*2-06-700474-3*, 474) Michelin.

Middle Atmosphere. Alan R. Plumb. 472p. 1989. 34.50 (*0-8176-2290-X*) Birkhauser.

Middle Atmosphere: Changes & Electrodynamics. Ed. by D. K. Chakrabarty & S. P. Gupta. (Advances in Space Research Ser.: 20/11). 160p. 1997. pap. 100.50 (*0-08-043308-1*, Pergamon Pr) Elsevier.

Middle Atmosphere Dynamics. Ed. by David G. Andrews et al. (International Geophysics Ser.: No. 40). 489p. 1987. pap. text 54.00 (*0-12-058576-6*) Acad Pr.

Middle Atmosphere Sciences: A Selection of Papers from the Symposium Organised by the IAMAP & IAGA on the Occasion of the XVIII General Assembly of the IUGG, Hamburg, Federal Republic of Germany, August 1983. Ed. by A. Ebel & P. C. Simon. 120p. 1985. pap. 36.00 (*0-08-032592-0*, Pergamon Pr) Elsevier.

Middle Babylonian Legal & Economic Texts from Ur. Oliver R. Gurney. (Illus.). 203p. 1983. 36.00 (*0-614-21867-5*, Pub. by Brit Sch Archaeol Iraq) David Brown.

Middle Beat: A Correspondent's View of Mexico, Guatemala, & El Salvador. Paul P. Kennedy. Ed. by Stanley R. Ross. LC 71-144045. (Columbia University, Center for Education in Asia, Publications). 255p. reprint ed. pap. 79.10 (*0-608-14883-0*, 202602900048) Bks Demand.

Middle Childhood: Practical Tips to Develop Greater Peace & Cooperation for Parents of Children Ages 7-12. James Herz. LC 98-205934. (Illus.). 216p. (Orig.). 1997. pap. 8.95 (*0-9658511-0-9*) Effred Family.

Middle Children. Rayda Jacobs. LC 94-229496. 168p. 1994. pap. 12.95 (*0-929005-59-7*, Pub. by Sec Story Pr) LPC InBook.

Middle Class. 2nd ed. Roger King et al. LC 81-199238. (Aspects of Modern Sociology: the Social Structure of Modern Britain Ser.). 286p. reprint ed. pap. 88.70 (*0-8357-2976-1*, 203923800011) Bks Demand.

Middle Class & Democracy in Socio-Historical Perspective. Ronald M. Glassman. LC 95-224478. (Studies in Human Society: No. 10). 250p. 1995. 89.00 (*90-04-10359-7*) Brill Academic Pubs.

Middle-Class Blacks in Britain: A Racial Fraction of a Class Group or a Class Fraction of a Racial Group? Sharon J. Daye. LC 93-29486. 1994. text 69.95 (*0-312-10638-6*) St Martin.

Middle Class Dreams. Stanley B. Greenberg. 338p. 1995. 25.00 (*0-614-32267-7*) Random.

Middle Class Dreams: The Politics & Power of the New American Majority. rev. ed. Stanley B. Greenberg. LC 96-60012. 370p. 1996. pap. 16.00 (*0-300-06712-7*) Yale U Pr.

Middle Class in Politics. Ed. by J. Garrard et al. 382p. 1978. text 82.95 (*0-566-00225-6*) Ashgate Pub Co.

Middle-Class Providence, 1820-1940. John S. Gilkeson. LC 85-43284. 391p. reprint ed. pap. 121.30 (*0-608-04623-X*, 206531000003) Bks Demand.

Middle Class Vote. John Bonham. LC 74-11985. (Illus.). 210p. 1974. reprint ed. lib. bdg. 59.50 (*0-8371-7709-X*, BOMI, Greenwood Pr) Greenwood.

Middle-Class Waifs: The Psychodynamic Treatment of Affectively Disturbed Children. Elaine V. Siegel. 280p. 1991. text 42.50 (*0-88163-098-5*) Analytic Pr.

Middle Classes in Dependent Countries. Ed. by Dale L. Johnson. LC 84-12713. (Class, State & Development Ser.: No. 3). 295p. reprint ed. pap. 91.50 (*0-8357-8435-5*, 203469800091) Bks Demand.

Middle Classes in Europe, 1789-1914: France, Germany, Italy & Russia. Pamela M. Pilbeam. LC 89-13220. 328p. (C). 1990. text 49.95 (*0-925065-29-3*); pap. text 25.95 (*0-925065-26-9*) Lyceum IL.

Middle Classes in Middle-Sized Cities: The Stratification & Political Position of Small Business & White. C. Wright Mills. (Reprint Series in Social Sciences). (C). 1993. reprint ed. pap. text 5.00 (*0-8290-2662-2*, S-198) Irvington.

Middle Colonies see English in America

***Middle Commentary of Aristotle's de Anima.** Abu Al-Walid Muhammad Ibn. Ed. by Alfred L. Ivry. (Islamic Translation Ser.). (ARA & ENG.). 300p. 2000. 29.95 (*0-8425-2473-8*) Brigham.

Middle Cypriot White Painted Pottery: An Analytical Study of the Decoration. David Frankel. (Studies in Mediterranean Archaeology: Vol. XLII). (Illus.). 140p. (Orig.). 1974. pap. 22.50 (*91-85058-60-2*, Pub. by P Astroms) Coronet Bks.

Middle Distance Running: Training & Competition. Cliff Temple. (Illus.). 160p. 1993. pap. 19.95 (*0-09-174815-1*, Pub. by S Paul) Trafalgar.

Middle Distances: Contemporary Theory, Technique & Training. 4th ed. Ed. by Jess Jarver. LC 97-138860. (Contemporary Track & Field Ser.). (Illus.). 150p. 1997. pap. 16.50 (*0-911521-49-6*) Tafnews.

Middle Dutch Prose Lancelot: A Study of the Rotterdam Fragments & Their Place in the French, German & Dutch Lancelot in Prose Tradition. O. S. H. Lie. 232p. 1987. text 81.25 (*0-444-85647-1*) Elsevier.

***Middle Ear.** Forrest Hamer. (California Poetry Ser.: Vol. 7). 80p. 2000. pap. 12.50 (*0-9666691-6-9*) Heyday Bks.

Middle Ear Fluid in Young Children, Consumer Version: Clinical Practice. 13p. 1994. pap. 25.00 (*0-16-061525-9*) USGPO.

An Asterisk (*) at the beginning of an entry indicates that the title is appearing for the first time.

Middle Ear Implant: Implantable Hearing Aids. Ed. by K. I. Suzuki. (Advances in Audiology Ser.: Vol. 4). (Illus.). x, 174p. 1988. 128.00 (*3-8055-4620-3*) S Karger.
Middle Ear Structures, Organogenesis & Congenital Defects. Ed. by B. Ars & P. Van Cauwenberge. LC 91-12019. (Illus.). 98p. 1991. pap. text 34.50 (*90-6299-074-6*, Pub. by Kugler) Kugler Pubns.
Middle East. Evan Anderson. LC 99-47555. 400p. (C). 1998. 99.99 (*0-415-07667-6*); pap. 29.99 (*0-415-07668-4*) Routledge.
Middle East. Ed. by Talal Asad & Roger Owen. LC 83-42527. (Sociology of "Developing Societies" Ser.). 240p. 1983. pap. 14.00 (*0-85345-637-2*, Pub. by Monthly Rev) NYU Pr.
Middle East. Michelle Breyer. (Thematic Unit Ser.). 80p. (J). (gr. 5-8). 1997. pap. 9.95 (*1-55734-573-2*) Tchr Create Mat.
Middle East. Ed. by John C. Campbell. 1976. 27.95 (*0-405-06660-0*) Ayer.
Middle East. Ed. by Virginia Danielson et al. (Illus.). 900p. 1999. text 165.00 (*0-8240-6042-3*) Garland.
Middle East. Griffin Trade Paperbacks Staff. (Let's Go 2000 Ser.). (Illus.). 736p. 1999. pap. 22.99 (*0-312-24667-6*) St Martin.
Middle East. Dilip Hiro. LC 96-12397. (International Government & Politics Ser.). 232p. 1996. pap. 37.95 (*1-57356-004-9*) Oryx Pr.
Middle East. Kublin. 1990. pap., teacher ed. 3.92 (*0-395-53615-4*) HM.
Middle East. Hyman Kublin. 1989. pap. 18.68 (*0-395-47081-1*) HM.
Middle East. Bernard Lewis. 448p. 1997. per. 15.00 (*0-684-83280-1*, Touchstone) S&S Trade Pap.
Middle East. Mary Tassin. LC 91-91351. (Illus.). 122p. 1992. pap. 14.95 (*0-9631179-0-4*) Penny Hill Rkshp.
Middle East. Jay Walz. LC 65-27595. (New York Times Byline Bks.). (C). 1972. 3.95 (*0-689-10279-8*) Atheneum Yung Read.
***Middle East.** Mary E. Williams. LC 99-10881. (Opposing Viewpoints Ser.). (Illus.). 224p. (YA). (gr. 9). 2000. pap. 13.96 (*0-7377-0132-3*) Greenhaven.
Middle East. rev. ed. Ed. by Michael Adams. LC 86-29274. (Handbooks to the Modern World Ser.). 883p. reprint ed. pap. 200.00 (*0-7837-1575-7*, 204186700024) Bks Demand.
Middle East. rev. ed. Frank Hill. (TravelCard Pac Ser.). 1992. 4.00 (*0-88699-021-1*) Travel Sci.
***Middle East.** rev. ed. Let's Go Staff. (Let's Go 2001 Ser.). (Illus.). 736p. 2000. pap. 22.99 (*0-312-24693-5*, St Martin Griffin) St Martin.
Middle East. 3rd ed. Armajani & Ricks. 448p. (C). 2001. pap. 38.67 (*0-13-976010-5*) P-H.
***Middle East.** 3rd ed. Andrew Humphreys et al. (Illus.). 896p. 2000. pap. 21.95 (*0-86442-701-8*) Lonely Planet.
Middle East. 8th ed. LC 94-17492. 512p. (C). (gr. 11). 1995. text 47.95 (*1-56802-038-4*) Congr Quarterly.
Middle East. 8th ed. Ed. by Daniel C. Diller & John L. Moore. LC 94-17492. 438p. (C). (gr. 11). 1995. pap. text 34.95 (*0-87187-999-9*) Congr Quarterly.
Middle East. 8th ed. Spencer. 240p. 2000. pap. 18.75 (*0-07-236588-9*) McGraw.
***Middle East.** 9th ed. LC 99-51565. 1999. 49.95 (*1-56802-101-1*); pap. 34.95 (*1-56802-100-3*) CQ Pr.
Middle East, 39 bks., Set. Ed. by John E. Woods et al. 1973. 1321.00 (*0-405-05310-X*) Ayer.
Middle East: A Brief History of the Last 2,000 Years. Bernard Lewis. (Illus.). 433p. 1996. 29.50 (*0-684-80712-2*) S&S Trade.
Middle East: A Geopolitical Study of the Region in the New Global Era. Richard Krooth & Minoo Moallem. LC 94-27413. 302p. 1995. lib. bdg. 38.50 (*0-89950-987-8*) McFarland & Co.
Middle East: A History. 5th ed. Sydney N. Fisher & William L. Ochsenwald. LC 96-42103. 464p. (C). 1996. pap. 35.94 (*0-07-021231-7*) McGraw.
Middle East: A History, Vol. 2. 5th ed. Sydney N. Fisher & William L. Ochsenwald. LC 96-42103. 560p. (C). 1996. pap. 35.94 (*0-07-021719-X*) McGraw.
Middle East: A Political Dictionary. 2nd ed. Lawrence Ziring. LC 92-15379. (Clio Dictionaries in Political Science Ser.). 450p. 1992. pap. text 29.95 (*0-87436-697-6*); lib. bdg. 60.00 (*0-87436-612-7*) ABC-CLIO.
Middle East: Abstracts & Index, 1978, Vol. 1. Ed. by Amy C. Lowenstein. 1979. 250.00 (*0-318-50002-7*) Northumberland Pr.
Middle East: Abstracts & Index, 1979, Vol. 2. Ed. by Amy C. Lowenstein. 1979. 250.00 (*0-318-50003-5*) Northumberland Pr.
Middle East: Abstracts & Index, 1980, Vol. 3. Ed. by Amy C. Lowenstein. 1980. 250.00 (*0-318-50004-3*) Northumberland Pr.
Middle East: Abstracts & Index, 1981, Vol. 4. Ed. by Amy C. Lowenstein. 1981. pap. 250.00 (*0-934565-00-7*) Northumberland Pr.
Middle East: Abstracts & Index, 1982, Vol. 5. Ed. by Amy C. Lowenstein. 1986. 250.00 (*0-318-49998-3*) Northumberland Pr.
Middle East: Abstracts & Index, 1983, Vol. 6. Ed. by Amy C. Lowenstein. 1988. 250.00 (*0-318-49999-1*) Northumberland Pr.
Middle East: Abstracts & Index, 1984, Vol. 7. Ed. by Amy C. Lowenstein. 1989. 250.00 (*0-318-50000-0*) Northumberland Pr.
Middle East: Abstracts & Index, 1985, Vol. 8. Ed. by Amy C. Lowenstein. 1990. 250.00 (*0-318-50001-9*) Northumberland Pr.
Middle East: Five Perspectives. Ed. by Margaret Pennar. (Information Papers: No. 7). 33p. (Orig.). (C). 1973. pap. 1.00 (*0-937694-23-1*) Assn Arab-Amer U Grads.
Middle East: Fourteen Islamic Centuries. 3rd ed. Glenn E. Perry. LC 96-33631. 362p. (C). 1996. pap. text 52.00 (*0-13-266339-7*) P-H.
Middle East: From the End of Empire to the End of the Cold War. P. J. Vatikiotis. LC 97-181171. 296p. (C). 1997. 65.00 (*0-415-15849-4*) Routledge.
Middle East: Issues & Events of 1978 from The New York Times Information Bank. Ed. by David Chaffetz & Mitchell Rapoport. LC 78-32140. (News in Print Ser.). 300p. 1979. lib. bdg. 30.95 (*0-405-12875-4*) Ayer.
Middle East: Issues & Events of 1979. Ed. by Janet Byrne. LC 80-1718. (News in Print Ser.). (Illus.). 1980. lib. bdg. 30.95 (*0-405-12878-9*) Ayer.
Middle East: Its Oil, Economies, & Investment Policies: A Guide to Sources of Financial Information. David Nicholas. LC 80-28555. 199p. 1981. lib. bdg. 49.95 (*0-313-22986-4*, NME/, Greenwood Pr) Greenwood.
Middle East: Opposing Viewpoints. Ed. by William Dudley. LC 91-43280. (Illus.). 264p. (YA). (gr. 10 up). 1992. pap. text 16.20 (*0-89908-160-6*) Greenhaven.
***Middle East: Opposing Viewpoints.** Mary E. Williams. LC 99-10881. (Opposing Viewpoints Ser.). (YA). (gr. 9-12). 2000. lib. bdg. 27.45 (*0-7377-0133-1*) Greenhaven.
Middle East: Quest for an American Policy. Ed. & Intro. by Willard A. Beling. LC 73-4281. (Illus.). 347p. (C). 1976. text 24.50 (*0-87395-228-6*) State U NY Pr.
Middle East: Special Studies, 1992-1994: Supplement. Compiled by Blair D. Hydrick. LC 95-26365. (Special Studies). (C). 1995. 2070.00 incl. mic. film (*1-55655-538-5*) U Pubns Amer.
Middle East: Struggle for a Homeland. Keith Greenberg. Ed. by Bruce S. Glassman. (Children in Crisis Ser.). (Illus.). 32p. (J). (gr. 3-5). 1996. lib. bdg. 16.95 (*1-56711-187-4*) Blackbirch.
Middle East: Ten Years after Camp David. Ed. by William B. Quandt. 450p. 1988. 44.95 (*0-8157-7294-7*); pap. 19.95 (*0-8157-7293-9*) Brookings.
Middle East: War Without End. Alain Gresh. (C). 1988. pap. 18.50 (*0-85315-662-X*, Pub. by Lawrence & Wishart) NYU Pr.
Middle East After Iraq's Invasion of Kuwait. Ed. by Robert O. Freedman. LC 93-18252. 416p. 1993. 49.95 (*0-8130-1214-7*); pap. 24.95 (*0-8130-1215-5*) U Press Fla.
Middle East after the Cold War. Ed. by William Harris & Louis S. Leland. 236p. 1996. pap. 45.00 (*0-614-22149-8*) Intl Spec Bk.
Middle East after the Cold War. Ed. by William Harris & Louis S. Leland, Jr. LC 97-206880. 236p. 1996. pap. 45.00 (*1-877133-13-2*, Pub. by Univ Otago Pr) Intl Spec Bk.
Middle East & Africa see International Dictionary of Historic Places
Middle East & Central Asia: An Anthropological Approach. 3rd ed. Dale F. Eickelman. LC 97-14080. 388p. 1997. pap. text 45.00 (*0-13-123019-0*) P-H.
Middle East & Development in a Changing World. Ed. by Donald F. Heisel. 164p. 1999. pap. 10.00 (*977-424-477-X*, Pub. by Am Univ Cairo Pr) Col U Pr.
Middle East & Europe. B. A. Roberson. LC 98-18945. 1998. write for info. (*0-415-14044-7*); pap. write for info. (*0-415-14045-5*) Routledge.
Middle East & North Africa see 1999 Political Risk Yearbook
Middle East & North Africa, Vol. 2. Ed. by Clive H. Schofield & Richard N. Schofield. (World Boundaries Ser.). (Illus.). 224p. (C). 1994. 85.00 (*0-415-08839-9*) Routledge.
Middle East & North Africa: A Political Geography. Alasdair Drysdale & Gerald H. Blake. LC 84-1095. (Illus.). 382p. 1985. pap. text 33.95 (*0-19-503538-0*) OUP.
Middle East & North Africa: Essays in Honor of J. C. Hurewitz. Ed. by Reeva S. Simon. 545p. 1990. text 75.00 (*0-231-07148-5*) Col U Pr.
Middle East & North Africa: Essays in Honor of J. C. Hurewitz. Ed. by Reeva S. Simon. 545p. (C). 1998. text 40.00 (*0-7881-5505-9*) DIANE Pub.
Middle East & North Africa: Governance, Democratization, Human Rights. Ed. by Paul Magnarella. (Contemporary Perspectives on Developing Societies Ser.). 240p. 1999. text 65.95 (*1-84014-913-2*, Pub. by Ashgate Pub) Ashgate Pub Co.
Middle East & North Africa: Medieval & Modern History. Ed. by Patricia J. Rosof et al. LC 82-11931. (Trends in History Ser.: Vol. 2, No. 3). 134p. 1983. text 39.95 (*0-917724-45-3*) Haworth Pr.
Middle East & North Africa in World Politics: A Documentary Record, Vol. 1. 2nd enl. rev. ed. J. C. Hurewitz. LC 74-83525. 640p. reprint ed. pap. 198.40 (*0-8357-3748-9*, 203647400001) Bks Demand.
Middle East & North Africa in World Politics: A Documentary Record, Vol. 2: British-French Supremacy, 1914-1945. 2nd ed. Ed. by J. C. Hurewitz. LC 74-83525. Vol. 2. 672p. 1979. 95.00 (*0-300-02203-4*) Yale U Pr.
Middle East & North Africa, 1995. 41st ed. 967p. 1995. 310.00 (*0-946653-99-2*) Intl Pubns Serv.
Middle East & North Africa, 1997. 43rd rev. ed. 1000p. 1996. 345.00 (*1-85743-030-1*, Pub. by EurP) Taylor & Francis.
Middle East & North Africa, 1996. 44th ed. 1995. 325.00 (*1-85743-011-5*, Pub. by EurP) Gale.
Middle East & North Africa, 1998. 44th ed. 1104p. 1997. 370.00 (*1-85743-037-9*, 110555, Pub. by EurP) Gale.
Middle East & North Africa, 1999. 45th ed. Europa Publications Staff. (Middle East & North Africa Ser.). 1100p. 1998. 405.00 (*1-85743-047-6*, GML00299-111507, Pub. by EurP) Gale.
Middle East & North Africa on File. Facts on File Staff. LC 94-44747. (Illus.). 288p. (YA). (gr. 7 up). 1995. ring bd. 165.00 (*0-8160-3106-1*) Facts on File.
***Middle East & North Africa Regional Set, 1999/2000, 18 vols., Set.** 2nd ed. Robert C. Kelly et al. (Illus.). 60p. 1999. pap. 600.00 (*1-58310-209-4*) CountryWatch.
***Middle East & North Africa 2000.** 46th ed. Gale Group Publishing Staff. (Illus.). 1100p. 1999. 574.00 (*1-85743-061-1*) EurP.
Middle East & Problems of Democracy. Heather Deegan. LC 93-4446. (Issues in Third World Politics Ser.). 160p. (C). 1994. pap. text 16.95 (*1-55587-455-X*) L Rienner.
Middle East & Problems of Democracy. Heather Deegan. Ed. by Vicky Randall. (Issues in Third World Politics Ser.). 160p. 1993. 9.00 (*0-335-15687-8*); pap. 2.00 (*0-335-15686-X*) OpUniv Pr.
Middle East & South Asia, 1996. 30th ed. Malcolm B. Russell. 251p. 1996. pap. 11.50 (*1-887985-00-X*) Stryker-Post.
Middle East & South Asia, 1998. 32nd ed. Malcolm B. Russell. (World Today Ser.). 1998. pap. 11.50 (*1-887985-14-X*) Stryker-Post.
***Middle East & South Asia, 99.** 33rd ed. Malcolm B. Russell. 1999. pap. 11.50 (*1-887985-21-2*) Stryker-Post.
Middle East & the Balkans under the Ottoman Empire: Essays on Economy & Society. Halil Inalcik. LC 91-70793. (Turkish Studies: Vol. 9). 487p. (C). 1993. pap. text 32.00 (*1-878318-04-7*) IN Univ Turkish.
Middle East & the Balkans under the Ottoman Empire: Selected Essays. (Turkish Studies). pap. 28.50 (*0-614-04312-3*) IN Univ Turkish.
Middle East & the European Common Market. Rouhollah K. Ramazani. LC 64-13718. 175p. reprint ed. 54.30 (*0-8357-9810-0*, 201365800086) Bks Demand.
Middle East & the Peace Process: The Impact of the Oslo Accords. Robert O. Freedman. LC 97-20336. 435p. 1998. pap. 29.95 (*0-8130-1554-5*) U Press Fla.
Middle East & the Trilateral Countries. Garret FitzGerald et al. (Triangle Papers: No. 22). 1981. 6.00 (*0-930503-28-7*) Trilateral Comm.
Middle East & the United States: A Historical & Political Reassessment. Ed. by David W. Lesch. 460p. (C). 1996. pap. 32.00 (*0-8133-2405-X*, Pub. by Westview) HarpC.
Middle East & the United States: A Historical & Political Reassessment. 2nd ed. Ed. by David W. Lesch. LC 98-40724. 496p. (C). 1999. pap. 32.00 (*0-8133-3559-0*, Pub. by Westview) HarpC.
Middle East & the United States: Images, Perceptions, & Policies. Ed. by Haim Shaked & Itamar Rabinovich. LC 80-14290. 510p. 1980. 49.95 (*0-87855-329-0*); pap. 24.95 (*0-87855-752-0*) Transaction Pubs.
Middle East & Turkey see World Architecture 1900-2000: A Critical Mosaic
Middle East at the Crossroads: Regional Forces & External Powers. Ed. by Janice Gross-Stein & David B. Dewitt. 300p. 1995. pap. 14.95 (*0-88962-201-9*) Mosaic.
Middle East at the Crossroads: The Changing Political Dynamics & the Foreign Policy. Ed. by Manochehr Dorraj. LC 99-24370. 320p. 1999. 52.00 (*0-7618-1390-X*) U Pr of Amer.
***Middle East at the Crossroads: The Changing Political Dynamics & the Foreign Policy.** Ed. by Manochehr Dorraj. LC 99-24370. 320p. 1999. pap. 34.50 (*0-7618-1391-8*) U Pr of Amer.
Middle East Bedside Book. Ed. by Tahir Shah. 287p. 1991. 29.00 (*0-86304-035-7*, Pub. by Octagon Pr) ISHK.
Middle East Bedside Book. Tahir Shah. 287p. 1992. pap. 15.00 (*0-86304-060-8*, Pub. by Octagon Pr) ISHK.
***Middle East Between the Great Powers: Anglo-American Conflict & Cooperation, 1952-7.** Tore T. Petersen. LC 00-26980. 2000. write for info. (*0-312-23481-3*) St Martin.
Middle East Bibliography. Sanford R. Silverburg. LC 91-26074. (Area Bibliographies Ser.: No. 1). 599p. 1992. 73.00 (*0-8108-2469-8*) Scarecrow.
Middle East Challenge, 1980-1985. Ed. by Thomas Naff. LC 81-5651. 192p. (Orig.). 1981. pap. 17.95 (*0-8093-1042-2*) S Ill U Pr.
Middle East City: Ancient Traditions Confront a Modern World. Ed. by Abdulaziz Y. Saqqaf. (Illus.). 393p. 1986. 34.95 (*0-943852-32-3*) Prof World Peace.
Middle East Conflicts. Francois Massoulie. LC 98-20065. (Illustrated Histories Ser.). (Illus.). 160p. 1999. pap. 15.00 (*1-56656-237-6*, Interlink Bks) Interlink Pub.
***Middle East Contemporary Survey, Vol. 21.** Ed. by Bruce Maddy-Weitzman. LC 78-648245. 840p. 2000. 99.00 (*0-8133-3762-3*) Westview.
***Middle East Contemporary Survey Vol. XX: 1996.** Bruce Maddy-Weitzman. 800p. 1998. text 135.00 (*0-8133-3582-5*, Pub. by Westview) HarpC.
Middle East Contemporary Survey, 1976-1977, Vol. 1. Ed. by Colin Legum. (Illus.). 684p. 1978. 245.00 (*0-8419-0323-9*) Holmes & Meier.
Middle East Contemporary Survey, 1977-1978, Vol. 2. Ed. by Colin Legum & Haim Shaked. LC 78-648245. (Illus.). 824p. 1979. 245.00 (*0-8419-0398-0*) Holmes & Meier.
Middle East Contemporary Survey, 1978-1979, Vol. 3. Ed. by Colin Legum & Haim Shaked. 1980. 245.00 (*0-8419-0514-2*) Holmes & Meier.
Middle East Contemporary Survey, 1979-1980, Vol. 4. Ed. by Colin Legum & Haim Shaked. LC 78-648245. (Illus.). 890p. 1982. 245.00 (*0-8419-0609-2*) Holmes & Meier.
Middle East Contemporary Survey, 1980-1981, Vol. 5. Ed. by Colin Legum et al. 896p. 1983. 245.00 (*0-8419-0825-7*) Holmes & Meier.
Middle East Contemporary Survey, 1981-1982, Vol. 6. Ed. by Colin Legum et al. 957p. 1984. 245.00 (*0-8419-0878-8*) Holmes & Meier.
Middle East Contemporary Survey, 1982-1983, Vol. 7. Ed. by Colin Legum et al. (Illus.). 950p. 1985. 245.00 (*0-8419-1014-6*) Holmes & Meier.
Middle East Country Studies. Randy L. Womack. (Illus.). 112p. 1991. student ed. 11.95 (*1-56500-024-2*) Gldn Educ.
Middle East Crisis. Hyman Lumer. 1967. pap. 0.25 (*0-87898-023-7*) New Outlook.
Middle East Crucible: Studies on the Arab-Israeli War of October 1973. Ed. by Naseer H. Aruri. (Monographs: No. 6). 479p. 1975. 15.00 (*0-914456-10-5*); pap. 7.95 (*0-914456-11-3*) Assn Arab-Amer U Grads.
***Middle East Dilemmas: Politics & Economics of Arab Integration.** Michael Hudson. LC 98-23052. 376p. 1998. pap. 19.50 (*0-231-11139-8*); lib. bdg. 49.50 (*0-231-11138-X*) Col U Pr.
Middle East Economic Handbook. 2nd ed. 1995. write for info. (*0-8103-9804-4*, 073062, Pub. by Euromonitor PLC) Gale.
Middle East Economic Papers. 1969. pap. 19.95 (*0-8156-6017-0*, Pub. by Am U Beirut) Syracuse U Pr.
Middle East Economy: Decline & Recovery. rev. ed. Charles P. Issawi. (Princeton Series on the Middle East). (Illus.). 320p. (C). 1995. pap. text 16.95 (*1-55876-103-9*) Wiener Pubs Inc.
Middle East Economy: Decline & Recovery. rev. ed. Charles P. Issawi. (Princeton Series on the Middle East). (Illus.). 320p. (C). 1996. text 39.95 (*1-55876-102-0*) Wiener Pubs Inc.
Middle East Foreign Policy: Issues & Processes. Ronald D. McLaurin. LC 82-13137. 325p. 1982. 45.00 (*0-275-90858-5*, C0858, Praeger Pubs) Greenwood.
Middle East Imbroglio: Status & Prospects. Ed. by P. S. Link. 298p. (C). 1996. lib. bdg. 95.00 (*1-56072-391-2*) Nova Sci Pubs.
Middle East Imperatives & Choices. Alon Ben-Meir. LC 75-26110. (Illus.). 1975. 14.95 (*0-915474-01-8*, Effective Learn) Decalogue Bks.
Middle East in China's Foreign Policy, 1949-1977. Y. Shichor. LC 78-58801. (International Studies). (Illus.). 272p. 1979. text 64.95 (*0-521-22214-1*) Cambridge U Pr.
Middle East in Crime Fiction. Reeva S. Simon. 224p. 1989. text 24.95 (*0-936508-20-5*) Barber Pr.
Middle East in Pictures, 4 Vols. Ghastgifvar E. Matson. 1980. 192.95 (*0-405-12212-8*, 19456) Ayer.
Middle East in Pictures, Vol. 4. Ghastgifvar E. Matson. 1980. 49.95 (*0-405-18868-4*) Ayer.
Middle East in Review, 1984-1985. Mazher A. Hameed. (Illus.). 147p. (Orig.). 1986. pap. 12.00 (*0-937783-01-3*) Mid East Assess.
Middle East in Search of Peace. rev. ed. Cathryn J. Long. (Headliners Ser.). (Illus.). 64p. (J). (gr. 5-8). 1996. lib. bdg. 23.40 (*0-7613-0105-4*) Millbrook Pr.
Middle East in the Middle Ages: The Early Mamluk Sultanate, 1250-1382. Robert Irwin. LC 85-26102. 191p. 1986. text 31.95 (*0-8093-1286-7*) S Ill U Pr.
***Middle East in the New Millennium.** Ed. by David J. Eaton. (Institute & Seminar Proceedings Ser.). 68p. (C). 2000. pap. 10.00 (*0-89940-113-9*) LBJ Sch Pub Aff.
***Middle East in the New Millennium: Economic Development & Business Law.** Gil Feiler. LC 00-39086. 2000. write for info. (*90-411-8844-4*) Kluwer Law Intl.
Middle East in the World Economy, 1800-1914. Roger Owen. 378p. 1993. text 19.95 (*1-85043-658-4*, Pub. by I B T) St Martin.
Middle East in the World Economy, 1800-1914. Roger Owen. 400p. 1987. pap. 25.00 (*0-416-03272-9*) Routledge.
Middle East in Transition: Studies in Contemporary History. Ed. by Walter Laqueur. LC 70-156676. (Essay Index Reprint Ser.). 1977. reprint ed. 31.95 (*0-8369-2367-7*) Ayer.
Middle East in World Politics. Ed. by Mohammed Ayoob. LC 81-169898. 217p. reprint ed. pap. 67.30 (*0-608-11744-7*, 201935900011) Bks Demand.
Middle East in World Politics: A Study in Contemporary International Relations. Ed. by Tareq Y. Ismael. LC 73-16637. 311p. reprint ed. pap. 96.50 (*0-608-15204-8*, 202739600055) Bks Demand.
Middle East Industrialisation: A Study of Saudi & Iranian Downstream Investment. Louis Turner & James Bedore. LC 79-89599. (Praeger Special Studies). (Illus.). 229p. 1979. 59.95 (*0-275-90432-6*, C0432, Praeger Pubs) Greenwood.
Middle East Intelligence Handbooks, 1943-1946, 5 vols., Set. Archives Research Ltd. Staff. (Illus.). 3178p. (C). 1987. reprint ed. lib. bdg. 995.00 (*1-85207-060-9*, Pub. by Archive Editions) N Ross.
Middle East into the Twenty-First Century: Studies on the Arab-Israeli Conflict, the Gulf Crisis. Chibli Mallat. 1998. pap. text 19.95 (*0-86372-224-5*, Pub. by Garnet-Ithaca) LPC InBook.
Middle East, Its Religion & Culture. Edward J. Jurji. LC 72-9809. 159p. 1973. reprint ed. lib. bdg. 55.00 (*0-8371-6597-0*, JUME, Greenwood Pr) Greenwood.
Middle East Legal Systems. S. H. Amin. 308p. (C). 1985. 210.00 (*0-946706-22-0*, Pub. by Royston Ltd) St Mut.
Middle East Master Map Kit: Their Lands & Ours. Ellen Fairbanks & D. Bodman. 39p. (J). (gr. 5 up). 1989. 14.95 (*0-930141-25-3*) World Eagle.
Middle East Materials for Teachers, Students, Non-Specialists. Pref. by Catherine E. Jones. 153p. (Orig.). 1988. pap. 10.00 (*0-9621344-0-6*) Mid East Outreach.
Middle East Materials in United Kingdom & Irish Libraries: A Directory: a MELCOM Guide to Libraries & Other Institutions in Britain & Ireland with Islamic & Middle Eastern Books & Materials. Ed. by Ian R. Netton. LC 82-23574. 136p. reprint ed. pap. 42.20 (*0-7837-5318-7*, 204505700005) Bks Demand.

M

An Asterisk (*) at the beginning of an entry indicates that the title is appearing for the first time.

Middle East Military Balance, Vol. 1, Pt. 3. MESSQ Staff. (Middle East Strategic Studies Quarterly: No. 8903). 176p. 1990. 40.50 (*0-08-040375-1*, Pergamon Pr) Elsevier.

***Middle East Military Balance: Annual Volume.** annuals Mark Heller. 365p. 1998. lib. bdg. 52.50 (*0-231-10893-1*) Col U Pr.

***Middle East Military Balance: 1997.** Mark Heller. 1999. 50.00 (*0-231-11464-8*) Col U Pr.

***Middle East Military Balance, 1999-2000.** Ed. by Shlomo Brom & Yiftah Shapir. LC 99-49269. (BCSIA Studies in International Security). (Illus.). 480p. 2000. 37.50 (*0-262-02478-0*) MIT Pr.

Middle East Military Balance 1996. Mark A. Heller. 452p. 1998. 50.00 (*0-231-10892-3*) Col U Pr.

***Middle East Monarchies: The Challenge of Modernity.** Ed. by Joseph Kostiner. LC 99-51384. 350p. 2000. lib. bdg. 59.95 (*1-55587-862-8*) L Rienner.

***Middle East Mosaic: Fragments of Life, Letters & History.** Ed. by Bernard Lewis. LC 99-10150. (Illus.). 512p. 2000. 35.00 (*0-679-45191-9*) Random.

Middle East Oil: A Redistribution of Values Arising from the Oil Industry. Mohamed B. Alumulhim. 352p. (C). 1991. lib. bdg. 62.00 (*0-8191-8179-X*) U Pr of Amer.

Middle East Oil: Issues & Problems. Benjamin Shwadran. 122p. 1977. 29.95 (*0-87073-597-7*); pap. 18.95 (*0-87073-598-5*) Transaction Pubs.

Middle East Oil & Gas. OECD (Int. Energy Agency) Staff. LC 96-175042. (ENG & FRE.). 350p. (Orig.). 1996. pap. 105.00 (*92-64-14387-4*, Pub. by Org for Econ) OECD.

Middle East Oil & the Energy Crisis. Jose Stork. LC 74-7786. 336p. reprint ed. pap. 104.20 (*0-7837-3912-5*, 204376000010) Bks Demand.

Middle East, Oil & the Great Powers. 3rd ed. Benjamin Shwadran. 630p. 1973. boxed set 21.95 (*0-87855-157-3*) Transaction Pubs.

Middle East Oil Decade & Beyond. Gad G. Gilbar. LC 97-201145. 144p. 1997. 45.00 (*0-7146-4734-9*, Pub. by F Cass Pubs) Intl Spec Bk.

Middle East on the Eve of Modernity: Aleppo in the Eighteenth-Century. Abraham Marcus. (Study of the Middle East Institute Ser.). 418p. (C). 1992. pap. 20.00 (*0-231-06595-7*) Col U Pr.

Middle East on the Eve of Modernity: Culture & Society in Eighteenth-Century Aleppo. Abraham Marcus. (Study of the Middle East Institute Ser.). (Illus.). 1989. text 57.50 (*0-231-06594-9*) Col U Pr.

Middle East Organizations in Washington, D. C. Ed. by David Colvin & Leslie Hunter. 104p. 1998. 12.00 (*0-916808-40-8*) Mid East Inst.

Middle East, Pacific Basin, & the United States: Refining & Petrochemicals. Ragaei E. Mallakh. LC 86-81024. (Illus.). 180p. 1986. pap. 36.00 (*0-918714-10-9*) Intl Res Ctr Energy.

***Middle East Patterns: Places, Peoples & Politics.** 3rd ed. Colbert C. Held. 528p. 2000. pap. 30.00 (*0-8133-3488-8*) Westview.

Middle East Peace Plans. Ed. by Willard A. Beling. (WVSS on the Middle East Ser.). (C). 1996. pap. text 22.50 (*0-8133-7125-2*) Westview.

Middle East Peace Process: Interdisciplinary Perspectives. Ed. by Ilan Peleg. LC 97-1208. (SUNY Series in Israeli Studies). 312p. (C). 1997. text 59.50 (*0-7914-3541-5*); pap. text 19.95 (*0-7914-3542-3*) State U NY Pr.

Middle East Peace Talks: Role Play Peacegames. David W. Felder. LC 95-90507. (Illus.). 102p. 1996. 24.95 (*0-910959-10-2*, B&G 10H); teacher ed. 44.95 (*0-910959-30-7*, B&G 10T) Wellington Pr.

Middle East Perspective. Bruce Barnes. (Illus.). 224p. (Orig.). (C). 1983. pap. text 7.00 (*0-913811-00-9*) Northeast A S.

Middle East Postwar Environment. Walid Khalidi. LC 91-75982. (IPS Papers). 50p. (Orig.). (C). 1991. pap. 3.95 (*0-88728-233-4*) Inst Palestine.

Middle East Record, Vols. 1-4. Ed. by Daniel Dishon. Incl. Vol. 2. 826p. 1961. (*0-87855-165-4*); Vol. 4. 920p. 1968. (*0-87855-167-0*); 69.95 (*0-685-04921-3*) Transaction Pubs.

Middle East Regional Issues: Role Play Peacegames. David W. Felder. (Illus.). 56p. 1996. pap. text 8.95 (*0-910959-51-X*, B&G 10B) Wellington Pr.

Middle East Remembered. John S. Badeau. LC 83-61202. 271p. 1983. 5.00 (*0-916808-21-1*) Mid East Inst.

***Middle East Remembered: Forged Identities, Competing Narratives, Contested Spaces.** Jacob Lassner. 430p. 1999. text 54.50 (*0-472-11083-7*, 11083) U of Mich Pr.

Middle East Review, 1989. 1993. pap. 29.95 (*0-8442-3398-6*, Passprt Bks) NTC Contemp Pub Co.

***Middle East Security in the Gulf.** 2000. write for info. (*0-582-35723-3*) Pearson Educ.

Middle East Sketches. Mark N. Katz. LC 97-14071. 166p. 1997. pap. 29.00 (*0-7618-0776-4*) U Pr of Amer.

Middle East Sources: A MELCOM Guide to Middle Eastern & Islamic Books & Materials in the United Kingdom & Irish Libraries. Ian R. Netton. LC 98-179259. 260p. 1998. 75.00 (*0-7007-1029-9*, Pub. by Curzon Pr Ltd) Paul & Co Pubs.

Middle East Studies: International Perspectives on the State of the Art. Ed. by Tareq Y. Ismael. LC 89-16279. 242p. 1990. 55.00 (*0-275-93300-8*, C3300, Praeger Pubs) Greenwood.

Middle East Terrorism: Current Threats & Future Prospects. Ed. by Yonah Alexander. LC 93-33931. 509p. 1994. 50.00 (*0-8161-7337-0*, G K Hall Lrg Type) Mac Lib Ref.

Middle East Terrorism: Selected Group Profiles. Yonah Alexander. (Illus.). 96p. (Orig.). (C). 1996. reprint ed. pap. text 35.00 (*0-7881-3515-5*) DIANE Pub.

Middle East Today. 6th ed. Don Peretz. LC 93-26376. 608p. 1994. 85.00 (*0-275-94575-8*, Praeger Pubs); pap. 26.95 (*0-275-94576-6*, Praeger Pubs) Greenwood.

Middle East Today: An Atlas of Reproducible Pages. Ed. by World Eagle Staff. (Today Ser.). (Illus.). 1997. ring bd. 49.95 (*0-930141-62-8*) World Eagle.

Middle East Wastewater Management. F. El-Gohary. (Water Science & Technology Ser.: 32). (Orig.). pap. 88.00 (*0-08-042889-4*, Pergamon Pr) Elsevier.

***Middle East Water Question: Hydropolitics & the Global Economy.** Tony Allan. 2000. text 59.50 (*1-86064-582-8*, Pub. by I B T) St Martin.

Middle East, 1940-1945 see British Documents on Foreign Affairs: Series B: Near & Middle East

***Middle Eastern.** Ed. by Lorenz Books Staff. 2000. pap. 9.95 (*0-7548-0165-9*, Lorenz Bks) Anness Pub.

Middle Eastern Candle Dancing, Vol. I, Bk. 22. Vicki Corona. (Celebrate the Cultures Ser.). (Illus.). 24p. 1989. pap. 14.95 (*1-58513-035-4*) Dance Fantasy.

Middle Eastern Cane Dancing, Vol. I, Bk. 17. Vicki Corona. (Celebrate the Cultures Ser.). (Illus.). 24p. 1989. pap. 14.95 (*1-58513-030-3*) Dance Fantasy.

Middle Eastern Cooking. Suzy Benghiat. 1993. 12.98 (*1-55521-940-3*) Bk Sales Inc.

Middle Eastern Cooking: A Practical Guide. Abdennour Samia. LC 97-144551. 1997. pap. text 17.95 (*977-424-401-X*, Pub. by Am Univ Cairo Pr) Col U Pr.

Middle Eastern Cooking: Over 100 Delicious Recipes. Christine Osborne. (Illus.). 152p. 1997. pap. 24.95 (*1-85375-257-6*, Pub. by Prion) Trafalgar.

Middle Eastern Cuisine. Sima O. Yassine. 1984. 24.95 (*0-86685-360-X*) Intl Bk Ctr.

Middle Eastern Economic Relations with the Soviet Union, Eastern Europe, & Mainland China. Robert L. Allen & Rowland Egger. LC 85-14822. 128p. 1985. reprint ed. lib. bdg. 59.50 (*0-313-23535-X*, ALMI, Greenwood Pr) Greenwood.

Middle Eastern Economy: Studies in Economics & Economic History. Ed. by Elie Kedourie. 185p. 1976. 39.50 (*0-7146-3074-8*, Pub. by F Cass Pubs) Intl Spec Bk.

Middle Eastern Environment. Ed. by Eric Watkins. (Illus.). 253p. 1995. pap. 39.50 (*1-898565-03-1*, Pub. by St Malo Pr) Antique Collect.

Middle Eastern Folk Dance Costumes, Vol. I, Bk. 20. Vicki Corona. (Celebrate the Cultures Ser.). (Illus.). 44p. 1990. pap. 15.95 (*1-58513-033-8*) Dance Fantasy.

Middle Eastern History. Ed. by Guity Nashat. (Selected Reading Lists & Course Outlines from Leading American Colleges & Universities Ser.). 300p. (Orig.). 1988. pap. 16.95 (*0-910129-70-3*) Wiener Pubs Inc.

Middle Eastern Investments in the U. S. Ibrahim A. Warde. 250p. 1985. pap. 95.00 (*0-88115-062-2*) I B P C Inc.

Middle Eastern Lectures. Ed. by Martin Kramer. (Middle East Studies). 130p. (Orig.). 1995. pap. text 12.95 (*0-8156-7057-5*, Pub. by Moshe Dayan Ctr) Syracuse U Pr.

Middle Eastern Lectures, No. 2. 125p. 1997. pap. 12.95 (*965-224-023-0*) Syracuse U Pr.

Middle Eastern Lectures, 1999, No. 3. Ed. by Martin Kramer. 129p. 1999. pap. 14.95 (*965-224-036-2*, Pub. by Moshe Dayan Ctr) Syracuse U Pr.

Middle Eastern Lives: The Practice of Biography & Self-Narrative. Ed. by Martin Kramer. LC 91-11277. (Contemporary Issues in the Middle East Ser.). 160p. 1991. text 34.95 (*0-8156-2548-0*) Syracuse U Pr.

***Middle Eastern Minorities: Between Integration & Conflict.** Moshe Maoz. LC 99-48682. (Policy Papers Ser.: No. 50). 111p. 1999. pap. 19.95 (*0-944029-33-7*) Wash Inst NEP.

Middle Eastern Muslim Women Speak. Ed. by Elizabeth W. Fernea & Basima Q. Bezirgan. (Illus.). 452p. 1977. pap. 18.95 (*0-292-75041-2*) U of Tex Pr.

Middle Eastern Politics & Ideas: A History from Within. Ed. by Moshe Maoz & Ilan Pappe. LC 95-62316. 256p. 1998. text 59.50 (*1-86064-012-5*, Pub. by I B T) St Martin.

Middle Eastern Recipes for Healthy Eating. Edward Matzaganian. 104p. 1998. pap. 17.95 (*0-931541-43-3*) Mancorp Pub.

Middle Eastern Security: Prospects for an Arms Control Regime. Ed. by Efraim Inbar & Shmuel Sandler. LC 95-12261. 200p. 1995. 39.50 (*0-7146-4644-X*, Pub. by F Cass Pubs); pap. 22.50 (*0-7146-4168-5*, Pub. by F Cass Pubs) Intl Spec Bk.

Middle Eastern Studies: Thirty Volume Index, 1964-1994. Ed. by Sylvia Kedourie. LC 94-38020. 116p. 1994. 45.00 (*0-7146-4590-7*, Pub. by F Cass Pubs) Intl Spec Bk.

Middle Eastern Tales. Samyr Souki. 1994. 15.00 (*0-533-10807-1*) Vantage.

Middle Eastern Themes: Papers in History & Politics. Jacob M. Landau. 309p. 1973. 49.50 (*0-7146-2969-3*, Pub. by F Cass Pubs) Intl Spec Bk.

Middle Eastern Village. Ed. by Richard Lawless. 320p. 1987. lib. bdg. 59.00 (*0-7099-1695-7*, Pub. by C Helm) Routldge.

Middle Eastern Women & the Invisible Economy. Ed. by Richard Lobban. LC 98-12588. (Illus.). 416p. 1998. 49.95 (*0-8130-1577-4*) U Press Fla.

Middle Education in the Middle Kingdom: The Chinese Junior High School in Modern Taiwan. Douglas C. Smith. LC 96-24463. 176p. 1997. 55.00 (*0-275-95641-5*, Praeger Pubs) Greenwood.

Middle Egyptian: An Introduction. Gertie Englund. 146p. (Orig.). 1988. pap. 79.50 (*91-506-0660-3*) Coronet Bks.

***Middle Egyptian: An Introduction to the Language & Culture of Hieroglyphs.** James P. Allen. (Illus.). 524p. (C). 1999. 74.95 (*0-521-65312-6*); pap. 29.95 (*0-521-77483-7*) Cambridge U Pr.

Middle English Anthology. Ed. by Ann S. Haskell. LC 89-5595. 548p. (C). 1985. reprint ed. pap. 21.95 (*0-8143-1798-7*) Wayne St U Pr.

Middle English Breton Lays. Ed. by Anne Laskaya & Eve Salisbury. (Middle English Texts Ser.). 1995. pap. 16.00 (*1-879288-62-1*) Medieval Inst.

Middle English Debate Poetry. Ed. by John Conlee. 329p. 1991. 42.00 (*0-937191-18-3*) Mich St U Pr.

Middle English Debate Poetry. Ed. by John Conlee. 376p. 1997. pap. text 15.95 (*0-937191-23-X*) Mich St U Pr.

Middle English Debate Poetry & the Aesthetics of Irresolution. Thomas L. Reed, Jr. 480p. 1990. text 43.00 (*0-8262-0733-2*) U of Mo Pr.

Middle English Dialectology: Essays on Some Principles & Problems. Margaret Laing. 272p. 1989. text 50.00 (*0-08-036404-7*, Pub. by Aberdeen U Pr) Macmillan.

Middle English Dictionary. Ed. by Gertrude P. Kurath. (Illus.). (C). 1956. pap. text 25.00 (*0-472-01011-5*, 01011) U of Mich Pr.

Middle English Dictionary. Ed. by Robert E. Lewis. (Illus.). (C). 1952. pap. text 25.00 (*0-472-01051-4*, 01051) U of Mich Pr.

Middle English Dictionary. Ed. by Robert E. Lewis. (Illus.). (C). 1953. pap. text 25.00 (*0-472-01052-2*, 01052) U of Mich Pr.

Middle English Dictionary. Ed. by Robert E. Lewis. (Illus.). (C). 1953. pap. text 25.00 (*0-472-01053-0*, 01053) U of Mich Pr.

Middle English Dictionary. Ed. by Robert E. Lewis. (Illus.). (C). 1953. pap. text 25.00 (*0-472-01061-1*, 01061) U of Mich Pr.

Middle English Dictionary. Ed. by Robert E. Lewis. (Illus.). (C). 1954. pap. text 25.00 (*0-472-01062-X*, 01062) U of Mich Pr.

Middle English Dictionary. Ed. by Robert E. Lewis. (Illus.). (C). 1954. pap. text 25.00 (*0-472-01063-8*, 01063) U of Mich Pr.

Middle English Dictionary. Ed. by Robert E. Lewis. (Illus.). (C). 1954. pap. text 25.00 (*0-472-01064-6*, 01064) U of Mich Pr.

Middle English Dictionary. Ed. by Robert E. Lewis. (Illus.). (C). 1956. pap. text 25.00 (*0-472-01013-1*, 01013); pap. text 25.00 (*0-472-01012-3*, 01012) U of Mich Pr.

Middle English Dictionary. Ed. by Robert E. Lewis. (Illus.). (C). 1957. pap. text 25.00 (*0-472-01022-0*, 01022); pap. text 25.00 (*0-472-01014-X*, 01014); pap. text 25.00 (*0-472-01023-9*, 01023) U of Mich Pr.

Middle English Dictionary. Ed. by Robert E. Lewis. (Illus.). (C). 1958. pap. text 25.00 (*0-472-01025-5*, 01025); pap. text 25.00 (*0-472-01024-7*, 01024) U of Mich Pr.

Middle English Dictionary. Ed. by Robert E. Lewis. (Illus.). (C). 1959. pap. text 25.00 (*0-472-01033-6*, 01033); pap. text 25.00 (*0-472-01032-8*, 01032); pap. text 25.00 (*0-472-01031-X*, 01031) U of Mich Pr.

Middle English Dictionary. Ed. by Robert E. Lewis. (Illus.). (C). 1960. pap. text 25.00 (*0-472-01034-4*, 01034) U of Mich Pr.

Middle English Dictionary. Ed. by Robert E. Lewis. (Illus.). (C). 1960. pap. text 25.00 (*0-472-01035-2*, 01035); pap. text 25.00 (*0-472-01036-0*, 01036) U of Mich Pr.

Middle English Dictionary. Ed. by Robert E. Lewis. (Illus.). (C). 1961. pap. text 25.00 (*0-472-01041-7*, 01041); pap. text 25.00 (*0-472-01042-5*, 01042) U of Mich Pr.

Middle English Dictionary. Ed. by Robert E. Lewis. (Illus.). (C). 1961. pap. text 25.00 (*0-472-01043-3*, 01043) U of Mich Pr.

Middle English Dictionary. Ed. by Robert E. Lewis. (Illus.). (C). 1962. pap. text 25.00 (*0-472-01044-1*, 01044) U of Mich Pr.

Middle English Dictionary. Ed. by Robert E. Lewis. (Illus.). (C). 1962. pap. text 25.00 (*0-472-01045-X*, 01045) U of Mich Pr.

Middle English Dictionary. Ed. by Robert E. Lewis. (Illus.). (C). 1963. pap. text 25.00 (*0-472-01071-9*, 01071) U of Mich Pr.

Middle English Dictionary. Ed. by Robert E. Lewis. (Illus.). (C). 1963. pap. text 25.00 (*0-472-01072-7*, 01072) U of Mich Pr.

Middle English Dictionary. Ed. by Robert E. Lewis. (Illus.). (C). 1964. pap. text 25.00 (*0-472-01073-5*, 01073) U of Mich Pr.

Middle English Dictionary. Ed. by Robert E. Lewis. (Illus.). (C). 1966. pap. text 25.00 (*0-472-01081-6*, 01081) U of Mich Pr.

Middle English Dictionary. Ed. by Robert E. Lewis. (Illus.). (C). 1966. pap. text 25.00 (*0-472-01082-4*, 01082) U of Mich Pr.

Middle English Dictionary. Ed. by Robert E. Lewis. (Illus.). (C). 1966. pap. text 25.00 (*0-472-01083-2*, 01083) U of Mich Pr.

Middle English Dictionary. Ed. by Robert E. Lewis. (Illus.). (C). 1966. pap. text 25.00 (*0-472-01084-0*, 01084) U of Mich Pr.

Middle English Dictionary. Ed. by Robert E. Lewis. (Illus.). (C). 1967. pap. text 25.00 (*0-472-01085-9*, 01085) U of Mich Pr.

Middle English Dictionary. Ed. by Robert E. Lewis. (Illus.). (C). 1968. pap. text 25.00 (*0-472-01091-3*, 01091) U of Mich Pr.

Middle English Dictionary. Ed. by Robert E. Lewis. (Illus.). (C). 1968. pap. text 25.00 (*0-472-01092-1*, 01092) U of Mich Pr.

Middle English Dictionary. Ed. by Robert E. Lewis. (Illus.). (C). 1969. pap. text 25.00 (*0-472-01101-4*, 01101) U of Mich Pr.

Middle English Dictionary. Ed. by Robert E. Lewis. (Illus.). (C). 1969. pap. text 25.00 (*0-472-01111-1*, 01111) U of Mich Pr.

Middle English Dictionary. Ed. by Robert E. Lewis. (Illus.). (C). 1970. pap. text 25.00 (*0-472-01121-9*, 01121) U of Mich Pr.

Middle English Dictionary. Ed. by Robert E. Lewis. (Illus.). (C). 1970. pap. text 25.00 (*0-472-01122-7*, 01122) U of Mich Pr.

Middle English Dictionary. Ed. by Robert E. Lewis. (Illus.). (C). 1971. pap. text 25.00 (*0-472-01123-5*, 01123) U of Mich Pr.

Middle English Dictionary. Ed. by Robert E. Lewis. (Illus.). (C). 1972. pap. text 25.00 (*0-472-01124-3*, 01124) U of Mich Pr.

Middle English Dictionary. Ed. by Robert E. Lewis. (Illus.). (C). 1973. pap. text 25.00 (*0-472-01125-1*, 01125) U of Mich Pr.

Middle English Dictionary. Ed. by Robert E. Lewis. (Illus.). (C). 1973. pap. text 25.00 (*0-472-01126-X*, 01126) U of Mich Pr.

Middle English Dictionary. Ed. by Robert E. Lewis. (Illus.). (C). 1975. pap. text 25.00 (*0-472-01131-6*, 01131) U of Mich Pr.

Middle English Dictionary. Ed. by Robert E. Lewis. (Illus.). (C). 1975. pap. text 25.00 (*0-472-01132-4*, 01132) U of Mich Pr.

Middle English Dictionary. Ed. by Robert E. Lewis. (Illus.). (C). 1975. pap. text 25.00 (*0-472-01133-2*, 01133) U of Mich Pr.

Middle English Dictionary. Ed. by Robert E. Lewis. (Illus.). (C). 1977. pap. text 25.00 (*0-472-01134-0*, 01134) U of Mich Pr.

Middle English Dictionary. Ed. by Robert E. Lewis. (Illus.). (C). 1977. pap. text 25.00 (*0-472-01135-9*, 01135) U of Mich Pr.

Middle English Dictionary. Ed. by Robert E. Lewis. (Illus.). (C). 1978. pap. text 25.00 (*0-472-01136-7*, 01136) U of Mich Pr.

Middle English Dictionary. Ed. by Robert E. Lewis. (Illus.). (C). 1978. pap. text 25.00 (*0-472-01141-3*, 01141) U of Mich Pr.

Middle English Dictionary. Ed. by Robert E. Lewis. (Illus.). (C). 1979. pap. text 25.00 (*0-472-01142-1*, 01142) U of Mich Pr.

Middle English Dictionary. Ed. by Robert E. Lewis. (Illus.). (C). 1979. pap. text 25.00 (*0-472-01143-X*, 01143) U of Mich Pr.

Middle English Dictionary. Ed. by Robert E. Lewis. (Illus.). (C). 1980. pap. text 25.00 (*0-472-01151-0*, 01151) U of Mich Pr.

Middle English Dictionary. Ed. by Robert E. Lewis. (Illus.). (C). 1980. pap. text 25.00 (*0-472-01152-9*, 01152) U of Mich Pr.

Middle English Dictionary. Ed. by Robert E. Lewis. (Illus.). (C). 1981. pap. text 25.00 (*0-472-01153-7*, 01153) U of Mich Pr.

Middle English Dictionary. Ed. by Robert E. Lewis. (Illus.). (C). 1981. pap. text 25.00 (*0-472-01154-5*, 01154) U of Mich Pr.

Middle English Dictionary. Ed. by Robert E. Lewis. (Illus.). (C). 1982. pap. text 25.00 (*0-472-01161-8*, 01161) U of Mich Pr.

Middle English Dictionary. Ed. by Robert E. Lewis. (Illus.). (C). 1982. pap. text 25.00 (*0-472-01162-6*, 01162) U of Mich Pr.

Middle English Dictionary. Ed. by Robert E. Lewis. (Illus.). (C). 1982. pap. text 25.00 (*0-472-01163-4*, 01163) U of Mich Pr.

Middle English Dictionary. Ed. by Robert E. Lewis. (Illus.). (C). 1983. pap. text 25.00 (*0-472-01164-2*, 01164) U of Mich Pr.

Middle English Dictionary. Ed. by Robert E. Lewis. (Illus.). (C). 1983. pap. text 25.00 (*0-472-01165-0*, 01165) U of Mich Pr.

Middle English Dictionary. Ed. by Robert E. Lewis. (Illus.). (C). 1983. pap. text 25.00 (*0-472-01166-9*, 01166) U of Mich Pr.

Middle English Dictionary. Ed. by Robert E. Lewis. (Illus.). (C). 1983. pap. text 25.00 (*0-472-01167-7*, 01167) U of Mich Pr.

Middle English Dictionary. Ed. by Robert E. Lewis. (Illus.). (C). 1984. pap. text 25.00 (*0-472-01168-5*, 01168) U of Mich Pr.

Middle English Dictionary. Ed. by Robert E. Lewis. (Illus.). (C). 1985. pap. text 25.00 (*0-472-01171-5*, 01171); pap. text 25.00 (*0-472-01181-2*, 01181) U of Mich Pr.

Middle English Dictionary. Ed. by Robert E. Lewis. (Illus.). (C). 1985. pap. text 25.00 (*0-472-01182-0*, 01182) U of Mich Pr.

Middle English Dictionary. Ed. by Robert E. Lewis. (Illus.). (C). 1985. pap. text 25.00 (*0-472-01183-9*, 01183) U of Mich Pr.

Middle English Dictionary. Ed. by Robert E. Lewis. (Illus.). (C). 1985. pap. text 25.00 (*0-472-01184-7*, 01184) U of Mich Pr.

Middle English Dictionary. Ed. by Robert E. Lewis. (Illus.). (C). 1986. pap. text 25.00 (*0-472-01185-5*, 01185) U of Mich Pr.

Middle English Dictionary. Ed. by Robert E. Lewis. (Illus.). (C). 1986. pap. text 25.00 (*0-472-01186-3*, 01186) U of Mich Pr.

Middle English Dictionary. Ed. by Robert E. Lewis. (Illus.). (C). 1986. pap. text 25.00 (*0-472-01191-X*, 01191) U of Mich Pr.

Middle English Dictionary. Ed. by Robert E. Lewis. (Illus.). (C). 1986. pap. text 25.00 (*0-472-01192-8*, 01192) U of Mich Pr.

Middle English Dictionary. Ed. by Robert E. Lewis. (Illus.). (C). 1987. pap. text 25.00 (*0-472-01193-6*, 01193) U of Mich Pr.

Middle English Dictionary. Ed. by Robert E. Lewis. (Illus.). (C). 1987. pap. text 25.00 (*0-472-01194-4*, 01194) U of Mich Pr.

Middle English Dictionary. Ed. by Robert E. Lewis. (Illus.). (C). 1987. pap. text 25.00 (*0-472-01195-2*, 01195) U of Mich Pr.

Middle English Dictionary. Ed. by Robert E. Lewis. (Illus.). (C). 1988. pap. text 25.00 (*0-472-01196-0*, 01196); pap. text 25.00 (*0-472-01197-9*, 01197) U of Mich Pr.

An Asterisk (*) at the beginning of an entry indicates that the title is appearing for the first time.

Middle English Dictionary. Ed. by Robert E. Lewis. (Illus.). (C). 1988. pap. text 25.00 (*0-472-01198-7*, 01198) U of Mich Pr.

Middle English Dictionary. Ed. by Robert E. Lewis. (Illus.). (C). 1988. pap. text 25.00 (*0-472-01199-5*, 01199) U of Mich Pr.

Middle English Dictionary. Ed. by Robert E. Lewis. (Illus.). (C). 1989. pap. text 25.00 (*0-472-01200-2*, 01200) U of Mich Pr.

Middle English Dictionary. Ed. by Robert E. Lewis. (Illus.). (C). 1989. pap. text 25.00 (*0-472-01201-0*, 01201) U of Mich Pr.

Middle English Dictionary. Ed. by Robert E. Lewis. (Illus.). (C). 1990. pap. text 25.00 (*0-472-01202-9*, 01202) U of Mich Pr.

Middle English Dictionary, Bk. 1. Ed. by Robert E. Lewis. (Illus.). (C). 1957. pap. text 25.00 (*0-472-01021-2*, 01021) U of Mich Pr.

***Middle English Dictionary, W.3.** Ed. by Robert E. Lewis. (Illus.). 128p. (C). 2000. pap. text 17.50 (*0-472-01229-0*, 01229) U of Mich Pr.

***Middle English Dictionary, W.4.** Ed. by Robert E. Lewis. (Illus.). 128p. (C). 2000. pap. text 17.50 (*0-472-01230-4*, 01230) U of Mich Pr.

Middle English Dictionary, W.5. (Illus.). 128p. (C). pap. text 17.50 (*0-472-01231-2*, 01231) U of Mich Pr.

Middle-English Dictionary: Containing Words Used by English Writers from the Twelfth to the Fifteenth Century. Francis H. Stratmann. Ed. by Henry Bradley. (ENM.). 732p. 1920. text 115.00 (*0-19-863106-5*) OUP.

Middle English Dictionary: Fascicle T.1. Ed. by Robert E. Lewis & Mary J. Williams. (C). 1993. pap. text 25.00 (*0-472-01211-8*, 01211) U of Mich Pr.

Middle English Dictionary: Fascicle T.10. Ed. by Robert E. Lewis & Mary J. Williams. 88p. (Orig.). 1997. pap. text 25.00 (*0-472-01220-7*, 01220) U of Mich Pr.

Middle English Dictionary: Fascicle T.2. Ed. by Robert E. Lewis & Mary J. Williams. (C). 1993. pap. text 25.00 (*0-472-01212-6*, 01212) U of Mich Pr.

Middle English Dictionary: Fascicle T.3. Ed. by Robert E. Lewis et al. 128p. 1994. pap. text 25.00 (*0-472-01213-4*, 01213) U of Mich Pr.

Middle English Dictionary: Fascicle T.4. Ed. by Robert E. Lewis et al. 128p. 1994. pap. text 25.00 (*0-472-01214-2*, 01214) U of Mich Pr.

Middle English Dictionary: Fascicle T.5. Ed. by Robert E. Lewis et al. 128p. 1995. pap. text 25.00 (*0-472-01215-0*, 01215) U of Mich Pr.

Middle English Dictionary: Fascicle T.7. Ed. by Robert E. Lewis & Mary J. Williams. 128p. (Orig.). 1996. pap. text 25.00 (*0-472-01217-7*, 01217) U of Mich Pr.

Middle English Dictionary: Fascicle T.8. Ed. by Robert E. Lewis & Mary J. Williams. 128p. (Orig.). 1996. pap. text 25.00 (*0-472-01218-5*, 01218) U of Mich Pr.

Middle English Dictionary: Fascicle T.9. Ed. by Robert E. Lewis & Mary J. Williams. 112p. (Orig.). 1997. pap. text 25.00 (*0-472-01219-3*, 01219) U of Mich Pr.

Middle English Dictionary: Fascicle U.1, Vol. U.1. Ed. by Robert E. Lewis & Mary J. Williams. 128p. (Orig.). 1997. pap. text 25.00 (*0-472-01221-5*, 01221) U of Mich Pr.

Middle English Dictionary: Fascicle U.2, Vol. U.2. Ed. by Robert E. Lewis & Mary J. Williams. 128p. (Orig.). 1998. pap. text 25.00 (*0-472-01222-3*, 01222) U of Mich Pr.

Middle English Dictionary: Plan & Bibliography. Ed. by Hans Kurath. (Illus.). (C). 1984. pap. text 25.00 (*0-472-01001-8*, 01001) U of Mich Pr.

Middle English Dictionary: Plan & Bibliography. Ed. by Robert E. Lewis. (Illus.). (C). 1985. pap. text 25.00 (*0-472-01002-6*, 01002) U of Mich Pr.

Middle English Dictionary: S.13. Ed. by Robert E. Lewis. (Illus.). (C). 1990. pap. text 25.00 (*0-472-01203-7*, 01203) U of Mich Pr.

Middle English Dictionary: S.14. Ed. by Robert E. Lewis. (Illus.). (C). 1990. pap. text 25.00 (*0-472-01204-5*, 01204) U of Mich Pr.

Middle English Dictionary: S.15. Ed. by Robert E. Lewis. (Illus.). (C). 1991. pap. text 25.00 (*0-472-01205-3*, 01205) U of Mich Pr.

Middle English Dictionary: S.16. Ed. by Robert E. Lewis. (Illus.). (C). 1991. pap. text 25.00 (*0-472-01206-1*, 01206) U of Mich Pr.

Middle English Dictionary: S.17. Ed. by Robert E. Lewis. (Illus.). (C). 1992. pap. text 25.00 (*0-472-01207-X*, 01207) U of Mich Pr.

Middle English Dictionary: S.18. Ed. by Robert E. Lewis. (Illus.). (C). 1992. pap. text 25.00 (*0-472-01208-8*, 01208) U of Mich Pr.

Middle English Dictionary: T.6. Ed. by Robert E. Lewis. LC 53-62158. (Illus.). 128p. (C). 1995. pap. text 25.00 (*0-472-01216-9*, 01216) U of Mich Pr.

Middle English Dictionary: U.1. Ed. by Robert E Lewis & Mary J. Williams. 128p. 1998. pap. text 25.00 (*0-472-01223-1*, 01223) U of Mich Pr.

***Middle English Dictionary: U.4.** Ed. by Robert E. Lewis. (Illus.). 128p. (C). 1998. pap. text 17.50 (*0-472-01224-X*, 01224) U of Mich Pr.

***Middle English Dictionary: V.1.** Ed. by Robert E. Lewis. 184p. 1999. pap. text 17.50 (*0-472-01225-8*, 01225) U of Mich Pr.

***Middle English Dictionary: W.1.** Ed. by Robert E. Lewis. 128p. 1999. pap. text 17.50 (*0-472-01227-4*, 01227) U of Mich Pr.

Middle English Dictionary: W.2. Ed. by Robert E. Lewis. 128p. 1999. pap. text 17.50 (*0-472-01228-2*, 01228) U of Mich Pr.

Middle English Genesis & Exodus: A Running Commentary on the Text of the Poem. Philip G. Buehler. LC 73-79277. (De Proprietatibus Litterarum, Ser. Practica: No. 74). 85p. 1974. pap. text 33.10 (*90-279-3082-1*) Mouton.

Middle English Historiography. Robert A. Albano. LC 92-38882. (American University Studies: English Language & Literature: Ser. IV, Vol. 168). 254p. (C). 1993. text 51.95 (*0-8204-2136-7*) P Lang Pubng.

Middle English Humorous Tales in Verse. Ed. by George H. McKnight. LC 77-144435. (Belles Lettres Ser. Section II: No. 1). reprint ed. 31.50 (*0-404-53611-5*) AMS Pr.

Middle English Humorous Tales in Verse. George H. McKnight. LC 78-128190. 211p. (C). 1971. reprint ed. 50.00 (*0-87752-131-X*) Gordian.

Middle English Ideal of Personal Beauty. Walter C. Curry. LC 70-180443. reprint ed. 32.50 (*0-404-01886-6*) AMS Pr.

Middle English Literature. Ed. by Charles W. Dunn & Edward T. Byrnes. LC 89-78116. 564p. 1990. text 30.00 (*0-8240-5298-6*, 1330); pap. text 20.95 (*0-8240-5297-8*, 1330) Garland.

Middle English Literature. Jack A. Bennett. Ed. by Douglas Gray. (Oxford History of English Literature Ser.: No. 1). 510p. 1990. reprint ed. pap. text 29.95 (*0-19-811970-4*) OUP.

Middle English Literature. 2nd ed. Alois Brandl & O. Zippel. LC 48-3315. 1980. 14.95 (*0-685-01051-1*) Chelsea Pub.

Middle English Literature: A Critical Study of the Romances, the Religious Lyrics, "Piers Plowman" George Kane. LC 79-14146. 252p. 1980. reprint ed. lib. bdg. 35.00 (*0-313-21992-3*, KAMI, Greenwood Pr) Greenwood.

Middle English Literature: British Academy Gollancz Lectures. Intro. by J. A. Burrow. 262p. 1990. pap. text 29.95 (*0-19-726085-3*) OUP.

Middle English Literature, 1100-1400. Jack A. Bennett. Ed. by Douglas Gray. (Oxford History of English Literature Ser.: Vol. I). 508p. 1990. text 59.00 (*0-19-812228-4*) OUP.

Middle English Lyrics. Ed. by Maxwell S. Luria & Richard L. Hoffman. (Critical Editions Ser.). (Illus.). 360p. (C). 1974. pap. text 12.50 (*0-393-09338-7*) Norton.

Middle English Lyrics. 2nd ed. Maxwell S. Luria. (Critical Editions Ser.). (C). Date not set. pap. write for info. (*0-393-96649-6*, Norton Paperbks) Norton.

Middle English 'Mirror' An Edition Based on Bodleian Library, MS Holkam Misc. 40. Kathleen M. Blumreich. (Medieval & Renaissance Texts & Studies: Vol. 182). 2000. write for info. (*0-86698-224-8*, MR182) MRTS.

Middle English Occupational Terms. B. Thuresson. (Lund Studies in English: Vol. 19). 1974. reprint ed. pap. 45.00 (*0-8115-0562-6*) Periodicals Srv.

Middle English Penitential Lyric. Frank A. Patterson. LC 11-26002. reprint ed. 31.50 (*0-404-04908-7*) AMS Pr.

Middle English Physiologus. Ed. by Hanneke Wirtjes. (Early English Text Society Ser.: No. 299). 160p. 1991. text 35.00 (*0-19-722301-X*, 60) OUP.

Middle English Poem Erthe upon Erthe. Ed. by H. M. Murray. (EETS Original Ser.: No. 141). 102p. 1964. reprint ed. 20.00 (*0-19-722141-6*, Pub. by EETS) Boydell & Brewer.

Middle English Poems. Tr. by Richard O'Connell. 1976. pap. 10.00 (*0-685-62624-5*) Atlantis Edns.

Middle English Poetry: An Anthology. Ed. by Lewis J. Owen & Nancy H. Owen. LC 76-138662. (Library of Literature). 1971. pap. 7.50 (*0-672-60984-3*, LL-12, Bobbs) Macmillan.

Middle English Prose: A Critical Guide to Major Authors & Genres. Ed. by A. S. Edwards. 440p. (C). 1984. text 60.00 (*0-8135-1001-5*) Rutgers U Pr.

Middle English Reader. Oliver F. Emerson. LC 75-41087. reprint ed. 47.50 (*0-404-14784-4*) AMS Pr.

Middle English Romances. Ed. by A. C. Gibbs. (York Medieval Texts Ser.). 180p. 1988. pap. 14.95 (*0-8101-0100-9*) Northwestern U Pr.

Middle English Romances. Stephen Sheperd. LC 94-36710. 514p. (C). 1994. pap. text 13.25 (*0-393-96607-0*) Norton.

Middle English Sea Terms, Pt. I. Bertil Sandahl. (Essays & Studies on English Language & Literature: Vol. 8). 1974. reprint ed. pap. 25.00 (*0-8115-0206-6*) Periodicals Srv.

Middle English Sea Terms Pt. II: Masts, Spars & Sails. Bertil Sandahl. (Essays & Studies on English Language & Literature: Vol. 20). 1958. pap. 25.00 (*0-8115-0218-X*) Periodicals Srv.

Middle English Sermons from Manuscript Roy, No. 18 B. Ed. by W. O. Ross. (EETS, OS Ser.: Vol. 209). 1974. reprint ed. 70.00 (*0-8115-3385-9*) Periodicals Srv.

Middle English Stanzaic Versions of the Life of Saint Anne. Ed. by R. E. Parker. (EETS, OS Ser.: No. 174). 1974. reprint ed. 40.00 (*0-527-00171-6*) Periodicals Srv.

Middle English Studies: Presented to Norman Davis in Honour of His Seventieth Birthday. Ed. by Douglas Gray & E. G. Stanley. (Illus.). 296p. (C). 1983. text 110.00 (*0-19-811183-5*) OUP.

Middle English Subject-Verb Cluster: A Quantitative Sunchronic Description. Andrew MacLeish. LC 68-23809. (Janua Linguarum, Ser. Practica: No. 26). (Orig.). (C). 1969. pap. text 73.10 (*90-279-0689-0*) Mouton.

Middle English Surnames of Occupation, 1100-1350. G. Fransson. (Lund Studies in English: Vol. 3). 1974. reprint ed. pap. 30.00 (*0-8115-0546-4*) Periodicals Srv.

Middle English Survey: Critical Essays. Ed. by Edward Vasta. LC 65-23514. 1965. 19.95 (*0-8290-1653-8*) Irvington.

Middle English Survey: Critical Essays. Ed. by Edward Vasta. LC 65-23514. (C). reprint ed. pap. text 7.95 (*0-8290-2379-8*) Irvington.

Middle English Translation de Macer Floridus de Viribus Herbarum. G. Frisk. (Essays & Studies on English Language & Literature: Vol. 3). 1974. reprint ed. pap. 35.00 (*0-8115-0201-5*) Periodicals Srv.

Middle English Translation of Trevet's Les Cronicles. Christine M. Rose. Ed. by Anthony Edwards. (Garland Medieval Texts Ser.). 500p. Date not set. text 75.00 (*0-8153-1424-8*) Garland.

Middle-English U & Related Sounds: Their Development in Early American English. Harold Whitehall. (LM Ser.: No. 19). 1939. pap. 25.00 (*0-527-00823-0*) Periodicals Srv.

Middle English Verse Romances. Ed. by Donald B. Sands. 408p. 1986. pap. text 19.95 (*0-85989-228-X*, Pub. by Univ Exeter Pr) Northwestern U Pr.

Middle English Weye of Paradys & the Middle French Voie de Paradis: A Parallel-Text Edition. F. N. Diekstra. LC 90-19288. (Medieval & Renaissance Authors Ser.: No. 1). (ENM & FEM., Illus.). xvi, 544p. 1991. 149.00 (*90-04-09118-1*) Brill Academic Pubs.

***Middle English Word Studies: A Word & Author Index.** Ed. by Jane Roberts & Louise Sylvester. 240p. 2000. 60.00 (*0-85991-606-5*) Boydell & Brewer.

Middle English Words for "Town" A Study of Changes in a Semantic Field. Ann-Marie Svensson. (Gothburg Studies in English: No. 70). (Illus.). 220p. 1997. pap. 52.50 (*91-7346-314-0*, Pub. by Almqvist Wiksell) Coronet Bks.

Middle Euphrates: A Topographical Itinerary. Alois Musil. LC 77-87086. (American Geographical Society Oriental Explorations & Studies: No. 3). reprint ed. 74.50 (*0-404-60233-9*) AMS Pr.

Middle Five: Indian Schoolboys of the Omaha Tribe. Francis La Flesche. LC 78-17409. (Illus.). xxiv, 156p. 1978. reprint ed. text 25.00 (*0-8032-2852-X*) U of Nebr Pr.

Middle Five: Indian Schoolboys of the Omaha Tribe. Francis La Flesche. LC 78-17409. (Illus.). xxiv, 156p. 1978. reprint ed. pap. text 12.00 (*0-8032-7901-9*, Bison Books) U of Nebr Pr.

Middle Fork: A Guide. Cort Conley & John Carrey. LC 80-17367. 1966. pap. 19.95 (*0-9603566-1-4*) Backeddy Bks.

Middle Fork Guide: Seattle Local Mountain Day Trips. Carl Dreisbach. LC 96-95107. (Illus.). 124p. 1998. pap. 11.95 (*0-942153-01-4*) Entropy Conserv.

Middle French Proverbs, Sentences, & Proverbial Phrases. James W. Hassell. x, 275p. pap. text 25.71 (*0-88844-361-7*) Brill Academic Pubs.

Middle French Translation of Bernard Gui's Shorter Historical Works by Jean Golein. Ed. by Thomas F. Coffey & Terrence J. McGovern. LC 93-15104. 660p. 1993. text 129.95 (*0-7734-9263-1*) E Mellen.

Middle Game in Chess. Eugene Znosko-Borovsky. (Illus.). 224p. 1980. reprint ed. pap. 6.95 (*0-486-23931-4*) Dover.

Middle Georgia on My Mind. Middle Georgia Girl Scout Council Staff. (Illus.). 1990. 10.00 (*0-87197-282-4*) Favorite Recipes.

Middle Grade Fantasy Novel, 2. Jane Yolen. 192p. (J). (gr. 3-7). 15.95 (*0-06-028736-5*) HarpC.

Middle Grade Fantasy Novel, Vol. 2. Jane Yolen. 192p. (J). (gr. 3-7). 4.95 (*0-06-440848-5*) HarpC Child Bks.

Middle Grade Novel. Corinne Demas. 196p. (gr. 3-7). 15.95 (*0-06-028725-X*) HarpC.

Middle Grade Novel. Corinne Demas. 196p. (J). (gr. 3-7). 4.95 (*0-06-440845-0*) HarpC Child Bks.

Middle Grade Teachers' Mathematical Knowledge & Its Relationship to Instruction: A Research Monograph. Judith T. Sowder et al. LC 97-34910. (SUNY Series, Reform in Mathematical Education). 224p. (C). 1998. text 65.50 (*0-7914-3841-4*); pap. text 21.95 (*0-7914-3842-2*) State U NY Pr.

Middle Grades Assessment Program: Leader's Manual. rev. ed. Gayle Dorman. Ed. by Robin Pulver. 136p. 1995. pap., teacher ed. 17.50 (*1-57482-717-0*) Search Inst.

Middle Grades Assessment Program: User's Manual. rev. ed. Gayle Dorman. 175p. 1995. pap. 9.00 (*1-57482-718-9*) Search Inst.

Middle Grades Mathematics Project. G. Lappan. 1986. text 82.50 (*0-201-21473-3*) Addison-Wesley.

***Middle Grades Mathematics Textbooks: A Benchmarks Based Evaluation.** American Association for the Advancement of Science Staff. LC 99-54400. 1999. write for info. (*0-87168-635-X*) AAAS.

Middle Grades Social Studies: Teaching & Learning for Active & Responsible Citizenship. 2nd ed. Michael G. Allen & Robert L. Stevens. LC 97-15612. 180p. (C). 1997. pap. text 30.00 (*0-205-27118-9*) Allyn.

Middle Grades Teacher's Handbook for Cooperative Learning. Terri Breeden & Janice Mosley. 160p. (Orig.). (J). (gr. 5-8). 1991. pap. text 14.95 (*0-86530-224-3*, IP 193-8) Incentive Pubns.

Middle Grenadines-Canouan to Carriacou. Wilson Ltd. Staff & Imray L. Norie. (C). 1987. 53.00 (*0-7855-5919-1*, Pub. by Laurie Norie & Wilson Ltd) St Mut.

Middle Ground: Coping with Physical & Emotional Pain. unabridged ed. John Guzman & Jean Dixen. (Illus.). 84p. (Orig.). 1996. pap. 14.95 (*0-9655573-0-8*) Ivory Tower CA.

Middle Ground: Indians, Empires & Republics in the Great Lakes Region, 1650-1815. Richard White. LC 92-5045. (Studies in North American Indian History). (Illus.). 560p. (C). 1991. text 85.00 (*0-521-37104-X*); pap. text 19.95 (*0-521-42460-7*) Cambridge U Pr.

Middle Grounds: Studies in Contemporary American Fiction. Alan Wilde. (Pennsylvania Studies in Contemporary American Fiction). 198p. 1987. text 35.95 (*0-8122-8069-5*) U of Pa Pr.

Middle Group of American Historians. John S. Bassett. LC 67-22070. (Essay Index Reprint Ser.). 1977. 23.95 (*0-8369-0175-4*) Ayer.

Middle Heart. Bette Bao Lord. 1997. mass mkt. 6.99 (*0-449-28808-0*); mass mkt. 6.99 (*0-449-22564-X*, Crest) Fawcett.

Middle Heart. Bette Bao Lord. 1997. pap. 12.00 (*0-449-91232-9*, Columbine) Fawcett.

Middle Heart. Bette Bao Lord. LC 95-36165. 352p. 1996. 25.00 (*0-394-53432-8*) Knopf.

Middle Helladic Village: Asine in the Argolid. Gullog C. Nordquist. (Uppsala Studies in Ancient Mediterranean & Near Eastern Civilizations: No. 16). (Illus.). 195p. (Orig.). 1987. pap. text 45.00 (*91-554-1971-2*, Pub. by Uppsala Univ Acta Univ Upsaliensis) Coronet Bks.

Middle High German Courtly Reader. 2nd ed. Ed. by Martin Joos & Frederick R. Whitesell. LC 73-16404. 367p. reprint ed. pap. 113.80 (*0-608-30833-1*, 200291200015) Bks Demand.

Middle High German Reader: With Grammar, Notes & Glossary. M. O. Walshe. 232p. (C). 1974. pap. text 26.00 (*0-19-872082-3*) OUP.

Middle High German Translations of the Regula Sancti Benedicti. Benedictus. Ed. & Intro. by Carl Selmer. (Mediaeval Academy of America Publications: Vol. 17). 1933. 40.00 (*0-527-01689-6*) Periodicals Srv.

Middle Innings: A Documentary History of Baseball, 1900-1948. Dean A. Sullivan. LC 97-36995. (Illus.). 250p. 1998. text 50.00 (*0-8032-4258-1*) U of Nebr Pr.

***Middle Innings: A Documentary History of Baseball, 1900-1948.** Ed. by Dean A. Sullivan. LC 97-36995. (Illus.). 250p. 2001. pap. 16.95 (*0-8032-9283-X*, Bison Books) U of Nebr Pr.

Middle is the Best Part. Lynette M. Samuel. Ed. & Created by Patty Baker. LC 97-93533. (Illus.). 32p. (J). (gr. 2-5). 1997. per. 15.95 (*0-9651270-2-8*) Bright Lamb.

Middle Kingdom. Adrienne Su. LC 96-40204. 80p. (Orig.). 1997. pap. 9.95 (*1-882295-15-3*) Alice James Bks.

Middle Kingdom. Andrea Barrett. Ed. by Jane Rosenman. 288p. 1992. reprint ed. pap. 12.00 (*0-671-72961-6*, WSP) PB.

Middle Kingdom: The Faerie World of Ireland. Dermot MacManus. (Illus.). 191p. 1973. 6.95 (*0-317-65888-3*, Pub. by Smyth) Dufour.

Middle Kingdom: The Faerie World of Ireland. Dermot MacManus. (Illus.). 191p. 1979. pap. 12.95 (*0-900675-82-9*, Pub. by Smyth) Dufour.

***Middle Knowledge: Theory & Applications.** Ed. by William Hasker et al. (Contributions to Philosophical Theology Ser.: Vol. 4). vii, 309p. 2000. pap. text 47.95 (*0-8204-4753-6*) P Lang Pubng.

Middle Land, Middle Way: A Pilgrim's Guide to the Buddha's India. S. Dhammika. 208p. 1992. 12.00 (*955-24-0095-3*, Pub. by Buddhist Pub Soc) Vipassana Res Pubns.

Middle Latency Response. Krause. 1998. 27.00 (*1-56593-201-3*) Singular Publishing.

Middle Length Discourses of the Buddha: A New Translation of the Majjhima Nikaya. Tr. by Bhikkhu Nanamoli & Bhikkhu Bodhi from PLI. LC 37-636. (Teachings of the Buddha Ser.). 1424p. (C). 1995. 60.00 (*0-86171-072-X*) Wisdom MA.

Middle Length Sayings, 3 vols. Tr. by I. B. Horner from PLI. (C). 1959. 119.50 (*0-86013-262-5*, Pub. by Pali Text) Elsevier.

Middle Length Sayings, 3 vols., 1. Tr. by I. B. Horner from PLI. (C). 1959. 43.90 (*0-86013-020-7*, Pub. by Pali Text) Elsevier.

Middle Length Sayings, 3 vols., 2. Tr. by I. B. Horner from PLI. (C). 1959. 43.90 (*0-86013-021-5*, Pub. by Pali Text) Elsevier.

Middle Length Sayings, 3 vols., 3. Tr. by I. B. Horner from PLI. (C). 1959. 43.90 (*0-86013-022-3*, Pub. by Pali Text) Elsevier.

Middle Level Education: An Annotated Bibliography, 16. Samuel Totten & Toni Sills-Briegel. LC 96-6136. (Bibliographies & Indexes in Education Ser.). 456p. 1996. lib. bdg. 89.50 (*0-313-29002-4*, Greenwood Pr) Greenwood.

Middle Level Map. Wilson Ltd. Staff & Imray L. Norie. (C). 1989. 50.00 (*0-85288-118-5*, Pub. by Laurie Norie & Wilson Ltd) St Mut.

Middle Level Map (Fenland) Derek Bowskill. (Illus.). 1997. 125.00 (*0-85288-367-6*, Pub. by Laurie Norie & Wilson Ltd) St Mut.

Middle Level Positions. Jack Rudman. (Career Examination Ser.: C-511). 1994. pap. 27.95 (*0-8373-0511-X*) Nat Learn.

Middle Level Principalship, Vol. 1. Jerry Valentine et al. 168p. (Orig.). (C). 1982. pap. 11.00 (*0-88210-132-3*) Natl Assn Principals.

Middle-Level Principalship: The Effective Middle-Level Principal, Vol. 2. James W. Keefe et al. Ed. by Thomas F. Koerner. 104p. (Orig.). 1983. pap. 11.00 (*0-88210-154-4*) Natl Assn Principals.

Middle Level Schools for the New Century. (C). 1999. pap. text 50.67 (*0-205-28977-0*, Longwood Div) Allyn.

Middle Level Teachers' Handbook: Becoming a Reflective Practitioner. Gilbert H. Hunt et al. LC 97-37556. (Illus.). 248p. 1998. text 51.95 (*0-398-06831-3*); pap. text 38.95 (*0-398-06832-1*) C C Thomas.

Middle Man. Dorothy B. Davis & Sara E. Davis. (Illus.). 36p. (J). (ps-2). 1993. 11.95 (*0-87178-570-6*, 8706) Brethren.

***Middle Management in Action: Practical Approaches to School Improvement.** Eric Ruding. LC 00-28424. 2000. pap. write for info. (*0-415-23155-8*) Routledge.

***Middle Management in Schools: How to Harmonize Managing & Teaching for an Effective School.** Sonia Blandford. 208p. 1998. pap. 54.50 (*0-273-61608-0*, Pub. by F T P-H) Trans-Atl Phila.

M

An Asterisk (*) at the beginning of an entry indicates that the title is appearing for the first time.

Middle Management in the Primary School: A Development Guide of Curriculum Leaders. Subject Managers & Senior Staff. 132p. 1995. pap. text 26.95 (*1-85346-344-2*, Pub. by David Fulton) Taylor & Francis.

Middle Managers: How to Survive & Thrive. M. Thompson & K. Harrison. 1996. pap. 129.00 (*1-85953-046-X*, Pub. by Tech Comm) St Mut.

Middle-Market Leveraged Financing Directory & Source Book. A. David Silver. 528p. 1990. 68.00 (*0-88730-408-7*, HarpBusn) HarpInfo.

Middle Miocene Pyramid Flora of Western Nevada. Daniel I. Axelrod. (Publications in Geological Sciences: Vol. 137). (C). 1993. pap. 19.95 (*0-520-09776-9*, Pub. by U CA Pr) Cal Prin Full Svc.

Middle Mississippi Exploitation of Animal Populations. Bruce D. Smith. LC 75-622031. (University of Michigan, Museum of Anthropology, Anthropological Papers: No. 57). 245p. reprint ed. pap. 76.00 (*0-608-14112-7*, 202429900037) Bks Demand.

Middle Mississippians: Encounters with the Prehistoric Amerindians. Ted Hirschfield. (University of Central Florida Contemporary Poetry Ser.). (Illus.). 72p. 1996. 19.95 (*0-8130-1399-2*); pap. 10.95 (*0-8130-1430-1*) U Press Fla.

Middle Mist. Mary Renault. 23.95 (*0-89244-080-5*, Queens House) Amereon Ltd.

M

***Middle Moffat.** Eleanor Estes. LC 00-37030. (Illus.). (J). 2001. write for info. (*0-15-202529-4*) Harcourt.

Middle Minoan III: A Time of Transition. Gisela Walberg. (Studies in Mediterranean Archaeology: Vol. XCVII). (Illus.). 180p. (Orig.). 1992. pap. 77.50 (*91-7081-037-0*, Pub. by P Astroms) Coronet Bks.

***Middle Mosaic: A Celebration of Reading, Writing & Reflective Practice at the Middle Level.** Elizabeth Close & Katherine D. Ramsey. LC 00-42378. 2000. write for info. (*0-8141-0034-1*) NCTE.

Middle Murphy. Mark Costello. (Illinois Short Fiction Ser.). 152p. 1991. 10.95 (*0-252-06319-8*); text 16.95 (*0-252-01795-1*) U of Ill Pr.

Middle of History? Towards a Synthesis Between Marxism & Functionalism. Jan Sollenius. 167p. 1992. 65.00 (*91-22-01478-0*) Coronet Bks.

Middle of My Journey. John R. Boyd. 240p. (Orig.). 1990. pap. 14.95 (*0-85640-438-1*, Pub. by Blackstaff Pr) Dufour.

Middle of Nowhere. Janet Lorimer. LC 95-76742. (Ten-Minute Thrillers Ser.). 32p. (YA). (gr. 6-12). 1995. pap. 2.95 (*0-7854-1068-6*, 40814) Am Guidance.

***Middle of Nowhere.** Ridley Pearson. LC 99-51670. 416p. 2000. 23.95 (*0-7868-6563-6*, Pub. by Hyperion) Time Warner.

Middle of Nowhere: A One-Act Play. Raleigh Marcell, Jr. (Illus.). 28p. 1982. pap. 3.25 (*0-88680-130-3*) I E Clark.

Middle of Nowhere Readalong. Janet Lorimer. (Ten-Minute Thrillers Ser.). 32p. (YA). (gr. 6-12). 1995. pap. 12.95 incl. audio (*0-7854-1079-1*, 40816) Am Guidance.

Middle of the Journey. Vincent Campo et al. (Illus.). 156p. write for info. (*0-318-56311-8*) V Campo.

Middle of the Journey. Intro. by Lionel Trilling. LC 79-3369. 384p. 1980. 14.95 (*0-15-159547-X*) Harcourt.

Middle of the Night. Robert Cormier. (J). 1995. 19.95 (*0-385-44629-2*) BDD Bks Young Read.

Middle of the Night. Bob Hartman. (What Was It Like Ser.). (Illus.). 24p. (J). (ps-2). 1993. 8.99 (*1-56476-042-1*, 6-3042, Victor Bks) Chariot Victor.

Middle of the Night. Bob Hartman & Michael McGuire. (J). (ps-3). 1994. 11.99 incl. audio (*7-900882-47-2*, 3-1214, Chariot Bks) Chariot Victor.

Middle of the Night: Samuel. Bob Hartman. Date not set. 11.99 incl. audio Chariot Victor.

Middle-Ordovician Crinoids from Southwestern Virginia & Eastern Tennessee, No. 283 see Bulletins of American Paleontology: Vol. 66

***Middle Palaeolithic Occupation of Europe.** Ed. by Wil Roebroeks & Clive Gamble. (Illus.). 240p. 1999. 65.00 (*90-73368-12-X*, Pub. by Leiden Univ Pr) David Brown.

Middle Paleolithic: Adaptation, Behavior & Variability. Ed. by Harold L. Dibble & Paul Mellars. (University Museum Monographs: University Museum Symposium Ser.: Nos. 78 & IV). (Illus.). 217p. (C). 1992. text 50.00 (*0-924171-07-3*) U Museum Pubns.

Middle Paleolithic Assemblage & Settlement Variability in West-Central Jordan. James M. Potter. (Anthropological Research Papers: No. 45). (Illus.). v, 57p. 1993. pap. 10.00 (*0-936249-08-0*) AZ Univ ARP.

Middle Paleolithic Site of Combe-Capelle Bas (France) Ed. by Harold L. Dibble & Michel Lenoir. LC 95-35093. (Illus.). xxi, 365p. 1995. 40.00 (*0-924171-38-3*) U Museum Pubns.

Middle Passage: A Novel. Charles R. Johnson. 160p. 1990. 17.95 (*0-689-11968-2*) Atheneum Yung Read.

Middle Passage: A Novel. Charles R. Johnson. 224p. 1998. pap. 11.00 (*0-684-85588-7*, Scribner Pap Fic) S&S Trade Pap.

Middle Passage: From Misery to Meaning in Midlife. James Hollis. 128p. 1995. pap. 16.00 (*0-919123-60-0*, Pub. by Inner City Bks) BookWorld.

Middle Passage: White Ships/Black Cargo. Illus. by Tom Feelings. 80p. (YA). (gr. 7 up). 1995. 50.00 (*0-8037-1804-7*, Dial Yng Read) Peng Put Young Read.

Middle Passages. Kamau Brathwaite. 90p. (Orig.). 1993. pap. 15.95 (*1-85224-224-8*, Pub. by Bloodaxe Bks) Dufour.

Middle Path - The Safest: The Religion of "Head & Heart" S. R. Parchment. 119p. 1996. reprint ed. spiral bd. 11.00 (*0-7873-0655-X*) Hlth Research.

Middle Path - The Safest: The Religion of "Head & Heart" S. R. Parchment. 120p. 1996. reprint ed. pap. 9.95 (*1-56459-790-3*) Kessinger Pub.

Middle Path Cookbook. Jay Disney. LC 98-48796. (Illus.). 308p. 1999. text 26.95 (*0-87951-921-5*, Pub. by Overlook Pr) Penguin Putnam.

Middle Path of a Life: Talks on the Practice of Insight Meditation. Dhiravamsa. LC 88-38455. 96p. (Orig.). 1989. pap. 9.95 (*0-931892-22-8*) B Dolphin Pub.

Middle Period, 1817-1858. John W. Burgess. LC 79-37301. (Black Heritage Library Collection). 1977. reprint ed. 41.95 (*0-8369-8938-4*) Ayer.

Middle Period in Latin American History: Values & Attitudes in the 17th-19th Centuries. Ed. by Mark D. Szuchman. LC 89-31959. 193p. 1989. lib. bdg. 40.00 (*1-55587-138-0*) L Rienner.

Middle Pillar: The Balance Between Mind & Magic. 3rd ed. Israel Regardie. LC 97-51493. (Illus.). 312p. 1998. pap. text 12.95 (*1-56718-140-6*) Llewellyn Pubns.

Middle Platonists: 80 B. C. to A. D. 220. rev. ed. John Dillon. 1996. pap. text 29.95 (*0-8014-8316-6*) Cornell U Pr.

Middle Power Internationalism: The North-South Dimension. Ed. by Cranford Pratt. 176p. (C). 1990. pap. 60.00 (*0-7735-0725-6*, Pub. by McG-Queens Univ Pr) CUP Services.

Middle Proterozoic Belt Supergroup, Western Montana. Ed. by Winston. (IGC Field Trip Guidebooks Ser.). 112p. 1989. 21.00 (*0-87590-667-2*, T334) Am Geophysical.

Middle Proterozoic to Cambrian Rifting, Central North America. Ed. by R. W. Ojakangas et al. LC 96-48160. (Special Papers: No. 312). 1997. pap. 100.00 (*0-8137-2312-4*) Geol Soc.

Middle Puget Sound & Hood Canal: Afoot & Afloat. 2nd rev. ed. Marge Mueller & Ted Mueller. LC 96-40917. (Afoot & Afloat Ser.). (Illus.). 224p. (Orig.). 1997. pap. 14.95 (*0-89886-498-4*) Mountaineers.

Middle Range Theory & the Study of Organizatons. Ed. by Craig C. Pinder & Larry F. Moore. 1980. lib. bdg. 118.50 (*0-89838-021-9*) Kluwer Academic.

Middle Readers Handbook. WLA, Youth Services Section Staff. 50p. 1993. 14.00 (*0-614-04667-X*) Wisc Lib Assn.

Middle School: A Bridge Between Elementary & Secondary School. 2nd ed. (What Research Says to the Teacher Ser.). 1988. pap. 3.95 (*0-8106-1079-5*) NEA.

***Middle School: Blackline Master Package.** (Overcoming Obstacles). 70p. (YA). (gr. 6-9). 1999. pap. text 11.50 (*1-929393-12-1*) Community for Ed.

Middle School - & Beyond. Paul S. George et al. LC 92-3662. 166p. (Orig.). 1992. pap. 17.95 (*0-87120-190-9*, 611-92016) ASCD.

Middle School Advisement. Ball. (J). (gr. 5-8). 1996. pap. text, wbk. ed. 24.95 (*1-55734-193-1*) Tchr Create Mat.

Middle School Art: Issues of Curriculum & Instruction. Ed. by Carole Henry. 128p. 1996. pap. text 22.00 (*0-937652-78-4*, 222) Natl Art Ed.

Middle School Assessment. Teacher Created Materials Staff. 1997. pap. text 14.95 (*1-55734-506-6*) Tchr Create Mat.

Middle School Blues. Lou Kassem. 192p. (J). (gr. 4-7). 1987. mass mkt. 3.99 (*0-380-70363-7*, Avon Bks) Morrow Avon.

Middle School Blues. Lou Kassem. 1987. 9.09 (*0-606-13608-8*, Pub. by Turtleback) Demco.

Middle School Case Studies: Challenges, Perceptions & Practices. Charles R. Watson. LC 96-11923. 1996. pap. text 30.00 (*0-13-197922-1*, Merrill Pub Co) Macmillan.

***Middle School Climate: A Study of Attitudes.** Joshua M. Gold et al. (Fastback Ser.: No. 455). 50p. 1999. pap. 3.00 (*0-87367-655-6*, FB# 455) Phi Delta Kappa.

Middle School Curriculum: From Rhetoric to Reality. James A. Beane. 132p. (C). pap. text 18.00 (*1-56090-073-3*) Natl Middle Schl.

Middle School Distinction. Louis G. Romano & Nicholas P. Georgiady. LC 97-69144. (Fastback Ser.: No. 418). 44p. 1997. pap. 3.00 (*0-87367-618-1*, FB#418) Phi Delta Kappa.

***Middle School English Teacher's Guide to Active Learning.** Marc Moeller & Victor Moeller. 200p. 2000. pap. text, teacher ed. 29.95 (*1-883001-87-0*) Eye On Educ.

Middle School Gets Married. Jamie Suzanne. (Sweet Valley Twins Ser.: No. 68). (J). (gr. 3-7). 1993. 8.60 (*0-606-05648-3*, Pub. by Turtleback) Demco.

Middle School Handbook. Harry Finks. 1990. pap. 27.00 (*0-934338-71-X*) NAIS.

Middle School-Junior High School Evaluative Criteria. 152p. 10.00 (*0-318-17480-4*) Mid St Coll & Schl.

Middle School Keyboarding. Dream Light Inc. (PB - Keyboarding Ser.). (J). (gr. k-8). 1997. pap., teacher ed. 15.95 (*0-538-66049-X*) S-W Pub.

Middle School Language Challenge. Phyllis Amerikaner. (Middle School Ser.). (Illus.). 128p. (J). (gr. 5-8). 1994. pap. 9.95 (*0-88160-272-8*, LW1011) Learning Wks.

Middle School Life Science. 7th ed. Jeffco Staff & Jefferson County School District Staff. 656p. 1990. boxed set 43.90 (*0-8403-5098-8*) Kendall-Hunt.

Middle School Life Science: Teacher's Guide. 7th ed. Jeffco Staff. 480p. 1991. teacher ed., ring bd. 69.90 (*0-8403-5099-6*) Kendall-Hunt.

Middle School Math Challenge. Daniel Ary. (Middle School Math Ser.). (Illus.). 136p. (J). (gr. 5-8). 1996. pap. 9.95 (*0-88160-267-1*, LW1018) Learning Wks.

Middle School Mathematician: Empowering Students to Achieve Success in Algebra & Geometry. Terri Breeden & Kathryn Dillard. Ed. by Leslie Britt. (Illus.). 128p. (Orig.). (J). (gr. 6-8). 1996. pap. text 12.95 (*0-86530-330-4*, IP 301-1) Incentive Pubns.

Middle School Matters: Tips from the Principal's Desk. ACSA Middle Grades Education Committee. 218p. 1998. ring bd. 70.00 (*0-943397-45-6*, 166) Assn Calif Sch Admin.

Middle School Maze. Cliff Schimmels. LC 96-24413. 156p. 1996. pap. 10.99 (*1-56476-431-1*) Chariot Victor.

Middle School Media Magic. Gloria Beadles. Ed. by Leslie Britt & Jan Keeling. LC 96-75149. (Illus.). 64p. (Orig.). (J). (gr. 5-8). 1995. pap. text 8.95 (*0-86530-339-8*, IP 310-2) Incentive Pubns.

Middle School Principal. Robert L. Herring et al. Ed. by Jerry J. Herman & Janice L. Herman. LC 95-1902. (Road Maps to Success Ser.). 80p. 1995. pap. 14.95 (*0-8039-6247-9*) Corwin Pr.

Middle School Science: Demonstrations, Activities, Labs. Salvatore M. Trento. 160p. (C). 1991. spiral bd. 35.95 (*0-8403-6614-0*) Kendall-Hunt.

Middle School Science & Technology: Investigating Diversity & Limits, Level B. BSCS Staff. 448p. 1993. pap. text, teacher ed. 79.90 (*0-8403-6679-5*) Kendall-Hunt.

Middle School Science & Technology: Investigating Diversity & Limits, Level B. BSCS Staff. 368p. 1995. boxed set 42.90 (*0-8403-6678-7*) Kendall-Hunt.

Middle School Science & Technology: Investigating Diversity & Limits Level B Teachers Guide & Resource Book. BSCS Staff. 336p. 1993. pap. text 66.90 (*0-8403-7497-6*) Kendall-Hunt.

Middle School Science & Technology: Investigating Patterns of Change Level A. BSCS Staff. 384p. 1995. boxed set 42.90 (*0-8403-6676-0*) Kendall-Hunt.

Middle School Science & Technology: Investigating Patterns of Change Level A Teacher's Edition. BSCS Staff. 338p. 1993. pap. text 66.90 (*0-8403-7496-8*); pap. text, teacher ed. 79.90 (*0-8403-6677-9*) Kendall-Hunt.

Middle School Science & Technology: Investigating Systems & Change, Level C. BSCS Staff. 528p. 1993. pap. text, teacher ed. 79.90 (*0-8403-6681-7*) Kendall-Hunt.

Middle School Science & Technology: Investigating Systems & Change, Level C. BSCS Staff. 496p. 1995. boxed set 42.90 (*0-8403-6680-9*) Kendall-Hunt.

Middle School Science & Technology Level C: Investigating Systems & Change. BSCS Staff. 464p. 1993. pap. text, teacher ed. 66.90 (*0-8403-7498-4*) Kendall-Hunt.

Middle School Science Challenge. Kathy Harbaugh. Ed. by Kimberley Clark. (Middle School Ser.). (Illus.). (Orig.). (J). (gr. 5-8). 1996. pap. 9.95 (*0-88160-273-6*, LW1012) Learning Wks.

Middle School Social Studies. Linda Schwartz. (J). (gr. 5-8). 1996. pap. text 9.95 (*0-88160-313-9*) Learning Wks.

Middle School Study Skills. Ernst. (Illus.). 144p. (J). (gr. 6-8). 1996. pap., wbk. ed. 14.95 (*1-55734-194-X*) Tchr Create Mat.

Middle School Teaching: A Guide to Methods & Resources. 3rd ed. Kellough. LC 98-19207. 452p. 1998. pap. text 59.00 (*0-13-919846-6*) P-H.

Middle School Vocabulary Challenge. Linda Schwartz. Ed. by Kimberley Clark. (Illus.). 136p. (J). (gr. 5-8). 1996. 9.95 (*0-88160-315-5*, LW1016) Learning Wks.

***Middle School Years: Achieving the Best Education for Your Child Grades 5-8.** Michele A. Hernandez. LC 99-86717. 320p. 2000. pap. 14.99 (*0-446-67562-8*) Warner Bks.

Middle Scots Poets: A Reference Guide. Walter Scheps & J. Anna Looney. (Reference Guides to Literature Ser.). 328p. 1986. 65.00 (*0-8161-8356-2*, Hall Reference) Macmillan.

***Middle Sister.** Amanda Christie. LC 99-68957. (7th Heaven Ser.). 132p. (J). (gr. 3-7). 2000. pap. 3.99 (*0-375-80336-X*, Pub. by Random Bks Yng Read) Random.

Middle Sized Church: Leader's Guide. Lyle E. Schaller & Joe Iaquinta. 1990. pap. 11.95 (*0-911866-18-3*) LifeSprings Res.

Middle-Sized Church: Problems & Prescriptions. Lyle E. Schaller. LC 84-12496. 160p. (Orig.). 1985. pap. 11.95 (*0-687-26948-2*) Abingdon.

Middle Son: A Novel. Deborah Iida. LC 95-33685. 228p. 1996. 18.95 (*1-56512-119-8*, 72119) Algonquin Bks.

Middle Son: A Novel. Deborah Iida. 224p. 1998. mass mkt. 6.99 (*0-425-16151-X*) Berkley Pub.

***Middle Son: A Novel.** Deborah Iida. 224p. 2000. pap. 12.95 (*0-425-17443-3*) Berkley Pub.

Middle Stone Age at Klasies River Mouth in South Africa. Ronald Singer & John J. Wymer. LC 81-16081. (Illus.). (C). 1996. 36.00 (*0-226-76103-7*) U Ch Pr.

Middle Stone Age at Klasies River Mouth in South Africa. Ronald Singer & John Wymer. LC 81-16081. (Illus.). 276p. reprint ed. pap. 85.60 (*0-608-09041-7*, 206967600005) Bks Demand.

Middle Tennessee on Foot: Hikes in the Woods & Walks on Country Roads. Robert Brandt. LC 97-52606. (Illus.). 1998. pap. 12.95 (*0-89587-212-9*) Blair.

Middle Tennessee Society Transformed, 1860-1870: War & Peace in the Upper South. Stephen V. Ash. LC 87-3337. (Illus.). 352p. 1988. text 50.00 (*0-8071-1400-6*) La State U Pr.

Middle Turkie Glosses of the Rylands: Interlinear Koran Translation. Ed. by E. Schutz & J. Eckmann. 358p. (C). 1976. 75.00 (*963-05-0984-9*, Pub. by Akade Kiado) St Mut.

Middle Ultraviolet: Its Science & Technology. Ed. by Alex E. Green. LC 66-22839. (Wiley Series in Pure & Applied Optics). 406p. reprint ed. pap. 125.90 (*0-608-10308-X*, 200739300062) Bks Demand.

Middle United States. rev. ed. Ed. by Christine J. Dillon. (My First Report Ser.). (Illus.). 54p. (J). (gr. 1-3). 1998. ring bd. 5.95 (*1-57896-021-5*, 1998) Hewitt Res Fnd.

Middle Voice. Suzanne Kemmer. LC 93-5762. (Typological Studies in Language (TSL): No. 23). xii, 300p. 1993. 89.00 (*1-55619-410-2*); pap. 32.95 (*1-55619-411-0*) J Benjamins Pubng Co.

Middle Voice in Modern Greek: Meaning & Function of an Inflectional Category. Linda Joyce Manney. LC 98-44715. (Studies in Language Companion Ser.: Vol. 48). xiii, 262p. 2000. 94.00 (*1-55619-934-1*) J Benjamins Pubng Co.

Middle Way: Voices of Anglicanism. Lee W. Gibbs. (Illus.). 136p. (Orig.). 1991. pap. 4.95 (*0-88028-120-0*, 1121) Forward Movement.

***Middle Way to God.** Garth L. Hallett. LC 99-21008. 176p. 2000. text 35.00 (*0-19-513268-8*) OUP.

Middle West. Danny Rendleman. 78p. (Orig.). 1995. pap. 10.00 (*1-56439-049-7*) Ridgeway.

Middle West: Its Meaning in American Culture. James R. Shortridge. LC 88-29991. (Illus.). xiv, 202p. 1989. 25.00 (*0-7006-0388-3*); pap. 14.95 (*0-7006-0475-8*) U Pr of KS.

Middle West Side by Ortho G. Cartwright & Mothers Who Must Earn by Katharine Anthony see West Side Studies

Middle Western Farm Novel in the Twentieth Century. Roy W. Meyer. LC 64-17221. 272p. 1965. reprint ed. pap. 84.40 (*0-608-02142-3*, 206281100003) Bks Demand.

***Middle Window.** Elizabeth Goudge. LC 99-73060. 304p. 1999. write for info. (*1-893766-06-3*) Aeon Pub Co.

Middle Window. Elizabeth Goudge. 1976. 25.95 (*0-8488-1344-8*) Amereon Ltd.

Middle Window. Elizabeth Goudge. 302p. 1976. lib. bdg. 26.95 (*0-89966-106-8*) Buccaneer Bks.

Middle Woodland Population of the Lower Illinois Valley. David L. Asch. LC 82-101264. (Scientific Papers: No. 1). (Illus.). 112p. 1976. 7.50 (*0-942118-00-6*); pap. 4.50 (*0-942118-01-4*) Ctr Amer Arche.

Middle Woodland Settlement & Ceremonialism in the Mid-South & Lower Mississippi Valley: Proceedings of the 1984 Mid-South Archaeological Conference. Ed. by Robert Mainfort. LC 89-60071. (Archaeological Report Ser.: No. 22). (Illus.). (Orig.). 1989. pap. text 10.00 (*0-938896-55-5*) Mississippi Archives.

Middle Works of John Dewey, 1899-1924, 15 vols. Incl. 1899-1901: Collected Articles & "The School & Society" & "The Educational Situation" Intro. by Joe R. Burnett. LC 76-7231. 480p. 1976. 52.00 (*0-8093-0753-7*); 1899-1901: Collected Articles & "The School & Society" & "The Educational Situation" Intro. by Joe R. Burnett. LC 76-7231. 385p. 1983. pap. 16.95 (*0-8093-1135-6*); 1902-1903: Essays on Logical Theory. Intro. by Sidney Hook. LC 76-7231. 471p. 1976. 52.00 (*0-8093-0754-5*); 1902-1903: Essays on Logical Theory. Intro. by Sidney Hook. LC 76-7231. 397p. 1983. pap. 16.95 (*0-8093-1136-4*); 1903-1906: Essays on the New Empiricism. Ed. by Patricia R. Baysinger. LC 76-7231. 495p. 1977. 52.00 (*0-8093-0775-8*); 1903-1906: Essays on the New Empiricism. Ed. by Patricia R. Baysinger. LC 76-7231. 347p. 1983. pap. 16.95 (*0-8093-1137-2*); 1907-1909: Essays on Pragmatism & Truth. Intro. by Lewis E. Hahn. LC 76-7231. 471p. 1977. 52.00 (*0-8093-0776-6*); 1907-1909: Essays on Pragmatism & Truth. Intro. by Lewis E. Hahn. LC 76-7231. 418p. 1983. pap. 14.95 (*0-8093-1138-0*); 1908: Essays on Ethics. Intro. by Charles L. Stevenson. LC 76-7231. 652p. 1978. 52.00 (*0-8093-0834-7*); 1908: Essays on Ethics. Intro. by Charles L. Stevenson. LC 76-7231. 584p. 1983. pap. 16.95 (*0-8093-1139-9*); 1910-1911. Intro. by H. S. Thayer. LC 76-7231. 597p. 1978. 52.00 (*0-8093-0835-5*); 1910-1911. Intro. by H. S. Thayer. LC 76-7231. 539p. 1985. pap. 16.95 (*0-8093-1256-5*); 1912-1914. Intro. by Ralph Ross. LC 76-7231. 575p. 1979. 52.00 (*0-8093-0881-9*); 1912-1914. Intro. by Ralph Ross. LC 76-7231. 533p. 1985. pap. 16.95 (*0-8093-1257-3*); 1915. Intro. by Sidney Hook. LC 76-7231. 582p. 1979. 52.00 (*0-8093-0882-7*); 1915. Intro. by Sidney Hook. LC 76-7231. 526p. 1985. pap. 16.95 (*0-8093-1258-1*); 1916. Intro. by Sidney Hook. LC 76-7231. 426p. 1980. 52.00 (*0-8093-0933-5*); 1916. Intro. by Sidney Hook. LC 76-7231. 408p. 1980. pap. 14.95 (*0-8093-1259-X*); 1916-1917. Intro. by Lewis E. Hahn. LC 76-7231. 575p. 1980. 52.00 (*0-8093-0934-3*); 1916-1917. Intro. by Lewis E. Hahn. LC 76-7231. 511p. 1985. pap. 16.95 (*0-8093-1260-3*); 1918-1919. Intro. by Oscar Handin & Lilian Handin. LC 76-7231. 491p. 1982. 52.00 (*0-8093-1003-1*); 1918-1919. Intro. by Oscar Handin & Lilian Handin. LC 76-7231. 447p. 1988. pap. 14.95; 1920. Intro. by Ralph Ross. LC 76-7231. 346p. 1982. 52.00 (*0-8093-1004-X*); 1920. Intro. by Ralph Ross. LC 76-7231. 322p. 1988. pap. 16.95 (*0-8093-1435-5*); 1921-1922. Intro. by Ralph Ross. LC 76-7231. 560p. 1983. 52.00 (*0-8093-1083-X*); 1921-1922. Intro. by Ralph Ross. LC 76-7231. 554p. 1985. pap. 14.95; 1922. Intro. by Murray G. Murphey. LC 76-7231. 352p. 1983. 52.00 (*0-8093-1084-8*); 1922. Intro. by Murray G. Murphey. LC 76-7231. 260p. 1985. pap. 14.95: 1923-1924. Intro. by Carl Cohen. LC 76-7231. 480p. 1983. 52.00 (*0-8093-1085-6*); 1923-1924. Intro. by Carl Cohen. LC 76-7231. 480p. 1988. pap. 16.95 (*0-8093-1438-X*); LC 76-7231. pap. write for info. (*0-318-55568-9*) S Ill U Pr.

Middle Years see Henry Adams

Middle Years see Works of Henry James Jr.: Collected Works

Middle Years. Paul E. Johnson. LC 70-154489. (Pocket Counsel Bks.). 64p. (Orig.). reprint ed. pap. 30.00 (*0-608-16327-9*, 202718300054) Bks Demand.

Middle Years: New Psychoanalytic Perspectives. John M. Oldham & Robert S. Liebert. 304p. (C). 1990. 37.50 (*0-300-04418-6*) Yale U Pr.

Middle Years: New Psychoanalytic Perspectives. Ed. by John M. Oldham & Robert S. Liebert. LC 89-8939. (Illus.). 311p. 1989. reprint ed. pap. 96.50 (*0-608-07841-7*, 205401700010) Bks Demand.

An Asterisk (*) at the beginning of an entry indicates that the title is appearing for the first time.

Middle Yukon River. Alaska Geographic Society Staff. Ed. by Penny Rennick. LC 72-92087. (Alaska Geographic Ser.: Vol. 17, No. 3). (Illus.). 96p. pap. 19.95 (*0-88240-194-7*) Alaska Geog Soc.

Middlebatchers: Throw a Party for the Marriage of Hetty Wish & Lester Leg, Vol. 1. Anna P. Barrett. Ed. by Shelia S. Darst. (Illus.). 118p. (Orig.). (J). (gr. 3-7). 1984. pap. 7.95 (*0-89896-105-X*) Larksdale.

Middleborough, Massachusetts, Vital Records, Vol. 1. Ed. by Barbara L. Merrick & Alicia C. Williams. 487p. 1986. text 35.00 (*0-942445-00-7*) MA Soc Mayflower Descendants.

Middleborough, Massachusetts, Vital Records, Vol. 2. Ed. by Barbara L. Merrick & Alicia C. Williams. 360p. 1990. text 35.00 (*0-942445-01-5*) MA Soc Mayflower Descendants.

Middlebury College. Photos by Kip Brundage. (First Edition Ser.). (Illus.). 112p. 1988. 39.00 (*0-916509-44-3*) Harmony Hse Pub.

Middlebury College Foreign Language Schools, 1915-1970: The Story of a Unique Idea. Stephen A. Freeman. (Orig.). 1975. pap. 15.95 (*0-910408-17-3*) Coll Store.

Middlegame Artistry. rev. ed. Eugene A. Furst. (Artistry Series of Chess Encyclopedias: Vol. 3). (Illus.). 1991. pap. 19.95 (*1-879394-00-6*, 885-213) Caissas Pr.

Middlegame Strategy: With the Carlsbad Pawn Structure. Robert Leininger. 155p. 1997. pap. 17.50 (*1-886846-07-3*) Pickard & Son.

Middleground: The American Public & the Abortion Debate. Bhavani Sitaraman. LC 93-49087. (Children of Poverty Ser.). 248p. 1994. text 20.00 (*0-8153-1572-4*) Garland.

***Middleman & Other Stories.** Bharati Mukherjee. 208p. 1999. pap. 12.00 (*0-8021-3650-8*, Grove) Grove-Atltic.

Middlemarch. 1991. pap. text. write for info. (*0-17-556698-4*) Addison-Wesley.

***Middlemarch.** George Eliot. (Classics Ser.). 2000. pap. 9.95 (*0-679-78331-8*) Modern Lib NY.

Middlemarch. Georgette Eliot. 1965. 3.95 (*0-671-00709-2*, Arco) Macmillan Gen Ref.

Middlemarch. George Eliot, pseud. 816p. 1985. mass mkt. 6.99 (*0-553-21180-3*, Bantam Classics) Bantam.

Middlemarch, 001. George Eliot, pseud. Ed. by G. S. Haight. LC 56-13878. (YA). (gr. 9 up). 1956. pap. 13.96 (*0-395-05105-3*, RivEd) HM.

Middlemarch, 2 vols. George Eliot, pseud. 240p. 1998. boxed set 14.95 (*3-89508-260-0*) Konemann.

Middlemarch. George Eliot, pseud. LC 83-22161. 1984. 10.95 (*0-318-37464-1*) Modern Lib NY.

Middlemarch. George Eliot, pseud. LC 92-50215. 1992. 19.00 (*0-679-60019-1*) Modern Lib NY.

Middlemarch. George Eliot, pseud. 1964. mass mkt. 6.95 (*0-451-51750-4*, CE1750, Sig Classics) NAL.

Middlemarch. George Eliot, pseud. Ed. by Bert G. Hornback. LC 76-22805. (Critical Editions Ser.). 770p. (C). 1977. pap. text 20.25 (*0-393-09210-0*) Norton.

Middlemarch. George Eliot, pseud. Ed. by David Carroll. (Clarendon Edition of the Novels of George Eliot). (Illus.). 910p. (C). 1987. text 175.00 (*0-19-812558-5*) OUP.

Middlemarch. George Eliot, pseud. Ed. & Notes by David Carroll. (Oxford World's Classics Ser.). 898p. 1998. pap. 8.95 (*0-19-283402-9*) OUP.

Middlemarch. George Eliot, pseud. LC 99-462505. (Oxford World's Classics Hardcovers Ser.). 944p. 1999. 14.00 (*0-19-210029-7*) OUP.

Middlemarch. George Eliot, pseud. Ed. by Margaret Harris. (Everyman Paperback Classics Ser.). 848p. (C). 1995. pap. 5.95 (*0-460-87561-2*, Everyman's Classic Lib) Tuttle Pubng.

Middlemarch. George Eliot, pseud. Ed. & Intro. by Rosemary Ashton. 880p. 1994. pap. 9.95 (*0-14-043388-0*, Penguin Classics) Viking Penguin.

Middlemarch. George Eliot, pseud. (Classics Library). 800p. 1998. pap. 3.95 (*1-85326-237-4*, 2374WW, Pub. by Wrdsworth Edits) NTC Contemp Pub Co.

Middlemarch. Kerry McSweeney. (Unwin Critical Library). 176p. 1984. text 39.95 (*0-04-800031-0*); pap. text 19.95 (*0-04-800032-9*) Routledge.

Middlemarch. Ed. by John Peck. LC 91-36461. (New Casebooks Ser.). 208p. 1992. text 45.00 (*0-312-07567-7*) St Martin.

Middlemarch. abr. ed. George Eliot, pseud. (Classics on Cassette Ser.). 1994. 24.00 incl. audio (*0-453-00879-8*, Pub. by Penguin-HghBrdg) Penguin Putnam.

Middlemarch. George Eliot, pseud. 1992. reprint ed. lib. bdg. 27.95 (*0-89968-277-4*, Lghtyr Pr) Buccaneer Bks.

Middlemarch: A Novel of Reform. George Eliot, pseud. Ed. by Bert G. Hornback. (Twayne's Masterwork Studies: No. 14). 168p. (C). 1988. pap. 13.95 (*0-8057-7981-7*, Twyne) Mac Lib Ref.

Middlemarch: An Authoritative Text, Backgrounds, Criticism. 2nd ed. George Eliot, pseud et al. Ed. by Bert G. Hornback. LC 99-35661. (Critical Editions Ser.). 688p. 1999. pap. 23.75 (*0-393-97452-9*) Norton.

Middlemarch: Masterpiece Theatre Edition. George Eliot, pseud. 816p. 1994. 15.00 (*0-679-60118-X*) Modern Lib NY.

Middlemarch, a Study of Provincial Life see Writings of George Eliot

Middlemarch from Notebook to Novel: A Study of George Eliot's Creative Method, 47. Jerome Beaty. LC 81-6588. 134p. 1981. reprint ed. lib. bdg. 45.00 (*0-313-22412-9*, BEMF, Greenwood Pr) Greenwood.

Middlemarch Notes. Brian Johnston. (Cliffs Notes Ser.). 112p. 1967. pap. 4.95 (*0-8220-0825-4*, Cliff) IDG Bks.

Middlemen & Brokers in Oceania. Ed. by William L. Rodman & Dorothy A. Counts. (ASAO Monographs: No. 9). 318p. (C). 1983. reprint ed. pap. text 23.00 (*0-8191-3468-6*) U Pr of Amer.

Middlemen in English Business, Particularly Between 1660-1760. Ray B. Westerfield. LC 68-30551. (Reprints of Economic Classics Ser.). 333p. 1968. reprint ed. 45.00 (*0-678-00447-1*) Kelley.

Middlemen of the Cameroon Rivers: The Duala & Their Hinterland, c.1600 - c.1960. Ralph A. Austen & Jonathan M. Derrick. (African Studies: No. 96). (Illus.). 270p. (C). 1999. text 64.95 (*0-521-56228-7*); pap. text 24.95 (*0-521-56664-9*) Cambridge U Pr.

MiddlePassages. Kamau Brathwaite. LC 93-17249. 128p. (Orig.). 1994. pap. 9.95 (*0-8112-1232-7*, NDP776, Pub. by New Directions) Norton.

Middleplots 4: A Book Talk Guide for Use with Readers Ages 8-12. John T. Gillespie & Corinne J. Naden. 434p. 1994. 45.00 (*0-8352-3446-0*) Bowker.

Middle Ages in French Literature, 1851-1900. Jannie R. Dakyns. (Oxford Modern Languages & Literature Monographs). 1973. 29.95 (*0-19-815522-0*) OUP.

Middlesbrough: The Growth of a Community. A. J. Pollard. LC 97-131020. 1998. 33.95 (*0-7509-1270-7*, Pub. by Sutton Pub Ltd) Intl Pubs Mktg.

Middlesex Canal Guide & Maps. Warbutton K. VerPlanck. (Illus.). 35p. (Orig.). 1996. pap. 17.00 (*0-9654490-0-9*) Middlesex Canal.

Middlesex County see Hagstrom Atlases

Middlesex County. Gary Karasik & Anna M. Aschkenes. (Illus.). 248p. 1999. 32.95 (*1-892724-06-5*) Am Historical Pr.

Middlesex County Marriage Records, 1853-1904 & Federal Census, 1880. Catherine M. Taylor. 352p. 1998. pap. 41.50 (*0-7884-0894-1*, T609) Heritage Bk.

***Middlesex County, New Jersey Deed Abstracts, Bk. 1.** Richard S. Hutchinson. 145p. 2000. pap. 27.50 (*0-7884-1434-8*, 1434) Heritage Bk.

Middlesex County, New Jersey Militia, 1791-1795: Compiled Records with Biographical Sketches of the Officers of Selected Companies, Including a Roster of the Middlesex County Militia, 1775-1783. Russell K. Dutcher, III. (Illus.). 275p. 1996. pap. 26.50 (*0-8063-4516-0*) Clearfield Co.

Middlesex County, Virginia, Court Orders, 1711-1713. LC 98-121885. 152p. 1997. spiral bd. 15.00 (*1-57445-037-9*) TLC Genealogy.

Middlesex County, Virginia, Deed Book 1 (1687-1750) & Miscellaneous Records (1752-1831) T.L.C. Genealogy Staff. 67p. (Orig.). 1993. pap., spiral bd. 12.00 (*1-886633-95-9*) TLC Genealogy.

Middlesex Water Company: A Business History. Mark E. Lender. 235p. 1994. 20.00 (*0-9642916-0-6*) Upland Press.

Middleton Zephyr. Pat Cook. 1995. 5.50 (*0-87129-501-6*, M89) Dramatic Pub.

Middleton's Tragedies. Samuel Schoenbaum. LC 71-128191. 275p. (C). 1970. reprint ed. 75.00 (*0-87752-132-8*) Gordian.

Middleton's "Vulgar Pasquin" Essays on "A Game of Chess" Trevor H. Howard-Hill. LC 94-31107. (Illus.). 344p. 1995. 45.00 (*0-87413-534-6*) U Delaware Pr.

Middletown. Robert S. Lynd & Helen M. Lynd. 562p. (C). 1959. pap. 15.00 (*0-15-659550-8*, Harvest Bks) Harcourt.

Middletown. Roger L. Miller & George C. Crout. LC 98-86558. (Images of America Ser.). (Illus.). 128p. 1998. pap. 16.99 (*0-7524-1287-6*) Arcadia Publng.

Middletown: A Biography. Franklin B. Williams. (Illus.). 201p. 1997. reprint ed. lib. bdg. 32.50 (*0-8328-6175-8*) Higginson Bk Co.

Middletown: The Making of a Documentary Film Series, Vol. 2. Dwight Hoover. (Visual Anthropology Ser.). xvii, 222p. 1992. text 96.00 (*3-7186-0543-0*, Harwood Acad Pubs); pap. text 32.00 (*3-7186-0542-2*, Harwood Acad Pubs) Gordon & Breach.

Middletown Families: Fifty Years of Change & Continuity. Theodore Caplow & Howard M. Bahr. LC 81-14757. 462p. 1982. reprint ed. pap. 131.70 (*0-608-00833-8*, 2061624) Bks Demand.

***Middletown in the 20th Century.** Randall Gabrielan. (Images of America Ser.). 128p. 1999. pap. 18.99 (*0-7524-1322-8*) Arcadia Publng.

Middletown Jews: The Tenuous Survival of an American Jewish Community. Ed. by Dan Rottenberg. LC 96-22779. (Illus.). 192p. 1998. pap. 12.95 (*0-253-21206-5*) Ind U Pr.

Middletown Photographs. E. F. Ball et al. Ed. by T. A. Sargent. (Illus.). 68p. (Orig.). 1984. pap. 5.00 (*0-915511-01-0*) Ball St U Mus Art.

Middletown Township, Vol. I. Randall Gabrielan. LC 95-163228. (Images of America Ser.). 128p. 1999. pap. 14.99 (*0-7524-0075-4*) Arcadia Publng.

Middletown Township, Vol. II. Randall Gabrielan. (Images of America Ser.). 128p. 1999. pap. 16.99 (*0-7524-0234-X*) Arcadia Publng.

Middletown Township, Vol. III. Randall Gabrielan. LC 97-199101. (Images of America Ser.). 128p. 1999. pap. 16.99 (*0-7524-0508-X*) Arcadia Publng.

Middleware. Daniel Serain. 1998. pap. 49.95 (*1-85233-011-2*) Spr-Verlag.

Middleware: Achieving Open Systems for the Enterprise. Paul Korzeniowski. LC 96-48282. (Illus.). 196p. 1997. pap. 275.00 (*1-56607-982-9*) Comput Tech Res.

Middleware Architectures for Client/Server Computing. James Martin & Joseph Leben. (C). 2001. text 48.00 (*0-13-238551-1*, Prentice Hall) P-H.

***Middleware Networks: Concept, Design & Deployment of Internet Infrastructure.** Michael Lerner. LC 00-35404. (International Series on Advances in Database Systems). 2000. write for info. (*0-7923-7840-7*) Kluwer Academic.

Middleware '98: IFIP International Conference on Distributed Systems Platforms & Open Distributed Processing. Nigel Davies et al. LC 98-43175. 1998. write for info. (*1-85233-088-0*) Spr-Verlag.

***Middleware 2000: IFIP/ACM International Conference on Distributed Systems Platforms & Open Distributed Processing New York, NY, April 4-7, 2000, Proceedings.** Ed. by Joseph Sventek & G. Coulson. LC 00-36583. (Lecture Notes in Computer Science Ser.: Vol. 1795). xi, 436p. 2000. pap. 72.00 (*3-540-67352-0*) Spr-Verlag.

Middling, Meddling, Muddling: Issues in Australian Foreign Policy. Ed. by Richard Leaver & David Cox. LC 97-192774. 304p. 1997. pap. 24.95 (*1-86448-305-9*, Pub. by Allen & Unwin Pty) Paul & Co Pubs.

Middling Planters of Ruxton, Maryland, 1694-1850. Joseph M. Coale. LC 96-47364. 1997. 24.95 (*0-938420-56-9*) MD Hist.

Middling Sort: Commerce, Gender & the Family in England, 1680-1780. Margaret R. Hunt. LC 96-18063. 358p. 1996. 48.00 (*0-520-20260-0*, Pub. by U CA Pr) Cal Prin Full Svc.

Middling Sort of People Vol. 1: Culture, Society, & Politics in England, 1550-1800. Jonathan Barry. 1994. text 55.00 (*0-312-12356-6*) St Martin.

***Middos: Stories for Children.** Menucha Fuchs. (Children's Learning Ser.: Vol. 12). (Illus.). (J). (ps-5). 2000. pap. 4.95 (*1-880582-64-3*) Judaica Pr.

Mideast after the Gulf War. Richard Steins. (YA). 1992. pap. 4.80 (*0-395-62471-1*) HM.

Mideast & Mediterranean Cuisines. Rose Dosti. LC 93-37394. 144p. 1993. pap. 9.95 (*1-55561-055-2*) Fisher Bks.

Mideast & North African Banks & Financial Institutions. 8th ed. Tyler Gregory Hicks. 70p. 1996. pap. 15.00 (*1-56150-170-0*) Intl Wealth.

Mideast & North African Banks & Financial Institutions. 9th ed. Tyler Gregory Hicks. 70p. 1998. pap. 15.00 (*1-56150-220-0*) Intl Wealth.

Mideast & North African Banks & Financial Institutions. 10th ed. Tyler Gregory Hicks. 70p. 1999. pap. 15.00 (*1-56150-271-5*) Intl Wealth.

***Mideast & North African Banks & Financial Institutions.** 11th ed. Tyler G. Hicks. 70p. 2000. pap. 15.00 (*1-56150-331-2*) Intl Wealth.

Mideast Arms Sales Debate. Marvin Feuerwerger. (Research Note Ser.: Vol. 3). 1978. reprint ed. pap. 10.00 (*0-86682-034-5*) Ctr Intl Relations.

Mideast Germany Map. 1996. 8.95 (*2-06-700418-2*, 418) Michelin.

Mideast Kaleidoscope. Louise O. Neaderland. (Illus.). 45p. 1983. 15.00 (*0-942561-05-8*) Bone Hollow.

Mideast Meets Midwest: Ethnographic Rugs from Midwest Collections. Intro. by Peter F. Stone. (Illus.). 180p. (Orig.). 1994. pap. 45.00 (*0-9639753-0-7*) Chicago Rug.

Mideast Treaty: Greatest Prophetic Fulfillment in 2,000 Years. Irvin Baxter, Jr. LC 94-70128. 160p. (Orig.). (C). 1994. pap. 12.50 (*0-941559-01-7*) Endtime Pub.

***Midfielders: Positional Play.** Allen Wade. (Illus.). 141p. 1999. pap. 12.95 (*1-890946-09-5*) Reedswain.

Midfielder's Moment: Politics, Literature, & Culture in Contemporary South Africa. Grant Farred. LC 99-45372. (Cultural Studies). 200p. (C). 1999. text 55.00 (*0-8133-3514-0*) Westview.

Midge & Fred. Brian Schatell. LC 82-48540. (Illus.). 32p. (J). (ps-2). 1983. lib. bdg. 11.89 (*0-397-32047-7*) HarpC Child Bks.

Midges. Alasdair Roberts. (Illus.). 126p. 1998. pap. 9.95 (*1-874744-79-3*, Pub. by Birlinn Ltd) Dufour.

Midges. Alasdair Roberts & Barbara Robertson. 126p. 1998. pap. 9.95 (*1-874744-63-7*, Pub. by Birlinn Ltd) Dufour.

Midges in Scotland. George Hendry. (Illus.). 84p. 1989. pap. 8.00 (*0-08-036595-7*, Pub. by Aberdeen U Pr) Macmillan.

Midges in Scotland. rev. ed. George Hendry. 84p. 1996. pap. 23.00 (*1-873644-61-2*, Pub. by Mercat Pr Bks) St Mut.

***Midget.** Tim Bowler. (Illus.). 160p. (YA). (gr. 7). 2000. 8.00 (*0-689-82909-4*) Aladdin.

Midget. Tim Bowler. LC 94-46963. 160p. (YA). (gr. 7 up). 1995. pap. 15.00 (*0-689-80115-7*) McElderry Bks.

Midget & Sprite Restoration, Preparation & Maintenence. Jim Tyler. (Illus.). 240p. 1993. pap. 39.95 (*1-85532-242-0*, Pub. by Osprey) Motorbooks Intl.

Midget MK 2 & MK 3 Parts Catalogue, 1962-74. British Leyland Motors. (Illus.). 280p. 1988. 55.00 (*0-8376-0513-X*) Bentley Pubs.

Midget Submarines of the Second World War. Paul Kemp. 1999. 55.00 (*1-86176-042-6*) Naval Inst Pr.

Midgie Purvis. Mary Chase. 1963. pap. 5.25 (*0-8222-0754-0*) Dramatists Play.

Mid/Heavy Duty Truck Electrical. Robert N. Brady. 560p. 1991. 105.00 (*0-13-385659-3*, 410101) P-H.

Midi. J. Law. 1992. pap. text 24.95 (*0-7195-5081-5*, Pub. by John Murray) Trafalgar.

MIDI: A Comprehensive Introduction, Vol. 7. 2nd ed. Joseph Rothstein. LC 94-45738. (Illus.). xvii, 268p. (C). 1995. pap. 28.95 (*0-89579-309-1*) A-R Eds.

Midi: Music Technology Access for VIPs. large type ed. Geraldine Page. (Ulverscroft Large Print Ser.). 95p. 1996. pap. 27.50 (*0-7089-4999-1*) Ulverscroft.

MIDI - The In's, Out's & Thru's. Jeff Rona. 96p. (Orig.). 1987. pap. 12.95 (*0-88188-560-6*, 00183495) H Leonard.

MIDI Book: Using MIDI & Related Interfaces. Steve De Furia & Joe Scacciaferro. (Syntharts Ser.). 104p. (Orig.). 1986. pap. 14.95 (*0-88188-515-0*, 00605600) H Leonard.

MIDI Book: Using MIDI & Related Interfaces. Steve DeFuria. (Illus.). (J). 1986. per. 14.95 incl. VHS (*0-88188-514-2*, HLO 8418400) H Leonard.

MIDI Companion. Jeff Rona. (Illus.). 96p. 1994. per. 14.95 (*0-7935-3077-6*, HL00183500) H Leonard.

Midi Drummer. David Grigger. (C). 1987. pap. 17.95 (*0-939067-50-1*) Alexander Pub.

Midi Files. Rob Young. 352p. 1996. pap. text 29.95 (*0-13-262403-6*) P-H.

MIDI for Musicians. Craig Anderton. 105p. 1986. pap. 17.95 (*0-8256-1050-8*) Omnibus NY.

MIDI for the Professional. Paul Lehrmann & Tim Tully. (Illus.). 240p. 1995. pap. 24.95 (*0-8256-1374-4*, AM91049) Music Sales.

Midi for the Technophobe. Paul White. (Illus.). 190p. 1997. pap. text 19.95 (*1-86074-193-2*, Pub. by Sanctuary Pubng) Music Sales.

Midi Guitar. Rey Sanchez. 1988. pap. 17.95 (*0-89898-544-7*, F2917GTX) Wrner Bros.

Midi Guitar & Synthesis. Youngblood. 96p. 1989. 14.95 (*0-88188-886-9*, 00330015) H Leonard.

MIDI Home Studio. Howard C. Massey. (Illus.). 96p. 1988. pap. 17.95 (*0-8256-1127-X*, AM67182) Music Sales.

MIDI Implementation Book. Steve DeFuria & Joe Scacciaferro. (Ferro Technologies Ser.). 208p. (Orig.). 1987. pap. 19.95 (*0-88188-558-4*, HL 00605601) H Leonard.

Midi in Revolution: A Study of Regional Political Diversity, 1789-1793. Hubert C. Johnson. LC 85-13839. (Illus.). 320p. reprint ed. pap. 99.20 (*0-608-06358-4*, 206671900008) Bks Demand.

MIDI Manual. David M. Huber. 250p. 1998. pap. text 27.95 (*0-240-80320-5*) Buttrwrth-Heinemann.

MIDI Manual. 2nd ed. David Miles Huber. 255p. 1999. pap. text 29.95 (*0-240-80330-2*, Focal) Buttrwrth-Heinemann.

***Midi Orchestrator's Handbook.** Dennis F. McCorkle. (Illus.). 64p. 1999. pap. 14.95 (*0-8256-1616-6*) Music Sales.

Midi Piano Library: Bach. 1994. 19.95 (*0-7119-3869-5*, AM91748) Omnibus NY.

Midi Piano Library: Classics. 1994. 19.95 (*0-7119-3873-3*, AM91752) Omnibus NY.

Midi Piano Library: Handel. 1994. 19.95 (*0-7119-3870-9*, AM91749) Omnibus NY.

Midi-Pyrenees. Delia Evans. LC 98-149718. (Blue Guide Ser.). (Illus.). 256p. 1995. pap. 15.95 (*0-393-31413-8*, Norton Paperbks) Norton.

Midi-Pyrenees Map. 1996. 8.95 (*2-06-700235-X*, 235) Michelin.

MIDI Resource Book. Steve DeFuria & Joe Scacciaferro. (Ferro Technologies Ser.). 148p. (Orig.). 1987. pap. 17.95 (*0-88188-587-8*, HL 00605602) H Leonard.

MIDI Sequencing for Musicians. Compiled by Keyboard Magazine Editors. 144p. 1989. per. 14.95 (*0-88188-911-3*, 00183491) H Leonard.

Midi Survival Guide. Vic Lennard. (Illus.). 96p. 1996. pap. 13.95 (*1-870775-28-7*, Pub. by PC Pubg) Cimino Pub Grp.

MIDI Systems & Control. 2nd expanded ed. Francis Rumsey. LC 94-191382. 256p. 2000. pap. text 42.95 (*0-240-51370-3*, Focal) Buttrwrth-Heinemann.

Midian, Moab, & Edom: The History & Archaeology of Late Bronze & Iron Age Jordan & North-West Arabia. Ed. by John F. Sawyer & David J. Clines. (Journal for the Study of the Old Testament Supplement Ser.: Vol. 24). 172p. 1983. 52.50 (*0-905774-48-5*, Pub. by Sheffield Acad); pap. 18.95 (*0-905774-49-3*, Pub. by Sheffield Acad) CUP Services.

Mididictionary of Science. Peter G. Mellett. LC 92-40594. (C). 1993. write for info. (*0-19-211680-0*) OUP.

Midland: A Venture in Literary Regionalism. Milton M. Reigelman. LC 75-28219. 154p. (Orig.). 1975. pap. text 9.95 (*0-87745-054-4*) U of Iowa Pr.

***Midland: Poems.** Kwame Dawes. 104p. 2000. 24.95 (*0-8214-1355-4*); pap. 12.95 (*0-8214-1356-2*) Ohio U Pr.

Midland - Odessa. San Antonio Cartographers Staff. 1995. 2.95 (*0-671-56288-6*) Macmillan.

Midland Genealogical Directory, 1985. (C). 1987. 50.00 (*0-7855-2091-0*, Pub. by Birmingham Midland Soc) St Mut.

Midland Illinois Dialect Patterns. Timothy C. Frazer. (Publications of the American Dialect Society: No. 73). 194p. 1987. pap. text 19.50 (*0-8173-0367-7*) U of Ala Pr.

Midland Septs & the Pale. F. R. Hitchcock. 311p. 1998. pap. 24.50 (*0-7884-0901-8*, H371) Heritage Bk.

Midland Swimmer. John Reibetanz. LC 97-104852. 112p. 1996. pap. 12.95 (*0-919626-86-6*, Pub. by Brick Bks) Genl Dist Srvs.

Midland Valley: Rails for Coal, Cattle & Crude. 2nd ed. Lloyd E. Stagner. (Illus.). 56p. (Orig.). 1998. reprint ed. pap. 15.95 (*0-942035-43-7*) South Platte.

Midlands. David Clark. LC 94-4452. (Battlefield Walks Ser.). (Illus.). 192p. 1996. pap. 17.95 (*0-7509-0258-2*, Pub. by Sutton Pub Ltd) Intl Pubs Mktg.

Midlands - The North Map. 1997. 8.95 (*2-06-700402-6*, 402) Michelin.

Midlands Invitational, 1997: Photography. Janet L. Farber & Joslyn Art Museum Staff. LC 97-42003. (Illus.). 62p. 1997. pap. 21.95 (*0-936364-27-0*) Joslyn Art.

Midlands Invitational, 1992: Installation. Graham W. Beal & Janet L. Farber. LC 92-46761. 1993. pap. 12.00 (*0-936364-22-X*) Joslyn Art.

***Midlands Invitational 2000: Works on Paper.** Midlands Invitational Staff et al. LC 00-30192. 2000. pap. write for info. (*0-936364-29-7*) Joslyn Art.

Midlands Mysteries. unabridged ed. Douglas Sugano & Kenneth Pickering. 182p. 1999. pap. 12.00 (*0-85343-615-0*, Pub. by J G Miller Ltd) Empire Pub Srvs.

Midlife: A Manual. Steven Estrine & Judith Estrine. 224p. 1999. text 21.95 (*1-86204-594-1*, Pub. by Element MA) Penguin Putnam.

Midlife: Meditations for Women. Maureen Brady. LC 94-24328. 1995. pap. 13.00 (*0-06-251148-3*, Pub. by Harper SF) HarpC.

Midlife, a Rite of Passage - The Wise Woman, a Celebration. Irene Fine. 120p. (Orig.). 1991. pap. 8.95 (*0-9608054-7-8*) Womans Inst-Cont Jewish Ed.

M

An Asterisk (*) at the beginning of an entry indicates that the title is appearing for the first time.

Midlife & Older Women in Latin America & the Caribbean. (ENG & SPA.). x, 424p. 1989. pap. text 50.00 (*92-75-12021-8*, 1630002) World Health.

Midlife Awakenings: Discovering the Gifts Life Has Given Us. Barbara Bartocci. LC 98-18814. 120p. 1998. pap. 8.95 (*0-87793-659-5*) Ave Maria.

Midlife Development. Lachman. 832p. (C). 2000. 89.95 (*0-471-33331-X*) Wiley.

Midlife Health: A Woman's Practical Guide to Feeling Good. Ada P. Kahn & Linda H. Holt. 384p. 1989. mass mkt. 5.99 (*0-380-70719-5*, Avon Bks) Morrow Avon.

Midlife Health: Every Woman's Guide to Feeling Good. Ada P. Kahn & Linda H. Holt. LC 86-19954. 276p. reprint ed. pap. 85.60 (*0-7837-1359-2*, 204150700021) Bks Demand.

Midlife in Your Face, Man! Midlife Questions for Men. David C. Regester. 278p. 1998. per., wbk. ed. 6.95 (*0-9663238-5-8*) Doc Reeg.

Midlife Journeys: A Traveler's Guide. Richard P. Olson. LC 96-30146. 312p. (Orig.). 1996. pap. 16.95 (*0-8298-1142-7*) Pilgrim OH.

***Midlife Lesbian Relationships: Friends, Lovers, Children & Parents.** Marcy Adelman. LC 00-31966. 2000. write for info. (*1-56023-142-4*) Harrington Pk.

Midlife Loss: Coping Strategies. Ed. by Richard A. Kalish. (Focus Editions Ser.: Vol. 107). 320p. (C). 1989. text 59.95 (*0-8039-3054-2*); pap. text 26.00 (*0-8039-3055-0*) Sage.

Midlife Loss: Coping Strategies. Ed. by Richard A. Kalish. LC 89-34764. (Sage Focus Edition Ser.). 328p. 1989. reprint ed. pap. 101.70 (*0-608-01721-3*, 206237600003) Bks Demand.

Midlife, Madness, or Menopause: Does Anyone Know What's Normal? Patricia Richter & Roger Duvivier. 264p. 1995. pap. 12.95 (*1-56561-059-8*) Wiley.

Midlife, Madness, or Menopause: Does Anyone Know What's Normal? Patricia J. Richter. 264p. 1995. pap. 12.95 (*0-471-34685-3*) Wiley.

***Midlife Man: A Not-So-Threatening Guide to Health & Sex for a Man at His Peak.** Art Hister. 224p. 2000. pap. 12.95 (*1-55054-756-9*, Greystone) DGL.

***Midlife Man: A Not-So-Threatening Guide to Health & Sex for Man at His Peak.** Art Hister. 1999. 19.95 (*1-55054-656-2*) DGL.

Midlife Mischief. Philippa Gregory. 240p. 1998. 24.00 (*0-7278-5379-1*) Severn Hse.

Midlife Myths: Issues, Findings, & Practice Implications. Ed. by Ski Hunter & Martin Sundel. (Sourcebooks for the Human Services Ser.: Vol. 7). 320p. (C). 1989. text 56.00 (*0-8039-2964-1*); pap. text 26.00 (*0-8039-2965-X*) Sage.

Midlife Orphan: Facing Life's Changes Now That Your Parents Are Gone. Jane Brooks. LC 99-191736. 228p. (Orig.). 1999. pap. 13.00 (*0-425-16693-7*) Berkley Pub.

Midlife Parenting: A Guide to Having & Raising Kids in Your 30s, 40s & Beyond. Christi Taylor-Jones. 240p. 1993. pap. 12.95 (*0-9636864-0-2*) Veracity Pr.

Midlife Queer: Autobiography of a Decade, 1971-1981. Martin Duberman. LC 98-28098. 240p. 1998. pap. 18.95 (*0-299-16024-6*) U of Wis Pr.

Midlife Women: Contemporary Issues. Joan M. Jacobson. LC 94-42098. 141p. 1995. pap. 38.75 (*0-86720-929-1*) Jones & Bartlett.

Midnight. Odie Hawkins. 224p. 1995. mass mkt. 4.95 (*0-87067-738-1*) Holloway.

Midnight. Dean Koontz. 1989. 12.60 (*0-606-01912-X*, Pub. by Turtleback) Demco.

Midnight. Mao Tun. 540p. 1979. pap. 17.95 (*0-88727-099-9*, Pub. by Foreign Lang Pr) Cheng & Tsui.

Midnight. large type ed. Dean Koontz. LC 89-77192. 780p. 1990. reprint ed. lib. bdg. 20.95 (*0-89621-965-8*) Thorndike Pr.

Midnight. Dean Koontz. 480p. 1989. reprint ed. mass mkt. 7.99 (*0-425-11870-3*) Berkley Pub.

Midnight. Yen-Ping Shen, pseud. Tr. by Meng-hsiung Hsu. LC 75-36237. 1976. reprint ed. 45.00 (*0-404-14485-3*) AMS Pr.

Midnight: A Cinderella Alphabet. Stephanie Perkal. LC 96-38241. (Illus.). 32p. (J). (gr. k-4). 1997. 15.95 (*1-885008-05-8*) Shens Bks.

***Midnight: Sunset Poetry.** Mary Hickey. 2000. pap. write for info. (*1-58235-410-3*) Watermrk Pr.

***Midnight Adventures of Kelly, Dot & Esmeralda.** John S. Goodall. LC 98-87823. (Illus.). 32p. (J). (ps-3). 1999. 8.95 (*0-689-82564-1*) McElderry Bks.

Midnight & Magnolias. Rebecca Paisley. 416p. (Orig.). 1992. mass mkt. 4.50 (*0-380-76566-7*, Avon Bks) Morrow Avon.

Midnight & Morning: An Account of the Adventist Awakening & the Founding of the Advent Christian Denomination. Clyde E. Hewitt. (Advent Christian History Ser.: Vol. 1). 326p. 1983. pap. 5.00 (*1-881909-10-7*) Advent Christ Gen Conf.

Midnight Angel. Lisa Kleypas. 384p. (Orig.). 1995. mass mkt. 6.50 (*0-380-77353-8*, Avon Bks) Morrow Avon.

***Midnight at Noon.** James Alderson. 1998. spiral bd. 6.00 (*1-929326-34-3*) Hal Bar Pubg.

***Midnight at the Camposanto: A Taos Mystery.** Mari Ulmer. LC 99-68781. 258p. 2000. 23.95 (*1-890208-30-2*) Poisoned Pen.

Midnight at the Lost & Found. Stacey Schuett. LC 93-23342. (Illus.). 1998. lib. bdg. write for info. (*0-679-94921-6*) Random.

Midnight at the Lost & Found. Stacey Shuett. LC 93-23342. (Illus.). 1999. write for info. (*0-679-84921-1*) Random.

Midnight at the Oasis. Angela McAllister. (Illus.). 32p. (J). (ps-2). 1995. 19.95 (*0-370-31884-6*, Pub. by Bodley Head) Trafalgar.

Midnight Baby: An Autobiography. Dory Previn. LC 76-20544. x, 246p. 1976. write for info. (*0-02-599000-4*) Macmillan.

Midnight Before Christmas: A Holiday Thriller. William Bernhardt. LC 98-20329. (The/Ben Kincaid "Justice" Ser.). 1998. 14.95 (*0-345-42810-2*) Ballantine Pub Grp.

Midnight Before Christmas: A Holiday Thriller. William Bernhardt. 1999. mass mkt. 5.99 (*0-345-42811-0*) Ballantine Pub Grp.

Midnight Blue. E. D'Arcy. 1997. mass mkt. 11.95 (*0-340-66644-7*, Pub. by Hodder & Stought Ltd) Trafalgar.

Midnight Blue. Dorothy Garlock. 368p. 1989. mass mkt. 5.99 (*0-446-35522-4*, Pub. by Warner Bks) Little.

Midnight Blue. Monica Jackson. 256p. 1997. mass mkt. 4.99 (*0-7860-0445-2*, Pinncle Kensgtn) Kensgtn Pub Corp.

Midnight Blue. large type ed. Dorothy Garlock. (Niagara Large Print Ser.). 1995. 29.50 (*0-7089-5809-5*) Ulverscroft.

Midnight Blue: The Sonja Blue Collection. Nancy A. Collins. LC 95-215664. (Illus.). 1995. pap. 14.99 (*1-56504-900-4*, 13000, Borealis) White Wolf.

Midnight Bride see Novia de Medianoche: Midnight Bride

Midnight Bride. Marlene Suson. 384p. (Orig.). 1995. mass mkt. 4.99 (*0-380-77851-3*, Avon Bks) Morrow Avon.

Midnight Bridge. Mary N. Korte. 1970. pap. 2.50 (*0-685-29874-4*) Oyez.

Midnight Bridge. Barbara McCauley. (Desire Ser.). 1996. per. 3.50 (*0-373-76028-0*, 1-76028-9) Silhouette.

***Midnight Butterfly.** Joan Elizabeth Lloyd. 224p. 2000. pap. 11.95 (*0-7867-0761-5*, Pub. by Carroll & Graf) Publishers Group.

Midnight Butterfly Sings. Ed. by John Minczeski. (Illus.). 164p. (Orig.). 1988. pap. 7.50 (*0-927663-01-5*) COMPAS.

***Midnight Cab: The Mystery of the Lost Child.** unabridged ed. Perf. by Canadian Broadcasting Company cast. 1999. audio 5.99 (*1-55204-615-X*, PAC-8615) Durkin Hayes Pub.

Midnight Caller. Horton Foote. 1959. pap. 3.25 (*0-8222-0755-9*) Dramatists Play.

Midnight Caller: 43 Light St. Rebecca York. (Intrigue Ser.: No. 534). 1999. per. 3.99 (*0-373-22534-2*, 1-22534-1) Harlequin Bks.

Midnight Carol: A Novel of How Charles Dickens Saved Christmas. Patricia K. Davis. LC 99-15886. 192p. 1999. text 16.95 (*0-312-24523-8*) St Martin.

***Midnight Carol: A Novel of How Charles Dickens Saved Christmas.** Patricia K. Davis. 2000. reprint ed. pap. 4.99 (*0-312-97698-4*, St Martins Paperbacks) St Martin.

***Midnight Champagne: A Novel.** A. Manette Ansay. LC 99-11467. 240p. 1999. 24.00 (*0-688-15244-9*, Wm Morrow) Morrow Avon.

***Midnight Champagne: A Novel.** A. Manette Ansay. 240p. 2000. pap. 13.00 (*0-380-72975-X*) Morrow Avon.

Midnight Chill. Barbara Siegal & Scott Siegal. Ed. by Patricia MacDonald. (Ghostworld Ser.). 176p. (Orig.). (J). 1991. per. 2.99 (*0-671-70905-4*, Archway) PB.

Midnight Cinderella: Way Out West. Eileen Wilks. 1999. per. 4.25 (*0-373-07921-4*, 1-07921-9) Silhouette.

Midnight Clear. Beth Garbo. (Illus.). 20p. 1998. 5.95 (*1-892373-15-7*, 99-15) Especially Bks.

Midnight Clear. Katherine Stone. 352p. 1999. mass mkt. 6.99 (*0-446-60678-2*, Pub. by Warner Bks) Little.

Midnight Clear: A Callahan Garrity Mystery. Kathy Hogan Trocheck. LC 98-20321. 288p. 1998. 23.00 (*0-06-017543-5*) HarpC.

Midnight Clear: A Callahan Garrity Mystery. Kathy Hogan Trocheck. 416p. 1999. mass mkt. 5.99 (*0-06-109800-0*) HarpC.

***Midnight Clear: A Holiday Anthology.** Leslie Esdaile et al. Ed. by Donna Hill. 2000. pap. 10.95 (*1-58571-039-3*, 909-105, Pub. by Genesis Press) BookWorld.

Midnight Clear: A Novel. William Wharton. LC 95-25713. 288p. 1996. pap. 12.95 (*1-55704-257-8*, Pub. by Newmarket) Norton.

Midnight Club. James Patterson. 256p. 1990. mass mkt. 5.99 (*0-8041-0597-9*) Ivy Books.

***Midnight Club.** James Patterson. 400p. 2000. mass mkt. 13.95 (*0-446-67641-1*, Pub. by Warner Bks) Little.

Midnight Club. Christopher Pike, pseud. Ed. by Patricia MacDonald. LC 93-20917. 224p. (J). 1994. mass mkt. 3.99 (*0-671-87263-X*, Archway) PB.

Midnight Club. Christopher Pike, pseud. Ed. by Patricia MacDonald. LC 93-20917. 256p. (YA). (gr. 9 up). 1994. 14.00 (*0-671-87255-9*, Archway) PB.

Midnight Club. Christopher Pike, pseud. (J). 1994. 9.09 (*0-606-05925-3*, Pub. by Turtleback) Demco.

Midnight Club. large type ed. James Patterson. LC 99-19337. (Large Print Book Ser.). 1999. pap. 23.95 (*1-56895-716-5*) Wheeler Pub.

Midnight Club. James Patterson. 368p. 1999. reprint ed. mass mkt. 6.99 (*0-446-60638-3*, Pub. by Warner Bks) Little.

Midnight Come. Michael D. Anthony. LC 98-46678. 304p. 1999. text 22.95 (*0-312-20058-7*) St Martin.

***Midnight Come Again: A Kate Shugak Novel.** Dana Stabenow. 304p. 2000. text 23.95 (*0-312-20596-1*, Minotaur) St Martin.

Midnight Confessions. Karen Leabo. (Intimate Moments Ser.). 1996. per. 3.99 (*0-373-07734-3*, 1-07734-6) Silhouette.

Midnight Court. Brian Merriman. 72p. 1990. pap. 14.95 (*0-86278-205-8*) Dufour.

Midnight Court. Brian Merriman. 1987. pap. 16.95 (*0-85342-658-9*) Dufour.

Midnight Court. Frank O'Connor. LC 74-6477. (English Literature Ser.: No. 33). 1974. lib. bdg. 75.00 (*0-8383-1896-7*) M S G Haskell Hse.

Midnight Court: Cuirt an Mhean-Oiche. 3rd ed. Brian Merriman. LC 96-111122. 1990. pap. 7.95 (*0-85342-244-3*) Dufour.

Midnight Court & the Adventures of a Luckless Fellow. Brian Merriman. Tr. by Percy A. Ussher from GAE. LC 75-28825. (Illus.). 80p. reprint ed. 24.50 (*0-404-13817-9*) AMS Pr.

Midnight Cowboy. Adrianne Lee. LC 96-3539. (Intrigue Ser.). 250p. 1996. per. 3.50 (*0-373-22354-4*, 1-22354-4) Harlequin Bks.

Midnight Cry: A Defense of William Miller & the Millerites. Francis D. Nichol. LC 72-8249. reprint ed. 52.00 (*0-404-11003-7*) AMS Pr.

Midnight Dancers. large type ed. Anne Maybury. LC 91-8483. 498p. 1991. reprint ed. lib. bdg. 20.95 (*1-56054-160-1*) Thorndike Pr.

***Midnight Diaries.** Boris Yeltsin. 2000. audio compact disk 34.95 (*1-56511-413-2*, Pub. by HighBridge) Penguin Putnam.

***Midnight Diaries.** Boris Yeltsin. (Illus.). 2000. 26.00 (*1-58648-011-1*) PublicAffairs NY.

Midnight Diary. R. L. Stine, pseud & Austin Fowler. (Fear Street Ser.). (YA). (gr. 7 up). 1984. per. 1.75 (*0-671-00876-5*) PB.

Midnight Doll. Maggie Glenn. (Illus.). 32p. (J). (gr. 1-3). 1997. 19.95 (*0-09-176218-9*, Pub. by Hutchnson) Trafalgar.

***Midnight Dreams.** Kayla Perrin. 1999. mass mkt. 4.99 (*1-58314-044-1*) BET Bks.

Midnight Dreary: The Mysterious Death of Edgar Allan Poe. John E. Walsh. LC 98-24043. (Illus.). 180p. 1998. 23.00 (*0-8135-2605-1*) Rutgers U Pr.

Midnight Dreary: The Mysterious Death of Edgar Allen Poe. John Evangelist Walsh. pap. 14.95 (*0-312-22732-9*) St Martin.

Midnight Economist. William R. Allen. 1996. pap. text 24.95 (*0-913878-57-X*) T Horton & Dghts.

Midnight Economist: Meditations on Truth & Public Policy. William R. Allen. LC 89-11242. 300p. (C). 1989. pap. 19.95 (*1-55815-055-2*) ICS Pr.

***Midnight Enchantment.** Nancy Gideon. 273p. 1999. pap. 8.50 (*1-893896-04-8*) Ima Jinn.

Midnight Examiner. William Kotzwinkle. 227p. 1997. pap. 12.95 (*1-56924-777-3*) Marlowe & Co.

***Midnight Fantasies.** Kimberly Raye. 400p. 2000. pap. 5.99 (*0-505-52392-2*, Love Spell) Dorchester Pub Co.

Midnight Fantasy. Jasmine Cresswell. LC 96-2429. (Temptation Ser.). 219p. 1996. per. 3.50 (*0-373-25674-4*, 1-25674-2) Harlequin Bks.

***Midnight Fantasy.** Ann Major. (Desire Ser.: Bk. 1304). 2000. mass mkt. 3.99 (*0-373-76304-2*, 1-76304-4) Silhouette.

***Midnight Farm.** (gr. k-3). 2000. per. 6.99 (*0-689-83888-3*) Aladdin.

Midnight Farm. Reeve Lindbergh. (J). 1995. 11.19 (*0-606-07869-X*) Turtleback.

Midnight Farm. Simon & Schuster Staff. LC 96-25568. (Illus.). 40p. (J). (ps-3). 1997. pap. 16.00 (*0-689-81237-X*) S&S Childrens.

Midnight Fire. Madeline Baker. 448p. 1996. mass mkt. 5.99 (*0-8439-4056-5*, Leisure Bks) Dorchester Pub Co.

Midnight Fire. Linda Ladd. 384p. 1991. mass mkt. 4.50 (*0-380-75696-X*, Avon Bks) Morrow Avon.

Midnight Fire, 1. Madeline Baker. 448p. 1999. reprint ed. mass mkt. 5.99 (*0-8439-4590-7*, Leisure Bks) Dorchester Pub Co.

***Midnight Fox.** (J). 1999. 9.95 (*1-56137-667-1*) Novel Units.

Midnight Fox. Betsy C. Byars. (Storybooks Ser.). (Illus.). 160p. (J). (gr. 3-7). 1981. pap. 4.99 (*0-14-031450-4*, PuffinBks) Peng Put Young Read.

Midnight Fox. Betsy C. Byars. (J). 1981. 9.09 (*0-606-01689-9*, Pub. by Turtleback) Demco.

Midnight Fox: A Study Guide. Estelle Kleinman. Ed. by J. Friedland & R. Kessler. (Novel-Ties Ser.). (J). (gr. 3-5). 1998. pap. text, student ed. 15.95 (*0-7675-0310-4*) Lrn Links.

Midnight Fridge. Bruce Glassman. LC 97-38431. (Illus.). 32p. (J). (ps-3). 1998. 16.95 (*1-56711-801-1*, Blackbirch Picturebk) Blackbirch.

Midnight Fright: A Collection of Ghost Stories. Watermill Press Staff. (J). (gr. 4-7). 1997. pap. 2.95 (*0-89375-405-6*) Troll Communs.

Midnight Frolic: A Ziegfeld Girl's True Story. Marcelle Earle & Arthur C. Homme. LC 99-71183. (Illus.). x, 312p. 1999. pap. 16.95 (*0-9671916-0-2*, 100) Twin Oaks NJ.

***Midnight Gamble.** Nancy Gideon. 288p. 2000. pap. 9.95 (*1-893896-14-5*) Ima Jinn.

Midnight Game see Strange Matter

Midnight Garden. Ed. by Ginny L. Ballor & Carrie Neumann. 40p. (Orig.). (C). 1996. pap. 3.00 (*1-882294-14-9*) Green Gate.

Midnight Ghosts. Emma Fischel. (Illustrated Spinechillers Ser.). (Illus.). 48p. (J). (gr. 4 up). 1991. lib. bdg. 13.95 (*0-88110-521-X*, Usborne) EDC.

Midnight Ghosts. Emma Fischel. (Illustrated Spinechillers Ser.). (Illus.). 48p. (J). (gr. 4-7). 1992. pap. 5.95 (*0-7460-0651-9*, Usborne) EDC.

***Midnight Hand.** Stewart. 2000. pap. 6.95 (*0-440-86348-1*, Pub. by Transworld Publishers Ltd) Trafalgar.

Midnight Heiress. Kate Frederick. 384p. 1989. mass mkt. 3.95 (*0-8217-2690-0*, Zebra Kensgtn) Kensgtn Pub Corp.

Midnight Heiress. large type ed. Kate Frederick. 592p. 1996. 27.99 (*0-7089-3540-0*) Ulverscroft.

Midnight Horse. Michelle Bates. (gr. 4-8). 1997. pap. text 3.95 (*0-7460-2486-X*, Usborne) EDC.

Midnight Horse. Michelle Bates. 112p. (J). (gr. 4-8). 1998. lib. bdg. 11.95 (*0-88110-907-X*) EDC.

Midnight Horse. Sid Fleischman. (J). 1995. pap. 4.99 (*0-440-91271-7*) BDD Bks Young Read.

Midnight Horse. Sid Fleischman. 96p. (J). (gr. 4-7). 1992. pap. 4.50 (*0-440-40614-5*) Dell.

Midnight Horse. Sid Fleischman. LC 89-23441. (Illus.). 84p. (J). (gr. 4-7). 1990. 16.00 (*0-688-09441-4*, Grenwillow Bks) HarpC Child Bks.

Midnight Horse. Sid Fleischman. 1990. 9.09 (*0-606-00887-X*, Pub. by Turtleback) Demco.

Midnight Hour. Jillian James. 1999. mass mkt. 3.99 (*1-85487-598-1*, Pub. by Scarlet Bks) London Brdge.

Midnight Hour. Karen Robards. LC 98-35730. 368p. 1999. 24.95 (*0-385-31971-1*) Delacorte.

Midnight Hour. Karen Robards. 454p. 1999. mass mkt. 6.99 (*0-440-22504-3*) Dell.

Midnight Hour. Karen Robards. LC 99-19339. (Wheeler Large Print Book Ser.). 1999. write for info. (*1-56895-719-X*, Wheeler) Wheeler Pub.

***Midnight Hour.** Mary Saums. 188p. 2000. 24.50 (*1-57072-107-6*, Silver Dagger); pap. 15.00 (*1-57072-123-8*, Silver Dagger) Overmountain Pr.

***Midnight Hour: As America Faces Its Final Crisis, the Choices Become Intensely Personal.** Celeste P. Walker & Eric Stoffle. Ed. by Jerry T. Thomas. LC 98-51965. 320p. 1999. pap. 12.99 (*0-8163-1698-8*) Pacific Pr Pub Assn.

Midnight Hour Encores. Bruce Brooks. LC 86-45035. 288p. (YA). (gr. 7 up). 1986. 14.00 (*0-06-020709-4*) HarpC Child Bks.

Midnight Hour Encores. Bruce Brooks. LC 86-45035. (Trophy Keypoint Bk.). 272p. (YA). (gr. 12 up). 1988. mass mkt. 4.95 (*0-06-447021-0*, HarpTrophy) HarpC Child Bks.

Midnight House & Other Tales. William F. Harvey. Ed. by R. Reginald & Douglas A. Menville. LC 75-46275. (Supernatural & Occult Fiction Ser.). 1976. reprint ed. lib. bdg. 21.95 (*0-405-08133-2*) Ayer.

Midnight Howl: Intermediate Level. Robin Bullock. 72p. 1997. pap. 11.95 (*0-7866-2072-2*, 96006) Mel Bay.

Midnight Ice. Cathie Linz. (Desire Ser.). 1994. per. 2.99 (*0-373-05846-2*, 5-05846-6) Silhouette.

Midnight in Paris. Francine Mandeville. (Lucky in Love Ser.: No. 9). 320p. 1992. mass mkt. 3.99 (*0-8217-3865-8*, Zebra Kensgtn) Kensgtn Pub Corp.

***Midnight in Ruby Bayou.** Elizabeth Lowell. LC 00-29198. 400p. 2000. 24.00 (*0-380-97405-3*, Wm Morrow) Morrow Avon.

***Midnight in Ruby Bayou.** large type ed. Elizabeth Lowell. 592p. 2000. 24.00 (*0-06-019740-4*) HarpC.

***Midnight in Savannah.** Darwin Porter. 500p. 2000. pap. 14.95 (*0-9668030-1-9*, Pub. by Georgia Literary) Bookazine Co Inc.

Midnight in Sicily: On Art, Feed, History, Travel, & la Cosa Nostra. Peter Robb. LC 97-41778. 326p. 1998. 25.95 (*0-571-19932-1*) Faber & Faber.

Midnight in Sicily: On Art, Feed, History, Travel, & la Cosa Nostra. Peter Robb. LC 98-41397. 1999. pap. 13.00 (*0-375-70458-2*) Vin Bks.

Midnight in the Cemetery. Cheryl Harness. LC 97-34552. (Illus.). 29p. (J). (gr. k-3). 1999. 16.00 (*0-689-80873-9*) S&S Bks Yung.

Midnight in the Century. Victor Serge. Tr. by Richard Greeman from FRE. 284p. 12.95 (*0-904613-95-X*) Writers & Readers.

Midnight in the Dollhouse. Marjorie F. Stover. 128p. (J). (gr. 4-6). 1992. pap. 2.95 (*0-590-44924-9*) Scholastic Inc.

Midnight in the Garden of Good & Evil. John Berendt. 35.00 (*0-679-44944-2*) Discovery.

Midnight in the Garden of Good & Evil. John Berendt. 1998. 25.00 (*0-676-54681-1*) Random.

Midnight in the Garden of Good & Evil: A Savannah Story. John Berendt. LC 93-3955. 400p. 1994. 25.00 (*0-679-42922-0*) Random.

Midnight in the Garden of Good & Evil: A Savannah Story. John Berendt. 386p. 1999. pap. 12.00 (*0-679-75152-1*) Vintage Publng.

Midnight in the Garden of Good & Evil: A Savannah Story. large type ed. John Berendt. 400p. 1995. pap. 20.00 (*0-679-76283-3*) Random Hse Lrg Prnt.

Midnight in the Mountains. Julie Lawson. LC 98-85282. (Illus.). 32p. (J). (gr. k-3). 1998. 14.95 (*1-55143-113-0*) Orca Bk Pubs.

Midnight Is a Lonely Place. large type ed. Barbara Erskine. LC 94-27311. 647p. 1994. lib. bdg. 24.95 (*0-8161-7479-2*, G K Hall Lrg Type) Mac Lib Ref.

Midnight Is a Place. Joan Aiken. 288p. (J). (gr. 4-7). 1993. pap. 2.95 (*0-590-45496-X*) Scholastic Inc.

Midnight Is a Place. Joan Aiken. (J). 1974. 8.05 (*0-606-05466-9*, Pub. by Turtleback) Demco.

Midnight Is Mine. large type ed. Leila Mackinlay. 1991. 27.99 (*0-7089-2540-5*) Ulverscroft.

Midnight Jewels. Jayne Ann Krentz. 384p. 1992. mass mkt. 4.99 (*0-445-36373-8*); mass mkt. 6.99 (*0-446-36373-1*, Pub. by Warner Bks) Little.

Midnight Jewels. Jayne Ann Krentz. 384p. 1998. mass mkt. 3.99 (*0-446-60684-7*, Pub. by Warner Bks) Little.

Midnight Jewels. Tavi White. 285p. 1992. 18.95 (*1-56062-187-7*) CIS Comm.

Midnight Jewels. large type ed. Jayne Ann Krentz. LC 96-38765. (Star-Romance Ser.). 391p. 1997. 23.95 (*0-7862-0909-7*) Five Star.

Midnight Journeys. Ed. by Bill Allen & Davi Dee. (Illus.). ii, 87p. 1995. pap. 9.95 (*1-893816-00-1*) Ozark Tri.

***Midnight Journeys.** Vicki Campbell-Crystal. 1999. pap. write for info. (*1-58235-229-1*) Watermrk Pr.

Midnight Kiss. Rebecca York. (Intrigue Ser.: 273). 1994. per. 2.99 (*0-373-22273-4*) Harlequin Bks.

***Midnight Kisses.** Kimberly Raye. (Time of Your Life Ser.). 400p. 2000. mass mkt. 5.99 (*0-505-52361-2*, Love Spell) Dorchester Pub Co.

Midnight Knocking at the Door. Tony Moffeit. (Illus.). 46p. 1998. 5.00 (*1-889289-50-7*) Ye Olde Font Shoppe.

An Asterisk (*) at the beginning of an entry indicates that the title is appearing for the first time.

Midnight Lady. Rosemary Rogers. LC 97-93179. 390p. 1997. mass mkt. 6.99 (*0-380-78605-2*, Avon Bks) Morrow Avon.

Midnight Lemonade. large type ed. Ann Goethe. LC 93-19762. 455p. 1993. lib. bdg. 22.95 (*1-56054-768-5*) Thorndike Pr.

Midnight Lion - Gustav Adolf. William Dallmann. 60p. 1997. reprint ed. pap. 3.50 (*1-891469-01-0*) Repristination.

Midnight Lord. Marlene Suson. 384p. (Orig.). 1995. mass mkt. 4.99 (*0-380-77852-1*, Avon Bks) Morrow Avon.

Midnight Louie's Pet Detectives. Ed. by Carole Nelson Douglas. LC 98-12431. 1998. 23.95 (*0-312-86435-3*, Pub. by Forge NYC) St Martin.

***Midnight Louie's Pet Detectives.** Carole Nelson Douglas. 352p. 2000. mass mkt. 6.99 (*0-8125-7901-1*) Tor Bks.

Midnight Lynching. large type ed. Terry Murphy. 256p. pap. 18.99 (*0-7089-5433-2*) Ulverscroft.

***Midnight Magic.** Avi. LC 98-50192. (Illus.). 192p. (YA). (gr. 5-9). 1999. 15.95 (*0-590-36035-3*, Pub. by Scholastic Inc) Penguin Putnam.

***Midnight Magic.** Gwynne Forster. 2000. pap. 8.95 (*1-58571-019-9*, 909-100, Pub. by Genesis Press) BookWorld.

Midnight Magic. Amy Gordon. LC 94-34967. (Illus.). 64p. (J). (gr. 1-5). 1997. 12.95 (*0-8167-3660-X*) BrdgeWater.

Midnight Magic. Amy Gordon. LC 94-34967. (Illus.). 64p. (J). (gr. 1-4). 1995. pap. 2.95 (*0-8167-3661-8*, Little Rainbow) Troll Communs.

Midnight Magic. Betina Krahn. 1995. pap. 4.99 (*0-8217-4994-3*) NAL.

Midnight Magic: Selected Short Stories of Bobbie Ann Mason. Bobbie Ann Mason. LC 97-36369. 320p. 1999. 25.00 (*0-88001-595-0*) HarpC.

***Midnight Magic: Selected Stories of Bobbie Ann Mason.** Intro. & Selected by Bobbie A. Mason. LC 97-36369. 301p. 1999. pap. 16.00 (*0-88001-657-4*) HarpC.

Midnight Man. Berlie Doherty. LC 98-3457. (Illus.). 32p. (J). (gr. k-3). 1998. 15.99 (*0-7636-0700-2*) Candlewick Pr.

***Midnight Man.** Loren D. Estleman. 288p. 2000. per. 14.00 (*0-7434-0002-X*, Pub. by ibooks) S&S Trade.

Midnight Man. Barbara Faith. (Intimate Moments Ser.). 1994. per. 3.50 (*0-373-07544-8*, 5-07544-5) Silhouette.

Midnight Man. Jack Higgins. 1996. mass mkt. 6.99 (*0-425-15731-8*) Berkley Pub.

***Midnight Man.** Stephen Laws. 264p. 2000. 35.00 (*0-9675157-1-8*); pap. write for info. (*0-9675157-2-6*, Silver Salamander Pr) Darkside.

Midnight Marquee Actors Series: Boris Karloff. Ed. by Gary J. Svehla & Susan Svehla. (Illus.). 320p. (Orig.). 1996. pap. 20.00 (*1-887664-07-6*) Midnght Marquee Pr.

***Midnight Mask: A Lover's Kiss.** Maria Greene. (Ballad Romances Ser.). 2000. mass mkt. 5.50 (*0-8217-6869-7*, Zebra Kensgtn) Kensgtn Pub Corp.

Midnight Masque. Jenna Ryan. (Intrigue Ser.). 1993. per. 2.99 (*0-373-22251-3*, 1-22251-2) Harlequin Bks.

Midnight Masquerade. Shirlee Busbee. 464p. 1988. mass mkt. 5.50 (*0-380-75210-7*, Avon Bks) Morrow Avon.

Midnight Masquerade. Meg-Lynn Roberts. 320p. 1996. mass mkt. 3.99 (*0-8217-4336-8*, Zebra Kensgtn) Kensgtn Pub Corp.

Midnight Masquerade. large type ed. Shirlee Busbee. (General Ser.). 606p. 1989. lib. bdg. 21.95 (*0-8161-4753-1*, G K Hall Lrg Type) Mac Lib Ref.

Midnight Mass. Paul Bowles. LC 81-4803. 176p. 1991. reprint ed. 17.50 (*0-87685-477-3*); reprint ed. pap. 12.50 (*0-87685-476-5*) Black Sparrow.

***Midnight Math.** Illus. by Peter Ledwon & Marilyn Mets. LC 99-37167. 32p. (J). (gr. 1-5). 2001. 15.95 (*0-8234-1530-9*) Holiday.

Midnight Matinee. R. J. Williams. LC 96-96124. (Illus.). 65p. (Orig.). (C). 1996. pap. 6.50 (*0-9652226-0-8*) Borderline Arts.

Midnight Meal & Other Essays about Doctors, Patients, & Medicine. Jerome Lowenstein. LC 96-26159. 144p. 1997. 18.00 (*0-300-06816-9*) Yale U Pr.

Midnight Meditations. 1998. pap. 9.99 (*0-8341-9833-9*) Lillenas.

Midnight Mimi. unabridged ed. Marie-Louise Gay. LC 95-150226. (Illus.). 32p. (J). (gr. k up). 1994. 11.95 (*0-7737-2815-5*) STDK.

***Midnight Mistress.** Ruth Owen. (Meet Me at Midnight Ser.). 320p. 2000. mass mkt. 5.99 (*0-553-57746-8*) Bantam.

Midnight Moods. Edmund E. Wells. (Orig.). pap. 1.00 (*0-686-30402-0*) WOS.

Midnight Moon. Stobie Piel. 368p. 1998. mass mkt. 5.50 (*0-505-52268-3*, Love Spell) Dorchester Pub Co.

Midnight Moon. Mildred Riley. 1995. mass mkt. 4.99 (*0-7860-0200-X*, Pinncle Kensgtn) Kensgtn Pub Corp.

Midnight Movies. rev. ed. J. Hoberman & Jonathan Rosenbaum. (Quality Paperbacks Ser.). (Illus.). 360p. 1991. reprint ed. pap. 14.95 (*0-306-80433-6*) Da Capo.

***Midnight Murder.** large type ed. John Morgan. 312p. 2000. pap. 18.99 (*0-7089-5680-7*, Linford) Ulverscroft.

Midnight Musings of Family Therapist. Carl A. Whitaker. 1989. 27.95 (*0-393-70084-4*) Norton.

Midnight Noon. Carol F. Laque. (Orig.). 1995. pap. 15.00 (*0-9619532-2-5*) Circumference Pr.

Midnight Oil: Work, Energy, War, 1973-1992. (Midnight Notes Collective Ser.). 333p. Date not set. 10.00 (*0-936756-96-9*) Autonomedia.

Midnight on Julia Street. Ciji Ware. 470p. 1999. mass mkt. 6.99 (*0-449-00187-3*, GM) Fawcett.

Midnight on the Farm. unabridged ed. Stephen E. Hume. (Illus.). 24p. (J). (ps-3). 1996. pap. 8.95 (*0-7737-5725-2*) STDK.

Midnight on the Moon. Mary Pope Osborne. (Magic Tree House Ser.: No. 8). (Illus.). (J). (gr. k-3). 1996. pap. 3.99 (*0-679-86374-5*) McKay.

Midnight on the Moon. Mary Pope Osborne. (Magic Tree House Ser.: No. 8). (Illus.). (J). (gr. k-3). 1996. lib. bdg. 11.99 (*0-679-96374-X*) McKay.

Midnight on the Moon. Mary Pope Osborne. (Magic Tree House Ser.: No. 8). (Illus.). (J). (gr. k-3). 1996. 9.84 (*0-606-10876-9*, Pub. by Turtleback) Demco.

Midnight on Your Left. John Godfrey. 1988. per. 7.50 (*0-935724-31-1*) Figures.

***Midnight Panther Vol. 1: I'll Love You to Death.** Yu Asagiri. 160p. 1998. pap. 15.95 (*1-56219-908-0*, CMX 06071) Central Pk Media.

***Midnight Panther Vol. 2: Feline Fanatics.** Yu Asagiri. (Illus.). 160p. 1999. pap. 15.95 (*1-56219-914-5*, CMX 06072) Central Pk Media.

***Midnight Panther Vol. 3: School Daze Yearbook.** Yu Asagiri. (Illus.). 120p. 1999. pap. 15.95 (*1-56219-915-3*, CMX 06073) Central Pk Media.

***Midnight Panther Vol. 4: Feudal Fantasy.** Yu Asagiri. (Illus.). 160p. 1999. pap. 15.95 (*1-56219-916-1*, CMX 06074) Central Pk Media.

Midnight Peril. Vicki Andrews. LC 98-208439. 247p. 1998. pap. 10.95 (*1-885478-27-5*, Pub. by Genesis Press) BookWorld.

Midnight Phone Calls. Eric Weiner. (Clue Ser.: No. 5). 112p. (J). (gr. 3-6). 1994. pap. 3.50 (*0-590-47804-4*) Scholastic Inc.

Midnight Phone Calls. Eric Weiner. (Clue Ser.: No. 5). (J). (gr. 3-6). 1994. 9.09 (*0-606-09611-6*, Pub. by Turtleback) Demco.

Midnight Piano Moods. Matt Dennis. pap. 12.95 (*0-943748-29-1*) Ekay Music.

Midnight Pillow Fight. Jan Ormerod. LC 92-53011. (Illus.). 32p. (J). (ps up). 1993. 14.95 (*1-56402-169-6*) Candlewick Pr.

Midnight Play. Kveta Pacovska. Tr. by Andrew Clements from GER. LC 94-26546.Tr. of Mitternacht Spiel. (Illus.). 48p. (J). (gr. k-3). 1994. 28.00 (*1-55858-252-5*, Pub. by North-South Bks NYC) Chronicle Bks.

Midnight Play. Kveta Pacovska. LC 93-16258.Tr. of Mitternacht Spiel. (Illus.). (J). (ps-8). 1993. 15.95 (*0-88708-317-X*, Picture Book Studio) S&S Childrens.

Midnight Plays. Leon Katz. 265p. 1992. 23.95 (*1-881053-00-8*); pap. 12.95 (*1-881053-01-6*) Wavecrest Bks.

Midnight Pleasures. Robert Bloch. 1991. pap. 3.95 (*0-8125-1574-9*, Pub. by Tor Bks) St Martin.

***Midnight Pleasures.** Eloisa James. 400p. 2000. 19.95 (*0-385-33361-7*) Delacorte.

Midnight Plumber. Maurice Procter. 1996. 19.50 (*0-7451-8682-3*, Black Dagger) Chivers N Amer.

Midnight Prey: Lawman. Caroline Burnes. (Intrigue Ser.). 1997. per. 3.75 (*0-373-22409-5*, 1-2409-6) Harlequin Bks.

Midnight Promise. Hebby Roman. 352p. 1998. mass mkt. 4.99 (*0-8217-6003-3*, Zebra Kensgtn) Kensgtn Pub Corp.

***Midnight Promises: (Conveniently Wed)** Eileen Wilks. (Intimate Moments Ser.: No. 982). 2000. per. 4.50 (*0-373-07982-6*, 1-07982-1) Harlequin Bks.

Midnight Raccoon Alarm. Jerry D. Thomas. LC 98-47397. (Great Stories for Kids Ser.). (J). 1999. 14.99 (*0-8163-1697-X*) Pacific Pr Pub Assn.

Midnight Raider. Shelly Thacker. 384p. (Orig.). 1992. mass mkt. 4.50 (*0-380-76293-5*, Avon Bks) Morrow Avon.

Midnight Raiders: The Story of the Allman Brothers Band. Scott Freeman. 1996. pap. 12.95 (*0-614-12555-3*) Little.

Midnight Rain. Elizabeth Turner. 384p. (Orig.). 1994. mass mkt. 4.50 (*0-380-77371-6*, Avon Bks) Morrow Avon.

Midnight Rainbow. Linda Howard. 1992. mass mkt. 4.59 (*0-373-48240-X*, 5-48240-1) Harlequin Bks.

Midnight Rainbow. Linda Howard. (Mira Bks.). 1996. per. 5.50 (*1-55166-153-5*, 0-66153-8, Mira Bks) Harlequin Bks.

***Midnight Rainbow.** large type ed. Donna Baker. LC 99-14746. 1999. pap. 25.95 (*0-7838-8618-7*, G K Hall Lrg Type) Mac Lib Ref.

***Midnight Redeemer.** Nancy Gideon. 2000. pap. 9.95 (*1-893896-17-X*) Ima Jinn.

Midnight Rescue. Adapted by C. Archer. LC 95-13160. (Christy Fiction Ser.: Vol. 4). 128p. (J). (gr. 5-9). 1995. mass mkt. 4.99 (*0-8499-3689-6*) Tommy Nelson.

Midnight Rescue. Lois W. Johnson. LC 96-45763. (Riverboat Adventures Ser.: No. 3). 176p. (J). (gr. 3-7). 1996. pap. 5.99 (*1-55661-353-9*) Bethany Hse.

***Midnight Ride.** Ed. by Bill Randles et al. (Illus.). 288p. 2000. pap. 14.99 (*1-885831-08-0*) Proclaim Pubng.

***Midnight Ride of Paul Revere.** Henry Wadsworth Longfellow. LC 99-54540. (Illus.). 32p. (J). (gr. 1-4). 2000. 16.95 (*0-7922-7674-4*, Pub. by Natl Geog) S&S Trade.

Midnight Ride of Thomas the Tank Engine. Reverend Wilbert V. Awdry. LC 93-26587. (Illus.). 16p. (J). (ps-3). 1994. pap. 5.99 (*0-679-85643-9*, Pub. by Random Bks Yng Read) Random.

Midnight Rider. Kat Martin. 372p. 1996. mass mkt. 5.99 (*0-312-95774-2*) St Martin.

Midnight Rider. Kat Martin. LC 97-47732. 1998. 24.95 (*0-7862-1380-9*) Thorndike Pr.

Midnight Rider. Laura Pender. 1994. per. 2.99 (*0-373-22280-7*, 1-22280-1) Harlequin Bks.

Midnight Rider. Krista Ruepp. Tr. by J. Alison James. LC 95-12321. (Illus.). 64p. (J). (gr. 2-4). 1995. 13.95 (*1-55858-494-3*, Pub. by North-South Bks NYC); lib. bdg. 13.88 (*1-55858-495-1*, Pub. by North-South Bks NYC) Chronicle Bks.

Midnight Rider. Krista Ruepp. Tr. by J. Alison James. LC 95-12321. (Illus.). 64p. (J). (gr. 2-4). 1995. pap. 5.95 (*1-55858-620-2*, Pub. by North-South Bks NYC) Chronicle Bks.

Midnight Rider Takes a Bride. Christine Rimmer. 1997. per. 3.50 (*0-373-76101-5*, 1-76101-4) Silhouette.

Midnight Riders: The Story of the Allman Brothers Band. Scott Freeman. 368p. 1996. pap. 13.95 (*0-316-29452-7*) Little.

***Midnight Robber.** Nalo Hopkinson. LC 99-43008. 336p. 2000. mass mkt. 13.95 (*0-446-67560-1*, Aspect) Warner Bks.

***Midnight Room.** Richard Montanari. 2001. write for info. (*0-380-97593-9*, Wm Morrow) Morrow Avon.

Midnight Rose. Robin L. Hatcher. 448p. (Orig.). 1999. mass mkt. 5.99 (*0-8439-4504-4*) Dorchester Pub Co.

Midnight Rose: Special Edition. Patricia Hagan. 2000. mass mkt. 2.99 (*0-06-108233-3*, Harp PBks) HarpC.

***Midnight Salvage: Poems 1995-1998.** Adrienne Rich. LC 98-19293. 96p. 1999. pap. 22.00 (*0-393-04682-6*) Norton.

Midnight Salvage: Poems 1995-1998. Adrienne Rich. 96p. 1999. pap. 11.00 (*0-393-31984-9*, Norton Paperbks) Norton.

Midnight Sandwiches at the Mariposa Express. Beatriz Rivera. LC 97-22187. 118p. 1997. pap. 11.95 (*1-55885-216-6*) Arte Publico.

Midnight Secrets. Janelle Taylor. 512p. 1993. mass mkt. 4.99 (*0-8217-4181-0*, Zebra Kensgtn) Kensgtn Pub Corp.

Midnight Secrets. Janelle Taylor. 1995. pap. 5.99 (*0-8217-5280-4*) NAL.

***Midnight Shadow.** Laurel O'Donnell. (Zebra Historical Romance Ser.). 320p. 2000. mass mkt. 5.99 (*0-8217-6617-1*, Zebra Kensgtn) Kensgtn Pub Corp.

***Midnight Shadows.** Martha Mier. 4p. 1999. pap. 2.50 (*0-7390-0288-0*, 18519) Alfred Pub.

***Midnight Side: A Novel.** Natasha Mostert. LC 00-25931. 256p. 2001. 24.00 (*0-688-17385-3*, Wm Morrow) Morrow Avon.

Midnight Skies. Crystal Barouche. (Arabesque Ser.). 352p. 1997. mass mkt. 4.99 (*0-7860-0465-7*, Pinncle Kensgtn) Kensgtn Pub Corp.

Midnight Sky. Stephen B. Castleberry & Susie L. Castleberry. (Farm Mystery Ser.). 160p. (YA). 1998. pap. 7.50 (*1-891907-06-9*) Castleberry.

Midnight Snack. Mercer Mayer. (Step into Reading Ser.: A Step 1 Book). (J). 1997. lib. bdg. 11.99 (*0-679-98706-1*, Pub. by Random Bks Yng Read) Random.

Midnight Snack. Mercer Mayer et al. LC 97-67476. (Step into Reading Ser.: A Step 1 Book). (Illus.). (J). (ps-3). 1997. pap. 3.99 (*0-679-88706-7*, Pub. by Random Bks Yng Read) Random.

Midnight Snack Cookbook. Christine Hibbard. (Illus.). 102p. (Orig.). 1983. pap. 8.00 (*0-930528-04-2*) Sassafras Pr.

Midnight Special. Ben Hunter. 1997. per. 18.00 (*0-671-01427-7*) PB.

***Midnight Special.** Larry Karp. 368p. 2001. 24.95 (*1-885173-51-2*, Pub. by Write Way) Midpt Trade.

Midnight Star. Catherine Coulter. 1986. mass mkt. 7.50 (*0-451-40446-7*, Onyx) NAL.

***Midnight Star.** large type ed. Catherine Coulter. LC 00-22867. 2000. 25.95 (*1-56895-862-5*) Wheeler Pub.

Midnight Stranger. Diana Whitney. (Intimate Moments Ser.). 1993. per. 3.50 (*0-373-07530-8*, 5-07530-4) Silhouette.

***Midnight Sun.** Lisa Tawn Bergren. LC 99-89444. (Northern Lights Ser.: Vol. 3). 384p. 2000. pap. 10.95 (*1-57856-113-2*) Waterbrook Pr.

Midnight Sun. Ramsey Campbell. 1992. mass mkt. 4.99 (*0-8125-1803-9*) Tor Bks.

Midnight Sun. Amanda Harte. 368p. 1999. mass mkt. 5.50 (*0-8439-4503-6*) Dorchester Pub Co.

***Midnight Sun.** Vella Munn. LC 99-45471. 1999. 24.95 (*0-7862-2244-1*) Mac Lib Ref.

Midnight Sun. Vasco Popa. Ed. by Stanley H. Barkan. Tr. by Branko Mikasinovich. (Review Chapbook Ser.: No. 28). (ENG & SER.). 48p. 1992. 15.00 (*0-89304-963-8*); pap. 5.00 (*0-89304-964-6*) Cross-Cultrl NY.

***Midnight Sun.** Elwood Reid. LC 00-22719. 288p. 2000. 23.95 (*0-385-49736-9*) Doubleday.

Midnight Sun: Mini Book. Vasco Popa. Ed. by Stanley H. Barkan. Tr. by Branko Mikasinovich. (Review Chapbook Ser.: No. 28). (ENG & SER.). 48p. 1992. 15.00 (*0-89304-965-4*); pap. 5.00 (*0-89304-966-2*) Cross-Cultrl NY.

Midnight Surrender. Nancy Gideon. 1995. mass mkt. 4.99 (*0-7860-0134-8*, Pinncle Kensgtn) Kensgtn Pub Corp.

Midnight Tales. Bram Stoker. Ed. by Peter Haining. LC 95-213085. (Illus.). 182p. 1995. pap. 22.95 (*0-7206-0971-2*, Pub. by P Owen Ltd) Dufour.

Midnight Tales. Bram Stoker. Ed. by Peter Haining. 182p. 1996. 30.00 (*0-7206-0777-9*, Pub. by P Owen Ltd) Dufour.

Midnight Tales: Seasonal Ghost Stories with Happy Endings. Lailee B. Van Dillen. Ed. by Antonia H. Ehlers. 138p. 1998. pap. 14.95 (*1-891165-07-0*) Sera Pub.

Midnight Teddies. Dana Kubick. (Little Book Cards Ser.). 32p. (J). (gr. 1-4). 1997. pap. text 3.29 (*0-7636-0217-5*) Candlewick Pr.

Midnight Temptation. Nancy Gideon. 384p. 1994. mass mkt. 4.99 (*0-7860-0054-6*, Pinncle Kensgtn) Kensgtn Pub Corp.

Midnight Tour: Cemetery Dance. Richard Laymon. 600p. 40.00 (*1-881475-40-9*) Cemetery Dance.

Midnight Train from Georgia. Glenda Sanders. (Temptation Ser.). 1996. per. 3.50 (*0-373-25703-1*, 1-25703-9) Harlequin Bks.

***Midnight Train Home.** Erika Tamar. LC 00-20355. (Illus.). 160p. (YA). (gr. 4-7). 2000. lib. bdg. 18.99 (*0-375-90159-0*, Pub. by Knopf Bks Yng Read) Random.

***Midnight Train Home.** Erika Tamar. LC 00-20355. (Illus.). 160p. (YA). (gr. 5-8). 2000. 16.95 (*0-375-80159-6*, Pub. by Knopf Bks Yng Read) Random.

Midnight Visit at Molly's House. Jirina Marton. (Illus.). 24p. (J). (ps-8). 1988. pap. 4.95 (*0-920303-98-6*, Pub. by Annick) Firefly Bks Ltd.

Midnight Waltz. Barbara Hazard. (Signet Regency Romance Ser.). 1999. mass mkt. 4.99 (*0-451-19813-1*) NAL.

Midnight Waltz. Jennifer Blake. 352p. 1995. reprint ed. 20.00 (*0-7278-4719-8*) Severn Hse.

Midnight Warrior. Iris Johansen. 384p. 1994. mass mkt. 6.99 (*0-553-29946-8*) Bantam.

Midnight Whispers. V. C. Andrews. 1992. 12.09 (*0-606-02201-5*, Pub. by Turtleback) Demco.

Midnight Whispers. large type ed. V. C. Andrews. LC 93-14808. 515p. 1993. lib. bdg. 23.95 (*0-8161-5655-7*, G K Hall Lrg Type) Mac Lib Ref.

Midnight Whispers. large type ed. V. C. Andrews. LC 93-14808. (Large Print Bks.). 515p. 1993. 19.95 (*0-8161-5656-5*, G K Hall Lrg Type) Mac Lib Ref.

Midnight Whispers, Vol. 5. V. C. Andrews. Ed. by Linda Marrow. 448p. 1992. mass mkt. 6.99 (*0-671-69516-9*) PB.

***Midnight Wilderness: Journeys in Alaska's Arctic National Wildlife Refuge.** Debbie Miller. LC 00-38039. 2000. pap. 14.95 (*0-88240-517-9*, Alaska NW Bks) Gr Arts Ctr Pub.

Midnight Wishes. Carla Cassidy. (Cheyenne Nights Ser.). 1997. per. 3.75 (*0-373-22415-X*, 1-22415-3) Harlequin Bks.

Midnights: A Year with the Wellfleet Police. Alec Wilkinson. 202p. 2000. pap. 12.95 (*1-886913-32-3*, Pub. by Ruminator Bks) Consort Bk Sales.

Midnight's Children. Salman Rushdie. 620p. 1995. 20.00 (*0-679-44462-9*) Knopf.

Midnight's Children. Salman Rushdie. 552p. (C). 1999. pap. 14.95 (*0-14-013270-8*) Viking Penguin.

***Midnight's Children 1980.** Salman Rushdie. 544p. 2000. pap. 15.95 (*0-14-028339-0*) Viking Penguin.

Midnight's Choice, Kate Thompson. 192p. (YA). 1999. 15.99 (*0-7868-0381-9*, Pub. by Hyperion) Time Warner.

Midnight's Choice. Kate Thompson. 240p. (J). 2000. pap. 5.99 (*0-7868-1266-4*, Pub. by Hyprn Ppbks) Little.

Midnight's Choice, No. 2. Kate Thompson. 192p. (J). 1999. lib. bdg. 16.49 (*0-7868-2329-1*, Pub. by Hyprn Child) Little.

Midnight's Daughter. Jesse Jones. 256p. 1992. mass mkt. 3.95 (*0-87067-324-6*, BH324) Holloway.

Midnight's Lady. Debra Falcon, pseud. 432p. 1995. mass mkt. 4.99 (*0-8217-0106-1*, Zebra Kensgtn); mass mkt. 4.99 (*0-7860-0106-2*, Pinncle Kensgtn) Kensgtn Pub Corp.

Midnights of the Soul: From Normandy to the Rhineland, the Personal War of a WWII Infantry Platoon Leader Told in Compelling & Bloody Details. William F. Arendt. LC 98-65169. (Illus.). 191p. 1998. pap. 11.90 (*0-9640235-1-2*) PRA.

***Midnight's Smiling.** large type ed. Alexandra Connor. 400p. 1999. 31.99 (*0-7089-4096-X*, Linford) Ulverscroft.

Midnite & Mark. Kathryn Weber. LC 83-8622. (Illus.). 64p. (Orig.). (J). (gr. 4-6). 1983. pap. 3.95 (*0-88100-021-3*) Ranch House Pr.

Midpoint & Other Poems. John Updike. 1969. 16.95 (*0-394-40383-5*) Knopf.

Midpoint Interpretation Simplified. Karen O. Savalan. LC 80-127755. 208p. 1978. 21.00 (*0-86690-155-8*, S1449-014) Am Fed Astrologers.

Midpoint Key to Chiron. Brooks. 98p. 1992. 13.00 (*0-86690-407-7*) Am Fed Astrologers.

Midpoint Love Simplified. Karen O. Savalan. 208p. 1980. 16.00 (*0-86690-156-6*, S1450-014) Am Fed Astrologers.

Midpoint Synastry Simplified. Karen O. Savalan. 192p. 1979. 15.00 (*0-86690-157-4*, S1451-014) Am Fed Astrologers.

Midquest: A Poem. Fred Chappell. LC 81-8474. 208p. 1981. pap. 16.95 (*0-8071-1580-0*) La State U Pr.

Midrange Computing's Top 25 Utilities. Ed. by Robin Klima. (Illus.). 448p. (Orig.). 1996. pap. 99.00 (*1-883884-35-7*, 564) Midrange Comput.

Midrasch Sifre Numeri: Voruntersuchungen zur Redaktionsgeschichte. Dagmar Borner-Klein. (Judentum und Umwelt Ser.: Bd. 39). (GER.). 104p. 1993. 31.80 (*3-631-45670-0*) P Lang Pubng.

Midrasch zur Eschatologie aus der Qumrangemeinde, 4QMidrEschat: Materielle Rekonstruktion, Textbestand, Gattung & Traditionsgeschichtliche Einordnung des durch 4Q174, Florilegium & 4Q177, Catena A, Reprasentierten Werkes aus den Qumranfunden. Annette Steudel. (Studies on the Texts of the Desert of Judah: No. 13). (GER.). xi, 237p. 1993. 113.50 (*90-04-09763-5*, NLG150) Brill Academic Pubs.

Midrash: An Introduction. Jacob Neusner. LC 89-18274. 256p. 1994. reprint ed. pap. text 25.00 (*1-56821-357-3*) Aronson.

Midrash: Rabbinic Lore. Harry Gersh & Robert L. Platzner. 64p. 1985. pap. 6.95 (*0-87441-412-1*) Behrman.

Midrash: The Search for a Contemporary Past. 2.00 (*0-686-99696-8*); pap. 3.00 (*0-686-96071-8*) USCJE.

Midrash & a Ma'aseh see Midrash & a Maaseh: An Anthology of Insights & Commentaries on the Weekly Torah Reading

Midrash & a Maaseh: An Anthology of Insights & Commentaries on the Weekly Torah Reading, 2 vols. A. Hanoch Teller & E. Marsi Tabak. Incl. Midrash & a Ma'aseh., **2 vols.** LC 96-32620. 408p. 1996. 43.95 (*1-881939-08-1*, Pub. by NYC Pub Co); Vol. II. Midrash & a Ma'aseh. LC 96-32620. 648p. 1996. boxed set (*1-881939-09-X*); 1996. 43.95 (*0-614-21720-2*) NYC Pub Co.

Midrash & Theory: Ancient Jewish Exegesis & Contemporary Literary Studies. David Stern. LC 96-1076. (Rethinking Theory Ser.). (Illus.). 160p. 1996. 49.95 (*0-8101-1122-5*) Northwestern U Pr.

M

Midrash & Theory: Ancient Jewish Exegesis & Contemporary Literary Studies. David Stern. (Rethinking Theory Ser.). 126p. 1998. pap. 19.95 (0-8101-1574-3) Northwestern U Pr.

Midrash Bet HaShem: The Alphabet. 3rd rev. ed. Shmuel Ben Aharon. (Illus.). 22p. 1986. pap. text. write for info. (0-9616488-1-3) Alef Bet Comns.

Midrash Criticism: Introduction & Appraisal. Charles L. Quarles. LC 97-37864. 176p. (C). 1997. 49.00 (0-7618-0924-4); pap. 27.50 (0-7618-0925-2) U Pr of Amer.

Midrash for Beginners. Edwin C. Goldberg. LC 96-4385. 96p. 1997. reprint ed. pap. 20.00 (1-56821-599-1) Aronson.

Midrash, Mishnah & Gemara: The Jewish Predilection for Justified Law. David W. Halivni. 176p. 1986. 35.95 (0-674-57370-6) HUP.

Midrash of Philo Vol. 1: The Oldest Recorded Midrash, Genesis II-XVII. Samuel Belkin. Ed. by Elazar Hurvitz. (HEB.). 1989. 49.50 (0-88125-149-6) Ktav.

Midrash on Proverbs. Tr. by Burton L. Visotzky from HEB. LC 91-22071. Vol. 27. 160p. (C). 1992. 37.00 (0-300-05107-7) Yale U Pr.

Midrash on Psalms, 2 vols. Tr. by William G. Braude. (Judaica Ser.: No. 13). 1959. 125.00 (0-300-00322-6) Yale U Pr.

Midrash Pesher of Habakkuk. William H. Brownlee. LC 76-30560. (Society of Biblical Literatur, Ser.: No. 24). 230p. reprint ed. pap. 71.30 (0-7837-5446-9, 204521100005) Bks Demand.

Midrash Rabbah, 10 vols., Set. 1999. reprint ed. 219.00 (0-900689-38-2) Soncino Pr.

Midrash Rabbah: Midrashim on the Pentateuch & the Five Scrolls with the Matnoth Kehunah Commentary, 2 vols., Set. deluxe ed. (ENG, HEB & YID.). 75.00 (0-87559-096-9) Shalom.

Midrash Tanhuma Vol. 1: Genesis, 2 vols. John T. Townsend. 800p. 1989. 69.50 (0-88125-087-2) Ktav.

Midrashic Comments on the Torah: Torah Thoughts for Sabbaths & Holidays. Abraham P. Bloch. 17.95 (0-88125-377-4) Ktav.

Midrashic Imagination: Jewish Exegesis, Thought, & History. Ed. by Michael Fishbane. LC 92-27070. 296p. (C). 1993. text 21.50 (0-7914-1521-X) State U NY Pr.

Midrashic Process: Tradition & Interpretation in Rabbinic Judaism. Irving Jacobs. LC 93-46182. 232p. (C). 1995. text 64.95 (0-521-46174-X) Cambridge U Pr.

Midrashim. David Curzon. (Review Jewish Writers Chapbook Ser.: No. 5). 1991. 15.00 (0-89304-347-8); pap. 5.00 (0-89304-348-6); audio 10.00 (0-685-49056-4); VHS 50.00 (0-685-49057-2) Cross-Cultrl NY.

Midrashim. limited ed. David Curzon. (Review Jewish Writers Chapbook Ser.: No. 5). 1991. 35.00 (0-685-49055-6) Cross-Cultrl NY.

Midrashim: Mini Book. David Curzon. (Review Jewish Writers Chapbook Ser.: No. 5). 1991. 15.00 (0-685-49053-X); pap. 5.00 (0-685-49054-8) Cross-Cultrl NY.

Midshipman Bolitho. Alexander Kent. LC 98-13529. (Richard Bolitho Novels Ser.: Vol. 1). 240p. 1998. pap. text 11.95 (0-935526-41-2) McBooks Pr.

Midshipman Bolitho & the Avenger. Alexander Kent. 1976. 19.95 (0-8488-1398-7) Amereon Ltd.

Midshipman Bolitho & the Avenger. Alexander Kent. 144p. 1990. reprint ed. lib. bdg. 25.95 (0-89966-732-5) Buccaneer Bks.

Midshipman in Gray. Ed. by R. Thomas Campbell. LC 97-23402. (Illus.). 220p. 1997. 24.95 (1-57249-061-6, Burd St Pr) White Mane Pub.

***Midshipman Quinn Collection: Four Complete Adventures.** Showell Styles. LC 99-66605. (Bethlehem Budget Bks.). (Illus.). 616p. (YA). (gr. 7 up). 1999. pap. 19.95 (1-883937-45-0, 45-0) Bethlehem ND.

Midshipman's Hope. David Feintuch. 400p. (Orig.). (J). 1994. reprint ed. mass mkt. 6.99 (0-446-60096-2, Pub. by Warner Bks) Little.

Midsommer Nights Dreame. William Shakespeare. Ed. by Patrick Tucker & Michael Holden. 166p. 1990. 95.00 (1-872680-00-3, Pub. by M H Pubns) St Mut.

Midsommer Nights Dreame. annot. ed. William Shakespeare. LC 97-9572. (Shakespeare Library). 192p. 1999. pap. 12.95 (1-55783-293-5) Applause Theatre Bk Pubs.

Midsommer Nights Dreame see New Variorum Edition of Shakespeare

Midsommer Nights Dreame: As It Hath Been Sundry Times Publikely Acted, by the Right Honourable, the Lord Chamberlaine His Servants. William Shakespeare. Ed. by T. O. Treadwell. LC 96-4595. (Shakespearean Originals Ser.). (C). 1996. pap. text 12.95 (0-13-355587-9) P-H.

Midstream: My Later Life. Helen A. Keller. LC 68-8063. (Illus.). 362p. 1969. reprint ed. lib. bdg. 59.50 (0-8371-0127-1, KELL, Greenwood Pr) Greenwood.

Midstream: My Later Life. Helen A. Keller. (American Biography Ser.). 362p. 1991. reprint ed. lib. bdg. write for info. (0-7812-8229-2) Rprt Serv.

Midstream: The Story of a Mother's Death & a Daughter's Renewal. Le Anne Schreiber. LC 96-17584. 320p. 1996. pap. 14.95 (1-55821-493-3) Lyons Pr.

Midsummer. Derek Walcott. LC 83-11563. 72p. 1984. pap. 10.00 (0-374-51863-7) FS&G.

Midsummer Bride. Louise Bergstrom. 1980. pap. 1.50 (0-373-58014-2) Harlequin Bks.

Midsummer Bride. Barbara L. Picard. (Illus.). 32p. (J). 1999. 16.95 (0-19-279879-0) OUP.

Midsummer Classic, 1993. Lee R. Schreiber. 112p. 1993. 24.95 (0-9638222-0-9) Maj Leag Baseball.

***Midsummer Lightning.** Kate Ivers. 304p. 2000. mass mkt. 5.99 (0-515-12884-8, Jove) Berkley Pub.

Midsummer Magic. Catherine Coulter. 1999. 26.00 (0-7278-5468-2, Pub. by Severn Hse) Chivers N Amer.

Midsummer Magic. large type ed. Juliet Gray. LC 94-9237. 190p. 1994. lib. bdg. write for info. (0-8161-5983-1, G K Hall Lrg Type) Mac Lib Ref.

Midsummer Magic. Catherine Coulter. (Historical Romance Ser.). 412p. 1998. reprint ed. mass mkt. 7.50 (0-451-40870-5, Topaz) NAL.

Midsummer Malice. M. D. Lake. (Peggy O'Neill Mystery Ser.). 256p. 1997. mass mkt. 5.99 (0-380-78759-8, Avon Bks) Morrow Avon.

Midsummer Moon. Laura Kinsale. 400p. 1987. reprint ed. mass mkt. 5.99 (0-380-75398-7, Avon Bks) Morrow Avon.

Midsummer Night. Mark Dunster. 22p. (Orig.). 1995. pap. 4.00 (0-89642-258-5) Linden Pubs.

Midsummer Night. Uwe Timm. Tr. by Peter Tegel from GER. LC 97-42140. 288p. 1998. 23.95 (0-8112-1372-2, Pub. by New Directions) Norton.

Midsummer Night. Uwe Timm. Tr. by Peter Tegel from GER. LC 97-42140. 288p. 2000. pap. 12.95 (0-8112-1420-6, Pub. by New Directions) Norton.

Midsummer Night Dream. Ed. by Cookson. 1991. pap. text. write for info. (0-582-07580-7, Pub. by Addison-Wesley) Longman.

***Midsummer Nightmare.** Kilworth. 2000. 26.95 (0-593-04029-5, Pub. by Transworld Publishers Ltd) Trafalgar.

Midsummer Nights: A Rock 'n' Roll Musical in Two Acts. Kevin Kuhn & Brian D. Leys. LC 98-191033. 92 p. 1996. write for info. (0-573-69514-8) S French Trade.

***Midsummer Night's Dream.** 1999. 11.95 (1-56137-519-5) Novel Units.

Midsummer Night's Dream. Bachman. (Shakespeare Ser.). 1995. pap., teacher ed. 6.99 (0-8442-5742-7) NTC Contemp Pub Co.

Midsummer Night's Dream. James Calderwood. LC 92-22796. (Twayne's New Critical Introduction to Shakespeare Ser.: No. 14). 224p. 1992. pap. 13.95 (0-8057-8734-8, Twayne) Mac Lib Ref.

***Midsummer Nights Dream.** Cass Foster. Ed. by Paul M. Howey. (Sixty-Minute Shakespeare Ser.). 75p. 2000. pap. 8.99 (1-877749-37-0) Five Star AZ.

Midsummer Night's Dream. Helen Hackett. (Writers & Their Works). (Illus.). 88p. (Orig.). 1997. pap. 18.95 (0-7463-0754-3, Pub. by Northcote House) Trans-Atl Phila.

Midsummer Night's Dream. Ed. by Judith M. Kennedy & Richard F. Kennedy. LC 99-21407. (Critical Tradition Ser.). 461p. (C). 1999. text 160.00 (0-485-81003-4, Pub. by Athlone Pr) Humanities.

Midsummer Night's Dream. Ed. by Markus & Jordan. 1993. text. write for info. (0-582-24590-7, Pub. by Addison-Wesley) Longman.

***Midsummer Night's Dream.** Barbara A. Mowat & Paul Werstine. 1999. per. 8.95 (0-671-04290-4) S&S Trade.

Midsummer Night's Dream. William Shakespeare. LC 81-19272. (Illustrated Classics Shakespeare Collection). 64p. 1994. pap. 4.95 (0-7854-0809-6, 40609) Am Guidance.

Midsummer Night's Dream. William Shakespeare. Ed. by John R. Brown. LC 81-19272. (Shakespeare Library). 192p. 1996. pap. 7.95 (1-55783-181-5) Applause Theatre Bk Pubs.

Midsummer Night's Dream. William Shakespeare. Ed. by David Bevington et al. LC 81-19272. (Classics Ser.). 144p. 1988. mass mkt. 4.95 (0-553-21300-8, Bantam Classics) Bantam.

Midsummer Night's Dream. William Shakespeare. Ed. by Alan Durband. (Shakespeare Made Easy Ser.). 1985. pap. 6.95 (0-8120-3584-4) Barron.

Midsummer Night's Dream. William Shakespeare. LC 81-19272. (Barron's Book Notes Ser.). 224p. 1985. pap. 2.95 (0-8120-3527-5) Barron.

***Midsummer Night's Dream.** William Shakespeare. (Literature Made Easy Ser.). 96p. (YA). 1999. pap. 4.95 (0-7641-0827-1) Barron.

Midsummer Night's Dream. William Shakespeare. (Illus.). 32p. (J). (gr. 2-4). 1996. 8.00 (1-85854-271-5) Brimax Bks.

Midsummer Night's Dream. William Shakespeare. Ed. by R. A. Foakes. LC 81-19272. (New Cambridge Shakespeare Ser.). 181p. 1985. text 44.95 (0-521-22194-3) Cambridge U Pr.

Midsummer Night's Dream. William Shakespeare. Ed. by R. A. Foakes. LC 81-19272. (New Cambridge Shakespeare Ser.). 181p. 1985. pap. text 11.95 (0-521-29389-8) Cambridge U Pr.

Midsummer Night's Dream. William Shakespeare. Ed. by Linda Buckle & Paul Kelley. LC 81-19272. (Cambridge School Shakespeare Ser.). (Illus.). 160p. (C). 1992. pap. 9.95 (0-521-40904-7) Cambridge U Pr.

Midsummer Night's Dream. William Shakespeare. Ed. by Trevor R. Griffiths. (Shakespeare in Production Ser.). (Illus.). 350p. (C). 1996. text 59.95 (0-521-44560-4); pap. text 19.95 (0-521-57565-6) Cambridge U Pr.

***Midsummer Night's Dream, Vol. 1.** William Shakespeare. 1999. pap. 4.95 (0-7910-4137-9) Chehalem.

Midsummer Night's Dream. William Shakespeare. (Illustrated Classic Book Ser.). (Illus.). 61p. (J). (gr. 3 up). 1998. pap. text 4.95 (1-56767-245-0) Educ Insights.

Midsummer Night's Dream. William Shakespeare. Ed. by Roma Gill. (Oxford School Shakespeare Ser.). (C). 1994. text 10.72 (0-669-40350-4) HM Trade Div.

Midsummer Night's Dream. William Shakespeare. Ed. by Ken Roy & Harriet Law. 1989. pap., student ed. 12.00 (0-7747-1267-8) Harcourt Schl Pubs.

Midsummer Night's Dream. William Shakespeare. Ed. by Alfred Alexander Evans. LC 68-97427. (London English Literature Ser.). 140 p. 1967. write for info. (0-340-07278-4) Hodder & Stought Ltd.

Midsummer Night's Dream. William Shakespeare. (YA). 1989. pap., student ed. 11.00 (0-03-031639-1) Holt R&W.

Midsummer Night's Dream. William Shakespeare. 1997. text 8.25 (0-03-051499-1) Holt R&W.

Midsummer Night's Dream. William Shakespeare. Ed. by Richard Adams. (J). 1990. pap. text 4.29 (0-582-01345-3, 78421) Longman.

Midsummer Night's Dream. William Shakespeare. Ed. by Roy Blatchford. (Literature Ser.). 1993. pap. 5.95 (0-582-08833-X, TG7664) Longman.

Midsummer Night's Dream. William Shakespeare. Ed. & Illus. by Diane Davidson. LC 83-12311. (Shakespeare on Stage Ser.: Vol. 5). 99p. (YA). (gr. 8-12). 1983. pap. 6.95 (0-934048-10-X) Lrn Links.

Midsummer Night's Dream. William Shakespeare. (Signet Classic Shakespeare Ser.). 208p. 1998. mass mkt. 3.95 (0-451-52696-1, Sig) NAL.

Midsummer Night's Dream. William Shakespeare. LC 81-19272. (Shakespeare Ser.). 184p. 1995. pap. 8.95 (0-8442-5741-9, 57419, Natl Textbk Co) NTC Contemp Pub Co.

***Midsummer Night's Dream.** William Shakespeare. 1999. 9.95 (1-56137-518-7) Novel Units.

Midsummer Night's Dream. William Shakespeare. Ed. by Peter Holland. LC 81-19272. (Oxford World's Classics Ser.). (Illus.). 284p. 1995. text 89.00 (0-19-812928-9) OUP.

Midsummer Night's Dream. William Shakespeare. Ed. by Thomas L. Berger. (Malone Society Reprints Ser.: Vol. 157). 80p. 1996. text 45.00 (0-19-729033-7) OUP.

Midsummer Night's Dream. William Shakespeare. Ed. by Peter Holland. (Oxford World's Classics Ser.). (Illus.). 284p. 1998. pap. 7.95 (0-19-283420-7) OUP.

***Midsummer Night's Dream.** William Shakespeare. (Big Works Collection). (Illus.). 1p. 1999. 29.95 (1-929142-00-5) One Page Bk.

Midsummer Night's Dream. William Shakespeare. Ed. by Paul Werstine & Barbara A. Mowat. LC 81-19272. (Folger Library General Reader's Shakespeare Ser.). (Illus.). 256p. 1993. per. 3.99 (0-671-72279-4, Folger Shake Ser) PB.

Midsummer Night's Dream. William Shakespeare. LC 81-19272. (Short Classics Ser.). (Illus.). 48p. (J). (gr. 4 up). 1983. pap. 7.45 (0-8172-2015-1) Raintree Steck-V.

Midsummer Night's Dream. William Shakespeare. Ed. by Harold F. Brooks. 1985. pap. 8.95 (0-416-17940-1) Routledge.

Midsummer Night's Dream. William Shakespeare. Ed. by Neil King. LC 81-19272. (Illustrated Shakespeare Ser.). (Illus.). 80p. 1995. pap. 17.95 (0-7487-0498-1, Pub. by S Thornes Pubs) Trans-Atl Phila.

Midsummer Night's Dream. William Shakespeare. Ed. by Dom Saliani. (Global Shakespeare Ser.). 1998. mass mkt. 11.95 (0-17-606617-9) S-W Pub.

Midsummer Night's Dream. William Shakespeare. LC 98-86158. 346p. 1999. text 39.95 (0-312-21822-2); pap. text 9.95 (0-312-16621-4) St Martin.

Midsummer Night's Dream. William Shakespeare. (Folger Library General Reader's Shakespeare Ser.). 1958. 9.09 (0-606-01078-5, Pub. by Turtleback) Demco.

Midsummer Night's Dream. William Shakespeare. (Shakespeare Made Easy Ser.). (J). 1985. 12.05 (0-606-01097-1, Pub. by Turtleback) Demco.

Midsummer Night's Dream. William Shakespeare. Ed. by John F. Andrews. LC 81-19272. (Everyman Shakespeare Ser.). 181p. 1993. pap. 3.95 (0-460-87246-X, Everyman's Classic Lib) Tuttle Pubng.

Midsummer Night's Dream. William Shakespeare. Ed. by A. L. Rowse. LC 84-5099. (Contemporary Shakespeare Ser.: Vol. I). 94p. (C). 1984. pap. text 3.45 (0-8191-3900-9) U Pr of Amer.

Midsummer Night's Dream. William Shakespeare. Ed. by Madeleine Doran. (Pelican Shakespeare Ser.). 130p. (YA). (gr. 9 up). 1959. pap. 3.95 (0-14-071418-9, Pelican Bks) Viking Penguin.

***Midsummer Night's Dream.** William Shakespeare. (Pelican Shakespeare Ser.). 128p. 2000. pap. 3.95 (0-14-071455-3, Pelican Bks) Viking Penguin.

Midsummer Night's Dream. William Shakespeare. (English Ser.). (C). 1999. mass mkt. 9.95 (0-17-443529-0) Wadsworth Pub.

Midsummer Night's Dream. William Shakespeare. (Classics Library). 88p. 1997. pap. 3.95 (1-85326-030-4, 0304WW, Pub. by Wrdsworth Edits) NTC Contemp Pub Co.

Midsummer Night's Dream. William Shakespeare & Sidney Homan. LC 70-15875. xvi, 54 p. 1970. write for info. (0-697-03910-2) Brown & Benchmark.

Midsummer Night's Dream. large type ed. William Shakespeare. LC 81-19272. 1991. pap. 24.95 (0-7089-4503-1, Charnwood) Ulverscroft.

Midsummer Night's Dream. William Shakespeare. LC 81-19272. (Thrift Editions Ser.). (Illus.). 80p. 1992. reprint ed. pap. 1.00 (0-486-27067-X) Dover.

Midsummer Night's Dream. William Shakespeare. 80p. 1999. reprint ed. pap. 6.95 (1-57002-108-2) Univ Publng Hse.

Midsummer Night's Dream. 2nd ed. William Shakespeare. (Illus.). 78p. 1993. pap. text 5.95 (0-19-585261-3) OUP.

Midsummer Night's Dream. 2nd ed. William Shakespeare. (English). 1979. pap. 11.95 (0-17-443606-8) Thomson Learn.

Midsummer Night's Dream. 2nd rev. ed. William Shakespeare. Ed. by Roma Gill. LC 81-19272. (Oxford School Shakespeare Ser.). (Illus.). 128p. (YA). (gr. 6 up). 1994. pap. text 7.95 (0-19-831975-4) OUP.

Midsummer Night's Dream. 3rd ed. William Shakespeare. Ed. by Harold F. Brooks. (Arden Shakespeare Ser.). 1979. mass mkt. 45.00 (0-416-17930-4, NO. 2629) Routledge.

Midsummer Night's Dream. 3rd ed. William Shakespeare. (English Ser.). (C). 1999. mass mkt. 45.00 (0-17-443562-2) Wadsworth Pub.

Midsummer Night's Dream: A One-Act Adaptation. William Shakespeare. LC 81-19272. (Illus.). 32p. (YA). (gr. 7 up). 1984. pap. 3.25 (0-88680-214-8) I E Clark.

Midsummer Night's Dream: A Unit Plan. Mary B. Collins. 158p. 1994. teacher ed., ring bd. 26.95 (1-58337-114-1) Teachers Pet Pubns.

Midsummer Night's Dream: Adapted for the Modern Stage. Adapted by Doug McClure. 64p. 1997. pap. 5.00 (0-87440-043-0) Bakers Plays.

Midsummer Night's Dream: Authorized Acting Edition. Ed. by Peter Brook. 193p. 1974. pap. 14.95 (0-87129-737-X, M26) Dramatic Pub.

Midsummer Night's Dream: Critical Essays. Ed. by Dorothea Kehler. LC 97-31433. (Shakespeare Criticism Ser.: Vol. 19). (Illus.). 504p. 1997. text 110.00 (0-8153-2009-4, H1900) Garland.

Midsummer Night's Dream: For Kids. Lois Burdett. (Shakespeare Can Be Fun Ser.). (Illus.). 64p. (J). (gr. 2 up). 1997. pap. 8.95 (1-55209-124-4); lib. bdg. 19.95 (1-55209-130-9) Firefly Bks Ltd.

Midsummer Night's Dream: Original Text & Modern Verse. William Shakespeare. Ed. by Alan Durband. (Shakespeare Made Easy Ser.). (Orig.). 1995. pap. 17.95 (0-7487-0278-4, Pub. by S Thornes Pubs) Trans-Atl Phila.

Midsummer Night's Dream: Reproducible Teaching Unit. rev. ed. James Scott. 31p. (YA). (gr. 7-12). 1995. teacher ed., ring bd. 29.50 (1-58049-066-2, TU29/U) Prestwick Hse.

Midsummer Night's Dream: Scofield,&Paul, Set. abr. ed. William Shakespeare. LC 67-567. 1991. audio 18.00 (1-55994-086-7, CPN 208, Caedmon) HarperAudio.

Midsummer Night's Dream: Shakespeare in Modern English. William Shakespeare. Ed. by John Hort & Leela Hort. LC 81-19272. (Shakespeare in Modern English Ser.). 40p. 1992. pap. 7.00 (0-948662-03-4, Pub. by Kabet Pr) Empire Pub Srvs.

Midsummer Night's Dream: Simply Shakespeare. Ed. by Jim Volz & Evelyn C. Case. (Illus.). 98p. (J). (gr. 3-6). 1989. 14.95 (0-929077-05-9); lib. bdg. 14.95 (0-317-93769-3) WaterMark Inc.

***Midsummer Night's Dream: The Arden Edition of the Works of William Shakespeare.** William Shakespeare. Ed. by Harold F. Brooks. 164p. 1998. write for info. (0-17-443605-X) Thomson Learn.

Midsummer Night's Dream, A Winter's Tale, The Tempest: Granville Barker's Prefaces to Shakespeare. William Shakespeare. Ed. by Granville Barker. 98p. 1995. pap. 6.95 (0-435-08654-5, 08654) Heinemann.

Midsummer Night's Dream Classicscript. abr. ed. William Shakespeare. Ed. & Intro. by William-Alan Landes. LC 98-14391. 55p. (Orig.). (YA). (gr. 6-12). 1998. pap. 6.00 (0-88734-529-8) Players Pr.

Midsummer Night's Dream for Kids. Lois Burdett. (Shakespeare Can Be Fun! Ser.). 1997. 14.15 (0-606-12767-4, Pub. by Turtleback) Demco.

Midsummer Night's Dream for Young People. William Shakespeare. Ed. & Illus. by Diane Davidson. LC 86-5957. (Shakespeare for Young People Ser.: Vol. 1). 64p. (J). (gr. 5-8). 1986. pap. 5.95 (0-934048-18-5) Lrn Links.

Midsummer Night's Dream-Jr. Style. Claire Jones & Bob Varga. 31p. (J). (gr. k-5). 1995. mass mkt. 4.00 (1-58193-167-0) Brown Bag Prods.

Midsummer Night's Dream Notes. Matthew W. Black. (Cliffs Notes Ser.). 64p. 1961. pap. 4.95 (0-8220-0057-1, Cliff) IDG Bks.

Midsummer Night's Dream Readalong. William Shakespeare. (Illustrated Classics Shakespeare Collection). 64p. 1994. pap. 14.95 incl. audio (0-7854-0825-8, 40611) Am Guidance.

Midsummer Night's Dreams: One Story, Many Tales. Ed. by M. Christian. 1998. mass mkt. 7.95 (1-56333-679-0, Rhinoceros) Masquerade.

***Midsummer Nights Fairy Tale.** Terri Windling & Wendy Froud. LC 99-31525. 52p. 1999. 18.00 (0-684-85559-3) S&S Trade.

Midsummer Night's Magic. Emma Craig et al. 368p. (Orig.). 1997. mass mkt. 5.50 (0-505-52209-8, Love Spell) Dorchester Pub Co.

Midsummer's Delight. Alicia Rasley. 320p. 1993. mass mkt. 3.99 (0-8217-4230-2, Zebra Kensgtn) Kensgtn Pub Corp.

Midsummer's Knight. Tori Phillips. (Historical Ser.). 304p. 1998. mass mkt. 4.99 (0-373-29015-2, 1-29015-4) Harlequin Bks.

Midsummer's Night Dream, Great Expectations, Prince & the Pauper & Moby Dick. Acclaim Books Staff. (Classics Illustrated Ser.). (Illus.). 1997. pap. text 179.64 (1-57840-018-X, Pub. by Acclaim Bks) Penguin Putnam.

***Midsummers Night's Dream: A Dual Edition.** James Scott. 80p. (YA). (gr. 7-12). 1999. pap., wbk. ed. 6.75 (1-58049-508-7, DK07A) Prestwick Hse.

Midsummers Night's Dream: Curriculum Unit. Center for Learning Network Staff & William Shakespeare. (Shakespeare Ser.). 69p. (YA). (gr. 9-12). 1992. spiral bd. 18.95 (1-56077-262-X) Ctr Learning.

Midterm Survey of Churched Development, 1985-1989. David Paulovich. Ed. by Irvin D. Weaver. 87p. 1990. pap. 5.00 (1-877736-09-0) MB Missions.

Midwater Fishes in the Eastern North Atlantic see Progress in Oceanography

Midway. Philip Sauvain. LC 92-29566. (Great Battles & Sieges Ser.). (Illus.). 32p. (YA). (gr. 6 up). 1993. lib. bdg. 21.00 (0-02-781090-9, Mac Bks Young Read) S&S Childrens.

An Asterisk (*) at the beginning of an entry indicates that the title is appearing for the first time.

Midway: The Battle that Doomed Japan. Mitsuo Fuchida & Masatake Okumiya. (War Library). 224p. 1986. mass mkt. 5.99 (0-345-34691-2) Ballantine Pub Grp.

Midway: The Battle that Doomed Japan. Mitsuo Fuchida & Masatake Okumiya. Ed. by Clarke H. Kawakami et al. LC 91-36652. (Classics of Naval Literature Ser.). (Illus.). 320p. 1992. 32.95 (1-55750-575-6) Naval Inst Pr.

***Midway: The Incredible Battle.** Walter Lord. (Illus.). 2000. pap. 12.99 (1-84022-236-0, Pub. by Wrdsworth Edits) Combined Pub.

Midway Campaign: December 7, 1941-June 6, 1942. rev. ed. Jack Greene. (Illus.). 256p. 1994. 22.95 (0-938289-11-X, 28911X) Combined Pub.

Midway Guide to Fishing & Diving Waypoints: Loran C & Global Positioning System Coordinates. Enrico Monti. (Illus.). 29p. 1997. pap. text 25.00 (1-890322-03-2) Monti & Assocs.

Midway in My Song: The Autobiography of Lotte Lehmann. Lotte Lehmann. (American Biography Ser.). 250p. 1991. reprint ed. lib. bdg. 69.00 (0-7812-8241-1) Rprt Serv.

Midway in My Song, the Autobiography of Lotte Lehmann. Lotte Lehmann. LC 73-107813. (Select Bibliographies Reprint Ser.). 1977. 26.95 (0-8369-5186-7) Ayer.

Midway, 1942. Mark Healy. (Campaign Ser.: Vol. 30). (Illus.). 96p. pap. 15.95 (1-85532-335-4, Pub. by Osprey) Stackpole.

Midway, 1942. Mark Healy. (Campaign Ser.: No. 30). (Illus.). 96p. 1994. pap. 14.95 (0-685-72283-X, 9529, Pub. by Osprey) Stackpole.

***Midwest.** Tracey Menges. (Annual Directory of American & Canadian Bed & Breakfasts Ser.: Vol. IV). (Illus.). 179p. 2000. pap. 9.95 (1-57748-774-5) Barbour Pub.

***Midwest.** 15th ed. Petersons. (Peterson's Colleges in the Midwest Ser.). 139-357p. 1999. pap. 17.95 (0-7689-0249-5) Petersons.

Midwest: Myth or Reality? A Symposium. Thomas T. McAvoy & Russel B. Nye. LC 61-10848. 104p. reprint ed. pap. 32.30 (0-608-15459-8, 202931100060) Bks Demand.

Midwest Aeronautical. Paul F. Gerhart. 82p. (C). 1996. pap. text. write for info. (0-03-075337-6); pap. text, teacher ed. write for info. (0-03-075338-4); write for info. (0-03-075339-2) Dryden Pr.

Midwest & the Heartland. Jill C. Wheeler. LC 94-10647. (America, This Land Is Your Land Ser.). (J). 1994. lib. bdg. 15.98 (1-56239-297-2) ABDO Pub Co.

Midwest & the Nation: Rethinking the History of an American Region. Andrew R. Cayton & Peter S. Onuf. LC 89-45479. (Midwestern History & Culture Ser.). 192p. 1990. 10.95 (0-253-31525-5) Ind U Pr.

Midwest Art Fairs, Vol. 10. 136p. 1999. pap. 7.95 (1-882975-11-1) New North.

Midwest at Noon. Graham Hutton. 377p. 1990. reprint ed. pap. 16.00 (0-87580-550-7, 90-045914) N Ill U Pr.

Midwest Childhood. Sherwood Anderson. 1993. reprint ed. lib. bdg. 89.00 (0-7812-5337-3) Rprt Serv.

***Midwest Directory.** 1999th ed. 1999. pap. write for info. (1-887528-48-2) Scott & Daughters.

***Midwest Directory 2000.** Ed. by Scott & Daughters Publishing Staff. (Workbook Ser.: Vol. 22). 2000. pap. 20.00 (1-887528-62-8) Scott & Daughters.

Midwest Families. Michael J. Kearney & Lisa Von Kaenel. LC 79-83599. 1979. 25.00 (0-9604688-0-3) Kearney.

Midwest Flood: Performances, Effects, & Control of Levees. (Illus.). 79p. (Orig.). 1996. pap. text 25.00 (0-7881-2884-1) DIANE Pub.

Midwest Folklore & Other Dances. Eric O. Johnson. LC 95-61646. 146p. 1995. pap. 18.00 (0-9648409-0-1) Urbana Cntry.

Midwest Gardener's Book of Lists. Susan McClure. LC 97-47321. 1998. pap. text 17.95 (0-87833-985-X) Taylor Pub.

Midwest Gardener's Handbook. Jan Riggenbach. 432p. 1999. pap. 24.95 (1-888608-13-7) Cool Springs Pr.

Midwest Gardens. Pamela Wolfe. LC 91-25570. (Illus.). 224p. 1991. 39.95 (1-55652-138-3) Chicago Review.

Midwest Gardens. Pamela Wolfe. LC 91-25570. (Illus.). 208p. 1997. pap. text 29.95 (1-55652-309-2) Chicago Review.

Midwest Gardner's Cookbook. Marian A Towne. LC 95-39893. (Illus.). 256p. 1996. 17.95 (0-253-21056-9) Ind U Pr.

Midwest Gem Fossil & Mineral Trails: Prairie States. rev. ed. June C. Zeitner. LC 97-78228. (Illus.). 128p. 1998. pap. 10.95 (0-935182-94-2) Gem Guides Bk.

Midwest Gem Fossil & Mineral Trails - Great Lakes States. rev. ed. June C. Zeitner. LC 99-72085. (Illus.). 128p. 1999. pap. 10.95 (1-889786-06-3) Gem Guides Bk.

Midwest Germany Map. 1996. 8.95 (2-06-700417-4, 417) Michelin.

Midwest Girls. Cherie Bennett. (Pageant Ser.: No. 2). 167p. (gr. 7-12). 1998. mass mkt. 4.50 (0-425-16378-4) Berkley Pub.

Midwest Haiku Anthology. Ed. by Randy Brooks & Lee Gurga. 128p. 1992. 15.00 (0-913719-94-3, High Coo Pr) Brooks Books.

Midwest in American Architecture. Ed. by John S. Garner. (Illus.). 280p. 1991. text 37.50 (0-252-01743-9) U of Ill Pr.

Midwest Landscape Design. Susan McClure. LC 98-43757. 1999. 34.95 (0-87833-218-9) Taylor Pub.

Midwest Medical Polymer & Device Conference: Regional Technical Conference, Sheraton International O'Hare, Rosemont, Illinois, September 26-28, 1983. Society of Plastics Engineers Staff. LC TP1185.M4S63. 190p. reprint ed. pap. 58.90 (0-608-13389-2, 202250900027) Bks Demand.

***Midwest Passage: How Traveling Close to Home Broadened My Horizons.** Marianne E. Goss. LC 00-190682. iv, 108p. 2000. pap. 11.95 (0-9679953-0-2) M E Goss.

Midwest Portraits: A Book of Memories & Friendships. Harry Hansen. (BCL1-PS American Literature Ser.). 357p. 1992. reprint ed. lib. bdg. 89.00 (0-7812-6626-2) Rprt Serv.

Midwest Research. Nancy E. Carlberg. (Illus.). 110p. (Orig.). 1991. pap. 5.00 (0-944878-11-3) Carlberg Pr.

Midwest Response to the New Federalism. Ed. by Peter K. Eisinger & William Gormley. LC 88-40185. (La Follette Public Policy Ser.). 333p. (Orig.). 1988. reprint ed. pap. 103.30 (0-608-01965-8, 206262000003) Bks Demand.

***Midwest Skiing: A Glance Back.** John Pontti & Kenneth Luostari. (Images of America Ser.). (Illus.). 128p. 2000. pap. 18.99 (0-7385-0124-7) Arcadia Publng.

Midwest Small Town Cookin' B. Carlson. (Illus.). 160p. 1994. spiral bd. 5.95 (1-57166-006-2) Hearts N Tummies.

***Midwest Studies in Philosophy Vol. 23: New Directions in Philosophy.** Ed. by Peter A. French & Howard K. Wettstein. 350p. 1999. 62.95 (0-631-21593-X); pap. text 29.95 (0-631-21691-X) Blackwell Pubs.

Midwest Symposium on Circuits & Systems 37th, 1994. IEEE, Circuits & Systems Society Staff. Ed. by IEEE, Institute of Electrical & Electronics Engine. LC 79-645128. 1450p. 1994. pap. text. write for info. (0-7803-2428-5, 94CH35731); lib. bdg. write for info. (0-7803-2429-3, 94CH35731); fiche. write for info. (0-7803-2430-7, 94CH35731) Inst Electrical.

***Midwest Tornadoes of May 3, 1999, Oklahoma & Kansas: Observations, Recommendations, & Technical Guidance.** (Illus.). 160p. 2000. pap. text 30.00 (0-7567-0003-5) DIANE Pub.

Midwest Transaction Guide, 14 vols. Samuel H. Young & Philip Gordon. 1980. ring bd. 1340.00 (0-8205-1404-7) Bender.

Midwest Tree Fruit Handbook. Ed. by R. A. Hayden et al. (Illus.). 46p. 1998. pap. text 20.00 (0-7881-4463-4) DIANE Pub.

Midwest Voter Registration Laws: A Comparative Overview. Jamie Cooper. 60p. 1990. 12.00 (0-685-56592-0) CPA Washington.

Midwest Weekends: Memorable Getaways in the Upper Midwest. Beth Gauper. 180p. 1996. pap. text 8.95 (0-8362-1444-7) Andrews & McMeel.

Midwest Wisdom: The Character of the Heartland. Patrick Caton. LC 97-71654. 168p. 1997. pap. 5.95 (1-56245-306-8) Great Quotations.

Midwestern Ascendancy in American Writing. Ronald Weber. LC 91-46602. (Midwestern History & Culture Ser.). 288p. 1992. 9.95 (0-253-36366-7) Ind U Pr.

***Midwestern Corn Festival: Ears Everywhere.** Lisa Gabbert. (Festivals! U. S. A. Ser.). (Illus.). 24p. (J). (gr. k-4). 1999. 17.26 (0-8239-5341-6, PowerKids) Rosen Group.

Midwestern Country Cookbook: Recipes & Remembrances from a Traditional Farmhouse. Marilyn Kluger. LC 92-39920. 304p. 1993. spiral bd. 14.95 (1-55958-297-9) Prima Pub.

Midwestern Home Cookery. Louis Szathmary et al. 1973. 15.95 (0-405-05052-6) Ayer.

Midwestern Junior League Cookbook. Ed. by Ann Seranne. 1978. 13.95 (0-679-51204-7) McKay.

***Midwestern Landscape Architecture.** William H. Tishler. LC 99-50980. (Illus.). 256p. 2000. text 37.50 (0-252-02593-8) U of Ill Pr.

Midwestern State University in Photographs. Louis J. Rodriguez. (Illus.). 1995. 25.00 (0-915323-07-9) Midwestern St U Pr.

Midwestern Tea Room Pleasures. Joyce Decherd. 200p. 1994. pap. write for info. (0-9642586-0-9) J Decherd.

Midwestern Women: Work, Community, & Leadership at the Crossroads. Ed. by Lucy E. Murphy & Wendy H. Venet. LC 97-4073. 1997. 39.95 (0-253-33307-5); pap. 19.95 (0-253-21133-6) Ind U Pr.

Midwich Cuckoos. John Wyndham. 189p. Date not set. 20.95 (0-8488-2421-0) Amereon Ltd.

Midwich Cuckoos. John Wyndham. 256p. 1993. reprint ed. lib. bdg. 31.95 (0-89968-387-8, Lghtyr Pr) Buccaneer Bks.

Midwife. Gay Courter. 536p. 1985. mass mkt. 6.99 (0-451-15623-4, Sig) NAL.

Midwife. Carolyn Davidson. (Historical Ser.). 1999. per. 4.99 (0-373-29075-6, 1-29075-8) Harlequin Bks.

Midwife & Other Poems on Caring. Marilyn Krysl. 60p. 1989. pap. 9.95 (0-88737-448-4) Natl League Nurse.

Midwife & Society: Perspectives, Policies & Practice. Anthea Symonds & Sheila C. Hunt. 241p. 1996. pap. 39.50 (0-333-63038-6, Pub. by Macmillan) Trans-Atl Phila.

Midwife & the Witch. Thomas R. Forbes. LC 79-8099. (Satanism Ser.). 224p. 1982. reprint ed. 34.50 (0-404-18411-1) AMS Pr.

Midwife Challenge. Ed. by Sheila Kitzinger. 288p. 1991. pap. 12.95 (0-04-440845-5) NYU Pr.

Midwife Challenge. Ed. by Sheila Kitzinger. 1989. pap. 12.95 (0-86358-235-4, Pub. by Pandora) Harper SF.

Midwife Chronicles. Shirley Windward. Ed. by Gwen Costa. LC 91-38820. (Orig.). 1992. pap. 13.95 (0-87949-331-3) Ashley Bks.

Midwife for Souls: Spiritual Care for the Dying. Kathy Kalina. LC 93-32153. 108p. (Orig.). 1993. pap. 5.95 (0-8198-4769-0) Pauline Bks.

Midwife Through the Dying Process: Stories of Healing & Hard Choices at the End of Life. Timothy E. Quill. LC 96-26475. 208p. 1996. 24.95 (0-8018-5516-0) Johns Hopkins.

Midwifery. Walsh. Date not set. text. write for info. (0-7216-4716-2) Harcourt.

Midwifery, 2 vols., Set. Pauline M. Sellers. 1995. pap. 92.25 (0-7021-2882-1, Pub. by Juta & Co) Gaunt.

Midwifery, Vol. 1. P. McCall Sellars. 1992. write for info. (0-7021-2925-9, Pub. by Juta & Co) Gaunt.

Midwifery, Vol. 2. P. McCall Sellars. 1992. write for info. (0-7021-2926-7, Pub. by Juta & Co) Gaunt.

Midwifery: Safe, Cost Effective Maternity Care for All Women & Babies. 4th ed. David Stewart et al. 87p. 1997. reprint ed. pap. 4.95 (0-934426-81-3) NAPSAC Reprods.

Midwifery & Childbirth in America. Judith P. Rooks. LC 97-12790. 592p. 1997. text 54.95 (1-56639-565-8) Temple U Pr.

Midwifery & Childbirth in America. Judith P. Rooks. 592p. 1999. pap. 34.95 (1-56639-711-1) Temple U Pr.

Midwifery & Herbs. Willa Shaffer. 1987. pap. 2.95 (0-913923-19-2) Woodland UT.

Midwifery & Medicine in Early Modern France: Louise Bourgeois. Wendy Perkins. 240p. 1996. text 55.00 (0-85989-471-1, Pub. by Univ Exeter Pr) Northwestern U Pr.

Midwifery & the Law. 1990. pap. 5.95 (0-914257-08-0) Mothering Magazine.

Midwifery & the Medicalization of Childbirth: Comparative Perspectives. Ed. by Edwin Van Teijlingen et al. LC 99-14711. 430p. 1999. lib. bdg. 59.00 (1-56072-680-6) Nova Sci Pubs.

Midwifery Handbook: A Practical Guide to Prenatal & Postpartum Care. Linda Wheeler. LC 96-49608. 320p. 1997. spiral bd. 31.95 (0-397-55360-9) Lppncott W & W.

Midwifery in Australia. Barclay. (C). 1998. pap. text 42.00 (0-443-05429-0) Harcourt.

Midwifery of the Soul: A Holistic Perspective on Psychoanalysis. Margaret Arden. 200p. 1998. 50.00 (1-85343-389-6, Pub. by Free Assoc Bks); pap. 21.50 (1-85343-391-8, Pub. by Free Assoc Bks) NYU Pr.

Midwifery Research Database Miriad Supplement, No. 1. Renfrew & McCormick. 60p. 1997. pap. text, suppl. ed. 42.00 (1-898507-46-5) Buttrwrth-Heinemann.

Midwifery Theory & Practice. Ed. by Philip K. Wilson. LC 96-794. (Childbirth Ser.: Vol. 1). (Illus.). 488p. 1996. reprint ed. text 94.00 (0-8153-2230-5) Garland.

Midwife's Apprentice. (Pathways to Critical Thinking Ser.). 32p. (YA). 1997. pap. text 19.95 (1-58303-035-2) Pthways Pubng.

Midwife's Apprentice. (Assessment Packs Ser.). 15p. 1998. pap. text 15.95 (1-58303-051-4) Pthways Pubng.

***Midwife's Apprentice.** 1999. 9.95 (1-56137-801-1) Novel Units.

***Midwife's Apprentice.** 2000. 11.95 (1-56137-802-X) Novel Units.

Midwife's Apprentice. Karen Cushman. LC 94-13792. 122p. (J). (gr. 6-9). 1995. 10.95 (0-395-69229-6, Clarion Bks) HM.

Midwife's Apprentice. Karen Cushman. (Trophy Bk.). (Illus.). 128p. (J). (gr. 12 up). 1996. pap. 5.95 (0-06-440630-X, HarpTrophy) HarpC Child Bks.

Midwife's Apprentice. Karen Cushman. 1996. 10.05 (0-606-09612-4, Pub. by Turtleback) Demco.

Midwife's Apprentice: A Study Guide. P. Street. Ed. by J. Friedland & R. Kessler. (Novel-Ties Ser.). (J). (gr. 5-7). 1997. pap. 15.95 (0-7675-0164-0) Lrn Links.

Midwife's Apprentice: A Unit Plan. Janine Sherman. 160p. 1998. teacher ed., ring bd. 26.95 (1-58337-211-3) Teachers Pet Pubns.

Midwife's Apprentice: L-I-T Guide. Charlotte Jaffe & Barbara Roberts. (J). (gr. 4-10). Date not set. pap. 8.95 (1-56644-015-7, 015-7AP) Educ Impress.

Midwife's Dilemma. large type ed. Lilian Darcy. 288p. 1996. 23.99 (0-263-14519-0, Pub. by Mills & Boon) Ulverscroft.

Midwife's Pharmacopeia. Claire Banister. LC 98-134173. 178p. 1997. pap. text 25.00 (1-898507-61-9) Buttrwrth-Heinemann.

Midwife's Practical Directory: Woman's Confidential Friend. Thomas Hersey. LC 73-20627. (Sex, Marriage & Society Ser.). 362p. 1974. reprint ed. 33.95 (0-405-05803-9) Ayer.

***Midwife's Song: A Story of Moses' Birth.** Brenda Ray. LC 00-102602. 256p. 2000. pap. 14.95 (0-9653966-8-1, Pub. by Karmichael Pr) Follett Library.

Midwife's Tale: An Oral History from Handywoman to Professional Midwife. Nicky Leap & Billie Hunter. (Illus.). 238p. 1993. pap. 20.95 (1-85727-041-X, Pub. by Scarlet Pr) LPC InBook.

Midwife's Tale: The Life of Martha Ballard, Based on Her Diary, 1785-1812. Laurel T. Ulrich. (Illus.). 464p. 1991. pap. 13.00 (0-679-73376-0) Vin Bks.

Midwife's Tale & Other Christmas Stories. W. Edward Harris. 80p. 1993. pap. 12.00 (0-9638864-2-8) Stonewrk Pr.

Midwinter. John Buchan. 1988. reprint ed. lib. bdg. 49.00 (0-7812-0467-4) Rprt Serv.

Midwinter. John Buchan. 1971. reprint ed. 59.00 (0-403-00878-6) Scholarly.

Midwinter Day. Bernadette Mayer. LC 98-54649. 119p. 1999. reprint ed. pap. 12.95 (0-8112-1406-0, NDP876, Pub. by New Directions) SPD-Small Pr Dist.

Midwinter Fires. Jeffery Beam. 20p. (Orig.). 1990. pap. 8.00 (0-9622572-3-0) French Broad.

Midwinter Fires. limited ed. Jeffery Beam. 20p. (Orig.). 1990. 25.00 (0-9622572-4-9); 50.00 (0-9622572-5-7) French Broad.

Midwinter Mourning: The Boyertown Opera House Fire, Vol. I. Mary J. Schneider. (Illus.). 200p. (Orig.). 1991. pap. 10.00 (0-9629218-0-7) MJS Pubns.

***Midwinter Murder: A Vivi Hartman Adventure.** Harriet K. Feder. LC 00-9706. (Illus.). 2001. write for info. (0-8225-0741-2) Lerner Pub.

Midwinter Music: A Scottish Anthology for the Festive Season. Marjory Greig & Marjorie Wilson. 176p. 1990. pap. 39.00 (1-898218-21-8) St Mut.

Midwinter Mysteries, Bk. 1. large type ed. Hilary Hale. (Magna Large Print Ser.). 1994. 27.99 (0-7505-0682-2, Pub. by Mgna Lrg Print) Ulverscroft.

Midwinter Mysteries, Bk. 2. large type ed. Hilary Hale. 297p. 1995. 27.99 (0-7505-0683-0, Pub. by Mgna Lrg Print) Ulverscroft.

Midwinter Pottery: A Revolution in British Tableware. Steven Jenkins. 1997. pap. 35.00 (0-903685-55-8, Pub. by R Dennis) Antique Collect.

Midwinter Rites of the Cayuga Long House. Frank G. Speck. LC 94-44361. xviii, 208p. 1995. pap. 8.95 (0-8032-9231-7, Bison Books) U of Nebr Pr.

Midwinter Transport. Anne Bromley. LC 85-70429. (Poetry Ser.). 80p. 1985. 20.95 (0-88748-016-0); pap. 11.95 (0-88748-017-9) Carnegie-Mellon.

Midwinter's Bliss. Cathleen Clare. 240p. (Orig.). 1995. mass mkt. 3.99 (0-380-77668-5, Avon Bks) Morrow Avon.

***Midwinter's Tale.** Andrew M. Greeley. 448p. 1999. mass mkt. 6.99 (0-8125-9025-2, Pub. by Forge NYC) St Martin.

Midwinter's Tale, No. 1. Andrew M. Greeley. LC 98-21183. 383p. 1998. 24.95 (0-312-86571-6, Pub. by Forge NYC) St Martin.

Midwinter's Tale: The Shooting Script. Kenneth Branagh. LC 95-45331. (Shooting Script Ser.). 144p. 1996. pap. 14.95 (1-55704-274-8, Pub. by Newmarket) Norton.

Midwives: A Novel. Christopher A. Bohjalian. 1998. 24.00 (0-609-60497-X) Crown Pub Group.

***Midwives: A Novel.** Christopher A. Bohjalian. 372p. 1998. pap. 13.00 (0-375-70677-1) Knopf.

Midwives: A Novel. Christopher A. Bohjalian. 400p. 1998. pap. 13.00 (0-679-77146-8) Vin Bks.

Midwives: A Novel. large type ed. Christopher A. Bohjalian. (Niagara Large Print Ser.). 1997. lib. bdg. 29.50 (0-7089-5880-X) Ulverscroft.

Midwives & Management. Rosemary E. Cross. 1996. pap. text 29.00 (1-898507-20-1) Buttrwrth-Heinemann.

Midwives & Mothers: The Re-Emergence of Midwifery in Canada. Elizabeth Allemang et al. 175p. Date not set. pap. 14.95 (0-929005-58-9, Pub. by Sec Story Pr) LPC InBook.

Midwives & Safer Motherhood. Murray. 1996. mass mkt. 24.00 (0-7234-2122-6) Mosby Inc.

Midwives Book: Or the Whole Art of Midwifry Discovered. Jane Sharp. Ed. by Elaine Hobby. LC 98-28773. (Women Writers in English 1350-1850 Ser.). (Illus.). 368p. 1999. pap. 19.95 (0-19-508653-8); text 49.95 (0-19-508652-X) OUP.

Midwives in History & Society. Jean Towler & Joan Bramall. LC 85-26508. (Illus.). 288p. (Orig.). 1986. pap. 33.00 (0-7099-2453-4, Pub. by C Helm) Routldge.

***Midwives of Seventeenth-Century London.** Doreen Evenden. (Cambridge Studies in the History of Medicine). (Illus.). 280p. (C). 2000. 64.95 (0-521-66107-2) Cambridge U Pr.

***Midwives of the Revolution: Female Bolsheviks & Women Workers in 1917.** Jane McDermid & Anna Hillyar. LC 99-21962. 304p. 1999. text 42.95 (0-8214-1289-2) Ohio U Pr.

Midwives' Pocket Reference. Sinclair. (C). 2000. pap. text. write for info. (0-7216-8168-9, W B Saunders Co) Harcrt Hlth Sci Grp.

Midwives, Research & Childbirth, Vol. 2. Ed. by Sarah Robinson & Ann Thomson. 256p. 1990. pap. 34.95 (0-412-31650-1, A4455) Chapman & Hall.

Midwives, Research & Childbirth, Vol. 3. Ed. by S. Robinson & A. M. Thomson. 1994. 45.00 (1-56593-043-6, 0291) Singular Publishing.

Midwives, Research & Childbirth, Vol. 4. Ed. by S. Robinson & A. M. Thomson. 288p. 1995. 44.75 (1-56593-289-7, 0613) Singular Publishing.

Midwives, Society & Childbirth: Debates & Controversies in the Modern Period. Ed. by Hilary Marland & Anne M. Rafferty. LC 96-41125. (Studies in the Social History of Medicine Ser.). 292p. (C). 1997. 74.95 (0-415-13328-9) Routledge.

Midwives to Nazism: University Professor in Weimar Germany, 1925-1933. Alice Gallin. LC 86-8792. viii, 134p. 1986. 16.95 (0-86554-202-3, MUP H186) Mercer Univ Pr.

Midwives to the Dying. Miriam Schneider & Jan S. Bernard. (Illus.). 64p. (Orig.). 1992. pap. 12.95 (0-9632553-0-4) Angels Work.

Midworld. Alan Dean Foster. 1987. mass mkt. 5.99 (0-345-35011-1, Del Rey) Ballantine Pub Grp.

Midworld. Alan Dean Foster. 1995. mass mkt. 5.99 (0-345-90816-3, Del Rey) Ballantine Pub Grp.

Midworld of Symbols & Functioning Objects. John W. Miller. 192p. 1982. reprint ed. 20.00 (0-393-01579-3) Norton.

Midworld of Symbols & Functioning Objects. John W. Miller. 192p. 1984. reprint ed. pap. 6.95 (0-393-30156-7) Norton.

Midyear Meeting Abstract Volume (Austin, TX) (Abstract Ser.: No. 4). 98p. 1987. pap. 14.00 (0-918985-70-6) SEPM.

MIE: Charles Pardosy, O. M. I., a Missionary of the Northwest, Missionary to the Yakima Indians in the 1850's & Tater with British Columbia Indians. Edward J. Kowrach. 336p. 1992. 24.95 (0-87770-501-1) Ye Galleon.

Miedo a Quererte: Angry Desire. Charlotte Lamb. (SPA.). 1997. per. 3.50 (0-373-33395-1, 1-33395-4) Harlequin Bks.

Miedo Al Amor (Fear to Love) Diana Mars. (Deseo Ser.). (SPA.). 1998. per. 3.50 (0-373-35226-3, 1-35226-9) Harlequin Bks.

Mieko & the Fifth Treasure. Eleanor Coerr. 80p. (J). 1994. pap. 4.50 (0-440-40947-0) Dell.

M

An Asterisk (*) at the beginning of an entry indicates that the title is appearing for the first time.

Mieko & the Fifth Treasure. Eleanor Coerr. LC 92-14660. 64p. (J). 1993. 14.95 (*0-399-22434-3*, G P Putnam) Peng Put Young Read.

Mieko & the Fifth Treasure. Eleanor Coerr. 1993. 9.19 (*0-606-07037-0*, Pub. by Turtleback) Demco.

Mielograma. Oliver D. Grin & Dorothy L. Bouwman. (Patient Education Ser.). (SPA., Illus.). 10p. (Orig.). 1992. pap. text 4.00 (*0-929689-53-4*) Ludann Co.

***Mielziner: Master of Modern Stage Design.** Mary C. Henderson. (Illus.). 288p. 2000. write for info. (*0-8230-8823-5*, Back Stage Bks) Watsn-Guptill.

Miembros de su Cuerpo. Gary Teja. (SPA.). 1992. pap. 3.00 (*1-55955-037-6*) CRC Wrld Lit.

Mien - English Mini-Books Set with Audio, 11 bks. Claudia Schwalm. (Illus.). (Orig.). (J). (gr. k-6). 1997. pap. 21.95 incl. audio (*0-614-24740-3*) Cultural Cnnect.

Mien Family. Sara Gogol. LC 95-48473. (Journey Between Two Worlds Ser.). (J). 1996. lib. bdg. 22.60 (*0-8225-3432-0*, Lerner Publctns) Lerner Pub.

Mien Family. Sara Gogol. (J). 1996. lib. bdg. 22.60 (*0-8225-3407-X*) Lerner Pub.

Mien Family. Sara Gogol. (Illus.). 56p. (J). (gr. 3-6). 1996. pap. text 8.95 (*0-8225-9745-4*) Lerner Pub.

Mien/English Mini-Books Set with Audio, 11 bks. Claudia Schwalm. (Illus.). (Orig.). 1997. pap. 21.95 incl. audio (*0-614-24472-2*) Cultural Cnnect.

***Mientras Dormias.** Carolyn Andrews. Vol. 212.Tr. of While You Sleep. (SPA.). 2000. per. 3.50 (*0-373-35342-1*, 1-35342-1) Harlequin Bks.

Mientras el Viene. Valentin Gonzalez. (Serie Discipulado - Discipleship Ser.).Tr. of While He Comes. (SPA.). 28p. 1992. pap. 1.99 (*1-56063-417-0*, 498254) Editorial Unilit.

Mientras Espera. George E. Verrilli & Anne M. Mueser. Tr. by Angela R. Sobrino. (Illus.). 192p. (Orig.). 1994. pap. 7.95 (*0-312-11027-8*) St Martin.

Mierda. Frances De T. Berger. 1990. pap. 9.95 (*0-452-26424-3*, Plume) Dutton Plume.

Mies Van Der Rohe. J. L. Cohen. (Illus.). 144p. 1995. pap. 29.99 (*0-419-20330-3*, E & FN Spon) Routledge.

Mies Van Der Rohe. Ludwig Glaeser. (Illus.). 88p. 1990. pap. 9.95 (*0-8109-6051-6*) Abrams.

Mies van der Rohe. 2nd ed. Werner Blaser. LC 97-13753. (Studio Paperback Ser.). (Illus.). 248p. 1997. pap. 29.95 (*3-7643-5619-7*, Pub. by Birkhauser) Princeton Arch.

Mies Van Der Rohe: A Critical Biography. Franz Schulze. LC 85-8488. (Illus.). xxiv, 380p. 1989. pap. text 28.00 (*0-226-74060-9*) U Ch Pr.

Mies Van Der Rohe: A Critical Biography. Franz Schulze. LC 85-8488. (Illus.). xxiv, 356p. 1994. 39.95 (*0-226-74059-5*) U Ch Pr.

Mies Van Der Rohe: Architect as Educator. Rolf Achilles. (Illus.). 168p. 1986. pap. 25.00 (*0-318-20183-6*, 31718-8); lib. bdg. 39.95 (*0-318-20182-8*, 31716-1) IL Inst Tech.

Mies Van Der Rohe: Architect As Educator. Ed. by Kevin P. Harrington. (Illus.). 184p. 1986. pap. 25.00 (*0-226-31718-8*) U Ch Pr.

Mies Van Der Rohe: Critical Essays. Ed. by Franz Schulze. (Illus.). 192p. 1989. 35.00 (*0-87070-569-5*) Mus of Modern Art.

***Mies Van der Rohe: Farnsworth House: Weekend House.** Werner Blaser. LC 99-42388. (Illus.). 84p. 1999. pap. 29.95 (*3-7643-6089-5*) Birkhauser.

***Mies Van Der Rohe: Farnsworth House: Weekend House = Wochenendhaus.** Werner Blaser. LC 99-42388. 1999. write for info. (*0-8176-6089-5*) Birkhauser.

***Mies Van der Rohe: Lake Shore Drive Apartments: High Rise Building.** Werner Blaser. LC 99-48031. (Illus.). 80p. 1999. pap. 29.95 (*3-7643-6090-9*) Birkhauser.

Mies Van Der Rohe: Stuttgart, Barcelona & Brno: Furniture & Architecture. (Illus.). 272p. 1999. 55.00 (*88-8118-395-1*, Pub. by Skira IT) Abbeville Pr.

Mies van der Rohe: The Art of Structure: Die Kunst Der Struktur. enl. rev. ed. Werner Blaser. LC 92-46540. xi, 227p. 1993. 45.70 (*0-8176-2848-7*, Pub. by Birkhauser) Princeton Arch.

Mies Van Der Rohe: West Meets East. Werner Blaser. (Illus.). 132p. 1996. 50.00 (*3-7643-5430-5*, Pub. by Birkhauser) Princeton Arch.

Mies Van Der Rohe Archive, Vol. 1. Ed. by Arthur Drexler. LC 86-9980. Pt. 1. 383p. 1986. text 225.00 (*0-8240-4025-2*) Garland.

Mies Van Der Rohe Archive, Vol. 3. Ed. by Arthur Drexler. LC 86-9980. Pt. 1. 511p. 1986. text 250.00 (*0-8240-4027-9*) Garland.

Mies Van Der Rohe Archive, Vol. 4. Ed. by Arthur Drexler. LC 86-9980. Pt. 1. 568p. 1986. text 275.00 (*0-8240-4028-7*) Garland.

Mies Van Der Rohe Archive: Alumni Memorial Hall, Field House Building, Gymnasium, Natatorium, & Other Buildings & Projects, Vol. 10: IIT, Vol. 3. Ed. by Franz Schulze. LC 86-9980. 312p. 1993. text 330.00 (*0-8240-5994-8*) Garland.

Mies Van Der Rohe Archive: Library & Administration Building, Vol. 9: IIT, Vol. 2. Ed. by Franz Schulze & George E. Danforth. LC 86-9980. 368p. 1993. text 330.00 (*0-8240-5993-X*) Garland.

Mies Van Der Rohe Archive: Metallurgical & Chemical Engineering Building (Perlstein Hall) & Other Buildings & Projects, Vol 11: IIT, Vol. 4. Ed. by Franz Schulze. LC 86-9980. 488p. 1993. text 330.00 (*0-8240-5995-6*) Garland.

Mies Van Der Rohe Archive: Resor House, Vol. 7. Ed. by Franz Schulze & George E. Danforth. LC 86-9980. 408p. 1992. text 330.00 (*0-8240-5174-2*) Garland.

Mies Van Der Rohe Archive: Robert F. Carr Memorial Chapel of Saint Savior, S. R. Crown Hall, & Other Buildings & Projects, Vol. 12: IIT, Vol. 5. Ed. by Franz Schulze. LC 86-9980. 528p. 1993. text 330.00 (*0-8240-5996-4*) Garland.

Mies Van Der Rohe Archive Vol. 13: Cantor Drive-In Restaurant, Farnsworth. Ed. by Franz Schulze & George E. Danforth. LC 86-9980. (Illustrated Catalog of the Mies Van Der Rohe Drawing in the Museum of Modern Art Ser.: Pt. II, 1938-1967, the American Work). (Illus.). 568p. 1993. text 330.00 (*0-8240-5997-2*) Garland.

Mies Van Der Rohe Archive Vol. 16: Convention Hall, Seagram Building (New York) & Other Buildings & Projects. Ed. by Franz Schulze & George E. Danforth. LC 86-9980. (Mies Van Der Rohe Archive Series: An Illustrated Catalog of the Mies Van Der Rohe Drawing in the Museum of Modern Art, Pt. II, 1938-1967, the American Work: Vol. 16). (Illus.). 696p. 1993. text 330.00 (*0-8153-0117-0*) Garland.

Mies Van Der Rohe Archive Supplementary Drawings, Vols. 5 & 6. Ed. by Franz Schulze. LC 86-9980. (Mies Van Der Rohe Archive Series: An Illustrated Catalog of the Miles Van Der Rohe Drawing in the Museum of Modern Art, Pt. II, 1938-1967). 504p. 1990. text 385.00 (*0-8240-5991-3*) Garland.

Mies Van Der Rohe Archive, Vol. 14: Algonquin Apartment Buildings, the Arts Club of Chicago, & Other Buildings & Projects. Ed. by Franz Schulze & George E. Danforth. LC 86-9980. Vol. 14. (Illus.). 544p. 1993. text 300.00 (*0-8240-5998-0*) Garland.

Mies Van Der Rohe Archive, 1910-1937, Vol. 2, Pt. I. Ed. by Arthur Drexler. LC 86-9980. 568p. 1987. text 303.00 (*0-8240-4026-0*) Garland.

Mies van der Rohe at Work. Peter Carter. (Illus.). 192p. 1999. pap. 29.95 (*0-7148-3896-9*) Phaidon Pr.

Mies Van Der Rohe: The European Works: An Architectural Monograph. Academy Architecture Books Staff et al. (Academy Architecture Ser.). (Illus.). 112p. 1986. 45.00 (*0-312-53214-8*); pap. 30.00 (*0-312-53215-6*) St Martin.

Mieux Ecrire en Francais: Livret du Professeur. 2nd ed. Michele R. Morris. LC 88-21287. 323p. (Orig.). (C). 1988. pap., teacher ed. 5.00 (*0-87840-226-8*) Georgetown U Pr.

Mieux Ecrire en Francais: Manuel de Composition et Guide Pratique a l'Usage des Etudiants Anglophones. 2nd ed. Michele R. Morris. LC 88-21287. 323p. (Orig.). (C). 1988. pap. text 14.95 (*0-87840-225-X*) Georgetown U Pr.

MIFE Christmas Book, Level 1. Gail Gilbert. 16p. 1981. 5.95 (*0-87166-587-5*, 93811) Mel Bay.

MIFE Christmas Book, Level 2. Gail Gilbert. 24p. 1981. pap. 5.95 (*0-87166-595-6*, 93812) Mel Bay.

MIFE Christmas Book, Level 3. Gail Gilbert. 28p. 1981. pap. 5.95 (*0-87166-602-2*, 93813) Mel Bay.

MIFE Reader, Level 1. Gail Gilbert. 32p. 1978. pap. 6.95 (*0-87166-580-8*, 93596) Mel Bay.

MIFE Reader, Level 2. Gail Gilbert. 32p. 1978. pap. 6.95 (*0-87166-588-3*, 93599) Mel Bay.

MIFE Solo Book, Level 1. Gail Gilbert. 32p. 1982. pap. 5.95 (*0-87166-583-2*, 93846) Mel Bay.

MIFE Workbook, Level 1. Gail Gilbert. 32p. 1978. pap. 6.95 (*0-87166-582-4*, 93598) Mel Bay.

MIFE Workbook, Level 2. Gail Gilbert. 32p. 1978. 5.95 (*0-87166-590-5*, 93601) Mel Bay.

Miffy. Dick Bruna. Ed. by Chikako Noma. LC 95-48495. (Illus.). 28p. (J). (ps-k). 1996. bds. 4.95 (*1-56836-151-3*) Kodansha.

***Miffy & Melanie.** Dick Bruna. (Illus.). 28p. (J). (ps-k). 2000. 4.95 (*1-56836-305-2*) Kodansha.

Miffy at Play: A Flip Book. Dick Bruna. LC 97-76169. (Illus.). 16p. (J). (ps-k). 1998. bds. 5.95 (*1-56836-223-4*) Kodansha.

Miffy at School. Dick Bruna. (Miffy Ser.). (Illus.). 32p. (J). (ps-1). 1997. bds. 4.95 (*1-56836-176-9*) Kodansha.

Miffy at the Museum. Dick Bruna. (Illus.). 28p. (J). (ps-k). 1998. 4.95 (*1-56836-270-6*) Kodansha.

Miffy at the Playground. Dick Bruna. Ed. by Chikako Noma. LC 96-11539.Tr. of Usako-Chan to Yuenchi. (Illus.). 28p. (J). (ps-k). 1996. 4.95 (*1-56836-159-9*) Kodansha.

Miffy at the Zoo. Dick Bruna. (Miffy Ser.). (Illus.). 32p. (J). (ps-1). 1997. bds. 4.95 (*1-56836-175-0*) Kodansha.

Miffy Goes Flying. Dick Bruna. (Illus.). 28p. (J). (ps-k). 1998. pap. 4.95 (*1-56836-221-8*) Kodansha.

Miffy Goes for a Walk. Dick Bruna. (J). (ps). 1998. 8.95 (*1-56836-269-2*) Kodansha.

Miffy Goes Outside. Dick Bruna. LC 97-73066. (Miffy Ser.). (Illus.). 14p. (J). (ps-3). 1997. bds. 5.95 (*1-56836-193-9*) Kodansha.

Miffy Helps at Home. Dick Bruna. (J). (ps). 1998. 4.95 (*1-56836-265-X*) Kodansha.

Miffy in the Hospital: A Storybook. Dick Bruna. (Illus.). 28p. (J). (ps-k). 1999. pap. 4.95 (*1-56836-297-8*) Kodansha.

Miffy in the Snow: A Storybook. Dick Bruna. (Illus.). 28p. (J). (ps-k). 1999. pap. 4.95 (*1-56836-296-X*) Kodansha.

Miffy in the Tent. Dick Bruna. 28p. (J). (ps-k). 1998. pap. 4.95 (*1-56836-218-8*) Kodansha.

Miffy Is Crying. Dick Bruna. (Illus.). 28p. (J). (ps-k). 1998. 4.95 (*1-56836-263-3*) Kodansha.

Miffy Likes to... Dick Bruna. LC 97-73065. (Miffy Ser.). (Illus.). 14p. (J). (ps-1). 1997. bds. 5.95 (*1-56836-194-7*) Kodansha.

Miffy Likes to Ride. Dick Bruna. (J). (ps). 1998. 8.95 (*1-56836-268-4*) Kodansha.

***Miffy Rides a Bike.** Dick Bruna. (Miffy Ser.). (Illus.). 28p. (ps-k). 1999. 4.95 (*1-56836-280-3*) Kodansha.

Miffy Tours the Zoo. Dick Bruna. (J). (ps). 1998. 4.95 (*1-56836-266-8*) Kodansha.

Miffy Visits the Zoo. Dick Bruna. (J). (ps). 1998. 8.95 (*1-56836-267-6*) Kodansha.

Miffy's Birthday. Dick Bruna. LC 97-71722. (Miffy Ser.). (Illus.). 28p. (J). (ps-k). 1997. bds. 4.95 (*1-56836-192-0*) Kodansha.

Miffy's Busy Morning: A Flip Book. Dick Bruna. (Miffy Ser.). (Illus.). 16p. (ps-k). 1999. 5.95 (*1-56836-288-9*) Kodansha.

***Miffy's Counting Book.** Dick Bruna. (Miffy Ser.). (Illus.). 20p. (ps-k). 1999. bds. 7.95 (*1-56836-281-1*) Kodansha.

Miffy's First Sleepover. Dick Bruna. (Miffy Ser.). (Illus.). 28p. (ps-k). 1999. 4.95 (*1-56836-279-X*) Kodansha.

Mig. (Hawkins Scribble Bks.). (Illus.). 16p. (J). 1996. 6.95 (*0-7894-1167-9*) DK Pub Inc.

Mig: Fifty Years of Secret Aircraft Design. R. A. Belyakov & Jacques Marmain. LC 93-4526. (Illus.). 479p. 1994. 49.95 (*1-55750-566-7*) Naval Inst Pr.

***MIG Aircraft since 1937.** Bill Gunston. 1999. 59.95 (*0-85177-884-4*) Conway.

MiG Aircraft since 1937. Bill Gunston & Yefim Gordon. (Putnam Aviation Ser.). (Illus.). 304p. 1998. 59.95 (*1-55750-541-1*) Naval Inst Pr.

Mig-15 to Freedom: Memoir of the Wartime North Korean Defector Who First Delivered the Secret Fighter Jet to the Americans in 1953. No Kum-Sok & J. Roger Osterholm. LC 96-27288. (Illus.). 231p. 1996. lib. bdg. 35.00 (*0-7864-0210-5*) McFarland & Co.

Mig Master: The Story of the F-8 Crusader. 2nd ed. Barrett Tillman. LC 89-13628. (Illus.). 288p. 1990. 27.95 (*0-87021-585-X*) Naval Inst Pr.

Mig-19 Farmer in Action. Hans-Heiri Stapfer. LC 94-215605. (Aircraft in Action Ser.). (Illus.). 58p. 1994. pap. 9.95 (*0-89747-311-6*) Squad Sig Pubns.

Mig Pilot. John Barron. 1980. 10.95 (*0-685-04285-5*) Readrs Digest Pr.

Mig Pilot: The Final Escape of Lieutenant Belenko. John Barron. 232p. 1981. mass mkt. 4.50 (*0-380-53868-7*, Avon Bks) Morrow Avon.

MIG Pilot - the Final Escape of Lieutenant Belenko see Pilot MIGa: Poslednii Polet Leitinanta Belenko

Mig Pilot Survival: Russian Aircrew Survival Equipment & Instruction. Alan R. Wise. LC 96-68819. (Illus.). 96p. (YA). (gr. 10-13). 1996. pap. 19.95 (*0-7643-0130-6*) Schiffer.

Mig the Pig. Colin Hawkins. (Hawkins Reading Ser.). (J). write for info. (*0-7894-0156-8*, 5-70602) DK Pub Inc.

Mig-21 Fishbed: The World's Most Widely Used Supersonic Fighter. Yefim Gordon & Bill Gunston. (Illus.). 144p. 1996. pap. 27.95 (*1-85780-042-7*) Specialty Pr.

Mig-25 Foxbat & Mig-31 Foxhound: Russia's Defensive Front Line. Yefim Gordon. 1998. pap. text 21.95 (*1-85780-064-8*) Specialty Pr.

MIGA: The Standard Setter of Investment Promotion Business. Akira Iida. LC 97-184246. 116p. 1997. pap. 22.00 (*0-8213-3959-1*, 13959) World Bank.

Miga & Foreign Direct Investment: Evaluating Developmental Impacts. Gerald T. West. LC 98-44282. 104p. 1998. 22.00 (*0-8213-4346-7*) World Bank.

Miga & Foreign Investment. Ibrahim F. Shihata. 1987. lib. bdg. 232.50 (*0-89838-903-8*) Kluwer Academic.

MIGA Roundtable on Foreign Direct Investment Policies in Africa: Proceedings & Lessons. Ed. by Ken Kwaku. LC 93-37605. 72p. 1994. pap. 22.00 (*0-8213-2685-6*, 12685) World Bank.

Might & Magic Compendium: The Authorized Strategy Guide to Games I-V. Caroline Spector. LC 93-85086. (Illus.). 400p. (Orig.). 1994. pap. 19.95 (*1-55958-325-8*) Prima Pub.

***Might & Magic VIII: Day of the Destroyer.** Ed. by Prima Temp Staff. LC 00-10174. (Official Strategy Guides Ser.). (Illus.). 396p. (YA). 2000. pap. 19.99 (*0-7615-2841-5*) Prima Pub.

***Might & Magic VII: For Blood & Honor - Prima's Official Strategy Guide.** Tom Ono. LC 99-70045. 240p. 1999. pap. 19.99 (*0-7615-2069-4*) Prima Pub.

Might & Magic VI: The Mandate of Heaven. Chapman Edward. LC 97-65823. (Secrets of the Game Ser.). 408p. 1998. per. 19.99 (*0-7615-1109-1*) Prima Pub.

Might & Right after the Cold War: Can Foreign Policy Be Moral? Michael Cromartie. 146p. (C). 1993. text 18.95 (*0-89633-180-6*) Ethics & Public Policy.

Might & Right in Antiquity. "Dike" I: From Homer to the Persian Wars. Hartvig Frisch. Tr. by Cyril C. Martindale. LC 75-13268. (History of Ideas in Ancient Greece Ser.). (Illus.). 1976. reprint ed. 23.95 (*0-405-07309-7*) Ayer.

Might As Well Be Dead. large type ed. Rex Stout. LC 95-49122. (Nightingale Ser.). 262p. 1997. lib. bdg. 18.95 (*0-7838-1570-0*, G K Hall Lrg Type) Mac Lib Ref.

Might in Flight: Daily Diary of the 8th Air Forces Hell's Angels, 303rd Bombardment Group. 2nd rev. ed. Harry D. Gobrecht. LC 97-60989. (Illus.). 928p. 1997. 75.00 (*0-9636155-1-3*) Bomb Group.

Might in Flight: Daily Diary of the 8th Air Forces Hell's Angels, 303rd Bombardment Group (H) Harry D. Gobrecht. LC 93-60095. (Illus.). 880p. 1993. 75.00 (*0-9636155-0-5*) Bomb Group.

Might Is Right. Ragnar Redbeard. 1972. 250.00 (*0-87700-187-1*) Revisionist Pr.

Might Is Right: The Survival of the Fittest. deluxe ed. Contrib. by Anton Lavey et al. 230p. (C). 1996. pap. 13.00 (*1-929399-02-2*) M Hunt Pubg.

Might, Mind & Strength: Autobiography of Eli Carlos Openshaw. Eli C. Openshaw et al. Ed. by Mark W. Lund. (Illus.). 442p. 1997. 30.00 (*0-9660894-0-5*, 9701) Eli Pr.

Might of Nations: World Politics in Our Time. 10th ed. John G. Stoessinger. LC 92-31307. 448p. (C). 1992. 43.13 (*0-07-061625-6*) McGraw.

Might of the Multinationals: The Rise & Fall of the Corporate Legend. Alex Rubner. LC 89-26526. 312p. 1990. 55.00 (*0-275-93531-0*, C3531, Greenwood Pr) Greenwood.

Might of the West. Lawrence Brown. 1962. 27.95 (*0-8392-1069-8*) Astor-Honor.

Mightier Than a Lord. Lain F. Grigor. 1985. 35.70 (*0-86152-030-0*, Pub. by Acair Ltd); pap. 23.70 (*0-7855-1337-X*, Pub. by Acair Ltd) St Mut.

Mightier Than the Sword. Robert T. Weiner. (Orig.). 1985. pap. 3.50 (*0-938558-16-1*) Maranatha.

Mightier Than the Sword: How the News Media Have Shaped American History. Rodger Streitmatter. 304p. (C). 1998. pap. text 25.00 (*0-8133-3211-7*, Pub. by Westview) HarpC.

Mightier Than the Sword: Powerful Writing in the Legal Profession. C. Edward Good. 258p. (Orig.). (C). 1997. reprint ed. pap. 19.95 (*0-9648247-0-1*) Word Store.

Mightier Than the Sword: The Journal As a Path to Men's Self-Discovery. Kathleen Adams. 256p. (Orig.). 1994. pap. 10.99 (*0-446-39464-5*) Warner Bks.

Mightiest of Them All: Memories of Grand Coulee Dam. rev. ed. L. Vaughn Downs. LC 93-37713. 160p. 1993. pap. 63.00 (*0-87262-935-X*, ASCE Press) Am Soc Civil Eng.

Mighty. Brian Porter. 645p. (C). 1991. text 34.95 (*1-881814-99-8*); pap. text 24.95 (*0-685-62417-X*) Pace Pr MA.

Mighty: A Study Guide. Estelle Kleinman. Ed. by J. Friedland & R. Kessler. (Novel-Ties Ser.). (J). (gr. 6-8). 1998. pap. text, student ed. 15.95 (*0-7675-0300-7*) Lrn Links.

Mighty: Trees. Frank Kubic. LC 95-71056. 18p. (YA). (gr. 8-12). 1996. pap. 4.50 (*0-9636320-5-1*) Nuggets Wisdom.

Mighty Acts of God. Arnold B. Rhodes. 1964. pap., student ed. 22.95 (*0-8042-9010-5*) Westminster John Knox.

***Mighty Acts of God.** rev. ed. Arnold B. Rhodes & W. Eugene March. 320p. 2000. pap. write for info. (*0-664-50076-5*, Pub. by Geneva Press) Presbyterian Pub.

Mighty Atom. Marie Corelli. 310p. 1972. reprint ed. spiral bd. 19.00 (*0-7873-0212-0*) Hlth Research.

Mighty Atom, 1906. Marie Corelli. 310p. 1996. reprint ed. pap. 17.95 (*1-56459-755-5*) Kessinger Pub.

Mighty Aztecs. Gene S. Stuart. Ed. by Donald J. Crump. LC 80-8102. (Special Publications Series 16: No. 2). (Illus.). 200p. 1981. lib. bdg. 12.95 (*0-87044-367-4*) Natl Geog.

Mighty Baptism: Race, Gender, & the Creation of American Protestantism. Susan Juster. Ed. by Lisa MacFarlane. (Illus.). 336p. 1996. pap. text 16.95 (*0-8014-8212-7*) Cornell U Pr.

Mighty Bernborough. Bill Sigley & Athol Mulley. 242p. (C). 1990. pap. 75.00 (*0-86439-103-X*, Pub. by Boolarong Pubns) St Mut.

***Mighty Big Book of Children's Songs.** (Big Books of Music Ser.: 354). 144p. 1999. otabind 12.95 (*0-634-00304-6*) H Leonard.

***Mighty Big Book of Jokes.** Craig Yoe. (Library O'Laughs). (Illus.). 288p. (J). (gr. 4-7). 2000. pap. 5.99 (*0-8431-7582-6*, Price Stern) Peng Put Young Read.

***Mighty Big Book of Riddles.** Craig Yoe. (Library O'Laughs). (Illus.). 288p. (J). (gr. 4-7). 2000. pap. 5.99 (*0-8431-7583-4*, Price Stern) Peng Put Young Read.

***Mighty Big River.** Chad Merriman. 1999. 19.00 (*0-7540-8071-4*, Gunsmoke) Chivers N Amer.

Mighty Boy. Carol Sonenklar. LC 99-11706. 128p. (J). (gr. 3-7). 1999. 15.95 (*0-531-30203-2*); lib. bdg. 16.99 (*0-531-33203-9*) Orchard Bks Watts.

Mighty Bugeaters: The First Decade of Nebraska Football, 1890-1899. David F. Harding. (Illus.). 52p. 1998. pap. 9.95 (*0-9668492-0-5*) Nebraska Cloth.

Mighty Casey: All-American, 7. Eugene C. Murdock. LC 83-16338. (Contributions to the Study of Popular Culture Ser.: No. 7). 164p. 1984. 45.00 (*0-313-24075-2*, MMC/, Greenwood Pr) Greenwood.

Mighty Cat: Russian Folk Tale Story Pak. Retold by K. Hollenbeck. (Graphic Learning Literature Program Series: Folk Tales). (ENG & SPA., Illus.). (J). 1992. 45.00 (*0-87746-265-8*) Graphic Learning.

Mighty Change. Ed J. Pinegar. pap. 11.98 (*1-55517-275-X*) CFI Dist.

***Mighty Change: An Anthology of Deaf American Writing.** Ed. by Christopher Krentz. 2000. 45.00 (*1-56368-098-X*); pap. 24.95 (*1-56368-101-3*) Gallaudet Univ Pr.

Mighty Chieftains see American Indians Series

Mighty Chieftains. Time-Life Books Editors. LC 93-22395. (American Indians Ser.). (Illus.). 184p. 1993. lib. bdg. write for info. (*0-8094-9430-2*) Time-Life.

Mighty Christ: Touching Glory. R. C. Sproul. 9.99 (*1-85792-148-8*, Pub. by Christian Focus) Spring Arbor Dist.

Mighty Dinosaurs. Kindersley Publishing Dorling. 1999. pap. text 3.95 (*0-7894-4784-3*) DK Pub Inc.

Mighty Dinosaurs. Judith Simpson. LC 96-15737. (Nature Company Young Discoveries Ser.). (Illus.). 32p. (J). 1999. 10.00 (*0-7835-4837-0*) Time-Life.

Mighty Dinosaurs. Time-Life Books Editors. (Nature Company Discoveries Library Sticker Activity Bks.). (Illus.). 16p. (gr. k-3). 1999. pap. 7.95 (*0-7835-4897-4*) Time-Life.

Mighty Ducks: The First Face-Off. Debra M. Zakarin. LC PZ7.Z2527Di 1997. (Disney Chapters Ser.). 64p. (J). (gr. 2-4). 1997. pap. 3.50 (*0-7868-4147-8*, Pub. by Disney Pr) Little.

Mighty Ducks D3: Junior Novelization. Jonathan Schmidt. LC 96-84565. (Illus.). 96p. (J). (gr. 2-5). 1996. pap. 4.95 (*0-7868-4102-8*, Pub. by Disney Pr) Little.

Mighty Eighth: The Air War in Europe As Told by the Men Who Fought It. Gerald Astor. 560p. 1998. mass mkt. 6.50 (*0-440-22648-1*) Dell.

Mighty Eighth: The Air War in Europe Told by the Men Who Fought It. Gerald Astor. LC 96-48594. (Illus.). 480p. 1997. pap. 26.95 (*1-55611-510-5*, Pub. by D I Fine) Penguin Putnam.

M

An Asterisk (*) at the beginning of an entry indicates that the title is appearing for the first time.

Mighty Eighth: Warpaint & Heraldry. Roger Freeman. LC 98-129817. (Illus.). 160p. 1998. 34.95 (*1-85409-373-8*, Pub. by Arms & Armour) Sterling.

Mighty Eighth in Art. Roger A. Freeman. (Illus.). 160p. pap. 24.95 (*1-85409-473-4*) Arms & Armour.

Mighty Eighth in Art. Roger A. Freeman. (Illus.). 160p. 1996. 39.95 (*1-85409-312-6*, Pub. by Arms & Armour) Sterling.

***Mighty Eighth in WWII: A Memoir.** J. Kemp McLaughlin. LC 00-28305. (Illus.). 248p. 2000. 22.00 (*0-8131-2178-7*) U Pr of Ky.

Mighty Endeavor: The American War in Europe. Charles B. MacDonald. (Illus.). 621p. 1992. reprint ed. pap. 16.95 (*0-306-80486-7*) Da Capo.

***Mighty Engine: The Printing Press & Its Impact.** Peter C. G. Isaac & Barry McKay. LC 00-40656. (Print Networks Ser.). (Illus.). 2000. write for info. (*1-58456-024-X*) Oak Knoll.

Mighty Engineering Feats. Harriet Salt. LC 71-86782. (Essay Index Reprint Ser.). 1977. 23.95 (*0-8369-1193-8*) Ayer.

Mighty Faith see Effective Faith: How to Be Like the Heros of Faith

Mighty Five. Victor I. Seroff. LC 77-126256. (Select Bibliographies Reprint Ser.). 1977. 21.95 (*0-8369-5483-1*) Ayer.

Mighty Fortress. Robert Deitmeyer. 1.25 (*0-687-05823-6*) Abingdon.

***Mighty Fortress.** Charles E. Williams. LC 99-91973. 2000. 25.00 (*0-7388-1456-3*); pap. 18.00 (*0-7388-1457-1*) Xlibris Corp.

Mighty Fortress in the Storm. Paulina M. Rustenburg-Bootsma. LC 92-29417. (Illus.). 174p. (YA). 1992. 10.90 (*0-921100-37-X*) Inhtce Pubns.

Mighty Fortress Is Our God. 1996. pap. 1.30 (*0-8341-9607-7*, AG-1020) Lillenas.

Mighty Fortress is Our God. Jim Cromarty. 1998. pap. 13.99 (*0-85234-411-2*, Pub. by Evangelical Pr) P & R Pubng.

Mighty Gents. Richard Wesley. 1979. pap. 5.25 (*0-8222-0756-7*) Dramatists Play.

Mighty Hand of God. Katherine Carter. 224p. 1991. pap. 8.95 (*0-89228-043-3*) Impact Christian.

***Mighty Hand of God.** Dale Evrist. 228p. 2000. pap. 12.99 (*0-88419-658-5*) Creation House.

Mighty Hugo Comes to Town: Hurricane. large type ed. Jereleen Hollimon-Miller. Ed. by Beverly Lutze. (Facing Your Fears Ser.). (Illus.). 32p. (J). (ps-5). 1997. pap. 9.95 (*0-9643500-0-9*) Jereleen.

Mighty in Spirit. Joseph Bagiackas. LC 82-72094. 54p. 1982. pap. 3.95 (*0-943780-00-4*, 8004) Greenlawn Pr.

***Mighty in Word & Deed: The Role of the Holy Spirit in Luke-Acts.** James B. Shelton. 196p. 2000. pap. 20.00 (*1-57910-321-9*) Wipf & Stock.

Mighty Is Your Hand: A Forty-Day Journey in the Company of Andrew Murray. Andrew Murray. Ed. by David Hazzard. LC 93-50653. (Rekindling the Inner Fire Ser.: No. 6). 16p. 1994. pap. 8.99 (*1-55661-369-5*) Bethany Hse.

Mighty Joe, Pew Prompter: Another Complete Book of Short Scenes for Sermons, Services & Special Seasons. (Pew Prompters Ser.). 1997. pap. 15.99 (*0-8341-9657-3*) Lillenas.

Mighty Joe Young. Carolyn Otto. LC 97-80191. (Junior Novelization Ser.). (Illus.). 96p. (J). (gr. 3-7). 1998. pap. 4.95 (*0-7868-4137-0*, Pub. by Disney Pr) Time Warner.

Mighty Joe Young. Che Rudko. LC PZ7.M6995735Wal 1998. (Golden Look-Look Ser.). 24p. 1998. pap. 3.29 (*0-307-13183-1*, 13183, Goldn Books) Gldn Bks Pub Co.

Mighty Like a River: The Black Church & Social Reform. Andrew Billingsley. LC 98-13875. (Illus.). 288p. 1999. 26.00 (*0-19-510617-2*) OUP.

***Mighty Little Lion Hunter.** Jana Carson. (We Both Read Ser.). (Illus.). 44p. (J). (gr. k-1). 2000. 7.99 (*1-891327-21-6*); pap. 3.99 (*1-891327-22-4*) Treas Bay Inc.

***Mighty Long Journey: Reflections on Racial Reconciliation.** Ed. by Timothy George & Robert Smith, Jr. 240p. 2000. pap. 17.99 (*0-8054-1820-2*) Broadman.

Mighty Mac: The Official Picture History of the Mackinac Bridge. Lawrence A. Rubin. LC 58-13847. (Illus.). 148p. 1986. reprint ed. pap. 13.95 (*0-8143-1817-7*) Wayne St U Pr.

***Mighty Machines.** LC 00-38341. 2000. lib. bdg. write for info. (*0-7894-6797-6*) DK Pub Inc.

***Mighty Machines.** Angela Royston. LC 00-25792. 2000. pap. 10.95 (*0-7534-5315-0*, Kingfisher) LKC.

Mighty Man Is He. Arthur Kober & George Oppenheimer. 1960. pap. 5.25 (*0-8222-0757-5*) Dramatists Play.

***Mighty Man of God: A Return to the Glory of Manhood.** Sam Laing. 160p. 1999. pap. 9.99 (*1-57782-118-1*) Discipleshp.

Mighty Man VS Almighty God: David & Goliath. 1995. pap. 9.98 (*1-886858-49-7*) Shepherds Tales.

Mighty Maps! Facts, Fun & Trivia to Develop Map Skills. Cindy Barden. Ed. by Judy Mitchell. (Illus.). 96p. (Orig.). (J). (gr. 3-6). 1995. pap., teacher ed. 9.95 (*1-57310-037-4*) Teachng & Lrning Co.

***Mighty Match-Ups.** (World Championship Wrestling - New World Order Ser.). (Illus.). 24p. 1999. pap. write for info. (*0-7666-0444-6*, Honey Bear Bks) Modern Pub NYC.

Mighty Maverick Magick: The Essence of Victorious Living. Al G. Manning. 180p. 1983. 12.95 (*0-941698-08-4*); pap. 6.95 (*0-941698-09-2*) Pan Ishtar.

Mighty Maze: A Study of Pope's an Essay on Man. Michael Srigley. (Studia Anglistica Upsaliensia Ser.: No. 87). 178p. (Orig.). 1994. pap. 42.50 (*91-554-3329-4*) Coronet Bks.

Mighty Menfolk. Carole B. Weatherford. (Illus.). 12p. (J). (ps-k). 1996. bds. 5.95 (*0-86316-253-3*) Writers & Readers.

***Mighty Midgets at War: The Saga of the LCS(L) Ships from Iwo Jima to Vietnam.** Robin L. Rielly. (Illus.). 2000. pap. 18.95 (*1-55571-522-2*, Hellgate Pr) PSI Resch.

Mighty Midwest Flood: Raging Rivers. Carmen Bredeson. LC 98-11728. (American Disasters Ser.). 48p. (YA). (gr. 4-10). 1999. lib. bdg. 18.95 (*0-7660-1221-2*) Enslow Pubs.

***Mighty Mighty Bosstones: Let's Face It.** 80p. 1998. otabind 19.95 (*0-7935-8737-9*) H Leonard.

***Mighty Mini Mind Bogglers.** K. Richards. LC 99-45675. 160p. 1999. pap. text 4.95 (*0-8069-1239-1*) Strlng Pub CA.

***Mighty Mini Rhyming Picture Puzzles.** Steve Ryan & American Mensa Limited Staff. LC 99-86833. 2000. 4.95 (*0-8069-2893-X*) Sterling.

Mighty Mini Success Sparklers: Education - Excellence - Einstein. Compiled by Ivy Conner. 16p. (Orig.). 1997. pap. text 3.00 (*1-878579-11-8*) SUN Pub Co.

Mighty Mini Success Sparklers: Goals - Success. Compiled by Ivy Conner. 16p. (Orig.). 1997. pap. text 3.00 (*1-878579-10-X*) SUN Pub Co.

Mighty Minis. 3rd ed. Chris Harvey. (Illus.). 320p. 1997. 39.95 (*1-85509-237-9*, Pub. by J H Haynes & Co) Haynes Manuals.

Mighty Minorities? Minorities in Early Christianity-Positions & Strategies. Ed. by David Hellholm et al. 220p. 1995. 34.00 (*82-00-22451-1*) Scandnvan Univ Pr.

Mighty Miss & Other Poems. Amy Boudreau. 1974. 4.95 (*0-614-30803-8*, BMIGHT) Claitors.

Mighty Missionaries. Elaine Cannon. 1994. pap. 1.95 (*0-88494-944-3*) Bookcraft Inc.

Mighty Mississippi. Amy Boudreau. 1967. pap. 3.00 (*0-685-08193-1*) Claitors.

Mighty Mogul. Lin Oliver. LC 99-28601. (Great Railway Adventures Ser.: Vol. 2;1). (Illus.). 32p. (J). (gr. k-4). 1999. 14.95 (*1-890647-56-X*); pap. 9.99 incl. audio (*1-890647-57-8*) Lrning Curve.

Mighty Monday Madness. Doug TenNapel & Mike Koelsch. (Strange Kid Chronicles Ser.: No. 1). (J). (gr. 2 up). 1998. pap. 3.99 (*0-590-05953-X*) Scholastic Inc.

Mighty Morphin Power Rangers: Adventure on Phaedos. Tor Books Staff. 1995. pap. 3.50 (*0-8125-4455-2*, Pub. by Tor Bks) St Martin.

Mighty Morphin Power Rangers: The Movie. Ed. by Carol Cuellar. 84p. (Orig.). (C). 1995. pap. text 16.95 (*0-89724-741-8*, PF9527) Wrner Bros.

Mighty Morphin Power Rangers: The Movie Scrapbook. Tor Books Staff. 1995. pap. 4.99 (*0-8125-4456-0*, Pub. by Tor Bks) St Martin.

Mighty Morphin Power Rangers: The Movie Storybook. Tor Books Staff. 1995. pap. 3.50 (*0-8125-4454-4*, Pub. by Tor Bks) St Martin.

Mighty Morphin Power Rangers Model Book. pap. 7.95 (*0-8431-3871-8*, Price Stern) Peng Put Young Read.

Mighty Morphin Power Rangers Scrapbook. Nancy E. Krulik. 32p. (J). (ps-3). 1994. pap. 3.95 (*0-590-48853-8*) Scholastic Inc.

Mighty Mountain. Archie Binns. 440p. 1951. 14.95 (*0-8323-0110-8*); pap. 9.95 (*0-8323-0259-7*) Binford Mort.

Mighty Mountain & the Three Strong Women. Irene Hedlund. LC 89-28052. (Illus.). 28p. (J). (gr. 2-5). 1990. 14.95 (*0-912078-86-3*) Volcano Pr.

Mighty Mountains. Finn Bevan. (Landscapes of Legend Ser.). (J). 1998. pap. text 6.95 (*0-516-26299-8*) Childrens.

Mighty Mountains: The Facts & the Fables. Finn Bevan. LC 96-48801. (Landscapes of Legend Ser.). (Illus.). (J). 1997. lib. bdg. 20.00 (*0-516-20348-7*) Childrens.

***Mighty Movies: Movie Poster Art from Hollywood's Greatest Adventure Epics & Spectaculars.** Lawrence Bassoff. LC 99-95159. (Illus.). 152p. 1999. pap. 35.00 (*1-886310-14-9*, Pub. by Bassoff Collect) SCB Distributors.

Mighty Myth. Great B. Lipson & Sidney Bolkosky. 152p. (J). (gr. 5-12). 1982. 13.99 (*0-86653-064-9*, GA 419) Good Apple.

***Mighty Oaks from Little Acorns Grow: The History of Norfolk Collegiate School.** Amy Waters Yarsinske. LC 00-40876. 2000. write for info. (*0-9653759-9-4*) Hallmark Publng.

Mighty Ocean. Melvin Berger. Ed. by Lauren Weidenman. (Ranger Rick Science Spectacular Ser.). (Illus.). 16p. (Orig.). (J). (gr. 2-4). 1996. pap. 16.95 (*1-56784-218-6*) Newbridge Educ.

Mighty Ocean: Student Book. Melvin Berger. Ed. by Lauren Weidenman. (Ranger Rick Science Spectacular Ser.). (Illus.). 16p. (Orig.). (J). (gr. 2-4). 1996. pap. 3.95 (*1-56784-243-7*) Newbridge Educ.

Mighty Ocean: Theme Pack. Melvin Berger. Ed. by Lauren Weidenman. (Ranger Rick Science Spectacular Ser.). (Illus.). (Orig.). (J). (gr. 2-4). 1996. pap. 36.90 (*1-56784-278-X*) Newbridge Educ.

Mighty Opposites: From Dichotomies to Differences in the Comparative Study of China. Lung-Hsi Chang. LC 98-26223. 248 p. 1999. write for info. (*0-8047-3259-0*) Stanford U Pr.

Mighty Opposites: From Dichotomies to Differences in the Comparative Study of China. Longxi Zhang. 256p. 1999. pap. text 17.95 (*0-8047-3471-2*) Stanford U Pr.

Mighty Prevailing Prayer. Wesley L. Duewel. 352p. 1990. pap. 14.99 (*0-310-36191-5*) Zondervan.

Mighty Prevailing Prayer see Oracion Poderosa Que Prevalece

Mighty Quinn. Candace Schuler. (Temptation Ser.: No. 397). 1992. mass mkt. 2.99 (*0-373-25497-0*, 1-25497-8) Harlequin Bks.

Mighty Quinn. Candace Schuler. (Men at Work Ser.: Vol. 34). 1998. mass mkt. 4.50 (*0-373-81046-6*, 1-81046-4) Harlequin Bks.

Mighty River: A Portrait of the Fraser. Richard C. Bocking. LC 97-23760. (Illus.). 304p. 1998. 29.95 (*0-295-97670-5*) U of Wash Pr.

***Mighty Rough Times I Tell You: Personal Accounts of Slavery in Tennessee.** Ed. by Andrea Sutcliffe. 103p. 2000. pap. 7.95 (*0-89587-226-9*) Blair.

Mighty Santa Fe. William H. Hooks. LC 92-17026. (Illus.). 32p. (J). (gr. k-3). 1993. lib. bdg. 14.95 (*0-02-744432-5*, Mac Bks Young Read) S&S Childrens.

***Mighty Skink.** Paul Shipton. LC 99-46186. 192p. (YA). (gr. 4-7). 2000. 15.95 (*0-688-17420-5*, Wm Morrow) Morrow Avon.

Mighty Slide. Allan Ahlberg. 96p. (YA). (gr. 7 up). 1990. pap. 7.95 (*0-14-032335-X*, Pub. by Pnguin Bks Ltd) Trafalgar.

Mighty Spiders! Fay Robinson. LC 95-10530. (Hello Reader! Ser.: Level 2). (Illus.). 32p. (J). (gr. k-2). 1996. pap. 3.50 (*0-590-26262-9*, Cartwheel) Scholastic Inc.

Mighty Spiders! Fay Robinson. (Hello, Reader! Ser.). 1996. 8.70 (*0-606-09613-2*, Pub. by Turtleback) Demco.

Mighty Stonewall. Frank E. Vandiver. LC 88-9642. (Military History Ser.: No. 9). (Illus.). 560p. 1992. reprint ed. 29.95 (*0-89096-384-3*) Tex A&M Univ Pr.

Mighty Stonewall. Frank E. Vandiver. LC 88-9642. (Military History Ser.: No. 9). (Illus.). 560p. 1995. reprint ed. pap. 17.95 (*0-89096-391-6*) Tex A&M Univ Pr.

Mighty Stories, Dangerous Rituals: Weaving Together the Human & the Divine. Herbert Anderson & Edward Foley. LC 97-21075. 1997. 21.95 (*0-7879-0880-0*) Jossey-Bass.

Mighty Tree. Dick Gackenbach. LC 91-12904. (Illus.). 32p. (J). (ps-3). 1992. 13.95 (*0-15-200519-6*, Gulliver Bks) Harcourt.

Mighty Tree. Dick Gackenbach. LC 91-12904. (Illus.). 32p. (J). (ps-3). 1996. pap. 5.00 (*0-15-201013-0*, Gulliver Bks) Harcourt.

Mighty Tree. Dick Gackenbach. 1996. 10.20 (*0-606-09614-0*, Pub. by Turtleback) Demco.

***Mighty U. S. Forces Versus a Little Man.** Gino Enas. LC 99-93644. 1999. pap. 12.95 (*0-533-13100-6*) Vantage.

Mighty Warrior: A Guide to Effective Prayer. Elizabeth Alves. 216p. 1998. pap. 10.99 (*0-8307-2333-1*) Gospel Lght.

Mighty Wave: Aspects of the 1978 Rebellion in Wexford. Ed. by Daire Keogh & Nicholas Furlong. LC 96-184601. 220p. 1996. 50.00 (*1-85182-253-4*, Pub. by Four Cts Pr); pap. 14.95 (*1-85182-254-2*, Pub. by Four Cts Pr) Intl Spec Bk.

Miglior Fabbro: The Cult of the Difficult in Daniel, Dante & Pound. James J. Wilhelm. LC 82-80304. (Ezra Pound Scholarship Ser.). (Illus.). 132p. (Orig.). 1982. 20.00 (*0-915032-03-1*); pap. 10.95 (*0-915032-04-X*) Natl Poet Foun.

Mignon G. Eberhart's Best Mystery Stories. Mignon G. Eberhart. 384p. 1989. mass mkt. 5.50 (*0-446-35932-7*, Pub. by Warner Bks) Little.

Mignonette Yin Cheng. Pref. by Evan M. Maurer. (Illus.). 46p. (Orig.). (C). 1988. pap. 5.00 (*0-912303-40-9*) Michigan Mus.

Mignot de la Voye: Treatise on Music. Ed. by A. Gruber. (Musical Theorists in Translation Ser.: Vol. 11). 96p. 1972. lib. bdg. 27.00 (*0-912024-31-3*) Inst Mediaeval Mus.

Migola Ligeula. Compiled by El Friedman. (HEB.). 379p. 1991. pap. 17.00 (*0-8266-5220-4*) Kehot Pubn Soc.

Migracion de Inmigrantes Indocumentados Mexicanos: Y la Politica para Gestionarla. John Carney & Angela Alcerro. (ENG & SPA., Illus.). 84p. (Orig.). 1995. pap. 6.00 (*1-879861-13-5*) Consensus Pubs.

Migracion Indocumentada de Mexico a Los Estados Unidos (Indocumented Migration from Mexico) Un Nuevo Enfoque. Juan D. Ruiz. LC 85-187805. (Seccion de Obras de Economia). (SPA.). 208p. 1984. pap. 9.99 (*968-16-1742-8*, Pub. by Fondo) Continental Bk.

Migracion y Etnicidad en Oaxaca. M. Musalem & O. Riosz Vazquez. Ed. by J. Corbett et al. (Vanderbilt University Publications in Anthropology: No. 43). (SPA.). 176p. (Orig.). 1992. pap. 12.75 (*0-935462-34-1*) VUPA.

Migraine. M. A. Budd. 1998. mass mkt. 7.00 (*0-7225-3326-8*, 902696Q) Thorsons PA.

Migraine. Ed. by F. Clifford Rose. (Illus.). xii, 280p. 1985. 152.25 (*3-8055-4039-6*) S Karger.

***Migraine.** Oliver W. Sacks. LC 99-33021. (Illus.). 368p. 1999. pap. 14.00 (*0-375-70406-X*) Vin Bks.

Migraine: A Spectrum of Ideas. Ed. by Merton Sandler & Geralyn M. Collins. (Illus.). 340p. 1990. 75.00 (*0-19-261810-5*) OUP.

Migraine: An Annotated Bibliography of Treatment Sources. Compiled by Gerald Wade. 41p. 1986. 12.00 (*0-937755-00-1*) Cypress Creek Pubns.

Migraine: Clinical & Research Aspects. J. N. Blau. LC 87-3801. (Series in Contemporary Medicine & Public Health). 680p. 1988. text 160.00 (*0-8018-3551-8*) Johns Hopkins.

Migraine: Everything You. Arthur Elkind. LC 97-93166. 256p. 1997. mass mkt. 5.99 (*0-380-79077-7*, Avon Bks) Morrow Avon.

Migraine: Everything You Need to Know. Valerie South. (Illus.). 220p. 1996. pap. 14.95 (*1-55013-784-0*) Firefly Bks Ltd.

Migraine: Manifestations, Pathogenesis, & Management. Robert A. Davidoff. LC 94-16409. (Contemporary Neurology Ser.: No. 42). (Illus.). 400p. (C). 1994. text 85.00 (*0-8036-2360-7*) OUP.

Migraine: Pharmacology & Genetics. Ed. by M. Sandler et al. (Illus.). 344p. 1996. text 56.00 (*1-86036-006-8*, Pub. by E A) OUP.

Migraine: Questions & Answers. Egilius L. Spierings. (Illus.). 120p. 1996. pap. 15.95 (*1-873413-60-2*) Merit Pub Intl.

Migraine: The Complete Guide. American Council for Headache Education Staff et al. LC 93-27843. 304p. 1994. pap. 12.95 (*0-440-50458-9*) Dell.

Migraine: The Evolution of a Common Disorder. Oliver W. Sacks. LC 78-128584. 220p. reprint ed. pap. 68.20 (*0-608-17281-2*, 202959100061) Bks Demand.

Migraine: Winning the Fight of Your Life. Charles W. Theisler. LC 94-66613. 176p. 1995. pap. 12.95 (*0-914984-63-2*, Pub. by Starburst) Natl Bk Netwk.

Migraine - Questions & Answers. 2nd ed. Egilius Spierings. 120p. 2000. pap. 17.95 (*1-873413-96-3*) Merit Pub Intl.

Migraine - What Works: A Complete Self Help Guide to Overcoming & Preventing Migraines. Joseph Kandel & David B. Sudderth. LC 95-21229. (Illus.). 224p. 1995. pap. text 14.00 (*0-7615-0087-1*) Prima Pub.

Migraine & Other Headaches. James W. Lance. 256p. 1999. per. 13.00 (*0-684-86846-6*) S&S Trade.

Migraine & Other Headaches. Marcia Wilkinson & Anne MacGregor. LC 98-43379. (ACP Home Medical Guides). 96p. 1999. pap. 6.95 (*0-7894-4164-0*, D K Ink) DK Pub Inc.

Migraine & Other Headaches: A Practical Guide to Understanding, Preventing & Treating Headaches. James W. Lance. 1998. pap. text. write for info. (*0-7318-0740-5*) Simon & Schuster.

Migraine & Other Headaches: The Vascular Mechanisms. Jes Olesen. (Frontiers in Headache Research Ser.: Vol. 1). 368p. 1991. text 99.50 (*0-88167-795-7*) Lppncott W & W.

Migraine Boy. Greg Fiering. (Illus.). 80p. 1996. pap. 7.95 (*0-312-14369-9*) St Martin.

Migraine Handbook. J. Lewis. pap. 15.95 (*0-09-181666-1*, Pub. by Random) Trafalgar.

Migraine Headache: Prevention & Treatment by Phytotherapy, Herbal Medicine. Ela Ronen & Bernice Baefour. 68p. (Orig.). 1993. pap. 15.95 (*0-9638677-0-9*) E M D Ent.

Migraine Headache Disease. Charles W. Theisler. LC 90-960. (Diagnostic & Management Strategies Ser.). 190p. 1990. 82.00 (*0-8342-0176-3*) Aspen Pub.

Migraine Headache Prevention & Management. Seymour Diamond. (Illus.). 256p. 1990. text 125.00 (*0-8247-8212-7*) Dekker.

Migraine Headaches & the Food You Eat: 200 Recipes for Relief. Agnes Peg Hartnell. 272p. 1997. pap. 12.95 (*0-471-34686-1*) Wiley.

Migraine Headaches & the Foods You Eat: 200 Recipes for Relief. Agnes P. Hartnell & G. Scott Tyler. LC 99-210386. 272p. (Orig.). 1997. pap. 12.95 (*1-56561-121-7*) Wiley.

Migraine in Perspective. 96p. pap. text 34.95 (*0-86471-053-4*, Pub. by Adis Intl) Lppncott W & W.

***Migraine in Women.** Anne MacGregor. 90p. 1999. 39.95 (*1-85317-744-X*, Pub. by Martin Dunitz) Blackwell Sci.

Migraine Killers That Zap Headaches Now. Douglas Hunt. 272p. 1998. pap. 19.95 (*0-9663040-0-4*) Rosebud Pubns.

Migraine Prevention. Victor A. Young. LC 78-61831. 156p. 1978. 3.95 (*0-9603694-0-6*) V Young.

Migraines: A Natural Approach. Sue Dyson. LC 98-84064. (Natural Approach Ser.). (Illus.). 240p. 1998. pap. 10.95 (*1-56975-140-4*) Ulysses Pr.

Migraines & More - Conquered. Louis M. Hale. 160p. 1987. 14.95 (*0-941219-75-5*) Phillips Pub MA.

Migrancy, Culture, Identity. Iain Chambers. LC 93-7863. (Illus.). 192p. (C). 1994. pap. 19.99 (*0-415-08802-X*) Routledge.

Migrant & Seasonal Farmworkers: Health Care Accessibility. Sandra Benavides-Vaello & Heather Setzler. (Working Paper Ser.: Vol. 76). 46p. 1994. pap. 5.50 (*0-89940-567-3*) LBJ Sch Pub Aff.

***Migrant Belongings: Memory, Space & Identity.** Anne-Marie Fortier. 224p. 2000. 65.00 (*1-85973-405-7*, Pub. by Berg Pubs); pap. 19.50 (*1-85973-410-3*, Pub. by Berg Pubs) NYU Pr.

Migrant Child Labour in India. S. N. Tripathy. LC 96-905621. 1996. pap. 130.00 (*81-7445-030-0*, Pub. by Print Hse) St Mut.

Migrant Children: Their Education. Association for Childhood Education International Staff. Ed. by Sylvia Sunderlin. LC 74-162482. 64p. reprint ed. pap. 30.00 (*0-608-13787-1*, 202063100018) Bks Demand.

***Migrant Cocoa-Farmers of Southern Ghana.** Polly Hill. (Classics in African Anthropology). 310p. 1999. pap. 26.95 (*3-8258-3085-3*, Pub. by CE24) Transaction Pubs.

***Migrant Daughter: Coming of Age as a Mexican American Woman.** Frances E. Tywoniak & Mario T. Garcma. LC 99-40594. 321p. 2000. 45.00 (*0-520-21914-7*, Pub. by U CA Pr); pap. 17.95 (*0-520-21915-5*, Pub. by U CA Pr) Cal Prin Full Svc.

Migrant Experience in Europe. write for info. (*0-8386-3617-9*) Fairleigh Dickinson.

Migrant Family. Larry D. Brimner. (In My Shoes Ser.). (Illus.). 40p. (J). (gr. 4-8). 1992. lib. bdg. 19.93 (*0-8225-2554-2*, Lerner Publctns) Lerner Pub.

Migrant Farm Worker Nutritional Manual. M. Alison Hull & Donna H. Runyan. (Illus.). 260p. (Orig.). (C). 1996. pap. text 50.00 (*0-7881-2658-X*) DIANE Pub.

Migrant Farm Workers: A Caste of Despair. Ronald L. Goldfarb. LC 81-6024. (Illus.). 254p. 1981. reprint ed. pap. 78.80 (*0-608-00028-0*, 206079400006) Bks Demand.

Migrant Farmer in the History of the Cape Colony, 1657-1842. Petrus J. Van der Merwe. Tr. by Roger B. Beck from AFR. LC 94-21649. (Illus.). 333p. (C). 1994. text 60.00 (*0-8214-1090-3*) Ohio U Pr.

Migrant Farmworker's Son. Silvia Gonzalez. 1996. 5.50 (*0-87129-551-2*, M90) Dramatic Pub.

M

An Asterisk (*) at the beginning of an entry indicates that the title is appearing for the first time.

M

Migrant Labour & Related Issues. Ed. by Vidyut Joshi. (C). 1987. 22.00 (*81-204-0199-9*, Pub. by Oxford IBH) S Asia.

Migrant Labour & Tribal Life: A Study of Conditions in the Bechuanaland Protectorate. Isaac Schapera. LC 74-15084. reprint ed. 32.50 (*0-404-12134-9*) AMS Pr.

*__Migrant Labour in Japan.__ Yoko Sellek. LC 00-34488. (Illus.). 2000. write for info. (*0-312-23775-8*) St Martin.

Migrant Labour in South Africa's Mining Economy: The Struggle for the Gold Mines' Labour Supply, 1890-1920. Alan H. Jeeves. 256p. 1985. 65.00 (*0-7735-0420-6*, Pub. by McG-Queens Univ Pr) CUP Services.

Migrant Missionary Story: The Autobiography of Giacomo Gambera. Ed. by Mary E. Brown. Tr. by Serafina M. Clarke & Thomas F. Carlesimo. LC 94-22750. 336p. 1994. 14.50 (*0-934733-85-6*) CMS.

Migrant Song: Politics & Process in Contemporary Chicano Literature. Teresa Mckenna. LC 96-25379. 1997. 27.50 (*0-292-76518-5*); pap. text 12.95 (*0-292-75188-5*) U of Tex Pr.

Migrant Soul: The Story of an American Ger. Avi Shafran. 272p. 1992. 17.95 (*0-944070-45-0*) Targum Pr.

Migrant Souls. Arturo Islas. 256p. 1991. pap. 8.95 (*0-380-71440-X*, Avon Bks) Morrow Avon.

Migrant Spirit. Bri M. Tiwari. 1999. write for info. (*0-609-60265-9*) Harmony Bks.

Migrant Women: Crossing Boundaries & Changing Identities. Ed. by Gina Buijs. LC 92-15999. (Cross-Cultural Perspectives on Women Ser.). 256p. 1993. 49.50 (*0-85496-729-X*); pap. 19.50 (*0-85496-869-5*, Pub. by Berg Pubs) NYU Pr.

Migrant Worker: A Boy from the Rio Grande Valley. Diane Hoyt-Goldsmith. LC 95-36779. (Illus.). 32p. (J). (gr. 4-6). 1996. 15.95 (*0-8234-1225-3*) Holiday.

Migrant Workers: Strangers in Our Midst. H. Monte Hill. LC 93-83907. 63p. 1999. pap. 8.00 (*1-882911-00-8*) Soc Science.

Migrant Workers in International Human Rights Law: Their Protection in Countries of Employment. Ryszard Cholewinski. LC 98-101421. 538p. (C). 1997. text 95.00 (*0-19-825992-1*) OUP.

Migrant Workers in Japan. Hiroshi Komai. Tr. by Jens Wilkinson from JPN. LC 94-40694. (Japanese Studies).Tr. of Gaikokujin rodosha teiju e no michi. (ENG & JPN.). 1995. write for info. (*0-7103-0499-4*) Routledge.

Migrants: Partners in International Cooperation. Marie-Helene Libercier & Hartmut Schneider. LC 97-102597. 60p. (Orig.). 1996. pap. 12.00 (*92-64-14907-4*, 41-96-06-1, Pub. by Org for Econ) OECD.

Migrants & Anthropologists Labour, Capital, & the Social Order. Ed. by Jerry Eades. 288p. (C). 1988. pap. text 34.99 (*0-422-61680-X*, Pub. by Tavistock) Routldge.

*__Migrants & Citizens: Demographic Change in the European State System.__ Rey Koslowski. 2000. 39.95 (*0-8014-3714-8*) Cornell U Pr.

Migrants & Refugees: Muslim & Christian Pakistani Families in Bristol. Patricia Jeffery. LC 75-25428. 229p. reprint ed. pap. 65.30 (*0-608-15742-2*, 2031674) Bks Demand.

Migrants & Refugees: The Moral Challenge. Ed. by Dietmar Mieth & Lisa S. Cahill. (Concilium Ser.). 1993. 15.00 (*0-88344-873-4*) Orbis Bks.

Migrants & Stay-at-Homes: A Comparative Study of Rural Migration from Michoacan, Mexico. Ina R. Dinerman. (Monographs: No. 5). 112p. (Orig.). (C). 1982. pap. 7.50 (*0-935391-43-6*, MN-05) UCSD Ctr US-Mex.

Migrants As Actors. Sharlene Hesse. (Illus.). 196p. 1981. text 27.00 (*0-8290-0301-0*) Irvington.

*__Migrants, Citizens & the State in Southern Africa.__ Jim Whitman. LC 99-53015. (Illus.). 2000. text 79.95 (*0-312-23108-3*) St Martin.

*__Migrants Ethnic Minorities.__ John Wrench. LC 99-11215. 1999. text 69.95 (*0-312-22187-8*) St Martin.

Migrants from the Promised Land. Zvi Sobel. 230p. (C). 1986. 39.95 (*0-88738-046-8*) Transaction Pubs.

Migrants, Immigrants, & Slaves: Racial & Ethnic Groups in America. George Henderson & Thompson Olasiji. 334p. (C). 1994. pap. text 23.50 (*0-8191-9738-6*) U Pr of Amer.

Migrants in Agricultural Development. Ed. by J. A. Mollett. 260p. (C). 1991. text 80.00 (*0-8147-5459-7*) NYU Pr.

Migrants in Europe: Problems of Acceptance & Adjustment. Arnold M. Rose. LC 76-76162. 206p. reprint ed. pap. 63.90 (*0-608-15979-4*, 203328700084) Bks Demand.

Migrants in Europe: The Role of the Family, Labor, & Politics, 12. Ed. by Hans C. Buechler & Judith-Maria Buechler. LC 86-25722. (Contributions in Family Studies: No. 12). 327p. 1987. 85.00 (*0-313-23236-9*, BUM/, Greenwood Pr) Greenwood.

Migrants, Minorities, & Health: Historical & Contemporary Studies. Lara V. Marks & Michael Worboys. LC 96-22911. (Studies in the Social History of Medicine Ser.). (Illus.). 264p. (C). 1997. 85.00 (*0-415-11213-3*) Routledge.

Migrants No More: Settlement & Survival in Mambwe Villages, Zambia. Johan Pottier. LC 88-9373. (International African Library). (Illus.). 224p. 1989. 36.95 (*0-253-33894-8*) Ind U Pr.

Migrants of Identity: Perceptions of 'Home' in a World in Movement. Ed. by Nigel Rapport & Andrew Dawson. LC 98-230639. (Ethnicity & Identity Ser.). 224p. 1998. 55.00 (*1-85973-994-6*, Pub. by Berg Pubs); pap. 19.50 (*1-85973-999-7*, Pub. by Berg Pubs) NYU Pr.

Migrants, Refugees, & Foreign Policy: U. S. & German Policies Toward Countries of Origin. Ed. by Rainer Munz & Myron Weiner. LC 97-2328. (Migration & Refugees: Vol. 2). 384p. 1997. 59.95 (*1-57181-087-0*) Berghahn Bks.

Migrants, Regional Identities & Latin American Cities. Teofilo Altamirano et al. LC 97-3401. (Society for Latin American Anthropology Publication Ser.). 1997. write for info. (*0-913167-79-7*) Am Anthro Assn.

Migrant's Story: The Struggle & Success of an Italian-Australian, 1920s-1960s. Osvaldo Bonutto. LC 94-185740. 99p. 1995. pap. 16.95 (*0-7022-2660-2*, Pub. by Univ Queensland Pr) Intl Spec Bk.

Migrants, Urban Poverty, & Instability in Developing Nations. Joan M. Nelson. LC 74-9752. (Harvard University. Center for International Affairs. Occasional Papers in International Affairs: No. 22). reprint ed. 27.50 (*0-404-54622-6*) AMS Pr.

Migrating to DB2. Lockwood Lyon. 254p. 1993. 52.00 (*0-471-58180-1*) Wiley.

*__Migrating from Access to MS SQL Server 7.__ Wrox Press Inc., Staff & Robert Smith. 700p. 2000. pap. 39.99 (*1-86100-328-5*) Wrox Pr Inc.

Migrating from Novell NetWare to Windows NT Server 4.0. Sue Plumley. LC 96-44767. 401p. 1997. pap. 29.95 (*0-471-17563-3*) Wiley.

Migrating from Oracle7.X to Oracle8i. David Austin. 500p. 1999. pap. text 39.99 (*0-672-31577-7*) Sams.

Migrating from Pascal to C++ Susan M. Merritt & Allen Stix. LC 96-11796. (Undergraduate Texts in Computer Science Ser.). 565p. 1996. 54.95 (*0-387-94730-2*) Spr-Verlag.

Migrating from X.400(84) to X.400(88) Jim Graigie & Jeroen Houttuin. 19p. (Orig.). (C). 1995. pap. text 25.00 (*0-7881-1939-7*) DIANE Pub.

Migrating Legacy Systems: Gateways, Interfaces, & the Incremental Approach. Michael L. Brodie & Michael Stonebraker. LC 95-19699. 210p. 1995. pap. text 42.95 (*1-55860-330-1*) Morgan Kaufmann.

Migrating to ATM. Bennett. (ITCP-UK Computer Science Ser.). 1997. pap. 43.99 (*1-85032-319-4*, VNR) Wiley.

Migrating to Object Technology. Ian Graham. 576p. (C). 1995. 49.95 (*0-201-59389-0*) Addison-Wesley.

Migrating to Office 95 & Office 97. Laura Monsen. LC 97-80900. 1998. 16.99 (*0-7897-1569-4*, Que New Media) MCP SW Interactive.

*__Migrating to Office 2000.__ Ed. by Que Staff. 250p. 2000. pap. 17.99 (*0-7897-2224-0*) Que.

Migrating to the Intranet & Microsoft Exchange. Randall Covill. LC 96-29966. 223p. 1997. pap. text 29.95 (*1-55558-172-2*) Buttrwrth-Heinemann.

Migrating to Windows, Vol. 1. David Kipping. 500p. 1995. pap. 39.95 (*1-55958-546-3*) Prima Pub.

Migrating to Windows NT. 2nd ed. Steve Heath. LC 97-222278. 343p. 1997. pap. text 46.95 (*1-55558-185-4*, Digital DEC) Buttrwrth-Heinemann.

Migrating to Windows NT 4.0. Sean K. Daily. LC 96-45904. 475p. (Orig.). 1997. pap. 39.95 (*1-882419-50-2*) News Four-Hund.

*__Migrating to Windows 2000 Server.__ Lars Klander. (Illus.). 576p. 2000. pap. 39.99 (*0-7821-2660-X*) Sybex.

*__Migrating to Windows 2000 Server for Dummies.__ Leonard Stearns. (For Dummies Ser.). 360p. 1999. pap. 24.99 incl. cd-rom (*0-7645-0459-2*) IDG Bks.

Migrating Words & Worlds: Pan-Africanism Updated. Ed. by E. Anthony Hurley et al. LC 98-41440. (ALA Annuals Ser.: No. 4). 380p. 1998. 69.95 (*0-86543-700-9*); pap. 19.95 (*0-86543-701-7*) Africa World.

Migration. Paul Bennett. (Nature's Secrets Ser.). (Illus.). 32p. (J). (gr. 1-5). 1994. lib. bdg. 21.40 (*1-56847-209-9*) Raintree Steck-V.

Migration. Michael Simms. LC 85-3727. 70p. 1985. 14.95 (*0-932576-27-3*); pap. 6.95 (*0-932576-28-1*) Breitenbush Bks.

Migration. John A. Jackson. LC 85-13098. (Aspects of Modern Sociology: Social Processes Ser.). 101p. reprint ed. pap. 31.40 (*0-7837-1600-1*, 204189200024) Bks Demand.

Migration: A Spatial Perspective. Swarnjit Mehta. (C). 1990. 19.00 (*81-7033-096-3*, Pub. by Rawat Pubns) S Asia.

Migration: Paths Through Time & Space. R. Robin Baker. (Illus.). 248p. (C). 1983. 39.95 (*0-8419-0868-0*) Holmes & Meier.

Migration: The Asian Experience. Ed. by Judith M. Brown & Rosemary Foot. LC 93-47025. 1994. text 75.00 (*0-312-09723-9*) St Martin.

Migration: The Biology of Life on the Move. Hugh Dingle. (Illus.). 480p. 1996. text 90.00 (*0-19-508962-6*); pap. text 45.00 (*0-19-509723-8*) OUP.

*__Migration: The Biology of Life on the Move.__ Hugh Dingle. (Illus.). 474p. 1999. reprint ed. pap. text 20.00 (*0-7881-6751-0*) DIANE Pub.

*__Migration: The Controversies & the Evidence.__ Ed. by Riccardo Faini et al. LC 98-55715. (Illus.). 380p. (C). 1999. 69.95 (*0-521-66233-8*) Cambridge U Pr.

Migration: United Kingdom. John Dewhurst. 1986. 44.00 (*90-6544-196-4*) Kluwer Law Intl.

Migration Across Time & Nations: Population Mobility in Historical Contexts. Ed. by Ira Glazier & Luigi De Rosa. LC 85-17615. (Illus.). 300p. (C). 1986. 54.00 (*0-8419-0994-6*) Holmes & Meier.

Migration & Anthropology: American Ethnological Society Proceedings, 1970. Ed. by Robert F. Spencer. LC 84-45506. 1988. reprint ed. pap. 55.00 (*0-404-62664-5*) AMS Pr.

Migration & Business Cycles. Harry Jerome. (General Ser.: No. 9). 258p. 1926. reprint ed. 67.20 (*0-87014-008-6*) Natl Bur Econ Res.

Migration & Change in Rural Zambia. Hans Hedlund & Mats Lundahl. (Research Report Ser.: No. 70). 107p. 1983. write for info. (*91-7106-220-3*, Pub. by Nordic Africa) Transaction Pubs.

*__Migration & Colonization in Human Microevolution.__ Alan G. Fix. LC 98-32340. (Studies in Biological & Evolutionary Anthropology: No. 24). (Illus.). 284p. (C). 1999. 69.95 (*0-521-59206-2*) Cambridge U Pr.

*__Migration & Development.__ 354p. 1999. 35.00 (*92-1-103600-3*) UN.

Migration & Development. Ronald Skeldon. (C). 1997. pap. text 36.80 (*0-582-23960-5*) Addison-Wesley.

Migration & Development: Dependence on South Africa--A Study of Lesotho. 2nd ed. Gabriele W. Strom. 174p. (Orig.). 1986. pap. text 33.00 (*91-7106-252-1*) Coronet Bks.

Migration & Development: Implications for Ethnic Identity & Political Conflict. Ed. by Helen I. Safa & Brian M. Du Toit. (World Anthropology Ser.). xvi, 336p. 1975. 35.40 (*90-279-7549-3*) Mouton.

Migration & Development Co-Operation. (Population Studies: No. 28). 1994. 18.00 (*92-871-2611-9*, Pub. by Council of Europe) Manhattan Pub Co.

Migration & Economic Development. Ed. by Klaus F. Zimmermann et al. LC 92-20312. (Population Economics Ser.). (Illus.). x, 165p. 1992. 107.95 (*0-387-55557-9*) Spr-Verlag.

Migration & Economic Development in Rhode Island. Kurt B. Mayer & Sidney Goldstein. LC 58-10480. 72p. 1958. reprint ed. 30.00 (*0-608-16581-6*, 202751700055) Bks Demand.

Migration & Economic Development of Kerala. K. V. Joseph. (C). 1988. 17.50 (*81-7099-092-0*, Pub. by Mittal Pubs Dist) S Asia.

Migration & Economic Integration in the Nordic Common Labour Market. Peter A. Fischer & Thomas Straubhaar. LC 98-167837. 248p. 1996. 30.00 (*92-9120-737-3*, Pub. by Nordic Coun Minsters) Bernan Associates.

Migration & Environment. Harry L. Shapiro. Ed. by Roger Daniels. LC 78-54852. (Asian Experience in North America Ser.). 1979. reprint ed. lib. bdg. 44.95 (*0-405-11310-2*) Ayer.

Migration & Ethnicity in Chinese History: Hakkas, Pengmin & Their Neighbors. Sow-Theng Leong & Tim Wright. LC 97-413. (Illus.). 274p. 1997. 42.50 (*0-8047-2857-7*) Stanford U Pr.

Migration & Ethnicity in Urban India. Susan Lewandowski. 1982. 18.00 (*0-8364-0833-0*, Pub. by Manohar) S Asia.

Migration & European Integration: The Dynamics of Inclusion & Exclusion. Robert Miles & Dietrich Thranhardt. 224p. 1995. 38.50 (*0-8386-3613-6*) Fairleigh Dickinson.

Migration & Fate of Pollutants in Soils & Subsoils. Ed. by Domenico Petruzzelli & Friedrich G. Helfferich. LC 92-45284. (NATO ASI Series G: Ecological Sciences: Vol. 32). 1993. 307.95 (*0-387-56041-6*) Spr-Verlag.

*__Migration & Gender in the Developed World.__ P.J. Boyle. LC 98-44333. 1999. write for info. (*0-415-17144-X*) Routledge.

Migration & Health: Towards an Understanding of the Health Care Needs of Ethnic Minorities. M. College. 210p. 1987. pap. text 17.00 (*92-890-1045-2*, 1340032) World Health.

Migration & Health in a Small Society: The Case of Tokelau. Albert F. Wessen et al. (Research Monographs on Human Population Biology: No. 8). (Illus.). 468p. 1992. 110.00 (*0-19-854262-3*) OUP.

Migration & Homing of Lymphoid Cells, Vol. I. Ed. by Alan Husband. 240p. 1988. 121.00 (*0-8493-6508-2*, QR185, CRC Reprint) Franklin.

Migration & Homing of Lymphoid Cells, 2 vols., Vol. II: A Common Mucosal Immune System Revisited. Ed. by Alan Husband. 224p. 1988. 113.00 (*0-8493-6509-0*, QR185, CRC Reprint) Franklin.

Migration & Integration in a Fortress Europe: A Policy Report. Klaus F. Zimmermann et al. 144p. 1997. pap. 14.95 (*1-898128-29-4*, Pub. by Ctr Econ Policy Res) Brookings.

Migration & Intercultural Education in Europe. Compiled by Ulrike Pornbacher. 180p. 1990. 49.00 (*1-85359-112-2*, Pub. by Multilingual Matters) Taylor & Francis.

Migration & Labor Market Adjustment. Ed. by Jouke Van Dijk et al. (C). 1989. lib. bdg. 171.00 (*0-7923-0026-2*) Kluwer Academic.

Migration & Meteorology: Flight Behaviour & the Atmospheric Environment of Migrant Pests. R. C. Rainey. (Illus.). 344p. 1990. 150.00 (*0-19-854541-X*) OUP.

Migration & Metropolis: An Empirical & Theoretical Analysis. Tony Fielding. (Progress in Planning Ser.: Vol. 39). 96p. 1995. pap. 51.50 (*0-08-042197-0*, Pergamon Pr) Elsevier.

*__Migration & Mobility in Britain Since the Eighteenth Century__ Colin G. Pooley. 419p. 1998. 85.00 (*1-85728-867-X*) Taylor & Francis.

Migration & Mobility in Britain Since the Eighteenth Century Colin G. Pooley & Jean Turnbull. LC 98-186667. xix, 419 p. 1998. write for info. (*1-85728-868-8*) UCL Pr Ltd.

Migration & Politics: The Impact of Population Mobility on American Voting Behavior. Thad A. Brown. LC 87-16240. xxii, 198p. (C). 1988. 45.00 (*0-8078-1765-1*) U of NC Pr.

Migration & Population Change in Europe. (UNIDIR Research Papers: No. 19). 86p. 20.00 (*92-9045-082-7*, E.GV.93.0.14) UN.

*__Migration & Public Policy.__ Ed. by Vaughan Robinson. LC 99-17120. (International Library of Studies on Migration: No. 8). 680p. 1999. 245.00 (*1-85898-922-1*) E Elgar.

Migration & Refugee Policies: An Overview. Ann Bernstein & Myron Weiner. LC 98-36010. 1999. write for info. (*1-85567-505-6*, Pub. by P P Pubs) CRC Pr.

Migration & Regional Development in the United States, 1950-1960. Paul J. Schwind. LC 77-138350. (University of Chicago, Department of Geography, Research Paper Ser.: No. 133). 183p. (Orig.). 1971. reprint ed. pap. 56.80 (*0-608-02287-X*, 206292800004) Bks Demand.

Migration & Regional Economic Integration in Asia. OECD Staff. LC 98-121824. (Proceedings Ser.). 180p. 1998. pap. 16.00 (*92-64-16039-6*, 81-98-01-1-P, Pub. by Org for Econ) OECD.

Migration & Remittances: Inter-Urban & Rural-Urban Linkages. Jayasri R. Chaudhuri. LC 92-34738. (Illus.). 328p. 1993. 38.95 (*0-8039-9458-3*) Sage.

*__Migration & Reorganization: The Pueblo IV Period in the American Southwest.__ Katherine A. Spielmann & E. Charles Adams. LC 98-74871. (Illus.). 1998. write for info. (*0-936249-09-9*) AZ Univ ARP.

Migration & Residential Mobility: Macro & Micro Approaches. Martin Cadwallader. LC 92-50246. (Illus.). 292p. (Orig.). (C). 1993. pap. text 19.95 (*0-299-13494-6*); lib. bdg. 45.00 (*0-299-13490-3*) U of Wis Pr.

Migration & Residential Mobility in the United States. Larry E. Long. LC 88-15758. (Population of the United States in the 1980s: A Census Monograph Ser.). 400p. 1988. 49.95 (*0-87154-555-1*) Russell Sage.

Migration & Restructuring in the United States: A Geographic Perspective. Ed. by Kavita Pandit & Suzanne D. Withers. LC 99-10342. 352p. 1999. pap. 34.95 (*0-8476-9393-7*) Rowman.

*__Migration & Restructuring in the United States: A Geographic Perspective.__ Ed. by Kavita Pandit & Suzanne D. Withers. LC 99-10342. 352p. 1999. text 69.00 (*0-8476-9392-9*) Rowman.

Migration & Settlement. Andrei Rogers & Frans Willekens. (C). 1980. text 33.00 (*0-8133-0103-3*) Westview.

Migration & Social Cohesion. Ed. by Steven Vertovec. LC 99-14857. (International Library of Studies on Migration: No. 7). 576p. 1999. 200.00 (*1-85898-868-3*) E Elgar.

Migration & Social Welfare: Report. Research Institute on the Social Welfare Consequen. LC 72-144344. 256p. reprint ed. pap. 79.40 (*0-608-15426-1*, 202927500059) Bks Demand.

*__Migration & Society in Britain, 1550-1830.__ Ian D. Whyte. LC 99-59336. 2000. write for info. (*0-312-23175-X*) St Martin.

Migration & the Inter-Industry Wage Structure in Germany. John P. Haisken-DeNew. LC 96-13405. (Population Economics Ser.). 211p. 1996. 78.00 (*3-540-60921-0*) Spr-Verlag.

Migration & the International Labour Market, 1850-1939. Ed. by Tim Hatton & Jeffrey Williamson. LC 94-3975. 336p. (C). 1994. pap. 29.99 (*0-415-10769-5*, B4226) Routledge.

Migration & the International Labour Market, 1850-1939. Ed. by Tim Hatton & Jeffrey Williamson. LC 94-3975. 368p. (C). (gr. 13). 1994. 90.00 (*0-415-10768-7*, B4226) Routledge.

Migration & the Labour Market in Asia: Prospects to the Year 2000. OECD Staff. LC 96-175582. (ENG & FRE.). 250p. (Orig.). 1996. pap. 40.00 (*92-64-14775-6*, Pub. by Org for Econ) OECD.

Migration & the New Europe. Ed. by Kimberly A. Hamilton. LC 93-32176. (Significant Issues Ser.: Vol. 15, No. 8). 115p. (Orig.). (C). 1994. pap. 8.95 (*0-89206-214-2*) CSIS.

Migration & the Origins of the English Atlantic World. Alison Games. LC 99-26018. (Historical Studies). 368p. 1999. 45.00 (*0-674-57381-1*) HUP.

Migration & Transformations: Regional Perspectives on New Guinea. Andrew J. Strathern & Gabriele Sturzenhofecker. LC 93-39287. 344p. (C). 1994. pap. 19.95 (*0-8229-5523-7*); text 59.95 (*0-8229-3782-4*) U of Pittsburgh Pr.

Migration & Transportation Social Spaces. Ed. by Ludger Pries. LC 98-72623. (Research in Ethnic Relations Ser.). 226p. 1998. text 61.95 (*1-84014-580-3*, Pub. by Ashgate Pub) Ashgate Pub Co.

Migration & Urban Unemployment in Dualistic Economic Development. Donald W. Jones. LC 75-35772. (University of Chicago Department of Geography Research Paper Ser.: Vol. 165). 184p. 1975. reprint ed. pap. 57.10 (*0-608-02432-5*, 206307500004) Bks Demand.

Migration & Urbanization: Models & Adaptive Strategies. Ed. by Brian M. Du Toit & Helen I. Safa. (World Anthropology Ser.). xii, 306p. 1975. 33.10 (*90-279-7579-5*) Mouton.

Migration & Urbanization in China. Ed. by Lincoln H. Day & Ma Xia. LC 93-29350. (Studies in Chinese Environment & Development Ser.). 264p. (C). (gr. 13). 1994. text 73.95 (*1-56324-338-5*, East Gate Bk) M E Sharpe.

Migration & Urbanization in the Ruhr Valley, 1821-1914. James H. Jackson, Jr. LC 96-51147. (Studies in Central European Histories). 368p. (C). 1997. text 85.00 (*0-391-04033-2*) Humanities.

Migration Art: A. D. 300-800. Katherine R. Brown. LC 95-13786. (Illus.). 1995. pap. 9.95 (*0-87099-750-5*) Metro Mus Art.

Migration Between California & Other States, 1985-1994. Hans Johnson & Richard Lovelady. 49p. 1995. pap. write for info. (*1-58703-041-1*, CRB-95-006) CA St Libry.

An Asterisk (*) at the beginning of an entry indicates that the title is appearing for the first time.

Migration-Canada: A Guide to Tax, Legal & Other Implications of Coming to, Investing in & Leaving Canada. H. Arnold Sherman & Jeffrey D. Sherman. 372p. 1985. 118.00 (*90-6544-208-1*) Kluwer Law Intl.

Migration, Citizenship & Ethno-National Identities in the European Union. Ed. by Marco Martiniello. (Research in Ethnic Relations Ser.). 224p. 1995. 72.95 (*1-85972-002-1*, Pub. by Avebry) Ashgate Pub Co.

Migration-Development Interelationships: The Case of the Philippines. Gianni Agostinelli. 33p. 1992. 5.00 (*0-934733-59-7*) CMS.

Migration, Diasporas & Transnationalism. Ed. by Steven Vertovec & Robin Cohen. LC 99-20054. (International Library of Studies on Migration: No. 9). 704p. 1999. 245.00 (*1-85898-869-1*) E Elgar.

Migration, Displacement & Identity in Post-Soviet Russia. Hilary Pilkington. LC 97-20608. 264p. (C). 1998. 90.00 (*0-415-15824-9*); pap. 29.99 (*0-415-15825-7*) Routledge.

Migration Dynamics & Labour Market Turnover see Progress in Planning

Migration, Ethnicity & Community. Ed. by Ernest Krausz. LC 79-93045. (Studies of Israeli Society: Vol. I). 324p. 1980. 39.95 (*0-87855-414-9*); pap. 18.95 (*0-87855-369-X*) Transaction Pubs.

***Migration, Free Trade & Regional Integration in North America.** Ed. by Jean-Pierre Garson. LC 99-177179. (OECD Proceedings Ser.). 316p. 1998. pap. 53.00 (*92-64-16188-0*, 8198121P) OECD.

Migration from Rural Areas: The Evidence from Village Studies. John Connell et al. 1977. 7.50 (*0-19-560789-9*) OUP.

Migration from the Russian Empire Vol. 3: Lists of Passengers Arriving at the Port of New York, May 1886-December 1887. Ed. by Ira A. Glazier. LC 95-75722. 521p. 1997. 50.00 (*0-8063-1539-3*) Genealog Pub.

Migration from the Russian Empire Vol. 4: Lists of Passengers Arriving at the Port of New York, January 1888-June 1889. Ed. by Ira A. Glazier. 519p. 1997. 50.00 (*0-8063-1540-7*) Genealog Pub.

Migration from the Russian Empire: Lists of Passengers Arriving at U. S. Ports Vol. 5: June 1889-July 1890. Ira A. Glazier. 550p. 1998. 50.00 (*0-8063-1583-0*) Genealog Pub.

Migration from the Russian Empire: Lists of Passengers Arriving at U. S. Ports Vol. 6: August 1890-June 1891. Ira A. Glazier. 499p. 1998. 50.00 (*0-8063-1584-9*) Genealog Pub.

Migration from Vermont. Lewis D. Stilwell. 1988. reprint ed. lib. bdg. 75.00 (*0-7812-0119-5*) Rprt Serv.

***Migration, Globalisation & Human Security.** David T. Graham & Nana Poku. LC 99-33643. (Research in Population & Migration Ser.). 224p. 2000. 85.00 (*0-415-18436-3*) Routledge.

Migration in China. Ed. by Borge Bakken. LC 98-216544. 160p. 1998. pap. 19.95 (*87-87062-57-7*, Pub. by NIAS) Paul & Co Pubs.

Migration in Colonial Spanish America. Ed. by David J. Robinson. (Cambridge Studies in Historical Geography: No. 16). (Illus.). 416p. (C). 1990. text 69.95 (*0-521-36281-4*) Cambridge U Pr.

Migration in Early America: The Virginia Quaker Experience. Larry D. Gragg. Ed. by Robert Berkhofer. LC 80-15188. (Studies in American History & Culture: No. 13). 143p. 1980. reprint ed. pap. 44.40 (*0-8357-1095-5*, 207009700064) Bks Demand.

Migration in European History, 2 vols., Set. Ed. by Colin Holmes. LC 96-18569. (International Library of Studies on Migration: Vol. 4). 1280p. (C). 1996. text 440.00 (*1-85898-421-1*) E Elgar.

Migration in Metropolitan Japan: Social Change & Political Behavior. James W. White. LC 82-82667. (Japan Research Monographs: No. 2). 322p. (Orig.). 1983. pap. 12.00 (*0-912966-53-X*) IEAS.

Migration in Seismic Prospecting. E. A. Kozlov. Tr. by B. B. Bhattacharya from RUS. (Russian Translation Ser.: No. 82). (Illus.). 279p. (C). 1990. text 110.00 (*90-6191-908-8*, Pub. by A A Balkema) Ashgate Pub Co.

Migration into Rural Areas: Theories & Issues. Paul Boyle & Keith Halfacree. LC 97-50257. 338p. 1998. 140.00 (*0-471-96989-3*) Wiley.

Migration, Jihad, & Muslim Authority in West Africa: The Futanke Colonies in Karta. John H. Hanson. LC 95-43340. (Illus.). 224p. 1996. text 39.95 (*0-253-33088-2*) Ind U Pr.

Migration Laws & Treaties: Immigration Laws & Regulations, Vol. 61. International Labour Office Staff. (I. L. O. Studies & Reports Series O: No. 3, Vol. 2). 1974. reprint ed. bds. 40.00 (*0-8115-3293-3*) Periodicals Srv.

Migration Legend of the Creek Indians. Albert S. Gatschet. LC 72-83460. (Library of Aboriginal American Literature: No. 4). reprint ed. 39.50 (*0-404-52184-3*) AMS Pr.

Migration, Migration History, History: Old Paradigms & New Perspectives. Ed. by Jan Lucassen & Leo Lucassen. (International & Comparative Social History Ser.: Vol. 4). 454p. 1997. 68.95 (*3-906756-86-6*, Pub. by P Lang) P Lang Pubng.

Migration, Migration History, History: Old Paradigms & New Perspectives. Ed. by Jan Lucassen & Leo Lucassen. LC 97-13081. (International & Comparative Social History Ser.: Vol. 4). 454p. (C). 1997. text 68.95 (*0-8204-3405-1*, Pub. by P Lang) P Lang Pubng.

***Migration, Migration History, History: Old Paradigms & New Perspectives.** 2nd ed. Jan Lucassen & Leo Lucassen. LC 99-210132. (International & Comparative Social History Ser.: Vol. 4). (Illus.). 454p. 1999. 53.95 (*0-8204-4227-5*) P Lang Pubng.

Migration, Mobility, & Aging. Southern Conference on Gerontology Staff. LC 74-19211. (Center for Gerontological Studies & Programs Ser.: No. 23). 186p. reprint ed. pap. 57.70 (*0-7837-4898-1*, 204456300004) Bks Demand.

Migration, Mobility, & Modernization. D. J. Siddle. (Illus.). 256p. 1998. 45.95 (*0-85323-883-9*, Pub. by Liverpool Univ Pr); pap. 23.95 (*0-85323-963-0*, Pub. by Liverpool Univ Pr) Intl Spec Bk.

Migration Models. Peter Congdon & John C. Stillwell. 308p. 1993. text 105.00 (*0-471-94804-7*, Pub. by P P Pubs) Wiley.

Migration of Asian Workers to the Arab World. 358p. 1987. 20.00 (*92-808-0555-X*, E.86.III.A.2) UN.

***Migration of Birds.** Frederick C. Lincoln. 117p. 1999. per. 8.00 (*0-16-061701-4*) USGPO.

Migration of Church Groups to Midwest: Routes & Sources. Ed. by Nita Neblock. (Illus.). 52p. 1987. pap. 5.00 (*0-913233-12-9*) AFRA.

***Migration of Clowns.** Carroll D. Short. 2000. pap. 12.95 (*1-880216-49-3*, Elliott Clark) Black Belt Communs.

Migration of Fines in Porous Media. Kartic Khilar & Scott Fogler. LC 98-38830. (Theory & Applications of Transport in Porous Media Ser.). 1998. 92.00 (*0-7923-5284-X*) Kluwer Academic.

Migration of Ghosts. Pauline Melville. LC 98-215800. 209p. 1998. write for info. (*0-7475-3675-9*) AMACOM.

Migration of Ghosts. Pauline Melville. 224p. 1999. 23.95 (*1-58234-020-X*) Bloomsbury Pubg.

***Migration of Ghosts.** Pauline Melville. 2000. pap. 13.95 (*1-58234-074-9*) Bloomsbury Pubg.

Migration of High Level Manpower from Developing to Developed Countries. F. J. Van Hoek. (Institute of Social Studies Publications). (Orig.). 1970. pap. text 9.25 (*90-279-1623-3*) Mouton.

Migration of Hydrocarbons in Sedimentary Basins: 3rd IFP Exploration & Production Research Conference, Carcans, 1987. Ed. by B. Doligez. (Illus.). 712p. (C). 1987. 775.00 (*2-7108-0540-5*, Pub. by Edits Technip) Enfield Pubs NH.

Migration of Intercultural Education in Europe. Ulrike Pornbacher et al. 1990. 49.00 (*1-85359-094-0*, Pub. by Multilingual Matters) Taylor & Francis.

Migration of Knowledge Workers Binod Khadria. LC 98-51515. 1999. write for info. (*81-7036-785-9*) Sage.

Migration of Knowledge Workers: Second-Generation Effects of India's Brain Drain. Binod Khadria. LC 98-51515. 1999. write for info. (*0-7619-9320-7*) Sage.

Migration of Labor. Oded Stark. 416p. 1993. pap. 33.95 (*1-55786-429-2*) Blackwell Pubs.

Migration of Moro: My Other Grandfather's Story. Roland R. Bianchi. LC 97-535. (Illus.). 112p. (Orig.). 1997. pap. 9.95 (*1-56474-209-1*) Fithian Pr.

Migration of Seismic Data. Ed. by Gerald H. Gardner. LC 85-61313. (Geophysics Reprint Ser.: No. 4). (Illus.). 472p. 1985. reprint ed. pap. 45.00 (*0-931830-35-4*, 464) Soc Expl Geophys.

Migration of Symbols & Their Relations to Beliefs & Customs. Donald A. MacKenzie. LC 73-121283. reprint ed. 28.00 (*0-404-04136-1*) AMS Pr.

Migration of Symbols, 1894. Goblet D'Alviella. 303p. 1994. reprint ed. pap. 19.95 (*1-56459-442-4*) Kessinger Pub.

***Migration of Willie Mackerels.** Mike Clarke. LC 99-66903. 160p. 2000. pap. 11.95 (*1-885003-30-7*, Pub. by R D Reed Pubs) Midpt Trade.

Migration of Women: Methodological Issues in the Measurement & Analysis of Internal & International Migration. 112p. 21.95 (*92-1-127005-7*, E.95.III.C.1) UN.

Migration Past, Migration Future: Germany & the United States. Ed. by Klaus J. Bade & Myron Weiner. LC 97-7505. (Migration & Refugees: Vol. 1). 176p. 1997. 29.95 (*1-57181-125-7*) Berghahn Bks.

***Migration Patterns & the Growth of High Poverty Neighborhoods, 1970-1990.** Lincoln Quillian. 49p. (C). 1999. pap. text 20.00 (*0-7881-8361-3*) DIANE Pub.

Migration Patterns of Young Adults in Nebraska. Jerome A. Deichert et al. (Nebraska Economic & Business Reports: No. 25). 1978. 5.00 (*0-686-28413-5*) Bur Busn Res U Nebr.

Migration Phenomena of Radionuclides into the Geosphere: A Critical Review of the Available Information, Vol. 5. B. S. Jensen. (Radioactive Waste Management Ser.). 152p. 1982. text 142.00 (*3-7186-0120-6*) Gordon & Breach.

Migration Policies in Europe & the United States. Ed. by Giacomo Luciani. LC 93-23464. 172p. (C). 1993. lib. bdg. 134.50 (*0-7923-2537-0*) Kluwer Academic.

***Migration Potential in Central & Eastern Europe.** 84p. 1999. 20.00 (*92-9068-087-3*) UN.

Migration Process: Capital, Gifts & Offerings among Overseas Pakistanis. Pnina Werbner. LC 89-35877. (Explorations in Anthropology Ser.). 403p. 1990. 25.00 (*0-85496-625-0*) Berg Pubs.

Migration Process in Britain & West Germany: Two Demographic Studies of Migrant Populations. Heather Booth. 100p. 1992. 67.95 (*1-85628-058-6*, Pub. by Avebry) Ashgate Pub Co.

Migration Processes & Patterns Vol. 1: Research Progress & Prospects. Ed. by Tony Champion & Tony Fielding. LC 91-34230. 272p. 1993. 140.00 (*0-471-94504-8*) Wiley.

Migration Processes in Soil & Groundwater Zone. Ludwig Luckner. 504p. 1991. lib. bdg. 110.00 (*0-87371-302-8*, L302) Lewis Pubs.

Migration, Remittances & Capital Flow: The Indian Experience. Deepak Nayyar. 144p. (C). 1994. 14.95 (*0-19-563345-8*) OUP.

Migration Return: A Bibliographical Overview. Anne M. Gaillard. 153p. 1994. 14.95 (*0-934733-77-5*) CMS.

Migration Settlement & Ethnic Associations. K. P. Kumaran. (C). 1992. 21.00 (*81-7022-390-3*, Pub. by Concept) S Asia.

Migration, Social Change, & Health: A Samoan Community in Urban California. Craig R. Janes. 216p. 1990. 39.50 (*0-8047-1789-3*) Stanford U Pr.

Migration, Socialism & the International Division of Labour: The Yugoslavian Experience. Carl-Ulrik Schierup. (Research in Ethnic Relations Ser.). 351p. 1990. text 77.95 (*1-85628-063-2*, Pub. by Avebry) Ashgate Pub Co.

Migration Solo. Lee H. Bahan. (Indiana Poetry Chapbook Contest Ser.: No. 1). 43p. 1989. pap. 3.95 (*1-880649-23-3*) Writ Ctr Pr.

Migration Studies: Evidence from Rural Field Studies. K. N. Yadava & Surendra Yadava. LC 98-900185. v, 173p. 1998. write for info. (*81-7541-008-6*) Shipra Pubns.

Migration Surveys in Low-Income Countries: Guidelines for Survey & Questionnaire Design. Richard E. Bilsborrow et al. LC 84-11354. 560p. 1984. 45.00 (*0-7099-3266-9*, Pub. by C Helm) Routldge.

Migration Tears: Poems about Transitions. Michael Kabotie. LC 87-50917. (Native American Literature Ser.). (Illus.). 60p. 1990. reprint ed. pap. 10.00 (*0-935626-32-8*) U Cal AISC.

***Migration Theory: Talking Across Disciplines.** Ed. by Caroline B. Brettell & James F. Hollifield. LC 99-87915. 224p. 2000. write for info. (*0-415-92610-6*); pap. write for info. (*0-415-92611-4*) Routledge.

Migration Theory & Fact. R. Paul Shaw. (Bibliography Ser.: No. 5). 1975. 24.00 (*1-55869-076-X*) Regional Sci Res Inst.

Migration to Shashemene: Ethnicity, Gender & Occupation in Urban Ethiopia. Gunilla Bjeren. (Illus.). xiv, 292p. (Orig.). 1985. pap. text 41.00 (*91-7106-245-9*, Pub. by Nordisk Afrikainstitutet) Coronet Bks.

Migration to the Arab World: Experience of Returning Migrants. 352p. 35.00 (*92-808-0745-5*, 90.III.A.11) UN.

***Migration und Mehrsprachigkeit: Der Sprachstand Turkischer Ruckkehrer Aus Deutschland.** Helmut Daller. (GER., Illus.). VIII, 201p. 1999. 37.95 (*3-631-34559-3*) P Lang Pubng.

Migration, Urbanisation & Development. Amarjit S. Oberi. (Background Paper for Training in Population, Human Resources & Development Planning Ser.: No. 5). vi, 108p. (Orig.). 1990. pap. 13.50 (*92-2-106129-9*) Intl Labour Office.

Migration, Urbanization & Development: New Directions & Issues. Ed. by Richard E. Bilsborrow. LC 97-31606. 544p. 1997. 137.50 (*0-7923-8032-0*) Kluwer Academic.

Migration Within the Empire see British Empire

Migration World Magazine Cumulative Index, 1973-1995. Marie-Christine Michaud. 43p. 1996. lib. bdg. 9.95 (*0-934733-99-6*) CMS.

Migrations. Marlene L. Groth. 1997. pap. write for info. (*1-57553-526-2*) Watermrk Pr.

Migrations. Ladybird Staff. (J). 1999. pap. 9.99 (*0-7214-5758-4*, Ladybrd) Penguin Putnam.

Migrations. Claire Needell. 32p. 1998. pap. 4.00 (*1-893032-03-5*) Jensen Daniels.

***Migrations: Humanity in Transition.** Photos & Text by Sebastiao Salgado. (Illus.). 432p. 2000. 100.00 (*0-89381-891-7*) Aperture.

Migrations: Wildlife in Motion. Barbara Sleeper. LC 94-25473. (Earthsong Collection). (Illus.). 168p. 1994. 60.00 (*0-941831-98-1*) Beyond Words Pub.

Migrations: Wildlife in Motion, Author's Ed. Photos by Art Wolfe. (EarthSong Collection). (Illus.). 192p. 1994. 80.00 (*0-614-19291-9*) Beyond Words Pub.

Migrations & Cultures: A World View. Thomas Sowell. 528p. 1997. pap. 18.00 (*0-465-04589-8*, Pub. by Basic) HarpC.

Migrations & Cultures: A World View. Thomas Sowell. 516p. (C). 1998. text 30.00 (*0-7881-5595-4*) DIANE Pub.

***Migrations et Migrants dans une Perspective Historique/Migrations & Migrants in Historical Perspective: Permanences et Innovations/ Permanancies & Innovations.** Ed. by Rene Leboutte. (FRE.). 313p. 2000. pap. text 34.95 (*0-8204-4660-2*) P Lang Pubng.

Migrations of Hawks. Donald S. Heintzelman. LC 85-45412. (Illus.). 383p. 1986. reprint ed. pap. 118.80 (*0-608-01063-4*, 205937100001) Bks Demand.

Migratory Bird Habitat on the Platte & North Platte Rivers in Nebraska. Paul J. Currier et al. Ed. by James Lewis. LC 86-61270. (Illus.). 177p. (Orig.). 1986. pap. text 11.00 (*0-938441-00-0*); lib. bdg. 21.00 (*0-938441-01-9*) PRWCT.

Migratory-Casual Worker. John N. Webb. LC 73-165690. (FDR & the Era of the New Deal Ser.). 1971. reprint ed. lib. bdg. 19.50 (*0-306-70339-4*) Da Capo.

Migratory Legends: List of Types with a Systematic Catalogue of the Norwegian Variants. Reidar T. Christiansen. Ed. by Richard M. Dorsen. LC 77-70585. (International Folklore Ser.). 1977. reprint ed. lib. bdg. 24.95 (*0-405-10087-6*) Ayer.

Migratory Worker & Family Life. Marion Hathway. LC 77-169386. (Family in America Ser.). 258p. 1977. reprint ed. 18.95 (*0-405-03863-1*) Ayer.

Migratory Workers of the Southwest: Consisting of "Migratory Cotton Pickers in Arizona" (1939), "The Pecan Shellers of San Antonio" (1940) & "Mexican Migratory Workers of South Texas" (1941), 3 vols. in 1. United States Works Progress Administration Staff. LC 78-10233. 1979. reprint ed. lib. bdg. 35.00 (*0-313-20685-6*, USMW) Greenwood.

Migueis--To the Seventh Decade. John A. Kerr, Jr. LC 77-12965. (Romance Monographs: No. 29). 1978. 25.00 (*84-399-7900-2*) Romance.

***Miguel.** Francois Doucet. (Coffragants Ser.). Orig. Title: Mes Yeux de l'Interieur (Mes Yeux D'Enfant). (FRE.). 64p. 1998. 12.95 (*2-921997-66-5*) Penton Overseas.

Miguel. 2nd rev. ed. Francois Doucet. Orig. Title: Mes Yeux de l'Interieur (Mes Yeux D'Enfant). 150p. 1998. reprint ed. pap. write for info. (*2-921892-47-2*) EAsa.

Miguel Aleman Contesta: Ensayo. Miguel Aleman. LC 75-620022. (Encuesta Politica, Mexico Ser.: No. 4). 68p. reprint ed. pap. 30.00 (*0-608-17159-X*, 202731800055) Bks Demand.

Miguel & Sarah: Close Friends & Cystic Fibrosis. large type ed. Andrea C. Dowell & Kathi R. Rokke. (Illus.). 22p. (J). (gr. k-4). 1999. pap. 8.00 (*0-9644972-1-2*) Chldrns Hosps.

Miguel & the Santero. Sandra E. Guzzo. LC 93-85233. (Illus.). 32p. (Orig.). (J). (gr. 1-6). 1995. pap. 3.95 (*0-937206-30-X*) New Mexico Mag.

***Miguel Angel.** Angelika Taschen. 1998. pap. 12.99 (*3-8228-7576-7*) Benedikt Taschen.

Miguel Angel Asturias, lo Ancestral en Su Obra Literaria. E. Leon Hill. 1972. 11.95 (*0-88303-007-1*); pap. 9.95 (*0-685-73211-8*) E Torres & Sons.

Miguel Angel Asturias's Archaeology of Return. Rene Prieto. LC 92-24500. (Studies in Latin American & Iberian Literature: Vol. 7). 319p. (C). 1993. text 64.95 (*0-521-43412-2*) Cambridge U Pr.

***Miguel Angel Campano.** Miguel Angel Campano. (Illus.). 212p. 2000. pap. 50.00 (*84-8026-126-9*) Dist Art Pubs.

Miguel Angel Roca. 2nd rev. ed. Oriol Bohigas et al. (Academy Architecture Ser.). (Illus.). 176p. 1986. pap. 24.95 (*0-312-53229-6*) St Martin.

***Miguel Bacelo: Works on Paper, 1979-1999.** Enrique Juncosa & Miquel Barcelo. (Illus.). 408p. 2000. 64.95 (*84-8003-180-8*, Pub. by Aldeasa) Dist Art Pubs.

Miguel de Cervantes: Spanish Writer. Jake Goldberg. (Hispanics of Achievement Ser.). (Illus.). 120p. (YA). (gr. 5 up). 1993. lib. bdg. 19.95 (*0-7910-1238-7*) Chelsea Hse.

Miguel de Cervantes's Don Quixote. Marcia Williams. 1995. 11.19 (*0-606-07439-2*) Turtleback.

Miguel de Unamuno. Demetrios Basdekis. LC 74-92029. (Columbia Essays on Modern Writers Ser.: No. 44). 48p. (Orig.). 1970. pap. text 12.00 (*0-231-03259-5*) Col U Pr.

Miguel de Unamuno. Julian Marias. Tr. by Frances M. Lopez-Morillas. LC 66-18251. 238p. 1966. reprint ed. pap. 73.80 (*0-7837-2296-6*, 205738400004) Bks Demand.

Miguel de Unamuno: The Agony of Belief. Martin Nozick. LC 81-47966. 238p. 1982. reprint ed. pap. 73.80 (*0-608-02510-0*, 206315400004) Bks Demand.

Miguel de Unamuno's Political Writings, 1918-1924 Vol. 1: La Anarquia Reinante (1918-1920) Ed. by G. D. Robertson. LC 95-36709. (Hispanic Literature Ser.: Vol. 31). 448p. 1996. text 109.95 (*0-7734-8846-4*) E Mellen.

Miguel de Unamuno's Political Writings, 1918-1924 Vol. 2: El Absolutismo en Acecho (1921-1922) Ed. by G. D. Robertson. LC 95-36709. (Hispanic Literature Ser.: Vol. 32). 520p. 1999. text 119.95 (*0-7734-8848-0*) E Mellen.

Miguel De Unamuno's Political Writings, 1918-1924 Vol. 3: Roto El Curadro (1923-1924) Miguel de Unamuno. Ed. by G. D. Robertson. LC 95-36709. (Hispanic Literature Ser.: Vol. 33). 324p. 1999. pap. 99.95 (*0-7734-8850-2*) E Mellen.

Miguel Delibes. Janet W. Diaz. (Twayne's World Authors Ser.). 1971. lib. bdg. 17.95 (*0-8290-0119-0*) Irvington.

Miguel Delibes: An Annotated Critical Bibliography. Glenn G. Meyers. LC 98-52551. (Author Bibliographies Ser.: No. 102). (Illus.). 352p. 1999. 50.00 (*0-8108-3626-2*) Scarecrow.

Miguel Hidalgo y Costilla: Father of Mexican Independence. Frank De Varona. (Hispanic Heritage Ser.). (J). 1993. 10.15 (*0-606-07870-3*) Turtleback.

Miguel Hidalgo y Costilla - Father of Mexican Independence. Frank De Varona. LC 92-36562. (Hispanic Heritage Ser.). (Illus.). 32p. (J). (gr. 2-4). 1993. lib. bdg. 19.90 (*1-56294-370-7*) Millbrook Pr.

Miguel Marmol. Roque Dalton. Tr. by Kathleen Ross & Richard Schaaf. LC 87-71397. 503p. 1987. 19.95 (*0-915306-68-9*) Curbstone.

Miguel Marmol. Roque Dalton. Tr. by Kathleen Ross & Richard Schaaf. LC 87-71397. 503p. 1988. pap. 12.95 (*0-915306-67-0*) Curbstone.

Miguel Mendez in Aztlan: Two Decades of Literary Production. Ed. by Gary D. Keller. LC 94-43636. (Illus.). 104p. (Orig.). (C). 1995. pap. 12.00 (*0-927534-53-3*) Biling Rev-Pr.

Miguel Najdorf: King of the King's Indian Defense. Nikolay Minev. (Illus.). 112p. 1997. pap. 14.95 (*0-9661889-1-8*) Chess Library.

Miguel Protocolos de Comunicaciones para Sistemas Abiertos. 400p. (C). 1995. pap. text 16.66 (*0-201-65396-6*) HEPC Inc.

Miguel Rio Branco: An Aperture Monograph. Contrib. by David L. Strauss. LC 98-84499. (Monographs). (Illus.). 136p. 1998. 68.00 (*0-89381-801-1*) Aperture.

Miguel Servet: Su Vida y Obra. Jose Baron Fernandez. (Nueva Austral Ser.: No. 92). (SPA.). 1991. pap. text 34.95 (*84-239-1892-0*) Elliots Bks.

Miguel Street. V. S. Naipaul. (Caribbean Writers Ser.). 172p. (C). 1974. pap. 7.95 (*0-435-98645-7*, 98645) Heinemann.

Miguel Street. V. S. Naipaul. 288p. 1977. pap. 11.95 (*0-14-003302-5*, Penguin Bks) Viking Penguin.

Miguel, the Shepherd Boy. Edith Witmer. (Illus.). 189p. (J). (gr. 3-6). 1992. 8.10 (*0-7399-0089-7*, 2237) Rod & Staff.

Miguel, the Shepherd Boy. Edith Witmer. Tr. by Maria Juana De Mejia. (SPA., Illus.). 220p. (J). (gr. 3-6). 1995. 6.90 (*0-7399-0090-0*, 2237.1) Rod & Staff.

M

Miguel Vicente Pata Caliente (Hot-Footed Miguel Vicente) Orlando Araujo.Tr. of Hot-Footed Miguel Vicente. (SPA., Illus.). 48p. (J). (gr. 3 up). Date not set. 11.95 (*980-257-102-4*, Pub. by Ediciones Ekare) Kane-Miller Bk.

Mihaia: The Prophet Rua Kenana & His Community at Māungapohatu. Judith Binney. 208p. 1996. pap. 39.95 (*1-86940-148-4*, Pub. by Auckland Univ) Paul & Co Pubs.

Mihigimanitka. large type ed. Veronica Michael & Frances Caole.Tr. of My Feelings. (ESK., Illus.). 8p. (J). (gr. k-3). 1999. pap. text 6.00 (*1-58084-130-9*) Lower Kuskokwim.

MIHU the Detective & the Mystery of the Blue Budgie. Chaiky Halpern. (Sifrei Rimom Ser.). 1987. pap. 2.95 (*0-87306-439-9*) Feldheim.

Mihu the Detective & the Mystery of the Missing Chometz. 1982. pap. 2.95 (*0-87306-168-3*) Feldheim.

Mijikenda. Johnson A. Mwangudza. (Kenya People Ser.). (Illus.). 37p. (YA). (gr. 6-9). 1991. pap. write for info. (*0-237-50490-1*) EVN1 UK.

Mijikenda. Tiyambe Zeleza. LC 94-25657. (Heritage Library of African Peoples). (Illus.). 64p. (YA). (gr. 7-12). 1995. lib. bdg. 16.95 (*0-8239-1767-3*) Rosen Group.

MIK Medical Information Kit: Your Memory File for Faster, Safer Health Care. Carol H. Jones. 48p. 1998. ring bd. 17.95 (*0-9664061-0-9*) Hlth Care Excell.

Mik-Shrok. Gloria Repp. LC 98-8838. 133p. (J). 1998. pap. 6.49 (*1-57924-069-0*) Bob Jones Univ.

Mika Hakkinen: McLaten's Flying Finn. Christopher Hilton. LC 97-70201. 1997. pap. text 24.95 (*1-85960-402-1*, Pub. by J H Haynes & Co) Motorbooks Intl.

Mika Lidov vs. Hal Heinrich. Kit Woolsey. 216p. 1995. pap. 25.00 (*1-880604-06-X*) Gammon Pr.

Mikado. (Vocal Score Ser.). 240p. 1986. pap. 14.95 (*0-88188-724-2*, 50337520) H Leonard.

Mikado. William Gilbert. 64p. 1999. reprint ed. pap. 6.95 (*1-57002-102-3*) Univ Publng Hse.

Mikado. William S. Gilbert. (Illus.). 64p. 1992. reprint ed. pap. text 1.50 (*0-486-27268-0*) Dover.

Mikado Chorus Parts. Gilbert & Sullivan. 48p. 1986. pap. 5.00 (*0-7935-3478-X*, 50337580) H Leonard.

Mikado in Full Score. W. S. Gilbert. 1999. pap. text 19.95 (*0-486-40626-1*) Dover.

Mikado Institution & Person. William E. Griffis. (Notable American Authors Ser.). 1992. reprint ed. lib. bdg. 75.00 (*0-7812-2970-7*) Rprt Serv.

Mikado: or The Town of Titipu. William S. Gilbert. Ed. by William-Alan Landes. LC 97-23922. 55p. 1997. pap. 10.00 (*0-88734-745-2*) Players Pr.

***Mikado Vocal Score.** William S. Gilbert & Arthur Sullivan. 2000. pap. 14.95 (*0-486-41163-X*) Dover.

Mikado's Empire. William E. Griffis. (Notable American Authors Ser.). 1992. reprint ed. lib. bdg. 75.00 (*0-7812-2958-8*) Rprt Serv.

Mikael's Magical Wave. Anne A. Roth. LC 96-32813. (Illus.). (J). 1997. write for info. (*1-56763-239-4*); pap. write for info. (*1-56763-240-8*) Ozark Pub.

***Mikaelson Untitled.** Ben Mikaelsen. (J). 2001. write for info. (*0-380-97745-1*) Morrow Avon.

***Mikayla - The Second Coming.** Photos by Cheryl Friberg. 385p. 1999. pap. 14.95 (*0-9676007-1-5*) Poverti Prod.

Mikayla's Victory, Vol. 29. Cynthia Bates. 100p. (J). (gr. 3-8). 1999. text 5.50 (*1-55028-638-2*, Pub. by J Lorimer) Orca Bk Pubs.

Mikdamot. Yizhar. Date not set. write for info. (*0-8050-5016-7*) H Holt & Co.

Mike see Early Phonetic Readers - Set D

Mike. Colleen L. Reece. LC 96-119772. 96p. (J). (gr. 4-7). 1995. pap. 5.99 (*0-8280-0879-5*) Review & Herald.

Mike. Tress. 24.99 (*0-89906-623-2*, MIKH); pap. 20.99 (*0-89906-624-0*, MIKP) Mesorah Pubns.

Mike & Doug Starn. Andy Grundberg & Sarah Rogers-Lafferty. (Illus.). 168p. 1990. pap. 27.95 (*0-917562-55-0*) Contemp Arts.

Mike & Else's Norwegian Songbook. 3rd ed. Mike Sevig & Else Sevig. (ENG & NOR., Illus.). 160p. 1999. reprint ed. pap. 19.95 (*0-9615394-0-2*) Skandisk.

Mike & Else's Swedish Songbook. Ed. by Mike Savig & Else Savig. (ENG & SWE., Illus.). 160p. 1997. pap. 19.95 (*1-57534-025-9*) Skandisk.

Mike & Lottie. Verna A. Wilkins. LC 93-6643. (Illus.). 32p. (J). (ps-3). 1993. pap. 2.95 (*1-870516-03-6*) Tamarind Bks.

Mike & Me. 2nd ed. Eric Boyd. 1996. mass mkt. 5.95 (*1-56333-419-4*, Badboy) Masquerade.

***Mike & Nick.** Mark Shleifer. LC 98-90762. (J). 1999. pap. 7.95 (*0-533-12913-3*) Vantage.

Mike & Nick & the Pumpkin Patch. Joan B. Barsotti. (Apple Hill Ser.: No. 1). (Illus.). 24p. (Orig.). (J). (ps-2). 1993. pap. 5.99 (*0-9642112-0-3*) Barsotti Bks.

Mike & Phani's Essential: C ++ Techniques. M. Hyman & P. Vaddadi. 300p. 1999. pap. 34.95 incl. cd-rom (*1-893115-04-6*) APress L P.

Mike & Psmith. P. G. Wodehouse. LC 98-117200. 190p. 1998. pap. 8.95 (*0-14-012447-0*) Viking Penguin.

Mike & the Bike. Illus. by Leoung O'Young. (Kids of Canada Ser.). 32p. (J). 1980. 12.95 (*0-88862-257-0*, Pub. by J Lorimer); pap. 5.95 (*0-88862-258-9*, Pub. by J Lorimer) Formac Dist Ltd.

Mike & the Magic Cookies. Jon Buller. (J). 1992. 9.15 (*0-606-12423-3*, Pub. by Turtleback) Demco.

Mike & the Marines. 2nd ed. Eric Boyd. 1997. reprint ed. mass mkt. 6.50 (*1-56333-497-6*, Badboy) Masquerade.

Mike & the Mechanics: Anthology. Ed. by Carol Cuellar. 124p. (Orig.). (C). 1993. pap. text 18.95 (*0-7692-0721-9*, VF1920) Wrner Bros.

Mike & the Prowler. Houghton Mifflin Company Staff. (Literature Experience 1993 Ser.). (J). (gr. 5). 1992. pap. 10.24 (*0-395-61816-9*) HM.

Mike & Tony Level 1, Blue: Best Friends. Harriet Ziefert. (Easy-to-Read Bks.). (Illus.). (J). (ps-2). 1994. pap. 3.99 (*0-14-036853-1*, PuffinBks) Peng Put Young Read.

Mike at Wrykyn. P. G. Wodehouse. LC 98-115815. 189p. 1998. pap. 9.95 (*0-14-012454-3*) Viking Penguin.

Mike Barry & the Kentucky Irish American: An Anthology. Ed. by Clyde F. Crews. LC 95-7902. (Illus.). 184p. 1995. text 25.00 (*0-8131-1898-0*) U Pr of Ky.

Mike Bolton's Favorite Alabama Jokes. 3rd ed. Mike Bolton. (Illus.). 64p. 1992. pap. 5.00 (*1-878561-11-1*) Seacoast AL.

Mike Bolton's Favorite Auburn Jokes. 3rd ed. Mike Bolton. (Illus.). 64p. (Orig.). 1992. pap. 5.00 (*1-878561-12-X*) Seacoast AL.

Mike Dime. large type ed. Barry Fantoni. 333p. 1982. 27.99 (*0-7089-0731-8*) Ulverscroft.

***Mike E. Meanderer Meets the Cow in the Flannel Nightgown.** Christine K. Trease. (Illus.). 21p. (J). (ps-7). 1999. 14.95 (*1-929450-02-8*) Lexico.

***Mike E. Meanderer Moves to the Country.** Christine K. Trease. (Illus.). 22p. (J). (ps-7). 1999. 14.95 (*1-929450-00-1*) Lexico.

Mike Fink. Illus. & Retold by Steven Kellogg. LC 91-46014. 48p. (J). (ps-3). 1992. 16.00 (*0-688-07003-5*, Wm Morrow) Morrow Avon.

Mike Fink. Steven Kellogg. 48p. (J). 1998. mass mkt. 5.95 (*0-688-13577-3*, Wm Morrow) Morrow Avon.

Mike Fink. Steven Kellogg. 1998. 11.15 (*0-606-13609-6*, Pub. by Turtleback) Demco.

Mike Fink. Emerson Bennett. LC 75-104415. reprint ed. lib. bdg. 22.50 (*0-8398-0162-9*) Irvington.

Mike Fink: King of Mississippi Keelboatmen. Walter Blair. LC 74-138143. (Illus.). 283p. 1971. reprint ed. lib. bdg. 35.00 (*0-8371-5600-9*, BLMF, Greenwood Pr) Greenwood.

***Mike Fright: How to Succeed in Media Interviews When Mike Wallace Comes Calling.** David Snell. Ed. by Christopher Snell. (Illus.). 125p. 1999. pap. 16.95 (*0-9671888-0-6*) Effect Commns.

Mike Gardner's Fish Have No Hands: Catching Tons of Fish in Bays & Estuaries. Mike Gardner. Ed. by Lisa Hanks. (Illus.). 192p. (Orig.). 1997. pap. 19.95 (*0-9649331-1-X*, Ragnars Bks) Galt Pubng.

Mike Gimbel's Baseball Player & Team Ratings. Mike Gimbel. 223p. (Orig.). 1990. pap. 8.95 (*0-9626748-0-X*) Boerum St Pr.

Mike Gimbel's Baseball Player & Team Ratings, 1991 Edition. LC 90-85559. 300p. 1991. pap. 10.95 (*0-9626748-1-8*) Boerum St Pr.

Mike Gimbel's Baseball Player & Team Ratings, 1992 Edition. 336p. 1991. pap. 14.95 (*0-9626748-2-6*) Boerum St Pr.

Mike Gimbel's Baseball Player & Team Ratings, 1993 Edition. Mike Gimbel. Ed. by Robert Johns. LC 90-167749. 336p. (Orig.). 1993. pap. 14.95 (*0-9626748-3-4*) Boerum St Pr.

Mike Gimbel's Baseball Player & Team Ratings, 1994 Edition. Mike Gimbel. LC 90-167749. 336p. (Orig.). 1994. pap. 14.95 (*0-9626748-4-2*) Boerum St Pr.

Mike Gimbel's Baseball Player & Team Ratings, 1995. Mike Gimbel. LC 90-167749. 1995. pap. 14.95 (*0-9626748-5-0*) Boerum St Pr.

Mike Glier Vol. 1: Garden Court. unabridged ed. Contrib. by Lucy R. Lippard et al. (Illus.). 56p. (Orig.). (C). 1995. pap. 15.00 (*0-614-13762-4*) Temple U Tyler Gal.

Mike Goes Trucking. Photos by Henry Horenstein. (Illus.). (J). 1988. write for info. (*0-318-62371-4*) HM.

Mike Gold: Dean of Am. Proletarian Literature. John Pyros. 218p. (Orig.). 1980. pap. 3.00 (*0-9604000-0-1*) Dramatika.

Mike Gonzo & the Almost Invisible Man. Bill Crider. (J). (gr. 2-4). 1996. mass mkt. 3.99 (*0-671-53652-4*) PB.

Mike Gonzo & the Sewer Monster. Bill Crider. (J). (gr. 2-4). 1996. mass mkt. 3.99 (*0-671-53651-6*) PB.

Mike Gonzo & the UFO Terror. Bill Crider. (YA). 1997. mass mkt. 3.99 (*0-671-53653-2*) PB.

***Mike Hailwood: A Motorcycle Racing Legend.** Mick Woollett. (Illus.). 208p. 2000. 49.95 (*1-85960-648-2*, 129518AE, Pub. by Haynes Manuals) Motorbooks Intl.

Mike Hammer: The Comic Strip, Vol. 2. Mickey Spillane, pseud. Ed. by Max Allan Collins & Catherine Yronwode. (U. S. Classics Ser.). (Illus.). 64p. 1985. pap. 5.95 (*0-912277-26-2*) K Pierce Bks.

Mike Henderson: Nineteen Ninety Adaline Kent Award Exhibition. Mark Van Proyen. 32p. 1990. pap. 5.00 (*0-930495-08-X*) San Fran Art Inst.

Mike Kelley. Mike Kelley & John Miller. Ed. by Miyoshi Barosh & William S. Bartman. (Illus.). 64p. 1992. pap. text 25.00 (*0-923183-09-4*) ART Pr NY.

Mike Kelley. Elisabeth Sussman et al. LC 93-13287. (Illus.). 1993. pap. write for info. (*0-87427-087-1*) Whitney Mus.

***Mike Kelley.** John C. Welchman. 1999. 29.95 (*0-7148-3834-9*) Phaidon Pr.

Mike Kelley: A Conversation. Thomas Kellein. 1996. pap. 14.95 (*3-89322-261-8*, Pub. by Edition Cantz) Dist Art Pubs.

***Mike Kelley 1985-1996.** Mike Kelley. (Illus.). 210p. 1999. pap. 32.00 (*84-89771-80-4*, 920781, Pub. by Actar) Dist Art Pubs.

Mike King Story. Mike King. LC 85-81940. (Illus.). 176p. (Orig.). 1985. 15.95 (*0-934672-33-4*) Good Bks PA.

Mike King Story. Mike King. LC 85-81940. (Illus.). 176p. (Orig.). 1985, reprint ed. pap. 5.95 (*0-934672-42-3*) Good Bks PA.

Mike Lawrence's Workbook on the Two-over-One System. Bergen. LC 90-159351. 189p. 1987. pap. 11.95 (*0-939460-35-1*) Devyn Pr.

Mike Leigh: Interviews. Ed. by Howie Movshovitz. LC 99-44200. (Conversations with Filmmakers Ser.). 256p. 2000. 45.00 (*1-57806-067-2*) U Pr of Miss.

Mike Leigh: Interviews. Ed. by Howie Movshovitz & Peter Brunette. LC 99-44200. (Conversations with Filmmakers Ser.). 256p. 2000. pap. 18.00 (*1-57806-068-0*) U Pr of Miss.

Mike Mandel: Making Good Time. Photos by Mike Mandel. 72p. (Orig.). 1992. 27.50 (*0-918290-00-7*) Eighteen Pubns.

Mike Mansfield, Majority Leader: A Different Kind of Senate, 1961-1976. Francis R. Valeo. LC 98-55373. (Illus.). 296p. (gr. 13). 1999. text 36.95 (*0-7656-0450-7*) M E Sharpe.

Mike McClintock's Home Sense Care & Repair Almanac. Mike McClintock. (Orig.). 1989. pap. 14.60 (*0-318-41624-7*) McGraw-Hill Prof.

Mike McClintock's Home Sense Care & Repair Almanac. Mike McClintock. (Illus.). 416p. (Orig.). 1989. 28.95 (*0-8306-0449-9*); pap. 19.95 (*0-8306-0349-2*) McGraw-Hill Prof.

Mike Mentzer's High Intensity Training Program: Secrets to Building Muscles in Minutes. Mike Mentzer. 40p. 1997. 39.95 incl. audio (*1-889462-02-0*) Advanced Research Pr.

Mike Monroney: Oklahoma Liberal. Bob Burke & Von R. Creel. Ed. by Kenny A. Franks & Gini Moore Campbell. LC 96-71238. (Oklahoma Statesmen Ser.: Vol. IV). (Illus.). 210p. 1997. 20.00 (*1-885596-04-9*) OK Heritage.

Mike Mulligan & His Steam Shovel. Virginia L. Burton. (Illus.). (J). (gr. k-3). 1939. lib. bdg. 11.95 (*0-395-06681-6*) HM.

Mike Mulligan & His Steam Shovel. Virginia L. Burton. (J). 1939. 11.15 (*0-606-01106-4*, Pub. by Turtleback) Demco.

Mike Mulligan & His Steam Shovel. unabridged ed. Virginia L. Burton. (Carry-Along Book & Cassette Favorites Ser.). 1p. (J). (ps-4). 1993. pap. 9.95 incl. audio (*0-395-66499-3*, 482618) HM.

Mike Mulligan & His Steam Shovel: A Study Guide. Garrett Christopher. Ed. by J. Friedland & R. Kessler. (Little Novel-Ties Ser.). (J). (gr. k-2). 1995. pap. text, student ed. 14.95 (*1-56982-237-9*) Lrn Links.

Mike Mulligan & His Steam Shovel: Story & Pictures, 001. Virginia L. Burton. (Sandpiper Books Ser.). (Illus.). 44p. (J). (ps-3). 1977. pap. 5.95 (*0-395-25939-8*) HM.

Mike Mulligan & His Steam Shovel: 60th Anniversary Edition. 60th ed. Virginia Lee Burton. (Sandpiper Books Ser.). (Illus.). 44p. (J). (ps-3). 1977. 14.95 (*0-395-16961-5*) HM.

Mike Mulligan y Su Maquina Maravillosa. Virginia L. Burton. 48p. (J). (ps-3). 1997. 16.00 (*0-395-86264-7*); pap. 5.95 (*0-395-86134-9*) HM.

Mike Mulligan y Su Maquina Maravillosa. Virginia Lee Burton. 1997. 11.15 (*0-606-12768-2*, Pub. by Turtleback) Demco.

***Mike Mulligan Y Su Maquina Maravillosa: Mike Mulligan & His Steam Shovel.** Virginia Lee Burton. (Illus.). 56p. (J). (gr. k-3). 1999. 9.95 (*0-618-01136-6*) HM.

Mike Myers. Connie Hull Dupont. LC 99-34328. (Illus.). 64p. 1999. 17.95 (*0-7910-5236-2*) Chelsea Hse.

Mike Myers. Lonnie Hull Dupont. LC 99-34328. (Galaxy of Superstars Ser.). (Illus.). 64p. (YA). (gr. 3-7). 1999. pap. 9.95 (*0-7910-5336-9*) Chelsea Hse.

***Mike Nelson's Movie Megacheese.** Michael J. Nelson. 288p. 2000. pap. 15.00 (*0-380-81467-6*) Morrow Avon.

Mike O'Garry's Pocket: Selected Short Stories. Tom McDevitt. 1986. pap. 6.00 (*0-933046-04-9*) Little Red Hen.

Mike Piazza. Brant James & Chelsea House Publishing Staff. LC 97-5504. (Baseball Legends Ser.). (Illus.). 64p. (J). (gr. 3 up). 1997. 15.95 (*0-7910-4379-7*) Chelsea Hse.

Mike Piazza: Hard-Hitting Catcher. Jeff Savage. LC 96-54063. 1997. lib. bdg. 19.93 (*0-8225-2895-9*) Lerner Pub.

Mike Piazza: Hard-Hitting Catcher. Jeff Savage. LC 96-54063. (Illus.). 64p. 1997. pap. 5.95 (*0-8225-9752-7*) Lerner Pub.

Mike Piazza: Mike & the Mets. Marty Noble. Ed. by Rob Rains. (Super Star Ser.). 96p. (J). 1999. pap. 4.95 (*1-58261-051-7*) Sprts Pubng.

Mike Piazza: Phenomenal Catcher. Tom Owens. LC 97-506. (Sports Greats Ser.). (J). 1997. lib. bdg. 17.27 (*0-8239-5089-1*, PowerKids) Rosen Group.

***Mike Richter: Gotham Goalie.** Mike Shalin. (SuperStar Ser.: Vol. 2). (Illus.). 96p. 1999. pap. 4.95 (*1-58261-149-1*, Pub. by Sprts Pubng) Partners-West.

Mike Rounds' Quick Tips for the Internet. Michael F. Rounds. 2p. 1998. pap. 9.95 (*1-891440-08-X*) CPM Systems.

Mike Sakamoto's Keiki Fishing Guide. Michael R. Sakamoto. (Illus.). 80p. (J). (gr. k-6). 1994. pap. 6.95 (*1-880188-77-5*) Bess Pr.

Mike Schmidt. Lois P. Nicholson. LC 94-23612. (Baseball Legends Ser.). (Illus.). 64p. (J). (gr. 3 up). 1995. lib. bdg. 15.95 (*0-7910-2173-4*) Chelsea Hse.

***Mike Schmidt: Philadelphia's Hall of Fame Third Baseman.** William C. Kashatus. LC 99-48776. (Illus.). 165p. 1999. pap. 22.50 (*0-7864-0713-1*) McFarland & Co.

Mike Schmidt Study: Hitting Theory, Skills, & Technique. Mike Schmidt & Rob Ellis. LC 93-77354. (Illus.). 176p. 1993. 22.95 (*0-9634609-1-9*); pap., student ed. 18.95 (*0-9634609-2-7*) McGriff & Bell.

Mike Schmidt Study: Youth Version. Mike Schmidt & Rob Ellis. LC 93-77353. (Mike Schmidt Study Ser.). (Illus.). 80p. (Orig.). (J). (gr. 4-10). 1991. pap. 9.95 (*0-9634609-3-5*) McGriff & Bell.

Mike Stern. Ed. by Dan Thress. LC 99-389532. (Ultimate Play along Ser.). 84p. (Orig.). 1996. pap. text 24.95 (*1-57623-404-5*, MMBK0065CD) Wrner Bros.

Mike Stern Guitar Transcriptions. 80p. 1992. per. 16.95 (*0-7935-1182-8*, 00673224) H Leonard.

Mike Swan, Sink or Swim. Deborah Heiligman. LC 97-28789. (Illus.). 48p. (J). 1998. 13.95 (*0-385-32522-3*) Delacorte.

Mike Swan, Sink or Swim. Deborah Heiligman. LC 97-28789. (Illus.). 48p. (J). (gr. 4-8). 1998. pap. 4.50 (*0-440-41435-0*) Dell.

Mike Swan, Sink or Swim. Deborah Heiligman. 1998. 9.70 (*0-606-13610-X*, Pub. by Turtleback) Demco.

Mike the Copycat: Adventures & Stories of Cat Tails. Veronica L. Cook. (Illus.). 50p. (Orig.). (J). (ps up). 1989. pap. text. write for info. (*0-318-66532-8*) Ronnie Two Pub.

***Mike the Mail Carrier.** large type ed. Beth Esh Smith. (LB Ser.). (Illus.). 8p. (J). (ps-1). 1999. pap. text 10.95 (*1-57332-157-5*); pap. text 10.95 (*1-57332-144-3*) HighReach Lrning.

Mike the Microbe. Ruth Simione. (Illus.). 38p. (J). (gr. 4-8). Date not set. pap. text 14.70 (*1-877960-23-3*) Kemtec Educ.

Mike Tyson: Money, Myth, Betrayal. Monteil Illingiworth. (Illus.). 410p. 1991. 22.95 (*1-55972-079-4*, Birch Ln Pr) Carol Pub Group.

Mike Tyson: The Release of Power. Reg Gutteridge. (Illus.). 224p. (Orig.). 1996. pap. text 14.95 (*1-895629-61-6*) Warwick Publ.

Mikelngur Tenqmiar (Little Bird) (Cupig) large type ed. Marie Hoover et al. (ESK., Illus.). 8p. (J). (gr. k-3). 1999. pap. text 6.00 (*1-58084-165-1*) Lower Kuskokwim.

Mike's Baby. Mary L. Baxter. (Desire Ser.). 1993. per. 2.89 (*0-373-05781-4*, 5-05781-5) Silhouette.

Mike's Basic Guide to Cabling Computers & Telephones in Homes & Apartments. Mike Gorman. (Mike's Basic Guide to Cabling Ser.: Vol. 2). (Illus.). 70p. 1998. spiral bd. 29.95 (*0-9660638-1-3*) Prairie Wind.

Mike's Best Summer. Leslie Dunkling. (American Structural Readers Stage Ser.: No. 1). (Illus.). 16p. 1989. pap. text 6.31 (*0-582-79885-X*, 75124) Longman.

Mike's Case. Christopher Schoggen. 32p. (YA). 1983. pap. 3.50 (*0-87129-689-6*, M56) Dramatic Pub.

Mike's Corner: Daunting Literary Snippets from Phish's Bassit. Michael Gordon. LC 96-48322. (Illus.). 148p. 1997. pap. 14.95 (*0-8212-2389-5*) Little.

Mike's First Haircut. Sharon Gordon. LC 87-10911. (Illus.). 32p. (J). (gr. k-2). 1988. lib. bdg. 13.05 (*0-8167-1113-5*) Troll Communs.

Mike's First Haircut. Sharon Gordon. LC 87-10911. (Illus.). 32p. (J). (gr. k-2). 1997. pap. 2.50 (*0-8167-1114-3*) Troll Communs.

Mike's First Haircut. enl. ed. Sharon Gordon. 1999. pap. text 16.95 (*0-8167-6274-0*) Troll Communs.

Mike's Guide to the Motor City: World Class Art, Architecture, History & Fun! In Detroit. Michael E. Fisher. LC 93-73825. (Illus.). 72p. (Orig.). 1993. pap. 4.95 (*0-9638877-0-X*) Glast Road Pr.

Mike's Kite. 93rd ed. 1993. pap. text 10.80 (*0-15-300320-0*, Harcourt Child Bks) Harcourt.

Mike's Lonely Summer: A Child's Guide to Divorce. Carolyn Nystrom. 48p. (J). (gr. 4-7). 1994. pap. 4.99 (*0-7459-2925-7*) Lion USA.

Mike's Lucky Day. Dunkling. 1984. pap. text. write for info. (*0-582-52973-5*, Pub. by Addison-Wesley) Longman.

Mike's Lucky Day, 1. Leslie Dunkling. (Longman Originals Ser.). 1996. pap. text 5.51 (*0-582-07499-1*) Addison-Wesley.

Mike's Mystery. Gertrude Chandler Warner. LC 60-8428. (Boxcar Children Ser.: No. 5). (Illus.). 128p. (J). (gr. 2-5). 1960. lib. bdg. 14.95 (*0-8075-5140-6*) A Whitman.

Mike's Mystery. Gertrude Chandler Warner. LC 60-8428. (Boxcar Children Ser.: No. 5). (Illus.). 128p. (J). (gr. 2-5). 1990. pap. 3.95 (*0-8075-5141-4*) A Whitman.

Mike's Mystery. Gertrude Chandler Warner. (Boxcar Children Ser.: No. 5). 128p. (J). (gr. 2-5). pap. 3.95 (*0-8072-1462-0*) Listening Lib.

Mike's Mystery. Gertrude Chandler Warner. (Boxcar Children Ser.: No. 5). (J). (gr. 2-5). 1988. 8.60 (*0-606-01921-9*, Pub. by Turtleback) Demco.

Mike's New Bike. Rose Greydanus. (Illus.). 32p. (J). (gr. k-2). 1980. lib. bdg. 13.05 (*0-89375-382-3*) Troll Communs.

Mike's New Bike. Rose Greydanus. (Illus.). 32p. (J). (gr. k-2). 1997. pap. 2.50 (*0-89375-282-7*) Troll Communs.

Mike's Oil Patch. Dorys Ward. 96p. (J). 1993. 12.95 (*0-89015-920-3*) Sunbelt Media.

Mike's Oil Patch. Dorys Ward. 96p. (J). 1997. pap. 7.95 (*1-57168-121-3*, Eakin Pr) Sunbelt Media.

Mike's Place, Every Monday & Raw Sienna. Michael E. Waldecki & Ronald E. Kittell. (Wild Dog Ser.: No. 1). 44p. (Orig.). 1986. pap. 4.95 (*0-933087-05-5*) Bottom Dog Pr.

Mikey & Mary Are Illiterate & Nobody Cares. Carol Ericson. LC 94-70139. 144p. 1994. pap. 9.95 (*0-9640157-2-2*) Excell Educ.

Mikey Goes Whale Watching. Joseph Allen. Ed. by M. D. Trout. (Illus.). 50p. (Orig.). (J). (gr. 1-5). 1986. pap. 8.95 (*0-917071-04-2*); lib. bdg. 13.50 (*0-917071-05-0*) Ocean Allen Pub.

Mikey Likes It. Michael Stephens. 110p. (Orig.). 1989. pap. 9.95 (*0-317-93027-3*) Emjay Pub Co.

Mikey Mite Goes to School. Gilles Gauthier. (First Novels Ser.). (Illus.). 58p. (J). (gr. 1-4). 1995. mass mkt. 3.99 (*0-88780-223-0*, Pub. by Formac Publ Co); bds. 14.95 (*0-88780-224-9*, Pub. by Formac Publ Co) Formac Dist Ltd.

***Mikey Mite's Best Present.** Gilles Gauthier. (First Novels). (Illus.). 58p. (J). 1998. bds. 14.95 (*0-88780-433-0*, Pub. by Formac Publ Co) Formac Dist Ltd.

Mikey Mite's Best Present. Gilles Gauthier. (First Novels). 58p. (J). (gr. 1-4). 1998. text 3.99 (*0-88780-432-2*, Pub. by Formac Publ Co) Formac Dist Ltd.

An Asterisk (*) at the beginning of an entry indicates that the title is appearing for the first time.

Mikey Mite's Big Problem. Gilles Gauthier. (First Novels Ser.). (Illus.). 60p. (J). (gr. 1-4). 1995. mass mkt. 3.99 (*0-88780-274-5*, Pub. by Formac Publ Co); bds. 14.95 (*0-88780-275-3*, Pub. by Formac Publ Co) Formac Dist Ltd.

Mikhail Bakhtin. Katerina Clark & Michael Holquist. (Illus.). 416p. 1986. pap. 18.95 (*0-674-57417-6*) Belknap Pr.

Mikhail Bakhtin. Tzvetan Todorov. Tr. by Wlad Godzich from FRE. LC 84-3636. (Theory & History of Literature Ser.: Vol. 13). 141p. 1984. pap. 12.95 (*0-8166-1291-9*) U of Minn Pr.

Mikhail Bakhtin: A Bibliography. Ed. by Joan Nordquist. (Social Theory: A Bibliographic Ser.: No. 12). 60p. (Orig.). 1988. pap. 20.00 (*0-937855-22-7*) Ref Rsch Serv.

***Mikhail Bakhtin: An Aesthetic for Democracy.** Ken Hirschkop. LC 99-16106. 352p. 2000. 74.00 (*0-19-815961-7*) OUP.

***Mikhail Bakhtin: An Aesthetic for Democracy.** Kenneth Hirschkop. LC 99-16106. 352p. 2000. 24.95 (*0-19-815960-9*) OUP.

Mikhail Bakhtin: An Annotated Bibliography. Harold Baker. Ed. by William Cain. (Bibliographies of Modern Critics & Critical Schools Ser.). 300p. Date not set. text 45.00 (*0-8153-1172-9*) Garland.

Mikhail Bakhtin: Between Phenomenology & Marxism. Steven Bird. (Studies in Natural Language Processing: No. 11). 205p. (C). 1995. pap. text 19.95 (*0-521-46647-4*) Cambridge U Pr.

Mikhail Bakhtin: Creation of a Prosaics. Gary S. Morson & Caryl Emerson. LC 90-39855. 560p. 1990. 57.50 (*0-8047-1821-0*); pap. 18.95 (*0-8047-1822-9*) Stanford U Pr.

Mikhail Bakhtin Two: A Bibliography. Ed. by Joan Nordquist. (Social Theory: A Bibliographic Ser.: No. 32). 64p. (Orig.). 1993. pap. 20.00 (*0-937855-63-4*) Ref Rsch Serv.

Mikhail Bakunin: A Study in the Psychology & Politics of Utopianism. Aileen Kelly. 1982. text 55.00 (*0-19-827244-8*) OUP.

Mikhail Baryshinikov. Alecia C. Townsend. LC 92-42547. (Arts Ser.). 112p. (YA). (gr. 1-8). 1993. lib. bdg. 25.27 (*0-86625-484-6*) Rourke Pubns.

Mikhail Bulgakov: Life & Interpretations. Anthony C. Wright. LC 78-3872. 334p. 1978. reprint ed. pap. 103.60 (*0-608-02226-8*, 202368100006) Bks Demand.

Mikhail Bulgakov: The Early Years. Edythe C. Haber. LC 97-42403. (Russian Research Center Studies). 320p. 1998. 45.00 (*0-674-57418-4*) HUP.

Mikhail Chekhov As Actor, Director, & Teacher. Lendley C. Black. LC 87-5995. (Theater & Dramatic Studies: No. 43). 130p. 1987. reprint ed. pap. 40.30 (*0-8357-1800-X*, 207059200004) Bks Demand.

Mikhail Glinka. David Brown. LC 84-19878. (Music Reprint Ser.). (Illus.). 342p. 1985. reprint ed. lib. bdg. 39.50 (*0-306-76247-1*) Da Capo.

Mikhail Gorbachev. Thomas Butson. (World Leaders Past & Present Ser.). (Illus.). 120p. (Orig.). (YA). (gr. 5 up). 1989. pap. 8.95 (*0-7910-0571-2*) Chelsea Hse.

Mikhail Gorbachev. Thomas Butson. (World Leaders Past & Present Ser.). (Illus.). 112p. (Orig.). (YA). (gr. 5 up). 1990. lib. bdg. 19.95 (*1-55546-200-6*) Chelsea Hse.

Mikhail Gorbachev. Michel Tatu. LC 91-73244. 155p. 1991. text 38.50 (*0-88033-197-6*, Pub. by East Eur Monographs) Col U Pr.

Mikhail Gorbachev - "A Road to the Future" Complete Text of the United Nations Address. Mikhail S. Gorbachev. LC 90-6832. (Peacewatch Editions Ser.). 48p. 1990. pap. 5.95 (*0-943734-13-4*) Ocean Tree Bks.

Mikhail Gorbachev, the Soviet Innovator. Steven Otfinoski. (Great Lives Ser.). (J). 1989. 9.05 (*0-606-01927-8*, Pub. by Turtleback) Demco.

Mikhail Kuzmin: A Life in Art. John E. Malmstad & N. A. Bogomolov. LC 98-44379. xvi, 463p. 1999. 49.95 (*0-674-53087-X*) HUP.

Mikhail Larionov & the Russian Avant-Garde. Anthony Parton. 280p. 1993. pap. text 31.95 (*0-691-02620-3*, Pub. by Princeton U Pr) Cal Prin Full Svc.

Mikhail Larionov & the Russian Avant-Garde. Anthony Parton. LC 92-20814. (Illus.). 216p. (C). 1993. text 80.00 (*0-691-03603-9*, Pub. by Princeton U Pr) Cal Prin Full Svc.

Mikhail Larionov, 1881-1964. Evgeni Kovtun. (Great Painters Ser.). (Illus.). 172p. 1997. 40.00 (*1-85995-296-8*) Parkstone Pr.

Mikhail Lermontov: A Hero of Our Time. Ed. by D. J. Richards. (Bristol Russian Texts Ser.). (RUS.). (C). 1992. reprint ed. pap. 20.95 (*1-85399-314-X*, Pub. by Brist Class Pr) Focus Pub-R Pullins.

Mikhail Lermontov: From Russia to the Caucasus. Robert Reid. Date not set. write for info. (*1-57181-995-9*) Berghahn Bks.

Mikhail Naimy: An Introduction. Nadeem N. Naimy. 1967. pap. 15.95 (*0-8156-6028-6*, Pub. by Am U Beirut) Syracuse U Pr.

Mikhail, Prince of Chernigov & Grand Prince of Kiev, 1224-1246. Martin Dimnik. (Illus.). xvi, 199p. pap. 18.29 (*0-88844-052-9*) Brill Academic Pubs.

Mikhail S. Gorbachev: An Intimate Biography. Donald Morrison. pap. 4.50 (*0-318-50012-4*, Sig) NAL.

Mikhail S. Gorbachev: An Intimate Biography. Ed. by Donald Morrison. 288p. 1988. 14.95 (*0-317-70076-6*, Sig) NAL.

Mikhail Vasil'evich Lomonosov on the Corpuscular Theory. Mikhail V. Lomonosov. Tr. by Henry M. Leicester. LC 73-95927. (Illus.). 297p. 1970. 30.00 (*0-674-57420-6*) HUP.

Mikhail Vrubel. Mikhail Guerman. (Great Painters Ser.). (Illus.). 176p. 1996. 40.00 (*1-85995-153-8*) Parkstone Pr.

Miki. Donna Barr. (Desert Peach Ser.: Vol. 26). (Illus.). 48p. 1996. pap. 4.95 (*1-892253-05-4*, Pub. by Fine Line) Last Gasp.

Miki & Maile: Moveable Hawaiian Paper Dolls. Wren. (Illus.). 24p. 1993. pap. 4.95 (*1-56647-045-5*) Mutual Pub HI.

Mikkai see Secret Rendezvous: A Novel

Mi'kmag Hieroglyph Prayers: Reading in North America's First Indigenous Script. David L. Schmidt & Murdena Marshall. (Illus.). 148p. 1995. pap. 16.95 (*1-55109-069-4*) Nimbus Publ.

Mi'kmaq: Peoples of the Maritimes. Stephen A. Davis. LC 96-950112. 1998. pap. text 10.95 (*1-55109-180-1*) Nimbus Publ.

Mi'kmaq: Resistance, Accommodation & Cultural Survival. Harald E. Prins. (Case Studies in Cultural Anthropology). 1997. pap. 25.00 (*0-03-053427-5*) Harcourt Coll Pubs.

Miko. Eric Van Lustbader. 544p. 1985. mass mkt. 5.95 (*0-449-20596-7*, Crest) Fawcett.

MIKON '98: 12th International Conference on Microwaves & Radar : Krakbow, Poland, May 20-22, 1998. International Conference on Microwaves & Radar Staff. LC 99-163005. 1998. pap. write for info. (*0-7803-5003-0*) Inst Electrical.

Mikoyan MiG-29 Fulcrum. Yefim Gordon. LC 99-58916. 304p. 1999. 39.95 (*0-7603-0764-4*) Motorbooks Intl.

Mikpon Exxonorion H Ariaematapion: The Priest's Service Book. Evagoras Constantinides. (Illus.). 426p. (C). 1989. 20.00 (*0-685-28020-9*) E Constantinides.

Mikro- & Makrookonomische Auswirkungen von Terminmarkten: Zur Synthese Zwischen Portfoliotheorie, Kapitalmarkttheorie, Optionspreistheorie & Futurebewertungstheorie. Carsten Kotas. (GER., Illus.). XXIII, 330p. 1996. 57.95 (*3-631-31006-4*) P Lang Pubng.

Mikrobiologischebodensanierung. 1995. 69.95 (*3-540-59014-5*) Spr-Verlag.

Mikrofiltration und Andere Tranfusions-Probleme in der Intensivmedizin. Ed. by H. Busch. (Beitraege zur Infusionstherapie und Klinische Ernaehrung Ser.: Band 3). (Illus.). 1979. pap. 15.00 (*3-8055-3057-9*) S Karger.

Mikropalaeontologische und Stratigraphische Untersuchungen Im Palaeocaen und Eocaen des Vicentin (Norditalien) Mit Besonderer Beruecksichtigung der Discocyclinen und Asterocyclinen. J. Schweighauser. (Illus.). 110p. 1972. reprint ed. 76.50 (*3-87429-031-X*, 014011, Pub. by Koeltz Sci Bks) Lubrecht & Cramer.

Mikroradiographische Untersuchungen zur Mineralisation der Knochen Fruehgeborener und junger Saeuglinge 1980. G. Mueller. (Journal: Acta Anatomica: Vol. 108, Suppl. 64). (Illus.). iv, 44p. 1981. pap. 39.25 (*3-8055-1719-X*) S Karger.

Mikrovaskul are Gewebetransplantation im Kopt-Hals-Bereich see Microvascular Tissure Transplant in the Head & Neck

Mikrozirkulation des Skelettmuskels. Ed. by K. Messmer & F. Hammersen. (Illus.). viii, 162p. 1985. pap. 64.50 (*3-8055-3919-3*) S Karger.

Mikrozirkulation in Malignen Tumoren. Ed. by P. W. Vaupel & F. Hammersen. (Mikrozirkulation in Forschung und Klinik; Progress in Applied Microcirculation Ser.: Vol. 2). (Illus.). vi, 126p. 1983. pap. 39.25 (*3-8055-3762-X*) S Karger.

Mikrozirkulation und arterielle Verschlusskrankheiten, Muenchen, November 1980. Ed. by K. Messmer & Bengt Fagrell. (Illus.). vi, 222p. 1982. pap. 42.75 (*3-8055-2417-X*) S Karger.

Mikrozirkulation und Entzuendung: Beziehungen Zwischen Gefaesswand Entzuendungszellen und Mediatoren. Ed. by K. Messmer & F. Hammersen. (Illus.). xvi, 358p. 1988. pap. 130.50 (*3-8055-4656-4*) S Karger.

Mik's Mammoth. Roy Gerrard. (Illus.). 32p. (J). (gr. k-3). 1990. 15.00 (*0-374-31891-3*) FS&G.

Mik's Mammoth. Roy Gerrard. LC 90-55189. (Illus.). 32p. (J). (ps-3). 1992. pap. 4.95 (*0-374-44843-4*) FS&G.

Mikvaos. (Mishnah Ser.: No. 4b). pap. 15.99 (*0-89906-331-4*, T4BP) Mesorah Pubns.

Mil Ano de Poesia Espanola. Planeta-Agostini. 1998. pap. 44.95 (*84-08-01733-0*) Planeta.

1,000 Errores Mas Frecuentes en Espanol. rev. unabridged ed. Jose Escarpanter. Orig. Title: Eso no se Escribe Asi: Los 1,000 Errores Mas Frecuentes en Espanol. (SPA., Illus.). 128p. 1993. pap. 5.95 (*1-893909-02-6*) Brickell Commun.

MIL-I-45208 Inspection System Manual: Including a Set of 28 Read to Use Control Forms & Instruction Guide: "How to Implement the System" Gunther B. Gumpp. 118p. 1995. ring bd. 250.00 incl. disk (*1-881006-39-5*) Qual Cont Systs Srvs.

Mil Ochocientos Noventa y Ocho: La Guerra Despues de la Guerra. Fernando Pico. LC 87-80624. (Coleccion Semilla). (SPA.). 215p. 1987. pap. 8.50 (*0-940238-25-X*) Ediciones Huracan.

Mil Pesos. John Galbreath. (Illus.). 72p. 1998. pap. 8.00 (*0-8059-4427-3*) Dorrance.

Mil Protagonistas de la Historia. Ed. by Espasa Staff. (SPA., Illus.). 622p. 1994. 34.95 (*84-239-5994-5*) Elliots Bks.

MIL-Q 9858 Quality Program: Including a Set of 36 Control Forms & Instruction Guide: "How to Implement the Program" Gunther B. Gumpp. 128p. 1995. ring bd. 295.00 incl. disk (*1-881006-40-9*) Qual Cont Systs Srvs.

MIL Sections 1-End, Vol. 127. 313p. 1999. write for info. (*0-327-06976-7*, 57752-12) LEXIS Pub.

MIL-SPEC, Ruggedized, & Commercially Rugged Computer Market: Purchasing Shifts Toward Commercial Products Offering Portability. Market Intelligence Staff. 322p. (Orig.). 1992. 1495.00 (*1-56753-071-0*) Frost & Sullivan.

Mil-Std-810D Dynamic Environments - Guidelines to Implementation - A Tutorial. Ed. by Edward A. Szymkowiak. 160p. 1985. 75.00 (*0-915414-80-5*) IEST.

Mil Voces: Blue. Para Celebrar. 11.00 (*0-687-43183-2*) Abingdon.

Mil Voces: Red. Para Celebrar. 11.00 (*0-687-43185-9*) Abingdon.

Mil y una Noches. (SPA.). 9.50 (*84-241-5612-9*) E Torres & Sons.

Mil y una Noches: Relatos Ilustrados. (SPA.). 10.00 (*84-241-5409-6*) E Torres & Sons.

Mila Eighteen. Leon Uris. 576p. 1983. mass mkt. 7.99 (*0-553-24160-5*) Bantam.

Milabs! Military Mind-Control & Alien Abductions. Helmut Lammer & Marion Lammer. LC 99-14041. (Illus.). 168p. 1999. 14.95 (*1-881532-18-6*) IllumiNet Pr.

Milad Mujtama': Shabakat Al-Alaqat Al-Ijtima Iyah. Malik Bin-Nabi. (Mushkilat al-Hadarah Ser.). 128p. 1986. pap. 3.95 (*1-57547-038-1*) Dar Al-Fikr.

Milady Alex! Diana G. Gallagher. (Secret World of Alex Mack Ser.: No. 15). (Orig.). (J). (gr. 3-6). 1984. pap. 1.75 (*0-671-00684-3*) PB.

***Milady Charlotte.** large type ed. Jean Plaidy, pseud. 368p. 2000. write for info. (*0-7089-4186-9*) Ulverscroft.

Milady Illustrated Cosmetology Dictionary. Bobbi R. Madry. (Illus.). 1985. 27.95 (*0-87350-412-7*) Milady Pub.

Milady's a Contemporary Approach to Permanent Waving. Mark E. Padgett. LC 93-28020. 142p. 1994. pap. 19.95 (*1-56253-101-8*) Milady Pub.

Milady's Art & Science of Nail Technology. Milady Publishing Company Staff. (SPA.). 224p. 1994. pap. 32.45 (*1-56253-156-5*) Milady Pub.

Milady's Black Cosmetology. Thomas Hayden & James D. Williams. (HAIR). (Illus.). 256p. 1991. pap. 28.95 (*0-87350-377-5*) Thomson Learn.

***Milady's Cosmetology Dictionary.** 3rd ed. Milady Staff. 2001. pap. 14.50 (*1-56253-667-2*) Milady Pub.

Milady's Esthetician's Guide to Business Management. Gambino. LC 93-4228. (NAILS). 320p. 1993. pap. 37.95 (*1-56253-127-1*) Thomson Learn.

Milady's Flash Cosmetology Dictionary. Milady Publishing Company Staff. 1996. 19.95 (*1-56253-372-X*) Milady Pub.

Milady's for Men Only: Styling & Techniques. Louise Cotter. LC 93-39834. 160p. 1994. pap. 34.95 (*1-56253-203-0*) Thomson Learn.

Milady's Guide to Becoming a Financially Solvent Salon. Leslie Edgerton & Glen Allie. LC 95-16204. (Illus.). 160p. 1996. pap. 26.95 (*1-56253-211-1*) Thomson Learn.

Milady's Guide to Owning & Operating a Nail Salon. Joanne L. Wiggins & Ron Wiggins. LC 93-28026. (NAILS). 150p. 1993. pap. 21.95 (*1-56253-201-4*) Thomson Learn.

Milady's Hair Coloring Techniques. Louise Cotter. LC 92-34815. (HAIR). 114p. 1993. pap. 27.75 (*1-56253-116-6*) Thomson Learn.

Milady's Hair Cutting: A Technical Guide: Men's, Women's, & Children's Cuts. Kenneth Young. LC 92-23133. (HAIR). 62p. 1992. pap. 16.95 (*1-56253-103-4*) Thomson Learn.

Milady's Life Management Skills for Cosmetology, Barber-Styling & Nail Technology. Catherine Lamb. LC 95-21218. (Career Development Ser.). (Illus.). 136p. 1996. 10.95 (*1-56253-252-9*) Thomson Learn.

Milady's Makeup Techniques. Pamela Taylor. LC 93-25665. (SKIN). 164p. 1993. pap. 31.95 (*1-56253-142-5*) Thomson Learn.

Milady's Nail Structure & Product Chemistry. Douglas D. Schoon. LC 95-10229. (NAILS). 128p. 1996. pap. 26.95 (*1-56253-239-1*) Thomson Learn.

Milady's Professional Instructor for Cosmetology, Barber-Styling, & Nail Technology. Linda J. Howe. LC 93-31648. (Career Development Ser.). 118p. 1994. pap. 32.25 (*1-56253-073-9*) Thomson Learn.

Milady's Razor Cutting. Kenneth Young. LC 93-28547. (HAIR). 46p. 1993. pap. 16.95 (*1-56253-180-8*) Thomson Learn.

Milady's Salon Receptionist's Handbook. Ventura & Judy Ventura. LC 93-3776. (SalonOvations Ser.). 208p. 1993. pap. 21.50 (*1-56253-044-5*) Milady Pub.

Milady's Skin Care & Cosmetic Ingredients Dictionary. Natalia Michalun & M. Varinia Michalun. LC 93-33822. (Career Development Ser.). 328p. 1994. pap. 22.50 (*1-56253-125-5*) Thomson Learn.

Milady's Skin Care Reference Guide. Mark Lees. LC 93-28236. (SKIN). 384p. 1993. pap. 39.95 (*1-56253-071-2*) Thomson Learn.

Milady's Standard Hair Coloring Manual & Activities Book: A Level System Approach. 2nd abr. rev. ed. Deborah Rangl. LC 97-10089. (Milady - Cosmetology). 208p. 1997. 27.95 (*1-56253-356-8*) Thomson Learn.

***Milady's Standard System of Salon Skills: Hairdressing : [Student] Course Book.** Marybeth Janssen & Milady Publishing Company Staff. LC 98-7543. xx, 607 p. 1999. write for info. (*1-56253-510-2*) Milady Pub.

Milady's Standard Textbook for Professional Estheticians. 8th ed. Joel Gerson. LC 98-20108. 1998. pap. 55.95 (*1-56253-359-2*) Thomson Learn.

Milady's Standard Textbook of Cosmetology see Texto General de Cosmetologia

Milady's Standard Textbook of Cosmetology. Milady Publishing Company Staff. LC 99-19654. 716p. 1999. 57.95 (*1-56253-466-1*) Thomson Learn.

Milady's Standard Textbook of Cosmetology. rev. ed. Milday Staff. 634p. 1994. pap. write for info. (*1-56253-210-3*); pap. write for info. (*1-56253-213-8*) Milady Pub.

Milady's Standard Textbook of Cosmetology: Practical Workbook-Answer Key. rev. ed. Milady Publishing Company Staff. 273p. 1995. text, teacher ed. 28.00 (*1-56253-219-7*) Milady Pub.

Milady's Standard Textbook of Cosmetology: Theory Workbook-Answer Key. rev. ed. Milady Publishing Company Staff. 130p. 1995. text, teacher ed. 29.95 (*1-56253-221-9*) Milady Pub.

Milady's Standard Textbook of Cosmetology, 1991. Milady Publishing Company Staff. 1980. pap. 13.50 (*1-56253-018-6*) Delmar.

Milady's Standard Textbook of Cosmetology, 1991. Milady Publishing Company Staff. 544p. 1991. student ed. 26.95 (*1-56253-008-9*) Delmar.

Milady's Standard Textbook of Cosmetology, 1991. Milady Publishing Company Staff. 544p. 1991. pap. 32.45 (*1-56253-003-8*) Delmar.

Milady's Standard Textbook of Cosmetology, 1991. Milady Publishing Company Staff. 544p. 1991. pap. 12.50 (*1-56253-059-3*) Delmar.

Milady's Standard Textbook of Cosmetology, 1991. Milady Publishing Company Staff. 1982. VHS 160.00 (*0-87350-659-6*) Milady Pub.

Milady's Standard Textbook of Cosmetology, 1991. Milady Publishing Company Staff. 1991. pap. 15.95 (*0-87350-443-7*) Milady Pub.

Milady's Standard Textbook of Cosmetology, 1991. 2nd ed. Milady Publishing Company Staff. 1991. pap. 1.00 (*1-56253-004-6*) Delmar.

Milady's Standard Textbook of Cosmetology, 1991. 2nd ed. Milady Publishing Company Staff. 544p. 1991. text 35.45 (*1-56253-001-1*) Delmar.

Milady's Standard Textbook of Professional Barber-Styling. 2nd rev. ed. Maura Sheahan & Milady Publishing Company Staff. LC 92-20470. 640p. 1993. 44.50 (*1-56253-104-2*) Milady Pub.

***Milady's Standard Textbook of Professional Barber-Styling.** 3rd ed. Maura T. Scali-Snipes. LC 98-20079. (Cosmetology Ser.). (C). 1998. pap., student ed. 57.95 (*1-56253-366-5*) Thomson Learn.

Milady's Standard Theory Workbook 91. 2nd ed. Lindquist. 160p. 1991. pap. 20.25 (*1-56253-005-4*) Milady Pub.

Milady's Theory & Practice of Therapeutic Massage. 2nd ed. Mark F. Beck. 693p. 1994. pap. 48.95 (*1-56253-120-4*) Thomson Learn.

Milady's Theory & Practice of Therapeutic Massage: Curriculum Guide. 2nd ed. Mark F. Beck. 3p. 1993. 2.75 (*1-56253-121-2*) Milady Pub.

Milady's Theory & Practice of Therapeutic Massage: Workbook-Answer Key. 2nd ed. Mark F. Beck. 161p. 1994. text, teacher ed. 20.00 (*1-56253-217-0*) Milady Pub.

Milady's Workbook for the Professional Instructor - Answers. Mary A. Clark. 105p. 1994. 28.00 (*1-56253-233-2*) Milady Pub.

Milady/Salon Ovation's in the Bag: Selling in the Salon. Carol Phillips. LC 94-6811. (Career Development Ser.). 320p. 1994. pap. 34.95 (*1-56253-236-7*) Thomson Learn.

Milagra de la Vida. Robert Wells.Tr. of Miracle of Life. (SPA.). 128p. 1995. pap. 6.99 (*0-8297-1983-0*) Vida Pubs.

Milagre no Rio Kwai. Ernest Gordon. Orig. Title: Miracle on the River Kwai. (POR.). 304p. 1986. pap. 6.95 (*0-8297-0538-4*) Vida Pubs.

Milagro & Other Stories. Patricia P. Martin. LC 95-32550. (Camino Del Sol Ser.). 92p. 1996. pap. 9.95 (*0-8165-1548-4*) U of Ariz Pr.

Milagro Beanfield War. John Nichols. 640p. 1987. mass mkt. 5.95 (*0-345-34446-4*) Ballantine Pub Grp.

Milagro Beanfield War. John Nichols. LC 96-96673. 1996. pap. 12.95 (*0-345-41016-5*) Ballantine Pub Grp.

Milagro Beanfield War. John Nichols. 464p. 2000. pap. 14.00 (*0-8050-6374-9*, Owl) H Holt & Co.

Milagro Beanfield War: Facsimile Anniversary Edition. John Nichols. (Illus.). 484p. 1995. 27.50 (*0-8050-2805-6*) H Holt & Co.

Milagro de la Gracia. John Hagee. Ed. by Lucretia Hobbs & Connie Reece. Tr. by Victoria Diaz from ENG. (SPA.). 40p. (Orig.). 1991. pap., per. 3.00 (*1-56908-004-6*) Global Evang.

Milagro de Maria. Jack W. Hayford.Tr. of Mary Miracle. (SPA.). 1995. 5.99 (*0-7899-0015-7*, 497456) Editorial Unilit.

Milagro de Vida. Edwin D. Roels. Tr. by Jane Compeau from ENG. (Friendship Ser.). (SPA., Illus.). 48p. 1992. pap. 0.70 (*1-882536-28-2*, A110-0015) Bible League.

Milagro en la Montana (Miracle on the Mountain) (SPA.). (J). 1993. 4.98 (*1-56173-930-8*, P000-9308) Pubns Intl Ltd.

Milagro es la Respuesta. rev. ed. Mike Francen. Ed. by Libros Desafio Staff. Tr. by Rogelio D. Diaz. (SPA., Illus.). 78p. 1994. reprint ed. pap. text 8.00 (*958-9354-06-8*) Francen Wrld.

Milagro Mas Grande Del Mundo. Mandino Og. (SPA.). 1997. pap. text 13.98 (*968-13-2010-7*) Libros Fronteras.

Milagro para su Matrimonio. John Osteen.Tr. of A Miracle for Your Marriage. (SPA.). 32p. 1996. mass mkt. 1.50 (*0-912631-72-4*) J O Pubns.

Milagros: A Book of Miracles. Helen Thompson. LC 98-11736. (Illus.). 96p. 1998. 15.95 (*0-06-251563-2*, Pub. by Harper SF) HarpC.

Milagros: Symbols of Hope. Nancy Walkup & Sharon Warwick. Ed. by Jenny Fiore. (Illus.). 1996. teacher ed. 93.00 incl. VHS (*0-945666-55-1*) Crizmac.

M

Milagros: Votive Offerings from the Americas. Martha Egan. (Illus.). 132p. 1991. pap. 19.95 (*0-89013-220-8*) Museum NM Pr.

Milagros de Jesus (Miracles of Jesus. Neff. (SPA.). (J). 1995. write for info. (*0-7899-0034-3*) Editorial Unilit.

Milagros de Nuestra Senora. Berceo. (SPA.). 148p. 1966. 9.95 (*0-8288-7025-X*, S3346) Fr & Eur.

Milagros de Nuestra Senora. Gonzalo D. Berceo. Ed. by Juan M. Cacho Blecva. (Nueva Austral Ser.: No. 103). (SPA.). 1991. pap. text 14.95 (*84-239-1903-X*) Elliots Bks.

Milagros de Nuestra Senora. Gonzalo De Berceo. Ed. by Daniel Devoto. 3.50 (*0-685-11394-9*) Fr & Eur.

Milagros en la Oracion. Quin Sherrer. 1999. pap. text 7.99 (*0-8297-1585-1*) Vida Pubs.

Milagros en Metal y en Cera de Puerto Rico. Teodoro Vidal. 1974. 20.00 (*0-9600714-1-5*) Edns Alba.

Milagros en Metal y en Cera de Puerto Rico. Teodoro Vidal. LC 73-90014. (SPA., Illus.). 190p. 1974. 20.00 (*0-8477-7141-5*) U of PR Pr.

Milagros Inagotables para Cristianos Agotados. Tr. by Eduardo Ramirez & Elvira Ramirez. (Nineteen Ninety-Eight Fifty-Day Spiritual Adventure Ser.). (SPA.). 1996. wbk. ed. 6.00 (*1-57849-039-1*) Mainstay Church.

M

Milagros Inexplicables. Van Diest.Tr. of Unsolved Miracles. 8.99 (*0-7899-0468-3*, 495034) Editorial Unilit.

Milagrosas Hierbas Cura. Heinerman. 1999. pap. text 13.95 (*0-13-011652-1*) P-H.

Milagrosas Hierbas Cura. John Heinerman. 1999. pap. text 24.95 (*0-13-011653-X*) P-H.

***Milagrosas Hierbas Curativas.** John Heinerman. (SPA.). 2000. pap. 14.00 (*0-7352-0212-5*) PH Pr.

Milagrosos Alimentos Curativos. Rex Adams. 1998. 24.95 (*0-13-921081-4*) P-H.

Milagrosos Alimentos Curativos. Rex Adams. 320p. (C). 1998. pap. text 13.95 (*0-13-921073-3*) P-H.

***Milagrosos Alimentos Curativos.** Rex Adams. (SPA.). 2000. pap. 14.00 (*0-7352-0195-1*) PH Pr.

***Milagrosos Alimentos Curativos de la Biblia.** Reese P. Dubin. 2000. pap. 13.95 (*0-13-083425-4*) P-H.

***Milagrosos Alimentos Curativos de la Biblia.** Reese P. Dubin. (SPA.). 2000. pap. 14.00 (*0-7352-0210-9*) PH Pr.

Milan. 1998. pap. text 24.95 (*88-422-0794-2*) Allemandi.

Milan. (Insight Compact Guides Ser.). 1996. pap. 12.95 (*0-614-12817-X*, Insight Trvl Guides) HM.

Milan. Insight Guides Staff. (Insight Guides). 1998. pap. text 7.95 (*0-88729-546-0*) Langenscheidt.

Milan. Jonathan Moberly. (Architecture Guides Ser.). (Illus.). 320p. 1998. pap. 5.95 (*3-8290-0472-9*, 520550) Konemann.

Milan. 3rd ed. Insight Guides Staff. (Insight Guides). 1998. pap. text 12.95 (*0-88729-914-8*) Langenscheidt.

***Milan.** 5th ed. Insight Guides Staff. 2000. pap. 12.95 (*0-88729-475-8*) Langenscheidt.

Milan: Phantasier I. Kone Music Inc. Staff. (Illus.). 1999. 9.95 (*963-9155-07-1*) Kone Music.

Milan & the Italian Lakes. 1999. pap. text 8.95 (*2-8315-6978-8*) Berlitz.

***Milan & the Lakes.** Eyewitness Books Staff. LC 99-53706. (Eyewitness Travel Guides Ser.). (Illus.). 240p. 2000. pap. 19.95 (*0-7894-5171-9*, D K Ink) DK Pub Inc.

Milan & Turin. Touring Club of Italy Staff. (Heritage Guides Ser.). (Illus.). 224p. 1999. pap. 16.95 (*88-365-1519-3*) Abbeville Pr.

Milan Approach to Family Therapy. Guido L. Burbatti & Laura Formenti. LC 87-19595. 221p. 1988. 40.00 (*0-87668-972-1*) Aronson.

Milan Approach to Family Therapy. Guido L. Burbatti & Laura Formenti. LC 87-19595. 232p. 1993. reprint ed. pap. 30.00 (*0-87668-161-5*) Aronson.

Milan, Biblioteca del Conservatorio Di Musica Giuseppe Verdi ("The Tarasconi Codex") Ed. by Howard Brown et al. LC 86-753537. (Renaissance Music in Facsimile Ser.: Vol. 11). 870115p. 1987. text 35.00 (*0-8240-1460-X*) Garland.

Milan Family Therapy: Variant & Invariant Methods. Esther Gelcer et al. LC 89-18346. 280p. 1990. 45.00 (*0-87668-807-5*) Aronson.

Milan Kunc. Milan Kunc. (Illus.). 120p. 1993. 45.00 (*3-89322-514-5*, Pub. by Edition Cantz) Dist Art Pubs.

Milan Kundera. Trensky. 1999. 22.95 (*0-8057-7814-4*, Twyne) Mac Lib Ref.

Milan Kundera & the Art of Fiction: Critical Essays. Ed. by Aron Aji. LC 92-6421. 368p. 1992. text 20.00 (*0-8153-0038-7*, H1156) Garland.

Milan Systemic Family Therapy: Conversations in Theory & Practice. Luigi Boscolo et al. LC 87-71985. 352p. 1987. 42.00 (*0-465-04596-0*, Pub. by Basic) HarpC.

Milanese-Italian Dictionary. Arrighi Cletto. (ITA.). 904p. 1983. 75.00 (*0-8288-7347-X*, 8820309645) Fr & Eur.

Milani-Comparetti Motor Development Screening Test for Infants & Young Children: A Manual. 3rd ed. Wayne Stuberg. 1992. reprint ed. spiral bd. 20.00 (*1-889843-02-4*) Munroe-Meyer Inst.

Milankovitch Sea-Level Changes, Cycles, & Reservoirs on Carbonate: Platforms in Greenhouse & Icehouse Worlds. J. Fred Read et al. LC 95-215854. (Short Course Notes Ser.: No. 35). (Illus.). 212p. (Orig.). 1995. pap. 55.00 (*1-56576-020-4*) SEPM.

Milano Papers: Essays in Societal Alternatives. Ed. by Michele Cangiani & Marguerite Mendell. (Critical Perspectives on Historic Issues Ser.: Vol. 7). 254p. 1995. 48.99 (*1-55164-023-6*, Pub. by Black Rose); pap. 19.99 (*1-55164-022-8*, Pub. by Black Rose) Consort Bk Sales.

Milatti Islami: Islamic Treatment for the Disease of Addiction. Zaid Imami. 76p. 1996. pap. 7.50 (*0-614-21554-4*, 782) Kazi Pubns.

Milbank Memorial Fund at Ninety. Ed. by Milbank Memorial Fund Staff. LC 96-150103. 144p. (Orig.). 1995. pap. write for info. (*1-887748-02-4*) Milbank Memorial.

Milbi: Aborigine Tales from Queensland. Gordon Staff. (Australian National University Press Ser.). 1980. 18.00 (*0-08-032938-1*, Pergamon Pr) Elsevier.

Milbourne Christopher Library. Christopher Maurine Brooks & George P. Hansen. LC 93-77302. 1994. write for info. (*0-915181-26-6*) Magic Words.

Milbridge Register, 1905: Town History & Directory. Mitchell & Campbell. 88p. 1997. reprint ed. pap. 17.50 (*0-8328-5871-4*) Higginson Bk Co.

Milcah Martha Moore's Book: A Commonplace Book of Early American Literature. Catherine L. Blecki & Karin A. Wulf. LC 96-37555. 1997. 45.00 (*0-271-01690-6*); pap. 14.95 (*0-271-01691-4*) Pa St U Pr.

Milcom, 1995. IEEE, Communications Society Staff. Ed. by IEEE Staff. LC 94-74517. 1388p. 1995. pap. text 184.00 (*0-7803-2489-7*, 95CH35750); lib. bdg. 184.00 (*0-7803-2490-0*, 95CB35750); fiche 184.00 (*0-7803-2491-9*, 95CM35750) Inst Electrical.

Milcom, 1997. IEEE Staff. 1800p. 1997. pap. text 274.00 (*0-7803-4249-6*); lib. bdg. write for info. (*0-7803-4250-X*) Inst Electrical.

Milcom, 1996: Conference Proceedings. IEEE (Communications Society) Staff. LC 96-78416. 1158p. 1996. pap. text. write for info. (*0-7803-3682-8*, 96CH36008); lib. bdg. write for info. (*0-7803-3683-6*, 96CB36008); fiche. write for info. (*0-7803-3684-4*, 96CM36008) Inst Electrical.

Milcom, 1993. IEEE, Communications Society Staff. Ed. by Institute of Electrical & Electronics Engineers, I. LC 92-56150. 1300p. 1993. pap. text. write for info. (*0-7803-0953-7*); lib. bdg. write for info. (*0-7803-0954-5*, 93CH3260-7); fiche. write for info. (*0-7803-0955-3*) Inst Electrical.

MILCOM '98: Proceedings, 3 vols. LC 98-84051. xxxv, 1083 p. 1998. pap. write for info. (*0-7803-4508-8*) IEEE Standards.

Mild Ale: History, Brewing Techniques, Recipes. David Sutula. LC 98-43604. (Classic Beer Style Ser.: Vol. 15). (Illus.). 200p. 1999. pap. 14.95 (*0-937381-68-3*) Brewers Pubns.

Mild & Bitter. Clyde A. Beakley. 44p. 1949. text 9.45 (*0-9636782-2-1*) C Beakley.

Mild & Bitter, Vol. 2. Clyde A. Beakley. 94p. 1966. text 12.45 (*0-9636782-9-9*) C Beakley.

Mild Brain Injury: A Special Issue of "Applied Neuropsychology" Ed. by Thomas L. Bennett & Michael J. Raymond. 83p. 1997. pap. write for info. (*0-8058-9868-9*) L Erlbaum Assocs.

Mild Day. William Bronk. LC 93-5346. 57p. (Orig.). 1993. pap. 9.95 (*1-883689-00-7*); lib. bdg. 29.95 (*1-883689-01-5*) Talisman Hse.

Mild Head Injury. Ed. by Harvey S. Levin et al. (Illus.). 304p. 1989. text 49.50 (*0-19-505301-X*) OUP.

***Mild Head Injury: A Guide to Management.** Philip Wrightson & Dorothy Gronwall. LC 99-19511. (Illus.). 194p. 1999. text 34.50 (*0-19-262939-5*) OUP.

Mild Hypertension: From Drug Trials to Practice. Ed. by T. Strasser & Detlev Ganten. LC 86-29679. 316p. 1987. reprint ed. pap. 98.00 (*0-608-00400-6*, 206111400007) Bks Demand.

Mild Hypertension: Recent Advances. Ed. by Franz Gross & Tomas Strasser. LC 83-11208. (Illus.). 445p. 1983. reprint ed. pap. 138.00 (*0-7837-9529-7*, 206027800005) Bks Demand.

Mild Majesty. Elwyn Davies. 164p. (C). 1987. 30.00 (*0-86383-450-7*, Pub. by Gomer Pr) St Mut.

Mild Reservationists & the League of Nations Controversy in the Senate. Herbert F. Margulies. LC 89-4702. 264p. 1989. text 39.00 (*0-8262-0693-X*) U of Mo Pr.

Mild Traumatic Brain Injury: A Clinician's Guide. Michael J. Raymond. LC 98-46594. 1999. 37.00 (*0-89079-809-5*) PRO-ED.

Mild Traumatic Brain Injury: A Therapy & Resource Manual. Elizabeth S. Green et al. LC 97-25314. (Neurogenic Communication Disorders Ser.). 282p. (Orig.). 1997. pap. 49.95 (*1-56593-827-5*, 1622) Thomson Learn.

Mild Voice of Reason: Deliberative Democracy & American National Government. Joseph M. Bessette. LC 93-30669. 256p. (C). 1994. 32.50 (*0-226-04423-8*) U Ch Pr.

Mild Voice of Reason: Deliberative Democracy & American National Government. Joseph M. Bessette. (American Politics & Political Economy Ser.). 1997. pap. text 15.95 (*0-226-04424-6*) U Ch Pr.

Milday's Art & Science of Nail Technology. rev. ed. Milday Staff. 272p. 1997. pap. write for info. (*1-56253-330-4*); pap., teacher ed., wbk. ed. write for info. (*1-56253-328-2*) Milady Pub.

***Mildenhall Treasure.** Roald Dahl. LC 00-24683. (Illus.). 80p. (J). (ps up). 2000. 22.95 (*0-375-81035-8*, Pub. by Knopf Bks Yng Read) Random.

Mildew: Poems from Hollywood. Mark Dunster. 19p. 1998. pap. 5.00 (*0-89642-416-2*) Linden Pubs.

Mildly Handicapped. Smith. Date not set. pap. text, teacher ed. write for info. (*0-314-96659-5*) West Pub.

Mildly Handicapped Conditions. Ed. by Margaret C. Wang et al. (Handbook of Special Education: Research & Practice Ser.: Vol. 2). 406p. 1988. 133.50 (*0-08-033384-2*, Pergamon Pr) Elsevier.

Mildred & Elsie. unabridged ed. Martha Finley. (Mildred Keith Collection: Vol. 3). 332p. (YA). 1997. reprint ed. 15.00 (*1-889128-33-3*) Mantle Ministries.

Mildred & Sam. Collicott. 40p. (J). (ps-2). lib. bdg. 14.89 (*0-06-026682-1*) HarpC Child Bks.

Mildred & Sam. Stefan Czernecki. 40p. (J). (ps-2). 14.95 (*0-06-026681-3*) HarpC Child Bks.

Mildred Ann Butler. Anne Crookshank. (Lives of Irish Artists Ser.). (Illus.). 36p. 1995. 7.95 (*0-948524-37-5*, Pub. by Town Hse) Roberts Rinehart.

Mildred at Home. unabridged ed. Martha Finley. (Mildred Keith Collection: Vol. 5). 1998. reprint ed. 15.00 (*1-889128-35-X*) Mantle Ministries.

Mildred at Roselands. unabridged ed. Martha Finley. (Mildred Keith Collection: Vol. 2). (Illus.). (YA). 1996. reprint ed. 15.00 (*1-889128-32-5*) Mantle Ministries.

Mildred Keith, Vol. 1. unabridged ed. Martha Finley. (Mildred Keith Collection). 303p. (YA). 1996. reprint ed. 12.00 (*1-889128-31-7*) Mantle Ministries.

Mildred Minturn: A Biography. Leslie Minturn Allison. (Illus.). 192p. pap. 13.95 (*0-9698752-3-1*) Sh1oreline.

Mildred Pierce. James M. Cain. 1976. 15.95 (*0-8488-1259-X*) Amereon Ltd.

Mildred Pierce. James M. Cain. (FRE.). 438p. 1977. pap. 11.95 (*0-7859-1848-5*, 2070369226) Fr & Eur.

Mildred Pierce. James M. Cain. (Vintage Crime Ser.). 1989. pap. 12.00 (*0-679-72321-8*) Vin Bks.

Mildred Pierce. Ranald MacDougall & James M. Cain. Ed. by Albert J. LaValley. LC 80-5107. (Warner Bros. Screenplay Ser.). (Illus.). 264p. 1980. 14.95 (*0-299-08370-5*) U of Wis Pr.

Mildred Pierce. large type ed. James M. Cain. 544p. 1988. 27.99 (*0-7089-1829-8*) Ulverscroft.

Mildred Pierce. James M. Cain. 489p. 1981. reprint ed. lib. bdg. 14.95 (*0-89968-233-2*, Lghtyr Pr) Buccaneer Bks.

Mildred Skinner Scrapbook, 1997. Loren E. Shuler. LC 97-91910. (Illus.). 78p. 1997. 35.00 (*1-890210-00-5*); pap. 20.00 (*1-890210-01-3*) Pyxis Prods.

***Mildred's Boys & Girls, 7 vols., Vol. 6.** Martha Finley. (Mildred Keith Collection Ser.). (J). 1999. reprint ed. 14.00 (*1-889128-36-8*) Mantle Ministries.

Mildred's Married Life. unabridged abr. ed. Martha Finley. (Mildred Keith Collection: No. 4). 320p. 1998. reprint ed. 15.00 (*1-889128-34-1*) Mantle Ministries.

Mildred's Memoirs & Notes. Mildred H. Johnson. Ed. & Illus. by Lance B. Johnson. 349p. 1996. ring bd. 40.00 (*0-9631328-5-7*) Come & See Minist.

***Mildred's New Daughter, 7 vols., Vol. 7.** unabridged ed. Martha Finley. (Mildred Keith Collection: Vol. 7). 1999. reprint ed. 14.00 (*1-889128-37-6*) Mantle Ministries.

Mile-a-Minute Afghans. Leisure Arts Staff. LC 96-76035. 128p. 1997. pap. 14.95 (*1-57486-043-7*) Oxmoor Hse.

Mile High & Three Feet Six Wide. Ken Fletcher. 32p. 1993. pap. 7.95 (*1-884567-00-2*) Mtn West Ent.

Mile High City: An Illustrated History of Denver. Thomas J. Noel. Ed. by Lori Parks. LC 97-71126. (Illus.). 550p. 1997. 49.95 (*1-886483-10-8*) Heritge Media.

***Mile High City: An Illustrated History of Denver.** 2nd rev. ed. Thomas Jacob Noel. Ed. by Lori M. Parks. (Illus.). 200p. 2000. pap. 29.95 (*1-886483-43-4*, Pub. by Heritge Media) Sunbelt Pubns.

***Mile High Club.** Kinky Friedman. 224p. 2000. 23.00 (*0-684-86486-X*) S&S Trade.

Mile High Denver: Coloring Book. Sandy Whelchel. (Illus.). 30p. (Orig.). (J). (gr. k-4). 1987. pap. 3.50 (*1-878406-02-7*) Parker Dstb.

Mile-High Love. Jane M. Choate. LC 98-96071. 192p. 1998. 18.95 (*0-8034-9297-9*) Bouregy.

Mile in Their Shoes. Dennis D. Baughman et al. Ed. by Cindy Harr et al. LC 95-4582. (Joe & Penny Heisel Ser.: United States of America Armed Forces Veterans Ser.: Vol. 2). 1995. 30.00 (*1-885851-08-1*) St Vincent Coll.

Mile in Their Shoes: Conversations with Veterans of World War II. Aaron Elson. Ed. by Susan English. 242p. 1998. pap. 17.95 (*0-9640611-2-0*) Chi Chi Pr.

Mile Stones of Life: Self-Esteem Essence of You. Ida Greene. 100p. (Orig.). (YA). (gr. 10 up). 1995. pap. text 10.00 (*1-881165-05-1*) People Skills.

Mile with Me. Mary J. Seversen. LC 89-11872. (Illus.). 196p. 1988. 60.00 (*0-9620708-0-7*) M J Seversen.

Mile Zero. Thomas Sanchez. LC 90-50248. (Vintage Contemporaries Ser.). 368p. 1990. pap. 14.00 (*0-679-73260-8*) Vin Bks.

Mileage Chart. Amoco Pathfinder Staff. 1992. pap. 2.25 (*0-671-84029-0*) Macmillan USA.

Milemarking I-80: San Francisco to New York. 2nd ed. Mary L. Kost. LC 94-75705. Orig. Title: Milepost I-80. (Illus.). 255p. 1994. pap. text 17.95 (*0-9633489-1-4*) Mile Pubns.

Milena. Margarete Buber-Neumann. Tr. by Ralph Manheim. LC 87-28718. (GER.). 213p. 1988. 18.95 (*0-8050-0748-2*) Seaver Bks.

Milena: The Tragic Story of Kafka's Great Love. Margarete Buber-Neumann. Tr. by Ralph Manheim from GER. LC 97-26760. 213p. 1997. pap. 12.45 (*1-55970-390-3*, Pub. by Arcade Pub Inc) Time Warner.

Milenio. Thomas Ice & Timothy Demy. (SPA.). 48p. 1997. pap. 2.99 (*0-8254-1344-3*, Edit Portavoz) Kregel.

Milenio: Mil Anos de Literatura Espanola. Mujica. 400p. pap. text 58.95 (*0-471-24112-1*) Wiley.

***Milepost: Alaska Trip Planner.** 52nd rev. ed. (Illus.). 768p. 2000. pap. 23.95 (*1-892154-02-1*) Morris Comms.

***Milepost: Alaska Trip Planner.** 53rd rev. ed. (Illus.). 768p. 2001. pap. 24.95 (*1-892154-05-6*) Morris Comms.

Milepost: Trip Planner for Alaska, Yukon Territory, British Columbia, Alberta & Northwest Territory. 51st ed. Vernon Publications Staff. (Milepost Ser.). (Illus.). 768p. 1999. pap. 23.95 (*1-892154-00-5*) Morris Comms.

Milepost I-80 see Milemarking I-80: San Francisco to New York

***Milepost Souvenir Log Book.** rev. ed. (Illus.). 80p. 2000. pap. 12.95 (*1-892154-04-8*) Morris Comms.

Milepost Spring '98 - Spring '99. 50th rev. ed. Ed. by Kris Graef. (Illus.). 768p. 1998. 50.00 (*1-878425-31-5*) Vernon Pubns.

Miler: An Autobiography. Steve Scott & Marc Bloom. LC 97-18565. 304p. 1997. 23.95 (*0-02-861677-4*) Macmillan.

Miles. Mark Dunster. LC 75-177113. (Rin Ser.: Pt. 39). 1974. 4.00 (*0-89642-025-6*) Linden Pubs.

Miles: The Autobiography. Miles Davis. 448p. 1990. per. 14.00 (*0-671-72582-3*) S&S Trade.

Miles: The Autobiography, Set. unabridged ed. Miles Davis & Quincy Troupe. 1995. 15.95 incl. audio (*0-944993-62-1*) Audio Lit.

***Miles Aircraft.** Rod Simpson. (Transport Ser.). 1999. pap. 18.99 (*0-7524-1091-1*) Arcadia Publng.

***Miles & Me: A Memoir.** Quincy Troupe. LC 99-54370. 256p. 2000. 19.95 (*0-520-21624-5*, Pub. by U CA Pr) Cal Prin Full Svc.

Miles & Miles de Palabras. 3rd ed. Ruth Bowdoin. (Bowdoin Method I Ser.). Orig. Title: Thousands & Thousands of Words. (SPA., Illus.). 30p. 1991. reprint ed. pap. write for info. (*1-55997-061-8*) Websters Intl.

Miles Away see Walk Across France

***Miles Away from Home.** Joan Cottle. LC 99-50609. (Illus.). (J). 2001. write for info. (*0-15-202212-0*) Harcourt.

Miles Champion: Compositional Bonbons Placate. 64p. 1996. pap. 14.95 (*1-85754-137-5*, Pub. by Carcanet Pr) Paul & Co Pubs.

Miles Chart Display, 2 vols. Betty T. Miles et al. 1980. 163.95 (*0-405-19072-7*, 19805) Ayer.

Miles Chart Display of Popular Music, Vol. 3. Martin J. Mukes & Daniel J. Miles. 400p. 1981. lib. bdg. 40.00 (*0-913920-04-5*) Convex Indus.

Miles Chart Display of Popular Music, 1955-1970 Vol. 1: Top 100. 3rd ed. Betty T. Miles et al. (Illus.). 1979. reprint ed. lib. bdg. 95.00 (*0-913920-03-7*) Convex Indus.

***Miles College: A Journey into Academic Excellence.** Miles College Staff. 314p. (C). 1999. per. 34.95 (*0-7872-6247-1*, 41624701) Kendall-Hunt.

***Miles Coverdale & the English Bible, 1488 - 1568.** Henry Guppy. 1999. pap. 8.00 (*1-58329-012-5*) Lazarus Minist.

Miles Davis. George R. Crisp. LC 96-26427. (Impact Biographies Ser.). 144p. (YA). (gr. 6 up). 1997. lib. bdg. 23.60 (*0-531-11319-1*) Watts.

Miles Davis. George R. Crisp. (Impact Biographies Ser.). 144p. (YA). (gr. 6 up). 1997. pap. text 9.95 (*0-531-15865-9*) Watts.

Miles Davis. Stuart Isacoff. 48p. pap. 14.95 (*0-8256-4079-2*, AM23227) Music Sales.

Miles Davis: Musician. Ed. by Nathan I. Huggins. (Black Americans of Achievement Ser.). (Illus.). 124p. (YA). (gr. 5 up). 1995. lib. bdg. 19.95 (*0-7910-2156-4*) Chelsea Hse.

***Miles Davis: The Definitive Biography.** Ian Carr. LC 99-29423. (Illus.). 658p. 1999. pap. 18.95 (*1-56025-241-3*, Thunders Mouth) Avalon NY.

Miles Davis: The Early Years. Bill Cole. LC 93-36391. 256p. 1994. reprint ed. pap. 13.95 (*0-306-80554-5*) Da Capo.

Miles Davis & David Liebman: Jazz Connections. Larry Fisher & Dave Liebman. LC 96-43510. (Studies in the History & Interpretation of Music: Vol. 53). 224p. 1997. text 89.95 (*0-7734-8771-9*) E Mellen.

Miles Davis Diary: The Life of Miles Davis, 1947-1961. Ken Vail. 184p. (Orig.). pap. 19.95 (*1-86074-159-2*, SG00622, Pub. by Sanctuary Pubng) Music Sales.

Miles Davis for B Trumpet. Stuart Isacoff. 48p. pap. 14.95 (*0-8256-4089-X*, AM24589) Music Sales.

Miles Davis for Beginners. Daryl Long. (Illus.). 100p. (Orig.). 1992. 18.00 (*0-86316-154-5*); pap. 9.00 (*0-86316-153-7*) Writers & Readers.

Miles Davis Reader. Ed. by Bill Kirchner. 256p. 1997. pap. 14.95 (*1-56098-802-9*); text 29.95 (*1-56098-774-X*) Smithsonian.

Miles Diamond & the Cretan Apollo. Derek Adams. (Adventures of Miles Diamond Ser.). (Orig.). 1997. mass mkt. 5.95 (*1-56333-381-3*, Badboy) Masquerade.

Miles Diamond & the Demon of Death. Derek Adams. (Orig.). 1995. mass mkt. 4.95 (*1-56333-251-5*, Badboy) Masquerade.

Miles Expedition of 1874-1875: An Eyewitness Account of the Red River Ear. J. T. Marshall. Ed. by Lonnie J. White. (Narratives of the American West Ser.: Vol. 1). (Illus.). 1971. 24.95 (*0-88426-014-3*) Encino Pr.

Miles Expedition of 1874-1875: An Eyewitness Account of the Red River War. J. T. Marshall. (American Biography Ser.). 74p. 1991. reprint ed. lib. bdg. 59.00 (*0-7812-8270-5*) Rprt Serv.

Miles Franklin: The Story of a Famous Australian. 2nd ed. Marjorie Barnard. (Illus.). 174p. 1989. pap. text 16.95 (*0-7022-2146-5*, Pub. by Univ Queensland Pr) Intl Spec Bk.

Miles from Home. Anna K. McCauley. 108p. 1984. pap. 3.95 (*0-9612430-0-7*) A K L M Pubns.

Miles from Nowhere: Round-the-World Bicycle Adventure. Barbara Savage. LC 83-13484. (Illus.). 340p. 1985. pap. 14.95 (*0-89886-109-8*) Mountaineers.

***Miles from Nowhere: Tales from America's Contemporary Frontier.** Dayton Duncan. (Illus.). 352p. 2000. pap. 16.95 (*0-8032-6627-8*, Bison Books) U of Nebr Pr.

Miles Gloriosus. 2nd rev. ed. Titus Maccius Plautus. Ed. by Mason Hammond et al. LC 73-122213. 140p. 1963. 24.45 (*0-674-57436-2*) HUP.

***Miles of Prairie.** 328p. 1999. pap. 10.00 (*0-9633479-5-0*, Pub. by Dummer Pub) Badger Bks Inc.

Miles of Smiles. Karl Davidson & Cassie Davidson. (Illus.). 96p. (Orig.). 1992. pap. text 7.95 (*0-9630884-1-6*) Team Effort.

Miles of Smiles! Backseat Games. Ed. by Pleasant Company Staff. (American Girl Library Ser.). 1999. pap. 1.95 (*1-56247-728-5*) Pleasant Co.

Miles of Smiles: Kids Pick the Funniest Poems. Bruce Lansky. LC 97-52095. (Illus.). 128p. (J). (gr. 2-8). 1998. lib. bdg. 16.00 (*0-689-82183-2*) Meadow Brook.

Miles of Smiles: Kids Pick the Funniest Poems. Bruce Lansky. LC 97-52095. (Illus.). (J). (gr. 3-7). 1998. 16.00 (*0-88166-313-1*) Meadow Brook.

Miles of Smiles: 101 Great Car Games & Activities. Carole T. Meyers. LC 91-458885. (Illus.). 128p. (Orig.). (J). (ps-11). 1992. pap. 8.95 (*0-917120-11-6*) Carousel Pr.

***Miles of Smiles with Poetry.** Mae D. Elms. (Illus.). 200p. (J). (gr. k-7). 2000. pap. 27.50 (*1-930002-09-2*) I&L Pubs.

Miles of Smiles, Years of Struggle: Stories of Black Pullman Porters. Jack Santino. LC 88-20981. (Illus.). 192p. 1989. text 24.95 (*0-252-01591-6*) U of Ill Pr.

Miles of Smiles, Years of Struggle: Stories of Black Pullman Porters. Jack Santino. (Illus.). 192p. 1991. pap. text 16.95 (*0-252-06194-2*) U of Ill Pr.

***Miles of Tiles.** Charles A. Radin. LC 99-20662. (Student Mathematical Library). 120p. 1999. pap. 16.00 (*0-8218-1933-X*) Am Math.

***Miles on the Bridge: And Other Poems.** Ruhama Veltfort. iv, 16p. 2000. pap. write for info. (*0-9674900-7-3*) Wordrunner.

***Miles' Song.** Alice McGill. LC 99-43157. 224p. (YA). (gr. 5-9). 2000. 15.00 (*0-395-97938-2*) HM.

Miles Standish. Susan Martins Miller. LC 99-20977. (Illus.). 26.27p. 1999. 16.95 (*0-7910-5350-4*) Chelsea Hse.

Miles Standish. Susan Martins Miller. (Colonial Leaders Ser.). (Illus.). 80p. (J). (gr. 3 up). 1999. pap. 8.95 (*0-7910-5693-7*) Chelsea Hse.

Miles to Go, Vol. 1. Richard Peterson. 1997. mass mkt. 6.50 (*0-312-96275-4*) St Martin.

Miles to Go: A Personal History of Social Policy. Daniel P. Moynihan. LC 96-8291. (Illus.). 245p. 1996. 22.95 (*0-674-57440-0*) HUP.

Miles to Go: A Personal History of Social Policy. Daniel P. Moynihan. (Illus.). 256p. 1997. reprint ed. pap. 14.95 (*0-674-57441-9*) HUP.

Miles to Go: A Status Report on Americans' Plans for Retirement. Steve Farkas & Jean Johnson. 38p. (Orig.). 1997. pap. 10.00 (*1-889483-45-1*) Public Agenda.

Miles to Go: Aging in Rural Virginia. Susan Garrett. LC 97-35306. (Age Studies). 175p. 1998. 22.95 (*0-8139-1799-9*) U Pr of Va.

Miles to Go Before I Sleep. Ed. by Nadia Giordana. (Illus.). 164p. (Orig.). (C). 1996. pap. text 29.99 (*1-886352-12-7*) Natl Poets Assn.

Miles to Go Before I Sleep: My Grateful Journey Back from the Hijacking of EgyptAir Flight 648. Jackie N. Pflug & Peter J. Kizilos. 230p. 19.95 (*1-56838-088-7*) Hazelden.

***Miles Wallingford.** James Fenimore Cooper. (Notable American Authors Ser.: Pt. I). 454p. 2000. reprint ed. lib. bdg. 79.00 (*0-7812-2399-7*) Rprt Serv.

Milesian Chief: A Romance, 4 vols., 2 bks., Set. Charles R. Maturin. LC 79-8172. reprint ed. 84.50 (*0-404-62038-8*) AMS Pr.

Milestone. Donna Lagerquist. 1998. pap. 15.00 (*0-310-67798-X*) Zondervan.

Milestone. Sayyid Qutb. 1981. pap. 8.50 (*0-934905-14-2*) Kazi Pubns.

Milestone Documents in the National Archives. rev. ed. National Archives & Records Administration Staff. LC 93-23047. Orig. Title: The Written Word Endures. (Illus.). 112p. 1995. pap. 12.00 (*0-911333-98-3*, 100006) National Archives & Recs.

Milestone in Education for Social Work: The Carnegie Experiment, 1954-1958. Alma E. Hartshorn. 1982. 40.00 (*0-7855-0543-1*, Pub. by Natl Inst Soc Work) St Mut.

Milestone Papers. Daniel Steele. pap. 7.99 (*0-88019-153-8*) Schmul Pub Co.

Milestone Planning for Successful Ventures: Mac. Bernard J. David. LC 94-29642. 1996. pap., teacher ed. 55.00 (*0-89426-861-9*) Course Tech.

Milestone Sampler: 15th Anniversary Anthology. Ed. by Naomi L. Madgett. (Illus.). 130p. (Orig.). (YA). (gr. 9-12). 1988. pap., per. 9.00 (*0-916418-74-X*) Lotus.

Milestone 70. Carol R. Murphy. (Orig.). 1989. pap. 4.00 (*0-87574-287-4*) Pendle Hill.

Milestones. Sayyid Qutb.Tr. of Ma alim fi at-Tariq. 303p. (Orig.). 1978. pap. 5.95 (*0-939830-07-8*, Pub. by IIFSO KW) New Era Publns MI.

Milestones. large type ed. Barbara Erskine. 480p. 1992. 27.99 (*0-7089-2605-3*) Ulverscroft.

Milestones. Arnold Bennett. LC 74-17129. (Collected Works of Arnold Bennett: Vol. 56). 1977. reprint ed. 19.95 (*0-518-19137-0*) Ayer.

Milestones. rev. ed. Sayyid Qutb.Tr. of Ma alim fi at-Tariq. (Orig.). 1991. pap. 9.00 (*0-89259-076-9*) Am Trust Pubns.

***Milestones: A Book of Days.** Jochanan Stenesh. (Illus.). 128p. 1999. 22.50 (*0-9633552-1-X*) Cogno Pr.

Milestones: A Chronology of Women's History. Doris L. Weatherford. LC 96-18359. 400p. 1997. 45.00 (*0-8160-3200-9*) Facts on File.

Milestones: A History of Cable Television. Ed. by Priscilla Walker & Matt Stump. (Illus.). 56p. 1998. pap. 28.95 (*1-891821-00-8*) Nat Cable Tele Ctr.

Milestones: A Pictorial History of Philippi, West Virginia 1844-1994. Jane Mattaliano & Lois G. Omonde. LC 94-17015. 1994. write for info. (*0-89865-902-7*) Donning Co.

Milestones: Memoirs, 1927-1977. Cardinal Joseph Ratzinger. LC 98-71929. 1998. pap. 12.95 (*0-89870-702-1*) Ignatius Pr.

Milestones: National Geographic Photographs. Ed. by Leah Bendavid-Val & Kim Heacox. LC 99-29397. (Illus.). 336p. 1999. per. 50.00 (*0-7922-7520-9*) Natl Geog.

Milestones, a Play in Three Acts. Arnold Bennett & Edward Knoblauch. LC 78-131624. 1971. reprint ed. 15.00 (*0-403-00511-6*) Scholarly.

***Milestones & Memories: Seasons of Change... SECURA's 100-Year Journey.** Sandra S. Wight. LC 00-90174. (Illus.). 104p. 2000. write for info. (*0-9678567-0-1*) SECURA Insurance.

Milestones & Millstones: Social Science at the National Science Foundation, 1945-1991. Otto N. Larsen. 292p. (C). 1991. text 44.95 (*0-88738-441-2*) Transaction Pubs.

Milestones, Etc. Getting Started. Kidasa Software, Inc. Staff. (Illus.). 120p. (C). 1995. 189.95 (*0-9623182-2-1*) KIDASA.

Milestones, Etc. User Manual. Kidasa Software, Inc. Staff. (Illus.). 250p. (C). 1995. 189.95 (*0-9623182-0-5*) KIDASA.

Milestones in American Literary History, 27. Robert E. Spiller. LC 76-47170. (Contributions in American Studies: No. 27). 152p. 1977. 49.95 (*0-8371-9403-2*, SMI/, Greenwood Pr) Greenwood.

Milestones in Analytical Chemistry. Analytical Chemistry, Washington Staff. LC 93-51082. 1994. 74.95 (*0-8412-2855-8*) Am Chemical.

***Milestones in Archaeology: An Encyclopedia.** Tim Murray. 2001. lib. bdg. 99.00 (*1-57607-186-3*) ABC-CLIO.

Milestones in Australian History. Robin Brown. Ed. by Richard Appleton. (Reference Books - Non-Fiction). (Illus.). 500p. (C). 1986. 40.00 (*0-8161-8820-3*, Hall Reference) Macmillan.

Milestones in Black American History, 16 vols., Set. (Illus.). (YA). (gr. 5 up). 1994. pap. 143.20 (*0-7910-3750-9*, Chelsea Juniors); lib. bdg. 319.20 (*0-7910-2250-1*) Chelsea Hse.

Milestones in Colour Printing, 1450-1850: With a Bibliography of Nelson Prints. Bamber Gascoigne. LC 96-28588. (Sandars Lectures in Bibliography). 133p. (C). 1997. text 59.95 (*0-521-55441-1*) Cambridge U Pr.

Milestones in Development: A Cumulative Index to Industrial Development, Site Selection Handbook & Related Publications Covering a Quarter-Century of Professional Contribution. Ed. by Jane Martin. 316p. 1981. 11.95 (*0-910436-16-9*) Conway Data.

Milestones in Environmental Physiology. Ed. by M. K. Yousef. (Progress in Biometeorology Ser.: Vol. 7). (Illus.). xxiv, 161p. 1989. 60.00 (*90-5103-032-0*, Pub. by SPB Acad Pub) Balogh.

Milestones in Geology. Ed. by M. J. Le Bas. (Geological Society Memoir Ser.: No. 16). 272p. 1995. 49.00 (*1-897799-24-1*, 247, Pub. by Geol Soc Pub Hse) AAPG.

Milestones in Glasnost & Perestroyka: The Economy. Ed. by Ed A. Hewett & Victor H. Winston. 522p. 1991. 49.95 (*0-8157-3622-3*); pap. 22.95 (*0-8157-3621-5*) Brookings.

Milestones in Gujarati Literature. Krishnalal M. Jhaveri. LC 98-904940. (C). 1993. text 20.00 (*81-206-0651-5*, Pub. by Asian Educ Servs) S Asia.

Milestones in Health & Medicine. Anne S. Harding. (Illus.). 272p. 2000. boxed set 59.95 (*1-57356-140-1*) Oryx Pr.

Milestones in Human Evolution. Ed. by Alan J. Almquist & Anne Manyak. (Illus.). 274p. (C). 1993. pap. text 16.95 (*0-88133-736-6*) Waveland Pr.

***Milestones in Hypertension, Issue No. 2.** Ed. by Claudia Stahl. 1999. write for info. (*1-57130-039-2*) Medicine Grp USA.

***Milestones in Hypertension, Vol. 4.** Ed. by Dave Varnum. 2000. write for info. (*1-57130-045-7*) Medicine Grp USA.

***Milestones in Hypertension: Special Focus: Cardioprotection, Issue No. 3.** Ed. by Claudia Stahl. 1999. write for info. (*1-57130-044-9*) Medicine Grp USA.

Milestones in Irish History. Ed. by Liam De Paor. 56p. (Orig.). 1998. pap. 10.95 (*1-85635-217-X*, Pub. by Mercier Pr) Irish Amer Bk.

Milestones in Leukemia Research & Therapy. Emil J. Freireich & Noreen A. Lemak. LC 90-5362. (Series in Contemporary Medicine & Public Health). (Illus.). 256p. 1991. text 60.00 (*0-8018-4130-5*) Johns Hopkins.

Milestones in Mass Communication Research. 4th ed. Shearon A. Lowery. (C). 1999. pap. text. write for info. (*0-8013-1795-9*) Longman.

Milestones in Mass Communication Research: Media Effects. 3rd ed. Shearon A. Lowery & Melvin L. DeFleur. LC 94-3707. 415p. (C). 1994. pap. text 56.00 (*0-8013-1437-2*) Longman.

Milestones in Medicine. New York Academy of Medicine Staff. LC 73-142681. (Essay Index Reprint Ser.). 1977. 21.95 (*0-8369-2119-4*) Ayer.

Milestones in Microbiology. 2nd rev. ed. Ed. by Thomas D. Brock. 274p. 1998. pap. 29.95 (*1-55581-142-6*) ASM Pr.

Milestones in Midwifery & the Secret Instrument: The Birth of the Midwifery Forceps. Walter Radcliffe. (Illus.). 193p. 1989. reprint ed. 75.00 (*0-930405-20-X*) Norman SF.

Milestones in Mission. William Rule, III. Ed. by Barbara R. Sugue. LC 98-65598. (Illus.). 352p. 1998. pap. 22.95 (*1-57736-092-3*) Providence Hse.

Milestones in Motion-Picture & Television Technology - the SMPTE 75th Anniversary Collection. Ed. by Jeffrey Friedman. 241p. 1991. 25.00 (*0-940690-19-5*) Soc Motion Pic & TV Engrs.

Milestones in 150 Years of the Chemical Industry, No. 96. W. A. Campbell. Ed. by H. L. Roberts. 1991. 87.00 (*0-85186-456-2*) CRC Pr.

Milestones in Rock Engineering: The Bieniawski Jubilee Collection. 438p. 1996. 123.00 (*90-5410-656-5*, Pub. by A A Balkema) Ashgate Pub Co.

Milestones in Science & Technology: The Ready Reference Guide to Discoveries, Inventions, & Facts. 2nd ed. Ellis Mount. LC 93-25679. (Illus.). 216p. 1993. 39.50 (*0-89774-671-6*) Oryx Pr.

Milestones in Social Work & Medicine. Ed. by Helen Rehr. LC 82-18542. 1982. pap. 8.95 (*0-317-04157-6*, Prodist) Watson Pub Intl.

Milestones in the British Accounting Literature. Compiled by R. H. Parker & Stephen A. Zeff. LC 95-52263. (New Works in Accounting History). 472p. 1996. reprint ed. text 109.00 (*0-8153-2272-0*) Garland.

Milestones in the Development of Social Work & Social Welfare. Robert L. Barker. LC 99-11809. 1999. write for info. (*0-87101-309-6*, NASW Pr) Natl Assn Soc Wkrs.

Milestones in the Life of a Jew. Donald G. Frieman. LC 65-15710. 1980. reprint ed. pap. 4.95 (*0-8197-0002-9*) Bloch.

Milestones in Twentieth Century African-American History. Alton Hornsby, Jr. (Illus.). 542p. 1993. 17.95 (*0-8103-9180-5*, 089173) Visible Ink Pr.

Milestones in Western Civilization Vol. 1: Selected Readings: Ancient Greece Through the Middle Ages. Ed. by Joan Mickelson-Gaughan. LC 90-46171. (Illus.). 447p. 1990. 52.00 (*0-8108-2188-5*) Scarecrow.

Milestones in Western Civilization Vol. 2: Selected Readings: The Renaissance Through Waterloo. Intro. by Joan Mickelson-Gaughan. LC 90-46171. 439p. 1991. 52.00 (*0-8108-2508-2*) Scarecrow.

Milestones in Western Civilization Vol. III: Selected Readings: 1815 to the Present. Ed. by Joan Mickelson-Gaughan. (Illus.). 552p. 1998. 57.50 (*0-8108-3205-4*) Scarecrow.

Milestones of Jazz. Linton Chiswick. 1997. 14.99 (*1-85833-764-X*, Pub. by CLib Bks) Whitecap Bks.

***Milestones of Medicine.** Reader's Digest Association Staff. LC 00-23050. (Eventful 20th Century Ser.). 2000. write for info. (*0-7621-0285-3*) RD Assn.

Milestones of Renewal: A Journey of Hope & Accomplishment. Ismail Serageldin. (Illus.). x, 64p. 1996. write for info. (*1-889676-00-4*) Consult Grp Intl.

***Milestones of Science.** Curt Suplee. LC 00-36149. (Illus.). 288p. 2000. write for info. (*0-7922-7906-9*) Natl Geog.

Milestones of Science: Epochal Books in the History of Science As Represented in the Library of the Buffalo Society of Natural Sciences. Ruth A. Sparrow. LC 71-173348. (Illus.). 307p. (C). 1972. 25.00 (*0-944032-41-9*) Buffalo SNS.

Milestones of Science: Epochal Books in the History of Science As Represented in the Library of the Buffalo Society of Natural Sciences. deluxe limited ed. Ruth A. Sparrow. LC 71-173348. (Illus.). 307p. (C). 1972. 100.00 (*0-944032-42-7*) Buffalo SNS.

***Milestones of the First Century of Flight.** F. Clifton Berry, Jr. 2000. 34.95 (*1-57488-311-9*) Brasseys.

Milestones: The Music & Times of Miles Davis. Jack Chambers. LC 98-28958. (Illus.). 816p. 1998. reprint ed. pap. 23.00 (*0-306-80849-8*) Da Capo.

Milestones Simplicity User Manual. Kidasa Software, Inc. Staff. (Illus.). 120p. 1995. 89.95 (*0-9623182-1-3*) KIDASA.

Milestones to God: Healing Mind & Emotions. Lori M. Poe. LC 89-92799. 260p. (Orig.). 1990. pap. 23.95 (*0-9624804-0-1*) Place Light.

Milestones to Maturity. Jack W. Hayford. LC 94-166268. (Spirit-Filled Life Study Guide Ser.). 1994. pap. 6.99 (*0-8407-8513-5*) Nelson.

Milestones to Shakespeare: A Study of the Dramatic Forms & Pageantry That Were the Prelude to Shakespeare. David Klein. 126p. text 22.95 (*0-8290-0188-3*) Irvington.

Milestones to Shakespeare: A Study of the Dramatic Forms & Pageantry That Were the Prelude to Shakespeare. David Klein. LC 76-99549. 126p. 1970. write for info. (*0-8057-5715-5*, Twyne) Mac Lib Ref.

Milet: Ergebnisse der Ausgrabungen und Untersuchungen Seit Dem Jahre 1989. Funde Aus Milet. Teil 1: Die Megarischen Becher. Anne U. Kossatz. xi, 144p. (C). 1990. lib. bdg. 246.15 (*3-11-010899-2*) De Gruyter.

Milet Redhouse Large Portable Dictionary. Serap Bezmez. 1997. pap. text 42.50 (*975-8176-03-X*) MLE Inc.

Milet Redhouse Mini Dictionary, Mini Ed. R. Avery. 1997. pap. text 8.50 (*975-8176-09-9*) MLE Inc.

Milet Redhouse Smaller Portable Dictionary. Serap Bezmez. 1997. pap. text 17.00 (*975-8176-01-3*) MLE Inc.

Milettes: Small French Dolls to Collect & Make. rev. ed. Mildred Seeley & Colleen Seeley. LC 93-84178. 80p. 1993. reprint ed. pap. 15.95 (*0-916809-62-5*) Scott Pubns MI.

Milford & Me. Patrick Lane. (Illus.). 32p. (J). 1989. pap. 6.95 (*0-919926-97-5*, Pub. by Coteau) Genl Dist Srvs.

Milford & Me. Patrick Lane. (Illus.). 32p. (J). (ps-7). 1989. pap. 11.95 (*0-919926-96-7*, Pub. by Coteau) Genl Dist Srvs.

Milford, MA. Historical Briefs, Inc. Staff. Ed. by Thomas Antonucci & Michael Antonucci. 176p. 1991. pap. 19.95 (*0-89677-030-3*) Hist Briefs.

Milford Zornes. Gordon T. McClelland & Milford Zornes. (Illus.). 70p. 1992. 27.50 (*0-914589-07-5*) Hillcrest Pr.

Milgrim on Licensing, 4 vols. Roger Milgram. 1991. ring bd. 250.00 (*0-8205-1743-7*) Bender.

Milgrim on Trade Secrets, 4 vols., Set. Roger M. Milgrim. 1967. ring bd. 1020.00 (*0-8205-1738-0*) Bender.

Milianthrus: The Dark Power. IGOOS Staff. 235p. 1994. 35.00 (*1-883147-77-8*); 35.00 (*1-883147-78-6*) Intern Guild ASRS.

Miliathros - Advanced Magic Quest Course: Dark Power Course. IGOOS Staff. (Illus.). 105p. 1994. 25.00 (*1-57179-033-0*) Intern Guild ASRS.

Milieu Divin. Pierre Teilhard De Chardin. 8.95 (*0-685-36583-2*) Fr & Eur.

Milieu Divin. Pierre Teilhard De Chardin. (Coll. Livre de vie). (FRE.). 192p. 1972. pap. 13.95 (*0-685-67478-9*, 2020005646) Fr & Eur.

Milieu Therapy: Significant Issues & Innovative Applications. Ed. by Jacquelyn Sanders. LC 93-15448. (Residential Treatment for Children & Youth Ser.: Vol. 10, No. 3). 121p. 1993. lib. bdg. 39.95 (*1-56024-409-7*) Haworth Pr.

Milinda Question: An Inquiry into Its Place in the History of Buddhism with a Theory As to Its Author. C. Rhys Davids. LC 78-72411. reprint ed. 22.50 (*0-404-17275-X*) AMS Pr.

Milindapanho, Being Dialogues Between King Milinda & the Buddhist Sage: The Pali Text to Which Has Now Been Appended a General Index...& An Index of Gathas. Milindapanha. reprint ed. 42.00 (*0-404-17348-9*) AMS Pr.

Milinda's Questions, 2 vols., Set. Tr. by I. B. Horner from PLI. (C). 1964. 65.00 (*0-86013-263-3*) Wisdom MA.

Milinda's Questions, Vol. 1. Tr. by I. B. Horner from PLI. (C). 1964. 36.50 (*0-86013-046-0*) Wisdom MA.

Milinda's Questions, Vol. 2. Tr. by I. B. Horner from PLI. (C). 1964. 36.50 (*0-86013-047-9*) Wisdom MA.

Milione di Marco Polo: Advanced Beginning. (ITA.). (C). 9.95 (*0-8442-8024-0*, X8024-0) NTC Contemp Pub Co.

Milit Arsystem & Sozialleben im Alten Preussen, 1713-1807 see Military System & Social Life in Old-Regime Prussia, 1713-1807: The Beginning of the Social Militarization of Prusso-German Society

Militaire Philosophe. Jacques A. Naigeon. 200p. 1978. reprint ed. write for info. (*3-487-06568-1*) G Olms Pubs.

Militancia Contra la Soledad. Felix Cordova-Iturregui. LC 87-83311. (Flor del Agua Ser.). (SPA.). 77p. 1987. 8.50 (*0-940238-95-0*) Ediciones Huracan.

Militancy, Market Dynamics, & Workplace Authority: The Struggle over Labor Process Outcomes in the U. S. Automobile Industry, 1946 to 1973. James R. Zetka, Jr. LC 93-48155. (SUNY Series in American Labor History). 293p. (C). 1994. text 59.50 (*0-7914-2065-5*); pap. text 19.95 (*0-7914-2066-3*) State U NY Pr.

Militant Agnostic. E. Haldeman-Julius. LC 95-13673. (Freethought Library). 132p. 1995. pap. 14.95 (*0-87975-974-7*) Prometheus Bks.

Militant & Triumphant: William Henry O'Connell & the Catholic Church in Boston, 1859-1944. James M. O'Toole. LC 91-50570. (C). 1993. pap. text 17.50 (*0-268-01403-5*) U of Notre Dame Pr.

Militant Church. Lester Sumrall. 160p. 1990. pap. 5.99 (*0-89274-712-9*, HH712) Harrison Hse.

Militant Hackwriter: French Popular Literature, 1800-1848 - Its Influence, Artistic & Political. Lucian Minor. 1975. 11.95 (*0-87972-105-7*) Bowling Green Univ Popular Press.

Militant Labor in the Philippines. Lois A. West. LC 96-41078. (Illus.). 256p. (C). 1997. 59.95 (*1-56639-491-0*) Temple U Pr.

Militant Man. Tom Franks. 144p. (Orig.). 1991. pap. 7.95 (*0-926044-51-6*) Mercedes Ministries.

Militant Mediator: Whitney M. Young, Jr. Dennis C. Dickerson. LC 97-43456. (Illus.). 416p. 1998. 32.50 (*0-8131-2058-6*) U Pr of Ky.

Militant Ministry: People & Pastors of the Early Church. Hans R. Weber. LC 64-12990. (Knubel-Miller Lectures for 1963). 120p. reprint ed. pap. 37.20 (*0-608-16336-8*, 202718600054) Bks Demand.

Militant Muse. Harri Webb. LC 99-211623. 200p. 1998. pap. 25.95 (*1-85411-212-0*, Pub. by Seren Bks) Dufour.

Militant Nationalism in the Punjab, 1919-1935. Kamlesh Mohan. 447p. 1986. 40.00 (*0-8364-1956-1*, Pub. by Manohar) S Asia.

Militant New World, 1607-1640. Darrett B. Rutman. Ed. by Richard H. Kohn. LC 78-22416. (American Military Experience Ser.). 1980. lib. bdg. 63.95 (*0-405-11890-2*) Ayer.

Militant South, 1800-1861. John H. Franklin. LC 56-10160. 333p. 1956. reprint ed. pap. 103.30 (*0-7837-6084-1*, 205913000007) Bks Demand.

Militant Worker: Class & Radicalism in France & America. Scott Lash. LC 83-25366. 260p. 1984. 36.50 (*0-8386-3224-6*) Fairleigh Dickinson.

Militant Workers: Labour & Class Conflict on the Clyde, 1900-1950. Ed. by R. Duncan. 200p. (C). 1989. pap. 30.00 (*0-7855-6974-X*, Pub. by J Donald) St Mut.

Militant Workers: Labour & Class Conflict on the Clyde, 1900-1950. R. Duncan & A. McIvor. 200p. (C). 1996. pap. 30.00 (*0-85976-373-0*, Pub. by J Donald) St Mut.

***Militant Zionism in America: The Rise & Impact of the Jabotinsky Movement in the U. S., 1926-1948.** Rafael Medoff. 2000. 39.95 (*0-8173-1071-1*) U of Ala Pr.

Militants & Migrants: Rural Sicilians Become American Workers. Donna R. Gabaccia. (Class & Culture Ser.). 352p. (Orig.). (C). 1988. text 45.00 (*0-8135-1318-9*); pap. text 20.00 (*0-8135-1356-1*) Rutgers U Pr.

Militararztlichen Bildungsanstalten Von Ihrer Grundung Bis Zur Gegenwart. Otto Schickert. (GER.). 1985. reprint ed. write for info. (*3-283-07697-9*) G Olms Pubs.

Militaria: A Study of German Helmets & Uniforms, 1729-1918. Jan K. Kube. Tr. by Edward Force from GER. LC 90-60467. (Illus.). 238p. 1990. 29.95 (*0-88740-243-7*) Schiffer.

Militarisation of Politics & Neo-Colonialism: The Nigerian Experience, 1966-1990. John S. Ikpuk. 128p. 1996. 25.00 (*1-85756-186-4*, Pub. by Janus Pubng) Paul & Co Pubs.

Militarisation of Politics & Society: Southeast Asian Experiences. Mathews G. Chunakara. 116p. 1998. reprint ed. pap. text 25.00 (*0-7881-1907-9*) DIANE Pub.

Militarism. Guglielmo Ferrero. LC 73-172547. 1972. reprint ed. 18.95 (*0-405-08500-1*) Ayer.

Militarism & Anti-Militarism. Karl Liebknecht. 1969. 29.50 (*0-86527-130-5*) Fertig.

Militarism & Anti-Militarism. Karl Liebknecht. 1972. 59.95 (*0-8490-0635-X*) Gordon Pr.

Militarism & Fascism in Japan. O. Tanin & E. Yohan. LC 72-136553. 320p. 1974. reprint ed. lib. bdg. 35.00 (*0-8371-5478-2*, TAMF, Greenwood Pr) Greenwood.

Militarism & Foreign Policy in Japan. Eric E. Causton. LC 78-63658. (Studies in Fascism: Ideology & Practice). reprint ed. 32.50 (*0-404-16918-X*) AMS Pr.

Militarism & Global Ecology. Gary E. McCuen. (Ideas in Conflict Ser.). (Illus.). 134p. (YA). (gr. 7-12). 1993. lib. bdg. 15.95 (*0-86596-086-0*) G E M.

Militarism & Organized Labor, 1900-1914. Philip S. Foner. LC 86-2770. (Studies in Marxism: Vol. 18). 133p. 1987. 17.95 (*0-930656-43-1*) MEP Pubns.

Militarism & Politics in Latin America: Peru from Sanchez Cerro to Sendero Luminoso, 111. Daniel M. Masterson. LC 90-23010. (Contributions in Military Studies Ser.: No. 111). 360p. 1991. 69.50 (*0-313-27213-1*, MLM, Greenwood Pr) Greenwood.

Militarism & Social Revolution in the Third World. Miles D. Wolpin. LC 81-65014. 272p. 1982. text 41.00 (*0-86598-021-7*) Rowman.

Militarism for America. Grover L. Hartman. (C). 1945. pap. 4.00 (*0-87574-025-1*) Pendle Hill.

Militarism, Imperialism, & Racial Accommodation: An Analysis & Interpretation of the Early Writings of Robert E. Park. Stanford M. Lyman. 360p. 1992. text 38.00 (*1-55728-219-6*) U of Ark Pr.

Militarism in Arab Society: An Historiographical & Bibliographical Sourcebook. John W. Jandora. LC 96-35019. 192p. 1997. lib. bdg. 65.00 (*0-313-29370-8*, Greenwood Pr) Greenwood.

Militarism in Developing Countries. Ed. by Kenneth Fidel. LC 74-20190. (Third World Ser.). 300p. 1975. pap. 21.95 (*0-87855-585-4*) Transaction Pubs.

Militarism in India: The Army & Civil Society in Consensus. Kundu. 230p. 1998. text 59.50 (*1-86064-318-3*) I B T.

Militarism in Modern China. Wou. (Australian National University Press Ser.). 1996. text. write for info. (*0-08-033031-2*, Pergamon Pr) Elsevier.

Militarism in Politics see Militarism, Politics, & Working Class Attitudes in Late Nineteenth Century Europe

Militarism, Politics, & Working Class Attitudes in Late Nineteenth Century Europe. Incl. Armee, Est-Elle, Doit-Elle Etre la Nation? Jules Bourelly. LC 75-147561. 1975. Army & the Democracy. LC 75-147561. 1975. Militarism in Politics. Jean De Bloch. LC 75-147561. 1975. Militarismus. F. Wiede. LC 75-147561. 1975. Working Men & War. Thomas Burt. LC 75-147561. 1975. LC 75-147561. (Library of War & Peace; Control & Limitation of Arms). 1975. Set lib. bdg. 46.00 (*0-8240-0335-7*) Garland.

Militarismus see Militarism, Politics, & Working Class Attitudes in Late Nineteenth Century Europe

Militarists, Merchants & Missionaries: United States Expansion in Middle America. Ed. by Edward H. Moseley & Eugene R. Huck. LC 68-14556. 184p. reprint ed. 57.10 (*0-8357-9620-5*, 205045000081) Bks Demand.

Militarization & Demilitarization in El Salvador's Transition to Democracy. Philip J. Williams & Knut Walter. LC 97-4920. (Latin American Ser.). 260p. 1998. pap. 19.95 (*0-8229-5646-2*); text 45.00 (*0-8229-4041-8*) U of Pittsburgh Pr.

Militarization, Gender & Reproductive Health in South Sudan. Jok M. Jok. LC 98-10057. 360p. 1998. text 99.95 (*0-7734-2235-8*) E Mellen.

Militarization of Mother India. Ravi Rikhya. 1990. 23.50 (*81-7001-060-8*, Pub. by Chanakya) S Asia.

Militarization of Space. P. Suares. 1998. mass mkt. 25.00 (*0-8041-1810-8*) Ivy Books.

Militarization of Space: U. S. Policy, 1945-1984. Paul B. Stares. LC 85-47501. (Cornell Studies in Security Affairs). 336p. (C). 1985. text 42.50 (*0-8014-1810-0*) Cornell U Pr.

Militarization of the U. S. - Mexico Border, 1978-1992: Low Intensity Conflict Doctrine Comes Home. Timothy J. Dunn. LC 94-42964. (Border & Migration Studies). (Illus.). xii, 307 p. (C). 1995. pap. 14.95 (*0-292-71580-3*) U of Tex Pr.

Militarization of the U. S. Mexico Border, 1978-1992: Low Intensity Conflict Doctrine Comes Home. Timothy J. Dunn. LC 94-42964. (Border & Migration Studies). (Illus.). 256p. (C). 1995. text 35.00 (*0-292-71579-X*) U of Tex Pr.

Militarization of the Western World: 1870 to the Present. Ed. by John R. Gillis. LC 88-36808. 212p. (C). 1989. text 35.00 (*0-8135-1449-5*); pap. text 16.00 (*0-8135-1450-9*) Rutgers U Pr.

Militarverwaltung in Den Von Den Osterreichisch-Ungarischen Truppen Besetzten Gebieten. Hugo Kerchnawe et al. (Wirtschafts-Und Sozialgeschichte des Weltkrieges (Osterreichische Und Ungarische Serie)). (GER.). 1928. 125.00 (*0-317-27522-4*) Elliots Bks.

Military. Sheldon M. Cohen. (Contemporary Ethical Issues Ser.). 1997. lib. bdg. 39.50 (*0-87436-880-4*) ABC-CLIO.

Military. Lila Summer & Samuel D. Woods. (Good Citizenship Ser.). (Illus.). 1997. pap., student ed. 5.95 (*0-8114-5581-5*) Raintree Steck-V.

Military - Rev. War, Record of Connecticut Men in the Military & Naval Service During the War of the Revolution, 1775-1783. (Illus.). 779p. 1995. reprint ed. lib. bdg. 79.50 (*0-8328-4652-X*) Higginson Bk Co.

Military Academy: Differences in Performance & Experience Between Men & Women, & Whites & Minorities at West Point. (Illus.). 63p. (Orig.). (C). 1994. pap. text 25.00 (*0-7881-1006-3*) DIANE Pub.

Military Academy: Gender & Racial Disparities. (Illus.). 64p. 1994. pap. text 45.00 (*1-57979-098-4*) DIANE Pub.

Military Academy As an Assimilating Institution. Sanford M. Dornbusch. (Reprint Series in Social Sciences). (C). 1993. reprint ed. pap. text 1.00 (*0-8290-2724-6*, S-73) Irvington.

Military Adventures of Charles O'Neil. Charles O'Neil. 1997. 29.95 (*1-885119-45-3*) Sarpedon.

Military Adventures of Charles O'Neil. Charles O'Neil. 272p. 1997. 80.00 (*1-873376-74-X*, Pub. by Spellmnt Pubs) St Mut.

Military Advisors in Korea: Kmag in Peace & War. Robert K. Sawer. 216p. 1962. per. 8.00 (*0-16-001867-6*) USGPO.

Military Affairs see Alaska Administrative Code 4/99 Supplement

Military Aid to Civil Authorities. David Fastabend et al. (Illus.). 51p. (C). 1999. reprint ed. pap. text 20.00 (*0-7881-7524-6*) DIANE Pub.

Military Aid to the Civil Power. Cassius Dowell. Ed. by Igor I. Kavass & Adolf Sprudzs. LC 72-75030. (International Military Law & History Ser.: Vol. 1). 330p. 1972. reprint ed. lib. bdg. 42.00 (*0-930342-38-0*, 300300) W S Hein.

Military Air & Space Communications, 1990. Ed. by John P. Hyde. LC 90-35081. (Illus.). 432p. (C). 1990. text 21.95 (*0-916159-21-3*) AFCEA Intl Pr.

Military Air Power. 1991. lib. bdg. 79.95 (*0-8490-4939-3*) Gordon Pr.

Military Air Transport Operations. K. Chapman. (Air Power: Aircraft, Weapons Systems & Technology Ser.: No. 6). (Illus.). 226p. 1989. 40.00 (*0-08-034749-5*, Pub. by Brasseys); 25.00 (*0-08-036255-9*, Pub. by Brasseys) Brasseys.

Military Aircraft. Christopher Chant. LC 99-30416. (World's Greatest Aircraft Ser.). (Illus.). 64p. 1999. 21.95 (*0-7910-5420-9*) Chelsea Hse.

Military Aircraft Accidents Around Western Massachusetts, 1941. Thomas E. Martin. LC 94-96095. 180p. 1995. pap. 18.95 (*0-9641015-0-5*) T E Martin.

***Military Aircraft Boneyards.** Nick Veronico. (Illus.). 128p. 2000. pap. 24.95 (*0-7603-0820-9*, 129833AP, Pub. by MBI Pubg) Motorbooks Intl.

Military Aircraft Insignia of the World. John Cochrane & Stuart Elliot. (Putnam Aviation Ser.). (Illus.). 144p. 1998. pap. 29.95 (*1-55750-542-X*) Naval Inst Pr.

Military Aircraft Library, 3 bks. David Baker. (Illus.). 288p. (J). (gr. 3-8). 1989. lib. bdg. 75.81 (*0-86592-350-7*) Rourke Enter.

Military Aircraft Library, 6 bks., Set II, Reading Level 5. David Baker. (Illus.). 288p. (J). (gr. 3-8). 1989. 83.70 (*0-685-58763-0*) Rourke Corp.

Military Aircraft Markings & Profiles Barry C. Wheeler. LC 93-150219. 191p. 1990. write for info. (*0-600-56976-4*, Pub. by Hamlyn Publishing Group Ltd) Sterling.

Military Aircraft Safety: Significant Improvements since 1975. (Illus.). 28p. (Orig.). (C). 1996. pap. text 15.00 (*0-7881-3018-8*) DIANE Pub.

Military Airlift: Options Exist for Meeting Requirements While Acquiring Fewer C-17's. Thomas J. Denomme et al. 62p. (C). 1999. reprint ed. pap. text 20.00 (*0-7881-4375-1*) DIANE Pub.

Military Airlift Command. Timothy Laur. LC 91-23951. (Illus.). 325p. 1994. 26.95 (*1-877853-15-1*) Nautical & Aviation.

Military Airpower: The CADRE Digest of Air Power Opinions & Thoughts. LC 90-45674. (Illus.). 224p. 1990. pap. 8.50 (*1-58566-034-5*) Air Univ.

Military Almanac of the United States. 1991. lib. bdg. 88.95 (*0-8490-4988-1*) Gordon Pr.

Military & Colonial Policy of the United States. Elihu Root. LC 70-121030. reprint ed. 47.50 (*0-404-05399-8*) AMS Pr.

Military & Conflict Between Cultures: Soldiers at the Interface. Ed. by James C. Bradford. LC 96-43015. (Military History Ser.: Vol. 50). (Illus.). 264p. (C). 1997. text 37.95 (*0-89096-743-1*) Tex A&M Univ Pr.

Military & Government Simulation, 1993. Ed. by Chinni. 74p. 1993. pap. 30.00 (*1-56555-053-6*, SMC93-1) Soc Computer Sim.

Military & Industrial Complexes. Nash. 2000. 25.00 (*0-465-04594-4*) HarpC.

Military & Militarism in Israeli Society. Ed. by Edna Lomsky-Feder & Eyal Ben-Ari. LC 99-10884. (SUNY Series in Israeli Studies). (Illus.). 320p. (C). 2000. pap. text 23.95 (*0-7914-4352-3*) State U NY Pr.

Military & Militarism in Israeli Society. Ed. by Edna Lomsky-Feder & Eyal Ben-Ari. LC 99-10884. (SUNY Series in Israeli Studies). (Illus.). 320p. (C). 2000. text 71.50 (*0-7914-4351-5*) State U NY Pr.

Military & Naval, Vol. 3. (British Parliamentary Papers). 720p. 1970. 96.00 (*0-7165-1282-3*, Pub. by Irish Acad Pr) Intl Spec Bk.

Military & Naval, Vol. 5. (British Parliamentary Papers). 904p. 1970. 75.00 (*0-7165-1315-3*, Pub. by Irish Acad Pr) Intl Spec Bk.

Military & Naval, Vol. 6. (British Parliamentary Papers). 814p. 1970. 90.00 (*0-7165-1316-1*, Pub. by Irish Acad Pr) Intl Spec Bk.

Military & Naval Vols. 1-6, 6 vols., Set. (British Parliamentary Papers). 1970. 730.00 (*0-614-16194-0*, Pub. by Irish Acad Pr) Intl Spec Bk.

Military & Naval Vols. 1-6, Vol. 1. (British Parliamentary Papers). 504p. 1970. 75.00 (*0-7165-0488-X*, Pub. by Irish Acad Pr) Intl Spec Bk.

Military & Naval Vols. 1-6, Vol. 2. (British Parliamentary Papers). 376p. 1970. 78.00 (*0-614-16195-9*, Pub. by Irish Acad Pr) Intl Spec Bk.

Military & Naval Vols. 1-6, Vol. 4. (British Parliamentary Papers). 536p. 1970. 94.00 (*0-7165-1313-7*, Pub. by Irish Acad Pr) Intl Spec Bk.

Military & Police Uniform Association. Ed. by Military & Police Uniform Assoc. Staff. (Gay Men in Uniform Ser.). (Illus.). 80p. (Orig.). 1997. pap. 30.00 (*0-614-04388-3*) L Wendruck.

Military & Political Career of Jose Joaquin de Herrera, 1792-1854, 7--7. Thomas E. Cotner. LC 69-19007. 336p. 1970. reprint ed. lib. bdg. 69.50 (*0-8371-1018-1*, TICH, Greenwood Pr) Greenwood.

Military & Political Power in China in the 1970's: Organization, Leadership, Political Strategy. Ed. by William W. Whitson. LC 78-189842. (Special Studies in International Politics & Government). 1972. 42.50 (*0-275-28293-7*) Irvington.

Military & Political Succession in China: Leadership, Institutions, Beliefs. M. D. Swaine. 290p. 1992. pap. 20.00 (*0-8330-1296-7*, R-4254) Rand Corp.

Military & Politics in Israel, 1948-1967: Nation Building & Role Expansion. 2nd rev. ed. Amos Perlmutter. (Illus.). 161p. 1977. 42.50 (*0-7146-2392-X*, Pub. by F Cass Pubs) Intl Spec Bk.

Military & Politics in Pakistan. Hasan-Askari Rizvi. 367p. 1989. text 30.00 (*81-220-0084-3*, Pub. by Konark Pubs Pvt Ltd) Advent Bks Div.

Military & Related Terms. 2nd ed. David Traynor. LC 91-73728. 306p. 1992. pap. 15.95 (*0-9629304-0-7*) DOT Pub.

Military & Social Significance of Ballad Singing in the English Civil War, 1642-1649. John M. Carter. 95p. (Orig.). 1980. pap. text 25.00 (*0-89126-095-1*) MA-AH Pub.

Military & Society: A Collection of Essays. Peter Karsten. 1998. 375.00 (*0-8153-2979-2*) Garland.

Military & Society: Reviews of Recent Research. Ed. by Patricia J. Rosof et al. LC 81-20073. (Trends in History Ser.: Vol. 2, No. 2). 120p. (C). 1982. text 39.95 (*0-917724-44-5*) Haworth Pr.

Military & Society in Colonial Peru, 1750-1810. Leon G. Campbell. LC 77-91650. (American Philosophical Society, Memoirs Ser.: No. 123). 272p. reprint ed. pap. 84.40 (*0-608-15297-8*, 202923400059) Bks Demand.

Military & Society in the Former Eastern Bloc. Ed. by Constantine Danopoulos & Daniel Zirker. LC 98-46210. 248p. 1998. 69.00 (*0-8133-3524-8*, Pub. by Westview) HarpC.

***Military & Society in 21st Century Europe: A Comparative Analysis.** Jurgen Kuhlmann & Jean Callaghan. LC 00-32555. 2000. write for info. (*0-7658-0062-4*) Transaction Pubs.

Military & Sporting Rifle Shooting. E. C. Crossman. (Library Classics). (Illus.). 536p. 1986. reprint ed. 45.00 (*0-935632-34-4*) Wolfe Pub Co.

Military & Strategic Policy: An Annotated Bibliography, 2. Compiled by Benjamin R. Beede. LC 89-25616. (Bibliographies & Indexes in Military Studies: No. 2). 355p. 1990. lib. bdg. 89.50 (*0-313-26000-1*, BMZ/, Greenwood Pr) Greenwood.

Military & the Making of Modern South Africa. Annette Seegers. 320p. 1996. text 65.00 (*1-85043-689-4*, Pub. by I B T) St Martin.

Military & the Media. Alan Hooper. 264p. 1982. text 69.95 (*0-566-00610-3*) Ashgate Pub Co.

Military & the Media: Why the Press Cannot Be Trusted to Cover a War. William V. Kennedy. LC 92-46555. 184p. 1993. 55.00 (*0-275-94191-4*, C4191, Praeger Pubs) Greenwood.

Military & the Media, 1962-1968. William M. Hammond. (Propaganda Analysis Ser.). 1989. lib. bdg. 79.95 (*0-8490-3976-2*) Gordon Pr.

Military & the South. Ed. by Bob Hall & Joseph Hughes. (Southern Exposure Ser.). (Illus.). 100p. (Orig.). (C). 1973. pap. 2.50 (*0-943810-00-0*) Inst Southern Studies.

Military & the State in Latin America. Alain Rouquie. Tr. by Paul E. Sigmund. 520p. 1987. 60.00 (*0-520-05559-4*, Pub. by U CA Pr) Cal Prin Full Svc.

Military & United States Indian Policy, 1865-1903. Robert Wooster. LC 94-43018. xiii, 268p. 1995. pap. 10.95 (*0-8032-9767-X*, Bison Books) U of Nebr Pr.

Military Annals of Lancaster, 1740-1865: Including Lists of Soldiers Serving in the Colonial & Revolutionary Wars. Henry S. Nourse. 402p. 1989. reprint ed. lib. bdg. 42.50 (*0-8328-0834-2*, MA0021) Higginson Bk Co.

Military Annals of Mississippi: Military Organizations Which Entered the Service of the Confederate States of America, from the State of Mississippi. J. C. Rietti. LC 75-45377. 196p. 1999. reprint ed. 25.00 (*0-87152-218-7*) Reprint.

Military Annals of Tennessee Vols. I & II: Confederate, 2 vols. Ed. by John B. Lindsley. (Illus.). 1634p. 1996. 100.00 (*1-56837-310-4*) Broadfoot.

Military Applications of Fiber Optics. rev. ed. IGIC, Inc. Staff. (Fiber Optics Reprint Ser.: Vol. 14). (Illus.). 504p. 1994. pap. 75.00 (*1-56851-063-2*) Info Gatekeepers.

Military Applications of Microelectromechanical Systems. Keith W. Brendley & Randall Steeb. LC 93-18546. 1993. pap. 13.00 (*0-8330-1344-0*, MR-175-OLD/AF/A) Rand Corp.

Military Applications of Modeling Selected Case Studies. Francis P. Hoeber. Ed. by Stephhen W. Leibholz. (Military Operations Research Ser.: Vol. 1). xviii, 222p. 1981. text 257.00 (*0-677-05840-3*) Gordon & Breach.

Military Architecture. Eugene E. Viollet-Le-Duc. 304p. 1991. 35.00 (*1-85367-078-2*, 5551) Stackpole.

Military Art of People's War: Selected Writings of General Vo Nguyen Giap. Vo Nguyen Giap. Ed. by Russell Stetler. LC 75-105317. 336p. reprint ed. pap. 104.20 (*0-608-11782-X*, 201925400011) Bks Demand.

Military Ascendancy & Political Culture: A Study of Indonesia's Golkar. Leo Suryadinata. (Monographs in International Studies, Southeast Asia Ser.: No. 85). (Illus.). 235p. 1989. pap. 18.00 (*0-89680-154-3*) Ohio U Pr.

Military Aspects of the Israeli-Arab Conflict. Ed. by Louis Williams. 265p. 1975. 44.95 (*0-87855-227-8*) Transaction Pubs.

***Military Aspects of the Vietnam Conflict.** Walter L. Hixson. LC 00-32926. (United States & the Vietnam War Ser.). 2000. write for info. (*0-8153-3532-6*) Garland.

Military Assistance: An Operational Perspective, 170. William H. Mott, IV. LC 98-17532. (Contributions in Military Studies Ser.: No. 170). 384p. 1999. 65.00 (*0-313-30729-6*, GM0729, Greenwood Pr) Greenwood.

Military Assistance in Recent Wars: The Dominance of the Superpowers, 122. Stephanie G. Neuman. LC 86-16911. (Washington Papers: No. 122). 199p. 1987. 45.00 (*0-275-92219-7*, C2219, Praeger Pubs) Greenwood.

Military Assistance to the Civil Authorities in Democracies: Case Studies & Perspectives. Ed. by NATO Defense College Staff. LC 96-38060. (Euro-Atlantic Security Studies: Vol. 4). 145p. 1996. pap. 35.95 (*3-631-30485-4*) P Lang Pubng.

Military Atlas of the First World War. Arthur Banks. (Illus.). 1997. 29.95 (*0-85052-563-2*, Pub. by Leo Cooper) Combined Pub.

Military Attache. Alfred Vagts. LC 66-14315. 422p. reprint ed. pap. 130.90 (*0-7837-0101-2*, 204037900016) Bks Demand.

Military Attrition: Better Data, Coupled with Policy Changes, Could Help the Services Reduce Early Separations. Carol Schuster. (Illus.). 75p. (C). 1999. text 20.00 (*0-7881-7732-X*) DIANE Pub.

Military Attrition: DOD Could Save Millions by Better Screening Enlisted Personnel. Sharon Cekala et al. (Illus.). 64p. (C). 1998. reprint ed. pap. text 20.00 (*0-7881-4334-4*) DIANE Pub.

Military Aviation Disasters. David Gero. LC 98-73715. (Illus.). 192p. 1998. 39.95 (*1-85260-574-X*, Pub. by P Stephens) Haynes Manuals.

Military Aviation Fuel Characteristics, 1917-1945. Robert Kerley. (International Fuels & Lubricants Meeting & Exposition, 1993 Ser.). 128p. 1993. pap. 19.00 (*1-56091-454-8*, SP-1008) Soc Auto Engineers.

Military Badge Collecting. 5th ed. John Gaylor. LC 98-178469. (Illus.). 294p. 1995. 39.95 (*0-85052-524-1*, Pub. by Leo Cooper) Trans-Atl Phila.

Military Badges & Insignia. Chelsea House Publishing Staff. (Concise Collection). 48p. (J). (gr. 3 up). 1997. 15.95 (*1-85627-792-5*) Chelsea Hse.

Military Badges & Insignia. Mark Lloyd. (Illus.). 46p. (gr. 8-12). 1999. text 20.00 (*0-7881-6443-0*) DIANE Pub.

Military Balance, 1988-89. 1989. pap. 29.50 (*0-08-037567-7*, Pergamon Pr) Elsevier.

Military Balance, 1989-1990. IISS Staff. (ANMB 89 Military Balance-IISS Annual Ser.). 260p. 1989. 70.00 (*0-08-040352-2*, Pergamon Pr); pap. 35.00 (*0-08-037569-3*, Pergamon Pr) Elsevier.

Military Balance, 1980-1981. International Institute for Strategic Studies Staff. LC UA0015.L65. 143p. reprint ed. pap. 44.40 (*0-608-12296-3*, 202515400042) Bks Demand.

Military Balance, 1995-1996. International Institute for Strategic Studies Staff. (International Institute for Strategic Studies). (Illus.). 322p. 1995. pap. text 75.00 (*0-19-828055-6*) OUP.

Military Balance 1999-2000. International Institute of Strategic Studies Staff. (International Institute for Strategic Studies). (Illus.). 320p. 1999. pap. text 135.00 (*0-19-922425-0*) OUP.

Military Balance, 1996-1997. International Institute for Strategic Studies Staff. (International Institute for Strategic Studies). (Illus.). 320p. 1996. pap. text 80.00 (*0-19-829217-1*) OUP.

Military Balance, 1990-1991. IISS Staff. 1990. 95.95 (*0-08-040376-X*, Pergamon Pr); pap. 44.95 (*0-08-040364-6*, Pergamon Pr) Elsevier.

Military Balance, 1979-1980. International Institute for Strategic Studies Staff. LC UA0015.L65. 143p. reprint ed. pap. 44.40 (*0-608-12114-2*, 202515300042) Bks Demand.

***Military Balance 2000/2001.** International Institute for Strategic Studies Staff. (Illus.). 320p. 2000. pap. text 135.00 (*0-19-929003-2*) OUP.

***Military Balance 1998-1999.** International Institute of Strategic Studies Staff. (International Institute for Strategic Studies). (Illus.). 320p. 1998. pap. text 100.00 (*0-19-922372-6*) OUP.

Military Ballistics: A Basic Manual. C. L. Farrar & D. W. Leeming. 225p. 1983. text 35.00 (*0-08-028342-X*, Pergamon Pr); pap. text 22.00 (*0-08-028343-8*, Pergamon Pr) Elsevier.

Military Ballistics: A Basic Manual. G. M. Moss et al. (Land Warfare: Brassey's New Battlefield Weapons & Technology Ser.: Vol. 12). (Illus.). 230p. 1994. pap. 21.95 (*1-85753-084-5*, Pub. by Brasseys) Brasseys.

***Military Ballooning During the Early Civil War.** Frederick S. Haydon. LC 99-44060. 2000. pap. 18.95 (*0-8018-6442-9*) Johns Hopkins.

Military Bases: Analysis of DOD's Recommendations & Selection Process for Closures & Realignments. Ed. by Harry E. Taylor et al. (Illus.). 113p. 1997. reprint ed. pap. text 30.00 (*0-7881-4114-7*) DIANE Pub.

Military Bases: Case Studies. (Illus.). 120p. 1995. pap. text 45.00 (*1-57979-116-6*) DIANE Pub.

Military Bases: Case Studies on Selected Bases Closed in 1988 & 1991. (Illus.). 120p. (Orig.). (C). 1996. pap. text 35.00 (*0-7881-2753-5*) DIANE Pub.

Military Bases: Lessons Learned from Prior Base Closure Rounds. David R. Warren et al. (Illus.). 64p. (C). 1998. pap. text 20.00 (*0-7881-7553-X*) DIANE Pub.

Military Bases: Letters & Requests Received on Proposed Closures & Realignments. (Illus.). 50p. 1997. reprint ed. pap. text 30.00 (*0-7881-3799-9*) DIANE Pub.

An Asterisk (*) at the beginning of an entry indicates that the title is appearing for the first time.

Military Bases: Review of DOD's 1998 Report on Base Realignment & Closure. Barry W. Holman. 52p. (C). 1999. text 20.00 (*0-7881-7919-5*) DIANE Pub.

Military Bases: Update on the Status of Bases Closed in 1988, 1991, & 1993. James F. Wiggins & John J. Klotz. (Illus.). 44p. (Orig.). (C). 1996. pap. text 25.00 (*0-7881-3643-7*) DIANE Pub.

Military Basing & U. S. - Soviet Military Balance in Southeast Asia: A Vietnam Legacy. Ed. by George K. Tanham & Alvin H. Bernstein. 200p. 1988. write for info. (*0-8448-1568-3*) Taylor & Francis.

Military Bibliography of the Civil War: General References, Armed Forces, & Campaigns & Battle, Vol. 3. Ed. by Charles E. Dornbusch. LC 72-137700. xv, 224p. 1989. reprint ed. 25.00 (*0-87104-117-0*) NY Pub Lib.

Military Bibliography of the Civil War: Regimental Publications & Personal Narratives, Vol. 1. Ed. by Charles E. Dornbusch. LC 72-137700. 528p. 1971. reprint ed. 35.00 (*0-87104-504-4*) NY Pub Lib.

Military Bibliography of the Civil War: Southern, Border, Western & Territories; Federal Troops; Union & Confederate Biographies, Vol. 2. Ed. by Charles E. Dornbusch. LC 61-15574. 270p. 1971. reprint ed. 30.00 (*0-87104-514-1*) NY Pub Lib.

Military Blunders. Michael Coffey. 320p. 2000. pap. 15.95 (*0-7868-8470-3*, Pub. by Hyperion) Time Warner.

Military Blunders. Saul David. LC 98-6806. (Illus.). 384p. 1998. pap. 11.95 (*0-7867-0504-3*) Carroll & Graf.

Military Blunders: Wartime Fiascoes from the Roman Age Through World War I. Steve Eden. 120p. 1995. 16.98 (*1-56799-175-0*, MetroBooks) M Friedman Pub Grp Inc.

Military Blunders II: The Twentiety Century. Steven Eden. 1996. 16.98 (*1-56799-388-5*, MetroBooks) M Friedman Pub Grp Inc.

Military Brats: Legacies of Childhood Inside the Fortress. Mary E. Wertsch. LC 91-76227. 478p. 1991. reprint ed. pap. 14.95 (*0-9639260-3-9*) Aletheia.

Military Buildup in the High North: American & Nordic Perspectives. Sverre Jervall & Kare Nyblom. (Illus.). 174p. (Orig.). 1987. pap. text 19.50 (*0-8191-5685-X*) U Pr of Amer.

Military-Bureaucracy Relationship in Nigeria: Public Policy Making & Implementation. Robert A. Dibie. LC 98-38257. 256p. 2000. 69.95 (*0-275-96447-7*, Praeger Pubs) Greenwood.

Military Buttons of the Gulf Coast, 1711-1830. Dan Jenkins. LC 74-185504. (Illus.). (Orig.). 1973. pap. 5.00 (*0-914334-01-8*) Museum Mobile.

***Military Campaigns of the 100 Years War.** Kelly DeVries. 2000. 39.95 (*0-7509-1804-7*, Pub. by Sutton Publng) Intl Pubs Mktg.

Military Campaigns of the Wars of the Roses. Philip A. Haigh. (Illus.). 206p. 1997. pap. 19.95 (*0-7509-1430-0*, Pub. by Sutton Pub Ltd) Intl Pubs Mktg.

Military Capabilities: Stronger Joint Staff Role Needed to Enhance Joint Military Training. (Illus.). 64p. (Orig.). (C). 1996. pap. text 20.00 (*0-7881-3238-5*) DIANE Pub.

Military Capacity & the Risk of War: China, India, Pakistan & Iran. Ed. by Eric H. Arnett. LC 96-30040. (A SIPRI Publication). (Illus.). 382p. 1997. text 65.00 (*0-19-829281-3*) OUP.

Military Career of Alexander Macomb & Alexander Macomb at Plattsburgh, N. Y. Allan S. Everest. (Illus.). 85p. 1989. pap. 15.95 (*1-890402-16-8*) Clinton Cnty Hist.

Military Careers: A Guide to Military Occupations & Selected Military Career Paths, 2 vols. 1995. lib. bdg. 600.00 (*0-8490-6868-1*) Gordon Pr.

Military Careers: Military Occupations & Selected Military Career Paths, 1995-1998. 439p. 1996. per. 46.00 (*0-16-061115-6*) USGPO.

***Military Challenges of Transatlantic Coalitions.** James P. Thomas. (Adelphi Papers: 333). 96p. 2000. pap. 24.95 (*0-19-929005-9*) OUP.

Military Chaplains Association. Turner Publishing Company Staff. (Illus.). 144p. Date not set. 49.95 (*1-56311-231-0*) Turner Pub KY.

Military Chemical & Biological Agents: Chemical & Toxicological Properties. James A. Compton. 440p. 1988. lib. bdg. 95.00 (*0-936923-11-3*) Telford Pr.

Military Chemistry & Chemical Compounds. 1995. lib. bdg. 260.95 (*0-8490-6556-9*) Gordon Pr.

***Military Child: Mobility & Education.** Mary M. Keller & Glynn T. Decoteau. (Fastback Ser.: No. 463). 40p. 2000. pap. 3.00 (*0-87367-663-7*) Phi Delta Kappa.

Military-Civilian Interactions. Weiss. LC 98-27504. 304p. 1998. 55.00 (*0-8476-8745-7*) Rowman.

Military-Civilian Interactions. Ed. by Weiss. LC 98-27504. 304p. 1998. pap. 18.95 (*0-8476-8746-5*) Rowman.

Military-Civilian Teamwork in Suicide Prevention: Armed Forces Strategies, Procedures & Responsibilities to Implement Their Policy That Suicide Prevention Is Everybody's Business. Meyer Moldeven. LC 88-90534. 272p. 1994. pap. 10.95 (*0-9615092-7-9*) M Moldeven.

Military Clip Art: Color Unit Patches. Tom Adkins. (Illus.). 32p. 1997. pap. text 12.95 incl. disk (*1-884778-26-7*) Old Mountain.

Military Clip Art Vol. I: Color Military Clip Art. Tom Adkins. (Illus.). 36p. 1997. pap. text 12.95 incl. disk (*1-884778-25-9*) Old Mountain.

Military Clipart: Air Assault. Tom Adkins. (Illus.). 48p. 1997. pap. text 16.95 incl. cd-rom (*1-884778-21-6*) Old Mountain.

Military Clipart: Army Line Art, Vol. 2. Tom Adkins. (Illus.). 44p. 1997. pap. text 12.95 (*1-884778-20-8*) Old Mountain.

Military Clipart: Rank Insignia. Tom Adkins. 36p. 1997. pap. text 16.95 incl. cd-rom (*1-884778-19-4*) Old Mountain.

Military Clipart: Soviet. Tom Adkins. (Illus.). 40p. 1997. pap. text 12.95 incl. disk (*1-884778-32-1*) Old Mountain.

Military Clipart: USAF Line Art, Vol. I. Tom Adkins. 40p. 1997. pap. text 16.95 incl. cd-rom (*1-884778-30-5*) Old Mountain.

Military Clipart: USMC Line Art, Vol. I. Tom Adkins. (Illus.). 48p. 1997. pap. text 12.95 incl. disk (*1-884778-31-3*) Old Mountain.

Military Clipart Vol. I: Army Line Art. Tom Adkins. (Illus.). 44p. 1997. pap. text 12.95 (*1-884778-18-6*) Old Mountain.

Military Cohesion: A Special Issue of Military Psychology. Ed. by A. David Mangelsdorff. 128p. 1998. pap. 24.50 (*0-8058-9809-3*) L Erlbaum Assocs.

***Military Collectibles.** Patrick Newell. LC 99-58093. (Cool Collectibles Ser.). (Illus.). 48p. (J). (gr. 4-7). 2000. pap. 6.95 (*0-516-23531-1*) Childrens.

Military Commander & the Law. 3rd ed. Ed. by Richard A. Gittins & Kirk L. Davies. (Illus.). 578p. (C). 1998. pap. text 50.00 (*0-7881-7260-3*) DIANE Pub.

Military Committee of the North Atlantic Alliance: A Study of Structure & Strategy. Douglas L. Bland. LC 90-7437. 288p. 1990. 65.00 (*0-275-93712-7*, C3712, Praeger Pubs) Greenwood.

Military Communications: A Test for Technology, 2 vols., Set. 1995. lib. bdg. 627.99 (*0-8490-6577-1*) Gordon Pr.

Military Compensation: Trends & Policy Options. Beth J. Asch & James R. Hosek. LC 99-230327. v, 50p. 1999. pap. 6.00 (*0-8330-2742-5*, DB-273-OSD) Rand Corp.

Military Concepts & Philosophy. Henry E. Eccles. LC 65-14457. 359p. reprint ed. pap. 111.30 (*0-608-30739-4*, 205051300084) Bks Demand.

Military Conquest of the Southern Plains. William H. Leckie. LC 63-17160. (Illus.). 295p. reprint ed. 91.50 (*0-8357-9736-8*, 201623600002) Bks Demand.

Military Conscription: An Economic Analysis of the Labour Component in the Armed Forces. S. Duindam. (Contributions to Economics Ser.). (Illus.). viii, 202p. 1999. pap. 53.00 (*3-7908-1203-X*) Spr-Verlag.

***Military Construction Appropriations for Fiscal Year 1999: Hearings Before a Subcommittee of the Committee on Appropriations, United States Senate, 105th Congress, 2nd Session, on H.R. 4059/s. 2160 ....** USGPO Staff. LC 99-170835. iii, 148, p. 1998. write for info. (*0-16-057578-8*) USGPO.

Military Construction Appropriations for 1999: Hearings Before a Subcommittee of the Committee on Appropriations, House of Representatives, One Hundred Fifth Congress, Second Session United States Government. LC 98-158187. 1998. write for info. (*0-16-057014-X*) USGPO.

Military Counselors Manual see What Choice Do We Have?: How States Manipulate Ballot Rules to Restrict Voter Choice

Military Coup d'Etat As a Political Process: Ecuador, 1948-1966. John S. Fitch. LC 76-47381. (Johns Hopkins University Studies in Historical & Political Science: No. 1). 260p. 1977. reprint ed. pap. 80.60 (*0-608-03729-X*, 206455400009) Bks Demand.

Military Coups in Sub-Saharan Africa: How to Justify Illegal Assumptions of Power. Staffan Wiking. 144p. 1983. write for info. (*91-7106-214-9*, Pub. by Nordic Africa) Transaction Pubs.

Military Crimes: Desertion see Military Crimes: Desertion & Desertion Quickfinder

Military Crimes: Desertion & Desertion Quickfinder. Edward M. Byrne. Incl. Military Crimes: Desertion. LC 97-92897. 427p. 1997. Not sold separately (*0-9656899-0-5*); Military Crimes: Desertion Quickfinder. LC 97-92898. 1171p. 1997. Not sold separately (*0-9656899-1-3*); 249.00 (*0-9656899-2-1*) LawQuest Pub.

Military Crimes: Desertion Quickfinder see Military Crimes: Desertion & Desertion Quickfinder

Military Criminal Justice: Practice & Procedure. 3rd ed. David A. Schlueter. 1220p. 1992. 110.00 (*0-87473-965-9*, MICHIE) LEXIS Pub.

Military Criminal Justice: Practice & Procedure. 4th ed. David A. Schlueter. 1239p. 1996. text 95.00 (*1-55834-344-X*, 66928-11, MICHIE) LEXIS Pub.

***Military Criminal Justice: Practice & Procedure.** 5th ed. David A. Schlueter. 1500p. 1999. write for info. (*0-327-04999-5*, 6692812) LEXIS Pub.

Military Criminal Justice: 1990 Cumulative Supplement. 2nd ed. David Schlueter. 1990. pap. write for info. (*0-87473-373-1*, 66914-10, MICHIE) LEXIS Pub.

Military Criminal Justice, 1998 Cumulative Supplement: Practice & Procedure. 4th ed. David A. Schlueter. 175p. 1998. pap., suppl. ed. write for info. (*0-327-00491-6*, 6692914) LEXIS Pub.

Military Criminal Procedure: Forms 1997. Schlueter et al. 485p. 1997. text 90.00 (*1-55834-453-5*, 66955-10, MICHIE) LEXIS Pub.

Military Criminal Procedure Forms: 1998 Supplement. David A. Schlueter et al. LC 96-79959. 200p. 1998. write for info. (*0-327-00237-9*, 66956-10) LEXIS Pub.

Military Criminal Procedure Forms: 1999 Cumulative Supplement. David A. Schleuter et al. 125p. 1999. write for info. (*0-327-01414-8*, 6695611) LEXIS Pub.

Military Crisis Management: U. S. Intervention in the Dominican Republic, 1965, 95. Herbert G. Schoonmaker. LC 89-38227. (Contributions in Military Studies Ser.: No. 95). (Illus.). 168p. 1990. 52.95 (*0-313-26685-9*, SMX/, Greenwood Pr) Greenwood.

Military Cryptanalysis, Pt. I. William F. Friedman. 149p. 1979. pap. 28.80 (*0-89412-044-1*) Aegean Park Pr.

Military Cryptanalysis, Pt. II. rev. ed. William F. Friedman. 155p. (C). 1984. pap. 28.80 (*0-89412-064-6*); lib. bdg. 38.30 (*0-89412-111-1*) Aegean Park Pr.

Military Cryptanalysis, Pt. III. William F. Friedman. 125p. 1993. pap. 32.80 (*0-89412-196-0*) Aegean Park Pr.

Military Cryptanalysis, Pt. IV. William F. Friedman. 195p. 1993. pap. 44.80 (*0-89412-198-7*) Aegean Park Pr.

Military Cryptanalytics, Pt. I, Vol. 2. William F. Friedman & Lambros D. Callimahos. 242p. 1985. pap. 34.80 (*0-89412-074-3*) Aegean Park Pr.

Military Cryptanalytics, Vol. 1, Pt. I. William F. Friedman & Lambros D. Callimahos. 235p. 1985. pap. 34.80 (*0-89412-073-5*) Aegean Park Pr.

Military Cryptanalytics, Vol. 1, Pt. II. William F. Friedman & Lambros D. Callimahos. 327p. 1985. pap. 42.80 (*0-89412-075-1*) Aegean Park Pr.

Military Cryptanalytics, Pt. II, Vol. II. William F. Friedman & Lambros D. Callimahos. 341p. (Orig.). 1985. pap. 42.80 (*0-89412-076-X*) Aegean Park Pr.

Military Customs & Traditions. Mark M. Boatner, III. LC 75-17189. (Illus.). 176p. 1976. reprint ed. lib. bdg. 35.00 (*0-8371-8299-9*, BOMCT, Greenwood Pr) Greenwood.

Military Data Processing & Microcomputers: Battlefield Weapons Systems & Technology, Vol. IX. J. W. Ward & G. N. Taylor. LC 82-13159. (Illus.). 225p. 1982. text 31.50 (*0-08-028338-1*, Pergamon Pr); pap. text 16.25 (*0-08-028339-X*, Pergamon Pr) Elsevier.

Military Deception & Strategic Surprise. Ed. by John Gooch & Amos Perlmutter. (Illus.). 200p. 1982. text 49.50 (*0-7146-3202-3*, Pub. by F Cass Pubs) Intl Spec Bk.

Military Dictionary. 399p. 1987. pap. text 40.00 (*0-941375-10-2*) DIANE Pub.

Military Dictionary. Henry L. Scott. LC 68-54782. 674p. 1970. reprint ed. lib. bdg. 35.00 (*0-8371-0648-6*, SCMD, Greenwood Pr) Greenwood.

Military Dimension: Mark II. David Drake. 1995. mass mkt. 5.99 (*0-671-87697-X*) Baen Bks.

Military Dioramas. Jerry Scutts. (Illus.). 64p. 1999. pap. 17.95 (*1-902579-24-0*, Pub. by Compendium) Motorbooks Intl.

Military District of Washington in the War Years, 1942-1945. abr. ed. William H. Cartwright & Louise E. Goeden. Ed. by William M. Offutt et al. 80p. (Orig.). 1995. pap. 4.00 (*0-9643819-1-5*) Innovat Game.

Military Doctrine & the American Character: Reflections on Air-Land Battle. Herbert I. London. LC 84-62054. (Agenda Paper Ser.: No. 14). 79p. reprint ed. pap. 30.00 (*0-7837-2122-6*, 204240400004) Bks Demand.

Military Doctrines for Central Europe. Swedish National Defence Research Institute. Ed. by Lars B. Wallin. 192p. (Orig.). 1986. pap. 47.50 (*0-317-65652-X*) Coronet Bks.

Military Draft: Selected Readings on Conscription. Ed. by Martin Anderson. LC 81-84641. (Publication Ser.: No. 258). 668p. 1982. 7.98 (*0-8179-7581-0*) Hoover Inst Pr.

Military Dress of the Peninsular War, 1800-1814. Martin Windrow. 1997. 39.95 (*1-872004-70-9*) Combined Pub.

Military Drum Beats for School & Drum Corps. George L. Stone. (Illus.). 48p. 1998. pap. text 5.50 (*1-892764-03-2*) G B Stone.

Military Dune Buggies see Land & Sea Series

Military Dune Buggies. Michael Green. (Land & Sea Ser.). (Illus.). (J). 1997. lib. bdg. 19.00 (*0-516-20514-5*) Childrens.

Military Effectiveness, 3 vols. Ed. by Allan R. Millett & Williamson Murray. 1988. write for info. (*0-318-62728-0*) Routledge.

Military Effectiveness, 3 vols., Vol. I: The First World War. Ed. by Allan R. Millett & Williamson Murray. 320p. 1988. 65.00 (*0-04-445053-2*) Routledge.

Military Effectiveness, 3 vols., Vol. II: The Interwar Period. Ed. by Allan R. Millett & Williamson Murray. 320p. 1988. 65.00 (*0-04-445054-0*) Routledge.

Military Effectiveness Vol. 1: The First World War. Ed. by Allan R. Millett & Williamson Murray. (Mershon Center Series on International Security & Foreign Policy). 384p. 1989. pap. text 24.95 (*0-04-445578-X*) Routledge.

Military Eitzen. 4th ed. K. Eitzen. (ENG & GER.). 547p. 1988. lib. bdg. 65.00 (*0-8288-3404-0*) Fr & Eur.

Military Electro-Optics Equipment Markets: Despite Peace Dividend, Numerous Segments Still Hot. Market Intelligence Staff. 174p. (Orig.). 1992. 1695.00 (*1-56753-065-6*) Frost & Sullivan.

Military Electromagnetic Compatibility Standards of the United States. John D. Osburn. LC 87-83430. (Electromagnetic Interference & Compatibility Ser.: Vol. 11). (Illus.). 340p. 1988. 45.00 (*0-944916-11-2*) emf-emi Control.

Military Elite & Social Change: Egypt since Napoleon. Morroe Berger. LC DT0100.B38. (Research Monograph: Center for International Studies, Woodrow Wilson School of Public & International Affairs: No. 6). 39p. reprint ed. pap. 30.00 (*0-608-14267-0*, 201572500097) Bks Demand.

Military Encyclopedia of Russia & Eurasia, Vol. 7. Ed. by David R. Jones. 242p. 1996. 40.00 (*0-87569-028-9*, UA770) Academic Intl.

Military Encylopaedic Dictionary. N. Ogarkov. (RUS.). 865p. (C). 1984. 150.00 (*0-7855-6739-9*, Pub. by Collets) St Mut.

Military Engineer: Journal of the Society of American Military Engineers. Ed. by Gordon T. Bratz. 80p. 4.00 (*0-318-16536-8*) Soc Am Mil Eng.

Military Engineering & Technology: Papers Presented at the 1982 American Military Institute Annual Meeting. 46p. 1984. pap. text 22.95 (*0-89126-127-3*) MA-AH Pub.

Military Enterprise & Technological Change: Perspectives on the American Experience. Ed. by Merritt Roe Smith. 408p. 1985. reprint ed. 48.00 (*0-262-19239-X*) MIT Pr.

Military Entomology Operational Handbook. 1991. lib. bdg. 79.95 (*0-8490-4113-9*) Gordon Pr.

Military Entomology Operational Handbook. 1995. lib. bdg. 256.95 (*0-8490-6630-1*) Gordon Pr.

Military Environmental Law Issues Seminar (1989) 133p. 1989. pap. text 15.00 (*1-56986-069-6*) Federal Bar.

Military Equation in Northeast Asia. Stuart E. Johnson & Joseph A. Yager. LC 78-20900. (Studies in Defense Policy). 99p. reprint ed. pap. 30.70 (*0-608-18003-3*, 205631000057) Bks Demand.

Military Equipment in Context. Ed. by C. Van Driel-Murray. (Journal of Roman Military Equipment Studies: Vol. 5). (Illus.). 258p. 1996. pap. 60.00 (*1-900188-19-8*, Pub. by Oxbow Bks) David Brown.

Military Errors of World War II. Kenneth Macksey. (Illus.). 256p. 1993. pap. 16.95 (*1-85409-199-9*) Sterling.

Military Errors of World War Two. Kenneth Macksey. (Illus.). 262p. 1998. pap. 9.95 (*0-304-35083-4*) Sterling.

Military Essays. Aeneas Tacticus. (Loeb Classical Library: No. 156). 19.95 (*0-674-99172-9*) HUP.

Military Establishment of the Yuan Dynasty. Ch'I-Ch'Ing Hsiao. (East Asian Monographs: No. 77). 350p. 1977. 30.00 (*0-674-57461-3*) HUP.

Military Ethics: Guidelines for Peace & War. N. Fotion & Gerard Elfstrom. 288p. (C). 1986. text 32.50 (*0-7102-0182-6*, Routledge Thoemms) Routledge.

Military Ethics: Reflections on Principles-the Profession of Arms, Military Leadership, Ethical Practices, War & Morality, Educating the Citizen-Soldier. Ed. by Malham M. Wakin & James Kempf. 250p. (Orig.). (C). 1994. pap. text 50.00 (*0-7881-1311-9*) DIANE Pub.

Military Evidentiary Foundations. Stephen A. Saltzburg et al. 468p. 1994. 75.00 (*1-55834-131-5*, 66895-10, MICHIE) LEXIS Pub.

Military Evidentiary Foundations: 1998 Cumulative Supplement. David A. Schlueter et al. 131p. 1998. pap. 75.00 (*0-327-00577-7*, 6689614) LEXIS Pub.

***Military Evidentiary Foundations, 1999 Cumulative Supplement: Pocketpart.** David A. Schlueter et al. 180p. 1999. suppl. ed. write for info. (*0-327-01722-8*, 6689615) LEXIS Pub.

Military Expansion, Economic Decline: The Impact of Military Spending on U. S. Economic Performance. expanded ed. Robert W. DeGrasse. LC 83-12680. (Illus.). 256p. 1983. reprint ed. pap. 79.40 (*0-7837-9964-0*, 206069100006) Bks Demand.

Military Expansion, Economic Decline: The Impact of Military Spending on U. S. Economic Performance. rev. ed. Robert W. DeGrasse, Jr. LC 83-12360. 260p. (gr. 13). 1983. pap. text 39.95 (*0-87332-260-6*) M E Sharpe.

Military Expenditure: The Political Economy of International Security. Saadet Deger & Somnath Sen. (SIPRI Strategic Issue Papers). (Illus.). 198p. 1991. text 48.00 (*0-19-829141-8*) OUP.

Military Expert in the Age of Reason. Christopher Duffy. 1998. pap. 12.99 (*1-85326-690-6*, Pub. by Wrdsworth Edits) Combined Pub.

Military Explosives. (Explosives & Ser.). 1989. lib. bdg. 250.00 (*0-8490-3978-9*) Gordon Pr.

Military Explosives. 1991. lib. bdg. 79.95 (*0-8490-4071-X*) Gordon Pr.

Military Factor in Nigeria, 1966-1985. Falola Toyin & A. Ajayi. Ed. by A. Alao & B. Babawale. LC 93-50870. (African Studies: Vol. 35). 252p. 1994. text 89.95 (*0-7734-9130-9*) E Mellen.

Military Factor in Social Change Vol. 1: From Provincial to Political Society. Henry Barbera. LC 97-20090. (State As Revolution Ser.). 280p. 1997. text 39.95 (*1-56000-342-1*) Transaction Pubs.

Military Factor in Social Change Vol. 2: The State As Revolution. Henry Barbera. LC 97-20090. 370p. 1998. text 49.95 (*1-56000-356-1*) Transaction Pubs.

Military Families: Adaptation to Change. Edna J. Hunter & Stephen D. Nice. LC 78-13067. (Praeger Special Studies). 278p. 1978. 65.00 (*0-275-90299-4*, C0299, Praeger Pubs) Greenwood.

***Military Family: A Practice Guide for Human Service Providers.** James A. Martin et al. LC 99-55036. 304p. 2000. 59.95 (*0-275-96540-6*) Greenwood.

Military Family Housing: Opportunities Exist to Reduce Costs & Mitigate Inequities. James Murphy. (Illus.). 46p. (Orig.). (C). 1996. pap. text 25.00 (*0-7881-3578-3*) DIANE Pub.

Military Family Housing in the U. S. (Illus.). 66p. (Orig.). (C). 1993. pap. text 20.00 (*0-7881-0008-4*) DIANE Pub.

Military Family in Peace & War. Ed. by Florence R. Kaslow. LC 93-14560. 296p. 1993. 58.00 (*0-8261-8270-4*) Springer Pub.

Military Fiber Optics & Communications, 1987: Washington, D. C. 1997. 100.00 (*0-614-26496-0*, 133M87) Info Gatekeepers.

Military Fiber Optics & Communications, 1988: Washington, D. C. 1997. 100.00 (*0-614-26502-9*, 133M88) Info Gatekeepers.

Military Fiber Optics & Communications, 1988: West Los Angeles. 1997. 100.00 (*0-614-26506-1*, MW88PR) Info Gatekeepers.

Military Fiber Optics & Communications, 1989: Washington, D. C. 1997. 125.00 (*0-614-26515-0*, M89PRC) Info Gatekeepers.

Military Flight Aptitude Tests. Solomon Wiener. (Illus.). 352p. 1989. pap. 17.00 (*0-13-583022-2*, Arco) Macmillan Gen Ref.

Military Flight Aptitude Tests. 2nd ed. Solomon Wiener. LC 94-7659. (Illus.). 352p. 1994. pap. 20.00 (*0-671-84821-6*) P-H.

Military Flight Aptitude Tests: Everything You Need To Score High On. 4th ed. Solomon Wiener. 368p. 1999. pap. text 24.95 (*0-02-863544-2*, Arco) Macmillan Gen Ref.

Military Force. Julian Lider. 360p. 1981. text 85.95 (*0-566-00296-5*) Ashgate Pub Co.

Military Force As an Instrument of U. S. Foreign Policy: The Case of America's Intervention in Lebanon, August 1982 - February 1984. Ralph A. Hallenbeck. LC 90-49218. 248p. 1991. 62.95 (*0-275-93710-0*, C3710, Praeger Pubs) Greenwood.

M

M

Military Fortifications: A Selective Bibliography, 4. Compiled by Dale E. Floyd. LC 91-24840. (Bibliographies & Indexes in Military Studies: No. 4). 384p. 1992. lib. bdg. 79.50 (*0-313-28220-X*, FLF, Greenwood Pr) Greenwood.

Military Franchise. Akin O. Akindele. 170p. 1993. pap. 14.95 (*1-880365-97-9*) Prof Pr NC.

Military Frontier. (Understanding Computers Ser.). 128p. (gr. 7). 1999. 16.95 (*0-8094-5729-6*) Time-Life.

Military Frontier. rev. ed. (Understanding Computers Ser.). (Illus.). 128p. 1991. lib. bdg. 25.93 (*0-8094-7611-8*) Time-Life.

Military Garden: Instructions for All Young Souldiers. James Achesone. LC 74-80157. (English Experience Ser.: No. 637). 36p. 1974. reprint ed. 15.00 (*90-221-0637-3*) Walter J Johnson.

Military Geography: For Professionals & the Public. John M. Collins. LC 98-24963. (Association of the U. S. Army Book Ser.). (Illus.). 460p. 1998. pap. 32.95 (*1-57488-180-9*) Brasseys.

Military Geography: For Professionals & the Public. John M. Collins. LC 97-34721. 1997. write for info. (*1-57906-002-1*) Natl Defense.

Military Geography for Professionals & the Public. John M. Collins. 459p. 1998. per. 39.00 (*0-16-049405-2*) USGPO.

Military Geology in War & Peace. James R. Underwood & Peter L. Guth. LC 98-7163. (Reviews in Engineering Geology Ser.: Vol. 13). 245p. 1998. 76.00 (*0-8137-4113-0*) Geol Soc.

***Military, Goverment & Aerospace Simulation.** Ed. by Michael J. Chinni. 188p. 1999. pap. 80.00 (*1-56555-168-0*) Soc Computer Sim.

Military, Government & Aerospace Simulation. Ed. by Michael J. Chinni. 200p. 1994. 80.00 (*1-56555-072-2*) Soc Computer Sim.

Military, Government & Aerospace Simulation. Ed. by Michael J. Chinni. 191p. 1995. 100.00 (*1-56555-075-7*, SS-27-4) Soc Computer Sim.

Military, Government & Aerospace Simulation. Ed. by Michael J. Chinni. 270p. 1996. 80.00 (*1-56555-093-5*, SS-28-3) Soc Computer Sim.

***Military, Government & Aerospace Simulation.** Ed. by Michael J. Chinni. (Simulation Ser.: Vol. 29, No. 4). 252p. 1998. 80.00 (*1-56555-120-6*, SS-29-4) Soc Computer Sim.

***Military, Government & Aerospace Simulation.** Ed. by Michael J. Chinni. Vol. 30. 236p. 1998. 50.00 (*1-56555-143-5*) Soc Computer Sim.

Military Government & the Movement Toward Democracy in South America. Ed. by Howard Handelman & Thomas G. Sanders. LC 80-8765. 416p. 1981. 15.95 (*0-253-10555-2*) Ind U Pr.

Military Government & the Movement Toward Democracy in South America. Ed. by Howard Handelman & Thomas G. Sanders. LC 80-8765. 416p. 1991. pap. text 11.95 (*0-253-23645-2*) Ind U Pr.

Military Government in the Territories Administered by Israel, 1967-1980 Vol. I: The Legal Aspects. Ed. by Meir Shamgar. 520p. 1986. 47.50 (*1-57588-332-5*, 304420) W S Hein.

Military Ground Rappelling Techniques. 1995. lib. bdg. 255.95 (*0-8490-6667-0*) Gordon Pr.

Military Handbook & Soldier's Manual of Information: Authentic Reproduction of 1861 Handbook. Orville J. Victor. 148p. 1994. pap. 9.95 (*0-9640619-3-7*) C W Heritage.

Military Handbooks of Arabia, 1913-1917, 10 vols., Set. Archive Editions Staff. (Illus.). 5140p. (C). 1988. reprint ed. lib. bdg. 1495.00 (*1-85207-080-3*, Pub. by Archive Editions) N Ross.

Military Helicopter Design Technology. Raymond W. Prouty. LC 97-28755. (Illus.). 148p. (C). 1998. reprint ed. text 38.50 (*1-57524-067-X*) Krieger.

Military Helicopter Doctrines of the Major Powers, 1945-1992: Making Decisions about Air-Land Warfare, 137. Matthew Allen. LC 92-32230. (Contributions in Military Studies Ser.: No. 137). 328p. 1993. 69.50 (*0-313-28522-5*, AMY, Greenwood Pr) Greenwood.

Military Helicopters. E. J. Everett-Heath et al. Ed. by R. G. Lee & Frank Hartley. (Land Warfare: Brassey's New Battlefield Weapons & Technology Ser.: Vol. 6). 177p. 1990. 40.00 (*0-08-037341-0*, Pub. by Brasseys); 25.00 (*0-08-036716-X*, Pub. by Brasseys) Brasseys.

Military Helicopters. P. G. Harrison. (Battlefield Weapons Systems & Technology Ser.: Vol. 11). 200p. 1985. pap. text 19.25 (*0-08-029959-8*, Pergamon Pr) Elsevier.

Military Helicopters. P. G. Harrison. (Battlefield Weapons Systems & Technology Ser.: Vol. XI). 200p. 1985. text 36.00 (*0-08-029958-X*, Pergamon Pr) Elsevier.

Military Heretics: The Unorthodox in Policy & Strategy. Ed. by B. J. McKercher & A. Hamish Ion. LC 93-14116. 256p. 1993. 62.95 (*0-275-94554-5*, C4554, Praeger Pubs) Greenwood.

Military Heroes of New Mexico Military Institute. Joseph D. Posz. LC 94-65906. (Illus.). 108p. 1994. 21.67 (*0-9641019-0-4*) N Mex Military.

Military History. (Illus.). 448p. 1991. 27.50 (*0-685-48206-5*) S&S Trade.

Military History & Atlas of the Napoleonic Wars. Vincent J. Esposito & John R. Elting. (Illus.). 400p. 1999. 80.00 (*1-85367-346-3*, Pub. by Greenhill Bks) Stackpole.

Military History & Atlas of the Napoleonic Wars. Vincent J. Esposito & John R. Elting. LC 77-14708. 1978. reprint ed. write for info. (*0-404-16950-3*) AMS Pr.

Military History & the Military Profession. Ed. by David A. Charters et al. LC 92-9114. 264p. 1992. 55.00 (*0-275-94072-1*, C4072, Praeger Pubs) Greenwood.

***Military History of Australia.** rev. ed. Jeffrey Grey. LC 98-54959. (Illus.). 320p. (C). 1999. 64.95 (*0-521-64283-3*); pap. 24.95 (*0-521-64483-6*) Cambridge U Pr.

***Military History of Boston's Harbor Islands: Massachusetts.** Gerald Butler. LC 00-104053. (Images of America Ser.). (Illus.). 128p. 2000. pap. 18.99 (*0-7385-0464-5*) Arcadia Publng.

***Military History of Canada: From Champlain to Kosovo.** 4th rev. ed. Desmond Morton. 368p. 2000. pap. 24.99 (*0-7710-6514-0*) McCland & Stewart.

Military History of Ceylon: An Outline. Anton Muttukumaru. 227p. (C). 1987. 36.00 (*81-7013-046-8*, Pub. by Navarang) S Asia.

***Military History of China.** Graff. 2000. 65.00 (*0-8133-3736-4*, Pub. by Westview) HarpC.

Military History of India. H. C. Kar. 1980. 17.50 (*0-8364-1588-4*) S Asia.

Military History of Ireland. Thomas Bartlett. Ed. by Keith Jeffrey. (Illus.). 592p. 1997. pap. text 27.95 (*0-521-62989-6*) Cambridge U Pr.

Military History of Ireland. Ed. by Thomas Bartlett & Keith Jeffery. (Illus.). 591p. (C). 1996. text 69.95 (*0-521-41599-3*) Cambridge U Pr.

Military History of Mississippi, 1803-1898. Dunbar Rowland. LC 78-2454. 704p. 1999. reprint ed. 47.50 (*0-87152-266-7*) Reprint.

Military History of Modern China, 1924 to 1949. Frederick F. Lio. LC 81-6577. 312p. 1981. reprint ed. lib. bdg. 59.75 (*0-313-23012-9*, LIMH, Greenwood Pr) Greenwood.

Military History of Russia. Kagan Higman. 1999. text Price not set. (*0-312-22635-7*) St Martin.

Military History of the Campaigns of 1882 in Egypt Prepared in the Intelligence Branch of the War Office. J. F. Maurice. 228p. (C). 1987. reprint ed. 110.00 (*0-7855-2218-2*, Pub. by Picton) St Mut.

Military History of the Third World since 1945: A Reference Guide. Claude C. Sturgill. LC 93-35391. 256p. 1994. lib. bdg. 75.00 (*0-313-28152-1*, Greenwood Pr) Greenwood.

Military History of the Western World, 3 vols. J. F. Fuller. Incl. Vol. 1. From the Earliest Times to the Battle of Lepanto. 602p. 1987. reprint ed. pap. 17.50 (*0-306-80304-6*); Vol. 2. From the Defeat of the Spanish Armada to the Battle of Waterloo. 562p. 1987. reprint ed. pap. 15.95 (*0-306-80305-4*); Vol. 3. From the American Civil War to the End of World War II. 666p. 1987. reprint ed. pap. 15.95 (*0-306-80306-2*); reprint ed. write for info. (*0-685-73875-2*) Da Capo.

Military History of Ulysses S. Grant, from April, 1861 to April, 1865. Adam Badeau. 1977. 79.95 (*0-8369-7150-7*, 7982) Ayer.

Military History of Wayne County: The County in the Civil War. Lewis H. Clark. (Illus.). 924p. 1997. reprint ed. lib. bdg. 92.50 (*0-8328-6272-X*) Higginson Bk Co.

Military History Official & Statistical Register of the State of Mississippi, Military History Only. Dunbar Rowland. 565p. 1995. reprint ed. lib. bdg. 59.50 (*0-8328-6546-X*) Higginson Bk Co.

Military History Symposium Series of the United States Air Force Academy. Ed. by Carl W. Reddel. (Orig.). 1993. write for info. (*1-879176-14-9*) Imprint Pubns.

***Military History Tennessee Army National Guard: Honoring Delta Company 1/278th ACR Loudon County.** Jess Walker. (Illus.). 93p. 1998. pap. write for info. (*1-882194-39-X*) TN Valley Pub.

Military History's Magazine Tenth Anniversary Index. Military History Magazine Staff. Ed. by C. Brian Kelly. (Illus.). (Orig.). (C). 1994. pap. text 21.95 (*1-884641-03-2*) Cowles Enthusiast.

Military Holsters of World War II. Eugene J. Bender. (Illus.). 215p. 1998. reprint ed. 45.00 (*1-884849-27-X*) R&R Bks.

Military Housing: Privatization off to a Slow Start & Continued Management Attention Needed. Carol Schuster. (Illus.). 57p. (C). 1999. pap. text 20.00 (*0-7881-7786-9*) DIANE Pub.

***Military Illustration.** M. Tamiya. (Illus.). 80p. (Orig.). 2000. reprint ed. pap. 39.95 (*4-7661-0404-8*, Pub. by Graphic-Sha) Bks Nippan.

Military Implications of United Nations Peacekeeping Operations. (Illus.). 100p. (Orig.). (C). 1994. pap. text 25.00 (*0-7881-1191-4*) DIANE Pub.

Military Implications of United Nations Peacekeeping Operations. (Orig.). 1997. lib. bdg. 250.95 (*0-8490-7641-2*) Gordon Pr.

Military Improvisations During the Russian Campaign. (Center for Military History Publication German Report Series, DA Pam: No. 104-1). (Illus.). 118p. (Orig.). 1996. reprint ed. pap. 5.00 (*0-16-001944-3*, S/N 008-029-00142-0) USGPO.

Military in African Politics. Ed. by John W. Harbeson. LC 86-30641. 208p. 1987. 55.00 (*0-275-92295-2*, C2295, Praeger Pubs) Greenwood.

Military in America: From the Colonial Era to the Present. 2nd rev. ed. Ed. by Peter Karsten. LC 79-7846. (Illus.). 480p. 1986. pap. 19.95 (*0-02-919190-4*) Free Pr.

Military in British India: The Development of British Land Forces in South Asia, 1600-1947. T. A. Heathcote. LC 94-18101. (Manchester History of the British Army Ser.). 1995. text 79.95 (*0-7190-3570-8*, Pub. by Manchester Univ Pr) St Martin.

Military in Contemporary Soviet Politics: An Institutional Analysis. Edward L. Warner, III. LC 77-83476. (Praeger Special Studies). 314p. 1978. 69.50 (*0-275-90320-6*, C0320, Praeger Pubs) Greenwood.

Military in Greek Politics: From Independence to Democracy. Thanos Veremis. 230p. 1997. 52.99 (*1-55164-105-4*, Pub. by Black Rose); pap. text 23.99 (*1-55164-104-6*, Pub. by Black Rose) Consort Bk Sales.

Military in Greek Politics: The 1909 Coup D'Etat. S. Victor Papacosma. LC 77-22391. 266p. reprint ed. pap. 82.50 (*0-7837-0505-0*, 204082900018) Bks Demand.

Military in Politics & Society in France & Germany in the Twentieth Century. Ed. by Klaus-Jurgen Muller et al. LC 94-46596. (German Historical Perspectives Ser.: Vol. 9). 176p. 1995. 37.50 (*0-85496-812-1*) Berg Pubs.

Military in the Development Process: A Guide to Issues. Nicole Ball. LC 81-21009. (Guides to Contemporary Issues Ser.: No. 2). 124p. (C). 1981. 17.95 (*0-941690-02-4*); pap. 10.95 (*0-941690-03-2*) Regina Bks.

Military in the Middle East: Problems in Society & Government. Sydney N. Fisher. LC 63-9001. (Ohio State University Graduate Institute for World Affairs Ser.: No. 1). 147p. reprint ed. pap. 45.60 (*0-608-30149-3*, 200051100028) Bks Demand.

Military in the Service of Society & Democracy, 153. Ed. by Daniella Ashkenazy. LC 93-28030. (Contributions in Military Studies Ser.: No. 153). 256p. 1994. 62.95 (*0-313-29004-0*, GM9004, Greenwood Pr) Greenwood.

Military in Your Backyard: How to Determine the Impact of Military Spending in Your Community. Randy Schutt. 176p. (Orig.). 1984. pap. 13.00 (*0-930471-00-8*) Ctr Econ Conversion.

Military Incapacity & What It Costs the Country. Charles Ellet. (Notable American Authors Ser.). 1992. reprint ed. lib. bdg. 75.00 (*0-7812-2796-8*) Rprt Serv.

Military Incompetence: Why the American Military Doesn't Win. Richard A. Gabriel. xii, 212p. 1986. pap. 10.95 (*0-374-52137-9*) FS&G.

Military-Industrial Complex: A Historical Perspective. Paul A. Koistinen. LC 79-20569. 168p. 1980. 39.95 (*0-275-90506-3*, C0506, Praeger Pubs) Greenwood.

Military-Industrial Complex: Eisenhower's Warning Three Decades Later. Ed. by Gregg B. Walker et al. LC 91-46428. (American University Studies: Political Science: Ser. X, Vol. 32). XV, 371p. (C). 1992. text 61.95 (*0-8204-1540-5*) P Lang Pubng.

Military-Industrial Complex: The Cases of Sweden & Japan. Masako Ikegami-Andersson. 154p. 1992. 72.95 (*1-85521-309-5*, Pub. by Dartmth Pub) Ashgate Pub Co.

Military-Industrial Complex & United States Foreign Policy. Ed. by Omer L. Carey. LC 71-8835. 74p. reprint ed. pap. 30.00 (*0-608-18354-7*, 203303500083) Bks Demand.

Military-Industrial Firm: A Practical Theory & Model. John F. Gorgol. LC 75-170024. (Special Studies in U. S. Economic, Social & Political Issues). 1972. 32.50 (*0-275-28229-5*) Irvington.

Military Industrialization & Economic Development: Theory & Historical Case Studies. Raimo Vayryen. 130p. 1992. 66.95 (*1-85521-286-2*, Pub. by Dartmth Pub) Ashgate Pub Co.

Military Innovation in the Interwar Period. Ed. by Allan R. Millett & Williamson Murray. 442p. 1998. pap. text 19.95 (*0-521-63760-0*) Cambridge U Pr.

Military Innovation in the Interwar Period. Ed. by Williamson Murray & Allan R. Millett. 442p. (C). 1996. text 74.95 (*0-521-55241-9*) Cambridge U Pr.

Military Institutions & Coercion in the Developing Nations: An Essay in Comparative Analysis. Morris Janowitz. LC 76-50462. (Orig.). 1993. lib. bdg. 8.00 (*0-226-39309-7*) U Ch Pr.

Military Institutions & Coercion in the Developing Nations: Expanded Edition of the Military in the Political Development of New Nations. Morris Janowitz. 232p. 1988. pap. text 15.95 (*0-226-39319-4*, Midway Reprint) U Ch Pr.

Military Institutions of the Romans. Flavia Vegetius Renatus. Ed. by Thomas Phillips. Tr. by John O. Clark from LAT. LC 84-23484. 114p. 1985. reprint ed. lib. bdg. 57.50 (*0-313-24690-4*, VEMI, Greenwood Pr) Greenwood.

Military Institutions on the Welsh Marches: Shropshire, AD 1066-1300. Frederick Suppe. (Studies in Celtic History: No. 14). (Illus.). 203p. (C). 1994. 75.00 (*0-85115-304-6*) Boydell & Brewer.

Military Intellectuals in Britain, 1918 to 1939. Robin D. Higham. LC 81-4917. xi, 267p. 1981. reprint ed. lib. bdg. 65.00 (*0-313-23008-0*, HIMI, Greenwood Pr) Greenwood.

Military Intelligence A History. Peter Gudgin. 1999. 36.00 (*0-7509-1870-5*) Bks Intl VA.

Military Intelligence: A Picture History. John Patrick Finnegan. LC 96-44554. (Center of Military History Publication Ser.: Vol. 60). (Illus.). 457p. 1998. boxed set 39.00 (*0-16-048828-1*) USGPO.

Military Intelligence: A Picture History. John Patrick Finnegan & Romana Danysh. 205p. 1993. boxed set 22.00 (*0-16-038020-0*) USGPO.

***Military Intelligence Blunders.** John Hughes Wilson. 384p. 2000. pap. 12.95 (*0-7867-0715-1*) Carroll & Graf.

Military Intelligence, 1870-1991: A Research Guide, 6. Jonathan M. House. LC 93-226. 184p. 1993. lib. bdg. 59.95 (*0-313-27403-7*, HMD/, Greenwood Pr) Greenwood.

***Military Intelligence (In the U. S. Army)** John Patrick Finnegan & Romana Danysh. (Illus.). 437p. (C). 2000. text 65.00 (*0-7881-8680-9*) DIANE Pub.

Military Intelligence Organizations. 1991. lib. bdg. 79.95 (*0-8490-4116-3*) Gordon Pr.

Military Intelligence Organizations. 1990. lib. bdg. 79.95 (*0-87700-889-2*) Revisionist Pr.

***Military Intelligence Story: A Photo History.** John P. Finnegan. 165p. 1998. boxed set 16.00 (*0-16-049335-8*) USGPO.

Military Intelligence Story: A Photographic History. 2nd ed. 153p. text. write for info. (*0-7881-8975-1*) DIANE Pub.

Military Intervenes: Case Studies in Political Development. Ed. by Henry S. Bienen. LC 67-31395. 176p. 1968. 25.00 (*0-87154-110-6*) Russell Sage.

Military Intervention: From Gunboat Diplomacy to Humanitarian Intervention. Andrew M. Dorman & Thomas G. Otte. (Illus.). 224p. 1995. text 81.95 (*1-85521-579-9*, Pub. by Dartmth Pub) Ashgate Pub Co.

Military Intervention in the 1990s. Richard M. Connaughton. LC 92-7938. (Operational Level of War Ser.). (Illus.). 208p. (C). 1993. pap. 27.99 (*0-415-07991-8*, A9791) Routledge.

Military Intervention in the Third World: Threats, Constraints, & Options. John H. Maurer & Richard H. Porth. LC 84-11685. (Foreign Policy Issues Ser.). 1984. 62.95 (*0-275-91223-X*, C1223, Praeger Pubs) Greenwood.

Military Investor's Handbook. Andrew C. Robertson. LC 85-70435. 179p. 1985. pap. 9.95 (*0-935871-00-4*) Global Man.

Military Jeeps, 1941 to 1945. T. Richards. 100p. 1985. pap. 17.95 (*0-946489-27-0*) Portrayal.

Military Journal of Major Ebenezer Denny: An Officer in the Revolutionary & Indian Wars. Ebenezer Denny. LC 70-140860. (Eyewitness Accounts of the American Revolution Ser.). 1971. reprint ed. 25.95 (*0-405-01214-4*) Ayer.

Military Journal of Major Ebenezer Denny: An Officer in the Revolutionary & Indian Wars, with an Introductory Memoir. Ebenezer Denny. (American Biography Ser.). 288p. 1991. reprint ed. lib. bdg. 69.00 (*0-7812-8105-9*) Rprt Serv.

Military Journal of the American Revolution. James Thacher. Ed. by Peter Decker. LC 74-79946. (Eyewitness Accounts of the American Revolution Ser.). (Illus.). 1978. reprint ed. 36.95 (*0-405-01184-9*) Ayer.

Military Journal of the American Revolution: From the Commencement to the Disbanding of the American Army, 1775-1783. 2nd unabridged ed. James Thacher. (Illus.). 576p. (C). 1998. reprint ed. pap. 21.95 (*0-87928-124-3*) Corner Hse.

Military Journals of Two Private Soldiers, 1758-1775. Ed. by Abraham Tomlinson. LC 70-117895. (Select Bibliographies Reprint Ser.). 1977. 18.95 (*0-8369-5348-7*) Ayer.

Military Journals of Two Private Soldiers, 1758-1775. A. Tomlinson. LC 75-146146. (Era of the American Revolution Ser.). 1971. reprint ed. lib. bdg. 19.50 (*0-306-70134-0*) Da Capo.

Military Justice Citations. Shepard's Citations, Inc. Staff. LC 85-1832. 1985. 235.00 (*0-685-10266-1*) Shepards.

Military Knife Combat. unabridged ed. W. Hock Hochheim. Ed. by Jane Eden. (Knife Fighting Encyclopedia Ser.: No. 2). (Illus.). 169p. 1999. pap. 24.95 (*0-9657302-1-2*, Pub. by Lauric Press) Herveys Bklink.

Military Knife Fighting. Robert K. Spear. (Illus.). 138p. (Orig.). 1991. pap. 9.95 (*0-9622627-6-5*) U Force Dynamics.

Military Landscape: Mathematical Models of Combat. Ed. by J. T. Dockery & A. E. Woodcock. 608p. 1995. boxed set 285.00 (*1-85573-077-4*, Pub. by Woodhead Pubng) Am Educ Systs.

Military Law & Precedents. William Winthrop. Ed. by Richard H. Kohn. LC 78-74061. (American Military Experience Ser.). 1980. reprint ed. lib. bdg. 80.95 (*0-405-11895-3*) Ayer.

***Military Law & Precedents.** 2nd rev. enl. ed. William Winthrop. LC 00-33592. 2000. write for info. (*1-57588-643-X*) W S Hein.

Military Law & Precedents, 2 vols., Set. 2nd ed. William Winthrop. Ed. by Igor I. Kavass & Adolf Sprudzs. LC 79-91717. (International Military Law & History Ser.: Vol. 11). 1116p. 1979. reprint ed. lib. bdg. 63.00 (*0-930342-72-0*, 301890) W S Hein.

Military Law at a Glance. B. S. Jain. 176p. (C). 1989. pap. 30.00 (*81-7002-051-4*, Pub. by Himalayan Bks) St Mut.

Military Law at a Glance: Handbook for Army Promotion Exams, 1989. 3rd ed. B. S. Jain. (C). 1989. 60.00 (*0-7855-4757-6*) St Mut.

Military Law in a Nutshell. 2nd ed. Charles A. Shanor & L. Lynn Hogue. (Nutshell Ser.). 370p. (C). 1996. pap. 22.95 (*0-314-06590-3*) West Pub.

Military Law in India. O. P. Sharma. (C). 1990. 100.00 (*0-89771-297-8*) St Mut.

Military Law Review. Government Printing Office Staff. pap. 12.00 (*0-16-010250-2*) USGPO.

Military Laws of the U. S. From the Civil War Through the War Powers Act of 1973: An Original Anthology. Ed. by Richard H. Kohn. LC 78-74063. (American Military Experience Ser.). 1979. lib. bdg. 44.95 (*0-405-11894-5*) Ayer.

Military Leaders. Macmillan Staff. (Macmillan Profiles Ser.). 1998. per. 75.00 (*0-02-864981-8*) Macmillan.

***Military Leaders in the Civil War.** Joseph B. Mitchell. 252p. 1999. pap. 40.00 (*1-86227-075-9*, Pub. by Spellmnt Pubs) St Mut.

Military Leaders of the Civil War. Patrick A. Tracey. LC 92-34346. (American Profiles Ser.). (Illus.). 128p. (YA). (gr. 5-12). 1993. 19.95 (*0-8160-2671-8*) Facts on File.

Military Leaders of the Civil War. Joseph B. Mitchell. LC 88-24681. (Illus.). 251p. 1988. reprint ed. pap. 10.95 (*0-939009-13-7*, EPM) Howell Pr VA.

Military Leaders of World War II. Walter Oleksy. LC 93-33641. (American Profiles Ser.). (Illus.). 160p. (J). (gr. 5-12). 1994. 19.95 (*0-8160-3008-1*) Facts on File.

Military Leaders since World War II, 1945-1990. C. W. Borklund. (American Profiles Ser.). (Illus.). 144p. 1992. lib. bdg. 17.95 (*0-8160-2606-8*) Facts on File.

Military Leadership. 1995. lib. bdg. 261.99 (*0-8490-8372-9*) Gordon Pr.

***Military Leadership: In Pursuit of Excellence.** Taylor. LC 99-48661. 2000. 25.00 (*0-8133-6839-1*) Westview.

Military Leadership: In Pursuit of Excellence. 3rd ed. William E. Rosenbach. Ed. by Robert L. Taylor. (C). 1996. pap. text 25.00 (*0-8133-3024-6*, Pub. by Westview) HarpC.

Military Leadership Vol. 3: An Organizational Behavior Perspective. Ed. by David D. Van Fleet et al. LC 85-23975. (Monographs in Organizational Behavior & Industrial Relations: Vol. 3). 327p. 1986. 78.50 (*0-89232-554-2*) Jai Pr.

***Military Leadership in India: The Twelve Captains.** V. K. Singh. 1998. 72.00 (*81-7049-074-X*) Manas Pubns.

Military Leadership in India: Vedic Period to Indo-Pak Wars. Rajendra Nath. 1990. 72.50 (*81-7095-018-X*, Pub. by Lancer India) S Asia.

Military Leadership to Prevent Military Coup. M. L. Chibber. 1987. 26.00 (*0-8364-2211-2*, Pub. by Lancer India) S Asia.

Military Legacy of the Civil War: The European Inheritance. Jay Luvaas. LC 88-27800. (Modern War Studies). (Illus.). xxx, 258p. 1988. pap. 14.95 (*0-7006-0379-4*) U Pr of KS.

Military Legitimacy: Might & Right in the New Millenium. Rudolph C. Barnes, Jr. LC 95-30804. 199p. (C). 1996. 45.00 (*0-7146-4624-5*, Pub. by F Cass Pubs) Intl Spec Bk.

Military Lessons of the Gulf War. Bruce W. Watson. LC 92-41768. 256p. 1993. pap. 14.95 (*1-85367-136-3*) Stackpole.

Military Life under Napoleon: The Memoirs of Captain Elzear Blaze. Elzear Blaze. 1997. 29.50 (*1-883476-06-2*, Pub. by Emperors Pr) Combined Pub.

Military Lifestyle & Children. Robin Wuebker-Battershell. (Family Forum Library). 16p. 1993. 1.95 (*1-56688-072-6*) Bur For At-Risk.

Military Living, Military RV, Camping & Recreation Areas Around the World. William R. Crawford et al. LC 97-10747. 1997. pap. write for info. (*0-914862-65-0*) Military Living Pubns.

Military Living's: Temporary Military Lodging Around the World. Ann C. Crawford et al. LC 97-17542. 1997. pap. write for info. (*0-914862-67-7*) Military Living Pubns.

Military Living's Assignment, Washington: A Guide to Washington Area Military Installations. William R. Crawford & Ann C. Crawford. LC 84-9111. vi, 122p. 1984. write for info. (*0-914862-06-5*) Military Living Pubns.

Military Living's California State Military Road Map. William R. Crawford & L. Ann Crawford. 1994. pap. write for info. (*0-914862-45-6*) Military Living Pubns.

Military Living's Desert Shield Commemorative Maps. William R. Crawford & Lela A. Crawford. 1991. pap. write for info. (*0-914862-27-8*) Military Living Pubns.

Military Living's Florida State Military Road Map. William R. Crawford & L. Ann Crawford. 1994. pap. write for info. (*0-914862-46-4*) Military Living Pubns.

Military Living's Mid-Atlantic United States Military Road Map. William R. Crawford & L. Ann Crawford. 1994. pap. write for info. (*0-914862-47-2*) Military Living Pubns.

***Military Living's Space-A Air Opportunities Around the World.** Ann Caddell Crawford & William Roy Crawford. LC 99-59039. 2000. write for info. (*0-914862-87-1*) Military Living Pubns.

Military Living's Temporary Military Lodging Around the World. Ann C. Crawford et al. LC 98-25190. 1998. 18.45 (*0-914862-72-3*) Military Living Pubns.

Military Living's Texas State Military Road Map. William R. Crawford & L. Ann Crawford. 1994. pap. write for info. (*0-914862-48-0*) Military Living Pubns.

***Military Logistics: The Third Dimension.** Parmodh Sarin. 416p. 2000. 42.00 (*81-7049-090-1*, Pub. by Manas Pubns) Nataraj Bks.

Military Man, Family Man: Crown Property? Ruth A. Jolly. 180p. 1987. 29.00 (*0-08-031204-7*, Pergamon Pr); pap. 14.91 (*0-08-031203-9*, Pergamon Pr) Elsevier.

Military Man, Family Man: Crown Property? 2nd rev. ed. Ruth A. Jolly. 167p. 1992. pap. 21.95 (*1-85753-005-5*, Pub. by Brasseys) Brasseys.

Military Manpower & National Security. Committee for Economic Development. LC 78-189538. 48p. 1972. pap. 1.00 (*0-87186-045-7*) Comm Econ Dev.

Military Marching: A Pictorial History. Ed. by James Edward Cramer. 172p. (C). 1992. 110.00 (*0-946771-79-0*, Pub. by Spellmnt Pubs) St Mut.

Military Market Basket see Lancaster County During the American Revolution Series

Military Market in the United States. American Marketing Association Staff & Murray L. Weidenbaum. LC 63-4878. 57p. reprint ed. pap. 30.00 (*0-608-30676-2*, 200217300011) Bks Demand.

Military Marxist Regimes in Africa. John Markakis. 250p. 1986. 42.50 (*0-7146-3295-3*, Pub. by F Cass Pubs) Intl Spec Bk.

***Military Mavericks: Extraordinary Men of Battle.** David Rooney. (Illus.). 2000. 27.95 (*0-304-35316-7*) Continuum.

Military Maxims of Napoleon. Napoleon Bonaparte. 256p. 1993. 24.95 (*0-947898-64-6*, 5553) Stackpole.

Military Maxims of Napoleon. David G. Chandler. LC 88-21781. 256p. 1988. 19.95 (*0-02-897171-X*) Macmillan.

Military Maxims of Napoleon. Napoleon Bonaparte. Ed. by David G. Chandler & William E. Cairnes. Tr. by George C. D'Aguilar from FRE. (Illus.). 253p. 1995. reprint ed. pap. 13.95 (*0-306-80618-5*) Da Capo.

Military Medals, Decorations & Orders of the United States & Europe: A Photographic Study to the Beginning of WW II. Robert Ball & Paul Peters. (Illus.). 184p. 1994. 45.00 (*0-88740-579-7*) Schiffer.

Military Medicine: Medical Subject Index of Current Progress with Research Bibliography. Roy R. Zimmerman. LC 88-47591. 150p. 1988. 47.50 (*0-88164-734-9*); pap. 44.50 (*0-88164-735-7*) ABBE Pubs Assn.

Military Memoirs of a Confederate: A Critical Narrative. Edward P. Alexander. (Illus.). 658p. 1993. reprint ed. pap. 17.95 (*0-306-80509-X*) Da Capo.

Military Memoirs of General John Pope. Ed. by Peter Cozzens & Robert Girardi. LC 98-13801. (Civil War America Ser.). (Illus.). 320p. 1998. 34.95 (*0-8078-2444-5*) U of NC Pr.

Military Memoirs of Marlborough's Campaigns, 1702-1712. Robert B. Parker et al. LC 98-19844. (Illus.). 276p. 1998. 34.95 (*1-85367-330-7*, Pub. by Greenhill Bks) Stackpole.

Military Men. Wyatt & Sheffield. 76.95 (*1-85928-145-1*) Ashgate Pub Co.

Military Metalurgy. Alistair Doig. (Illus.). 152p. 1998. 40.00 (*1-86125-061-4*, Pub. by Inst Materials) Ashgate Pub Co.

Military Mindlessness: An Informal Compendium. Ed. by Raymond Horricks. 256p. (C). 1993. text 32.95 (*1-56000-105-4*) Transaction Pubs.

Military Minutes of the Council of Appointment of the State of New York, 3 vols., Set, Vols. 1-3. Hugh Hastings. (Illus.). 3038p. 1994. reprint ed. lib. bdg. 280.00 (*0-8328-3805-5*) Higginson Bk Co.

Military Misfortunes: The Anatomy of Failure in War. Eliot A. Cohen & John Gooch. 1990. 29.95 (*0-02-906060-5*) Free Pr.

Military Misfortunes: The Anatomy of Failure in War. Eliot A. Cohen & John Gooch. LC 90-50491. 320p. 1991. pap. 13.00 (*0-679-73296-9*) Vin Bks.

Military Money Guide. P. J. Budahn. 144p. 1996. pap. 10.95 (*0-8117-2557-X*) Stackpole.

Military Motions. American Bar Association, General Practice Staff. LC 86-72226. 27p. 1986. pap. 14.95 (*0-89707-269-3*, 515-0063) Amer Bar Assn.

Military Motorcycles see Land & Sea Series

Military Motorcycles. Michael Green. (Land & Sea Ser.). (Illus.). (J). 1997. 19.00 (*0-516-20515-3*) Childrens.

Military Mountaineering. 1995. lib. bdg. 250.99 (*0-8490-6638-7*) Gordon Pr.

Military Music of the American Revolution. Raoul F. Camus. (Illus.). 231p. 1993. 16.95 (*0-918048-10-9*) Integrity.

Military-Naval Encyclopedia of Russia & the Soviet Union, Vols. 1-6. Ed. by David R. Jones. (MNERSU Ser.). 10.00 (*0-685-73096-4*) Academic Intl.

Military Obedience. N. Keijzer. 349p. 1978. lib. bdg. 99.00 (*90-286-0508-8*) Kluwer Academic.

Military Objectives in Soviet Foreign Policy. Michael McGwire. LC 86-24932. 530p. 1987. 49.95 (*0-8157-5552-X*); pap. 19.95 (*0-8157-5551-1*) Brookings.

Military Occupation & Diplomacy: Soviet Troops in Romania, 1944-1958. Sergiu Verona. LC 91-26601. 224p. 1992. text 42.95 (*0-8223-1171-2*) Duke.

Military Occupational Analysis: A Special Issue of "Military Psychology", Vol. 8, No. 2, 1996. Bennett et al. 1996. pap. 20.00 (*0-8058-9925-1*) L Erlbaum Assocs.

Military 100: A Ranking of the Most Influential Military Leaders of All Time. Michael L. Lanning. (Illus.). 372p. 1999. text 27.00 (*0-7881-6038-9*) DIANE Pub.

Military 100: Ranking of the Most Influential Military Leaders of All Time. Michael L. Lanning. (Illus.). 352p. Date not set. 27.50 (*0-8065-1828-6*, Citadel Pr) Carol Pub Group.

Military Opeartions, Gallipoli, 2 vols., Set. C. F. Aspinall-Oglander. (Great War Ser.). (Illus.). 602p. reprint ed. 89.95 (*0-89839-175-X*) Battery Pr.

Military Operation, 1861-1864: Fayetteville, West Va. & Lynchburg Va. Campaign. Milton W. Humphreys. 103p. 1991. 14.95 (*1-881413-00-4*) Thomas In-Prints.

***Military Operations: Impact of Operations Other Than War on the Services Varies.** Ed. by Steven H. Sternlieb. (Illus.). 64p. (C). 1999. pap. text 20.00 (*0-7881-8490-3*) DIANE Pub.

Military Operations & Maritime Preponderance: Their Relations & Interdependence. C. E. Callwell. Ed. & Intro. by Colin S. Gray. LC 97-102933. (Classics of Sea Power Ser.). (Illus.). 512p. 1996. 39.95 (*1-55750-341-9*) Naval Inst Pr.

Military Operations, East Africa. 11th ed. Charles Hordern. (Great War Ser.: No. 11). 720p. 1990. reprint ed. 49.95 (*0-89839-158-X*) Battery Pr.

Military Operations, Egypt & Palestine, Vol. I. George MacMunn & Cyril Falls. (Great War Ser.: Vol. 46). (Illus.). 469p. 1996. reprint ed. 49.95 (*0-89839-241-1*) Battery Pr.

Military Operations, Egypt & Palestine, Vol. II, Pt. I. Cyril B. Falls. (Great War Ser.: No. 44). (Illus.). 496p. 1996. reprint ed. 49.95 (*0-89839-239-X*) Battery Pr.

Military Operations, Egypt & Palestine, Vol. II, Pt. II. Cyril B. Falls. (Great War Ser.: No. 45). (Illus.). 408p. 1996. reprint ed. 49.95 (*0-89839-240-3*) Battery Pr.

Military Operations, France & Belgium, 1917, Vol. II. James E. Edmonds. (Great War Ser.: No. 16). (Illus.). 576p. reprint ed. 49.95 (*0-89839-166-0*) Battery Pr.

Military Operations, France & Belgium, 1914, Vol. I. James E. Edmonds. (Great War Ser.: No. 43). (Illus.). 577p. 1996. 49.95 (*0-89839-233-0*) Battery Pr.

Military Operations, France & Belgium, 1914, Vol. II. James E. Edmonds. (Great War Ser.). (Illus.). 593p. 1995. reprint ed. 49.95 (*0-89839-232-2*) Battery Pr.

Military Operations, France & Belgium, 1915, Vol. I. James E. Edmonds. (Great War Ser.: No. 36). (Illus.). 433p. 1995. reprint ed. 49.95 (*0-89839-218-7*) Battery Pr.

Military Operations, France & Belgium, 1915, Vol. II. James E. Edmonds. (Great War Ser.: No. 49). (Illus.). 640p. 1995. reprint ed. 49.95 (*0-89839-245-4*) Battery Pr.

Military Operations, France & Belgium, 1916, Vol. I. James E. Edmonds. (Great War Ser.: No. 26). (Illus.). 632p. reprint ed. 49.95 (*0-89839-185-7*) Battery Pr.

Military Operations, France & Belgium, 1916, Vol. II. Wilfred Miles. (Great War Ser.: No. 19). (Illus.). 654p. reprint ed. 49.95 (*0-89839-169-5*) Battery Pr.

Military Operations, France & Belgium, 1916 Vol. I: Appendices. James E. Edmonds. (Great War Ser.: No. 33). 240p. 1995. reprint ed. 39.95 (*0-89839-226-8*) Battery Pr.

Military Operations, France & Belgium, 1916 Vol. II: Maps & Appendices. Wilfrid Miles. (Great War Ser.: No. 34). 135p. 1994. reprint ed. 39.95 (*0-89839-207-1*) Battery Pr.

Military Operations, France & Belgium, 1917, Vol. I. Cyril B. Falls. (Great War Ser.: No. 23). 664p. reprint ed. 49.95 (*0-89839-180-6*) Battery Pr.

Military Operations, France & Belgium, 1917: The Battle of Cambrai, Vol. III. Wilfrid Miles. (Great War Ser.: No. 13). (Illus.). 432p. reprint ed. 49.95 (*0-89839-162-8*) Battery Pr.

Military Operations, France & Belgium, 1917 Vol. I: Appendices. Cyril B. Falls. (Great War Ser.: No. 30). 176p. 1994. 39.95 (*0-89839-202-0*) Battery Pr.

Military Operations, France & Belgium, 1918, Vol. I. James E. Edmonds. (Great War Ser.: No. 37). (Illus.). 648p. 1995. reprint ed. 49.95 (*0-89839-219-5*) Battery Pr.

Military Operations, France & Belgium, 1918, Vol. II. James E. Edmonds. (Great War Ser.: No. 38). (Illus.). 656p. 1995. reprint ed. 49.95 (*0-89839-223-3*) Battery Pr.

Military Operations, France & Belgium, 1918, Vol. III. James E. Edmonds. (Great War Ser.: No. 35). (Illus.). 417p. 1994. 49.95 (*0-89839-211-X*) Battery Pr.

Military Operations, France & Belgium, 1918, Vol. IV. James E. Edmonds. (Great War Ser.: No. 27). (Illus.). 688p. 1993. reprint ed. 54.95 (*0-89839-191-1*) Battery Pr.

Military Operations, France & Belgium, 1918, Vol. V. James E. Edmonds. (Great War Ser.: No. 28). (Illus.). 760p. 1993. reprint ed. 54.95 (*0-89839-192-X*) Battery Pr.

Military Operations, France & Belgium, 1918 Vol. I: Appendices. James E. Edmonds. (Great War Ser.: No. 32). 160p. 1994. reprint ed. 39.95 incl. reel tape (*0-89839-204-7*) Battery Pr.

Military Operations in Burma, 1890 to 1892: Letters from J. K. Watson. James K. Watson. Ed. by B. R. Pearn. LC 67-9137. (Cornell University, Southeast Asia Program, Data Paper Ser.: No. 64). 100p. reprint ed. pap. 31.00 (*0-608-11731-5*, 201047100028) Bks Demand.

Military Operations in Eastern Maine & Nova Scotia During the Revolution. Frederic Kidder. 336p. 1997. reprint ed. lib. bdg. 42.00 (*0-8328-5458-1*) Higginson Bk Co.

Military Operations in Georgia During the War Between the States. Charles C. Jones, Jr. & Joseph B. Cumming. (Illus.). 38p. 1993. reprint ed. pap. 10.95 (*1-56869-040-1*) Oldbuck Pr.

Military Operations in Hanover County, Virginia, 1861-1865. John M. Gabbert. (Illus.). 130p. (Orig.). (C). 1989. pap. write for info. (*0-318-65244-7*) J M Gabbert.

Military Operations in Jefferson County, Virginia & West Virginia, 1861-1865. Ed. by Charles S. Adams. 52p. 1994. pap. 6.95 (*1-888256-00-1*) CS Adams.

***Military Operations in Low Intensity Conflict.** Ed. by Barry Leonard. 150p. 1999. reprint ed. pap. text 35.00 (*0-7881-7894-6*) DIANE Pub.

Military Operations, Italy, 1915-1919. James E. Edmonds. (Great War Ser.: No. 15). (Illus.). 504p. reprint ed. 49.95 (*0-89839-165-2*) Battery Pr.

Military Operations, Macedonia, Vol. I. Cyril Falls. (Great War Ser.: Vol. 47). (Illus.). 472p. 1996. reprint ed. 49.95 (*0-89839-242-X*) Battery Pr.

Military Operations, Macedonia, Vol. II. Cyril Falls. (Great War Ser.: Vol. 48). (Illus.). 381p. 1997. reprint ed. 49.95 (*0-89839-243-8*) Battery Pr.

Military Operations of General Beauregard: In the War Between the States, 1861 to 1865, 2 vols. Alfred Roman. (Illus.). 1994. reprint ed. pap. 17.95 (*0-306-80551-0*) Da Capo.

Military Operations of General Beauregard Vol. 1: In the War Between the States, 1861 to 1865, 2 vols. Alfred Roman. (Illus.). 614p. 1994. reprint ed. write for info. (*0-306-80546-4*) Da Capo.

Military Operations of General Beauregard Vol. 2: In the War Between the States, 1861 to 1865, 2 vols. Alfred Roman. (Illus.). 715p. 1994. reprint ed. 17.95 (*0-306-80547-2*) Da Capo.

Military Operations on Urbanized Terrain. 1995. lib. bdg. 259.99 (*0-8490-6637-9*) Gordon Pr.

Military Operations Research: Quantitative Decision Making. N. K. Jaiswal. LC 96-53961. 400p. (C). 1997. lib. bdg. 140.00 (*0-7923-9858-0*) Kluwer Academic.

Military Operations Research Society Membership Directory. Ed. by Michael P. Cronin. (Orig.). 1996. pap. write for info. (*0-930473-02-7*) Military Opera Res.

Military Operations, Togoland & the Cameroons, 1918, Vol. III. F. J. Moberly. (Great War Ser.: No. 44). (Illus.). 584p. 1995. reprint ed. 69.95 (*0-89839-235-7*) Battery Pr.

Military Order of the Loyal Legion of the United States, 70 vols. Contrib. by William Marvel. (Illus.). 1996. reprint ed. 2400.00 (*1-56837-001-6*) Broadfoot.

Military Order of the Loyal Legion of the United States, Vols. I-IV. Ed. by Janet B. Hewett. 1448p. 1985. 300.00 (*1-56837-341-4*) Broadfoot.

Military Order of World Wars. Turner Publishing Company Staff. LC 95-60320. (Illus.). 208p. 1995. 49.95 (*1-56311-184-5*) Turner Pub KY.

Military Orders: Fighting for the Faith & Caring for the Sick. Ed. by Malcolm Barber. (Illus.). 432p. 1994. text 98.95 (*0-86078-438-X*, Pub. by Variorum) Ashgate Pub Co.

Military Orders: From the Twelfth to the Early Fourteenth Centuries. Alan Forey. 280p. (Orig.). 1992. text 60.00 (*0-8020-2805-5*); pap. text 18.95 (*0-8020-7680-7*) U of Toronto Pr.

Military Orders Vol. 2: Welfare & Warfare. Helen Nicholson. 412p. 1998. text 101.95 (*0-86078-679-X*, Pub. by Ashgate Pub) Ashgate Pub Co.

Military Orders & Crusades. Alan Forey. (Collected Studies: No. CS 432). 328p. 1994. 101.95 (*0-86078-398-7*, Pub. by Variorum) Ashgate Pub Co.

Military Organizations, Complex Machines: Modernization in the U. S. Armed Services. Chris C. Demchak. LC 90-55731. (Cornell Studies in Security Affairs). 224p. 1991. text 39.95 (*0-8014-2468-2*) Cornell U Pr.

Military Origins of Industrialization & International Trade Rivalry. Gautam Sen. 288p. 1995. pap. 22.50 (*1-85567-239-1*) Bks Intl VA.

Military Paintings of Terence Cuneo. Gerald Landy. (Illus.). 192p. 60.00 (*1-872727-51-4*) Pincushion Pr.

Military Pay Gaps & Caps. James R. Hosek et al. LC 94-4160. 1994. pap. 13.00 (*0-8330-1514-1*, MR-368-P&R) Rand Corp.

Military Pay Muddle. Martin Binkin. LC 75-4422. (Studies in Defense Policy). 66p. 1975. pap. 8.95 (*0-8157-0961-7*) Brookings.

Military Periodicals: United States & Selected International Journals & Newspapers. Ed. by Michael E. Unsworth. LC 89-25902. 448p. 1990. lib. bdg. 115.00 (*0-313-25920-8*, UHM/, Greenwood Pr) Greenwood.

Military Personnel. (My Ancestors--My Heroes Ser.: Vol. 49). (J). (gr. 3-4). 2000. write for info. (*1-893091-48-1*) F R Parker.

***Military Personnel: Actions Needed to Better Define Pilot Requirements & Promote Retention.** Marke Gebicke & Brenda S. Farrell. (Illus.). 72p. (C). 2000. pap. text 20.00 (*0-7881-8725-2*) DIANE Pub.

Military Personnel: High Aggregate Personnel Levels Maintained Throughout Drawdown. (Illus.). 43p. (Orig.). (C). 1996. pap. text 20.00 (*0-7881-3243-1*) DIANE Pub.

Military Personnel Measurement: Testing, Assignment, Evaluation. Ed. by Martin F. Wiskoff & Glenn M. Rampton. LC 89-3691. 229p. 1989. 59.95 (*0-275-92924-8*, C2924, Praeger Pubs) Greenwood.

Military Persuasion: Deterrence & Provocation in Crisis & War. Stephen J. Cimbala. LC 93-1202. 1994. 50.00 (*0-271-01005-3*); pap. 18.95 (*0-271-01006-1*) Pa St U Pr.

Military Philosophers see Dance to the Music of Time: Third Movement

***Military Philosophers.** large type unabridged ed. Anthony Powell. 287p. 1999. 25.95 (*0-7531-5822-1*, 158221, Pub. by ISIS Lrg Prnt) ISIS Pub.

Military Phrasebook for Iraqi Arabic. Margerat K. Nydell. 72p. 1990. pap. text 9.95 (*0-9628410-0-5*) DLS VA.

Military Physicians: Dod's Medical School & Scholarship Program. (Illus.). 93p. (Orig.). (C). 1996. pap. text 25.00 (*0-7881-2751-9*) DIANE Pub.

Military Physicians: DOD's Medical School & Scholarship Program. (Illus.). 94p. 1995. pap. text 35.00 (*1-57979-121-2*) DIANE Pub.

Military Pistols of Japan. 3rd ed. Fred L. Honeycutt, Jr. LC 91-90245. (Illus.). 168p. 1991. 42.00 (*0-9623208-4-6*) F L Honeycutt Jr.

***Military Planning & the Origins of the Second World War in Europe.** Ed. by B. J. C. McKercher & Roch Legault. LC 99-52826. 224p. 2000. 62.00 (*0-275-96158-3*, C6158, Praeger Pubs) Greenwood.

Military Planning for Defense of the United Kingdom, 1814-1870, 91. Michael S. Partridge. LC 88-20637. (Contributions in Military Studies Ser.: No. 91). 248p. 1989. 65.00 (*0-313-26871-1*, PMY/, Greenwood Pr) Greenwood.

Military Planning Today: Calculus or Charade? Carl H. Builder. LC 93-28129. 1993. pap. 15.00 (*0-8330-1425-0*, MR-293-AF) Rand Corp.

Military Police. 1997. lib. bdg. 250.99 (*0-8490-8218-8*) Gordon Pr.

***Military Police.** Michael Green. (Serving Your Country Ser.). (Illus.). 48p. (YA). (gr. 5 up). 2000. lib. bdg. 21.26 (*0-7368-0473-0*, Capstone Bks) Capstone Pr.

Military Police: A Professional Bulletin for the Military Police Corps Regiment. Government Printing Office Staff. 1986. pap. 6.50 (*0-16-010358-4*) USGPO.

Military Police Corps[0012] 50th Year. 52p. pap. text 25.00 (*0-7881-2172-3*) DIANE Pub.

Military Police Guide to the Federal Criminal Code, 1999-2000. Barbara J. Birkland & Steven T. Kernes. 247p. 1996. pap. 15.20 (*0-937935-43-3*) Justice Syst Pr.

Military Police Operations. 1989. lib. bdg. 250.00 (*0-8490-3979-7*) Gordon Pr.

Military Police Working Dogs. 1986. lib. bdg. 250.00 (*0-8490-3824-3*) Gordon Pr.

Military Politics from Bonaparte to the Bourbons: The Life & Death of Michel Ney, 1769-1815. Raymond Horricks. LC 94-17380. 286p. (C). 1994. pap. 24.95 (*1-56000-767-2*) Transaction Pubs.

Military Politics in Nigeria: Economic Development & Political Stability. Theophilus O. Odetola. LC 76-58232. (Illus.). 180p. 1975. text 34.95 (*0-87855-100-X*) Transaction Pubs.

M

Military Power: Land Warfare in Theory & Practice. Ed. by Brian H. Reid. LC 96-54594. 272p. (C). 1997. 42.50 (*0-7146-4768-3*, Pub. by Irish Acad Pr); pap. 22.00 (*0-7146-4325-4*, Pub. by Irish Acad Pr) Intl Spec Bk.

Military Power & Policy in Asian States: China, India, Japan. Ed. by Onkar Marwah & Jonathan D. Pollack. LC 79-16241. (Special Studies in Military Affairs). 1983. text 44.00 (*0-89158-407-2*) Westview.

Military Power in a Free Society. Henry E. Eccles. LC 79-10928. 290p. (C). 1979. text 8.50 (*0-9637973-8-7*) Naval War Coll.

Military Preparations of the Arab Community in Palestine, 1945-1948. Haim Levenberg. LC 92-18785. 281p. 1993. text 52.50 (*0-7146-3439-5*, Pub. by F Cass Pubs) Intl Spec Bk.

Military Prepositioning: Army & Air Force Programs Need to be Reassessed. Ed. by Mark E. Gebicke. (Illus.). 72p. (C). 1999. pap. text 20.00 (*0-7881-7770-2*) DIANE Pub.

Military Presence on the Gulf Coast. (Gulf Coast History & Humanities Conference Publications Ser.). 1978. pap. 10.00 (*0-940836-11-4*) U of S AL.

Military Prime Contract Wards: Fiscal Year 1995. (Illus.). 60p. (Orig.). 1996. pap. text 30.00 (*0-7881-3506-6*) DIANE Pub.

Military Procurement Fraud Seminar. 182p. 1987. pap. text 5.00 (*1-56986-162-5*) Federal Bar.

Military Procurement Fraud Seminar. 222p. 1988. pap. text 10.00 (*1-56986-163-3*) Federal Bar.

Military Production & Innovation in Spain, Vol. 2, Issue 2. Jordi Molas-Gallart. LC 92-30353. 212p. 1992. text 101.00 (*3-7186-5280-3*) Gordon & Breach.

Military Propaganda: Psychological Warfare & Operations. Ed. by Ronald D. McLaurin. LC 81-22638. 379p. 1982. 59.95 (*0-275-90859-3*, C0859, Praeger Pubs) Greenwood.

Military Psychiatry: A Comparative Perspective, 57. Ed. by Richard A. Gabriel. LC 86-12107. (Contributions in Military Studies Ser.: No. 57). 225p. 1986. 55.00 (*0-313-25491-5*, GML/, Greenwood Pr) Greenwood.

Military Psychiatry: Preparing in Peace for War. Ed. by Franklin D. Jones et al. (Textbook of Military Medicine. Part I, Warfare, Weaponry, & the Casualty: Vol. 1). 1994. write for info. (*0-614-32111-5*) AFIP DC.

Military Psychology: An Introduction. Christopher Cronin. (Illus.). 324p. (C). 1997. text 42.00 (*0-536-00565-6*) Pearson Custom.

Military Quiz Book. John Pimlott. 128p. 1993. pap. 9.95 (*1-85367-151-7*, 5425) Stackpole.

Military Quotation Book. James Charlton. 1990. text 14.95 (*0-312-04350-3*) St Martin.

Military R&D after the Cold War: Proceedings of the NATO Advanced Research Workshop, Budapest Hungary, 27-31 August, 1994. Ed. by Philip Gummett. LC 96-26718. (NATO Advanced Science Instituten-Partnership Ser.: Sub-Series 4). 216p. (C). 1996. lib. bdg. 129.00 (*0-7923-4139-2*) Kluwer Academic.

Military Readiness: Concepts, Choices, Consequences. Richard K. Betts. LC 94-44266. 280p. (C). 1995. 42.95 (*0-8157-0906-4*); pap. 18.95 (*0-8157-0905-6*) Brookings.

Military Readiness: Data & Trends for January 1990 to March 1995. 23p. (Orig.). (C). 1996. pap. text 15.00 (*0-7881-2867-1*) DIANE Pub.

Military Readiness: Reports to Congress Provide Few Details on Deficiencies & Solutions. Mark E. Gebicke. (Illus.). 46p. 1999. pap. text 20.00 (*0-7881-7969-1*) DIANE Pub.

Military Rebellion in Argentina: Between Coups & Consolidation. Deborah L. Norden. LC 95-32285. (Illus.). vii, 240p. (C). 1996. text 45.00 (*0-8032-3339-6*); pap. text 25.00 (*0-8032-8369-5*, Bison Books) U of Nebr Pr.

Military Reconnaissance Market (U. S.) Market Intelligence Staff. 350p. 1992. 2600.00 (*1-56753-865-7*, A2521) Frost & Sullivan.

Military Record of Louisiana: Including Biographical & Historical Papers Relating to the Military Organizations of the State. Napier Bartlett. LC 64-11967. 260p. 1996. pap. 17.95 (*0-8071-2078-2*) La State U Pr.

Military Recruiting: DOD Could Improve Its Recruiter Selection & Incentive Systems. Ed. by Carol R. Schuster. 55p. (C). 1999. pap. text 20.00 (*0-7881-7694-3*) DIANE Pub.

Military Recruiting: More Innovative Approaches Needed. (Illus.). 86p. (Orig.). 1994. pap. text 40.00 (*1-57979-122-0*) DIANE Pub.

Military Recruiting: More Innovative Approaches Needed. (Illus.). 85p. (Orig.). (C). 1995. pap. text 30.00 (*0-7881-1706-8*) DIANE Pub.

Military Recruiting Outlook: Recent Trends in Enlistment Propensity & Conversion of Potential Enlisted Supply. Bruce R. Orvis et al. LC 96-48738. xvii, 68p. 1997. pap. 15.00 (*0-8330-2461-2*, MR-677-A/OSO) Rand Corp.

Military Reform & Society in New Granada, 1773-1808. Allan J. Kuethe. LC 77-21908. (University of Florida Latin American Monographs: No. 22). 1978. 19.95 (*0-8130-0570-1*) U Press Fla.

Military Reforms of Nicholas I: The Origins of the Modern Russian Army. Frederick W. Kagan. LC 98-44711. 352p. 1999. text 49.95 (*0-312-21928-8*) St Martin.

Military Regalia. Will Fowler. 80p. 1993. 6.98 (*1-55521-843-1*) Bk Sales Inc.

Military Regimes & Development: A Comparative Analysis in African Societies. Olatunde Odetola. 240p. (C). 1982. pap. text 16.95 (*0-04-301154-3*) Routledge.

Military Regimes & the Press in Nigeria, 1966-1993: Human Rights & National Development. Chris W. Ogbondah. 200p. (Orig.). (C). 1994. pap. text 29.50 (*0-8191-8835-2*) U Pr of Amer.

Military Religion in Roman Britain. Georgia L. Irby-Massie. LC 99-36882. (Mnemosyne, Supplements Ser.). (Illus.). 408p. 1999. 109.00 (*90-04-10848-3*) Brill Academic Pubs.

Military Religious Orders of the Middle Ages: Knights Templar. 2nd ed. F. C. Woodhouse. (Illus.). 727p. 1997. reprint ed. 35.00 (*1-57179-071-3*) Intern Guild ASRS.

Military Remongton Rolling Block Rifle. 4th rev. ed. George J. Layman. (Illus.). 148p. 2001. reprint ed. pap. 24.95 (*1-877704-32-6*) Pioneer Pr.

Military Retirement: Possible Changes Merit Further Evaluation. Ed. by Sharon Cekala. (Illus.). 53p. (C). 1999. reprint ed. pap. text 20.00 (*0-7881-7857-1*) DIANE Pub.

Military Retirement: Social, Economic & Mental Health Dilemmas. John S. McNeil et al. (Illus.). 156p. 1983. text 50.00 (*0-86598-078-0*) Rowman.

Military Revolution? Military Change & European Society, 1550-1800. Black. Ed. by Richard Overy et al. (Studies in European History Ser.). 1996. text 11.95 (*0-333-51906-X*, Pub. by Macmillan) St Martin.

Military Revolution: Military Innovation & the Rise of the West, 1500-1800. 2nd ed. Geoffrey Parker. (Illus.). 284p. (C). 1996. pap. 22.95 (*0-521-47958-4*) Cambridge U Pr.

Military Revolution Debate: Readings on the Military Transformation of Early Modern Europe. Ed. by Clifford J. Rogers. (History & Warfare Ser.). (C). 1995. pap. 34.00 (*0-8133-2054-2*, Pub. by Westview) HarpC.

Military Revolution in Sixteenth-Century Europe. David Eltis. 182p. 1998. pap. 24.50 (*1-86064-352-3*, Pub. by I B T) St Martin.

Military Rifles of Japan. 5th ed. Fred L. Honeycutt, Jr. & F. Patt Anthony. LC 96-77531. (Illus.). 208p. 1996. 42.00 (*0-9623208-7-0*) F L Honeycutt Jr.

Military Roads see Historic Highways of America...with Maps & Illustrations

Military Role of Nuclear Weapons: Perceptions & Misperceptions. Robert S. McNamara. (CISA Working Papers: No. 45). 41p. (Orig.). 1984. pap. 15.00 (*0-86682-058-2*) Ctr Intl Relations.

Military Roll, Stanislaus County, California, 1895. Compiled & Intro. by Cecil E. Kilroy. LC 92-97214. 75p. (Orig.). 1992. 10.00 (*0-9617906-1-X*) M F Kilroy.

Military Rule in Chile: Dictatorship & Oppositions. Ed. by J. Samuel Valenzuela & Arturo Valenzuela. LC 85-9797. 345p. 1986. reprint ed. pap. 107.00 (*0-608-03678-1*, 206450400009) Bks Demand.

Military Rule in Latin America. Karen L. Remmer. 208p. 1989. 39.95 (*0-04-445479-1*) Routledge.

Military Rules of Evidence: 1986, 1990 Supplement. 2nd ed. Saltzburg et al. 1990. text 95.00 (*0-87215-969-8*, 66905-10, MICHIE) LEXIS Pub.

Military Rules of Evidence Manual. 3rd ed. Stephen A. Saltzburg et al. 1096p. 1992. suppl. ed. 20.00 (*0-87473-844-X*, MICHIE) LEXIS Pub.

Military Rules of Evidence Manual. 4th ed. Stephen A. Saltzburg et al. LC 97-74883. 1237p. 1997. 95.00 (*1-55834-642-2*) LEXIS Pub.

Military Rules of Evidence Manual: 1990 Cumulative Supplement. 4th ed. Stephen A. Saltzburg et al. 1990. pap. 95.00 (*0-87473-292-1*, 66909-10, MICHIE) LEXIS Pub.

Military Rules of Evidence Manual: 1998 Supplement. 4th ed. Stephen A. Saltzburg et al. 1998. 95.00 (*0-327-00115-1*, 66900-14) LEXIS Pub.

Military Rules of Evidence Manual, 1999 Cumulative Supplement. 4th ed. Stephen A. Saltzburg et al. 160p. 1999. pap. write for info. (*0-327-01325-7*, 6690015) LEXIS Pub.

*__Military RV, Camping & Outdoor Recreation Around the World Including Golf Courses & Marinas.__ William R. Crawford. LC 98-31698. 1998. write for info. (*0-914862-74-X*) Military Living Pubns.

Military Sales to Israel & Egypt: U. S. - Financed Procurements. (Illus.). 52p. (Orig.). (C). 1994. pap. text 25.00 (*0-7881-0458-6*) DIANE Pub.

Military Satellite Communications: Milstar Program Issues & Cost-Saving Opportunities. (Illus.). 54p. (Orig.). (C). 1995. pap. text 20.00 (*0-7881-1856-0*) DIANE Pub.

Military Schools & Courses of Instruction in the Science & Art of War. Compiled by Henry Barnard. LC 68-54786. 960p. 1970. reprint ed. lib. bdg. 145.00 (*0-8371-1325-3*, BAMS, Greenwood Pr) Greenwood.

Military Sealift Command: Weak Controls & Management of Contractor-Operated Ships. (Illus.). 45p. (Orig.). (C). 1996. pap. text 15.00 (*0-7881-2925-2*) DIANE Pub.

Military Secrets. Lindsay Welsh. (Orig.). 1996. mass mkt. 5.95 (*1-56333-397-X*, Rosebud) Masquerade.

Military Service in American Life since World War II: An Overview. Albert D. Klassen, Jr. (Report Ser.: No. 117). 1966. 15.00 (*0-932132-09-X*) Natl Opinion Res.

Military Service in the United States. Ed. by Brent Scowcroft. LC 81-22744. 226p. 1982. 11.95 (*0-13-583062-1*) Am Assembly.

Military Service in the United States. American Assembly Staff. Ed. by Brent Scowcroft. LC 81-22744. (Illus.). 245p. reprint ed. pap. 76.00 (*0-608-18004-1*, 202798100057) Bks Demand.

Military Service Records: A Select Catalog of National Archives Microfilm Publications. National Archives & Records Administration Staff. 330p. 1985. pap. text 3.50 (*0-911333-07-X*, 200028) National Archives & Recs.

Military Services & Genealogical Records of Soldiers of Blair County, Pennsylvania (from Revolutionary War to WW I) Floyd G. Hoenstine. (Illus.). 426p. 1997. reprint ed. lib. bdg. 48.00 (*0-8328-7160-5*) Higginson Bk Co.

Military Sex: True Homosexual Stories, Vol. 3. Ed. by Winston Leyland. 160p. (Orig.). 1993. pap. 14.95 (*0-943595-41-X*) Leyland Pubns.

Military Side of Japanese Life. Malcolm D. Kennedy. LC 72-9091. (Illus.). 367p. 1973. reprint ed. lib. bdg. 35.00 (*0-8371-6574-1*, KEJL, Greenwood Pr) Greenwood.

Military Signal Communications, Vol. 1. Paul J. Scheips. 1980. 40.95 (*0-405-13194-1*) Ayer.

Military Signal Communications, Vol. 2. Paul J. Scheips. 40.95 (*0-405-13197-6*) Ayer.

Military Signal Communications: An Original Anthology, 2 vols., Set. Ed. by Paul J. Scheips & Christopher H. Sterling. LC 80-483. (Historical Studies in Telecommunications). (Illus.). 1980. lib. bdg. 78.95 (*0-405-13193-3*) Ayer.

Military Simulation & Training Systems Market: Increased Networking Propels Mission Simulation. Market Intelligence Staff. 251p. 1993. 1695.00 (*1-56753-447-3*) Frost & Sullivan.

Military Simulation Markets. 2nd ed. (Market Intelligence - Related Special Reports). 695.00 (*0-7106-1836-0*) Janes Info Group.

Military Simulations Markets. 695.00 (*0-7106-1212-5*) Janes Info Group.

Military Situation in the Far East: U. S. Congress, Senate Committee on Armed Services & the Committee on Foreign Relations, 5 vols., Set. LC 78-22402. (American Military Experience Ser.). 1979. reprint ed. lib. bdg. 248.50 (*0-405-11878-3*) Ayer.

*__Military Small Arms of the 20th Century.__ 7th rev. expanded ed. Ian V. Hogg & John S. Weeks. LC 73-83466. (Illus.). 416p. 2000. pap. 24.95 (*0-87341-824-7*) Krause Pubns.

Military Sociology. Charles H. Coates & Roland J. Pellegrin. 1965. pap. text 14.95 (*0-686-00733-6*) Md Bk Exch.

Military Soils Engineering. 1995. lib. bdg. 255.99 (*0-8490-6611-5*) Gordon Pr.

Military Space. Lyn Dutton et al. (Air Power: Aircraft, Weapons Systems & Technology Ser.). (Illus.). 200p. 1990. 40.00 (*0-08-037346-1*, 3004, Pub. by Brasseys) Brasseys.

Military Space - Air Opportunities Air Route Map. William R. Crawford & Lela A. Crawford. 1995. pap. write for info. (*0-914862-52-9*) Military Living Pubns.

Military Space-A: Air Opportunities Around the World. William R. Crawford & Ann C. Crawford. Ed. by Donna L. Russell. LC 98-10819. 1998. pap. 19.95 (*0-914862-69-3*) Military Living Pubns.

Military Space-A Air Basic Training & Reader Trip Reports. Ann C. Crawford & William R. Crawford. Ed. by Donna L. Russell. LC 97-29517. 1995. pap. write for info. (*0-914862-66-9*) Military Living Pubns.

*__Military Space-A Air Basic Training & Reader Trip Reports.__ William Roy Crawford & Ann Caddell Crawford. LC 00-31891. 2000. write for info. (*0-914862-89-8*) Military Living Pubns.

Military Space Forces: The Next 50 Years. John M. Collins. (Illus.). 236p. (C). 1997. reprint ed. text 25.00 (*0-7881-5091-X*) DIANE Pub.

Military Spending & Industrial Decline: A Study of the American Machine Tool Industry, 68. Anthony DiFilippo. LC 85-27144. (Contributions in Economics & Economic History Ser.: No. 68). (Illus.). 211p. 1986. 55.00 (*0-313-25179-7*, DMI/) Greenwood.

Military Stability & European Stability: Ten Years from Now. Lutz Unterseher. (Project on Defense Alternatives Research Monograph Ser.: Vol. 2). 50p. 1993. pap. 10.00 (*1-881677-06-0*) Commonwlth Inst.

Military Staff: Its History & Development. James D. Hittle. LC 74-34478. 326p. 1975. reprint ed. lib. bdg. 35.00 (*0-8371-7952-1*, HIMS, Greenwood Pr) Greenwood.

Military Standard 1246C (MIL-STD-1246C) Product Cleanliness Levels & Contamination Control Program. 20p. 1993. 60.00 (*0-685-69158-8*) IEST.

Military Standards Drawing Set, 20 vols., Set. 1993. ring bd. 995.00 (*1-57053-065-3*) Global Eng Doc.

*__Military, State & Society in Pakistan.__ Hasan Askari Rizvi. LC 99-55831. 2000. 79.95 (*0-312-23193-8*) St Martin.

Military-State-Society Symbiosis, 5. Ed. by Peter Karsten. LC 98-42475. (Military & Society Ser.: Vol. 5). 368p. 1998. reprint ed. 85.00 (*0-8153-3237-8*) Garland.

Military Strategies for Sustainment of Nutrition & Immune Function in the Field. Institute of Medicine Staff. 722p. 1999. pap. 80.00 (*0-309-06345-0*) Natl Acad Pr.

Military Strategy: A General Theory of Control. J. C. Wylie. Ed. by Wayne P. Hughes, Jr. (Classics of Sea Power Ser.). 200p. 1989. 34.95 (*0-87021-362-8*) Naval Inst Pr.

Military Strategy & Political Interests: The Soviet Union & the United States. Roman Kolkowicz. (CISA Working Papers: No. 30). 40p. (Orig.). 1981. pap. 15.00 (*0-86682-029-9*) Ctr Intl Relations.

Military Strategy & the Origins of the First World War: An International Security Reader. rev. ed. Ed. by Steven E. Miller et al. 360p. 1991. pap. text 19.95 (*0-691-02349-2*, Pub. by Princeton U Pr) Cal Prin Full Svc.

Military Strategy of the Soviet Union: A History. David M. Glantz. LC 91-43411. 360p. 1992. 54.50 (*0-7146-3435-2*, Pub. by F Cass Pubs) Intl Spec Bk.

Military Support for Youth Development: An Exploratory Analysis. Beth J. Asch. LC 94-24606. 51p. (Orig.). 1995. pap. text 7.50 (*0-8330-1588-5*, MR-497-A/RC) Rand Corp.

Military Survey of 1522 for Babergh Hundred. John F. Pound. (Suffolk Records Society Ser.: No. XXVIII). 166p. 1986. 45.00 (*0-85115-438-7*) Boydell & Brewer.

Military Swords of Japan, 1868-1945. Richard Fuller & Ron Gregory. (Illus.). 128p. 1993. pap. 16.95 (*1-85409-183-2*) Sterling.

Military System & Social Life in Old-Regime Prussia, 1713-1807: The Beginning of the Social Militarization of Prusso-German Society. Otto B. Usch. Tr. by John G. Gagliardo. LC 96-3390. (Studies in Central European Histories). Orig. Title: Milit Arsystem & Sozialleben im Alten Preussen, 1713-1807. 160p. 1996. 39.95 (*0-391-03984-9*) Humanities.

Military Technology, Pt. 7, The Gunpowder Epic see Science & Civilisation in China

*__Military Technology & Defence Industrialisation: The Indian Experience.__ Samir K. Sen. LC 99-940234. 208p. 2000. 29.00 (*81-7049-103-7*, Pub. by Manas Pubns) Nataraj Bks.

Military Technology & Defense Manpower. Martin Binkin. LC 85-48204. (Studies in Defense Policy). 143p. 1986. 28.95 (*0-8157-0978-1*); pap. 10.95 (*0-8157-0977-3*) Brookings.

Military Telegraph During the Civil War in the United States, 2 vols. William R. Plum. LC 74-4690. (Telecommunications Ser.). 1566p. 1974. reprint ed. 60.95 (*0-405-06053-X*) Ayer.

Military Telemedicine On-Line Today, 1995 National Forum. LC 94-75388. 192p. 1996. pap. 50.00 (*0-8186-5860-6*, PR05860) IEEE Comp Soc.

Military Threats: A Systematic Historical Analysis of the Determinants of Success, 36. Peter Karsten et al. LC 83-8552. (Contributions in Military History Ser.: No. 36). (Illus.). 166p. 1984. 52.95 (*0-313-23825-1*, KAR/, Greenwood Pr) Greenwood.

Military Timepieces. Marvin E. Whitney. (Illus.). 667p. 1992. 75.00 (*0-918845-14-9*) Am Watchmakers.

Military Tokens of the U. S., 2 vols. Paul Cunningham. (Illus.). 461p. 1998. 49.95 (*0-945008-01-5*) MI Exonumia Pubs.

Military Trade. Steven Zeeland. LC 98-31595. (Illus.). 301p. 1999. 49.95 (*0-7890-0402-X*, Harrington Park); pap. 19.95 (*1-56023-924-7*, Harrington Park) Haworth Pr.

Military Tradition in Ukrainian History: Its Role in the Construction of Ukraine's Armed Forces. Kostiantyn P. Morozov et al. (Papers in Ukrainian Studies). (Illus.). 93p. 1995. pap. text 5.00 (*0-916458-73-3*) Harvard Ukrainian.

Military Training: Is It Effective for Technical Specialties? (Illus.). 103p. (Orig.). (C). 1994. pap. text 35.00 (*0-7881-0311-3*) DIANE Pub.

*__Military Training: Management & Oversight of Joint Combined Exchange Training.__ Ed. by Carol Schuster. (Illus.). 67p. (C). 1999. pap. text 20.00 (*0-7881-8489-X*) DIANE Pub.

Military Training: Potential to Use Lessons Learned to Avoid Past Mistakes Is Largely Untapped. 49p. (Orig.). (C). 1996. pap. text 20.00 (*0-7881-3036-6*) DIANE Pub.

*__Military Training in the British Army, 1940-1944: From Dunkirk to D-Day.__ Timothy Harrison Place. LC 00-31480. (Military History & Policy Ser.). (Illus.). 2000. write for info. (*0-7146-5037-4*, Pub. by F Cass Pubs) Intl Spec Bk.

Military Training Technology: Systematic Approaches. Ed. by Hendrick W. Ruck & John A. Ellis. LC 85-9459. 253p. 1985. 49.95 (*0-275-90008-8*, C0008, Praeger Pubs) Greenwood.

Military Transition Series. Rob Black. Ed. by Becky Dean et al. 60p. 1998. reprint ed. pap. 14.95 (*1-891726-13-7*) Aviation Info.

Military Transport: Trucks & Transporters. T. J. O'Malley. LC 94-41840. (Greenhill Military Manuals Ser.: Vol. 3). (Illus.). 160p. 1995. 19.95 (*1-85367-202-5*, Pub. by Greenhill Bks) Stackpole.

Military Tribunals & International Crimes. John A. Appleman. LC 76-152589. (Illus.). 421p. 1972. reprint ed. lib. bdg. 75.00 (*0-8371-6022-7*, APMT, Greenwood Pr) Greenwood.

Military Trucks see Land & Sea Series

Military Trucks. Michael Green. (Land & Sea Ser.). (J). 1997. 19.00 (*0-516-20516-1*) Childrens.

Military Uniforms. Jacob Kobelt. LC 82-3659. 24p. 1982. lib. bdg. write for info. (*0-86592-706-5*) Rourke Enter.

Military Use of Drugs Not Yet Approved by the FDA for CW/BW Defense: Lessons from the Gulf War. Richard A. Rettig. LC 98-31679. (Illus.). 120p. 1999. pap. 15.00 (*0-8330-2683-6*, MR-1018/9-OSD) Rand Corp.

Military Use of Land: A History of the Defense Estate. John Childs. 302p. 1998. pap. 45.95 (*3-906757-66-8*) P Lang Pubng.

Military Use of Land: A History of the Defense Estate. John Childs. LC 97-32733. 302p. (C). 1998. pap. 45.95 (*0-8204-3410-8*) P Lang Pubng.

Military Uses of Literature: Fiction & the Armed Forces in the Soviet Union. Mark Hooker. LC 95-43318. 256p. 1996. 65.00 (*0-275-95563-X*, Praeger Pubs) Greenwood.

*__Military Vehicles.__ Francois Verlinden. (Publications: Vol. II). (Illus.). 48p. 2000. pap. 14.95 (*1-930607-47-4*) Verlinden Prod.

Military Vehicles of the Reichswehr. Wolfgang Fleischer. (Illus.). 48p. 1996. pap. 9.95 (*0-7643-0166-7*) Schiffer.

Military Vehicles (Ordnance Corps Responsibility, TM 9-28000-1, 1953) With Changes to 1956. U. S. Army Staff. (Illus.). 294p. 1995. pap. 25.00 (*0-938242-26-1*) Portrayal.

Military Veterans PTSD Reference Manual. I. S. Parrish. 244p. 1999. pap. 19.95 (*0-7414-0077-4*) Buy Books.

An Asterisk (*) at the beginning of an entry indicates that the title is appearing for the first time.

Military Weather Calculations for the Nato Theater: Weather & Warplanes VIII. R. E. Huschke et al. LC 80-36722. xv, 129 p. 1980. 10.00 (*0-8330-0245-7*) Rand Corp.

Military Withdrawal from Politics: A Comparative Study. Talukder Maniruzzaman. LC 86-28741. (Wilson Center Series on International Security Studies). 272p. 1987. text 34.95 (*0-88730-147-9*, HarpBusn) HarpInfo.

Military World. Ed. by Scott Morris. LC 92-22286. (Using & Understanding Maps Ser.). (Illus.). 48p. (YA). (gr. 5 up). 1993. lib. bdg. 17.95 (*0-7910-1808-3*) Chelsea Hse.

Military Writings. Leon Trotsky. Tr. by John G. Wright et al. LC 72-92843. 160p. 1969. reprint ed. pap. 15.95 (*0-87348-029-5*) Pathfinder NY.

Military Writings. Leon Trotsky. Tr. by John G. Wright et al. LC 72-92843. 160p. 1971. reprint ed. lib. bdg. 45.00 (*0-87348-030-9*) Pathfinder NY.

Military Years. Bobby Owens. LC 93-90793. 80p. 1994. 25.00 (*1-884308-09-0*); pap. text 15.00 (*1-884308-10-4*) Enlisted Ldrship.

Militerrorism: On the Morality of Combating Terror with Terror. J. Landrum, Jr. LC 95-23001. (Critical Questions Ser.). 1996. text 9.95 (*0-7734-8909-6*) E Mellen.

Militia. James B. Whisker. LC 92-17294. 216p. 1992. lib. bdg. 89.95 (*0-7734-9553-3*) E Mellen.

Militia & the National Guard in America since Colonial Times: A Research Guide, 7. Jerry M. Cooper. LC 93-14047. (Research Guides in Military Studies: No. 7). 200p. 1993. lib. bdg. 65.00 (*0-313-27721-4*, CMN/, Greenwood Pr) Greenwood.

Militia in Antebellum South Carolina Society. Jean M. Flynn. LC 91-11379. (Illus.). 214p. 1991. 25.00 (*0-87152-446-5*) Reprint.

Militia in Twentieth Century America: A Symposium. Ed. by Morgan Norval. 252p. (Orig.). 1985. pap. 9.95 (*0-317-19795-9*) Gun Ownrs Fund.

Militia Lists & Musters, 1757-1876: A Directory of Holdings in the British Isles. 3rd ed. J. S. W. Gibson & Mervyn Medlycott. LC 98-72242. 48 p. 1999. pap. 8.50 (*0-8063-1567-9*) Genealog Pub.

Militia Man: Circa 1740. Intro. by Peter R. Schaaphok. (Illus.). 100p. (Orig.). 1995. reprint ed. pap. 8.00 (*0-9633659-3-2*) US Hist Res Srv.

Militia Movement. Ed. by Charles P. Cozic. LC 96-44910. (At Issue Ser.). (J). (gr. 5-12). 1996. pap. 11.20 (*1-56510-541-9*) Greenhaven.

Militia Movement. Ed. by Charles P. Cozic. LC 96-44910. (At Issue Ser.). (J). (gr. 5-12). 1996. lib. bdg. 18.70 (*1-56510-542-7*) Greenhaven.

Militia Movement: Fighters of the Far Right Ben Sonder. LC 99-20321. 2000. 25.00 (*0-531-11405-8*) Watts.

***Militia Movement: Fighters of the Far Right.** Ben Sonder. (YA). 2000. pap. 8.95 (*0-531-16466-7*) Watts.

Militia Movement & Hate Groups in America. Ed. by Gary E. McCuen. (Ideas in Conflict Ser.). (Illus.). 176p. (YA). (gr. 7-12). 1996. lib. bdg. 15.95 (*0-86596-135-2*) G E M.

Militia Movement in America: Before & after Oklahoma City. Tricia Andryszewski. LC 96-32178. (Illus.). 128p. (YA). (gr. 7 up). 1997. lib. bdg. 22.40 (*0-7613-0119-4*) Millbrook Pr.

Militia Movement in the United States: Hearing Before the Committee on the Judiciary, U. S. Senate. Ed. by Arlen Specter. (Illus.). 144p. (C). 1999. reprint ed. pap. text 25.00 (*0-7881-3823-5*) DIANE Pub.

Militia Threat: Terrorists Among Us. R. L. Snow. LC HV6432.S67 1999. (Illus.). 248p. (C). 1999. 24.95 (*0-306-46001-7*, Kluwer Plenum) Kluwer Academic.

Militiaman, Volunteer & Professional: The Air National Guard & the American Military Tradition. Charles Joseph Gross. 252p. 1996. boxed set 30.00 (*0-16-048302-6*) USGPO.

Militiamen, Rangers & Redcoats: The Military in Georgia, 1754-1776. James M. Johnson. LC 91-27412. (Illus.). 144p. (C). 1993. 25.00 (*0-86554-379-8*, H319) Mercer Univ Pr.

Militias. Gail B. Stewart. LC 97-23362. (Overview Ser.). (Illus.). (YA). (gr. 4-12). 1997. lib. bdg. 22.45 (*1-56006-501-X*) Lucent Bks.

Militias: Armed & Dangerous. Kathlyn Gay. LC 97-12528. (Issues in Focus Ser.). (Illus.). 112p. (YA). (gr. 6 up). 1997. lib. bdg. 20.95 (*0-89490-902-9*) Enslow Pubs.

Militias in America: A Reference Handbook. Neil A. Hamilton. LC 96-26538. (Contemporary World Issues Ser.). 235p. 1996. lib. bdg. 45.00 (*0-87436-859-6*) ABC-CLIO.

Milk. John M. Bennett. 6p. (Orig.). 1990. pap. 2.00 (*0-935350-20-9*) Luna Bisonte.

Milk. Claire Llewellyn. LC 97-39803. (What's for Lunch? Ser.). (J). 1998. 20.00 (*0-516-20840-3*) Childrens.

Milk. Claire Llewellyn. Ed. by Helaine Cohen. (What's for Lunch? Ser.). (Illus.). 32p. (J). 1998. pap. 6.95 (*0-516-26221-1*) Childrens.

Milk. Jillian Powell. LC 96-49126. (Everyone Eats Ser.). (Illus.). 32p. (J). (gr. 2-6). 1997. lib. bdg. 22.83 (*0-8172-4766-1*) Raintree Steck-V.

Milk. Sharon Shebar. Ed. by Dan Wasserman. (Ten Word Book Ser.). (Illus.). (J). (gr. k-1). 1979. 9.95 (*0-89868-067-0*); pap. 3.95 (*0-89868-078-6*) ARO Pub.

Milk: History & Genealogy of the Milk-Milks Family. Grace Croft et al. 308p. 1992. reprint ed. pap. 47.00 (*0-8328-2365-1*); reprint ed. lib. bdg. 57.00 (*0-8328-2364-3*) Higginson Bk Co.

Milk: The Deadly Poison. unabridged ed. Robert Cohen. LC 97-94585. (Illus.). 317p. 1998. 24.95 (*0-9659196-0-9*) Argus Pub.

Milk: The Vital Force. Ed. by International Dairy Congress, XXII Organizing Comm. 1987. lib. bdg. 271.00 (*90-277-2331-1*) Kluwer Academic.

Milk & Dairy Product Technology. Edgar Spreer. LC 98-135838. (Food Science & Technology Ser.). (Illus.). 504p. 1998. text 135.00 (*0-8247-0094-5*) Dekker.

Milk & Dairy Products: Properties & Processing. Ionel Rosenthal. (Illus.). 218p. 1991. 125.00 (*3-527-27989-X*, Wiley-VCH) Wiley.

Milk & Dairy Products Market see Agricultural Review for Europe, 1983 & 1984

Milk & Dairy Products Markets, Vol. III. (Agricultural Review for Europe Ser.: No. 37). 42p. pap. 17.00 (*92-1-116622-5*) UN.

Milk & Honey. (Vocal Score Ser.). 240p. 1982. per. 45.00 (*0-88188-035-3*, 00384250) H Leonard.

Milk & Honey. Bridgewater Book Co., Staff. (Victorian Kitchen Ser.). 41p. 1995. write for info. (*1-57215-053-X*) World Pubns.

Milk & Honey. Faye Kellerman. 1998. mass mkt. 6.99 (*0-449-00313-2*, Crest) Fawcett.

Milk & Honey: A Collection of Poems. Margaret C. Cuda. (Illus.). 48p. (Orig.). 1994. pap. 6.95 (*1-881692-07-8*) Trillium WV.

Milk & Honey: A Novel. Elizabeth Jolley. LC 86-4896. 185p. 1986. pap. 8.95 (*0-89255-103-8*) Persea Bks.

Milk & Honey: A Year of Jewish Holidays. Jane Yolen. LC 93-44474. (Illus.). 80p. (J). (gr. 2-5). 1996. 21.95 (*0-399-22652-4*, G P Putnam) Peng Put Young Read.

Milk & Honey: Vocal Selections. (Illus.). 28p. 1982. pap. 7.95 (*0-88188-096-5*, 00384251) H Leonard.

Milk & Lactation: Proceedings of the Symposium, Campione, Sept. 1973. Symposium, Campione Staff. Ed. by N. Kretchmer et al. (Modern Problems in Pediatrics Ser.: Vol. 15). (Illus.). 250p. 1975. 85.25 (*3-8055-2056-5*) S Karger.

Milk & Milk Products Dictionary, English, French, German. Christophe Schneider. (ENG, FRE, GER & SPA.). 1994. 295.00 (*0-7859-9994-9*) Fr & Eur.

Milk & Milk Research: Medical & Scientific Index with Reference Bibliography. American Health Research Institute Staff. LC 88-47595. 150p. 1988. 47.50 (*0-88164-746-2*); pap. 44.50 (*0-88164-747-0*) ABBE Pubs Assn.

Milk & Mortality: The Connection Between Milk Drinking & Coronary Heart Disease. David B. Gordon. (Illus.). viii, 208p. 1999. 35.00 (*0-9671605-0-2*) Gordon Bks.

Milk & Yogurt. Hazel King. LC 97-44110. (Food in Focus Ser.). (Illus.). 32p. (YA). (gr. 1-5). 1998. 14.95 (*1-57572-657-2*) Heinemann Lib.

Milk-Based Soaps: Making Natural, Skin-Nourishing Soap. Casey Makela. Ed. by Deborah Balmuth. LC 97-30670. (Herbal Body Ser.). (Illus.). 96p. 1997. pap. 12.95 (*0-88266-984-2*, Storey Pub) Storey Bks.

Milk Book. (J). 1997. bds. 1.99 (*1-56987-870-6*) Warner Bros Wrldwide.

Milk Cartel in Ohio. Porter. (Case; Hb - Economics Ser.). 1997. mass mkt. 3.75 (*0-538-85806-0*) S-W Pub.

Milk Cartons: Bible Activities for Church & Home. L. Stroup. (Creative Factor Ser.). 1993. pap. 5.95 (*0-8272-9021-7*) Chalice Pr.

Milk Composition, Production & Biotechnology. Ed. by R. A. Welch et al. LC 96-48879. (Biotechnology in Agriculture Ser.: No. 18). (Illus.). 592p. (C). 1997. text 120.00 (*0-85199-161-0*) OUP.

Milk Dictionary English-German-Spanish-French. C. Scheider. 426p. 1996. 135.00 (*3-86022-173-6*, Pub. by Behrs Verlag) IBD Ltd.

Milk Does Not Do a Body Good. Daniel A. Twogood. 23p. (Orig.). 1996. pap. 7.95 (*0-9631125-1-1*) Wilhelmina.

Milk Farm: An Erotic Novel. Luc Milne. 160p. 1996. pap. 14.95 (*0-943595-61-4*) Leyland Pubns.

Milk for Babes. John Cotton. (Works of John Cotton Ser.). 1990. reprint ed. lib. bdg. 79.00 (*0-7812-2318-0*) Rprt Serv.

Milk-Free Kitchen: Living Well Without Dairy Products. Beth Kidder. 480p. 1995. pap. 16.95 (*0-8050-1836-0*, Owl) H Holt & Co.

Milk: From Cow to Carton see Leche: De la Vaca Al Envase (Milk: From Cow to Carton)

Milk from Cow to Carton. Aliki. (Let's Read-&-Find-Out Science Ser.). 1992. 10.15 (*0-606-09615-9*, Pub. by Turtleback) Demco.

***Milk from Cow to Carton.** Aliki. (Illus.). (J). 1999. pap. 12.20 (*0-8335-9083-9*) Econo-Clad Bks.

Milk from Cow to Carton. rev. ed. Aliki. LC 91-23807. (Trophy Let's Read-&-Find-Out Science Bk.: Stage 2). (Illus.). 32p. (J). (ps-3). 1992. pap. 4.95 (*0-06-445111-9*, HarpTrophy) HarpC Child Bks.

Milk Glass Book. Frank Chiarenza & James Slater. LC 98-29623. 208p. 1998. 49.95 (*0-7643-0661-8*) Schiffer.

Milk Horses: A Memoir. Rebecca Newth. Ed. by Martha Estes. LC 98-85089. 160p. 1998. pap. 12.95 (*0-9664290-0-1*) Lost Creek Pr.

Milk Hygiene: Report of the FAO-WHO Expert Committee on Milk Hygiene, 3rd, Geneva, 1969. FAO-WHO Expert Committee on Milk Hygiene. (Technical Reports: No. 124). (ENG & SPA.). 54p. 1957. pap. 3.00 (*92-4-120124-X*) World Health.

Milk Hygiene: Report of the FAO-WHO Expert Committee on Milk Hygiene, 3rd, Geneva, 1969. FAO-WHO Expert Committee on Milk Hygiene. (Technical Reports: No. 453). 82p. 1970. pap. text 5.00 (*92-4-120453-2*, 1100453) World Health.

***Milk in My Coffee.** Eric Jerome Dickey. 2000. pap. 12.95 (*0-451-20100-0*, Sig) NAL.

***Milk in My Coffee.** Eric Jerome Dickey. LC 98-5258. 320p. 1998. 23.95 (*0-525-94385-4*, Dutton Child) Peng Put Young Read.

Milk in My Coffee. Eric Jerome Dickey. 1999. reprint ed. mass mkt. 6.99 (*0-451-19406-3*, Sig) NAL.

Milk Intolerances & Rejection. Ed. by J. Delmont. (Illus.). x, 170p. 1983. pap. 121.75 (*3-8055-3546-5*) S Karger.

Milk is Not for Every Body: Living with Lactose Intolerance. Steve Carper. LC 95-9950. 304p. 1995. 27.95 (*0-8160-3127-4*) Facts on File.

Milk Makers. Gail Gibbons. LC 84-20081. (Illus.). 32p. (J). (gr. k-3). 1985. lib. bdg. 16.00 (*0-02-736640-5*, Mac Bks Young Read) S&S Childrens.

Milk Makers. Gail Gibbons. (Reading Rainbow Bks.). (J). 1987. 10.15 (*0-606-02787-4*, Pub. by Turtleback) Demco.

Milk Makers. Gail Gibbons. LC 86-22148. (Illus.). 32p. (J). (ps-3). 1987. reprint ed. mass mkt. 5.99 (*0-689-71116-6*) Aladdin.

Milk, Meat & Strong Meat of the Bible: Deep Spiritual Nutrition. Evan McDirmit & Marilynn McDirmit. (Illus.). 416p. (Orig.). (C). 1995. pap. 12.95 (*0-9623953-2-3*) Eagle Pubn Co.

Milk, Meat Biscuits & the Terraqueous Machine: The Story of Gail Borden. Mary D. Wade. Ed. by Melissa Roberts. (Illus.). 64p. (J). (gr. 4-7). 1995. pap. 5.95 (*1-57168-014-4*) Sunbelt Media.

Milk, Money, & Madness: The Culture & Politics of Breastfeeding. Naomi Baumslag & Dia L. Michels. LC 95-14975. (Illus.). 288p. 1995. 26.95 (*0-89789-407-3*, Bergin & Garvey) Greenwood.

Milk Mustache Book: A Behind-the-Scenes Look at America's Favorite Advertising Campaign. Jay Schulberg. LC 98-21663. 155p. (YA). (gr. 8-12). 1998. pap. 18.00 (*0-345-42729-7*) Ballantine Pub Grp.

Milk of Amnesia. Leandro Katz. (Illus.). 24p. 1985. pap. 10.00 (*0-939784-11-4*) CEPA Gall.

Milk of Human Kindness E. X. Ferrars. LC 96-30931. 278 p. 1997. write for info. (*0-7451-6950-3*) Chivers N Amer.

Milk of Inquiry. Wayne Koestenbaum. LC 98-50497. 144p. 1999. pap. 16.50 (*0-89255-239-5*) Persea Bks.

Milk of the Word. Peter Barnes. 80p. (Orig.). 1985. pap. 5.99 (*0-85151-434-0*) Banner of Truth.

Milk Production in the Tropic. Chamberlain. 1990. pap. text. write for info. (*0-582-77513-2*, Pub. by Addison-Wesley) Longman.

Milk Products & Eggs. Widdows & M. E. McCance. 1989. 66.00 (*0-85186-366-3*) CRC Pr.

Milk Proteins. Ed. by C. A. Barth & E. Schlimme. 240p. 1989. 54.00 (*0-387-91349-1*) Spr-Verlag.

Milk Quality. F. Harding. 166p. 1996. 105.00 (*0-8342-1345-1*) Aspen Pub.

Milk Quotas: European Community & United Kingdom Law. Michael Cardwell. 258p. 1996. text 65.00 (*0-19-825940-9*) OUP.

Milk Quotas in the European Community. Ed. by A. Burrell. 214p. (C). 1989. 55.00 (*0-85198-640-4*) OUP.

Milk Recipes from Nuts & Seeds. Edith V. Edwards. LC 97-80510. 107 p. 1998. per. 9.95 (*1-57258-099-2*) Teach Servs.

Milk Rock. John E. Kaufman. (J). 1995. write for info. (*0-8050-2814-5*) H Holt & Co.

Milk Run. 1988. 18.00 (*0-915269-09-0*) Windgate Pr.

Milk Snakes. W. P. Mara. (Illus.). 64p. 1995. pap. text 9.95 (*0-7938-0250-4*, RE107) TFH Pubns.

Milk Sugar Dilemma: Living with Lactose Intolerance. 2nd rev. ed. Sherlyn Skinner & Richard A. Martens. LC 85-234985. (Illus.). 260p. 1987. pap. 13.95 (*0-936741-01-5*) Medi-Ed Pr.

Milk, Sulphate & Alby Starvation. Martin Millar. LC 95-149417. 152p. 1989. pap. 13.95 (*1-85702-214-9*) Trafalgar.

Milk Thief, 1. Paul Henry. LC 99-219625. 64p. 1999. pap. text 17.95 (*1-85411-240-6*) Seren Bks.

Milk Thistle. Woodland Publishing Staff. (Woodland Health Ser.). 1999. pap. text 3.95 (*1-885670-24-9*) Woodland UT.

***Milk Thistle: A Step-by-Step Guide.** Jill Nice & Jill Rosemary Davies. (In a Nutshell Ser.). 2000. 7.95 (*1-86204-710-3*, Pub. by Element MA) Penguin Putnam.

Milk Thistle: The Liver Herb. 2nd ed. Christopher Hobbs. Ed. by Beth Baugh. LC 97-49613. (Illus.). 53p. (Orig.). 1992. pap. text 3.95 (*0-9618470-6-9*) Botanica CA.

Milk Train Doesn't Stop Here Anymore. Tennessee Williams. 1964. pap. 5.25 (*0-8222-0758-3*) Dramatists Play.

Milkfish Production Dualism in the Philippines: A Multi-Disciplinary Perspective on Continous Low Yields & Constraints to Aquaculture Development. K. C. Chong et al. (ICLARM Technical Reports: No. 15). (Illus.). 70p. (Orig.). 1984. pap. 10.50 (*971-10-2210-9*, Pub. by ICLARM) Intl Spec Bk.

***Milking & Milk Production of Dairy Sheep & Goats.** F. Barillet. (Illus.). 571p. 1999. 114.00 (*90-74134-64-5*) Wageningen Pers.

Milking Black Bull: 12 Gay Black Poets. Alden Reimonenq et al. LC 95-725. 168p. 1995. pap. 12.00 (*1-880729-11-3*) Vega Pr.

Milking in November. Judith B. Goodenough. 74p. (Orig.). 1990. pap. 9.95 (*0-932662-87-0*) St Andrews NC.

Milking Jug. George Wallace. Ed. by Stanley H. Barkan. (Review Long Island Writers Chapbook Ser.: No. 1). (Illus.). 48p. 1989. 15.00 (*0-89304-250-1*, CCC600); pap. 5.00 (*0-89304-251-X*); audio 10.00 (*0-89304-254-4*) Cross-Cultrl NY.

Milking Jug: Mini Book. George Wallace. Ed. by Stanley H. Barkan. (Review Long Island Writers Chapbook Ser.: No. 1). (Illus.). 48p. 1989. 15.00 (*0-89304-252-8*); pap. 5.00 (*0-89304-253-6*) Cross-Cultrl NY.

Milking Machine Guide. Paul Dettloff. (Illus.). 164p. 1998. spiral bd. 16.95 (*0-9632897-2-1*) Million Mile.

***Milking Machines: By Hal Rogers.** Hal Rogers. LC 99-89470. 2000. lib. bdg. write for info. (*1-56766-753-8*) Childs World.

Milking the Public: Political Scandals of the Dairy Lobby from LBJ to Jimmy Carter. Michael McMenamin & Walter McNamara. LC 80-11546. 312p. 1980. text 36.95 (*0-88229-552-7*) Burnham Inc.

Milkmaid & Her Pail see Lechera y Su Cubeta

Milkmaid & Her Pail. Carol Barnett. (Illus.). 64p. (J). (ps-3). 1994. 7.95 (*0-8442-9421-7*, Natl Textbk Co) NTC Contemp Pub Co.

Milkmaid & Her Pail. Carol Barnett. (StoryLand Fables Ser.). (Illus.). 48p. (J). (ps-4). 1995. 8.95 (*0-8442-9433-0*) NTC Contemp Pub Co.

Milkman's Boy. Donald Hall. LC 97-14170. (Illus.). 32p. (J). (ps-3). 1997. 15.95 (*0-8027-8463-1*); lib. bdg. 16.85 (*0-8027-8465-8*) Walker & Co.

Milkman's Matinee. John J. Dorfner. 121p. (Orig.). 1994. pap. 9.95 (*0-9636046-8-6*) Cooper St Pubns.

***Milksnakes & Tricolored Kingsnakes.** Richard D. Bartlett & Patricia P. Bartlett. LC 99-42835. (Reptile Keepers Ser.). 48p. 2000. pap. 5.95 (*0-7641-1128-0*) Barron.

Milkweed. Mary Gardner. LC 94-14469. 320p. 1994. 18.00 (*0-918949-46-7*) Martz.

Milkweed. Mary Gardner. LC 94-14469. 320p. 1995. pap. 11.00 (*0-918949-45-9*) Martz.

Milkweed & Winkles: A Wild Child's Cookbook. Elizabeth M. Hulbert. Ed. by Laura Beal. LC 95-61437. (Illus.). 56p. (Orig.). (J). (gr. 2-4). 1995. pap. 8.00 (*1-883650-28-3*) Windswept Hse.

***Milkweed Bugs: Life Cycles.** Donna Schaffer. LC 98-53032. (Life Cycles Ser.). (Illus.). 24p. (J). 1999. 15.93 (*0-7368-0208-8*, Bridgestone Bks) Capstone Pr.

Milkweed Butterflies: Their Cladistics & Biology. P. R. Ackery & Richard I. Vane-Wright. LC 83-7334. (Illus.). 450p. 1984. 79.50 (*0-8014-1688-4*) Cornell U Pr.

Milkweed Charley: The Saltsman's Hotel Caper. Doris H. Masi. 54p. 1997. pap. 8.95 (*1-886623-02-3*) Canal Side Pubs.

Milkweed Ladies. Louise McNeill. LC 88-1334. 136p. (Orig.). 1989. pap. 10.95 (*0-8229-5406-0*) U of Pittsburgh Pr.

Milky Way. Jon Anderson. LC 82-11491. (American Poetry Ser.: No. 25). 175p. 1985. pap. 8.50 (*0-88001-007-X*) HarpC.

Milky Way. Muriel Jensen. (Tyler Ser.: No. 9). 1999. mass mkt. write for info. (*0-373-82509-9*, 0-82509-1) Harlequin Bks.

Milky Way. 5th ed. Bart J. Bok & Priscilla F. Bok. LC 80-22544. (Harvard Books on Astronomy). (Illus.). 364p. (C). 1981. 46.50 (*0-674-57503-2*) HUP.

Milky Way: Contemporary Sculpture in New York. Stephen Westfall. Ed. by Shoshana Blank. (Illus.). 16p. (Orig.). 1989. pap. write for info. (*0-318-65455-5*) Shoshana Wayne Gall.

Milky Way: The Structure & Development of Our Star System. Ludwig Kuhn. LC 82-2820. (Illus.). 161p. reprint ed. pap. 50.00 (*0-8357-4272-5*, 203707000002) Bks Demand.

Milky Way As a Galaxy. Ivan King et al. (Illus.). 448p. (C). 1990. text 44.50 (*0-935702-62-8*) Univ Sci Bks.

Milky Way Galaxy. Leonid S. Marochnik. 512p. 1995. text 160.00 (*2-88124-931-0*) Gordon & Breach.

Milky Way Galaxy. Ed. by Hugo Van Woerden et al. 1985. pap. text 90.00 (*90-277-1920-9*); lib. bdg. 197.00 (*90-277-1919-5*) Kluwer Academic.

Milky Way Galaxy & Statistical Cosmology, 1890-1924. Erich R. Paul. LC 92-36530. (Illus.). 278p. (C). 1993. text 54.95 (*0-521-35363-7*) Cambridge U Pr.

Milky Way Railroad. Kenji Miyazawa. Tr. by Joseph Sigrist & D. M. Stroud from JPN. (Illus.). 160p. (J). (gr. 7-12). 1996. pap. 11.95 (*1-880656-26-4*) Stone Bridge Pr.

Mill. Bruce Butterfield. 2001. 25.00 (*0-06-019103-1*) HarpC.

***Mill.** Bruce Butterfield. 2002. pap. 13.00 (*0-06-093057-8*, Perennial) HarperTrade.

Mill, 001. David Macaulay. (Illus.). 128p. (J). (gr. 6 up). 1983. 18.00 (*0-395-34830-7*) HM.

Mill. David Macaulay. 128p. (J). (ps up). 1989. pap. 8.95 (*0-395-52019-3*, Sandpiper) HM.

***Mill.** Rade B. Vukmir. LC 99-26069. (Illus.). 456p. 1999. 42.00 (*0-7618-1415-9*) U Pr of Amer.

***Mill: General Philosophy.** Sanchez-Valencia. 2001. 166.95 (*0-7546-2068-9*) Ashgate Pub Co.

Mill: Texts, Commentaries. expanded rev. ed. John Stuart Mill. Ed. & Selected by Alan Ryan. LC 96-7642. 365p. (C). 1996. pap. text 11.25 (*0-393-97009-4*) Norton.

***Mill: The History & Future of Naturally Powered Buildings.** David Larkin. (Illus.). 2000. 50.00 (*0-7893-0501-1*) Universe.

Mill: Utilitarianism. Ed. by Oskar Piest. 88p. (C). 1957. pap. text 5.20 (*0-02-395670-4*, Macmillan Coll) P-H.

Mill & Mansion: A Study of Architecture & Society in Lowell, Massachusetts, 1820-1865. 2nd ed. John Coolidge. LC 92-14978. (Illus.). 336p. 1993. reprint ed. pap. 18.95 (*0-87023-819-1*) U of Mass Pr.

Mill & Mine: The CF&I in the Twentieth Century. H. Lee Scamehorn. LC 91-3966. (Illus.). x, 271p. 1992. text 50.00 (*0-8032-4214-X*) U of Nebr Pr.

Mill & Religion: Contemporary Responses to Three Essays on Religion. Ed. & Intro. by Alan P. Sell. LC 98-157969. (Key Issues Ser.). 250p. 1997. 72.00 (*1-85506-541-X*) Thoemmes Pr.

Mill & Religion: Contemporary Responses to Three Essays on Religion. Ed. & Intro. by Alan P. Sell. LC 98-157969. (Key Issues Ser.: Vol. 17). 250p. 1997. pap. 24.00 (*1-85506-542-8*) Thoemmes Pr.

Mill & the Moral Character of Liberalism. Ed. by Eldon J. Eisenach. LC 98-8534. 344p. 1998. 48.50 (*0-271-01836-4*); pap. 18.95 (*0-271-01837-2*) Pa St U Pr.

Mill & Town in South Carolina, 1880-1920. David L. Carlton. LC 82-7753. xii, 313p. (C). 1982. pap. text 19.95 (*0-8071-1059-0*) La State U Pr.

Mill at Philipsburg Manor, Upper Mills, & A Brief History of Milling. Charles Howell & Allan Keller. LC 75-7156. (Illus.). 192p. 1977. 15.00 (*0-912882-22-0*) Sleepy Hollow.

M

Mill Control & Control Systems: Quality & Testing, Environmental, Corrosion, Electrical. (Pulp & Paper Manufacture Ser.: Vol. 9). 430p. 1992. text 81.56 (*1-895288-28-2*) Pulp & Paper.

***Mill Cottage.** large type ed. Barbara Whitnell. 224p. 2000. 31.99 (*0-7089-4176-1*) Ulverscroft.

Mill Creek: An Unnatural History of an Urban Stream. Stanley Hedeen. (Illus.). 226p. (Orig.). 1995. pap. 15.00 (*0-9643436-0-6*, Blue Heron OH) Riv Unltd Mill.

Mill Creek Journal: Ashland, Oregon, 1850-1860. Kay Atwood. (Illus.). 216p. 1987. pap. 15.95 (*0-685-24088-6*) K Atwood.

Mill Creek Memories. John Russell. (Illus.). 104p. 1995. pap. 7.00 (*0-87012-533-8*) McClain.
The history of Mill Creek, West Virginia, is told by the author with the aid of maps & photos to give the reader an in-depth look at the small town & its heritage. *Publisher Paid Annotation.*

Mill Creek Site & Pattern Recognition in Historical Archaeology. Patrick E. Martin. (Archaeological Completion Reports: No. 10). (Illus.). 265p. (Orig.). 1985. pap. 16.00 (*0-911872-54-X*) Mackinac St Hist Pks.

Mill Family: The Labor System in the Southern Cotton Textile Industry. Cathy L. McHugh. (Illus.). 160p. 1988. text 60.00 (*0-19-504299-9*) OUP.

Mill Hill Fathers in West Cameroon: Education, Health & Development, 1884-1970. Bernard F. Booth. LC 93-45913. 284p. 1995. 64.95 (*1-883255-41-4*, U Pr W Africa); pap. 44.95 (*1-883255-40-6*, U Pr W Africa) Intl Scholars.

***Mill Hill Pilot.** William J. Blanton. 193p. 1998. 23.95 (*1-57087-375-5*) Prof Pr NC.

Mill Iron Site. Ed. by George Frison. LC 95-49369. (Illus.). 248p. (C). 1996. 34.95 (*0-8263-1676-X*) U of NM Pr.

Mill of Luck & Plenty: And Other Stories. Ioan Slavici. Tr. by Eugenia Farca from RUM. 250p. (C). 1994. 37.00 (*0-88033-248-4*, 351, Pub. by East Eur Monographs) Col U Pr.

Mill on Bentham & Coleridge. John Stuart Mill. LC 82-15854. 168p. (C). 1983. reprint ed. lib. bdg. 42.50 (*0-313-23740-9*, MIOB, Greenwood Pr) Greenwood.

Mill on Liberty. John Stuart Mill. (C). 1997. pap. text. write for info. (*0-321-02591-1*) Addson-Wesley Educ.

Mill on Liberty. Jonathan Riley. LC 97-35429. (Routledge Philosophy Guidebooks Ser.). 256p. (C). 1998. pap. 12.99 (*0-415-14189-3*) Routledge.

Mill on Liberty: A Defence. 2nd ed. John Gray. 192p. (C). 1996. pap. 22.99 (*0-415-12474-3*) Routledge.

Mill on Liberty: Jonathan Riley. Jonathan Riley. LC 97-35429. (Philosophy Guidebooks Ser.). 256p. (C). 1998. 50.00 (*0-415-14188-5*) Routledge.

Mill on the Boot: The Story of the St. Paul & Tacoma Lumber Company. Murray Morgan. LC 82-16107. (Illus.). 286p. 1982. 19.95 (*0-295-95949-5*) U of Wash Pr.

Mill on the Boot: The Story of the St. Paul & Tacoma Lumber Company. Murray Morgan. LC 82-16107. (Illus.). 296p. 1985. pap. 17.50 (*0-295-96273-9*) U of Wash Pr.

Mill on the Boot: The Story of the St. Paul & Tacoma Lumber Company. Murray Morgan. LC 82-16107. (Illus.). 286p. 1982. 19.95 (*0-685-38498-5*) Wash St Hist Soc.

Mill on the Floss. George Eliot, pseud. 1976. 30.95 (*0-8488-0483-X*) Amereon Ltd.

Mill on the Floss, 001. George Eliot, pseud. Ed. by G. S. Haight. LC 62-16032. (YA). (gr. 9 up). 1972. pap. 13.96 (*0-395-05151-7*, RivEd) HM.

Mill on the Floss. George Eliot, pseud. (Cloth Bound Pocket Ser.). 240p. 1998. 7.95 (*3-89508-461-1*) Konemann.

Mill on the Floss. George Eliot, pseud. Ed. by Peter Cairns. 1988. pap. 5.72 (*0-582-33169-2*, 72063) Longman.

Mill on the Floss. George Eliot, pseud. 96p. 1994. pap. 12.95 (*1-85459-276-9*, M88, Pub. by N Hern Bks) Theatre Comm.

Mill on the Floss. George Eliot, pseud. 1965. mass mkt. 5.95 (*0-451-52396-2*) NAL.

Mill on the Floss. George Eliot, pseud. Ed. by Gordon S. Haight. (Clarendon Edition of the Novels of George Eliot). (Illus.). 516p. (C). 1980. text 130.00 (*0-19-812560-7*) OUP.

Mill on the Floss. George Eliot, pseud. Ed. by Gordon S. Haight. (Oxford World's Classics Ser.). 566p. 1998. pap. 7.95 (*0-19-283364-2*) OUP.

Mill on the Floss. George Eliot, pseud. LC 87-202458. 1981. 11.05 (*0-606-03858-2*, Pub. by Turtleback) Demco.

Mill on the Floss. George Eliot, pseud. Ed. by A. S. Byatt. 696p. 1980. pap. 8.95 (*0-14-043120-9*, Penguin Classics) Viking Penguin.

Mill on the Floss. George Eliot, pseud. (Classics Library). 512p. pap. 3.95 (*1-85326-074-6*, 0746WW, Pub. by Wrdsworth Edits) NTC Contemp Pub Co.

Mill on the Floss. large type ed. George Eliot, pseud. 562p. 1991. 24.95 (*1-85089-383-7*, Pub. by ISIS Lrg Prnt) Transaction Pubs.

Mill on the Floss see Writings of George Eliot

Mill on the Floss: A Natural History. Rosemary Ashton. (Twayne's Masterwork Studies: No. 54). 144p. (C). 1990. 23.95 (*0-8057-9406-9*, Twayne); per. 13.95 (*0-8057-8134-X*, Twyne) Mac Lib Ref.

Mill on the Floss: Authoritative Text, Backgrounds, Criticism. George Eliot, pseud. Ed. by Carol T. Christ. LC 93-13151. (Critical Editions Ser.). 613p. (C). 1993. pap. text 18.25 (*0-393-96332-2*) Norton.

Mill on the Floss Notes. William Holland. (Cliffs Notes Ser.). 96p. 1966. pap. 4.95 (*0-8220-0834-3*, Cliff) IDG Bks.

Mill on the Roeliff Jansen Kill: Two Hundred Fifty Years of American Industrial History. Roeliff Jansen Historical Society Staff. Ed. by Harold Faber. LC 93-79570. (Illus.). 144p. 1993. pap. 15.00 (*0-9628523-9-2*) Blk Dome Pr.

Mill on the Third River: A History of the Davey Company Makers of Binders Board since 1842. Helen B. Cushman. Ed. by Robert Burnett & Donald Bagger. (Illus.). 147p. (C). 1992. write for info. (*0-9628551-0-3*) Davey NJ.

Mill River: River Mill: With Associated Music. Bob Chaplin. (Illus.). 60p. 1997. 45.00 (*0-89822-120-X*) Visual Studies.

Mill Town, 1723-1804. Edwin Harrington. (Illus.). 75p. (Orig.). 1994. pap. 8.00 (*0-941066-08-8*) Hillside Pr.

Mill Valley: The Early Years. Barry Spitz. LC 96-92299. (Illus.). 272p. 1996. 35.00 (*0-9620715-8-7*) Potrero Meadow Pub.

***Millais.** Peter Funnell. LC 98-67804. 1999. pap. text 35.00 (*0-691-00720-9*, Pub. by Princeton U Pr) Cal Prin Full Svc.

***Millais: Portraits.** Peter Funnell. LC 98-67804. 1999. 65.00 (*0-691-00719-5*, Pub. by Princeton U Pr) Cal Prin Full Svc.

Millais: Three Generations in Nature, Art & Sport. 45.00 (*0-948253-28-2*) Sportmans Pr.

Millais & His Works. Marion H. Spielmann. LC 74-148306. reprint ed. 34.50 (*0-404-06175-3*) AMS Pr.

Millard Fillmore. Jane C. Casey. LC 87-35183. (Encyclopedia of Presidents Ser.). (Illus.). 100p. (J). (gr. 3 up). 1988. lib. bdg. 24.00 (*0-516-01353-X*) Childrens.

Millard Fillmore. Paul Joseph. LC 98-16241. (United States Presidents Ser.). 32p. (J). 1999. lib. bdg. 18.60 (*1-57765-235-5*, Checkerboard Library) ABDO Pub Co.

***Millard Fillmore.** Robert J. Scarry. (Illus.). 512p. 2000. 75.00 (*0-7864-0869-3*) McFarland & Co.

Millard Fillmore: Biography of a President. Robert J. Rayback. Ed. by Katherine E. Speirs. LC 91-78015. (Signature Ser.). (Illus.). 470p. 1992. reprint ed. 32.50 (*0-945707-04-5*) Amer Political.

Millard Fillmore: Thirteenth President of the United States. Kevin J. Law. Ed. by Richard G. Young. LC 89-25651. (Presidents of the United States Ser.). (Illus.). 128p. (J). (gr. 5-9). 1990. lib. bdg. 19.93 (*0-944483-61-5*) Garrett Ed Corp.

Millard on Channel Analysis: The Key to Share Price Prediction. Brian J. Millard. LC 96-46490. 212p. 1997. pap. 48.50 (*0-471-96845-5*) Wiley.

Millard on Profitable Charting Techniques. 2nd ed. Brian J. Millard. LC 96-47782. 222p. 1997. pap. 48.50 (*0-471-96846-3*) Wiley.

Millard on Traded Options. 2nd ed. Brian J. Millard. LC 96-46656. 212p. 1997. pap. 48.50 (*0-471-96780-7*) Wiley.

Millay at 100: A Critical Reappraisal. Ed. by Diane P. Freedman. LC 94-12823. 240p. (C). 1995. 36.95 (*0-8093-1973-X*) S Ill U Pr.

Millbrook: A Narrative of the Early Years of American Psychedelianism, Recension of 1997. rev. ed. Art Kleps. LC 95-7217. (Illus.). 222p. 1998. pap. 25.00 (*0-9600388-6-8*) Orig Kleptonian.

***Millburn - Short Hills: New Jersey.** Owen Lampe. LC 00-100181. (Images of America Ser.). (Illus.). 128p. 2000. pap. 18.99 (*0-7385-0413-0*) Arcadia Publng.

Millcroft Inn Cookbook. Fredy Stamm. 128p. 1987. pap. write for info. (*0-88984-108-X*) Porcup Quill.

Mille et un Fantomes. Alexandre Dumas. (FRE.). 238p. 1980. pap. 7.95 (*0-7859-5573-9*) Fr & Eur.

Mille et Une Annees de la Nostalgie. Rachid Boudjedra. (Folio Ser.: No. 1998). (FRE.). 1988. pap. 14.95 (*2-07-038087-4*) Schoenhof.

Mille et une Nuits, Vol. I. unabridged ed. Tr. by Antoine Galland. (FRE.). Date not set. reprint ed. pap. 8.95 (*2-87714-362-7*, Pub. by Bookking Intl) Distribks Inc.

Mille et une Nuits, Vol. II. unabridged ed. Tr. by Antoine Galland. (FRE.). Date not set. reprint ed. pap. 8.95 (*2-87714-363-5*, Pub. by Bookking Intl) Distribks Inc.

Mille et une Nuits, Vol. III. unabridged ed. Tr. by Antoine Galland. (FRE.). Date not set. reprint ed. pap. 8.95 (*2-87714-364-3*, Pub. by Bookking Intl) Distribks Inc.

Mille et une Nuits, Vol. IV. unabridged ed. Tr. by Antoine Galland. (FRE.). Date not set. reprint ed. pap. 8.95 (*2-87714-361-9*, Pub. by Bookking Intl) Distribks Inc.

Mille Francs de Recompense. Victor Hugo. 4.95 (*0-686-54081-6*) Fr & Eur.

Mille Lacs - Thirty Years on the Big Lake: Memoirs & Secrets of a Walleye Fishing Guide. Joe Fellegy. (Illus.). 272p. 1990. pap. 9.95 (*0-9626907-0-8*) Mille Lacs Pr.

Mille Miglia: The Postwar Years. Motorbooks Staff. 1998. 29.95 (*88-7911-188-4*) Giorgio Nada Editore.

Mille Neuf Cent Trente-Nuef-Mille Neuf Cent Quarante-Cinc: Poemes. Jules Supervielle. (FRE.). 166p. 1946. pap. 10.95 (*0-7859-1328-9*, 2070261433) Fr & Eur.

Milled Coinage of England, 1662-1946. Ed. by Howard W. Linecar. 1971. 22.00 (*0-932106-61-7*) S J Durst.

Millefiori Beads from the West African Trade. John Picard & Ruth Picard. (Beads from the West African Trade Ser.: Vol. VI). (Illus.). 88p. (Orig.). 1991. pap. 25.00 (*0-9622884-1-1*) Picard African.

Millel Plus. Bob Blankenship. 276p. 1994. pap. text 35.00 (*0-9633774-4-2*) Cherokee Roots.

Millenarian Anthologies see Millennium in America: From the Puritan Migration to the Civil War

Millenarian Bolshevism, 1900 to 1920. David G. Rowley. (Modern European History Ser.). 392p. 1987. text 15.00 (*0-8240-8061-0*) Garland.

Millenarian Movements in Historical Context. Michael J. St. Clair. LC 91-36655. 386p. 1992. text 25.00 (*0-8153-0218-5*) Garland.

Millenarian Piety of Roger Williams. W. Clark Gilpin. LC 78-20786. 1979. lib. bdg. 19.00 (*0-226-29397-1*) U Ch Pr.

Millenarian Piety of Roger Williams. W. Clark Gilpin. LC 78-20786. 222p. reprint ed. pap. 68.90 (*0-608-09310-6*, 205418400004) Bks Demand.

Millenarian Rebellion in China: The Eight Trigrams Uprising of 1813. Susan Naquin. LC 75-18180. (Yale Historical Publications: Miscellany: No. 108). (Illus.). 398p. reprint ed. pap. 123.40 (*0-8357-8224-7*, 203384100087) Bks Demand.

Millenarian Vision, Capitalist Reality: Brazil's Contestado Rebellion, 1912-1916. Todd A. Diacon. LC 91-521. 215p. 1991. pap. text 19.95 (*0-8223-1167-4*); lib. bdg. 45.50 (*0-8223-1157-7*) Duke.

***Millenarian World of Early Mormonism.** Grant Underwood. 224p. 1999. pap. text 17.95 (*0-252-06826-2*) U of Ill Pr.

Millenarianism & Peasant Politics in Vietnam. Hue-Tam H. Tai. (East Asian Monographs: No. 99). (Illus.). 240p. 1983. 46.50 (*0-674-57555-5*) HUP.

Millenary. Raeburn Miller. Ed. by Richard Katrovas & Maxine Cassin. LC 85-63468. (Journal Press Bks.: Louisiana Legacy). 88p. (Orig.). 1986. pap. 12.00 (*0-938498-06-1*) New Orleans Poetry.

Millenial Debate: Owen vs. Campbell see Millennium in America: From the Puritan Migration to the Civil War

***Millenial Dogs on Main Street: Another Litter.** Tom Clyde. 160p. 1999. pap. 13.95 (*0-9668829-1-1*) Giardia Springs.

Millenishocks: Abandoning the Chase: Hints on How the Turn of the Century Will Reorient Our Priorities. Twin Michaels. LC 98-88308. (Illus.). 144p. 1998. pap. 19.99 (*0-9667846-6-9*, HRH326) Metro Ventures.

***Millenium.** Lv. 3. (C). 2000. 7.00 (*0-582-43285-5*) Addison-Wesley.

Millenium. Felipe Fernandez-Armesto. 864p. 1996. mass mkt. 29.95 (*0-385-25612-4*) Doubleday.

Millenium. Douglas E. Winter. 1999. pap. 22.95 (*0-525-93557-6*) NAL.

***Millenium: A Comedy of the Year 2000.** Upton Sinclair. 272p. 2000. pap. 14.95 (*1-58322-021-6*) Seven Stories.

Millenium: Aspects from Another Angle. George Sprague. 70p. 1997. pap. 8.95 (*1-57502-634-1*, PO1795) Morris Pubng.

Millenium: Christianity & Russia (AD 988-1988) Ed. by Albert Leong. LC 90-46791. 224p. 1990. pap. 13.95 (*0-88141-080-2*) St Vladimirs.

Millenium: What It Is Not, & What It Is. George P. Fletcher. pap. 5.00 (*0-87377-007-2*) GAM Pubns.

Millenium Falcon. Mouse Works Staff. 4p. (J). 1997. 4.98 (*1-57082-640-4*, Pub. by Mouse Works) Time Warner.

Millenium Fears, Fantasies & Facts: Astrologers Look Toward 2000. Maritha Pottenger et al. 157p. 1998. pap. 12.95 (*0-935127-62-3*) ACS Pubns.

Millenium Hall. Sarah. Scott. (Virago Modern Classics Ser.). 272p. 1986. mass mkt. 6.95 (*0-14-016143-0*, Penguin Bks) Viking Penguin.

Millenium Hall: Sarah Scott. Ed. by Gary Kelly. 260p. 1995. 12.95 (*1-55111-015-6*) Broadview Pr.

Millenium Judgement or Jubilee. Brian Daley. LC 97-14056. (Illus.). 42p. (J). 1997. pap. 2.95 (*0-8198-4796-8*) Pauline Bks.

***Millenium Man: New & Selected Poems.** unabridged ed. Craig Easley. (Cimarron Poetry Ser.). 46p. 2000. pap. 5.00 (*0-9653587-5-5*) Meridien Pr.

***Millenium Membership: How to Attract & Keep Members in the New Marketplace.** Mark Levin. LC 99-50222. (Illus.). xvi, 151p. 1999. pap. 35.00 (*0-88034-163-7*) Am Soc Assn Execs.

Millenium, Messiahs & Mayhem: Contemporary Apocalyptic Movements. Ed. by Thomas Robbins & Susan J. Palmer. LC 97-12408. 332p. (C). 1997. 75.00 (*0-415-91648-8*); pap. 19.99 (*0-415-91649-6*) Routledge.

***Millenium Myth.** Ed. by N. T. Wright. LC 99-29665. 128p. 1999. pap. 12.95 (*0-664-25841-7*) Westminster John Knox.

Millennium #1: The Frenchman: This Title Was Remaindered 1/98Smitrovich,&Bill, Set. abr. ed. Elizabeth Hand. 1997. audio 18.00 (*0-694-51832-8*) HarperAudio.

Millenium of Faith: Christianity in Russia, 988-1988. Francis House. LC 88-3256. Orig. Title: The Russian Phoenix. (Illus.). 133p. 1988. pap. 10.95 (*0-88141-073-X*) St Vladimirs.

Millenium of Family Change: Feudalism to Capitalism in North Western Europe. Wally Seccombe. 304p. (C). 1995. pap. 20.00 (*1-85984-052-3*, C0512, Pub. by Verso) Norton.

***Millenium Pin Book Walt Disney World Exclusive.** Disney Staff. 1999. 8.95 (*0-7868-6612-8*, Pub. by Disney Pr) Time Warner.

***Millenium Project.** Cal Glover. LC 98-12659. 224p. 1998. pap. 14.95 (*0-943972-63-9*) Homestead WY.

Millenium Prophecies. Mark Thurston. LC 97-181156. 192p. 1997. pap. 12.00 (*1-57566-143-8*) Kensgtn Pub Corp.

***Millenium Stocks.** Richard C. Dorf. LC 99-45048. 239p. 1999. 39.95 (*1-57444-250-3*) St Lucie Pr.

Millenium Strategies Workbook: Preparing for the Future. BSW Consulting, Inc. Staff. 63p. 1998. pap., wbk. ed. 79.95 (*1-56829-094-2*) Med Group Mgmt.

Millennial Activities in Late Thirteenth-Century Albi, France. Kathryn M. Karrer. LC 96-17598. (Studies in French Civilization: Vol. 11). 100p. 1997. text 59.95 (*0-7734-8819-7*) E Mellen.

***Millennial Afterlives: A Retrospective.** Stratis Haviaras. 44p. 2000. pap. 15.00 (*1-887196-06-4*) Wells Col Pr.

Millennial Blues, from "Apocalypse Now" to "The Edge" see Blood Poets: A Cinema of Savagery, 1958-1998

Millennial Blues, from "Apocalypse Now" to "The Matrix" see Blood Poets: A Cinema of Savagery, 1958 - 1999

***Millennial Capitalism & the Culture of Neoliberalism.** Ed. by Jean Comaroff. 320p. 2000. pap. 12.00 (*0-8223-6480-8*) Duke.

***Millennial Child: Transforming Education in the Twenty-First Century.** Eugene Schwartz. LC 99-36524. 320p. 1999. pap. 19.95 (*0-88010-465-1*) Anthroposophic.

***Millennial City: A New Urban Paradigm for 21st Century America.** Ed. by Myron Magnet. LC 99-88326. 448p. 2000. text 27.50 (*1-56663-285-4*, Pub. by I R Dee) Natl Bk Netwk.

Millennial Dawnism: The Blasphemous Religion. I. M. Haldeman. 80p. 1988. reprint ed. pap. 2.95 (*1-883858-43-7*) Witness CA.

Millennial Deception: Angels, Aliens & the Antichrist. Timothy J. Dailey. LC 95-16266. 240p. (gr. 10). 1995. pap. 11.99 (*0-8007-9233-5*) Chosen Bks.

Millennial Dreams: Contemporary Culture & Capital in the North. Paul Smith. LC 97-5093. 1997. 60.00 (*1-85984-918-0*, Pub. by Verso); pap. 19.00 (*1-85984-038-8*, Pub. by Verso) Norton.

Millennial Expectations & Jewish Liberties: A Study of the Efforts to Convert the Jews in Britain, up to the Mid-Nineteenth Century Mel Scult. LC 78-317829. (Studies in Judaism in Modern Times). xvi, 153p. 1978. write for info. (*90-04-05066-3*) Brill Academic Pubs.

***Millennial Fables: Seven Ahort Stories That Can Only Cause Trouble.** Richard Gloff. LC 00-190422. 120p. 2000. 25.00 (*0-7388-1681-7*); pap. 18.00 (*0-7388-1682-5*) Xlibris Corp.

Millennial Fever & the End of the World. George Knight. LC 93-25531. 384p. 1993. pap. 14.99 (*0-8163-1176-5*) Pacific Pr Pub Assn.

Millennial Generation: Leading Today's Youth into the Future. Vaughn J. Featherstone. LC 99-10519. 180p. 1999. 18.95 (*1-57345-524-5*) Deseret Bk.

Millennial Harbinger - Index. David McWhirter. LC 81-65031. (Millennial Harbinger Ser.). 776p. (C). 1981. 19.99 (*0-89900-228-5*) College Pr Pub.

Millennial Impulse in Michigan, 1830-1860: The Second Coming in the Third New England. Nathan G. Thomas. (Studies in American Religion: Vol. 44). 150p. 1989. write for info. (*0-88946-646-7*) E Mellen.

***Millennial Journal.** James Magorian. LC 00-90544. 64p. 2000. pap. 12.00 (*0-930674-54-5*) Black Oak.

Millennial Landscape: The Ethics & Aesthetics of Dealing with the Landscape, 1. David Jacques. 1999. 59.50 (*1-870673-28-X*) Antique Collect.

Millennial Leap: Launching a Strategic, City Wide Youth Ministry Model for the 21st Century. Mike King. Date not set. pap. 20.00 (*0-9678689-0-4*) KCYFC.

Millennial Maze: Sorting Out Evangelical Options. Stanley J. Grenz. LC 92-14865. 284p. (Orig.). 1992. pap. 13.99 (*0-8308-1757-3*, 1757) InterVarsity.

Millennial Myths: Paintings by Lynn Randolph. Marilyn Zeitlin et al. (Illus.). 64p. 1998. pap. 18.95 (*0-9644646-5-9*) Ariz St U Art Mus.

Millennial New World. Frank Graziano. LC 98-36634. 376p. 1999. 45.00 (*0-19-512432-4*) OUP.

Millennial Optimism & Despair see Millennium in America: From the Puritan Migration to the Civil War

Millennial Project: Colonizing the Galaxy - in 8 Easy Steps. Marshall T. Savage. LC 92-27807. (Illus.). 520p. (Orig.). 1993. pap. 18.95 (*0-9633914-9-6*); lib. bdg. 24.95 (*0-9633914-8-8*) Empyrean Pub.

Millennial Project: Colonizing the Galaxy in 8 Easy Steps. Marshall T. Savage. 512p. 1994. pap. 16.95 (*0-316-77163-5*) Little.

Millennial Project: Postcards. Marshall Savage. 1994. pap. write for info. (*0-316-77167-8*) Little.

Millennial Project Poster. Marshall Savage. 1994. pap. write for info. (*0-316-77131-7*) Little.

Millennial Run: An LDS Novel to Celebrate the Year 2000. Wayne Hunter. 273p. 1999. pap. 20.00 (*0-9671312-0-0*) Pillar Pr CA.

***Millennial Scriptions: The Ashen Book of Logres.** David C. D. Gansz. 253p. 2000. 25.00 (*0-9626046-5-8*) OtherWind Pr.

Millennial Seduction: A Skeptic Confronts Apocalyptic Culture. Lee Quinby. LC 98-46230. 1999. 39.95 (*0-8014-3592-7*); pap. 16.95 (*0-8014-8601-7*) Cornell U Pr.

***Millennial Spring: Eight New Oregon Poets.** Ed. by Peter Sears & Michael Malan. 112p. 1999. pap. 12.95 (*0-936085-42-8*, Pub. by Blue Heron OR) Consort Bk Sales.

***Millennial Visions: Essays on Twentieth-Century Millenarianism.** Ed. by Martha F. Lee. LC 99-88489. 240p. 2000. 64.00 (*0-275-96690-9*, C6690, Praeger Pubs) Greenwood.

***Millennial Visions & Earthly Pursuits: The Israelite House of David.** Robert C. Myers. LC 99-492276. (Illus.). 31p. 1999. pap. 8.95 (*0-9660808-9-0*) Berrien Cnty.

Millennial World Order: Discover the Spirit, Philosophy & Conditions of the Coming 1,000 Year Utopian Age. Frank J. Sherosky. 224p. 1998. pap. 16.95 (*1-890170-04-6*) Strategic MI.

Millennialism: An International Bibliography. Theodore T. Daniels. LC 91-39298. 692p. 1992. text 35.00 (*0-8240-7102-6*, SS667) Garland.

Millennialism: The Two Major Views. Charles L. Feinberg. 1985. 15.99 (*0-88469-166-7*) BMH Bks.

Millennialism & Social Theory. Gary North. LC 90-47609. 393p. 1990. 14.95 (*0-930464-49-4*) Inst Christian.

An Asterisk (*) at the beginning of an entry indicates that the title is appearing for the first time.

Millennialism & Violence. Ed. by Michael Barkun. (Political Violence Ser.). 177p. (Orig.). 1996. 35.00 (*0-7146-4708-X*, Pub. by F Cass Pubs); pap. 18.50 (*0-7146-4250-9*, Pub. by F Cass Pubs) Intl Spec Bk.

Millennialism of Cotton Mather: An Historical & Theological Analysis. John S. Erwin. LC 89-48625. (Studies in American Religion: Vol. 45). 248p. 1990. lib. bdg. 89.95 (*0-88946-645-9*) E Mellen.

***Millennialism, Persecution & Violence.** Ed. by Catherine Wessinger. LC 99-16575. 416p. 1999. 49.95 (*0-8156-2809-9*) Syracuse U Pr.

***Millennialism, Persecution & Violence: Historical Cases.** Catherine Wessinger. LC 99-16575. 416p. 2000. pap. text 29.95 (*0-8156-0599-4*) Syracuse U Pr.

Millennialism, Utopianism, & Progress. Theodore Olson. 1981. text 45.00 (*0-8020-5506-0*) U of Toronto Pr.

***Millennials Rising: The Next American Generation.** Neil Howe. 304p. 2000. pap. 14.00 (*0-375-70719-0*) Vin Bks.

***Millennimania.** Martin Weber. 127p. 1998. pap. 5.95 (*1-57847-058-7*) Genl Conf Svnth-day.

***Millennium.** Anderson. 336p. 2000. text 15.95 (*0-312-87394-8*) Forge NYC.

Millennium. Jack Anderson. 416p. 1995. mass mkt. 5.99 (*0-8125-2258-3*, Pub. by Tor Bks) St Martin.

Millennium. Andrews & Mcmeel Staff. (Little Bks.). (Illus.). 80p. 1998. 4.95 (*0-8362-5222-5*) Andrews & McMeel.

Millennium. Fernandez Armesto. (Illus.). 816p. 1996. per. 18.00 (*0-684-82536-8*) S&S Trade.

Millennium. Hakim Bey. 1996. pap. 7.00 (*1-57027-045-7*) Autonomedia.

Millennium. Loraine Boettner. 1991. pap. 8.99 (*0-87552-113-4*) P & R Pubng.

Millennium. Daniel Cohen. (YA). 1999. mass mkt. 3.99 (*0-671-01562-1*) PB.

***Millennium.** DK Publishing Staff. (Dk Sticker Gift Box Ser.). 1999. 9.99 (*0-7894-4794-0*); pap. 6.99 (*0-7894-4796-7*) DK Pub Inc.

***Millennium.** Havoc Publishing Staff. 1999. 8.00 (*1-57977-618-3*) Havoc Pub.

Millennium. Maybury D. Lewis. 1999. pap. 15.00 (*0-14-012432-2*, Viking) Viking Penguin.

Millennium. Gordon Lindsay. (Revelation Ser.: Vol. 15). 1962. 2.50 (*0-89985-048-0*) Christ for the Nations.

***Millennium.** Time Magazine Editors. (Illus.). 160p. 2000. 24.95 (*1-883013-97-6*) Natl Bk Netwk.

Millennium. John Varley. 264p. (Orig.). 1999. pap. text 12.95 (*0-441-00677-9*) ACE.

Millennium. John Varley. (Orig.). 1989. mass mkt. 4.99 (*0-441-53183-0*) Ace Bks.

Millennium: A History of the Last Thousand Years. Felipe Fernandez-Armesto. (Illus.). 816p. 1995. 34.50 (*0-684-80361-5*) S&S Trade.

Millennium: A Latin Reader AD, 374-1374. Ed. by F. E. Harrison. (LAT.). 254p. 1991. reprint ed. 20.00 (*0-86516-191-7*) Bolchazy-Carducci.

***Millennium: A Record Book about the Turn of the Millennium.** Havoc Publishing Staff. 1999. write for info. (*1-57977-143-2*) Havoc Pub.

Millennium: A Rough Guide to the Year 2000. Nick Hanna. LC 99-176671. (Rough Guides Ser.). 224p. 1998. pap. 8.95 (*1-85828-314-0*, Penguin Bks) Viking Penguin.

Millennium: A Rough Guide to the Year 2000. 2nd ed. Nick Hanna. (Rough Guides Ser.). 1999. pap. 8.95 (*1-85828-405-8*) Penguin Putnam.

***Millennium: Apocalypse, Antichrist, & Old English Monsters, c. 1000.** Zacharias Thundy. LC 98-73773. 319p. 1998. 29.95 (*0-940121-51-4*) Cross Cultural Pubns.

Sophisticated & insightful, this book celebrates the dawning of a new millennium by chronicling the narrative story of the first millennium. By reviewing both Western & Eastern literary traditions, this work offers a new appreciation for the apocalyptic dimensions of the world's folklore & mythology. The volume clearly demonstrates that the story of our future resides in our narrative. ***Publisher Paid Annotation.***

***Millennium: Architecture Studio.** (Illus.). 256p. 2000. 65.00 (*1-86470-021-1*, Pub. by Images) Antique Collect.

***Millennium: Daryl Jackson.** (Illus.). 256p. 2000. 65.00 (*1-86470-049-1*, Pub. by Images) Antique Collect.

***Millennium: Force Majeure, Vol. 5.** Lewis Gannett. 240p. 1998. mass mkt. 5.99 (*0-06-105816-5*, HarperPrism) HarpC.

Millennium: Glimpses into the 21st Centuty. Alberto Villoldo. LC 80-53147. 1981. 15.00 (*0-87477-145-5*) Putnam Pub Group.

***Millennium: Its 500 Most Famous People.** Arther Trace. LC 99-91443. 2000. 25.00 (*0-7388-0786-9*); pap. 18.00 (*0-7388-0787-7*) Xlibris Corp.

***Millennium: Kisho Kurokawa.** (Illus.). 256p. 2000. 65.00 (*1-86470-019-X*, Pub. by Images) Antique Collect.

Millennium: My Reflections on the End of One Era & the Beginning of Another. Ed. by Andrews & McMeel Staff. 1998. 14.95 (*0-8362-8298-1*) Andrews & McMeel.

Millennium: Peace, Promises, & the Day They Take Our Money Away. abr. ed. Texe Marrs. (Illus.). 272p. (Orig.). 1990. pap. 10.95 (*0-9620086-5-6*) Living Truth Pubs.

***Millennium: SOM.** (Illus.). 256p. 2000. 65.00 (*1-86470-018-1*, Pub. by Images) Antique Collect.

***Millennium: The Thousand Year Reign of King Jesus.** George Otis. 2000. 18.99 (*1-57778-127-9*) Albury Pub.

Millennium: The Wild & the Innocent. Jorge Zamacona. 256p. 2000. mass mkt. 5.99 (*0-06-105817-3*, HarperPrism) HarpC.

Millennium: Tools for the Coming Changes. Lyssa Royal. 205p. 1999. pap. 13.95 (*0-9631320-3-2*, Pub. by Royal Priest) ACCESS Pubs Network.

***Millennium: Tribal Wisdom & the Modern World.** David Maybury-Lewis. (Illus.). 397p. 1999. reprint ed. text 25.00 (*0-7881-6418-X*) DIANE Pub.

***Millennium: Twenty First Century Orange County** Marge Bitetti. LC 98-67812. 170p. 1998. write for info. (*1-881547-27-2*) Pioneer Pubns.

***Millennium: Weeds, Vol. 3.** Victor Koman. 288p. 1998. mass mkt. 5.99 (*0-06-105837-8*, HarperPrism) HarpC.

***Millennium Agenda: The Goals & Deceptions of the New Age Movement in the 21st Century.** Jeff Justus. LC 99-97821. (Illus.). 208p. 2000. pap. 12.95 (*0-9676350-0-4*) Cleff Pubg.

Millennium Approaches. Dennis E. Hensley. 240p. 1998. mass mkt. 5.99 (*0-380-78703-2*, Avon Bks) Morrow Avon.

***Millennium Aptitude Test: Entrance Exam for the 21st Century.** Dennis McClellan. 200p. 2000. pap. 15.95 (*0-9673439-0-9*) InSync Commn.

***Millennium Art.** Taschen America Staff. (Illus.). 2000. pap. 4.99 (*3-8228-6086-7*) Taschen Amer.

Millennium Baby: Baby, It's Cold Outside; One-Night Stand Baby; Baby Jane Doe. Kristine Rolofson et al. (Promo Ser.). 2000. per. 5.99 (*0-373-83418-7*, 1-83418-3) Harlequin Bks.

Millennium Baby's First Year. Deni Bown. (Illus.). 56p. 1999. 17.95 (*1-56458-851-3*) DK Pub Inc.

***Millennium Bible: Complete Commentary on All Scripture Passages Related to the Second Coming.** William Edward Biederwolf. 728p. 1999. pap. 6.99 (*1-58558-002-3*) Global Pubs.

***Millennium Blitzkrieg.** Martin Cole. LC 99-93990. 279p. 2000. pap. 13.95 (*0-533-13213-4*) Vantage.

Millennium Bomb: Countdown to a 400 Billion Pound Cata$trophe. Simon Reeve & Colin McGhee. (Illus.). 195p. 1999. pap. 15.95 (*1-883319-82-X*) Frog Ltd CA.

Millennium Book of Prophecy: 777 Visions & Predictions from Nostradamus, Edgar Cacye & Gurdjieff. John Hogue. 400p. 1997. pap. 14.00 (*0-06-251498-9*, Pub. by Harper SF) HarpC.

***Millennium Bug: A Pictorial Scrapbook of the Volkswagen Beetle.** Keith Seume. (Illus.). 160p. 1999. 29.95 (*0-7603-0818-7*, 129262AP, Pub. by MBI Pubg) Motorbooks Intl.

Millennium Bug: Banking & the Year 2000 Computer Problem. Ed. by James A. Leach. 167p. (C). 1999. pap. text 25.00 (*0-7881-7840-7*) DIANE Pub.

Millennium Bug: Banking & the Year 2000 Computer Problem Hearing Before the Committee on Banking & Financial Services, House of Representatives, 105th Congress, First Session, November 4, 1997. LC 98-160843. iii, 167p. 1997. write for info. (*0-16-056227-9*) USGPO.

Millennium Bug: How to Survive the Coming Chaos. Michael S. Hyatt. LC 98-11505. 286p. 1998. 24.95 (*0-89526-373-4*) Regnery Pub.

Millennium Bug: How to Survive the Coming Chaos. Michael S. Hyatt. LC 99-12311. (Illus.). 304p. 1999. reprint ed. pap. 13.00 (*0-7679-0374-9*) Broadway BDD.

***Millennium Bug: Is This the End of the World As We Know It?** Jon Paulien. Ed. by B. Russell Holt. LC 99-30888. 128p. 1999. pap. 9.99 (*0-8163-1755-0*) Pacific Pr Pub Assn.

***Millennium Bug Debugged: The Story Behind All the Y2K Sensationalism.** Hank Hanegraaff. LC 99-6769. 1999. pap. 8.99 (*0-7642-2339-9*) Bethany Hse.

Millennium Candidate: A New Approach to Getting the Job That's Right for You. Kathy Wilson. 224p. 1999. pap. 14.95 (*1-86204-380-9*, Pub. by Element MA) Penguin Putnam.

Millennium Career Force. Jack L. Fadely. Ed. by Virginia Hosler. 232p. (Orig.). 1991. pap. text 17.50 (*0-934293-10-4*) Huber-Copeland Pub.

Millennium Champagne & Sparkling Wine Guide. Tom Stevenson. LC 98-17158. 192p. 1998. pap. 19.95 (*0-7894-3561-6*) DK Pub Inc.

Millennium Children: Tales of the Shift. Caryl Dennis. Ed. by Parker Whitman. (Orig.). 1997. pap. 18.00 (*0-9627845-1-6*) Rainbows Unltd.

***Millennium Children's Library, Set.** Irene D. H. Sasman. (Illus.). (J). (gr. 2-3). 1999. pap. 99.95 (*1-56831-989-4*) Lrning Connect.

***Millennium Children's Library Set.** Irene D. H. Sasman. (Illus.). 1999. pap. 99.95 (*1-56831-987-8*) Lrning Connect.

***Millennium Children's Library Set, Set.** Irene D. H. Sasman. (Illus.). (J). (gr. 4-8). 1999. pap. 99.95 (*1-56831-990-8*) Lrning Connect.

Millennium Clues for the Clueless: God's Word in Your World. Illus. by Elwood Smith. (Clues for the Clueless Ser.). 256p. 1999. pap. 8.99 (*1-57748-566-1*) Barbour Pub.

Millennium Collection of Old Ukrainian Books at the University of Toronto Library: A Catalogue. Edward Kasinec et al. LC 85-240386. ix, 36p. 1984. write for info. (*0-7727-5105-6*) U of Toronto Pr.

***Millennium Cookbook: Extraordinary Vegetarian Cuisine.** Good Housekeeping Editors. 2000. write for info. (*0-688-17807-3*, Hearst) Hearst Commns.

Millennium Cookbook: Extraordinary Vegetarian Cuisine. Eric Tucker et al. LC 97-38978. (Illus.). 272p. 1998. pap. 19.95 (*0-89815-899-0*) Ten Speed Pr.

Millennium Countdown: A Practical Guide to Preparing Your Business for the Year 2000. Lynn Craig & Mike Kusminak. 150p. 1998. pap. 14.95 (*0-7494-2887-2*) Kogan Page Ltd.

Millennium Crisis. Bradford Morgan. LC 98-89502. 375p. 1998. text 25.00 (*0-7388-0235-2*); pap. text 15.00 (*0-7388-0236-0*) Xlibris Corp.

Millennium Culture. Nell Leach. pap. 12.00 (*1-84166-025-6*, Pub. by Ellipsis) Norton.

Millennium Edition of the Decoded New Testament: Origins & History of the Paradosis or Secret Tradition of the Oral Law Called the Gospel, with Commentary on the Canonical New Testament, Apocrypha, Pseudepigrapha, Old Testament, Dead Sea Scrolls, Ancient Fragments, & Other Religious Texts. rev. ed. Gene Savoy. LC 83-80523. (Sacred Teachings of Light Ser.: Codex II). Orig. Title: The Decoded New Testament. (Illus.). 207p. 1983. text 39.50 (*0-936202-06-8*) Intl Comm Christ.

Millennium Edition of the Essaei Document: Secrets of an Eternal Race. rev. ed. Gene Savoy. LC 83-83221. Orig. Title: The Essaei Document. (Illus.). xii, 140p. 1983. text 39.50 (*0-936202-07-6*) Intl Comm Christ.

Millennium Effect. Kathryn Harwig. LC 96-67011. (Illus.). 200p. 1996. pap. 12.95 (*0-9638822-2-8*) Spring Pr MN.

***Millennium Elvis - As Good As It Gets - Larger Than Life.** Paul Lichter. (Illus.). 140p. 2000. 65.00 (*1-929137-01-X*) Jesse Bks.

Millennium Eve. unabridged ed. Kenny Love. LC 98-91378. 320p. 1998. 24.95 (*0-9663064-0-6*, MT-01) Mys-Tech.

***Millennium Experience.** Jim Parton. 2000. pap. 24.95 (*0-00-220169-0*, Pub. by HarpC) Trafalgar.

Millennium Eyewitness: A Thousand Years of History Written by Those Who Were There. Brian Stone. (Illus.). 1998. pap. 16.95 (*0-7499-1883-7*, Pub. by Piatkus Bks) London Brdge.

Millennium Falcon: 3-D Excitement on Every Page. John Whitman. (Illus.). 12p. (J). 1997. 15.95 (*0-316-93591-3*) Little.

Millennium Fever. Jack Marshall. LC 96-2773. 96p. (Orig.). 1996. pap. 11.95 (*1-56689-054-3*) Coffee Hse.

***Millennium Fever.** Julia Ward. 224p. (Orig.). 1999. pap. text 9.95 (*0-352-33368-5*) Virgin Bks.

***Millennium File.** Eric Vaughn. 276p. 2000. 22.95 (*0-9669930-2-0*, Pub. by Stonehall Pubg) BookMasters.

***Millennium Fitness: Reshaping the Body & Mind.** Timothy Ghazaleh. 226p. 1999. pap. write for info. (*0-7392-0425-4*, PO3639) Morris Pubng.

Millennium Girl. Coerte V. W. Felske. LC 99-15935. 304p. 1999. text 24.95 (*0-312-24217-4*) St Martin.

***Millennium Girl.** Coerte V. W. Felske. 368p. 2000. reprint ed. mass mkt. 6.99 (*0-312-97697-6*, St Martins Paperbacks) St Martin.

Millennium Girls: Today's Girls Around the World. Sherrie A. Inness. LC 98-28142. 304p. 1998. 60.00 (*0-8476-9136-5*) Rowman.

Millennium Girls: Today's Girls Around the World. Sherrie A. Inness. LC 98-28142. (Illus.). 325p. 1998. pap. 17.95 (*0-8476-9137-3*, Pub. by Rowman) Natl Bk Netwk.

Millennium Guide: Parties, Events & Festivals Around the World. Richard Knight. 224p. 1998. pap. write for info. (*1-873756-20-8*, Pub. by Trailblazer) Seven Hills Bk.

***Millennium Guide for Pilgrims to the Holy Land.** James H. Charlesworth. LC 00-8353. 2000. 16.95 (*0-941037-93-2*, BIBAL Press) D & F Scott.

Millennium Hotel. Mark Rudman. LC 96-26572. (Wesleyan Poetry Ser.). 201p. 1996. pap. 14.95 (*0-8195-2230-9*, Wesleyan Univ Pr); text 35.00 (*0-8195-2229-5*, Wesleyan Univ Pr) U Pr of New Eng.

Millennium III, Century XXI: A Retrospective on the Future. Peter N. Stearns. LC 98-30419. 208p. 1998. pap. text 24.00 (*0-8133-3457-8*, Pub. by Westview) HarpC.

Millennium in America: From the Puritan Migration to the Civil War, 41 vols. Incl. Elhanan Winchester Vols. 20 & 21. LC 78-67596. 115.00 (*0-404-60943-0*); Puritan Doctrine of the Last Judgment. LC 78-67512. (*0-404-60902-3*); Signs of the Times Vols. 18 & 19: The Late Eighteenth Century. LC 78-67595. 115.00 (*0-404-60942-2*); 78-067587. French & Indian Wars. LC 78-67587. (*0-404-60912-0*); Vol. 1. Puritan Interpretation of Scripture. LC 78-67510. (*0-404-60901-5*); Vol. 3. Puritan Vision of New Jerusalem. LC 78-67513. (*0-404-60903-1*); Vol. 4. Increase Mather: Selected Works. LC 78-67514. (*0-404-60904-X*); Vol. 5. Samuel Willard: Selected Works. LC 78-67515. (*0-404-60905-8*); Vol. 6. Cotton Mather. LC 78-67516. (*0-404-60906-6*); Vol. 7. Representative Writings of the Eighteenth Century: Scriptural Interpretations. LC 78-67517. (*0-404-60907-4*); Vol. 8. Representative Writings of the Eighteenth Century: Applications of Prophecy. LC 78-67518. (*0-404-60908-2*); Vol. 9. Earthquakes of the Apocalypse. LC 78-67519. (*0-404-60909-0*); Vol. 10. Edwardian Revivalism from the Great Awakening to the Revolution. LC 78-67520. (*0-404-60910-4*); Vol. 11. Charles Chauncy. LC 78-67586. (*0-404-60911-2*); Vol. 13. Sermons of the American Revolution. LC 78-67588. (*0-404-60913-9*); Vol. 14. Celebration of Nationhood. LC 78-67590. (*0-404-60914-7*); Vol. 15. Loyalist Millenarians. LC 78-67591. (*0-404-60915-5*); Vol. 16. Poems on the Rising Glory of America. LC 78-67592. (*0-404-60916-3*); vol. 17. Interpretations of the French Revolution. LC 78-67599. (*0-404-60917-1*); Vol. 18. Signs of the Times: The Late Eighteenth Century. (*0-404-60918-X*); Vol. 19. Signs of the Times: The Late Eighteenth Century. (*0-404-60919-8*); Vol. 20. Elhanan Winchester. (*0-404-60920-1*); Vol. 21. Elhanan Winchester. (*0-404-60921-X*); Vol. 22. Timothy Dwight: Selected Writings. LC 78-67598. (*0-404-60922-8*); Vol. 23. Representative Writings of the Early Nineteenth Century (1800-1839) LC 78-67600. (*0-404-60923-6*); Vol. 24. Garden of the West. LC 78-67601. (*0-404-60924-4*); Vol. 25. Three Women Prophets: Harriet Livermore. LC 78-67603. (*0-404-60925-2*); Vol. 26. Three Women Prophets: Phoebe Palmer. LC 78-67604. (*0-404-60926-0*); Vol. 27. Three Women Prophets: Ellen Gould White. LC 78-67605. (*0-404-60927-9*); Vol. 28. Allegorical Narratives. LC 78-67606. (*0-404-60928-7*); Vol. 29, Pt. 1. Slavery & Abolition. LC 78-67607. (*0-404-60929-5*); Vol. 30, Pt. 2. Slavery & Abolition. LC 78-67608. (*0-404-60930-9*); Vol. 31. Millennial Optimism & Despair. LC 78-67610. (*0-404-60931-7*); Vol. 32. Hymns to Millennium. LC 78-67611. (*0-404-60932-5*); Vol. 33. Millenarian Anthologies. LC 78-67612. (*0-404-60933-3*); Vol. 34. Elias Smith: Selected Writings. LC 78-67613. (*0-404-60934-1*); Vol. 35. Elias Boudinot. LC 78-67614. (*0-404-60935-X*); Vol. 36. Ethan Smith: Selected Writings. LC 78-67615. (*0-404-60936-8*); Vol. 37. Lyman Beecher: Selected Works. LC 78-67616. (*0-404-60937-6*); Vol. 38. Millenial Debate: Owen vs. Campbell. LC 78-67618. (*0-404-60938-4*); Vol. 39. George Duffield: Selected Works. LC 78-67619. (*0-404-60939-2*); Vol. 40. William Miller: Selected Works. LC 78-67620. (*0-404-60940-6*); Vol. 41. Representative Writings, 1840-1860. LC 78-67621. (*0-404-60941-4*); write for info. (*0-318-50660-2*) AMS Pr.

Millennium Intelligence: Understanding & Conducting Competitive Intelligence in the Digital Age. Ed. by Jerry P. Miller. 2000. pap. 29.95 (*0-910965-28-5*, CyberAge Bks) Info Today Inc.

Millennium Journal. Affinity Publishing Editors. 384p. 1999. 6.95 (*1-928684-06-8*, Pub. by Affinity Pubg) BookWorld.

Millennium Journal: Once Every Thousand Years. Abby Bogomolny. 144p. 1998. wbk. ed. 12.95 (*0-9650665-1-7*) Burning Bush CA.

Millennium Journal: Sports. Affinity Publishing Editors. 384p. 1999. 6.95 (*1-928684-00-9*, Pub. by Affinity Pubg) BookWorld.

M

***Millennium Lectures: The Coming Together of the Common Law & the Civil Law.** Ed. by B. S. Markesinis. 256p. 2000. 54.00 (*1-84113-068-0*, Pub. by Hart Pub) Intl Spec Bk.

***Millennium Madness: Super Edition.** Pocket Books Staff. (Sabrina, the Teenage Witch Ser.: Vol. 29). 368p. (J). (gr. 7-12). 2000. per. 4.99 (*0-671-02820-0*, Archway) PB.

***Millennium Madness: 2000 Ways to Mark the Moment.** Annemarie Marek & Debbie Berens. 120p. 1999. pap. 17.95 (*0-9674401-0-6*) Marek Company.

***Millennium Madness Vol. 1: The Future Is Now.** Randall Bedwell. Ed. by Mardy Fones. LC 99-70380. 128p. 1999. pap. 6.95 (*1-887654-74-7*) Premium Pr TN.

Millennium Man. W. Joseph Wyatt. LC 97-90568. 196p. (J). (gr. 8-12). 1999. 24.00 (*0-9663622-4-1*) Thrd Millennum.

Millennium Man. W. Joseph Wyatt. LC 97-90568. 196p. (YA). (gr. 8-12). 1999. pap. 12.00 (*0-9663622-0-9*) Thrd Millenum.

***Millennium Man, Vol. 1.** Kim Kindrad. 1999. mass mkt. 9.95 (*1-55279-024-X*) Picasso Publ.

Millennium Management: "Better, Faster, Cheaper" Strategies for Managing 21st Century Healthcare Organizations. Russell C. Coile. LC 98-19872. 215p. 1998. 49.00 (*1-56793-084-0*) Health Admin Pr.

Millennium Mania. Charles Cook. 150p. (Orig.). 1980. pap. 2.50 (*0-933672-68-3*, C-1914) Star Bible.

Millennium Mania: Fascinating Facts, Quotes, & Trivia for the Dawn of the 21st Century. Stephen Fowler. LC 98-15896. 374p. 1998. pap. 5.95 (*0-8362-6976-4*) Andrews & McMeel.

Millennium Mars: The Terraforming Calendar for Mars. limited ed. James M. Graham & Kandis Elliot. (Illus.). 54p. 1998. spiral bd. 30.00 (*0-9666458-0-4*) Inst Implied Sci.

Millennium Meltdown: The 2000 Computer Crisis. Jeffrey. 249p. 1998. pap. 13.99 (*0-921714-48-3*, Pub. by Fon3tier Res) Spring Arbor Dist.

***Millennium Membership Directory with CD.** 608p. 2000. per. 99.00 incl. audio compact disk (*0-7872-5827-X*) Kendall-Hunt.

***Millennium Messages.** Barbara Coller. Ed. by Janie M. Welker. 24p. 1999. pap. text. write for info. (*1-879195-10-0*) Heckscher Mus.

***Millennium Miracle.** Josie Metcalfe. (Readers Choice Ser.). 2000. mass mkt. 4.50 (*0-373-51123-X*, 1511237) Harlequin Bks.

Millennium Mode: Fashion Forecasts from 40 Top Designers. Roberta Wolf. (Illus.). 144p. 1999. 50.00 (*0-8478-2114-5*, Pub. by Rizzoli Intl) St Martin.

Millennium Myth: Love & Death at the End of Time. Michael Grosso. (Illus.). 384p. 1995. 22.00 (*0-8356-0711-9*, Quest) Theos Pub Hse.

Millennium Myth: Love & Death at the End of Time. Michael Grosso. (Illus.). 384p. 1997. pap. 16.00 (*0-8356-0734-8*, Quest) Theos Pub Hse.

Millennium Myth: The Ever-Ending Story. Sean O'Shea & Meryl Walker. Ed. by Nancy Brand. LC 98-23121. (Illus.). (Orig.). 1998. lib. bdg. 26.95 (*0-89334-274-2*) Humanics Ltd.

Millennium Novel. Date not set. mass mkt. 23.00 (*0-06-105279-5*) HarpC.

Millennium of Buddhist Logic. Alex Wayman. LC 99-932712. (Buddhist Tradition Ser.). (ENG, SAN & TIB.). 349p. 1999. pap. 200.00 (*81-208-1646-3*, Pub. by Motilal Bnarsidass) St Mut.

Millennium of Classical Persian Poetry. Wheeler M. Thackston. 212p. 1996. pap. 20.00 (*0-614-21651-6*, 784) Kazi Pubns.

Millennium of Jesus Christ: An Exposition of the Revelation for All Ages. David W. Hall. 380p. 1998. pap. 19.95 (*0-9650367-6-6*) Covenant Fnd.

***Millennium of Praise.** David G. Browne. 171p. 1999. pap. 9.99 (*1-84030-062-0*) Emerald House Group Inc.

Millennium of the Book: Production, Design & Illustration in Manuscript & Print 900-1900. Ed. by Robin Myers & Michael Harris. LC 94-30712. (Publishing Pathways Ser.: No. 8). (Illus.). 192p. 1995. 30.00 (*1-884718-07-8*) Oak Knoll.

Millennium Organization. Harrison Owen. LC 94-94260. (Illus.). 174p. (Orig.). 1994. pap. 20.00 (0-9618205-4-3) Abbott Pub.

Millennium Paper Doll Book. Phyllis Amerikaner. 1998. pap. 9.95 (0-88160-319-8) Learning Wks.

***Millennium Parkers' Prediction Pack.** Julia Parker & Derek Parker. LC 99-30470. 80p. 1999. pap. 29.95 (0-7894-4611-1) DK Pub Inc.

Millennium Party Book: 1001 Great Ideas. Lauren Floodgate. LC 98-54600. 128p. 1999. 19.95 (0-7894-4181-0) DK Pub Inc.

Millennium Philadelphia: The Last 100 Years. Philadelphia Inquirer Staff. LC 99-19970. (Illus.). 256p. 1999. 29.95 (0-940159-53-8) Camino Bks.

Millennium Pope: A Novel of Spiritual Journey. Frederick J. Luhmann. 288p. 1999. pap. write for info. (0-7392-0135-2, PO3057) Morris Pubng.

Millennium Postponed. Edward Hyams. LC 74-186806. x, 277p. 1974. write for info. (0-436-20996-9) M Secker & Warburg.

***Millennium Primer: Take Charge of Your Life.** Jo Condrill. LC 99-91315. (Illus.). xv, 193p. 1999. 24.95 (0-9661414-5-8) GoalMinds.

Millennium Project. Joseph Massucci. 368p. 2000. mass mkt. 5.99 (0-8439-4460-9, Leisure Bks) Dorchester Pub Co.

Millennium Prophecies. Brian Innes. LC 98-27576. (Unsolved Mysteries Ser.). 48p. (J). (gr. 3). 1999. pap. 6.95 (0-8172-5848-5) Raintree Steck-V.

Millennium Prophecies. A. Tad Mann. 1995. pap. 7.95 (1-85230-685-8, Pub. by Element MA) Penguin Putnam.

Millennium Rage: Survivalists, White Supremacists & the Doomsday Prophecy. Philip Lamy. LC 96-32896. (Illus.). 306p. (C). 1996. 25.95 (0-306-45409-2, Plenum Trade) Perseus Pubng.

Millennium Reader. Terry Hirschberg & Stuart Hirschberg. LC 96-27752. 701p. 1997. pap. text, suppl. ed. 37.00 (0-13-454217-7) P-H.

Millennium Reader. 2nd ed. Composed by Stuart Hirschberg & Terry Hirschberg. LC 99-19182. 828p. 1999. pap. text 36.80 (0-13-012099-5) P-H.

Millennium Resolutions: 100 Things to Do Before, During & after the Millennium! Gary R. Blair. 48p. 1998. pap. 6.95 (1-889770-06-X, MLR) GoalsGuy.

***Millennium Rising.** Jane Jensen. LC 99-31285. 430p. 1999. 24.00 (0-345-43034-4, Del Rey) Ballantine Pub Grp.

***Millennium Seven.** Frank E. Stranges. LC 98-157401. (Illus.). 1998. write for info. (0-933470-15-0) Intl Evang.

Millennium Shows. Philip E. Baruth. 160p. (Orig.). 1994. pap. 12.95 (0-9637025-5-6) Albion Bks.

Millennium Star Atlas, 3 vols. Roger W. Sinnott & Michael A. Perryman. Incl. Vol. I: 0 - 8 Hours. LC 97-2552. (Illus.). 552p. 1997. 84.95 (0-933346-81-6); Vol. II: 8 - 16 Hours. LC 97-2552. (Illus.). 540p. 1997. 84.95 (0-933346-82-4); Vol. III: 16 - 24 Hours. LC 97-2552. (Illus.). 540p. 1997. 84.95 (0-933346-83-2); LC 97-2552. 1997. Set boxed set 249.00 (0-933346-84-0) Sky Pub.

Millennium Superworld. R. Chris Connolly. 155p. 1997. reprint ed. pap. 8.95 (0-9666506-0-3) Megiddo Pr.

Millennium Survival Kit: Your Guide to Surviving the End of This Millennium & Navigating the Next. John L. Hoff. 36p. 1998. boxed set 29.95 (0-9667889-0-7) Mandula Resources.

Millennium Tablets. John McIntosh. 177p. 1996. pap. 14.95 (0-929385-78-0) Light Tech Pubng.

***Millennium Threat: 221 Days & Counting.** LC 99-229475. 1999. write for info. (0-10-266399-8) Statnry Office.

Millennium Time Bomb: How to Prepare & Survive the Coming Technological Disaster. Charles H. Coppes. LC 98-75121. 25690-075121p. 1998. pap. 12.99 (1-56384-158-4) Huntington Hse.

Millennium Time Capsule. Carlton Books Staff. 1999. pap. 24.95 (1-85868-647-4, Pub. by Carlton Bks Ltd) Natl Bk Netwk.

Millennium Trail. large type ed. Peter M. Fotheringham. (Large Print Ser.). 384p. 1996. 27.99 (0-7089-3645-8) Ulverscroft.

***Millennium 20th Century Day by Day.** D K Publishing Staff. (DK Millennium Ser.). 1542p. 1999. 49.95 (0-7894-4640-5) DK Pub Inc.

Millennium 2000: A Positive Approach. Louise L. Hay. LC 99-26150. 1999. pap. 7.00 (1-56170-658-2) Hay House.

***Millennium 2000: Rapture or Jubilee.** Donald J. Sneen. LC 99-96537. 76p. 1999. pap. 7.95 (1-886513-00-7) Kirk Hse Pubs.

***Millennium Virus.** John Bassett. (Illus.). 183p. 1999. pap. 9.95 (1-891899-50-3) Derivations.

***Millennium Woman: A Guideline to Personal Security & Financial Prosperity for Today's Woman.** Michael O'Shaughnessy. LC 99-95065. (Illus.). 200p. 2000. pap. 15.95 (0-9674788-0-4, 1000) M OShaughnessy.

***Millennium World Atlas.** 432p. 1999. 70.00 (0-528-84175-0) Rand McNally.

Millennium World Map. 1995. 7.95 (0-528-83716-8) Rand McNally.

***Millennium Year by Year.** rev. ed. Ed. by DK Publishing Staff. (Illus.). 2000. 29.95 (0-7894-6539-6) DK Pub Inc.

Millennium's Dawn. Ed Stewart. LC 94-5080. 480p. 1994. pap. 11.99 (1-56476-345-5, 6-3345, Victor Bks) Chariot Victor.

Millennium's End: Contemporary & Near-Future Role-Playing Game. 2nd ed. Charles Ryan. (Illus.). 192p. (Orig.). 1993. pap. 20.00 (0-9628748-5-X) Chameleon Eclectic.

***Millennium's End: Poems.** Michael J. Bugeja. LC 99-41809. 120p. 2000. 20.00 (0-9662299-3-2, Pub. by Archer Books) Midpt Trade.

Millennium's End GM Screen & 1999 Datasource. Charles Ryan. (Illus.). 32p. (Orig.). 1992. pap. text 11.95 (0-9628748-2-5) Chameleon Eclectic.

Millennium's End GM's Companion. Charles Ryan. (Illus.). 144p. (Orig.). 1995. pap. 15.00 (0-9628748-7-6) Chameleon Eclectic.

Millennium's Eve. Ed Stewart. 448p. 1993. pap. 12.99 (1-56476-133-9, 6-3133, Victor Bks) Chariot Victor.

Millenniums of Moonbeams: A Definitive History & Anthology of Chinese Poetry, 3 vols., Set. Robert W. Clack. 995p. 1975. lib. bdg. 900.00 (0-87968-445-3) Gordon Pr.

Miller. Regine Pernoud. Tr. by Dominique Clift from ITA. LC 96-28160. (Day With Ser.). (Illus.). (YA). 1997. lib. bdg. 22.60 (0-8225-1914-3, Runestone Pr) Lerner Pub.

Miller: Collected Plays, Vol. 1. Arthur Miller. 439p. 1957. 17.95 (0-670-13597-6) Viking Penguin.

Miller: Collected Plays, Vol. 2. Arthur Miller. LC 80-52008. 704p. 1981. 17.95 (0-670-13598-4) Viking Penguin.

Miller: "Death of a Salesman" Brenda Murphy. (Plays in Production Ser.). (Illus.). xix, 246 p. (C). 1995. pap. text 18.95 (0-521-47865-0) Cambridge U Pr.

Miller: Product Liability & Safety Encyclopaedia. C. J. Miller et al. ring bd. write for info. (0-406-00758-6, MPLSISET, MICHIE) LEXIS Pub.

Miller Analogies Test, (MAT) Jack Rudman. (Admission Test Ser.: ATS-18). 300p. 1994. pap. 29.95 (0-8373-5018-2) Nat Learn.

Miller & Friedenthal's Quick Review on Civil Procedure. 3rd ed. Publishing West Staff. (Sum & Substance Quick Review Ser.). 1998. pap. 19.95 (1-57793-050-9) West Pub.

Miller & His Donkey; The Greedy Dog, 2 bks. in 1. (Aesop's Fables - Two in One Tales Ser.). (Illus.). 24p. (Orig.). (J). (gr. 1-4). 1993. pap. 2.50 (1-56144-304-2, Honey Bear Bks) Modern Pub NYC.

***Miller & Refunds Probably.** 6th ed. Ed. by Johnson & Miller. LC 99-53236. (Illus.). 622p. 1999. text 104.33 (0-13-014158-5) P-H.

Miller & Simmons Families: Genealogy & History Documents, 2 vols., Set. 2nd ed. Compiled by William R. Shurtleff. 620p. 1993. spiral bd. 69.95 (0-942515-04-8) Pine Hill CA.

Miller & Starr California Real Estate Desk Set. 2nd ed. Harry D. Miller & Marvin B. Starr. LC 98-131973. 1997. write for info. (0-8321-0087-0) West Group.

***Miller Boy & The Donkey.** Brian Wildsmith. (Illus.). 32p. 2000. pap. 8.95 (0-19-272400-2) OUP.

Miller, Bukowski, & Their Enemies: Essays on Contemporary Culture. William Joyce. LC 96-85582. 144p. 1997. pap. 12.00 (1-888105-11-9) Avisson Pr.

Miller Comprehensive GAAP Guide. Martin A. Miller. (Miller Accounting Ser.). 1000p. 1988. pap. 50.00 (0-15-601790-3); pap. 35.00 (0-15-601791-1) Harcourt.

Miller Comprehensive GAAP Guide, 1990. Martin A. Miller. 1989. pap. 40.00 (0-685-33321-3) Harcourt.

Miller Comprehensive GAAS Guide. Martin A. Miller & Larry P. Bailey. (Miller Accounting Ser.). 1400p. 1988. pap. 55.00 (0-15-601792-X); pap. 40.00 (0-15-601793-8) Harcourt.

Miller Comprehensive GAAS Guide, 1990. Martin A. Miller. 1989. pap. 40.00 (0-685-33322-1) Harcourt.

Miller Comprehensive Governmental GAAP Guide. Larry P. Bailey. (Miller Accounting Ser.). 1100p. 1988. pap. 50.00 (0-15-601784-9); pap. 40.00 (0-15-601789-X) Harcourt.

Miller Comprehensive Governmental GAAP Guide, 1990. Larry P. Bailey. 1989. pap. 40.00 (0-685-33323-X) Harcourt.

Miller Dynasty. deluxe rev. ed. Mark L. Dees. 560p. 1993. write for info. (0-9638084-1-9) Hippodrome.

Miller Dynasty. 2nd rev. ed. Mark L. Dees. (Illus.). 564p. 1993. 129.50 (0-9638084-0-0) Hippodrome.

Miller Family: An Address Delivered Before the Miller Re-Union at N. Waldoboro, Maine, Sept. 7, 1904, with Genealogy. Frank B. Miller. (Illus.). 47p. 1995. reprint ed. pap. 10.00 (0-8328-4562-0); reprint ed. lib. bdg. 20.00 (0-8328-4561-2) Higginson Bk Co.

Miller Family: Descendants of Frank Miller. F. B. Miller. (Illus.). 174p. 1991. reprint ed. pap. 37.00 (0-8328-2087-3); reprint ed. lib. bdg. 47.00 (0-8328-2086-5) Higginson Bk Co.

***Miller Family Cookbook.** D. Miller. (Illus.). 167p. 1999. spiral bd. 9.95 (0-9670704-2-2) Abana Bks.

Miller Family History: Descendants of Solomon S. Miller. Mary Hershberger & Barbara Christner. (Illus.). 85p. 6.00 (0-686-95513-7) O R Miller.

Miller Family History, 1821 to 1980. Incl. Vol. I. Descendants of Eli S. Miller & Marie Kaufman. Vol. II. Descendants of Isaac S. Miller. Rachel Troyer & Fannie Erb. (Illus.). 126p. 6.00 (0-686-95510-2) O R Miller.

Miller 400 see NASCAR!

***Miller GAAP Implementation Manual.** Jan R. Williams & Joseph V. Carcello. 1000p. 2000. pap. 79.00 (0-15-607229-7) Harcourt Prof.

***Miller Governmental GAAP Guide.** Larry P. Bailey. 1400p. 2000. pap. 79.00 (0-15-607230-0) Harcourt Prof.

Miller Governmental GAAP Guide: A Comprehensive Interpretation of All Current Promulgated Governmental Generally Accepted Accounting. 99th ed. Larry P. Bailey. (Governmental GAAP Guide (Miller) Ser.). (Illus.). 1400p. (C). 1998. pap. 69.00 (0-15-606317-4, Pub. by Harcourt Coll Pubs) Harcourt.

Miller, His Son & the Donkey Pop up Book. 10p. (J). (gr. 4-7). 1991. 9.95 (0-8167-2200-5) Troll Communs.

Miller Hud Audit Procedures Guide. 98th ed. Janet Holland & George Georgiades. 400p. (C). 1998. pap. 113.00 (0-15-606286-0, Pub. by Harcourt Coll Pubs) Harcourt.

Miller in Eighteenth-Century Virginia. Colonial Williamsburg Foundation Staff. (Historic Trades Ser.). (Illus.). 32p. (Orig.). 1958. pap. 2.95 (0-910412-19-7) Colonial Williamsburg.

Miller-Keane Encyclopedia & Dictionary of Medicine, Nursing & Allied Health. 5th ed. Benjamin F. Miller. 1992. text 25.95 (0-7216-3456-7, W B Saunders Co) Harcrt Hlth Sci Grp.

Miller-Keane Encyclopedia & Dictionary of Medicine, Nursing & Allied Health. 6th ed. Ed. by Thomas Eoyang. 2080p. 1997. text 29.95 (0-7216-6278-1, W B Saunders Co) Harcrt Hlth Sci Grp.

Miller Masks: A Novel in Stories. Neil D. Isaacs. LC 99-12245. 208p. 2000. pap. 12.95 (1-56474-308-X) Fithian Pr.

Miller Mitch/Community Songbook. 128p. (Orig.). 1962. pap. 9.95 (0-7692-1041-4, CN0027) Wrner Bros.

Miller Not-for-Profit Organization Audits. Warren Ruppel. 1998. pap. 130.00 (0-15-606215-1) Harcourt Coll Pubs.

Miller Not-for-Profit Organization Audits: Electronic Workpapers & Reference Guide. Warren Ruppel. (Illus.). 851p. 1999. pap. 137.00 incl. cd-rom (0-15-606875-3) Harcourt.

***Miller Not-For-Profit Reporting.** Mary F. Foster et al. 500p. 2000. pap. 79.00 (0-15-607226-2) Harcourt Prof.

Miller Not-For-Profit Reporting: GAAP, Tax, Financial, & Regulatory Requirements. 99th ed. Mary F. Foster. (Illus.). 529p. (C). 1998. pap. 69.00 (0-15-606318-2, Pub. by Harcourt Coll Pubs) Harcourt.

Miller of Old Church. Ellen Glasgow. (Collected Works of Ellen Glasgow). 432p. 1998. reprint ed. lib. bdg. 108.00 (1-58201-637-2) Classic Bks.

Miller on Managing: "Straight Talk on the Ups & Downs, Do's & Don'ts of Managing a Water Utility. William H. Miller. (Illus.). 180p. (C). 1992. 26.00 (0-89867-619-3, 10056) Am Water Wks Assn.

Miller Paralegal Today. Date not set. pap. text, teacher ed. write for info. (0-314-05433-2) West Pub.

Miller, Reiter & Robbins: Three New Poets. Derek Miller et al. 1991. 15.00 (0-914610-96-1); pap. 9.00 (0-914610-95-3) Hanging Loose.

Miller Single Audits. 98th ed. Rhett D. Harrell. 1998. pap. 127.00 (0-15-606223-2, Pub. by Harcourt Coll Pubs) Harcourt.

Miller Williams & the Poetry of the Particular. Ed. by Michael Burns. 152p. (C). 1991. text 27.50 (0-8262-0807-X) U of Mo Pr.

Miller 2000 Audit Procedures: Electronic Workpapers & Reference Guide. 99th ed. George Georgiades. 667p. 1999. pap. 131.00 incl. cd-rom (0-15-606871-0, Pub. by Harcourt Coll Pubs) Harcourt.

***Miller 2000 Compilations & Reviews: Electronic Workpapers & Reference Guide.** Bailey. 903p. (C). 1999. pap. 131.00 incl. cd-rom (0-15-606873-7, Pub. by Harcourt Coll Pubs) Harcourt.

Millere. Sketch of Miller (English) & Calhoun-Miller (Scotch-Irish) Families, with Their Genealogy. Florence M. Miller. 196p. 1996. reprint ed. pap. 29.50 (0-8328-5244-9); reprint ed. lib. bdg. 39.50 (0-8328-5243-0) Higginson Bk Co.

Miller/Hull Partnership. Ed. by Oscar R. Ojeda. (Ten Houses Ser.). (Illus.). 108p. 1999. pap. 25.00 (1-56496-450-7) Rockport Pubs.

Miller's Anatomy of the Dog. 3rd ed. Howard E. Evans. LC 92-32950. (Illus.). 1056p. 1993. text 99.00 (0-7216-3200-9, W B Saunders Co) Harcrt Hlth Sci Grp.

***Miller's Annotated Competition Law.** Russell V. Miller. 800p. 2000. pap. 66.50 (0-455-21707-6, Pub. by LBC Info Servs) Gaunt.

***Miller's Annotated Trade Practices Act.** 21st ed. Russell V. Miller. 1300p. 2000. pap. 60.00 (0-455-21706-8, Pub. by LBC Info Servs) Gaunt.

Miller's Annotated Trade Practices Act, 1997. 18th ed. Russell V. Miller. 834p. 1997. pap. 48.00 (0-455-21481-6, Pub. by LawBk Co) Gaunt.

Miller's Antiques & Collectibles: The Facts at Your Fingertips. 1999. pap. 10.95 (1-85732-179-0, Pub. by Mitchell Beazley) Antique Collect.

Miller's Antiques & Collectibles: The Facts at Your Fingertips. Lita Solis-Cohen. (Illus.). 176p. 1994. pap. 10.95 (1-85732-583-4, Pub. by Millers Pubns) Antique Collect.

Miller's Antiques Checklist: Clocks. John Mighell. LC 96-139075. (Illus.). 192p. 1993. 15.95 (1-85732-945-7, Pub. by Millers Pubns) Antique Collect.

Miller's Antiques Checklist: Jewellery. Ed. by Stephen Giles. (Antique Collectors' Club Ser.). (Illus.). 192p. 1997. 15.95 (1-85732-816-7, Pub. by Mitchell Beazley) Antique Collect.

Miller's Antiques Checklist: Pottery. Gordon Lang. LC 96-147009. (Illus.). 192p. 1995. 15.95 (1-85732-408-0, Pub. by Millers Pubns) Antique Collect.

Miller's Antiques Checklist: Toys & Games. Hugo Marsh. (Illus.). 192p. 1995. 14.95 (1-85732-273-8, Pub. by Millers Pubns) Antique Collect.

Miller's Antiques Encyclopedia: The Definitive Reference on Antiques & Collectibles. Ed. by Judith Miller. (Illus.). 560p. 1998. 70.00 (1-85732-747-0, Pub. by Millers Pubns) Antique Collect.

***Miller's Antiques Shops, Fairs & Auctions 2000.** Miller's Publications Staff. (Illus.). 2000. pap. 24.95 (1-84000-209-3) Millers Pubns.

Miller's Art Nouveau & Art Deco: Buyer's Guide. Judith Miller & Martin Miller. LC 96-147591. (Illus.). 400p. 1995. 29.95 (1-85732-685-7, Pub. by Millers Pubns) Antique Collect.

Millers Bolt: A Modern Business Parable. Thomas Stirr. 1997. write for info. (0-201-12750-4); pap. text 120.00 (0-201-30449-X) Addison-Wesley.

Millers Bolt: A Modern Business Parable. Thomas Stirr. LC 96-40935. 262p. 1997. pap. 12.00 (0-201-14379-8) Addison-Wesley.

***Miller's Ceramics Buyer's Guide.** Miller's Publications Staff. (Illus.). 384p. 2000. 29.95 (1-84000-267-0, Pub. by Millers Pubns) Antique Collect.

***Miller's Ceramics of the '20s & '30s: A Collector's Guide.** Frankie Liebe & Frankie Leibe. (Illus.). 100p. 1999. 11.95 (1-84000-161-5) Antique Collect.

Miller's Chinese & Japanese Collectables: Buyer's Guide. Ed. by Peter Waine & Jo Wood. LC 99-233824. (Illus.). 320p. 1999. 29.95 (1-84000-127-5) Antique Collect.

Miller's Classic Motorcycles, 1997. Ed. by Mick Walker. 1997. 19.95 (1-85732-821-3, Pub. by Reed Illust Books) Antique Collect.

Miller's Classic Motorcycles Price Guide, 1995. 1995. 17.95 (1-85732-541-9) Antique Collect.

Miller's Classic Motorcycles Price Guide, 1996. Judith Miller & Martin Miller. (Illus.). 176p. 1996. 17.95 (1-85732-658-X, Pub. by Reed Illust Books) Antique Collect.

Miller's Classic Motorcycles Price Guide, 1998-1999. Judith Miller & Mick Walker. (Illus.). 176p. 1997. 19.95 (1-84000-009-0, Pub. by Millers Pubns) Antique Collect.

Miller's Classic Motorcycles Price Guide, 1999-2000: 1999-2000 Edition. Ed. by Mick Walker. (Miller's Classic Motorcycles Price Guide Ser.). (Illus.). 176p. 1998. 19.95 (1-84000-058-9, Pub. by Millers Pubns) Antique Collect.

Miller's Classic Motorcycles Yearbook 2000. annuals Ed. by Mick Walker. (Illus.). 176p. 1999. 19.95 (1-84000-175-5, Pub. by Millers Pubns) Antique Collect.

Miller's Clinical Case Companion. Neal H. Cohen. 1994. pap. 49.95 (0-443-08961-2) Church.

Miller's Clocks & Barometers: Buyer's Guide. Ed. by Derek Roberts. (Illus.). 320p. 1997. 29.95 (1-85732-990-2, Pub. by Millers Pubns) Antique Collect.

Miller's Collectables, 1999-2000. (Illus.). 496p. 29.95 Antique Collect.

Miller's Collectables Price Guide, 1997-1998. Ed. by Madeleine Marsh. (Antique Collectors' Club Ser.). (Illus.). 496p. 1997. 29.95 (1-85732-860-4, Pub. by Mitchell Beazley) Antique Collect.

Miller's Collectables Price Guide, 1996-1997. Judith Miller & Martin Miller. (Illus.). 496p. 1996. 25.00 (1-85732-752-7) Antique Collect.

Miller's Collectables Price Guide, 1995-1996, Vol. VI. Judith Miller. (Illus.). 497p. 1995. 25.00 (1-85732-542-7, Pub. by Reed Illust Books) Antique Collect.

***Miller's Collectable Price Guide 1999-2000.** Ed. by Madaleine Marsh. (Illus.). 496p. 1999. 29.95 (1-84000-128-3) Millers Pubns.

Miller's Collectables Price Guide, 1998-99. annuals Miller's Publication Staff & Madeleine Marsh. (Miller's Antiques Checklist Ser.). 496p. 1998. 29.95 (1-84000-055-4, Pub. by Millers Pubns) Antique Collect.

***Miller's Collectables Price Guide 2000-2001.** Miller's Publications Staff. (Illus.). 496p. 2000. 29.95 (1-84000-238-7, Pub. by Millers Pubns) Antique Collect.

Miller's Collecting Books. Catherine Porter. (Illus.). 192p. text 35.00 (1-85732-543-5, Pub. by Millers Pubns) Antique Collect.

Miller's Collecting Books. Catherine Porter. LC 96-141828. (Illus.). 192p. 1996. 30.00 (1-85732-766-7, Pub. by Reed Illust Books) Antique Collect.

***Miller's Collecting Fashion & Accessories.** Carol Harris. Ed. by Madeleine Marsh. (Illus.). 191p. 2000. 24.95 (1-84000-212-3, Pub. by Millers Pubns) Antique Collect.

Miller's Collecting Furniture: The Facts at Your Fingertips. Christopher Payne. (Illus.). 192p. 1996. 19.95 (1-85732-877-9, Pub. by Reed Illust Books) Antique Collect.

Miller's Collecting Furniture: The Facts at Your Fingertips. Christopher Payne & Janet Gleeson. (Miller's Antiques Checklist Ser.). 1998. 19.95 (1-84000-053-8, Pub. by Millers Pubns) Antique Collect.

***Miller's Collecting Glass: The Facts At Your Fingertips.** Sarah Yates. (Illus.). 176p. 2000. 19.95 (1-84000-191-7, Pub. by Millers Pubns) Antique Collect.

***Miller's Collecting Kitchenware.** Christina Bishop. (Illus.). 144p. 1999. 25.00 (1-85732-565-6, Pub. by Millers Pubns) Antique Collect.

Miller's Collecting Kitchenware. Christina Bishop. LC 96-141831. (Illus.). 144p. 1996. 25.00 (1-85732-767-5, Pub. by Reed Illust Books) Antique Collect.

Miller's Collecting Pottery & Porcelain: The Facts at Your Fingertips. Gordon Lang. (Illus.). 192p. 1997. 19.95 (1-84000-040-6, Pub. by Millers Pubns) Antique Collect.

***Miller's Collecting Science & Technology.** Janet Gleeson. (Illus.). 160p. 1999. write for info. (1-84000-079-1, Pub. by Millers Pubns) Antique Collect.

Miller's Collecting Silver: The Facts at Your Fingertips. Jill Bace. (Illus.). 176p. 1999. 19.95 (1-84000-143-7, Pub. by Millers Pubns) Antique Collect.

***Miller's Collecting Silver: The Facts At Your Fingertips.** Jill Bace. (Illus.). 1999. 19.95 (1-84000-231-X) Mitchell Beazley.

Miller's Collecting Teddy Bears & Dolls: The Facts at Your Fingertips. Alison Beckett. (Illus.). 176p. 1996. 19.95 (1-85732-893-0, Pub. by Reed Illust Books) Antique Collect.

***Miller's Collecting Textiles.** Patricia Frost. (Illus.). 160p. 2000. 35.00 (1-84000-203-4, Pub. by Millers Pubns) Antique Collect.

Miller's Collecting the 1950s. Madeleine Marsh. (Illus.). 144p. 1997. 26.95 (1-85732-605-9, Pub. by Mitchell Beazley) Antique Collect.

***Miller's Collecting the 1960s.** Madeleine Marsh. 1999. 26.95 (1-84000-258-1) Millers Pubns.

Miller's Collecting the 1960s. Madeleine Marsh. (Illus.). 144p. 1999. 26.95 (1-84000-081-3, Pub. by Millers Pubns) Antique Collect.

Miller's Collector's Cars, 1996-1997. (Illus.). 352p. 1996. 35.00 (*1-85732-820-5*, Pub. by Reed Illust Books) Antique Collect.

Miller's Collector's Cars, 1995-1996. Judith Miller. (Illus.). 352p. 1995. 35.00 (*1-85732-559-1*, Pub. by Reed Illust Books) Antique Collect.

Miller's Collectors Cars Price Guide, 1999-2000: 1999-2000 Edition. Ed. by Dave Selby. (Miller's Collectors' Cars Price Guide Ser.). (Illus.). 352p. 1998. 35.00 (*1-84000-057-0*) Millers Pubns.

Miller's Collector's Cars Price Guide, 1998-1999. Judith Miller & Dave Selby. (Illus.). 352p. 1997. 35.00 (*1-84000-008-2*, Pub. by Millers Pubns) Antique Collect.

Miller's Collectors Cars Yearbook 2000. annuals Ed. by Dave Selby. (Illus.). 354p. 1999. 35.00 (*1-84000-174-7*, Pub. by Millers Pubns) Antique Collect.

***Miller's Collector's Guide: Postcards.** Chris Connor. (Illus.). 64p. 2000. pap. 9.95 (*1-84000-190-9*, Pub. by Millers Pubns) Antique Collect.

***Miller's Collector's Guides: Paperweights of the 19th & 20th Centuries.** Anne Metcalf. (Illus.). 64p. 2000. pap. 9.95 (*1-84000-309-X*, Pub. by Millers Pubns) Antique Collect.

***Miller's Collector's Guides: Smoking Accessories.** Sarah Yates. (Illus.). 64p. 2000. pap. 9.95 (*1-84000-187-9*, Pub. by Millers Pubns) Antique Collect.

Miller's Comprehensive GAAS Guide, 1987. Miller Accounting Staff. 1987. 42.00 (*0-317-64875-6*); pap. 32.00 (*0-317-64876-4*) Harcourt.

Miller's Dance. Winston Graham. Date not set. lib. bdg. 22.95 (*0-8488-1016-3*) Amereon Ltd.

***Miller's Daughters.** Edward Hewitt. 248p. 2000. 31.99 (*0-7089-4205-9*) Ulverscroft.

Miller's Furniture Buyer's Guide: Late Georgian to Edwardian. Leslie Gillham. (Miller's Antiques Checklist Ser.). 400p. 1998. 29.95 (*1-84000-054-6*, Pub. by Millers Pubns) Antique Collect.

Miller's Golf Memorabilia. Sara Fabian-Baddiel. (Illus.). 160p. 1994. 24.95 (*1-85732-350-5*) Antique Collect.

Miller's Guide to the Dissection of the Dog. 4th ed. Howard E. Evans & Alexander DeLahunta. 420p. 1995. text 39.00 (*0-7216-5748-6*, W B Saunders Co) Harcrt Hlth Sci Grp.

Miller's International Antiques Price Guide 2000: Professional Handbook. Ed. by Elizabeth Norfolk. (Miller's International Antiques Price Guide Ser.). (Illus.). 808p. 1998. 35.00 (*1-84000-060-0*, Pub. by Millers Pubns) Antique Collect.

Miller's International Antiques Price Guide, 1996. Judith Miller & Martin Miller. (Illus.). 808p. 1995. 35.00 (*1-85732-746-2*, Pub. by Millers Pubns) Antique Collect.

Miller's International Antiques Price Guide, 1997. Judith Miller & Martin Miller. (Illus.). 808p. 1996. 35.00 (*1-85732-892-2*, Pub. by Reed Illust Books) Antique Collect.

Miller's International Antiques Price Guide, 1998. Judith Miller. (Illus.). 808p. 1997. 35.00 (*1-84000-039-2*, Pub. by Mitchell Beazley) Antique Collect.

Miller's International Antiques Price Guide 2000. Ed. by Elizabeth Norfolk. (Illus.). 808p. 1999. 35.00 (*1-84000-230-1*, Pub. by Millers Pubns) Antique Collect.

Miller's Manual: A Research Guide to the Mayor French: Canadian Genealogical Resources: What They Are & How to Use Them. Douglas J. Miller. 195p. 1997. pap. 19.95 (*1-886560-47-1*, 097091) Quintin Pub RI.

Miller's Picture Price Guide, 1996. Judith Miller & Martin Miller. (Illus.). 400p. 1995. 30.00 (*1-85732-609-1*, Pub. by Reed Illust Books) Antique Collect.

Miller's Pine & Country Furniture: Buyer's Guide. Judith Miller & Martin Miller. (Illus.). 400p. 1995. 29.95 (*1-85732-684-9*, Pub. by Reed Illust Books) Antique Collect.

Miller's Pocket Antiques Fact File: Essential Information for Dealers, Collectors & Enthusiasts. Judith Miller. (Illus.). 192p. 1994. 12.95 (*0-85533-689-7*) Mitchell Beazley.

Miller's Pocket Dictionary of Antiques: An Authoritative Reference Guide for Dealers, Collectors, & Enthusiasts. Judith Miller & Martin Miller. (Illus.). 160p. 1990. 10.95 (*0-85533-760-5*, Pub. by Millers Pubns) Antique Collect.

***Miller's Popular Glass of the 19th & 20th Centuries.** Raymond Notley. (Illus.). 64p. 2000. pap. 9.95 (*1-84000-188-7*, Pub. by Millers Pubns) Antique Collect.

Miller's Pottery & Porcelain Marks. Gordon Lang. LC 96-139077. (Illus.). 400p. 1995. 15.95 (*1-85732-615-6*, Pub. by Reed Illust Books) Antique Collect.

***Miller's Powder Compacts.** Juliette Edwards. (Illus.). 64p. 2000. pap. 9.95 (*1-84000-186-0*, Pub. by Millers Pubns) Antique Collect.

Miller's Prologue & Tale. Geoffrey Chaucer. Ed. by J. Winny. LC 76-132283. (Selected Tales from Chaucer Ser.). 108p. 1971. pap. text 10.95 (*0-521-08033-9*) Cambridge U Pr.

Miller's Rock & Pop Memorabilia. Stephen Maycock. (Illus.). 160p. 1997. 24.95 (*1-85732-270-3*, Pub. by Millers Pubns) Antique Collect.

Miller's Royal Memorabilia. Eric Knowles. (Illus.). 176p. 1994. 24.95 (*1-85732-167-7*) Antique Collect.

Miller's Silver & Sheffield Plate Marks: Including a Guide to Makers & Styles. John Bly. Ed. by Judith Miller & Martin Miller. (Illus.). 192p. 1993. pap. 12.95 (*1-85732-096-4*, Pub. by Millers Pubns) Antique Collect.

Miller's Standard Insurance Policies Annotated. 4th ed. Susan J. Miller & Philip Lefebvre. LC 93-197619. 1998. 495.00 (*0-9639112-5-2*) Legal Res Systs.

Miller's Time: A Legacy of OSU Basketball, 1971-1989 K. J. White. LC 97-75636. 142 p. 1997. pap. 15.95 (*1-888803-07-X*) Lenswrk.

Miller's Traditional English Christmas. Judith Miller. LC 96-173386. 160p. 1997. 19.95 (*1-85732-995-3*, Pub. by Millers Pubns) Antique Collect.

Miller's 20th Century Ceramics. Paul Atterbury & Ellen P. Denker. (Illus.). 256p. 1999. 40.00 (*1-84000-034-1*) Antique Collect.

Miller's Understanding Antiques. Ed. by Judith Miller & Martin Miller. (Illus.). 272p. 1993. pap. 19.95 (*1-85732-001-8*, Pub. by Millers Pubns) Antique Collect.

Miller's Understanding Antiques. rev. ed. Judith Miller & Martin Miller. (Antique Collectors' Club Ser.). (Illus.). 256p. 1997. 27.95 (*1-85732-857-4*, Pub. by Mitchell Beazley) Antique Collect.

Miller's Victoriana to Art Deco: A Collector's Guide. Eric Knowles. (Illus.). 1993. 35.00 (*1-85732-176-6*, Pub. by Millers Pubns) Antique Collect.

Millersburg Glass. Marie McGee. Ed. by James Measell. (Illus.). 128p. 1995. pap. 29.95 (*1-57080-005-7*) Antique Pubns.

Millet Crop-Loss Assessment Methods. N. D. Jago. 1993. pap. 50.00 (*0-85954-354-4*, Pub. by Nat Res Inst) St Mut.

Millet Pests of the Sahel: An Identification Guide. M. Matthews & N. D. Jago. 80p. 1993. pap. 45.00 (*0-85954-331-5*, Pub. by Nat Res Inst) St Mut.

Millet Pests of the Sahel: Biology, Monitoring & Control. N. D. Jago. 66p. 1993. pap. 39.00 (*0-85954-349-8*, Pub. by Nat Res Inst) St Mut.

Millhands & Preachers: A Study of Gastonia. Liston Pope. (Studies in Religious Education: No. 15). (Illus.). (J). 1965. reprint ed. pap. 22.50 (*0-300-00182-7*) Yale U Pr.

Milliardaire Antique: Herode Atticus et Sa Famille. Paul Graindor. Ed. by Moses I. Finley. LC 79-4977. (Ancient Economic History Ser.). (FRE., Illus.). 1979. reprint ed. lib. bdg. 25.95 (*0-405-12364-7*) Ayer.

Milliardaire Sans Bagages. Beverly Barton. (Rouge Passion Ser.: Vol. 472). 1998. mass mkt. 3.50 (*0-373-37472-0*, 1-37472-7) Harlequin Bks.

Millicent: A Mystery. Veronica Ross. 256p. mass mkt. 7.99 (*1-55128-042-6*, Pub. by Mercury Bk) LPC InBook.

Millicent & the Wind. Robert Munsch. (Illus.). 32p. (J). (gr. k-3). 1984. lib. bdg. 15.95 (*0-920236-98-7*, Pub. by Annick) Firefly Bks Ltd.

Millicent & the Wind. Robert Munsch. (Illus.). 32p. (J). (gr. k-3). 1984. pap. 5.95 (*0-920236-93-6*, Pub. by Annick) Firefly Bks Ltd.

Millicent & the Wind. Robert Munsch. (Annikins Ser.: Vol. 7). (Illus.). 32p. (J). (ps-2). 1989. pap. 0.99 (*1-55037-010-3*, Pub. by Annick) Firefly Bks Ltd.

Millicent & the Wind. Robert Munsch. (Munsch for Kids Ser.). (J). 1984. 10.15 (*0-606-02788-2*, Pub. by Turtleback) Demco.

Millie. Linda Jennings. (Illus.). 24p. (J). (ps). 1994. pap. 9.99 (*1-881445-32-1*) Sandvik Pub.

Millie & the Fugitive. Liz Ireland. (Historical Ser.). 1996. per. 4.99 (*0-373-28930-8*, 1-28930-5) Harlequin Bks.

Millie & the Mermaid. Penny Ives. (Illus.). 32p. (J). pap. 9.95 (*0-14-055635-4*, Pub. by Pnguin Bks Ltd) Trafalgar.

***Millie-Christine: Fearfully & Wonderfully Made.** Joanne Martell. LC 99-52515. (Illus.). 304p. 2000. 17.95 (*0-89587-194-7*); pap. 12.95 (*0-89587-188-2*) Blair.

***Millie Donohue in Bodie.** Douglas Westfall & Millie Donohue. (Illus.). 250p. 2000. 24.95 (*1-891030-07-8*) Paragon Agency.

Millie Milkweed Seed Meets the Genny Geranium Gang. Wayne J. Cernobous. (Illus.). 46p. (Orig.). (J). (gr. k-5). 1984. pap. 5.95 (*0-9615065-0-4*) Kinnickinnic Pr.

Millie's China. Edie Lambert. 240p. 1998. pap. 9.95 (*0-939497-48-4*) Promise Pub.

Millie's Fimo Notebook. Millie Beachum. Ed. by Valerie Bernardino. (Illus.). 16p. (Orig.). 1991. pap. 3.95 (*0-938685-07-4*) Dees Delights.

Millie's Jewish Kitchen. Joyce LaFray & Millie Kushnir. Ed. by B. J. Altschul. LC 97-62108. 105 p. 1982. 0.95 (*0-942084-03-9*) SeaSide Pub.

Millie's Secret. Gyo Fujikawa. (Illus.). 16p. (J). (ps). 1989. bds. 6.95 (*1-55987-006-0*, Sunny Bks) J B Comns.

Milligan Case. Ed. by Samuel Klaus. (American Trials Ser.). 473p. 1997. reprint ed. 144.50 (*1-56169-345-6*) Gaunt.

Millikan's School: A History of the California Institute of Technology. Judith R. Goodstein. (Illus.). 288p. 1991. 25.00 (*0-393-03017-2*) Norton.

Millikin Poems: A Personal Look at College Life. (Illus.). 128p. (Orig.). 1996. pap. 10.00 (*0-9655326-0-7*) PureWater Pr.

Millimeter & Microwave Engineering for Communications & Radar: Proceedings of Conference Held 10-11 January 1994, San Diego, California, Sponsored by SPIE--the International Society for Optical Engineering. Ed. by James C. Wiltse & Society of Photo-Optical Instrumentation Engineers. 1994. 30.00 (*0-8194-1505-7*) SPIE.

Millimeter & Submillimeter Wave Spectroscopy of Solids. Ed. by George Gruener. LC 97-28346. (Topics in Applied Physics Ser.: Vol. 74). (Illus.). xii, 240p. 1997. 99.95 (*3-540-62860-6*) Spr-Verlag.

Millimeter & Submillimeter Waves. Ed. by F. A. Benson. LC 77-489384. (Illus.). 579p. reprint ed. pap. 179.50 (*0-608-14721-4*, 202572300046) Bks Demand.

Millimeter & Submillimeter Waves & Applications III, Vol. 2842. Ed. by Mohammed N. Afsar. 650p. 1996. 94.00 (*0-8194-2230-4*) SPIE.

Millimeter & Submillimeter Waves & Applications IV, Vol. 3465. Ed. by Mohammed N. Afsar. 1998. 124.00 (*0-8194-2920-1*) SPIE.

Millimeter Wave & Infrared Multisensor Design & Signal Processing. Larry A. Klein. LC 97-12574. 520p. 1997. 114.00 (*0-89006-764-3*) Artech Hse.

Millimeter-Wave Astronomy: Molecular Chemistry & Physics in Space: Proceedings of the 1996 INAOE Summer School of Millimeter-Wave Astronomy. INAOE Summer School of Millimeter-Wave Astronomy Staff. LC 98-52738. (Astrophysics & Space Science Library). 1999. write for info. (*0-7923-5581-4*) Kluwer Academic.

Millimeter Wave Engineering & Applications. Prakash Bhartia & Inder J. Bahl. LC 83-12404. 736p. 1984. 245.00 (*0-471-87083-8*) Wiley.

Millimeter Wave Measurement & Modeling of Terrain Scattering. Fawwaz T. Ulaby. LC TK7876.. (University of Michigan Final Reports: No. 026247-1-F). 116p. reprint ed. pap. 36.00 (*0-7837-3211-2*, 204321400007) Bks Demand.

Millimeter-Wave Microstrip & Printed Circuit Antennas. Prakash Bhartia et al. LC 90-1126. (Artech House Antenna Library). 336p. 1991. reprint ed. pap. 104.20 (*0-608-01349-8*, 206208900002) Bks Demand.

Millimeter Wave Optical Dielectric Integrated Guides & Circuits. Shiban K. Koul. LC 96-34530. 563p. 1997. 98.50 (*0-471-16841-6*) Wiley.

Millimeter Wave Radar. Ed. by Stephen L. Johnston. LC 80-53388. (Artech Radar Library). 673p. reprint ed. pap. 200.00 (*0-608-14989-6*, 202595700047) Bks Demand.

Millimeter-Wave Radar Clutter. Nicholas C. Currie et al. LC 92-12921. (Radar Library). 240p. 1992. text 58.00 (*0-89006-345-1*) Artech Hse.

Millimeter-Waves & Applicable Interfaces. (Tech Edge Ser.). (Illus.). 125p. 1990. 25.00 (*0-944916-16-3*) emf-emi Control.

Millimetre & Submillimetre Astronomy. Ed. by R. D. Wolstencroft & W. Butler Burton. (C). 1988. text 206.50 (*90-277-2763-5*) Kluwer Academic.

Millimetre-Wave Optics, Devices & Systems. James C. Lesurf. (Illus.). 268p. 1990. 130.00 (*0-85274-129-4*) IOP Pub.

Milliner's Apprentice: Girlhood in Edwardian Yorkshire. Hazel Wheeler. (Illus.). 128p. 1997. pap. 17.95 (*0-7509-1330-4*, Pub. by Sutton Pub Ltd) Intl Pubs Mktg.

***Millinery: Feathers, Fruits & Flowers.** Ed. by Jules Kliot & Kaethe Kliot. (Illus.). 256p. 2000. 20.00 (*1-891656-23-6*, LE80) Lacis Pubns.

Millinery for Children. Woman's Institute of Domestic Arts & Sciences. (Illus.). 25p. 1999. reprint ed. pap. 8.95 (*0-9669077-3-6*) Judith M Pubg.

Millinery for Every Woman. Georgina K. Kaye. 1992. 24.00 (*0-916896-43-9*) Lacis Pubns.

Milling & Milling Methods. 76p. 1988. pap. text 20.00 (*0-87263-323-3*) SME.

Milling Machine. David J. Gingery. LC 80-66142. (Build Your Own Metalworking Shop from Scrap Ser.). (Illus.). 160p. 1982. pap. 9.95 (*1-878087-03-7*) D J Gingery.

Milling Machine Explained. Leo Rizzo. LC 73-732667. 1984. student ed. 7.00 (*0-8064-0221-0*, 502) Bergwall.

Milling Metal Made Easy. Colvin. (Illus.). 140p. 1991. reprint ed. pap. 16.00 (*1-877767-34-4*) Univ Publng Hse.

Milling, Methods & Machines. Ed. by Brian K. Lambert. LC 82-61032. (Manufacturing Update Ser.). (Illus.). 268p. reprint ed. pap. 83.10 (*0-8357-6483-4*, 203585400097) Bks Demand.

Milling One. 1987. 50.00 (*0-85083-011-7*) St Mut.

Milling Operations in the Lathe. Tubal Cain. (Workshop Practice Ser.: No. 5). (Illus.). 128p. (Orig.). 1984. pap. 18.50 (*0-85242-840-5*, Pub. by Nexus Special Interests) Trans-Atl Phila.

Milling Two. 1983. 50.00 (*0-7855-2877-6*) St Mut.

Million - Dollar Cowboy. Martha Shields. LC 99-11203. 1999. 25.95 (*0-7862-1878-9*) Mac Lib Ref.

Million a Minute: Inside the Mega-Money, High-Tech World of Traders. Hillary Davis. LC 98-28133. 304p. 1998. 27.00 (*0-88730-941-0*) HarpC.

Million & One Love Strategies. Marie Papillion. 1995. mass mkt. 5.99 (*0-312-95466-2*) St Martin.

Million & One Love Strategies: How to Be Irresistible to the Opposite Sex! Marie Papillion. 343p. 1998. pap. text 15.00 (*0-7881-5628-4*) DIANE Pub.

Million & White: Family Proceedings: a Guide for Urgent Business & Emergencies. Clive Million & Ken White. 1997. write for info. (*0-406-99294-0*, MWGUB, MICHIE) LEXIS Pub.

Million Cheers: One Hundred Years of Wyoming Cowboy Football. Steve Weakland. Ed. by Margaret Marron. (Illus.). 176p. 1993. 29.95 (*0-9638252-0-8*) U Wyo Football.

Million Clinical Multiaxial Inventory: A Clinical Research Information Synthesis. Ed. by Robert J. Craig. 312p. 1993. text 69.95 (*0-8058-1145-1*) L Erlbaum Assocs.

Million Dollar Automobiles: Ninety Years. Burgess D. Wise. 1989. 17.98 (*1-55521-411-8*) Bk Sales Inc.

Million Dollar Autos. Jerry Street. 1992. 12.98 (*1-55521-798-2*) Bk Sales Inc.

Million Dollar Aviator. Miles E. Gibson. 109p. (Orig.). 1976. pap. text 9.95 (*0-942306-04-X*) Diversified Pub Co.

Million Dollar Baby: A Hot Time in the Old Town Tonight. Craig Sodaro. (Illus.). 60p. (Orig.). 1987. pap. 4.00 (*0-88680-275-X*) I E Clark.

***Million Dollar Backfield: The San Francisco 49ers in the 1950s.** Dave Newhouse. 250p. (C). 2000. pap. 16.95 (*1-58394-007-3*) Frog Ltd CA.

Million Dollar Bear. William Kotzwinkle. LC 93-6262. (Illus.). 48p. (J). (ps-3). 1995. lib. bdg. 17.99 (*0-679-95295-0*, Pub. by Knopf Bks Yng Read) Random.

Million Dollar Blackjack. Ken Uston. (Illus.). 330p. 1982. 18.95 (*0-914314-08-4*) Carol Pub Group.

Million Dollar Blackjack. Ken Uston. (Illus.). 348p. 1992. pap. 18.95 (*0-89746-068-5*) Gambling Times.

Million Dollar Book Writing Formula: It Can Make You Rich (Even if You Can't Write!) Larry Oxenham. (Illus.). 156p. (Orig.). 1988. 14.95 (*0-943813-02-6*) Page One Pub.

Million-Dollar Bride: Wedding Dress Trilogy. Karen T. Whittenburg. LC 96-2471. (American Romance Ser.). 248p. 1996. per. 3.75 (*0-373-16621-4*, 1-16621-4) Harlequin Bks.

***Million Dollar Bucket: And Other Stories about Your Favorite Sports.** (Sports Shorts Ser.). 160p. 2000. pap. 5.95 (*0-7373-0433-2*, 04332W, Pub. by Lowell Hse) NTC Contemp Pub Co.

***Million Dollar Car & $250,000 Pizza: How Every Dollar You Save Builds Your Financial Future.** Allyson Lewis. LC 99-54458. (Illus.). 322p. 2000. pap. 18.95 (*0-7931-3593-1*) Dearborn.

Million Dollar Closing Techniques. \Million Dollar Round Table Center for Productivity Staff. LC 99-22889. 262p. 1999. pap. 16.95 (*0-471-32551-1*) Wiley.

Million Dollar Consulting: The Professional's Guide to Growing a Practice. 2nd rev. ed. Alan Weiss. LC 97-28334. (Illus.). 320p. 1997. 29.95 (*0-07-069629-2*); pap. 14.95 (*0-07-069628-4*) McGraw.

Million-Dollar Cowboy: Cowboys to the Rescue. Martha Shields. (Romance Ser.). 1998. per. 3.50 (*0-373-19346-7*, 1-19346-5) Silhouette.

Million-Dollar Frauds. Gary McKechnie. Ed. by Lee A. Campbell. LC 99-162916. 113p. 1998. write for info. (*0-89413-402-7*) Inst Inter Aud.

Million Dollar Gamble see **Micro Adventure Series**

Million Dollar Golf Game: With Help of Computer-Type Self-Programming. (Illus.). 1997. 14.50 (*1-885170-04-1*) Walden Press.

Million-Dollar Guide to Business & Real Estate Loan Sources. Tyler Gregory Hicks. 200p. 1998. pap. 25.00 (*1-56150-230-8*) Intl Wealth.

Million-Dollar Guide to Business & Real Estate Loan Sources. 8th ed. Ed. by Tyler Gregory Hicks. 200p. 1996. pap. 25.00 (*1-56150-180-8*) Intl Wealth.

Million-Dollar Guide to Business & Real Estate Loan Sources. 10th ed. Tyler Gregory Hicks. 200p. 1999. pap. 25.00 (*1-56150-281-2*) Intl Wealth.

***Million-Dollar Guide to Business & Real Estate Loan Sources.** 11th ed. Tyler G. Hicks. 200p. 2000. pap. 25.00 (*1-56150-341-X*) Intl Wealth.

Million Dollar Habits. Robert J. Ringer. 320p. 1991. mass mkt. 6.99 (*0-449-21878-3*, Crest) Fawcett.

Million Dollar Highway: Colorado's Most Spectacular Seventy Miles. Marvin Gregory & P. David Smith. LC 97-219416. (Illus.). 96p. 1997. 19.95 (*1-890437-01-8*) Western Reflections.

***Million Dollar Hole.** Michael Casey. 80p. 2001. pap. 12.95 (*0-914061-86-0*) Orchises Pr.

Million Dollar Home-Based Businesses: Successful Entrepreneurs. Sunny Baker & Kim Baker. 228p. 1993. pap. 9.95 (*1-55850-246-7*) Adams Media.

***Million-Dollar Horse.** Bonnie Bryant. (Saddle Club Ser.: No. 92). (Illus.). 160p. (J). (gr. 4-6). 2000. pap. 4.50 (*0-553-48696-9*, Skylark BDD) BDD Bks Young Read.

Million-Dollar Man: How to Marry. Vivian Leiber. 1997. per. 3.75 (*0-373-16672-9*, 1-16672-7) Harlequin Bks.

Million-Dollar Mare. Alison Hart. (Riding Academy Ser.: No. 3). (J). 1996. pap. 3.99 (*0-679-88118-2*, Bullseye Bks) Random Bks Yng Read.

Million Dollar Marriage. Maggie Shayne. (Fortunes of Texas Ser.: Vol. 1). 1999. per. 4.50 (*0-373-65030-2*, 1-65030-8) Harlequin Bks.

Million-Dollar Marriage: Whirlwind Weddings. Eva Rutland. (Romance Ser.: Vol. 3518). 1998. per. 3.50 (*0-373-03518-7*, 1-03518-7) Harlequin Bks.

Million-Dollar Marriage: Whirlwind Weddings. large type ed. Eva Rutland. (Larger Print Ser.: Vol. 364). 1998. per. 3.50 (*0-373-15764-9*, 1-15764-3) Harlequin Bks.

***Million Dollar Mermaid.** Esther Williams & Digby Diehl. LC 00-35096. (Illus.). 416p. 2000. pap. 14.00 (*0-15-601135-2*) Harcourt.

***Million Dollar Mermaid.** Esther Williams & Digby Diehl. LC 99-35872. (Illus.). 320p. 1999. 25.50 (*0-684-85284-5*) Simon & Schuster.

***Million Dollar Mermaid.** large type ed. Esther Williams. (Biography Ser.). (Illus.). 2000. 29.95 (*0-7862-2360-X*) Thorndike Pr.

Million Dollar Mistake. D.L. Carey. (Distress Call 911 Ser.). 1996. 9.09 (*0-606-10786-X*, Pub. by Turtleback) Demco.

Million Dollar Mistake: Distress Call 911. 5th ed. Diane L. Carey. (Distress Call 911 Ser.: No. 5). 192p. (YA). (gr. 7 up). 1996. pap. 3.99 (*0-671-00095-0*) PB.

Million-Dollar Mommy. Jacqueline Diamond. 1997. per. 3.75 (*0-373-16674-5*, 1-16674-3) Harlequin Bks.

Million Dollar Movie. Michael Powell. (Illus.). 626p. 1995. 30.00 (*0-614-32303-7*) Random.

Million Dollar Nightmare. Franklin W. Dixon. Ed. by Ann Greenberg. (Hardy Boys Mystery Stories Ser.: No. 103). 160p. (Orig.). (J). (gr. 3-6). 1990. pap. 3.99 (*0-671-69272-0*, Minstrel Bks) PB.

Million Dollar Prospecting Techniques. \Million Dollar Round Table Center for Productivity Staff. LC 99-25931. 262p. 1999. pap. 16.95 (*0-471-32550-3*) Wiley.

Million Dollar Rock. Roland W. Abbott. 82p. 1994. pap. 7.95 (*1-895387-47-7*) Creative Bk Pub.

Million Dollar Sales Letters for Your Own Use & Profit. 16p. 1992. pap. 5.00 (*0-915665-26-3*) Premier Publishers.

Million Dollar Salespeople: Success Stories of Top Sales Performers. 2nd ed. Lisa Coleman. 152p. 1996. reprint ed. pap. 14.95 (*0-9660493-0-6*) Scrivo Inc.

Million Dollar Secret: Create the Business of Your Dreams!! Take Action!! large type ed. John Comandari. Ed. by Lisa Comandari. 70p. 1997. pap. 8.95 (*0-9666913-0-X*) Diamond Enterprises.

M

Million Dollar Selling. Dan Sherman. (Illus.). 200p. 1997. pap. 14.95 (0-9651436-2-7) D Sherman & Assocs.

Million Dollar Selling Techniques. \Million Dollar Round Table Center for Productivity Staff. LC 99-25932. 246p. 1999. pap. 16.95 (0-471-32549-X) Wiley.

Million Dollar Shot. Gutman. 120p. (J). (gr. 3-7). 1997. pap. 4.95 (0-7868-1220-6, Pub. by Hyperion) Time Warner.

Million-Dollar Tattoo. Earl Emerson. 1997. mass mkt. 5.99 (0-345-40067-4) Ballantine Pub Grp.

***Million Dollar Valentine.** Rita C. Estrada. (Temptation Ser.: No. 766). 2000. per. 3.99 (0-373-25866-6, 1-25866-4, Harlequin) Harlequin Bks.

Million Dollars for Your Hangover see Rational Behavioral Alcoholic-Relapse Prevention Treatment Method: An Illustrated Guide for the New Self-Help Treatment Techniques for Alcoholics & Other Substance Abusers

Million Family Menus. Robert Carrier. 232p. 1996. 19.99 (1-57215-194-3, JG1194) World Pubns.

Million Fires: A Novel. Rajesh Gill. (New World Literature Ser.: No. 50). (C). 1992. pap. 11.00 (81-7018-704-4, Pub. by BR Pub) S Asia.

Million Fish . . . More or Less. Patricia C. McKissack. (Illus.). 40p. (J). (gr. k-4). 1996. pap. 6.99 (0-679-88086-0) Random.

Million Fish . . . More or Less. Patricia C. McKissack. 1996. 12.19 (0-606-09616-7, Pub. by Turtleback) Demco.

M

Million for Your Thoughts: The Industry-Funded Campaign Against the FDA by Conservative Think Tanks. Public Citizen Staff. 53p. (Orig.). 1996. pap. 20.00 (0-937188-57-3) Pub Citizen.

Million Heirs. John V. Childers, Jr. LC 98-28110. 200p. 1998. 20.00 (0-910019-76-2) Lghthse Pub Gp.

***Million Man March: Book of the American Dead.** P. J. Brown. 2000. pap. 9.95 (0-533-13099-9) Vantage.

Million Man March: The Untold Story. LaRon D. Bennett, Sr. Ed. by Katie Garcia. LC 97-126601. 128p. (Orig.). 1996. pap. 10.95 (0-9653831-0-5) BHse Publng.

Million Man March - Day of Absence: A Commemorative Anthology Speeches, Commentary, Photography. Ed. by Haki R. Madhubuti & Maulana Karenga. 172p. 1996. pap. text 19.95 (0-88378-188-3) Third World.

Million Man March Print. J. D. Howard. 1996. pap. text 10.00 (1-878647-27-X) APU Pub Grp.

Million Man March/Day of Absence: Mission Statement. Maulana Karenga. 22p. 1995. pap. 3.00 (0-943412-19-6) Univ Sankore Pr.

***Million Miles over Kansas City.** Charles Gray. 136p. 2000. 18.95 (1-58597-040-9) Leathers Pub.

Million Moms & Mine. Leah Komaiko & Kids. (Illus.). 28p. (J). 1992. 11.95 (0-9634893-0-5); pap. 5.95 (0-9634893-1-3) L Claiborne.

Million Open Doors. John Barnes. 320p. 1993. mass mkt. 4.99 (0-8125-1633-8, Pub. by Tor Bks) St Martin.

Million Pound Bank-Note see Creative Short Stories

Million Pound Strike. Jim Arnison. 86p. 1971. pap. 14.95 (0-8464-0631-4) Beekman Pubs.

Million Selling Records from the 1900s to the 1980s: An Illustrated Directory. Joseph Murrells. (Illus.). 528p. 1985. pap. 9.95 (0-685-09767-6, Arco) Macmillan Gen Ref.

***Million-to-One Team: Why the Chicago Cubs Haven't Won a Pennant since World War II.** George Castle. 2000. 29.95 (1-888698-31-4) Diamond Communications.

Million Truths: A Decade in China. Linda Jakobson. LC 98-20765. (Illus.). 224p. 1998. 24.95 (0-87131-873-3) M Evans.

***Million Truths: A Decade in China.** Linda Jakobson. 352p. 2000. pap. 17.95 (0-87131-919-5) M Evans.

Million under One: One Man's Perspective on the Million Man March. J. R. Fenwick. Ed. by Justin W. Fenwick & Willette Fenwick. LC 96-178190. (Illus.). 157p. (Orig.). 1996. pap. 15.00 (0-9646262-1-7) TPFS Pr.

Million Visions of Peace: Wisdom from the Friends of Old Turtle. Jennifer Garrison & Andrew Tubesing. LC 95-69777. (Illus.). 160p. (Orig.). 1995. pap. 9.95 (1-57025-079-0) Pfeifer-Hamilton.

Millionaire. Mikhail P. Artsybashev. Tr. by Percy Pinkerton. LC 78-103491. (Short Story Index Reprint Ser.). 1977. 20.95 (0-8369-3233-1) Ayer.

***Millionaire: John Law; the Philanderer, Gambler, Killer Who Invented Modern Finance.** Janet Gleeson. 304p. 2000. 23.00 (0-684-87295-1) Simon & Schuster.

***Millionaire Affair.** Sophie Weston. (Presents Ser.). 2000. mass mkt. 3.99 (0-373-12089-3) Harlequin Bks.

Millionaire & the Cowgirl. Lisa Jackson. (Fortune's Children Ser.). 1996. per. 4.50 (0-373-50178-1, 1-50178-2) Harlequin Bks.

Millionaire Bachelor. Susan Mallery. 1998. per. 4.25 (0-373-24220-4, 1-24220-5, Mira Bks) Harlequin Bks.

***Millionaire Bootcamp: Basic Training.** Thomas G. Psillas. 325p. 1999. pap. 24.95 (0-9674683-0-2) Tamion.

Millionaire Dad see Padre Millonario

Millionaire Dad. Leanne Banks. (Desire Ser.). 1998. per. 3.75 (0-373-76166-X, 1-76166-7) Silhouette.

Millionaire from Nazareth. Catherine Ponder. (Millionaires of the Bible Ser.). 1979. pap. 11.95 (0-87516-370-X) DeVorss.

Millionaire Joshua. Catherine Ponder. LC 77-86719. (Millionaires of the Bible Ser.). 1978. pap. 11.95 (0-87516-253-3) DeVorss.

Millionaire Kit: Surprisingly Simple Strategies for Building Real Wealth. Stephen L. Nelson. LC 98-16182. 224p. 1998. pap. 29.95 (0-8129-3004-5, Times Bks) Crown Pub Group.

Millionaire Manager. Curtis W. Symonds. 108p. 1993. 39.95 (0-9631056-0-4) Financial Pub.

Millionaire Meets His Match: Women to Watch. Patricia Seeley. (Silhouette Romance Ser.: No. 1329). 1998. per. 3.50 (0-373-19329-7, 1-19329-1) Harlequin Bks.

Millionaire Mentality. Dexter Yager. (Illus.). 130p. 1983. pap. 6.95 (0-932877-07-9); pap. 6.95 (0-932877-39-7) InterNET Serv.

Millionaire Mentality. Dexter R. Yager, Sr. (ENG & KOR., Illus.). 123p. 1983. pap. 7.95 (0-932877-42-7) InterNET Serv.

Millionaire Mentality (La Mentalidad Millonaria) Dexter Yager. (SPA., Illus.). 128p. 1997. pap. 7.95 (0-932877-40-0) InterNET Serv.

Millionaire Mentality (Nootpoiiia Ekatommypioyxoy) Dexter Yager. (ENG & GRE., Illus.). 136p. 1983. pap. 7.95 (0-932877-43-5) InterNET Serv.

***Millionaire Mind.** Thomas J. Stanley. 2000. 26.95 (0-7407-0357-9) Andrews & McMeel.

***Millionaire Mind.** large type ed. Thomas J. Stanley. LC 00-33494. 2000. write for info. (0-7838-9125-3, G K Hall Lrg Type) Mac Lib Ref.

Millionaire Mindset: Secret Strategies of Self-Made Millionaires. Michael M. Kiefer. (Illus.). 24p. (Orig.). 1996. pap. 10.00 (0-9645934-3-2) Kiefer Enterprises.

Millionaire Moses. Catherine Ponder. LC 77-71459. (Millionaires of the Bible Ser.). 1977. pap. 11.95 (0-87516-232-0) DeVorss.

***Millionaire Next Door.** T. J. Stanley & W. D. Danko. 1999. per. 14.00 (0-671-77530-8) Aladdin.

Millionaire Next Door. large type ed. Thomas J. Stanley & William D. Danke. LC 98-46515. 1999. 30.00 (0-7838-0448-2) Mac Lib Ref.

Millionaire Next Door: The Surprising Secrets of America's Wealthy. Thomas J. Stanley & William D. Danke. 272p. 1998. per. 14.00 (0-671-01520-6) PB.

Millionaire Next Door: The Surprising Secrets of America's Wealthy. Thomas J. Stanley & William D. Danko. LC 96-76497. 256p. 1996. 22.00 (1-56352-330-2) Longstreet.

Millionaire on Her Doorstep: Twins on the Doorstep. Stella Bagwell. (Romance Ser.: No. 1368). 1999. per. 3.50 (0-373-19368-8, 1-19368-9) Silhouette.

***Millionaire She Married.** Christine Rimmer. 2000. mass mkt. 4.50 (0-373-24322-7) Harlequin Bks.

Millionaire Sourcebook. Noel Clark. 1971. 15.00 (0-579-80030-X) Claitors.

***Millionaire Takes a Bride.** Pamela Toth. (Special Edition Ser.: Bk. 1353). 2000. mass mkt. 4.50 (0-373-24353-7, 1-24353-4) Silhouette.

Millionaires & Grub Street: Comrades - Contacts in the Last Half Century. James H. Bridge. LC 68-8441. (Essay Index Reprint Ser.). (Illus.). 1977. reprint ed. 23.95 (0-8369-0253-X) Ayer.

Millionaires & Managers: Structure of U. S. Financial Oligarchy. Leo Lempert. (Illus.). 1969. pap. 22.00 (0-8464-0632-2) Beekman Pubs.

Millionaires Are Coming! Pete Billac. Ed. by Sharon Davis. LC 98-86954. (Illus.). 120p. 1998. pap. 9.95 (0-943629-36-5) Swan Pub.

Millionaire's Baby. Phyllis Halldorson. (Special Edition Ser.: No. 1145). 1997. per. 3.99 (0-373-24145-3, 1-24145-4) Harlequin Bks.

Millionaire's Baby. Diana Hamilton. (Presents Ser.). 1998. per. 3.75 (0-373-11956-9, 0-11956-0) Harlequin Bks.

Millionaire's Bible: How to Start Your Own Business. rev. ed. Monroe C. Babcock. LC 87-81480. 171p. (Orig.). 1987. pap. 12.95 (0-87208-201-6) Shoeless Pub.

Millionaire's Christmas Wish. Shawna Delacorte. (Desire Ser.: No. 1187). 1998. per. 3.75 (0-373-76187-2, 1-76187-3) Silhouette.

***Millionaires' Club: How to Start & Run Your Own Investment Club - And Make Your Money Grow!** Carolyn M. Brown. 256p. 2000. pap. 19.95 (0-471-36938-1) Wiley.

Millionaire's Dinner Party: An Adaptation of the Cena Trimalchionis of Petronius. Maurice G. Balme. (Illus.). 96p. 1974. pap. text 18.95 (0-19-912025-0) OUP.

Millionaires Handbook. Peter Miller. 1998. pap. 6.95 (1-57636-061-X) SunRise Pbl.

***Millionaires' Handbook: Sage Advice for Success in Business & Life.** H. Peter R. Miller. 196p. 2000. pap. 9.95 (0-915009-70-6, Pub. by World Leis Corp) Midpt Trade.

***Millionaire's Instant Baby.** Allison Leigh. (Special Edition Ser.). 2000. per. 4.50 (0-373-24312-X) Silhouette.

***Millionaire's Mistress.** 1999. per. write for info. (0-373-15323-6) S&S Trade.

Millionaire's Mistress. large type ed. Miranda Lee. 1999. 21.95 (0-263-15809-8, G K Hall & Co) Mac Lib Ref.

Millionaire's Mistress: Presents Passion. Miranda Lee. (Presents Ser.: No. 2026). 1999. per. 3.75 (0-373-12026-5, 1-12026-0) Harlequin Bks.

Millionaire's Notebook: How Ordinary People Achieve Extraordinary Success. Steven K. Scott. LC 95-40929. 288p. 1996. pap. 11.00 (0-684-80303-8, Fireside) S&S Trade Pap.

Millionaires of Genesis. Catherine Ponder. (Millionaires of the Bible Ser.). 224p. 1976. pap. 11.95 (0-87516-215-0) DeVorss.

***Millionaire's Proposition, No. 141.** Natalie Patrick. (Romance Ser.). 1999. mass mkt. 3.50 (0-373-19413-7) Silhouette.

Millionaire's Row. Norman Katkov. 1996. mass mkt. 5.99 (0-451-18852-7) NAL.

Millionaires Row. Peggy M. Petkus. 1989. mass mkt. 4.50 (0-8217-2763-X, Zebra Kensgtn) Kensgtn Pub Corp.

Millionaire's Secret. Tom Harken. (Illus.). 192p. 1998. 16.99 (0-7852-7727-7) Nelson.

Millionaire's Secrets: Life Lessons in Wisdom & Wealth. Mark Fisher. 240p. 1996. 18.95 (0-684-80281-3) S&S Trade.

***Millionaire's Virgin: The Greek Tycoons.** Anne Mather. (Presents Ser.: Bk. 2109). 2000. per. 3.99 (0-373-12109-1, 1-12109-4) Harlequin Bks.

***Millionaire's Waitress Wife.** Carolyn Zane. (Romance Ser.: Bk. 1482). 2000. mass mkt. 3.50 (0-373-19482-X) Silhouette.

Millionaire's Woman. large type ed. Tessa Barclay. (Charnwood Large Print Ser.). 1996. 27.99 (0-7089-8886-5, Charnwood) Ulverscroft.

Millions & Billions of Years Ago: Dating Our Earth & Its Life. Norman F. Smith. LC 92-42744. (Venture Bks.). (Illus.). 128p. (YA). (gr. 7-12). 1993. lib. bdg. 24.00 (0-531-12533-5) Watts.

***Millions for Defense: The Subscription Warships of 1798.** Frederick C Leiner. LC 99-15206. 1999. 36.95 (1-55750-508-X) Naval Inst Pr.

***Millions Like Us? British Culture in the Second World War.** Ed. by Nicky Hayes & Jeff Hill. 240p. 1999. 39.95 (0-85323-763-8); pap. 19.95 (0-85323-773-5) Liverpool Univ Pr.

Millions Now Dying Will Never Live: A Scriptural Investigation of Russellism As Propagated by the International Bible Students. J. O'Hair. 22p. 1988. reprint ed. pap. 1.95 (1-883858-52-6) Witness CA.

Millions Now Living Will Never Die! Joseph F. Rutherford. 128p. 1985. reprint ed. pap. 5.95 (1-883858-29-1) Witness CA.

Millions of Cats. Wanda Ga'g. LC 28-21571. (Illus.). 32p. (J). (ps-3). 1996. pap. 4.99 (0-698-11363-2, PapStar) Peng Put Young Read.

Millions of Cats. Wanda Ga'g. (Illus.). (J). 1956. 13.99 (0-399-23315-6) Putnam Pub Group.

Millions of Cats. Wanda Ga'g. (J). 1977. 10.15 (0-606-01817-4, Pub. by Turtleback) Demco.

Millions of Memories. Linda Abrev. 150p. 1999. 15.99 (0-9670865-0-7) Millions Memos.

Millions of Miles to Mars. Joseph W. Kelch. LC 93-33798. (Illus.). (J). (gr. 3 up). 1995. 16.95 (0-671-88249-X, Julian Messner); pap. 9.95 (0-671-88250-3, Julian Messner) Silver Burdett Pr.

***Millions of Monarchs, Bunches of Beetles: How Bugs Find Strength in Numbers.** Gilbert Waldbauer. LC 99-42453. (Illus.). 272p. 2000. 24.95 (0-674-00090-0) HUP.

Millions of Snowflakes. Mary McKenna-Siddals. LC 97-47733. (Illus.). (J). (ps-k). 1998. 13.00 (0-395-71531-8, Clarion Bks) HM.

***Millionth Circle: How to Change Ourselves & the World.** Jean Shinoda Bolen. LC 99-23769. 168p. 1999. 14.95 (1-57324-176-8) Conari Press.

Millionth Moon. W. Edmund Hood. (J). 1997. pap. 15.00 (0-9647539-1-X) QDP Pubng.

***Millipedeology.** Michael Elsohn Ross. (Backyard Buddies Ser.). (Illus.). 48p. (J). (gr. 1-4). 2000. pap. 6.95 (1-57505-436-1, First Ave Edns) Lerner Pub.

***Millipedeology.** Michael Elsohn Ross. LC 99-35398. (Backyard Buddies Ser.). (Illus.). 48p. (J). (gr. 1-4). 2000. 19.93 (1-57505-398-5, Carolrhoda) Lerner Pub.

***Millipedes: Life Cycles.** Donna Schaffer. LC 98-53002. (Life Cycles Ser.). (Illus.). 24p. (J). 1999. 15.93 (0-7368-0210-X, Bridgestone Bks) Capstone Pr.

Millipedes & Centipedes of Ohio. Stephen R. Williams & Robert A. Hefner. (Bulletin Ser.: No. 18). 1928. pap. text 2.00 (0-86727-017-9) Ohio Bio Survey.

Millisecond Pulsars: A Decade of Surprise; Proceedings. Ed. by A. S. Fruchter et al. LC 95-75016. (Astronomical Society of the Pacific Conference Ser.: Vol. 72). 442p. 1995. 34.00 (0-937707-91-0) Astron Soc Pacific.

Millennium Prophecies. Brian Innes. LC 98-27576. (Unsolved Mysteries Ser.). (J). 1999. 24.26 (0-8172-5486-2) Raintree Steck-V.

Millon Inventories: Clinical & Personality Assessment. Theodore Millon. LC 97-7702. 553p. 1997. lib. bdg. 60.00 (1-57230-184-8, 0184) Guilford Pubns.

***Millonario Sorprendente.** Jan Hudson.Tr. of Surprising Millionaire. (ENG & SPA.). 2000. per. 3.50 (0-373-35320-0) Harlequin Bks.

***Millrat.** enl. ed. Michael Casey. 54p. 1999. pap. 6.00 (0-938566-81-4, Pub. by Adastra Pr) SPD-Small Pr Dist.

Millroy the Magician. Paul Theroux. 1996. pap. 11.00 (0-449-91197-7) Fawcett.

Mills: Andrew Mills & His Descendants. E. M. Taylor. 150p. 1991. reprint ed. pap. 23.00 (0-8328-2226-4); reprint ed. lib. bdg. 33.00 (0-8328-2225-6) Higginson Bk Co.

Mills: The Mills, Cope & Related Families of Georgia. Thomas H. Goddard & John H. Goddard, Sr. (Illus.). 326p. 1993. reprint ed. pap. 51.00 (0-8328-2971-4); reprint ed. lib. bdg. 61.50 (0-8328-2970-6) Higginson Bk Co.

Mills' Atlas of 1825. Ed. by Robert Mills. 1979. reprint ed. 100.00 (0-87844-021-6) Sandlapper Pub Co.

Mills-Bakeries of Ostia: Description & Interpretation. Ed. by J. T. Bakker. (Dutch Monographs on Ancient History & Archaeology: Vol. 21). 225p. 1999. 135.00 (90-5063-058-8, Pub. by Gieben) J Benjamins Pubng Co.

Mills Consoles. Richard M. Bueschel. (Coin-Op Collector's Ser.). (Illus.). 110p. (Orig.). 1994. spiral bd. 24.95 (1-885160-00-3) Coin-Op Classics.

Mill's Constitutional Annotations: A Compendium of the Law Especially Applicable to State Constitutions & Adapted to the Constitution of Colorado & Cross-Reference to the Constitutions of Other States. J. Warner Mills. viii, 444p. 1992. reprint ed. 55.00 (0-8377-2441-4, Rothman) W S Hein.

Mills, Frazier & Allied Families. Margaret M. Frazier. LC 78-88161. (Illus.). 258p. 1979. 20.00 (0-87012-348-3) McClain.

Mill's Life: From the Domesday Book to the Millenium. Charles Llewellyn. LC 98-70056. (Illus.). 198p. 1999. 29.95 (1-86105-105-0, Pub. by Robson Bks) Parkwest Pubns.

Mills, Mansions, & Mergers: The Life of William M. Wood. 2nd ed. Edward G. Roddy. LC 82-81081. (Illus.). 148p. 1997. reprint ed. pap. text 15.00 (0-937474-04-5) Am Textile Hist.

Mill's Moral, Political & Legal Philosophy. Ed. by C. L. Ten. LC 99-28314. (International Library of Critical Essays in the History of Philosophy). 510p. 1999. text 166.95 (1-84014-432-7, Pub. by Ashgate Pub) Ashgate Pub Co.

Mills. My North Carolina Heritage: Col. Ambrose Mills, a Soldier in the King's Army During the American Revolution, His Ancestry & Descendants: A Genealogy of the No. Carolina Cos. Buncombe, Henderson, Madison, Polk, Rutherford, Yancey 1650-1995, Including the Primary Families of Edney &, Vol. 5. Marshall L. Styles. (Illus.). 221p. 1996. reprint ed. lib. bdg. 44.00 (0-8328-5413-1) Higginson Bk Co.

Mills. My North Carolina Heritage: Col. Ambrose Mills, a Soldier in the King's Army During the American Revolution, His Ancestry & Desscendants: A Genealogy of the No. Carolina Cos. Buncombe, Henderson, Madison, Polk, Rutherford, Yancey 1650-1995, Including the Primary Families of Edney,& Styles, Vol. 5. Marshall L. Styles. (Illus.). 221p. 1996. reprint ed. pap. 34.00 (0-8328-5414-X) Higginson Bk Co.

Mills of Rockingham County. Janet B. Downs & Pat T. Ritchie. Ed. & Photos by Earl J. Downs. (Illus.). 464p. 1997. 35.00 (0-9664149-0-X) Harrisonburg-Rockingham.

Mills of Rockingham County, Vol. II. Janet B. Downs & Pat T. Ritchie. Ed. & Photos by Earl J. Downs. LC 98-71290. (Illus.). 688p. 1998. 45.00 (0-9664149-2-6) Harrisonburg-Rockingham.

Mills of the Forties Operator's Companion. Dan Post. (The/Yesteryear Series). (Illus.). 192p. 1980. 12.95 (0-934422-28-1, BKS-100274) Mead Pub Corp.

Mills of the Forties Operator's Companion. Ed. by Dan R. Post. LC 79-53627. (Slot Machines of Yesteryear Ser.). (Illus.). 1980. 21.95 (0-911160-75-2) Post Group.

Mills of the Thirties Operator's Companion. Dan Post. (The/Yesteryear Series). (Illus.). 192p. 1979. 12.95 (0-934422-27-3, BKS-100273) Mead Pub Corp.

Mills of the Thirties Operator's Companion. Ed. by Dan R. Post. LC 79-53627. (Slot Machines of Yesteryear Ser.). (Illus.). 1979. 21.95 (0-911160-73-6) Post Group.

Mill's "On Liberty" Critical Essays. Ed. by Gerald Dworkin. LC 97-1792. (Critical Essays on the Classics Ser.). 206p. 1997. 36.00 (0-8476-8488-1); pap. 13.95 (0-8476-8489-X) Rowman.

Mill's Utilitarianism: Critical Essays. Ed. by David Lyons. LC 97-29038. (Critical Essays on the Classics Ser.). 244p. 1998. 36.00 (0-8476-8783-X); pap. 15.95 (0-8476-8784-8) Rowman.

***Millspaugh-Milspaw Family in America.** 3rd ed. Ann Millspaugh Huff & Francis Corwin Millspaugh. LC 99-61633. 1999. write for info. (0-89725-371-X, Penobscot Pr) Picton Pr.

Millstaetter Genesis- und Physiologus-Handschrift. fac. ed. Intro. by A. Kracher. (Codices Selecti B Ser.: Vol. X). (GER.). 334p. 1967. 213.00 (3-201-00744-7, Pub. by Akademische Druck-und) Balogh.

Millstone. Margaret Drabble. LC 98-20928. (C). 1998. pap. 12.00 (0-15-600619-7, Harvest Bks) Harcourt.

Millstone & Hammer: The Origins of Water Power. M. J. Lewis. 200p. 1998. pap. 25.00 (0-85958-657-X, Pub. by Univ of Hull Pr) Paul & Co Pubs.

***Millstone Justice.** Florence B. Smith. 170p. 1999. pap. 7.00 (1-893463-24-9) F B Smith.

***Millstone Manufacture in Virginia: Interviews with the Last Two Brush Mountain Millstone Makers.** Charles D. Hockensmith et al. LC 99-67085. (Illus.). 112p. 1999. pap. 10.95 (0-943335-17-5) Marblehead Pub.

Millstones & Milestones: The Career of B. F. Dillingham, 1844-1918. Paul T. Yardley. LC 81-11506. 350p. 1981. reprint ed. pap. 108.50 (0-608-00526-6, 206140500008) Bks Demand.

Millstones & Milestones Vol. 1: Impressions That Guide Our Lives. Al Schalow. 104p. (Orig.). 1997. pap. 12.95 (0-9654963-2-5) Medwag Pub.

Milltown. Milltown Centennial Staff. (Images of America Ser.). 1995. pap. 16.99 (0-7524-0238-2) Arcadia Publng.

Milltown Natural: Essays & Stories form a Life. Richard Hague. (Working Lives Ser.). 184p. 1997. 19.95 (0-933087-44-6) Bottom Dog Pr.

Milltown Natural: Essays & Stories from a Life. Richard Hague. (Working Lives Ser.). 184p. 1997. pap. 10.95 (0-933087-43-8) Bottom Dog Pr.

Millville. Nancy Van Doren James. (Images of America Ser.). (Illus.). 128p. 1998. pap. 16.99 (0-7524-0962-X) Arcadia Publng.

Millways of Kent. John K. Morland. 1958. pap. 14.95 (0-8084-0219-6) NCUP.

Millwork Handbook. John E. Hiro. LC 92-45042. (Illus.). 288p. 1993. pap. 19.95 (0-8069-8698-0) Sterling.

Millwright, Level 1. National Center for Construction Education & Reseach Staff. (Wheels of Learning Ser.). (C). 1996. pap. text, teacher ed. 50.00 (0-13-245762-8) P-H.

Millwright, Level 2. National Center for Construction Education & Reseach Staff. (Wheels of Learning Ser.). (C). 1996. student ed., ring bd. 80.00 (0-13-265810-0) P-H.

Millwright, Level 3. (C). 1996. pap. text, teacher ed. 80.00 (0-13-245804-7) P-H.

Millwright, Level 3. National Center for Construction Education & Reseach Staff. (Wheels of Learning Ser.). 1996. student ed., ring bd. 80.00 (0-13-265828-3) P-H.

Millwright, Level 3. National Center for Construction Education & Reseach Staff. (Wheels of Learning Ser.). (C). 1996. teacher ed., ring bd. 80.00 (0-13-265414-8) P-H.

An Asterisk (*) at the beginning of an entry indicates that the title is appearing for the first time.

Millwright, Level 4. National Center for Construction Education & Reseach Staff. (Wheels of Learning Ser.). (C). 1996. teacher ed., ring bd. 80.00 (*0-13-265422-9*); student ed., ring bd. 80.00 (*0-13-265836-4*) P-H.

Millwright, Level 5. National Center for Construction Education & Reseach Staff. (Wheels of Learning Ser.). (C). 1996. student ed., ring bd. 80.00 (*0-13-265844-5*) P-H.

Millwright: Instructor's Guide, Level 1. National Center for Construction Education & Reseach Staff. (Wheels of Learning Ser.). (C). 1996. teacher ed., ring bd. 50.00 (*0-13-265398-2*) P-H.

Millwright: Instructor's Guide, Level 4. (C). 1996. teacher ed., per. 80.00 (*0-13-245820-9*) P-H.

Millwright: Instructor's Guide, Level 5. (C). 1996. teacher ed., per. 80.00 (*0-13-245846-2*) P-H.

Millwright: Level Two, Level 2. rev. ed. NCCER Staff. 488p. (C). 1997. pap. text, teacher ed. 80.00 (*0-13-772245-1*, Prentice Hall) P-H.

Millwright: Trainee Guide, Level 1. National Center for Construction Education & Reseach Staff. (Wheels of Learning Ser.). (C). 1996. pap. text, student ed. 50.00 (*0-13-266438-0*) P-H.

Millwright: Trainee Guide, Level 4. National Center Construction Staff. (C). 1996. per. 80.00 (*0-13-245812-8*) P-H.

Millwright Level Three: Trainee Guide, Level 1. National Center for Construction Education & Reseach Staff. (Wheels of Learning Ser.). (C). 1996. student ed., per. 50.00 (*0-13-245754-7*) P-H.

Millwright Level Three: Trainee Guide, Level 3. National Center for Construction Education & Reseach Staff. (Wheels of Learning Ser.). (C). 1996. student ed., per. 80.00 (*0-13-245796-2*) P-H.

Millwright Level Two: Instructor's Guide, Level 2. (C). 1996. teacher ed., per. 80.00 (*0-13-245788-1*) P-H.

***Millwright Trainee, Level 2.** rev. ed. NCCER Staff. 1998. pap. text 80.00 (*0-13-770900-5*) P-H.

Millwrights & Mechanics Guide. 4th ed. Carl A. Nelson. 1040p. 1989. 34.95 (*0-02-588591-X*, Aude IN) IDG Bks.

Milly. P. Goodhart. (Illus.). (J). text 22.95 (*0-340-67273-0*, Pub. by Hodder & Stought Ltd); mass mkt. 7.95 (*0-340-67274-9*, Pub. by Hodder & Stought Ltd) Trafalgar.

***Milly & Tilly: The Story of a Town Mouse & a Country Mouse.** Kate Summers. (Picture Puffin Ser.). (Illus.). 32p. (J). (ps-3). 2000. pap. 5.99 (*0-14-056724-0*, PuffinBks) Peng Put Young Read.

Milly-Molly-Mandy Storybook. Joyce Lakester Brisley. LC 97-76184. (Milly-Molly-Mandy Ser.). (Illus.). 224p. (J). (gr. k-3). 1998. 13.95 (*1-85697-493-6*) LKC.

***Milly of the Rovers.** Harriet Castor. (Illus.). 96p. (J). 1998. pap. 7.95 (*0-14-037839-1*, Pub. by Pnguin Bks Ltd) Trafalgar.

Milly Stories: Corpses, Carnations, the Weirdness Index, and, of Course, Aunt Gloria. Janice Lindsay. LC 97-36066. 131p. (J). (gr. 4-7). 1998. 15.95 (*0-7894-2491-6*) DK Pub Inc.

Milly's Wedding. Kate Summers. LC 98-50396. (J). (ps-1). 1999. 15.99 (*0-525-46046-2*, Dutton Child) Peng Put Young Read.

Milly's Wedding. Kate Summers & Maggie Kneen. (J). 1999. 15.99 (*1-85881-360-3*) NAL.

Milne Problem with Anisotropic Scattering: Proceedings. Ed. by M. V. Maslennikov. (Proceedings of the Steklov Institute of Mathematics Ser.: No. 97). 161p. 1969. pap. 59.00 (*0-8218-1897-X*, STEKLO/97) Am Math.

Milner Gray. Avril Blake. 100p. 1987. 60.00 (*0-85072-158-X*) St Mut.

Milner's Cases & Materials on Contracts. 3rd ed. S. M. Waddams. LC 75-151396. 1977. text 40.00 (*0-8020-2273-1*) U of Toronto Pr.

Milner's Cases & Materials on Contracts. 3rd ed. James B. Milner. Ed. by S. M. Waddams. LC 75-151396. 915p. reprint ed. pap. 200.00 (*0-7837-1049-6*, 204136100020) Bks Demand.

Milner's Young Men: The Kindergarten in Edwardian Imperial Affairs. Walter Nimocks. LC 68-8588. 248p. reprint ed. pap. 76.90 (*0-608-11980-6*, 202342900033) Bks Demand.

Milo. Jennifer Bassett. (Illus.). 32p. 1998. pap. text 4.95 (*0-19-421963-1*) OUP.

Milo & Brownville Town Register, 1905: Town Histories & Directories. Compiled by Mitchell et al. (Illus.). 120p. 1997. reprint ed. pap. 15.00 (*0-8328-5872-2*) Higginson Bk Co.

Milo & Roger: A Magical Life. Arthur Brandon. 424p. 1999. 37.00 (*0-945296-24-X*) Hermetic Pr.

Milo & the Magical Stones see Mats und die Wundersteine

Milo & the Magical Stones see Justine et la Pierre de Feu

Milo & the Magical Stones see Gaia e la Pietra di Fuoco

Milo & the Magical Stones. Marcus Pfister. (Illus.). (J). 1997. 189.50 (*1-55858-792-6*) North-South Bks NYC.

***Milo & the Magical Stones.** Marcus Pfister. (JPN., Illus.). (J). 1998. 18.95 (*4-06-261981-4*, Pub. by North-South Bks NYC) Chronicle Bks.

Milo & the Magical Stones: A Book with 2 Endings. Marcus Pfister. Tr. by Marianne Martens. LC 97-7543. (Illus.). 32p. (J). (gr. k-3). 1997. 18.95 (*1-55858-682-2*, Pub. by North-South Bks NYC) Chronicle Bks.

Milo & the Magical Stones: A Book with 2 Endings see Milo y las Piedras Magicas: Un Libro Con Dos Finales

***Milo & the Mysterious Island.** Marcus Pfister. (Illus.). 32p. (gr. k-3). 2000. 18.95 (*0-7358-1352-3*) North-South Bks NYC.

Milo Reno, Farmers Union Pioneer: The Story of a Man & a Movement. Roland A. White. Ed. by Dan C. McCurry & Richard E. Rubenstein. LC 74-30664. (American Farmers & the Rise of Agribusiness Ser.). (Illus.). 1975. reprint ed. 21.95 (*0-405-06840-9*) Ayer.

Milo Talon. Louis L'Amour. 224p. 1981. mass mkt. 4.50 (*0-553-24763-8*) Bantam.

Milo y las Piedras Magicas: Un Libro Con Dos Finales. Marcus Pfister.Tr. of Milo & the Magical Stones: A Book with 2 Endings. (SPA., Illus.). 32p. (J). (gr. k-3). 1997. 18.95 (*1-55858-721-7*, Pub. by North-South Bks NYC) Chronicle Bks.

Milocca: A Sicilian Village. rev. ed. Charlotte G. Chapman. (Illus.). 256p. (C). 1971. text 32.95 (*0-87073-764-3*) Transaction Pubs.

Miloli's Orchids. Alisandra Jezek. (Publish-a-Book Contest Ser.). (Illus.). 32p. (J). (gr. 1-6). 1990. lib. bdg. 22.83 (*0-8172-2784-9*) Raintree Steck-V.

Milon Kis: Pocket Hebrew Dictionary. 10th ed. Even Shushan & Dov Harden. (Illus.). 662p. 1998. reprint ed. pap. 6.00 (*1-880880-30-X*) Israeli Trad.

Milooka Chronicles, Bk. 1. Turock Dash. 126p. (J). (gr. 3-8). 1996. pap. 3.95 (*1-890081-57-4*) T D Publng.

Milos Forman: A Bio-Bibliography, 1. Thomas J. Slater. LC 87-7494. (Bio-Bibliographies in the Performing Arts Ser.: No. 1). 206p. 1987. lib. bdg. 55.00 (*0-313-25392-7*, SRF, Greenwood Pr) Greenwood.

Milos Forman Stories. Antonin J. Liehm. LC 73-92806. (Illus.). 201p. reprint ed. pap. 62.40 (*0-608-18128-5*, 203278200081) Bks Demand.

Milo's Friends in the Dark. Craig T. Ploetz. (Illus.). 32p. (J). (ps-4). 1992. lib. bdg. 11.95 (*1-882172-00-0*) Milo Prods.

Milo's Great Invention. Andrew Clements. (Ways to Communicate Ser.). 24p. (J). (gr. 1-2). 1995. 19.97 (*0-8172-5159-6*) Raintree Steck-V.

Milo's Great Invention. Andrew Clements. LC 97-25473. (Illus.). (J). 1998. write for info. (*0-8172-7288-7*) Raintree Steck-V.

Milo's Toothache. Ida Luttrell. (Illus.). 40p. (J). (gr. k-3). 1997. pap. 3.99 (*0-14-038429-4*) Viking Penguin.

Milo's Trip to the Museum with Grandpa. Craig T. Ploetz. (J). (ps-3). 1994. 11.95 (*1-882172-01-9*) Milo Prods.

***Milosevic: Portrait of a Tyrant.** Dusko Doder & Louise Branson. LC 99-41729. 291p. 1999. 25.00 (*0-684-84308-0*) Free Pr.

***Milosevic Regime Versus Serbian Democracy & Balkan Stability: Hearings Before the Commission on Security & Cooperation in Europe.** Ed. by Christopher H. Smith. 68p. 2000. reprint ed. pap. text 20.00 (*0-7567-0156-2*) DIANE Pub.

***Milosz's ABC's.** Czeslaw Milosz. Tr. by Madeline Levine from POL. 256p. 2001. 24.00 (*0-374-19977-9*) FS&G.

Milovan Djilas: A Revolutionary As a Writer. Dennis Reinhartz. (East European Monographs: No. 89). 112p. 1981. text 58.00 (*0-914710-83-4*, Pub. by East Eur Monographs) Col U Pr.

Milovan Djilas: An Annotated Bibliography, 1928-1975. Michael M. Milenkovitch. LC 76-20364. 50p. reprint ed. pap. 30.00 (*0-608-11434-0*, 201649900026) Bks Demand.

Milspeak: A Dictionary of International Military Acronyms & Abbreviations. Andy Lightbody & Joe Poyer. 91p. (Orig.). 1986. pap. 5.95 (*1-882391-00-4*) N Cape Pubns.

Milt Larsen's Magical Mystery Tour of Hollywood's Most Amazing Landmark, the Magic Castle. Carol Marie. LC 98-72807. 295 p. 1997. write for info. (*0-9661005-0-6*) Brookledge Corp.

***Milton.** Hayde Ardalan. (Illus.). 40p. 2000. 7.95 (*0-8118-2762-3*) Chronicle Bks.

Milton. Paul Buchanan & Anthony Sammarco. (Images of America Ser.). 128p. 1996. pap. 16.99 (*0-7524-0286-2*) Arcadia Publng.

Milton. Rose Macaulay. LC 74-7050. (Studies in Milton: No. 22). 1974. lib. bdg. 75.00 (*0-8383-1911-4*) M S G Haskell Hse.

Milton. Gillian Newsum. (Illus.). 96p. 1991. 28.95 (*1-872082-20-3*, Pub. by Kenilworth Pr) Half Halt Pr.

Milton. Stopford A. Brooke. LC 70-39534. reprint ed. 19.50 (*0-404-01108-X*) AMS Pr.

Milton. Thomas Babington Macaulay. (BCL1-PR English Literature Ser.). 155p. 1992. reprint ed. lib. bdg. 69.00 (*0-7812-7386-2*) Rprt Serv.

Milton. Mark Pattison. (BCL1-PR English Literature Ser.). 227p. 1992. reprint ed. lib. bdg. 79.00 (*0-7812-7388-9*) Rprt Serv.

Milton. Walter Raleigh. LC 67-13336. 1972. reprint ed. 19.95 (*0-405-08873-6*) Ayer.

Milton. Walter Raleigh. (BCL1-PR English Literature Ser.). 286p. 1992. reprint ed. lib. bdg. 79.00 (*0-7812-7389-7*) Rprt Serv.

Milton: A Study in Form & Ideology. Christopher Kendrick. 250p. 1986. 29.95 (*0-416-01251-5*, 9847) Routledge.

Milton: Complete Short Poems. 2nd ed. John Carey. (Laep Ser.). 531p. (C). 1997. pap. 88.00 (*0-582-01984-2*) Addison-Wesley.

Milton: Critical Heritage, 2 vols., Set. Ed. by John T. Shawcross. Incl. John Milton Vol. 2: 1732 - 1801. 452p. (C). 1996. 140.00 (*0-415-13421-8*); Vol. 1. John Milton Vol. 1: 1628 - 1731. 288p. (C). 1996. 125.00 (*0-415-13420-X*); 740p. (C). 1996. Set text, boxed set 250.00 (*0-415-13419-6*) Routledge.

Milton: Man & Thinker. Denis Saurat. LC 73-153352.Tr. of La/Pensee De Milton. reprint ed. 31.50 (*0-404-05565-6*) AMS Pr.

Milton: Paradise Lost. 2nd ed. John Milton. Ed. by Alastair Fowler. LC 97-51835. (Annotated English Poets Ser.). 704p. (C). 1998. pap. 39.06 (*0-582-21518-8*) Addison-Wesley.

Milton: Poems. John Milton. 1996. 12.50 (*0-679-45099-8*) McKay.

Milton: Poet of Exile. 2nd ed. Louis L. Martz. LC 86-7772. 356p. 1986. pap. 22.00 (*0-300-03736-8*) Yale U Pr.

Milton Vol. I: A Biography. 2nd ed. William R. Parker. LC 96-16384. (Illus.). 690p. 1996. text 90.00 (*0-19-812889-4*) OUP.

Milton Vol. II: A Biographical Commentary. 2nd ed. William R. Parker. (Illus.). 878p. 1996. text 110.00 (*0-19-812900-9*) OUP.

Milton, a Bibliography for the Years, 1624-1700. Ed. by John T. Shawcross. LC 84-653. (Medieval & Renaissance Texts & Studies: Vol. 30). 464p. 1984. 36.00 (*0-86698-064-4*, MR30) MRTS.

Milton, a Bibliography for the Years, 1624-1700: Addenda & Corrigenda. Ed. by John T. Shawcross. (Medieval & Renaissance Texts & Studies: Vol. 30A). 40p. 1990. pap. 7.00 (*0-86698-081-4*, MR30A) MRTS.

Milton, A Poem, Vol. 5. William Blake. (Blake's Illuminated Bks.). 1998. pap. 29.95 (*0-691-00148-0*, Pub. by Princeton U Pr) Cal Prin Full Svc.

Milton Acorn & His Works. Ed Jewinski. (Canadian Author Studies). 54p. (C). 1990. pap. 9.95 (*1-55022-062-4*, Pub. by ECW) Genl Dist Srvs.

Milton Agonistes. Edward H. Visiak. (Studies in Milton: No. 22). (C). 1970. reprint ed. pap. 39.95 (*0-8383-0102-9*) M S G Haskell Hse.

Milton Agonistes: A Metaphysical Criticism. Edward H. Visiak. (BCL1-PR English Literature Ser.). 104p. 1992. reprint ed. lib. bdg. 69.00 (*0-7812-7390-0*) Rprt Serv.

Milton among the Philosophers: Poetry & Materialism in Seventeenth-Century England. Stephen M. Fallon. LC 90-55729. 280p. 1991. text 45.00 (*0-8014-2495-X*) Cornell U Pr.

Milton & Augustine: Patterns of Augustinian Thought in Milton's Paradise Lost. Peter A. Fiore. LC 80-17854. 144p. 1981. 28.50 (*0-271-00269-7*) Pa St U Pr.

Milton & Freewill: An Essay in Criticism & Philosophy. William Myers. 256p. 1987. 65.00 (*0-7099-4620-1*) Routledge.

Milton & Heresy. Ed. by Stephen B. Dobranski et al. LC 97-35243. 293p. (C). 1998. 59.95 (*0-521-63065-7*) Cambridge U Pr.

Milton & His Poetry. William Henry Hudson. LC 79-120964. (Poetry & Life Ser.). reprint ed. 16.00 (*0-404-52518-0*) AMS Pr.

***Milton & Isaiah: A Journey Through the Drama of Salvation in "Paradise Lost"** Youngwon Park. LC 99-46192. (Seventeenth-Century Texts & Studies: Vol. 5). 160p. (C). 2000. text 47.95 (*0-8204-4288-7*) P Lang Pubng.

Milton & Jakob Boehme. Margaret L. Bailey. LC 65-15885. (Studies in Comparative Literature: No. 35). 1969. reprint ed. lib. bdg. 75.00 (*0-8383-0505-9*) M S G Haskell Hse.

Milton & Midrash. Golda Werman. LC 94-25463. 266p. 1995. 54.95 (*0-8132-0821-1*) Cath U Pr.

***Milton & Milton Mills.** Sarah M. Ricker. (Images of America Ser.). 1999. pap. 18.99 (*0-7524-1267-1*) Arcadia Publng.

***Milton & Modernity: Politics, the Individual & Paradise Lost.** Matthew Jordan. LC 00-42053. 2000. write for info. (*0-312-23600-X*) St Martin.

Milton & Paradise Lost. N. Bogholm. LC 74-7116. (Studies in Milton: No. 22). 1974. lib. bdg. 75.00 (*0-8383-1968-8*) M S G Haskell Hse.

***Milton & Religious Controversy: Satire & Polemic in Paradise Lost.** John N. King. (Illus.). 247p. (C). 2000. 59.95 (*0-521-77198-6*) Cambridge U Pr.

Milton & Republicanism. Ed. by David Armitage et al. (Ideas in Context Ser.: No. 35). (Illus.). 296p. (C). 1996. text 59.95 (*0-521-55178-1*) Cambridge U Pr.

Milton & Republicanism. Ed. by David Armitage et al. LC 99-162521. (Ideas in Context Ser.: No. 35). (Illus.). 296p. (C). 1998. pap. 22.95 (*0-521-64648-0*) Cambridge U Pr.

Milton & the Art of Sacred Song: Essays. Ed. by J. Max Patrick & Roger H. Sundell. LC 78-65014. 168p. 1979. reprint ed. pap. 52.10 (*0-7837-9792-3*, 206052100005) Bks Demand.

Milton & the Big Freeze. Tony Garth. (Microscopic Milton Ser.). 24p. 1996. pap. 4.99 (*1-900207-11-7*, Pub. by Splash) Assoc Pubs Grp.

Milton & the Book of Revelation: The Heavenly Cycle. Austin C. Dobbins. LC 73-22715. (Studies in the Humanities: No. 7). (Illus.). 176p. 1975. pap. 54.60 (*0-7837-8370-1*, 205918000009) Bks Demand.

Milton & the Bubble Bath. Tony Garth. (Microscopic Milton Ser.). 24p. 1996. pap. 4.99 (*1-900207-01-X*, Pub. by Splash) Assoc Pubs Grp.

Milton & the Culture of Violence. Michael Lieb. LC 93-32279. 288p. 1994. text 37.50 (*0-8014-2903-X*) Cornell U Pr.

***Milton & the Death of Man: Humanism on Trial in Paradise Lost.** Harold Skulsky. LC 99-51869. 264p. 2000. 44.50 (*0-87413-719-5*) U Delaware Pr.

Milton & the Drama of History: Historical Vision, Iconoclasm & the Literary Imagination. David Loewenstein. (Illus.). 207p. (C). 1990. text 69.95 (*0-521-37253-4*) Cambridge U Pr.

Milton & the Dust Collection. Tony Garth. (Microscopic Milton Ser.). 24p. 1996. pap. 4.99 (*1-900207-16-8*, Pub. by Splash) Assoc Pubs Grp.

Milton & the English Mind. Francis Hutchinson. LC 74-7187. (Studies in Milton: No. 22). 1974. lib. bdg. 75.00 (*0-8383-1906-8*) M S G Haskell Hse.

Milton & the Hermeneutics Journey. Gale H. Carrithers, Jr. & James D. Hardy, Jr. LC 94-6781. 264p. 1994. text 37.50 (*0-8071-1876-1*) La State U Pr.

Milton & the Imperial Vision. Ed. by Balachandra Rajan & Elizabeth Sauer. LC 98-40119. (Medieval & Renaissance Literary Studies). 376p. 1999. 58.00 (*0-8207-0303-6*) Duquesne.

Milton & the Kitten. Tony Garth. (Microscopic Milton Ser.). 24p. 1996. pap. 4.99 (*1-900207-06-0*, Pub. by Splash) Assoc Pubs Grp.

Milton & the Line of Vision. Ed. by Joseph A. Wittreich. LC 75-12215. (Illus.). 301p. 1975. reprint ed. pap. 93.40 (*0-7837-9800-8*, 206052900005) Bks Demand.

Milton & the Literature of Travel. Robert R. Cawley. LC 72-114095. (Princeton Studies in English: No. 32). 163p. (C). 1970. reprint ed. 45.00 (*0-87752-015-1*) Gordian.

Milton & the Masque Tradition: The Early Poems, Arcades & Comus. John G. Demaray. LC 68-14254. 212p. reprint ed. pap. 65.80 (*0-7837-2250-8*, 205733800004) Bks Demand.

Milton & the Middle Ages. Ed. by John Mulryan. LC 81-694400. 192p. 1982. 29.50 (*0-8387-5036-2*) Bucknell U Pr.

Milton & the Miltonic Dryden. Anne Ferry. LC 68-25608. 238p. reprint ed. pap. 73.80 (*0-7837-2258-3*, 205734600004) Bks Demand.

Milton & the Muses. E. R. Gregory. LC 86-30842. (Illus.). 190p. 1989. pap. 58.90 (*0-608-05140-3*, 206570100005) Bks Demand.

***Milton & the Natural World: Science & Poetry in "Paradise Lost"** Karen L. Edwards. LC 99-11230. (Illus.). 279p. (C). 2000. 59.95 (*0-521-64359-7*) Cambridge U Pr.

Milton & the Paradoxes of Renaissance Heroism. John M. Steadman. LC 86-20080. 280p. 1987. text 40.00 (*0-8071-1332-8*) La State U Pr.

Milton & the Postmodern. Herman Rapaport. LC 82-21935. 284p. 1983. reprint ed. pap. 88.10 (*0-608-01853-8*, 206250300003) Bks Demand.

Milton & the Puritan Dilemma, 1641-1660. Arthur E. Barker. LC 58-3195. (University of Toronto, Department of English Studies & Texts: No. 1). 464p. reprint ed. pap. 143.90 (*0-608-16544-1*, 202635700049) Bks Demand.

Milton & the Revolutionary Reader. Sharon Achinstein. LC 94-6647. (Literature in History Ser.). 344p. 1994. text 39.50 (*0-691-03490-7*, Pub. by Princeton U Pr) Cal Prin Full Svc.

Milton & the Rise of Russian Satanism. Valentin Boss. 254p. 1991. text 60.00 (*0-8020-5795-0*) U of Toronto Pr.

Milton & the Sense of Tradition. Christopher Grose. LC 88-1707. 240p. (C). 1988. 35.00 (*0-300-04171-3*) Yale U Pr.

Milton & the Sons of God: The Divine Image in Milton's Epic Poetry. Hugh MacCallum. 335p. 1986. text 40.00 (*0-8020-5679-2*) U of Toronto Pr.

Milton & the Tangles of Neaera's Hair: The Making of the 1645 Poems. Stella P. Revard. LC 97-360. 304p. 1997. spiral bd. 44.95 (*0-8262-1100-3*) U of Mo Pr.

Milton & the Theme of Fame. R. B. Jenkins. (Studies in English Literature: Vol. 77). 1973. pap. text 17.70 (*90-279-2529-1*) Mouton.

Milton, Aristocrat & Rebel: The Poet & His Politics. Perez Zagorin. 176p. (C). 1993. 60.00 (*1-878822-99-3*, Pub. by Univ Rochester Pr) Boydell & Brewer.

***Milton, Authorship & the Book Trade.** Stephen B. Dobranski. LC 98-44373. (Illus.). 264p. (C). 1999. 54.95 (*0-521-64192-6*) Cambridge U Pr.

Milton Avery. Robert Hobbs. LC 89-11022. (Illus.). 264p. 1990. 85.00 (*0-933920-95-4*, Pub. by Hudson Hills) Natl Bk Netwk.

Milton Avery: Works from the Nineteen Fifties. Marla Price. LC 90-61490. (Illus.). 48p. (Orig.). 1990. 19.95 (*0-929865-05-7*) Mod Art Mus Ft Worth.

Milton Avery Prints, 1933 to 1955. Harry H. Lunn, Jr. 99p. 1973. pap. 50.00 (*1-55660-121-2*) A Wofsy Fine Arts.

Milton Avery Prints, 1933-1955: With an Original Etching. limited ed. Harry H. Lunn, Jr. (Illus.). 99p. 1973. boxed set 400.00 (*1-55660-159-X*) A Wofsy Fine Arts.

Milton Babbitt: Words about Music. Ed. by Stephen Dembski & Joseph N. Straus. LC 86-40455. (Illus.). 208p. 1987. text 27.95 (*0-299-10790-6*) U of Wis Pr.

Milton Berle's Private Joke File. Milton Berle. 672p. 1992. pap. 21.00 (*0-517-58716-5*, Crown) Crown Pub Group.

Milton Brown & the Founding of Western Swing. Cary Ginell. LC 93-29364. (Music in American Life Ser.). 360p. 1994. text 29.95 (*0-252-02041-3*) U of Ill Pr.

Milton Cross New Encyclopedia of the Great Composers & Their Music, 2 vols., Set. Milton Cross & David Ewen. LC 70-87097. 1969. boxed set 35.00 (*0-385-03635-3*) Doubleday.

Milton, 1805-1833. Edwin Harrington. (Illus.). 37p. (Orig.). 1994. pap. 8.00 (*0-941066-11-8*) Hillside Pr.

Milton Encyclopedia, 9 vols. Ed. by William B. Hunter, Jr. Incl. Vol. 1. A-B. 40.00 (*0-8387-1834-5*); Vol. 2. C-Ec. 40.00 (*0-8387-1835-3*); Vol. 3. Ed-Hi. 40.00 (*0-8387-1836-1*); Vol. 4. Ho-La. 40.00 (*0-8387-1837-X*); Vol. 5. Le-N. 40.00 (*0-8387-1838-8*); Vol. 6. O-Po. 40.00 (*0-8387-1839-6*); Vol. 7. Pr-Sl. 40.00 (*0-8387-1840-X*); Vol. 8. Sm-Z. 40.00 (*0-8387-1841-8*); Vol. 9. 176p. 1984. 40.00 (*0-8387-5053-2*); write for info. (*0-318-51247-5*) Bucknell U Pr.

Milton Friedman: Critical Assessments, 4 vols., Set. Ed. by John C. Wood & Ronald N. Woods. (Critical Assessments Ser.). (Illus.). 2016p. (C). (gr. 13). 1990. text, boxed set 700.00 (*0-415-02005-0*, A4191) Routledge.

Milton Friedman: Economics in Theory & Practice. Abraham Hirsch & Neil De Marchi. LC 89-20266. 336p. 1991. reprint ed. pap. text 25.95 (*0-472-08167-5*, 08167) U of Mich Pr.

Milton Friedman's Monetary Framework: A Debate with His Critics. Milton Friedman et al. Ed. by Robert J. Gordon. LC 73-92599. xii, 208p. 1975. pap. text 16.00 (*0-226-26408-4*, P619) U Ch Pr.

Milton Glaser: Graphic Design. Milton Glaser. (Illus.). 242p. 1998. pap. 39.95 (*0-87951-188-5*, Pub. by Overlook Pr) Penguin Putnam.

Milton Harris: Chemist, Innovator, & Entrepreneur. Ed. by Miklos M. Breuer. LC 82-13926. 170p. 1982. pap. text 22.00 (*0-8412-0740-2*, Pub. by Am Chemical) OUP.

M

An Asterisk (*) at the beginning of an entry indicates that the title is appearing for the first time.

Milton Hershey: Chocolate King, Town Builder. Charnan Simon. LC 97-24560. (Community Builders Ser.). 48p. 1998. 23.00 (*0-516-20389-4*) Childrens.

***Milton Hershey: Chocolate King, Town Builder.** Charnan Simon. Ed. by Sarah DeCapua. (Community Builders Ser.). (Illus.). 48p. (J). 1998. pap. 6.95 (*0-516-26330-7*) Childrens.

Milton in Context: The Seventeenth Century: Annotated Chronology, Genealogical Tables, & Selected Bibliographies. Michael R. Collings. 400p. (C). 1998. 50.00 (*1-886405-61-1*, Zarahemla Motets) White Crow Pr.

Milton in Deutschland: Seine Rezeption Im Latein-und Deutschs Schrifttum Zwischen, 1651-1732. Hans-Dieter Kreuder. (Quellen und Forschungen zur Sprach und Kulturgeschichte der Germanischen Voelker). 257p. (C). 1971. 104.60 (*3-11-003685-1*) De Gruyter.

Milton in Early America. George F. Sensabaugh. LC 79-14332. 322p. 1979. 75.00 (*0-87752-180-8*) Gordian.

Milton in Government. Robert T. Fallon. LC 92-17716. (Illus.). 312p. (C). 1993. 45.00 (*0-271-00904-7*) Pa St U Pr.

Milton in Italy: Contexts, Images, Contradictions. Ed. by Mario A. Di Cesare. (Medieval & Renaissance Texts & Studies: Vol. 90). 616p. 1991. 40.00 (*0-86698-103-9*, MR90) MRTS.

M

Milton, Man & Thinker. Denis Saurat. LC 76-121151. (Studies in Milton: No. 22). 1970. reprint ed. lib. bdg. 75.00 (*0-8383-1093-1*) M S G Haskell Hse.

***Milton, Massachusetts Cemetery Catalogue.** Ed. by Charles D. Townsend. 80p. 2000. reprint ed. pap. 25.00 (*1-878545-53-1*) ACETO Bookmen.

Milton Memorial Lectures, 1909. Percy Ames. LC 65-15895. (Studies in Milton: No. 22). 1969. reprint ed. lib. bdg. 75.00 (*0-8383-0501-6*) M S G Haskell Hse.

***Milton Moose Finds a Home.** large type ed. Michael Mackniak. (Illus.). 36p. (J). (gr. 1-4). 2000. 18.95 (*1-57532-221-8*) Press-Tige Pub.

Milton, My Father's Dog. Eric Copeland. LC 93-61795. (Illus.). 24p. (J). (gr. 1-5). 1994. 13.95 (*0-88776-339-1*) Tundra Bks.

Milton Obote. Kenneth Ingham. LC 93-22702. 1994. 37.50 (*0-415-05542-3*) Routledge.

Milton on Education. John Milton. Ed. & Intro. by Oliver M. Ainsworth. LC 75-112640. 22.5p. reprint ed. 49.50 (*0-404-00298-6*) AMS Pr.

Milton on Education: The Tractate of Education with Supplementary Extracts from Other Writings of Milton. John Milton. Ed. by Oliver M. Ainsworth. LC 70-145185. 1971. reprint ed. 18.00 (*0-403-01110-8*) Scholarly.

Milton on Education: The Tractatte of Education. John Milton. (BCL1-PR English Literature Ser.). 369p. 1992. reprint ed. lib. bdg. 89.00 (*0-7812-7378-1*) Rprt Serv.

Milton Papers. David H. Stevens. LC 75-176438. reprint ed. 20.00 (*0-404-06262-8*) AMS Pr.

Milton: Paradise Lost. Alastair Fowler. (Annotated English Poets Ser.). (Illus.). 649p. (C). 1989. reprint ed. pap. text 46.00 (*0-582-48455-3*, 73261) Longman.

Milton, Poet of Duality: A Study of Semiosis in the Poetry & the Prose. R. A. Shoaf. LC 92-36794. 254p. 1993. pap. 19.95 (*0-8130-1192-2*) U Press Fla.

Milton Poetical Works. John Milton. (Poetry Library). 496p. 1998. pap. 7.95 (*1-85326-410-5*, 4105WW, Pub. by Wrdsworth Edits) NTC Contemp Pub Co.

Milton Re-Viewed: Ten Essays. Edward Le Comte. LC 91-1083. 160p. 1991. text 10.00 (*0-8153-0306-8*, 1446) Garland.

Milton Resnick: Monuments. Edward M. Gomez. (Illus.). 26p. 1997. pap. 20.00 (*0-944680-54-2*) R Miller Gal.

Milton Resnick Paintings, 1945-1985. (Illus.). 100p. 1985. pap. 14.95 (*0-936080-14-0*) Cont Arts Museum.

Milton S. Eisenhower: Educational Statesman. Stephen E. Ambrose & Richard H. Immerman. LC 83-4. (Illus.). 351p. 1983. reprint ed. pap. 108.90 (*0-608-05921-8*, 206625700008) Bks Demand.

Milton S. Eisenhower Years at Kansas State University. Ed. by Virginia M. Quiring. 120p. 1986. 25.00 (*0-685-18353-X*) Friends Lib KSU.

Milton S. Eisenhower Years at Kansas State University. limited ed. Ed. by Virginia M. Quiring. 120p. 1986. 50.00 (*0-9616658-0-7*) Friends Lib KSU.

Milton S. Hershey. Katherine B. Shippen. 20.95 (*0-8488-1164-X*) Amereon Ltd.

***Milton Spenser & the Epic Tradition.** Cook. 208p. 1999. pap. 19.95 (*0-7546-0048-3*) Ashgate Pub Co.

Milton, Spenser & the Epic Tradition. Patrick J. Cook. 208p. 1996. 65.95 (*1-85928-271-7*, Pub. by Scolar Pr) Ashgate Pub Co.

Milton Studies see Milton Studies

Milton Studies, Vol. I-XXV. Ed. by James D. Simmonds. Incl. Milton Studies Vol. VII: "Eyes Fast Fix't" Ed. by Albert C. Labriola & Michael Lieb. LC 69-12335. (Illus.). 323p. 1975. text 49.95 (*0-8229-3305-5*); Milton Studies Vol. XI: The Presence of Milton. Ed. by B. Rajan. LC 69-12335. (Illus.). 143p. 1978. text 49.95 (*0-8229-3373-X*); Milton Studies Vol. XVII: Composite Orders: The Genres of Milton's Last Poems. Ed. by Richard S. Ide & Joseph A. Wittreich. LC 69-12335. 332p. 1983. text 49.95 (*0-8229-3473-6*); Milton Studies Vol. XIX: Urbane Milton: The Latin Poetry. Ed. by James A. Freeman & Anthony Low. LC 69-12335. (Illus.). 320p. 1984. text 49.95 (*0-8229-3492-2*); Vol. I. Milton Studies. LC 69-12335. 192p. 1969. reprint ed. text 49.95 (*0-8229-3174-5*); Vol. II. Milton Studies. LC 69-12335. 230p. 1970. text 49.95 (*0-8229-3194-X*); Vol. III. Milton Studies. LC 69-12335. (Illus.). 224p. 1971. text 49.95 (*0-8229-3218-0*); Vol. IV. Milton Studies. LC 69-12335. (Illus.). 215p. 1972. text 49.95 (*0-8229-3244-X*); Vol. V. Milton Studies. LC 69-12335. (Illus.). 308p. 1973. text 49.95 (*0-8229-3272-5*); Vol. VI. Milton Studies. LC 69-12335. 306p. 1974. text 49.95 (*0-8229-3288-1*); Vol. VIII. Milton Studies. LC 69-12335. (Illus.). 291p. 1975. text 49.95 (*0-8229-3310-1*); Vol. IX. Milton Studies. LC 69-12335. 275p. 1976. text 49.95 (*0-8229-3329-2*); Vol. X. Milton Studies. LC 69-12335. (Illus.). 215p. 1976. text 49.95 (*0-8229-3356-X*); Vol. XII. Milton Studies. LC 69-12335. (Illus.). 304p. 1979. text 49.95 (*0-8229-3376-4*); Vol. XIII. Milton Studies. LC 69-12335. 317p. 1979. text 49.95 (*0-8229-3404-3*); Vol. XIV. Milton Studies. LC 69-12335. (Illus.). 255p. 1980. text 49.95 (*0-8229-3429-9*); Vol. XV. Milton Studies. LC 69-12335. (Illus.). 255p. 1981. text 49.95 (*0-8229-3449-3*); Vol. XVI. Milton Studies. LC 69-12335. 220p. 1982. text 49.95 (*0-8229-3465-5*); Vol. XVIII. Milton Studies. LC 69-12335. 300p. 1983. text 49.95 (*0-8229-3484-1*); Vol. XX. Milton Studies. LC 69-12335. (Illus.). 245p. 1988. text 49.95 (*0-8229-3497-3*); Vol. XXI. Milton Studies. LC 69-12335. 327p. 1986. text 49.95 (*0-8229-3524-4*); Vol. XXII. Milton Studies. LC 69-12335. (Illus.). 270p. 1986. text 49.95 (*0-8229-3541-4*); Vol. XXIII. Milton Studies. LC 69-12335. (Illus.). 290p. 1988. text 49.95 (*0-8229-3558-9*); Vol. XXIV. Milton Studies. LC 69-12335. (Illus.). 296p. 1988. text 49.95 (*0-8229-3591-0*); Vol. XXV. Milton Studies. LC 69-12335. (Illus.). 272p. 1990. text 49.95 (*0-8229-3625-9*); Vols. I-XII. Milton Studies Index. Beth E. Luey. LC 69-12335. 120p. 1980. text 49.95 (*0-8229-3389-6*); LC 69-12335. (Milton Studies). write for info. (*0-318-56123-9*) U of Pittsburgh Pr.

Milton Studies, Vol. XXVI. Ed. by James D. Simmonds. LC 69-12335. (Illus.). 272p. 1991. text 49.95 (*0-8229-3654-2*) U of Pittsburgh Pr.

Milton Studies, Vol. 29. Ed. by Albert C. Labriola. LC 69-12335. 208p. (C). 1993. text 49.95 (*0-8229-3732-8*) U of Pittsburgh Pr.

Milton Studies, Vol. 30. Ed. by Albert C. Labriola. (Illus.). 224p. 1994. text 49.95 (*0-8229-3772-7*) U of Pittsburgh Pr.

Milton Studies, Vol. 31. Ed. by Albert C. Labriola. 242p. (C). 1995. text 49.95 (*0-8229-3861-8*) U of Pittsburgh Pr.

Milton Studies, Vol. 32. Ed. by Albert C. Labriola. 272p. (C). 1996. text 49.95 (*0-8229-3914-2*) U of Pittsburgh Pr.

Milton Studies, Vol. 35. Ed. by Albert C. Labriola. (Illus.). 380p. 1998. text 50.00 (*0-8229-4038-8*) U of Pittsburgh Pr.

Milton Studies, Vol. 36. Albert C. Labriola. (Illus.). 286p. 1998. text 50.00 (*0-8229-4073-6*) U of Pittsburgh Pr.

Milton Studies, Vol. VII, "Eyes Fast Fix't" see Milton Studies

Milton Studies, Vol. XI, The Presence of Milton see Milton Studies

Milton Studies, Vol. XVII, Composite Orders: The Genres of Milton's Last Poems see Milton Studies

Milton Studies, Vol. XIX, Urbane Milton: The Latin Poetry see Milton Studies

Milton Studies Index see Milton Studies

Milton Studies 34. Ed. by Albert C. Labriola. 256p. 1996. text 49.95 (*0-8229-3958-4*) U of Pittsburgh Pr.

***Milton Studies 39, 39 vols., Vol. 39.** Ed. by Albert C. Labriola. (Milton Studies: Vol. 39). 312p. 2001. 50.00 (*0-8229-4130-9*) U of Pittsburgh Pr.

Milton Studies 37. Ed. by Albert C. Labriola. 320p. (C). 2000. text 50.00 (*0-8229-4106-6*) U of Pittsburgh Pr.

Milton Studies 33: The Miltonic Samson. Ed. by Albert C. Labriola & Michael Lieb. (Illus.). 240p. 1995. text 49.95 (*0-8229-3949-5*) U of Pittsburgh Pr.

Milton Studies 27. James D. Simmonds. LC 69-12335. (Illus.). 296p. (C). 1992. text 49.95 (*0-8229-3683-6*) U of Pittsburgh Pr.

Milton the Early Riser. Robert Kraus. LC 81-9460. (Illus.). 32p. (J). (ps-3). 1987. pap. 6.99 (*0-671-66911-7*) S&S Bks Yung.

Milton the Early Riser. Robert Kraus. (J). 1972. 12.19 (*0-606-02795-5*, Pub. by Turtleback) Demco.

Milton to Ouida: A Collection of Essays. Bonamy Dobree. 198p. 1970. 26.00 (*0-7146-2393-8*, Pub. by F Cass Pubs) Intl Spec Bk.

Milton Unbound: Controversy & Reinterpretation. John P. Rumrich. (Illus.). 204p. (C). 1996. text 54.95 (*0-521-55173-0*) Cambridge U Pr.

Milton Warren's Favorite Recipes: Specialties from the Ice House Restaurant of Virginia Beach. Sally W. Warren & Milton Warren. 166p. 1993. pap. text 18.50 (*0-9639733-0-4*) S Warren.

Miltonic Moment. J. Martin Evans. LC 97-53104. (Studies in the English Renaissance). 176p. (C). 1998. 32.95 (*0-8131-2060-8*) U Pr of Ky.

Miltonic Setting Past & Present. Eustace M. Tillyard. LC 83-45900. 1949. 29.50 (*0-404-20257-8*, PR3588) AMS Pr.

Milton's Adam & Eve: Fallible Perfection. George Musacchio. LC 90-49694. (American University Studies: English Language & Literature: Ser. IV, Vol. 118). XII, 216p. (C). 1991. text 37.95 (*0-8204-1326-7*) P Lang Pubng.

Milton's Biblical & Classical Imagery: Poetry & Exegetical Tradition. John M. Steadman. LC 84-1667. (Duquesne Studies: Language & Literature Ser.: Vol. 5). 258p. 1984. text 28.00 (*0-8207-0161-0*) Duquesne.

Milton's Brief Epic: The Genre, Meaning, & Art of "Paradise Regained" Barbara K. Lewalski. LC 66-10282. (Brown University Bicentennial Publications). 448p. reprint ed. pap. 127.70 (*0-7837-2620-1*, 2042956) Bks Demand.

Milton's Burden of Interpretation. Dayton Haskin. LC 93-50526. 344p. (C). 1994. text 44.95 (*0-8122-3281-X*) U of Pa Pr.

***Milton's Christmas.** Hayde Ardalan. LC 00-8932. (Illus.). (J). 2000. pap. write for info. (*0-8118-2842-5*) Chronicle Bks.

Milton's "Comus" Family Piece. William B. Hunter, Jr. LC 82-50824. xvi, 101p. 1983. 25.00 (*0-87875-257-9*) Whitston Pub.

Milton's Contemporary Reputation. William R. Parker. LC 70-122996. (Studies in Milton: No. 22). 1970. reprint ed. lib. bdg. 75.00 (*0-8383-1129-6*) M S G Haskell Hse.

Milton's Dramatic Poems. 6th rev. ed. John Milton. Ed. by Geoffrey Bullough & Margaret Bullough. LC 85-3986. 224p. (C). 1958. pap. 8.95 (*0-485-61009-4*, Pub. by Athlone Pr) Humanities.

Milton's Earthly Paradise: A Historical Study of Eden. Joseph E. Duncan. LC 71-187167. (Minnesota Monographs in the Humanities: No. 5). (Illus.). 347p. reprint ed. pap. 107.60 (*0-8357-8953-5*, 203321800085) Bks Demand.

Milton's Editors & Commentators. Ants Oras. LC 67-31494. (Studies in Milton: No. 22). 1969. reprint ed. lib. bdg. 75.00 (*0-8383-0604-7*) M S G Haskell Hse.

Milton's Elisions. Robert O. Evans. LC 66-63842. (University of Florida Humanities Monographs: No. 21). 76p. reprint ed. pap. 30.00 (*0-7837-4990-2*, 204465700004) Bks Demand.

Milton's English Poetry: Being Entries from a Milton Encyclopedia. Intro. by William B. Hunter, Jr. LC 85-47666. 248p. 1986. 32.50 (*0-8387-5096-6*) Bucknell U Pr.

Milton's Epic Voice: The Narrator in Paradise Lost. Anne Ferry. LC 83-4839. xx, 206p. 1983. pap. text 8.50 (*0-226-24468-7*) U Ch Pr.

Milton's Epics & the Book of Psalms. Mary A. Radzinowicz. LC 88-34383. 245p. 1989. reprint ed. pap. 76.00 (*0-608-07122-6*, 206734800009) Bks Demand.

Milton's Eyesight & the Chronology of His Works. Heinrich Mutschmann. LC 75-163458. (Studies in Milton: No. 22). 1971. reprint ed. lib. bdg. 75.00 (*0-8383-1325-6*) M S G Haskell Hse.

Milton's "First Couple" Love & Alienation in Paradise Lost. Hilda U. Stubbings. LC 94-92443. 350p. (C). Date not set. lib. bdg. 55.00 (*1-880622-06-8*) Rubena Pr.

Milton's God. William Empson. LC 78-14409. 280p. 1979. reprint ed. lib. bdg. 35.00 (*0-313-21021-7*, EMMG, Greenwood Pr) Greenwood.

Milton's Grand Style. Christopher Ricks. 164p. (C). 1978. pap. text 16.95 (*0-19-812090-7*) OUP.

Milton's History of Britain: Republican Historiography in the English Revolution. Nicholas Von Maltzahn. (Illus.). 256p. 1992. text 65.00 (*0-19-812897-5*) OUP.

Milton's House of God: The Invisible & Visible Church. Stephen R. Honeygosky. LC 92-38869. 272p. (C). 1993. text 39.95 (*0-8262-0876-2*) U of Mo Pr.

Milton's Imperial Epic: Paradise Lost & the Discourse of Colonialism. J. Martin Evans. (Illus.). 232p. 1996. text 37.50 (*0-8014-3211-1*) Cornell U Pr.

Milton's Kinesthetic Vision in Paradise Lost. Elizabeth E. Fuller. LC 81-65862. 320p. 1983. 45.00 (*0-8387-5027-3*) Bucknell U Pr.

Milton's Knowledge of Music. Sigmund G. Spaeth. LC 72-8052. (Music Reprint Ser.). 186p. 1973. reprint ed. lib. bdg. 29.50 (*0-306-70535-4*) Da Capo.

Milton's Languages: The Impact of Multilingualism on Style. John K. Hale. 262p. (C). 1997. text 54.95 (*0-521-58353-5*) Cambridge U Pr.

Milton's Legacy in the Arts. Ed. by Albert C. Labriola & Edward Sichi, Jr. LC 86-43037. (Illus.). 239p. 1988. 30.00 (*0-271-00497-5*) Pa St U Pr.

Milton's Literary Craftsmanship: A Study of a Brief History of Muscovia. Robert R. Cawley. LC 65-25136. (Princeton Studies in English: No. 24). 103p. 1965. reprint ed. 45.00 (*0-87752-016-X*) Gordian.

Milton's Marilyn. Milton H. Greene. (Illus.). 225p. 1995. 50.00 (*0-9646873-3-X*) Moss Run Pubs.

Milton's Marilyn. Photos by Milton H. Greene. (Illus.). 220p. 1998. 19.95 (*3-8238-0366-2*) te Neues.

Milton's Paradise Regained: Two Eighteenth-Century Critiques, 2 vols. in 1. Richard Meadowcourt & Charles Dunster. LC 76-161937. 344p. 1971. reprint ed. 50.00 (*0-8201-1087-6*) Schol Facsimiles.

Milton's Paradise with Reference to the Hexameral Background. Mary I Corcoran. LC 45-3381. 159p. reprint ed. pap. 49.30 (*0-608-18735-6*, 202951800061) Bks Demand.

Milton's Pastoral Vision: An Approach to "Paradise Lost" John R. Knott, Jr. LC 79-145576. 1992. lib. bdg. 15.00 (*0-226-44846-0*) U Ch Pr.

Milton's Poetic Art: A Mask, Lycidas, & Paradise Lost. John Reesing. LC 68-17632. 222p. reprint ed. 68.90 (*0-8357-9166-1*, 201701100006) Bks Demand.

Milton's Poetry of Independence: Five Studies. George H. McLoone. LC 98-33975. (Illus.). 160p. 1999. 32.50 (*0-8387-5403-1*) Bucknell U Pr.

Milton's Prose. Corns. LC 97-36419. 1998. 32.00 (*0-8057-4530-0*, Twyne) Mac Lib Ref.

Milton's Prosody with a Chapter on Accentual Verse & Notes. Robert S. Bridges. (BCL1-PR English Literature Ser.). 119p. 1992. reprint ed. lib. bdg. 69.00 (*0-7812-7380-3*) Rprt Serv.

Milton's Punctuation & Changing English Usage, 1582-1676. Mindele A. Treip. LC 77-16752. xiv, 189p. 1970. write for info. (*0-416-13650-8*) Routledge.

Milton's Rabbinical Readings. Harris F. Fletcher. LC 67-30701. 344p. 1967. reprint ed. 50.00 (*0-87752-034-8*) Gordian.

Milton's Rabbinical Readings. Harris F. Fletcher. (BCL1-PR English Literature Ser.). 334p. 1992. reprint ed. lib. bdg. 89.00 (*0-7812-7382-X*) Rprt Serv.

Milton's Samson Agonistes. Christian E. Kreipe. 1972. 59.95 (*0-8490-0638-4*) Gordon Pr.

Milton's Semitic Studies & Some Manifestations of Them in His Poetry. Harris F. Fletcher. LC 66-29575. 155p. 1966. reprint ed. 50.00 (*0-87752-035-6*) Gordian.

Milton's Sonnets: An Annotated Bibliography, 1900-1992. Ed. by Edward Jones. LC 94-20238. (Medieval & Renaissance Texts & Studies: Vol. 122). 160p. 1997. reprint ed. 20.00 (*0-86698-127-6*, MR122) MRTS.

Milton's Sonnets & the Ideal Community. Anna K. Nardo. LC 79-17221. 227p. reprint ed. pap. 70.40 (*0-7837-1824-1*, 204202400001) Bks Demand.

Milton's Spenser: The Politics of Reading. Maureen Quilligan. LC 83-45149. 256p. 1983. 37.50 (*0-8014-1590-X*) Cornell U Pr.

Milton's Technique of Source Adaptation. Grant McColley. 50p. (C). 1938. reprint ed. pap. 39.95 (*0-8383-0053-7*) M S G Haskell Hse.

Milton's Tercentenary. Henry A. Beers. LC 73-39421. reprint ed. 19.50 (*0-404-00725-2*) AMS Pr.

Milton's Theatrical Epic: The Invention & Design of Paradise Lost. John G. Demaray. LC 79-23139. (Illus.). 179p. 1980. 23.50 (*0-674-57615-2*) HUP.

Milton's Theory of Poetry & Fine Art: And Essay. Ida Langdon. (BCL1-PR English Literature Ser.). 342p. 1992. reprint ed. lib. bdg. 89.00 (*0-7812-7385-4*) Rprt Serv.

Milton's Use of Du Bartas. George C. Taylor. 129p. (C). 1934. reprint ed. lib. bdg. 75.00 (*0-8383-0632-2*) M S G Haskell Hse.

Milton's Warring Angels: A Study of Critical Engagements. William Kolbrener. LC 96-23377. 226p. (C). 1997. text 54.95 (*0-521-58104-4*) Cambridge U Pr.

Milton's Wisdom: Nature & Scripture in Paradise Lost. John Reichert. LC 92-20087. 312p. (C). 1992. text 47.50 (*0-472-10324-5*, 10324) U of Mich Pr.

Miluim Maarei Mekomos Lisofer Mishne Torah. (HEB.). 400p. 1993. 17.00 (*0-8266-5311-1*) Kehot Pubn Soc.

***Milwaukee.** Richard Prestor. (Images of America Ser.). 128p. 1999. pap. 18.99 (*0-7385-0309-6*) Arcadia Publng.

Milwaukee: At the Gathering of the Waters. Harry H. Anderson & Frederick I. Olson. LC 81-65676. (Illus.). 224p. 1981. 32.95 (*0-938076-06-X*) Milwaukee Cty Hist Soc.

Milwaukee: The History of a City. Bayrd Still. LC 83-45888. 1948. 62.50 (*0-404-20246-2*, F589) AMS Pr.

Milwaukee - Wisconsin: Heimat in the Heartland. Bert Lachner. Ed. by Trudi Paradis. Tr. by Claudia Becker et al. LC 95-76780. (ENG & GER., Illus.). 224p. 1995. 45.00 (*0-9640659-2-4*) Lachner & Assocs.

Milwaukee Architecture: A Guide to Notable Buildings. Joseph Korom. LC 95-4057. (Illus.). 208p. 1995. pap. 18.95 (*1-879483-27-0*) Prairie Oak Pr.

Milwaukee Autumns Can Be Lethal. Kathleen A. Barrett. LC 98-96230. (Milwaukee Mystery Ser.: Bk. 3). 192p. 1998. 18.95 (*0-8034-9308-8*, Avalon Bks) Bouregy.

Milwaukee Braves: A Baseball Eulogy. Bob Buege. LC 88-70552. (Illus.). 415p. 1988. 19.95 (*1-882134-34-6*); pap. 12.95 (*1-882134-26-5*) Douglas Amer Sports Pubns.

Milwaukee Brewers. Bob Italia. LC 96-17919. (America's Game Ser.). (Illus.). 32p. (J). (gr. 3-8). 1997. lib. bdg. 15.95 (*1-56239-684-6*) ABDO Pub Co.

Milwaukee Bucks see Pro Basketball Today

Milwaukee Bucks. Bob Italia. LC 96-39611. (Inside the NBA Ser.). (Illus.). 32p. (J). (gr. 3-8). 1997. lib. bdg. 16.95 (*1-56239-764-8*) ABDO Pub Co.

Milwaukee Chefs Book. William Struns. Ed. by R. McMinn. 120p. (Orig.). 1989. pap. text 6.95 (*0-935201-84-X*) Affordable Adven.

Milwaukee County, Wisconsin Censuses of 1846 & 1847. T.L.C. Genealogy Staff. LC 91-67268. 104p. (Orig.). 1991. spiral bd. 12.00 (*1-57445-011-5*) TLC Genealogy.

Milwaukee Eats. Cari Taylor-Carlson. 1993. 10.95 (*0-9629452-2-6*) Serendpty Ink.

***Milwaukee Entertainment, 2000.** (Illus.). 950p. 1999. pap. 35.00 (*1-58553-040-9*, 0032) Enter Pubns.

Milwaukee Evaluation of Daily Living Skills: Evaluation in Long-Term Psychiatric Care (MEDLS) Carol A. Leonardelli. LC 88-42542. 136p. 1988. pap. 25.00 (*1-55642-039-0*) SLACK Inc.

Milwaukee Family Fun & Adventure Guide. Barbara McCaig & Lynn D. Soli. (Illus.). 67p. (Orig.). 1985. pap. 7.95 (*0-935201-02-5*) Affordable Adven.

Milwaukee for Free (or the Next Thing to It!) Susan Rice. LC 97-12640. 144p. 1997. pap. 8.95 (*1-879483-37-8*) Prairie Oak Pr.

Milwaukee Murders, Nightmare in Apartment 213: The True Story. Don Davis. 1991. mass mkt. 6.50 (*0-312-92840-8*) St Martin.

Milwaukee Project: Preventing Mental Retardation in Children at Risk. Howard L. Garber. 464p. (C). 1988. 15.00 (*0-940898-16-0*) Am Assn Mental.

Milwaukee Road: Steam Locomotives & Trains 1930-1954. Robert K. Durham. LC 98-73837. (Steam Ser.: Vol. 14). (Illus.). 66p. 1998. pap. 21.00 (*1-891427-02-4*) Durham Publng.

Milwaukee Road Color Guide to Freight & Passenger Equipment, Vol. 1. Doug Nighswonger & William F. Stauss. LC 98-66805. (Illus.). 128p. 1998. 49.95 (*1-58248-011-7*) Morning NJ.

Milwaukee Road 1850-1960 Photo Archive. Ed. by P. A. Letourneau. LC 96-76223. (Photo Archive Ser.). (Illus.). 128p. 1996. pap. 29.95 (*1-882256-61-1*) Iconografix.

Milwaukee Road in Color, Vol. 1. William A. Raia. (Illus.). 1995. 49.95 (*1-878887-46-7*) Morning NJ.

Milwaukee Road in Color Vol. 2: City of Milwaukee. Jeffrey M. Koeller. (Illus.). 1996. 49.95 (*1-878887-62-9*) Morning NJ.

Milwaukee Road in Color Vol. 3: Wisconsin & Michigan. William F. Strauss. (Illus.). 128p. 1997. 49.95 (*1-878887-85-8*) Morning NJ.

An Asterisk (*) at the beginning of an entry indicates that the title is appearing for the first time.

Milwaukee Road in Idaho: A Guide Book to Sites & Locations. Stanley W. Johnson. (Illus.). 232p. (Orig.). 1997. pap. 14.95 (*0-9643647-5-1*) Mus North Idaho.

Milwaukee Road in Its Hometown: In & Around the City of Milwaukee. Jim Scribbins. LC 98-109807. (Golden Years Ser.). (Illus.). 128p. (Orig.). 1997. pap. 18.95 (*0-89024-315-8*, 01080, Kalmbach Books) Kalmbach.

Milwaukee Road Revisited. Stanley W. Johnson. LC 96-31786. 251p. 1997. 29.95 (*0-89301-198-3*) U of Idaho Pr.

Milwaukee Road Steam Power. John Tigges. Ed. by Marion Harris. LC 94-12067. (Illus.). 208p. 1994. text 57.00 (*0-933449-22-4*) Transport Trails.

Milwaukee Streets: The Stories Behind Their Names. Carl Baehr. LC 94-94149. 1994. pap. 19.95 (*0-9640204-4-0*) Cream City Pr.

Milwaukee Summers Can Be Deadly. Kathleen A. Barrett. LC 97-93461. (Milwaukee Mystery Ser.: Bk. 2). 192p. 1997. 17.95 (*0-8034-9239-1*, Avalon Bks) Bouregy.

Milwaukee Symposia for Church Composers: A Ten Year Report. Archdiocese of Milwaukee Staff. 16p. 1992. pap. 4.95 (*0-912405-43-0*, Pastoral Press) OR Catholic.

Milwaukee Symposia for Church Composers: A Ten-Year Report. Ed. by Edward Foley & Gabe Huck. 32p. (Orig.). 1992. pap. 4.00 (*0-929650-91-3*, REPORT) Liturgy Tr Pubns.

Milwaukee Symposium: Refining the Methodology for Comparing U. S. & Foreign Educational Credentials. Ann Fletcher et al. LC 98-3077. (PIER World Education Ser.). 1998. write for info. (*1-57858-005-6*) Am Assn Coll Registrars.

Milwaukee, the Cream City Observed. Steve Slaske. LC 80-84244. (Illus.). 58p. 1980. pap. 10.00 (*0-9605294-0-3*) Preserv Ink.

Milwaukee Walks. Cari Taylor-Carlson. 1992. reprint ed. 8.95 (*0-9629452-0-X*) Serendpty Ink.

Milwaukee, WI. (Streetfinder Ser.). (Illus.). 1995. pap. 12.95 (*0-528-91121-X*) Rand McNally.

Milwaukee Winters Can Be Murder. Kathleen A. Barrett. LC 96-96756. (Milwaukee Mystery Ser.: Bk. 1). 192p. 1996. 18.95 (*0-8034-9224-3*, Avalon Bks) Bouregy.

Milwaukee, Wisconsin. Ed. by Gousha, H. M., Staff. 1995. pap. 2.95 (*0-671-50243-3*, H M Gousha) Prntice Hall Bks.

Milwaukee's East Side. Phil Fisher. LC 86-70030. (Illus.). 68p. (Orig.). 1986. pap. 17.95 (*0-9616168-0-6*) Brady St Pr.

Milwaukee's Finest Fish Frys. Barbara McCaig & Lynn D. Soli. LC 85-73789. (Illus.). 75p. 1986. pap. 3.95 (*0-935201-07-6*) Affordable Adven.

Milwaukee's Italians: The Early Years. Mario A. Carini. Ed. by Austin Goodrich. (Illus.). 180p. 1999. pap. 12.95 (*0-9670696-0-2*) Italian Comm Ctr Milwaukee.

Milwaukee's New Architecture: A Downtown Trail. David Reed. (Publications in Architecture & Urban Planning: No. R86-2). (Illus.). 6p. 1986. 1.00 (*0-938744-48-8*) U of Wis Ctr Arch-Urban.

***Mim & the Klan: Atbosier Quaker Farm Family's Story.** Cynthia Stanley Russell. LC 99-65568. (Illus.). 108p. 1999. 18.95 (*1-57860-036-7*) Guild Pr IN.

Mimamsa Sutras of Jaimini. Mohan L. Sandal. 1022p. 1988. 59.95 (*0-318-37147-2*) Asia Bk Corp.

Mimamsa Sutras of Jaimini. Jaimini. Tr. by Mohan L. Sandal. LC 73-3820. (Sacred Books of the Hindus: No. 27-28). (ENG & SAN.). reprint ed. 104.00 (*0-404-57827-6*) AMS Pr.

***Mimamsa Sutras of Jaimini.** T. Sandal. 1999. reprint ed. pap. 14.00 (*81-208-1129-1*, Pub. by Motilal Bnarsidass) S Asia.

Mimbres: Art & Archaeology. Jesse W. Fewkes. LC 89-6869. (Illus.). 192p. 1989. reprint ed. pap. 16.95 (*0-936755-10-5*) Avanyu Pub.

Mimbres Archaeology of the Upper Gila, New Mexico. Stephen H. Lekson. LC 89-20538. (Anthropological Papers: No. 53). 116p. (Orig.). 1990. pap. 35.95 (*0-8165-1164-0*) U of Ariz Pr.

Mimbres Designs. deluxe ed. Fred Kabotie. (Illus.). 1982. 925.00 (*0-915998-13-0*) Lime Rock Pr.

Mimbres During the Twelfth Century Abandonment, Continuity, & Reorganization. Margaret C. Nelson. LC 98-40197. 1999. 35.00 (*0-8165-1868-8*) U of Ariz Pr.

Mimbres Indian Treasure: In the Land of Baca. Roy H. Evans et al. LC 85-65. (Illus.). 352p. 1985. 29.95 (*0-913504-93-9*) Lowell Pr.

Mimbres Mogollon Archaeology: Charles C. Di Peso's Excavations at Wind Mountain. Anne I. Woosley. (Illus.). 463p. (C). 1996. 55.00 (*0-8263-1674-3*) U of NM Pr.

Mimbres Pottery: Ancient Art of the American Southwest. J. J. Brody et al. LC 83-10812. (Illus.). 132p. 1983. 39.95 (*0-933920-46-6*, Pub. by Hudson Hills) Natl Bk Netwk.

Mime. Jean Dorcy. 1961. pap. 10.95 (*0-8315-0045-X*) Speller.

Mime: Basics for Beginners. Cindie Straub & Matthew Straub. LC 84-11694. (Illus.). (J). (ps-12). 1984. pap. 13.95 (*0-8238-0263-9*) Kalmbach.

Mime: Techniques & Class Formats: A Movement Program for the Visually Handicapped. Maravene S. Loeschke. LC PN2071.G4.L6. (American Foundation for the Blind Practice Ser.). 79p. reprint ed. pap. 30.00 (*0-7837-0132-2*, 204042000016) Bks Demand.

Mime & Beyond: The Silent Outcry. Samuel Avital. (Illus.). 173p. (Orig.). 1990. pap. 17.00 (*0-934252-10-6*) Players Pr.

Mime & Masks. Roberta Nobleman. (Illus.). 151p. 1979. pap. 8.95 (*0-932720-46-3*); write for info. (*0-932720-47-1*) New Plays Inc.

Mime Book. Claude Kipnis. Ed. by Neil Kleinman. LC 88-23248. (Illus.). 208p. 1988. reprint ed. pap. text 14.95 (*0-916260-55-0*, B124) Meriwether Pub.

Mime Ministry: An Illustrated, Easy-to-Follow Guidebook for Organizing, Programming & Training a Troupe of Christian Mimes. Susie K. Toomey. Ed. by Arthur L. Zapel & Kathy Pijanowski. LC 85-63774. (Illus.). 176p. 1986. pap. 12.95 (*0-916260-37-2*, B198) Meriwether Pub.

Mime, Speaking: Poems. Thomas Gardner. LC 92-12071. 68p. 1992. pap. 14.95 (*0-7734-0044-3*) E Mellen.

Mime Time: 45 Complete Routines for Everyone. 2nd ed. Happy Jack Feder. LC 92-25611. (Illus.). 208p. (YA). (gr. 9-12). 1992. pap. 12.95 (*0-916260-73-9*, B101) Meriwether Pub.

Mime Workbook. Samuel Avital. (Illus.). 158p. Date not set. pap., wbk. ed. write for info. (*0-88734-638-3*) Players Pr.

Mimekor Yisrael: Classical Jewish Folktales. Ed. by Dan Ben-Amos et al. Tr. by I. M. Lask. LC 88-46028. 560p. 1991. 24.95 (*0-253-31158-6*) Ind U Pr.

Mimekor Yisreal: Selected Classical Jewish Folktales. Ed. by Dan Ben-Amos et al. Tr. by I. M. Lask. LC 88-46029. 288p. 1990. 31.95 (*0-253-31156-X*); pap. 13.95 (*0-253-20588-3*, MB 588) Ind U Pr.

Mimes & Fragments. Herodas. Ed. by W. R. Connor. LC 78-18580. (Greek Texts & Commentaries Ser.). (Illus.). 1979. reprint ed. lib. bdg. 39.95 (*0-405-11423-0*) Ayer.

Mimes on Miming: An Anthology of Writings on the Art of Mime. Ed. by Bari Rolfe. (Illus.). 256p. (C). 1980. 15.95 (*0-915572-32-X*); pap. 8.95 (*0-915572-31-1*) Panjandrum.

Mimesis. Erich Auerbach. (SPA.). pap. 16.99 (*968-16-0282-X*, Pub. by Fondo) Continental Bk.

Mimesis: Culture, Art, Society. Gunter Gebauer & Christopher Wulf. Tr. by Don Reneau from GER. LC 95-36928. 400p. 1996. pap. 19.95 (*0-520-08459-4*, Pub. by U CA Pr) Cal Prin Full Svc.

Mimesis: The Representation of Reality in Western Literature. Erich Auerbach. Tr. by Willard R. Trask. 576p. 1953. pap. text 17.95 (*0-691-01269-5*, 124, Pub. by Princeton U Pr) Cal Prin Full Svc.

Mimesis & Alterity: A Particular History of the Senses. Michael Taussig. 288p. (C). (gr. 13). 1992. pap. 20.99 (*0-415-90687-3*, A7365) Routledge.

Mimesis & Indirectionies. Sheila Murnaghan. 0.00 (*0-691-06844-5*) Princeton U Pr.

***Mimesis & Its Romantic Reflections.** Frederick Burwick. LC 99-53720. 2000. write for info. (*0-271-02037-7*) Pa St U Pr.

Mimesis & Metaphor: An Inquiry into the Genesis & Scope of Conrad's Symbolic Imagery. Donald C. Yelton. 1967. pap. text 46.15 (*90-279-0279-8*) Mouton.

Mimesis & the Human Animal: On the Biogenetic Foundations of Literary Representation. Robert F. Storey. LC 96-30678. (Rethinking Theory Ser.). 352p. 1996. 75.00 (*0-8101-1457-7*); pap. 19.95 (*0-8101-1458-5*) Northwestern U Pr.

Mimesis As Make-Believe: On the Foundations of the Representational Arts. Kendall Walton. (Illus.). 472p. Date not set. pap. 23.95 (*0-674-57603-9*) HUP.

Mimesis As Make-Believe: On the Foundations of the Representational Arts. Kendall Walton. (Illus.). 480p. 1990. 42.50 (*0-674-57619-5*) HUP.

Mimesis Begriff in der Griechischen Antike, Vol. 153. M. Kardaun. 78p. 1993. pap. 40.75 (*0-444-85765-6*) Elsevier.

Mimesis, from Mirror to Method, Augustine to Descartes. Ed. by John D. Lyons & Stephen G. Nichols, Jr. LC 82-40340. 287p. 1982. reprint ed. pap. 89.00 (*0-608-02322-1*, 206296300004) Bks Demand.

Mimesis, Genres & Post-Colonial Discourse: Deconstructing Magic Realism Jean-Pierre Durix. LC 98-3656. viii, 206 p. 1998. write for info. (*0-333-73224-3*, Pub. by Macmillan) St Martin.

Mimesis in Contemporary Theory-An Interdisciplinary Approach Vol. 1: The Literary & Philosophical Debate. Ed. by Giuseppe Mazzotta & Mihai I. Spariosu. LC 84-14494. (Cultura Ludens Ser.: No. 1:1). 1985. pap. 39.95 (*0-915027-14-3*) J Benjamins Pubng Co.

Mimesis, Masochism, & Mime: The Politics of Theatricality in Contemporary French Thought. Ed. by Timothy Murray. LC 97-601. 328p. (C). 1997. text 52.50 (*0-472-09635-4*, 09635); pap. text 21.95 (*0-472-06635-8*, 06635) U of Mich Pr.

Mimesis on the Move: Theodor W. Adorno's Concept of Imitation. Karla L. Schultz. (New York University Ottendorfer Series: Neue Folge: Vol. 36). 204p. 1990. pap. 32.00 (*3-261-04208-7*) P Lang Pubng.

Mimesis, Semiosis & Power: Mimesis in Contemporary Theory: An Interdisciplinary Approach, Vol. 2. Ed. by Ronald Bogue. LC 84-14494. (Cultura Ludens Ser.: Vol. 1: 2). viii, 210p. 1991. 59.00 (*1-55619-150-2*) J Benjamins Pubng Co.

Mimesis und Historische Erfahrung: Untersuchungen Zur Mimesistheorie Walter Benjamins. Seong M. Choi. (Europaische Hochschulschriften Ser.: Reihe 1, Bd. 1591). (GER.). 246p. 1996. 44.95 (*3-631-31153-2*) P Lang Pubng.

Mimesis und Poiesis Poetologische zum Bildungsroman. Monika Schrader. (Quellen und Forschungen zur Sprach und Kulturgeschichte der Germanischen Voelker). (GER.). 367p. (C). 1975. 89.25 (*3-11-005904-5*) De Gruyter.

Mimesis y Cultura en la Ficcion: Teoria de la Novela. Gonzalo Navajas. (Monagrafias A Ser.: No. 115). (SPA.). 214p. (C). 1985. 58.00 (*0-7293-0212-1*, Pub. by Tamesis Bks Ltd) Boydell & Brewer.

Mimetic Desire: Essays on Narcissism in German Literature from Romanticism to Post Modernism. Ed. by Jeffrey Adams & Eric Williams. LC 95-2819. (GERM Ser.). x, 226p. (C). 1995. 60.00 (*1-879751-91-7*) Camden Hse.

Mimetic Disillusion: Eugene O'Neill, Tennessee Williams & U. S. Dramatic Realism. Anne Fleche. LC 96-24510. 152p. 1997. pap. text 19.95 (*0-8173-0838-5*) U of Ala Pr.

Mimetic Reflections: A Study in Hermeneutics, Theology, & Ethics. William Schweiker. LC 89-85847. xiii, 267p. 1990. pap. 19.95 (*0-8232-1254-8*) Fordham.

Mimi & Jean-Paul's Cajun Mardi Gras. Alice W. Couvillon & Elizabeth Moore. LC 95-31612. (Illus.). 32p. (J). (ps-3). 1996. 14.95 (*1-56554-069-7*) Pelican.

Mimi & the Dream House. Martin Waddell. LC 95-67988. (Illus.). 32p. (J). (ps-1). 1998. pap. 3.99 (*0-7636-0587-5*) Candlewick Pr.

Mimi & the Ginger Princess. William Pasnak. (Blue Kite Adventure Ser.). (Illus.). 117p. (J). (gr. 3-6). bds. 16.95 (*1-55028-107-0*) Formac Dist Ltd.

Mimi & the Picnic. Martin Waddell. LC 95-71370. (Illus.). 32p. (J). (ps-1). 1998. pap. 3.99 (*0-7636-0588-3*) Candlewick Pr.

Mimi Letters & Other Poems. Emmy Johnson. (Illus.). 72p. (Orig.). 1992. pap. 6.95 (*0-938711-15-6*) Tecolote Pubns.

Mimi Makes a Splash. Agnes Rosenthiel. Ed. by Sandy Stryker. LC 91-11286. (Mimi Ser.). (Illus.). 48p. (Orig.). (J). (ps-4). 1991. pap. 6.95 (*0-911655-51-4*) Advocacy Pr.

Mimi Sheraton's U.S. Restaurant Guide. Mimi Sheraton. LC 91-8205. 1992. pap. 12.95 (*0-13-587585-4*) P-H.

Mimi Smith: Steel Wool Politics. Judith Tannenbaum. (Illus.). 36p. 1994. pap. 12.00 (*0-88454-073-1*) U of Pa Contemp Art.

Mimi Takes Charge. Agnes Rosenthiel & Angnes Rosenthiel. Ed. & Tr. by Penelope C. Paine. Ed. by Sandy Stryker. LC 91-11285. (Mimi Ser.). (Illus.). 48p. (Orig.). (J). (ps-4). 1991. pap. 6.95 (*0-911655-50-6*) Advocacy Pr.

Mimi the Selfish Kitten. Time-Life Books Editors. (Child's First Library of Values). (Illus.). 30p. 1996. 14.95 (*0-7835-1301-1*) Time-Life.

Mimiamben des Herondas. Otto Crusius. xvi, 206p. 1967. reprint ed. 50.00 (*0-318-70904-X*) G Olms Pubs.

Mimic Fires: Accounts of Early Long Poems on Canada. D. M. Bentley. 368p. (C). 1994. 60.00 (*0-7735-1200-4*, Pub. by McG-Queens Univ Pr) CUP Services.

Mimicry & the Evolutionary Process. Lincoln P. Brower. (Illus.). 136p. 1988. pap. text 18.00 (*0-226-07608-3*) U Ch Pr.

Mimicry & the Evolutionary Process. Lincoln P. Brower. (Illus.). 136p. 1996. lib. bdg. 36.00 (*0-226-07607-5*) U Ch Pr.

Miminal Access Coloproctology. Ed. by Maurice E. Arregui & Jonathan M. Sackier. LC 94-45687. 1995. 130.00 (*1-870905-68-7*, Radcliffe Med Pr) Scovill Paterson.

Mimi's Christmas. Martin Waddell. LC 97-6760. (Illus.). 32p. (Orig.). (J). (ps-2). 1997. pap. 3.99 (*0-7636-0413-5*) Candlewick Pr.

Mimi's Cookies. Dennis B. Harris. Ed. by Kay Harris. (Illus.). 44p. (J). (gr. 1-5). 1997. 12.95 (*1-890022-03-9*) Lfestyle Min.

Mimi's First Mardi Gras. Alice Couvillon & Elizabeth Moore. LC 91-24006. (Illus.). 32p. (J). (ps-3). 1992. 14.95 (*0-88289-840-X*) Pelican.

***Mimi's Ghost.** Tim Parks. (Illus.). 2001. 24.95 (*1-55970-556-6*, Pub. by Arcade Pub Inc) Time Warner.

Mimi's Tutu. Tynia Thomassie. (Illus.). (J). (ps-3). 1996. 14.95 (*0-614-15759-5*) Scholastic Inc.

Mimmy & Sophie. Miriam Cohen. LC 97-15683. (Illus.). 40p. (YA). (gr. k up). 1999. 16.00 (*0-374-34988-6*) FS&G.

Mimola ou l'Histoire d'une Cassette: Petit Tableau de Moeurs Locales. 2nd ed. Antoine Innocent. (B. E. Ser.: No. 14). (FRE.). 1935. 35.00 (*0-8115-2965-7*) Periodicals Srv.

Mimologics. Gerard Genette. Tr. by Thais E. Morgan from FRE. LC 94-28679. (Stages Ser.). Orig. Title: Mimologiques. (Illus.). lxvi, 446p. 1995. text 85.00 (*0-8032-2129-0*); pap. text 35.00 (*0-8032-7044-5*) U of Nebr Pr.

Mimologiques see Mimologics

Mimosa. Amy Carmichael. 1992. mass mkt. 5.99 (*0-87508-074-X*) Chr Lit.

Mimosa. Laura Kramer. (Illus.). (J). (ps-2). 1997. 15.95 (*0-614-28879-7*) Pippin Bks.

Mimosa. Bill Schermbrucker. 320p. 1988. pap. 16.95 (*0-88922-254-1*, Pub. by Talonbks) Genl Dist Srvs.

Mimosa & Other Poems. Mary DiMichele. 46p. 1995. reprint ed. pap. 9.95 (*0-88962-131-4*) Mosaic.

Mimosa Sky. large type ed. Annecy Scott. (Linford Romance Library). 240p. 1996. pap. 16.99 (*0-7089-7839-8*, Linford) Ulverscroft.

Mimosaceae (Leguminosae-Mimosoideae) Index. rev. ed. Ed. by C. Kalkman et al. (Flora Malesiana Series I: Vol. 11, Pt. 1). (Illus.). 226p. 1992. pap. 47.00 (*90-71236-16-1*, Pub. by Rijksherbarium) Balogh.

***Mimosoideae of South-East Asia: MAC-WIN-Version.** Ed. by J. W. A. Ridder & I. De Kort. 2000. cd-rom 59.95 (*3-540-14705-5*) Spr-Verlag.

Mimoun. Rafael Chirbes. (Masks Ser.). 144p. 1993. pap. 12.99 (*1-85242-220-3*) Serpents Tail.

Mimus. Hermann Reich. xii, 900p. 1974. reprint ed. write for info. (*3-487-05109-5*) G Olms Pubs.

Min Ajl Al-Taghyir. Malik Bin-Nabi. (Mushkilat al-Hadarah Ser.). 144p. 1995. pap. 4.95 (*1-57547-211-2*) Dar Al-Fikr.

Min-Yo & the Moon Dragon. Elizabeth Hillman. LC 89-36462. (Illus.). 32p. (J). (ps-3). 1992. 14.95 (*0-15-254230-2*, Harcourt Child Bks) Harcourt.

Min-Yo & the Moon Dragon. Elizabeth Hillman. 1996. 10.20 (*0-606-09617-5*, Pub. by Turtleback) Demco.

***Mina.** Elaine Bergstrom. 2000. mass mkt. 5.99 (*0-441-00662-0*) Ace Bks.

Mina. Marie Kiraly. 336p. (Orig.). 1994. mass mkt. 5.99 (*0-425-14359-7*) Berkley Pub.

Mina & the Bear. Sabine Jorg. LC 98-44744. (Illus.). (J). (gr. k-3). 1999. lib. bdg. 16.88 (*0-7358-1037-0*, Pub. by North-South Bks NYC) Chronicle Bks.

Mina & the Bear. Sabine Jorg. LC 98-44744. (Illus.). 48p. (J). (gr. k-3). 1999. 16.95 (*0-7358-1036-2*, Pub. by North-South Bks NYC) Chronicle Bks.

Mina Loy: Woman & Poet. Ed. by Maeera Shreiber & Keith Tuma. LC 96-72053. (Man & Poet Ser.). 606p. 1998. pap. 24.95 (*0-943373-43-3*); text 50.00 (*0-943373-42-5*) Natl Poet Foun.

Mina P. Shaughnessy: Her Life & Work. Jane Maher. LC 96-37306. (Illus.). 331p. (Orig.). 1997. pap. 25.95 (*0-8141-5029-2*) NCTE.

Mina und Otto: Ein Lese-und Schreiblehrgang in Deutsch als Fremdsprache. Deutsch als Zweitsprache fuer Kinder: Schuelerbuch. J. Douvitsas-Gamst & S. Xanthos-Kretzschmer. (GER.). 141p. (J). 1989. pap. text 18.00 (*3-12-675030-3*, Pub. by Klett Edition) Intl Bk Import.

Mina und Otto: Lehrerhandbuch. J. Douvitsas-Gamst & S. Xanthos-Kretzschmer. (GER.). 93p. (J). 1989. pap. text 19.00 (*3-12-675033-8*, Pub. by Klett Edition); audio 22.50 (*3-12-675034-6*, Pub. by Klett Edition) Intl Bk Import.

Mina und Otto: Schreiblehrgang 1, Vereinf. Ausgangs. J. Douvitsas-Gamst & S. Xanthos-Kretzschmer. (GER.). 64p. (J). 1990. pap. text 11.75 (*3-12-675035-4*, Pub. by Klett Edition) Intl Bk Import.

Mina und Otto: Schreiblehrgang 2, Vereinf. Ausgangs. J. Douvitsas-Gamst & S. Xanthos-Kretzschmer. (GER.). 64p. (J). 1990. pap. text 11.75 (*3-12-675036-2*, Pub. by Klett Edition) Intl Bk Import.

Mina und Otto Level 1: Schreiblehrgang. J. Douvitsas-Gamst & S. Xanthos-Kretzschmer. (GER.). 64p. (J). 1989. pap. text 11.75 (*3-12-675031-1*, Pub. by Klett Edition) Intl Bk Import.

Mina und Otto Level 2: Schreiblehrgang. J. Douvitsas-Gamst & S. Xanthos-Kretzschmer. (GER.). 64p. (J). 1989. pap. text 11.75 (*3-12-675032-X*, Pub. by Klett Edition) Intl Bk Import.

Minah. Bronwyn Bancroft. 1998. pap. 6.95 (*0-207-19169-7*) HarpC.

Minamata. Jeanne Finley & Aileen Smith. (Illus.). 24p. 1981. pap. 3.00 (*0-938262-05-X*) Ctr Creat Photog.

***Minamata & the Struggle for Democracy in Postwar Japan.** Timothy S. George. 194p. 2000. 45.00 (*0-674-00364-0*) HUP.

Minangkabau & Negri Sembilan: Socio-Political Structure in Indonesia. Jan P. Josselin De Jong. LC 77-86994. reprint ed. 39.50 (*0-404-16732-2*) AMS Pr.

Minangkabau Response to Dutch Colonial Rule in the 19th Century, Vol. 60. Elizabeth E. Graves. 157p. 1981. pap. 7.50 (*0-87763-000-3*) Cornell Mod Indo.

Minaret: Symbol of Islam. Jonathan M. Bloom. (Oxford Studies in Islamic Art: Vol. VII). (Illus.). 216p. 1990. text 65.00 (*0-19-728013-7*) OUP.

***Minarets: Poems from Hollywood.** Mark Dunster. 11p. 1999. pap. 5.00 (*0-89642-928-8*) Linden Pubs.

Minarets of Cairo. D. B. Abouseif. 1985. pap. 20.00 (*977-424-035-9*, Pub. by Am Univ Cairo Pr) Col U Pr.

Minarets of Vienna. Barbara Lefcowitz. Ed. by Clarinda Harriss. 80p. 1996. pap. 10.00 (*0-932616-54-2*) Brick Hse Bks.

Minas & the Fish. Olga Pastuchiv. LC 96-24861. (Illus.). 32p. (J). 1997. 14.95 (*0-395-79756-X*) HM.

Minas del Retorno see Gambusino

Minas Del Rey Salomon. (Spanish Children's Classics Ser.: No. 800-8). (SPA.). (J). 1990. boxed set 3.50 (*0-7214-1402-8*, Ladybrd) Penguin Putnam.

Minas Gerais in the Brazilian Federation, 1889-1937. John D. Wirth. LC 76-23373. (Illus.). xx, 322p. 1977. 47.50 (*0-8047-0932-7*) Stanford U Pr.

Minas Lived by the Sea. Olga Pastuchiv. LC 97-10126. 96p. (J). (ps-4). 1998. 16.00 (*0-395-72290-X*) HM.

***Mina's Spring of Colors.** Rachna Gilmore. 148p. 2000. pap. text 7.95 (*1-55041-534-4*) Fitzhenry & W Ltd.

Mina's Story: Memoir of the Holocaust. Mina Deutsch. LC 96-145562. (Illus.). 184p. 1994. pap. 14.95 (*1-55022-212-0*, Pub. by ECW) Genl Dist Srvs.

Minature Victorian Lamps. Marjorie Hasulbus. LC 96-3807. 192p. 1996. 39.95 (*0-88740-931-8*) Schiffer.

Minchah/Maariv: Ashkenaz. pap. 2.99 (*0-89906-894-4*, SMAP) Mesorah Pubns.

Minchah/Maariv: Sefard. pap. 2.99 (*0-89906-895-2*, SMSP) Mesorah Pubns.

***Minchiate Tarot: The 97-Card Tarot of the Renaissance, Complete with the 12 Astrological Signs & the 4 Elements.** Brian Williams. LC 99-28904. (Illus.). 272p. 1999. boxed set 35.00 (*0-89281-651-1*) Inner Tradit.

Mind. Baker & Dewar. (What's the Big Idea Ser.). 1996. mass mkt. 8.95 (*0-340-65588-7*, Pub. by Hodder & Stought Ltd) Trafalgar.

Mind. Slim Goodbody. (Wonderful You Ser.). (Illus.). 32p. (J). (gr. k-2). 1996. 14.95 (*1-57749-020-7*) Fairview Press.

Mind. Ed. by Daniel Robinson. LC 98-11810. (Oxford Readers Ser.). 400p. (Orig.). (C). 1998. pap. text 22.95 (*0-19-289308-4*) OUP.

Mind. John X. Pyne. 408p. 1998. reprint ed. pap. 29.95 (*0-7661-0463-X*) Kessinger Pub.

Mind, Vol. 20. Readings Research Dept. Staff. (Library). 346p. 1986. lib. bdg. 22.95 (*0-87604-180-2*, 1120) ARE Pr.

Mind: An Essay on Human Feeling. abr. ed. Susanne K. Langer & Arthur C. Danto. LC 88-45414. 464p. (C). 1988. pap. 17.95 (*0-8018-3706-5*); text 55.00 (*0-8018-3705-7*) Johns Hopkins.

Mind: An Essay on Human Feeling, 3 vols., Vol. 1. Susanne K. Langer. (Illus.). 512p. 1970. pap. 16.95 (*0-8018-1150-3*) Johns Hopkins.

An Asterisk (*) at the beginning of an entry indicates that the title is appearing for the first time.

Mind: An Essay on Human Feeling, 3 vols., Vol. 2. Susanne K. Langer. LC 66-26686. 412p. 1974. pap. 16.95 (*0-8018-1607-6*) Johns Hopkins.

Mind: An Essay on Human Feeling, 3 vols., Vol. 3. Susanne K. Langer. 264p. 1984. pap. 16.95 (*0-8018-2511-3*) Johns Hopkins.

Mind: Introduction to Cognitive Science. Paul R. Thagard. (Illus.). 225p. 1996. 24.00 (*0-262-20106-2*, Bradford Bks) MIT Pr.

Mind: Its Origin, Evolution, Structure & Functioning. Malcolm I. Hale. (Illus.). 300p. (Orig.). 1989. pap. 7.95 (*0-9623691-0-1*) Hale-Van Ruth.

Mind: Its Properties & Multiple Facets. Yogi Bhajan & Gurucharan S. Khalsa. Ed. by Sat K. Khalsa. (Illus.). 224p. 1998. pap. 19.95 (*0-9639991-6-8*) KRI.

Mind: Our Greatest Gift. Ed. by Margaret Leuverink. (Mananam Ser.). (Illus.). 111p. 1995. 7.00 (*1-880687-09-7*) Chinmaya Pubns.

Mind: Perception & Thought in Their Constructive Aspects. Paul Schilder. LC 72-165805. (Select Bibliographies Reprint Ser.). 1977. reprint ed. 29.95 (*0-8369-5962-0*) Ayer.

Mind: Reactive & Creative. 2nd ed. Sangharakshita. 25p. (Orig.). 1995. pap. 3.95 (*0-904766-23-3*) Windhorse Pubns.

Mind: The Master Power. 3rd rev. ed. Charles Roth. LC 97-10435. 210p. 1999. 9.95 (*0-87159-209-6*) Unity Bks.

Mind - Body - Spirit. Burma D. Stewart. Ed. by Larry Woods & Burma Lynn Stewart. (Illus.). 120p. 1998. pap. 19.95 (*0-9663474-0-4*) Weston Publ.

***Mind - Mood Pill Book: A Concise Guide to the Most Widely Used Psychiatric Drugs.** Robert E. Hales & Dianne Hales. 384p. 2000. pap. 19.95 (*0-553-38004-4*) Bantam Dell.

Mind Abuse: Media Violence in an Information Age. Rose A. Dyson. 1999. 48.99 (*1-55164-153-4*, Pub. by Black Rose) Consort Bk Sales.

Mind Abuse: Media Violence in an Information Age. Rose Anne Dyson. 250p. 1999. pap. 19.99 (*1-55164-152-6*, Pub. by Black Rose) Consort Bk Sales.

Mind According to Vedanta. Swami Satprakashananda. 181p. 1996. 4.95 (*81-7120-650-6*, Pub. by Ramakrishna Math) Vedanta Pr.

Mind Aerobics. Warren L. Oberholser. (Illus.). 176p. 1992. pap. 10.00 (*0-9633500-0-5*) WarVic Prods.

Mind Aerobics: The Fundamentals of Memory Fitness. Phil Bruchi. Ed. by Robin Levinson. LC 97-210287. (Illus.). x, 102p. (Orig.). 1997. pap. 14.95 (*0-9656555-0-4*) Mind Aerobics.

Mind Aflame: The Theological Vision of One of the World's Great Theologians: Emile Mersch. James Arraj. LC 94-17658. 100p. (Orig.). 1994. pap. 10.00 (*0-914073-08-7*) Inner Growth Bks.

Mind Al-Quran Builds. S. A. Latif. 200p. 1983. 8.50 (*1-56744-330-3*) Kazi Pubns.

Mind Alone & in Groups: Archetypes, Myths & Rituals: The Deepest Patterns of the Mind. Richard L. Crews. 46p. (C). 1988. pap. text. write for info. (*0-945864-05-1*) Columbia Pacific U Pr.

Mind Alone & in Groups: Individuality in a Cultural Context: The Culmination of Mental Activities. Richard L. Crews. 28p. (C). 1988. pap. text. write for info. (*0-945864-07-8*) Columbia Pacific U Pr.

Mind Alone & in Groups: Psychology & Semantics: The Causes & Mechanisms of Mental Function. Richard L. Crews. 67p. (C). 1988. pap. text. write for info. (*0-945864-06-X*) Columbia Pacific U Pr.

Mind-Altering Drugs: Use, Abuse & Treatment. Richard C. Stephens. LC 86-10192. (Law & Criminal Justice Ser.: Vol. 9). 133p. 1987. pap. 41.30 (*0-7837-8968-8*, 204974900003) Bks Demand.

Mind-Altering Drugs: Use, Abuse & Treatment. Richard T. Stephens. (Law & Criminal Justice Ser.: Vol. 9). (Illus.). 136p. (Orig.). 1986. pap. text 18.95 (*0-8039-2667-7*) Sage.

Mind-Altering Drugs Desk Reference: A Guide to the History, Uses & Effects of Psychoactive Drugs. 2nd rev. ed. Mary Rekowski et al. Ed. by Karen Bankston & Terri Holzhecht. 346p. 1998. ring bd. 25.95 (*1-882145-04-6*) U WI Clearinghse.

Mind Always in Motion: The Autobiography of Emilio Segre. Emilio Segre. (C). 1993. 38.00 (*0-520-07627-3*, Pub. by U CA Pr) Cal Prin Full Svc.

Mind & Art of Chaucer. John S. Tatlock. LC 66-10987. 126p. 1966. reprint ed. 35.00 (*0-87752-109-3*) Gordian.

Mind & Art of Henry Miller. fac. ed. William A. Gordon. LC 67-12215. 264p. 1967. reprint ed. pap. 81.90 (*0-7837-7921-6*, 204767700008) Bks Demand.

Mind & Art of Jonathan Swift. Richardo Quintana. 1990. 16.50 (*0-8446-1370-3*) Peter Smith.

Mind & Art of Poe's Poetry. John P. Fruit. LC 70-85908. reprint ed. 27.50 (*0-404-02629-X*) AMS Pr.

Mind & Art of Victorian England. Ed. by Josef L. Altholz. LC 75-22686. 254p. reprint ed. pap. 78.80 (*0-7837-2980-4*, 205747400006) Bks Demand.

Mind & Beyond. Time-Life Books Editors. Ed. by Jim Hicks. (Mysteries of the Unknown Ser.). (Illus.). 144p. 1991. 12.95 (*0-8094-6525-6*) Time-Life.

Mind & Blood: The Collected Poems of John Finlay. John Finlay. Ed. by David Middleton. LC 92-8290. 128p. 1992. 15.00 (*0-936784-99-7*) J Daniel.

Mind & Body. Cecilia Tan. (Illus.). 224p. (Orig.). 2000. pap. 14.95 (*1-885865-21-X*) Circlet Pr.

Mind & Body: A History of the American Psychosomatic Society. Dorothy Levenson. LC 94-5786. 1994. write for info. (*0-683-05840-1*) Lppncott W & W.

Mind & Body: East Meets West. Seymour Kleinman. LC 85-19710. (Big Ten Body of Knowledge Symposium Ser.: No. 15). (Illus.). 191p. 1986. reprint ed. pap. 59.30 (*0-608-07113-7*, 206734000009) Bks Demand.

Mind & Body: The Psychology of Physical Illness. Stephen A. Green. LC 85-13496. 221p. reprint ed. pap. 68.60 (*0-8357-7807-X*, 203617900002) Bks Demand.

Mind & Body: The Reality of Winning. Sue Humphrey. 64p. (Orig.). 1986. pap. 8.95 (*0-932741-04-5*) Championship Bks & Vid Prodns.

Mind & Body Health Handbook: How to Use Your Mind & Body to Relieve Stress, Overcome Illness & Enjoy Healthy Pleasures. 2nd rev. ed. David S. Sobel & Robert Ornstein. LC 98-4698. 284p. 1998. pap. 16.95 (*0-9651040-1-X*) DRx.

Mind & Body Medicine. Daniel Goleman. 1995. pap. 14.95 (*0-89043-840-4*) Consumer Reports.

Mind & Body or Mental States & Physical Conditions. William W. Atkinson. 208p. 1998. reprint ed. pap. 19.95 (*0-7661-0274-2*) Kessinger Pub.

***Mind & Body Spaces: Geographies of Illness Impairment & Disability.** Ed. by Ruth Butler & Hester Parr. (Critical Geographies Ser.). (Illus.). 320p. (Orig.). (C). 1999. pap. 29.99 (*0-415-17903-3*); text 90.00 (*0-415-17902-5*) Routledge.

Mind & Brain. Ed. by Roberta Conlan. LC 93-1152. (Journey Through the Mind & Body Ser.). (Illus.). 144p. 1993. lib. bdg. 17.99 (*0-7835-1001-2*) Time-Life.

Mind & Brain: A Dialogue on the Mind-Body Problem. Rocco J. Gennaro. LC 95-46249. 72p. 1996. pap. text 5.95 (*0-87220-332-8*); lib. bdg. 24.95 (*0-87220-333-6*) Hackett Pub.

Mind & Brain: A Theory of Determinism, Vol. 1. Ted Honderich. 410p. 1990. pap. text 27.00 (*0-19-824282-4*) OUP.

Mind & Brain: Principles of Neuropsychology. Alberta S. Gilinsky. LC 83-24740. 550p. 1984. 65.00 (*0-275-91170-5*, C1170, Praeger Pubs) Greenwood.

Mind & Brain: The Many-Faceted Problems. 2nd ed. John C. Eccles. LC 82-83242. 349p. 1986. pap. 12.95 (*0-89226-032-7*) Paragon Hse.

Mind & Brain: or The Correlation of Consciousness, 2 vols. Thomas Laycock. LC 75-16715. (Classics in Psychiatry Ser.). (Illus.). 1976. reprint ed. 75.95 (*0-405-07443-3*) Ayer.

Mind & Brain Sciences in the 21st Century. Ed. by Robert L. Solso. LC 96-43751. (Illus.). 374p. 1997. 38.50 (*0-262-19385-X*, Bradford Bks) MIT Pr.

Mind & Brain Sciences in the 21st Century. Ed. by Robert L. Solso. (Illus.). 1999. pap. text 20.00 (*0-262-69223-6*) MIT Pr.

Mind & Cancer Prognosis. Ed. by Basil A. Stoll. LC 79-40643. 213p. reprint ed. pap. 66.10 (*0-608-17593-5*, 203043800069) Bks Demand.

Mind & Cognition. William G. Lycan. 340p. 1990. pap. text 34.95 (*0-631-16763-3*) Blackwell Pubs.

Mind & Cognition: An Anthology. 2nd ed. Ed. by William Lycan. LC 98-35450. (Blackwell Philosophy Anthologies Ser.). 630p. 1999. 64.95 (*0-631-21204-3*); pap. 34.95 (*0-631-20545-4*) Blackwell Pubs.

Mind & Common Sense: Philosophical Essays on Common Sense Psychology. Ed. by Radu J. Bogdan. 218p. (C). 1991. text 69.95 (*0-521-40201-8*) Cambridge U Pr.

Mind & Cosmos: Essays in Contemporary Science & Philosophy. Ed. by Robert G. Colodny. LC 83-21662. (CPS Publications in Philosophy of Science). (Illus.). 380p. (C). 1984. pap. text 31.00 (*0-8191-3650-6*); lib. bdg. 57.00 (*0-8191-3649-2*) U Pr of Amer.

Mind & Destiny: A Social Approach to Psychoanalytic Theory. Robert Seidenberg & Hortence S. Cochrane. LC 64-16918. 1964. 39.95 (*0-8156-2061-6*) Syracuse U Pr.

Mind & Face of Nazi Germany: An Anthology. Ed. by N. Gangulee. LC 78-63671. (Studies in Fascism: Ideology & Practice). 200p. 1979. reprint ed. 24.50 (*0-404-16528-1*) AMS Pr.

Mind & Faith of Justice Holmes: His Speeches, Essays, Letters, & Judicial Opinions. Intro. by Max Lerner. 500p. 1989. pap. 24.95 (*0-88738-765-9*) Transaction Pubs.

Mind & Heart for Wellness. Louise Giroux. 256p. 1998. pap. 9.95 (*1-896836-19-4*) NStone Publ.

Mind & Heart in Human Sexual Behavior: Owning & Sharing Our Personal Truths. Alan P. Bell. LC 97-33435. (Illus.). 408p. 1997. 40.00 (*0-7657-0135-9*) Aronson.

Mind & Heart of the Church: Papers Presented at a Conference Sponsored by the Wethersfield Institute. Wethersfield Institute Staff. Ed. & Pref. by Ralph McInerny. LC 92-70554. 130p. 1992. pap. 7.95 (*0-89870-406-5*) Ignatius Pr.

Mind & Heart of the Negotiator. Leigh Thompson. LC 97-25122. 359p. (C). 1997. 62.00 (*0-13-270950-3*) P-H.

***Mind & Heart of the Negotiator.** 2nd ed. Leigh L. Thompson. LC 00-40666. 2000. write for info. (*0-13-017964-7*) P-H.

Mind & Immunity: Behavioral Immunology. Steven Locke & Mady Hornig-Rohan. LC 83-81107. 258p. 1983. 79.50 (*0-275-91400-3*, C1400, Praeger Pubs) Greenwood.

Mind & Its Control. Swami Budhananda. 112p. (Orig.). 1972. pap. 1.95 (*81-7505-034-9*, Pub. by Advaita Ashrama) Vedanta Pr.

Mind & Its Depths. Richard Wollheim. LC 92-12738. 224p. 1993. 31.50 (*0-674-57611-X*) HUP.

Mind & Its Depths. Richard Wollheim. 224p. 1994. pap. 18.00 (*0-674-57612-8*) HUP.

Mind & Its Discontents: An Essay in Discursive Psychiatry. Grant Gillett. 462p. 1999. text 55.00 (*0-19-852313-0*) OUP.

Mind & Its Education. George H. Betts. LC 77-164694. reprint ed. 29.50 (*0-404-00789-9*) AMS Pr.

Mind & Its Treatment: A Psychoanalytic Approach. Veikko Tahka. LC 92-49559. 509p. 1993. 72.50 (*0-8236-3367-5*) Intl Univs Pr.

Mind & Its World. Gregory McCulloch. LC 97-33896. (Problems of Philosophy Series: Their Past & Present). 264p. (C). 1995. pap. 24.99 (*0-415-12205-8*, C0419) Routledge.

Mind & Its World. Gregory McCulloch. LC 94-33896. (Problems of Philosophy Series: Their Past & Present). 264p. (C). (gr. 13). 1995. 75.00 (*0-415-09330-9*, C0418) Routledge.

***Mind & Labor on the Farm in Black-Earth Russia, 1861-1914.** David Kerans. 400p. (C). 2000. 51.95 (*963-9116-94-7*) Ctrl Europ Univ.

Mind & Language: An Interdisciplinary Reader. Ed. by Heimir Geirsson & Michael Losonsky. (Illus.). 600p. (C). 1996. pap. 31.95 (*1-55786-671-6*) Blackwell Pubs.

Mind & Materialism. Geoffrey Madell. 176p. 1988. 45.00 (*0-85224-575-0*, Pub. by Edinburgh U Pr) Col U Pr.

Mind & Materialism. Geoffrey Madell. 160p. 1991. pap. text 22.00 (*0-85224-602-1*, Pub. by Edinburgh U Pr) Col U Pr.

Mind & Matter. Jenny Bryan. LC 93-71714. (Body Talk Ser.). (Illus.). 48p. (YA). (gr. 5 up). 1993. lib. bdg. 13.95 (*0-87518-588-6*, Dillon Silver Burdett) Silver Burdett Pr.

Mind & Matter: Man's Changing Concepts of the Material World. Cecil J. Schneer. LC 88-8915. (History of Science & Technology Reprint Ser.). (Illus.). 319p. 1988. reprint ed. pap. 98.90 (*0-608-00133-3*, 206091400006) Bks Demand.

Mind & Media: The Effects of Television, Video Games, & Computers. Patricia Greenfield. LC 83-18644. (Developing Child Ser.). (Illus.). 232p. 1984. 29.00 (*0-674-57620-9*); pap. text 6.95 (*0-674-57621-7*) HUP.

Mind & Mental Factors in Early Buddhist Psychology. Amol K. Barua. (C). 1990. text 21.00 (*81-85119-54-6*, Pub. by Northern Bk Ctr) S Asia.

Mind & Method of the Historian. Emmanuel Le Roy-Ladurie. Tr. by Sian Reynolds & Ben Reynolds. LC 81-449. (Illus.). vi, 310p. (C). 1984. pap. 12.95 (*0-226-47325-2*) U Ch Pr.

Mind & Method of the Historian. Emmanuel Le Roy-Ladurie. Tr. by Sian Reynolds & Ben Reynolds. LC 81-449. 320p. (C). 1997. lib. bdg. 31.50 (*0-226-47326-0*) U Ch Pr.

Mind & Modes. Prem Kirpal. 124p. (C). 1989. 65.00 (*81-209-0164-9*, Pub. by Pitambar Pub) St Mut.

Mind & Mood of Aging: Mental Health Problems of the Community Elderly in New York & London. Barry J. Gurland et al. LC 83-294. 192p. 1983. text 49.95 (*0-917724-28-3*) Haworth Pr.

Mind & Morality: An Examination of Hume's Moral Psychology. John Bricke. LC 95-46828. 274p. (C). 1996. text 45.00 (*0-19-823589-5*, Clarendon Pr) OUP.

***Mind & Morality: An Examination of Hume's Moral Psychology.** John Bricke. 2000. pap. 19.95 (*0-19-825011-8*) OUP.

Mind & Morals: Essays on Ethics & Cognitive Science. Ed. by Larry May et al. (Illus.). 325p. 1996. 42.50 (*0-262-13313-X*, Bradford Bks); pap. text 21.00 (*0-262-63165-2*, Bradford Bks) MIT Pr.

Mind & Movement. Tony Crisp. 108p. 1987. pap. 9.95 (*0-85207-182-5*, Pub. by C W Daniel) Natl Bk Netwk.

Mind & Movement: The Practice of Coex. Tony Crisp. 200p. (Orig.). pap. 14.95 (*0-8464-4255-8*) Beekman Pubs.

***Mind & Muscle: An Owner's Handbook.** Elizabeth Langford. 253p. 1999. 45.00 (*90-5350-883-X*, Pub. by Garant Uitgevers) Gaunt.

Mind & Muscle: Fitness for All of You. Phil Kaplan. (Orig.). 1995. pap. 24.95 (*1-887463-24-0*) Grt Atltc.

Mind & Performance: A Comparative Study of Learning in Mammals, Birds, & Reptiles. Harold K. Fink. LC 70-138229. (Illus.). 113p. 1972. reprint ed. lib. bdg. 55.00 (*0-8371-5586-X*, FIMI, Greenwood Pr) Greenwood.

Mind & Philosophers. John Lachs. LC 87-2076. 256p. (Orig.). 1987. pap. 17.50 (*0-8265-1222-4*) Vanderbilt U Pr.

Mind & Poetry of Gerard Manley Hopkins. Bernard Kelly. LC 77-119087. (Studies in Poetry: No. 38). 1970. reprint ed. lib. bdg. 75.00 (*0-8383-1083-4*) M S G Haskell Hse.

Mind & Social Practice: Selected Writings by Sylvia Scribner. Ed. by Ethel Tobach et al. (Learning in Doing: Social, Cognitive & Computational Perspectives Ser.). (Illus.). 450p. (C). 1997. text 69.95 (*0-521-46203-7*); pap. text 24.95 (*0-521-46767-5*) Cambridge U Pr.

Mind & Society, 4 vols., Set. Vilfredo Pareto. Ed. by Arthur Livingston. Tr. by Andrew Bongiorno. LC 78-63704. (Studies in Fascism: Ideology & Practice). reprint ed. , 300.00 (*0-404-16990-2*) AMS Pr.

Mind & Society Fads. Frank Hoffmann & William G. Bailey. LC 91-4079. (Illus.). 285p. 1992. pap. 14.95 (*1-56023-010-X*, Harrington Park); lib. bdg. 49.95 (*1-56024-178-0*) Haworth Pr.

Mind & Sociocultures: An Analysis of Religious & Dissenting Movements: Zoroastrianism & the Indian Religions, Vol. 1. Kevin R. Shepherd. LC 96-132159. 995p. 1995. 125.00 (*0-9525089-0-7*, Pub. by Philo Pr) St Mut.

Mind & Spirit of John Peter Altgeld. John P. Altgeld. Ed. by Henry M. Christman. LC 70-128200. (Essay Index Reprint Ser.). 1977. 18.95 (*0-8369-1860-6*) Ayer.

Mind & Spirit of John Peter Altgeld: Selected Writings & Addresses. John P. Altgeld. Ed. by Henry M. Christman. LC 70-128200. (Essay Index Reprint Ser.). 185p. reprint ed. lib. bdg. 17.00 (*0-8290-0801-2*) Irvington.

Mind & Sports. Mike Spino & Herbert R. Kohl. write for info. (*0-318-58234-1*) P-H.

Mind & Supermind. N. C. Panda. 1996. 88.00 (*81-246-0053-8*, Pub. by DK Pubs Ind) S Asia.

Mind & the American Civil War: A Meditation on Lost Causes. Lewis P. Simpson. LC 80-13911. (Walter Lynwood Fleming Lectures in Southern History). 128p. 1989. text 22.50 (*0-8071-1555-X*) La State U Pr.

Mind & the American Civil War: A Meditation on Lost Causes. Lewis P. Simpson. LC 89-30159. 128p. 1998. pap. 9.95 (*0-8071-2266-1*) La State U Pr.

Mind & the Body Politic. Elisabeth Young-Bruehl. 256p. 1989. 42.50 (*0-415-90117-0*, A2428) Routledge.

Mind & the Brain: A Multi-Aspect Interpretation. J. H. Ornstein. 183p. 1972. pap. text 99.50 (*90-247-1339-0*) Kluwer Academic.

Mind & the Film: A Treatise on the Psychological Factors in the Film. Gerard F. Buckle. LC 70-112573. (Literature of Cinema, Ser. 1). 1978. reprint ed. 11.95 (*0-405-01604-2*) Ayer.

Mind & the Machine: Philosophical Aspects of Artificial Intelligence. Steve Torrance. LC 84-12845. (Artificial Intelligence Ser.). 213p. 1984. text 39.95 (*0-470-20104-5*) P-H.

Mind & the Physical World: A Psychologist's Exploration of Modern Physical Theory. Douglas M. Snyder. (Illus.). xi, 159p. (Orig.). 1996. pap. 13.95 (*0-9653689-0-4*) Tailor Pr.

Mind & the Sword. J. W. Stein. 14.95 (*0-317-18414-8*) NCUP.

Mind & the Way: Buddhist Reflections on Life. Ajahn Sumedho. LC 95-30703. (Illus.). 228p. (Orig.). 1995. pap. 16.95 (*0-86171-081-9*) Wisdom MA.

Mind & the World Order: Outline of a Theory of Knowledge. Clarence Irving Lewis. 446p. 1991. pap. 9.95 (*0-486-26564-1*) Dover.

Mind & Variability. Patrick McNamara. LC 98-31365. 184p. 1999. 55.00 (*0-275-96383-7*) Greenwood.

Mind & Vision. 7th ed. R. S. Agarwal. 269p. 1996. pap. 9.95 (*81-7058-218-0*, Pub. by SAA) E-W Cultural Ctr.

***Mind & Will of the Lord: Indexed Discourses of Brigham Young Speaking in General Conferences.** Brigham Young. 1999. pap. 25.95 (*1-55517-418-3*) CFI Dist.

***Mind & Will of the Lord: Indexed Discourses of John Taylor Speaking in General Conferences.** John Taylor. 1999. pap. 12.95 (*1-55517-432-9*) CFI Dist.

***Mind & Will of the Lord: Indexed Discourses of Wilford Woodruff Speaking in General Conferences.** Wilford Woodruff. 1999. pap. 12.95 (*1-55517-443-4*) CFI Dist.

***Mind & Will of the Lord: Joseph Smith.** Harold W. Pease. (Illus.). 2000. pap. 12.95 (*0-9701358-0-7*) Wstwood Bks.

***Mind & Will of the Lord: Lorenzo Snow.** Harold W. Pease. (Illus.). 2000. pap. 7.95 (*0-9701358-1-5*) Wstwood Bks.

Mind & World. John McDowell. LC 93-44418. 208p. (C). 1994. text 33.50 (*0-674-57609-8*, MCDMIN) HUP.

Mind & World. John McDowell. LC 96-22268. 224p. 1996. pap. 17.50 (*0-674-57610-1*) HUP.

Mind As Action. James V. Wertsch. LC 97-25636. (Illus.). 224p. (C). 1998. text 29.95 (*0-19-511753-0*) OUP.

Mind As Behavior & Studies in Empirical Idealism. Edgar A. Singer. LC 75-3386. (Philosophy in America Ser.). reprint ed. 45.00 (*0-404-59382-8*) AMS Pr.

Mind As Mirror & the Mirroring of Mind: Buddhist Reflections on Western Phenomenology. Steven W. Laycock. LC 93-41539. 337p. (C). 1994. text 64.50 (*0-7914-1997-5*); pap. text 21.95 (*0-7914-1998-3*) State U NY Pr.

***Mind as Mosaic: The Robot in the Machine.** Bruce H. Hinrichs. Ed. by Sidney Jackson. (Illus.). 384p. (C). 2000. pap. 20.00 (*0-9660111-9-8*) J Press.

Mind as Motion: Explorations in the Dynamics of Cognition. Ed. by Robert F. Port & Timothy Van Gelder. LC 94-23127. 602p. 1995. 65.00 (*0-262-16150-8*, Bradford Bks) MIT Pr.

Mind As Motion: Explorations in the Dynamics of Cognition. Ed. by Robert F. Port & Timothy Van Gelder. (Illus.). 602p. 1998. reprint ed. pap. text 32.50 (*0-262-66110-1*, Bradford Bks) MIT Pr.

Mind Assassins. large type ed. Rozella Roberts. 201p. (Orig.). 1992. pap. 9.95 (*0-9633452-0-6*) Roxanne Unltd.

Mind at Ease: Barbara Pym & Her Novels. Robert Liddell. 144p. 1989. 30.00 (*0-7206-0731-0*, Pub. by P Owen Ltd) Dufour.

Mind at Large: Knowing in the Technological Age. Paul Levinson. Ed. by Frederick Ferre et al. 271p. 1998. pap. 25.75 (*0-7623-0018-3*) Jai Pr.

Mind at Work. W. T. Singleton. (Illus.). 368p. (C). 1989. text 95.00 (*0-521-26579-7*) Cambridge U Pr.

Mind Awake: An Anthology of C. S. Lewis. Ed. by Clyde S. Kilby. LC 80-14133. 252p. (C). 1980. pap. 11.00 (*0-15-659772-1*) Harcourt.

Mind Bafflers. George Summers. LC 97-39948. (Illus.). 128p. 1997. 5.95 (*0-8069-9867-9*) Sterling.

Mind Behind the Musical Ear: How Children Develop Musical Intelligence. Jeanne Bamberger. 304p. (C). 1991. text 52.00 (*0-674-57607-1*) HUP.

Mind Behind the Musical Ear: How Children Develop Musical Intelligence. Jeanne Bamberger. (Illus.). 304p. 1995. pap. text 20.50 (*0-674-57606-3*, BAMMIX) HUP.

Mind Bender. William Saxon. 256p. (Orig.). 1989. pap. 3.95 (*0-380-75597-1*, Avon Bks) Morrow Avon.

Mind Benders: Instructions & Detailed Solutions. Anita Harnadek. 58p. (Orig.). 1982. pap. 10.95 (*0-89455-205-8*) Crit Think Bks.

Mind Benders: The Gradual Revolution & Scottish Independence. James G. Stuart. 180p. 1982. 50.00 (*0-85335-232-1*, Pub. by Stuart Titles Ltd) St Mut.

Mind Benders A1: Deductive Thinking Skills. Anita Harnadek. 32p. (gr. 2 up). 1978. pap. 8.95 (*0-89455-017-9*) Crit Think Bks.

Mind Benders A2: Deductive Thinking Skills. Anita Harnadek. 32p. (gr. 2 up). 1978. pap. 8.95 (*0-89455-018-7*) Crit Think Bks.

Mind Benders A3: Deductive Thinking Skills. Anita Harnadek. 32p. (gr. 3 up). 1981. pap. 8.95 (*0-89455-121-3*) Crit Think Bks.

An Asterisk (*) at the beginning of an entry indicates that the title is appearing for the first time.

Mind Benders A4: Deductive Thinking Skills. Anita Harnadek. 32p. (gr. 3 up). 1981. pap. 8.95 (0-89455-123-X) Crit Think Bks.

Mind Benders B1: Deductive Thinking Skills. Anita Harnadek. 32p. (gr. 6 up). 1978. pap. 8.95 (0-89455-019-5) Crit Think Bks.

Mind Benders B2: Deductive Thinking Skills. Anita Harnadek. 32p. (gr. 6 up). 1978. pap. 8.95 (0-89455-020-9) Crit Think Bks.

Mind Benders B3: Deductive Thinking Skills. Anita Harnadek. 32p. (gr. 6 up). 1981. pap. 8.95 (0-89455-125-6) Crit Think Bks.

Mind Benders B4: Deductive Thinking Skills. Anita Harnadek. 32p. (gr. 6 up). 1981. pap. 7.95 (0-89455-127-2) Crit Think Bks.

***Mind Benders C1: Deductive Thinking Skills.** 2nd expanded anniversary ed. Anita Harnadek. 40p. (Orig.). (gr. 8 up). 1999. pap. 8.95 (0-89455-021-7) Crit Think Bks.

Mind Benders C2: Deductive Thinking Skills. Anita Harnadek. 32p. (gr. 8 up). 1978. pap. 8.95 (0-89455-022-5) Crit Think Bks.

Mind Benders C3: Deductive Thinking Skills. Anita Harnadek. 32p. (gr. 8 up). 1981. pap. 8.95 (0-89455-129-9) Crit Think Bks.

***Mind Benders Warm Up: Deductive Thinking Skills.** 2nd expanded anniversary ed. Anita Harnadek. 32p. (Orig.). (J). (gr. k up). 1999. pap. 8.95 (0-89455-038-1) Crit Think Bks.

Mind-Bending Challenging Logic, No. 1. Lagoon Bks Staff. (Mind-Bending Puzzle Bks.). (Illus.). 96p. 1998. 6.95 (1-899712-24-0, Pub. by Lagoon Bks) Midpt Trade.

Mind-Bending Challenging Optical Puzzles. Lagoon Books Staff. 1999. 6.95 (1-899712-69-0) Lagoon Bks.

Mind-Bending Classic Logic Puzzles, No. 1. Lagoon Bks Staff. (Mind-Bending Puzzle Bks.). (Illus.). 96p. 1994. 6.95 (1-899712-18-6, Pub. by Lagoon Bks) Midpt Trade.

Mind-Bending Conundrums & Puzzles, No. 1. Lagoon Bks Staff. (Mind-Bending Puzzle Bks.). (Illus.). 96p. 1994. 6.95 (1-899712-03-8, Pub. by Lagoon Bks) Midpt Trade.

Mind-Bending Lateral Thinking Puzzles, 1, No. 1. Lagoon Bks Staff. (Mind-Bending Puzzle Bks.). (Illus.). 96p. 1994. 6.95 (1-899712-06-2, Pub. by Lagoon Bks) Midpt Trade.

Mind-Bending Lateral Thinking Puzzles by Des Machale, No. 1. Des Machale. (Mind-Bending Puzzle Bks.). (Illus.). 96p. 1998. 6.95 (1-899712-23-2, Pub. by Lagoon Bks) Midpt Trade.

Mind-Bending Maze Puzzles. Lagoon Books Staff. 1999. 6.95 (1-899712-72-0) Lagoon Bks.

Mind-Bending Puzzles: A Bundle of Bogglers to Baffle Your Brain!, Vol. I. Terry Stickels. 96p. 1998. pap. 12.00 (0-7649-0690-9) Pomegranate Calif.

***Mind-Bending Puzzles: A Storehouse of Stumpers!, Vol. III.** Terry Stickels. 1999. pap. 12.00 (0-7649-1025-6) Pomegranate Calif.

Mind-Bending Puzzles: More Bushels of Brillance to Boggle Your Brain!, Vol. II. Terry Stickels. 96p. 1998. pap. 12.00 (0-7649-0691-7) Pomegranate Calif.

***Mind-Bending Puzzles: Provocative Posers!, Vol. IV.** Terry Stickels. 1999. pap. 12.00 (0-7649-1026-4) Pomegranate Calif.

***Mind-Bending Puzzles Vol. 1: Knowledge Cards.** Terry H. Stickels. 48p. 1998. pap. 9.95 (0-7649-0325-X) Pomegranate Calif.

***Mind-Bending Puzzles Vol. 2: Knowledge Cards.** Terry H. Stickels. 48p. 1998. pap. 9.95 (0-7649-0378-0) Pomegranate Calif.

***Mind-Bending Puzzles Vol. 3: Knowledge Cards.** Terry H. Stickels. 48p. 1998. pap. 9.95 (0-7649-0701-8) Pomegranate Calif.

***Mind-Bending Puzzles Vol. 4: Knowledge Cards.** Terry H. Stickels. 48p. 1998. pap. 9.95 (0-7649-0968-1) Pomegranate Calif.

***Mind-Bending Puzzles Vol. 5: Knowledge Cards.** Terry H. Stickels. 48p. 1998. pap. 9.95 (0-7649-1054-X) Pomegranate Calif.

***Mind-Bending Puzzles Vol. 6: Knowledge Cards.** Terry H. Stickels. 48p. 1998. pap. 9.95 (0-7649-1055-8) Pomegranate Calif.

Mind Blower. Marco Vassi. 221p. 1993. pap. 16.95 (0-933256-82-5) Second Chance.

Mind-Blowing Mammals. Leslee Elliott. LC 94-26052. (Amazing Animals Ser.). (Illus.). 64p. (Orig.). (J). (gr. 3-6). 1994. 14.95 (0-8069-1270-7) Sterling.

Mind-Blowing Mammals. Leslee Elliott. (Amazing Animals Ser.). (Illus.). 64p. (Orig.). (J). (gr. 3-6). 1995. pap. 9.95 (0-8069-1271-5) Sterling.

Mind-Body: A Categorical Relation. H. Tristram Engelhardt. 179p. 1974. pap. text 65.00 (90-247-1550-4) Kluwer Academic.

Mind-Body: A Pluralistic Interpretation of Mind-Body Interaction under the Guidelines of Time, Space, & Movement, 46. Adrian C. Moulyn. LC 90-47286. (Contributions in Philosophy Ser.: No. 46). 192p. 1991. 62.95 (0-313-27351-0, MMU/, Greenwood Pr) Greenwood.

Mind Body & Health: Toward an Integral Medicine. Ed. by James S. Gordon et al. 269p. 1984. 43.95 (0-89885-150-5, Kluwer Acad Hman Sci); pap. 21.95 (0-89885-188-2, Kluwer Acad Hman Sci) Kluwer Academic.

Mind, Body & Immunity. Rachel Charles. 1996. pap. 9.99 (0-7493-2416-3) Buttrwrth-Heinemann.

Mind, Body & Society: Life & Mentality in Colonial Bengal. Ed. by Rajat K. Ray. LC 96-900190. (Illus.). 498p. 1996. text 35.00 (0-19-563757-7) OUP.

Mind, Body & Soul. Troy Aikman. 1998. 50.00 (1-892049-10-4) Benchmark Press.

Mind, Body & Soul: The Body Shop Book of Well Being, Vol. 1. The Body Shop Staff. (Illus.). 256p. 1998. 25.00 (0-8212-2560-X, Pub. by Bulfinch Pr) Little.

Mind, Body & Soul in Balance. Juliet Mills. (Illus.). 140p. 1993. pap. 10.00 (1-879371-45-6) Pub Mills.

Mind-Body Communication: The Secrets of Total Wellness. Robert B. Stone. 1994. 16.00 incl. audio (0-671-50589-0) S&S Trade.

Mind-Body Communication in Hypnosis. Milton H. Erickson. Ed. by Ernest L. Rossi & Margaret O. Ryan. (Seminars, Workshops & Lectures of Milton H. Erickson: Vol. 3). (Illus.). 314p. 1986. 19.95 (0-8290-3156-1); text 39.50 incl. audio (0-8290-1805-0); audio 20.00 (0-8290-3161-8) Irvington.

Mind-Body Connection. Patricia Wellingham-Jones. (Illus.). 52p. (Orig.). 1989. pap. 10.00 (0-939221-00-4) Wellingham-Jones.

***Mind-Body Fitness for Dummies.** Therese Iknoian. 384p. 2000. pap. 19.99 (0-7645-5304-6) IDG Bks.

Mind-Body Identity Theories. Cynthia MacDonald. 256p. 1989. 45.00 (0-415-03347-0, A3659) Routledge.

Mind Body in Action: MBA - Multi-Dimensional Health & Fitness. Steve Beard. (Illus.). 165p. (Orig.). 1995. pap. 15.95 (0-9642982-9-5) NuLife Pubg.

Mind-Body Magic: Creative Activities for Any Audience. Martha Belknap. LC 96-35696. 160p. (Orig.). 1997. pap. 21.95 (1-57025-126-6) Whole Person.

Mind-Body Maturity: Psychological Approaches to Sports, Exercise, & Fitness. Louis Diamant. 304p. 1991. 79.95 (0-89116-892-3) Hemisp Pub.

Mind-Body Medicine: A Clinician's Guide to Psychoneuroimmunology. Alan Watkins. 314p. (C). 1997. pap. text 35.00 (0-443-05526-2) Church.

Mind Body Medicine Vol. 1: The Stages of Healing. Lewis E. Mehl & Gayle H. Peterson. (Frontiers of Consciousness Ser.). (Illus.). 250p. write for info. (0-8290-2468-9) Irvington.

Mind Body Medicine Vol. 2: The Language of Healing. Lewis E. Mehl & Gayle H. Peterson. (Frontiers of Consciousness Ser.). 250p. write for info. (0-8290-2469-7) Irvington.

Mind-Body Problem. Rebecca Goldstein. 256p. 1993. pap. 12.95 (0-14-017245-9, Penguin Bks) Viking Penguin.

Mind-Body Problem: A Guide to the Current Debate. Ed. by Richard Warner & Tadeusz Szubka. (Illus.). 304p. 1994. pap. 28.95 (0-631-19086-4) Blackwell Pubs.

Mind-Body Problem: A Psychobiological Approach. Mario Bunge. (Foundations & Philosophy of Science & Technology Ser.: Vol. 1). (Illus.). 245p. 1980. 121.00 (0-08-024720-2, Pub. by Pergamon Repr) Franklin.

Mind-Body Problem: An Opinionated Introduction. D. M. Armstrong. LC 99-19443. (Focus Ser.). 184p. 1999. mass mkt. 20.00 (0-8133-9057-5) Westview.

***Mind-Body Problem: An Opinionated Introduction.** D. M. Armstrong. LC 99-19443. (Focus Ser.). 184p. 1999. 60.00 (0-8133-9056-7) Westview.

Mind-Body Problems: Psychotherapy with Psychosomatic Disorders. Janet S. Finell. LC 96-38977. 376p. 1997. 70.00 (1-56821-654-8) Aronson.

***Mind, Body, Spirit: A Practical Guide to Natural Therapies for Health & Well-Being.** Ed. by Lorenz Books Staff. (Illus.). 2000. 35.00 (0-7548-0447-X, Lorenz Bks) Anness Pub.

Mind-Body-Spirit: Connecting with Your Creative Self. Mary Braheny & Diane Halperin. 64p. 1989. 7.95 (1-55874-039-2) Health Comm.

Mind-Body Therapies: A Select Bibliography of Books in English. R. Monro et al. 176p. 1987. text 90.00 (0-7201-1811-5) Continuum.

Mind-Body Therapy: Methods of Ideodynamic Healing in Hypnosis. Ernest L. Rossi & David B. Cheek. 544p. 1994. pap. 24.95 (0-393-31247-X) Norton.

Mind-Bogglers. Lagoon Bks Staff. (Illus.). 96p. 1996. 6.95 (1-899712-44-5, Pub. by Lagoon Bks) Midpt Trade.

Mind Bogglers for Juniors. Gary Miller. 38p. (J). 1991. student ed. 1.95 (1-882449-00-2) Messenger Pub.

Mind-Boggling Astronomy. Steven R. Wills. LC 96-104953. (Illus.). 160p. 1995. pap. text 19.50 (0-942389-11-5) Cobblestone Pub Co.

Mind Boggling Mazes. (J). 1987. pap. 1.49 (0-671-63853-X) Litle Simon.

Mind-Boggling Mazes: Forty Graphic & Three-D Labyrinths. Dave Phillips. (Illus.). 1979. pap. 3.95 (0-486-23798-2) Dover.

***Mind-Boggling Problems of Philosophy.** 8th ed. John L. Safko. 528p. (C). 2000. spiral bd. 42.95 (0-7872-7340-6) Kendall-Hunt.

Mind Boosters. Ray Sahelian. 300p. 2000. pap. 14.95 (0-312-19584-2, Thomas Dunne) St Martin.

Mind, Brain, & Adaptation in the 19th Century: Cerebral Localization & Its Biological Context from Gall to Ferrier. Robert M. Young. (History of Neuroscience Ser.: No. 3). 304p. 1990. text 39.95 (0-19-506389-9) OUP.

Mind, Brain & Behavior. Bloom. 2000. pap. text, student ed. write for info. (0-7167-2802-8) W H Freeman.

Mind, Brain & Computer: An Introduction to Cognitive Science. Komatsu. (Psychology Ser.). 2001. pap. text. write for info. (0-534-36594-9) Brooks-Cole.

Mind, Brain & Function: Essays in the Philosophy of Mind. J. I. Biro & Robert W. Shahan. LC 81-40296. 208p. 1982. 29.95 (0-8061-1783-4) U of Okla Pr.

Mind, Brain & Human Potential: The Quest for an Understanding of Self. Brian Lancaster. 204p. 1993. pap. 17.95 (1-85230-209-7, Pub. by Element MA) Penguin Putnam.

Mind, Brain & the Environment, Vol. 199. Bryan Cartledge. LC 97-37602. (Linacre Lectures, 1995-1996). (Illus.). 198p. 1998. text 59.00 (0-19-854992-X) OUP.

Mind Brain Behavior: Discussions of B. F. Skinner & J. R. Searle. Ilham Dilman. 128p. (C). 1988. lib. bdg. 49.95 (0-415-00006-8) Routledge.

Mind, Brain, Behavior: The Mind-Body Problem & the Philosophy of Psychology. Martin Carrier & Juergen Mittelstrass. x, 314p. (C). 1991. lib. bdg. 98.50 (3-11-012876-4, 159-91) De Gruyter.

Mind, Brain, Behavior: The Mind-Body Problem & the Philosophy of Psychology. Martin Carrier & Juergen Mittelstrass. x, 314p. (C). 1995. pap. text 29.95 (3-11-014954-0) De Gruyter.

Mind-Brain Continuum: Sensory Processes. Ed. by Rodolfo R. Llinas & Patricia S. Churchland. (Illus.). 329p. (C). 1996. 52.50 (0-262-12198-0, Bradford Bks) MIT Pr.

Mind Breaths: Poems, 1972-1977. Allen Ginsberg. LC 77-541. (Pocket Poets Ser.: No. 35). 1978. pap. 8.95 (0-87286-092-2) City Lights.

Mind Bugs: The Origins of Procedural Misconception. Kurt Vanlehn. (Learning, Development & Conceptual Change Ser.). 368p. 1990. 35.00 (0-262-22036-9, Bradford Bks) MIT Pr.

Mind Builder for Self-Confidence & Self-Identity: For Students Grades 6-8. Dewatha Graham. (Illus.). 40p. (J). (gr. 6-8). 1995. pap. 8.00 (0-8059-3678-5) Dorrance.

Mind Change: The Overcomer's Handbook. 2nd ed. Thomas Jones. 170p. 1997. pap. 9.99 (1-57782-022-3) Discipleshp.

Mind Changer. James White. LC 98-23620. 304p. 1998. 23.95 (0-312-86663-1, Pub. by Tor Bks) St Martin.

***Mind Changer.** James White. 1999. mass mkt. 6.99 (0-8125-4196-0, Pub. by Tor Bks) St Martin.

Mind, Character, & Personality: Guidelines to Mental & Spiritual Health, 2 vols., 1. Ellen Gould Harmon White. 1978. 12.99 (0-8127-0148-8) Review & Herald.

Mind, Character, & Personality: Guidelines to Mental & Spiritual Health, 2 vols., 2. Ellen Gould Harmon White. (Christian Home Library). 1978. 12.99 (0-8127-0149-6) Review & Herald.

Mind Child Architecture. Ed. by John C. Baird & Anthony D. Lutkus. LC 81-69937. 224p. reprint ed. pap. 69.50 (0-7837-0371-6, 204069100018) Bks Demand.

Mind Children: The Future of Robot & Human Intelligence. Hans Moravec. (Illus.). 176p. 1988. pap. text 14.95 (0-674-57618-7) HUP.

Mind Coach: How to Teach Children & Teenagers to Think Positive & Feel Good. Daniel G. Amen. (Illus.). 40p. (Orig.). 1997. pap. 19.95 (1-886554-07-2) MindWrks.

Mind, Code & Context: Essays in the Pragmatics of Language. Thomas Givon. (Harry-Whitaker-Neuropsychology & Neurolinguistics Ser.). 472p. 1989. text 99.95 (0-89859-607-6) L Erlbaum Assocs.

***Mind-Conditioning System Vol. 1: Your Complete Guide to Achieving Personal Power, Success, Wealth.** large type ed. Mushtaq H. Jaafri. (Illus.). 86p. 1998. pap. 20.00 (1-892189-01-1) Mushtaq Pub.

***Mind-Conditioning System Vol. 2: Discover the System That Will Change Your Life...** large type ed. Mushtaq H. Jaafri. (Illus.). 86p. 1999. pap. 20.00 (1-892189-02-X) Mushtaq Pub.

Mind Conscripted: A Collection of Poems with One Song. David Ferguson. 32p. (Orig.). 1994. pap. 6.95 (1-885902-01-8) Printable Arts.

Mind Control. Melvin Berger. LC 82-46004. 128p. (J). (gr. 5 up). 1985. 12.89 (0-690-04348-1) HarpC Child Bks.

Mind Control. Shirley Greenslade. 94p. 1996. pap. write for info. (1-886799-05-9) Agape Word.

Mind Control. Emilio Guzman. write for info. (0-913343-25-0) Inst Psych Inc.

Mind Control & UFOs: Casebook on Alternative. 3rd ed. Jim Keith. LC 99-11139. 236p. 1999. pap. 14.95 (1-881532-17-8) IllumiNet Pr.

Mind Control, Oswald & JFK: Were We Controlled? Kenn Thomas. 1997. pap. 16.00 (0-932813-46-1) Adventures Unltd.

Mind Control Wars: They Promise Immortality Using New Human-Alien Technologies That Could Trigger the Apocalypse. Bernie Nelson. LC 94-77607. 240p. (Orig.). 1995. pap. 12.95 (0-9641923-0-6) Lightword Pubng.

Mind Control Within the United States. unabridged ed. Kai Bashir. 325p. (Orig.). 1997. write for info. (0-9658174-1-5); pap. 18.00 (0-9658174-0-7) Kai Bashir.

Mind Control-World Control. Jim Keith. 1997. pap. 14.95 (0-932813-45-3) Adventures Unltd.

***Mind Controllers.** Armen Victorian & Thomas Gray. 1999. pap. 14.95 (1-883319-96-X) Frog Ltd CA.

Mind Crime of August Saint: A Novel. Alain Arias-Misson. 420p. 1993. 22.95 (0-932511-78-3); pap. 11.95 (0-932511-79-1) Fiction Coll.

Mind, Culture & Activity: Seminal Papers from the Laboratory of Comparative Human Cognition. Ed. by Michael Cole et al. (Illus.). 516p. (C). 1997. text 59.95 (0-521-55238-9); pap. text 21.95 (0-521-55823-9) Cambridge U Pr.

Mind Cure. Robert A. Kloner. 276p. 1998. 10.00 (0-9626020-5-1) Le Jacq Commns.

Mind Cure in New England: From the Civil War to World War I. Gail T. Parker. LC 72-92704. 209p. reprint ed. pap. 64.80 (0-608-15383-4, 202925400059) Bks Demand.

Mind Design II: Philosophy, Psychology, Artificial Intelligence. 2nd enl. rev. ed. Ed. by John Haugland. LC 96-45188. (Illus.). 488p. 1997. 45.00 (0-262-08259-4, Bradford Bks); pap. text 22.50 (0-262-58153-1, Bradford Bks) MIT Pr.

Mind Detox: How to Cleanse Your Mind & Coach Yourself to Inner Power. Deborah Marshall Warren. 1999. pap. 15.00 (0-7225-3647-X) Thorsons PA.

***Mind Doesn't Work That Way: The Scope & Limits of Computational Psychology.** Jerry Fodor. LC 99-89687. (Illus.). 184p. 2000. 21.00 (0-262-06212-7) MIT Pr.

Mind Drugs. Margaret Hyde. 1999. 14.99 (0-525-65257-4) NAL.

Mind Drugs, Vol. VI. 6th ed. Margaret O. Hyde. LC 98-20392. 144p. (J). (gr. 7 up). 1998. 23.90 (0-7613-0970-5, Copper Beech Bks) Millbrook Pr.

Mind-Energy, Lectures & Essays. Henri Bergson. Tr. by H. Wildon Carr from FRE. LC 74-28922. 262p. 1975. reprint ed. lib. bdg. 59.50 (0-8371-7931-9, BEEN, Greenwood Pr) Greenwood.

Mind Expanders: Provoking Creativity in Individuals & Organizations. H. J. Harrington et al. LC 97-36698. 1997. write for info. (0-07-027069-4) McGraw.

Mind-Expanding Grits: Defining Southernness. Mell Johnson. (Illus.). 96p. 1998. pap. 7.95 (0-87651-144-2) Southern U Pr.

Mind Field. Gregory Corso. 56p. (Orig.). 1989. pap. 5.95 (0-937815-26-8) Hanuman Bks.

Mind Field: A Personal Essay. 3rd ed. Robert E. Ornstein. LC 95-81219. 144p. 1996. reprint ed. pap. 15.00 (1-883536-00-6, Malor Bks) ISHK.

Mind Fields. Harlan Ellison & Jacek Yerka. LC 94-236491. (Illus.). 72p. 1994. pap. 24.95 (0-9623447-9-6) Morpheus Intl.

Mind Fields: Reflections on the Science of Mind & Brain. Malcolm A. Jeeves. (Illus.). 134p. 1994. pap. 9.99 (0-8010-5227-0) Baker Bks.

Mind-Find. Wilanne S. Belden. LC 87-11979. 191p. (YA). (gr. 7 up). 1988. 14.95 (0-15-254270-1) Harcourt.

Mind Flex - the Mindset. Frank Horton. 236p. 1994. pap. text 14.95 (0-9644602-0-3) Porter Enter.

Mind Food & Smart Pills. Ross R. Pelton. 1989. mass mkt. 13.95 (0-385-26139-X) Doubleday.

Mind Food & Smart Pills: A Sourcebook for the Vitamins, Herbs & Drugs That Can Increase Intelligence, Improve Memory & Prevent Brain Aging. Ross Pelton & Taffy C. Pelton. 336p. 1989. pap. 13.95 (0-385-26138-1) Doubleday.

Mind for Missions. Paul Borthwick. LC 87-62360. 168p. (Orig.). 1987. pap. 9.00 (0-89109-191-2) NavPress.

Mind for Pool. Philip B. Capelle. 1999. pap. text 19.95 (0-9649204-1-7) Billiards Pr.

Mind for Tomorrow: Facts, Values & The Future. David Stover & Erika Erdmann. LC 99-32093. 224p. 2000. 59.95 (0-275-96634-8) Greenwood.

Mind for Trade. Andre Norton & Sherwood Smith. (Solar Queen Ser.). 1998. mass mkt. 5.99 (0-8125-5273-3, Pub. by Tor Bks) St Martin.

Mind for Trade. large type ed. Andre Norton & Sherwood Smith. LC 97-52119. 1998. 23.95 (0-7838-8432-X, G K Hall & Co) Mac Lib Ref.

Mind-Forg'd Manacles: A History of Madness from the Restoration to the Regency. Roy Porter. LC 87-8703. 424p. 1988. 49.50 (0-674-57617-9) HUP.

Mind-Forg'd Manacles: Slavery & the English Romantic Poets. Joan Baum. LC 93-45722. xiv, 253p. (C). 1994. lib. bdg. 29.50 (0-208-02187-6, Archon Bks) Shoe String.

Mind-Forged Manacles. Michael Yatron. 216p. 1986. 10.95 (0-317-38755-3) Adelphi Pr.

Mind-Forged Manacles. Michael Yatron. 207p. 1987. 10.95 (0-9615832-0-7) Adelphi Pr PA.

Mind Forged Manacles: Cults & Spiritual Bondage. Thomas W. Case. 277p. (Orig.). 1993. pap. 15.95 (0-614-07026-0) Fidelity Pr.

Mind Game: Witchdoctors & Psychiatrists. E. Fuller Torrey. LC 87-70297. 236p. 1994. 50.00 (0-87668-689-7) Aronson.

Mind Games. W. James Harmeyer. LC 99-47820. (C). 1999. pap. 14.95 (0-7668-1280-4) Thomson Learn.

Mind Games. C. J. Koehler. (WWL Mystery Ser.: Bk. 309). 1999. mass mkt. 4.99 (0-373-26309-0, 1-26309-4, Harlequin) Harlequin Bks.

Mind Games. Anthony D. Parnell. LC 96-84121. 88p. 1997. pap. 12.95 (0-9644205-1-1) Dreams & Visions.

Mind Games: American Culture & the Birth of Psychotherapy. Eric Caplan. LC 98-16999. (Medicine & Society Ser.). 246p. 1998. 35.00 (0-520-21169-3, Pub. by U CA Pr) Cal Prin Full Svc.

Mind Games: Are We Obsessed with Therapy? Robert A. Baker. LC 96-3035. (Illus.). 476p. 1996. 29.95 (1-57392-071-1) Prometheus Bks.

Mind Games: Mental Fitness for Tennis. Jason Whitmore & John Whitmore. 64p. (J). pap. 5.95 (1-901881-70-9, Pub. by Element MA) Penguin Putnam.

Mind Games: The Guide to Inner Space. rev. ed. Robert Masters & Jean Houston. LC 98-20231. (Illus.). 208p. 1998. pap. 14.00 (0-8356-0753-4, Pub. by Theos Pub Hse) Natl Bk Netwk.

Mind Grenades. 1996. pap. 34.95 (0-688-15159-0, Wm Morrow) Morrow Avon.

Mind Grenades: Manifestos from the Future. Ed. by John Plunkett & Louis Rossetto. LC 96-207698. (Illus.). 160p. (Orig.). 1996. pap. 32.95 (1-888869-00-3) Wired Bks.

Mind Has No Sex? Women in the Origins of Modern Science. Londa Schiebinger. (Illus.). 368p. 1990. pap. text 17.95 (0-674-57625-X, SCHMIX) HUP.

Mind, History, & Dialectic: The Philosophy of R. G. Collingwood. Louis O. Mink. LC 87-6143. (Wesleyan Paperback Ser.). 287p. 1987. reprint ed. pap. 89.00 (0-608-02995-5, 206306200007) Bks Demand.

Mind-Hold. Wilanne S. Belden. LC 86-19370. 256p. 1987. 14.95 (0-15-254280-9) Harcourt.

***Mind, Immunity & Health: The Science of Psychoneuroimmunology.** Philip Evans et al. (Key Texts in the Psychology of Health & Illness: Vol. 1). 256p. 2000. 55.00 (1-85343-486-8, Pub. by Free Assoc Bks); pap. 25.00 (1-85343-487-6, Pub. by Free Assoc Bks) Intl Spec Bk.

An Asterisk (*) at the beginning of an entry indicates that the title is appearing for the first time.

Mind in a Physical World: An Essay on the Mind-Body Problem & Mental Causation. Jaegwon Kim. LC 98-24346. (Representation & Mind Ser.). (Illus.). 156p. 1998. 25.00 (*0-262-11234-5*, Bradford Bks) MIT Pr.
***Mind in a Physical World: An Essay on the Mind-Body Problem & Mental Causation.** Jaegwon Kim. LC 98-24346. (Representation & Mind Ser.). (Illus.). 160p. 2000. reprint ed. pap. 15.00 (*0-262-61153-8*) MIT Pr.
Mind in Action. Jeff Coulter. LC 89-11106. 200p. (C). 1989. pap. 17.50 (*0-391-03657-2*) Humanities.
Mind in Action. Bede Rundle. LC 97-18544. 314p. (C). 1997. text 70.00 (*0-19-823691-3*) OUP.
Mind in Art: Cognitive Foundations for Art Education. Charles M. Dorn. LC 98-35913. 272p. 1998. 69.95 (*0-8058-3078-2*); pap. 27.50 (*0-8058-3079-0*) L Erlbaum Assocs.
Mind in Buddhist Psychology: The Necklace of Clear Understanding, an Elucidation of the Workings of Mind & Mental Events. Ye-Shes Rgyal-Mtshan. Tr. by Herbert V. Guenther & Leslie S. Kawamura from TIB. LC 74-24373. (Tibetan Translation Ser.: Vol. 3). (Illus.). 164p. 1975. pap. 12.95 (*0-913546-06-2*) Dharma Pub.
Mind in Conflict. Charles Brenner. LC 82-21391. v, 266p. (Orig.). 1982. 40.00 (*0-8236-3365-9*) Intl Univs Pr.
Mind in Context: Interactionist Perspectives on Human Intelligence. Ed. by Robert J. Sternberg & Richard K. Wagner. LC 93-221756. (Illus.). 259p. (C). 1994. pap. text 19.95 (*0-521-42287-6*) Cambridge U Pr.
Mind in Context: Interactionist Perspectives on Human Intelligence. Ed. by Robert J. Sternberg & Richard K. Wagner. LC 93-221756. (Illus.). 259p. (C). 1994. text 59.95 (*0-521-41114-9*) Cambridge U Pr.
Mind in Creation: Essays on English Romantic Literature in Honour of Ross G. Woodman. Ed. by J. Douglas Kneale. 192p. 1992. 60.00 (*0-7735-0898-8*, Pub. by McG-Queens Univ Pr) CUP Services.
Mind in Disorder: Psychoanalytic Models of Pathology. John E. Gedo. 264p. 1987. text 39.95 (*0-88163-068-3*) Analytic Pr.
Mind in Evolution. Leonard T. Hobhouse. 435p. 100.00 (*1-85506-688-2*) Thoemmes Pr.
Mind in Evolution. Leonard T. Hobhouse. LC 73-2968. (Classics in Psychology Ser.). 1974. reprint ed. 29.95 (*0-405-05140-9*) Ayer.
Mind in Motion. Katherine H. Granville. (Illus.). 42p. (Orig.). 1991. pap. text 14.00 (*0-9623897-0-6*) Catalyst Pr.
***Mind in Prison: The Memoir of a Son & Soldier in the Third Reich.** Bruno Manz. LC 99-86468. (Illus.). 288p. 2000. 24.95 (*1-57488-242-2*) Brasseys.
Mind in Science. Richard Gregory. 1983. pap. 35.00 (*0-14-013742-4*, Pub. by Pnguin Bks Ltd) Trafalgar.
Mind in Sleep: Psychology & Psychophysiology. 2nd ed. Ed. by Steven J. Ellman & John Antrobus. LC 90-39136. (Series on Personality Processes). 588p. 1991. 175.00 (*0-471-52556-1*) Wiley.
Mind in Society: The Development of Higher Psychological Processes. L. S. Vygotsky. Ed. by Michael Cole et al. LC 77-26023. (Illus.). 173p. 1978. pap. 15.95 (*0-674-57629-2*) HUP.
Mind in Sport: Directing Energy Flow into Success. Kenneth E. Jennings. (Illus.). 299p. 1993. pap. 25.15 (*0-7021-2910-0*, Pub. by Juta & Co) Intl Spec Bk.
Mind in the World: The Marxist Psychology of Self-Actualization. David Lethbridge. LC 91-37124. (Studies in Marxism: Vol. 26). 186p. 1992. 39.95 (*0-930656-61-X*); pap. 19.95 (*0-930656-62-8*) MEP Pubns.
Mind in Tibetan Buddhism. Lati Rinbochay. Ed. by Elizabeth S. Napper. LC 86-3799. 184p. (C). 1980. lib. bdg. 16.95 (*0-937938-02-5*) Snow Lion Pubns.
***Mind into Matter: A New Alchemy of Science & Spirit.** Fred Alan Wolf. (Illus.). 150p. 2000. pap. 12.95 (*0-9661327-6-9*, Pub. by Moment Pt Pr) ACCESS Pubs Network.
Mind Invaders: A Reader in Psychic Warfare, Cultural Sabotage & Semiotic Terrorism. Stewart Home. LC 97-65848. 1998. pap. text 15.99 (*1-85242-560-1*) Serpents Tail.
Mind Is It: Meditation, Prayer, Healing, & the Psychic. Charles C. Wise, Jr. LC 77-82923. 191p. (Orig.). 1978. pap. 3.75 (*0-917023-02-1*) Magian Pr.
Mind Is Not the Heart: Recollections of a Woman Physician. Eva J. Salber. LC 88-33557. xvi, 284p. 1993. text 49.95 (*0-8223-0910-6*) Duke.
Mind Is Not the Heart: Recollections of a Woman Physician. Eva J. Salber. LC 88-33557. (Illus.). 304p. 1993. pap. 16.95 (*0-8223-1365-0*) Duke.
Mind Is Our World. Baba Hari Dass. (Essays on the Search for Peace in Daily Life Ser.: Vol. 2). 16p. (Orig.). 1992. pap. 3.00 (*0-918100-15-1*) Sri Rama.
Mind Jogger. Hal Z. Bennett. LC 85-28943. 144p. (Orig.). 1986. pap. 7.95 (*0-89087-455-7*) Celestial Arts.
Mind Joggers, Vol. 1. Sandy Minor. 83p. 1993. spiral bd. 13.95 (*1-879633-13-2*) Eldersong.
Mind Joggers, Vol. 2. Sandy Minor. 81p. 1995. spiral bd. 13.95 (*1-879633-21-3*) Eldersong.
Mind Joggers, Vol. 3. Sandra L. Minor. 83p. 1997. spiral bd. 13.95 (*1-879633-29-9*, P215) Eldersong.
Mind Joggers! 5 to 15-Minute Activities That Make Kids Think. Susan S. Petreshene. (Illus.). 224p. 1985. pap. text 27.95 (*0-87628-583-3*) Ctr Appl Res.
Mind Kill. Richard La Plante. 320p. 1999. mass mkt. 6.99 (*0-8125-8405-8*, Pub. by Tor Bks) St Martin.
Mind Kill. large type ed. Richard La Plante. 464p. 1998. 29.99 (*0-7089-3954-6*) Ulverscroft.
Mind, Language & Reality see Philosophical Papers
Mind, Language & Society: Doing Philosophy in the Real World. John R. Searle. 175p. 2000. 21.00 (*0-465-04519-7*, Pub. by Basic) HarpC.
Mind, Language & Society: Philosophy in the Real World. John R. Searle. 1999. pap. 13.00 (*0-465-04521-9*, Pub. by Basic) HarpC.
Mind Like a Mirror. Lee Robertson. Ed. by Kim D. Lansford. LC 92-61739. (Illus.). (Orig.). pap. 15.00 (*0-9623377-8-1*) Thermopylae.
***Mind Like His: Developing the Character of Christ.** Mike Nappa & Amy Nappa. 272p. 2000. 4.97 (*1-57748-835-0*) Barbour Pub.
Mind-Lines: Lines for Changing Minds. L. Michael Hall & Bobby G. Bodenhamer. 1997. pap. 19.95 (*1-890001-15-5*) Empowerment Tech.
Mind Links: The Psychology of Golf. Tom Kubistant. LC 94-93878. 161p. 1994. pap. text 29.95 (*0-9643842-0-5*) Perf & Prod.
Mind Machines You Can Build. G. Harry Stine. LC 91-27801. (Illus.). 208p. (Orig.). 1995. pap. 15.95 (*1-56087-075-3*) Top Mtn Pub.
Mind-Made Disease: A Clinician's Guide to Recent Research. Ed. by R. Rosser. (Journal of Psychosomatic Research: No. 25). (Illus.). 144p. 1982. pap. 30.00 (*0-08-027957-0*, Pergamon Pr) Elsevier.
***Mind Magic.** Betty Shine. 2000. pap. 8.95 (*0-552-13671-9*, Pub. by Transworld Publishers Ltd) Trafalgar.
Mind Magic: A Wheelchair Excursion Through Time & Space. Lesley Einer. (Illus.). 6p. (Orig.). 1997. pap. 4.50 (*0-9620822-6-0*) Sage Shadow Pr.
Mind Magic Kit. Jonn Mumford. LC 97-44746. 128p. 1998. boxed set 15.95 (*1-56718-475-8*) Llewellyn Pubns.
Mind Magnet. Paul Ellsworth. 158p. 1996. reprint ed. spiral bd. 14.00 (*0-7873-0308-9*) Hlth Research.
Mind Magnet: How to Unify & Intensify Your Natural Faculties for Efficiency, Health & Success. Paul Ellsworth. 160p. 1998. reprint ed. pap. 12.95 (*0-7661-0449-4*) Kessinger Pub.
Mind, Man, & Machine. 2nd ed. Paul T. Sagal. LC 94-21166. 67p. (Orig.). (C). 1994. lib. bdg. 24.95 (*0-87220-264-X*) Hackett Pub.
Mind, Man, & Machine: A Dialogue. 2nd ed. Paul T. Sagal. 67p. (C). 1994. pap. text 5.95 (*0-87220-263-1*) Hackett Pub.
Mind Map: Your Guide to Prosperity & Fulfillment. Sanford B. Frumker. LC 93-79635. 180p. 1993. pap. 16.95 (*1-883974-11-9*) Hlth Assocs.
Mind Map Book: How to Use Radiant Thinking to Maximize Your Brain's Untapped Potential. Tony Buzan & Barry Buzan. 320p. 1996. pap. 22.95 (*0-452-27322-6*, Plume) Dutton Plume.
Mind Massage: 60 Creative Visualizations. Marlene Maundril. 1997. pap. 19.95 (*1-86163-005-0*, Pub. by Capall Bann Pubng) Holmes Pub.
Mind Master. Larry Townsend. (Orig.). 1994. mass mkt. 4.95 (*1-56333-209-4*, Badboy) Masquerade.
Mind Mastery Meditations. Valerie V. Hunt. (Illus.). 126p. (Orig.). 1997. pap. text, wbk. ed. 14.95 (*0-9643988-2-6*) Malibu Pubng.
Mind, Materiality & History: Essays in Fijian Ethnography Christina Toren. LC 99-26827. 1999. pap. write for info. (*0-415-19577-2*) Routledge.
***Mind, Materiality & History: Essays in Fijian Ethnography.** Christina Toren. LC 99-26827. 1999. write for info. (*0-415-19576-4*) Routledge.
Mind, Matter, & Gravitation. Haakon Forwald. LC 72-97212. (Parapsychological Monographs: No. 11). 1969. pap. 5.00 (*0-912328-15-0*) Parapsych Foun.
Mind, Matter, & Method: Essays in Philosophy & Science in Honor of Herbert Feigl. Ed. by Paul K. Feyerabend & Grover Maxwell. LC 66-13467. 530p. reprint ed. pap. 164.30 (*0-8357-8954-3*, 203322000085) Bks Demand.
Mind, Matter, & Quantum Mechanics. Henry P. Stapp. LC 93-8407. (Illus.). 248p. 1993. 39.95 (*0-387-56289-3*) Spr-Verlag.
Mind, Matter, Motion: Prescription Running, Your Animal Therapy in the 21st Century. 2nd ed. Eugene R. Smith & Elaine N. Smith. LC 82-99857. (Philosophy & Lifestyle Ser.). (Illus.). 264p. (Orig.). 1983. reprint ed. pap. 10.00 (*0-9608910-0-5*) Mind-Matter-Motion.
Mind Matters. Marguerite Iwersen. LC 80-67158. 123p. (Orig.). 1981. pap. 5.50 (*0-87516-421-8*) DeVorss.
Mind Matters. Jerry Kelly. LC 99-165237. 1998. pap. 9.99 (*1-56043-317-5*, Treasure Hse) Destiny Image.
Mind Matters: A Tribute to Allen Newell. Ed. by David M. Steier & Tom Mitchell. (Carnegie Mellon Symposia on Cognition Ser.). 464p. 1996. pap. 45.00 (*0-8058-1364-0*); text 99.95 (*0-8058-1363-2*) L Erlbaum Assocs.
Mind Matters: Consciousness & Choice in a Quantum World. David Hodgson. (Illus.). 496p. 1993. reprint ed. pap. text 19.95 (*0-19-824068-6*) OUP.
Mind Matters: Exploring the World of Artificial Intelligence. James Patrick Hogan. 1997. 24.00 (*0-614-28202-0*, Del Rey) Ballantine Pub Grp.
Mind Matters: Psychological Medicine in Holistic Practice. J. R. Millenson. LC 94-61963. (Illus.). 337p. (Orig.). (C). 1995. pap. text 29.95 (*0-939616-21-1*) Eastland.
Mind Matters: Seven SportPsych Steps to Maximize Performance. Daniel S. Kirschenbaum. 208p. (Orig.). 1997. pap. 19.95 (*1-884125-29-8*) Cooper Pubng.
Mind Matters: Teaching for Thinking. Dan Kirby & Carol Kuykendall. LC 90-27201. 233p. (Orig.). (C). 1991. pap. text 25.00 (*0-86709-276-9*, 0276, Pub. by Boynton Cook Pubs) Heinemann.
Mind Matters in Selling. unabridged ed. Jeffrey Offenburger & Nancy Constant. 20p. pap. text 69.50 incl. audio (*0-88432-175-4*, S29600) Audio-Forum.
***Mind Mazes for Kids.** Robert Allen. (Mensa Ser.). (Illus.). 224p. (J). (gr. 4-7). 2000. mass mkt. 4.50 (*0-439-10843-8*) Scholastic Inc.
Mind Me & Love the Lord: Life with Granny. Ric Mandes. 160p. 1996. write for info. (*0-9652800-1-2*) Mandes Pub.
Mind Me Good Now! A Caribbean Folktale. Lynette Comissiong. (Illus.). 32p. (J). (ps-4). 1997. pap. 6.95 (*1-55037-482-6*, Pub. by Annick) Firefly Bks Ltd.
Mind Me Good Now! Caribbean Folktale. Lynette Comissiong. (Illus.). 32p. (J). (ps-4). 1997. 16.95 (*1-55037-483-4*, Pub. by Annick) Firefly Bks Ltd.
Mind, Meaning & Mathematics: Essays on the Philosophical Views of Husserl & Frege. Ed. by Leila Haaparanta. LC 94-317. (Synthese Library: Vol. 237). 292p. (C). 1994. lib. bdg. 140.00 (*0-7923-2703-9*, Pub. by Kluwer Academic) Kluwer Academic.
Mind, Meaning, & Mental Disorder: The Nature of Causal Explanation in Psychology & Psychiatry. Derek Bolton. 416p. 1996. pap. text 45.00 (*0-19-262936-0*) OUP.
Mind, Meaning & Mental Disorder: The Nature of Causal Explanation in Psychology & Psychiatry. Derek Bolton & Jonathan Hill. (Illus.). 406p. (C). 1996. text 89.50 (*0-19-261504-1*) OUP.
Mind, Meaning & Metaphysics: The Philosophy & Theory of Language of Anton Marty. Ed. by Kevin Mulligan. 304p. (C). 1990. lib. bdg. 191.50 (*0-7923-0578-7*, Pub. by Kluwer Academic) Kluwer Academic.
Mind Medicine: The Secret of Powerful Healing. Uri Geller & Lulu Appleton. 224p. 1999. text 24.99 (*1-86204-477-5*, Pub. by Element MA) Penguin Putnam.
Mind Meld, Vol. 82. John Vornholt. (Star Trek Ser.). 1997. per. 5.99 (*0-671-00258-9*, Pocket Books) PB.
Mind, Method, & Conditionals: Selected Essays. Frank Jackson. LC 97-50010. 296p. (C). 1998. 65.00 (*0-415-16574-1*) Routledge.
Mind Monsters. Randles. 1990. pap. 9.95 (*0-85030-829-1*, Pub. by Aqrn Pr) Harper SF.
Mind Mood Foods. Ed. by Reader's Digest Editors. LC 98-44148. 1998. 24.95 (*0-7621-0104-0*) Login Bros.
Mind, Movement & Psychotherapy. Seymour Halpern. LC 99-182775. 314p. 1997. 24.95 (*0-8488-2125-4*) Amereon Ltd.
Mind Movers: Creative Homework Assignments Grades 3-6. Diane Hart. 1986. text 19.20 (*0-201-20090-2*) Addison-Wesley.
***Mind Munchies: An Assortment of Delicious Brain Snacks!** Gary R. Blair. 80p. 2000. pap. 6.95 (*1-889770-63-9*) GoalsGuy.
Mind-Murders. Janwillem Van de Wetering. LC 96-29658. (Soho Crime Ser.). 224p. 1997. pap. 12.00 (*1-56947-092-8*) Soho Press.
Mind, Muscle & Motion Studies of Instrument Performing & Conducting. Donald W. Stauffer. (Illus.). 207p. 1988. pap. 19.95 (*1-929263-02-3*) Stauffer Pr.
Mind-Muscle: Fitness for All of You see Transform!: The Final Fitness Solution
Mind, Music & Imagery: Unlocking the Treasures of Your Mind. Stephanie Merritt. LC 95-43181. 256p. (Orig.). 1996. pap. 13.95 (*0-944031-62-5*) Aslan Pub.
Mind Myths: Exploring Popular Assumptions about the Mind & Brain. Sergio Della Sala. LC 98-38574. 310p. 1999. pap. 38.95 (*0-471-98303-9*) Wiley.
Mind Noir & el Siglo de Oro. Susan S. Nash. 20p. (Orig.). 1995. pap. 5.00 (*0-9535350-5-3*) Luna Bisonte.
Mind Object: Precocity & Pathology of Self Sufficiency. Ed. by Edward G. Corrigan & Pearl-Ellen Gordon. LC 95-9997. 1995. 50.00 (*1-56821-480-4*) Aronson.
Mind Obstacle Course. Mensa Publications Staff. 1998. pap. text 7.99 (*0-7858-0955-4*) Bk Sales Inc.
Mind of a Fox. Howard E. Greager. LC 89-90613. 200p. 1993. 15.95 (*0-9634407-2-1*) H E Greager.
Mind of a Manager, Soul of a Leader. Craig R. Hickman. 304p. 1992. pap. 24.95 (*0-471-56934-8*) Wiley.
Mind of a Mnemonist: A Little Book about a Vast Memory. Aleksandr R. Luria. LC 86-33487. 160p. 1987. pap. text 7.95 (*0-317-59999-2*) HUP.
Mind of a Mnemonist: A Little Book about a Vast Memory. Aleksandr R. Luria. LC 86-31847. 160p. 1987. pap. 14.95 (*0-674-57622-5*) HUP.
Mind of a Savant: Language Learning & Modularity. Neil Smith & Ianthi Tsimpli. (Illus.). 256p. (C). 1995. pap. 26.95 (*0-631-19017-1*) Blackwell Pubs.
Mind of a Trader: Lessons in Trading Strategies from the World's Leading Traders. Alpesh B. Patel. 288p. 1997. 34.95 (*0-273-63006-7*) F T P-H.
Mind of Africa. W. E. Abraham. LC 63-9733. (Nature of Human Society Ser.). 1966. pap. text 3.00 (*0-226-00086-9*, P233) U Ch Pr.
Mind of African Strategists: A Study of Kalabari Management Practice. Nimi Wariboko. LC 96-26297. (Illus.). 152p. 1997. 29.50 (*0-8386-3706-X*) Fairleigh Dickinson.
Mind of America, 1820-1860. Rush Welter. LC 74-14976. 621p. reprint ed. pap. 192.60 (*0-8357-6214-9*, 203461100090) Bks Demand.
Mind of Aristotle: A Study in Philosophical Growth. John M. Rist. (Phoenix Supplementary Volumes Ser.). 361p. 1989. text 60.00 (*0-8020-2692-3*) U of Toronto Pr.
Mind of Black Africa. Dickson A. Mungazi. LC 95-34094. 296p. 1996. 65.00 (*0-275-95260-6*, Praeger Pubs); pap. 21.95 (*0-275-95429-3*, Praeger Pubs) Greenwood.
Mind of Christ. Anthony Duncan. 1993. pap. 14.95 (*1-85230-185-6*, Pub. by Element MA) Penguin Putnam.
Mind of Christ. Ed. by Lynn Gardner. LC 87-70890. 274p. 1987. 9.99 (*0-89900-224-2*) College Pr Pub.
Mind of Christ. T. W. Hung & Claude V. King. 224p. 1994. pap. text 12.95 (*0-8054-9870-2*, LifeWy Press) LifeWay Christian.
Mind of Christ. T. W. Hunt & Claude V. King. 229p. 1996. pap. text 10.95 (*0-7673-0000-9*, LifeWy Press) LifeWay Christian.
***Mind of Christ.** Dennis F. Kinlaw. LC 98-72659. 128p. 1998. pap. 12.50 (*0-916035-93-X*, Pub. by Evangel Indiana) BookWorld.
Mind of Christ: The Transforming Power of Thinking His Thoughts. T. W. Hunt. 1997. pap. 11.99 (*0-8054-6349-6*) Broadman.
Mind of Clover: Essays in Zen Buddhist Ethics. Robert Aitken. LC 84-60680. 202p. (Orig.). 1982. pap. 12.00 (*0-86547-158-4*) N Point Pr.
Mind of David Hume. Oliver A. Johnson. LC 94-24329. 392p. 1995. pap. text 24.95 (*0-252-06456-9*) U of Ill Pr.
Mind of David Hume: A Companion Book to Book 1 of a Treatise of Human Nature. Oliver A. Johnson. LC 94-24329. 392p. 1995. text 59.95 (*0-252-02156-8*) U of Ill Pr.
Mind of Edmund Gurney. Gordon Epperson. LC 96-52921. 176p. 1997. 32.50 (*0-8386-3720-5*) Fairleigh Dickinson.
Mind of Frederick Douglass. Waldo E. Martin, Jr. LC 84-5140. (Illus.). xii, 334p. 1986. reprint ed. 49.95 (*0-8078-1616-7*); reprint ed. pap. 18.95 (*0-8078-4148-X*) U of NC Pr.
***Mind of God.** Jack Meyer. 1999. 20.00 (*0-9672197-0-1*) CrocusplusDBR.
Mind of God: The Scientific Basis for a Rational World. Paul Davies. 256p. 1993. pap. 12.00 (*0-671-79718-2*, Touchstone) S&S Trade Pap.
Mind of God & the Works of Man. Edward Craig. LC 87-1514. 362p. 1987. text 69.00 (*0-19-824933-0*) OUP.
Mind of God & the Works of Man. Edward Craig. 364p. 1997. reprint ed. pap. text 21.00 (*0-19-823682-4*) OUP.
Mind of God (1917) Elwin L. House. 190p. 1998. reprint ed. pap. 19.95 (*0-7661-0350-1*) Kessinger Pub.
Mind of Her Own. Veronica M. Boyle. LC 98-94029. 1999. 18.95 (*0-533-12959-1*) Vantage.
Mind of Its Own: Tourette's Syndrome, a Story & a Guide. Ruth D. Bruun & Bertel Bruun. (Illus.). 192p. (C). 1994. 32.50 (*0-19-506587-5*) OUP.
Mind of Jeremy Bentham. David J. Manning. LC 84-6551. 118p. 1984. reprint ed. lib. bdg. 39.75 (*0-313-22579-6*, MAMJ, Greenwood Pr) Greenwood.
Mind of Jesus. William Barclay. (C). 1990. pap. 30.00 (*0-85305-291-3*, Pub. by Arthur James) St Mut.
Mind of Jesus. William Barclay. LC 61-7332. 352p. 1976. reprint ed. pap. 18.00 (*0-06-060451-4*, RD143, Pub. by Harper SF) HarpC.
Mind of John Keats. Clarence D. Thorpe. (BCL1-PR English Literature Ser.). 209p. 1992. reprint ed. lib. bdg. 79.00 (*0-7812-7575-X*) Rprt Serv.
Mind of John Knox. Richard G. Kyle. 350p. 1984. 25.00 (*0-87291-164-0*) Coronado Pr.
Mind of John Locke: A Study of Political Theory in Its Intellectual Setting. Ian Harris. 445p. (C). 1994. text 74.95 (*0-521-35603-2*) Cambridge U Pr.
Mind of John Locke: A Study of Political Theory in Its Intellectual Setting. Ian Harris. 445p. (C). 1998. pap. text 24.95 (*0-521-63872-0*) Cambridge U Pr.
Mind of John Meredith. Francis Gerard. (Black Dagger Crime Ser.). 1990. 18.50 (*0-86220-794-0*, C1034, Black Dagger) Chivers N Amer.
Mind of Jung: An Explanation of Jungian Theosophy. Stephen C. Byrnes. (Illus.). v, 140p. 1998. pap. 8.95 (*1-891530-01-1*) Centaur Bks.
Mind of Mahatma Gandhi. Mohandas Karamchand Gandhi. Ed. by R. K. Prabhu & U. R. Rao. 613p. 1988. 25.00 (*0-934676-75-5*) Greenlf Bks.
Mind of Mahatma Gandhi, Vol. 1. Mohandas Karamchand Gandhi. Ed. by R. K. Prabhu & U. R. Rao. 1997. 29.95 (*0-9651800-3-4*) Free Hand.
Mind of Mahatma Gandhi, Vol. 2. M. K. Gandhi. Ed. by R. K. Prabhu & U. R. Rao. 1997. 29.95 (*0-9651800-4-2*) Free Hand.
Mind of Mahatma Gandhi, Vol. 3. M. K. Gandhi. Ed. by R. K. Prabhu & U. R. Rao. 1997. 29.95 (*0-9651800-5-0*) Free Hand.
Mind of Mahatma Gandhi: Authorized U. S. Edition in 3 Volumes, 3 vols. M. K. Gandhi. Ed. by R. K. Prabhu & U. R. Rao. Incl. Vol. 1. 1997. pap. 14.95 (*0-9651800-6-9*); Vol. 2. 1997. pap. 14.95 (*0-9651800-7-7*); Vol. 3. 1997. pap. 14.95 (*0-9651800-8-5*); 42.95 (*0-9651800-9-3*) Free Hand.
Mind of Man: Being a Natural System of Mental Philosophy. Alfred Smee. LC 78-72825. (Brainedness, Handedness, & Mental Abilities Ser.). (Illus.). reprint ed. 39.50 (*0-404-60893-0*) AMS Pr.
Mind of Mankind: Human Imagination, the Source of Mankind's Tremendous Power! Donald L. Hamilton. LC 96-92329. (Illus.). 1997. pap. 12.95 (*0-9649265-1-2*) Suna Press.
Mind of Max Scheler. Manfred S. Frings. LC 97-4682. (Studies in Philosophy: No. 14). 328p. (Orig.). 1997. pap. 35.00 (*0-87462-613-7*) Marquette.
Mind of My Mind. Octavia E. Butler. 224p. 1994. reprint ed. mass mkt. 5.99 (*0-446-36188-7*, Pub. by Warner Bks) Little.
Mind of My Own. E. Maxwell. 23.00 (*0-685-69284-1*) HarperTrade.
Mind of Napoleon: A Selection of His Written & Spoken Words. Ed. by J. Christopher Herold. LC 55-9068. 1961. pap. text 25.50 (*0-231-08523-0*) Col U Pr.
Mind of Napoleon: A Study of Napoleon, Mr. Roosevelt, & the Money Power. R. MacNair Wilson. 1972. 250.00 (*0-8490-0639-2*) Gordon Pr.
***Mind of One's Own.** 2nd ed. Louise Antony. 416p. 2001. pap. 25.00 (*0-8133-6607-0*, Pub. by Westview) HarpC.
Mind of One's Own: A Kleinian View of Self & Object. Robert A. Caper. LC 98-25734. (New Library of Psychoanalysis Ser.). 208p. (C). (gr. 13). 1998. 85.00 (*0-415-19911-5*, D6620); pap. 29.99 (*0-415-19912-3*, D6624) Routledge.
Mind of Primitive Man. rev. ed. Franz Boas. LC 83-10869. 254p. (C). 1983. reprint ed. lib. bdg. 77.50 (*0-313-24004-3*, BOMP, Greenwood Pr) Greenwood.
Mind of Robert Louis Stevenson. Robert Louis Stevenson. Ed. by Roger Ricklefs. LC 72-99651. (Essay Index Reprint Ser.). 1977. 19.95 (*0-8369-1430-9*) Ayer.

An Asterisk (*) at the beginning of an entry indicates that the title is appearing for the first time.

M

Mind of Society: From a Fruitful Analogy of Minsky to a Prodigious Idea of Teilhard de Chardin. Yvon Provencal. (World Futures General Evolution Studies: Vol. 12). 124p. 1998. text 29.00 (*90-5700-514-X*, ECU38, Harwood Acad Pubs) Gordon & Breach.

Mind of Tennyson: His Thoughts on God Freedom & Immortality. Elias H. Sneath. LC 77-114099. 204p. (C). 1970. reprint ed. 50.00 (*0-87752-102-6*) Gordian.

Mind of the Bible-Believer. rev. ed. Edmund D. Cohen. LC 86-42574. 438p. 1988. pap. 22.95 (*0-87975-495-8*) Prometheus Bks.

***Mind of the C. E. O.** Jeffrey E. Garten. 2001. 25.00 (*0-465-02615-X*, Pub. by Basic) HarpC.

Mind of the Cat. Gary Brodsky. 1990. 5.98 (*1-55521-698-6*) Bk Sales Inc.

Mind of the Cells. SATPREM Staff. Tr. by Luc Venet from FRE. LC 82-15659.Tr. of Le Mental Des Cellules. 215p. 1982. pap. 8.95 (*0-938710-06-0*) Inst Evolutionary.

Mind of the Child, 2 vols. William Preyer. LC 73-2985. (Classics in Psychology Ser.). 1977. reprint ed. 47.95 (*0-405-05156-5*) Ayer.

Mind of the Church in the Formation of Sisters: Selections from Addresses Given During the Six Regional Conferences & the First National Meeting of the Sister Formation Conference, 1954-1955. Sister Ritamary. LC 56-9888. 312p. reprint ed. pap. 96.80 (*0-7837-5579-1*, 204536700005) Bks Demand.

Mind of the Dog. F. J. Buytendijk. LC 73-2964. (Classics in Psychology Ser.). 1977. reprint ed. 20.95 (*0-405-05137-9*) Ayer.

Mind of the Donor. George Barna. LC 94-227088. 85p. (Orig.). 1993. pap., spiral bd. 129.00 (*1-882297-04-0*) Barna Res Grp.

Mind of the Fathers. George S. Bebis. LC 93-50532. 147p. 1994. pap. 9.95 (*0-916586-73-1*, Pub. by Holy Cross Orthodox) BookWorld.

Mind of the Fathers: Essays in Patristic Studies. George S. Bebis. LC 93-50532. 1994. pap. 9.95 (*0-917651-73-1*) Holy Cross Orthodox.

Mind of the Founder: Sources of the Political Thought of James Madison. rev. ed. James Madison. Ed. by Marvin Meyers. LC 80-54466. 516p. 1981. pap. 23.00 (*0-87451-201-8*) U Pr of New Eng.

Mind of the Horse. R. H. Smythe. 123p. 1997. 6.98 (*0-7858-0874-4*) Bk Sales Inc.

Mind of the Juror As Judge of the Facts: or The Layman's View of the Law. Albert S. Osborn. xv, 239p. 1982. reprint ed. 40.00 (*0-8377-0926-1*, Rothman) W S Hein.

Mind of the Magic. Holly Lisle. 320p. 1995. per. 5.99 (*0-671-87654-6*) Baen Bks.

Mind of the Maker. Dorothy L. Sayers. LC 72-106698. 229p. 1971. reprint ed. lib. bdg. 59.50 (*0-8371-3372-6*, SAMM, Greenwood Pr) Greenwood.

Mind of the Maker. Dorothy L. Sayers. 256p. 1987. reprint ed. pap. 13.00 (*0-06-067077-0*, Pub. by Harper SF) HarpC.

Mind of the Market: A Study of Stock Market Philosophies, Their Uses & Their Implications. Charles W. Smith. LC 81-1820. 218p. 1981. 30.00 (*0-8476-6983-1*) Rowman.

***Mind of the Market: Spiritual Lessons for the Active Investor.** F. J. Chu. LC 99-47002. 149p. 1999. 30.00 (*0-87034-133-2*) Fraser Pub Co.

Mind of the Middle Ages: An Historical Survey: A. D. 200-1500. 3rd rev. ed. Frederick B. Artz. LC 79-16259. 600p. 1980. reprint ed. pap. text 28.00 (*0-226-02840-2*, P859) U Ch Pr.

Mind of the Monster: The Mentality of Atrocity in the World Today & in the New Age Ahead. Richard Ventura. LC 98-90050. 452p. 1998. pap. write for info. (*1-57502-730-5*, PO2042) Morris Pubng.

Mind of the Murderer. Manfred S. Guttmacher. LC 72-10849. (Select Bibliographies Reprint Ser.). 1977. reprint ed. 21.95 (*0-8369-7111-6*) Ayer.

Mind of the Negro As Reflected in Letters Written During the Crisis, 1800-1860. Carter G. Woodson. (BCL1 - U. S. History Ser.). 672p. 1991. reprint ed. lib. bdg. 109.00 (*0-7812-6083-3*) Rprt Serv.

Mind of the Ninja. Kirtland C. Peterson. (Illus.). 320p. (Orig.). 1986. pap. 18.95 (*0-8092-4951-0*, 495100, Contemporary Bks) NTC Contemp Pub Co.

Mind of the Old South. rev. ed. Clement Eaton. LC 67-11648. (Walter Lynwood Fleming Lectures). (Illus.). x, 348p. 1964. pap. text 19.95 (*0-8071-0120-6*) La State U Pr.

Mind of the Political Terrorist. Richard M. Pearlstein. LC 90-9134. 237p. 1991. 45.00 (*0-8420-2345-3*) Scholarly Res Inc.

***Mind of the Raven: Investigations & Adventures with Wolf-Birds.** Bernd Heindrich. (Illus.). 416p. 2000. pap. 13.00 (*0-06-093063-2*) HarpC.

Mind of the Raven: Investigations & Adventures with Wolf-Birds. Bernd Heinrich. LC 99-18129. (Illus.). 400p. 1999. 25.00 (*0-06-017447-1*) HarpC.

Mind of the South. W. J. Cash. 1992. 26.00 (*0-8446-6632-7*) Peter Smith.

Mind of the South. W. J. Cash. LC 91-50042. 464p. 1991. pap. 14.00 (*0-679-73647-6*) Vin Bks.

Mind of the South: Fifty Years Later. Ed. by Charles W. Eagles. LC 92-17130. (Chancellor's Symposium on Southern History Ser.). 192p. 1992. text 40.00 (*0-87805-580-0*); pap. text 17.95 (*0-87805-581-9*) U Pr of Miss.

Mind of the Soviet Fighting Man: A Quantitative Survey of Soviet Soldiers, Sailors, & Airmen. Richard A. Gabriel. LC 83-18520. 156p. 1984. lib. bdg. 55.00 (*0-313-24187-2*, GMS/, Greenwood Pr) Greenwood.

Mind of the Strategist: The Art of Japanese Business. Kenichi Ohmae. LC 81-18630. (Illus.). 304p. 1991. pap. 12.95 (*0-07-047904-6*) McGraw.

***Mind of the Universe: The Current Worldview & Our Image of God.** Mariano Artigas. LC 99-37740. 475p. 1999. 22.95 (*1-890151-32-7*) Templeton Fnd.

Mind of the Wing. Herbert F. West. LC 75-134155. (Essay Index Reprint Ser.). 1977. 21.95 (*0-8369-2087-2*) Ayer.

Mind of Thomas Jefferson. Randall. 1999. text 25.00 (*0-8050-3795-0*) St Martin.

Mind of Whittier: A Study of Whittier's Fundamental Religious Ideas. C. Hawkins. LC 73-6984. (American Literature Ser.: No. 49). 1973. reprint ed. lib. bdg. 75.00 (*0-8383-1700-6*) M S G Haskell Hse.

Mind of William Paley: A Philosopher & His Age. D. L. LeMahieu. LC 75-22547. 229p. reprint ed. pap. 71.00 (*0-7837-6172-4*, 204589400009) Bks Demand.

Mind of Winter: Wallace Stevens, Meditation & Literature. William W. Bevis. LC 88-19814. (Critical Essays in Modern Literature Ser.). 356p. 1988. reprint ed. pap. 110.40 (*0-608-00898-2*, 206169200010) Bks Demand.

Mind of Your Newborn Baby. 3rd ed. David Chamberlain. LC 97-46583. Orig. Title: Babies Remember Birth. 225p. 1998. reprint ed. pap. 14.95 (*1-55643-264-X*) North Atlantic.

Mind of Your Own. Betty Shine. 1999. pap. 13.95 (*0-00-653019-2*) Collins SF.

***Mind on Cyberstats.** Utts & Lawrence R. Heckard. 2002. pap. 53.00 (*0-534-37934-6*) Wadsworth Pub.

Mind on Fire: A Christian's Character Before God. Blaise Pascal. (Classics of Faith & Devotion Ser.: No. 3). 32p. 1997. pap. 9.99 (*1-55661-831-X*) Bethany Hse.

***Mind on Paper.** unabridged ed. Elizabeth Peterson. (Illus.). 20p. 1999. spiral bd. 7.50 (*1-929326-41-6*) Hal Bar Pubg.

Mind on Statistics. Utts. (Statistics Ser.). 2000. 50.00 (*0-534-35935-3*) PWS Pubs.

Mind One, Pt. 1. Terrill M. Burke. LC 95-90145. 208p. (Orig.). (YA). (gr. 6 up). 1993. pap. 9.99 (*1-880485-61-3*) Alpha-Dolphin.

Mind One, Pt. 2. Terrill M. Burke. LC 95-90145. 165p. (Orig.). (YA). (gr. 6 up). 1996. pap. 9.99 (*1-880485-58-3*) Alpha-Dolphin.

Mind Only School & Buddhist Logic. Ed. by Doboom Tulku. (C). 1990. 19.50 (*81-85179-49-2*, Pub. by Aditya Prakashan) S Asia.

Mind-Opening Training Games: Activities to Help Groups Learn How to Learn, Tap Their Right-Brain Power & "Think Outside the Box" Rex Davies & David McDermott. 205p. 1996. pap. 69.95 (*0-07-913053-4*) McGraw.

Mind Out of Matter: Topics in the Physical Foundations of Consciousness & Cognition. Gregory R. Mulhauser. LC 98-22509. (Studies in Cognitive Systems). 1998. 120.00 (*0-7923-5103-7*) Kluwer Academic.

Mind over Back Pain. John E. Sarno. 1986. mass mkt. 6.50 (*0-425-12700-1*) Berkley Pub.

Mind over Back Pain. John E. Sarno. (Illus.). 124p. 1986. mass mkt. 6.50 (*0-425-08741-7*) Berkley Pub.

***Mind over Back Pain.** John E. Sarno. 1999. pap. 12.00 (*0-425-17523-5*) Berkley Pub.

Mind over Golf: How to Use Your Head to Lower Your Score. Richard Coop. 194p. 1997. 12.95 (*0-02-861683-9*) Macmillan.

Mind over Golf: How to Use Your Head to Lower Your Score. Richard Coop & Bill Fields. Ed. by Rick Wolff. 256p. 1993. 20.00 (*0-02-527830-4*) Macmillan.

Mind over Labor. Carl Jones. 208p. 1988. pap. 18.99 (*0-14-046762-9*, Penguin Bks) Viking Penguin.

Mind over Ladder: Corporate Dehumanization & My Battle for Sanity. Beth Stance. 120p. 1998. pap. 9.95 (*0-9665674-0-4*) B Stance.

***Mind over Machine.** Hubert L. Dreyfus. 2000. per. 16.95 (*0-7432-0551-0*) S&S Trade.

Mind over Machine: The Power of Human Intuition & Expertise in the Era of the Computer. Hubert L. Dreyfus & Stuart E. Dreyfus. 256p. 1988. pap. 17.95 (*0-02-908061-4*) Free Pr.

Mind over Malignancy: Living with Cancer. Wayne D. Gersh et al. LC 97-66076. 168p. (Orig.). 1997. pap. 12.95 (*1-57224-082-2*) New Harbinger.

***Mind over Manners: Poems, Discussion & Activities about Responsible Behavior: Grades 4-6.** Greta B. Lipson. Ed. by Judy Mitchell. (Illus.). 112p. 1999. pap., teacher ed. 10.95 (*1-57310-186-9*) Teachng & Lrning Co.

Mind over Markets: Power Trading with Market Generated Information. James F. Dalton. (Illus.). 345p. 1999. reprint ed. pap. 29.95 (*0-934380-53-8*) Traders Pr.

Mind over Markets: Power Trading with Market Generated Information. James F. Dalton et al. 350p. 1993. reprint ed. per. 27.50 (*1-55738-489-4*, Irwn Prfssnl) McGraw-Hill Prof.

Mind over Marriage. Rebecca Daniels. (Intimate Moments Ser.). 1997. per. 3.99 (*0-373-07765-3*, 1-07765-0) Silhouette.

Mind over Mass! Conquering Your Fat Genes Forever. Alex Glozman. Ed. by Marilyn Bruno. (Illus.). 190p. 1999. pap. 14.95 (*0-9668971-0-2*, 107) New Times Publ.

Mind over Math: Put Yourself on the Road to Success by Freeing Yourself from Math Anxiety. J. Warren & Stanley Kogelman. 256p. (C). 1979. reprint ed. pap. 9.95 (*0-07-035281-X*) McGraw.

Mind over Matter. (Mysteries of the Unknown Ser.). (Illus.). 160p. 1988. lib. bdg. 23.27 (*0-8094-6337-7*) Time-Life.

***Mind over Matter.** Nora Roberts. LC 00-37795. 2000. pap. write for info. (*0-7862-2604-8*) Thorndike Pr.

Mind over Matter. D. Scott Rogo. 1988. 7.95 (*0-85030-485-7*, Pub. by Aqrn Pr) HarpC.

Mind over Matter. large type ed. Ranulph Fiennes. (Illus.). 1995. 27.99 (*0-7089-3310-6*) Ulverscroft.

Mind over Matter: A Comprehensive Guide to Discovering Your Psychic Powers. Loyd Auerbach. LC 96-165065. 1996. pap. 14.00 (*1-57566-047-4*) Kensgtn Pub Corp.

Mind over Matter: Higher Martial Arts. Siao Weija. Tr. by Thomas Cleary from CHI. LC 93-40427. 102p. (Orig.). (C). 1994. pap. 12.95 (*1-883319-15-3*) Frog Ltd CA.

***Mind over Matter: Personal Choices for a Lifetime of Fitness.** Susan Cantwell. 176p. 1999. 16.95 (*0-7737-3216-0*) Stoddart Publ.

***Mind over Matter: Personal Choices for a Lifetime of Fitness.** Susan Cantwell & Silken Laumann. 176p. 1999. pap. 16.95 (*0-7737-6059-8*, Pub. by Stoddart Publ) Genl Dist Srvs.

Mind over Matter: Recasting the Role of Materials in Our Lives. Gary Gardner & Payal Sampat. Ed. by Jane A. Peterson. LC 98-61749. 80p. 1998. pap. 5.00 (*1-878071-46-7*) Worldwatch Inst.

Mind over Matter: The Epic Crossing of the Antarctic Continent. Ranulph Fiennes. (Illus.). 322p. 1998. pap. text 13.00 (*0-7881-5242-4*) DIANE Pub.

Mind over Matter: The Images of Pink Floyd. Storm Thorgerson. (Illus.). 176p. 1997. text 39.95 (*1-86074-206-8*, Pub. by Sanctuary Pubng) Music Sales.

***Mind over Matter: The Images of Pink Floyd.** rev. ed. Storm Thorgerson. (Illus.). 176p. 2000. pap. text 30.00 (*1-86074-268-8*) Music Sales.

Mind over Media: Creative Thinking Skills for Electronic Media. Mark Von Wodtke. LC 92-27328. (C). 1993. pap. text 36.51 (*0-07-067633-X*) McGraw.

Mind over Media: Everybody's Ultimate Authority on Media Access from an Insider's Point of View. Colleen Patrick. 184p. (Orig.). 1988. pap. 13.00 (*0-935529-04-7*) Comprehen Health Educ.

Mind over Mood: Change How You Feel by Changing the Way You Think. Dennis Greenberger & Christine A. Padesky. LC 95-8223. (Illus.). 243p. 1995. pap. text 21.00 (*0-89862-128-3*, 2128) Guilford Pubns.

Mind over Murder. William X. Kienzle. (Father Koesler Mystery Ser.: No. 3). 1989. mass mkt. 5.99 (*0-345-35667-5*) Ballantine Pub Grp.

Mind over Murder. Bill Pomidor. (Cal & Plato Marley Mystery Ser.). 1998. mass mkt. 5.99 (*0-451-19216-8*, Sig) NAL.

Mind over Murder: DNA & Other Forensic Adventures. Jack Batten. (Illus.). xvi, 260p. 1996. 27.99 (*0-7710-1066-4*) McCland & Stewart.

Mind over Murder: DNA & Other Forensic Adventures. Jack Batten. (Illus.). 280p. 1997. pap. text 14.95 (*0-7710-1069-9*) McCland & Stewart.

Mind over Tennis-Canc. A. Loehr. 1982. 13.50 (*0-671-45026-3*) S&S Trade.

Mind over Water: Lessons on Life from the Art of Rowing. Craig Lambert. LC 98-34450. 160p. 1998. 22.00 (*0-395-85716-3*) HM.

***Mind over Water: Lessons on Life from the Art of Rowing.** Craig Lambert. 160p. 1999. pap. 12.00 (*0-618-00184-0*, Mariner Bks) HM.

Mind Play: The Creative Uses of Fantasy. Jerome L. Singer & Ellen Switzer. 1980. 13.95 (*0-13-198069-6*, Spectrum IN); pap. 4.95 (*0-13-198051-3*, Spectrum IN) Macmillan Gen Ref.

Mind Pool. Charles Sheffield. Orig. Title: The Nimrod Hunt. 432p. 2000. reprint ed. mass mkt. 6.99 (*0-671-72165-8*) PB.

Mind Portals to Superconsciousness: A Spiritual Sojourn to God. Gerald Kuwada. (Self-Mastery III Ser.). 150p. 1997. 17.95 (*0-9643386-3-7*) Self Mastery.

Mind Power. Jana Nolan. 120p. 1997. pap. 12.95 (*0-944851-10-X*) Earth Star.

Mind Power: Picture Your Way to Success in Business. Gini G. Scott. 200p. (C). 1987. text 24.95 (*0-13-583527-5*) P-H.

Mind Power: The Secret of Mental Magic. limited ed. William W. Atkinson. reprint ed. 15.00 (*0-911662-27-8*) Yoga.

Mind Power: The Secret of Mental Magic. William W. Atkinson. 444p. 1997. reprint ed. pap. 29.95 (*0-7661-0091-X*) Kessinger Pub.

Mind-Power: The Ultimate 15-Second Formula to Transform Your Life Forever. J. Lee Boothby. 322p. (Orig.). 1997. pap. 23.95 (*0-9652926-0-6*) Mind-Power.

Mind Power into the 21st Century: Techniques for Success & Happiness. John Kehoe. 160p. 1997. pap. text 12.95 (*0-9697551-4-7*, Pub. by Z1oetic) Assoc Pubs Grp.

Mind Power Techniques: How to Make Your Mind Work for You. 1991. lib. bdg. 74.95 (*0-8490-4643-2*) Gordon Pr.

Mind Power to Better Golf. unabridged ed. Robert J. Rotella & Coop. 25p. pap. text 34.50 incl. audio (*0-88432-187-8*, S01820) Audio-Forum.

Mind-Powered Job Hunt. Christopher Van Kleeck. 1995. pap. text 14.95 incl. audio (*0-88432-830-9*, S04080) Audio-Forum.

Mind Prey. John Sandford, pseud. 354p. 1996. mass mkt. 7.50 (*0-425-15289-8*) Berkley Pub.

Mind Prey. large type ed. John Sandford, pseud. 1995. 25.95 (*1-56895-233-3*) Wheeler Pub.

Mind Probe-Hypnosis. Irene Hickman. 200p. (Orig.). 1983. 10.95 (*0-915689-01-4*); pap. 6.95 (*0-915689-00-6*) Hickman Systems.

Mind Program: How to Raise Your Mental Age. rev. ed. Paul M. Gluchowsky. Ed. by Betty Rudd. LC 93-79381. 342p. (YA). 1994. 23.95 (*1-878398-13-X*) Blue Note Pubns.

Mind Rape. Edna Kimball. 176p. 1994. pap. 8.00 (*1-57087-058-6*) Prof Pr NC.

Mind Reader. Victoria Cole. (Intimate Moments Ser.). 1993. per. 3.50 (*0-373-07510-3*, 5-07510-6) Silhouette.

Mind Reader. Brian Freemantle. LC 98-4484. 480p. 1998. text 25.95 (*0-312-18654-1*) St Martin.

***Mind Reader.** Pete Johnson. 1999. 16.95 (*0-7540-6069-1*) Chivers N Amer.

Mind Reader. Jan Slepian. LC 97-10573. 144p. (J). (gr. 5-7). 1997. 15.95 (*0-399-23150-1*, Philomel) Peng Put Young Read.

Mind Reader. R. L. Stine, pseud. Ed. by Patricia MacDonald. (Fear Street Ser.: No. 27). 176p. (J). (gr. 7 up). 1994. mass mkt. 3.99 (*0-671-78600-8*, Archway) PB.

Mind Reader. R. L. Stine, pseud. (Fear Street Ser.: No. 27). (YA). (gr. 7 up). 1994. 9.09 (*0-606-07038-9*, Pub. by Turtleback) Demco.

Mind Reader: A Mystery. Walter A. Roberts. LC 73-18600. reprint ed. 42.50 (*0-404-11410-5*) AMS Pr.

***Mind Reader: Blackmail.** large type ed. Pete Johnson. (Illus.). (J). 2000. pap. write for info. (*0-7540-6087-X*) Chivers N Amer.

Mind Readers. Margery Allingham. 272p. 1990. pap. 3.95 (*0-380-70570-2*, Avon Bks) Morrow Avon.

Mind Readers. Margery Allingham. 286p. 1998. lib. bdg. 23.95 (*1-56723-012-1*) Yestermorrow.

Mind Reading Magic Tricks. Bob Longe. LC 95-26204. (Illus.). 96p. 1996. 4.95 (*0-8069-3896-X*) Sterling.

Mind Readings: Introductory Selections on Cognitive Science. Ed. by Paul Thagard. LC 97-38748. (Illus.). 356p. 1998. pap. text 20.00 (*0-262-70067-0*, Bradford Bks) MIT Pr.

***Mind Reconstruction to Avoid Self-Destruction.** Lauretha Brown Ward. LC 99-97758. 2000. pap. 8.95 (*0-533-13473-0*) Vantage.

M

Mind Regained: How Mind Functions As a Real Cause in the Material World. Edward Pols. LC 98-9482. 176p. 1998. 29.95 (*0-8014-3531-5*) Cornell U Pr.

Mind Remakes Your World. Ed. by Ernest Holmes & Maude A. Lathem. 238p. 1997. pap. 25.00 (*0-89540-338-2*, SB-338) Sun Pub.

Mind Renewed by God: Truths That Will Forever Change the Way You Think, Feel, & Live. Kimball Hodge. LC 98-16022. 1998. pap. 9.99 (*1-56507-934-5*) Harvest Hse.

Mind Ride. Stephanie Wade. 64p. 1991. per. 5.00 (*0-8187-0132-3*) Harlo Press.

Mind Riot: Coming of Age in Comix. Karen D. Hirsch. LC 96-48073. 128p. (YA). (gr. 7 up). 1997. per. 9.99 (*0-689-80622-1*) Aladdin.

Mind Scapes. Wesly J. Sokotoski. 1997. pap. write for info. (*1-57553-505-X*) Watermrk Pr.

***Mind Scapes: The Virtual Reality Game Book.** 2nd rev. ed. Andromeda Knecht. 1999. pap. 14.95 (*1-929589-21-2*) Branching Leaf.

Mind, Science, & History. Ed. by Howard E. Kiefer & Milton K. Munitz. LC 69-14642. (Contemporary Philosophic Thought Ser.: Vol. 2). 333p. reprint ed. pap. 103.30 (*0-608-10185-0*, 201011200068) Bks Demand.

Mind Sciences: Christian Science; Religious Science; Unity School of Christianity. Todd Ehrenborg. LC 95-2140. (Guide to Cults & Religious Movements Ser.). 96p. 1995. pap. 5.99 (*0-310-48861-3*) Zondervan.

***Mind Sculpture: Unlocking Your Brain's Untapped Potential.** Ian Robertson. 272p. 2000. 27.00 (*0-88064-221-1*) Fromm Intl Pub.

Mind, Self & Interiority. Thomas Duddy. 208p. 1995. text 72.95 (*1-85972-153-2*, Pub. by Avebry) Ashgate Pub Co.

Mind, Self, & Society: From the Standpoint of a Social Behaviorist. George Herbert Mead. Ed. by Charles W. Morris. 448p. 1967. pap. text 15.95 (*0-226-51668-7*) U Ch Pr.

Mind Sense: Fine Tuning Your Intellect & Intuition--A Practical Workbook. Kathlyn Rhea. 214p. 1988. pap. 12.95 (*0-89087-529-4*) Celestial Arts.

Mind Series. Alan C. Walter. Ed. by Beverly Miles. 13p. (Orig.). 1995. pap. text 1.79 (*1-57569-025-X*) Wisdom Pubng.

Mind-Set Management: The Psychology of Effective Management. Samuel A. Culbert. (Illus.). 368p. 1996. 30.00 (*0-19-509746-7*) OUP.

Mind Shampoo: For the Conditioned Mind. Dyne N. Shaffron. Ed. by Nancy Earle. LC 95-75210. 160p. (Orig.). 1996. pap. 12.95 (*1-886836-30-2*) Black Diamnd.

Mind-Sharpening Lateral Thinking Puzzles. Edward Harshman. LC 96-29530. (Illus.). 96p. 1997. 4.95 (*0-8069-9432-0*) Sterling.

***Mind-Shifting.** unabridged ed. Earl C. Engelhardt. (Illus.). 200p. 1998. spiral bd. 24.95 (*0-615-11419-9*) E C Engelhardt.

Mind Sights: Original Visual Illusions, Ambiguities, & Other Anomalies, with a Commentary on the Play of Mind Perception & Art. Roger N. Shepard. (Illus.). 288p. (C). 1990. pap. text 21.95 (*0-7167-2133-3*) W H Freeman.

Mind Skills Assessment. Mike Woodcock & Dave Francis. 440p. 1998. ring bd. 691.95 (*0-566-08082-6*, Pub. by Gower) Ashgate Pub Co.

Mind Skills for Managers. Samuel A. Malone. LC 96-15513. 240p. 1997. 51.95 (*0-566-07817-1*, Pub. by Gower) Ashgate Pub Co.

Mind Snare. Gayle Greeno. 352p. 1997. mass mkt. 5.99 (*0-88677-749-6*, Pub. by DAW Bks) Penguin Putnam.

Mind, Soul & Spirit: An Inquiry into the Spiritual Derailments of Modern Life. Ronald E. Puhek. 148p. 1998. pap. 10.00 (*1-892590-02-6*) Out Your Bk.

Mind Sparklers Bk. 1: Fireworks for Igniting Creativity in Young Minds. Robert E. Myers. (Illus.). 94p. 1997. pap. 17.95 (*1-882664-32-9*) Prufrock Pr.

Mind Sparklers Bk. 2: Fireworks for Igniting Creativity in Young Minds. Robert E. Myers. (Illus.). 1998. pap. 17.95 (*1-882664-33-7*) Prufrock Pr.

Mind States: An Introduction to Light & Sound Technology. unabridged ed. Michael Landgraf. LC 97-97223. (Illus.). 92p. 1997. pap. 12.98 (*0-9662596-0-2*) Little Minnies.

Mind Stretchers, Bk. C. Michael J. Hult & Heather Rankin Eagles. 1997. 24.00 (*81-209-0834-1*, Pub. by Pitambar Pub) St Mut.

Mind Stretchers, Bk. A. Michael J. Hult & Heather Rankin Eagles. 1997. 24.00 (*81-209-0832-5*, Pub. by Pitambar Pub) St Mut.

Mind Stretchers, Bk. B. Michael J. Hult & Heather Rankin Eagles. 1997. 24.00 (*81-209-0833-3*, Pub. by Pitambar Pub) St Mut.

***Mind-Stretching Thinking Activities.** 96p. (J). (gr. 1-6). 1999. 12.95 (*0-8167-2600-0*) Troll Communs.

Mind-Stretching Thinking Activities: Grades 1-6. Troll Books Staff. 96p. 1999. pap. text 12.95 (*0-8167-2588-8*) Troll Communs.

Mind Styles Model: Theory, Principles & Practice. Anthony F. Gregorc. 28p. 1998. pap. 5.00 (*0-934481-06-7*) Gregorc Assocs.

Mind-Surfer. Mark Leon. 272p. (Orig.). 1995. mass mkt. 4.99 (*0-380-77582-4*, Avon Bks) Morrow Avon.

Mind Teaches the Brain. rev. ed. Caleb Gattegno. 1988. pap. 16.95 (*0-87825-067-0*) Ed Solutions.

Mind Test. Rita Aero & Elliot Weiner. LC 81-2341. (Illus.). 192p. (Orig.). 1981. pap. 17.95 (*0-688-00401-6*, Quil) HarperTrade.

Mind That Feeds upon Infinity: The Deep Self in English Romantic Poetry. Jean Hall. LC 90-55871. 192p. 1991. 35.00 (*0-8386-3430-3*) Fairleigh Dickinson.

M

Mind That Found Itself. 5th ed. Clifford W. Beers. LC 80-5256. (Contemporary Community Health Ser.). 228p. (C). 1981. reprint ed. pap. 15.95 (*0-8229-5324-2*) U of Pittsburgh Pr.

Mind That Found Itself: An Autobiography. Clifford W. Beers. (American Biography Ser.). 205p. 1991. reprint ed. lib. bdg. 69.00 (*0-7812-8017-6*) Rprt Serv.

Mind That's Mine. Mel Levine et al. Ed. by Ruth Brown. (Illus.). 74p. 1997. pap. text, student ed. write for info. (*1-891000-01-2*); teacher ed., ring bd. 65.00 (*1-891000-02-0*) All Kinds Minds.

Mind That's Mine: A Program to Help Young Learners Learn about Learning. Mel Levine et al. Ed. by Ruth Brown. 1997. 370.00 (*1-891000-00-4*) All Kinds Minds.

Mind, the Brain & Complex Adaptive Systems. Harold Morowitz & Jerome L. Singer. 256p. (C). 1995. pap. 38.00 (*0-201-40986-0*) Addison-Wesley.

Mind, the Brain & Complex Adaptive Systems. Ed. by Harold Morowitz & Jerome L. Singer. LC 94-44256. (Proceedings: Vol. 22). 237p. (C). 1995. 61.00 (*0-201-40988-7*) Addison-Wesley.

***Mind the Doors: Long Short Stories.** Zinovy Zinik. 288p. 2001. 22.00 (*1-893956-04-0*) Context Bks.

***Mind the Gap: Promoting A Transatlantic Revolution in Military Affairs.** David C. Gompert. 104p. 1999. per. 5.25 (*0-16-061224-1*) USGPO.

***Mind the Gap: Promoting a Transatlantic Revolution in Military Affairs.** David C. Gompert et al. 91p. 1999. pap. text 25.00 (*0-7881-8089-4*) DIANE Pub.

Mind the Horse. Reginald H. Smythe. LC 65-22225. 1979. 9.95 (*0-317-54406-3*) Viking Penguin.

Mind the Stop: A Brief Guide to Punctuation. G. V. Carey. (Illus.). (J). pap. 11.95 (*0-14-051072-9*, Pub. by Pnguin Bks Ltd) Trafalgar.

***Mind to Magic.** Betty Shine. (J). 2000. pap. 8.95 (*0-552-13378-7*, Pub. by Transworld Publishers Ltd) Trafalgar.

Mind to Mind: A Novel. Seikan Hasegawa. LC 98-47120. (Companions of Zen Training Ser.). (Illus.). 1024p. 1999. 40.00 (*0-915556-35-9*) Great Ocean.

Mind to Murder. P. D. James. 1985. mass mkt. 3.50 (*0-446-31395-5*, Pub. by Warner Bks) Little.

Mind to Murder. P. D. James. 1987. mass mkt. 3.95 (*0-446-34828-7*, Pub. by Warner Bks) Little.

Mind to Murder. P. D. James. 256p. 1988. mass mkt. 6.99 (*0-446-31480-3*, Pub. by Warner Bks) Little.

Mind to Murder. large type ed. P. D. James. LC 93-36328. 304p. 1994. pap. 17.95 (*0-8161-5645-X*, G K Hall Lrg Type) Mac Lib Ref.

Mind Tool: Computers & Their Impact on Society Language Free Version. 5th ed. Neill Graham. Ed. by Marshall. 430p. (C). 1989. pap. text 50.75 (*0-314-47608-3*) West Pub.

Mind Tools: Powerful Techniques For Improving Your Creativity & Think Skills. James Manktelo. 1999. pap. 17.95 (*0-7494-2537-7*) Kogan Page Ltd.

Mind Tools: The Five Levels of Mathematical Reality. Rudy Rucker. (Illus.). 352p. 1988. pap. 14.00 (*0-395-46810-8*) HM.

Mind Tools: The Science of Artificial Intelligence. Fred Bortz. LC 92-16653. (Venture Bks.). (Illus.). 144p. (YA). (gr. 7-12). 1992. lib. bdg. 24.00 (*0-531-12515-7*) Watts.

Mind Training: A Practical System for Developing Self Confidence, Memory, Mental Concentration & Character. Victor G. Rocine. 1996. reprint ed. spiral bd. 18.50 (*0-7873-0734-3*) Hlth Research.

Mind Transfer. Janet Asimov. 1988. 17.95 (*0-8027-6748-6*) Walker & Co.

Mind Travelers: Portraits of Famous Psychics & Healers of Today. Loretta Washburn. LC 95-131054. 132p. (Orig.). 1994. pap. 10.95 (*1-57174-004-X*) Hampton Roads Pub Co.

Mind Trek: Exploring Consciousness, Time & Space Through Remote Viewing. Joe McMoneagle. (Illus.). 264p. 1993. pap. 12.95 (*1-878901-72-9*) Hampton Roads Pub Co.

Mind Tuning: Cause & Effect. Dayton Fandray & Jack Nolan. Ed. by Cindy Drolet. (Mind Tuning Ser.). 40p. (Orig.). 1992. pap. text 14.95 (*0-9609464-7-0*, 8300) Imaginart Intl.

Mind Tuning: Likely or Not? Jack Nolan & Dayton Fandray. Ed. by Cindy Drolet et al. (Mind Tuning Ser.). 46p. (Orig.). (YA). 1996. pap. text 14.95 (*1-883315-17-4*, 8303) Imaginart Intl.

Mind Tuning: Relevant or Not. Dayton Fandray & Jack Nolan. Ed. by Cindy Drolet. (Mind Tuning Ser.). 45p. 1993. pap. text 14.95 (*1-883315-02-6*, 8301) Imaginart Intl.

Mind Tuning: Suggest & Guess. large type ed. Jack Nolan & Dayton Fandray. Ed. by Michael Rule. (Mind Tuning Ser.). 56p. (Orig.). 1995. pap. text 14.95 (*1-883315-11-5*, 8302) Imaginart Intl.

Mind under Par. unabridged ed. David F. Wright. (Illus.). 250p. (Orig.). 1997. pap. 24.95 (*1-888787-00-7*, 002) Behvr Change.

Mind Underlies Spacetime: The Infinite-System Model of Connected Existence. 2nd ed. Daniel Cowan. 1988. 17.00 (*0-915878-08-9*); pap. 12.00 (*0-915878-07-0*) Joseph Pub Co.

Mind Unfolded: Essays on Psychology's Historic Texts. Daniel N. Robinson. LC 78-58510. 539p. 1978. pap. 19.95 (*0-313-27077-5*, P7077); lib. bdg. 85.00 (*0-313-27076-7*, U7076) Greenwood.

Mind, Value, & Culture: Essays in Honor of E. M. Adams. Ed. by Daniel Weissbord. x, 408p. (Orig.). 1989. pap. text 12.00 (*0-917930-41-X*); lib. bdg. 30.00 (*0-917930-96-7*) Ridgeview.

Mind, Value & Reality. John H. McDowell. LC 97-38090. 384p. 1998. 35.00 (*0-674-57613-6*) HUP.

Mind Vs. Computer: Was Dreyfus Winograd Right? Ed. by M. Gams. LC 97-75036. (Frontiers in Artificial Intelligence Applications Ser.: Vol. 43). 200p. Date not set. pap. 75.00 (*90-5199-357-9*) IOS Press.

Mind Wars. Ron Dalrymple. 175p. 1981. text 12.95 (*0-935882-02-2*) Celestial Gifts.

***Mind Waves.** Betty Shine. 2000. pap. 8.95 (*0-552-13998-X*, Pub. by Transworld Publishers Ltd) Trafalgar.

Mind What Stirs in your Heart. Teresina R. Havens. LC 92-61204. 32p. (Orig.). 1992. pap. 4.00 (*0-87574-304-8*) Pendle Hill.

Mind with Reason. Robert Villetto. Ed. by Kathryn Hall. LC 94-60482. 208p. 1994. pap. 12.00 (*1-56664-066-0*) WorldComm.

Mind Within the Net: Models of Learning, Thinking & Acting. Manfred Spitzer. LC 98-10911. (Illus.). 320p. 1999. 27.50 (*0-262-19406-6*, Bradford Bks) MIT Pr.

***Mind Within the Net: Models of Learning, Thinking & Acting.** Manfred Spitzer. (Illus.). 376p. 2000. reprint ed. pap. 17.95 (*0-262-69236-8*) MIT Pr.

***Mind Works - The Psychology of Golf Learning Program.** Cory Vanthuyne. LC 99-56. (Illus.). 85p. 1999. spiral bd. 19.47 (*1-55212-305-7*) Trafford Pub.

Mind Writing Slogans. Allen Ginsberg. (Orig.). 1994. pap. 75.00 (*0-931659-19-1*) Limberlost Pr.

Mind Writing Slogans. limited ed. Allen Ginsberg. (Orig.). 1994. 50.00 (*0-931659-20-5*) Limberlost Pr.

Mind Your Body. Howard. LC 98-13030. 320p. 1998. pap. 14.95 (*0-312-18767-X*) St Martin.

Mind Your Colour: The 'Coloured' Stereotype in South African Literature. Vernon A. February. 248p. 1991. pap. 16.95 (*0-7103-0386-6*, A4926) Routledge.

Mind Your Health. Betty L. Randolph. Ed. by Success Education Institute International Staff. (Health Ser.). 1989. 14.98 incl. audio (*1-55909-250-5*, 380P); Price not set. incl. audio Randolph Tapes.

Mind Your Local Business. Eurofi Staff. 235p. (C). 1988. 150.00 (*0-907304-31-1*, Pub. by Eurofi) St Mut.

Mind Your Manners! Peggy Parish. LC 93-11732. 1994. 10.15 (*0-606-06572-5*, Pub. by Turtleback) Demco.

Mind Your Manners. Peggy Parish. LC 93-11732. (Illus.). 56p. (J). (gr. 1-4). 1994. reprint ed. mass mkt. 5.95 (*0-688-13109-3*, Wm Morrow) Morrow Avon.

Mind Your Manners: Managing Business Cultures in Europe. John Mole. 236p. 1996. reprint ed. pap. 17.95 (*1-85788-085-4*) Nicholas Brealey.

Mind Your Manners, Ben Bunny: A Life-the-Flap Book about Table Manners. Mavis Smith. (Illus.). 24p. (J). (ps-4). 1998. bds. 8.95 (*0-590-06844-X*) Scholastic Inc.

Mind Your Manor: A Guide to Organizing Your Personal Finances. James P. Fredenberg. 150p. 1998. ring bd. 29.95 (*0-9663102-0-9*) Cavan Pub.

Mind Your Musical Manners. 3rd ed. 80p. 1995. pap. 8.95 (*0-7935-5274-5*, 00841043) H Leonard.

Mind Your Musical Manners, on & off Stage: A Handbook of Stage Etiquette. Claudette Sorel. 80p. 1996. pap. 8.95 (*0-614-19989-1*) H Leonard.

Mind Your Own Business. M. C. Millman. LC 94-70753. 200p. (YA). 1994. 15.95 (*1-56062-264-4*) CIS Comm.

Mind Your Own Business. Michael Rosen. LC 74-9969. (Illus.). 96p. (J). (gr. 3 up). 1974. 26.95 (*0-87599-209-9*) S G Phillips.

Mind Your Own Business: Getting Started As an Entrepreneur. LaVerne L. Ludden & Bonnie Maitlen. LC 93-6007. 212p. 1993. pap. 9.95 (*1-56370-083-2*, MYOB) JIST Works.

Mind Your Own Business: My Turf, Your Space, Our Place. Donald Akutagawa & Terry Whitman. Ed. by Lynne E. Lewis. LC 94-66620. 220p. (Orig.). 1994. pap. write for info. (*0-614-05037-5*) Brownell & Carroll.

Mind Your Own Business: People, Performance & Profits. Jim Sullivan. LC 99-23635. 160p. 1999. pap. 14.95 (*0-86730-766-8*) Lebhar Friedman.

Mind Your Own Business: Rules, Guidelines, Examples, Stories & Exhortations. Murray Raphel. 1992. 19.95 (*0-9624808-4-3*) Raphel Mktg.

Mind Your Own Business! The Best Businesses You Can Start Today for under Five Hundred Dollars. Income Opportunities Editors & Stephen Wagner. 252p. (Orig.). 1992. pap. 6.95 (*1-55850-153-3*) Adams Media.

Mind Your Own Business, Kristy! Ann M. Martin. (Baby-Sitters Club Ser.: No. 107). 1997. 9.09 (*0-606-11067-4*, Pub. by Turtleback) Demco.

Mind Your Own Business, Kristy!, Vol. 107. Ann M. Martin. (Baby-Sitters Club Ser.: No. 107). 1997. pap. text 3.99 (*0-590-69213-5*, Little Apple) Scholastic Inc.

Mind Your P's & Q's: Your B's, D's & S's Too! Mary I. Lennon. LC 97-92243. (Illus.). 32p. (Orig.). (J). (gr. k-3). 1998. mass mkt., per. 6.25 (*0-9658531-0-1*) Acrospire Bk.

Mindanao: Land of Unfulfilled Promise. Ed. by Mark Turner. 268p. (Orig.). 1992. pap. 17.50 (*971-10-0502-6*, Pub. by New Day Pub) Cellar.

Mindanao: Philippines Earthquake, August 17, 1976. James L. Stratta et al. 106p. 1977. pap. 12.00 (*0-318-16322-5*, EP-25) Earthquake Eng.

Mindanderings. Bob Stanish. (Illus.). 112p. (J). (gr. 4-9). 1990. 11.99 (*0-86653-526-8*, GA1140) Good Apple.

Mindbend. Robin Cook. LC 85-5804. 352p. 1986. mass mkt. 7.99 (*0-451-14108-3*, Sig) NAL.

Mindbenders. N. Fisk. mass mkt. 8.95 (*0-340-71020-9*, Pub. by Hodder & Stought Ltd) Trafalgar.

Mindbenders Mirror. Dorling Kindersley Staff. 1996. write for info. (*0-7894-1016-8*) HM.

***Mindbenders Stories to Warp Your Brain.** Shusterman. 128p. 1998. mass mkt. 3.99 (*0-8125-3872-2*) Tor Bks.

Mindbenders 3-D. Dorling Kindersley Staff. 1996. write for info. (*0-7894-1017-6*) HM.

Mindblindness: An Essay on Autism & Theory of Mind. Simon Baron-Cohen. (Learning, Development & Conceptual Change Ser.). 300p. 1995. 33.00 (*0-262-02384-9*, Bradford Bks) MIT Pr.

Mindblindness: An Essay on Autism & Theory of Mind. Simon Baron-Cohen. (Learning, Development & Conceptual Change Ser.). (Illus.). 300p. 1997. reprint ed. pap. text 16.50 (*0-262-52225-X*, Bradford Bks) MIT Pr.

Mind/Body Health: The/Effects of Attitudes, Emotions & Relationships. Brent Q. Hafen et al. LC 95-13437. 656p. 1995. pap. text 53.00 (*0-205-17211-3*) Allyn.

Mind/Body Integration: Essential Readings in Biofeedback. E. Peper et al. LC 78-27224. (Illus.). 606p. (C). 1979. 90.00 (*0-306-40102-9*, Plenum Trade) Perseus Pubng.

Mindbody Prescription: Healing the Body, Healing the Pain. John E. Sarno. LC 97-41031. 240p. 1998. 22.00 (*0-446-52076-4*, Pub. by Warner Bks) Little.

Mindbody Prescription: Healing the Body, Healing the Pain. John E. Sarno. 240p. 1999. mass mkt. 14.00 (*0-446-67515-6*, Pub. by Warner Bks) Little.

Mindbridge. Joe Haldeman. 208p. 1978. pap. 2.95 (*0-380-01689-3*, Avon Bks) Morrow Avon.

Mindbridge. Joe Haldeman. LC 75-26185. 186p. 1976. 25.00 (*0-89366-143-0*) Ultramarine Pub.

Mindcoil. Wendy Pini. (Elfquest Reader's Collection: Vol. 14-A). 1999. pap. 11.95 (*0-936861-50-9*, Pub. by Warp Graphics) Midpt Trade.

***Minden, Louisiana.** John Agan. (Images of America Ser.). (Illus.). 128p. 2000. pap. 18.99 (*0-7385-0580-3*) Arcadia Publng.

Minder: The Story of the Courtship, Call & Conflicts of John Ledger, Minder & Minister, 1900. Frederick R. Smith. Ed. by Robert L. Wolff. (Victorian Fiction Ser.). 1976. lib. bdg. 73.00 (*0-8240-1590-8*) Garland.

***Mindestpreise und Abnahmezwang Als Beitrag zum Europaischen Umweltschutz? Deutsches Stromeinspeisungsgesetz und EG-Vertrag.** Kai Gent. (Europaische Hochschulschriften Ser: Bd. 2767). 232p. 1999. 42.95 (*3-631-35691-9*) P Lang Pubng.

Mindfield: New & Selected Poems. Gregory Corso. LC 99-178252. (Illus.). 288p. 1998. pap. 13.95 (*1-56025-201-4*, Thunders Mouth) Avalon NY.

Mindfield: New & Selected Poems. aut. limited ed. Gregory Corso. (Illus.). 288p. Date not set. pap. 300.00 (*0-938410-90-3*, Thunders Mouth) Avalon NY.

Mindfield: New & Selected Poems. limited ed. Gregory Corso. 288p. 1997. 50.00 (*0-938410-96-2*, Thunders Mouth) Avalon NY.

Mindfield Years (Billy Pyrene's Biography of Ned) Vol. 1: The Sycamore Trees. Billy Tripp. 725p. (Orig.). 1996. pap. 17.00 (*0-9652238-0-9*) Mindfield Pr.

Mindfields. Gillian Walker. 288p. 1997. 37.00 (*0-465-09555-0*) Basic.

Mindfire: Dialogues in the Other Future. Ed. by Alexander Blair-Ewart. 360p. pap. (*1-895897-43-2*) Somerville Hse.

Mindful Abyss Springing in the Distance. unabridged ed. Lewis C. Brooks, III. Ed. by Lana M. Wegeng. (Illus.). 26p. 1998. pap. 8.50 (*1-892651-01-7*) Columbia Pubns.

***Mindful Cook: Finding Awareness, Simplicity, & Freedom in the Kitchen.** Isaac Cronin. LC 99-20374. (Illus.). 224p. 1999. 19.95 (*0-375-50275-0*) Villard Books.

***Mindful Corporation.** Leadership Press Staff et al. 224p. 2000. 25.00 (*0-9648466-7-5*, Pub. by Leadrship Pr) Gulf Pub.

Mindful Inquiry in Social Research. Valerie M. Bentz & Jeremy J. Shapiro. LC 98-19720. 216p. 1998. 56.00 (*0-7619-0408-5*); pap. write for info. (*0-7619-0409-3*) Sage.

Mindful Learning: Teaching Self-Discipline & Academic Accomplishment. David B. Strahan. LC 97-37448. 224p. 1997. pap. 19.95 (*0-89089-932-0*) Carolina Acad Pr.

***Mindful Money Guide: Creating Harmony Between Your Values & Your Finances.** Marshall Glickman. LC 98-43543. 320p. 1999. pap. 13.00 (*0-345-43050-6*) Ballantine Pub Grp.

***Mindful of Butterflies.** Bernard Jackson. (Illus.). 160p. 1999. 45.00 (*1-85776-339-4*, Pub. by Book Guild Ltd) Trans-Atl Phila.

Mindful of Famine: Religious Climatology of the Warao Indians. Johannes Wilbert. LC 96-32031. (Religions of the World Ser.). (Illus.). 330p. (C). 1996. pap. 19.95 (*0-945454-11-2*) Harvard U Wrld Relig.

Mindful of Others: Teaching Children to Teach. Suzanne Brady & Suzie Jacobs. LC 93-48126. 222p. 1994. pap. text 23.00 (*0-435-08356-2*, 08356) Heinemann.

***Mindful Parenting Stress Reduction.** (C). 2000. VHS. write for info. (*0-205-32659-5*) Allyn.

***Mindful School: How to Grade for Learning** Ken O'Connor. LC 98-61156. xiv, 192p. 1999. write for info. (*1-57517-123-6*) SkyLght.

Mindful Spontaneity: Lessons in the Feldenkrais Method. Ruthy Alon. 300p. (Orig.). (C). 1995. pap. 22.95 (*1-55643-185-6*) North Atlantic.

Mindful Spontaneity: Moving in Tune with Nature: Lessons in the Feldenkrais Method. Ruthy Alon. 284p. (Orig.). 1990. pap. write for info. (*1-85327-050-4*, Pub. by Prism Pr) Assoc Pubs Grp.

***Mindful Traveler: A Guide to Journaling & Transformative Travel.** Jim Currie. (Illus.). 160p. 2000. pap. 16.95 (*0-8126-9421-X*) Open Court.

Mindful Worker: Learning & Working into the 21st Century. Curtis Miles. LC 94-78037. 246p. (Orig.). 1994. pap. text 19.95 (*0-943202-46-9*) H & H Pub.

Mindfulness. Ellen J. Langer. 1989. 16.30 (*0-201-09502-5*) Addison-Wesley.

Mindfulness. Ellen J. Langer. 1990. pap. 12.50 (*0-201-52341-8*) Addison-Wesley.

Mindfulness & Home: Poetry & Prose from a Prairie Landscape. Photos by Anne Dunham. (Illus.). 115p. (Orig.). 1997. pap. write for info. (*0-9636224-4-7*) Rose Hill Bks.

Mindfulness & Meaningful Work: Explorations in Right Livelihood. Ed. by Claude F. Whitmyer. 289p. (Orig.). 1994. pap. 18.00 (*0-938077-54-6*) Parallax Pr.

Mindfulness in Plain English. Henepola Gunaratana. LC 92-33407. 208p. 1994. pap. 14.95 (*0-86171-064-9*) Wisdom MA.

Mindfulness Meditation: Cultivating the Wisdom of Your Body & Mind. Jon Kabat-Zinn. 1995. 17.00 incl. audio (*0-671-53724-5*) S&S Trade.

Mindfulness Meditation Workshop: Exercises & Meditations. Jon Kabat-Zinn. 119p. 1995. 24.95 incl. audio (*1-879323-34-6*) Sound Horizons AV.

Mindfulness of Breathing. Nagabodhi. 36p. (Orig.). 1995. pap. write for info. (*0-904766-99-3*) Windhorse Pubns.

Mindfulness of Breathing. Bhikkhu Nanamoli. 126p. 1982. 4.20 (*955-24-0167-4*, Pub. by Buddhist Pub Soc) Vipassana Res Pubns.

Mindfulness with Breathing: A Manual for Serious Beginners. Ajahn B. Bhikkhu. Tr. by Santikaro Bhikkhu. 160p. 1996. pap. 14.95 (*0-86171-111-4*) Wisdom MA.

Mindgame. Laura Pender. (Intrigue Ser.: No. 177). 1992. per. 2.79 (*0-373-22177-0*, 1-22177-9) Harlequin Bks.

***Mindgames.** Ivan Moscovich. 2000. 95.20 (*0-7611-2083-1*) Workman Pub.

***Mindgames.** Ivan Moscovich. (MindGames Ser.). (Illus.). 24p. 2000. 5.95 (*0-7611-2018-1*) Workman Pub.

***Mindgames: Phil Jackson's Long Strange Journey.** Roland Lazenby. 256p. 2000. 23.95 (*0-8092-9707-8*, Contemporary Bks) NTC Contemp Pub Co.

Mindglow. Bob Stanish. (Illus.). 96p. (J). (gr. 3-12). 1986. student ed. 11.99 (*0-86653-346-X*, GA 693) Good Apple.

Mindhunter: Inside the FBI's Elite Serial Crime Unit. John E. Douglas. 1997. mass mkt. 3.99 (*0-671-01375-0*) PB.

Mindhunter: Inside the FBI's Elite Serial Crime Unit. John E. Douglas & Mark Olshaker. 416p. 1996. per. 6.99 (*0-671-52890-4*) PB.

Mindhunter: Inside the FBI's Elite Serial Crime Unit. John E. Douglas & Mark Olshaker. (Illus.). 384p. 1995. 24.00 (*0-684-80376-3*) Scribner.

***Minding a Sacred Place.** Ed. by Sunnie Empie. Tr. by Hart W. Empie. (Illus.). 2001. 60.00 (*1-931025-03-7*) Boulder Hse.

Minding God's Business. Ray S. Anderson. LC 86-6367. 164p. (Orig.). reprint ed. pap. 50.90 (*0-8357-4351-9*, 203717800007) Bks Demand.

Minding God's Business. Ray S. Anderson. 156p. (Orig.). 1992. reprint ed. pap. 18.00 (*0-9602638-7-X*) Fuller Seminary.

***Minding Her Own Business.** 3rd ed. Jan Zobel. LC 99-46341. 208p. 1999. pap. 10.95 (*1-58062-200-3*) Adams Media.

Minding Her Own Business: The Self-Employed Woman's Guide to Taxes & Recordkeeping. 2nd ed. Jan Zobel. (Illus.). 208p. 1998. pap. 16.95 (*0-9654778-9-4*) EastHill Pr.

Minding Mind: A Course in Basic Meditation. Tr. by Thomas Cleary. LC 94-27845. 180p. (Orig.). 1995. pap. 11.95 (*1-57062-004-0*, Pub. by Shambhala Pubns) Random.

***Minding Minds: Evolving a Reflexive Mind by Interpreting Others.** Radu J. Bogdan. LC 99-30174. (Illus.). 310p. 2000. 35.00 (*0-262-02467-5*) MIT Pr.

Minding Minutes with Minute Minders: More Than 150 Activities to Stimulate Creative Thinking. Troy W. Cole. (Illus.). 96p. (J). (gr. k-9). 1994. 11.99 (*0-86653-795-3*, GA1489) Good Apple.

Minding My Own Business: An Autobiography. Percy Muir. (Illus.). 240p. 1991. reprint ed. 35.00 (*0-938768-28-X*) Oak Knoll.

Minding Nature: The Philosophers of Ecology. David Macauley. LC 95-39862. (Democracy & Ecology Ser.). 355p. 1996. pap. text 18.95 (*1-57230-059-0*, 0059); lib. bdg. 43.95 (*1-57230-058-2*, 0058) Guilford Pubns.

***Minding Organization: Bring the Future to the Present & Turn Creative Ideas into Business Solutions.** Moshe F. Rubinstein & Iris R. Firstenberg. LC 99-22803. 224p. 1999. 27.95 (*0-471-34781-7*) Wiley.

Minding Our Lives: Women from the South & North Reconnected Ecology & Health. Ed. by Vandana Shiva. 164p. 1993. pap. text 80.00 (*81-85107-51-3*, Pub. by Print Hse) St Mut.

Minding Ruth. Aidan C. Mathews. 68p. 1983. pap. 12.95 (*0-904011-40-2*) Dufour.

An Asterisk (*) at the beginning of an entry indicates that the title is appearing for the first time.

***Minding the Body: Clinical Uses of Somatic Awareness.** Donald Bakal. LC 98-55170. 228p. 1999. 30.00 (1-57230-435-9) Guilford Pubns.

Minding the Body: Women & Literature in the Middle Ages, 800-1500. Adam Potkay. LC 96-36468. 1997. 33.00 (0-8057-8981-2, Twyne) Mac Lib Ref.

Minding the Body: Women Writers on Body & Soul. Ed. by Patricia Foster. 336p. 1995. pap. 12.95 (0-385-47167-X, Anchor NY) Doubleday.

Minding the Body, Mending the Mind. Joan Borysenko. 256p. 1988. pap. 15.95 (0-553-34556-7) Bantam.

Minding the Body, Mending the Mind. Joan Borysenko. 1988. 11.00 incl. audio (0-671-66778-5, Sound Ideas) S&S Trade.

Minding the Carbon Store: Weighing U. S. Forestry Strategies to Slow Global Warming. Mark C. Trexler. 75p. 1991. pap. 20.00 (0-915825-48-1, TRMCP) World Resources Inst.

Minding the Children: Child Care in America from Colonial Times to the Present. Geraldine Youcha. LC 94-33096. 413p. 1995. 26.00 (0-684-19336-1) S&S Trade.

***Minding the Close Relationship: A Theory of Relationship Enhancement.** John H. Harvey & Julia Omarzu. LC 98-51562. (Illus.). 240p. (C). 1999. 39.95 (0-521-63318-4) Cambridge U Pr.

***Minding the Darkness: A Poem for the Year 2000.** Peter Dale Scott. 2000. pap. 21.95 (0-8112-1454-0, Pub. by New Directions) Norton.

Minding the Earth: Thinly Disguised Essays on Human Ecology. Joseph W. Meeker. LC 87-83609. (Illus.). 110p. (Orig.). 1988. pap. 8.95 (0-931735-01-7) Latham Found Pubn.

***Minding the Gap: Epistemology & Philosophy of Science in the Two Traditions.** Christopher Norris. LC 99-86484. 368p. 2000. 39.95 (1-55849-255-0) U of Mass Pr.

Minding the Helm: Marine Navigation & Piloting. National Research Council Staff. 528p. (C). 1994. text 54.95 (0-309-04829-X) Natl Acad Pr.

Minding the Kids: A Practical Guide to Employing Nannies, Caregivers, Baby Sitters, & Au Pairs. Ruth Elliot & James Savage. 562p. 1990. pap. 9.95 (0-685-31173-2) P-H.

***Minding the Law.** Anthony G. Amsterdam & Jerome S. Bruner. LC 00-25428. 448p. 2000. 35.00 (0-674-00289-X) HUP.

Minding the Other's Mind: The Factor of Control & Dominance in Contemporary Relationships. Gerald Alper. LC 96-39510. 124p. 1997. 39.95 (1-57309-101-4); pap. 24.95 (1-57309-100-6) Intl Scholars.

Minding the Soul: Pastoral Counseling as Remembering. James B. Ashbrook. 300p. 1995. pap. 24.00 (0-8006-2673-7, 1-2673) Augsburg Fortress.

Minding the Store: A Memoir. Stanley Marcus. LC 97-13287. (Illus.). 383p. 1998. 29.95 (1-57441-039-3) UNTX Pr.

Minding the Sun. Robert Pack. LC 95-31080. 112p. 1996. pap. 11.95 (0-226-64408-1); lib. bdg. 35.00 (0-226-64407-3) U Ch Pr.

Minding the Temple of the Soul: Balancing Body, Mind & Spirit through Traditional Jewish Prayer, Movement & Meditation. Tamar Frankiel & Judy Greenfeld. LC 96-32990. (Illus.). 184p. (Orig.). 1997. pap. 16.95 (1-879045-64-8) Jewish Lights.

Minding the Underworld: Clayton Eshleman & Late Postmodernism. Paul Christensen. LC 91-2933. 250p. (C). 1991. 25.00 (0-87685-822-1); pap. 15.00 (0-87685-821-3) Black Sparrow.

Minding the Whole Person: Cultivating a Healthy Lifestyle from Youth Through the Senior Years. William F. Haynes. LC 94-12238. 178p. 1994. pap. 14.95 (0-8294-0778-2) Loyola Pr.

Minding Women: Reshaping the Educational Realm. Ed. by Holly Gelfond & Christine A. Woyschner. LC 97-77122. (Reprint Ser.: Vol. 30). 250p. (C). 1997. pap. text 24.95 (0-916690-32-6) Harvard Educ Rev.

Minding Your Body: 100 Ways to Eat Well & Live Positively, Includes Recipes. Joseph S. Rechtschaffen & Robert Carola. 256p. 1995. 18.00 (1-56836-076-2) Kodansha.

Minding Your Business: Legal Issues & Practical Answers for Managing Workplace Privacy. Lynn Outwater & Michael Lotito. 160p. 1997. pap. 35.00 (0-939900-57-2) Soc Human Resc Mgmt.

Minding Your Business Manners: Etiquette Tips for Presenting Yourself Professionally in Every Business Situation. Marjorie Brody & Barbara Pachter. Ed. by Kelly Scanlon. LC 95-71779. (Illus.). 110p. 1996. pap. 12.95 (1-57294-014-X, 12-0026) SkillPath Pubns.

Minding Your Business with MapInfo. Angela Whitener & Jeff Davis. LC 97-43201. 312p. (C). 1998. pap. 45.95 (1-56690-151-0) Thomson Learn.

Minding Your Money: Personal, Money Management & Investment Strategies. Patricia Stallworth. LC 99-36584. 208p. 1998. pap. 14.95 (1-58151-002-0) BookPartners.

Minding Your Own Business: A Common Sense Guide to Home Management & Industry. large type unabridged ed. Raymond S. Moore & Dorothy N. Moore. LC 90-44989. xii, 267p. (Orig.). 1994. pap. 11.95 (0-7852-7830-3) Moore Fnd.

Minding Your Own Business: Arthur Andersen Answers the 101 Toughest Questions about Family Business. Barbara B. Buchholz et al. LC 99-34102. 256p. 1999. text 24.00 (0-7352-0038-6) PH Pr.

Mindkill. Richard La Plante. LC 98-3147. 320p. 1998. text 23.95 (0-312-86055-2) St Martin.

Mindmapping. Joyce Wycoff. 1991. pap. 12.95 (0-425-12780-X) Berkley Pub.

Mindmaster. Clive Gifford. (Spinechillers Fiction Ser.). 128p. (Orig.). (J). (gr. 3-7). 1997. pap. 3.95 (0-7460-2470-3, Usborne); lib. bdg. 11.95 (0-88110-935-5, Usborne) EDC.

Mindoro & Beyond: Stories. N. V. M. Gonzalez. 200p. (Orig.). (C). 1990. pap. 25.75 (971-10-0278-7, Pub. by New Day Pub) Cellar.

Mindoro Highlanders: The Life of the Swidden Agriculturist. Yasushi Kikuchi. (Illus.). 128p. (Orig.). 1984. pap. 12.50 (971-10-0156-X, Pub. by New Day Pub) Cellar.

Mindpower & the Spiritual Dimension. R. Haw. 1981. pap. 20.00 (0-933062-30-3) R H Sommer.

Mindquakes, Stories to Shatter Your Brain. Neal Shusterman. 1996. 9.09 (0-606-11625-7, Pub. by Turtleback) Demco.

Mindrobics: How to Be Happy for the Rest of Your Life. Steve Simms. LC 96-110892. 172p. (Orig.). 1995. pap. 12.95 (0-9648210-0-1) Attitude-Lifter Enter.

Minds Alive: Teachers as Scholars. Bernadette A. Colley et al. (Illus.). 80p. 1999. pap. 12.00 (0-931989-12-4, J W Boarman) Coun Basic Educ.

***Minds & Bodies: An Introduction with Readings.** Robert Wilkinson. 224p. 2000. 65.00 (0-415-21239-1); pap. 19.99 (0-415-21240-5) Routledge.

Minds & Bodies: Philosophers & Their Ideas. Colin McGinn. LC 96-27353. (Philosophy of Mind Ser.). 272p. 1997. 39.95 (0-19-511355-1) OUP.

Minds & Money: The Mental Health Business in America. Leo H. Bradman & David T. Volz. Ed. by Ronald C. Harshman. LC 93-60952. 350p. 1994. 38.00 (1-883945-04-6); pap. 24.00 (1-883945-00-3) UniPsych Pr.

Minds at War: The Poetry & Experience of the First World War. Ed. by David Roberts. (Illus.). 412p. 1996. pap. 28.50 (0-9528969-0-7, Pub. by Saxon Bks) Trans-Atl Phila.

Minds Behind the Brain: A History of the Pioneers & Their Discoveries. Stanley Finger. LC 99-17110. (Illus.). 384p. 2000. 35.00 (0-19-508571-X) OUP.

Mind's Best Work: A New Psychology of Creative Thinking. D. N. Perkins. (Illus.). 325p. 1981. pap. 17.00 (0-674-57624-1) HUP.

Mind's Bodies: Thought in the Act. Berel Lang. LC 94-48037. 162p. (C). 1995. text 39.50 (0-7914-2553-3); pap. text 12.95 (0-7914-2554-1) State U NY Pr.

Minds, Brains & Computers - The Foundations of Cognitive Science: An Anthology. Ed. by Robert Cummins & Denise D. Cummins. LC 99-30789. (Philosophy Anthologies Ser.). (Illus.). 576p. (C). 1999. text 74.95 (1-55786-876-X) Blackwell Pubs.

***Minds, Brains & Computers - The Foundations of Cognitive Science: An Anthology.** Ed. by Robert Cummins & Denise D. Cummins. LC 99-30789. (Philosophy Anthologies Ser.). (Illus.). 576p. (C). 1999. pap. text 39.95 (1-55786-877-8) Blackwell Pubs.

Minds, Brains & People. T. E. Wilkerson. 1974. 12.50 (0-19-824510-6) OUP.

Minds, Brains & Science. John R. Searle. 112p. 1986. pap. text 10.50 (0-674-57633-0) HUP.

Minds, Causes & Mechanisms: A Case Against Physicalism. Josep E. Corbi & Josep L. Prades. LC 99-16131. (Aristotelian Society Monographs: Vol. 17). 288p. 1999. text 64.95 (0-631-21801-7) Blackwell Pubs.

***Minds, Causes & Mechanisms: A Case Against Physicalism.** Josep E. Corbi & Josep L. Prades. LC 99-16131. (Aristotelian Society Monographs: Vol. 17). 288p. 1999. pap. text 29.95 (0-631-21802-5) Blackwell Pubs.

Mind's Ear. Bruce Adolphe. LC 91-35028. 72p. (Orig.). 1991. pap. 9.95 (0-918812-71-2, SE0183) MMB Music.

Mind's Empire: Myth & Form in George Chapman's Narrative Poems. Raymond B. Waddington. LC 74-6841. 235p. reprint ed. pap. 72.90 (0-608-14999-3, 202588300046) Bks Demand.

***Mind's Eye.** Paul Fleischman. LC 99-20844. 108p. (YA). (gr. 7 up). 2000. 15.95 (0-8050-6314-5) H Holt & Co.

***Mind'S Eye.** Paul Fleischman. (YA). 2001. mass mkt. 5.50 (0-440-22901-4) BDD Bks Young Read.

Mind's Eye. Jeane Gardner & Ernest N. Hart, Jr. 1997. pap. 12.95 (0-87012-572-9) McClain.
An insightful look into life & love through the art of poetry. ***Publisher Paid Annotation.***

***Mind's Eye: An Eye of the Beholder Collection.** Peter Kuper. (Illus.). 128p. 2000. 11.95 (1-56163-259-7, Comics Lit) NBM.

Mind's Eye: Essays. Edmund C. Blunden. LC 67-28745. (Essay Index Reprint Ser.). 1977. 20.95 (0-8369-0218-1) Ayer.

Mind's Eye: Imagery in Everyday Life. Robert Sommer. 1994. pap. text. write for info. (0-86651-259-4) Seymour Pubns.

Mind's Eye: Using Pictures Creatively in Language Learning. Alan Maley et al. 64p. 1981. pap. text, teacher ed. 14.95 (0-521-23333-X) Cambridge U Pr.

***Mind's Eye: Writings on Photography & Photographers.** Henri Cartier-Bresson. Ed. by Michael L. Sand. LC 99-64610. (Illus.). 112p. 1999. 19.95 (0-89381-875-5) Aperture.

Mind's Eye Geometry. Ivan Moscovich. (Illus.). (J). 1996. pap. 8.50 (0-906212-98-7, Pub. by Tarquin Pubns) Parkwest Pubns.

Mind's Eye, Mind's Truth: FSA Photography Reconsidered. James Curtis. (American Civilization Ser.). 1991. pap. 24.95 (0-87722-823-X) Temple U Pr.

***Mind's Eye Theatre: The Sabbat Guide.** Justin Achilli. 2000. pap. 14.95 (1-56504-732-X) White Wolf.

***Mind's Eye Theatre Journal.** Contrib. by Carol Bowen. (Mind's Eye Theatre Ser.: Vol. 4). (Illus.). 80p. 1999. pap. 7.95 (1-56504-780-X, 5404) White Wolf.

***Mind's Eye Theatre Journal.** Wolf White White Wolf Publishing Staff. (Mind's Eye Theatre Ser.: Vol. 3). (Illus.). 80p. 1999. pap. 7.95 (1-56504-779-6, 5403) White Wolf.

***Minds Eye Theatre Journal, No. 1.** Wolf White Wolf Publishing Staff. (Mind's Eye Theatre Ser.). 80p. 1999. pap. 7.95 (1-56504-777-X, 5401) White Wolf.

***Minds Eye Theatre Journal, No. 2.** Wolf White Wolf Publishing Staff. (Mind's Eye Theatre Ser.). 80p. 1999. pap. 7.95 (1-56504-778-8, 5402) White Wolf.

Mind's Eye Theatre Prop Deck. 14.95 (1-56504-679-X) White Wolf.

Mind's Fate. Robert Coles. 1996. pap. 14.95 (0-614-20826-2) Little.

Minds for the Making: The Role of Science in American Education, 1750-1990. Scott L. Montgomery. LC 93-38389. 316p. 1994. pap. text 18.95 (0-89862-188-7); lib. bdg. 42.00 (0-89862-189-5) Guilford Pubns.

Mind's I. Doug Hofstadter. 512p. 1985. pap. 17.95 (0-553-34584-2, New Age Bks) Bantam.

***Mind's I.** Doug Hofstadter. 2000. pap. 20.00 (0-465-03091-2, Pub. by Basic) HarpC.

Minds, Ideas, & Objects: Essays on the Theory of Representation in Modern Philosophy. Ed. by P. D. Cummins & G. Zoeller. (North American Kant Society Studies in Philosophy: Vol. 2). vi, 378p. (Orig.). 1992. pap. text 27.00 (0-924922-13-3); lib. bdg. 49.00 (0-924922-63-X) Ridgeview.

Minds in Many Pieces: Revealing the Spiritual Side of Multiple Personality Disorder. 2nd rev. ed. Ralph Allison & Ted Schwarz. LC 98-96785. 220p. 1999. pap. 29.95 (0-9668949-0-1) CIE Publ.

Minds in Motion: A Kinesthetic Approach to Teaching Elementary Curriculum. Susan Griss. LC 97-49593. 130p. 1998. pap. 19.50 (0-325-00034-4) Heinemann.

Minds in Motion: Using Museums to Expand Creative Thinking. 3rd ed. LC 96-30100. 186p. 1997. 14.95 (1-880192-21-7) Caddo Gap Pr.

Minds in Play: Computer Game Design As a Context for Children's Learning. Yasmin B. Kafai. 352p. 1995. 69.95 (0-8058-1512-0); pap. 34.50 (0-8058-1513-9) L Erlbaum Assocs.

***Minds in the Making: Essays in Honor of David R. Olson.** Ed. by Janet Wilde Astington. LC 99-58778. (Illus.). 288p. 2000. text 59.95 (0-631-21805-X, Pub. by Blackwell Publishers); pap. text 27.95 (0-631-21806-8, Pub. by Blackwell Publishers) Blackwell Pubs.

***Mind's Landscape: An Introduction to Philosophy of Mind.** Samuel Guttenplan. 2000. 62.95 (0-631-20217-X); pap. 27.95 (0-631-20218-8) Blackwell Pubs.

***Minds, Machines & Evolution.** James Patrick Hogan. 1999. mass mkt. 6.99 (0-671-57843-X) Baen Bks.

***Minds, Machines & the Multiverse: The Quest for the Quantum Computer.** Julian Brown. LC 99-56638. 464p. 2000. 27.00 (0-684-81481-1) S&S Trade.

***Mind's Matter: An Intellectual Autobiography.** Stanley L. Jaki. 2000. 24.95 (1-882926-49-8) ISI Books.

Mind's New Science: A History of Cognitive Revolution. Howard Gardner. LC 87-47555. 448p. 1987. pap. 20.00 (0-465-04635-5, Pub. by Basic) HarpC.

Minds of Billy Milligan. Daniel Keyes. 448p. 1995. mass mkt. 5.99 (0-553-26381-1) Bantam.

Minds of Birds. Alexander F. Skutch. LC 95-4645. (Louise Lindsey Merrick Natural Environment Ser.: No. 23). (Illus.). 200p. (C). 1996. 29.95 (0-89096-671-0) Tex A&M Univ Pr.

Minds of Birds. Alexander F. Skutch. LC 95-4645. (Louise Lindsey Merrick Natural Environment Ser.: No. 23). (Illus.). 200p. (C). 1997. pap. 19.95 (0-89096-759-8) Tex A&M Univ Pr.

Minds of Blue Souls of Gold: What's the Point II. Michael Levy. 128p. 1999. pap. 9.95 (0-9668069-1-3) Point of Life Inc.

Minds of Man. Joel Friedlander. Date not set. pap. write for info. (0-936385-19-7) J Friedlander.

Minds of Robots: Sense Data, Memory Images & Behavior in Conscious Automata. James T. Culbertson. LC 63-7256. (Illus.). 480p. reprint ed. 148.80 (0-8357-9690-6, 201173400079) Bks Demand.

Minds of the West: Ethnocultural Evolution in the Rural Middle West, 1830-1917. Jon Gjerde. LC 96-22213. 442p. (gr. 13). 1997. 45.00 (0-8078-2312-0) U of NC Pr.

Minds of the West: Ethnocultural Evolution in the Rural Middle West, 1830-1917. Jon Gjerde. LC 96-22213. (Illus.). 442p. 1999. pap. 19.95 (0-8078-4807-7) U of NC Pr.

Minds of Their Own: Thinking & Awareness in Animals. Lesley J. Rogers. 212p. 1998. pap. 19.00 (0-8133-9065-6, Pub. by Westview) HarpC.

Minds-On Fun for Fall. Judy Beach & Kathleen Spencer. (J). (gr. k-4). 1991. pap. 10.99 (0-86653-948-4) Fearon Teacher Aids.

Minds-On Fun for Spring. Judy Beach & Kathleen Spencer. (J). (gr. k-4). 1991. pap. 10.99 (0-86653-946-8) Fearon Teacher Aids.

Minds-On Fun for Summer. Judy Beach & Kathleen Spencer. (J). (gr. k-4). 1991. pap. 10.99 (0-86653-945-X) Fearon Teacher Aids.

Minds-On Fun for Winter. Judy Beach & Kathleen Spencer. (J). (gr. k-4). 1991. pap. 10.99 (0-86653-947-6) Fearon Teacher Aids.

Minds on Math. 1994. teacher ed. write for info. (0-201-83009-4) Addison-Wesley.

***Minds On Math: Grade 8 Ontario Edition Independent.** 1999. student ed. write for info. (0-201-43996-4) Addison-Wesley.

Mind's Past. Michael S. Gazzaniga. LC 97-32505. 263p. 1998. 22.50 (0-520-21320-3, Pub. by U CA Pr) Cal Prin Full Svc.

***Mind's Past.** Michael S. Gazzaniga. LC 97-32505. 263p. 2000. pap. text 14.95 (0-520-22486-8, Pub. by U CA Pr) Cal Prin Full Svc.

Mind's Road to God: Bonaventura. George Boas. 72p. (C). 1953. pap. text 7.33 (0-02-311250-6, Macmillan Coll) P-H.

Mind's Staircase: Stages in the Development of Human Intelligence. Ed. by Robbie Case. 424p. 1992. pap. 45.00 (0-8058-1190-7); text 79.95 (0-8058-0324-6) L Erlbaum Assocs.

Mind's We: Contextualism in Cognitive Psychology. Dianne F. Gillespie. LC 91-39988. 232p. (C). 1992. 26.95 (0-8093-1675-7) S Ill U Pr.

Mindscape: Exploring the Reality of Thought Forms. Bruce A. Vance. LC 90-50201. 232p. 1990. pap. 9.95 (0-8356-0660-0, Quest) Theos Pub Hse.

Mindscape of Art: Dimensions of the Psyche in Fiction, Drama & Film. Roy Huss. LC 82-49280. (Illus.). 224p. 1986. 35.00 (0-8386-3182-7) Fairleigh Dickinson.

Mindscapes. Amy Maid. LC 82-9904. 67p. (J). (gr. 3-8). 1983. pap. 11.95 (0-8290-1001-7) Irvington.

Mindscapes: Philosophy, Science, & the Mind. Ed. by Martin Carrier & Peter Machamer. LC 98-116300. (Pittsburgh-Konstanz Series in the Philosophy & History of Science). 372p. (C). 1997. text 75.00 (0-8229-3986-X) U of Pittsburgh Pr.

Mindscapes: Poetry & Computer Art. Ann Gasser. (Illus.). 40p. (Orig.). 1994. pap. 3.95 (1-884257-06-2) AGEE Keyboard.

Mindscapes: The Epistemology of Magoroh Maruyama. Ed. by Michael T. Caley & Daiyo Sawada. 256p. 1994. text 48.00 (2-88124-442-4) Gordon & Breach.

Mindscapes: The Geographies of Imagined Worlds. Ed. by George E. Slusser & Eric S. Rabkin. LC 88-18299. (Alternatives Ser.). 316p. (C). 1989. text 31.95 (0-8093-1454-1) S Ill U Pr.

***Mindscapes: The Virtual Reality Gamebook.** Prophet Andromeda. Ed. by Sherry Knecht. (Illus.). 85p. (Orig.). 1999. pap. 12.95 (1-929589-09-3) Branching Leaf.

Mindscapes in Management: Use of Individual Differences in Multicultural Management. Magoroh Maruyama. 160p. 1994. 41.95 (1-85521-367-2, Pub. by Dartmth Pub) Ashgate Pub Co.

MindScience: An East-West Dialogue. Dalai Lama XIV et al. Ed. by Daniel Goleman & Robert Thurman. LC 91-30288. (Illus.). 137p. 1993. pap. 13.95 (0-86171-066-5) Wisdom MA.

Mindset: Win Place Show. Fred J. Kruger. Ed. by Lynne E. Lewis. 126p. (Orig.). 1995. pap. write for info. (1-885487-05-3) Brownell & Carroll.

Mindset for the New Generation Organization. Martin Nasser & Frank Vivier. (Illus.). 169p. (C). 1993. pap. text 41.45 (0-7021-2879-1, Pub. by Juta & Co) Intl Spec Bk.

Mindset for Winning: A 4-Step Mental Training Program for Athletes. John D. Curtis. (Illus.). 120p. 1989. student ed. 9.95 (0-9611456-5-X, Coulee Press); pap. 9.95 (0-9611456-3-3, Coulee Press) Adastra Pub.

Mindset for Winning: Coaching Manual. John D. Curtis. 130p. 1989. 39.95 (0-9611456-7-6, Coulee Press) Adastra Pub.

Mindset for Winning Athlete's Log. John D. Curtis. 50p. 1989. pap. 7.95 (0-9611456-6-8, Coulee Press) Adastra Pub.

***Mindset of a Martial Artist.** Dean Alan Clerc. (Illus.). 113p. 2000. pap. text 10.85 (1-58500-420-0) First Bks Lib.

Mindsets: The Role of Culture & Perception in International Relations. 2nd rev. ed. Glen Fisher. LC 97-35904. 228p. (Orig.). 1997. pap. text 18.95 (1-877864-54-4) Intercult Pr.

Mindsets Factor in Ethnic Conflict: A Cross-Cultural Agenda. Glen Fisher. LC 98-5153. 123p. (C). 1998. pap. text 15.95 (1-877864-60-9) Intercult Pr.

Mindshadow. J. M. Dillard. (Star Trek Ser.: No. 27). 1989. mass mkt. 5.50 (0-671-70420-6, Pocket Star Bks) PB.

MindShadows. Diane Conrad. (Illus.). 70p. (Orig.). 1996. pap. 8.00 (0-614-32386-X) Phantsml Pr.

Mindshift: The Employee Handbook for Understanding the Changing World of Work. Price Pritchett. 60p. 1996. pap. text 5.95 (0-944002-50-1) Pritchett Assocs.

Mindshifts: A Brain-Based Process for Restructuring Schools & Renewing Education. rev. ed. Geoffrey Caine et al. LC 98-34855. 1998. 37.00 (1-56976-091-8) Zephyr Pr AZ.

MindShifts: Brain-Based Process for Restructuring Schools & Renewing Education. Geoffrey Caine et al. LC 94-27925. 280p. 1995. pap. 35.00 (1-56976-007-1) Zephyr Pr AZ.

***Mindsight: Near-Death & Out-Of-Body Experiences in the Blind.** Kenneth Ring. 1999. pap. 12.95 (0-9669630-0-8) W James Ctr.

Mindsnakes: Solving the N-Queen's Problem with One Pawn. Richard Butner. (Illus.). 32p. (Orig.). 1988. pap. 4.95 (0-929133-01-3) Barefoot Pr.

Mindspan. Gordon Rupert Dickson. 288p. (Orig.). 1986. mass mkt. 4.99 (0-671-65580-9) Baen Bks.

Mindspeakers' Call. Gayle Greeno. (Ghatti's Tale Ser.: Bk. 2). 512p. (Orig.). 1994. mass mkt. 5.99 (0-88677-579-5, Pub. by DAW Bks) Penguin Putnam.

Mindspell. Kay N. Smith. 288p. 1984. mass mkt. 2.95 (0-345-31766-1, Ballantine) Ballantine Pub Grp.

Mindstar Rising. Peter F. Hamilton. 438p. 1993. pap. 16.95 (0-330-32376-8, Pub. by Pan) Trans-Atl Phila.

Mindstar Rising. Peter F. Hamilton. 1997. mass mkt. 6.99 (0-8125-9056-2, Pub. by Tor Bks) St Martin.

Mindstorms. Baum. write for info. (0-07-135252-X) McGraw.

Mindstorms: Children, Computers & Powerful Ideas. 2nd ed. Seymour A. Papert. LC 92-53249. 230p. 1999. pap. 14.00 (0-465-04674-6, Pub. by Basic) HarpC.

Mindstorms: Stories to Blow Your Mind. Neal Shusterman. 128p. (YA). (gr. 5 up). 1996. pap. text 3.99 (0-8125-5197-4, Pub. by Tor Bks) St Martin.

M

An Asterisk (*) at the beginning of an entry indicates that the title is appearing for the first time.

Mindstorms: Stories to Blow Your Mind. Neal Shusterman. 1996. mass mkt. 3.99 (*0-8125-5198-2*, Pub. by Tor Bks) St Martin.

Mindstorms, Stories to Blow Your Mind. Neal Shusterman. 1996. 9.09 (*0-606-11626-5*, Pub. by Turtleback) Demco.

Mindstretchers. Wordwright. Incl. Level 1., **3 vols.** (gr. 1-3). pap. 9.95 (*0-8224-4501-8*); Level 1., **3 vols.** (gr. 1-3). pap. 9.95 Level 1., **3 vols.** (gr. 1-3). pap. 9.95 (*0-8224-4503-4*); Level 1., **3 vols.** (gr. 1-3). pap. 9.95 (*0-8224-4504-2*); write for info. (*0-318-56618-4*) Fearon Teacher Aids.

Mindstretchers, 4 vols., Level 2. Pat Carr & Steve Tracey. Incl. Enchantments. 1983. pap. 5.95 (*0-8224-4508-5*); Great Explorations. 1983. pap. 5.95 (*0-8224-4507-7*); Star Gazing. 1983. pap. 5.95 (*0-8224-4505-0*); (J). (gr. 4-6). 1983. pap. write for info. (*0-318-57166-8*) Fearon Teacher Aids.

Mindstretching Puzzles. Terry H. Stickels. LC 94-26373. (Illus.). 96p. 1994. pap. 5.95 (*0-8069-0694-4*) Sterling.

Mindstrings & How to Pull Them: Psychological Tactics for the Sales Professional That Guarantee Unlimited Success. unabridged ed. Kevin L. Hogan & Mark N. Cohen. Ed. by Elsom Eldridge, Jr. (Illus.). 200p. 1998. pap. 19.95 (*0-9662966-7-2*) Best-Sellers Pub.

Mindsword's Story. Fred Saberhagen. (The Sixth Book of the Lost Swords Ser.: No. 6). 1991. mass mkt. 4.50 (*0-8125-1118-2*, Pub. by Tor Bks) St Martin.

Mindszenty the Man. Joseph Vecsey & Phyllis Schlafly. LC 72-93906. 1972. 2.00 (*0-934640-04-1*) Pere Marquette.

Mindtraps: Unlocking the Key to Investment Success. 2nd ed. Roland Barach. 260p. Date not set. reprint ed. 34.95 (*0-935219-07-2*) Intl Trading Mastery.

Mindtwisters: Stories That Play with Your Head. Neal Shusterman. (J). (gr. 6-9). 1997. pap. text 4.99 (*0-8125-5199-0*, Pub. by Tor Bks) St Martin.

Mindual of Philosopher G. 2nd rev. ed. 82p. 1986. pap. 7.95 (*0-9617048-0-2*) Philosopher Pr.

Mindwalking: Guide to Psionics. Ed Stark. 1999. 18.95 (*0-7869-1384-3*, Pub. by TSR Inc) Random.

***MindWalking Step by Step: Words & Music That Help You Find Your Path.** Mary H. Frakes. (MindPaths Ser.). 242p. 1999. pap. 18.50 (*0-9667879-2-7*, MindWalks) Life Lessons.

***MindWalks: 100 Easy Ways to Relieve Stress, Stay Motivated, & Nourish.** Mary H. Frakes. LC 98-96770. 244p. 1999. pap. 8.95 (*0-9667879-4-3*) Life Lessons.

***Mindware: An Introduction to the Philosophy of Cognitive Science.** Andy Clark. (Illus.). 240p. (C). 2000. pap. 18.95 (*0-19-513857-0*); text 45.00 (*0-19-513856-2*) OUP.

Mindwatching: Why We Behave the Way We Do. Hans J. Eysenck & Michael Eysenck. 385p. 1997. pap. 13.95 (*1-85375-194-4*) Trafalgar.

MindWealth: Turning Knowledge into Assets. Janet Slemko. LC 98-74713. 208p. 1999. pap. 15.95 (*1-58151-027-6*) BookPartners.

Mindworks. Kevin Siembieda. Ed. by Alex Marciniszyn et al. (Rifts Sourcebook Ser.: No. 3). (Illus.). 112p. (Orig.). (YA). (gr. 8 up). 1994. pap. 12.95 (*0-916211-69-X*, 812) Palladium Bks.

Mindworks: How to Be a More Creative & Critical Thinker. Charleen W. Swansea. 82p. (Orig.). 1990. pap. text 14.95 (*0-943274-05-2*) SC Ed Comm Inc.

Mindworks: NLP Tools for Building a Better Life. Anne Linden & Kathrin Perutz. LC 98-227920. 368p. 1998. pap. 6.99 (*0-425-16624-4*) Berkley Pub.

Mindworks: Time & Conscious Experience. Ernst Poppel. 208p. 1988. 17.95 (*0-15-152190-5*) Harcourt.

Mindy: Farmer's Daughter, Farmer's Wife. Mildred Gaasland. (Illus.). 166p. (Orig.). 1994. pap. 9.95 (*0-9639777-1-7*) Pekin Pubns.

Mindy Gets Her Reward & Other Stories for Children. Ester G. Shemtov. (Illus.). 62p. (Orig.). (YA). reprint ed. pap. 7.00 (*0-8266-0366-1*, Merkos LInyonei Chinuch) Kehot Pubn Soc.

Mindy Wise. Marilyn Kaye. 144p. (J). (gr. 5). 1993. pap. 3.50 (*0-380-71879-0*, Avon Bks) Morrow Avon.

Mindy's Mysterious Miniature. Jane L. Curry. (J). (gr. 4-7). 1990. 20.25 (*0-8446-6433-2*) Peter Smith.

***Mine.** D. M. Badowich. (Illus.). 16p. (J). (ps-3). 1999. pap. 5.95 (*1-894303-19-9*) RRP.

Mine! Jill Gorey & Barbara Herndon. (Rugrats Books for Parents Ser.: Vol. 2). (Illus.). 64p. (ps-3). 1999. per. 8.00 (*0-671-02638-0*, PB Hardcover) PB.

Mine. Jessica Jones. Ed. by Susan Fryer & Gina Bakan. Date not set. pap. 24.95 (*0-9670829-2-7*) Realizing Potential.

***Mine.** Andy Young. 28p. 2000. pap. 5.00 (*0-9663846-7-9*) Lavender Ink.

Mine. Robert R. McCammon. Ed. by Bill Grose. 496p. 1991. reprint ed. per. 6.99 (*0-671-73944-1*) PB.

Mine: A Backpack Baby Story. Miriam Cohen. LC 99-70750. (Illus.). 12p. (J). 1999. bds. 6.95 (*1-887734-59-7*) Star Brght Bks.

Mine! A Sesame Street Book about Sharing. Linda Hayward. (Classic Board Bks.). (Illus.). (J). (ps-k). 1997. bds. 5.99 (*0-614-28919-X*) Random Bks Yng Read.

Mine, All Mine: A Book about Pronouns. Ruth Heller. LC 97-10051. (Illus.). 48p. (J). (gr. k-3). 1997. 17.95 (*0-448-41606-9*, G & D) Peng Put Young Read.

Mine, All Mine: A Book about Pronouns. Ruth Heller. (Ruth Heller's World of Nature Ser.). 48p. 1999. pap. 6.99 (*0-698-11797-2*, PuffinBks) Peng Put Young Read.

Mine & Yours Are Hers: Retrieving Women's History from Rabbinic Literature. Tal Ilan. LC 97-29996. (Arbeiten zur Geschichte des Antiken Judentums und des Urchristentums Ser.: No. 41). 320p. 1997. 112.50 (*90-04-10860-2*) Brill Academic Pubs.

Mine Angels Round About: Mormon Missionary Evacuation from Western Germany - 1939. Terry B. Montague. 13.50 (*0-685-30414-0*) Roylance Pub.

Mine Boy. Peter Abrahams. (African Writers Ser.). 192p. (C). 1989. pap. 9.95 (*0-435-90562-7*, 90562) Heinemann.

Mine Classic Board Books. Linda Hayward. (Sesame Street Bks.). (J). 1997. 5.99 (*0-679-88345-2*, Pub. by Random Bks Yng Read) Random.

Mine-Countermine Operations. 1990. lib. bdg. 79.95 (*0-8490-3982-7*) Gordon Pr.

***Mine Design.** John R. Sturgul. LC 99-48032. 1999. pap. write for info. (*0-87335-181-9*) SMM&E Inc.

Mine Disasters & Mine Rescue. M. A. Ramlu. (Illus.). 408p. (C). 1991. text 123.00 (*90-6191-964-9*, Pub. by A A Balkema) Ashgate Pub Co.

Mine-Duty Fuses, UL 198M. 3rd ed. (C). 1995. pap. text 95.00 (*1-55989-661-2*) Underwrtrs Labs.

Mine Electrical Fitter. 1973. 28.00 (*0-8464-4404-6*) Beekman Pubs.

Mine Enemy Grows Older. Alexander King. 1993. reprint ed. lib. bdg. 19.95 (*1-56849-160-3*) Buccaneer Bks.

Mine Environmental Engineering, I. Mritunjoy Sengupta. 288p. 1989. lib. bdg. 195.00 (*0-8493-4958-3*, TN29) CRC Pr.

Mine Environmental Engineering, Vol. II. Mritunjoy Sengupta. 240p. 1989. lib. bdg. 195.00 (*0-8493-4957-5*, TN295) CRC Pr.

Mine Environmental Engineering, Vols. I-II. Mritunjoy Sengupta. 1989. write for info. (*0-318-66742-8*) CRC Pr.

Mine Eyes Have Seen. Richard Goldstein. LC 97-6445. 1997. pap. 14.00 (*0-684-81599-0*, Touchstone) S&S Trade Pap.

Mine Eyes Have Seen. Ann Rinaldi. LC 97-10680. 288p. (J). (gr. 7-12). 1997. 16.95 (*0-590-54318-0*) Scholastic Inc.

Mine Eyes Have Seen: Dr. Martin Luther King Jr.'s Final Journey. D'Army Bailey. Ed. by David Lyons. LC 93-16660. (Illus.). 144p. 1993. 29.95 (*1-881096-02-5*) Towery Pub.

***Mine Eyes Have Seen: Into the Millennium: An Anthology of African American Poetry.** Ed. by Kimmika Williams & Lois Moses. 61p. 2000. pap. 8.00 (*0-9626216-6-8*) Three Goat Pubns.

Mine Eyes Have Seen the Glory: A Journey into the Evangelical Subculture in America. Randall H. Balmer. 264p. 1989. 19.95 (*0-685-47315-5*) OUP.

Mine Eyes Have Seen the Glory: A Journey into the Evangelical Subculture in America. enl. ed. Randall H. Balmer. 320p. 1993. pap. text 14.95 (*0-19-507985-X*) OUP.

Mine Eyes Have Seen the Glory: Combat Diaries of Union Sergeant Hamlin Alexander Coe. Ed. & Intro. by David Coe. LC 74-5896. 240p. 1975. 32.50 (*0-8386-1492-2*) Fairleigh Dickinson.

Mine Eyes Have Seen the Glory: The Victory of the Lamb in the Book of Revelation. Gordon Ferguson. (Practical Exposition Ser.). 198p. 1996. pap. 11.99 (*1-884553-92-3*) Discipleshp.

Mine Fields. Bill Burke. 120p. 1995. 50.00 (*0-932526-50-0*) Nexus Pr.

Mine Fields. deluxe ed. Bill Burke. 1995. 300.00 (*0-932526-79-9*) Nexus Pr.

Mine Fires. 218p. 1996. pap. 69.95 (*0-929531-35-3*) Intertec.

***Mine for All Time.** Julia Hanlon. 2000. mass mkt. 5.99 (*0-8217-6523-X*, Zebra Kensgtn) Kensgtn Pub Corp.

Mine Forever. Carol Finch, pseud. 384p. 1999. mass mkt. 5.99 (*0-8217-6114-5*) Kensgtn Pub Corp.

Mine Forever. Richard. 1989. pap. 14.95 (*0-340-49641-X*, Pub. by Hodder & Stought Ltd) Trafalgar.

Mine Hoisting. M. A. Ramlu. LC 99-227028. (Illus.). 586p. (C). 1996. text 149.00 (*90-5410-298-5*, Pub. by A A Balkema) Ashgate Pub Co.

Mine Hydrology. fac. ed. Roy E. Williams et al. LC 86-60202. (Illus.). 181p. 1986. reprint ed. pap. 56.20 (*0-7837-7844-9*, 204760300007) Bks Demand.

Mine in the Sky: The History of California's Pine Creek Tungsten Mine & the People Who Were Part of It. 2nd rev. ed. Joseph M. Kurtak. (Illus.). 234p. 1998. pap. 19.95 (*1-888125-34-9*) Publ Consult.

Mine Induced Subsidence: Effects on Engineered Structures. Ed. by H. J. Siriwardane. (Symposium Proceedings Ser.). 216p. 1988. 23.00 (*0-87262-649-0*) Am Soc Civil Eng.

Mine Intercom Messages from the Realms of Light. Thedra. 176p. 1989. pap. 7.95 (*0-941131-04-1*) ASSK Pub.

Mine Investment Analysis. Donald W. Gentry & Thomas J. O'Neill. LC 84-51346. (Illus.). 510p. 1984. 47.00 (*0-89520-429-0*, 429-0) SMM&E Inc.

Mine Management. D. A. Sloan. (Illus.). 450p. (gr. 13). 1983. text 114.00 (*0-412-24070-X*, NO. 6762) Chapman & Hall.

Mine Mechanization & Automation: Proceedings of the Second International Symposium on Mine Mechanization & Automation, Lulea, Sweden 7-10 June 1993. Ed. by Gunnar Almgren et al. (Illus.). 827p. (C). 1993. text 181.00 (*90-5410-314-0*, Pub. by A A Balkema) Ashgate Pub Co.

***Mine, Mine, Mine!** Illus. by Joan Holub. (All by Myself Bks.). 16p. (J). 2000. 6.95 (*1-58260-019-8*) Infnty Plus One.

Mine of Her Own: Women Prospectors in the American West, 1850-1950. Sally Zanjani. LC 96-24533. (Illus.). xii, 375p. 1997. text 32.50 (*0-8032-4914-4*) U of Nebr Pr.

***Mine of Her Own: Women Prospectors in the American West, 1850-1950.** Sally Zanjani. LC 96-24533. (Illus.). 375p. 2000. pap. 17.95 (*0-8032-9916-8*, Bison Books) U of Nebr Pr.

Mine Planning & Equipment Selection: Proceedings of the International Symposium, Calgary, November 3-4, 1988. Ed. by Raj K. Singhal. 548p. (C). 1988. text 226.00 (*90-6191-819-7*, Pub. by A A Balkema) Ashgate Pub Co.

Mine Planning & Equipment Selection, 1995: Proceedings of the 4th International Symposium on Mine Planning & Equipment Selection, Sao Paulo, Brazil, 1995. Ed. by R. K. Singhal. (Illus.). 1136p. (C). 1995. text 175.00 (*90-5410-569-0*, Pub. by A A Balkema) Ashgate Pub Co.

Mine Planning & Equipment Selection, 1996: Proceedings of the 5th International Symposium, Sao Paulo, Brazil, 22-24 October 1996. Ed. by W. T. Hennies et al. (Illus.). 732p. (C). 1996. text 181.00 (*90-5410-827-4*, Pub. by A A Balkema) Ashgate Pub Co.

Mine Planning & Equipment Selection 1990: Proceedings of the 2nd International Symposium, Calgary, Alberta, 7-9 November 1990. Ed. by Raj K. Singhal & Marion Vavra. (Illus.). 543p. (C). 1990. text 168.00 (*90-6191-159-1*, Pub. by A A Balkema) Ashgate Pub Co.

Mine Planning & Equipment Selection 1997: Proceedings of the Sixth International Symposium, Ostrava, Czech Republic, 3-6 September 1997. Ed. by V. Strakos et al. LC 99-496369. (Illus.). 1038p. (C). 1997. text 146.00 (*90-5410-915-7*, Pub. by A A Balkema) Ashgate Pub Co.

***Mine Planning & Equipment Selection 1998 7th Intl.** Singhal. 830p. 1998. 122.00 (*90-5809-011-6*) Ashgate Pub Co.

Mine Plant. Benjamin F. Tillson. LC 38-31588. (Rocky Mountain Fund Ser.). 399p. reprint ed. pap. 123.70 (*0-608-14265-4*, 202220600025) Bks Demand.

Mine Run Campaign. Martin Graham & George Skoch. (Illus.). 130p. 1987. 19.95 (*0-930919-48-3*) H E Howard.

Mine Safety (Select Papers) Proceedings of the 27th International Conference on Safety in Mines Research Institute, New Delhi, 20-22 February 1997. Ed. by Bharat B. Dhar & B. C. Bhowmick. (Illus.). 624p. (C). 1997. text 162.00 (*90-5410-738-3*, Pub. by A A Balkema) Ashgate Pub Co.

***Mine Science & Technology 1999: Proceedings of the '99 International Symposium, Beijing, 29-31 August 1999.** Ed. by Heping Xie & Tad S. Golosinski. (Illus.). 834p. 1999. text 120.00 (*90-5809-067-1*, Pub. by A A Balkema) Ashgate Pub Co.

Mine Simulation: Proceedings of the First International Symposium on Mine Simulation Via the Internet, 2-13 December 1996. G. N. Panagiotou & J. R. Sturgul. (Illus.). 200p. (C). 1997. text 110.00 incl. cd-rom (*90-5410-863-0*, Pub. by A A Balkema) Ashgate Pub Co.

Mine Site Concept in Seabed Mining. (Seabed Minerals Ser.: Vol. 4). 150p. 1987. lib. bdg. 83.00 (*0-86010-396-X*) G & T Inc.

Mine Subsidence. fac. ed. Ed. by Madan M. Singh. LC 86-61784. (Illus.). 156p. 1986. reprint ed. pap. 48.40 (*0-7837-7848-1*, 204760700007) Bks Demand.

Mine to Make a Mine: Financing the Colorado Mining Industry, 1859-1902. Joseph E. King. LC 76-51655. 240p. 1977. 29.95 (*0-89096-034-8*) Tex A&M Univ Pr.

Mine to Take. Dara Joy. 400p. 1998. mass mkt. 5.99 (*0-8439-4446-3*, Leisure Bks) Dorchester Pub Co.

***Mine to Win: An Anthology of Heroic Poems.** Ed. by Kimberly Kanigel. 128p. 2000. 14.95 (*0-9676995-0-9*) Ideal Studios.

Mine Ventilation: Second Us-addendum. Pierre F. Mousset-Jones. 1985. 104.00 (*90-6191-648-8*) Ashgate Pub Co.

Mine Ventilation: U. S. Mine Ventilation Symposium, Reno, Nevada, 2nd, 23-25 September 1985, Vol. 1. Ed. by Pierre F. Mousset-Jones. (C). 1985. text 188.00 (*90-6191-611-9*, Pub. by A A Balkema) Ashgate Pub Co.

Mine Ventilation & Air Conditioning. 3rd ed. Howard L. Hartman. LC 97-547. 752p. 1997. 98.95 (*0-471-11635-1*) Wiley.

Mine Ventilation Engineering. fac. ed. C. J. Hall. LC 80-70415. (Illus.). 352p. 1981. reprint ed. pap. 109.20 (*0-7837-7859-7*, 204761800007) Bks Demand.

Mine Ventilation Symposium: Proceedings of the 1st, March 29-31, 1982, the University of Alabama, University (Tuscaloosa), Alabama. fac. ed. Mine Ventilation Symposium Staff. Ed. by Howard L. Hartman. LC 82-71996. (Illus.). 324p. 1982. reprint ed. pap. 100.50 (*0-7837-7857-0*, 204761600007) Bks Demand.

Mine Warfare at Sea. Howard S. Levie. 236p. (C). 1992. lib. bdg. 111.00 (*0-7923-1526-X*) Kluwer Academic.

Mine Warfare in the Russo-Soviet Navy. Jeffrey K. Bray. (Illus.). 200p. (Orig.). 1996. pap. 34.80 (*0-89412-253-3*, M-22) Aegean Park Pr.

Mine Warfare Technology. Louis Gerken. LC 89-2. (Illus.). 300p. (C). 1989. 50.00 (*0-9617163-1-2*) Amer Scientific.

Mine Waste Management. Richard D. Ellison. Ed. by Ian P. G. Hutchison. 672p. 1992. boxed set 136.95 (*0-87371-746-5*) CRC Pr.

Mine Water Pollution, No. 2. Ed. by P. E. Odendaal. (Water Science & Technology Ser.: Vol. 15). (Illus.). 180p. 1983. pap. 44.00 (*0-08-030423-0*, Pergamon Pr) Elsevier.

Mine Will, Said John. rev. ed. Helen V. Griffith. LC 91-32476. (Illus.). 32p. (J). (ps-3). 1980. lib. bdg. 13.93 (*0-688-10958-6*, Wm Morrow) Morrow Avon.

Mine with the Iron Door. Harold Bell Wright. 352p. Date not set. 25.95 (*0-8488-2508-X*) Amereon Ltd.

Mine with the Iron Door: A Romance. Harold Bell Wright. (Collected Works of Harold Bell Wright). 338p. 1999. reprint ed. lib. bdg. 98.00 (*1-58201-891-X*) Classic Bks.

Mine Work: A Novel. Jim Davidson. LC 99-6251. 312p. 1999. pap. 17.95 (*0-87421-275-8*) Utah St U Pr.

Mine Your Own Business. Casey Cannon & Don Meyer. LC 97-38980. 256p. (C). 1997. pap. text 41.99 (*0-13-890757-9*) P-H.

Minear, Descendants of John Minear (1732-1781) C. J. Maxwell. 232p. 1993. reprint ed. pap. 36.50 (*0-8328-3244-8*); reprint ed. lib. bdg. 46.50 (*0-8328-3243-X*) Higginson Bk Co.

Mined It! A Fairy Tale with Mineral Content. Jeanette M. Harris & Peter W. Harben. 60p. (J). (gr. 1-12). 1992. pap. text 12.98 (*0-9632303-0-1*) Butternut Bks.

Mined-Land Rehabilitation. Dennis L. Law. 198p. (C). 1984. text 39.95 (*0-442-25987-5*) Krieger.

Minefields in the Way: Growing Up in America. Kathie L. Lauderdale et al. LC 98-73820. (Illus.). 112p. 1998. pap. 19.95 (*1-879774-17-8*) ICA Pub Co.

Minefields in Their Hearts: The Mental Health of Children in War & Communal Violence. Ed. by Roberta J. Apfel & Bennett Simon. LC 96-10976. 256p. 1996. 37.50 (*0-300-06570-1*) Yale U Pr.

***Minehead District - A Concise Account of the Geology: Geological Memoir for 1:50 000 Sheet 278 & Part of Sheet 294 (England & Wales)** R. A. Edwards. (British Geological Survey Ser.). (Illus.). xii, 128p. 1999. 70.00 (*0-11-884544-6*, Pub. by Statnry Office) Balogh.

Mineheads. Hilla Becher & Bernd Becher. LC 97-72280. (Illus.). 180p. 1997. 75.00 (*0-262-02430-6*) MIT Pr.

***Minehunters, Patrol Boats & Logistics.** Lema Publications Staff. 1999. pap. text 16.95 (*84-95323-14-1*) LEMA.

Mineola Twins. Paula Vogel. 1998. pap. 5.25 (*0-8222-1622-1*) Dramatists Play.

Miner. Natsume Soseki, pseud. Tr. by Jay Rubin from JPN. LC 87-26711. 200p. 1988. 32.50 (*0-8047-1460-6*) Stanford U Pr.

***Miner, Preacher, Doctor, Teacher: A Turn-of-the-19th-Century Odyssey from Ann Arbor, Michigan to Ketchikan, Alaska, to a Pioneering Medical Career in Oakland, California.** Frederic M. Loomis. (Illus.). 128p. 2000. pap. 19.50 (*0-9625429-9-7*, Pub. by Hardscratch Pr) Partners-West.

Miner Was a Bishop: The Pioneer Years of Patrick Manogue in California & Nevada, 1854-1895. William Breault. (Illus.). 158p. 1988. pap. 20.00 (*0-910845-34-4*, 536) Landmark Ent.

Mineral- und Thermalgewasser - Allgemeine Balneogeologie, Band 7. Gert Michel. (Lehrbuch der Hydrogeologie Ser.). xii, 397p. 1998. 88.00 (*3-443-01011-3*, Pub. by Gebruder Borntraeger) Balogh.

Mineral Absorption in the Monogastric GI Tract: Chemical, Nutritional, & Physiological Aspects. Ed. by F. R. Dintzis & J. A. Laszlo. (Advances in Experimental Medicine & Biology Ser.). (Illus.). 208p. 1989. 69.50 (*0-306-43200-5*, Plenum Trade) Perseus Pubng.

Mineral Admixtures. 88p. 1993. 32.50 (*0-685-72218-6*, C-22BOW6) ACI.

Mineral & Energy Resources. 2nd ed. Douglas G. Brookins. (C). 1996. 44.00 (*0-02-315081-5*, Macmillan Coll) P-H.

Mineral & Energy Resources: Current Status & Future Trends. Kula C. Misra. (Studies in Geology). (Illus.). 276p. (Orig.). (C). 1986. pap. text 15.00 (*0-910249-13-X*) U of Tenn Geo.

Mineral & Metal Neurotoxicology. Ed. by Masayuki Yasui et al. LC 96-5735. 480p. 1996. boxed set 169.95 (*0-8493-7664-5*) CRC Pr.

Mineral & Nuclear Fuels of the Indian Subcontinent & Burma. J. Coggin Brown & A. K. Key. 1976. 38.00 (*0-19-560172-6*) OUP.

Mineral & Rock Deformation: Laboratory Studies - The Paterson Volume. Ed. by Bruce E. Hobbs & H. C. Heard. (Geophysical Monograph Ser.: Vol. 36). 352p. 1986. 40.00 (*0-87590-062-3*) Am Geophysical.

Mineral & Rock Resources of Ghana. Kesse. 1985. 175.00 (*90-6191-622-4*) Ashgate Pub Co.

Mineral & Rock Resources of Ghana. G. O. Kesse. 624p. (C). 1985. text 162.00 (*90-6191-589-9*, Pub. by A A Balkema) Ashgate Pub Co.

Mineral Aspects of Dentistry. F. C. Driessens. (Monographs in Oral Science: Vol. 10). (Illus.). xvi, 216p. 1982. 128.75 (*3-8055-3469-8*) S Karger.

Mineral Bioprocessing: Proceedings of the Conference Mineral Bioprocessing Held in Santa Barbara, California, June 16-22, 1991. Ed. by Ross W. Smith & Manoranjan Misra. LC 91-51127. (Illus.). 510p. 1991. pap. 158.10 (*0-608-04887-9*, 206557900004) Bks Demand.

Mineral Classification of Soils. Ed. by James A. Kittrick. (Special Publications: No. 16). 178p. 1985. pap. 10.50 (*0-89118-777-4*) Soil Sci Soc Am.

Mineral Collector's Handbook. Barry Krause. (Illus.). 192p. 1998. pap. 14.95 (*0-8069-0873-4*) Sterling.

Mineral Commodity Summaries. 1994. lib. bdg. 256.00 (*0-8490-5795-7*) Gordon Pr.

***Mineral Commodity Summaries, 1998.** 199p. 1998. per. 16.00 (*0-16-061636-0*) USGPO.

Mineral Commodity Summaries, 1996. 195p. (Orig.). (C). 1996. pap. text 40.00 (*0-7881-3630-5*) DIANE Pub.

Mineral Commodity Summaries, 1995. 204p. 1995. per. 15.00 (*0-16-061629-8*) USGPO.

Mineral Cycling in Southeastern Ecosystems: Proceedings. Ed. by Fred G. Howell et al. LC 75-33463. (ERDA Symposium Ser.). 920p. 1975. pap. 31.00 (*0-87079-022-6*, CONF-740513); fiche 9.00 (*0-87079-276-8*, CONF-740513) DOE.

Mineral Deposits: From Their Origin to Their Environmental Impacts: Proceedings: Biennial SGA Meeting (3d: 1995: Prague, Czech Republic) Bohdan Kribek & Karel Zak. Ed. by Jan Pasava. (Illus.). 1048p. (C). 1995. text 194.00 (*90-5410-550-X*, TN272, Pub. by A A Balkema) Ashgate Pub Co.

***Mineral Deposits: Proceedings of the 5th Biennial SGA Meeting & IAGOD 10th Quadrennial Symposium, London, August 1999, 2 vols.** Ed. by Christopher Stanley. (Illus.). 1500p. 1999. text 137.50 (*90-5809-068-X*) A A Balkema.

An Asterisk (*) at the beginning of an entry indicates that the title is appearing for the first time.

Mineral Deposits: Research & Exploration - Where Do They Meet? Proceedings of the 4th Biennial SGA Meeting, Turku, Finland, 11-13 August 1997. Ed. by Heikki Papunen. (Illus.). 1008p. (C). 1997. text 162.00 (*90-5410-889-4*, Pub. by A A Balkema) Ashgate Pub Co.

Mineral Deposits & Geology of Central Colorado. Ed. by Bryant. (IGC Field Trip Guidebooks Ser.). 80p. 1989. 21.00 (*0-87590-645-1*, T129) Am Geophysical.

Mineral Deposits & the Evolution of the Biosphere: Report of the Dahlem Workshop. Ed. by H. D. Holland & M. Schidlowski. (Dahlem Workshop Reports: Vol. 3). (Illus.). 333p. 1982. 29.00 (*0-387-11328-2*) Spr-Verlag.

Mineral Deposits of Europe Vol. 2: Southeast Europe. Ed. by F. W. Dunning et al. 304p. 1982. text 98.00 (*0-900488-63-8*) IMM-North Am.

Mineral Deposits of the Alps & of the Alpine Epoch in Europe. Ed. by H. J. Schneider. (Special Publications of the Society for General Microbiology: No. 3). (Illus.). 410p. 1983. 91.95 (*0-387-12231-1*) Spr-Verlag.

Mineral Deposits of the Erzgebirge/Krusne Hory: Germany/Czech Republic. Reviews & Results of Recent Investigations. Dietrich D. Klemm. Ed. by Kurt Von Gehlen. LC 95-120401. (Monograph Series on Mineral Deposits: No. 31). vii, 230p. 1994. 76.00 (*3-443-12031-8*, Pub. by Gebruder Borntraeger) Balogh.

Mineral Deposits of the World: Bores, Industrial Minerals, & Rocks. Ed. by Mirko Vanecek. LC 93-3432. (Developments in Economic Geology Ser.: Vol. 28). 538p. 1994. 247.75 (*0-444-98667-7*) Elsevier.

Mineral Deposits Within the European Community. Ed. by J. Boissonnas & P. Omenetto. (Special Publications of the Society for General Microbiology). (Illus.). 530p. 1988. 161.00 (*0-387-18201-2*) Spr-Verlag.

Mineral Development & Land Use. (Mineral Law Ser.). 1995. student ed., ring bd. 125.00 (*0-929047-55-9*) Rocky Mtn Mineral Law Found.

Mineral Development in Latin America. (Mineral Law Ser.). 600p. 1997. wbk. ed. 125.00 (*0-929047-70-2*) Rocky Mtn Mineral Law Found.

Mineral Development in the 80s: Prospects & Problems. British-North American Committee. LC 76-53628. 64p. 1977. 3.00 (*0-902594-29-X*) Natl Planning.

Mineral Economics. Sinha & Sharma. (C). 1991. 12.00 (*81-204-0331-2*, Pub. by Oxford IBH) S Asia.

Mineral Economy of Mexico. 1994. lib. bdg. 250.00 (*0-8490-9065-2*) Gordon Pr.

Mineral Economy of Mexico. 1996. lib. bdg. 250.75 (*0-8490-5995-X*) Gordon Pr.

Mineral, Energy & Ground-Water Resources of San Juan County, Utah. Robert W. Gloyn et al. LC 96-622170. (Special Study of the Utah Geological Survey Ser.: No. 86). (Illus.). 39p. (Orig.). 1995. pap. 10.00 (*1-55791-205-X*, SS-86) Utah Geological Survey.

Mineral Energy Resource Evaluation: Probabilistic Methods. F. P. Agterberg. write for info. (*0-318-56737-7*) Elsevier.

Mineral Exploration Decisions, a Guide to Economic Analysis & Modeling. Deverle P. Harris. LC 89-36771. 464p. 1990. 175.00 (*0-471-51017-3*) Wiley.

Mineral Exploration, Mining, & Processing Patents, 1979. fac. ed. Oliver S. North. LC 80-66760. (Illus.). 143p. 1980. reprint ed. pap. 44.40 (*0-7837-7850-3*, 204760900007) Bks Demand.

Mineral Exploration, Mining, & Processing Patents, 1980. fac. ed. Oliver S. North. LC 66-23725. (Illus.). 141p. 1982. reprint ed. pap. 43.80 (*0-7837-7851-1*, 204761000007) Bks Demand.

Mineral Facts & Problems: A Complete Reference, 2 vols., Set. 1991. lib. bdg. 600.00 (*0-8490-4357-3*) Gordon Pr.

Mineral Fertilizer Production & the Environment: A Guide to Reducing the Environmental Impact of Fertilizer Production. (Technical Reports: No. 26). 150p. 1997. pap. 40.00 (*92-807-1640-9*) UN.

Mineral Fibers & Health. F. D. Liddell & Klara Miller. (Illus.). 376p. 1991. lib. bdg. 229.00 (*0-8493-6646-1*, RC1231) CRC Pr.

*__Mineral Fillers in Thermoplastics I: Raw Materials & Processing.__ Ed. by J. Jancar. (Illus.). 250p. 1998. 179.00 (*3-540-64621-3*) Spr-Verlag.

Mineral Foreign Trade of the United States in the 20th Century: A Study in Mineral Economics. Bruce C. Netschert. Ed. by Stuart Bruchey. LC 76-39836. (Nineteen Seventy-Seven Dissertations Ser.). (Illus.). 1977. lib. bdg. 47.95 (*0-405-09916-9*) Ayer.

Mineral Impurities in Coal Combustion: Behavior, Problems, & Remedial Measures. Erich Raask. LC 83-26400. (Illus.). 467p. 1985. 132.00 (*0-89116-362-X*) Hemisp Pub.

Mineral Industries of Asia & the Pacific. (Illus.). 380p. (Orig.). (C). 1994. pap. text 65.00 (*0-7881-0507-8*) DIANE Pub.

Mineral Industries of Asia & the Pacific, 2 vols. (Orig.). 1994. lib. bdg. 395.00 (*0-8490-8575-6*) Gordon Pr.

Mineral Industries of Europe & Central Eurasia, 2 vols., Set. 1994. lib. bdg. 555.99 (*0-8490-5792-2*) Gordon Pr.

Mineral Industries of Europe & U. S. S. R. 1994. lib. bdg. 295.95 (*0-8490-9044-X*) Gordon Pr.

Mineral Industries of Latin America. 1991. lib. bdg. 250.00 (*0-8490-4365-4*) Gordon Pr.

Mineral Industries of Latin America & Canada. 1994. lib. bdg. 275.95 (*0-8490-9043-1*) Gordon Pr.

Mineral Industries of Latin America & Canada, 2 vols. 1994. lib. bdg. 395.00 (*0-8490-8576-4*) Gordon Pr.

Mineral Industries of the Middle East. (Illus.). 125p. (Orig.). (C). 1994. pap. text 55.00 (*0-7881-0578-7*) DIANE Pub.

Mineral Industry of the United States: A State-by-State Survey, 2 vols., Set. (Metals & Minerals Ser.). 1993. lib. bdg. 625.95 (*0-8490-9017-2*) Gordon Pr.

Mineral Investment Conditions in Selected Countries of the Asia-Pacific Region. (ST-ESCAP Ser.: No. 1197). 361p. 85.00 (*92-1-119666-3*) UN.

Mineral Land Surveying. James Underhill. (Illus.). 218p. 1979. reprint ed. 50.00 (*0-910845-05-0*, 619) Landmark Ent.

Mineral Law. rev. ed. Terry S. Maley. (Illus.). 936p. 1996. pap. 65.00 (*0-940949-04-0*) Mineral Pubns.

Mineral Law, Teacher's Manual to Accompany Cases & Materials On. Barlow Burke, Jr. et al. (American Casebook Ser.). 175p. (C). 1995. pap. text, teacher ed. write for info. (*0-314-04809-X*) West Pub.

Mineral Licks, Geophagy, & Biogeochemistry of North American Ungulates. Robert L. Jones & Harold C. Hanson. LC 84-10849. (Illus.). 311p. 1985. reprint ed. pap. 96.50 (*0-608-00178-3*, 206096000006) Bks Demand.

Mineral Matter & Ash in Coal. Ed. by Karl S. Vorres. LC 86-3556. (ACS Symposium Ser.: Vol. 301). 552p. 1986. reprint ed. pap. 171.20 (*0-608-03847-4*, 206429400008) Bks Demand.

Mineral Metabolism: An Advanced Treatise, 3 vols. Ed. by C. L. Comar & Felix Bronner. Incl. Vol. 1, Pt. A. Principles, Processes & Systems. 1960. 72.00 (*0-12-183201-5*); Vol. 1, Pt. B. Principles, Processes & Systems. 1961. 84.00 (*0-12-183241-4*); Vol. 2, Pt. A. Elements. 1964. 94.00 (*0-12-183202-3*); Vol. 2, Pt. B. Elements. 1962. 88.00 (*0-12-183242-2*); Vol. 3. Supplementary Volume. 1969. 84.00 (*0-12-183250-3*); 342.00 (*0-685-00058-3*) Acad Pr.

Mineral Mine Safety Laws of Virginia: 1998 Edition. Ed. by Christine Giesecke. LC 99-188688. 1998. pap. write for info. (*0-327-06099-9*, 35495-13) LEXIS Pub.

*__Mineral Mine Safety Laws of Virginia: 1999 Edition.__ 50p. 1999. pap. 10.00 (*0-327-08952-0*, 3549) LEXIS Pub.

Mineral Nutrients in Tropical Forests & Savannah Ecosystems. J. Proctor. 1989. 125.00 (*0-632-02559-X*) Blackwell Sci.

Mineral Nutrition of Conifer Seedlings. Ed. by R. Van Den Driessche. 288p. 1990. lib. bdg. 239.00 (*0-8493-5971-6*, QP519) CRC Pr.

Mineral Nutrition of Crops: Fundamental Mechanisms & Implications. Ed. by Zdenko Rengel. LC 98-48697. (Illus.). 399p. (C). 1999. lib. bdg. 149.95 (*1-56022-880-6*, Food Products) Haworth Pr.

Mineral Nutrition of Food Legumes in Thailand, with Particular Reference to Micronutrients. Ed. by R. W. Bell et al. 1990. pap. 60.00 (*1-86320-014-2*, Pub. by ACIAR) St Mut.

Mineral Nutrition of Fruit Crops. T. K. Bose & S. K. Mitra. 850p. (C). 1986. 118.00 (*81-85109-44-3*, Pub. by Naya Prokash) S Asia.

Mineral Nutrition of Higher Plants. 2nd ed. Horst Marschner. (Illus.). 912p. 1995. pap. text 62.00 (*0-12-473543-6*) Acad Pr.

Mineral Nutrition of Livestock. 3rd ed. Eric J. Underwood & N. Suttle. LC 99-11802. 624p. 2000. text 140.00 (*0-85199-128-9*) OUP.

Mineral Nutrition of Trees: A Symposium. Duke University, School of Forestry Staff. LC SD0390.D85. (Duke University, School of Forestry Bulletin Ser.: No. 15). (Illus.). 200p. reprint ed. pap. 62.00 (*0-7837-6042-6*, 204585500008) Bks Demand.

*__Mineral Palace.__ Heidi Julavits. LC 00-24221. (Illus.). 400p. 2000. 23.95 (*0-399-14622-9*) Putnam Pub Group.

Mineral Physics - Point Defects in Minerals, Vol. 1. Ed. by R. N. Schock. (Geophysical Monograph Ser.: Vol. 31). 240p. 1985. 25.00 (*0-87590-056-9*) Am Geophysical.

Mineral Physics & Crystallography: A Handbook of Physical Constants. Ed. by T. J. Ahrens. LC 95-3663. (AGU Reference Shelf Ser.: Vol. 2). 400p. 1995. 65.00 (*0-87590-852-7*) Am Geophysical.

Mineral Position of the United States, 1975-2000. Eugene N. Cameron. LC 72-7983. 181p. 1973. reprint ed. pap. 56.20 (*0-608-01924-0*, 206257900003) Bks Demand.

Mineral Processing. G. Tarjan. (C). 1986. 210.00 (*963-05-4143-2*, Pub. by Akade Kiado) St Mut.

Mineral Processing, Vol. 2. Ghosh Tarjan. 782p. (C). 1986. 500.00 (*0-7855-4999-4*, Pub. by Collets) St Mut.

Mineral Processing: Environment, Health & Safety, 11. B. A. Hancock & M. R. L. Pan. (Illus.). 448p. write for info. (*0-87339-436-4*) Minerals Metals.

Mineral Processing & the Environment. G. P. Gallios & K. A. Matis. LC 98-20974. (NATO Science Ser.). 1998. 195.00 (*0-7923-5085-5*) Kluwer Academic.

Mineral Processing at a Crossroads: Problems & Prospects. B. A. Wills & R. W. Barley. 1986. text 218.00 (*90-247-3410-X*) Kluwer Academic.

Mineral Processing Design. Ed. by Baki Yarar & Z. M. Dogan. 1987. text 233.00 (*90-247-3472-X*) Kluwer Academic.

Mineral Processing in ASEAN. Bruce McKern. Ed. by Praipol Koomsup. 1988. pap. text 34.95 (*0-04-330384-6*, Pub. by Allen & Unwin Pty) Paul & Co Pubs.

Mineral Processing Lab Manual. lab manual ed. 70.00 (*0-87849-082-5*, Pub. by Trans T Pub) Enfield Pubs NH.

Mineral Processing Plant Design. Ed. by Andrew L. Mular & Roshan B. Bhappu. LC 77-26531. 897p. reprint ed. pap. 200.00 (*0-608-14285-9*, 201742000005) Bks Demand.

Mineral Processing Plant Design. 2nd ed. Mineral Processing Plant Design Symposium Staff. Ed. by Andrew L. Mular & Roshan B. Bhappu. LC 79-57345. 960p. reprint ed. pap. 200.00 (*0-8357-3418-8*, 203967500013) Bks Demand.

Mineral Processing Technology. Wills. 1981. text 66.00 (*0-08-027322-X*, Pergamon Pr) Elsevier.

Mineral Processing Technology. 3rd ed. Willis. (International Series on Materials Science & Technology). 1985. text 73.00 (*0-08-031160-1*, Pergamon Pr) Elsevier.

*__Mineral Processing Technology.__ 7th ed. Wills. 2000. pap. 66.95 (*0-7506-4450-8*) Buttrwrth-Heinemann.

Mineral Processing Technology: An Introduction to the Practical Aspects of Ore Treatment & Mineral Recovery. B. A. Wills. LC 80-41698. (International Series on Materials Science & Technology: Vol. 29). (Illus.). 450p. 1981. pap. text 20.00 (*0-08-027323-8*, Pergamon Pr) Elsevier.

Mineral Processing Technology: An Introduction to the Practical Aspects of Ore Treatment & Mineral Recovery. 2nd ed. B. A. Wills. LC 80-41698. (International Series on Materials Science & Technology: Vol. 29). (Illus.). 450p. 1985. pap. text 21.00 (*0-08-031159-8*, Pergamon Pr) Elsevier.

Mineral Processing Technology: An Introduction to the Practical Aspects of Ore Treatment & Mineral Recovery. 6th ed. B. A. Wills. LC 97-15498. 272p. 2000. pap. text 56.95 (*0-7506-2838-3*) Buttrwrth-Heinemann.

Mineral Production Costs Vol. I: Analysis & Mangement. Bruce Cavender. LC 98-54796. 192p. 1999. 69.00 (*0-87335-174-6*, 174-6) SMM&E Inc.

Mineral Profile of the Muslim World. K. M. Aslam. LC 95-930659. 602p. 1995. write for info. (*969-487-007-0*) Buttrwrth-Heinemann.

Mineral Range Railroad. (Copper Country Local History Ser.: Vol. 43). (Illus.). 128p. 1993. 3.00 (*0-942363-42-6*) C J Monette.

Mineral Recognition. Iris Vanders & Paul F. Kerr. LC 66-25223. 382p. reprint ed. pap. 118.50 (*0-608-15377-X*, 205635400060) Bks Demand.

Mineral Reference Manual. (C). (gr. 13). 1990. text 20.95 (*0-412-07811-2*) Chapman & Hall.

Mineral Reference Manual. Ernest H. Nickel. 1990. pap. 16.95 (*0-442-00344-7*) Chapman & Hall.

Mineral Resource Evaluation II: Methods & Case Histories, No. 2. Ed. by M. K. Whateley & P. K. Harvey. (Geological Society Special Publication Ser.: No. 79). (Illus.). 272p. 1994. 108.00 (*1-897799-06-3*, 298, Pub. by Geol Soc Pub Hse) AAPG.

Mineral Resource Management by Personal Computer. Ed. by Ta M. Li et al. LC 86-63422. 180p. (Orig.). reprint ed. pap. 55.80 (*0-8357-2566-9*, 204025600015) Bks Demand.

Mineral Resources. W. H. Dennen. (Illus.). 380p. (C). 1989. 85.00 (*0-8448-1569-1*) Taylor & Francis.

Mineral Resources: A System Analytical & Functional Approach. L. Kapolyi. LC 87-17360. (Illus.). xvi, 316p. 1987. 93.95 (*0-387-82008-6*) Spr-Verlag.

Mineral Resources: Economics & the Environment. Stephen E. Kesler. 392p. (C). 1994. 48.80 (*0-02-362842-1*, Macmillan Coll) P-H.

Mineral Resources: Federal Coal-Leasing Program Needs Strengthening. (Illus.). 118p. (Orig.). (C). 1995. pap. text 35.00 (*0-7881-1682-7*) DIANE Pub.

Mineral Resources A-Z. Robert L. Bates. LC 90-34301. 128p. (YA). (gr. 6 up). 1991. lib. bdg. 20.95 (*0-89490-244-X*) Enslow Pubs.

Mineral Resources Appraisal: Mineral Endowment, Resources & Potential Supply: Concepts, Methods & Cases. DeVerle P. Harris. LC 83-11445. (Oxford Geological Science Ser.). (Illus.). (C). 1984. 72.00 (*0-19-854456-1*) OUP.

Mineral Resources Development & the Environment. (ST-ESCAP Ser.: No. 1192). 163p. 45.00 (*92-1-119670-1*) UN.

Mineral Resources' Extraction, Environmental Protection & Land-Use Planning in the Industrial & Developing Countries. Ed. by P. Arndt & G. W. Luettig. x, 338p. (C). 1987. pap. text 59.00 (*3-510-65132-4*, Pub. by E Schweizerbartsche) Balogh.

Mineral Resources of Africa. A. Williams Postel. (African Handbooks Ser.: Vol. 2). (Illus.). iv, 106p. 1943. pap. 10.00 (*0-686-24091-X*) U Museum Pubns.

Mineral Resources of China. (CHI & ENG.). 391p. 1994. 205.00 (*7-80090-091-6*, Pub. by HUWEI Cnslts) Am Overseas Bk Co.

Mineral Resources of Mesa County: A Model Study. abr. ed. Stephen D. Schwochow. (Resource Ser.: No. 2). (Illus.). 110p. (Orig.). 1978. pap. 10.00 (*1-884216-25-0*) Colo Geol Survey.

Mineral Resources of South Texas: Region Served Through the Port of Corpus Christi. R. A. Maxwell. (Reports of Investigations: RI 43). (Illus.). 140p. 1962. pap. 3.50 (*0-686-29333-9*) Bur Econ Geology.

Mineral Resources of the Pacific Rim: Proceedings of the Special Programming by the Minerals Resource Management Committee During the First International SME-AIME Fall Meeting, Honolulu, Hawaii, September 5-9, 1982. Ed. by Ta M. Li et al. LC 82-71990. (Illus.). 237p. reprint ed. pap. 73.50 (*0-7837-1217-0*, 204174800023) Bks Demand.

Mineral Resources of the State of New York. David H. Newland. 315p. 1993. reprint ed. lib. bdg. 89.00 (*0-7812-5150-8*) Rprt Serv.

Mineral Resources Potential of Antarctica. Ed. by G. A. Dreschhoff & John F. Splettstoesser. (Antarctic Research Ser.: No. 51). 327p. 1990. 53.00 (*0-87590-174-3*) Am Geophysical.

Mineral Resources Potential of the Earth: Proceedings of the 2nd International Symposium, Held in Hannover, Federal Republic of Germany, at the Federal Institute for Geosciences & Mineral Resources, April 18-20, 1979. Ed. by F. Bender. (Illus.). v, 156p. 1980. pap. text 32.00 (*3-510-65093-X*, Pub. by E Schweizerbartsche) Balogh.

Mineral Resources Technician. (Career Examination Ser.: C-3640). pap. 29.95 (*0-8373-3640-6*) Nat Learn.

Mineral-Rock Handbook. Paul D. Proctor et al. LC 89-205367. (Illus.). 272p. (Orig.). 1989. lib. bdg. 14.95 (*0-9625042-0-3*) Paulmar.

*__Mineral Royalties: Royalties in the Western States & in Major Mineral-Producing Countries.__ Robert W. Wilson. 66p. (C). 1999. reprint ed. pap. text 20.00 (*0-7881-8241-2*) DIANE Pub.

Mineral Scale Formation & Inhibition: Proceedings of an American Chemical Society Symposium in Washington, D.C., August 21-26, 1994. Z. Amjad. (Illus.). 368p. (C). 1996. text 125.00 (*0-306-45195-6*, Kluwer Plenum) Kluwer Academic.

Mineral Severance Taxes in Western States: Economic, Legal, & Policy Considerations, Vol. 75, No. 3. Sandra L. Blackstone. Ed. by Jon W. Raese. LC 80-29698. (Colorado School of Mines Quarterly Ser.). (Illus.). 39p. 1981. pap. text 8.00 (*0-317-06078-3*) Colo Sch Mines.

Mineral Sisters Play Hide-&-Seek. Lynne Hudgins. (Nature's Natives Ser.). 24p. (J). (gr. 3-6). 1996. text 3.50 (*1-889203-03-3*) L Hudgins.

Mineral Spectroscopy: A Tribute to Roger G. Burns. Ed. by M. D. Dyar et al. LC 96-77227. (Special Publication: No. 5). (Illus.). xiv, 400p. (C). 1996. write for info. (*0-941809-04-8*) Geochemical Soc.

*__Mineral Supplement.__ 1999. ring bd. 45.00 (*1-893997-03-0*) Am Oil Chemists.

Mineral Title Examination III, 1. (Mineral Law Ser.). 738p. 1992. student ed. 125.00 (*0-929047-29-X*) Rocky Mtn Mineral Law Found.

Mineral-Water Interface Geochemistry. Ed. by M. F. Hochella, Jr. & Art F. White. (Reviews in Mineralogy Ser.: Vol. 23). 1990. reprint ed. per. 36.00 (*0-939950-28-6*) Mineralogical Soc.

*__Mineral-Water Interfacial Reactions: Kinetics & Mechanisms.__ Donald L. Sparks et al. LC 98-34534. (ACS Symposium Ser.: No. 715). (Illus.). 448p. 1998. text 135.00 (*0-8412-3593-7*, Pub. by Am Chemical) OUP.

Mineral Wealth & Economic Development. Ed. by John E. Tilton. LC 91-46042. 121p. 1992. pap. text 22.50 (*0-915707-62-4*) Resources Future.

Mineral Wealth of Saudia Arabia. Christopher Spencer & Octave Farra. 128p. (C). 1995. 72.00 (*0-907151-13-2*, Pub. by IMMEL Pubng) St Mut.

*__Mineral Wealth of the Ocean: A Treatise on Distribution, Origin, Exploration, Mining & Management of Sea Floor Non-Living Resources.__ Anil K. Ghosh & Ranadhir Mukhopadhyay. (Illus.). 249p. (C). 1999. text 75.00 (*90-5410-797-9*, Pub. by A A Balkema) Ashgate Pub Co.

Mineral Yearbook, 3 vols. 1997. lib. bdg. 999.75 (*0-8490-6070-2*) Gordon Pr.

Minerale: Bestimmen Nach Aeusseren Kennzeichen. R. H. Hochleitner et al. vi, 390p. 1996. 59.00 (*3-510-65164-2*, Pub. by E Schweizerbartsche) Balogh.

*__Mineralization in Natural & Synthetic Biomaterials Vol. 599: Materials Research Society Symposium Proceedings.__ Ed. by P. Li et al. (Materials Research Society Symposium Proceedings Ser.). 2000. text 86.00 (*1-55899-507-2*) Materials Res.

Mineralization in Silicic Calderas: Questa, New Mexico, & San Juan Mountains, Colorado. Ed. by Bethke. (IGC Field Trip Guidebooks Ser.). 88p. 1989. 13.00 (*0-87590-654-0*, T320) Am Geophysical.

Mineralocorticoids & Hypertension. K. A. Meurer. Ed. by W. Kaufman et al. (International Boehringer Mannheim Symposia Ser.). (Illus.). 225p. 1983. 56.95 (*0-387-12391-1*) Spr-Verlag.

Mineralogical Applications of Crystal Field Theory. 2nd ed. Roger G. Burns. (Cambridge Topics in Mineral Physics & Chemistry Ser.: No. 5). (Illus.). 575p. (C). 1993. text 89.95 (*0-521-43077-1*) Cambridge U Pr.

Mineralogical Record Index, 1970-1983, Vols. 1-14. Ed. by Friends of Mineralogy Staff. (Illus.). 246p. (Orig.). 1985. pap. text 21.00 (*0-9614396-1-0*) Friends Mineralogy.

Mineralogie. 1995. 41.95 (*0-387-56680-5*) Spr-Verlag.

Mineralogy. Hibbard. 2001. 69.25 (*0-07-234572-1*) McGraw.

Mineralogy. Perkins. LC 97-36445. 484p. (C). 1997. 86.00 (*0-02-394501-X*, Macmillan Coll) P-H.

Mineralogy. 2nd ed. R. V. Dietrich et al. LC 82-16008. 561p. (C). 1983. text 38.40 (*0-7167-1424-8*) W H Freeman.

Mineralogy see Proceedings of the 30th International Geological Congress

Mineralogy: Proceedings of the 27th International Geological Congress, Vol. 10. International Geological Congress Staff. 306p. 1984. lib. bdg. 85.00 (*90-6764-019-0*, Pub. by VSP) Coronet Bks.

Mineralogy - Applications to the Minerals Industry: Proceedings of the Paul F. Kerr Memorial Symposium, New York, New York, February 28, 1985. fac. ed. Kerr, Paul F. Memorial Symposium Staff. Ed. by Donald M. Hausen & Otto C. Kopp. LC 85-71781. (Illus.). 295p. 1985. reprint ed. pap. 91.50 (*0-7837-7864-3*, 204762200007) Bks Demand.

Mineralogy & Geology of Rare Earths in China. Zhang Peishan et al. 242p. 1996. 99.50 (*90-6764-220-7*, Pub. by VSP) Coronet Bks.

Mineralogy & Petrology see Apollo Eleven Lunar Science Conference, Jan., 1970: Proceedings

Mineralogy, Chemistry, & Physics of Tropical Soils with Variable Charge Clays. Goro Uehara & Gavin P. Gillman. (Tropical Agriculture Ser.). 1981. pap. text 57.00 (*0-89158-484-6*) Westview.

Mineralogy Dictionary, German-Russian, 2 Vols. (GER & RUS.). 633p. 1976. 49.95 (*0-8288-5742-3*, M9112) Fr & Eur.

Mineralogy of Arizona. 3rd ed. John W. Anthony et al. Ed. by Wendell E. Wilson. LC 94-18765. (Illus.). 508p. 1995. pap. 37.00 (*0-8165-1555-7*) U of Ariz Pr.

Mineralogy of Arizona. 3rd ed. John W. Anthony et al. Ed. by Wendell E. Wilson. LC 94-18765. (Illus.). 508p. 1995. 77.00 (*0-8165-1579-4*) U of Ariz Pr.

Mineralogy of Hyperagpaitic Alkaline Rocks. A. P. Khomyakov. (Illus.). 234p. 1995. text 115.00 (*0-19-854836-2*) OUP.

M

An Asterisk (*) at the beginning of an entry indicates that the title is appearing for the first time.

Mineralogy Students. 2nd ed. Maurice Hugh Battey. 1996. text 42.00 (0-582-44005-X) Addison-Wesley.

Minerals. Rupert Hochleitner. (Mini Fact Finders Ser.). 1990. pap. 4.95 (0-8120-4456-8) Barron.

Minerals. Rupert Hochleitner. 240p. 1994. pap. 14.95 (0-8120-1777-3) Barron.

Minerals. Greg H. Quinn. 32p. (J). (gr. 4-6). 1995. pap. 4.95 (0-590-48487-7) Scholastic Inc.

Minerals. George W. Robinson. LC 94-6344. (Illus.). 208p. 1994. 40.00 (0-671-88002-0) S&S Trade.

*Minerals. Jon Tillman. (Pocket Healing Bks.). (Illus.). 72p. 2000. pap. 4.95 (965-494-115-5) Astrolog Pub.

*Minerals: Nutrition & Metabolism. Donald Oberleas et al. LC 99-93616. 1999. pap. 34.95 (0-533-13086-7) Vantage.

Minerals: What Your Body Really Needs & Why. George L. Redmon. LC 99-18141. 196p. 1998. pap. 10.95 (0-89529-863-5, Avery) Penguin Putnam.

Minerals & Gems from the American Museum of Natural History. George E. Harlow & Joseph J. Peters. LC 94-10365. (Tiny Folios Ser.). (Illus.). 336p. 1995. pap. 11.95 (1-55859-273-3) Abbeville Pr.

Minerals & How to Study Them. 3rd rev. ed. Edward S. Dana. LC 49-7833. 333p. 1949. reprint ed. pap. 103.30 (0-7837-3437-9, 205775900008) Bks Demand.

Minerals & Men: An Exploration of the World of Minerals & Metals, Including Some of the Major Problems That Are Posed. 2nd ed. James M. McDivitt & Gerald Manners. LC 73-8138. xiii, 175p. 1974. pap. 15.95 (0-8018-1827-3) Resources Future.

Minerals & Metals in Ancient India, 2 vols., Set. Arun K. Biswas & Sulekha Biswas. (C). 1996. 210.00 (81-246-0048-1, Pub. by DK Pubs Ind) S Asia.

Minerals & Metals Trade in the Asia-Pacific Region. 223p. 75.00 (92-1-119664-7, E.94.II.F.28) UN.

Minerals & Metals Trade in the Asia-Pacific Region. (ST-ESCAP Ser.: No. 1247). 233p. 1995. 75.00 (0-614-08387-7) UN.

Minerals & Metals Trading. (ST - ESCAP Ser.: No. 1268). 184p. 75.00 (92-1-119672-8) UN.

Minerals & Reactions at the Atomic Scale: Transmission Electron Microscopy. Ed. by P. Buseck. (Reviews in Mineralogy Ser.: Vol. 27). 1992. per. 28.00 (0-939950-32-4) Mineralogical Soc.

*Minerals Commodity Summary, 2000. 199p. 2000. per. 24.00 (0-16-059201-1) USGPO.

Minerals, Energy & Economic Development in China. James P. Dorian. (Illus.). 304p. 1994. text 75.00 (0-19-828744-5) OUP.

Minerals for Grazing Ruminants in Tropical Regions. 3rd ed. L. R. McDowell. LC 97-20222. (Bulletin Ser.). 1997. write for info. (0-916287-23-8) Univ Fla Food.

Minerals in Animal & Human Nutrition: Comparative Aspects to Human Nutrition. Lee R. McDowell. Ed. by Tony J. Cunha. (Animal Feeding & Nutrition Ser.). (Illus.). 524p. (C). 1992. text 104.00 (0-12-483369-1) Acad Pr.

Minerals in Food & Nutritional Topics. Ed. by Geoffrey H. Bourne. (World Review of Nutrition & Dietetics Ser.: Vol. 46). (Illus.). xii, 260p. 1985. 191.50 (3-8055-4058-2) S Karger.

Minerals in Health, Science & Research: Index of Modern Information. Betty J. Wysocki. LC 88-47861. 150p. 1988. 47.50 (0-88164-934-1); pap. 44.50 (0-88164-935-X) ABBE Pubs Assn.

Minerals in Soil Environments. 2nd ed. Ed. by J. B. Dixon & S. B. Weed. (Book Ser.: No. 1). 1264p. 1989. 90.00 (0-89118-787-1) Soil Sci Soc Am.

Minerals in the World Economy. 1994. lib. bdg. 250.00 (0-8490-9066-0) Gordon Pr.

Minerals in the World Economy. 1994. lib. bdg. 250.00 (0-8490-5724-8) Gordon Pr.

Minerals in Thin Section. Dexter Perkins & Kevin R. Henke. LC 99-11429. 125p. (C). 1999. spiral bd. 44.00 (0-13-010997-5) P-H.

Minerals Industries of Africa. 1994. lib. bdg. 350.00 (0-8490-5725-6) Gordon Pr.

Minerals Industries of the Middle East. 1994. lib. bdg. 250.00 (0-8490-5726-4) Gordon Pr.

Minerals Industry of ASEAN. Bruce McKern. Ed. by Praipol Koomsup. 1988. pap. text 37.95 (0-04-301284-1, Pub. by Allen & Unwin Pty) Paul & Co Pubs.

Minerals Industry Taxation Policies for Asia & the Pacific. (ST-ESCAP Ser.: No. 1200). 170p. 50.00 (92-1-119665-5) UN.

Minerals Investment under the Shari'A Law. Walied M. El-Malik. (International Energy & Resources Law & Policy Ser.). 176p. (C). 1993. lib. bdg. 98.00 (1-85333-907-5) Kluwer Academic.

Minerals of Arizona: A Field Guide for Collectors. Neil R. Bearce. LC 98-44239. (Illus.). 224p. 1999. pap. 19.00 (0-945005-33-4) Geoscience Pr.

Minerals of California. Arthur S. Eakle. 1992. reprint ed. lib. bdg. 75.00 (0-7812-5029-3) Rprt Serv.

Minerals of Colorado. Edwin B. Eckel. LC 97-14815. (Illus.). 860p. 1997. text 150.00 (1-55591-365-2) Fulcrum Pub.

Minerals of New Mexico. rev. ed. Stuart A. Northrop. 1959. 34.95 (0-8263-0079-0) U of NM Pr.

Minerals of New Mexico. 3rd ed. Stuart A. Northrop. LC 95-25171. (Illus.). 356p. 1996. 34.95 (0-8263-1662-X) U of NM Pr.

Minerals of the World. Alain Eid & Michel Viard. (Illus.). 192p. 1997. 22.98 (0-7858-0824-8) Bk Sales Inc.

Minerals of the World. Walter Schumann. (Illus.). 224p. 1998. 14.95 (0-8069-8571-2) Sterling.

Minerals of the World Table. Compiled by P. Lof. 1983. 25.00 (0-444-42135-1) Elsevier.

*Minerals, Supplements & Vitamins: The Essential Guide. H. Winter Griffith. LC 99-53244. (Illus.). 208p. 1999. pap. 9.95 (1-55561-229-6) Fisher Bks.

*Minerals Yearbook: Area Reports, Vol. 3. 202p. 1998. per. 20.00 (0-16-061635-2) USGPO.

*Minerals Yearbook: Area Reports, Vol. 3. 252p. 1998. per. 20.00 (0-16-061640-9) USGPO.

*Minerals Yearbook: Area Reports, International, 1995, Mineral Industries of Africa & the Middle East, Vol. 3. 230p. 1998. per. 19.00 (0-16-061638-7) USGPO.

Minerals Yearbook: Area Reports, International 1995, Mineral Industries of Asia & the Pacific, Vol. 3. 178p. 1997. per. 16.00 (0-16-048985-7) USGPO.

Minerals Yearbook: Area Reports, International, 1995, Mineral Industries of Europe & Central Eurasia, Vol. 3. 239p. 1997. per. 20.00 (0-16-049008-1) USGPO.

Minerals Yearbook 1995: Metals & Minerals, 1995, Vol. 1. 947p. 1997. boxed set 65.00 (0-16-049167-3) USGPO.

Minerals Yearbook 1995: Mineral Industries of Latin America & Canada, Vol. 3. 188p. 1997. per. 17.00 (0-16-049043-X) USGPO.

Minerals Yearbook 1996-Domestic: Area Reports, Vol.2. Arnold Tanner. 327p. 1997. per. 27.00 (0-16-049294-7) USGPO.

*Minerals Yearbook, Area Reports: Domestic, 1998, Vol. 2. 336p. 2000. per. 31.00 (0-16-059103-1) USGPO.

*Minerals Yearbook, Area Reports: International, 1997, Africa & The Middle East, Vol. 3. 278p. 2000. per. 25.00 (0-16-059118-X) USGPO.

*Minerals Yearbook, Metals & Minerals, 1997, Vol. 1. 1044p. 2000. per. 73.00 (0-16-059039-6) USGPO.

*Minerals Yearbook, Metals & Minerals, 1996, Vol. 1. 996p. 1998. boxed set 74.00 (0-16-061639-5) USGPO.

*Minerals Yearbook, 1997: Latin America & Canada, Vol. 3. 188p. 1999. per. 18.00 (0-16-059200-3) USGPO.

*Minerals Yearbook, 1996: Mineral Industries of Latin America & Canada, Vol. 3. 201p. 1998. per. 16.00 (0-16-061641-7) USGPO.

Mineralogy & Geology of Rare Earths in China. Ed. by Zhang Peishan et al. LC 98-109791. (Solid Earth Sciences Research in China Ser.). (Illus.). 209p. 1996. 49.95 (7-03-004904-7, Pub. by Sci Pr) Lubrecht & Cramer.

Miners. Charles L. Convis. (True Tales of the Old West Ser.: Vol. 8). (Illus.). ii, 62p. 1998. pap. 7.95 (0-9651954-8-1) Pioneer Pr NV.

Miners. Rick Steber. (Tales of the Wild West Ser.: Vol. 9). (Illus.). 60p. 1990. pap. 4.95 (0-945134-09-6); lib. bdg. 14.95 (0-945134-87-8) Bonanza Pub.

Miners: One Union, One Industry: A History of the National Union of Mineworkers, 1939-1946. Robert P. Arnot. LC 78-40603. 240p. reprint ed. pap. 74.40 (0-608-14647-1, 202330600032) Bks Demand.

Miners: The History of Sports at University of Texas at El Paso. Bob Ingram & Ray Sanchez. LC 97-75964. (Illus.). 168p. 1998. 19.95 (0-9623471-5-9) Mesa Pub Corp.

Miners - In Crisis & War: A History of the Miner's Federation of Great Britain from 1930 Onwards. Robert P. Arnot. 451p. 1961. 49.50 (0-678-08024-0) Kelley.

Miners, Adult Education & Community Service, 1920-1984. Graham Mee. (C). 1985. 65.00 (1-85041-006-2, Pub. by Univ Nottingham) St Mut.

Miners Against Racism. Francis. (C). 1984. pap. 19.50 (0-85315-577-1, Pub. by Lawrence & Wishart) NYU Pr.

Miners & Millhands: Work, Culture & Politics in Princely Mysore. Janaki Nair. LC 98-12773. 308p. (C). 1998. 44.95 (0-7619-9251-0) Sage.

Miner's & Prospector's Reference Handbook. Ray Seibert. Ed. by Ruth Seibert. (Illus.). 103p. (Orig.). 1996. pap. 11.95 (0-9652246-0-0) R-S Bks.

Miners & Travelers Guide. John Mullan. Ed. by Kimberly R. Brown & Glen Adams. (Illus.). 178p. 1991. reprint ed. 19.95 (0-87770-502-X) Ye Galleon.

Miner's & Travelers' Guide to Oregon, Washington, Idaho, Montana, Wyoming, & Colorado. John Mullan. LC 72-9461. (Far Western Frontier Ser.). (Illus.). 158p. 1978. reprint ed. 18.95 (0-405-04989-7) Ayer.

*Miner's Canary. Brown. 2001. pap. text. write for info. (0-7167-3390-0) W H Freeman.

Miner's Canary: Unraveling the Mysteries of Extinction. Niles Eldridge. LC 93-50185. (Science Library). 272p. (C). 1994. pap. 15.95 (0-691-03655-1, Pub. by Princeton U Pr) Cal Prin Full Svc.

Miner's Flame Light Book. Henry A. Pohs. LC 92-97415. (Illus.). 833p. 1995. 89.50 (0-9641165-0-2) Flame Pubng.

Miner's Freedom: Study of the Working Life in a Changing Industry. Carter Goodrich. Ed. by Leon Stein. LC 77-70498. (Illus.). 1977. reprint ed. lib. bdg. 23.95 (0-405-10169-4) Ayer.

Miners Getting Off the Graveyard: Poems. Walter Hall. (Burning Deck Poetry Ser.). 1978. 15.00 (0-930900-07-3); pap. 4.00 (0-930900-08-1) Burning Deck.

Miners' Justice: Migration, Law & Order on the Alaska-Yukon Frontier, 1873-1902. Thomas Stone. (American University Studies Anthropology & Sociology: Ser. XI, Vol. 34). X, 308p. (C). 1988. text 39.50 (0-8204-0577-9) P Lang Pubng.

Miners, Merchants, & Farmers in Colonial Colombia. Ann Twinam. (Latin American Monographs: No. 57). 205p. (C). 1982. text 22.00 (0-292-72034-3) U of Tex Pr.

Miners, Merchants & Farmers in Colonial Colombia. Ann Twinam. LC 82-11054. (Latin American Monographs: Vol. 57). (Illus.). 205p. reprint ed. pap. 63.60 (0-608-08651-7, 206917400003) Bks Demand.

Miners, Merchants, & Maids. Suzanne Hilton. (Settling the West Ser.). (Illus.). 96p. (J). (gr. 5-8). 1995. lib. bdg. 20.40 (0-8050-2998-2) TFC Bks NY.

Miners, Merchants & Midwives: Michigan's Upper Peninsula Italians. Russell M. Magnaghi. LC 87-70604. 113p. (Orig.). 1987. pap. 7.95 (0-942879-00-7) Belle Fontaine Pr.

Miners, Millhands, & Mountaineers: Industrialization of the Appalachian South, 1880-1930. Ronald D. Eller. LC 81-16020. (Twentieth-Century America Ser.). (Illus.). 298p. (C). 1982. pap. 16.95 (0-87049-341-8) U of Tenn Pr.

Miners of Decazeville: A Genealogy of Deindustrialization. Donald Reid. (Illus.). 336p. 1985. 38.50 (0-674-57634-9) HUP.

Miners of Windber: The Struggles of New Immigrants for Unionization, 1890s-1930s. Mildred A. Beik. LC 95-47701. 1996. 65.00 (0-271-01566-7); pap. 22.95 (0-271-01567-5) Pa St U Pr.

Miners on Strike: Class Solidarity & Division in Britain. Andrew J. Richards. LC 96-34875. 256p. 1997. 55.00 (1-85973-172-4, Pub. by Berg Pubs); pap. 19.50 (1-85973-177-5, Pub. by Berg Pubs) NYU Pr.

Miner's Pale Children. W. S. Merwin. 1995. pap. 12.95 (0-8050-2870-6) H Holt & Co.

Miner's Rule - A More Definitive Approach. Al Meyer. (Technical Papers: Vol. 95FTM8). (Illus.). 6p. 1995. pap. text 30.00 (1-55589-657-X) AGMA.

Miner's Sunday, 1849. Charles B. Gillespie. Ed. by William R. Jones. (Illus.). 18p. 1976. reprint ed. pap. 2.00 (0-89646-005-3) Vistabooks.

Miners, Unions & Politics, 1910-1947. Ed. by Alan Campbell et al. (Illus.). 320p. 1996. 78.95 (1-85928-269-5, Pub. by Scolar Pr) Ashgate Pub Co.

Minerva & the Muse: A Life of Margaret Fuller. Joan Von Mehren. LC 94-18663. (Illus.). 416p. (C). 1995. 40.00 (0-87023-941-4) U of Mass Pr.

Minerva & the Muse: A Life of Margaret Fuller. Joan Von Mehren. LC 94-18663. (Illus.). 408p. 1996. pap. 20.95 (1-55849-015-9) U of Mass Pr.

Minerva at Fifty: The Jubilee History of the Society of Industrial Artists & Designers, 1930 to 1980. Ed. by James Holland. 96p. (C). 1989. 59.00 (0-903696-16-9, Pub. by Hurtwood Pr Ltd) St Mut.

Minerva Britanna: or A Garden of Heroical Devises. Henry Peacham. LC 73-171783. (English Experience Ser.: No. 407). 232p. 1971. reprint ed. 45.00 (90-221-0407-9) Walter J Johnson.

Minerva-Handbuecher Archive: Archive im deutschsprachigen Raum, 2 vols. 2nd ed. 1418p. (C). 1974. 434.65 (3-11-001955-8) De Gruyter.

Minerva Lane. large type ed. Glover Judith. 1995. 27.99 (0-7505-0794-2, Pub. by Mgna Lrg Print) Ulverscroft.

Minerva Louise. Janet Morgan Stoeke. LC 87-24458. (Illus.). 24p. (J). (ps-1). 1988. 14.99 (0-525-44374-6, 01063-320, Dutton Child) Peng Put Young Read.

*Minerva Louise & Her Farmyard Friends: A Minerva Louise Sticker Storybook. Janet Morgan Stoeke. (Illus.). 16p. (J). 2000. pap. 4.99 (0-525-46329-1, Dutton Child) Peng Put Young Read.

Minerva Louise at School. Janet Morgan Stoeke. LC 95-52173. (Illus.). 24p. (J). (ps-1). 1996. 13.99 (0-525-45494-2, Dutton Child) Peng Put Young Read.

*Minerva Louise at School, Vol. 1. Janet Morgan Stoeke. 1999. pap. 5.99 (0-14-056287-7, PuffinBks) Peng Put Young Read.

*Minerva Louise at the Fair. Janet Morgan Stoeke. (Illus.). 24p. (J). (ps-1). 2000. 14.99 (0-525-46439-5, Dutton Child) Peng Put Young Read.

Minerva! The Story of an Artist with a Mission. Elaine Cannon. 1997. 19.95 (1-57008-377-0) Bookcraft Inc.

Minerva Wakes. Holly Lisle. 288p. 1994. per. 4.99 (0-671-72202-6) Baen Bks.

*Minerva's Marquis. Sheila Walsh. 352p. 1999. 20.99 (1-85389-958-5) Ulverscroft.

Minerva's Message: Stabilizing the French Revolution. Martin S. Staum. LC 98-121901. (Illus.). 360p. 1996. 49.95 (0-7735-1442-2, Pub. by McG-Queens Univ Pr) CUP Services.

Minerva's Owl. Harold Adams Innis. LC AZ0515.Z5I55. 31p. reprint ed. pap. 30.00 (0-608-10766-2, 201425500096) Bks Demand.

Minerva's Stepchild. large type ed. Helen Forrester. Orig. Title: Twopence to Cross the Mersey. 1990. 18.95 (0-7089-1140-4) Ulverscroft.

*Mines. Jennifer Maiden. 104p. 1999. pap. text 15.95 (90-5704-046-8) Gordon & Breach.

Mines & Minie Balls: Weapons of the Civil War. Jean F. Blashfield. LC 96-32157. (First Bks.). (J). 1997. lib. bdg. 22.00 (0-531-20273-9) Watts.

Mines & Quarries: General Report & Analysis see Census of the United States: 13th Decennial Census, 1910

Mines & Quarries of the Indians of California, Vol. 40:3. fac. ed. R. F. Heizer & A. E. Treganza. (California Journal of Mines & Geology Ser.). (Illus.). (C). 1944. reprint ed. pap. text 9.06 (1-55567-672-3) Coyote Press.

Mine's Bigger Than Yours: EGO - The Arterial Blockage of Business. Steve Hance. 145p. (Orig.). 1996. pap. 14.50 (0-911119-69-8) Ctr Intgrtd Prodctvty.

Mines, Manufactures & Ouvriers du Valenciennois au XVIII Siecle: Contribution a l'Histoire du Travail Dans l'Ancuenne France, 2 vols. Philippe Guignet. Ed. by Stuart Bruchey. LC 77-77172. (Dissertations in European Economic History Ser.). (FRE., Illus.). 1978. lib. bdg. 75.95 (0-405-10785-4) Ayer.

Mines, Miners & Minerals of Western North Carolina's Mountain Empire. Lowell Presnell. LC 98-36574. (Illus.). 272p. 1998. pap. 14.95 (1-56664-135-7) WorldComm.

Mines, Murders, & Grizzlies: Tales of California's Ventura Back Country. rev. ed. Charles F. Outland. LC 69-19561. (Illus.). 151p. 1986. pap. 17.50 (0-87062-173-4) A H Clark.

Mines of Battle Mountain, Reese River, Aurora & Other Western Nevada Districts. J. M. Hill. 200p. 1982. pap. 19.95 (0-913814-63-6) Nevada Pubns.

Mines of Behemoth. Michael Shea. 256p. 1997. per. 5.99 (0-671-87847-6) Baen Bks.

Mines of Cardiganshire (Metalliferous & Associated Minerals, 1845-1913) Roger Burt et al. 92p. 1990. 65.00 (0-9507624-5-8, Pub. by Northern Mine Res) St Mut.

Mines of Cherry Creek, Ely Range & Other Eastern Nevada Districts. J. M. Hill. (Illus.). 214p. 1982. pap. 14.95 (0-913814-65-2) Nevada Pubns.

Mines of Churchill & Mineral Counties. William Vanderburg. (Illus.). 128p. 1988. pap. 14.95 (0-913814-73-3) Nevada Pubns.

Mines of Clark County. William Vanderburg. (Illus.). 96p. 1988. pap. 14.95 (0-913814-70-9) Nevada Pubns.

Mines of Colorado. Ovando J. Hollister. LC 72-9452. (Far Western Frontier Ser.). (Illus.). 454p. 1973. reprint ed. 28.95 (0-405-04980-3) Ayer.

Mines of Death Valley. L. Burr Belden. 1996. pap. 4.50 (0-87505-410-2) Borden.

Mines of Flintshire & Denbighshire, Vol. 10. Roger Burt et al. 192p. 1992. pap. text 25.95 (0-85989-371-5, Pub. by Univ Exeter Pr) Northwestern U Pr.

Mines of Humboldt & Pershing Counties. William Vanderburg. 120p. 1988. pap. 14.95 (0-913814-71-7) Nevada Pubns.

Mines of Julian. Helen Ellsberg. 1986. pap. 4.50 (0-87505-412-9) Borden.

Mines of Lander & Eureka Counties. William Vanderburg. (Illus.). 1988. pap. 14.95 (0-913814-72-5) Nevada Pubns.

Mines of Newent & Ross. Pound House Staff. (C). 1985. text 40.00 (0-906885-06-X, Pub. by Pound Hse) St Mut.

Mines of Ouray (Colorado) County. rev. ed. Frank A. Rice. Ed. by Jack L. Benham. (Illus.). 56p. (Orig.). 1980. reprint ed. pap. 3.95 (0-941026-05-1) Bear Creek Pub.

Mines of Shropshire & Montgomeryshire with Cheshire, Vol. 9. 144p. 1990. pap. text 21.99 (0-85989-343-X, Pub. by Univ Exeter Pr) Northwestern U Pr.

Mines of Silver & Gold in the Americas. Ed. by Peter Bakewell. LC 96-237. (Expanding World Ser.: Vol. 19). 420p. 1997. 138.95 (0-86078-513-0, Pub. by Variorum) Ashgate Pub Co.

Mines of the Dillsburg, Pennsylvania Area: And Related Enterprises. Robert F. Gayman. (Illus.). 96p. 1995. 30.00 (0-9648050-0-6); pap. 10.00 (0-9648050-1-4) Nrthrn York Cnty.

Mines of the East Fork. John W. Robinson. 1980. pap. 4.50 (0-87505-417-X) Borden.

Mines of the Eastern Sierra. Mary DeDecker. 1996. pap. 4.50 (0-87505-411-0) Borden.

Mines of the Goldfield, Bullfrog & Other Southern Nevada Districts. F. L. Ransome. (Illus.). 144p. 1983. pap. 19.95 (0-913814-60-1) Nevada Pubns.

Mines of the High Desert. R. D. Miller. 1996. pap. 4.50 (0-87505-413-7) Borden.

Mines of the Mojave. Ron Miller & Peggy Miller. 1996. pap. 4.50 (0-87505-414-5) Borden.

Mines of the San Bernardino. John W. Robinson. 1986. pap. 4.50 (0-87505-415-3) Borden.

Mines of the San Gabriels. John W. Robinson. 1986. pap. 4.50 (0-87505-416-1) Borden.

Mines of the Silver Peak Range, Kawich Range & Other Southernwestern Nevada Districts. S. H. Ball. 218p. 1983. pap. 14.95 (0-913814-61-X) Nevada Pubns.

Mines of Tuscarora, Cortez & Other Northern Nevada Districts. William H. Emmons. 220p. 1982. pap. 14.95 (0-913814-64-4) Nevada Pubns.

Mine's the Best. Crosby N. Bonsall. (My First I Can Read Bks.). (Illus.). (J). (ps-k). 1973. 14.89 (0-06-020577-6, 133480) HarpC Child Bks.

Mine's the Best. Crosby N. Bonsall. (My First I Can Read Bks.). (Illus.). 32p. (J). (ps-k). 1973. lib. bdg. 14.89 (0-06-020578-4) HarpC Child Bks.

Mine's the Best. Crosby N. Bonsall. (My First I Can Read Bks.). (J). (ps-k). 1997. 8.95 (0-606-11627-3, Pub. by Turtleback) Demco.

Mine's the Best. Crosby N. Bonsall. LC 95-12405. (My First I Can Read Bks.). (Illus.). 32p. (J). (ps-k). 1997. reprint ed. pap. 3.95 (0-06-444213-6, HarpTrophy) HarpC Child Bks.

Mine's the Best. rev. ed. Crosby N. Bonsall. (My First I Can Read Bks.). (Illus.). 32p. (J). (ps-k). 1996. lib. bdg. 15.89 (0-06-027091-8) HarpC Child Bks.

Mineshaft Nights. Leo Cardini. Ed. by Jerry Douglas. (Illus.). 183p. (Orig.). 1990. pap. 10.95 (0-943383-01-3) FirstHand Ltd.

Minesite Recultivation. Joe Wisniewski et al. Ed. by Reinhard F. Huttl. LC 96-35783. 160p. (C). 1996. text 88.00 (0-7923-4245-3) Kluwer Academic.

Minesta's Vision: A Centenary Collection of Grace Cooke's Writing. Grace Cooke. (Illus.). 60p. (Orig.). 1992. pap. (0-85487-089-X) White Eagle.

Minestrone. Fred Waage. 34p. 1983. pap. 7.95 (0-944754-03-1) Pudding Hse Pubns.

Minesweeper & Terran Girls Make Wonderful Wives. Gary Lovisi & James Reasoner. (Gryphon Double Novel Ser.: No. 8). 1995. per. 12.00 (0-936071-40-0) Gryphon Pubns.

Minesweepers of the Royal Canadian Navy, 1938-1945. Ken Macpherson. (Illus.). 110p. 1993. 24.95 (0-920277-55-1, Pub. by Vanwell Publ) Howell Pr VA.

Minetown, Milltown, Railtown: Life in Canadian Communities of Single Industry. Rex A. Lucas. LC 70-166934. 450p. reprint ed. pap. 139.50 (0-8357-4158-3, 203693200007) Bks Demand.

Ming: Finding a Footpath Through Literature. Abigail Silver. (Textworks Ser.). (Illus.). ix, 91p. (YA). (gr. 6-12). 1995. ring bd. 39.95 (1-58284-022-9, Thoughtful Educ) Silver Strong.

 An Asterisk (*) at the beginning of an entry indicates that the title is appearing for the first time.

Ming & I. Tamar Myers. LC 97-93174. 256p. 1997. mass mkt. 5.99 (*0-380-79255-9*, Avon Bks) Morrow Avon.

Ming & Qing Historical Studies in the People's Republic of China. Ed. by Frederic Wakeman, Jr. (China Research Monographs: No. 17). 210p. 1981. pap. 10.00 (*0-912966-27-0*) IEAS.

Ming Breakfast: Grits & Scrambled Moments. Photos by Ming Smith. (Illus.). 1992. write for info. (*0-9634666-0-7*) De Ming Dynasty.

Ming History: An Introductory Guide to Research. Edward L. Farmer et al. (Ming Studies Research Ser.). 358p. 1994. pap. 36.00 (*1-886108-02-1*) UMN Ming Studies.

Ming Ling. Stephen Cosgrove. (Serendipity Ser.). 1986. 9.15 (*0-606-02415-8*, Pub. by Turtleback) Demco.

Ming Lo Moves the Mountain. Arnold Lobel. (J). 1993. 10.15 (*0-606-05926-1*, Wm Morrow) Morrow Avon.

Ming Lo Moves the Mountain. Arnold Lobel. LC 92-47364. (Illus.). 32p. (J). (ps-3). 1993. mass mkt. 5.95 (*0-688-10995-0*, Wm Morrow) Morrow Avon.

Ming-Qing Conflict, 1619-1683: A Historiography & Source Guide. Lynn A. Struve. LC 98-39736. 1998. 40.00 (*0-924304-37-5*) Assn Asian Studies.

Ming Society: T'ai-ho County, Kiangsi, Fourteenth to Seventeenth Centuries. John W. Dardess. LC 96-3631. (Illus.). 313p. 1997. 48.00 (*0-520-20425-5*, Pub. by U CA Pr) Cal Prin Full Svc.

Ming Studies in Japan, 1961-1981: A Classified Bibliography. Richard T. Wang. (Ming Studies Research Ser.). 108p. 1985. pap. 14.00 (*1-886108-01-3*) UMN Ming Studies.

Ming Tombs. Ann Paludan. (Images of Asia Ser.). (Illus.). 94p. (C). 1991. 15.95 (*0-19-585003-3*) OUP.

Mingei see **Folk Arts & Crafts of Japan**

Minghella: Plays One. Anthony Minghella. 292p. (C). 1992. pap. 14.95 (*0-413-66580-1*, A0659, Methuen Drama) Methn.

Mingled Chime: An Autobiography. Thomas Beecham. LC 76-40182. (Music Ser.). 1976. reprint ed. 39.50 (*0-306-70791-8*) Da Capo.

Mingled Chime: An Autobiography. Thomas Beecham. LC 76-40238. 330p. 1977. reprint ed. lib. bdg. 35.00 (*0-8371-9274-9*, BEMCH, Greenwood Pr) Greenwood.

Mingled Chime, an Autobiography. Thomas Beecham. (Music Book Index Ser.). 330p. 1992. reprint ed. lib. bdg. 89.00 (*0-7812-9462-2*) Rprt Serv.

Mingled Measure Diaries, 1953-1972. James Lees-Milne. 325p. 1996. 45.00 (*0-7195-5362-8*, Pub. by John Murray) Trafalgar.

Mingled Roots: A Guide for Jewish Grandparents of Interfaith Grandchildren. Sunie Levin. (Illus.). 84p. (Orig.). 1992. pap. 13.95 (*0-9632259-0-1*) Bnai Brith Wom.

Mingled Yarn: Autobiographical Sketches. Henry M. Tomlinson. LC 71-134146. (Essay Index Reprint Ser.). 1977. reprint ed. 19.95 (*0-8369-2254-9*) Ayer.

Mingling Minds: Phineas P. Quimby's Science of Health & Happiness. Ervin Seale. 160p. (Orig.). 1997. pap. 9.95 (*0-87516-703-9*) DeVorss.

Mingling of God with Man: The Testimony of Church History. Bill Freeman. 100p. (Orig.). 1992. pap. 3.00 (*0-914271-37-7*) Mnstry Pubns.

Mingling of Streams Vols. 1-9: An Anthology of Poems Selected from "The Poet's Voice" Ed. by Fred Beake. 243p. pap. write for info. (*3-7052-0912-4*, Pub. by Poetry Salzburg) Intl Spec Bk.

Mingling of the Canadian & American Peoples, Vol. I, Historical. Marcus L. Hansen. Tr. by John B. Brebner. LC 78-129400. (American Immigration Collection. Series 2). (Illus.). 1970. reprint ed. 19.95 (*0-405-00553-9*) Ayer.

Mingo & Other Sketches in Black & White. Joel Chandler Harris. LC 70-83911. (Black Heritage Library Collection). 1977. 18.95 (*0-8369-8696-2*); 22.95 (*0-8369-3395-8*) Ayer.

Mingo & Other Sketches in Black & White. Joel Chandler Harris. LC 76-104477. 273p. reprint ed. pap. text 7.50 (*0-8290-5206-2*); reprint ed. lib. bdg. 15.50 (*0-8290-0764-4*) Irvington.

Mingo & Other Sketches in Black & White. Joel Chandler Harris. (Notable American Authors Ser.). 1992. reprint ed. lib. bdg. 75.00 (*0-7812-3017-9*) Rprt Serv.

***Mingo y Yo.** Karen M. Rogers. Tr. by Ana M. Alvarado. (Think-Kids Book Collection).Tr. of Max & Me. (SPA., Illus.). 16p. (J). (gr. 1-4). 2000. pap. 2.95 (*1-58237-050-8*) Creat Think.

Mingqiileg. large type ed. Kelly J. Lincoln.Tr. of Making a Grass Basket. (ESK., Illus.). 16p. (J). (gr. k-3). 1999. pap. text 21.00 (*1-58084-063-9*) Lower Kuskokwim.

Mingqiller Tapernarneg. large type ed. Kelly J. Lincoln.Tr. of Making a Grass Basket. (ESK., Illus.). 16p. (J). (gr. k-3). 1999. pap. text 21.00 (*1-58084-110-4*) Lower Kuskokwim.

Mingrelian Conspiracy. Michael Pearce. 192p. 1998. mass mkt. 8.95 (*0-00-649778-0*, Pub. by HarpC) Trafalgar.

Ming's Kingdom. Nicol Williamson. LC 96-156077. 246p. 1997. 24.95 (*0-09-179222-3*, Pub. by Hutchinson) Trafalgar.

Mingulay: An Island & Its People. Ben Buxton. LC 96-140549. (Illus.). 200p. pap. 21.95 (*1-874744-24-6*, Pub. by Birlinn Ltd) Dufour.

Mingus: A Critical Biography. Brian Priestley. LC 83-26155. (Quality Paperbacks Ser.). (Illus.). 320p. 1984. pap. 11.95 (*0-306-80217-1*) Da Capo.

Mingus - Mingus: Two Memoirs. Janet Coleman & Al Young. LC 88-38524. 160p. 1989. 14.95 (*0-88739-067-6*) Creat Arts Bk.

Mingus - Mingus: Two Memoirs. Janet Coleman & Al Young. LC 91-23247. (Illus.). 164p. 1991. reprint ed. pap. 10.95 (*0-87910-149-0*) Limelight Edns.

Minguyaq Elitnauryartuq. Sandi Nicori.Tr. of Julie Goes to School. (ESK., Illus.). 8p. (J). (gr. k-3). 1998. pap. text 6.00 (*1-58084-039-6*) Lower Kuskokwim.

Minh Man Rules. Eric Minh Tang & Ed Ifkovic. (J). (gr. 7-9). 2000. pap. 9.99 (*0-88092-419-5*) Royal Fireworks.

Minha Mao Esquerda: Poemas. unabridged ed. Gloria Melo. Ed. by Peregrinacao Publications Staff. (Poetry/ Poesia Ser.: No. 5). (POR.). 96p. 1998. boxed set 12.00 (*1-889358-14-2*, 10) Peregrinacao.

Minhagim: The Customs & Ceremonies of Judaism, Their Origins & Rationale. 6th ed. Abraham Chill. LC 78-62153. (Illus.). 339p. 1980. 24.95 (*0-87203-076-8*); pap. 17.50 (*0-87203-077-6*) Hermon.

Minhah & Maariv Service. Tr. by Ben Z. Bokser. 45p. 1958. pap. 3.00 (*0-88482-125-0*) Hebrew Pub.

Minhah Le-Nahum: Biblical & Other Studies Presented to Nahum M. Sarna in Honour of His 70th Birthday. Ed. by Michael Fishbane & Marc Brettler. (JSOT Supplement Ser.: No. 154). 337p. 1993. 85.00 (*1-85075-419-5*, Pub. by Sheffield Acad) CUP Services.

Minhaj et Talibin: A Manual of Muhammadan Law According to the School of Shafii. Mahiudin A. Nawawi. 1992. reprint ed. 72.00 (*81-7013-097-2*, Pub. by Navarang) S Asia.

Minhas Marheshes: Commentary on Genesis. P. S. Pollak. (ENG & HEB.). 12.00 (*0-87559-101-9*) Shalom.

***Mini.** Jon Pressnell. (Album Ser.: No. 299). (Illus.). 32p. 1999. pap. 5.25 (*0-7478-0235-1*, Pub. by Shire Pubns) Parkwest Pubns.

Mini: Guide to Purchase & DIY Restoration. 2nd ed. Lindsay Porter. LC 96-75169. (Illus.). 304p. 1996. 36.95 (*0-85429-971-8*, Pub. by J H Haynes & Co) Motorbooks Intl.

Mini: The Complete Story. James Rupert. (Illus.). 200p. 1997. 35.95 (*1-86126-047-4*, Pub. by Cro1wood) Motorbooks Intl.

Mini: The Design Icon of a Generation. L. J. Setright. LC 99-491029. (Illus.). 224p. 1999. text 29.95 (*1-85227-815-3*, Pub. by Virgin Bks) Motorbooks Intl.

***Mini: The Racing Story.** John Baggott. (Illus.). 232p. 2000. 44.95 (*1-86126-254-X*, 129771AE, Pub. by Cro1wood) Motorbooks Intl.

***Mini Address Book, Assorted Guatemalan Fabrics.** Photos by Joshua Gerak. 96p. 1999. 2.49 (*1-892985-09-8*) Adventure Imports.

***Mini Address Book, Assorted Indonesian Batik Fabrics.** Photos by Joshua Gerak. 96p. 1999. 2.99 (*1-892985-10-1*) Adventure Imports.

***Mini Address Book, Hemp Fabric, Stamped.** Photos by Joshua Gerak. 96p. 1999. 3.49 (*1-892985-11-X*) Adventure Imports.

Mini-Adventures in First Day Cover Collecting. Monte Eiserman. 10p. 1996. pap. 3.00 (*1-879390-26-4*) AFDCS.

Mini Afrikaans - English - Afrikaans: Bilingual General Dictionary. 11th rev. ed. M. S. Kritzinger. (AFR & ENG.). 431p. 1988. 14.95 (*0-627-01581-6*) Fr & Eur.

Mini & Microcomputer Systems: An Introduction. 2nd ed. M. G. Hartley et al. (Macmillan Computer Science Ser.). (Illus.). 385p. (C). 1989. text 90.00 (*0-333-41758-5*); pap. text 36.00 (*0-333-41759-3*) Scholium Intl.

Mini & Microcomputers & Their Applications: Proceedings of the International Symposium Held in Lugano, Switzerland, June 19-21, 1990. Ed. by M. H. Hamza. 352p. 1990. 92.00 (*0-88986-150-1*, 161) Acta Pr.

Mini & Microcomputers & Their Applications - Mimi, 1983: Proceedings, ISMM Symposium, Lugano, Switzerland, June 21-24, 1983. Ed. by M. H. Hamza. 189p. 1983. 60.00 (*0-88986-047-5*, 056) Acta Pr.

Mini & Microcomputers & Their Applications - Mimi, 1983: Proceedings, ISMM Symposium, San Antonio, Texas, U. S. A., December 12-13, 1983. Ed. by M. H. Hamza. 156p. 1983. 65.00 (*0-88986-054-8*, 061) Acta Pr.

Mini & Microcomputers & Their Applications - Mimi, 1983: Proceedings, ISMM Symposium, San Francisco, U. S. A., May 16-17, 1983. Ed. by M. H. Hamza. 112p. 1983. 50.00 (*0-88986-044-0*, 052) Acta Pr.

Mini & Microcomputers & Their Applications - Mimi, 1984: Proceedings, ISMM Symposium, Bari, Italy, June 5-8, 1984. Ed. by G. Mastronardi. 289p. 1984. 85.00 (*0-88986-058-0*, 065) Acta Pr.

Mini & Microcomputers & Their Applications - Mimi, 1984: Proceedings, ISMM Symposium, San Francisco, U. S. A., June 5-6, 1984. Ed. by M. H. Hamza. 78p. 1984. 35.00 (*0-88986-060-2*) Acta Pr.

Mini & Microcomputers & Their Applications - Mimi, 1985: Proceedings, IASTED Symposium, Montreal, Canada, June 3-5, 1985. Ed. by P. J. Zsombor-Murray et al. 230p. 1985. 85.00 (*0-88986-082-3*, 088) Acta Pr.

Mini & Microcomputers & Their Applications - Mimi, 1985: Proceedings, ISMM Symposium, Sant Feliu de Guixols, Spain, June 25-28, 1985. Ed. by E. Luque. LC 91-343. (Illus.). 518p. 1985. 108.00 (*0-88986-121-8*, 077) Acta Pr.

Mini & Microcomputers & Their Applications - Mimi, 1986: Proceedings of the ISMM Symposium, Austin, Texas, U. S. A., November 10-12, 1986. Ed. by A. S. Gouda & M. H. Hamza. 157p. 1986. 50.00 (*0-88986-094-7*, 096) Acta Pr.

Mini & Microcomputers & Their Applications - Mimi, 1987: Proceedings of the ISMM Symposium, Lugano, Switzerland, June 29-July 1, 1987. Ed. by M. H. Hamza. 203p. 1987. 72.00 (*0-88986-124-2*, 125) Acta Pr.

Mini & Microcomputers & Their Applications - Mimi, 1988: Proceedings of the ISMM Symposium, Sant Feliu de Guixols, Spain, June 27-30, 1988. Ed. by E. Luque. 680p. 1988. 125.00 (*84-7488-121-8*, 148) Acta Pr.

Mini & Microcomputers & Their Applications - Mimi, 1989: Proceedings of ISMM Symposium, Zurich, Switzerland, June 26-29, 1989. Ed. by M. H. Hamza. 369p. 1989. 95.00 (*0-88986-123-4*, 142) Acta Pr.

Mini & Microcomputers in Control, Filtering & Signal Processing - Mimi '84: Proceedings, ISMM Symposium, Las Vegas, U. S. A., December 10-12, 1984. Ed. by M. H. Hamza. 182p. 1984. 65.00 (*0-88986-066-1*, 083) Acta Pr.

Mini & Mini Cooper 1959-95. Chilton Automotive Editorial Staff. (Porter Manuals Ser.). (Illus.). 128p. (C). 1998. pap. 24.95 (*1-899238-01-8*, Pub. by Porter Pub) Nichols Pub.

Mini Atlas, Britain: Britain in Your Pocket, 1991. 91st rev. ed. John Bartholomew. (Illus.). 1987. pap. 15.95 (*0-7028-0789-3*) Brtholomew.

Mini Atlas of Britain. deluxe ed. Bartholomew Staff. (Illus.). pap. 15.95 (*0-7028-1203-X*) Brtholomew.

Mini-Atlas of Cats of the World. Andrew De Prisco & James B. Johnson. (Illus.). 448p. 1991. text 23.95 (*0-86622-627-3*, TS-152) TFH Pubns.

Mini-Atlas of Dog Breeds. Andrew De Prisco. (Illus.). 576p. 1990. 35.95 (*0-86622-091-7*, H-1106) TFH Pubns.

Mini-Atlas of Snakes. John Coborn. (Illus.). 736p. 1994. 59.95 (*0-86622-601-X*, TS193) TFH Pubns.

Mini Baby Counter. Annette Natow & Jo-Ann Heslin. 208p. 1999. per. 3.99 (*0-671-02563-5*) PB.

Mini-Baccarat & Roulette Guide for Women. Dee Richards. Ed. by Debby Frerichs. 50p. 1996. 10.95 (*1-890244-02-3*) D&D Pubns.

Mini-Cheers: Carving Miniature Santas. Photos & Text by Jeffrey B. Snyder. LC 95-7246. (Illus.). 64p. (Orig.). 1995. pap. 12.95 (*0-88740-824-9*) Schiffer.

Mini Classics: Baskets. Chitra Publications Staff. Ed. by Janice P. Johnson. LC 95-33336. (Illus.). 20p. (Orig.). 1995. pap. 6.95 (*1-885588-05-4*) Chitra Pubns.

Mini Classics: Flowers. Chitra Publications Staff. Ed. by Joanne S. Nolt. LC 95-35542. (Illus.). 20p. (Orig.). 1995. pap. 6.95 (*1-885588-08-9*) Chitra Pubns.

Mini Classics: Log Cabin. Chitra Publications Staff. Ed. by Joanne S. Nolt. LC 95-35541. (Illus.). 20p. (Orig.). 1995. pap. 6.95 (*1-885588-06-2*) Chitra Pubns.

Mini Computers. Charles A. Jortberg. LC 96-28296. (Kids & Computers Ser.). (Illus.). (J). (gr. 4-8). 1997. lib. bdg. 15.95 (*1-56239-726-5*) ABDO Pub Co.

Mini-Concordancer 5.25. Longman Publishing Staff. Date not set. pap. text. write for info. (*0-582-03816-2*, Pub. by Addison-Wesley) Longman.

Mini-Concordancer 3.5. Longman Publishing Staff. Date not set. pap. text. write for info. (*0-582-06343-4*, Pub. by Addison-Wesley) Longman.

Mini-Consults in Dermatology: Gross & Microscopic Symposium, Vol. III. American Academy of Dermatology Staff & Tom Pearson. (gr. 13). 1996. text 169.00 (*0-8151-1552-0*) Mosby Inc.

Mini Cooper the Real Thing. John Tipler. (Illus.). 160p. 1994. 39.95 (*1-874105-22-7*, Pub. by Vloce Pub) Motorbooks Intl.

Mini Core Concepts 98. 5th ed. Long & Grauer. 1997. pap. text 5.40 (*0-13-095389-X*) P-H.

Mini Course in Training Design. William A. Welch. (Illus.). 120p. (Orig.). 1997. pap. 25.00 (*0-9658204-0-8*) Behav Mgmt Assocs.

Mini Day Trips: Withlacoochee State Forest. Joan L. Scalpone. 64p. 1995. pap. 6.95 (*0-929198-13-1*) Mini DayTrip Bks.

Mini Day Trips: 150 Day Trips in & Around Orlando, Florida. Joan L. Scalpone. 64p. 1989. pap. 7.95 (*0-929198-07-7*) Mini DayTrip Bks.

Mini Day Trips: 150 Day Trips Southeast Florida. Joan L. Scalpone. 64p. (Orig.). 1988. pap. 7.95 (*0-929198-06-9*) Mini DayTrip Bks.

Mini Day Trips Vol. 7: Apalachicola, Florida. Joan L. Scalpone. (Illus.). 64p. (Orig.). 1997. pap. 7.95 (*0-929198-15-8*) Mini DayTrip Bks.

Mini Day Trips Miami, FL Vol. 1: Keys "N" Glades. Joan L. Scalpone. (Illus.). 64p. 1998. pap. 8.95 (*0-929198-19-0*) Mini DayTrip Bks.

Mini Day Trips Panhandle: 150 Daytrips. Joan L. Scalpone. (Illus.). 64p. 1991. pap. 6.95 (*0-929198-10-7*) Mini DayTrip Bks.

Mini Daytrips: 150 Day Trips-Northeast, Florida. Joan L. Scalpone. 64p. (Orig.). 1986. pap. 7.95 (*0-929198-01-8*) Mini DayTrip Bks.

Mini Daytrips: 150 Day Trips-Southwest, Florida. Joan L. Scalpone. 64p. (Orig.). 1984. pap. 7.95 (*0-929198-00-X*) Mini DayTrip Bks.

Mini Daytrips: 150 Day Trips-Tampa-Big Bend, Florida. Joan L. Scalpone. 72p. (Orig.). 1986. pap. 7.95 (*0-929198-02-6*) Mini DayTrip Bks.

Mini de Arte - Cezanne. (Mini de Arte/Art Minis Ser.). (Illus.). 96p. 2000. pap. 4.95 (*3-8290-2949-7*, 540954) Konemann.

Mini de Arte - Dali. (Mini de Arte/Art Minis Ser.). (Illus.). 96p. 2000. pap. 4.95 (*3-8290-2954-3*, 540803) Konemann.

Mini de Arte - Malewitsch. (Mini de Arte/Art Minis Ser.). (Illus.). 96p. 2000. pap. 4.95 (*3-8290-2955-1*, 541077) Konemann.

Mini de Arte - Michelangelo. (Mini de Arte/Art Minis Ser.). (Illus.). 96p. 2000. pap. 4.95 (*3-8290-2951-9*, 540800) Konemann.

Mini de Arte - Monet. (Mini de Arte/Art Minis Ser.). (Illus.). 96p. 2000. pap. 4.95 (*3-8290-2956-X*, 540796) Konemann.

Mini de Arte - Picasso. (Mini de Arte/Art Minis Ser.). (Illus.). 96p. 2000. pap. 4.95 (*3-8290-3297-8*, 540801) Konemann.

Mini de Arte - Pollock. (Mini de Arte/Art Minis Ser.). (Illus.). 96p. 2000. pap. 4.95 (*3-8290-2952-7*, 541078) Konemann.

Mini de Arte - Schiele. (Mini de Arte/Art Minis Ser.). (Illus.). 96p. 2000. pap. 4.95 (*3-8290-2957-8*, 541079) Konemann.

Mini de Arte - Toulouse Lautrec. (Mini de Arte/Art Minis Ser.). (Illus.). 96p. 2000. pap. 4.95 (*3-8290-2953-5*, 541080) Konemann.

Mini de Arte - Van Gogh. (Mini de Arte/Art Minis Ser.). (Illus.). 96p. 2000. pap. 4.95 (*3-8290-2958-6*, 540795) Konemann.

Mini Diccionario Microinformatico. R. Tapias. (SPA.). 182p. 1986. 19.95 (*0-8288-1366-3*, S 15694) Fr & Eur.

Mini Dictionary. Webster's New World Staff & Joyce L. Vedral. 640p. 1997. 5.95 (*0-02-861885-8*) Macmillan.

Mini Dictionary of Arabic Synonyms. Wagdy Rizk Ghali. (ARA.). 320p. 1997. pap. 14.95 (*0-86685-693-5*) Intl Bk Ctr.

Mini Dictionary of English - Korean, Korean - English: Romanized. Gene S. Rhie & B. J. Jones. (ENG & KOR.). 780p. 1995. pap. 16.50 (*1-56591-011-7*) Hollym Intl.

Mini Easter Activity Book. Robin Currie. (Illus.). 48p. (J). (gr. 1-5). 1993. pap. 2.99 (*0-7459-2149-3*) Lion USA.

Mini-Encyclopedia of Public Domain Songs. annuals BZ-Rights Stuff, Inc. Staff. 126p. 1998. ring bd. 299.00 (*1-884286-00-3*) BZ-Rights Stuff.

Mini-Encyclopedia of Wine: Minienciclopedia del Vino. Hugh Johnson. (SPA.). 207p. 1985. 19.95 (*0-8288-1180-6*, S60511) Fr & Eur.

Mini English - Thai - English Dictionary. G. Allison. (ENG & THA.). 460p. 1979. pap. 16.95 (*0-8288-4820-3*, M9900) Fr & Eur.

Mini-Esher Collection. (Illus.). 18p. 1993. pap. text 25.00 (*1-56762-048-5*) Modern Learn Pr.

Mini-14: The Plinker, Hunter, Assault, & Everything Else Rifle. Duncan Long. (Illus.). 120p. 1987. pap. 17.00 (*0-87364-407-7*) Paladin Pr.

Mini Fourteen Exotic Weapons System. 1985. pap. 18.00 (*0-87364-250-3*) Paladin Pr.

Mini-14 Exotic Weapons System. (Exotic Weapons Systems Ser.). (Illus.). 80p. 1982. pap. 15.00 (*0-87364-527-8*) Paladin Pr.

Mini-14 Super Systems. Duncan Long. (Illus.). 200p. 1991. pap. 16.95 (*0-87364-589-8*) Paladin Pr.

Mini Fun-Way Band Book: Piano - Conductor. (Beginning Band Ser.). 1990. 7.95 (*0-685-32005-7*, M451) Hansen Ed Mus.

Mini Fun-Way Orchestra Book. P. Gordon. (Beginning Orchestra Ser.). 1990. 6.95 (*0-685-32001-4*, S012) Hansen Ed Mus.

***Mini Guide to Mushrooms.** Konemann Inc. Staff. (Illus.). 384p. 2000. pap. 9.95 (*3-8290-2905-5*) Konemann.

Mini Guide to Purchase & DIY Restoration. 2nd ed. Lindsay Porter. 1996. 36.95 (*0-524-29971-4*) Am Theol Lib.

Mini-Guide to the Contents of the Books of the Bible. J. R. Miller. pap. 0.99 (*0-87377-163-X*) GAM Pubns.

Mini Guinness Bodhran, INSTRUMENT. pap. 75.00 (*0-7866-0894-3*, 95191IWW) Mel Bay.

Mini Historias Biblicas: The German Bible Society Mini Bible Story Books. Angus. (SPA.). 1995. write for info. (*0-7899-0079-3*); write for info. (*0-7899-0080-7*); write for info. (*0-7899-0081-5*); write for info. (*0-7899-0082-3*); write for info. (*0-7899-0083-1*); write for info. (*0-7899-0084-X*); write for info. (*0-7899-0085-8*); write for info. (*0-7899-0086-6*) Editorial Unilit.

Mini House Spring. 1997. 9.95 (*0-7611-1333-9*) Workman Pub.

Mini-Hydropower. Ed. by M. Gottschalk. (UNESCO Energy Engineering Learning Program Ser.). 322p. 1997. pap. 94.95 (*0-471-96264-3*) Wiley.

Mini Journal - Yellow. Cassandra Eason. (Masquerade Ser.). 128p. 1995. 4.50 (*0-8069-3960-5*) Sterling.

***Mini Las Vegas.** Bob Sehlinger. 208p. 1999. pap. 10.95 (*0-02-863266-4*) Macmillan.

Mini-Lessons: A Sampler. School Renaissance Institute Staff. (Reading Renaissance Library). (Illus.). 83p. 1998. pap., teacher ed. 14.95 (*0-9646404-4-9*) Schl Ren Inst.

Mini Lessons for Revisions: How to Teach Writing Skills, Language Usage, Grammar, & Mechanics in the Writing Process. Susan Geye. 93p. 1997. pap. text 17.95 (*1-888842-04-0*, 1030) Absey & Co.

Mini Lessons That Teach. Joan Clemmons & Lois Laase. (Illus.). 1996. pap. 16.95 (*0-590-49643-3*) Scholastic Inc.

Mini Maestro Presents the Tic-Toc Clocks. large type ed. Janet E. Osen. (Illus.). 30p. (J). (ps-k). 15.95 (*0-9700489-0-4*) Little Fiddle.

***Mini Manual for New Owners: A Guided Tour for the First-Time Miniature Horse Owner.** Illus. by Toni M. Leland. 66p. 1999. pap. 21.95 (*1-887932-05-4*, Small Horse Pr) Equine Graph Pubng.

Mini-Map '93: A Practical Application & Standards to Manufacturing Cell Networks. McMillan & Gardner. 300p. 1994. pap. 60.00 (*0-9639941-0-7*) Open I T.

Mini-Marchen: Dramatizations of Popular Fairy Tales. Douglas Hall & Herbert Lederer. (GER.). 54p. 1997. ring bd. 10.00 (*0-942017-47-1*, 04-64346) Amer Assn Teach German.

Mini-Marketing: How to Sell Yourself, Your Products, & Your Services Using a Low Cost, Common-Sense Approach. (Illus.). 161p. 1997. 19.95 (*0-9661878-0-6*) RKA Pub.

Mini-Maxi Trails: Florida. Joan L. Scalpone. (Illus.). 64p. 1997. pap. 8.95 (*0-929198-17-4*) Mini DayTrip Bks.

Mini Medical Encyclopedia: Mini-Encyclopedie Medicale. 8th ed. P. Letonturier. (FRE.). 416p. 1984. 25.00 (*0-8288-1816-9*, M8935) Fr & Eur.

Mini Memories: For Image Bearers. Joanne Wallace. (Illus.). 112p. (Orig.). 1995. pap. 7.00 (*1-880527-03-0*) J Wallace Sem.

M

An Asterisk (*) at the beginning of an entry indicates that the title is appearing for the first time.

*Mini Metro Chicago. Michael E. Brown. (Illus.). 1998. 1.95 (0-935039-56-2) Stwise Maps.
*Mini Metro London. Michael E. Brown. (Illus.). 1998. 1.95 (0-935039-33-3) Stwise Maps.
*Mini Metro Los Angeles. Michael E. Brown. (Illus.). 1998. 1.95 (0-935039-11-2) Stwise Maps.
*Mini Metro Manhattan Bus/Subway. Michael E. Brown. (Illus.). 1998. 1.95 (0-935039-00-7) Stwise Maps.
*Mini Metro Paris. Michael E. Brown. (Illus.). 1998. 1.95 (0-935039-32-5) Stwise Maps.
*Mini Metro San Francisco. Michael E. Brown. (Illus.). 1998. 1.95 (0-935039-18-X) Stwise Maps.
*Mini Metro Washington D. C. Michael E. Brown. (Illus.). 1998. 1.95 (0-935039-34-1) Stwise Maps.
Mini Michaelis Dicionario: English-Portuguese. Michaelis. 1999. pap. 13.95 (85-06-01595-2) Midwest European Pubns.
*Mini Michaelis Dicionario Frances-Portugues/Portugues-Frances. Michaelis. 1999. pap. 13.95 (85-06-01725-4) Midwest European Pubns.
Mini-Mickey. Bob Sehlinger. (Unofficial Guide to Walt Disney World Ser.). 1997. pap. 10.95 (0-02-861558-1) Macmillan.
Mini-Mickey: The Pocket-Size Unofficial Guide to Walt Disney World, 1999 Edition. Ed. by Frommer's Staff. (Disney Miniature Ser.). 320p. 1998. pap. 10.95 (0-02-862764-4, Pub. by Macmillan) S&S Trade.
Mini Mickey: The Pocket-Sized Unofficial Guide to Walt Disney World. Bob Sehlinger. 310p. 1999. pap. 10.95 (0-02-863040-8) Macmillan.
*Mini Mickey: The Pocket-Sized Unofficial Guide to Walt Disney World 2001. Bob Sehlinger. (Illus.). 312p. 2000. pap. 10.99 (0-7645-6250-9) IDG Bks.
Mini Mickey, 2001: The Pocket-sized Unofficial Guide. 336p. 1900. 10.95 (0-02-863799-2) Macmillan.
Mini Midrash & a Maaseh: An Anthology of Insights & Commentaries for Youngsters on the Weekly Torah Reading: Including Stories & Illustrations, 2 vols. Hanoch Teller. LC 98-27180. (J). 1998. 36.95 (1-881939-12-X, Pub. by NYC Pub Co) Feldheim.
Mini-Mills vs. Integrated & Foreign Producers. S. Moskowitz. 183p. 1998. 2500.00 (0-945235-63-1) Lead Edge Reports.
Mini Mini More, Vol. 2. Terri Brown & Nancy Brown. 48p. 1985. pap. text 6.50 (1-56770-151-5) S Scheewe Pubns.
Mini Module Manual. S. Leonard Dart & Eldred Tubbs F. 1976. pap. text 3.00 (0-915242-17-6) Pygmalion Pr.
Mini-Module, No. MS1: Skillbuilding in Medicine-Surgery. Ed. by American Association for Medical Transcription Sta. (Exploring Transcription Practices Ser.). 16p. (C). 1993. text, student ed. 30.00 incl. audio (0-935229-18-3) Am Assoc Med.
Mini-Module, No. MS3: Skillbuilding in Medicine-Surgery. Ed. by American Association for Medical Transcription Sta. (Exploring Transcription Practices Ser.). 16p. (C). 1995. text, student ed. 30.00 incl. audio (0-935229-26-4) Am Assoc Med.
Mini-Module, No. R1: Skillbuilding in Radiology. Ed. by American Association for Medical Transcription Sta. (Exploring Transcription Practices Ser.). 16p. (C). 1993. student ed. 30.00 incl. audio (0-935229-19-1) Am Assoc Med.
Mini-Module, No. R2: Skillbuilding in Radiology. Ed. by American Association for Medical Transcription Sta. (Exploring Transcription Practices Ser.). 16p. (C). 1994. text, student ed. 30.00 incl. audio (0-935229-24-8) Am Assoc Med.
Mini-Moments for Christmas: Forty Bright Spots to Enhance the Holidays. Robert Strand. LC 96-69685. (Mini-Moments to Give Ser.: Vol. 4). 112p. 1996. pap. 5.99 (0-89221-330-2) New Leaf.
Mini-Moments for Fathers. Robert Strand. LC 95-73127. (Mini Moments to Give Ser.: Vol. 2). 112p. 1996. pap. 5.99 (0-89221-317-5) New Leaf.
Mini-Moments for Graduates: Forty Bright Spots to Light the Path of a Graduate. Robert Strand. LC 95-73128. (Mini Moments to Give Ser.: Vol. 3). 112p. 1996. pap. 5.99 (0-89221-318-3) New Leaf.
Mini-Moments for Leaders: Forty Bright Spots to Encourage Those in Leadership. Robert Strand. LC 96-69686. (Mini-Moments to Give Ser.: Vol. 5). 112p. 1996. pap. 5.99 (0-89221-331-0) New Leaf.
Mini-Moments for Mothers. Robert Strand. LC 95-73130. (Mini Moments to Give Ser.: Vol. 1). 112p. 1996. pap. 5.99 (0-89221-316-7) New Leaf.
Mini Moments with Angels. Robert Strand. LC 97-68954. (Mini Moments to Give Ser.: Vol. 6). 112p. 1997. pap. 5.99 (0-89221-359-0) New Leaf.
Mini Mughals. Muni Lal. (Illus.). 340p. 1990. text 37.50 (81-220-0174-2, Pub. by Konark Pubs Pvt Ltd) Advent Bks Div.
Mini-Myths & Maxi-Words. Susan K. Weiler. (J). 1986. pap. text 9.99 (0-88334-191-3, 76156) Longman.
Mini Nuke Conspiracy. Hounam. 1999. pap. 12.95 (0-14-025733-0) Viking Penguin.
Mini Nutritional Assessment (MNA) Research & Practice in the Elderly: 1st Nestle Clinical & Performance Nutrition Workshop, Mini Nutritional Assessment (MNA) - MNA in the Elderly, Lausanne, October 1997. Ed. by B. J. Vellas et al. LC 99-18247. (Nestle Nutrition Workshop Series : Clinical & Performance Programme). (Illus.). 196p. 1999. 137.50 (3-8055-6803-7) S Karger.
Mini Owners Survival Manual. J. Tyler. (Illus.). 144p. Date not set. 19.95 (1-85532-610-8, Pub. by Ospry) Stackpole.
Mini Oxford School Dictionary. Hawkins. 704p. pap. write for info. (0-19-910333-X) OUP.
Mini Pocket Dictionaries: Arabic-English. Wagdi Rizk Ghali. 1996. pap. 3.95 (0-86685-718-4) Intl Bk Ctr.
Mini Pocket Dictionaries: English-Arabic. Wagdi Rizk Ghali. 1996. pap. 3.95 (0-86685-717-6) Intl Bk Ctr.
Mini Pocket Dictionaries: English-Arabic & Arabic-English. Wagdi Rizk Ghali. 1996. pap. 5.95 (0-86685-719-2) Intl Bk Ctr.
Mini Prayers That Prevail. Richard. LC 97-150890. 1996. pap. text 5.99 (0-932081-35-5) Victory Hse.
Mini Quilt Celebrations. Elizabeth Chandler & Joanne Donahue. (Illus.). 28p. (Orig.). 1995. pap. 15.95 (0-9636371-4-2) Lizanne Pub.
Mini Quilts from Traditional Designs. Adele Corcoran & Caroline Wilkinson. LC 95-24068. (Illus.). 128p. 1995. 27.95 (0-8069-1322-3) Sterling.
Mini Quilts from Traditional Designs. Adele Corcoran & Caroline Wilkinson. (Illus.). 128p. 1997. pap. 16.95 (0-8069-1323-1) Sterling.
Mini-Reef Aquarium. Richard F. Stratton. (Illus.). 64p. 1996. 19.95 (0-7938-0112-5, WW002) TFH Pubns.
Mini Reference Center, 4 vols., Set. 1992. boxed set 24.95 (0-528-83702-8) Rand McNally.
Mini Restoration: Preperation - Restoration & Maintenance. Jim Taylor. (Illus.). 240p. 1992. pap. 39.95 (1-85532-229-3, Pub. by Ospry) Motorbooks Intl.
*Mini Restoration Manual. Porter. (Illus.). 304p. 2000. 36.95 (1-85960-440-4, Pub. by Haynes Manuals) Motorbooks Intl.
*Mini Rough Guide Edinburgh. 2nd ed. Rough Guides Staff. (Illus.). 2000. pap. 9.95 (1-85828-505-4) Viking Penguin.
*Mini Rough Guide to Boston. 2nd ed. Rough Guides Staff. (Miniguides Ser.). (Illus.). 352p. 2000. pap. 9.95 (1-85828-521-6, Pub. by Rough Guides) Penguin Putnam.
Mini Rough Guide to Budapest. Charles Hebbert & Dan Richardson. (Illus.). 288p. 1999. 11.95 (1-85828-431-7, Pub. by Rough Guides) Penguin Putnam.
*Mini Rough Guide to Dublin. 2nd ed. Rough Guides Staff. (Illus.). 336p. 2000. pap. 9.95 (1-85828-504-6, Pub. by Rough Guides) Penguin Putnam.
Mini Rough Guide to Honolulu: Including Waikiki & All of Oahu. Rough Guides Staff. 208p. 1999. pap. 9.95 (1-85828-402-3) Penguin Putnam.
*Mini Rough Guide to Jerusalem 2000. Rough Guides Staff. (Miniguides Ser.). (Illus.). 2000. pap. 9.95 (1-85828-579-8, Rough Guides) Viking Penguin.
Mini Rough Guide to Lisbon. Matthew Hancock. (Illus.). 272p. 1998. pap. 9.95 (1-85828-297-7) Viking Penguin.
*Mini Rough Guide to Lisbon. 2nd ed. Rough Guides Staff. (Illus.). 2000. pap. 9.95 (1-85828-514-3, Rough Guides) Viking Penguin.
Mini Rough Guide to Madrid. Simon Baskett. (Illus.). 256p. 1998. pap. 9.95 (1-85828-353-1) Viking Penguin.
Mini Rough Guide to Maui. Rough Guides Staff. 240p. 1999. pap. 9.95 (1-85828-401-5) Penguin Putnam.
Mini Rough Guide to Melbourne. Stephen Townsend. (Illus.). 304p. 1999. 9.95 (1-85828-454-6, Pub. by Rough Guides) Penguin Putnam.
Mini Rough Guide to New Orleans. Samantha Cook. (Illus.). 288p. 1999. 9.95 (1-85828-440-6, Pub. by Rough Guides) Penguin Putnam.
Mini Rough Guide to St. Lucia. Sasha Heseltine & Karl Luntta. (Mini Rough Guide Ser.). (Illus.). 224p. 1998. pap. 9.95 (1-85828-329-9, Pub. by Rough Guides) Penguin Putnam.
Mini Rough Guide to Sydney. Margo Daly. (Illus.). 304p. 1999. 9.95 (1-85828-453-8, Pub. by Rough Guides) Penguin Putnam.
Mini Rough Guide to the Big Island of Hawaii. 2nd ed. Rough Guides Staff. (Illus.). 256p. 1999. pap. 9.95 (1-85828-485-6) Penguin Putnam.
*Mini Rough Guide to Toronto. Rough Guides Staff. (Miniguides Ser.). 544p. 1999. pap. 9.95 (1-85828-414-7, Pub. by Rough Guides) Penguin Putnam.
Mini Sagas: From the Daily Telegraph Competition. Intro. by Victoria Glendinning. LC 98-112176. 256p. 1998. pap. 14.25 (0-7509-1594-3, Pub. by Sutton Pub Ltd) Intl Pubs Mktg.
Mini-Scam: Reading Level 3-4. (Stormy Night Stories Ser.). 16p. 1993. 2.50 (0-88336-075-6) New Readers.
Mini-Sets Caption Books & Math Caption Books. Keep Books Organization Staff. (Illus.). 8p. (ps-5). pap. write for info. (1-893986-05-5) Keep Bks.
Mini-Sets Caption Books & Nursery Rhymes. Keep Books Organization Staff. (Illus.). (ps-5). pap. write for info. (1-893986-04-7) Keep Bks.
Mini-Sets 5 & Math Concepts. Keep Books Organization Staff. (Illus.). 8p. (ps-5). pap. write for info. (1-893986-15-2) Keep Bks.
Mini-Sets Letters, Words & Phonics. Keep Books Organization Staff. (Illus.). 8p. (ps-5). pap. write for info. (1-893986-17-9) Keep Bks.
Mini-Sets 1 & 2. Keep Books Organization Staff. (Illus.). (ps-5). pap. write for info. (1-893986-01-2) Keep Bks.
Mini-Sets Spanish Caption Books & Spanish Nursery Rhymes. Keep Books Organization Staff. (SPA., Illus.). 8p. (ps-5). pap. write for info. (1-893986-16-0) Keep Bks.
Mini-Sets 3 & 4. Keep Books Organization Staff. (Illus.). 8p. (ps-5). pap. write for info. (1-893986-14-4) Keep Bks.
Mini Sims Temporaries: Modern Office Simulations, 2 vols. Rosemarie McCauley. 232p. (Orig.). 1979. teacher ed. write for info. (0-672-97168-2) Macmillan.
Mini Sims Temporaries: Modern Office Simulations, 2 vols., 1. Rosemarie McCauley. 232p. (Orig.). 1979. pap. text. write for info. (0-672-97167-4) Macmillan.
Mini Sims Temporaries: Modern Office Simulations, 2 vols., 2. Rosemarie McCauley. 232p. (Orig.). 1979. pap. text. write for info. (0-672-97424-X) Macmillan.
Mini Sprint/Micro Sprint Racing Technology. Steve Smith. (Illus.). 93p. 1989. pap. text 17.95 (0-936834-67-6) S S Autosports.
Mini Story of the Root Children. Sibylle Von Olfers. 1998. 6.99 (0-86315-248-1, Pub. by Floris Bks) Gryphon Hse.
Mini Thesaurus. Webster's New World Staff & Joyce L. Vedral. 416p. 1997. 4.95 (0-02-862062-3) Macmillan.
Mini Tiny Tots. 5.98 (0-317-38606-9) Gick.
Mini Walks on the Mesa: A Story for Children. Ursula Cooper. LC 89-4448. (Illus.). 32p. (Orig.). (J). (gr. 3-6). 1989. pap. 6.95 (0-86534-133-8) Sunstone Pr.
Mini-World Video, 4 vols., Vol. 1. Jill Sazanami. 39p. 1992. pap. text 49.95 incl. VHS (1-881486-00-1) Sierra Media.
Mini-World Video, 4 vols., Vol. 2. Jill Sazanami. 38p. 1992. pap. text 49.95 incl. VHS (1-881486-01-X) Sierra Media.
Mini-World Video, 4 vols., Vol. 3. Jill Sazanami. 34p. 1992. pap. text 49.95 incl. VHS (1-881486-02-8) Sierra Media.
Mini-World Video, 4 vols., Vol. 4. Jill Sazanami. 53p. 1992. pap. text 49.95 incl. VHS (1-881486-03-6) Sierra Media.
Mini-World Video, 4 vols.; set, Vols. 1-4. Jill Sazanami. 1992. pap. text 169.00 incl. VHS (1-881486-04-4) Sierra Media.
Mini-World Video Textbook, Vol. 1. Jill Sazanami. 39p. 1992. pap. text 5.95 (1-881486-05-2) Sierra Media.
Mini-World Video Textbook, Vol. 2. Jill Sazanami. 38p. 1992. pap. text 5.95 (1-881486-06-0) Sierra Media.
Mini-World Video Textbook, Vol. 3. Jill Sazanami. 34p. 1992. pap. text 5.95 (1-881486-07-9) Sierra Media.
Mini-World Video Textbook, Vol. 4. Jill Sazanami. 53p. 1992. pap. text 5.95 (1-881486-08-7) Sierra Media.
Mini-World Video Textbook, Vols. 1-4. Jill Sazanami. 1992. teacher ed. 3.95 (1-881486-09-5) Sierra Media.
Miniatrue Mania. Shirley Liby. (Illus.). 80p. 1992. spiral bd. 14.95 (1-890952-05-2) S Liby Pubns.
Miniatura: or The Art of Limning. Edward Norgate et al. LC 96-43520. 304p. 1997. 65.00 (0-300-06913-8) Yale U Pr.
Miniaturas. Berta Montalvo. LC 88-84023. (Coleccion Espejo de Paciencia). (SPA., Illus.). 38p. (Orig.). 1991. pap. 6.00 (0-89729-522-6) Ediciones.
Miniature & Putting Courses: Insights & Opportunities. unabridged ed. (NGF Info Pacs Ser.). (Illus.). 97p. (Orig.). 1999. pap. 45.00 (1-57701-034-5, 99LB048) Natl Golf.
Miniature Antique Furniture: Doll House & Children's Furniture from the United States & Europe. Herbert F. Schiffer & Peter B. Schiffer. (Illus.). 266p. (Orig.). 1995. 49.95 (0-88740-882-6) Schiffer.
Miniature Arts of the Southwest. Nancy N. Schiffer. LC 91-60665. (Illus.). 64p. 1991. pap. 12.95 (0-88740-317-4) Schiffer.
Miniature Baltimore Album Quilts: 28 Embroidered & Embellished Block Designs. Jenifer Buechel. Ed. by Melissa Lowe. LC 96-30983. (Illus.). 96p. (Orig.). 1997. pap. 17.95 (1-56477-176-8, B290) Martingale & Co.
Miniature Bearing Technologies in the U. S. S. R. (The Institute VNIPP & NIIChasprom) Alexander Radin. Ed. by Andreas Tamberg. 151p. (Orig.). 1986. pap. text 75.00 (1-55831-038-X) Delphic Associates.
Miniature Beer Bottles & Go-Withs: A Price Guide & Reference Manual for Miniature Beer Collectables, Includes 1990 Update. Robert E. Kay. LC 80-81282. (Illus.). 166p. (Orig.). 1980. pap. 15.00 (0-9604218-0-7) K & K Pubs.
Miniature Bobbin Lace. Roz Snowdon. (Illus.). 176p. 1998. pap. text 14.95 (1-86108-086-7) Guild Master.
*Miniature Bonsai. Herb L. Gustafson. (Illus.). 2000. pap. 19.95 (0-8069-0983-8) Sterling.
Miniature Bull Terrier. Barbara J. Andrews. (Illus.). 96p. 1997. 19.95 (0-7938-0768-9, RX118) TFH Pubns.
*Miniature Cars. Julie Beyer. (High Interest Bks.). (Illus.). (J). 2000. 19.00 (0-516-23332-7) Childrens.
*Miniature Cars. Julie Beyer. LC 99-40449. (High Interest Bks.). (Illus.). 48p. (J). (gr. 4-7). 2000. pap. 6.95 (0-516-23532-X) Childrens.
*Miniature Cars. Julie Beyer. LC 99-40449. (Cool Collectibles Ser.). (Illus.). 2000. pap. write for info. (0-531-17620-7) Watts.
Miniature Crocheting & Knitting for Dollhouses. Rosemary Drysdale. (Illus.). 48p. 1982. pap. 3.95 (0-486-23964-0) Dover.
Miniature Decorative Patterns. William Veasey. LC 83-51777. (Blue Ribbon Pattern Ser.: Bk. VI). (Illus.). 64p. 1984. pap. 14.95 (0-88740-000-0) Schiffer.
*Miniature Dolls' Houses in 1/24th Scale: A Complete Guide to Making & Furnishing Houses. Derek Rowbottom. (Illus.). 2000. 29.95 (0-7153-0836-X) D & C Pub.
Miniature Donkey Foaling Manual. Bonnie Gross. (Illus.). 148p. (J). (gr. 3-12). 1995. pap. 27.95 (0-9658547-1-X) Miniat Donkey.
Miniature Duck Decoys for Woodcarvers: Easy-to-Use Templates & Complete Instructions for Making 16 Decorative Carvings. Anthony Hillman. (Illus.). 40p. (Orig.). 1985. pap. 6.95 (0-486-24936-0) Dover.
*Miniature Edition Joy of Cooking Keepsake. Irma R. Rombauer et al. (Illus.). 2000. 9.95 (0-7624-0842-1) Running Press Min.
*Miniature Embroidery for the Georgian Dolls' House. Pamela Warner. (Illus.). 2000. pap. 21.95 (1-86108-136-7) Guild Master.
Miniature Embroidery for the Victorian Dolls' House. Pamela Warner. LC 99-494970. 184p. 1999. pap. 19.95 (1-86108-095-6, Pub. by Guild Master) Sterling.
Miniature Emergency Vehicles. Edward Force. LC 85-50878. (Illus.). 236p. 1985. pap. 14.95 (0-88740-031-0) Schiffer.
*Miniature Empires. James Minahan. 360p. 1999. lib. bdg. 80.00 (1-57958-133-1) Fitzroy Dearborn.
Miniature Empires: A Historical Dictionary of the Newly Independent States. James Minahan. LC 98-13979. 360p. 1998. lib. bdg. 75.00 (0-313-30610-9, Greenwood Pr) Greenwood.
Miniature Epic in Vandal Africa. David. F. Bright. LC 87-40211. 320p. 1987. 37.50 (0-8061-2075-4) U of Okla Pr.
Miniature Fashions, 1750-1770, Vol. 7. Susan B. Sirkis. (Wish Booklets Ser.). 36p. 1971. pap. 5.95 (0-913786-07-1) Wish Bklets.
Miniature Fashions, 1848-1880-1896. Susan B. Sirkis. (Wish Booklets Ser.: Vol. 8). (Illus.). 48p. (Orig.). 1971. pap. 5.95 (0-913786-08-X) Wish Bklets.
*Miniature Floral Victorian Design Photo Album. (Montague House Photograph Albums Ser.). 1999. 5.99 (1-55853-505-5) Rutledge Hill Pr.
Miniature Golf. Nina Garfinkel & Maria Reidelbach. (Illus.). 96p. 1987. 27.50 (0-89659-684-2) Abbeville Pr.
Miniature Harmonica. Arnold. (Illus.). 1995. pap. 14.95 (0-940168-30-8) Boxwood.
Miniature Horse. Gail LaBonte. LC 89-26046. (Remarkable Animals Ser.). (Illus.). 60p. (J). (gr. 3 up). 1990. lib. bdg. 13.95 (0-87518-424-3, Dillon Silver Burdett) Silver Burdett Pr.
Miniature Horse: The Complete Guild to the Fascinating World of Miniatures. Jill Swedlow Coffey. (Illus.). 1992. reprint ed. pap. 16.95 (0-944963-02-1) Glastonbury CA.
Miniature Horse in Review: A Collection of Articles on Miniature Horses, 1. rev. ed. Ed. by Toni M. Leland. LC 95-74741. (Illus.). 136p. (Orig.). 1999. pap. text 21.95 (1-887932-04-6) Equine Graph Pubng.
Miniature Horse in Review Vol. 2: A Collection of Articles on Miniature Horses. rev. ed. Ed. by Toni M. Leland. (Illus.). 144p. 1998. pap. 23.95 (1-887932-08-9, Small Horse Pr) Equine Graph Pubng.
Miniature Horses see Learning about Horses Series
Miniature Horses. Charlotte Wilcox. (Learning about Horses Ser.). (Illus.). (J). 1997. 19.00 (0-516-20518-8) Childrens.
Miniature Horses: Their Care, Breeding & Coat Colors. Barbara Naviaux. Ed. by Joanne Abramson. LC 98-87725. (Illus.). 272p. 1999. 42.00 (0-9635964-1-1) Raintree Pubns.
Miniature Illustrations of Alisher Navoi's Works of the XV-XIXth Centuries. E. Yu Yusupov. 150p. 1982. 240.00 (0-7855-1654-9) St Mut.
Miniature Lamps. Frank Smith & Ruth Smith. LC 68-57930. (Illus.). 285p. 1981. reprint ed. 29.95 (0-916838-44-7) Schiffer.
*Miniature Lamps. 2nd ed. Ruth E. Smith. (Illus.). 249p. 2000. 29.95 (0-7643-1094-1) Schiffer.
Miniature Lamps II. Ruth E. Smith. LC 82-50618. (Illus.). 249p. 1982. 28.50 (0-916838-65-X) Schiffer.
Miniature Living Bonsai Landscapes: The Art of Saikei. Herb L. Gustafson. LC 94-13707. (Illus.). 192p. 1994. 29.95 (0-8069-0734-7) Sterling.
Miniature Masterpieces: Mosaic Glass, 1838-1924. Giovanni Sarpellon et al. LC 97-127407. (Illus.). 192p. 1997. 75.00 (3-7913-1454-8, Pub. by Prestel) te Neues.
Miniature Merchant Ships: A Guide to Waterline Ship Modelling in 1/1200 Scale. John Bowen. LC 97-132234. (Illus.). 240p. 1997. 38.95 (0-85177-659-0, Pub. by Brasseys) Brasseys.
Miniature Murder Mystery. large type ed. Peter Chambers. (Dales Large Print Ser.). 240p. 1996. pap. 18.99 (1-85389-655-1, Dales) Ulverscroft.
Miniature Needlepoint Carpets, 1. Janet Granger. 133p. 1999. pap. 14.95 (1-86108-023-9, Pub. by Guild Master) Sterling.
Miniature Needlepoint Rugs for Dollhouses Charted for Easy Use. Susan McBaine. (Illus.). 40p. (Orig.). 1976. pap. 3.95 (0-486-23388-X) Dover.
Miniature Orchids & How to Grow Them. enl. rev. ed. Rebecca T. Northen. LC 95-36243. (Illus.). 192p. 1996. reprint ed. pap. 14.95 (0-486-28920-6) Dover.
*Miniature Painting: A Complete Guide to Techniques, Mediums & Superface. Joan Cornish Willies. (Illus.). 143p. 1999. pap. text 25.00 (0-7881-6787-1) DIANE Pub.
Miniature Painting & Painters of Persia, India & Turkey, 2 vols. F. R. Martin. (C). 1993. 94.00 (81-85557-13-6) S Asia.
Miniature Painting in Ottoman Baghdad. Rachel Milstein. (Islamic Art & Architecture Ser.: No. 5). (Illus.). 268p. (C). 1989. text 55.00 (0-939214-60-1) Mazda Pubs.
Miniature Painting in the Armenian Kingdom of Cilicia from the Twelfth to the Fourteenth Century, 2 vols. Sirarpie Der Nersessian. LC 92-14829. (Dumbarton Oaks Studies: No. 31). (Illus.). 882p. 1993. 165.00 (0-88402-202-1, DEMP, Dumbarton Rsch Lib) Dumbarton Oaks.
Miniature Perfume Bottles. Glinda Bowman. LC 94-65619. (Illus.). 160p. (Orig.). 1994. pap. text 29.95 (0-88740-628-9) Schiffer.
Miniature Perfume Bottles: Minis, Mates, & More. Jeri L. Ringblum. LC 96-6012. (Illus.). 264p. 1996. pap. 24.95 (0-7643-0038-5) Schiffer.
Miniature Pigs. Pat Storer. (Complete Pet Owner's Manual Ser.). 1992. pap. 6.95 (0-8120-1356-5) Barron.
*Miniature Pinscher. Howell Book House Staff. LC 99-39657. 96p. 1999. pap. 7.95 (1-58245-136-2) Howell Bks.
Miniature Pinscher. Rose Radel. LC 98-37225. (Owner's Guide to a Happy, Healthy Pet Ser.). (Illus.). 160p. 1998. 9.95 (0-87605-229-4) Howell Bks.
*Miniature Pinscher: The Reigning King of Toys. Jacklyn E. Hungerland. LC 00-38315. (Illus.). 256p. 2000. 24.95 (1-58245-141-9) Howell Bks.
Miniature Pinscher Champions, 1952-1992. Jan Linzy. (Illus.). 175p. 2001. pap. 36.95 (1-55893-008-6) Camino E E & Bk.
Miniature Pinschers, AKC Rank No. 23. Evelyn Miller. (KW Dog Ser.). (Illus.). 1996. pap. 9.95 (0-7938-2358-7, KW162S) TFH Pubns.
Miniature Pinschers: Everything about Purchase, Care, Nutrition, Breeding, Behavior, & Training with Color Photos. D. Caroline Coile. (Complete Pet Owner's Manual Ser.). 1996. pap. 6.95 (0-8120-9346-1) Barron.

An Asterisk (*) at the beginning of an entry indicates that the title is appearing for the first time.

Miniature Political Economies: The Survival Strategies of the Poor. Abdul Aziz et al. LC 97-903882. 129p. 1997. pap. 100.00 (*81-7533-040-6*, Pub. by Print Hse) St Mut.

Miniature Portrait Collection of the Carolina Art Association. Martha R. Severens. Ed. by Charles L. Wyrick, Jr. (Illus.). 232p. 1984. pap. 17.50 (*0-910326-19-3*) Carolina Art.

Miniature Pullovers, Bk. 2. 2nd ed. 1994. 7.00 (*0-9634890-1-1*) B Lampen Knit.

Miniature Quilts. Adele Corcoran. Date not set. write for info. (*1-897954-55-7*) Sterling.

Miniature Quilts: Connecting New & Old Worlds. Tina Gravatt. LC 96-28026. (Illus.). 80p. (Orig.). 1996. pap. 14.95 (*0-89145-877-8*, 4752, Am Quilters Soc) Collector Bks.

Miniature Quilts with Vintage Style. Joyce Libal. Ed. by Debbie Hearn. (Illus.). 32p. 1999. pap. 12.95 (*1-885588-28-3*) Chitra Pubns.

Miniature Reef Aquarium. Cliff W. Emmens. 1989. 17.95 (*0-86622-661-3*, TS-119) TFH Pubns.

Miniature Rooms: The Thorne Rooms at the Art Institute of Chicago. Fannia Weingartner & Bruce H. Boyer. LC 83-8788. (Illus.). 168p. 1983. reprint ed. 40.00 (*0-89659-407-6*) Art Inst Chi.

Miniature Rooms: The Thorne Rooms at the Art Institute of Chicago. 6th ed. Fannia Weingartner & Bruce H. Boyer. LC 83-8788. (Illus.). 168p. 1983. reprint ed. pap. 24.95 (*0-89659-408-4*) Art Inst Chi.

Miniature Roses. Sergio Baradat & Saxon Holt. LC 97-30393. 1998. 14.95 (*0-8118-1844-6*) Chronicle Bks.

***Miniature Roses.** Lin Hawthorne. (New Plant Library). 1999. 11.95 (*0-7548-0124-1*, Lorenz Bks) Anness Pub.

Miniature Roses: Their Care & Cultivation. Sean McCann. (Illus.). 144p. 1996. pap. 17.95 (*0-304-34799-X*, Pub. by Cassell) Sterling.

Miniature Satellite Dishes: The New Digital Television. 2nd ed. Frank Baylin. (Illus.). 128p. 1995. pap. text 20.00 (*0-917893-24-7*) Baylin Pubns.

Miniature Schnauzer. Janice A. Pisano. (Illus.). 224p. 1995. 9.95 (*0-7938-1184-8*, KW042) TFH Pubns.

Miniature Schnauzer: Owner's Guides to a Happy, Healthy Pet. Jeanette Stark. (Owner's Guide to a Happy Healthy Pet Ser.). (Illus.). 160p. 1996. 12.95 (*0-87605-397-5*) Howell Bks.

Miniature Schnauzer Champions, 1952-1987. Camino E. E. & Bk. Co. Staff. (Illus.). 200p. 1989. pap. 36.95 (*0-940808-84-6*) Camino E E & Bk.

Miniature Schnauzers. Beverly Pisano. 1998. pap. text 9.95 (*0-7938-2336-6*) TFH Pubns.

Miniature Schnauzers. Karla S. Rugh. LC 96-44416. 1997. pap. 6.95 (*0-8120-9739-4*) Barron.

***Miniature Schnauzers: A New Owner's Guide.** Charlotte Schwartz. LC 99-205967. 1998. 12.95 (*0-7938-2796-5*) TFH Pubns.

Miniature Schnauzers Today. Peter Newman. LC 97-34517. 176p. 1997. 29.95 (*0-87605-239-1*) Howell Bks.

Miniature Schnauzers Today. Peter Newman. 176p. 1998. 27.95 (*0-87605-275-8*) Macmillan.

Miniature Sculpture from the Athenian Agora. Dorothy B. Thompson. (Excavations of the Athenian Agora Picture Bks.: No. 3). (Illus.). 32p. 1959. pap. 3.00 (*0-87661-603-1*) Am Sch Athens.

Miniature Sweaters, Bk. I. 2nd ed. Betty Lampen. 1990. 7.00 (*0-9634890-0-3*) B Lampen Knit.

Miniature Thermoplastics Sculpture. Zach M. Arnold. 232p. (Orig.). 1996. pap. 14.95 (*0-940168-39-1*) Boxwood.

Miniature to Masterpiece: Perfect Piecing Secrets from a Prizewinning Quiltmaker. Nancy Srebro-Johnson. Ed. by Mark Wilber & Rebecca Wilber. (Illus.). 80p. (Orig.). 1990. student ed. 14.95 (*0-9627646-0-4*) R C W Publng.

Miniature Trees: Their Care & Maintenance. Charles Harnett. (Secrets of Bonsai Ser.). (Illus.). 190p. (Orig.). pap. 14.95 (*0-9630959-0-0*) Bonsai East.

Miniature Vehicles. Robert S. Young. LC 92-33010. (Collectibles Ser.). (Illus.). 72p. (YA). (gr. 5 up). 1993. lib. bdg. 13.95 (*0-87518-518-5*, Dillon Silver Burdett) Silver Burdett Pr.

Miniature Vertebrates: The Implications of Small Body Size. Peter J. Miller. (Symposia of the Zoological Society of London Ser.: Vol. 69). (Illus.). 348p. 1996. text 125.00 (*0-19-857787-7*, Clarendon Pr) OUP.

Miniatures. Richard Walker. 1998. 15.95 (*1-85514-267-8*) Natl Port Gall.

Miniatures: An Illustrated Selection of over 100 Subjects from the Ashmolean's Collection. Richard Walker. (Illus.). 80p. 1997. 19.95 (*1-85444-077-2*, 0772, Pub. by Ashmolean Mus) A Schwartz & Co.

Miniatures: An Illustrated Selection of over 100 Subjects from the Ashmolean's Collections. Richard Walker. (Illus.). 80p. 1997. pap. 12.95 (*1-85444-078-0*, 0780, Pub. by Ashmolean Mus) A Schwartz & Co.

Miniatures. Cooper-Hewitt Museum. Ed. by Nancy Aakre. LC 82-72762. (Smithsonian Illustrated Library of Antiques). (Illus.). 128p. (Orig.). 1983. 9.95 (*0-910503-45-1*) Cooper-Hewitt Museum.

Miniatures: Dictionary & Guide. Daphne Foskett. (Illus.). 704p. 1987. 99.50 (*1-85149-063-9*) Antique Collect.

Miniatures: 250 Years of the English Miniature. Richard Walker. (Illus.). 96p. 1998. pap. 15.95 (*1-85514-242-2*, Pub. by Natl Port Gall) Antique Collect.

Miniatures & Silhouettes: Modes & Manners Supplement. Max Von Boehn. LC 70-145772. (Illus.). 224p. 1972. reprint ed. 21.95 (*0-405-08279-7*, Pub. by Blom Pubns) Ayer.

Miniatures Battles. (Star Wars Miniatures Ser.). 18.00 (*0-87431-206-X*, 40090) West End Games.

Miniatures Battles. (Star Wars Miniatures Ser.). 128p. 1991. 18.00 (*0-87431-144-6*, 40044) West End Games.

Miniatures Battles Starter Set. (Star Wars Miniatures Ser.). boxed set 35.00 (*0-87431-264-7*, 40210) West End Games.

Miniatures Companion. (Star Wars Miniatures Ser.). 15.00 (*0-87431-216-7*, 40070) West End Games.

Miniatures for Guitar. L. Boyd. 56p. 1994. pap. 14.95 (*0-7935-2339-7*, 00699385); pap. 17.95 (*0-7935-2340-0*, 00699386) H Leonard.

Miniatures for Tuba & Piano. Barton Cummings. (Contemporary Instrumental Ser.: No. 5). 9p. 1991. pap. text 7.00 (*1-56571-000-2*) PRB Prods.

Miniatures from the Heart Judges' Choice. Chitra Publications Staff. Ed. by Joanne S. Nolt. LC 94-45253. (Illus.). 40p. (Orig.). 1995. pap. 9.95 (*1-885588-00-3*) Chitra Pubns.

Miniatures in Judaeo-Persian Manuscripts. Vera Basch Moreen. (Bibliographica Judaica Ser.: No. 9). 56p. 1985. pap. 15.00 (*0-87820-907-7*) Hebrew Union Coll Pr.

Miniatures in Music. Prod. by Zobeida Perez. 20p. (Orig.). (J). 1994. pap. 17.00 (*0-89898-749-0*, BMR05077) Wrner Bros.

Miniatures in the Collection of Her Majesty the Queen: The 18th & 19th Centuries. Richard Walker. (Pictures in the Collection of Her Majesty the Queen). (Illus.). 571p. (C). 1992. text 250.00 (*0-521-30781-3*) Cambridge U Pr.

Miniatures in the Gospels of St. Augustine: Corpus Christi College Ms. 286. Francis Wormald. LC 54-4312. (Sandars Lectures in Bibliography). (Illus.). 67p. reprint ed. pap. 25.00 (*0-608-30132-9*, 2051474) Bks Demand.

Miniatures of French History. Hilaire Belloc. 300p. 1990. reprint ed. pap. 14.95 (*0-89385-035-7*) Sugden.

Miniaturization Technologies. (Illus.). 48p. (Orig.). (C). 1992. pap. text 25.00 (*1-56806-118-8*) DIANE Pub.

***Miniaturized Systems with Micro-Optics & MEMS.** Ed. by M. E. Motamedi & Rolf Goering. 434p. 1999. pap. text 92.00 (*0-8194-3475-2*) SPIE.

Miniaturized Systems with Micro-Optics & Micromechanics II, Vol. 3008. Ed. by M. Edward Motamedi et al. LC 97-175321. 382p. 1997. 89.00 (*0-8194-2419-6*) SPIE.

Miniaturized Systems with Micro-Optics & Micromechanics III, Vol. 3276. Ed. by M. Edward Motamedi & Rolf Goering. LC 98-226760. 290p. 1998. 69.00 (*0-8194-2715-2*) SPIE.

Minibeasts As Pets. Elaine Landau. LC 97-17372. (True Books--Animals Ser.). 1997. lib. bdg. 21.00 (*0-516-20388-6*) Childrens.

Minibeasts As Pets. Elaine Landau. LC 97-17372. (True Bks.). (J). 1998. pap. text 6.95 (*0-516-26268-8*) Childrens.

Minibike Mystery: Read-Along. Gutman & Johnson. (Illus.). 32p. (J). (gr. 3-6). 1984. pap. 9.95 (*0-87386-296-1*) Jan Prods.

Minibikes. Lori K. Pupeza. LC 98-10606. (Ultimate Motorcycle Ser.). (J). 1998. lib. bdg. 14.98 (*1-57765-002-6*) ABDO Pub Co.

Minicomputer to the Rescue! Denita Keagy. LC 87-62051. (Mini-Rora Adventures Ser.). (Illus.). 36p. (J). (gr. k-5). 1987. lib. bdg. 10.95 (*0-944027-01-6*) New Memories.

Minicomputers: A Reference Book for Engineers, Scientists & Managers. Yacup Paker. (Abacus Bks.). 506p. 1981. text 249.00 (*0-85626-188-2*) Gordon & Breach.

Minicomputers: Low-cost Computer Power for Management. Donald P. Kenney. LC 72-92752. 207p. reprint ed. pap. 64.20 (*0-608-12164-9*, 202391500034) Bks Demand.

Minicomputers in Industrial Control: An Introduction. Ed. by Thomas J. Harrison. LC 77-93080. (Illus.). 381p. reprint ed. pap. 118.20 (*0-7837-5156-7*, 204488500004) Bks Demand.

Minidicionario da Lingua Portuguesa. Ed. by Melhoramentos. (POR.). 568p. 1992. 24.95 (*0-7859-9313-4*) Fr & Eur.

***Minidictionary for Nurses.** 4th ed. Tanya A. McFerran. LC 98-24055. 1998. write for info. (*0-19-860204-9*) OUP.

Minidictionary of Geography. Susan Mayhew. LC 93-46664. (Oxford Minireference Ser.). (Illus.). 320p. 1994. pap. write for info. (*0-19-211692-4*) OUP.

Minidisc. Roger Verlinden. 112p. 1996. pap. text 32.95 (*0-240-51444-0*, Focal) Buttrwrth-Heinemann.

***Minidrill: Fifteen Projects.** John Everett. (Illus.). 2000. pap. 17.95 (*1-86108-137-5*) Guild Master.

Miniguide to ISO 9000. John T. Rabbitt & Peter A. Bergh. 59p. 1995. pap. 4.50 (*0-527-76302-0*) Productivity Inc.

***Minikin.** Stephen Cosgrove. (Illus.). 32p. (Orig.). (ps-3). 2000. pap. 4.99 (*0-8431-7629-6*, Price Stern) Peng Put Young Read.

Minilaparotomy under Local Anaesthesia: A Curriculum for Doctors & Nurses, Participant's Handbook. AVSC International Staff. Ed. by Ruth Mullen. (Illus.). 72p. 1995. student ed. 8.00 (*1-885063-08-3*) AVSC Int.

Minilaparotomy under Local Anaesthesia: A Curriculum for Doctors & Nurses, Trainer's Package. AVSC International Staff. Ed. by Ruth Mullen. (Illus.). 140p. 1993. pap. text 75.00 (*1-885063-07-5*) AVSC Int.

Minilibros - Rey Rollo. David McKee. (SPA., Illus.). (J). (ps-1). boxed set 7.95 (*980-257-191-1*, Pub. by Ediciones Ekare) Kane-Miller Bk.

Minima Ethnographica. Jackson. LC 97-49428. 216p. 1998. pap. text 17.00 (*0-226-38946-4*); lib. bdg. 40.00 (*0-226-38945-6*) U Ch Pr.

Minima Media. 208p. 1996. 40.00 (*0-614-18125-9*, 610451, Pub. by Plitt Druck-und) Dist Art Pubs.

Minima Media. (Illus.). 208p. 1996. 40.00 (*3-9802395-7-8*, Pub. by Plitt Druck-und) Dist Art Pubs.

Minimaksnye Algoritmy v Zadachakh Chislennogo Analiza see Minimax Models in the Theory of Numerical Methods

Minimal Access Cardiothoracic Surgery. Anthony P. Yim et al. Ed. by Richard Lampert. LC 99-36532. (Illus.). 655p. (C). 1999. text 295.00 (*0-7216-7723-1*, W B Saunders Co) Harcrt Hlth Sci Grp.

Minimal Access General Surgery. David Rosin. LC 93-41152. 1994. 95.00 (*1-870905-72-5*, Radcliffe Med Pr) Scovill Paterson.

Minimal Access Gynaecology. Ed. by Stephen Grochmal. LC 94-37495. 1994. 120.00 (*1-870905-73-3*, Radcliffe Med Pr) Scovill Paterson.

Minimal Access Medicine & Surgery. David Rosin. 1993. 89.95 (*1-870905-67-9*, Radcliffe Med Pr) Scovill Paterson.

Minimal Access Orthopedics. David Hunt. LC 95-1976. 1996. 90.00 (*1-870905-58-X*, Radcliffe Med Pr) Scovill Paterson.

Minimal Access Surgery for Nurses & Technicians. Ed. by Fiona A. Hall. LC 94-8610. 1994. 47.50 (*1-870905-63-6*, Radcliffe Med Pr) Scovill Paterson.

Minimal Access Surgical Oncology. Ed. by Frederick Greene & David Rosin. LC 95-5161. 1995. 150.00 (*1-85775-080-2*, Radcliffe Med Pr) Scovill Paterson.

Minimal Access Thoracic Surgery. K. Mannccke. (Illus.). 296p. 1999. text 110.00 (*0-412-81600-8*, Pub. by E A) OUP.

Minimal Art: A Critical Anthology. Ed. by Gregory Battcock. LC 94-32628. 1995. 22.50 (*0-520-20147-7*, Pub. by U CA Pr) Cal Prin Full Svc.

Minimal Art: Critical Perspectives. F. Colpitt. LC 92-23902. (Illus.). 248p. 1993. reprint ed. pap. 16.95 (*0-295-97236-X*) U of Wash Pr.

***Minimal Art: Eine Kritische Retrospektive.** 2nd ed. Gregor Stemmrich. (GER., Illus.). 720p. 1998. text 30.00 (*3-364-00354-8*, Verlag Kunst) Gordon & Breach.

Minimal Brain Dysfunction: A Prospective Study. Paul L. Nichols & Ta-Chuan Chen. LC 80-18739. 352p. 1981. text 69.95 (*0-89859-074-4*) L Erlbaum Assocs.

Minimal Brain Dysfunction: Facts or Fiction. Ed. by Alex F. Kalverboer et al. (Advances in Biological Psychiatry Ser.: Vol. 1). (Illus.). 1978. 34.00 (*3-8055-2864-7*) S Karger.

Minimal Competency Testing. Peter W. Airasian et al. LC 79-3994. (Illus.). 248p. 1979. 39.95 (*0-87778-138-9*) Educ Tech Pubns.

Minimal Contrast: Read Aloud Stories with Activities. Lynn Krupa. Ed. by Sharon G. Webber. (Illus.). 236p. (J). (ps-2). 1996. spiral bd., wbk. ed. 30.95 (*1-58650-042-2*, BK-235) Super Duper.

Minimal Contrast Phonics Test. Nita Sundbye. 40p. 1998. pap. 29.95 (*0-9659517-4-X*) Curriculum Solns.

Minimal Degrees of Unsolvability & the Full Approximation Construction. Richard L. Epstein. LC 75-20308. (Memoirs Ser.: No. 3/162). 136p. 1975. pap. 21.00 (*0-8218-1862-7*, MEMO/3/162) Am Math.

Minimal Family. Jan E. Dizard & Howard Gadlin. LC 90-10801. 304p. 1992. 35.00 (*0-87023-728-4*); pap. 17.95 (*0-87023-804-3*) U of Mass Pr.

Minimal Fictions. Richard Kostelanetz. LC 94-70883. 100p. 1994. pap. 9.95 (*1-878580-06-X*) Asylum Arts.

***Minimal Graphics: The Powerful New Look of Graphic Design.** Catharine Fishel. 2000. 45.00 (*1-56496-628-3*) Rockport Pubs.

Minimal Ideas: Syntactic Studies in the Minimalist Framework. Ed. by Werner Abraham et al. LC 96-26359. (Linguistik Aktuell/Linguistics Today Ser.: Vol. 12). xii, 364p. 1996. pap. 29.95 (*1-55619-231-2*); lib. bdg. 89.00 (*1-55619-230-4*) J Benjamins Pubng Co.

***Minimal Interiors.** Ann Mcardle. (Interiors Ser.). (Illus.). 112p. 1999. pap. 19.99 (*1-56496-612-7*) Rockport Pubs.

Minimal Invasive Surgery (MIS) Disposable Devices Markets. (Market Research Reports). 1995. write for info. (*0-614-96231-5*) Theta Corp.

Minimal Invasive Surgery (MIS) Disposable Devices Markets. (Market Research Reports: No. 417). (Illus.). 195p. 1995. pap. 795.00 (*0-614-09919-6*) Theta Corp.

Minimal Model Approach & Determinants of Glucose Tolerance. Ed. by Richard N. Bergman & Jennifer C. Lovejoy. LC 97-18553. (Pennington Center Nutrition Ser.: Vol. 7). 424p. 1997. text 90.00 (*0-8071-2238-6*) La State U Pr.

Minimal Neopasia. Ed. by Ekkehard Grundmann & L. Beck. (Recent Results in Cancer Research Ser.: Vol. 106). (Illus.). 208p. 1988. 106.00 (*0-387-18455-4*) Spr-Verlag.

Minimal Networks. Alexander O. Ivanov. 432p. 1994. boxed set 134.95 (*0-8493-8642-X*, QA166) CRC Pr.

Minimal Politics. Maurice Berger. (Illus.). 200p. 1997. pap. 14.95 (*1-890761-00-1*) Dist Art Pubs.

Minimal Processing of Foods & Process Optimization--An Interface. Ed. by R. Paul Singh & Fernanda A. R. Oliveira. LC 94-4206. (Food Engineering & Manufacturing Ser.). 544p. 1994. boxed set 177.95 (*0-8493-7903-2*) CRC Pr.

Minimal Projections in Banach Spaces: Problems of Existence & Uniqueness & Their Application. W. Odyniec & G. Lewicki. (Lecture Notes in Mathematics Ser.: Vol. 1449). (Illus.). viii, 168p. 1990. 35.95 (*0-387-53197-1*) Spr-Verlag.

Minimal Rationality. Christopher Cherniak. 176p. 1990. reprint ed. pap. text 14.50 (*0-262-53087-2*, Bradford Bks) MIT Pr.

Minimal Residual Disease in Acute Leukemia. Ed. by B. Lowenberg & A. Hagenbeek. (Developments in Oncology Ser.). 382p. 1984. text 211.50 (*0-89838-630-6*) Kluwer Academic.

Minimal Residual Disease in Acute Leukemia, 1986. Ed. by A. Hagenbeek & B. Lowenberg Hagenbeek. (Developments in Oncology Ser.). 1986. lib. bdg. 170.50 (*0-89838-799-X*) Kluwer Academic.

Minimal Self: Psychic Survival in Troubled Times. Christopher Lasch. LC 84-4103. 352p. 1985. reprint ed. pap. 12.95 (*0-393-30263-6*) Norton.

Minimal Surface I: Boundary Value Problems. U. Dierkes et al. LC 90-27155. 507p. 1992. 135.95 (*0-387-53169-6*) Spr-Verlag.

***Minimal Surfaces** Tobias H. Colding. LC 99-72225. (Lecture Notes in Mathematics 4 Ser.). 124p. 1999. write for info. (*0-9658703-3-2*) NYU Courant.

Minimal Surfaces. Ed. by A. T. Fomenko. LC 91-640741. (Advances in Soviet Mathematics Ser.: Vol. 15). 342p. 1993. 137.00 (*0-8218-4116-5*, ADVSOV/15C) Am Math.

Minimal Surfaces & Functions of Bounded Variation. E. Guisti. (Monographs in Mathematics: No. 80). 240p. 1984. 91.50 (*0-8176-3153-4*) Birkhauser.

Minimal Surfaces in IR Cube. J. L. Barbosa & A. G. Colares. (Lecture Notes in Mathematics Ser.: Vol. 1195). x, 124p. 1990. 31.95 (*0-387-16491-X*) Spr-Verlag.

Minimal Surfaces in Riemannian Manifolds. Min Ji & Guang Y. Wang. LC 93-17168. (Memoirs of the American Mathematical Society Ser.: No. 495). 50p. 1993. pap. 25.00 (*0-8218-2560-7*, MEMO/104/495) Am Math.

Minimal Surfaces, Stratified Multivarifolds, & the Plateau Problem. Dao Trong Thi & A. Fomenko. LC 90-22932. (Translations of Mathematical Monographs). 404p. 1991. text 158.00 (*0-8218-4536-5*, MMONO/84) Am Math.

Minimal Words in a Minimal Syntax: Word Formation in Swedish. Gunlog Josefsson. LC 98-13794. (Linguistik Aktuell/Linguistics Today Ser.: Vol. 19). ix, 199p. 1998. 75.00 (*1-55619-903-1*) J Benjamins Pubng Co.

Minimalism. Atrium. 1999. pap. 35.00 (*0-688-16222-3*, Wm Morrow) Morrow Avon.

Minimalism. David Batchelor. (Movements in Modern Art Ser.). (Illus.). 80p. (C). 1998. pap. 15.00 (*0-521-62759-1*) Cambridge U Pr.

Minimalism: Art of Circumstance. Kenneth Baker. (Illus.). 144p. 1997. 45.00 (*0-89659-887-X*) Abbeville Pr.

Minimalism: Origins. Edward Strickland. LC 93-18396. (Illus.). 320p. (C). 1993. lib. bdg. 31.95 (*0-253-35499-4*) Ind U Pr.

***Minimalism: Origins.** Edward Strickland. (Illus.). 320p. 2000. pap. 17.95 (*0-253-21388-6*) Ind U Pr.

***Minimalism: Themes & Movements.** James Meyer. 2000. 69.95 (*0-7148-3460-2*) Phaidon Pr.

***Minimalism & the Short Story - Raymond Carver, Amy Hempel & Mary Robinson.** Cynthia W. Hallett. LC 99-16645. (Studies in Comparative Literature: Vol. 28). 168p. 1999. text 79.95 (*0-7734-7936-8*) E Mellen.

Minimalism Beyond the Nurnberg Funnel. John M. Carroll. LC 97-36124. (Illus.). 428p. 1998. 49.50 (*0-262-03249-X*, 175-98) MIT Pr.

Minimalism, Scope, & VP Structure. Thomas Stroik. LC 96-4512. 192p. 1996. 39.95 (*0-8039-5960-5*); pap. 17.95 (*0-8039-5961-3*) Sage.

***Minimalismus: Leonid Dobycins Prosa im Kontext der Totalitaren Asthetik.** Caroline Schramm. (Slavische Literaturen. Texte und Abbandlungen. BD. 19 Ser.). 297p. 1999. 52.95 (*3-631-34252-7*) P Lang Pubng.

Minimalist Analysis. Howard Lasnik. LC 98-35453. (Generative Syntax Ser.). 224p. 1999. 64.95 (*0-631-21093-8*); pap. 29.95 (*0-631-21094-6*) Blackwell Pubs.

***Minimalist Approach to Intrasentential Code Switching.** rev. ed. Jeff MacSwan. LC 98-51959. (Outstanding Dissertations in Linguistics Ser.). 329p. 1999. 71.00 (*0-8153-3274-2*) Garland.

***Minimalist Cooks at Home: Recipes That Give You More Flavor from Fewer Ingredients in Less Time.** Mark Bittman. LC 99-36291. (Illus.). 288p. 2000. 25.00 (*0-7679-0361-7*) Broadway BDD.

Minimalist Garden. Christopher Bradley-Hole. LC 99-32815. (Illus.). 208p. 1999. text 50.00 (*1-58093-055-7*, Pub. by Monacelli Pr) Penguin Putnam.

Minimalist Griller Handbook. Oliver Abel. (Illus.). 208p. 1998. pap. 16.00 (*0-8059-4523-7*) Dorrance.

***Minimalist Interiors.** Joaquin Rossell. (Illus.). 176p. 2000. pap. write for info. (*0-8230-6636-3*) Watsn-Guptill.

Minimalist Mobile Robotics: A Colony-Style Architecture for an Artificial Intelligence. Ed. by Jonathan H. Connell. (Perspectives in Artificial Intelligence Ser.: Vol. 5). 192p. 1990. text 47.00 (*0-12-185230-X*) Acad Pr.

***Minimalist Parameter: Selected Papers from the Open Linguistics Forum, Ottawa, 21-23 March, 1997.** Open Linguistics Forum Staff. Ed. by Galina M. Alexandrova & Olga Arnaudova. LC 99-88575. (Current Issues in Linguistic Theory Ser.: Vol. 192). viii, 374p. 2000. 79.00 (*1-55619-970-8*) J Benjamins Pubng Co.

Minimalist Program. Noam Chomsky. (Current Studies in Linguistics). 426p. (Orig.). 1995. pap. text 24.00 (*0-262-53128-3*) MIT Pr.

Minimalist Vision of Transcendence: A Naturalist Philosophy of Religion. Jerome A. Stone. LC 91-33858. (SUNY Series in Religious Studies). 262p. (C). 1992. pap. text 21.95 (*0-7914-1160-5*) State U NY Pr.

Minimalists. K. Robert Schwartz. LC 96-196303. (Twentieth Century Composers Ser.). (Illus.). 240p. 1996. pap. text 19.95 (*0-7148-3381-9*, Pub. by Phaidon Press) Phaidon Pr.

Minimally Invasive Abdominal Surgery. Ed. by K. Kremer et al. (Illus.). 396p. 2000. 199.00 (*0-86577-639-3*) Thieme Med Pubs.

Minimally Invasive Cardiac Surgery. Ed. by Robbin G. Cohen. LC 99-10903. 359p. 1999. 245.00 (*0-942219-79-1*) Quality Med Pub.

Minimally Invasive Cardiac Surgery. Ed. by Gerard M. Guiraudon. (Cardiac Surgery Grand Rounds Ser.: Vol. 1). (Illus.). 2000. write for info. (*0-87993-688-6*, Futura Media) Futura Pub.

Minimally Invasive Cardiac Surgery, Vol. II. Mehmet C. Oz & Daniel Goldstein. LC 98-30788. (Contemporary Cardiology Ser.: Vol. 2). 256p. 1998. 125.00 (*0-89603-635-9*) Humana.

***Minimally Invasive Endonasal Sinus Surgery: Principles, Techniques, Results, Complications, Revision Surgery.** Werner G. Hosemann. LC 99-52609. (Illus.). 2000. 99.00 (*0-86577-907-4*) Thieme Med Pubs.

Minimally Invasive Neurosurgery I. Ed. by B. L. Bauer & D. Hellwig. (Acta Neurochirugica - Supplementum Ser.: Vol. 54). 200p. 1992. 108.00 (*0-387-82321-2*) Spr-Verlag.

Minimally Invasive Neurosurgery II. Ed. by B. L. Bauer & D. Hellwig. (Acta Neurochirugica - Supplementum Ser.: Vol. 61). 115p. 1995. 88.00 (*0-387-82593-2*) Spr-Verlag.

Minimally Invasive Restorations with Bonding. Michel Degrange & Jean-Francois Roulet. LC 96-37504. (Illus.). 280p. 1997. 98.00 (*0-86715-327-X*) Quintessence.

***Minimally Invasive Spine Surgery: A Surgical Manual.** Ed. by H. Mayer. 290p. 2000. (*3-540-65631-6*) Spr-Verlag.

Minimally Invasive Surgery: Principles & Outcomes. Ed. by Charles Andrus et al. 416p. 1998. text 83.00 (*90-5702-261-3*, ECU107, Harwood Acad Pubs) Gordon & Breach.

Minimally Invasive Surgery & New Technology. Ed. by Felicien M. Steichen & Roger Welter. LC 93-38895. (Illus.). 763p. 1993. 130.00 (*0-942219-51-1*) Quality Med Pub.

Minimally Invasive Surgery in Gastrointestinal Cancer. Ed. by Miguel A. Cuesta & Alexander G. Nagy. LC 93-29876. (Illus.). 1993. text 120.00 (*0-443-04987-4*) Church.

Minimally Invasive Surgery of the Foregut. Ed. by Jeffrey H. Peters & Tom R. DeMeester. LC 94-31703. (Illus.). 334p. 1994. text 115.00 (*0-942219-62-7*) Quality Med Pub.

Minimally Invasive Techniques for Neurosurgery: Current Status & Future Perspectives. Ed. by D. Hellwig & B. L. Bauer. LC 97-34546. (Acta Neurochirurgica Supplementum Ser.: Vols. 1 & 2). (Illus.). 305p. 1997. text. write for info. (*3-540-63299-9*) Spr-Verlag.

Minimally Invasive Techniques in Neurosurgery. Stephen J. Haines & Alan R. Cohen. (Illus.). 286p. 1995. 85.00 (*0-683-02000-5*) Lppncott W & W.

Minimally Invasive Therapy of the Brain. Antonio A. De Salles & Robert B. Lufkin. LC 96-44702. 1996. 189.00 (*0-86577-641-5*) Thieme Med Pubs.

Minimally Invasive Therapy of the Liver & Biliary System. J. G. McNulty. LC 93-42224. (Illus.). 205p. 1994. 115.00 (*0-86577-514-1*) Thieme Med Pubs.

***Minimally Processed Fruits & Vegetables: Fundamental Aspects & Applications.** Stella M. Alzamora et al. LC 00-38113. (Illus.). 2000. write for info. (*0-8342-1672-8*) Aspen Pub.

Minimally Processed Refrigerated Fruits & Vegetables. Ed. by Robert C. Wiley. LC 93-40071. 1994. write for info. (*0-442-23834-7*) Chapman & Hall.

Minimanual see Works Manual, Version 8, An Introduction & Beyond to Vectorworks

Minimanual - An Introduction & Beyond to Minicad: For Version 7. Janis Kent. LC 98-228649. (Illus.). xxviii, 630p. 1998. pap. 65.00 (*0-9651981-4-6*) Improbability Pr.

Minimax. Anna Livia. LC 90-42350. 224p. 1991. pap. 9.95 (*0-933377-11-8*, Pub. by Eighth Mount Pr); lib. bdg. 22.95 (*0-933377-12-6*, Pub. by Eighth Mount Pr) Consort Bk Sales.

Minimax Algebra. R. A. Cuninghame-Green. LC 79-1314. (Lecture Notes in Economics & Mathematical Systems Ser.: Vol. 166). 1979. 28.00 (*0-387-09113-0*) Spr-Verlag.

Minimax & Applications. Panos M. Pardalos. LC 95-30189. (Nonconvex Optimization & Its Applications Ser.: Vol. 4). 308p. (C). 1995. text 154.50 (*0-7923-3615-1*) Kluwer Academic.

Minimax & Monotonicity. S. Simons. LC 98-37797. (Lecture Notes in Mathematics Ser.: Vol. 1693). xi, 172p. 1998. pap. 33.00 (*3-540-64755-4*) Spr-Verlag.

Minimax Diet & Nutrition Book: Maximum Nutrition, Minimum Calories. David A. Phillips. LC 88-6937. 160p. (Orig.). 1988. pap. 8.95 (*0-88007-165-6*) Woodbridge Pr.

Minimax Methods for Image Reconstruction. A. Korostelev & A. Tsybakov. LC 93-18028. (Lecture Notes in Statistics Ser.: Vol. 82). 1993. 39.00 (*0-387-94028-6*) Spr-Verlag.

Minimax Methods in Critical Point Theory with Applications to Differential Equations. P. Rabinowitz. LC 86-7847. (CBMS Regional Conference Series in Mathematics: No. 65). 110p. 1986. reprint ed. pap. 19.00 (*0-8218-0715-3*, CBMS/65) Am Math.

Minimax Models in the Theory of Numerical Methods. Aleksei G. Sukharev. LC 92-16531. (Theory & Decision Library. Series B, Mathematical & Statistical Methods: Vol. 21).Tr. of Minimaksnye Algoritmy v Zadachakh Chislennogo Analiza. 1992. lib. bdg. 193.50 (*0-7923-1821-8*) Kluwer Academic.

Minimax Solutions in Sampling from Finite Populations. S. Gabler. Ed. by J. O. Berger et al. (Lecture Notes in Statistics Ser.: Vol. 64). v, 132p. 1990. 31.95 (*0-387-97358-3*) Spr-Verlag.

Minimax Theorems. LC 96-19919. (Progress in Nonlinear Differential Equations & Their Applications Ser.). 1996. write for info. (*3-7643-3913-6*) Birkhauser.

Minimax Theorems. Michel Willem. LC 96-19919. (Progress in Nonlinear Differential Equations & Their Applications Ser.: Vol. 24). 165p. 1996. 49.50 (*0-8176-3913-6*) Birkhauser.

Minimax Theorems & Qualitative Properties of the Solutions of Hemivariational Inequalities. D. Motreanu. LC 98-45178. (Nonconvex Optimization & Its Applications Ser.). 12p. 1999. 156.00 (*0-7923-5456-7*) Kluwer Academic.

Minimax Theory & Applications. Biagio Ricceri & S. Simons. LC 98-6569. (Nonconvex Optimization & Its Applications Ser.). 1998. 119.00 (*0-7923-5064-2*) Kluwer Academic.

Minimax under Transportation Constrains. A. A. Mironov & Vladimir I. Surkov. LC 99-11149. (Applied Optimization Ser.). 1999. write for info. (*0-7923-5609-8*) Kluwer Academic.

Minimisation of the Physical & Sexual Abuse of Children. Goddard & Hiller. 56.95 (*1-85628-940-0*) Ashgate Pub Co.

Minimization Methods for Non-Differentiable Functions & Applications. N. Z. Shor. Tr. by K. C. Kiwiel & A. Ruszczynski from RUS. (Computational Mathematics Ser.: Vol. 3). 170p. 1985. 104.95 (*0-387-12763-1*) Spr-Verlag.

Minimization of Computational Costs of Non-Analogue Monte Carlo Methods. G. A. Mikhailov. 220p. (C). 1992. text 43.00 (*981-02-0707-7*) World Scientific Pub.

Minimization of Radioactive Waste from Nuclear Power Plants & the Back End of the Nuclear Fuel Cycle. I.A.E.A. Staff. LC 96-146474. (Technical Reports: Vol. 337): 84p. 1995. pap. text 40.00 (*92-0-101195-4*, STI/DOC/377, Pub. by IAEA) Bernan Associates.

Minimizing Chlorate Ion Formation in Drinking Water When Hypochlorite Ion Is the Chlorinating Agent. (Illus.). 180p. 1995. pap. 98.00 (*0-89867-781-5*, 90675) Am Water Wks Assn.

Minimizing Earthquake Damage: A Guide for Water Utilities. Donald B. Ballantyne. (Illus.). 98p. 1994. pap. 30.00 (*0-89867-750-5*, 20326) Am Water Wks Assn.

Minimizing Electrical Susceptibility to Power. W. Imes. (Electrical Engineering Ser.). 1992. write for info. (*0-442-01056-7*, VNR) Wiley.

Minimizing Emissions from MSW Incinerators. Clarke. 1998. write for info. (*0-87371-629-9*, L629) Lewis Pubs.

Minimizing Employee Exposure to Toxic Chemical Releases. Ralph W. Plummer et al. LC 87-12213. (Pollution Technology Review Ser.: No. 145). (Illus.). 257p. 1988. 44.00 (*0-8155-1131-0*) Noyes.

Minimizing Gear Noise Excitation. M. Nielsen et al. (1985 Fall Technical Meeting: Vol. 85FTM12). 19p. 1985. pap. text 30.00 (*1-55589-105-5*) AGMA.

***Minimizing Harm.** Edward Rubin. 224p. 1999. pap. 24.00 (*0-8133-6804-9*) Westview.

Minimizing High Risk Parenting. Ed. by Valerie J. Sasserath. (Pediatric Round Table Ser.: No. 7). 1983. 10.00 (*0-931562-07-4*) J & J Consumer Prods.

Minimizing Independent Contractor Disputes. Nina Yablok. Ed. by Marie Hagelstein. 98p. 1994. pap. text 65.00 (*0-88124-765-0*, BU-32810) Cont Ed Bar-CA.

Minimizing Medical Mistakes. Richard K. Riegelman. 1991. 32.95 (*0-316-74523-5*, Little Brwn Med Div) Lppncott W & W.

Minimizing Premature Cracking in Asphaltic Concrete Pavement. (National Cooperative Highway Research Program Report Ser.: No. 195). 51p. 1978. 6.00 (*0-309-02855-8*, NR195) Transport Res Bd.

Minimizing Reflex & Reaction Time. Health for Life Staff. 24p. 1988. pap. 11.95 (*0-685-72102-7*) Health Life.

Minimizing Risk. George C. Belev. 156p. (Orig.). 1995. pap. 37.45 (*0-940343-68-1*, MRIS) Natl Contract Mgmt.

Minimizing the Impact of Alternative Recording Methods on the Consolidation Process - "Conversion to Complete Equity" Michael S. Luehlfing. 21p. 1995. pap. text 19.50 (*0-933179-09-X*) Bus Account Pubns.

Minimizing the Risk of Legionella in Cooling Towers & Other HVAC Equipment. Matthew R. Freije. LC 98-92505. 18p. 1998. pap. 19.00 (*0-9649926-3-9*, 304) HC Info Res.

Minimizing Waste, Maximizing Recycling. Brenda A. Platt. 34p. 1994. 6.00 (*0-614-18036-8*) Inst Local Self Re.

Minims. D. Norel Thims. 70p. 1993. pap. 8.00 (*0-9631902-1-0*) Canonymous.

Minims. Tom Weller. 1982. pap. text 2.95 (*0-685-42446-4*) HM.

Minimum. John Pawson. LC 97-190858. (Illus.). 272p. 1996. 95.00 (*0-7148-3262-6*, Pub. by Phaidon Press) Phaidon Pr.

Minimum: Mini Edition. John Pawson. LC 99-214641. (Illus.). 320p. 1998. 18.00 (*0-7148-3817-9*); 18.00 (*0-7148-5011-X*) Phaidon Pr.

Minimum Albanian - Polish, Polish - Albanian Dictionary. M. Jeziorski. (ALB & POL.). 1992. pap. write for info. (*0-8288-7280-5*) Fr & Eur.

Minimum Animal Populations. Ed. by Hermann Remmert. LC 93-34010. 1995. 96.95 (*0-387-56684-8*) Spr-Verlag.

Minimum Business Attributes Tutor. Roderick A. Ward & Eric J. Ward. Ed. by Carla L. Ward. (Illus.). 148p. 1998. pap. text 35.00 (*0-9663294-0-6*) McLaughlin & Ward.

Minimum Business Attributes Tutor: Case Studies. Roderick A. Ward & Eric J. Ward. Ed. by Carla L. Ward. 64p. 1998. pap. text 20.00 (*0-9663294-1-4*) McLaughlin & Ward.

Minimum Competence, Maximum Choice: Educational Vouchers for Children Who Need Them Most. Barbara Lerner. (C). 1982. text 22.50 (*0-8290-0414-9*) Irvington.

Minimum Conflict: Guidelines for Planning the Use of American Humid Tropic Environments. 35.00 (*0-8270-2658-7*) OAS.

Minimum Cost of Living in Nebraska, Vol. I-II. Douglas O. . Love. 1986. 20.00 (*0-317-46859-6*) Bur Busn Res U Nebr.

Minimum Design Loads for Buildings & Other Structures. 232p. 1995. pap. 72.00 (*0-7844-0092-X*) Am Soc Civil Eng.

Minimum Design Loads for Buildings & Other Structures. American Society of Civil Engineers Staff. LC 94-3854. 134p. 1994. pap. 44.00 (*0-87262-904-X*) N K Gregg.

Minimum Design Loads for Buildings & Other Structures: ASCE 7-88 (Formerly ANSI A58.1) LC 90-1065. 108p. 1990. pap. text 26.00 (*0-87262-742-X*) Am Soc Civil Eng.

***Minimum Detectable Concentrations with Typical Radiation Survey Instruments for Various Contaminants & Field Conditions.** E. W. Abelquist. 168p. 1998. per. 15.00 (*0-16-062744-3*) USGPO.

Minimum Distributions from Retirement Plans. Charles W. McKenzie. 311p. 1993. ring bd. 49.95 (*0-9638660-0-1*) Actuarial Assocs.

Minimum Entropy Control for Time-Varying Systems. Marc A. Peters & Pablo A. Iglesias. LC 96-45332. (Systems & Control Ser.). 185p. 1996. 49.50 (*0-8176-3972-1*) Birkhauser.

Minimum Entropy H Control. D. Mustafa & K. Glover. Ed. by M. Thoma & A. Wyner. (Lecture Notes in Control & Information Sciences: Vol. 146). (Illus.). ix, 144p. 1990. 37.95 (*0-387-52947-0*) Spr-Verlag.

***Minimum Essentials of English.** 2nd rev. ed. Fred Obrecht. LC 98-74451. 72p. 1999. ring bd. 6.95 (*0-7641-0745-3*) Barron.

Minimum French. W. Leon Wiley & Henry A. Grubbs. (ENG & FRE.). 142p. 1963. 9.95 (*0-8288-6973-1*) Fr & Eur.

Minimum French. W. Leon Wiley & Henry A. Grubbs. 1935. text 17.95 (*0-89197-634-5*); pap. text 10.95 (*0-89197-610-8*) Irvington.

Minimum Impatience Theorems for Recursive Economic Models. Gerhard Sorger. LC 92-21404. (Lecture Notes in Economics & Mathematical Systems Ser.: Vol. 390). 1992. 45.95 (*0-387-56022-X*) Spr-Verlag.

Minimum Intervention & Life Cycle Costing Etc. B. Songhurst. 1989. 130.00 (*90-6314-593-4*, Pub. by Lorne & MacLean Marine) St Mut.

Minimum Japanese - Polish, Polish - Japanese Dictionary. K. Adachi. (JPN & POL.). 1992. write for info. (*0-8288-7282-1*) Fr & Eur.

Minimum Level of Unemployment & Public Policy. Frank C. Pierson. LC 80-26536. 194p. 1980. pap. text 12.00 (*0-911558-75-6*) W E Upjohn.

Minimum of Italian Grammar & Answer Key. Valentine Giamatti. (C). 1964. pap. 10.95 (*0-913298-28-X*) S F Vanni.

Minimum Polish - Greek, Greek - Polish Dictionary. M. T. Kamburelli. (GRE & POL.). 1992. write for info. (*0-8288-7281-3*) Fr & Eur.

Minimum Price Fixing in the Bituminous Coal Industry. Waldo E. Fisher & Charles M. James. (Conference on Price Research Ser.: No. 5). 555p. 1955. reprint ed. 144.50 (*0-87014-191-0*) Natl Bur Econ Res.

Minimum Rates of Wages Fixed under the Minimum Wages Act, 1948, as on 1.7.1997. R. K. Subrahmanya. LC 98-915819. xv, 190p. 1998. write for info. (*81-7646-056-7*) BR Pub.

Minimum Reinforcement in Concrete Members. A. Carpinteri. LC 99-18029. (International Series on Structural Integrity). 212p. 1999. 101.50 (*0-08-043022-8*, Pergamon Pr) Elsevier.

Minimum Standards for Property Management Accounting Software, 1995. 32p. 1995. pap. 27.00 (*1-57203-045-3*) Inst Real Estate.

Minimum Tillage Farming No-Tillage Farming. 1995. 18.95 (*0-944605-00-1*) Lessiter Pubns.

Minimum Topside Facilities for Deepwater Marginal Fields. Shah Rustam. 1989. 125.00 (*90-6314-566-7*, Pub. by Lorne & MacLean Marine) St Mut.

Minimum Topside Facilities for Deepwater Marginal Fields. Shah Rustam. (C). 1989. 95.00 (*0-7855-6719-4*, Pub. by Lorne & MacLean Marine) St Mut.

Minimum Wage, Bk. 1. Bob Fingerman. 72p. 1995. pap. 9.95 (*1-56097-187-8*) Fantagraph Bks.

Minimum Wage, Bk. 2. Bob Fingerman. 1998. pap. text 12.95 (*1-56097-286-6*) Fantagraph Bks.

Minimum Wage: An Analysis of the Issues. (Research Monographs). 200p. (C). 1991. 395.00 (*0-85292-479-8*, Pub. by IPM Hse) St Mut.

Minimum Wage & Overtime Pay Answer Book. 64p. 1996. pap. 12.95 (*0-614-26841-9*, 22096BLS01) CCH INC.

Minimum Wage in the Restaurant Industry. William T. Alpert. LC 86-8111. 175p. 1986. 55.00 (*0-275-92085-2*, C2085, Praeger Pubs) Greenwood.

Minimum Wage Law: Who Benefits, Who Loses? see Series on Public Issues

Minimum Wage Maximum Results. Robert McIntosh. 1997. pap. 12.95 (*1-887938-26-5*) Preston-Speed.

***Minimum Wage, Maximum Results: Finding, Hiring, Training & Bringing Out the Best in Your Employees.** 2nd rev. ed. Robert K. McIntosh. 160p. 2000. pap. 20.00 (*1-893435-04-0*, Williams Custom Pub) Lakeshore Comm.

Minimum Wage Regulations in Retail Trade. Belton M. Fleisher. LC 80-39895. (AEI Studies: No. 307). 143p. reprint ed. pap. 44.40 (*0-8357-4507-4*, 203736400008) Bks Demand.

Minimum Wages. Hans F. Sennholz. 22p. 1988. pap. 2.00 (*0-910884-20-X*) Libertarian Press.

Minimum Wages: Issues & Evidence. Finis Welch. LC 78-13477. (AEI Studies: No. 206). 56p. reprint ed. pap. 30.00 (*0-8357-4510-4*, 203736700008) Bks Demand.

Minimum Wages Act. P. L. Malik. 1985. 150.00 (*0-7855-1445-7*) St Mut.

Minimum Wages Act with Central & U. P. Rules & Notification Fixing Minimum Wages in Various Industries & Establishments. 7th ed. Ed. by P. L. Malik. (C). 1991. 95.00 (*0-7855-5483-1*) St Mut.

Minimum Wages Act with Central & U. P. Rules & Notifications Fixing Minimum Wages in Various Industries & Establishments. Ed. by P. L. Malik. (C). 1987. 50.00 (*0-7855-5264-2*) St Mut.

Minimum Wages & On-the-Job Training. Masanori Hashimoto. LC 81-1435. (AEI Studies: No. 311). (Illus.). 83p. reprint ed. pap. 30.00 (*0-8357-4509-0*, 203736600008) Bks Demand.

***Minimum Wages & Workweeks in Africa, 1999.** Compiled by Icon Group International. (Illus.). 168p. 1999. ring bd. 1680.00 incl. audio compact disk (*0-7418-1952-X*) Icon Grp.

***Minimum Wages & Workweeks in Asia & Oceana, 1999.** Compiled by Icon Group International. (Illus.). 116p. 1999. ring bd. 1160.00 incl. audio compact disk (*0-7418-1969-4*) Icon Grp.

***Minimum Wages & Workweeks in Europe, 1999.** Compiled by Icon Group International. (Illus.). 152p. 1999. ring bd. 1520.00 incl. audio compact disk (*0-7418-1955-4*) Icon Grp.

***Minimum Wages & Workweeks in Latin America & The Caribbean, 1999.** Compiled by Icon Group International. (Illus.). 109p. 1999. ring bd. 1090.00 incl. audio compact disk (*0-7418-1966-X*) Icon Grp.

***Minimum Wages & Workweeks in the Middle East, 1999.** Compiled by Icon Group International. (Illus.). 81p. 1999. ring bd. 810.00 incl. audio compact disk (*0-7418-1975-9*) Icon Grp.

Minimum Wages, Fringe Benefits, & Working Conditions. Walter J. Wessels. LC 80-25643. (AEI Studies: No. 304). (Illus.). 109p. reprint ed. pap. 33.80 (*0-8357-4508-2*, 203736500008) Bks Demand.

Minimum Wages in Central & Eastern Europe: From Protection to Destitution. Ed. by Guy Standing & Daniel Vaughan-Whitehead. (Illus.). 192p. (C). 1996. pap. 21.95 (*1-85866-043-2*) Ctrl Europ Univ.

Minimum-Worterbuch: Deutsch - Polnisch, Polnisch - Deutsch. J. Jozwicki. (GER & POL.). 557p. 1980. pap. 7.95 (*0-8288-4709-6*, M9218) Fr & Eur.

***Minimus: Starting Out in Latin.** Barbara Bell. (Cambridge Latin Texts Ser.). 80p. (C). 2000. pap., student ed. 17.95 (*0-521-65960-4*) Cambridge U Pr.

***Minimus: Starting Out in Latin.** Barbara Bell. (Cambridge Latin Texts Ser.). 80p. (C). 2000. teacher ed. 59.95 (*0-521-65961-2*) Cambridge U Pr.

MININEC Broadcast Professional for Windows. John W. Rockway & James C. Logan. 187p. 1995. pap. 390.00 incl. 3.5 hd (*1-887438-00-9*) EM Scientific.

MININEC Broadcast Professional for Windows. John W. Rockway & James C. Logan. LC 96-85405. (Illus.). 239p. 1996. pap. 790.00 (*1-887438-01-7*) EM Scientific.

MININEC Broadcast Professional for Windows. John W. Rockway & James C. Logan. 1997. pap. 125.00 incl. 3.5 hd (*1-887438-02-5*) EM Scientific.

Mining. Jane Drake & Ann Love. LC 96-932204. (Canada at Work Ser.). (Illus.). (J). (gr. 2-4). 1997. 14.99 (*1-55074-337-6*) Kids Can Pr.

***Mining.** Ann Love & Jane Drake. (America at Work Ser.). (Illus.). 31p. (J). (gr. 2). 1999. 12.95 (*1-55074-508-5*, Pub. by Kids Can Pr) Genl Dist Srvs.

Mining Advance into the Inland Empire. William J. Trimble. 254p. 1986. 19.95 (*0-87770-088-5*) Ye Galleon.

Mining Agreements III. (Mineral Law Ser.). 1991. student ed. 125.00 (*0-929047-25-5*) Rocky Mtn Mineral Law Found.

Mining America: The Industry & the Environment, 1800-1980. Duane A. Smith. LC 93-13337. (Illus.). 224p. 1994. reprint ed. pap. 19.95 (*0-87081-306-4*) Univ Pr Colo.

Mining & Agriculture in Highland Bolivia: Ecology, History, & Commerce among the Jukumanis. Ricardo A. Godoy. LC 90-35214. (Arizona Studies in Human Ecology). 169p. 1990. 33.50 (*0-8165-1169-1*) U of Ariz Pr.

Mining & Coking of Coal: Proceedings of the 2nd Conference, Pittsburgh Meeting, October 6-7, 1980, Vol. 1- 1980. Iron & Steel Society of AIME Staff. LC 81-109760. 71p. reprint ed. pap. 30.00 (*0-608-14336-7*, 201969600014) Bks Demand.

Mining & Indigenous Peoples in Australasia. Ed. by John Connell & Richard Howitt. (Illus.). 216p. 1992. pap. text 28.00 (*0-424-00177-2*) OUP.

Mining & Industrial Applications of Low Density Explosives. E. G. Baranov et al. LC 99-226661. (Illus.). 126p. (C). 1996. text 65.00 (*90-5410-295-0*, Pub. by A A Balkema) Ashgate Pub Co.

Mining & Its Environmental Impact. Ed. by R. E. Hester & R. M. Harrison. (Issues in Environmental Science & Technology Ser.: Vol. 1). 164p. 1994. 42.00 (*0-85404-200-8*, R4200) CRC Pr.

Mining & Mineral Laws of South Africa. B. L. Franklin. 853p. 1982. boxed set 360.00 (*0-409-02898-3*, SA, MICHIE) LEXIS Pub.

Mining & Mineral Processing Wastes: Proceedings of the Western Regional Symposium on Mining & Mineral Processing Wastes, Berkeley, California, May 30-June 1, 1990. Western Regional Symposium Mining & Mineral Wastes. Ed. by Fiona M. Doyle. LC 90-61107. 287p. reprint ed. pap. 89.00 (*0-7837-1267-7*, 204140600020) Bks Demand.

Mining & Quarrying. Ed. by ICC Information Group Staff. 1987. 750.00 (*1-85319-041-1*, Pub. by ICC Info Group Ltd) St Mut.

Mining & Quarrying Trends in the Metals & Industrial Minerals Industries. (Metals & Minerals Ser.). 1993. lib. bdg. 253.95 (*0-8490-8992-1*) Gordon Pr.

Mining & Quarrying Trends in the Metals & Industrial Minerals Industries. (Metals & Minerals Ser.). 1993. lib. bdg. 263.95 (*0-8490-9018-0*) Gordon Pr.

Mining & Structural Adjustment: Studies on Zimbabwe & Tanzania. Chachage S. Chachage et al. (Research Report Ser.: No. 92). 112p. 1993. 16.95 (*91-7106-340-4*, Pub. by Nordic Africa) Transaction Pubs.

Mining & the Environment: International Perspectives on Public Policy. Ed. by Roderick G. Eggert. (Illus.). 172p. (C). 1994. pap. text 25.00 (*0-915707-72-1*) Resources Future.

An Asterisk (*) at the beginning of an entry indicates that the title is appearing for the first time.

Mining & the Politics of Risk: Political Risk Insurance in the Mining Industry. Roger Moody. 200p. (Orig.). 1997. pap. 24.95 (*90-5727-006-4*, Pub. by Uitgeverij Arkel) LPC InBook.

Mining at the Surface. (C). 1990. pap. 30.00 (*0-85025-325-X*, Pub. by Tor Mark Pr) St Mut.

Mining Camp Days. Emil Billeb. (Illus.). 229p. 1968. pap. 12.95 (*0-913814-05-9*) Nevada Pubns.

Mining Camps: A Study in American Frontier Government. Charles H. Shinn. Ed. by R. W. Paul. 1990. 16.50 (*0-8446-0909-9*) Peter Smith.

Mining-Camps: A Study in American Frontier Government. Charles H. Shinn. 1992. reprint ed. lib. bdg. 75.00 (*0-7812-5087-0*) Rprt Serv.

Mining Camps & Ghost Towns: Along the Lower Colorado in Arizona & California. Frank Love. LC 73-86960. (Great West & Indian Ser.: Vol. 42). (Illus.). 240p. 24.95 (*0-87026-031-6*) Westernlore.

Mining Camps Speak: A New Way to Explore the Ghost Towns of the American West. Beth Sagstetter & Bill Sagstetter. LC 98-212796. (Illus.). 283p. 1998. pap. 19.95 (*0-9645824-1-4*) BenchMark CO.

Mining Claims & Sites on Federal Lands. 29p. 1996. pap. 1.25 (*0-16-061707-3*) USGPO.

Mining Coal. John Davey. (Junior Reference Ser.). (Illus.). 64p. (J). (gr. 6 up). 1976. 15.95 (*0-7136-1596-6*) Dufour.

Mining Community in Northern New Spain: The Parral Mining District. Robert C. West. LC 76-29398. reprint ed. 37.50 (*0-404-15331-3*) AMS Pr.

Mining Dictionary (Glosario de Terminos Mineros) Prieto P. Diaz. (ENG & SPA.). 291p. 1995. pap. 39.00 (*84-7719-506-4*) IBD Ltd.

Mining Districts & Mineral Resources of Nevada. Francis G. Lincoln. (Illus.). 1982. pap. 14.95 (*0-913814-48-2*) Nevada Pubns.

Mining Economics & Strategy. Ian Runge. LC 98-24661. (Illus.). 312p. 1998. pap. 83.00 (*0-87335-165-7*, 165-7) SMM&E Inc.

Mining Engineering Analysis. Christopher J. Bise. LC 85-62660. (Illus.). 160p. (C). 1986. text 61.00 (*0-87335-057-X*, 057-X) SMM&E Inc.

Mining Engineering Monuments As a Cultural Heritage: Report of the Bochum Colloquy (Federal Republic of Germany) Council of Europe Staff. (Cultural Heritage Ser.: No. 15). 1989. 18.00 (*92-871-1740-3*, Pub. by Council of Europe) Manhattan Pub Co.

Mining Engineers & the American West: The Lace-Boot Brigade, 1849-1933. Clark C. Spence. (Illus.). 420p. 1993. reprint ed. pap. 29.95 (*0-89301-167-3*) U of Idaho Pr.

Mining Environment: Proceedings of the First World Mining Environment Congress. Ed. by Bharat B. Dhar & D. N. Thakur. LC 99-227031. (Illus.). 416p. (C). 1996. text 91.00 (*90-5410-715-4*, Pub. by A A Balkema) Ashgate Pub Co.

Mining Environmental Handbook: Effects of Mining on the Environment & American Environmental Control. J. J. Marcus. 950p. 1997. 168.00 (*1-86094-029-3*) World Scientific Pub.

***Mining Equipment - Components in Brazil: A Strategic Entry Report, 1996.** Compiled by Icon Group International Staff. (Illus.). 169p. 1999. ring bd. 1690.00 incl. audio compact disk (*0-7418-1324-6*) Icon Grp.

***Mining Equipment & Services in India: A Strategic Entry Report, 1998.** Compiled by Icon Group International Staff. (Country Industry Report). (Illus.). 194p. 1999. ring bd. 1940.00 incl. audio compact disk (*0-7418-0266-X*) Icon Grp.

***Mining Equipment & Services in Vietnam: A Strategic Entry Report, 1996.** Compiled by Icon Group International Staff. (Illus.). 151p. 1999. ring bd. 1510.00 incl. audio compact disk (*0-7418-1325-4*) Icon Grp.

***Mining Equipment & Technology in India: A Strategic Entry Report, 1995.** Compiled by Icon Group International Staff. (Illus.). 193p. 1999. ring bd. 1930.00 incl. audio compact disk (*0-7418-1617-2*) Icon Grp.

***Mining Equipment in Argentina: A Strategic Entry Report, 1998.** Compiled by Icon Group International Staff. (Country Industry Report). (Illus.). 146p. 1999. ring bd. 1460.00 incl. audio compact disk (*0-7418-0512-X*) Icon Grp.

***Mining Equipment in Chile: A Strategic Entry Report, 2000.** Compiled by Icon Group International. (Illus.). 115p. 1999. ring bd. 1150.00 incl. audio compact disk (*0-7418-2203-2*) Icon Grp.

***Mining Equipment in Egypt: A Strategic Entry Report, 1998.** Compiled by Icon Group International Staff. (Country Industry Report). (Illus.). 162p. 1999. ring bd. 1620.00 incl. audio compact disk (*0-7418-0267-8*) Icon Grp.

Mining Equipment in Mexico: A Strategic Entry Report, 1997. Compiled by Icon Group International Staff. (Illus.). 148p. 1999. ring bd. 1480.00 incl. audio compact disk (*0-7418-1057-3*) Icon Grp.

***Mining Equipment in Peru: A Strategic Entry Report, 1996.** Compiled by Icon Group International Staff. (Illus.). 141p. 1999. ring bd. 1410.00 incl. audio compact disk (*0-7418-1326-2*) Icon Grp.

Mining Equipment in Saudi Arabia: A Strategic Entry Report, 1997. Compiled by Icon Group International Staff. (Illus.). 132p. 1999. ring bd. 1320.00 incl. audio compact disk (*0-7418-1058-1*) Icon Grp.

***Mining Equipment in Vietnam: A Strategic Entry Report, 1998.** Compiled by Icon Group International Staff. (Country Industry Report). (Illus.). 153p. 1999. ring bd. 1530.00 incl. audio compact disk (*0-7418-0268-6*) Icon Grp.

Mining Equipment MFRS. Ed. by ICC Information Group Staff. 1987. 700.00 (*1-85319-040-3*, Pub. by ICC Info Group Ltd) St Mut.

Mining for Gold on the Internet: How to Find Investment & Financial Information on the Internet. Mary Ellen Bates. 300p. 2000. pap. 24.95 (*0-07-134981-2*) McGraw.

Mining for the Future: Trends & Expectations. Ed. by World Mining Congress, Chinese Committee. (International Academic Publishers Ser.). (Illus.). 1200p. 1990. 315.00 (*0-08-040189-9*, Pub. by IAP) Elsevier.

Mining Geostatistics. Andre G. Journel & C. J. Huijbregts. 600p. 1981. pap. text 84.00 (*0-12-391056-0*) Acad Pr.

Mining Gold to Mining Wallets Central City, Colorado, 1859-1999. Alan Granruth. (Illus.). 176p. 1999. 29.95 (*0-9672916-0-7*) Gilpin County.

Mining Group Gold: How to Cash in on the Collaborative Brain Power of a Group. 2nd rev. ed. Thomas A. Kayser. LC 95-2846. 178p. 1995. 24.95 (*0-7863-0429-4*, Irwn Prfssnl) McGraw-Hill Prof.

Mining in Chile's Norte Chico: Journal of Charles Lambert, 1825-1830. John Mayo & Simon Collier. LC 98-29741. (Dellplain Latin American Studies: No. 36). 248p. 1998. text 55.00 (*0-8133-3584-1*, Pub. by Westview) HarpC.

Mining in Cornwall: A Pictorial Record, 1850-1960, 2 vols., Vol. 1: Camborne-Redruth Area. J. H. Trounson. (C). 1989. 45.00 (*0-907566-83-9*, Pub. by Dyllansow Truran) St Mut.

Mining in Cornwall: A Pictorial Record, 1850-1960, 2 vols., Vol. 2: St. Just-Camborne Area. J. H. Trounson. (C). 1989. 45.00 (*1-85033-049-2*, Pub. by Dyllansow Truran) St Mut.

Mining in The Americas: Stories & History. Helmut Waszkis. 304p. 1993. 89.95 (*1-85573-131-2*, Pub. by Woodhead Pubng) Am Educ Systs.

Mining in the Arctic: Proceedings of the 1st International Symposium on Mining in the Arctic, Fairbanks, 17-19 July 1989. Ed. by Sukumar Bandopadhyay & F. J. Skudrzyk. 256p. (C). 1989. text 168.00 (*90-6191-899-5*, Pub. by A A Balkema) Ashgate Pub Co.

Mining in the Arctic: Proceedings of the 2nd International Symposium on Mining in the Arctic, Fairbanks, Alaska, 19-22 July 1992. Ed. by Sukumar Bandopadhyay & Michael G. Nelson. (Illus.). 326p. (C). 1992. text 128.00 (*90-5410-078-8*, Pub. by A A Balkema) Ashgate Pub Co.

***Mining in the Artic: Proceedings of the 5th International Symposium, Yellowknife, NWT, Canada, 14-17 June, 1998.** Ed. by John E. Udd & A. J. Keen. 196p. (C). 1999. pap. 95.00 (*90-5809-098-1*, Pub. by A A Balkema) Ashgate Pub Co.

Mining in the East Midlands, 1550-1947. A. R. Griffin. 338p. 1971. 35.00 (*0-7146-2585-X*, Pub. by F Cass Pubs) Intl Spec Bk.

Mining in the Netherlands East Indies. Alex L. Ter Braake. Ed. by Mira Wilkins. LC 76-29762. (European Business Ser.). (Illus.). 1977. reprint ed. lib. bdg. 17.95 (*0-405-09777-8*) Ayer.

Mining in the West. Dave Pearson. LC 95-20554. 166p. (gr. 10). 1996. pap. 24.95 (*0-88740-933-4*) Schiffer.

Mining Industries, 1899-1939: A Study of Output, Employment, & Productivity. Harold Barger & Sam H. Schurr. LC 72-2833. (Use & Abuse of America's Natural Resources Ser.). 474p. 1972. reprint ed. 33.95 (*0-405-04502-6*) Ayer.

Mining Industries, 1899-1939: A Study of Output, Employment, & Productivity. Harold Barger & Sam H. Schurr. LC 75-19694. (National Bureau of Economic Research Ser.). (Illus.). 1975. reprint ed. 35.95 (*0-405-07575-8*) Ayer.

Mining Industries, 1899-1939: A Study of Output, Employment, & Productivity. Harold Barger & Sam H. Schurr. (General Ser.: No. 43). 474p. 1944. reprint ed. 123.30 (*0-87014-042-6*) Natl Bur Econ Res.

Mining Industry, 4 vols. Ed. by Trevor Boyns. (Tauris Industrial Histories Ser.). (Illus.). 1650p. 1997. text 625.00 (*1-86064-072-9*, Pub. by I B T) St Martin.

***Mining Industry Equipment in Australia: A Strategic Entry Report, 1997.** Compiled by Icon Group International Staff. (Country Industry Report). (Illus.). 137p. 1999. ring bd. 1370.00 incl. audio compact disk (*0-7418-0269-4*) Icon Grp.

***Mining Industry Equipment in Canada: A Strategic Entry Report, 1997.** Compiled by Icon Group International Staff. (Country Industry Report). (Illus.). 138p. 1999. ring bd. 1380.00 incl. audio compact disk (*0-7418-0270-8*) Icon Grp.

***Mining Industry Equipment in Chile: A Strategic Entry Report, 1996.** Compiled by Icon Group International Staff. (Illus.). 116p. 1999. ring bd. 1160.00 incl. audio compact disk (*0-7418-1327-0*) Icon Grp.

***Mining Industry Equipment in Guatemala: A Strategic Entry Report, 1998.** Compiled by Icon Group International Staff. (Country Industry Report). (Illus.). 109p. 1999. ring bd. 1090.00 incl. audio compact disk (*0-7418-0513-8*) Icon Grp.

***Mining Industry Equipment in Mexico: A Strategic Entry Report, 1996.** Compiled by Icon Group International Staff. (Illus.). 157p. 1999. ring bd. 1570.00 incl. audio compact disk (*0-7418-1328-9*) Icon Grp.

Mining Industry Equipment in Peru: A Strategic Entry Report, 1997. Compiled by Icon Group International Staff. (Illus.). 139p. 1999. ring bd. 1390.00 incl. audio compact disk (*0-7418-0871-4*) Icon Grp.

***Mining Industry Equipment in Ukraine: A Strategic Entry Report, 1995.** Compiled by Icon Group International Staff. (Illus.). 199p. 1999. ring bd. 1990.00 incl. audio compact disk (*0-7418-1618-0*) Icon Grp.

Mining International Yearbook, 1988. Longman Publishing Staff. 1988. pap. text. write for info. (*0-582-00431-4*, Pub. by Addison-Wesley) Longman.

Mining Law: A Study in Perpetual Motion. John D. Leshy. LC 86-42610. 521p. 1987. 50.00 (*0-915707-26-8*) Resources Future.

Mining Law & Regulations of Mexico, 1992-1993. Fausto C. Miranda & John C. Lacy. 263p. 1993. pap., student ed. 125.00 incl. disk (*0-929047-37-0*, MEX2) Rocky Mtn Mineral Law Found.

Mining Law in Western Australia. 2nd ed. Michael Hunt & Michael Lewis. 374p. 1993. 79.00 (*1-86287-108-6*, Pub. by Federation Pr) Gaunt.

Mining Lease Handbook. George E. Reeves. 300p. 1992. pap., student ed. 135.00 (*0-929047-32-X*, ML) Rocky Mtn Mineral Law Found.

Mining Men. Otis E. Young, Jr. LC 74-15148. (Illus.). 308p. 1974. 9.95 (*0-913504-18-1*) Lowell Pr.

Mining Planning & Equipment Selection, 1994: Proceedings of the 3rd International Symposium, Istanbul, Turkey, 18-20 October 1994. Ed. by A. G. Pasamehmetoglu et al. (Illus.). 964p. (C). 1994. text 162.00 (*90-5410-327-2*, Pub. by A A Balkema) Ashgate Pub Co.

***Mining Pollution Control Equipment in Indonesia: A Strategic Entry Report, 1998.** Compiled by Icon Group International Staff. (Country Industry Report). (Illus.). 165p. 1999. ring bd. 1650.00 incl. audio compact disk (*0-7418-0540-5*) Icon Grp.

***Mining Projects at Work.** Gordon L. Webster. LC 98-31592. 1999. 61.95 (*0-566-07982-8*) Ashgate Pub Co.

Mining Rights in Colorado. R. S. Morrison. 331p. 1996. 85.00 (*1-56169-216-6*) Gaunt.

Mining Science & Technology: Proceedings of an International Symposium Organized by the China Institute of Mining & Technology September 1985. 1430p. 1987. 70.00 (*0-87849-059-0*, Pub. by Trans T Pub) Enfield Pubs NH.

Mining Science & Technology, 1996: Proceedings of the '96 International Symposium, Xuzhou, Jiangsu, China, 16-18 October 1996. Ed. by Guo Yuguang & Tad S. Golosinski. (Illus.). 848p. (C). 1996. 181.00 (*90-5410-825-8*, Pub. by A A Balkema) Ashgate Pub Co.

Mining Sites in Cornwall & South-West Devon. Barry Atkinson. 96p. (C). 1989. text 50.00 (*1-85022-044-1*, Pub. by Dyllansow Truran) St Mut.

Mining Strategy for Latin American & the Caribbean. LC 96-45104. (Technical Papers: No. 345). 128p. 1997. pap. 8.95 (*0-8213-3816-1*, 13816) World Bank.

Mining Systems Adjusted to High Rock Pressure Conditions: Proceedings of the Plenary Scientific Session of the International Bureau of Strata Mechanics, World Mining Congress, Varna, 9th, 18-21 June 1985. A. Kidybinski & M. Kwasniewski. 360p. (C). 1986. text 168.00 (*90-6191-658-5*, Pub. by A A Balkema) Ashgate Pub Co.

Mining Technology for Energy Resources: Advances for the '80's: Presented at the 1978 Energy Technology Conference & Exhibition, Houston, Texas, November 6-9, 1978. Energy Technology Conference & Exhibition Staff. Ed. by Arfon H. Jones. LC 78-67410. 78p. reprint ed. pap. 30.00 (*0-8357-8740-0*, 203362900087) Bks Demand.

Mining the Darkness. Stephen Stepanchev. LC 74-31285. 107p. (Orig.). 1974. pap. 10.00 (*0-87685-222-3*) Black Sparrow.

***Mining the Document Warehouse.** Mark Kempster. 88p. 1998. spiral bd. 100.00 (*0-89258-340-1*, C141) Assn Inform & Image Mgmt.

Mining the Earth. John E. Young. 70p. (Orig.). 1992. pap. 5.00 (*1-878071-11-4*) Worldwatch Inst.

Mining the Fields: Farmworkers Fight Back. John C. Leggett. (Illus.). 133p. (Orig.). (C). 1991. text 34.95 (*0-9625270-0-9*); pap. text 24.95 (*0-9625270-1-7*) Raritan Inst.

Mining the Hard Rock in the Silverton San Juans: A Sense of Place, a Sense of Time. John Marshall. LC 96-94414. (Illus.). 224p. 1996. 34.95 (*0-9632028-2-0*) Simpler Way.

***Mining the Internet: Information Gathering & Research on the Net.** Brian Clegg. 1999. pap. 16.95 (*0-7494-3025-7*) Kogan Page Ltd.

***Mining the Middle Ground: Developing Mid-Level Managers for Strategic Change.** David N. Williams. LC 00-40282. 2000. write for info. (*1-57444-295-3*) St Lucie Pr.

Mining the Nation's Brain Trust. Fred E. Grissom, Jr. 1992. pap. 22.75 (*0-201-55156-X*) Addison-Wesley.

Mining the Nation's Brain Trust: How to Put Federally-Funded Research to Work for You. Fred E. Grissom, Jr. & Richard M. Chapman. (Illus.). 208p. (C). 1992. pap. 30.00 (*0-201-55015-6*) Addison-Wesley.

Mining the Seam. Arline R. Thorn. 32p. 1992. pap. 3.95 (*1-881692-00-0*) Trillium WV.

Mining the Silver Lining: Taking Triumph from Tragedy. Billy J. Branson. 224p. (Orig.). 1988. pap. 9.95 (*0-925048-00-3*) Sun-Coyote Pr.

Mining the Sky. John S. Lewis. (Illus.). 288p. 1997. pap. 15.00 (*0-201-32819-4*) Addison-Wesley.

***Mining the Soul: From the Inside Out.** Robin Robertson. (Illus.). 288p. 2000. pap. 18.95 (*0-89254-055-9*, Pub. by Nicolas-Hays) Weiser.

Mining Town: The Photographic Record of T. N. Barnard & Nellie Stockbridge from the Coeur d'Alenes. Hart & Nelson. (Illus.). 190p. (C). 1993. pap. 19.95 (*0-295-97254-8*) U of Wash Pr.

Mining Underground. J. A. Buckley. (C). 1989. pap. text 35.00 (*0-85025-316-0*, Pub. by Tor Mark Pr) St Mut.

Mining Urban Wastes: The Potential for Recycling. Cynthia Pollock. LC 87-50357. 52p. (Orig.). 1987. pap. 5.00 (*0-916468-77-1*) Worldwatch Inst.

Mining Ventures in Developing Countries Pt. 2: Analysis of Projects Agreements, English Translation. E. Schanze. 281p. 48.00 (*90-6544-038-0*) Kluwer Academic.

Mining Very Large Databases with Parallel Processing. Alex A. Freitas & Simon H. Lavington. LC 97-41615. (The Kluwer International Series on Advances in Database Systems: No. 9). 224p. 1997. text 115.50 (*0-7923-8048-7*) Kluwer Academic.

Mining Wisdom. Patricia Holland. (J). pap., teacher ed. 49.95 (*0-614-18233-6*, M300) Let Us Tch Kids.

Mining Wisdom Puppet Skit Package. (J). pap. 44.00 incl. audio (*0-614-18223-9*, 3MS1) Let Us Tch Kids.

Mining Wisdom Puppet Skits. (J). pap., teacher ed. 14.95 (*0-614-18236-0*) Let Us Tch Kids.

Mining Wisdom Puppet Tapes. (J). pap., teacher ed. 19.95 (*0-614-18235-2*) Let Us Tch Kids.

Mining with Backfill: Proceedings of the International Symposium, Lulea, 7-9 June 1983. Ed. by S. Granholm. 472p. (C). 1983. text 207.00 (*90-6191-509-0*, Pub. by A A Balkema) Ashgate Pub Co.

Minions of the Moon. Richard Bowes. LC 98-43981. (Illus.). 320p. 1999. 23.95 (*0-312-86566-X*, Pub. by Tor Bks) St Martin.

***Minions of the Moon.** Richard Bowes. 320p. 2000. pap. text 13.95 (*0-312-87228-3*, Pub. by Tor Bks) St Martin.

Minions of the Race. Anne Paolucci. 1978. pap. 2.95 (*0-918680-09-3*) Griffon House.

Minipets. Raintree. 1999. 95.88 (*0-8172-5591-5*) Raintree Steck-V.

***MiniPlanner: A Novel.** Abba Dewasar. 250p. 2000. pap. 12.95 (*1-57344-115-5*, Pub. by Cleis Pr) Publishers Group.

M

Minireviews of the Neurosciences from Life Sciences, Vols. 13-15. Ed. by Bernard B. Brodie & R. Bressler. LC 75-8733. 493p. 1975. 225.00 (*0-08-019724-8*, Pub. by Pergamon Repr) Franklin.

Minirhizotron Observation Tubes: Methods & Applications for Measuring Rhizosphere Dynamics. H. M. Taylor. (ASA Special Publications: No. 50). 144p. 1987. 24.00 (*0-89118-093-1*) Am Soc Agron.

Minis, Micros & Terminals for Libraries & Information Services: Proceedings of the Conference. Ed. by Alan Gilchrist. LC 82-10088. (British Computer Society Workshop Ser.). (Illus.). 129p. reprint ed. pap. 40.00 (*0-608-17858-6*, 203267800080) Bks Demand.

Minisink Patent. Armand S. La Potin. Ed. by Stuart Bruchey. LC 78-56697. (Management of Public Lands in the U. S. Ser.). 1979. lib. bdg. 25.95 (*0-405-11340-4*) Ayer.

Minispec Residential Construction Specifications. J. Hardy LeGwin. 150p. 1991. ring bd. 79.00 (*1-55701-306-3*) BNI Pubns.

Minispec Residential Construction Specifications: PC Version for IBM. J. Hardy LeGwin. 150p. 1991. ring bd. 99.00 (*1-55701-304-7*) BNI Pubns.

Minispec Residential Construction Specifications: PC Version for MAC. J. Hardy LeGwin. 150p. 1991. 99.00 (*1-55701-305-5*) BNI Pubns.

***Minister, a Priest & a Rabbi...** Alan Tapper & Peter R. Press. LC 99-40476. 2000. pap. 10.95 (*0-7407-0503-2*) Andrews & McMeel.

Minister As Crisis Counselor. rev. ed. David L. Switzer. LC 85-15827. 304p. (C). 1986. pap. 15.95 (*0-687-26954-7*) Abingdon.

Minister As Diagnostician: Personal Problems in Pastoral Perspective. Paul W. Pruyser. LC 76-8922. 144p. 1976. pap. 14.95 (*0-664-24123-9*) Westminster John Knox.

Minister As Shepherd. rev. ed. Charles Jefferson. LC 98-223220. 170p. 1998. mass mkt. 5.99 (*0-87508-706-X*, 706) Chr Lit.

***Minister Everyone Could Respect: 2 Cor.8-13.** Charles R. Swindoll. 1998. pap. 6.95 (*1-57972-189-3*) Insight Living.

Minister from Kansas. Gustave A. Gabelmann. 138p. 1996. pap. text 8.00 (*1-884680-01-1*) Gabelmann Pr.

Minister: His Character & His Struggles see **Ministro: Su Persona y Sus Luchas**

Minister in Oman: A Personal Narrative. Neil M. Innes. (Arabia Past & Present Ser.: Vol. 22). (Illus.). 304p. 1987. 35.00 (*0-900891-89-0*) Oleander Pr.

Minister Louis Farrakhan Vintage, 1970: The Presentation of the N. O. I. Solution to Congress of African People 1970. unabridged ed. Ed. by H. Khalif Khalifah. 40p. (Orig.). 1996. pap. 3.95 (*1-56411-153-9*, 4BBG0155) Untd Bros & Sis.

Minister, Mazen, Metallforscher: Carl Heinrich von Sickingen (1737-1791) und Seine Versuche Uber die Platina (1782) Leben und Werk Eines Laienforschers Im Zeitalter der Aufklarung. Eva Flegel. (Europaische Hochschulschriften Ser.: Reihe 3, Bd. 753). (GER., Illus.). XI, 230p. 1997. 44.95 (*3-631-31562-7*) P Lang Pubng.

Minister of Others Affairs. Jay O'Callahan. (J). (gr. 2 up). 1984. 10.00 incl. audio (*1-877954-03-9*) Artana Prodns.

Minister of Relief: Harry Hopkins & the Depression. Searle F. Charles. LC 74-2585. (Illus.). 286p. 1974. reprint ed. lib. bdg. 35.00 (*0-8371-7407-4*, CHMR, Greenwood Pr) Greenwood.

Minister to Minister Vol. I: Alternative Services for All Occasions. Cayli H. Levitan. 100p. (Orig.). 1992. pap. 13.95 (*0-9632747-0-8*) C H Levitan.

***Ministere de Puissance: Un Manuel pour les Predicateurs Pentecotistes.** Denny Miller. (Discovery Ser.).Tr. of Power Ministry. (FRE.). 142p. 1999. pap. text. write for info. (*2-912377-07-2*, Editions SAFT) Africa Theolog Trng.

Ministerial Acts of the Church of the Lutheran Brethren. rev. ed. Luther Larson & Warren Olsen. Ed. by David Rinden. 145p. 1993. ring bd. 14.95 (*0-943167-28-0*) Faith & Fellowship Pr.

***Ministerial & Common Priesthood in the Eucharistic Celebration: The Proceedings of the 1998 4th International Colloquium of Historical, Canonica.** Ed. by St. Austin Press Staff. 256p. 1999. pap. 22.95 (*1-901157-86-5*) St Austin.

Ministerial Competency Report. Steve Clapp. (Practice of Ministry Ser.). 123p. (Orig.). 1982. pap. 8.00 (*0-914527-10-X*) C-Four Res.

Ministerial Education in the American Methodist Movement. Gerald O. McCulloh. LC 80-69028. (Informed Ministry Series, Two Hundred Years of American Methodist Thought: 200 Years of American Methodist Thought). 342p. (Orig.). 1980. pap. 3.95 (*0-938162-00-4*) United Meth Educ.

Ministerial Ethics see Etica Ministerial

Ministerial Ethics: A Guide for Spirit-Filled Leaders. T. Burton Pierce. Ed. by Stanley M. Horton. LC 96-3636. 288p. 1996. 19.95 (*0-88243-320-2*) Gospel Pub.

Ministerial Ethics: Being a Good Minister in a Not-So-Good World. Joe E. Trull & James E. Carter. LC 92-36291. 1993. 14.99 (*0-8054-1056-2*, 4210-56) Broadman.

Ministerial Ethics & Etiquette. I. Parker Maxey. 1987. pap. 14.99 (*0-88019-222-4*) Schmul Pub Co.

Ministerial Ethics & Etiquette. rev. ed. Nolan B. Harmon. LC 87-12604. 176p. 1987. pap. 13.95 (*0-687-27034-0*) Abingdon.

Ministerial Responsibility. Ed. by Geoffrey Marshall. (Oxford Readings in Politics & Government Ser.). 186p. 1989. 45.00 (*0-19-827580-3*); pap. 16.95 (*0-19-827579-X*) OUP.

Ministerial Training in 18th Century New England. Mary L. Gambrell. (Columbia University. Studies in the Social Sciences: No. 428). reprint ed. 20.00 (*0-404-51428-6*) AMS Pr.

M

***Ministering Angels.** large type ed. Anthea Cohen. 336p. 1999. pap. 20.99 (*1-85389-929-1*, Dales) Ulverscroft.

Ministering Cross-Culturally: An Incarnational Model for Personal Relationships. Sherwood G. Lingenfelter & Marvin K. Mayers. LC 86-71157. 128p. 1986. pap. 9.99 (*0-8010-5632-2*) Baker Bks.

Ministering Deliverance. Paul Fernandez. 110p. (Orig.). 1993. pap. 6.95 (*0-89228-108-1*) Impact Christian.

Ministering in the Gifts of the Spirit. Larry Keefauver. 64p. 1997. pap., student ed. 6.99 (*0-88419-495-7*) Creation House.

Ministering in the Secular University: A Guide for Christian Professors & Staff. Joseph M. Mellichamp. LC 97-26127. 1997. write for info. (*0-929510-09-7*) Lewis & Stanley.

Ministering in the Spirit & Strength of Jesus (II Corinthians, I & II Timothy, Titus) Thomas Nelson Publishers Staff. LC 98-145860. (Spirit-Filled Life Bible Discovery Guides Ser.: Vol. B20). 160p. pap. 6.99 (*0-7852-1204-3*) Nelson.

Ministering Inner Healing. 1988. pap. text 6.95 (*0-917726-90-1*) Hunter Bks.

Ministering Spirits Sent Forth. Brian K. McCallum. Ed. by Phyllis Mackall. 225p. 1997. pap. 8.95 (*0-9620883-3-1*) McCallum Ministries.

***Ministering Through Spiritual Gifts.** Charles Stanley. LC 99-229506. (In Touch Study Ser.). 112p. 1999. pap. 7.99 (*0-7852-7287-9*) Nelson.

Ministering to Abortion's Aftermath. Bill Banks & Sue Banks. 144p. (Orig.). 1982. pap. 5.95 (*0-89228-057-3*) Impact Christian.

Ministering to Families. Royce Money. LC 86-72162. 300p. 1987. pap. 10.95 (*0-915547-92-9*) Abilene Christ U.

Ministering to God: The Reach of the Heart. Victoria Brooks. 166p. 1995. pap. 8.00 (*1-886296-10-3*, VB1-001) Arrow Publications.

Ministering to the Brokenhearted. Kenneth E. Hagin, Jr. 1987. 1.00 (*0-89276-721-9*) Faith Lib Pubns.

Ministering to the House or to God. Watchman. 47p. 1998. pap. 1.00 (*1-57593-869-3*, 18-062-001) Living Stream Ministry.

***Ministering to the Lord: The Power of His Presence.** Roxanne Brant. 96p. 2000. pap. 7.99 (*0-88368-611-2*) Whitaker Hse.

Ministering to Today's Adults. Kenneth O. Gangel. LC 98-39063. (Swindoll Leadership Library). 1999. 24.99 (*0-8499-1361-6*) Word Pub.

Ministering to Today's Adults Supersaver ed., 1. Kenneth O. Gangel. (Swindoll Leadership Library). 1999. 19.97 (*0-8499-1595-3*) Word Pub.

Ministering to Your Family. Kenneth E. Hagin. 1986. pap. 3.95 (*0-89276-407-4*) Faith Lib Pubns.

Ministering to Your Pastor. Toby Awasum. LC 97-174159. 168p. 1997. pap. 10.99 (*1-56043-288-8*, Treasure Hse) Destiny Image.

Ministering to Youth: A Guide for Parents, Teachers & Youth Workers. Michael G. Wensing. LC 82-11382. 120p. (Orig.). 1982. pap. 4.95 (*0-8189-0444-5*) Alba.

Ministering with the Earth. Mary E. Moore. LC 97-44507. 160p. 1998. pap. 19.99 (*0-8272-2323-4*) Chalice Pr.

Ministering Within the Church Towards the Third Millennium Vol. 7, No. 6: Proceedings of the Sixth International Assembly of Priests' Representatives from English-Speaking Countries. David McLaughlin. (Illus.). 16p. (Orig.). 1996. pap. 3.00 (*0-9653675-2-5*) NFPC.

Ministerio de Cristo en Jerusalen, Libro 2. Francis Breisch, Jr. (SPA.). 142p. pap. 6.00 (*1-55883-020-0*, 6700-0520C) Libros Desafio.

Ministerio de Cristo en Palestina, Libro 1. Francis Breisch, Jr. (SPA.). 192p. pap. 6.00 (*1-55883-019-7*, 6700-0510C) Libros Desafio.

Ministerio de Cristo Hasta lo Ultimo de la Tierra, Libro 3. Francis Breisch, Jr. (SPA.). 168p. pap. 6.00 (*1-55883-021-9*, 6700-0530C) Libros Desafio.

Ministerio de la Diaconia. H. R. Perez.Tr. of Deacon's Ministry. (SPA.). pap. 10.99 (*0-7899-0326-1*, 491048) Editorial Unilit.

Ministerio de la Hospitalidad. James A. Comiskey. Tr. by Colette J. Dees. (Ministry Ser.). (SPA.). 48p. 1994. pap. 1.95 (*0-8146-2070-1*) Liturgical Pr.

Ministerio de la Oracion Intercesora. Andrew Murray.Tr. of Ministry of Intercessory Prayer. (SPA.). 176p. (Orig.). 1985. pap. 7.99 (*0-88113-207-1*) Caribe Betania.

Ministerio de Liberacion. Jorge Ovando.Tr. of Liberation Ministry. (SPA.). 80p. 1996. 2.99 (*0-89922-294-3*, C033-2943) Caribe Betania.

Ministerio de los Lectores. James A. Wallace. Tr. by Colette J. Dees. (Ministry Ser.). (SPA.). 48p. 1994. pap. 2.95 (*0-8146-2041-8*) Liturgical Pr.

Ministerio de los Monaguillos. Michael Kwatera. Tr. by Colette J. Dees. (Ministry Ser.). (SPA.). 48p. 1994. pap. 1.95 (*0-8146-2174-0*) Liturgical Pr.

Ministerio de los Santos. Jose D. Camacho.Tr. of Ministry of the Saints. (SPA.). 224p. 1992. pap. 6.99 (*1-56063-390-5*, 498544) Editorial Unilit.

Ministerio del Drama y la Pantomima. Judy Whitener.Tr. of Ministry of Drama & Pantomime. (SPA.). 1994. pap., teacher ed. 6.50 (*0-311-11076-2*) Casa Bautista.

Ministerio del Pastor-Consejero: Pastoral Care & Counseling. James E. Giles. (SPA.). 224p. 1992. pap. 11.50 (*0-311-42084-2*) Casa Bautista.

Ministerio en el Infierno. David Wilkerson. (SPA.). 1998. pap. 5.99 (*0-8297-0376-4*) Vida Pubs.

Ministerio Ideal, 2 vols., 1. Charles H. Spurgeon. (SPA.). 200p. 1993. reprint ed. 8.99 (*0-85151-410-3*) Banner of Truth.

Ministerio Ideal, 2 vols., 2. Charles H. Spurgeon. (SPA.). 234p. 1993. reprint ed. 8.99 (*0-85151-411-1*) Banner of Truth.

Ministerio Juvenil Dinamico. J. Burns.Tr. of Youth Builder. (SPA.). 100. pap. 13.99 (*0-7899-0314-8*, 497392) Editorial Unilit.

Ministerio Profetico. Juan J. Churruarin. 1998. pap. text 5.99 (*0-8297-0724-7*) Vida Pubs.

Ministers. 31p. 1996. pap. 3.50 (*0-16-061964-5*) USGPO.

Ministers: Market Segment Specialization Program-Audit Technique Guide. 36p. 1995. pap. 13.10 (*1-57402-107-9*) Athena Info Mgt.

Ministers' Accounts II of the Earldom of Cornwall, 1296-7. L. M. Midgley. (Camden Third Ser.). 35.00 (*0-86193-068-1*) David Brown.

Ministers & Generals: Politics & the Canadian Militia, 1868-1904. Desmond Morton. LC 79-135208. 272p. reprint ed. pap. 84.40 (*0-608-30834-X*, 201437400090) Bks Demand.

Ministers & Members in the New Zealand Parliament. G. A. Wood. LC 96-208419. 128p. 1996. 24.95 (*1-877133-00-0*, Pub. by Univ Otago Pr) Intl Spec Bk.

Ministers & Ministries: A Functional Analysis. Richard Rose. LC 86-23739. (Illus.). 296p. 1987. text 65.00 (*0-19-827486-6*) OUP.

Ministers & Parliament: Accountability in Theory & Practice. Diana Woodhouse. LC 93-30851. 330p. 1994. text 65.00 (*0-19-827892-6*, Clarendon Pr) OUP.

Minister's Annual Manual, 1997-1998: For Preaching & Worship Planning. Clyde Steckel et al. Ed. by Sharilyn A. Figueroa. 500p. (Orig.). 1997. pap. text 23.95 (*1-885361-04-1*) Logos Prods.

Minister's Annual Manual, 1998-99: For Preaching & Worship Planning. Clyde Steckel et al. Ed. by Sharilyn Figueroa. 500p. 1998. pap. 23.95 (*1-885361-22-X*) Logos Prods.

***Ministers at the Millennium: A Survey of Ministers in Churches of Christ.** Douglas A. Foster et al. LC 00-102020. 180p. 2000. pap. 14.95 (*0-89112-062-9*) Abilene Christ U.

Minister's Cat. Hamish Whyte. (Illus.). 64p. 1996. pap. 22.00 (*1-873644-10-8*, Pub. by Mercat Pr Bks) St Mut.

Minister's Cat. Hamish Whyte & Barbara Robertson. (Aberdeen University Press Bks.). (Illus.). 56p. 1991. pap. 5.00 (*0-08-041208-4*, Pub. by Aberdeen U Pr) Macmillan.

Minister's Cat: An A-Z of Cats in Verse. Douglas Kynoch. (Illus.). 1990. pap. 21.00 (*1-898218-18-8*) St Mut.

Minister's Cat, ABC see Gold Star First Readers

Minister's Charge. William Dean Howells. (Notable American Authors Ser.). 1992. reprint ed. lib. bdg. 75.00 (*0-7812-3239-2*) Rprt Serv.

Minister's Charge: or The Apprenticeship of Lemuel Barker. William Dean Howells. 18.00 (*0-403-00024-6*) Scholarly.

Minister's Compass see Brujula Para el Ministro Evangelico

Minister's Guide for Special Occasions. Ed. by Zeno C. Tharp. 1996. reprint ed. 12.99 (*0-87148-553-2*) Pathway Pr.

Minister's Guide to Financial Planning. Kenneth M. Meyer. 160p. 1987. pap. 7.95 (*0-310-34621-5*, 18421P) Zondervan.

Minister's Handbook. G. C. Ministerial Association Staff. 282p. 1997. 10.95 (*1-57847-005-6*) Genl Conf Svnth-day.

Minister's Handbook. Lewis F. Shaffer. 529p. (Orig.). (C). 1991. pap. write for info. (*0-929389-06-9*) Son Shine Ministries.

Minister's Handbook. Orlando L. Tibbetts. 224p. 1986. 12.00 (*0-8170-1088-2*) Judson.

Minister's Handbook of Mental Disorders. Joseph W. Ciarrocchi. LC 93-11092. (Integration Bks.). 224p. 1993. pap. 16.95 (*0-8091-3403-9*) Paulist Pr.

Ministers in Training Manual. James Pierce & Stacia Pierce. 60p. 1996. wbk. ed. 39.95 (*1-886880-11-5*) Life Changers.

Ministers Journey Through Adultry. Edward D. Hernandez. LC 97-93110. 120p. (Orig.). 1997. pap. 10.00 (*1-57502-448-9*, P01347) Morris Pubng.

***Minister's Library.** Cyril Barber. 1999. 79.99 (*1-57822-050-5*) Bible Companion.

Minister's Library, Vol. 1. Cyril J. Barber. LC 84-25500. 510p. 1974. 24.99 (*0-8024-5296-5*) Loizeaux.

Minister's Library, Vol. 2. C. J. Barber. 1985. 24.99 (*0-8024-5299-X*) Loizeaux.

Minister's Little Devotional Book. Stan Toler & H. B. London, Jr. LC 98-220955. 320p. 1997. 14.99 (*1-56292-374-9*) Honor Bks OK.

Minister's Little Instruction Book: Timeless Wisdom & Practical Advice for Ministers & Lay L. Stan Toler. 160p. 1998. pap. text 7.99 (*0-8341-1762-2*) Beacon Hill.

Minister's Manual see Manuel Del Ministro

Minister's Manual. Ed. by John Rempel. 242p. 1998. pap. 24.95 (*0-87303-320-5*); pap. 32.95 incl. disk (*0-87303-327-2*) Faith & Life.

Minister's Manual. 6th ed. Ed. by Herbert L. Beierle. 283p. (C). 1997. pap. 14.95 (*0-940480-03-4*) UNIPress.

Minister's Manual: King James Version. rev. ed. Owen Alderfer. 1970. reprint ed. 8.95 (*0-916035-04-2*) Evangel Indiana.

Minister's Manual: New International Version. Owen Alderfer. 192p. 1991. 10.95 (*0-916035-47-6*) Evangel Indiana.

Ministers Manual: 1999 Edition. James W. Cox. 1998. 19.95 (*0-7879-4250-2*) Jossey-Bass.

Ministers Manual: 1999 Edition. 74th ed. Ed. by James W. Coy. (Religion in Practice Ser.). 375p. 1998. 19.95 (*0-7879-4205-7*) Jossey-Bass.

Minister's Manual: 2000 Edition. James W. Cox. 448p. 1999. 21.00 (*0-7879-4546-3*) Jossey-Bass.

Minister's Manual for Funerals. Al Cadenhead, Jr. LC 87-14616. 208p. 1987. 16.99 (*0-8054-2317-6*, 4223-17) Broadman.

Ministers Manual, 1988. 73rd ed. Ed. by James W. Cox. LC 25-21658. (Religion in Practice Ser.). 1997. 19.95 (*0-7879-0882-7*) Jossey-Bass.

Ministers Manual Ser., 3 vols., Set. Compiled by William E. Pickthorn. Incl. Vol. 1. Services for Special Occasions. LC 65-13222. 132p. 1965. 7.99 (*0-88243-547-7*, 02-0547); Vol. 2. Services for Weddings & Funerals. LC 65-13222. 130p. 1965. 7.99 (*0-88243-548-5*, 02-0548); Vol. 3. Services for Ministers & Workers. LC 65-13222. 134p. 1965. 7.99 (*0-88243-549-3*, 02-0549); LC 65-13222. 1965. 22.99 (*0-88243-544-2*, 02-0544) Gospel Pub.

***Minister's Manual 2001.** James W. Cox. 448p. 2000. 21.00 (*0-7879-5002-5*) Jossey-Bass.

Minister's Marriage Manual. Compiled by S. W. Hutton. LC 67-18181. 96p. (C). 1968. 12.99 (*0-8010-4031-0*) Baker Bks.

Ministers' Minders: Political Advisors in National Governments. James Walter. 304p. 1987. 36.00 (*0-19-554590-7*) OUP.

Minister's of Grace: Women in the Early Church. Judith Long. 151p. (C). 1996. pap. 39.95 (*0-85439-298-X*, Pub. by St Paul Pubns) St Mut.

Ministers of Reform: The Progressives' Achievement in American Civilization, 1889-1920. Robert M. Crunden. 320p. 1985. pap. text 14.95 (*0-252-01167-8*) U of Ill Pr.

Ministers of the Crown. Rodney Brazier. 414p. 1997. text 90.00 (*0-19-825988-3*) OUP.

Ministers of the Gospel. Carlo M. Martini. 1989. pap. 6.95 (*0-8245-0959-5*) Crossroad NY.

Ministers of the Gospel. Ed. by Carlo M. Martini. (C). 1988. 39.00 (*0-85439-220-3*, Pub. by St Paul Pubns) St Mut.

Ministers of Your Joy: Reflections on Priestly Spirituality. Joseph Ratzinger & Board of St. Paul Editorial Staff. 128p. (C). 1996. pap. 39.95 (*0-85439-287-4*, Pub. by St Paul Pubns) St Mut.

Minister's Prayer Book: An Order of Prayers & Readings. Ed. by John W. Doberstein. LC 85-16212. 512p. 1986. 22.00 (*0-8006-0760-0*, 1-760, Fortress Pr) Augsburg Fortress.

Minister's Seal see Two Plays of Ancient India

Minister's Service Book. Myer Pearlman. 147p. 1990. 7.99 (*0-88243-551-5*, 02-0551) Gospel Pub.

Minister's Service Manual. Clyne W. Buxton. 1985. text 11.99 (*0-87148-584-2*) Pathway Pr.

Minister's Service Manual. S. W. Hutton. 230p. 1963. 16.99 (*0-8010-4035-3*) Baker Bks.

Minister's Task & Calling in the Sermons of Jonathan Edwards. Helen Westra. LC 85-29694. (Studies in American Religion: Vol. 17). 400p. 1986. lib. bdg. 99.95 (*0-88946-661-0*) E Mellen.

Minister's Wife. Delia Parr. 320p. 1998. mass mkt. 5.99 (*0-312-96650-4*) St Martin.

Minister's Wife, 3 vols., 2 bks., Set. Margaret O. Oliphant. LC 79-8185. reprint ed. 84.50 (*0-404-62098-1*) AMS Pr.

Minister's Wooing. Harriet Beecher Stowe. Ed. & Intro. by Susan K. Harris. LC 99-19095. 480p. 1999. pap. 13.95 (*0-14-043702-9*, PuffinBks) Peng Put Young Read.

Minister's Wooing. Harriet Beecher Stowe. (BCL1-PS American Literature Ser.). 578p. 1992. reprint ed. lib. bdg. 99.00 (*0-7812-6872-9*) Rprt Serv.

Minister's Wooing. Harriet Beecher Stowe. (Notable American Authors Ser.). 1999. reprint ed. lib. bdg. 125.00 (*0-7812-8959-9*) Rprt Serv.

Minister's Wooing. Harriet Beecher Stowe. LC 77-13796. (Illus.). 578p. (C). 1996. reprint ed. pap. 17.00 (*0-917482-12-3*) Rutgers U Pr.

Minister's Wooing. Harriet Beecher Stowe. reprint ed. 14.00 (*0-403-00187-0*) Scholarly.

***Ministramos al Templo Ministramos a Dios, Vol. 10.** Watchman Nee. 1999. pap. 10.00 (*0-7363-0305-7*) Living Stream Ministry.

Ministrando con Musica. B. J. Gramm.Tr. of Ministry Through Music. 4.99 (*0-7899-0466-7*, 495031) Editorial Unilit.

Ministries of Mercy: The Call of the Jericho Road. 2nd ed. Timothy J. Keller. LC 97-19767. 236p. 1997. pap. 9.99 (*0-87552-217-3*) P & R Pubng.

Ministries Specialties Test. Corinne Ware. pap. 10.00 (*1-56699-170-6*) Alban Inst.

Ministries Weekend. rev. ed. Robert D. Noble. 138p. (Orig.). 1993. pap., student ed. 20.00 (*0-944687-13-X*) Gather Family Inst.

Ministro: Su Persona y Sus Luchas. K. Silva & Suarez.Tr. of Minister: His Character & His Struggles. (SPA.). pap. 4.50 (*1-56063-501-0*, 498464) Editorial Unilit.

Ministro Negro Imi IDX. 1994. 29.99 (*0-8297-2061-8*) Vida Pubs.

Ministry. T. Austin-Sparks. 1999. pap. 29.95 (*0-940232-66-9*) Seedsowers.

Ministry. Joseph T. Lienhard. Ed. by Thomas Halton. LC 83-83154. (Message of the Fathers of the Church Ser.: Vol. 8). 183p. 1984. pap. 11.95 (*0-8146-5320-0*) Liturgical Pr.

Ministry: A Theological, Pastoral Handbook. Richard P. McBrien. LC 86-43011. 128p. 1988. pap. 12.00 (*0-06-065324-8*, Pub. by Harper SF) HarpC.

Ministry: How Japan's Most Powerful Institution Endangers World Markets. Peter Hartcher. LC 97-27489. 320p. 1998. 24.95 (*0-87584-785-4*, HBS Pr) Harvard Busn.

Ministry: How Japan's Most Powerful Institution Endangers World Markets. Harvard Business School Press Staff. 288p. 1997. 14.95 (*0-07-105065-5*) McGraw.

Ministry: It's Not Just for Ministers. Gary Morsch & Eddy Hall. 128p. (Orig.). 1993. pap. 8.99 (*0-8341-1510-7*) Beacon Hill.

Ministry: Lay Ministry in the Roman Catholic Church, Its History & Theology. Kenan B. Osborne. LC 92-40299. 720p. 1993. pap. 29.95 (*0-8091-3371-7*) Paulist Pr.

Ministry: What's Right? What's Wrong? Paul E. Paino. 48p. 1992. pap. 4.95 (*1-882357-02-7*) P E Paino Minist.

Ministry, a Way of Life. Miriam Hellman. 16p. 1992. 2.00 (*1-891309-04-8*) Prophetic DC.

Ministry & Authority in the Catholic Church. Edmund Hill. 1990. pap. 14.95 (*0-225-66527-1*, 6355, Pub. by G Chapman) Morehouse Pub.

***Ministry & Community: Recognizing, Healing & Preventing Ministry Impairment.** Len Sperry. LC 99-42557. 136p. 2000. pap. 11.95 (*0-8146-2723-4*) Liturgical Pr.

Ministry & Leadership: Adult Workshops. Center for Learning Network Staff. (Adult Workshops Ser.). 88p. 1989. pap. text 15.95 (*1-56077-039-2*) Ctr Learning.

Ministry & Meaning: A Religious History of Catholic Health Care in the United States. Christopher J. Kauffman. LC 95-1123. 384p. 1995. 29.95 (*0-8245-1459-9*) Crossroad NY.

Ministry & Medicine in Human Relations. New York Academy of Medicine Staff. Ed. by Iago Galdston. LC 77-142682. (Essay Index Reprint Ser.). 1977. 19.95 (*0-8369-2120-8*) Ayer.

Ministry & Mission: Theological Reflections for the Life of the Church. James F. Hopewell et al. Ed. by Barbara B. Taylor. 192p. (Orig.). 1985. pap. 9.95 (*0-935311-00-9*) Post Horn Pr.

Ministry & Music. Robert H. Mitchell. LC 77-20815. 164p. 1978. pap. 17.95 (*0-664-24186-7*) Westminster John Knox.

Ministry & Solitude: The Ministry of Laity & Clergy in Church & Society. James C. Fenhagen. 128p. 1984. 10.45 (*0-8164-0498-4*) Harper SF.

Ministry & Spirituality: Reaching Out, Creativity Ministry. Henri J. M. Nouwen. LC 96-84430. 240p. 1996. 29.00 (*0-8264-0910-5*) Continuum.

Ministry & the American Legal System: A Guide for Clergy, Lay Workers, & Congregations. Richard B. Couser. LC 92-34214. 360p. 1993. 42.00 (*0-8006-2603-6*, 1-2603, Fortress Pr) Augsburg Fortress.

Ministry & the Law: What You Need to Know. Mary A. Shaughnessy. LC 97-44065. 128p. 1998. pap. 8.95 (*0-8091-3789-5*) Paulist Pr.

Ministry & the Miraculous: A Case Study at Fuller Theological Seminary. Lewis B. Smedes. 68p. 1992. reprint ed. pap. 10.00 (*1-881266-09-5*) Fuller Seminary.

Ministry & Theology: Studies for the Church & Its Leaders. John C. Thomas. 179p. 1996. pap. 10.99 (*0-87148-600-8*) Pathway Pr.

Ministry & Theology in Global Perspective: Contemporary Challenges for the Church. Ed. by Don A. Pittman et al. 542p. (Orig.). 1996. pap. 35.00 (*0-8028-0844-1*) Eerdmans.

Ministry Anointing of Governments. John J. Eckhardt. 64p. 1991. 5.00 (*0-9630567-0-0*) Crusaders Minist.

Ministry Anointing of Helps. John J. Eckhardt. 27p. 1991. 3.00 (*0-9630567-1-9*) Crusaders Minist.

Ministry Anointing of the Apostle. John J. Eckhardt. 56p. (Orig.). 1993. 5.00 (*0-9630567-6-X*) Crusaders Minist.

Ministry Anointing of the Prophet. John J. Eckhardt. 39p. 1991. 5.00 (*0-9630567-2-7*) Crusaders Minist.

***Ministry Anyone Could Trust: A Study of 2 Corinthians 1-7.** Charles R. Swindoll. 127p. 1998. pap., student ed. 5.95 (*1-57972-188-5*) Insight Living.

Ministry at the Margins: The Prophetic Mission of Women, Youth & the Poor. Cheryl J. Sanders. LC 96-43164. 108p. (Orig.). 1997. pap. 10.99 (*0-8308-1997-5*, 1997) InterVarsity.

Ministry Burnout. Ed. by John A. Sanford. (C). 1990. pap. 24.00 (*0-85305-262-X*, Pub. by Arthur James) St Mut.

Ministry Burnout. John A. Sanford. 128p. 1992. pap. 12.95 (*0-664-25352-0*) Westminster John Knox.

Ministry by the People: Theological Education by Extension. Ed. by F. Ross Kinsler. LC 83-210665. 348p. (Orig.). reprint ed. pap. 107.90 (*0-8357-2680-0*, 204021600015) Bks Demand.

Ministry for a New Time: Case Study for Change. James C. Fenhagen. LC 95-78601. (Once & Future Church Ser.). 190p. 1995. pap. 15.95 (*1-56699-156-0*, AL165) Alban Inst.

Ministry for Retired Persons: A Simple Narrative of the Evolvement of a Concept. Clinton W. Bradford. LC 87-50591. 123p. (Orig.). 1987. pap. 2.50 (*0-9618924-0-4*) Reily Mem Univ.

An Asterisk (*) at the beginning of an entry indicates that the title is appearing for the first time.

Ministry Gift Error. Tom Bynum. Ed. by Tanya C. Stokes. 62p. (Orig.). 1991. pap. 6.95 (*0-9627849-8-2*) Temperance Pub Hse.

Ministry Gifts. Kenneth E. Hagin. 74p. 1992. pap. 6.95 (*0-89276-087-7*) Faith Lib Pubns.

Ministry Gifts: Apostles, Prophets, Evangelists, Pastors, Teachers. Tr. of Les Dons du Ministere. (SPA.). 111p. 1995. spiral bd. 12.95 (*0-941975-62-2*); spiral bd. 12.95 (*0-941975-63-0*) Powerhouse.

Ministry Gifts: Apostles, Prophets, Evangelists, Pastors, Teachers. rev. ed. A. L. Gill. 112p. (Orig.). 1995. pap., student ed. 9.95 (*0-941975-36-3*) Powerhouse.

Ministry Helps in Acts. Richard P. Belchen. 72p. (C). reprint ed. pap. 6.95 (*0-925703-62-1*) Crown MA.

Ministry Helps in Amos. Richard P. Belcher. 48p. 1995. pap. 6.95 (*1-883265-16-9*) Richbarry Pr.

Ministry Helps in Ephesians. Richard P. Belcher. 44p. 1996. pap. 6.95 (*1-883265-18-5*) Richbarry Pr.

Ministry Helps in Galatians. Richard P. Belcher. 50p. 1996. pap. 6.95 (*1-883265-17-7*) Richbarry Pr.

Ministry Helps in Hosea. Richard P. Belcher. 60p. (Orig.). 1993. pap. 6.95 (*1-883265-08-8*) Richbarry Pr.

Ministry Helps in Isaiah. Richard P. Belcher. 132p. 1994. pap. 6.95 (*1-883265-15-0*) Richbarry Pr.

Ministry Helps in John. Richard P. Belchen. 60p. pap. 6.95 (*0-925703-18-4*) Crown MA.

***Ministry Helps in Thessalonians.** Richard P. Belcher. 70p. 2000. pap. write for info. (*1-883265-20-7*) Richbarry Pr.

Ministry Ideabank. John H. Krahn & Betty J. Foster. 136p. (Orig.). 1981. pap. text 7.25 (*0-89536-488-3*, 1314) CSS OH.

Ministry Ideabank III. Betty J. Foster & John H. Krahn. (Orig.). 1987. pap. 9.25 (*0-89536-895-1*, 7881) CSS OH.

Ministry in an Oral Culture: Living with Will Rogers, Uncle Remus, & Minnie Pearl. Tex Sample. LC 93-23713. 128p. (Orig.). 1994. pap. 17.95 (*0-664-25506-X*) Westminster John Knox.

Ministry in Community. J. Farmer. (Louvain Theological & Pastoral Monographs). 1993. pap. text 25.00 (*0-8028-0573-6*) Eerdmans.

Ministry in Daily Life: A Practical Guide for Congregations. William E. Diehl. LC 96-85342. 118p. 1996. pap. 14.25 (*1-56699-172-2*, AL174) Alban Inst.

Ministry in Modern Singapore: The Effects of Modernity on the Church. Chang K. Wrong et al. LC 97-945836. xi, 254p. 1997. write for info. (*981-00-8898-1*) Miscell Pubs.

Ministry in the Church: A Historical & Pastoral Approach. Paul Bernier. LC 92-64051. 336p. (Orig.). 1992. pap. 16.95 (*0-89622-536-4*) Twenty-Third.

Ministry in the Countryside. A. Bowden. LC 75-153122. par. 21.95 (*0-264-67321-2*) Continuum.

Ministry in the New Testament. David L. Bartlett. LC 93-19849. (Overtures to Bibical Theology Ser.). 224p. 1993. pap. 19.00 (*0-8006-1565-4*, 1-1565) Augsburg Fortress.

Ministry Kit. Dorothy Miller. 34p. 1997. pap., wbk. ed. 9.95 incl. VHS (*1-878993-02-X*) Jeremiah Films.

Ministry Nuts & Bolts: What They Don't Teach Pastors in Seminary. Aubrey Malphurs. LC 97-41092. 192p. 1997. pap. 11.99 (*0-8254-3190-5*) Kregel.

Ministry of a Wife. June Boisselier. LC 89-92037. 316p. (Orig.). 1993. pap. 11.95 (*0-9625705-4-0*) Revival Pubns.

Ministry of Affliction. 2nd ed. B. R. Hicks. (Illus.). 127p. 1988. reprint ed. pap. 7.95 (*1-58363-058-9*, CM-0503) Christ Gospel.

Ministry of Angels. Gordon Lindsay. 1964. 1.95 (*0-89985-018-9*) Christ for the Nations.

Ministry of Art. Ralph A. Cram. LC 67-30203. (Essay Index Reprint Ser.). 1977. 19.95 (*0-8369-0347-1*) Ayer.

Ministry of Believers. Emeric A. Lawrence. (Ministry Ser.). 28p. (Orig.). 1982. pap. text 1.95 (*0-8146-1276-8*) Liturgical Pr.

Ministry of Caring: Leader's Guide. rev. ed. Duane A. Ewers. LC 99-61196. 68p. 1999. pap., teacher ed. 12.95 (*0-88177-290-9*, DR290) Discipleship Res.

Ministry of Caring: Participant's Workbook. rev. ed. Duane A. Ewers & Fritz Mutti. LC 99-90318. 88p. 1999. pap. 14.95 (*0-88177-289-5*, DR289) Discipleship Res.

Ministry of Cheerfulness. large type ed. Jesse Duplantis. 80p. 1994. pap. 5.99 (*0-89274-799-4*, HH-799) Harrison Hse.

Ministry of Christian Teaching. Donald S. Aultman. 111p. 1981. pap. 3.95 (*0-87148-555-9*) Pathway Pr.

Ministry of Communion. Michael Kwatera. (Ministry Ser.). (Illus.). 48p. 1983. pap. text 1.95 (*0-8146-1292-X*) Liturgical Pr.

Ministry of Consolation: A Parish Guide for Comforting the Bereaved. Terence P. Curley. LC 93-10315. 80p. (Orig.). 1993. pap. 3.95 (*0-8189-0651-0*) Alba.

Ministry of Consolation: Involving Your Parish in the Order of Christian Funerals. Rose M. Cover et al. LC 96-36774. 136p. (Orig.). 1997. pap. text 14.95 (*0-8146-2460-X*, Liturg Pr Bks) Liturgical Pr.

Ministry of Counseling. Carol R. Murphy. (C). 1952. pap. 4.00 (*0-87574-067-7*) Pendle Hill.

Ministry of Defense: Performance Report 1996-97, Command Paper 3781. (Command Papers (All) Ser.: No. 81011068). 1997. 25.00 (*0-10-137812-2*, HM78122, Pub. by Statnry Office) Bernan Associates.

Ministry of Development in Evangelical Perspective: A Symposium on the Social & Spiritual Mandate. Ed. by Carl F. Henry & Robert L. Hancock. LC 78-27821. 109p. 1979. pap. 5.95 (*0-87808-164-X*) William Carey Lib.

Ministry of Drama & Pantomime see Ministerio del Drama y la Pantomima

Ministry of Evangelization. Susan Blum. (Ministry Ser.). 80p. (C). 1988. pap. 1.95 (*0-8146-1599-6*) Liturgical Pr.

Ministry of Fasting. Zacharias T. Fomum. 1991. 14.95 (*0-533-08281-1*) Vantage.

Ministry of Fear. Graham Greene. 224p. 1993. pap. 10.95 (*0-14-018536-4*, Penguin Classics) Viking Penguin.

Ministry of Finance: Bureaucratic Practices & the Transformation of the Japanese Economy. J. Robert Brown. LC 98-23644. 288p. 1999. 65.00 (*1-56720-230-6*, Quorum Bks) Greenwood.

Ministry of God's Word. Watchman Nee. Tr. by Stephen Kaung. 282p. 1971. 8.00 (*0-935008-27-6*); pap. 6.00 (*0-935008-28-4*) Christian Fellow Pubs.

Ministry of Healing. Ellen Gould Harmon White. (ASI Ser.). 224p. 1990. pap. 1.10 (*0-8163-1007-6*) Pacific Pr Pub Assn.

Ministry of Healing. Ellen Gould Harmon White. 1942. reprint ed. 12.99 (*0-8163-0124-7*, 13540-0) Pacific Pr Pub Assn.

Ministry of Healing Vol. 1: Direction for Healthful Living. Ellen Gould Harmon White. 300p. (C). 1995. reprint ed. pap. 9.95 (*1-883012-56-2*, RP1301) Remnant Pubns.

Ministry of Healing for Black America. abr. ed. Ellen Gould Harmon White. Ed. by W. H. Frazier. (Illus.). 192p. 1998. mass mkt. 5.95 (*1-886002-15-0*) Foy Inst Pr.

Ministry of Helps Handbook. Buddy Bell. 128p. (Orig.). 1990. pap. 7.99 (*0-89274-766-8*, HH766) Harrison Hse.

Ministry of Hope. Roy A. Heath. 320p. 1996. 24.95 (*0-7145-3015-8*) M Boyars Pubs.

Ministry of Hospital Chaplains: Patient Satisfaction. Ed. by Larry VandeCreek & Marjorie A. Lyons. LC 97-30300. 64p. 1997. 24.95 (*0-7890-0357-0*, Haworth Pastrl) Haworth Pr.

Ministry of Hospitality. Sylvia C. Deck. LC 97-148973. (Pastoral Ministry Ser.). 70p. (Orig.). 1996. pap. 8.95 (*1-55612-951-3*, LL951) Sheed & Ward WI.

Ministry of Hospitality, 20 vols., Set. James A. Comiskey. (Ministry Ser.). 48p. (C). 1989. pap. 1.95 (*0-8146-1812-X*) Liturgical Pr.

Ministry of Illusion: Nazi Cinema & Its Afterlife. Eric Rentschler. LC 96-11731. (Illus.). 480p. 1996. 62.50 (*0-674-57639-X*); pap. 26.00 (*0-674-57640-3*) HUP.

Ministry of Intercession. Murray. 1996. pap. 6.99 (*1-85792-145-3*, Pub. by Christian Focus) Spring Arbor Dist.

Ministry of Intercession. Andrew Murray. 204p. 1982. mass mkt. 5.99 (*0-88368-114-5*) Whitaker Hse.

Ministry of Intercession. B. E. Underwood. 1992. pap. 5.95 (*0-911866-25-6*) LifeSprings Res.

Ministry of Intercession: A Plea for More Prayer. Andrew Murray. 159p. 1987. pap. 3.95 (*0-310-55082-3*, 19008P) Zondervan.

Ministry of Intercession: Leader's Guide. Shirley G. Spencer. 1992. pap. 11.95 (*0-911866-26-4*) LifeSprings Res.

Ministry of Intercessory Prayer see Ministerio de la Oracion Intercesora

Ministry of Intercessory Prayer. rev. ed. Andrew Murray. LC 81-18011. 16p. 1981. pap. 7.99 (*0-87123-353-3*) Bethany Hse.

***Ministry of Irish Dissent, 1650-1800.** Ed. by Kevin Herlihy. 128p. 1999. 39.95 (*1-85182-451-0*, Pub. by Four Cts Pr); pap. 19.95 (*1-85182-452-9*, Pub. by Four Cts Pr) Intl Spec Bk.

Ministry of Jesus. (Life of Jesus Pict-O-Graph Ser.). (Illus.). (J). 1981. 10.99 (*0-7847-1025-2*, 02225) Standard Pub.

Ministry of Law in the Church Today. Kevin E. McKenna. LC 98-38658. 112p. 1999. 30.00 (*0-268-01441-8*, Pub. by U of Notre Dame Pr) Chicago Distribution Ctr.

Ministry of Lectors. James Wallace. (Ministry Ser.). 48p. 1981. pap. 1.95 (*0-8146-1229-6*) Liturgical Pr.

Ministry of Lies: The Truth Behind the Nation of Islam's "The Secret Relationship Between Blacks & Jews" Harold Brackman. LC 94-7173. (Illus.). 160p. 1994. pap. 10.00 (*1-56858-016-9*) FWEW.

Ministry of Meetings: The Apostolic Diaries of Rudger Clawson. limited ed. Rudger Clawson. Ed. by Stan Larson. LC 92-5901. (Significant Mormon Diaries Ser.: No. 6). (Illus.). 844p. 1993. 85.00 (*0-941214-96-6*) Signature Bks.

Ministry of Missions to African Independent Churches: Papers Presented at the Conference on Ministry to African Independent Churches, July 1986, Abidjan, Cote d'Iviore. 2nd ed. Ed. by David A. Shank. 291p. 1989. reprint ed. pap. text 21.50 (*1-877736-04-X*) MB Missions.

Ministry of Music. Kenneth W. Osbeck. LC 61-14865. 192p. 1975. pap. 11.99 (*0-8254-3410-6*) Kregel.

Ministry of Music in the Black Church. J. Wendell Mapson, Jr. 1984. pap. 12.00 (*0-8170-1057-2*) Judson.

Ministry of Musicians. Edward J. McKenna. (Ministry Ser.). 40p. (Orig.). 1981. pap. 1.95 (*0-8146-1295-4*) Liturgical Pr.

Ministry of Nurture: How to Build Real-Life Faith into Your Kids. Duffy Robbins. 192p. 1990. pap. 14.99 (*0-310-52581-0*) Zondervan.

Ministry of Peter, John & Paul. A. E. Booth. 1982. pap. 1.95 (*0-88172-004-6*) Believers Bkshelf.

Ministry of Philanthropy: A Collection of Stories about How Giving Changes People's Lives. Jeff Scoggins. 120p. 1999. pap. write for info. (*0-9643585-2-2*) Philanthropic Srv.

Ministry of Reconciliation: Spirituality & Strategies. Robert J. Schreiter. LC 98-14532. 125p. (Orig.). 1998. pap. 15.00 (*1-57075-168-4*) Orbis Bks.

Ministry of Reconciliation in the Christian Church of North America. Guy BonGiovanni. 23p. (Orig.). (C). 1983. pap. 2.00 (*0-912981-03-2*) Hse BonGiovanni.

Ministry of Servers. Michael Kwatera. (Ministry Ser.). (Illus.). 48p. (Orig.). (J). (gr. 6-8). 1982. pap. 1.95 (*0-8146-1300-4*) Liturgical Pr.

***Ministry of Sound Book.** 1998. pap. text 22.95 (*0-7472-7636-6*, Pub. by Headline Bk Pub) Trafalgar.

Ministry of Teaching Toddlers. Lynda T. Boardman. 96p. (Orig.). 1983. pap. 7.99 (*0-8341-0820-8*) Beacon Hill.

Ministry of the Cantor. James Hansen. (Ministry Ser.). 48p. 1985. pap. 1.95 (*0-8146-1387-X*) Liturgical Pr.

Ministry of the Christian School Guidance Counselor: Pupil Personnel Services in the Christian School. James W. Deuink. (Illus.). 175p. 1985. pap. 8.50 (*0-89084-273-6*, 023416) Bob Jones Univ.

Ministry of the Church: Image of Pastoral Care. Joseph J. Allen. LC 86-22037. 232p. (Orig.). 1986. pap. 11.95 (*0-88141-044-6*) St Vladimirs.

Ministry of the Dispossessed: Learning from the Farm Worker Movement. Pat Hoffman. LC 86-51483. 176p. (Orig.). 1987. pap. 8.95 (*0-941181-00-6*) Wallace Pr CA.

Ministry of the Dispossessed: Study Guide. Pat Hoffman. 13p. (Orig.). 1987. pap. text 2.00 (*0-941181-01-4*) Wallace Pr CA.

Ministry of the Liturgical Environment. Thomas G. Simons & James M. Fitzpatrick. (Ministry Ser.). 48p. (Orig.). 1984. pap. 2.95 (*0-8146-1354-3*) Liturgical Pr.

Ministry of the New Testament & the Teaching & Fellowship of the Apostles. Witness Lee. 33p. 1993. pap. 3.25 (*0-87083-722-2*, 15-047-001) Living Stream Ministry.

Ministry of the Sacristan: Preparing & Maintaining the Liturgical Space, 20 vols., Set. Frank Winkels. (Ministry Ser.). 64p. 1989. pap. 1.95 (*0-8146-1810-3*) Liturgical Pr.

Ministry of the Saints see Ministerio de los Santos

Ministry of the Spirit. A. J. Gordon. LC 85-27503. 144p. 1964. reprint ed. pap. 7.99 (*0-87123-843-8*) Bethany Hse.

Ministry of Ushering. Mark Moore. 64p. 1986. pap. 5.99 (*0-8341-1143-8*) Beacon Hill.

Ministry of Ushers. Gregory F. Smith. (Ministry Ser.). 30p. (Orig.). 1980. pap. 1.95 (*0-8146-1207-5*) Liturgical Pr.

Ministry of Women. Roberta Hestenes. Date not set. 12.99 (*0-8499-0522-2*) Word Pub.

Ministry of Women in the Church. Elisabeth Behr-Sigel. LC 89-63746. 235p. 1990. per. 8.95 (*0-9618545-6-1*) Oakwood Pubns.

Ministry on the Cutting Edge. Richard Ezell. LC 95-8343. 112p. 1995. pap. 7.99 (*0-8254-2526-3*) Kregel.

Ministry on the Fireline. Ray S. Anderson. Tr. by Sharman Hsiao. (Theology Ser.). 265p. 1996. pap. 12.95 (*1-885216-04-1*) Evan Formosan.

Ministry on the Fireline: A Practical Theology for an Empowered Church. Ray S. Anderson. 235p. (Orig.). 1998. reprint ed. pap. 18.00 (*0-9602638-8-8*) Fuller Seminary.

***Ministry Partners in Senior Housing: A Shared Vision for Service: Principles for Catholic-Sponsored Assisted Living & Senior Housing.** Catholic Health Association of the United States Staff & Catholic Charities USA Staff. LC 99-203064. 8 p. 1998. pap. write for info. (*0-87125-250-3*) Cath Health.

Ministry Planning & Goal Setting. Ted Engstrom. 1988. 164.95 incl. VHS (*1-57052-015-1*) Chrch Grwth VA.

Ministry Through Music see Ministrando con Musica

Ministry to Bereaved Families & Ministry with the Elderly Facilitator Manual. Vickie Kaczmarek. 22p. 1988. pap. text 14.95 (*1-882472-04-7*) Comm Grief Ctr.

Ministry to Bereaved Families Student Manual. Vickie Kaczmarek. 31p. 1988. student ed. 7.95 (*1-882472-05-5*) Comm Grief Ctr.

Ministry to Marriage. William P. Steinhauser et al. (Marriage & Marriage Preparation Ser.). (Illus.). 68p. 1993. 7.95 (*0-940679-07-8*) CCOC.

***Ministry to Muslim Women: Longing to Call Them Sisters.** Frank Love et al. LC 00-31228. 2000. pap. write for info. (*0-87808-338-3*) William Carey Lib.

Ministry to the Divorced. Joseph E. Norris. (Ministry Ser.). 64p. 1990. pap. 1.95 (*0-8146-1923-1*) Liturgical Pr.

Ministry to the Divorced: Guidance, Structure & Organization That Promote Healing in the Church. Sue Richards & Stanley Hagemeyer. 112p. 1986. pap. 8.95 (*0-310-20051-2*, 9604P) Zondervan.

Ministry to the Homebound. Kent C. Miller. (Healing Presence Ser.). 176p. (Orig.). (C). 1995. pap. text 29.95 (*0-89390-268-3*) Resource Pubns.

Ministry to the Imprisoned. Joan Campbell. (Ministry Ser.). 48p. 1989. pap. 2.95 (*0-8146-1789-1*) Liturgical Pr.

Ministry to the Incarcerated. Henry G. Covert. LC 95-8780. 185p. (Orig.). 1995. pap. 16.95 (*0-8294-0860-6*) Loyola Pr.

Ministry to the Sick. Ed. by Leo Malania. 192p. 1988. 10.95 (*0-89869-205-9*) Church Pub Inc.

Ministry to the Sick. Gerald R. Niklas & Charlotte Stefanics. LC 82-4083. 153p. (Orig.). 1982. pap. 7.95 (*0-8189-0429-1*) Alba.

Ministry to the Single Person. Merrill Morse. (Ministry Ser.). 56p. 1988. pap. text 1.95 (*0-8146-1586-4*) Liturgical Pr.

***Ministry We Need.** R. Baxter. 1998. pap. text 6.99 (*0-946462-51-8*) Grace Pubns Trust.

Ministry with Senior Adults. Melvin Shrout. 88p. 1981. pap. 5.99 (*0-8341-0736-8*) Nazarene.

Ministry with the Aging: Designs, Challenges, Foundations. Ed. by William M. Clements. 274p. 1989. pap. text 19.95 (*0-86656-934-0*) Haworth Pr.

Ministry with the Elderly Student Manual. Vickie Kaczmarek. 27p. 1988. student ed. 7.95 (*1-882472-09-8*) Comm Grief Ctr.

Ministry with Young Adults: The Search for Intimacy. Ed. by Julie Garber. LC 91-31651. 111p. 1992. reprint ed. pap. 34.50 (*0-608-04183-1*, 206491800011) Bks Demand.

Ministry with Youth in Crisis. Harley Atkinson. LC 96-45209. 270p. (Orig.). 1997. pap. 24.95 (*0-89135-099-3*) Religious Educ.

Ministry, Word, & Sacraments: An Enchiridion. Martin Chemitz. Tr. by Luther Poellot. 1981. pap. 23.00 (*0-570-03295-4*, 15-2730) Concordia.

Ministry Years, Vol. 1. Keith Green. 244p. 1997. otabind 16.95 (*0-7935-7980-5*) H Leonard.

Minitab DOS. 2nd ed. Robert L. Schaefer. (C). 1994. pap. text, student ed. 42.00 (*0-201-82048-X*) Addison-Wesley.

Minitab Guide. 2nd ed. Kilman Shin. (Irwin Statistical Software Ser.). 408p. (C). 1995. text 20.54 (*0-256-20658-9*, Irwn McGrw-H) McGrw-H Hghr Educ.

Minitab Guide Statistics. Meyer & Krueger. LC 97-227381. 416p. (C). 1997. pap. text 26.40 (*0-13-784232-5*) P-H.

***Minitab Guide to Statistics.** 2nd ed. Ruth Meyer. 403p. 2001. pap. 24.00 (*0-13-014156-9*) P-H.

Minitab Handbook. 2nd ed. Joiner et al. (C). 1985. pap. 17.50 (*0-87150-470-7*, 36G8505) PWS Pubs.

Minitab Handbook. 3rd ed. Barbara F. Ryan & Brian L. Joiner. 448p. 1994. pap. 31.95 (*0-534-21240-9*) Wadsworth Pub.

***Minitab Handbook.** 4th ed. Barbara F. Ryan & Brian L. Joiner. LC 00-39732. 2000. pap. write for info. (*0-534-37093-4*) Brooks-Cole.

Minitab Handbook: With Release 8. 2nd rev. ed. Barbara F. Ryan et al. 409p. 1992. pap. 24.50 (*0-534-93366-1*) Wadsworth Pub.

Minitab Handbook A Course In Bus Stat 2e. 2nd ed. Mendenhall. (Business Statistics). 1988. 13.50 (*0-534-91522-1*) Brooks-Cole.

Minitab Handbook for Business & Economics. Robert B. Miller. 628p. (C). 1987. pap. 18.50 (*0-87150-092-2*, 36G01210) PWS Pubs.

Minitab Handbook (revised) 2nd ed. Barbara F. Ryan et al. (Statistics Software). 379p. 1988. pap. 20.25 (*0-534-91579-5*) Wadsworth Pub.

Minitab Macintosh. 2nd ed. Robert L. Schaefer. (C). 1994. pap. text, student ed. 38.00 (*0-201-82052-8*) Addison-Wesley.

Minitab Man Introd Statistics. Anthony A. Salvia. (C). 1989. pap. text, teacher ed. 24.50 (*0-03-040469-X*) Harcourt Coll Pubs.

Minitab Manual Essentials of Statistics F/behaviorial Sci. 3rd ed. Gravetter & Wallnau. (Psychology Ser.). 1998. pap. text 7.50 (*0-534-36453-5*) Wadsworth Pub.

Minitab Manual Statistics for Behavioral. 4th ed. Gravetter. (Psychology Ser.). (C). 1996. mass mkt. 4.00 (*0-314-08500-9*) Brooks-Cole.

***Minitab Manual Statistics for Behavioral.** 5th ed. Gravetter & Wallnau. (Psychology Ser.). 1999. pap. text 4.50 (*0-534-37078-0*) Wadsworth Pub.

Minitab Student Handbook. Barbara F. Ryan et al. LC 75-41977. (C). 1976. pap. 14.25 (*0-87150-359-X*) PWS Pubs.

Minitab Sup Stat/Prob Mod Life. 5th ed. Newmark. (C). 1992. pap. text, suppl. ed. 22.00 (*0-03-076299-5*) Harcourt Coll Pubs.

Minitab Supplement to Accompany Introductory Statistics 88330. 5th ed. Niel Weiss. 272p. 1998. pap. text 22.00 (*0-201-88324-4*) Addison-Wesley.

Minitab Win 3.5 Single Pk. Minitab Inc. Staff. Ed. by Julia Berrisford. 1p. 1994. 66.00 (*0-201-59157-X*) Addison-Wesley.

Minitab Workbook. 5th ed. Watson & Billingsley. (C). 1993. pap. text, wbk. ed. 17.20 (*0-205-14864-6*) Allyn.

Minitex & Illinet: Two Library Networks. Michael J. LaCroix. (Occasional Papers: No. 178). 1987. pap. 2.50 (*0-685-34541-6*) U of Ill Grad Sch.

Minitutorial - A Hop, Skip & Jump into Minicad: For Version 6. Janis Kent. (Illus.). x, 214p. 1996. pap. 38.00 (*0-9651981-1-1*) Improbability Pr.

Minivanity: An Adam Collection. Brian Basset. (Illus.). 128p. 1995. pap. 8.95 (*0-8362-0417-4*) Andrews & McMeel.

Miniver Cheevy & Other Poems. Edwin Arlington Robinson. LC 95-8708. (Thrift Editions Ser.). 64p. (Orig.). 1995. reprint ed. pap. text 1.00 (*0-486-28756-4*) Dover.

Miniversity: Ideas for Student Activities & Projects. Ed. by Jackie Rough. 32p. (Orig.). 1989. pap. 10.00 (*0-88210-237-0*, 6208902) Natl Assn Student.

Minjung-Theologie Ahn Byungmus von Ihren Voraussetzungen Her Dargestellt. Sunhee Lee. (Europaische Hochschulschriften Ser.: Reihe 23, Bd. 443). (GER.). XVII, 266p. 1991. 55.80 (*3-631-44459-1*) P Lang Pubng.

Minjung's English - Korean & Korean - English Dictionary. Minjung's Editorial Staff. LC 90-86010. (ENG & KOR.). 1689p. 1997. 37.50 (*0-930878-02-7*) Hollym Intl.

Mink, a Fink, a Skating Rink: What Is a Noun? Brian P. Cleary. 1999. write for info. (*0-8225-2109-1*) Lerner Pub.

Mink, a Fink, a Skating Rink: What Is a Noun? Brian P. Cleary. LC 98-46384. (Words Are Categorical Ser.). (Illus.). 32p. (J). (gr. 2-4). 1999. 12.95 (*1-57505-402-7*, Carolrhoda); pap. text 5.95 (*1-57505-417-5*, Carolrhoda) Lerner Pub.

Mink Coat. Hoffman. pap. text. write for info. (*0-8050-2403-4*) St Martin.

Mink Coats Don't Trickle Down: The Economic Attack on Women & People of Color. Randy Albelda et al. LC 87-63363. 64p. 1988. pap. 5.00 (*0-89608-328-4*) South End Pr.

Mink Manual: A Common Sense Approach to Mink Trapping. 1990. pap. 9.95 (*1-879206-14-5*) Outdoor World Pr.

Mink, Mary & Me. Clarence Ferguson. (American Autobiography Ser.). 248p. 1995. reprint ed. lib. bdg. 79.00 (*0-7812-8517-8*) Rprt Serv.

Mink Raising. L. Adams. (Illus.). 222p. 1979. pap. 4.00 (*0-936622-15-6*) A R Harding Pub.

An Asterisk (*) at the beginning of an entry indicates that the title is appearing for the first time.

Mink Trapper's Guide. 2nd rev. ed. Richard E. Faler, Jr. LC 94-32568. (Illus.). 240p. 1996. pap. 14.95 (*1-881399-10-9*) Beaver Pond P&P.

Mink Trapping. A. R. Harding. (Illus.). 171p. pap. 4.00 (*0-936622-16-4*) A R Harding Pub.

***Mink Was Already Dead.** Henry Beard et al. LC 00-20108. 96p. 2000. pap. 7.95 (*0-7611-1636-2*) Workman Pub.

***Minke Whales: Worldlife Library.** A. Rus Hoelzel & S. Jonathan Stern. LC 99-89957. (WorldLife Library). (Illus.). 48p. 2000. pap. 12.95 (*0-89658-490-9*) Voyageur Pr.

Minkowski Geometry. A. C. Thompson. (Encyclopedia of Mathematics & Its Applications Ser.: No. 55). (Illus.). 352p. (C). 1996. text 64.95 (*0-521-40472-X*) Cambridge U Pr.

Minks. Lynn M. Stone. LC 94-46896. (Wild Animals of the Woods Ser.). (J). (gr. 2-6). 1995. lib. bdg. 14.60 (*1-57103-095-6*) Rourke Pr.

Minkus Specialized American Stamp Catalog. rev. ed. Ed. by Richard L. Sine. (Illus.). 540p. 1993. 27.95 (*0-912236-19-1*, Minkus Pubns) Novus Debut.

Minn of the Mississippi, 001. Holling C. Holling. (Illus.). 96p. (J). (gr. 4-6). 1951. 20.00 (*0-395-17578-X*) HM.

Minn of the Mississippi. Holling C. Holling. (Illus.). 88p. (J). (gr. 4-6). 1978. pap. 11.95 (*0-395-27399-4*) HM.

Minn of the Mississippi. Holling Clancy Holling. 1951. 17.15 (*0-606-01647-3*, Pub. by Turtleback) Demco.

***Minna Cooks Caribbean: A Calorie Counter's Guide.** 2nd rev. ed. Nyla Y. Morrison. (Illus.). 124p. 2000. spiral bd. 14.95 (*0-9701777-1-2*) Morrison Artistic.

Minna No Kao see Animal Faces

Minna Von Barnhelm. Gotthold Ephraim Lessing. Ed. by Kenneth J. Northcott. LC 70-189867. (German Literary Classics in Translation Ser.). 1973. pap. text 1.95 (*0-226-47342-2*, P488) U Ch Pr.

Minna Von Barnhelm. Gotthold Ephraim Lessing. Tr. & Intro. by Kenneth J. Northcott. LC 70-189867. (German Literary Classics in Translation Ser.). 116p. (C). 1992. lib. bdg. 10.00 (*0-226-47341-4*) U Ch Pr.

Minna von Barnhelm or the Soldier's Fortune. Gotthold Ephraim Lessing. Tr. by Arnold P. Grunwald. LC 98-90813. 1999. pap. 8.95 (*0-533-12925-7*) Vantage.

Minna's Story: The Secret Love of Dr. Sigmund Freud. Kathleen Daniels. (Illus.). 280p. 1992. 18.95 (*0-929173-08-2*) Health Press.

Minneapolis - St. Paul: Linked to the Future. Barbara Flanagan & Amy Hanson. LC 96-29990. (Urban Tapestry Ser.). 1997. 44.95 (*1-881096-39-4*) Towery Pub.

Minneapolis - St. Paul: People, Place, & Public Life. John S. Adams & Barbara J. VanDrasek. LC 93-2836. 248p. (C). 1993. 26.95 (*0-8166-2236-1*) U of Minn Pr.

Minneapolis & St. Louis in Color. Gene Green. LC 96-76547. (Illus.). 1996. 49.95 (*1-878887-65-3*) Morning NJ.

Minneapolis & St. Paul. Access Press Staff. (Illus.). 256p. 1998. pap. 19.00 (*0-06-277234-1*, Access Trvl) HarpInfo.

Minneapolis Meeting (DPF '96) Proceedings of the 9th Meeting of the APS Division of Particles & Fields Minneapolis, U. S. A. 10-15 August, 1996, 2 vols., Set. Ed. by K. Heller & D. Reeder. LC 98-14015. 1500p. 1998. 168.00 (*981-02-3461-9*) World Scientific Pub.

Minneapolis Meeting, DPF 96: Twin Cities Campus, University of Minnesota, Minneapolis, U. S. A., 10-15 August, 1996. American Physical Society Staff et al. LC 98-14015. 1998. 168.00 (*981-02-3969-6*) World Scientific Pub.

***Minneapolis Metro Business Directory, 1999-2000.** rev. ed. American Business Directories Staff. 2896p. 1999. boxed set 495.00 incl. cd-rom (*0-7687-0199-6*) Am Busn Direct.

Minneapolis-Moline: A History of Its Formation & Operations. Norman F. Thomas. LC 75-41783. (Companies & Men: Business Enterprises in America Ser.). 1976. 33.95 (*0-405-08098-0*) Ayer.

***Minneapolis-Moline Farm Tractors.** Chester Peterson & Rod Beemer. LC 00-28179. (Farm Tractor Histories Ser.). (Illus.). 128p. 2000. 24.95 (*0-7603-0625-7*, 130117AP, Pub. by MBI Pubg) Motorbooks Intl.

Minneapolis-Moline Tractors. Al Sayers. LC 96-13071. (Enthusiast Color Ser.). (Illus.). 96p. 1996. pap. 12.95 (*0-7603-0047-X*) MBI Pubg.

Minneapolis-Moline Tractors, 1870 to 1969. Andrew Morland & Charles H. Wendel. (Farm Tractor Color History Ser.). (Illus.). 128p. 1990. pap. 21.95 (*0-87938-468-9*) MBI Pubg.

Minneapolis-Moline U Series Photo Archive. Ed. by P. A. Letourneau. LC 93-79371. (Photo Archive Ser.). (Illus.). 141p. 1993. pap. text 29.95 (*1-882256-07-7*) Iconografix.

Minneapolis Riverfront: Vision & Implementation. (Illus.). 56p. (Orig.). 1996. pap. 27.00 (*0-9652618-0-8*) Cuningham Grp.

Gousha City Metro Map: Minnesota: Minneapolis/St. Paul. 2nd ed. Gousha, H. M., Editors. 1989. pap. 2.25 (*0-671-87981-2*, H M Gousha) Prntice Hall Bks.

Minneapolis-St. Paul JobBank. 11th ed. Adams Media Corporation Staff. Ed. by Marcie Dipietro. (Illus.). 304p. 1999. pap. 16.95 (*1-58062-151-1*) Adams Media.

Minneapolis Teamsters Strike of 1934. Philip A. Korth. LC 94-46315. 1995. 27.00 (*0-87013-385-3*) Mich St U Pr.

Minneapolis, the Story of a City. Writers Program, Minnesota Staff. LC 73-3629. reprint ed. 29.50 (*0-404-57930-2*) AMS Pr.

Minneapolis/st. Paul Minnesota. Rand McNally Staff. 1997. pap. 5.95 (*0-528-97152-2*) Rand McNally.

***Minneburg Beitrage Zu einer Funktionsgeschichte der Allegorie im Spaten Mittelalter: Mit der Erstedition der Prosafassung.** Anja Sommer. (Mikrokosmos. Beitrage zur Literaturwissenschaft und Bedeutungsforschung Ser.). 312p. 1999. 48.95 (*3-631-35134-8*) P Lang Pubng.

Minnehaha County, South Dakota. Bob Kolbe. (Illus.). 668p. 1987. 50.00 (*0-88107-104-8*) Curtis Media.

Minnehaha Creek - Living Waters. Jane K. Halleberg. 1995. pap. 18.95 (*0-911506-23-3*) Thueson.

***Minneota, Minnesota: The Heart Can Be Filled Anywhere on Earth.** Bill Holm. 2001. pap. 13.95 (*1-57131-251-X*) Milkweed Ed.

Minnesang: Mittelhochdeutsche Texte Mit Uebertragung und Anmerkungen. Ed. by Helmut Brackert. (GEH & GER.). 352p. 1996. pap. 18.00 (*3-596-26485-5*, Pub. by Fischer Tasch) Intl Bk Import.

Minnesinger Heinrich Von Morungen: An Introduction to His Songs. R. W. Fisher. LC 96-41997. 284p. 1996. pap. 49.95 (*1-57309-116-2*); text 69.95 (*1-57309-117-0*) Intl Scholars.

Minnesota see From Sea to Shining Sea

Minnesota see One Nation Series

***Minnesota.** (Switched on Schoolhouse Ser.). (Illus.). (J). 2000. pap. 24.95 (*0-7403-0275-2*) Alpha AZ.

Minnesota. Capstone Press Geography Department Staff. (One Nation Ser.). 1997. 19.00 (*0-516-20530-7*) Childrens.

Minnesota. Compass American Staff. LC 96-3086. (Compass American Guides Ser.). 348p. 1997. pap. 18.95 (*1-878867-48-2*, Compass Amrcn) Fodors Travel.

***Minnesota.** Jim Fizzell. (Midwest Fruit & Vegetables Ser.). (Illus.). 2000. pap. 19.95 (*1-930604-11-4*) Cool Springs Pr.

Minnesota. Martin Hintz. LC 98-50074. (America the Beautiful Ser.). (J). 2000. 32.00 (*0-516-21040-8*) Childrens.

Minnesota. Paul Joseph. LC 97-11734. (United States Ser.). (Illus.). 32p. (J). 1998. lib. bdg. 19.93 (*1-56239-863-6*, Checkerboard Library) ABDO Pub Co.

Minnesota. A. P. Porter. Ed. by Lerner Geography Department Staff. (Hello U. S. A. Ser.). (Illus.). 72p. (J). (gr. 3-6). 1992. lib. bdg. 19.93 (*0-8225-2718-9*, Lerner Publctns) Lerner Pub.

Minnesota. R. Conrad Stein. LC 90-35384. (America the Beautiful Ser.). (Illus.). 144p. (J). (gr. 4 up). 1990. lib. bdg. 28.00 (*0-516-00469-7*) Childrens.

Minnesota. Kathleen Thompson. LC 87-16405. (Portrait of America Library). 48p. (YA). (gr. 4-8). 1996. pap. 5.95 (*0-8114-7448-8*) Raintree Steck-V.

Minnesota. Kathleen Thompson. LC 87-16405. (Portrait of America Library). (Illus.). 48p. (YA). (gr. 3-6). 1996. lib. bdg. 22.83 (*0-8114-7343-0*) Raintree Steck-V.

***Minnesota.** 2nd ed. William E. Lass. (Illus.). 336p. 2000. pap. 15.95 (*0-393-31971-7*) Norton.

Minnesota, 5 vols., Set. R. Stefoff. (Celebrate the States Ser.). 144p. (YA). 1997. 35.64 (*0-7614-0658-1*, Benchmark NY) Marshall Cavendish.

Minnesota: A Cold Love Affair. Ed Fischer. (Illus.). 72p. 1995. pap. 5.95 (*0-9624482-1-4*) E Fischer.

***Minnesota: A Guide to Unique Places.** 5th ed. John G. Shepard. (Off the Beaten Path Ser.). (Illus.). 2000. pap. 12.95 (*0-7627-0798-4*) Globe Pequot.

Minnesota: A History. 2nd ed. William E. Lass. LC 97-34650. (Illus.). 336p. 1998. 27.50 (*0-393-04628-1*) Norton.

Minnesota: A History of the State. 2nd ed. Theodore C. Blegen. LC 75-6116. (Illus.). xiv, 731p. 1975. 29.95 (*0-8166-0754-0*) U of Minn Pr.

Minnesota: A Photographic Celebration. American Geographic Publishing Staff. (Illus.). 96p. (Orig.). 1989. pap. 14.95 (*0-938314-76-9*) Am Wrld Geog.

Minnesota: A State Guide. Federal Writers' Project Staff. (American Guidebook Ser.). 545p. 1938. reprint ed. 89.00 (*0-403-02173-1*) Somerset Pub.

Minnesota: A State Guide. Federal Writers' Project Staff & Writers Program-WPA Staff. (American Guide Ser.). 1989. reprint ed. lib. bdg. 69.00 (*0-7812-1022-4*, 1022) Rprt Serv.

Minnesota: Facts & Symbols. Bill McAuliffe. LC 98-43014. 1999. 14.00 (*0-531-11803-7*) Capstone Pr.

Minnesota: Hello U. S. A. A. P. Porter. (Illus.). 72p. (J). 1996. pap. text 5.95 (*0-8225-9735-7*) Lerner Pub.

Minnesota: Off the Beaten Path: A Guide to Unique Places. 4th ed. John G. Shepard. LC 98-35299. (Off the Beaten Path Ser.). (Illus.). 288p. 1998. pap. 12.95 (*0-7627-0270-2*) Globe Pequot.

Minnesota: State of Beauty. 2nd ed. James LaVigne & Charles Wechsler. (Illus.). 96p. 1992. pap. 6.98 (*0-931714-12-5*, Pub. by Nodin Pr) Bookmen Inc.

Minnesota: The State & It's Educational System. Harold L. Hodgkinson. 12p. 1989. 12.00 (*0-937846-69-4*) Inst Educ Lead.

Minnesota - Collected Works of Federal Writers Project. Federal Writers' Project Staff. 1991. reprint ed. lib. bdg. 98.00 (*0-7812-5637-2*) Rprt Serv.

Minnesota - Wisconsin Golfers Travel Guide. Ed. by Roy H. Rasmussen. 40p. (Orig.). 1992. pap. 6.95 (*0-940703-05-X*) RSG Pub MI.

Minnesota A to Z: Coloring Book. Hetty Mitchell. (Illus.). (J). 1992. pap. 3.50 (*0-87351-284-7*) Minn Hist.

Minnesota Adjutant General's Report of 1866. LC 97-34358. 470p. 1997. pap. 45.00 (*0-915709-39-2*) Pk Geneal Bk.

Minnesota Administrative Procedure. 2nd ed. George A. Beck et al. LC 98-61176. 450p. 1998. ring bd. 115.00 (*0-9666567-0-9*) Weekend Pubns.

***Minnesota Adoption Law & Practice.** 775p. 1999. pap. 95.00 (*0-327-09783-3*, 2700110) LEXIS Pub.

Minnesota Advising Corporations & Other Business Organizations. Martin J. Costello et al. 1994. ring bd., suppl. ed. 48.50 (*0-614-03161-3*, MICHIE) LEXIS Pub.

***Minnesota Almanac 2000.** John Brekke. (Illus.). 2000. pap. 15.95 (*0-942072-05-7*) John L Brekke & Sons.

Minnesota & Dacotah: In Letters Descriptive of a Tour Through the Northwest... Christopher C. Andrews. LC 75-81. (Mid-American Frontier Ser.). 1975. reprint ed. 19.95 (*0-405-06850-6*) Ayer.

Minnesota & Dakotah: In Letters Descriptive of a Tour Through the North-West in the Autumn of 1856. C. C. Andrews. (Illus.). 216p. 1997. reprint ed. lib. bdg. 29.00 (*0-8328-6795-0*) Higginson Bk Co.

Minnesota & Manitoba One Hundred Years Ago. Powell & Van Dyke. (Historical Ser.). (Illus.). 1977. pap. 3.50 (*0-89540-056-1*, SB-056) Sun Pub.

Minnesota & Other State Greats (Biographies) Carole Marsh. (Carole Marsh Minnesota Bks.). (Illus.). (J). (gr. 3 up). 1994. pap. 19.95 (*1-55609-661-5*); lib. bdg. 29.95 (*1-55609-660-7*); disk 29.95 (*1-55609-662-3*) Gallopade Intl.

Minnesota Architect: The Life & Work of Clarence H. Johnston. Paul Clifford Larson. (Illus.). 224p. 1996. 35.00 (*1-890434-35-3*) Afton Hist Soc.

Minnesota Arrowhead Country. Writers Program, Minnesota Staff. LC 73-3630. (American Guide Ser.). reprint ed. 16.50 (*0-404-57931-0*) AMS Pr.

Minnesota Atlas. John M. Hanson. 216p. 1990. pap. 24.95 (*0-934860-61-0*) Adventure Pubns.

Minnesota Atlas & Gazetteer. 2nd ed. DeLorme. LC 94-675209. (Atlas & Gazetteer Ser.). (Illus.). 96p. (Orig.). 1997. pap. 16.95 (*0-89933-222-6*, AA-000017-000) DeLorme Map.

Minnesota Attorney's/Paralegal's/Secretary's Handbook, 1997. 20th ed. Ed. by Jean M. Walburg. (Attorney's/Paralegal's/Secretary's Handbooks Ser.). 666p. 1997. ring bd. 47.00 (*0-927573-44-X*); ring bd. 47.00 (*0-927573-50-4*) Mariposa Pub.

Minnesota Automotive Directory. Ed. by T. L. Spelman. 1985. 24.95 (*1-55527-019-0*) Auto Contact Inc.

Minnesota Aviation History, 1857-1945. Noel E. Allard & Gerald N. Sandvick. (Illus.). 296p. 1993. 39.95 (*0-9637807-0-0*); pap. 29.95 (*0-9637807-1-9*) MAHB Pubng.

Minnesota Bandits, Bushwackers, Outlaws, Crooks, Devils, Ghosts, Desperadoes & Other Assorted & Sundry Characters! Carole Marsh. (Carole Marsh Minnesota Bks.). (Illus.). (J). (gr. 3 up). 1994. pap. 19.95 (*0-7933-0622-1*); lib. bdg. 29.95 (*0-7933-0623-X*); disk 29.95 (*0-7933-0624-8*) Gallopade Intl.

Minnesota Biking Guide. Barbara McCaig. Ed. by Gretchen Vanderboom. 100p. (Orig.). 1989. pap. text 5.95 (*0-935201-78-5*) Affordable Adven.

Minnesota "BIO" Bingo! 24 Must Know State People for Kids to Learn about While Having Fun! Carole Marsh. (Bingo! Ser.). (Illus.). (J). (gr. 2-8). 1998. pap. 14.95 (*0-7933-8591-1*) Gallopade Intl.

Minnesota Biographical Dictionary. LC 93-29200. 1993. 79.00 (*0-403-09945-5*) Somerset Pub.

Minnesota Birds. James Kavanagh. (Pocket Naturalist Ser.). (Illus.). 1999. 5.95 (*1-889903-81-7*, Pub. by Waterford WA) Falcon Pub Inc.

Minnesota Bookstore Book: A Surprising Guide to Our State's Bookstores & Their Specialties for Students, Teachers, Writers & Publishers. Carole Marsh. (Carole Marsh Minnesota Bks.). (Illus.). 1994. pap. 19.95 (*0-7933-2925-6*); lib. bdg. 29.95 (*0-7933-2924-8*); disk 29.95 (*0-7933-2926-4*) Gallopade Intl.

Minnesota Bride Magazine Wedding Planner. Minnesota Bride Magazine, Inc. Staff. (Illus.). 120p. 1998. pap. 14.95 (*0-9663558-0-6*) Tiger Oak.

Minnesota Business Almanac: Minnesota's Guide to Business, 1996-1997. Ed. by Jon Olson. (Illus.). 740p. (Orig.). 1996. pap. write for info. (*0-9641908-7-7*) MSP Communs.

Minnesota Business Almanac: Minnesota's Guide to Business, 1997-1998. Ed. by John Farmer. (Illus.). 1997. write for info. (*0-9641908-8-5*) MSP Communs.

***Minnesota Business Directory, 1999-2000.** rev. ed. American Business Directories Staff. 1920p. 1999. boxed set 520.00 incl. cd-rom (*0-7687-0157-0*) Am Busn Direct.

Minnesota Census Index, 1880, Vol. 1. Ronald V. Jackson. (Illus.). lib. bdg. 130.00 (*0-89593-551-1*, Accel Indexing) Genealogical Srvcs.

Minnesota Census Index, 1880, Vol. 2. Ronald V. Jackson. (Illus.). lib. bdg. 130.00 (*0-89593-552-X*, Accel Indexing) Genealogical Srvcs.

Minnesota Charter Schools. (Illus.). 65p. (Orig.). (C). 1995. pap. text 20.00 (*0-7881-1889-7*) DIANE Pub.

Minnesota Christmas Anthology: Selections from Literature & History of Christmas Past in Minnesota. Ed. by Stephen E. Engels. (State Anthologies Ser.: No. 1). (Illus.). (Orig.). 1991. reprint ed. pap. 10.95 (*0-9621085-0-2*) Partridge Pr.

Minnesota Christmas Book. Patricia C. Johnston. LC 85-90344. (Illus.). 96p. 1985. text 27.50 (*0-942934-08-3*) Johnston Pub.

Minnesota Civil Practice. Clasen. 1998. ring bd. write for info. (*0-327-00184-4*, 81207-13) LEXIS Pub.

Minnesota Civil Practice. William J. Keppel & Douglas D. McFarland. 1994. ring bd., suppl. ed. 65.00 (*0-614-03153-2*, MICHIE) LEXIS Pub.

Minnesota Civil Practice. 2nd ed. John Miller. 1995. text 73.75 (*0-86678-862-X*, 81740-10, MICHIE) LEXIS Pub.

Minnesota Civil Practice, 4 Vols. 3rd ed. Douglas D. McFarland & William J. Keppel. 314.00 (*0-327-12453-9*) LEXIS Pub.

***Minnesota Civil Practice, 4 vols.** 3rd ed. Douglas D. McFarland & William J. Keppel. Incl. Vol. 1. Minnesota Civil Practice. 3rd ed. 1999. (*0-327-04994-4*); Vol. 2. Minnesota Civil Practice. 3rd ed. 1999. (*0-327-04995-2*); Vol. 3. Minnesota Civil Practice. 3rd ed. 1999. (*0-327-04996-0*); Vol. 4. Minnesota Civil Practice. 3rd ed. 1999. (*0-327-04997-9*); 700p. 1999. write for info. (*0-327-04998-7*) LEXIS Pub.

Minnesota Civil Practice, No. 98:2. Douglas D. McFarland & William J. Keppel. 480p. 1998. pap. write for info. (*0-327-00717-6*, 8174118) LEXIS Pub.

Minnesota Civil Practice, 4 vols., Set. 2nd ed. Douglas D. McFarland & William J. Keppel. 2560p. 1994. 295.00 (*0-86678-858-1*, 81736-10, MICHIE) LEXIS Pub.

Minnesota Civil Practice see Minnesota Civil Practice

Minnesota Civil Practice: 1999 Cumulative Supplement. 2nd ed. Douglas McFarland & William Keppel. 350p. 1999. pap. write for info. (*0-327-01362-1*, 8174119) LEXIS Pub.

Minnesota Classic Christmas Trivia: Stories, Recipes, Activities, Legends, Lore & More! Carole Marsh. (Carole Marsh Minnesota Bks.). (Illus.). (J). (gr. 3 up). 1994. pap. 19.95 (*0-7933-0625-6*); lib. bdg. 29.95 (*0-7933-0626-4*); disk 29.95 (*0-7933-0627-2*) Gallopade Intl.

Minnesota Coastales. Carole Marsh. (Carole Marsh Minnesota Bks.). (Illus.). (J). (gr. 3 up). 1994. pap. 19.95 (*1-55609-655-0*); lib. bdg. 29.95 (*1-55609-654-2*); disk 29.95 (*1-55609-656-9*) Gallopade Intl.

Minnesota Coastales! Carole Marsh. (Carole Marsh Minnesota Bks.). (J). 1994. lib. bdg. 29.95 (*0-7933-7288-7*) Gallopade Intl.

Minnesota Collections. Allan J. Zlimen. LC 79-87463. (Minnesota Practice Systems Library). 1980. ring bd. 120.00 (*0-317-00452-2*) West Group.

Minnesota Collections. Allan J. Zlimen. LC 79-87463. (Minnesota Practice Systems Library). 1993. suppl. ed. 22.50 (*0-317-03176-7*) West Group.

Minnesota Collects. Text by Jack El-Hai. LC 92-18368. (Illus.). ix, 117p. 1992. pap. 14.95 (*0-87351-280-4*) Minn Hist.

Minnesota Community: Country & Town in Transition. Lowry Nelson. LC 60-10191. 185p. reprint ed. pap. 57.40 (*0-608-18647-3*, 205589300039) Bks Demand.

Minnesota Compiled Laws Annotated. write for info. (*0-318-57497-7*) West Pub.

Minnesota Condemnation Law. Robert J. Lindall et al. 450p. 1992. suppl. ed. 35.00 (*0-685-74268-7*, MICHIE); ring bd. 115.00 (*0-86678-646-5*, MICHIE) LEXIS Pub.

***Minnesota Cookbook.** Golden West Publishers Staff. 1999. pap. text 6.95 (*1-885590-44-X*) Golden West.

Minnesota Cooking. B. Carlson. (Illus.). 160p. 1994. spiral bd. 5.95 (*1-57166-000-3*) Hearts N Tummies.

Minnesota Corporation Law & Practice. John H. Matheson & Philip S. Garon. LC 92-32448. (National Corporation Law Ser.). 1992. 110.00 (*0-13-145996-1*) Aspen Law.

Minnesota Corporations Practice Manual, 1986-1993. Bert Black. 400p. 1993. ring bd. 78.00 (*0-86678-501-9*, MICHIE); suppl. ed. 37.50 (*1-56257-818-9*, MICHIE) LEXIS Pub.

***Minnesota Crime in Perspective 2000.** Ed. by Kathleen O'Leary Morgan & Scott E. Morgan. 22p. 2000. spiral bd. 19.00 (*0-7401-0322-9*) Morgan Quitno Corp.

Minnesota Crime Perspective, 1998. Ed. by Kathleen O'Leary Morgan & Scott E. Morgan. 20p. 1998. pap. 19.00 (*1-56692-922-9*) Morgan Quitno Corp.

Minnesota Crime Perspectives, 1999. Kathleen O'Leary Morgan. 22p. 1999. spiral bd. 19.00 (*0-7401-0122-6*) Morgan Quitno Corp.

Minnesota Crimes & Defenses. Butterworth Staff. 300p. 1993. ring bd., suppl. ed. 37.00 (*0-614-03154-0*, MICHIE) LEXIS Pub.

Minnesota "Crinkum-Crankum" A Funny Word Book about Our State. Carole Marsh. (Carole Marsh Minnesota Bks.). (Illus.). (J). 1994. pap. 19.95 (*0-7933-4878-1*); lib. bdg. 29.95 (*0-7933-4877-3*); disk 29.95 (*0-7933-4879-X*) Gallopade Intl.

Minnesota Days: Our Heritage in Stories, Art & Photos. Ed. by Michael Dregni. LC 99-20679. (Illus.). 1999. 35.00 (*0-89658-421-6*) Voyageur Pr.

Minnesota Dingbats! A Fun Book of Games, Stories, Activities & More about Our State That's All in Code! for You to Decipher, Bk. 1. Carole Marsh. (Carole Marsh Minnesota Bks.). (Illus.). (J). (gr. 3-12). 1994. pap. 19.95 (*0-7933-3843-3*); lib. bdg. 29.95 (*0-7933-3842-5*); disk 29.95 (*0-7933-3844-1*) Gallopade Intl.

Minnesota Dissolution of Marriage. William E. Haugh. LC 79-91150. (Minnesota Practice Systems Library). 1979. ring bd. 120.00 (*0-317-00443-3*) West Group.

Minnesota Dissolution of Marriage. William E. Haugh. LC 79-91150. (Minnesota Practice Systems Library). 1993. suppl. ed. 62.50 (*0-317-03174-0*) West Group.

Minnesota Divorce Revolution: A Plain English Explanation of Current Minnesota Divorce Law. Jeanette A. Frederickson & Court C. Holton. Ed. by Cheryl Lennon & Susan Oliphant. 100p. (Orig.). 1989. pap. 8.95 (*0-9622587-0-9*) Regency MN.

Minnesota Divorce Revolution: A Plain English Explanation of Minnesota Divorce Law. 2nd ed. Jeanette A. Frederickson et al. 150p. Date not set. pap. 14.95 (*0-9622587-1-7*) Regency MN.

Minnesota Employment Laws: A Compendium of Minnesota Statutes Relating to Employment, Wages & Benefits, Discrimination, Termination, Workplace, Safety, Etc. Minnesota Staff. LC 96-128548. xxxiii, 763 p. 1996. write for info. (*0-314-08243-3*) West Pub.

Minnesota Environmental Law Handbook. 2nd ed. Dorsey & Whitney Staff. 360p. 1994. pap. text 89.00 (*0-86587-377-1*) Gov Insts.

Minnesota Evidence Trialbook, Issue 11. 75p. 1998. ring bd. write for info. (*0-327-00697-8*, 8175521) LEXIS Pub.

Minnesota Evidence Trialbook, Vol. 9. Bertrand Portinsky. 90p. 1997. ring bd. 79.00 (*0-86678-278-8*, 81755-19, MICHIE) LEXIS Pub.

Minnesota Evidence Trialbook, 1987-1990. Bertrand Poritsky. 210p. 1994. spiral bd. 65.00 (*0-86678-279-6*, MICHIE); ring bd., suppl. ed. 39.00 (*0-86678-004-1*, MICHIE) LEXIS Pub.

An Asterisk (*) at the beginning of an entry indicates that the title is appearing for the first time.

Minnesota Evidentiary Foundations. Roger C. Park et al. LC 96-75722. 1996. 80.00 (*1-55834-353-9*, 66836-10, MICHIE) LEXIS Pub.

Minnesota Evidentiary Foundations: 1998 Cumulative Supplement. Roger C. Park et al. 32p. 1998. pap. 80.00 (*0-327-00572-6*, 6683711) LEXIS Pub.

Minnesota Facts & Factivities. Carole Marsh. (Carole Marsh State Bks.). (Illus.). (J). (gr. 4-7). 1996. pap., teacher ed. 19.95 (*0-7933-7893-1*, C Marsh) Gallopade Intl.

Minnesota Facts & Symbols. Bill McAuliffe. LC 98-43014. (States & Their Symbols Ser.). (J). 1999. write for info. (*0-7368-0219-3*) Capstone Pr.

Minnesota Family Law. Edward L. Winer. 1994. write for info. (*1-56257-726-3*, MICHIE) LEXIS Pub.

Minnesota Family Law Journal. Ed. by Stephen L. Liebo. 125.00 (*0-327-12455-5*) LEXIS Pub.

Minnesota Family Law Journal. Edward L. Winer et al. Ed. by Stephen L. Liebo. 16p. 1980. 120.00 (*0-86678-051-3*, 81759-10, MICHIE) LEXIS Pub.

Minnesota Family Law Practice Manual, 2 vols. 2nd ed. Cathy Gorlin. 1997. ring bd. 169.00 (*0-327-03938-8*, 81764, MICHIE) LEXIS Pub.

Minnesota Family Law Practice Manual, Issue 49. Ed. by Gorlin. 1998. ring bd. 145.00 (*0-327-00190-9*, 81768-29) LEXIS Pub.

Minnesota Family Law Practice Manual, Issue 52. Gorlin. 175p. 1998. ring bd. write for info. (*0-327-00719-2*, 8176832) LEXIS Pub.

Minnesota Family Law Practice Manual, Issue 53. 150p. 1999. ring bd., suppl. ed. write for info. (*0-327-01062-2*, 8176833) LEXIS Pub.

Minnesota Family Law Practice Manual, Issue 54. Cathy E. Gorlin. 100p. 1999. ring bd. 70.00 (*0-327-01145-9*, 8176834) LEXIS Pub.

***Minnesota Family Law Practice Manual, Issue 55.** 100p. 1999. ring bd. write for info. (*0-327-01373-7*, 8176835) LEXIS Pub.

Minnesota Family Law Practice Manual, No. 50. Gorlin. 150p. 1998. ring bd. write for info. (*0-327-00323-5*, 81768-30) LEXIS Pub.

Minnesota Family Law Practice Manual, Vol. 1. 2nd ed. Cathy Gorlin. 1997. ring bd. write for info. (*0-86678-953-7*, 81766-26, MICHIE) LEXIS Pub.

Minnesota Family Law Practice Manual, 1990-1994. Ed. by Cathy E. Gorlin. 1994. ring bd., suppl. ed. 32.00 (*0-614-03155-9*, MICHIE) LEXIS Pub.

Minnesota Family Law Practice Manual, 1990-1994. 2nd ed. Ed. by Cathy E. Gorlin. 400p. 1991. spiral bd. 145.00 (*0-86678-276-1*, 81764-10, MICHIE) LEXIS Pub.

Minnesota Family Practice Manual, 2 vols., Issue 51. Davidson. Ed. by Gorlin. 150p. 1998. ring bd. write for info. (*0-327-00540-8*, 8176831) LEXIS Pub.

Minnesota Farmer-Laborism: The Third-Party Alternative. Millard L. Gieske. LC 79-1115. (Illus.). 401p. reprint ed. pap. 124.40 (*0-8357-8955-1*, 203322300085) Bks Demand.

Minnesota Fastmap. 4th ed. Gousha, H. M., Editors. 1995. pap. 4.95 (*0-671-53776-8*, H M Gousha) Prntice Hall Bks.

Minnesota Fats: Never Behind the Eight Ball. Fred Walther. LC 98-19528. 182p. 1998. pap. 14.95 (*1-888608-54-4*) Cool Springs Pr.

Minnesota Fats on Pool. Minnesota & Fats. 1976. 17.95 (*0-8488-1555-6*) Amereon Ltd.

Minnesota Federal Census Index, 1840. Ronald V. Jackson. (Illus.). 1982. lib. bdg. 38.00 (*0-89593-808-1*, Accel Indexing) Genealogical Srvcs.

Minnesota Federal Census Index, 1850. Ronald V. Jackson. (Illus.). 1981. lib. bdg. 67.00 (*0-89593-810-3*, Accel Indexing) Genealogical Srvcs.

Minnesota Federal Census Index, 1860. Ronald V. Jackson. (Illus.). lib. bdg. 84.00 (*0-89593-679-8*, Accel Indexing) Genealogical Srvcs.

Minnesota Federal Census Index, 1870 (Every Name), 2 vols., Set. Ronald V. Jackson. (Illus.). 1979. lib. bdg. 200.00 (*0-89593-680-1*, Accel Indexing) Genealogical Srvcs.

Minnesota Festival Fun for Kids! Carole Marsh. (Carole Marsh Minnesota Bks.). (Illus.). (J). (gr. 3-12). 1994. pap. 19.95 (*0-7933-3996-0*); lib. bdg. 29.95 (*0-7933-3995-2*) Gallopade Intl.

Minnesota Festival Fun for Kids! Carole Marsh. (Carole Marsh Minnesota Bks.). (Illus.). (YA). (gr. 3-12). 1994. disk 29.95 (*0-7933-3997-9*) Gallopade Intl.

Minnesota Fortune Cookies. 5th ed. Yogi Blair. 26p. (YA). (gr. 11 up). 1993. pap. 8.95 (*0-930366-73-5*) Northcountry Pub.

***Minnesota Free: The State's Best No-Charge Attractions.** Jim Morse. 271p. 1998. pap. 14.95 (*0-931714-78-8*, Pub. by Nodin Pr) Bookmen Inc.

***Minnesota Gardening, 2000.** Deborah Brown. Ed. by Kathleen Cleberg. (Illus.). 30p. 1999. pap. 9.95 (*1-888440-07-4*) U MN Ext Serv.

Minnesota Gardens: An Illustrated History. Susan Davis Price. 168p. 1995. 35.00 (*1-890434-36-1*) Afton Hist Soc.

Minnesota "GEO" Bingo! 38 Must Know State Geography Facts for Kids to Learn While Having Fun! Carole Marsh. (Bingo! Ser.). (Illus.). (J). (gr. 2-8). 1998. pap. 14.95 (*0-7933-8592-X*) Gallopade Intl.

Minnesota Golfing Insider. 96p. (Orig.). 1996. pap. 6.95 (*0-9647179-1-3*) Star MN.

Minnesota Golfing Insider, 1997. 1997. 5.95 (*0-9647179-3-X*) Star MN.

Minnesota Government! The Cornerstone of Everyday Life in Our State! Carole Marsh. (Carole Marsh Minnesota Bks.). (Illus.). (J). (gr. 3-12). 1996. pap. 19.95 (*0-7933-6251-2*); lib. bdg. 29.95 (*0-7933-6250-4*); disk 29.95 (*0-7933-6252-0*) Gallopade Intl.

Minnesota Governments Performance Standards, 1990. Ed. by Greg Michels. (Governments Performance Standards Ser.). (Illus.). 150p. 1990. text 125.00 (*1-55507-490-1*) Municipal Analysis.

***Minnesota Guide.** Ann G. Lewis. LC 99-31529. (Illus.). 320p. 1999. pap. 21.95 (*1-55591-362-8*) Fulcrum Pub.

Minnesota Handbook for 1856-1857. Nathan H. Parker. LC 75-114. (Mid-American Frontier Ser.). 1975. reprint ed. 16.95 (*0-405-06880-8*) Ayer.

***Minnesota Health Care in Perspective 2000.** Ed. by Kathleen O'Leary Morgan & Scott E. Morgan. 21p. 2000. spiral bd. 19.00 (*0-7401-0222-2*) Morgan Quitno Corp.

Minnesota Health Care Perspective, 1998. Ed. by Kathleen O'Leary Morgan & Scott E. Morgan. 20p. 1998. pap. 19.00 (*1-56692-822-2*) Morgan Quitno Corp.

Minnesota Health Care Perspective, 1999. Kathleen O'Leary Morgan. 21p. 1999. spiral bd. 19.00 (*0-7401-0072-6*) Morgan Quitno Corp.

Minnesota Heat: The Heat Minnesotans Get When They Go Someplace Else. Bob Rueff. (Illus.). 176p. (Orig.). 1997. pap. 14.95 (*0-9656395-0-9*) RM Pub.

Minnesota Heritage Cookbook: Hand-Me-Down-Recipes, Vol. 1. Ed. by Sue Zelickson et al. LC 79-52859. (Illus.). 174p. 1979. 15.95 (*0-9602796-0-1*) Am Cancer Minn.

Minnesota Heritage Cookbook I: Hand-Me-Down Recipes, No. I. American Cancer Society, Minnesota Div. Staff. LC 93-71690. (Illus.). 1993. spiral bd. 15.95 (*0-87197-374-X*) Favorite Recipes.

Minnesota Heritage Cookbook II: Look What's Cooking Now!, No. II. American Cancer Society, Minnesota Div. Staff. LC 93-71761. (Illus.). 1993. spiral bd. 15.95 (*0-87197-375-8*) Favorite Recipes.

Minnesota "HISTO" Bingo! 42 Must Know State History Facts for Kids to Learn While Having Fun! Carole Marsh. (Bingo! Ser.). (Illus.). (J). (gr. 2-8). 1998. pap. 14.95 (*0-7933-8593-8*) Gallopade Intl.

Minnesota History! Surprising Secrets about Our State's Founding Mothers, Fathers & Kids! Carole Marsh. (Carole Marsh Minnesota Bks.). (Illus.). (J). (gr. 3-12). 1996. pap. 19.95 (*0-7933-6098-6*); lib. bdg. 29.95 (*0-7933-6097-8*); disk 29.95 (*0-7933-6099-4*) Gallopade Intl.

Minnesota History Center. Brian Horrigan. LC 96-11606. (Illus.). 32p. 1996. pap. 7.95 (*0-87351-330-4*) Minn Hist.

Minnesota Hot Air Balloon Mystery. Carole Marsh. (Carole Marsh Minnesota Bks.). (Illus.). (J). (gr. 2-9). 1994. 29.95 (*0-7933-2525-0*); pap. 19.95 (*0-7933-2526-9*); disk 29.95 (*0-7933-2527-7*) Gallopade Intl.

Minnesota Hot Zones! Viruses, Diseases, & Epidemics in Our State's History. Carole Marsh. (Hot Zones! Ser.). (Illus.). (J). (gr. 3-12). 1998. pap. 19.95 (*0-7933-8898-8*); lib. bdg. 29.95 (*0-7933-8897-X*) Gallopade Intl.

Minnesota House of Representatives & the Professionalization of Politics. Theodore Reuter. LC 94-982. 244p. (Orig.). 1994. pap. 28.50 (*0-8191-9452-2*); lib. bdg. 54.00 (*0-8191-9451-4*) U Pr of Amer.

Minnesota Impressionists. Rena N. Coen. LC 96-36446. (Illus.). 96p. 1996. 35.00 (*0-9639338-6-8*) Afton Hist Soc.

Minnesota in a Century of Change: The State & Its People since 1900. Ed. by Clifford E. Clark, Jr. LC 89-30925. (Illus.). xiv, 607p. 1989. 35.95 (*0-87351-234-0*); pap. 24.95 (*0-87351-238-3*) Minn Hist.

Minnesota in Books for Young Readers: An Annotated Bibliography. Grace Swenson. 1975. pap. 10.00 (*0-87018-076-2*) Ross.

Minnesota in Maps: A Trailblazer Atlas. Constance J. Sansome. (Illus.). 32p. (J). (gr. 3 up). 1990. 17.95 (*0-9626025-0-7*); pap. 12.95 (*0-9626025-1-5*) Trailblazer Bks.

Minnesota in My Heart. rev. ed. Victoria L. Estrem & Helen Lesman. (Illus.). 120p. 1992. spiral bd. (*1-879127-16-4*) Lighten Up Enter.

***Minnesota in Our Time: A Photographic Portrait.** George Slade. LC 00-27091. (Illus.). 160p. 2000. 45.00 (*0-87351-382-7*, Borealis Book); pap. 27.50 (*0-87351-383-5*) Minn Hist.

Minnesota in Perspective, 1998. Ed. by Kathleen O'Leary Morgan & Scott E. Morgan. 24p. 1998. pap. 19.00 (*1-56692-872-9*) Morgan Quitno Corp.

Minnesota in Perspective, 1999. Ed. by Kathleen O'Leary Morgan. 26p. 1999. spiral bd. 19.00 (*1-56692-972-5*) Morgan Quitno Corp.

***Minnesota in Perspective 2000.** Ed. by Kathleen O'Leary Morgan & Scott E. Morgan. 26p. 2000. spiral bd. 19.00 (*0-7401-0272-9*) Morgan Quitno Corp.

Minnesota in the Civil & Indian Wars, 1861-1865, 2 vols., Set. 1498p. 1994. reprint ed. lib. bdg. 149.50 (*0-8328-3969-8*) Higginson Bk Co.

***Minnesota in the Civil War: An Illustrated History.** Kenneth Carley. LC 00-40180. (Illus.). 2000. write for info. (*0-87351-387-8*) Minnesota Historical Society.

Minnesota Indian Dictionary for Kids! Carole Marsh. (Carole Marsh State Bks.). (J). (gr. 2-9). 1996. 29.95 (*0-7933-7713-7*, C Marsh); pap. 19.95 (*0-7933-7714-5*, C Marsh) Gallopade Intl.

Minnesota Infant Death Investigation Guidelines (For Infants 0 to 24 Months Old): Background & Implementation for Local Investigative Personnel. 82p. pap. text. write for info. (*0-7881-8714-7*) DIANE Pub.

Minnesota Insurance Law. Clarance E. Hagglund et al. 230p. (Orig.). 1995. pap. 17.50 (*0-9631290-2-3*) Common Law.

***Minnesota Investment & Business Guide: Business, Investment, Export-Import Opportunities, 50 vols., Vol. 23.** Global Investment Center, USA Staff. (U. S. Regional Investment & Business Library-99: Vol. 23). (Illus.). 350p. (Orig.). 1999. pap. 59.95 (*0-7397-1122-9*) Intl Business Pubns.

Minnesota Jeopardy! Answers & Questions about Our State! Carole Marsh. (Carole Marsh Minnesota Bks.). (Illus.). (J). (gr. 3-12). 1994. pap. 19.95 (*0-7933-4149-3*); lib. bdg. 29.95 (*0-7933-4148-5*); disk 29.95 (*0-7933-4150-7*) Gallopade Intl.

Minnesota Job Seeker's Sourcebook: The Complete Statewide Guide to Job-Seeking Support Services. 3rd rev. ed. Ed. by Pati Gelfman. 288p. 1996. pap. 21.95 (*0-9629615-2-3*) Resource Pub Grp MN.

Minnesota "Jography" A Fun Run Thru Our State. Carole Marsh. (Carole Marsh Minnesota Bks.). (Illus.). (J). (gr. 3 up). 1994. pap. 19.95 (*1-55609-643-7*); lib. bdg. 29.95 (*1-55609-642-9*); disk 29.95 (*1-55609-644-5*) Gallopade Intl.

Minnesota Jury Instruction Guides, Criminal (CRIMJIG), Vol. 10. 2nd ed. Minnesota District Judges Association, Committee o. LC 85-51063. (Minnesota Practice Ser.). 510p. 1985. 59.50 (*0-685-13436-9*) West Pub.

Minnesota Kid's Cookbook: Recipes, How-To, History, Lore & More. Carole Marsh. (Carole Marsh Minnesota Bks.). (Illus.). (J). (gr. 3 up). 1994. pap. 19.95 (*0-7933-0634-5*); lib. bdg. 29.95 (*0-7933-0635-3*); disk 29.95 (*0-7933-0636-1*) Gallopade Intl.

Minnesota, Land of Lakes & Innovation: Entering the 21st Century. Nood Reynolds. LC 98-71769. (Illus.). 416p. 1998. 49.95 (*1-882933-21-4*) Cherbo Pub Grp.

Minnesota Land Owner Maps & Directories. Compiled by Mary H. Bakeman. LC 94-22062. 1994. text. write for info. (*0-915709-16-3*) Pk Geneal Bk.

Minnesota Land Surveying Law: Questions & Answers. John E. Keen. 50p. (C). 1995. pap. text 25.00 (*1-56569-030-3*) Land Survey.

Minnesota Lectures on Extragalactic Neutral Hydrogen, Vol. 106. Ed. by Evan P. Skillman. (ASP Conference Series Proceedings). 408p. 1996. 44.00 (*1-886733-26-0*) Astron Soc Pacific.

Minnesota Lectures on the Structure & Dynamics of the Milky Way. Ed. by R. M. Humphreys. (ASP Conference Series Proceedings: Vol. 39). 156p. 1993. 34.00 (*0-937707-58-9*) Astron Soc Pacific.

Minnesota Legal Form for Commercial Real Estate. John Miller. 1995. ring bd. 69.95 (*0-917126-89-0*, 81772-10, MICHIE) LEXIS Pub.

Minnesota Legal Forms, 8 vols., Set. 1981. ring bd. 450.00 incl. disk (*0-86678-942-1*, MICHIE) LEXIS Pub.

Minnesota Legal Forms: Bankruptcy. Michael C. Wagner & Cass S. Weil. 360p. ring bd. 69.95 incl. disk (*0-917126-91-2*, MICHIE) LEXIS Pub.

Minnesota Legal Forms: Bankruptcy. Michael C. Wagner & Cass S. Weil. 360p. 1993. suppl. ed. 25.00 (*0-86678-044-0*, MICHIE) LEXIS Pub.

Minnesota Legal Forms: Bankruptcy. Cass S. Weil. 360p. 1994. ring bd. 69.95 incl. disk (*0-614-05899-6*, MICHIE) LEXIS Pub.

Minnesota Legal Forms: Commercial Real Estate. John M. Miller. Date not set. lib. bdg. 69.95 (*0-327-01029-0*, 81772, MICHIE) LEXIS Pub.

Minnesota Legal Forms: Commercial Real Estate. John M. Miller. 180p. 1982. ring bd. 69.95 incl. disk (*0-917126-88-2*, MICHIE) LEXIS Pub.

Minnesota Legal Forms: Commercial Real Estate. John M. Miller. 180p. 1993. ring bd. 69.95 incl. disk (*0-614-05900-3*, MICHIE); ring bd., suppl. ed. 35.00 (*0-614-03156-7*, MICHIE); suppl. ed. 35.00 (*0-685-70860-8*, MICHIE) LEXIS Pub.

Minnesota Legal Forms: Creditors' Remedies. Thomas F. Miller. 190p. 1994. ring bd., wbk. ed. 69.95 incl. disk (*0-614-05901-1*, MICHIE) LEXIS Pub.

Minnesota Legal Forms: Creditors' Remedies, 1981-1993. Thomas F. Miller. (Minnesota Legal Forms Ser.). 200p. 1994. ring bd., suppl. ed. 39.00 (*0-685-74347-0*, MICHIE) LEXIS Pub.

Minnesota Legal Forms: Criminal Law Forms. Rick E. Mattox. 240p. 1993. ring bd., wbk. ed. 69.95 incl. disk (*0-614-05902-X*, MICHIE) LEXIS Pub.

Minnesota Legal Forms: Family Law. Daniel M. McLean. Date not set. ring bd. 95.00 (*0-327-00986-1*, 81794, MICHIE) LEXIS Pub.

Minnesota Legal Forms: Family Law. Daniel W. McLean. 240p. ring bd. 50.00 incl. disk (*0-917126-85-8*, 81795-10, MICHIE) LEXIS Pub.

Minnesota Legal Forms: Family Law. Daniel W. McLean. 240p. 1994. ring bd. 69.95 incl. digital audio (*0-614-05903-8*, MICHIE); ring bd., suppl. ed. 40.00 (*0-614-03157-5*, MICHIE) LEXIS Pub.

Minnesota Legal Forms: Minnesota Limitations Manual. 2nd ed. Publisher's Editorial Staff. 352p. 1989. ring bd. 95.00 (*0-86678-835-2*, MICHIE) LEXIS Pub.

Minnesota Legal Forms: Personal Injury. Gary Stoneking. 150p. 1994. ring bd. 69.95 incl. disk (*0-614-05904-6*, MICHIE) LEXIS Pub.

Minnesota Legal Forms: Probate. Jeffrey D. Bates & Jeffrey M. Hucek. Date not set. ring bd. 95.00 (*0-327-01031-2*, 81804, MICHIE) LEXIS Pub.

Minnesota Legal Forms: Probate. 4th ed. Rev. by Jeffrey M. Hucek. 180p. 1993. ring bd. 69.95 incl. disk (*0-614-05905-4*, MICHIE) LEXIS Pub.

Minnesota Legal Forms: Residential Real Estate. Kathleen M. Roer. 1981. ring bd. 95.00 (*0-327-00988-8*, 81810, MICHIE) LEXIS Pub.

Minnesota Legal Forms: Residential Real Estate. Kathleen M. Roer. 150p. 1994. ring bd. 69.95 incl. disk (*0-614-05906-2*, MICHIE) LEXIS Pub.

***Minnesota Legal Forms: Residential Real Estate, Issue 15.** Kathleen M. Roer. 100p. 1999. ring bd. write for info. (*0-327-01691-4*, 8181116) LEXIS Pub.

Minnesota Legal Forms Issue 14: Probate. 30p. 1998. ring bd. write for info. (*0-327-00669-2*, 8180614) LEXIS Pub.

Minnesota Legal Forms Issue 14: Residential Real Estate. Kathleen M. Roer. Ed. by Neil B. Davidson. 40p. 1998. ring bd. write for info. (*0-327-00513-0*, 8181115) LEXIS Pub.

Minnesota Legal Forms Issue 17: Family Law. Daniel W. McLean. Ed. by Neil Davidson. 50p. 1998. ring bd. write for info. (*0-327-00552-1*, 8179517) LEXIS Pub.

Minnesota Legal Forms, 1981-1993: Criminal Law Forms. Rick E. Mattox. (Minnesota Legal Forms Ser.). 240p. ring bd. 69.95 incl. disk (*0-917126-83-1*, MICHIE) LEXIS Pub.

Minnesota Legal Forms, 1981-1993: Criminal Law Forms. Rick E. Mattox. (Minnesota Legal Forms Ser.). 240p. 1993. suppl. ed. 28.50 (*0-86678-030-0*, MICHIE) LEXIS Pub.

Minnesota Legal Forms, 1981-1993: Personal Injury. Gary Stoneking. 1993. ring bd., suppl. ed. 25.00 (*0-614-03159-1*, MICHIE) LEXIS Pub.

Minnesota Legal Forms, 1981-1993: Probate. James D. Bates. 180p. ring bd. 69.95 incl. disk (*0-917126-97-1*, MICHIE) LEXIS Pub.

Minnesota Legal Forms, 1981-1993: Probate. James D. Bates. 180p. 1993. ring bd., suppl. ed. 25.00 (*0-685-49511-6*, MICHIE) LEXIS Pub.

Minnesota Legal Forms, 1981-1993: Residential Real Estate. Kathleen M. Roer. 200p. ring bd. 69.95 incl. disk (*0-917126-86-6*, 81810-10, MICHIE) LEXIS Pub.

Minnesota Legal Forms, 1981-1993: Residential Real Estate. Kathleen M. Roer. 200p. 1994. ring bd., suppl. ed. 39.00 (*0-685-52223-7*, MICHIE) LEXIS Pub.

Minnesota Legal Research Guide. Arlette M. Soderberg & Barbara J. Golden. LC 85-80035. xvii, 298p. 1985. pap. 25.00 (*0-89941-438-9*, 303630); lib. bdg. 37.50 (*0-89941-428-1*, 303630) W S Hein.

Minnesota Library Book: A Surprising Guide to the Unusual Special Collections in Libraries Across Our State for Students, Teachers, Writers & Publishers - Includes Reproducible Mailing Labels Plus Activities for Young People! Carole Marsh. (Carole Marsh Minnesota Bks.). (Illus.). 1994. pap. 19.95 (*0-7933-3075-0*); lib. bdg. 29.95 (*0-7933-3074-2*); disk 29.95 (*0-7933-3076-9*) Gallopade Intl.

Minnesota Limitations Manual, No. 10. Davidson. 60p. 1998. ring bd. write for info. (*0-327-00320-0*, 83042-14) LEXIS Pub.

Minnesota Limitations Manual, 1989-1992. Butterworth Staff. 1994. ring bd., suppl. ed. 42.00 (*0-614-03160-5*, MICHIE) LEXIS Pub.

Minnesota Limitations Manual, 1989-1992. 2nd ed. Butterworth Staff. 350p. 1994. spiral bd. 85.00 (*0-86678-040-8*, MICHIE) LEXIS Pub.

Minnesota Lodging Directory: Directory of Motels, Hotels, & Bed & Breakfasts in Minnesota 1989. Illus. by Susan Brue. (Orig.). 1988. pap. 1.95 (*0-927290-00-6*) Lodging Unlimited.

Minnesota Manufacturers Register. 16th rev. ed. Ed. by Frank Lambing. 1998. 106.00 (*1-58202-054-X*) Manufacturers.

Minnesota Math! How It All Adds up in Our State. Carole Marsh. (Carole Marsh Minnesota Bks.). (Illus.). (YA). (gr. 3-12). 1996. pap. 19.95 (*0-7933-6557-0*); lib. bdg. 29.95 (*0-7933-6556-2*) Gallopade Intl.

Minnesota Mechanics' Liens Practice Manual, 1987-1991. James E. Snoxell. 180p. 1991. ring bd. 85.00 (*0-86678-488-8*, MICHIE) LEXIS Pub.

Minnesota Media Book: A Surprising Guide to the Amazing Print, Broadcast & Online Media of Our State for Students, Teachers, Writers & Publishers - Includes Reproducible Mailing Labels Plus Activities for Young People! Carole Marsh. (Carole Marsh Minnesota Bks.). (Illus.). 1994. pap. 19.95 (*0-7933-3231-1*); lib. bdg. 29.95 (*0-7933-3230-3*); disk 29.95 (*0-7933-3232-X*) Gallopade Intl.

Minnesota Mining & Manufacturing (3M) A Report on the Company's Environmental Policies & Practices. (Illus.). 28p. (C). 1994. reprint ed. pap. text 40.00 (*0-7881-0923-5*, Coun on Econ) DIANE Pub.

Minnesota Misdemeanor & Moving Traffic Violations, Vol. ISS.11. Costello et al. 328p. 1996. ring bd. 165.00 (*0-86678-933-2*, 81819-15, MICHIE) LEXIS Pub.

Minnesota Misdemeanors & Moving Traffic Violations. Costello et al. 1998. ring bd. 165.00 (*0-327-00145-3*, 81819-18) LEXIS Pub.

Minnesota Misdemeanors & Moving Traffic Violations, 2 Vols. 3rd ed. Martin J. Costello et al. 184.00 (*0-327-12457-1*) LEXIS Pub.

***Minnesota Misdemeanors & Moving Traffic Violations, 2 vols.** 3rd ed. Martin J. Costello et al. Incl. Vol. 1. Minnesota Misdemeanors & Moving Traffic Violations. 3rd ed. 600p. 1999. ring bd. (*0-327-04905-7*); Vol. 2. Minnesota Misdemeanors & Moving Traffic Violations. 3rd ed. 600p. 1999. ring bd. (*0-327-04906-5*, 8181820); 1200p. 1999. ring bd. write for info. (*0-327-04904-9*) LEXIS Pub.

Minnesota Misdemeanors & Moving Traffic Violations, 2 vols., No. 15. Costello et al. 300p. 1998. ring bd. 165.00 (*0-327-00771-0*, 8181919) LEXIS Pub.

Minnesota Misdemeanors & Moving Traffic Violations see Minnesota Misdemeanors & Moving Traffic Violations

Minnesota Misdemeanors & Moving Traffic Violations, 1990-1992, 2 vols. 2nd ed. Martin J. Costello et al. suppl. ed. write for info. (*0-250-40723-X*, MICHIE) LEXIS Pub.

M

An Asterisk (*) at the beginning of an entry indicates that the title is appearing for the first time.

Minnesota Misdemeanors & Moving Traffic Violations, 1990-1992, 2 vols., Set. 2nd ed. Martin J. Costello et al. 700p. 1994. spiral bd. 165.00 (*0-86678-932-4*, 81815-10, MICHIE) LEXIS Pub.
Minnesota Model: The Evolution of the Multidisciplinary Approach to Addiction Recovery. Jerry Spicer. LC 92-44556. 178p. 1993. 17.95 (*0-89486-862-2*, 5148A) Hazelden.
Minnesota Moods. Linda Zurflieh. (Illus.). 23p. (Orig.). 1995. pap. text 8.95 (*0-9653717-0-0*) New Heart Pub.
Minnesota Moon. John Olive. 48p. (Orig.). 1990. 5.95 (*0-317-91359-X*) Playsmith.
***Minnesota Mornings: Comfort & Cuisine.** LC 99-68651. (Illus.). 144p. 2000. pap. 15.95 (*0-942495-95-0*) Palmer Pubns Inc.
Minnesota Mortality Schedule, 1880. Ronald V. Jackson. 1992. 57.00 (*0-89593-850-2*, Accel Indexing) Genealogical Srvcs.
Minnesota Mortality Schedule, 1850. Ronald V. Jackson. 1992. 47.00 (*0-89593-847-2*, Accel Indexing) Genealogical Srvcs.
Minnesota Mortality Schedule, 1860. Ronald V. Jackson. 1992. 47.00 (*0-89593-848-0*, Accel Indexing) Genealogical Srvcs.
Minnesota Mortality Schedule, 1870. Ronald V. Jackson. 1992. 49.00 (*0-89593-849-9*, Accel Indexing) Genealogical Srvcs.
Minnesota Multiphasic Personality Inventory (MMPI) Index of Modern Authors & Subjects with Guide for Rapid Research. Remley L. Rannigan. 200p. 1991. 47.50 (*1-55914-280-4*); pap. 44.50 (*1-55914-281-2*) ABBE Pubs Assn.
Minnesota Mummy, Don't You Try to Tut Tut Me. Al Blair. 8p. 1990. pap. 3.95 (*0-930366-44-1*) Northcountry Pub.
Minnesota Mystery Van Takes Off! Bk. 1: Handicapped Minnesota Kids Sneak off on a Big Adventure. Carole Marsh. (Carole Marsh Minnesota Bks.). (Illus.). (J). (gr. 3-12). 1994. 29.95 (*0-7933-5030-1*); pap. 19.95 (*0-7933-5031-X*); disk 29.95 (*0-7933-5032-8*) Gallopade Intl.
Minnesota No Fault Auto Insurance, Vol. ISS.6. Michael Steenson. 122p. 1997. ring bd. 60.00 (*0-86678-670-8*, 81827-11, MICHIE) LEXIS Pub.
Minnesota No-Fault Automobile Insurance, Issue 8. 75p. 1998. ring bd., suppl. ed. write for info. (*0-327-00519-X*, 8182713) LEXIS Pub.
Minnesota No-Fault Automobile Insurance, 1989-1993. Michael K. Steenson. 1994. ring bd., suppl. ed. 60.00 (*0-614-03162-1*, MICHIE) LEXIS Pub.
Minnesota No-Fault Automobile Insurance, 1989-1993, 2 vols., Set. 2nd ed. Michael K. Steenson. 700p. 1994. spiral bd. 155.00 (*0-86678-669-4*, 81823-10, MICHIE) LEXIS Pub.
Minnesota Nonprofit Directory. Ed. by Norah Davies & Jon Pratt. 420p. (Orig.). 1988. pap. 24.75 (*0-929080-04-1*) MN Council Nonprofits.
***Minnesota Notes on Jordan Algebras & Their Applications.** Max Koecher et al. LC 99-44596. (Lecture Notes in Mathematics Ser.: Vol. 1710). ix, 173p. 1999. pap. 36.80 (*3-540-66360-6*) Spr-Verlag.
Minnesota Objections at Trial. Ronald L. Carlson et al. 200p. 1992. pap. 39.50 (*0-88063-824-9*, 81875, MICHIE) LEXIS Pub.
Minnesota Objections at Trial. Carlson et al. 200p. 1992. pap. text 39.50 (*0-327-03912-4*, 81875-10, MICHIE) LEXIS Pub.
Minnesota on My Mind. Paul Gruchow. LC 89-80765. (America on My Mind Ser.). (Illus.). 120p. 1989. 29.95 (*0-937959-70-7*) Falcon Pub Inc.
Minnesota Plan: Recommendations for Preventing Gross Human Rights Violations in Kosovo. MN. Advocates for Human Rights Staff. 8p. (Orig.). 1993. pap. 5.00 (*0-614-16435-4*) MN Advocates.
Minnesota Policy Blueprint: A Project of Center of the American Experiment. Mitchell B. Pearlstein & Annette Meeks. Ed. by Brooke Benson. (Illus.). 400p. 1999. pap. write for info. (*1-892845-00-8*, Pub. by MSP Communs) Bookmen Inc.
Minnesota Politics & Government. Daniel J. Elazar et al. LC 99-20478. (Politics & Governments of the American States Ser.). (Illus.). 304p. 1999. text 45.00 (*0-8032-1852-4*) U of Nebr Pr.
***Minnesota Politics & Government.** Daniel J. Elazar et al. LC 99-20478. (Politics & Governments of the American States Ser.). (Illus.). 304p. 1999. pap. text 25.00 (*0-8032-6714-2*) U of Nebr Pr.
Minnesota Practice Vol. 3A: General Rules of Practice for the District Court Annotated, 1994 Edition. David F. Herr & Laurie K. Fett. LC 94-215531. xxxiii, 532 p. 1994. pap. text. write for info. (*0-314-04238-5*) West Pub.
Minnesota Practice Jury Instruction Guides: Misdemeanor & Gross Misdemeanor. Hvass & Albrecht. 224p. 1986. pap. 14.00 (*0-317-52117-9*) West Pub.
Minnesota Probate. Mark D. Helland. LC 79-91151. (Minnesota Practice Systems Library). 1979. ring bd. 120.00 (*0-317-00447-6*) West Group.
Minnesota Probate. Mark D. Helland. LC 79-91151. (Minnesota Practice Systems Library). 1991. suppl. ed. 62.50 (*0-317-03175-9*) West Group.
Minnesota Probate Law Digest, 3 vols., 1. rev. ed. Ed. by James W. Forbess. 1992. write for info. (*0-318-69301-1*, MICHIE) LEXIS Pub.
Minnesota Probate Law Digest, 3 vols., 2. rev. ed. Ed. by James W. Forbess. 1992. write for info. (*0-318-69302-X*, MICHIE) LEXIS Pub.
Minnesota Probate Law Digest, 3 vols., 3. rev. ed. Ed. by James W. Forbess. 1992. write for info. (*0-318-69303-8*, MICHIE) LEXIS Pub.
Minnesota Public Health Goals, 1995. Ed. by Barry Leonard. (Illus.). 185p. 1998. pap. text 35.00 (*0-7881-7186-0*) DIANE Pub.
Minnesota Publishers & Producers Directory. (Communication Ser.). 104p. 1985. pap. 18.00 (*0-318-19316-7*) More Info.
Minnesota Quiz Bowl Crash Course! Carole Marsh. (Carole Marsh Minnesota Bks.). (Illus.). (J). (gr. 3 up). 1994. pap. 19.95 (*1-55609-658-5*); lib. bdg. 29.95 (*1-55609-657-7*); disk 29.95 (*1-55609-659-3*) Gallopade Intl.
Minnesota Rag. Fred W. Friendly. LC 82-40157. 272p. 1982. pap. 7.96 (*0-394-71241-2*) Vin Bks.
Minnesota Real Estate. Gordon W. Shumaker & Clinton R. McLagan. LC 79-91152. (Minnesota Practice Systems Library). 1981. ring bd. 120.00 (*0-317-00439-5*) West Group.
Minnesota Real Estate. Gordon W. Shumaker & Clinton R. McLagan. LC 79-91152. (Minnesota Practice Systems Library). 1992. suppl. ed. 50.00 (*0-317-03173-2*) West Group.
Minnesota Residential Real Estate. James D. Olson. 1994. ring bd., suppl. ed. 45.00 (*0-318-68686-4*, MICHIE) LEXIS Pub.
Minnesota Residential Real Estate, Issue 15. Kathleen M. Roer. Ed. by Neil Davidson. 210p. 1998. ring bd. write for info. (*0-327-00505-X*, 8185025) LEXIS Pub.
Minnesota Residential Real Estate, Issue 16. James D. Olson. 210p. 1999. ring bd. write for info. (*0-327-01083-5*, 8185026) LEXIS Pub.
***Minnesota Residential Real Estate, Issue 17.** James D. Olson. Ed. by Neil Davidson. 150p. 1999. ring bd. write for info. (*0-327-01698-1*, 8185027) LEXIS Pub.
Minnesota Residential Real Estate, 2 vols., Set. James D. Olson. 980p. 1994. spiral bd. 179.00 (*0-88063-862-1*, 81846-10, MICHIE) LEXIS Pub.
Minnesota Retirement & Relocation Guide. large type ed. (Retirement & Relocation Guides Ser.). (Illus.). 350p. Date not set. pap. 24.95 (*1-56559-144-5*) HGI-Over Fifty.
Minnesota Rock & Roll Novelties for People Who Aren't Deaf Yet. Allen M. Blair. 13p. 1987. pap. 7.25 (*0-930366-11-5*) Northcountry Pub.
Minnesota Rollercoasters! Carole Marsh. (Carole Marsh Minnesota Bks.). (Illus.). (J). (gr. 3-12). 1994. pap. 19.95 (*0-7933-5294-0*); lib. bdg. 29.95 (*0-7933-5293-2*) Gallopade Intl.
Minnesota Rollercoasters! Carole Marsh. (Carole Marsh Minnesota Bks.). (Illus.). (YA). (gr. 3-12). 1994. disk 29.95 (*0-7933-5295-9*) Gallopade Intl.
Minnesota School Trivia: An Amazing & Fascinating Look at Our State's Teachers, Schools & Students! Carole Marsh. (Carole Marsh Minnesota Bks.). (Illus.). (J). (gr. 3 up). 1994. pap. 19.95 (*0-7933-0631-0*); lib. bdg. 29.95 (*0-7933-0632-9*); disk 29.95 (*0-7933-0633-7*) Gallopade Intl.
Minnesota Seasons: Classic Tales of Life Outdoors. Ed. by Scott Bestul. (Illus.). 240p. 1998. 22.95 (*0-9653381-4-2*) Cabin Bkshelf.
Minnesota Sentencing Guidelines Commission: Report to the Legislature on the Mandatory Minimum Law for Weapons. (Illus.). 41p. (Orig.). (C). 1995. pap. text 20.00 (*0-7881-1878-1*) DIANE Pub.
Minnesota Sentencing Guidelines Commission: Report to the Legislature, 1994. (Illus.). 35p. (Orig.). (C). 1994. pap. text 25.00 (*0-7881-1383-6*) DIANE Pub.
Minnesota Sentencing Guidelines Commission: Summary of 1989 Sentencing Practices for Convicted Felons. (Illus.). 57p. (Orig.). (C). 1993. pap. text 20.00 (*1-56806-829-8*) DIANE Pub.
Minnesota Shouts, Stomps, & Syncopated Hollers. Al Blair. 54p. 1988. pap. 9.75 (*0-930366-50-6*) Northcountry Pub.
Minnesota Silly Basketball Sportsmysteries, Vol. I. Carole Marsh. (Carole Marsh Minnesota Bks.). (Illus.). (J). (gr. 3 up). 1994. pap. 19.95 (*0-7933-0628-0*); lib. bdg. 29.95 (*0-7933-0629-9*); disk 29.95 (*0-7933-0630-2*) Gallopade Intl.
Minnesota Silly Basketball Sportsmysteries, Vol. II. Carole Marsh. (Carole Marsh Minnesota Bks.). (Illus.). (J). (gr. 3 up). 1994. pap. 19.95 (*0-7933-1721-5*); lib. bdg. 29.95 (*0-7933-1720-7*); disk 29.95 (*0-7933-1722-3*) Gallopade Intl.
Minnesota Silly Football Sportsmysteries, Vol. I. Carole Marsh. (Carole Marsh Minnesota Bks.). (Illus.). (J). (gr. 3 up). 1994. pap. 19.95 (*1-55609-649-6*); lib. bdg. 29.95 (*1-55609-648-8*); disk 29.95 (*1-55609-650-X*) Gallopade Intl.
Minnesota Silly Football Sportsmysteries, Vol. II. Carole Marsh. (Carole Marsh Minnesota Bks.). (Illus.). (J). (gr. 3 up). 1994. pap. 19.95 (*1-55609-652-6*); lib. bdg. 29.95 (*1-55609-651-8*); disk 29.95 (*1-55609-653-4*) Gallopade Intl.
Minnesota Silly Trivia! Carole Marsh. (Carole Marsh Minnesota Bks.). (Illus.). (J). (gr. 3 up). 1994. pap. 19.95 (*1-55609-640-2*); lib. bdg. 29.95 (*1-55609-639-9*); disk 29.95 (*1-55609-641-0*) Gallopade Intl.
Minnesota Solid Waste Management: Selected Economic & Financial Issues. (Illus.). 48p. (Orig.). (C). 1993. pap. text 30.00 (*1-56806-742-9*) DIANE Pub.
Minnesota Spelling Bee! Score Big by Correctly Spelling Our State's Unique Names. Carole Marsh. (Carole Marsh Minnesota Bks.). (Illus.). (YA). (gr. 3-12). 1996. pap. 19.95 (*0-7933-6710-7*); lib. bdg. 29.95 (*0-7933-6709-3*) Gallopade Intl.
Minnesota Standoff: The Politics of Deadlock. Rod Searle. (Illus.). (Orig.). 1990. pap. 12.95 (*0-9627120-0-0*) Alton Pr.
***Minnesota State Credit Directory, 2000 Edition.** rev. ed. American Business Directories Staff. 464p. 1999. boxed set 165.00 incl. cd-rom (*0-7687-0309-3*) Am Busn Direct.
Minnesota State Government Spending. Cindy Berquirt. (Illus.). 20p. 1996. pap. 3.00 (*1-877889-14-8*) League Wmn Voters MN.
Minnesota State Parks. Barbara McCaig & Raster Vanderboom. (Illus.). 100p. (Orig.). 1989. pap. text 5.95 (*0-935201-68-8*) Affordable Adven.
Minnesota State Rules of Evidence with Objections. Anthony J. Bocchino et al. 208p. 1994. pap. 22.95 (*1-55681-399-6*) Natl Inst Trial Ad.
Minnesota Statutes Annotated. write for info. (*0-318-57498-5*) West Pub.
Minnesota Strip. Micheal Collins. 1988. pap. 3.95 (*0-373-97093-5*) Harlequin Bks.
Minnesota Suite. Thom Tammaro. 24p. 1996. reprint ed. 3.00 (*0-941127-19-2*) Dacotah Terr Pr.
Minnesota Supplement to Street Law. 51st ed. Nicel. (HA - Social Studies). 1997. pap. 52.95 (*0-314-22324-X*) S-W Pub.
Minnesota Survival. Betty L. Hall & Marlowe G. Severson. 160p. (Orig.). (gr. 10-12). 1979. pap. text 5.84 (*0-03-046901-5*) Westwood Pr.
Minnesota Symposia on Child Psychology, Vol. 1. Ed. by John P. Hill. LC 67-30520. 251p. reprint ed. pap. 77.90 (*0-608-14646-3*, 205587600001) Bks Demand.
Minnesota Symposia on Child Psychology, Vol. 2. Hill. 1997. 36.00 (*0-89859-393-X*) L Erlbaum Assocs.
Minnesota Symposia on Child Psychology, Vol. 3. Hill. 1997. 36.00 (*0-89859-394-8*) L Erlbaum Assocs.
Minnesota Symposia on Child Psychology, Vol. 4. Hill. 1997. pap. 36.00 (*0-89859-395-6*) L Erlbaum Assocs.
Minnesota Symposia on Child Psychology, Vol. 5. Hill. 1997. 36.00 (*0-89859-396-4*) L Erlbaum Assocs.
Minnesota Symposia on Child Psychology, Vol. 6. A. D. Pick. Ed. by Ann Masten. 1973. 36.00 (*0-89859-397-2*) L Erlbaum Assocs.
Minnesota Symposia on Child Psychology, Vol. 7. A. D. Pick. Ed. by Ann Masten. 1974. 36.00 (*0-89859-398-0*) L Erlbaum Assocs.
Minnesota Symposia on Child Psychology, Vol. 8. A. D. Pick. Ed. by Ann Masten. 1975. 36.00 (*0-89859-399-9*) L Erlbaum Assocs.
Minnesota Symposia on Child Psychology, Vol. 9. A. D. Pick. Ed. by Ann Masten. 1976. 36.00 (*0-89859-400-6*) L Erlbaum Assocs.
Minnesota Symposia on Child Psychology, Vol. 10. A. D. Pick. Ed. by Ann Masten. 1977. 36.00 (*0-89859-401-4*) L Erlbaum Assocs.
Minnesota Symposia on Child Psychology, Vol. 11. Ed. by W. A. Collins. 286p. 1978. 59.95 (*0-89859-113-9*) L Erlbaum Assocs.
Minnesota Tax Handbook, 1999. rev. ed. John P. James. Ed. by Richard E. Jenis. 192p. 1999. pap. text 35.75 (*0-7811-0194-8*) Res Inst Am.
Minnesota Territorial Census Index, 1849, Vol. 1. Ronald V. Jackson. (Illus.). lib. bdg. 34.00 (*0-89593-809-X*, Accel Indexing) Genealogical Srvcs.
Minnesota Territorial Census Index, 1849, Vol. 2. Ronald V. Jackson. 1991. 34.00 (*0-89593-657-7*, Accel Indexing) Genealogical Srvcs.
Minnesota Territory in Postmarks, Letters & History. Floyd E. Risvold. LC 85-73113. (Illus.). 329p. 1985. 65.00 (*0-916675-01-7*) L H Hartmann.
Minnesota, the North Star State. William W. Folwell. LC 72-3767. (American Commonwealths Ser.: No. 19). reprint ed. 39.50 (*0-404-57219-7*) AMS Pr.
Minnesota, the Spirit of the Land. Douglas Wood. LC 95-4107. (Illus.). 144p. 1995. 19.95 (*0-89658-310-4*) Voyageur Pr.
Minnesota Theatre: From Old Fort Snelling to the Guthrie. Frank M. Whiting. LC 88-60421. (Illus.). 231p. (Orig.). 1988. pap. 17.95 (*0-9617767-2-2*) Pogo Pr.
Minnesota Timberwolves see Pro Basketball Today
Minnesota Timberwolves. Paul Joseph. LC 97-3812. (Inside the NBA Ser.). (Illus.). 32p. (J). (gr. 3-8). 1997. lib. bdg. 16.95 (*1-56239-765-6*) ABDO Pub Co.
Minnesota Timeline: A Chronology of Minnesota History, Mystery, Trivia, Legend, Lore & More. Carole Marsh. (Carole Marsh Minnesota Bks.). (Illus.). (J). (gr. 3-12). 1994. pap. 19.95 (*0-7933-5945-7*); lib. bdg. 29.95 (*0-7933-5944-9*); disk 29.95 (*0-7933-5946-5*) Gallopade Intl.
Minnesota Times & Tastes: Recipes & Menus Seasoned with History from the Minnesota Governor's Residence. Ed. by Jean Steiner. 1994. 24.95 (*0-9606852-1-9*) One Thousand Six Summit Avenue.
Minnesota Trivia. Laurel Winter. LC 90-19588. 192p. (Orig.). 1990. pap. 6.95 (*1-55853-092-4*) Rutledge Hill Pr.
Minnesota Twins. Paul Joseph. LC 96-22380. (Illus.). 32p. (J). (gr. 3-8). 1997. 16.48 (*1-56239-670-6*) ABDO Pub Co.
***Minnesota Twins: The First 40 Years.** Stew Thornley. LC 00-9364. (Illus.). (J). 2001. write for info. (*0-8225-3699-4*) Lerner Pub.
Minnesota 2000! Coming Soon to a Calendar Near You - The 21st Century! - Complete Set of AL 2000 Items. Carole Marsh. (Two Thousand! Ser.). (Illus.). (J). (gr. 3-12). 1998. pap. 75.00 (*0-7933-9355-8*); lib. bdg. 85.00 (*0-7933-9356-6*) Gallopade Intl.
Minnesota 2000! Coming Soon to a Calendar near You--The 21st Century! Carole Marsh. (Two Thousand! Ser.). (Illus.). (J). (gr. 3-12). 1998. pap. 19.95 (*0-7933-8745-0*); lib. bdg. 29.95 (*0-7933-8744-2*) Gallopade Intl.
Minnesota UFO's & Extraterrestrials! A Look at the Sightings & Science in Our State. Carole Marsh. (Carole Marsh Minnesota Bks.). (Illus.). (J). (gr. 3-12). 1997. pap. 19.95 (*0-7933-6404-3*); lib. bdg. 29.95 (*0-7933-6403-5*) Gallopade Intl.
Minnesota Underfoot: A Field Guide to Minnesota's Geology. Constance J. Sansome. LC 97-4139. (Illus.). 224p. (Orig.). 1990. reprint ed. pap. 16.95 (*0-89658-036-9*) Voyageur Pr.
Minnesota Vikings. Bob Italia. LC 95-36978. (Illus.). 32p. (J). (gr. 3-8). 1996. lib. bdg. 15.98 (*1-56239-530-0*) ABDO Pub Co.
Minnesota Vikings. Minnesota Vikings Staff. Ed. by CWC Sports Inc. (NFL Team Yearbooks Ser.). (Illus.). (J). (gr. 1-12). 1998. pap. 9.99 (*1-891613-14-6*) Everett Sports.
***Minnesota Vikings.** 3rd rev. ed. Julie Nelson. (Pro Football Today Ser.). (Illus.). 32p. (YA). (gr. 3-12). 2000. lib. bdg. 22.60 (*1-58341-049-X*, Creat Educ) Creative Co.
Minnesota Vikings Facts & Trivia. John Holler. 1998. pap. text 9.99 (*0-9667300-0-3*) Ravenstone Grp.
Minnesota Wills & Estate Planning. Susan L. Neumeyer. 400p. 1993. spiral bd. 105.00 (*1-56257-262-8*, MICHIE) LEXIS Pub.
Minnesota Writes: Poetry. Ed. by Jim Moore & Cary Waterman. LC 87-200754. 240p. (Orig.). 1987. pap. 11.95 (*0-915943-21-2*) Milkweed Ed.
MinnesotaCare: A Progress Report on the Coordination of Medical Assistance & the MinnesotaCare Plan. (Illus.). 94p. (Orig.). (C). 1994. pap. text 35.00 (*0-7881-0380-6*) DIANE Pub.
Minnesotans in the Spanish American War & the Phillipine Insurrection. Ed. by Antona H. Richardson. 232p. 1998. pap. 25.00 (*0-9659271-1-3*, 981) Paduan Pr.
Minnesota's Amphibians & Reptiles: Proceedings of a Symposium. John J. Moriarty et al. 75p. 1997. pap. 9.95 (*1-885209-08-8*) Serpents Tale.
Minnesota's Ethnic Language Schools: Potential for the 80's: Proceedings of the Conference. LC 81-83985. viii, 79p. 1983. pap. text 8.00 (*0-932833-04-7*) Immig His Res.
Minnesota's Irish. Patricia C. Johnston. LC 83-83014. (Illus.). 100p. 1984. 12.95 (*0-942934-07-5*) Johnston Pub.
Minnesota's Literary Visitors. John T. Flanagan. LC 92-50850. (Illus.). 248p. 1993. reprint ed. pap. 13.95 (*1-880654-01-6*) Pogo Pr.
Minnesota's Mining Accidents, 1900-1920 & Mining Deaths, 1889-1990. Compiled by Stina B. Green. LC 95-36665. (Illus.). 55p. (Orig.). 1995. pap. 13.00 (*0-915709-20-1*) Pk Geneal Bk.
Minnesota's (Most Devastating!) Disasters & (Most Calamitous!) Catastrophies! Carole Marsh. (Carole Marsh Minnesota Bks.). (Illus.). (J). (gr. 3 up). 1994. pap. 19.95 (*0-7933-0619-1*); lib. bdg. 29.95 (*0-7933-0620-5*); disk 29.95 (*0-7933-0621-3*) Gallopade Intl.
Minnesota's Natural Heritage: An Ecological Perspective. John R. Tester. Ed. by Mary Keirstead. LC 94-45153. 1995. 29.95 (*0-8166-2133-0*) U of Minn Pr.
Minnesota's Pathways Souvenir Books. (Orig.). Date not set. pap. text. write for info. (*1-56944-128-6*) Terrell Missouri.
Minnesota's Programs for Troubled Gamblers. Patrick J. McCormack. (Illus.). 61p. (Orig.). (C). 1995. pap. text 25.00 (*0-7881-2121-9*) DIANE Pub.
Minnesota's Roadkill Cookbook. Bruce Carlson. (Illus.). 112p. 1992. pap. 7.95 (*1-878488-74-0*) Quixote Pr IA.
Minnesota's Rocks & Waters: A Geological Story. George Schwartz et al. LC 54-6370. (Minnesota Geological Survey Bulletin Ser.: No. 37). 384p. reprint ed. pap. 119.10 (*0-608-12440-0*, 205591100039) Bks Demand.
Minnesota's St. Croix River Valley & the Anoka Sandplain: A Guide to Native Habitats. Daniel S. Wovcha et al. LC 94-40951. (Illus.). 1995. 29.95 (*0-8166-2483-6*); pap. 19.95 (*0-8166-2484-4*) U of Minn Pr.
Minnesota's State Capitol: The Art & Politics of a Public Building. Neil B. Thompson. LC 74-4326. (Publications of the Minnesota Historical Society: No. 9). (Illus.). 108p. 1974. reprint ed. pap. 33.50 (*0-608-06679-6*, 206687600009) Bks Demand.
Minnesota's State Parks: How to Get There - What to Do - Where to Do It. Anne Arthur. 280p. 1998. pap. 14.95 (*1-885061-51-X*) Adventure Pubns.
Minnesota's Statewide Strategy for Drug & Violent Crime Control. (Illus.). 75p. (Orig.). (C). 1993. pap. text 30.00 (*1-56806-805-0*) DIANE Pub.
Minnesota's Statewide Strategy for Drug & Violent Crime Control. (Illus.). 75p. (Orig.). (C). 1995. pap. text 30.00 (*0-7881-2259-2*) DIANE Pub.
Minnesota's Twentieth Century: Stories of Extraordinary Everyday People. D. J. Tice. LC 99-29883. 256p. 1999. 29.95 (*0-8166-3428-9*, Pub. by U of Minn Pr) Chicago Distribution Ctr.
***Minnesota's Twentieth Century: Stories of Extraordinary Everyday People.** D. J. Tice. LC 99-29883. 1999. pap. write for info. (*0-8166-3429-7*) U of Minn Pr.
Minnesota's Unsolved Mysteries (And Their "Solutions") Includes Scientific Information & Other Activities for Students. Carole Marsh. (Carole Marsh Minnesota Bks.). (Illus.). (J). (gr. 3-12). 1994. pap. 19.95 (*0-7933-5792-6*); lib. bdg. 29.95 (*0-7933-5791-8*); disk 29.95 (*0-7933-5793-4*) Gallopade Intl.
Minnesota's Vanishing Outhouse: A Collection of Illustrations & Stories about a Rapidly Vanishing Institution in Minnesota, the Little Outhouse Out Back. Bruce Carlson. (Illus.). 168p. (Orig.). 1991. pap. 9.95 (*1-878488-26-0*) Quixote Pr IA.
Minnesota's World War II Combat Connected Naval Casualties: Navy, Marine Corps, Coast Guard. Park Genealogical Books Staff. Ed. by Mary H. Bakeman. LC 96-31751. 1996. pap. 12.50 (*0-915709-27-9*) Pk Geneal Bk.
Minnesota's WW Two Army War Dead. Ed. by Mary H. Bakeman. 40p. 1994. pap. 9.50 (*0-915709-14-7*) Pk Geneal Bk.

Minnetaka Indian Boy. J. Gordon Bergquist. (Illus.). 150p. (Orig.). 1985. pap. text 9.75 (0-9615483-0-4) Bergquist Pub.

Minnie. Annie M. Schmidt. Tr. by Lance Salway from DUT. LC 93-35924. (Illus.). 172p. (J). (gr. 3-7). 1993. pap. 6.95 (1-57131-600-0) Milkweed Ed.

Minnie. Annie M. Schmidt. Tr. by Lance Salway from DUT. LC 93-35924. (Illus.). 172p. (J). (gr. 3-7). 1994. 14.95 (1-57131-601-9) Milkweed Ed.

Minnie: My Coloring Book. (Mickey & Friends Ser.). (J). 1.09 (0-307-08671-2, 08671) Gldn Bks Pub Co.

***Minnie & Moo & the Musk of Zorro.** Denys Cazet. LC 00-21280. (Illus.). 48p. (J). (ps-3). 2000. pap. 3.95 (0-7894-2653-6) DK Pub Inc.

***Minnie & Moo & the Musk of Zorro.** Denys Cazet. LC 00-21280. (Illus.). 48p. (ps-3). 2000. 12.95 (0-7894-2652-8) DK Pub Inc.

***Minnie & Moo & the Thanksgiving Tree.** Denys Cazet. LC 00-21278. (Illus.). 48p. (ps-3). 2000. pap. 3.95 (0-7894-2655-2) DK Pub Inc.

***Minnie & Moo & the Thanksgiving Tree.** Denys Cazet. LC 00-21278. (Illus.). 48p. (ps-3). 2000. 12.95 (0-7894-2654-4) DK Pub Inc.

Minnie & Moo Go Dancing. Cazet. (J). (gr. 1-3). Date not set. 3.95 (0-7894-2536-X) DK Pub Inc.

Minnie & Moo Go Dancing. Denys Cazet. LC 97-39416. (Illus.). 47p. (J). (gr. 1-3). 1998. 12.95 (0-7894-2515-7) DK Pub Inc.

***Minnie & Moo Go to Paris.** Denys Cazet. LC 98-47421. 48p. (J). 1999. pap. 3.95 (0-7894-3928-X) DK Pub Inc.

***Minnie & Moo Go to Paris, Vol. 4.** Denys Cazet. LC 98-47421. 48p. (J). 1999. 12.95 (0-7894-2595-5) DK Pub Inc.

Minnie & Moo Go to the Moon. Denys Cazet. (J). (gr. 1-3). 1998. write for info. (0-7894-2537-8) DK Pub Inc.

Minnie & Moo Go to the Moon. Denys Cazet. LC 97-39417. (Illus.). 48p. (J). (gr. 1-3). 1998. 3.95 (0-7894-2516-5) DK Pub Inc.

Minnie & Moo Save the Earth, Vol. 3. Denys Cazet. LC 98-47394. 48p. (J). 1999. 12.95 (0-7894-2594-7); pap. 3.95 (0-7894-3929-8) DK Pub Inc.

Minnie & the Mick: The Go-Go White Sox Challenge the Fabled Yankee Dynasty, 1951 to 1964. Bob Vanderberg. (Illus.). 272p. 1996. 25.00 (1-888698-02-0) Diamond Communications.

Minnie Evans: Artist. Ed. by Charles M. Lovell & Erwin Hester. (Illus.). 72p. (Orig.). 1993. pap. 24.50 (0-9636759-0-7) East Carolin Mus.

Minnie Mae: My Story. Minnie M. Robinson. LC 96-17295. (Life Stories Ser.). 62p. (Orig.). 1996. pap. 3.95 (1-56212-181-2) CRC Pubns.

Minnie Mouse. Mouseworks Staff. LC 99-161550. (Friendly Tales Ser.). (Illus.). (J). 1998. 6.99 (1-57082-930-6, Pub. by Mouse Works) Time Warner.

Minnie Muskrat. Katherine Oana. Ed. by Tate Baird. LC 88-51856. (Fables for Today Ser.). (Illus.). 16p. (Orig.). (J). (ps). 1989. pap. 5.52 (0-914127-10-1) Univ Class.

Minnie Mysteries: The Butterscotch Bandit. Cathy Hapka. LC 96-79778. (Look-Look Bks.: Vol. 1). (Illus.). 24p. (J). (ps-3). 1997. pap. 3.29 (0-307-12849-0, 12849, Goldn Books) Gldn Bks Pub Co.

Minnie Mysteries: The Dognapper. Cathy Hapka. LC 96-79779. (Look-Look Bks.: Vol. 2). (Illus.). 24p. (J). (ps-3). 1997. pap. 3.29 (0-307-12850-4, 12850, Goldn Books) Gldn Bks Pub Co.

Minnie Mysteries: The Flower Prowler. Cathy Hapka. LC 97-76906. (Look-Look Bks.). (Illus.). 24p. (J). 1998. pap. 3.29 (0-307-13190-4, 13190, Goldn Books) Gldn Bks Pub Co.

Minnie Mysteries: The Noisy Attic. Catherine Hapka. LC 99-158615. (Look-Look Bks.). 24p. (J). (ps-3). 1998. pap. text 3.29 (0-307-13188-2, 13188, Goldn Books) Gldn Bks Pub Co.

Minnie Negoro: A Retrospective. Contrib. by Anthony Terenzio. (Illus.). 12p. Date not set. 4.50 (0-614-10430-0) W Benton Mus.

Minnie P. Blair: Days Remembered of Folsom & Placerville, California; Banking & Farming in Goldfield, Tonopah, & Fallon, Nevada. Intro. by Mary E. Glass. 156p. 1968. lib. bdg. 36.50 (1-56475-047-7); fiche. write for info. (1-56475-048-5) U NV Oral Hist.

***Minnie's Costume Party Discovery Lift the Flap.** Ellen Weiss. 16p. (J). 2000. 5.99 (0-7364-1036-8, Pub. by Mouse Works) Time Warner.

***Minnie's Sacrifice, Sowing & Reaping, Trial & Triumph.** Frances E. W. Harper. 2000. pap. 14.00 (0-8070-6233-2) Beacon Pr.

Minnie's Sacrifice, Sowing & Reaping, Trial & Triumph: Three Rediscovered Novels. Frances Ellen Watkins Harper. Ed. by Frances Smith Foster. 336p. (C). 1995. pap. 12.95 (0-8070-8333-X) Beacon Pr.

Minnie's Small Wonders see Walt Disney's Read & Grow Library

Minnie's Surprise Trip see Walt Disney's Read & Grow Library

***Minnie's Tea Party.** Jill Wright. Ed. by Anthony Boyd. (Minnie's Adventures Ser.). (Illus.). 32p. (J). (gr. k-2). 1999. 12.00 (0-9672839-0-6); pap. 8.00i (0-9672839-1-4) Starry Puddle Pubng.

***Minnie's Tea Party.** Illus. by Ed Murrieta & Diana Wakeman. 18p. (ps-1). 1999. reprint ed. text 10.00 (0-7881-6632-8) DIANE Pub.

Minnie's Yom Kippur Birthday. Marilyn Singer. LC 85-14193. (Illus.). 32p. (J). (ps-3). 1989. 12.95 (0-06-025846-2) HarpC Child Bks.

Minnisota Tax Handbook, 1998. rev. ed. John P. James. 160p. 1997. pap. text 45.00 (0-7811-0183-2) Res Inst Am.

Minnow: The Children's Story Annual. Donna Sinclair. (Illus.). 128p. (J). 1996. pap. 9.95 (1-55145-067-4) NStone Publ.

Minnow among Tritons: Mrs. S. T. Coleridge's Letters to Thomas Poole, 1799-1834. Sara Coleridge. Ed. by Stephen Potter. LC 75-38028. reprint ed. 34.50 (0-404-56737-1) AMS Pr.

Minnow Knits: Uncommon Clothes to Knit for Kids. Jil Eaton. LC 95-24990. (Illus.). 128p. 1996. pap. 16.95 (1-887374-09-4) Lark Books.

Minnow on the Say. Philippa Pearce. LC 98-52078. (Illus.). 256p. (YA). (gr. 5-9). 2000. 16.95 (0-688-17098-6, Grenwillow Bks) HarpC Child Bks.

Minnowknits, Too: 26 Uncommon Knits for Kids, Big & Small. Jennifer L. Eaton. LC 97-15495. 1998. 25.00 (0-517-70785-3) Crown.

Minnows: Seining & Trapping. Richard E. Faler, Jr. (Illus.). 28p. 1995. pap. 4.50 (1-881399-01-X) Beaver Pond P&P.

***Minnows & Shotgun Shells: Northwoods Hunting & Fishing Tales.** Illus. by Bill Thornley. 197p. 2000. pap. 8.95 (1-885548-05-2) Boot Prints.

***Minnows in the Bath & Other Doggie Treats: An Above-Average Collection of Dog Cartoons for Dog.** Jerry Van Amerongen. (Illus.). 2000. pap. text 9.95 (0-7407-0579-2) Andrews & McMeel.

Mino School of Swordsmiths: A Monograph. Yasu Kizu. 14p. 1991. pap. 4.95 (0-910704-16-3) Hawley.

Minoan: An Mycenaen Art. Reynold Higgins. LC 84-51312. (World of Art Ser.). (Illus.). 216p. 1985. pap. 14.95 (0-500-20184-6, Pub. by Thames Hudson) Norton.

Minoan & Mycenaean Art. 2nd rev. ed. Reynold Higgins. LC 97-60252. (World of Art Ser.). (Illus.). 216p. 1997. pap. 14.95 (0-500-20303-2, Pub. by Thames Hudson) Norton.

Minoan Architectural Design: Formation & Signification. Donald Preziosi. LC 82-22415. (Approaches to Semiotics Ser.: No. 63). xxxi, 522p. 1983. 133.85 (90-279-3409-6) Mouton.

***Minoan Architecture: A Contextual Analysis.** Louise A. Hitchcock. (Illus.). 272p. 2000. 72.50 (91-7081-192-X, Pub. by P Astroms) Coronet Bks.

***Minoan Buildings in Areas B, C, D & F.** Philip P. Betancourt et al. LC 99-6974. (PSEIRA Ser.). 1999. write for info. (0-924171-74-X) U Museum Pubns.

Minoan Conical Cups: Form, Function & Significance. Carole Gillis. (Studies in Mediterranean Archaeology: Vol. LXXXIX). (Illus.). 210p. (Orig.). 1990. pap. 77.50 (91-7081-010-9, Pub. by P Astroms) Coronet Bks.

Minoan Crafts Vol. 1: Tools & Techniques: An Introduction. R. D. Evely. (Studies in Mediterranean Archaeology: Vol. XCII:1). (Illus.). 307p. (Orig.). 1993. pap. 127.50 (91-7081-009-5, Pub. by P Astroms) Coronet Bks.

Minoan Crete. Elizabeth McLellan. Ed. by Kenneth McLeish & Valerie McLeish. (Aspects of Greek Life Ser.). (Illus.). 64p. (Orig.). (gr. 7-12). 1976. pap. text 9.00 (0-582-20671-5, 70818) Longman.

Minoan Distance: The Symbolism of Travel in D. H. Lawrence. Lovel D. Clark. LC 80-18844. 428p. 1980. 42.00 (0-8165-0707-4) U of Ariz Pr.

Minoan-Mycenaean Religion. Martin P. Nilsson. LC 70-162300. 1950. pap. 25.00 (0-8196-0273-6) Biblo.

Minoan Religion: A Bibliography. Compiled by Inger M. Ruud. (Studies in Mediterranean Archaeology & Literature: No. 141). 124p. (Orig.). 1996. pap. 42.50 (91-7081-162-8, Pub. by P Astroms) Coronet Bks.

Minoan Sacrificial Ritual: Cult Practice & Symbolism. Nanno Marinatos. (Acta Instituti Rengi Sueciae Ser.: Series 8, IX). (Illus.). 78p. (Orig.). 1986. pap. 34.50 (91-85086-95-9, Pub. by P Astroms) Coronet Bks.

Minoan Seals see Mediterranean Studies

Minoans: Life in Bronze Age Crete. Rodney Castleden. (Illus.). 272p. (C). 1993. pap. 22.99 (0-415-08833-X, B0410) Routledge.

***Minoans & Mycenaeans: Flavours of Their Time.** Ed. by Yannis Tzedakis & Holley Martlew. (Illus.). 287p. 1999. pap. 57.95 (960-7254-80-5, Pub. by Production Kapon) David Brown.

Minol Araki. Claudia Brown et al. LC 98-50148. 1999. write for info. (0-910407-36-3) Phoenix Art.

Minolta Classic Cameras. Robert E. Mayer. (Magic Lantern Guides). (Illus.). 176p. (Orig.). (C). 1998. pap. 19.95 (1-883403-17-0, H 195, Silver Pixel Pr) Saunders Photo.

Minolta Dynax 7000. 2nd ed. Hove Foto Books Staff. LC 70-7673. (Illus.). 220p. 1993. text 19.95 (0-86343-165-8, Pub. by Hove Foto) Watsn-Guptill.

Minolta Dynax/Maxxum 5xi. (User's Guides Bks.). (Illus.). 220p. text 19.95 (0-906447-51-8, Pub. by Hove Foto) Watsn-Guptill.

Minolta Dynax/Maxxum 9xi. Hove Foto Books Staff. (Illus.). 220p. 1993. pap. text 19.95 (1-874031-15-0, Pub. by Hove Foto) Watsn-Guptill.

Minolta Dynax/Maxxum 700si. Hove Foto Books Staff. (Illus.). 220p. 1996. pap. text 19.95 (1-874031-46-0, Pub. by Hove Foto) Watsn-Guptill.

Minolta Dynax/Maxxum 7000i. Hove Foto Books Staff. LC 70-1609. (Illus.). 220p. 1993. pap. text 19.95 (0-86343-160-7, Pub. by Hove Foto) Watsn-Guptill.

Minolta Dynax/Maxxum 7xi. (User's Guides Bks.). (Illus.). 220p. pap. 19.95 (0-906447-92-5, Pub. by Hove Foto) Watsn-Guptill.

Minolta Dynax/Maxxum 600si. Hove Foto Books Staff. (Illus.). 220p. 1996. pap. text 19.95 (1-874031-60-6, Pub. by Hove Foto) Watsn-Guptill.

Minolta Dynax/Maxxum 3000i/5000i. (User's Guides Bks.). (Illus.). 220p. pap. 19.95 (0-906447-67-4, Pub. by Hove Foto) Watsn-Guptill.

Minolta Dynax/Maxxum 3xi/Xisp. (User's Guides Bks.). (Illus.). 220p. pap. 19.95 (0-906447-96-8, Pub. by Hove Foto) Watsn-Guptill.

Minolta 8000i. (User's Guides Bks.). (Illus.). 220p. pap. 19.95 (0-906447-66-6, Pub. by Hove Foto) Watsn-Guptill.

Minolta Maxxum 800SI, 400SI & 300SI. Thomas Maschke & Peter K. Burian. (Magic Lantern Guides Ser.). (Illus.). 176p. Date not set. pap. 19.95 (1-883403-57-X, Silver Pixel Pr) Saunders Photo.

Minolta Maxxum 700si/500si/400si/300si. 3rd rev. ed. Peter K. Burian & Thomas Maschke. Tr. by Hayley Ohlig from GER. (Magic Lantern Guides Ser.). (Illus.). 176p. (Orig.). (C). 1997. pap. 19.95 (1-883403-08-1, H 122, Silver Pixel Pr) Saunders Photo.

Minolta Maxxum 600si. Thomas Maschke & Peter K. Burian. Tr. by Hayley Ohlig from GER. (Magic Lantern Guides Ser.). (Illus.). 176p. (Orig.). (C). 1995. pap. 19.95 (1-883403-34-0, H 120, Silver Pixel Pr) Saunders Photo.

Minolta Maxxum XTSI HTSI. Tom Maskell. LC 98-36468. (Magic Lantern Guides Ser.). 160 p. 1999. pap. 19.95 (1-883403-54-5, Silver Pixel Pr) Saunders Photo.

Minolta X300/X700/X-370N/X9. (User's Guides Bks.). (Illus.). 220p. pap. 19.95 (0-906447-72-0, Pub. by Hove Foto) Watsn-Guptill.

Minor Agreements in a Horizontal-Line Synopsis. F. Neirynck. (Studiorum Novi Testamenti Auxilia: No. 15). 103p. (Orig.). 1991. pap. 24.00 (90-6186-457-7, Pub. by Leuven Univ) Coronet Bks.

Minor & Fragmentary Sentences of a Corpus of Spoken English. Elizabeth Bowman. LC 66-63898. (General Publications: Vol. 42). (Orig.). 1966. pap. text 16.00 (0-87750-130-0) Res Inst Inner Asian Studies.

Minor & Trace Elements in Breast Milk: Report of a Joint WHO/IAEA Collaborative Study. WHO Staff. 171p. 1989. 30.00 (92-4-156121-1) World Health.

Minor Apocalypse. Tadeusz Konwicki. Tr. by Richard Lourie from POL. LC 98-54885. 244p. 1999. reprint ed. pap. 12.95 (1-56478-217-4) Dalkey Arch.

Minor Archeologies. Lori Baker. (Isthmus Project Ser.). 24p. 1999. pap. 5.00 (0-945926-52-9) Paradigm RI.

Minor Attic Orators, Vol. 1. Tr. by K. J. Maidment. Incl. Antiphon & Andocides. (Loeb Classical Library: No. 308). 15.50 (0-674-99340-3) HUP.

Minor Attic Orators, Vol. 2. Tr. by J. O. Burtt. Incl. Demades. Dinarchus. Hyperides. Lycurgus. (Loeb Classical Library: No. 395). 15.50 (0-674-99434-5) HUP.

Minor Authors of the Corpus Tibullianum. John Yardley. (Latin Commentaries Ser.). 57p. (Orig.). (C). 1992. pap. text 6.00 (0-929524-74-8) Bryn Mawr Commentaries.

Minor Ballet Composers: Biographical Sketches of 66 Underappreciated Yet Significant Contributors to the Body of Western Ballet Music. Bruce R. Schueneman. Ed. & Contrib. by William E. Studwell. LC 97-6729. 118p. 1997. 39.95 (0-7890-0323-6) Haworth Pr.

Minor Casualties. Robert Chrisman. 60p. 1993. pap. 10.00 (0-916418-82-0) Lotus.

Minor Characters. Joyce Johnson. Ed. by Jane Rosenman. 277p. 1990. pap. 7.95 (0-671-72790-7) PB.

Minor Characters: A Beat Memoir. Joyce Johnson. LC 99-462665. 288p. 1999. pap. 13.95 (0-14-028357-9) Viking Penguin.

Minor Constituents in the Middle Atmosphere. Tatsuo Shimazaki. 1986. text 262.00 (90-277-2107-6) Kluwer Academic.

Minor Declamations Ascribed to Quintilian. Ed. by Michael Winterbottom. LC 84-1737. xxxiii, 622p. 1984. 246.15 (3-11-006769-2) De Gruyter.

Minor Demons. Bruce Graham. 1992. pap. 5.25 (0-8222-1340-0) Dramatists Play.

Minor Dialect Areas of the Upper Midwest; A Tentative Bibliography of Kentuch Speech; The Language of Jazz Musicians. Harold B. Allen et al. (Publications of the American Dialect Society: No. 30). 48p. 1958. pap. 4.80 (0-8173-0630-7) U of Ala Pr.

***Minor Elements 2000: Processing & Environmental Aspects of As, Sb, Se, Te & Bi.** Courtney Young. LC 00-20846. (Illus.). 2000. pap. write for info. (0-87335-199-1) SMM&E Inc.

Minor Emergencies. Buttarovoli. LC 99-40670. 1999. pap. text 34.95 (0-323-00756-2) Mosby Inc.

Minor English Poets, 1660-1780: A Selection from Alexander Chalmer's "The Works of the English Poets" 1810. Alexander Chalmers. 1972. 60.95 (0-405-12602-6); 60.95 (0-405-12603-4); 60.95 (0-405-12605-0); 60.95 (0-405-12606-9); 60.95 (0-405-12607-7); 60.95 (0-405-12608-5); 60.95 (0-405-12609-3) Ayer.

Minor English Poets, 1660-1780: A Selection from Alexander Chalmer's "The Works of the English Poets" 1810. Alexander Chalmers & David P. French. 1972. 60.95 (0-405-12604-2) Ayer.

Minor English Poets, 1660-1780: A Selection from Alexander Chalmer's "The English Poets" David P. French & Alexander Chalmers. 1972. 599.00 (0-405-12600-X, 867) Ayer.

Minor English Poets, 1660-1780: A Selection from Alexander Chalmer's "The Works of the English Poets" 1810. Alaxander Chalmers. 1972. 60.95 (0-405-12601-8) Ayer.

Minor Forest Products. S. S. Negi. (C). 1992. 125.00 (81-7136-038-6, Pub. by Periodical Expert) St Mut.

Minor Head Trauma. Ed. by Steven Mandel et al. LC 92-49619. (Illus.). 347p. 1993. 139.00 (0-387-97943-3) Spr-Verlag.

Minor Heresies. John J. Espey. (American Autobiography Ser.). 202p. 1995. reprint ed. lib. bdg. 79.00 (0-7812-8513-5) Rprt Serv.

Minor Heresies, Major Departures: A China Mission Boyhood. John J. Espey. LC 93-24516. 357p. (C). 1994. 30.00 (0-520-08250-8, Pub. by U CA Pr) Cal Prin Full Svc.

***Minor Histocompatibility Antigens: From the Laboratory to the Clinic.** Derry Roopenian & Elizabeth Simpson. LC 99-31656. (Molecular Biology Intelligence Unit Ser.). 225p. 1999. 99.00 (1-57059-599-2) Landes Bioscience.

Minor Illness Manual. Gina Johnson et al. LC 97-3787. 1997. write for info. (1-85775-285-6, Radcliffe Med Pr) Scovill Paterson.

Minor in Name Only: The History of the Adirondack Red Wings. Mike Kane. LC 94-67273. (Illus.). 231p. 1994. 19.95 (1-57167-004-1) Sports Pub.

Minor in Possession. J. A. Jance. LC 89-91871. (J.P. Beaumont Ser.). 336p. 1990. mass mkt. 6.99 (0-380-75546-7, Avon Bks) Morrow Avon.

Minor Injuries Unit Handbook: A Guide for A&E Senior House Officers Emergency Nurse Practitioners & General Practitioners. Matthew Cooke et al. LC 98-26929. 194p. 1998. pap. text 28.00 (0-7506-3451-0) Buttrwrth-Heinemann.

Minor Knickerbockers. Kendall B. Taft. LC 72-111113. (Play Anthology Reprint Ser.). 1977. 30.95 (0-8369-8206-1) Ayer.

Minor Latin Poets, Vol. I. Ed. by E. H. Warmington. (Loeb Classical Library: No. 284). (ENG & LAT.). 434p. 1934. 18.95 (0-674-99314-4) HUP.

Minor Latin Poets II. rev. ed. Tr. by John W. Duff & A. M. Duff from LAT. (Loeb Classical Library: No. 434). 434p. 1935. text 15.50 (0-318-42567-X) HUP.

Minor Laws of Major Importance: A Guide to Federal & State Child Labor Laws. Bryna S. Eraser et al. (Cross Case Report & Case Studies). 100p. 1994. pap. text, teacher ed. 10.95 (0-614-24552-4) Natl Inst Work.

Minor League: Photographs by Andrea Modica. Ed. by Constance Sullivan. (Photographers at Work Ser.). (Illus.). 60p. (Orig.). 1993. pap. 16.95 (1-56098-290-X) Smithsonian.

Minor League: Step-by-Step Guide to Understanding Investment Basics. Terilyn A. Davenport. LC 94-65046. 320p. (Orig.). 1996. 29.95 (1-884573-08-8); pap. 19.95 (1-884573-11-8) S-By-S Pubns.

Minor League Baseball & Local Economic Development. Arthur T. Johnson. LC 92-15713. (Sport & Society Ser.). 300p. (C). 1993. text 34.95 (0-252-01865-6) U of Ill Pr.

Minor League Baseball & Local Economic Development. Arthur T. Johnson. 296p. (C). 1995. pap. text 15.95 (0-252-06502-6) U of Ill Pr.

***Minor League Baseball Standings: All North American Leagues Through 1998.** Benjamin Barrett Sumner. 726p. 2000. 55.00 (0-7864-0781-6) McFarland & Co.

Minor League Baseball Stars. 128p. 1978. 5.00 (0-685-11659-X) Soc Am Baseball Res.

Minor League Baseball Stars. rev. ed. Ed. by L. Robert Davids. (Illus.). 128p. 1984. 5.00 (0-910137-12-9) Soc Am Baseball Res.

Minor League Baseball Stars, Vol. II. Ed. by L. Robert Davids. (Illus.). 158p. 1985. pap. 5.00 (0-910137-13-7) Soc Am Baseball Res.

Minor League Baseball Stars, Vol. III. L. Robert Davids. 184p. 1992. pap. 9.95 (0-910137-49-8) Soc Am Baseball Res.

Minor League Baseball Towns of Michigan: Adrian to Ypsilanti. Marc Okkonen. (Illus.). 186p. 1997. pap. 16.95 (1-882376-43-9) Thunder Bay Pr.

***Minor League Fall Classics: From the Junior World Series to the Triple A World Series.** Bob Bailey. 380p. 2001. spiral bd. 24.95 (1-893392-03-1) Baseball Pr Bks.

***Minor League Handbook 2000.** 9th ed. STATS Inc. Staff. 410p. 1999. pap. 19.95 (1-884064-72-8) STATS.

Minor League Register. Lloyd Johnson. 1994. 42.95 (0-9637189-2-4); pap. 34.95 (0-9637189-3-2) Baseball Amer.

***Minor League Scouting Notebook 2000.** 6th ed. STATS Inc. Staff. 352p. 2000. pap. 19.95 (1-884064-75-2) STATS.

Minor Lives: A Collection of Biographies. Annotated & with an Introduction on John Nichols & the Antiquarian & Anecdotal Movements of the Late Eighteenth Century. John Nichols. Ed. by Edward L. Hart. LC 73-131470. 402p. reprint ed. pap. 124.70 (0-7837-4473-0, 204418100001) Bks Demand.

Minor Masters, Bk. 1. Ed. by Frances Clark & Louise Goss. 16p. 1983. pap. text 3.50 (0-913277-05-3) Summy-Birchard.

Minor Masters, Bk. 2. Ed. by Frances Clark & Louise Goss. 16p. 1983. pap. text 3.50 (0-913277-06-1) Summy-Birchard.

Minor Masters, Bk. 3. Ed. by Frances Clark & Louise Goss. 16p. 1983. pap. text 3.50 (0-913277-07-X) Summy-Birchard.

Minor Miracles. Sandra G. Shapard. LC 93-72937. (Illus.). 64p. (Orig.). 1995. pap. 9.95 (1-56883-043-2) Colonial Pr AL.

Minor Miracles: The Legend & Lure of Minor League Baseball. David Pietrusza. LC 95-8592. (Illus.). 256p. 1995. 22.95 (0-912083-82-4) Diamond Communications.

Minor Mlabri: A Hunter-Gatherer Language of Northern Indochina. Jergen Rischel. 350p. 1995. 98.00 (87-7289-294-3, Pub. by Mus Tusculanum) Paul & Co Pubs.

Minor Murder: Manuscript Edition. Mary Orr & Reginald Denham. 1967. pap. 13.00 (0-8222-0760-5) Dramatists Play.

Minor Objects. Gladys R. Davidson. (Corinth Ser.: Vol. 12). (Illus.). xvi, 366p. 1987. reprint ed. 60.00 (0-87661-122-6) Am Sch Athens.

Minor Papers on the Currency Question, 1809-1823. David Ricardo. 1979. 21.95 (0-405-10624-6) Ayer.

Minor Pentatonic Scales for Guitar. 24p. 1995. pap. 5.95 (0-7935-4370-3, 00695014) H Leonard.

Minor Pentatonic Sclaes for Guitar see Pentatonicas Menores Escalas Para Guitarra

M

An Asterisk (*) at the beginning of an entry indicates that the title is appearing for the first time.

Minor Players, Major Dreams. Brett Mandel. LC 96-32437. (Illus.). xvi, 243p. 1997. pap. 16.95 (*0-8032-8232-X*, A Bison Orig) U of Nebr Pr.

Minor Poems. Alexander Pope. Ed. by Norman Ault. (Twickenham Ser.). 514p. 1964. 97.50 (*0-416-47750-X*) Elliots Bks.

Minor Poems. Michael Drayton. (Select Bibliographies Reprint Ser.). 1977. reprint ed. 21.95 (*0-8369-6853-0*) Ayer.

Minor Poems, Pt. 1. Geoffrey Chaucer. Ed. by Alfred David & George B. Pace. LC 80-5943. (Variorum Edition of the Works of Geoffrey Chaucer, The Canterbury Tales Ser.: Vol. V). 200p. 1982. 49.95 (*0-8061-1629-3*) U of Okla Pr.

Minor Poems of John Lydgate. John Lydgate. (BCL1-PR English Literature Ser.). 1992. reprint ed. lib. bdg. write for info. (*0-7812-7185-1*) Rprt Serv.

Minor Poems of John Lydgate, Pt. I. John Lydgate. Ed. by J. N. MacCracken. (EETS, OS Ser.: Nos. 107 & 192). 1974. reprint ed. 40.00 (*0-527-00308-5*) Periodicals Srv.

Minor Poems of John Lydgate, Pt. II. John Lydgate. Ed. by J. N. MacCracken. (EETS, OS Ser.: Nos. 107 & 192). 1974. reprint ed. 30.00 (*0-527-00193-7*) Periodicals Srv.

Minor Poems of Stephen Hawes. Stephen Hawes. Ed. by Florence W, Gluck & Alice B. Morgan. (OS 271 Ser.: No. 271). (Illus.). 1974. 15.95 (*0-19-722273-0*) OUP.

Minor Poems of the Vernon MS, Pt. 1. Ed. by C. Horstmann. (EETS, OS Ser.: No. 98). 1974. reprint ed. 65.00 (*0-527-00099-X*) Periodicals Srv.

Minor Poems of the Vernon MS, Pt. 2. Ed. by F. J. Furnivall. (EETS, OS Ser.: No. 117). 1974. reprint ed. 55.00 (*0-527-00101-5*) Periodicals Srv.

Minor Poets of the Caroline Period, 3 vols., Set. George E. Saintsbury. (BCL1-PR English Literature Ser.). 1992. reprint ed. lib. bdg. 225.00 (*0-7812-7138-X*) Rprt Serv.

Minor Prophecies: The Literary Essay in the Culture Wars. Geoffrey H. Hartman. 252p. (C). 1991. 40.50 (*0-674-57636-5*) HUP.

Minor Prophets see Profetas Menores

Minor Prophets. Elizabeth Achtemeier. LC 96-31321. (New International Biblical Commentary Ser.: Vol. 17). 390p. (C). 1996. pap. 11.95 (*0-943575-05-2*) Hendrickson MA.

Minor Prophets. Charles L. Feinberg. pap. 19.99 (*0-8024-5305-8*, 216) Moody.

Minor Prophets. John T. Ferrier. 250p. 1976. text 12.50 (*0-900235-40-3*) Order Of The Cross.

Minor Prophets. Michael H. Floyd. LC 99-29802. 649p. 1999. pap. 49.00 (*0-8028-4452-9*) Eerdmans.

Minor Prophets. H. A. Ironside. LC 98-20506. (Ironside Commentaries Ser.). 464p. 1998. pap. 9.99 (*0-87213-411-3*) Loizeaux.

Minor Prophets. Compiled by A. E. Knoch. 141p. 1979. pap. 5.00 (*0-910424-25-X*) Concordant.

Minor Prophets, 3. Ed. by Thomas Edward McComiskey. 1468p. 1996. 115.00 (*0-8010-1124-8*) Baker Bks.

Minor Prophets, 1. James M. Boice. 1988. pap. 17.99 (*0-310-21551-X*) Zondervan.

Minor Prophets, Vol. 2. James M. Boice. 1988. pap. 17.99 (*0-310-21581-1*) Zondervan.

Minor Prophets see Old Testament Commentaries

Minor Prophets: An Exegetical & Expository Commentary (Obadiah-Habakkuk), 2. Ed. by Thomas E. McComiskey. LC 91-38388. 420p. (C). 1993. 44.99 (*0-8010-6307-8*) Baker Bks.

Minor Prophets: An Exegetical & Expository Commentary (Zephaniah-Malachi), 3. Ed. by Thomas Edward McComiskey. LC 91-38388. 528p. (C). 1998. 44.99 (*0-8010-2055-7*) Baker Bks.

Minor Prophets: An Expositional Commentary, 2 vols. in 1. James M. Boice. LC 96-40998. 544p. 1996. reprint ed. pap. 21.99 (*0-8254-2148-9*) Kregel.

Minor Prophets: An Expositional Commentary (Hosea-Jonah), Vol. 1. James M. Boice. 272p. 1984. 17.95 (*0-310-21550-1*, 10423) Zondervan.

Minor Prophets: An Expositional Commentary (Micah-Malachi), Vol. 2. James M. Boice. 1986. 17.95 (*0-310-21580-3*, 10424) Zondervan.

Minor Prophets: Blueprints for 28 Messages Built upon God's Word. Loren D. Deckard. (Sermon Starters Ser.). 64p. 1999. 5.99 (*0-7847-0934-3*, 23012) Standard Pub.

Minor Prophets: Hosea, Joel, Amos, Obadiah, Jonah, Micah. Gordon Lindsay. (Old Testament Ser.: Vol. 36). 1968. 1.95 (*0-89985-156-8*) Christ for the Nations.

Minor Prophets: Nahum, Habakkuk, Zephaniah, Haggai, Zechariah, Malachi. Gordon Lindsay. (Old Testament Ser.: Vol. 37). 1968. 1.95 (*0-89985-157-6*) Christ for the Nations.

Minor Prophets: Teacher's Guide. Joel Schroeder. 1980. 6.50 (*0-8100-0401-1*, 22N0830) WELS Board.

Minor Prophets Vol. 1: An Exegetical & Expository Commentary (Hosea, Joel & Amos), 1. Ed. by Thomas E. McComiskey. LC 91-38388. 520p. (gr. 13). 1992. 44.99 (*0-8010-6285-3*) Baker Bks.

Minor Prophets in the Light of Christian Science. Max Kappeler. LC 64-36062. 214p. 1962. 16.00 (*0-85241-041-7*) Kappeler Inst Pub.

Minor Prophets, Major Themes. Daniel Berrigan. 400p. 1995. pap. 19.95 (*1-879175-17-7*) Fortkamp.

Minor Readings & the Illustrator of Ultimate Meaning. Tr. by Ven Nanamoli from PLI. (C). 1960. 37.00 (*0-86013-023-1*, Pub. by Pali Text) Elsevier.

***Minor Respondent.** Linda Nanos. 313p. 1999. pap. 16.95 (*0-9674090-0-4*) B & Nanos.

Minor Standard Gauge Railways. Ed. by R. W. Kidner. 64p. (C). 1985. 39.00 (*0-85361-264-1*) St Mut.

Minor Surgery: A Text & Atlas. 2nd ed. John S. Brown. (Illus.). 344p. (C). (gr. 13). 1992. mass mkt. 99.95 (*0-412-44910-2*, Chap & Hall NY) Chapman & Hall.

Minor Surgery: A Text & Atlas. 2nd ed. John S. Brown & John Alexander-Williams. LC 92-49983. 1992. write for info. (*0-442-31713-1*) Chapman & Hall.

Minor Surgery: A Text & Atlas. 3rd ed. J. S. Brown. LC 96-84210. (Illus.). 448p. 1996. text 75.00 (*0-412-75060-0*, Pub. by E A) OUP.

Minor Surgery in Orthodontics. Ed. by Jean-Paul Schatz & Jean-Pierre Joho. LC 92-21763. (Illus.). 188p. 1992. text 98.00 (*0-86715-248-6*) Quint Pub Co.

Minor Surgery in Practice. Vija K. Sodera. LC 93-31378. (Illus.). 378p. (C). 1995. text 74.95 (*0-521-44466-7*) Cambridge U Pr.

Minor Surgical Procedures in Remote Areas. Ed. by Jean Rigal. (Medecins Sans Frontieres - Hatier Ser.). 172p. 1989. vinyl bd. 23.95 (*2-218-02163-3*) Hatier Pub.

Minor Tractates of the Talmud. Isidore Epstein. 480p. 1965. 35.00 (*0-900689-86-2*) Bloch.

Minor Traditions of British Mythology. Lewis Spence. LC 72-84001. 1972. reprint ed. 34.95 (*0-405-08989-9*) Ayer.

Minor Traditions of British Mythology. Lewis Spence. 176p. 1996. reprint ed. pap. 17.95 (*1-56459-528-5*) Kessinger Pub.

***Minor Traumatic Brain Injury Handbook: Diagnosis & Treatment.** Gary W. Jay. 376p. 2000. boxed set 79.95 (*0-8493-1955-2*) CRC Pr.

Minor Upanishads. Tr. by Swami Madhavananda. 1970. pap. 2.00 (*81-7505-104-3*, Pub. by Advaita Ashrama) Vedanta Pr.

Minor Voice among Megaliths, Lost Violin & Other Poems. Rufus Goodwin. 80p. (Orig.). 1990. pap. 12.50 (*0-9628429-0-7*) Urban Pr.

Minor White: The Eye That Shapes. Peter C. Bunnell. Ed. by Jill Guthrie. LC 88-83824. (Illus.). 310p. 1989. pap. text 25.00 (*0-943012-09-0*) Prince U Art.

Minor Works. Tr. by W. S. Hett. (Loeb Classical Library: No. 307). 528p. 1936. 18.95 (*0-674-99338-1*) HUP.

Minor Works. Lactantius. Tr. by Mary F. McDonald. LC 64-18669. (Fathers of the Church Ser.: Vol. 54). 245p. 1965. 17.95 (*0-8132-0054-7*) Cath U Pr.

Minor Works see Oxford Illustrated Jane Austen

Minor Works, Alterations, Repairs & Maintenance. 7th ed. Ed. by Tweeds. (Spon's Contractors' Handbooks). 448p. (Orig.). 1994. pap. text 43.00 (*0-419-18540-2*, E & FN Spon) Routledge.

Minor Works of Cornelius Von Bynkershoek see De Domino Maris Dissertatio

Minor Writings of Charles Dickens. Frederic G. Kitton. LC 71-148805. reprint ed. 39.50 (*0-404-08873-2*) AMS Pr.

Minor Writings of Charles Dickens. Frederic G. Kitton. LC 72-129341. (Studies in Fiction: No. 34). 1970. reprint ed. lib. bdg. 75.00 (*0-8383-1144-X*) M S G Haskell Hse.

Minorca, the Illusory Prize: A History of the British Occupation of Minorca Between 1708 & 1802. Desmond Gregory. LC 89-45528. (Illus.). 296p. 1990. 45.00 (*0-8386-3389-7*) Fairleigh Dickinson.

Minorcans of Florida: Their History, Language, & Culture. Philip D. Rasico. LC 90-30600. (Illus.). 200p. (C). 1990. pap. 24.95 (*1-877633-07-0*) Luthers.

Minorities. Gisela Meier. LC 91-11651. (Women Today Ser.). 64p. (J). (gr. 5-7). 1991. lib. bdg. 17.95 (*0-86593-124-0*); lib. bdg. 17.27 (*0-685-59203-0*) Rourke Corp.

Minorities. Ed. by Mary E. Williams. LC 97-37077. (Current Controversies Ser.). (YA). (gr. 5-12). 1997. pap. 16.20 (*1-56510-680-6*); lib. bdg. 26.20 (*1-56510-681-4*) Greenhaven.

Minorities: A Changing Role in American Society. 10th rev. ed. Ed. by Abbey M. Begun et al. (Information Plus Reference Ser.). (Illus.). 180p. 1998. pap. text 26.95 (*1-57302-077-X*) Info Plus TX.

Minorities: America's Rich Culture. 3rd rev. ed. Ed. by Virginia Peterson et al. (Information Plus Compact Reference Ser.). (Illus.). 84p. 1998. pap. text 14.95 (*1-57302-070-2*) Info Plus TX.

Minorities: Community & Identity. Ed. by C. Fried. (Dahlem Workshop Reports: Vol. 27). (Illus.). 430p. 1983. 55.00 (*0-387-12747-X*) Spr-Verlag.

Minorities, Aging & Health. Ed. by Kyriakos S. Markides & Manuel R. Miranda. LC 97-4841. 384p. 1997. 59.95 (*0-8039-5973-7*); pap. 28.95 (*0-8039-5974-5*) Sage.

Minorities & Cancer. Ed. by L. A. Jones. (Illus.). 360p. 1989. 105.00 (*0-387-96950-0*) Spr-Verlag.

Minorities & Criminality. R. Barri Flowers. LC 90-6716. 229p. 1990. 39.95 (*0-685-46010-X*, Greenwood Pr); pap. 19.95 (*0-275-93604-X*, B3604, Praeger Pubs) Greenwood.

Minorities & Criminality, 21. R. Barri Flowers. LC 88-5707. (Contributions in Criminology & Penology Ser.: No. 21). 229p. 1988. 49.95 (*0-313-25366-8*, FMI/, Greenwood Pr) Greenwood.

Minorities & Family Therapy. Ed. by George W. Saba et al. LC 89-26981. (Journal of Psychotherapy & the Family: Vol. 6, Nos. 1 & 2). 237p. (C). 1990. reprint ed. 49.95 (*0-86656-777-1*) Haworth Pr.

Minorities & Family Therapy. Ed. by George W. Saba et al. LC 89-26981. (Journal of Psychotherapy & the Family: Vol. 6, Nos. 1 & 2). 237p. 1995. reprint ed. pap. 19.95 (*1-56024-565-4*) Haworth Pr.

Minorities & Girls in School: Effects on Achievement & Performance. David Johnson. LC 97-4857. (Leaders in Psychology Ser.). 1997. 44.00 (*0-7619-0828-5*); pap. 19.95 (*0-7619-0829-3*) Sage.

Minorities & Marketing: Research Challenges. Ed. by Alan R. Andreasen & Frederick D. Sturdivant. LC 77-6819. 150p. reprint ed. pap. 46.50 (*0-608-13067-2*, 201462600093) Bks Demand.

Minorities & Media: Diversity & the End of Mass Communication. Clint C. Wilson & Felix Gutierrez. 250p. (C). 1985. text 39.95 (*0-8039-2454-2*); pap. text 18.95 (*0-8039-2455-0*) Sage.

Minorities & Media: Diversity & the End of Mass Communication see Race, Multiculturalism & the Media: From Mass to Class Communication

Minorities & Newspapers: A Survey of Readership Research. Virginia D. Fielder & Leonard P. Tipton. 62p. 1988. 2.25 (*0-318-33450-X*) Nwspaper Assn Amer.

Minorities & Policy Studies. Ed. by Michael Preston & Marian L. Palley. (C). 1978. pap. 15.00 (*0-918592-29-1*) Pol Studies.

Minorities & the American City. David N. Alloway. LC 79-124683. 124p. 1970. pap. 13.50 (*0-685-45320-0*) St Aedans Pr & Bk.

Minorities & the American Dream: A Bicentennial Perspective. Warren Marr & Mayhelle Ward. 1976. 19.95 (*0-405-09117-6*, 19461) Ayer.

Minorities & the American Political System. Ed. by B. Ramesh Babu. (C). 1989. 21.00 (*81-7003-108-7*, Pub. by S Asia Pubs) S Asia.

Minorities & the Canadian State. Ed. by Neil Nevitte & Allan Kornberg. 320p. 1994. 24.95 (*0-88962-278-7*); pap. 14.95 (*0-88962-277-9*) Mosaic.

Minorities & the Military: A Cross National Study in World Perspective, 6. Warren L. Young. LC 81-4246. (Contributions in Ethnic Studies: No. 6). 357p. 1982. 65.00 (*0-313-22900-7*, YMG/, Greenwood Pr) Greenwood.

***Minorities & the State in the Arab World.** Ed. by Ofra Bengio & Gabriel Ben-Dor. LC 98-37994. 224p. 1998. lib. bdg. 49.95 (*1-55587-647-1*) L Rienner.

Minorities at Risk: A Global View of Ethnopolitical Conflict. Ted R. Gurr. LC 92-45737. 1993. pap. text 24.95 (*1-878379-24-0*) US Inst Peace.

Minorities at Risk: A Global View of Ethnopolitical Conflict. Ted R. Gurr. LC 92-45737. 1996. reprint ed. 37.50 (*1-878379-25-9*) US Inst Peace.

***Minorities Claims: From Autonomy to Succession.** Welhengama. 2000. 84.95 (*0-7546-1077-2*) Ashgate Pub Co.

Minorities in a Democracy: The Indian Experience James Massey. LC 99-932118. 224 p. 1999. write for info. (*81-7304-282-9*) S Asia.

Minorities in American Higher Education: Recent Trends, Current Prospects, & Recommendations. Alexander W. Astin. LC 81-48663. (Jossey-Bass Series in Higher Education). 285p. reprint ed. pap. 88.40 (*0-7837-2510-8*, 204266900006) Bks Demand.

Minorities in Central & Eastern Europe. 1994. 12.00 (*92-871-2560-0*, Pub. by Council of Europe) Manhattan Pub Co.

***Minorities in Europe: Croatia, Estonia & Slovakia.** Ed. by Snezana Trifunovska. 240p. 1999. text 87.00 (*90-6704-117-3*, Pub. by TMC Asser Pr) Kluwer Law Intl.

***Minorities in European Cities: The Dynamics of Social Integration & Social Exclusion at the Neighborhood Level.** Sophie Body-Gendrot & Marco Martiniello. LC 99-54922. 2000. 65.00 (*0-312-23132-6*) St Martin.

Minorities in Higher Education. Thomas Smith. 38p. 1997. pap. 4.75 (*0-16-048996-2*) USGPO.

Minorities in Higher Education. Lars G. Bjork & Manuel J. Justiz. LC 91-11397. 416p. 1994. reprint ed. pap. text 34.95 (*1-57356-211-4*) Oryx Pr.

Minorities in India: Protection & Welfare. Rajendra Pandey. 288p. (C). 1997. 42.00 (*81-7024-873-6*, Pub. by APH Pubng) Nataraj Bks.

Minorities in Juvenile Justice. Ed. by Kimberly K. Leonard et al. LC 95-15769. 242p. (C). 1995. 48.00 (*0-8039-7264-4*) Sage.

Minorities in Juvenile Justice. Ed. by Kimberly K. Leonard et al. 232p. (C). 1995. pap. 22.95 (*0-8039-7265-2*) Sage.

Minorities in Phoenix: A Profile of Mexican American, Chinese American, & African American Communities, 1860-1992. Bradford Luckingham. LC 94-8103. 258p. 1994. 39.50 (*0-8165-1457-7*) U of Ariz Pr.

Minorities in Public Higher Education: At a Turning Point. American Association of State Colleges & Universit. LC 87-17554. 72p. (Orig.). (C). 1988. pap. text 13.00 (*0-88044-083-X*); lib. bdg. 25.50 (*0-88044-093-7*) AASCU Press.

Minorities in Revolt. Dominick J. Coyle. LC 81-65866. (Illus.). 256p. 1983. 38.50 (*0-8386-3120-7*) Fairleigh Dickinson.

Minorities in the Arab World. Albert H. Hourani. LC 77-87665. reprint ed. write for info. (*0-404-16402-1*) AMS Pr.

***Minorities in the Balkans.** Vladimir Ortakovski. LC 00-23470. 300p. 2000. 95.00 (*1-57105-129-5*) Transnatl Pubs.

Minorities in the Middle: A Cross-Cultural Analysis. Walter P. Zenner. LC 90-39846. (SUNY Series in Ethnicity & Race in American Life). 224p. (C). 1991. text 59.50 (*0-7914-0642-3*); pap. text 19.95 (*0-7914-0643-1*) State U NY Pr.

Minorities in the Middle East: A History of Struggle & Self-Expression. Mordechai Nisan. LC 91-52512. 312p. 1991. lib. bdg. 45.00 (*0-89950-564-3*) McFarland & Co.

Minorities in the Open Society: Prisoners of Ambivalence & Containment. Geoff Densch. (Reports of the Institute of Community Studies). 256p. 1986. text 37.50 (*0-7102-0898-7*, 08987, Routledge Thoemms) Routledge.

***Minorities in the Ottoman Empire: A Reconsideration.** Ed. by Molly Greene. (Princeton Series on the Middle East). 160p. 2000. pap. text 16.95 (*1-55876-228-0*) Wiener Pubs Inc.

Minorities in the Sunbelt. Franklin J. James. 276p. 1984. pap. 1.00 (*0-88285-096-2*) Ctr Urban Pol Res.

Minorities in Wartime: National & Racial Groupings in Europe, North America, & Australia During the Two World Wars. Ed. by Panikos Panayi. LC 92-15669. 280p. 1993. 39.50 (*0-85496-339-1*) Berg Pubs.

Minorities, Migrants, & Crime: Diversity & Similarity Across Europe & the United States. Ed. by Ineke H. Marshall. LC 97-4758. 280p. 1997. text 49.95 (*0-7619-0334-8*); pap. text 22.95 (*0-7619-0335-6*) Sage.

Minorities, Mullahs & Modernity: Reshaping Community in the Late Soviet Union. Mark Saroyan & Edward W. Walker. LC 97-19310. (Research Ser.). 1997. pap. text 22.95 (*0-87725-195-9*) U of Cal IAS.

Minorities of Northern China: A Survey. Henry G. Schwarz. LC 84-5239. (Studies on East Asia: V. 17). xiii, 309p. 1984. reprint ed. pap. 15.00 (*0-914584-96-0*) WWUCEAS.

Minorities of Southwest China: An Introduction to the Yi (Lolo) & Related Peoples & an Annotated Bibliography. Alain Y. Dessaint. LC 80-80017. (Bibliographies Ser.). 381p. 1980. 25.00 (*0-87536-250-8*) HRAFP.

Minorities on India's West Coast: History & Society. Ed. by Anirudha Gupta. xix, 231p. 1991. 27.00 (*81-85163-22-7*, Pub. by Kalinga) Nataraj Bks.

Minorities, Schools, & Politics: Essays. Donald G. Creighton et al. LC 76-436561. (Canadian Historical Readings Ser.: No. 7). 123p. reprint ed. pap. 38.20 (*0-8357-6374-9*, 203572800096) Bks Demand.

Minorities Today. William L. Katz. LC 92-47438. (History of Multicultural America Ser.). (Illus.). 96p. (YA). (gr. 6-8). 1993. lib. bdg. 27.11 (*0-8114-6281-1*) Raintree Steck-V.

Minorities Today. William L. Katz. 96p. (YA). (gr. 7 up). 1994. pap. 6.95 (*0-8114-2918-0*) Raintree Steck-V.

Minorities under Communism: Nationalities As a Source of Tension among Balkan Communist States. Robert R. King. LC 72-95184. 336p. reprint ed. pap. 104.20 (*0-7837-2288-5*, 205737600004) Bks Demand.

Minoritized Space: An Inquiry into the Spatial Order of Things. Michel S. Laguerre. LC 99-19278. 152p. 1999. pap. 15.00 (*0-87772-387-7*) UCB IGS.

Minority Access to Higher Education: An Analysis of a Pipeline Approach Through Neighborhood Learning Centers - the Minnesota Experiment. Patrick A. Roch. LC 94-4719. 156p. (Orig.). (C). 1994. lib. bdg. 48.00 (*0-8191-9496-4*) U Pr of Amer.

Minority Access to Higher Education: An Analysis of a Pipeline Approach Through Neighborhood Learning Centers - the Minnesota Experiment. Patrick A. Roche. LC 94-4719. 156p. (Orig.). (C). 1994. pap. text 24.50 (*0-8191-9497-2*) U Pr of Amer.

Minority Aging: Sociological & Social Psychological Issues, 8. Ed. by Ron C. Manuel. LC 82-930. (Contributions in Ethnic Studies: No. 8). 285p. 1982. 55.00 (*0-313-22541-9*, MAG/, Greenwood Pr) Greenwood.

Minority Alzheimer's Caregivers: Removing Barriers to Community Services. J Neil Henderson et al. LC 89-64011. 100p. 1989. student ed., ring bd. 20.00 (*0-9622070-1-2*) USF SGC.

Minority & Ethnic Issues in the Divorce Process. Ed. by Craig A. Everett. LC 87-35988. (Journal of Divorce: Vol. 11, No. 2). (Illus.). 127p. 1988. text 39.95 (*0-86656-784-4*) Haworth Pr.

***Minority & Group Rights in the New Millennium.** Bill Bowring & Deidre Fottrell. LC 99-48138. 1999. 111.00 (*90-411-1013-5*) Kluwer Law Intl.

Minority & Women's Complete Scholarship Book. Student Services L. L. C. Staff. LC 97-32078. 192p. 1998. pap. 18.95 (*1-57071-193-3*) Sourcebks.

Minority Business Information Resources Directory (MBIRD) 100p. 1997. 32.00 (*1-885786-07-7*) Try Us Res.

Minority Business Programs & Disparity Studies. 82p. 1994. 20.00 (*0-933729-67-7*, No. 3018) Natl League Cities.

Minority Business Today. 44p. 1992. pap. write for info. (*0-16-038144-4*) USGPO.

Minority Children in American Society. Scott-Jones. 2000. pap. 65.00 (*0-8133-3093-9*) HarpC.

Minority Children in Therapy. Ho Man Keung. 224p. (C). 1992. text 48.00 (*0-8039-3912-4*); pap. text 22.95 (*0-8039-3913-2*) Sage.

Minority Education: Anthropological Perspectives. Ed. by Evelyn Jacob et al. (Social & Policy Issues in Education Ser.). 296p. (C). 1993. pap. 24.95 (*0-89391-937-3*); text 73.25 (*0-89391-868-7*) Ablx Pub.

Minority Education: From Shame to Struggle. Ed. by Jim Cummins & Tove Skutnabb-Kangas. 1988. 99.00 (*1-85359-004-5*, Pub. by Multilingual Matters); pap. 34.90 (*1-85359-003-7*, Pub. by Multilingual Matters) Taylor & Francis.

Minority Education & Ethnic Survival. Michael Byram. 208p. 1986. 79.00 (*0-905028-55-4*, MM20, Pub. by Multilingual Matters); pap. 29.95 (*0-905028-54-6*, Pub. by Multilingual Matters) Taylor & Francis.

Minority Enterprise Development. Nancy McCrea. Ed. by Jenny Murphy. 46p. (Orig.). 1989. pap. 21.50 (*0-317-04808-2*) Natl Coun Econ Dev.

Minority Enterprise in the Nineties: A Questionable Future? Ed. by Rudy Winston. (Illus.). 320p. (Orig.). 1992. write for info. (*0-9614387-0-3*) Babson Coll.

Minority Executives' Handbook. 20th rev. ed. Randolph W. Cameron. LC 94-12488. (Illus.). 282p. 1997. reprint ed. pap. 11.95 (*1-56743-021-X*, Amistad) HarperTrade.

Minority Faiths & the American Protestant Mainstream. Ed. by Jonathan D. Sarna. LC 97-4617. 480p. 1997. text 46.50 (*0-252-02293-9*); pap. text 21.95 (*0-252-06647-2*) U of Ill Pr.

Minority Families in the United States: A Multicultural Perspective. 2nd ed. Ronald L. Taylor. LC 97-35834. 300p. 1997. pap. text 44.00 (*0-13-269564-2*) P-H.

***Minority Funding Set: 2001-2003.** Gail A. Schlachter & R. David Weber. 2001. lib. bdg. 126.00 (*1-58841-011-0*) Ref Serv Pr.

An Asterisk (*) at the beginning of an entry indicates that the title is appearing for the first time.

Minority Funding Set, 1999-2001, 4 vols. Gail A. Schlachter & R. David Weber. 1999. lib. bdg. 126.00 (0-918276-84-5) Ref Serv Pr.

Minority Group Influence: Agenda Setting, Formulation, & Public Policy, 333. Ed. by Paula D. McClain. LC 93-7707. (Contributions in Political Science Ser.: No. 333). 232p. 1993. 62.95 (0-313-29036-9, GM9036, Greenwood Pr) Greenwood.

Minority Group Threat, Crime, & Policing: Social Context & Social Control. Pamela I. Jackson. LC 88-31927. 168p. 1989. 49.95 (0-275-92983-3, C2983, Praeger Pubs) Greenwood.

***Minority Health in America: Findings & Policy Implications from the Commonwealth Fund Minority Health Survey** Carol J. Hogue et al. LC 99-30914. 2000. write for info. (0-8018-6299-X) Johns Hopkins.

Minority Health Issues for an Emerging Majority: The 4th National Forum on Cardiovascular Health, Pulmonary Disorders, & Health Resources. Ed. by Shiriki Kumanyika & John Karefa-Smart. (Illus.). 129p. (C). 1998. pap. text 25.00 (0-7881-7292-1) DIANE Pub.

Minority Hiring & Promotion Practices Within Federal Law Enforcement Agencies: Hearing Before the Subcommittee on Investigations of the Committee on Post Office & Civil Service, House or Representatives, 102 Congress, 2nd Session, October 1, 1992. USGPO Staff. LC 93-135500. iii, 221 p. 1992. write for info. (0-16-039695-6) USGPO.

Minority Identities & the Nation State. Ed. by Gurpreet Mahajan & D. L. Sheth. LC 99-939173. 344p. 2000. text 29.95 (0-19-564541-3) OUP.

Minority Language & Literature: Retrospective & Perspective. Ed. by Dexter Fisher. LC 78-100162. 160p. reprint ed. pap. 49.60 (0-608-15492-X, 202967900062) Bks Demand.

Minority Languages & Bilingualism: Case Studies in Maintenance & Shift. Robert C. Williamson. 192p. (C). 1991. text 73.25 (0-89391-766-4) Ablx Pub.

Minority Languages in Europe - Past & Present: A Classified Bibliography. Reiner Pogarell. viii, 208p. 1983. 72.35 (3-11-009783-4) Mouton.

Minority Languages Today. Einar Haugen et al. 256p. 1991. reprint ed. pap. 35.00 (0-85224-642-0, Pub. by Edinburgh U Pr) Col U Pr.

Minority Marketing: Research Perspectives for the 1990's: Proceedings of the Minority Marketing Conference Presented by the Academy of Marketing Science & the University of Southern Mississippi, Long Beach, MS, October 14-16, 1993. fac. ed. Academy of Marketing Science Staff. Ed. by Robert L. King. LC HF5411.. (Special Conference Ser.: No. 6). 125p. 1993. reprint ed. pap. 38.80 (0-7837-8115-6, 204792200008) Bks Demand.

***Minority Medical Students: Taking My Place in Medicine.** Carmen Webb. LC 00-8370. (Surviving Medical School Ser.). 2000. write for info. (0-7619-1809-4) Sage.

Minority Mental Health. Jones Staff. (C). 1982. text. write for info. (0-03-047056-0) Harcourt Coll Pubs.

Minority Migrants in the Urban Community: Mexican-American & Negro Adjustment to Industrial Society. Lyle W. Shannon & Magdaline Shannon. LC 72-84055. (Illus.). 352p. reprint ed. pap. 109.20 (0-608-10909-6, 202195800026) Bks Demand.

Minority Nationalism & European Integration. Peter S. Lynch. LC 97-140251. 228p. 75.00 (0-7083-1377-9, Pub. by Univ Wales Pr) Paul & Co Pubs.

***Minority of One.** Henry Goldberg. LC 00-131651. 288p. 2000. write for info. (1-57197-224-2, Pub. by Pentland Pr) Assoc Pubs Grp.

Minority of One. Bruce H. Smith. 144p. (C). 1990. pap. text 44.95 (0-9627882-0-1) Bradley Mann.

Minority Organizations: A National Directory. 4th ed. 690p. 1997. pap. 49.95 (0-89434-176-6, F112) Ferguson.

Minority-Owned High-Tech Businesses. 3rd ed. Ed. by Thomas D. Johnson. 390p. 1994. pap. 145.00 (0-933527-45-4) Business Research.

Minority Party Politics in a Multinational State: The German Social Democrats of Czechoslovakia, 1918-1938. Nancy M. Wingfield. (East European Monographs: No. 259). 238p. 1989. text 55.50 (0-88033-156-9, Pub. by East Eur Monographs) Col U Pr.

Minority People in the Age of Nation States. Ed. by Gerard Chaliand. (C). 1989. 22.50 (81-202-0275-9, Pub. by Ajanta) S Asia.

Minority Peoples Age Ntn States. Chaliand. (C). 49.95 (0-7453-0276-9); pap. 15.95 (0-7453-0286-6, Pub. by Pluto GBR) Stylus Pub VA.

Minority Perspectives: Papers. Dale R. Marshall et al. LC 78-186473. (Governance of Metropolitan Regions Ser.: No. 2). 76p. reprint ed. pap. 30.00 (0-7837-3042-X, 202382000034) Bks Demand.

Minority Politics & Ideologies in the United States. Jane H. Bayes. Ed. by Victor Jones. LC 82-17698. (Chandler & Sharp Publications in Political Science Ser.). 144p. (Orig.). (C). 1982. pap. text 9.95 (0-88316-551-1) Chandler & Sharp.

***Minority Politics at the Millennium.** Katherine Underwood & Richard A. Keiser. LC 99-52031. (Reference Library of Social Science). 1999. write for info. (0-8153-3519-9) Garland.

Minority Presence in American Literature, 1600-1900, 2 vols., 1. Ed. by Philip Butcher. LC 77-5687. 1977. pap. 12.95 (0-88258-061-2) Howard U Pr.

Minority Presence in American Literature, 1600-1900, 2 vols., 2. Ed. by Philip Butcher. LC 77-5687. 1977. pap. 12.95 (0-88258-100-7) Howard U Pr.

Minority Presence in American Literature, 1600-1900, 2 vols., Set. Ed. by Philip Butcher. LC 77-5687. 1977. pap. 20.50 (0-88258-104-X) Howard U Pr.

Minority Question in Europe: Texts & Commentary. Ed. by Florence Benoit-Rohmer. LC 97-175949. 180p. 1996. pap. 15.00 (92-871-2932-0, Pub. by Council of Europe) Manhattan Pub Co.

Minority Recruiting, IEC Enterprises, Inc. Staff. LC 96-113938. 128p. 1995. pap. text, per. 17.95 (0-7872-1560-0) Kendall-Hunt.

Minority Recruitment Data: An Analysis of Baccalaureate Degree Production in the United States. Donald R. Deskins, Jr. LC 83-19159. 832p. (C). 1984. 95.50 (0-86598-145-0) Rowman.

Minority Religions in America. rev. ed. William J. Whalen. LC 81-3664. 222p. (Orig.). 1981. pap. 8.95 (0-8189-0413-5) Alba.

Minority Report. Bernard A. De Voto. LC 71-142619. (Essay Index Reprint Ser.). 1977. 23.95 (0-8369-2105-4) Ayer.

***Minority Report.** Philip K. Dick. 1999. pap. text 14.95 (0-8065-2168-6, Citadel Pr) Carol Pub Group.

Minority Report. Andrew Herron. 352p. (C). 1989. 75.00 (0-7855-6816-6, Pub. by St Andrew) St Mut.

Minority Report. 3rd ed. Anthony G. Dworkin & Rosalind J. Dworkin. LC 98-87890. (C). 1998. pap. text 56.00 (0-03-047534-1, Pub. by Harcourt Coll Pubs) Harcourt.

Minority Report: Confessions of an Unrepentant Non-Conformist. Andrew Herron. 352p. (C). 1990. text 60.00 (0-7152-0638-9) St Mut.

Minority Report: H. L. Mencken's Notebooks. H. L. Mencken. LC 97-4116. (Maryland Paperback Bookshelf Ser.). 296p. 1997. reprint ed. pap. 15.95 (0-8018-5658-2) Johns Hopkins.

Minority Representation & the Quest for Voting Equality. Bernard N. Grofman et al. (Illus.). 184p. (C). 1992. text 49.95 (0-521-39128-8) Cambridge U Pr.

Minority Representation & the Quest for Voting Equality. Bernard N. Grofman et al. (Illus.). 184p. (C). 1994. pap. text 17.95 (0-521-47764-6) Cambridge U Pr.

Minority Responses. Ed. by Minako Kurpkawa. LC 81-40764. 384p. 1981. pap. text 26.00 (0-8191-1818-4) U Pr of Amer.

Minority Rights: A Comparative Analysis, 104. Jay A. Sigler. LC 83-5580. (Contributions in Political Science Ser.: No. 104). 245p. 1983. 52.95 (0-313-23400-0, SMR/, Greenwood Pr) Greenwood.

Minority Rights: A Socio-Linguistic Analysis of Group Conflicts in Eastern Region of India. Snehamoy Chakladar. (C). 1987. 14.00 (81-7074-011-8, Pub. by KP Bagchi) S Asia.

Minority Rights in the 'New' Europe. Peter Cumper & Steven C. Wheatley. LC 98-47104. 1999. 135.00 (90-411-1124-7) Kluwer Law Intl.

Minority Rights, Majority Rule. Sarah A. Binder. 250p. 1997. text 59.95 (0-521-58239-3); pap. text 18.95 (0-521-58792-1) Cambridge U Pr.

***Minority Rules.** Louisa Schein. LC 99-36861. (Body, Commodity & Text Ser.). 352p. 2000. pap. 19.95 (0-8223-2444-X) Duke.

Minority Self-Employment in North Carolina. Lance Freeman. 1997. write for info. (0-9633115-5-7) NC Inst Min Econ Devel.

Minority Shareholders' Protection. S. H. Goo. 162p. 1994. pap. 40.00 (1-874241-04-X, Pub. by Cavendish Pubng) Gaunt.

Minority Shareholders' Remedies. Elizabeth J. Boros. (Illus.). 386p. 1996. text 89.00 (0-19-825975-1) OUP.

Minority Small Business & Capital Ownership Development Program, 2 vol. set. 1995. lib. bdg. 599.99 (0-8490-6546-1) Gordon Pr.

Minority Small Business & Capital Ownership Development Program, 2 vols. 1997. lib. bdg. 600.95 (0-8490-6090-7) Gordon Pr.

Minority Small Business & Capital Ownership Development Program, 2 vols., Set. 1993. lib. bdg. 598.95 (0-8490-8923-9) Gordon Pr.

Minority Small Business & Capital Ownership Development Program, 4 vols., Set. 1995. lib. bdg. 1299.99 (0-8490-6776-6) Gordon Pr.

Minority Small Business & Capital Ownership Development Program, 2 vols., Set. 1996. lib. bdg. 755.99 (0-8490-5965-8) Gordon Pr.

Minority Small Business & Capital Ownership Development Program, Vols. 1-2. E. A. Patrick. 2 Bks. (1056p. 1990. ring bd. 38.00 (0-16-027829-5) USGPO.

Minority Student Graduate School Information Kit. 53p. (C). 1992. pap. 3.50 (1-887284-07-9) Natl Consortium.

Minority Student Opportunities in U. S. & Canadian Medical Schools. 13th rev. ed. Ed. by Lily M. Johnson. 400p. (C). 1996. pap. 7.50 (1-57754-001-8) Assn Am Med Coll.

Minority Student Services Delivery System: Self Evaluation Instrument. Charles A. Taylor. LC 89-36321. 1989. 12.50 (0-935483-08-X) Praxis Pubs.

Minority Student Services Delivery System Self-Evaluation Instrument. Charles A. Taylor. 42p. (Orig.). 1987. pap. 12.50 (0-935483-04-7) Praxis Madison.

Minority Teacher Supply & Demand. 1990. 12.00 (0-89333-070-1) AACTE.

Minority Verdict: Experiences of a Catholic Public Servant. Maurice Hayes. (Illus.). 304p. 1995. pap. 25.00 (0-85640-548-5, Pub. by Blackstaff Pr) Dufour.

Minority View of How to Campaign for Political Office. Roosevelt Baums. Ed. by Nancy Augst & Michelle Mathews. (Illus.). 76p. (Orig.). 1982. pap. 4.95 (0-934138-00-1) Rosey-Royce.

Minority Voice in Educational Reform: An Analysis by Minority & Women College of Education Deans. Louis A. Castenell & Jill M. Tarule. LC 96-52286. (Social & Policy Issues in Education). 1997. 73.25 (1-56750-318-7); pap. 24.95 (1-56750-319-5) Ablx Pub.

Minority Vote Dilution. Ed. by Chandler Davidson. LC 84-10883. 298p. 1989. pap. 14.95 (0-88258-176-7) Howard U Pr.

***Minority Women in Science: Forging the Way.** Keiko E. Suda et al. (Illus.). 94p. 2000. pap., teacher ed. 25.00 (1-878550-68-3); pap., student ed. 6.50 (1-878550-67-5) Inter Dev Res Assn.

Minors. Neil J. Sullivan. 1991. pap. 12.95 (0-312-05470-X) St Martin.

Minors - The Law & Practice: The Juvenile Courts - The Offences - The Role of the Local Authorities. Kenneth W. Pain. 293p. 1987. 136.00 (1-85190-030-6, Pub. by Fourmat Pub) St Mut.

Minor's Holiday Big Band. Date not set. 40.00 (0-7935-4831-4, 00000792) H Leonard.

Minos, Leges, Epinomis, Epistulae, Definitiones see Opera

Minotaur. Stephen Coonts. 448p. 1990. mass mkt. 6.99 (0-440-20742-8) Dell.

Minotaur. Bernard Evslin. (Monsters of Mythology Ser.). (Illus.). 104p. 1987. lib. bdg. 19.95 (1-55546-237-5) Chelsea Hse.

Minotaur. John Farris. 384p. 1985. pap. 3.95 (0-8125-8258-6, Pub. by Tor Bks) St Martin.

Minotaur. large type ed. Stephen Coonts. LC 90-10806. 719p. 1990. 13.95 (0-89621-982-8) Thorndike Pr.

Minotaur. large type ed. Stephen Coonts. LC 90-10806. 719p. 1990. reprint ed. 21.95 (1-56054-020-6) Thorndike Pr.

Minotaur: Poetry & the Nation State. Tom Paulin. 256p. (C). 1992. 35.50 (0-674-57637-3) HUP.

***Minotaur: Sir Arthur Evans & the Archaeology of the Minoan Myth.** Joseph Alexander MacGillivray. (Illus.). 352p. 2000. text 26.00 (0-8090-3035-7) FS&G.

Minotaur of Knossos. Roberta Angeletti. (Journey Through Time Ser.). (Illus.). 32p. (J). (gr. 3-5). 1999. 16.95 (0-19-521557-5) OUP.

***Minotaur Takes a Cigarette Break.** Steven Sherrill. LC 99-59651. 312p. 2000. 19.95 (0-89587-197-1) Blair.

Minotaur Trilogy: Crysilver Bell, the Forest of Forever, Day of the Minotaur. Thomas B. Swann. (Illus.). 464p. 1996. reprint ed. 50.00 (0-9641476-1-0) M D Hargreaves.

Minotaure, 4 vols., Set. Ed. by Albert Skira & E. Teriade. LC 68-9227. (Contemporary Art Ser.: Nos. 1-13). (FRE., Illus.). 1969. reprint ed. 218.95 (0-405-00700-0) Ayer.

Minotaure, 4 vols., Vol. 1. Ed. by Albert Skira & E. Teriade. LC 68-9227. (Contemporary Art Ser.: Nos. 1-13). (FRE., Illus.). 1969. reprint ed. 62.95 (0-405-00701-9) Ayer.

Minotaure, 4 vols., Vol. 2. Ed. by Albert Skira & E. Teriade. LC 68-9227. (Contemporary Art Ser.: Nos. 1-13). (FRE., Illus.). 1969. reprint ed. 62.95 (0-405-00702-7) Ayer.

Minotaure, 4 vols., Vol. 3. Ed. by Albert Skira & E. Teriade. LC 68-9227. (Contemporary Art Ser.: Nos. 1-13). (FRE., Illus.). 1969. reprint ed. 62.95 (0-405-00703-5) Ayer.

Minotaure, 4 vols., Vol. 4. Ed. by Albert Skira & E. Teriade. LC 68-9227. (Contemporary Art Ser.: Nos. 1-13). (FRE., Illus.). 1969. reprint ed. 62.95 (0-405-00704-3) Ayer.

Minotaur's Lament. Stephen Gomez. (Illus.). 112p. (Orig.). 1995. pap. 12.95 (1-56474-146-X) Fithian Pr.

Minotaur's Tale. Alan Davison. (Illus.). 80p. (Orig.). 1992. pap. 11.95 (1-878574-42-6) Dark Horse Comics.

Minou. Mindy Bingham. LC 86-26539. (Illus.). 64p. (J). (ps up). 1987. 14.95 (0-911655-36-0) Advocacy Pr.

Minoxidil (Rogaine) Index of New Information with Authors & Subjects. rev. ed. Science & Life Consultants Association Staff. LC 31-242. 105p. 1994. 47.50 (0-7883-0342-2); pap. 44.50 (0-7883-0343-0) ABBE Pubs Assn.

Minpins. Roald Dahl. (J). 1991. 17.00 (0-670-84168-4, Viking Child) Peng Put Young Read.

Minpins. Roald Dahl. (Illus.). 48p. (J). (ps-3). 1994. pap. 5.99 (0-14-054970-6, PuffinBks) Peng Put Young Read.

Minpins. Roald Dahl. 1993. 11.19 (0-606-07039-7, Pub. by Turtleback) Demco.

Minerals Bioprocessing II. Ed. by D. S. Holmes & R. W. Smith. LC 95-78349. (Illus.). 338p. 1995. 20.00 (0-87339-301-5, 3015) Minerals Metals.

Minsk Ghetto. Hersh Smolar. Tr. by Max Rosenfeld from YID. 1988. 16.95 (0-89604-068-2, Holocaust Library); pap. 10.95 (0-89604-069-0, Holocaust Library) US Holocaust.

Minspi. Okey Onuzo. 385p. 1998. pap. 7.00 (1-880608-08-1, LL-BK-06) Life Link.

Minstrel: And Selected Poems. Stephen M. Ryder. Ed. by Anna L. Ganz. 85p. (Orig.). 1997. pap. 12.95 (0-9654867-0-2) Bennington NY.

Minstrel: My Adventure in Newspapering. Jim Klobuchar. LC 97-11088. 1997. pap. 17.95 (0-8166-2991-9) U of Minn Pr.

Minstrel: The Progress of Genius. James Beattie. LC 78-67646. (Scottish Enlightenment Ser.). reprint ed. 44.00 (0-404-17176-1) AMS Pr.

Minstrel & the Dragon Pup. Rosemary Sutcliff. LC 92-53012. (Illus.). (J). (ps up). 1996. pap. 6.99 (1-56402-603-5) Candlewick Pr.

Minstrel & the Dragon Pup. Rosemary Sutcliff. 1996. 12.19 (0-606-09618-3, Pub. by Turtleback) Demco.

Minstrel Banjo Vol. 1: Briggs Banjo Instructor. Joseph Weidlich & Tom Briggs. LC 98-114430. (Illus.). 96p. (Orig.). 1997. pap. 12.95 (1-57424-040-4) Centerstream Pub.

Minstrel Banjo Briggs Banjo Instructor. (bri). Date not set. pap. text 12.95 (0-7935-8631-3) H Leonard.

Minstrel Boy. Sharon Stewart. 168p. (YA). (gr. 7 up). 1997. pap. 7.95 (0-929141-54-7) Napoleon Publ.

Minstrel Gags & End Men's Handbook. LC 77-91097. (American Humorists Ser.). reprint ed. lib. bdg. 42.50 (0-8398-1261-2) Irvington.

Minstrel in the Tower. Gloria Skurzynski. LC 87-26614. (Stepping Stone Bks). (Illus.). 64p. (J). (gr. 4-7). 1988. pap. 3.99 (0-394-89598-3, Pub. by Random Bks Yng Read) Random.

Minstrel in the Tower. Gloria Skurzynski. 1988. 9.44 (0-606-12424-1) Turtleback.

Minstrel in the Tower Study Guide. Rebecca Gilleland. 48p. (J). (gr. 2-4). 1993. student ed., ring bd. 9.99 (1-58609-118-2) Progeny Pr WI.

Minstrel of Love: A Biography of Satguru Sant Keshavadas. Michael Makowsky. (Illus.). 334p. (Orig.). 1980. pap. 12.00 (0-942508-20-3) Vishwa.

Minstrel of the Yukon. John Hines. (American Autobiography Ser.). 231p. 1995. reprint ed. lib. bdg. 79.00 (0-7812-8556-9) Rprt Serv.

Minstrel-Show Songs. Steven Foster. LC 72-169646. (Earlier American Music Ser.: No. 14). 1980. reprint ed. lib. bdg. 25.00 (0-306-77314-7) Da Capo.

Minstrel Tales from Southeastern Turkey. Wolfram Eberhard. Ed. by Richard M. Dorson. LC 80-793. (Folklore of the World Ser.). 1981. reprint ed. lib. bdg. 17.95 (0-405-13332-4) Ayer.

Minstrels. Michael Hemmingson. 148p. 1997. pap. 10.00 (1-882633-23-7) Permeable.

Minstrels & Angels: Carvings of Musicians in Medieval English Churches. Jeremy Montagu & Gwen Montagu. LC 97-38360. (Reference Books in Music: Vol. 33). (Illus.). 212p. 1998. 36.00 (0-914913-40-9, Fallen Lef Pr); pap. 19.95 (0-914913-41-7, Fallen Lef Pr) Scarecrow.

M

Minstrel's Notes: Stories & Sermons on Worship in Spirit & in Truth & Music Theory & Technique for the Acoustic Guitar. John J. Frank. 71p. (YA). (gr. 10 up). 1996. pap. text. write for info. (1-887835-11-3) Minstrel Missions.

Minstrels of the Dawn: The Folk-Protest Singer As a Cultural Hero. Jerome L. Rodnitzky. LC 76-4520. 214p. 1976. text 34.95 (0-88229-284-6); pap. text 24.95 (0-88229-427-X) Burnham Inc.

***Minstrels Playing: Music in Early English Religious Drama II.** Richard Rastall. 464p. 2000. 110.00 (0-85991-585-9) Boydell & Brewer.

***Minstrel's Tale.** Berit I. Haahr. (Illus.). 256p. (YA). (gr. 7). 2000. 15.95 (0-385-32713-7, Delacorte Pr Bks) BDD Bks Young Read.

***Minstrel's Tale.** Joslin. 1999. 16.95 (0-7459-3965-1, Pub. by Lion Pubng) Trafalgar.

Minstrelsy: Poems from Hollywood. Mark Dunster. 15p. 1998. pap. 5.00 (0-89642-473-1) Linden Pubs.

Minstrelsy of the Scottish Border, 4 vols., Set. Sir Walter Scott. Ed. by T. F. Henderson. 2000. reprint ed. 150.00 (1-55888-189-1) Omnigraphics Inc.

***Mint.** Deni Bown & Kate Ferry-Swainson. LC 99-42983. (Herb Library). 2000. pap. 12.95 (1-58290-016-7) Jrny Editions.

Mint Cookie Miracles. Nancy S. Levene. LC 88-11902. (Alex Ser.). 120p. (J). (gr. 3-7). 1988. pap. 4.99 (1-55513-514-5, Chariot Bks) Chariot Victor.

***Mint Cookies Miracles.** Nancy Simpson. LC 88-11902. (Alex Ser.). (Illus.). 128p. (J). (gr. 2-5). 2000. pap. 4.99 (0-7814-3373-8) Chariot Victor.

Mint Julep Murder. Carolyn G. Hart. 256p. 1996. mass mkt. 6.50 (0-553-57202-4) Bantam.

Mint Juleps, Wisteria, & Queers: Gay & Lesbian Culture in the South. Ed. by Jim Baxter. (Illus.). 64p. (Orig.). 1988. pap. 5.00 (0-943810-38-8) Southern Exposure.

Mint, Spice & Other Aromatic Teas. Scentouri Staff. (Scentouri Recipe Bks.). 1984. ring bd. 21.95 (0-318-01386-X) Prosperity & Profits.

Mint Tea. Christine Craig. (Caribbean Writers Ser.). 144p. 1993. pap. 9.95 (0-435-98932-4, 98932) Heinemann.

Minto Pyramid Principle: Logic in Writing, Thinking, & Problem Solving. Barbara Minto. LC 95-94799. (Illus.). 275p. 1996. 80.00 (0-9601910-3-8); pap. 60.00 (0-9601910-4-6) Minto Intl Inc.

Minton. Joan Jones. (Shire Album Nineteen Seventy Ser.). (Illus.). 32p. 1989. pap. 25.00 (0-7478-0151-7, Pub. by Shire Pubns) Lubrecht & Cramer.

Minton. Joan Jones. (Album Ser.: No. 279). (Illus.). 32p. 1995. pap. 4.75 (0-7478-0304-8, Pub. by Shire Pubns) Parkwest Pubns.

Minton: The First 200 Years of Design. Joan Jones. (Illus.). 392p. 1993. 140.00 (1-85310-283-0, Pub. by Swan Hill Pr) Antique Collect.

Mintons Tiles. Ed. by Chris Blanchett. 1997. pap. 19.95 (0-903685-50-7, Pub. by R Dennis) Antique Collect.

***Minty.** Alan Schroeber. (Illus.). 32p. (J). (ps-3). 2000. pap. 6.99 (0-14-056196-X, PuffinBks) Peng Put Young Read.

Minty: A Story of Young Harriet Tubman. Alan Schroeder. LC 95-23499. (Illus.). 40p. (J). (gr. k-4). 1996. 16.99 (0-8037-1888-8, Dial Yng Read) Peng Put Young Read.

Minty Alley. C. L. R. James. 1997. pap. text 17.00 (1-57814-000-5) Rnd McNally Custom.

Minty Alley. C. L. R. James. LC 97-21362. 248p. 1997. reprint ed. pap. 17.00 (1-57806-027-3) U Pr of Miss.

Minty Mixtures. Alexander Bryce. 1997. pap. write for info. (1-57553-651-X) Watermrk Pr.

Mintzberg on Management: Inside Our Strange World of Organizations. Henry Mintzberg. 256p. 1989. 40.00 (0-02-921371-1) Free Pr.

Minuci Felicis. rev. ed. Ed. by Kytzler. (LAT.). 1992. pap. 21.95 (3-8154-1539-X, T1539, Pub. by B G Teubner) U of Mich Pr.

Minucias del Lenguaje (Details of the Language) Jose G. Moreno de Alba. (SPA.). 560p. 1992. pap. 19.99 (968-16-3718-6, Pub. by Fondo) Continental Bk.

Minucius Felix - Concordantia in Minuci Felicis Octavium. Menucius Felix. Ed. by B. Kytzler & Dietmar Najock. (Alpha-Omega, Reihe A Ser.: Vol. LXXII). (GER.). x, 423p. 1991. write for info. (3-487-09395-2) G Olms Pubs.

An Asterisk (*) at the beginning of an entry indicates that the title is appearing for the first time.

M

Minuet. Jennie Gallant. (Coventry Romance Ser.: No. 66). 224p. 1980. pap. 1.75 (*0-449-50097-7*, Coventry) Fawcett.

Minuet: A Critical Survey of French & English Literary Ideas in the 18th Century. Frederick C. Green. LC 75-158504. 1971. reprint ed. 49.00 (*0-403-01296-1*) Scholarly.

Minuet & Gavotte. 1990. 10.00 (*0-685-32110-X*, 77-190) Hansen Ed Mus.

Minuet Opus I. Joseph DiEdwardo. 18p. (Orig.). (J). (gr. k-12). 1996. pap. 12.95 (*0-9641468-3-5*) M DiEdwardo Pubng.

***Minuit Dans Le Jardin Du Bien Et Du Mal.** 4th ed. John Berendt. 1998. pap. 12.95 (*2-266-07518-7*) Distribks Inc.

Minus a Shamus. large type ed. Anthony Graham. 368p. 1988. 27.99 (*0-7089-1865-4*) Ulverscroft.

Minus Green Plus. limited ed. Graham Everett. 40p. (Orig.). 1995. pap. 7.00 (*0-935252-52-5*) Street Pr.

***Minus Man.** Lew McCreary. LC 99-43716. 256p. 1999. reprint ed. pap. 12.00 (*0-8021-3674-5*, Pub. by Grove-Atltic) Publishers Group.

***Minus 148 Degrees.** 3rd ed. Art Davidson. 1999. pap. text 14.95 (*0-89886-687-1*) Mountaineers.

Minus 148 Degrees: First Winter Ascent of Mt. McKinley. 2nd enl. rev. ed. Art Davidson. (Illus.). 254p. 1987. pap. 14.95 (*0-938567-00-4*) Mountaineers.

Minus Stress. George E. Soroka. 1997. pap. text 15.00 (*1-889122-51-3*) Ariel Starr.

Minus Stress: The Mini Book. George E. Soroka. LC 96-96351. 50p. 1997. 7.95 (*1-889122-50-5*, Pub. by Ariel Starr) ACCESS Pubs Network.

Minus Time. 2nd ed. Catherine Bush. (High Risk Ser.). 320p. 1995. pap. 12.99 (*1-85242-408-7*, High Risk Bks) Serpents Tail.

Minus Time: A Novel. Catherine Bush. LC 92-32822. 352p. 1993. 19.45 (*1-56282-881-9*, Pub. by Hyperion) Time Warner.

***Minute beyond This Moment.** Matt Fisk. 40p. 2000. pap. 6.50 (*1-886467-57-9*) WJM Press.

Minute Boys of Bunker Hill. rev. ed. Edward Stratemeyer. LC 98-84149. (Illus.). 316p. (J). (gr. 4-8). 1998. pap. 14.95 (*1-890623-05-9*) Lost Classics.

Minute Boys of Lexington. Edward Stratemeyer. LC 96-77551. (Illus.). x, 294p. (YA). (gr. 4 up). 1997. reprint ed. pap. 14.95 (*0-9652735-3-9*) Lost Classics.

Minute Brand Rice Fast Fabulous Meals. (Favorite All Time Recipes Ser.). (Illus.). 96p. 1993. spiral bd. 3.50 (*1-56173-372-5*, 2007900) Pubns Intl Ltd.

Minute by Minute: A History of the Baltimore Monthly Meetings of Friends, Homewood & Stony Run. Barbara C. Mallonee et al. (Illus.). 308p. (Orig.). 1992. pap. 17.00 (*0-9635053-1-9*) Baltimore Monthly.

Minute DOS. Joseph Addante. (Illus.). 192p. 1997. spiral bd. 24.95 incl. 3.5 hd (*0-9657970-0-7*) EDP Software.

Minute Man: A Ballad of the Shot Heard Round the World. limited ed. Margaret Sidney. (Illus.). 32p. 1991. reprint ed. 25.00 (*0-9627608-1-1*) Estabrook Pr.

Minute Man: A Ballad of the Shot Heard Round the World. Margaret Sidney. (Illus.). 32p. 1991. reprint ed. pap. 11.95 (*0-9627608-0-3*) Estabrook Pr.

Minute Math Drills: Grade 1-3. Ed. by Matthew Lamoreaux. (Illus.). 64p. (J). (gr. 1-3). 1998. pap. text 8.95 (*0-88724-453-X*, CD-0901) Carson-Dellos.

Minute Math Drills: Grade 3-6. Ed. by Matthew Lamoreaux. (Illus.). 64p. (J). (gr. 3-6). 1998. pap. text 8.95 (*0-88724-454-8*, CD-0902) Carson-Dellos.

Minute Meditations for Each Day. Bede Naegele. (Spiritual Life Ser.). 1982. vinyl bd. 6.25 (*0-89942-190-3*, 190/09) Catholic Bk Pub.

Minute Meditations for Men. Bob Barnes. LC 97-44732. 224p. 1998. pap. 9.99 (*1-56507-863-2*) Harvest Hse.

Minute Meditations for Women. Emilie Barnes. LC 99-21701. 250p. 1999. pap. 9.99 (*0-7369-0101-9*) Harvest Hse.

Minute Meditations from the Popes. Jude Winkler. (Illus.). 1993. 6.25 (*0-89942-175-X*, 175/09) Catholic Bk Pub.

Minute Men: The First Fight - Myths & Realities of the American Revolution. John R. Galvin. (Association of the U. S. Army Book Ser.). 279p. 1989. 26.95 (*0-08-036733-X*, 3667M) Brasseys.

Minute Men: The First Fight - Myths & Realities of the American Revolution. John R. Galvin. (Association of the U. S. Army Book Ser.). 279p. 1996. pap. 19.95 (*1-57488-049-7*) Brasseys.

Minute Messages: 60 Seconds of Inspiration. Garnett\Simpson-Grief. 105p. 1998. pap. 10.00 (*1-893425-00-2*) Simnett Pub.

***Minute Minders.** Sue R. Abegglen. (Illus.). 96p. (YA). (gr. 5). 1998. pap. text 10.95 (*1-58037-071-3*, Pub. by M Twain Media) Carson-Dellos.

***Minute Monologues for Kids.** Ruth Mae Roddy. 2000. pap. write for info. (*0-940669-45-5*, Pub. by Dramaline Pubns) Distributors.

Minute Motivator. Rebecca Clark & King Duncan. (Orig.). 1996. pap. write for info. (*0-936497-19-X*) Seven Worlds.

Minute Motivators: Instant Insights for Leaders. Stan Toler. 148p. 1996. pap. 9.99 (*0-8341-1634-0*) Beacon Hill.

***Minute of Angle.** Terri Nice. (Illus.). 132p. 1999. pap. 11.95 (*0-7414-0314-5*) Buy Books.

Minute of Silence. Larry Reiner. LC 90-34659. 268p. 1990. lib. bdg. 18.95 (*0-9626148-0-7*) Integra Pr.

Minute Taker's Handbook. 2nd ed. Jane Watson. (Self-Counsel Reference Ser.). (Illus.). 136p. 1999. pap. 10.95 (*1-55180-236-8*) Self-Counsel Pr.

Minute to Smile. Ruth Wind. (Special Edition Ser.: No. 742). 1992. per. 3.39 (*0-373-09742-5*, 5-09742-3) Harlequin Bks.

Minuteman: Restoring an Army of the People. Gary Hart. LC 98-12302. 224p. 1998. 22.50 (*0-684-83809-5*) S&S Trade.

***Minuteman: The Military Career of General Robert S. Beightler.** John Kennedy Ohl. 280p. (YA). 2000. 59.95 (*1-55587-923-3*) L Rienner.

Minutemen & Their World. Robert A. Gross. (American Century Ser.). 256p. 1976. pap. 12.00 (*0-8090-0120-9*) Hill & Wang.

Minutemen News. unabridged ed. Joseph P. Berry. 326p. (Orig.). 1997. pap. 19.00 (*0-9657898-0-2*) Legend Bks.

Minutes. Simon Mort. 128p. 1991. text 56.95 (*0-566-02708-9*, Pub. by Gower) Ashgate Pub Co.

Minutes & Correspondence of the Academy of Natural Sciences of Philadelphia: 1812-1924, Microfilm Publication Guide. Ed. by Maurice E. Phillips. (Special Publication: No. 7). 92p. (Orig.). 1967. pap. 5.00 (*0-910006-35-0*) Acad Nat Sci Phila.

Minutes & Documents of the Cabinet Meetings of President Eisenhower, 1953-1961. Dwight D. Eisenhower et al. LC 86-892620. (Presidential Documents Ser.). 10p. 1980. write for info. (*0-89093-355-3*) U Pubns Amer.

Minutes & Documents of the Cabinet Meetings of President Johnson. Paul Kesaris. LC 86-892619. (Presidential Documents Ser.). 17 p. 1980. write for info. (*0-89093-387-1*) U Pubns Amer.

Minutes & Report of Committee Recommendations: Census Advisory Committees. 130p. (Orig.). (C). 1994. pap. text 40.00 (*0-7881-0775-5*) DIANE Pub.

Minutes de Sable-Memorial. Alfred Jarry. (FRE.). 249p. 1977. pap. 11.95 (*0-7859-4606-3*) Fr & Eur.

Minutes de Sable-Memorial: Avec: Cesar Antechrist. Alfred Jarry. 1978. 4.50 (*0-686-54208-8*) Fr & Eur.

Minutes de Sable-Memorial: Cesar-Antichrist. Alfred Jarry. (Poesie Ser.). (FRE.). 1977. pap. 9.95 (*2-07-031835-4*) Schoenhof.

Minutes for Men. (Illus.). 36p. (Orig.). 1997. mass mkt. write for info. (*0-9658371-9-X*) M Goloversic.

Minutes from the Blue Route. Tom Donaghy. LC 98-115338. 1997. pap. 5.25 (*0-8222-1608-6*) Dramatists Play.

Minutes from the Great Women's Coffee Club. Angela Beasley. 1997. pap. text 6.95 (*1-887655-33-6*) Walnut Gr Pr.

Minutes of a Conspiracy Against the Liberties of America. William Wightman. LC 79-76554. (Eyewitness Accounts of the American Revolution Ser.). 1969. reprint ed. 13.95 (*0-405-01145-8*) Ayer.

Minutes of Council Northern Department of Rupert Land, 1821-1831. Ed. by R. H. Fleming. (Hudson's Bay Record Society Publications: Vol. 3). 1974. reprint ed. pap. 65.00 (*0-8115-3177-5*) Periodicals Srv.

Minutes of Evidence of the Committee Appointed to Consider & Report Whether Any & What Changes Should Be Made in the Method of Recruiting for, the Conditions of Service of, & the Rates of Pay, Pensions, & Allowances of the Police Forces of England, Wales & Scotland. Police Conditions of Service Committee. LC 70-156282. (Police in Great Britain Ser.). 1971. reprint ed. 72.95 (*0-405-03393-1*) Ayer.

Minutes of Evidence of the Royal Commission upon the Duties of the Metropolitan Police, 3 vols. Royal Commission upon the Duties of the Metropolit. LC 70-156285. (Police in Great Britain Ser.). 1971. reprint ed. 217.95 (*0-405-03396-6*) Ayer.

Minutes of Meetings of the National Security Council. Paul Kesaris et al. LC 88-14424. 5 p. 1988. write for info. (*0-89093-939-X*) U Pubns Amer.

Minutes of Meetings of the National Security Council: With Special Advisory Reports National Security Council (U.S.) Staff et al. LC 86-892100. 3 p. 1982. write for info. (*0-89093-462-2*) U Pubns Amer.

Minutes of Meetings of the National Security Council, 3rd Supplement. 3rd ed. National Security Council (U.S.) Staff et al. LC 96-32873. 1996. suppl. ed. 965.00 (*1-55655-600-4*) U Pubns Amer.

***Minutes of Proceedings of the Joint Committee on Statutory Instruments Session 1: House of Lords Paper 3 Session 1998-99.** (House of Lords Papers (All) Ser.). 1999. 18.00 (*0-10-400399-5*, HM03995, Pub. by Statnry Office) Bernan Associates.

Minutes of Telephone Conversations of John Foster Dulles & of Christian Herter, 1953-1961. John F. Dulles et al. LC 86-892621. (Presidential Documents Ser.). 11 p. 1980. write for info. (*0-89093-356-1*) U Pubns Amer.

Minutes of the Aberdeen Philosophical Society, 1758-1773. Ed. by H. Lewis Ulman. (Illus.). 264p. 1990. pap. text 26.00 (*0-08-040932-6*, Pub. by Aberdeen U Pr) Macmillan.

Minutes of the Board of Proprietors of the Eastern Division of New Jersey from 1685-1705, Vol. I. Board of Proprietor Staff. 280p. 1985. reprint ed. 30.00 (*0-614-30724-4*) NJ Hist Soc.

Minutes of the Board of Proprietors of the Eastern Division of New Jersey from 1764 to 1794, Vol. IV. Ed. by Maxine N. Lurie & Joanne R. Walroth. LC 84-42826. xlii, 522p. 1985. 30.00 (*0-911020-11-X*) NJ Hist Soc.

Minutes of the Commissioners for Detecting & Defeating Conspiracies in the State of New York, 3 vols. in 2, Set. Ed. by Victor H. Paltsits. LC 72-8752. (American Revolutionary Ser.). 1972. reprint ed. lib. bdg. 110.00 (*0-8398-1574-3*) Irvington.

Minutes of the Council & General Court of Colonial Virginia. 2nd ed. Ed. by Henry R. McIlwaine. LC 79-13080. xviii, 668p. 1979. reprint ed. 29.95 (*0-88490-077-0*) Library of VA.

Minutes of the Court of Albany, Rensselaerswyck & Schenectady, 1668-80, 2 vols. Ed. & Tr. by A. J. Van Laer. 886p. 1997. reprint ed. lib. bdg. 94.50 (*0-8328-6096-4*) Higginson Bk Co.

Minutes of the District Court of Nacogdoches County (Texas) Emma B. Reeves. (Minute Bk. A). 152p. (Orig.). 1981. pap. 12.50 (*0-911013-06-7*) E B Reeves.

Minutes of the Executive Board of the Congress of Industrial Organizations, 1935-1955: The Cio & Industrial Unionism in America. Robert H. Zieger et al. LC 94-48460. (Research Collections in Labor Studies). 18p. 1991. write for info. (*1-55655-390-0*) U Pubns Amer.

Minutes of the Executive Boards of the Burgomasters of New Amsterdam. Ed. by Berthold Fernow. LC 71-112544. (Rise of Urban America Ser.). 1970. reprint ed. 13.95 (*0-405-02453-3*) Ayer.

Minutes of the Hudson's Bay Company, 1671-1674. Ed. by E. E. Rich. (Hudson's Bay Record Society Publications: Vol. 5). 1974. reprint ed. pap. 65.00 (*0-8115-3179-1*) Periodicals Srv.

Minutes of the Hudson's Bay Company, 1679-1684, Pt. 1. Ed. by E. E. Rich. (Hudson's Bay Record Society Publications: Vol. 8). 1974. reprint ed. pap. 65.00 (*0-8115-3182-1*) Periodicals Srv.

Minutes of the Last Meeting. Gene Fowler, Jr. 287p. reprint ed. lib. bdg. 23.95 (*0-89190-496-4*, Rivercity Pr) Amereon Ltd.

Minutes of the Lead Pencil Club: Pulling the Plug on the Electronic Revolution. Ed. by Bill Henderson. LC 96-67278. 234p. 1996. 22.00 (*0-916366-84-7*, Pub. by Pushcart Pr) Norton.

Minutes of the Lead Pencil Club: Pulling the Plug on the Electronic Revolution. Ed. by Bill Henderson. LC 96-67278. 234p. 1996. pap. 12.50 (*0-916366-20-0*, Pub. by Pushcart Pr) Norton.

Minutes of the Michigan Commission on Indian Affairs, 1956-1977, Vols. 1 & 2. Ed. by James R. Hillman. 850p. 1991. 89.95 (*0-931649-00-5*); lib. bdg. 79.95 (*0-685-38797-6*) Hillman Pubns.

Minutes of the Presbyterian Church in America, 1706-1788. text. write for info. (*0-685-84634-2*) Presby Hist.

Minutes of the Proceedings of the Greenville Ladies' Association in Aid of the Volunteers of the Confederate Army. Greenville Ladies' Association Staff. Ed. by James W. Patton. LC 77-15995. (Duke University. Trinity College Historical Society. Historical Papers: No. 21). 1970. reprint ed. 30.00 (*0-404-51771-4*) AMS Pr.

Minutes of the Proceedings of the National Negro Conventions, 1830-1864. Ed. by Howard H. Bell. LC 72-105552. (American Negro His History & Literature Ser.: No. 3). 1970. reprint ed. 27.95 (*0-405-01916-5*) Ayer.

Minutes of the Rainbow Circle. Michael Freeden. (Camden Fourth Ser.: No. 38). 390p. 27.00 (*0-86193-120-3*) David Brown.

Minutes of the Testimony Taken Before John Q. Wilson, Joseph Eaton, & Morris Woodruff, Committee from the General Assembly, to Inquire into the Condition of the Connecticut State Prison. Connecticut General Assembly Staff. LC 74-3819. (Criminal Justice in America Ser.). 1974. reprint ed. 15.95 (*0-405-06140-4*) Ayer.

Minutes of the Vestry of St. Helen's Parish, South Carolina, 1726-1812. Alexander S. Salley, Jr. 296p. 1958. reprint ed. 20.00 (*0-89308-295-3*) Southern Hist Pr.

Minutes of the Vienna Psychoanalytic Society, 4 vols. Ed. by Herman Nunberg & Ernst Federn. Incl. Vol. 1. 1906-1908. LC 62-15591. 1963. text 70.00 (*0-8236-3380-2*); Vol. 2. 1908-1910. LC 62-15591. 1963. text 70.00 (*0-8236-3400-0*); Vol. 3. 1910-1911. LC 62-15591. 1963. text 70.00 (*0-8236-3401-9*); Vol. 4. 1912-1918. LC 62-15591. 1963. text 70.00 (*0-8236-3402-7*); LC 62-15591. 1963. text. write for info. (*0-318-53692-7*) Intl Univs Pr.

Minutes to Midnight: Nuclear Weapons Protest in America. Frances B. McCrea. (Violence, Cooperation, & Peace Ser.). 240p. (C). 1989. text 55.00 (*0-8039-3417-3*); pap. text 24.95 (*0-8039-3418-1*) Sage.

Minutiae: Poems from Hollywood. Mark Dunster. 11p. 1998. pap. 5.00 (*0-89642-531-2*) Linden Pubs.

Minutos de Sabiduria. large type ed. Torres Pastorino. (SPA., Illus.). 310p. 1997. pap. 5.98 (*968-13-2342-4*, Pub. by Edit Diana) Libros Fronteras.

Minx. Julia Quinn. LC 96-96077. 352p. 1996. mass mkt. 5.99 (*0-380-78562-5*, Avon Bks) Morrow Avon.

Minx of Mayfair. Bess Willingham. 288p. 1998. pap. 4.99 (*0-8217-5914-0*) Kensgtn Pub Corp.

Minyan: Ten Principles for Living a Life of Integrity. Rabbi R. Shapiro. LC 96-51604. 208p. 1997. pap. 14.00 (*0-609-80055-8*) Bell T.

Minyan Miracle: A Jewish Tradition - A Daily Blessing. I. Alan Cohen. 1993. pap. 9.95 (*1-55673-585-5*) CSS OH.

Minyan of Comfort: Evening Services for the House of Mourning. Ed. by Jonathan D. Levine. 1990. 10.95 (*0-87677-078-2*) Prayer Bk.

Minyans for a Prairie City: The Politics of Chicago Jewry, 1850-1940. Edward H. Mazur. LC 90-3294. (European Immigrants & American Society Ser.). 456p. 1990. reprint ed. text 30.00 (*0-8240-0297-0*) Garland.

Mio & Other Plays for Young People. Shauneille Perry & Donald Jackson. LC 73-92790. (J). (gr. 4 up). 1976. 5.95 (*0-89388-154-6*) Okpaku Communications.

Mio Cid del Taller Alfonsi: Version en Prosa en la Primera Cronica General y en la Cronica. Ed. by Nancy Joe Dyer. (Ediciones Criticas Ser.: Vol. 6). (SPA.). 237p. 1995. 23.00 (*0-936388-72-2*) Juan de la Cuesta.

Mio Cid Studies. Ed. by A. D. Deyermond. (Monagrafias A Ser.: No. 59). (SPA.). 210p. (C). 1977. 51.00 (*0-7293-0023-4*, Pub. by Tamesis Bks Ltd) Boydell & Brewer.

Mio Marito e l'Altra Famiglia: Level A. Dacia Maraini. pap. text 7.95 (*0-88436-922-6*) EMC-Paradigm.

Mio Marito Guglielmo see My Beloved Marconi

Mio Nonno Jack Lo Squartatore see My Grandfather Jack the Ripper

Mio Primo Grieg Piano Solo - My First Grieg: Piano Solo. E. Grieg.Tr. of My First Grieg. (ITA.). 1987. pap. 5.95 (*0-7935-5529-9*) H Leonard.

Miocene & Oligocene Petroleum Reservoirs of the Santa Maria & Santa Barbara-Ventura Basins, California. Ed. by Margaret A. Keller & Mary K. McGowen. (Core Workshop Notes Ser.: No. 14). (Illus.). 400p. (Orig.). 1990. pap. text 62.00 (*0-918985-84-6*) SEPM.

***Miocene Arrow.** Sean McMullen. 2000. pap. write for info. (*0-312-87547-9*) St Martin.

***Miocene Arrow.** Sean McMullen. 416p. 2000. 27.95 (*0-312-87054-X*, Pub. by Tor Bks) St Martin.

Miocene Floras from the Middlegate Basin, West-Central Nevada. Daniel I. Axelrod. LC 84-2414. (University of California Publications in Entomology: No. 129). 311p. 1985. pap. 96.50 (*0-7837-7467-2*, 204918900010) Bks Demand.

Miocene Foraminifera of the Coastal Plain of the Eastern U. S. J. A. Cushman & E. D. Cahill. 1971. reprint ed. 15.00 (*0-934454-64-7*) Lubrecht & Cramer.

Miocene Mammals of the Split Rock Area, Granite Mountains Basin, & Central Wyoming. Jens Munthe. (UC Publications in Geological Sciences). 1989. pap. 25.00 (*0-520-09706-8*, Pub. by U CA Pr) Cal Prin Full Svc.

Miocene Non-Marine Diatoms from the Yakima Region in South Central Washington. S. L. Van Landingham. (Illus.). 1965. pap. 28.00 (*3-7682-5414-3*) Lubrecht & Cramer.

Miocene Ocean: Paleoceanography & Biogeography. Ed. by James P. Kennett. LC 85-14851. (Geological Society of America Ser.: Vol. 163). (Illus.). 353p. 1985. reprint ed. pap. 109.50 (*0-608-07713-5*, 206780100010) Bks Demand.

Miocene Purple Mountain Flora of Western Nevada. Daniel I. Axelrod. LC 94-32291. (University of California Publications in Geological Sciences Ser.: No. 139). 1995. 16.95 (*0-520-09797-1*, Pub. by U CA Pr) Cal Prin Full Svc.

Miocene Stratigraphy: An Integrated Approach, Vol. 15. Ed. by Alessandro Montanari et al. LC 97-19654. (Developments in Palaeontology & Stratigraphy Ser.). 694p. 1997. 247.00 (*0-444-82498-7*) Elsevier.

Miocene Stratigraphy of California. Robert M. Kleinpell. LC 39-3024. (Illus.). 526p. reprint ed. pap. 163.10 (*0-608-08733-5*, 206937200004) Bks Demand.

***Miocene (10-12 MA) Evergreen Laurel-Oak Forest from Carmel Valley, California.** Daniel I. Axelrod. LC 00-21952. (Publications in Geological Sciences: Vol. 145). (Illus.). 36p. 2000. pap. 13.00 (*0-520-09839-0*, Pub. by U CA Pr) Cal Prin Full Svc.

***Miorita: An Icon of Romanian Culture.** Ed. by Ernest H. Latham, Jr. (Illus.). 96p. 1999. 49.95 (*973-9432-04-2*, Pub. by Ctr Romanian Studies) Intl Spec Bk.

***Mipam: The First Tibetan Novel.** 4th rev. ed. Lama Yongden. LC 99-52397. (Illus.). 396p. 1999. pap. text 12.95 (*0-943389-33-X*) Snow Lion-SLG Bks.

***Mipham's Beacon of Certainty: Illuminating the View of Dzogchen, the Great Perfection.** John W. Pettit. LC 99-33810. (Studies in Indian & Tibetan Buddhism: Vol. 2). 576p. 1999. pap. 28.95 (*0-86171-157-2*, Pub. by Wisdom MA) Natl Bk Netwk.

MIPS Programmer's Handbook. Erin Farquhar & Philip J. Bunce. LC 94-396. 562p. (Orig.). (C). 1993. pap. text 48.95 (*1-55860-297-6*) Morgan Kaufmann.

MIPS RISC Architecture. 2nd ed. Gerry Kane & Joseph Heinrich. 544p. 1991. pap. 66.00 (*0-13-590472-2*) P-H.

MIPS RISC Architecture Siemens. Kane Stry. 352p. 1999. pap. text. write for info. (*0-13-584210-7*) P-H.

MIPS R4000 User's Manual. Silicon Graphics Incorporated Staff. 1993. pap. text 48.00 (*0-13-105925-4*) P-H.

MIPS-X RISC Microprocessor. Ed. by Paul Chow. (C). 1989. text 126.00 (*0-7923-9045-8*) Kluwer Academic.

Miqueas: Profeta para Latino America. Fernando Santillana. LC 97-35837. (SPA.). 186p. 1997. 74.95 (*1-57309-194-4*) Intl Scholars.

Miqueas: Profeta para Latino America. Fernando B. Santillana. LC 97-35837. (SPA.). 108p. 1997. pap. 54.95 (*1-57309-193-6*) Intl Scholars.

Miquel Barcelo, 1987-1997. Pep Subiros et al. (Illus.). 302p. 1998. 38.00 (*84-89698-82-1*, Pub. by Actar) Dist Art Pubs.

Miquon Math Lab Series: Complete Home School. rev. ed. Lore Rasmussen. Incl. Blue Book. 1977. pap. text 5.95 (*0-913684-52-X*); First Grade Diary. Robert Hightower. 218p. 1977. 5.95 (*0-913684-67-8*); Green Book. 1977. pap. text 5.95 (*0-913684-53-8*); Lab Sheet Annotations. Peter Rasmussen & Robert Hightower. 372p. 1977. 13.95 (*0-913684-64-3*); Notes to Teachers. 53p. 1977. 3.95 (*0-913684-62-7*); Orange Book. 1977. pap. text 5.95 (*0-913684-50-3*); Purple Book. 1977. pap. text 5.95 (*0-913684-55-4*); Red Book. 1977. pap. text 5.95 (*0-913684-51-1*); Yellow Book. 1977. pap. text 5.95 (*0-913684-54-6*); (J). (gr. 1-4). 1977. 53.95 (*1-55953-195-9*) Key Curr Pr.

Mir: A Novel of Virtual Reality. Alexander Besher. LC 98-3496. 320p. 1998. 23.00 (*0-684-83087-6*) S&S Trade.

Mir Rusky: The World of the Russians. ACTR Staff. 504p. 1997. text 54.95 (*0-7872-2471-5*, 41247101) Kendall-Hunt.

An Asterisk (*) at the beginning of an entry indicates that the title is appearing for the first time.

Mir Russkikh: The World of the Russians Exercise Book. Corlac. 192p. 1997. per. 29.95 (*0-7872-2733-1*, 41273301) Kendall-Hunt.

Mir Space Station. Neal Bernards. LC 98-18246. (Above & Beyond Ser.). (Illus.). 32p. (YA). (gr. 4 up). 2000. lib. bdg. 21.30 (*1-58340-049-4*) Smart Apple.

Mir Taqi Mir: Selected Poetry. K. C. Kanda. (C). 1997. write for info. (*81-207-1850-X*) Sterling Pubs.

Mir Trogn A Gezang Yiddish Songbook: Favorite Yiddish Songs. Eleanor G. Mlotek. 239p. 1977. pap. 19.95 (*0-685-05910-3*) Jwsh Bk Ctr Wrkmns Cir.

***Mira.** Michael Grejniec. Tr. by Alis Alejandro. LC 99-18977.Tr. of Look. (SPA., Illus.). 32p. (J). (ps-2). 1999. pap. 6.95 (*0-7358-1207-1*, Pub. by North-South Bks NYC) Chronicle Bks.

***Mira.** Michael Grejniec. Tr. by Alis Alejandro. LC 99-18977.Tr. of Look. (SPA., Illus.). 32p. (J). (ps-3). 1999. 15.95 (*0-7358-1206-3*, Pub. by North-South Bks NYC) Chronicle Bks.

***Mira & the Stone Tortoise.** Melinda Lilly & Charles Reasoner. LC 99-12113. 1999. write for info. (*1-57103-264-9*) Rourke Pr.

Mira Calligraphiae Monumenta: A 16th-Century Calligraphic Manus. Lee Hendrix & Thea Vignau-Wilberg. LC 91-42741. (Illus.). 412p. 1992. 135.00 (*0-89236-212-X*, Pub. by J P Getty Trust) OUP.

Mira Conquistador. Martin Ancel. 1974. 19.95 (*0-685-52987-8*); pap. 15.95 (*0-930400-00-3*) Pleasure Trove.

Mira los Colores. (Mi Gran Librito Gordo Ser.). (SPA.). 1995. bds. 2.98 (*1-85854-300-2*) Brimax Bks.

Mira Que Luna. May Garelick. (SPA., Illus.). (J). (ps-3). 1998. pap. 4.95 (*1-57255-510-6*) Mondo Pubng.

Mira y Escucha. (Mi Gran Librito Gordo Ser.). (SPA.). 1995. bds. 2.98 (*1-85854-299-5*) Brimax Bks.

Mirabeau. Barbara Luttrell. LC 90-39621. 317p. (C). 1990. 36.95 (*0-8093-1705-2*) S Ill U Pr.

Mirabeau. Louis Barthou. LC 72-7091. (Select Bibliographies Reprint Ser.). 1977. reprint ed. 26.95 (*0-8369-6923-5*) Ayer.

Mirabeau. Antonina Vallentin. Tr. by E. W. Dickes. LC 70-122070. (Illus.). vi, 542p. 1973. reprint ed. 49.50 (*0-678-03173-8*) Kelley.

Mirabeau B. Lamar: President of Texas. Elizabeth D. Morgan. LC 94-2641. (Illus.). 96p. (J). (gr. 4-5). 1995. 12.95 (*0-89015-963-7*, Eakin Pr) Sunbelt Media.

Mirabeau Buonaparte Lamar, Troubadour & Crusader. Herbert P. Cambrell. 1993. reprint ed. lib. bdg. 75.00 (*0-7812-5930-4*) Rprt Serv.

Mirabelle House. George Bedard. Ed. by Mary Inbody & Dahk Knox. (Illus.). 116p. 1996. pap. 11.95 (*1-881116-83-2*) Black Forest Pr.

Mirabelle's Country Club for Cats & Other Poems. Norma Sadler. (Illus.). 48p. (J). (gr. 2-7). 1986. pap. 9.95 (*0-9617206-0-3*) Riverstone Pr.

Mirabilia. James D. Sanderson. LC 95-67197. 265p. 1995. pap. 13.95 (*1-884787-01-0*) Colonia Bks.

Mirabilia Urbis Romae see Marvels of Rome

Mirable Dictu: Representations of the Marvelous in Medieval & Renaissance Epic. Douglas Biow. LC 96-3475. (Stylus Ser.). (Illus.). 216p. (C). 1996. text 42.50 (*0-472-10691-0*, 10691) U of Mich Pr.

Miracle on 34th Star. Valentine Davies. LC 98-72387. (Illus.). 144p. (ps-3). 1998. 9.99 (*1-57866-027-0*) Galahad Bks.

Miracle. Ed. by Wolfgang Hageney. (ENG, FRE, GER, ITA & SPA., Illus.). 112p. 1984. pap. 21.95 (*88-7070-040-2*) Belvedere USA.

Miracle. Muriel Jensen. (Men at Work Ser.: Vol. 36). 1998. mass mkt. 4.50 (*0-373-81048-2*, 1-81048-0) Harlequin Bks.

Miracle. Osho. LC 97-208944. (Zen Ser.). 288p. 1989. 12.95 (*3-89338-053-1*, Pub. by Rebel Hse) Oshos.

Miracle. Deborah Smith. 464p. 1991. mass mkt. 6.50 (*0-553-29107-6*) Bantam.

Miracle. Katherine Sutcliffe. 384p. (Orig.). 1995. mass mkt. 6.50 (*0-515-11546-0*, Jove) Berkley Pub.

***Miracle: The Story of the First Christmas.** Kelly S. Heaps & Susan Dunn. LC 99-43477. (Holy Bear's Travel Ser.). (Illus.). 32p. (J). (gr. k-5). 1999. pap. 7.95 (*1-885628-31-5*) Buckaroo Bks.

Miracle a Day. Spangle. (SPA.). 1996. 10.95 (*0-8297-0354-3*) Vida Pubs.

Miracle a Day: Stories of Heavenly Encounters. Ann Spangler. 192p. 1996. 13.99 (*0-310-20794-0*) Zondervan.

Miracle a Universe. Lawrence Wechler. LC 97-52199. 311p. 1998. pap. 15.00 (*0-226-89394-4*) U Ch Pr.

Miracle after Miracle. Tom Fettke & Linda Rebuck. 68p. 1982. 5.99 (*0-8341-9474-0*, MB-505) Lillenas.

Miracle & a Privilege: Recounting a Half-Century of Surgical Advance. Francis D. Moore. (Illus.). 488p. (Orig.). (C). 1995. 29.95 (*0-309-05188-6*, Joseph Henry Pr) Natl Acad Pr.

***Miracle & Mission: The Authentication of Missionaries & Their Message in the Longer Ending of Mark.** James A. Kelhoffer. (Wissenshaftliche Untersuchungen zum Neuen Testament Ser.). 570p. 1999. 117.50 (*3-16-147243-8*, Pub. by JCB Mohr) Coronet Bks.

***Miracle & Other Christmas Stories.** Connie Willis. LC 99-15686. 336p. 1999. 19.95 (*0-553-11111-6*) Bantam.

***Miracle & Other Christmas Stories.** Connie Willis. 2000. mass mkt. 6.99 (*0-553-58048-5*) Bantam.

Miracle & the Tree. Joe Winter. Date not set. pap. 7.95 (*0-900977-54-X*, Pub. by Anvil Press) Dufour.

Miracle Art: Trick Cartoons. Vic Lockman. (Illus.). 48p. (Orig.). (YA). (gr. 8 up). 1992. pap. 6.00 (*0-936175-19-2*) V Lockman.

Miracle at Blowing Rock. Wanda Z. Larson. Ed. by Ruth Bard. (Illus.). 20p. (Orig.). 1992. pap. 4.95 (*0-9628584-2-0*) Blue Uncrn.

Miracle at Clements' Pond. Patricia Pendergraft. LC 86-30283. 192p. (J). (gr. 5 up). 1987. pap. 13.95 (*0-399-21438-0*, Philomel) Peng Put Young Read.

Miracle at Crowhurst. Ed. by George Bennett. (C). 1990. pap. 40.00 (*0-85305-178-X*, Pub. by Arthur James) St Mut.

Miracle at Indian River. Alden Nowlan. 132p. 1982. pap. 8.95 (*0-7720-1402-7*) Genl Dist Srvs.

Miracle at Kitty Hawk: The Letters of Wilbur & Orville Wright. Wilbur Wright & Orville Wright. Ed. by Fred C. Kelly. (Illus.). 508p. 1996. pap. 16.95 (*0-306-80671-1*) Da Capo.

Miracle at Kitty Hawk: The Letters of Wilbur & Orville Wright. Ed. by Fred C. Kelly. LC 74-169424. (Literature & History of Aviation Ser.). 1979. reprint ed. 30.95 (*0-405-03769-4*) Ayer.

***Miracle at Manassas.** Martin Harmon. 112p. 2000. pap. write for info. (*0-8059-4967-4*) Dorrance.

Miracle at Midway. Gordon W. Prange et al. (Illus.). 384p. 1983. pap. 18.95 (*0-14-006814-7*, Penguin Bks) Viking Penguin.

Miracle at Philadelphia. Catherine D. Bowen. 368p. Date not set. 26.95 (*0-8488-2565-9*) Amereon Ltd.

Miracle at Philadelphia: The Story of the Constitutional Convention, May to September 1787. Catherine D. Bowen. 346p. 1986. reprint ed. pap. 16.95 (*0-316-10398-5*) Little.

Miracle at San Juan. Richard Tevis. (Illus.). 64p. (Orig.). 1983. pap. 5.95 (*0-930277-00-7*) Tres Amigos Pubns.

***Miracle at Sea: The Sinking of the Zamzam & Our Family's Astrounding Rescue.** Eleanor Anderson. (Illus.). 148p. 2000. pap. 16.00 (*0-9663966-3-4*) Quiet Waters.

Miracle at the Manger. H. Owen. 1990. pap. 6.95 (*1-55897-038-X*) Brentwood Music.

Miracle at the Plate. Matt Christopher. (Illus.). 129p. (J). (gr. 3-6). 1989. pap. 3.95 (*0-316-13926-2*) Little.

Miracle at the Plate. Matt Christopher. (J). 1967. 9.05 (*0-606-04275-X*, Pub. by Turtleback) Demco.

Miracle at Willowcreek. Annette LeBox. (Illus.). 172p. 1998. pap. 7.95 (*1-896764-04-5*, Pub. by Sec Story Pr) LPC InBook.

Miracle at Woolworth's. Ellen T. Johnston-Hale. 65p. Date not set. pap. 8.95 (*1-879934-15-9*) St Andrews NC.

Miracle Baby. Shawna Delacorte. (Desire Ser.). 1995. per. 2.99 (*0-373-05905-1*, 1-05905-4) Silhouette.

Miracle Baby. Janice K. Johnson. (Nine Months Later Ser.). 1997. per. 3.99 (*0-373-70736-3*, 1-70736-3) Harlequin Bks.

Miracle Birth Stories of Very Premature Babies: Little Thumbs Up! Timothy Smith. LC 98-36762. 216p. 1999. pap. 15.95 (*0-89789-635-1*, Bergin & Garvey) Greenwood.

Miracle Child. Kayla Daniels. (Special Edition Ser.). 1994. per. 3.50 (*0-373-09911-8*, 1-09911-8) Harlequin Bks.

Miracle Child: Genetic Mother, Surrogate Womb. Cheryl Saban. LC 92-85167. 268p. 1993. pap. 14.95 (*0-88282-172-5*) New Horizon NJ.

Miracle Children. Duncan Dyason. 1998. pap. 6.99 (*0-340-72184-7*, Pub. by Hodder & Stought Ltd) Trafalgar.

Miracle Christ see Cristo de los Milagros

Miracle Cure. Michael Palmer. LC 98-4884. 496p. 1999. reprint ed. mass mkt. 7.50 (*0-553-57662-3*) Bantam.

Miracle Cure: A Novel. large type ed. Michael Palmer. LC 98-24433. 1998. 26.95 (*1-56895-612-6*) Wheeler Pub.

Miracle Cures: Dramatic New Scientific Discoveries Revealing the Healing Powers of Herbs, Vitamins, & Other Natural Remedies. Jean Carper. 308p. 1998. text 25.00 (*0-7881-5907-0*) DIANE Pub.

Miracle Cures: Dramatic New Scientific Discoveries Revealing the Healing Powers of Herbs, Vitamins, & Other Natural Remedies. Jean Carper. LC 97-13747. 320p. 1998. pap. 14.00 (*0-06-098436-8*, Perennial) HarperTrade.

Miracle Cures: Dramatic New Scientific Discoveries Revealing the Healing Powers of Herbs, Vitamins, & Other Natural Remedies. abr. ed. Jean Carper. 1997. audio 12.00 (*0-694-51848-4*, CPN 10112) HarperAudio.

Miracle Cures: Dramatic New Scientific Discoveries Revealing the Healing Powers of Herbs, Vitamins, & Other Natural Remedies. large type ed. Jean Carper. LC 97-43877. (Large Print Bks.). 1998. 26.95 (*1-56895-516-2*) Wheeler Pub.

Miracle Cures for the New Millennium. I. Am. (God's Words for the New Millennium Ser.: Vol. 9). (Illus.). Date not set. pap. 19.95 (*1-892177-59-5*, Lightning Source) Heaven Earth.

Miracle Dad. Toni Collins. 1997. per. 42.00 (*0-373-91008-8*) Silhouette.

Miracle de la Rose. Jean Genet. (FRE.). 1977. pap. 11.95 (*0-8288-3648-5*, M5696) Fr & Eur.

Miracle de la Rose. Jean Genet. (Folio Ser.: No. 887). (FRE.). pap. 9.95 (*2-07-036887-4*) Schoenhof.

Miracle Diet. Carol Rumens. 64p. 1998. pap. 15.95 (*1-85224-418-6*, Pub. by Bloodaxe Bks) Dufour.

Miracle Diet: 14 Days to New Vigor & Health. Earl F. Updike. 282p. (Orig.). 1995. pap. 12.95 (*1-887437-00-2*) Best Possible Hlth.

Miracle Diet Cookbook. Ethel C. Updike & Earl F. Updike. 464p. (Orig.). 1995. pap. 16.95 (*1-887437-01-0*) Best Possible Hlth.

Miracle Drugs: How They Work & What You Should Know about Them. Frank Minirth et al. 312p. 1996. pap. 12.99 (*0-7852-7865-6*) Nelson.

***Miracle Evangelism.**Tr. of Evangelismo de Milagres. (POR.). 110p. 1999. spiral bd. 12.95 (*0-941975-50-9*) Powerhouse.

Miracle Evangelism. John Ezekiel. (SPA.). 110p. (Orig.). 1993. spiral bd. 12.95 (*0-941975-17-7*) Powerhouse.

Miracle Evangelism: God's Plan to Reach the World. John Ezekiel. 112p. 1996. reprint ed. pap. 9.95 (*0-941975-38-X*) Powerhouse.

Miracle Every Day: Triumph & Transformation in the Lives of Single Mothers. Marita Golden. LC 98-30942. 144p. 1999. pap. 9.95 (*0-385-48315-5*, Anchor NY) Doubleday.

Miracle Exercises That Can Save Your Life! 11th rev. ed. Edwin Flatto. Orig. Title: Encyclopedia of Therapeutic Exercises. (Illus.). 394p. 1998. pap. 19.95 (*0-935540-05-9*) Plymouth Pr.

Miracle Food Cures from the Bible. Reese P. Dubin. LC 99-19393. xix, 410p. 1999. text 24.95 (*0-13-621269-7*) P-H.

Miracle Food of the East: The Story of the Wakame Spore. Alex Durate. 95p. 1995. pap. text 8.00 (*1-891036-02-5*) Nutri Tapes.

Miracle Foods Cookbook: Easy, Low-Cost Recipes & Menus with Antioxidant Rich Vegetables & Fruits That Help You Lose Weight, Enhance Your Immune System, Fight Disease, & Slow the Aging Process. M. J. Smith. 304p. 1994. pap. 12.95 (*1-56561-056-3*) Wiley.

Miracle Foods Cookbook: Easy, Low-Cost Recipes & Menus with Antioxidant Rich Vegetables & Fruits That Help You Lose Weight, Enhance Your Immune System, Fight Disease, & Slow the Aging Process. M. J. Smith. 304p. 1995. pap. 12.95 (*0-471-34687-X*) Wiley.

Miracle for a Madonna. large type ed. Barbara Cartland. (Magna Large Print Ser.). 227p. 1997. 27.99 (*0-7505-1108-7*, Pub. by Mgna Lrg Print) Ulverscroft.

Miracle for Bryan. Jude Randal. (Romance Ser.). 1994. pap. 2.75 (*0-373-08986-4*, 5-08986-7) Silhouette.

Miracle for Christmas. Grace Green. (Romance Ser.: No. 404). 1998. pap. 3.50 (*0-373-17404-7*, 1-17404-4) Harlequin Bks.

Miracle for Our Time: Studies in Esoteric Christianity. Lona Truding. 96p. 1994. pap. 12.95 (*0-904693-22-8*, Pub. by Temple Lodge) Anthroposophic.

Miracle for Your Marriage. John Osteen. 32p. 1988. mass mkt. 1.50 (*0-912631-38-4*) J O Pubns.

Miracle from the Streets. Cherie A. Potts. LC 96-34387. 160p. 1997. pap. 10.99 (*0-8163-1360-1*) Pacific Pr Pub Assn.

Miracle Game. Josef Skvorecky. 435p. 1992. pap. 10.95 (*0-393-30849-9*) Norton.

Miracle Hand Around the World. Anna E. McGhie. 1989. pap. 8.99 (*0-88019-251-8*) Schmul Pub Co.

Miracle Healing Foods. Heinerman. 1998. text 27.95 (*0-13-012577-6*) P-H.

Miracle Healing from China . . . Qugong. Effie Chow. LC 94-96177. 258p. 1994. pap. 15.95 (*0-9636979-5-1*) MediPress.

Miracle Healing Power of Chelation Therapy. Intro. by Morton Walker. (Illus.). 257p. 1984. 18.95 (*0-915421-00-3*) Fischer Pub.

Miracle Healing Power Through Nature's Pharmacy. William L. Fischer. Ed. by Juilene McKnight-Osborne. LC 85-81689. (Illus.). 202p. (Orig.). 1986. pap. 17.95 (*0-915421-04-6*) Fischer Pub.

Miracle Heart: The Ultimate Guide to Preventing & Curing Heart Disease with Diet & Supplements. Jean Carper. 336p. 2000. mass mkt. 5.99 (*0-06-101383-8*) HarpC.

Miracle Heidi: When Doctors Couldn't . . . God Could! Vickie B. Watson. (Illus.). 272p. (Orig.). (YA). 1996. pap. 12.99 (*0-9654974-0-2*) Sterling Pr Int.

Miracle Herbs. Stephen Holt. LC 98-4556. 208p. 1998. 19.95 (*1-55972-463-3*, Birch Ln Pr) Carol Pub Group.

***Miracle Herbs: How Herbs Combine With Modern Medicine to Treat Cancer, Heart Disease & Aids.** Stephen Holt. 1999. pap. 14.95 (*0-8065-2124-4*, Citadel Pr) Carol Pub Group.

Miracle Hormones . . . Naturally. Paul Yanick. 256p. 1998. pap. 13.00 (*1-57566-197-7*, Knsington) Kensgtn Pub Corp.

Miracle Hour: A Method of Prayer That Will Change Your Life. 14th ed. Linda Schubert. 39p. (Orig.). 1991. reprint ed. pap. 2.00 (*0-9632643-0-3*) L Schubert.

Miracle in a Shoe Box. Franklin Graham. (Illus.). 32p. (J). (ps-4). 1998. pap. 7.97 (*0-7852-6034-X*) Tommy Nelson.

Miracle in Bethlehem. Lynda F. Richwine. 24p. 1969. pap. 4.50 (*0-8341-9725-1*) Nazarene.

Miracle in Bethlehem. Lynda R. Richwine. 1969. 4.99 (*0-685-68589-6*, MC-21) Lillenas.

Miracle in Darien. Bob Slosser. LC 79-83791. 268p. 1985. pap. 10.99 (*0-88270-427-3*) Bridge-Logos.

Miracle in East Harlem. S. W. Fliegel & M. MacGuire. 1994. pap. 12.00 (*0-8129-6354-7*) Random.

Miracle in Milan. Vittorio De Sica. LC 68-30777. (Illus.). 120p. 1968. 16.95 (*0-910278-09-1*) Boulevard.

Miracle in Motion. S. Storey. 1995. pap. 8.00 (*0-927936-33-X*) Vincom Pubng Co.

Miracle in My Arms: Prayers for a New Mother. Shelley S. Sateren. 160p. 1995. pap. 9.99 (*0-8066-2726-3*, 9-2726) Augsburg Fortress.

Miracle in Natal: Revolution by Ballot-Box. Ed. by Alan Thorold. (Pamphlets Ser.: No. 7). 64p. 1995. pap. text 5.00 (*1-891754-06-8*) Prickly Pear Pmphlts NA.

***Miracle in New York.** Donn Clendenon. (Illus.). 190p. 1999. pap. write for info. (*1-57579-167-6*) Pine Hill Pr.

***Miracle in Paradise.** Carolina Garcia-Aguilera. (Lupe Solano Mystery Ser.). 352p. 2000. mass mkt. 5.99 (*0-380-80738-6*) Morrow Avon.

***Miracle in Paradise: A Lupe Solano Mystery, Vol. 1.** Carolina Garcia-Aguilera. LC 99-32209. (Lupe Solano Mystery Ser.). 288p. 1999. 23.00 (*0-380-97779-6*, Avon Bks) Morrow Avon.

Miracle in Seville. James A. Michener. LC 94-10187. (Illus.). 1995. 25.00 (*0-685-72068-3*) Random.

Miracle in Stone: The Great Pyramid of Egypt. Joseph A. Seiss. 250p. 1996. reprint ed. spiral bd. 17.50 (*0-7873-0762-9*) Hlth Research.

Miracle in Stone: or The Great Pyramid of Egypt, 1877. Joseph A. Seiss. 250p. 1996. reprint ed. pap. 16.50 (*1-56459-820-9*) Kessinger Pub.

Miracle in the Bethlehem Inn. Mary L. Warstler. 1996. pap. 6.50 (*1-55673-634-7*) CSS OH.

Miracle in the Christmas City: Playscript. Nellie McCaslin. LC 93-2602. 16p. (J). 1993. pap. 5.00 (*0-88734-437-2*) Players Pr.

Miracle in the Cornfield. Joseph Trombello. (Illus.). 210p. 1999. pap. 14.95 (*0-9669815-1-0*) J Trombello.

Miracle in the Cornfield. Joseph Trombello. Ed. by Sara McPherson. Tr. by Al Haynes. (Illus.). 210p. 1999. text 23.95 (*0-9669815-0-2*) J Trombello.

Miracle in the Early Christian World: A Study in Sociohistorical Method. Howard C. Kee. LC 83-4004. 332p. reprint ed. pap. 103.00 (*0-7837-2350-4*, 208024900004) Bks Demand.

Miracle in the Glass. Ruthann Crosby. Ed. by Ellen F. Godfrey et al. (Illus.). 32p. (Orig.). 1996. pap. 19.95 incl. audio (*0-9649962-0-0*) Gabriels Gthrings.

Miracle in the Glass: To Save a Life Is to Save the World. large type ed. Ruthann Crosby. (Illus.). 48p. (J). (gr. 3-6). 1998. pap. 14.95 (*1-888125-26-8*) Publ Consult.

Miracle in the Making. William Floyd & Bruce Hayman. 220p. 1995. 11.00 (*0-614-06705-7*) Budlong.

Miracle in the Mirror. Mark Buntain et al. LC 81-70999. (Illus.). 16p. 1982. reprint ed. mass mkt. 4.99 (*0-87123-352-5*) Bethany Hse.

M

***Miracle in the Morning.** Mary Erickson. 32p. 2000. 12.99 (*0-7814-3386-X*) Chariot Victor.

Miracle in the Morning: The Wonderful Story of Easter. Mary E. Erickson. LC 92-20260. 32p. (J). 1994. 11.99 (*0-7814-0779-6*, Chariot Bks) Chariot Victor.

Miracle in the Void: Free Energy, UFO's & Other Scientific Revelations. Brian O'Leary. 262p. 1997. pap. 9.95 (*0-9647826-0-X*) Kamapua a Pr.

***Miracle in You.** Arethia Gilliam. 80p. 1999. pap. 10.00 (*1-892525-14-3*) ACW Press.

Miracle in Your Mouth. rev. ed. Mike Francen. (Illus.). 94p. (J). (gr. 7). 1998. pap. 6.00 (*1-888079-16-9*) Francen Wrld.

Miracle Language. Richard Lederer. 272p. 1999. pap. 12.00 (*0-671-02811-1*, PB Trade Paper) PB.

Miracle Maker. Mary Joslin. LC 99-203696. 1999. 12.99 (*0-7459-4081-1*) Lion USA.

Miracle Makers: Miraculous Stories, Prayer & Praise. Mary Talken. 144p. (Orig.). 1997. text 8.95 (*0-9619510-4-4*); pap. text 5.95 (*0-9619510-3-6*) M Talken.

Miracle Man. Terry Bisson. (X-Files Ser.). 144p. (J). 1998. pap. 4.50 (*0-06-447192-6*) HarpC Child Bks.

Miracle Man. Nolan Ryan. 314p. 1993. mass mkt. 5.99 (*0-8499-3507-5*) Word Pub.

Miracle Man. Sharon Sala. (Intimate Moments Ser.). 1995. per. 3.75 (*0-373-07650-9*, 1-07650-4) Silhouette.

***Miracle Man: A Novel.** Ben Shrank. LC 98-47671. 304p. 1999. pap. 13.00 (*0-688-16771-3*, Wm Morrow) Morrow Avon.

Miracle Man: Nolan Ryan, the Autobiography. large type ed. Nolan Ryan & Jerry Jenkins. LC 92-33582. 333p. 1993. 16.95 (*0-8161-5606-9*, G K Hall & Co) Mac Lib Ref.

Miracle Man of Japan: The Life & Work of Masaharu Taniguchi, One of the Most Influential Spiritual Leaders of Our Time. Roy E. Davis. (Illus.). 160p. (Orig.). pap. 3.00 (*0-87707-048-2*) CSA Pr.

Miracle Manual: An Evangelism & Prayer Handbook for the 1 Million Souls Campaign. R. W. Schambach. 306p. 1996. pap. 15.00 (*1-888361-11-5*) Power Publns.

Miracle Meals: 8 Nights of Chanukah Food & Fun. Madeline Wikler & Judye Groner. LC 87-17325. (Illus.). 64p. (J). (gr. k up). 1987. spiral bd. 6.95 (*0-930494-71-7*) Kar-Ben.

Miracle Medicine Foods. Rex Adams. 228p. (C). 1979. pap. text 9.95 (*0-13-585471-7*) P-H.

Miracle Medicine Herbs. Richard M. Lucas. 224p. (C). 1991. text 24.95 (*0-13-585142-4*, Busn); pap. text 10.95 (*0-13-585134-3*, Busn) P-H.

Miracle Medicines of the Rainforest: A Doctor's Revolutionary Work with Cancer & AIDS Patients. Thomas David. Tr. by J. Michal Beasley from GER. LC 97-22873. (Illus.). 144p. 1997. pap. 19.95 (*0-89281-746-1*) Inner Tradit.

Miracle Method: A Radically New Approach to Problem Drinking. Scott Miller. 192p. 1996. pap. 13.00 (*0-393-31533-9*) Norton.

Miracle Method: A Radically New Approach to Problem Drinking. Scott D. Miller & Insoo K. Berg. 160p. 1995. 19.95 (*0-393-03740-1*) Norton.

Miracle Mile. Ed Ochester. LC 83-72900. 1984. pap. 11.95 (*0-915604-89-2*) Carnegie-Mellon.

Miracle Mile. Ed Ochester. LC 83-72900. 1984. 20.95 (*0-915604-88-4*) Carnegie-Mellon.

Miracle Ministry of the Prophet. Christian Harfouche. 100p. (Orig.). 1993. pap. text 9.00 (*0-9634451-5-4*) Power House Pub.

Miracle Mirrored: The Dutch Republic in European Perspective. Ed. by Karel Davids & Jan Lucassen. (Illus.). 559p. (C). 1996. text 80.00 (*0-521-46247-9*) Cambridge U Pr.

Miracle Moments. J. Jason Browne. (Illus.). 176p. (Orig.). 1994. pap. 11.95 (*0-9642667-0-9*) Visionary Pr.

Miracle Moments. Linda Schubert. (Orig.). 1999. pap. 2.00 (*0-9632643-5-4*) L Schubert.

Miracle Mongers & Their Methods: A Complete Expose. Harry Houdini. LC 92-43234. (Illus.). 256p. (C). 1993. reprint ed. pap. 17.95 (*0-87975-817-1*) Prometheus Bks.

***Miracle Mountain: Where Volunteers Left Their Mark.** D. Jay Walsh. (Illus.). 132p. 1998. pap. 7.95 (*1-888796-15-4*) ABWE Pubng.

Miracle Muffins: Amazingly Delicious Treats Without All That Fat! Patty A. Neeley. (Illus.). 160p. 1996. pap., per. 12.00 (0-7615-0423-0) Prima Pub.

Miracle Named Jesus. Gary Holloway. LC 97-1838. 1997. pap. 7.99 (0-89900-780-5) College Pr Pub.

Miracle Nutrient: Coenzyme Q10. Emile G. Bliznakov & Gerry Hunt. 256p. 1986. mass mkt. 6.99 (0-553-26233-5) Bantam.

Miracle Nutrient Cookbook. Tamara Holt. 1995. pap. 12.00 (0-671-89893-0, Fireside) S&S Trade Pap.

Miracle Nutrient Cookbook: 100 Delicious Antioxidant-Enriched Recipes & Menu Suggestions for Optimum Health. Tamara Holt & Maureen Callahan. LC 95-3830. 224p. 1995. pap. 12.00 (0-684-80238-4, Fireside) S&S Trade Pap.

Miracle of a Christmas Doll. Scholastica I. Njoku. (Ngozi of Africa Ser.: No. 1). (Illus.). 29p. (J). (gr. k up). 1986. per. 5.95 (0-9617833-0-3) S I NJOKU.

Miracle of Abduction. Intro. by William J. Williams & Dennis Murray. LC 84-82540. 160p. (Orig.). (C). 1985. 12.95 (0-930371-02-X); pap. 8.95 (0-930371-03-8) Epistemics.

Miracle of Abduction: Applied Epistemology As a Method of Inquiry. William J. Williams. LC 84-82540. 159p. 1985. reprint ed. pap. 49.30 (0-608-05712-6, AU0049100007) Bks Demand.

Miracle of Agape Love. Joseph F. Manning. 160p. 1977. mass mkt. 5.99 (0-88368-079-3) Whitaker Hse.

Miracle of Aloe Vera: Everything You Should Know about Aloe. Ben Mattingly. LC 97-12785. (Illus.). 192p. Date not set. per. 12.00 (0-7615-0861-9) Prima Pub.

Miracle of America Study Guide. W. Cleon Skousen. (Illus.). xx, 187p. (Orig.). 1981. pap. 7.50 (0-88080-007-0) Natl Ctr Constit.

Miracle of Believing. 100p. 1985. 9.95 (0-930061-05-5) Interspace Bks.

Miracle of Birth. Consumer Guide Editors. (Illus.). 128p. 1993. 9.98 (0-88176-560-0, 3201900) Pubns Intl Ltd.

Miracle of Castel Di Sangro. Joe McGinniss. LC GV943.6.C35M35 1999. 416p. (gr. 8). 1999. 25.00 (0-316-55736-6) Little.

***Miracle of Castel di Sangro.** Joe McGinniss. 2000. pap. write for info. (0-316-56603-9) Back Bay Pr.

***Miracle of Castel di Sangro.** Joe McGinniss. LC 99-58210. 416p. 2000. pap. 14.95 (0-7679-0599-7) Broadway BDD.

***Miracle of Castel di Sangro.** Joe McGinniss. 1998. write for info. (0-316-56615-2) Little.

Miracle of Castel di Sangro. Joe McGinniss. 1999. write for info. (0-316-56229-7) Little.

Miracle of Change. Dennis Wholey. 1998. per. 14.00 (0-671-51890-9, PB Trade Paper) PB.

Miracle of Change: The Path to Self Discovery & Spiritual Growth. Dennis Wholey. LC 96-36364. 1997. 23.00 (0-671-51891-7) PB.

***Miracle of Change: The Path to Self-Discovery & Spiritual Growth.** Dennis Wholey. 285p. 1999. reprint ed. text 23.00 (0-7881-6307-8) DIANE Pub.

Miracle of Charismatic Healing. Andy O'Neill. 190p. 1997. pap. 11.95 (1-85635-136-X, Pub. by Mercier Pr) Irish Amer Bk.

Miracle of Color Healing: Aura-Soma Therapy As the Mirror of the Soul. Vicky Wall. 208p. 1993. reprint ed. pap. 12.00 (1-85538-289-X, Pub. by Aqrn Pr) Harper SF.

Miracle of Colour Healing. Vicky Wall. 1990. pap. 12.95 (0-85030-895-X, Pub. by Aqrn Pr) Harper SF.

Miracle of Connecticut. Ellsworth S. Grant. (Illus.). 323p. 1992. pap. 24.00 (1-881264-03-3) Connecticut Bk.

Miracle of Connecticut. 2nd ed. Ellsworth S. Grant. Ed. by Oliver O. Jensen. (Illus.). 335p. 1995. 32.00 (1-881264-06-8) Conn Hist Soc.

Miracle of Dialogue. Reuel L. Howe. 1984. 6.95 (0-86683-886-4, SP9) Harper SF.

Miracle of Dr. George Washington Carver, Vol. 1. James A. Lewis. (Illus.). 68p. (Orig.). 1987. pap. 10.00 (0-9617322-3-7) Flat Surface.

Miracle of Dunkirk. Walter Lord. (Wordsworth Collection). 452p. 1997. pap. 11.95 (1-85326-685-X, Pub. by Wrdsworth Edits) Combined Pub.

Miracle of Easter. (Children's Bible Stories Ser.). (Illus.). 24p. (J). 1993. 4.98 (0-7853-0266-2) Pubns Intl Ltd.

Miracle of Easter. Group Publishing Staff. (Bible Big Books Ser.). (Illus.). 14.99 (1-55945-576-4) Group Pub.

***Miracle of Eosa.** 256p. 2000. pap. 17.95 (0-9700515-0-6) Milrose Pubns.

Miracle of Existence. Henry Margenau. LC 83-4972. xii, 143p. 1984. pap. 17.00 (1-881987-03-5) Ox Bow.

***Miracle of Faith: Eastern Baptist Theological Seminary Celebrates Seventy-Five Years.** Randall L. Frame. LC 99-89240. 2000. write for info. (1-57864-096-2) Donning Co.

Miracle of Fasting: Proven Throughout History for Physical, Mental & Spiritual Rejuvenation. Patricia Bragg & Paul C. Bragg. (Illus.). 272p. 1999. pap. 8.95 (0-87790-036-1, Pub. by Hlth Sci) Natl Bk Netwk.

Miracle of Flight. rev. ed. Stephen Dalton. (Illus.). 184p. 1999. 40.00 (1-55209-378-6) Firefly Bks Ltd.

Miracle of Forgetness: A Novel. Robert F. Smith. LC 97-41895. 284p. 1997. pap. 9.95 (1-56236-235-6, Pub. by Aspen Bks) Origin Bk Sales.

Miracle of Forgiveness. Spencer W. Kimball. 1969. 17.95 (0-88494-192-2) Bookcraft Inc.

Miracle of Forgiveness. Spencer W. Kimball. 1979. pap. 8.95 (0-88494-444-1) Bookcraft Inc.

Miracle of Garlic. Paavo O. Airola. 48p. 1984. pap. 3.95 (0-932090-08-7) Health Plus.

Miracle of Grace. John Hagee. Ed. by Lucretia Hobbs & Connie Reece. 47p. (Orig.). 1991. pap., per. 3.00 (1-56908-003-8) Global Evang.

Miracle of Healing Hands: The Complete Guide to Ancient Yogic Healing & Massage Techniques. Waheguru S. Khalsa. Ed. by John Ricker. LC 99-163918. (Illus.). 240p. 1997. pap. 34.95 (0-9658497-4-0) Rishi Knot.

Miracle of Imagination. Neville W. Goddard. Ed. by Margaret R. Broome. LC 90-84286. 163p. (Orig.). 1990. pap. 12.95 (1-56296-000-8) Canterbury Hse.

Miracle of Intervale Avenue: The Story of a Jewish Congregation in the South Bronx. Jack Kugelmass. (Illus.). 277p. 1996. pap. 18.00 (0-231-10307-7) Col U Pr.

Miracle of Islamic Science. K. Ajram. 200p. 1993. pap. 12.95 (0-911119-43-4) Knowledge Hse.

Miracle of Israel. Gordon Lindsay. 3.95 (0-89985-188-6) Christ for the Nations.

Miracle of Jesus & the Theology of Miracles. Rene Latourelle. 1988. pap. 14.95 (0-8091-2997-3) Paulist Pr.

Miracle of Language. Richard Lederer. Ed. by Jane Rosenman. 272p. 1992. reprint ed. mass mkt. 5.99 (0-671-70940-2) PB.

Miracle of Learning: How to Inspire Children. Anne Marfey & Cathy Gayron. (Illus.). 90p. 1998. pap. 17.95 (0-9667733-0-6) Windflower Pub.

Miracle of Learning: Irish Manuscripts, Their Uses & Their Owners, 800-1760. Ed. by Toby C. Barnard et al. LC 97-14761. (Illus.). 303p. 1997. text 86.95 (1-85928-293-8, Pub. by Ashgate Pub) Ashgate Pub Co.

Miracle of Life see **Milagra de la Vida**

Miracle of Life. Merce Parramon. (Invisible World Ser.). (Illus.). 32p. (J). (gr. 4 up). 1994. lib. bdg. 15.95 (0-7910-2130-0) Chelsea Hse.

Miracle of Life: A Parent & Child book about Life. Stephanie Jeffs. (Illus.). 32p. (J). (gr. 1-4). 1997. 12.95 (0-687-08720-1) Abingdon.

Miracle of Life: Baby's First Year. Tyndale House Publishers Staff. (Illus.). 55p. 1998. 18.99 (0-8423-3651-6) Tyndale Hse.

Miracle of Life: Devotions for Expectant Mothers. Robert G. Wells et al. (Illus.). 144p. 1993. 19.99 (0-310-54960-4) Zondervan.

***Miracle of Life: Science Facts.** Lionel Bender. (Illus.). 108p. (YA). 1999. reprint ed. text 25.00 (0-7881-6832-0) DIANE Pub.

Miracle of Love: General Authorities Counsel on Life & Love. C. Douglas Beardall & Jewel N. Beardall. 126p. (Orig.). 1993. pap. 8.95 (1-882371-01-1) LDS Bk Pubns.

Miracle of Love: General Authorities Counsel on Love & Life. Ed. by Jewel Beardall. (Personal Enrichment Ser.). 108p. (Orig.). 1991. write for info. (0-929985-57-5) Jackman Pubng.

Miracle of Love: Stories about Neem Karoli Baba. Ram Dass. (Illus.). 432p. (Orig.). 1995. reprint ed. pap. 17.95 (1-887474-00-5) Hanuman Found.

Miracle of Love: The Gift of Life. Edwin D. Roels. (Friendship Ser.). (Illus.). 48p. (Orig.). 1993. reprint ed. pap. 0.70 (1-882536-06-1, A100-0022) Bible League.

Miracle of Love Pt. III: Reflections of the Christ Mind. Paul Ferrini. LC 97-197726. 192p. 1997. pap. 12.95 (1-879159-23-6) Heartways Pr.

Miracle of Marriage. Judith A. Brumbaugh. (Illus.). 250p. (Orig.). 1996. pap. 13.00 (0-9624603-8-9) Comt Restoration Fam.

Miracle of Marriage. Bill Panko & Margaret Panko. 48p. 1994. pap. 4.95 (1-885342-00-4) Creative Ways.

Miracle of Mata Ortiz: Juan Quezada & the Potters of Northern Chihuahua. Walter P. Parks. 142p. 1994. pap. 19.95 (0-9637655-0-7) Coulter Pr.

Miracle of Mercy: Filling the World with the Love of God. Terry Rush. LC 99-19367. 200p. 1999. 14.99 (1-58229-010-5) Howard Pub LA.

Miracle of Mind Dynamics. James F. Murphy. (C). 1972. pap. text 9.95 (0-13-585398-2, Reward) P-H.

Miracle of Mind Power. Dan Custer. 263p. (C). 1985. reprint ed. pap. 9.95 (0-930298-20-9) Westwood Pub Co.

Miracle of Mindfulness, Set. abr. ed. Thich Nhat Hanh. 1994. audio 18.00 (0-694-51462-4, CPN 2438) HarperAudio.

Miracle of Mindfulness: A Manual on Meditation. gif. ed. Thich Nhat Hahn. Tr. by Mobi Ho. (Illus.). 224p. 1996. 17.00 (0-8070-1232-7) Beacon Pr.

Miracle of Mindfulness: An Introduction to the Practice of Meditation. Thich Nhat Hahn & Tom Hallock. Tr. by Mobi Ho from VIE. LC 87-42852. Orig. Title: The Miracle of Mindfulness: A Manual on Meditation. 160p. 1999. pap. 12.00 (0-8070-1239-4) Beacon Pr.

Miracle of Mindfulness: A Manual on Meditation see **Miracle of Mindfulness: An Introduction to the Practice of Meditation**

Miracle of Motivation. George Shinn. 272p. 1994. mass mkt. 5.99 (0-8423-3967-1) Tyndale Hse.

Miracle of MSM: The Natural Solution for Pain. Stanley W. Jacob et al. LC 98-48592. 256p. 1999. 19.95 (0-399-14474-9, G P Putnam) Peng Put Young Read.

***Miracle of MSM: The Natural Solution for Pain.** Stanley W. Jacob et al. 1999. reprint ed. pap. 12.00 (0-425-17265-1) Berkley Pub.

Miracle of Music Therapy. Edith H. Boxill. LC 99-164236. (Illus.). 212p. 1997. pap. text 22.00 (0-9624080-8-5) Barcelona Pubs.

Miracle of Names: A 500 Word Description of Your Character. Clayne Conings et al. LC 94-67155. 220p. (Orig.). (YA). (gr. 10). 1996. pap. 13.95 (1-887472-03-7) Sunstar Pubng.

Miracle of Natural Hormones. 2nd rev. ed. David Brownstein. (Illus.). 204p. 1999. pap. 14.95 (0-9660882-0-4) Med Alternat.

Miracle of New Life: Minibook. Bill Basansky. 48p. 1992. pap. 1.00 (0-89274-896-6, HH-896) Harrison Hse.

Miracle of Personal Leadership: Revolutionary New Personal Leadership Secrets to Energize & Empower Your Work & Life. Ray Russell. LC 95-77750. 304p. 1995. boxed set 26.95 (0-7872-0603-2) Kendall-Hunt.

Miracle of Prayer. Pat Boone. 1989. 8.95 (0-310-22131-5) Zondervan.

Miracle of Prayer. Guideposts Magazine Staff. 192p. 1993. 6.99 (0-517-08784-7) Random Hse Value.

Miracle of Prayer. Rosemary E. Guiley. Ed. by Claire Zion. 192p. (Orig.). 1995. pap. 14.00 (0-671-75692-3) PB.

Miracle of Print: An Exhibition on the Art of the Printed Word. James P. Bixler & Bernard P. Margolis. 84p. 1993. pap. 6.00 (1-884003-02-8) Frnds Pikes Peak.

Miracle of Psycho Command Power: The New Way to Riches, Love & Happiness. Scott Reed. 1972. 17.95 (0-13-585679-5, Reward) P-H.

Miracle of Rare Design. Mike Resnick. 256p. 1996. pap. write for info. (0-614-05523-7); mass mkt. 5.99 (0-8125-2424-1, Pub. by Tor Bks) St Martin.

Miracle of Right Thought. Orison S. Marden. 339p. 1996. pap. 28.00 (0-89540-311-0, SB-311) Sun Pub.

Miracle of Saint Nicholas. Gloria Whelan. LC 97-73496. (Golden Key Bks.). (Illus.). 32p. (J). (ps up). 1997. 12.95 (1-883937-18-3) Bethlehem ND.

Miracle of Salvation. Carroll J. Thompson. (Illus.). 178p. (Orig.). 1986. pap. 9.95 (1-55630-010-7) Brentwood Comm.

***Miracle of Sponsorship: Recovery Stories of Hope & Renewal.** Karen Casey. 250p. 2000. pap. 15.00 (1-56838-553-6) Hazelden.

Miracle of Survival: A Holocaust Memoir. Herbert Boucher. (Illus.). 196p. 1997. pap. 12.95 (0-943376-64-5) Magnes Mus.

Miracle of the Age: The Great Pyramid of Gizeh. Worth Smith. 160p. 1996. reprint ed. spiral bd. 14.00 (0-7873-0805-6) Hlth Research.

Miracle of the Bells. Russell Janney. 1993. reprint ed. lib. bdg. 29.95 (1-56849-135-2) Buccaneer Bks.

Miracle of the Christmas Child. Penelope J. Stokes. 128p. 1999. 12.99 (0-8499-5420-7) Word Pub.

Miracle of the Hills. Kay S. Holt. LC 98-172854. vi, 353p. 1997. write for info. (1-883570-31-X) Craigmiles & Assocs.

***Miracle of the Illumination of All Consciences.** Thomas W. Petrisko. (Illus.). 176p. 2000. pap. 10.95 (1-891903-25-X) St Andrew Prodns.

Miracle of the Killer Bees: 12 Senators Who Changed Texas Politics. Robert Heard. LC 81-90115. (Illus.). 124p. 1981. pap. 10.00 (0-937642-01-0) Honey Hill.

***Miracle of the Loaves & Fishes.** Broughton. 20p. (J). 2000. pap. text. write for info. (0-307-16036-X) Gldn Bks Pub Co.

Miracle of the Loaves & Fishes. Illus. by Kirsten Soderlind. LC 96-13150. (Family Time Bible Stories Ser.). 28p. (J). (ps-2). 1999. 4.95 (0-7835-4632-7) Time-Life.

Miracle of the Met. Quaintance Eaton. LC 82-7256. (Music Reprint Ser.). (Illus.). xii, 490p. 1982. reprint ed. lib. bdg. 49.50 (0-306-76168-8) Da Capo.

Miracle of the Mind. Judith DeMaleissye-Melun & D. L. Chapman. 1986. pap. write for info. (1-893310-03-5) Science of Understand.

***Miracle of the Myrrh.** Marci Alborghetti. LC 00-20551. (Illus.). 32p. (J). (gr. k-4). 2000. 16.95 (1-890817-16-3, Pub. by Winslow Pr) Publishers Group.

Miracle of the Phoenix. Kathryn Breese-Whiting. 96p. (Orig.). 1995. pap. 14.95 (0-9647989-0-5, Voice Phoenix Pr) Phoenix Inst.

***Miracle of the Red Roses.** Rafael A. Alvarado. LC 99-91867. 2000. 25.00 (0-7388-1348-6); pap. 18.00 (0-7388-1349-4) Xlibris Corp.

Miracle of the Rose. Jean Genet. Tr. by Bernard Frechtman from FRE. LC 66-58157. 344p. 1988. pap. 11.95 (0-8021-3088-7, Grove) Grove-Atltic.

Miracle of the Sacred Scroll: A Novel of Hope & Inspiration. Johan Christian. LC 97-68721. Orig. Title: The Merchant from Bethelehem. 112p. 1997. 14.95 (0-914984-73-X) Starburst.

Miracle of the Scarlet Thread. Richard Booker. (Illus.). 168p. 1991. reprint ed. pap. 10.99 (0-914903-26-8) Destiny Image.

Miracle of the 2nd Advent: The Emerging New Christianity. Gene Savoy & Ileana Isfan. LC 84-81232. (Illus.). 68p. 1984. text 14.50 (0-936202-04-1) Intl Comm Christ.

Miracle of the Shoebox Baby. S. S. Edward. 64p. (YA). (gr. 5-12). 1993. pap. 8.95 (1-883500-23-0) RAMSI Bks.

Miracle of the Sun at Medjugorje. Charles R. Toye. 112p. (Orig.). 1988. pap. 6.95 (0-9619732-1-8) Send Your Spirit Pub.

Miracle of Theism. John L. Mackie. 276p. 1983. pap. text 24.95 (0-19-824682-X) OUP.

Miracle of Tithing. Mark Victor Hansen. 64p. 1983. pap. 3.95 (1-878549-05-7, 604) M V Hansen.

Miracle of 8 Pennies. 28p. 1997. pap. 3.00 (1-883164-05-2) Delphi Intl.

Miracle on a Mountain: The Story of a College. Lucile Bogue. LC 87-17947. (Illus.). 166p. (Orig.). 1987. pap. 9.95 (0-89407-086-X) Strawberry Hill.

Miracle on Alaska Street. A. J. Wagner. (Illus.). 87p. (Orig.). (J). (gr. 1-8). 1996. pap. 12.95 (0-9657771-0-3) Raven Graphix.

***Miracle on Boswell Road: True Stories of Unexpected Acts of Love.** John M. Eades. 2000. pap. text 9.99 (1-57748-848-2) Barbour Pub.

Miracle on Harding Road. Dora B. Platt. (Illus.). 136p. 1989. lib. bdg. write for info. (0-9623777-0-8) Saint Thomas Hospital.

Miracle on I-40. rev. ed. Curtiss A. Matlock. (Illus.). 126p. 1999. pap. 11.95 (0-9654499-2-0, Madeira Bks) Windows on Hist.

Miracle on 10th Street: And Other Christmas Writings. Madeleine L'Engle. LC 98-24322. 144p. 1998. 16.99 (0-87788-531-1, H Shaw Pubs) Waterbrook Pr.

Miracle on the East Ridge, Vol. 1. Patrick J. Kearney. Ed. by Cheri Crowley-Meier & Karen McGrath-Sullivan. LC TX2-967-289. (Illus.). 128p. 1990. text 12.95 (0-9661688-1-X, 03991805) Skyhigh.

Miracle on the Mountain: A True Tale of Faith & Survival. Mike Couillard et al. LC 97-29978. 256p. 1998. mass mkt. 20.00 (0-380-97392-8, Avon Bks) Morrow Avon.

Miracle on the Mountain: A True Tale of Faith & Survival. Mike Couillard et al. LC 97-29978. 256p. 1999. mass mkt. 5.99 (0-380-78979-5, Avon Bks) Morrow Avon.

Miracle on the Potomac: The Kennedy Center from the Beginning. Ralph E. Becker. (Illus.). 240p. 1989. 24.95 (0-910155-15-1) Bartleby Pr.

Miracle on the River Kwai see **Milagre no Rio Kwai**

Miracle on the Road. Jane Taylor. 1997. pap. 2.99 (1-85792-296-4, Pub. by Christian Focus) Spring Arbor Dist.

***Miracle on the Road: The Story of Paul.** Christian Focus Publishing Staff. (Bible Wise Ser.). 2000. pap. 2.99 (1-85792-344-8) Christian Focus.

Miracle on the Sepik. 2nd ed. Clarence Hall. (Illus.). 100p. 1980. pap. 3.95 (0-685-01806-7) Full Gospel.

Miracle on the Sepik. 2nd ed. Clarence Hall. (Illus.). 100p. 1981. pap. 3.95 (0-685-01900-4) Gift Pubns.

Miracle on the 17th Green: A Novel about Life, Love, Family, Miracles...& Golf. James Patterson & Peter De Jonge. 160p. (gr. 8). 1996. 16.95 (0-316-69331-6) Little.

Miracle on the 17th Green: A Novel about Life, Love, Family, Miracles...& Golf. James Patterson & Peter De Jonge. 160p. 1999. pap. 10.00 (0-316-69335-9, Back Bay) Little.

***Miracle on Theodore's Street.** Lisa Funari-Willever. (Illus.). 32p. 1998. pap. 6.95 (1-889383-09-0) Angel Publns NJ.

Miracle on 34th Street. Valentine Davies. LC 47-4221. 120p. 1947. 13.95 (0-15-160239-5) Harcourt.

Miracle on 34th Street. Valentine Davies. (Illus.). (J). (gr. k up). 1984. 16.95 (0-15-254526-3, Harcourt Child Bks) Harcourt.

Miracle on 34th Street. Valentine Davies. LC 84-3742. (Illus.). 128p. (ps-3). 1987. pap. 13.00 (0-15-254528-X, Voyager Bks) Harcourt.

Miracle on 34th Street. Valentine Davies. 160p. 1994. pap. 9.95 (0-15-600198-5) Harcourt.

Miracle on 34th Street. Valentine Davies. 76p. 1996. pap. 5.60 (0-87129-707-8, M96) Dramatic Pub.

Miracle on 34th Street M-TV. Francine Hughes. 32p. (J). (ps-3). 1994. pap. 2.95 (0-590-22507-3) Scholastic Inc.

Miracle on 34th Street. Valentine Davies. reprint ed. lib. bdg. 17.95 (0-88411-934-3) Amereon Ltd.

Miracle on 34th Street. Valentine Davies. 128p. 1992. reprint ed. lib. bdg. 17.95 (0-89968-313-4, Lghtyr Pr) Buccaneer Bks.

Miracle on 34th Street, Gift Edition. Valentine Davies. (Illus.). 146p. 1991. pap. 9.95 (0-15-660455-8, Harvest Bks) Harcourt.

Miracle on 34th Street: A Hollywood Classic. Sarah P. Danielson. (Illus.). 112p. 1993. 14.98 (0-8317-4284-4) Smithmark.

Miracle on 33rd Street: The New York Knickerbockers' Championship Season, 1969-70. Phil Berger. LC 93-39326. (Illus.). 258p. 1994. pap. 14.95 (1-56858-008-8) FWEW.

Miracle on Tyne Street: The Channel Nine Story. Rex Heading. LC 97-172509. 124 p. 1996. write for info. (1-86254-390-9, Pub. by Wakefield Pr) BHB Intl.

Miracle or Design? Lessons from the East Asian Experience. Albert Fishlow et al. LC 94-12155. (Policy Essay Ser.: No. 11). 128p. 1994. pap. 13.95 (1-56517-015-6) Overseas Dev Council.

Miracle Play in England. Sidney M. Clarke. LC 65-15874. 1970. reprint ed. lib. bdg. 75.00 (0-8383-0529-6) M S G Haskell Hse.

Miracle Plays of Mathura. Norvin Hein. LC 75-99826. (Illus.). 325p. reprint ed. pap. 100.80 (0-8357-2801-3, 203375100087) Bks Demand.

Miracle Power see **Poder Milagroso**

Miracle Power for Infinite Riches. Joseph Murphy. (C). 1974. pap. text 9.95 (0-13-585612-4, Parker Publishing Co) P-H.

Miracle Protein: Secret of Natural Cell-Tissue Rejuvenation. Carlson Wade. 1976. 12.95 (0-13-585653-1, Reward); pap. 4.95 (0-13-585588-8, Reward) P-H.

***Miracle Recipes.** Lynne Fitzgerald. (Illus.). 94p. 1999. spiral bd. 9.95 (0-9678953-0-8) Miracl Recipe.

Miracle Road. Ed. by Jerry Shaw & Annie Shaw. LC 98-60707. 176p. 1998. pap. 10.95 (1-57921-119-4, Pub. by WinePress Pub) BookWorld.

Miracle Santa's Beard. Helen C. Mercurio. Ed. by Mary M. Mercurio. (Illus.). 29p. (J). 1985. 12.00 (0-9616079-0-4) Tiffany Pub.

Miracle Settles the Issue. Mike Francen. 117p. 1997. pap. 8.00 (1-888079-13-4, MF-913) Francen Wrld.

Miracle Signs & Wonders. Marilyn Hickey. pap. 24.95 (1-56441-029-3) M Hickey Min.

Miracle Spiritology. Al G. Manning. LC 75-19350. 1975. 13.95 (0-13-585745-7) Pan Ishtar.

Miracle Stories from the Bible. Ruth R. Brand & Charles Mills. LC 96-52247. (Professor Appleby & the Maggie B. Tapes Ser.: Vol. 5). 128p. (J). 1997. pap. 8.99 (0-8280-0961-9) Review & Herald.

Miracle Stories of the Early Christian Tradition. Gerd Theissen. 324p. 1998. 49.95 (0-567-09314-X) Bks Intl VA.

Miracle Strain. Michael Cordy. 400p. 1998. mass mkt. 6.99 (0-380-73042-1, Avon Bks) Morrow Avon.

An Asterisk (*) at the beginning of an entry indicates that the title is appearing for the first time.

Miracle Strain: Larson,&Darrell, Set. abr. ed. Michael Cordy. 1997. audio. write for info. (*0-694-51859-X*, 395357, Pub. by HarperAudio) Lndmrk Audiobks.

Miracle Strip. Nancy Bartholomew. LC 98-7330. 256p. 1998. text 22.95 (*0-312-19299-1*) St Martin.

Miracle Strip: A Sierra Lavotini Mystery. Nancy Bartholomew. 256p. 1999. pap. 5.99 (*0-312-97095-1*, Minotaur) St Martin.

Miracle Superfood: Wild Blue-Green Algae. Gillian McKeith. (Good Health Guides Ser.). 48p. (Orig.). 1996. pap. 3.95 (*0-87983-729-2*, 37292K, Keats Publng) NTC Contemp Pub Co.

Miracle Through the Fire. rev. ed. Tommy D. Hudson & Judy C. Hudson. LC 96-53151. 216p. 1997. pap. 8.99 (*1-56722-202-1*) Word Aflame.

Miracle to Meltdown in Asia: Business, Government & Society. Norman Flynn. (Illus.). 192p. 2000. text 70.00 (*0-19-829552-9*); pap. text 24.95 (*0-19-829553-7*) OUP.

Miracle Town: Creating America's Bavarian Village in Leavenworth, Washington. Ted Price. LC 96-92027. (Illus.). 208p. 1997. 40.00 (*0-9651206-1-9*); pap. 24.95 (*0-9651206-0-0*) Price & Rodgers.

Miracle Tree. Christobel Mattingley. LC 86-4541. (Illus.). 28p. (J). (gr. 3 up). 1986. 11.95 (*0-15-200530-7*, Gulliver Bks) Harcourt.

Miracle under the Oaks: The Revival of Nature in America. William K. Stevens. LC 94-31436. (Illus.). 1995. 22.00 (*0-671-78042-5*) PB.

Miracle under the Oaks: The Revival of Nature in America. William K. Stevens. 352p. 1996. pap. 12.00 (*0-671-78045-X*, PB Trade Paper) PB.

Miracle Victory over the Flesh-Eating Bacteria. David L. Cowles & Delys Cowles. LC 96-39228. 160p. 1997. pap. 10.95 (*0-87905-809-9*) Gibbs Smith Pub.

Miracle Wife: Kids & Kisses. Day Leclaire. (Romance Ser.: Vol. 3523). 1998. per. 3.50 (*0-373-03523-3*, 1-03523-7) Harlequin Bks.

Miracle Wife: Kids & Kisses. large type ed. Day Leclaire. (Larger Print Ser.: Vol. 369). 1998. per. 3.50 (*0-373-15769-X*, 1-15769-2) Harlequin Bks.

***Miracle Wife: Kids & Kisses.** large type ed. Day Leclaire. (Harlequin Ser.). 1999. 21.95 (*0-263-16079-3*) Mills & Boon.

Miracle Woman's Secret. Josephine C. Trust. 96p. 1949. reprint ed. pap. 3.00 (*1-892203-07-3*, 8, Superet Pr) Mother Trust.

Miracle Worker. (J). Date not set. pap. 13.32 (*0-395-85806-2*) HM.

Miracle Worker. (J). 1997. text 15.96 (*0-395-85803-8*) HM.

***Miracle Worker.** 1998. 11.95 (*1-56137-531-4*) Novel Units.

***Miracle Worker.** 1999. 9.95 (*1-56137-183-1*) Novel Units.

Miracle Worker. William Gibson. 128p. (J). (gr. 6-9). 1984. mass mkt. 5.99 (*0-553-24778-6*) Bantam.

Miracle Worker. William Gibson. 1975. 10.60 (*0-606-01082-3*, Pub. by Turtleback) Demco.

Miracle Worker: A Study Guide. Anne Spencer. Ed. by J. Friedland & R. Kessler. (Novel-Ties Ser.). (J). (gr. 6-8). 1994. pap. text, student ed. 15.95 (*1-56982-074-0*) Lrn Links.

Miracle Worker: A Unit Plan. Janine Sherman. 170p. 1998. teacher ed., ring bd. 26.95 (*1-58337-201-6*) Teachers Pet Pubns.

Miracle Worker: Curriculum Unit. Center for Learning Network Staff & William Gibson. (Drama Ser.). 84p. (YA). (gr. 9-12). 1990. spiral bd. 18.95 (*1-56077-117-8*) Ctr Learning.

Miracle Worker: Reproducible Teaching Unit. rev. ed. James Scott. 32p. (YA). (gr. 7-12). 1988. teacher ed., ring bd. 29.50 (*1-58049-067-0*, TU30/U) Prestwick Hse.

Miracle-Working Power of Love. Ron Roth. 99p. 1986. pap. 5.00 (*1-893869-13-X*) Celbrtng Life.

Miracle Year: An Expectant Parents' Guide to the Miraculous Six Months Before - & after - the Birth of Their First Baby. Lanie Carter & Lauren S. Ostrow. 224p. 1992. pap. 8.00 (*0-671-70432-X*) PB.

***Miracle Years: A Cultural History of West Germany, 1949-1968.** Hanna Schissler. LC 00-39974. (Illus.). 448p. 2000. pap. 22.95 (*0-691-05820-2*) Princeton U Pr.

***"Miracle" Years: A Cultural History of West Germany, 1949-1968.** Hanna Schissler. (Illus.). 448p. 2001. 65.00 (*0-691-05819-9*) Princeton U Pr.

Miraclemind. Karen Henderson. 1993. pap. 10.50 (*1-55673-588-X*, 7987) CSS OH.

Miracles. (St. Joseph's Coloring Bks.). (Illus.). 32p. (Orig.). (J). (ps-3). 1988. pap. 0.99 (*0-89942-686-7*, 686/00) Catholic Bk Pub.

***Miracles.** 352p. (Orig.). 1999. pap. 12.95 (*1-929440-00-6*, 3000) Nautilus Pubg Co.

Miracles. (Group Bible Study Ser.). (Orig.). 1995. pap. 4.95 (*1-883419-93-X*) Serendipty Hse.

Miracles. Alain-Fournier. (FRE.). 223p. 1988. pap. 11.95 (*0-7859-3144-9*, 2253047066) Fr & Eur.

Miracles. C. Stephen Byrum. (Controversial Biblical Texts Ser.). 133p. 1991. 11.95 (*0-924234-23-7*) Milton Pub.

Miracles. Robbie Castleman. 80p. 1996. pap. 4.99 (*0-87788-555-9*, H Shaw Pubs) Waterbrook Pr.

Miracles. Don Fearheiley. 240p. (Orig.). 1994. mass mkt. 4.99 (*0-380-77652-9*, Avon Bks) Morrow Avon.

Miracles. Tobsha Learner. (Orig.). pap. 14.95 (*0-86819-557-X*, Pub. by Currency Pr) Accents Pubns.

***Miracles.** C. S. Lewis. 1999. pap. 7.00 (*0-8054-2045-2*) Broadman.

Miracles. C. S. Lewis. 240p. 1996. per. 7.00 (*0-684-82379-9*, Touchstone) S&S Trade Pap.

Miracles. John T. Osborne. (Illus.). 90p. (J). 1988. pap. text 5.75 (*0-929918-00-2*) Midstates Pub.

Miracles. Charles H. Spurgeon. (Spurgeon Collection: Vol. 3). 235p. 1998. pap. 9.99 (*1-889893-19-6*) Emerald House Group Inc.

Miracles. Students of St. Mary's School Staff. (Illus.). 96p. 1999. pap. 8.95 (*0-9650315-8-6*) Glacier Publng.

Miracles. F. Richard Thomas. (Illus.). 50p. 1996. pap. 12.50 (*0-945950-09-8*) Canoe Pr MI.

Miracles. Stuart Wilde. LC 97-53047. 64p. 1998. pap. 5.00 (*1-56170-540-3*) Hay House.

Miracles. Stuart Wilde. LC 88-17144. 40p. 1983. pap. 4.50 (*0-930603-01-X*) White Dove NM.

Miracles: A Jewish Perspective. Ronald H. Isaacs. LC 97-9519. 168p. 1997. 25.00 (*0-7657-9950-2*) Aronson.

Miracles: A Parascientific Exploration of Wondrous Phenomena. D. Scott Rogo. (Illus.). 384p. 1991. pap. 14.00 (*1-85538-055-2*, Pub. by Aqrn Pr) Harper SF.

Miracles: A 21st Century Interpretation. Josef Imbach. LC 98-60894. 240p. 1998. pap. 14.95 (*0-87243-239-4*) Templegate.

Miracles! More Than Believing : Supernatural Events are Happening Today. William Carr Blood. LC 95-83204. xiii, 93 p. 1995. write for info. (*1-56043-573-9*) Destiny Image.

Miracles: Opposing Viewpoints. Michael Arvey. LC 90-39156. (Great Mysteries Ser.). (Illus.). 112p. (J). (gr. 5-8). 1990. lib. bdg. 22.45 (*0-89908-084-7*) Greenhaven.

Miracles: Orthodox Homilies on Miracles in Nature, Man, Holy Scripture, History of Nations & the Church. Augoustinos N. Kantiotes. Tr. by Asterios Gerostergios. LC 98-70455. 268p. 1998. pap. 17.95 (*1-884729-37-1*) Inst Byzantine.

Miracles: Signs & Wonders. Serendipty House Staff. (301 Depth Bible Study Ser.). 1998. pap. text 4.95 (*1-57494-107-0*) Serendipty Hse.

Miracles: Signs of God's Glory. Douglas Connelly. (Life Guide Bible Studies). 64p. 1999. pap. 4.99 (*0-8308-3087-1*, 3087) InterVarsity.

Miracles: The Process of Creation & Healing. Thom Stecher. (Illus.). 165p. (Orig.). 1996. pap. 11.95 (*0-9650624-0-6*) T Stecher Assocs.

Miracles: The Sculptures of William Edmondson. Ed. by John E. Ollman. LC 94-73210. (Illus.). 60p. Date not set. pap. 15.00 (*0-9621506-3-0*) Fleisher Ollman Gallery.

Miracles: What the Bible Really Says. Douglas Connelly. LC 96-43161. 168p. (Orig.). 1997. pap. 9.99 (*0-8308-1959-2*, 1959) InterVarsity.

Miracles along the Way. Bob Christensen & Lynne Christensen. 91p. (Orig.). 1992. pap. 5.95 (*1-886045-03-8*) Covenant Marriages.

Miracles & Monasteries of 17th-Century Ukraine. Tr. by Dana R. Miller et al from ENG. (Harvard Library of Early Ukrainian Literature: Vol. 10). 350p. (C). 2000. text 39.95 (*0-916458-81-4*) Harvard Ukrainian.

***Miracles & Marriage.** large type ed. Meredith Webber. 288p. 1999. 25.99 (*0-263-15897-7*, Pub. by Mills & Boon) Ulverscroft.

Miracles & Messengers. Catherine L. Baynard. 287p. 1998. pap. 12.95 (*0-9667971-0-8*) Linkpoint.

Miracles & Metaphors. Mirza Abu'l-Fadl. Tr. by Juan R. Cole from ARA. (Illus.). 220p. 1982. pap. 19.95 (*0-933770-22-7*) Kalimat.

Miracles & Mistletoe. Cait London. 1995. per. 3.25 (*0-373-05968-X*, 1-05968-2) Silhouette.

Miracles & Modern Spiritualism. rev. ed. Alfred R. Wallace. LC 75-7409. (Perspectives in Psychical Research Ser.). 1975. reprint ed. 21.95 (*0-405-06996-0*) Ayer.

Miracles & Modern Thought. Norman L. Geisler. LC 82-6999. 168p. 1982. pap. 8.45 (*0-310-44681-3*) Probe Bks.

Miracles & Other Happenings. Betty S. McCoy. (Illus.). 80p. 1993. pap. write for info. (*0-935648-42-9*) Halldin Pub.

Miracles & Other Ordinary Things. Lana J. Ford. (Illus.). 382p. (Orig.). 1995. pap. 19.95 (*0-929686-04-7*) Temple Golden Pubns.

Miracles & Other Poems. Vincent Byrne. LC 78-65634. 1979. pap. 6.95 (*0-8159-6216-9*) Devin.

Miracles & Parables of Christ. Richard C. Trench. (Classic Library). 650p. 1996. 21.99 (*0-529-10633-7*, MPC) World Publng.

Miracles & Parables of Our Lord, 3. Charles H. Spurgeon. 2000p. 1995. 95.00 (*0-8010-8291-9*) Baker Bks.

Miracles & Pilgrims: Popular Beliefs in Medieval England. Ronald C. Finucane. LC 94-41007. 248p. 1995. pap. 19.95 (*0-312-12528-3*) St Martin.

***Miracles & Pilgrims: Popular Beliefs in Medieval England.** Ronald C. Finucane. 248p. 2000. reprint ed. pap. 17.00 (*0-7881-9342-2*) DIANE Pub.

Miracles & Prophecies in Nineteenth-Century France. Thomas A. Kselman. (Illus.). 312p. 1983. 45.00 (*0-8135-0963-7*) Rutgers U Pr.

Miracles & Rubies. Clare Cooper. 69p. (J). (gr. 4). 1992. pap. 7.95 (*0-8464-4847-5*) Beekman Pubs.

Miracles & the Medieval Mind: Theory, Record, & Event, 1000 to 1215. Benedicta Ward. LC 81-23106. (Middle Ages Ser.). (Illus.). 300p. 1982. pap. 20.95 (*0-8122-1228-2*) U of Pa Pr.

Miracles & the Modern Religious Imagination. Robert B. Mullin. LC 96-13505. 336p. 1996. 35.00 (*0-300-06696-1*) Yale U Pr.

Miracles & Wonders. Tom Seims. (In the Picture with Jesus Ser.). (Illus.). 32p. (Orig.). (J). 1993. 8.99 (*1-56476-046-4*, 6-3046, Victor Bks) Chariot Victor.

Miracles & Wonders. Tom Siems & Arbuckle. (J). 1995. 12.99 incl. audio Chariot Victor.

Miracles & Wonders: Musicals for Chanukah & Purim. Debbie Friedman. 1992. audio 6.95 (*1-890161-15-2*) Sounds Write.

Miracles & Wonders: Musicals for Chanukah & Purim. Debbie Friedman. (Illus.). 1992. audio 9.95 (*1-890161-14-4*) Sounds Write.

Miracles & Wonders: Musicals for Chanukah & Purim. Debbie Friedman. Ed. & Frwd. by Randee Friedman. (Illus.). 66p. 1992. pap. 18.95 (*0-9626286-1-1*) Sounds Write.

Miracles & Wonders: Musicals for Chanukah & Purim. Debbie Friedman. (Illus.). 1995. audio compact disk 15.95 (*1-890161-16-0*) Sounds Write.

Miracles Are Guaranteed: A Step-by-Step Guide to Restoring Love, Being Free & Creating a Life That Works. Bill Ferguson. 1992. pap. 10.95 (*1-878410-20-2*) Return Heart.

***Miracles Are Still Happening.** A. L. Gill & Joyce Gill. LC 00-9596. 160p. 2000. pap. 12.99 (*0-88368-620-1*) Whitaker Hse.

***Miracles Around Us: How to Recognize God at Work Today.** Ron Rhodes. 250p. 2000. pap. 9.99 (*0-7369-0211-2*) Harvest Hse.

Miracles at the Inn. Auguste R. Black. (Illus.). 24p. (Orig.). (J). (gr. 1-12). 1990. pap. 4.95 (*0-9628010-1-1*) A R Black.

***Miracle's Boys.** Jacqueline Woodson. LC 99-40050. 192p. (YA). (gr. 5-9). 2000. 15.99 (*0-399-23113-7*, G P Putnam) Peng Put Young Read.

Miracles Can Happen to You: Power of Visual Imagery. 3rd ed. Lew Miller. LC 85-61118. 72p. (Orig.). 1986. reprint ed. pap. 5.45 (*0-9615752-0-4*) Milbeck Pr.

Miracles de la Pensee. 1984. 18.50 (*2-920083-06-6*) Edns Roseau.

Miracles Do Happen. Briege McKenna. 1992. mass mkt. 5.99 (*0-312-92972-2*) St Martin.

Miracles Do Happen: A Physician's Experiences with Alternative Medicine. C. Norman Shealy. 288p. 1995. pap. 15.95 (*1-85230-688-2*, Pub. by Element MA) Penguin Putnam.

Miracles Do Happen: God Can Do the Impossible. Briege McKenna & Henry Libersat. LC 95-46595. 170p. 1987. pap. 9.99 (*0-89283-316-5*, Charis) Servant.

Miracles Do Happen! Monthly Meditations for African Americans. rev. ed. Anthony Milan. 48p. 1994. pap. 6.95 (*0-913543-41-1*) African Am Imag.

Miracles Do Happen: The Best-Selling Account of One Woman's Ministry in the Church Today. Briege McKenna & Henry Libersat. 142p. 1989. pap. 22.00 (*0-86217-253-5*, Pub. by Veritas Pubns) St Mut.

Miracles, Duels, & Cide Hamete's Morrish Dissent. Juergen Hahn. 42.50 (*0-916379-96-5*) Scripta.

Miracles from Heaven. unabridged ed. Barbara Duffey. Orig. Title: In Search of Miracles. 180p. 1998. lib. bdg. 13.95 (*0-9659477-1-8*, 2) Elysian Ent.

Miracles Galore. Eithne A. Nunez. 1998. pap. 9.99 (*1-873796-67-6*) Review & Herald.

***Miracles Happen, 1.** Carole Whang Schutter. 1999. pap. text 9.95 (*0-9672747-0-2*) Miracle Pubg.

Miracles Happen to Women Who Believe in Love. Elza Shinfeld. (Illus.). 180p. 1998. pap. 7.95 (*965-494-048-5*, Pub. by Astrolog Pub) Assoc Pubs Grp.

***Miracles Happen When Women Pray.** Joy Haney. 1999. pap. 9.95 (*1-880969-35-1*) Schl Prophet.

Miracles Happen When You Pray: True Stories of the Remarkable Power of Prayer. LC 97-1878. 192p. 1997. 10.99 (*0-310-20997-8*) Zondervan.

Miracles in Black. John Wengentz. 1987. pap. 7.99 (*0-88019-225-9*) Schmul Pub Co.

Miracles in Greco-Roman Antiquity: A Sourcebook. Wendy Cotter. LC 98-19320. 1999. write for info. (*0-415-11863-8*); pap. 23.99 (*0-415-11864-6*) Routledge.

Miracles in Jewish & Christian Antiquity: Imagining Truth. Ed. by John C. Cavadini. LC 99-35187. (Notre Dame Studies in Theology: Vol. 3). 240p. 1999. 35.00 (*0-268-01217-2*, Pub. by U of Notre Dame Pr) Chicago Distribution Ctr.

***Miracles in Jewish & Christian Antiquity: Imagining Truth.** Ed. by John C. Cavadini. LC 99-35187. (Notre Dame Studies in Theology: Vol. 3). 256p. 2000. reprint ed. pap. 25.00 (*0-268-03453-2*, Pub. by U of Notre Dame Pr) Chicago Distribution Ctr.

Miracles in Maggody: An Arly Hanks Mystery. Joan Hess. 288p. 1996. mass mkt. 5.99 (*0-451-40656-7*) NAL.

Miracles in My Life: Tales of a Happy Wanderer. Fred A. Birchmore. LC 96-14854. (Illus.). 136p. 1997. 19.95 (*1-887813-30-6*) Cucumber Island.

Miracles in Natoma's Kitchen: Healthy Low Fat Downhome Cooking. Natoma Riley. 362p. 1995. 17.95 (*1-886246-04-1*) Alpha LifeSpan.

Miracles in Our Midst. Richard L. Scott et al. 1996. 12.95 (*0-9646872-3-2*) Wessex House.

Miracles in the Atomic Age? John R. Terry. 200p. 1993. pap. 7.50 (*0-933704-98-4*) Dawn Pr.

Miracles in the Kitchen: Delicious & Nutritious Replacements for Junk Foods. Regina E. Lorr. LC 91-60773. 304p. (Orig.). 1992. pap. 12.95 (*0-914711-09-1*) Rishis Inst.

Miracles in the Last Days. 1992. pap. 14.95 (*1-880364-06-9*) New Sarov.

Miracles in the Light of Science & History 166. A. Huelster. 166p. 1998. reprint ed. pap. 17.95 (*0-7661-0507-5*) Kessinger Pub.

Miracles in the Making: Scientific Evidence for the Effectiveness of Prayer. Robert N. Miller. 1996. 13.95 (*0-89804-097-3*); pap. 9.95 (*0-89804-096-5*) Ariel GA.

Miracles in the Middle: Men Who Live the Promise in Midlife. Richard Bimler & Theodore W. Schroeder. LC 96-44487. 288p. 1997. pap. 10.99 (*0-570-04890-7*, 12-3307) Concordia.

Miracles Lately Wrought by the Intercession of the Glorious Virgin Marie at Mont-Aigu. Philips Numan. LC 76-370285. (English Recusant Literature, 1558-1640 Ser.). 298 p. 1975. write for info. (*0-85967-231-X*) Scolar Pr.

Miracles, Mysteries, & Prayer I: Kabbalah. Berg. (RUS.). 224p. 1997. pap. 11.95 (*0-924457-93-7*) Res Ctr Kabbalah.

Miracles, Mysteries, & Prayer II: Kabbalah. Berg. (RUS., Illus.). 224p. 1997. pap. 11.95 (*0-924457-94-5*) Res Ctr Kabbalah.

Miracles, Mysteries & Prayer I. Philip S. Berg. (ENG.). 12p. 1993. pap. 11.95 (*0-924457-83-X*); pap. 11.95 (*0-924457-84-8*); pap. 11.95 (*0-924457-85-6*); pap. 11.95 (*0-924457-88-0*) Res Ctr Kabbalah.

Miracles, Mysteries & Prayer II. Philip S. Berg. (ENG.). 12p. 1993. pap. 11.95 (*0-924457-90-2*); pap. 11.95 (*0-924457-86-4*); pap. 11.95 (*0-924457-87-2*); pap. 11.95 (*0-924457-89-9*) Res Ctr Kabbalah.

Miracles of Card Play. Terence Reese & David Bird. 160p. 1998. pap. 17.95 (*0-575-06594-X*, Pub. by V Gollancz) Trafalgar.

Miracles of Christ. Dmitri Royster. LC 98-56027. 1999. write for info. (*0-88141-193-0*) St Vladimirs.

Miracles of Christ, Pt. I, Vol. 2. Gordon Lindsay. (Miracles in the Bible Ser.: Vol. 7). 1979. 2.95 (*0-89985-960-7*) Christ for the Nations.

Miracles of Christ, Pt. II, Vol. 3. Gordon Lindsay. (Miracles in the Bible Ser.: Vol. 7). 1979. 2.95 (*0-89985-961-5*) Christ for the Nations.

Miracles of Christmas. Agatha Christie. LC 97-15467. 145p. 1997. 16.99 (*0-87788-563-X*, H Shaw Pubs) Waterbrook Pr.

Miracles of Divine Discipline, Vol. 7 of 7. Gordon Lindsay. (Miracles in the Bible Ser.: Vol. 7). 1977. 1.95 (*0-89985-184-3*) Christ for the Nations.

Miracles of God: Gifts of Mercy. Jean Vogler. LC 95-79995. 216p. (Orig.). 1995. pap. 15.00 (*0-938041-63-0*) Arc Pr AR.

Miracles of Grace: Inspiring Stories of What God Has Done in Human Lives. Jon T. Murphree. 137p. (Orig.). 1996. pap. 7.95 (*1-885729-08-1*) Toccoa Falls.

Miracles of Jesus. (Children's Bible Stories Ser.). (Illus.). 24p. (J). 1993. 4.98 (*0-7853-0267-0*) Pubns Intl Ltd.

Miracles of Jesus. Tomie De Paola. (Illus.). (J). (ps-3). 1987. pap. 8.95 (*0-8234-1211-3*) Holiday.

Miracles of Jesus. Illus. & Retold by Tomie De Paola. LC 86-18297. 32p. (J). (gr. 4-7). 1987. lib. bdg. 16.95 (*0-8234-0635-0*) Holiday.

Miracles of Jesus. James Harpur & Marcus Braybrooke. LC 96-29132. (Bible Wisdom for Today Ser.). 1997. 14.95 (*0-89577-907-2*, Pub. by RD Assn) Penguin Putnam.

Miracles of Jesus. Lawrence G. Lovasik. (Saint Joseph Picture Bks.). 1978. pap. 1.25 (*0-89942-279-9*, 279-00) Catholic Bk Pub.

Miracles of Jesus. Joseph Rhymer. 152p. (C). 1996. pap. 39.95 (*0-85439-387-0*, Pub. by St Paul Pubns) St Mut.

***Miracles of Jesus.** Ellyn Sanna. (Young Reader's Christian Library). (Illus.). 224p. (J). (gr. 3-7). 2000. pap. 1.39 (*1-57748-723-0*) Barbour Pub.

***Miracles of Jesus.** Alfons Weiser. 112p. 2000. pap. 8.00 (*0-687-09020-2*) Abingdon.

***Miracles of Jesus, Vol. 8.** Amberly Neese. (Pulse Ser.). 2000. pap. 14.99 (*0-8307-2509-1*) Gospel Lght.

Miracles of Jesus: And Other Bible Stories. Retold by Selina Hastings. (Bible Stories Ser.). (Illus.). 64p. (J). (gr. 4-7). 1996. pap. 5.95 (*0-7894-1194-6*) DK Pub Inc.

Miracles of Jesus: Then & Now. Alfons Weiser. Ed. by Robert J. Karris. Tr. by David L. Tiede. (Hearld Biblical Bklts.). 1972. pap. 1.00 (*0-8199-0211-X*, Frncscn Herld) Franciscan Pr.

***Miracles of Jesus & Their Flip Side: Cycle A, B, & C.** Jerry L. Schmalenberger. LC 00-35792. 2000. disk 9.95 (*0-7880-1711-X*) CSS OH.

***Miracles of Jesus & Their Flip Side: Cycles A, B & C: Miracle Narratives from the Revised Common Lectionary...** Jerry L. Schmalenberger. LC 00-35792. 98p. 2000. pap. 9.95 (*0-7880-1710-1*) CSS OH.

Miracles of Jesus Christ. Lester Sumrall. 63p. (C). 1986. pap. text 10.00 (*0-937580-99-6*) Sumrall Pubng.

Miracles of Jesus for Children. Savary. (J). 1980. pap. 2.50 (*0-88271-155-5*) Regina Pr.

***Miracles of Mentoring: The Joy of Investing in the Future.** Thomas W. Dortch, Jr. LC 99-89128. 224p. 2000. 22.95 (*0-385-49991-4*) Doubleday.

Miracles of Military Medicine. Albert Q. Maisel. LC 70-167382. (Essay Index Reprint Ser.). 1977. reprint ed. 23.95 (*0-8369-2561-0*) Ayer.

Miracles of Mind: Exploring Nonlocal Consciousness & Spiritual Healing. Russell Targ & Jane Katra. LC 97-31591. (Illus.). 352p. 1998. 24.95 (*1-57731-070-5*) New Wrld Lib.

Miracles of Mind: Exploring Nonlocal Consciousness & Spiritual Healing. 2nd rev. ed. Russell Targ & Jane Katra. LC 97-31591. (Illus.). 360p. 1999. pap. 15.95 (*1-57731-097-7*) New Wrld Lib.

Miracles of Minerals: The Human Need for 90 Plus Elements from a Cell's Point of View. Albert E. Carter. 224p. (Orig.). 1995. pap. text 14.95 (*1-887995-00-5*) Amer Institute Res.

Miracles of Nature. Jo Hollingsworth. 36p. 1997. pap. 11.95 (*1-57377-001-9*) Easl Pubns.

Miracles of Our Lady. Gonzalo De Berceo. Tr. by Richard T. Mount & Annette G. Cash. LC 97-2119. (Illus.). 176p. 1997. 24.95 (*0-8131-2019-5*) U Pr of Ky.

***Miracles of Our Lady of Rocamadour: Analysis & Translation.** Marcus Bull. LC 99-37959. 256p. 1999. 75.00 (*0-85115-765-3*, Suffolk Records Soc) Boydell & Brewer.

Miracles of Our Lord. Charles C. Ryrie. LC 88-16608. 186p. 1988. reprint ed. 14.99 (*0-87213-742-2*) Loizeaux.

Miracles of Our Lord (a duplex) George MacDonald. 440p. 1995. reprint ed. 24.00 (*1-881084-59-0*) Johannesen.

Miracles of Rare Device: The Poet's Sense of Self in Nineteenth-Century Poetry. Fred Kaplan. LC 73-38818. 192p. reprint ed. pap. 59.60 (*0-608-17875-6*, 203271300080) Bks Demand.

Miracles of St. Anthony Mary Claret. Juan Echevarria. LC 92-61033. 318p. 1992. reprint ed. pap. 15.00 (*0-89555-473-9*) TAN Bks Pubs.

Miracles of St. Artemios: A Collection of Miracle Stories by an Anonymous Author of Seventh Century Byzantium. Tr. & Comment by V. S. Crisafulli. LC 96-47378. xxii, 319p. 1996. 122.50 (*90-04-10574-3*) Brill Academic Pubs.

Miracles of St. James. Ed. by Linda Davidson et al. Tr. by Maryjane Dunn et al from LAT. LC 96-14801. (Illus.). 150p. (Orig.). 1996. pap. 17.50 (*0-934977-38-0*) Italica Pr.

*__Miracles of St. John Capistan.__ Stanko Andric. 2000. 49.95 (*963-9116-68-8*) Ctrl Europ Univ.

Miracles of the Apostles, Vol. 4 of 7. Gordon Lindsay. (Miracles in the Bible Ser.: Vol. 4). 1977. 1.95 (*0-89985-181-9*) Christ for the Nations.

Miracles of the Bells. Russell Fanney. 508p. Date not set. 31.95 (*0-8488-2620-5*) Amereon Ltd.

Miracles of the Bible. large type ed. Sitare Ltd. Staff. Ed. by Alistair MacLean. (Yesterday & Tomorrow Bible Cartoon Ser.). (Illus.). 75p. (YA). 1996. spiral bd. 10.00 (*0-940178-83-4*) Sitare.

*__Miracles of the Heart.__ Monica Coglas. LC 99-68311. 240p. 2000. pap. 12.99 (*1-57921-264-6*) WinePress Pub.

Miracles of the Holy Qur'an. unabridged ed. Rachad El-Moussaoui. 270p. 1992. 35.00 (*1-893581-04-7*) Muhammad Islamic.

Miracles of the Mind: How to Use the Power of Your Mind for Healing & Prosperity. Byron Gentry & Mary Gentry. LC 98-39135. 1998. 14.95 (*1-56825-044-4*) Rainbow Books.

Miracles of Urine Therapy. C. P. Mithal. 82p. 1990. pap. 4.95 (*0-8464-4821-1*) Beekman Pubs.

Miracles of Urine Therapy: Nature's Natural Nectar to Cure Diseases. S. K. Sharma. (Illus.). 122p. 1999. pap. 7.95 (*0-8464-4938-2*) Beekman Pubs.

Miracles on Main Street. Veronica Ray. 1996. mass mkt. 5.50 (*0-312-95700-9*, Pub. by Tor Bks) St Martin.

Miracles on Maple Hill. Virginia Sorensen. (Illus.). (J). (gr. 4-7). 1984. 7.66 (*0-15-254560-3*, 836109) Harcourt.

Miracles on Maple Hill. Virginia Sorensen. LC 89-38864. 192p. (J). (gr. 3-7). 1990. pap. 4.95 (*0-15-254561-1*, Odyssey) Harcourt.

Miracles on Maple Hill. Virginia Aeggertsenn Sorensen. (Odyssey Classic Ser.). (J). 1956. 11.10 (*0-606-04005-6*, Pub. by Turtleback) Demco.

Miracles on Park Avenue: A Technique for Treating Acute & Chronic Pain. Albert B. Gerber. 192p. 1986. 14.95 (*0-8184-0387-X*) Carol Pub Group.

Miracles on Tap. Frank Duff. 1961. pap. 5.00 (*0-910984-15-8*) Montfort Pubns.

Miracles on the Border: Retablos of Mexican Migrants to the United States. Jorge Durand & Douglas S. Massey. LC 94-32080. (Illus.). 216p. 1995. pap. 25.95 (*0-8165-1497-6*); lib. bdg. 52.00 (*0-8165-1471-2*) U of Ariz Pr.

*__Miracles One at a Time.__ Andy Andrews. 2000. pap. 12.95 (*0-9629620-8-2*) Lightning Crown Pub.

*__Miracles Still Happen: My Faith Took Me to My Miracles.__ Doris Wallace. 50p. 1999. pap. 10.00 (*1-893303-08-X*) Trinity.

Miracles Still Happen in Brindavan. Anil Mohan & Kripavikshu. (Illus.). vi, 240p. 1991. 21.00 (*81-85318-55-7*, Pub. by H K Pubs & Dist) Nataraj Bks.

*__Miracles That I Have Seen.__ William A. Ward. LC 99-222807. 252p. 1998. pap. 12.99 (*1-884369-79-0*) McDougal Pubng.

Miracles, the Glory of God. Bill Panko & Margaret Panko. 250p. (Orig.). Date not set. pap. 19.95 (*1-885342-17-9*) Creative Ways.

Miracles, the Prelude to Glory. Bill Panko & Margaret Panko. 250p. (Orig.). Date not set. pap. 19.95 (*1-885342-16-0*) Creative Ways.

Miracles, the Speaking of Glory. Bill Panko & Margaret Panko. 250p. (Orig.). Date not set. pap. 19.95 (*1-885342-19-5*) Creative Ways.

Miracles, the Working of Glory. Bill Panko & Margaret Panko. 250p. (Orig.). Date not set. pap. 19.95 (*1-885342-18-7*) Creative Ways.

Miracles to Share. Kinoshita & Sanderson. 65p. (J). (ps up). 1983. pap. 5.00 (*0-318-57338-5*) Coleman Pub.

Miracles Today: True Stories of Divine Healing. Henry Libersat. LC 99-33944. 194p. 1999. pap. 10.99 (*1-56955-107-3*, Charis) Servant.

Miracles with Love. Jean Osborne. 61p. (Orig.). 1982. write for info. (*0-915631-02-4*) Osborne.

Miraculous Breakthroughs for Prostate & Impotency Problems. rev. ed. William L. Fischer. Ed. by Rebekah Schreffler. (Illus.). 222p. 1994. 24.95 (*0-915421-19-4*) Fischer Pub.

*__Miraculous Catch of Fish, 1.__ Patricia A. Hoffman. 1999. 8.99 (*0-570-05565-2*) CPH Preserv Soc.

Miraculous Child. Alvi Currier. 1997. 14.95 (*3-9500271-2-2*, Pub. by Basic Luka) Conciliar Pr.

Miraculous Day of Amalia Gomez. John Rechy. 256p. 1993. pap. 11.45 (*1-55970-203-6*, Pub. by Arcade Pub Inc) Time Warner.

Miraculous Gopal. Illus. by Padmavati D. Dasi. (Gopal Trilogy Ser.: No. 2). 48p. (J). (gr. k-4). 1999. 14.95 (*1-886069-18-2*, 1211, Pub. by Mandala Pub Grp) Words Distrib.

*__Miraculous Healing & You: Student Guide.__ Henry Wildeboer. LC 99-37885. (What the Bible Teaches, What You Need to Know Ser.). 95p. 1999. pap., student ed. 9.95 (*1-56212-417-X*, 150620) CRC Pubns.

*__Miraculous Healing on You: Leader's Guide.__ Leonard Kuyuenhover. (What the Bible Teaches, What You Need to Know Ser.). 66p. 1999. pap., teacher ed. 11.95 (*1-56212-418-8*, 150625) CRC Pubns.

Miraculous Heart: With Ikan, the Angel of the Rainbow. Jamie A. Modesco. (Illus.). 49p. (Orig.). (J). (gr. 4 up). 1995. pap. 12.95 (*0-9638758-4-1*) Brockton Pubng.

Miraculous Images of Our Lady: 100 Famous Catholic Portraits & Statues. Joan C. Cruz. LC 92-62149. (Illus.). 441p. (Orig.). 1993. pap. 20.00 (*0-89555-484-4*) TAN Bks Pubs.

Miraculous Images of Our Lord. Joan C. Cruz. (Illus.). 235p. 1995. pap. 13.50 (*0-89555-496-8*) TAN Bks Pubs.

Miraculous Journey of Mahomet. Marie-Rose Seguy. LC 77-5140. (Illus.). 1977. 40.00 (*0-8076-0868-8*) Braziller.

Miraculous Laws of Universal Dynamics. Al G. Manning. 1964. pap. 6.95 (*0-317-46046-3*) Pan Ishtar.

Miraculous Living. Shoni Labowitz. 336p. 1998. per. 12.00 (*0-684-83556-8*) S&S Trade.

Miraculous Living: A Guided Journey Through the 10 Gates of the Tree of Life. Shoni Labowitz. LC 96-19269. 336p. 1996. 22.50 (*0-684-81444-7*) S&S Trade.

Miraculous Makeover of Lizard Flanagan. Carol Gorman. LC 94-1279. (Trophy Bk.). 192p. (J). (gr. 3-7). 1996. pap. 4.95 (*0-06-440570-2*, HarpTrophy) HarpC Child Bks.

Miraculous Makeover of Lizard Flanagan. Carol Gorman. 1996. 9.60 (*0-606-09619-1*, Pub. by Turtleback) Demco.

Miraculous Medal: The Story of Our Lady's Appearances to Saint Catherine of Laboure. Mary F. Windeatt. LC 90-71823. (Stories of the Saints for Young People Ages 10 to 100 Ser.). Orig. Title: The Medal: The Story of Saint Catherine Laboure. (Illus.). 107p. (J). (gr. 5-9). 1994. reprint ed. pap. 7.00 (*0-89555-417-8*) TAN Bks Pubs.

Miraculous Milk Cow: More Tales My Great, Great Grandfather Might Tell about Life in a Ghetto in Russia in the Time of the Czars. Herman I. Kantor & Eric Larson. LC 94-5097. (Illus.). 176p. (Orig.). 1994. 18.95 (*1-56474-094-3*); pap. 9.95 (*1-56474-095-1*) Fithian Pr.

Miraculous Moments. Betty A. Killian. (Illus.). 125p. (Orig.). pap. 6.95 (*0-9634748-0-4*) Killian Min.

*__Miraculous Mystery: Reflections, Devotions & Awakenings.__ Tom Beyer. LC 99-96236. (Illus.). vi, 182p. 2000. mass mkt. 14.00 (*0-9672498-0-5*) OneSelf Pubg.

Miraculous Realm of God's Love. K. Copeland. 1987. pap. 5.95 (*0-938458-11-6*) K Copeland Pubns.

Miraculous Realm of God's Love. Kenneth Copeland. 71p. 1987. pap. 5.95 (*0-88114-784-2*) K Copeland Pubns.

Miraculous Retribution: A Study & Translation of T'ang Lin's Ming-pao Chi. Donald E. Gjertson. LC 89-82216. 305p. 1989. 35.00 (*0-87725-318-8*) U of Cal IAS.

Miraculous Simplicity: Essays on R. S. Thomas. Ed. by William V. Davis. LC 92-24609. 288p. 1993. text 26.00 (*1-55728-265-X*) U of Ark Pr.

Miraculous Stories from the Japanese Buddhist Tradition: The Nihon Ryoiki of the Monk Kyokai. Tr. & Anno. by Kyoko M. Nakamura. 344p. (C). 1997. text 49.00 (*0-7007-0449-3*, Pub. by Curzon Pr Ltd) UH Pr.

Miraculous Tales of the Lotus Sutra from Ancient Japan: The Dainihonkoku Hokeky Okenki of Priest Chingen. Chingen. Tr. & Anno. by Yoshiko K. Dykstra. LC 86-30744. 180p. 1987. reprint ed. pap. 51.30 (*0-608-00530-4*, 2061409) Bks Demand.

Miraculous Teacher: Ivan Galamian & the Meadowmount Experience. Elizabeth A. H. Green et al. (Illus.). xiv, 180p. 1993. text 27.50 (*0-9637170-0-6*, 1905S) Am String Tchrs.

Miraculous World of Your Unborn Baby. Nikki Bradford. LC 97-46417. 160p. 1998. pap. 14.95 (*0-8092-2928-5*, 292850, Contemporary Bks) NTC Contemp Pub Co.

*__Miraculously Builded in Our Hearts: A Dartmouth Reader.__ Ed. by Edward Connery Lathem & David M. Shribman. 422p. 1999. 35.00 (*1-58465-054-0*) U Pr of New Eng.

Mirad, Boy from Bosnia. Bont. (Longman Literature Ser.). 1995. pap. text. write for info. (*0-582-24949-X*, Pub. by Addison-Wesley) Longman.

Mirada a los Tipos Psichologicos: Una Descripcion de las Preferencias Dadas Por el Indicador de Tipos Psicologicos Myers-Briggs (MBTI) Earle C. Page. Tr. by Raymond A. Moody from ENG. LC 93-40958. (SPA., Illus.). 41p. 1993. pap. 5.75 (*0-935652-18-3*) Ctr Applications Psych.

Mirada al Espacio. David Glover. Tr. by Maria T. Sanz. (Biblioteca de Descubrimientos Ser.). (SPA., Illus.). 32p. (J). (gr. k-4). 1998. 11.95 (*1-58087-007-4*) C D Stampley Ent.

Mirada Biblica a la Familia. Luis Palau & James C. Dobson. (Serie Enfoque a la Familia - Focus on the Family Ser.).Tr. of Biblical Look at the Family. (SPA.). 20p. 1992. pap. 1.99 (*1-56063-348-4*, 497440) Editorial Unilit.

Mirada de los Sonambulos. Ana M. Fagundo. LC 94-70869. (Coleccion Interamer). (SPA.). 96p. (Orig.). 1994. pap. 13.00 (*0-89729-731-8*) Ediciones.

Miradas Ardientes: Burning Look, Vol. 419. Eva Rutland. (Harlequin Bianca Ser.). (SPA.). 1997. per. 3.50 (*0-373-33419-2*, 1-33419-2) Harlequin Bks.

Mirador: My Term As Hitler's Guest. John Burton. 163p. 1986. 39.00 (*0-7212-0766-9*, Pub. by Regency Pr GBR) St Mut.

Mirage. Perry Brass. Ed. by Tom Laine. LC 71-73116. (Ki Chronicles Ser.: Bk. 1). 219p. 1991. pap. 10.95 (*0-9627123-1-0*) Belhue Pr.

Mirage. Soheir Kashoggi. 1997. mass mkt. 6.99 (*0-614-20507-7*) Forge NYC.

Mirage. Soheir Khashoggi. 1997. mass mkt. 6.99 (*0-8125-5094-3*, Pub. by Forge NYC) St Martin.

Mirage. Soheir Khashoggi. 1997. 12.09 (*0-606-13081-0*, Pub. by Turtleback) Demco.

Mirage. Caragh M. O'Brien. LC 97-94018. 192p. 1997. 18.95 (*0-8034-9256-1*, Avalon Bks) Bouregy.

*__Mirage.__ Donald S. Passman. 336p. 2000. 25.95 (*0-446-52724-6*) Warner Bks.

Mirage. Boris Vallejo & Doris Vallejo. LC 96-61055. (Illus.). 128p. 1997. pap. 22.95 (*1-56025-139-5*, Thunders Mouth) Avalon NY.

Mirage. F. Paul Wilson & Matthew J. Costello. 352p. 1997. mass mkt. 6.99 (*0-446-60473-9*, Pub. by Warner Bks) Little.

*__Mirage: Dance of the Sun.__ 2nd ed. Jerome Brooke. (Mirage Bks.). 42p. 1999. pap. 4.00 (*0-9674487-0-0*) Good SAMAR.

Mirage: Enigmas of Race, Difference & Desire. David A. Bailey. LC 96-131527. (Illus.). 112p. 1996. pap. 18.95 (*0-905263-84-7*) Dist Art Pubs.

Mirage: The Soldiers' Story of Desert Storm. J. T. Terranova. Ed. by Kirstin Scott. 272p. 1995. pap. 19.95 (*0-9653103-0-2*) Noble Press.

Mirage Land: Images of Nevada. Wilbur S. Shepperson & Ann Harvey. LC 91-34066. (Wilbur S. Shepperson Series in History & Humanities). 216p. 1992. 21.95 (*0-87417-191-1*) U of Nev Pr.

Mirage of Continuity: Reconfiguring Academic Information Resources for the 21st Century. Council on Library & Information Resources Staff et al. Ed. by Brian L. Hawkins & Patricia Battin. LC 98-28434. 301p. 1998. 25.00 (*1-887334-59-9*) Coun Lib & Info.

Mirage of Health: Utopias, Progress, & Biological Change. Rene Jules Dubos. 236p. 1987. pap. 16.00 (*0-8135-1260-3*); text 35.00 (*0-8135-1259-X*) Rutgers U Pr.

Mirage of Modernization. Boris Kagarlitsky. Tr. by Renfrey Clarke from RUS. 352p. (C). 1995. text 38.00 (*0-85345-911-8*, Pub. by Monthly Rev); pap. text 18.00 (*0-85345-912-6*, Pub. by Monthly Rev) NYU Pr.

Mirage of Oil Protection. Robert L. Bradley, Jr. LC 88-25125. 284p. 1989. 41.00 (*0-8191-7202-2*); pap. 22.00 (*0-8191-7203-0*) U Pr of Amer.

*__Mirage of Power.__ Mubashir Hasan. 367p. 2000. text 24.95 (*0-19-579300-5*) OUP.

Mirage Revealed: A Review of the Mirage Edition of Magic the Gathering. Scott Johns. LC 97-225395. 208p. 1997. pap. 14.95 (*1-55622-561-X*) Wordware Pub.

Mirage Spartiate Pt. 1: Etude sur l'Idealisation de Sparte dans l'Antiquite Greque de ' Origine Jusqu'aux Cyniques, 2 vols. Francois Ollier. LC 72-7903. (Greek History Ser.). (FRE.). 1979. reprint ed. 53.95 (*0-405-04799-1*) Ayer.

Mirages de la Farce: Fete des Fous, Bruegel et Moliere. Thierry Boucquey. LC 90-28663. (Purdue University Monographs in Romance Languages: Vol. 33). (FRE., Illus.). xviii, 158p. 1991. 53.00 (*1-55619-085-9*); pap. 22.95 (*1-55619-086-7*) J Benjamins Pubng Co.

Mirages of Development: Science & Technology for the Third Worlds. Jean-Jacques Salomon & Andre Lebeau. LC 92-40754. 224p. 1993. lib. bdg. 42.00 (*1-55587-368-5*) L Rienner.

Mirages of Marriage. William J. Lederer & Don D. Jackson. LC 67-16608. 1968. 21.95 (*0-393-08400-0*) Norton.

Mirages of Marriage. William J. Lederer & Don D. Jackson. 1990. pap. 14.95 (*0-393-30632-1*) Norton.

Mirages of Transition: The Peruvian Altiplano, 1780-1930. Nils Jacobsen. LC 92-33342. 1993. 60.00 (*0-520-07938-8*, Pub. by U CA Pr); pap. 30.00 (*0-520-08291-5*, Pub. by U CA Pr) Cal Prin Full Svc.

Miramar. 2nd enl. ed. Naguib Mahfouz. Tr. by Fatma Moussa-Mahmoud. LC 89-20627. (ARA.). 156p. 1996. reprint ed. pap. 12.00 (*1-57889-037-3*) Passeggiata.

Miramar: U. K. Edition. Naguib Mahfouz. 192p. 1993. pap. 7.99 (*0-385-26941-2*) Doubleday.

Mirame, Puedo Cantar Mas! Look, I Can Sing More!, Vol. 5. Gale Mackey. (Look, I Can Talk! Ser.: Vol. 5). (SPA.). xx, 59p. (gr. 4-12). 1997. pap. 12.95 incl. audio Command Performance.

Mirame, Puedo Cantar Mas! Look, I Can Sing More!, Vol. 5. Gale Mackey & Contee Seely. (Look, I Can Talk! Ser.: Vol. 5). (SPA.). xx, 59p. (gr. 4-12). 1997. pap. 19.95 incl. audio (*0-929724-31-3*, 31-3) Command Performance.

Mirame, Todavia Estoy Hablando: Look, I'm Still Talking!, Vol. 3. Blaine Ray & Joe Neilson. (Look, I Can Talk! Ser.). (SPA., Illus.). vi, 72p. (Orig.). (YA). (gr. 9-12). 1994. pap. text 12.95 (*0-929724-22-4*, 22-4) Command Performance.

Miramichi Magic. Photos by Cathy Carnahan. LC 96-950144. (Illus.). 112p. 1996. bds. 29.95 (*0-88780-380-6*, Pub. by Formac Publ Co) Formac Dist Ltd.

Miramichi, New Brunswick, Canada Earthquake Sequence of 1982: A Preliminary Report. Ed. by Anne E. Stevens. 99p. 1983. pap. 12.00 (*0-318-17284-4*, EP-53) Earthquake Eng.

Miramichi River, NB. Paul Marriner. (River Journal Ser.: Vol. 4, No. 4). (Illus.). 48p. 1997. pap. 15.95 (*1-57188-055-0*) F Amato Pubns.

Miramichi Seasons. Cathy Carnahan. LC 98-95022. (Illus.). 128p. 1998. write for info. (*0-88780-468-3*) FMC.

Miranda. Linda Lael Miller. (Springwater Seasons Ser.: Bk. 3). 1999. mass mkt. 3.99 (*0-671-02686-0*) PB.

*__Miranda.__ large type ed. Vicki Page. LC 98-33778. 162p. 1999. write for info. (*0-7540-3532-8*) Chivers N Amer.

Miranda. large type ed. Vicki Page. LC 98-33778. 1999. 30.00 (*0-7838-0359-1*, G K Hall Lrg Type) Mac Lib Ref.

Miranda. Grace Livingston Hill. reprint ed. lib. bdg. 21.95 (*0-89190-042-X*, Rivercity Pr) Amereon Ltd.

*__Miranda: Springwater Seasons, Bk. 3.__ large type ed. Linda Lael Miller. LC 99-36091. (Thorndike Americana Ser.). 1999. 26.95 (*0-7862-2159-3*) Thorndike Pr.

Miranda: The Craft of Functional Programming. Simon Thompson. LC 95-23970. 480p. (C). 1995. pap. text 51.00 (*0-201-42279-4*) Addison-Wesley.

Miranda & the Frogs see Miranda y las Ranas

Miranda & the Movies. Jane Kendall. LC 98-36607. 256p. (J). 1999. pap. 6.00 (*0-15-202057-8*) Harcourt.

Miranda Debate: Law, Justice, & Policing. Ed. by Richard A. Leo & George C. Thomas, III. LC 98-9496. (Illus.). 352p. 1998. text 55.00 (*1-55553-338-8*) NE U Pr.

*__Miranda Debate: Law, Justice & Policing.__ Ed. by Richard A. Leo & George C. Thomas, III. LC 98-9496. 352p. 2000. pap. text 24.95 (*1-55553-422-8*) NE U Pr.

Miranda Encuentra una Campanita. Illus. by Tom Hirst. (Cuentame un Cuento Ser.).Tr. of Miranda Finds a Bell. (ENG & SPA.). 24p. (J). (ps-1). 1995. 2.98 (*1-85854-338-X*) Brimax Bks.

Miranda Finds a Bell see Miranda Encuentra una Campanita

Miranda Goes to Hollywood. Jane Kendall. LC 98-30912. 256p. (YA). 1999. 16.00 (*0-15-202059-4*) Harcourt.

Miranda Goose see Miranda la Gansa

Miranda, Her Litel Booke. Darley Mitchell. (Illus.). 1998. pap. 20.00 (*0-9631809-1-6*) Castle MI.

Miranda Is Lost see Miranda Se Pierde

Miranda la Gansa. Illus. by Tom Hirst. (Cuentame un Cuento Ser.).Tr. of Miranda Goose. (ENG & SPA.). 24p. (J). (ps-1). 1995. 2.98 (*1-85854-336-3*) Brimax Bks.

Miranda of the Island. large type ed. Sally James. 1991. 27.99 (*0-7089-2368-2*) Ulverscroft.

Miranda Said Murder. large type ed. Martin Carroll. (Linford Mystery Library). 224p. 1988. pap. 16.99 (*0-7089-6620-9*, Linford) Ulverscroft.

Miranda Se Pierde. Illus. by Tom Hirst. (Cuentame un Cuento Ser.).Tr. of Miranda Is Lost. (ENG & SPA.). 24p. (J). (ps-1). 1995. 2.98 (*1-85854-337-1*) Brimax Bks.

Miranda v Arizona. John Hogrogian. LC 98-50357. (Famous Trials Ser.). (Illus.). (J). (gr. 4-12). 1999. 22.45 (*1-56006-471-4*) Lucent Bks.

Miranda vs. Arizona: Rights of the Accused. Gail Blasser Riley. LC 93-34380. (Landmark Supreme Court Cases Ser.). (Illus.). 128p. (YA). (gr. 6 up). 1994. lib. bdg. 20.95 (*0-89490-504-X*) Enslow Pubs.

Miranda vs. Arizona: You Have the Right to Remain Silent. Paul B. Wice. LC 95-45284. (Historic Supreme Court Cases Ser.). (Illus.). 160p. (YA). (gr. 9-12). 1996. lib. bdg. 24.00 (*0-531-11250-0*) Watts.

Miranda vs. Arizona, 1966: Suspects' Rights. Susan D. Gold. (Supreme Court Decisions Ser.). (Illus.). 96p. (YA). (gr. 6 up). 1995. lib. bdg. 18.90 (*0-8050-3915-5*) TFC Bks NY.

Miranda y las Ranas. Illus. by Tom Hirst. (Cuentame un Cuento Ser.).Tr. of Miranda & the Frogs. (ENG & SPA.). 24p. (J). (ps-1). 1995. 2.98 (*1-85854-339-8*) Brimax Bks.

Miranda's Folly. large type ed. Rachelle Edwards. (Linford Romance Library). 320p. 1997. pap. 16.99 (*0-7089-5185-6*) Ulverscroft.

Miranda's Last Stand. Gloria Whelan. LC 99-21189. (Illus.). 144p. (J). (gr. 3-7). 1999. 14.95 (*0-06-028251-7*) HarpC Child Bks.

*__Miranda's Last Stand.__ Gloria Whelan. LC 99-21189. (Illus.). 144p. (J). (gr. 3-7). 1999. lib. bdg. 14.89 (*0-06-028252-5*) HarpC Child Bks.

*__Miranda's Last Stand.__ Gloria Whelan. LC 99-21189. 144p. (J). (gr. 3-7). 2000. pap. 4.95 (*0-06-442097-3*, HarpTrophy) HarpC Child Bks.

Miranda's Magic Garden. Linda Atnip. LC 97-9928. (Illus.). 32p. (J). (ps-7). 1997. 19.95 (*1-885394-21-7*) Bluestar Communs.

Miranda's Masquerade. large type ed. Meg Alexander. (Mills & Boon Large Print Ser.). 350p. 1997. 23.99 (*0-263-15239-1*, Pub. by Mills & Boon) Ulverscroft.

Miranda's Outlaw. Katherine Garbera. (Desire Ser.). 1998. per. 3.75 (*0-373-76169-4*, 1-76169-1) Silhouette.

Miranda's Viking. Maggie B. Shayne. 1994. per. 3.50 (*0-373-07568-5*) Silhouette.

Mirando Hacia Arriba en Medio de la Enfermedad (Looking up . . . While Lying Down) John E. Biegert. (Looking up Ser.).Tr. of Looking Up While Lying Down (Thoughts, Poems & Prayers for Those in the Hospital). (SPA.). 24p. (Orig.). 1983. pap. 1.95 (*0-8298-0663-6*) Pilgrim OH.

Mirandola Dormir (Watching Her Sleep) Persefone, 2 vols. in 1. Homero Aridjis. (SPA.). 295p. 1992. pap. 17.99 (*968-16-3932-4*, Pub. by Fondo) Continental Bk.

Mirandy & Brother Wind. Patricia C. McKissack. LC 87-349. (Illus.). 32p. (J). (ps-3). 1988. 17.00 (*0-394-88765-4*, Pub. by Knopf Bks Yng Read) Random.

Mirandy & Brother Wind. Patricia C. McKissack. LC 87-349. (Dragon Tales Ser.). (Illus.). (J). (ps-3). 1997. pap. 6.99 (*0-679-88333-9*, Pub. by Random Bks Yng Read) Random.

Mirandy & Brother Wind. Patricia C. McKissack. (J). 1996. 12.19 (*0-606-10877-7*, Pub. by Turtleback) Demco.

*__Miraposa.__ Francisco Jimenez. (SPA.). 2000. pap. 5.95 (*0-618-07036-2*) HM.

*__Mirari Vos: On Liberalism & Religious Indifferentism.__ Gregory XVI, pseud. 19p. 1998. reprint ed. pap. 2.95 (*0-935952-47-0*) Angelus Pr.

*__Mira's Food Planner/Journal.__ Mira K. Coone. 68p. 1999. 4.95 (*1-928824-00-5*) JMC Pubg.

Mirati Sikandari: A Study of Medieval History of Gujarat. Fazlullah L. Faridi. 1990. reprint ed. 52.00 (*81-85326-18-5*, Pub. by Vintage) S Asia.

Mircea Eliade: The Mythical Narrative. Eugen Simion. 320p. 1999. 42.50 (*0-88033-436-3*, 538, Pub. by East Eur Monographs) Col U Pr.

Mircea Eliade: The Romanian Roots, 1907-1945, 2 vols., Set. Mac L. Ricketts. (East European Monographs: No. 248). 1453p. 1988. text 276.00 (*0-88033-145-3*, Pub. by East Eur Monographs) Col U Pr.

Mircea Eliade & the Dialectic of the Sacred. Thomas J. Altizer. LC 73-15398. 219p. 1975. reprint ed. lib. bdg. 35.00 (*0-8371-7196-2*, ALME, Greenwood Pr) Greenwood.

An Asterisk (*) at the beginning of an entry indicates that the title is appearing for the first time.

Mircea Eliade et la Coincidence des Opposes ou l'Existence en Duel. Shafique Keshavjee. (FRE.). 498p. 1993. 33.95 (*3-906750-83-3*, Pub. by P Lang) P Lang Pubng.

Mircea Eliade's Vision for a New Humanism. John D. Cave. 232p. 1993. text 55.00 (*0-19-507434-3*) OUP.

*__Mircobial Telecourse__ 272p. 1999. pap., student ed. 28.13 (*0-07-237426-8*) McGraw.

Mircobiology. 3rd ed. Lansing Prescott & John P. Harley. 368p. (C). 1996. text, student ed. 25.62 (*0-697-21871-6*, WCB McGr Hill) McGrw-H Hghr Educ.

Mircroelectric Controls. (Science at Work Ser.). Date not set. pap. text. write for info. (*0-582-34926-5*, Pub. by Addison-Wesley) Longman.

MIRD: Radionuclide Data & Decay Schemes. rev. ed. David Weber et al. LC 89-11355. (Illus.). 447p. 1989. 63.00 (*0-932004-32-6*) Soc Nuclear Med.

MIRD Cellular S Values: Self-Absorbed Dose per Unit Cumulated Activity for Selected Radionuclides & Monoenergetic Electron & Alpha Particle Emitters Incorporated into Different Cell Compartments. SNM MIRD Committee. LC 96-51086. 1997. pap. text 70.00 (*0-932004-46-6*) Soc Nuclear Med.

MIRD Head & Brain Dosimetry: Absorbed Fractions of Energy & Absorbed Dose Per Unit Cumulated Activity Within Pediatric & Adult Head & Brain Models for Use in Nuclear Medicine Internal Dosimetry. Lionel G. Bouchet et al. (Illus.). 206p. 1999. pap. 70.00 (*0-932004-70-9*, Pub. by Soc Nuclear Med) Matthews Medical Bk Co.

MIRD Primer for Absorbed Dose Calculations. rev. ed. Ed. by Robert Loevinger et al. LC 91-4858. (Illus.). 128p. 1991. text 49.00 (*0-932004-38-5*) Soc Nuclear Med.

Mirena - The Levonorgestrel Intrauterine System: The New Contraceptive Option for Parous Women. Ed. by E. D. Johansson. LC 97-46788. (Illus.). 86p. 1998. 35.00 (*1-85070-037-0*) Prthnon Pub.

Mirette on the High Wire. Emily Arnold McCully. (Illus.). 32p. (J). (ps-3). 1992. 15.95 (*0-399-22130-1*, G P Putnam) Peng Put Young Read.

Mirette on the High Wire. Emily Arnold McCully. LC 91-36324. (Illus.). 32p. (J). (ps-3). 1997. pap. 5.99 (*0-698-11443-4*, PapStar) Peng Put Young Read.

Mirette on the High Wire. Emily Arnold McCully. LC 91-36324. (J). 1997. 11.15 (*0-606-11628-1*, Pub. by Turtleback) Demco.

Mirex. (Environmental Health Criteria Ser.: No. 44). 70p. 1984. pap. text 15.00 (*92-4-154184-9*, 1160044) World Health.

Mirex Health & Safety Guide. WHO Staff. (Health & Safety Guides: No. 39). 28p. 1990. 5.00 (*92-4-151039-0*) World Health.

Miriam see Young Readers Christian Library

Miriam. Beatrice Gormley. LC 98-17761. (J). Date not set. write for info. (*0-8028-5153-3*) Eerdmans.

*__Miriam.__ Patrick Henden. 240p. 1999. mass mkt. 7.95 (*1-56201-136-7*) Blue Moon Bks.

Miriam. Iris Rosofsky. LC 87-45859. (Charlotte Zolotow Bk.). 192p. (YA). (gr. 7 up). 1988. 11.95 (*0-06-024853-X*) HarpC Child Bks.

Miriam. Violet Wesson. (C). 1990. text 35.00 (*0-7223-2507-X*, Pub. by A H S Ltd) St Mut.

Miriam: A Novel. Beatrice Gormley. LC 98-17761. 192p. (YA). (gr. 4-9). 1999. pap. 6.00 (*0-8028-5156-8*) Eerdmans.

Miriam: The Southern Belle Who Became the First Woman Governor Of Texas. Carl R. McQueary & May N. Paulissen. Ed. by Ed Eakin. LC 94-4455. 400p. 1995. 27.95 (*0-89015-971-8*) Sunbelt Media.

Miriam Adahan Handbook: Living with Kids Parents at Their Best. Miriam Adahan. 250p. 1994. 12.95 (*1-56871-050-X*) Targum Pr.

Miriam Adahan Handbook: Nobody's Perfect - Maintaining Emotional Health, Vol. 1. Miriam Adahan. 263p. 1994. 12.95 (*1-56871-047-X*) Targum Pr.

Miriam Amanda Ferguson: First Woman Governor of Texas: Her Life Story Presented Through the Clothes She Wore. Nelda Patteson. LC 94-92139. (Women of Texas Ser.: 2). (Illus.). (Orig.). (J). (gr. 4-8). 1994. pap. 14.95 (*0-9629001-1-7*) Smiley Co.

Miriam & the Baby Moses. Illus. by Tammie Lyon. LC 99-203960. 12p. (J). (ps). 1999. bds. 3.99 (*0-310-97577-8*) Zondervan.

Miriam Coffin: or The Whale-Fisherman. Joseph C. Hart. 368p. 1995. text 19.95 (*0-9638910-5-7*) Mill Hill Pr.

Miriam Coffin: or The Whale-Fisherman. Joseph C. Hart. (C). 1972. reprint ed. text 29.50 (*0-8422-8071-5*) Irvington.

Miriam Coffin: or The Whale-Fisherman. Joseph C. Hart. (C). 1986. reprint ed. pap. text 6.95 (*0-8290-1872-7*) Irvington.

Miriam Colon, Actor & Theater Founder. Mayra Fernandez. (Illus.). (J). (gr. 1-4). 1994. pap. 6.35 (*0-8136-5271-5*); lib. bdg. 63.60 (*0-8136-5265-0*) Modern Curr.

Miriam Colon, Actriz y Fundadora de Teatro. Mayra Fernandez. (SPA., Illus.). (J). (gr. 1-4). 1994. pap. 6.35 (*0-8136-5299-5*); lib. bdg. 17.55 (*0-8136-5293-6*) Modern Curr.

Miriam Laufer: A Retrospective. Intro. by Diana Morris. LC 81-66864. (Illus.). 80p. 1981. pap. text 12.95 (*0-940220-04-0*) Asylums Pr-Language.

Miriam Mary & Me: Women in the Bible. Lois M. Wilson. 256p. 1996. pap. 15.95 (*1-55145-082-8*) NStone Publ.

*__Miriam, Moses' Sister.__ Theresa Morin. (Little Bible Bks.). (Illus.). 24p. (J). (ps-1). 2000. 1.99 (*1-57748-685-4*) Barbour Pub.

Miriam of Nazareth. unabridged ed. Ann S. Zoll. LC 96-83428. (Illus.). v, 200p. (Orig.). 1996. pap. 10.95 (*1-888937-01-7*, Echos of Bks) Echos of Life.

Miriam Schapiro: Shaping the Fragments of Art & Life. Thalia Gouma-Peterson. LC 99-18149. (Illus.). 160p. 1999. 45.00 (*0-8109-4377-8*, Pub. by Abrams) Time Warner.

*__Miriam Schapiro: Works on Paper: A 30 Year Retrospective.__ Miriam Schapiro et al. LC 98-61729. 72p. 1999. 20.00 (*0-911611-14-2*) Tucson Mus Art.

Miriam Shapiro: The Politics of the Decorative. Tracey Bashkoff. (Illus.). 15p. 1992. pap. 5.00 (*0-933793-21-9*) Guild Hall.

Miriam Waddington & Her Works. Peter Stevens. (Canadian Author Studies). 51p. (C). 1985. pap. 9.95 (*0-920802-87-7*, Pub. by ECW) Genl Dist Srvs.

Miriam Watches Baby Moses: A Story of Faith & Loyalty. Mary Manz Simon. LC 98-38567. (Prince of Egypt Ser.). 32p. (J). (ps-3). 1998. 8.99 (*0-8499-5851-2*) Tommy Nelson.

Miriam's Cookbook. Carrie Bender. Ed. by Mary C. Meyer. LC 97-51939. (Illus.). 112p. 1998. spiral bd. 9.99 (*0-8361-9086-6*) Herald Pr.

Miriam's Cup: A Passover Story. Fran Manushkin. LC 96-2480. (Illus.). 32p. (J). (gr. k-4). 1998. 15.95 (*0-590-67720-9*) Scholastic Inc.

*__Miriam's Daughters: Jewish Latin American Women Poets.__ Ed. by Marjorie Agosin. Tr. by Roberta Gordenstein. (SPA & ENG.). 224p. 2000. pap. 16.00 (*1-890932-13-2*, Pub. by Sherman Asher Pub) Partners-West.

Miriam's Dilemma. Donna Adee. (Miriam Ser.: No. 1). (Illus.). 160p. (J). (gr. 6-10). 1997. pap. 8.95 (*0-9654272-1-8*) Harvest KS.

Miriam's Gift: A Mother's Blessing - Then & Now. Rosemary Mild. LC 98-40757. (Illus.). 176p. 1999. pap. 12.95 (*1-56474-295-4*) Fithian Pr.

Miriam's Gift: Book & Keepsake. Prod. by Dream Works Staff. LC 98-30081. (Prince of Egypt Ser.). 32p. (J). (gr. 1-4). 1998. 9.99 (*0-525-46052-7*, PuffinBks) Peng Put Young Read.

Miriam's Gift Book & Keepsake. Tommy Nelson Publishers Staff. (Prince of Egypt Ser.). (J). 1998. 9.99 (*0-8499-5895-4*) Tommy Nelson.

Miriam's Holiday. Gail Gilkey. (Illus.). 32p. (J). (gr. k-5). 1998. pap. 5.95 (*0-9662983-1-4*) Windy Hill Pr.

Miriam's Journal Set, 5 bks. Carrie Bender. 1996. pap. 39.95 (*0-8361-9023-8*) Herald Pr.

Miriam's Kitchen: A Memoir. Elizabeth Ehrlich. LC 97-11473. 369p. 1997. 24.95 (*0-670-86908-2*) Viking Penguin.

Miriam's Kitchen: A Memoir. Elizabeth Ehrlich. LC 97-11473. 370p. 1998. pap. 13.95 (*0-14-026759-X*) Viking Penguin.

*__Miriam's Song: A Memoir.__ Miriam Mathabane. LC 00-26552. 320p. 2000. 24.50 (*0-684-83303-4*) Simon & Schuster.

Miriam's Tambourine: Jewish Folktales from Around the World. Ed. by Howard Schwartz. (Illus.). 428p. 1988. pap. 16.95 (*0-19-282136-9*) OUP.

Miridae of Ohio. S. A. Watson. (Bulletin Ser.: No. 16). 1928. pap. text 3.00 (*0-86727-015-2*) Ohio Bio Survey.

Mirko y el Mamut (Mirko & the Mammoth) Elisabeth Heck. (SPA.). (J). (gr. 5-6). 1995. pap. 5.99 (*968-16-4725-4*, Pub. by Fondo) Continental Bk.

Mirk's Festial: A Collection of Homilies. T. Erbe. (EETS, ES Ser.: No. 96). 1974. reprint ed. 63.00 (*0-527-00296-8*) Periodicals Srv.

Mirlo. Noelle Granger.Tr. of Blackbird. (SPA., Illus.). (J). (gr. k-1). 6.95 (*980-257-220-9*, Pub. by Ediciones Ekare) Kane-Miller Bk.

Miro. Jacques Dupin. (Great Monographs). (Illus.). 480p. 1993. 500.00 (*84-343-0727-8*) Elliots Bks.

Miro. Walter Erben. (Big Art Ser.). 1998. 19.99 (*3-8228-7217-2*) Taschen Amer.

*__Miro.__ Walter Erben. 1999. 19.99 (*3-8228-7369-1*) Taschen Amer.

Miro. Walterf Erben. 1994. pap. 19.99 (*3-8228-0112-7*) Taschen Amer.

Miro. Walterf Erben. (SPA.). 1996. pap. 19.99 (*3-8228-0219-0*) Taschen Amer.

Miro. Janis Mink. (Basic Ser.). 1994. pap. 9.99 (*3-8228-9649-7*) Taschen Amer.

Miro. Janis Mink. (SPA.). 1996. pap. 9.99 (*3-8228-0685-4*) Taschen Amer.

Miro. Roland Penrose. LC 85-50751. (World of Art Ser.). (Illus.). 1985. pap. 14.95 (*0-500-20099-8*, Pub. by Thames Hudson) Norton.

Miro. Nicholas Ross. LC 95-35420. (Famous Artists Ser.). (Illus.). 32p. (J). (gr. 5 up). 1995. 11.95 (*0-8120-6535-2*); pap. 6.95 (*0-8120-9427-1*) Barron.

Miro. Nicholas Ross. (Famous Artists Ser.). 1995. 12.15 (*0-606-08822-9*, Pub. by Turtleback) Demco.

Miro: A Toute Epreuve. Paul Eluard. LC 84-45389. 104p. 1993. pap. 29.50 (*0-8076-1330-4*) Braziller.

Miro: Earth & Sky see Art for Children

Miro: Exhibition Catalogue of Paintings, Sculpture & Graphics. Henry T. Hopkins. (Illus.). 96p. 1981. pap. 25.00 (*0-8150-0012-X*) Wittenborn Art.

Miro di Tenebra see Wall of Darkness

Miro, les Essencies de la Terra. Illus. by Joan Miro. (CAT.). 1993. 7500.00 (*0-614-00037-8*) Elliots Bks.

Miro, les Essencies de la Terra. limited ed. Illus. by Joan Miro. (CAT.). 1993. 7500.00 (*0-614-00143-9*) Elliots Bks.

Miro Lithographs. Joan Miro. (Art Library). (Illus.). 48p. (Orig.). 1983. pap. 4.95 (*0-486-24437-7*) Dover.

Miro Lithographs, 1976-1981, Vol. 6. Patrick Cramer. (Illus.). 292p. 1992. 270.00 (*1-55660-190-5*) A Wofsy Fine Arts.

Miro Lithographs, 1972-1975, Vol. 5. Patrick Cramer. (Illus.). 192p. 1992. 250.00 (*1-55660-189-1*) A Wofsy Fine Arts.

Miro Litografo, 4 vols., Set. Fernand Mourlot et al. (SPA., Illus.). 926p. 1981. 1900.00 (*1-55660-227-8*) A Wofsy Fine Arts.

Miro Mirror Poems. Robley E. Whitson. 55p. 1995. pap. 12.00 (*1-55605-260-X*) Wyndham Hall.

Miro on Mallorca. Barbara Catoir et al. (Pegasus Library). (Illus.). 128p. 1995. 25.00 (*3-7913-1483-1*, Pub. by Prestel) te Neues.

Miro Postcard Book. 1995. pap. 5.99 (*3-8228-9389-7*) Taschen Amer.

Miro Poster Book. Taschen Staff. (Illus.). 1995. pap. 8.99 (*3-8228-9378-1*) Taschen Amer.

Miro 95: Proceeding of the Final Workshop on Multimedia Information Retrieval : Glasgow, Scotland, 18-20 September 1995. British Computer Society Staff. Ed. by Ian Ruthven. LC 96-22046. (Electronic Workshops in Computing Ser.). 9p. 1996. pap. 54.50 (*3-540-14582-6*) Spr-Verlag.

Miroir des Limbes: La Corde et les Souris, Tome 2. Andre Malraux. (Folio Ser.: No. 731). (FRE.). 1986. pap. 13.95 (*2-07-036731-2*) Schoenhof.

Miroir des Limbes: La Corde et les Souris, Vol. 2. Andre Malraux. (FRE.). 1986. pap. 16.95 (*0-8288-3713-9*, M11056) Fr & Eur.

Miroir des Limbes Vol. 1: Antimemoires. Andre Malraux. (FRE.). 1972. pap. 17.95 (*0-8288-3712-0*, F110871) Fr & Eur.

Miroir des Simples Ames see Marguerite Porete: The Mirror of Simple Souls

*__Miroir du Soleil.__ Rony Blain. 98p. 2000. pap. 15.00 (*1-886699-31-3*) Five Corners.

Miroirs de l'Infini see Mirrors of Infinity: The French Formal Garden & 17th Century Metaphysics

Miroku - Maitreya. Taruho Inagaki. Tr. by Kenji Yuda from JPN.Tr. of Maitreya. 58p. (Orig.). 1996. pap. 5.00 (*1-887289-24-0*) Rodent Pr.

Miron Sima: Woodcuts. Ed. by Grace C. Grossman. 28p. (Orig.). 1977. pap. 7.00 (*0-935982-23-X*, JMJ-04) Spertus Coll.

Miro's Dream. E. J. Gold & Iven Lourie. Ed. by Linda Corriveau. (Fine Art Ser.). (Illus.). 120p. 1988. pap. 16.95 (*0-89556-055-0*) Gateways Bks & Tapes.

Miro's Engravings, 1961-1973: With Two Original Woodcuts. Jacques Dupin. (Illus.). 248p. 1989. 375.00 (*1-55660-248-0*) A Wofsy Fine Arts.

Miro's Engravings, 1928-1960: A Catalogue Raisonne with Two Original Woodcuts. Jacques Dupin. (Illus.). 192p. 1984. 375.00 (*1-55660-058-5*) A Wofsy Fine Arts.

Miro's Illustrated Books. Patrick Cramer. (Illus.). 680p. 1989. boxed set 395.00 (*1-55660-102-6*) A Wofsy Fine Arts.

Miro's Lithographs, 1953 to 1972, 4 Vols. Raymond Queneau et al. (Illus.). 1000p. 1981. 2950.00 (*0-915346-83-4*) A Wofsy Fine Arts.

Miroslaw Balka: 36,6. Miroslaw Balka. (Illus.). 44p. 1993. pap. 15.00 (*0-941548-25-2*) Ren Soc U Chi.

Mirounga: A Guide to Elephant Seals. 2nd rev. ed. Sheri Howe. Ed. & Photos by Frank S. Balthis. (Illus.). 50p. (Orig.). 1997. pap. 5.95 (*0-918355-04-4*) Firehole Pr.

Mirour de l'Omme: The Mirror of Mankind. John Gower. Tr. by William B. Wilson. (Medieval Texts & Studies: No. 5). 411p. 1992. text 62.00 (*0-937191-17-5*) Mich St U Pr.

Mirour Of Mans Saluacioune. Henry. 347p. 1987. 105.95 (*0-85967-716-8*) Ashgate Pub Co.

Mirrikh: or A Woman from Mars. Francis W. Doughty. Ed. by R. Reginald & Douglas A. Menville. LC 75-46267. (Supernatural & Occult Fiction Ser.). (Illus.). 1976. lib. bdg. 23.95 (*0-405-08125-1*) Ayer.

Mirro & Marble: Poetry of Iain Crichton Smith. Carol Gow. (C). 1993. pap. 36.00 (*0-86334-070-9*, Pub. by Saltire Soc) St Mut.

Mirrons, Nos. 1-110, the Lounger, Nos. 1-101 see Mirror & the Lounger

Mirror. Robert Creeley. (Illus.). 24p. (Orig.). (C). 1988. pap. 20.00 (*0-922668-01-9*) SUNYB Poetry Rare Bks.

Mirror. Christina Darling. LC 96-84953. (Illus.). 32p. (J). (gr. k). 1997. 16.00 (*0-374-34720-4*) FS&G.

Mirror. Lynn Freed. (Illus.). 219p. 1999. pap. 11.95 (*0-345-42689-4*) Ballantine Pub Grp.

Mirror. David Hollis & Dotty Hollis. 180p. (YA). 1994. pap. 9.95 (*0-9640894-0-8*) BPCOA.

Mirror. deluxe limited ed. Robert Creeley. (Illus.). 24p. (Orig.). (C). 1988. 35.00 (*0-922668-02-7*) SUNYB Poetry Rare Bks.

Mirror. Marlys Millhiser. (Illus.). 304p. 1997. reprint ed. pap. 14.95 (*0-915230-15-1*) Rue Morgue.

*__Mirror: A History.__ Sabine Melchior-Bonnet. Tr. by Katharine Jewett from FRE. 2001. 27.50 (*0-415-92447-2*) Routledge.

Mirror: Advice on the Presence of Awareness. Namkhai Norbu. LC 96-36348. 80p. 1995. pap. text 9.95 (*1-886449-10-4*) Barrytown Ltd.

Mirror: Psychoanalytic Perspectives. Ed. by Bornstein. (Psychoanalytic Inquiry Ser.: Vol. 5, No. 2). 1995. 20.00 (*0-88163-974-5*) Analytic Pr.

*__Mirror: The Fiction & Essays of Koda Aya.__ Ann Sherif. LC 99-10672. 264p. 1999. 42.00 (*0-8248-1899-7*) UH Pr.

*__Mirror: The Fiction & Essays of Koda Aya.__ Ann Sherif. LC 99-10672. 224p. 1999. pap. 16.95 (*0-8248-2181-5*) UH Pr.

Mirror & Man. Benjamin Goldberg. LC 85-718. 272p. 1985. pap. 84.40 (*0-7837-8437-6*, 204924100010) Bks Demand.

Mirror & Memory. Richard P. Heitzenrater. 1989. pap. 14.95 (*0-687-27069-3*) Abingdon.

Mirror & Pattern. Carobeth Laird. LC 83-62710. 1984. 25.00 (*0-939046-30-X*) Malki Mus Pr.

Mirror & the Killer-Queen: Otherness in Literary Language. Gabriele Schwab. (Theories of Contemporary Culture Ser.: Vol. 18). 240p. 1996. 35.00 (*0-253-33037-8*) Ind U Pr.

Mirror & the Killer-Queen: Otherness in Literary Language. Gabriele Schwab. (Theories of Contemporary Culture Ser.: Vol. 18). 240p. 1996. pap. text 15.95 (*0-253-21051-8*) Ind U Pr.

Mirror & the Lamp: Romantic Theory & the Critical Tradition. Meyer H. Abrams. (Illus.). 406p. 1971. reprint ed. pap. text 16.95 (*0-19-501471-5*) OUP.

Mirror & the Lounger. Ed. by Henry Mackenzie. LC 78-67534. (Scottish Enlightenment Ser.). Orig. Title: The Mirrons, Nos. 1-110, the Lounger, Nos. 1-101. reprint ed. 32.50 (*0-404-17675-5*) AMS Pr.

Mirror & the Magic. Carol S. Saxe. 448p. (Orig.). 1996. mass mkt. 5.99 (*0-505-52086-9*, Love Spell) Dorchester Pub Co.

Mirror & the Skylight. Colin Evans. 1987. 35.00 (*0-7855-1882-7*) St Mut.

Mirror & the Word: Modernism, Literary Theory, & Georg Trakl. Eric B. Williams. LC 92-24242. (Texts & Contexts Ser.). x, 350p. (C). 1993. text 50.00 (*0-8032-4756-7*) U of Nebr Pr.

Mirror & Veil: The Historical Dimension of Spenser's "Faerie Queene" Michael O'Connell. LC 77-1733. 234p. reprint ed. pap. 72.60 (*0-7837-3754-8*, 204357100010) Bks Demand.

M

Mirror Book: English, American & European. Herbert F. Schiffer. LC 83-61252. (Illus.). 256p. 1983. 45.00 (*0-916838-82-X*) Schiffer.

Mirror Bride. Robyn Donald. 1997. per. 3.50 (*0-373-11865-1*, 1-11866-0) Harlequin Bks.

Mirror by Design: Using Reflection to Transform Space. Pamela Heyne. LC 95-51484. (Illus.). 203p. 1996. 85.00 (*0-471-11833-8*) Wiley.

Mirror by the Road: A Transforming Journey of Spirituality in Everyday Life. Peter Oppenheimer. (Illus.). 208p. (Orig.). 1988. pap. 12.95 (*0-945925-03-4*) Inner Wealth Pr.

*__Mirror Crack'd.__ Agatha Christie. 2000. mass mkt. 5.99 (*0-451-19989-8*, Sig) NAL.

Mirror Crack'd from Side to Side. Agatha Christie. 240p. 1992. mass mkt. 5.99 (*0-06-100285-2*, Harp PBks) HarpC.

Mirror Dance. Lois McMaster Bujold. 592p. 1995. per. 6.99 (*0-671-87646-5*) Baen Bks.

Mirror Dance. Elisabeth Kyle. 1999. pap. 31.00 (*0-671-77489-1*, Pocket Books) PB.

Mirror Dance: Identity in a Women's Community. Susan Krieger. LC 82-19424. 224p. 1983. pap. 19.95 (*0-87722-314-9*) Temple U Pr.

Mirror Dances. Louis Hammer. LC 86-2907. (Illus.). 64p. (Orig.). 1986. pap., per. 15.00 (*0-912767-08-1*) Intertxt AK.

Mirror Driven Through Nature. William Zaranka. (Vagrom Chap Bk.: No. 18). 52p. 1981. pap. 4.95 (*0-935552-00-6*) Sparrow Pr.

Mirror Explorations. Peggy McLean. (Illus.). 52p. (J). (gr. 1-5). 1993. pap. text 8.95 (*1-882293-01-0*, A-1685) Activity Resources.

Mirror for Americans: Likeness of the Eastern Seaboard, 1810. Ralph H. Brown. LC 67-27449. (American Scene Ser.). 1968. reprint ed. 45.00 (*0-306-70974-0*) Da Capo.

Mirror for French Poetry, 1840 to 1940. Ed. by Cecily Mackworth. LC 71-76946. (Granger Index Reprint Ser.). 1977. 19.95 (*0-8369-6027-0*) Ayer.

Mirror for Gotham: New York As Seen by Contemporaries from Dutch Days to the Present. 2nd ed. Bayrd Still. LC 94-17970. (Illus.). xxxiv, 417p. 1994. 35.00 (*0-8232-1528-8*); pap. 19.95 (*0-8232-1529-6*) Fordham.

Mirror for Humanity: A Concise Introduction to Cultural Anthropology. Conrad P. Kottak. LC 95-15382. 317p. (C). 1995. pap. 34.38 (*0-07-035783-8*) McGraw.

Mirror for Humanity: A Concise Introduction to Cultural Anthropology. 2nd ed. Conrad P. Kottak. LC 98-18645. 336p. 1998. pap. 30.00 (*0-07-290171-3*) McGraw.

Mirror for Man: The Relation of Anthropology to Modern Life. Clyde Kluckhohn. LC 85-1120. (Classics of Anthropology Ser.). 333p. 1985. pap. 103.30 (*0-608-05642-1*, 206609600006) Bks Demand.

*__Mirror for Marriage__ Roger W. Axford. LC 99-194509. 85p. 1999. write for info. (*1-893453-05-7*) Media Prods.

Mirror for Observers. Edgar Pangborn. 1993. reprint ed. lib. bdg. 18.95 (*0-89968-358-4*, Lghtyr Pr) Buccaneer Bks.

Mirror for Princes from India. Ed. by Ernst J. Grube. (C). 1991. 36.00 (*81-85026-16-5*, Pub. by Marg Publns) Art Media Resources.

Mirror for Ruffians. Philip Lindsay. LC 72-303. (Essay Index Reprint Ser.). 1977. reprint ed. 23.95 (*0-8369-2799-0*) Ayer.

Mirror for Socialism: Soviet Criticisms of China. Gilbert Rozman. LC 84-42902. 307p. 1985. reprint ed. pap. 95.20 (*0-7837-9436-3*, 206017800004) Bks Demand.

Mirror for Witches. Esther Forbes. 21.95 (*0-8488-0050-8*) Amereon Ltd.

Mirror for Witches. Esther Forbes. (Cassandra Edition Ser.). (Illus.). 215p. 1985. reprint ed. pap. 9.00 (*0-89733-154-0*) Academy Chi Pubs.

Mirror Group PLC & Midland Independent Newspapers PLC: A Report on the Propose Monopolies & Mergers Commission Report, Command Paper 3762. (Command Papers (All) Ser.: No. 81011068). 1997. 35.00 (*0-10-137622-7*, HM76227, Pub. by Statnry Office) Bernan Associates.

*__Mirror Guide to Buying House IBD.__ 1998. write for info. (*0-13-915794-8*) P-H.

*__Mirror Guide to Investment IBD.__ 1998. write for info. (*0-13-915828-6*) P-H.

*__Mirror Guide to Managing Your Money IBD.__ 1998. write for info. (*0-13-915802-2*) P-H.

M

Mirror Hate: The Convergent Ideology of Northern Ireland Paramilitaries, 1966-1992. Richard Davis. LC 94-27123. 1994. 77.95 (*1-85521-558-6*, Pub. by Dartmth Pub) Ashgate Pub Co.

Mirror Image. Melinda Cross. (Presents Ser.). 1993. per. 2.89 (*0-373-11535-0*, 1-11535-1) Harlequin Bks.

Mirror Image. Lucille Fletcher. 224p. 1990. pap. 3.95 (*0-380-70770-5*, Avon Bks) Morrow Avon.

Mirror Image. Shirley Hailstock. 304p. 1998. pap. 4.99 (*0-7860-0521-1*, Pinncle Kensgtn) Kensgtn Pub Corp.

***Mirror Image.** Danielle Steel. 560p. 1999. mass mkt. 7.99 (*0-440-22477-2*) Dell.

Mirror Image. Danielle Steel. LC 98-16828. 432p. 1998. 26.95 (*0-385-31509-0*) Doubleday.

***Mirror Image.** large type ed. Brian Battison. 408p. 1999. 31.99 (*0-7089-4129-X*) Ulverscroft.

Mirror Image. large type ed. Melinda Cross. 1992. reprint ed. 18.95 (*0-263-13027-4*) Mac Lib Ref.

Mirror Image. limited aut. ed. Danielle Steel. 432p. 1998. 200.00 (*0-385-33343-9*) Delacorte.

Mirror Image. Sandra Brown. 448p. 1990. reprint ed. mass mkt. 7.99 (*0-446-35395-7*, Pub. by Warner Bks) Little.

Mirror Image: The Influence of the Daguerreotype on American Society. Richard Rudisill. LC 79-137880. 354p. reprint ed. pap. 109.80 (*0-608-12048-0*, 202467800038) Bks Demand.

Mirror Image: 12 Ways to Becoming More Christlike. Beacon Hill Press Staff. 44p. 1999. pap. text, teacher ed. 5.50 (*0-8341-1723-1*) Beacon Hill.

Mirror Image: 12 Ways to Becoming More Christlike. Beacon Hill Press Staff. 128p. 1999. pap. text, student ed. 6.50 (*0-8341-1722-3*) Beacon Hill.

Mirror Images. Mike Van Fleteren. 167p. 1993. pap. 5.95 (*0-9638397-3-X*) Blue Water.

Mirror Images: Carma Riera's Joc de Miralls. Carme Riera. Tr. by Cristina De la Torre from CAT. LC 93-9535. (Catalan Studies: Vol. 9).Tr. of Joc de Miralls. 182p. 1993. 29.95 (*0-8204-2077-8*) P Lang Pubng.

Mirror Images: Looking at Our Reflections to Transform Our Lives. Gabrielle Sarfaty & Gayle Knowles. (Illus.). 124p. 1997. pap. 12.95 (*1-880047-49-7*) Creative Des.

Mirror Images: Teaching Writing in Black & White. Jane Zeni et al. LC 94-22330. 515p. 1994. pap. text 29.00 (*0-435-08821-1*, 08821) Heinemann.

Mirror Images: Women, Surrealism & Self-Representation. Ed. by Whitney Chadwick. LC 97-46576. (Illus.). 154p. 1998. pap. text 35.00 (*0-262-53157-7*) MIT Pr.

Mirror Images Vol. 1: Mirrors of Life. Phyllis Adams-Crymes. Ed. by Hardbound, Inc., Staff. Date not set. pap. 8.95 (*1-930659-00-8*) P Adams-Crymes.

Mirror in Parchment: The Luttrell Psalter & the Making of Medieval England. annuals Michael Camille. LC 98-13986. (Illus.). 416p. 1998. 40.00 (*0-226-09240-2*) U Ch Pr.

Mirror in the Roadway. Frank O'Connor. LC 77-117886. (Select Bibliographies Reprint Ser.). 1977. 24.95 (*0-8369-5339-8*) Ayer.

Mirror in the Shrine: American Encounters with Meiji Japan. Robert A. Rosenstone. LC 87-31053. (Illus.). 336p. 1988. text 39.00 (*0-674-57641-1*) HUP.

Mirror in the Shrine: American Encounters with Meiji Japan. Robert A. Rosenstone. 336p. 1991. pap. 18.00 (*0-674-57642-X*, ROSMIX) HUP.

Mirror in the Text. Lucien Dallenbach. Tr. by Jeremy Whiteley & Emma Hughes. LC 89-4898. 280p. 1989. 47.95 (*0-226-13491-1*) U Ch Pr.

***Mirror Magic: Level B.** Steck-Vaughn Company Staff. (Read All about It Ser.). (Illus.). (J). 2000. pap. 4.95 (*0-8114-3769-8*) Raintree Steck-V.

Mirror Makers: A History of American Advertising & Its Creators. Stephen R. Fox. LC 97-9235. 416p. 1997. 18.95 (*0-252-06659-6*) U of Ill Pr.

Mirror Manipulations: Hidden Images - Unique Quilts. Gail Valentine. (Illus.). 96p. 1999. pap. 21.95 (*0-9671328-1-9*) Valentine Designs.

Mirror Maze. William Bayer. 400p. 1995. mass mkt. 5.99 (*0-515-11523-1*, Jove) Berkley Pub.

Mirror Me. Joan Albarella. (Illus.). 50p. 1973. pap. 3.00 (*0-914620-01-0*) Alpha Pr.

Mirror Mimes Mankind's Mind. A. M. Onoapoi. LC 96-94708. 56p. (Orig.). 1996. pap. 12.05 (*0-9654513-1-3*) Think Pen.

Mirror Mind: Zen-Christian Dialogue. 2nd ed. William S. Johnston. LC 80-8350. x, 181p. 1990. pap. 17.00 (*0-8232-1255-6*) Fordham.

Mirror, Mirror. Margareta Bergman. Tr. by Veronica Ralston from SWE. LC 98-230638. 256p. 1998. 29.95 (*0-7206-1046-X*, Pub. by P Owen Ltd) Dufour.

Mirror, Mirror. M. T. Coffin. (Spinetinglers Ser.). 1997. 9.09 (*0-606-10878-5*, Pub. by Turtleback) Demco.

Mirror, Mirror. Donna Julian. 1996. mass mkt. 5.99 (*0-451-18867-5*, Sig) NAL.

***Mirror Mirror.** Carol Kafka. 402p. 2000. pap. 14.95 (*0-929093-06-2*, Pub. by GRM Assocs) Allnce Hse.

Mirror, Mirror. Marilyn M. McAuley & Alice Gray. 144p. (Orig.). 1985. pap. 6.70 (*0-310-42951-X*, 11344P) Zondervan.

***Mirror Mirror.** Pendergrast. 2000. 26.00 (*0-465-05470-6*, Pub. by Basic); pap. 15.00 (*0-465-05471-4*, Pub. by Basic) HarpC.

Mirror Mirror. Patricia Scanlan. LC 98-120452. 396 p. 1997. write for info. (*1-85371-767-3*) Poolbeg Pr.

Mirror, Mirror. Valerie Stephens. 352p. 1994. mass mkt. 4.50 (*0-8217-4782-7*, Zebra Kensgtn) Kensgtn Pub Corp.

***Mirror, Mirror.** Linda Randall Wisdom. 2001. mass mkt. 4.50 (*0-373-27119-0*, 1-27119-6) Silhouette.

Mirror, Mirror, Vol. 9. A. G. Cascone. (Deadtime Stories Ser.). 1997. pap. 3.50 (*0-8167-4260-X*) Troll Communs.

Mirror, Mirror, Vol. 18. M. T. Coffin. (Spinetinglers Ser.). (J). 1997. pap. 3.99 (*0-380-78611-7*, Avon Bks) Morrow Avon.

***Mirror, Mirror: Forty Folktales for Mothers & Daughters to Share.** Jane Yolen & Heidi E. Stemple. LC 99-46891. 254p. (J). 2000. 24.95 (*0-670-88907-5*, Viking Child) Peng Put Young Read.

Mirror, Mirror: Reflections of the Sacred Self. Patricia Telesco. 202p. 1999. pap. 10.95 (*1-881542-51-3*) Blue Star Prodns.

Mirror, Mirror: Terse Verse for Seasoned Citizens. Vi Bercovitch. (Illus.). 66p. pap. (*0-9695180-5-6*) Sh1oreline.

Mirror, Mirror on the Easel: Caesar Cirigliano. Ed. by Mary Dawson. LC 98-211629. (Illus.). 192p. 1998. 40.00 (*1-85756-393-X*, Pub. by Janus Pubng) Paul & Co Pubs.

Mirror, Mirror, On the Floor! Evan Skolnick. (Snow White & the Seven Dwarfs Ser.). (J). 1998. pap. text 4.50 (*1-57840-165-8*, Pub. by Acclaim Bks) Penguin Putnam.

Mirror, Mirror on the Wall. Ken Hemphill. 176p. (Orig.). 1992. pap. 8.99 (*0-8054-1037-6*, 4210-37) Broadman.

Mirror, Mirror on the Wall... Who Is in There after All. Beverly Toney-Walter. 180p. 1998. pap. 24.95 (*1-890168-19-X*) Cobra Pub Co.

Mirror, Mirror, on the Wall: Women Writers Explore the Fairy Tales That Have Changed Their Lives. Ed. by Kate Bernheimer. LC 97-42242. 368p. 1998. pap. 14.00 (*0-385-48681-2*, Anchor NY) Doubleday.

Mirror, Mirror on the Wall, Have I Got News for You: An A to Z Faith Lift for Your Sagging Self-Esteem. Liz Curtis Higgs. LC 97-25326. 132p. 1997. pap. 9.99 (*0-7852-7109-0*) Nelson.

Mirror, Mirror on the Wall, Who Am I Fooling. 45p. 1986. pap. 2.00 (*0-934803-42-0*) J Van Impe.

Mirror Murder. Marjaree Mayne. 276p. 1996. pap. 5.99 (*1-888701-10-2*) Jarrett Pr.

Mirror of a People. Ed. by Sheldon Oberman & Elaine Newton. 256p. 1985. pap. 10.95 (*0-920657-00-1*, Pub. by Coteau) Genl Dist Srvs.

Mirror of a Soul. Helena E. Ruhnau. LC 81-67864. (Illus.). 80p. (Orig.). 1981. pap. 7.95 (*0-941036-04-9*) Colleasius Pr.

Mirror of Alchemy. Roger Bacon. Ed. by Michael Charles. 1992. reprint ed. pap. 6.95 (*1-55818-146-6*) Holmes Pub.

Mirror of Alchemy: Alchemical Ideas & Images in Manuscripts & Books from Antiquity to the 17th Century. Gareth Roberts. (Illus.). 128p. 1995. pap. text 24.95 (*0-8020-7660-2*) U of Toronto Pr.

Mirror of Alchemy: Alchemical Ideas & Images in Manuscripts & Books from Antiquity to the 17th Century. Gareth Roberts. (Illus.). 128p. 1995. text 55.00 (*0-8020-0710-4*) U of Toronto Pr.

Mirror of America: Literary Encounters with the National Parks. Ed. by David Harmon. 188p. 1989. 25.00 (*0-911797-50-5*); pap. 14.95 (*0-911797-51-3*) Roberts Rinehart.

Mirror of American Education: Race, Religion & Politics in Mississippi, 1860-1880. Broadus B. Jackson. LC 97-61411. 500p. (Orig.). (C). 1997. pap. text 39.99 (*1-886017-08-5*) Town Sq Bks.

Mirror of Art, Critical Studies. Charles Baudelaire. Ed. by Jonathan Mayne. LC 77-10247. (Illus.). reprint ed. 32.50 (*0-404-16303-3*) AMS Pr.

Mirror of Awakening: A Spiritual Visionary's Adventures with Sex, God, & Unspeakable Wonders. P. Davis. Ed. by M. Houston. LC 92-81050. (Illus.). 186p. (Orig.). 1992. pap. 19.95 (*0-9632307-0-0*) New Cent Pdns.

Mirror of Brass: The Compensation & Working Conditions of College & University Administrators. Mark H. Ingraham & Francis P. King. LC 68-9832. 350p. reprint ed. pap. 108.50 (*0-608-13887-8*, 202372400033) Bks Demand.

Mirror of Buddhism. Ed. by Harcharan S. Sobti. (C). 1997. 40.00 (*81-86339-41-8*, Pub. by Eastern Bk Linkers) S Asia.

Mirror of Charity. Aelred of Rievaulx. Tr. by Elizabeth Connor from LAT. (Fathers Ser.: No. 17).Tr. of Speculum Caritatis. 352p. 1990. pap. 14.95 (*0-87907-717-4*) Cistercian Pubns.

Mirror of Coitus: An Edition with English Translation & Edition of the Fifteenth-Century Speculum al Foderi. Ed. & Tr. by Michael Solomon. (Medieval Spanish Medical Texts Ser.: No. 29). (SPA.). xxviii, 142p. 1990. 12.50 (*0-940639-48-3*) Hispanic Seminary.

Mirror of Conflict: The Black Press & Major Issues of Jewish Concern. Harold Brackman. (Simon Wiesenthal Center Special Reports). 40p. (Orig.). 1988. pap. 10.00 (*0-943058-07-4*) S Wiesenthal Ctr.

Mirror of Confusion: The Representation of French History in English Renaissance Drama. Andrew M. Kirk. Ed. by Raymond Waddington. LC 96-19446. (Garland Studies in the Renaissance: Vol. 6). 240p. 1996. text 50.00 (*0-8153-2091-4*, H1928) Garland.

Mirror of Destiny. Andre Norton. LC 94-32818. 400p. 1995. 22.00 (*0-688-13988-4*, Avon Bks) Morrow Avon.

Mirror of Destiny. Andre Norton. 400p. 1996. mass mkt. 6.50 (*0-380-77976-5*, Avon Bks) Morrow Avon.

***Mirror of Destiny.** Andre Norton. 2000. 22.00 (*0-380-97249-2*) Morrow Avon.

Mirror of Dreams. Yvonne Lehman. (White Dove Romance Ser.: No. 3). 16p. (J). 1996. mass mkt. 4.99 (*1-55661-707-0*) Bethany Hse.

Mirror of Empire: Dutch Marine Art of the Seventeenth Century. Ed. by George S. Keyes. (Illus.). 458p. (C). 1990. text 119.95 (*0-521-39328-0*) Cambridge U Pr.

Mirror of England: English Puritan Views of Foreign Nations, 1618-1640. Marvin A. Breslow. LC 70-89966. (Historical Studies: No. 84). 189p. 1970. 17.95 (*0-674-57638-1*) HUP.

Mirror of Existence: Stepping into Wholeness. Christine R. Page. (Illus.). 144p. 1996. pap. 14.50 (*0-85207-294-5*, Pub. by C W Daniel) Natl Bk Netwk.

Mirror of Faith. William of St. Thierry. Ed. by E. Rozanne Elder. Tr. by Thomas X. Davis from LAT. LC 78-12897. (Cistercian Fathers Ser.). (Illus.). 1979. 14.95 (*0-87907-315-2*) Cistercian Pubns.

Mirror of Gesture. Ananda Coomaraswamy & Gopala K. Duggirala. (C). 1997. 14.00 (*81-215-0021-4*, Pub. by M Manoharial) Coronet Bks.

Mirror of God's Love: Sacramental Marriage & the Difference It Makes. John Freund & JoAnn H. Hunter. 64p. (Orig.). 1991. pap. 3.95 (*0-8146-6060-6*, Pueblo Bks) Liturgical Pr.

Mirror of Her Dreams. Stephen R. Donaldson. (The Wizards of Fantasy Promotion). 640p. 1987. mass mkt. 6.99 (*0-345-34697-1*, Del Rey) Ballantine Pub Grp.

Mirror of Herodotus: The Representation of the Other in the Writing of History. Francois Hartog. Tr. by Janet Lloyd. (New Historicism: Studies in Cultural Poetics: No. 5). 1988. 60.00 (*0-520-05487-3*, Pub. by U CA Pr) Cal Prin Full Svc.

Mirror of Human Culture Sketches. Kottak. 1996. 33.50 (*0-07-913258-8*) McGraw.

Mirror of Ideas (Le Miroir des Idees) Michel Tournier. Tr. by Jonathan F. Krell. LC 97-23303. (Stages Ser.).Tr. of Le Miroir des Id Ees. 136p. 1998. text 30.00 (*0-8032-4430-4*) U of Nebr Pr.

Mirror of Justice: Literary Reflections of Legal Crises. Theodore J. Ziolkowski. LC 96-28326. xiv, 322p. 1997. text 47.50 (*0-691-02683-1*, Pub. by Princeton U Pr) Cal Prin Full Svc.

Mirror of Language: A Study in the Medieval Theory of Knowledge. rev. ed. Marcia L. Colish. LC 83-3599. 356p. 1983. reprint ed. pap. 110.40 (*0-608-02688-3*, 206334100004) Bks Demand.

Mirror of Language: The Debate on Bilingualism. Kenji Hakuta. LC 85-45313. 272p. 1987. pap. 17.50 (*0-465-04637-1*, Pub. by Basic) HarpC.

Mirror of Lida Sal: Tales Based on Mayan Myths & Guatemalan Legends. Miguel Angel Asturias. Tr. by Gilbert Alter-Gilbert from SPA. LC 96-35864. 126p. (C). 1997. pap. 14.95 (*0-935480-83-8*) Lat Am Lit Rev Pr.

Mirror of Life: Exercise Equipment for Your Spirit. Athena S. Andreu. Date not set. pap., wbk. ed. 19.95 (*1-892645-00-9*, MOL) Phx Rising.

Mirror of Medieval Culture: Saint Peter Hymns of the Middle Ages. Joseph A. Szoverffy. (Connecticut Academy of Arts & Sciences Ser., Trans.: Vol. 42). 1965. pap. 79.50 (*0-685-22889-4*) Elliots Bks.

***Mirror of Merlin.** T. A. Barron. LC 99-13043. 245p. (J). (gr. 5). 1999. 19.99 (*0-399-23455-1*) Peng Put Young Read.

Mirror of Mind. Russel W. McDougal. LC 76-17152. 1977. pap. 8.95 (*0-917694-01-5*) Open Window.

Mirror of Mindfulness. Tsele N. Rangdrol. 144p. 1996. pap. 14.00 (*962-7341-18-5*, Pub. by Rang Jung Yshe) Bookpeople.

Mirror of Modernity: Invented Traditions of Modern Japan. Stephen Vlastos. LC 97-7897. (Twentieth-Century Japan Ser.). 300p. 1998. 45.00 (*0-520-20621-5*, Pub. by U CA Pr); pap. 17.00 (*0-520-20637-1*, Pub. by U CA Pr) Cal Prin Full Svc.

***Mirror of Monsters: (The Christabel)** deluxe ed. Alex S. Defazio. (Illus.). 200p. 1999. pap. 17.99 (*0-9676282-0-2*) Elixir Prods.

Mirror of Monsters & Prodigies. Pamela Ditchoff. LC 95-18247. 250p. (Orig.). 1995. pap. 12.95 (*1-56689-035-7*) Coffee Hse.

Mirror of Music, 1844-1944, 2 Vols, Set. Percy A. Scholes. LC 71-124255. (Select Bibliographies Reprint Ser.). 1977. 90.95 (*0-8369-5443-2*) Ayer.

Mirror of Music, 1844-1944: Music Book Index, 2 vols., Set. Percy A. Scholes. 1993. reprint ed. lib. bdg. 150.00 (*0-7812-9578-5*) Rprt Serv.

Mirror of Nature. Robertson Davies. (Illus.). 132p. 1996. pap. text 12.95 (*0-8020-7939-3*) U of Toronto Pr.

Mirror of Nature. Robertson Davies. LC 83-196795. (Alexander Lectures: No. 1982). (Illus.). 144p. reprint ed. pap. 44.70 (*0-8357-6359-5*, 203571300096) Bks Demand.

Mirror of Our Anguish: A Study of Luigi Pirandello's Narrative Works. Douglas Radcliff-Unstead. 329p. 1978. 39.50 (*0-8386-1930-4*) Fairleigh Dickinson.

Mirror of Our Souls: Selected Poems from Bermuda & Her People. Inspirational Writers Association Staff. LC 90-60201. (Illus.). 176p. (Orig.). 1990. pap. 8.52 (*0-88100-069-8*) Natl Writ Pr.

Mirror of Our Times: More Than a Century. BNC Staff. 1997. per. 22.95 (*1-57571-003-X*) Birm News.

Mirror of Production. Jean Baudrillard. Tr. by Mark Poster. LC 74-82994. (C). 1975. pap. 14.00 (*0-914386-06-9*) Telos Pr.

Mirror of Relationship: Love, Sex, & Chastity: A Selection of Passages for the Study of the Teachings of J. Krishnamurti. Jiddu Krishnamurti. Ed. by Douglas Evans & Frode Steen. 134p. 1992. per. 10.95 (*1-888004-05-3*) Krishnamurti.

Mirror of Self-Supremacy or Svatantrya-Darpana. B. N. Pandit. (C). 12.50 (*81-215-0559-3*, Pub. by M Manoharial) Coronet Bks.

Mirror of Simple Souls. Marguerite Porete et al. LC 98-54869. (Texts in Medieval Culture Ser.). 1999. pap. text 24.00 (*0-268-01435-3*) U of Notre Dame Pr.

Mirror of Simple Souls. Margaret Porette. LC 98-54869. (Texts in Medieval Culture Ser.: Vol. 6). (C). 1999. pap. 24.00 (*0-268-01431-0*) U of Notre Dame Pr.

***Mirror of Spain, 1500-1700: The Formation of a Myth.** J. N. Hillgarth. 1087p. (C). 1999. text 72.50 (*0-472-11092-6*, 11092) U of Mich Pr.

Mirror of Sumari. Suzan K. Anderson. (Illus.). 32p. (J). (ps-6). 1985. 13.95 (*0-942494-93-8*, #129) Coleman Pub.

Mirror of the Artist: Northern Renaissance Art in Its Historical Context. Craig Harbison. LC 94-48786. (The Perspectives Ser.). (Illus.). 176p. 1995. 16.95 (*0-8109-2728-4*, Pub. by Abrams) Time Warner.

Mirror of the Artist: Northern Renaissance Art in Its Historical Context. Craig Harbison. LC 94-48786. 176p. 1995. pap. text 16.40 (*0-13-368549-7*) P-H.

Mirror of the Body. Anna Kaye & Don C. Matchan. LC 77-8717. (Illus.). 160p. (Orig.). 1978. pap. 6.95 (*0-89407-010-X*) Strawberry Hill.

Mirror of the Divine: Art in the Baha'i World Community. Ludwig Tuman. (Illus.). 336p. 1993. pap. 29.95 (*0-85398-333-X*) G Ronald Pub.

Mirror of the Earth: The World Landscape in Sixteenth-Century Flemish Painting. Walter S. Gibson. LC 88-29308. (Illus.). 361p. 1989. reprint ed. pap. 112.00 (*0-608-07642-2*, 205995900010) Bks Demand.

Mirror of the Indies: A History of Dutch Colonial Literature. Rob Nieuwenhuys. Ed. by E. M. Beekman. Tr. by Frans Van Rosevelt from DUT. LC 82-4755. (Library of the Indies).Tr. of Oost-indische Spiegel. 368p. 1982. text 40.00 (*0-87023-368-8*) U of Mass Pr.

Mirror of the Indies: A History of Dutch Colonial Literature. Robert Nieuwenhuys.Tr. of Oost-indische Spiegel. 202p. 1999. pap. 22.95 (*962-593-509-6*) Tuttle Pubng.

Mirror of the Intellect: Essays on Traditional Science & Sacred Art. Titus Burckhardt. Ed. & Tr. by William Stoddart from GER. 269p. 1987. 26.95 (*0-946621-08-X*, Pub. by Islamic Texts) Intl Spec Bk.

Mirror of the Intellect: Essays on Traditional Science & Sacred Art. Ed. & Tr. by Titus Burckhardt. Tr. by William Stoddart. LC 87-10103. (SUNY Series in Islam). 269p. 1987. text 21.50 (*0-88706-683-6*) State U NY Pr.

Mirror of the Martyrs. John S. Oyer & Robert S. Kreider. LC 90-71117. (Illus.). 96p. 1999. pap. 9.95 (*1-56148-003-7*) Good Bks PA.

Mirror of the Marvelous: The Classic Surrealist Work on Myth. Pierre Mabille. Tr. by Jody Gladding from FRE. LC 98-14998. (Illus.). 256p. 1998. 25.00 (*0-89281-650-3*, Inner Trad) Inner Tradit.

Mirror of the Medieval World. William D. Wixom. LC 98-43426. (Illus.). 320p. 1999. 60.00 (*0-8109-6514-3*, Pub. by Abrams) Time Warner.

Mirror of the Medieval World. William D. Wixom. LC 98-43426. 1999. write for info. (*0-87099-786-6*) Metro Mus Art.

***Mirror of the Medieval World.** William D. Wixom. LC 98-43426. 10p. 1999. write for info. (*0-87099-785-8*) Metro Mus Art.

Mirror of the Ministry in Modern Novels. Horton Davies. LC 70-111824. (Essay Index Reprint Ser.). 1977. 21.95 (*0-8369-1601-8*) Ayer.

Mirror of the New Christians. Francisco Machado. Ed. by F. Talmage & M. Vieira. 344p. pap. text 45.14 (*0-88844-036-7*) Brill Academic Pubs.

Mirror of the Sea. Joseph Conrad. Date not set. lib. bdg. 19.95 (*0-8488-1669-2*) Amereon Ltd.

Mirror of the Sea. Joseph Conrad. LC 87-62517. 196p. 1988. pap. 10.95 (*0-910395-34-9*) Marlboro Pr.

Mirror of the Sea & a Personal Record. Joseph Conrad. (Oxford World's Classics Ser.), 216p. 2000. pap. 8.95 (*0-19-283748-6*) OUP.

Mirror of the Sky: Songs of the Bauls of Bengal. 2nd rev. ed. Deben Bhattacharya. LC 98-45834. (Illus.). 288p. 1999. pap. 24.95 incl. audio compact disk (*0-934252-89-0*, Pub. by Hohm Pr) SCB Distributors.

***Mirror of the Soul.** Meggita Brown. 67p. 2000. 15.95 (*0-7541-1280-2*) Minerva Pr.

Mirror of Time: Images of Aging & Dying, 7. Joan M. Boyle & James E. Morriss. LC 86-33631. (Contributions to the Study of Aging Ser.: No. 7). 237p. 1987. 55.00 (*0-313-25597-0*, BYM/, Greenwood Pr) Greenwood.

Mirror on Mirror: Translation, Imitation, Parody. Reuben A. Brower. LC 74-80442. (Studies in Comparative Literature: No. 34). 224p. 1974. 28.00 (*0-674-57645-4*) HUP.

Mirror on Still Water: A Journey to the Heart of Love. Joel Wright. LC 98-191383. xii, 340 p. 1997. write for info. (*0-87418-325-1*, Mind & Miracles) Coleman Pub.

Mirror on the Stage: The Pulitzer Plays As an Approach to American Drama. Thomas P. Adler. LC 86-21170. 192p. 1987. 39.95 (*0-911198-84-9*) Purdue U Pr.

Mirror on the Town Hall. Jan LaFont. 150p. (Orig.). 1982. pap. 3.50 (*0-9603596-3-X*) Fontastic.

Mirror on the Wall. large type ed. C. W. Reed. (Dales Large Print Ser.). 365p. 1996. pap. 18.99 (*1-85389-685-3*, Dales) Ulverscroft.

Mirror Our Children See. Edward H. Pauley & Robert C. Larson. 144p. 1995. 7.99 (*0-8499-5159-3*) Word Pub.

Mirror Painting & Silvering. 3rd ed. reprint ed. 4.50 (*0-939608-42-1*) Campana Art.

Mirror Planet. Eve Bunting. (Author's Signature Collection). (Illus.). 40p. (J). (gr. 3-8). 1992. lib. bdg. 12.79 (*0-89565-767-8*) Childs World.

Mirror Puzzle Book. Marion Walter. (Illus.). 32p. (J). (gr. 2 up). 1985. pap. 7.50 (*0-906212-39-1*, Pub. by Tarquin Pubns) Parkwest Pubns.

Mirror Racing. Guy Wilkins. 96p. (C). 1990. text 59.00 (*0-906754-45-3*, Pub. by Fernhurst Bks) St Mut.

***Mirror Suite.** Scott N. Kaeff. 38p. 2000. pap. 10.00 (*0-9671385-3-1*) Diabolical Kitten.

***Mirror Symmetry** C. Voisin. LC 99-35675. (Panoramas et Synthaeses Ser.). 1999. write for info. (*0-8218-1947-X*) Am Math.

An Asterisk (*) at the beginning of an entry indicates that the title is appearing for the first time.

*Mirror Symmetry & Algebraic Geometry. David A. Cox & Sheldon Katz. LC 98-55564. (Mathematical Surveys & Monographs). xxi, 469p. 1999. write for info. (0-8218-1059-6) Am Math.

Mirror Symmetry III: Conference Proceedings on Complex Geometry & Mirror Symmetry, 1996. Ed. by Duong H. Phong. LC 98-37643. (IP Studies in Advanced Mathematics: Vol. 10). 312p. 1999. 42.00 (0-8218-1193-2) Am Math.

Mirror Symmetry I. Ed. by Shing-Tung Yau. LC 98-35520. (AMS/IP Studies in Advanced Mathematics: Vol. 9). 444p. 1998. 49.00 (0-8218-0665-3) Am Math.

Mirror Symmetry II, Vol. II. Ed. by Brian Greene. LC 96-32938. (AMS-IP Studies in Advanced Mathematics: Vol. 1). (Illus.). 844p. (C). Date not set. text 85.00 (0-8218-0634-3, AMSIP/1) Am Math.

Mirror Talk: Genres of Crisis in Contemporary Autobiography. Susanna Egan. LC 99-17970. 296p. 1999. pap. text 19.95 (0-8078-4782-8) U of NC Pr.

Mirror Talk: Genres of Crisis in Contemporary Autobiography. Susanna Egan. LC 99-17970. (Illus.). 296p. 1999. lib. bdg. 49.95 (0-8078-2499-2) U of NC Pr.

Mirror to Geneva. George E. Slocombe. LC 70-121506. (Essay Index Reprint Ser.). 1977. 23.95 (0-8369-1852-5) Ayer.

Mirror to Kathleen's Face: Education in Independent Ireland, 1922-1960. Donald H. Akenson. 240p. (C). 1975. 39.95 (0-7735-0203-3, Pub. by McG-Queens Univ Pr) CUP Services.

Mirror to Nature: Reflections on Science, Scientists & Society. Peter M. Knudtson. 224p. 1991. 28.95 (0-7737-2467-2) Genl Dist Srvs.

Mirror to Nature: Transformations in Drama & Aesthetics, 1660-1732. Rose A. Zimbardo. LC 86-1336. 256p. reprint ed. pap. 79.40 (0-7837-5816-2, 204548300006) Bks Demand.

Mirror to Physiology: A Self-Survey of Physiological Science. American Physiological Society & R. W. Gerard. LC 58-10348. 384p. reprint ed. pap. 119.10 (0-608-16745-2, 202639400049) Bks Demand.

Mirror to the Cage: 3 Contemporary Hungarian Plays. Ed. & Tr. by Clara Gyorgyey from HUN. LC 92-27577. 272p. 1993. text 33.00 (1-55728-267-6) U of Ark Pr.

*Mirror to the Distorted Nazi Value System: Primary Source Documents. Ed. by Richard Kalfus. 129p. 1999. pap. text 31.95 (0-87411-962-6, Copley Custom Pub Grp) Copley Pub.

Mirror to the Light. Thompson. 1990. pap. 10.95 (0-904575-19-5) Sigo Pr.

Mirror to the Safe. Greg Keeler. 36p. 1998. pap. 12.00 (0-931659-41-8) Limberlost Pr.

Mirror to the Safe. limited ed. Greg Keeler. 36p. 1998. 45.00 (0-931659-42-6) Limberlost Pr.

Mirror to the Sky. Mark S. Geston. 240p. 1993. mass mkt. 4.99 (0-380-71703-4, Avon Bks) Morrow Avon.

*Mirror to the Sky. Mark S. Geston. 2000. 22.00 (0-380-97213-1) Morrow Avon.

Mirror to the Son of Heaven: Wei Cheng at the Court of T'ang T'ai-tsung. Howard J. Wechsler. LC 74-76649. (Yale Historical Publications: Miscellany: No. 105). 272p. reprint ed. pap. 84.40 (0-608-11663-7, 202205200024) Bks Demand.

Mirror Universe Saga. Mike W. Barr. Ed. by Bob Greenberger. (Illus.). 192p. 1992. mass mkt. 19.95 (0-930289-96-X) DC Comics.

Mirror up to Nature: The Technique of Shakespeare's Tragedies. Virgil K. Whitaker. LC 65-15370. 342p. reprint ed. 106.10 (0-8357-9192-0, 201500900096) Bks Demand.

Mirror up to Shakespeare: Essays in Honor of G. R. Hibbard. Ed. by Jack C. Gray. LC 84-217778. 325p. reprint ed. pap. 100.80 (0-8357-3660-1, 203638700003) Bks Demand.

Mirror Wall. Richard Murphy. 64p. 1989. 13.95 (0-916390-36-5); pap. 7.95 (0-916390-35-7) Wake Forest.

*Mirror Wars. Nancy C. Harris. LC 99-75919. 128p. 1999. pap. 15.00 (0-916620-40-9) Portals Pr.

*Mirror, Window: An Artbabe Collection. Jessica Abel. (Illus.). 2000. pap. 12.95 (1-56097-384-6) Fantagraph Bks.

Mirror World: An Illustrated Novel. Tad Williams. write for info. (0-06-105546-8) HarpC.

Mirror Worlds: or The Day Software Puts the Universe in a Shoebox . . . How It Will Happen & What It Will Mean. David Gelernter. (Illus.). 256p. (C). 1991. text 30.00 (0-19-506812-2) OUP.

Mirror Writing. MacDonald Critchley. LC 78-72793. reprint ed. 42.50 (0-404-60857-4) AMS Pr.

*Mirrored Images: American Anthropology & Popular Culture, 1960-1980. Susan R. Trencher. LC 99-36904. 232p. 2000. 59.95 (0-89789-673-4, Bergin & Garvey) Greenwood.

Mirrored Lives: Aging Children & Elderly Parents. Tom Koch. LC 90-7457. 240p. 1990. 21.95 (0-275-93671-6, C3671, Praeger Pubs) Greenwood.

Mirrored Memories. 1991. write for info. (0-9629580-0-X) Col Cnty NY.

Mirroring Belief: Marguerite de Navarre's Devotional Poetry. Gary Ferguson. 240p. 1992. 68.00 (0-7486-0347-6, Pub. by Edinburgh U Pr) Col U Pr.

Mirroring the Sky: A Postclassic K'iche-Maya Cosmology. Jose A. Valbuena. LC 96-75031. (Illus.). 108p. (Orig.). (C). 1996. pap. 25.00 (0-911437-24-X) Labyrinthos.

Mirror/Mirror - An International Office Simulation. Ristau. (GB - Basic Business Ser.). 1994. mass mkt., wbk. ed. 16.95 (0-538-62384-5) S-W Pub.

Mirrors. Vicki Bennett. 119p. (C). 1990. pap. 60.00 (0-86439-146-3, Pub. by Boolarong Pubns) St Mut.

Mirrors. Naguib Mahfouz. Tr. by Roger Allen. LC 76-47306. 1977. pap. 16.00 (0-88297-016-X) Bibliotheca.

Mirrors. Herand Markarian. (Illus.). 102p. (Orig.). 1996. pap. 10.00 (0-9654126-0-1) Hamazkayin Armenian.

Mirrors. Howard McCord. (Illus.). 1973. pap. 5.00 (0-685-37097-6) Stone-Marrow Pr.

Mirrors. John O'Brien. 1982. 3.50 (0-87129-540-7, M53) Dramatic Pub.

Mirrors. Bernie Zubrowski. LC 91-29142. (Illus.). 96p. (J). (gr. 5 up). 1992. pap. 6.95 (0-688-10591-2, Wm Morrow) Morrow Avon.

Mirrors, Vol. 144. Marcel Cohen. Tr. by Jason Weiss. (Green Integer Ser.: No. 7). 224p. 1998. pap. 12.95 (1-55713-313-1) Green Integer.

Mirrors: A Reflection in One-Act. Jerome McDonough. (Illus.). 32p. (YA). (gr. 7 up). 1987. pap. 3.25 (0-88680-278-4) I E Clark.

Mirrors: Finding Out about the Properties of Light. Bernie Zubrowski. LC 91-29142. (Illus.). 96p. (J). (gr. 3 up). 1992. lib. bdg. 13.93 (0-688-10592-0, Wm Morrow) Morrow Avon.

Mirrors: Finding Out about the Properties of Light. Bernie Zubrowski. (J). 1992. 12.05 (0-606-02753-X, Pub. by Turtleback) Demco.

Mirrors: Portrait of a Lesbian Transsexual. Geri Nettick & Beth Elliot. (Orig.). 1996. mass mkt. 6.95 (1-56333-435-6, Rhinoceros) Masquerade.

Mirrors: Reflections of a Woman's Soul. Laura Y. Bowman. LC 89-80576. (Orig.). 1989. pap. 9.95 (0-9622404-0-0) Lu-Bow Pub.

Mirrors & Holographic Labyrinths: The Process of a New Aesthetic Synthesis in John Banville's Work. Laura Izarra. 324p. 1998. 74.95 (1-57309-258-4); pap. 54.95 (1-57309-257-6) Intl Scholars.

Mirrors & Masks. Anselm Strauss. LC 78-300956. 1970. reprint ed. pap. 7.00 (0-686-24891-0) Sociology Pr.

Mirrors & Masks: The Search for Identity. Anselm Strauss. LC 96-38934. 200p. (Orig.). 1997. pap. text 19.95 (1-56000-935-7) Transaction Pubs.

Mirrors Are Lonely. Judith B. Richardson. (Illus.). 95p. (YA). (gr. 6-9). 1992. 10.95 (0-9611374-4-4) Woods Hole Hist.

Mirrors Beneath the Earth: Short Fiction by Chicano Writers. Ed. by Ray Gonzalez. LC 92-27664. 331p. (Orig.). 1992. pap. 13.95 (1-880684-02-0) Curbstone.

*Mirror's Edge. Carol Davis & Esther D. Reese. (Quantum Leap Ser.: No. XVIII). 2000. mass mkt. 6.99 (0-425-17351-8) Berkley Pub.

Mirrors for Behavior III: An Anthology of Observation Instruments. Ed. by Anita Simon & E. Gil Boyer. LC 67-31735. (Illus.). 1974. 29.95 (0-686-21834-5) Comm Materials.

Mirror's Image. Francis Grose & Dan Cragg. LC 76-56970. (Illus.). 1978. 9.50 (0-913896-10-1) Owlswick Pr.

Mirrors, Images & Reflections of Love. LaVerne Thomas. (Illus.). 68p. 1997. pap. write for info. (1-57502-628-7, PO 1786) Morris Pubng.

*Mirrors in Mind. Richard Gregory. 320p. 1998. pap. 24.95 (0-14-017118-5, Pub. by Pnguin Bks Ltd) Trafalgar.

Mirrors in Mind. Richard Gregory. (Illus.). 304p. 1997. text 21.60 (0-7167-4511-9) W H Freeman.

Mirrors in Time: A Psycho-Spiritual Journey Through the Jewish Year. Joel D. Ziff. LC 96-43830. 360p. 1996. 40.00 (0-7657-5977-2) Aronson.

Mirrors in Time, Leaves in the Wind. Nancy Heanly. 128p. 1986. 40.00 (0-7223-1997-5, Pub. by A H S Ltd) St Mut.

Mirrors Kill. large type ed. Jack Curtis. LC 95-13855. 550p. 1995. lib. bdg. 25.95 (0-7838-1298-1, G K Hall Lrg Type) Mac Lib Ref.

Mirrors, Mice, & Mustaches: A Sampling of Superstitions & Popular Beliefs in Texas. George D. Hendricks. LC 80-27405. 126p. 1981. reprint ed. pap. 7.95 (0-87074-075-X) SMU Press.

Mirrors of American Culture. Paul Deane. LC 91-30998. 275p. 1991. 34.50 (0-8108-2460-4) Scarecrow.

Mirrors of Astonishment: Poems. Rachel Hadas. LC 92-9877. 64p. (C). 1992. 25.00 (0-8135-1899-7); pap. 11.95 (0-8135-1900-4) Rutgers U Pr.

Mirrors of Celestial Grace: Patristic Theology in Spenser's Allegory. Harold L. Weatherby. 256p. 1993. text 50.00 (0-8020-0548-9) U of Toronto Pr.

*Mirrors of Destruction: War, Genocide & Modern Identity. Omer Bartov. LC 99-39974. 304p. 2000. 35.00 (0-19-507723-7) OUP.

Mirrors of Disaster: A Chronicle of the Spanish Military Conquest of America. Gerard Chaliand. Tr. by A. M. Berrett from FRE. LC 93-30414. (Illus.). 300p. 1994. 35.00 (0-9628715-6-7) Blue Crane Bks.

Mirrors of Downing Street. Harold Begbie. LC 79-121448. (Essay Index Reprint Ser.). 1977. 20.95 (0-8369-1695-6) Ayer.

Mirrors of Fate: A Journey into Past Lives. Joanne E. Moleski. (Illus.). 158p. (Orig.). 1988. pap. 9.95 (1-882053-00-1) Tamaris Pub Hse.

*Mirrors of God. rev. ed. Joseph W. Goetz. (Illus.). 116p. 1999. pap. 6.95 (0-88028-213-4, 1543) Forward Movement.

Mirrors of Illusion. Edward A. Storer. LC 78-64054. (Des Imagistes: Literature of the Imagist Movement Ser.). reprint ed. 27.50 (0-404-17104-4) AMS Pr.

Mirrors of Indian Buddhism. K. Krishna Murthy. (C). 1991. text 28.50 (81-85067-72-4, Pub. by Sundeep Prak) S Asia.

Mirrors of Infinity: The French Formal Garden & 17th Century Metaphysics. Allen S. Weiss. LC 95-15886.Tr. of Miroirs de l'Infini. (Illus.). 112p. (Orig.). 1995. pap. 14.95 (1-56898-050-7) Princeton Arch.

Mirrors of Madness: Patroling the Psychic Border. Bruce Luske. (Social Problems & Social Issues Ser.). 143p. 1990. pap. text 24.95 (0-202-30423-X); lib. bdg. 47.95 (0-202-30422-1) Aldine de Gruyter.

Mirrors of Magic: Evoking the Spirit of Dewponds. P. Heselton. (Orig.). 1997. pap. 22.95 (1-898307-84-9, Pub. by Capall Bann Pubng) Holmes Pub.

Mirrors of Memory. David A. Wilson. 120p. (Orig.). 1996. pap. 10.00 (0-934852-42-1) Lorien Hse.

Mirrors of Mind: An Introduction to Humanities. 2nd ed. Charles Roberts et al. 320p. 1991. pap. text 24.95 (0-88725-158-7) Hunter Textbks.

Mirrors of Minds: Patterns of Experience in Educational Computing. Ed. by Roy D. Pea & Karen Sheingold. LC 87-1274. (Cognition & Computing Ser.). 336p. 1987. pap. 39.50 (0-89391-423-1); text 73.25 (0-89391-422-3) Ablx Pub.

Mirrors of 1932. Ray T. Tucker. LC 78-121508. (Essay Index Reprint Ser.). 1977. 20.95 (0-8369-1779-0) Ayer.

Mirrors of Our Playing: Paradigms & Presences in Modern Drama. Thomas R. Whitaker. LC 98-58110. 320p. 1999. text 49.50 (0-472-11025-X, 11025) U of Mich Pr.

*Mirrors of Paradise: The Gardens of Fernando Caruncho. Guy Cooper & Gordon Taylor. (Illus.). 224p. 2000. 65.00 (1-58093-071-9, Pub. by Monacelli Pr) Penguin Putnam.

Mirrors of the Hidden Wisdom: Threads of Theosophy in Literature - I. W. Emmett Small et al. (Study Ser.: No. 7). 122p. 1981. pap. 8.50 (0-913004-42-1) Point Loma Pub.

Mirrors of the Sea. Sally Wentworth. (Presents Ser.). 1994. per. 2.99 (0-373-11634-9, 1-11634-2) Harlequin Bks.

Mirrors of the Soul. Kahlil Gibran. 1993. 4.98 (1-55521-896-2) Bk Sales Inc.

Mirrors of the Soul. Kahlil Gibran. 1999. pap. text 6.99 (0-7858-1071-4) Bk Sales Inc.

Mirrors of the Soul. Kahlil Gibran. 1972. pap. 6.95 (0-8065-0270-3, Citadel Pr) Carol Pub Group.

Mirrors of Transformation: The Self in Relationships. Marita Digney. Ed. by Dolores E. Brien. LC 94-49053. (PAJA Papers). 1995. pap. write for info. (1-882275-06-3) Rnd Table Pr.

Mirrors of Truth: Reflections of Living Mastery. Frederic Lionel. Tr. by Wise Thinking Staff from FRE. 128p. (Orig.). 1991. pap. 10.95 (0-944135-10-2) Archedigm Pubns.

Mirrors of Wall Street. LC 77-152198. (Essay Index Reprint Ser.). 1977. reprint ed. 20.95 (0-8369-2247-6) Ayer.

Mirrors of Washington. Clinton W. Gilbert. LC 79-156649. (Essay Index Reprint Ser.). 1977. reprint ed. 23.95 (0-8369-2363-4) Ayer.

Mirrors of Washington. Clinton W. Gilbert. LC 79-156649. (Essay Index Reprint Ser.). (Illus.). 256p. reprint ed. lib. bdg. 18.50 (0-8290-0477-7) Irvington.

Mirrors of Your Castle. Micki Avila. (Illus.). 38p. 1993. pap. 5.95 (1-891634-02-X) Azure Pr.

Mirrors of Your Castle, Vol. II. Micki Avila. (Illus.). 95p. 1997. pap. 9.95 (1-891634-03-8) Azure Pr.

Mirrors on the Maghrib: Critical Reflections on Paul & Jane Bowles & Other American Writers in Morocco. Ed. by R. Kevin Lacey & Francis Poole. LC 96-5758. 226p. 1996. 50.00 (0-88206-087-2) Caravan Bks.

Mirrorshades. Bruce Sterling. 1988. mass mkt. 5.99 (0-441-53382-5) Ace Bks.

Mirrorsun Rising: Book Two of Greatwinter. Sean McMullen. LC 95-218557. (Greatwinter Ser.: Vol. 2). 332p. 1995. pap. 10.00 (1-875346-14-7, Pub. by Aphelion) Firebird Dist.

Mirrorwork. Mimi Khalvati. LC 95-189495. 96p. 1995. pap. 14.95 (1-85754-114-6, Pub. by Carcanet Pr) Paul & Co Pubs.

Mirrorwork: 50 Years of Indian Writing, 1947-1997. Salman Rushdie & Elizabeth West. LC 97-19595. 1997. pap. 15.00 (0-8050-5710-2) H Holt & Co.

Mirrorwork: 50 Years of Indian Writing, 1947-1997. Ed. by Salman Rushdie & Elizabeth West. LC 97-19595. 566p. 1997. 30.00 (0-8050-5709-9) H Holt & Co.

Mirrour of Justices: Written Originally in the Old French, Long Before the Conquest; And Many Things Added - To Which Is Added the Diversity of Courts & Their Jurisdiction. Andrew Horne. xix, 337p. 1969. reprint ed. 45.00 (0-8377-2227-6, Rothman) W S Hein.

Mirrour of Justices: Written Originally in the Old French Long Before the Conquest to Which Is Added, the Diversity of Courts & Their Jurisdiction. Andrew Horn. LC 68-54748. xix, 337p. 1968. reprint ed. 13.50 (0-678-04527-5) Kelley.

Mirrour of Monsters. William Rankins. (English Stage Ser.: Vol. 9). 1973. lib. bdg. 61.00 (0-8240-0592-9) Garland.

Mirth: Poems from Hollywood. Mark Dunster. 11p. 1998. pap. 5.00 (0-89642-539-8) Linden Pubs.

Mirth & Morality of Shakespeare's Holy Fools. Sandra J. Pyle. LC 97-47267. (Studies in British Literature: Vol. 33). 284p. 1998. text 89.95 (0-7734-8480-9) E Mellen.

*Mirth for the Millennium: Inspirational Wit & Cartoons. Cal Samra & Rose Samra. LC 99-33686. (Holy Humor Ser.). 128p. 1999. pap. 6.95 (1-57856-283-X) Waterbrook Pr.

Mirth of a Nation: America's Great Dialect Humor. Ed. by Walter Blair & Raven I. McDavid, Jr. LC 81-16403. 331p. 1983. reprint ed. pap. 102.70 (0-7837-2975-8, 205747900006) Bks Demand.

Mirth of a Nation: The Best Contemporary Humor. Ed. by Michael J. Rosen. LC 99-44293. 656p. 2000. pap. 15.00 (0-06-095321-7, Perennial) HarperTrade.

Mirth of Yore: Contours of Fantasy. Illus. by Darin Davis et al. LC 90-70743. 96p. (Orig.). 1990. pap. 7.95 (0-9627030-0-1, 1001) Starlance Pubns.

Mirthful Kombat. John Byrne. 128p. 1995. 2.50 (0-09-941471-6) Random.

MIRV & the Arms Race: An Interpretation of Defense Strategy. Ronald L. Tammen. LC 73-9065. (Special Studies in International Politics & Government). 1973. 42.50 (0-275-28749-1) Irvington.

*Mirza Ghalib: A Creative Biography. Natalia Prigarina. Tr. by M. Osama Faruqi. 400p. 2000. 29.95 (0-19-577945-2) OUP.

MIS: Concepts & Design. 2nd ed. Robert G. Murdick. (Illus.). 672p. 1986. text 50.00 (0-13-586322-8) P-H.

*Mis Amigos Alumno, Vol. 10, No. 3. Tr. & Prod. by Life Publishers International Staff. (Vida Nueva Ser.). (SPA., Illus.). 32p. (J). (gr. 1-3). 2001. pap., student ed. write for info. (0-7361-0179-9) Life Pubs Intl.

*Mis Amigos Alumno, Vol. 10, No. 4. Tr. & Prod. by Life Publishers International Staff. (Vida Nueva Ser.). (SPA., Illus.). 26p. (J). (gr. 1-3). 2001. pap., student ed. write for info. (0-7361-0180-2) Life Pubs Intl.

*Mis Amigos Alumno Vol. 9: June to August 2000. (SPA., Illus.). 32p. (J). (gr. 1-3). 1999. pap. write for info. (0-7361-0109-8) Life Pubs Intl.

*Mis Amigos Alumno Vol. 9: March to May 2000. (SPA., Illus.). 32p. (J). (gr. 1-3). 1999. pap. write for info. (0-7361-0108-X) Life Pubs Intl.

Mis Amigos Alumno, Dec 1999 a Feb 2000, Vol. 9 Tomo. Life Publishers International Staff. (SPA., Illus.). 32p. (J). (gr. 1-3). 1999. pap., student ed. write for info. (0-7361-0061-X) Life Pubs Intl.

*Mis Amigos Alumno, Dec. 2000 to Feb. 2001, Vol. 10. Prod. by Life Publishers International Staff. (SPA., Illus.). 32p. (gr. 1-3). 2000. pap., student ed. write for info. (0-7361-0139-X) Life Pubs Intl.

Mis Amigos Alumno, Sep 99 a Nov 99, Vol. 9 Tomo. Life Publishers International Staff. (SPA., Illus.). 32p. (J). (gr. 1-3). 1999. pap., student ed. write for info. (0-7361-0060-1) Life Pubs Intl.

*Mis Amigos Alumno, Sept. 2000 to Nov. 2000, Vol. 10. Prod. by Life Publishers International Staff. (SPA., Illus.). 32p. (gr. 1-3). 2000. pap., student ed. write for info. (0-7361-0138-1) Life Pubs Intl.

*Mis Amigos Ayudas Visuales, Vol. 10. Prod. by Life Publishers International Staff. (SPA., Illus.). 26p. 2000. pap., teacher ed. write for info. (0-7361-0137-3) Life Pubs Intl.

*Mis Amigos Ayudas Visuales, Vol. AMI-04. Tr. & Prod. by Life Publishers International Staff. (Vida Nueva Ser.). (SPA., Illus.). 26p. (J). (gr. 1-3). 2001. pap. write for info. (0-7361-0178-0) Life Pubs Intl.

*Mis Amigos Ayudas Visuales Vol. AMI-02: March to August 2000. (SPA., Illus.). 26p. 1999. pap. write for info. (0-7361-0110-1) Life Pubs Intl.

Mis Amigos Ayudas Visuales, Sep 1999 a Feb 2000, No. AMI-01. Life Publishers International Staff. (SPA., Illus.). 26p. (J). (gr. 1-3). 1999. pap. write for info. (0-7361-0062-8) Life Pubs Intl.

Mis Amigos Maestro, Vol. 9, Sept. 1999. Life Publishers International Staff. (Illus.). 1999. pap., teacher ed. write for info. (0-7361-0063-6) Life Pubs Intl.

*Mis Amigos Maestro, Vol. 10, No. 3. Tr. & Prod. by Life Publishers International Staff. (Vida Nueva Ser.). (SPA., Illus.). 112p. 2001. pap., teacher ed. write for info. (0-7361-0177-2) Life Pubs Intl.

*Mis Amigos Maestro: March to August 2000. (SPA.). 112p. 1999. pap., teacher ed. write for info. (0-7361-0111-X) Life Pubs Intl.

*Mis Amigos Maestro, Sept. 2000 to Feb. 2001, Vol. 10. Prod. by Life Publishers International Staff. (SPA., Illus.). 112p. 2000. pap., teacher ed. write for info. (0-7361-0136-5) Life Pubs Intl.

*MIS & LAN Manager's Guide to Advanced Telecommunications. Leo A. Wrobel. LC TK5105.7.W76 1999. (Illus.). 1999. pap. 50.00 (0-7695-0099-4, IEEE Inst Elec) IEEE Comp Soc.

Mis Cinco Sentidos. Aliki. (Let's Read-&-Find-Out Science Ser.).Tr. of My Five Senses. (SPA.). (J). 1995. 11.40 (0-606-07873-8) Turtleback.

Mis Cinco Sentidos. Joy Evans & Jo E. Moore. Tr. by Liz Wolfe & Dora Ficklin from ENG. (Science Mini-Unit Ser.). (SPA., Illus.). 16p. (J). (gr. 1-3). 1992. pap. text 6.95 (1-55799-233-9, EMC 035) Evan-Moor Edu Pubs.

Mis Cinco Sentidos: Cuento de un Leon. Judy Nayer. Tr. by Argentina Palacios. (Spanish Whole Language Big Bks.).Tr. of My Five Senses. (SPA., Illus.). 16p. (Orig.). (J). (ps-2). 1994. pap. 16.95 (1-56784-094-9) Newbridge Educ.

Mis Cuatro Puntos Cardinales. Luis M. Martinez. Ed. by Sergio A. Sardinas. LC 98-89801. (Coleccion Cuba y Sus Jueces Ser.). (SPA., Illus.). 160p. (Orig.). 1999. pap. 13.00 (0-89729-891-8) Ediciones.

MIS Design Variables & Decision Making Performance: A Simulation Experiment. A. Milton Jenkins. LC 82-21858. (Management Information Systems Ser.: No. 3). 269p. reprint ed. pap. 83.40 (0-8357-1399-7, 207039600088) Bks Demand.

*Mis Dos Luces. Felix Padilla. Ed. by Rebecca Padilla. (SPA., Illus.). 32p. 1999. 16.00 (0-9675413-1-X) Libros Latin Treas.

*Mis-Education of the Negro. Carter G. Woodson. 240p. 2000. pap. 9.50 (0-913543-70-5, Pub. by African Am Imag) IPG Chicago.

Mis-Education of the Negro. Carter G. Woodson. (YA). 1990. pap. 12.95 (0-87498-001-1) Assoc Pubs DC.

Mis-Education of the Negro. Carter G. Woodson. 207p. (C). 1993. pap. 8.95 (0-317-05270-5) Hakims Pubs.

Mis-Education of the Negro. Carter G. Woodson. LC 77-24332. reprint ed. 10.00 (0-404-16027-1) AMS Pr.

Mis-Education of the Negro. Carter G. Woodson. 230p. (C). 1990. reprint ed. 19.95 (0-86543-170-1); reprint ed. pap. 9.95 (0-86543-171-X) Africa World.

Mis Encuentros Con Jesus. Nicole Gausseron. 1997. pap. text 16.98 (970-05-0640-1) Grijalbo Edit.

*Mis Enigmas Favoritos. J. J. Benitez. (SPA.). 1998. pap. 6.50 (84-01-46558-3, Pub. by Plaza) Lectorum Pubns.

M

Mis Juguetes. Illus. by Stephanie Longfoot. (Juega y Aprende Ser.).Tr. of My Playthings. (ENG & SPA.). 12p. (J). (ps). 1995. bds. 3.98 (*1-85854-335-5*) Brimax Bks.

Mis' Luci. 2nd rev. ed. Beverly Rose. LC 96-79733. (Rosebrier Collection: Vol. 1). (Illus.). 46p. (J). (ps-2). 1997. 17.50 (*0-9655612-2-4*) Laurel Pub SC.

Mis Padres Me Estan Volviendo Loco. Joyce L. Vedral. (SPA.). 159p. (gr. 4-7). 1997. pap. text 12.98 (*968-13-2970-8*) Edit Diana.

Mis Primeras 500 Palabras. Illus. by Stephanie Ryder.Tr. of My First 500 Words. (ENG & SPA.). 64p. (J). (ps-1). 1995. 7.98 (*1-85854-340-1*) Brimax Bks.

Mis Primeras Letras: Libro de Lectura y Escritura Para Primer Ano, Letra Script y Ligada. 2nd ed. Carmen G. Basurto & Jose Luis Castillo Basurto. (SPA., Illus.). 127p. 1997. pap. 12.98 (*968-24-5347-X*) Trillas.

Mis Primeras Palabras en Ingles. Illus. by Nadine Piette. (Pequenos Libros Ser.). (ENG & SPA.). 60p. (J). (ps). 1994. reprint ed. 3.95 (*970-607-187-3*, Larousse LKC) LKC.

Mis Primeros Conocimentos. Illus. by Nadine Piette. (Pequenos Libros Ser.). (SPA.). 60p. (J). (ps). 1993. reprint ed. 3.95 (*970-607-188-1*, Larousse LKC) LKC.

Mis Primeros Cuentos. Pablo Ozaeta. Ed. by Marjorie Frank & Luz P. Lono. LC 75-16546. (Illus.). (J). (gr. 4-8). 1991. pap., teacher ed. 10.60 (*0-8325-9641-8*, Natl Textbk Co) NTC Contemp Pub Co.

Mis Primeros Cuentos. Pablo Ozaeta. Ed. by Marjorie Frank & Luz P. Lono. LC 75-16546. (Illus.). (J). (gr. 4-8). 1994. pap., student ed. 6.60 (*0-8325-9642-6*, Natl Textbk Co) NTC Contemp Pub Co.

Mis Primeros Cuentos. Pablo Ozaeta. Ed. by Marjorie Frank & Luz P. Lono. LC 75-16546. (Illus.). (J). (gr. 4-8). 1995. 76.60 (*0-8325-9640-X*, Natl Textbk Co) NTC Contemp Pub Co.

Mis Primeros Treinta Momentos a Solas Con Dios. Ty Saltzgiver. (SPA.). Date not set. 2.50 (*0-9616562-4-7*) Salt Resources Inc.

Mis-Reading the Creative Impulse: The Poetic Subject in Rimbaud & Claudel, Restaged. Adrianna M. Paliyenko. LC 96-35091. 1997. 34.95 (*0-8093-2122-X*) S Ill U Pr.

***Mis Recuerdos.** Alma Flor Ada. (Puertas al Sol Ser.). (SPA., Illus.). 1999. pap. text 4.95 (*1-58105-414-9*) Santillana.

***Mis Relaciones con el General Batista.** Roberto Fernandez Miranda. LC 99-68366. (Coleccion Cuba y sus Jueces). (SPA., Illus.). 223p. 1999. pap. 19.95 (*0-89729-910-8*) Ediciones.

Mis Relaciones con Maximo Gomez. Orestes Ferrara. LC 86-83193. (Coleccion Cuba y sus Jueces). 315p. 1987. pap. 14.95 (*0-89729-431-9*) Ediciones.

***Mis Relatos.** Alma Flor Ada. (Puertas al Sol Ser.). (SPA., Illus.). 1999. pap. text 4.95 (*1-58105-416-5*) Santillana.

MIS Spanish-English Clinical Medical Translator. LC 99-164692. 93 p. 1998. write for info. (*1-891953-00-1*) Medical Info.

***Mis Tres Adioses a Cuba: Diario de Dos Viajes.** Ani Mestre. LC 98-62433. (SPA., Illus.). 213p. 1999. pap. 16.00 (*0-89729-895-0*) Ediciones.

MIS-X - Top Secret. A. R. Wichtrich. LC 97-65969. (Illus.). 114p. 1997. 21.95 (*1-57197-067-3*) Pentland Pr.

Misa de Mariachi. Carlos Amezcua. (SPA.). 12p. 1978. write for info. (*0-614-04899-0*) Mex Am Cult.

Misa de Tepeyac. Carlos Rosas. (SPA.). write for info. (*0-614-04900-8*) Mex Am Cult.

Misa Mesa Musa: Liturgy in the U. S. Hispanic Church. Ed. by Alan Hommerding & Ken Davis. LC 97-195472. (Illus.). (Orig.). 1997. pap. text 6.95 (*0-937690-37-6*) Wrld Lib Pubns.

Misadministration of Radioactive Material in Medicine - Scientific Background. Intro. by Charles B. Meinhold. LC 91-35005. (Commentary Ser.: No. 7). 49p. 1991. pap. text 25.00 (*0-929600-22-3*) NCRP Pubns.

***Misadventure of Salem Jack & Finnigan Reeves.** William M. Harmening. 202p. (YA). 2000. pap. write for info. (*0-9639377-1-5*) Big Rock Pr.

Misadventures in the (213) Dennis Hensley. LC 98-4990. 304p. 1998. 24.00 (*0-688-15452-2*, Wm Morrow) Morrow Avon.

***Misadventures in the (213)** Dennis Hensley. 304p. 1999. pap. 14.00 (*0-688-17128-1*, Wm Morrow) Morrow Avon.

Misadventures of an American Abroad: Big Brother Exposed. Albert E. Tyrrell. Ed. by Mary E. Rose. (Illus.). 680p. (Orig.). 1990. 21.95 (*0-9626055-0-6*) Terril Pub.

Misadventures of Sherlock Holmes. John Lennon. 1991. 16.95 (*0-8065-1245-8*) Carol Pub Group.

Misadventures of Sherlock Holmes. John Lennon et al. Ed. by Sebastian Wolfe. 1991. pap. 10.95 (*0-8065-1235-0*) Carol Pub Group.

Misadventures of Silk & Shakespeare. Winfred Blevins. LC 85-18207. (Frontier Library). 250p. 1985. 13.95 (*0-915463-26-1*, Frontier Libr) Jameson Bks.

Misadventures of Tim McPick: A Gay Comedy. Daniel Curzon. LC 75-32707. 1980. reprint ed. pap. 4.95 (*0-930650-02-6*) IGNA Books.

***Misadventures of Tron Bonne.** Christine Cain. LC 99-66299. (Official Strategy Guides Ser.). (Illus.). 96p. 2000. pap. 14.99 (*0-7615-2579-3*) Prima Pub.

Misadventures of Wags & Freckles Kid-Pak: A Lesson in the Dangers of Alcohol. rev. ed. James Bosco. Ed. by Ann Lupo. (Life-Skill Builder Educational Ser.). (Illus.). 28p. (J). (ps-3). 1991. pap. text 3.95 (*1-56230-136-5*); pap. text 4.95 incl. audio (*1-56230-126-8*) Syndistar.

Misalignment of Exchange Rates: Effects on Trade & Industry. Richard C. Marston. (National Bureau of Economic Research Project Report Ser.). (Illus.). x, 328p. 1988. lib. bdg. 48.00 (*0-226-50723-8*) U Ch Pr.

Misalliance. George Bernard Shaw. 1957. pap. text. write for info. (*0-573-61955-7*) S French Trade.

Misanthrope. Moliere. Date not set. lib. bdg. 14.95 (*0-8488-1655-2*) Amereon Ltd.

Misanthrope. Moliere. Tr. by Richard Wilbur from FRE. 1965. pap. 5.25 (*0-8222-1389-3*) Dramatists Play.

Misanthrope. Moliere. LC 96-172587. 98p. 1996. pap. 10.95 (*0-571-17909-6*) Faber & Faber.

Misanthrope. Moliere. Tr. by Charles H. Wall from FRE. LC 93-16948. 1993. pap. 7.00 (*0-88734-267-1*) Players Pr.

Misanthrope. Moliere. 49.95 incl. audio (*0-685-21217-3*); pap. 7.95 (*0-685-34239-5*) Fr & Eur.

Misanthrope. Moliere. (Coll. Class. du Theatre). (FRE., Illus.). 1965. pap. 7.95 (*0-8288-9943-6*, F40016) Fr & Eur.

Misanthrope. Moliere. (Absolute Classics Ser.). 92p. 1998. pap. 12.95 (*1-84002-032-6*, Pub. by Oberon Bks Ltd) Theatre Comm.

Misanthrope. Moliere. (Thrift Editions Ser.). 64p. 1992. reprint ed. pap. 1.00 (*0-486-27065-3*) Dover.

Misanthrope: A Modern English Adaptation. Tony Harrison. LC 73-83157. 1975. 15.95 (*0-89388-112-0*); pap. 9.95 (*0-89388-113-9*) Okpaku Communications.

Misanthrope: Reproducible Teaching Unit. James Scott. 30p. (YA). (gr. 7-12). 1995. teacher ed., ring bd. 29.50 (*1-58049-068-9*, TU62/U) Prestwick Hse.

Misanthrope & Other French Classics. Ed. by Eric Bentley. (Eric Bentley's Dramatic Repertoire Ser.). 330p. 1986. pap. 10.95 (*0-936839-19-8*) Applause Theatre Bk Pubs.

Misanthrope & Other Plays. Incl. Doctor in Spite of Himself. Moliere. Tr. by John Wood. 1959. Imaginary Invalid. Moliere. Tr. by John Wood. 1959. Sicilian. Moliere. Tr. by John Wood. 1959. Tartuffe. (Classics Ser.). 288p. (Orig.). (YA). (gr. 9 up). 1959. Set pap. 8.95 (*0-14-044089-5*, Penguin Classics) Viking Penguin.

Misanthrope & Other Plays. Moliere. Tr. by Donald M. Frame. (Orig.). 1968. mass mkt. 6.95 (*0-451-52415-2*, CE1721, Sig Classics) NAL.

***Misanthrope & Other Plays: A New Selection.** Moliere. (Penguin Classics Ser.). 320p. 2000. pap. 8.95 (*0-14-044730-X*, Penguin Bks) Viking Penguin.

Misanthrope & Tartuffe. Richard Wilbur. LC 65-29707. (Illus.). 336p. (C). 1965. pap. 12.00 (*0-15-660517-1*, Harvest Bks) Harcourt.

Misanthrope, Moliere: Critical Monographs in English. David Whitton. 96p. 1993. pap. 40.00 (*0-85261-280-X*, Pub. by Univ of Glasgow) St Mut.

Misanthrope Ou la Philanthropie de l'Honnete Homme Classique. Salwa E. Mishriky. (Currents in Comparative Romance Languages & Literatures Ser.). (FRE.). XVIII, 237p. (C). 1995. text 49.95 (*0-8204-2398-X*) P Lang Pubng.

Misapprehensions. E. A. Markham. 96p. 1995. pap. 17.95 (*0-85646-271-3*, Pub. by Anvil Press) Dufour.

Misapprehensions & Other Poems. Edmund Pennant. 80p. (Orig.). 1984. pap. 5.95 (*0-931642-15-9*) Lintel.

Misbegotten. James Richardson. LC 98-87020. 192p. 2000. pap. 11.95 (*1-56315-169-3*) SterlingHse.

***Misbegotten Anguish: A Theology & Ethics of Violence.** Cheryl Kirk-Duggan. 2001. pap. 29.99 (*0-8272-2327-7*) Chalice Pr.

Misbegotten King. Anne K. Bush. 368p. (Orig.). 1997. mass mkt. 5.99 (*0-446-60331-7*, Pub. by Warner Bks) Little.

Misbegotten Match. Rita Boucher. 192p. 1994. mass mkt. 3.99 (*0-380-77714-2*, Avon Bks) Morrow Avon.

***Misbehaving Saint.** Florence B. Smith. 315p. 1999. pap. 8.00 (*1-893463-30-3*) F B Smith.

Misc Neighborhood Reader. Ferrre. 1997. 24.00 (*0-374-92490-2*, Sunburst Bks) FS&G.

***Miscalculations.** Elizabeth Mansfield. 304p. 2000. mass mkt. 5.99 (*0-515-12834-1*, Jove) Berkley Pub.

Miscarriage. Eileen McGrath. 1997. pap. 3.95 (*0-7829-0752-0*, 661-009 12500) T More.

Miscarriage: A Man's Book. Rick Wheat. Ed. by Joy Johnson. 24p, 1995. pap. 3.50 (*1-56123-082-0*, MMBC) Centering Corp.

Miscarriage: A Quiet Grief. Nelson Kraybill & Ellen Kraybill. (Visitation Pamphlet Ser.). 16p. (Orig.). 1990. pap. 2.99 (*0-8361-3531-8*) Herald Pr.

Miscarriage: For Parents Experiencing Fetal Death. rev. ed. Joy Johnson & S. M. Johnson. LC 98-45174. (Illus.). 24p. 1980. pap. 3.50 (*1-56123-007-3*, MISC) Centering Corp.

Miscarriage: Sharing the Grief, Facing the Pain, Healing the Wounds. Walter Williamson. 1987. 14.95 (*0-8027-0947-8*) Walker & Co.

Miscarriage: The Facts. 2nd ed. Gillian C. Lachelin. LC 95-39063. (Facts Ser.). (Illus.). 96p. (C). 1996. pap. text 19.95 (*0-19-262613-2*) OUP.

Miscarriage: Women Sharing from the Heart. Marie Allen & Shelly Marks. LC 92-22852. 272p. 1993. pap. 17.95 (*0-471-54834-0*) Wiley.

Miscarriage: Your Questions Answered. Ursula Markham. LC 98-29524. (Element Guide Ser.). 128p. 1999. pap. 9.95 (*1-86204-297-7*, Pub. by Element MA) Penguin Putnam.

Miscarriage - A Shattered Dream. rev. ed. Sherokee Ilse & Linda H. Burns. 64p. 1995. pap. 9.95 (*0-9609456-3-6*) Wintergrn.

Miscarriage of Justice: An Irish Family's Story of Wrongful Conviction As IRA Terrorists. rev. ed. Anne Maguire et al. (Illus.). 188p. 1994. pap. 10.95 (*1-57098-006-3*) Roberts Rinehart.

Miscarriage of Marriage. Andrew Telford. pap. 1.45 (*0-686-12750-1*) Grace Pub Co.

***Miscarriages, Abortions & Still-Born Babies: In the House of God.** Lorna Wren. 49p. 1999. pap. 7.99 (*1-57921-243-3*) WinePress Pub.

Miscarriages Can Be Prevented: Hope & Help for Couples Who Thought They Could Never Have a Baby. William Matzner et al. (Illus.). 110p. 1998. pap. write for info. (*1-57502-778-X*, P02153) Morris Pubng.

***Miscarriages of Justice: A Review of Justice in Error.** Ed. by Clive Walker & Keir Starmer. 402p. 1999. 45.00 (*1-85431-687-7*, Pub. by Blackstone Pr) Gaunt.

Miscast: Negotiating the Presence of the Bushmen. Ed. by Pipa Skotnes. (Illus.). 383p. 1998. pap. 49.95 (*0-7992-1652-6*) Ctr Con Resol.

Miscasting Mandamus in Georgia Local Government Law. R. Perry Sentell, Jr. 132p. 1988. pap. 5.95 (*0-89854-138-7*) U of GA Inst Govt.

Miscegenation. David G. Croly. LC 70-104435. reprint ed. lib. bdg. 42.00 (*0-8398-0281-1*) Irvington.

Miscegenation: The Theory of the Blending of the Races. David Croly. 60p. 1995. pap. 7.50 (*0-88092-199-4*, 1994, Kav Bks) Royal Fireworks.

Miscegenation Blues: Voices of Mixed Race Women. Ed. by Carol Camper. LC 95-156038. (Illus.). 416p. 1994. per. 19.95 (*0-920813-95-X*) Sister Vis Pr.

Miscegenation in the Ante-Bellum South. James H. Johnston. LC 70-144642. reprint ed. 20.00 (*0-404-00178-5*) AMS Pr.

Miscelanea, Meditations, Memoratives. Elizabeth Grymeston. LC 79-84114. (English Experience Ser.: No. 933). 68p. 1979. reprint ed. lib. bdg. 20.00 (*90-221-0933-X*) Walter J Johnson.

Miscelaneas Campesinas (Decimas Cubanas) Coleccion Espejo de Paciencia Ser. Oscar Guerra & Dario Espina Perez. LC 86-82092. 215p. (Orig.). 1987. pap. 12.00 (*0-89729-412-2*) Ediciones.

Miscelanies see Three Prose Works

Miscellanea see Works of Robert Louis Stevenson, Valima Edition

***Miscellanea, 1.** Ahmad Nawaz. LC 00-133577. 180p. 2000. pap. 10.00 (*1-58225-379-X*) Ananta Prakashani.

***Miscellanea, 2.** Ahmad Nawaz. LC 00-133577. 71p. 2000. pap. 10.00 (*1-58225-380-3*) Ananta Prakashani.

Miscellanea Celtica in Memoriam Henrich Wagner. Ed. by Seamus M. Mathuna & Ailbhe O. Corrain. LC 98-116831. (Acta Universitatis Upsaliensis Studia Celtica Upsaliensia: No. 2). (Illus.). 366p. 1997. 67.50 (*91-554-3951-9*, Pub. by Almqvist Wiksell) Coronet Bks.

Miscellanea Hibernica. Kuno Meyer. 1998. pap. 10.00 (*0-89979-100-X*) British Am Bks.

***Miscellanea Indo-Europea.** Edgar C. Palome et al. (Journal of Indo-European Studies Monographs: Vol. 33). 314p. (C). 1999. pap. text 48.00 (*0-941694-71-2*) Inst Study Man.

Miscellanea Mathematica. Ed. by Peter J. Hilton et al. xiii, 326p. 1992. 42.95 (*0-387-54174-8*) Spr-Verlag.

Miscellanea Moreana: Essays for Germain Marc'hadour. Ed. by Clare M. Murphy et al. (Medieval & Renaissance Texts & Studies: Vol. 61). 608p. 1989. 50.00 (*0-86698-045-8*, MR61) MRTS.

Miscellanea Musica Celtica. James Travis. (Wissenschaftliche Abhandlungen-Musicological Studies: Vol. 14). 80p. 1969. lib. bdg. 27.00 (*0-912024-84-4*) Inst Mediaeval Mus.

Miscellanea Opera, Vol. 24. Compiled by Charles H. Parsons. 1987. write for info. (*0-88946-421-9*) E Mellen.

Miscellanea Philosophica et Historia Graece. Theodorus Metochites. Ed. by C. Muller. 854p. 1921. reprint ed. lib. bdg. 95.00 (*0-685-13372-9*, Pub. by AM Hakkert) Coronet Bks.

Miscellanea the Pick of the Four Judges: Miscellanies & Later Writings. M. Hidayatullah. (C). 1989. 150.00 (*0-7855-3689-2*) St Mut.

***Miscellaneous.** (Ironworking Lev 2 Ser.). 1999. teacher ed., ring bd. 12.00 (*0-13-019303-8*) P-H.

Miscellaneous see Works of Samuel Johnson

Miscellaneous, A1. Anita Harnadek. (Algebra Word Problems). 32p. (Orig.). (YA). (gr. 9 up). 1988. pap. 6.95 (*0-89455-339-9*) Crit Think Bks.

Miscellaneous B1. Anita Harnadek. 32p. (Orig.). (YA). (gr. 10 up). 1988. pap. 6.95 (*0-89455-340-2*) Crit Think Bks.

Miscellaneous C1. Anita Harnadek. 32p. (Orig.). (YA). (gr. 10 up). 1988. pap. 6.95 (*0-89455-341-0*) Crit Think Bks.

Miscellaneous - Peter Pilgrim. Robert M. Bird. (Works of Robert Montgomery Bird). 1989. reprint ed. lib. bdg. 79.00 (*0-7812-1995-7*) Rprt Serv.

***Miscellaneous - The Algerine Captive.** Royall Tyler. (Notable American Authors Ser.). 1999. reprint ed. lib. bdg. 125.00 (*0-7812-9861-X*) Rprt Serv.

Miscellaneous - The Italian Sketch Book. Henry T. Tuckerman. (Notable American Authors Ser.). 1999. reprint ed. lib. bdg. 125.00 (*0-7812-9849-0*) Rprt Serv.

Miscellaneous - The Life of Benjamin Harrison. Lewis Wallace. (Notable American Authors Ser.). 1999. reprint ed. lib. bdg. 125.00 (*0-7812-9871-7*) Rprt Serv.

Miscellaneous - The South: A Tour of Its Battlefields & Ruined Cities. John T. Trowbridge. (Notable American Authors). 1999. reprint ed. lib. bdg. 125.00 (*0-7812-9819-9*) Rprt Serv.

Miscellaneous Alabama Newspaper Abstracts, Vol. 1. Michael Kelsey et al. 256p. (Orig.). 1995. pap. text 21.00 (*0-7884-0238-2*) Heritage Bk.

Miscellaneous Alabama Newspaper Abstracts, Vol. 2. Michael Kelsey et al. LC 95-211997. iv, 352p. (Orig.). 1996. pap. 32.00 (*0-7884-0589-6*, K151) Heritage Bk.

Miscellaneous Archaeological Studies in the ANAMAX-Rosemont Land Exchange Area see ANAMAX-Rosemont Project

Miscellaneous Bible Records, Principally New Jersey Families. Compiled by Agnes F. Risley. (Illus.). 151p. 1997. reprint ed. pap. 22.00 (*0-8328-6031-X*) Higginson Bk Co.

Miscellaneous Boards & Commissions see Alaska Administrative Code--Register 151 Supplement (October 1999)

Miscellaneous Boards & Commissions see Alaska Administrative Code--Register 150 Supplement (July 1999)

Miscellaneous Boards & Commissions, Binder 8, TITLE 20. write for info. (*0-327-06380-7*) LEXIS Pub.

Miscellaneous Church & Cemetery Records from Columbia County, Pennsylvania. Compiled by Schuylkill Roots Staff. 80p. 1990. pap. text 9.50 (*1-55856-051-3*, 390) Closson Pr.

Miscellaneous Church Music. Ed. by Ernest Warburton. (Johann Christian Bach, 1735-1782 The Collected Works). 275p. 1989. text 94.00 (*0-8240-6073-3*) Garland.

Miscellaneous Collected Papers see Vaisesika Sutras of Kanada: With Commentary of Sankara Misra & Extracts from Gloss, of Jayanarayana & Notes from Commentary of Candrakanta

Miscellaneous Contributions to Punch, The Fat Contributor Papers, Novels by Eminent Hands, Sketches & Travels in London, Mr. Brown's Letters to His Nephew, The Proser Papers, Etc. see Complete Works of William Makepeace Thackeray

Miscellaneous Coptic Texts in the Dialect of Upper Egypt, 2 vols. Ed. by E. A. Wallis Budge. LC 77-3587. (Coptic Texts Ser.: Vol. 5). (Illus.). reprint ed. 150.00 (*0-404-11555-1*) AMS Pr.

Miscellaneous Discourses Concerning the Dissolution & Changes of the World. John Ray. (Anglistica & Americana Ser.: No. 10). 259p. 1968. reprint ed. 50.70 (*0-685-66508-9*, 05102001) G Olms Pubs.

Miscellaneous Docket Index Suffolk County, Massachusetts: Probate Records, 1639-1866. Ed. by Melinde L. Sanborn. 32p. 1997. pap. 5.00 (*0-89725-333-7*, 1855) Picton Pr.

Miscellaneous Essays. George E. Saintsbury. LC 72-39114. (Essay Index Reprint Ser.). 1977. reprint ed. 26.95 (*0-8369-2718-4*) Ayer.

Miscellaneous Facts, Confessions, & Observations. Eugene Field. (Notable American Authors Ser.). 1992. reprint ed. lib. bdg. 75.00 (*0-7812-2653-8*) Rprt Serv.

Miscellaneous Foods: Supplement to McCance & Widdowson's "The Composition of Foods" 5th ed. Ed. by W. Chan et al. 193p. 1994. pap. 63.00 (*0-85186-360-4*, R6360) CRC Pr.

Miscellaneous History of New London, Ct. from the Records & Papers of the New London Historical Society: Includes the Early Whaling Industry of New London, Famous Old Tavern, Facts & Reminiscence, & More. 110p. 1994. reprint ed. pap. 15.00 (*0-8328-4403-9*) Higginson Bk Co.

Miscellaneous Inscriptions in the Yale Babylonian Collection. Albert T. Clay. LC 78-63530. (Yale Oriental Series: Babylonian Texts: No. 1). (Illus.). 232p. reprint ed. 42.00 (*0-404-60251-7*) AMS Pr.

Miscellaneous Keyboard Works: Toccatas, Fugues & Other Pieces. Composed by Johann Sebastian Bach. 304p. 1991. pap. 15.95 (*0-486-26681-8*) Dover.

Miscellaneous Land Exchange & Boundary Adjustment Bills: Hearing Before the Subcommittee on Forests & Public Land Management of the Committee On Energy & Natural Resources, United States Senate, One Hundred Fifth Congress, First Session, on S. 541, S. 587, S. 588, S. 589, S. 590, S. 591, S. 750, S. 785, S. 881, June 18, 1997. United States Staff. LC 98-108460. (S. Hrg. Ser.). 38 p. 1997. write for info. (*0-16-055580-9*) USGPO.

Miscellaneous Laws Riser Hook. Scott Turow. 1996. text. write for info. (*0-374-94832-1*) FS&G.

Miscellaneous Light Artillery (1st Virginia, Wise, Middlesex, Hanover, Magruder, Manchester, Campbell Long Island Artillery) Robert H. Moore. (Virginia Regimental Histories Ser.). (Illus.). 141p. 1998. 19.95 (*1-56190-105-9*) H E Howard.

Miscellaneous Manuscripts. Ed. by Elise B. Jorgens. (English Song 1600-1675 Ser.). 232p. 1987. text 25.00 (*0-8240-8241-9*) Garland.

Miscellaneous Masonic Documents. Ed. by Gerry L. Prinsen. 58p. 1998. reprint ed. pap. 12.95 (*0-7661-0692-6*) Kessinger Pub.

Miscellaneous New Mexico Public Land Bills, Cave Creek Canyon Mining Withdrawal, El Camino Real Para Los Texas National Trails System Study: Hearing Before the Subcommittee on Public Lands, National Parks, & Forests of the Committee on Energy & Natural Resources, United States Senate, 103 Congress, 1st Session, on S. 294, S. 310, S. 313, S. 643, H.R 38, S. 836, S. 983, S. 1049, H.R. 698, H.r. 843, June 16, 1993. USGPO Staff. LC 94-113943. iii, 131 p. 1993. write for info. (*0-16-041597-7*) USGPO.

Miscellaneous Notes on Plato. G. J. De Vries. (Mededelingen der Koninklijke Nederlandse Akademie van Wetenschappen, Afd. Letterkunde Ser.: No. 38(1)). 1975. pap. text 8.75 (*0-7204-8294-1*) Elsevier.

Miscellaneous Observations Connected with the Physical Sciences. Emanuel Swedenborg. Tr. & Intro. by Charles E. Strutt. (Illus.). 168p. 1976. reprint ed. 12.95 (*0-915221-21-7*) Swedenborg Sci Assn.

Miscellaneous Papers in Paleopathology. Ed. by William D. Wade. (Technical Ser.). 60p. 1967. pap. 1.25 (*0-685-69760-6*, TS-7) Mus Northern Ariz.

Miscellaneous Papers on Archaeology. S. Ragir et al. (Contributions of the University of California Archaeological Research Facility: No. 14). 125p. (C). 1972. reprint ed. pap. text 13.75 (*1-55567-590-5*) Coyote Press.

Miscellaneous Papers, Principally Illustrative of Events in the Reigns of Queen Mary & King James Sixth. Ed. by William J. Duncan. LC 79-164807. (Maitland Club, Glasgow. Publications: No. 26). reprint ed. 32.50 (*0-404-52981-X*) AMS Pr.

An Asterisk (*) at the beginning of an entry indicates that the title is appearing for the first time.

Miscellaneous Papers, 1672-1865: Now First Printed from the Manuscript in the Collections of the Virginia Historical Society. Ed. by Robert A. Brock. LC 72-14425. (Virginia Historical Society. Collections First Ser.: No. 6). reprint ed. 27.50 (*0-404-57656-7*) AMS Pr.

Miscellaneous Pesticides: The Evaluation of Carcinogenic Risks to Humans. (IARC Monographs: No. 30). 424p. 1983. text 72.00 (*92-832-1230-4*) World Health.

Miscellaneous Poems. George Gordon Byron. Ed. by Jerome J. McGann & Alice Levine. LC 89-29116. (Manuscripts of the Younger Romantics & the Bodleian Shelley Manuscripts: Vol. IV). 276p. 1988. text 50.00 (*0-8240-6253-1*) Garland.

*__Miscellaneous Poems.__ Susanna Haswell Rowson. (Notable American Authors Ser.). 1999. reprint ed. lib. bdg. 125.00 (*0-7812-8842-8*) Rprt Serv.

Miscellaneous Poetry, Prose & Translations from Bodleian, Vol. XXI. Percy Bysshe Shelley. Ed. by E. B. Murray. LC 95-23011. (The Bodleian Shelley Manuscripts Ser.). 576p. 1995. text 297.00 (*0-8153-1156-7*) Garland.

Miscellaneous Proceedings in the Surrogate's Court. 220p. 1994. pap. 30.00 (*0-614-26744-7*, 1411); pap. 175.00 incl. VHS (*0-614-26745-5*, 3411) NYS Bar.

Miscellaneous Prose & Verse. Nathaniel Hawthorne & Claude M. Simpson. Ed. by Thomas Woodson et al. LC 94-31078. (Centenary Edition of the Works of Nathaniel Hawthorne Ser.: Vol. XXIII). 752p. 1995. text 95.00 (*0-8142-0644-1*) Ohio St U Pr.

Miscellaneous Prose of Sir Philip Sidney. Philip Sidney. Ed. by Jan A. Van Dorsten & Katherine Duncan-Jones. (Oxford English Texts Ser.). 1973. 29.00 (*0-19-811880-5*) OUP.

Miscellaneous Readings. Ed. by Lewis B. Monroe. LC 71-38603. (Granger Index Reprint Ser.). 1977. 23.95 (*0-8369-6335-0*) Ayer.

*__Miscellaneous Rights Encyclopedia.__ (C). 1999. pap. write for info. (*0-13-585935-2*) P-H.

Miscellaneous Studies in History of Music. Oscar G. Sonneck. LC 70-127897. reprint ed. 32.50 (*0-404-06155-9*) AMS Pr.

Miscellaneous Studies in Mexican Prehistory. Michael W. Spence et al. (Anthropological Papers Ser.: No. 45). (Illus.). vi, 170p. (Orig.). 1972. pap. 2.00 (*0-932206-43-3*) U Mich Mus Anthro.

Miscellaneous Studies in the History of Music. Oscar G. Sonneck. LC 68-9192. (Music Reprint Ser.). 344p. 1968. reprint ed. lib. bdg. 45.00 (*0-306-71163-X*) Da Capo.

Miscellaneous Studies in the History of Music. Oscar G. Sonneck. 344p. 1990. reprint ed. lib. bdg. 79.00 (*0-7812-9016-3*) Rprt Serv.

Miscellaneous Texas Newspaper Abstracts - Deaths, Vol. 1. Michael Kelsey et al. 271p. (Orig.). 1995. pap. 22.00 (*0-7884-0321-4*) Heritage Bk.

Miscellaneous Texas Newspaper Abstracts - Deaths, Vol. 2. Michael Kelsey et al. 455p. (Orig.). 1998. pap. 32.00 (*0-7884-0781-3*, K152) Heritage Bk.

Miscellaneous Theological Works. Emanuel Swedenborg. Tr. by J. Whitehead. LC 76-46143. ix, 712p. 1996. 20.00 (*0-87785-283-9*) Swedenborg.

Miscellaneous Tracts Relating to Natural History, Husbandry, & Physick: Calender of Flora Is Added. Carl Linnaeus. Ed. by Frank N. Egerton, 3rd. LC 77-74237. (History of Ecology Ser.). 1978. reprint ed. lib. bdg. 31.95 (*0-405-10406-5*) Ayer.

Miscellaneous Treaty Series, Great Britain, 1997 No. 7: Comprehensive Nuclear-Test-Ban Treaty with Annexes & Protocol. 16p. 1997. pap. 19.00 (*0-10-136652-3*, HM66523, Pub. by Statnry Office) Bernan Associates.

Miscellaneous Verdicts. Anthony Powell. 510p. 1992. 38.50 (*0-226-67710-9*) U Ch Pr.

Miscellaneous Water Projects & Hydroelectric Project Extensions: Hearing Before the Subcommittee on Water & Power of the Committee on Energy & Natural Resources, United States Senate, One Hundred Fifth Congress, Second Session, on S. 1398, S. 2041, S. 2087, S. 2140, S. 2142, H.r. 2165, H.r. 2217, H.r. 2841, June 16, 1998. United States. LC 98-214933. 51 p. 1998. write for info. (*0-16-057515-X*) USGPO.

Miscellaneous Water Projects & Small Reclamation Projects Act of 1956: Hearing Before the Subcommittee on Water & Power of the Committee on Energy & Natural Resources, United States Senate, One Hundred Fifth Congress, First Session, on S. 725, S. 777, S. 841, S. 1230, H.r. 848, H.r. 1184, H.r. 1217, October 7, 1998. United States. LC 98-159812. 108 p. 1998. write for info. (*0-16-056194-9*) USGPO.

Miscellaneous Works, 5 vols. Edward Gibbon. Ed. by John Sheffield. LC 76-171363. (Illus.). reprint ed. 395.00 (*0-404-02830-6*) AMS Pr.

Miscellaneous Works. David Humphreys. LC 68-24210. 432p. 1968. reprint ed. 60.00 (*0-8201-1028-0*) Schol Facsimiles.

Miscellaneous Works: Some Gospel Truths Opened, a Vindication of Some Gospel Truths Opened, & a Few Sighs from Hell, Vol. 1. John Bunyan. Ed. by T. L. Underwood & Roger Sharrock. (Oxford English Texts Ser.). (Illus.). 458p. 1980. 115.00 (*0-19-812730-8*) OUP.

Miscellaneous Works of John Bunyan Vol. 3: Christian Behavior, the Holy City, the Resurrection of the Dead. John Bunyan. Ed. by James S. McGee. (Oxford English Texts Ser.). (Illus.). 512p. 1987. 95.00 (*0-19-812731-6*) OUP.

Miscellaneous Works of John Bunyan Vol. 4: A Defence of the Doctrine of Justification, A Confession of My Faith, Differences in Judgment about Water-Baptism, Peaceable Principles & True, A Case of Conscience Resolved, Questions about the Nature & Perpetuity of the Seventh-Day-Sabbath. John Bunyan. Ed. by Ted L. Underwood. (Oxford English Texts Ser.). (Illus.). 464p. 1990. 115.00 (*0-19-812732-4*) OUP.

Miscellaneous Works of John Bunyan Vol. 5: The Barren Fig-Tree, The Strait Gate, The Heavenly Foot-Man. John Bunyan. Ed. by Graham Midgley. (Oxford English Texts Ser.). (Illus.). 224p. 1986. 85.00 (*0-19-812733-2*) OUP.

Miscellaneous Works of John Bunyan Vol. 6: The Poems, Vol. 6. John Bunyan. Ed. by E. G. Midgley. (Oxford English Texts Ser.). (Illus.). 470p. 1980. 115.00 (*0-19-812734-0*) OUP.

Miscellaneous Works of John Bunyan Vol. 7: Solomon's Temple Spiritualized, The House of the Forest of Lebanon, The Water of Life, Vol. 7. John Bunyan. Ed. by Graham Midgley. (Oxford English Texts Ser.). (Illus.). 288p. 1989. 95.00 (*0-19-812735-9*) OUP.

Miscellaneous Works of John Bunyan Vol. 8: Instruction for the Ignorant; Light for Them That Sit in Darkness; Saved by Grace; Come, Welcome to Jesus Christ. John Bunyan. Ed. by Richard L. Greaves. (Oxford English Texts Ser.). (Illus.). 470p. 1979. 98.00 (*0-19-812736-7*) OUP.

Miscellaneous Works of John Bunyan Vol. 9: A Treatise of the Fear of God, the Greatness of the Soul, a Holy Life, Vol. 9. John Bunyan. Ed. by Richard L. Greaves. (Oxford English Texts Ser.). (Illus.). 412p. 1981. 118.00 (*0-19-812737-5*) OUP.

Miscellaneous Works of John Bunyan Vol. 10: Seasonable Counsel & a Discourse upon the Pharisee & the Publicane. John Bunyan. Ed. by Owen C. Watkins. (Oxford English Texts Ser.). (Illus.). 304p. 1988. 79.00 (*0-19-812738-3*) OUP.

Miscellaneous Works of John Bunyan Vol. 11: Good News for the Vilest of Men; The Advocateship of Jesus Christ. John Bunyan. Ed. by Richard L. Greaves. (Oxford English Texts Ser.). (Illus.). 276p. 1985. 75.00 (*0-19-812739-1*) OUP.

Miscellaneous Works of John Bunyan Vol. 13: Israel's Hope Encouraged; The Desire of the Righteous Granted; The Saints Privilege & Profit; Christ a Compleat Saviour; The Saints Knowledge of Christ's Love; Of Antichrist, & His Ruine, Vol. 13. John Bunyan. Ed. by W. R. Owens & Roger Sharrock. (Illus.). 576p. (C). 1994. 110.00 (*0-19-812368-X*) OUP.

Miscellaneous Works to French & Italian Texts. Ed. by Ernest Warburton. (Johann Christian Bach, 1735-1782 The Collected Works). 325p. 1990. text 127.00 (*0-8240-6065-2*) Garland.

Miscellaneous Writings. Andrew Carnegie. Ed. by Burton J. Hendrick. LC 68-58777. (Essay Index Reprint Ser.). 1977. 44.95 (*0-8369-0105-3*) Ayer.

Miscellaneous Writings. H. P. Lovecraft. Ed. & Intro. by S. T. Joshi. LC 94-27323. (Illus.). xiv, 570p. 1995. 32.95 (*0-87054-168-4*) Arkham.

Miscellaneous Writings. John Stuart Mill. Ed. & Intro. by John M. Robson. (Collected Works of John Stuart Mill: Vol. 31). 462p. 1989. text 85.00 (*0-8020-2728-8*) U of Toronto Pr.

Miscellaneous Writings. Mary Baker Eddy. 490p. (C). 1992. reprint ed. pap. 14.95 (*0-930227-18-2*) Bookmark CA.

Miscellaneous Writings. Mary M. Eddy. (Notable American Authors Ser.). 1992. reprint ed. lib. bdg. 75.00 (*0-7812-2758-5*) Rprt Serv.

Miscellaneous Writings see Complete Works of Henry Fielding

Miscellaneous Writings, 1883-1896. Mary Baker Eddy. 471p. reprint ed. pap. 16.00 (*0-87952-040-X*) Writings of Mary Baker.

Miscellaneous Writings of Horatio Greenough. Horatio Greenough. LC 75-1118. 72p. 1975. lib. bdg. 50.00 (*0-8201-1152-X*) Schol Facsimiles.

Miscellaneous Writings of J. H. Tilden, M. D. J. H. Tilden. 232p. 1996. reprint ed. spiral bd. 21.00 (*0-7873-1083-2*) Hlth Research.

Miscellaneous Writings of the Late Hon. Joseph P. Bradley, Associate Justice of the Supreme Court of the United States: With a Sketch of His Life by His Son, Charles Bradley & a Review of His "Judicial Record" & an Account of His "Dissenting Opinions" William D. Lewis. Ed. & Compiled by Charles Bradley. xii, 435p. 1986. reprint ed. 50.00 (*0-8377-0876-1*, Rothman) W S Hein.

Miscellaneous Writings on Slavery. William Jay. (Select Bibliographies Reprint Ser.). 1977. 31.95 (*0-8369-5288-X*) Ayer.

Miscellanies. Austin Dobson. LC 67-28749. (Essay Index Reprint Ser.: Second Series). 1977. 20.95 (*0-8369-0380-3*) Ayer.

Miscellanies. William E. Channing. (Works of William Ellery Channing II). 1990. reprint ed. lib. bdg. 79.00 (*0-685-27700-3*) Rprt Serv.

Miscellanies. Austin Dobson. LC 73-100820. (Second Ser.). reprint ed. 27.50 (*0-404-02140-9*) AMS Pr.

Miscellanies. Austin Dobson. (BCL1-PR English Literature Ser.). 364p. 1992. reprint ed. lib. bdg. 89.00 (*0-7812-7041-3*) Rprt Serv.

Miscellanies. Austin Dobson. (BCL1-PR English Literature Ser.: Second Series). 277p. 1992. reprint ed. lib. bdg. 79.00 (*0-7812-7042-1*) Rprt Serv.

Miscellanies. Austin Dobson. 1889. reprint ed. 10.00 (*0-403-00250-8*) Scholarly.

Miscellanies. Ralph Waldo Emerson. (Notable American Authors Ser.). 1992. reprint ed. lib. bdg. 75.00 (*0-7812-2809-3*) Rprt Serv.

Miscellanies, Second Series. Austin Dobson. LC 79-108474. 1970. reprint ed. 16.00 (*0-403-00206-0*) Scholarly.

Miscellanies, 2 vols., Set. Harriet Martineau. LC 79-148342. reprint ed. 71.00 (*0-404-08887-2*) AMS Pr.

Miscellanies: Literary & Historical, 2 vols. Archibald P. Rosebery. LC 71-152211. (Essay Index Reprint Ser.). 1977. reprint ed. 47.95 (*0-8369-2253-0*) Ayer.

Miscellanies by Henry Fielding, Esq., Vol. 1. Henry Fielding. Ed. by Henry K. Miller. LC 71-184366. (Wesleyan Edition of the Works of Henry Fielding). 346p. reprint ed. pap. 107.30 (*0-7837-2622-8*, 204295800001) Bks Demand.

Miscellanies by Henry Fielding, Esq., Vol. 2. Henry Fielding. Ed. by Hugh Amory. LC 71-184366. (Works of Henry Fielding Ser.). 442p. 1993. text 85.00 (*0-8195-5254-2*, Wesleyan Univ Pr) U Pr of New Eng.

Miscellanies by Henry Fielding, Esq. Vol. 3: Jonathan Wild. Henry Fielding. Ed. by Hugh Amory. LC 71-184366. (Works of Henry Fielding). (Illus.). 414p. 1997. text 75.00 (*0-8195-5298-4*, Wesleyan Univ Pr) U Pr of New Eng.

Miscellanies Critical, Imaginative & Juridical: Contributed to Blackwell's Magazine, 2 vols. Samuel Warren. 992p. 1996. reprint ed. 125.00 (*0-8377-2785-5*, Rothman) W S Hein.

Miscellanies of the Fuller Worthies' Library, 4 vols. Intro. & Notes by Alexander B. Grosart. LC 70-129362. (Fuller Worthies' Library). reprint ed. 306.00 (*0-404-02670-2*) AMS Pr.

Miscellany. Andrew C. Bradley. LC 72-76894. (Essay Index Reprint Ser.). 1977. 21.95 (*0-8369-0005-7*) Ayer.

Miscellany. Andrew C. Bradley. (BCL1-PR English Literature Ser.). 267p. 1992. reprint ed. lib. bdg. 79.00 (*0-7812-7009-X*) Rprt Serv.

Miscellany: Poems from Hollywood. Mark Dunston. 11p. 1998. pap. 5.00 (*0-89642-444-8*) Linden Pubs.

Miscellany - A Journal of the Transactions & Occurrences in the ASettlement of Massachusetts & Other New England Colonies. John Wintrop. (Notable American Authors Ser.). 1999. reprint ed. lib. bdg. 125.00 (*0-7812-7779-5*) Rprt Serv.

Miscellany - The Liberties of the Massachusetts in New England. Nathaniel Ward. (Notable American Authors Ser.). 1999. reprint ed. lib. bdg. 125.00 (*0-7812-9880-6*) Rprt Serv.

Miscellany by Mark. Mark Sonnenfeld. (Illus.). 54p. 1994. pap. 4.00 (*0-9632820-6-9*) M Sonnenfeld.

*__Miscellany Macabre: Tales of the Unknown.__ Ken Cowley. (Illus.). 75p. 1999. pap. 14.95 (*0-9524153-6-4*, Pub. by BFS) Firebird Dist.

Miscellany of American Christianity: Essays in Honor of H. A. Shelton Smith. Stuart C. Henry. LC 63-14288. 398p. reprint ed. pap. 123.40 (*0-608-15080-0*, 202620200048) Bks Demand.

Miscellany of Etceteras. Ed. by Hazel S. Greenberg. 220p. 1992. ring bd. 20.00 (*0-614-03005-6*) Amer Forum.

Miscellany of Hebrew Literature, 2 vols., Pt. 1. Ed. by Society of Hebrew Literature Staff & Albert Lowy. LC 72-97298. 1975. lib. bdg. 65.00 (*0-8371-4623-2*, LOMH) Greenwood.

Miscellany of Hebrew Literature, 2 vols., Vol. 1. Ed. by Society of Hebrew Literature Staff & Albert Lowy. LC 72-97298. 1975. lib. bdg. 45.00 (*0-8371-2622-3*, LOMI) Greenwood.

Miscellany of Hebrew Literature, 2 vols., Vol. 2. Ed. by Society of Hebrew Literature Staff & Albert Lowy. LC 72-97298. 1975. lib. bdg. 45.00 (*0-8371-2623-1*, LOMJ) Greenwood.

Miscellany of Men. G. K. Chesterton. LC 73-90624. (Essay Index Reprint Ser.). 1977. 23.95 (*0-8369-1281-0*) Ayer.

Miscellany of Men. G. K. Chesterton. LC 74-84061. (G. K. Chesterton Reprint Ser). 1969. 22.95 (*0-8023-1224-1*) Dufour.

Miscellany of Men. G. K. Chesterton. 1988. reprint ed. lib. bdg. 49.00 (*0-7812-0168-3*) Rprt Serv.

Miscellany of the Maitland Club, 4 vols. Maitland Club Staff. Ed. by Alexander Macdonald et al. LC 72-982. (Maitland Club, Glasgow. Publications: No. 25). reprint ed. 165.00 (*0-404-52971-2*) AMS Pr.

Miscellany of Words. Clayton Stabnow. 78p. (Orig.). 1996. pap. 8.00 (*1-57502-154-4*) Morris Pubng.

Miscellany on Nicholas of Cusa. Jasper Hopkins. LC 93-72933. xii, 312p. (C). 1994. text 23.00 (*0-938060-43-0*) Banning Pr.

Miscellany, 1759 to 1763. Ed. by William Shenstone. LC 78-16381. 163p. 1978. reprint ed. lib. bdg. 55.00 (*0-313-20591-4*, SHMI, Greenwood Pr) Greenwood.

Miscellany Two. Emyr Humphreys. 146p. 1981. 16.95 (*0-907476-05-8*); pap. 9.95 (*0-907476-06-6*) Dufour.

Misch Kohn: Beyond the Tradition. Jo Farb Hernandez. (Illus.). 297p. 1999. 60.00 (*0-8109-6381-7*, Pub. by Abrams) Time Warner.

Mischa Elman & the Romantic Style. Allan Kozinn. xiv, 406p. 1990. text 23.00 (*3-7186-0497-3*) Gordon & Breach.

Mischeefs Mysterie: Or, Treasons Masterpeece, No. 317. Francis Herring. Tr. by J. Vicars from LAT. LC 79-171763. 122p. 1971. reprint ed. 25.00 (*90-221-0317-X*) Walter J Johnson.

Mischeefs Mysterie: or Treasons Masterpeece. Gloria Vanjak. (Illus.). 1990. pap. text 10.00 (*1-878180-00-2*) De Ville Gal.

*__Mischief.__ Douglas Clegg. 368p. 2000. pap. 5.99 (*0-8439-4766-7*, Leisure Bks) Dorchester Pub Co.

Mischief. Catherine Hart. 384p. (Orig.). 1995. mass mkt. 5.99 (*0-380-77731-2*, Avon Bks) Morrow Avon.

Mischief. Ed McBain, pseud. 352p. 1994. mass mkt. 5.99 (*0-380-71384-5*, Avon Bks) Morrow Avon.

Mischief. Amanda Quick, pseud. 384p. 1997. mass mkt. 6.50 (*0-553-57190-7*) Bantam.

Mischief. large type ed. Amanda Quick, pseud. LC 96-20873. 1996. lib. bdg. 20.00 (*0-7862-0781-7*) Thorndike Pr.

Mischief. large type ed. Amanda Quick, pseud. LC 96-20873. 1997. pap. 24.95 (*0-7862-0782-5*) Thorndike Pr.

Mischief. Charlotte Armstrong. LC 87-82448. 148p. 1987. reprint ed. pap. 4.95 (*0-930330-72-2*) Intl Polygonics.

Mischief. unabridged ed. Mary Blaylock. Ed. by Peter Schmidt. LC 97-178984. (Illus.). 216p. (YA). (gr. 9 up). 1997. 20.95 (*0-9654440-0-7*) Ironwood Pr AZ.

Mischief & Eve: A Halloween Beginning. Jane Bedell. (Illus.). 22p. (J). (gr. 2-4). 1998. pap. 3.99 (*0-9665837-0-1*) J M Bedell.

Mischief & Marriage. Emma Darcy. 1996. per. 3.50 (*0-373-11815-5*, 1-11815-7) Harlequin Bks.

Mischief & Mayhem: A Nabob's Daughter; Heir Apparent. Janet Edmonds & Petra Nash. LC 95-6890. (Promo Ser.). 443p. 1995. per. 4.99 (*0-373-31217-2*, 1-31217-2) Harlequin Bks.

Mischief & Mercy: Tales of the Saints. Jean McClung. LC 93-2487. (Illus.). 224p. (YA). (gr. 7 up). 1993. pap. 10.95 (*1-883672-02-3*) Tricycle Pr.

*__Mischief at Frinton Park.__ large type ed. Freda M. Long. 384p. 2000. pap. 18.99 (*0-7089-5635-1*, Linford) Ulverscroft.

Mischief in the Catskills: A Ward Eastman Mystery with Five Short Stories. Norman J. Van Valkenburgh. LC 98-24034. 159p. 1998. pap. 12.50 (*0-935796-94-0*, 94) Purple Mnt Pr.

*__Mischief in the Sun: The Making & Unmaking of "The Loved One"__ Robert M. Davis. LC 97-60171. viii, 136p. (C). 1999. 28.50 (*0-87875-494-6*) Whitston Pub.

Mischief, Mad Mary, & Me. Dawn Knight. LC 96-23212. (Illus.). 96p. (J). (gr. 3 up). 1997. 15.00 (*0-688-14865-4*, Grenwillow Bks) HarpC Child Bks.

Mischief, Mad Mary, & Me. Dawn Knight. LC 96-23212. (Illus.). 96p. (gr. 2-6). 1998. mass mkt. 3.99 (*0-380-73135-5*, Avon Bks) Morrow Avon.

Mischief Makers. Nettie Jones. 1991. pap. 9.00 (*0-679-72785-X*) McKay.

*__Mischief Marketing: How the Rich, Famous, & Successful Really Got Their Careers & Business Going (And How You Can, Too)__ Raymond Simon. 224p. 2000. pap. 16.95 (*0-8092-2590-5*, 259050, Contemporary Bks) NTC Contemp Pub Co.

Mischief, Mishaps & Mirth. Marjorie Hitt. 70p. (Orig.). 1996. pap. 5.95 (*1-57502-224-9*, P0883) Morris Pubng.

Mischief of Sin. Thomas Watson. Ed. by Don Kistler. 163p. 1994. reprint ed. 16.95 (*1-877611-85-9*) Soli Deo Gloria.

Mischief on Daisy Hill. Charles M. Schulz. (Illus.). 32p. (J). (ps-3). 12.95 (*0-915696-15-0*) Determined Prods.

Mischiefs That Ought Justly to Be Apprehended from a Whig-Government. Bernard Mandeville. LC 92-544. (Augustan Reprints Ser.: No. 174). 1975. reprint ed. 14.50 (*0-404-70174-4*, DA503) AMS Pr.

Mischievious Acts & Repercussions. Sam Chekwas & R. M. Soccolich. 176p. 1998. pap. 13.00 (*1-885778-45-7*) Seaburn.

Mischievous Maid. Rebecca Robbins. 256p. (Orig.). 1993. mass mkt. 3.99 (*0-380-77336-8*, Avon Bks) Morrow Avon.

Mischievous Miss. Irene L. Black. 1991. mass mkt. 3.95 (*0-8217-3519-5*, Zebra Kensgtn) Kensgtn Pub Corp.

Mischievous Miss Murphy. Kasey Michaels. (Regency Romance Ser.). 176p. 1987. pap. 2.95 (*0-380-89907-8*, Avon Bks) Morrow Avon.

Mischievous Molly. Dorothy D. Moore. LC 95-60902. (Illus.). 48p. (J). (gr. 1-5). 1995. pap. 9.95 (*1-883650-25-9*) Windswept Hse.

Mischievous Monkey Caper. Georgette Livingston. LC 96-97013. (Jennifer Gray Veterinarian Mystery Ser.: Bk. 7). 192p. 1996. 18.95 (*0-8034-9183-2*, Avalon Bks) Bouregy.

Mischievous Pastime: Digging in Cyprus in the Nineteenth Century. Elizabeth Goring. (Illus.). 108p. 1994. pap. 16.95 (*0-948636-11-4*, 6114, Pub. by Natl Mus Scotland) A Schwartz & Co.

Mischka's Tale. Robert Griffin. LC 96-90598. 500p. 1997. 25.00 (*1-889314-11-0*); pap. 12.00 (*1-889314-12-9*) Windhover Pub.

Mischling, Second Degree: My Childhood in Nazi Germany. Ilse Koehn. 1977. 11.09 (*0-606-04477-9*, Pub. by Turtleback) Demco.

Mischna: Text, Ubersetzung und Ausfuhrliche Erklarung mit Eingehenden Gesschichtlichten und Sprachelichen Einleitungen und Textkritischen Anhangen. Ed. by Karl Rengstorf et al. (GER.). x, 188p. (Orig.). (C). 1991. pap. text 104.65 (*3-11-012464-5*, 147-91) De Gruyter.

Miscible Processes, No. II. (SPE Reprint Ser.). 727p. 1985. reprint ed. pap. 20.00 (*0-89520-326-X*, EORRPT018) Soc Petrol Engineers.

Miscibles. Mary Gribble. LC 97-61800. (Illus.). 88p. 1997. pap. 8.00 (*1-886467-25-0*) WJM Press.

Miscommunication: Finding Our Way. C. David Mortensen. LC 96-35714. 368p. 1997. pap. 21.95 (*0-8039-7376-4*) Sage.

Miscommunication: Finding Our Way. C. David Mortensen & Carter M. Ayres. LC 96-35714. 368p. 1997. 46.00 (*0-8039-7375-6*) Sage.

Miscommunication & Problematic Talk. Ed. by Nikolas Coupland et al. (Illus.). 432p. 1991. 55.00 (*0-8039-4032-7*); pap. 26.95 (*0-8039-4033-5*) Sage.

Miscommunication & Problematic Talk. Ed. by Nikolas Coupland et al. LC 90-22484. (Illus.). 384p. 1991. reprint ed. pap. 119.10 (*0-608-01715-9*, 206237000003) Bks Demand.

Miscomprehension of Televised Communications. Jacob Jacoby et al. 208p. 1987. pap. text 19.95 (*0-8058-0215-0*) L Erlbaum Assocs.

Misconceiver. Lucy Ferriss. LC 97-9989. 1997. 22.50 (*0-684-80092-6*) S&S Trade.

Misconceiving Canada: The Struggle for National Unity. Ed. by Kenneth McRoberts. LC 97-183213. 288p. (Orig.). 1997. pap. text 35.00 (*0-19-541233-8*) OUP.

Misconceiving Mothers: Legislators, Prosecutors & the Politics of Prenatal Drug Exposure. Laura E. Gomez. LC 97-1634. (Gender, Family & the Law Ser.). 256p. 1997. 59.95 (*1-56639-557-7*); pap. 19.95 (*1-56639-558-5*) Temple U Pr.

M

M

Misconception. Margaret Pargeter. (Scarlet Ser.). 1997. mass mkt. 3.99 (*1-85487-997-9*, Pub. by Scarlet Bks) London Brdge.

Misconception. David Shifrin. LC 97-77763. 328p. 1997. pap. 14.95 (*0-9663679-0-1*) Hatikvah Pr.

***Misconception.** Becker Walt William. 2001. write for info. (*0-688-17685-2*, Wm Morrow) Morrow Avon.

Misconceptions about Radiation, Facts Are Stranger Than Fiction in Hiroshima, Nagasaki, Marshall Islands, No. 1. Robert J. Lemke & Karen K. Diedrich. (Illus.). 1994. pap. 35.00 (*0-9645418-3-1*) F T Cua.

Misconceptions & Simple Truths in Dressage. L. M. Van Schaik. 135p. 1990. 52.00 (*0-85131-489-9*, Pub. by J A Allen) St Mut.

Misconceptions of Mind & Freedom. Irving Thalberg. 248p. (C). 1984. pap. text 22.00 (*0-8191-3540-2*) U Pr of Amer.

Misconduct & Mysteries: Short Vowel II Sequence. Ellis Richardson. (Read Aloud Ser.: Bk. 9). 28p. (Orig.). 1990. pap. text 4.00 (*1-56775-026-5*, SVIIS9-4) ISM Teach Systs.

Misconduct Cases Book. David W. O'Brien. LC 85-51769. 501p. (Orig.). 1985. 49.00 (*0-9602204-1-0*) Winterbrook.

Misconduct in Employment. B. R. Ghaiye. 1065p. 1977. suppl. ed. 375.00 (*0-7855-1382-5*) St Mut.

Misconduct in Employment. B. R. Ghaiye. (C). 1989. 210.00 (*0-7855-5124-7*) St Mut.

Miscreant. Jean Cocteau. 164p. 1975. 29.95 (*0-7206-5480-7*, Pub. by P Owen Ltd) Dufour.

Miscsellanea Critica. Carel G. Cobet. xv, 616p. 1981. reprint ed. 130.00 (*3-487-07127-4*) G Olms Pubs.

***Misdeeds at Marriston.** Mary Gaul. 2000. 19.95 (*1-929085-48-6*); pap. 4.95 (*1-929085-47-8*) Rgncy Pr.

***Misdeeds at Marriston.** large type ed. Mary Gaul. 2000. pap. 19.95 (*1-929085-51-6*) Rgncy Pr.

Misdemeanor Crime: Trivial Criminal Pursuit. John H. Lindquist. LC 87-34664. (Studies in Crime, Law & Justice: No. 4). 197p. reprint ed. pap. 61.10 (*0-7837-6584-3*, 204614900011) Bks Demand.

Misdiagnosis: Woman As a Disease. Karen M. Hicks. LC 93-48592. 256p. 1994. pap. 19.95 (*1-882606-10-8*) Peoples Med Soc.

Misdirection. Kevin Riordan. (Adventure Ser.: No. 1). (Orig.). 1994. pap. 10.00 (*1-888636-04-1*) Sara Ranchouse.

Misdirection: The Secret to Successful Magic. unabridged ed. Mark Alexander. Ed. by Bruce Fife. LC 98-49941. (Illus.). 64p. 1998. pap. 10.00 (*0-941599-36-1*, Pub. by Piccadilly Bks) Empire Pub Srvs.

Misdirection Conspiracy: or Who Really Killed the American Dream? (Exposed by Reality Investing) Kenneth Coleman. LC 82-50091. (Illus.). 216p. 1983. pap. 12.95 (*0-942632-00-1*) Seraphim Pr.

Mise a Mort. Louis Aragon. (FRE.). 256p. 1978. pap. 16.95 (*0-7859-1728-4*, 2070363147) Fr & Eur.

Mise a Mort. Louis Aragon. (Folio Ser.: No. 314). (FRE.). pap. 12.95 (*2-07-036314-7*) Schoenhof.

***Mise en Memoire de la Science.** P. Abir-Am. (FRE.). 336p. 1998. pap. text 44.00 (*90-5709-007-4*, edit archives) Gordon & Breach.

Mise en Pratique. Favrod. 1995. wbk. ed. write for info. (*0-201-82237-7*) Addison-Wesley.

***Mise En Pratique.** 3rd ed. 2000. teacher ed. write for info. (*0-201-71047-1*) Addison-Wesley.

***Mise en Pratique.** 3rd ed. Lynn Penrod. (FRE.). 208p. 2000. pap. text, wbk. ed. write for info. (*0-201-65413-X*) Addison-Wesley.

Mise en Pratique: Manuel de Grammaire et d'Expression Ecrite. 3rd ed. Morrison. 544p. (Orig.). 2000. pap. 59.95 (*0-201-61449-9*) Addison-Wesley.

***Mise-en-Scene.** Claude Ollier. Tr. & Afterword by Dominic Di Bernardi. LC 87-73069. 256p. 2000. pap. 12.50 (*1-56478-232-8*, Pub. by Dalkey Arch) Chicago Distribution Ctr.

Mise en Scene: Photographs by Claude Cahun, Tacita Dean, & Virginia Nimarkoh. David Bate & Francois Leperlier. (Illus.). 64p. 1995. 14.95 (*0-905263-59-6*) Dist Art Pubs.

Miseducation: Preschoolers at Risk. David Elkind. LC 86-82790. 240p. 1987. pap. 15.00 (*0-394-75634-7*) Knopf.

***Miseducation of Lauryn Hill.** 80p. 1999. otabind 16.95 (*0-634-00245-7*) H Leonard.

Miseducation of the Black Child. Nathan Hare & Julia Hare. 131p. 1991. pap. 10.50 (*0-614-07455-X*) Black T T.

Miseducation of the Negro. Carter G. Woodson. 224p. (Orig.). reprint ed. pap. 9.95 (*1-56411-041-9*) Untd Bros & Sis.

Misenchanted Sword. Lawrence Watt-Evans. (The Wizards of Fantasy Promotion). 304p. (Orig.). 1985. mass mkt. 4.99 (*0-345-31822-6*, Del Rey) Ballantine Pub Grp.

Miser. 1977. pap. 4.95 (*0-8120-0138-9*) Barron.

Miser. Moliere. 1942. 5.50 (*0-87129-454-0*, M28) Dramatic Pub.

Miser. Moliere. 1993. pap. 5.25 (*0-8222-1341-9*) Dramatists Play.

Miser. Roland Reed. (J). (gr. 4-12). 1973. 6.00 (*0-87602-158-5*) Anchorage.

Miser. large type ed. Lesley Egan. 1984. 15.95 (*0-7089-1069-6*) Ulverscroft.

Miser. 2nd rev. ed. Mark Dunster. 39p. (Orig.). 1982. pap. 4.00 (*0-89642-093-0*) Linden Pubs.

Miser & George Dandin: Two Plays. Moliere. Tr. by Albert Bermel. (Actor's Moliere Ser.: Vol. 1). 176p. 1987. pap. 6.95 (*0-936839-75-9*) Applause Theatre Bk Pubs.

Miser & Other Plays. Moliere. Tr. by John Wood. Incl. Don Juan. 1953. Love's the Best Doctor. 1953. That Scoundrel Scapin. 1953. Would-Be Gentleman. 1953. (Classics Ser.). 288p. (Orig.). (YA). (gr. 9 up). 1953. Set pap. 8.95 (*0-14-044036-4*, Penguin Classics) Viking Penguin.

***Miser & Other Plays: A New Selection.** Moliere. (Penguin Classics Ser.). 336p. 2000. pap. 8.95 (*0-14-044728-8*, Penguin Bks) Viking Penguin.

Miser Hoadley's Secret: A Detective Story. Arthur W. Marchmont. 1976. lib. bdg. 14.85 (*0-89968-067-4*, Lghtyr Pr) Buccaneer Bks.

Miser of Mexico. Carlos Morton. LC 93-19388. (Orig.). 1993. pap. 6.00 (*0-88734-270-1*) Players Pr.

Miser on the Mountain: A Nisqually Legend of Mount Rainier. Nancy Luenn. LC 96-42392. (Illus.). 32p. (J). (gr. 1-12). 1997. 15.95 (*1-57061-082-7*) Sasquatch Bks.

Miserable Mill. Lemony Snicket & Brett Helquist. LC 99-42695. (Series of Unfortunate Events : Vol. 4). (Illus.). 208p. (YA). (gr. 4-7). 2000. 8.95 (*0-06-440769-1*) HarpC Child Bks.

***Miserable Mill.** Lemony Snicket & Brett Helquist. LC 99-42695. Vol. 4. (Illus.). 208p. (YA). (gr. 4-7). 2000. lib. bdg. 14.89 (*0-06-028315-7*) HarpC Child Bks.

Miserable Miracle: La Mescaline. Henri Michaux. (FRE.). 1991. pap. 10.95 (*0-7859-3381-6*) Fr & Eur.

Miserables. 64p. 1997. pap. 10.95 (*0-7935-5837-9*) H Leonard.

***Miserables.** (YA). 2000. 11.95 (*1-56137-757-0*) Novel Units.

***Miserables.** 2000. 9.95 (*1-56137-756-2*) Novel Units.

Miserables. Tr. by Munir Ba'Albaki. (ARA.). 200p. pap. 14.95 (*0-86685-758-3*) Intl Bk Ctr.

Miserables. Edward Behr. 1996. pap. 21.45 (*1-55970-370-9*, Pub. by Arcade Pub Inc) Time Warner.

Miserables. Kathryn M. Grossman. 1996. 29.00 (*0-8057-8350-4*, Hall Reference) Macmillan.

Miserables. Kathryn M. Grossman. (Illus.). 144p. 1996. pap. 14.95 (*0-8057-7832-2*, Hall Reference) Macmillan.

Miserables. Victor Hugo. (J). 1976. 25.95 (*0-8488-0535-6*) Amereon Ltd.

Miserables. Victor Hugo. (J). 1998. mass mkt. 5.99 (*0-449-45834-2*) Ballantine Pub Grp.

Miserables. Victor Hugo. (J). 1987. pap. 5.50 (*0-87129-287-4*, L57) Dramatic Pub.

Miserables. Victor Hugo. Tr. by Charles E. Wilbour. LC 98-156450. 1432p. (J). 1998. 22.00 (*0-375-40317-5*) Everymns Lib.

Miserables. Victor Hugo. 336p. (J). 1982. mass mkt. 5.99 (*0-449-30002-1*) Fawcett.

Miserables. Victor Hugo. Tr. by Charles E. Wilbour. LC 96-96722. (J). 1996. pap. 11.00 (*0-449-91167-5*) Fawcett.

Miserables. Victor Hugo. (J). 1951. write for info. (*0-318-63491-0*) Fr & Eur.

Miserables. Victor Hugo. Ed. by Maurice Allem. (FRE.). 1808p. (J). 1976. lib. bdg. 125.00 (*0-7859-3757-9*, 2070102645) Fr & Eur.

Miserables. Victor Hugo. Tr. by Charles E. Wilbour. LC 92-50220. 1280p. (J). 1992. 22.00 (*0-679-60012-4*) Modern Lib NY.

Miserables. Victor Hugo. LC 86-62313. (Signet Classics Ser.). 1463p. (J). 1987. pap. 7.95 (*0-451-52526-4*, Sig Classics) NAL.

Miserables. Victor Hugo. LC 94-15411. (Step into Classics Ser.). (Illus.). 106p. (J). (gr. 4-7). 1995. pap. 3.99 (*0-679-86668-X*) Random.

Miserables. Victor Hugo. (J). 1964. 11.09 (*0-606-02836-6*, Pub. by Turtleback) Demco.

Miserables. Victor Hugo. Tr. & Intro. by Norman Denny. (Classics Ser.). 1,248p. (J). 1982. pap. 11.95 (*0-14-044430-0*, Penguin Classics) Viking Penguin.

Miserables. Monica Kulling. LC 94-15411. (Bullseye Step into Classics Ser.). 1995. 9.09 (*0-606-09539-X*, Pub. by Turtleback) Demco.

Miserables. Monarch Staff & Victor Hugo. (C). 3.95 (*0-671-00844-7*, Arco) Macmillan Gen Ref.

Miserables. abr. ed. Victor Hugo. Ed. by Paul Benichou. Tr. by Charles E. Wilbour. 544p. (J). (gr. 11 up). 1983. per. 5.99 (*0-671-50439-8*, WSP) PB.

Miserables. deluxe ed. Victor Hugo. Ed. by Allen. (Pleiade Ser.). (FRE.). (J). 84.95 (*2-07-010264-5*) Schoenhof.

Miserables. Victor Hugo. 528p. (J). 1990. reprint ed. lib. bdg. 49.95 (*0-89966-452-0*) Buccaneer Bks.

Miserables. rev. ed. (FRE.). 32p. 1991. pap. 14.95 (*0-7935-4889-6*, 00360287) H Leonard.

Miserables, 3 tomes, I. Victor Hugo. (Folio Ser.: Nos. 348, 349, & 350). (FRE.). (J). 1951. pap. 10.95 (*2-07-036348-1*) Schoenhof.

Miserables, 3 tomes, II. Victor Hugo. (Folio Ser.: Nos. 348, 349, & 350). (FRE.). (J). 1951. pap. 10.95 (*2-07-036349-X*) Schoenhof.

Miserables, 3 tomes, III. Victor Hugo. (Folio Ser.: Nos. 348, 349, & 350). (FRE.). 1951. pap. 10.95 (*2-07-036350-3*) Schoenhof.

Miserables, No. 114. 48p. 1987. pap. 9.95 (*0-7935-2523-3*, 00243425) H Leonard.

Miserables, Vol. 1. Victor Hugo. (FRE.). 1973. pap. 11.95 (*0-7859-2306-3*, 2070363481) Fr & Eur.

Miserables, Vol. 1. Victor Hugo. LC 94-15411. 1990. pap. 12.95 (*0-7859-2876-6*) Fr & Eur.

Miserables, Vol. 1. Victor Hugo. (Classics Library). (J). pap. 3.95 (*1-85326-085-1*, 0851WW, Pub. by Wrdsworth Edits) NTC Contemp Pub Co.

Miserables, Vol. I. unabridged ed. Victor Hugo. (FRE.). (J). 1996. pap. 7.95 (*2-87714-296-5*, Pub. by Bookking Intl) Distribks Inc.

Miserables, Vol. 2. Victor Hugo. (FRE.). 1973. pap. 11.95 (*0-7859-2633-X*, 207036349X) Fr & Eur.

Miserables, Vol. 2. Victor Hugo. (FRE.). (J). 1990. pap. 12.95 (*0-7859-3385-9*) Fr & Eur.

Miserables, Vol. 2. Victor Hugo. (Classics Library). (J). 1997. pap. 3.95 (*1-85326-050-9*, 0509WW, Pub. by Wrdsworth Edits) NTC Contemp Pub Co.

Miserables, Vol. II. unabridged ed. Victor Hugo. (FRE.). (J). 1996. pap. 7.95 (*2-87714-301-5*, Pub. by Bookking Intl) Distribks Inc.

Miserables, Vol. 3. Victor Hugo. (FRE.). 1973. pap. 11.95 (*0-7859-2307-1*, 2070363503) Fr & Eur.

Miserables, Vol. III. unabridged ed. Victor Hugo. (FRE.). (J). 1996. pap. 7.95 (*2-87714-302-3*, Pub. by Bookking Intl) Distribks Inc.

Miserables: Classics of French Literature. Jean E. Peyrazat. (C). 1987. pap. text 14.80 (*0-13-530668-X*) P-H.

Miserables: Curriculum Unit. Center for Learning Network Staff & Victor Hugo. (Novel Ser.). 98p. (YA). (gr. 9-12). 1992. reprint ed. spiral bd. 18.95 (*1-56077-255-7*) Ctr Learning.

Miserables: The Musical Sensation. (HL Piano Solo Ser.). (Illus.). 72p. 1991. otabind 15.95 (*0-7935-0058-3*, 00290271) H Leonard.

***Miserables: Viola Selections.** 16p. 1998. pap. 5.95 (*0-7935-9662-9*) H Leonard.

Miserables Notes. George Klin. (Cliffs Notes Ser.). 120p. 1968. pap. 4.95 (*0-8220-0735-5*, Cliff) IDG Bks.

Misere! Charlie Brown. Charles M. Schulz. (Peanuts Ser.). (FRE.). (J). 1985. 4.95 (*0-8288-4515-8*) Fr & Eur.

Miseres du Present: Richesse du Possible see Reclaiming Work: Beyond the Wage-Based Society

Misericordes. Philippe Bosser. 1984. 29.95 (*0-7859-8157-8*, 2-86853-000-1) Fr & Eur.

Misericordia. unabridged ed. Benito Perez Galdos. (SPA.). 284p. 1999. pap. 7.95 (*84-410-0009-3*, Pub. by Bookking Intl) Distribks Inc.

Misericordia. 2nd ed. Benito P. Galdos. Ed. by Adrian Murdoch. Tr. by Charles De Latis from SPA. (European Classics). 280p. 1997. reprint ed. pap. 14.99 (*1-873982-85-2*, Pub. by Dedalus) Subterranean Co.

Misericordia De Dios. Kenneth Copeland. Tr. by Copeland, Kenneth, Publications Staff. (SPA.). 47p. (Orig.). 1986. pap. 3.95 (*0-88114-726-5*) K Copeland Pubns.

***Miseries of Enforced Marriage.** George Wilkins. 1999. pap. 15.00 (*0-87830-103-8*) Routledge.

Miseries of Enforced Marriage. George Wilkins. LC 73-133763. (Tudor Facsimile Texts. Old English Plays Ser.: No. 118). reprint ed. 59.50 (*0-404-53418-X*) AMS Pr.

Miseries of Enforced Marriage, 1607. George Wilkins. (Malone Society Ser.). (Illus.). 93p. 1963. text 39.95 (*0-19-729010-8*) OUP.

Miserly Moms: Living on One Income in a Two Income Economy. 2nd ed. Jonni McCoy. 256p. 1996. pap. 9.99 (*1-888306-14-9*, Full Quart Pr) Holly Hall.

***Miser's Daughter.** W. H. Ainsworth. 252p. 2000. pap. 9.95 (*0-594-02926-0*) Eightn Hundrd.

Misers, Shrews & Polygamists: Sexuality & Male-Female Relations in Eighteenth-Century China. Keith McMahon. LC 94-33072. (Illus.). 384p. 1995. text 54.95 (*0-8223-1555-6*); pap. text 19.95 (*0-8223-1566-1*) Duke.

Misery. Suzanne Heller. LC 64-15778. (Illus.). 96p. 1995. pap. 6.95 (*0-8397-5802-2*) Eriksson.

***Misery.** Stephen King. 1999. 13.95 (*84-01-49997-6*) Plaza.

Misery. Stephen King. 1987. 12.09 (*0-606-03859-0*, Pub. by Turtleback) Demco.

Misery. Stephen King. LC 86-40504. 310p. 1987. 29.95 (*0-670-81364-8*) Viking Penguin.

Misery. Stephen King. 352p. (C). 1998. reprint ed. mass mkt. 6.99 (*0-451-16952-2*) Addson-Wesley Educ.

Misery. unabridged ed. Stephen King. 1995. pap. 30.00 incl. audio (*0-453-00927-1*, 102508, Pub. by Penguin-HghBrdg) Lndmrk Audiobks.

Misery & Company. Candace Clark. LC 96-34946. 300p. (C). 1997. 29.95 (*0-226-10756-6*) U Ch Pr.

Misery & Company: Sympathy in Everyday Life. Candace Clark. LC 96-34946. 1998. pap. text 18.00 (*0-226-10757-4*) U Ch Pr.

Misery & Its Causes. Edward T. Devine. LC 70-137161. (Poverty U. S. A. Historical Record Ser.). 1973. reprint ed. 20.95 (*0-405-03100-9*) Ayer.

***Misery Express.** Ralph Cotton. 2000. mass mkt. 5.99 (*0-451-19999-5*, Sig) NAL.

Misery Guts. Morris Gleitzman. LC 92-22570. 160p. (J). (gr. 3-7). 1995. pap. 5.00 (*0-15-200026-7*) Harcourt.

Misery Guts. Morris Gleitzman. (J). (gr. 3-7). 1995. 10.35 (*0-606-07874-6*) Turtleback.

Misery Guts. large type ed. Morris Gleitzman. 1993. 33.50 (*0-614-09844-0*, L-34136-00) Am Printing Hse.

Misery Guts. 94th ed. Morris Gleitzman. LC 92-22570. (J). 1994. text 17.70 (*0-15-302254-X*) Harcourt.

Misery in the Name of Freedom: The United States in Nicaragua, 1909-1988. Al Burke. LC 88-6740. (Illus.). 200p. (Orig.). (C). 1988. pap. 8.95 (*0-929004-01-9*, E183.8.N5B87) Sea Otter Pr.

Misery Loves. Martin Ott. 32p. (Orig.). 1994. pap. 4.00 (*1-881168-49-2*) Red Danceflr.

Misery Loves Company. Christine Beatty. (Illus.). 80p. 1993. pap. 6.95 (*0-9637406-0-1*) Glamazon Pr.

Misery Loves Maggody. Joan Hess. 304p. 2000. reprint ed. per. 6.99 (*0-671-01684-9*) PB.

Misery Loves Maggody: An Arly Hanks mystery. Joan Hess. LC 98-28728. (Arly Hanks Mystery Ser.). 285p. 1999. 22.00 (*0-684-84562-8*) S&S Trade.

Mises: An Annotated Bibliography, 1902-1981. Ed. by Bettina B. Greaves & Robert W. McGee. 407p. 1993. lib. bdg. 29.95 (*0-910614-79-2*) Foun Econ Ed.

Mises: An Annotated Bibliography, 1982-1993, Update. Ed. by Bettina B. Greaves. 238p. 1995. lib. bdg. 29.95 (*1-57246-004-0*) Foun Econ Ed.

Mises Made Easier: A Glossary for Ludwig von Mises' Human Action. rev. ed. Percy L. Greaves, Jr. xviii, 158p. 1990. pap. 15.00 (*0-930902-30-0*) Free Market.

Mises Made Easier: A Glossary for Ludwig von Mises' Human Action. 2nd rev. ed. Percy L. Greaves, Jr. xviii, 158p. 1990. 25.00 (*0-930902-29-7*) Free Market.

Misfire: The History of How America's Small Arms Have Failed Our Military. William H. Hallahan. (Illus.). 512p. 1994. 30.00 (*0-684-19359-0*, Scribners Ref) Mac Lib Ref.

Misfit. Chief Little Summer & Warm Night Rain. (Illus.). 300p. (YA). (gr. 8-12). 1991. 14.95 (*1-880440-03-2*) Piqua Pr.

Misfit. Robert Heinleim. 20.95 (*0-89190-849-8*) Amereon Ltd.

Misfit. John Newman. 228p. 1999. pap. 14.95 (*0-7392-0051-8*, PO2846) Morris Pubng.

Misfit. Nancy Rue. LC 97-24445. (Christian Heritage Ser.: Vol. 1). 192p. (J). (gr. 3-13). 1998. pap. 5.99 (*1-56179-560-7*) Focus Family.

Misfit: Haunting of the Human, Unveiling the Divine. Larry Lewis. LC 96-51865. 150p. (Orig.). 1997. pap. 13.00 (*1-57075-122-6*) Orbis Bks.

Misfit: Short Vowel II Sequence. Ellis Richardson & Barbara DiBenedetto. (Read Aloud Ser.: Bk. 10). 32p. (Orig.). 1991. pap. text 4.00 (*1-56775-027-3*, SVIIS10-5) ISM Teach Systs.

***Misfit Maid.** Elizabeth Bailey. 352p. 2000. 26.99 (*0-263-16364-4*, Pub. by Mills & Boon) Ulverscroft.

***Misfit Soldier: A War Story, 1914-1932.** Ed. by Joanna Bourke. LC 99-197993. 96p. 1999. pap. 12.95 (*1-85918-188-0*, Pub. by Cork Univ) Intl Spec Bk.

***Misfits.** Serge Toubiana. 2000. 29.95 (*0-7148-3936-1*) Phaidon Pr.

Misfits: An Original Screenplay, Directed by John Huston. Arthur Miller et al. Ed. by George P. Garrett et al. LC 71-135273. (Film Scripts Ser.). (Illus.). 1989. pap. 19.95 (*0-89197-850-X*) Irvington.

***Misfits! Baseball's Worst Ever Team.** 2nd rev. ed. J. Thomas Hetrick. Orig. Title: Misfits! The Cleveland Spiders in 1899. (Illus.). ii, 216p. 1999. pap. 19.95 (*1-929763-00-X*, 1) Pocol Pr.

Misfits in the Public Schools. William M. Cruickshank et al. LC 69-13137. 230p. reprint ed. pap. 71.30 (*0-8357-3989-9*, 203668700005) Bks Demand.

Misfits! The Cleveland Spiders in 1899: A Day-by-Day Narrative of Baseball Futility. J. Thomas Hetrick. LC 90-50826. (Illus.). 224p. 1991. pap. 25.95 (*0-89950-608-9*) McFarland & Co.

Misfits! The Cleveland Spiders in 1899 see Misfits! Baseball's Worst Ever Team

Misfortune. 2nd ed. Gary Kern. LC 88-28071. 228p. 1997. pap. 13.00 (*0-89370-941-7*) Xenos Riverside.

Misfortune Cookie. Dan Greenberg. LC 98-24099. (Zack Files: No. 13). (Illus.). 64p. (J). (gr. 2-5). 1998. mass mkt. 3.99 (*0-448-41748-0*, G & D) Peng Put Young Read.

Misfortune Teller. Murphy & Sapir. (Destroyer Ser.: No. 115). 1999. per. 5.99 (*0-373-63230-4*, 1-63230-6, Harlequin) Harlequin Bks.

Misfortune's Friend. 2nd ed. Sarah Aldridge. LC 84-29610. 296p. (Orig.). 1996. reprint ed. pap. 8.95 (*0-9646648-2-8*) A&M Bks.

Misfortunes of Arthur. Thomas Hughes et al. LC 76-133682. (Tudor Facsimile Texts. Old English Plays Ser.: No. 56). reprint ed. 59.50 (*0-404-53356-6*) AMS Pr.

Misfortunes of Arthur: A Critical, Old-Spelling Edition. rev. ed. Ed. by Brian J. Corrigan. LC 92-31784. (Renaissance Imagination Ser.). 256p. 1992. text 35.00 (*0-8153-1088-9*) Garland.

Misfortunes of Colette. 1997. mass mkt. 7.95 (*1-56333-564-6*) Masquerade.

Misfortunes of Nigel. Fiona Pitt-Kethley. 176p. 1991. 29.95 (*0-7206-0830-9*, Pub. by P Owen Ltd) Dufour.

Misfortunes of Prosperity: An Introduction to Modern Political Economy. Daniel Cohen. Tr. by Jacqueline Lindenfeld. LC 94-47022.Tr. of Infortunes de la Prosperite. (ENG & FRE.). 186p. 1995. 26.50 (*0-262-03230-9*) MIT Pr.

***Misfortunes of Virtue & Other Early Tales.** Marquis de Sade. Tr. by David Coward. (Oxford World's Classics Ser.). 330p. 1999. pap. 10.95 (*0-19-283695-1*) OUP.

***Misgivings: My Mother, My Father, Myself.** C. K. Williams. LC 99-53290. 176p. 2000. 21.00 (*0-374-19984-1*) FS&G.

Misguided Faith. Norvel Hayes. (Mini-Bks.). 32p. 1988. pap. 1.00 (*0-89274-483-9*, HH-483) Harrison Hse.

Misguiding Lights? Stephen Miller. (Dialog Ser.). 44p. 1991. pap., teacher ed. 5.50 (*0-8341-1279-5*); pap., student ed. 6.50 (*0-8341-1280-9*) Beacon Hill.

Mish Mosh. Arnold Smith. LC 96-92750. 272p. (Orig.). 1996. pap. 9.00 (*0-9653899-2-8*) Digi Print.

Misha: A Memoire of the Holocaust Years. Misha Defonseca. (Illus.). 265p. 1997. 24.95 (*0-9635257-7-8*) Mt Ivy Pr.

Misha Black. Avril Blake. 108p. (Orig.). 1987. 65.00 (*0-85072-152-0*) St Mut.

Misha the Minstrel. Michelle Edwards. LC 84-62336. (Illus.). 21p. (J). (gr. 3-7). 1985. 8.95 (*0-930100-19-0*) Holy Cow.

Mishell's Textbook of Infertility, Contraception & Reproductive Endocrinology. 4th ed. Rogerio A. Lobo et al. LC 96-52003. (Illus.). 896p. 1997. 175.00 (*0-86542-385-7*) Blackwell Sci.

Mishima. Luis Canales. (Illus.). 40p. 1986. pap. 7.75 (*0-933704-55-0*) Dawn Pr.

***Mishima: A Biography.** John Nathan. (Illus.). 352p. 2000. pap. text 17.00 (*0-306-80977-X*) Da Capo.

Mishima: A Biography. John Nathan. LC 74-12184. xx, 300 p. 1974. write for info. (*0-316-59844-5*) Little.

Mishima ou le Vision du Vide. Marguerite Yourcenar. (FRE.). 128p. 1981. 33.95 (*0-7859-0451-4*, 2070238873) Fr & Eur.

Mishirimiau: Modulo 1. 1994. write for info. (*92-806-3042-3*) U N I C E.
Mishirimiau: Modulo 2. 1994. write for info. (*92-806-3043-1*) U N I C E.
Mishirimiau: Modulo 3. 1994. write for info. (*92-806-3045-8*) U N I C E.
Mishka: From One Job to Another. Tod Thilleman. 200p. (Orig.). (C). 1992. pap. 15.95 (*0-923389-02-4*) Meet Eyes Bind.
Mishka & Plishka. Longford. LC 95-14692. (J). 1996. 16.00 (*0-689-80244-7*) Aladdin.
Mishkat al-Masabih, 3 vol. set. Abu Muhammad Baghawi. Tr. by Abdul Hameed Siddiqui. (ARA & ENG.). 950p. (C). 1988. text 59.00 (*1-56744-328-1*) Kazi Pubns.
Mishkat al-Masabih, 2 vols. Robson. 1994. 59.00 (*1-56744-141-6*) Kazi Pubns.
Mishkat ul-Anwar. Helen Gardner. 1990. pap. 4.95 (*1-56744-140-8*) Kazi Pubns.
Mishkin's Economics of Money & Banking. 5th ed. Mishkin. (C). 1998. text. write for info. (*0-321-02844-9*) Addison-Wesley.
Mishloach Matanot Laevyonim see Mitzvah of the Month
Mishmash, 001. Molly Cone. 128p. (J). (gr. 4-7). 1962. 16.00 (*0-395-06711-1*) HM.
***Mishmash.** Molly Cone. (Illus.). 128p. (J). 2000. pap. 4.95 (*0-618-05482-0*) HM.
Mishmash: Poems from Hollywood. Mark Dunster. 11p. 1998. pap. 5.00 (*0-89642-513-4*) Linden Pubs.
Mishmash & the Sauerkraut Mystery. Molly Cone. (Illus.). (J). (gr. 4-6). 1974. pap. 0.95 (*0-395-18556-4*) HM.
***Mishmash & the Substitute Teacher.** Molly Cone. (Illus.). 96p. (J). 2000. pap. 4.95 (*0-618-05483-9*) HM.
Mishna Berurah, Vol. 3A. 1980. 20.95 (*0-87306-233-7*) Feldheim.
Mishna Berurah, Vol. 3A. large type ed. 1980. 25.95 (*0-87306-198-5*) Feldheim.
Mishna Berurah: Laws of Shabbath, Section, 325-344, Sec. 325-344, Vol. 3-D. 1986. 20.95 (*0-87306-409-7*) Feldheim.
Mishna Berurah: Laws of Shabbath, Section, 325-344, Sec. 325-344, Vol. 3-D. large type ed. 1986. 25.95 (*0-87306-408-9*) Feldheim.
Mishna Berurah Vol. 2C: Covering Chapters 202-241 of Shulchan Aruch Orach Chaim. Chaim-Chofet. Tr. by Aviel Orenstein from HEB. 458p. 1989. 22.95 (*0-87306-503-4*) Feldheim.
Mishna Berurah Vol. 2C: Covering Chapters 202-241 of Shulchan Aruch Orach Chaim. large type ed. Chaim-Chofet. Tr. by Aviel Orenstein from HEB. 458p. 1989. 26.95 (*0-87306-502-6*) Feldheim.
Mishnah, 7 vols. Tr. by Philip Blackman. (ENG & HEB.). 4050p. 1962. 125.00 (*0-910818-00-2*) Judaica Pr.
Mishnah. Tr. by Herbert Danby. 876p. 1933. text 69.00 (*0-19-815402-X*) OUP.
Mishnah: A New Translation. Jacob Neusner. 1162p. (C). 1991. reprint ed. pap. 35.00 (*0-300-05022-4*) Yale U Pr.
Mishnah: An Introduction. Jacob Neusner. LC 88-38460. 256p. 1994. reprint ed. pap. text 25.00 (*1-56821-358-1*) Aronson.
Mishnah: Pirkay Avot-Ethics of the Fathers. (Home Study Program Ser.: No. 401). 7.00 (*0-686-96126-9*) USCJE.
Mishnah: Religious Perspectives. Jacob Neusner. LC 99-30517. (Handbook of Oriental Studies). 272p. 1999. 88.50 (*90-04-11492-0*) Brill Academic Pubs.
***Mishnah: Social Perspectives.** Jacob Neusner. LC 99-30516. (Handbook of Oriental Studies: Vol. 46). (Illus.). xviii, 270p. 1999. text 94.50 (*90-04-11491-2*) Brill Academic Pubs.
Mishnah: The Oral Law. Robert L. Platzner. 64p. 1995. pap., teacher ed. 6.95 (*0-87441-390-7*) Behrman.
Mishnah & Tosefta, 2 vols. Alberdina Houtman. LC 97-167059. (Texte und Studien zum Antiken Judentum Ser.: Vol. 59). 347p. 1997. 137.50 (*3-16-146638-1*, Pub. by JCB Mohr) Coronet Bks.
Mishnah-Berakoth, Peah, Demai. 1871st ed. Y. D. Herzog. (ENG & HEB.). 482p. 1980. 15.00 (*0-900689-18-8*) Soncino Pr.
Mishnah Berurah, Vol. 3B. Yisroel Meir Ha-Cohen. Tr. by Aharon Feldman & Aviel Orenstein. 402p. 1981. 19.95 (*0-87306-276-0*) Feldheim.
Mishnah Berurah, Vol. 3B. large type ed. Yisroel Meir Ha-Cohen. Tr. by Aharon Feldman & Aviel Orenstein. 402p. 1981. 25.95 (*0-87306-275-2*) Feldheim.
Mishnah Berurah, Vol. 3C. large type ed. Yisroel Meir Ha-Cohen. Tr. by Aviel Orenstein from HEB. 1984. 27.95 (*0-87306-350-3*) Feldheim.
Mishnah Berurah, Vol. 3C. large type ed. Yisroel Meir Ha-Cohen. Tr. by Aviel Orenstein from HEB. 1984. 27.95 (*0-87306-351-1*) Feldheim.
Mishnah Berurah, Vol. 5A. large type ed. Chofetz Chaim Staff. 25.95 (*0-87306-710-X*) Feldheim.
Mishnah Berurah, Vol. 5B. Chofetz Chaim Staff. 22.95 (*0-87306-712-6*) Feldheim.
Mishnah Berurah, Vol. 5B. large type ed. Chofetz Chaim Staff. 28.95 (*0-87306-713-4*) Feldheim.
Mishnah Berurah, Vol. 5C. Chofetz Chaim Staff. 22.95 (*0-87306-778-9*) Feldheim.
Mishnah Berurah, Vol. 5C. large type ed. Chofetz Chaim Staff. 28.95 (*0-87306-777-0*) Feldheim.
Mishnah Berurah, Vol. 6A. Chofetz Chaim Staff. 22.95 (*0-87306-862-9*) Feldheim.
Mishnah Berurah, Vol. 6A. large type ed. Chofetz Chaim Staff. 27.95 (*0-87306-861-0*) Feldheim.
Mishnah Berurah, Vol. 6B. Chofetz Chaim Staff. 22.95 (*0-87306-942-0*) Feldheim.
Mishnah Berurah, Vol. 6B. large type ed. Chofetz Chaim Staff. 27.95 (*0-87306-943-9*) Feldheim.
Mishnah Berurah Vol. 1A: Laws of Daily Conduct. Tr. by Aviel Orenstein. 1993. 20.95 (*0-87306-604-9*) Feldheim.
Mishnah Berurah Vol. 1A: Laws of Daily Conduct. large type ed. Tr. by Aviel Orenstein. 1993. 25.95 (*0-87306-603-0*) Feldheim.
Mishnah Berurah Vol. 1B: Laws of Tefillin. Tr. by Aviel Orenstein. 1993. 20.95 (*0-87306-623-5*) Feldheim.
Mishnah Berurah Vol. 1B: Laws of Tefillin. large type ed. Tr. by Aviel Orenstein. 1993. 25.95 (*0-87306-624-3*) Feldheim.
Mishnah Berurah Vol. 1C: Laws of Daily Prayer. Tr. by Aviel Orenstein. 1991. 22.95 (*0-87306-552-2*) Feldheim.
Mishnah Berurah Vol. 1C: Laws of Daily Prayer. large type ed. Tr. by Aviel Orenstein. 1991. 27.95 (*0-87306-551-4*) Feldheim.
Mishnah Berurah Vol. 1D: Laws of Daily Prayer. Tr. by Aviel Orenstein. 1991. 20.95 (*0-87306-554-9*) Feldheim.
Mishnah Berurah Vol. 1D: Laws of Daily Prayer. large type ed. Tr. by Aviel Orenstein. 1991. 25.95 (*0-87306-553-0*) Feldheim.
Mishnah Berurah Vol. 2B: Covering Chapters 157-201 of the Shulchan Aruch Orach Chaim. Ed. by Aviel Orenstein. (HEB.). 570p. 1988. 22.95 (*0-87306-445-3*) Feldheim.
Mishnah Berurah Vol. 2B: Covering Chapters 157-201 of the Shulchan Aruch Orach Chaim. large type ed. Ed. by Aviel Orenstein. (HEB.). 570p. 1988. 28.95 (*0-87306-444-5*) Feldheim.
Mishnah-Kodashim Vol. 1: Zevachim. Hersh Goldwurm. Tr. by Y. Danziger. (ArtScroll Mishnah Ser.). (Illus.). 328p. 1988. 22.99 (*0-89906-301-2*) Mesorah Pubns.
Mishnah-Kodashim Vol. 1B: Menachos. Matis Roberts. Ed. by Naftali Kempler & Yehezkel Danziger. (ArtScroll Mishnah Ser.). 302p. 1989. 22.99 (*0-89906-303-9*) Mesorah Pubns.
Mishnah-Kodashim Vol. 2A: Chullin. Avrohom Y. Rosenberg. Ed. by H. Danziggen. (ArtScroll Mishnah Ser.). (Illus.). 286p. 1989. 22.99 (*0-89906-305-5*) Mesorah Pubns.
Mishnah Kodashim Vol. 3A: Arachin. A. J. Rosenberg. Ed. by Y. Danziger & Y. Adelman. (Artscroll Mishanh Ser.). 1991. 22.99 (*0-89906-312-8*) Mesorah Pubns.
Mishnah-Moed: Eruvin-Beitzah. Hersh GoldWurm. Ed. by Y. Danziger & A. Gold. (ArtScroll Mishnah Ser.). (Illus.). 374p. 1986. 22.99 (*0-89906-262-8*) Mesorah Pubns.
Mishnah-Moed: Shabbos. A. Y. Rosenberg. Ed. by Y. Danziger & A. Gold. (ArtScroll Mishnah Ser.). (Illus.). 396p. 1982. 22.95 (*0-89906-250-4*) Mesorah Pubns.
Mishnah-Moed Vol. 2: Pesachim-Shekalim. Hersh Goldworm. (ArtScroll Mishnah Ser.). 416p. 1981. 22.95 (*0-89906-254-7*) Mesorah Pubns.
Mishnah-Moed Vol. 3: Rosh Hashana-Yoma-Succah. Hersh Goldwurm et al. (ArtScroll Mishnah Ser.). 1980. 22.99 (*0-89906-256-3*) Mesorah Pubns.
Mishnah-Nashim: Gittin-Kiddushin. M. Roberts & T. Z. Arem. (ArtScroll Mishnah Ser.). (Illus.). 314p. 1986. 22.99 (*0-89906-283-0*) Mesorah Pubns.
Mishnah-Nashim: Kesubos. A. Y. Rosenberg. Ed. by T. Z. Arem. (ArtScroll Mishnah Ser.). (Illus.). 258p. 1984. 22.99 (*0-89906-277-6*) Mesorah Pubns.
Mishnah-Nashim: Nazir-Sotah. M. Rabinovitch & Y. Kalatsky. Ed. by Y. Danziger. (ArtScroll Mishnah Ser.). (Illus.). 400p. 1985. 22.99 (*0-89906-281-4*) Mesorah Pubns.
Mishnah-Nashim: Nedarim. M. Rabinovitch. Ed. by T. Z. Arem. (ArtScroll Mishnah Ser.). (Illus.). 238p. 1985. 22.99 (*0-89906-279-2*) Mesorah Pubns.
Mishnah-Nashim: Yevamos. Y. Rabinowitz. Ed. by Y. Danziger. (ArtScroll Mishnah Ser.). (Illus.). 364p. 1984. 22.99 (*0-89906-275-X*) Mesorah Pubns.
Mishnah-Nezikin: Bava Basra. M. Roberts. Ed. by Y. Danziger. (ArtScroll Mishnah Ser.). (Illus.). 240p. 1986. 22.99 (*0-89906-293-8*) Mesorah Pubns.
Mishnah-Nezikin: Bava Kamma. A. Y. Rosenberg. Ed. by T. Z. Arem. (ArtScroll Mishnah Ser.). 240p. 1986. 22.99 (*0-89906-289-X*) Mesorah Pubns.
Mishnah-Nezikin: Bava Metzia. A. Y. Rosenberg. Ed. by T. Z. Arem. (ArtScroll Mishnah Ser.). (Illus.). 264p. 22.99 (*0-89906-291-1*) Mesorah Pubns.
Mishnah-Nezikin: Makkos/Shevos. A. Y. Rosenberg. Ed. by G. Finkel. (ArtScroll Mishnah Ser.). (Illus.). 310p. 1987. 22.99 (*0-89906-297-0*) Mesorah Pubns.
Mishnah-Nezikin: Sanhedrin. M. Roberts. Ed. by Y. Danzinger. (ArtScroll Mishnah Ser.). (Illus.). 206p. 1987. 22.99 (*0-89906-295-4*) Mesorah Pubns.
Mishnah-Nezikin Vol. 3B: Avodah Zarah-Horayos. Hillel Danziger. Ed. by Naftali Kempler. (ArtScroll Mishnah Ser.). 228p. 1988. 22.99 (*0-89906-299-7*) Mesorah Pubns.
Mishnah-Seder Moed Vol. 4: Tranis-Megillah-Moed Katan-Chaggigah. Avrohom Y. Rosenberg. (ArtScroll Mishnah Ser.). 352p. 1979. 22.99 (*0-89906-258-X*) Mesorah Pubns.
Mishnah-Zeraim: Sheviis. M. Rabinnovitch & Hersh Goldwurm. Ed. by Y. Danziger. (ArtScroll Mishnah Ser.). (Illus.). 254p. 1987. 22.99 (*0-89906-326-8*) Mesorah Pubns.
Mishnayoth Tohoroth, 2 vols. (ENG & HEB.). 36.00 (*0-910218-88-9*) Bennet Pub.
Mishnayoth Tohoroth. 1989. 29.95 (*1-871055-00-8*) Soncino Pr.
Mishnayoth Zeraim, 2 vols. (ENG & HEB.). 30.00 (*0-910218-52-8*) Bennet Pub.
Mishnayoth Zeraim. 1989. 29.95 (*1-871055-05-9*) Soncino Pr.
Mishne Torah Hilchot Avodat Kochavim (The Laws of Star Worship & Statues) Maimonides. Tr. & Comment by Eliyahu Touger. (Mishneh Torah Ser.: 3). 239p. 1990. 20.00 (*0-940118-67-X*) Moznaim.
Mishne Torah Hilchot Berachot - Hilchot Milah Laws of Blessings Laws of Circumcision. Maimonides. Tr. & Comment by Eliyahu Touger. (Mishneh Torah Ser.: 8). 256p. 1991. 20.00 (*0-940118-69-6*) Moznaim.
Mishne Torah Hilchot Eruvin, Hilchot Sh'vitat Asor Hilchot Sh'vitat Yom Tov: Laws of Eruvin, Laws of Resting on the 10th of Tishrie, Laws of Resting on Yom Tov. Maimonides. (Mishneh Torah Ser.: Vol. 11). (Illus.). 316p. 1993. 20.00 (*0-940118-93-9*) Moznaim.
Mishne Torah Hilchot Gittin Vol. 17: Laws of Divorce. Maimonides. Tr. by Eliyahu Touger from HEB. (Mishneh Torah Ser.). (Illus.). 247p. 1995. 20.00 (*1-885220-02-2*) Moznaim.
Mishne Torah Hilchot Ishut: Laws Pertaining to Marriage. Maimonides. Ed. & Tr. by Eliyahu Touger. (Mishneh Torah Ser.: Vol. 16). (HEB.). 337p. 1994. 20.00 (*1-885220-01-4*) Moznaim.
Mishne Torah Hilchot Shabbat Pt. 1: Laws of Shabbat. Maimonides. Tr. & Comment by Eliyahu Touger. (Mishneh Torah Ser.: 9). 296p. 1992. 20.00 (*0-940118-71-8*) Moznaim.
Mishne Torah Hilchot Shabbat Pt. 2: Laws of Shabbat. Maimonides. (Mishneh Torah Ser.). 358p. 1993. 20.00 (*0-940118-81-5*) Moznaim.
Mishne Torah Hilchot Shekalim Hilchot Kiddush Hachodesh: Laws of Shekalim & Laws of Son the Sanctification of the New Moon. Maimon Idies. Ed. & Tr. by Eliyahu Touger from HEB. (Mishneh Torah Ser.: Vol. 14). (Illus.). 255p. 1992. 20.00 (*0-940118-82-3*) Moznaim.
Mishne Torah Hilchot Ta'aniot Hilchot Megillah & Chanukah: Laws of Fasts, Laws of Reading the Megillah & of Chanukah. Maimonides. Tr. & Comment by Eliyahu Touger. (Mishneh Torah Ser.: 15). 189p. 1991. 20.00 (*0-940118-70-X*) Moznaim.
Mishne Torah Hilchot Tefilah Pt. 2: Laws of Prayer & Priestly Blessings. Maimonides. Tr. by Eliyahu Touger from HEB. (Mishneh Torah Ser.: 6). 232p. 1989. 20.00 (*0-940118-30-0*) Moznaim.
Mishne Torah Hilchot Tefillin U'Mezuza Lu'Sefer Torah: Hilchot Tzizit Laws of Tefillin, Mezuza & Torah Scrolls, Laws of Tzitzit. Maimonides. Tr. & Comment by Eliyahu Touger. (Mishneh Torah Ser.: 7). 139p. 1990. 20.00 (*0-940118-68-8*) Moznaim.
Mishne Torah Hilchot Yesodei HaTorah: The Laws (Which Are the) Foundations of the Torah. Maimonides. Tr. & Comment by Eliyahu Touger. (Mishneh Torah Ser.: 1). 300p. 1989. 20.00 (*0-940118-41-6*) Moznaim.
Mishne Torah Hilchot Yibbum Va'chalitza, Hilchot Na'Arahmh Betula, Hilchot Sotah: Laws of Yibbum Va'chalitza, Laws of a Virgin Maiden, Laws Pertaining to a Sotah. Maimonides. (Mishneh Torah Ser.: No. 18). (Illus.). 237p. 1995. 20.00 (*1-885220-04-9*) Moznaim.
Mishne Torah Seder Nezikin: Book of Damages. Maimonides. Tr. by Eliyahu Touser. 607p. 1997. 32.00 (*1-885220-18-9*) Moznaim.
Mishneh Torah Hilchos Chametz U'Matzah: Laws of Chametz & Matzah. Maimonides. Tr. & Comment by Eliyahu Touger. (Mishneh Torah Ser.: 12). 198p. 1988. 20.00 (*0-940118-21-1*) Moznaim.
Mishneh Torah Hilchos Melachim V'Milchomoteihem: Laws of Kings & Their Wars. Maimonides. Tr. & Comment by Eliyahu Touger. (Mishneh Torah Ser.). 263p. 1987. 20.00 (*0-940118-34-3*) Moznaim.
Mishneh Torah Hilchot Bais Habechira: Laws of (God's) Chosen House. Maimonides. Tr. & Comment by Eliyahu Touger. (Mishneh Torah Ser.). 223p. 1986. 20.00 (*0-940118-19-X*) Moznaim.
Mishneh Torah Hilchot De'ot - Hilchot Talmud Torah: Laws of De'ot - Personality Development Laws of Torah Study. Maimonides. Tr. & Comment by Eliyahu Touger. (Mishneh Torah Ser.: 2). 304p. 1989. 20.00 (*0-940118-23-8*) Moznaim.
Mishneh Torah Hilchot Kriat Shema Hilchot Tefilah Pt. 1: Laws of Kriat Shema & Laws of Prayer. Maimonides. Tr. & Comment by Boruch Kaplan. (Mishneh Torah Ser.: 5). 224p. 1989. 20.00 (*0-940118-24-6*) Moznaim.
Mishneh Torah Hilchot Shofar, Sukkah, VE Lulav: Laws of the Shofar Sukah & Lulav. Maimonides. Tr. & Comment by Eliyahu Touger. (Mishneh Torah Ser.: 13). 231p. 1988. 20.00 (*0-940118-42-4*) Moznaim.
Mishneh Torah Hilchot Teshuvah: Laws of Repentance. Maimonides. Tr. & Comment by Eliyahu Touger. (Mishneh Torah Ser.: 4). 241p. 1987. 20.00 (*0-940118-20-3*) Moznaim.
Mishneh Torah Series, 25 vols., Set. Maimonides. Tr. by Eliyahu Touger. 1989. 510.00 (*0-940118-18-1*) Moznaim.
Misho School: Kakubana Style. K. Hihara. 1996. pap. 10.95 (*4-07-973263-5*) Shufu No.
Misho Tells a Story: A Potawatomi Fable. Jack Wooldridge. (Potawatomi Fables Ser.: Vol. 10). (Illus.). 32p. (J). (gr. 1-5). 1998. pap. 7.00 (*1-887963-13-8*) Pota Pr.
Mishomis Book: The Voice of the Ojibway. unabridged ed. Edward Benton-Banai. LC 80-138057. (Illus.). 114p. 1988. pap. 19.95 (*1-893487-00-8*) Indian Country.
Mishoryu: Love & Flowers. S. Nakayama. 1996. pap. 10.95 (*4-07-973317-8*) Shufu No.
Mishoryu: Scandinavian Glass. S. Nakayama. 1996. pap. 10.95 (*4-07-973300-3*) Shufu No.
Mishoryu: Shinka Style. B. Nakayama. 1996. pap. 10.95 (*4-07-973323-2*) Shufu No.
Mishpochah Matters. David Brickner. LC 96-3075. 1996. pap. 7.00 (*1-881022-24-2*) Purple Pomegranate.
Mishpokhe: A Study of New York City Jewish Family Clubs. William E. Mitchell. (New Babylon Studies in the Social Sciences: No. 30). (Illus.). 1978. 41.55 (*3-10-800287-2*) Mouton.
Misia. Arthur Gold & Robert Fizdale. (FRE.). 416p. 1992. pap. 13.95 (*0-7859-2484-1*, 2070375226) Fr & Eur.
Mision: Matrimonio. Jackie Merritt. (SPA.). 1996. per. 3.50 (*0-373-35161-5*, 1-35161-8) Harlequin Bks.
Mision de los Negocios. Andrew Campbell & Kiran Tawadey. (SPA.). 411p. 1992. pap. 34.00 (*84-7978-035-5*, Pub. by Ediciones Diaz) IBD Ltd.
***Mision en el Planeta Paradiso (Star Quest)** (ENG & SPA., Illus.). 32p. (YA). (gr. 3 up). 2000. pap. 9.95 (*0-7460-3888-7*, Usborne) EDC.
Mision Mundial, 3 vols., Set. Jonathan Lewis.Tr. of World Mission. (SPA.). 16.99 (*0-685-74961-4*, 498481) Editorial Unilit.
Mision Mundial, Tomo 3. Jonathan Lewis.Tr. of World Mission. (SPA.). 47p. 1987. pap., teacher ed. 2.50 (*1-56063-538-X*, 498680) Editorial Unilit.
Mision Mundial, Vol. I. Jonathan Lewis.Tr. of World Mission. (SPA.). 47p. 1987. pap. 5.99 (*1-56063-065-5*, 498478); pap., teacher ed. 2.50 (*1-56063-536-3*, 498678) Editorial Unilit.
Mision Mundial, Vol. 2. Jonathan Lewis.Tr. of World Mission. (SPA.). 47p. 1987. pap. 5.99 (*1-56063-066-3*, 498479) Editorial Unilit.
Mision Mundial, Vol. II. Jonathan Lewis.Tr. of World Mission. (SPA.). 40p. 1993. pap., teacher ed. 2.50 (*1-56063-537-1*, 498679) Editorial Unilit.
Mision Mundial, Vol. 3. Jonathan Lewis.Tr. of World Mission. (SPA.). 47p. 1987. pap. 5.99 (*1-56063-067-1*, 498480) Editorial Unilit.
Misiones en la Iglesia Local. Jeff Stam. (SPA.). 80p. pap. 4.95 (*1-55883-092-8*, 6724-4510C) Libros Desafio.
Misiones Latinas para el Siglo XXI. Tr. of Latin Mission for the 21st Century. 5.99 (*0-7899-0446-2*, 498663) Editorial Unilit.
Misiones Mundiales. J. Lewis.Tr. of World Missions. (SPA.). 85p. 1985. pap. 3.50 (*1-56063-397-2*, 498547) Editorial Unilit.
Misiones Mundiales (Missions Now) Crucial para Esta Generacion (This Generation) Greenway. (SPA.). 133p. write for info. (*1-56063-767-6*) Editorial Unilit.
Misionologia. Larry D. Pate.Tr. of From Every People to Every People. (SPA.). 1996. pap. 14.99 (*0-8297-0470-1*) Vida Pubs.
Miskatonic University. Ed. by Martin H. Greenberg. 1996. pap. 5.99 (*0-88677-722-4*, Pub. by DAW Bks) Penguin Putnam.
***Misko.** Alvena Vajdak Seckar. LC 99-55377. (Illus.). 159p. (J). 1999. pap. 15.00 (*0-86516-465-7*) Bolchazy-Carducci.
Mislah Oh! A Tribute to William Barnabas Moore of Charlotteville, Tobago. Ed. by Nathan Moore. (Illus.). x, 166p. (Orig.). 1997. pap. 13.95 (*0-9657359-0-7*) Phoenyx Binding.
Misleading Cases. Alan R. White. (Illus.). 160p. 1991. text 55.00 (*0-19-825688-4*) OUP.
Misleading Cases in the Common Law. 4th ed. A. P. Herbert. xii, 236p. 1989. reprint ed. 45.00 (*0-8377-2242-X*, Rothman) W S Hein.
Misleading Ladies. Cynthia Smith. (Casebook of Emma Rhodes Ser.). 1997. mass mkt. 5.99 (*0-425-16112-9*, Prime Crime) Berkley Pub.
Misleading or Deceptive Conduct: Issues & Trends. Ed. by Colin Lockhart. 312p. 1996. 79.00 (*1-86287-154-X*, Pub. by Federation Pr) Gaunt.
Misleading Symptoms. large type ed. Lilian Darcy. (Mills & Boon Large Print Ser.). 288p. 1997. 22.50 (*0-263-15229-4*, Pub. by Mills & Boon) Ulverscroft.
Misled. Susan L. Holbrook. 120p. 2000. pap. 9.95 (*0-88995-215-9*, Pub. by Red Deer) Genl Dist Srvs.
Misli o Bogosluzhenii Pravoslavnoi Tserkvi. Saint John Kronstadt.Tr. of Thoughts on the Divine Services of the Orthdox Church. 141p. 1954. 5.00 (*0-317-28907-1*) Holy Trinity.
Misma. Luis Mario. LC 88-81864. (Coleccion Espejo de Paciencia). (SPA.). 131p. (Orig.). 1990. pap. 9.95 (*0-89729-498-X*) Ediciones.
Mismanaged Care: How Corporate Medicine Jeopardizes Your Health. Michael E. Makover. LC 98-38860. 296p. 1998. 26.00 (*1-57392-248-X*) Prometheus Bks.
Mismanaged Trade? Strategic Policy & the Semiconductor Industry. Kenneth Flamm. 472p. (C). 1996. 59.95 (*0-8157-2846-8*); pap. 24.95 (*0-8157-2847-6*) Brookings.
Mismanagement Issues at the Charleston, South Carolina & Pittsburgh, Pennsylvania Veterans Affairs Medical Centers: Hearing Before the Subcommittee Oversight & Investigations of the Committee on Veterans' Affairs, House of Representatives, 105th Congress, First Session, October 23, 1997. LC 98-168061. iii, 191p. 1998. write for info. (*0-16-056530-8*) USGPO.
Mismanagement of Indian Economy. Bepin Behari. (C). 1991. 23.50 (*81-7018-659-5*, Pub. by BR Pub) S Asia.
Mismanaging America: The Rise of the Anti-Analytic Presidency. Walter Williams. LC 90-38704. (Studies in Government & Public Policy). xvi, 184p. 1990. 25.00 (*0-7006-0446-4*); pap. 14.95 (*0-7006-0538-X*) U Pr of KS.
(Mis)Managing the System: How to Change the System. Wesley G. Matthei. LC 94-73196. 368p. (Orig.). 1997. pap. 19.95 (*0-9658493-0-9*) Nusystems.
Mismapping the Underworld: Daring & Error in Dante's Comedy. John W. Kleiner. LC 93-19358. xviii, 182p. 1994. 32.50 (*0-8047-2143-2*) Stanford U Pr.
Mismatch & Labour Mobility. Ed. by Fiorella P. Schioppa. (Illus.). 521p. (C). 1991. text 80.00 (*0-521-40243-3*) Cambridge U Pr.
Mismatch Explanations of European Unemployment: A Critical Evaluation. Horst Entorf. Ed. by J. V. Hagen et al. LC 98-16485. (European & Transatlantic Studies). (Illus.). x, 206p. 1998. 84.95 (*3-540-64056-8*) Spr-Verlag.
***Mismatch Negativity.** Ed. by R. Naatanen. (Audiology & Neuro-Otology Ser.: 5). (Illus.). 150p. 2000. pap. 39.25 (*3-8055-7100-3*) S Karger.

M

Mismatched Mommy? Mary A. Wilson. (American Romance Ser.). 1996. per. 3.75 (*0-373-16652-4*, 1-16652-9) Harlequin Bks.

Mismeasure of Desire: The Science, Theory & Ethics of Sexual Orientation. Edward Stein. LC HQ76.25.S69 1999. (Illus.). 400p. 1999. 35.00 (*0-19-509995-8*) OUP.

Mismeasure of Man. Stephen Jay Gould. 352p. 1993. pap. 9.95 (*0-393-31067-1*) Norton.

Mismeasure of Man. Stephen Jay Gould. LC 95-44442. 1996. 25.00 (*0-393-03972-2*) Norton.

Mismeasure of Man. Stephen Jay Gould. (Illus.). 400p. 1996. pap. 15.95 (*0-393-31425-1*) Norton.

Mismeasure of Woman. Carol Tavris. 1998. 25.75 (*0-8446-6959-8*) Peter Smith.

Mismeasure of Women: Why Women Are Not the Better Sex, the Inferior Sex, or the Opposite Sex. Carol Tavris. 400p. 1993. pap. 14.00 (*0-671-79749-2*, Touchstone) S&S Trade Pap.

Mismeasurement of Economic Growth. Martin J. Bailey. 27p. 1991. pap. 9.95 (*1-55815-150-8*) ICS Pr.

***Miso & Soybean Chiang: Bibliography & Sourcebook, 1st Century B. C. to 1999.** Compiled by William Shurtleff & Akiko Aoyagi. LC 99-88367. Date not set. pap. write for info. (*1-928914-03-9*) Soyfoods Center.

Miso Production: The Book of Miso, Vol. II. rev. ed. William Shurtleff & Akiko Aoyagi. LC 76-19599. (Soyfoods Production Ser.: No. 1). (Illus.). 80p. 1980. pap. 39.95 (*0-933332-00-9*) Soyfoods Center.

Misogynie Oder Philogynie? Philologisch-Theologische Untersuchungen Zum Wortfeld Frau Bei Augustinus. Silvia Soennecken. (Kontexte Ser.: Bde. 13). (GER.). 193p. 1993. 36.95 (*3-631-46069-4*) P Lang Pubng.

Misogynies: Reflections on Myths & Malice. Joan Smith. 208p. 1992. pap. 8.00 (*0-449-90676-0*) Fawcett.

Misogynous Economies. Laura C. Mandell. LC 99-17695. (Illus.). 256p. 1999. 42.00 (*0-8131-2116-7*) U Pr of Ky.

Misogyny, Cultural Nihilism & Oppositional Politics: Contemporary Chinese Experimental Fiction. Tonglin Lu. LC 94-22076. viii , 236p. 1995. 39.50 (*0-8047-2463-6*); pap. 14.95 (*0-8047-2464-4*) Stanford U Pr.

Misogyny in Literature: An Essay Collection. Ed. by Katherine A. Ackley. LC 92-5103. (Illus.). 424p. 1992. text 20.00 (*0-8240-9774-2*, H1398) Garland.

Misogyny in the Movies: The De Palma Question. Kenneth MacKinnon. LC 88-40607. (Illus.). 224p. 1990. 38.50 (*0-87413-376-9*) U Delaware Pr.

Misogyny in the Western Philosophical Tradition: A Reader. Ed. by Beverly Clack. LC 98-34341. 320p. (C). 1999. pap. 22.99 (*0-415-92182-1*, D5989) Routledge.

Misogyny in the Western Philosophical Tradition: A Reader. Ed. by Beverly Clack. LC 98-34341. 320p. (C). (gr. 13). 1999. 75.00 (*0-415-92181-3*, D5985) Routledge.

Misogyny, Misandry, & Misanthropy. Ed. by R. Howard Bloch & Frances Ferguson. (Representation Bks.: No. 3). 1989. pap. 14.95 (*0-520-06546-8*, Pub. by U CA Pr) Cal Prin Full Svc.

Misoso: Once upon a Time Tales from Africa. Illus. by Reynold Ruffins. LC 92-43288. 96p. (J). (gr. k-5). 1994. 19.00 (*0-679-83430-3*, Pub. by Knopf Bks Yng Read) Random.

Misperceptions of Economic Phenomena. F. E. Brown & A. R. Oxenfeldt. LC 72-79606. 1977. 26.95 (*0-89197-851-8*) Irvington.

Misplaced Blame: The Real Roots of Population Growth. Alan T. Durning & Christopher D. Crowther. Ed. by Ellen W. Chu. LC 95-68006. (New Report Ser.: No. 5). 41p. (Orig.). (YA). (gr. 11-12). 1997. pap. 9.95 (*1-886093-05-9*) NW Environ Watch.

Misplaced City: Jericho's Ancient Geography: 8 Miles North of the Traditional Site. Edward Weaver. (Illus.). 224p. (Orig.). 1997. pap. 14.95 (*0-9656384-5-6*) NorRem Pub.

Misplaced Corpse. A. E. Martin. (Crime Classics Ser.). 207p. 1999. pap. 9.95 (*1-86254-281-3*, Pub. by Wakefield Pr) BHB Intl.

Misplaced Hopes, Misspent Millions (Farmland Assessments) 45p. 1972. 7.00 (*0-943136-08-3*) Ctr Analysis Public Issues.

Misplaced Ideas: Essays on Brazilian Culture. Roberto Schwartz. (Critical Studies in Latin American Culture). 256p. (C). 1992. pap. 22.00 (*0-86091-576-X*, Pub. by Verso) Norton.

Misplaced Legion: Book One of the Videssos Cycle. Harry Turtledove. (Orig.). 1987. mass mkt. 5.99 (*0-345-33067-6*, Del Rey) Ballantine Pub Grp.

Misplaced Loyalties. Esther Menaker. LC 94-24042. 1995. pap. 21.95 (*1-56000-816-4*) Transaction Pubs.

Misplaced Loyalty. large type ed. Jenny Ashe. (Magna Large Print Ser.). 300p. 1997. 27.99 (*0-7505-1055-2*) Ulverscroft.

***Misplaced Loyalty: Why U. S.-Born Africans Don't Believe They Are Africans Anymore.** 125p. 1999. pap. 15.00 (*0-9659612-2-2*) M P Fancher.

Misplaced Psyche Lauran Paine. LC 96-30932. 1997. write for info. (*0-7451-6955-4*) Chivers N Amer.

***Misplaced Trust.** Peter Willoughby. 148p. 1999. 75.00 (*0-9533599-5-6*, Pub. by Gostick Hall) Gaunt.

Misquitoes. Cheryl Peterson & Cheryl Coughlan. Ed. by Gail Saunders-Smith. LC 98-43745. (Illus.). 24p. 24.00 (*0-7368-0243-6*, Pebble Bks) Capstone Pr.

Misread Record: The Deluge & Its Cause. 2nd rev. ed. Isaac N. Vail. 88p. 1996. reprint ed. spiral bd. 8.00 (*0-7873-0905-2*) Hlth Research.

Misread Record: or The Deluge & Its Cause, 1921. Issac N. Vail. 88p. 1996. reprint ed. pap. 6.95 (*1-56459-963-9*) Kessinger Pub.

Misreading Jane Eyre: A Postformalist Paradigm. Jerome Beaty. LC 96-2288. (Theory & Interpretation of Narrative Ser.). 259p. 1996. text 37.50 (*0-8142-0692-1*) Ohio St U Pr.

Misreading Reading: The Bad Science That Hurts Children. Gerald Coles. LC 99-55073. 144p. pap. text 15.00 (*0-325-00060-3*) Heinemann.

Misreading the African Landscape: Society & Ecology in the Forest-Savanna Mosaic. James Fairhead & Melissa Leach. LC 95-52318. (African Studies: No. 90). (Illus.). 372p. (C). 1996. text 64.95 (*0-521-56353-4*); pap. text 23.95 (*0-521-56499-9*) Cambridge U Pr.

***Misreading the Chinese Character: Images in Euroamerican Drama to 1925.** Dave Williams. LC 99-33958. (Asian Thought & Culture Ser.: Vol. 40). 296p. 2000. text 54.95 (*0-8204-4559-2*) P Lang Pubng.

Misreading the Public. I. M. Destler & Steven Kull. LC 98-40102. 1998. 44.95 (*0-8157-1766-0*) Brookings.

Misreading the Public. I. M. Destler & Steven Kull. LC 98-40102. xiv, 312p. 1999. pap. 18.95 (*0-8157-1765-2*) Brookings.

Misreadings. Umberto Eco. Tr. by William Weaver from ITA. LC 93-249. (Helen & Kurt Wolff Bk.). 192p. 1993. pap. 13.00 (*0-15-660752-2*) Harcourt.

Misreadings: Fall '95. Umberto Eco. 1995. pap. 12.95 (*0-15-600371-6*) Harcourt.

Misregulating Television: Network Dominance & the F. C. C. Stanley M. Besen et al. LC 84-8738. viii, 202p. 1985. 24.00 (*0-226-04415-7*) U Ch Pr.

Misregulating Television: Network Dominance & the F. C. C. Stanley M. Besen et al. LC 84-8738. viii, 210p. 1986. pap. text 12.00 (*0-226-04416-5*) U Ch Pr.

Misrepresentation Case: In a Changing Life & Health Insurance Climate. LC 90-83103. 98p. 1990. pap. 34.95 (*0-89707-579-X*, 519-0204, ABA Tort) Amer Bar Assn.

Misrepresentation in Railroad Affairs. George F. Kennan. Ed. by Stuart Bruchey. LC 80-1323. (Railroads Ser.). 1981. reprint ed. lib. bdg. 15.95 (*0-405-13798-2*) Ayer.

Misrepresentation in the Marketplace & Beyond: Ethics under Siege. Ed. by Peggy C. Askins. LC 95-23795. 1995. 20.00 (*0-929851-69-2*) Am Assn Coll Registrars.

Misrepresentations: Shakespeare & the Materialists. Graham Bradshaw. 322p. 1993. text 45.00 (*0-8014-2890-4*); pap. text 17.95 (*0-8014-8129-5*) Cornell U Pr.

Misrepresentations Corrected & Truth Vindicated. Jonathan Edwards. (Notable American Authors Ser.). 1992. reprint ed. lib. bdg. 75.00 (*0-7812-2770-4*) Rprt Serv.

Miss Abernathy's Concise Slave Training Manual. Christina Abernathy. 96p. (Orig.). 1996. pap. text 11.95 (*0-9639763-9-7*) Greenery Pr.

Miss Adams, Country Teacher. Treva A. Strait. 1991. pap. 8.95 (*0-934904-25-1*) J & L Lee.

***Miss Adventure.** George Garagonne. 1999. pap. 14.95 (*1-56097-289-0*, Pub. by Fantagraph Bks); pap. 14.95 (*1-56097-290-4*, Pub. by Fantagraph Bks) Seven Hills Bk.

***Miss Alaineus: A Vocabulary Disaster.** Debra Frasier. LC 98-48937. (Illus.). 32p. (ps-3). 2000. 16.00 (*0-15-202163-9*, Harcourt Child Bks) Harcourt.

Miss Alice M & Her Dragon: Recovery of a Hidden Talent. Margaret I. Little. (Illus.). 68p. 1998. pap. text 14.95 (*1-883881-30-7*, 30-7) S Freud RT&PF.

Miss Alma: Friend of Missions. Beth Branyon. LC 96-68864. (Little MISSionary Bks.). (Illus.). 32p. (Orig.). (J). (gr. 5-8). 1996. pap. 8.95 (*1-57736-012-5*) Providence Hse.

Miss America. Howard Stern. 592p. 1996. mass mkt. 7.99 (*0-06-109550-8*, Harp PBks) HarpC.

Miss America: In Pursuit of the Crown. Ann-Marie Bivans. (Illus.). 232p. 1998. reprint ed. text 27.00 (*0-7881-5572-5*) DIANE Pub.

***Miss America Cookbook: Favorite Recipes from All 50 States.** Ann-Marie Bivans. (Illus.). 256p. 1999. reprint ed. text 20.00 (*0-7881-6710-3*) DIANE Pub.

***Miss America, 1945: Bess Myerson & the Year That Changed Our Lives.** Susan Dworkin. LC 98-18445. 240p. 1999. pap. 18.95 (*1-55704-381-7*, Pub. by Newmarket) Norton.

Miss Annie. rev. ed. Omar Fletcher. 224p. (Orig.). 1984. mass mkt. 2.25 (*0-87067-242-8*, BH242) Holloway.

Miss Annie's Secret: The Story of Annie Armstrong. Jimmye Winter. (Orig.). (J). (gr. 4-6). 1987. pap. text 5.95 (*1-56309-310-3*) Womans Mission Union.

Mrs. Armitage & the Big Wave. Illus. by Quentin Blake. LC 97-15420. 32p. (J). (gr. k-3). 1998. 15.00 (*0-15-201642-2*) Harcourt.

Miss Astbury & Milordo. large type ed. Irene Northan. (Linford Romance Library). 304p. 1996. pap. 16.99 (*0-7089-7973-4*) Ulverscroft.

Miss Ayr of Virginia & Other Stories. Julia Magruder. LC 77-110207. (Short Story Index Reprint Ser.). 1977. 23.95 (*0-8369-3358-3*) Ayer.

Miss Ballard's Inspiration. William Dean Howells. (Notable American Authors Ser.). 1992. reprint ed. lib. bdg. 75.00 (*0-7812-3258-9*) Rprt Serv.

Miss Behavior's Book of Etiquette David Greenberg. 2001. write for info. (*0-316-32618-6*) Little.

Miss Bertha: Woman of Revival. Lewis A. Drummond. 304p. 1996. 12.99 (*0-8054-1164-X*, 4211-64) Broadman.

Miss Bertha & the Yankee & Other Stories. Wilkie Collins. reprint ed. lib. bdg. 18.95 (*0-89190-248-1*, Rivercity Pr) Amereon Ltd.

Miss Best's Etiquette for Young People. Alyse Best. 1990. pap. write for info. (*0-945033-02-8*) PEP Pr.

Miss Biddlewick Gets Even with Santa. Donna Shavatt & Eve Shavatt. LC 98-88360. (Illus.). 32p. (J). 1999. pap. 9.95 (*1-56167-480-X*) Am Literary Pr.

Miss Billy. Eleanor H. Porter. 1976. lib. bdg. 16.25 (*0-89968-103-4*, Lghtyr Pr) Buccaneer Bks.

Miss Billy-Married. Eleanor H. Porter. 1976. lib. bdg. 16.75 (*0-89968-104-2*, Lghtyr Pr) Buccaneer Bks.

Miss Billy's Decision. Eleanor H. Porter. 1976. lib. bdg. 16.25 (*0-89968-105-0*, Lghtyr Pr) Buccaneer Bks.

Miss Bindergarten Celebrates the 100th Day of Kindergarten. Joseph Slate. LC 98-10486. (Illus.). 32p. (J). (ps-1). 1998. 16.99 (*0-525-46000-4*, Dutton Child) Peng Put Young Read.

***Miss Bindergarten Stays Home from Kindergarten.** Joseph Slate. (Illus.). (J). 2000. 15.99 (*0-525-46396-8*, Dutton Child) Peng Put Young Read.

Miss Bindergarten's Craft Center, 1. Joseph Slate. (Illus.). 24p. 1999. pap. 17.99 (*0-525-46257-0*, Dutt) Dutton Plume.

Miss Bishop. Bess S. Aldrich. 336p. 1975. reprint ed. lib. bdg. 25.95 (*0-88411-255-1*) Amereon Ltd.

Miss Bishop. Bess S. Aldrich. LC 86-6969. iv, 337p. 1986. reprint ed. pap. 14.95 (*0-8032-5909-3*, Bison Books) U of Nebr Pr.

Miss Buncle's Book. D. E. Stevenson. 335p. 1981. reprint ed. lib. bdg. 25.95 (*0-89966-168-8*) Buccaneer Bks.

Miss Bunkley's Book: The Testimony of an Escaped Novice see Nun Who Escaped: A True Story

***Miss Bunting: A Novel.** large type ed. Angela M. Thirkell. 432p. 1999. 31.99 (*0-7505-1341-1*, Pub. by Mgna Lrg Print) Ulverscroft.

Miss Bunting: A Novel. Angela M. Thirkell. (Illus.). 336p. 1996. reprint ed. pap. 12.95 (*1-55921-174-1*) Moyer Bell.

Miss Buxley: Sexism in Beetle Bailey? Mort Walker. 96p. 1982. pap. 4.95 (*0-940420-01-5*) Comicana.

Miss Carlyle's Curricle, 1 vol. Karen Harbaugh. (Regency Romance Ser.). 214p. 1999. mass mkt. 4.99 (*0-451-19536-1*, Sig) NAL.

Miss Carter & the Ifrit. Alice E. Burton. Ed. by Douglas Melville & R. Reginald. LC 77-84239. (Lost Race & Adult Fantasy Ser.). 1978. reprint ed. lib. bdg. 19.95 (*0-405-10987-3*) Ayer.

***Miss Chadwick's Companion.** Melinda McRae. (Signet Regency Romance Ser.). 2000. mass mkt. 4.99 (*0-451-19857-3*, Sig) NAL.

***Miss Chambers Takes Charge.** Joy Reed. (Zebra Regency Romance Ser.). 2000. mass mkt. 4.99 (*0-8217-6581-7*, Zebra Kensgtn) Kensgtn Pub Corp.

Miss Charity's Case. Jo A. Ferguson. 224p. 1996. mass mkt. 4.50 (*0-8217-5238-3*, Zebra Kensgtn) Kensgtn Pub Corp.

Miss Charlotte Surrenders. Cathy G. Thacker. LC 95-6953. (American Romance Ser.). 248p. 1995. per. 3.50 (*0-373-16568-4*, 1-16568-7) Harlequin Bks.

***Miss Charlotte Surrenders.** Cathy G. Thacker. 2000. mass mkt. 4.50 (*0-373-82222-7*, 1-82222-0) Harlequin Bks.

***Miss Charming's Book of Bar Amusements.** Cheryl Charming. (Illus.). 144p. 2000. pap. 12.00 (*0-609-80508-8*, CBK029000, Three Riv Pr) Crown Pub Group.

Miss Circo Comes Apart at the Seams. Frances M. Thompson. (Illus.). 18p. (Orig.). (J). (gr. k-3). 1986. pap. 3.95 (*0-9616207-0-6*) Bks By Brooks.

Miss Clam & Miss Claw. Bruce Gerig. 1972. write for info. (*0-318-64123-2*) Poets Pr.

Miss Clare Remembers. Miss Read. 1996. 24.95 (*0-614-14677-1*, G K Hall Lrg Type) Mac Lib Ref.

Miss Clare Remembers. Miss Read. 1996. 24.95 (*0-614-14676-3*, G K Hall Lrg Type) Mac Lib Ref.

Miss Clare Remembers. large type ed. Miss Read. 276p. 1996. 24.95 (*0-7838-1658-8*, G K Hall Lrg Type) Mac Lib Ref.

Miss Coffin & Mrs. Blood: Poems of Art & Madness. Sandy Diamond. LC 94-70717. (Illus.). 80p. (Orig.). (C). 1994. pap. 15.00 (*0-88739-104-4*) Creat Arts Bk.

Miss Columbia's Public School. Charles H. Pullen. LC 70-85687. (American Fiction Reprint Ser.). 1977. 17.95 (*0-8369-7016-0*) Ayer.

Miss Conchita Gray Paws: A Tale for Cat Lovers of All Ages. William J. Gough. (Illus.). 68p. 1998. write for info. (*0-7541-0066-9*, Pub. by Minerva Pr) Unity Dist.

Miss Cornett's Courtship. Cathlynn R. Dodson. LC 97-97200. (Illus.). 95p. 1997. pap. 8.95 (*0-9662279-0-5*) Hummingbird Hse.

***Miss Cranston: Patron of Charles Rennie Mackintosh.** Ed. by Perilla Kinchin. (Illus.). 96p. 1999. pap. 8.95 (*1-901663-13-2*, Pub. by Natl Mus Scotland) A Schwartz & Co.

***Miss Cuchifrito, Ballerina.** Deborah Gregory. (Cheetah Girls Ser.: No. 10). 96p. (J). (gr. 3-7). 2001. pap. 3.99 (*0-7868-1476-4*, Jump at the Sun) Hyprn Child.

Miss Daisy Celebrates Tennessee. James A. Crutchfield & Winette Sparkman. LC 95-79050. (Illus.). 266p. 1997. 19.95 (*0-9656547-0-2*) Side Dish.

Miss Daisy Celebrates Tennessee. Daisy King et al. LC 95-79050. (Illus.). 288p. 1995. 19.95 (*1-881576-54-X*, Hillsboro Pr) Providence Hse.

Miss Daisy Cooks Light: The Healthy Revelation. Daisy King. LC 94-19582. (Illus.). 288p. 1994. 17.95 (*1-55853-300-1*) Rutledge Hill Pr.

Miss Daisy Entertains. Daisy King. LC 86-14262. 180p. 1985. reprint ed. spiral bd. 9.95 (*0-934395-16-0*) Rutledge Hill Pr.

***Miss Darby's Debut, Vol. 1.** Marilyn Clay. (Zebra Regency Romance Ser.). 1999. mass mkt. 4.99 (*0-8217-6357-1*, Zebra Kensgtn) Kensgtn Pub Corp.

Miss Darby's Duenna. Sheri C. South. 224p. 1999. pap. 12.95 (*0-9668005-1-6*) PrinnyWorld.

Miss Dennis School of Writing: And Other Lessons from a Woman's Life. Alice Steinbach. Ed. by Bruce Bortz. LC 96-85002. 234p. 1996. 22.95 (*0-9631246-2-5*) Bancroft MD.

Miss Dirt: The Dustman's Daughter. Allan Ahlberg. (Illus.). 24p. (J). pap. 6.95 (*0-14-037882-0*, Pub. by Pnguin Bks Ltd) Trafalgar.

Miss Doctor. Elizabeth Seifert. 1973. lib. bdg. 23.95 (*0-88411-024-9*) Amereon Ltd.

Miss Dorothy's Bookmobile. Gloria M. Houston. 32p. 15.95 (*0-06-029155-9*); pap. 5.95 (*0-06-443726-4*); lib. bdg. 15.89 (*0-06-029156-7*) HarpC.

Miss Dose: The Doctor's Daughter. Allan Ahlberg. (Illus.). (J). 1988. pap. 6.95 (*0-14-032346-5*, Pub. by Pnguin Bks Ltd) Trafalgar.

Miss Doyle's Level 1. Hanson. (International Reader's Library). (J). 1991. mass mkt. 11.95 (*0-8384-3419-3*) Heinle & Heinle.

Miss Drayton's Crusade. Elizabeth Barron. 240p. (Orig.). 1986. mass mkt. 2.95 (*0-446-30172-8*, Pub. by Warner Bks) Little.

Miss Elizabeth B. Mitchell. Jean Lindsay. (C). 1989. pap. text 40.00 (*1-85821-023-2*, Pub. by Pentland Pr) St Mut.

Miss Eliza's Gentleman Caller. Marilyn Clay. 256p. 1998. mass mkt. 4.99 (*0-8217-6064-5*, Zebra Kensgtn) Kensgtn Pub Corp.

Miss Ellen's Zoo Critters Scribble Art. Linda Boudreaux Montgomery. (Illus.). 20p. (J). (gr. 1-6). 1996. pap. text 4.95 (*1-890113-11-5*) LB Collection.

Miss Ellie's Purple Sage Saloon. Jerrie Hurd. 1995. mass mkt. 5.99 (*0-671-51909-3*) PB.

Miss Eloise: First Lady of Foreign Missions. Beth Branyon. LC 96-68862. (Little MISSionary Bks.: Vol. 1). (Illus.). 32p. (Orig.). (J). (gr. 3-4). 1996. pap. 8.95 (*1-881576-78-7*) Providence Hse.

Miss Emily: Emily Howland, Teacher of Freed Slaves, Suffragist & Friend of Susan B. Anthony & Harriet Tubman. Mildred D. Myers. LC 98-60582. (Illus.). 240p. 1998. pap. 12.95 (*1-881539-20-2*) Tabby Hse Bks.

Miss Emily Martine & Other Stories. Lynn K. Thorsen. 236p. 1989. pap. 11.95 (*0-8283-1928-6*) Branden Bks.

Miss Emmaline & the Archangel. Rachel Lee. (Intimate Moments Ser.). 1993. mass mkt. 3.39 (*0-373-07482-4*, 5-07482-8) Silhouette.

Miss Emma's Way. Jack W. Boone. 292p. 1998. pap. 14.95 (*1-880719-06-1*) Grafco Prods.

Miss Emma's Wild Garden. Anna G. Hines. LC 96-6291. (J). 1996. write for info. (*0-614-13395-5*, Grenwillow Bks); lib. bdg. write for info. (*0-614-13394-7*, Grenwillow Bks) HarpC Child Bks.

Miss Emma's Wild Garden. Anna G. Hines. LC 96-6291. (Illus.). 24p. (J). (ps up). 1997. 15.00 (*0-688-14692-9*, Grenwillow Bks); lib. bdg. 14.93 (*0-688-14693-7*, Grenwillow Bks) HarpC Child Bks.

Miss Etta's Arkansas Spring: A Novel. George Imbragulio. LC 98-27398. 176p. 1999. pap. 9.95 (*1-56474-283-0*) Fithian Pr.

Miss Evers' Boys. David Feldshuh. 1995. pap. 5.25 (*0-8222-1464-4*) Dramatists Play.

Miss Fannie: Leader for WMU. Beth Branyon. LC 98-65214. (Little MISSionary Bks.). 32p. (J). (gr. 3-5). 1998. pap. 8.95 (*1-57736-094-X*) Providence Hse.

Miss Fannie's Hat. Jan Karon. LC 97-43481. (Illus.). 32p. (J). (ps-2). 1998. 16.95 (*0-8066-3526-6*, 9-3526) Augsburg Fortress.

Miss Fannie's Hat. Jan Karon. (Illus.). 32p. (J). 1999. pap. 17.99 incl. audio (*0-8066-3835-4*, 9-3835, Augsburg) Augsburg Fortress.

Miss Farnsworth. Willard Simms. 1971. pap. 3.25 (*0-8222-0761-3*) Dramatists Play.

Miss Firecracker Contest. Beth Henley. 1985. pap. 5.25 (*0-8222-0762-1*) Dramatists Play.

Miss Florence & the Artists of Old Lyme. Arthur Heming. (Illus.). 69p. 1971. 15.00 (*1-880897-08-3*) Lyme Hist.

Miss Flowers. large type ed. Joanne Wall. (Christmas Ornaments Ser.: No. 1). (Illus.). 34p. (Orig.). (J). (ps up). 1994. pap. 12.95 (*0-9644283-0-X*) M J Wall.

Miss Fogarty's Fabulous Cake: An Old Irish Folk Song. Illus. & Adapted by Catharine O'Neill. LC 95-41642. (J). 1997. write for info. (*0-316-89086-3*) Little.

Miss Fontenot. Stephen Bly. LC 98-46369. (Heroines of the Golden West Ser.: No. 3). 224p. 1999. pap. 10.99 (*1-58134-074-5*) Crossway Bks.

***Miss Fontenot.** large type ed. Stephen Bly. LC 99-33512. 1999. 24.95 (*0-7838-8729-9*, G K Hall Lrg Type) Mac Lib Ref.

Miss Fortune's Folly. Dawn A. Poore. 256p. 1992. mass mkt. 3.50 (*0-8217-3913-1*, Zebra Kensgtn) Kensgtn Pub Corp.

Miss Fourth of July, Goodbye. Christopher G. Janus. 224p. 1990. pap. 12.95 (*0-934831-00-9*) Sheffield Bks.

Miss Gabriel's Gambit. Rita Boucher. 224p. (Orig.). 1993. mass mkt. 3.99 (*0-380-77090-3*, Avon Bks) Morrow Avon.

Miss Garbo: An Unusual Dog. Janiece M. Beinke. (Illus.). 20p. (J). (gr. 1-4). 1998. pap. 8.95 (*1-880726-14-9*) Turnage Pub.

Miss Gathercole's Girls. large type ed. Judy Gardiner. (Magna Large Print Ser.). 561p. 1997. 27.50 (*0-7505-1091-9*) Thorndike Pr.

Miss Gator's School House, 6 bks., Set. Robert Kraus. (Illus.). (J). (gr. k-3). 1989. pap. 17.70 (*0-671-94106-2*, Julian Messner); lib. bdg. 35.70 (*0-671-94105-4*, Julian Messner) Silver Burdett Pr.

Miss Giardino. Dorothy Bryant. LC 78-54280. 160p. 1978. pap. 9.95 (*0-931688-01-9*) Feminist Pr.

Miss Giardino. Dorothy Bryant. LC 78-54280. 192p. 1997. reprint ed. pap. 11.95 (*1-55861-174-6*); reprint ed. lib. bdg. 32.00 (*1-55861-180-0*) Feminist Pr.

Miss Gomez & the Brethren. William Trevor. LC 96-9798. 256p. 1997. pap. 11.95 (*0-14-025264-9*, Penguin Bks) Viking Penguin.

Miss Grace's House. Jacqueline Woodson. (Illus.). 32p. (J). Date not set. lib. bdg. 16.49 (*0-7868-2380-1*, Pub. by Disney Pr) Little.

Miss Grace's House. Jacqueline Woodson. (Illus.). 32p. (J). (ps-4). Date not set. 15.99 (*0-7868-0430-0*, Pub. by Disney Pr) Little.

Miss Grundy Doesn't Teach Here Anymore: Popular Culture & the Composition Classroom. Diane Penrod. LC 97-25941. 1997. pap. 25.00 (*0-86709-438-9*, Pub. by Boynton Cook Pubs) Heinemann.

Miss Gunton of Poughkeepsie see Works of Henry James Jr.: Collected Works

An Asterisk (*) at the beginning of an entry indicates that the title is appearing for the first time.

*Miss Hallberg's Butterfly Garden. Gay Bishop. LC 99-97783. (Illus.). 32p. (J). (ps-6). 2000. pap. 10.95 (0-9676839-0-4) Pinevine Pr.

Miss Hamilton's Hero. Nancy Lawrence. 224p. 1999. mass mkt. 4.99 (0-8217-6154-4) Kensgtn Pub Corp.

Miss Happiness & Miss Flower. Rumer Godden. 112p. lib. bdg. 14.89 (0-06-029193-1) HarpC.

Miss Harcourt's Dilemma. Anne Ashley. 1999. per. 4.99 (0-373-30332-7, . 1-30332-0) Harlequin Bks.

Miss Harriet. Guy de Maupassant. 1978. pap. 10.95 (0-7859-2892-8) Fr & Eur.

Miss Harriet. Guy de Maupassant. (Folio Ser.: No. 1036). (FRE.). pap. 8.95 (2-07-037036-4) Schoenhof.

Miss Harriett, & Other Stories Vol. 6: Collected Novels & Stories. Guy de Maupassant. Ed. by Ernest A. Boyd. LC 71-157790. (Short Story Index Reprint Ser.). 1977. reprint ed. 18.95 (0-8369-3902-6) Ayer.

Miss Hartwell's Dilemma. Carola Dunn. 224p. 1988. 17.95 (0-8027-1041-7) Walker & Co.

Miss Hartwell's Dilemma. large type ed. Carola Dunn. LC 90-10939. 341p. 1990. reprint ed. 18.95 (1-56054-014-1) Thorndike Pr.

Miss Haycroft's Suitors. Emily Hendrickson. (Signet Regency Romance Ser.). 1999. mass mkt. 4.99 (0-451-19834-4) NAL.

Miss Henrietta: Lady of Many Firsts. Beth Branyon. LC 96-68865. (Little MISSionary Bks.). (Illus.). 32p. (Orig.). (J). (gr. 3-5). 1996. pap. 8.95 (1-57736-013-3) Providence Hse.

Miss Hickory. Carolyn S. Bailey. (Illus.). (J). (gr. 4-7). 1946. 16.99 (0-670-47940-3, Viking Child) Peng Put Young Read.

Miss Hickory. Carolyn S. Bailey. LC 46-7275. (Illus.). (J). (gr. 4-7). 1977. pap. 4.99 (0-14-030956-X, PuffinBks) Peng Put Young Read.

Miss Hickory. Carolyn Sherwin Bailey. (J). 1977. 10.09 (0-606-04008-0, Pub. by Turtleback) Demco.

Miss Hickory, Set. abr. ed. Carolyn S. Bailey. (J). (gr. 4-7). 1972. pap. 15.95 incl. audio (0-670-47945-4) Live Oak Media.

Miss High Heels. 176p. 1990. mass mkt. 4.95 (0-929654-62-5, 20) Blue Moon Bks.

Miss High Heels. 2nd ed. Alizarin Lake. 1998. reprint ed. mass mkt. 6.95 (1-56333-632-4) Masquerade.

*Miss Hildy's Missing Cape Caper. Lois Grambling. LC 99-13129. (Step into Reading Ser.). (Illus.). 48p. (J). (gr. k-3). 2000. pap. 3.99 (0-375-80196-0, Pub. by Random Bks Yng Read); lib. bdg. 11.99 (0-375-90196-5, Pub. by Random Bks Yng Read) Random.

Miss Ima & the Hogg Family. Gwen C. Neeley. (Illus.). 96p. (J). (gr. 7 up). 1992. pap. 8.95 (0-937460-79-6) Hendrick-Long.

*Miss Jesmond's Heir. large type ed. Paula Marshall. 320p. 1999. 25.99 (0-263-16220-6, Pub. by Mills & Boon) Ulverscroft.

Miss Jessie: Missionary Nurse in China. Beth Branyon. LC 96-68863. (Little MISSionary Bks.: Vol. 2). (Illus.). 32p. (Orig.). (J). (gr. 3-4). 1996. pap. 8.95 (1-881576-77-9) Providence Hse.

Miss Jessie's Place. Gene Schulze. 300p. 1997. write for info. (0-614-14043-9) Houston Hse.

Miss Josephine's Secret Walk. Yuji Kobayashi. (J). 1998. 12.95 (0-671-75226-X) S&S Bks Yung.

Miss Josephine's Secret Walk. Yuji Kobayashi. 1987. 11.95 (0-310-57080-8, 16108) Zondervan.

Miss Julia & Ghosts. August Strindberg & Henrik Ibsen. Ed. & Tr. by Thaddeus Torp. (Crofts Classics). 128p. 1992. pap. text 4.95 (0-88295-128-9) Harlan Davidson.

*Miss Julia Speaks Her Mind. large type ed. Ann B. Ross. LC 99-46320. 1999. 26.95 (0-7862-2255-7) Thorndike Pr.

*Miss Julia Speaks Her Mind: A Novel. Ann B. Ross. LC 98-52489. 288p. 1999. 23.00 (0-688-16788-8, Wm Morrow) Morrow Avon.

*Miss Julia Speaks Her Mind: A Novel. Ann B. Ross. 288p. 2000. pap. 13.00 (0-688-17775-1) Morrow Avon.

Miss Julie see Three Plays

Miss Julie. August Strindberg. Tr. by Truda Stockenstron. LC 95-49227. (Plays for Performance Ser.). 64p. 1996. pap. 7.95 (1-56663-109-2, Pub. by I R Dee); lib. bdg. 15.95 (1-56663-110-6, Pub. by I R Dee) Natl Bk Netwk.

Miss Julie. August Strindberg. 96p. (C). 1992. pap. 10.95 (0-413-66610-7, A0652, Methuen Drama) Methn.

Miss Julie. August Strindberg. Ed. by William-Alan Landes. Tr. by S. H. Landes. LC 96-35906. 55p. 1996. pap. 7.00 (0-88734-303-1) Players Pr.

Miss Julie. unabridged ed. August Strindberg. 64p. 1992. reprint ed. pap. text 1.50 (0-486-27281-8) Dover.

Miss Julie & Other Plays. August Strindberg. Ed. & Tr. by Michael Robinson. LC 98-15458. (Oxford World's Classics Ser.). 362p. 1999. pap. 10.95 (0-19-283317-0) OUP.

*Miss Julie, David Mamet Fan Club & Other Plays. Lance Tait. 292p. 2000. pap. 16.00 (0-9656184-9-8) Enfield Pubs NH.

Miss Jump the Jockey. Allan Ahlberg. (Illus.). 24p. (J). (gr. 3-6). 1980. pap. 6.95 (0-14-031241-2, Pub. by Pnguin Bks Ltd) Trafalgar.

Miss Kate: Kate Douglas Wiggin in San Francisco. limited ed. Lois Rather. (Illus.). 1980. 35.00 (0-686-26424-X) Rather Pr.

Miss Kittie Hays: Grand Lady of the Frontier. Ted Wilkerson & Evelyn Wilkerson. Ed. by Susan Novak. LC 93-81020. (Illus.). 112p. (Orig.). 1994. pap. 9.95 (1-882420-12-8, 1-882420-12-8) Hearth KS.

Miss Kitty Mystery. Shannon M. Leppard. LC 97-21041. (Adventures of Callie Ann Ser.: No. 4). 8p. (J). 1997. pap. 3.99 (1-55661-816-6) Bethany Hse.

Miss Know-It-All & the Magic House. Carol B. York. (Illus.). (J). (gr. 3-7). 1989. pap. 2.75 (0-318-41641-7, Skylark BDD) BDD Bks Young Read.

Miss Lane's Class see Early Phonetic Readers - Set E

Miss Laughinghouse & the Reluctant Mystic: The Collected Poems of Judith Morley. Judith Morley. (Orig.). 1995. pap. 12.00 (0-9628181-6-X) Black Thistle Pr.

Miss Lavinia's Call. Grace Livingston Hill. 20.95 (0-89190-069-1) Amereon Ltd.

Miss Lenora When Last Seen & 15 Other Stories. Peter Taylor. 1963. 15.00 (0-8392-1070-1) Astor-Honor.

Miss Leslie's Behaviour Book: A Guide & Manual for Ladies. Eliza Leslie. LC 72-2611. (American Women Ser.: Images & Realities). 340p. 1974. reprint ed. 24.95 (0-405-04465-8) Ayer.

*Miss Leslie's Directions for Cookery. unabridged ed. Eliza Leslie. LC 98-55116. 1999. reprint ed. pap. 14.95 (0-486-40614-8) Dover.

Miss Leslie's Secrets: What Every Bride Should Know. Eliza Leslie. Ed. by James A. Franks & Elizabeth McKenzie. (Cookbook Ser.). 528p. 1999. 18.95 (0-9657173-2-1) Wld Goose Pr.

Miss Li'l' Tweetty. Louise C. Pyrnelle. LC 72-4705. (Black Heritage Library Collection). 1977. reprint ed. 28.95 (0-8369-9122-2) Ayer.

Miss Little Britches: A Story of Junior Rodeo. Bonny S. Speer. LC 99-70387. 141p. (YA). (gr. 4 up). 1999. mass mkt. 11.95 (1-889683-12-4) Reliance Pr.

Miss Liz's Passion. Sherryl Woods. (Men at Work Ser.: Vol. 14). 1998. per. 4.50 (0-373-81026-1) Harlequin Bks.

Miss Lizzy's Legacy. Peggy Moreland. (Desire Ser.). 1995. per. 3.25 (0-373-05921-3, 1-05921-1) Silhouette.

Miss Lockharte's Letters, No. 1. Barbara Metzger. 1998. mass mkt. 4.99 (0-449-00170-9) Fawcett.

Miss Lonely Hearts. adapted ed. Nathanael West. 1959. pap. 5.25 (0-8222-0763-X) Dramatists Play.

Miss Lonelyhearts & the Day of the Locust. Nathanael West. LC 97-39828. 1998. 15.50 (0-679-60278-X) Modern Lib NY.

Miss Lonelyhearts & the Day of the Locust. Nathanael West. LC 62-16924. 1962. pap. 8.95 (0-8112-0215-1, NDP125, Pub. by New Directions) Norton.

Miss Lou. Edward P. Roe. (Notable American Authors Ser.). 1999. reprint ed. lib. bdg. 125.00 (0-7812-8824-X) Rprt Serv.

Miss Louise Bos & Animal Friends. Cathy Prather. LC 98-92173. (Illus.). 136p. (J). (ps-6). 1998. text 29.95 (0-9666959-0-9) Cathy Prather.

Miss Lucie. Charles Walker. LC 93-23195. (National Baptist Great Personalities Ser.: Vol. 2). 1993. 8.95 (0-910683-20-4) Townsnd-Pr.

Miss Ludington's Sister. Edward Bellamy. LC 71-104414. reprint ed. lib. bdg. 39.50 (0-8398-0161-0) Irvington.

Miss Lulu Bett. Zona Gale. 1994. lib. bdg. 24.95 (1-56849-439-4) Buccaneer Bks.

Miss Lulu Bett. Zona Gale. LC 76-26895. 264p. 1976. reprint ed. lib. bdg. 35.00 (0-8371-9021-5, GALB, Greenwood Pr) Greenwood.

Miss Lulu Bett - Birth. Zona Gale. Ed. by Marv Balousek. 384p. (Orig.). 1994. pap. 12.95 (1-878569-19-8) Badger Bks Inc.

Miss M. R. Kate Harris. LC 95-62003. 152p. (Orig.). 1995. pap. 10.00 (0-913510-68-8) Wizards.

Miss Mabel's Table. Deborah Chandra. LC 93-9137. (Illus.). 32p. (J). (ps-3). 1994. 14.95 (0-15-276712-6, Harcourt Child Bks) Harcourt.

Miss MacIntosh, My Darling, Vol. 1. Marguerite Young. LC 92-12145. 616p. 1993. reprint ed. pap. 15.00 (1-56478-013-9) Dalkey Arch.

Miss MacIntosh, My Darling, Vol. 2. Marguerite Young. LC 92-12145. 600p. 1993. reprint ed. pap. 15.00 (1-56478-014-7) Dalkey Arch.

Miss Mackenzie, 2 vols. Anthony Trollope. Ed. by N. John Hall. LC 80-1862. (Selected Works of Anthony Trollope). 1981. reprint ed. lib. bdg. 71.95 (0-405-14143-2) Ayer.

Miss Mackenzie: (trollope 1998) Skilton. 48.00 (1-870587-48-0) Ashgate Pub Co.

*Miss Maitland's Letters. Martha Kirkland. (Regency Romance Ser.). 2000. mass mkt. 4.99 (0-451-19973-1, Sig) NAL.

Miss Malarkey Doesn't Live in Room 10. Judy Finchler. 1996. 12.15 (0-606-10879-3, Pub. by Turtleback) Demco.

Miss Malarkey Doesn't Live in Room 10. Judy Finchler. LC 94-48703. (Illus.). 32p. (J). (ps-3). 1995. lib. bdg. 15.85 (0-8027-8387-2) Walker & Co.

Miss Malarkey Doesn't Live in Room 10. Judy Finchler. LC 94-48703. (Illus.). 32p. (J). (ps-3). 1995. 14.95 (0-8027-8386-4) Walker & Co.

Miss Malarkey Doesn't Live in Room 10. Judy Finchler. (Illus.). 32p. (J). (gr. k-3). 1996. pap. 5.95 (0-8027-7498-9) Walker & Co.

Miss Malarkey Won't Be in Today. Judy Finchler. LC 97-48729. (Illus.). 32p. (J). (gr. k-3). 1998. 15.95 (0-8027-8652-9); lib. bdg. 16.85 (0-8027-8653-7) Walker & Co.

*Miss Malarkey Won't Be in Today. Judy Finchler. (Illus.). 32p. (J). (gr. k-3). 2000. reprint ed. pap. 6.95 (0-8027-7591-8) Walker & Co.

Miss Manner's Basic Training. Judith Martin. 1999. 20.01 (0-609-60052-4) Crown Pub Group.

Miss Manners Basic Training: Eating. Judith Martin. 1997. 15.00 (0-614-28222-5) Crown Pub Group.

Miss Manner's Basic Training: The Right Thing to Say. Judith Martin. LC 97-28967. 192p. 1998. 17.00 (0-609-60051-6) Crown Pub Group.

Miss Manner's Basics: Eat. Judith Martin. LC 97-186937. 1997. 15.00 (0-517-70186-3, Crown) Crown Pub Group.

Miss Manners' Citizens Guide to Civility. Judith Martin. LC 99-13072. 1999. pap. 18.00 (0-609-80158-9) Three Rivers Pr.

Miss Manners' Guide to Domestic Tranquillity: The Authoritative Manual for Every Civilized Household, However Harried. Judith Martin. LC 99-22824. 448p. 1999. 30.00 (0-517-70165-0) Random Hse Value.

*Miss Manners' Guide to Domestic Tranquillity: The Authoritative Manual for Every Civilized Household, However Harried. Judith Martin. (Illus.). 448p. 2000. reprint ed. pap. 18.00 (0-609-80539-8, Three Riv Pr) Crown Pub Group.

Miss Manners' Guide to Excruciatingly Correct Behavior. Judith Martin. 768p. 1991. 14.99 (0-88365-781-3) Galahad Bks.

Miss Manners' Guide to Raising Perfect Children. Judith Martin. 432p. 1993. 10.99 (0-88365-838-0) Galahad Bks.

Miss Manner's Guide to the Turn-of-the-Millenium. Judith Martin. 768p. 1990. per. 17.00 (0-671-72228-X) S&S Trade.

Miss Manners on Weddings. Judith Martin. LC 98-40684. 224p. 1999. 16.00 (0-609-60431-7) Crescent Books.

Miss Manners Rescues Civilization: From Sexual Harassment, Frivolous Lawsuits, Drive-By Shootings & Other Lapses in Civilization. Judith Martin. 1996. 30.00 (0-614-95749-4, Crown) Crown Pub Group.

Miss Manner's Weddings. Judith Martin. 1999. 11.20 (0-517-88608-1) Random.

Miss Mapp. E. F. Benson. LC 98-37623. 232p. 1999. pap. 11.95 (1-55921-275-6) Moyer Bell.

*Miss Mapp, Set. unabridged ed. E. F. Benson. 1999. 41.95 incl. audio (1-55685-587-7) Audio Bk Con.

Miss Marcie's Mischief. Lindsay Randall. 224p. 1995. mass mkt. 3.99 (0-8217-4814-9, Zebra Kensgtn) Kensgtn Pub Corp.

Miss Marianne Woods & Miss Jane Pirie Against Dame Helen Cumming Gordon. Ed. by Jonathan N. Katz. LC 75-13707. (Homosexuality: Lesbians & Gay Men in Society, History & Literature Ser.). 1975. reprint ed. 44.95 (0-405-07403-4) Ayer.

Miss Marjoribanks. Margaret Oliphant. LC 99-461808. 1999. pap. 12.95 (0-14-043630-8, PuffinBks) Peng Put Young Read.

Miss Marple: The Complete Short Stories. Agatha Christie. 352p. 1986. pap. 12.95 (0-425-09486-3) Berkley Pub.

Miss Mary Bobo's Boarding House Cookbook. Pat Mitchamore. LC 94-23511. (Illus.). 256p. 1994. 17.95 (1-55853-314-1) Rutledge Hill Pr.

Miss Mary Cassatt: Paintings & the Graphic Arts. Intro. by Frederick A. Sweet. (Illus.). 15p. (Orig.). (C). 1967. pap. 4.00 (0-943526-29-9) Parrish Art.

Miss Mary Cassatt, Impressionist from Pennsylvania. Frederick A. Sweet. LC 66-13423. (Illus.). 302p. reprint ed. pap. 93.70 (0-608-10951-7, 200486800046) Bks Demand.

Miss Mary Ellen: Watching God Work. Beth Branyon. LC 98-65215. (Little MISSionary Bks.). 32p. (J). (gr. 3-5). 1998. pap. 8.95 (1-57736-093-1) Providence Hse.

Miss Mary Mac All Dressed in Black: Tongue Twisters, Jump-Rope Rhymes, & Other Children's Lore from New England. Scott E. Hastings, Jr. 128p. (Orig.). (J). 1990. pap. 8.95 (0-87483-156-3) August Hse.

*Miss Mary Mack. Mary Ann Hoberman & Nadine Bernard Westcott. (J). 2001. bds. 5.95 (0-316-36642-0) Little.

Miss Mary Mack: A Hand-Clapping Rhyme. Mary A. Hoberman. LC 96-34829. (Illus.). 32p. (J). (gr. k-3). 1998. 14.95 (0-316-93118-7) Little.

Miss Mary Mack: And Other Children's Street Rhymes. Joanna Cole & Stephanie Calmenson. LC 89-37266. (Illus.). 64p. (J). (ps-3). 1990. mass mkt. 7.95 (0-688-09749-9, Wm Morrow) Morrow Avon.

Miss Mary Mack: And Other Children's Street Rhymes. Joanna Cole & Stephanie Calmenson. LC 89-37266. (Illus.). 64p. (J). (ps-3). 1990. 11.89 (0-688-08330-7, Wm Morrow) Morrow Avon.

Miss Mary Mack Big Book: Black & White Nellie Edge I Can Read & Sing Big Book. Illus. by Tani Draper. (J). (ps-2). 1994. pap. text 20.00 (0-922053-36-7) N Edge Res.

Miss Mary McLeod Bethune: The Life of a Beautiful African American Woman. Charlotte T. Durant. Ed. by Ethel Pye. (Illus.). 40p. (Orig.). (J). (ps-1). 1992. pap. 4.00 (0-913678-21-X) New Day Pr.

Miss Maxwell Becomes a Mom. Donna Clayton. (Romance Ser.). 1997. per. 3.25 (0-373-19211-8, 1-192111) Silhouette.

Miss May Sinclair: A Biographical & Critical Introduction. Theophilus E. M. Boll. LC 72-414. 332p. 1973. 45.00 (0-8386-1156-7) Fairleigh Dickinson.

Miss McKirdys Daughter. Barbara Kinghorn. 336p. 1996. 22.95 (0-312-14016-9) St Martin.

Miss Melville Regrets. Evelyn E. Smith. 1987. mass mkt. 5.99 (0-449-21259-9, Crest) Fawcett.

Miss Melville Regrets. large type ed. Evelyn E. Smith. 1989. 27.99 (0-7089-2110-8) Ulverscroft.

Miss Melville Rides a Tiger. large type ed. Evelyn E. Smith. LC 92-22861. (General Ser.). 334p. 1993. 20.95 (0-8161-5559-3, G K Hall Lrg Type) Mac Lib Ref.

Miss Melville Runs for Cover. Evelyn E. Smith. LC 92-54982. 256p. 1996. pap. 19.95 (1-55611-361-7, Pub. by D I Fine) Penguin Putnam.

Miss Meow Pageant. Richardo Keens-Douglas. (Illus.). 32p. (J). (ps-3). 1998. pap. 6.95 (1-55037-536-9, Pub. by Annick Pr); lib. bdg. 16.95 (1-55037-537-7, Pub. by Annick Pr) Firefly Bks Ltd.

Miss Meredith's Marriage. Lindsay Randall. 288p. 1995. mass mkt. 3.99 (0-8217-5051-8, Zebra Kensgtn) Kensgtn Pub Corp.

Miss Merry. Nora S. McNab. 210p. 1993. pap. 11.95 (0-942323-19-X) N Amer Heritage Pr.

Miss Miles: or A Tale of Yorkshire Life 60 Years Ago. Mary Taylor. 496p. 1991. pap. 12.95 (0-19-506492-5) OUP.

*Miss Millie. Beckie Countryman. (Illus.). 12p. (J). 2000. pap. 3.00 (0-9650312-7-6) Cosmo Starr.

Miss Minerva & William Green Hill. Frances B. Calhoun. LC 75-20498. (Tennesseana Editions Ser.). (Illus.). 246p. 1976. 16.95 (0-87049-182-2) U of Tenn Pr.

Miss Minerva & William Green Hill. Emma S. Sampson. 275p. (YA). 1992. reprint ed. lib. bdg. 21.95 (0-89966-922-0) Buccaneer Bks.

Miss Molly's Secret Adventure. Annette Sultemeier. Ed. by Laredo Publishing Staff. LC 98-13216. (Illus.). 19p. (J). (ps-3). 1998. pap. 9.95 (0-9662426-0-2) A Sultemeier.

Miss Moppet. (Classic Tales Ser.). (Illus.). 24p. (J). 1993. 4.98 (1-56173-595-7) Pubns Intl Ltd.

Miss Moppet. Illus. by Pat Schoonover & Anita Nelson. (Classic Tales Ser.). 24p. (J). (gr. 2-4). 1992. lib. bdg. 11.95 (1-56674-020-7, HTS Bks) Forest Hse.

Miss Morissa: Doctor of the Gold Trail. Mari Sandoz. LC 79-23761. vi, 249p. 1980. reprint ed. pap. 10.00 (0-8032-9118-3, Bison Books) U of Nebr Pr.

Miss Mouse Gets Dressed: A Book & Toy Set. Elizabeth Worsley. (Illus.). 10p. (J). (ps). 1996. 9.95 (0-8050-4868-5, B Martin BYR) H Holt & Co.

Miss Mouse Takes Off. Jan Omerod. (J). Date not set. 14.95 (0-688-17870-7, Wm Morrow) Morrow Avon.

Miss Mouse Takes Off. Jan Ormerod. (J). Date not set. lib. bdg. 14.89 (0-688-17871-5, Wm Morrow) Morrow Avon.

M

*Miss Mouse's Day. Jan Ormerod. LC 99-27641. (J). 2000. 14.95 (0-688-16333-5, Wm Morrow); lib. bdg. 14.89 (0-688-16334-3, Wm Morrow) Morrow Avon.

Miss Muffet. S & J Products Int., Inc. Staff. (Mother Goose & Then Some Ser.). (Illus.). 12p. (Orig.). (J). (ps). 1995. pap. 5.45 incl. audio (1-884851-17-7) S&J Prods.

Miss Muffins Lost: The Polly Guidorzi Story As Told to Thel Spencer. Thel Spencer & Polly Guidorzi. LC 94-37558. (Illus.). 181p. 1994. pap. 9.95 (0-87714-180-0) Denlingers.

*Miss Muriel & Other Stories. Ann Petry. LC 99-35548. 304p. 1999. pap. 13.00 (0-618-00709-1) HM.

Miss Myrtle's Boy: A Collection of Southeast Arkansas Memories. Charles L. Larance. LC 98-61619. 238p. 1998. 19.95 (0-9667665-0-4); pap. 12.95 (0-9667665-1-2) Windchimes MO.

Miss Nan: Beloved Rebel. Margaret L. Smith. (Illus.). 467p. 1986. 16.95 (0-932807-20-8) Overmountain Pr.

Miss Natalie's Garden: A Gullah Gullah Island Sticker Book. Ronald Daise & Natalie E. Daise. (Illus.). 24p. (J). (ps-2). 1996. 4.99 (0-689-80830-5) S&S Childrens.

Miss Nelson Has a Field Day. Harry Allard. (Miss Nelson Ser.). (Illus.). 32p. (J). (ps-3). 1985. 15.00 (0-395-36690-9) HM.

Miss Nelson Has a Field Day. Harry Allard. (Miss Nelson Ser.). (Illus.). 32p. (J). (ps-3). 1988. pap. 5.95 (0-395-48654-8, Sandpiper) HM.

Miss Nelson Has a Field Day. Harry Allard. (Carry-Along Book & Cassette Favorites Ser.). (Illus.). 1p. (J). (ps-3). 1989. pap. 9.95 incl. audio (0-395-52138-6, 480440) HM.

Miss Nelson Has a Field Day. Harry Allard. (Miss Nelson Ser.). (Illus.). (J). (ps-3). 1985. 11.15 (0-606-04276-8, Pub. by Turtleback) Demco.

Miss Nelson Is Back. Harry Allard. (Carry-Along Book & Cassette Favorites Ser.). (Illus.). 1p. (J). (ps-6). 1988. pap. 9.95 incl. audio (0-395-48872-9, 480436) HM.

Miss Nelson Is Back. Harry Allard. (Miss Nelson Ser.). (Illus.). (J). (ps-3). 1982. 10.15 (0-606-02538-3, Pub. by Turtleback) Demco.

Miss Nelson Is Back. Harry Allard & James Marshall. (Illus.). 32p. (J). (ps-3). 1982. 15.00 (0-395-32956-6) HM.

Miss Nelson Is Back. Harry Allard & James Marshall. (Miss Nelson Ser.). (Illus.). 32p. (J). (ps-3). 1986. pap. 5.95 (0-395-41668-X) HM.

*Miss Nelson Is Back; Miss Nelson Is Missing. (J). 1999. 9.95 (1-56137-032-0) Novel Units.

Miss Nelson is Missing see Senorita Nelson Ha Desaparecido

Miss Nelson Is Missing! Harry Allard. (Miss Nelson Ser.). (SPA., Illus.). 32p. (J). (ps-3). 1998. 16.00 (0-395-90009-3) HM.

Miss Nelson Is Missing! Harry Allard. (Miss Nelson Ser.). (Illus.). (J). (ps-3). 1977. 10.15 (0-606-04400-0, Pub. by Turtleback) Demco.

Miss Nelson Is Missing!, 001. Harry Allard & James Marshall. (Miss Nelson Ser.). (Illus.). 32p. (J). (ps-3). 1977. 16.00 (0-395-25296-2) HM.

Miss Nelson Is Missing!, 001. Harry Allard & James Marshall. LC 76-55918. (Miss Nelson Ser.). (Illus.). 32p. (J). (ps-3). 1985. pap. 5.95 (0-395-40146-1) HM.

Miss Nelson Is Missing! unabridged ed. Harry Allard. (Carry-Along Book & Cassette Favorites Ser.). 1p. (J). (gr. 4-8). 1993. pap. 9.95 incl. audio (0-395-66498-5, 480429) HM.

Miss Nelson Is Missing! A Study Guide. Garrett Christopher. Ed. by J. Friedland & R. Kessler. (Little Novel-Ties Ser.). (J). (gr. k-2). 1993. pap. text, student ed. 14.95 (0-88122-948-2) Lrn Links.

Miss New Zealand: Selected Poems Jenny Bornholdt. LC 98-144030. 127 p. 1997. write for info. (0-86473-323-2) Victoria Univ Pr.

Miss Nobody: A Novel. Tomek Tryzna. Tr. by Tomek Trzeciak from POL. LC 98-7235. Orig. Title: Panna Nikt. 304p. 1998. 23.00 (0-385-48939-0) Doubleday.

Miss Nomer's Guide to Painfully Incorrect English. Alan Axelrod. LC 98-217135. 1998. mass mkt. 6.99 (0-425-16422-5) Berkley Pub.

Miss Nowhere Diner. Kathleen Potts. 75p. 1998. pap. (0-87129-876-7, MA4) Dramatic Pub.

Miss Nume of Japan. Onoto Watanna. 224p. 1998. pap. text 15.95 (0-8018-6108-X) Johns Hopkins.

Miss O: My Life in Dance. Betty Oliphant. LC 97-100358. (Illus.). 288p. 1996. 22.95 (0-88801-210-1, Pub. by Turnstone Pr) Genl Dist Srvs.
Miss O'Keeffe. Christen Taylor Patten. LC 91-22431. 203p. (C). 1992. 18.95 (0-8263-1322-1) U of NM Pr.
Miss O'Keeffe. Christine T. Patten & Alvaro Cardona-Hine. (Illus.). 203p. 1998. pap. 12.95 (0-8263-1961-0) U of NM Pr.
Miss Opal's Auction. Vizurraga. LC 99-33610. (Illus.). 32p. (ps-2). 1999. 15.95 (0-8050-5891-5) H Holt & Co.
Miss Ophelia. large type ed. Mary B. Smith. LC 97-48405. (Core Ser.). 447p. 1998. 26.95 (0-7838-8402-8, G K Hall & Co) Mac Lib Ref.
Miss Ophelia. large type ed. Mary B. Smith. LC 97-48405. 1998. pap. write for info. (0-07-838402-8) McGraw.
***Miss Ophelia.** Mary Burnett Smith. 288p. 1998. reprint ed. pap. 13.00 (0-688-16357-2, Quil) HarperTrade.
Miss Ophelia: A Novel. Mary B. Smith. LC 98-23520. 277p. 1997. 24.00 (0-688-15234-1, Wm Morrow) Morrow Avon.
Miss or Mrs?; The Haunted Hotel; The Guilty River. Wilkie Collins. Ed. by Norman Page & Toru Sasaki. LC 98-22118. (Oxford World's Classics Ser.). 400p. 1999. pap. 10.95 (0-19-283307-3) OUP.
Miss P & Me. Florence McNeil. LC 83-48819. 128p. (J). (gr. 5-7). 1984. 11.95 (0-06-024136-5) HarpC Child Bks.
Miss Panda in Australia. Ambika Mathur-Kamat. (Illus.). 16p. (J). (gr. k-2). 1998. pap. 8.00 (0-8059-4316-1) Dorrance.
Miss Panda in China. Ambika Mathur-Kamat. (Miss Panda Ser.). (Illus.). 40p. (J). (ps-5). 2000. pap. 10.00 (1-886383-98-7, Little Blue) Pride & Imprints.
Miss Panda in Egypt. Ambika Mathur-Kamat. (Miss Panda Ser.). (Illus.). 40p. (J). (ps-5). 2000. pap. 10.00 (1-886383-99-5, Little Blue) Pride & Imprints.
***Miss Panda in Great Britain.** Ambika Mathur. (Miss Panda Ser.). (Illus.). 40p. (J). (ps-5). 2000. pap. 10.00 (1-883573-01-7, Little Blue) Pride & Imprints.
Miss Parkworth, & 3 Short Stories. Edward C. Booth. LC 72-125204. (Short Story Index Reprint Ser.). 1977. 19.95 (0-8369-3571-3) Ayer.
Miss Penny & Mr. Grubbs. Lisa Campbell Ernst. (Illus.). 40p. (J). (ps-2). 1995. mass mkt. 4.95 (0-689-80035-5) Aladdin.
Miss Penny & Mr. Grubbs. Lisa Campbell Ernst. (J). 1995. 10.15 (0-606-07875-4) Turtleback.
Miss Piggy, Bk. 2. Henson, Jim, Production Staff. (J). 1999. text 11.99 (0-670-86109-X) Viking Penguin.
Miss Piggy's Mixed-Up Christmas. Mary Maguire. (Muppet Lift-the-Flap Book Ser.). 16p. (J). (gr. k-3). 1999. pap. 6.99 (0-14-056539-6, PuffinBks) Peng Put Young Read.
Miss Pink at the Edge of the World. Gwen Moffat. 208p. 1995. 19.50 (0-7451-8667-X, Black Dagger) Chivers N Amer.
Miss Pink at the Edge of the World. large type ed. Gwen Moffat. 368p. 1995. 27.99 (0-7089-3379-3) Ulverscroft.
Miss Pinkerton. Mary Roberts Rinehart. 272p. 1998. mass mkt. 5.99 (1-57566-255-8, Knsington) Kensgtn Pub Corp.
Miss Pinkerton. Mary Roberts Rinehart. reprint ed. lib. bdg. 24.95 (0-89190-327-5, Rivercity Pr) Amereon Ltd.
Miss Plympton's Peril. Sheila Rabe. 208p. (Orig.). 1994. mass mkt. 3.99 (0-515-11453-7, Jove) Berkley Pub.
Miss Polly Had a Dolly. Kath Mellentin & Tim Wood. (Illus.). 20p. (J). 1997. 14.95 (0-7641-7057-0) Barron.
Miss Primrose's Husband. Agnes Adam. LC 98-55441. 28p. 1999. pap. 5.00 (0-88734-828-9) Players Pr.
Miss Prim's Untamable Cowboy. Carolyn Zane. 1997. per. 3.25 (0-373-19248-7, 1-19248-3) Silhouette.
***Miss Prudence Pennypack's a Month of Manners.** Karen Rupprecht. (Illus.). 40p. (J). (ps-4). 2000. pap. (1-893116-13-1) Baltimore Sun.
***Miss Prudence Pennypack's Perfectly Proper.** Karen Rupprecht. (Illus.). 68p. (J). (ps-4). 1999. 16.95 (1-893116-09-3) Baltimore Sun.
Miss Purdy's Problem. Mary Chesely. Ed. by Jane Weinberger. LC 93-61195. (Illus.). 48p. (J). (ps-4). 1994. pap. 7.95 (0-932433-75-8) Windswept Hse.
Miss Pym Disposes. Josephine Tey. 223p. Date not set. 21.95 (0-8488-2408-3) Amereon Ltd.
Miss Pym Disposes. Josephine Tey. LC 98-17682. 240p. 1998. per. 11.00 (0-684-84751-5) S&S Trade Pap.
Miss Pym Disposes. large type ed. Josephine Tey. LC 98-51098. 1999. 25.95 (0-7862-1778-2) Thorndike Pr.
Miss Pym Disposes. Josephine Tey. LC 79-19665. 1981. reprint ed. lib. bdg. 16.00 (0-8376-0447-8) Bentley Pubs.
***Miss Ravenel's Conversion from Secession to Loyalty.** John W. De Forest. LC 99-36933. (Penguin Classics Ser.). 544p. 2000. pap. 14.95 (0-14-043757-6, Penguin Bks) Viking Penguin.
Miss Ravenel's Conversion from Secession to Loyalty see Collected Works of John W. De Forest
Miss Ravenel's Conversion from Secession to Loyalty. John W. De Forest. (Collected Works of John W. De Forest). 1988. reprint ed. lib. bdg. 59.00 (0-7812-1153-0) Rprt Serv.
Miss Ravenel's Conversion from Secession to Loyalty. John W. De Forest. LC 98-20846. xxi, 466p. 1998. reprint ed. pap. 20.00 (0-8032-6615-4, DEFMIX) U of Nebr Pr.
Miss Read's Christmas. Read. Date not set. lib. bdg. 21.95 (0-8488-1701-X) Amereon Ltd.
Miss Read's Country Cooking. Miss Read. (Illus.). 248p. 1992. 20.00 (0-89733-373-X) Academy Chi Pubs.
***Miss Rhythm: The Autobiography of Ruth Brown, Rhythm & Blues Legend.** Ruth Brown & Andrew Yule. (Illus.). 360p. (Orig.). 1999. reprint ed. text 24.00 (0-7881-6331-0) DIANE Pub.
Miss Rhythm: The Autobiography of Ruth Brown, Rhythm & Blues Legend. Ruth Brown & Andrew Yule. LC 98-31733. (Illus.). 368p. (Orig.). 1999. reprint ed. mass mkt. 15.95 (0-306-80888-9, Pub. by Da Capo) HarpC.
Miss Rogan Poems. Esther Odzer. (Illus.). 96p. (Orig.). 1984. pap. 4.76 (0-9613572-0-7) E Odzer.
***Miss Rumphius.** 2000. 9.95 (1-56137-258-7) Novel Units.
Miss Rumphius. Barbara Cooney. LC 82-2837. (Illus.). 32p. (J). (gr. k-3). 1982. 15.99 (0-670-47958-6, Viking Child) Peng Put Young Read.
Miss Rumphius. Barbara Cooney. (Illus.). (J). (ps-3). 1994. pap. 9.99 incl. audio (0-14-095026-5, PuffinBks) Peng Put Young Read.
Miss Rumphius. Barbara Cooney. (Picture Puffin Ser.). (J). 1985. 10.19 (0-606-00345-2, Pub. by Turtleback) Demco.
Miss Rumphius: A Study Guide. Garrett Christopher. Ed. by J. Friedland & R. Kessler. (Little Novel-Ties Ser.). (J). (gr. k-2). 1995. pap. text, student ed. 14.95 (1-56982-238-7) Lrn Links.
Miss Rumphius Literature Mini-Unit. Janet Lovelady. (Illus.). 32p. (J). (gr. 2-4). 1989. student ed. 4.95 (1-56096-003-5) Mari.
Miss Saigon, No. 314. M. Schonberg. 64p. 1991. pap. 10.95 (0-7935-1009-0, 00102191) H Leonard.
Miss Saigon, Vol. 336. Bo Schonberg. 64p. 1992. pap. 6.95 (0-7935-1013-9, 00001605) H Leonard.
Miss Saigon: Big Note for Piano. 72p. 1993. otabind 14.95 (0-7935-1978-0, 00222560) H Leonard.
Miss Saigon: Easy Piano. (Easy Play Ser.). 72p. 1992. per. 14.95 (0-7935-1010-4, 00222537) H Leonard.
Miss Scrooge: Under the Mistletoe. Toni Collins. (Romance Ser.). 1994. per. 2.75 (0-373-19050-6, 1-19050-3) Silhouette.
Miss Sedgewick & the Spy. 1950. 30.00 (0-7862-2215-8) Five Star.
***Miss Seeton by Moonlight.** large type ed. Hamilton Crane. LC 99-462229. (Mystery Ser.). 336p. 2000. 27.95 (0-7862-2481-9) Thorndike Pr.
Miss Seeton Cracks the Case. Hamilton Crane. 1991. mass mkt. 4.99 (0-425-12676-5) Berkley Pub.
Miss Seeton Goes to Bat. Hamilton Crane. LC 99-32537. 1999. 26.95 (0-7862-2065-1) Thorndike Pr.
Miss Seeton Goes to Bat. Hamilton Crane & Heron Carvic. 208p. 1993. mass mkt. 4.99 (0-425-13576-4) Berkley Pub.
Miss Seeton Rocks the Cradle. Hamilton Crane. 208p. (Orig.). 1992. mass mkt. 4.99 (0-425-13400-8) Berkley Pub.
Miss Seeton Rules. Hamilton Crane. 272p. 1995. mass mkt. 4.99 (0-425-15006-2, Prime Crime) Berkley Pub.
Miss Seeton's Finest Hour, 1 vol. Hamilton Crane. 259p. 1999. mass mkt. 5.99 (0-425-17026-8, Prime Crime) Berkley Pub.
Miss Silver Comes to Stay: A Miss Maud Silver Mystery. Patricia Wentworth. 22.95 (0-88411-749-9) Amereon Ltd.
Miss Silver Deals with Death: A Miss Silver Mystery. Patricia Wentworth. 21.95 (0-8488-1218-2) Amereon Ltd.
Miss Silver's Past. Josef Skvorecky. 175p. 1985. reprint ed. pap. 7.50 (0-88001-074-6) HarpC.
Miss Spider's ABC: New Board Book Edition. David Kirk. LC 97-48415. (Miss Spider Ser.). (Illus.). 32p. (J). (ps-2). 1998. 16.95 (0-590-28279-4, Pub. by Scholastic) Scholastic Inc.
***Miss Spider's ABC: New Board Book Edition.** David Kirk. LC 99-71214. (Miss Spider Ser.). (Illus.). 32p. (J). (ps-k). 2000. bds. 8.95 (0-439-13747-0, Scholastic Ref) Scholastic Inc.
Miss Spider's New Car. David Kirk. Ed. by Antoinette White. (Miss Spider Ser.). (Illus.). 32p. (J). (ps-2). 1997. 16.95 (0-614-30105-X) Callaway Edns.
Miss Spider's New Car. David Kirk. LC 97-744. (Miss Spider Ser.). (Illus.). 32p. (J). (ps-2). 1997. 16.95 (0-590-30713-4) Scholastic Inc.
Miss Spider's New Car. David Kirk. LC 98-30514. (Miss Spider Ser.). (Illus.). 32p. (J). (ps-k). 1999. 8.95 (0-439-04675-0) Scholastic Inc.
Miss Spider's Tea Party. David Kirk. Ed. by Antoinette White. LC 93-15710. (Miss Spider Ser.). (Illus.). 31p. (J). (ps-2). 1994. 16.95 (0-590-47724-2, Scholastic Hardcover) Scholastic Inc.
Miss Spider's Tea Party: The Counting Book. David Kirk. Ed. by Antoinette White. LC 96-7029. (Miss Spider Ser.). (Illus.). 34p. (J). (ps-k). 1997. bds. 8.95 (0-590-06519-X) Scholastic Inc.
Miss Spider's Wedding. David Kirk. Ed. by Antoinette White. LC 94-42096. (Miss Spider Ser.). (Illus.). 32p. (J). (ps-2). 1995. 16.95 (0-590-56866-3, Scholastic Hardcover) Scholastic Inc.
Miss Sue & the Sheriff. Robert B. House. LC 51-23911. 128p. reprint ed. pap. 39.70 (0-7837-2452-7, 204260500005) Bks Demand.
Miss Suzy's Easter Surprise. Miriam Young. LC 89-37842. (Illus.). 48p. (J). (ps-3). 1990. pap. 4.95 (0-689-71374-6) Aladdin.
***Ms. Taken.** Jo Leigh. (Temptation Ser.). 2000. mass mkt. 3.99 (0-373-25909-3, 1259092) Harlequin Bks.
Miss Taken's Identity. David LaRochelle. (Mad Mysteries Ser.: Vol. 8). (Illus.). 48p. (J). (gr. 2-4). 1998. pap. 3.50 (0-8431-7849-3, Price Stern) Peng Put Young Read.
***Miss Tappety (Tock) the Tap Dance Teaching Clock.** large type ed. Sitare Ltd. Staff. Ed. by MacLean. (Opening the Million Dollar Doors of Show Business Ser.: Vol. 9). (Illus.). 100p. (YA). (gr. 8-11). 1999. pap. 10.00 (0-940178-62-1, CJE 1011) Sitare.
Miss Teen Sweet Valley. Kate William. (Sweet Valley High Ser.: No. 76). (YA). (gr. 7 up). 1991. 8.60 (0-606-04976-2, Pub. by Turtleback) Demco.
Miss Temptation. Kurt Vonnegut, Jr. 25p. 1993. pap. 3.50 (0-87129-334-X, M82) Dramatic Pub.
Miss Tempy's Watchers. unabridged ed. Sarah Orne Jewett. 1994. lib. bdg. 18.95 incl. audio (1-883049-48-2) Sound Room.
Miss Tempy's Watchers, Set. unabridged ed. Sarah Orne Jewett. (Jewett Ser.). 1994. 16.95 incl. audio (1-883049-42-3, 390232, Pub. by Sound Room) Lndmrk Audiobks.
Miss Thornrose & the Rake. Geraldine Burrows. LC 99-33907. (Romances Ser.). 1999. 24.95 (0-7862-2043-0, Five Star MI) Mac Lib Ref.
***Miss Tibbles Investigates.** April Kihlstrom. (Regency Romance Ser.). 224p. 2000. mass mkt. 4.99 (0-451-20040-3, Sig) NAL.
Miss Tina Did It: And Other Fresh Looks at Modern Fiction. Joseph J. Waldmeir. LC 97-28923. (Locust Hill Literary Studies: No. 22). 1997. lib. bdg. 28.00 (0-933951-76-0) Locust Hill Pr.
Miss Tizzy. Libba M. Gray. LC 92-8409. (Illus.). 40p. (J). (ps-2). 1993. 15.00 (0-671-77590-1) S&S Bks Yung.
Miss Tizzy. Libba M. Gray. (Illus.). 32p. (J). 1998. mass mkt. 5.99 (0-689-81897-1) S&S Childrens.
Miss Tizzy. Libba M. Gray. 1998. 11.19 (0-606-13611-8, Pub. by Turtleback) Demco.
Miss Tonks Turns to Crime. large type ed. Marion Chesney. LC 93-29303. (Poor Relation Ser.: Vol. 2). 251p. 1994. lib. bdg. 17.95 (0-8161-5898-3, G K Hall Lrg Type) Mac Lib Ref.
Miss Ulysses from Puka-Puka. Florence Frisbie. (American Autobiography Ser.). 241p. 1995. reprint ed. lib. bdg. 79.00 (0-7812-8523-2) Rprt Serv.
Miss Undine's Living Room. James Wilcox. LC 86-46109. 1994. reprint ed. lib. bdg. 21.95 (1-56849-522-6) Buccaneer Bks.
Miss Vera's Finishing School for Boys Who Want to Be Girls: Tips, Tales, & Teachings from the Dean of the World's First Cross-Dressing Academy. Veronica Vera. LC 97-18736. (Illus.). 208p. (Orig.). 1997. pap. 14.95 (0-385-48456-9, Main St Bks) Doubleday.
Miss Viola & Uncle Ed Lee. Alice F. Duncan. LC 95-30292. (Illus.). 40p. (J). (ps-3). 1999. 16.00 (0-689-80476-8) Atheneum Yung Read.
Miss Violet's Shining Day. Jane Breskin Zalben. LC 94-70687. (Illus.). 32p. (J). (ps-2). 1995. 14.95 (1-56397-234-4) Boyds Mills Pr.
Miss Wickham's Betrothal. Nancy Richards-Akers. 224p. (Orig.). 1992. mass mkt. 3.99 (0-380-76532-2, Avon Bks) Morrow Avon.
Miss Willie. Janice H. Giles. 1976. 22.95 (0-8488-1012-0) Amereon Ltd.
Miss Willie. Janice H. Giles. 272p. 1994. 30.00 (0-8131-1885-9); pap. 17.00 (0-8131-0831-4) U Pr of Ky.
***Miss Wyoming.** Douglas Coupland. LC 99-15212. 320p. 1999. 23.00 (0-375-40734-0) Pantheon.
***Miss Wyoming.** Douglas Coupland. 2001. pap. 13.00 (0-375-70723-9) Vin Bks.
Miss Yonkers Goes Bonkers. Mike Thaler. (Illus.). 32p. (J). (gr. 2). 1994. pap. 3.99 (0-380-77510-7, Avon Bks) Morrow Avon.
Miss Yonkers Goes Bonkers. Mike Thaler. (Young Camelot Bks.). (YA). 1994. 9.19 (0-606-06573-3, Pub. by Turtleback) Demco.
Miss Zukas & Island Murd. Jo Dereske. 224p. 1995. mass mkt. 5.99 (0-380-77031-8, Avon Bks) Morrow Avon.
Miss Zukas & Library M. Jo Dereske. 224p. 1994. mass mkt. 5.99 (0-380-77030-X, Avon Bks) Morrow Avon.
Miss Zukas & Raven. Jo Dereske. LC 96-96492. 256p. 1996. mass mkt. 5.99 (0-380-78243-X, Avon Bks) Morrow Avon.
Miss Zukas & Stroke of D. Jo Dereske. (Miss Zukas Ser.: No. 3). 224p. 1995. mass mkt. 5.99 (0-380-77033-4, Avon Bks) Morrow Avon.
***Miss Zukas in Death's Shadow.** Jo Dereske. 224p. 1999. mass mkt. 5.99 (0-380-80472-7, Avon Bks) Morrow Avon.
***Miss Zukas Shelves the Evidence.** Jo Dereske. 2000. mass mkt. 5.99 (0-380-80474-3) Morrow Avon.
Missa "Ancor Che Col Partire" see Complete Works of Philippe De Monte
Missa "Aspice Domine" see Complete Works of Philippe De Monte
Missa Breva: A Capella. G. Palestrina. (LAT.). 32p. 1986. pap. 3.95 (0-7935-4904-3, 50324020) H Leonard.
Missa "Cum Sit Omnipotens Rector Olympi" see Complete Works of Philippe De Monte
Missa de "Requiem" see Complete Works of Philippe De Monte
Missa "Inclina Cor Meum" see Complete Works of Philippe De Monte
Missa "La Dolce Vista" see Complete Works of Philippe De Monte
Missa "Nasce la Pena Mia" see Complete Works of Philippe De Monte
Missa "O Altitudo Divitiarum" see Complete Works of Philippe De Monte
Missa Pange Lingua. Des Prez Josquin. LC 76-22703. (Early Musical Masterworks Ser.). 76p. reprint ed. pap. 30.00 (0-8357-3883-3, 203661500004) Bks Demand.
Missa "Quando Lieta Sperai" see Complete Works of Philippe De Monte
Missa Quaternis Vocibus see Complete Works of Philippe De Monte
Missa "Quomodo Dilexi" see Complete Works of Philippe De Monte
Missa "Reviens Vers Moi" see Complete Works of Philippe De Monte
Missa Sex Vocum, Ex Cod. Bibl. Municipalis Norimbergensis see Complete Works of Philippe De Monte
Missa Sine Nomine see Complete Works of Philippe De Monte
Missa "Sine Nomine", 8 Vocum see Complete Works of Philippe De Monte
Missa "Sine Nomine", 5 Vocum see Complete Works of Philippe De Monte
Missa Sine Nomine, No. 2 see Complete Works of Philippe De Monte
Missa "Sine Nomine", 6 Vocum see Complete Works of Philippe De Monte
Missa Solemnis: A Celebration in Poetry for 3 Voices. Robley E. Whitson. LC 93-87687. 112p. pap. text 12.00 (1-55605-235-9) Wyndham Hall.
Missa Solemnis in Full Score. Ludwig van Beethoven. 272p. pap. 15.95 (0-486-26894-2) Dover.
Missa Super "Cara la Vita Mia" see Complete Works of Philippe De Monte
Missa "Ultimi Miei Sospiri" see Complete Works of Philippe De Monte
Missal: The Order of Mass in English. National Conference of Catholic Bishops. Ed. by Kevin O. Johnson. LC 96-72375. 50p. 1997. pap. 4.00 (0-9653660-2-2) Pangaeus Pr.
Missal of Robert of Jumieges. Ed. by H. A. Wilson. LC 94-34594. (Henry Bradshaw Society Ser.: Vol. XI). (C). 1994. 99.00 (1-870252-09-8, Henry Bradshaw Soc) Boydell & Brewer.
Missale Hervoiae Ducis Spalatensis Croatico-Glagoliticum. fac. ed. Comment by V. Stefanic et al. (Codices Selecti A Ser.: Vol. XXXIV). (GER., Illus.). 494p. 1973. lthr. 2203.00 (3-201-00830-3, Pub. by Akademische Druck-und) Balogh.
Missale Romanum. (Illus.). 1120p. 1996. reprint ed. 310.00 (0-912141-43-3) Roman Cath Bks.
Missalettes & the Mass. Wilton Gregory. 1981. pap. 2.00 (0-915866-12-9) Am Cath Pr.
Missbrauchte Aufklarung? Schriften zum Preuphischen Religionsedikt vom 9. Juli 1788. 258p. 1996. write for info. (3-487-10239-0) G Olms Pubs.
Missed Blessings. Sue S. Nickel. 1993. 9.95 (0-9637015-0-9) Crossover OK.
Missed Connections: Hard of Hearing in a Hearing World. Barbara Stenross. LC 98-30716. (Illus.). 128p. 1999. 39.50 (1-56639-681-6); pap. 16.95 (1-56639-682-4) Temple U Pr.
Missed It by That Much: Baseball Players who Challenged the Record Books. Victor Debs, Jr. LC 98-7486. (Illus.). 252p. 1998. pap. 29.95 (0-7864-0508-2) McFarland & Co.
Missed Opportunities: The Rise & Fall of Jamaica's Edward Seaga. Timothy Ashby. 40p. 1989. pap. 5.00 (1-55813-031-4) Hudson Instit IN.
Missed Opportunities? The Role of Security Assurances in Nuclear Non-Proliferation. Ed. by Virginia I. Foran. 215p. (C). 1997. pap. 14.95 (0-87003-067-1) Brookings.
Missed Opportunities: The Story of Canada's Broadcasting Policy. Marc Raboy. 488p. (C). 1990. pap. 27.95 (0-7735-0775-2, Pub. by McG-Queens Univ Pr); lib. bdg. 65.00 (0-7735-0743-4, Pub. by McG-Queens Univ Pr) CUP Services.
Misselthwaite. large type ed. Susan Moody. (Charnwood Large Print Ser.). 624p. 1996. 27.99 (0-7089-8914-4) Ulverscroft.
***Mrs. Hippo's Pizza Parlor.** Vivian French. (Illus.). 48p. (J). 2000. pap. 3.95 (0-7534-5289-8, Kingfisher) LKC.
Mrs. Morgan's Lawn. Barney Saltzberg. LC 92-54873. (Illus.). 32p. (J). (gr. k-3). 1993. lib. bdg. 13.89 (1-56282-424-4, Pub. by Hyprn Child) Little.
Mrs. Morgan's Lawn. Barney Saltzberg. LC 92-54873. (Illus.). 32p. (J). (gr. k-3). 1993. 13.95 (1-56282-423-6, Pub. by Hyprn Child) Time Warner.
Mrs. Morgan's Lawn. Barney Saltzberg. LC 92-54873. (Illus.). 32p. (J). (gr. k-3). 1998. pap. 4.95 (0-7868-1294-X, Pub. by Hyprn Child) Time Warner.
Mrs. Morgan's Lawn. Barney Saltzberg. 32p. 1998. pap. 4.95 (0-7868-1365-2, Pub. by Hyprn Ppbks) Little.
Mrs. Moskowitz & the Sabbath Candlesticks. Amy Schwartz. (Illus.). 32p. (J). (gr. k-5). 1983. pap. 4.95 (0-8276-0231-6) JPS Phila.
Misshapen. Robert Budde. LC 98-136744. 216p. 1997. pap. 13.95 (1-896300-22-7) NeWest Pubs.
Misshapen Banana. Richard Morris. 1990. pap. 3.50 (0-938979-36-1) EG Bksellers.
Missile Aerodynamics. Jack N. Nielsen. LC 88-15223. (Illus.). 450p. (C). 1988. reprint ed. text 40.00 (0-9620629-0-1) Nielsen Engineering & Res Inc.
Missile & Space Race. Alan J. Levine. LC 93-23673. 256p. 1994. 59.95 (0-275-94451-4, Praeger Pubs) Greenwood.
Missile Crisis in Cuba. Keith Eubank. LC 99-25624. (Anvil Ser.). 235p. (C). 2000. pap. text 19.50 (0-89464-890-X) Krieger.
Missile Crisis of October 1962 see Cuba-Caribbean Missile Crisis of October 1962
Missile Defense Controversy: Strategy, Technology, & Politics, 1955-1972. Ernest J. Yanarella. LC 76-46034. 248p. 1977. 29.95 (0-8131-1355-5) U Pr of Ky.
Missile Defenses & Western European Security: NATO Strategy, Arms Control, & Deterrence, 81. Robert M. Soofer. LC 88-16394. 188p. 1988. 55.00 (0-313-26351-5, SRO/, Greenwood Pr) Greenwood.
Missile Gap: A Study of the Formulation of Military & Political Policy. Edgar M. Bottome. LC 77-129964. 265p. 1975. 29.50 (0-8386-7734-7) Fairleigh Dickinson.
Missile Guidance & Pursuit: Kinematics, Dynamics & Control. N. A. Shneydor. 264p. 1998. 65.00 (1-898563-43-8, Pub. by Horwood Pub) Paul & Co Pubs.
Missile Inbound: The Attack on the "Stark" in the Persian Gulf. Jeffrey L. Levinson & Randy L. Edwards. LC 97-2087. (Illus.). 176p. 1997. 28.95 (1-55750-517-9) Naval Inst Pr.

An Asterisk (*) at the beginning of an entry indicates that the title is appearing for the first time.

Missile Proliferation in the Information Age: Hearing Before the Subcommittee on International Security, Proliferation & Federal Services of the Committee on Governmental Affairs, United States Senate, One Hundred Fifth Congress, First Session, September, 22, 1997. United States Government. LC 98-133404. (S. Hrg. Ser.). iii, 47 p. 1997. write for info. (*0-16-055938-3*) USGPO.

Missile Summer. Martin Booth. (C). 1988. 30.00 (*0-904524-36-1*, Pub. by Rivelin Grapheme Pr) St Mut.

Missile Wounds of the Head & Neck, Vol. I. Ed. by Bizhan Aarabi et al. 270p. 95.00 (*1-879284-64-2*) Am Assn Neuro.

Missile Wounds of the Head & Neck, Vol. II. Ed. by Bizhan Aarabi et al. 196p. 95.00 (*1-879284-66-9*) Am Assn Neuro.

Missiles & the Revolution in Warfare. Nels A. Parson. LC 62-19221. (Illus.). 255p. reprint ed. pap. 79.10 (*0-608-30818-8*, 200282500014) Bks Demand.

Missiles in Cuba: A Decision-Making Game. Dan Caldwell. (CISE Learning Packages in International Studies). (Illus.). 38p. (Orig.). 1979. pap. text 3.50 (*0-936876-35-2*) LRIS.

Missiles in Cuba: Kennedy, Khrushchev, Castro & the 1962 Crisis. Mark J. White. LC 96-54620. (American Ways Ser.). 192p. 1997. 22.50 (*1-56663-155-6*, Pub. by I R Dee); pap. text 12.95 (*1-56663-156-4*, Pub. by I R Dee) Natl Bk Netwk.

Missiles, Masks & Miracles: Personal Accounts of the Invisible Shield Protecting Israel During the Gulf War. Sam Veffer. (Illus.). 130p. Date not set. pap. 11.00 (*1-881927-08-3*, Pub. by Leviathan OH) Natl Bk Netwk.

Missiles of October. Robert S. Thompson. 400p. 1993. pap. 14.00 (*0-671-87176-5*, Touchstone) S&S Trade Pap.

Missiles, Reactors & Civil Liberties: Against the Nuclear State. Ed. by Gari Donn. 1981. 20.00 (*0-906502-04-7*, Pub. by NCCL) St Mut.

Missiles to Learning: Beyond the Left/Right Brain. Beverly B. Casebeer. Ed. by Betty Lou Kratoville. LC 96-208557. (Illus.). 206p. (Orig.). 1996. pap. 18.00 (*1-57128-018-9*, 018-9) Acad Therapy.

Missing. Kate Chester. (Hear No Evil Ser.: No. 2). 1996. mass mkt. 3.99 (*0-590-67327-0*) Scholastic Inc.

Missing! Kate Chester. (Hear No Evil Ser.). (J). 1996. 9.09 (*0-606-09399-0*, Pub. by Turtleback) Demco.

Missing! Hannah Kuraoka. 147p. (Orig.). (J). (gr. 6-8). 1995. mass mkt. 3.99 (*0-380-77374-0*, Avon Bks) Morrow Avon.

Missing. R. L. Stine, pseud. (Fear Street Ser.: No. 2). 224p. (YA). (gr. 7 up). 1990. per. 3.99 (*0-671-69410-3*, Archway) PB.

Missing. R. L. Stine, pseud. (Fear Street Ser.: No. 2). (YA). (gr. 7 up). 1990. 9.09 (*0-606-01954-5*, Pub. by Turtleback) Demco.

Missing!! Wesley Wood. LC 96-96914. (Illus.). viii, 248p. (Orig.). 1996. pap. 12.00 (*0-9653736-0-6*) Angels of Today.

Missing. Michelle Herman. LC 89-38340. 154p. reprint ed. pap. 47.80 (*0-608-09685-7*, 206980000006) Bks Demand.

Missing: A Social History of Glasgow & Gloucester. Andrew O'Hagan. 208p. 1996. 20.00 (*1-56584-335-5*, Pub. by New Press NY) Norton.

Missing: One Bride. Alice Sharpe. (Romance Ser.). 1997. per. 3.25 (*0-373-19212-6*, 1-19212-9) Silhouette.

***Missing: One Stuffed Rabbit.** Maryann Cocca-Leffler. (Illus.). 32p. (J). (gr. k-3). 2000. pap. 6.95 (*0-8075-5162-7*) A Whitman.

Missing! Stranger Abduction: Teaching Your Child How to Escape. Robert Stuber. LC 93-48404. 95p. 1994. pap. 6.95 (*0-918606-12-8*) Heidelberg Graph.

Missing - Kissing: 2 Plays - Missing Marisa & Kissing Christine. John P. Shanley. 1997. pap. 5.25 (*0-8222-1590-X*) Dramatists Play.

Missing a Voice: Critical Pedagogy & the Possibilities of Democratic Teaching. Linda McNeil. 1997. pap. 17.95 (*0-8133-2624-9*) Westview.

Missing, Abducted, Runaway, & Thrown Away Children in America: First Report: Numbers & Characteristics, National Incidence Studies. David Finkelhor et al. (Illus.). 379p. (Orig.). (C). 1996. pap. text 50.00 (*0-7881-2651-2*) DIANE Pub.

Missing & Murdered Children. Margaret O. Hyde. LC 97-23355. (Impact Book Ser.). 112p. (J). 1998. 24.00 (*0-531-11384-1*) Watts.

Missing Angel Juan. Francesca Lia Block. LC 92-38299. (Illus.). 144p. (YA). (gr. 7 up). 1993. 14.89 (*0-06-023007-X*) HarpC Child Bks.

Missing Angel Juan. Francesca Lia Block. LC 92-38299. (Trophy Bk.). 144p. (J). (gr. 12 up). 1995. pap. 4.95 (*0-06-447120-9*, HarpTrophy) HarpC Child Bks.

Missing Angel Juan. Francesca Lia Block. (J). 1995. 9.60 (*0-606-08463-0*, Pub. by Turtleback) Demco.

Missing at Tenoclock. Arthur Williams. LC 93-38034. 216p. 1994. 19.95 (*0-8027-3185-6*) Walker & Co.

Missing Bananas. Richard Scarry. Richard Scarry Best Board Books Ever Ser.: Vol. 4). Orig. Title: Big Trouble for Bananas Gorilla. (Illus.). 12p. (J). (ps-3). 2000. bds. 5.99 (*0-689-81643-X*, Simon Spot) Litle Simon.

Missing Beauty. Teresa Carpenter. 1989. mass mkt. 5.99 (*0-7860-0449-5*, Pinncle Kensgtn) Kensgtn Pub Corp.

Missing, Believed Lost: The Great British Film Search. Ed. by Allen Eyles. (Illus.). 112p. 1993. pap. 31.95 (*0-85170-306-2*, Pub. by British Film Inst) Ind U Pr.

Missing Bishop. Ross H. Spencer. (Illus.). 270p. 1985. 15.45 (*0-89296-121-X*, Pub. by Mysterious Pr) Little.

Missing Bonds, Vol. 1. Bruce W. Most. 288p. 1997. mass mkt. 5.99 (*0-312-96273-8*) St Martin.

Missing Boy & the Escapee, Pt. 2. Jean C. Charles. LC 83-70229. 50p. 1984. pap. 3.50 (*0-9610796-8-1*) Adelphi Pr.

Missing Bride. E.D.E.N. Southworth. (Notable American Authors Ser.). 1999. reprint ed. lib. bdg. 125.00 (*0-7812-8900-9*) Rprt Serv.

Missing Bureaucrat. Hans Scherfig. Tr. by Frank Hugus from DAN. LC 88-10899.Tr. of Den forsvundne fuldmaegtig. 207p. (Orig.). 1988. 17.95 (*0-940242-26-5*); pap. 8.95 (*0-940242-25-7*) Fjord Pr.

***Missing Cat.** Felicity Brooke & Jo Litchfield. (Illus.). 16p. (ps-3). 2000. lib. bdg. 13.95 (*1-58086-226-8*) EDC.

***Missing Cat.** Ed. by Felicity Brooks & Jo Litchfield. (Easy Reading Ser.). (Illus.). 16p. (J). (ps-3). 2000. pap. 5.95 (*0-7460-3027-4*, Pub. by Usbrne Pbng UK) EDC.

Missing Cat: English-Spanish. Berlitz Kids Editors. (Berlitz Kids Ser.). (ENG & SPA., Illus.). 64p. (J). (gr. k-4). pap. text 16.95 incl. audio (*2-8315-5710-0*) Berlitz.

Missing Cat: French-English. Berlitz Kids Editors. (Berlitz Kids Ser.). (ENG & FRE., Illus.). 64p. (J). (gr. k-4). 1996. pap. text 16.95 incl. audio (*2-8315-5711-9*) Berlitz.

Missing Cat: German-English. Berlitz Kids Editors. (Berlitz Kids Ser.). (ENG & GER., Illus.). 64p. (J). (gr. k-4). 1996. pap. text 16.95 incl. audio (*2-8315-5712-7*) Berlitz.

Missing Cat: Italian-English. Berlitz Kids Editors. (Berlitz Kids Ser.). (ENG & ITA., Illus.). 64p. (J). (gr. k-4). 1996. pap. text 16.95 incl. audio (*2-8315-5713-5*) Berlitz.

Missing Cat: Spanish-English. Berlitz Kids Editors. (Berlitz Kids Ser.). (ENG & SPA., Illus.). 64p. (J). (gr. k-4). 1996. pap. text 16.95 incl. audio (*2-8315-5714-3*) Berlitz.

Missing Cat Caper. Lochie Fowler. LC 97-211830. 192p. (Orig.). 1997. pap. write for info. (*0-9657192-6-X*) Feline Familia.

Missing Century. E. Peters. LC 99-223615. 1998. 43.95 (*90-6831-985-X*, Pub. by Peeters Pub) Bks Intl VA.

Missing Chapter. large type ed. Robert Goldsborough. LC 93-47302. 342p. 1994. lib. bdg. 21.95 (*0-7862-0166-5*) Thorndike Pr.

Missing Chapters: Women Staff at the University of Western Australia 1963-1987. Patricia Crawford & Myrna Tonkinson. pap. 9.95 (*0-86422-073-1*, Pub. by Univ of West Aust Pr) Intl Spec Bk.

Missing Child in Liberal Theory: Towards a Covenant Theory of Family, Community Welfare & the Civic State. John O'Neill. 136p. 1994. text 40.00 (*0-8020-0627-2*); pap. text 14.95 (*0-8020-7586-X*) U of Toronto Pr.

Missing Children. Loren W. Christensen. (The Family Ser.). (Illus.). 64p. (J). (gr. 7 up). 1990. lib. bdg. 17.95 (*0-86593-076-7*) Rourke Corp.

Missing Children. Loren W. Christensen. (Family Ser.). (Illus.). 64p. (YA). (gr. 7 up). 1990. lib. bdg. 12.95 (*0-685-46440-7*) Rourke Corp.

***Missing Children.** B. J. Rowley. (Light Traveler Adventure Ser.: Vol. 3). 256p. (YA). 2000. pap. 13.95 (*0-9700103-3-8*) Goldn Wings.

Missing Children: A Psychological Approach to Understanding the Causes & Consequences of Stranger & Non-Stranger Abduction of Children. James N. Tedisco & Michele A. Paludi. LC 95-18494. (SUNY Series, the Psychology of Women). (Illus.). 161p. (C). 1996. text 59.50 (*0-7914-2879-6*); pap. text 19.95 (*0-7914-2880-X*) State U NY Pr.

Missing Children: The Law Enforcement Response. Ed. by Martin L. Forst. (Illus.). 250p. 1990. pap. 37.95 (*0-398-06125-4*) C C Thomas.

Missing Children: The Law Enforcement Response. Ed. by Martin L. Forst. (Illus.). 250p. (C). 1990. text 54.95 (*0-398-05681-1*) C C Thomas.

Missing Chums. Franklin W. Dixon. (Hardy Boys Mystery Stories Ser.: No. 4). (Illus.). 210p. (J). (gr. 3-6). 1996. reprint ed. 14.95 (*1-55709-147-1*, Pub. by Applewood) Consort Bk Sales.

Missing Chums. rev. ed. Franklin W. Dixon. (Hardy Boys Mystery Stories Ser.: No. 4). (Illus.). 180p. (J). (gr. 4-7). 1930. 5.99 (*0-448-08904-1*, G & D) Peng Put Young Read.

Missing Clue. Gaby Waters. (Whodunnits Ser.). (Illus.). 48p. (J). (gr. 4 up). 1999. lib. bdg. 12.95 (*0-88110-523-6*, Usborne) EDC.

Missing Coin. R. Woodman. (Look 'N See Ser.). (J). 1995. 0.99 (*1-85792-136-4*, Pub. by Christian Focus) Spring Arbor Dist.

Missing Combination Mystery. Eric D. Stoffle & Jerry D. Thomas. LC 95-50445. (Shoebox Kids Ser.: No. 4). 93p. (J). (gr. 2-5). 1996. pap. 6.99 (*0-8163-1276-1*) Pacific Pr Pub Assn.

Missing Connection Between Business & Universities. Ernest A. Lynton. (ACE-Oryx Series on Higher Education). (Illus.). 192p. 1984. 27.95 (*0-02-919280-3*) Free Pr.

Missing Continents. Ariel Dorfman. 1999. pap. 19.95 (*0-670-84453-5*) Viking Penguin.

Missing Crown. Galila Ben-Uri. (Illus.). 223p. (J). (gr. 5-7). 1988. 15.95 (*0-935063-41-2*); pap. 12.95 (*0-935063-42-0*) CIS Comm.

Missing Diagnosis. C. Orian Truss. 175p. (Orig.). 1983. reprint ed. pap. 8.95 (*0-9615758-0-8*) Missing Diag.

Missing Diagnosis. 2nd ed. C. Orian Truss. 175p. (Orig.). 1986. 25.00 (*0-9615758-2-4*) Missing Diag.

Missing Duchess. large type ed. Alanna Knight. 1996. pap. 20.95 (*0-7838-1650-2*, G K Hall Lrg Type) Mac Lib Ref.

Missing Earring. unabridged ed. 269p. 1998. pap. 15.95 (*1-892896-14-1*) Buy Books.

Missing Eden. Wendi Lee. 1999. per. 4.99 (*0-373-26301-5*) Harlequin Bks.

Missing Element in Church Development. Paul E. Paino. 224p. 1992. pap. 12.95 (*1-882357-03-5*) P E Paino Minist.

Missing Face. Osonye T. Onwueme. LC 96-95387. (Musical Drama for the Voices of Color Ser.). 76p. (Orig.). (YA). (gr. 5 up). 1997. pap. 10.00 (*1-57579-053-X*, 1) Pine Hill Pr.

Missing Frames. Photos by Mikhail Lemkhin. LC 95-1321. (Illus.). 72p. (Orig.). 1995. pap. 24.00 (*1-55779-083-3*) Hermitage Pubs.

Missing from Action: A Powerful Historical Response to the Crisis among American Men. 2nd rev. ed. Weldon M. Hardenbrook & Terry Somerville. Orig. Title: Missing from Action: Vanishing Manhood in America. 320p. 1996. pap. 14.95 (*1-888212-00-4*) Conciliar Pr.

Missing from Action: Vanishing Manhood in America see Missing from Action: A Powerful Historical Response to the Crisis among American Men

Missing from Home. large type ed. Peter N. Walker. (Linford Mystery Library). 352p. 1993. pap. 16.99 (*0-7089-7344-2*, Linford) Ulverscroft.

***Missing Gator of Gumbo Limbo.** (J). 1999. 9.95 (*1-56137-700-7*) Novel Units.

Missing 'Gator of Gumbo Limbo. Jean Craighead George. LC 91-20779. (Trophy Bk.). 160p. (J). (gr. 3-7). 1993. pap. 4.95 (*0-06-440434-X*, HarpTrophy) HarpC Child Bks.

Missing 'Gator of Gumbo Limbo: An Ecological Mystery. Jean Craighead George. LC 91-20779. 176p. (J). (gr. 4-7). 1992. 15.95 (*0-06-020396-X*) HarpC Child Bks.

Missing 'Gator of Gumbo Limbo: An Ecological Mystery. Jean Craighead George. (J). 1993. 10.05 (*0-606-05467-7*, Pub. by Turtleback) Demco.

Missing Girls. Lois Metzger. LC 98-18817. 208p. (YA). (gr. 5-9). 1999. 15.99 (*0-670-87777-8*) Viking Penguin.

Missing Half of the Church: The Concept of the Care Fellowship Ministry. Chester M. Wright. 112p. (Orig.). 1989. pap. 7.95 (*0-932345-00-X*) Antioch Publishes.

Missing Head Mystery. Carole Marsh. LC 79-55447. (History Mystery Ser.). (Illus.). (Orig.). (J). (gr. 3-9). 1994. 29.95 (*1-55609-179-6*); pap. 19.95 (*0-935326-01-4*) Gallopade Intl.

Missing Head Mystery: Classroom Gamebook. Carole Marsh. (Carole Marsh Bks.). (Illus.). (Orig.). (J). (gr. 3-6). 1994. pap. 19.95 (*0-935326-84-7*) Gallopade Intl.

Missing Head Mystery Set. Carole Marsh. (Carole Marsh Mysteries Ser.). 1994. teacher ed. 125.00 (*0-7933-6944-4*) Gallopade Intl.

Missing Head of Damasceno Monteiro. Antonio Tabucchi. Tr. by Patrick Creagh. LC 98-31263. (ITA.). 192p. 2000. 23.95 (*0-8112-1393-5*, Pub. by New Directions) Norton.

Missing Headlines: Selected Speeches. Emeka Anyaoku. LC 98-144389. (Illus.). 352p. 1997. 36.95 (*0-85323-812-X*, Pub. by Liverpool Univ Pr); pap. 22.95 (*0-85323-822-7*, Pub. by Liverpool Univ Pr) Intl Spec Bk.

Missing Heir: The Autobiography of Kylie Tennant. Kylie Tennant. LC 86-162772. viii, 190 p. 1986. write for info. (*0-333-41509-4*) Macmillan.

Missing Horse Mystery. James Greene & Carolyn Keene. (Nancy Drew Mystery Stories Ser.: No. 145). 147p. (J). (gr. 3-7). 1998. pap. 3.99 (*0-671-00754-8*) PB.

Missing Hour. Dawn Stewardson. (Intrigue Ser.). 1998. per. 3.99 (*0-373-22470-2*, 1-22470-8) Harlequin Bks.

Missing Impossible. Paul Trevillion. 128p. 1999. text 19.95 (*0-670-86951-1*) Viking Penguin.

Missing in Action: A World War II Memoir. Nick Moramarco. LC 98-19973. (Illus.). 128p. (Orig.). 1999. pap. 10.95 (*1-56474-269-5*) Fithian Pr.

Missing in Action: An RCAF Navigator's Story. John D. Harvie. LC 96-112711. (Illus.). 272p. 1995. 34.95 (*0-7735-1350-7*, Pub. by McG-Queens Univ Pr) CUP Services.

Missing in Action & Presumed Dead. Rashidah Ismaili. LC 91-78394. 112p. 1992. 24.95 (*0-86543-296-1*); pap. 9.95 (*0-86543-297-X*) Africa World.

Missing in Action, Ww II: Mission No. 70. James J. Bollich. LC 98-93703. 229 p. 1998. write for info. (*0-9643275-4-6*) J J Bollich.

Missing in Manhattan. Mary Higgins Clark et al. 1994. mass mkt. 4.99 (*0-425-14203-5*) Berkley Pub.

Missing in the Mountains. T. S. Fields. LC 99-40048. (J). (gr. 4-6). 1999. pap. text. write for info. (*0-87358-741-3*, Rising Moon Bks) Northland AZ.

Missing Japanese Festival Dolls. Judith M. Austin. (GlobalFriends Adventures Ser.). (Illus.). 64p. (J). (gr. 2-6). 1997. pap. 5.95 (*1-58056-004-0*, GlobalFr Pr) GlobalFriends.

Missing Jesus. Paul M. Miller. 57p. 1984. 4.99 (*0-8341-9373-6*, MC-262) Lillenas.

Missing Jesus: A Christmas Story & Nativity Figure Set. Gary L. Whetstone. (Illus.). 24p. (J). (gr. 2-4). 1998. pap. 45.00 (*0-937739-33-2*) Roman IL.

Missing Jew: New & Selected Poems. rev. ed. Rodger Kamenetz. LC 91-68488. 102p. 1992. 18.95 (*1-877770-56-6*); pap. 12.50 (*1-877770-57-4*); audio 12.95 (*1-877770-59-0*) Time Being Bks.

Missing Joseph. Elizabeth George. LC 92-35630. 567p. 1994. mass mkt. 7.50 (*0-553-56604-0*) Bantam.

Missing Lane. Mathu Wayne. LC 97-9915. 1997. pap. 9.95 (*1-877633-37-2*) Luthers.

Missing Link. Sydney Cross. 358p. 1994. write for info. (*0-9639626-0-4*) Prescott Png.

Missing Link: A Gil Yates Private Investigator Novel. Alistair Boyle. LC 94-78009. 224p. 1995. 19.95 (*0-9627297-3-6*) A A Knoll Pubs.

Missing Link? A Persuasive New Look at Heart Disease As It Relates to Mercury. Michael F. Ziff & Sam Ziff. (Illus.). 184p. (Orig.). 1991. pap. 12.00 (*0-941011-08-9*) Bio-Probe.

Missing Link: An Historical Accounting of Jacob Waltz & the Dutchman's Lost Gold. H. Henry Sheffer, III. 155p. 1994. pap. 12.95 (*1-885162-47-2*) Norseman.

Missing Link: Between Genesis Creation & Scientific Findings. B. R. Hicks. 309p. 1988. 19.95 (*1-58363-059-7*, EO-0702) Christ Gospel.

***Missing Link: Found.** Christina Gerwitz & Felice Gerwitz. (Truth Seeker's Mystery Ser.: Vol. 1). 192p. (YA). (gr. 7-12). 2000. pap. 7.99 (*0-9700385-9-3*) Media Angels.

Missing Link? Nuclear Proliferation & the International Mobility of Russian Nuclear Experts. LC 96-216399. (UNIDIR Research Papers: No. 35). 46p. 1995. 12.00 (*92-9045-104-1*, E.GV.95.0.18) UN.

Missing Link: Reflections on Philosophy & Spirit. Sydney Banks. 160p. 1998. 12.95 (*0-9681645-0-1*); lthr. 19.95 (*0-9681645-2-8*) Lone Pine.

Missing Link: The Facts about Glyconutrients. Neecie Moore. LC 99-198149. 288p. 1999. pap. 14.95 (*0-9660700-0-3*, Pub. by Validation Pr) ACCESS Pubs Network.

***Missing Link: The Image of Man in Contemporary Photography.** Ed. by Christopho Doswald. (Illus.). 328p. 2000. 65.00 (*3-908163-12-9*, Pub. by Edit Stemmle) Abbeville Pr.

Missing Link: West European Neutrals & Regional Security. Ed. by Richard E. Bissell & Curt Gasteyger. LC 89-17010. (Duke Press Policy Studies). (Illus.). 270p. 1990. text 42.95 (*0-8223-0953-X*) Duke.

Missing Link in Modern Spiritualism. A. Leah Underhill. LC 75-36923. (Occult Ser.). (Illus.). 1976. reprint ed. 41.95 (*0-405-07977-X*) Ayer.

Missing Link in Your Relationship with God. Robert Hellmann. 114p. (Orig.). 1996. pap. 10.24 (*0-9654071-0-1*) Wrd of Truth.

Missing Link: or The Negro's Ethnological Status. Gottlieb C. Hasskarl. LC 77-144636. reprint ed. 32.00 (*0-404-00170-X*) AMS Pr.

Missing Links. Vincent J. Begley. 224p. 1988. 15.95 (*0-933905-17-3*); pap. 9.95 (*0-933905-06-8*) Claycomb Pr.

Missing Links. Rick Reilly. 288p. 1997. pap. 12.95 (*0-385-48886-6*, Main St Bks) Doubleday.

***Missing Links.** Daniel Wexler. LC 99-87515. (Illus.). 224p. 2000. 35.00 (*1-886947-60-0*) Sleepng Bear.

Missing Links: Gender Equity in Science & Technology for Development. U. N. Commission on Science & Technology for Development Staff. 200p. 1995. pap. 24.95 (*0-912917-37-7*) UNIFEM.

Missing Links: Technology & Environmental Improvement in the Industrializing World. large type ed. George R. Heaton et al. 52p. 1994. pap. 20.00 (*0-915825-80-5*) World Resources Inst.

Missing Links Discovered in Assyrian Tablets. E. Raymond Capt. LC 84-72709. (Illus.). 256p. (C). 1985. 16.00 (*0-934666-17-2*); pap. 11.00 (*0-934666-15-6*) Artisan Pubs.

Missing Links in the JFK Assassination: Evidence of Conspiracy & Coverup. Ralph D. Thomas. (Illus.). 200p. 1992. pap. text 35.00 (*0-918487-60-9*) Thomas Investigative.

Missing Lynx. David Zawalski. (Illus.). 40p. 1998. pap. 16.00 (*0-9657670-2-7*) D Johnson Pub.

Missing Lynx: Finally, a Speak-in-Public Learning System for High School Students. Stephen M. Gower. LC 98-94138. 160p. (YA). (gr. 9 up). 1998. 20.00 (*1-880150-79-4*) Lectern Pub.

Missing Magical Energy. Shahastra. LC 82-99874. (Magical Rainbow Ser.). (Illus.). 64p. (J). (ps-7). 1982. pap. 8.95 (*0-686-38241-2*) Magical Rainbow.

Missing Majority: The Recruitment of Women As State Legislative Candidates. David Niven. LC 97-26173. 208p. 1998. 59.95 (*0-275-96073-0*, Praeger Pubs) Greenwood.

***Missing Man.** Cassutt. 448p. 2000. mass mkt. 6.99 (*0-8125-7786-8*, Pub. by Tor Bks) St Martin.

Missing Man. Michael Cassutt. LC 98-22541. 352p. 1998. 24.95 (*0-312-86620-8*, Pub. by Forge NYC) St Martin.

Missing Map of Pirate's Haven. Sigmund Brouwer. (Accidental Detective Ser.: Vol. 5). 132p. (J). (gr. 3-7). 1995. pap. text 5.99 (*1-56476-374-9*, 6-3374, Victor Bks) Chariot Victor.

Missing Marlene. Evan Marshall. 320p. 1999. text 20.00 (*1-57566-420-8*) Kensgtn Pub Corp.

***Missing Marlene.** Evan Marshall. (Jane Stuart & Winky Mystery Ser.). 2000. mass mkt. 5.99 (*1-57566-555-7*) Kensgtn Pub Corp.

Missing Marx. 1992. 36.00 (*0-85345-827-8*, Pub. by Monthly Rev); pap. 16.00 (*0-85345-828-6*, Pub. by Monthly Rev) NYU Pr.

***Missing May.** 2000. 9.95 (*1-56137-590-X*) Novel Units.

Missing May. Cynthia Rylant. 96p. (YA). (gr. 7 up). 1993. pap. 5.50 (*0-440-40865-2*) Dell.

Missing May. Cynthia Rylant. LC 91-23303. 96p. (YA). (gr. 6 up). 1992. 14.95 (*0-531-05996-0*); lib. bdg. 15.99 (*0-531-08596-1*) Orchard Bks Watts.

Missing May. Cynthia Rylant. (J). 1992. 9.60 (*0-606-05468-5*, Pub. by Turtleback) Demco.

Missing May: A Study Guide. Garrett Christopher. Ed. by J. Friedland & R. Kessler. (Novel-Ties Ser.). (J). (gr. 4-6). 1994. pap. text, student ed. 15.95 (*1-56982-060-0*) Lrn Links.

Missing May: L-I-T Guide. Charlotte Jaffe & Barbara Roberts. (J). (gr. 4-10). Date not set. pap. 8.95 (*1-56644-982-0*, 982-0AP) Educ Impress.

Missing May & The Summer of the Swans: Curriculum Unit. Center for Learning Network Staff et al. (Novel Ser.). 64p. (YA). (gr. 4-9). 1994. spiral bd. 18.95 (*1-56077-314-6*) Ctr Learning.

Missing Measures: Modern Poetry & the Revolt Against Meter. Timothy Steele. LC 89-34918. 350p. 1990. pap. 18.00 (*1-55728-126-2*) U of Ark Pr.

Missing Members. 2nd ed. Anca Vlasopolos. 217p. 1991. mass mkt. 4.95 (*0-9629611-0-8*) Corridors Pr.

Missing Memories. Assorted. 1995. per. 5.50 (*0-373-20110-9*) Harlequin Bks.

Missing Message of Revelation: Natural Catastrophes Ordained by God. Judy Becker. (Illus.). 374p. (Orig.). 1986. pap. 9.95 (*0-9617493-0-X*) Judy Becker.

M

Missing Middle: Working Families & the Future of American Social Policy. Theda Skocpol. LC 99-37842. 256p. 2000. 25.95 (0-393-04822-5) Norton.

***Missing Middle: Working Families & the Future of American Social Policy.** Theda Skocpol. 224p. 2000. reprint ed. pap. 15.95 (0-393-32113-4, Norton Paperbks) Norton.

Missing Millions: Why & How Africa Is Underdeveloped. Kinfe Abraham. 1995. 49.95 (0-86543-352-6); pap. 16.95 (0-86543-353-4) Africa World.

Missing Minikin. Alan Wheatley. (Skinny Bks.). 1998. pap. 3.95 (0-207-19093-3) HarpC.

Missing Minx. large type ed. Richard Goyne. 432p. 1998. pap. 17.99 (0-7089-5389-1, Linford) Ulverscroft.

Missing Missionary. Mark Weinrich. (Illus.). 24p. (Orig.). (J). (gr. k-3). 1993. pap. 4.99 (0-87509-518-6) Chr Pubns.

***Missing Mittens.** Stuart J. Murphy. LC 99-41334. (MathStart Ser.). 40p. (J). (ps-2). 2001. pap. 4.95 (0-06-446733-3, HarpTrophy) HarpC Child Bks.

***Missing Mittens.** Stuart J. Murphy. LC 99-41334. (MathStart Ser.). 40p. (YA). (ps up). 2001. 15.95 (0-06-028026-3); lib. bdg. 15.89 (0-06-028027-1) HarpC Child Bks.

Missing Mobster Millions & Other Gangland Gold. Thomas P. Terry. (Illus.). 45p. (Orig.). 1980. pap. 5.95 (0-939850-06-0) Spec Pub.

Missing Moment: How the Unconscious Shapes Modern Science. Robert Pollack. LC 99-26241. 240p. 1999. 25.00 (0-395-70985-7) HM.

***Missing Mooch.** Gilles Gauthier. (Early Readers Ser.). (Illus.). 64p. (J). (gr. 1-4). 1999. mass mkt. 3.99 (0-88780-484-5) Formac Publ Co.

Missing Moon. Noel Tyl. (Illus.). 180p. 1979. pap. 4.95 (0-87542-797-9) Llewellyn Pubns.

Missing Mother Goose. Stephen Krensky. (J). 1988. 15.00 (0-385-26277-9) Doubleday.

Missing Mr. Mosley. John Greenwood. (Mosley Mystery Ser.). 192p. 1985. 13.95 (0-8027-5618-2) Walker & Co.

***Missing Mummy.** Ron Roy. (J). 2001. mass mkt. 11.99 (0-375-90268-6, Pub. by Random Bks Yng Read); mass mkt. 3.99 (0-375-80268-1, Pub. by Random Bks Yng Read) Random.

Missing Music. Mouse Works Staff. (Illus.). 18p. (J). 1997. 3.98 (1-57082-672-2, Pub. by Mouse Works) Time Warner.

Missing Myna. C. Arthur Bundrant. (Illus.). 100p. (Orig.). (J). (gr. 6). 1996. pap. 6.95 (1-57502-142-0) Morris Pubng.

Missing on Castaway Island. Joan R. Biggar. LC 97-12850. (Megan Parnell Mysteries Ser.). (J). (gr. 5-9). 1997. pap. text 5.99 (0-570-05015-4, 56-1842) Concordia.

Missing One Stuffed Rabbit. Maryann Cocca-Leffler. LC 97-18203. (Illus.). 32p. (J). (gr. k-3). 1998. lib. bdg. 14.95 (0-8075-5161-9) A Whitman.

***Missing Organizational Linkages: Tools for Cross-Level Research.** Paul S. Goodman. LC 00-8798. (Foundations for Organizational Science Ser.). 2000. write for info. (0-7619-1618-0) Sage.

Missing Pages in American History: Revealing the Services of Negroes in the Early Wars in the United States of America, 1641-1815. Laura E. Wilkes. LC 72-7728. reprint ed. 27.50 (0-404-06948-7) AMS Pr.

Missing Patient. J. L. Lu. 1978. pap. 2.75 (0-9601768-0-2) J L Lu.

Missing Peace. M. Hencher. 0.30 (0-614-11455-1, Pub. by Christian Focus) Spring Arbor Dist.

Missing Person. Mary Evans. LC 98-19232. 160p. (C). 1999. 75.00 (0-415-09975-7) Routledge.

Missing Person. Samuel Wi Fussell. 1995. 21.00 (0-671-78739-X) S&S Trade.

Missing Person. Sara Pfoutz. 1999. pap. 3.95 (0-14-036254-1, Viking) Viking Penguin.

***Missing Person.** Mary Jane Staples. 2000. 25.95 (0-593-03641-7, Pub. by Transworld Publishers Ltd); pap. 8.95 (0-552-14230-1, Pub. by Transworld Publishers Ltd) Trafalgar.

Missing Person. large type ed. Frances Ferguson. 560p. 1995. 27.99 (0-7089-3241-X) Ulverscroft.

Missing Person: A Radio Play. Karen H. Anderson et al. (Intermediate Listening Ser.: No. 1). (Illus.). 92p. (Orig.). 1983. pap. text 29.40 (0-582-79789-6, 75043) Longman.

Missing Person Package. Karen H. Anderson et al. (Intermediate Listening Ser.: No. 1). (Illus.). 92p. 1989. pap. text 40.50 incl. audio (0-582-79814-0, 75064) Addison-Wesley.

Missing Persons. Fay Faron. LC 96-51861. (Howdunit Ser.). 272p. 1997. pap. 16.99 (0-89879-790-X, Wrtrs Digest Bks) F & W Pubns Inc.

***Missing Persons.** Hartmut Lange. 2000. write for info. (1-902881-26-5, Pub. by Toby Pr Ltd); pap. 15.95 (1-902881-27-3, Pub. by Toby Pr Ltd) Toby Pr.

Missing Persons. Craig Lucas. 1996. pap. 5.25 (0-8222-1474-1) Dramatists Play.

Missing Persons. Louise O. Neaderland. 32p. 1988. spiral bd. 15.00 (0-942561-10-4) Bone Hollow.

Missing Persons. B. Swanton et al. 284p. 1988. pap. 20.00 (0-642-13587-8, Pub. by Aust Inst Criminology) Advent Bks Div.

Missing Persons: A Critique of the Social Sciences. Mary Douglas & Steven Ney. LC 98-12747. 237p. 1998. 24.95 (0-520-20752-1, Pub. by U CA Pr) Cal Prin Full Svc.

Missing Persons: The Impossibility of Auto/Biography. Mary Evans. 1999. pap. 22.99 (0-415-09976-5) Routledge.

Missing Persons & Mistaken Identities: Women & Gender in Ancient Israel. Phyllis A. Bird. LC 97-27404. (Overtures to Biblical Theology Ser.). 320p. 1997. pap. 20.00 (0-8006-3128-5, Fortress Pr) Augsburg Fortress.

Missing Persons & Other Essays. Heinrich Boll. Tr. by Leila Vennewitz from GER. LC 94-10930. (European Classics Ser.). 290p. 1994. reprint ed. 39.95 (0-8101-1177-2); reprint ed. pap. 13.95 (0-8101-1162-4) Northwestern U Pr.

Missing Persons U. S. A: How to Hunt down & Find Anyone, Anywhere. Roger Willard. (Illus.). 88p. 1994. pap. 15.00 (0-87364-771-8) Paladin Pr.

Missing Picture: Alternative Contemporary Photography in the Soviet Union. John P. Jacob et al. LC 90-50869. (Illus.). 56p. 1990. pap. 10.00 (0-938437-35-6) MIT List Visual Arts.

Missing Piece. Lee Ezell. 139p. 1992. pap. 9.99 (0-89283-797-7, Vine Bks) Servant.

Missing Piece. Shel Silverstein. LC 75-37408. (Ursula Nordstrom Bk.). (Illus.). 112p. (J). 1976. lib. bdg. 15.89 (0-06-025672-9) HarpC Child Bks.

Missing Piece. Shel Silverstein. LC 75-37408. (Ursula Nordstrom Bk.). (Illus.). 112p. (YA). (gr. 2 up). 1976. 15.95 (0-06-025671-0) HarpC Child Bks.

***Missing Piece in Greece.** Linda Lowery Keep. (Hannah & the Angels Ser.: No. 9). (Illus.). 128p. (J). (gr. 3-7). 2000. pap. 3.99 (0-375-80257-6) Random Bks Yng Read.

Missing Piece Meets the Big O. Shel Silverstein. LC 80-8721. (Illus.). 112p. (J). (gr. 2 up). 1981. lib. bdg. 15.89 (0-06-025658-3) HarpC Child Bks.

Missing Piece Meets the Big O. Shel Silverstein. LC 80-8721. (Illus.). 104p. (J). (gr. 4-7). 1981. 15.95 (0-06-025657-5) HarpC Child Bks.

Missing Pieces. 1997. mass mkt. 6.99 (0-440-29554-8) Dell.

Missing Pieces. Lucille C. Campbell. (J). (gr. 4-12). 1992. pap. text 9.97 (0-937659-55-X) GCT.

Missing Pieces. Joy Fielding. 432p. 1998. mass mkt. 6.99 (0-440-22287-7) Doubleday.

Missing Pieces. Carole W. Holden. 223p. mass mkt. 4.99 (1-55197-172-0) Picasso Publ.

Missing Pieces. Norma F. Mazer. LC 94-39271. (Illus.). 208p. (YA). (gr. 7 up). 1995. 16.00 (0-688-13349-5, Wm Morrow) Morrow Avon.

Missing Pieces. Norma F. Mazer. 144p. (YA). (gr. 7 up). 1996. mass mkt. 4.50 (0-380-72289-5, Avon Bks) Morrow Avon.

Missing Pieces. Norma Fox Mazer. 1996. 9.60 (0-606-09620-5, Pub. by Turtleback) Demco.

Missing Pieces. Irving K. Zola. 1983. pap. 22.95 (0-87722-311-4) Temple U Pr.

Missing Pieces. large type ed. Joy Fielding. LC 97-34306. 1997. 24.95 (1-56895-491-3, Compass) Wheeler Pub.

Missing Pieces: A Coroner's Companion. Kathryn Rantala. LC 98-30614. (Illus.). 128p. 1999. pap. 11.95 (0-938075-28-4) Ocean View Bks.

Missing Pieces: How to Investigate Ghosts, UFOs, Psychics, & Other Mysteries. Robert A. Baker & Joe Nickell. LC 92-3439. 339p. (C). 1992. 27.95 (0-87975-729-9) Prometheus Bks.

Missing Pieces in the Weight Loss Puzzle. Martha B. Beveridge. Ed. by Terrisa Bruce-Phipps. 71p. (Orig.). 1996. pap. 9.95 (1-889237-01-9) Options Now.

Missing Pony Pal. Jeanne Betancourt. (Pony Pals Ser.: No. 16). (Illus.). 96p. (J). (gr. 2-5). 1997. pap. text 3.50 (0-590-37459-1) Scholastic Inc.

Missing Popcorn. Mary Landis. (Illus.). 160p. 1975. 7.65 (0-7399-0079-X, 2335) Rod & Staff.

Missing, Presumed Dead. large type ed. J. M. Gregson. (Magna Large Print Ser.). 320p. 1998. 29.99 (0-7505-1249-0, Pub. by Mgna Lrg Print) Ulverscroft.

***Missing Reels: Lost Films of American & European Cinema.** Harry Waldman. LC 99-88007. (Illus.). 319p. 2000. 55.00 (0-7864-0724-7) McFarland & Co.

Missing Scientist. 1988. pap. 4.95 (0-19-581015-5) OUP.

Missing Scientist. 2nd ed. Ed. by D. H. Howe. (Illus.). 94p. 1993. pap. text 5.95 (0-19-585398-9) OUP.

Missing Secret Diary of Admiral Byrd. (Illus.). 68p. 1992. pap. 12.95 (0-938294-91-1) Inner Light.

Missing Sex. M. Ward. (C). 1990. 25.00 (1-85594-030-2) St Mut.

Missing Shapes Mix-Up see Walt Disney's Read & Grow Library

Missing Sheep. R. Woodman. (Look 'N See Ser.). (J). 1995. 0.99 (1-85792-137-2, Pub. by Christian Focus) Spring Arbor Dist.

Missing since Monday. Ann M. Martin. LC 86-45390. 176p. (YA). (gr. 7 up). 1987. pap. 3.99 (0-590-43136-6) Scholastic Inc.

Missing since Monday. Ann M. Martin. (J). 1986. 9.09 (0-606-03617-2, Pub. by Turtleback) Demco.

Missing Sisters. Gregory Maguire. LC 97-24112. 164p. (J). 1998. pap. 4.95 (0-7868-1273-7, Pub. by Hyperion) Time Warner.

***Missing Sisters.** Gregory Macguire. 1998. 10.05 (0-606-13612-6, Pub. by Turtleback) Demco.

Missing Sixth. Mark Graham. 1992. 22.95 (0-15-160576-9) Harcourt.

Missing Socrates: Problems of Plato's Writing. Jay Farness. 216p. 1991. 35.00 (0-271-00722-2) Pa St U Pr.

Missing Son. R. Woodman. (Look 'N See Ser.). (J). 1995. 0.99 (1-85792-135-6, Pub. by Christian Focus) Spring Arbor Dist.

***Missing Spanish Creoles.** John H. McWhorter. LC 99-41957. 283p. 2000. 45.00 (0-520-21999-6, Pub. by U CA Pr) Cal Prin Full Svc.

***Missing Stories: An Oral History of Ethnic & Minority Groups in Utah.** Leslie G. Kelen & Eileen Hallet Stone. (Illus.). 528p. 2000. pap. 24.95 (0-87421-293-6) Utah St U Pr.

Missing Stratum: Technical School Education in England, 1900-1990s. Michael Sanderson. LC 93-39429. 256p. (C). 1994. text 85.00 (0-485-11442-9) Humanities.

Missing Sunflowers. Maggie Stern. LC 96-7148. (Illus.). 32p. (J). (gr. k up). 1997. 15.00 (0-688-14873-5, Greenwillow Bks) HarpC Child Bks.

***Missing Susan.** Sharyn McCrumb. 2000. mass mkt. 6.99 (0-345-91578-X) Ballantine Pub Grp.

Missing Susan. large type ed. Sharyn McCrumb. LC 92-46703. (General Ser.). 408p. 1993. pap. 18.95 (0-8161-5566-6, G K Hall Lrg Type) Mac Lib Ref.

Missing Susan. Sharyn McCrumb. 1992. reprint ed. mass mkt. 5.99 (0-345-37945-4) Ballantine Pub Grp.

***Missing Suspect.** Laura Coburn. 1998. mass mkt. 6.99 (0-451-40642-7, Onyx) NAL.

Missing Tablets & Unknown Oracles. Mueller et al. 50p. 1996. pap. text 5.00 (1-879665-20-4) Cyborg Prods.

Missing the Lifeboat? Gyeorgos C. Hatonn. (Phoenix Journals). 221p. 1994. pap. 6.00 (1-56935-033-7) Phoenix Source.

Missing the Meaning? A Cognitive Neuropsychological Study of Processing of Words by an Aphasic Patient. David Howard & Sue Franklin. (Issues in the Biology of Language & Cognition Ser.). 192p. 1989. 27.50 (0-262-08178-4, Bradford Bks) MIT Pr.

Missing the Moment. Grace Thompson. 320p. 1995. 20.00 (0-7278-4761-9) Severn Hse.

Missing the Piano. Adam Rapp. 160p. (YA). (gr. 7 up). 1994. 14.99 (0-670-95340-7, Viking Child) Peng Put Young Read.

Missing the Piano. Adam Rapp. (J). 1996. 10.09 (0-606-09621-3, Pub. by Turtleback) Demco.

Missing Tooth. Joanna Cole. LC 88-1903. (Step into Reading Ser.: A Step 2 Book). (Illus.). 48p. (J). (ps-3). 1988. pap. 3.99 (0-394-89279-8, Pub. by Random Bks Yng Read) Random.

Missing Tooth. Joanna Cole. (Step into Reading Ser.: A Step 2 Book). (J). (gr. 1-3). 1988. 9.19 (0-606-03860-4, Pub. by Turtleback) Demco.

Missing Transport Networks in Europe. Peter Nijkamp et al. 224p. 1994. 78.95 (1-85628-674-6, Pub. by Avebry) Ashgate Pub Co.

Missing Truth Vol. 1: Angelic Revelations Replace 16 Centuries of Blind Faith. Cornelia Shakour. LC 96-84374. 224p. (Orig.). 1997. 17.95 (0-9652258-8-7) Concorde Pub NJ.

Missing Verse. Robert J. Walker. 30p. 1994. pap. 2.95 (0-9642553-1-6) In His Name.

Missing Video. Dave Gustaveson. (Reel Kids Adventures Ser.: Bk. 1). 143p. (J). (gr. 3-8). 1993. pap. 5.99 (0-927545-60-8) YWAM Pub.

Missing Voices: The Experience of Motherhood. Stephanie Brown et al. (Illus.). 312p. 1995. pap. text 29.95 (0-19-553378-X) OUP.

Missing Woman. Michael Z. Lewin. 1991. mass mkt. 4.99 (0-446-40026-2, Mysterious Paperbk) Warner Bks.

Missing Women & Others: Stories. June Spence. LC 97-32906. 208p. 1998. 21.95 (1-57322-098-1, Riverhead Books) Putnam Pub Group.

Missing Women & Others: Stories. June Spence. 208p. 1999. reprint ed. pap. 12.00 (1-57322-737-4, Riverhd Trade) Berkley Pub.

Missing Words: The Family Handbook on Adult Hearing Loss. Kay Thomsett & Eve Nickerson. LC 93-668. 254p. 1993. 24.95 (1-56368-023-8) Gallaudet Univ Pr.

Missing Workforce: Managing Absenteeism. Andrew Sargent. 160p. (C). 1989. 65.00 (0-85292-411-9, Pub. by IPM Hse) St Mut.

***Missing World.** Margot Livesey. LC 99-35785. 352p. 2000. 23.00 (0-375-40581-X) Knopf.

***Missing You.** (Rock & Pop Classics: Vol. 13). (Illus.). 30p. 2000. write for info. (1-892207-42-7) Intl Masters Pub.

Missing You. Ed. by Helen Exley. (Miniature Square Bks.). (Illus.). 64p. 1996. 6.00 (1-85015-690-5) Exley Giftbooks.

Missing You: You're Never Really Far from Me. Dean Walley. 1979. pap. 2.50 (0-8378-5019-3) Gibson.

Missio Moscovitica Vol. 178: The Role of the Jesuits in the Westernization of Russia 1582-1689. Jan J. Santich. (American University Studies: Series IX). VII, 255p. (C). 1996. text 46.95 (0-8204-2758-6) P Lang Pubng.

Missiological Education for the 21st Century: The Book, the Circle, & the Sandals. Ed. by J. Dudley Woodberry et al. LC 96-25646. (American Society of Missiology Ser.: No. 23). 335p. (Orig.). 1996. pap. 15.00 (1-57075-089-0) Orbis Bks.

***Missiological Implications of Epistemological Shifts: Affirming Truth in a Modern World.** Paul G. Hiebert. LC 98-48832. (Christian Mission & Modern Culture Ser.). 152p. 1998. pap. 13.00 (1-56338-259-8) TPI PA.

Missiology: An Introduction to the Foundation, History, & Strategies of World Missions. Ed. by John M. Terry et al. LC 98-3541. 768p. 1998. text 38.99 (0-8054-1075-9) Broadman.

Missiology - Its Subject-Matter & Method: A Study of Mission-Doers in Madagascar. Laurent W. Ramambason. LC 99-15095. (Studies in the Intercultural History of Christianity: Vol. 116). 208p. 1999. pap. text 37.95 (0-8204-4320-4) P Lang Pubng.

Missiology & the Social Sciences: Contributions, Cautions, & Conclusions. Ed. by Edward Rommen & Gary Corwin. LC 96-34634. (Evangelical Missiological Society Ser.). 1996. 8.95 (0-87808-378-2) William Carey Lib.

***Missiology: Its Subject-Matter & Method: A Study of Mission-Doers in Madagascar.** Laurent W. Ramambason. 208p. 1999. pap. 37.95 (3-631-34602-6) P Lang Pubng.

Mission. Richard C. Holbrooke. 1998. 0.25 (0-8129-2877-6, Times Bks) Crown Pub Group.

Mission. Ed. by Randy McKean & Kay S. McKean. 154p. 1994. pap. 7.99 (1-884553-29-X) Discipleshp.

Mission. large type ed. Layne Kenric. (Dales Western Ser.). 183p. 1992. pap. 18.99 (1-85389-355-2, Pub. by Mgna Lrg Print) Ulverscroft.

Mission: Addition. Loreen Leedy. (Illus.). (J). (gr. k-3). 1997. pap. 6.95 (0-8234-1412-4) Holiday.

Mission: An American Congressman's Voyage in Space. Jamie Buckingham. (Illus.). 220p. 1988. 19.95 (0-15-105556-4) Harcourt.

***Mission: An Essential Guide.** Carlos F. Cardoza-Orlandi. 1999. 15.00 (0-687-05472-9) Abingdon.

Mission: Apline Redoubt. Alexander Molnar, Jr. LC 98-89529. 375p. 1998. text 25.00 (0-7388-0241-7); pap. text 15.00 (0-7388-0242-5) Xlibris Corp.

Mission: Children. Marisa Carroll. (Hometown Reunion Ser.). 1997. per. 4.50 (0-373-82560-9, Harlequin) Harlequin Bks.

Mission: Earth: Voyage to the Home Planet. Thomas D. Jones & June A. English. LC 95-17474. 48p. (J). (gr. 3-10). 1996. 16.95 (0-590-48571-7) Scholastic Inc.

Mission: Impossible: Prima's Official Strategy Guide. Steve Honeywell. LC 98-66958. (Secrets of the Games Ser.). 96p. 1998. per. 12.99 (0-7615-1774-X) Prima Pub.

Mission: Improbable. Looney Tune Books Staff. (Looney Tunes Ser.). 1999. text 12.99 (0-8289-1026-X) Viking Penguin.

Mission: Irresistible. Sharon Sala. write for info. (0-373-15328-7) Harlequin Bks.

***Mission: Irresistible.** Sharon Sala. (Intimate Moments Ser.: Bk. 1016). 2000. mass mkt. 4.50 (0-373-27086-0, 1-27086-7) Silhouette.

Mission: Make-Over. large type ed. Penny Jordan. (Thorndike Harlequin Romance Ser.). 1998. 21.95 (0-263-15587-0, Pub. by Mills & Boon) Thorndike Pr.

Mission: Motherhood. Jule McBride. 1997. per. 3.75 (0-373-16693-1, 1-16693-3) Harlequin Bks.

Mission: The Small Church Reaches Out. Anthony Pappas & Scott Planting. LC 93-1337. (Small Church in Action Ser.). 128p. 1993. pap. 12.00 (0-8170-1174-9) Judson.

***Mission - Gegenstand der Praktischen Theologie? Die Missionstatigkeit der Kirche in Den Pastoraltheologischen Lehrbuchern Von der Aufklarung Bis Zum Zweiten Vatikanum Mit Einem Beitrag Von Ottmar Fuchs.** Franz Weber. 253p. 1999. 45.95 (3-631-34620-4) P Lang Pubng.

Mission a Rome. Jules Romains, pseud. (FRE., Illus.). 356p. 1958. pap. 14.95 (0-7859-1402-1, 2080506161) Fr & Eur.

Mission Accomplished. Albert E. Allen. LC 97-90878. 1998. pap. 12.95 (0-533-12502-2) Vantage.

***Mission Accomplished: A Practical Guide to Risk Management for Nonprofit.** 2nd ed. Peggy M. Jackson et al. 78p. 1999. pap., wbk. ed. 25.00 (1-893210-01-4) Nonprof Risk Mgmt Ctr.

Mission Accomplished: The Story of the VII Corps, United States Army, in the War Against Germany, 1944-1945. VII Corps, U. S. Army Staff. (World War II Monograph Ser.: Vol. 26). (Illus.). 71p. 1998. 27.95 (1-57638-113-7, M26); pap. 17.95 (1-57638-112-9, M26) Merriam Pr.

Mission Accomplished: The Work of Christ. Michael S. Horton. 1990. pap. 9.99 (0-85234-277-2, Pub. by Evangelical Pr) P & R Pubng.

Mission Accomplished: The Workbook. Peggy M. Jackson et al. 69p. 1997. pap., wbk. ed. 15.00 (0-9637120-6-3) Nonprof Risk Mgmt Ctr.

Mission-Addition. Loreen Leedy. LC 96-37149. (Illus.). 32p. (J). (gr. k-3). 1997. lib. bdg. 16.95 (0-8234-1307-1) Holiday.

Mission Adventures in Many Lands: Stories for Children. J. Lawrence Driskill. LC 92-15689. (Illus.). 212p. (J). (gr. 3-8). 1992. pap. 11.95 (0-932727-56-5); lib. bdg. 19.95 (0-932727-57-3) Hope Pub Hse.

***Mission Agendas in the New Century: A Summary of the Congress on the World Mission of the Church - St. Paul '98.** Roland E. Miller. 80p. 2000. pap. text 3.50 (1-886513-31-7) Kirk Hse Pubs.

Mission Albania: Ten Years of Vital Christian Work for the Albanian People. unabridged ed. Ed. by David M. Young. 80p. (Orig.). 1996. mass mkt. 6.99 (1-85792-278-6, Pub. by Christian Focus) Spring Arbor Dist.

Mission Alive! Gailyn Van Rheenen. LC 94-70221. 94p. 1994. pap. 3.95 (0-89112-157-9) Abilene Christ U.

Mission among the Blackfeet, Vol 112. Howard L. Harrod. (Civilization of the American Indian Ser.). 1999. pap. text 19.95 (0-8061-3153-5) U of Okla Pr.

Mission & Betrayal, 1940-1945: Working with Franklin Roosevelt to Help Save Britain & Europe. Rene De Chambrun. LC 92-35463. (Publication Ser.: Vol. 414). (Illus.). 228p. (C). 1993. text 33.95 (0-8179-9221-9); pap. text 18.95 (0-8179-9222-7) Hoover Inst Pr.

Mission & Business Philosophy. Andrew Campbell & Kiran Tawadey. 242p. 1993. pap. text 47.95 (0-7506-0509-X) Buttrwrth-Heinemann.

Mission & Catechesis: Alexander de Rhodes & Inculturation in the Seventeenth Century Vietnam. Peter C. Phan. LC 97-42447. (Faith & Culture Ser.). 300p. 1998. 50.00 (1-57075-166-8) Orbis Bks.

Mission & Change: Institutional Mission & Its Application to the Management of Further & Higher Education. Graham Peeke. LC 94-19796. 146p. 1994. pap. 39.95 (0-335-19338-2) OpUniv Pr.

Mission & Change: Institutional Mission & Its Application to the Management of Further & Higher Education. Graham Peeke. LC 94-19796. 160p. 1994. 122.00 (0-335-19337-4) Taylor & Francis.

Mission & Conversion: Proselytizing in the Religious History of the Roman Empire. Martin Goodman. 208p. 1996. pap. text 22.00 (0-19-826387-2) OUP.

Mission & Meaning: Essays Presented to Peter Cotterell. Ed. by Anthony Billington et al. xvi, 375p. 1995. reprint ed. pap. 25.00 (0-85364-676-7, Pub. by Paternoster Pub) OM Literature.

M

An Asterisk (*) at the beginning of an entry indicates that the title is appearing for the first time.

Mission & Message of Ramalinga Swamy. T. Dayanandan Francis. (C). 1990. 17.00 (*81-208-0661-1*, Pub. by Motilal Bnarsidass) S Asia.

Mission & Method: The Early Nineteenth-Century French Public Health Movement. Ann F. La Berge. (Cambridge History of Medicine Ser.). (Illus.). 396p. (C). 1992. text 80.00 (*0-521-40406-1*) Cambridge U Pr.

Mission & Ministry: A History of Virginia Theological Seminary. John E. Booty. LC 95-7419. (Illus.). 416p. 1995. 34.95 (*0-9644169-1-3*) Morehouse Pub.

Mission & Tamil Society: Social & Religious Change in South India 1840-1900. Henriette Bugge. LC 95-114743. (SIAS Monographs: No. 65). 220p. (C). 1996. pap. text 38.00 (*0-7007-0292-X*, Pub. by Curzon Pr Ltd) UH Pr.

Mission: Animal Watch: Super Coloring Book. Golden Books Staff. 56p. (ps-3). 1999. pap. text 2.29 (*0-307-28020-9*) Gldn Bks Pub Co.

***Mission Apollo.** Lewis Kerr. (Illus.). 32p. 1998. pap. 6.95 (*0-19-422804-5*) OUP.

Mission Arlington Story: Tillie's Vision. Erma H. Mathis. 80p. (Orig.). 1996. pap. 11.95 (*1-889730-02-5*, SPI0038) Scripta Pubng.

***Mission at the Dawn of the 21st Century: A Vision for the Church.** Ed. by Paul V. Martinson. LC 99-33588. 416p. 1999. pap. 15.95 (*1-886513-30-9*) Kirk Hse Pubs.

Mission Audacieuse. Joceline Sanschagrin. (Novels in the Roman Jeunesse Ser.). (FRE.). 96p. (J). (gr. 4-7). 1991. pap. 8.95 (*2-89021-156-8*, Pub. by La Courte Ech) Firefly Bks Ltd.

***Mission-Based Management: Leading Your Not-for-Profit in the 21st Century.** 2nd ed. Peter C. Brinckerhoff. 300p. 2000. 34.95 (*0-471-39013-5*) Wiley.

Mission-Based Management: Leading Your Not-for-Profit into the 21st Century. Peter C. Brinckerhoff. LC 94-28766. 272p. 1994. 29.95 (*0-931712-15-7*) Wiley.

***Mission-Based Management: Leading Your Not-for-Profit into 21st Century.** Peter C. Brinckerhoff. LC 98-25938. (Nonprofit Law, Finance, & Management Ser.). 272p. 1998. 52.95 (*0-471-29691-0*) Wiley.

Mission-Based Management Discussion Leader's Guide. Peter C. Brinckerhoff. (Mission-Based Management Ser.). 37p. 1995. spiral bd. 19.95 (*0-931712-17-3*) Wiley.

Mission-Based Marketing. Peter C. Brinckerhoff. LC 97-29488. (Mission-Based Management Ser.). 1997. 34.95 (*0-931712-23-8*) Wiley.

***Mission-Based Marketing: How Your Not-for-Profit Can Succeed in a More Competitive World.** Peter C. Brinckerhoff. LC 98-25934. (Nonprofit Law, Finance, & Management Ser.). 224p. 1998. 52.95 (*0-471-29693-7*) Wiley.

Mission Bells That Never Rang. Max Kurillo & E. M. Tuttle. 1995. pap. 8.00 (*0-87505-407-2*) Borden.

Mission Berlin. Ted Allbeury. 1986. 15.95 (*0-8027-0892-7*) Walker & Co.

Mission-Book of the Congregation of the Most Holy Redeemer. Redemptorist Pastoral Pubns. Staff & Alfonso M. Liguori. 1978. 42.95 (*0-405-10843-5*, 11848) Ayer.

Mission Child. Maureen F. McHugh. LC 98-8774. 400p. 1998. 20.00 (*0-380-97456-8*, Eos) Morrow Avon.

***Mission Child.** Maureen F. McHugh. LC 98-8774. 384p. 1999. mass mkt. 6.99 (*0-380-79122-6*, Avon Bks) Morrow Avon.

Mission, Church, & Sect in Oceania. Ed. by James A. Boutilier et al. (ASAO Monographs: No. 6). (Illus.). 514p. 1984. reprint ed. pap. text 40.50 (*0-8191-3838-X*); reprint ed. lib. bdg. 68.00 (*0-8191-3837-1*) U Pr of Amer.

Mission Cottes au Sud-Cameroun (1905-1908) A. Cottes. (B. E. Ser.: No. 145). (FRE.). 30.00 (*0-8115-3066-3*) Periodicals Srv.

Mission Critical: Death of the Phoenix: A Novel. Paul Chafe. 264p. 1996. mass mkt. 5.99 (*0-7615-0234-3*) Prima Pub.

Mission Critical: Re-Energizing Christianity for the First Demonstration of the Kingdom of God. Eugene C. Shults, Sr. (Illus.). 196p. 1996. pap. 14.50 (*0-9650250-6-3*) PRO-King Bks.

***Mission Critical: Realizing the Promise of Enterprise Systems.** Thomas H. Davenport. 2000. 29.95 (*0-87584-906-7*, HBS Pr) Harvard Busn.

Mission Critical: The Official Strategy Guide. Rick Barba. 1995. pap. text 19.95 (*0-7615-0177-0*) Prima Pub.

Mission Critical: The 7 Strategic Traps That Derail Even the Smartest Companies. Joseph C. Picken & Gregory G. Dess. LC 96-23782. 300p. 1996. text 29.95 (*0-7863-0969-5*, Irwn Prfssnl) McGraw-Hill Prof.

***Mission Critical Active Directory: Architecting a Secure & Scalable Infrastructure.** Micky Balladelli & Jan de Clercq. 512p. 2000. pap. 44.95 (*1-55558-240-0*, Digital DEC) Buttrwrth-Heinemann.

Mission Critical Computer Resources Management Guide. 1995. lib. bdg. 255.95 (*0-8490-7550-5*) Gordon Pr.

***Mission Critical Internetworking Security.** Syngress Media, Inc. Staff. 656p. 2000. pap. 59.95 (*1-928994-20-2*) Syngress.

Mission Critical Java Management: Business Strategies, Applications, & Development. Gregory Dennis. LC 98-8514. 272p. (C). 1998. pap. text 34.95 (*0-201-32573-X*) Addison-Wesley.

***Mission-Critical Microsoft Exchange 2000: Building Highly Available Messaging & Knowledge Management.** Jerry Cochran. (Illus.). 320p. 2000. pap. 34.95 (*1-55558-233-8*, Digital DEC) Buttrwrth-Heinemann.

Mission Critical Operating Systems. Ed. by A. K. Agrawala et al. LC 91-33762. (Studies in Computer & Communications Systems: Vol. 1). 392p. (gr. 12). 1992. 75.00 (*90-5199-069-3*, Pub. by IOS Pr) IOS Press.

Mission Critical Systems Management. Yuval Lirov. LC 97-3634. 640p. (C). 1997. 33.80 (*0-13-240292-0*) P-H.

***Mission Critical Windows 2000 Server Administration.** Syngress Media, Inc. Staff. 560p. 2000. pap. 49.95 (*1-928994-16-4*) Syngress.

Mission Culture on the Upper Amazon: Native Tradition, Jesuit Enterprise, & Secular Policy in Moxos, 1660-1880. David Block. LC 93-24620. (Illus.). xiii, 240p. 1994. text 40.00 (*0-8032-1232-1*) U of Nebr Pr.

Mission der Brudergemeinde in Suriname und Berbice Im Achtzehnten Jahrhundert, 3 vols. Fritz Staehelin. (Zinzendorf, Materialien und Dokumente Ser.: Reihe 2, Bd. XXVIII). (GER.). xlviii, 1264p. 1997. reprint ed. 560.00 (*3-487-10436-9*) G Olms Pubs.

Mission Design & Implementation of Satellite Constellations. Ha Van Der Jozej. LC 98-35403. (Space Technology Proceedings Ser.). 1998. 226.00 (*0-7923-5210-6*) Kluwer Academic.

Mission down Under. Linda Lowery Keep. LC 97-39285. (Hannah & the Angels Ser.: No. 1). 127p. (J). (gr. 3-6). 1998. pap. 3.99 (*0-679-89081-5*, Pub. by Random Bks Yng Read) Random.

***Mission-Driven Organization: From Mission Statements to a Thriving Organization, Here's Your Blueprint for Building an Inspired.** Mark Sobol et al. 237p. 1999. pap. 14.95 (*0-7615-1881-9*) Prima Pub.

Mission Earth: Modeling & Simulation for a Sustainable Future. Ed. by A. Martin Wildberger. (Illus.). 114p. (Orig.). 1995. pap. 60.00 (*1-56555-041-2*, ME-95) Soc Computer Sim.

Mission Earth: Modeling & Simulation for a Sustainable Global System. Ed. by Mark Clymer & Carlos Mechoso. 96p. 1997. pap. 60.00 (*1-56555-106-0*, ME-97) Soc Computer Sim.

***Mission Earth 1998.** Ed. by Achim Sydow & Jin-Yi Yu. 116p. 1998. 30.00 (*1-56555-139-7*) Soc Computer Sim.

Mission Failure & Survival. Charles C. McBride. (Illus.). 192p. (Orig.). 1989. pap. 17.95 (*0-89745-125-2*) Sunflower U Pr.

Mission: Faithful: A Christian Adventure Novel. N. Kay Carlson. 225p. 1999. pap. 7.95 (*0-9665487-2-8*) T Carlson.

Mission for Margaret see Saint Margaret Mary: And the Promises of the Sacred Heart of Jesus

Mission for Peace: Point 4 in Iran. William E. Warne. LC 98-42782. 336p. 1999. 28.00 (*0-936347-84-8*) IBEX.

Mission for the People: The Story of La Purisima. Mary Ann Fraser. LC 97-2692. 38p. 1998. 15.95 (*0-8050-5050-7*) H Holt & Co.

Mission Friends Guide. Kathy Burns. Ed. by Cindy McClain. 42p. (Orig.). 1995. pap. text 3.95 (*1-56309-131-3*, W958105) Womans Mission Union.

Mission Friends Planbook. Ed. by Cindy McClain. (Illus.). 39p. (Orig.). 1995. pap. text 2.95 (*1-56309-134-8*, W958106) Womans Mission Union.

Mission from Mount Yoda. Paul Davids. (Star Wars: No. 4). 128p. (YA). (gr. 4-7). 1993. pap. 4.50 (*0-553-15890-2*) Bantam.

Mission from Mount Yoda. Paul Davids. (Star Wars: No. 4). (YA). (gr. 4 up). 1993. 9.09 (*0-606-02755-6*, Pub. by Turtleback) Demco.

Mission from Mount Yoda. Paul Davids. (Star Wars: No. 4). (YA). (gr. 4 up). 1999. 9.50 (*0-7607-0447-3*, Pub. by Turtleback) Demco.

Mission from Mount Yoda see Star Wars

***Mission from Zeus.** Daniel J. Fingeroth. (Young Hercules Ser.: Vol. 1). 176p. (YA). 2000. per. 3.99 (*0-671-03553-3*, Archway) PB.

Mission Furniture: From the American Arts & Crafts Movement. Paul Royka. LC 97-80044. (Illus.). 256p. 1997. 69.95 (*0-88740-987-3*) Schiffer.

Mission Furniture: How to Make It. Popular Mechanics Co. Staff. (Illus.). vii, 342p. 1980. pap. 8.95 (*0-486-23966-7*) Dover.

Mission Furniture of L. & J. G. Stickley. rev. ed. Ed. by Stephen Gray. (Mission Furniture Catalogues Ser.: No. 6). 208p. 1989. pap. 20.00 (*0-940326-12-4*) Turn of Cent.

Mission Furniture You Can Build: Authentic Techniques & Designs for the Home Woodworker. John D. Wagner. Ed. by Barry Estabrook. LC 97-15962. (Illus.). 144p. 1997. pap. 20.00 (*1-57630-040-4*, Chapters Bks) HM.

Mission Handbook, 1998-2000. Ed. by John A. Siewert & Edna G. Valdez. 500p. 1998. pap. 49.95 (*1-887983-02-3*) MARC.

Mission: Impossible. Peter Barsocchini. 1996. mass mkt. 5.99 (*0-671-54921-9*) PB.

Mission Impossible. Beth Goobie. (Northern Lights Young Novels Ser.). 160p. (YA). (gr. 10 up). 1994. pap. 8.95 (*0-88995-114-4*, Pub. by Red Deer) Genl Dist Srvs.

Mission Impossible. Janet McHenry. 48p. (J). 1996. mass mkt. 3.99 (*0-7814-0255-7*) Chariot Victor.

***Mission Impossible.** Prima Publishing Staff. (Official Strategy Guides Ser.). (Illus.). 94p. (YA). 1999. pap. 12.99 (*0-7615-2758-3*) Prima Pub.

Mission Impossible: Ring of Fire. Tom Philbin. 1996. mass mkt. 5.99 (*0-671-00233-3*) PB.

Mission Impossible: The Aztec Imperative. James Luceno. 1996. mass mkt. 5.99 (*0-671-00232-5*) PB.

Mission Impossible: The Tokyo Mandate. Anthony Bruno. 1996. mass mkt. 5.99 (*0-671-00231-7*) PB.

Mission Impossible: The Unreached Nosu on China's Frontier. Ralph R. Covell. LC 89-19918. (Illus.). 310p. 1990. pap. 12.95 (*0-932727-35-2*); lib. bdg. 17.95 (*0-932727-38-7*) Hope Pub Hse.

Mission: Impractical. David A. McIntee. (Doctor Who Ser.). 1998. pap. 5.95 (*0-563-40592-9*) BBC.

Mission Improbable: The World Community on a U. N. Compound in Somalia. Helen Fogarassy et al. LC 98-48275. 3p. 1999. 45.00 (*0-7391-0020-3*) Lxngtn Bks.

Mission Improbable: Using Fantasy Documents to Tame Disasters. Lee B. Clarke. LC 98-40808. 216p. 1991. pap. text 14.95 (*0-226-10942-9*) U Ch Pr.

***Mission Improbable: Using Fantasy Documents to Tame Disasters.** Lee B. Clarke. LC 98-40808. 216p. 1999. 25.00 (*0-226-10941-0*) U Ch Pr.

Mission in a Pluralist World. Ed. by Aasulv Lande & Werner Ustorf. (Studies in the Intercultural History of Christianity: Vol. 97). 193p. 1996. pap. 42.95 (*3-631-49430-0*) P Lang Pubng.

Mission in a Pluralist World. Ed. by Aasulv Lande & Werner Ustorf. LC 95-52830. (Studies in the Intercultural History of Christianity: Bd. 97). 193p. 1996. pap. 42.95 (*0-8204-2973-2*, BV2063) P Lang Pubng.

Mission in Art: Recent Holocaust Works in America. Vivian Thompson. LC 88-10038. 155p. 1988. pap. 19.95 (*0-86554-309-7*, MUP/P055) Mercer Univ Pr.

Mission in Bold Humility: David Bosch's Work Considered. Ed. by Willem Saayman & Klippies Kritzinger. LC 96-46650. 250p. (Orig.). 1996. pap. 20.00 (*1-57075-087-4*) Orbis Bks.

Mission in Christ's Way: A Gift, a Command, an Assurance. Lesslie Newbigin. 48p. 1988. pap. 2.95 (*0-377-00190-2*) Friendship Pr.

Mission in Christ's Way: Bible Studies. Lesslie Newbigin. (Mission Ser.: No. 8). 48p. (Orig.). 1987. pap. 2.90 (*2-8254-0900-6*) Wrld Coun Churches.

Mission in der Industrie: Die Geschichte Kirchlicher Industrie- und Sozialarbeit in Grobbritannien. Bernd Fechner. (Erfahrung und Theologie Ser.: Bd. 25). (GER.). 266p. 1995. 46.95 (*3-631-48630-8*) P Lang Pubng.

Mission in Dialogue: The Sedos Research Seminar on the Future of Mission, March 8-19, 1981, Rome, Italy. SEDOS Research Seminar on the Future of Mission St. Ed. by Mary Motte & Joseph R. Lang. LC 82-2258. 704p. 1982. reprint ed. pap. 200.00 (*0-7837-9819-9*, 206054800005) Bks Demand.

Mission in Life. Edward Hunter-Blair. 148p. (C). 1989. pap. text 45.00 (*0-946270-39-2*, Pub. by Pentland Pr) St Mut.

Mission in Mufti: Brazil's Military Regimes, 1964-1985, 255. Wilfred A. Bacchus. LC 89-26069. (Contributions in Political Science Ser.: No. 255). (Illus.). 184p. 1990. 52.95 (*0-313-25535-0*, BMM/, Greenwood Pr) Greenwood.

Mission in Palestine, 1948 to 1952. Pablo De Azcarate. LC 66-30659. 1966. 3.00 (*0-916808-07-6*) Mid East Inst.

Mission in the Marketplace. Jeffrey W. Comment. Ed. by Jim Hughey & Shifra Stein. (Illus.). 200p. (Orig.). Date not set. pap. 11.95 (*0-9647405-0-8*) MITM.

Mission in the New Testament: An Evangelical Approach. Ed. by William J. Larkin, Jr. & Joel F. Williams. LC 97-38902. (American Society of Missiology Ser.: No. 27). 176p. (Orig.). 1998. pap. 20.00 (*1-57075-169-2*) Orbis Bks.

***Mission in the Old Testament: Israel as a Light to the Nations.** Walter C. Kaiser. LC 99-50219. 112p. 2000. pap. 8.99 (*0-8010-2228-2*) Baker Bks.

***Mission in Today's World.** Donal Dorr. 308p. 2000. pap. 20.00 (*1-57075-339-3*) Orbis Bks.

Mission Incomprehensible: The Linguistic Barrier to Effective Police Co-Operation in Europe. Roy D. Ingleton. LC 93-29933. 186p. 1994. 69.00 (*1-85359-214-5*, Pub. by Multilingual Matters); pap. 24.95 (*1-85359-213-7*, Pub. by Multilingual Matters) Taylor & Francis.

Mission Jupiter: The Spectacular Journey of the Galileo Space Probe. Daniel Fischer. LC 99-31342. (Illus.). 256p. 1999. 30.00 (*0-387-98764-9*) Spr-Verlag.

Mission la Concepcion Parisima. Zephyrin Engelhardt. 144p. (Orig.). 1986. 15.00 (*0-87461-066-4*); pap. 7.50 (*0-87461-067-2*) McNally & Loftin.

Mission (La Mision) Spanish. Ed. by Kay S. McKean & Randy McKean. (Daily Power Ser.). 154p. 1995. pap. 7.99 (*1-884553-61-3*) Discipleshp.

Mission La Purisima Concepcion see Missions of California

Mission Legacies: Biographical Studies of Leaders of the Modern Missionary Movements. Ed. by Gerald H. Anderson et al. LC 94-16771. (American Society of Missiology Ser.: Vol. 19). 640p. 1994. 38.00 (*0-88344-964-1*) Orbis Bks.

Mission Management Vol. 1: A New Synthesis. Ed. by Roger J. Bulger et al. 25.00 (*1-879694-13-1*) AAH Ctrs.

Mission Management Vol. 2: A New Synthesis. Ed. by Elaine R. Rubin. LC 98-19149. 1998. pap. 30.00 (*1-879694-12-3*) AAH Ctrs.

Mission Mania: A Cartoonist's View of the Best 2 Years of Life. Val C. Bagley. (Illus.). 98p. (Orig.). 1980. pap. 6.98 (*0-88290-140-0*) Horizon Utah.

Mission Marchand, 1895 to 1899. Marc Michel. (Monde d'Outre Mer Passe & Present, Etudes Ser.: No. 36). (Illus.). 1972. pap. 49.25 (*90-279-7153-6*) Mouton.

Mission Mathematics 5-8: Linking Aerospace & the NCTM Standards. Ed. by Vincent F. O'Connor & Michael C. Hynes. LC 97-42145. (Illus.). 136p. 1997. pap. 22.95 (*0-87353-435-2*) NCTM.

Mission Mathematics K-6: Linking Aerospace & the NCTM Standards. Ed. by Mary Ellen Hynes. LC 97-8167. (Illus.). 120p. (J). (gr. k-6). 1997. pap. 22.95 (*0-87353-434-4*) NCTM.

Mission Mathematics 9-12: Linking Aerospace & the NCTM Standards. Peggy House & Mary J. Aiken. LC 97-12780. (Illus.). 121p. (YA). (gr. 9-12). 1997. pap. 22.95 (*0-87353-436-0*) NCTM.

Mission Matters. Ed. by Lynne Price et al. (Studies in the Intercultural History of Christianity: Vol. 103). 232p. 1997. pap. 44.95 (*3-631-31513-9*) P Lang Pubng.

Mission Matters. Ed. by Lynne Price et al. (Studies in the Intercultural History of Christianity: Vol. 103). 232p. 1997. pap. 44.95 (*0-8204-3265-2*) P Lang Pubng.

Mission Matters: A Report on the Future of Voluntary Health Care Institutions. J. David Seay & Bruce C. Vladeck. 47p. 1987. 5.00 (*0-934459-36-3*) United Hosp Fund.

Mission: Mayhem. Franklin W. Dixon. Ed. by Ruth Ashby. LC 00-1314. (Hardy Boys Casefiles Ser.: No. 93). 160p. (YA). (gr. 7-12). 1994. pap. 3.99 (*0-671-88204-X*, Archway) PB.

Mission: Mayhem. Franklin W. Dixon. (Hardy Boys Casefiles Ser.: No. 93). (YA). (gr. 6 up). 1994. 9.09 (*0-606-07002-8*, Pub. by Turtleback) Demco.

Mission Memoirs: A Collection of Photographs, Illustrations & Late Twentieth-Century Reflections of California's Past. Terry Ruscin. LC 99-20322. (Illus.). 200p. 1999. 50.00 (*0-932653-30-8*) Sunbelt Pubns.

Mission Mobilizers Handbook. Ed. by Dave Imboden. (Illus.). 135p. 1996. pap. 8.95 (*0-87808-270-0*, WCL270-0) William Carey Lib.

Mission Moments: Laugh-Filled Missionary Cartoons. Ryan Stoker. (Illus.). 96p. 1992. pap. 7.98 (*0-88290-454-X*) Horizon Utah.

Mission Music of California. Ed. by Arthur Bienbar. Tr. by Owen F. Da Silva. LC 77-16531. (Music Reprint Ser.). (Illus.). 1978. reprint ed. lib. bdg. 39.50 (*0-306-77524-7*) Da Capo.

Mission Nuestra Senora de la Soledad see Missions of California

Mission Number Three: Missing in Action. Charles A. Fisher et al. LC 98-4278. 98p. 1998. 25.00 (*1-885851-11-1*) St Vincent Coll.

Mission of Art. Alex Grey. LC 98-16930. 280p. 1999. 27.50 (*1-57062-396-1*, Pub. by Shambhala Pubns) Random.

Mission of Danger. Clarias Burns. 185p. (Orig.). 1996. pap. 4.95 (*0-9645041-1-1*) Cntryside Pub.

Mission of Gravity. Hal Clement. 1993. reprint ed. lib. bdg. 18.95 (*0-89968-336-3*, Lghtyr Pr) Buccaneer Bks.

Mission of Israel. Jacob Baal-Teshuva. 1963. 10.95 (*0-8315-0046-8*) Speller.

Mission of Jane, Set. unabridged ed. Edith Wharton. (Edith Wharton Ser.). 1994. 16.95 incl. audio (*1-883049-15-6*, 390233, Pub. by Sound Room) Lndmrk Audiobks.

Mission of Jane: Library Edition. unabridged ed. Edith Wharton. 1994. lib. bdg. 18.95 incl. audio (*1-883049-36-9*) Sound Room.

Mission of Murder. large type ed. Robert Charles. (Linford Mystery Library). 416p. 1998. pap. 17.99 (*0-7089-5221-6*, Linford) Ulverscroft.

Mission of San Luis Rey de Francia see Missions of California

Mission of Sorrows: Jesuit Guevari & the Pimas, 1691-1767. John L. Kessell. LC 79-101098. 240p. reprint ed. pap. 74.40 (*0-608-13659-X*, 205524800011) Bks Demand.

Mission of Spiritual Science & of Its Building at Dornach, Switzerland. Rudolf Steiner. 63p. 1993. reprint ed. spiral bd. 8.00 (*0-7873-0824-2*) Hlth Research.

Mission of Spiritual Science & of Its Building at Dornach, Switzerland (1916) Rudolf Steiner. 63p. 1996. reprint ed. pap. 6.95 (*1-56459-705-9*) Kessinger Pub.

Mission of the Church in Methodist Perspective: The World Is My Parish. Ed. by Alan G. Padgett. LC 92-34032. (Studies in the History of Missions: Vol. 10). 196p. 1992. text 79.95 (*0-7734-9157-0*) E Mellen.

Mission of the Columbia. Jean B. Bolduc. 144p. 1979. 19.95 (*0-87770-216-0*) Ye Galleon.

Mission of the Messiah. Tim Gray. Ed. by Leon J. Suprenant, Jr. 150p. 1998. pap. 9.95 (*0-9663223-1-2*) Emmaus Road.

Mission of The Messiah (Three) Ed. by Chung H. Kwak. (Home Study Course). 40p. (Orig.). (C). 1980. pap. 4.00 (*0-910621-12-8*) HSA Pubns.

Mission of the Prophets. Adrienne Von-Speyr. LC 96-83644. 125p. 1996. pap. text 9.95 (*0-89870-593-2*) Ignatius Pr.

Mission of the Redeemer: Redemptoris Missio. John Paul, II, pseud. 125p. pap. 4.95 (*0-8198-4746-1*) Pauline Bks.

Mission of the University. Jose Ortega y Gasset. 120p. (C). 1991. pap. text 24.95 (*1-56000-560-2*) Transaction Pubs.

Mission of the Wind. R. D. Schmidt et al. 40p. (Orig.). (C). 1996. pap. 3.00 (*1-882294-09-2*) Green Gate.

Mission of Theology & Theology As Mission. J. Andrew Kirk. LC 96-49155. (Christian Mission & Modern Culture Ser.). 64p. (Orig.). 1996. pap. 7.00 (*1-56338-189-3*) TPI PA.

Mission of This Generation: Messages from the Universal House of Justice to Baha'i Youth. Universal House of Justice Staff. 128p. 1997. pap. 12.95 (*1-870989-72-4*) Bahai.

Mission on the Ho Chi Minh Trail: Mature, Myth & War in Vietnam. Richard L. Stevens. LC 95-10198. (Illus.). 288p. 1995. 24.95 (*0-8061-2768-6*) U of Okla Pr.

Mission on the Margins. Mary Beasley. 110p. 1998. pap. 13.95 (*0-7188-2966-2*, Lutterworth-Parkwest) Parkwest Pubns.

Mission on the Mesa: History of St. Paul United Methodist Church, Pueblo, Colorado. O. Ray Dodson. (Orig.). 1994. pap. text 10.95 (*0-9620550-6-9*, Prairie Heritage Pr) Dodson Assocs.

Mission on the Rhine: Reeducation & De-Nazification in American-Occupied Germany. James F. Tent. LC 82-4896. 388p. (C). 1983. pap. text 16.00 (*0-226-79358-3*) U Ch Pr.

Mission on the Way: Issues in Mission Theology. Charles Van Engen. LC 96-41593. 306p. (C). 1996. pap. 24.99 (*0-8010-2090-5*) Baker Bks.

Mission Overseas: A Handbook for U. S. Families in Developing Countries. Harold D. Guither & W. N. Thompson. LC 76-76828. 300p. 1969. pap. text 12.50 (*0-252-00017-X*) U of Ill Pr.

Mission Padre. David Stienecker. LC 94-743. (How They Lived Ser.). 32p. (J). (gr. 3-8). 1994. lib. bdg. 21.27 (*1-55916-040-3*) Rourke Bk Co.

An Asterisk (*) at the beginning of an entry indicates that the title is appearing for the first time.

Mission Planner: So You Want to Take Your Kids on a Mission Trip. Mark Schaufler. 20p. 1996. spiral bd. 2.00 (*1-886904-31-6*) MST Minist.

Mission Possible. Blanchard. 1999. pap. 14.95 (*0-07-134827-1*) McGraw.

Mission Possible. Deborah S. Koch et al. LC 98-145478. (Orig.). 1998. pap. text. write for info. (*1-886949-13-1*) Union Inst.

Mission Possible. Marilyn Laszlo. LC 98-25029. 1998. 9.99 (*0-8423-3881-0*) Tyndale Hse.

Mission Possible. D. Marsh. 1997. pap. 7.00 (*0-7601-1523-0*) Brentwood Music.

Mission Possible. Raymond Murn. 1973. pap. 2.50 (*0-8341-1021-0*) Nazarene.

Mission Possible: Adventures in Faith. Liz VonSeggen. (Illus.). 131p. 1998. pap. text 30.00 (*1-58302-050-0*, BTU-11) One Way St.

Mission Possible: Becoming a World Class Organization While There's Still Time. Kenneth Blanchard & Terry Waghorn. LC 96-77499. 220p. 1996. 22.00 (*0-07-005940-3*) McGraw.

Mission Possible: Churches Supporting Fragile Families. Ed. by Ruth Graham. 34p. (Orig.). 1992. reprint ed. pap. 5.95 (*0-934513-78-3*) Natl Crime DC.

***Mission Possible: True Stories of Special Pet Adoptions from the San Francisco SPCA.** Edwin Sayres. 2000. 17.99 (*0-7645-6237-1*) IDG Bks.

M

***Mission Primer: Four Steps to an Effective Mission Statement.** Richard D. O'Hallaron & David R. O'Hallaron. LC 99-91651. 136p. 2000. per. 19.00 (*0-9676635-0-4*) Mission Inc.

Mission Quest: Quest for Character. Charlene Gray. (MissionsQuest Ser.). (Illus.). 24p. (YA). (gr. 10). 1998. pap. text 3.95 (*1-56309-242-5*, W986114) Womans Mission Union.

Mission Quest: Quest for Courage. Julie Massey. (MissionsQuest Ser.). 24p. (J). (gr. 8). 1998. pap. text 3.95 (*1-56309-240-9*, W986112) Womans Mission Union.

Mission Quest: Quest for Creativity. Charlene Gray. (MissionsQuest Ser.). 24p. (YA). (gr. 9). 1998. pap. text 3.95 (*1-56309-241-7*, W986113) Womans Mission Union.

Mission Quest: Quest for Excellence. Cindy Gaskins. (Illus.). 24p. (YA). (gr. 11). 1998. pap. text 3.95 (*1-56309-243-3*, W986115) Womans Mission Union.

Mission Quest: Quest for Vision. Cindy Gaskins. (MissionsQuest Ser.). 24p. (YA). (gr. 12). 1998. pap. text 3.95 (*1-56309-244-1*, W986116) Womans Mission Union.

Mission Quest Journal: Quest Reflections. DeAnna Sanders. (MissionsQuest Ser.). (Illus.). 118p. (J). (gr. 11). 1998. pap. text 9.95 (*1-56309-262-X*, W986124) Womans Mission Union.

Mission Record of the California Indians. fac. ed. A. L. Kroeber. (University of California Publications in American Archaeology & Ethnology: Vol. 8: 1). 27p. (C). 1908. reprint ed. pap. text 3.13 (*1-55567-180-2*) Coyote Press.

***Mission S. T. A. R. (Space Travel & Recreation)** Candy Cain Spahr. 50p. (J). (gr. k-6). 2000. pap. 4.00 (*1-58193-189-1*) Brown Bag Prods.

Mission San Antonio de Padua see Missions of California

Mission San Buenaventura see Missions of California

Mission San Carlos Borromeo del Rio Carmela see Missions of California

Mission San Diego de Alcala see Missions of California

Mission San Fernando Rey de Espana see Missions of California

Mission San Francisco de Asis see Missions of California

Mission San Francisco de Solano see Missions of California

Mission San Gabriel Arcangel see Missions of California

Mission San Jose de Guadalupe see Missions of California

Mission San Juan Bautista see Missions of California

Mission San Juan Capistrano see Missions of California

Mission San Luis Obispo de Tolosa see Missions of California

Mission San Miguel Arcangel see Missions of California

Mission San Rafael Arcangel see Missions of California

Mission Santa Barbara see Missions of California

Mission Santa Clara de Asia see Missions of California

Mission Santa Cruz see Missions of California

Mission Santa Ines see Missions of California

Mission Santa Ines. Zephyrin Engelhardt. LC 85-23977. (Missions & Missionaries of California Ser.). (Illus.). 202p. (Orig.). 1986. reprint ed. 16.50 (*0-87461-063-X*); reprint ed. pap. 7.50 (*0-87461-062-1*) McNally & Loftin.

Mission Santa Ines: The Hidden Gem. Cresencia Olmstead & Dale Olmstead. LC 95-661321. (Illus.). 25p. (Orig.). 1995. pap. 8.95 (*0-9646858-0-9*) Old Mission Santa Ines.

Mission Scientifique au Mexique et dans l'Amerique Centrale . . . Recherches Zoologiques: Etude des Batraciens de l'Amerque Centrale. Paul Brocchi. Ed. by Keir B. Sterling. LC 77-81099. (Biologists & Their World Ser.). (Illus.). 1978. reprint ed. lib. bdg. 19.95 (*0-405-10681-5*) Ayer.

Mission Scientifique au Mexique et dans l'Amerique Centrale . . . Recherches Zoologiques: Etude Sur les Reptiles, Avec Atlas, 2 vols. Auguste H. Dumeril et al. Ed. by Keir B. Sterling. LC 77-81098. (Biologists & Their World Ser.). (FRE., Illus.). 1978. reprint ed. lib. bdg. 121.95 (*0-405-10680-7*) Ayer.

Mission Statement Book: 301 Corporate Mission Statements from America's Top Companies. rev. ed. Jeffrey Abrahams. LC 99-23607. 640p. 1999. pap. text 21.95 (*1-58008-132-0*) Ten Speed Pr.

Mission Statements: A Guide to the Corporate & Nonprofit Sectors. John W. Graham & Wendy Havlick. LC 94-540. (Reference Library of Social Science: Vol. 900). 576p. 1994. text 99.00 (*0-8153-1297-0*) Garland.

***Mission Statements for College Libraries.** 2nd rev. ed. Compiled by Jamie Hastreiter et al. LC 99-34722. (CLIP Notes Ser.: Vol. 28). 110p. (C). 1999. pap. 22.00 (*0-8389-8047-3*) Assn Coll & Res Libs.

Mission Stories from Around the World: Stories for Children. J. Lawrence Driskill. LC 93-39413. 178p. (J). (gr. 4-8). 1994. pap. 11.95 (*0-932727-71-9*); lib. bdg. 19.95 (*0-932727-72-7*) Hope Pub Hse.

Mission Success! Og Mandino. 176p. (Orig.). 1987. mass mkt. 6.99 (*0-553-26500-8*) Bantam.

Mission Tales in the Days of the Dons. Harrie R. Forbes. LC 71-128735. (Short Story Index Reprint Ser.). (Illus.). 1977. 23.95 (*0-8369-3626-4*) Ayer.

***Mission, The Method, This Magic: The Insight on Network Marketing.** large type ed. James Morrison & Stewart Taub. 184p. 2000. pap. 19.95 (*0-9676131-0-8*) Millennium DE.

Mission 3:16 Devotional. Carman. 144p. 1998. pap. 9.99 (*1-57778-098-1*, Pub. by Albury Pub) Appalach Bk Dist.

Mission Through a Woman's Eyes. Olivia Casberg. LC 84-27232. 120p. (Orig.). 1985. pap. 6.95 (*0-933380-31-3*) Olive Pr Pubns.

Mission to Abisko: Stories & Myths in the Creation of Scientific "Truth" John L. Casti. Ed. by Anders Karlqvist. 1998. 25.00 (*0-7382-0002-6*) Perseus Pubng.

***Mission to Abisko: Stories & Myths in the Creation of Scientific "Truth"** Ed. by John L. Casti & Anders Karlqvist. 208p. 1999. pap. text 13.00 (*0-7382-0167-7*, Pub. by Perseus Pubng) HarpC.

***Mission to America: A History of Saint Vincent Archabbey, the First Benedictine Monastery in the United States.** Jerome Oetgen. LC 99-34694. 2000. 39.95 (*0-8132-0957-9*) Cath U Pr.

Mission to America: 5 Islamic Sectarian Communities in North America. Yvonne Y. Haddad & Jane I. Smith. LC 93-18255. (Illus.). 232p. 1993. 49.95 (*0-8130-1216-3*); pap. 19.95 (*0-8130-1217-1*) U Press Fla.

Mission to Argana. large type ed. Jean Marsh. (Lythway Ser.). 200p. 1990. 19.95 (*0-7451-1127-0*, G K Hall Lrg Type) Mac Lib Ref.

Mission to Asia. Christopher Dawson. (Medieval Academy Reprints for Teaching Ser.). 228p. 1981. reprint ed. pap. text 13.95 (*0-8020-6436-1*) U of Toronto Pr.

Mission to Bhutan: Nation in Transition. B. S. Das. (C). 1995. 21.00 (*0-7069-9470-1*, Pub. by Vikas) S Asia.

Mission to Civilize: The Republican Idea of Empire in France & West Africa, 1895-1930. Alice L. Conklin. LC 97-9868. 446p. 1997. 55.00 (*0-8047-2999-9*) Stanford U Pr.

***Mission to Civilize: The Republican Idea of Empire in France & West Africa, 1895-1930.** Alice L. Conklin. 2000. pap. text 24.95 (*0-8047-4012-7*) Stanford U Pr.

Mission to Educate: A History of the Educational Work of the Scottish Presbyterian Mission in East Nigeria, 1846-1960. William H. Taylor. LC 96-32131. (Studies of Religion in Africa). xii, 281p. 1996. 110.00 (*90-04-10713-4*) Brill Academic Pubs.

Mission to India: From Confrontation to Cooperation. Stanley Kalpage. LC 96-912023. (C). 1997. 28.00 (*81-259-0218-X*, Pub. by Vikas) S Asia.

***Mission to Japan: Travels Through a Missionary Career** Theodore O. Cox. LC 99-180084. 187 p. 1998. write for info. (*1-55630-874-4*) Brentwood Comm.

Mission to Kala. Mongo Beti. (African Writers Ser.). 192p. (C). 1964. pap. 8.95 (*0-435-90013-7*, 90013) Heinemann.

Mission to Korea: Thirty-Eight Years Below the Thirty-Eighth. Joe B. Hopper. LC 98-68425. (Illus.). 288p. 1999. pap. 18.95 (*1-57736-127-X*) Providence Hse.

Mission to Latin America: The Successes & Failures of a Twentieth-Century Crusade. Gerald M. Costello. LC 78-12974. 319p. reprint ed. pap. 98.90 (*0-8357-8956-X*, 203357000086) Bks Demand.

Mission to Lianna. 64p. 1992. pap., per. 10.00 (*0-87431-123-3*, 40052) West End Games.

***Mission to Malaspiga.** large type ed. Evelyn Anthony. LC 00-35833. 370p. 2000. lib. bdg. 27.95 (*1-58547-042-2*) Ctr Point Pubg.

Mission to Mankind: A Cosmic Autobiography. Robert E. Birdsong. LC 74-18195. 1975. 6.35 (*0-917108-12-4*); pap. 3.50 (*0-917108-08-6*) Sirius Bks.

Mission to Mars & Beyond. Vince DeSomma. Ed. by William H. Goetzmann. (World Explorers Ser.). (Illus.). 120p. (YA). (gr. 5 up). 1992. lib. bdg. 19.95 (*0-7910-1325-1*) Chelsea Hse.

Mission to Mexico: A Tale of British Diplomacy in the 1820s. Henry McKenzie-Johnstone. 300p. 1992. text 59.50 (*1-85043-555-3*, Pub. by I B T) St Martin.

Mission to Millboro. Marge Rieder. LC 93-6003. (Illus.). 208p. 1993. pap. 13.00 (*0-931892-59-7*) B Dolphin Pub.

***Mission to Millions.** Victor Maxwell. 183p. 2000. pap. 9.99 (*1-84030-069-8*, Ambassador-Emerald) Emerald House Group Inc.

Mission to Moscow. Ed. by David Culbert. (Warner Bros. Screenplay Ser.). (Illus.). 280p. 1980. 14.95 (*0-299-08380-2*); pap. 9.95 (*0-299-08384-5*) U of Wis Pr.

Mission to Planet Earth: Background & Issues: Public Policy Workshop Report. 45p. 1990. pap. 14.95 (*1-56347-201-5*, PP-10) AIAA.

***Mission to Planet X: Internet Coach.** 2nd rev. ed. APTE Staff. (Illus.). 81p. 1999. spiral bd. 25.00 (*1-889651-53-2*) APTE.

Mission to Pomerania Where Bonhoeffer Met the Holocaust: A History & Traveler's Journal. 2nd expanded ed. Jane Pejsa. LC 00-91150. (Illus.). 100p. 2000. pap. 14.95 (*0-9612776-7-X*) Kenwood Pub.

Mission to Seduce. Sally Wentworth. (Presents Ser.: No. 2018). 1999. per. 3.75 (*0-373-12018-4*, 1-12018-7) Harlequin Bks.

Mission to Serve: The Life of John A. Scherzer & the Birth of Fellowship Square Foundation. Jack Erickson. (Illus.). 112p. (Orig.). 1989. pap. 8.95 (*0-941397-03-3*) Redbrick Pr.

Mission to Shanghai: The Life of Medical Service of Dr. Josiah C. McCracken. Helen M. Fulcher. LC 95-60506. (Illus.). xii, 276p. 1995. 12.95 (*0-9646018-1-8*) Tiffin Pr ME.

Mission to Sonora. Rebecca Cramer. 298p. 1998. pap. 10.95 (*1-881542-50-5*) Book World Inc.

***Mission to the Arctic.** Nicola Baxter. (Dorling Kindersley Readers). 48p. (J). (gr. 2-3). 2000. 12.95 (*0-7894-6095-5*, D K Ink); pap. text 3.95 (*0-7894-5459-9*, D K Ink) DK Pub Inc.

Mission to the Catskills: A History of Immanuel Lutheran Church of Delhi, New York. Paul R. Hinlicky. 96p. 1991. pap. text 10.00 (*1-881579-02-6*) Theophilus Pr.

Mission to the Jews. Harman. 1996. pap. 16.99 (*1-85792-258-1*, Pub. by Christian Focus) Spring Arbor Dist.

***Mission to the Lord Sophy of Persia (1539-1542) Translated with Introduction & Notes.** 2nd ed. Michele Membre. Ed. by A. H. Morton. 144p. (C). 1999. pap. 32.00 (*0-906094-43-7*, Pub. by Gibb Memorial Trust) David Brown.

Mission to the Planets: The Illustrated Story of Man's Exploration of the Solar System. Patrick Moore. 1990. 24.95 (*0-393-02872-0*) Norton.

Mission to the Space Station. Christopher Carrie. (Crayola Color & Activity Ser.). (Illus.). 40p. (J). (gr. k up). 1990. 1.59 (*0-86696-247-6*) Binney & Smith.

Mission to Yenan: American Liaison with the Chinese Communists, 1944-1947. Carolle J. Carter. LC 96-53110. (Illus.). 296p. 1997. 39.95 (*0-8131-2015-2*) U Pr of Ky.

Mission Trail. Photos by Michael R. Moses. (Illus.). 24p. (Orig.). 1997. pap. 10.00 (*0-944551-14-9*) Sundance Pr TX.

Mission 21: Level III Sampler. Brusic. (Tech & Industrial Education Ser.). 1991. pap. write for info. (*0-8273-4896-7*) Delmar.

Mission 2000: A Document to Direct Off-Highway Motor Vehicle Recreation into the Twenty-First Century. 16p. pap. text 10.00 (*0-9999013-2-X*) DIANE Pub.

Mission 2000 - Year B: Daily Meditations Based on the Lectionary, Cycle B. Mark Link. (Mark Link, S. J., Library). 412p. 1993. pap. 8.95 (*0-7829-0048-8*, 22046) Res Christian Liv.

Mission 2009. 1990. 10.00 (*0-914422-19-7*) Glenmary Res Ctr.

Mission und Kirche in Sambia (1875-1994) Aleksander Bejger. (Europaische Hochschulschriften Ser.: Reihe 23, Bd. 584). (GER., Illus.). 818p. 1996. 114.95 (*3-631-30154-5*) P Lang Pubng.

***Mission Values & Leadership Styles in Credit Unions.** Ramon J. Aldag & David Antonioni. 90p. 1999. pap. 100.00 (*1-880572-42-7*, 1752-54) Filene Res.

Mission with a Difference: The Exploits of 71 Mountain Brigade. P. N. Kathpalia. 126p. 1986. 16.50 (*0-685-67629-3*, Pub. by Lancer India) Nataraj Bks.

Mission Without a Mandate: U. S. Foreign Aid after the Cold War. Steven W. Hook. (Pew Case Studies in International Affairs). 50p. (C). 1997. pap. text 3.50 (*1-56927-378-2*) Geo U Inst Dplmcy.

Mission Work in Today's World: Insights & Outlook. J. Samuel Hofman. LC 92-72007. 288p. (Orig.). 1993. 8.95 (*0-87808-234-4*, WCL234-4) William Carey Lib.

Mission Write. Lucy K. Berardi. (Illus.). (Orig.). (J). (gr. 7-8). 1978. pap. 1.80 (*0-915441-00-4*); pap., student ed. 1.80 (*0-915441-01-2*); student ed. 1.00 (*0-915441-04-7*); 15.00 (*0-915441-02-0*); 15.00 (*0-915441-03-9*); 1.00 (*0-915441-05-5*); 1.00 (*0-915441-06-3*); 15.00 (*0-915441-07-1*) Mission Write.

***Mission Year Book.** Mark S. J. Link. 1999. pap. 8.95 (*0-88347-457-3*, Pub. by T More) BookWorld.

Mission Ziffoid. Michael Rosen. LC 98-33760. (Illus.). (J). (ps-k). 1999. pap. text 3.29 (*0-7636-0806-8*) Candlewick Pr.

Mission Ziffoid. Michael Rosen. LC 98-33760. (Illus.). 24p. (YA). (ps up). 1999. text 10.99 (*0-7636-0805-X*) Candlewick Pr.

Mission Zone. M. Ellis. 1999. pap. text 10.99 (*1-85792-446-0*) Christian Focus.

***Missional Church: The People of God Sent on a Mission.** Ed. by Darrell L. Guder. LC 97-32962. (Gospel & Our Culture Ser.). 288p. 1998. pap. 26.00 (*0-8028-4350-6*) Eerdmans.

Missionaries. (Bible People Ser.). 80p. 1996. pap. 5.95 (*0-687-05558-X*) Abingdon.

Missionaries & a Hindu State: Travancore 1858-1936. Koji Kawashima. LC 98-903529. (Illus.). 264p. 1998. text 26.00 (*0-19-564318-6*) OUP.

Missionaries & Managers: American Influences on European Management Education, 1945-1960. Ed. by T. R. Gourvish & N. Tiratsoo. LC 98-2899. 208p. 1998. text 69.95 (*0-7190-5156-8*, Pub. by Manchester Univ Pr) St Martin.

Missionaries & Mandarins: Feminist Engagement with Development Institutions. Ed. by Carol Miller & Shahra Razavi. 96p. 1998. pap. 17.50 (*1-85339-434-3*, Pub. by Intermed Tech) Stylus Pub VA.

Missionaries Go Home? A Sociological Interpretation of an African Response to Christian Missions. E. M. Uka. 315p. 1989. pap. 48.00 (*3-261-03874-8*) P Lang Pubng.

Missionaries, Miners, & Indians: Spanish Contact with the Yaqui Nation of Northwestern New Spain, 1533-1820. Evelyn Hu-DeHart. LC 81-14658. (Illus.). 160p. reprint ed. pap. 49.60 (*0-7837-1907-8*, 204211100001) Bks Demand.

Missionaries, Monks & Martyrs. Luke Veronis. 168p. (Orig.). 1994. pap. 9.95 (*1-880971-00-3*) Light&Life Pub Co MN.

Missionaries Need to Know God. Grant Von Harrison. 21p. (Orig.). 1991. write for info. (*0-318-68390-3*) Jackman Pubng.

Missionaries of Revolution: Soviet Advisers & Nationalist China, 1920-1927. C. Martin Wilbur & Julie L. How. (Illus.). 928p. (Orig.). 1992. pap. 29.95 (*0-674-57653-5*) HUP.

Missionaries of Revolution: Soviet Advisors & Nationalist China, 1920-1927. rev. ed. C. Martin Wilbur & Julie L. How. LC 88-19124. (Illus.). 928p. 1989. 87.95 (*0-674-57652-7*) HUP.

Missionaries of Science: The Rockefeller Foundation & Latin America. Ed. by Marcos Cueto. LC 93-24416. (Philanthropic Studies). 196p. (C). 1994. 24.95 (*0-253-31583-2*) Ind U Pr.

Missionaries of the Book: The American Library Profession & the Origins of United States Cultural Diplomacy, 54. Gary E. Kraske. LC 84-27914. (Contributions in Librarianship & Information Science Ser.: No. 54). (Illus.). 293p. 1985. 59.95 (*0-313-24351-4*, KMB/) Greenwood.

Missionaries, Rebellion & Proto-Nationalism: James Long of Bengal. Geoffrey Oddie. (SOAS London Studies on South Asia Ser.: Vol. 16). 260p. (C). 1998. text 47.00 (*0-7007-1028-0*, Pub. by Curzon Pr Ltd) UH Pr.

Missionaries to Match Our Message. Ezra Taft Benson. 1990. pap. 5.95 (*0-88494-779-3*) Bookcraft Inc.

Missionaries to the Skeptics: Christian Apologists for the Twentieth Century C. S. Lewis, E. J. Carnell, & Reinhold Niebuhr. John A. Sims. 288p. (C). 1995. pap. text 22.95 (*0-86554-496-4*, MUP/P130) Mercer Univ Pr.

Missionaries to Yourselves: African Catechists Today. Ed. by Aylward Shorter & Eugene Kataza. LC 73-182576. 222p. reprint ed. pap. 68.90 (*0-8357-8957-8*, 203351500086) Bks Demand.

Missionary. Alex Cathcart. LC 88-61440. 256p. (Orig.). 1988. pap. 12.95 (*0-948275-48-0*) Dufour.

Missionary. John Weld. 180p. 1980. 15.00 (*0-89002-176-7*); pap. 7.95 (*0-89002-175-9*) Am Hist Pr.

Missionary: An Indian Tale, 3 vols. in 1. Sydney O. Morgan. LC 80-20308. 208p. 1980. reprint ed. 50.00 (*0-8201-1358-1*) Schol Facsimiles.

Missionary Adventures of Bob & Arty. Jeff Barth. Ed. by Marge Barth. LC 99-179428. (Mission Alaska! Ser.: Vol. 3). (Illus.). 293p. (J). (gr. 4-12). 1998. pap. 10.00 (*0-9624067-8-3*) Parable Pub.

Missionary Adventures of Bob & Arty Vol. 1: In Search of the Lost Missionary. Jeff Barth. Ed. by Marge Barth. LC 99-179416. (Illus.). 240p. (J). (gr. 4-12). 1997. pap. 10.00 (*0-9624067-6-7*) Parable Pub.

Missionary Adventures of Bob & Arty Vol. 2: Trapped in an Abandoned Mine. Jeff Barth. Ed. by Marge Barth. LC 99-179419. (Illus.). 192p. (J). (gr. 4-12). 1997. pap. 10.00 (*0-9624067-7-5*) Parable Pub.

Missionary Adventures of Bob & Arty Vol. 4: The Storm! Jeff Barth. Ed. by Marge Barth. (Illus.). 392p. (J). (gr. 4-12). 1999. pap. 10.00 (*1-891484-01-X*) Parable Pub.

***Missionary & the Libertine.** Ian Buruma. LC 99-53744. 320p. 2000. 22.95 (*0-375-50222-X*) Random.

Missionary As a Cultural Interpreter. Jonna L. Mandelbaum. (American University Studies: Series 7, Vol. 46). 220p. 1989. 34.00 (*0-8204-0692-9*) P Lang Pubng.

Missionary Care: Counting the Cost for World Evangelization. Ed. by Kelly S. O'Donnell. LC 92-72009. 560p. (Orig.). (C). 1992. pap. text 13.95 (*0-87808-233-6*, WCL233-6) William Carey Lib.

Missionary Cartoon: Two by Two, Missionary Moments, 2 bks., Set. Ryan Stoker & Darold L. Westover. 1994. pap. 14.98 (*0-88290-460-4*) Horizon Utah.

Missionary Censuses of Hawaii. Robert C. Schmitt. (Pacific Anthropological Records Ser.: No. 20). 50p. 1973. pap. 3.00 (*0-910240-66-3*) Bishop Mus.

Missionary Congregation, Leadership & Liminality. Alan J. Roxburgh. LC 96-49154. (Christian Mission & Modern Culture Ser.). 80p. 1997. pap. 7.00 (*1-56338-190-7*) TPI PA.

Missionary Conquest: The Gospel & Native American Cultural Genocide. George E. Tinker. 192p. 1993. pap. 15.00 (*0-8006-2576-5*, 1-2576) Augsburg Fortress.

Missionary Conspiracy: Letters to a Postmodern Hindu. Francis A. Schaeffer & Vishal Mangalwadi. write for info. (*81-86701-03-6*) MacLaurin Inst.

***Missionary Conspiracy: Letters to a Postmodern Hindu.** Vishal Mangalwadi. 320p. 1998. reprint ed. pap. 16.99 (*1-85078-327-6*, Pub. by O M Pubng) OM Literature.

Missionary Conspiracy: Letters to a Postmodern Hindu. 2nd rev. ed. Intro. by Vishal Mangalwadi. LC 96-903508. 488p. 1996. 23.50 (*81-86701-00-1*, Pub. by Nivedit Good Bks) MacLaurin Inst.

Missionary Conversations with Protestant Sectarians. Kyrill Archpriest Zaits. 49p. (Orig.). 1985. pap. 2.00 (*0-317-30291-4*) Holy Trinity.

Missionary Dialogues. Patricia Pinegar & Ed J. Pinegar. pap. 10.95 (*1-55517-317-9*) CFI Dist.

Missionary Discipleship: The Story of R. E. & Ella Thompson. R. E. Thompson et al. (Illus.). 42p. (Orig.). 1982. pap. 3.95 (*0-942726-00-6*) Mission Trng.

Missionary Earthkeeping. Ed. by Calvin B. DeWitt & Ghillean T. Prance. (C). 1992. lib. bdg. 30.00 (*0-86554-390-9*, H318) Mercer Univ Pr.

Missionary Emphasis of Lukan Pneumatology. John M. Penney. (JPTS Ser.: Vol. 12). 143p. 1997. pap. 13.95 (*1-85075-800-X*, Pub. by Sheffield Acad) CUP Services.

An Asterisk (*) at the beginning of an entry indicates that the title is appearing for the first time.

Missionary Encounters: Sources & Issues. Ed. by Robert A. Bickers & Rosemary Seton. 264p. (C). 1996. 68.50 (*0-7007-0369-1*, Pub. by Curzon Pr Ltd); pap. 29.95 (*0-7007-0370-5*, Pub. by Curzon Pr Ltd) Paul & Co Pubs.

Missionary Enterprise in China & America. Ed. by John K. Fairbank. LC 74-82191. (Studies in American-East Asian Relations: No. 6). (Illus.). 442p. 1974. 32.00 (*0-674-57655-1*) HUP.

Missionary Factor in Ethiopia: Papers from a Symposium on the Impact of European Missions on Ethiopian Society, Lund University, August, 1996, Ed. by Richard Friedli et al. (Studies in the Intercultural History of Christianity: Vol. 110). 215p. 1998. 37.95 (*3-631-33259-9*) P Lang Pubng.

Missionary Factor in Ethiopia: Papers from a Symposium on the Impact of European Missions on Ethiopian Society, Lund University, August, 1996. Ed. by Getatchew Haile et al. LC 98-47874. (Studies in the Intercultural History of Christianity: Vol. 110). 215p. (C). 1998. pap. 37.95 (*0-8204-3588-0*) P Lang Pubng.

Missionary Grams: Cartoons for Missionaries. Val C. Bagley. 64p. 1980. pap. 6.98 (*0-88290-538-4*, 2032) Horizon Utah.

Missionary Handbook. Lazar Puhalo. 42p. (Orig.). Date not set. pap. 5.50 (*1-879038-57-9*, 9027) Synaxis Pr.

Missionary Handbook. Lazar Puhalo. 49p. (Orig.). 1985. pap. text 3.00 (*0-911523-00-6*) Synaxis Pr.

Missionary Handbook: Hints, Tips, & Smart Advice for Missionaries. Douglas C. Beardall. Ed. & Pref. by Jewel N. Beardall. 238p. (Orig.). 1995. pap. 11.95 (*1-882371-05-4*) LDS Bk Pubns.

Missionary Herald: Reports from Northern Iraq (1833-1870) Ed. by Kamal S. Salibi & Yusuf K. Khoury. 1760p. 1997. 230.00 (*0-88206-205-0*) Caravan Bks.

Missionary Herald: Reports from Ottoman Syria (1819-1870) Ed. by Kamàl S. Salibi & Yusuf K. Khoury. 2244p. 1995. 300.00 (*0-88206-204-2*) Caravan Bks.

Missionary Heroes of Africa. James H. Morrison. LC 79-89010. 267p. 1969. reprint ed. lib. bdg. 59.50 (*0-8371-1738-0*, MOM&) Greenwood.

Missionary Kit: Hints, Tips & Smart Advice for Missionaries. C. Douglas Beardall & Jewel N. Beardall. 208p. 1992. pap. 9.95 (*1-882371-00-3*) LDS Bk Pubns.

Missionary Landscapes in the Dark Continent. James Johnston. LC 72-3911. (Black Heritage Library Collection). 1977. reprint ed. 28.95 (*0-8369-9100-1*) Ayer.

Missionary Lives: A Study in Canadian Missionary Biography & Autobiography. Terrence L. Craig. LC 97-8352. (Studies in Christian Mission: Vol. 19). 152p. 1997. text 68.50 (*90-04-10815-7*) Brill Academic Pubs.

Missionary Lives: Papua, 1874-1914. Diane Langmore. LC 88-26131. (Pacific Islands Monographs: No. 6). (Illus.). 430p. 1989. text 36.00 (*0-8248-1163-1*) UH Pr.

Missionary Medicine in China: A Study of Two Canadian Protestant Missions in China Before 1937. Yuet-Wah Cheung. LC 88-173. (Illus.). 192p. (C). 1988. lib. bdg. 38.00 (*0-8191-6901-3*) U Pr of Amer.

Missionary Messages. rev. ed. A. B. Simpson. LC 87-71136. 1987. mass mkt. 7.99 (*0-87509-765-0*) Chr Pubns.

Missionary Methods: St. Paul's or Ours? Roland Allen. 184p. 1962. pap. 12.00 (*0-8028-1001-2*) Eerdmans.

Missionary Mind & American East Asia Policy, 1911-1915. James Reed. (East Asian Monographs: No. 104). 300p. 1983. 30.00 (*0-674-57657-8*) HUP.

Missionary Moments. Phyllis Cammack. LC 66-30364. (Illus.). 134p. 1966. 6.50 (*0-913342-09-2*) Barclay Pr.

Missionary Movement in American Catholic History. Angelyn Dries. LC 97-32083. (American Society of Missiology Ser.: No. 26). 400p. 1998. pap. 20.00 (*1-57075-167-6*) Orbis Bks.

Missionary Movement in Christian History: Studies in the Transmission of Faith. Andrew F. Walls. LC 95-51175. 250p. (Orig.). 1996. pap. 20.00 (*1-57075-059-9*) Orbis Bks.

Missionary Movement of the 19th & 20th Centuries & Its Encounter with India: A Historico-Theological Investigation with Three Case Studies. Isaac Padinjarekuttu. LC 95-139262. (European University Studies: Series 23, Vol. 527). XIII, 305p. 1995. pap. 52.95 (*3-631-47415-6*) P Lang Pubng.

Missionary Notebook. Harold C. Anderson. 75p. 1998. pap. text 6.59 (*1-57636-056-3*) SunRise Pbl.

Missionary of Moderation: Henry Melchior Muhlenberg & the Lutheran Church in English America. Leonard R. Riforgiato. LC 78-75203. 256p. 1970. 36.50 (*0-8387-2379-9*) Bucknell U Pr.

***Missionary Outreach of the West Indian Church: Jamaican Baptist Missions to West Africa in the Nineteenth Century.** Horace O. Russell. (Research in Religion & Family Ser.: Vol. 3). 344p. 2000. pap. text 38.95 (*0-8204-3063-3*) P Lang Pubng.

Missionary Pilgrimage. Charles W. Ranson. LC 88-7021. (Illus.). 212p. reprint ed. pap. 65.80 (*0-8357-4367-5*, 203719600007) Bks Demand.

Missionary Position: Mother Teresa in Theory & Practice. Christopher Hitchens. (Illus.). 120p. 1997. pap. 13.00 (*1-85984-054-X*, Pub. by Verso) Norton.

Missionary Position: The Ideology of Mother Teresa. Christopher Hitchens. LC 95-45694. 98p. 1995. 19.00 (*1-85984-929-6*, Pub. by Verso) Norton.

Missionary Program Builder, No. 2. 1954. 4.50 (*0-685-68754-6*, MP-202) Lillenas.

Missionary Program Builder, No. 3. Compiled by Evelyn Stenbock. 40p. 1980. 4.99 (*0-8341-9297-7*, MP-203) Lillenas.

Missionary Program Builder, No. 4. Compiled by Paul M. Miller. 36p. 1990. pap. 4.50 (*0-8341-9747-2*, MP-204) Nazarene.

Missionary Program Builder 03. Evelyn Stenbock. 1991. pap. 4.99 (*0-00-154184-6*) Lillenas.

Missionary Reference Library. Deseret Book Company Staff. 2234p. pap. 20.95 (*0-87579-951-5*) Deseret Bk.

Missionary Responses to Tribal Religions at Edinburgh, 1910. J. Stanley Friesen. LC 94-17919. (Studies in Church History: Vol. 1). XV, 222p. (C). 1996. text 49.95 (*0-8204-2552-4*) P Lang Pubng.

Missionary Rivalry & Educational Expansion in Nigeria, 1885-1945. Magnus O. Bassey. LC 99-12629. (Studies in the History of Missions: Vol. 15). 204p. 1999. text 89.95 (*0-7734-8153-2*) E Mellen.

Missionary Scrapbook Kit - Elder: Preserving the Precious. Charles English. 72p. 1993. 17.95 (*1-885425-01-5*) Restorat Source.

Missionary Scrapbook Kit - Sister: Preserving the Precious. Charles English. (Best Years of My Life - My Mission Ser.). 72p. 1994. 17.95 (*1-885425-00-7*) Restorat Source.

Missionary Sheriff. Alice French. LC 70-75777. (Short Story Index Reprint Ser.). (Illus.). 1977. 19.95 (*0-8369-3002-9*) Ayer.

Missionary Stories & the Millers. Mildred A. Martin. (Miller Family Ser.). (Illus.). 208p. (J). (gr. 3 up). 1993. 9.50 (*0-9627643-7-X*) Green Psturs Pr.

Missionary Stories & the Millers. Mildred A. Martin. (Miller Family Ser.). (Illus.). 208p. (J). (gr. 3 up). 1993. pap. 6.00 (*0-9627643-4-5*) Green Psturs Pr.

Missionary Story Sketches: Folk-Lore from Africa. Alexander P. Camphor. LC 79-173603. (Black Heritage Library Collection). 1977. reprint ed. 28.95 (*0-8369-8915-5*) Ayer.

Missionary Strategies. Ed. by Rhema Ministerial Association International Staff. 120p. 1995. pap. 14.95 (*0-89276-957-2*) Faith Lib Pubns.

Missionary Success in the Island of Formosa, 2 vols. William Campbell, Jr. 1000p. 1996. reprint ed. 75.00 (*957-638-299-8*) Oriental Bk Store.

Missionary That's Right. Mark Weinrich. (Missionary - That's Me! Ser.). (Illus.). 32p. (J). (ps-2). 1995. pap. 4.99 (*0-87509-559-3*) Chr Pubns.

Missionary to Tanganyika, 1877-1888. Edward C. Hore. Ed. by James B. Wolf. 200p. 1971. 45.00 (*0-7146-2924-3*, Pub. by F Cass Pubs) Intl Spec Bk.

Missionary to the Malagasy: The Madagascar Diary of the Rev. Charles T. Price, 1875-1877. Ed. by Arnold H. Price. (American University Studies: History: Ser. IX, Vol. 60). 273p. (C). 1989. text 48.00 (*0-8204-1083-7*) P Lang Pubng.

Missionary to the Mountain West: The Reminiscences of Episcopal Bishop Daniel S. Tuttle, 1866-1886. Daniel S. Tuttle. LC 87-8225. 516p. 1987. reprint ed. pap. 160.00 (*0-7837-8565-8*, 204938000011) Bks Demand.

Missionary Travels & Researches in South Africa. David Livingstone. LC 72-5439. (Select Bibliographies Reprint Ser.). 1977. reprint ed. 68.95 (*0-8369-6918-9*) Ayer.

Missionary Treasure. Mark Weinrich. (Missionary-That's Me! Ser.). (Illus.). 30p. (J). 1994. pap. 4.99 (*0-87509-519-4*) Chr Pubns.

Missionary Voices. H. Robert Cowles & K. Neill Foster. 272p. 1996. mass mkt. 5.99 (*0-87509-682-4*) Chr Pubns.

Missionary Who Forgot His Name. Gary Allen. (Illus.). 145p. (Orig.). 1994. pap. 8.00 (*1-882775-06-6*) Selva Edit.

Missionary's Ghost. P. J. Neri. LC 98-149722. (Hawaii Chillers Ser.: No. 3). 104p. (Orig.). (J). (gr. 3-6). 1997. pap. 4.95 (*1-57306-029-1*) Bess Pr.

Missionary's Little Quote Book. R. Dale Jeffery. LC 97-222590. 1997. pap. 9.95 (*1-57734-136-8*, 01112961) Covenant Comms.

Missionary's Position. Gary Buslik. LC 98-60334. 312p. 1999. pap. 12.95 (*0-9665513-0-3*) Sunny Bk.

Missionnaires au Quotidien a Tahiti: Les Picpuciens en Polynesie au XIXe Siecle. Pierre-Yves Toullelan. (Studies in Christian Mission). (FRE.). 260p. 1995. text 113.00 (*90-04-10100-4*) Brill Academic Pubs.

MissionQuest: Quest for Confidence. Julie Massey. (MissionsQuest Ser.). (Illus.). 24p. (YA). (gr. 7 up). 1998. pap. text 3.95 (*1-56309-239-5*, W986111) Womans Mission Union.

Missions. (FRE.). 1989. 3.95 (*0-86508-377-0*) BCM Pubn.

***Missions.** Paul Borthwick. (LifeGuide Bible Studies). 2000. pap. 4.99 (*0-8308-3090-1*) InterVarsity.

Missions. Lynn M. Stone. LC 93-18638. (Old America Ser.). (Illus.). 32p. (J). (gr. 3-6). 1993. lib. bdg. 21.27 (*0-86625-445-5*) Rourke Pubns.

Missions: A Family Affair. Jack B. Scott. 1985. pap. 4.95 (*0-934688-15-X*) Great Comm Pubns.

Missions: A Family Affair, Leader's Guide. (Orig.). 1985. pap. text 3.95 (*0-934688-20-6*) Great Comm Pubns.

Missions: Biblical Foundations & Contemporary Strategies. Gailyn VanRheenen. LC 96-15860. 240p. 1996. 22.99 (*0-310-20809-2*) Zondervan.

***Missions: Home & Abroad.** Delmar R. Guynes. (Spiritual Discovery Ser.). 121p. 1998. pap. 9.95 (*0-88243-226-5*, 02-0226) Gospel Pub.

***Missions: Home & Abroad.** Delmar R. Guynes. (Spiritual Discovery Ser.). 109p. 1998. pap. 4.95 (*0-88243-126-9*, 02/0126) Gospel Pub.

Missions: 52 Creative Methods for Teaching Christ's Message. Phyllis Wezeman & Kenneth Wezeman. 84p. 1993. pap. 14.95 (*1-877871-50-8*) Ed Ministries.

Missions - California's Heritage, 21 bks. Mary N. Boule. Ed. by Nancy N. Kenyon. (Illus.). 1988. pap. 79.00 (*1-877599-21-2*) Merryant Pubs.

Missions - California's Heritage No. 1: Mission San Diego de Alcala. Mary N. Boule. (Illus.). 24p. (Orig.). (J). (gr. 4-6). 1988. pap. 6.95 (*1-877599-00-X*) Merryant Pubs.

Missions - California's Heritage No. 2: Mission San Carlos Borromeo de Carmelo. Mary N. Boule. (Illus.). 24p. (Orig.). (J). (gr. 4-6). 1988. pap. 6.95 (*1-877599-01-8*) Merryant Pubs.

Missions - California's Heritage No. 3: Mission San Antonio de Padua. Mary N. Boule. (Illus.). 24p. (Orig.). (J). (gr. 4-6). 1988. pap. 6.95 (*1-877599-02-6*) Merryant Pubs.

Missions - California's Heritage No. 4: Mission San Gabriel Arcangel. Mary N. Boule. (Illus.). 24p. (Orig.). (J). (gr. 4-6). 1988. pap. 6.95 (*1-877599-03-4*) Merryant Pubs.

Missions - California's Heritage No. 5: Mission San Luis Obispo de Tolosa. Mary N. Boule. (Illus.). 24p. (Orig.). (J). (gr. 4-6). 1988. pap. 6.95 (*1-877599-04-2*) Merryant Pubs.

Missions - California's Heritage No. 6: Mission San Francisco de Asis. Mary N. Boule. (Illus.). 24p. (Orig.). (J). (gr. 4-6). 1988. pap. 6.95 (*1-877599-05-0*) Merryant Pubs.

Missions - California's Heritage No. 7: Mission San Juan Capistrano. Mary N. Boule. (Illus.). 24p. (Orig.). (J). (gr. 4-6). 1988. pap. 6.95 (*1-877599-06-9*) Merryant Pubs.

Missions - California's Heritage No. 8: Mission Santa Clara de Asis. Mary N. Boule. (Illus.). 24p. (Orig.). (J). (gr. 4-6). 1988. pap. 6.95 (*1-877599-07-7*) Merryant Pubs.

Missions - California's Heritage No. 9: Mission San Buenaventura. Mary N. Boule. (Illus.). 24p. (Orig.). (J). (gr. 4-6). 1988. pap. 6.95 (*1-877599-08-5*) Merryant Pubs.

Missions - California's Heritage No. 10: Mission Santa Barbara. Mary N. Boule. (Illus.). 24p. (Orig.). (J). (gr. 4-6). 1988. pap. 6.95 (*1-877599-09-3*) Merryant Pubs.

Missions - California's Heritage No. 11: Mission la Purisima Concepcion. Mary N. Boule. (Illus.). 24p. (Orig.). (J). (gr. 4-6). 1988. pap. 6.95 (*1-877599-10-7*) Merryant Pubs.

Missions - California's Heritage No. 12: Mission Santa Cruz. Mary N. Boule. (Illus.). 24p. (Orig.). (J). (gr. 4-6). 1988. pap. 6.95 (*1-877599-11-5*) Merryant Pubs.

Missions - California's Heritage No. 13: Mission Nuestra Senora de la Soledad. Mary N. Boule. (Illus.). 20p. (Orig.). (J). (gr. 4-6). 1988. pap. 6.95 (*1-877599-12-3*) Merryant Pubs.

Missions - California's Heritage No. 14: Mission San Jose. Mary N. Boule. (Illus.). 28p. (Orig.). (J). (gr. 4-6). 1988. pap. 6.95 (*1-877599-13-1*) Merryant Pubs.

Missions - California's Heritage No. 15: Mission San Juan Bautista. Mary N. Boule. (Illus.). 24p. (Orig.). (J). (gr. 4-6). 1988. pap. 6.95 (*1-877599-14-X*) Merryant Pubs.

Missions - California's Heritage No. 16: Mission San Miguel Arcangel. Mary N. Boule. (Illus.). 24p. (Orig.). (J). (gr. 4-6). 1988. pap. 6.95 (*1-877599-15-8*) Merryant Pubs.

Missions - California's Heritage No. 17: Mission San Fernando Rey de Espana. Mary N. Boule. (Illus.). 24p. (Orig.). (J). (gr. 4-6). 1988. pap. 6.95 (*1-877599-16-6*) Merryant Pubs.

Missions - California's Heritage No. 18: Mission San Luis Rey de Francia, 21 Bks. Mary N. Boule. (Illus.). 24p. (Orig.). (J). (gr. 4). 1988. pap. 6.95 (*1-877599-17-4*) Merryant Pubs.

Missions - California's Heritage No. 19: Mission Santa Ines. Mary N. Boule. (Illus.). 24p. (Orig.). (J). (gr. 4-6). 1988. pap. 6.95 (*1-877599-18-2*) Merryant Pubs.

Missions - California's Heritage No. 20: Mission San Rafael Arcangel. Mary N. Boule. (Illus.). 24p. (Orig.). (J). (gr. 4-6). 1988. pap. 6.95 (*1-877599-19-0*) Merryant Pubs.

Missions - California's Heritage No. 21: Mission San Francisco Solano. Mary N. Boule. (Illus.). 24p. (Orig.). (J). (gr. 4-6). 1988. pap. 6.95 (*1-877599-20-4*) Merryant Pubs.

Missions Alive: Experiential Games for Youth. David Howard. Ed. by Becky Nelson. 46p. (YA). (gr. 7-12). 1993. pap. text 5.95 (*1-56309-071-6*, C936107, Wrld Changers Res) Womans Mission Union.

Missions & Ecumenical Expressions see Modern American Protestantism & Its World

Missions & Medals - The Medals & Ribbons of the United Nations: United Nations Service Medals & Decorations. Lawrence Borts. LC 96-76063. (Illus.). 96p. 1997. 24.95 (*1-884452-31-0*); pap. 19.95 (*1-884452-30-2*) MOA Press.

Missions & Missionaries in the Pacific. Ed. by Char Miller. LC 85-5074. (Symposium Ser.: Vol. 14). 136p. 1986. lib. bdg. 69.95 (*0-88946-705-6*) E Mellen.

Missions & Missionaries of California, 4 vols. Zephyrin Englehardt. 1992. reprint ed. lib. bdg. 300.00 (*0-7812-5031-5*) Rprt Serv.

Missions & Money: Affluence As a Western Missionary Problem. Jonathan J. Bonk. LC 90-48231. (American Society of Missiology Ser.). xxi, 170 p. 1991. pap. 20.00 (*0-88344-718-5*) Orbis Bks.

***Missions & Psychoheresy.** Martin Bobgan & Deidre Bobgan. LC 00-190743. 168p. 2000. pap. 10.00 (*0-941717-17-8*) EastGate Pubs.

Missions & Regional Characteristics of the Early Church. Ed. by Everett Ferguson. LC 92-41449. (Studies in Early Christianity: Vol. 12). (Illus.). 384p. 1993. text 70.00 (*0-8153-1072-2*) Garland.

Missions & Service Projects, 8 vols., Vol. 6. Ed. by Jim Burns. (Fresh Ideas Ser.). 153p. (YA). 1999. pap. 16.99 (*0-8307-1879-6*, Gospel Light) Gospel Lght.

Missions & Society in the Leeward Islands, 1810-1850: An Ecclesiastical & Social Analysis. David U. Farquhar. (Illus.). 273p. (C). 1993. text 30.00 (*0-685-63303-9*) Mt Prospect Pr.

Missions, Basic: Questions & Answers. (BMC Teaching Bks.). (Illus.). 10p. (Orig.). (J). (gr. 1-8). 1970. pap. text 4.50 (*0-86508-156-5*) BCM Pubn.

Missions by the Book: How to Find & Evangelize Lost People of Every Culture. Tom Stebbins. LC 95-83058. (Illus.). 324p. (Orig.). 1996. pap. 11.99 (*0-87509-656-5*) Chr Pubns.

Missions Day Camp: Biovocational Missionaries. Alice Bates. Ed. by Karen Gross. 23p. (J). (gr. 1-6). 1992. pap. text 2.95 (*1-56309-058-9*, W927106) Womans Mission Union.

***Missions de Paix et le Canada: Enseignements des Conflits au Nicaragua, Cambodge et en Somalie.** Robert Miller et al. (FRE.). 1999. pap. 17.50 (*0-88936-872-4*, Pub. by IDRC Bks) Stylus Pub VA.

Missions Events with a Sizable Difference: Ning Events for Small & Large Churches. Lottie Crim & Katsy McAlister. Ed. by Becky Nelson. 35p. 1993. pap. text 4.95 (*1-56309-073-2*, W933122) Womans Mission Union.

Missions Growth: A Case Study on Finnish Free Foreign Missions. Lauri Ahonen. LC 84-12636. 73p. (Orig.). 1984. pap. 5.95 (*0-87808-335-9*) William Carey Lib.

***Missions in a New Millennium: Changes & Challenges in World Outreach.** Ed Glenny. 2000. pap. 14.99 (*0-8254-2698-7*) Kregel.

***Missions in Photogravure: The Old Missions of California in Photography.** Ed. by Joseph A. Hofmann. (Special Bks.: Vol. 2). (Illus.). vii, 54p. 1998. reprint ed. pap. 5.95 (*1-891030-02-7*) Paragon Agency.

***Missions in the Age of the Spriit.** John V. York. 272p. 2000. 11.99 (*0-88243-464-0*, 02-0464) Gospel Pub.

Missions in the Local Church. rev. ed. Ed. by Melbourne E. Cuthbert & Jeannie Lockerbie. 237p. (Orig.). 1998. pap. text 8.95 (*1-888796-06-5*) ABWE Pubng.

Missions in the 21st Century: Getting Your Church into the Game. Tom Telford & Lois Shaw. LC 97-44697. 176p. 1998. pap. 11.99 (*0-87788-578-8*, H Shaw Pubs) Waterbrook Pr.

Missions of a University in a Small Country. Millard W. Hansen. 168p. 1975. 5.00 (*0-8477-2426-3*) U of PR Pr.

Missions of California, 21 bks. Incl. Mission La Purisima Concepcion. Kim Ostrow. LC 99-19531. (Illus.). 64p. (J). (gr. k-4). 1999. lib. bdg. 17.95 (*0-8239-5498-6*, PowerKids); Mission Nuestra Senora de la Soledad. Kim Ostrow. LC 99-23211. (SPA., Illus.). 64p. (J). (gr. 4). 1999. lib. bdg. 17.95 (*0-8239-5500-1*, PowerKids); Mission of San Luis Rey de Francia. Jennifer Quasha. LC 99-20441. (Illus.). 64p. (J). (gr. 4). 1999. lib. bdg. 16.01 (*0-8239-5504-4*, PowerKids); Mission San Antonio de Padua. Kim Serafin. LC 99-27378. (Illus.). 64p. (J). (gr. 4). 1999. lib. bdg. 17.95 (*0-8239-5489-7*, PowerKids); Mission San Buenaventura. Amy Margaret. LC 98-46485. (Illus.). 64p. (J). (gr. 4). 1999. lib. bdg. 17.95 (*0-8239-5496-X*, PowerKids); Mission San Carlos Borromeo del Rio Carmela. Kathleen J. Edgar & Susan E. Edgar. LC 99-19098. (Illus.). 64p. (J). (gr. 4). 1999. lib. bdg. 17.95 (*0-8239-5488-9*, PowerKids); Mission San Diego de Alcala. Kathleen J. Edgar & Susan E. Edgar. LC 99-19096. (Illus.). 64p. (J). (gr. 4). 2000. lib. bdg. 25.27 (*0-8239-5487-0*, PowerKids); Mission San Fernando Rey de Espana. Jacqueline Ching. LC 99-21539. (Illus.). 64p. (J). (gr. 4). 1999. lib. bdg. 17.95 (*0-8239-5503-6*, PowerKids); Mission San Francisco de Asis. Kathleen J. Edgar & Susan E. Edgar. LC 99-25062. (Illus.). 64p. (J). (gr. 4). 1999. lib. bdg. 17.95 (*0-8239-5492-7*, PowerKids); Mission San Francisco de Solano. Allison Stark Draper. LC 99-21447. (Illus.). 64p. (J). (gr. 4). 1999. lib. bdg. 17.95 (*0-8239-5507-9*, PowerKids); Mission San Gabriel Arcangel. Alice McGinty. LC 99-19097. (Illus.). 64p. (J). (gr. 4). 2000. lib. bdg. 25.27 (*0-8239-5490-0*, PowerKids); Mission San Jose de Guadalupe. Amy Margaret. LC 99-24610. (Illus.). 64p. (J). (gr. 4). 1999. lib. bdg. 17.95 (*0-8239-5495-1*, PowerKids); Mission San Juan Bautista. Allison Stark Draper. LC 99-24063. (Illus.). 64p. (J). (gr. 4). 1999. lib. bdg. 17.95 (*0-8239-5501-X*, PowerKids); Mission San Juan Capistrano. Kathleen J. Edgar & Susan E. Edgar. LC 99-31530. (Illus.). 64p. (J). (gr. 4). 1999. lib. bdg. 17.95 (*0-8239-5493-5*, PowerKids); Mission San Luis Obispo de Tolosa. Kathleen J. Edgar & Susan E. Edgar. LC 99-21305. (Illus.). 64p. (J). (gr. 4). 1999. lib. bdg. 17.95 (*0-8239-5491-9*, PowerKids); Mission San Miguel Arcangel. Kathleen J. Edgar & Nancy A. Edgar. LC 99-20507. (Illus.). 64p. (J). (gr. 4). 1999. lib. bdg. 17.95 (*0-8239-5502-8*, PowerKids); Mission San Rafael Arcangel. Jacqueline Ching. LC 99-23212. (Illus.). 64p. (J). 1999. lib. bdg. 17.95 (*0-8239-5506-0*, PowerKids); Mission Santa Barbara. Amy Margaret. LC 99-27379. (Illus.). 64p. (J). (gr. 4). 1999. lib. bdg. 17.95 (*0-8239-5497-8*, PowerKids); Mission Santa Clara de Asia. Amy Margaret. LC 99-17433. (Illus.). 64p. (J). (gr. 4). 1999. lib. bdg. 17.95 (*0-8239-5494-3*, PowerKids); Mission Santa Cruz. Kim Ostrow. LC F869.S48O88 1999. (Illus.). 64p. (J). (gr. 4). 1999. lib. bdg. 17.95 (*0-8239-5499-4*, PowerKids); Mission Santa Ines. Jacqueline Ching. LC 99-21540. (Illus.). 64p. (J). (gr. 4). 1999. lib. bdg. 17.95 (*0-8239-5505-2*, PowerKids); (Illus.). (J). (gr. 4). Set lib. bdg. 530.67 Rosen Group.

Missions of California. Ed. by Phyllis R. Emert. LC 97-77590. (Perspectives on History Ser.: Pt. III). (Illus.). 68p. 1997. pap. 6.95 (*1-57960-016-6*) Disc Enter Ltd.

Missions of California. Melba Levick & Stanley Young. (Illus.). 138p. 1988. pap. 16.95 (*0-87701-540-6*) Chronicle Bks.

Missions of California. Stanley Young. 1998. pap. 18.95 (*0-8118-1938-8*) Chronicle Bks.

Missions of California: A Legacy of Genocide. Rupert Costo & Jeannette H. Costo. 248p. (C). 1987. pap. 11.50 (*0-317-64539-0*) Indian Hist Pr.

Missions of Jesus & the Disciples According to the Fourth Gospel: With Implications for the Fourth Gospel's Purpose & the Mission of the Contemporary Church. Andreas J. Kostenberger. LC 97-35709. 266p. 1997. pap. 30.00 (*0-8028-4255-0*) Eerdmans.

An Asterisk (*) at the beginning of an entry indicates that the title is appearing for the first time.

Missions of Los Angeles. Dianne MacMillan. (J). (gr. 4-7). 1999. pap. 5.95 (0-8225-9834-5) Lerner Pub.

Missions of monterey Bay. Emily Abbink. (J). (gr. 4-7). 1999. pap. 5.95 (0-8225-9835-3) Lerner Pub.

Missions of New Mexico since 1776. John L. Kessell. LC 79-4934. (Illus.). 288p. reprint ed. pap. 89.30 (0-8357-4643-7, 203757400008) Bks Demand.

Missions of Northern Sonora: A 1935 Field Documentation Relating Piman Indians to the Material Culture of the Hispanic Southwest. Notes & Pref. by Buford Pickens. LC 92-30728. (Southwest Center Ser.). (Illus.). 198p. (Orig.). 1993. pap. 15.95 (0-8165-1356-2); lib. bdg. 31.95 (0-8165-1342-2) U of Ariz Pr.

Missions of San Antonio. Emilie Toepperwein & Fritz A. Toepperwein. pap. text 1.95 (0-910722-12-9) Highland Pr.

Missions of San Francisco. Tekla White. (J). (gr. 4-7). 1999. pap. 5.95 (0-8225-9836-1) Lerner Pub.

Missions of Southern Coast. Nancy Lemke. (J). (gr. 4-7). pap. 5.95 (0-8225-9837-X) Lerner Pub.

Missions of Spanish Florida. David H. Thomas. LC 90-23656. (Spanish Borderlands Sourcebooks Ser.: Vol. 23). 536p. 1991. reprint ed. text 30.00 (0-8240-2098-7) Garland.

Missions of the Central Coast. June Behrens. (J). (gr. 4-7). pap. 5.95 (0-8225-9832-9) Lerner Pub.

Missions of the Central Coast. June Behrens. LC 95-2875. (California Missions Ser.). (Illus.). (J). 1996. lib. bdg. 23.93 (0-8225-1930-5, Lerner Publctns) Lerner Pub.

Missions of the College Curriculum: A Contemporary Review with Suggestions: A Commentary. Carnegie Foundation for the Advancement of Teachin. LC 77-84320. (Carnegie Council Ser.). (Illus.). 344p. reprint ed. pap. 106.70 (0-8357-4872-3, 203780400009) Bks Demand.

Missions of the Inland Valleys. Pauline Brower. (J). (gr. 4-7). pap. 5.95 (0-8225-9833-7) Lerner Pub.

Missions of the Inland Valleys. Pauline Brower. LC 95-2844. (California Missions Ser.). (J). 1996. lib. bdg. 23.93 (0-8225-1929-1, Lerner Publctns) Lerner Pub.

Missions of the Los Angeles Area. Dianne MacMillan. LC 95-16717. (California Missions Ser.). 80p. (J). (gr. 4-7). 1996. lib. bdg. 23.93 (0-8225-1927-5, Lerner Publctns) Lerner Pub.

Missions of the Monterey Bay Area. Emily Abbink. LC 95-2843. (California Missions Ser.). (J). 1996. lib. bdg. 23.93 (0-8225-1928-3, Lerner Publctns) Lerner Pub.

Missions of the San Francisco Bay Area. Tekla N. White. LC 95-8714. 80p. (J). (gr. 4-7). 1996. lib. bdg. 23.93 (0-8225-1926-7, Lerner Publctns) Lerner Pub.

Missions of the Southern Coast. Nancy Lemke. LC 95-16619. (California Missions Ser.). 80p. (J). (gr. 4-7). 1996. lib. bdg. 23.93 (0-8225-1925-9, Lerner Publctns) Lerner Pub.

Missions on the Go for Preschoolers. Nell Branum. (Illus.). 16p. (J). (ps-k). 1997. pap. text 18.95 (1-56309-223-9, N978101, New Hope) Womans Mission Union.

Missions Remembered: Recollections of the World War II Air War. Men of the Middle Tennessee WWII Fighter Pilots As. LC 97-48517. (Illus.). 220p. 1998. 22.95 (0-07-001649-6) McGraw.

Missions Resource Handbook. Morris G. Watkins. 128p. (Orig.). (YA). (gr. 7 up). 1987. pap. 9.95 (0-939925-05-2) R C Law & Co.

Missions Schools in Batakland, Indonesia, 1861-1940. Jan S. Aritonang. Ed. & Tr. by Robert R. Boehlke. LC 93-41413. (Studies in Christian Mission: Vol. 10). 450p. 1993. 124.50 (90-04-09967-0, NLG190) Brill Academic Pubs.

Missions to the Calusa. Ed. & Tr. by John H. Hann. (Columbus Quincentenary Series - Ripley B. Bullen). 560p. (C). 1991. 24.95 (0-8130-1075-6) U Press Fla.

Missions to the Moon & Exploring the Cold Universe: Proceedings of EI, EI/B3 & E3 Symposia of COSPAR Scientific Commissions Band E Which were Held During Thirtieth COSPAR Scientific Assembly, Hamburg, Germany 11-21 July 1994. Ed. by B. H. Foing et al. 224p. 1996. pap. 92.75 (0-08-042904-1, Pergamon Pr) Elsevier.

Missions to the Sun, Vol. 2804. Ed. by David M. Rust. 314p. 1996. 85.00 (0-8194-2192-8) SPIE.

Missions to the Sun II, Vol. 3442. Ed. by Clarence M. Korendyke. LC 99-211212. 1998. 59.00 (0-8194-2897-3) SPIE.

MissionsQuest: Leading the Quest. Pam Smith. 14p. 1998. pap. text 3.95 (1-56309-238-7, W986117) Womans Mission Union.

***MissionsQuest: Quest Challenges - Book of Recognition & Commissioning Services.** DeAnna Sanders. Ed. by Jan Turrentine. (Illus.). 52p. 1998. pap. 11.99 (1-56309-282-4) Womans Mission Union.

MissionsQuest Devotional Book: Character Questions. Karen Dockrey. (MissionsQuest Ser.). 113p. (J). (gr. 10). 1998. pap. text 9.95 (1-56309-263-8, W986123) Womans Mission Union.

Mississauga: City of Excellence. Ric McDonald et al. LC 97-21428. 304p. 1997. 39.00 (1-885352-64-6); pap. text. write for info. (1-885352-65-4) Community Comm.

Mississippi see From Sea to Shining Sea

Mississippi see Great Rivers

***Mississippi.** (Switched on Schoolhouse Ser.). (Illus.). (J). 2000. pap. 24.95 (0-7403-0276-0) Alpha AZ.

Mississippi. Charles Davis & Linda Davis. LC 98-19618. (America the Beautiful Ser.). 144p. (YA). (gr. 5-8). 1999. write for info. (0-516-20688-5) Childrens.

Mississippi. Dennis B. Fradin. (From Sea to Shining Sea Ser.). (J). 1997. pap. 5.95 (0-516-26200-9) Childrens.

Mississippi. Theodor Geus. LC 89-16466. (Illus.). 184p. 1989. 50.00 (0-8131-1713-5) U Pr of Ky.

Mississippi. Paul Joseph. LC 97-22674. (U. S. Ser.). (Illus.). 32p. 1998. lib. bdg. 19.93 (1-56239-883-0, Checkerboard Library) ABDO Pub Co.

Mississippi. Patricia K. Kummer. LC 98-13543. (One Nation Ser.). (Illus.). 48p. (J). (gr. 3-7). 1998. 19.00 (0-7368-0021-2, Cpstone High Low) Capstone Pr.

Mississippi. Ken Kuron. LC 91-17884. 1992. 21.95 (0-399-22134-4) Putnam Pub Group.

Mississippi. John F. Prevost. LC 98-11984. (Rivers Ser.). (J). 2002. lib. bdg. 19.92 (1-57765-102-2) ABDO Pub Co.

Mississippi. Anna Ready. LC 92-31056. (Hello U. S. A. Ser.). (Illus.). 72p. (J). (gr. 3-6). 1993. lib. bdg. 19.93 (0-8225-2743-X, Lerner Publctns) Lerner Pub.

***Mississippi.** Anna Ready. (Hello U. S. A. Ser.). (Illus.). 72p. (J). (gr. 3-6). 2000. pap. 5.95 (0-8225-9788-8, First Ave Edns) Lerner Pub.

Mississippi. Diane Siebert. (J). 1924. 16.95 (0-688-16445-5, Wm Morrow); lib. bdg. 16.89 (0-688-16446-3, Wm Morrow) Morrow Avon.

Mississippi. Kathleen Thompson. LC 87-16440. (Portrait of America Library). 48p. (J). (gr. 4-8). 1996. pap. 5.95 (0-8114-7449-6) Raintree Steck-V.

Mississippi. Kathleen Thompson. LC 87-16440. (Portrait of America Library). (Illus.). 48p. (J). (gr. 3-6). 1996. lib. bdg. 22.83 (0-8114-7344-9) Raintree Steck-V.

Mississippi, 23. Capstone Press Geography Staff. (One Nation Ser.). 1999. 19.00 (0-516-21477-2) Childrens.

Mississippi, 5 vols. , Set. D. Shirley. LC 98-19496. (Celebrate the States Ser.: Group 6). (Illus.). 144p. (YA). (gr. 4 up). 1999. lib. bdg. 35.64 (0-7614-0664-6, Benchmark NY) Marshall Cavendish.

Mississippi see American Slave: A Composite Autobiography, Supplement Series 1

Mississippi: A Guide to the Magnolia State. Federal Writers' Project Staff. (American Guidebook Ser.). 545p. 1938. reprint ed. 89.00 (0-403-02174-X) Somerset Pub.

Mississippi: A Guide to the Magnolia State. Federal Writers' Project Staff & Writers Program-WPA Staff. (American Guide Ser.). 1989. reprint ed. lib. bdg. 69.00 (0-7812-1023-2, 1023) Rprt Serv.

Mississippi: An American Journey. Anthony Walton. 1997. pap. 13.00 (0-679-77741-5) Vin Bks.

Mississippi: Off the Beaten Path: A Guide to Unique Places. 2nd ed. Marlo C. Kirkpatrick. LC 98-53480. (Off the Beaten Path Ser.). (Illus.). 225p. 1999. pap. text 12.95 (0-7627-0407-1) Globe Pequot.

Mississippi: Sketches of Counties, Towns, Events, Institutions & Persons Arranged in Cyclopedic Form, 4 vols., 1. Ed. by Dunbar Rowland. LC 76-73. 1976. reprint ed. 37.50 (0-87152-220-9) Reprint.

Mississippi: Sketches of Counties, Towns, Events, Institutions & Persons Arranged in Cyclopedic Form, 4 vols., 2. Ed. by Dunbar Rowland. LC 76-73. 1976. reprint ed. 37.50 (0-87152-221-7) Reprint.

Mississippi: Sketches of Counties, Towns, Events, Institutions & Persons Arranged in Cyclopedic Form, 4 vols., Vol. 3. Ed. by Dunbar Rowland. LC 76-73. 1976. reprint ed. 37.50 (0-87152-222-5) Reprint.

Mississippi: Sketches of Counties, Towns, Events, Institutions & Persons Arranged in Cyclopedic Form, 4 vols., Vol. 4. Ed. by Dunbar Rowland. LC 76-73. 1976. reprint ed. suppl. ed. 37.50 (0-87152-223-3) Reprint.

Mississippi: Storm Center of Secession, 1856-1861. Percy L. Rainwater. LC 72-84188. (American Scene, Comments & Commentators Ser.). 1969. reprint ed. lib. bdg. 29.50 (0-306-71614-3) Da Capo.

Mississippi: The Blues Today. Robert Nicholson. LC 98-40012. (Illus.). 192p. (Orig.). 1999. mass mkt. 25.00 (0-306-80883-8, Pub. by Da Capo) HarpC.

Mississippi Almanac: The Ultimate Reference on the State of Mississippi. James L. Cox. 560p. (Orig.). 1995. pap. 25.00 (0-9643545-0-0) Comp Search & Res.

Mississippi Alphabet. Laurie Parker. LC 98-23274. 1998. 5.95 (0-937552-92-5) Quail Ridge.

Mississippi & Ohio Rivers. Charles Ellet. (Notable American Authors Ser.). 1992. reprint ed. lib. bdg. 75.00 (0-7812-2794-1) Rprt Serv.

Mississippi & Ohio Rivers, Containing Plans for the Protection of the Delta from Inundation & Investigations. Charles Ellet. LC 70-125738. (American Environmental Studies). 1974. reprint ed. 25.95 (0-405-02663-3) Ayer.

Mississippi & Other State Greats (Biographies) Carole Marsh. (Carole Marsh Mississippi Bks.). (Illus.). (J). (gr. 3 up). 1994. pap. 19.95 (1-55609-726-3); lib. bdg. 29.95 (1-55609-725-5); disk 29.95 (1-55609-727-1) Gallopade Intl.

Mississippi & the Compromise of 1850. Cleo C. Hearon. LC 70-168958. reprint ed. 37.50 (0-404-00061-4) AMS Pr.

Mississippi Appellate Practice. Luther T. Munford. 450p. 1995. 170.00 (0-9619323-1-7) On Point Pr.

Mississippi Artist: A Self Portrait. Karl Wolfe. LC 79-18098. 170p. 1997. pap. text 10.95 (0-87805-106-6) U Pr of Miss.

Mississippi As a Province, Territory & State, with Biographical Notices of Eminent Citizens. John F. Claiborne. LC 78-2291. (Illus.). 568p. 1999. reprint ed. 45.00 (0-87152-264-0) Reprint.

***Mississippi Atlas & Gazetteer.** David Delorme. LC 99-462941. 1998. pap. text 16.95 (0-89933-223-4) DeLorme Map.

Mississippi Automotive Directory. Ed. by T. L. Spelman. 1985. 24.95 (1-55527-020-4) Auto Contact Inc.

Mississippi Back Roads: Notes on Literature & History. Elmo Howell. (Illus.). 350p. 1998. pap. 19.95 (0-9622026-6-5) E Howell.

Mississippi Bandits, Bushwackers, Outlaws, Crooks, Devils, Ghosts, Desperadoes & Other Assorted & Sundry Characters! Carole Marsh. (Carole Marsh Mississippi Bks.). (Illus.). (J). (gr. 3 up). 1994. pap. 19.95 (0-7933-0647-7); lib. bdg. 29.95 (0-7933-0648-5); disk 29.95 (0-7933-0649-3) Gallopade Intl.

Mississippi Basin. Justin Winsor. LC 70-39703. (Select Bibliographies Reprint Ser.). 1977. reprint ed. 26.95 (0-8369-9949-5) Ayer.

Mississippi Beau. Jo Beecher Prather. LC 93-50614. (Illus.). 32p. (J). (gr. 4-5). 1995. pap. 8.95 (0-89015-961-0) Sunbelt Media.

***Mississippi BIG Activity Book.** Carole Marsh. (Mississippi Experience! Ser.). (Illus.). (J). (gr. k-5). 2000. pap. 9.95 (0-7933-9558-5) Gallopade Intl.

Mississippi "BIO" Bingo! 24 Must Know State People for Kids to Learn about While Having Fun! Carole Marsh. (Bingo! Ser.). (Illus.). (J). (gr. 2-8). 1998. pap. 14.95 (0-7933-8594-6) Gallopade Intl.

Mississippi Blues. Kathleen A. Goonan. LC 97-21892. 512p. 1997. text 25.95 (0-312-85917-1) St Martin.

***Mississippi Blues.** Kathleen A. Goonan. 1999. mass mkt. write for info. (0-8125-4466-8) Tor Bks.

Mississippi Blues. Kathleen A. Goonan. 1999. pap. 15.95 (0-312-86893-6, Pub. by Tor Bks) St Martin.

Mississippi Bookstore Book: A Surprising Guide to Our State's Bookstores & Their Specialties for Students, Teachers, Writers & Publishers. Carole Marsh. (Carole Marsh Mississippi Bks.). (Illus.). 1994. pap. 19.95 (0-7933-2928-0); lib. bdg. 29.95 (0-7933-2927-2); disk 29.95 (0-7933-2929-9) Gallopade Intl.

Mississippi Bridge. Mildred D. Taylor. (Illus.). 64p. (J). (gr. 4-7). 1992. pap. 3.99 (0-553-15992-5, Skylark BDD) BDD Bks Young Read.

***Mississippi Bridge.** Mildred D. Taylor. (Illus.). 64p. (YA). (gr. 4-7). 2000. pap. 4.99 (0-14-130817-6, PuffinBks) Peng Put Young Read.

Mississippi Bridge. Mildred D. Taylor. 1992. 9.19 (0-606-00528-5, Pub. by Turtleback) Demco.

Mississippi Bridge: A Study Guide. K. M. Fischer. Ed. by J. Friedland & R. Kessler. (Novel-Ties Ser.). (J). (gr. 3-5). 1997. pap. text 15.95 (0-7675-0155-1) Lrn Links.

***Mississippi Brigade of Brig. Gen. Joseph R. Davis: A Geographical Account of Its Campaigns & a Biographical Account of Its Personalities, 1861-1865.** T. P. Williams. (Illus.). 291p. 2000. 34.95 (0-89029-335-X) Morningside Bkshop.

Mississippi Bubble. Emerson Hough. 1976. lib. bdg. 19.25 (0-89968-042-9, Lghtyr Pr) Buccaneer Bks.

***Mississippi Business Directory (2000)** American Business Directories Staff et al. 1,088p. 2000. boxed set 415.00 incl. cd-rom (0-7687-0211-9) Am Busn Direct.

Mississippi Census Index 1880. (Illus.). lib. bdg. write for info. (0-89593-390-X, Accel Indexing) Genealogical Srvcs.

Mississippi Census Index 1880 Mortality Schedule. (Illus.). lib. bdg. 50.00 (0-89593-391-8, Accel Indexing) Genealogical Srvcs.

Mississippi Census Index 1850 Slave Schedule. (Illus.). 1988. lib. bdg. 79.00 (0-89593-397-7, Accel Indexing) Genealogical Srvcs.

Mississippi Census Index 1850 Mortality Schedule. (Illus.). lib. bdg. 44.00 (0-89593-385-3, Accel Indexing) Genealogical Srvcs.

Mississippi Census Index 1805 Jefferson & Wilkinson Counties. (Illus.). lib. bdg. 45.00 (0-89593-681-X, Accel Indexing) Genealogical Srvcs.

Mississippi Census Index 1890: Union Veterns. Ronald V. Jackson. (Illus.). lib. bdg. 59.00 (0-89593-685-2, Accel Indexing) Genealogical Srvcs.

Mississippi Census Index 1870. (Illus.). lib. bdg. 360.00 (0-89593-388-8, Accel Indexing) Genealogical Srvcs.

Mississippi Census Index 1870 Mortality Schedule. (Illus.). lib. bdg. 40.00 (0-89593-389-6, Accel Indexing) Genealogical Srvcs.

Mississippi Census Index 1860 Slave Schedule. (Illus.). 1990. lib. bdg. 109.00 (0-89593-387-X, Accel Indexing) Genealogical Srvcs.

Mississippi Census Index 1860 Mortality Schedule. (Illus.). 1981. lib. bdg. 44.00 (0-89593-386-1, Accel Indexing) Genealogical Srvcs.

Mississippi Census Index 1860. Ronald V. Jackson. (Illus.). 1985. lib. bdg. 180.00 (0-89593-684-4, Accel Indexing) Genealogical Srvcs.

Mississippi Challenge. Walter. (J). 1996. pap. 6.95 (0-02-045641-7) Macmillan.

Mississippi Challenge. Mildred P. Walter. (J). (gr. 7). 1996. pap. 6.95 (0-689-80307-9) Aladdin.

Mississippi Challenge. Mildred P. Walter. LC 92-6718. (Illus.). 256p. (YA). (gr. 6 up). 1992. lib. bdg. 18.95 (0-02-792301-0, Bradbury S&S) S&S Childrens.

Mississippi Challenge. Mildred Pitts Walter. 1996. 12.05 (0-606-09622-1, Pub. by Turtleback) Demco.

Mississippi Chariot. Robinet. (J). 1998. pap. 3.99 (0-87628-571-X) Ctr Appl Res.

Mississippi Chariot. Harriet Gillem Robinet. 1997. 9.09 (0-606-11629-X, Pub. by Turtleback) Demco.

Mississippi Chariot. Harriette G. Robinet. LC 94-11092. 128p. (J). (gr. 4-7). 1994. 14.95 (0-689-31960-6) Aladdin.

Mississippi Chariot. Harriette G. Robinet. 128p. (J). 1997. per. 3.99 (0-689-80632-9) Aladdin.

Mississippi Chinese: Between Black & White. 2nd ed. James W. Loewen. 240p. (C). 1988. reprint ed. pap. text 12.50 (0-88133-312-3) Waveland Pr.

Mississippi Choctaws at Play: The Serious Side of Leisure. Kendall A. Blanchard. LC 80-26527. 248p. 1981. text 24.95 (0-252-00866-9) U of Ill Pr.

Mississippi Civil Procedure. Jeffrey Jackson. Ed. by Karen Morgan. LC 95-81582. 600p. 1996. text. write for info. (0-7620-0023-6) West Group.

Mississippi Classic Christmas Trivia: Stories, Recipes, Activities, Legends, Lore & More. Carole Marsh. (Carole Marsh Mississippi Bks.). (Illus.). (J). (gr. 3 up). 1994. pap. 19.95 (0-7933-0650-7); lib. bdg. 29.95 (0-7933-0651-5); disk 29.95 (0-7933-0652-3) Gallopade Intl.

Mississippi Coastales. Carole Marsh. (Carole Marsh Mississippi Bks.). (J). 1994. lib. bdg. 29.95 (0-7933-7289-5) Gallopade Intl.

Mississippi Coastales. Carole Marsh. (Carole Marsh Mississippi Bks.). (Illus.). (J). (gr. 3 up). 1994. pap. 19.95 (1-55609-122-2); lib. bdg. 29.95 (1-55609-720-4); disk 29.95 (1-55609-721-2) Gallopade Intl.

***Mississippi Code Annotated, 1999 Cumulative Supplement, 22 vols.** annot. ed. Incl. Mississippi Code Annotated, 1999 Cumulative Supplement: Statutory Tables. annot. ed. 315p. 1999. (0-327-09039-1, 54625-10); Mississippi Code Annotated, 1999 Cumulative Supplement Vol. 1: U. S. Constitution, MS Constitution, T. 1 - Laws & Statutes. annot. ed. 70p. 1999. (0-327-09018-9, 54601-10); Mississippi Code Annotated, 1999 Cumulative Supplement Vol. 2: T. 3 - State Sovereignty, Jurisdiction & Holidays, T. 5 - Legislative Department, T. 7 - Executive Department, T. 9 - Courts, T. 11 - Civil Practice & Procedure. annot. ed. 310p. 1999. (0-327-09019-7, 54602-10); Mississippi Code Annotated, 1999 Cumulative Supplement Vol. 3: T. 11 - Civil Practice & Procedure. annot. ed. 3p. 1999. (0-327-09020-0, 54603-10); Mississippi Code Annotated, 1999 Cumulative Supplement Vol. 4: T. 11 - Civil Practice & Procedure, T. 13 - Evidence, Process & Juries. annot. ed. 360p. 1999. (0-327-09021-9, 54604-10); Mississippi Code Annotated, 1999 Cumulative Supplement Vol. 5: T. 15 - Limitations of Actions & Prevention of Frauds, T. 17 - Local Government; Provisions Common to Counties & Municipalities, T. 19 - Counties & County Officers. annot. ed. 220p. 1999. (0-327-09022-7, 54605-10); Mississippi Code Annotated, 1999 Cumulative Supplement Vol. 6: T. 21 - Municipalities, T. 23 - Elections. annot. ed. 340p. 1999. (0-327-09023-5, 54606-10); Mississippi Code Annotated, 1999 Cumulative Supplement Vol. 8: T. 27 Taxation & Finance. annot. ed. 220p. 1999. (0-327-09024-3, 54608-10); Mississippi Code Annotated, 1999 Cumulative Supplement Vol. 9: T. 27 Taxation & Finance; T. 29 - Public Lands, Buildings & Property; T. 31 - Public Business, Bonds & Oligations; T. 33 - Military Affairs. annot. ed. 420p. 1999. (0-327-09025-1, 54609-10); Mississippi Code Annotated, 1999 Cumulative Supplement Vol. 10: T. 35 - War Veterans & Pensions; T. 37 - Education; T. 39 - Libraries, Arts, Archives & History. annot. ed. 315p. 1999. (0-327-09026-X, 54610-10); Mississippi Code Annotated, 1999 Cumulative Supplement Vol. 11: T. 41 - Public Health. annot. ed. 360p. 1999. (0-327-09027-8, 54611-10); Mississippi Code Annotated, 1999 Cumulative Supplement Vol. 11A: T. 43 - Public Welfare; T. 45 - Public Safety & Good Order; T. 47 - Prisons & Prisoners; Probation & Parole. annot. ed. 430p. 1999. (0-327-09028-6, 54612-10); Mississippi Code Annotated, 1999 Cumulative Supplement Vol. 13: T. 55 - Parks & Recreation; T. 57 - Planning, Research & Development. annot. ed. 150p. 1999. (0-327-09029-4, 54614-10); Mississippi Code Annotated, 1999 Cumulative Supplement Vol. 13A: T. 59 - Ports, Harbors, Landings & Watercraft; T. 61 - Aviation; T. 63 - Motor Vehicles & Traffic Regulations. annot. ed. 130p. 1999. (0-327-09030-8, 54615-10); Mississippi Code Annotated, 1999 Cumulative Supplement Vol. 14: T. 65 - Highways, Bridges & Ferries; T. 67 - Alcoholic Beverages; T. 69 - Agriculture, Horticulture, & Animals. annot. ed. 390p. 1999. (0-327-09031-6, 54616-10); Mississippi Code Annotated, 1999 Cumulative Supplement Vol. 15: T. 71 - Labor & Industry; T. 73 - Professions & Vocations. annot. ed. 420p. 1999. (0-327-09032-4, 54610-10); Mississippi Code Annotated, 1999 Cumulative Supplement Vol. 16: T. 75 0 Regulation of Trade, Commerce & Investments. annot. ed. 270p. 1999. (0-327-09033-2, 54618-10); Mississippi Code Annotated, 1999 Cumulative Supplement Vol. 16A: T. 75 - Regulation of Trade, Commerce & Investments. annot. ed. 400p. 1999. (0-327-09034-0, 54619-10); Mississippi Code Annotated, 1999 Cumulative Supplement Vol. 17: T. 75 -Regulation of Trade, Commerce & Investments; T. 77 - Public Utilities & Carriers. annot. ed. 420p. 1999. (0-327-09035-9, 54620-10); Mississippi Code Annotated, 1999 Cumulative Supplement Vol. 18: T. 77 - Public Utilities & Carriers; T. 79 - Corporations, Associations, & Partnerships; T. 81 - Banks & Financial Institutions. annot. ed. 370p. 1999. (0-327-09036-7, 54621-10); Mississippi Code Annotated, 1999 Cumulative Supplement Vol. 20: T. 91 - Trusts & Estates; T. 93 - Domestic Relations; T. 95 - Torts. annot. ed. 220p. 1999. (0-327-09037-5, 54623-10); Mississippi Code Annotated, 1999 Cumulative Supplement Vol. 21: T. 97 - Crimes; T. 99 - Criminal Procedure. annot. ed. 420p. 1999. (0-327-09038-3, 54624-10); 8000p. 1999. write for info. (0-327-09017-0, 4459510) LEXIS Pub.

Mississippi Code Annotated, 1999 Cumulative Supplement: Statutory Tables see Mississippi Code Annotated, 1999 Cumulative Supplement

Mississippi Code Annotated, 1999 Cumulative Supplement, Vol. 1, U. S. Constitution, MS Constitution, T. 1 - Laws & Statutes see Mississippi Code Annotated, 1999 Cumulative Supplement

Mississippi Code Annotated, 1999 Cumulative Supplement, Vol. 2, T. 3 - State Sovereignty, Jurisdiction & Holidays, T. 5 - Legislative Department, T. 7 - Executive Department, T. 9 - Courts, T. 11 - Civil Practice & Procedure see Mississippi Code Annotated, 1999 Cumulative Supplement

An Asterisk (*) at the beginning of an entry indicates that the title is appearing for the first time.

Mississippi Code Annotated, 1999 Cumulative Supplement, Vol. 3, T. 11 - Civil Practice & Procedure see Mississippi Code Annotated, 1999 Cumulative Supplement

Mississippi Code Annotated, 1999 Cumulative Supplement, Vol. 4, T. 11 - Civil Practice & Procedure, T. 13 - Evidence, Process & Juries see Mississippi Code Annotated, 1999 Cumulative Supplement

Mississippi Code Annotated, 1999 Cumulative Supplement, Vol. 5, T. 15 - Limitations of Actions & Prevention of Frauds, T. 17 - Local Government; Provisions Common to Counties & Municipalities, T. 19 - Counties & County Officers see Mississippi Code Annotated, 1999 Cumulative Supplement

Mississippi Code Annotated, 1999 Cumulative Supplement, Vol. 6, T. 21 - Municipalities, T. 23 - Elections see Mississippi Code Annotated, 1999 Cumulative Supplement

Mississippi Code Annotated, 1999 Cumulative Supplement, Vol. 8, T. 27 Taxation & Finance see Mississippi Code Annotated, 1999 Cumulative Supplement

Mississippi Code Annotated, 1999 Cumulative Supplement, Vol. 9, T. 27 Taxation & Finance; T. 29 - Public Lands, Buildings & Property; T. 31 - Public Business, Bonds & Oligations; T. 33 - Military Affairs see Mississippi Code Annotated, 1999 Cumulative Supplement

Mississippi Code Annotated, 1999 Cumulative Supplement, Vol. 10, T. 35 - War Veterans & Pensions; T. 37 - Education; T. 39 - Libraries, Arts, Archives & History see Mississippi Code Annotated, 1999 Cumulative Supplement

Mississippi Code Annotated, 1999 Cumulative Supplement, Vol. 11, T. 41 - Public Health see Mississippi Code Annotated, 1999 Cumulative Supplement

Mississippi Code Annotated, 1999 Cumulative Supplement, Vol. 11A, T. 43 - Public Welfare; T. 45 - Public Safety & Good Order; T. 47 - Prisons & Prisoners; Probation & Parole see Mississippi Code Annotated, 1999 Cumulative Supplement

Mississippi Code Annotated, 1999 Cumulative Supplement, Vol. 13, T. 55 - Parks & Recreation; T. 57 - Planning, Research & Development see Mississippi Code Annotated, 1999 Cumulative Supplement

Mississippi Code Annotated, 1999 Cumulative Supplement, Vol. 13A, T. 59 - Ports, Harbors, Landings & Watercraft; T. 61 - Aviation; T. 63 - Motor Vehicles & Traffic Regulations see Mississippi Code Annotated, 1999 Cumulative Supplement

Mississippi Code Annotated, 1999 Cumulative Supplement, Vol. 14, T. 65 - Highways, Bridges & Ferries; T. 67 - Alcoholic Beverages; T. 69 - Agriculture, Hortlculture, & Animals see Mississippi Code Annotated, 1999 Cumulative Supplement

Mississippi Code Annotated, 1999 Cumulative Supplement, Vol. 15, T. 71 - Labor & Industry; T. 73 - Professions & Vocations see Mississippi Code Annotated, 1999 Cumulative Supplement

Mississippi Code Annotated, 1999 Cumulative Supplement, Vol. 16, T. 75 0 Regulation of Trade, Commerce & Investments see Mississippi Code Annotated, 1999 Cumulative Supplement

Mississippi Code Annotated, 1999 Cumulative Supplement, Vol. 16A, T. 75 - Regulation of Trade, Commerce & Investments see Mississippi Code Annotated, 1999 Cumulative Supplement

Mississippi Code Annotated, 1999 Cumulative Supplement, Vol. 17, T. 75 -Regulation of Trade, Commerce & Investments; T. 77 - Public Utilities & Carriers see Mississippi Code Annotated, 1999 Cumulative Supplement

Mississippi Code Annotated, 1999 Cumulative Supplement, Vol. 18, T. 77 - Public Utilities & Carriers; T. 79 - Corporations, Associations, & Partnerships; T. 81 - Banks & Financial Institutions see Mississippi Code Annotated, 1999 Cumulative Supplement

Mississippi Code Annotated, 1999 Cumulative Supplement, Vol. 20, T. 91 - Trusts & Estates; T. 93 - Domestic Relations; T. 95 - Torts see Mississippi Code Annotated, 1999 Cumulative Supplement

Mississippi Code Annotated, 1999 Cumulative Supplement, Vol. 21, T. 97 - Crimes; T. 99 - Criminal Procedure see Mississippi Code Annotated, 1999 Cumulative Supplement

***Mississippi Code of 1972 Annotated - Court Rules: 1999 Edition.** 900p. 1999. Price not set. (0-327-09629-2, 4459010) LEXIS Pub.

***Mississippi Code of 1972 Annotated Vol. 1: 2000 Advance Code Service.** 50p. 1999. pap. write for info. (0-327-09943-7, 4462110) LEXIS Pub.

***Mississippi Code of 1972 Annotated - Replacement Volume 19A (T83 ch 39-end, T84-89) Vol. 19A: Insurance; Debtor-Creditor Relationship; etc.** 750p. 1999. Price not set. (0-327-09518-0, 4456610) LEXIS Pub.

Mississippi Code of 1972, 26 vols., Set. LC 72-86599. 1991. suppl. ed. 732.00 (0-318-57146-3) West Group.

***Mississippi Code of 1972 Annotated, Replacement Volume 7: Public Officers & Employees, Public Records.** 1200p. 1999. Price not set. (0-327-09043-X, 4452911) LEXIS Pub.

***Mississippi Code of 1972 Annotated, 1999 Replacement Volume 12: Conservation & Ecoloby, Water, Etc.** 1350p. 1999. Price not set. (0-327-09041-3, 4454411) LEXIS Pub.

***Mississippi Code of 1972 Annotated, 1999 Replacement Volume 19: Insurance, Debtor-Creditor Relationship, Etc.** 1400p. 1999. Price not set. (0-327-09042-1, 4456411) LEXIS Pub.

Mississippi Confederate Pension Applications, A-G. Betty C. Wiltshire. 362p. (Orig.). 1994. pap. 25.00 (1-885480-01-6) Pioneer Pubng.

Mississippi Confederate Pension Applications, H-O. Betty C. Wiltshire. 312p. (Orig.). 1995. pap. 25.00 (1-885480-05-9) Pioneer Pubng.

Mississippi Confederate Pension Applications, P-Z. Betty C. Wiltshire. 324p. (Orig.). 1995. pap. 25.00 (1-885480-06-7) Pioneer Pubng.

Mississippi Cookbook. Ed. by Mississippi Cooperative Extension Service, Home Ec. LC 74-185345. 476p. 1972. pap. 17.95 (0-87805-381-6) U Pr of Miss.

***Mississippi County Court Records.** May W. McBee. LC 67-29601. 94p. 1999. reprint ed. pap. 16.50 (0-8063-0218-6) Clearfield Co.

***Mississippi Court Records, 1799-1835.** J. Estelle King. LC 69-17129. 205p. 1999. reprint ed. pap. 21.50 (0-8063-0203-8) Clearfield Co.

***Mississippi Crime in Perspective 2000.** Ed. by Kathleen O'Leary Morgan & Scott E. Morgan. 22p. 2000. spiral bd. 19.00 (0-7401-0323-7) Morgan Quitno Corp.

Mississippi Crime Perspective, 1998. Ed. by Kathleen O'Leary Morgan & Scott E. Morgan. 20p. 1998. pap. 19.00 (1-56692-923-7) Morgan Quitno Corp.

Mississippi Crime Perspectives, 1999. Kathleen O'Leary Morgan. 22p. 1999. spiral bd. 19.00 (0-7401-0123-4) Morgan Quitno Corp.

***Mississippi Criminal & Traffic Law Manual: 1999 Edition.** 931p. 1999. pap. 38.00 (0-327-09949-6, 2730510) LEXIS Pub.

Mississippi "Crinkum-Crankum" A Funny Word Book about Our State. Carole Marsh. (Carole Marsh Mississippi Bks.). (Illus.). (J). 1994. pap. 19.95 (0-7933-4881-1); lib. bdg. 29.95 (0-7933-4880-3); disk 29.95 (0-7933-4882-X) Gallopade Intl.

Mississippi Delta. Jason Cooper. LC 95-12305. (Natural Wonders Ser.). (J). (gr. 2-6). 1995. lib. bdg. 14.60 (1-57103-016-6) Rourke Pr.

Mississippi Delta & the World: The Memoirs of David L. Cohn. David L. Cohn. Ed. by James C. Cobb. LC 94-24290. (Library of Southern Civilization). (Illus.). 312p. 1995. 24.95 (0-8071-1991-1) La State U Pr.

Mississippi Dingbats! Bk. 1: A Fun Book of Games, Stories, Activities & More about Our State That's All in Code! for You to Decipher. Carole Marsh. (Carole Marsh Mississippi Bks.). (Illus.). (J). (gr. 3-12). 1994. pap. 19.95 (0-7933-3846-8); lib. bdg. 29.95 (0-7933-3845-X); disk 29.95 (0-7933-3847-6) Gallopade Intl.

Mississippi Early Census, Vol. 1. Ronald V. Jackson. 1981. lib. bdg. 43.00 (0-89593-729-8, Accel Indexing) Genealogical Srvcs.

Mississippi Early Census, Vol. 2. Ronald V. Jackson. 1984. lib. bdg. 43.00 (0-89593-730-1, Accel Indexing) Genealogical Srvcs.

Mississippi 1840 Census Vol. 1: Alphabetically Listed by Surnames. Ed. by Thomas E. Coyle. 551p. 1990. pap. text 60.00 (1-56088-011-2) Coyle Data Co.

Mississippi Environmental Law Handbook. Daniel Coker Horton & Bell Staff et al. 145p. 1994. pap. text 79.00 (0-86587-309-7) Gov Insts.

***Mississippi Experience Pocket Guide.** Carole Marsh. (Mississippi Experience! Ser.). (Illus.). (J). 2000. pap. 6.95 (0-7933-9554-2) Gallopade Intl.

Mississippi Facts & Factivities. Carole Marsh. (Carole Marsh State Bks.). (Illus.). (J). (gr. 4-7). 1996. pap., teacher ed. 19.95 (0-7933-7895-8, C Marsh) Gallopade Intl.

***Mississippi Facts & Symbols.** Karen Bush Gibson. LC 00-22920. (States & Their Symbols Ser.). (Illus.). 24p. (J). (ps-3). 2000. lib. bdg. 15.93 (0-7368-0640-7, Hilltop Bks) Capstone Pr.

Mississippi Family: "Seven Generations of Mississippi Women" Barbara Johnson & Mary Sikora. 224p. 1987. mass mkt. 2.50 (0-87067-272-X, BH272) Holloway.

Mississippi Farmers, 1840 to 1860. H. Weaver. 1990. 16.50 (0-8446-1468-8) Peter Smith.

Mississippi Federal Census Index 1820. Ronald V. Jackson. LC 77-85971. 1981. lib. bdg. 48.00 (0-89593-076-5, Accel Indexing) Genealogical Srvcs.

Mississippi Federal Census Index 1830. Ronald V. Jackson. LC 77-85972. (Illus.). 1976. lib. bdg. 56.00 (0-89593-077-3, Accel Indexing) Genealogical Srvcs.

Mississippi Federal Census Index 1850. Ronald V. Jackson. LC 77-85975. (Illus.). 1976. lib. bdg. 99.00 (0-89593-079-X, Accel Indexing) Genealogical Srvcs.

Mississippi Federal Census Index 1840. Ronald V. Jackson. (Illus.). lib. bdg. 62.00 (0-89593-683-6, Accel Indexing) Genealogical Srvcs.

Mississippi Federal Census Index, 1810 (Enumerations) Ronald V. Jackson. (Illus.). 1986. lib. bdg. 43.00 (0-89593-682-8, Accel Indexing) Genealogical Srvcs.

Mississippi Festival Fun for Kids! Carole Marsh. (Carole Marsh Mississippi Bks.). (Illus.). (J). (gr. 3-12). 1994. pap. 19.95 (0-7933-3999-5); lib. bdg. 29.95 (0-7933-3998-7) Gallopade Intl.

Mississippi Festival Fun for Kids! Carole Marsh. (Carole Marsh Mississippi Bks.). (Illus.). (YA). (gr. 3-12). 1994. disk 29.95 (0-7933-4000-4) Gallopade Intl.

Mississippi Flood of 1993. Karin L. Badt. LC 94-9493. (Cornerstones to Freedom Ser.). (Illus.). 32p. (J). (gr. 3-6). 1994. lib. bdg. 19.50 (0-516-06680-3) Childrens.

***Mississippi Forests & Forestry.** James E. Fickle. LC 00-35166. (Illus.). 384p. 2001. 35.00 (1-57806-308-6) U Pr of Miss.

Mississippi Gardener's Guide: The What, Where, When, How & Why of Gardening in Mississippi. Norman Winter. LC 99-50052. (Illus.). 264p. 1999. pap. 19.95 (1-888608-44-7) Cool Springs Pr.

Mississippi "GEO" Bingo! 38 Must Know State Geography Facts for Kids to Learn While Having Fun! Carole Marsh. (Bingo! Ser.). (Illus.). (J). (gr. 2-8). 1998. pap. 14.95 (0-7933-8595-4) Gallopade Intl.

Mississippi Going North. Sanna A. Baker. LC 95-52923. (Illus.). 32p. (J). (gr. k-4). 1996. lib. bdg. 15.95 (0-8075-5164-3) A Whitman.

Mississippi Government! The Cornerstone of Everyday Life in Our State! Carole Marsh. (Carole Marsh Mississippi Bks.). (Illus.). (J). (gr. 3-12). 1996. pap. 19.95 (0-7933-6254-7); lib. bdg. 29.95 (0-7933-6253-9); disk 29.95 (0-7933-6255-5) Gallopade Intl.

Mississippi Government & Politics: Modernizers vs. Traditionalists. Dale Krane & Stephen D. Shaffer. LC 91-24025. (Politics & Governments of the American States Ser.). (Illus.). xx, 367p. 1992. pap. text 22.00 (0-8032-7758-X) U of Nebr Pr.

Mississippi Government & Politics: Modernizers vs. Traditionalists. Dale Krane & Stephen D. Shaffer. LC 91-24025. (Politics & Governments of the American States Ser.). (Illus.). xx, 367p. 1992. text 50.00 (0-8032-2715-9) U of Nebr Pr.

Mississippi Governments Performance Standards, 1990. Ed. by Greg Michels. (Governments Performance Standards Ser.). (Illus.). 150p. 1990. text 125.00 (1-55507-491-X) Municipal Analysis.

***Mississippi Gulf Coast: Portrait of a People.** Charles L. Sullivan & Murella H. Powell. (Illus.). 264p. 1999. 32.95 (1-892724-02-2) Am Historical Pr.

Mississippi Headwaters Guide Book: A Guide to the Natural, Cultural, Scenic, Scientific & Recreational Values of the Mississippi River's First 400 Miles. Molly MacGregor. LC 96-127602. (Illus.). 88p. (Orig.). 1995. pap. 15.00 (0-9645849-1-3) MS Headwaters.

***Mississippi Health Care in Perspective 2000.** Ed. by Kathleen O'Leary Morgan & Scott E. Morgan. 21p. 2000. spiral bd. 19.00 (0-7401-0223-0) Morgan Quitno Corp.

Mississippi Health Care Perspective, 1998. Ed. by Kathleen O'Leary Morgan & Scott E. Morgan. 20p. 1998. pap. 19.00 (1-56692-823-0) Morgan Quitno Corp.

Mississippi Health Care Perspective, 1999. Kathleen O'Leary Morgan. 21p. 1999. spiral bd. 19.00 (0-7401-0073-4) Morgan Quitno Corp.

***Mississippi High.** Jack Dukes. 296p. 2000. pap. 19.95 (0-9700270-0-1) Wild Dove Pub.

Mississippi "HISTO" Bingo! 42 Must Know State History Facts for Kids to Learn While Having Fun! Carole Marsh. (Bingo! Ser.). (Illus.). (J). (gr. 2-8). 1998. pap. 14.95 (0-7933-8596-2) Gallopade Intl.

Mississippi Historical & Biographical Index, Vol. 1. Ronald V. Jackson. LC 78-53705. (Illus.). 1984. lib. bdg. 30.00 (0-89593-188-5, Accel Indexing) Genealogical Srvcs.

Mississippi History: Stories. Steve Yarbrough. 176p. (C). 1994. pap. 16.95 (0-8262-0967-X) U of Mo Pr.

Mississippi History! Surprising Secrets about Our State's Founding Mothers, Fathers & Kids! Carole Marsh. (Carole Marsh Mississippi Bks.). (Illus.). (J). (gr. 3-12). 1996. pap. 19.95 (0-7933-6101-X); lib. bdg. 29.95 (0-7933-6100-1); disk 29.95 (0-7933-6102-8) Gallopade Intl.

Mississippi Home-Places: Notes on Literature & History. Elmo Howell. (Illus.). 1988. pap. 14.95 (0-9622026-0-6) E Howell.

Mississippi Homespun: Nineteenth Century Textiles & the Women Who Made Them. Mary Lohrenz & Anita A. Stamper. (Illus.). 79p. 1989. pap. 15.00 (0-938896-56-3) Mississippi Archives.

Mississippi Hot Air Balloon Mystery. Carole Marsh. (Carole Marsh Mississippi Bks.). (Illus.). (J). (gr. 2-9). 1994. 29.95 (0-7933-2534-X); pap. 19.95 (0-7933-2535-8); disk 29.95 (0-7933-2536-6) Gallopade Intl.

Mississippi Hot Zones! Viruses, Diseases, & Epidemics in Our State's History. Carole Marsh. (Hot Zones! Ser.). (Illus.). (J). (gr. 3-12). 1998. pap. 19.95 (0-7933-8901-1); lib. bdg. 29.95 (0-7933-8900-3) Gallopade Intl.

Mississippi in Perspective, 1998. Ed. by Kathleen O'Leary Morgan & Scott E. Morgan. 24p. 1998. pap. 19.00 (1-56692-873-7) Morgan Quitno Corp.

Mississippi in Perspective, 1999. Ed. by Kathleen O'Leary Morgan. 26p. 1999. spiral bd. 19.00 (1-56692-973-3) Morgan Quitno Corp.

***Mississippi in Perspective 2000.** Ed. by Kathleen O'Leary Morgan & Scott E. Morgan. 26p. 2000. spiral bd. 19.00 (0-7401-0273-7) Morgan Quitno Corp.

Mississippi Index of Wills, 1800 to 1900. Betty C. Wiltshire. 224p. 1989. pap. 25.00 (1-55613-219-0) Heritage Bk.

Mississippi Indian Dictionary for Kids! Carole Marsh. (Carole Marsh State Bks.). (J). (gr. 2-9). 1996. 29.95 (0-7933-7716-1, C Marsh); pap. 19.95 (0-7933-7717-X, C Marsh) Gallopade Intl.

***Mississippi Investment & Business Guide: Business, Investment, Export-Import Opportunities, 50 vols., Vol. 24.** Global Investment Center, USA Staff. (U. S. Regional Investment & Business Library-99: Vol. 24). (Illus.). 350p. (Orig.). 1999. pap. 59.95 (0-7397-1123-7) Intl Business Pubns.

Mississippi Invitational. Rene P. Barilleaux et al. Ed. by Kathy L. Greenberg. LC 99-10848. (Illus.). 48p. 1999. pap. 10.00 (1-887422-02-1) Miss Mus Art.

Mississippi Invitational. Nina Felshin. Ed. by Rene P. Barilleaux & Ginger Tucker. LC 97-6580. (Illus.). 48p. (Orig.). 1997. pap. text 10.00 (1-887422-01-3) Miss Mus Art.

***Mississippi Jeopardy.** Carole Marsh. (Mississippi Experience! Ser.). (Illus.). (J). (gr. 2-6). 2000. pap. 7.95 (0-7933-9556-9) Gallopade Intl.

Mississippi Jeopardy! Answers & Questions about Our State! Carole Marsh. (Carole Marsh Mississippi Bks.). (Illus.). (J). (gr. 3-12). 1994. pap. 19.95 (0-7933-4152-3); lib. bdg. 29.95 (0-7933-4151-5); disk 29.95 (0-7933-4153-1) Gallopade Intl.

***Mississippi Jography.** Carole Marsh. (Mississippi Experience! Ser.). (Illus.). (J). (gr. 2-6). 2000. pap. 7.95 (0-7933-9557-7) Gallopade Intl.

Mississippi "Jography" A Fun Run Thru Our State. Carole Marsh. (Carole Marsh Mississippi Bks.). (Illus.). (J). (gr. 3 up). 1994. pap. 19.95 (1-55609-091-9); lib. bdg. 29.95 (1-55609-709-3); disk 29.95 (1-55609-715-8) Gallopade Intl.

Mississippi John Hurt. Ed. by Aaron Stang. 100p. (Orig.). (C). 1993. pap. text 20.95 (0-7692-0953-X, F3176GTXCD) Wrner Bros.

Mississippi Kid's Cookbook: Recipes, How-To, History, Lore & More. Carole Marsh. (Carole Marsh Mississippi Bks.). (Illus.). (J). (gr. 3 up). 1994. pap. 19.95 (0-7933-0659-0); lib. bdg. 29.95 (0-7933-0660-4); disk 29.95 (0-7933-0661-2) Gallopade Intl.

M

Mississippi Kite. Eric G. Bolen & Dan Flores. LC 93-3657. (Corrie Herring Hooks Ser.: No. 25). (Illus.). 128p. (C). 1993. 17.95 (0-292-75148-6) U of Tex Pr.

Mississippi Land Surveying Law: Questions & Answers. John E. Keen. 46p. (C). 1995. pap. text 25.00 (1-56569-031-1) Land Survey.

Mississippi Law Journal, 1928-1994/95, 66 vols., Set. 1996. 3080.00 (0-8377-9114-6, Rothman) W S Hein.

Mississippi Library Book: A Surprising Guide to the Unusual Special Collections in Libraries Across Our State for Students, Teachers, Writers & Publishers - Includes Reproducible Mailing Labels Plus Activities for Young People! Carole Marsh. (Carole Marsh Mississippi Bks.). (Illus.). 1994. pap. 19.95 (0-7933-3078-5); lib. bdg. 29.95 (0-7933-3077-7); disk 29.95 (0-7933-3079-3) Gallopade Intl.

Mississippi-Louisiana Border Country: History of Rodney Mississippi & Environs. Marie Logan. 1974. 35.00 (0-87511-072-X) Claitors.

Mississippi Manufacturers Directory 1987. 1987. 35.00 (0-317-58439-1) MS Res & Dev Ctr.

Mississippi Manufacturers Register. 5th rev. ed. Ed. by Frank Lambing. 1999. 66.00 (1-58202-055-8) Manufacturers.

Mississippi Marriages, Early to 1825. Liahona Research, Inc. Staff. Ed. by Jordan Dodd. 117p. 1991. lib. bdg. 35.00 (1-877677-35-3) Herit Quest.

Mississippi Math! How It All Adds up in Our State. Carole Marsh. (Carole Marsh Mississippi Bks.). (Illus.). (YA). (gr. 3-12). 1996. pap. 29.95 (0-7933-6559-7); pap. 19.95 (0-7933-6560-0) Gallopade Intl.

Mississippi Mayhem. David Thompson. (Davy Crockett Ser.: No. 4). 176p. (Orig.). 1997. mass mkt. 3.99 (0-8439-4278-9, Leisure Bks) Dorchester Pub Co.

Mississippi Media Book: A Surprising Guide to the Amazing Print, Broadcast & Online Media of Our State for Students, Teachers, Writers & Publishers - Includes Reproducible Mailing Labels Plus Activities for Young People! Carole Marsh. (Carole Marsh Mississippi Bks.). (Illus.). 1994. pap. 19.95 (0-7933-3234-6); lib. bdg. 29.95 (0-7933-3233-8); disk 29.95 (0-7933-3235-4) Gallopade Intl.

Mississippi Methodists, 1799-1983: A Moral People "Born of Conviction" Ray Holder. 11.95 (0-9612932-0-9); pap. 8.95 (0-9612932-1-7) Maverick Prints.

Mississippi Mind: A Personal Cultural History of an American State. Gayle G. Yates. LC 89-28630. 320p. 1990. 30.00 (0-87049-643-3) U of Tenn Pr.

Mississippi Miss. Emma Goldrick. (Romance Ser.: No. 134). 1991. per. 2.75 (0-373-03134-3) Harlequin Bks.

Mississippi Miss. large type ed. Emma Goldrick. 1991. reprint ed. lib. bdg. 19.95 (0-263-12621-8) Mac Lib Ref.

Mississippi Mud. Edward Humes. (Illus.). 416p. 1994. 22.50 (0-671-88998-2) S&S Trade.

Mississippi Mud: A True Story from a Corner of the Deep South. Edward Humes. 448p. 1995. per. 6.99 (0-671-53505-6) PB.

Mississippi Mud: 3 Prairie Journals. Ann Turner. LC 95-10850. (Illus.). 48p. (J). (gr. 2-5). 1997. 15.95 (0-06-024432-1); lib. bdg. 16.89 (0-06-024433-X) HarpC Child Bks.

***Mississippi Mystery Series, 7 vols.** Phil Hardwick. (Illus.). 1999. pap. 49.95 (1-893062-13-9) Quail Ridge.

Mississippi Mystery Van Takes Off! Bk. 1: Handicapped Mississippi Kids Sneak Off on a Big Adventure. Carole Marsh. (Carole Marsh Mississippi Bks.). (Illus.). (J). (gr. 3-12). 1994. 29.95 (0-7933-5033-6); pap. 19.95 (0-7933-5034-4); disk 29.95 (0-7933-5035-2) Gallopade Intl.

Mississippi Newspaper Obituaries, 1862-1875. Betty C. Wiltshire. 253p. 1994. pap. 22.50 (1-885480-00-8) Pioneer Pubng.

Mississippi Newspaper Obituaries, 1876-1885. Betty C. Wiltshire. LC 99-214378. 260p. 1998. pap. 25.00 (1-885480-27-X) Pioneer Pubng.

***Mississippi 1999 Advance Sheets ALS, No. 3.** 1000p. 1999. write for info. (0-327-08717-X, 44613-10) LEXIS Pub.

Mississippi 1999 Advance Sheets: MS 99 ALS, Vol. 2. 800p. 1999. pap. write for info. (0-327-08531-2, 44612-10) LEXIS Pub.

Mississippi 1999 Advance Sheets Pamphlet No. 1: MS 99 ALS. 500p. 1999. pap. write for info. (0-327-08524-X, 44611-10) LEXIS Pub.

***Mississippi, 1999 Index, Vol. 1 & 2.** Incl. Mississippi, 1999 Index Vol. 1: Index A to I. 1115p. 1999. (*0-327-08999-7*, 44587-10); Mississippi, 1999 Index Vol. 2: Index J to Z. 1115p. 1999. (*0-327-09000-6*, 44588-10); 2246p. 1999. Price not set. (*0-327-08897-4*, 4458610) LEXIS Pub.

Mississippi, 1999 Index, Vol. 1, Index A to I see Mississippi, 1999 Index

Mississippi, 1999 Index, Vol. 2, Index J to Z see Mississippi, 1999 Index

***Mississippi 1972 Code Annotated 1999 Annotation Citator.** 1700p. 1999. Price not set. (*0-327-09755-8*, 4135510) LEXIS Pub.

Mississippi Observed. Sheree Hightower & Cathie Stanga. Ed. by Carol Cox. LC 94-19079. (Illus.). 144p. 1994. 45.00 (*0-87805-727-7*) U Pr of Miss.

***Mississippi Odyssey.** Chris Markham. (Illus.). 145p. 2000. pap. 11.95 (*0-595-09123-7*) iUniversecom.

Mississippi Patent Models. Ed. by Patti C. Black. (Illus.). 24p. 1981. pap. 3.50 (*0-938896-32-6*) Mississippi Archives.

Mississippi Penal Code Annotated, with Cd-rom: 1999 Edition. 47.50 incl. cd-rom (*0-327-19743-9*) LEXIS Pub.

Mississippi Portraiture. Vera J. Speakes & Estill C. Pennington. LC 87-61368. (Illus.). 326p. 1987. 35.00 (*0-935903-02-X*) Lauren Rogers.

Mississippi Provincial Archives: French Dominion, 3 vols. Mississippi Department of Archives and History Sta. Ed. by Dunbar Rowland & A. G. Sanders. LC 72-172737. reprint ed. 315.00 (*0-404-07370-0*) AMS Pr.

Mississippi Provincial Archives: French Dominion, 1729-1748, Vol. IV. Ed. by Patricia Kay Galloway et al. LC 82-17267. (Library of Southern Civilization). 424p. 1984. text 60.00 (*0-8071-1068-X*) La State U Pr.

Mississippi Provincial Archives: French Dominion, 1749-1763, Vol. V. Ed. by Patricia Kay Galloway et al. LC 82-17267. (Library of Southern Civilization). 424p. 1984. text 60.00 (*0-8071-1069-8*) La State U Pr.

Mississippi Public Policy Think Tank: Creating a Blueprint for Responsible Public Policy in the Management of Compulsive Gambling. Elizabeth M. George. 36p. 1995. reprint ed. spiral bd. 15.00 (*1-930467-00-1*, LA Zarus) MN Coun Gambling.

Mississippi Question, 1985 to 1803. Arthur P. Whitaker. 1990. 14.50 (*0-8446-1476-9*) Peter Smith.

Mississippi Quiz Bowl Crash Course! Carole Marsh. (Carole Marsh Mississippi Bks.). (Illus.). (J). (gr. 3 up). 1994. pap. 19.95 (*1-55609-723-9*); lib. bdg. 29.95 (*1-55609-722-0*); disk 29.95 (*1-55609-724-7*) Gallopade Intl.

Mississippi Rebel in the Army of Northern Virginia: The Civil War Memoirs of Private David Holt. Ed. by Thomas D. Cockrell & Michael B. Ballard. LC 95-30226. (Illus.). 384p. (C). 1996. 34.95 (*0-8071-1981-4*) La State U Pr.

Mississippi Retirement & Relocation Guide. large type ed. (Retirement & Relocation Guides Ser.). (Illus.). 350p. Date not set. pap. 24.95 (*1-56559-145-3*) HGI-Over Fifty.

Mississippi River. Casa Bonechi. 128p. text 14.95 (*88-8029-420-2*, Pub. by Bonechi) Eiron.

Mississippi River. Allan Fowler. LC 98-43961. (Rookie Read-About Geography Ser.). (Illus.). 32p. (J). (gr. 1-2). 1999. 19.00 (*0-516-21557-4*) Childrens.

***Mississippi River.** Allan Fowler. (Rookie Read-About Geography Ser.). (J). 2000. pap. text 5.95 (*0-516-26556-3*) Childrens.

***Mississippi River.** Maria Mudd-Ruth. LC 99-49873. (Ecosystems of North America Ser.). (Illus.). (J). 2001. lib. bdg. 27.07 (*0-7614-0934-3*, Benchmark NY) Marshall Cavendish.

Mississippi River. Tom Weil. (U. S. A. Guides Ser.). (Illus.). 514p. 1993. pap. 16.95 (*0-7818-0142-7*) Hippocrene Bks.

Mississippi River. unabridged ed. Rebecca Pittman. (Illus.). 128p. 1996. pap. 15.95 (*0-934520-96-8*, PPB 0006) Cartwheel Co.

***Mississippi River: From the Northern Pines to the Tropical Mangroves.** Peter Lourie. LC 98-88235. (Illus.). 48p. (YA). (gr. 2-5). 2000. 17.95 (*1-56397-756-7*) Boyds Mills Pr.

Mississippi River: Nature Culture & Travel Sites along the "Mighty Mississip" Tom Weil. (Travel Guides Ser.). 425p. 1992. 24.95 (*0-7818-0030-7*) Hippocrene Bks.

Mississippi River Activity Guide for Kids. abr. ed. Pat Middleton. (Illus.). 30p. (J). (gr. 4-7). 1993. pap. 6.95 (*0-9620823-5-X*) Heritage WI.

Mississippi River Cookin' Book. Bruce Carlson. (Illus.). 214p. (Orig.). 1989. spiral bd. 11.95 (*1-878488-09-0*) Hearts N Tummies.

***Mississippi River Country Tales: A Celebration of 500 Years of Deep Sixth History.** Jim Fraiser. 168p. 1999. pap. 14.95 (*0-9627737-1-9*) Persimmon Pr MS.

***Mississippi River Country Tales: A Celebration of 500 Years of Deep South History.** Jim Fraiser. LC 00-35948. (Illus.). (J). 2000. pap. write for info. (*1-56554-787-X*) Pelican.

Mississippi River Delta: Legal-Geomorphologic Evaluation of Historic Shoreline Changes. David J. Morgan. (Geoscience & Man Ser.: Vol. 16). (Illus.). 104p. 1977. pap. 15.00 (*0-938909-15-0*) Geosci Pubns LSU.

Mississippi River Getaways. (Midwest Living Ser.). 144p. 1998. pap. 14.95 (*0-696-20787-7*) Meredith Bks.

Mississippi River Po' Folk. Pat Wallace. Ed. & Illus. by Bruce Carlson. 173p. (Orig.). 1990. pap. 9.95 (*1-878488-30-9*) Quixote Pr IA.

Mississippi River Tales. Front Porch Favorites Staff. Date not set. lib. bdg. 19.95 (*0-8488-1706-0*) Amereon Ltd.

Mississippi Road Atlas. LC 97-2089. (Illus.). 40.00 (*0-87805-997-0*) U Pr of Miss.

Mississippi Road Atlas. University of Mississippi. LC 97-2089. (Illus.). pap. 20.00 (*0-87805-990-3*) U Pr of Miss.

Mississippi Rogue. Clay Tanner. (Chance Ser.: No. 6). 176p. (Orig.). 1987. pap. 2.50 (*0-380-75165-8*, Avon Bks) Morrow Avon.

Mississippi Rollercoasters! Carole Marsh. (Carole Marsh Mississippi Bks.). (Illus.). (J). (gr. 3-12). 1994. pap. 19.95 (*0-7933-5297-5*); lib. bdg. 29.95 (*0-7933-5296-7*) Gallopade Intl.

Mississippi Rollercoasters! Carole Marsh. (Carole Marsh Mississippi Bks.). (Illus.). (YA). (gr. 3-12). 1994. disk 29.95 (*0-7933-5298-3*) Gallopade Intl.

Mississippi Roots & Records Vol. 1: Claiborne, Co. Joyce S. Bridges & Wanda V. Head. 100p. 1994. pap. text 16.00 (*1-57088-035-2*) J&W Ent.

Mississippi Roots & Records Vol. 2: Tishomingo County. Joyce S. Bridges & Wanda V. Head. 100p. 1995. pap. text 16.00 (*1-57088-036-0*) J&W Ent.

Mississippi Roots & Records - Copiah County, Vol. 3. Joyce S. Bridges & Wanda V. Head. 97p. 1994. pap. text 16.00 (*1-57088-037-9*) J&W Ent.

Mississippi Roots & Records - Franklin County, Vol. 4. Joyce S. Bridges & Wanda V. Head. 104p. 1994. pap. text 16.00 (*1-57088-038-7*) J&W Ent.

Mississippi Roots & Records - Madison County, Vol. 5. Joyce S. Bridges & Wanda V. Head. 102p. 1994. pap. text 16.00 (*1-57088-039-5*) J&W Ent.

Mississippi Roots n' Records - WPA County Maps, Vol. 6. Joyce S. Bridges & Wanda V. Head. 81p. 1997. pap. 16.00 (*1-57088-047-6*) J&W Ent.

Mississippi Scenes: Notes on Literature & History. Elmo Howell. (Illus.). 330p. (Orig.). 1992. pap. 16.95 (*0-9622026-2-2*) E Howell.

Mississippi School Trivia: An Amazing & Fascinating Look at Our State's Teachers, Schools & Students! Carole Marsh. (Carole Marsh Mississippi Bks.). (Illus.). (J). (gr. 3 up). 1994. pap. 19.95 (*0-7933-0656-6*); lib. bdg. 29.95 (*0-7933-0657-4*); disk 29.95 (*0-7933-0658-2*) Gallopade Intl.

Mississippi Schoolmaster. Henrietta Matson. LC 72-1511. (Black Heritage Library Collection). 1977. reprint ed. 25.95 (*0-8369-9035-8*) Ayer.

Mississippi Silly Basketball Sportsmysteries, Vol. I. Carole Marsh. (Carole Marsh Mississippi Bks.). (Illus.). (J). (gr. 3 up). 1994. pap. 19.95 (*0-7933-0653-1*); lib. bdg. 29.95 (*0-7933-0654-X*); disk 29.95 (*0-7933-0655-8*) Gallopade Intl.

Mississippi Silly Basketball Sportsmysteries, Vol. II. Carole Marsh. (Carole Marsh Mississippi Bks.). (Illus.). (J). (gr. 3 up). 1994. pap. 19.95 (*0-7933-1732-0*); lib. bdg. 29.95 (*0-7933-1731-2*) Gallopade Intl.

Mississippi Silly Basketball Sportsmysteries, Vol. II. Carole Marsh. (Carole Marsh Mississippi Bks.). (Illus.). (J). (gr. 3 up). 1997. disk 29.95 (*0-7933-1733-9*) Gallopade Intl.

Mississippi Silly Football Sportsmysteries, Vol. I. Carole Marsh. (Carole Marsh Mississippi Bks.). (Illus.). (J). (gr. 3 up). 1994. pap. 19.95 (*1-55609-712-3*); lib. bdg. 29.95 (*1-55609-711-5*); disk 29.95 (*1-55609-713-1*) Gallopade Intl.

Mississippi Silly Football Sportsmysteries, Vol. II. Carole Marsh. (Carole Marsh Mississippi Bks.). (Illus.). (J). (gr. 3 up). 1994. pap. 19.95 (*1-55609-718-2*); lib. bdg. 29.95 (*1-55609-717-4*); disk 29.95 (*1-55609-719-0*) Gallopade Intl.

Mississippi Silly Trivia! Carole Marsh. (Carole Marsh Mississippi Bks.). (Illus.). (J). (gr. 3 up). 1994. pap. 19.95 (*1-55609-039-0*); lib. bdg. 29.95 (*1-55609-708-5*); disk 29.95 (*1-55609-714-X*) Gallopade Intl.

Mississippi Small Claims Court: A Comprehensive Guide on Your Own. William D. Eshee, Jr. 250p. 1993. pap. write for info. (*0-9636223-0-7*) Rockwell Pr.

Mississippi Soldiers: Revolutionary, 1812, Indian & Mexican Wars. Betty C. Wiltshire. LC 99-214382. 96p. 1998. pap. 12.00 (*1-885480-29-6*) Pioneer Pubng.

Mississippi Solo: A River Quest. Eddy L. Harris. LC 98-24706. 256p. 1998. pap. 12.95 (*0-8050-5903-2*, Owl) H Holt & Co.

Mississippi Soundex for Collier Surname, 1880: With Various Spellings. Compiled by Berniece Douglas Coyle. 4p. 1989. pap. text 2.00 (*1-882111-89-3*) Coyle Data Co.

Mississippi Spelling Bee! Score Big by Correctly Spelling Our State's Unique Names. Carole Marsh. (Carole Marsh Mississippi Bks.). (Illus.). (YA). (gr. 3-12). 1996. pap. 19.95 (*0-7933-6713-1*); lib. bdg. 29.95 (*0-7933-6712-3*) Gallopade Intl.

Mississippi State Census Index 1818. (Illus.). lib. bdg. 40.00 (*0-89593-392-6*, Accel Indexing) Genealogical Srvcs.

Mississippi State Census Index, 1820-1825. (Illus.). lib. bdg. 55.00 (*0-89593-393-4*, Accel Indexing) Genealogical Srvcs.

Mississippi State Census Index, 1830-1837. (Illus.). lib. bdg. 50.00 (*0-89593-394-2*, Accel Indexing) Genealogical Srvcs.

Mississippi State Census Index, 1840-1841. (Illus.). lib. bdg. 55.00 (*0-89593-395-0*, Accel Indexing) Genealogical Srvcs.

Mississippi State Census Index, 1845. (Illus.). lib. bdg. 55.00 (*0-89593-396-9*, Accel Indexing) Genealogical Srvcs.

Mississippi State Census Index 1853. (Illus.). lib. bdg. 90.00 (*0-89593-398-5*, Accel Indexing) Genealogical Srvcs.

Mississippi State Census Index 1866. (Illus.). lib. bdg. 105.00 (*0-89593-399-3*, Accel Indexing) Genealogical Srvcs.

Mississippi State Constitution: A Reference Guide, 12. John W. Winkle, III. LC 92-21357. (Reference Guides to the State Constitutions of the United States Ser.: No. 12). 200p. 1993. lib. bdg. 69.50 (*0-313-27295-6*, WMS, Greenwood Pr) Greenwood.

Mississippi Steamboat Era in Historic Photographs: Natchez to New Orleans, 1870-1920. Ed. by Joan W. Gandy & Thomas H. Gandy. 128p. 1987. pap. 11.95 (*0-486-25260-4*) Dover.

Mississippi Steamboatman: The Story of Henry Miller Shreve. Edith McCall. LC 85-13795. (Walker's American History Series for Young People). (Illus.). 115p. (J). (gr. 5-8). 1986. 11.95 (*0-8027-6597-1*) Walker & Co.

Mississippi Stories. Beverly Carradine. 1989. reprint ed. pap. 11.99 (*0-88019-243-7*) Schmul Pub Co.

***Mississippi Stories for Young People: A Look at the Past.** Craig Skates. (YA). 1999. pap. 6.95 (*1-893062-07-4*) Quail Ridge.

Mississippi Survival. Betty L. Hall & Walter E. Sistrunk. 160p. (Orig.). (gr. 10-12). 1979. pap. text 5.84 (*0-03-055511-6*) Westwood Pr.

***Mississippi Territory in the War of 1812.** Eron Rowland. 249p. 1999. 25.00 (*0-8063-0301-8*) Clearfield Co.

Mississippi Timeline: A Chronology of Mississippi History, Mystery, Trivia, Legend, Lore & More. Carole Marsh. (Carole Marsh Mississippi Bks.). (Illus.). (J). (gr. 3-12). 1994. pap. 19.95 (*0-7933-5948-1*); lib. bdg. 29.95 (*0-7933-5947-3*); disk 29.95 (*0-7933-5949-X*) Gallopade Intl.

Mississippi to Madrid: Memoir of a Black American in the Abraham Lincoln Brigade. James Yates. LC 88-62370. (Illus.). 183p. (Orig.). (C). 1989. 19.95 (*0-940880-19-9*); pap. 9.95 (*0-940880-20-2*) Open Hand.

Mississippi Trial Handbook. 2nd ed. Stanford Young. Ed. by Karen Morgan. LC 95-79069. xxv, 1133 p. 1995. text 120.00 (*0-7620-0002-3*) West Group.

Mississippi 2000! Coming Soon to a Calendar Near You - The 21st Century! - Complete Set of AL 2000 Items. Carole Marsh. (Two Thousand! Ser.). (Illus.). (J). (gr. 3-12). 1998. pap. 75.00 (*0-7933-9357-4*); lib. bdg. 85.00 (*0-7933-9358-2*) Gallopade Intl.

Mississippi 2000! Coming Soon to a Calendar near You--The 21st Century! Carole Marsh. (Two Thousand! Ser.). (Illus.). (J). (gr. 3-12). 1998. pap. 19.95 (*0-7933-8748-5*); lib. bdg. 29.95 (*0-7933-8747-7*) Gallopade Intl.

Mississippi UFO's & Extraterrestrials! A Look at the Sightings & Science in Our State. Carole Marsh. (Carole Marsh Mississippi Bks.). (Illus.). (J). (gr. 3-12). 1997. pap. 19.95 (*0-7933-6407-8*); lib. bdg. 29.95 (*0-7933-6406-X*) Gallopade Intl.

Mississippi United Methodist Churches: Two Hundred Years of Heritage & Hope. William L. Jenkins. LC 98-66284. (Illus.). 256p. 1998. 29.95 (*1-57736-104-0*) Providence Hse.

Mississippi Valley Architecture: Houses of the Lower Mississippi Valley. Stanley Schuler. LC 83-51744. (Illus.). 240p. 1984. 30.00 (*0-916838-96-X*) Schiffer.

Mississippi Valley Beginnings: An Outline of the Early History of the Earlier West. Henry E. Chambers. (Illus.). 389p. 1997. reprint ed. lib. bdg. 42.50 (*0-8328-6821-3*) Higginson Bk Co.

Mississippi Valley Beginnings: An Outline of the Early History of the Earlier West. Henry E. Chambers. (BCL1 - United States Local History Ser.). 389p. 1991. reprint ed. text 89.00 (*0-7812-6303-4*) Rprt Serv.

***Mississippi Valley in the Civil War.** John Fiske. (Illus.). 468p. 1999. reprint ed. pap. 34.00 (*0-7884-1223-X*, F371) Heritage Bk.

Mississippi Valley in the Civil War. John Fiske. (Notable American Authors Ser.). 1992. reprint ed. lib. bdg. 75.00 (*0-7812-2861-1*) Rprt Serv.

Mississippi Valley's Great Yellow Fever Epidemic of 1878. Kaled J. Bloom. LC 93-2965. 296p. (C). 1993. text 40.00 (*0-8071-1824-9*) La State U Pr.

Mississippi Vistas. Louis D. Brodsky. LC 90-70684. (Mississippi Trilogy Ser.: Vol. 1). 91p. 1990. pap. 12.50 (*1-877770-73-6*); pap. 19.95 incl. audio (*1-877770-15-9*); audio 12.95 (*1-877770-14-0*) Time Being Bks.

Mississippi Vistas Vol. 1: A Mississippi Trilogy. Louis D. Brodsky. LC 90-70684. 91p. 1990. 18.95 (*1-877770-12-4*) Time Being Bks.

***Mississippi Wildlife, Fisheries & Parks Law Book, 1999 Cumulative Supplement.** Ed. by LEXIS Law Publishing Editors. 363p. 2000. pap. 17.00 (*0-327-10660-3*, 2528010) LEXIS Pub.

Mississippi Workers' Compensation Laws & Rules, 1999. annot. ed. Ed. by LEXIS Law Publishing Editors. 280p. pap. 30.00 (*0-327-19728-5*) LEXIS Pub.

Mississippi Writers: An Anthology. Ed. by Dorothy Abbott. LC 90-28947. (Center for the Study of Southern Culture Ser.). 1991. pap. 19.95 (*0-87805-503-7*); text 37.50 (*0-87805-479-0*) U Pr of Miss.

Mississippi Writers Vol. 2: Reflections of Childhood & Youth: Nonfiction. Ed. by Dorothy Abbott. LC 84-5131. (Center for the Study of Southern Culture Ser.). 736p. 1986. text 37.50 (*0-87805-233-X*) U Pr of Miss.

Mississippi Writers Vol. 3: Reflections of Childhood & Youth - Poetry. Ed. by Dorothy Abbott & Rosellen Brown. LC 84-5131. (Center for the Study of Southern Culture Ser.). 1987. text 37.50 (*0-87805-235-6*) U Pr of Miss.

Mississippi Writers Vol. 4: Reflections of Childhood & Youth, Drama. Ed. by Dorothy Abbott. LC 84-5131. 1991. pap. 19.95 (*0-87805-238-0*); text 37.50 (*0-87805-237-2*) U Pr of Miss.

Mississippi Writers Directory & Literary Guide. Aleda Shirley et al. (Illus.). 128p. (Orig.). 1995. pap. 6.00 (*0-9647848-0-7*) U MS CSSC.

Mississippi Writers Talking Vol. 1: Interviews with Eudora Welty, Shelby Foote, Elizabeth Spencer, Barry Hannah, Beth Henley. John G. Jones. LC 81-23057. 204p. reprint ed. pap. 63.30 (*0-8357-4344-6*, 203714700001) Bks Demand.

Mississippi Writings: Tom Sawyer; Life on the Mississippi; Huckleberry Finn; Pudd'nhead Wilson. Mark Twain, pseud. Ed. by Guy Cardwell. LC 82-9917. 1126p. 1982. 30.00 (*0-940450-07-0*, Pub. by Library of America) Penguin Putnam.

Mississippian Communities & Households. Ed. by J. Daniel Rogers & Bruce D. Smith. LC 94-44049. (Illus.). 320p. 1995. pap. text 29.95 (*0-8173-0768-0*) U of Ala Pr.

Mississippian Emergence. Ed. by Bruce D. Smith. LC 89-22000. (Illus.). 272p. 1990. text 50.00 (*0-87474-844-5*) Smithsonian.

Mississippian Exploitative Strategies: A Southeast Missouri Example. R. Barry Lewis. Ed. by W. Raymond Wood. LC 73-620254. (Research Ser.: No. 11). (Illus.). 63p. (Orig.). 1974. pap. 5.00 (*0-943414-12-1*) MO Arch Soc.

Mississippian Faunas of Western Canada. Samuel J. Nelson. LC QE0729.N36. (Geological Association of Canada. Special Paper: No. 2). 100p. reprint ed. pap. 31.00 (*0-608-18711-9*, 202783700056) Bks Demand.

Mississippian Mortuary Practices. Lynne G. Goldstein. LC 82-101139. (Scientific Papers Ser.: No. 4). (Illus.). 196p. 1980. pap. 9.00 (*0-942118-08-1*) Ctr Amer Arche.

Mississippian Oolites & Modern Analogs. Ed. by Brian D. Keith & Charles W. Zuppann. (Studies in Geology: No. 35). (Illus.). ix, 265p. 1993. pap. 29.00 (*0-89181-043-9*, 580) AAPG.

Mississippian Political Economy. J. Muller. LC 97-16721. (Interdisciplinary Contributions to Archaeology Ser.). (Illus.). 472p. (C). 1997. 95.00 (*0-306-45529-3*, Plenum Trade) Perseus Pubng.

Mississippian Political Economy. Jon Muller. LC 97-16721. (Interdisciplinary Contributions to Archaeology Ser.). (Illus.). 472p. (C). 1997. pap. 47.00 (*0-306-45675-3*, Plenum Trade) Perseus Pubng.

Mississippian Towns & Sacred Spaces: Searching for an Architectural Grammar. R. Barry Lewis. LC 98-19772. 1999. pap. text 29.95 (*0-8173-0947-0*) U of Ala Pr.

Mississippian Village Textiles at Wickliffe. Penelope B. Drooker. LC 92-4722. 312p. (C). 1992. pap. text 29.95 (*0-8173-0592-0*) U of Ala Pr.

Mississippi's Forest Products Industry: Performance & Contribution to the State's Economy, 1970 to 1980. Con H. Schallau et al. (Illus.). 32p. 1988. reprint ed. pap. 4.20 (*0-89904-928-1*, Ecosytems Resrch) Crumb Elbow Pub.

Mississippi's (Most Devastating!) Disasters & (Most Calamitous!) Catastrophies! Carole Marsh. (Carole Marsh Mississippi Bks.). (Illus.). (J). (gr. 3 up). 1994. pap. 19.95 (*0-7933-0643-4*); lib. bdg. 29.95 (*0-7933-0645-0*); disk 29.95 (*0-7933-0646-9*) Gallopade Intl.

Mississippi's Old Capitol: Biography of a Building. John R. Skates. LC 90-621746. (Illus.). 240p. 1990. boxed set 29.95 (*0-938896-59-8*) Mississippi Archives.

Mississippi's Unsolved Mysteries (& Their "Solutions") Includes Scientific Information & Other Activities for Students. Carole Marsh. (Carole Marsh Mississippi Bks.). (Illus.). (J). (gr. 3-12). 1994. pap. 19.95 (*0-7933-5795-0*); lib. bdg. 29.95 (*0-7933-5794-2*); disk 29.95 (*0-7933-5796-9*) Gallopade Intl.

Missives. Douglas J. Cusine & Robert Rennie. 230p. 1993. boxed set 60.00 (*0-406-00593-1*, UK, MICHIE) LEXIS Pub.

Missles at Jarmah. R. C. McField. Ed. by Gwen Costa. LC 90-43990. 1991. pap. 14.95 (*0-87949-310-0*) Ashley Bks.

Missoni. (Made in Italy Ser.: No. 1). (Illus.). 128p. 1997. 19.95 (*3-927258-47-4*) Gingko Press.

Missoula-Bitterroot Valley Diner's Club Menu Book, 1997-1998. 4th ed. Peter S. Addeo & Carolyn Addeo. (Illus.). 125p. 1997. pap. text 24.95 (*1-890019-02-X*) Big Sky Pubns.

***Missoula-Bitterroot Valley Diner's Club, 1999-2000.** 6th deluxe ed. Peter Addeo. Ed. by Carol Addeo. (Illus.). 114p. 1999. pap. 24.95 (*1-890019-10-0*) Big Sky Pubns.

Missouri see From Sea to Shining Sea

Missouri see One Nation Series

***Missouri.** (Switched on Schoolhouse Ser.). (J). 2000. pap. 24.95 (*0-7403-0277-9*) Alpha AZ.

Missouri. Capstone Press, Geography Department Staff. (One Nation Ser.). (Illus.). 48p. (J). (gr. 3-7). 1997. lib. bdg. 19.00 (*0-516-20928-0*) Childrens.

***Missouri.** Jim Fizzell. (Midwest Fruit & Vegetables Ser.). (Illus.). 2000. pap. 19.95 (*1-930604-14-9*) Cool Springs Pr.

Missouri. Martin Hintz. LC 98-27785. (America the Beautiful Ser.). 144p. (YA). (gr. 5-8). 1999. 32.00 (*0-516-20836-5*) Childrens.

Missouri. Rita C. LaDoux. (Hello U. S. A. Ser.). (Illus.). 72p. (J). (gr. 3-6). 1991. lib. bdg. 19.93 (*0-8225-2710-3*, Lerner Publctns) Lerner Pub.

Missouri. Kathleen Thompson. LC 95-49530. (Portrait of America Library). 48p. (J). (gr. 4-8). 1996. pap. 5.95 (*0-8114-7451-8*) Raintree Steck-V.

Missouri. Kathleen Thompson. (Portrait of America Library). (Illus.). 48p. (J). (gr. 3-6). 1996. lib. bdg. 22.83 (*0-8114-7345-7*) Raintree Steck-V.

Missouri. Stanley Vestal. LC 96-25529. (Illus.). xii, 384p. 1996. pap. 15.00 (*0-8032-9616-9*, Bison Books) U of Nebr Pr.

Missouri. Anne Welsbacher. LC 97-18131. (United States Ser.). (Illus.). 32p. 1998. lib. bdg. 19.93 (*1-56239-884-9*, Checkerboard Library) ABDO Pub Co.

An Asterisk (*) at the beginning of an entry indicates that the title is appearing for the first time.

Missouri: A Guide to the 'Show Me' State. Federal Writers' Project Staff. LC 72-84486. (American Guidebook Ser.). 1981. reprint ed. 89.00 (*0-403-02175-8*) Somerset Pub.

Missouri: A Guide to the "Show Me" State. Federal Writers' Project Staff & Writers Program-WPA Staff. (American Guide Ser.). 1989. reprint ed. lib. bdg. 89.00 (*0-7812-1024-0*, 1024) Rprt Serv.

Missouri: A History. Paul C. Nagel. LC 88-27761. xiv, 210p. 1988. pap. 9.95 (*0-7006-0386-7*) U Pr of KS.

***Missouri: Fun Facts & Games.** Susan Royals. (Fun Facts & Games Bks.). (Illus.). 64p. (J). 2000. pap. text 5.59 (*1-892920-21-2*) G H B Pubs.

Missouri: Off the Beaten Path: A Guide to Unique Places. 4th ed. Patti Ann Delano & Cathy Johnson. LC 98-8063. (Off the Beaten Path Ser.). (Illus.). 256p. 1998. pap. 12.95 (*0-7627-0192-7*) Globe Pequot.

Missouri: State Map. Rand McNally Staff. 1998. write for info. (*0-528-97405-X*) Rand McNally.

Missouri: The Heart of the Nation. 2nd ed. William E. Parrish et al. (Illus.). 423p. 1992. pap. text 24.95 (*0-88295-887-9*) Harlan Davidson.

Missouri: The Show Me State on the Eve of the 21st Century. Ann Wylie et al. (Illus.). 414p. 1999. 39.95 (*1-882933-24-9*) Cherbo Pub Grp.

Missouri: The WPA Guide to the "Show Me" State. Federal Writers' Project Staff. LC 98-4818. Orig. Title: Missouri: A Guide to the "Show Me" State. (Illus.). 652p. 1998. reprint ed. pap. 24.95 (*1-883982-23-5*) MO Hist Soc.

Missouri: Then & Now. Perry McCandless & William E. Foley. 48p. 1992. 3.50 (*0-8262-0830-4*) U of Mo Pr.

Missouri: Then & Now. rev. ed. Perry McCandless & William E. Foley. LC 90-32545. (Illus.). 328p. (J). (gr. 4). 1992. text 19.95 (*0-8262-0825-8*) U of Mo Pr.

Missouri - From Sea to Shining Sea. Dennis B. Fradin. LC 93-32675. (From Sea to Shining Sea Ser.). (Illus.). 64p. (J). (gr. 3-5). 1995. pap. 5.95 (*0-516-43825-5*) Childrens.

***Missouri - Off the Beaten Path: A Guide to Unique Places.** 5th ed. Patti DeLano. (Off the Beaten Path Ser.). (Illus.). 2000. pap. 12.95 (*0-7627-0777-1*) Globe Pequot.

Missouri, a Bone of Contention. Lucien Carr. LC 72-3761. (American Commonwealths Ser.: No. 11). reprint ed. 39.00 (*0-404-57211-1*) AMS Pr.

Missouri: A Guide to the "Show Me" State see Missouri: The WPA Guide to the "Show Me" State

Missouri, an Index to the 1830 Census. Bobbie J. McLane & Capitola Glazner. 191p. (Orig.). 1966. pap. 25.00 (*0-929604-05-9*) Arkansas Ancestors.

Missouri & North Arkansas Railroad Strike. Orville T. Gooden. LC 68-57567. (Columbia University. Studies in the Social Sciences: No. 275). reprint ed. 29.50 (*0-404-51275-5*) AMS Pr.

Missouri & Other State Greats (Biographies) Carole Marsh. (Carole Marsh Missouri Bks.). (Illus.). (J). (gr. 3 up). 1994. pap. 19.95 (*1-55609-749-2*); lib. bdg. 29.95 (*1-55609-748-4*); disk 29.95 (*1-55609-750-6*) Gallopade Intl.

Missouri Approved Jury Instructions (mai) 5th ed. Stephen H. Ringkamp et al. LC 96-61666. lxxvii, 783 p. 1996. write for info. (*0-314-21604-9*) West Pub.

Missouri Atlas & Gazetteer. Delorme Staff. LC 98-675234. (Map Ser.). (Illus.). 1998. pap. 16.95 (*0-89933-224-2*, AA-001247-000) DeLorme Map.

Missouri Attorney's/Paralegal's/Secretary's Handbook, 1997. 11th ed. Ed. by Jean Walburg. (Attorney's/ Paralegal's/Secretary's Handbooks Ser.). 646p. 1996. ring bd. 55.00 (*0-927573-49-0*) Mariposa Pub.

Missouri Attorney's/Paralegal's/Secretary's Handbook, 1997. 11th ed. Ed. by Jean M. Walburg. (Attorney's/Paralegal's/Secretary's Handbooks Ser.). 676p. 1996. ring bd. 55.00 (*0-927573-43-1*) Mariposa Pub.

Missouri Automotive Directory. Ed. by T. L. Spelman. 1985. 24.95 (*1-55527-021-2*) Auto Contact Inc.

Missouri Bandits, Bushwackers, Outlaws, Crooks, Devils, Ghosts, Desperadoes & Other Assorted & Sundry Characters! Carole Marsh. (Carole Marsh Missouri Bks.). (Illus.). (J). (gr. 3 up). 1994. pap. 19.95 (*0-7933-0671-X*); lib. bdg. 29.95 (*0-7933-0672-8*); disk 29.95 (*0-7933-0673-6*) Gallopade Intl.

Missouri Basic Essential Skills Test (BEST) Jack Rudman. (Admission Test Ser.: ATS-64). 1994. pap. 23.95 (*0-8373-5064-6*) Nat Learn.

Missouri "BIO" Bingo! 24 Must Know State People for Kids to Learn about While Having Fun! Carole Marsh. (Bingo! Ser.). (Illus.). (J). (gr. 2-8). 1998. pap. 14.95 (*0-7933-8597-0*) Gallopade Intl.

Missouri Biographical Dictionary: People of All Times & All Places Who Have Been Important to the History & Life of the State. LC 93-36116. 1993. 79.00 (*0-403-09957-9*) Somerset Pub.

Missouri Birds. James Kavanagh. (Pocket Naturalist Ser.). (Illus.). 1999. 5.95 (*1-889903-92-2*, Pub. by Waterford WA) Falcon Pub Inc.

Missouri Birth & Death Records, Vol. 1. Sherida K. Eddlemon. 435p. (Orig.). 1995. pap. 31.50 (*0-7884-0297-8*) Heritage Bk.

Missouri Birth & Death Records, Vol. 2. Sherida K. Eddlemon. 223p. (Orig.). 1999. pap. 23.50 (*0-7884-1147-0*, E102) Heritage Bk.

Missouri Blood Trail. large type ed. Terry Murphy. (Linford Western Library). 224p. 1996. pap. 16.99 (*0-7089-7886-X*) Ulverscroft.

Missouri Bookstore Book: A Surprising Guide to Our State's Bookstores & Their Specialties for Students, Teachers, Writers & Publishers. Carole Marsh. (Carole Marsh Missouri Bks.). (Illus.). 1994. pap. 19.95 (*0-7933-2931-0*); lib. bdg. 29.95 (*0-7933-2930-2*); disk 29.95 (*0-7933-2932-9*) Gallopade Intl.

Missouri Bound. Roger L. MacBride. LC PZ7.M12255Mi 1999. (Little House Chapter Bks.: No. 1). (Illus.). 80p. (J). (gr. k-2). 1999. lib. bdg. 14.89 (*0-06-027953-2*) HarpC.

Missouri Bound. Roger L. MacBride. LC PZ7.M12255Mi 1999. (Little House Chapter Bks.: No. 1). (Illus.). 80p. (J). (gr. k-2). 1999. mass mkt. 4.25 (*0-06-442087-6*) HarpC Child Bks.

Missouri Brothers in Gray: The Reminiscences & Letters of William J. & John P. Bull. Ed. by Michael E. Banasik. LC 97-77924. (Unwritten Chapters of the Civil War West of the River Ser.: No. 1). (Illus.). 190p. 1998. pap. 12.95 (*0-9628936-8-4*) Pr Camp Pope.

***Missouri Business Directory, 1999-2000.** American Business Directories Staff. 2176p. 1999. boxed set 520.00 incl. cd-rom (*0-7687-0147-3*, 1048-7301) Am Busn Direct.

***Missouri Business Directory (2000-2001)** American Business Directories Staff et al. 2,176p. 2000. boxed set 520.00 incl. cd-rom (*0-7687-0232-1*) Am Busn Direct.

Missouri Cancer Control Resource Directory. 131p. (Orig.). (C). 1993. pap. text 35.00 (*1-56806-307-5*) DIANE Pub.

Missouri Causes of Action: Torts. Richard J. Mehan & Robert H. Dierker. 400p. 1993. spiral bd. 95.00 (*1-56257-326-8*, MICHIE) LEXIS Pub.

Missouri Cemetery Inscription Sources: Print & Microform. Elizabeth G. Kot & Shirley P. Thomson. LC 95-60350. 800p. (Orig.). 1995. pap. 55.00 (*0-9641213-3-6*) Indices Pubng.

Missouri Census Index 1860, Vol. 1. (Illus.). 1986. lib. bdg. 190.00 (*0-89593-401-9*, Accel Indexing) Genealogical Srvcs.

Missouri Census Index 1860, Vol. 2. (Illus.). 1986. lib. bdg. 190.00 (*0-89593-402-7*, Accel Indexing) Genealogical Srvcs.

Missouri Census Index 1850 Slave Schedule. (Illus.). 1988. lib. bdg. 79.00 (*0-89593-400-0*, Accel Indexing) Genealogical Srvcs.

Missouri Census Index 1860, Mortality Schedule, Vol. 1. (Illus.). lib. bdg. 38.00 (*0-89593-405-1*, Accel Indexing) Genealogical Srvcs.

Missouri Census Index 1860 Slave Schedule. (Illus.). 1990. lib. bdg. 79.00 (*0-89593-404-3*, Accel Indexing) Genealogical Srvcs.

Missouri Census Index 1860 St. Louis. (Illus.). lib. bdg. 255.00 (*0-89593-403-5*, Accel Indexing) Genealogical Srvcs.

Missouri Census Index 1870 North Federal. (Illus.). lib. bdg. 340.00 (*0-89593-406-X*, Accel Indexing) Genealogical Srvcs.

Missouri Census Index 1870 South Federal. (Illus.). lib. bdg. 340.00 (*0-89593-408-6*, Accel Indexing) Genealogical Srvcs.

Missouri Census Index 1870 St. Louis & Jackson Counties. (Illus.). lib. bdg. 290.00 (*0-89593-407-8*, Accel Indexing) Genealogical Srvcs.

Missouri Census Index 1890 Union Vets. (Illus.). lib. bdg. write for info. (*0-89593-409-4*, Accel Indexing) Genealogical Srvcs.

Missouri Challenge: The Real Golfer's Guide. Jerry McCarty et al. (Illus.). 109p. (Orig.). 1993. per. 7.95 (*0-9651906-0-9*) Lily Pubns.

Missouri Citations, Statutes, 5 vols. Shepard's Citations, Inc. Staff. suppl. ed. 625.00 (*0-686-89817-6*) Shepards.

Missouri Civil Procedure Forms. Arianna S. Huffington. 1993. disk 50.00 (*0-614-03772-7*, MICHIE) LEXIS Pub.

Missouri Civil Procedure Forms. Margaret M. Mooney & Alan D. Pratzel. 500p. 1994. spiral bd. 209.00 (*0-87189-066-6*, MICHIE); ring bd., suppl. ed. 87.00 (*0-685-74598-8*, MICHIE) LEXIS Pub.

Missouri Civil Procedure Forms, Issue 8. Mooney & Pratzel. 1995. ring bd. 159.00 (*0-327-03927-2*, 81899-10, MICHIE) LEXIS Pub.

***Missouri Civil Procedure Forms, Issue 10.** Margaret M. Mooney & Alana D. Pratzel. 100p. 1999. ring bd. write for info. (*0-327-01693-0*, 8190215) LEXIS Pub.

Missouri Civil Procedure Forms, No. 9. Mooney & Pratzel. 100p. 1998. ring bd. write for info. (*0-327-00321-9*, 81902-14) LEXIS Pub.

Missouri Classic Christmas Trivia: Stories, Recipes, Activities, Legends, Lore & More. Carole Marsh. (Carole Marsh Missouri Bks.). (Illus.). (J). (gr. 3 up). 1994. pap. 19.95 (*0-7933-0674-4*); lib. bdg. 29.95 (*0-7933-0675-2*); disk 29.95 (*0-7933-0676-0*) Gallopade Intl.

Missouri Coastales. Carole Marsh. (Carole Marsh Missouri Bks.). (J). 1994. lib. bdg. 29.95 (*0-7933-7290-9*) Gallopade Intl.

Missouri Coastales. Carole Marsh. (Carole Marsh Missouri Bks.). (Illus.). (J). (gr. 3 up). 1994. pap. 19.95 (*1-55609-743-3*); lib. bdg. 29.95 (*1-55609-742-5*); disk 29.95 (*1-55609-744-1*) Gallopade Intl.

Missouri Connection. LC 96-34567. (J). 1997. write for info. (*1-56763-269-6*); pap. write for info. (*1-56763-270-X*) Ozark Pub.

Missouri Contracts Litigation. Robert H. Dierker & Richard J. Mehan. Ed. by Monique C. Leahy. LC 96-76213. (Practitioner's Ser.). 800p. 1996. text. write for info. (*0-7620-0054-6*) West Group.

Missouri Cooking. B. Carlson. (Illus.). 160p. 1994. spiral bd. 5.95 (*1-57166-001-1*) Hearts N Tummies.

Missouri Corporate Forms, 2 vols. Charles F. Myers & Edward M. Dolson. 1993. suppl. ed. 89.00 (*0-685-74599-6*, MICHIE) LEXIS Pub.

Missouri Corporate Forms, Issue No. 9. Myers & Dolson. 200p. 1998. ring bd. write for info. (*0-327-00626-9*, 8191314) LEXIS Pub.

Missouri Corporate Forms, 2 vols., Set. Charles F. Myers & Edward M. Dolson. 1100p. 1994. spiral bd. 239.00 (*0-87189-067-4*, 81905-10, MICHIE) LEXIS Pub.

Missouri Corporate Forms: Practice. Charles F. Myers. 1993. disk 95.00 (*0-614-03773-5*, MICHIE) LEXIS Pub.

Missouri Corporate Practice & Forms: The Bryan Cave Manual, 2 vols. Thomas VanDyke & Jack Epps. LC 98-31603. 1348p. 1998. ring bd. 275.00 (*1-57400-041-1*) Data Trace Pubng.

Missouri Corporation Law & Practice. write for info. (*0-318-60805-7*) MO Bar.

Missouri Corporation Law & Practice. 2nd ed. Charles Hansen & Don G. Lents. (National Corporation Law Ser.). 1992. ring bd. 126.00 (*0-13-072331-2*) Aspen Law.

***Missouri Corporation Law & Practice.** 3rd rev. ed. Charles Hansen & Don G. Lents. LC 99-59015. 1072p. 1999. ring bd. 125.00 (*1-881758-65-6*) Tower Pub ME.

Missouri Court Rules Handbook: Local Rules of the 44 Judicial Circuit Courts of Missouri. Ed. by Butterworths Staff. 1994. ring bd., suppl. ed. 49.50 (*0-614-03774-3*, MICHIE) LEXIS Pub.

***Missouri Crime in Perspective 2000.** Ed. by Kathleen O'Leary Morgan & Scott E. Morgan. 22p. 2000. spiral bd. 19.00 (*0-7401-0324-5*) Morgan Quitno Corp.

Missouri Crime Perspective, 1998. Ed. by Kathleen O'Leary Morgan & Scott E. Morgan. 20p. 1998. pap. 19.00 (*1-56692-924-5*) Morgan Quitno Corp.

Missouri Crime Perspectives, 1999. Kathleen O'Leary Morgan. 22p. 1999. spiral bd. 19.00 (*0-7401-0124-2*) Morgan Quitno Corp.

Missouri Crime Survey. Missouri Association for Criminal Justice Staff. LC 68-55778. (Criminology, Law Enforcement, & Social Problems Ser.: No. 10). 1968. reprint ed. 30.00 (*0-87585-010-3*) Patterson Smith.

***Missouri Criminal & Traffic Law Manual, 1999-2000.** annuals Michie Staff. 992p. 2000. text 32.00 (*0-327-10429-5*, MICHIE) LEXIS Pub.

Missouri "Crinkum-Crankum" A Funny Word Book about Our State. Carole Marsh. (Carole Marsh Missouri Bks.). (Illus.). (J). 1994. pap. 19.95 (*0-7933-4884-6*); lib. bdg. 29.95 (*0-7933-4883-8*); disk 29.95 (*0-7933-4885-4*) Gallopade Intl.

Missouri Dingbats! Bk. 1: A Fun Book of Games, Stories, Activities & More about Our State That's All in Code! for You to Decipher. Carole Marsh. (Carole Marsh Missouri Bks.). (Illus.). (J). (gr. 3-12). 1994. pap. 19.95 (*0-7933-3849-2*); lib. bdg. 29.95 (*0-7933-3848-4*); disk 29.95 (*0-7933-3850-6*) Gallopade Intl.

Missouri Divorce Handbook: A Comprehensive Guide to Dissolution of Marriage & Legal Separation in Missouri. Curtis E. Harding, 3rd. (Divorce Ser.). 198p. 1994. pap. text 29.95 (*1-883079-10-1*) Legal Writes.

Missouri Domestic Relations Forms. Karen Johnson. 1994. disk 50.00 (*0-614-03775-1*, MICHIE) LEXIS Pub.

Missouri Domestic Relations Forms. John A. Turcotte, Jr. & Michael C. Walther. LC 87-1445. 500p. 1987. spiral bd. 209.00 (*0-87189-068-2*, MICHIE) LEXIS Pub.

Missouri Domestic Relations Forms. John A. Turcotte, Jr. & Michael C. Walther. LC 87-1445. 1994. suppl. ed. 79.00 (*0-685-73874-4*, MICHIE) LEXIS Pub.

Missouri Domestic Relations Forms. Turcotte & Walther. 1997. ring bd. write for info. (*0-327-03925-6*, 81929-10, MICHIE) LEXIS Pub.

***Missouri Domestic Relations Forms, Issue 11.** John A. Turcott, Jr. & Michael C. Walther. 100p. 1999. ring bd. write for info. (*0-327-01679-5*, 8193215) LEXIS Pub.

Missouri Domestic Relations Forms, No. 10. Turcotte & Walther. 75p. 1998. ring bd. write for info. (*0-327-00327-8*, 81932-14) LEXIS Pub.

Missouri Early Census, Vol. 1. Ronald V. Jackson. (Illus.). lib. bdg. 35.00 (*0-89593-731-X*, Accel Indexing) Genealogical Srvcs.

***Missouri Employment: Guide to Employment Laws, Regulations & Practices, Issue 10.** 3rd ed. Mark S. Summers. 121p. 1999. ring bd. write for info. (*0-327-01376-1*, 8196520) LEXIS Pub.

Missouri Environmental Law Handbook. 3rd rev. ed. Armstrong, Teasdale, Schlafly & Staff et al. 436p. 1997. pap. text 95.00 (*0-86587-574-X*, 574) Gov Insts.

Missouri Estate Planning, Will Drafting & Estate Administration, No. 10. Cornfeld & Brody. 100p. 1998. ring bd. write for info. (*0-327-00326-X*, 81939-15) LEXIS Pub.

Missouri Estate Planning, Will Drafting & Estate Administration Forms. Dave L. Cornfeld & Lawrence Brody. 1994. suppl. ed. 89.00 (*0-685-74625-9*, MICHIE) LEXIS Pub.

***Missouri Estate Planning, Will Drafting & Estate Administration Forms, Issue 11.** Dave L. Cornfeld & Lawrence Brody. 100p. 1999. ring bd. write for info. (*0-327-01533-0*, 8193916) LEXIS Pub.

Missouri Estate Planning, Will Drafting & Estate Administration Forms, 2 vols., Set. Dave L. Cornfeld & Lawrence Brody. 1200p. 1994. spiral bd. 318.00 (*0-87189-069-0*, 81935-10, MICHIE) LEXIS Pub.

Missouri Evidence, 2 vols. Spencer A. Gard. LC 85-50755. 1985. 190.00 (*0-318-11861-0*) West Group.

Missouri Evidence, 2 vols. Spencer A. Gard. LC 85-50755. 1993. suppl. ed. 55.00 (*0-317-03263-1*) West Group.

Missouri Evidentiary Foundations. John C. O'Brien et al. 327p. 1994. 75.00 (*1-55834-177-3*, 65355-10, MICHIE) LEXIS Pub.

Missouri Evidentiary Foundations: 1998 Cumulative Supplement. Edward A. Imwinkelried et al. 120p. (C). 1998. suppl. ed. 75.00 (*0-327-00282-4*, 6535613) LEXIS Pub.

Missouri Evidentiary Foundations, 1999 Cumulative Supplement Vol. 1: Pocketpart. Eugene K. Buckley et al. 150p. write for info. (*0-327-01655-8*, 6535614) LEXIS Pub.

***Missouri Experience Pocket Guide.** Carole Marsh. (Missouri Experience! Ser.). (Illus.). (J). 2000. pap. 6.95 (*0-7933-9570-4*) Gallopade Intl.

Missouri Facts & Factivities. Carole Marsh. (Carole Marsh State Bks.). (Illus.). (J). (gr. 4-7). 1996. pap., teacher ed. 19.95 (*0-7933-7897-4*, C Marsh) Gallopade Intl.

Missouri Facts & Symbols. Emily McAuliffe. LC 99-25346. (States & Their Symbols Ser.). 2000. 14.60 (*0-7368-0377-7*, Hlltop Bks) Capstone Pr.

Missouri Facts & Symbols. Emily McAuliffe. (States & Their Symbols Ser.). 1999. 15.00 (*0-531-12003-1*) Watts.

Missouri Family Histories & Genealogies: A Bibliography. Donald M. Hehir. xvi, 224p. (Orig.). 1996. pap. 20.00 (*0-7884-0542-X*, H142) Heritage Bk.

Missouri Federal Census Index 1840. Ronald V. Jackson. LC 77-85977. (Illus.). 1976. lib. bdg. 69.00 (*0-89593-081-1*, Accel Indexing) Genealogical Srvcs.

Missouri Federal Census Index 1850. Ronald V. Jackson. LC 77-85978. (Illus.). 1976. lib. bdg. 125.00 (*0-89593-082-X*, Accel Indexing) Genealogical Srvcs.

Missouri Federal Census Index 1820. Ronald V. Jackson. (Illus.). lib. bdg. 49.00 (*0-89593-686-0*, Accel Indexing) Genealogical Srvcs.

Missouri Federal Census Index, 1830. Ronald V. Jackson. LC 77-85976. (Illus.). 1981. lib. bdg. 47.00 (*0-89593-080-3*, Accel Indexing) Genealogical Srvcs.

Missouri Festival Fun for Kids! Carole Marsh. (Carole Marsh Missouri Bks.). (Illus.). (J). (gr. 3-12). 1994. pap. 19.95 (*0-7933-4002-0*); lib. bdg. 29.95 (*0-7933-4001-2*) Gallopade Intl.

Missouri Festival Fun for Kids! Carole Marsh. (Carole Marsh Missouri Bks.). (Illus.). (YA). (gr. 3-12). 1994. disk 29.95 (*0-7933-4003-9*) Gallopade Intl.

Missouri Folk Heroes of the Nineteenth Century. Ed. by F. Mark McKiernan & Roger D. Launius. (Illus.). 1989. pap. 2.00 (*0-8309-0547-2*) Herald Pub Hse.

Missouri Gardener's Guide: The What, Where, When, How & Why of Gardening in Missouri. Mike Miller. (Illus.). 424p. 1998. pap. 19.95 (*1-888608-50-1*) Cool Springs Pr.

Missouri Genealogical Gleanings No. 5: 1840 & Beyond. Sherida K. Eddlemon. 255p. 1998. pap. 24.00 (*0-7884-0984-0*, E115) Heritage Bk.

Missouri Genealogical Gleanings Vol. 4: 1840 & Beyond. Sherida K. Eddemon. 232p. 1998. pap. 20.00 (*0-7884-0805-4*, E114) Heritage Bk.

Missouri Genealogical Gleanings 1840 & Beyond, Vol. 1. Sherida K. Eddlemon. 258p. (Orig.). 1994. pap. text 22.00 (*0-7884-0001-0*) Heritage Bk.

Missouri Genealogical Gleanings 1840 & Beyond, Vol. 2. Sherida K. Eddlemon. 233p. (Orig.). 1990. pap. text 22.00 (*0-7884-0233-1*) Heritage Bk.

Missouri Genealogical Gleanings 1840 & Beyond, Vol. 3. Sherida K. Eddlemon. xiv, 256p. (Orig.). 1996. pap. 25.00 (*0-7884-0552-7*, E133) Heritage Bk.

Missouri Genealogical Records & Abstracts, Vol. 5, 1755-1839. Sherida K. Eddlemon. xxii, 275p. (Orig.). 1993. pap. text 23.00 (*1-55613-769-9*) Heritage Bk.

Missouri Genealogical Records & Abstracts, 1621-1839, Vol. 6. Sherida K. Eddlemon. xvi, 234p. (Orig.). 1996. pap. 21.00 (*0-7884-0543-8*, E132) Heritage Bk.

Missouri Genealogical Records & Abstracts, 1741-1839, Vol. 4. Sherida K. Eddlemon. xxii, 272p. (Orig.). 1992. pap. text 21.00 (*1-55613-654-4*) Heritage Bk.

Missouri Genealogical Records & Abstracts, 1752-1839, Vol. 2. Sherida K. Eddlemon. 284p. (Orig.). 1990. pap. 22.50 (*1-55613-362-6*) Heritage Bk.

Missouri Genealogical Records & Abstracts, 1787-1839, Vol. 3. Sherida K. Eddlemon. (Missouri Genealogical Records & Abstracts Ser.). 274p. (Orig.). 1991. pap. 20.00 (*1-55613-447-9*) Heritage Bk.

Missouri Genealogical Research. George K. Schweitzer. 235p. 1997. pap. 15.00 (*0-913857-19-X*) Genealog Sources.

Missouri "GEO" Bingo! 38 Must Know State Geography Facts for Kids to Learn While Having Fun! Carole Marsh. (Bingo! Ser.). (Illus.). (J). (gr. 2-8). 1998. pap. 14.95 (*0-7933-8598-9*) Gallopade Intl.

Missouri Geology: Three Billion Years of Volcanoes, Seas, Sediments, & Erosion. A. G. Unklesbay & Jerry D. Vineyard. (Illus.). 208p. (Orig.). (C). 1992. pap. 22.50 (*0-8262-0836-3*) U of Mo Pr.

Missouri Ghosts: Spirits, Haunts & Related Lore. Joan Gilbert. (Show Me Missouri Ser.). (Illus.). 230p. (Orig.). 1997. pap. 14.95 (*0-9646625-7-4*, MG3470) Pebble Pub.

Missouri Golf Directory, 1999. Grimes. pap. 20.00 (*1-893304-00-0*, Pub. by Golf Dir Inc) Booksource.

Missouri Government! The Cornerstone of Everyday Life in Our State! Carole Marsh. (Carole Marsh Missouri Bks.). (Illus.). (J). (gr. 3-12). 1996. pap. 19.95 (*0-7933-6257-1*); lib. bdg. 29.95 (*0-7933-6256-3*); disk 29.95 (*0-7933-6258-X*) Gallopade Intl.

Missouri Government & Politics. enl. rev. ed. Ed. by Richard J. Hardy et al. (Illus.). 480p. 1995. pap. text 24.95 (*0-8262-0990-4*) U of Mo Pr.

Missouri Governments Performance Standards, 1990. Ed. by Greg Michels. (Governments Performance Standards Ser.). (Illus.). 150p. 1990. text 125.00 (*1-55507-492-8*) Municipal Analysis.

Missouri Harmony: or A Collection of Psalm & Hymn Tunes, & Anthems. Allen D. Carden. LC 93-41235. xx, 240p. 1994. pap. 12.00 (*0-8032-6114-4*, Bison Books) U of Nebr Pr.

***Missouri Health Care in Perspective 2000.** Ed. by Kathleen O'Leary Morgan & Scott E. Morgan. 21p. 2000. spiral bd. 19.00 (*0-7401-0224-9*) Morgan Quitno Corp.

Missouri Health Care Perspective, 1998. Ed. by Kathleen O'Leary Morgan & Scott E. Morgan. 20p. 1998. pap. 19.00 (*1-56692-824-9*) Morgan Quitno Corp.

Missouri Health Care Perspective, 1999. Kathleen O'Leary Morgan. 21p. 1999. spiral bd. 19.00 (*0-7401-0074-2*) Morgan Quitno Corp.

M

Missouri "HISTO" Bingo! 42 Must Know State History Facts for Kids to Learn While Having Fun! Carole Marsh. (Bingo! Ser.). (Illus.). (J). (gr. 2-8). 1998. pap. 14.95 (*0-7933-8599-7*) Gallopade Intl.

Missouri Historic Sites Catalogue. Ed. by Dorothy J. Caldwell. LC 63-63854. (Illus.). 199p. 1963. 15.00 (*0-614-14522-8*) SHS MO.

Missouri Historical & Biographical Index, Vol. 1. Ronald V. Jackson. LC 78-53706. (Illus.). 1984. lib. bdg. 30.00 (*0-89593-189-3*, Accel Indexing) Genealogical Srvcs.

Missouri Historical Tour Guide. rev. ed. D. Ray Wilson. LC 94-79191. (Illus.). 288p. 1995. pap. 15.00 (*0-614-02482-X*) Crossroads Comm.

Missouri Historical Tour Guide: A Guide to the Historical Places & Personalities of the... 3rd ed. D. Ray Wilson. (Illus.). 288p. 1995. pap. 15.00 (*0-916445-22-4*) Crossroads Comm.

Missouri History! Surprising Secrets about Our State's Founding Mothers, Fathers & Kids! Carole Marsh. (Carole Marsh Missouri Bks.). (Illus.). (J). (gr. 3-12). 1996. pap. 19.95 (*0-7933-6104-4*); lib. bdg. 29.95 (*0-7933-6103-6*); disk 29.95 (*0-7933-6105-2*) Gallopade Intl.

Missouri Homestead. T. L. Tedrow. (Days of Laura Ingalls Wilder Ser.). 1992. 10.09 (*0-606-12241-9*, Pub. by Turtleback) Demco.

Missouri Hot Air Balloon Mystery. Carole Marsh. (Carole Marsh Missouri Bks.). (Illus.). (J). (gr. 2-9). 1994. 29.95 (*0-7933-2543-9*); pap. 19.95 (*0-7933-2544-7*); disk 29.95 (*0-7933-2545-5*) Gallopade Intl.

Missouri Hot Zones! Viruses, Diseases, & Epidemics in Our State's History. Carole Marsh. (Hot Zones! Ser.). (Illus.). (J). (gr. 3-12). 1998. pap. 19.95 (*0-7933-8904-6*); lib. bdg. 29.95 (*0-7933-8903-8*) Gallopade Intl.

Missouri in Perspective, 1998. Ed. by Kathleen O'Leary Morgan & Scott E. Morgan. 24p. 1998. pap. 19.00 (*1-56692-874-5*) Morgan Quitno Corp.

Missouri in Perspective, 1999. Ed. by Kathleen O'Leary Morgan. 26p. 1999. spiral bd. 19.00 (*1-56692-974-1*) Morgan Quitno Corp.

***Missouri in Perspective 2000.** Ed. by Kathleen O'Leary Morgan & Scott E. Morgan. 26p. 2000. spiral bd. 19.00 (*0-7401-0274-5*) Morgan Quitno Corp.

Missouri in the Federal System. 3rd ed. Stephen S. Chen. 240p. (Orig.). (C). 1986. pap. text 26.00 (*0-8191-5498-9*) U Pr of Amer.

Missouri Indian Dictionary for Kids! Carole Marsh. (Carole Marsh State Bks.). (J). (gr. 2-9). 1996. 29.95 (*0-7933-7719-6*, C Marsh); pap. 19.95 (*0-7933-7720-X*, C Marsh) Gallopade Intl.

***Missouri Investment & Business Guide: Business, Investment, Export-Import Opportunities, 50 vols., Vol. 25.** Global Investment Center, USA Staff. (U. S. Regional Investment & Business Library-99: Vol. 25). (Illus.). 350p. (Orig.). 1999. pap. 59.95 (*0-7397-1124-5*) Intl Business Pubns.

***Missouri Jeopardy.** Carole Marsh. (Missouri Experience! Ser.). (Illus.). (J). (gr. 2-6). 2000. pap. 7.95 (*0-7933-9572-0*) Gallopade Intl.

Missouri Jeopardy! Answers & Questions about Our State! Carole Marsh. (Carole Marsh Missouri Bks.). (Illus.). (J). (gr. 3-12). 1994. pap. 19.95 (*0-7933-4155-8*); lib. bdg. 29.95 (*0-7933-4154-X*); disk 29.95 (*0-7933-4156-6*) Gallopade Intl.

***Missouri JobBank.** 3rd ed. Contrib. by Adam Media Corporation Staff. (JobBank Ser.). 336p. 2000. pap. 16.95 (*1-58062-380-8*) Adams Media.

Missouri JobBank: 1999 Edition. 2nd ed. Ed. by Adams Media Corporation Staff. (JobBank Ser.). 336p. 1998. pap. 16.95 (*1-58062-083-3*) Adams Media.

***Missouri Jography.** Carole Marsh. (Missouri Experience! Ser.). (Illus.). (J). (gr. 2-6). 2000. pap. 7.95 (*0-7933-9573-9*) Gallopade Intl.

Missouri "Jography" A Fun Run Thru Our State. Carole Marsh. (Carole Marsh Missouri Bks.). (Illus.). (J). (gr. 3 up). 1994. pap. 19.95 (*1-55609-731-X*); lib. bdg. 29.95 (*1-55609-730-1*); disk 29.95 (*1-55609-732-8*) Gallopade Intl.

Missouri Juvenile Law. Missouri Bar Staff. write for info. (*0-318-61044-2*) MO Bar.

Missouri-Kansas-Texas in Color. Ray George. (Illus.). 128p. 1994. 49.95 (*1-878887-28-9*) Morning NJ.

Missouri Kid's Cookbook: Recipes, How-To, History, Lore & More. Carole Marsh. (Carole Marsh Missouri Bks.). (Illus.). (J). (gr. 3 up). 1994. pap. 19.95 (*0-7933-0683-3*); lib. bdg. 29.95 (*0-7933-0684-1*); disk 29.95 (*0-7933-0685-X*) Gallopade Intl.

Missouri Land Surveying Law: Questions & Answers. John E. Keen. 52p. (C). 1995. pap. text 25.00 (*1-56569-032-X*) Land Survey.

Missouri Land Use Law & Practice, 2 vols. Michael T. White. LC 93-22950. 1300p. 1993. ring bd. 185.00 (*1-56257-282-2*, MICHIE) LEXIS Pub.

Missouri Landscapes: Designs from Nature. Kevin Sink. Ed. by Jane Cigard. LC 98-93186. (Illus.). 96p. 1998. 34.95 (*0-9664964-0-X*); 175.00 (*0-9664964-1-8*) Designs from Nature.

Missouri Lawyer. John Barker. (American Autobiography Ser.). 391p. 1995. reprint ed. lib. bdg. 89.00 (*0-7812-8451-1*) Rprt Serv.

Missouri Library Book: A Surprising Guide to the Unusual Special Collections in Libraries Across Our State for Students, Teachers, Writers & Publishers - Includes Reproducible Mailing Labels Plus Activities for Young People! Carole Marsh. (Carole Marsh Missouri Bks.). (Illus.). 1994. pap. 19.95 (*0-7933-3081-5*); lib. bdg. 29.95 (*0-7933-3080-7*); disk 29.95 (*0-7933-3082-3*) Gallopade Intl.

Missouri Limited Liability Company Forms & Practice Manual. Dale G. Schedler. LC 95-33422. 710p. 1996. ring bd. 219.90 (*1-57400-004-7*) Data Trace Pubng.

Missouri Manufacturers Register. 12th rev. ed. Ed. by Frank Lambing. 1998. 101.00 (*1-58202-056-6*) Manufacturers.

Missouri Marriages Before 1840. Susan Ormesher. LC 82-81219. 317p. 1998. reprint ed. pap. 28.50 (*0-8063-0985-7*, Pub. by Clearfield Co) ACCESS Pubs Network.

Missouri Marriages, Early to 1825. Liahona Research, Inc. Staff. Ed. by Jordan Dodd. 67p. 1991. lib. bdg. 25.00 (*1-877677-37-X*) Herit Quest.

Missouri Marriages Index, 1826-1850. Liahona Research Staff. 870p. lib. bdg. 145.00 (*1-877677-16-7*) Herit Quest.

Missouri Math! How It All Adds up in Our State. Carole Marsh. (Carole Marsh Missouri Bks.). (Illus.). (YA). (gr. 3-12). 1996. pap. 19.95 (*0-7933-6563-5*); lib. bdg. 29.95 (*0-7933-6562-7*) Gallopade Intl.

Missouri Media Book: A Surprising Guide to the Amazing Print, Broadcast & Online Media of Our State for Students, Teachers, Writers & Publishers - Includes Reproducible Mailing Labels Plus Activities for Young People! Carole Marsh. (Carole Marsh Missouri Bks.). (Illus.). 1994. pap. 19.95 (*0-7933-3237-0*); lib. bdg. 29.95 (*0-7933-3236-2*); disk 29.95 (*0-7933-3238-9*) Gallopade Intl.

Missouri Mule: His Origin & Times. Melvin Bradley. LC 93-73481. (Illus.). 540p. 1998. pap. 35.00 (*0-933842-26-0*, UED99) Extension Div.

Missouri Music. Ernst C. Krohn. LC 65-23398. (Music Ser.). xlvi, 380p. 1971. reprint ed. lib. bdg. 47.50 (*0-306-70932-5*) Da Capo.

Missouri Mystery Van Takes Off! Bk. 1: Handicapped Missouri Kids Sneak off on a Big Adventure. Carole Marsh. (Carole Marsh Missouri Bks.). (Illus.). (J). (gr. 3-12). 1994. 29.95 (*0-7933-5036-0*); pap. 19.95 (*0-7933-5037-9*); disk 29.95 (*0-7933-5038-7*) Gallopade Intl.

Missouri Notary Law Primer. 5th ed. National Notary Association Editors. 124p. 1996. pap. 16.00 (*0-933134-81-9*) Natl Notary.

Missouri Objection at Trial. Carlson & Bright. 200p. 1993. pap. text 39.50 (*0-327-03968-X*, 81943-10, MICHIE) LEXIS Pub.

Missouri Objections at Trial. Ronald L. Carlson et al. LC 93-11002. 200p. 1993. pap. 39.50 (*0-250-42765-6*, MICHIE) LEXIS Pub.

Missouri One Hundred Years Ago. Compiled by Skip Whitson. (Historical Ser.). (Illus.). 1976. pap. 4.50 (*0-89540-029-4*, SB-029) Sun Pub.

Missouri Pacific Diesel Power. Kevin N. EuDaly. (Illus.). 192p. 1995. 59.95 (*0-9659040-2-4*) White River Prodns.

***Missouri Pacific Lines.** Patrick C. Dorin. (Illus.). 160p. 2000. 28.95 (*1-883089-54-9*, 130613AE, Pub. by TLC VA) Motorbooks Intl.

Missouri Pacific Northwest: A History of the Kansas City Northwestern Railroad. I. E. Quastler. (Illus.). 136p. 1994. pap. 31.95 (*0-942035-30-5*) South Platte.

Missouri Pacific River & Prairie Rails: The MoPac in Nebraska. Michael M. Bartels. (Illus.). 204p. 1997. 56.95 (*0-942035-39-9*) South Platte.

***Missouri Palace.** large type ed. S. J. Rodgers. 256p. 1999. pap. 18.99 (*0-7089-5500-2*, Linford) Ulverscroft.

Missouri Parks Guide. Chris Boyer. Ed. by Barbara McCarg. 100p. (Orig.). 1988. pap. text 5.95 (*0-935201-32-7*) Affordable Adven.

Missouri Personal Injury & Torts. Robert H. Dierker & Richard J. Mehan. Ed. by Monique C. Leahy. LC 96-75996. (Practitioner's Ser.). 800p. 1996. text. write for info. (*0-7620-0053-8*) West Group.

Missouri Pioneers: New Madrid County. Ed. by Audrey L. Woodruff. 32p. (Orig.). 1995. pap. 12.50 (*0-9644858-5-0*) Boyd Pub Co.

Missouri Playwrights' Anthology of Prize-Winning Plays. Pamela S. Berlin et al. Ed. by Robert E. Knittel. LC 81-82168. 383p. (Orig.). 1981. pap. 8.95 (*0-933038-01-1*) Grass Hooper Pr.

Missouri Quiz Bowl Crash Course! Carole Marsh. (Carole Marsh Missouri Bks.). (Illus.). (J). (gr. 3 up). 1994. pap. 19.95 (*1-55609-746-8*); lib. bdg. 29.95 (*1-55609-745-X*); disk 29.95 (*1-55609-747-6*) Gallopade Intl.

Missouri Real Estate Forms, 2 vols. Richard W. Scarritt & Michael C. Kirk. 1993. suppl. ed. 79.00 (*0-685-74600-3*, MICHIE) LEXIS Pub.

Missouri Real Estate Forms, Issue 7. Michael C. Kirk & Richard W. Scarritt. 300p. 1998. ring bd. write for info. (*0-327-00507-6*, 8195213) LEXIS Pub.

Missouri Real Estate Forms, 2 vols., Set. Richard W. Scaritt & Michael C. Kirk. 900p. 1988. spiral bd. 239.00 (*0-87189-070-4*, 81948-10, MICHIE) LEXIS Pub.

Missouri Real Estate Forms: Practice. Richard W. Scarritt. 1993. disk 75.00 (*0-614-03776-X*, MICHIE) LEXIS Pub.

Missouri Real Estate Practice, 2 vols. 3rd ed. write for info. (*0-318-61828-1*) MO Bar.

Missouri River. Stanley Vestal. 1995. write for info. (*0-8050-4825-1*) H Holt & Co.

Missouri River Country of Montana & North Dakota. Tom Thayer. LC 97-72082. (Rocky Mountain Ser.). 133 p. 1997. write for info. (*0-9652439-3-1*) Montana Speaks.

Missouri River Country of Montana & North Dakota. Tom Thayer. LC 97-72082. (Rocky Mountain Ser.: Vol. 2). 133p. 1997. 34.95 (*0-9652439-2-3*) Montana Speaks.

Missouri Roadsides: The Traveler's Companion. Bill Earngey. LC 95-616. (Illus.). 360p. (C). 1995. pap. 19.95 (*0-8262-1021-X*) U of Mo Pr.

***Missouri Rocks & Minerals: Fun Facts & Games.** Judy Oetting. (Fun Facts & Games Bks.). (Illus.). 64p. (J). 2000. pap. text 5.95 (*1-892920-24-7*) G H B Pubs.

Missouri Rollercoasters! Carole Marsh. (Carole Marsh Missouri Bks.). (Illus.). (J). (gr. 3-12). 1994. pap. 19.95 (*0-7933-5300-9*); lib. bdg. 29.95 (*0-7933-5299-1*) Gallopade Intl.

Missouri Rollercoasters! Carole Marsh. (Carole Marsh Missouri Bks.). (Illus.). (YA). (gr. 3-12). 1994. disk 29.95 (*0-7933-5301-7*) Gallopade Intl.

***Missouri School Days.** Roger Lea Macbride. (J). 2001. pap. write for info. (*0-06-442110-4*, HarpTrophy); lib. bdg. write for info. (*0-06-028555-9*) HarpC Child Bks.

Missouri School Trivia: An Amazing & Fascinating Look at Our State's Teachers, Schools & Students! Carole Marsh. (Carole Marsh Missouri Bks.). (Illus.). (J). (gr. 3 up). 1994. pap. 19.95 (*0-7933-0680-9*); lib. bdg. 29.95 (*0-7933-0681-7*); disk 29.95 (*0-7933-0682-5*) Gallopade Intl.

***Missouri Senior Citizen's Guide to Health Care.** annuals 2000. pap. 19.95 (*1-928937-01-2*) Eagle Pbg Inc.

Missouri Silly Basketball Sportsmysteries, Vol. I. Carole Marsh. (Carole Marsh Missouri Bks.). (Illus.). (J). (gr. 3 up). 1994. pap. 19.95 (*0-7933-0677-9*); lib. bdg. 29.95 (*0-7933-0678-7*) Gallopade Intl.

Missouri Silly Basketball Sportsmysteries, Vol. I. Carole Marsh. (Carole Marsh Missouri Bks.). (Illus.). (J). (gr. 3 up). 1997. disk 29.95 (*0-7933-0679-5*) Gallopade Intl.

Missouri Silly Basketball Sportsmysteries, Vol. II. Carole Marsh. (Carole Marsh Missouri Bks.). (Illus.). (J). (gr. 3 up). 1994. pap. 19.95 (*0-7933-1741-X*); lib. bdg. 29.95 (*0-7933-1740-1*); disk 29.95 (*0-7933-1742-8*) Gallopade Intl.

Missouri Silly Football Sportsmysteries, Vol. I. Carole Marsh. (Carole Marsh Missouri Bks.). (Illus.). (J). (gr. 3 up). 1994. pap. 19.95 (*1-55609-737-9*); lib. bdg. 29.95 (*1-55609-736-0*) Gallopade Intl.

Missouri Silly Football Sportsmysteries, Vol. II. Carole Marsh. (Carole Marsh Missouri Bks.). (Illus.). (J). (gr. 3 up). 1994. pap. 19.95 (*1-55609-740-9*); lib. bdg. 29.95 (*1-55609-739-5*); disk 29.95 (*1-55609-741-7*) Gallopade Intl.

Missouri Silly Trivia! Carole Marsh. (Carole Marsh Missouri Bks.). (Illus.). (J). (gr. 3 up). 1994. pap. 19.95 (*1-55609-100-1*); lib. bdg. 29.95 (*1-55609-728-X*); disk 29.95 (*1-55609-729-8*) Gallopade Intl.

Missouri Spelling Bee! Score Big by Correctly Spelling Our State's Unique Names. Carole Marsh. (Carole Marsh Missouri Bks.). (Illus.). (YA). (gr. 3-12). 1996. pap. 19.95 (*0-7933-6716-6*); lib. bdg. 29.95 (*0-7933-6715-8*) Gallopade Intl.

***Missouri State Credit Directory, 2000 Edition.** rev. ed. American Business Directories Staff. 528p. 1999. boxed set 175.00 incl. cd-rom (*0-7687-0310-7*) Am Busn Direct.

***Missouri State Fair: Images of a Midwestern Tradition.** Richard Gaskell. 128p. 2000. 24.95 (*0-8262-1273-5*) U of Mo Pr.

Missouri Story: A Deluge of Strangers, 1 Vol. 2nd ed. Charles M. Evans. Ed. by Laura C. Evans. LC 86-80083. (Illus.). 271p. 1986. 27.50 (*0-937181-02-1*) Charlemarie.

Missouri Studies. Darryl Stacy. 24p. 1999. pap. text, teacher ed. 9.95 (*0-911981-52-7*) Cloud Pub.

Missouri Studies: Government & Constitution. Darryl Stacy & Richard Dohn. (Illus.). 124p. (J). (gr. 7-9). 1999. reprint ed. text 24.95 (*0-911981-75-6*) Cloud Pub.

Missouri Supreme Court: From Dred Scott to Nancy Cruzan. Gerald T. Dunne. (Illus.). 240p. 1993. text 34.95 (*0-8262-0826-6*) U of Mo Pr.

Missouri Survival. Betty L. Hall & Verlin M. Abbott. 160p. (Orig.). (gr. 10-12). 1979. pap. text 5.84 (*0-03-046911-2*) Westwood Pr.

Missouri Timeline: A Chronology of Missouri History, Mystery, Trivia, Legend, Lore & More. Carole Marsh. (Carole Marsh Missouri Bks.). (Illus.). (J). (gr. 3-12). 1994. pap. 19.95 (*0-7933-5951-1*); lib. bdg. 29.95 (*0-7933-5950-3*); disk 29.95 (*0-7933-5952-X*) Gallopade Intl.

Missouri to Oregon in 1860. August V. Kautz. 1995. pap. 9.95 (*0-87770-556-9*) Ye Galleon.

Missouri Town, 1855: A Program in Architectural Preservation. LaVoone B. Moore. (Illus.). 109p. 1987. pap. 14.95 (*0-932845-26-6*) Lowell Pr.

Missouri Trivia. Ernie Couch. LC 92-32523. 192p. (Orig.). 1992. pap. 6.95 (*1-55853-203-X*) Rutledge Hill Pr.

Missouri 2000! Coming Soon to a Calendar Near You - The 21st Century! - Complete Set of AL 2000 Items. Carole Marsh. (Two Thousand! Ser.). (Illus.). (J). (gr. 3-12). 1998. pap. 75.00 (*0-7933-9359-0*); lib. bdg. 85.00 (*0-7933-9360-4*) Gallopade Intl.

Missouri 2000! Coming Soon to a Calendar near You--The 21st Century! Carole Marsh. (Two Thousand! Ser.). (Illus.). (J). (gr. 3-12). 1998. pap. 19.95 (*0-7933-8751-5*); lib. bdg. 29.95 (*0-7933-8750-7*) Gallopade Intl.

Missouri U. S. 66 Tour Book. C. H. Curtis. LC 94-94615. 274p. 1994. pap. 19.95 (*0-9633863-4-4*) Curtis Ent.

Missouri UFO's & Extraterrestrials! A Look at the Sightings & Science in Our State. Carole Marsh. (Carole Marsh Missouri Bks.). (Illus.). (J). (gr. 3-12). 1997. pap. 19.95 (*0-7933-6410-8*); lib. bdg. 29.95 (*0-7933-6409-4*) Gallopade Intl.

Missouri Worker's Compensation, 2 vols. Jerry Kenter. LC 84-80828. (Missouri Practice Systems Library). 1992. suppl. ed. 125.00 (*0-317-03254-2*) West Group.

Missouri Worker's Compensation, 2 vols. 2nd ed. Monique C. Leahy & Jerry Kenter. LC 96-78600. (Lawyers Cooperative Practice Guide Ser.). 1996. write for info. (*0-7620-0113-5*) West Group.

Missouri Worker's Compensation, 2 vols., Set. Jerry Kenter. LC 84-80828. (Missouri Practice Systems Library). 1984. ring bd. 220.00 (*0-318-03859-5*) West Group.

***Missouri's Big Activity Book.** Carole Marsh. (Missouri Experience! Ser.). (Illus.). (J). (gr. k-5). 2000. pap. 9.95 (*0-7933-9574-7*) Gallopade Intl.

Missouri's Black Heritage. rev. ed. Gary R. Kremer & Antonio F. Holland. LC 93-20175. 272p. (C). 1993. pap. 17.95 (*0-8262-0905-X*) U of Mo Pr.

Missouri's Black Heritage. rev. ed. Ed. by Gary R. Kremer & Antonio F. Holland. LC 93-20175. (Illus.). 272p. (C). 1993. text 34.95 (*0-8262-0904-1*) U of Mo Pr.

***Missouri's Confederate: Claiborne Fox Jackson & the Creation of Southern Identity.** Christopher Phillips. LC 00-21061. (Missouri Biography Ser.). (Illus.). 360p. 2000. 29.95 (*0-8262-1272-7*) U of Mo Pr.

Missouri's Early Home Remedies. Betty Hams et al. (Illus.). 181p. (Orig.). 1992. pap. text 9.95 (*1-878488-53-8*) Quixote Pr IA.

Missouri's Literary Heritage for Children & Youth: An Annotated Bibliography of Books about Missouri. Alice I. Fitzgerald. LC 81-3030. (Illus.). 272p. 1981. text 30.00 (*0-8262-0346-9*) U of Mo Pr.

Missouri's (Most Devastating!) Disasters & (Most Calamitous!) Catastrophies! Carole Marsh. (Carole Marsh Missouri Bks.). (Illus.). (J). (gr. 3 up). 1994. pap. 19.95 (*0-7933-0668-X*); lib. bdg. 29.95 (*0-7933-0669-8*); disk 29.95 (*0-7933-0670-1*) Gallopade Intl.

Missouri's Roadkill Cookbook. Bruce Carlson. (Illus.). 110p. (Orig.). 1991. pap. 7.95 (*1-878488-44-9*) Quixote Pr IA.

Missouri's Unsolved Mysteries (& Their "Solutions") Includes Scientific Information & Other Activities for Students. Carole Marsh. (Carole Marsh Missouri Bks.). (Illus.). (J). (gr. 3-12). 1994. pap. 19.95 (*0-7933-5798-5*); lib. bdg. 29.95 (*0-7933-5797-7*); disk 29.95 (*0-7933-5799-3*) Gallopade Intl.

Misspecification Tests in Econometrics: The Lagrange Multiplier Principle & Other Approaches. L. G. Godfrey. (Econometric Society Monographs: No. 16). 264p. (C). 1991. pap. text 28.95 (*0-521-42459-3*) Cambridge U Pr.

Misspeller's Guide: Find Correct Spellings Fast Sort Out Sound-Alikes Avoid Confusables. Joel Schroeder & Ruth Schroeder. Ed. by Kelly Scanlon & Jane D. Guthrie. LC 95-72993. 202p. 1996. pap. 12.95 (*1-57294-006-9*, 12-0018) SkillPath Pubns.

***Misssing Link.** Charlyne Dickerson. 2000. pap. 8.95 (*1-58571-037-7*, 909-110, Pub. by Genesis Press) BookWorld.

Missy: Joy & Pain. Hazel G. Snowden. 270p. 1999. 20.95 (*0-9671596-0-1*); pap. 12.95 (*0-9671596-1-X*) Hazel Snowden.

***Missy the Mutt.** 2nd rev. ed. Frederick Spain. (Illus.). i, 28p. (J). (ps-6). 1999. 12.95 (*1-929792-00-X*) Roehm Pubs.

***Missy the Mutts Surprise Birthday Party.** Frederick Spain. (Illus.). i, 26p. (J). (ps-6). 1999. 12.95 (*1-929792-02-6*) Roehm Pubs.

Missy's Proposition. Maris Soule. (Romance Ser.: No. 864). 1992. per. 2.69 (*0-373-08864-7*, 5-08864-6) Silhouette.

***Mist: A Tragicomic Novel.** Miguel de Unamuno & Warner Fite. LC 99-55817. 2000. pap. 15.00 (*0-252-06894-7*) U of Ill Pr.

Mist No. 3: The Captain's Table. Dean W. Smith & Benjamin Sisko. (Star Trek Ser.: Vol. 3). 271p. 1998. mass mkt. 6.50 (*0-671-01471-4*) PB.

Mist & Stone. Maggie Sansone. audio 10.98 (*1-56222-898-6*, 95025C); audio compact disk 15.98 (*1-56222-899-4*, 95025CD) Mel Bay.

Mist & Stone. Maggie Sansone. 48p. 1993. pap. 9.95 (*1-56222-895-1*, 95025) Mel Bay.

Mist & Stone. Maggie Sansone. 48p. 1993. pap. 19.95 incl. audio (*0-7866-1181-2*, 95025P); pap. 24.95 incl. audio compact disk (*0-7866-1180-4*, 95025CDP) Mel Bay.

Mist Around the Moon. large type ed. Mary Mackie. (Dales Large Print Ser.). 1996. pap. 18.99 (*1-85389-609-8*, Dales) Ulverscroft.

Mist Before the Morning Wind: Rufus Crook Gates. Stephen H. Cobb. 1997. pap. 19.95 (*0-910119-46-5*) SOCO Pubns.

Mist in Glen Torran. large type ed. Amanda Doyle. 288p. 1984. 27.99 (*0-7089-1099-8*) Ulverscroft.

Mist in the Mirror. Hill. (Longman Literature Ser.). 1995. pap. text. write for info. (*0-582-25399-3*, Pub. by Addison-Wesley) Longman.

Mist in the Mirror. large type ed. Susan Hill. 1995. 27.99 (*0-7089-3367-X*) Ulverscroft.

Mist in Three-D Sound. abr. ed. Stephen King. 1986. audio 15.00 (*0-671-62138-6*) PB.

Mist in Three-D Sound: The Compact Disc Nightmare Edition. abr. ed. Stephen King. 1993. audio 15.00 (*0-671-87475-6*) S&S Audio.

Mist of Memories. Pat Stephenson. 1991. pap. 9.95 (*0-938645-58-7*) In His Steps.

Mist of Yesterday. 2nd rev. ed. Guido C. Levetto. Ed. by William E. Todd. 157p. 1997. reprint ed. pap. 10.50 (*0-9667870-1-3*) G C Levetto.

Mist on the Lake. June Montgomery. 4p. Date not set. pap. 2.50 (*0-7390-0719-X*, 19701) Alfred Pub.

***Mist on the Mountain.** Kathleen Day. 255p. 1999. pap. 13.95 (*0-9675071-0-3*) Daybreak Lake.

Mist on the River: Remembrances of Dan Bailey. Charles F. Waterman. (Illus.). 195p. 1986. 19.95 (*0-917253-0-3*) Yellow Pr MT.

***Mist over the Mersey.** Andrews. (J). 2000. pap. 8.95 (*0-552-14058-9*, Pub. by Transworld Publishers Ltd) Trafalgar.

Mist over the Mountains: Appalachia & Its People. Raymond Bial. (Illus.). 48p. (J). 1997. 14.95 (*0-395-73569-6*) HM.

***Mist over the Rice Fields: Burma & Korea.** John Neville Shipster. 2000. 29.95 (*0-85052-742-2*, Pub. by Pen & Sword Bks Ltd) Combined Pub.

Mistakable French. Philip Thody & Howard E. Evans. 1986. pap. 9.95 (*0-685-54094-4*, Scribners Ref) Mac Lib Ref.

An Asterisk (*) at the beginning of an entry indicates that the title is appearing for the first time.

Mistakable French: Faux Amis & Key Words. 2nd ed. Philip Thody & Howard Evans. 224p. 1998. reprint ed. pap. 12.95 (*0-7818-0649-6*) Hippocrene Bks.

Mistake & Unjust Enrichment. George E. Palmer. LC 93-78321. (Historical Reprints in Jurisprudence Ser.). 128p. 1993. reprint ed. 38.50 (*0-89941-840-6*, 307850) W S Hein.

Mistake-Free Management: Communicating Successfully in All Business Situations. Allan Krieff. 576p. (C). 1996. text 29.95 (*0-13-210766-X*) P-H.

Mistake Making: The Addiction to Shame. Kenneth L. Artiss. LC 93-3020. (Illus.). 302p. (C). 1993. text 22.50 (*0-9615865-1-6*) Psych Bks.

Mistake Making: With Sections on Stuttering & Psychotherapy. Kenneth L. Artiss. 298p. 1996. pap. text 34.50 (*0-7618-0309-2*) U Pr of Amer.

Mistake-Proofing for Operators: The ZQC System. Shigeo Shingo & Productivity Press Staff. LC 96-2756. (Shopfloor Ser.). 1996. pap. 25.00 (*1-56327-127-3*) Productivity Inc.

Mistaken Adversary. Penny Jordan. (Presents Ser.). 1994. per. 2.99 (*0-373-11625-X*, 1-11625-0) Harlequin Bks.

Mistaken Adversary. Penny Jordan. (Promo Ser.). 1999. per. 4.50 (*0-373-21974-1*, 1-21974-0) Harlequin Bks.

Mistaken Adversary. large type ed. Penny Jordan. 1992. 18.95 (*0-263-13096-7*) Mac Lib Ref.

Mistaken Beliefs about Relapse. Terence T. Gorski & Merlene Miller. 32p. 1988. pap. text 4.00 (*0-8309-0511-1*) Herald Pub Hse.

Mistaken Bride. Brittany Young. 1997. per. 3.99 (*0-373-24076-7*, 1-24076-1) Silhouette.

Mistaken Extinction: Dinosaur Evolution & the Origin of Birds. Lowell Dingus. 1998. 37.00 incl. cd-rom (*0-7167-3385-4*) St Martin.

Mistaken Extinction: Dinosaur Evolution & the Origin of Birds. Lowell Dingus. 1998. 37.00 incl. cd-rom (*0-7167-3384-6*) W H Freeman.

***Mistaken Extinction: Dinosaur Evolution & the Origin of Birds.** Lowell Dingus & Timothy Rowe. 2000. pap. 18.95 (*0-7167-4165-2*) W H Freeman.

Mistaken for a Mistress. Jacqueline Baird. 1997. per. 3.50 (*0-373-11915-1*, 1-11915-5) Harlequin Bks.

Mistaken for a Mistress. large type ed. Jacqueline Baird. (Harlequin Romance Ser.). 1997. 20.95 (*0-263-15165-4*) Mac Lib Ref.

Mistaken Identification: The Eyewitness, Psychology & the Law. Brian L. Cutler & Steven D. Penrod. (Illus.). 300p. (C). 1995. pap. text 19.95 (*0-521-44572-8*) Cambridge U Pr.

***Mistaken Identities.** Peter McDonald. 240p. 2000. pap. 24.95 (*0-19-818687-8*) OUP.

Mistaken Identities. Ed. by Abigail Solomon-Godeau. LC 92-43801. (ENG & GER., Illus.). 80p. 1993. pap. 20.00 (*0-942006-23-2*) U of CA Art.

Mistaken Identities: Poetry & Northern Ireland. Peter McDonald. 236p. 1997. text 65.00 (*0-19-818422-0*) OUP.

***Mistaken Identities: The Second Wave of Controversy over "Political Correctness"** Ed. by Cyril Levitt et al. LC 99-22413. 339p. 1999. pap. text 29.95 (*0-8204-4137-6*) P Lang Pubng.

Mistaken Identity. Michael J. Dunn. 290p. mass mkt. 4.99 (*1-55197-259-X*) Picasso Publ.

Mistaken Identity! Diana G. Gallagher. (Secret World of Alex Mack Ser.: No. 5). (J). (gr. 3-6). 1996. pap. 3.99 (*0-671-55778-5*, PB Trade Paper) PB.

***Mistaken Identity.** Merline Lovelace. (Intimate Moments Ser.: Vol. 987). 2000. mass mkt. 4.50 (*0-373-07987-7*) Silhouette.

Mistaken Identity. Joyce Pope. LC 91-17136. (Curious Creatures Ser.). (Illus.). 48p. (J). 1992. lib. bdg. 5.00 (*0-8114-3152-5*) Raintree Steck-V.

Mistaken Identity. Nayantara Sahgal. LC 88-29143. 224p. 1989. 16.95 (*0-8112-1093-6*, Pub. by New Directions) Norton.

Mistaken Identity. Nayantara Sahgal. LC 88-29143. 224p. 1992. pap. 10.95 (*0-8112-1207-6*, NDP742, Pub. by New Directions) Norton.

Mistaken Identity. Lisa Scottoline. LC 98-43200. 496p. 1999. 24.00 (*0-06-018747-6*) HarpC.

Mistaken Identity. Lisa Scottoline. 592p. 2000. mass mkt. 7.50 (*0-06-109611-3*) HarpC.

Mistaken Identity. large type ed. Lisa Scottoline. LC 99-14749. 704p. 1950. 30.00 (*0-7862-1976-9*) Mac Lib Ref.

***Mistaken Identity.** large type ed. Lisa Scottoline. LC 99-14749. 1999. 29.95 (*0-7862-1975-0*, G K Hall & Co) Mac Lib Ref.

***Mistaken Identity: Burton,&Kate, Set.** abr. ed. Lisa Scottoline. 1999. audio 18.00 (*0-694-52110-8*, 394823, Pub. by HarperAudio) Lndmrk Audiobks.

Mistaken Identity: The Supreme Court & the Politics of Minority Representation. Keith J. Bybee. LC 97-51799. 206p. 1998. text 35.00 (*0-691-01729-8*, Pub. by Princeton U Pr) Cal Prin Full Svc.

Mistaken Lights. Gary Schroeder. LC 85-50796. (Illus.). 58p. 1985. pap. 7.00 (*0-933573-00-6*) Wayland Pr.

Mistaken Lights. limited ed. Gary Schroeder. LC 85-50796. (Illus.). 58p. 1985. 15.00 (*0-933573-01-4*) Wayland Pr.

Mistaken Reasons see Motivos Equivocados: Mistaken Reasons

Mistaken Seven: Eyewitness Identification of the "Gentlemen Bandit" R. Buckhout. (Monographs: No. CR-48). 1985. 4.00 (*1-55524-049-6*) Ctr Respon Psych.

Mistaken Widow. Cheryl St. John. (Historical Ser.: Vol. 429). 304p. 1998. per. 4.99 (*0-373-29029-2*, 1-29029-5) Harlequin Bks.

***Mistakes.** Sharon Dolin. (Poetry New York Pamphlet Ser.: No. 24). 18p. 1999. pap. 5.00 (*0-923389-40-7*) Meet Eyes Bind.

Mistakes Made & Lessons Learned: Overcoming Obstacles to Successful Program Planning. Ed. by Thomas J. Sork. LC 85-644750. (New Directions for Adult & Continuing Education Ser.: No. ACE 49). 1990. pap. 22.00 (*1-55542-783-9*) Jossey-Bass.

Mistakes Social Scientists Make. Seltzer. 157p. 1995. pap. text 14.95 (*0-312-12003-6*) St Martin.

Mistakes That Worked: 40 Familiar Inventions & How They Came to Be. Charlotte Foltz-Jones. (Illus.). 78p. (J). (gr. 3-7). 1994. pap. 11.95 (*0-385-32043-4*) BDD Bks Young Read.

Mistakes That Worked: 40 Familiar Inventions & How They Came to Be. Charlotte Foltz-Jones. (Illus.). 81p. (YA). (gr. 6-12). 1998. pap. text 11.00 (*0-7881-5769-8*) DIANE Pub.

Mistakes to Avoid in English. Howard. 1987. pap. text. write for info. (*0-582-65791-1*, Pub. by Addison-Wesley) Longman.

Mistakes You Make at Bridge. Terence Reese & Roger Trezel. (Master Bridge Ser.). 160p. 1984. pap. 13.95 (*0-575-05785-8*, Pub. by V Gollancz) Trafalgar.

Mistaking Africa. Curtis A. Keim. LC 99-21972. 2000. mass mkt. 22.00 (*0-8133-3509-4*) HarpC.

***Mistaking Africa: Curiosities & Inventions of the American Mind.** Curtis Keim. LC 99-21972. 256p. 1999. 65.00 (*0-8133-3508-6*) Westview.

Misteaching of Academic Discourse: The Politics of Language in the Classroom. Lilia I. Bartolome. LC 98-9693. (C). 1998. text 60.00 (*0-8133-3144-7*, Pub. by Westview) HarpC.

Misteaks & How to Find Them Before the Teacher Does. Barry Cipra. 70p. 1983. pap. text 5.95 (*0-8176-3083-X*) Birkhauser.

Misteaks & How to Find Them Before the Teacher Does. 2nd ed. Barry Cipra. 66p. 1989. pap. text 13.00 (*0-12-174695-X*) Acad Pr.

***Misteaks [sic] & How to Find Them Before the Teacher Does: A Calculus Supplement.** 3rd ed. Barry Cipra. LC 00-24778. (Illus.). 88p. 2000. 5.95 (*1-56881-122-5*) AK Peters.

Mistel: The Piggy-Back Aircraft of the Luftwaffe. Hans-Peter Dabrowski. (Illus.). 52p. 1994. pap. 9.95 (*0-88740-668-8*) Schiffer.

Misteltherapie & Immunologische Forschung: Arbeitstagung, Hercecke, Mai, 1996. Ed. by Arndt Buessing et al. (Journal Ser.: Vol. 3, Supplement 1, 1996). (GER., Illus.). iv, 20p. 1996. pap. 40.00 (*3-8055-6445-7*) S Karger.

Mr. Absalom Billingslea & Other Georgia Folk. Richard M. Johnston. LC 72-110203. (Short Story Index Reprint Ser.). 1977. 26.95 (*0-8369-3354-0*) Ayer.

Mr. Alaska: The Chuck West Story. Charles B. West. LC 85-50666. 1993. 19.95 (*0-933319-12-6*) Weslee Pub.

Mr. Alaska: The Chuck West Story Forty Years of Alaska Tourism, 1945-1985. Charles B. West. LC 85-50666. (Illus.). 153p. (Orig.). 1986. 17.95 (*0-933319-10-X*); pap. 9.95 (*0-933319-11-8*) Weslee Pub.

Mr. Alfred, M. A. George Friel. (Classics Ser.). 179p. 1996. pap. 9.95 (*0-86241-163-7*, Pub. by Canongate Books) Interlink Pub.

Mr. American. George MacDonald Fraser. LC 98-6917. 585p. 1998. pap. 15.95 (*0-7867-0554-X*) Carroll & Graf.

Mister & Me. Kimberly W. Holt. LC 97-40329. (Illus.). 80p. (J). (gr. 2-6). 1998. 14.99 (*0-399-23215-X*) Putnam Pub Group.

***Mister & Me.** Kimberly Willis Holt. (Illus.). 80p. (J). (gr. 2-5). 2000. pap. 3.99 (*0-698-11869-3*, PuffinBks) Peng Put Young Read.

Mr. & Mrs. Bo Jo Jones. Ann Head. (Illus.). 192p. (YA). (gr. 9-12). 1968. mass mkt. 4.99 (*0-451-16319-2*, Sig) NAL.

Mr. & Mrs. Bo Jo Jones. Ann Head. (J). 1968. 10.09 (*0-606-01102-1*, Pub. by Turtleback) Demco.

Mr. & Mrs. Kevin Wade. 1984. pap. 5.25 (*0-8222-0778-8*) Dramatists Play.

Mr. & Mrs. Charles Dickens: His Letters to Her. Charles Dickens. Ed. by Walter Dexter. LC 72-1331. (Studies in Dickens: No. 52). 1972. reprint ed. lib. bdg. 75.00 (*0-8383-1429-5*) M S G Haskell Hse.

***Mr. & Mrs. Gifts from the Heart.** Dolley Carlson. LC 99-39105. (Illus.). 64p. 2000. 12.99 (*0-7814-3381-9*) Chariot Victor.

Mr. & Mrs. Job. Ellen Van Wolde. 1997. pap. 23.00 (*0-334-02712-8*) TPI PA.

Mr. & Mrs. Mephistopheles & Son. Michael Lopes. 44p. 1975. pap. 2.50 (*0-913218-42-1*) Dustbooks.

***Mr. & Mrs. President: From the Trumans to the Clintons.** 2nd rev. ed. Gil Troy. LC 99-87805. (Illus.). 472p. 2000. pap. text 17.95 (*0-7006-1034-0*) U Pr of KS.

Mr. & Ms. Tana Reiff. LC 94-79116. (That's Life Ser.: Bk. 8). 96p. (YA). (gr. 6-12). 1994. pap. 4.95 (*0-7854-1093-7*, 40708) Am Guidance.

Mr. & Ms. Stories: Short Novels. Jaime P. Espiritu. LC 98-92090. 350p. 1998. pap. 15.00 (*0-9666975-0-2*) Petradome Enter.

Mr. Anderson's Monument: Stories of Meridian Street, Lincoln Mill & Lincoln Village. Tillman Hill. Ed. by Bill Easterling. (Illus.). 128p. (C). 1996. 19.95 (*0-916039-09-9*) Kaylor & Kaylor.

Mister Andrews School, 1837-1842: Students' Journal Transcript. Ellen Swartzlander. (Illus.). 126p. 1958. boxed set 2.00 (*0-910302-07-3*) Bucks Co Hist.

Mr. Ape. Dick King-Smith. LC 97-40235. (Illus.). 144p. (J). (gr. 4-6). 1998. 16.00 (*0-517-70986-4*); lib. bdg. 17.99 (*0-517-70987-2*) Crown Pub Group.

Mr. Ape. Dick King-Smith. (Illus.). 144p. (J). (gr. 3-5). 1999. pap. 4.99 (*0-375-80206-1*, Pub. by Knopf Bks Yng Read) Random.

Mr. Arashi's Amazing Freak Show. Suehiro Maruo. (Illus.). 160p. 1991. pap. 10.95 (*0-922233-06-3*) Blast Bks.

Mr. Arkadin. Orson Welles. 23.95 (*0-8488-0774-X*) Amereon Ltd.

Mr. Arkadin. Orson Welles. 1987. pap. 3.50 (*0-8217-2145-3*) NAL.

Mr. Atomic Energy: Congressman Chet Holifield & Atomic Energy Affairs, 1945-1974, 241. Richard W. Dyke. LC 89-12005. (Contributions in Political Science Ser.: No. 241). 467p. 1989. 65.00 (*0-313-26244-6*, DYM/, Greenwood Pr) Greenwood.

Mr. Attorney: The Attorney General for Ontario in Court, Cabinet & Legislature, 1791-1899. Paul Romney. 456p. 1986. text 47.50 (*0-8020-3431-4*) U of Toronto Pr.

Mr. Austin's Commercial Bartending Basics. Patrick R. Dunn. Orig. Title: Professional Bartending Basics. (Illus.). 62p. (Orig.). 1985. reprint ed. pap. 4.95 (*0-9613869-1-6*) Texas Cedar Pr.

Mister B. Donald F. Lippert. (Illus.). 32p. (J). (ps). 1989. write for info. (*0-318-64642-0*) Pastel Pubns.

Mr. B: or Comforting Thoughts about the Bison: A Critical Biography of Robert Benchley, 35. Wes D. Gehring. LC 92-24262. (Contributions to the Study of Popular Culture Ser.: No. 35). 288p. 1992. 59.95 (*0-313-25242-4*, GBY, Greenwood Pr) Greenwood.

Mr. Baldwin, I Presume: James Baldwin - Chinua Achebe: A Meeting of the Minds. Ernest A. Champion. 176p. (C). 1995. pap. text 28.50 (*0-7618-0043-3*) U Pr of Amer.

Mr. Baldwin, I Presume: James Baldwin - Chinua Achebe: A Meeting of the Minds. Ernest A. Champion. 176p. (C). 1995. lib. bdg. 47.00 (*0-7618-0042-5*) U Pr of Amer.

Mr. Banker, Meet Your Customer. 2nd ed. 1997. 2.18 (*0-7863-1263-7*, Irwn Prfssnl) McGraw-Hill Prof.

Mr. Barry's Etchings. Daniel Archer & Walter Bullock. 1950. pap. 5.25 (*0-8222-0779-6*) Dramatists Play.

***Mr. Baruch.** Margaret L. Coit. LC 00-40404. 2000. pap. write for info. (*1-58798-021-5*) Beard Bks.

Mr. Baseball see Bank Street Ready-to-Read Books: Levels 1, 2 & 3

Mr. Baseball. William H. Hooks. (Bank Street Ready-to-Read Ser.). 48p. (J). (ps-3). 1991. pap. 4.50 (*0-553-35303-9*) Bantam.

Mr. Baseball. Alex Jordon. (Illus.). (J). 1991. mass mkt. 3.95 (*0-553-53078-X*) BDD Bks Young Read.

Mr. Bass's Planetoid. Eleanor Cameron. (Illus.). (J). (gr. 3-7). 1958. 14.95 (*0-316-12525-3*, Joy St Bks) Little.

Mr. Bear Says a Spoonful for You. Debi Gliori. (Mr. Bear Says Board Bks.). (Illus.). 10p. (J). (ps up). 1997. 4.99 (*0-689-81519-0*) Litle Simon.

Mr. Bear Says Are You There, Baby Bear? A Lift-the-Flap Book. Debi Gliori. LC 97-52502. (Illus.). 22p. (J). (ps-k). 1999. 9.95 (*0-531-30182-6*) Orchard Bks Watts.

Mr. Bear Says Good Night. Debi Gliori. (Mr. Bear Says Board Bks.). (Illus.). 10p. (J). (ps up). 1997. 4.99 (*0-689-81518-2*) Litle Simon.

Mr. Bear Says I Love You. Debi Gliori. (Mr. Bear Says Board Bks.). (Illus.). 10p. (J). (ps up). 1997. 4.99 (*0-689-81517-4*) Litle Simon.

Mr. Bear Says Peek-a-Boo. Debi Gliori. (Mr. Bear Says Board Bks.). (Illus.). 10p. (J). (ps up). 1997. 4.99 (*0-689-81516-6*) Litle Simon.

***Mr. Bear to the Rescue.** Debi Gliori. LC 99-51524. (Illus.). 32p. (J). 2000. 15.95 (*0-531-30276-8*) Orchard Bks Watts.

Mr. Bear's Apple Tree. A. J. Wood. LC 97-12879. (Magic Shapes Ser.). (Illus.). 24p. (J). (ps-k). 1997. 9.95 (*0-7613-0293-X*) Millbrook Pr.

Mr. Bedford & the Muses. Gail Godwin. 240p. 1984. mass mkt. 4.95 (*0-380-69377-1*, Avon Bks) Morrow Avon.

***Mr. Beetle.** Satoshi Tada. LC 00-9697. (Illus.). (J). 2001. lib. bdg. write for info. (*1-57505-561-9*, Carolrhoda) Lerner Pub.

Mr. Belinsky's Bagels. Ellen Schwartz. LC 97-27057. (Illus.). 32p. (ps-3). 1998. 15.95 (*0-88106-256-1*, Talewinds) Charlesbridge Pub.

Mr. Benihana: The Rocky Aoki Story. Miyuki Takahashi. 1997. pap. text 12.95 (*0-9634335-7-1*) Mangajin.

***Mr. Benson.** 2nd rev. ed. John Preston. 1998. mass mkt. 6.95 (*1-56333-636-7*, Badboy) Masquerade.

Mr. Bernds Goes to Hollywood: My Early Life & Career in Sound Recording at Columbia with Frank Capra & Others. Edward Bernds. LC 98-47142. (Filmmakers Ser.: No. 65). (Illus.). 312p. 1999. 45.00 (*0-8108-3602-5*) Scarecrow.

***Mr. Betts & Mr. Potts.** Rod Hull. (Illus.). 32p. (J). (ps-5). 2000. 15.99 (*1-84148-106-8*) Barefoot Bks NY.

Mr. Big. (Play-It-Like-It-Is Guitar Ser.). pap. 19.95 (*0-89524-486-1*); pap. 16.95 (*0-89524-510-8*); pap. 19.95 (*0-89524-647-3*, Pub. by Cherry Lane); pap. 17.95 (*0-89524-754-2*) Cherry Lane.

Mr. Big: Bump Ahead. (Play-It-Like-It-Is Guitar Ser.). 1994. pap. 19.95 (*0-89524-809-3*) Cherry Lane.

Mr. Big - Hey Man Guitar/Vocal. 85p. (YA). pap. 19.95 (*1-57560-007-2*, Pub. by Cherry Lane) H Leonard.

Mr. Big Brother see Bank Street Ready-to-Read Books: Levels 1, 2 & 3

Mr. Big Brother. William H. Hooks. LC 98-7827. (Bank Street Ready-to-Read Ser.). (Illus.). 32p. (J). 1999. pap. 4.50 (*0-553-37586-5*) Bantam.

Mr. Bill's ABC in Poetry. Bill Garrison. (Illus.). 62p. (Orig.). (J). (gr. k-2). 1996. pap. 12.95 (*0-9653576-0-0*) B Garrison.

Mr. Bill's Handbook of Signals for Letter Sounds. Bill Garrison. Ed. by Nancy Wilkes. LC 96-95110. (Illus.). v, 91p. (Orig.). (J). 1997. pap. text 17.95 (*0-9653576-3-5*) B Garrison.

Mister Blake's Walking Stick. Edward Eggleston. (Collected Works of Edward Eggleston). (YA). 1988. reprint ed. lib. bdg. 59.00 (*0-7812-1170-0*) Rprt Serv.

Mr. Blandings Builds His Dream House. Eric Hodgins. LC 86-32268. (Illus.). 239p. 1999. reprint ed. pap. 14.95 (*0-89733-245-8*) Academy Chi Pubs.

Mr. Bligh's Bad Language: Passion, Power & Theater on the "Bounty. Greg Dening. (Illus.). 459p. (C). 1992. text 54.95 (*0-521-38370-6*) Cambridge U Pr.

Mr. Bligh's Bad Language: Passion, Power & Theatre on the "Bounty" Greg Dening. (Canto Book Ser.). (Illus.). 459p. (C). 1994. pap. 11.95 (*0-521-46718-7*) Cambridge U Pr.

Mr. Bliss, 001. J. R. R. Tolkien. (Illus.). 112p. 1983. 13.95 (*0-395-32936-1*) HM.

Mr. Blue. Myles Connolly. LC 90-31948. 97p. 1990. 10.95 (*0-911519-20-3*) Richelieu Court.

Mr. Blue. Jacques Poulin. Tr. by Sheila Fischman from FRE. 160p. (Orig.). 1993. pap. 13.95 (*1-55065-039-4*, Pub. by Vehicule Pr) Genl Dist Srvs.

Mister Blue Jeans. Maryann N. Weidt. 1997. pap. 5.75 (*0-15-307547-3*) Harcourt.

Mr. Blue Jeans: A Story about Levi Strauss. Maryann N. Weidt. (Creative Minds Ser.). (Illus.). 64p. (J). (gr. 3-6). 1990. lib. bdg. 19.95 (*0-87614-421-0*, Carolrhoda) Lerner Pub.

Mr. Blue Jeans: A Story about Levi Strauss. Maryann N. Weidt. (Illus.). 56p. (J). (gr. 3-6). 1992. pap. 5.95 (*0-87614-588-8*, First Ave Edns) Lerner Pub.

Mr. Blueberry. Cullinan. 1994. text 13.90 (*0-15-302316-3*) Harcourt.

Mister Bluefin. J. B. Drori. 180p. (Orig.). 1986. pap. 12.95 (*0-940391-00-7*) Scopus Bks.

Mr. Boffin. Laurence Schorsch. (Illus.). 32p. (J). (gr. k-3). 1993. 6.95 (*1-56288-353-4*) Checkerboard.

Mister Boffo: The First Decade. Joe Martin. LC 95-83103. (Illus.). 128p. (Orig.). 1996. pap. 9.95 (*0-8362-1442-0*) Andrews & McMeel.

Mister Boffo Shrink Wrapped. Joe Martin. (Illus.). 208p. 1995. pap. 10.95 (*0-8362-1777-2*) Andrews & McMeel.

Mr. Boggle's Peculiar Day: A Visual-Perception Book. Time-Life Books Editors. Ed. by Neil Kagan & Elizabeth Ward. (Early Learning Program Ser.). (Illus.). 56p. (J). (ps-2). 1992. write for info. (*0-8094-9311-X*) Time-Life.

Mr. Boggle's Peculiar Day: A Visual-Perception Book. Time-Life Books Editors. Ed. by Neil Kagan & Elizabeth Ward. (Early Learning Program Ser.). (Illus.). 56p. (J). (ps-2). 1992. lib. bdg. write for info. (*0-8094-9312-8*) Time-Life.

Mr. Bojangles: The Biography of Bill Robinson. Jim Haskins & N. R. Mitgang. (Illus.). 320p. 2000. reprint ed. pap. 14.00 (*1-56649-113-4*) Welcome Rain.

Mister Bonaparte of Corsica. John K. Bangs. LC 70-166657. (Illus.). 1971. reprint ed. 19.00 (*0-403-01416-6*) Scholarly.

***Mr. Bones.** Jean Westcott. 90p. (YA). 2000. pap. 5.99 (*1-57532-298-6*, Pub. by Press-Tige Pub) Am Wholesale.

Mr. Boston. 1997. mass mkt. 9.99 (*0-446-67439-7*, Pub. by Warner Bks) Little.

Mr. Boston Bar. Sunset Books Staff. 1991. mass mkt. 7.95 (*0-446-11424-3*) Warner Bks.

Mr. Boston Official Bartender's & Party Guide. (Illus.). 272p. 1994. reprint ed. mass mkt. 9.99 (*0-446-67042-1*, Pub. by Warner Bks) Little.

Mr. Boston's Official Bartender's Guide. 272p. 1988. mass mkt. 7.95 (*0-446-38763-0*, Pub. by Warner Bks) Little.

***Mr. Bounce.** Roger Hargreaves. (Illus.). 32p. (J). (gr. k-3). 2000. pap. 2.99 (*0-8431-7562-1*, Price Stern) Peng Put Young Read.

Mr. Bradley's Day of Surprises. Stanley D. Eitzen et al. LC 96-231939. 24p. (J). (ps-3). 1996. 4.99 (*0-689-80423-7*) Litle Simon.

Mr. Bridge: A Novel. Evan S. Connell. LC 81-81513. 367p. 1990. reprint ed. pap. 9.95 (*0-86547-054-5*) N Point Pr.

Mr. Bristol's Barn: With Excerpts from Mr. Blinn's Diary. John Szarkowski. LC 96-27198. (Illus.). 72p. 1997. 16.95 (*0-8109-4286-0*, Pub. by Abrams) Time Warner.

Mr. Britling see Works of H. G. Wells

Mr. Brodrick's Army. deluxe ed. Winston L. S. Churchill. LC 76-26305. (Illus.). 120p. 1973. 18.50 (*0-917684-03-6*) Churchilliana.

Mr. Brodrick's Army & For Free Trade, 2 bks. Winston L. S. Churchill. LC 76-26306. (Facsimile Set Editions Ser.). (Illus.). 1977. reprint ed. lib. bdg. 28.50 (*0-685-87406-0*) Churchilliana.

Mr. Brooks & the Australian Trade: Imperial Business in the Nineteenth Century. Frank Broeze. 384p. 1993. 49.95 (*0-522-84574-6*, Pub. by Melbourne Univ Pr) Paul & Co Pubs.

Mr. Brooks Goes to Bethlehem. McMahan. 1994. pap. 6.95 (*1-55897-831-3*) Brentwood Music.

Mr. Brown Can Moo! Can You? Dr. Seuss's Book of Wonderful Noises. Dr. Seuss, pseud et al. LC 96-68776. (Bright & Early Bks.). (Illus.). 20p. (J). (ps-k). 1996. 4.99 (*0-679-88282-0*, Pub. by Random Bks Yng Read) Random.

***Mr. Browne & the Rose Show: A Child's Perception of "Different"** M. Beatryce Shaw. 40p. (J). (gr. k-4). 2000. pap. 7.95 (*1-929234-02-3*) Schooner Pubns.

***Mr. Browne's Roses: A Story of Early Childhood Color Awareness.** M. Beatryce Shaw. 36p. (J). (gr. k-4). 1999. pap. 7.95 (*1-929234-03-1*) Schooner Pubns.

Mister B's Land. LaJoyce Martin. LC 98-34552. 219p. 1998. pap. 8.99 (*1-56722-222-6*) Word Aflame.

Mr. Bubble Gum see Bank Street Ready-to-Read Books: Levels 1, 2 & 3

Mr. Buchanan's Administration on the Eve of the Rebellion. James Buchanan. (American Biography Ser.). 296p. 1991. reprint ed. lib. bdg. 69.00 (*0-7812-8049-4*) Rprt Serv.

M

Mister Buchanan's Administration on the Eve of the Rebellion. James Buchanan. LC 70-107795. (Select Bibliographies Reprint Ser.). 1977. 27.95 (*0-8369-5212-X*) Ayer.

Mr. Buck: The Autobiography of Nash Buckingham. T. Nash Buckingham. Ed. by Steven R. Smith. LC 90-81090. (Illus.). 288p. 1990. 40.00 (*0-924357-15-0*, 61200-A) Countrysport Pr.

Mr. Buck: The Autobiography of Nash Buckingham. deluxe limited ed. T. Nash Buckingham. Ed. by Steven R. Smith. LC 90-81090. (Illus.). 288p. 1990. lthr. 70.00 (*0-924357-16-9*, 61200-B); lthr. 100.00 (*0-924357-17-7*, 61205-B) Countrysport Pr.

Mr. Bug's Phonics: Level 1 Student Book. Catherine Y. Eisele et al. (Illus.). 1997. pap. text, student ed. 8.95 (*0-19-435252-8*) OUP.

Mr. Bug's Phonics 1: Level 1 Teacher's Book. Catherine Y. Eisele et al. (Illus.). 48p. 1998. pap. text, teacher ed. 10.95 (*0-19-435250-1*) OUP.

Mr. Bug's Phonics 2. Catherine Y. Eisele et al. (Illus.). 62p. 1997. pap. text, teacher ed. 10.95 (*0-19-435356-7*) OUP.

Mr. Bug's Phonics 2: Level 2 Student Book. Catherine Y. Eisele et al. (Illus.). 80p. 1998. pap. text, student ed. 8.95 (*0-19-435259-5*) OUP.

Mr. Bumble. Kim Kennedy. 1999. pap. text 5.99 (*0-7868-1353-9*, Pub. by Hyperion) Time Warner.

Mr. Bumble. Kim Kennedy. LC 96-35465. (Illus.). 32p. (J). (ps-3). 1997. 15.95 (*0-7868-0263-4*, Pub. by Hyprn Child); lib. bdg. 15.89 (*0-7868-2293-7*, Pub. by Hyprn Child) Little.

***Mr. Bunny's Big Cup O' Java.** Carlton Egrement. (Illus.). 128p. (C). 1999. pap. text 14.95 (*0-201-61563-0*) Addison-Wesley.

***Mr. Bunny's Guide to Activex.** Carlton Egremont. LC 99-181638. 112p. (C). 1998. pap. text 14.95 (*0-201-48536-2*) Addison-Wesley.

***Mr. Busy.** Roger Hargreaves. (Mr. Men & Little Miss Ser.). (Illus.). 32p. (J). (ps-3). 2000. pap. 2.99 (*0-8431-7600-8*, Price Stern) Peng Put Young Read.

Mr. Campion & Others. Margery Allingham. 272p. 1991. pap. 3.95 (*0-380-70579-6*, Avon Bks) Morrow Avon.

Mr. Campion's Farthing. Margery Allingham & Youngman Carter. 191p. 1990. mass mkt. 3.95 (*0-88184-667-8*) Carroll & Graf.

Mr. Campion's Lucky Day & Other Stories. Margery Allingham. 240p. 1992. mass mkt. 3.95 (*0-88184-890-5*) Carroll & Graf.

Mr. Campion's Quarry. Margery Allingham & Youngman Carter. 240p. 1991. mass mkt. 3.95 (*0-88184-724-0*) Carroll & Graf.

Mr. Capone: The Real - & Complete - Story of Al Capone. Robert J. Schoenberg. LC 92-5228. 1993. pap. 16.00 (*0-688-12838-6*, Quil) HarperTrade.

Mr. Carey's Garden. Jane Cutler. LC 93-13720. (Illus.). 32p. (J). (ps-3). 1996. 14.95 (*0-395-68191-X*) HM.

Mister Carlyle, My Patient. James L. Halliday. LC 73-18125. (English Literature Ser.: No. 33). 1974. lib. bdg. 75.00 (*0-8383-1737-5*) M S G Haskell Hse.

Mr. Cat. Ruth Corrin. LC 91-20236. (Illus.). 32p. (J). (ps-3). 1991. 13.95 (*0-940793-89-X*, Crocodile Bks) Interlink Pub.

Mr. Chairman: A Guide to Meeting Procedure & Forms of Address. 5th ed. Marjorie Puregger. 1989. pap. text 16.95 (*0-7022-1769-7*, Pub. by Univ Queensland Pr) Intl Spec Bk.

***Mr. Chairman: The Journal of a Congressional Appropriator.** William Lehman. LC 99-49038. 728p. 2000. pap. 47.50 (*0-7618-1559-7*) U Pr of Amer.

Mr. Charles Booth's Inquiry: Life & Labour of the People in London Reconsidered. Rosemary O'Day & David Englander. LC 93-356. 256p. 1993. 55.00 (*1-85285-079-5*) Hambledon Press.

Mr. Chatterbox. Roger Hargreaves. (Mr. Men & Little Miss Ser.). (Illus.). 32p. 1997. pap. 2.99 (*0-8431-7807-8*, Price Stern) Peng Put Young Read.

Mr. Cheap's Atlanta: Bargains, Factory Outlets, Off-Price Stores, Deep Discount Stores, Cheap Eats, Cheap Places to Stay, & Cheap Fun Things to Do. Mark Waldstein. LC 93-43270. (Mr. Cheap Ser.). 304p. 1994. pap. 9.95 (*1-55850-292-0*) Adams Media.

Mr. Cheap's Boston. 2nd ed. Mark Waldstein. Ed. by Tami M. Forman & Andy Richardson. 1995. pap. 9.95 (*1-55850-556-3*) Adams Media.

Mr. Cheap's Chicago: Bargains, Factory Outlets, Off-Price Stores, Deep Discount Stores, Cheap Eats, Cheap Places to Stay, & Cheap Fun Things to Do. Mark Waldstein. LC 93-43271. (Mr. Cheap Ser.). 304p. (Orig.). 1994. pap. 9.95 (*1-55850-291-2*) Adams Media.

***Mr. Cheap's Chicago: Shopping Bargains, Factory Outlets, Off-Price Stores, Discount Stores, Cheap Eats, Cheap Places to Stay & Affordable Fun Things to Do.** 2nd ed. Adams Media Editors. (Mr. Cheap's Ser.). 320p. 2000. pap. 9.95 (*1-58062-374-3*) Adams Media.

***Mr. Cheap's New York.** 2nd ed. Editors of Adams Media Corporation. 320p. 2000. pap. 9.95 (*1-58062-271-2*) Adams Media.

Mr. Cheap's New York: Bargains, Factory Outlets, Off-Price Stores, Deep Discount Stores, Cheap Eats, Cheap Places to Stay, & Cheap Fun Things to Do. Mark Waldstein. (Mr. Cheap Ser.). 448p. 1993. pap. 9.95 (*1-55850-256-4*) Adams Media.

Mr. Cheap's San Francisco: Bargains, Factory Outlets, Off-Price Stores, Deep Discount Stores, Cheap Eats, Cheap Places to Stay, & Cheap Fun Things to Do. Mark Waldstein. LC 94-16132. 1994. pap. 8.95 (*1-55850-388-9*) Adams Media.

Mr. Cheap's Seattle. Mark Waldstein. 304p. 1995. pap. 9.95 (*1-55850-445-1*) Adams Media.

Mr. Cheap's Washington, D. C. Bargains, Factory Outlets, Off-Price Stores, Deep Discount Stores, Cheap Eats, Cheap Places to Stay, & Cheap Fun Things to Do. Mark Waldstein. (Mr. Cheap's Ser.). 352p. (Orig.). 1996. pap. 9.95 (*1-55850-415-X*) Adams Media.

Mr. China's Son: A Villager's Life. Liyi He & Claire A. Chik. 312p. (C). 1993. pap. 28.00 (*0-8133-1730-4*, Pub. by Westview) HarpC.

Mr. Chips. Laura McGee Kvasnosky. LC 95-38986. 32p. (J). 1996. 15.00 (*0-374-35092-2*) FS&G.

Mr. Christian. William Kinsolving. 1997. 23.00 (*0-07-158770-5*) McGraw.

Mr. Christian. large type ed. William Kinsolving. LC 96-17812. (Large Print Bks.). 1996. 25.95 (*1-56895-339-9*) Wheeler Pub.

Mister Christmas. Linda Cajio. 251p. 1997. per. 3.75 (*0-373-16704-0*, 1-16704-8) Harlequin Bks.

Mr. Cibber of Drury Lane. Richard H. Barker. LC 71-160002. reprint ed. 32.50 (*0-404-00654-X*) AMS Pr.

Mr. Civil Rights: The Story of Thurgood Marshall. Nancy Whitelaw. LC 95-10481. (Notable Americans Ser.). (Illus.). 124p. (YA). (gr. 5 up). 1995. lib. bdg. 17.95 (*1-883846-10-2*) M Reynolds.

Mr. Clark's Summer. Gilles Tibo. 24p. 1992. pap. 8.00 (*0-385-25331-1*) Doubleday.

Mr. Claude. Ada M. Holland. LC 83-40502. (Illus.). 160p. 1984. 12.50 (*0-89096-182-4*) Tex A&M Univ Pr.

Mr. Clemens & Mark Twain: A Biography. Justin E. Kaplan. 432p. 1991. per. 15.00 (*0-671-74807-6*, Touchstone) S&S Trade Pap.

Mr. Clemens & Mr. Brown. Sally Netzel. 83p. Date not set. pap. write for info. (*0-87129-820-1*, MC1) Dramatic Pub.

***Mr. Clumsy.** Roger Hargreaves. (Illus.). 32p. (ps-3). 2000. pap. 2.99 (*0-8431-7617-2*, Price Stern) Peng Put Young Read.

Mr. Clutterbus. Cecily Matthews. LC 92-34257. (Voyages Ser.). (Illus.). (J). 1993. 4.25 (*0-383-03642-9*) SRA McGraw.

Mr. Cogito. Zbigniew Herbert. Tr. by John Carpenter & Bogdana Carpenter from POL. LC 92-37992. (Modern European Poets Ser.). 62p. 1993. 22.95 (*0-88001-330-3*) HarpC.

***Mr. Commitment.** Mike Gayle. 320p. 2000. 22.95 (*0-385-50100-5*) Doubleday.

Mr. Creep the Crook. Allan Ahlberg. (Illus.). 24p. (J). 1988. pap. 6.95 (*0-14-032345-7*, Pub. by Pnguin Bks Ltd) Trafalgar.

Mr. Crewe's Career. Winston L. S. Churchill. (BCL1-PS American Literature Ser.). 498p. 1992. reprint ed. lib. bdg. 99.00 (*0-7812-6686-6*) Rprt Serv.

Mr. Crispy's Story of the First Candy Canes, Vol. 1. 2nd rev. ed. Sally R. Manley. LC TXU775-417. (Illus.). 32p. (J). (gr. k-4). 1997. 16.95 (*0-9655303-0-2*) Sunny Lane.

Mr. Crumblestone's Eden. large type ed. Alan S. Well. (Linford Mystery Library). 384p. 1997. pap. 16.99 (*0-7089-5027-2*, Linford) Ulverscroft.

Mr. Cuckoo. Becky Bloom. LC 97-43650. (Illus.). 32p. (J). (gr. k-4). 1998. 15.95 (*1-57255-626-9*) Mondo Pubng.

Mr. Cue's Zoo: Phonics & Cued Speech. Gustav Katschka. (Illus.). 53p. (J). (gr. k-5). 1998. spiral bd. 30.00 (*1-892917-05-X*) N Coast Cued.

Mr. Dalloway. Robin Lippincott. LC 98-31006. 232p. 1999. pap. 13.95 (*1-889330-29-9*, Pub. by Sarabande Bks) Consort Bk Sales.

***Mr. Darwin's Shooter.** Roger McDonald. LC 98-36819. 365p. 1999. 25.00 (*0-87113-733-X*, Atlntc Mnthly) Grove-Atltic.

***Mr. Darwin's Shooter.** Roger McDonald. 384p. 2000. pap. 13.95 (*0-14-028859-7*, Penguin Bks) Viking Penguin.

Mr. Darwin's Voyage. Linda J. Altman. (People in Focus Ser.). (Illus.). (YA). (gr. 5 up). 1995. pap. 7.95 (*0-382-24962-3*, Dillon Silver Burdett) Silver Burdett Pr.

Mr. Darwin's Voyage. Linda J. Altman. LC 94-27367. (J). (gr. 1-8). 1995. 13.95 (*0-87518-609-2*, Dillon Silver Burdett) Silver Burdett Pr.

Mr. Davies & the Baby. Charlotte Voake. LC 95-11338. (Illus.). 32p. (J). (ps-3). 1997. reprint ed. pap. 4.99 (*0-7636-0122-5*) Candlewick Pr.

***Mr. Daydream.** Roger Hargreaves. (Illus.). 32p. (J). (gr. k-3). 2000. pap. 2.99 (*0-8431-7563-X*, Price Stern) Peng Put Young Read.

Mr. December: (Mail Order Men) Heather Macallister. (Temptation Ser.: No. 711). 1998. per. 3.75 (*0-373-25811-9*, 1-25811-0) Harlequin Bks.

***Mr. Dickens Hits Town.** Jan Mark. (Illus.). 64p. (YA). (gr. 4-7). 1999. 16.95 (*0-88776-468-1*) Tundra Bks.

***Mr. Dimock Explores the Mysteries of the East: An American in India.** Edward Cameron Dimock. LC 98-43901. 224p. 1999. 18.95 (*1-56512-153-8*, 72153) Algonquin Bks.

***Mr. Dineen's Careful Parade.** Thomas McCarthy. 176p. 2000. pap. 22.95 (*0-85646-320-5*, Pub. by Anvil Press) Dufour.

Mr. Dinosaur see Bank Street Ready-to-Read Books: Levels 1, 2 & 3

Mr. Don & Mr. Dimple. Michael Whittaker. (Illus.). 44p. (Orig.). (J). (gr. k-4). 1997. pap., per. 5.95 (*1-889832-01-4*) Auburn Pub.

Mr. Donaghue Investigates. Anna Shone. 1997. per. 4.99 (*0-373-26238-8*, 0-26238-6, Wrldwide Lib) Harlequin Bks.

Mr. Donkey. Joanne Wall. (Christmas Ornaments Ser.). (Illus.). 34p. (Orig.). (J). (ps up). 1996. pap. 12.95 (*0-9644283-4-2*) M J Wall.

Mr. Doodle Had a Poodle. Jane Belk Moncure. LC 87-15808. (Magic Castle Readers Ser.). (Illus.). 32p. (J). (ps-2). 1988. lib. bdg. 21.36 (*0-89565-409-1*) Childs World.

Mr. Dooley - Wise & Funny - We Need Him Now. Finley P. Dunne & Barbara C. Schaaf. 310p. (Orig.). 1987. pap. 8.95 (*0-942936-11-6*) Lincoln-Herndon Pr.

Mr. Dooley & Mr. Dunne: A Study of Finley Peter Dunne & His Mr. Dooley. Edward Ifkovic. 1979. lib. bdg. 250.00 (*0-87700-265-7*) Revisionist Pr.

Mr. Dooley & the Chicago Irish: An Anthology. Ed. by Charles Fanning. LC 76-6339. (Irish Americans Ser.). 1979. 41.95 (*0-405-09334-9*) Ayer.

Mr. Dooley & the Chicago Irish: The Autobiography of a Nineteenth-Century Ethnic Group. Finley P. Dunne. Ed. by Charles Fanning. LC 87-13228. 357p. 1976. reprint ed. pap. 110.70 (*0-7837-9106-2*, 204990800004) Bks Demand.

Mr. Dooley in Peace & in War. Finley P. Dunne. LC 88-20662. (Prairie State Bks.). 176p. 1988. 11.95 (*0-252-06040-7*) U of Ill Pr.

Mr. Dooley in Peace & War. Finley P. Dunne. 1972. 250.00 (*0-87968-249-3*) Gordon Pr.

Mr. Dooley in the Hearts of His Countrymen. Finley P. Dunne. 1972. 250.00 (*0-87968-248-5*) Gordon Pr.

Mr. Dooley in the Hearts of His Countrymen. Finley P. Dunne. 1968. reprint ed. 13.00 (*0-403-00096-3*) Scholarly.

Mr. Dooley's Opinions. Finley P. Dunne. 1973. 250.00 (*0-87968-161-6*) Gordon Pr.

Mr. Dooley's Opinions. Finley P. Dunne. 1977. reprint ed. 59.00 (*0-403-08562-4*) Scholarly.

Mr. Dooley's Philosophy. Finley P. Dunne. LC 73-10444. (American Humorists Ser.). 267p. reprint ed. lib. bdg. 22.00 (*0-8398-0376-1*) Irvington.

Mr. Doppler Is Survived by Those Who Loved Him. J. Delgado-Figueroa. LC 94-73721.Tr. of Sus Desconsolados Deudos, al Comunicar la Sensible Perdida de Quien en Vida Fuera Frederick Doppler. (SPA.). 133p. 1995. pap. 7.95 (*0-9643486-1-6*) Hispanic Caribbean.

***Mr. Dream Merchant.** Erroll J. Bailey. 280p. (J). (gr. 7-12). 2000. 15.95 (*1-902618-30-0*, Pub. by Element Childrns) Penguin Putnam.

Mr. Dream Merchant: A Novel. Erroll J. Bailey. LC 97-45795. 224p. 1998. 19.95 (*1-86204-192-X*, Pub. by Element MA) Penguin Putnam.

Mr. Dress-Up's Fifty More Things to Make & Do. Ernie Coombs & Shelley Tanaka. (Illus.). 62p. 1991. pap. 9.95 (*0-7737-5460-1*) Genl Dist Srvs.

Mister Du Quesne, & Other Essays. John D. Beresford. LC 68-24845. (Essay Index Reprint Ser.). 1977. 19.95 (*0-8369-0200-9*) Ayer.

Mr. Dunn Browne's Experiences in the Army: The Civil War Letters of Samuel W. Fiske. Samuel W. Fiske. Ed. by Stephen W. Sears. LC 98-14100. (North's Civil War Ser.: Vol. 6). xiii, 254p. 1998. 27.50 (*0-8232-1833-3*) Fordham.

Mr. Dutch: The Arkansas Traveler. Beach Leighton. LC 91-60004. (Illus.). 263p. 1991. 19.95 (*0-915611-44-9*) Sports Pub.

Mr. Duvall Reports the News. Jill D. Duvall. (Our Neighborhood Ser.). (J). pap. 6.95 (*0-516-26150-9*) Childrens.

Mr. Duvall Reports the News. Jill D. Duvall. LC 96-34915. (Our Neighborhood Ser.). (Illus.). (J). 1997. lib. bdg. 19.50 (*0-516-20316-9*) Childrens.

Mr. Easy: Man of the Month, Hawk's Way. Cait London. (Desire Ser.). 1995. mass mkt. 3.25 (*0-373-05919-1*, 1-05919-5) Silhouette.

Mr. Ed Rose' Industrial Relations. Ed Rose. (C). 1997. pap. text. write for info. (*0-201-34299-5*) Addison-Wesley.

Mr. Ego Versus You. Bruce Jameson. 104p. 1986. pap. 40.00 (*0-7223-1981-9*, Pub. by A H S Ltd) St Mut.

Mr. Eighty Percent. James Sherman. 1987. pap. 5.25 (*0-8222-0780-X*) Dramatists Play.

Mr. Elephant. Joanne Wall. (Christmas Ornaments Ser.). (Illus.). 34p. (Orig.). (J). (ps up). 1996. pap. 12.95 (*0-9644283-5-0*) M J Wall.

Mister Eliot among the Nightingales. L. Grudin. LC 78-174691. (Studies in T. S. Eliot: No. 11). 1972. reprint ed. lib. bdg. 49.00 (*0-8383-1346-9*) M S G Haskell Hse.

Mr. Euchre: And Other Northwoods Fables. Bill Kruger. (Illus.). 36p. (Orig.). 1995. pap. 9.00 (*0-9651817-0-7*) Sunwood Mills.

Mr. Everybody's Musical Apartment, Bk. 1. Myles Feltenberger. LC 92-96919. (Illus.). 40p. (J). 1993. pap. 9.95 (*0-9634218-0-8*) Myles Music.

Mr. Everybody's Musical Apartment, Bk. 2. large type ed. Myles Feltenberger. (Illus.). 46p. (J). (gr. k-4). 1996. pap. 10.95 (*0-9634218-1-6*) Myles Music.

***Mr. Everybody's Musical Apartment Bk. 3: A Note-Teaching Musical Story.** large type ed. Myles Feltenberger. (Illus.). 62p. (ps-6). 1999. pap. 12.95 (*0-9634218-2-4*) Myles Music.

Mr. Family. Margot Early. (Superromance Ser.). 1996. mass mkt. 3.99 (*0-373-70711-8*, 1-70711-6) Harlequin Bks.

Mr. Farmer & His Animals. Judy S. Mason. Ed. by Nita Scoggan. (Illus.). 52p. (Orig.). (J). (gr. 3 up). 1987. pap. 3.95 (*0-910487-11-1*) Royalty Pub.

Mr. Fidgit's Big Day. Merry B. Robbins. LC 96-27666. (Illus.). (J). 1997. write for info. (*1-56763-293-9*); pap. write for info. (*1-56763-294-7*) Ozark Pub.

Mr. Fine Goes to the Eye Doctor. Michael L. Sirken. 28p. (J). (ps-4). 1993. pap. 2.95 (*0-9635483-0-1*) Sirken Pubns.

Mr. Fine, Porcupine. Fanny Joly. LC 97-9689. (Illus.). 32p. (J). (ps-1). 1997. 12.95 (*0-8118-1842-X*) Chronicle Bks.

Mister Fish & the Alabama Claims: A Chapter in Diplomatic History. J. Bancroft Davis. (Select Bibliographies Reprint Ser.). 1977. 19.95 (*0-8369-5067-4*) Ayer.

Mr. Fish & the Alabama Claims: A Chapter in Diplomatic History. J. C. Davies. LC 71-95065. (Select Bibliographies Reprint Ser.). 158p. 1972. reprint ed. lib. bdg. 18.00 (*0-8290-0485-8*) Irvington.

Mister Fish Takes A Wife. Demond Wilson. 1999. write for info. (*1-878898-23-X*) Christian Pub.

Mr. Fishrat. deluxe limited ed. Robert Darling. (Alaska Christmas Ser.: No. II). (Illus.). 17p. 1992. 50.00 (*0-9630863-8-3*); pap. 20.00 (*0-9630863-7-5*) Limner Pr.

***Mr. Fix-It: 101 Answers to the Most Commonly Asked Questions about Repairing Your Home.** Lou Manfredini. Ed. by Kathy Neumeyer. LC 99-69007. (Illus.). 156p. 2000. pap. 14.99 (*1-892866-22-6*) Rare Air.

Mr. Fixit's Magnet Machine. Richard Scarry. LC 97-39942. (Read-It-Yourself Ser.: No. 1). 32p. (J). 1998. mass mkt. 3.99 (*0-689-81624-3*, Simon Spot) Little Simon.

***Mr. Fixit's Mix-Ups.** Richard Scarry. (Richard Scarry's On the Go Books). (Illus.). 12p. (J). (ps-k). 1998. 5.99 (*0-689-81559-X*) S&S Trade.

Mr. Fluxus: A Collective Portrait of George Maciunas. Ed. by Emmett Williams & Ann Noel. LC 97-61643. (Illus.). 352p. 1998. 34.95 (*0-500-97461-6*, Pub. by Thames Hudson) Norton.

Mr. Food Cookbook. Art Ginsberg. (Illus.). 128p. 1986. spiral bd. 8.95 (*0-9615951-1-6*) Ginsburg Ent.

Mr. Food Cooks Chicken. Art Ginsburg. LC 93-8502. (Illus.). 157p. 1993. 11.95 (*0-688-11600-0*, Wm Morrow) Morrow Avon.

Mr. Food from My Kitchen to Yours: Recipes & Stories from Home. Art Ginsburg. (Illus.). 288p. 1996. 14.95 (*0-688-14512-4*, Wm Morrow) Morrow Avon.

Mr. Food Simply Chocolate. Art Ginsburg. 1996. 12.00 (*0-688-14419-5*, Wm Morrow) Morrow Avon.

Mr. Food's Italian Kitchen. Art Ginsburg. LC 97-19705. 256p. 1997. 14.95 (*0-688-14396-2*, Wm Morrow) Morrow Avon.

Mr. Food's Simple Southern Favorites. Art Ginsburg. LC 97-28594. (Mr. Food Ser.). (Illus.). 256p. 1997. 14.95 (*0-688-14580-9*, Wm Morrow) Morrow Avon.

Mister Fortune Speaking. Henry C. Bailey. LC 78-140325. (Short Story Index Reprint Ser.). 1977. 20.95 (*0-8369-3717-1*) Ayer.

Mr. Fortune Speaking. H. C. Bailey. 269p. 1977. reprint ed. lib. bdg. 12.95 (*0-89966-276-5*) Buccaneer Bks.

Mr. Fothergill's Plot: His Conspirators Martin Armstrong, H. R. Barbor, Elizabeth Bowen & Others. John Fothergill. 1977. 21.95 (*0-8369-4243-4*, 6054) Ayer.

Mr. Francis' Wife. Sandy Gills. LC 97-48910. 260p. 1997. 9.99 (*1-56476-689-6*, Victor Bks) Chariot Victor.

Mr. Froude & Mr. Carlyle. David Wilson. LC 75-122460. (English Biography Ser.: No. 31). 360p. 1970. reprint ed. lib. bdg. 64.95 (*0-8383-0904-6*) M S G Haskell Hse.

Mr. Frumble's Pickle Car. Richard Scarry. (Richard Scarry's on the Go Bks.). (Illus.). 12p. (J). (ps-k). 1998. 5.99 (*0-689-81558-1*) S&S Childrens.

Mr. Frumble's ABC. Richard Scarry. (Busy World of Richard Scarry Ser.). (Illus.). 14p. (J). (ps-k). 1998. 4.99 (*0-689-81653-7*) S&S Childrens.

Mr. Frumble's Bedtime Stories. Richard Scarry. (Illus.). 64p. (J). (gr. k-3). 1997. 10.95 (*0-689-81538-7*) S&S Trade.

Mr. Frumble's New Cars. Richard Scarry. (Illus.). 32p. (J). (ps-1). 1995. 3.25 (*0-689-80369-9*) S&S Childrens.

Mr. Funfiddle's Christmas: Singer's Activity Book. Dennis Allen & Nan Allen. 1995. pap. 3.99 (*0-8341-9308-6*, MC-92) Nazarene.

Mr. Funny. Roger Hargreaves. (Mr. Men & Little Miss Ser.). (Illus.). 32p. (gr. k-3). 1997. pap. 2.99 (*0-8431-7808-6*, Price Stern) Peng Put Young Read.

Mr. Garbage see Bank Street Ready-to-Read Books: Levels 1, 2 & 3

Mr. Garbage. William H. Hooks. LC 95-19072. (Bank Street Ready-to-Read Ser.). (Illus.). (J). 1996. pap. 3.99 (*0-553-09747-4*) Bantam.

***Mister Gariety, Himself: A Tale of Some Incredulity.** Peg Elliott Mayo. (Illus.). 258p. 1999. pap. 25.00 (*1-880797-04-6*) RiverVoice Pr.

Mr. Gay's London. Alan P. Herbert. LC 75-25258. (Illus.). 136p. 1976. reprint ed. lib. bdg. 55.00 (*0-8371-4805-7*, HEGL, Greenwood Pr) Greenwood.

Mr. George Jean Nathan Presents. George J. Nathan. LC 75-120099. 310p. 1975. 25.00 (*0-8386-7967-6*) Fairleigh Dickinson.

Mister George Jean Nathan Presents. George J. Nathan. LC 70-145205. 1971. reprint ed. 18.00 (*0-403-03648-8*) Scholarly.

Mr. Gilhooley. Liam O'Flaherty. 288p. (Orig.). 1997. pap. 11.95 (*0-86327-289-4*, Pub. by Wolfhound Press); pap. 11.95 (*0-86327-641-5*, Pub. by Wolfhound Press) Irish Amer Bk.

Mr. Glencannon Ignores the War. Guy Gilpatric & B. J. Clemons. Ed. by Walter W. Jaffe. 1976. 18.95 (*0-8488-0801-0*) Amereon Ltd.

Mr. Glencannon Ignores the War. Guy Gilpatric. Ed. by Walter W. Jaffee. LC 95-82068. (Glencannon Stories Ser.). (Illus.). xviii, 206p. 1996. reprint ed. 50.00 (*0-9637586-7-5*) Glencannon Pr.

Mister Glover's Groton: The Chronicle of Groton, VT - 1789-1978. Waldo Glover. LC 78-9592. (Illus.). 1978. 13.95 (*0-914016-53-9*) Phoenix Pub.

Mr. Goat's Bad Good Idea: Three Stories. Marileta Robinson. LC 77-26601. (J). (gr. 1-4). 1979. 11.50 (*0-690-03862-3*) HarpC Child Bks.

***Mister God, This Is Anna.** Fynn. 2000. pap. 7.50 (*0-345-44155-9*) Ballantine Pub Grp.

Mister God, This is Anna. Anna Fynn. 188p. 1985. mass mkt. 5.99 (*0-345-32722-5*) Ballantine Pub Grp.

Mister God, This Is Anna. large type ed. Fynn. LC 91-29229. 285p. 1991. reprint ed. lib. bdg. 16.95 (*1-56054-250-0*) Thorndike Pr.

An Asterisk (*) at the beginning of an entry indicates that the title is appearing for the first time.

Mr. Gonopolis & His Twelve Holsteins: A Christmas Story. Uncle Hyggly, pseud. LC 85-51650. (Mr. Gonopolis Ser.: No 1.). (Illus.). 44p. 1986. pap. 8.95 (*0-935583-01-7*) Wounded Coot.

Mr. Goolis: The Chicken That Woke Up. large type ed. Laura B. Hawbecker. (Illus.). 15p. (J). (ps-1). 1996. pap. 7.95 (*0-9644829-9-1*) Ding Dong Pr.

Mr. Goolis: The Chicken That Woke Up. large type unabridged ed. Laura B. Hawbecker. (Illus.). 15p. (J). (ps-1). 1996. 12.95 (*0-9644829-8-3*) Ding Dong Pr.

Mister Got to Go: The Cat That Wouldn't Leave. Lois Simmie. (Illus.). 32p. (J). (ps-3). 1998. pap. 7.95 (*0-88995-157-8*, Pub. by Red Deer) Genl Dist Srvs.

Mr. Green Peas. Judith Caseley. LC 93-24183. (Illus.). 32p. (J). (ps-3). 1995. 14.93 (*0-688-12860-2*, Grenwillow Bks) HarpC Child Bks.

***Mr. Green Peas.** Judith Caseley. 1998. mass mkt. 4.95 (*0-688-16092-1*, Wm Morrow) Morrow Avon.

Mr. Gronkle's Christmas Book. Richard Scarry. (J). 2000. mass mkt. 10.95 (*0-689-81656-1*) S&S Childrens.

Mr. Grumpy's Outing: Big Book. John Burningham. LC 77-159507. (Illus.). 32p. (J). (ps-3). 1995. pap. 19.95 (*0-8050-3854-X*) H Holt & Co.

Mr. Gumpy's Motor Car. John Burningham. LC 75-4582. (Illus.). 48p. (J). (ps-3). 1976. lib. bdg. 17.89 (*0-690-00799-X*) HarpC Child Bks.

Mr. Gumpy's Motor Car. John Burningham. (Illus.). (J). (ps-3). 1993. 18.82 (*0-690-00798-1*, 175231) HarpC Child Bks.

Mr. Henry. Laura Allen. (J). 1924. write for info. (*0-688-16653-9*); lib. bdg. write for info. (*0-688-16654-7*) Lothrop.

Mister Henry. large type ed. James V. Miller. (Linford Western Library). 277p. (Orig.). 1989. pap. 16.99 (*0-7089-6679-9*, Linford) Ulverscroft.

Mr. Henshaw. Cullinan. (J). 1994. text 20.20 (*0-15-302223-X*, Harcourt Child Bks) Harcourt.

Mr. Hobbes' Journey to Magic Mountain. John Wolski. (Illus.). 32p. (J). (gr. k-4). 1996. 3.95 (*0-9648333-0-1*) Magic Mtn Enter.

Mr. Hobbs' Vacation. adapted ed. Edward Streeter. 1963. pap. 5.25 (*0-8222-0782-6*) Dramatists Play.

Mr. Hodge & Mr. Hazard. Elinor H. Wylie. 256p. 1982. reprint ed. 7.95 (*0-89733-113-3*) Academy Chi Pubs.

Mr. Holland's Opus. 64p. 1996. per. 14.95 (*0-7935-6436-0*) H Leonard.

Mr. Horrox & the Gratch. James Reeves. LC 91-13326. (Illus.). 32p. (J). (gr. 1-6). 1991. 13.95 (*0-922984-08-5*) Wellington IL.

Mister, I Am the Band! Buddy Rich - His Life & Travels. Doug Meriwether. LC 97-42489. 464p. 1998. per. 49.95 (*0-7935-8243-1*, HL00330320) H Leonard.

Mr. Impossible. Roger Hargreaves. (Mr. Men & Little Miss Ser.). (Illus.). 32p. (J). (gr. k-3). 1998. pap. 2.50 (*0-8431-7420-X*) Putnam Pub Group.

Mister Incoul's Misadventures. Edgar E. Saltus. LC 68-54292. reprint ed. 37.50 (*0-404-05504-4*) AMS Pr.

Mr. Incoul's Misadventures. Edgar E. Saltus. (BCL1-PS American Literature Ser.). 221p. 1992. reprint ed. lib. bdg. 79.00 (*0-7812-6848-6*) Rprt Serv.

Mr. Incoul's Misadventures. Edgar E. Saltus. LC 70-131823. 1970. reprint ed. 15.00 (*0-403-00710-0*) Scholarly.

Mister Isaacs. Francis M. Crawford. LC 71-92607. (BCL Ser. I). 1969. reprint ed. 37.50 (*0-404-01835-1*) AMS Pr.

Mr. Isaacs. Francis M. Crawford. (Works of Francis Marion Crawford). 1990. reprint ed. lib. bdg. 79.00 (*0-685-44767-7*) Rprt Serv.

Mister Isaacs: A Tale of Modern India. Francis M. Crawford. 1882. 9.00 (*0-403-00015-7*) Scholarly.

Mr. Ives' Christmas. Oscar Hijuelos. LC 95-38434. 256p. 1997. pap. 13.00 (*0-06-092754-2*) HarpC.

Mr. Jack Hamlin's Mediation. Bret Harte. LC 72-10783. (Short Story Index Reprint Ser.). 1977. reprint ed. 24.95 (*0-8369-4218-3*) Ayer.

***Mr. Jack Hamlins Mediation.** Bret Harte. (Works of Bret Harte: Vol. 12). 508p. 1999. reprint ed. lib. bdg. 90.00 (*0-7812-7844-9*) Rprt Serv.

Mister Javelin: Guy Hadsall at American Motors. Guy Hadsall. Ed. by Patrick R. Foster & Samuel Fiorani. LC 98-90869. (Illus.). 1999. pap. 24.95 (*0-9668943-0-8*) SAH Pr.

Mr. Jefferson. Albert J. Nock. LC 82-83562. 228p. 1983. pap. 14.95 (*0-87319-024-6*) Hallberg Pub Corp.

Mr. Jefferson's University: A History. Virginius Dabney. LC 81-3392. (Illus.). 642p. 1981. pap. text 16.95 (*0-8139-1213-X*) U Pr of Va.

Mr. Jelly Bean, No. 1. 2nd ed. Ed Garehime. Tr. by American Red Cross Staff. LC 77-82261. 64p. (J). (ps-4). 1979. 9.95 (*0-918822-01-7*) Deem Corp.

Mr. Jelly's Business: Murder down Under. Arthur W. Upfield. (Napoleon Bonaparte Mysteries Ser.). reprint ed. lib. bdg. 24.95 (*0-89190-558-8*, Rivercity Pr) Amereon Ltd.

Mr. Jeremy Fisher. (Classic Tales Ser.). (Illus.). 24p. (J). 1993. 4.98 (*1-56173-596-5*) Pubns Intl Ltd.

Mr. Jeremy Fisher. Illus. by Pat Schoonover & Anita Nelson. (Classic Tales Ser.). 24p. (J). (gr. 2-4). 1992. lib. bdg. 11.95 (*1-56674-019-3*, HTS Bks) Forest Hse.

Mr. Jings. Mark Dunster. 80p. (Orig.). 1975. pap. 4.00 (*0-89642-027-2*) Linden Pubs.

Mr. John's Technique for Successful Holistic Black Hair Growth. John L. Jackson. 53p. 1992. pap. text 9.95 (*0-9634204-0-2*) J L Jackson.

Mister Johnson. adapted ed. Joyce Cary. 1969. pap. 5.25 (*0-8222-0764-8*) Dramatists Play.

Mister Johnson. Joyce Cary. LC 88-35710. 1994. reprint ed. lib. bdg. 21.95 (*1-56849-517-X*) Buccaneer Bks.

Mister Johnson: Novel. Joyce Cary. LC 88-35710. (New Directions Classics Ser.). 228p. 1989. pap. 9.95 (*0-8112-1030-8*, NDP657, Pub. by New Directions) Norton.

Mr. Jones, Meet the Master: Sermons & Prayers by Peter Marshall. Ed. by Catherine Marshall. 192p. (gr. 11). 1987. pap. 8.99 (*0-8007-5095-0*) Revell.

Mister Junior. Lael T. Wertenbaker. LC 92-76147. (Illus.). 186p. 1993. pap. write for info. (*0-912650-08-7*) Brookdale Pr.

Mr. Justice Black, Absolutist on the Court. James J. Magee. LC 79-11555. (Virginia Legal Studies). 232p. reprint ed. pap. 72.00 (*0-608-18803-4*, 203018800067) Bks Demand.

Mr. Justice Black & His Critics. Tinsley E. Yarbrough. LC 88-16184. 340p. 1988. text 54.95 (*0-8223-0866-5*) Duke.

Mr. Justice Brandeis. Ed. by Felix Frankfurter. LC 73-37766. (American Constitutional & Legal History Ser). (Illus.). 232p. 1972. reprint ed. lib. bdg. 27.50 (*0-306-70430-7*) Da Capo.

Mr. Justice Brennan & Freedom of Expression. W. Wat Hopkins. LC 91-8753. (Praeger Series in Political Communication). 208p. 1991. 47.95 (*0-275-93363-6*, C3363, Praeger Pubs) Greenwood.

Mr. Justice Cardozo: A Liberal Mind in Action. Joseph P. Pollard. LC 95-80916. viii, 327p. 1995. reprint ed. 75.00 (*0-89941-999-2*, 309020) W S Hein.

Mister Justice Cardozo: A Liberal Mind in Action. Joseph P. Pollard. LC 75-98790. 327p. 1970. reprint ed. lib. bdg. 65.00 (*0-8371-2815-3*, POJD, Greenwood Pr) Greenwood.

Mr. Justice Frankfurter & the Constitution. Philip B. Kurland. LC 77-133259. 1994. lib. bdg. 20.00 (*0-226-46405-9*) U Ch Pr.

***Mr. Justice Holmes.** Francis Biddle. 216p. 1999. reprint ed. 68.00 (*1-56169-484-3*) Gaunt.

Mr. Justice Holmes. Francis Biddle. LC 86-15042. (Illus.). 215p. 1986. reprint ed. lib. bdg. 75.00 (*0-313-25215-7*, BIJH, Greenwood Pr) Greenwood.

Mr. Justice Murphy: A Political Biography. Howard J. Woodford. LC 68-11444. 600p. 1968. reprint ed. pap. 186.00 (*0-7837-9350-2*, 206009200004) Bks Demand.

Mr. Justice Rehnquist, Judicial Activist: The Early Years. Donald E. Boles. LC 87-3295. 161p. 1987. reprint ed. pap. 50.00 (*0-608-00049-3*, 206081500006) Bks Demand.

Mr. Kaiser Goes to Washington: The Rise of a Government Entrepreneur. Stephen B. Adams. LC 96-53391. (Luther Hartwell Hodges Series on Business, Society & the State). 251p. (gr. 13). 1997. 45.00 (*0-8078-2358-9*) U of NC Pr.

Mr. Kalogo's Factory. Junior African Writers Staff & Carolyn B. Mitchell. (Junior African Writers Ser.). (Illus.). 80p. (J). (gr. 3 up). 1995. pap. 4.95 (*0-7910-3021-0*) Chelsea Hse.

Mister King. large type ed. Raija Siekkinen. Tr. by Tim Steffa from FIN. (Illus.). 1993. 9.50 (*0-614-09845-9*, L-34084-00) Am Printing Hse.

Mr. Kipling's Army: All the Queen's Men. Byron Farwell. 1987. pap. 11.95 (*0-393-30444-2*) Norton.

Mr. Klein Goes to Wall Street. Andrew Klein. 1998. write for info. (*0-201-32807-0*) Addison-Wesley.

Mr. Knife, Miss Fork, No. 2. Douglas Messerli. Vol. 2. (Illus.). 196p. 1999. pap. 10.95 (*1-55713-401-4*, Pub. by Sun & Moon CA) Consort Bk Sales.

Mr. Knife, Miss Fork No. 1: A Biannual of International Poetry. Ed. by Douglas Messerli. 130p. 1998. pap. 10.95 (*1-55713-345-X*) Sun & Moon CA.

Mr. Knocky. Jack Ziegler. LC 91-34145. (Illus.). 32p. (J). (gr. k-3). 1993. lib. bdg. 14.95 (*0-02-793725-9*, Mac Bks Young Read) S&S Childrens.

Mr. Koala's Steam Train. A. J. Wood. LC 97-12878. (Magic Shapes Ser.). (Illus.). 24p. (J). (ps-k). 1997. 9.95 (*0-7613-0294-8*) Millbrook Pr.

Mr. Law's Unlawfulness of the Stage Entertainment Examin'd. S. Philomusus. (English Stage Ser.: Vol. 50). 1977. lib. bdg. 55.00 (*0-8240-0633-X*) Garland.

Mr. Lawson's Gamble. William Keegan. 250p. 1991. text 34.95 (*0-340-50978-3*, Pub. by Hodder & Stought Ltd) Trafalgar.

Mister Leprosy. large type ed. Phyllis Thompson. 384p. 1983. 27.99 (*0-7089-1064-5*) Ulverscroft.

Mr. Lincoln. Herbert Mitgang. 58p. 1982. pap. 5.60 (*0-87129-703-5*, M58) Dramatic Pub.

Mister Lincoln: A Drama in 2 Acts. Herbert Mitgang. LC 81-8895. 67p. 1982. 11.95 (*0-8093-1034-1*) S Ill U Pr.

***Mr. Lincoln's Bridge Builders: The Right Hand of American Genius.** Phillip M. Thienel. 288p. 2000. 40.00 (*1-57249-198-1*, WM Books) White Mane Pub.

Mr. Lincoln's Camera Man: Mathew B. Brady. Roy Meredith. LC 73-92262. (Illus.). 368p. 1946. reprint ed. pap. 18.95 (*0-486-23021-X*) North South Trader.

Mr. Lincoln's City: An Illustrated Guide to the Civil War Sites of Washington. Richard M. Lee. LC 81-3267. (Illus.). 176p. 1981. pap. 17.95 (*0-914440-48-9*, EPM) Howell Pr VA.

Mr. Lincoln's Whiskers. Karen Winnick. LC 95-83973. (Illus.). 32p. (J). (ps-3). 1996. 15.95 (*1-56397-485-1*) Boyds Mills Pr.

Mr. Lincoln's Whiskers. Karen Winnick. LC 95-83973. (Illus.). 32p. (J). (gr. k-3). 1999. pap. 7.95 (*1-56397-805-9*) Boyds Mills Pr.

Mr. Love & Justice. Colin MacInnes. 128p. 1995. pap. write for info. (*0-7490-0186-0*) Allison & Busby.

Mr. Loverman. Mary Lyons. 1997. per. 3.50 (*0-373-11868-6*, 1-11868-6) Harlequin Bks.

Mr. Loverman. large type ed. Mary Lyons. (Mills & Boon Large Print Ser.). 288p. 1997. 23.99 (*0-263-14852-1*) Ulverscroft.

***Mister Lowry.** Tony Ross. (Illus.). 40p. 1999. 11.95 (*1-902970-02-0*, Pub. by Lowry Pr) Antique Collect.

Mr. Lunch Borrows a Canoe. J. Otto Seibold. (J). 1997. 11.19 (*0-606-12995-2*, Pub. by Turtleback) Demco.

Mr. Lunch Borrows a Canoe. J. Otto Seibold & Vivian Walsh. (Illus.). 40p. (J). (ps up). 1997. pap. 5.99 (*0-14-055375-4*, PuffinBks) Peng Put Young Read.

Mr. Lunch Takes a Plane Ride. J. Otto Seibold. 1997. 10.19 (*0-606-11645-1*, Pub. by Turtleback) Demco.

Mr. Lunch Takes a Plane Ride. Vivian Walsh & J. Otto Seibold. (Illus.). 40p. (J). (ps-3). 1993. 16.99 (*0-670-84775-5*, Viking Child) Peng Put Young Read.

***Mr. Macgregor.** large type ed. Alan Titchmarsh. 416p. 1999. 31.99 (*0-7089-9104-1*) Ulverscroft.

Mr. Majeika. Humphrey Carpenter. 96p. (J). (gr. 3-6). 1985. pap. 7.95 (*0-14-031677-9*, Pub. by Pnguin Bks Ltd) Trafalgar.

Mr. Majeika & the Dinner Lady. Humphrey Carpenter. (J). 1993. pap. 7.95 (*0-14-032762-2*, Pub. by Pnguin Bks Ltd) Trafalgar.

***Mr. Majeika & the Ghost Train.** Humphrey Carpenter. (Illus.). (J). 1998. pap. 7.95 (*0-14-036641-5*, Pub. by Pnguin Bks Ltd) Trafalgar.

Mr. Majeika & the School Book. Humphrey Carpenter. (Illus.). (J). 1993. pap. 7.95 (*0-14-034834-4*, Pub. by Pnguin Bks Ltd) Trafalgar.

***Mr. Majeika & the School Caretaker.** Humphrey Carpenter. 96p. (J). 1998. pap. 7.95 (*0-14-037123-0*, Pub. by Pnguin Bks Ltd) Trafalgar.

Mr. Majeika & the School Inspector. Humphrey Carpenter. (Illus.). 96p. (J). (gr. 3-6). 1993. pap. 7.95 (*0-14-036288-6*, Pub. by Pnguin Bks Ltd) Trafalgar.

Mr. Majeika & the School Play. Humphrey Carpenter. (Illus.). 96p. (J). (gr. 3-6). 1993. pap. 7.95 (*0-14-034358-X*, Pub. by Pnguin Bks Ltd) Trafalgar.

***Mr. Majeika Vanishes.** Humphrey Carpenter. (Illus.). 96p. (J). 1998. pap. 7.95 (*0-14-037840-5*, Pub. by Pnguin Bks Ltd) Trafalgar.

Mr. Majeika's Postbag. Humphrey Carpenter. (Illus.). pap. 7.95 (*0-14-036648-2*, Pub. by Pnguin Bks Ltd) Trafalgar.

Mr. Majestyk. Elmore Leonard. 224p. 2000. mass mkt. 6.99 (*0-440-23610-X*) Dell.

Mr. Majestyk. Elmore Leonard. 192p. 1986. mass mkt. 5.99 (*0-445-40228-8*, Mysterious Paperbk) Warner Bks.

Mr. Mani. Abraham B. Yehoshua. Tr. by Hillel Halkin. 384p. 1993. pap. 14.00 (*0-15-662769-8*, Harvest Bks) Harcourt.

Mr. Marble's Moose. D. J. May. (Illus.). 52p. (J). (ps-3). 1993. 9.99 (*0-8499-0969-4*) Tommy Nelson.

Mr. McCamey-- Claude W. Brown: Life of a West Texas Oil Man. Peggy N. Nash & R. Nash. LC 94-37570. 120p. 1995. 15.96 (*0-89015-976-9*, Eakin Pr) Sunbelt Media.

Mr. McGhee You've Done It Again. rev. ed. Bruce Campbell Adamson. Ed. by Donald G. Knight et al. (Oswald's Closest Friend Ser.: Vol. 2). (Illus.). 83p. 1996. 15.00 (*1-892501-05-8*) B C Adamson.

Mr. McGill Goes to Town. Jim Aylesworth. LC 89-31111. (Illus.). 32p. (J). (gr. k-2). 1995. pap. 4.95 (*0-8050-2096-9*, Owlet BYR) H Holt & Co.

Mr. McGillicuddy's Clocks. Elizabeth Best. LC 93-26928. (Voyages Ser.). (Illus.). (J). 1994. 4.25 (*0-383-03765-4*) SRA McGraw.

***Mr. McGinnis's New Shoes.** Phyllis Adams-Crymes. Ed. by Hardbound, Inc., Staff. (Children's Diary Ser.: Vol. 1). (Illus.). 27p. 2000. 17.00 (*1-930659-01-6*) P Adams-Crymes.

Mr. McGregor's Garden Sticker Activity Book. Cathy Beylon. (J). pap. 1.00 (*0-486-29793-4*) Dover.

Mr. McMouse. Leo Lionni. LC 92-8963. (Illus.). 40p. (J). (ps-1). 1992. 15.00 (*0-679-83890-2*, Pub. by Knopf Bks Yng Read) Random.

Mr. Mead & His Garden. John V. Lord. LC 74-20766. (Illus.). (J). (gr. k-3). 1975. lib. bdg. 6.95 (*0-395-20278-7*) HM.

Mr. Meeson's Will. H. Rider Haggard. LC 75-32747. (Literature of Mystery & Detection Ser.). (Illus.). 1976. reprint ed. 24.95 (*0-405-07876-5*) Ayer.

Mr. Mel Order, Set, Nos. 101-120. Don P. Smith. (Big-Little Reports Ser.: Nos. 101-120). (Illus.). 1976. 10.00 (*0-937514-06-3*, 788783, New Era Pub) World Merch Import.

Mister Mergenthwirker's Lobblies, & Other Fantastic Tales. Nelson S. Bond. LC 74-121523. (Short Story Index Reprint Ser.). 1977. 20.95 (*0-8369-3479-2*) Ayer.

Mr. Merritt's Ditch. Roberta Styran & Robert Taylor. Ed. by Noel Hudson. (Illus.). 152p. 1992. pap. 19.95 (*1-55046-005-6*, Pub. by Boston Mills) Genl Dist Srvs.

Mr. Messy. Roger Hargreaves. (Mr. Men & Little Miss Ser.). (Illus.). 32p. (J). (gr. k-3). 1998. pap. 2.99 (*0-8431-7421-8*) Putnam Pub Group.

Mr. Michel's War: From Manila to Mukden: An American Naval Officer's War with the Japanese, 1941-1945. John J. Michel. LC 97-28805. (Illus.). 352p. 1998. 26.95 (*0-89141-643-9*) Presidio Pr.

Mr. Midshipman Easy. Frederick Marryat. Date not set. lib. bdg. 24.95 (*0-8488-1678-1*) Amereon Ltd.

Mr. Midshipman Easy. Frederick Marryat. LC 98-6699. 368p. 1998. pap. 30.00 (*0-8050-5988-1*) H Holt & Co.

***Mr. Midshipman Easy.** Frederick Marryat. 252p. 2000. pap. 9.95 (*0-594-01690-8*) Eighth Hundrd.

Mr. Midshipman Easy. Frederick Marryat. LC 97-15354. (Classics of Nautical Fiction Ser.). 352p. 1997. reprint ed. pap. 14.95 (*0-935526-40-4*) McBooks Pr.

Mr. Midshipman Easy. Frederick Marryat. LC 89-13600. (Classics of Naval Literature Ser.). 448p. 1990. reprint ed. 32.95 (*0-87021-590-6*) Naval Inst Pr.

Mr. Midshipman Hornblower. C. S. Forester. 1991. lib. bdg. 21.95 (*1-56849-053-4*) Buccaneer Bks.

Mr. Midshipman Hornblower. C. S. Forester. (YA). (gr. 7 up). 1950. 17.95 (*0-316-28909-4*) Little.

Mr. Midshipman Hornblower. abr. ed. C. S. Forester. pap. text 16.95 incl. audio (*1-85998-975-6*) Trafalgar.

Mr. Midshipman Hornblower. large type ed. C. S. Forester. 1994. lib. bdg. 18.95 (*0-7862-0284-X*) Thorndike Pr.

Mr. Midshipman Hornblower. C. S. Forester. LC 98-164278. 310p. 1984. reprint ed. pap. 13.00 (*0-316-28912-4*) Little.

***Mr. Mike: The Life & Work of Michael O'Donoghue.** Dennis Perrin. (Illus.). 448p. 1999. pap. 13.50 (*0-380-72832-X*, Avon Bks) Morrow Avon.

Mr. Mint's Insider's Guide to Investing in Baseball Cards & Collectibles. Alan Rosen & Doug Garr. 1991. mass mkt. 8.99 (*0-446-39252-9*, Pub. by Warner Bks) Little.

***Mr. Modem's Internet Guide for Seniors.** Richard Sherman. LC 99-63317. (Illus.). 448p. 1999. pap. 19.99 (*0-7821-2580-8*) Sybex.

Mr. Mojo Risin' Jim Morrison: The Last Holy Fool. David Dalton. 1991. pap. 13.95 (*0-312-05899-3*) St Martin.

Mr. Monster see Bank Street Ready-to-Read Books: Levels 1, 2 & 3

Mr. Monster Vol. 1: His Books of Forbidden Knowledge. limited ed. Michael T. Gilbert. (Illus.). 196p. 1996. 50.00 (*1-56924-827-3*) Marlowe & Co.

Mr. Moon & Miss Sun/The Herdsman & the Weaver. Ed. by Mark Mueller. (Korean Folk Tales for Children Ser.: Vol. 2). (Illus.). 45p. (J). (gr. 2-5). 1990. lib. bdg. 10.95 (*0-930878-72-8*) Hollym Intl.

Mr. Moonlight. 19.95 (*0-89524-999-5*) Cherry Lane.

Mr. Moto Is So Sorry. John P. Marquand. 1976. 17.95 (*0-89387-016-1*) Amereon Ltd.

***Mr. Muddle's Little Green Book: A Guide for Hunting Lost Golf Balls.** Harrison H. Farley. (Illus.). 40p. 1999. 12.00 (*0-9670461-0-6*) Haasf Pubns.

Mr. Mumble. Peter Catalanotto. LC 89-48940. (Illus.). 32p. (J). (ps-2). 1990. 16.95 (*0-531-05880-8*) Orchard Bks Watts.

Mr. Mumble. Peter Catalanotto. LC 89-48940. (Illus.). 32p. (J). (ps-2). 1994. pap. 5.95 (*0-531-07052-2*) Orchard Bks Watts.

Mister Munchausen. John K. Bangs. LC 78-81261. (Short Story Index Reprint Ser.). 1977. 19.95 (*0-8369-3013-4*) Ayer.

Mr. Munday & the Space Creatures. Bonnie Pryor. (J). (gr. k-3). 1991. pap. 4.95 (*0-671-73620-5*) S&S Bks Yung.

Mr. Murder. Dean Koontz. LC 93-33653. 496p. 1994. mass mkt. 7.99 (*0-425-14442-9*) Berkley Pub.

Mr. Murder. large type ed. Dean Koontz. LC 93-33653. 715p. 1994. lib. bdg. 25.95 (*0-7862-0106-1*) Thorndike Pr.

Mr. Mysterious & Company. Sid Fleischman. LC 96-41225. (Illus.). 160p. (J). (gr. 3-7). 1997. mass mkt. 4.95 (*0-688-14922-7*, Grenwillow Bks) HarpC Child Bks.

Mr. Mysterious & Company. Sid Fleischman. LC 96-41225. (Illus.). 160p. (J). (gr. 5-9). 1997. 15.00 (*0-688-14921-9*, Grenwillow Bks) HarpC Child Bks.

Mr. Mysterious & Company. Sid Fleischman. 1997. 10.05 (*0-606-12433-0*, Pub. by Turtleback) Demco.

Mr. Nick's Knitting. Margaret Wild. LC 88-35778. (Illus.). 32p. (J). (ps-3). 1989. 12.95 (*0-15-200518-8*, Gulliver Bks) Harcourt.

Mr. Nick's Knitting. Margaret Wild. LC 88-35778. (ACE., Illus.). 32p. (J). (ps-3). 1994. pap. 4.95 (*0-15-200116-6*, Gulliver Bks) Harcourt.

Mr. Nobody's Eyes. Michael Morpurgo. 1999. pap. 3.95 (*0-14-034265-6*, Viking) Viking Penguin.

Mr. Noisy, Vol. 3653. Rozanne L. Williams. (Emergent Reader Bks.). 16p. 1994. pap. 1.75 (*0-916119-67-X*) Creat Teach Pr.

Mr. Noisy, Vol. 3696. Rozanne L. Williams. (Emergent Reader Big Bks). (Illus.). 16p. (J). (gr. k-2). 1995. pap. 12.98 (*1-57471-058-3*) Creat Teach Pr.

Mr. Noisy Builds a House, Vol. 3909. Luella Connelly. Ed. by Rozanne L. Williams. (Social Studies Learn to Read Ser.). (Illus.). 8p. (J). (ps-2). 1996. pap. 1.75 (*1-57471-128-8*, 3909) Creat Teach Pr.

Mr. Noisy Builds a House, Vol. 3966. Luella Connelly. Ed. by Rozanne L. Williams. (Social Studies Big Bks.). (Illus.). 8p. (J). (ps-2). 1997. pap. 8.98 (*1-57471-174-1*, 3966) Creat Teach Pr.

Mr. Noisy's Book of Patterns, Vol. 3705. Rozanne L. Williams. (Emergent Reader Bks). (Illus.). 8p. (J). (gr. k-2). 1995. pap. 1.75 (*0-916119-96-3*) Creat Teach Pr.

Mr. Noisy's Book of Patterns, Vol. 3762. Rozanne L. Williams. (Emergent Reader Big Bks.). (Illus.). 8p. (J). (gr. k-2). 1996. pap. 8.98 (*1-57471-100-8*) Creat Teach Pr.

Mr. Noisy's Helpers, Vol. 3931. Rozanne L. Williams. (Social Studies Learn to Read Ser.). (Illus.). 16p. (J). (ps-2). 1996. pap. 2.75 (*1-57471-136-9*, 3931) Creat Teach Pr.

Mr. Noisy's Helpers, Vol. 3974. Rozanne L. Williams. (Social Studies Big Bks.). (Illus.). 16p. (J). (ps-2). 1997. pap. 12.98 (*1-57471-182-2*, 3974) Creat Teach Pr.

Mr. Nonsense. rev. ed. Roger Hargreaves. (Mr. Men & Little Miss Ser.). (Illus.). 32p. (J). (gr. k-3). 1998. pap. 2.50 (*0-8431-7839-6*, Price Stern) Peng Put Young Read.

Mr. Noon: Cambridge Lawrence Edition. D. H. Lawrence. Ed. by Lindeth Vasey. LC 97-150723. 1997. pap. 12.95 (*0-14-018973-4*) Viking Penguin.

Mr. North Carolina: Life & Times of a Great Legislator. James R. Adams. (Illus.). 300p. 21.95 (*0-9618060-4-4*) Sheer Joy Pr.

Mr. Numb Gums. Diana Stoneberg. (Illus.). 12p. (J). (gr. k-3). 1995. write for info. (*0-9642796-3-0*) Snapping Turtle.

Mr. Obvious. James Lileks. 1995. pap. 5.50 (*0-671-73705-8*) S&S Trade.

Mr. Once-upon-a-Time. Remy Simard. Tr. by David Homel. (Illus.). 32p. (J). (ps-3). 1998. pap. 6.95 (*1-55037-538-5*, Pub. by Annick Pr); lib. bdg. 16.95 (*1-55037-539-3*, Pub. by Annick Pr) Firefly Bks Ltd.

Mr. Opp. Alice H. Rice. 336p. 25.95 (*0-8488-1132-1*) Amereon Ltd.

M

M

Mr. Opposite Pumpkin: Pasitos English Language Development Books, Vol. 5. Darlyne F. Schott. (Pasitos Hacia la Lectura Ser.). 15p. (J). (gr. k-1). 1990. pap. text 11.50 (*1-56537-064-3*) D F Schott Educ.

Mr. Ouine. Georges Bernanos. (Illus.). 288p. 1999. pap. 17.95 (*0-525-24492-1*, Dutt) Dutton Plume.

Mr. Pak Buys a Story. Carol J. Farley. LC 96-34411. (Illus.). 32p. (J). (gr. k-2). 1997. lib. bdg. 15.95 (*0-8075-5178-3*) A Whitman.

Mr. Pak Buys a Story. Carol Farley. (Prairie Paperback Bks.). (Illus.). 32p. (J). (gr. k-2). 1999. pap. 6.95 (*0-8075-5179-1*) A Whitman.

Mr. Palomar. Italo Calvino. Tr. by William Weaver. 144p. 1986. pap. 11.00 (*0-15-662780-9*, Harvest Bks) Harcourt.

Mr. Palomar. Italo Calvino. Tr. by William Weaver from ITA. LC 85-5490. (Helen & Kurt Wolff Bk.). 144p. 1985. reprint ed. 12.95 (*0-15-162835-1*) Harcourt.

Mr. Pam Pam & the Hullabazoo. Trish Cooke. LC 93-32382. (Illus.). 32p. (J). (ps up). 1994. 14.95 (*1-56402-411-3*) Candlewick Pr.

Mr. Panda's Painting. Anne Rockwell. LC 92-9220. (Illus.). 32p. (J). (ps-1). 1993. lib. bdg. 14.95 (*0-02-777451-1*, Mac Bks Young Read) S&S Childrens.

Mr. Parker Pyne, Detective. large type ed. Agatha Christie. 296p. 1989. lib. bdg. 19.95 (*0-8161-4563-6*, G K Hall Lrg Type) Mac Lib Ref.

Mr. Parker Pyne, Detective. large type ed. Agatha Christie. (Agatha Christie Ser.). 296p. 1990. pap. 13.95 (*0-8161-4564-4*, G K Hall Lrg Type) Mac Lib Ref.

Mister Pasta's Healthy Cookbook: More Than 150 Delicious, Low-Fat Pastas, Pasta Sauces... Rick Rodgers. LC 94-6664. 260p. 1994. 15.95 (*0-688-13077-1*, Wm Morrow) Morrow Avon.

Mr. Pasta's Healthy Pasta Cookbook: More Than 150 Delicious, Low-Fat Pastas, Pasta Sauces, & Pasta Meals! Rick Rodgers. 272p. 1996. reprint ed. pap. 12.00 (*0-688-14953-7*, Wm Morrow) Morrow Avon.

Mr. Patapoum's First Trip. Gilles Tibo & Francois Vaillancourt. (Illus.). 32p. 1993. pap. 5.95 (*1-55037-294-7*, Pub. by Annick) Firefly Bks Ltd.

Mr. Patapoum's First Trip. Gilles Tibo & Francois Vaillancourt. (Illus.). 32p. (J). (ps). 1993. lib. bdg. 15.95 (*1-55037-293-9*, Pub. by Annick) Firefly Bks Ltd.

Mr. Paul & Mr. Luecke Build Communities. Alice K. Flanagan. LC 98-44690. (Our Neighborhood Ser.). 32p. (J). (gr. 1-2). 1999. 19.50 (*0-516-21131-5*) Childrens.

***Mr. Paul & Mr. Lueke Build Communities.** Alice K. Flanagan. (Our Neighborhood Ser.). (J). 2000. pap. text 6.95 (*0-516-26540-7*) Childrens.

Mr. Peale's Bones. Tracey West. LC 93-41620. (Stories of the States Ser.). (Illus.). 64p. (J). (gr. 4-6). 1994. lib. bdg. 14.95 (*1-881889-50-5*) Silver Moon.

Mister Peale's Mammoth. Samuel Epstein. 16.95 (*0-8488-0079-6*) Amereon Ltd.

Mr. Peale's Museum: Charles Willson Peale & the First Popular Museum of Natural Science. Charles C. Sellers. (Barra Bks.). (Illus.). 1980. 14.95 (*0-393-05700-3*) Norton.

***Mister Perfect.** 1999. write for info. (*0-671-02757-3*) S&S Trade.

***Mr. Perfect.** Linda Howard. 384p. 2000. 24.95 (*0-671-03406-5*, PB Hardcover) PB.

***Mr. Persnickety & Cat Lady.** Paul B. Johnson. LC 99-56557. (Illus.). 32p. (J). (gr. k-2). 2000. 16.95 (*0-531-30283-0*) Orchard Bks Watts.

***Mr. Persnickety & Cat Lady.** Paul Brett Johnson. LC 99-56557. (Illus.). 32p. (J). (gr. k-2). 2000. 16.99 (*0-531-33283-7*) Orchard Bks Watts.

***Mr. Phillips.** John Lanchester. 304p. 2000. 23.95 (*0-399-14604-0*, Marion Wood) Putnam Pub Group.

Mr. Pickwick's Pilgrimages. Walter Dexter. LC 72-3637. (Studies in Dickens: No. 52). 1972. reprint ed. lib. bdg. 75.00 (*0-8383-1587-9*) M S G Haskell Hse.

Mr. Pickwick's Promise. Charles Dickens. Ed. & Frwd. by William-Alan Landes. LC 97-27757. 55p. 1997. pap. 6.00 (*0-88734-709-6*) Players Pr.

Mr. Pig & Family. Lillian Hoban. LC 80-7771. (I Can Read Bks.). (Illus.). 64p. (J). (ps-3). 1980. 9.95 (*0-06-022383-9*) HarpC Child Bks.

Mr. Pin: The Chocolate Files. Mary E. Monsell. Ed. by Patricia MacDonald. (Illus.). 64p. (J). 1992. reprint ed. per. 2.99 (*0-671-74085-7*, Minstrel Bks) PB.

***Mr Pink-Whistle Has Some Fun.** Enid Blyton. (Enid Blyton's Happy Days Ser.). (Illus.). 96p. (J). (gr. 1-4). 2000. pap. 6.95 (*0-7475-4345-3*, Pub. by Blmsbury Pub) Trafalgar.

***Mr. Pipes & the British Hymn Makers.** Douglas Bond. (Illus.). 236p. (YA). (gr. 7-12). 1999. pap. text 9.95 (*1-930092-12-1*) Christian Liberty.

Mr. Polk's Army: The American Military Experience in the Mexican War. Richard B. Winders. LC 96-37753. (Military History Ser.: Vol. 51). (Illus.). 288p. (C). 1997. text 34.95 (*0-89096-754-7*) Tex A&M Univ Pr.

Mr. Polk's War: American Opposition & Dissent, 1846-1848. John H. Schroeder. LC 73-2049, (Illus.). 201p. reprint ed. pap. 62.40 (*0-8357-6227-0*, 203427300089) Bks Demand.

Mister Pope & Other Poems. Allen Tate. LC 77-128896. (Select Bibliographies Reprint Ser.). 1977. 12.95 (*0-8369-5516-1*) Ayer.

Mr. Popper's Penguins. 44p. (J). 1998. 9.95 (*1-56137-177-7*, NU1777) Novel Units.

***Mr. Popper's Penguins.** 1999. 11.95 (*1-56137-716-3*) Novel Units.

Mr. Poppers Penguins. (J). 1991. pap. 3.50 (*0-440-80257-1*) BDD Bks Young Read.

Mr. Popper's Penguins. Richard Atwater. 139p. (J). (gr. 4-7). 1992. pap. 4.95 (*0-316-05843-2*) Little.

Mr. Popper's Penguins. Richard Atwater. (J). 1988. 10.05 (*0-606-02218-X*, Pub. by Turtleback) Demco.

Mr. Popper's Penguins. Richard Atwater & Florence Atwater. (Illus.). 139p. (J). (gr. 4-6). 1988. 16.95 (*0-316-05842-4*) Little.

Mr. Popper's Penguins. Scholastic, Inc. Staff. (Literature Guide Ser.). (J). 1997. pap. text 3.95 (*0-590-36645-9*) Scholastic Inc.

Mr. Popper's Penguins: A Study Guide. Gloria Levine. (Novel-Ties Ser.). (J). (gr. 3-5). 1989. pap. text, teacher ed., student ed. 15.95 (*0-88122-049-3*) Lrn Links.

Mr. Potato Goes to Washington. Ed. by Dutton Childrens Books Staff. (J). 1999. 6.99 (*0-525-45626-0*, Dutton Child) Peng Put Young Read.

Mr. Potato Head: Come Fry with Me. Sean Kelly. 1998. pap. 14.95 (*0-375-75119-X*) Villard Books.

***Mr. Potato Head: Giddyap, Cowspud!** Lucia Monfried. (Illus.). (J). 2000. pap. 4.99 (*0-525-46339-9*, Dutton Child) Peng Put Young Read.

Mr. Potato Head: My Life Story As Told to Sean Kelly. Sean Kelly. 80p. 1999. 14.95 (*0-375-50215-7*) Villard Books.

***Mr. Potato Head & Cinderspud.** Lucia Monfried. (Illus.). (J). 2000. pap. 3.49 (*0-525-46341-0*, Dutton Child) Peng Put Young Read.

Mister Potato Head & the Mixed-up Groceries, 1. Playskool Books Staff. (J). (ps-2). 1999. 2.99 (*0-525-46194-9*, Dutton Child) Peng Put Young Read.

***Mr. Potato Head Leads the Parade.** Lucia Monfried. (Illus.). (J). 2000. pap. 3.49 (*0-525-46342-9*, Dutton Child) Peng Put Young Read.

***Mr. Potato Head Learns to Dance.** Created by Hasboro, Inc. Staff. 1999. 6.99 (*0-525-46236-8*, Playskool) Peng Put Young Read.

Mister Potato Head Makes His Lunch, 1 vol. Playskool Books Staff. (YA). (ps up). 1999. pap. 5.99 (*0-525-46190-6*, Dutton Child) Peng Put Young Read.

Mister Potato Head: Space Spud! With Stickers, 1. Playskool Books Staff. (J). (ps-2). 1999. 4.99 (*0-525-46193-0*, Dutton Child) Peng Put Young Read.

Mister Potato Head's Busy Beach Day: Sticker Storybooks, 1 vol. Playskool Books Staff. (J). (ps-2). 1999. 4.99 (*0-525-46192-2*, Dutton Child) Peng Put Young Read.

Mister Potato Head's Missing Sock, 1. Playskool Books Staff. (J). (ps-2). 1999. 2.99 (*0-525-46195-7*, Dutton Child) Peng Put Young Read.

***Mr. Potato Head's Wonderful Wedding.** Lucia Monfried. (Illus.). (J). 2000. pap. 4.99 (*0-525-46340-2*, Dutton Child) Peng Put Young Read.

Mr. Potato's Neighborhood. Playskool, Staff. (J). 1999. 9.99 (*0-525-45810-7*) NAL.

Mr. Potter's Pet. Dick King-Smith. LC 95-4874. (Illus.). 128p. (J). (gr. 2-5). 1996. 13.95 (*0-7868-0174-3*, Pub. by Hyprn Child) Time Warner.

Mr. Potter's Pet. Dick King-Smith. LC 95-21784. (Illus.). 128p. (J). (gr. 2-5). 1997. reprint ed. pap. 3.95 (*0-7868-1206-0*, Pub. by Hyprn Ppbks) Little.

Mr. President. George A. Sullivan. LC 96-27396. 160p. (J). (gr. 5-7). 1997. mass mkt. 3.99 (*0-590-13671-2*) Scholastic Inc.

Mr. President: A Book of U. S. Presidents. Steve Sullivan. 160p. (J). (gr. 4-6). 1998. pap. 2.95 (*0-590-46540-6*) Scholastic Inc.

Mr. President: An Introduction to American History. Maurice P. Ashley. LC 79-38317. (Biography Index Reprint Ser.). 1977. reprint ed. 25.95 (*0-8369-8115-4*) Ayer.

Mr. President: A Spiritual Journey. rev. ed. Colin D. Mallard. LC 95-90227. 336p. (Orig.). 1996. pap. 16.95 (*0-9646040-5-1*) Wild Duck Pubng.

***Mr. Preston.** John Sauro. 100p. 1999. pap. 10.95 (*1-929416-21-0*) Magner Pubg.

Mr. Principal, Your Activity Period Sucks. Cecil Mosenson. (Illus.). (Orig.). 1991. pap. 11.95 (*0-9629935-0-6*) Woodruff PA.

Mr. Prohack: A Comedy in Three Acts. Arnold Bennett & Edward Knoblock. Date not set. write for info. (*0-518-19139-7*) NY Times Lib.

Mr. Prohack: A Comedy in Three Acts. Arnold Bennett. LC 74-17128. (Collected Works of Arnold Bennett: Vol. 58). 1977. reprint ed. 25.95 (*0-518-19138-9*) Ayer.

Mr. Punch. Neil Gaiman. Ed. by Karen Berger. (Illus.). 96p. 1995. mass mkt. 15.95 (*1-56389-246-4*, Pub. by DC Comics) Time Warner.

Mr. Punch the Cuckold. Ramon Del Valle-Inclan. Ed. by Warner & Keown. 1991. 59.95 (*0-85668-541-0*, Pub. by Aris & Phillips); pap. 22.00 (*0-85668-542-9*, Pub. by Aris & Phillips) David Brown.

Mr. Puntila & His Man Matti. Bertolt Brecht. Ed. by Ralph Manheim. Tr. & Intro. by John Willett. LC 94-13982. 176p. 1997. pap. 9.70 (*1-55970-280-X*, Pub. by Arcade Pub Inc) Time Warner.

Mr. Putter & Tabby Bake the Cake. Cynthia Rylant. LC 94-9557. (Illus.). 44p. (J). (gr. 1-5). 1994. 12.00 (*0-15-200205-7*) Harcourt.

Mr. Putter & Tabby Bake the Cake. Cynthia Rylant. LC 94-9557. (J). 1994. 10.15 (*0-606-09640-X*, Pub. by Turtleback) Demco.

Mr. Putter & Tabby Bake the Cake, Vol. 3. Cynthia Rylant. LC 94-9557. (Illus.). 44p. (J). (gr. 1-5). 1994. pap. 5.95 (*0-15-200214-6*) Harcourt.

Mr. Putter & Tabby Books. Cynthia Rylant. (J). 1994. 19.80 (*0-15-201279-6*) Harcourt.

Mr. Putter & Tabby Fly the Plane. Cynthia Rylant. LC 95-48786. (Illus.). 44p. (J). (gr. 1-5). 1997. pap. 5.00 (*0-15-201060-2*) Harcourt.

Mr. Putter & Tabby Fly the Plane. Cynthia Rylant. LC 95-48786. (Illus.). 44p. (J). 1997. 11.00 (*0-15-256253-2*) Harcourt.

Mr. Putter & Tabby Fly the Plane. Cynthia Rylant. 1997. 10.20 (*0-606-12773-9*, Pub. by Turtleback) Demco.

***Mr. Putter & Tabby Paint the Porch.** Cynthia Rylant. (Illus.). 44p. (J). (gr. 1-4). 2000. 13.00 (*0-15-201787-9*, Harcourt Child Bks) Harcourt.

Mr. Putter & Tabby Pick the Pears. Cynthia Rylant. LC 94-11259. (Mr. Putter & Tabby Ser.). (Illus.). 44p. (J). (gr. 1-5). 1995. pap. 6.00 (*0-15-200246-4*, Harcourt Child Bks) Harcourt.

Mr. Putter & Tabby Pick the Pears. Cynthia Rylant. LC 94-11259. (J). 1995. 11.20 (*0-606-09641-8*, Pub. by Turtleback) Demco.

Mr. Putter & Tabby Pick the Pears. abr. ed. Cynthia Rylant. LC 94-11259. (Mr. Putter & Tabby Ser.). (Illus.). 44p. (J). (gr. 1-5). 1995. 12.00 (*0-15-200245-6*, Harcourt Child Bks) Harcourt.

Mr. Putter & Tabby Row the Boat. Cynthia Rylant. LC 93-41832. (Illus.). 44p. (C). 1997. pap. 6.00 (*0-15-201059-9*, Harcourt Child Bks) Harcourt.

Mr. Putter & Tabby Row the Boat. Cynthia Rylant. LC 93-41832. (Illus.). 44p. (J). 1997. 11.00 (*0-15-256257-5*) Harcourt.

Mr. Putter & Tabby Take the Train. Cynthia Rylant. LC 97-23471. (Illus.). 44p. (J). (ps-2). 1998. 13.00 (*0-15-201786-0*) Harcourt.

***Mr. Putter & Tabby Take the Train.** Cynthia Rylant. (Early Chapter Bks.). (Illus.). 44p. (J). (gr. 1-4). 2000. pap. 6.00 (*0-15-202389-5*, Harcourt Child Bks) Harcourt.

Mr. Putter & Tabby Toot the Horn. Cynthia Rylant. LC 96-41768. (Illus.). 44p. (J). (gr. k-2). 1998. 13.00 (*0-15-200244-8*) Harcourt.

Mr. Putter & Tabby Toot the Horn. Cynthia Rylant. LC 96-41768. (Illus.). 44p. (J). 1999. pap. 5.95 (*0-15-200247-2*, Voyager Bks) Harcourt.

Mr. Putter & Tabby Walk the Dog. Cynthia Rylant. LC 93-21467. (Illus.). 44p. (J). (gr. 1-6). 1994. 13.00 (*0-15-256259-1*) Harcourt.

Mr. Putter & Tabby Walk the Dog. Cynthia Rylant. LC 93-21467. (Illus.). 44p. 1994. pap. 6.00 (*0-15-200891-8*) Harcourt Bindery Inc.

Mr. Putter & Tabby Walk the Dog. Cynthia Rylant. LC 93-21467. 1994. 11.20 (*0-606-06585-7*, Pub. by Turtleback) Demco.

Mr. Pye. Mervyn Peake. LC 83-19497. (Illus.). 288p. 1984. 15.95 (*0-87951-955-X*, Pub. by Overlook Pr) Penguin Putnam.

Mr. Rabbit & the Lovely Present. Charlotte Zolotow. LC 62-7590. (Charlotte Zolotow Bk.). (Illus.). 40p. (J). (ps-3). 1962. 15.95 (*0-06-026945-6*) HarpC Child Bks.

Mr. Rabbit & the Lovely Present. Charlotte Zolotow. LC 62-7590. (Trophy Picture Bk.). (Illus.). 40p. (J). (ps-3). 1977. pap. 5.95 (*0-06-443020-0*, HarpTrophy) HarpC Child Bks.

Mr. Rabbit & the Lovely Present. Charlotte Zolotow. (Illus.). (J). (gr. k-3). 1987. 24.95 incl. audio (*0-87499-047-5*) Live Oak Media.

Mr. Rabbit & the Lovely Present. Charlotte Zolotow. (J). 1962. 10.15 (*0-606-00349-5*, Pub. by Turtleback) Demco.

Mr. Rabbit & the Lovely Present. unabridged ed. Charlotte Zolotow. (Illus.). (J). (gr. k-3). 1987. pap. 15.95 incl. audio (*0-87499-046-7*) Live Oak Media.

Mr. Rabbit & the Lovely Present, 4 bks., Set. unabridged ed. Charlotte Zolotow. (Illus.). (J). (gr. k-3). 1987. pap., teacher ed. 33.95 incl. audio (*0-87499-048-3*) Live Oak Media.

Mr. Raccoon & His Friends. Eugene J. McCarthy. (Illus.). 100p. (J). 1992. reprint ed. 16.00 (*0-89733-377-2*); reprint ed. pap. 6.95 (*0-89733-374-8*) Academy Chi Pubs.

Mr. Radagast Makes an Unexpected Journey. Sharon Nastick. LC 80-8107. (Illus.). 96p. (J). (gr. 3-7). 1981. 10.95 (*0-690-04050-4*); lib. bdg. 11.89 (*0-690-04051-2*) HarpC Child Bks.

Mr. Rain: The Grate Rain. abr. large type ed. Kambiz Azordegan. (Tootee's Magical Stories Ser.: Vol. 4). (Illus.). 40p. (J). 1998. 9.95 (*1-890571-28-8*) Parrot Prod.

Mr. Raja's Neighborhood. Jeff Greenwald. LC 86-19647. (Illus.). 128p. (Orig.). 1987. pap. 9.95 (*0-936784-22-9*) J Daniel.

Mr. Red Tape. L. K. Jha. 1987. 17.50 (*0-8364-2064-0*, Pub. by Allied Pubs) S Asia.

Mr. Reez's Sneezes. Curtis Parkinson. (Illus.). 24p. (J). (ps-2). 1999. pap. 5.95 (*1-55037-556-3*, Pub. by Annick Pr); text 15.95 (*1-55037-557-1*, Pub. by Annick Pr) Firefly Bks Ltd.

Mr. Revere & I. Robert Lawson. (Illus.). 152p. (J). (gr. 3-6). 1988. pap. 5.95 (*0-316-51729-1*) Little.

Mr. Rickey. Robert Gregory. 1999. pap. 10.00 (*0-14-017228-9*, Viking); pap. 22.00 (*0-670-84625-2*) Viking Penguin.

Mr. Right. Carolyn Banks. LC 98-34202. 352p. 1999. 25.00 (*0-933256-91-4*) Second Chance.

***Mr. Right Is Out There: The Gay Man's Guide to Finding & Maintaining Love.** unabridged ed. Kenneth D. George. LC 00-29280. 178p. 2000. pap. 13.95 (*1-55583-506-6*, Pub. by Alyson Pubns) Consort Bk Sales.

Mister Roberts see Best American Plays: Third Series, 1945-51

Mister Roberts see Six Modern American Plays

Mr. Roberts. Thomas Heggen. 20.95 (*0-88411-696-4*) Amereon Ltd.

Mister Roberts. Joshua Logan & Thomas Heggen. 1951. pap. 5.25 (*0-8222-0765-6*) Dramatists Play.

Mister Roberts. Thomas Heggen. 230p. 1983. reprint ed. lib. bdg. 16.95 (*0-89966-445-8*) Buccaneer Bks.

Mister Roberts. Thomas Heggen. Ed. by Jack Sweetman. LC 92-9422. (Classics of Naval Literature Ser.). 200p. 1992. reprint ed. 32.95 (*1-55750-723-6*) Naval Inst Pr.

Mr. Rockefeller's Roads: The Untold Story of Acadia's Carriage Roads & Their Creator. Ann R. Roberts. LC 90-84029. (Illus.). 184p. 1990. pap. 14.95 (*0-89272-296-7*) Down East.

Mister Rodgers: How Families Grow. Head & Richard Rodgers. 1993. pap. 7.95 (*0-7935-2643-4*, 00815006) H Leonard.

Mister Rogers - You Are Special. (MusicTivity Ser.). (Illus.). 32p. (Orig.). (J). 1994. pap. 12.95 incl. cd-rom (*0-7935-2924-7*, 00815026) H Leonard.

Mister Rogers - You Are Special. Mister Rogers. (MusicTivity Ser.). (Illus.). 32p. (Orig.). (J). 1994. pap. 9.95 incl. audio (*0-7935-2925-5*, 00815025) H Leonard.

Mr. Rogers Bedtime. (J). 1993. audio 8.98 (*0-7935-2636-1*) H Leonard.

Mr. Rogers Meets the Leather Queen. Jessica Flemming & Bill Tyson. LC 93-85264. (Illus.). 160p. (Orig.). 1993. pap. 12.95 (*1-883445-03-5*) Plain Brown.

Mister Rogers' Neighborhood: Children, Television, & Fred Rogers. Ed. by Mark Collins & Margaret M. Kimmel. (Illus.). 249p. 1996. pap. 16.95 (*0-8229-5652-7*) U of Pittsburgh Pr.

Mister Rogers' Neighborhood: Children, Television, & Fred Rogers. Ed. by Mark Collins & Margaret M. Kimmel. LC 95-48461. (Illus.). 249p. (C). 1996. text 27.95 (*0-8229-3921-5*) U of Pittsburgh Pr.

Mister Rogers' Plan & Play Book. 400p. 1993. pap. 17.95 (*0-7935-2645-0*, 00815008) H Leonard.

Mister Rogers' Playbook. 1993. pap. 7.95 (*0-7935-2646-9*, 00815005) H Leonard.

Mister Roger's Songbook. (Songs for Kids Ser.). (Illus.). 80p. (Orig.). (J). 1994. pap. 10.95 (*0-7935-2928-X*, 00815027) H Leonard.

Mister Rogers Songbook, No. 260. 56p. 1994. pap. 8.95 (*0-7935-3185-3*, 00102322) H Leonard.

Mister Rogers Talks with Parents. Fred Rogers & Barry Head. 320p. 1993. pap. 7.95 (*0-7935-2642-6*, 00815004) H Leonard.

Mr. Rogers You're Growing. (J). 1993. audio 8.98 (*0-7935-2635-3*) H Leonard.

Mr. Ron's Favorite Animals. Sarah Albee. (Peek 'n' Seek Board Bks.). (Illus.). 14p. (J). (ps-k). 1997. 4.99 (*0-689-81301-5*) S&S Childrens.

***Mr. Roopratna's Chocolates: Winning Stories of the Rhys Davies Prize.** Ed. by Cary Archard. 160p. 1999. pap. 17.95 (*1-85411-267-8*, Pub. by Seren Bks) Dufour.

Mr. Rutledge of South Carolina. Richard Barry, Sr. LC 71-146851. (Select Bibliographies Reprint Ser.). 1980. reprint ed. 26.95 (*0-8369-5618-4*) Ayer.

***Mister St. John.** Loren D. Estleman. (Orig.). 1999. mass mkt. 5.99 (*0-515-12657-8*, Jove) Berkley Pub.

Mr. Salesman. Diane Keaton. (Illus.). 96p. 1993. 45.00 (*0-944092-26-8*) Twin Palms Pub.

Mr. Sammler's Planet. Saul Bellow. 352p. 1996. pap. 13.95 (*0-14-018936-X*, Penguin Classics) Viking Penguin.

Mr. Sampath: The Printer of Malgudi. R. K. Narayan. LC 80-27352. 220p. (C). 1981. pap. 10.95 (*0-226-56839-3*) U Ch Pr.

Mister Sandman: A Novel. Barbara Gowdy. LC 97-28209. (C). 1998. pap. 12.00 (*0-15-600577-8*) Harcourt.

Mister Sandman: A Novel. Barbara Gowdy. 288p. 24.95 (*1-895897-54-8*); pap. 13.95 (*1-895897-76-9*) Somerville Hse.

Mister Sandman: A Novel. Barbara Gowdy. LC 96-43870. 268p. 1997. 24.00 (*1-883642-33-7*) Steerforth Pr.

Mr. Santizo's Tasty Treats! Alice Flanagan & Romie Flanagan. LC 97-16399. (Our Neighborhood Ser.). 32p. 1998. 19.50 (*0-516-20771-7*) Childrens.

Mister Satan's Apprentice: A Blues Memoir. Adam Gussow. LC 98-17671. (Illus.). 416p. 1998. 25.00 (*0-679-45022-X*) Pantheon.

***Mister Satan's Apprentice: A Blue's Memoir.** Adam Gussow. 2000. pap. 15.00 (*0-679-77177-8*) Vin Bks.

Mr. Scott's Guide to the Enterprise. Shane Johnson. 1989. per. 14.00 (*0-671-70498-2*) PB.

Mr. Scrooge - Mus. Charles Dickens et al. 72p. 1963. pap. 5.95 (*0-87129-605-5*, M01) Dramatic Pub.

Mr. Secretary Thurloe: Cromwell's Secretary of State, 1652-1660. Philip Aubrey. LC 89-45379. 272p. 1990. 38.50 (*0-8386-3388-9*) Fairleigh Dickinson.

Mr. Secretary Walsingham & the Policy of Queen Elizabeth, 3 vols., Set. Conyers Read. LC 75-41223. reprint ed. 225.00 (*0-404-13490-4*) AMS Pr.

Mr. Semolina Semolinus. Anthony L. Manna & Christodoula Mitakidou. LC 96-1924. (Illus.). 40p. (J). (ps up). 1997. 15.00 (*0-689-81093-8*) S&S Childrens.

***Mr. Shadow.** Anthony DiGiacomo. 200p. 2000. pap. 6.00 (*1-58265-022-5*, 0113) Orphan Press.

***Mr. Silly.** Roger Hargreaves. (Illus.). 32p. (J). (gr. k-3). 2000. pap. 2.99 (*0-8431-7564-8*, Price Stern) Peng Put Young Read.

Mr. Silly's Friend: Quotations from Chainsaw Mike. Mike Harris. (Illus.). 100p. 1997. pap. 9.99 (*1-55022-343-7*, Pub. by ECW) LPC InBook.

Mr. Silver & Mrs. Gold. Dale B. Fink. LC 79-15924. (Illus.). 32p. (J). (ps-3). 1980. 16.95 (*0-87705-447-9*, Kluwer Acad Hman Sci) Kluwer Academic.

Mr. Skeffington. Elizabeth Von Arnim. lib. bdg. 21.95 (*0-8488-1877-6*) Amereon Ltd.

Mr. Skinny. Roger Hargreaves. pap. 2.99 (*0-8431-7618-0*, Price Stern) Peng Put Young Read.

***Mr. Slow.** Roger Hargreaves. (Mr. Men & Little Miss Ser.). (Illus.). 32p. (J). (ps-3). 2000. pap. 2.99 (*0-8431-7601-6*, Price Stern) Peng Put Young Read.

Mr. Small. Roger Hargreaves. (Mr. Men & Little Miss Ser.). (Illus.). 32p. (J). (gr. k-3). 1997. pap. 2.99 (*0-8431-7811-6*, Price Stern) Peng Put Young Read.

Mr. Smith. Louis Bromfield. Date not set. lib. bdg. 23.95 (*0-8488-1958-6*) Amereon Ltd.

An Asterisk (*) at the beginning of an entry indicates that the title is appearing for the first time.

Mr. Smith Goes to Tokyo: Japanese Cinema under the American Occupation, 1945-1952. Kyoko Hirano. LC 92-7033. (Studies in the History of Film & Television). (Illus.). 400p. 1994. pap. text 16.95 (*1-56098-402-3*) Smithsonian.

Mr. Snow. Roger Hargreaves. 32p. 1999. pap. 2.99 (*0-8431-7502-8*, Price Stern) Peng Put Young Read.

Mr. Social Security: The Life of Wilbur J. Cohen. Edward D. Berkowitz. LC 94-39964. (Illus.). 416p. 1995. 34.95 (*0-7006-0707-2*) U Pr of KS.

Mister Socialism: Norman Thomas, His Life & Times. Dwight Steward. LC 73-87815. 224p. 1974. 7.95 (*0-8184-0162-1*) Carol Pub Group.

***Mr. Spaceman.** Robert Olen Butler. LC 99-46822. 224p. 2000. 24.00 (*0-8021-1660-4*, Pub. by Grove-Atltic) Publishers Group.

Mr. Speaker: The Biography of Tom Murphy. Richard Hyatt. LC 99-52291. (Illus.). 326p. 1999. 27.95 (*0-86554-607-X*, H458) Mercer Univ Pr.

Mr. Splitfoot. large type ed. Helen McCloy. (Keating's Choice Ser.). 287p. 1992. 24.95 (*1-85089-493-0*, Pub. by ISIS Lrg Prnt) Transaction Pubs.

Mr. Spooner's in the Well: And Other Massachusetts Mysteries. Curt Norris. LC 97-24785. 160p. (Orig.). 1997. pap. 12.95 (*0-924771-90-9*, Covered Brdge Pr) Douglas Charles Ltd.

Mr. Standfast. John Buchan. 19.95 (*0-8488-0927-0*) Amereon Ltd.

Mr. Standfast. John Buchan. (Classics Library). 400p. 1998. pap. 3.95 (*1-85326-225-0*, 2250WW, Pub. by Wrdsworth Edits) NTC Contemp Pub Co.

Mr. Standfast. John Buchan. LC 77-144916. 374p. 1928. reprint ed. 69.00 (*0-403-00879-4*) Scholarly.

Mister Standfast. John Buchan. 1988. reprint ed. lib. bdg. 69.00 (*0-7812-0165-9*) Rprt Serv.

***Mr. Stanley of Estes Park.** James H. Pickering. LC 00-40051. 2000. pap. write for info. (*1-886727-05-8*) Stanley Mus.

Mr. Strang Picks up the Pieces: Reading Level 3-4. (Stormy Night Stories Ser.). 16p. 1993. 2.50 (*0-88336-079-9*) New Readers.

Mr. Strong. Roger Hargreaves. 32p. 1999. pap. 2.99 (*0-8431-7501-X*, Price Stern) Peng Put Young Read.

Mr. Stumpguss Is a Third Grader. Kathleen Duey. (Illus.). 80p. (Orig.). (J). 1992. pap. 3.50 (*0-380-76939-5*, Avon Bks) Morrow Avon.

Mr. Stupid Goes to Washington: A Political Satire. Jamie Malanowski. LC 92-15474. 224p. 1992. 16.95 (*1-55972-132-4*, Birch Ln Pr) Carol Pub Group.

Mr. Sugar Came to Town (La Visita del Sr. Azucar) Cruz Gomez & Harriet Rohmer. (ENG & SPA., Illus.). 32p. (YA). (ps-3). 1996. reprint ed. pap. 7.95 (*0-89239-141-3*) Childrens Book Pr.

Mr. Sugar Came to Town (La Visita del Sr. Azucar) Tr. by Rosalma Zubizarreta. LC 88-38781.Tr. of La Visita del Senor Azucar. (ENG & SPA., Illus.). 32p. (YA). (ps-3). 1989. 15.95 (*0-89239-045-X*) Childrens Book Pr.

Mr. Sweetums Wears Pink. Charlotte Hutchinson & Brenda Jones. (Illus.). 24p. (J). (ps-3). 1994. pap. 5.95 (*0-921556-18-7*, Pub. by Gynergy-Ragweed) U of Toronto Pr.

Mr. Taft's School: The First Century. Richard H. Lovelace. (Illus.). 208p. 1989. 20.00 (*0-9624435-0-6*) Taft Schl.

Mr. Tall & Mr. Small. Barbara Brenner. LC 93-8256. (Illus.). (J). 1995. write for info. (*0-8050-2757-2*) H Holt & Co.

Mr. Tall Cactus & His Shorter, Prickly Neighbors. Daniel Lonsberry. LC 96-78886. (Illus.). 32p. (J). (ps-4). 1997. pap. write for info. (*0-9658255-1-5*) Magic Carpet Rides.

Mr. Tanen's Ties. Maryann Cocca-Leffler. LC 98-33762. (Illus.). 32p. (J). (gr. k-3). 1999. lib. bdg. 14.95 (*0-8075-5301-8*) A Whitman.

Mr. Tasker's Gods. Theodore F. Powys. LC 72-145246. 320p. 1972. reprint ed. 39.00 (*0-403-01161-2*) Scholarly.

Mr. Thank You So Muchly. Mary M. Durland. (Illus.). 32p. (J). (gr. k-2). 1994. 8.95 (*0-9643013-0-X*) Hidden Brook Pr.

Mr. Theodore Mundstock. Ladislav Fuks. LC 91-2988. 216p. 1991. 10.95 (*0-941423-62-X*) FWEW.

***Mr. Tim's Tips for New Teachers.** Tim Bedley. (Illus.). 32p. 1999. spiral bd. 12.95 (*0-9667145-1-2*) Inspiring Teachers Pubg.

Mr. Tite's Belongings. Nick Warburton. 1999. pap. 4.99 (*0-14-054443-7*) NAL.

Mister Tommy Dove & Other Stories. Margaret W. Deland. LC 75-94716. (Short Story Index Reprint Ser.). 1977. 20.95 (*0-8369-3095-9*) Ayer.

Mr. Tompkins in Paperback. George Gamow. (Canto Book Ser.). (Illus.). 202p. (C). 1993. pap. 10.95 (*0-521-44771-2*) Cambridge U Pr.

Mr. Tree & the Little Girl. European Language Institute Staff. (Tell & Sing a Story Ser.). (Illus.). 27p. (J). (gr. k-2). 1992. pap. 19.95 (*88-85148-62-X*, Pub. by Europ Lang Inst) Midwest European Pubns.

***Mr. Trelawney's Proposal.** large type ed. Mary Brendan. 1999. 25.99 (*0-263-15911-6*, Pub. by Mills & Boon) Ulverscroft.

Mr. Tubbs' Civil War. Nat Brandt & Charles Tubbs. LC 96-21719. (Illus.). 240p. 1996. 34.95 (*0-8156-0391-6*, BRMT) Syracuse U Pr.

Mr. Tucket. Gary Paulsen. (J). 1995. pap. 5.99 (*0-440-91053-6*) BDD Bks Young Read.

Mr. Tucket. Gary Paulsen. Vol. 1. 192p. (YA). (gr. 5-9). 1995. pap. 4.50 (*0-440-41133-5*, YB BDD) BDD Bks Young Read.

Mr. Tucket. Gary Paulsen. (J). 1996. pap. 5.99 (*0-440-91097-8*) BDD Bks Young Read.

Mr. Tucket. Gary Paulsen. LC 93-31180. 176p. (J). 1994. 15.95 (*0-385-31169-9*) Delacorte.

***Mr. Tucket.** Gary Paulsen. (Illus.). (J). (gr. 4-7). 2000. mass mkt. 2.99 (*0-375-80680-6*, Pub. by Random Bks Yng Read) Random.

Mr. Tucket. Gary Paulsen. 1995. 9.85 (*0-606-07895-9*) Turtleback.

Mr. Turkey. large type ed. Judy Mullican. (Cuddle Bks.). (Illus.). 7p. (J). (ps-k). 1998. pap. text 10.95 (*1-57332-126-5*) HighReach Lrning.

Mr. Turtle's Award. John Schmidt. LC 96-692422. (Illus.). 24p. (Orig.). (J). (ps-3). 1996. pap. 7.00 (*0-9639132-2-0*) Path Pubng.

Mr. Tutt at His Best. Arthur Train. 24.95 (*0-89190-583-9*) Amereon Ltd.

Mr. Tutt Comes Home. Arthur Train. 352p. Date not set. 25.95 (*0-8488-2497-0*) Amereon Ltd.

***Mr Twiddle in Trouble Again.** Enid Blyton. (Enid Blyton's Happy Days Ser.). (Illus.). 96p. (J). (gr. 1-4). 2000. pap. 6.95 (*0-7475-4355-0*, Pub. by Blmsbury Pub) Trafalgar.

Mr. Twister. Robert Hinson. vi, 42p. (Orig.). (J). (gr. 6-9). 1997. pr. 6.95 (*1-885926-07-3*) Dyn-Novel.

Mister Ubiquity. Donald Levering. 30p. 1997. pap. 7.95 (*0-944754-50-3*) Pudding Hse Pubns.

Mr. Underbed. Chris Riddell. (Illus.). 32p. (J). (ps-1). 1998. pap. 9.95 (*0-86264-786-X*, Pub. by Andersen Pr) Trafalgar.

Mr. Valentine. Vicki L. Thompson. (Temptation Ser.). 1997. per. 3.50 (*0-373-25724-4*, 1-25724-5) Harlequin Bks.

Mr. Verlin's Zono Comix. Rik Livingston. LC 87-50993. (Showcase Comic Ser.: No. 2). (Illus.). 128p. (Orig.). 1988. pap. 7.95 (*0-917976-76-2*) Thunder Baas Pr.

Mr. Vertigo. Paul Auster. 256p. 1995. pap. 12.95 (*0-14-023190-0*, Penguin Bks) Viking Penguin.

Mr. W & I. Caroline Webster. (American Autobiography Ser.). 264p. 1995. reprint ed. lib. bdg. 79.00 (*0-7812-8660-3*) Rprt Serv.

Mr. Was. Pete Hautman. 224p. (YA). (gr. 7 up). 1996. 16.00 (*0-689-81068-7*) S&S Bks Yung.

Mr. Was. Pete Hautman. 240p. (YA). 1998. per. 3.99 (*0-689-81914-5*) S&S Childrens.

Mr. Was. Pete Hautman. (J). 1998. 9.09 (*0-606-13625-8*, Pub. by Turtleback) Demco.

Mr. Washington's Travelling Music. James H. Nelesen. 32p. (J). (ps-4). 1987. 8.99 (*0-570-04151-1*, 56-1611) Concordia.

Mr. Wason I Think. Roy Tricker. 166p. 1995. pap. 12.95 (*0-85244-291-2*, 6356, Pub. by Gra1cewing) Morehouse Pub.

Mr. White's Confession. Robert Clark. LC 98-18717. 341p. 1998. text 24.00 (*0-312-19217-7*, Picador USA) St Martin.

Mr. White's Confession. Robert Clark. LC 98-18717. 341p. 1999. pap. 14.00 (*0-312-20426-4*, Picador USA) St Martin.

Mr. White's Confession. large type ed. Robert Clark. (Basic Ser.). 436p. 1999. 27.95 (*0-7862-1733-2*) Thorndike Pr.

***Mr. Wiggle's Book.** Paula M. Craig. LC 00-22243. (Illus.). (J). 2000. write for info. (*1-56822-975-5*) Instruct Fair.

Mr. William Prynn-His Defence of Stage-Plays: Retraction of a Former Book of His Called 'Histrio-Mastix' (English Stage Ser.: Vol. 15). 1977. lib. bdg. 55.00 (*0-8240-0598-8*) Garland.

Mr. William Shakespeare: His Comedies, Histories & Tragedies Set Out by Himself in Quarto, 10 vols., Set. William Shakespeare. Ed. by Edward Capell. LC 68-55093. reprint ed. 470.00 (*0-404-05830-2*) AMS Pr.

Mr. Williams & Miss Wood. Max Wilk. 1990. pap. 5.25 (*0-8222-0783-4*) Dramatists Play.

Mr. Willowby's Christmas Tree. Robert Barry. 32p. Date not set. 16.95 (*0-8488-2206-4*) Amereon Ltd.

Mr. Willowby's Christmas Tree. Robert Barry. (Illus.). 32p. (J). (ps-2). 1992. pap. 6.99 (*0-440-40726-5*, YB BDD) BDD Bks Young Read.

***Mr. Willowby's Christmas Tree.** Robert Barry. (Illus.). (J). 2000. 17.99 (*0-385-90006-6*) Doubleday.

***Mr. Willowby's Christmas Tree.** Robert Barry. (Illus.). (J). 2000. 15.95 (*0-385-32721-8*) Random Bks Yng Read.

Mr. Willowby's Christmas Tree. Robert Barry. (Illus.). 32p. (J). 1992. reprint ed. lib. bdg. 18.95 (*0-89966-935-2*) Buccaneer Bks.

Mr. Wilson's Cabinet of Wonder. Lawrence Weschler. 1996. pap. 12.00 (*0-679-76489-5*) Vin Bks.

Mr. Wink & His Shadow, Ned. Dick Gackenbach. LC 82-47711. (Illus.). 32p. (J). (gr. 1-4). 1983. 11.95 (*0-06-021969-6*) HarpC Child Bks.

Mister Wizard's Four Hundred Experiments in Science. rev. ed. Don Herbert & Hy Ruchlis. (Science-Math Projects Ser.). (Illus.). (gr. 4-10). 1983. reprint ed. pap. 9.95 (*0-87594-012-9*); reprint ed. lib. bdg. 14.95 (*0-87594-343-8*) Book-Lab.

Mr. Wizard's Supermarket Science. Don Herbert. LC 79-27217. (Illus.). 96p. (J). (gr. 4-7). 1980. pap. 10.00 (*0-394-83800-9*, Pub. by Random Bks Yng Read) Random.

***Mr. Wolf's Pancakes.** Jan Fearnley. 32p. (J). (gr. k-2). 2000. 14.95 (*1-888444-76-2*) Little Tiger.

Mr. Wonderful: Vocal Selections. Ed. by Carol Cuellar. 28p. (Orig.). (C). 1989. pap. text 9.95 (*0-7692-0767-7*, VF1603) Wrner Bros.

Mr. Wright. Lauryn Chandler. (Romance Ser.). 1993. pap. 2.69 (*0-373-08936-8*, 5-08936-2) Silhouette.

Mr. Wright. large type ed. Lauryn Chandler. LC 93-31004. 269p. 1994. lib. bdg. 14.95 (*0-7862-0125-8*) Thorndike Pr.

Mr. Wroe's Virgins. Jane Rogers. LC 99-10232. 288p. 1999. text 24.95 (*0-87951-702-6*, Pub. by Overlook Pr) Penguin Putnam.

***Mr. Wroe's Virgins: A Novel.** Jane Rogers. 288p. 2000. pap. 13.00 (*0-618-06613-6*, Mariner Bks) HM.

***Mr. Wrong.** Terry Campbell. LC 99-38418. (Romances Ser.). 1999. 24.95 (*0-7862-2154-2*) Five Star.

Mr. Wrong. Geeta Kingsley. (Romance Ser.). 1994. pap. 2.75 (*0-373-08985-6*, 5-08985-9) Silhouette.

Mr. Wrong! Mary A. Wilson. 1997. per. 3.75 (*0-373-16700-8*, 1-16700-6) Harlequin Bks.

***Mr. Wrong: A User's Guide or How to Use a Guy.** Cindy Walker. LC 99-49341. 2000. write for info. (*0-688-17847-2*, Wm Morrow) Morrow Avon.

Mr. X. Nick Gaitano. 272p. 1995. 21.00 (*0-671-50010-4*) S&S Trade.

***Mr. X.** Peter Straub. 544p. 2000. mass mkt. 7.99 (*0-449-14990-0*) Ballantine Pub Grp.

Mr. X. Peter Straub. LC 98-47688. 512p. 1999. 25.95 (*0-679-40138-5*) Random House.

Mr. X from Planet X: And Other Animules. Robert Kahla. (Animules Ser.). (Illus.). 64p. (J). pap. 8.95 (*1-882820-00-2*) Cracked Egg.

Mr. Yee Fixes Cars. Alice Flanagan. LC 97-11863. (Our Neighborhood Ser.). (Illus.). 32p. (J). 1998. 19.50 (*0-516-20772-5*) Childrens.

Mr. Yee Fixes Cars. Alice K. Flanagan. Ed. by Dana Rau. (Our Neighborhood Ser.). (Illus.). 32p. (J). 1998. pap. 6.95 (*0-516-26297-1*) Childrens.

Mister, You Got Yourself a Horse: Tales of Old-Time Horse Trading. Ed. by Roger L. Welsch. LC 81-436. xii, 207p. 1981. pap. 9.00 (*0-8032-9717-3*, Bison Books) U of Nebr Pr.

Mr. Zamboni's Dream Machine. Francois Gravel. (Blue Kite Adventure Ser.). (Illus.). 40p. (J). (gr. 2 up). 1995. pap. 6.95 (*1-55028-402-9*); bds. 16.95 (*1-55028-403-7*) Formac Dist Ltd.

Mr. Zenger's Malice & Falshood: Six Issues of the New York Weekly Journal, 1733-34. Stephen Botein. (AAS Facsimiles Ser.: No. 3). 48p. 1985. pap. 10.00 (*0-912296-73-9*, 42175) Oak Knoll.

***Mister Zoo: The Life & Legacy of Dr. Charles Schroeder.** Douglas G. Myers. LC 99-61695. (Illus.). 304p. 1999. 28.00 (*0-911461-15-9*) Zoological Soc.

Misteries de Osiris: La Iniciacion del Antiguo Egipto. 2nd ed. R. Swinburne Clymer. 278p. 1978. pap. 8.95 (*0-932785-57-3*) Philos Pub.

Misterio de Cristo. Thomas Keating.Tr. of Mystery of Christ. (SPA.). 144p. 1999. pap. 12.95 (*0-8264-1173-8*) Continuum.

Misterio de la Isla de las Especias. Richard Keens-Douglas.Tr. of Nutmeg Princess. (SPA., Illus.). 32p. (J). (ps-2). 1992. pap. 6.95 (*1-55037-260-2*, Pub. by Annick) Firefly Bks Ltd.

Misterio de la Llave, Level 1. Elena Moreno. (Leer en Espanol Ser.). (SPA.). (C). 1998. pap. 5.95 (*84-294-4040-2*) Santillana.

***Misterio de la Providencia.** John Flavel. Ed. by Hervey Mockford. Tr. by Thomas Montgomery & Omar Ibanez Negrete. Orig. Title: God Willing. (SPA.). 62p. 1999. pap. 1.39 (*1-928980-10-4*) Pub Faro.

Misterio de la Vide e de la Muerta. Jan Van Rijckenborgh. (SPA.). 1987. pap. 7.50 (*90-70196-35-2*) Rosycross Pr.

Misterio de la Virgen de Guadalupe. J. J. Benitez. 1995. 22.95 (*84-08-02559-7*) Planeta.

Misterio de las Bienaventuranzas. Jan Van Rijckenborgh. (SPA.). 76p. 1988. pap. 13.00 (*84-300-8340-5*) Rosycross Pr.

Misterio de Salem's Lot. Stephen King. 1999. 13.95 (*84-01-47456-6*) Plaza.

Misterio Mas Grande del Mundo. Mandino Og. (SPA.). 1997. pap. 15.98 (*968-13-3005-6*, Pub. by Edit Diana) Libros Fronteras.

Misterios de los Dias Postreros, Vol. 1. Impe Jack Van. (SPA.). 229p. 1998. pap. 9.99 (*0-88113-529-1*) Caribe Betania.

Misterios del Senor Burdick (The Mysteries of Harris Burdick) Chris Van Allsburg. (SPA.). 16p. (J). (gr. 1-3). 1997. 12.99 (*968-16-5114-6*, Pub. by Fondo) Continental Bk.

Misterioso. Raynor Carroll. 4p. 1996. pap. 2.95 (*1-891188-06-2*) Batterie Music.

Misterioso. Gilbert Sorrentino. LC 89-7707. 282p. 1989. 19.95 (*0-916583-43-0*) Dalkey Arch.

***Misterioso: Poems.** Sascha Feinstein. 96p. 2000. 24.00 (*1-55659-145-4*); pap. 14.00 (*1-55659-136-5*) Copper Canyon.

Misterioso Origen Del Cristianismo: Ensayo en Religion Comparativa. Rafael Polanco. (SPA., Illus.). 423p. (Orig.). 1989. pap. write for info. (*0-318-65960-3*) R Polanco.

Misteriosos Poderes Curativos de Dios: Medicina Natural de Santa Hildegard. Hertzka Jottfried. Tr. by Elsa Sifontes from GER. (SPA.). 139p. 1994. mass mkt. 9.95 (*0-9639727-0-7*, 001) St Hildegard.

Mistero Della Pizza Scomparsa: Teenage Mutant Ninja Turtles. Stephen Murphy. Tr. by DigiPro Staff from ENG. (Comes to Life Bks.).Tr. of Mystery of the Missing Pizza. (ITA.). 16p. (J). (ps-2). 1994. write for info. (*1-883366-96-8*) YES Ent.

Mistero Delle Pizze Scomparse: Teenage Mutant Ninja Turtles. Stephen Murphy. Tr. by DigiPro Staff from ENG. (Comes to Life Bks.).Tr. of Mystery of the Missing Pizza. (SPA.). 16p. (J). (ps-2). 1994. write for info. (*1-57234-008-8*) YES Ent.

Mistero Dell'Oasi Addormentata: Advanced Beginning. (ITA.). (C). 9.95 (*0-8442-8036-4*, X8036-4) NTC Contemp Pub Co.

Misti. Guy de Maupassant. pap. 9.95 (*0-685-23907-1*, 2156) Fr & Eur.

Mistica Ciudad de Dios (1670) Augustine M. Esposito. 1990. 36.50 (*0-916379-67-1*) Scripta.

Mistler's Exit. Louis Begley. 1999. pap. 12.00 (*0-449-00422-8*) Ballantine Pub Grp.

Mistler's Exit. Louis Begley. LC 98-14566. 224p. 1998. 22.00 (*0-375-40262-4*) Random.

Mistletoe. Karen Ball et al. LC 96-222597. 300p. 1996. pap. 9.99 (*1-57673-013-1*, Palisades OR) Multnomah Pubs.

Mistletoe. Ed. by H. Franz. (Journal: Oncology: Vol. 1, Suppl. 1). (Illus.). vi, 70p. 1986. pap. 24.50 (*3-8055-4465-0*) S Karger.

Mistletoe & Holly. Janet Dailey. 1993. mass mkt. 4.99 (*0-671-87508-6*, Pocket Books) PB.

Mistletoe & Holly: Easy Piano. 96p. 1992. pap. 10.95 (*0-7692-1172-0*, PF0799) Wrner Bros.

Mistletoe & Mayhem. Richard Dalby. 1993. 8.98 (*1-55521-972-1*) Bk Sales Inc.

Mistletoe & Mischief. Patricia Wynn. (Regency Romance Ser.). 1993. per. 2.99 (*0-373-31210-5*, 1-31210-7) Harlequin Bks.

Mistletoe & the Sword. Anya Seton. 24.95 (*0-89190-442-5*) Amereon Ltd.

Mistletoe Bride. Linda Varner. 1996. per. 3.25 (*0-373-19193-6*, 1-19193-1) Silhouette.

***Mistletoe Daddy: Sex Single Dads.** Jacqueline Diamond. (American Romance Ser.: Vol. 804). 1999. mass mkt. 3.99 (*0-373-16804-7*) Harlequin Bks.

***Mistletoe Girl & Other Christmas Stories.** Ethel Pochocki & Peter LaGue. LC 99-48856. (Illus.). 64p. 1999. 15.95 (*0-939516-47-0*) Forest Peace.

Mistletoe Kiss. Neels. 1997. per. 3.25 (*0-373-15729-0*) Harlequin Bks.

Mistletoe Kiss. Betty A. Neels. (Romance Ser.: No. 3483). 1997. per. 3.25 (*0-373-03483-0*, 1-03483-4) Harlequin Bks.

Mistletoe Kisses, 3 bks. in 1. Andrea Edwards et al. 1998. mass mkt. 5.99 (*0-373-20153-2*, 1-20153-2) Harlequin Bks.

***Mistletoe Kittens.** Jo Ann Ferguson. (Regency Romance Ser.). 256p. 1999. mass mkt. 4.99 (*0-8217-6303-2*, Zebra Kensgtn) Kensgtn Pub Corp.

***Mistletoe Magic.** Betty Neels et al. 2000. mass mkt. 6.50 (*0-373-83440-3*) Harlequin Bks.

Mistletoe Man. Kathleen O'Brien. 1996. per. 3.50 (*0-373-11853-8*, 1-11853-8) Harlequin Bks.

***Mistletoe Man: A China Bayles Mystery.** Susan Wittig Albert. LC 99-87021. 2000. 21.95 (*0-425-17673-8*) Berkley Pub.

Mistletoe Marriage. Jeanne Allan. 1996. per. 3.25 (*0-373-03437-7*, 1-03437-0) Harlequin Bks.

Mistletoe Marriage. large type ed. Jeanne Allan. (Hitched Ser.). 1996. per. 3.25 (*0-373-15683-9*) Harlequin Bks.

Mistletoe Marriages: Rendezvous; The Wolf & the Lamb; Christmas in the Valley; Keeping Christmas. Elaine Barbieri et al. 1994. per. 4.99 (*0-373-83309-1*, 1-83309-4) Harlequin Bks.

***Mistletoe Mayhem.** Kate Huntington. 224p. 2000. mass mkt. 4.99 (*0-8217-6739-9*, Zebra Kensgtn) Kensgtn Pub Corp.

Mistletoe Mischief. Alyssa Dean. LC 97-13816. (Love & Laughter Ser.: No. 33). 187p. 1997. per. 3.50 (*0-373-44033-2*) Harlequin Bks.

***Mistletoe Mischief.** Sandra Heath. 2000. mass mkt. 4.99 (*0-451-20147-7*, Sig) NAL.

Mistletoe Mistress. Helen Brooks. 1999. 21.95 (*0-263-15953-1*, G K Hall & Co) Mac Lib Ref.

Mistletoe Murder. Leslie Meier. (Lucy Stone Mystery Ser.). Orig. Title: Mail-order Murder. 224p. 1998. mass mkt. 5.99 (*1-57566-370-8*, Knsington) Kensgtn Pub Corp.

Mistletoe Mysteries. Compiled by Charlotte MacLeod. 256p. 1989. 16.45 (*0-89296-400-6*) Mysterious Pr.

Mistletoe Mysteries. Compiled by Charlotte MacLeod. 256p. 1990. mass mkt. 5.50 (*0-445-40920-7*, Pub. by Warner Bks) Little.

Mistletoes of Africa. S. Linington & D. Wiens. (Illus.). 370p. 1998. 130.00 (*1-900347-56-3*, Pub. by Royal Botnic Grdns) Balogh.

Mistral. Rob Lyle. 1953. 49.50 (*0-686-50050-4*) Elliots Bks.

Mistral's Daughter. Judith Krantz. 592p. 1984. mass mkt. 7.50 (*0-553-25917-2*) Bantam.

Mistreatment & Sexual Abuse of Children see Maltrato y Abuso Sexual de Ninos

Mistreatment of Elderly People. Ed. by Peter Decalmer & Frank Glendenning. (Illus.). 224p. (C). 1993. text 59.95 (*0-8039-8712-9*); pap. text 19.95 (*0-8039-8713-7*) Sage.

Mistreatment of Elderly People. 2nd ed. Peter Decalmer & Frank Glendenning. LC 97-66778. 256p. 1997. text 85.00 (*0-7619-5262-4*); pap. text 29.95 (*0-7619-5263-2*) Sage.

Mistress. Vivienne La Fay. (Black Lace Ser.). 272p. (Orig.). 1996. mass mkt. 5.95 (*0-352-33057-0*, Pub. by Virgin Bks) London Bridge.

Mistress. Alan Marshfield. Date not set. pap. 7.95 (*0-900977-42-6*, Pub. by Anvil Press) Dufour.

Mistress. Amanda Quick, pseud. 384p. 1995. mass mkt. 6.99 (*0-553-56940-6*) Bantam.

***Mistress.** Susan Wiggs. 2000. mass mkt. 6.50 (*1-55166-610-3*, 1-66610-6, Mira Bks) Harlequin Bks.

***Mistress.** large type ed. Angela Drake. 496p. 2000. 31.99 (*0-7505-1508-2*, Pub. by Mgna Lrg Print) Ulverscroft.

Mistress: A Novel. Philippe Tapon. LC 98-27679. 192p. 1999. 23.95 (*0-525-94461-3*, W Abrahams Bks) Dutton Plume.

***Mistress: A Novel.** Philippe Tapon. 2000. pap. 12.95 (*0-452-28058-3*, Plume) Dutton Plume.

Mistress: Histories, Myths & Interpretations of the "Other Woman" Victoria Griffin. 320p. 1999. 25.95 (*1-58234-053-6*) Bloomsbury Pubg.

***Mistress & Maid: Jiaohongji.** Cheng-Shun Meng & Cyril Birch. LC 00-34583. (Translations from the Asian Classics). 2000. pap. 17.50 (*0-231-12169-5*) Col U Pr.

Mistress & Mother. Lynne Graham. (Presents Ser.: No. 1937). 1998. per. 3.75 (*0-373-11937-2*, 1-11937-9) Harlequin Bks.

Mistress & Mother. large type ed. Lynne Graham. (Harlequin Ser.). 285p. 1998. 20.95 (*0-263-15376-2*) Thorndike Pr.

M

An Asterisk (*) at the beginning of an entry indicates that the title is appearing for the first time.

Mistress & the Slave. Intro. by Michael R. Goss. 160p. 1995. 34.95 (*1-897767-09-9*, Pub. by Delectus Bks) Xclusiv Distrib.

Mistress Anne. Carolly Erickson. LC 98-17233. 1998. pap. 14.95 (*0-312-18747-5*, Pub. by Tor Bks) St Martin.

***Mistress Assignment: Society Weddings.** Penny Jordan. (Presents Ser.: No. 2061). 1999. per. 3.75 (*0-373-12061-3*, 1-12061-7) Harlequin Bks.

***Mistress Assignment: Society Weddings.** large type ed. Penny Jordan. 1999. 21.95 (*0-263-16137-4*) P-H.

Mistress at the Hall. large type ed. Eileen Knowles. (Linford Romance Library). 320p. 1997. pap. 16.99 (*0-7089-5080-9*, Linford) Ulverscroft.

Mistress Branican. Jules Verne. (Illus.). 8.95 (*0-686-55935-5*) Fr & Eur.

Mistress Bride: Society Weddings. Michelle Reid. (Presents Ser.: No. 2056). 1999. per. 3.75 (*0-373-12056-7*, 1-12056-7) Harlequin Bks.

***Mistress Bride: Society Weddings.** large type ed. Michelle Reid. (Romance Ser.). 1999. 21.95 (*0-263-16247-8*) Mills & Boon.

Mistress by Arrangement. Helen Bianchin. (Romance Ser.). 1999. per. 3.75 (*0-373-12049-4*, 1-12049-2) Harlequin Bks.

***Mistress by Arrangement.** large type ed. Helen Bianchin. (Thorndike Harlequin Romance Ser.). 2000. 22.95 (*0-263-16367-9*) Mills & Boon.

M

Mistress Cavalier. large type ed. Janis Coles. 336p. 1996. 27.99 (*0-7089-3533-8*) Ulverscroft.

Mistress Davenant. Arthur Acheson. (Works of Arthur Acheson). v, 332p. 1985. reprint ed. 49.00 (*0-7812-0818-1*) Rprt Serv.

***Mistress Deception: Presents Passion.** Susan Napier. (Presents Ser.: Bk. 2111). 2000. per. 3.99 (*0-373-12111-3*, 1-12111-0) Harlequin Bks.

***Mistress for a Night.** Diana Hamilton. (Presents Ser.). 2000. per. 3.99 (*0-373-12094-X*) Harlequin Bks.

Mistress for Hire. large type ed. Angela Devine. 288p. 1996. 23.99 (*0-263-14508-5*, Pub. by Mills & Boon) Ulverscroft.

***Mistress Manual: A Good Girl's Guide to Female Dominance.** Mistress Lorelei. 220p. 2000. 15.95 (*1-890159-19-0*) Greenery Pr.

Mistress Masham's Repose. T. H. White. 160p. (J). 1998. 24.95 (*1-85149-700-5*) Antique Collect.

Mistress Material. Sharon Kendrick. 1997. per. 3.50 (*0-373-11867-8*, 1-11867-8) Harlequin Bks.

Mistress Mine. 3rd ed. Valentina Cilescu. (Orig.). 1997. reprint ed. mass mkt. 6.50 (*1-56333-502-6*, Rosebud) Masquerade.

Mistress Mississippi. Louis D. Brodsky. LC 90-72139. (Mississippi Trilogy Ser.: Vol. 3). 125p. 1992. pap. 12.50 (*1-877770-37-X*) Time Being Bks.

Mistress Mississippi Vol. 3: A Mississippi Trilogy. Louis D. Brodsky. LC 90-72139. 125p. 1992. 18.95 (*1-877770-36-1*) Time Being Bks.

Mistress of Blackstone. large type ed. Mary Williams. 480p. 1992. 27.99 (*0-7089-2599-5*) Ulverscroft.

Mistress of Deception. Miranda Lee. LC 96-2778. (Presents Ser.). 186p. 1996. per. 3.50 (*0-373-11791-4*, 1-11791-0) Harlequin Bks.

***Mistress of Elvan Hall.** Mary Jane Warmington. 280p. 2000. 18.99 (*0-7089-5663-7*) Ulverscroft.

Mistress of Fortune. large type ed. Sheila Lancaster. 576p. 1984. 27.99 (*0-7089-1113-7*) Ulverscroft.

Mistress of Her Fate. large type ed. Julia Byrne. 350p. 1996. 23.99 (*0-263-14521-2*, Pub. by Mills & Boon) Ulverscroft.

***Mistress of Her Own Thoughts: Ella Freeman Sharpe & the Practice of Psychoanalysis.** Ed. by Maurice J. Whelan. 260p. 2000. pap. 29.99 (*1-900877-26-0*, Pub. by Rebus Pr Ltd) Intl Spec Bk.

Mistress of Justice. Jeffery Deaver. 400p. 1993. mass mkt. 6.50 (*0-553-29733-3*) Bantam.

Mistress of Luke's Folly. large type ed. Elizabeth Elgin. LC 97-24397. (Paperback Ser.). 281p. 1997. pap. text 21.95 (*0-7838-8261-0*, G K Hall Lrg Type) Mac Lib Ref.

***Mistress of Madderlea.** large type ed. Mary Nichols. 320p. 1999. 25.99 (*0-263-16151-X*, Pub. by Mills & Boon) Ulverscroft.

Mistress of Martinscombe. large type ed. Jan Tempest. (Romance Ser.). 304p. 1992. 11.50 (*0-7089-2651-7*) Ulverscroft.

Mistress of Melthorpe. large type ed. Alan Bloom. (Ulverscroft Large Print Ser.). 352p. 1997. 27.99 (*0-7089-3859-0*) Ulverscroft.

Mistress of Mishap. Cathleen Clare. 256p. (Orig.). 1992. mass mkt. 3.99 (*0-380-76815-1*, Avon Bks) Morrow Avon.

Mistress of Monticello. Anne M. Westlake. 268p. (Orig.). 1997. pap. 12.00 (*0-9657673-0-2*) Elkwood Pub.

Mistress of Polrudden. large type ed. E. V. Thompson. (Charnwood Large Print Ser.). 784p. 1995. 27.99 (*0-7089-8821-0*, Charnwood) Ulverscroft.

Mistress of Riversdale: The Plantation Letters of Rosalie Stier Calvert, 1795-1821. Margaret L. Callcott. (Maryland Paperback Bookshelf Ser.). (Illus.). 432p. 1992. reprint ed. pap. 16.95 (*0-8018-4399-5*) Johns Hopkins.

***Mistress of Rosecliffe.** Rexanne Becnel. 304p. 2000. mass mkt. 6.50 (*0-312-97402-7*, St Martins Paperbacks) St Martin.

Mistress of Sin. Sue Rich. 1994. mass mkt. 5.50 (*0-671-79408-6*) PB.

Mistress of Spices: A Novel. Chitra Banerjee Divakaruni. LC 96-23767. 388p. 1998. pap. 12.95 (*0-385-48238-8*, Anchor NY) Doubleday.

Mistress of the Bones. T. J. MacGregor. LC 95-10123. 352p. 1995. 21.45 (*0-7868-6106-1*, Pub. by Hyperion) Time Warner.

Mistress of the Darkened Rooms & Other Short Stories. Ruth W. Schuler. (Illus.). 76p. 1988. pap. 8.00 (*0-910083-23-1*) Heritage Trails.

Mistress of the Empire. Raymond E. Feist. 688p. 1993. mass mkt. 6.99 (*0-553-56118-9*, Spectra) Bantam.

Mistress of the Groom. Susan Napier. 1997. per. 3.50 (*0-373-11918-6*, 1-11918-6) Harlequin Bks.

Mistress of the Groom. large type ed. Susan Napier. (Harlequin Romance Ser.). 288p. 1998. 20.95 (*0-263-15403-3*) Thorndike Pr.

Mistress of the House: Women of Property in the Victorian Novel. Tim Dolin. LC 97-29550. (Nineteenth Century Ser.). 168p. 1997. text 61.95 (*1-85928-184-2*, Pub. by Ashgate Pub) Ashgate Pub Co.

Mistress of the House, Mistress of Heaven: Women in Ancient Egypt. Glenn Markoe et al. LC 96-9376. (Illus.). 240p. 1996. 50.00 (*1-55595-129-5*) Hudson Hills.

***Mistress of the Sheikh.** Sandra Marton. (Presents Ser.: Bk. 2136). 2000. mass mkt. 3.99 (*0-373-12136-9*, 1-12136-7) Harlequin Bks.

Mistress of the Waters. Janeen O'Kerry. (Love Spell Ser.). 320p. 1999. mass mkt. 4.99 (*0-505-52309-4*, Love Spell) Dorchester Pub Co.

Mistress of Udolpho: The Life of Ann Radcliffe. Rictor Norton. LC 98-8412. 1998. 75.00 (*0-7185-0201-9*); pap. 19.95 (*0-7185-0202-7*) Bks Intl VA.

Mistress Pat. L. M. Montgomery. (J). 1976. 23.95 (*0-8488-1103-8*) Amereon Ltd.

Mistress Pat. L. M. Montgomery. 288p. (YA). 1997. mass mkt. 3.99 (*0-7704-2246-2*) Bantam.

***Mistress to a Millionaire.** large type ed. Helen Brooks. (Thorndike Harlequin Romance (Large Print) Ser.). 2000. 22.95 (*0-263-16440-3*) Mac Lib Ref.

Mistress to an Age: A Life of Madame de Stael. J. Christopher Herold. LC 75-18399. (Illus.). 500p. 1975. reprint ed. lib. bdg. 35.00 (*0-8371-8339-1*, HEMTA, Greenwood Pr) Greenwood.

Mistresses: The Free Woman-The Unfree Man. Susan Kedgley & Wendy James. LC 74-17678. 176p. 1975. 5.95 (*0-672-52035-4*, Bobbs) Macmillan.

Mistresses & Slaves: Plantation Women in South Carolina, 1830-80. Marli F. Weiner. LC 96-45830. 400p. 1997. text 45.95 (*0-252-02322-6*); pap. text 19.95 (*0-252-06623-5*) U of Ill Pr.

Mistresses & Wives, Husbands & Other Lives. Izhar Patkin. (Illus.). 288p. 1998. 40.00 (*0-8478-5783-2*, Pub. by Rizzoli Intl) St Martin.

Mistresses of King George IV. M. J. Levy. LC 96-144880. (Illus.). 224p. 1996. 34.95 (*0-7206-0956-9*, Pub. by P Owen Ltd) Dufour.

Mistresses of the White House: Narrator's Tale of a Pageant First Ladies. Irene Gerlinger. 125p. 1977. 18.95 (*0-8369-8015-8*) Ayer.

Mistrusting Refugees. Ed. by E. Valentine Daniel & John Knudsen. LC 95-18975. 330p. 1996. 50.00 (*0-520-08898-0*, Pub. by U CA Pr); pap. 18.95 (*0-520-08899-9*, Pub. by U CA Pr) Cal Prin Full Svc.

Mists & Magic. Dorothy Edwards. 1997. 12.95 (*0-7188-2537-3*, Lutterworth-Parkwest) Parkwest Pubns.

Mists & Megaliths of Michael in the Mount. Gladys R. Lennox. 1986. 39.00 (*0-7223-2036-1*, Pub. by A H S Ltd); pap. 35.00 (*0-7223-2091-4*, Pub. by A H S Ltd) St Mut.

Mists of Avalon. Marion Zimmer Bradley. 896p. 1987. pap. 14.00 (*0-345-35049-9*, Del Rey) Ballantine Pub Grp.

***Mists of Avalon.** Marion Zimmer Bradley. 2000. 30.00 (*0-345-44118-4*) Ballantine Pub Grp.

Mists of Dragon Lore: The Toltec Teachings. Theun Mares. (Toltec Teachings Ser.: Vol. 3). 1998. pap. 16.95 (*1-919792-02-3*) Lionheart Pub OH.

Mists of Eden: Nature's Last Paradise. Erica Sherman. Ed. by Nancy R. Thatch. LC 98-14468. (Books for Students by Students). (Illus.). 29p. (J). (gr. 5-12). 1998. lib. bdg. 15.95 (*0-933849-69-9*) Landmark Edns.

Mists of Fear. large type ed. John Creasey. 436p. 1973. 27.99 (*0-85456-161-7*) Ulverscroft.

Mists of Mbinda: Kate's Busy Life Concealed the Soul of a Woman Lonely for Love. Corrine Vanderwerff. LC 97-29678. 1997. 6.97 (*0-8163-1404-7*) Pacific Pr Pub Assn.

Mists of Regret: Culture & Sensibility in Classic French Film. Dudley Andrew. LC 09-415486. 384p. 1995. text 65.00 (*0-691-05686-2*, Pub. by Princeton U Pr); pap. text 24.95 (*0-691-00883-3*, Pub. by Princeton U Pr) Cal Prin Full Svc.

Mists of Remembrance. large type ed. Betty O'Rourke. (Linford Romance Library). 256p. 1992. pap. 16.99 (*0-7089-7135-0*, Linford) Ulverscroft.

Mists over Mosley. John Greenwood. 192p. 1986. 15.95 (*0-8027-5642-5*) Walker & Co.

Misty. V. C. Andrews. (Wildflowers Ser.: No. 1). (YA). 1999. mass mkt. 3.99 (*0-671-02800-6*, Pocket Books) PB.

***Misty.** large type ed. V. C. Andrews. LC 99-46976. (G. K. Hall Core Ser.). (YA). 1999. 26.95 (*0-7838-8802-3*, G K Hall Lrg Type) Mac Lib Ref.

***Misty: A Motherus Journey Through Sorrow to Healing.** Carole Gift Page. 160p. 2000. mass mkt. 6.99 (*0-8007-8688-2*, Spire) Revell.

Misty - Misty of Chincoteague. Marguerite Henry. 1996. pap. text 7.95 (*84-279-3218-9*) Lectorum Pubns.

Misty Dreamer. Kevin Ragubir. LC 97-90464. 72p. 2000. pap. 8.95 (*0-533-12414-X*) Vantage.

***Misty Mourning.** Rett MacPherson. 2000. 22.95 (*0-312-26619-7*) St Martin.

Misty of Chincoteague. Henry. (J). 1998. per. 2.65 (*0-689-82170-0*) S&S Childrens.

Misty of Chincoteague. Marguerite Henry. (Illus.). (J). (gr. 4). 1995. 9.00 (*0-395-73241-7*) HM.

Misty of Chincoteague. Marguerite Henry. LC 47-11404. (Illus.). 176p. (J). (gr. 3-7). 1990. lib. bdg. 15.00 (*0-02-743622-5*, Mac Bks Young Read) S&S Childrens.

Misty of Chincoteague. Marguerite Henry. (J). 1997. 100.00 (*0-689-81377-5*) S&S Childrens.

Misty of Chincoteague. Marguerite Henry. (J). 1991. 9.05 (*0-606-04009-9*, Pub. by Turtleback) Demco.

***Misty of Chincoteague.** Marty Beatty Sanders. (Illus.). 48p. 1999. pap., teacher ed. 7.95 (*1-57690-624-8*, TCM2624) Tchr Create Mat.

***Misty of Chincoteague.** gif. ed. Marguerite Henry. LC 00-30763. (Illus.). (J). 2000. write for info. (*0-689-83926-X*) S&S Childrens.

Misty of Chincoteague. Marguerite Henry. LC 90-27237. (Illus.). 176p. (J). (gr. 3-7). 1991. reprint ed. mass mkt. 3.95 (*0-689-71492-0*) Aladdin.

Misty of Chincoteague, Vol. 1. Marguerite Henry. 1999. pap. 2.99 (*0-689-82993-0*) S&S Childrens.

Misty of Chincoteague: A Study Guide. Lorraine Sintetos. Ed. by J. Friedland & R. Kessler. (Novel-Ties Ser.). (J). (gr. 3-5). 1995. pap. text, student ed. 15.95 (*1-56982-288-3*) Lrn Links.

Misty the Kitten with Her Friends. Cindy Thoman. (Illus.). 16p. (J). (gr. k-3). 1996. pap. 7.00 (*0-8059-3728-5*) Dorrance.

Misty the Manatee. Veronica A. Lupsewicz. Ed. by Jane Weinberger. LC 93-61193. (Illus.). 46p. (J). (ps-4). 1996. pap. 9.95 (*0-932433-96-0*) Windswept Hse.

***Misty Trail: Life in the Early Years of This Century.** Florence Foley Miller. LC 99-91222. 322p. 1999. 25.00 (*0-7388-0680-3*); pap. 18.00 (*0-7388-0681-1*) Xlibris Corp.

Misty Treasury. O'Henry. (J). 1997. 11.95 (*0-689-82046-1*) S&S Bks Yung.

Misty's Black Tunnel. Nona Freeman. Ed. by Nell Perry. 108p. 1992. pap. 6.00 (*1-878366-05-X*) Nonas Bk Sales.

Misty's Twilight. Marguerite Henry. LC 91-42582. (Illus.). 144p. (J). (gr. 3-7). 1996. per. 3.99 (*0-689-80393-1*) Aladdin.

***Misty's Twilight.** Marguerite Henry. (2000 Kids Picks Ser.). 144p. (J). (gr. 4-7). 2000. mass mkt. 2.99 (*0-689-83868-9*) Aladdin.

Misty's Twilight. Marguerite Henry. LC 91-42582. 1996. 9.09 (*0-606-11630-3*, Pub. by Turtleback) Demco.

Misty/Till Loved You & Great. 128p. (Orig.). 1989. pap. 11.95 (*0-7692-1042-2*, VF1538) Wrner Bros.

Misunderstanding see Caligula & Three Other Plays

Misunderstanding: The Crux of Professional Liability Exposures. (Illus.). 15p. 5.00 (*0-614-05182-7*, MCPL06751M) ASFE.

Misunderstanding Media. Brian Winston. (Illus.). 424p. 1986. 34.50 (*0-674-57663-2*) HUP.

Misunderstanding of Nature: Poetry. Sophie C. Black. LC 93-23114. 96p. 1994. 22.50 (*1-55597-190-3*); pap. 12.00 (*1-55597-201-2*) Graywolf.

Misunderstanding Science? The Public Reconstruction of Science & Technology. Ed. by Alan Irwin & Brian Wynne. (Illus.). 240p. (C). 1996. text 69.95 (*0-521-43268-5*) Cambridge U Pr.

Misunderstandings of the Self. Victor Raimy. LC 74-28917. (Jossey-Bass Behavioral Science Ser.). 232p. reprint ed. pap. 72.00 (*0-8357-6884-8*, 203793600009) Bks Demand.

Misunderstood Caudillo: Miguel Ydigoras Fuentes & the Failure of Democracy in Guatemala. Roland H. Ebel. LC 97-29764. (Tulane Studies in Political Science: No. 21). 376p. (C). 1997. text 64.00 (*0-7618-0888-4*) U Pr of Amer.

Misunderstood Child: A Guide for Parents of Learning Disabled Children. 3rd ed. Larry Silver. 1998. write for info. (*0-8129-2985-3*, Times Bks) Crown Pub Group.

Misunderstood Child: Understanding & Coping with Your Child's Learning Disabilities. 3rd ed. Larry B. Silver. LC 97-51664. 288p. 1998. pap. 15.00 (*0-8129-2987-X*, Times Bks) Crown Pub Group.

Misunderstood Economy. Eisner. 1995. pap. 14.95 (*0-07-103635-0*) McGraw.

Misunderstood Economy: What Counts & How to Count It. Robert Eisner. 240p. 1995. pap. 14.95 (*0-87584-642-4*) Harvard Busn.

Misunderstood Economy: What Counts & How to Count It. Harvard Business Review Staff. 224p. 1994. 25.00 (*0-07-103576-1*) McGraw.

Misunderstood Jesus: Ten Lost Keys to Life. Clyde Fant. 176p. 1996. pap. 16.00 (*1-57312-015-4*) Smyth & Helwys.

Misunderstood Miracle: Industrial Development & Political Change in Japan. David Friedman. LC 87-47855. (Cornell Studies in Political Economy). (Illus.). 280p. 1988. pap. text 16.95 (*0-8014-9479-6*) Cornell U Pr.

Misunderstood Texts of Scripture Expounded & Explained: The Doctrine of the Higher Life Thereby Verified. Asa Mahan. 181p. 1996. pap. 9.99 (*0-88019-358-1*) Schmul Pub Co.

Misuse of Drugs. Ed. by British Medical Association Staff. 160p. 1997. text 24.00 (*90-5702-259-1*, Harwood Acad Pubs); pap. text 20.00 (*90-5702-260-5*, Harwood Acad Pubs) Gordon & Breach.

Misuse of Drugs. Don Mathias. 251p. 1988. pap. 54.00 (*0-409-78816-3*, NZ, MICHIE) LEXIS Pub.

Misuse of Drugs, Suppl. 1. P. Bucknell & H. Ghodse. (Criminal Law Library). 128p. 1986. pap. 8.25 (*0-08-033081-9*) Macmillan.

Misuse of Drugs, Supplement 2. P. Bucknell & H. Ghodse. (Criminal Law Library). 192p. 1988. pap. 18.00 (*0-08-033107-6*) Macmillan.

Misuse of Drugs, Supplement No. 3. P. Bucknell & H. Ghodse. (Criminal Law Library). 192p. 1989. pap. 30.00 (*0-08-036914-6*) Macmillan.

Misuse of Drugs & Supplement 3: Combined Set, WCLL 2. P. Bucknell & H. Ghodse. (Criminal Law Library). 632p. 1989. 100.00 (*0-08-036915-4*, Pergamon Pr) Elsevier.

Misuse of Drugs & the Law. P. Bucknell. (Library of Criminal Law Ser.). 352p. 1986. 54.00 (*0-08-039203-2*, Pergamon Pr) Elsevier.

Misuse of HUD Community Development Block Grant Funds: Hearings before the Employment & Housing Subcommittee of the Committee on Government Operations, House of Representatives, One Hundred Second Congress, First & Second Sessions, October 21, 1991, & March 18, 1992. United States. LC 94-117528. iv, 376 p. 1993. write for info. (*0-16-040185-2*) USGPO.

Misuse of Persons: Analyzing Pathological Dependency. Stanley J. Coen. 344p. 1992. text 49.95 (*0-88163-139-6*) Analytic Pr.

Misuse of Psychiatry in the Criminal Courts: Competency to Stand Trial. Group for the Advancement of Psychiatry Staff. LC KF9242.. (Group for the Advancement of Psychiatry, Symposium Ser.: No. 89). 70p. reprint ed. pap. 30.00 (*0-608-14393-6*, 202183300023) Bks Demand.

Misuse of Psychotropic Drugs. Royal College of Psychiatrists Staff. Ed. by Robin Murray et al. LC RM0146.M67. (Special Publication: No. 1). 116p. reprint ed. pap. 36.00 (*0-7837-0998-6*, 204130400020) Bks Demand.

Misused Statistics. 2nd ed. Jaffe et al. LC 98-25625. (Illus.). 280p. 1998. text 49.75 (*0-8247-0211-5*) Dekker.

Miswak. Uthman Hutchinson. LC 95-80047. (Children Stories Project Ser.). (Illus.). 24p. (J). (gr. 1 up). 1995. pap. 3.95 (*0-915957-50-7*) amana pubns.

Mit & the Weed. Alan M. Hofmeister et al. (Reading for All Learners Ser.). (Illus.). (J). pap. write for info. (*1-56861-113-7*) Swift Lrn Res.

***Mit Aufrichtiger Feder Meist Gegenwartig Aufgezeichnet: RU & Beta; Landberichte Deutscher Reisender Vom 16, Bis Zum 19, Jahrhundert.** Romualda Poljakov. (Deutsch-Russische Literaturbeziehungen - Forschungen und Materialien Ser.). 218p. 1999. 37.95 (*3-631-34921-1*) P Lang Pubng.

Mit Bildern Lernen. Theo Scherling & Hans F. Schuckall. 192p. 1990. 35.00 (*3-468-49995-7*) Langenscheidt.

Mit Bogova u Predpovijesti Hrvatske. Ivo Omrcanin. (CRO.). 158p. (Orig.). 1993. pap. 10.00 (*1-878716-09-3*) Ivor Pr.

MIT Catalog of Computer Science & Artificial Intelligence. Massachusetts Institute of Technology Library Staf. 850p. 1988. 245.00 (*0-8161-0480-8*, G K Hall & Co) Mac Lib Ref.

MIT Class of 1948: Fiftieth Reunion Book. Ed. by Sonny Monosson. (Illus.). 450p. 1998. pap. 40.00 (*0-9660524-9-8*) Monosson Technologies.

Mit Deutsch Spielen, Bk. 1. European Language Institute Staff. (Multilanguage Ser.). (GER., Illus.). 71p. (Orig.). (J). (gr. 2-6). 1997. pap. 12.95 (*88-85148-49-2*, Pub. by Europ Lang Inst) Distribks Inc.

Mit Deutsch Spielen, Bk. 2. European Language Institute Staff. (Multilanguage Ser.). (GER., Illus.). 71p. (Orig.). (J). (gr. 2-6). 1997. pap. 12.95 (*88-85148-96-4*, Pub. by Europ Lang Inst) Distribks Inc.

MIT Dictionary of Modern Economics. 4th ed. Ed. by David W. Pearce. (Illus.). 486p. 1992. 46.00 (*0-262-16132-X*); pap. text 21.50 (*0-262-66078-4*) MIT Pr.

Mit Dir, Statt Gegen Dich: Ein Feministisch-Theologischer Beitrag zur Relationalen Selbstvergewisserung der Frauen in Einer Androzentrischen Kultur. Verena Klotz. (Europaische Hochschulschriften Ser.: Reihe 23, Bd. 392). (GER.). 513p. 1990. 82.80 (*3-631-42850-2*) P Lang Pubng.

MIT Encyclopedia of the Cognitive Sciences. Ed. by Robert A. Wilson & Frank Keil. (Illus.). 1312p. 1999. 149.95 (*0-262-23200-6*, Bradford Bks) MIT Pr.

MIT Encyclopedia of the Japanese Economy. Robert C. Hsu. LC 93-34556. 432p. 1994. 52.50 (*0-262-08227-6*) MIT Pr.

MIT Encyclopedia of the Japanese Economy. 2nd ed. Robert C. Hsu. LC 99-19441. (Illus.). 550p. 1999. 60.00 (*0-262-08280-2*) MIT Pr.

Mit Erfolg zum Zertifikat: Testheft. Hubert L. Eichheim & G. Storch. (GER.). (C). 1992. audio 29.00 (*3-12-675368-X*, Pub. by Klett Edition) Intl Bk Import.

Mit Erfolg zum Zertifikat: Testheft. Hubert Eichheim & G. Storch. (GER.). 140p. (C). 1992. pap. text 17.75 (*3-12-675369-8*, Pub. by Klett Edition) Intl Bk Import.

Mit Erfolg zum Zertifikat Deutsch als Fremdsprache: Uebungsbuch. Hubert Eichheim. (GER.). 160p. (C). 1992. pap. text 20.00 (*3-12-675365-5*, Pub. by Klett Edition) Intl Bk Import.

Mit Erfolg zum Zertifikat Deutsch als Fremdsprache: Uebungsbuch. Hubert Eichheim & G. Storch. (GER.). (C). 1992. audio 32.00 (*3-12-675366-3*, Pub. by Klett Edition) Intl Bk Import.

MIT Guide to Science & Engineering Communication. James G. Paradis & Muriel Zimmerman. (Illus.). 300p. 1997. 31.50 (*0-262-16142-7*) MIT Pr.

Mit Hippokrates zur Organgewinnung? Medizinische Ethik und Sprache. Ed. by Horst D. Scholosser. (Frankfurter Forschungen zur Kultur- und Sprachwissenschaft Ser.: Band 1). (GER.). 278p. 1998. pap. 48.95 (*3-631-33006-5*) P Lang Pubng.

Mit Is Wet. Alan M. Hofmeister et al. (Reading for All Learners Ser.). (Illus.). (J). pap. write for info. (*1-56861-108-0*) Swift Lrn Res.

Mit Kreuzwortratseln Deutsch Lernen, Bk. 1. European Language Institute Staff. (Multilanguage Ser.). (GER., Illus.). 96p. (Orig.). (J). (gr. 2-6). 1997. pap. 12.95 (*88-85148-15-8*, Pub. by Europ Lang Inst) Distribks Inc.

An Asterisk (*) at the beginning of an entry indicates that the title is appearing for the first time.

Mit Kreuzwortratseln Deutsch Lernen, Bk. 2. European Language Institute Staff. (Multilanguage Ser.). (GER., Illus.). 96p. (Orig.). (J). (gr. 2-6). 1997. pap. 12.95 (*88-85148-20-4*, Pub. by Europ Lang Inst) Distribks Inc.

Mit Kreuzwortratseln Deutsch Lernen, Bk. 3. European Language Institute Staff. (Multilanguage Ser.). (GER., Illus.). 96p. (Orig.). (J). (gr. 6-10). 1997. pap. 12.95 (*88-85148-25-5*, Pub. by Europ Lang Inst) Distribks Inc.

MIT Lincoln Laboratory: Technology in the National Interest. Eva C. Freeman. LC 94-74574. (Illus.). 300p. 1995. lib. bdg. write for info. (*0-9645720-0-1*) Lincoln Lab.

MIT Marine-Related Research Directory, 1993-1994. Ed. by John Moore. write for info. (*1-56172-008-9*) MIT Sea Grant.

MIT Wavelength Tables, Vol. 1. 2nd ed. Ed. by George R. Harrison. 464p. 1939. 105.00 (*0-262-08002-8*) MIT Pr.

MIT Wavelength Tables: Wavelengths by Element, Vol. 2. Ed. by Frederick M. Phelps, III. 816p. 1982. 105.00 (*0-262-16087-0*) MIT Pr.

Mit Zaum und Zugel Mub Man Ihr Ungestum Bandigen - Ps 32,9: Ein Beitrag zur Christlichen Hebraistik und Antijudischen Polemik im Mittelalter. Ursula Ragacs. (Judentum und Umwelt Ser.: Bd. 65). (GER.). 202p. 1997. 44.95 (*3-631-31916-9*) P Lang Pubng.

Mita P 'Arriba, Mita P'Abajo. Hugo Hanriot. Ed. by SLUSA Staff. (SPA.). 118p. 1980. pap. 6.00 (*0-9606758-2-5*, TX525-786) SLUSA.

Mitakuye Oyasin: We Are All Related. A. C. Ross. LC 97-161684. (Illus.). 215p. (Orig.). 1989. pap. 12.00 (*0-9621977-0-X*) Wiconi Waste.

Mitarbeiter des Zeitgeistes? Die Auseinandersetzung Uber die Zeitgemabheit Als Kriterium Kirchlichen Handelns und die Kriterien Theologischer Entscheidungen in der Reformierten Kirche Ungarns, 1967-1992. Ed. by Zoltan Balog & Gerhard Sauter. (Beitrage zur Theologischen Urteilsbildung Ser.: Bd. 3). (GER.). 277p. 1997. 54.95 (*3-631-31636-4*) P Lang Pubng.

Mitbestimmung, Property-Rights-Ansatz & Transaktionskostentheorie: Eine Okonomische Analyse. Torsten Ganske. (GER., Illus.). XVII, 260p. 1996. 54.95 (*3-631-30510-9*) P Lang Pubng.

Mitch: On the Tail End of the Old West. Dean Krakel. (Illus.). 172p. 1982. pap. 18.00 (*0-318-15390-4*) Natl Cowboy Hall of Fame.

Mitch & Amy. Beverly Cleary. LC 67-10041. 224p. (J). (gr. 3-7). 1991. mass mkt. 4.99 (*0-380-70925-2*, Wm Morrow) Morrow Avon.

Mitch & Amy. Beverly Cleary. LC 67-10041. (Illus.). 224p. (J). (gr. 4-7). 1991. 15.00 (*0-688-10806-7*, Wm Morrow) Morrow Avon.

Mitch & Amy. Beverly Cleary. (J). 1991. 9.60 (*0-606-04747-6*, Pub. by Turtleback) Demco.

Mitch Miller. Edgar Lee Masters. (Collected Works of Edgar Lee Masters). 269p. 1999. reprint ed. lib. bdg. 98.00 (*1-58201-771-9*, c0771) Classic Bks.

Mitch Murray Book of One-Liners for Wedding Speeches & How to Use Them. Mitch Murray. 128p. (Orig.). 1994. pap. 18.95 (*0-572-01896-7*, Pub. by W Foulsham) Trans-Atl Phila.

***Mitch Murray's Handbook for the Terrified Speaker.** Mitch Murray. 2000. pap. 14.95 (*0-572-02459-2*) W Foulsham.

***Mitch Murray's One Liners for Business: How to Use Them in Your Speech.** Mitch Murray. 2000. pap. 14.95 (*0-572-02495-9*) Foulsham UK.

Mitchell: The Mitchell Record. C. B. Mitchell. (Illus.). 183p. 1992. reprint ed. pap. 27.00 (*0-8328-2288-4*); reprint ed. lib. bdg. 37.00 (*0-8328-2287-6*) Higginson Bk Co.

***Mitchell & Ruff: An American Profile in Jazz.** William Zinsser. 170p. 2000. reprint ed. pap. 14.95 (*0-9664913-4-3*, Pub. by Paul Dry Bks) IPG Chicago.

Mitchell Auto Body Repair Tech Manual. Duffy Scharff. 1997. pap. 12.00 (*0-7668-0632-4*) Delmar.

Mitchell Automotive Braking Systems. Mitchell International Inc. Staff. 208p. 1989. pap. 28.00 (*0-13-585480-6*) P-H.

Mitchell Beazley Pocket Guide to Garden Plants. Hugh Johnson et al. (Pocket Guides to Gardening Ser.). (Illus.). 100p. 1995. 12.95 (*1-85732-576-1*, Pub. by Reed Illust Books) Antique Collect.

Mitchell Beazley Pocket Guide to Gardening. Alan Titchmarsh & Mitchell Beazley. (Pocket Guides to Gardening Ser.). 100p. 1995. 12.95 (*1-85732-579-6*, Pub. by Reed Illust Books) Antique Collect.

Mitchell Beazley Pocket Guide to Indoor Plants. George Seddon & Mitchell Beazley. (Pocket Guides to Gardening Ser.). (Illus.). 100p. 1995. 12.95 (*1-85732-578-8*, Pub. by Reed Illust Books) Antique Collect.

Mitchell Beazley Pocket Guide to Old-Fashioned Roses. Orietta Sala & Mitchell Beazley. (Pocket Guides to Gardening Ser.). (Illus.). 100p. 1995. 12.95 (*1-85732-577-X*, Pub. by Reed Illust Books) Antique Collect.

Mitchell Beazley Red Wine Guide: A Complete Introduction to Choosing Red Wines. Jim Ainsworth. (Illus.). 192p. 1999. 21.95 (*1-84000-196-8*, Pub. by Mitchell Beazley) Antique Collect.

Mitchell Beazley White Wine Guide: A Complete Introduction to Choosing White Wines. Jim Ainsworth. (Illus.). 192p. 1999. 21.95 (*1-84000-197-6*, Pub. by Mitchell Beazley) Antique Collect.

Mitchell Brothers. Warren Hinckle. 1993. 23.00 (*0-679-41215-8*) McKay.

Mitchell County, Iowa. Leona Montag. (Illus.). 484p. 1989. 55.00 (*0-88107-151-X*) Curtis Media.

Mitchell D. Fardle. Lucinda Taylor. LC 93-28987. (Voyages Ser.). (Illus.). (J). 1994. 4.25 (*0-383-03761-1*) SRA McGraw.

***Mitchell Family Magazine: Genealogical, Historical & Biographical.** fac. ed. Ed. by Wm. M. Clemens. 96p. 1999. reprint ed. 28.00 (*0-8328-9981-X*); reprint ed. pap. 18.00 (*0-8328-9982-8*) Higginson Bk Co.

Mitchell Family of Tipton County, Tennessee: Their Antecedents in Colonial Southside Virginia, Including Jones & Bishop - & Their Numerous Descendents. Helen Goggans et al. (Illus.). 24p. 1990. 40.00 (*0-9626207-0-X*) Mitchell Family.

Mitchell-Giurgola Architects. (Master Architect Series II). (Illus.). 256p. 59.95 (*1-875498-50-8*) AIA Press.

Mitchell Guide to Diagnostics: Engine Performance, 1983-94 Cars, Light Trucks & Vans: Toyota/Lexus. Mitchell International Staff. LC 95-108937. 1994. write for info. (*0-8470-1442-8*) Mitchell Manuals Inc.

Mitchell Is Moving. Marjorie Weinman Sharmat. LC 85-47782. (Ready-to-Read Ser.: Level 2). (Illus.). 48p. (J). (ps-3). 1996. pap. 3.99 (*0-689-80876-3*) Aladdin.

Mitchell Is Moving. Marjorie Weinman Sharmat. LC 85-47782. (Ready-to-Read Ser.: Level 2). (Illus.). 48p. (J). (gr. k-4). 1996. mass mkt. 15.00 (*0-689-80875-5*) S&S Bks Yung.

Mitchell is Moving. Marjorie Weinman Sharmat. LC 78-6816. (Ready-to-Read Ser.). (J). 1978. 9.19 (*0-606-03861-2*, Pub. by Turtleback) Demco.

***Mitchell is Moving.** unabridged ed. Marjorie Weinman Sharmat. (Illus.). (J). (gr. k-2). 1998. pap. 15.95 incl. audio (*0-87499-425-X*) Live Oak Media.

***Mitchell is Moving, 4 bks., Set.** Marjorie Weinman Sharmat. (Illus.). (J). (gr. k-2). 1998. pap., teacher ed. 29.95 incl. audio (*0-87499-427-6*) Live Oak Media.

Mitchell Kennerley Imprint: A Bibliography. Daniel Boice. (Pittsburgh Series in Bibliography). (Illus.). 272p. 1996. 75.00 (*0-8229-3948-7*) U of Pittsburgh Pr.

Mitchell Leisen, Hollywood Director. expanded rev. ed. David Chierichetti. 1995. pap. text 19.95 (*0-929330-04-8*) Photoventures Co.

Mitchell Leisen, Hollywood Director. rev. ed. David Chierichetti. 1994. pap. 19.95 (*1-880756-07-2*) Riverwood Pr.

Mitchell Madison Group: A USWeb/CKS Company: The WetFeet.com Insider Guide. 2000th ed. WetFeet.com Staff. (Insider Guides Ser.). 51p. 1999. per. 25.00 (*1-58207-044-X*) WetFeet.

Mitchell, Pioneer of Air Power. Isaac D. Levine. LC 71-169426. (Literature & History of Aviation Ser.). 1972. reprint ed. 33.95 (*0-405-03777-5*) Ayer.

Mitchell, Taylor & Talbot on Confiscation & the Proceeds of Crime. 2nd ed. Andrew R. Mitchell et al. LC 98-230453. (Criminal Law Library). lxi, 778 p. 1997. write for info. (*0-421-56750-3*) Sweet & Maxwell.

Mitchell Tolle: American Artist. Garry Barker. 168p. 1992. 99.95 (*0-9644951-0-4*) Painted Treas.

Mitchell vs. Hughes: Negligence. 2nd rev. ed. John J. Sullivan. 116p. 1992. pap. 22.95 (*1-55681-320-1*) Natl Inst Trial Ad.

Mitchells: Five for Victory. Hilda Van Stockum. LC 94-79549. (Hilda Van Stockum Family Collection). (Illus.). 250p. (J). (gr. 4-10). 1995. reprint ed. pap. 12.95 (*1-883937-05-1*, 05-1) Bethlehem ND.

Mitchells Enviro & Service. Burberry. (C). 1997. pap. 62.95 (*0-582-24521-4*, Pub. by Addison-Wesley) Longman.

Mitchells Intro Building. Osbourn. (C). 1997. pap. 49.95 (*0-582-30200-5*, Pub. by Addison-Wesley) Longman.

Mitchell's Materials. 5th ed. Alan Everett. (C). 1994. pap. text 49.95 (*0-582-21923-X*, Pub. by Addison-Wesley) Longman.

Mitchell's Structure & Fabric, Vol. 1. 5th ed. Jack S. Foster. (Illus.). 260p. (C). 1994. pap. text 49.95 (*0-582-21605-2*, Pub. by Addison-Wesley) Trans-Atl Phila.

Mitchell's Structure & Fabric, Vol. 2. 5th ed. Jack S. Foster & Raymond Harington. (Illus.). 432p. (C). 1994. pap. text 52.95 (*0-582-21865-9*, Pub. by Addison-Wesley) Trans-Atl Phila.

Mitchelville: Experiment in Freedom. Michael Trinkley. (Illus.). 12p. 1995. pap. 1.00 (*1-58317-009-X*) Chicora Found.

***Mitchum: In His Own Words.** Ed. by Jerry Roberts. (Illus.). 240p. 2000. 28.95 (*0-87910-292-6*) Limelight Edns.

Eastern Visions: The Poetry of Central-East Europe. Ed. by Bradley R. Strahan. (International Anthologies Ser.). (Illus.). 52p. (Orig.). (C). 1997. pap. 7.00 (*0-938872-22-2*) Black Buzzard.

Mites: Ecology, Evolution & Behaviour. D. Eric Walters & Proctor. (CABI Publishing Ser.). 332p. 1999. 70.00 (*0-85199-375-3*) OUP.

***Mites of Australia: A Checklist & Bibliography.** B. Halliday. (Monographs on Invertebrate Taxonomy: Vol. 5). (Illus.). 317p. 1998. 120.00 (*0-643-06370-6*, Pub. by CSIRO) Accents Pubns.

Mitford Archives, Vol. 1. Francis W. Steer. 83p. 1961. 40.00 (*0-900801-23-9*) St Mut.

Mitford Archives, Vol. 2. Francis W. Steer. 67p. 1970. 45.00 (*0-900801-02-6*) St Mut.

Mitford Years: At Home in Mitford: A Light in the Window: These High, Green Hills. Jan Karon. (Mitford Years Ser.: Vol. 1-3). (Illus.). 1999. pap. 51.80 (*0-14-771256-4*) Viking Penguin.

Mitford's Japan: The Memoirs & Recollections, 1866-1906, of Algernon Bertram Mitford, the First Lord Redesdale. Ed. by Hugh Cortazzi. LC 85-15805. 270p. (C). 1985. text 36.50 (*0-485-11275-2*, Pub. by Athlone Pr) Humanities.

Mithai: Collection of Traditional Indian Sweets. Pramila Parmar. 1999. reprint ed. 16.00 (*81-85944-88-1*, Pub. by UBS Pubs) S Asia.

Mithani & Wheeler: The Disqualification of Company Directors. Abbas Mithani & Sally Wheeler. 570p. 1995. write for info. (*0-406-04362-0*, MICHIE) LEXIS Pub.

Mithradates Eupator, Koenig von Pontos: Mit Berichtigung und Nachtraegen Ins Deutsche Uebersetzt. Theodore Reinach. Tr. by A. Goetz. (GER.). 488p. 1975. reprint ed. lib. bdg. 125.00 (*3-487-05585-6*) G Olms Pubs.

Mithraic Mysteries Restored & Modernized: A Drama of Interior Initiation. Kenneth S. Guthrie. 216p. 1996. reprint ed. spiral bd. 16.00 (*0-7873-0362-3*) Hlth Research.

Mithraic Mysteries Restored & Modernized: A Drama of Interior Inititation. Kenneth S. Guthrie. 216p. 1993. reprint ed. pap. 14.95 (*1-56459-366-5*) Kessinger Pub.

Mithraic Ritual. G. R. Mead. 1994. pap. 6.95 (*1-55818-288-8*) Holmes Pub.

Mithras: Mysteries & Initiations Rediscovered. D. Jason Cooper. LC 96-10326. (Illus.). 192p. 1996. pap. 12.95 (*0-87728-865-8*) Weiser.

Mithriac Ritual. G. R. Mead. 77p. (Orig.). 1992. reprint ed. pap. 9.95 (*1-56459-117-4*) Kessinger Pub.

Mithridate. Jean Racine. (FRE., Illus.). 146p. 1992. pap. 10.95 (*0-7859-1255-X*, 2038701474) Fr & Eur.

MITI & the Japanese Miracle: The Growth of Industrial Policy, 1925-1975. Chalmers A. Johnson. LC 81-51330. xvi, 303p. 1982. 47.50 (*0-8047-1128-3*); pap. 16.95 (*0-8047-1206-9*) Stanford U Pr.

Miti E. Leggende: Myths & Legends, 4 vols. Ed. by Raffaele Pettazzoni & Kees W. Bolle. LC 77-79151. (Mythology Ser.). (ITA.). 1978. reprint ed. lib. bdg. 204.95 (*0-405-10560-6*) Ayer.

Miti, Leggende E Superstizioni Del Medio Evo, 2 vols. in 1. Arturo Graf. xxiv, 710p. 1985. reprint ed. write for info. (*3-487-07643-8*) G Olms Pubs.

Miticas Harley-Davidson. (Illus.). 450p. 1999. 39.95 (*3-89508-897-8*, 540186) Konemann.

Mitigating Bird Collisions. pap. 40.00 (*0-931032-33-4*) Edison Electric.

Mitigating Circumstances. Nancy Taylor Rosenberg. 448p. 1993. mass mkt. 6.99 (*0-451-17672-3*, Sig) NAL.

Mitigating Effects of Access Problems in Persian Gulf Contingencies. Paul K. Davis et al. LC 97-45901. (Illus.). 144p. 1999. pap. 15.00 (*0-8330-2570-8*, MR-915-OSD) Rand Corp.

Mitigating Misery: An Inquiry into the Political & Humanitarian Aspects of U. S. & Global Refugee Policy. Robert F. Gorman. LC 93-16035. 362p. (Orig.). (C). 1993. pap. text 29.50 (*0-8191-9176-0*); lib. bdg. 57.50 (*0-8191-9175-2*) U Pr of Amer.

Mitigating Natural Disasters. 164p. 1990. 30.00 (*92-1-132019-4*, 90.III.M.1) UN.

Mitigating Reactor Core Damage-BWR. (Illus.). 418p. 1981. teacher ed. 595.00 (*0-87683-076-9*); ring bd. 79.50 (*0-87683-075-0*) GP Courseware.

Mitigating Reactor Core Damage-PWR. (Illus.). 390p. 1981. teacher ed. 595.00 (*0-87683-078-5*); ring bd. 79.00 (*0-87683-077-7*) GP Courseware.

Mitigating the Impact of Impending Earthquakes: Earthquakes Prognostics Strategy Transferred into Practice. Ed. by Andreas Vogel & Klaus Brandes. (Illus.). 420p. (C). 1998. text 104.00 (*90-5410-801-0*, Pub. by A A Balkema) Ashgate Pub Co.

Mitigating the Millennium: Proceedings of a Seminar on Community Participation & Impact Measurement in Disaster Preparedness & Mitigation Programmes. Ed. by Jane Scobie. (Illus.). 74p. (C). 1998. pap. text 30.00 (*0-7881-7465-7*) DIANE Pub.

Mitigating Transport Pollution in Developing Countries: An Analysis of the Fuels Reformulation Option. Lakdasa Wijetilleke & Rapti Goonesekere. LC 98-30949. (World Bank Technical Paper Ser.). 1998. write for info. (*0-8213-4328-9*) World Bank.

***Mitigation & Cost Reduction Act of 1998.** LC 99-170819. iii, 130p. 1998. write for info. (*0-16-057621-0*) USGPO.

Mitigation Banking: Theory & Practice. Ed. by Douglas R. Porter et al. 225p. (Orig.). (C). 1996. pap. text 55.00 (*1-55963-371-9*) Island Pr.

Mitigation of Slavery. Ed. by William Dickson. LC 78-79013. (Black Heritage Library Collection). 1977. 26.95 (*0-8369-8655-5*) Ayer.

Mitigation Patterns of Adult Bull Trout in the Metoluis River & Lake Billy Chinook, Oregon. Steven L. Thiesfeld et al. 30p. 1998. reprint ed. pap. 4.00 (*0-89904-867-6*, Cascade Geog Soc) Crumb Elbow Pub.

Mitla Zapotec Texts: Folklore Texts in Mexican Indian Languages 3. Ed. by Morris Stubblefield & Carol Stubblefield. LC 93-86272. (Language Data, Amerindian Ser.: Vol. 12). 148p. (Orig.). 1995. pap. 15.75 (*0-88312-700-8*) S I L Intl.

Mitlesen-Mitteilen. 2nd ed. Wells. (C). 1994. 47.50 incl. audio (*0-03-010208-1*) Harcourt.

Mitlesen-Mitteilen 2E. 2nd ed. Larry D. Wells. (Illus.). 288p. (C). 1994. pap. text 46.00 (*0-03-072471-6*) Harcourt Coll Pubs.

Mito de Bourne. Robert Ludlum. 1998. pap. 12.95 (*84-08-00021-7*) Planeta.

Mito de Cofresi en la Narrativa Antillana. Roberto Fernandez-Valledor. LC 77-16653. (Coleccion Mente y Palabra). (Illus.). 149p. 1978. 5.00 (*0-8477-0557-9*); pap. 4.00 (*0-8477-0556-0*) U of PR Pr.

Mito de Edipoen la Tragedia Barroca Espanola Vol. 5: No Hay Resistencia a los Hados. Alejandro Arboreda. LC 92-46060. (Iberica Ser.: Vol. 5). (SPA.). 219p. (C). 1995. text 49.95 (*0-8204-1833-1*) P Lang Pubng.

Mito de Maria. Cesar Vidal. (Illus.). 192p. (Orig.). 1995. pap. 8.50 (*0-937958-46-8*) Chick Pubns.

Mito de Quetzalcoatl (The Myth of Quetzalcoatl) 2nd ed. Enrique Florescano. (SPA.). 182p. 1995. pap. 12.99 (*968-16-3993-6*, Pub. by Fondo) Continental Bk.

Mito del Acto Sexual Seguro. John Ankerberg & Weldon.Tr. of Myth about Safe Sex. (SPA.). pap. 9.99 (*1-56063-577-0*, 497725) Editorial Unilit.

Mito del Romance. Tr. of Myth of Romance. 1997. pap. text 7.99 (*0-88113-462-7*) Caribe Betania.

Mito e Historia. Miguel De Ferdinandy. (SPA.). 320p. 1995. pap. 17.95 (*0-8477-0214-6*) U of PR Pr.

Mito, Exilio y Demonios. Luis N. Rivera Pagan. (SPA.). 138p. 1997. pap. write for info. (*0-929441-99-0*) Pubns Puertorriquenas.

Mito Guadalupano see **Myth of the Virgin of Guadalupe**

Mito y Existencia. 2nd ed. Ludwig Schajowicz. LC 89-30505. (SPA.). 415p. 1990. pap. 12.75 (*0-8477-2830-7*) U of PR Pr.

Mitochondria. Scheffler. LC 99-23312. 367p. 1999. 99.95 (*0-471-19422-0*) Wiley.

Mitochondria. Alexander Tzagoloff. LC 81-23373. (Cellular Organelles Ser.). 358p. (C). 1982. 75.00 (*0-306-40799-X*, Plenum Trade); pap. 42.50 (*0-306-40778-7*, Plenum Trade) Perseus Pubng.

Mitochondria: DNA, Proteins & Disease. Ed. by V. Darley-Usmar & A. H. Shapira. LC 94-129580. (Portland Press Research Monographs: Vol. 5). (Illus.). xi, 286p. (C). 1994. text 102.00 (*1-85578-042-9*, Pub. by Portland Pr Ltd) Ashgate Pub Co.

Mitochondria: Structure, Biogenesis & Transducing Functions. Henry Tedeschi. (Cell Biology Monographs: Vol. 4). (Illus.). 180p. 1976. 87.95 (*0-387-81317-9*) Spr-Verlag.

***Mitochondria & Cell Death.** Guy Brown. 1999. 75.00 (*0-691-05026-0*) Princeton U Pr.

Mitochondria, Chloroplasts & Bacterial Membranes. J. N. Prebble. LC 80-40777. (Illus.). 392p. reprint ed. pap. 121.60 (*0-8357-6216-5*, 203450600090) Bks Demand.

Mitochondria 1983: Nucleo-Mitochondrial Interactions, Proceedings of a Conference Held in Schliersee, Germany, July 19-23, 1983. Ed. by R. J. Schweyen et al. LC 83-26341. xxv, 648p. 1984. 219.25 (*3-11-009871-7*) De Gruyter.

Mitochondria 1977: Genetics & Biogenesis of Mitochondria. Ed. by W. Bandlow et al. (C). 1977. 215.40 (*3-11-007321-8*) De Gruyter.

Mitochondrial Biogenesis & Breakdown. Valentin N. Luzikov. Tr. by Alexander V. Galkin from RUS. LC 84-12157. 378p. 1985. 95.00 (*0-306-10979-4*, Kluwer Plenum) Kluwer Academic.

Mitochondrial Biogenesis & Breakdown. Valentin N. Luzikov. Ed. by Donald B. Roodyn. Tr. by Alexander V. Galkin. LC 84-12157. (Illus.). 378p. 1985. reprint ed. pap. 117.20 (*0-608-05420-8*, 206588900006) Bks Demand.

Mitochondrial Biogenesis & Genetics, Pt. A. Ed. by Giuseppe M. Attardi et al. (Methods in Enzymology Ser.: Vol. 260). (Illus.). 540p. 1995. text 95.00 (*0-12-182161-7*) Acad Pr.

Mitochondrial Biogenesis & Genetics, Pt. B. Ed. by Giuseppe M. Attardi et al. (Methods in Enzymology Ser.: Vol. 264). (Illus.). 621p. 1996. text 95.00 (*0-12-182165-X*) Acad Pr.

Mitochondrial Diseases: Models & Methods. Ed. by Patrick Lestienne. LC 99-25405. (Illus.). 350p. 1999. 156.00 (*3-540-64177-7*) Spr-Verlag.

***Mitochondrial Disorders in Neurology.** A. H. Schapira & Dimauro. 288p. 2001. 95.00 (*0-7506-7288-9*) Buttrwrth-Heinemann.

Mitochondrial DNA in Human Pathology. Ed. by Salvatore DiMauro & Douglas C. Wallace. LC 92-49034. 218p. 1993. text 58.00 (*0-7817-0006-X*) Lppncott W & W.

Mitochondrial DNA Mutations in Aging, Disease & Cancer. Ed. by Keshav K. Singh. LC 97-50433. (Biotechnology Intelligence Unit Ser.). 346p. 1997. 175.00 (*3-540-64342-7*) Spr-Verlag.

Mitochondrial Free Radical Theory of Aging. Aubrey D. N. J. de Grey. LC QP86.D4 1999. (Molecular Biology Intelligence Unit Ser.: Vol. 9). 212p. 1999. 99.00 (*1-57059-564-X*) Landes Bioscience.

Mitochondrial Genes. Ed. by Piotr Slonimski et al. LC 81-68894. (Cold Spring Harbor Monographs: No. 12). 520p. reprint ed. pap. 161.20 (*0-7837-2000-9*, 204227400002) Bks Demand.

Mitochondrial Inhibitors & Neurodegenerative Disorders. Ed. by Paul R. Sanberg et al. LC 98-55467. (Contemporary Neuroscience Ser.). 360p. 1999. 125.00 (*0-89603-805-X*) Humana.

Mitochondriale Genexpression Bei Pilzen: Molekulare Analysen zur Nukleozytoplasmatischen Wechselwirkung. Ute Heinen. (Dissertationes Botanicae Ser.: Band 166). (GER., Illus.). viii, 107p. 1991. pap. 36.00 (*3-443-64078-8*, Pub. by Gebruder Borntraeger) Balogh.

Mitochondriale Genomveraenderungen und Altern: Struktur und Funktion eines Lineraren Plasmides einer Langlebigen Mutante Von Podospora Anserina. Josef Hennanns. (Bibliotheca Mycologica: Vol. 142). (GER., Illus.). 100p. 1992. 36.00 (*3-443-59043-8*, Pub. by Gebruder Borntraeger) Balogh.

Mitochondrion in Health & Disease. D. D. Tyler. 557p. 1991. 249.00 (*0-471-18792-5*, Wiley-VCH) Wiley.

Mitochondrion in Health & Disease. David D. Tyler. 557p. 1992. 125.00 (*1-56081-046-7*, Wiley-VCH) Wiley.

Mitologia Clasica. 2nd ed. A. Ruiz De Elvira. (SPA.). 540p. 1993. 100.00 (*84-249-0204-1*) Elliots Bks.

Mitologia Militar Chilena: Surrealismo Desde el Superego. Hernan Vidal. (Literature & Human Rights Ser.: Vol. 6). (SPA.). 170p. (Orig.). 1989. pap. 10.00 (*1-877660-03-5*) IFTSOIL.

Mitos en las Relaciones Mexico-E. U. (Myths in the Mexico-U. S. Relations) Esther Schumacher. (SPA.). 1995. pap. 23.99 (*968-16-4514-6*, Pub. by Fondo) Continental Bk.

Mitos y Leyendas de los Aztecas, Incas y Mayas (Myths & Legends of the Aztecs, Incas & Mayas) Walter Krickeberg. (SPA.). 268p. 1968. 19.99 (*968-16-0581-0*, Pub. by Fondo) Continental Bk.

Mitos y Leyendas Latino Americanas. 2nd ed. Jario Camacho. 1992. 10.15 (*0-606-10486-0*, Pub. by Turtleback) Demco.

M

An Asterisk (*) at the beginning of an entry indicates that the title is appearing for the first time.

Mitosenes & Related Antitumor Drugs: Rational Drug Design of Cytostatic Agents. Marc Maliepaard. (Medical Intelligence Unit Ser.). 139p. 1995. 99.00 (*1-57059-335-3*) Landes Bioscience.

Mitosis. Abramoff. Date not set. 1.20 (*0-7167-9015-7*) W H Freeman.

Mitosis. Helms. 1997. 1.50 (*0-7167-9312-1*) W H Freeman.

Mitosis. Ed. by Jeremy S. Hyams & B. R. Brinkley. 350p. 1989. text 136.00 (*0-12-363420-2*) Acad Pr.

Mitosis & Cytokinesis. Evert. 1998. 1.50 (*0-7167-9352-0*) W H Freeman.

Mitotes of John Igo. John Igo. (Poets Ser.). 56p. 1989. pap. 4.95 (*0-943373-13-1*) Natl Poet Foun.

Mitoxantrone for Injection Concentrate: Clinical Use in Bladder Cancer. Ed. by Chris Fellner. 7p. (Orig.). 1996. write for info. (*1-57130-020-1*) Medicine Grp USA.

Mitoxantrone for Injection Concentrate: Clinical Use in Hormone-Resistant Prostate Cancer. Ed. by Chris Fellner. 7p. (Orig.). 1996. write for info. (*1-57130-019-8*) Medicine Grp USA.

Mitoxantrone for Injection Concentrate: Clinical Use in Leukemia. Ed. by Chris Fellner. (Orig.). 1995. pap. write for info. (*1-57130-015-5*) Medicine Grp USA.

Mitoxantrone for Injection Concentrate: Clinical Use in Ovarian Cancer. Ed. by Chris Fellner. (Orig.). 1996. write for info. (*1-57130-017-1*) Medicine Grp USA.

Mitra & Aryaman. Paul Thieme. (Connecticut Academy of Arts & Sciences Ser., Trans.: Vol. 41). 1957. pap. 59.50 (*0-685-22893-2*) Elliots Bks.

Mitra-Varuna: An Essay on Two Indo-European Representations of Sovereignty. Georges Dumezil. Tr. by Derek Coltman from FRE. LC 87-34052. 189p. 1988. 26.95 (*0-942299-12-4*); pap. 13.50 (*0-942299-13-2*) Zone Bks.

*__Mitral Valve: Floppy Mitral Valve, Mitral Valve Prolapse, Mitral Valvular Regurgitation.__ 2nd rev. ed. Ed. by Harisios Boudoulas & Charles F. Wooley. (Illus.). 780p. 2000. 145.00 (*0-87993-448-4*) Futura Pub.

Mitral Valve Prolapse. (Landmark Ser.). 1979. 25.50 (*0-8422-4123-X*) Irvington.

Mitral Valve Prolapse. Richard B. Devereux. 350p. 1996. text. write for info. (*0-7817-0199-6*) Lppncott W & W.

Mitral Valve Prolapse: The Heart with a Different Beat. rev. ed. Nancy Tkaczuk. Ed. & Illus. by Nancy R. Hull. LC 86-22549. 16p. (Orig.). 1992. pap. text 6.50 (*0-939838-20-6*) Pritchett & Hull.

Mitration & Politics: The Impact of Population Mobility on American Voting Behavior. Thad A. Brown. LC 87-16240. (Illus.). 220p. reprint ed. pap. 68.20 (*0-608-08605-3*, 206912800003) Bks Demand.

Mitre & Crook. Bryan Houghton. 216p. 1994. text 12.95 (*0-912141-08-5*) Roman Cath Bks.

Mitreo dei Castra Peregrinorum: S. Stefano Rotondo. Elisa Lissi-Caronna. (Etudes Preliminaires aux Religions Orientales dans l'Empire Romain Ser.: Vol. 104). (Illus.). viii, 52p. 1986. pap. 71.00 (*90-04-07493-7*) Brill Academic Pubs.

Mitrofanovs Deflection. Victor Charushin. 1998. pap. 13.50 (*1-886846-12-X*) Pickard & Son.

Mitsou ou Comment l'Esprit Vient aux Filles. Sidonie-Gabrielle Colette. (FRE.). 1987. pap. 10.95 (*0-7859-3139-2*) Fr & Eur.

Mitsuaki Iwago's Penguins. Mitsuaki Iwago. LC 96-5622. (Illus.). 120p. 1996. pap. 19.95 (*0-8118-1440-8*) Chronicle Bks.

Mitsuaki Iwago's Whales. Mitsuaki Iwago. LC 96-119861. (Illus.). 96p. 1994. 29.95 (*0-8118-0585-9*); pap. 17.95 (*0-8118-0557-3*) Chronicle Bks.

Mitsubishi: Eclipse, 1990-98. Chilton Automotive Editorial Staff. (Total Car Care Ser.). (C). 1998. pap. 22.95 (*0-8019-8957-4*) Thomson Learn.

Mitsubishi: I&T Shop Manual - Models MT160, MT160D, MT180, MT180D, MT180H, MT180HD, MT210, MT210D, MT250, MT250D, MT300, MT300D. (Illus.). 80p. Date not set. reprint ed. pap. 24.95 (*0-87288-442-2*, M-1) Intertec Pub.

Mitsubishi: Its Challenge & Strategy. Yasua Mishima. LC 89-15451. (Industrial Development & the Social Fabric Ser.: Vol. 11). 350p. 1990. 73.25 (*1-55938-031-4*) Jai Pr.

Mitsubishi & the N. Y. K., 1870-1914: Business Strategy in the Japanese Shipping Industry. William D. Wray. (East Asian Monographs: No. 108). (Illus.). 325p. 1984. 40.00 (*0-674-57665-9*) HUP.

Mitsubishi A6M-1/2/-2N Zero-Sen of the Japanese Naval Air Service. rev. ed. Richard M. Bueschel. LC 95-67278. (Illus.). 80p. 1995. pap. 14.95 (*0-88740-754-4*) Schiffer.

Mitsubishi Cars & Trucks, 1983-89. Chilton Automotive Editorial Staff. LC 88-43191. (Illus.). 944p. 1990. pap. text 22.95 (*0-8019-7947-1*) Nichols Pub.

Mitsubishi Colt Automotive Repair Manual: 1982 Through 1990. Marc Scribner & John H. Haynes. LC 97-80264. (Haynes Automotive Repair Manual Ser.). 1997. write for info. (*1-56392-279-7*) Haynes Manuals.

Mitsubishi Eclipse, 1990-93. Chilton Automotive Editorial Staff. (Illus.). 800p. 1993. pap. 22.95 (*0-8019-8415-7*) Nichols Pub.

*__Mitsubishi-Galant/Mirage/Diamante 1990-2000.__ Chilton Automotive Editorial Staff. (Total Car Care Repair Manual Ser.). (C). 2000. pap. text 22.95 (*0-8019-9315-6*) NP-Chilton.

Mitsubishi Ki-67/Ki-109 HIRYU in Japanese Army Air Force Service. Richard M. Bueschel. LC 97-66914. 48p. 1997. pap. 14.95 (*0-7643-0350-3*) Schiffer.

Mitsubishi Lancer Automotive Repair Manual Larry Warren et al. LC 97-81292. (Haynes Automotive Repair Manual Ser.). 1998. write for info. (*1-56392-280-0*) Haynes Manuals.

Mitsubishi Magna Automotive Repair Manual. Eric Godfrey & John Harold Haynes. LC 97-73896. (Haynes Automotive Repair Manual Ser.). 1997. write for info. (*1-56392-268-1*); write for info. (*1-56392-269-X*) Haynes Manuals.

Mitsubishi Melody. John O'Donnell. Ed. by Genie Lester. 300p. 1997. pap. 14.95 (*0-9656874-0-6*) Bookmarkers Friend.

Mitsubishi Motors in Illinois: Global Strategies, Local Impacts. Margaret L. Chapman et al. LC 94-46195. 152p. 1995. 57.95 (*0-89930-972-0*, Quorum Bks) Greenwood.

Mitsubishi, 1985-89. Chilton Automotive Editorial Staff. 544p. (C). 1991. pap. 16.95 (*0-8019-8220-0*) Thomson Learn.

Mitsubishi Pajero Automotive Repair Manual. Larry Warren & John Harold Haynes. LC 97-80265. (Haynes Auto Repair Manual Ser.). 1997. write for info. (*1-56392-281-9*) Haynes Manuals.

Mitsubishi Pick-Ups & Montero 1983-1995. Chilton Automotive Editorial Staff. LC 94-69448. (Illus.). 928p. (C). 1996. pap. 22.95 (*0-8019-8666-4*) Thomson Learn.

*__Mitsubishi Type I Rikko Betty Units of World War 2.__ Osamu Tagaya. (Combat Aircraft Ser.: Vol. 22). (Illus.). 112p. 2000. pap. 19.95 (*1-84176-082-X*, 130589AE, Pub. by Ospry) Motorbooks Intl.

Mitsubishi/Nakajima G3M1/2/3 96 Rikko L3Y1/2 in Japanese Naval Air Service. Richard M. Bueschel. LC 96-70489. (Illus.). 64p. 1997. pap. 14.95 (*0-7643-0148-9*) Schiffer.

Mitt Magic: Finger Plays for Finger Puppets. Lynda S. Roberts. (Illus.). 89p. (Orig.). (ps-1). 1986. pap. 12.95 (*0-87659-111-X*) Gryphon Hse.

Mitt Man: A Novel. Mel Taylor. LC 98-38984. 352p. 1999. 24.00 (*0-688-16094-8*, Wm Morrow) Morrow Avon.

Mitteilungen des Gersamtarchivs der Deutschen Juden. (GER.). ix, 837p. 1992. write for info. incl. fiche (*0-318-70563-X*) G Olms Pubs.

Mittelaelterliche Ueberlieferungen Von Dagobert I, Vol. 62. Christoph Wehrli. (Geist und Werk der Zeiten Ser.). (GER.). 386p. 1982. 54.00 (*3-261-04914-6*) P Lang Pubng.

Mittelalter. Hans Delbruck. LC 80-2677. reprint ed. 63.50 (*0-404-18559-2*) AMS Pr.

Mittelalterliche Grabbild: Figuerliche Grabbilder des 11.bis 15. Kurt Bauch. (Illus.). 376p. (C). 1976. 415.40 (*3-11-004482-X*) De Gruyter.

Mittelalterliches Hausbuch. (GER.). xii, 53p. 1986. reprint ed. write for info. (*3-487-07721-3*) G Olms Pubs.

Mittelalterliches und Fruhneuzeitliches Reit- und Fahrzubehor aus dem Besitz der Kunstsammlungen der Veste Coburg. Axel Gelbhaar. (Nova Hippologica Ser.). (Illus.). 284p. 1997. reprint ed. 90.00 (*3-487-08380-9*) G Olms Pubs.

Mittelatterlichen Munzen. Reichmann & Co. Staff. (ENG & GER., Illus.). 151p. 1977. 15.00 (*0-915018-32-2*) Attic Bks.

Mitteleuropa: Between Europe & Germany. Ed. by Peter Katzenstein. LC 97-29740. 304p. 1997. 59.95 (*1-57181-124-9*) Berghahn Bks.

Mitteleuropa: History & Prospects. Ed. by Peter M. Stirk. (Studies in European Unity). 256p. 1994. 50.00 (*0-7486-0449-9*, Pub. by Edinburgh U Pr) Col U Pr.

Mitteleuropa & German Politics: 1848 to the Present. Jorg Brechtefeld. LC 95-52081. 240p. 1996. text 59.95 (*0-312-15841-6*) St Martin.

Mittelgriechische Sprichworter. Karl Krumbacher. 272p. 1969. reprint ed. write for info. (*0-318-71263-6*) G Olms Pubs.

Mittelhochdeutsche Glossare und Vokabulare in Schweizerischen Bibliotheken bis 1500. Heinrich Haenger. (Quellen und Forschungen zur Sprach und Kulturgeschichte der Germanischen Voelker: NF 44). 88p. (C). 1972. 78.45 (*3-11-003542-1*) De Gruyter.

Mittelhochdeutsche Grammatik. Helmut De Boor & Roswitha Wisniewski. 208p. 1997. text 14.00 (*3-11-015742-X*) De Gruyter.

Mittelhochdeutsche Grammatik. 9th ed. Helmut De Boor & Roswitha Wisniewski. (Sammlung Goeschen Ser.: Vol. 2209). (C). 1984. pap. text 15.25 (*3-11-010191-2*) De Gruyter.

Mittelhochdeutsche Minne - und Aventiureromane. Klaus Ridder. 400p. 1998. 116.00 (*3-11-015414-5*) De Gruyter.

Mittelhochdeutsche Minnereden II. Deutschen Akademie der Wissenschaften Staff & Gerhard Thiele. (Deutsche Texte des Mittelalters Ser.: Band XLI). (GER.). xxviii, 249p. 1967. write for info. (*3-296-17224-6*, Pub. by Weidmann) Lubrecht & Cramer.

*__Mittelhochdeutsche Minnereden und Minneallegorien der Prager Handschrift R VI Fc 26.__ Michael Mareiner. 1999. 52.95 (*3-906763-15-3*, Pub. by P Lang) P Lang Pubng.

Mittelhochdeutsches Woerterbuch, 4 vols. Benecke. (GER.). 1195.00 (*0-7859-7434-2*, 3777604666) Fr & Eur.

Mittelhochdeutsches Woerterbuch: Index, 4 vols. Benecke. (GER.). 1990. 995.00 (*0-7859-7433-4*, 3777604674) Fr & Eur.

Mittelirische Verslehren see Irische Texte: Mit Uebersetzung und Woerterbuch

Mittelmeerische Welt Als Geistige Landschaft und Geschichtsraum Im Fruhwerk von Albert Camus: Mit Ausblicken Auf Paul Valery, Giuseppe Tomasi di Lampedusa und Gottfried Benn. Claudia Lehmann. (Philosophie Ser.: Bd. 558). (GER.). 193p. 1998. 37.95 (*3-631-32626-2*) P Lang Pubng.

Mittelstufe, Moderner Deutscher Sprachgebrauch ein Lehrgang Fuer Fort see Deutsche Sprachlehre Fuer Auslaender

Mitten. Alvin R. Tresselt. LC 64-14436. (Illus.). 30p. (J). (ps-3). 1964. lib. bdg. 14.93 (*0-688-51053-1*) Lothrop.

Mitten. rev. ed. Alvin R. Tresselt. LC 64-14436. (Illus.). 40p. (J). (ps-3). 1989. mass mkt. 5.95 (*0-688-09238-1*, Wm Morrow) Morrow Avon.

Mitten: A Ukrainian Folktale. Jan Brett. (Illus.). 32p. (J). (ps-3). 1989. 15.95 (*0-399-21920-X*, G P Putnam) Peng Put Young Read.

Mitten: A Ukrainian Folktale. Jan Brett. (Illus.). 36p. (J). (ps). 1996. bds. 7.95 (*0-399-23109-9*, G P Putnam) Peng Put Young Read.

*__Mitten: A Ukrainian Folktale.__ gif. ed. Jan Brett. (Illus.). 32p. (J). 1998. boxed set 14.99 (*0-399-23360-1*) Putnam Pub Group.

Mitten: An Old Ukrainian Folktale. Alvin R. Tresselt. (J). 1989. 10.15 (*0-606-04277-6*, Pub. by Turtleback) Demco.

Mitten Book: Delightful Swedish Country Mitten Patterns. Inger Gottfridsson & Ingrid Gottfridsson. (Illus.). 140p. 1987. pap. 8.95 (*0-937274-36-4*) Lark Books.

Mitten Recycling Pattern, Royal Neck Attire & String Potpourri Pattern Poems. Patterns by Alfreda Staff. 1984. pap. text 5.00 (*0-318-04428-5*) Prosperity & Profits.

*__Mitten Strings for God: Reflections for Mothers in a Hurry.__ Katrina Kenison. LC 99-44625. (Illus.). 240p. 2000. 16.95 (*0-446-52531-6*, Pub. by Warner Bks) Little.

Mitten Tree. Candace Christiansen. LC 96-53358. (Illus.). (J). (gr. 1). 1997. 16.95 (*1-55591-349-0*) Fulcrum Pub.

*__Mittens.__ Brighter Vision Staff. 1999. pap. text 2.50 (*1-55254-070-7*) Brighter Vision.

*__Mittens.__ Clare Newberry. LC 97-62211. (Newberry Ser.). (Illus.). 32p. (J). (ps-3). 1998. 9.98 (*0-7651-9059-1*) Smithmark.

Mittens. Jean Warren. Ed. by Kathleen Cubley. (Sticker Book Ser.). (Illus.). 32p. (J). (ps). 1998. pap. 3.95 (*1-57029-222-1*, 3712) Totline Pubns.

Mittens, Mittens, & More Mittens! Laura Maryon. LC 98-60944. (Illus.). 32p. (J). (ps-4). 1998. pap. 11.99 (*1-57921-138-0*, Pub. by WinePress Pub) BookWorld.

Mittens, Peanut, Robbie, & Friends. Orpha N. Wilson. LC 97-91079. (J). 1998. 10.95 (*0-533-12557-X*) Vantage.

Mitternacht Spiel see Midnight Play

Mitterrand: A Political Biography. Wayne Northcutt. LC 91-29986. 416p. 1992. 42.95 (*0-8419-1295-5*) Holmes & Meier.

Mitterrand Era: Policy Alternatives & Political Mobilization in France. Ed. by Anthony Daley. 360p. (C). 1996. text 50.00 (*0-8147-1872-8*) NYU Pr.

Mitterrand Legacy & the Future of French Security Policy. (Illus.). 68p. 1995. pap. text 30.00 (*1-57979-173-5*) DIANE Pub.

Mitterrand Legacy & the Future of French Security Policy. Ronald Tiersky. (Illus.). 67p. (C). 1996. pap. text 25.00 (*0-7881-2714-4*) DIANE Pub.

Mitterrand's France. Ed. by Sonia Mazey & Michael Newman. 256p. 1987. lib. bdg. 67.50 (*0-7099-4648-1*, Pub. by C Helm) Routldge.

Mittheilungen Aus Altdeutschen Handschriften. Anton E. Schonbach. (GER.). 626p. 1976. reprint ed. write for info. (*3-487-05985-1*) G Olms Pubs.

Mittleider Basics Course. Jacob R. Mittleider. write for info. (*1-929982-04-6*) Food For Every.

*__Mittleider Gardening Course.__ Jacob R. Mittleider. (Illus.). 268p. 1999. pap. 29.95 (*1-929982-03-8*) Food For Every.

Mittleider Grow-Box Gardens. Jacob R. Mittleider. LC 78-52953. Orig. Title: More Food from Your Garden. (Illus.). 194p. 1975. reprint ed. mass mkt. 16.95 (*1-929982-02-X*) Food For Every.

Mittrin. Mark Dunster. 15p. (Orig.). 1987. pap. 4.00 (*0-89642-151-1*) Linden Pubs.

Mitverschulden des Patienten Im Arzthaftungsrecht. Jens Goben. (Recht und Medizin Ser.: Vol. 39). XIII, 180p. 1998. pap. 37.95 (*3-631-31574-0*) P Lang Pubng.

Mitzi's Office Jokes. E. C. Stangland. 1981. 2.00 (*0-9602692-6-6*) Norse Pr.

Mitzvah. Jacob Neusner. (J). (gr. 6-8). pap. 7.95 (*0-317-70156-8*) Behrman.

*__Mitzvah.__ Aaron Zelman & L. Neil Smith. 245p. (YA). (gr. 7 up). 1999. mass mkt. 7.95 (*0-9642304-3-7*) Jews Preserv Firearms.

Mitzvah: Basic Jewish Ideas. Jacob Neusner. (Ser.). (Orig.). (J). (gr. 6-8). 1981. pap. 6.95 (*0-940646-25-0*) Rossel Bks.

Mitzvah Girl. Beverly Geller. LC 99-52666. 24p. (J). 1999. 12.95 (*965-229-203-6*) Gefen Pub Hse.

Mitzvah Is Something Special. Phyllis R. Eisenberg. LC 77-25664. (Illus.). 32p. (J). (gr. k-4). 1978. 12.95 (*0-06-021807-X*) HarpC Child Bks.

Mitzvah Mouse: Children Do Good Deeds. David R. Goodman. 24p. (J). 1992. 8.95 (*965-229-069-6*, Pub. by Gefen Pub Hse) Gefen Bks.

Mitzvah of the Month, 13 vols, Set. Incl. No. 1. Kriyat Shema al Hametah. pap. 1.00 No. 2. Mishloach Matanot Laevyonim. pap. 1.00 No. 3. Maot Chittim. pap. 1.00 No. 4. Sefirat Haomer. pap. 1.00 No. 5. Talmud Torah. pap. 1.00 No. 6. Hanukat Habayit. pap. 1.00 No. 7. Tzedakah. pap. 1.00 No. 8. Shamor V'Zachor et Yom Hashabbat L'Kadsho. pap. 1.00 No. 9. Bikkur Cholim. pap. 1.00 No. 10. Kibbud Av V'Em. pap. 1.00 No. 11. Tallit. pap. 1.00 No. 12. Lo T'Kallel Cheresh V'Lifnay Iver lo Titen Michshol. pap. 1.00 No. 13. Eesor L'Shon Hara. pap. 1.00 Set pap. 10.50 (*0-686-95940-X*) USCJE.

Mitzvos We Can Do. Tzipa Rosenthal. (ArtScroll Youth Ser.). (Illus.). 32p. (J). (gr. 1-8). 1982. 13.99 (*0-89906-775-1*); pap. 9.99 (*0-89906-776-X*) Mesorah Pubns.

Mitzvot. Amye Rosenberg. (Illus.). 30p. (J). (gr. 1-5). pap. text 4.95 (*0-87441-387-7*) Behrman.

Mitzvot: A Sourcebook for the 613 Commandments. Ronald H. Isaacs. LC 96-13668. 280p. 1996. 35.00 (*1-56821-900-8*) Aronson.

MIW History Set, 6 vols. Ed. by World Book Staff. 1998. write for info. (*0-7166-4609-9*) World Bk.

MIW Science Set, 14 vols. Ed. by World Book Staff. 1999. write for info. (*0-7166-4730-3*) World Bk.

Miwok Balanophagy: Implications for the Cultural Development of Some California Acorn-Eaters. Peter J. Mayer. (Archaeological Research Facility, Dept. of Anthropology, Miscellaneous Papers, Berkeley CA). 43p. (C). 1976. pap. 4.38 (*1-55567-648-0*) Coyote Press.

Miwok Cults. fac. ed. Edward W. Gifford. (University of California Publications in American Archaeology & Ethnology: Vol. 18: 3). 19p. (C). 1926. reprint ed. pap. text 2.50 (*1-55567-234-5*) Coyote Press.

Miwok Indians. Kim Covert. (Native Peoples Ser.). (J). 1998. 14.00 (*0-516-21355-5*) Childrens.

Miwok Material Culture. Samuel A. Barrett & E. W. Gifford. (Public Museum of the City of Milwaukee, Bulletins Ser.: No. 2). (Illus.). 260p. (C). 1933. pap. text 27.50 (*1-55567-740-1*) Coyote Press.

Miwok Material Culture: Indian Life of the Yosemite Region. Samuel A. Barrett & Edward W. Gifford. LC 76-43652. (Illus.). 261p. 1982. reprint ed. pap. 7.95 (*0-939666-12-X*) Yosemite Assn.

Miwok Moieties. fac. ed. E. W. Gifford. (University of California Publications in American Archaeology & Ethnology: Vol. 12: 4). 56p. (C). 1916. reprint ed. pap. text 6.88 (*1-55567-203-5*) Coyote Press.

Miwok Myths. fac. ed. E. W. Gifford. (University of California Publications in American Archaeology & Ethnology: Vol. 12: 8). 55p. (C). 1917. reprint ed. pap. text 6.56 (*1-55567-205-1*) Coyote Press.

Mix & Match. Lorenz Books Staff. (Let's Look Ser.). (Illus.). 96p. (J). 1998. pap. 4.95 (*1-85967-520-4*, Lorenz Bks) Anness Pub.

*__Mix & Match.__ Lorenz Books Staff. (Illus.). (J). 2000. 16.95 (*0-7548-0379-1*, Lorenz Bks) Anness Pub.

*__Mix & Match Animal & Star Signs.__ Richard Craze. (Illus.). 128p. 2000. spiral bd. 24.95 (*0-7641-5302-1*) Barron.

Mix & Match Assortment. Barron's Educational Editors. 1999. 24.95 (*0-7641-7313-8*) Barron.

Mix & Match Astrology. Lori Reid. 128p. 1997. 24.95 (*0-7641-5054-5*) Barron.

Mix & Match Book of Dinosaurs. George Sanders. LC 92-168128. (Illus.). 12p. (J). (ps-3). 1992. reprint ed. pap. 8.99 (*0-671-76911-1*) Litle Simon.

*__Mix-&-Match Color Guide to Annuals & Perennials.__ 200p. 2001. 24.95 (*0-7370-0629-3*) Time-Life Educ.

Mix & Match Designer's Colors. 80p. 1991. 34.99 (*1-56496-009-9*) Rockport Pubs.

Mix & Match Designer's Type. 80p. 1992. 34.99 (*1-56496-010-2*) Rockport Pubs.

Mix & Match Fashions: Story Book & Key Chain Craft Kit. Rita Balducci. (Barbie Mix & Match Bks.). (Illus.). 16p. (J). (gr. k-3). 1999. spiral bd. 7.99 (*1-57584-334-X*, Pub. by Rdrs Digest) S&S Trade.

Mix & Match Gardening. Lindsey Thomas. LC 98-6395. (Illus.). 144p. 1998. 24.95 (*0-7641-5118-5*) Barron.

Mix & Match Ideas for Preschool Ministry. Ed. by Jan Kershner. LC 97-1963. 120p. (Orig.). 1997. pap. 14.99 (*0-7644-2021-6*) Group Pub.

Mix & Match Jokes. Viki Woodworth. LC 92-38580. (Funny Side Up Ser.). (Illus.). 24p. (J). (gr. 1-4). 1995. lib. bdg. 19.93 (*1-56766-063-0*) Childs World.

*__Mix & Match Scrap Quilting.__ Ed. by Jeanne Stauffer & Sandra L. Hatch. 176p. 2000. 19.95 (*1-882138-59-7*) Hse White Birches.

*__Mix & Match Sun & Moon Signs.__ Richard Craze. (Illus.). 128p. 2000. spiral bd. 24.95 (*0-7641-5304-8*) Barron.

Mix Design Methods for Asphalt Concrete MS-2. 6th ed. 92p. 1994. 15.00 (*0-317-05939-4*) Asphalt Inst.

Mix It Up. Jackie Gannaway. 32p. 1997. pap. 3.95 (*1-885597-21-5*) Cookbook Cup.

Mix It Up! The Science of Chemistry. Kids Publishing Science. 1999. pap. text 6.95 (*1-891418-15-7*) Science Kids.

*__Mix Me a Murder.__ large type ed. Leo Grex. 304p. 1999. pap. 18.99 (*0-7089-5505-3*, Linford) Ulverscroft.

Mix-of-Voices in Human Services Contracting. Marsi Fein. 242p. (Orig.). 1995. pap. 20.00 (*1-886949-06-9*) Union Inst.

Mix of Years. William S. Morse. LC 97-26811. 1997. pap. 20.00 (*0-9642213-5-7*) Moose Cntry.

Mix or Match. Tegan James. 1998. mass mkt. 3.99 (*1-85487-593-0*, Pub. by Scarlet Bks) London Brdge.

*__Mix-Up Counting Book.__ Goldern Books Staff. (Illus.). (J). 2000. 9.99 (*0-307-10614-4*) Gldn Bks Pub Co.

Mix Your Own Acrylics. Jill Mirza & Nick Harris. (Artist's Library Ser.). 64p. (Orig.). 1997. pap. 7.95 (*1-56010-224-1*, AL28) W Foster Pub.

Mix Your Own Acrylics. Jill Mizra & Nick Harris. 64p. 1995. 6.98 (*0-7858-0266-5*) Bk Sales Inc.

Mix Your Own Oils. Jeremy Galton. 64p. 1995. 6.98 (*0-7858-0264-9*) Bk Sales Inc.

Mix Your Own Oils. Ed. by Jeremy Galton. (Artist's Library Ser.). 64p. 1997. pap. 7.95 (*1-56010-250-0*, AL29) W Foster Pub.

Mix Your Own Watercolors. John Lidzey. 64p. 1995. 6.98 (*0-7858-0265-7*) Bk Sales Inc.

Mix Your Own Watercolors. John Lidzey. (Artist's Library Ser.). 64p. 1997. pap. 7.95 (*1-56010-223-3*, AL27) W Foster Pub.

Mixail Soloxov in Yugoslavia: Reception & Literary Impact. Robert F. Price. (East European Monographs: No. 4). 180p. 1973. text 69.00 (*0-231-03748-1*, Pub. by East Eur Monographs) Col U Pr.

Mixe of Oaxaca: Religion, Ritual, & Healing. Frank J. Lipp. (Illus.). 275p. 1998. pap. 16.95 (*0-292-74705-5*) U of Tex Pr.

An Asterisk (*) at the beginning of an entry indicates that the title is appearing for the first time.

Mixed & Hybrid Finite Element Methods. M. Fortin & F. Brezzi. Ed. by R. L. Graham et al. (Computational Mathematics Ser.: Vol. 15). (Illus.). ix, 350p. 1991. 75.95 (*0-387-97582-9*) Spr-Verlag.

Mixed & Matched: Interreligious Courtship & Marriage in Northern Ireland. Raymond M. Lee. (Class, Ethnicity, Gender, & the Democratic Nation Ser.: Vol. 2). 154p. (C). 1992. lib. bdg. 39.50 (*0-8191-8480-2*) U Pr of Amer.

Mixed & Pure Forest Plantations in the Tropics & Subtropics. 158p. 1992. 19.00 (*92-5-103216-5*, F32165, Pub. by FAO) Bernan Associates.

Mixed Banking & Economic Growth in Germany, 1850-1931. Holger L. Engberg. Ed. by Stuart Bruchey. LC 80-2806. (Dissertations in European Economic History Ser.). (Illus.). 1981. lib. bdg. 29.95 (*0-405-13990-X*) Ayer.

Mixed Blessing. 1986. mass mkt. 4.50 (*0-446-73365-2*, Pub. by Warner Bks) Little.

Mixed Blessing. Helen Van Slyke. 1990. pap. 27.50 (*0-449-08491-4*) Fawcett.

***Mixed Blessing: Impact of the American Colonial Experience on Politics & Society in the Philippines.** Ed. by Hazel M. McFerson. Vol. 41. 2001. write for info. (*0-313-30791-1*) Greenwood.

Mixed Blessing of Financial Inflows: Transition Countries in Comparative Perspective. Ed. by Janos Gacs et al. LC 98-31843. 272p. 1999. 90.00 (*1-84064-038-3*) E Elgar.

Mixed Blessings. William Christopher & Barbara Christopher. 240p. 1990. mass mkt. 4.95 (*0-380-70999-6*, Avon Bks) Morrow Avon.

Mixed Blessings. Paula Ripple Comin. LC 98-37485. 160p. 1999. pap. 9.95 (*0-87793-666-8*) Ave Maria.

***Mixed Blessings.** Rick Hamlin. LC 99-50403. 304p. 2000. pap. 10.99 (*0-7642-2326-7*) Bethany Hse.

***Mixed Blessings.** Rick Hamlin. LC 00-32538. 2000. write for info. (*0-7862-2750-8*) Thorndike Pr.

Mixed Blessings. D. K. Jones. 76p. (Orig.). 1997. pap. 6.95 (*0-9640186-1-6*) Ginabean Bks.

Mixed Blessings. Danielle Steel. 384p. 1992. 23.50 (*0-385-29910-9*) Delacorte.

Mixed Blessings. Danielle Steel. 432p. 1993. mass mkt. 6.99 (*0-440-21411-4*) Dell.

Mixed Blessings. limited ed. Danielle Steel. 384p. 1992. 150.00 (*0-385-30664-4*) Delacorte.

Mixed Blessings. 2nd ed. Barbara Brown Taylor. LC 98-36650. 144p. 1998. 10.95 (*1-56101-162-2*) Cowley Pubns.

Mixed Blessings: An Almost Ordinary Life in Hitler's Germany. Heinz R. Kuehn. LC 88-4744. (Illus.). 240p. 1989. 19.95 (*0-8203-1046-8*) U of Ga Pr.

Mixed Blessings: Gender & Religious Fundamentalism Cross Culturally. Ed. by Judy Brink & Joan Mencher. 264p. (C). 1996. pap. 20.99 (*0-415-91186-9*) Routledge.

Mixed Blessings: Intensive Care for Newborns. Jeanne H. Guillemin & Lynda L. Holmstrom. 336p. 1990. reprint ed. pap. text 19.95 (*0-19-506659-6*) OUP.

***Mixed Blessings: New Art in a Multicultural America.** Lucy R. Lippard. 2000. pap. 27.95 (*1-56584-573-0*, Pub. by New Press NY) Norton.

Mixed Blessings: Overcoming the Stumbling Blocks in an Interfaith Marriage. Paul Cowan & Rachel Cowan. 288p. 1988. pap. 13.95 (*0-14-011189-1*, Penguin Bks) Viking Penguin.

Mixed Blessings of Success: The Hecht Company & Department Store Branch Development after World War II. Richard Longstreth. (Occasional Papers: No. 014). (Illus.). 15p. (Orig.). 1995. pap. 7.50 (*1-888028-26-2*) GWU Ctr WAS.

Mixed Blood. Marilyn Bates. 36p. 1998. pap. 6.00 (*0-9663293-4-1*) Main St Rag.

Mixed Blood: Intermarriage & Ethnic Identity in Twentieth-Century America. Paul R. Spickard. LC 89-31235. 544p. 1989. reprint ed. pap. 168.70 (*0-608-07439-X*, 206766600009) Bks Demand.

Mixed Blood: Intermarriage & Ethnic Identity in Twentieth-Century America. Paul R. Spickard. LC 89-31235. 544p. (C). 1991. reprint ed. pap. 22.95 (*0-299-12114-3*) U of Wis Pr.

Mixed-Bloods & Tribal Dissolution: Charles Curtis & the Quest for Indian Identity. William E. Unrau. LC 89-31799. (Illus.). xii, 244p. 1989. 27.50 (*0-7006-0395-6*) U Pr of KS.

Mixed-Bloods, Apaches, & Cattle Barons: Documents for a History of the Livestock Economy on the White Mountain Reservation, Arizona. Thomas R. McGuire. (Archaeological Ser.: Vol. 142). (Illus.). 227p. 1980. 13.95 (*1-889747-56-4*) Ariz St Mus.

Mixed Boundary Value Problems of Potential Theory & Their Applications in Engineering. V. I. Fabrikant. (C). 1991. text 264.50 (*0-7923-1157-4*) Kluwer Academic.

Mixed Breed: An Owner's Guide to a Happy Healthy Pet. Jeanette Stark. (Illus.). 160p. 1996. 12.95 (*0-87605-399-1*) Howell Bks.

***Mixed Breed Cats: A Complete Pet Owner's Manual.** Karen Leigh Davis. LC 99-15226. 104p. 1999. pap. text 6.95 (*0-7641-0805-0*) Barron.

Mixed Carbonate-Siliciclastic Sequences. A. J. Lomando & P. M. Harris. (Core Workshop Notes Ser.: Vol. 15). 568p. 1991. pap. 71.00 (*0-918985-87-0*) SEPM.

Mixed Categories. Claire Lefebvre & Pieter Muysken. (C). 1988. lib. bdg. 127.00 (*1-55608-050-6*) Kluwer Academic.

Mixed Class Kit: Individual Sets in a Kit. Marion W. Stuart. text, teacher ed. write for info. (*0-943343-45-3*) Lrn Wrap-Ups.

Mixed Class Kit: 12 Sets of Each to a Kit. Marion W. Stuart. text, teacher ed. write for info. (*0-943343-46-1*) Lrn Wrap-Ups.

Mixed Company. James Crichton. 160p. (C). 1988. pap. text 29.00 (*0-7152-0626-5*) St Mut.

Mixed Company. Clay Franklin. 100p. 1959. 5.00 (*0-573-60070-8*) French.

Mixed Company. John C. Robertson. LC 77-107735. (Essay Index Reprint Ser.). 1977. 20.95 (*0-8369-1533-X*) Ayer.

Mixed Company. Alan Shapiro. LC 95-35099. (Phoenix Poets Ser.). 90p. 1996. pap. 11.95 (*0-226-75031-0*); lib. bdg. 35.00 (*0-226-75030-2*) U Ch Pr.

Mixed Convection Heat Transfer, 1993. Ed. by M. Keyhani & R. Kumar. (HTD Ser.: Vol. 247). 96p. 1993. 35.00 (*0-7918-1160-3*, G00804) ASME.

Mixed Couples. James Prideaux. 1981. pap. 5.25 (*0-8222-0766-4*) Dramatists Play.

Mixed Courts of Egypt. Mark S. Hoyle. (Arab & Islamic Laws Ser.). (C). 1991. lib. bdg. 126.50 (*1-85333-321-2*, Pub. by Graham & Trotman) Kluwer Academic.

Mixed Crystals. A. I. Kitaigorodsky. (Solid-State Sciences Ser.: Vol. 33). (Illus.). 400p. 1984. 102.95 (*0-387-10922-6*) Spr-Verlag.

Mixed Design of Integrated Circuits & Systems. Ed. by Andrzej Napieralski et al. LC 97-48316. 256p. 1998. lib. bdg. 110.00 (*0-7923-8116-5*) Kluwer Academic.

Mixed Doubles. Kathryn Bellamy. (Scarlet Ser.). 1997. mass mkt. 3.99 (*1-85487-988-X*, Pub. by Scarlet Bks) London Brdge.

Mixed Doubles. Z. Verdier. 1999. mass mkt. 6.95 (*0-352-33312-X*) BLA4.

Mixed Doubles. large type ed. Ann Purser. LC 98-44589. 1999. 30.00 (*0-7862-1712-X*) Thorndike Pr.

Mixed Drinks: Take a Poetic Drink : a Drink of Poetry. Delsue O. Welch. LC 98-90005. 91p. 1998. write for info. (*0-9662526-0-8*) Welch Pub.

Mixed Economic Progress of Immigrants. Robert F. Schoeni et al. LC 96-21392. 138p. (Orig.). 1996. pap. text 15.00 (*0-8330-2390-X*, MR-763-IF/FF) Rand Corp.

Mixed Economies in Europe: An Evolutionary Perspective on Their Emergence, Transition & Regulation. Ed. by Wolfgang Blaas & John Foster. (European Association for Evolutionary Political Economy Ser.). 320p. 1993. 95.00 (*1-85278-728-7*) E Elgar.

Mixed Economy: Proceedings of Section F (economics) of The British Association for The Advancement of Science, Salford, 1980. Eric Roll & British Association for the Advancement of Science Staff. LC 82-174648. 233 p. 1982. write for info. (*0-333-31540-5*) Macmillan.

Mixed Economy & Liberalization: A Study of Bihar. Sharat Kumar. (C). 1992. 20.00 (*81-7001-089-6*, Pub. by Chanakya) S Asia.

***Mixed Effects Models in S & S-Plus.** Jose C. Pinheiro & Douglas M. Bates. LC 99-53566. (Statistics & Computing Ser.). (Illus.). 552p. 2000. 69.95 (*0-387-98957-9*) Spr-Verlag.

Mixed Emotions. Charlotte Vale Allen. 250p. 1998. pap. 20.00 (*0-9657437-8-0*) Isld Nation.

Mixed Emotions. Charlotte Vale Allen. 1991. 19.00 (*0-7278-4159-9*) Severn Hse.

Mixed Emotions. Richard Baer. LC 95-230940. 1994. pap. 5.25 (*0-8222-1395-8*) Dramatists Play.

Mixed Emotions. Greg Child. 1994. 24.75 (*0-8446-6745-5*) Peter Smith.

Mixed Emotions. David Muschell. 24p. 1990. pap. 3.50 (*0-87129-010-3*, M77) Dramatic Pub.

Mixed Emotions. Charlotte Vale Allen. 260p. 1998. reprint ed. 22.95 (*1-892738-13-9*, Pub. by Isld Nation) Brodart.

Mixed Emotions: Certain Steps Toward Understanding Ambivalence. Andrew J. Weigert. LC 90-9888. (SUNY Series in the Sociology of Emotions). 197p. (C). 1991. pap. text 21.95 (*0-7914-0601-6*) State U NY Pr.

Mixed Emotions: Mountaineering Writings of Greg Child. Greg Child. 272p. 1993. pap. 14.95 (*0-89886-363-5*) Mountaineers.

Mixed Feelings. Cynthia Ehrlich. 1999. pap. 17.95 (*0-525-24786-6*) NAL.

Mixed Feelings: Feminism, Mass Culture & Victorian Sensationalism. Ann Cvetkovich. LC 92-4457. x, 227p. (C). 1992. pap. text 19.00 (*0-8135-1857-1*) Rutgers U Pr.

Mixed Finite Element Method. A. Poceski. (Lecture Notes in Engineering Ser.: Vol. 72). (Illus.). 352p. 1992. 100.95 (*0-387-54916-1*) Spr-Verlag.

Mixed-Flow Hydrodynamics, Vol. 1. Ed. by Nicholas P. Cheremisinoff. (Advances in Engineering Fluid Mechanics Ser.: Vol. 11). (Illus.). 914p. 1996. 155.00 (*0-88415-256-1*, 5256) Gulf Pub.

Mixed Fortunes. William A. Hayward. (C). 1989. text 40.00 (*0-948929-17-0*) St Mut.

Mixed Fruits. Les Thurston. Ed. by Ruth Campbell. (Illus.). 96p. (Orig.). 1994. pap. 5.00 (*1-885761-00-7*) Turner Geriatric.

Mixed-Gas Diving. 1997. lib. bdg. 251.99 (*0-8490-8127-0*) Gordon Pr.

Mixed Harvest: The Second Great Transformation in the Rural North, 1870-1930. Hal S. Barron. LC 96-51451. (Studies in Rural Culture). 320p. (gr. 13). 1997. 19.95 (*0-8078-4659-7*); lib. bdg. 55.00 (*0-8078-2354-6*) U of NC Pr.

Mixed Hodge Structures & Singularities. Valentine S. Kulikov. LC 97-11978. (Tracts in Mathematics Ser.: No. 132). (Illus.). 150p. (C). 1998. text 44.95 (*0-521-62060-0*) Cambridge U Pr.

***Mixed-Income Housing: In Memory of Donald Terner.** Ed. by Langley C. Keyes & Jill Khadduri. (Illus.). 92p. (C). 1999. reprint ed. pap. text 20.00 (*0-7881-8272-2*) DIANE Pub.

Mixed International Arbitration: Studies in Arbitration between States & Private Persons. 436p. 1993. text 100.00 (*0-521-46318-1*) Cambridge U Pr.

Mixed International Arbitration: Studies in Arbitration Between States & Private Persons. Stephen J. Toope. 436p. (C). 1990. 130.00 (*0-949009-81-4*, Pub. by Grotius Pubns Ltd) St Mut.

Mixed Language Programming for Windows. Matthew Telles. LC 94-13388. 1994. pap. 39.95 incl. disk (*1-55851-332-9*, M&T Bks) IDG Bks.

***Mixed Legacy of Charlotte Perkins Gilman.** Catherine Golden & Joanna S. Zangrando. LC 99-43538. 240p. 2000. 39.50 (*0-87413-688-1*) U Delaware Pr.

Mixed Matches: How to Create Successful Interracial, Interethnic & Interfaith Marriages. Joel Crohn. 304p. (Orig.). 1995. pap. 13.00 (*0-449-90961-1*) Fawcett.

***Mixed Media.** Jose M. Parramon. 95p. 1999. pap. 18.95 (*84-89730-95-4*) LEMA.

Mixed Media Cookbook. write for info. (*0-918386-33-0*) W Benton Mus.

Mixed Medicine Bag: Original Folk-Tales from a Black Wampanaoag Culture, the Red Book, Vol. 2. Mwalimu. Ed. by Shirley Nurse et al. (YA). 1999. pap. 7.00 (*0-9662428-1-5*) Talking Drum Pr.

Mixed Medicine Bag Vol. 4: Original Folk-Tales from a Black Wampanaoag Culture, the Gold Book. Mwalimu. Ed. by Shirley Nurse & Katherine Brown. 49p. (YA). 1998. pap. 8.00 (*0-9662428-0-7*) Talking Drum Pr.

***Mixed-Member Electoral Systems: The Best of Both Worlds?** Martin P. Wattenberg & Matthew Shugart. (Comparative Politics Ser.). 450p. 2000. text 55.00 (*0-19-924079-5*) OUP.

Mixed Men. A. E. Van Vogt. 1976. reprint ed. lib. bdg. 21.95 (*0-88411-975-0*) Amereon Ltd.

Mixed Messages. Linda Lael Miller. 1996. per. 5.50 (*1-55166-164-0*, Mira Bks) Harlequin Bks.

Mixed Messages. Dawn Stewardson. (Superromance Ser.: No. 827). 1999. per. 4.25 (*0-373-70827-0*, 1-70827-0) Harlequin Bks.

Mixed Messages: A Survey of the Foreign Policy Views of America's Leaders. Steve Farkas & Will Friedman. 32p. (Orig.). 1995. pap. 8.50 (*1-889483-22-2*) Public Agenda.

***Mixed Messages: American Politics & International Organization, 1919-1999.** Edward C. Luck. LC 99-6514. 1999. pap. 19.95 (*0-8157-5307-1*) Brookings.

***Mixed Messages: American Politics & International Organization 1919-1999.** Edward C. Luck. LC 99-6514. 1999. 49.95 (*0-8157-5308-X*) Brookings.

Mixed Messages: Light Heavyweight Verse. Henry C. Lindgren. LC 96-85147. 48p. (Orig.). 1996. pap. 10.00 (*0-9653126-0-7*) ChkeCherry Pr.

Mixed Methodology: Combining Qualitative & Quantitative Approaches. Abbas Tashakkori & Charles Teddlie. LC 98-9042. (Applied Social Research Methods Ser.). 185p. 1998. 49.95 (*0-7619-0070-5*); pap. 19.95 (*0-7619-0071-3*) Sage.

***Mixed-Mode Crack Behavior.** Ed. by Keith J. Miller & David L. McDowell. LC 99-37767. (STP Ser.: Vol. 1359). (Illus.). 335p. 1999. pap. text 150.00 (*0-8031-2602-6*, STP 1359) ASTM.

Mixed Mode Crack Propagation. Ed. by G. C. Sih & P. S. Theocaris. 410p. (C). 1981. text 141.50 (*90-286-2691-3*) Kluwer Academic.

Mixed-Mode Simulation. Resve A. Saleh & A. Richard Newton. (C). 1990. text 103.50 (*0-7923-9107-1*) Kluwer Academic.

Mixed-Mode Simulation & Analog Multilevel Simulation. Resve Ssaleh et al. LC 94-20345. (International Series in Engineering & Computer Science, VLSI, Computer Architecture, & Digital Screen Processing). 320p. (C). 1994. text 126.00 (*0-7923-9473-9*) Kluwer Academic.

Mixed Motives. Marc Levine. LC 98-4734. (Mathematical Surveys & Monographs). 515p. 1998. 125.00 (*0-8218-0785-4*, SURV-LEVINE) Am Math.

Mixed Motives & Algebraic K-Theory. U. Jannsen. (Lecture Notes in Mathematics Ser.: Vol. 1400). xiii, 246p. 1990. 43.95 (*0-387-52260-3*) Spr-Verlag.

Mixed Motives & Their Realization in Derived Categories. Annette Huber. Ed. by A. Dold & F. Takens. (Lecture Notes in Mathematics Ser.: Vol. 1604). 207p. 1995. 45.95 (*3-540-59475-2*) Spr-Verlag.

Mixed Motives, Uncertain Outcomes: Defense Conversion in China. Ed. by Jorn Brommelhorster & John Frankenstein. LC 96-27539. 280p. 1996. lib. bdg. 58.00 (*1-55587-710-9*, 877109) L Rienner.

Mixed Multitude: The Struggle for Toleration in Colonial Pennsylvania. Sally Schwartz. (American Social Experience Ser.: No. 9). 396p. (C). 1989. pap. text 20.00 (*0-8147-7882-8*) NYU Pr.

Mixed News: The Public/Civic/Communitarian Journalism Debate. Ed. by Jay Black. LC 96-48127. (LEA's Communication Ser.). 225p. 1996. 59.95 (*0-8058-2542-8*); pap. 27.50 (*0-8058-2543-6*) L Erlbaum Assocs.

Mixed Numbers. Globe Fearon Staff. 1991. pap. 8.95 (*0-8224-4489-5*) Globe Fearon.

Mixed Numbers see Key to Fractions Series

Mixed Nuts. Nancy Manera & Simon J. Donoghue. 1983. 5.50 (*0-87129-576-8*, M59) Dramatic Pub.

Mixed Oxide Fuel (MOX) Exploitation & Destruction in Power Reactors: Proceedings of the NATO Advanced Research Workshop, Obninsk, Russia, October 16-19, 1994. Ed. by Erich R. Merz et al. LC 95-12380. (NATO Advanced Science Institutes: Vol. 2). 320p. (C). 1995. text 173.50 (*0-7923-3473-6*) Kluwer Academic.

Mixed Pasture. Evelyn Underhill. LC 68-8501. (Essay Index Reprint Ser.). 1977. 19.95 (*0-8369-0958-5*) Ayer.

Mixed Plastics Recycling Technology. Bruce A. Hegberg et al. LC 91-44920. (Illus.). 207p. 1992. 89.00 (*0-8155-1297-X*) Noyes.

Mixed Poisson Processes. Jan Grandell. LC 97-67481. 268p. 1997. lib. bdg. 64.95 (*0-412-78700-8*, QA273, Chap & Hall CRC) CRC Pr.

Mixed Problems for Partial Differential Equations with Quasihomogeneous Principal Part. Simon G. Gindikin & L. R. Volevich. Tr. by V. M. Polsov from RUS. LC 95-20515. (Translations of Mathematical Monographs: Vol. 147). 233p. 1995. text 99.00 (*0-8218-4617-5*, MMONO/147) Am Math.

Mixed Problems for the Wave Equation in Coordinate Domains. A. M. Blokhin & D. L. Tkachev. LC 98-28355. 1998. 95.00 (*1-56072-592-3*) Nova Sci Pubs.

Mixed Race: Ethnicity in Early America. Ed. by Frank Shuffleton. LC 92-43927. 296p. (C). 1993. pap. text 22.00 (*0-19-507523-4*) OUP.

Mixed Race Children: A Study of Identity. Anne Wilson. LC 86-28732. 172p. 1987. text 55.00 (*0-04-370168-X*); pap. text 18.95 (*0-04-370169-8*) Routledge.

Mixed Reality - Merging Real & Virtual Worlds: International Symposium on Mixed Reality, Yokohama, March 9-11, 1999. Ed. by Y. Ohta & H. Tamura. 400p. 1999. 75.00 (*3-540-65623-5*) Spr-Verlag.

Mixed-Signal Design Seminar. Analog Devices Engineering Staff. Ed. by Walt Kester. (Analog Devices Technical Reference Bks.). (Illus.). 392p. (Orig.). 1991. pap. text 22.00 (*0-916550-08-7*) Analog Devices.

Mixed Signal VLSI: A Management Overview. Donald T. Comer. (C). 1994. pap. text 19.99 (*0-9638049-1-X*) Array Pubng.

***Mixed Signal VLSI Wireless Design.** Emad N. Farag & Mohamed I. Elmasry. LC 99-46689. 1999. write for info. (*0-7923-8687-6*) Kluwer Academic.

***Mixed Signals.** Liz Curtis Higgs. LC 98-40625. 390p. 1999. pap. 12.99 (*1-57673-401-3*, Alabaster) Multnomah Pubs.

Mixed Signals: The Prospects for Global Television News. Richard Parker. LC 95-19651. 105p. (C). 1995. pap. 7.95 (*0-87078-374-2*) Century Foundation.

Mixed Signals: We Went All the Way. Charles Chirchirillo. Ed. by Frank Young. LC 98-60413. 364p. 1998. 35.50 (*1-885001-12-6*) Via Press.

Mixed Skills in Math. Ideal Instructional Fair Staff. 1999. pap. text 10.95 (*1-56822-858-9*); pap. text 10.95 (*1-56822-859-7*); pap. text 10.95 (*1-56822-860-0*); pap. text 10.95 (*1-56822-861-9*) Instruct Fair.

Mixed-Species Association of Cercopithecus Monkeys in the Kakamega Forest, Kenya. Marina Cords. LC 86-30822. (University of California Publications in Zoology: Vol. 117). 123p. 1987. reprint ed. pap. 38.20 (*0-608-00714-5*, 206148800009) Bks Demand.

Mixed Student Young Choir: Essential Repertoire Level One. 192p. 1995. 12.95 (*0-7935-4223-5*, 08740070) H Leonard.

Mixed Surfactant Systems. Keizo Ogino & K. Abe. (Surfactant Science Ser.: Vol. 46). (Illus.). 472p. 1992. text 199.00 (*0-8247-8796-X*) Dekker.

Mixed Surfactant Systems: Developed from a Symposium: Sponsored by the ACS Division of Colloid & Surface Chemistry at the 65th Colloid & Surface Science Symposium, Norman, Oklahoma, June 17-19, 1991. Ed. by Paul M. Holland & Donn N. Rubingh. LC 92-26167. (ACS Symposium Ser.: Vol. 501). (Illus.). 451p. 1992. text 110.00 (*0-8412-2468-4*, Pub. by Am Chemical) OUP.

Mixed Type Equations. John Rassias. 312p. (C). 1986. 160.00 (*0-7855-4980-3*, Pub. by Collets) St Mut.

Mixed-Up Chameleon. Eric Carle. (J). 1984. 12.15 (*0-606-03618-0*, Pub. by Turtleback) Demco.

Mixed-Up Chameleon. rev. ed. Eric Carle. LC 83-45950. (Trophy Picture Bk.). (Illus.). 32p. (J). (ps-3). 1988. reprint ed. pap. 6.95 (*0-06-443162-2*, HarpTrophy) HarpC Child Bks.

Mixed-Up Chameleon Board Book. Eric Carle. 32p. (J). (ps up). 1998. 7.95 (*0-694-01147-9*) HarpC Child Bks.

Mixed-Up Chameleon Coloring Book. Carle. 32p. (J). Date not set. 3.95 (*0-694-00713-7*, HarpFestival) HarpC Child Bks.

Mixed-Up Chameleon Revised. 2nd ed. Eric Carle. LC 83-45950. (Illus.). 32p. (J). (ps-3). 1984. 15.95 (*0-690-04396-1*); lib. bdg. 15.89 (*0-690-04397-X*) HarpC Child Bks.

Mixed-Up Chameleon Sticker Book. Eric Carle. LC 75-5505. (Illus.). 32p. (J). (ps-2). 1993. 7.95 (*0-694-00448-0*, HarpFestival) HarpC Child Bks.

Mixed up Farm. Christopher Carrie. (Crayola Coloring Storybks.). (Illus.). 32p. (Orig.). (J). (ps). 1990. 1.99 (*0-86696-236-0*) Binney & Smith.

Mixed-Up Magic. Gail Herman. 80p. 1999. pap. 3.99 (*0-553-48681-0*) Bantam.

Mixed-Up Matrimony. Diana Mars. (Desire Ser.). 1995. per. 3.25 (*0-373-05942-6*, 1-05942-7) Silhouette.

Mixed-Up Max. Dick King-Smith. LC 97-220042. (Planet Reader First Chapter Bks.). (Illus.). 64p. (J). (gr. 2-5). 1998. pap. 2.95 (*0-8167-4437-8*) Troll Communs.

Mixed-Up Max. Dick King-Smith. 1998. 8.15 (*0-606-13613-4*, Pub. by Turtleback) Demco.

Mixed up Monsters. Jill B. Bruce. (Illus.). 32p. (J). 1997. 14.95 (*0-86417-834-4*, Pub. by Kangaroo Pr) Seven Hills Bk.

Mixed-Up Pup. Corey Maxwell. (Paw Island Presents...Ser.). (Illus.). 16p. (J). (ps-3). 1997. pap. 8.95 (*1-890145-01-7*) PetCare.

***Mixed-Up Pup.** Corey Maxwell. (Illus.). 32p. 1999. 12.95 (*1-890145-03-3*, Paw Island Ent) PetCare.

Mixed-Use Development Handbook. Dean Schwanke. LC 86-51443. (Community Builders Handbook Ser.). 364p. 1987. 64.95 (*0-87420-665-0*, M24) Urban Land.

Mixed-Use Development Projects in North America: Project Profiles. James Thomas Black et al. LC 82-84338. 96p. (Orig.). reprint ed. pap. 30.00 (*0-8357-8598-X*, 203497400091) Bks Demand.

Mixed-Use Developments: New Ways of Land Use. Robert E. Witherspoon et al. LC 75-37217. (Urban Land Institute, Technical Bulletin Ser.: No. 71). 210p. reprint ed. pap. 65.10 (*0-608-11921-0*, 202323600032) Bks Demand.

M

An Asterisk (*) at the beginning of an entry indicates that the title is appearing for the first time.

Mixed-Valence Compounds: Theory & Applications in Chemistry, Physics, Geology & Biology. Ed. by David B. Brown. (NATO Advanced Study Institute, C. Mathematical & Physical Sciences Ser.: No. 58). 525p. 1980. text 234.00 (90-277-1152-6) Kluwer Academic.

Mixed Valency Systems: Applications in Chemistry Physics & Biology. Ed. by Kosmas Prassides. 464p. (C). 1991. text 234.00 (0-7923-1381-X) Kluwer Academic.

Mixed Voices: Contemporary Poems about Music. Ed. by Emilie Buchwald & Ruth Roston. LC 91-15082. (Illus.). 190p. 1991. 14.95 (0-915943-82-4) Milkweed Ed.

Mixed Waste Risk Assessment. William R. Rish & David A. Waite. Date not set. 65.00 (0-87371-633-7) Lewis Pubs.

Mixed Waste III: Proceedings of the Third International Symposium, Baltimore MD, August 7-10. Ed. by Betty R. Love et al. (Illus.). 800p. 1995. pap. text 75.00 (1-882345-04-5) Cognizant Comm.

Mixed Wine Drinks: 700 Recipes for Punches, Hot Drinks, Coolers & Cocktails. 2nd ed. Adam Ramos & Joseph R. Ramos. LC 74-25080. (Illus.). 160p. 1990. pap. 9.95 (0-02-003504-7) Macmillan.

Mixed with Love. Ed. by Cheryl Matthews & Karen Hailey. 250p. (Orig.). 1985. pap. 11.00 (0-685-08482-5) Chattanooga Christ.

Mixedblood Messages: Literature, Film, Family, Place. Louis Owens. LC 98-5361. (American Indian Literature & Critical Studies: No. 26). (Illus.). 252p. 1998. 27.95 (0-8061-3051-2) U of Okla Pr.

Mixing. Multimedia Development Services Staff. (Plant Fundamentals Ser.: Vol. VII, Module III). (Illus.). 1995. teacher ed. 49.95 (1-57431-063-1); student ed. 30.00 (1-57431-023-2) Tech Trng Systs.

Mixing: Properties & Examples. Paul Doukhan. LC 93-47442. (Lecture Notes in Statistics Ser.: Vol. 85). 160p. 1994. pap. 29.00 (0-387-94214-9) Spr-Verlag.

Mixing: Theory & Practice, 3 vols., Vol. 1. Ed. by Vincent W. Uhl & Joseph B. Gray. 1966. text 174.00 (0-12-706601-2) Acad Pr.

Mixing: Theory & Practice, 3 vols., Vol. 2. Ed. by Vincent W. Uhl & Joseph B. Gray. 1967. text 174.00 (0-12-706602-0) Acad Pr.

Mixing & Compounding of Polymers: Theory & Practice. Ed. by Ica Manas-Zloczower & Zehev Tadmor. LC 93-33468. (Progress in Polymer Processing Ser.). 982p. 1993. 179.00 (1-56990-156-2) Hanser-Gardner.

***Mixing & Crystallization.** Bhaskar Sen Gupta & Shaliza Ibrahim. 352p. 2000. 149.00 (0-7923-6200-4) Kluwer Academic.

Mixing & Dispersion in Stably Stratified Flows. Ed. by Peter A. Davies. LC 99-229769. (Institute of Mathematics & Its Applications Conference Ser.; New Ser.: 68). (Illus.). 660p. 1999. text 225.00 (0-19-850015-7) OUP.

Mixing & Spreading of Medoc see Progress in Oceanography

Mixing & Transport in the Environment: A Memorial Volume for Catherine M. Allen (1954-1991) Ed. by Keith J. Beven et al. 474p. 1994. 205.00 (0-471-94142-5) Wiley.

***Mixing Business...with Baby.** Diana Whitney. 2001. mass mkt. 3.50 (0-373-19490-0, 1-19490-1) Silhouette.

***Mixing Cement.** Peter Tomassi. Ed. by Phyllis J. Green. LC 99-72908. 72p. 1999. pap. 28.00 (0-9654569-4-3, 99-2) Thunder Rain.

***Mixing Cement.** Peter Tomassi. Ed. by Phyllis Jean Green. LC 99-72908. 72p. 1999. pap. 13.95 (0-9654569-3-5, 99-2) Thunder Rain.

Mixing Colors. Tessa Krailing. LC 96-85320. (Art Handbooks). (Illus.). 96p. 1996. 9.95 (0-8120-6619-7) Barron.

***Mixing Colors: Oil.** Parramon's Editorial Team Staff. LC 99-20235. (Learning to Paint Ser.). (Illus.). 64p. 1999. pap. 13.95 (0-7641-0889-1) Barron.

Mixing Colors: Oil, Vol. 2. Ed. by Parramon's Editorial Staff. (Art Handbooks). (Illus.). 96p. 1998. 9.95 (0-7641-5087-1) Barron.

Mixing Colors & Materials to Use. Walter Foster. (How to Draw & Paint Ser.). (Illus.). 32p. (Orig.). 1989. pap. 6.95 (1-56010-046-X, HT056) W Foster Pub.

***Mixing Colors 3: Dry Techniques.** Parramon's Editorial Team Staff. (Art Handbooks). (Illus.). 96p. 2000. pap. 9.95 (0-7641-5227-0) Barron.

Mixing Engineer's Handbook. Bobby Owsinski. LC 99-62534. 180p. 1999. pap. text 34.95 (0-87288-723-5) Intertec Pub.

Mixing in Coagulation & Flocculation. Ed. by Appiah Amirtharajah et al. 440p. 1991. 125.00 (0-89867-561-8, 90580) Am Water Wks Assn.

Mixing in Continuous Flow Systems. E. Bruce Nauman & B. A. Buffham. LC 82-24858. (Wiley-Interscience Publications). (Illus.). 299p. 1983. reprint ed. pap. 92.70 (0-7837-2369-5, 204005500006) Bks Demand.

Mixing in Estuaries & Coastal Seas. Ed. by Charitha Pattiaratchi. LC 96-175. (Coastal & Estuarine Studies: Vol. 50). 1996. 70.00 (0-87590-264-2) Am Geophysical.

Mixing in Inland & Coastal Waters. Hugo B. Fischer et al. 1979. text 83.00 (0-12-258150-4) Acad Pr.

Mixing in Polymer Processing. Ed. by Chris J. Rauwendaal. (Plastics Engineering Ser.: Vol. 23). (Illus.). 488p. 1991. text 225.00 (0-8247-8521-5) Dekker.

Mixing in the Process Industries. 2nd ed. Ed. by N. Harnby et al. LC 92-17528. (Illus.). 432p. 2000. pap. text 69.95 (0-7506-3760-9) Buttrwrth-Heinemann.

Mixing Memory & Desire: The Waste Land & Modern British Novels. Fred D. Crawford. LC 82-477. 170p. 1982. 28.50 (0-271-00308-1) Pa St U Pr.

Mixing Messages: Graphic Design in Contemporary American Culture. Ellen Lupton. LC 96-18695. (Illus.). 176p. 1996. 55.00 (1-56898-098-1); pap. 35.00 (1-56898-099-X) Princeton Arch.

Mixing Methods: Qualitative & Quantitative Research. Julia Braner. 192p. 1995. pap. 31.95 (1-85972-116-8, Pub. by Avebry) Ashgate Pub Co.

Mixing Methods: Qualitative & Quantitative Research. Julia Brannen. 192p. 1992. 83.95 (1-85628-184-1, Pub. by Avebry) Ashgate Pub Co.

Mixing of Liquids by Mechanical Agitation, Vol. 1. Ed. by Jaromir J. Ulbrecht & Gary K. Patterson. LC 85-5253. (Chemical Engineering: Concepts & Reviews Ser.). x, 346p. 1985. text 332.00 (2-88124-112-3) Gordon & Breach.

***Mixing of Solids.** Hermann Gericke. 176p. 2000. 75.00 (0-7923-6229-2) Kluwer Academic.

Mixing Sequences of Random Variables & Probabilistic Number Theory. Walter Philipp. LC 52-42839. (Memoirs Ser.: No. 1/114). 102p. 1971. pap. 16.00 (0-8218-1814-7, MEMO/1/114) Am Math.

Mixing the Races in Hawaii: A Study of the Coming Neo-Hawaiian American Race. Sidney L. Gulick. LC 75-35194. reprint ed. 36.00 (0-404-14222-2) AMS Pr.

Mixing the Waters: Environment, Politics, & the Building of the Tennessee-Tombigbee Waterway. Jeffrey K. Stine. LC 93-23563. (Series on Technology & the Environment). (Illus.). 336p. (C). 1993. text 39.95 (0-9622628-5-4); pap. text 21.95 (0-9622628-6-2) U Akron Pr.

Mixing Two Languages: French-Dutch Contact in a Comparative Perspective. Jeanine Treffers-Daller. (Topics in Sociolinguistics Ser.: No. 9). xii, 300p. (C). 1994. lib. bdg. 106.15 (3-11-013837-9) Mouton.

Mixing Watercolors. Parramon's Editorial Team. LC 97-42795. (Learn to Paint Ser.). (Illus.). 64p. 1998. pap. 13.95 (0-7641-0551-5) Barron.

Mixing Zone Models for Submerged Discharges. I. K. Tsanis & C. Valeo. LC 94-68175. 184p. 1994. text 81.00 (1-56252-286-8, 3625) Computational Mech MA.

Mixquiahuala Letters. Ana Castillo. LC 86-70701. 132p. 1986. 20.00 (0-916950-67-0) Biling Rev-Pr.

Mixquiahuala Letters. Ana Castillo. 144p. 1992. pap. 11.00 (0-385-42013-7, Anchor NY) Doubleday.

Mixquiahuala Letters & Sapogonia. Ana Castillo. 368p. 1994. pap. 13.00 (0-385-47080-0, Anchor NY) Doubleday.

MiXtake Files: A Fan's Guide to the X-Files. Michael French. 1998. pap. 15.95 (1-84024-008-3, Pub. by Summers) Howell Pr VA.

Mixteca: Su Cultura e Historia Prehispanicas. 4th ed. Barbro Dahlgren. 312p. 1990. pap. 9.20 (968-36-0692-X, UN037) UPLAAP.

Mixteca - Puebla: Discoveries & Research in Mesoamerican Art & Archaeology. Ed. by H. B. Nicholson & Eloise Q. Keber. LC 92-70648. (Illus.). 264p. (Orig.). 1994. pap. 55.00 (0-911437-38-X) Labyrinthos.

Mixtery: A Festschrift for Anthony Braxton. Ed. by Graham Lock. 1995. pap. 19.95 (1-873012-97-7, Pub. by Stride Pubns) SPD-Small Pr Dist.

Mixture As Before. W. Somerset Maugham. LC 75-26134. (Works of W. Somerset Maugham). 1977. reprint ed. 23.95 (0-405-07855-2) Ayer.

Mixture Formation for Spark Ignition Engines. H. P. Lenz. 416p. 1992. 19.00 (1-56091-188-3, R-113) Soc Auto Engineers.

Mixture Models: Theory, Geometry & Applications. Bruce Lindsay. LC 94-75430. (NSF-CBMS Regional Conference Series in Probability & Statistics: Vol. 5). (Illus.). 163p. (C). 1995. pap. 25.00 (0-940600-32-3) Inst Math.

Mixture of Frailties. Robertson Davies. 384p. 1980. pap. 12.95 (0-14-016791-9, Penguin Bks) Viking Penguin.

Mixture Preparation in SI & Diesel Engines. 1997. 43.00 (0-7680-0008-4, SP-1280) Soc Auto Engineers.

Mixtures. Anita Harnadek. 32p. (Orig.). (YA). (gr. 8 up). 1988. pap. 6.95 (0-89455-336-4) Crit Think Bks.

Mixtures & Minerals Reactions. S. Saxena & J. Ganguly. (Minerals & Rocks Ser.: Vol. 19). (Illus.). 290p. 1987. 94.95 (0-387-17667-5) Spr-Verlag.

Mixtures in Chemistry. T. Harrison & M. Murphy. 1972. text 1.05 (0-13-586008-3) P-H.

Mixturism. rev. ed. James M. Carroll. 184p. (Orig.). 1996. pap. 7.95 (0-89826-068-X) Natl Paperback.

Miyagi-Ken-Oki, Japan Earthquake, June 12, 1978. Ed. by Peter I. Yanev. 165p. 1978. pap. 12.00 (0-318-16324-1, EP-27) Earthquake Eng.

Miyake: Making Things. Issey Miyake. Ed. by Herve Chandes. (Illus.). 192p. 1999. 49.95 (3-908247-08-X, Pub. by Scalo Pubs) Dist Art Pubs.

Miyanmin: Human Ecology of a Papua New Guinea Society. George E. Morren. LC 85-20817. (Studies in Cultural Anthropology: Vol. 9). (Illus.). 373p. 1986. reprint ed. pap. 115.70 (0-608-07368-7, 206759600009) Bks Demand.

***Miyon & the Mountain Spirit.** Adrienne J. De Dumas. (J). (gr. k-3). 1999. pap. 6.95 (0-533-13057-3) Vantage.

Miz Berlin Walks. Jane Yolen. LC 95-45866. (Illus.). 32p. (J). (ps-3). 1997. 15.95 (0-399-22938-8, Philomel) Peng Put Young Read.

***Miz Berlin Walks.** Jane Yolen. (Illus.). 32p. (J). (ps-3). 2000. pap. 6.99 (0-698-11845-6, PuffinBks) Peng Put Young Read.

Miz Fannie Mae's Fine New Easter Hat. Melissa Milich. LC 96-14233. (Illus.). 32p. (J). (gr. k-3). 1997. 14.95 (0-316-57159-8) Little.

Miz Lena's Backyard. Jan Villarrubia. 1994. pap. 5.50 (0-87129-302-1, M85) Dramatic Pub.

'Miz Liz Do You Dye Your Hair? Zoe Rexroad. 140p. (Orig.). (J). (gr. 5-6). 1997. pap. 6.95 (1-57502-490-X, P01457) Morris Pubng.

Mize & Kathy, Vol. 15. James Humphrey. LC 98-147466. 80p. 1998. pap. 17.00 (0-936641-25-8) Poets Alive Pr.

Mizlansky/Zilinsky or "Schmucks" Jon R. Baitz. 1998. pap. 5.25 (0-8222-1680-9) Dramatists Play.

Mizlansky/Zilinsky or "Schmucks" Jon Robin Baitz. 112p. 1998. pap. 10.95 (1-55936-160-3, Pub. by Theatre Comm) Consort Bk Sales.

Mizner's Florida: American Resort Architecture. Donald W. Curl. LC 83-22205. (American Monograph Newhouse Ser.). (Illus.). 264p. 1987. pap. text 17.50 (0-262-53068-6) MIT Pr.

Mizo Polity & Political Modernisation: Pre-Colonial & Colonial Institutions. Chitta Ranjan Nag. LC 98-903446. 1998. 20.00 (81-259-0451-4, Pub. by Vikas) S Asia.

Mizo Society in Transition. Chitta R. Nag. (C). 28.00 (0-7069-6963-4, Pub. by Vikas) S Asia.

***Mizora: A Prophecy.** Mary E. Bradley Lane. Ed. & Intro. by Jean Pfaelzer. LC 00-24976. 146p. 2000. pap. text 14.95 (0-8156-2839-0) Syracuse U Pr.

Mizora: A World of Women. Mary E. Bradley Lane. LC 99-34330. (Bison Frontiers of Imagination Ser.). 147p. 1999. pap. 9.95 (0-8032-7992-2) U of Nebr Pr.

Mizu. deluxe limited ed. Mei-Mei Berssenbrugge. 1990. pap. 75.00 (0-685-56973-X) Chax Pr.

Mizuumi see Lake

***Mizzly Fitch: The Light, the Sea, the Storm.** 2nd ed. Murray A. Pura. 1999. reprint ed. pap. 18.95 (1-57383-127-1, Regent Coll Pub) Regent College.

Mizzy & Zizzy Learn to Share. Zachary X. King & Barbara Tompkins-Brown. (Mizzy & Zizzy Ser.). (Illus.). 32p. 1996. 14.99 (1-886290-00-8); pap. 6.99 (1-886290-01-6) J Brown Ent.

Mizzy & Zizzy Learn to Share. Zachary X. King & Barbara Tompkins-Brown. (Mizzy & Zizzy Ser.). (Illus.). 32p. (J). 1996. lib. bdg. 21.99 (1-886290-13-X) J Brown Ent.

MI92--Technologies, Economics, Information for Global Partnership Realignments: Presented at Manufacturing International '92 March 29-april 1, 1992, Dallas, Texas / D. R. Durham et al. LC 92-160696. ix, 499p. 1992. write for info. (0-7918-0763-0) ASME.

MK Process at 50 Years No. 60: A Powerful Tool for Astrophysical Insight. Ed. by C. J. Corbally et al. 440p. 1994. 34.00 (0-937707-79-1) Astron Soc Pacific.

MK Spectral Clasifications: 5th General Catalogue. William Buscombe. LC 81-9555. 250p. (Orig.). 1981. pap. text 10.00 (0-939160-03-X) NWU Astro.

MK Spectral Clasifications: 13th General Catalogue. William Buscombe & Bruce E. Foster. 213p. (Orig.). (C). 1998. pap. 30.00 (0-939160-10-2) NWU Astro.

MkLinux: Microkernel Linux for the Power Macintosh. Ed. by Rich Morin. 350p. Date not set. write for info. incl. audio compact disk (1-881957-24-1) PT Freeware.

Mko Valley: A Potawatomi Fable. Jack Wooldridge. (Potawatomi Fables Ser.). (Illus.). 29p. (J). 1997. pap. 7.00 (1-887963-11-1) Pota Pr.

ML for the Working Programmer. 2nd ed. L. C. Paulson. (Illus.). 494p. (C). 1996. text 80.00 (0-521-57050-6); pap. text 35.95 (0-521-56543-X) Cambridge U Pr.

ML with Concurrency: Design, Analysis, Implementation & Application. Ed. by Flemming Nielson. LC 96-35926. (Monographs in Computer Science). 255p. 1997. 49.95 (0-387-94875-9) Spr-Verlag.

***MLA Directory of Periodicals: Complete International Listings.** 9th ed. 970p. 1999. text 130.00 (0-87352-833-6) Modern Lang.

***MLA Directory of Periodicals: Periodicals Published in the Americas.** 9th ed. 430p. 1999. pap. text 35.00 (0-87352-834-4) Modern Lang.

MLA Directory of Scholarly Presses in Language & Literature. Ed. by James L. Harner. x, 295p. (Orig.). 1996. pap. 23.00 (0-87352-681-3, S302P); lib. bdg. 45.00 (0-87352-680-5, S302C) Modern Lang.

MLA Guide to the Job Search: A Handbook for Departments & for Ph.D.s & Ph.D. Candidates in English & Foreign Languages. enl. expanded rev. ed. English Showalter et al. LC 96-43252. Orig. Title: A Career Guide, the MLA Guide to the Job Search. ix, 156p. (Orig.). 1996. pap. 10.00 (0-87352-682-1, W333P) Modern Lang.

MLA Handbook for Writers of Research Papers. 5th ed. Joseph Gibaldi. LC 99-18319. (Illus.). 332p. 1999. pap. 14.75 (0-87352-975-8) Modern Lang.
Since the publication of the first edition in 1977, the MLA Handbook has sold over four million copies worldwide. The fifth edition of the MLA Handbook is revamped for the Internet age. A complete toolbox for online research, this edition offers guidance in: finding research materials online; judging the quality of information on the Internet; using expanded & updated MLA formats to document a wide variety of online sources; preparing texts in electronic form. The MLA Handbook's authoritative guidelines on research practices & MLA style are enhanced in other ways. New topics have been added & citation examples, list of suggested writing guides & appendix of reference works by field have been expanded & updated. Large print edition also available.
Publisher Paid Annotation.

MLA Handbook for Writers of Research Papers. 5th large type ed. Joseph Gibaldi. LC 99-13998. 1999. pap. text 22.00 (0-87352-976-6) Modern Lang.

MLA International Bibliography of Books & Articles on the Modern Languages & Literatures. Incl. 1978. 1045p. 1979. (0-87352-413-6); 834p. 1973. (0-87352-213-3); 723p. 1970. (0-87352-409-8); 1980. 1304p. 1981. (0-87352-422-5); 1979. 1061p. 1980. 200.00 (0-318-59662-8) Modern Lang.

MLA International Bibliography of Books & Articles on the Modern Languages & Literatures, 1981: Listings & Author Index. xxxviii, 1141p. 1983. lib. bdg. 500.00 (0-87352-431-4) Modern Lang.

MLA International Bibliography of Books & Articles on the Modern Languages & Literatures, 1981: Subject Index. 1519p. 1983. lib. bdg. 450.00 (0-87352-429-2) Modern Lang.

MLA International Bibliography of Books & Articles on the Modern Languages & Literatures, 1983: Listings & Author Index. xi, 1312p. 1984. lib. bdg. 500.00 (0-87352-449-7) Modern Lang.

MLA International Bibliography of Books & Articles on the Modern Languages & Literatures, 1983: Subject Index. 1776p. 1984. lib. bdg. 450.00 (0-87352-451-9) Modern Lang.

MLA International Bibliography of Books & Articles on the Modern Languages & Literatures, 1984: Listings & Author Index. xxxvi, 1176p. 1985. lib. bdg. 500.00 (0-87352-455-1) Modern Lang.

MLA International Bibliography of Books & Articles on the Modern Languages & Literatures, 1984: Subject Index. 1496p. 1985. lib. bdg. 450.00 (0-87352-456-X) Modern Lang.

MLA International Bibliography of Books & Articles on the Modern Languages & Literatures, 1985: Listings & Author Index. xxxii, 1187p. 1986. lib. bdg. 500.00 (0-87352-463-2) Modern Lang.

MLA International Bibliography of Books & Articles on the Modern Languages & Literatures, 1985: Subject Index. 1510p. 1986. lib. bdg. 450.00 (0-87352-464-0) Modern Lang.

MLA International Bibliography of Books & Articles on the Modern Languages & Literatures, 1986: Listings & Author Index. xl, 1224p. 1987. lib. bdg. 500.00 (0-87352-473-X) Modern Lang.

MLA International Bibliography of Books & Articles on the Modern Languages & Literatures, 1986: Subject Index. 1476p. 1987. lib. bdg. 450.00 (0-87352-474-8) Modern Lang.

MLA International Bibliography of Books & Articles on the Modern Languages & Literatures, 1987: Listings & Author Index. xxxviii, 1223p. 1988. lib. bdg. 500.00 (0-87352-612-0) Modern Lang.

MLA International Bibliography of Books & Articles on the Modern Languages & Literatures, 1987: Subject Index. 1490p. 1988. lib. bdg. 450.00 (0-87352-613-9) Modern Lang.

MLA International Bibliography of Books & Articles on the Modern Languages & Literatures, 1988: Listings & Author Index. xxxix, 1329p. 1989. lib. bdg. 500.00 (0-87352-620-1) Modern Lang.

MLA International Bibliography of Books & Articles on the Modern Languages & Literatures, 1988: Subject Index. 1548p. 1989. lib. bdg. 450.00 (0-87352-621-X) Modern Lang.

MLA International Bibliography of Books & Articles on the Modern Languages & Literatures, 1989: Listings & Author Index. xxxix, 1276p. 1990. lib. bdg. 500.00 (0-87352-631-7) Modern Lang.

MLA International Bibliography of Books & Articles on the Modern Languages & Literatures, 1989: Subject Index. 1506p. 1990. lib. bdg. 450.00 (0-87352-632-5) Modern Lang.

MLA International Bibliography of Books & Articles on the Modern Languages & Literatures, 1990: Listings & Author Index. xxxix, 1209p. 1991. lib. bdg. 500.00 (0-87352-640-6) Modern Lang.

MLA International Bibliography of Books & Articles on the Modern Languages & Literatures, 1990: Subject Index. 1396p. 1991. lib. bdg. 450.00 (0-87352-641-4) Modern Lang.

MLA International Bibliography of Books & Articles on the Modern Languages & Literatures, 1991: Listings & Author Index. l, 1302p. 1992. lib. bdg. 500.00 (0-87352-648-1) Modern Lang.

MLA International Bibliography of Books & Articles on the Modern Languages & Literatures, 1991: Subject Index. 1600p. 1992. lib. bdg. 450.00 (0-87352-649-X) Modern Lang.

MLA International Bibliography of Books & Articles on the Modern Languages & Literatures, 1992: Listings & Author Index. l, 1779p. 1993. lib. bdg. 500.00 (0-87352-658-9) Modern Lang.

MLA International Bibliography of Books & Articles on the Modern Languages & Literatures, 1992: Subject Index. 1324p. 1993. lib. bdg. 450.00 (0-87352-659-7) Modern Lang.

MLA International Bibliography of Books & Articles on the Modern Languages & Literatures, 1993: Listings & Author Index. l, 1276p. 1994. lib. bdg. 500.00 (0-87352-667-8) Modern Lang.

MLA International Bibliography of Books & Articles on the Modern Languages & Literatures, 1993: Subject Index. 1430p. 1994. lib. bdg. 450.00 (0-87352-668-6) Modern Lang.

MLA International Bibliography of Books & Articles on the Modern Languages & Literatures, 1994: Listings & Author Index. liv, 1309p. 1995. lib. bdg. 500.00 (0-87352-676-7) Modern Lang.

MLA International Bibliography of Books & Articles on the Modern Languages & Literatures, 1994: Subject Index. 1506p. 1995. lib. bdg. 450.00 (0-87352-677-5) Modern Lang.

MLA International Bibliography of Books & Articles on the Modern Languages & Literatures, 1995: Listings & Author Index. lv, 1327p. 1996. lib. bdg. 500.00 (0-87352-684-8) Modern Lang.

MLA International Bibliography of Books & Articles on the Modern Languages & Literatures, 1996: Listings & Author Index. lvi, 1389p. 1997. lib. bdg. 500.00 (0-87352-692-9) Modern Lang.

MLA International Bibliography of Books & Articles on the Modern Languages & Literatures, 1996: Subject Index. 1694p. 1997. lib. bdg. 450.00 (*0-87352-693-7*) Modern Lang.

MLA Salary Survey. Compiled by Health Science Library, Status & Economic Interest. 1995. pap. 60.00 (*0-912176-38-5*) Med Lib Assn.

MLA Style Manual & Guide to Scholarly Publishing. 2nd ed. Joseph Gibaldi. LC 97-49983. xxviii, 343p. 1998. 25.00 (*0-87352-699-6*, S181C) Modern Lang.

MLA Style Manual & Guide to Scholarly Publishing. 2nd large type ed. Joseph Gibaldi & Modern Language Association of America Staff. LC 99-10534. 343p. 1999. 25.00 (*0-87352-977-4*) Ferguson.

M'Lady Witch. Christopher Stasheff. 256p. (Orig.). 1994. mass mkt. 5.99 (*0-441-00113-0*) Ace Bks.

Mlecchas in Early India. Aloka Parasher. (C). 1991. 29.50 (*0-685-59768-7*, Pub. by M Manoharial) S Asia.

M'Liss. Bret Harte. (Jamestown Classics Ser.). 1995. pap., teacher ed. 7.32 (*0-89061-049-5*, Jamestwn Pub); pap., student ed. 5.99 (*0-89061-048-7*, Jamestwn Pub) NTC Contemp Pub Co.

***MLM Binary Plan: A Comprehensive Look at Network Marketing's Most Controversial.** Ray H. Duncan. Ed. by Joy R. Duncan. (Illus.). 64p. 1999. 9.95 (*1-929746-01-6*) Double Dia.

MLM: Caution & Confidence: A Business Lawyer Looks at the Nature of Both the Beauty & the Beast. Roger Himes. 192p. 1996. pap. 16.95 (*1-888554-75-4*) Lamplighter Bks.

MLM 400 Resource Directory: 1999 Edition. Ed. by Maryelle Huber. 384p. 1999. pap. 49.95 (*1-892366-08-8*) KAAS Publ.

MLM 400 Resource Directory 1998. 6th ed. Ed. by Maryelle Huber. 416p. 1998. pap. 49.95 (*1-892366-05-3*) KAAS Publ.

MLM Magic Multilevel Marketing: How an Ordinary Person Can Build an Extra-Ordinary Networking Business from Scratch. 2nd ed. Venus C. Andrecht. Ed. by Summer Andrecht. LC 91-61552. (Illus.). 274p. (C). 1993. pap. 16.95 (*0-941903-07-9*, 3000) Ransom Hill.

MLM Magic Workbook: Companion Workbook to the Award Winning Book MLM Magic-How an Ordinary Person Can Build an Extra Ordinary Networking Business from Scratch. Venus C. Andrecht. Ed. by Summer Andrecht. 112p. (Orig.). 1994. pap. 18.95 (*0-941903-11-7*) Ransom Hill.

***MLM Road Map: A Step-by-Step System of Building a Network Marketing Dowline.** Ray H. Duncan. Ed. by Joy R. Duncan. (Illus.). 128p. 1999. 19.95 (*1-929746-00-8*) Double Dia.

MLP Manual. G. J. Ross. 1980. 11.20 (*0-317-52206-X*, Pub. by Rothamsted Stats) Parkwest Pubns.

Mls Accounting Module 2. L. Paden Neeley. (SWC-Accounting). (C). 1999. mass mkt. 47.95 (*0-538-26645-7*) S-W Pub.

MLS College Keyboarding: Basic Course. 12th ed. Duncan & Susie H. Vanhuss. (TE - Keyboarding Ser.). 1991. pap., student ed. 6.95 (*0-538-70139-0*) S-W Pub.

MLS College Keyboarding: Document Production, Advanced. 12th ed. Duncan & Susie H. Vanhuss. (TE - Keyboarding Ser.). (C). 1990. mass mkt. 36.00 (*0-538-70138-2*) S-W Pub.

MLS College Keyboarding: Formatting, Intermediate. 12th ed. Duncan & Susie H. Vanhuss. (TE - Keyboarding Ser.). (C). 1990. mass mkt. 36.00 (*0-538-70129-3*) S-W Pub.

***Mm.** Kelly Doudna. LC 00-28880. (Alphabet Ser.). (Illus.). (J). 2000. write for info. (*1-57765-406-4*) ABDO Pub Co.

Mm. Series on Fractals Vol. 1: Midgets on the Spike. A. G. Davis Philip et al. 160p. 1991. 29.00 (*0-933485-14-X*) L Davis Pr.

MMBI Handbook: Money & Me Inventory. Gayle R. Martinez. viii, 43p. 1997. pap. 6.50 (*1-892351-01-3*) Rose Petal.

***MMDI Amex Tax Guide.** American Express Staff. 96p. 1999. pap. 3.50 (*0-06-105912-9*) HarpC.

***MMDI Total Packers.** 160p. 1998. pap. 7.95 (*0-06-105892-0*) HarpC.

***MMDI Total Quarterback.** Bernard Ireland. 144p. 1998. pap. 7.95 (*0-06-105891-2*) HarpC.

***MMDI Total Steelers.** 160p. 1998. pap. 7.95 (*0-06-105894-7*) HarpC.

***MMDI Total Super Bowl.** Bernard Ireland. 160p. 1998. pap. 7.95 (*0-06-105885-8*) HarpC.

MMDS (Wireless Cable) Installation Manual. DeFrank Baylin et al. (Illus.). 326p. 1996. pap. 40.00 (*0-917893-28-X*) Baylin Pubns.

Mme. Blavatsky Defended. Iverson L. Harris. 174p. (Orig.). 1971. pap. 5.00 (*0-913004-01-4*) Point Loma Pub.

Mme. de Stael. Renee Winegarten. LC 85-13104. (Women's Ser.). (Illus.). 133p. 1987. pap. 13.50 (*0-907582-74-5*) Berg Pubs.

MMF: The Practitioner's Guide. H. Daniels. 1994. ring bd. write for info. (*0-409-02169-5*, MICHIE) LEXIS Pub.

MMG - Music Mind Games. 432p. (J). 1992. pap. 24.95 (*0-89898-561-7*, MY1945) Wrner Bros.

MMIC - Monolithic Microwave Integrated Circuits, Vol. 1. Yasuo Mitsui. (Japanese Technology Reviews Ser.: Vol. 2). viii, 130p. 1989. text 104.00 (*2-88124-286-3*) Gordon & Breach.

MMIC Design. Ed. by Ian Robertson. (Circuits & Systems Ser.: No. 7). 502p. 1995. boxed set 95.00 (*0-85296-816-7*, CS007) INSPEC Inc.

MMIC Design: GaAs FETs & HEMTs. Peter H. Ladbrooke. LC 88-34959. (Artech House Microwave Library). (Illus.). 394p. 1989. reprint ed. pap. 122.20 (*0-7837-9696-X*, 206042600005) Bks Demand.

***MMIXware: A RISC Computer for the Third Millenium.** Ed. by D. E. Knuth. LC 99-88774. (Lecture Notes in Computer Science Ser.: Vol. 1750). ix, 550p. 2000. pap. 59.00 (*3-540-66938-8*) Spr-Verlag.

***Mmm, Cookies!** Robert Munsch. LC 99-46966. (Illus.). 32p. (J). (ps-3). 2000. 11.95 (*0-590-89603-2*, Cartwheel) Scholastic Inc.

MMM... Skyscraper I Love You: Tomato. Karl Hyde & John Warwicker. (Illus.). 192p. 1998. pap. 24.95 (*1-873968-58-2*) Gingko Press.

Mmmm---Cookies! Simple Subtraction. Monica Weiss. LC 91-18648. (Frimble Family First Learning Adventures Ser.). (Illus.). 24p. (J). (gr. k-2). 1997. pap. 3.50 (*0-8167-2487-3*) Troll Communs.

Mmmmiami: Tempting Tropical Tastes for Home Cooks Everywhere. Martin Kotkin et al. LC 97-43884. (Illus.). 352p. 1998. 27.50 (*0-8050-5673-4*) H Holt & Co.

MMPI: A Comprehensive, Annotated Bibliography, 1940-1964 (Minnesota Multiphasic Personality Inventory) Earl S. Taulbee et al. LC 72-87108. viii, 603p. 1977. 50.00 (*0-87875-037-1*) Whitston Pub.

MMPI: A Contemporary Normative Study of Adolescents. Robert C. Colligan & Kenneth P. Offord. Ed. by Glenn R. Caddy. (Developments in Clinical Psychology Ser.). 640p. (C). 1992. pap. 49.50 (*0-89391-985-3*); text 125.00 (*0-89391-872-5*) Ablx Pub.

MMPI: Clinical & Research Trends. Ed. by Charles S. Newmark. LC 79-17777. (Praeger Special Studies). 464p. 1979. 49.95 (*0-03-048926-1*, Praeger Pubs) Greenwood.

MMPI: Used with Specific Populations. Greene. (C). 1989. pap. text 72.95 (*0-205-10104-6*) Allyn.

MMPI-A: Assessing Adolescent Psychopathology. Robert P. Archer. 472p. (C). 1992. text 39.95 (*0-8058-1113-3*) L Erlbaum Assocs.

MMPI-A: Assessing Adolescent Psychopathology. 2nd ed. Robert P. Archer. 512p. (C). 1996. 39.95 (*0-8058-2343-3*) L Erlbaum Assocs.

MMPI-A Casebook. Robert P. Archer et al. LC 94-5851. 223p. 1994. pap. 33.00 (*0-911907-14-9*) Psych Assess.

MMPI-A Content Scales: Assessing Psychopathology in Adolescents. Carolyn L. Williams et al. 192p. (C). 1992. text 29.95 (*0-8166-2144-6*) U of Minn Pr.

MMPI Codebook for Counselors. Lewis E. Drake & E. R. Oetting. LC 59-10187. 148p. reprint ed. pap. 45.90 (*0-8357-3330-0*, 203955500018) Bks Demand.

MMPI Handbook, Vol. 2. rev. ed. W. Grant Dahlstrom et al. LC 74-172933. 600p. 1975. reprint ed. pap. 186.00 (*0-608-00835-4*, 206162600010) Bks Demand.

MMPI Handbook: Clinical Interpretation, Vol. 1. rev. ed. W. Grant Dahlstrom et al. LC 74-172933. (Illus.). 1972. text 49.95 (*0-8166-0589-0*) U of Minn Pr.

MMPI (Minnesota Multiphasic Personality Inventory) in Testing, Medicine & Psycology: Guidebook for Reference & Research. rev. ed. Remley L. Rannigan. 150p. 1998. 47.50 (*0-7883-1070-4*); pap. 44.50 (*0-7883-1071-2*) ABBE Pubs Assn.

MMPI, MMPI-2 & MMPI-A in Court: A Practical Guide for Expert Witnesses & Attorneys. Kenneth S. Pope et al. LC 92-35352. 400p. 1993. 59.95 (*1-55798-182-5*) Am Psychol.

MMPI, MMPI-2, & MMPI-A in Court: A Practical Guide for Expert Witnesses & Attorneys. 2nd rev. ed. Kenneth S. Pope et al. LC 99-29100. 473p. 2000. 69.95 (*1-55798-590-1*, 431-729A) Am Psychol.

MMPI-168 Code Book. Ken R. Vincent et al. Ed. by Glenn R. Caddy. LC 84-2936. (Developments in Clinical Psychology Ser.). 200p. 1984. text 73.25 (*0-89391-189-5*) Ablx Pub.

MMPI Patterns of American Minorities. W. Grant Dahlstrom et al. 440p. 1986. text 44.95 (*0-8166-1530-6*) U of Minn Pr.

MMPI Treatment. Steven Rouse. Date not set. pap. 9.95 (*0-8166-3026-7*) U of Minn Pr.

***MMPI-2: An Interpretive Manual.** 2nd ed. Roger L. Greene. LC 99-20373. 696p. (C). 1999. 70.00 (*0-205-28416-7*) Allyn.

MMPI-2: Assessing Personality & Psychopathology. 3rd ed. John R. Graham. LC 99-12573. (Illus.). 528p. (C). 1999. text 54.00 (*0-19-511481-7*) OUP.

***MMPI-2 Correlates for Outpatient Community Mental Health Settings.** John R. Graham et al. LC 99-20293. 616p. 1999. 60.00 (*0-8166-2564-6*, Pub. by U of Minn Pr) Chicago Distribution Ctr.

MMPI-2 in Psychological Treatment. James N. Butcher. (Illus.). 208p. (C). 1990. text 32.95 (*0-19-506344-9*) OUP.

MMPI-2 Tutorial Workbook. Robert R. Reilly & Barbara A. Reilly. 212p. 1991. pap. text 22.00 (*0-89079-267-4*, 1510) PRO-ED.

MMS: The Communication Language of Manufacturing. Consortium CCE-CNMA Staff. (Research Reports ESPRIT, Project 7096, CCE-CNMA: Vol. 2). 185p. 1996. pap. 37.00 (*3-540-59061-7*) Spr-Verlag.

MMS - No Laughing Matter: Male Menopausal Syndrome. Dave Block. (Illus.). 52p. 1993. pap. 1.50 (*0-9639812-0-X*) Laid Back Ent.

MMXXVI - The Vision. Gerard Pannell. LC 93-84363. (Illus.). 12p. (Orig.). (YA). 1993. pap. 9.50 (*1-883588-00-6*) PAAS Pr.

Mn Manganese, Vol. A2. (Illus.). xi, 180p. 1993. 795.00 (*0-387-93665-3*) Spr-Verlag.

Mn Manganese: A 3 a Minerals (Oxides of Type M3O4) see Gmelin: Handbook of Inorganic & Organometallic Chemistry

Mn Manganese Pt. A, Section 5b1: History, Occurrence: Mineral (MO2-Type Tunnel Oxides) 8th ed. (Gmelin Ser.). (Illus.). xi, 250p. 1996. 1077.00 (*3-540-93746-3*) Spr-Verlag.

MN Roy: The Man. J. B. Wadia. 1984. 9.50 (*0-8364-1126-9*, Pub. by Popular Prakashan) S Asia.

MNC to 2010: The Networked Organisation. 1997. write for info. (*0-614-25481-7*) Econ Intel.

Mnemata: Papers in Memory of Nancy M. Waggoner. Ed. by William E. Metcalf. (Illus.). 115p. 1991. 20.00 (*0-89722-243-1*) Am Numismatic.

Mnemonics for Anatomy Students: A Guide to Memory Aids for the Students of Anatomy. David J. Gerrick. 1975. pap. 4.00 (*0-916750-38-8*) Dayton Labs.

Mnemonics for Math. Bernetta Gresko. (Illus.). 22p. (J). (gr. k-5). 1994. pap. 4.95 (*0-939155-17-6*) Sunset Prods.

Mnemonics Rhetoric & Poetics for Medics, Vol. I. Robert L. Bloomfield & Ted Chandler. 1983. pap. 11.50 (*0-9612242-1-5*) Harbinger Med Pr NC.

Mnemonics Rhetoric & Poetics for Medics, Vol. II. Carolyn F. Pedley et al. (Illus.). 175p. (Orig.). 1984. pap. 10.95 (*0-9612242-3-1*) Harbinger Med Pr NC.

Mnemonics Rhetoric & Poetics for Medics, Vol. III. Robert L. Bloomfield & Carolyn F. Pedley. (Illus.). 165p. 1990. pap. 9.75 (*0-9612242-6-6*) Harbinger Med Pr NC.

Mnemonotechnics. Alan Davies. 28p. (Orig.). 1982. pap. 5.50 (*0-937013-12-9*) Potes Poets.

MNM Team Building Process for Printers. Michael P. O'Connor & Becky Erickson. LC 91-90250. 250p. 1991. pap. 39.95 (*0-9629366-7-7*) Old Stone Pub.

Mnogoezichen Rechik po Informatika i Kompiuturna Tekhnika see Elsevier's Dictionary of Computer Science & Mathematics

Mnogosetochnye Metody Konechnykh Elementov see Multigrid Methods for Finite Elements

Mo' James R. Granger, Jr. LC 89-50093. (Illus.). 244p. (Orig.). 1989. pap. 12.95 (*0-945023-01-4*) Uraeus Pub.

MO: Causes & Consequences. F. J. Breedon & P. G. Fisher. LC HG0230.3. (Working Papers: No. 20). 44p. 1993. pap. 30.00 (*0-7837-8447-3*, 204925200010) Bks Demand.

Mo: Mohamed Amin: Frontline Cameraman. Brian Tetley. (C). 1988. 80.00 (*1-869828-03-8*, Pub. by Moonstone Bks) St Mut.

***Mo: The Life & Times of Morris K. Udall.** Donald W. Carson & James W. Johnson. LC 00-9255. 2001. write for info. (*0-8165-2049-6*) U of Ariz Pr.

***Mo: Tibetan Divination System.** rev. ed. Jamgon Mipham. 168p. 2000. pap. text. write for info. (*1-55939-147-2*) Snow Lion Pubns.

Mo & His Friends. Mary Pope Osborne. (Easy-to-Read Bks.: Level 2). (Illus.). 48p. (J). (gr. k-3). 1996. pap. 3.99 (*0-14-036202-9*, PuffinBks) Peng Put Young Read.

Mo & His Friends. Mary Pope Osborne. (Puffin Easy-to-Read Ser.). 1996. 8.70 (*0-606-09623-X*, Pub. by Turtleback) Demco.

Mo Artists Guide: Compendium of Missouri Artists. Dan Woodward. Ed. by Maureen Ramsey-Woodward. 100p. 1993. 12.95 (*1-882935-01-2*) Westphalia.

Mo Jo Woman: A Conjuring of Poems. Dee Frances. 65p. pap. 17.95 (*1-885519-74-5*) DDDD Pubns.

***Mo-Kan Ghosts: True Supernatural Stories of the Missouri-Kansas Area.** Maurice Schwalm. 176p. 1999. pap. 14.95 (*1-893407-02-0*, Pub. by Toad Hall PA) ACCESS Pubs Network.

Mo Molybdenum: Organomolybdenum Coumpounds, Pt. 11: Mononuclear Compounds. 8th ed. (Gmelin Handbook of Inorganic & Organometallic Chemistry Ser.). (Illus.). xii, 395p. 1996. 1640.00 (*3-540-93743-9*) Spr-Verlag.

Mo Molybdenum Pt. 13: Organomolybdenum Compounds: Mononuclear Compounds. 8th ed. (Gmelin Ser.). (Illus.). xi, 253p. 1996. 1084.00 (*3-540-93744-7*) Spr-Verlag.

Mo Organomolybdenum Compounds. 8th ed. (Gmelin Handbook of Inorganic & Organometallic Chemistry Ser.: Pt. 7). (Illus.). xi, 368p. 1991. 1380.00 (*0-387-93625-4*) Spr-Verlag.

Mo Organomolybdenum Compounds see Gmelin: Handbook of Inorganic & Organometallic Chemistry

Mo Organomolybdenum Compounds, Heteronuclear Compounds. 8th ed. (Gmelin Handbuch der Anorganischen Chemie Ser.: Pt. 9, Suppl.). (Illus.). xiii, 332p. 1993. 1410.00 (*0-387-93670-X*) Spr-Verlag.

Mo Them Rong Lon Con Duong. Tinh Thuy. (VIE.). 33p. 1996. pap. 6.00 (*1-891667-38-6*) La Boi Soc.

Mo Tzu: Basic Writings. Mo Tzu. Tr. by Burton Watson. LC 63-20339. (Translations from the Oriental Classics Ser.). 140p. (Orig.). 1963. pap. text 17.00 (*0-231-08608-3*) Col U Pr.

Mo Tzu's Religious Blueprint for a Chinese Utopia: The Will & the Way. Scott Lowe. LC 92-4366. 200p. 1992. lib. bdg. 79.95 (*0-7734-9490-1*) E Mellen.

Mo Vaughn: Angel on a Mission. Michael Shalin. Ed. by Rob Rains. (Super Star Ser.). 96p. (J). 1999. pap. 4.95 (*1-58261-046-0*) Sprts Pubng.

Mo Vaughn: Big Mo. Andrew Santella. (Sports Stars Ser.). (Illus.). 48p. (J). (gr. 2-8). 1996. lib. bdg. 19.00 (*0-516-04369-2*) Childrens.

Mo' Yo' Mama! Snap C. Pop & Kid Rank. LC 96-166677. 128p. (Orig.). 1996. pap. 8.00 (*0-425-15214-6*) Berkley Pub.

Moa see Extinct Species Collection

Moa-Hunters of New Zealand: Sportsmen of the Stone Age. Thomas L. Buick. LC 75-35242. reprint ed. 39.50 (*0-404-14417-9*) AMS Pr.

***Moab: An Atlas of Moab, Utah's Greatest Off-Road Bicycle Rides.** Lee Bridgers. (Mountain Bike America Guidebks.). (Illus.). 288p. 2000. pap. 17.95 (*0-7627-0702-X*) Globe Pequot.

Moab Area Mt. Bike Map, UT. rev. ed. Ed. by Trails Illustrated Staff. (Illus.). 1997. 6.99 (*0-925873-62-4*) Trails Illustrated.

Moab Country Day Hikes. F. A. Barnes & M. M. Barnes. LC 95-83944. (Canyon Country Ser.: No. 43). (Illus.). 48p. (Orig.). 1996. pap. 6.00 (*0-925685-25-9*) Canyon Country Pubns.

***Moab Is My Washpot.** Stephen Fry. 376p. 2000. pap. 13.00 (*1-56947-202-5*) Soho Press.

Moab Is My Washpot: An Autobiography. Stephen Fry. LC 98-46177. (Illus.). 352p. 1999. 24.00 (*0-375-50264-5*) Random House.

Moab, Utah: A Travelguide to Slickrock Bike Trail & Mountain Biking Adventures. Bob Ward. LC 95-5687. (Illus.). 240p. 1995. pap. 15.00 (*1-879415-11-9*) Mtn n Air Bks.

Moabit Sonnets. Albrecht Haushofer. Tr. by M. Herter Norton. 1978. pap. 3.95 (*0-393-04532-3*) Norton.

Moak 4 State Regional Exhibition, 1996. Donald D. Perry. (Illus.). 16p. (Orig.). 1996. pap. 3.00 (*0-934306-15-X*) Springfield.

Moaner's Bench. Mars Hill. LC 97-53078. 384p. 1998. 24.00 (*0-06-019102-3*, HarperFlamingo) HarpC.

Moaner's Bench: A Novel. Mars Hill. LC 97-53078. 384p. 1999. pap. 14.00 (*0-06-093058-6*) HarpC.

Moanin' Low: A Discography of Female Popular Vocal Recordings, 1920-1933, 67. Ross Laird. LC 96-21947. (Discographies Ser.: Vol. 67). 768p. 1996. lib. bdg. 105.00 (*0-313-29241-8*, Greenwood Pr) Greenwood.

***Moaning Bones: African-American Ghost Stories.** James Haskins. LC 98-14275. (Illus.). (J). (gr. 2 up). 1998. 14.00 (*0-688-16021-2*) Lothrop.

Moaning Lizzy. Loretta B. Staley. iv, 250p. Date not set. pap. 12.50 (*1-891142-04-6*) Book Bench.

Moans & Groans & Dinosaur Bones. Judy Delton. (Pee Wee Scouts Ser.: No. 31). (Illus.). 112p. (J). 1997. pap. 3.99 (*0-440-40982-9*, YB BDD) BDD Bks Young Read.

Moans & Groans & Dinosaur Bones. Judy Delton. (Pee Wee Scouts Ser.). 1997. 9.09 (*0-606-11726-1*, Pub. by Turtleback) Demco.

Moans, Groans & Skeleton Bones: Fun Songs & Activities for Kids. Cheryl Lavender. (MusicTivity Ser.). (Illus.). 32p. (Orig.). (J). 1993. pap. 9.95 (*0-7935-2372-9*, HL00330605) H Leonard.

Moas. Katie Beck. Ed. by Nancy R. Thatch. LC 99-18079. (Books for Students by Students). (Illus.). 29p. (J). (gr. 4-7). 1999. lib. bdg. 15.95 (*0-933849-73-7*) Landmark Edns.

Mob. Abigail Child. LC 94-67492. 96p. 1994. 9.50 (*1-882022-21-1*) O Bks.

Mob: Organized Crime in America. John Burgess. 70p. (Orig.). (YA). (gr. 7-12). 1996. pap. 6.95 (*1-57515-094-8*) PPI Pubng.

Mob: Rule & Riots. Lucy De Bruyn. 1984. 39.00 (*0-7212-0611-5*, Pub. by Regency Pr GBR) St Mut.

Mob Intent on Death: The NAACP & the Arkansas Riot Cases. Richard C. Cortner. LC 85-29511. 280p. 1988. reprint ed. pap. 86.80 (*0-608-02309-4*, 206295000004) Bks Demand.

Mob Lawyer: Including the Inside Account of Who Killed Jimmy Hoffa & JFK. Frank Ragano & Selwyn Raab. Ed. by Barbara Grossman & Nicholas Pileggi. (Illus.). 320p. 1994. text 22.00 (*0-684-19568-2*, Scribners Ref) Mac Lib Ref.

Mob Magic. P. N. Elrod et al. Ed. by Brian Thomsen & Martin H. Greenberg. 1998. pap. 5.99 (*0-88677-821-2*, Pub. by DAW Bks) Penguin Putnam.

***Mob Rule: Official Strategy Guide.** BradyGames Staff. 216p. 1999. pap. 19.99 (*1-56686-911-0*) Brady Pub.

***Mob Stories.** Allen R. May. 2000. 19.95 (*1-56072-779-9*, Nova Kroshka Bks) Nova Sci Pubs.

Mob Violence in India. S. L. Prachand. 144p. 1979. 12.95 (*0-318-37211-8*) Asia Bk Corp.

Mobbing: Emotional Abuse in the American Workplace. Noa Davenport et al. (Illus.). 216p. 1999. pap. 14.95 (*0-9671803-0-9*, Pub. by Civil Society) BookMasters.

Mobeetie. Illus. by Bill Izzard. vii, 105p. 1996. pap. 10.00 (*1-891584-03-0*) Tangleaire Pr.

Mobel in Ton: Untersuchungen Zur Archaologischen und Religionsgeschichtlichen Bedeutung der Terrakottamodelle von Tischen, Stuhlen und Betten aus dem Alten Orient. Nadja Cholidis. (Altertumskunde des Vorderen Orients Ser.: Vol. 1). (GER., Illus.). xii, 323p. 1992. text 86.00 (*3-927120-10-3*, Pub. by UGARIT) Eisenbrauns.

Moberg's Emigrant Novels & the Journals of Andrew Peterson. Roger McKnight. Ed. by Franklyn D. Scott. LC 78-15196. (Scandinavians in America Ser.). 1979. lib. bdg. 23.95 (*0-405-11649-7*) Ayer.

Mobfather. George Anastasia. 320p. 1994. mass mkt. 4.99 (*0-7860-0043-0*, Pinncle Kensgtn) Kensgtn Pub Corp.

MOBICOM, 95: 1st International Conference on Mobile Computing. 236p. 1995. pap. text 34.00 (*0-89791-814-2*, 533952) Assn Compu Machinery.

MOBICOM 97: MOBICOM 97: The Third Annual ACN/IEEE International Conference on Mobile Computing. 270p. 1997. 40.00 (*0-89791-988-2*, 533971) Assn Compu Machinery.

MOBICOM, 96: 2nd International Conference on Mobile Computing & Networking. 216p. 1996. pap. text 30.00 (*0-89791-872-X*, 533961) Assn Compu Machinery.

Mobie-Diq. Marie Redonnet. Tr. by Dan McGillicuddy from FRE. LC 95-71282. 96p. (Orig.). 1995. pap. 10.95 (*0-9648671-0-9*) DM Pubng.

Mobifunk-Lexikon: Telecommunications Von A-Z. 3rd ed. Hans Gusbeth. (GER.). 158p. 1992. 59.95 (*0-7859-8465-8*, 3772366449) Fr & Eur.

Mobil Collectibles: Chasing the Red Horse. Robert Bender & Tammy Cannoy-Bender. LC 98-89679. (Illus.). 160p. 1999. pap. 29.95 (*0-7643-0782-7*) Schiffer.

Mobil Corp. A Report on the Company's Environmental Policies & Practices. (Illus.). 42p. (C). 1994. reprint ed. pap. text 40.00 (*0-7881-0980-4*, Coun on Econ) DIANE Pub.

Mobil Food Vendors: Market Segment Specialization Program-Audit Technique Guide. 146p. 1995. pap. 37.85 (*1-57402-113-3*) Athena Info Mgt.

M

An Asterisk (*) at the beginning of an entry indicates that the title is appearing for the first time.

M

Mobil Highway Atlas 1994. Mobil Oil Corporation Staff. 1993. pap. 4.95 (0-671-86427-0, P-H Travel) Prntice Hall Bks.

Mobil IP: Design Principles & Practices: Design Principles & Practices. Charles E. Perkins. LC 97-35781. (Wireless Communications Ser.). 304p. (C). 1997. 49.99 (0-201-63469-4, Prentice Hall) P-H.

Mobil Pocket Atlas, 1994. Mobil Oil Corporation Staff. 1993. pap. 2.50 (0-671-79987-8, P-H Travel) Prntice Hall Bks.

Mobil Road Atlas Trip Planning Guide 1994. Mobil Oil Corporation Staff. 1993. pap. 7.95 (0-671-79986-X, P-H Travel) Prntice Hall Bks.

Mobil Travel Guide, 7 bks. Incl. California & West. Rand McNally Staff. 1991. Great Lakes Area. Mid-Atlantic States. Rand McNally Staff. 1991. 10.95 North Eastern States. Rand McNally Staff. 1991. 10.95 Northwest & Great Plains. Rand McNally Staff. 1991. 10.95 Southeastern States. Rand McNally Staff. 1991. 10.95 Southwest & South Central. Rand McNally Staff. 1991. 14.00 1991. write for info. (0-318-56391-6) Wehman.

Mobil Travel Guide: America's Best Hotels & Restaurants, 1995-1996. Fodor's Staff. 1996. pap. text 10.00 (0-614-10723-7) Fodors Travel.

Mobil 1999: Colorado. Fodor Staff. (Mobil Travel Guides Ser.). 1999. pap. write for info. (0-679-00242-1) Fodors Travel.

MobilCom '94. Market Intelligence Staff. 248p. 1994. 595.00 (1-56753-933-5) Frost & Sullivan.

Mobile. Michel Butor. (FRE.). 1991. pap. 24.95 (0-7859-2951-7) Fr & Eur.

Mobile. Michel Butor. (Imaginaire Ser.). (FRE.). pap. 19.95 (2-07-072530-8) Schoenhof.

Mobile. San Antonio Cartographers Staff. 1995. 2.95 (0-671-56278-9) Macmillan.

Mobile: A Gulf Coast Treasure. Foncie Bullard et al. Ed. by James E. Turner & Lenita Gilreath. LC 94-30172. (Illus.). 240p. 1994. pap. 24.95 (1-885352-01-8) Community Comm.

Mobile Academy of the Performing Arts for Children of Rural South East Arkansas. Herbert Zipper. 1969. 15.00 (0-318-21716-3) NGCSA.

Mobile Agents. William R. Cockayne & Michael Zyda. LC 97-1595. 250p. (C). 1997. pap. text 48.00 incl. cd-rom (0-13-858242-4) P-H.

Mobile Agents: First International Workshop, MA 97, Berlin, Germany, April 1997: Proceedings, Vol. 121. Kurt Rothermel & R. Popescu-Zeletin. LC 97-13203. (Lecture Notes in Computer Science Ser.). 1997. pap. write for info. (3-540-62803-7) Spr-Verlag.

Mobile Agents: 2nd International Workshop, MA '98, Stuttgart, Germany, September 9-11, 1998: Proceedings, Vol. 147. Kurt Rothermel & Fritz Hohl. LC 98-39444. (Lecture Notes in Computer Science Ser.). 1998. pap. 49.00 (3-540-64959-X) Spr-Verlag.

Mobile Agents & Security. Ed. by Giovanni Vigna. LC 98-36069. (Lecture Notes in Computer Science Ser.: Vol. 1419). 257p. 1998. pap. 49.00 (3-540-64792-9) Spr-Verlag.

Mobile Alchemy. Boruk Glasgow. 64p. 1978. write for info. (0-318-64124-0) Poets Pr.

Mobile Alternative Demilitarization Technologies. LC 97-18877. 1997. text 174.00 (0-7923-4591-6) Kluwer Academic.

***Mobile & Handheld Phones in Australia: A Strategic Entry Report, 1996.** Compiled by Icon Group International Staff. (Illus.). 142p. 1999. ring bd. 1420.00 incl. audio compact disk (0-7418-1468-4) Icon Grp.

Mobile & Handheld Phones in Australia: A Strategic Entry Report, 1997. Compiled by Icon Group International. (Country Industry Report). (Illus.). 152p. 1999. ring bd. 1520.00 incl. audio compact disk (0-7418-0375-5) Icon Grp.

***Mobile & Personal Communication Services & Systems.** Raj Pandya. LC 99-31330. (Series on Digital & Mobile Communications). 1999. 59.95 (0-7803-4708-0) IEEE Standards.

Mobile & Personal Communications: Proceedings of the 2nd Joint COST 227-231 Workshop on Mobile & Personal Communications, Florence, Italy, 20-21 April 1995. Ed. by E. Del Re. 382p. 1995. text 190.00 (0-444-82328-X) Elsevier.

Mobile & Personal Satellite Communications: Proceedings of the 1st European Workshop on Mobile-Personal Satcoms (EMPS 94) Ed. by F. Ananasso & F. K. Vatalaro. LC 95-2516. 348p. 1996. 59.00 (3-540-19933-0) Spr-Verlag.

Mobile & Personal Satellite Communications: Proceedings of the 2nd European Workshop on Mobile Personal SATCOMS EMPS' 96. F. K. Vatalaro & F. Ananasso. LC 96-43787. (Illus.). 582p. 1996. pap. 89.00 (3-540-76111-X) Spr-Verlag.

Mobile & Personal Satellite Communications 3: Proceeding of the 3rd European Workshop on Mobile/Personal Satcoms. Ed. by M. Ruggieri. LC 98-44133. (Illus.). xii, 428p. 1998. pap. 109.00 (1-85233-045-7) Spr-Verlag.

***Mobile & Rapidly Assembled Structures III.** Ed. by A. Samartin et al. (Advances in Architecture Ser.). 350p. 2000. 173.00 (1-85312-817-1, 8163, Pub. by WIT Pr) Computational Mech MA.

Mobile & Rapidly Assembled Structures II. Ed. by F. Escrig & C. A. Brebbia. LC 96-83649. 448p. 1996. 192.00 (1-85312-398-6, 3986, Pub. by WIT Pr) Computational Mech MA.

Mobile & the Eastern Shore. Nancy Gaillard et al. (Images of America Ser.). 1999. pap. 16.99 (0-7524-0546-2) Arcadia Publng.

Mobile & Wireless Communications Equipment in France: A Strategic Entry Report, 1997. Compiled by Icon Group International Staff. (Illus.). 142p. 1999. ring bd. 1420.00 incl. audio compact disk (0-7418-0921-4) Icon Grp.

***Mobile & Wireless Communications Networks: Proceedings of the IFIP - TC6/European Union Networking 2000 International Workshop, MWCN 2000, Paris, France, May 2000.** Cambyse Guy Omidyar. LC 00-33819. (Lecture Notes in Computer Science). 2000. pap. write for info. (3-540-67543-4) Spr-Verlag.

Mobile & Wireless Networks. Ulysses D. Black. LC 96-11741. 384p. 1996. 60.00 (0-13-440546-3) P-H.

Mobile Antenna Systems Handbook. Ed. by K. Fujimoto & J. R. James. LC 94-7672. 617p. 1994. 115.00 (0-89006-539-X) Artech Hse.

Mobile Applications Design & Development. Glenn Froemming. 1998. 69.95 (0-8493-2545-5) CRC Pr.

Mobile Barrages & Intakes on Sediment Transporting Rivers. Maurice Bouvard. 320p. 1991. 136.00 (90-6191-150-8, Pub. by A A Balkema) Ashgate Pub Co.

Mobile Bay: From 5 Sea Chanties for Voice & Piano. C. Dougherty. 12p. 1995. pap. 3.95 (0-7935-3834-3, 50482272) H Leonard.

Mobile Bay & the Mobile Campaign: The Last Great Battles of the Civil War. Chester G. Hearn. LC 92-50891. (Illus.). 272p. 1998. pap. 20.00 (0-7864-0574-0) McFarland & Co.

Mobile Bay Tales: Essays & Stories about a Region. Ed. by Tom Franklin & Barry Nowlin. 200p. 1991. 25.00 (0-685-40749-7); pap. 9.95 (0-685-40750-0) Soft Teach Inc.

Mobile Cadets, 1845 to 1945: A Century of Honor & Fidelity, Anonymous Manuscript. Ed. by William S. Coker. LC 92-42668. 1992. 30.00 (1-882695-04-6) Patagonia Pr.

Mobile Capital & the Structure of Development in Latin America. James E. Mahon. LC 95-17440. 232p. 1996. 48.50 (0-271-01525-X); pap. 18.95 (0-271-01526-8) Pa St U Pr.

Mobile Cellular Telecommunications Systems. 2nd ed. W. Lee. (Illus.). 664p. 1995. 69.95 (0-07-038089-9) McGraw.

Mobile Collector's & Price Guide. Wayne Henderson. LC 98-34414. (Illus.). 128p. 1998. pap. 19.95 (0-7603-0534-X, 127170AP) MBI Pubg.

Mobile Communication Satellites: Theory & Applications. Tom Logsdon. (Illus.). 277p. 1995. 55.00 (0-07-038476-2) McGraw.

Mobile Communication Service Markets: Enhanced Offerings Expand User-Base. Market Intelligence Staff. 396p. 1993. 1695.00 (1-56753-465-1) Frost & Sullivan.

Mobile Communication Systems. J. D. Parsons. 292p. 1989. text 115.00 (0-470-21213-6) Halsted Pr.

Mobile Communications. A. Jagoda & M. De Villepin. Tr. by J. C. Nelson from FRE. (Series in Communication & Distributed Systems). 184p. 1993. 105.00 (0-471-93906-4) Wiley.

Mobile Communications. F. F. Mazda. (Illus.). 350p. 1996. pap. text 32.95 (0-240-51458-0, Focal) Buttrwrth-Heinemann.

***Mobile Communications.** Jocker Schiller. 400p. (C). 1999. pap. text 49.95 (0-201-39836-2) Addison-Wesley.

Mobile Communications: Advanced Systems & Components. Ed. by Christoph Gunther. LC 94-8267. (Lecture Notes in Computer Science Ser.: Vol. 783). xv, 564p. 1994. 79.95 (0-387-57856-0) Spr-Verlag.

Mobile Communications Design Fundamentals. 2nd ed. Lee. 372p. 1993. pap. text 98.95 (0-471-00747-1) Wiley.

Mobile Communications Design Fundamentals. 2nd ed. William C. Lee. LC 92-21130. (Series in Telecommunications). 400p. 1993. 98.95 (0-471-57446-5) Wiley.

Mobile Communications Engineering. William C. Lee. (Illus.). 480p. 1982. 70.00 (0-07-037039-7) McGraw.

Mobile Communications Engineering. 2nd ed. William C. Lee. LC 97-30668. (Telecommunications Ser.). (Illus.). 689p. 1997. 65.00 (0-07-037103-2) McGraw.

***Mobile Communications Equipment in Austria: A Strategic Entry Report, 1996.** Compiled by Icon Group International Staff. (Illus.). 103p. 1999. ring bd. 1030.00 incl. audio compact disk (0-7418-1469-2) Icon Grp.

Mobile Communications Handbook. Ed. by Jerry D. Gibson. (Electrical Engineering Handbook Ser.). 592p. 1995. boxed set 94.95 (0-8493-8573-3, 8573) CRC Pr.

***Mobile Communications Handbook.** Jerry D. Gibson. (Illus.). 1999. pap. text (0-8493-2167-0, Chap & Hall CRC) CRC Pr.

Mobile Communications Handbook. 2nd ed. Jerry D. Gibson. 720p. 1999. boxed set 95.00 (0-8493-8597-0) CRC Pr.

Mobile Communications Handbook 2nd ed. Jerry D. Gibson. LC 99-17897. (Electrical Engineering Handbook Ser.). 1999. write for info. (3-540-64836-4) CRC Pr.

Mobile Communications in Mexico: A Strategic Entry Report, 1997. Compiled by Icon Group International Staff. (Illus.). 144p. 1999. ring bd. 1440.00 incl. audio compact disk (0-7418-1102-2) Icon Grp.

Mobile Computing. Agrawal. 1997. lib. bdg. 115.00 (0-7923-9929-3) Kluwer Academic.

Mobile Computing. Ed. by Tomasz Imielinski & Henry F. Korth. (International Series in Engineering & Computer Science, Natural Language Processing & Machine Translation). 752p. (C). 1996. text 176.00 (0-7923-9697-9) Kluwer Academic.

Mobile Computing: A Systems Integrator's Handbook. Chandler Dhawan. LC 96-33611. (s). (Illus.). 452p. 1996. pap. 60.00 (0-07-016769-9) McGraw.

***Mobile Computing Environments for Multimedia Systems** B. Prabhakaran & Mohsen Kavehrad. LC 99-31815. 1999. write for info. (0-7923-8549-7) Kluwer Academic.

Mobile Control of Distributed Parameter Systems. A. G. Butkovsky & A. M. Pustyl'nikov. (Engineering Science Ser.). 310p. 1987. text 94.95 (0-470-20817-1) P-H.

Mobile Crane Operations Level One. NCCER Staff. 1997. pap. text, teacher ed. 50.00 (0-13-909664-7, Prentice Hall); pap. text, student ed. 50.00 (0-13-909631-0, Prentice Hall); teacher ed., ring bd. 50.00 (0-13-909672-8, Prentice Hall); student ed., ring bd. 50.00 (0-13-909649-3, Prentice Hall) P-H.

***Mobile Data Access: Proceedings of the 1st International Conference, MDA '99, Hong Kong, China, December, 1999.** International Conference on Mobile Data Access Staff. Ed. by Hong Va Leong et al. LC 99-88578. (Lecture Notes in Computer Science Ser.: 1748). x, 245p. 2000. pap. write for info. (3-540-66878-0) Spr-Verlag.

Mobile Data & Wireless LAN Technologies. Rifaat A. Dayem. LC 97-156866. 336p. (C). 1997. 69.00 (0-13-839051-7) P-H.

Mobile Data Communications Equipment. Frost & Sullivan Staff. Date not set. write for info. (0-7889-0467-1, 2893) Frost & Sullivan.

***Mobile Data Management & Applications** Jin Jing & Anupam Joshi. LC 99-33653. 1999. write for info. (0-7923-8596-9) Kluwer Academic.

Mobile Dentistry: Establishing a Thriving Practice. J. Edward Murphy, Jr. 1996. 49.95 (0-87814-468-4) PennWell Bks.

Mobile DJ Handbook: How to Start & Run a Profitable Mobile Disc Jockey Service. Stacy Zemon. LC 97-645. 160p. 1997. pap. 21.95 (0-240-80266-7, Focal) Buttrwrth-Heinemann.

Mobile DNA. Ed. by Douglas E. Berg & Martha M. Howe. (Illus.). 990p. 1989. 89.00 (1-55581-005-5) ASM Pr.

Mobile Domain Boundaries. Ed. by E. K. Salje. 200p. 1994. pap. text 504.00 (2-88124-969-8) Gordon & Breach.

Mobile Drilling Units of the World, 1997-1998. Ed. by Oilfield Publications, Inc. Staff. (Illus.). 910p. 1997. pap. 383.00 (1-870945-97-2) Oilfield Publns.

Mobile Farmers: An Ethnoarchaeological Approach to Settlement Organization among the Raramuri of Northwestern New Mexico. Martha Graham. LC 94-6297. (Ethnoarchaeological Ser.: No. 3). (Illus.). viii, 113p. 1994. pap. 18.00 (1-879621-16-9); lib. bdg. 29.50 (1-879621-17-7) Intl Mono Prehstry.

Mobile Food Vendors. 144p. 1996. pap. 14.00 (0-16-061977-7) USGPO.

Mobile Genetic Elements: Frontiers in Molecular Biology. Ed. by David Sherratt. (Frontiers in Molecular Biology Ser.). (Illus.). 192p. 1995. text 105.00 (0-19-963405-X); pap. text 55.00 (0-19-963404-1) OUP.

Mobile Guerrilla Force. James C. Donahue. 1997. mass mkt. 6.99 (0-312-96164-2) St Martin.

Mobile Guerrilla Force: With the Special Forces in War Zone D. James C. Donahue. LC 95-37395. (Naval Institute Special Warfare Ser.). (Illus.). 228p. 1996. 29.95 (1-55750-172-6) Naval Inst Pr.

Mobile Health Unit. unabridged ed. S. Gianinazzi. 1998. pap. 14.95 (1-893336-22-0) B Newton.

Mobile Home Parks, Pt. 2. Max S. Wehrly. LC 72-79132. (Urban Land Institute, Technical Bulletin Ser.: No. 68). 136p. reprint ed. pap. 42.20 (0-608-14458-4, 202504200002) Bks Demand.

Mobile Home Parks: An Analysis of Characteristics, Pt. 1. Robinson Newcomb. LC 76-167878. (Urban Land Institute, Technical Bulletin Ser.: No. 66). 80p. reprint ed. pap. 30.00 (0-608-14292-1, 201735700007) Bks Demand.

Mobile Homes. Rudy Burckhardt. Ed. by Kenward Elmslie. LC 79-90670. (Illus.). 1980. 15.00 (0-915990-18-0); pap. 7.50 (0-915990-19-9) Z Pr.

***Mobile Hydraulic Technology.** (Illus.). 428p. (C). 2000. pap. 79.00 (1-55769-039-1) Parker Hannifin.

Mobile Hydraulics Manual. Frederick C. Wood. (Illus.). (C). 1998. text 50.00 (0-9634162-5-1) Vickers Inc Trng Ctr.

Mobile Information Systems. Ed. by John Walker. (Telecom Management Library). 388p. 1990. text 83.00 (0-89006-340-0) Artech Hse.

Mobile IP: The Internet Unplugged. James Solomon. LC 97-223529. 384p. (C). 1997. 49.99 (0-13-856246-6) P-H.

Mobile Juice & Smoothie Bar Business Plan. 2nd ed. Juice Gallery Staff. (Illus.). 120p. 1998. reprint ed. ring bd. 359.95 (1-58291-001-4) Juice Gallery.

Mobile Mardi Gras Annual, 1948, Vol. 1, No. 2. Eugene Walter. Ed. by Cameron M. Plummer. (Illus.). 32p. (YA). (gr. 7 up). 1948. pap. 10.00 (0-940882-05-1) HB Pubns.

Mobile Men: Limits to Social Change in Urban Punjab. Satish Saberwal. (C). 1990. 28.50 (81-85425-10-8, Pub. by Manohar) S Asia.

Mobile Mise En Scene: A Critical Analysis of the Theory & Practice of Long Take Camera Movement in the Narrative Film. L. Bacher. LC 77-22904. (Dissertations on Film Ser.). 1978. lib. bdg. 26.95 (0-405-10750-1) Ayer.

Mobile, Multi-Community Waste Wood Processing Facilities: Implementation Manual. (Illus.). 107p. (C). 1998. reprint ed. pap. text 30.00 (0-7881-4257-7) DIANE Pub.

***Mobile Multimedia Communications: Proceedings of the Third International Workshop Held in Princeton, New Jersey, September 25-27, 1996.** D. J. Goodman & D. Raychaudhuri. LC 97-40565. (Illus.). 324p. (C). 1998. 95.00 (0-306-45772-5, Plenum Trade) Perseus Pubng.

***Mobile Networks & Computing.** Illus. by Sanguthevar Rajasekaran et al. (DIMACS Ser.: Vol. 52). 313p. 2000. 99.00 (0-8218-1547-4) Am Math.

Mobile Object Systems Towards the Programmable Internet: 2nd International Workshop, MOSAE96. Ed. by Jan Vitek et al. LC 97-13128. (Lecture Notes in Computer Science Ser.: No. 1222). 250p. 1997. pap. 49.00 (3-540-62852-5) Spr-Verlag.

Mobile Particulate Systems: Proceedings of the NATO Advanced Study Institute, Cargese, Corsica, France, July 4-15, 1994. NATO Advanced Study Institute on Mobile Particulat. Ed. by Elisabeth Guazzelli. LC 95-9886. (NATO Advanced Science Institutes Series C: Vol. 287). 408p. (C). 1995. text 217.50 (0-7923-3437-X) Kluwer Academic.

Mobile Pastoralists: Development Planning & Social Change in Oman. Dawn Chatty. (Illus.). 256p. 1996. pap. 19.50 (0-231-10549-5) Col U Pr.

***Mobile Phone Etiquette.** Peter Laufer. 2000. pap. 8.95 (1-873668-17-1, Pub. by Take That Bks) Trafalgar.

Mobile Police Patlabor. Masami Yuki. (Illus.). 192p. 1998. pap. 15.95 (1-56931-287-7, Cadence Bks) Viz Commns Inc.

Mobile Police Patlabor: Basic Training. Masami Yuki. (Illus.). 192p. 1998. pap. text 15.95 (1-56931-337-7) Viz Commns Inc.

Mobile Processing in Distributed & Open Environments. Peter Sapaty. LC 98-33728. 432p. 1999. 84.95 (0-471-19572-3, Wiley-Interscience) Wiley.

Mobile Production Systems of the World. Oilfield Publications Limited Staff. (Vessels of the World Ser.). (Illus.). 400p. (C). 1994. pap. 355.00 (1-870945-66-2) Oilfield Publns.

Mobile Productions Systems of the World, 1997-1998. Oilfield Publishing Staff. (Illus.). 400p. 1997. pap. 383.00 (1-870945-93-X) Oilfield Publns.

Mobile Radio Communications. Raymond Steele. 792p. 1994. 89.95 (0-7803-1102-7, PC4572) Inst Electrical.

Mobile Radio Communications. 2nd ed. Ray Steele & Lajos Hansos. LC 99-13155. 1090p. 1999. 195.00 (0-471-97806-X) Wiley.

Mobile Radio Networks. Bernd Walke. LC 98-50609. 892p. 1999. 195.00 (0-471-97595-8) Wiley.

Mobile Radio Networks, Fundamental, Security & Operation. Sam Tabbane. LC 99-54639. 640p. 1999. 93.00 (1-58053-009-5) Artech Hse.

Mobile Radio Propagation Channel. J. D. Parsons. 328p. 1996. 180.00 (0-471-96415-8) Wiley.

***Mobile Radio Propagation Channel.** 2nd ed. J. D. Parsons. LC 00-32482. 2000. write for info. (0-471-98857-X) Wiley.

Mobile Radio Technology. Gordon White. 272p. 1994. pap. text 39.95 (0-7506-2491-4) Buttrwrth-Heinemann.

Mobile Receptor Hypothesis: Membrane Receptor Lateral Movement in Signal Transduction. David A. Jans. LC 97-5905. (Molecular Biology Intelligence Unit Ser.). 1997. 99.00 (1-57059-437-6) Landes Bioscience.

Mobile Riverine Force. Turner Publishing Company Staff. 216p. Date not set. 52.50 (1-56311-382-1) Turner Pub KY.

***Mobile Robot Localization & Map Building - A Multisensor Fusion Approach.** Jose A. Castellanos & Juan D. Tardos. 224p. 2000. 125.00 (0-7923-7789-3) Kluwer Academic.

***Mobile Robotics: A Practical Introduction.** Ulrich Nehmzow. LC 99-43763. (Applied Computing Ser.). xii, 244p. 1999. pap. 49.95 (1-85233-173-9, Pub. by Spr-Verlag) Spr-Verlag.

Mobile Robots: Inspiration to Implementation. 2nd ed. Joseph L. Jones et al. LC 98-42605. (Illus.). 486p. 1998. 32.00 (1-56881-097-0) AK Peters.

***Mobile Robots XIV.** Ed. by Douglas W. Gage & Howie M. Choset. 1999. pap. text 72.00 (0-8194-3431-0) SPIE.

Mobile Robots XI & Automated Vechile Control Systems, Vol. 2903. Ed. by Chase H. Kenyon & Pushkin Kachroo. 202p. 1997. 46.00 (0-8194-2305-X) SPIE.

Mobile Robots XII, Vol. 3210. Ed. by Douglas W. Gage. 154p. 1998. 48.00 (0-8194-2642-3) SPIE.

Mobile Robots XIII & Intelligent Transportation Systems, Vol. 3525. Ed. by Howie M. Choset et al. 478p. 1999. 89.00 (0-8194-2986-4) SPIE.

Mobile Satellite Communications. Shingo Ohmori et al. LC 97-41708. 1997. 99.00 (0-89006-843-7) Artech Hse.

***Mobile Satellite Communications Handbook.** Roger Cochetti. 342p. 1998. 105.00 (0-471-29778-X) Wiley.

Mobile Scheduled Castes: Rise of a New Middle Class. Nandu. (C). 1988. 27.50 (81-7075-007-5, Pub. by Hindustan) S Asia.

Mobile Scot: Emigration & Migration, 1861-1911. Jeanette M. Brock. 190p. 1998. pap. 75.00 (0-85976-453-2, Pub. by J Donald) St Mut.

Mobile Sextet. Caldwell Delaney. (Illus.). 187p. 1981. 15.00 (0-940882-15-9) HB Pubns.

Mobile Source Emissions Included Polycyclic Organic Species. Ed. by D. Rondia et al. 1983. text 184.00 (90-277-1633-1) Kluwer Academic.

Mobile Spectacle: Variable Perspective in Manzoni's "I Promessi Sposi" Clareece G. Godt. LC 93-3462. (Studies in Italian Culture: Vol. 12). XVI, 167p. (C). 1998. text 42.95 (0-8204-2134-0) P Lang Pubng.

***Mobile Suit Gundam 0079.** Kazuhisa Kondo. (Illus.). (J). 2000. pap. 15.95 (1-56931-466-7, Viz Comics) Viz Commns Inc.

Mobile Telecommunications: Emerging European Markets. Ed. by Jurgen Muller et al. LC 94-37148. 323p. 1994. 83.00 (0-89006-796-1) Artech Hse.

Mobile Telecommunications: Standards, Regulations & Applications - Wireless Communications Engineering. Rudi Bekkers. LC 98-41588. 1998. 99.00 (0-89006-806-2) Artech Hse.

An Asterisk (*) at the beginning of an entry indicates that the title is appearing for the first time.

Mobile Telecommunications Equipment in Dominican Republic: A Strategic Entry Report, 1997. Compiled by Icon Group International Staff. (Country Industry Report). (Illus.). 106p. 1999. ring bd. 1060.00 incl. audio compact disk (*0-7418-0565-0*) Icon Grp.

Mobile Telecommunications Factbook. Nathan J. Muller. LC 97-52227. 445p. 1998. pap. 29.95 (*0-07-044461-7*) McGraw.

***Mobile Telecommunications in Sweden: A Strategic Entry Report, 1996.** Compiled by Icon Group International Staff. (Illus.). 100p. 1999. ring bd. 1000.00 incl. audio compact disk (*0-7418-1470-6*) Icon Grp.

***Mobile Telecommunications Networking with ANSI-41.** Michael D. Gallagher. (Telecom Engineering Ser.). 2000. 75.00 (*0-07-135231-7*) McGraw.

Mobile Telecommunications Networking with IS-41. Randall A. Snyder & Michael D. Gallagher. LC 96-51017. (Telecommunications Ser.). (Illus.). 431p. 1997. 69.00 (*0-07-063314-2*) McGraw.

Mobile Telephone Handsets in Taiwan: A Strategic Entry Report, 1998. Compiled by Icon Group International. (Country Industry Report). (Illus.). 116p. 1999. ring bd. 1160.00 incl. audio compact disk (*0-7418-0361-5*) Icon Grp.

Mobile Telephones in Italy: A Strategic Entry Report, 1997. Compiled by Icon Group International. (Country Industry Report). (Illus.). 138p. 1999. ring bd. 1380.00 incl. audio compact disk (*0-7418-0362-3*) Icon Grp.

Mobile Telephones in Italy: A Strategic Entry Report, 1997. Compiled by Icon Group International Staff. (Illus.). 124p. 1999. ring bd. 1240.00 incl. audio compact disk (*0-7418-0922-2*) Icon Grp.

Mobiles & Other Paper Windcatchers. Noel Fiarotta & Phyllis Fiarotta. LC 96-11997. (Illus.). 80p. 1996. 17.95 (*0-8069-8106-7*) Sterling.

Mobiles Replacement. 1969. 29.16 (*0-07-521154-8*) McGraw.

Mobilian Jargon: Linguistic & Sociohistorical Aspects of a Native American Pidgin. Emanuel J. Drechsel. LC 96-20837. (Illus.). 412p. 1997. text 59.00 (*0-19-824033-3*) OUP.

Mobilian Trade Language. James M. Crawford. LC 78-13149. 150p. reprint ed. pap. 46.50 (*0-608-11957-1*, 202316700032) Bks Demand.

Mobilier 18e Siecle: Dictionnaire Ebenistes, Menuisiers. P. Kjellberg. (FRE.). 1998. 995.00 (*0-320-00205-5*) Fr & Eur.

Mobilier en Pierre de Bouqras: Utilisation de la Pierre dans un Site Neolithique sur le Moyen Euphrate (Syrie) J. J. Roodenberg. vii, 207p. 1986. pap. text 52.50 (*90-6258-061-0*, Pub. by Netherlands Inst) Eisenbrauns.

Mobilier Francais de XVIIIe Siecle: Dictionnaire des Ebenistes et des Menusiers. Denise Ledoux-Lebard. (FRE.). 736p. 1991. 450.00 (*0-8288-7315-1*, 285917088X) Fr & Eur.

Mobilier Francais du XVIII Siecle. P. Kjellberg. (FRE.). 896p. 1991. 450.00 (*0-8288-7314-3*, 2859170871) Fr & Eur.

Mobilisation de L'Epargne (French-Savings Mobilization) WCCU (World Council of Credit Unions, Inc.) Staff. 160p. (C). 1990. pap. text, per. 10.00 (*0-8403-6264-1*) Kendall-Hunt.

Mobilisation of the Nervous System. David S. Butler. (Illus.). 265p. 1991. text 83.00 (*0-443-04400-7*) Church.

Mobilisation of the Spine: A Primary Handbook of Clinical Methods. 5th ed. Gregory P. Grieve. (Illus.). 426p. (Orig.). 1991. pap. text 60.00 (*0-443-04236-5*) Church.

Mobilising Foreign Investment for Development see Developing with Foreign Investment

Mobilising the Novel: The Literature of Imperialism & the First World War. Johan A. Hoglund. LC 98-116205. (Acta Universitatis Upsaliensis - Studia Anglistica Upsaliensia 99). 198p. 1997. pap. 54.50 (*91-554-4068-1*, Pub. by Uppsala Univ Acta Univ Uppsaliensis) Coronet Bks.

Mobilising Jargon: Bringing Strategy to Life. John Bray et al. LC 95-10147. 320p. (C). 1995. pap. text 24.95 (*0-13-148891-0*) P-H.

***Mobilitatsverhalten und Verkehrsteilnahme Alterer Menschen: Auswirkungen auf Kompetenz und Lebensgestaltung.** Regina Ernst. (Europaische Hochschulschriften Ser.: Reihe 22). 224p. 1999. 35.95 (*3-631-34869-X*) P Lang Pubng.

Mobility: Processes, Computers & Agents. Dejan S. Milojicic. LC 99-10175. 704p. (C). 1999. pap. text 39.95 (*0-201-37928-7*) Addison-Wesley.

Mobility: Theory & Practice. Werner Schneider et al. LC 92-403. (Flexibook Ser.). 1992. 9.50 (*0-86577-435-8*) Thieme Med Pubs.

Mobility & Degradation of Organic Contaminants in Subsurface Environments. Warren J. Lyman. 416p. 1992. boxed set 104.95 (*0-87371-800-3*) Lewis Pubs.

Mobility & Economic Self-Sufficiency of Section 8 Participants in Rural Areas. Housing Assistance Council Staff. 80p. 1997. 4.50 (*1-58064-025-7*) Housing Assist.

Mobility & Migration: East Anglian Founders of New England, 1629-1640. Roger Thompson. LC 93-22735. 328p. (Orig.). 1994. lib. bdg. 40.00 (*0-87023-893-0*) U of Mass Pr.

Mobility & Migration of Labour in the European Union & Their Specific Implications for Young People. Alexandros Tassinopoulos et al. LC 98-234486. (Cedefop Document Ser.). 126 p. 1998. 13.00 (*92-828-4143-X*, Pub. by Comm Europ Commun) Bernan Associates.

Mobility & Modernity: Migration in Germany, 1820-1988. Steve Hochstadt. LC 98-40110. (Social History, Popular Culture, & Politics in Germany Ser.). 352p. 1999. text 52.50 (*0-472-10944-8*, 10944) U of Mich Pr.

Mobility & Proximity in Biomarkers. S. Damjanovich. 352p. 1994. lib. bdg. 210.00 (*0-8493-4931-1*, QH601) CRC Pr.

Mobility & Recognition in Cell Biology: Proceedings of the FEBS Lecture Course, University of Konstanz. FEBS Lecture Course Staff. Ed. by Horst Sund & Ces Veeger. xii, 586p. 1983. 146.15 (*3-11-009536-X*) De Gruyter.

Mobility & Territoriality: Social & Spatial Boundaries among Foragers, Fishers, Pastoralists & Peripatetics. Ed. by Michael J. Casimir & Aparna Rao. 256p. 1991. 39.50 (*0-85496-739-7*) Berg Pubs.

Mobility & the Small Town, 1900 to 1930. Norman T. Moline. LC 79-133029. (Research Papers: No. 132). (Illus.). 1971. pap. text 14.50 (*0-89065-039-X*, 132) U Ch Pr.

Mobility & Transport for Elderly & Disabled Persons, Vol. 13. C. E. Norrbom. (Transportation Studies). xv, 1152p. 1991. text 638.00 (*2-88124-763-6*) Gordon & Breach.

Mobility & Transport for Elderly & Handicapped Persons. Ed. by Norman Ashford et al. (Transportation Studies: Vol. 2). xi, 383p. 1982. text 228.00 (*0-677-16380-0*) Gordon & Breach.

***Mobility & Transportation in the Elderly.** Ed. by K. Warner Schaie & Martin Pietrucha. LC 99-54280. (Societal Impact on Aging Ser.). (Illus.). 324p. 2000. text 44.95 (*0-8261-1309-5*) Springer Pub.

Mobility for Special Needs. Juliet M. Stone. (Special Needs in Ordinary Schools Ser.). (Illus.). 192p. 1995. 100.00 (*0-304-33067-1*); pap. 33.95 (*0-304-33065-5*) Continuum.

Mobility Forum: Journal of the Air Mobility Command. Government Printing Office Staff. 1997. pap. 18.00 (*0-16-010215-4*) USGPO.

Mobility in Russian & Soviet Military Thought & Practice see SAFRA Papers

Mobility of Labor & Capital: A Study in International Investment & Labor Flow. Saskia Sassen. (Illus.). 236p. (C). 1990. pap. text 19.95 (*0-521-38672-1*) Cambridge U Pr.

Mobility of the Negro. Edward E. Lewis. LC 68-58603. (Columbia University. Studies in the Social Sciences: No. 342). reprint ed. 20.00 (*0-404-51342-5*) AMS Pr.

Mobility Plus . . . A Reference Guide. 2nd ed. Ed. by Center for Mobility Resources Staff. 773p. 1999. pap. 259.60 (*0-9643934-0-9*, D5503; D5504) Ctr Mobility Res.

Mobility, Subjective Deprivation & Ethnic Hostility. Morris Janowitz & Robert K. Merton. Ed. by Harriet Zuckerman. LC 79-9007. (Dissertations on Sociology Ser.). 1980. lib. bdg. 26.95 (*0-405-12975-0*) Ayer.

Mobility Tables. Michael Hout. LC 83-60605. (Quantitative Applications in the Social Sciences Ser.: Vol. 31). 93p. 1983. 10.95 (*0-8039-2056-3*) Sage.

Mobility Technology Planning Forum III. 76p. 1997. 49.00 (*1-56091-981-7*, SP-1269) Soc Auto Engineers.

Mobility Training for People with Disabilities: Children & Adults with Physical, Mental, Visual & Hearing Impairments Can Learn to Travel. William Goodman. (Illus.). 144p. 1989. pap. 28.95 (*0-398-06356-7*) C C Thomas.

Mobility Training for People with Disabilities: Children & Adults with Physical, Mental, Visual & Hearing Impairments Can Learn to Travel. William Goodman. (Illus.). 144p. (C). 1989. text 40.95 (*0-398-05572-6*) C C Thomas.

Mobilizaiton of Muslim Women in Egypt. Ghada H. Talhami. 192p. 1996. 49.95 (*0-8130-1429-8*) U Press Fla.

Mobilization: The United States Army in World War 2. 50th anniversary ed. 23p. 1994. pap. 1.25 (*0-16-045118-3*) USGPO.

Mobilization for Evangelism. Mit Medina. pap. 4.95 (*1-884213-00-6*) Vision Christ.

Mobilization for the Neurologically Involved Child: Assessment & Application Strategies for Pe. Sandra Brooks-Scott. 1997. pap. text 54.00 (*0-12-785061-9*) Acad Pr.

Mobilization of Intellect: French Scholars & Writers During the Great War. Martha Hanna. LC 95-42544. 320p. 1996. 44.50 (*0-674-57755-8*) HUP.

Mobilization of the U. S. in World War II: How the Government, Military & Industry Prepared for War. V. R. Cardozier. LC 94-48001. 277p. 1995. lib. bdg. 42.50 (*0-7864-0076-5*) McFarland & Co.

Mobilization, Participation & Democracy in America. Steven J. Rosenstone & John M. Hansen. LC 92-34552. (New Topics in Politics Ser.). (Illus.). 333p. (Orig.). (C). 1993. pap. text 28.00 (*0-02-403660-9*, Macmillan Coll) P-H.

Mobilizing Against AIDS. enl. rev. ed. Eve K. Nichols. LC 88-30100. (Illus.). 387p. 1989. 40.50 (*0-674-57763-9*); pap. text 12.95 (*0-674-57762-0*) HUP.

Mobilizing Against Nuclear Energy: A Comparison of Germany & the United States. Christian Joppke. 324p. 1994. 48.00 (*0-520-07813-6*, Pub. by U CA Pr) Cal Prin Full Svc.

Mobilizing America: Robert P. Patterson & the War Effort, 1940-1945. Keith E. Eiler. LC 97-24827. (Illus.). 544p. 1998. 35.00 (*0-8014-2276-0*) Cornell U Pr.

Mobilizing Consent: Public Opinion & American Foreign Policy, 1937-1947. Michael Leigh. LC 75-44656. 187p. 1976. 49.95 (*0-8371-8772-9*, LMC/, Greenwood Pr) Greenwood.

Mobilizing Domestic Capital Markets for Infrastructure Financing: International Experience & Lessons from China. Anjali Kumar et al. LC 97-28969. (Discussion Paper Ser.: No. 377). 104p. 1997. pap. 22.00 (*0-8213-4038-7*, 14038) World Bank.

Mobilizing for Chaos: The Story of the New Propaganda. Oscar W. Riegel. LC 72-4677. (International Propaganda & Communications Ser.). 231p. 1972. reprint ed. 20.95 (*0-405-04761-4*) Ayer.

Mobilizing for Peace: The Antinuclear Movements in Western Europe. Thomas R. Rochon. LC 88-9876. (Illus.). 254p. 1988. reprint ed. pap. 78.80 (*0-608-07155-2*, 206738000009) Bks Demand.

Mobilizing for the War Effort, 1940. Ed. by Aaron Klieman & Adrian L. Klieman. LC 90-45364. (American Zionism Ser.: Vol. 8). 456p. 1991. text 45.00 (*0-8240-7356-8*) Garland.

Mobilizing Human Potential: The Challenge of Unemployment. 80p. 1989. pap. 13.95 (*92-1-126011-6*, E89.111.B.2) UN.

Mobilizing Human Resources. Richard Pinder. 1995. pap. 7.95 (*1-56229-415-6*) Pneuma Life Pub.

Mobilizing Human Resources in the Arab World. R. Paul Shaw. (Arab World Ser.). 288p. 1983. 55.00 (*0-7103-0040-9*) Routledge.

Mobilizing Human Resources in the Arab World. R. Paul Shaw. 270p. 1985. pap. 22.50 (*0-7103-0137-5*) Routledge.

Mobilizing Illinois: Governor's Commission on Gangs Final Report. Jim Ryan. (Illus.). 126p. (C). 1998. pap. text 25.00 (*0-7881-7440-1*) DIANE Pub.

Mobilizing Interest Groups in America: Patrons, Professions, & Social Movements. Jack L. Walker, Jr. 272p. 1991. pap. text 18.95 (*0-472-08164-0*, 08164) U of Mich Pr.

Mobilizing Interest Groups in America: Patrons, Professions & Social Movements. Jack L. Walker, Jr. 272p. 1991. text 49.50 (*0-472-10276-1*, 10276) U of Mich Pr.

Mobilizing Invisible Assets. Hiroyuki Itami. (Illus.). 200p. 1991. pap. 18.50 (*0-674-57771-X*) HUP.

Mobilizing Local Communities. Alf Ronnby. 400p. 1996. 101.95 (*1-85972-189-3*, Pub. by Avebry) Ashgate Pub Co.

Mobilizing Private Sector Resources for Infrastructure. 143p. 19.95 (*92-1-119773-2*) UN.

Mobilizing Resentment: Conservative Resurgence from the John Birch Society to the Promise Keepers. Jean Hardisty. LC 99-28147. 208p. 1999. 25.00 (*0-8070-4316-8*) Beacon Pr.

***Mobilizing Resentment: Conservative Resurgence from the John Birch Society to the Promise Keepers.** Jean Hardisty. 304p. 2000. pap. 17.50 (*0-8070-4317-6*) Beacon Pr.

***Mobilizing Resources & Generating Competencies.** Ed. by Peter Karnoe et al. 368p. 1999. 38.00 (*87-16-13466-4*, Pub. by Copenhagen Busn Schl) Bks Intl VA.

Mobilizing Resources for District-Wide Middle-Grades Reform. Holly Hatch & Kathryn A. Hytten. LC 97-36916. 1997. pap. write for info. (*1-56090-118-7*) Natl Middle Schl.

Mobilizing Social Movement Organization: The Formation, Institionalization & Effectiveness of Economical Urban Ministries. James Davidson. (Monographs: No. 6). 1985. pap. 8.00 (*0-932566-05-7*) Soc Sci Stud Rel.

Mobilizing Technology for World Development. Jairam Ramesh. LC 79-53493. 234p. 1979. 69.50 (*0-275-90410-5*, C0410, Praeger Pubs) Greenwood.

Mobilizing Technology for World Development. Ed. by Jairam Ramesh & Charles Weiss, Jr. LC 79-5349. 240p. 1979. pap. 6.95 (*0-03-055451-9*) Overseas Dev Council.

Mobilizing the Army of God. Rick Joyner. 248p. 1996. mass mkt. 5.99 (*0-88368-376-8*) Whitaker Hse.

Mobilizing the Community: Local Politics in the Era of the Global City. Robert Fisher & Joseph Kling. (Urban Affairs Annual Review Ser.: Vol. 41). 390p. (C). 1993. text 62.00 (*0-8039-4247-8*); pap. text 26.00 (*0-8039-4248-6*) Sage.

***Mobilizing the Information Society: A View from Europe.** Robin Mansell & W. Edward Steinmueller. (Illus.). 600p. 2000. text 105.00 (*0-19-829556-1*) OUP.

Mobilizing the Masses: Building Revolution in Henan. Odoric Y. Wou. LC 93-20624. xi , 478p. 1994. 49.50 (*0-8047-2142-4*) Stanford U Pr.

Mobilizing the Modern War: The Political Economy of American Warfare, 1865-1919. Paul A. Koistinen. LC 97-19148. (Modern War Studies). 416p. 1997. 45.00 (*0-7006-0860-5*) U Pr of KS.

Mobilizing to Strengthen Neighborhoods: Profile from 13 Community Foundations. Ed. by David Scheie et al. 68p. 1997. pap. 15.00 (*0-9624428-6-0*) Rainbow Research.

Mobilizing U. S. Industry in World War II. Alan L. Gropman. 167p. (Orig.). (C). 1997. pap. text 35.00 (*0-7881-3646-1*) DIANE Pub.

Mobilizing United States Industry in World War 2: Myth & Reality. Alan L. Gropman. 167p. 1996. per. 10.00 (*0-16-061187-3*) USGPO.

Mobilizing Women for War: German & American Propaganda. Leila J. Rupp. LC 77-85562. (Illus.). 256p. reprint ed. pap. 79.40 (*0-8357-3698-9*, 203642200003) Bks Demand.

Mobilizing Women-Power. Harriot S. Blatch. LC 74-75231. (United States in World War I Ser.). (Illus.). iv, 195p. 1974. reprint ed. lib. bdg. 26.95 (*0-89198-094-6*) Ozer.

Mobius & His Band: Mathematics & Astronomy in Nineteenth-Century Germany. Ed. by John Fauvel et al. LC 92-46692. (Illus.). 178p. 1993. text 38.00 (*0-19-853969-X*) OUP.

Mobius Functions, Incidence Algebras & Power Series Representations. A. Dur. (Lecture Notes in Mathematics Ser.: Vol. 1202). xi, 134p. 1986. 35.95 (*0-387-16771-4*) Spr-Verlag.

Mobius I Rulebook. Ugly John Carver. 1990. 4.00 (*0-940244-86-1*) Flying Buffalo.

Mobius on Emerging Markets. 2nd ed. Mark Mobius. 256p. 1996. 35.00 (*0-273-62284-6*) F T P-H.

Mobius Stripper. Bana Witt. 96p. (Orig.). 1992. pap. 8.95 (*0-916397-23-8*) Manic D Pr.

Mob's Daily Number: Organized Crime & the Numbers Gambling Industry. Don Liddick. LC 98-37050. 1998. write for info. (*0-7618-1266-0*); pap. write for info. (*0-7618-1267-9*) U Pr of Amer.

***Mobsters & Thugs: Quotes from the Underworld.** Olindo Romeo Chiocca. (Prose Ser.: No. 50). 128p. 2000. pap. 13.00 (*1-55071-104-0*, , Pub. by Guernica Editions) Paul & Co Pubs.

Mobutu or Chaos? The United States & Zaire, 1960-1990. Michael G. Schatzberg. 126p. (C). 1991. pap. text 14.00 (*0-685-54252-1*); lib. bdg. 29.75 (*0-685-47831-9*) For Policy Res.

Mobutu or Chaos? The United States & Zaire, 1960-1990. Michael G. Schatzberg. 126p. 1991. 37.50 (*0-8191-8130-7*); pap. 18.50 (*0-8191-8131-5*) U Pr of Amer.

***Moby: Rock the Body.** Alan Wood. 128p. 2000. pap. write for info. (*1-58754-002-9*, Pub. by Olmstead Pr) LPC Group.

Moby Dick see Serie Illustrada, "Now Age"

Moby Dick. (J). 9.95 (*1-56156-308-0*) Kidsbks.

Moby Dick. 496p. 1997. pap. 3.95 (*1-85326-574-8*, Pub. by Wrdsworth Edits) NTC Contemp Pub Co.

Moby Dick. Ed. by Carol Hagerty. (Classics Ser.: Set II). 77p. (YA). (gr. 5-12). 1998. pap. text 7.95 (*1-56254-258-3*, SP2583) Saddleback Pubns.

Moby Dick. Herman Melville. Date not set. lib. bdg. 49.95 (*0-8488-0183-0*) Amereon Ltd.

Moby Dick. Herman Melville. (Cyber Classics Ser.). 486p. 1997. pap. text 14.95 (*1-55701-195-8*) BNI Pubns.

Moby Dick. Herman Melville. Ed. & Intro. by Charles C. Walcutt. 608p. (YA). (gr. 7-12). 1981. mass mkt. 4.95 (*0-553-21311-3*, Bantam Classics) Bantam.

Moby Dick. Herman Melville. 61p. (YA). (gr. 7 up). 1998. pap. 5.50 (*0-87129-782-5*, M68) Dramatic Pub.

Moby Dick, 001. Herman Melville. Ed. by Alfred Kazin. LC 56-14087. (YA). (gr. 9 up). 1956. pap. 13.96 (*0-395-05108-8*, RivEd) HM.

Moby Dick. Herman Melville. Ed. by Donna Carlson. (Illustrated Classics Ser.). (Illus.). 128p. (J). 1992. pap. 2.95 (*1-56156-093-6*) Kidsbks.

Moby Dick. Herman Melville. (Cloth Bound Pocket Series). 240p. 1998. 7.95 (*3-89508-088-8*) Konemann.

***Moby Dick.** Herman Melville. (Classics Ser.). 2000. pap. 11.95 (*0-679-78327-X*) Modern Lib NY.

Moby Dick. Herman Melville. (C). 1967. pap. text 16.00 (*0-393-09670-X*) Norton.

Moby Dick. Herman Melville. LC 97-11062. (Oxford Illustrated Classics Ser.). (Illus.). 104p. (J). (gr. 4 up). 1997. 25.00 (*0-19-274156-X*) OUP.

Moby Dick. Herman Melville. Ed. & Intro. by Tony Tanner. (Oxford World's Classics Ser.). 656p. 1998. pap. 6.95 (*0-19-283385-5*) OUP.

***Moby Dick.** Herman Melville. (Oxford World's Classics Hardcovers Ser.). 640p. 2000. 18.00 (*0-19-210041-6*) OUP.

Moby Dick. Herman Melville. Ed. by Irwin Shapiro. LC 73-75458. (Now Age Illustrated Ser.). (Illus.). 64p. (J). (gr. 5-10). 1973. pap. 2.95 (*0-88301-099-2*) Pendulum Pr.

***Moby Dick.** Herman Melville. (SPA.). 1998. pap. 15.95 (*84-08-02226-1*) Planeta.

Moby Dick. Herman Melville. Ed. by Malvina Vogel. (Great Illustrated Classics Ser.: Vol. 16). (Illus.). 240p. (J). (gr. 3-6). 1990. 9.95 (*0-86611-967-1*) Playmore Inc.

Moby Dick. Herman Melville. (American Collection Short Classics). (J). (gr. 4-7). 1993. pap. 4.95 (*0-8114-6834-8*) Raintree Steck-V.

Moby Dick. Herman Melville. LC 00-502456. (Illus.). 600p. 1999. per. 5.99 (*0-671-02835-9*) S&S Trade.

Moby Dick. Herman Melville. 640p. 1998. mass mkt. 5.99 (*0-8125-4156-1*, Pub. by Tor Bks) St Martin.

Moby Dick. Herman Melville. LC 87-16788. (Illus.). 48p. (J). (gr. 3-6). 1996. pap. 4.95 (*0-8167-1208-5*) Troll Communs.

Moby Dick. Herman Melville. (Classics Library). 608p. pap. 3.95 (*1-85326-008-8*, 0088WW, Pub. by Wrdsworth Edits) NTC Contemp Pub Co.

Moby-Dick. Herman Melville. (J). (gr. 8). 1996. mass mkt. 3.99 (*0-8125-4307-6*, Pub. by Tor Bks) St Martin.

Moby-Dick. Herman Melville. 1955. 10.05 (*0-606-01084-X*, Pub. by Turtleback) Demco.

Moby-Dick. Herman Melville. Ed. by A. Robert Lee. 512p. 1993. pap. 3.95 (*0-460-87307-5*, Everyman's Classic Lib) Tuttle Pubng.

Moby Dick. Herman Melville. LC 96-27942. (Illus.). 32p. (J). (gr. k-3). 1997. 16.00 (*0-374-34997-5*) FS&G.

Moby Dick. Herman Melville et al. (Classics Illustrated Ser.). (Illus.). 52p. (YA). pap. 4.95 (*1-57209-003-0*) Classics Int Ent.

Moby Dick. Bernice Selden. LC 87-16788. (Troll Illustrated Classics). (Illus.). (J). 1988. 10.15 (*0-606-03619-9*, Pub. by Turtleback) Demco.

Moby Dick. Guy Williams. LC 91-51103. (Orig.). (J). 1992. pap. 5.00 (*0-88734-414-3*) Players Pr.

Moby Dick. abr. ed. Herman Melville. 1991. audio 17.00 (*1-55994-394-7*, DCN 2077) HarperAudio.

Moby-Dick. abr. ed. Herman Melville. 1996. pap. 23.95 incl. audio (*0-14-086172-6*, Png AudioBks) Viking Penguin.

Moby Dick. large type ed. Herman Melville. 1997. pap. 21.95 (*1-55701-219-9*) BNI Pubns.

Moby Dick. Herman Melville. 687p. 1983. reprint ed. lib. bdg. 35.95 (*0-89966-478-4*) Buccaneer Bks.

Moby Dick. rev. ed. Herman Melville. LC 98-6469. 555p. 1998. mass mkt. 4.95 (*0-451-52699-6*, Sig Classics) NAL.

M

An Asterisk (*) at the beginning of an entry indicates that the title is appearing for the first time.

Moby Dick. rev. ed. Herman Melville. Ed. by Robert J. Dixson. (American Classics Ser.: Bk. 2). (gr. 9 up). 1987. audio 65.00 (*0-13-024662-X*, 58219) Prentice ESL.

Moby Dick. unabridged ed. Herman Melville. (Classics Ser.). (YA). (gr. 11 up). 1964. mass mkt. 3.95 (*0-8049-0033-7*, CL-33) Airmont.

***Moby-Dick.** 2nd ed. Herman Melville. (Critical Editions Ser.). 1999. pap. 11.50 (*0-393-97283-6*) Norton.

Moby Dick. 2nd ed. Herman Melville. (Illustrated Classic Book Ser.). (Illus.). 61p. (J). (gr. 3 up). 1998. reprint ed. pap. text 4.95 (*1-56767-235-3*) Educ Insights.

Moby Dick, 2 cass., Set. (Read-Along Ser.). (YA). 1986. pap., student ed. 34.95 incl. audio (*0-88432-967-4*, S23908) Audio-Forum.

Moby Dick, Tome I. Herman Melville. (FRE.). 1980. pap. 11.95 (*0-7859-4134-7*) Fr & Eur.

Moby Dick, Tome II. Herman Melville. 1980. pap. 11.95 (*0-7859-4135-5*) Fr & Eur.

***Moby Dick: Heston,&Charlton, Set.** abr. ed. Herman Melville. 95p. 1998. audio 18.00 (*0-694-52018-7*, Caedmon) HarperAudio.

Moby Dick: Ishmael's Mighty Book. Kerry McSweeney. (Twayne's Masterwork Studies: No. 3). 120p. (C). 1986. 23.95 (*0-8057-7954-X*, Twyne); pap. 13.95 (*0-8057-8002-5*, Twyne) Mac Lib Ref.

Moby Dick: Or the Whale. Herman Melville. LC 92-50222. (Illus.). 864p. 1992. 21.00 (*0-679-60010-8*) Modern Lib NY.

Moby Dick: Or the Whale. Herman Melville. Ed. by Hershel Parker & G. Thomas Tanselle. (Northwestern-Newberry Edition of the Writings of Herman Melville: Vol. 6). 1043p. (C). 1988. 99.95 (*0-8101-0268-4*); pap. text 29.95 (*0-8101-0269-2*) Northwestern U Pr.

Moby Dick: Or the Whale. annot. ed. Herman Melville. Ed. by Howard P. Vincent & Luther S. Mansfield. (Complete Works of Herman Melville Ser.). 909p. 1962. 29.95 (*0-87532-001-5*) Hendricks House.

Moby Dick: Or the Whale. Herman Melville. LC 81-40320. (Illus.). 600p. 1981. reprint ed. 55.00 (*0-520-04354-5*, Pub. by U CA Pr); reprint ed. 395.00 (*0-520-04549-1*, Pub. by U CA Pr); reprint ed. pap. 24.95 (*0-520-04548-3*, Pub. by U CA Pr) Cal Prin Full Svc.

Moby Dick: Or the Whale. rev. ed. Herman Melville. LC 92-19289. (Illus.). 624p. 1993. pap. 16.99 (*0-14-039084-7*, Penguin Classics) Viking Penguin.

Moby Dick: Or the White Whale. Herman Melville. (Oxford Illustrated Classics Ser.). (Illus.). 104p. 1998. reprint ed. pap. 12.95 (*0-19-278153-7*) OUP.

Moby Dick: Original Lithographs by Leonard Baskin. Herman Melville. (Illus.). 20p. 1970. boxed set 1200.00 (*1-55660-295-2*) A Wofsy Fine Arts.

***Moby Dick & Peace: Melvilles "Gospel of the Century" Revisited: The Influence of the China Trade, Orientalism & Universalism on Melville's romanticism.** D. J. Ferrantello. (Illus.). 128p. (C). 2000. pap. 19.95 (*0-9678903-0-6*) Open Sky Pr.

Moby Dick Index-Concordance (Adjunct) Compiled by Eugene F. Irey. (Complete Works of Herman Melville Ser.). 172p. 1978. 17.95 (*0-87532-035-X*) Hendricks House.

Moby Dick (Melville) J. Reed. (Barron's Book Notes Ser.). (C). 1984. pap. 2.50 (*0-8120-3428-7*) Barron.

Moby Dick, Notes. James L. Roberts. (Cliffs Notes Ser.). 104p. 1961. pap. 4.95 (*0-8220-0852-1*, Cliff) IDG Bks.

Moby Dick: or The Catfish. Illus. by David Boyd. LC 98-66373. (Trailer Park Classics Ser.: Vol. 1). 80p. 1998. pap. 8.95 (*1-56352-530-5*) Longstreet.

Moby Dick Readalong. Herman Melville. (Illustrated Classics Collection 1). 64p. 1994. pap. 14.95 incl. audio (*0-7854-0709-X*, 40351) Am Guidance.

Moby Dick Student Activity Book. Marcia Sohl & Gerald Dackerman. (Now Age Illustrated Ser.). (Illus.). (J). (gr. 4-10). 1976. pap. 1.25 (*0-88301-181-6*) Pendulum Pr.

Moby Dick Study Guide. Ed. by Carol Hagerty. (Classics Ser.: Set II). 48p. (YA). (gr. 5-12). 1998. student ed. 17.95 (*1-56254-259-1*, SP2591) Saddleback Pubns.

Moby Dog. Alexander Steele. LC 97-73759. (Adventures of Wishbone Ser.: No. 10). (Illus.). 144p. (J). (gr. 3-6). 1998. mass mkt. 3.99 (*1-57064-305-9*, Big Red) Lyrick Pub.

Moby Dog see Adventures of Wishbone

MOBY-Molecular Modelling on the PC: Version 1.6 with Handbook in English. U. Howeler. 330p. 1996. 655.00 incl. disk (*3-540-14529-X*); 1303.00 incl. disk (*3-540-14528-1*) Spr-Verlag.

MOBY Version 1.4 with a Handbook in English: Molecular Modelling on the PC. U. Howeler. (Illus.). 1990. 605.00 incl. disk (*0-387-14062-X*) Spr-Verlag.

MOBY. Version 1.4 with a Handbook in English: Molecular Modelling on the PC. U. Howeler. 1991. 998.00 incl. 3.5 hd, 5.25 hd (*0-387-14206-1*) Spr-Verlag.

Moc Hoa: A Vietnam Medical-Military Adventure. Larry P. Kammholz. LC 89-91084. (Illus.). 104p. (Orig.). 1990. pap. 23.80 (*0-9622696-4-6*) Starboard Pub.

Mocambique. Ake Magnusson. 38p. 1969. write for info. (*91-7106-003-0*, Pub. by Nordic Africa) Transaction Pubs.

Mocassins & Red Shoes. Ed. by Paula Sundet. (Illus.). 104p. 1997. pap. 2.95 (*1-888213-09-4*) Eastern National.

Moccasin Goalie. William R. Brownridge. (Illus.). 32p. (J). (ps-3). 1996. reprint ed. pap. 6.95 (*1-55143-054-1*) Orca Bk Pubs.

Moccasin Maker. E. Pauline Johnson & A. Lavonne Ruoff. LC 98-18679. (Illus.). 272p. 1998. pap. 12.95 (*0-8061-3079-2*) U of Okla Pr.

Moccasin Maker. E. Pauline Johnson. LC 86-6930. 272p. 1987. reprint ed. pap. 84.40 (*0-608-00729-3*, 206150500009) Bks Demand.

Moccasin Ranch see Collected Works of Hamlin Garland

Moccasin Ranch. Hamlin Garland. (Collected Works of Hamlin Garland). 1988. reprint ed. lib. bdg. 59.00 (*0-7812-1239-1*) Rprt Serv.

Moccasin Speaks: Living as Captives of the Dog Soldier Warriors, Red River War, 1874-1875. Arlene F. Jauken. Ed. by Linda Dageforde. LC 97-45174. 352p. 1998. 24.95 (*1-886225-26-5*, 5000) Dageforde Pub.

Moccasin Telegraph & Other Indian Tales. W. P. Kinsella. LC 83-48894. (Nonpareil Bks.: Vol. 72). 192p. 1994. pap. 12.95 (*0-87923-981-6*) Godine.

Moccasin Trail. Eloise J. McGraw. (Newbery Library). 256p. (J). (gr. 5-9). 1986. pap. 4.99 (*0-14-032170-5*, PuffinBks) Peng Put Young Read.

Moccasin Trail. Eloise J. McGraw. (Puffin Newbery Library). (J). 1986. 10.09 (*0-606-01321-0*, Pub. by Turtleback) Demco.

Moccasins. Emerson Alston. LC 99-64517. 128p. (YA). (gr. 8-12). 2000. pap. 7.95 (*1-56315-220-7*, Pub. by SterlingHse) Natl Bk Netwk.

Moccasins & Sneakers. Beverly Amstutz. (Illus.). 24p. (J). (gr. k-7). 1980. pap. 3.50 (*0-937836-02-8*) Precious Res.

Moccasins & Their Relation to Arctic Footwear. Gudmund Hatt. LC 18-6197. (American Anthropological Association Memoirs Ser.: No. 15). 1916. 25.00 (*0-527-00514-2*) Periodicals Srv.

Mocedades Del Cid. Guillen De Castro. (SPA.). 246p. 1963. 10.50 (*0-8288-7053-5*) Fr & Eur.

Mocedades Del Cid. Guillen De Castro. (SPA.). 269p. 1968. 11.95 (*0-8288-7176-0*, S29015) Fr & Eur.

***Mochaccino.** Ed. by Rally Jones. 230p. (C). 2000. pap. 14.95 (*0-9676706-3-2*) Robbie Jones.

Moche. Garth Bawden. (Peoples of America Ser.). (Illus.). 288p. 1997. 44.95 (*1-55786-520-5*) Blackwell Pubs.

***Moche.** Garth Bawden. (Peoples of America Ser.). (Illus.). 384p. 1999. pap. 27.95 (*0-631-21863-7*) Blackwell Pubs.

***Moche Fineline Painting: Its Evolution & Its Artists.** Christopher B. Donnan & Donna McClelland. (Illus.). 320p. (C). 1999. 70.00 (*0-930741-78-1*); pap. 39.00 (*0-930741-79-X*) UCLA Fowler Mus.

Moche Warrior: An Archaeological Mystery. Lyn Hamilton. LC 98-41519. 321p. 1999. 21.95 (*0-425-16809-3*, Prime Crime) Berkley Pub.

***Moche Warrior: An Archaeological Mystery.** Lyn Hamilton. 2000. reprint ed. mass mkt. 6.50 (*0-425-17308-9*, Prime Crime) Berkley Pub.

Mochila de Lin. 3rd ed. Helen Lester. Tr. by Alma F. Ada. (Dejame Leer).Tr. of Lin's Backpack. (SPA., Illus.). 8p. (J). (ps-1). 1995. bds. 2.95 (*0-673-36291-4*, GoodYrBooks) Addson-Wesley Educ.

Mocho. Jose Donoso. 1998. pap. 19.95 (*968-19-0334-X*) Santillana.

Mock Applique. Sara A. Nephew. LC 95-67105. (Illus.). 72p. (Orig.). 1995. pap. 5.00 (*0-9621172-4-2*) Clearview Triangle.

Mock Champagne Ingredient Substitution Recipe Book. Cookbook Consortium Staff. 1984. ring bd. 19.95 (*0-318-04313-0*) Prosperity & Profits.

Mock Fandango. Ray DiPalma. 20p. 1991. pap. 5.00 (*1-55713-114-7*) Sun & Moon CA.

Mock Kings in Medieval Society & Renaissance Drama. Sandra Billington. (Illus.). 300p. 1991. text 90.00 (*0-19-811967-4*, 1894) OUP.

Mock Revolt. Vera Cleaver & Bill Cleaver. LC 75-151467. 160p. (J). (gr. 6 up). 1971. lib. bdg. 12.89 (*0-397-31238-5*) HarpC Child Bks.

Mock Rock: The Guide to Indoor Climbing. Sharon C. Urquhart. Ed. by Werner A. Riefling. LC 94-68861. (Illus.). 128p. (Orig.). 1995. pap. 12.95 (*1-879706-63-6*) Paper Chase.

Mock Trial: A Student "How To" Textbook. Mary Winn & William H. Bennett. 81p. (YA). (gr. 7-12). 1998. pap. text 39.00 (*1-889510-37-8*) Chmpionship Debate.

Mock Trial Teacher's Guide. William H. Bennett. (Illus.). 92p. 1998. pap. text 12.00 (*1-889510-38-6*) Chmpionship Debate.

Mockbee Coker: Thought & Process. Ed. by Lori Ryker. (Illus.). 128p. (Orig.). 1995. pap. 27.95 (*1-56898-042-6*) Princeton Arch.

Mockers & Mocked: Comparative Perspectives on Differentiation, Convergence, & Diversity in Higher Education. Ed. by V. Lynn Meek et al. LC 96-7875. (Issues in Higher Education Ser.: Vol. 7). 240p. 1996. text 85.00 (*0-08-042563-1*, Pergamon Pr) Elsevier.

Mockery Bird. large type ed. Gerald Durrell. 1983. 15.95 (*0-7089-0901-9*) Ulverscroft.

Mockery in Spanish Golden Age Literature: Analysis of Burlesque Representation. Kimberly Contag. LC 96-8239. 260p. 1996. pap. text 32.00 (*0-7618-0374-2*); lib. bdg. 52.00 (*0-7618-0373-4*) U Pr of Amer.

Mockery of Justice: The True Story of the Sheppard Murder Case. Cynthia L. Cooper. LC 97-201401. 1997. mass mkt. 7.99 (*0-451-40763-6*, Onyx) NAL.

Mockery of Justice: The True Story of the Sheppard Murder Case. Cynthia L. Cooper & Sam R. Sheppard. LC 95-15809. 1995. 30.00 (*1-55553-241-1*) NE U Pr.

Mocking.... see Campaign Comedy: Political Humor from Clinton to Kennedy

Mocking Desire. Drago Jancar. Tr. by Michael Biggins from ENG. LC 98-15527. (Writings from an Unbound Europe Ser.). 288p. 1998. text 44.95 (*0-8101-1553-0*); pap. text 14.95 (*0-8101-1554-9*, Marlboro) Northwestern U Pr.

Mocking Justice: Vermont's Biggest Drug Scandal. Hamilton E. Davis. LC 89-61952. 256p. 1989. reprint ed. pap. 12.95 (*0-933050-76-3*) New Eng Pr VT.

Mocking Stones. Drumbeat Publishing Staff. Date not set. pap. text. write for info. (*0-582-78568-5*, Pub. by Addison-Wesley) Longman.

Mockingbird. Allan Ahlberg. LC 97-18207. (Illus.). 24p. (J). (ps-1). 1998. 14.99 (*0-7636-0439-9*) Candlewick Pr.

Mockingbird. Robin W. Doughty. LC 88-736. (Corrie Herring Hooks Ser.: No. 11). (Illus.). 80p. (YA). (gr. 10-12). 1988. 17.95 (*0-292-75099-4*) U of Tex Pr.

Mockingbird. Robin W. Doughty. (Corrie Herring Hooks Ser.). (Illus.). 80p. 1995. pap. 8.95 (*0-292-71584-6*) U of Tex Pr.

Mockingbird. Sean Stewart. LC 97-36468. 272p. 1998. 21.95 (*0-441-00547-0*) Ace Bks.

***Mockingbird.** Sean Stewart. 2000. pap. 14.00 (*0-441-00644-2*) Ace Bks.

***Mockingbird.** Walter Tevis. 275p. 1999. pap. 11.95 (*0-345-43162-6*) Ballantine Pub Grp.

Mockingbird: A Mother, a Child, a Murder. Gregg Olsen. 336p. 1995. mass mkt. 5.99 (*0-446-60095-4*, Pub. by Warner Bks) Little.

Mockingbird - Litmus. Larry Tomoyasu. 32p. (Orig.). 1990. pap. 3.00 (*0-926935-47-X*) Runaway Spoon.

Mockingbird in the Gum Tree: A Literary Gallimaufry. Louis Decimus Rubin, Jr. LC 90-27597. 281p. 1991. 27.50 (*0-8071-1680-7*) La State U Pr.

Mockingbird Mystery. Marianne Hering. LC 98-26432. (White House Adventures Ser.: Vol. 1). (J). 1998. pap. text 3.99 (*0-7814-3065-8*) Chariot Victor.

Mockingbird Song. Berthe Amoss. LC 87-45272. 128p. (J). (gr. 4-7). 1988. 12.95 (*0-06-020061-8*) HarpC Child Bks.

Mockingbird Wish Me Luck. Charles Bukowski. 160p. 1998. reprint ed. 20.00 (*0-87685-139-1*); reprint ed. pap. 14.00 (*0-87685-138-3*) Black Sparrow.

***Mockingbird Years: A Life In & Out of Therapy.** Emily Fox Gordon. LC 99-87907. 256p. 2000. 24.00 (*0-465-02727-X*, Pub. by Basic) HarpC.

Mockingbirds. Kenyetta Coner. Ed. by Lyn Richards. LC 98-93014. 250p. 1988. pap. 11.00 (*0-9665005-0-4*) Fifty-Two Wks.

Mocktail Alcohol-Free Cocktails Guide. American Bartenders' Association Staff & James P. Starcevic. 28p. (Orig.). 1988. pap. text 5.95 (*0-916689-87-5*) Am Bartenders.

Mocrocirculation in Circulatory Disorders. Ed. by K. Messmer et al. (Illus.). 552p. 1988. 160.00 (*0-387-70034-X*) Spr-Verlag.

Mocsines de Agua. Sherie Bargar & Linda Johnson. (Culebras Ser.).Tr. of Cottonmouths. 24p. (J). (gr. k-4). 1994. lib. bdg. 10.95 (*0-86593-332-4*) Rourke Corp.

Moctezuma Xocoyotzin. Meza Otilia. (SPA.). 1997. pap. 11.98 (*968-409-586-4*) Edamex.

Moctezuma's Mexico: Visions of the Aztec World. David Carrasco & Eduardo M. Moctezuma. Ed. by Scott Sessions. LC 92-11993. (Illus.). 200p. 1992. 49.95 (*0-87081-263-7*) Univ Pr Colo.

MOCVD Challenge Vol. 1: A Survey of GaInAsP-InP for Photonic & Electronic Applications. M. Razheghi. (Illus.). 340p. 1989. 184.00 (*0-85274-161-8*) IOP Pub.

MOCVD Challenge Vol. 2: A Study of GaInAsP-GaAs for Photonic & Electronic Device Applications. M. Razeghi. (Illus.). 443p. 1995. 231.00 (*0-7503-0309-3*) IOP Pub.

Mod Evidence, Set. Mueller. 1813p. 1995. 135.00 (*0-316-59002-9*, Aspen Law & Bus) Aspen Pub.

Mod-4 by Chris: Model 4 Owner's Manual for LS-DOS 6.3. Christopher Fara. 232p. 1989. pap., student ed. 24.95 (*1-880099-03-9*) Microdex Bkshelf.

Mod Moleculr Photochmsty. Nicholas J. Turro. 1981. pap. text 31.95 (*0-8053-9354-4*) Benjamin-Cummings.

Mod-III by Chris: Model III Owner's Manual for LDOS 5.3. Christopher Fara. 234p. 1989. pap., student ed. 24.95 (*1-880099-02-0*) Microdex Bkshelf.

Mod Two Cohomology Structure of Certain Fibre Spaces. William S. Massey & F. P. Peterson. LC 52-42839. (Memoirs Ser.: No. 1/74). 97p. 1967. pap. 16.00 (*0-8218-1274-2*, MEMO/1/74) Am Math.

Mod-3 by Chris for TRSDOS. Christopher Fara. 210p. 1989. pap., student ed. 24.95 (*1-880099-01-2*) Microdex Bkshelf.

Moda & Gioielli: Together Against Aids. (ITA., Illus.). 160p. 1998. pap. 79.95 (*88-7813-806-1*) Gingko Press.

MODA 5 - Advances in Model-Oriented Data Analysis & Experimental Design: Proceedings of the 5th International Workshop in Marseilles, France, June 22-26, 1998. Ed. by A. C. Atkinson et al. LC 98-21609. (Contributions to Statistics Ser.). (Illus.). xvi, 300p. 1998. pap. 73.00 (*3-7908-1111-4*) Spr-Verlag.

Modal Accompaniment of Plain Chant. Edwin Evans. 145p. 1991. reprint ed. lib. bdg. 69.00 (*0-7812-9347-2*) Rprt Serv.

Modal Analysis & Testing. (C). 1930. text. write for info. (*0-06-041713-7*) Allyn.

***Modal Analysis & Testing.** Nuno Manuel Mendes Maia & J. M. Montalvdao e Silva. LC 99-26683. (NATO Science Ser.). 1999. write for info. (*0-7923-5893-7*) Kluwer Academic.

Modal & Temporal Properties of Processes. Colin Stirling. 1999. 49.95 (*0-387-98717-7*) Spr-Verlag.

Modal Assignment in Northern Tonaries. Paul Merkley. (Wissenschaftliche Abhandlungen-Musicological Studies: Vol. 56). 1992. lib. bdg. 100.00 (*0-931902-72-X*) Inst Mediaeval Mus.

Modal Counterpoint: Renaissance Style. Peter Schubert. LC 98-22175. (Illus.). 336p. (C). 1999. spiral bd. 39.95 (*0-19-510912-0*) OUP.

Modal Expressions in English. Michael R. Perkins. LC 83-11890. 192p. 1983. text 73.25 (*0-89391-209-3*) Ablx Pub.

***Modal Interpretation of Quantum Mechanics.** Guido Bacciagaluppi. 220p. (C). 2000. 64.95 (*0-521-62200-X*) Cambridge U Pr.

Modal Interpretation of Quantum Mechanics. Dennis G. Dieks & Pieter E. Vermaas. LC 98-35400. (Western Ontario Series in Philosophy of Science). 1998. 135.00 (*0-7923-5207-6*) Kluwer Academic.

Modal Jams & Theory: Using the Modes for Solo Guitar. Dave Celentano. (Illus.). 40p. (Orig.). 1993. pap. text 17.95 incl. cd-rom (*0-931759-76-5*) Centerstream Pub.

Modal Logic. Alexander Chagrov & Michael Zakharyaschev. LC 97-185365. (Oxford Logic Guides Ser.: No. 35). (Illus.). 624p. (C). 1997. 140.00 (*0-19-853779-4*) OUP.

Modal Logic & Process Algebra. Ed. by Alban Ponse et al. (CSLI Lecture Notes Ser.). 352p. 1995. 64.95 (*1-881526-95-X*) CSLI.

Modal Logic & Process Algebra: A Bisimulation Perspective. Ed. by Alban Ponse et al. (CSLI Lecture Notes Ser.). 352p. 1995. pap. 23.95 (*1-881526-96-8*) CSLI.

Modal Method. Chris Theriault. Ed. by Byron Duckwall. (Getting into the Guitar Ser.). (Illus.). 78p. 1992. pap. 12.50 (*1-883617-02-2*) Evergreen Music.

Modal Personality Structure of the Tuscarora Indians. Anthony F. Wallace. (Bureau of American Ethnology Bulletins Ser.). 120p. 1995. lib. bdg. 79.00 (*0-7812-4150-2*) Rprt Serv.

Modal Rhythm. Bryan Gillingham. (Wissenschaftliche Abhandlungen-Musicological Studies: Vol. 46). (ENG.). 133p. 1986. 40.00 (*0-931902-52-5*) Inst Mediaeval Mus.

Modal Testing & Model Refinement: Presented by the Winter Annual Meeting of the American Society of Mechanical Engineers, Boston, Massachusetts, November 13-18, 1983. American Society of Mechanical Engineers Staff. Ed. by David F. Chu. LC 83-72721. (AMD Ser.: Vol. 59). 165p. pap. 51.20 (*0-7837-0207-8*, 204050300017) Bks Demand.

Modale Syllogismen, Moegliche Welten, Essentialismus: Eine Analyse Der Aristotelischen Modallogik. Ulrich Nortmann. (Perspektiven der Analytischen Philosophie - Perspectives in Analytical Philosophy Ser.: No. 9). (GER.). x, 427p. (C). 1996. lib. bdg. 192.60 (*3-11-014660-6*) De Gruyter.

Modales - Manners. Aliki. 1996. 10.95 (*84-261-2795-9*) Lectorum Pubns.

Modales y Vida Social: Preguntas y Respuestas. Lietty Raventos de Pubillones Staff. (SPA.). 157p. (Orig.). 1994. pap. 9.95 (*0-931839-19-X*) Miami Herald.

Modalidades Del Caso y Del Proceso Juridico En el Drama Hispanoamericano. Teresa B. Rodriguez. LC 89-83954. (SPA.). 141p. (Orig.). 1991. pap. 19.00 (*0-89729-534-X*) Ediciones.

Modalitat Im Kontrast: Ein Beitrag Zur Ubersetzungsorientierten Modalpartikelforschung Anhand des Deutschen und des Franzosischen. Cornelia Feyrer. (Europaische Hochschulschriften Ser.: Reibe 21, Band 202). (GER.). 311p. 1998. 51.95 (*3-631-32360-3*) P Lang Pubng.

Modalitat Nachsprechen: Materialien Fur Dysarthrie-, Dysprosodie- Und Aphasiebehandlung. Berthold Simons. (Illus.). 104p. 1998. 22.95 (*3-631-33996-8*) P Lang Pubng.

Modalites de Planification Agricole en Afrique Francophone Subsaharienne. (FRE.). 166p. 1988. 20.00 (*92-5-202631-2*, FF44, Pub. by FAO) Bernan Associates.

Modalites d'Institution et de Fonctionnement d'Une Banque Centrale Supranationale: Le Cas de la Banque Centrale Europeenne. Sergio Rossi. (Publications Universitaires Europeennes Ser.: Series 5, Vol. 2013). (FRE., Illus.). xxii, 452p. 1997. 57.95 (*3-906754-85-5*, Pub. by P Lang) P Lang Pubng.

Modalities: Philosophical Essays. Ruth B. Marcus. 288p. 1995. pap. text 24.95 (*0-19-509657-6*) OUP.

Modality & English Modals. 2nd ed. F. R. Palmer. (Linguistics Library). 224p. (C). 1989. pap. text 16.95 (*0-582-03486-8*, 78294) Longman.

Modality & Meaning. William G. Lycan. (Studies in Linguistics & Philosophy). 334p. (C). 1994. lib. bdg. 117.50 (*0-7923-3006-4*, Pub. by Kluwer Academic) Kluwer Academic.

Modality & Meaning. William G. Lycan. (Studies in Linguistics & Philosophy). 334p. (C). 1995. pap. text 64.00 (*0-7923-3007-2*, Pub. by Kluwer Academic) Kluwer Academic.

An Asterisk (*) at the beginning of an entry indicates that the title is appearing for the first time.

Modality in Grammar & Discourse. Ed. by Joan Bybee & Suzanne Fleischman. LC 95-17034. (Typological Studies in Language: No. 32). viii, 575p. 1995. pap. 37.95 (*1-55619-640-7*); lib. bdg. 125.00 (*1-55619-639-3*) J Benjamins Pubng Co.

Modality in Language Acquisition (Modalite et Acquisition des Langues) Ed. by Norbert Dittmar & Astrid Reich. LC 93-45800. (Sociolinguistics & Language Contact Ser.: Band 6). (ENG & FRE.). xxiv, 382p. (C). 1993. lib. bdg. 145.00 (*3-11-012378-9*) De Gruyter.

Modality, Mood & Aspect in Spoken Arabic: With Special Reference to Egypt & the Levant. Terence F. Mitchell & Shahir El-Hassan. 320p. (C). 1994. text 93.50 (*0-7103-0405-6*, A5603) Routledge.

Modality, Morality & Belief: Essays in Honor of Ruth Barcan Marcus. Ed. by Walter Sinnott-Armstrong et al. 288p. (C). 1995. text 80.00 (*0-521-44082-3*) Cambridge U Pr.

Modality, Probability, & Rationality: A Critical Examination of Alvin Platinga's Philosophy. James F. Sennett. LC 91-31768. (American University Studies: Philosophy: Ser. V, Vol. 129). 192p. (C). 1992. text 35.95 (*0-8204-1666-5*) P Lang Pubng.

Modallogik des Aristoteles in den Analytica Priora A: Zur Modernen Deutung Der Aristotelischen Logik. Friedemann Buddensiek. (Zur Modernen Deutung der Aristotelischen Logic Ser.: Bd. 6). (GER.). xii, 144p. 1994. write for info. (*3-487-09888-1*) G Olms Pubs.

Modalverben. Buscha et al. 55p. 1989. 13.00 (*3-324-00511-6*) Langenscheidt.

***Modbelisation du Climat Dela Terre et de Sa Variabilitbe (Modeling the Earth's Climate & Its Variability)** W. R. Holland et al. LC 99-58846. (Les Houches Summer School Proceedings Ser.). (FRE & ENG.). 592p. 1999. 190.50 (*0-444-50338-2*) Elsevier.

Mode & Meaning of "Bowulf," Margaret E. Goldsmith. LC 78-489490. xi, 282 p. 1970. write for info. (*0-485-11110-1*, Pub. by Athlone Pr) Humanities.

Mode & Sport. Ed. by Wolfgang Hageney. (ENG, FRE, GER, ITA & SPA., Illus.). 200p. 1988. 59.95 (*88-7070-070-4*) Belvedere USA.

Mode Illustree Fashion Plates in Full Color. Ed. by Florence Leniston. Tr. by JoAnne Olian. LC 97-22623. (Illus.). 64p. 1997. pap. 12.95 (*0-486-29819-1*) Dover.

Mode in Ancient Greek Music. R. P. Winnington-Ingram. 98p. 1936. reprint ed. lib. bdg. 34.00 (*0-685-13814-3*, Pub. by AM Hakkert) Coronet Bks.

Mode in Costume. 2nd ed. R. Turner Wilcox. (Illus.). 480p. 1974. pap. 18.00 (*0-684-13913-8*, SL547, Scribners Ref) Mac Lib Ref.

Mode in Javanese Music. Susan P. Walton. LC 86-33232. (Monographs in International Studies, Southeast Asia Ser.: No. 79). 278p. 1986. pap. text 15.00 (*0-89680-144-6*) Ohio U Pr.

Mode-Locking in Solid-State & Semiconductor Lasers. M. S. Demokan. LC 82-8610. (Electronic & Electrical Engineering Research Ser.: No. 1). (Illus.). 239p. reprint ed. pap. 74.10 (*0-8357-6217-3*, 203422100089) Bks Demand.

Mode-Locking of Lasers see Progress in Quantum Electronics

Mode of Action. Ed. by H. Schoenfeld & Alain L. De Weck. (Antibiotics & Chemotherapy Ser.: Vol. 17). 1971. 45.25 (*3-8055-1225-2*) S Karger.

***Mode of Action & Development of Resistance to Human Immunodeficiency Virus Inhibitors That Are Targeted at Early Stages of Infection.** Jose A. Este. (Acta Biomedica Lovaniensia Ser.: Vol. 190). (Illus.). 202p. 1999. pap. (*90-6186-943-9*, Pub. by Leuven Univ) Coronet Bks.

Mode of Action of Autonomic Drugs. Budh D. Bhagat. LC 78-58696. (Illus.). 170p. 1979. text 32.95 (*0-932126-00-6*); pap. text 29.50 (*0-932126-01-4*) Graceway.

Mode of Information: Poststructuralism & Social Context. Mark Poster. LC 90-34770. 188p. 1990. pap. text 19.95 (*0-226-67596-3*); lib. bdg. 48.00 (*0-226-67595-5*) U Ch Pr.

Mode of Melancholy: A Study of William Styron's Novels. Elisabeth Herion-Sarafidis. (Studia Anglistica Upsaliensia Ser.: No. 92). 176p. 1995. pap. 39.50 (*91-554-3517-3*) Coronet Bks.

***Mode of Parody: An Essay at Definition & Six Studies.** Bond Johnson. (Analysen und Dokumente. Beitrage zur Neueren Literatur Ser.: Vol. 40). iv, 218p. 2000. pap. 32.95 (*0-8204-4380-8*) P Lang Pubng.

***Mode of Parody: An Essay at Definition & Six Studies, 40.** Bond Johnson. Ed. by Leonhard M. Fiedler. (Illus.). 218p. 2000. 32.95 (*3-631-35729-X*) P Lang Pubng.

Mode of the Mountain Man. William W. Johnstone. 288p. 1995. mass mkt. 4.50 (*0-8217-5014-3*, Zebra Kensgtn) Kensgtn Pub Corp.

Mode Selective Chemistry. Ed. by Joshua Jortner et al. (C). 1991. text 283.50 (*0-7923-1421-2*) Kluwer Academic.

Mode und Revolution: Deutschland, 1848/49. Isabella Belting. (Historische Texte und Studien). (Illus.). 234p. 1997. 70.00 (*3-487-10314-1*) G Olms Pubs.

Mode, 1924. Ed. by Wolfgang Hageney. (ENG, FRE, GER, ITA & SPA., Illus.). 120p. 1984. pap. 24.95 (*88-7070-042-9*) Belvedere USA.

Mode, 1938. Ed. by Wolfgang Hageney. (ENG, FRE, GER, ITA & SPA., Illus.). 120p. 1986. pap. 24.95 (*88-7070-044-5*) Belvedere USA.

Modeh Ani Means Thank You. Ruth Lipson. (Illus.). (J). (ps-2). 1986. 10.95 (*0-87306-392-9*) Feldheim.

Model. Michael Gross. (Illus.). 524p. 1995. 25.00 (*0-614-32316-9*, Wm Morrow) Morrow Avon.

***Model: Selected Writings of Kenneth Seaforth McKenzie.** Richard Rossiter. 2000. pap. 34.95 (*1-876268-34-4*, Pub. by Univ of West Aust Pr) Intl Spec Bk.

Model: The Complete Guide for Men & Women. Marie A. Boyd. (Illus.). Date not set. pap. 25.95 (*0-87314-200-4*) Peter Glenn.

Model: The Ugly Business of Beautiful Women. Michael Gross. (Illus.). 524p. 1998. pap. text 20.00 (*0-7881-5922-4*) DIANE Pub.

Model: The Ugly Business of Beautiful Women. Michael Gross. 624p. 1996. mass mkt. 7.50 (*0-446-60346-5*, Pub. by Warner Bks) Little.

***Model - Escort.** John Butler. (Illus.). 285p. 1999. pap. 12.95 (*1-891855-07-7*, STARbks Pr) FL Lit Foundation.

Model A Ford Judging Standards & Restoration Guidelines, Incl. 1995 updates. 250p. 1989. ring bd. 25.00 (*0-318-14915-X*) Model A.

Model A Ford Mechanics Handbook. Les Andrews. LC 97-9151. (Illus.). 424p. 1997. pap. 32.95 (*0-9658240-0-4*, MHDC 970915-1) Cottage Hill.

Model A Ford Service Bulletins Complete. Ford Motor Company Staff. Ed. by Dan R. Post. LC 72-90821. (Illus.). 320p. 1957. 15.95 (*0-911160-28-0*) Post Group.

***Model A Ford Troubleshooting & Diagnostics.** Les Andrews. (Illus.). 200p. 2000. pap. 26.00 (*0-9658240-1-2*, TDDC 031500-0) Cottage Hill.

Model A Miseries & Cures. Mary Moline. 230p. 1999. pap. 22.00 (*0-913444-00-6*, A 384 267) M Moline.

***Model Accounting & Financial Policies & Procedures for Chambers of Commerce.** Edward J. McMillan. 170p. 2000. pap. 59.00 (*1-930270-01-1*) Harwood.

Model Accounting & Financial Policies & Procedures Handbook: For Not-for-Profit Organizations. rev. ed. Edward J. McMillan. LC 99-32096. (ASAE Financial Management Ser.). 1999. pap. 50.00 incl. cd-rom (*0-88034-157-2*) Am Soc Assn Execs.

Model Accounts. Arthur Young. 1987. pap. 39.95 (*0-85258-245-5*) Chapman & Hall.

Model-Actor's Dictionary. James A. Conrad. LC 88-60886. 160p. (Orig.). 1988. pap. 9.95 (*0-944957-00-5*) Rivercross Pub.

Model Adaptations for Image Coding. M. J. Reinders. (Illus.). x, 148p. (Orig.). 1995. pap. 59.50 (*90-407-1203-4*, Pub. by Delft U Pr) Coronet Bks.

Model Aeroplane Building: Sketch by Sketch. 2nd ed. Peter Holland. (Illus.). 215p. (Orig.). 1997. pap. 24.50 (*1-85486-148-4*) Nexus Special Interests.

Model Agreements for Corporate Counsel. 2100p. 1993. 385.00 incl. 3.5 hd (*0-929576-99-3*, 122/157) Busn Laws Inc.

Model-Aided Diagnosis of Mechanical Systems: Fundamentals, Detection, Localization, & Assessment. H. G. Naptke & Czes A. Cempel. LC 96-25712. 1996. write for info. (*0-387-61065-0*) Spr-Verlag.

Model-Aided Diagnosis of Mechanical Systems: Fundamentals, Detection, Localization, & Assessment. H. G. Natke & Czes A. Cempel. LC 96-25712. 330p. 1996. 129.50 (*3-540-61065-0*) Spr-Verlag.

***Model Aircraft Aerodynamics.** 4th ed. Martin Simons. (Illus.). 350p. 2000. pap. 29.50 (*1-85486-190-5*, 130185AP, Pub. by Nexus Special Interests) Motorbooks Intl.

Model Aircraft Tips & Techniques: An Illustrated Guide. Mike Ashey. LC 97-223551. (Illus.). 112p. (Orig.). 1997. pap. 16.95 (*0-89024-266-6*, 12165, Kalmbach Books) Kalmbach.

Model Airplane Racing. Julie C. Morgan. LC 78-172149. (Speed Sports Bks.). (Illus.). (YA). (gr. 7 up). 1972. 11.95 (*0-397-31295-4*) HarpC Child Bks.

Model Airplanes & American Boy: Collection of Articles from American Boy, 1927-1934. 160p. 1982. pap. text 19.00 (*0-913457-00-0*) Model Aero.

Model & Talent 2000: The International Directory of Model & Talent Agencies & Schools. Tricia Blount. 200p. 2000. 29.95 (*0-87314-143-1*, Pub. by Peter Glenn) SCB Distributors.

***Model & Talent 2001: The International Directory of Model & Talent Agencies & Schools.** Ed. by Tricia Blount. 240p. 2001. pap. 29.95 (*0-87314-144-X*, Pub. by Peter Glenn) SCB Distributors.

Model Apartment. Donald Margulies. 1990. pap. 5.25 (*0-8222-0767-2*) Dramatists Play.

Model Assisted Survey Sampling. Jan H. Wretman et al. (Series in Statistics). (Illus.). xv, 694p. 1997. reprint ed. 65.95 (*0-387-97528-4*) Spr-Verlag.

Model-Based Computer Vision. Rodney A. Brooks. LC 84-2416. (Computer Science: Artificial Intelligence Ser.: No. 14). (Illus.). 162p. reprint ed. pap. 50.30 (*0-8357-1526-4*, 207035100088) Bks Demand.

Model-Based Control of a Robot Manipulator. Chae An et al. (Artificial Intelligence Ser.). 248p. 1988. 42.50 (*0-262-01102-6*) MIT Pr.

***Model-Based Decision Support Methodology with Environmental Applications.** Andrzej Wierzbicki et al. LC 00-38932. (Mathematical Modelling--Theory & Applications Ser.). (Illus.). 2000. pap. write for info. (*0-7923-6327-2*, Kluwer Plenum) Kluwer Academic.

***Model-Based Depth Imaging.** Stuart W. Fagin. Ed. by Roger A. Young. (Course Notes Ser.: No. 10). (Illus.). 173p. 1998. pap. text 75.00 (*1-56080-085-2*) Soc Expl Geophys.

Model-Based Design & Evaluation of Interactive Applications. Fabio Patern. LC 99-12334. (Applied Computing Ser.). (Illus.). 205p. 1999. 49.95 (*1-85233-155-0*, Pub. by Spr-Verlag) Spr-Verlag.

Model-Based Fuzzy Control: Fuzzy Gain Schedulers & Sliding Mode Fuzzy Control. Rainer Palm et al. LC 96-47571. 184p. 1997. 44.95 (*3-540-61471-0*) Spr-Verlag.

Model-Based Image Matching Using Location. Henry S Baird. (Association for Computing Machinery Distinguished Dissertation Ser.: 1984). (Illus.). 115p. 1985. 25.00 (*0-262-02220-6*) MIT Pr.

Model Based Process Control. Y. Arkun et al. (IFAC Workshop Ser.: Vol. 82). 465p. 1989. 94.00 (*0-08-035735-0*, Pergamon Pr) Elsevier.

Model-Based Reasoning about Learner Behavior. Ed. by K. De Koning. LC 97-77019. 240p. Date not set. 81.00 (*90-5199-368-4*, 368-4) IOS Press.

***Model-Based Reasoning in Scientific Discovery.** Lorenzo Magnani et al. LC 99-44860. 354p. 1999. write for info. (*0-306-46292-3*) Kluwer Academic.

Model-Based Resolution. Arnold J. Den Dekker. (Illus.). 157p. 1997. pap. 45.00 (*90-407-1548-3*, Pub. by Delft U Pr) Coronet Bks.

Model Based Software Engineering. G. Bruno & Bala. (ITCP-UK Computer Science Ser.). (C). 1994. mass mkt. 42.95 (*0-412-48670-9*) Chapman & Hall.

Model-Based Systems Engineering. A. Wayne Wymore. 736p. 1993. boxed set 120.95 (*0-8493-8012-X*, TA168) CRC Pr.

Model Behavior: A Novel & 7 Stories. Jay McInerney. LC 98-27859. 275p. 1998. 24.00 (*0-679-42846-1*) Knopf.

***Model Behavior: A Novel & 7 Stories.** Jay McInerney. 2000. pap. 11.00 (*0-679-74953-5*) Vin Bks.

Model Bible Building Village see Modelos de Construcciones Biblicas

Model Boat Building: The Lobster Boat. Steve Rogers & Patricia S. Rogers. LC 94-66369. (Illus.). 64p. (Orig.). 1994. pap. 12.95 (*0-88740-642-4*) Schiffer.

Model Boat Building: The Skipjack. Steve Rogers & Patricia Staby-Rogers. (Illus.). 64p. (YA). (gr. 10-13). 1996. pap. 14.95 (*0-88740-937-7*) Schiffer.

Model Boat Building: The Spritsail Skiff. Steve Rogers & Patricia Staby-Rogers. LC 93-85082. (Illus.). 64p. 1992. pap. 12.95 (*0-88740-534-7*) Schiffer.

Model Boat Building Made Simple. Steve Rogers. LC 91-67007. (Illus.). 64p. 1992. pap. 12.95 (*0-88740-388-3*) Schiffer.

Model Boats from the Tomb of Tutankhamun Vol. 9: Tutankhamuns Tombs. Jones Staff. 126p. 1990. 110.00 (*0-900416-49-1*, Pub. by Aris & Phillips) David Brown.

Model Bride. Pamela Bauer. (Superromance Ser.). 1993. mass mkt. 3.39 (*0-373-70548-4*, 1-70548-2) Harlequin Bks.

Model Building & Finishing Guide. Gordon McComb. (Illus.). 128p. (Orig.). 1989. pap. write for info. (*0-938545-05-1*) Jennings & Keefe.

Model Building & Forecasting for Business Economics. (C). 1993. write for info. (*0-8087-9498-1*) Pearson Custom.

Model Building for Decision Analysis. Patrick Rivett. LC 79-40739. (Illus.). 184p. reprint ed. pap. 57.10 (*0-8357-4687-9*, 205234200008) Bks Demand.

***Model Building in Mathematical Programming.** Paul Williams. 368p. 1999. pap. 65.00 (*0-471-99788-9*) Wiley.

Model Buildings Masterclass. Roy Porter. (Illus.). 128p. 1997. 29.95 (*1-85915-063-2*, Pub. by W & G) Motorbooks Intl.

Model Business Corporation Act. Jonathan R. Macey. 530p. 1991. ring bd. 95.00 (*0-13-596628-0*) Aspen Law.

Model Business Corporation Act: Official Text with Official Comments & Statutory Cross-References. 3rd ed. American Bar Association Staff. LC 98-13878. 1998. 395.00 (*1-57073-424-0*) Amer Bar Assn.

Model Business Corporation Act Annotated, 3 vols. Robert W. Hamilton & Seth Searcy. 1985. suppl. ed. 225.00 (*0-317-29378-8*, #H43899) Harcourt.

Model Business Corporation Act Annotated, 4 vols. 3rd ed. ABA, Business Law Staff. 1985. write for info. (*0-318-65480-6*, H43899) P-H.

Model Business Corporation Act Annotated, 1984: Professional Corporation Supplement: Close Corporation Supplement. 3rd ed. American Bar Association Staff. LC 98-14871. 1998. 150.00 (*1-57073-555-7*); 150.00 (*1-57073-556-5*); 150.00 (*1-57073-558-1*); 150.00 (*1-57073-559-X*) Amer Bar Assn.

Model Business Corporation Act Annotated, 1984: Professional Corporation Supplement: Close Corporation Supplement. 3rd ed. American Bar Association Staff. LC 98-14871. 1998. 150.00 (*1-57073-557-3*) Amer Bar Assn.

Model Business Plan. P. W. Meerstadt & Daphne Batty. 1995. pap. 30.00 (*1-873868-29-4*) BAAF.

Model Business Plans for Product Businesses. William A. Cohen. 352p. 1995. 89.95 (*0-471-03030-9*); pap. 22.95 (*0-471-03028-7*) Wiley.

Model Business Plans for Service Businesses. William A. Cohen. LC 94-41827. 352p. 1995. 75.00 (*0-471-03037-6*) Wiley.

Model Car Building: Advanced Techniques. Dennis Doty. (Illus.). 128p. 1988. pap. 10.95 (*0-8306-9395-5*, 3095) McGraw-Hill Prof.

Model Car Building: Getting Started. Dennis Doty. (Illus.). 128p. 1988. pap. 10.95 (*0-8306-9385-8*, 3085) McGraw-Hill Prof.

Model Cars. Kathy Carre & Mir Tamim Ansary. LC 96-39411. (Cool Collections). (J). 1998. 18.50 (*1-57572-116-3*) Heinemann Lib.

Model Categories. Mark Hovey. LC 98-34539. (Mathematical Surveys & Monographs: Vol. 63). 207p. 1998. 54.00 (*0-8218-1359-5*) Am Math.

Model Chart of Accounts: An Expandable Structure for Law Offices. 90p. 1990. pap. 39.95 (*0-89707-615-X*, 511-0284) Amer Bar Assn.

Model Checking. E. M. Clarke et al. LC 99-17979. (Illus.). 305p. 1999. 50.00 (*0-262-03270-8*) MIT Pr.

Model Children: Inside the Republic of Red Scarves. Paul Thorez. Tr. by Nancy Cadet from FRE. 190p. 1991. pap. 10.00 (*0-936756-18-7*) Autonomedia.

Model Choice & the Value of Travel Time. Ian G. Heggie. (Illus.). 1976. 36.00 (*0-19-828404-7*) OUP.

Model City of the New South: Anniston, Alabama, 1872-1900. 2nd ed. Grace H. Gates. LC 95-21058. (Illus.). 336p. (C). 1996. reprint ed. pap. text 24.95 (*0-8173-0818-0*) U of Ala Pr.

Model Clause Library. Illus. by Edith N. Chase & Yolaine Lefebvre. 32p. 55.00 (*0-614-05184-3*, MCL11943.0M) ASFE.

Model Clause Library. 2nd rev. exp. expanded ed. Jean-Marc Hachey. 100.00 incl. disk (*0-614-05185-1*) ASFE.

Model Code of Evidence. Mason Ladd et al. xxiii, 435p. 1942. 63.50 (*0-686-91052-4*, 5070) Am Law Inst.

Model Code of Judicial Conduct for State Administrative Law Judges. LC 96-177608. 23p. 1995. pap. 5.00 (*1-57073-254-X*, 302-0003, ABA Judicial Admin) Amer Bar Assn.

Model Code of Judicial Conduct (1990) 42p. 1990. pap. 9.95 (*0-89707-614-1*, 561-0097) Amer Bar Assn.

Model Code of Pre-Arraignment Procedure: Official Draft-Complete Text & Commentary. Institutional Staff. LC 75-39890. xxii, 767p. 1975. 35.00 (*0-8318-5101-5*, 5101) Am Law Inst.

Model Code of Professional Responsibility & Code of Judicial Conduct: As Amended August, 1980. American Bar Association Staff. LC 83-202790. v, 71p. 1982. pap. 12.95 (*0-685-08534-1*, 561-0010) Amer Bar Assn.

M

Model Compliant Standard Operating Procedures for Administrative Enforcement. Date not set. write for info. (*1-893091-72-4*) F R Parker.

Model Compliant Standard Operating Procedures for Advertising & Promotional Literature. Date not set. write for info. (*1-893091-71-6*) F R Parker.

Model Compliant Standard Operating Procedures for Biological Vaccines Current Good Manufacturing Practices. Date not set. write for info. (*1-893091-74-0*) F R Parker.

Model Compliant Standard Operating Procedures for Biological Vaccines in Good Clinical Practices. Date not set. write for info. (*1-893091-73-2*) F R Parker.

Model Compliant Standard Operating Procedures for Medical Device Current Good Manufacturing Practices. Date not set. write for info. (*1-893091-77-5*) F R Parker.

Model Compliant Standard Operating Procedures for Medical Device Manufacturers Current Good Clincial Practices. Date not set. write for info. (*1-893091-76-7*) F R Parker.

Model Compliant Standard Operating Procedures for Pharmaceutical Drug Manufacturers Good Clinical Practices. Date not set. pap. text. write for info. (*1-893091-05-8*) F R Parker.

Model Compliant Standard Operating Procedures for Pharmaceutical Drug Manufacturers Good Laboratory Practices. Date not set. pap. text. write for info. (*1-893091-04-X*) F R Parker.

Model Compliant Standard Operating Procedures for Pharmaceutical Drugs, Current Good Manufacturing Practices. Date not set. write for info. (*1-893091-75-9*) F R Parker.

Model Conditions for the Carriage of Goods by Road in the U. K. Institute of Purchasing & Supply Staff & FTA Staff. (C). 1990. 100.00 (*0-7855-5735-0*, Pub. by Inst Pur & Supply) St Mut.

Model Conditions for the Supply of Liquid Fuels. Institute of Purchasing & Supply Staff. (C). 1989. 70.00 (*0-7855-5734-2*, Pub. by Inst Pur & Supply) St Mut.

Model Conditions of Contract When Using the Services of a Travel Agent. Institute of Purchasing & Supply Staff. (C). 1989. 80.00 (*0-7855-5736-9*, Pub. by Inst Pur & Supply) St Mut.

Model Constitution. Anthony C. Ibbott. 44p. 1991. pap. 2.50 (*0-9625291-2-5*) A C Ibbott Fndtn.

Model Constitution & Bylaws. 32p. 1981. pap. 2.00 (*0-8100-0145-4*, 04N1210) Northwest Pub.

Model Construction Specification for Asphalt Concrete & Other Plant Mix Types. 7th ed. (Illus.). 64p. 1984. pap. 8.00 (*0-318-13395-4*, SS-1) Asphalt Inst.

Model Construction with GPSS-Fortran Version 3. B. Schmidt. (Advances in Simulation Ser.). 300p. 1987. 67.95 (*0-387-96503-3*) Spr-Verlag.

Model Contract Language & Analysis see Human Relations & Industrial Relations Books & Management Tools

Model Cookbook. Frances Willey. LC 95-94617. (Illus.). 528p. 1990. reprint ed. pap. 29.95 (*0-9647286-0-5*) Beegee-LT.

Model Country: Jose Batlle y Ordonez of Uruguay, 1907-1915. Milton I. Vanger. LC 80-50489. (Illus.). 448p. (Orig.). reprint ed. pap. 138.90 (*0-8357-6523-7*, 203589400097) Bks Demand.

Model Crime. Carolyn Keene. Ed. by Ann Greenberg. (Nancy Drew Files: No. 51). 160p. (YA). (gr. 6 up). 1990. mass mkt. 3.75 (*0-671-70028-6*, Archway) PB.

Model Crime. Carolyn Keene. (Nancy Drew Files: No. 51). (YA). (gr. 6 up). 1990. 8.85 (*0-606-04479-5*, Pub. by Turtleback) Demco.

Model Culture: Photographs, 1975-1996. Ed. by Steven Jenkins et al. (Illus.). 96p. (Orig.). 1996. pap. 21.95 (*0-933286-71-6*, 620282) Frnds Photography.

Model Curriculum & Teaching Guide for the Instruction of the Homemaker. Home Health Aide Staff. 1990. 85.00 (*0-317-99927-3*) Natl Homecaring.

Model Curriculum for Bridge-the-Gap Programs. Institutional Staff. Ed. by Marilyn V. Yarbrough. 90p. 1988. pap. 3.25 (*0-8318-0604-4*, B604) Am Law Inst.

Model Curriculum for Computer Information Systems. 67p. write for info. (*0-318-17044-2*) AITP.

An Asterisk (*) at the beginning of an entry indicates that the title is appearing for the first time.

Model Curriculum Standards, Program Framework, & Progress Guide for Industrial & Technology Education in California. California Department of Education Staff. 324p. 1990. pap. 16.00 (*0-8011-0864-0*) Calif Education.

Model Daily Field Report for Geotechnical Field Observation. 16p. 30.00 (*0-614-05201-7*, MDFR02923.5M) ASFE.

Model Description, Irradiation, Erythropoietic Stimulation see Mathematical Modeling of Cell Proliferation: Stem Cell Regulation in Hemopoiesis

Model Design & Building. Boy Scouts of America. (Illus.). 56p. (YA). (gr. 6-12). 1964. pap. 2.90 (*0-8395-3280-6*, 33280) BSA.

Model Development & Optimization. Viktor V. Ivanov. LC 99-11148. (Applied Optimization Ser.). 1999. write for info. (*0-7923-5610-1*) Kluwer Academic.

Model Development Plan: New Strategies & Perspectives. David H. Lempert & Kim McCarty. LC 95-2225. 320p. 1998. pap. 24.95 (*0-275-96360-8*, Praeger Pubs) Greenwood.

Model Development Plan: New Strategies & Perspectives. David H. Lempert et al. LC 95-2225. 320p. 1995. 65.00 (*0-275-95068-9*) Greenwood.

Model Dialogues. Ed. by William M. Clark. LC 70-109138. (Granger Index Reprint Ser.). 1977. 17.95 (*0-8369-6122-6*) Ayer.

Model Discrimination for Nonlinear Regression Models. Borowiak. (Statistics: Textbooks & Monographs: Vol. 101). (Illus.). 200p. 1989. text 135.00 (*0-8247-8053-1*) Dekker.

Model Drainage Manual. AASHTO Staff. (Design & Traffic Ser.). (Illus.). 1368p. (Orig.). (C). 1991. pap. text 235.00 (*1-56051-010-2*, MDM-1) AASHTO.

Model Drama - Theatre Curriculum: Philosophy, Goals & Objectives. American Alliance for Theatre & Education Staff. 106p. (Orig.). 1987. pap. text 12.50 (*0-87602-027-9*) Anchorage.

Model Electronic Payments Agreement & Commentary (For Domestic Credit Transfers) LC 92-73872. 72p. 1992. pap. 9.95 (*0-89707-806-3*, 545-0009, ABA Sci Tech) Amer Bar Assn.

Model Employee Handbook for California Businesses. Margaret H. Edwards & Barbara C. Strikker. Ed. by Marie Hagelstein. 72p. 1994. pap. text 20.00 (*0-88124-784-7*, BU-31911) Cont Ed Bar-CA.

Model Employee Handbook for Staff Leasing Services. T. Joe Willey. LC 88-717792. 160p. (C). 1988. 150.00 (*0-944308-06-6*) Aegis Consulting.

Model Employee Policies for Indiana Employees. 3rd ed. Bose McKinney & Evans Attorneys at Law Staff. LC 99-193986. 149p. 1998. pap. 89.00 (*1-883698-21-9*) IN Chamber Comm.

Model Employee Policies for Indiana Employers: With Legal Commentary. Bose McKinney & Evans Attorneys at Law Staff. 132p. 1995. pap., per. 36.00 (*1-883698-07-3*) IN Chamber Comm.

Model Employee Policies for Indiana Employers: With Legal Commentary. 2nd ed. Bose McKinney & Evans Attorneys at Law Staff. 116p. 1996. per. 48.00 (*1-883698-11-1*) IN Chamber Comm.

Model Employer. Gerald S. Hartman & Gregory W. Homer. LC 96-76770. 876p. (Orig.). 1996. pap., per. 150.00 (*0-935165-52-5*) GWU Gov Contracts.

Model Employment Contracts. Michael Owen & Jan J. Kinzie. (Executive Performance Ser.). 40p. (Orig.). 1993. pap. 69.00 (*1-889394-04-1*) Credit Union Execs.

Model Engine Construction. J. Alexander. 1986. reprint ed. pap. 15.95 (*0-917914-44-9*) Lindsay Pubns.

Model Engineering: A Foundation Course. Peter Wright. (Illus.). 414p. 1997. pap. 42.50 (*1-85486-152-2*, Pub. by Nexus Special Interests) Trans-Atl Phila.

Model Engineer's Handbook. 3rd ed. Tubal Cain. (Illus.). 250p. 1996. pap. 22.50 (*1-85486-134-4*, Pub. by Nexus Special Interests) Trans-Atl Phila.

Model English-Chinese Dictionary with Illustrative Examples. Commercial Press Staff. (CHI & ENG., Illus.). 1674p. 1979. 24.95 (*0-8288-4821-1*, M9274) Fr & Eur.

Model Entrepreneurship Programs. Ed. by Novella Ross & Paula Kurth. 283p. 1986. 18.00 (*0-318-23569-2*, SN 53) Ctr Educ Trng Employ.

Model Equipment Lease-Purchase & Security Agreement for North Carolina Local Governments. A. Fleming Bell, II. 81p. (Orig.). (C). 1985. pap. text 12.00 (*1-56011-102-X*, 85.17) Institute Government.

Model Equity Compensation Plans. Ed. by Scott Rodrick. 1999. ring bd. 75.00 (*0-926902-37-7*) NCEO.

Model ESA Report. Ruth Maran. 70.00 incl. disk (*0-614-05203-3*) ASFE.

Model ESOP. rev. ed. Corey Rosen & Ron Ludwig. 78p. 1999. pap. 75.00 (*0-926902-05-9*) NCEO.

*__Model Father.__ Raymond G. Barber. 22p. 1999. pap. write for info. (*0-87398-571-0*) Sword of the Lord.

Model Federal Rules of Disciplinary Enforcement. Center for Professional Responsibility Staff. 15p. 1978. pap. 7.95 (*0-685-19032-3*, 720-0012-01) Amer Bar Assn.

Model Financial Statements for Public & Private Companies. 3rd ed. Stoy-Hayward Staff. 1993. pap. 70.00 (*0-406-01649-6*, MICHIE) LEXIS Pub.

Model Firefighter's Contract: A Labor Perspective. Will Aitchison. LC 97-211698. 215p. 1994. pap. 29.95 (*1-880607-08-5*) Labor Rel Info.

Model Firefighter's Contract: A Management Perspective. Richard Whitmore. LC 97-211686. 154p. 1994. pap. 29.95 (*1-880607-09-3*) Labor Rel Info.

Model Flight. Martin Simons. (Illus.). 140p. (Orig.). 1988. pap. 21.50 (*0-85242-938-X*) Nexus Special Interests.

Model Flirt. Created by Francine Pascal. (Sweet Valley High Ser.: No. 130). 208p. (YA). (gr. 7 up). 1997. mass mkt. 3.99 (*0-553-57064-1*, Sweet Valley) BDD Bks Young Read.

*__Model for a Better Future.__ Kim Alexis & James D. Denney. LC 98-31532. 224p. 1999. 16.99 (*0-7852-7456-1*) Nelson.

Model for Culture: Holsterbro-A Study of Cultural Policy & Theatre in a Danish Town. Ingvar Holm et al. (Illus.). 224p. 1985. pap. text 33.50 (*91-22-00762-8*) Coronet Bks.

Model for Deriving the Transfer Rate: Report of the Transfer Assembly Project. Ed. by Enid B. Jones. 1991. pap. 5.00 (*0-87117-245-3*, 1335) Comm Coll Pr Am Assn Comm Coll.

Model for Determining Total Warehousing Costs. Thomas W. Speh. 33p. 1991. pap., wbk. ed. 30.00 incl. disk (*1-892663-13-9*) WERC.

Model for Leadership - The Lubavitcher Rebbes. Chaim Dalfin. 224p. 1998. pap. 14.95 (*1-880880-26-1*) Israeli Trad.

Model for Leading Change: Making Acquisition Reform Work. Charles L. Beck. 136p. 1997. per. 10.00 (*0-16-061209-8*) USGPO.

Model for the Flow of Students Through the Swiss University System. Hanspeter Kriesi. (University Studies: Sociology: Ser. 22, Vol. 21). 368p. 1977. 48.00 (*3-261-02126-8*) P Lang Pubng.

Model for the Reinvented Higher Education System. Babak Armajani et al. 1994. 10.00 (*0-614-13562-1*) SHEEO.

Model Foreign Investment Law with Annotations. Don Wallace, Jr. & Robert B. Shanks. 128p. 1996. pap. 60.00 (*90-411-0986-2*) Kluwer Law Intl.

Model Foreign Investment Law with Annotations. annot. ed. Don Wallace, Jr. et al. pap. 35.00 (*0-935328-81-5*) Intl Law Inst.

*__Model Forest Nursery.__ 1998. pap. 120.00 (*0-7855-7666-5*) St Mut.

Model Form International Operating Agreement: An Analysis & Interpretation of the 1995 Form. Andrew B. Derman. LC 97-70751. (Section of Natural Resources, Energy, & Environmental Law Monograph Ser.). ix, 146 p. 1997. write for info. (*1-57073-430-5*) Amer Bar Assn.

Model Forms of Contract for Electrical & Mechanical Plant. Brian Eggleston. 272p. 1995. 99.95 (*0-632-03803-9*, Pub. by Blckwll Scitfc UK) Blackwell Sci.

Model Forms of Transfer of Technology Agreements. 75p. 1991. 25.00 (*92-1-106253-5*, 91.III.E.3) UN.

Model Four Semester Syllabus for Transcultural Theology Overseas. Ed. by Michael C. Kirwen. LC 86-8618. 224p. 1986. lib. bdg. 89.95 (*0-88946-047-7*) E Mellen.

Model-Free Curve Estimation. Michael E. Tarter & Michael D. Lock. LC 93-38411. 290p. (gr. 13). 1993. ring bd. 68.95 (*0-412-04251-7*, Chap & Hall CRC) CRC Pr.

Model Funds Transfer Services Agreement & Commentary. LC 94-72690. 88p. 1994. pap. 44.95 (*1-57073-034-2*, 507-0276) Amer Bar Assn.

Model Generation in Electronic Design. Ed. by Jean-Michel Berge et al. LC 95-11943. (Current Issues in Electronic Modeling CIEM Ser.: Vol. 1). 168p. (C). 1995. text 120.50 (*0-7923-9568-9*) Kluwer Academic.

Model Governing Body Rules of Procedure. Ed. by Don A. Morrison. 30p. student ed. 29.00 (*0-927160-05-6*) Sound Resc Mgmt.

Model Horses. Carol Gilbert. 1996. 25.95 (*0-87605-749-0*) Howell Bks.

Model Income Tax Treaties. 2nd ed. Kees Van Raad. (Orig.). 1990. 28.00 (*90-6544-505-6*) Kluwer Law Intl.

Model Inquiries into Nature in the Schoolyard: The Mints Book. Ed. by Frank Taylor et al. (Illus.). 290p. (Orig.). 1997. pap. text 18.95 (*1-884549-06-3*) VA Mus Natl Hist.

Model Interrogatories. 2nd ed. Kevin R. Culhane. 1997. ring bd. 119.00 incl. disk (*0-938065-33-5*) James Pub Santa Ana.

Model Job Descriptions for Business. Don A. Morrison. 400p. ring bd. 139.00 (*0-927160-10-2*) Sound Resc Mgmt.

Model Judicial Article, 1995 Edition. LC 95-213668. 1995. pap. 3.00 (*1-57073-167-5*, 394-0006, ABA Judicial Admin) Amer Bar Assn.

Model Jury Charges - Civil. 4th ed. New Jersey Supreme Court Committee on Model Jury C. 813p. 1992. ring bd. 75.00 (*0-685-65971-2*) NJ Inst CLE.

Model Jury Charges - Criminal. 3rd ed. New Jersey Supreme Court Committee on Model Jury C. 658p. 1990. ring bd. 75.00 (*0-939457-03-2*) NJ Inst CLE.

Model Jury Charges - Criminal. 3rd ed. New Jersey Supreme Court Committee on Model Jury C. 658p. 1991. suppl. ed. 39.00 (*0-685-58685-5*) NJ Inst CLE.

Model Jury Charges - Criminal. 3rd ed. New Jersey Supreme Court Committee on Model Jury C. 658p. 1992. suppl. ed. 39.00 (*0-685-58686-3*) NJ Inst CLE.

Model Jury Instructions for Business Tort Litigation. LC 87-73181. 192p. 1988. 29.95 (*0-89707-333-9*, 531-0056) Amer Bar Assn.

Model Jury Instructions for Business Tort Litigation: A Project of the Business Torts Litigation Committee, Subcommittee on Jury Instructions, Section of Litigation. 3rd ed. American Bar Association Staff. LC 96-19560. 1996. pap. write for info. (*1-57073-336-8*) Amer Bar Assn.

Model Jury Instructions for Employment Litigation. LC 93-73416. 384p. 1994. pap. 80.00 (*0-89707-925-6*, 531-0107, ABA Litigation) Amer Bar Assn.

Model Jury Instructions for Securities Litigation. LC 95-81711. 200p. 1996. pap. 80.00 (*0-89707-924-8*, 531-0208, ABA Litigation) Amer Bar Assn.

*__Model Jury Instructions for Surety Cases.__ Robert C. Niesley. LC 00-42147. 2000. write for info. (*1-57073-837-8*) Amer Bar Assn.

Model Jury Instructions for Use in the District Court. rev. ed. Committee on Juries of Six Staff. 1995. ring bd. 125.00 incl. disk (*0-944490-94-8*) Mass CLE.

Model Jury Instructions for Use in the District Court, 1997 Supplement: With Forms on Disk. Committee on Juries of Six. LC 95-78127. 72p. 1997. ring bd., suppl. ed. 39.50 (*1-57589-047-X*, 97-06.16-SP) Mass CLE.

Model Land Development Code: Official Draft. Institutional Staff. 524p. 1976. 35.00 (*0-8318-5080-9*, 5080) Am Law Inst.

Model Law Enforcement Contract: A Labor Perspective. 3rd ed. Will Aitchison. LC 99-462511. 414p. 1999. pap. 29.95 (*1-880607-14-X*) Labor Rel Info.

*__Model Law Enforcement Contract: A Management Perspective.__ 2nd ed. Richard Whitmore. 228p. (Orig.). 1999. pap. 29.95 (*1-880607-15-8*) Labor Rel Info.

Model Laws, Regulations & Guidelines. 2800p. (C). 1995. ring bd. 250.00 (*0-89382-320-1*) Nat Assn Insurance.

Model Laws, Regulations & Guidelines, 4 vols. 13th rev. ed. 3000p. (C). 1997. ring bd. 295.00 (*0-89382-443-7*, MDL-ZM) Nat Assn Insurance.

Model Laws, Regulations & Guidelines, 4 vols., Set. rev. ed. Ed. by National Association of Insurance Commissioners St. 1992. ring bd. 250.00 (*0-9601244-1-1*) Nat Assn Insurance.

Model Laws, Regulations & Guidelines, 4 vols., Set. 12th ed. Ed. by Carolyn Johnson. (Orig.). 1996. pap. 295.00 (*0-89382-386-4*, MDL-ZM) Nat Assn Insurance.

Model Leader: A Fully Functioning Person. William D. Hitt. LC 92-39347. 232p. 1993. 24.95 (*0-935470-62-X*) Battelle.

Model Letters & Memos: A Handbook for Scientists & Engineers. Ronald Tepper. LC 95-45547. 236p. 1996. 59.95 (*0-471-13917-3*) Wiley.

Model Living Standards Measurement Study Survey Questionnaire for the Countries of the Former Soviet Union. Raylynn Oliver. LC 97-19577. (Living Standards Measurement Survey Working Paper Ser.: No. 130). 144p. 1997. pap. 22.00 (*0-8213-3934-6*, 13934) World Bank.

Model Locomotive from Scratch. B. Terry Aspin. (Illus.). 92p. (Orig.). 1998. pap. 27.50 (*1-85486-165-4*) Nexus Special Interests.

Model Makers. Gary Loftiss. Ed. by Carolyn Loftiss. (Illus.). 460p. 1995. pap. text 19.95 (*0-9642120-9-9*) Chiffon Pubs.

Model Making. Madison Square Press Staff. 1924. 35.00 (*0-688-16924-4*, Wm Morrow) Morrow Avon.

Model Making. Raymond F. Yates. 1985. reprint ed. pap. 14.95 (*0-917914-32-5*) Lindsay Pubns.

*__Model Making: A Basic Guide.__ Martha Sutherland. LC 99-25280. 144p. 1999. pap. 17.50 (*0-393-73042-5*, Norton Paperbks) Norton.

Model Making for Mechanics. 1996. lib. bdg. 355.95 (*0-8490-8331-1*) Gordon Pr.

Model Manual: Everything You Need to Know about Modelling. Sandra Morris. (Illus.). 200p. 1997. 24.95 (*0-297-83585-8*, Pub. by Weidenfeld & Nicolson) Trafalgar.

Model Marriage. Jo Ann Ferguson. 256p. 1998. pap. 4.99 (*0-8217-5954-X*) Kensgtn Pub Corp.

Model Mechanics: A New Interpretation of Nature. Ken H. Seto. Ed. by Toni E. Weaver. LC 96-157119. 200p. (C). 1995. 22.95 (*0-9647136-0-8*) KHS Pubng.

Model Mechanics: A New Interpretation of Nature see Physics of Absolute Motion

*__Model Membranes: From Biophysics to Materials Science.__ Knoll, Mpi F Polymer Forschung Staff (Germany). 300p. 1999. 185.00 (*3-527-29442-2*) Wiley.

Model Memoirs: And Other Sketches from Simple to Serious. Stephen Leacock. LC 77-156678. (Essay Index Reprint Ser.). 1977. reprint ed. 32.95 (*0-8369-2434-7*) Ayer.

Model Mind: How the Mind Moves Matter. Peter K. Bros. (Copernican Ser.: Vol. 4). 370p. (Orig.). 1993. pap. 14.95 (*0-9627769-2-0*) Fin Bk Partners.

Model Mind: What the Mind Is & How It Works. 2nd rev. ed. Peter K. Bros. (Copernican Ser.: Vol. 4). Orig. Title: Model Mind: How the Mind Moves Matter. 114p. 1998. pap. 14.95 (*0-9627769-8-X*) Fin Bk Partners.

Model Mind: How the Mind Moves Matter see Model Mind: What the Mind Is & How It Works

Model Mothers: Jewish Mothers & Maternity Provision in East London 1870-1939. Lara V. Marks. (Oxford Historical Monographs). (Illus.). 342p. 1994. text 59.00 (*0-19-820454-X*) OUP.

Model Mystique Unraveled. Dann Parra. 96p. 1996. pap. 29.95 (*0-9643162-7-7*) Dancyn Pubng.

Model, Myth or Miracle? A Reassessment of the East Asian Experience. Beatrice Weder. 72p. 1998. pap. 9.95 (*92-808-1018-9*, Pub. by UN Univ Pr) Brookings.

Model, Myth, or Miracle: Reassessing the Role of Governments in the East Asian Experience Beatrice Weder. LC 99-10729. 1999. 9.95 (*92-808-1030-8*) UN Univ Pr.

Model Neural Networks & Behavior. Allen I. Selverston. LC 85-6351. 570p. 1985. 120.00 (*0-306-41949-1*, Plenum Trade) Perseus Pubng.

Model Occupation: The Channel Islands under German Rule, 1940-1945. Madeleine Bunting. (Illus.). 384p. 1998. pap. 15.95 (*0-00-637973-7*, Pub. by HarpC) Trafalgar.

Model of an Agricultural Household: Theory & Evidence. Howard N. Barnum & Lyn Squire. LC 78-21397. (World Bank Staff Occasional Papers: No. 27). 119p. reprint ed. pap. 36.90 (*0-7837-4252-5*, 204394200012) Bks Demand.

Model of Band Society. B. J. Williams. (Memoir Ser.: No. 29). 152p. 1974. pap. 9.00 (*0-932839-04-5*) Soc Am Arch.

Model of Building Society Interest Setting. Joanna Paisley. LC 95-3185. (Bank of England, Economics Division. Working Paper Ser.: No. 22). (Illus.). 40p. reprint ed. pap. 30.00 (*0-608-20162-6*, 207142600011) Bks Demand.

Model of Community Policing: The Singapore Story. David H. Bayley. (Illus.). 35p. 1996. reprint ed. pap. text 15.00 (*0-7881-2669-5*) DIANE Pub.

Model of Elementary Statistics. Simon & Freund. 1997. pap. text, student ed. 22.00 (*0-13-858317-X*) P-H.

Model of Human Occupation: Theory & Application. 2nd ed. Ed. by Gary Kielhofner. LC 95-7615. (Illus.). 416p. 1995. pap. 48.00 (*0-683-04601-2*) Lppncott W & W.

Model of Its Kind, Vol. 1. A. Mcgehee Harvey et al. LC 88-46064. 384p. 1989. reprint ed. pap. 119.10 (*0-608-03688-9*, 206451400001) Bks Demand.

Model of Its Kind, Vol. 2. A. Mcgehee Harvey et al. LC 88-46064. 182p. 1989. reprint ed. pap. 56.50 (*0-608-03689-7*, 206451400002) Bks Demand.

Model of Love: A Study in Philosophical Theology. Vincent Brummer. LC 92-42300. 261p. (C). 1993. text 64.95 (*0-521-44463-2*); pap. text 18.95 (*0-521-44909-X*) Cambridge U Pr.

Model of Price Mechanism. Ante Farm. (Swedish Institute for Social Research Ser.: No. 1). 86p. (Orig.). 1986. pap. text 33.00 (*91-22-00834-9*) Coronet Bks.

Model of Simple Competition. Joel E. Cohen. LC 66-23470. (Annals of the Computation Laboratory of Harvard University Ser.: No. 41). 150p. 1966. reprint ed. pap. 46.50 (*0-7837-2237-0*, 205732700004) Bks Demand.

Model of Societies & Social Decision Functions. A. Camacho. 1982. lib. bdg. 112.50 (*90-277-1407-X*) Kluwer Academic.

*__Model of Tatarstan.__ Ravil Bukharaev. LC 99-37895. 251p. 1999. text 39.95 (*0-312-22829-5*) St Martin.

Model of the Brain. John Z. Young. 1964. 35.00 (*0-19-857333-2*) OUP.

Model of the Building Society Sector. fac. ed. J. B. Wilcox. LC 86-24703. (Bank of England, Discussion Papers: No. 23). (Illus.). 37p. 1985. pap. 30.00 (*0-7837-7643-8*, 204739600007) Bks Demand.

Model of the Muslim Youth in the Story of Prophet Yusuf. Mahmud S. Saeed. (ARA.). 32p. (YA). pap. write for info. (*1-882837-28-2*) W A M Y Intl.

Model of the Universe: Space-Time, Probability, & Decision. Storrs McCall. (Clarendon Library of Logic & Philosophy). (Illus.). 344p. 1994. text 55.00 (*0-19-824053-8*) OUP.

Model of the Universe: Space-Time, Probability, & Decision. Storrs McCall. (Clarendon Library of Logic & Philosophy). (Illus.). 338p. 1996. pap. text 19.95 (*0-19-823622-0*) OUP.

Model of U. K. Non-Oil ICCs' Direct Investment. E. J. Pentecost. LC HG4502.. (Bank of England. Discussion Papers: No. 30). 58p. reprint ed. pap. 30.00 (*0-7837-5374-8*, 204513800005) Bks Demand.

Model Office Practice Set. 2nd ed. Fred C. Archer & Jeffrey R. Stewart, Jr. 1975. text 12.96 (*0-07-002306-9*) McGraw.

Model Order Reduction Techniques with Application in Electrical Engineering. L. Fortuna et al. LC 92-13086. (Illus.). xii, 232p. 1992. 192.95 (*0-387-19761-3*) Spr-Verlag.

Model-Oriented Data Analysis. Ed. by V. Fedorov & H. J. Lauter. (Lecture Notes in Economics & Mathematical Systems Ser.: Vol. 297). vi, 239p. 1987. 38.70 (*0-387-18596-8*) Spr-Verlag.

Model Oriented Data-Analysis. Ed. by H. P. Wynn et al. (Contributions to Statistics Ser.). (Illus.). 287p. 1993. 71.95 (*0-387-91457-9*) Spr-Verlag.

Model Oriented Data-Analysis: A Survey of Recent Methods: Proceedings of the 2nd IIASA-Workshop in St. Kyrik, Bulgaria May 28-June 1, 1990. Ed. by V. Fedorov et al. (Contributions to Statistics Ser.). (Illus.). xii, 248p. 1992. 65.95 (*0-387-91422-6*) Spr-Verlag.

Model-Oriented Design of Experiments. V. V. Fedorov & Peter Hackl. LC 97-15703. (Lecture Notes in Statistics Ser.: Vol. 125). 1997. pap. 29.95 (*0-387-98215-9*) Spr-Verlag.

Model Partnership Agreement for New York Law Firms. Ed. by Carl S. Koerner. 92p. (Orig.). 1989. pap. 30.00 (*0-942954-11-4*) NYS Bar.

*__Model Patient: My Life as an Incurable Wise-ass.__ Karen Duffy. 288p. 2000. 24.00 (*0-06-019725-0*, Pub. by HarperTrade) HarpC.

Model Penal Code: Complete Statutory Text. Institutional Staff. 1962. 40.00 (*0-8318-5788-9*, 5788) Am Law Inst.

Model Penal Code & Commentaries. Institutional Staff. 1985. 110.00 (*0-8318-5089-2*, 5089) Am Law Inst.

Model-Perinatal Autopsy Protocol. MacPherson. (Illus.). 60p. 1995. pap. text 10.00 (*1-881041-16-6*) Am Registry Path.

Model Personnel Policies for Business. Ed. by Don Morrison. 180p. ring bd. 89.00 (*0-927160-09-9*) Sound Resc Mgmt.

Model Plan for Implementation of Title I of the Americans with Disabilities Act: The Human Resource Perspective. Kay Robinson. (ADA Practice Ser.). 24p. 1994. pap. 9.00 (*0-934753-90-3*) LRP Pubns.

Model Plumbing Codes: A Comparison Study. Ed. by Robert J. DeCurtins. 1176p. 1997. 122.95 (*1-891255-02-9*) Am Soc Plumb Eng.

Model Policies for Small & Medium Public Libraries. Jeanette Larson & Herman L. Totten. LC 98-7917. 214p. 1998. pap. 40.00 (*1-55570-343-7*) Neal-Schuman.

Model Pooh Kit. (J). 1999. 12.95 (*0-7868-3223-1*, Pub. by Disney Pr) Time Warner.

Model Position Descriptions. 50.00 (*0-614-18091-0*) CHRIE.

Model Position Descriptions for the Foodservice Industry. 90p. 1992. pap. 33.00 (*0-614-31125-X*, MG999) Natl Restaurant Assn.

An Asterisk (*) at the beginning of an entry indicates that the title is appearing for the first time.

Model Positive Pay Services Agreement & Commentary. American Bar Association Staff. LC 99-34479. 1999. write for info. (*1-57073-691-X*) Amer Bar Assn.

Model Practices in Service Delivery in Child & Family Mental Health. Ed. by Michael C. Roberts. 456p. 1996. text 79.95 (*0-8058-1651-8*) L Erlbaum Assocs.

Model Practices in Service Delivery in Child & Family Mental Health. Ed. by Michael C. Roberts. 456p. 1996. pap. text 45.00 (*0-8058-1652-6*) L Erlbaum Assocs.

Model Prayer: How to Pray. J. Gordon Henry. 102p. (Orig.). 1996. pap. 5.00 (*0-9656424-1-0*) J G H Minist.

Model Predictive Control. E. F. Camacho & C. Bordons. Ed. by M. Grimble & M. Johnson. LC 98-4205. (Advanced Textbooks in Control & Signal Processing Ser.). 300p. 1999. pap. text 54.95 (*3-540-76241-8*) Spr-Verlag.

Model Predictive Control. Carlos E. Garcia et al. 300p. (C). 1996. boxed set 52.00 (*0-13-590506-0*) P-H.

Model Predictive Control in the Process Industry. E. F. Camacho & C. Bordons. LC 94-47060. (Advances in Industrial Control Ser.). (Illus.). 239p. 1995. 54.50 (*3-540-19724-9*) Spr-Verlag.

Model Procedures for Police Interrogation. Gerald M. Caplan. 27p. (Orig.). (C). 1995. pap. text 10.00 (*0-7881-2011-5*) DIANE Pub.

Model Procedures Guide: Industrial Incident Management. Ed. by Shirley Ayers. 20p. 1993. pap. 20.00 (*0-945790-07-4*) Detrick Lawrence.

Model Procedures Guide for Emergency Medical Incidents. National Fire Service Incident Management System Committee & Model Procedures Committee. Ed. by Michael A. Wieder. (Illus.). 116p. 1997. pap. text 21.00 (*0-87939-137-5*, 36005) IFSTA.

Model Procedures Guide for High-Rise Firefighting. National Fire Service Incident Management System Committee & Model Procedures Committee. Ed. by Michael A. Wieder. (Illus.). 144p. 1997. pap. text 23.00 (*0-87939-136-7*, 36004) IFSTA.

Model Procedures Guide for Structural Firefighting. National Fire Service Incident Management System Committee. (Illus.). 72p. 1993. pap. text 14.00 (*0-87939-108-1*) IFSTA.

Model Procurement Ordinance for Local Governments. 45p. 1982. pap. 8.50 (*0-89707-094-1*, 539-0032-01) Amer Bar Assn.

Model Program for Schools of Professional Accountancy. Robert W. McGee. LC 86-28226. 206p. (Orig.). 1987. pap. text 22.50 (*0-8191-6095-4*) U Pr of Amer.

Model Program for Serving LEP Students: Videotape & Facilitator's Guide. Joan E. Friedenberg. 1991. 49.50 (*0-317-04054-5*, LT71) Ctr Educ Trng Employ.

Model Programs for Instruction. Edward L. Vockell. (Illus.). 304p. (C). 1987. pap. text 21.95 (*0-8359-4682-7*) P-H.

Model Proposals. Barbara Darraugh. vi, 110p. 1998. pap. 50.00 (*1-892725-30-4*) Building Serv.

Model-Prototype Correlation of Hydraulic Structures. Ed. by Philip H. Burgi. (Symposium Proceedings Ser.). 488p. 1988. 49.00 (*0-87262-669-5*) Am Soc Civil Eng.

Model Radio Control Yachts. Trevor Reece. (Illus.). 176p. 1989. pap. 24.50 (*0-85242-972-X*, Pub. by Nexus Special Interests) Trans-Atl Phila.

Model Railroad Bridges & Trestles. Model Railroader Magazine Staff. Ed. by Michael Emmerich. (Illus.). 152p. (Orig.). 1992. per. 19.95 (*0-89024-128-7*, 12101) Kalmbach.

Model Railroad Electronics 1, Vol. 1. Rutger Friberg. (Illus.). 96p. 1995. pap. 16.00 (*91-85496-96-0*) Marklin Inc.

***Model Railroad Resources Handbook: A Where-to-Find-It Guide for the Hobbyist.** Ed. by Allan Miller. (Illus.). 192p. 2000. pap. 16.95 (*0-87341-887-5*) Krause Pubns.

Model Railroad Scenery & Detailing. Albert A. Sorensen. (Illus.). 368p. 1990. pap. 19.95 (*0-8306-3420-7*, 3420) McGraw-Hill Prof.

Model Railroader Cyclopedia Vol. 1: Steam Locomotives. Linn Westcott. 49.95 (*0-89024-001-9*, 01001) Kalmbach.

Model Railroader Cyclopedia Vol. 2: Diesel Locomotives. Bob Hayden. (Illus.). 160p. 34.95 (*0-89024-547-9*, 01033) Kalmbach.

Model Railroader's Catalogue. Melinda Corey. 265p. 1991. per. 19.95 (*0-671-70949-6*, Fireside) S&S Trade Pap.

Model Railroader's Guide to Intermodal Equipment & Operations. Jeff Wilson. LC 98-207306. (Illus.). 80p. 1998. pap. 15.95 (*0-89024-313-1*, 12190, Kalmbach Books) Kalmbach.

Model Railroading. Michael E. Goodman. LC 91-15853. (Hobby Guides Ser.). (Illus.). 48p. (J). (gr. 5-6). 1993. lib. bdg. 12.95 (*0-89686-620-3*, Crstwood Hse) Silver Burdett Pr.

Model Railroading in Small Spaces. Mat Chibbaro. LC 97-225323. (Illus.). 96p. (Orig.). 1997. pap. 16.95 (*0-89024-295-X*, 12176, Kalmbach Books) Kalmbach.

Model Railroading Made "E-Z" with Bachmann's E-Z Track System. Robert Schleicher. 32p. 1995. pap. 3.95 (*0-9647098-0-5*) Bachmann Indust.

Model Railroading with Athearn Locomotives & Cars. Ed. by Robert Schleicher. (Illus.). 98p. 1989. pap. text 9.95 (*0-9612692-3-5*) Rocky Mntn Pub Co.

Model Railroading's Guide to Model Photography. Bruce N. Nall. Ed. by Randall B. Lee. (Illus.). 64p. 1993. pap. 8.95 (*0-9612692-8-6*) Rocky Mntn Pub Co.

Model Railroading's Guide to Modeling & Detailing Diesels, Vol. I. Ed. by Randall B. Lee. (Illus.). 88p. 1991. pap. 9.95 (*0-9612692-4-3*) Rocky Mntn Pub Co.

Model Railroading's Guide to Modeling & Detailing Diesels, Vol. II. Ed. by Randall B. Lee. (Illus.). 128p. 1993. pap. 14.95 (*0-9612692-7-8*) Rocky Mntn Pub Co.

Model Railroading's Guide to the Norfolk & Western Railway: Williamson Terminal - 1953. Vern French. (Illus.). 100p. 1992. pap. 12.95 (*0-9612692-6-X*) Rocky Mntn Pub Co.

Model Railroading's Guide to the Railway Express. V. S. Roseman. 100p. 1992. pap. 12.95 (*0-9612692-5-1*) Rocky Mntn Pub Co.

Model Railway Design Manual. C. J. Freezer. (Illus.). 160p. 1996. 19.95 (*1-85260-538-3*) P Stephens.

Model Railway Manual: A Step by Step Guide to Building a Layout. C. J. Freezer. (Illus.). 192p. 1994. 32.95 (*1-85260-501-4*, Pub. by J H Haynes & Co) Motorbooks Intl.

Model Railways. Cyril J. Freegie. 1996. 6.98 (*0-7858-0603-2*) Bk Sales Inc.

***Model Rebels: The Rise & Fall of China's Richest Village.** Bruce Gilley. LC 00-22321. 2000. pap. write for info. (*0-520-22533-3*) U CA Pr.

Model Record-Keeping Manual for Small Water Companies. NARUC Staff Subcommittee on Water. 95p. 1978. 5.00 (*0-317-01666-0*) NARUC.

Model Residents Utility Services Regulations. 117p. 1984. 9.25 (*0-685-30189-3*, 36,398) NCLS Inc.

Model Rocket Computer Programs: Malewicki Closed-Form Altitude, Coefficient of Drag & Center of Pressure. Charles E. Rogers & Jerry Irvine. 1983. 39.95 (*0-912468-12-2*) CA Rocketry.

***Model Rocket Design & Construction: How to Create & Build Unique & Exciting Model Rockets That Work!** 2nd rev. ed. Timothy S. Van Milligan. LC TL844.V36 2000. (Illus.). 160p. (YA). (gr. 6-12). 2000. pap. 23.95 (*0-9653620-1-9*, 1001) Apogee Compnts.

Model Rocketry Handbook. Stuart Lodge. (Illus.). 125p. (Orig.). 1990. pap. 19.95 (*1-85486-047-X*) Nexus Special Interests.

Model Rockets from Design to Launch. Douglas J. Malewicki & Donald C. Schwenn. 1976. teacher ed. 9.95 (*0-912468-15-7*, MRDTL-T); student ed. 9.95 (*0-912468-16-5*, MRDTL-S) CA Rocketry.

Model Rules for Judicial Disciplinary Enforcement. 75p. 1995. pap. 12.00 (*1-57073-137-3*, 561-0122) Amer Bar Assn.

Model Rules for Lawyer Disciplinary Enforcement. 83p. 1993. pap. 15.95 (*0-317-31062-3*, 561-0115) Amer Bar Assn.

Model Rules of Professional Conduct. American Bar Association Staff & Center for Professional Responsibility Staff. LC 93-73874. viii, 165p. 1994. write for info. (*0-89707-933-7*) Amer Bar Assn.

Model Rules of Professional Conduct. American Bar Association Staff & Center for Professional Responsibility Staff. LC 97-80168. viii, 153 p. 1997. write for info. (*1-57073-511-5*) Amer Bar Assn.

Model Rules of Professional Conduct. Center for Professional Responsibility Staff. LC 95-80482. 176p. 1995. pap. 15.95 (*1-57073-235-3*, 561-0120) Amer Bar Assn.

Model Rules of Professional Conduct for Federal Lawyers (1990) 48p. 1990. pap. text 15.00 (*1-56986-079-3*) Federal Bar.

Model Sailplanes Without Myth or Magic. Tony Upso. LC 92-76107. 170p. 1993. pap. 18.95 (*0-9636034-0-X*) Beefsteak Mines.

***Model Security Policies, Plans & Procedures.** John Fay. LC 99-22511. 317p. 1999. write for info. (*0-7506-7183-1*) Buttrwrth-Heinemann.

Model Selection & Inference: A Practical Information Theoretic Approach. D. A. Anderson & K. P. Burnham. LC 98-13046. (Illus.). 320p. 1998. 69.95 (*0-387-98504-2*) Spr-Verlag.

Model Sense Concepts: Home Study Reference Guide to Personal Improvement & Modeling Basics. Pamela D. Gibson. Ed. by Glenn J. Gibson. 136p. 1990. pap. text 19.95 (*0-9626320-6-6*) Rated P&G.

***Model Ship: It's Purpose & History.** Norman Napier Boyd. 1999. 49.50 (*1-85149-327-1*) Antique Collect.

Model Ships & Boats. Ed. by Nexus Special Interests Staff. (Planbooks Series 3). (Illus.). 32p. (Orig.). 1995. pap. 13.95 (*1-85486-158-1*, Pub. by Nexus Special Interests) Trans-Atl Phila.

Model Ships from Scratch. Scott Robertson. (Illus.). 190p. 1994. 34.95 (*1-55750-589-6*) Naval Inst Pr.

Model Shipwright: An Anthology 1972-1997. John Bowen. (Conway Classics Ser.). 1998. 32.95 (*0-85177-729-5*) Brasseys.

Model Soldier Manual. Peter J. Blum. (Illus.). (Orig.). 1971. pap. 6.00 (*0-912364-03-3*) Imrie-Risley.

Model Solving in Mathematical Programming. Williams. 1993. pap. text 56.50 (*0-471-93722-3*) Wiley.

Model Specification for Tunneling. 152p. 1997. 71.00 (*0-7277-2588-2*) Am Soc Civil Eng.

Model Standards. Graves. 1997. pap. text. write for info. (*0-201-62879-1*) Addison-Wesley.

Model Standards for Adult Education Instructors. California Department of Education Staff. (English-As-a-Second Language Ser.). 88p. 1992. pap. 11.25 (*0-8011-1046-7*) Calif Education.

Model Steam Engines. Bob Gordon. (Album Ser.: No. 32). (Illus.). 32p. pap. 6.25 (*0-85263-906-6*, Pub. by Shire Pubns) Parkwest Pubns.

Model Steam Locomotive: A Complete Treatise on Design & Construction. Martin Evans. (Illus.). 208p. 1983. pap. 33.50 (*0-85242-817-0*, Pub. by Nexus Special Interests) Trans-Atl Phila.

Model Student Essays. 4th ed. Gallaher. 104p. (C). 1997. pap. 6.67 (*0-13-645516-6*, Macmillan Coll) P-H.

Model Subdivision Regulations, Planning, & Law. 2nd ed. Robert H. Freilich & Michael M. Shultz. LC 93-71516. 392p. 1995. lib. bdg. 62.95 (*0-918286-88-3*, Planners Press) Am Plan Assn.

Model Survey of Computer Services. 36p. pap. 15.00 (*92-1-161336-1*) UN.

Model Systems in Signal Transduction. Ed. by Shirish Shenolikar & Angus C. Nairn. LC QP0625.N89A3. (Advances in Second Messenger & Phosphoprotein Research Ser.: Vol. 27). (Illus.). 223p. 1993. reprint ed. pap. 69.20 (*0-608-07271-0*, 206749900009) Bks Demand.

Model Systems of Development & Aging of the Nervous System. Ed. by Antonia Vernadakis. (C). 1987. text 210.50 (*0-89838-838-4*) Kluwer Academic.

Model T Ford. Bruce W. McCalley. LC 93-80697. (Illus.). 614p. 1994. 39.95 (*0-87341-293-1*, TF01) Krause Pubns.

Model T Ford. Christopher Simonds. (Turning Points in American History Ser.). (Illus.). 64p. (YA). (gr. 5 up). 1991. pap. 11.00 (*0-382-24117-7*); lib. bdg. 17.95 (*0-382-24122-3*) Silver Burdett Pr.

***Model T Ford.** Jonathan Wood. 1999. pap. 25.00 (*0-7478-0432-X*, Pub. by Shire Pubns) St Mut.

Model Tax Convention: Four Related Studies. OECD Staff. 104p. (Orig.). 1992. pap. 24.00 (*92-64-13801-3*) OECD.

Model Tax Convention on Income & on Capital June 1998, Condensed Version. OECD Staff. 308p. 1998. pap. 35.00 (*92-64-16115-5*, 23 98 51 1 P, Pub. by European Conference Ministers Transp) OECD.

Model Tax Convention on Income & on Capital, 1995 Update. (ENG & FRE.). (Orig.). Date not set. pap. 40.00 (*0-614-11583-3*, Pub. by Org for Econ) OECD.

Model Theoretic Algebra with Particular Emphasis on Fields, Rings, Modules, Vol. 2. C. U. Jensen & H. Lenzing. xiv, 444p. 1989. text 274.00 (*2-88124-717-2*) Gordon & Breach.

Model-Theoretic Logics. Ed. by J. Barwise & Solomon Feferman. (Perspectives in Mathematical Logic Ser.). (Illus.). 750p. 1985. 318.95 (*0-387-90936-2*) Spr-Verlag.

Model Theory. Wilfrid Hodges. (Encyclopedia of Mathematics & Its Applications Ser.: No. 42). (Illus.). 786p. (C). 1993. text 125.00 (*0-521-30442-3*) Cambridge U Pr.

***Model Theory.** Maria Manzano. Tr. by Ruy J. G. B. de Queiroz. (Oxford Logic Guides Ser.: No. 37). (Illus.). 263p. 1999. text 75.00 (*0-19-853851-0*) OUP.

Model Theory. 3rd enl. ed. C. C. Chang & H. Jerome Keisler. (Studies in Logic & the Foundations of Mathematics: No. 73). xvi,650p. 1990. 169.50 (*0-444-88054-2*, North Holland) Elsevier.

***Model Theory, Algebra & Geometry.** Ed. by Deidre Haskell et al. LC 00-20294. (Mathematical Sciences Research Institute Publications: No. 39). 250p. (C). 2000. 49.95 (*0-521-78068-3*) Cambridge U Pr.

Model Theory & Algebraic Geometry: An Introduction to E. Hrushovski's Proof of the Geometric Mordell-Lang Conjecture, Vol. 169. Elisabeth Bouscaren. LC 98-38720. (Lecture Notes in Mathematics Ser.). 211p. 1999. pap. 41.00 (*3-540-64863-1*) Spr-Verlag.

***Model Theory & Applications.** LC 99-32567. (American Mathematical Society Translations Ser.). 1999. write for info. (*0-8218-1092-8*) Am Math.

Model Theory & Linear Extreme Points in the Numerical Radius Unit Ball. Michael A. Dritschel & Hugo J. Woerdeman. LC 97-21323. (Memoirs of the American Mathematical Society Ser.: Vol. 129, No. 615). 62p. 1997. pap. 34.00 (*0-8218-0651-3*) Am Math.

Model Theory & Modules. M. Y. Prest. (London Mathematical Society Lecture Note Ser.: No. 130). 400p. 1988. pap. text 64.95 (*0-521-34833-1*) Cambridge U Pr.

Model Theory for Modal Logic: Kripke Models for Modal Predicate Calculi. K. A. Bowen. (Synthese Library: Vol. 127). 137p. 1978. text 85.50 (*90-277-0929-7*, D Reidel) Kluwer Academic.

Model Theory of Fields. D. Marker et al. (Lecture Notes in Logic Ser.: Vol. 5). 154p. 1996. pap. 39.00 (*3-540-60741-2*) Spr-Verlag.

Model Theory of Groups & Automorphism Groups. Ed. by David M. Evans. LC 97-10532. (London Mathematical Society Lecture Note Ser.: No. 244). (Illus.). 228p. (C). 1997. pap. text 39.95 (*0-521-58955-X*) Cambridge U Pr.

Model Title Standards. Lewis M. Simes & Clarence B. Taylor. (Michigan Legal Publications). 99p. 1976. 30.00 (*1-57588-333-3*, 301480) W S Hein.

Model to Determine Benefits Obtainable from the Management of Riverine Fisheries of Bangladesh. M. Ahmed. (ICLARM Technical Reports: No. 28). 133p. 1991. per. write for info. (*971-8709-08-8*, Pub. by ICLARM) Intl Spec Bk.

Model Ts, Pep Chapels, & a Wolf at the Door: Kansas Teenagers, 1900-1941. Ed. by Marilyn I. Holt. (Illus.). 290p. (Orig.). (YA). (gr. 5 up). 1994. pap. 19.00 (*0-936352-11-6*) U of KS Cont Ed.

Model Tuberculosis Exposure Control Plan. Terry J. Gile. LC TX 4-345-292. 36p. 1996. wbk. ed. 69.00 (*0-9625414-4-3*) Clinical Lab Mgmnt Assn.

Model Tuberculosis Exposure Control Plan (Workbook & Training Kit) Terry J. Gile. LC TX 4-347-587. 85p. 1996. ring bd., wbk. ed. 125.00 (*0-9625414-6-X*) Clinical Lab Mgmnt Assn.

Model Utah Jury Instructions - Civil, 1993 Edition. Utah State Bar Model Jury Instructions Staff. 736p. 1993. pap. 60.00 (*1-55834-093-9*, 67675-10, MICHIE) LEXIS Pub.

Model Validation in Sparta. Beverly Watkins et al. Ed. by Robert H. Lafferty & John H. House. (Illus.). 300p. 1986. pap. 6.00 (*1-56349-052-8*, RR25) AR Archaeol.

Model Valuation, Plant Costs & Continuing Property Records Manual. 68p. 1974. 7.50 (*0-318-15009-3*) NARUC.

Model Warplanes, 1996: Golden Era, Vol. 2. John C. Fredriksen. (Hobby Bibliographies Ser.). 50p. (Orig.). 1996. pap. 15.00 (*1-888665-02-5*) Dollar Scholar.

Model Warplanes, 1996: Jet Age, Vol. 5. John C. Fredriksen. (Hobby Bibliographies Ser.). 50p. (Orig.). 1996. pap. 15.00 (*1-888665-05-X*) Dollar Scholar.

Model Warplanes, 1996: Second World War-Allied, Vol. 4. John C. Fredriksen. (Hobby Bibliographies Ser.). 50p. (Orig.). 1996. pap. 15.00 (*1-888665-04-1*) Dollar Scholar.

Model Warplanes, 1996: Second World War-Axis, Vol. 3. John C. Fredriksen. (Hobby Bibliographies Ser.). 50p. (Orig.). 1996. pap. 15.00 (*1-888665-03-3*) Dollar Scholar.

Model Warplanes, 1996: World War One, Vol. 1. John C. Fredriksen. (Hobby Bibliographies Ser.). 50p. (Orig.). 1995. pap. 15.00 (*1-888665-01-7*) Dollar Scholar.

Model Welfare States: Politics & Policies in Social Democratic Scandanavia. Eric S. Einhorn & John Logue. LC 88-27098. 354p. 1989. 75.00 (*0-275-92450-5*, C2450, Praeger Pubs); pap. 25.95 (*0-275-93188-9*, B3188, Praeger Pubs) Greenwood.

***Model Wife.** Arthur Ollman. LC 99-17301. (Illus.). 212p. 1999. 65.00 (*0-8212-2170-1*, Pub. by Bulfinch Pr) Little.

Model Witness Examinations. Paul M. Sandler & James K. Archibald. LC 97-888. 1997. pap. 54.00 (*1-57073-426-7*) Amer Bar Assn.

Model World & Other Co. Michael Chabon. 208p. 1992. reprint ed. pap. 12.00 (*0-380-71099-4*, Avon Bks) Morrow Avon.

Modeler's Guide to Scale Automotive Finishes. unabridged ed. Pat Covert. LC 97-152892. (Illus.). 88p. (Orig.). 1997. pap. 17.95 (*0-89024-265-8*, 12162, Kalmbach Books) Kalmbach.

Modeles Asymptotiques de la Mecanique des Fluides I. R. K. Zeytounian. (Lecture Notes in Physics Ser.: Vol. 245). ix, 260p. 1986. pap. 26.00 (*0-387-16447-2*) Spr-Verlag.

Modeles Clinico-Pharmacologiques pour l'Experimentation de Corticoides a Usage Externe. H. Wendt & P. J. Frosch. (Illus.). 64p. 1982. pap. 28.75 (*3-8055-3548-1*) S Karger.

Modeling. Ted Kowalski. (C). 1994. pap. text. write for info. (*0-8013-1336-8*) Longman.

Modeling: Simulation. Eyman. (West Engineering Ser.). 1988. pap., student ed. 8.00 (*0-534-93875-2*) PWS Pubs.

Modeling: Totally Exposed. Marsha D. Faulkenberry. LC 97-92526. (Illus.). 144p. 1997. pap. 19.95 (*0-9660437-0-7*) M Doll & Assocs.

Modeling a Likeness in Clay. Daisy Grubbs. (Illus.). 160p. 1982. 27.50 (*0-8230-3094-6*) Watsn-Guptill.

Modeling Air-Lake Interaction: Physical Background. Ed. by S. S. Zilitinkevich. (Research Reports in Physics). (Illus.). xi, 129p. 1991. 79.95 (*0-387-52988-8*) Spr-Verlag.

Modeling, Analysis & Control of Dynamic Elastic Multi-Link Structures. John E. Lagnese et al. LC 94-3096. (Systems & Control Ser.). 388p. 1994. 78.50 (*0-8176-3705-2*) Birkhauser.

Modeling, Analysis & Control of Dynamic Systems. William J. Palm. 370p. (C). 1983. pap. text, suppl. ed. 25.00 (*0-471-88581-9*) Wiley.

Modeling, Analysis, & Design of Water Distribution Systems. Lee Cesario. (Illus.). 328p. 1995. 84.00 (*0-89867-758-0*, 20296) Am Water Wks Assn.

***Modeling, Analysis & Simulation of Computer & Telecommunication Systems: Proceedings of the 7th International Symposium, College Park, Maryland, 1999.** 400p. 1999. 125.00 (*0-7695-0381-0*) IEEE Comp Soc.

Modeling, Analysis, Design, & Control of Stochastic Systems. Vidyadhar G. Kulkarni. Ed. by G. Casella et al. LC 98-52791. (Texts in Statistics Ser.). 400p. 1999. text 69.95 (*0-387-98725-8*) Spr-Verlag.

Modeling & Advanced Control for Process Industries: Applications to Paper Making Processes. Ming Rao et al. LC 94-26235. (Advances in Industrial Control Ser.). (Illus.). 297p. 1994. 59.95 (*0-387-19881-4*) Spr-Verlag.

Modeling & Analysis: An Introduction to System Performance Evaluation Methodology. Hisashi Kobayashi. LC 77-73946. (IBM Systems Programming Ser.). (Illus.). 1978. text. write for info. (*0-201-14457-3*) Addison-Wesley.

Modeling & Analysis in Biomedicine: Proceedings of the 4th Course of the International School of Pure & Applied Biostructure, Erice, Italy, Oct. 18-27,1982. Ed. by C. Nicolini. 552p. 1984. 108.00 (*9971-950-81-2*) World Scientific Pub.

Modeling & Analysis of Computer Communications Networks. J. F. Hayes. LC 84-16107. (Applications of Communications Theory Ser.). (Illus.). 414p. (C). 1984. 69.50 (*0-306-41782-0*, Plenum Trade) Perseus Pubng.

Modeling & Analysis of Conventional Defense in Europe: Assessment of Improvement Options. Ed. by Reiner K. Huber. LC 85-23233. 224p. 1986. 75.00 (*0-306-42227-1*, Plenum Trade) Perseus Pubng.

Modeling & Analysis of Diffusive & Advective Processes in Geosciences. W. E. Fitzgibbon & M. F. Wheeler. LC 92-16400. (Miscellaneous Bks.: No. 34). vii, 233p. 1992. pap. 47.25 (*0-89871-299-8*) Soc Indus-Appl Math.

Modeling & Analysis of Dynamic Systems. 2nd ed. Charles M. Close & Dean K. Frederick. 704p. 1994. text 100.95 (*0-471-12517-2*) Wiley.

Modeling & Analysis of Linear Physical Systems. J. F. Lindsay & V. Ramachandran. (Illus.). 780p. (C). 1990. text 69.95 (*0-929704-19-3*) Weber Systems.

Modeling & Analysis of Local Area Network. P. J. Fortier. 1989. 48.00 (*0-387-96832-6*) Spr-Verlag.

Modeling & Analysis of Local Area Networks. Ed. by Paul J. Fourtier. 314p. 1990. boxed set 94.95 (*0-8493-7405-7*, Q) CRC Pr.

Modeling & Analysis of Manufacturing Systems. Ronald G. Askin & Charles R. Standridge. LC 92-35014. 480p. 1993. text 97.95 (*0-471-51418-7*) Wiley.

M

An Asterisk (*) at the beginning of an entry indicates that the title is appearing for the first time.

M

Modeling & Analysis of Stochastic Systems. Vidyadhar G. Kulkarni. LC 95-15182. 624p. (gr. 13). 1996. ring bd. 64.95 (*0-412-04991-0*, Chap & Hall CRC) CRC Pr.

Modeling & Applications. 2nd rev. ed. David P. Lawrence. (Graphing Calculator Connection Ser.). (Illus.). 100p. 1998. spiral bd. 23.95 (*1-58108-008-5*) Pencil Point.

*__Modeling & Computation of Boundary-Layer Flows: Laminar, Turbulent & Transitional Boundary Layers in Incompressible Flows__ Tuncer Cebeci. LC 98-45815. 1998. pap. text 95.00 (*3-540-65010-5*) Spr-Verlag.

Modeling & Computation of Boundary-Layer Flows: Laminar, Turbulent & Transitional Boundary Layers in Incompressible Flows Tuncer Cebeci & J. Cousteix. LC 98-45815. 1998. write for info. (*0-9668461-0-9*) Horizons Pubg.

Modeling & Computation of Equilibria. Harker. 356p. 1999. write for info. (*0-12-325255-5*) Acad Pr.

Modeling & Control in Biomedical Systems: Proceedings of the International Federation of Automatic Control Symposium, Gavelston, Texas, U. S. A., 27-30 March 1994. Ed. by B. W. Patterson & International Federation of Automatic Control, Tri. LC 94-3756. 598p. 1994. pap. 105.75 (*0-08-042224-1*, Pergamon Pr) Elsevier.

*__Modeling & Control of Adaptive Mechanical Structure.__ (Proceedings Ser.). 468p. 1999. 99.00 (*0-7680-0448-9*, P-345) Soc Auto Engineers.

Modeling & Control of Biotechnical Processes, 1992, 2nd IFAC Symposium & Computer Applications in Fermentation Technology: Selected Papers from the IFAC & 5th International Conference, Keystone, Colorado, 29 March-2 April 1992. Ed. by M. Nazmul Karim & George Stephanopoulos. LC 92-37411. 480p. 1992. 173.00 (*0-08-041710-8*, Pergamon Pr) Elsevier.

Modeling & Control of Casting & Welding Processes: Proceedings of the 3rd Conference on Modeling of Casting & Welding Processes. Sponsored by the Engineering Foundation & Held on January 12-17, 1986, in Santa Barbara, CA. Conference on Modeling of Casting & Welding Proces. Ed. by Sindo Kou & Robert Mehrabian. LC 86-16402. (Illus.). 636p. reprint ed. pap. 197.20 (*0-8357-8522-X*, 203481900091) Bks Demand.

Modeling & Control of Constrained Mechanical Systems. Alessandro Astofi. 1999. 65.00 (*0-8176-4077-0*) Spr-Verlag.

Modeling & Control of Electric Power Plants: Proceedings of the IFAC Workshop, Como, Italy, 22-23 September 1983. Ed. by C. Maffezzoni. (IFAC Publication). 176p. 1984. 78.00 (*0-08-031163-6*, Pub. by Pergamon Repr) Franklin.

Modeling & Control of Kraft Production Systems for Pulp Production, Chemical Recovery, & Energy Conservation: Proceedings of a Symposium Held by the Pulp & Paper Division of the Instrument Society of American at the ISA-75 Industry Oriented Conference & Exhibit, Milwaukee, WI, October 8-9, 1975. Symposium on Modeling & Control of Kraft Productio. Ed. by Theodore J. Williams & Robert A. Holm. LC 76-373580. (Illus.). 294p. reprint ed. pap. 91.20 (*0-8357-4430-2*, 203726100008) Bks Demand.

Modeling & Control of Logical Discrete Event Systems. Ratnesh Kumar. (International Series in Engineering & Computer Science, Natural Language Processing & Machine Translation). 160p. (C). 1994. lib. bdg. 87.50 (*0-7923-7938-1*) Kluwer Academic.

Modeling & Control of Logical Discrete Event Systems. Ratnesh Kumar & Vijay K. Garg. LC 94-39722. (International Series in Engineering & Computer Science: Vol. 300). 143p. 1994. text 124.50 (*0-7923-9538-7*) Kluwer Academic.

Modeling & Control of Marine Craft: Proceedings of the International Conference, Held at Exeter, U. K., 18-20 April 1990. Ed. by M. M. Pourzanjani & G. N. Roberts. 432p. 1991. mass mkt. 150.95 (*1-85166-592-7*) Elsevier.

Modeling & Control of Ventilation: Proceedings of the London Conference on Modeling & Control of Ventilation Held in Egham, Surrey, England, September 17-20, 1994, Vol. 393. Ed. by Stephen J. Semple & Lewis Adams. (Illus.). 388p. 1996. 110.00 (*0-306-45180-8*, Kluwer Plenum) Kluwer Academic.

Modeling & Data Treatment in the Pharmaceutical Sciences. J. T. Carstensen. LC 96-60624. 235p. 1996. text 169.95 (*1-56676-440-8*) Technomic.

Modeling & Design of Twisted Tube Heat Exchangers. B.V. Dziubenko. LC 99-44188. 1998. write for info. (*1-56700-123-8*) Begell Hse.

Modeling & Diagnositcs in SI & Diesel Engines. (Special Publications). 100p. 1999. pap. 49.00 (*0-7680-0424-1*, SP-1460) Soc Auto Engineers.

Modeling & Diagnostics in Diesel Engines. 1996. 61.00 (*1-56091-862-4*, SP-1205) Soc Auto Engineers.

*__Modeling & Diagnostics in Diesel Engines.__ (Special Publications). 230p. 1999. 109.00 (*0-7680-0488-8*, SP-1480) Soc Auto Engineers.

*__Modeling & Diagnostics in SI Engines.__ (Special Publications). 200p. 1999. 109.00 (*0-7680-0489-6*, SP-1481) Soc Auto Engineers.

Modeling & Differential Equations in Biology. Burton. (Lecture Notes in Pure & Applied Mathematics Ser.: Vol. 58). (Illus.). 292p. 1980. pap. text 130.00 (*0-8247-7133-8*) Dekker.

Modeling & Forecasting Demand in Tourism. Stephen F. Witt & Christine Witt. (Illus.). 195p. 1991. text 65.00 (*0-12-760740-4*) Acad Pr.

Modeling & Identification of Dynamic Systems. Naresh K. Sinha & Boguslaw Kuzsta. 368p. 1983. text 64.95 (*0-442-28162-5*, VNR) Wiley.

Modeling & Inversion of the Radar Response of Vegetation Canopies. Paul F. Polatin. LC QC0973.. (University of Michigan Reports: No. RL899). 240p. reprint ed. pap. 74.40 (*0-7837-6781-1*, 204661100003) Bks Demand.

Modeling & Lab Manual for Differential Equations. Anton. (Mathematics Ser.). 2002. mass mkt. 32.95 (*0-534-34130-6*) Brooks-Cole.

Modeling & Management of Resources under Uncertainty. Ed. by T. Vencent et al. (Lecture Notes in Biomathematics Ser.: Vol. 72). 318p. 1987. pap. text 53.00 (*0-387-17999-2*) Spr-Verlag.

Modeling & Managing Shallow Lake Eutrophication. Ed. by G. Van Straten & Laszlo Somlyody. (Illus.). x, 386p. 1986. 99.00 (*0-387-16227-5*) Spr-Verlag.

*__Modeling & Measurement of Sliding Friction for Gear Analysis.__ M. Vaishya & D. R. Houser. (Technical Papers: Vol. 99FTMS1). 12p. 1999. pap. 30.00 (*1-55589-757-6*) AGMA.

Modeling & Optimization of Fermentation Processes. B. Volesky & J. Votruba. LC 92-9915. (Process Simulation & Modeling Ser.: Vol. 1). 266p. 1992. 173.00 (*0-444-89588-4*) Elsevier.

Modeling & Optimization of the Lifetime of Technologies. Natali Hritonenko & Yuri Yatsenko. (Applied Optimization Ser.: Vol. 4). 1996. text 144.00 (*0-7923-4014-0*) Kluwer Academic.

Modeling & Optimization with GINO. Judith Liebman et al. (Illus.). 200p. (C). 1986. pap. text, mass mkt. 54.75 incl. 3.5 hd (*0-89426-157-6*) Course Tech.

Modeling & Parameter Estimation in Respiratory Control. Ed. by Michael C. Khoo. LC 90-7301. (Illus.). 220p. (C). 1990. text 95.00 (*0-306-43530-6*, Kluwer Plenum) Kluwer Academic.

Modeling & Prediction: Honoring Seymour Geisser. Geisser, Seymour Geisser et al. LC 96-19132. 464p. 1996. 65.95 (*0-387-94808-2*) Spr-Verlag.

Modeling & Simulating Communication Networks: A Hands-on Approach Using Opnet. Irene Katzela. LC 98-25085. 116p. 1998. pap. 34.80 (*0-13-915737-9*) P-H.

Modeling & Simulating Sensory Response for Real & Virtual Environments. Ed. by John D. Illgen. LC 98-226762. (Proceedings of SPIE Ser.: Vol. 3367). 144p. 1998. 59.00 (*0-8194-2816-7*) SPIE.

Modeling & Simulation. Hartmut Bossel. LC 94-1847. (Illus.). 504p. (C). 1994. text 65.00 incl. disk (*1-56881-033-4*) AK Peters.

Modeling & Simulation: Linking Entertainment & Defense. National Research Council Staff. LC 97-68732. 175p. 1997. pap. text 29.00 (*0-309-05842-2*) Natl Acad Pr.

*__Modeling & Simulation Based Engineering, 2 vols.__ Ed. by Satya N. Atluri & P. E. O'Donoghue. (Illus.). 2209p. (C). 1998. 625.00 (*0-9657001-2-7*) Tech Sci Pr.

Modeling & Simulation in Chemical Engineering. Roger G. Franks. 411p. 1972. 193.00 (*0-471-27535-2*) Wiley.

Modeling & Simulation in Science & Mathematics Education. W. Feurzeig & Nancy Roberts. Ed. by B. Hannon & M. Ruth. LC 99-10025. (Modeling Dynamic System Ser.). (Illus.). 392p. 1999. 79.95 incl. cd-rom (*0-387-98316-3*) Spr-Verlag.

Modeling & Simulation in Science, Engineering & Technology. Ed. by Nicola Bellomo. Date not set. write for info. (*0-614-26638-6*) Birkhauser.

Modeling & Simulation of Dynamic Systems. Robert L. Woods & Kent L. Lawrence. 521p. (C). 1997. 105.00 (*0-13-337379-7*) P-H.

Modeling & Simulation of Embedded Systems. Ed. by Crosbie & Crawford. 205p. 1996. pap. 60.00 (*1-56555-048-X*, EMB-95) Soc Computer Sim.

Modeling & Simulation of High Speed VLSI Interconnects. Ed. by M. S. Nakhla. 108p. (C). 1994. text 106.00 (*0-7923-9441-0*) Kluwer Academic.

Modeling & Simulation of Higher-Power Laser Systems IV, Vol. 2989. Ed. by Usamah O. Farrukh. LC 98-103953. 282p. 1997. 69.00 (*0-8194-2400-5*) SPIE.

*__Modeling & Simulation of Mineral Processing Systems.__ R. Peter King. 492p. 2000. 72.95 (*0-7506-4884-8*) Buttrwrth-Heinemann.

Modeling & Simulation of Mixed Analog-Digital Systems. Ed. by Brian N. Antao. LC 96-8201. (Kluwer International Series in Engineering & Computer Science). 136p. (C). 1996. text 103.00 (*0-7923-9738-X*) Kluwer Academic.

Modeling & Simulation of Power System Harmonics. Paulo F. Ribeiro. 1999. audio compact disk 138.00 (*0-7803-4597-5*) IEEE Standards.

Modeling & Simulation on Microcomputers, 1988. Ed. by Joe E. Hilber. (Illus.). 148p. (Orig.). (C). 1988. pap. 36.00 (*0-911801-26-X*, MSM88) Soc Computer Sim.

Modeling & Simulation on Microcomputers, 1990. Ed. by Vijay Madisetti. 138p. 1990. pap. 40.00 (*0-911801-64-2*, MSM90) Soc Computer Sim.

Modeling & Simulation Technologies Conference Held August, 1997 at New Orleans, Louisiana. 1997. 220.00 (*1-56347-236-8*, CP9712(9991)) AIAA.

*__Modeling & Talent World Book.__ Platinum Media Inc. Staff. Ed. by Laura Huhn & Michael Dillon. 320p. 1999. per. 44.95 (*0-9670588-0-5*) Platinum Media.

*__Modeling & Using Context: Proceedings, 2nd International & Interdisciplinary Conference, CONTEXT'99, Trento, Italy, September 9-11, 1999.__ Ed. by P. Bouquet et al. LC 99-44750. (Lecture Notes in Artificial Intelligence Ser.: Vol. 1688). xii, 528p. 1999. pap. 79.00 (*3-540-66432-7*) Spr-Verlag.

Modeling & Visualizing Interiors: Autocad Release 13, Autovision Release 2. Kingsley K. Wu. LC 97-13768. 355p. 1997. spiral bd. 63.00 (*0-13-530932-8*) P-H.

Modeling As a Career. Donna Dudish-Dozier. 74p. 1993. pap. 10.00 (*0-9634826-1-0*) New Hope AL.

Modeling As Negotiating: The Political Dynamics of Computer Models in the Public Process. William Dutton & Kenneth L. Kraemer. Ed. by Melvin J. Voigt. LC 84-28429. (Communication & Information Science Ser.). 280p. 1985. text 73.25 (*0-89391-261-1*) Ablx Pub.

Modeling Axisymmetric Flows: Dynamics of Films, Jets, & Drops. Stanley Middleman. LC 95-2196. (Illus.). 299p. 1995. text 63.00 (*0-12-494950-9*) Acad Pr.

Modeling Biological Phosphorus Removal in Activated Sludge Systems. D. Brdanovic. (IHE Thesis Ser.: No. 17). 251p. (C). 1998. text 42.00 (*90-5410-415-5*, Pub. by A A Balkema) Ashgate Pub Co.

Modeling Bounded Rationality. Ariel Rubinstein. LC 97-40481. (Zeuthen Lecture Book Ser.). 220p. 1997. 29.95 (*0-262-18187-8*) MIT Pr.

Modeling Bounded Rationality. Ariel Rubinstein. LC 97-40481. (Zeuthen Lecture Bks.). (Illus.). 224p. 1997. pap. text 16.95 (*0-262-68100-5*) MIT Pr.

Modeling by Object-Driven Linear Elemental Relations: A User's Guide for MODLER, September 1992. Harvey J. Greenberg. (Computer Science Interface Ser.). 176p. 1993. lib. bdg. 127.00 (*0-7923-9323-6*) Kluwer Academic.

Modeling Chemical Transport in Soils: Natural & Applied Contaminants. Ed. by Hossein Ghadiri & Calvin W. Rose. 240p. 1992. lib. bdg. 95.00 (*0-87371-747-3*, L747) Lewis Pubs.

Modeling Chocolate Made Easy: A Decorating Guide. Peggy Alter & Sharon Solomon. 44p. 1995. pap. text 4.95 (*0-9648004-0-3*) Confection Art.

Modeling Clay: 20 Decorative Projects to Create for the Home, 1. Penny Boylan. (Inspirations Ser.). 1999. 12.95 (*1-85967-887-4*) Anness Pub.

*__Modeling Common-Cause Failures in Probabilistic Risk Assessment.__ A. Mosleh. 203p. 1998. per. 17.00 (*0-16-062974-8*) USGPO.

Modeling Complex Computer & Communication Systems: A Domain-Oriented Design Framework. Oryal Tanir. LC 96-9381. (Illus.). 288p. 1996. 55.00 (*0-07-063312-6*) McGraw.

Modeling Complex Data for Creating Information. Ed. by J. E. DuBois & N. D. Gershon. LC 96-18690. (Data & Knowledge in a Changing World Ser.). (Illus.). 271p. 1996. 117.00 (*3-540-61069-3*) Spr-Verlag.

Modeling Complex Phenomena. Ed. by Lui Lam & V. Naroditsky. (Woodward Conference Ser.). (Illus.). 320p. 1992. 96.95 (*0-387-97821-6*) Spr-Verlag.

Modeling Complex Turbulent Flows. M. D. Salas et al. LC 99-10167. (ICASE/IARC Interdisciplinary Series in Science & Engineering). 1999. write for info. (*0-7923-5590-3*) Kluwer Academic.

Modeling Components of Hydrologic Cycle. Ed. by Vijay P. Singh. LC 81-71291. 1982. 42.00 (*0-918334-46-2*) WRP.

*__Modeling Consciousness Across the Disciplines.__ Ed. by J. Scott Jordan. LC 99-45035. (Illus.). 376p. 1999. 57.50 (*0-7618-1523-6*) U Pr of Amer.

Modeling Cost & Performance for Military Enlistment: Report of a Workshop. Commission on Behavioral & Social Sciences & Educa. Ed. by Bert F. Green & Anne S. Mavor. 172p. (Orig.). (C). 1994. pap. text 29.00 (*0-309-05041-3*) Natl Acad Pr.

Modeling Creativity & Knowledge-Based Creative Design. Ed. by John S. Gero & Mary L. Maher. 360p. 1993. text 79.95 (*0-8058-1153-2*) L Erlbaum Assocs.

Modeling Crop Photosynthesis - From Biochemistry to Canopy. K. J. Boote. (Special Publication Ser.: Vol. 19). 140p. 1991. 25.00 (*0-89118-533-X*) Crop Sci Soc Am.

Modeling Delivery of Landslide Materials to Streams. Tim J. Ward. (Illus.). 38p. (Orig.). (C). 1995. pap. text 20.00 (*0-7881-2363-7*) DIANE Pub.

Modeling Density-Driven Flow in Porous Media: Basics, Numerics, Software. E. O. Holzbecher. LC 98-20099. (Illus.). 305p. 1998. 84.95 incl. cd-rom (*3-540-63677-3*) Spr-Verlag.

Modeling, Design, Analysis, Simulation & Evaluation. Ching-Fang Lin. 640p. (C). 2001. 56.00 (*0-13-596388-5*) P-H.

Modeling Design Objects & Processes. T. Yagiu. Ed. by Jose L. Encarnacao. (Symbolic Computation - Computer Graphics Ser.). (Illus.). 336p. 1991. 101.95 (*0-387-53671-X*) Spr-Verlag.

Modeling Dinosaurs see Draw, Model & Paint

Modeling Discourse Topic: Sequential Relations & Strategies in Expository Text. Dionysis Goutsos. LC 96-23722. (Advances in Discourse Processes Ser.: Vol. 59). (Illus.). 350p. 1996. pap. 42.50 (*1-56750-218-0*); text 78.50 (*1-56750-217-2*) Ablx Pub.

Modeling Disease Transmission & Its Prevention by Disinfection. Ed. by Christon J. Hurst. (Illus.). 424p. (C). 1996. text 100.00 (*0-521-48131-7*) Cambridge U Pr.

Modeling Dissolved Ozone Behavior in Ozone Contactors. Philip C. Singer et al. LC 99-14007. 1999. write for info. (*0-89867-992-3*) Am Water Wks Assn.

Modeling Dynamic Biological Systems. Bruce M. Hannon & Matthias Ruth. LC 96-38281. (Modeling Dynamic Systems Ser.). (Illus.). 344p. 1997. 59.95 (*0-387-94850-3*) Spr-Verlag.

Modeling Dynamic Economic Systems. Matthias Ruth & Bruce M. Hannon. LC 96-38303. (Modeling Dynamic Systems Ser.). (Illus.). 312p. 1997. 59.95 (*0-387-94849-X*) Spr-Verlag.

Modeling Dynamic Systems 9th ed. Doornik & Hendry. 1997. pap. text 46.95 (*1-86152-058-1*) Thomson Learn.

Modeling Dynamic Transportation Networks: An Intelligent Transportation System Oriented Approach. Bin Ran & David E. Boyce. LC 96-18806. 356p. 1996. 99.50 (*3-540-61139-8*) Spr-Verlag.

Modeling Dynamics Phenomena in Molecular & Cellular Biology. Lee A. Segel. LC 83-15172. 304p. 1984. pap. text 31.95 (*0-521-27477-X*) Cambridge U Pr.

Modeling Economic Inefficiency Caused by Public Transit Subsidies. Kofi Obeng et al. LC 96-40535. 216p. 1997. 65.00 (*0-275-95851-5*, Praeger Pubs) Greenwood.

Modeling Economic Management & Policy Issues of Water in Irrigated Agriculture. Ariel Dinar. LC 95-44596. 264p. 1996. 59.95 (*0-275-95017-4*, Praeger Pubs) Greenwood.

Modeling Engineering Systems: PC-Based Techniques & Design Tools. Jack W. Lewis. LC 93-40319. (Illus.). 288p. 1994. pap. 29.95 incl. cd-rom (*1-878707-08-6*) LLH Tech Pub.

Modeling Environmental Effects on Crack Growth Processes: Proceedings of a Symposium Sponsored by the Corrosion & Environmental Effects & Mechanical Metallurgy Committee, Held at the Fall Meeting of the Metallurgical Society in Toronto, Canada, October 13-17, 1985. Metallurgical Society of AIME Staff. Ed. by Russell H. Jones & W. W. Gerberich. LC 86-12512. 393p. reprint ed. pap. 121.90 (*0-7837-4075-1*, 205247200011) Bks Demand.

Modeling Environmental Policy. Lisa A. McDonald. Ed. by Wade E. Martin. LC 96-51423. (Natural Resource Management & Policy Ser.). 216p. (C). 1997. lib. bdg. 115.50 (*0-7923-9855-6*) Kluwer Academic.

Modeling Equitable Behavior in the Classroom: Training Module V. Norma Milanovich. (Illus.). 53p. 1995. pap. text 8.50 (*1-878550-14-4*) Inter Dev Res Assn.

Modeling, Estimation & Control of Systems with Uncertainty: Proceedings of a Conference Held in Sopron, Hungary, September 1990. Ed. by G. B. Di Masi et al. (Progress in Systems & Control Theory Ser.: Vol. 10). ix, 467p. 1991. 127.50 (*0-8176-3580-7*) Birkhauser.

Modeling Experimental & Observational Data. Clifford E. Lunneborg. 1994. teacher ed. write for info. incl. disk (*0-534-21427-4*) Brooks-Cole.

Modeling Financial Assets with Alternative Stable Models. Stefan Mittnik & S. Rachev. (Financial Economics Ser.). 874p. 2000. 95.00 (*0-471-95314-8*) Wiley.

Modeling for All Scales. Odum. 448p. (C). 1999. text 79.95 (*0-12-524170-4*) Acad Pr.

Modeling for AutoCAD Designer. Sandra Dobek & Ryan Ranschaert. LC 95-43381. 256p. (C). 1996. text 22.75 (*0-256-21376-3*, Irwn McGrw-H) McGrw-H Hghr Educ.

Modeling for Campaign Analysis: Lessons for the Next Generation of Models, Executive Summary. Richard J. Hillestad et al. LC 96-33349. 33p. 1996. pap. text 7.50 (*0-8330-2438-8*, MR-710-AF) Rand Corp.

Modeling for Design Using AutoCAD. Stewart. LC 96-26726. (General Engineering Ser.). 558p. (C). 1996. mass mkt. 50.95 (*0-534-95220-8*) PWS Pubs.

Modeling for Design Using AutoCAD AME & AutoSurf. Michael D. Stewart et al. LC 94-3190. 558p. (C). 1995. mass mkt. 62.95 (*0-534-93489-7*) PWS Pubs.

Modeling for Design Using Silverscreen. James E. Bolluyt. (Engineering Ser.). 28.95 (*0-534-93336-X*) PWS Pubs.

Modeling for Government & Business. Ed. by C. A. Van Bochove et al. 1977. lib. bdg. 110.50 (*90-207-0732-9*) Kluwer Academic.

Modeling for Learning Organization. Ed. by John D. Morecroft. LC 94-17395. (System Dynamics Ser.). (Illus.). 400p. 1994. 45.00 (*1-56327-060-9*) Productivity Inc.

*__Modeling for Quan Analysisf Winter 99 Jit.__ (C). 1999. 37.17 (*0-536-60287-5*) Pearson Custom.

Modeling for Reliability Analysis: Markov Modeling for Reliability, Maintainability, Safety, & Supportability Analysis of Complex Systems. Paul Pukite & Jan Pukite. LC 97-46570. (Series on Engineering of Complex Computer Systems). 288p. 1998. pap. 89.95 (*0-7803-3482-5*) Inst Electrical.

Modeling for Synthesis. Berge. (Current Issues in Electronic Modeling (CIEM) Ser.). Date not set. lib. bdg. write for info. (*0-7923-9877-7*) Kluwer Academic.

Modeling Functions & Graphs. 2nd ed. Bruce Yoshiwara. (Mathematics Ser.). 1996. mass mkt., student ed. 17.50 (*0-534-95042-6*) PWS Pubs.

*__Modeling Functions & Graphs.__ 3rd ed. Droyan Yoshiwara. (Mathematics Ser.). 2001. 18.00 (*0-534-37321-6*) Brooks-Cole.

Modeling, Functions & Graphs: Algebra for College Students. Katherine Franklin & Irving Drooyan. 626p. (C). 1990. mass mkt. 54.50 (*0-534-13284-7*) PWS Pubs.

Modeling, Functions & Graphs: Algebra for College Students. 2nd ed. Irving Drooyan et al. (Mathematics Ser.). 1995. mass mkt. 81.95 (*0-534-94560-0*) PWS Pubs.

Modeling, Functions & Graphs: Algebra for College Students. 2nd ed. Bruce Yoshiwara & Katherine Yoshiwara. (Mathematics Ser.). 1996. pap., student ed. 19.95 (*0-534-94575-9*) PWS Pubs.

*__Modeling, Functions, Graphs: Algebra for College Students.__ 3rd ed. Yoshiwara. 2000. pap. 64.95 (*0-534-36832-8*) Brooks-Cole.

Modeling Global Positioning System Effects in the TLC/NLC Model. Patrick D. Allen. LC 94-20919. 1994. pap. 13.00 (*0-8330-1559-1*, MR-393-AF/A) Rand Corp.

Modeling Growth & Individual Differences in Spatial Tasks. Hoben Thomas & Arnold Lohaus. (Monographs of the Society for Research on Child Development). 200p. 1993. pap. text 15.00 (*0-226-79602-7*) U Ch Pr.

Modeling Growth & Yield of Multipurpose Tree Species. Ed. by Norma Adams & Foster Cady. 57p. 1988. pap. 10.00 (*0-933595-17-4*) Winrock Intl.

Modeling Handbook: The Complete Guide to Breaking into Local, Regional & International Modeling. 3rd ed. Eve Matheson. 240p. 1995. pap. 12.00 (*0-8050-3830-2*, Owl) H Holt & Co.

An Asterisk (*) at the beginning of an entry indicates that the title is appearing for the first time.

Modeling Handbook: The Complete Guide to Breaking into Local, Regional & International Modeling. 4th ed. Eve Matheson. 192p. 2000. pap. 15.95 (*0-87314-300-0*, Pub. by Peter Glenn) SCB Distributors.

Modeling Healthy Behavior: Actions & Attitudes in Schools. Judy C. Berryman & Kathryn W. Breighner. LC 93-4787. 1993. 24.95 (*1-56071-357-7*) ETR Assocs.

Modeling Highlights: Modeling Locally, Statewide & Nationally - Experience What Modeling Can Do for You. Pamela Blanchard. (Illus.). 100p. (Orig.). 1993. pap. 14.95 (*0-9638373-0-3*) Ritz Pubng.

Modeling HIV Transmission & AIDS in the United States. Herbert W. Hethcote & James W. Van Ark. LC 92-27862. (Lecture Notes in Biomathematics Ser.: Vol. 95). xi, 234p. 1992. 58.95 (*0-387-55904-3*) Spr-Verlag.

Modeling How One Parent Started Her Children. Susan M. Halter. LC 97-94557. (Illus.). viii, 140p. 1998. pap. 29.95 (*0-9659634-8-9*, Modeling 1) Believe In Yourself.

Modeling Human Error in Structural Design & Construction. Ed. by Andrzej S. Nowak. (Workshop Proceedings Ser.). 200p. 1986. 28.00 (*0-87262-558-3*) Am Soc Civil Eng.

Modeling Human Organizational Behavior: Application to Military Simulations. National Research Council Staff. Ed. by Richard W. Pew & Anne S. Mavor. LC 98-19705. 424p. 1998. pap. text 47.00 (*0-309-06096-6*) Natl Acad Pr.

Modeling Hydrologic Processes. Ed. by Hubert J. Morel-Seytoux et al. LC 78-68497. 1979. 35.00 (*0-918334-27-6*) WRP.

Modeling, Identification & Simulation of Dynamical Systems. P. P. Van den Bosch & A. C. Van der Klauw. LC 94-19228. 208p. 1994. boxed set 89.95 (*0-8493-9181-4*) CRC Pr.

***Modeling, Identification, Signal Processing, Adaptive Control Vol. H, Pt. 2.** Ed. by H. F. Chen et al. 510p. 1999. pap. 126.00 (*0-08-043220-4*) Elsevier.

***Modeling, Identification, Signal Processing I, Vol. H.** Ed. by H. F. Chen & B. Wahlberg. 480p. 1999. pap. 126.00 (*0-08-043219-0*) Elsevier.

Modeling in Analog Design. Ed. by Jean-Michel Berge. (Current Issue in Electronic Modeling CIEM Ser.). 176p. (C). 1995. text 120.50 (*0-7923-9569-7*) Kluwer Academic.

***Modeling in Applied Sciences: A Kinetic Theory Approach.** Ed. by Nicola Bellomo & M. Pulvirenti. LC 99-57789. (Modeling & Simulation in Science, Engineering & Technology Ser.). (Illus.). 464p. 1999. 79.95 (*0-8176-4102-5*, Pub. by Birkhauser) Spr-Verlag.

***Modeling in Clay.** Patricia Liversain. (Illus.). 80p. 2000. pap. 19.95 (*0-233-99549-8*, Pub. by Andre Deutsch) Trafalgar.

Modeling in Clay. Dorothy Arthur. (Illus.). 128p. 1993. reprint ed. pap. 29.95 (*1-889250-03-1*) Gentle Br.

Modeling in Combustion Science: Proceedings of the U. S.-Japan Seminar Held in Kapaa, Kuai, Hawaii, 24-29 July 1994. Ed. by John D. Buckmaster & Tadao Takeno. LC 95-15163. (Lecture Notes in Physics Ser.: Vol. 449). 369p. 1995. 92.95 (*3-540-59224-5*) Spr-Verlag.

Modeling in Computer Graphics: Methods & Applications: 2nd Working Conference on Modeling in Computer Graphics, Genova, Italy, June 28 - July 2, 1993. Ed. by Bianca Falcidieno & Toshiyasu L. Kunii. LC 93-16065. (IFIP Series on Computer Graphics). (Illus.). xi, 477p. 1993. 158.95 (*0-387-56529-9*) Spr-Verlag.

Modeling in Computer Graphics: Proceedings of the IFIP WG 5.10 Working Conference Tokyo, Japan, April 8-12, 1991. Ed. by Toshiyasu L. Kunii et al. (IFIP Series on Computer Graphics). (Illus.). 400p. 1991. 107.95 (*0-387-70076-5*) Spr-Verlag.

Modeling in Diesel & SI Engines. 224p. 1995. 61.00 (*1-56091-707-5*, SP-1123) Soc Auto Engineers.

Modeling in South Florida. limited ed. Cynthia W. Wright. (Illus.). 100p. 1986. pap. 9.95 (*0-937961-00-0*) Williams-Wright Pub.

***Modeling in the Neurosciences: From Ionic Channels to Neural Networks.** Roman R. Poznanski. 555p. 1999. text 95.00 (*90-5702-284-2*, Harwood Acad Pubs) Gordon & Breach.

Modeling in Urban & Regional Economics. Alex Anas. Ed. by Jacques Lesourne & Hugo Sonnenschein. (Fundamentals of Pure & Applied Economics Ser.: Vol. 26). viii, 134p. 1987. pap. text 62.00 (*3-7186-0467-1*) Gordon & Breach.

Modeling in Wax for Jewelry & Sculpture. Lawrence Kallenberg. LC 80-70384. (Illus.). 252p. 1981. text 32.95 (*0-8019-6896-8*) Krause Pubns.

***Modeling in Wax for Jewelry & Sculpture.** 2nd rev. ed. Lawrence Kallenberg. LC 80-70384. (Illus.). 256p. 2000. pap. 34.95 (*0-87341-851-4*) Krause Pubns.

Modeling in Welding, Hot Powder Forming, & Casting. Ed. by Lennart Karlsson. LC 97-75011. 200p. 1997. 139.00 (*0-87170-616-4*, 06639GZ) ASM.

Modeling Integers, Unit VI. Albert B. Bennett et al. (Math & the Mind's Eye Ser.). (Illus.). 31p. (C). 1989. teacher ed., ring bd. 10.00 (*1-886131-18-X*, ME6) Math Lrning.

Modeling International Conflict. Ed. by F. C. Zagare. iv, 168p. 1990. pap. text 48.00 (*2-88124-396-7*) Gordon & Breach.

Modeling Japanese-American Trade: A Study of Asymmetric Interdependence. Peter A. Petri. (Economic Studies: No. 156). (Illus.). 232p. 1984. 20.00 (*0-674-57810-4*) HUP.

Modeling Laminar Flame Propagation in Premixed Gases. Charles Westbrook & James A. Miller. (Combustion Science & Technology Ser.). 365p. 1983. pap. text 332.00 (*0-677-06545-0*) Gordon & Breach.

Modeling Large Resource Development Projects in an Open Economy: The Case of Australia's North West Shelf Gas Project. Kenneth W. Clements & Robert A. Greig. (Studies in Urban & Resource Economics). (Illus.). xviii, 151p. 1994. 36.00 (*0-943893-10-0*) Blackstone.

Modeling Longitudinal & Multiple-Group Data: Practical Issues, Applied Approaches & Specific Examples. Ed. by Todd D. Little et al. LC 99-52417. 300p. 1999. 65.00 (*0-8058-3054-5*) L Erlbaum Assocs.

Modeling Magnetospheric Plasma. Ed. by T. E. Moore & J. H. Waite. (Geophysical Monograph Ser.: Vol. 44). 344p. 1989. 38.00 (*0-87590-070-4*) Am Geophysical.

Modeling Magnetospheric Plasma Processes. Ed. by G. R. Wilson. (Geophysical Monograph Ser.: Vol. 62). 182p. 1991. 42.00 (*0-87590-028-3*, GM062761X) Am Geophysical.

Modeling Manufacturing Systems: From Aggregate Planning to Real-Time Control. Ed. by P. Brandimarte & A. Villa. LC 99-21014. (Illus.). x, 215p. 1999. 74.95 (*3-540-65500-X*) Spr-Verlag.

Modeling Marine Systems, Vol. I. Ed. by Alan M. Davies. 312p. 1989. boxed set 195.00 (*0-8493-4221-X*, GC10) CRC Pr.

Modeling Marine Systems, Vol. 2. Davies. 456p. 1990. boxed set 249.00 (*0-8493-4222-8*, GC10) CRC Pr.

Modeling, Mesh Generation & Adaptive Numerical Methods for Partial Differential Equations. Ed. by Ivo Babuska et al. LC 95-17342. (IMA Volumes in Mathematics & Its Applications Ser.: Vol. 75). (Illus.). 502p. 1995. 79.95 (*0-387-94542-3*) Spr-Verlag.

Modeling Methods for Environmental Engineers. Isam M. Abdel-Magid et al. LC 96-4980. 496p. 1996. disk 85.00 (*1-56670-172-4*, L1172) Lewis Pubs.

Modeling Microprocessor Performance. Bibiche Geuskens & K. Rose. LC 98-21864. 195p. 1998. write for info. (*0-7923-8214-5*) Kluwer Academic.

Modeling Microwave Backscatter from Discontinuous Tree Canopies. Kyle C. McDonald & Fawaaz T. Ulaby. LC G 0070.. (Technical Reports: No. 026511-2-T). 377p. reprint ed. pap. 116.90 (*0-7837-1390-8*, 204157100021) Bks Demand.

Modeling Military Miniatures with Kim Jones Tools, Tips & Techniques: Tips, Tools, & Techniques. Photos & Text by Jeffrey B. Snyder. LC 95-2446. (Illus.). 80p. (Orig.). 1995. pap. 14.95 (*0-88740-883-4*) Schiffer.

***Modeling Mineral & Energy Markets.** Walter C. Labys. LC 98-46233. 6p. 1999. write for info. (*0-7923-8372-9*) Kluwer Academic.

Modeling Monetary Economies. Bruce Champ & Scott Freeman. LC 93-9879. 272p. 1993. text 81.95 (*0-471-57948-3*) Wiley.

Modeling Multigroup Populations. R. Schoen. LC 87-25714. (Demographic Methods & Population Analysis Ser.). (Illus.). 320p. (C). 1987. 49.50 (*0-306-42649-8*, Plenum Trade) Perseus Pubng.

Modeling Nature: Episodes in the History of Population Ecology. Sharon E. Kingsland. LC 85-1414. (Science & Its Conceptual Foundations Ser.). (Illus.). x, 268p. 1995. 29.95 (*0-226-43726-4*) U Ch Pr.

Modeling Nature: Episodes in the History of Population Ecology. 2nd ed. Sharon E. Kingsland. 316p. 1995. pap. text 16.95 (*0-226-43728-0*) U Ch Pr.

Modeling Nature with Cellular Automata Using Mathematica. Richard J. Gaylord & Kazume Nishidate. LC 96-5727. 260p. 1996. pap. 39.95 (*0-387-94620-9*) Spr-Verlag.

Modeling NMR Chemical Shifts: Gaining Insights into Structure & Environment. Ed. by Julio C. Facelli & Angel C. De Dios. LC 99-24229. (ACS Sympmosium Ser.: No. 732). 368p. 1999. text 130.00 (*0-8412-3622-4*, Pub. by Am Chemical) OUP.

Modeling North American Economic Integration. Ed. by Patrick J. Kehoe & Timothy J. Kehoe. (Advanced Studies in Theoretical & Applied Econometrics: Vol. 31). 1995. lib. bdg. 118.00 (*0-7923-3751-4*) Kluwer Academic.

Modeling Nutrient & Moisture Cycling in Tropical Forests. I. G. Noij et al. (Tropenbos Technical Ser.: No. 4). (Illus.). 195p. 1993. pap. 40.00 (*90-5113-016-3*, Pub. by Backhuys Pubs) Balogh.

Modeling of Adsorption & Diffusion of Vapors in Zeolites. Jan-Baptist W. Loos. (Illus.). 211p. 1997. pap. 52.50 (*90-407-1533-5*, Pub. by Delft U Pr) Coronet Bks.

Modeling of Batteries & Fuel Cells: Proceedings of the Symposium on Modeling of Batteries & Fuel Cells, Phoenix, AZ, 1991. Ed. by R. E. White et al. LC 91-75763. (Electrochemical Society Proceedings Ser.: No. 91-10). 141p. 1991. reprint ed. pap. 127.50 (*0-7837-6486-3*, 205251600012) Bks Demand.

Modeling of Cancer Genesis & Prevention. N. Voiculetz et al. (Illus.). 288p. 1991. lib. bdg. 177.00 (*0-8493-6379-9*, RC268) CRC Pr.

Modeling of Casting & Welding Processes: Proceedings of a Symposium. Metallurgical Society of AIME Staff. Ed. by Harold D. Brody & Diran Apelian. LC 81-83753. (Conference Proceedings Ser.). (Illus.). 567p. reprint ed. pap. 175.80 (*0-608-17717-2*, 203012400067) Bks Demand.

Modeling of Casting, Welding & Advanced Solidification Processes No. 5: Proceedings of the 5th International Conference on Modeling of Casting & Welding Processes, Held in Davos, Switzerland, September 16-21, 1990. International Conference on Modeling of Casting &. Ed. by Michel Pappaz et al. LC 91-60687. (Illus.). 856p. 1991. pap. 200.00 (*0-608-04977-8*, 206559400004) Bks Demand.

Modeling of Casting, Welding & Advanced Solidification Processes No. 6: Proceedings of the 6th Conference in a Series on Modeling, Casting, & Welding Processes, Held in Palm Coast, FL, March 21-26, 1993. International Conference on Modeling of Casting &. Ed. by T. S. Piwonka et al. LC 93-77480. (Illus.). 777p. 1993. reprint ed. pap. 200.00 (*0-7837-9140-2*, 204994000004) Bks Demand.

Modeling of Casting, Welding & Advanced Solidification Processes VII. Ed. by M. Cross & J. Campbell. (Illus.). 1036p. 1995. 20.00 (*0-87339-297-3*, 2973) Minerals Metals.

Modeling of Chemical Vapor Deposition of Tungsten Films. Chris R. Kleijn & Christoph Werner. LC 92-44681. (Progress in Numerical Simulation for Microelectronics Ser.: Vol. 2). xii, 126p. 1993. 81.50 (*0-8176-2858-4*) Birkhauser.

Modeling of Composites, Processing & Properties: A Collection of Papers from the 1996 TMS Annual Meeting & Exhibition in Anaheim, California, February 4-8, 1996. Ed. by S. P. Chen & Mary P. Anderson. (Illus.). 77p. 1996. pap. 54.00 (*0-87339-321-X*, 321X) Minerals Metals.

Modeling of Conformal Antennas on Doubly Curved Platforms & Their Interactions with Aircraft Platforms: Annual Progress Report. T. Ozdemir et al. LC TL0694.A6. (University of Michigan Reports: No. 031307-5-T). 96p. 1995. reprint ed. pap. 30.00 (*0-608-02396-5*, 206303700004) Bks Demand.

Modeling of Curves & Surfaces in CAD - CAM. M. Hosaka. Ed. by Jose L. Encarnacao et al. (Computer Graphics - Systems & Applications Ser.). (Illus.). xxi, 358p. 1992. 93.95 (*0-387-53974-3*) Spr-Verlag.

Modeling of Defects & Fracture Mechanics. Ed. by G. Herrmann. (CISM International Centre for Mechanical Sciences Ser.: No. 331). vii, 206p. 1994. 54.95 (*0-387-82487-1*) Spr-Verlag.

Modeling of Design Ideas. Rodriquez. 1992. student ed. 18.75 (*0-07-053393-8*) McGraw.

Modeling of Design Ideas: Graphics & Visualization Techniques for Engineers. Walter E. Rodriguez. 1992. text. write for info. (*0-07-079744-7*) McGraw.

Modeling of Design Ideas: Graphics & Visualization Techniques for Engineers. Walter E. Rodriguez. (C). 1992. text 40.00 (*0-07-053394-6*) McGraw.

Modeling of Dynamic Systems. Lennart Ljung & Torkel Glad. 368p. 1994. 63.80 (*0-13-597097-0*) P-H.

Modeling of Electrical Overstress in Integrated Circuits. Carlos H. Diaz et al. LC 94-31195. (International Series in Engineering & Computer Science, Natural Language Processing & Machine Translation). 176p. (C). 1994. text 113.00 (*0-7923-9505-0*) Kluwer Academic.

Modeling of Environment Flow Systems. Ed. by R. A. Bajura & T. B. Morrow. 88p. 1983. pap. text 20.00 (*0-317-02634-8*, H00281) ASME.

Modeling of Flood Propagation over Initially Dry Areas: Proceedings of the Specialty Conference Held in Milan, Italy at ENEL-DSR-CRIS, 29 June - 1 July 1994. American Society of Civil Engineers Staff. Ed. by Paolo Molinaro & Luigi Natale. LC 94-19397. 384p. 1994. 31.00 (*0-7844-0035-0*) Am Soc Civil Eng.

Modeling of In Situ Techniques for Treatment of Contaminated Soil: Soil Vapor Extraction, Sparging, & Bioventing. David Wilson. LC 95-60515. 587p. 1995. pap. text 79.95 (*1-56676-234-0*) Technomic.

Modeling of Indoor Air Quality & Exposure. Ed. by Niren L. Nagda. LC 93-31561. (Special Technical Publication Ser.: No. 1205). (Illus.). 310p. 1993. 65.00 (*0-8031-1875-9*, STP1205) ASTM.

Modeling of Inhalation Exposure to Vapors: Uptake, Distribution, & Elimination, 2 vols. Ed. by Vera Fiserova-Bergerova. 1983. write for info. (*0-318-57044-0*, RA1245) Franklin.

Modeling of Inhalation Exposure to Vapors: Uptake, Distribution, & Elimination, 2 vols., Vol. I. Ed. by Vera Fiserova-Bergerova. 184p. 1983. 104.00 (*0-8493-6315-2*) Franklin.

Modeling of Inhalation Exposure to Vapors: Uptake, Distribution, & Elimination, 2 vols., Vol. II. Ed. by Vera Fiserova-Bergerova. 192p. 1983. 108.00 (*0-8493-6316-0*) Franklin.

Modeling of Large-Scale Energy Systems: Proceedings of the IIASA-IFAC Symposium, Laxenburg, Austria, Feb. 25-29, 1980, Vol. 11. Ed. by Wolf Hafele & L. K. Kirchmayer. LC 80-41554. (IIASA Proceedings Ser.: Vol 11). 350p. 1981. 213.00 (*0-08-025696-1*, Pub. by Pergamon Repr) Franklin.

Modeling on Micros & Workstations, 1991. 10th ed. Ed. by Thomas A. Rathburn. 104p. 1991. pap. 48.00 (*0-911801-84-7*, MSM-91) Soc Computer Sim.

Modeling of Monthly Intermittent Streamflow Processes. (Illus.). 153p. (Orig.). (C). 1993. pap. text 35.00 (*1-56806-470-5*) DIANE Pub.

Modeling of Nature: The Philosophy of Science & the Philosophy of Nature in Synthesis. William A. Wallace. LC 96-5378. (Illus.). 337p. (C). 1996. text 59.95 (*0-8132-0859-9*); pap. text 34.95 (*0-8132-0860-2*) Cath U Pr.

Modeling of Plume Rise & Dispersion - The University of Salford Model: U. S. P. R. B. Henderson-Sellers. (Lecture Notes in Engineering Ser.: Vol. 25). viii, 113p. 1987. 23.95 (*0-387-17355-2*) Spr-Verlag.

Modeling of Polymer Processing: Recent Developments. A. I. Isayev. 328p. 1991. 86.50 (*1-56990-043-4*) Hanser-Gardner.

Modeling of Precipitation-Based Drought Characteristics over California. H. W. Shen & G. Q. Tabios, III. 100p. (Orig.). 1996. pap. text. write for info. (*0-614-13324-6*) U Cal CWWR.

Modeling of SI & CI Engines: 1996 International Congress & Exposition. LC 96-207901. (Special Publications). 284p. 1996. pap. 99.00 (*1-56091-798-9*, SP-1168) Soc Auto Engineers.

Modeling of SI & Diesel Engines. 250p. 1998. 85.00 (*0-7680-0150-1*) Soc Auto Engineers.

***Modeling of SI Engines.** (Special Publications). 402p. 2000. 109.00 (*0-7680-0561-2*, SP-1511) Soc Auto Engineers.

Modeling of the Kinetics of Suspension Crystallizers: A New Model for Secondary Nucleation. Ruairi O. Meadhra. (Illus.). 199p. (Orig.). 1995. pap. 59.50 (*90-407-1190-9*, Pub. by Delft U Pr) Coronet Bks.

***Modeling Our World: The ESRI Guide to Geodatabase Design.** Michael Zieler. (Illus.). 200p. 1999. pap. text 29.95 (*1-879102-62-5*) ESR Inst.

Modeling Percentages & Ratios, Unit VII. Albert B. Bennett et al. (Math & the Mind's Eye Ser.). (Illus.). 52p. (C). 1991. teacher ed., ring bd. 10.00 (*1-886131-19-8*, ME7) Math Lrning.

Modeling Plant & Soil Systems. J. T. Ritchie & R. J. Hanks. (Agronomy Monograph Ser.: Vol. 31). 565p. 1991. 30.00 (*0-89118-106-7*) Am Soc Agron.

Modeling Policy Outcomes: Decision Making at Local Transit Agencies. D. Ellerman. (Topics in Transportation Ser.). 256p. 1989. 115.00 (*90-6764-123-5*, Pub. by VSP) Coronet Bks.

Modeling Problems in Crack Tip Mechanics. Ed. by Jerzy T. Pinders. 1984. text 173.50 (*90-247-3067-8*) Kluwer Academic.

Modeling Projects For Math Before Calc. Laughbaum. (Math). 1996. mass mkt. 28.95 (*0-534-94636-4*) PWS Pubs.

M

Modeling Rationality, Morality & Evolution. Peter Danielson. (Vancouver Studies in Cognitive Science: Vol. 7). 480p. 1998. pap. text 29.95 (*0-19-512550-9*) OUP.

Modeling Rationality, Morality & Evolution. Peter A. Danielson. (Vancouver Studies in Cognitive Science: Vol. 7). 480p. 1999. text 70.00 (*0-19-512549-5*) OUP.

Modeling Rationals, Unit IV. Albert B. Bennett et al. (Math & the Mind's Eye Ser.). (Illus.). 92p. (C). 1988. teacher ed., ring bd. 10.00 (*1-886131-16-3*, ME4) Math Lrning.

Modeling Reactive Systems with Statecharts: The Stalmate Approach. David Harel & Michal Politi. LC 98-17831. 258p. 1998. 65.00 (*0-07-026205-5*) McGraw.

Modeling Real & Complex Numbers, Unit XII. Eugene Maier & L. Ted Nelson. (Math & the Mind's Eye Ser.). (Illus.). 91p. 1996. ring bd. 10.00 (*1-886131-41-4*, ME12) Math Lrning.

***Modeling Reality with Functions: Graphical, Numerical, Analytical.** Gene Fiorini & Jacob Miller. 238p. (C). 1999. spiral bd. 31.95 (*0-7872-6428-8*, 41642801) Kendall-Hunt.

Modeling Sensorineural Hearing Loss. Ed. by Walter Jesteadt. LC 96-49676. 432p. 1997. 99.95 (*0-8058-2230-5*) L Erlbaum Assocs.

Modeling, Simulation, & Control of Flexible Manufacturing Systems: A Petri Net Approach. 400p. 1998. 47.00 (*981-02-3029-X*) World Scientific Pub.

Modeling, Simulation, & Visualization of Sensory Response for Defense Applications. Ed. by Nickolas L. Faust & John D. Illgen. LC 98-118519. 24p. 1997. pap. 59.00 (*0-8194-2500-1*) SPIE.

Modeling, Simulation, Testing & Measurements for Solar Energy Systems: Presented at the Winter Annual Meeting of ASME, San Francisco, CA., December 10-15, 1978. American Society of Mechanical Engineers Staff. Ed. by J. M. Nash & J. T. Smok. LC 78-67977. 107p. reprint ed. pap. 33.20 (*0-608-12625-X*, 202418300035) Bks Demand.

Modeling Spatiotemporal Dynamics in Ecology. Jordi Bascompte & Ricard V. Sole. LC 97-26698. (Environmental Intelligence Unit (SV) Ser.). 216p. 1998. 112.00 (*1-57059-505-4*) Landes Bioscience.

Modeling Spatiotemporal Dynamics in Ecology. Ed. by Jordi Bascompte & Ricard V. Sole. LC 97-26698. (Environmental Intelligence Unit (SV) Ser.). (Illus.). 216p. 1998. 112.00 (*3-540-63449-5*) Spr-Verlag.

***Modeling Structural Change in the United States Textile Industry** Shu-Chin Yang & Barry K. Goodwin. LC 99-31726. (Studies on Industrial Productivity). 1999. write for info. (*0-8153-3396-X*) Garland.

***Modeling Survival Data: Extending the Cox Model.** T. Therneau & P. Grambsch. (Statistics for Biology & Health Ser.). 376p. 2000. 69.95 (*0-387-98784-3*) Spr-Verlag.

Modeling Synthesis & Rapid Prototyping with the VERILOG HDL. CILETTI. LC 99-10494. 727p. 1999. text 105.00 (*0-13-977398-3*) S&S Trade.

Modeling Techniques & Tools for Computer Performance Evaluation. Ed. by R. Puigjaner & D. Potier. (Illus.). 466p. 1989. 110.00 (*0-306-43368-0*, Plenum Trade) Perseus Pubng.

Modeling Techniques for Successful Data Warehousing & Data Marts. Earl Hadden. (Illus.). 22p. 1997. pap. 195.00 (*1-892815-23-0*) Patricia Seybold.

Modeling Techniques for Uncertain Systems: Proceedings of a Conference Held in Soporon, Hungary, July 1992. Ed. by Alexander B. Kurzhanski & Vladimir M. Veliov. LC 93-49802. (Progress in Systems & Control Theory Ser.: Vol. 18). (Illus.). 304p. 1994. 98.00 (*0-8176-3746-X*) Birkhauser.

Modeling Techniques in Materials Science & Engineering. L. Subramanian & M. Katagiri. (Illus.). Date not set. text. write for info. (*0-8247-0084-8*) Dekker.

Modeling Techniques in SI & CI Engines. 1996. 59.00 (*1-56091-821-7*, SP-1178) Soc Auto Engineers.

Modeling the AIDS Epidemic: Planning, Policy, & Prediction. Margaret L. Brandeau. Ed. by Edward H. Kaplan. LC 93-23684. 656p. 1994. text 99.00 (*0-7817-0164-3*) Lppncott W & W.

Modeling the AIDS Epidemic: Planning, Policy & Prediction. Ed. by Edward H. Kaplan & Margaret L. Brandeau. LC 93-23684. (Illus.). 656p. reprint ed. pap. 200.00 (*0-608-09758-6*, 206993100007) Bks Demand.

Modeling the Deformation of Crystalline Solids: Proceedings of a Symposium Jointly Sponsored by the ASM-MSD Computer Simulation Committee & the TMS-AIME Shaping & Forming Committee, Held at the Annual Meeting of the Minerals, Metals & Materials Society in New Orleans, Louisiana, February 17-21, 1991. Minerals, Metals & Materials Society Staff. Ed. by Terry C. Lowe et al. LC 91-62769. (Illus.). 700p. 1991. reprint ed. pap. 200.00 (*0-7837-9139-9*, 204993900004) Bks Demand.

Modeling the Demand for Cocaine. S. M. Everingham & C. Peter Rydell. 79p. 1994. pap. 15.00 (*0-8330-1553-2*, MR-332) Rand Corp.

Modeling the Distribution & Intergenerational Transmission of Wealth. Ed. by James D. Smith. LC 80-15537. (National Bureau of Economic Research Ser.). 344p. 1980. lib. bdg. 46.00 (*0-226-76454-0*) U Ch Pr.

Modeling the Dynamics of Living Systems: Nonlinear Phenomena & Pattern Formation. Erik Mosekilde & Ole G. Mouritsen. (Series in Synergetics: Vol. 65). 1994. write for info. (*0-387-58480-3*); 75.95 (*3-540-58480-3*) Spr-Verlag.

Modeling the Earth for Oil Exploration. Helbig. 812p. 1994. 181.50 (*0-08-042419-8*, Pergamon Pr) Elsevier.

Modeling the Economic Performance of Yugoslavia. James H. Gapinski et al. LC 89-16130. 311p. 1989. 69.50 (*0-275-93385-7*, C3385, Praeger Pubs) Greenwood.

M

Modeling the Enterprise: From Business Processes, to Business Oblects, to Systemarchitecture, to Code. Ed. by Prentice-Hall Staff. (C). 1999. pap. text 55.00 (*0-13-013783-9*) P-H.

Modeling the Environment: An Introduction to System Dynamics Modeling. Andrew Ford. LC 99-18909. 416p. (C). 1999. pap. 40.00 (*1-55963-601-7*); text 70.00 (*1-55963-600-9*) Island Pr.

Modeling the Environment with Arcview GIS. Benjamin R. Hayes. LC 99-19954. (C). 2001. text. write for info. (*1-56690-162-6*) Thomson Learn.

Modeling the Environmental Fate of Microorganisms. Ed. by Christon J. Hurst. (Illus.). 302p. 1991. text 59.00 (*1-55581-031-4*) ASM Pr.

Modeling the External Risks of Airports for Policy Analysis. Stephen D. Brady & Richard J. Hillestad. LC 95-34933. (MR-605-EAC/VW Ser.). 76p. (Orig.). 1995. pap. text 13.00 (*0-8330-2299-7*, MR-605-EAC) Rand Corp.

Modeling the Figure in Clay. Bruno Lucchesi. (Illus.). 144p. 1996. pap. text 19.95 (*0-8230-3096-2*) Watsn-Guptill.

Modeling the Fiji Economy. Mark Sturton. (Research Reports: No. 12). 153p. (Orig.). 1990. pap. text 8.00 (*0-86638-113-9*) EW Ctr HI.

Modeling the Head in Clay. Bruno Lucchesi. (Illus.). 160p. 1996. pap. text 19.95 (*0-8230-3099-7*) Watsn-Guptill.

Modeling the Hydrogen Bond. Ed. by Douglas A. Smith. LC 94-31645. (Symposium Ser.: No. 569). (Illus.). 304p. 1994. text 82.00 (*0-8412-2981-3*, Pub. by Am Chemical) OUP.

Modeling the Interactions of Trace Metals & Aquatic Humic Materials. Massachusetts Institute of Technology Staff. 150p. 1984. write for info. (*0-318-60404-3*) Intl Copper.

Modeling the Market: New Theories & Techniques. Sergio Focardi & Caroline Jonas. (Illus.). 289p. (C). 1997. 55.00 (*1-883249-12-0*) F J Fabozzi.

Modeling the Mechanical Response of Structural Materials: Proceedings, Annual Meeting of the Minerals, Metals & Materials Society, San Antonio, Texas, 1998. Ed. by Eric M. Taleff & Rao K. Mahidhara. LC 97-75880. (Illus.). 280p. 1998. 88.00 (*0-87339-392-9*, TA418) Minerals Metals.

Modeling the Metabolic & Physiologic Activities of Microorganisms. Ed. by Christon J. Hurst. LC 92-3482. 296p. 1992. 110.00 (*0-471-54271-7*) Wiley.

Modeling the Offshore Environment. Ed. by Society for Underwater Technology Staff. (C). 1987. lib. bdg. 228.00 (*0-86010-862-7*, Pub. by Graham & Trotman) Kluwer Academic.

Modeling the Stripping & Volatilization of Voc in Wastewater Collection & Treatment Systems, Project 91-TFT-1, 1998. John P. Bell. LC 98-89662. 1998. write for info. (*0-9662553-6-4*) Wtr Environ Res.

Modeling the World in a Spreadsheet: Environmental Simulation on a Microcomputer. Timothy J. Cartwright. 364p. (C). 1993. text 55.00 (*0-8018-4596-3*); pap. text 34.95 (*0-8018-4597-1*) Johns Hopkins.

Modeling Trade Policy: Applied General Equilibrium Assessments of NAFTA. Ed. by Joseph F. Francois & Clinton R. Shiells. LC 93-43808. (Illus.). 368p. (C). 1994. text 64.95 (*0-521-45003-9*) Cambridge U Pr.

Modeling Vapor-Liquid Equilibria: Cubic Equations of State & Their Mixing Rules. Hasan Orbey & Stanley I. Sandler. LC 97-43340. (Series in Chemical Engineering). (Illus.). 250p. (C). 1998. text 80.00 (*0-521-62027-9*) Cambridge U Pr.

Modeling Water Quality in Drinking Water Distribution Systems. Robert M. Clark & W. M. Grayman. LC 98-36443. 231p. 1998. write for info. (*0-89867-972-9*) Am Water Wks Assn.

Modeling Weapons & Accessories for Military Miniatures. Kim Jones & Jeffrey B. Snyder. LC 96-22301. 1996. pap. 16.95 (*0-7643-0128-4*) Schiffer.

Modeling Whole Numbers, Unit III. Albert B. Bennett et al. (Math & the Mind's Eye Ser.). (Illus.). 56p. (C). 1988. teacher ed., ring bd. 10.00 (*1-886131-15-5*, ME3) Math Lrning.

Modeling with an Analog Hardware Description Language. H. Alan Mantooth. (International Series in Engineering & Computer Science, Natural Language Processing & Machine Translation). 296p. (C). 1994. text 139.00 (*0-7923-9516-6*) Kluwer Academic.

Modeling with AutoCAD: Release 13 for Windows. Robert McFarlane. LC 97-167017. 248p. 1997. pap. 49.95 (*0-470-23737-6*) Wiley.

Modeling with Function, 6 vols., Vol. 5. Dossey. 1996. pap. text 20.00 (*0-435-07111-4*) Heinemann.

Modeling with NLP. Robert Dilts. LC 98-66554. 324p. 1998. 27.95 (*0-916990-41-9*) META Pubns.

Modell Assisi. Gerda Riedl. 344p. 1997. text 99.00 (*3-11-015814-0*) De Gruyter.

Modell und Vorlage der Synoptiker. Peter L. Hofrichter. (Theologische Texte und Studient Ser.: Bd. 6). (GER.). 205p. 1997. 40.00 (*3-487-10371-0*) G Olms Pubs.

***Modellbildung Im Forschungsbereich Sprachliche Sozialisation: Zur Systematik des Erwerbs Narrativer, Begrifflicher und Literaler Fahigkeiten.** Dagmar Wolf. (Theorie und Vermittlung der Sprache. Bd. 32 Ser.). 443p. 2000. 52.95 (*3-631-35459-2*) P Lang Pubng.

***Modelldiagnose in der Bayesschen Inferenz.** Reinhard Vonthein. (Illus.). 149p. 1999. 31.95 (*3-631-34610-7*) P Lang Pubng.

Modelle der Materialistische Dialektik: Beitrage der Bochumer Dialektik-Arbeitsgemeinschaft. Ed. by H. Kimmerle. 340p. 1978. text 155.50 (*90-247-2105-9*) Kluwer Academic.

Modelle Interdisziplinaeren Handelns: 25 Jahre Department Chirurgie Basel. Ed. by U. Laffer et al. (Basler Beitraege zur Chirurgie Ser.: Vol. 5). (Illus.). viii, 162p. 1992. pap. 85.25 (*3-8055-5708-6*) S Karger.

Modellierung. 1995. 54.00 (*0-387-00776-8*) Spr-Verlag.

Modelling. 1994. 8.95 (*1-85391-355-3*) Merehurst Ltd.

Modelling. Joan Jones. LC 95-60780. (Fun to Do Ser.). (Illus.). 32p. (J). (gr. 3 up). 1995. lib. bdg. 15.95 (*1-887238-03-4*) Fitzgerald.

Modelling Analysis & Control of Thin Plates. J. L. Lions & John E. Lagnese. (Recherches en Mathematiques Appliquees Ser.: Vol. 6). 185p. 1990. 45.95 (*0-387-51550-X*) Spr-Verlag.

Modelling & Adaptive Control. Christopher I. Byrnes. Ed. by Alexander B. Kurzhanski. (Lecture Notes in Control & Information Sciences: Vol. 105). 390p. 1988. 68.95 (*0-387-19019-8*) Spr-Verlag.

Modelling & Analysis of Large Systems. Ed. by Arabinda Tripathy. (C). 1991. text 28.00 (*81-204-0593-5*, Pub. by Oxford IBH) S Asia.

Modelling & Analysis of Reinforced Concrete Structures for Dynamic Loading. Ed. by C. Meyer. (CISM International Centre for Mechnical Sciences Ser.: Suppl. 346). (Illus.). ix, 250p. 1998. pap. 67.00 (*3-211-82919-9*) Spr-Verlag.

Modelling & Application of Stochastic Processes. Uday B. Desai. 1986. text 127.00 (*0-89838-177-0*) Kluwer Academic.

Modelling & Applications of Transport Phenomena in Porous Media. Ed. by Jacob Bear & J. M. Buchlin. 396p. (C). 1991. text 215.00 (*0-7923-1443-3*) Kluwer Academic.

Modelling & Assessing Second Language Acquisition. Ed. by Kenneth Hyltenstam & Manfred Pienemann. 400p. 1985. 99.00 (*0-905028-42-2*, MM18, Pub. by Multilingual Matters); pap. 49.00 (*0-905028-41-4*, Pub. by Multilingual Matters) Taylor & Francis.

Modelling & Computation for Applications in Mathematics, Science, & Engineering. Ed. by Joseph W. Jerome. LC 98-224248. (Numerical Mathematics & Scientific Computation Ser.). (Illus.). 232p. 1998. text 95.00 (*0-19-850080-7*) OUP.

Modelling & Computer Methods in Molecular Biology & Genetics. Ed. by N. A. Kolchanov & Vadim A. Ratner. 475p. (C). 1993. lib. bdg. 175.00 (*1-56072-077-8*) Nova Sci Pubs.

Modelling & Control. Xuyan. (IFAC Postprint Ser.). 218p. 1994. pap. 79.25 (*0-08-042588-7*, Pergamon Pr) Elsevier.

***Modelling & Control Dynamic.** Barker. (C). 1999. pap. text. write for info. (*0-582-08377-X*, Pub. by Addison-Wesley) Longman.

Modelling & Control in Biomedical Systems. Ed. by E. Carson & Derek A. Linkens. LC 97-42725. (IFAC Postprint Ser.). 1997. pap. text. write for info. (*0-08-042601-8*, Pergamon Pr) Elsevier.

Modelling & Control in Biomedical Systems: Proceedings of the IFAC Symposium, Venice, Italy, April 6-8, 1988. Ed. by C. Cobelli & L. Mariani. (IFAC Proceedings Ser.). (Illus.). 683p. 1988. pap. 30.00 (*0-08-036609-0*, Pergamon Pr) Elsevier.

Modelling & Control in Biomedical Systems: Proceedings of the IFAC Symposium, Venice, Italy, April 6-8, 1988. Ed. by C. Cobelli & L. Mariani. (IFAC Proceedings Ser.: 8901). (Illus.). 686p. 1989. 301.00 (*0-08-035732-6*, Pergamon Pr) Elsevier.

Modelling & Control in Solid Mechanics. Alexander M. Khludnev & J. Sokolowski. (International Series of Numerical Mathematics; Vol. 122). 384p. 1997. 120.00 (*3-7643-5238-8*) Spr-Verlag.

Modelling & Control in Solid Mechanics. Alexander M. Khludnev et al. LC 96-52344. (International Series of Numerical Mathematics). 1997. 120.00 (*0-8176-5238-8*) Birkhauser.

Modelling & Control of Activated Sludge Processes: Selected Proceedings of the IAWQ International Specialized Seminar Held in Copenhagen, Denmark, August 22-24, 1994. Ed. by M. Henze & W. Gujer. (Water Science & Technology Ser.). (Illus.). 274p. 1995. pap. 115.00 (*0-08-042648-4*, Pergamon Pr) Elsevier.

Modelling & Control of Biotechnical Processes: Proceedings of the Symposium, 1st, Helsinki, Finland, Aug., 1982. IFAC Symposium Staff & A. Halme. (IFAC Proceedings Ser.). 296p. 1983. 83.00 (*0-08-029978-4*, Pergamon Pr) Elsevier.

Modelling & Control of Casting & Welding Processes IV: Proceedings of the 4th International Conference. International Conference on Modeling of Casting &. Ed. by Anthony Giamei & G. J. Abbaschian. LC 88-62443. 1002p. reprint ed. pap. 200.00 (*0-7837-1970-1*, 205244800001) Bks Demand.

Modelling & Control of Dynamic Flows in Communication Networks. J. Filipiak. (Communications & Control Engineering Ser.). 240p. 1988. 104.95 (*0-387-18292-6*) Spr-Verlag.

Modelling & Control of Electrical Machines: New Trends. R. Le Doeuff & J. Robert. (Illus.). x,312p. 1991. 140.00 (*0-444-88732-6*) Elsevier.

Modelling & Control of Mechanical Systems: Proceedings of the Workshop Imperial College, London, U. K., 17-20 June 1997. Ed. by A. Astolfi et al. 340p. 1997. text 84.00 (*1-86094-058-7*) World Scientific Pub.

Modelling & Control of Mechanisms & Robots: Bertinoro, Italy, 22-26 July 1996. Claudio Melchiorri & Antonio E. Tornambè. LC 96-21727. 304p. 1996. write for info. (*981-02-2724-8*) World Scientific Pub.

Modelling & Control of National Economies, 1995. L. Vlacic et al. LC 97-197109. (IFAC Postprint Ser.). 506p. 1996. pap. write for info. (*0-08-042376-0*, Pergamon Pr) Elsevier.

***Modelling & Control of Robot Manipulators.** L. Sciavicco & Bruno Siciliano. LC 99-462018. (Advanced Textbooks in Control & Signal Processing Ser.). xxiii, 377p. 2000. pap. 45.00 (*1-85233-221-2*) Spr-Verlag.

Modelling & Decisions in Economics: Essays in Honor of Franz Ferschl. Ed. by U. Leopold-Wildburger et al. LC 99-30479. (Illus.). viii, 298p. 1999. 79.95 (*3-7908-1219-6*) Spr-Verlag.

Modelling & Empirical Evaluation of Labour Supply Behaviour. I. Woittiez. Ed. by Dieter Bos et al. (Studies in Contemporary Economics). (Illus.). viii, 232p. 1991. 47.95 (*0-387-54054-7*) Spr-Verlag.

***Modelling & Estimation of Measurement Errors.** Michele Neuilly. Tr. by Derek J. Pike from FRE. (Illus.). 704p. 1999. 198.00 (*1-898298-59-9*, Pub. by Intercept UK) Spr-Verlag.

Modelling & Global Change Studies on Critical Environment Regions. Lawrence Klein & Lo Fu-Chen. LC 97-102305. 100p. 1995. pap. text 35.00 (*92-808-0880-X*, UNUP-0880) UN Inst Train & Res.

Modelling & Graphics in Science & Technology. Ed. by J. C. Teixeira & J. Rix. (Beitrage zur Graphischen Datenverarbeitung Ser.). 188p. 1996. pap. text 64.95 (*3-540-60244-5*) Spr-Verlag.

Modelling & Identification in Robotics. Krzysztof Kozlowski. LC 97-51769. (Advances in Industrial Control Ser.). (Illus.). xii, 184p. 1998. 64.95 (*3-540-76240-X*) Spr-Verlag.

Modelling & Inverse Problems of Control for Distributed Parameter Systems: Proceedings of IFIP (W.G. - .2) - IIASA Conference, Laxenburg, Austria, July 1989. Ed. by Alexander B. Kurzhanski & Irena Lasiecka. (Lecture Notes in Control & Information Sciences: Vol. 154). (Illus.). 192p. 1991. 49.95 (*0-387-53583-7*) Spr-Verlag.

Modelling & Knowledge Basis IX. Ed. by P. J. Charrell & H. Jaakkola. (Frontiers in Artificial Intelligence & Applications Ser.: Vol. 45). 1998. 98.00 (*90-5199-396-X*, Pub. by IOS Pr) IOS Press.

***Modelling & Microbiology of Activated Sludge Processes.** Ed. by M. Henze et al. (Water Science & Technology Ser.). 264p. 1999. pap. 163.00 (*0-08-043399-5*, Pergamon Pr) Elsevier.

Modelling & Motion Capture Techniques for Virtual Environments: International Workshop, Captech'98, Geneva, Switzerland, November 1998: Proceedings: International Workshop, Captech '98, Geneva, Switzerland, November 26-27, 1998: Proceedings, 153. CAPTECH '98 Staff et al. LC 98-49869. (Lecture Notes in Computer Science Ser.). 271 p. 1998. pap. 49.00 (*3-540-65353-8*) Spr-Verlag.

Modelling & Painting Figures. Jerry Scutts. (Illus.). 64p. 1999. pap. 17.95 (*1-902579-23-2*) Compendium.

Modelling & Performance Evaluation Methodology: Proceedings of the International Seminar, Paris, France, January 24-26, 1983. Ed. by Francois L. Baccelli & G. Fayolle. (Lecture Notes in Control & Information Sciences: Vol. 60). (ENG & FRE., Illus.). vii, 653p. 1984. 73.95 (*0-387-13288-0*) Spr-Verlag.

Modelling & Performance Evaluation of ATM Technology: Proceedings of the IFIP TC6 Task Group - WG6.4 International Workshop on Performance of Communication Systems, Martinique, French Caribbean Island. Ed. by Harry G. Perros et al. LC 93-22898. (IFIP Transactions C: Communication Systems Ser.: Vol. 15). 500p. 1993. 163.75 (*0-444-81512-0*, North Holland) Elsevier.

Modelling & Planning for Sensor Based Intelligent Robot Systems. Ed. by Horst Bunke et al. (Series in Machine Perception & Artificial Intelligence: Vol. 21). 550p. 1995. text 99.00 (*981-02-2238-6*) World Scientific Pub.

Modelling & Prediction of the Upper Layers of the Ocean. Ed. by Eric B. Kraus. 1977. 153.00 (*0-08-020611-5*, Pub. by Pergamon Repr) Franklin.

Modelling & Sculpting Animals. Edouard Lanteri. (Illus.). 352p. 1985. reprint ed. pap. 8.95 (*0-486-25007-5*) Dover.

Modelling & Sculpting the Human Figure. Edouard Lanteri. (Illus.). 480p. 1985. reprint ed. pap. 10.95 (*0-486-25006-7*) Dover.

Modelling & Simulation. Ed. by C. W. De Silva & M. H. Hamza. 297p. 1995. 90.00 (*0-88986-222-2*, 210) Acta Pr.

Modelling & Simulation. M. H. Hamza. 598p. 1995. 170.00 (*0-88986-218-4*, 228) Acta Pr.

Modelling & Simulation. Ed. by M. H. Hamza. 466p. 1996. 120.00 (*0-88986-201-X*, 238) Acta Pr.

Modelling & Simulation. Ed. by M. H. Hamza. LC 97-18481. (Series on Modelling & Simulation). (Illus.). 544p. 1997. pap. 130.00 (*0-88986-221-4*) Acta Pr.

Modelling & Simulation: Proceedings, IASTED Symposium, Lugano, Switzerland, June 21-24, 1983. Ed. by M. H. Hamza. 403p. 1983. 85.00 (*0-88986-048-3*, 054) Acta Pr.

Modelling & Simulation: Proceedings, IASTED Symposium, Lugano, Switzerland, June 21-24, 1983. Ed. by M. H. Hamza. 470p. 1985. 95.00 (*0-88986-079-3*, 091) Acta Pr.

Modelling & Simulation in Air Traffic Management. L. Bianco et al. LC 97-22629. (Transportation Analysis Ser.). xii, 202p. 1997. text. write for info. (*3-540-63093-7*) Spr-Verlag.

Modelling & Simulation in the Social Sciences, from the Philosophy of Sciences Point of View. Rainer Hegselmann et al. LC 96-9070. (Theory & Decision Library). 320p. 1996. lib. bdg. 144.00 (*0-7923-4125-2*) Kluwer Academic.

***Modelling & Simulation in Thermal & Chemical Engineering: A Bond Graph Approach.** Jean U. Thoma & B. Ould Bouamama. LC 99-58791. (Illus.). xiv, 219p. 2000. 59.95 (*3-540-66388-6*) Spr-Verlag.

***Modelling & Simulation 95 ESM '95.** Ed. by Miroslav Snorek et al. 867p. 1998. 100.00 (*1-56555-080-3*, ESM-95) Soc Computer Sim.

Modelling & Simulation of Human Behaviour in System Control. Peitro C. Cacciabue. LC 97-51768. (Advances in Industrial Control Ser.). (Illus.). xxvi, 358p. 1998. 69.95 (*3-540-76233-7*) Spr-Verlag.

Modelling & Simulation of Macroeconomic Systems: Use of Quantitative Modes for Analyzing Macroeconomic Reform Policies with Application to China, India & Vietnam. Economic & Social Commission for Asia & the Pacific Staff. 145p. 1997. pap. 35.00 (*92-1-119774-0*) UN.

Modelling & Simulation of Neurons & Neural Networks with Temporal-Pattern Learning Capability. C. Torras. (Lecture Notes in Biomathematics Ser.: Vol. 63). vii, 227p. 1985. 39.95 (*0-387-16046-9*) Spr-Verlag.

Modelling & Simulation of Power Generation Plants. A. W. Ordys et al. LC 94-27489. (Advances in Industrial Control Ser.). 1994. 75.95 (*0-387-19907-1*) Spr-Verlag.

Modelling & Simulation of Robot Manipulators: A Parallel Processing Approach. Albert Y. Zomaya. LC 92-19666. (Series in Robotics & Automated Systems: No. 8). 312p. 1993. text 55.00 (*981-02-1043-4*) World Scientific Pub.

Modelling & Simulation of Thin-Film Processing. Ed. by Cynthia A. Volkert et al. (Symposium Proceedings Ser.: Vol. 389). 382p. 1995. text 91.00 (*1-55899-292-8*) Materials Res.

Modelling & Solution Techniques for Multiphase Flow. A. V. Jones. (Ispra Courses on Nuclear Engineering & Technology Ser.: Vol. 7). xii, 588p. 1987. text 436.00 (*3-7186-0474-4*) Gordon & Breach.

Modelling, Applications & Applied Problem Solving: Teaching Mathematics in Real Context. Werner Blum et al. 1989. text 59.95 (*0-470-21570-4*) P-H.

Modelling Aqueous Corrosion: From Individual Pits to System Management - Proceedings of the NATO Advanced Research Workshop, Manadon, Plymouth, U. K., September 6-8, 1993, Vol. 266. Ed. by Kenneth R. Trethewey & Pierre R. Roberage. LC 94-10375. 476p. (C). 1994. text 285.00 (*0-7923-2820-5*) Kluwer Academic.

Modelling Auditory Processing & Organisation. Martin Cooke. (Distinguished Dissertations in Computer Science Ser.: No. 7). (Illus.). 134p. (C). 1993. text 44.95 (*0-521-45094-2*) Cambridge U Pr.

Modelling Binary Data. D. Collett. 384p. (gr. 13). 1991. per. 52.95 (*0-412-38800-6*, A6276, Chap & Hall CRC) CRC Pr.

Modelling Biological Populations in Space & Time. Ed. by Eric Renshaw. (Cambridge Studies in Mathematical Biology: No. 11). 421p. (C). 1993. pap. text 35.95 (*0-521-44855-7*) Cambridge U Pr.

Modelling Brain Function: The World of Attractor Neural Networks. Daniel J. Amit. (Illus.). 528p. (C). 1989. text 64.95 (*0-521-36100-1*) Cambridge U Pr.

Modelling British English Intonation: An Analysis by Resynthesis of British English Intonation. J. R. De Pijper. (Netherlands Phonetic Archives Ser.). xii, 150p. 1983. pap. 34.65 (*90-6765-003-X*) Mouton.

Modelling Change in Environmental Systems. Ed. by A. J. Jakeman et al. LC 93-27491. 606p. 1995. pap. 110.00 (*0-471-95780-1*) Wiley.

***Modelling Change in Integrated Economic & Environmental Systems.** S. Mahendrarajah & M. J. McAleer. Ed. by A. J. Jakeman. LC 98-55968. 412p. 1999. 140.00 (*0-471-98544-9*) Wiley.

***Modelling Changes in Understanding: Case Studies in Physical Reasoning.** Daniel Kayser & Stella Vosniadou. LC 99-35714. (Advances in Learning & Instruction Ser.). 312p. 1999. 82.00 (*0-08-043454-1*, Pergamon Pr) Elsevier.

Modelling Coastal Sea Processes: Proceedings of the International Ocean & Atmosphere Pacific Conference. Ed. by John Noye. 390p. 1999. 68.00 (*981-02-3556-9*) World Scientific Pub.

Modelling Cognition. Ed. by Peter Morris. LC 86-28229. (Illus.). 325p. 1987. reprint ed. pap. 100.80 (*0-608-05289-2*, 206582700001) Bks Demand.

Modelling Covariances & Latent Variables Using EQS. G. Dunn et al. (Illus.). 208p. (Orig.). 1993. ring bd. 41.95 (*0-412-48990-2*, Chap & Hall CRC) CRC Pr.

Modelling Crop-Weed Interactions. Ed. by M. J. Kropff & H. H. Van Laar. (Illus.). 304p. 1993. text 90.00 (*0-85198-745-1*) OUP.

An Asterisk (*) at the beginning of an entry indicates that the title is appearing for the first time.

Modelling Database Dynamics: Selected Papers from the 4th International Workshop on Foundations of Models & Languages for Data & Objects, Volkse, Germany 19-22 October 1992. 4th ed. Udo W. Lipeck & Bernhard Thalheim. LC 93-3307. (Workshops in Computing Ser.). 1993. 66.95 (*0-387-19803-2*) Spr-Verlag.

Modelling Drainage-Wire Section. Pira Staff. 1998. 110.00 (*1-85802-196-0*, Pub. by Pira Pub) Bks Intl VA.

Modelling Dynamic Non-Linear Relationships. Clive Granger & Timo Terasvirta. (Advanced Texts in Econometrics Ser.). (Illus.). 198p. (C). 1993. pap. text 29.95 (*0-19-877320-X*) OUP.

Modelling Early Christianity: Social-Scientific Studies of the New Testament in Its Context. Ed. by Philip F. Esler. LC 95-1434. (Illus.). 368p. (C). 1995. pap. 27.99 (*0-415-12981-8*) Routledge.

Modelling Early Christianity: Social-Scientific Studies of the New Testament in Its Context. Ed. by Philip F. Esler. LC 95-1434. (Illus.). 368p. (C). (gr. 13). 1995. 85.00 (*0-415-12980-X*) Routledge.

Modelling Economic Series: Readings in Econometric Methodology. Ed. by C. W. Granger. (Advanced Texts in Econometrics Ser.). (Illus.). 426p. 1991. reprint ed. pap. text 35.00 (*0-19-828736-4*, 11103) OUP.

Modelling Epidemics: An Introduction. D. J. Daley & J. Gani. LC 98-44051. (Cambridge Studies in Mathematical Biology: No. 14). (Illus.). 200p. (C). 1999. text 44.95 (*0-521-64079-2*) Cambridge U Pr.

Modelling, Estimation & Control of the Soaking Pit: An Example of the Development & Application of Some Modern Control Techniques to Industrial Processes. Yong-Zai Lu & Theodore J. Williams. LC 83-101. (Illus.). 482p. reprint ed. pap. 149.50 (*0-8357-2998-2*, 203926600011) Bks Demand.

Modelling Extremal Events: For Insurance & Finance. Paul Embrechts et al. Ed. by I. Karatzas & M. Yor. LC 97-12308. (Applications of Mathematics Ser.: No. 33). (Illus.). 645p. 1997. 79.00 (*3-540-60931-8*) Spr-Verlag.

Modelling Extremal Events: With a View Towards Insurance & Finance. P. Embrechts. 1996. 79.00 (*0-387-60931-8*) Spr-Verlag.

Modelling Financial Derivatives with "Mathematicar" William Shaw. LC 99-191745. (Illus.). 548p. (C). 1999. text 150.00 (*0-521-59233-X*) Cambridge U Pr.

Modelling Fixed Income Securities & Interest Rate Options. Robert A. Jarrow. LC 95-38518. (Finance Ser.). 1995. write for info. (*0-07-032373-9*) McGraw.

Modelling Fixed Income Securities & Interest Rate Options. Robert A. Jarrow. LC 95-38518. (McGraw-Hill Finance Guides Ser.). 224p. (C). 1995. text 71.56 incl. disk (*0-07-912253-1*) McGraw.

Modelling Fluctuating Populations. R. M. Nisbet & W. S. Gurney. LC 81-14668. 393p. reprint ed. pap. 121.90 (*0-608-17609-5*, 203045900069) Bks Demand.

Modelling for Added Value. Ed. by R. Macredie et al. LC 98-3911. (Illus.). 260p. 1998. pap. 89.95 (*3-540-76108-X*) Spr-Verlag.

Modelling for Financial Decisions. Ed. by R. Flavell et al. (Studies in Financial Modelling). (Illus.). 248p. 1991. 87.95 (*0-387-54253-1*) Spr-Verlag.

Modelling for Management: Simulation in Support of Systems Thinking, 2 vols., Set. Ed. by George P. Richardson. (International Library of Management Ser.). (Illus.). 900p. 1995. text 389.95 (*1-85521-697-3*, Pub. by Dartmth Pub) Ashgate Pub Co.

Modelling for Management Vols. I & II: Simulation in Support of Systems Thinking, 2 vols. Ed. by George P. Richardson. (International Library of Management). (Illus.). 976p. 1997. pap. 89.95 (*1-85521-888-7*, Pub. by Ashgate Pub) Ashgate Pub Co.

Modelling for Population & Sustainable Development. Ed. by A. J. Gilbert & L. C. Braat. (Illus.). 288p. 1991. 95.00 (*0-415-06187-3*, A5549) Routledge.

***Modelling Forest Development.** Klaus Von Gadow & Gangying Hui. LC 98-47440. (Forestry Sciences Ser.: Vol. 57). 213p. 1998. 108.00 (*0-7923-5488-5*) Kluwer Academic.

Modelling Forest Growth & Yield: Applications to Mixed Tropical Forests. J. Vanclay. LC 95-161797. (Illus.). 336p. 1994. text 90.00 (*0-85198-913-6*) OUP.

Modelling Frequency & Count Data. J. K. Lindsey. (Oxford Statistical Science Ser.: No. 15). (Illus.). 300p. 1995. text 65.00 (*0-19-852331-9*) OUP.

Modelling, Functions & Graphs: Algebra for College Students. 2nd ed. Yoshiwara. 1996. mass mkt. 50.00 (*0-534-94573-2*) Brooks-Cole.

Modelling Global Change: The Art of Integrated Assessment Modelling. Marco Janssen. LC 97-51675. (Advances in Ecological Economics Ser.). 288p. 1998. 85.00 (*1-85898-763-6*) E Elgar.

Modelling Groundwater Flow. Jacob Bear. (Theory & Applications of Transport in Porous Media Ser.). 1987. pap. text 59.00 (*1-55608-015-8*) Kluwer Academic.

Modelling Hot Deformation of Steels. Ed. by J. G. Lenard. (Illus.). viii, 145p. 1989. 76.95 (*0-387-50754-X*) Spr-Verlag.

Modelling Human Speech Comprehension: A Computational Approach. E. J. Briscoe. (Cognitive Science Ser.). 272p. 1987. text 69.95 (*0-470-21032-X*) P-H.

Modelling, Identification & Control. Ed. by M. H. Hamza. 470p. 1994. 120.00 (*0-88986-183-8*, 207) Acta Pr.

Modelling, Identification & Control. Ed. by M. H. Hamza. 430p. 1996. 140.00 (*0-88986-193-5*, 236) Acta Pr.

Modelling, Identification & Control. Ed. by M. H. Hamza. LC 97-18404. (Illus.). 438p. 1997. pap. 140.00 (*0-88986-217-6*) Acta Pr.

Modelling, Identification & Control - MIC '84: Proceedings, IASTED Symposium, Innsbruck, Austria, February 14-17, 1984. Ed. by M. H. Hamza. 300p. 1984. 75.00 (*0-88986-056-4*, 063) Acta Pr.

Modelling, Identification & Control - MIC '85: Proceedings, IASTED Symposium, Grindelwald, Switzerland, February 19-22, 1985. Ed. by M. H. Hamza. 367p. 1985. 95.00 (*0-88986-074-2*, 085) Acta Pr.

Modelling, Identification & Control - MIC '86: Proceedings, IASTED Symposium, Innsbruck, Austria, February 18-21, 1986. Ed. by M. H. Hamza. 272p. 1986. 80.00 (*0-88986-087-4*, 101) Acta Pr.

Modelling, Identification & Control - MIC '87: Proceedings, IASTED Symposium, Grindelwald, Switzerland, February 17-20, 1987. Ed. by M. H. Hamza. 464p. 1987. 98.00 (*0-88986-106-4*, 110) Acta Pr.

Modelling, Identification & Control - MIC '89: Proceedings, IASTED Symposium, Grindewald, Switzerland, February 7-10, 1989. Ed. by M. H. Hamza. 448p. 1989. 100.00 (*0-88986-113-7*, 132) Acta Pr.

Modelling in Aquatic Chemistry. Ed. by Ingmarr Grenthe & Ignasi Puigdomenech. 726p. 1997. pap. 185.00 (*92-64-15569-4*, 66-97-07-1, Pub. by Org for Econ) OECD.

Modelling in Clay: And other Materials. Dorothy Arthur. (Illus.). 128p. 1997. pap. text. write for info. (*90-5703-921-4*, Harwood Acad Pubs) Gordon & Breach.

Modelling in Ecotoxicology. Ed. by Sven E. Jorgensen. (Developments in Environmental Modelling Ser.: No. 16). 360p. 1990. 153.75 (*0-444-88699-0*) Elsevier.

Modelling in Environmental Chemistry, Developments in Environmental Chemistry, Vol. 17. Sven E. Jorgensen. 506p. 1991. 247.75 (*0-444-88605-2*) Elsevier.

Modelling in Geography: A Mathematical Approach. R. W. Thomas & R. J. Huggett. (Illus.). 338p. 1980. 56.00 (*0-389-20049-2*, N6840); pap. 26.50 (*0-389-20050-6*, N6841) B&N Imports.

Modelling in Geomechanics. F. P. Glushikhim et al. Ed. by M. S. Zlotnikov. Tr. by A. Jaganmohan from RUS. (Russian Translation Ser.: No. 97). (ENG., Illus.). 253p. 1993. text 123.00 (*90-5410-219-5*, Pub. by A A Balkema) Ashgate Pub Co.

***Modelling in Health Care Finance A Compendium of Quantitative Techniques for Health Care Finance.** Michael Cichon. 1999. 60.00 (*92-2-110862-7*) Intl Labour Office.

***Modelling Indirect Taxes & Tax Reform.** John Creedy. LC 99-45040. 232p. 2000. 80.00 (*1-84064-264-5*) E Elgar.

Modelling Interest-Free Economy. M. Anwer. 1992. pap. 12.95 (*1-56744-142-4*) Kazi Pubns.

Modelling Interest-Free Economy: A Study in Macro-Economics & Development. Muhammad Anwar. LC 87-82481. (Islamization of Knowledge Ser.: No. 4). 140p. (Orig.). (C). 1987. text 15.75 (*0-912463-78-3*); pap. text 8.00 (*0-912463-11-2*) IIIT VA.

Modelling Large Systems. P. C. Roberts. 120p. 1978. 31.00 (*0-85066-170-6*) Taylor & Francis.

***Modelling Learning in Economics.** Thomas Brenner. LC 99-14860. 352p. 1999. 100.00 (*1-84064-134-7*) E Elgar.

Modelling Longitudinal & Spatially Correlated Data: Methods, Applications & Future Directions, Vol. 122. T. G. Gregoire. LC 97-9855. (Lecture Notes in Statistics Ser.). 1997. pap. 44.95 (*0-387-98216-7*) Spr-Verlag.

***Modelling Macroeconomic Adjustment with Growth in Developing Economies.** Sushanta K. Mallick. 218p. 2000. text 65.95 (*0-7546-1180-9*, Pub. by Ashgate Pub) Ashgate Pub Co.

Modelling Macroscopic Phenomena at Liquid Boundaries. Ed. by W. Kosinski & A. I. Murdoch. (CISM International Centre for Mechanical Sciences Ser.: No. 318). (Illus.). 288p. 1992. 65.95 (*0-387-82327-1*) Spr-Verlag.

Modelling Marine Processes. Philip Dyke. LC 96-3937. 1996. write for info. (*0-614-12742-4*) P-H.

Modelling Methods & Scientific Computation. Nicola Bellomo. 512p. 1994. boxed set 89.95 (*0-8493-8331-5*) CRC Pr.

***Modelling Molecular Structures.** 2nd ed. Hinchliffe. 2000. pap. text. write for info. (*0-471-48993-X*) Wiley.

Modelling Money Market Interest Rates. J. S. Fleming & D. G. Barr. LC HG0226.. (Bank of England. Discussion Papers. Technical Ser.: No. 24). 18p. reprint ed. pap. 30.00 (*0-7837-5375-6*, 204513900005) Bks Demand.

Modelling Nature: Episodes in the History of Population Ecology. Sharon E. Kingsland. (Science & Its Conceptual Foundations Ser.). (Illus.). x, 268p. 1993. pap. text 11.95 (*0-226-43727-2*) U Ch Pr.

Modelling Non-Linear Wave Processes. Yu A. Berezin. Tr. by L. Ya Yuzina from RUS. 189p. 1987. lib. bdg. 155.00 (*90-6764-075-1*, Pub. by VSP) Coronet Bks.

Modelling Nonlinearities in the German Stock Market. Sophie Robe. LC 99-32380. (European University Studies: Vol. 2472, No. 5). (Illus.). XII, 165p. 1999. pap. text 39.95 (*0-8204-4330-1*) P Lang Pubng.

***Modelling Nutrient Utilizatino in Farm Animals.** Ed. by J. P. McNamara et al. (Cabi Publishing Ser.). 384p. 2000. text 100.00 (*0-85199-449-0*) OUP.

Modelling Oceanic Climate Interactions. Ed. by David L. Anderson & Jurgen Willebrand. LC 93-26021. (NATO ASI Series I: Global Environmental Change: Vol. 11). 1993. 198.00 (*0-387-56855-7*) Spr-Verlag.

Modelling of Activated Sludge Systems. Derin Orhon & Nazik Artan. (Illus.). 585p. 1994. 116.95 (*1-56676-101-8*) Technomic.

Modelling of Atmospheric Flow Fields. Ed. by Demetri P. Lalas & Corrado F. Ratto. LC 95-45327. 768p. 1996. write for info. (*981-02-2509-1*) World Scientific Pub.

Modelling of Biological Wastewater Treatment: Proceedings of an IAWPRC Specialized Seminar Held in Copenhagen, 28-30 August 1985. M. Henze. 204p. 1986. pap. 52.00 (*0-08-034635-9*, Pergamon Pr) Elsevier.

Modelling of Biomolecular Structures & Mechanisms: Proceedings of the Jerusalem Symposium on Quantum Chemistry & Biochemistry (27th: 1994: Jerusalem, Israel) Ed. by Alberte Pullman et al. LC 94-32858. (The Jerusalem Symposia on Quantum Chemistry & Biochemistry Ser.: Vol. 27). 479p. 1995. text 217.50 (*0-7923-3102-8*) Kluwer Academic.

Modelling of Chemical Reaction Systems: Proceedings. Ed. by Klaus H. Ebert. (Chemical Physics Ser.: Vol. 18). (Illus.). 389p. 1981. 63.95 (*0-387-10983-8*) Spr-Verlag.

Modelling of Concrete Performance: Hydration, Microstructure Formation, & Mass Transport. Koichi Maekawa et al. LC 98-31036. 1999. 110.00 (*0-419-24200-7*, E & FN Spon) Routledge.

Modelling of Energy Forestry: Growth, Water Relations & Economics. K. L. Perttu. 209p. (C). 1991. pap. 175.00 (*81-7089-134-5*, Pub. by Intl Bk Distr) St Mut.

Modelling of Engineering Heat Transfer Phenomena. Ed. by Bengt Sunden & Mohammad Faghri. LC 97-80255. (Developments in Heat Transfer Ser.: Vol. 2). 384p. 1998. 184.00 (*1-85312-450-8*, 4508, Pub. by WIT Pr) Computational Mech MA.

Modelling of Extremal Events in Insurance & Finance. P. Embrechts. 400p. 1996. text. write for info. (*0-412-75690-0*, Chap & Hall NY) Chapman & Hall.

Modelling of Furnaces & Combustors, Vol. 2. E. E. Kahil. (Abacus Bks.). 260p. 1982. text 131.00 (*0-85626-303-6*) Gordon & Breach.

Modelling of Interface Carrier Transport for Device Simulation. Dietmar Schroeder. LC 94-9605. (Computational Microelectronics Ser.). 1994. 149.95 (*0-387-82539-8*) Spr-Verlag.

Modelling of Livestock Production Systems. Ed. by S. Korver & J. A. Van Arendonk. (Current Topics in Veterinary Medicine & Animal Science Ser.). (C). 1988. text 130.50 (*0-89838-373-0*) Kluwer Academic.

Modelling of Material Behavior & Design. Ed. by J. D. Embury & A. W. Thompson. LC 89-63256. 283p. reprint ed. pap. 87.80 (*0-7837-5644-5*, 205249600005) Bks Demand.

Modelling of Material Damage & Failure of Structures: Theory & Applications. J. Skrzypek & A. Ganczarski. Ed. by V. I. Babitsky & J. Wittenburg. (Foundations of Engineering Mechanics Ser.). (Illus.). 320p. 1998. 94.00 (*3-540-63725-7*) Spr-Verlag.

Modelling of Metal Forming Processes. Ed. by Jean-Loup Chenot & E. O'Nate. (C). 1988. text 201.00 (*90-247-3748-6*) Kluwer Academic.

Modelling of Microstructure & Its Potential for Studying Transport Properties & Durability: Proceedings of the NATO Advanced Research Workshop, Saint-Remy-les-Chevreuse, France, July 10-13, 1994. Ed. by Hammlin Jennings et al. LC 95-47423. (NATO Advanced Science Institutes Series C: No. 304). 576p. (C). 1996. text 291.00 (*0-7923-3852-9*) Kluwer Academic.

Modelling of Mine Structures: Proceedings of the 10th Plenary Scientific Session of the International Bureau of Strata Mechanics - World Mining Congress, Stockholm, June 4, 1987. Ed. by A. Kidybinski & M. Kwasniewski. (Illus.). viii, 184p. 1988. lib. bdg. 110.00 (*90-6191-847-2*, Pub. by A A Balkema) Ashgate Pub Co.

Modelling of Minerals & Silicated Materials. Ed. by Bernard Silvi. LC 96-49690. (Molecular Organization & Engineering Ser.). 344p. (C). 1997. text 160.50 (*0-7923-4333-6*) Kluwer Academic.

Modelling of Oxidation Processes. N. M. Emanuel & D. Gal. 436p. (C). 1986. 430.00 (*0-7855-6296-6*, Pub. by Collets) St Mut.

Modelling of Oxidation Processes Prototype: The Oxidation of Ethylbenzene. N. M. Emanuel & D. Gal. 436p. (C). 1986. 150.00 (*963-05-3878-4*, Pub. by Akade Kiado) St Mut.

Modelling of Structure & Properties of Molecules. Azonimir B. Maksic. 390p. 1987. text 75.95 (*0-470-21010-9*) P-H.

Modelling of Systems with Small Observation Sets. J. M. Maciejowski. (Lecture Notes in Control & Information Sciences: Vol. 10). (Illus.). 1978. 24.95 (*0-387-09004-5*) Spr-Verlag.

Modelling of the Impact Response of Fibre-Reinforced Composites: 6th Progress Report. University of Oxford, Dept. of Engineering Science. 139p. 1991. 29.95 (*0-87762-820-3*) Technomic.

Modelling of Transport Phenomena in Crystal Growth. Ed. by J. S. Szmyd & K. Suzuki. (Developments in Heat Transfer Ser.). 300p. 2000. 157.00 (*1-85312-735-3*, 7353, Pub. by WIT Pr) Computational Mech MA.

***Modelling of Transport Processes in Soils: At Various Scales in Time & Space.** J. Feyen. (Illus.). 786p. 2000. pap. 146.00 (*90-74134-76-9*) Wageningen Pers.

Modelling of Water Waves in Shallow Channels. A. Nachbin. LC 92-75036. (Topics in Engineering Ser.: Vol. 13). 160p. 1993. 95.00 (*1-56252-062-8*, 1355) Computational Mech MA.

Modelling of World Economic Development. 56p. pap. 7.50 (*92-1-109115-2*, E.88.II.C.2) UN.

***Modelling People: Proceedings IEEE International Workshop, Kerkyra, Greece 1999.** LC 99-65083. 103p. 1999. 100.00 (*0-7695-0362-4*) IEEE Comp Soc.

Modelling Phase Equilibria: Thermodynamic Background & Practical Tools. Stanislaw Malanowski & Andrzej Anderko. (Series in Chemical Engineering: No. 1793). 328p. 1992. 79.95 (*0-471-57103-2*) Wiley.

Modelling Plant Growth & Development. D. A. Charles-Edwards et al. 1987. pap. text 46.00 (*0-12-169362-7*) Acad Pr.

Modelling Policy Analysis. Iwan J. Azis. 55.95 (*1-84014-587-0*) Ashgate Pub Co.

Modelling Potential Crop Growth Processes: Textbook with Exercises. J. Goudriaan & H. H. Van Laar. LC 91-39505. (Current Issues in Production Ecology Ser.: Vol. 2). 1994. lib. bdg. 127.00 (*0-7923-3219-9*) Kluwer Academic.

***Modelling Radiocesium in Lakes & Coastal Areas.** 228p. 2000. 106.00 (*0-7923-6245-4*) Kluwer Academic.

Modelling Reality & Personal Modelling. R. Flavell. (Contributions to Management Science Ser.). (Illus.). vi, 407p. 1993. pap. 89.00 (*0-387-91446-3*) Spr-Verlag.

Modelling Robotic & Flexible Manufacturing Systems. I. M. Makarov. 1990. 109.00 (*0-89116-964-4*) Hemisp Pub.

Modelling, Robustness & Sensitivity Reduction in Control Systems. Ed. by R. F. Curtain. (NATO Asi Series F: Vol. 34). x, 492p. 1987. 119.95 (*0-387-17845-7*) Spr-Verlag.

Modelling Seasonality. Ed. by Svend Hylleberg. (Advanced Texts in Econometrics Ser.). (Illus.). 488p. 1992. text 85.00 (*0-19-877317-X*); pap. text 39.95 (*0-19-877318-8*) OUP.

Modelling, Simulation & Identification. Ed. by Y. Kagawa. 271p. 1994. 95.00 (*0-88986-202-8*) Acta Pr.

Modelling, Simulation & Optimization. Ed. by M. H. Hamza. (Series on Modelling & Simulation). 1996. 50.00 (*0-88986-197-8*, 242) Acta Pr.

Modelling, Simulation & Optimization. Ed. by M. H. Hamza. LC 97-18564. (Series on Modelling & Simulation). (Illus.). 374p. 1997. 140.00 (*0-88986-238-9*) Acta Pr.

Modelling, Simulation & Optimization: Proceedings of the International Symposium Held in Montreal, Canada, May 22-24, 1990. Ed. by Z. Jacyno. 242p. 1990. 75.00 (*0-88986-146-3*, 160) Acta Pr.

Modelling, Simulation, & Optimization of Industrial Fixed Bed Catalytic Reactors. S. S. E. H. Elnashaie & S. S. Elshishini. LC 92-29469. (Topics in Chemical Engineering Ser.: Vol. 7). xxiii, 478p. 1994. text 170.00 (*2-88124-883-7*) Gordon & Breach.

Modelling, Simulation, Policy Planning & Economics - Energy '83: Proceedings, IASTED Symposium, San Francisco, U. S. A., May 16-18, 1983. Ed. by M. H. Hamza. 201p. 1983. 60.00 (*0-88986-042-4*, 050) Acta Pr.

Modelling Sintering Processes with Boundary Elements. A. R. M. Primo. (Topics in Engineering Ser.). 270p. 2000. 143.00 (*1-85312-754-X*, 754X, Pub. by WIT Pr) Computational Mech MA.

***Modelling Soil-Biosphere Interactions.** Christopher Muller. LC 99-35159. (CABI Publishing Ser.). 220p. 1999. text 65.00 (*0-85199-353-2*, Pub. by C A B Intl) OUP.

Modelling Soil Erosion by Water. John Boardman et al. LC 98-10582. (NATO ASI Ser.: Vol. 55). (Illus.). 542p. 1998. 199.00 (*3-540-64034-7*) Spr-Verlag.

Modelling Soil-Water-Structure Interactions: Proceedings of the International Symposium, Delft, 29 August - 2 September, 1988. Ed. by P. A. Kolkman & J. Lindenberg. 800p. (C). 1988. text 136.00 (*90-6191-815-4*, Pub. by A A Balkema) Ashgate Pub Co.

Modelling Spatial Knowledge on a Linguistic Basis: Theory - Prototype - Integration. K. U. Carstensen et al. (Lecture Notes in Artificial Intelligence: Vol. 481). ix, 138p. 1991. 23.00 (*0-387-53718-X*) Spr-Verlag.

***Modelling Spatial Processes: The Identification & Analysis of Spatial Relationships in Regression Residuals by Means of Moran's I.** M. Tiefelsdorf. LC QA278.2.T52 1999. (Lecture Notes In Earth Sciences: Vol. 87). (Illus.). 186p. 2000. pap. 76.00 (*3-540-66208-1*) Spr-Verlag.

Modelling Stock Market Volatility: Bridging the Gap to Continuous Time. Ed. by Peter H. Rossi. (Illus.). 485p. 1996. text 59.95 (*0-12-598275-5*) Morgan Kaufmann.

Modelling Storage Systems. M. Satyanarayanan. LC 86-1312. (Computer Science: Computer Architecture & Design Ser.: No. 5). 272p. reprint ed. pap. 84.40 (*0-8357-1742-9*, 207041600088) Bks Demand.

Modelling Survival Data. D. Collett. LC 99-26358. (Illus.). 350p. (gr. 13). 1994. text 63.95 (*0-412-44880-7*) Chapman & Hall.

Modelling Survival Data in Medical Research. D. Collett. (Illus.). 368p. (gr. 13). 1993. per. 47.95 (*0-412-44890-4*, Chap & Hall CRC) CRC Pr.

Modelling Systems: Practical Tools & Techniques for Software Development. John Fitzgerald & Peter G. Larsen. (Illus.). 286p. (C). 1998. text 85.00 (*0-521-62605-6*); pap. text 39.95 (*0-521-62348-0*) Cambridge U Pr.

Modelling Techniques for Financial Markets & Bank Management. Ed. by M. Bertocchi et al. (Contributions to Management Science Ser.). x, 296p. 1996. pap. 78.00 (*3-7908-0928-4*) Spr-Verlag.

Modelling the Accumulation & Distribution of Wealth. Ed. by Denis Kessler & Andre Masson. 352p. 1988. 69.00 (*0-19-828523-X*) OUP.

Modelling the Early Human Mind. Ed. by Paul Mellars & Kathleen Gibson. (Monographs Ser.). (Illus.). x, 229p. 1996. 50.00 (*0-9519420-1-8*, Pub. by McDonald Inst) David Brown.

Modelling the Economy & the Environment. Ed. by Bjarne Madsen et al. LC 96-13010. (Illus.). 352p. 1996. text 127.00 (*3-540-60780-3*) Spr-Verlag.

Modelling the Effects of Blasting on Rock Breakage. V. A. Borovikov. Tr. by I. F. Vanyagin from RUS. LC 99-226794. (Russian Translation Ser.: No. 114). (Illus.). 250p. (C). 1995. text 104.00 (*90-5410-222-5*, Pub. by A A Balkema) Ashgate Pub Co.

M

An Asterisk (*) at the beginning of an entry indicates that the title is appearing for the first time.

M

Modelling the Effects of Logging on the Water Balance of a Tropical Rain Forest: A Study in Guyana. V. G. Jetten. (Tropenbos Technical Ser.: No. 6). (Illus.). 196p. 1994. pap. 30.00 (*90-5113-018-X*, Pub. by Backhuys Pubs) Balogh.

Modelling the Effects of Spatial Variability on Radionuclide Miigration. NEA Staff. 320p. 1998. pap. 74.00 (*92-64-16099-X*, 66 98 09 1 P, Pub. by European Conference Ministers Transp) OECD.

Modelling the Human Impact on Nature: Systems Analysis of Environmental Problems. Richard J. Huggett. LC 93-12093. (Illus.). 224p. 1993. pap. text 35.00 (*0-19-874171-5*) OUP.

Modelling the Impact of Climate Change on Rice Production in Asia. Ed. by R. B. Matthews et al. (Illus.). 304p. 1995. text 105.00 (*0-85198-959-4*) OUP.

Modelling the Kinetics of Reduction by Temperature Programming. Ahmed Tarfaoui. (Illus.). 175p. (Orig.). 1996. pap. 57.50 (*90-407-1342-1*, Pub. by Delft U Pr) Coronet Bks.

Modelling the Labour Market. Ed. by Michael Beenstock. 250p. (gr. 13). 1988. text 110.00 (*0-412-28830-3*) Chapman & Hall.

Modelling the Legal Decision Process for Information Technology Applications in Law. Georgios N. Yannopoulos. LC 97-46619. (Law & Electronic Commerce Ser.). 364p. 1998. 109.00 (*90-411-0540-9*) Kluwer Law Intl.

Modelling the Mind. Ed. by K. A. Said et al. 224p. 1990. text 55.00 (*0-19-824973-X*) OUP.

Modelling the Phoneme: The Trends in East European Phonemic Theory. F. H. Kortlandt. (Janua Linguarum, Ser. Major: No. 68). 177p. 1972. text 75.40 (*90-279-2109-1*) Mouton.

Modelling the Sterling Effective Exchange Rate Using Expectations & Learning. S. G. Hall. LC HG3823.. (Bank of England. Discussion Papers. Technical Ser.: No. 33). 22p. reprint ed. pap. 30.00 (*0-7837-5376-4*, 204514000005) Bks Demand.

Modelling the Stress-Strain Relationship in Work Settings. Meni Koslowsky. LC 97-45074. (Progress in Psychology Ser.). (Illus.). 232p. (C). 1998. 75.00 (*0-415-15320-4*) Routledge.

Modelling the U. K. Economy in a Stock-Flow Consistent Manner. E. P. Davis. LC HG1581.D57. (Bank of England. Discussion Papers. Technical Ser.: No. 14). 123p. reprint ed. pap. 38.20 (*0-8357-4084-6*, 203677500005) Bks Demand.

Modelling Transport. 2nd ed. Juan De Dios Ortuzar & Luis G. Willumsen. 454p. 1996. pap. 75.00 (*0-471-96534-0*) Wiley.

Modelling Uncertain Data. Ed. by Hans Bandemer. 171p. 1993. pap. 69.95 (*3-05-501578-9*) Wiley.

Modelling under Uncertainty, 1986: Proceedings of the 1st International Conference on Modelling under Uncertainty Held at the Fulmer Research Institute, Stoke Poges, Slough, 16-18, 1986. International Conference on Modelling under Uncert. Ed. by S. B. Jones & D. G. Davies. LC 89-123131. (Institute of Physics Conference Ser.: No. 80). 341p. reprint ed. pap. 105.80 (*0-7837-3248-1*, 204326700007) Bks Demand.

Modelling Welfare State Reform. G. M. Gelauff & J. J. Graafland. LC 94-26529. 308p. 98.50 (*0-444-81886-3*, North Holland) Elsevier.

Modelling with AutoCAD Release 14: For Windows 95 & Windows NT. R. McFarlane. LC 99-167905. 256p. 1998. pap. 44.95 (*0-470-32898-3*) Halsted Pr.

Modelling with Circular Motion. School Mathematics Project Staff. (Mathematics Series: Ages 16-19). 107p. (C). 1993. pap. text 11.95 (*0-521-40889-X*) Cambridge U Pr.

Modelling with Differential & Difference Equations. Glenn Fulford et al. LC 97-180614. (Australian Mathematical Society Lecture Ser.). (Illus.). 415p. (C). 1997. text 80.00 (*0-521-44069-6*); pap. text 29.95 (*0-521-44618-X*) Cambridge U Pr.

Modelling with Differential Equations. D. N. Burghes & M. S. Borrie. LC 80-41936. (Mathematics & Its Applications Ser.). 172p. 1982. pap. text 41.95 (*0-470-27360-7*) P-H.

Modelling with Differential Equations in Chemical Engineering. Stanley M. Walas. (Chemical Engineering Ser.). 544p. 1991. text 175.00 (*0-7506-9012-7*) Buttrwrth-Heinemann.

Modelling with Force & Motion. School Mathematics Project Staff. (Mathematics Series: Ages 16-19). 142p. (C). 1992. pap. text 11.95 (*0-521-40891-1*) Cambridge U Pr.

Modelling with Generalized Stochastic Petri Nets. M. Ajmone Marsan et al. (Series in Parallel Computing). 324p. 1995. 120.00 (*0-471-93059-8*) Wiley.

Modelling with Mathematics in Primary & Secondary Schools: Modelling with Mathematics in Primary & Secondary Schools. J. Mason & J. Davis. 78p. (C). 1995. pap. 40.00 (*0-7300-1265-4*, ECT404, Pub. by Deakin Univ) St Mut.

Modelling with Ordinary Differential Equations. T. P. Dreyer. LC 93-9636. 304p. 1993. per. 84.95 (*0-8493-8636-5*, QA401) CRC Pr.

Modelling with Projectiles. Derek Hart & Tony Croft. (Mathematics & Its Applications Ser.). 152p. 1988. text 41.95 (*0-470-21085-0*) P-H.

Modello: A Story of Hope for the Inner-City & Beyond. Jack Pransky. Ed. by Ronni Wood. 160p. 1998. pap. 32.00 (*0-9659057-1-3*) NEHRI Pubns.

Modell's Drugs in Current Use & New Drugs, 1998. 44th ed. Ed. by Elizabeth A. Duthie. 288p. 1998. 27.95 (*0-8261-7657-7*) Springer Pub.

Modell's Drugs in Current Use & New Drugs 1999. 45th ed. Ed. by Elizabeth A. Duthie. 304p. 1999. pap. 29.95 (*0-8261-7658-5*) Springer Pub.

Modelmania: The Working Model's Manual. Karl Preston. LC 98-92863. (Illus.). 232p. 1998. pap. 21.95 (*0-9641513-5-9*) Dog Gone Bks.

Modelo Antiguo see Modelo Antiguo: A Novel of Mexico City

Modelo Antiguo: A Novel of Mexico City. Luis E. Reyes. Tr. by Sharon Franco & Joe Hayes. LC 97-28170.Tr. of Modelo Antiguo. 160p. (Orig.). 1997. pap. 11.95 (*0-938317-32-6*) Cinco Puntos.

Modelo de Antiguia: Caracteristicas de una Iglesia Efectiva. Ken Hemphill.Tr. of Antioch Effect. (SPA.). 208p. 1996. pap. text 10.99 (*0-311-17037-4*) Casa Bautista.

***modelo de Dios para "la Iglesia" Una Exposicio'n Sobre la Naturaleza y Proposito de la Iglesia.** Eddie Cloer. Orig. Title: God's Design for "the Church". 260p. 1999. pap. 2.50 (*0-945441-33-9*) Res Pubns AR.

Modelo Economico de Puerto Rico. Jorge Freyre. LC 78-4191. (Illus.). 270p. 1979. 20.00 (*0-913480-39-8*); pap. 13.00 (*0-913480-40-1*) Inter Am U Pr.

Modelo Profetas de Esperanza see Prophets of Hope Model: A Weekend Workshop

Modelo Profetas de Esperanza. Carmen Cervantes et al. (Profetas de Esperanza Ser.: Vol. 3). (SPA., Illus.). 72p. 1997. pap. text 4.95 (*0-88489-515-7*) St Marys.

Modelos de Construcciones Biblicas, Vol. I. C. Gordon Stowell.Tr. of Model Bible Building Village. (SPA.). 92p. 1992. pap. 12.99 (*1-56063-401-4*, 498608) Editorial Unilit.

Modelos de Construcciones Biblicas, Vol. II. C. Gordon Stowell.Tr. of Model Bible Building Village. 12.99 (*0-7899-0283-4*, 498764) Editorial Unilit.

Modelos Dialogicos en la Narrativa de Benito Perez Galdos. Alicia G. Andreu. LC 89-31929. (Purdue University Monographs in Romance Languages: Vol. 27). (SPA.). xvi, 126p. 1989. 38.00 (*1-55619-057-3*); pap. 19.95 (*1-55619-058-1*) J Benjamins Pubng Co.

Modelos para el Proceso de Ensenanza-Aprendizaje. LeRoy Ford. Tr. by Nelda B. DeGaydou & Jorge E. Diaz from ENG.Tr. of Design for Teaching & Training. (SPA., Illus.). 320p. (Orig.). 1986. pap. 10.99 (*0-311-11042-8*) Casa Bautista.

Modelos para Orar. David Y. Cho.Tr. of Patterns of Prayer. (SPA.). 112p. 1995. pap. 5.99 (*0-8297-1859-1*) Vida Pubs.

***Modelos y Teorias de Enfermeri.** 4th ed. Ed. by Ann Marriner-Tomey. (C). 1999. text 40.02 (*84-8174-348-8*) Mosby Inc.

Models see Craft Workshop Series

Models. (Jump Ser.). (Illus.). 36p. (J). (gr. 2-6). pap. write for info. (*1-882210-36-0*) Action Pub.

Models. Helen McNiven & Peter McNiven. LC 94-22442. (First Arts & Crafts Ser.). (Illus.). 32p. (J). (gr. 1-6). 1994. 21.40 (*1-56847-214-5*) Raintree Steck-V.

Models. Keith Newell. LC 98-4529. (Arts & Crafts Skills Ser.). 31p. 1998. lib. bdg. 6.95 (*0-516-26451-6*) Childrens.

Models. Keith Newell. LC 98-4529. (Arts & Crafts Skills Ser.). (J). 1999. 21.00 (*0-516-21205-2*) Childrens.

***Models.** Lola M. Schaefer. LC 00-36476. (Illus.). (J). 2000. write for info. (*0-7368-0731-4*) Capstone Pr.

Models. Ed. by Marx W. Wartofsky. (Boston Studies in the Philosophy of Science: No. 1, Vol. 2). 416p. 1979. pap. text 62.50 (*90-277-0947-5*, D Reidel); lib. bdg. 100.50 (*90-277-0736-7*, D Reidel) Kluwer Academic.

Models: Sittings, 1979-1988. Marco Glaviano. (Illus.). 120p. 1988. 39.95 (*1-55824-068-3*) At-A-Glance Consumer.

Models, Algebras & Proofs: Proceedings Latin-American Symposium on Mathematical Logic,1996, Bogota, Colombia. Ed. by Xavier Caicedo & Carlos H. Montenegro. LC 98-45734. (Illus.). 472p. 1998. pap. text 165.00 (*0-8247-1970-0*) Dekker.

Models & Computability. Ed. by S. Barry Cooper & John K. Truss. LC 99-19677. (London Mathematical Society Lecture Note Ser.: No. 259). 300p. (C). 1999. pap. text 44.95 (*0-521-63550-0*) Cambridge U Pr.

***Models & Contacts: Arabic Literature & its Impact on Medieval Jewish Culture.** Rina Drory. 240p. 2000. 73.00 (*90-04-11738-5*) Brill Academic Pubs.

Models & Critical Pathways in Clinical Nursing: Conceptual Frameworks for Care Planning. 2nd ed. Ed. by Mike Walsh. (Illus.). 270p. 1998. pap. write for info. (*0-7020-2188-1*) Bailliere Tindall.

Models & Experiments in Risk & Rationality. Ed. by Bertrand R. Munier. (Theory & Decision Library B). 450p. (C). 1994. lib. bdg. 156.00 (*0-7923-3031-5*) Kluwer Academic.

***Models & Friends: Photobooks.** Kenn Duncan. (Illus.). 1998. 44.95 (*3-925443-73-8*) Janssen.

Models & Great Basin Prehistory: A Symposium. Don D. Fowler et al. (Desert Research Institute Publications in the Social Sciences: No. 12). (Illus.). 220p. (Orig.). (C). 1977. reprint ed. pap. text 23.13 (*1-55567-622-7*) Coyote Press.

Models & Integrations Vol. 3: Rochester Symposium on Developmental Psychopathology. Ed. by Dante Cicchetti & Sheree L. Toth. (Illus.). 352p. 1991. 85.00 (*1-878822-04-7*) Univ Rochester Pr.

Models & Interpretations: Selected Essays. J. A. Barnes. 281p. (C). 1990. text 80.00 (*0-521-36653-4*) Cambridge U Pr.

Models & Measurement of Welfare & Inequality. Ed. by Wolfgang Eichhorn. LC 94-34352. 1994. write for info. (*3-540-58051-4*) Spr-Verlag.

Models & Measurement of Welfare & Inequality. Ed. by Wolfgang Eichhorn. LC 94-34352. 1994. 180.95 (*0-387-58051-4*) Spr-Verlag.

Models & Metaphors in Language Teacher Training: Loop Input & Other Strategies. Tessa Woodward. (Teacher Training & Development Ser.). (Illus.). 255p. (C). 1991. pap. text 20.95 (*0-521-37773-0*) Cambridge U Pr.

Models & Methods for the Genetic Analysis of Pedigree Data. Ed. by J. Ott. (Journal: Reprint from Human Heredity Ser.: Vol. 42, No. 1, 1992). (Illus.). 92p. 1993. 39.25 (*3-8055-5762-0*) S Karger.

Models & Methods for Writing about Literature. 2nd ed. Marilyn J. Kurata. 172p. (C). 1996. pap. text 29.95 (*0-7872-2627-0*) Kendall-Hunt.

Models & Methods in Few-Body Physics: Proceedings of the 8th Annual School on the Models & Methods in Few-Body Physics Held in Lisboa, Portugal, October 13-18, 1986. Ed. by L. S. Ferretra et al. (Lecture Notes in Physics Ser.: Vol. 273). xix, 674p. 1987. 90.95 (*0-387-17647-0*) Spr-Verlag.

Models & Methods in Regional Exchange. Ed. by Robert E. Fry. (SAA Papers: No. 1). 160p. 1980. pap. 12.00 (*0-932839-05-3*) Soc Am Arch.

Models & Methods in the Philosophy of Science: Selected Essays. Patrick C. Suppes. LC 93-14714. (Synthese Library: Vol. 226). 528p. (C). 1993. lib. bdg. 188.00 (*0-7923-2211-8*, Pub. by Kluwer Academic) Kluwer Academic.

Models & Mirrors: Towards an Anthropology of Public Events. rev. ed. Don Handelman. LC 98-30855. (Illus.). 384p. 1998. pap. 18.95 (*1-57181-165-6*) Berghahn Bks.

Models & Modelers of Hydrogen. Akhlesh Lakhtakia. 400p. 1996. text 58.00 (*981-02-2302-1*) World Scientific Pub.

Models & Moments: Paintings & Drawings by John Koch. Edward Bryant. (Illus.). 52p. 1977. pap. 5.00 (*0-911209-11-5*) Palmer Mus Art.

Models & Parameters for Environmental Radiological Assessments. DOE Technical Information Center Staff. Ed. by Charles W. Miller. LC 84-14255. (DOE Critical Review Ser.). 157p. 1984. pap. 12.00 (*0-87079-517-1*, DOE/TIC-11468); fiche 9.00 (*0-87079-516-3*, DOE/TIC-11468) DOE.

Models & Prototypes: How to Make Architectural & New Product Models. T. Kojima et al. (Illus.). 160p. 1991. pap. 44.95 (*4-7661-0617-2*, Pub. by Graphic-Sha) Bks Nippan.

Models & Reality in Economics. Steven Rappaport. LC 97-43551. (Advances in Economic Methodology Ser.). 232p. 1998. 85.00 (*1-85898-575-7*) E Elgar.

Models & Sets, Pt. 1. Ed. by G. H. Muller & M. M. Richter. (Lecture Notes in Mathematics Ser.: Vol. 1103). viii, 484p. 1984. 59.95 (*0-387-13900-1*) Spr-Verlag.

Models & Stratigraphy of Mid-Cretaceous Reef Communities, Gulf of Mexico. Robert W. Scott. LC 90-214984. (Concepts in Sedimentology & Paleontology Ser.: Vol. 2). (Illus.). 106p. 1990. reprint ed. pap. 32.90 (*0-608-05674-X*, 206619000006) Bks Demand.

Models & Techniques in Computer Animation. Ed. by Nadia M. Thalmann & Daniel Thalmann. LC 93-10965. (CGS Computer Animation Ser.). (Illus.). viii, 293p. 1993. 99.95 (*0-387-70124-9*) Spr-Verlag.

Models & Techniques in Medical Imaging Research. Eric N. Milne et al. LC 82-13141. 596p. 1983. 115.00 (*0-275-91404-6*, C1404, Praeger Pubs) Greenwood.

Models & the Crystalline State. Clyde R. Metz. Ed. by H. Anthony Neidig. (Modular Laboratory Program in Chemistry Ser.). 16p. (C). 1988. pap. text 1.50 (*0-87540-351-4*, STRC 351-4) Chem Educ Res.

***Models & Tools for Managing Development Processes.** Bernhard Westfechtel. LC 99-88398. (Lecture Notes in Computer Science Ser.: Vol. 1646). xiv, 418p. 2000. pap. 69.00 (*3-540-66756-3*) Spr-Verlag.

Models & Trends in Religious Education. Gail T. McKenna. LC 98-60277. 160p. 1998. pap. 19.95 (*0-89622-928-9*) Twenty-Third.

***Models as Mediators: Perspectives on Natural & Social Science.** Ed. by Mary Morgan & Margaret Morrison. LC 98-41630. (Ideas in Context Ser.: No. 52). (Illus.). 401p. (C). 1999. 64.95 (*0-521-65097-6*); pap. 24.95 (*0-521-65571-4*) Cambridge U Pr.

Model's Black Book to Success. Rosalind Anthony. 100p. 1994. pap. text 15.00 (*0-9640693-0-X*) Lord & Jediah.

Models Close-Up. David Bailey. (Illus.). 192p. 1999. pap. 29.95 (*0-7893-0255-1*, Pub. by Universe) St Martin.

Models, Concepts & Information. Magnus Boman. (International Series in Computer Science). 304p. 1997. pap. 52.00 (*0-13-514879-0*, Prentice Hall) P-H.

Model's Edge. Nicholette Winston. LC 98-89498. 375p. 1998. text 25.00 (*0-7388-0245-X*); pap. text 15.00 (*0-7388-0246-8*) Xlibris Corp.

Models, Evaluations & Information Systems for Planners. Ed. by Jean Perraton & Richard Baxter. LC 75-326945. (Cambridge University Centre for Land Use & Built Form Studies Conference Proceedings: No. 1). 316p. reprint ed. pap. 98.00 (*0-608-13086-9*, 202521500043) Bks Demand.

Models for Analysis of Social Policy: An Introduction. Ed. by Ron Haskins & James J. Gallagher. LC 81-12856. (Child & Family Policy Ser.). 256p. 1981. text 73.25 (*0-89391-084-8*) Ablx Pub.

Models for Analyzing Comparative Advantage. David A. Kendrick. (C). 1989. lib. bdg. 106.00 (*0-7923-0528-0*) Kluwer Academic.

Models for Assessing Drug Absorption & Metabolism. Ed. by Ronald T. Borchardt et al. (Pharmaceutical Biotechnology Ser.: Vol. 8). (Illus.). 436p. (C). 1996. text 95.00 (*0-306-45243-X*, Kluwer Plenum) Kluwer Academic.

Models for Biomedical Research: A New Perspective. National Research Council (U. S.) Staff. LC 85-60945. 192p. reprint ed. pap. 59.60 (*0-8357-3451-X*, 203971200013) Bks Demand.

Models for Carbonate Stratigraphy from Miocene Reef Complexes of Mediterranean Regions. Ed. by Evan K. Franseen et al. LC 96-180334. (Concepts in Sedimentology & Paleontology Ser.: No. 5). (Illus.). 402p. 1996. pap. text 83.00 (*1-56576-033-6*) SEPM.

Models for Change in Social Group Work. Marian F. Fatout. (Modern Applications of Social Work Ser.). 231p. 1992. pap. text 27.95 (*0-202-36078-4*); lib. bdg. 48.95 (*0-202-36077-6*) Aldine de Gruyter.

Models for Christian Higher Education: Strategies for Success in the Twenty-First Century. Ed. by Richard T. Hughes & William B. Adrian. LC 96-37653. 472p. (Orig.). 1997. pap. 30.00 (*0-8028-4121-X*) Eerdmans.

Models for Concrete Structures. American Concrete Institute Staff. LC 79-103139. (American Concrete Institute Publication: SP-24). (Illus.). 503p. reprint ed. pap. 156.00 (*0-608-10959-2*, 202276000029) Bks Demand.

***Models for Concurrency.** Uri Abraham. 250p. 1999. text 60.00 (*90-5699-199-X*, Harwood Acad Pubs) Gordon & Breach.

***Models for Decision Making.** Denardo. (C). 2000. pap. text, student ed. write for info. (*0-471-33281-X*) Wiley.

Models for Discrete Data. Daniel Zelterman. 248p. 1999. text 65.00 (*0-19-852436-6*) OUP.

Models for Effective Writing. Ed. by J. Karl Nicholas & James R. Nicholl. LC 93-11808. 1994. write for info. (*0-205-40017-5*) Allyn.

***Models for Effective Writing.** 2nd ed. J. Karl Nicholas & James R. Nicholl. LC 99-14599. 416p. 1999. pap. text 34.00 (*0-205-30292-0*) Allyn.

Models for Effective Writing. 2nd ed. Karl J. Nicholas. (C). 1999. pap. text. write for info. (*0-205-31562-3*) Allyn.

Models for Embryonic Periodicity. L. I. Held, Jr. (Monographs in Developmental Biology: Vol. 24). (Illus.). viii, 120p. 1994. pap. 26.25 (*3-8055-6008-7*) S Karger.

Models for Energy Policy. Ed. by Jean-Baptiste Lesourd et al. LC 95-813. (New International Studies in Economic Modelling Ser.). 288p. (C). (gr. 13). 1995. 115.00 (*0-415-12975-3*) Routledge.

Models for Flow Systems & Chemical Reactors. Chin-Yung Wen & Liang-tseng Fan. LC 74-83417. (Chemical Processing & Engineering Ser.: Vol. 3). 584p. reprint ed. pap. 181.10 (*0-608-16694-4*, 202781900054) Bks Demand.

Models for Fulfilling Missions: Discovering Strategies for Passing on the Bread. Gary L. Royer. 203p. 1997. pap. text 9.95 (*0-9656825-0-1*) G L Royer.

Models for Genetics. Wolfgang Balzer & Chris M. Dawe. (Illus.). 183p. 1997. pap. 42.95 (*3-631-31876-6*) P Lang Pubng.

Models for Genetics. Wolfgang Balzer & Chris M. Dawe. LC 97-19725. (Illus.). 183p. 1997. pap. 42.95 (*0-8204-3283-0*) P Lang Pubng.

Models for Improving College Teaching: A Faculty Resource. Jon E. Travis. Ed. by Jonathan D. Fife. LC 96-78491. (ASHE-ERIC Higher Education Reports: No. 95-6). (Illus.). 100p. (Orig.). 1996. pap. 24.00 (*1-878380-70-2*) GWU Grad Schl E&HD.

Models for Individualized Instruction. William D. Georgiades & Donald C. Clark. LC 73-22495. text 30.50 (*0-8422-5164-2*) Irvington.

Models for Infectious Human Diseases: Their Structure & Relation to Data. Ed. by V. Isham & G. Medley. LC 95-23452. (Publications of the Newton Institute: No. 6). (Illus.). 514p. (C). 1996. text 74.95 (*0-521-45339-9*) Cambridge U Pr.

Models for Innovation Diffusion. Vijay Mahajan & Robert A. Peterson. (Quantitative Applications in the Social Sciences Ser.: Vol. 48). 1985. 10.95 (*0-8039-2136-5*) Sage.

Models for Interpretation of Scripture. John Goldingay. 1995. pap. 22.00 (*0-8028-0145-5*) Eerdmans.

Models for Large Integrated Circuits. Patrick Dewilde & Zhen-Qiu Ning. (C). 1990. text 103.50 (*0-7923-9115-2*) Kluwer Academic.

Models for Management: The Structure of Competence. Jay Hall. 520p. (C). 1988. pap. text 19.95 (*0-945804-11-3*) Woodstead Pr.

Models for Management: The Structure of Competence. Ed. by John A. Shtogren. LC 79-93291. (Illus.). 520p. (C). 1981. pap. write for info. (*0-937932-00-0*) Teleometrics.

Models for Managing Regional Water Quality. Ed. by Robert Dorfman et al. LC 72-87770. (Illus.). 471p. 1973. 43.00 (*0-674-57825-2*) HUP.

Models for Measuring Quality in Managed Care: Analysis & Impact. Ed. by Jonathan Seltzer & David Nash. (Medical Outcomes & Guidelines Practice Library II). (Illus.). 384p. (Orig.). 1997. pap. 145.00 (*1-57987-001-5*) Faulkner & Gray.

Models for Mental Disorder: Conceptual Models in Psychiatry. 3rd ed. Peter J. Tyrer & Derek Steinberg. LC 97-41382. 158p. 1998. pap. 43.95 (*0-471-97433-1*) Wiley.

Models for Ministry: Creative Administration in the Local Church. Raymond B. Knudsen. LC BV0652.K6. 106p. (Orig.). reprint ed. pap. 32.90 (*0-7837-1956-6*, 204217300001) Bks Demand.

Models for Multidisciplinary Arrangements: A State-by-State Review of Options. American Psychological Association Staff & McDermott, Will & Emery Staff. LC 96-27361. (APA Practitioner's Toolbox Ser.). 135p. 1996. 29.95 (*1-55798-363-1*) Am Psychol.

Models for Multispecies Management. T. Rodseth. LC 98-16486. (Contributions to Economics Ser.). (Illus.). viii, 246p. 1998. pap. 67.00 (*3-7908-1001-0*) Spr-Verlag.

Models for Mutual & Spiritual Parents & the Child's Responsibility to the Parents. B. R. Hicks. (Illus.). 71p. 1997. pap. 5.00 (*1-58363-060-0*, PS-8803) Christ Gospel.

Models for Psychotherapy: A Primer. Ed. by J. D. Haldane et al. 96p. 1983. pap. text 10.00 (*0-08-028446-9*, Pergamon Pr) Elsevier.

An Asterisk (*) at the beginning of an entry indicates that the title is appearing for the first time.

Models for Public Sculpture in America: Cast in the Shadow. Jennifer A. Gordon. (Illus.). 88p. 1985. pap. 25.00 (*1-55660-184-0*) A Wofsy Fine Arts.

Models for Repeated Measurements. J. K. Lindsey. (Oxford Statistical Science Ser.: No. 10). (Illus.). 432p. 1993. text 69.00 (*0-19-852299-1*) OUP.

***Models for Repeated Measurements.** 2nd ed. J. K. Lindsey. LC 99-33069. 19. (Illus.). 528p. 1999. text 75.00 (*0-19-850559-0*) OUP.

Models for Smooth Infinitesimal Analysis. G. E. Reyes & Izak Moerdijk. (Illus.). x, 399p. 1990. 95.95 (*0-387-97489-X*) Spr-Verlag.

***Models for the Millennium: Great Basin Anthropology Today.** Ed. by Charlotte Beck. LC 99-45381. (Illus.). 314p. 1999. 65.00 (*0-87480-593-7*) U of Utah Pr.

Models for the Multitudes: Social Values in the American Popular Novel, 1850-1920, 3. Karol L. Kelley. LC 86-15004. (Contributions to the Study of Childhood & Youth Ser.: No. 3). 209p. 1987. 55.00 (*0-313-23514-7*, KMM/, Greenwood Pr) Greenwood.

Models for Thermodynamic & Phase Equilibria Calculations. Stanley I. Sandler. (Chemical Industries Ser.: Vol. 52). (Illus.). 704p. 1993. text 250.00 (*0-8247-9130-4*) Dekker.

Models for Uncertainty in Educational Testing. N. Wermuth & K. Krickeberg. LC 95-8145. (Springer Series in Statistics). 300p. 1995. 54.95 (*0-387-94513-X*) Spr-Verlag.

Models for Undergraduate Research in Mathematics. Ed. by Lester J. Senechal. (MAA Notes Ser.). 208p. (Orig.). 1990. pap. text 5.00 (*0-88385-070-2*, NTE-18) Math Assn.

Models for Writers. 6th ed. Paul A. Eschholz. LC 97-65207. 528p. 1997. pap. text 32.95 (*0-312-15310-4*) St Martin.

Models for Writers: Short Essays for Composition. 2nd ed. Ed. by Paul A. Eschholz & Alfred F. Rosa. LC 85-61290. 400p. (C). 1986. pap. text 12.00 (*0-312-53592-9*) St Martin.

Models for Writers: Short Essays for Composition. 6th ed. Alfred F. Rosa. 1999. pap. text 10.00 (*0-312-17960-X*) St Martin.

Models for Writers Developmental Exercises & ESL Workbook. 6th ed. Rosa & Eschholz. pap. text, wbk. ed. 26.95 (*0-312-17953-7*) St Martin.

Models for Writing. 5th ed. Alfred F. Rosa. 1994. pap. text, teacher ed. 21.50 (*0-312-10122-8*) St Martin.

Models in Archaeology. Ed. by David L. Clarke. 1972. 120.00 (*0-416-16540-0*, NO. 2144) Routledge.

Models in Dermatology, Vol. 4. Ed. by Howard I. Maibach & N. J. Lowe. x, 298p. 1989. 321.75 (*3-8055-4761-7*) S Karger.

Models in Dermatology, 1987, Vol. 3. Ed. by Howard I. Maibach & N. J. Lowe. xvi, 204p. 1987. 217.50 (*3-8055-4239-9*) S Karger.

Models in Financial Management. 5th ed. Martin. (C). 1991. 16.00 (*0-13-060906-4*, Macmillan Coll) P-H.

Models in Geomorphology. M. Woldenberg. (Binghamton Symposia in Geomorphology: International Ser.: No. 14). 400p. (C). 1985. text 90.00 (*0-04-551075-X*) Routledge.

Models in Plant Physiology & Biochemistry, Vol. 1. D. Newman & K. Wilson. LC 87-9363. 160p. 1987. reprint ed. 95.00 (*0-8493-4343-7*, CRC Reprint) Franklin.

Models in Plant Physiology & Biochemistry, Vol. 2. D. Newman & K. Wilson. LC 87-9363. 176p. 1987. reprint ed. 101.00 (*0-8493-4344-5*, CRC Reprint) Franklin.

Models in Plant Physiology & Biochemistry, Vol. 3. D. Newman & K. Wilson. LC 87-9363. 152p. 1987. reprint ed. 91.00 (*0-8493-4345-3*, CRC Reprint) Franklin.

Models in Process: A Rhetoric & Reader. William J. Kelly. 443p. (C). 1988. pap. text 30.00 (*0-02-363090-6*, Macmillan Coll) P-H.

Models in the Mind: Perspective, Theory & Application. Ed. by Yvonne Rogers et al. (Computers & People Ser.). (Illus.). 330p. 1992. text 79.95 (*0-12-592970-6*) Acad Pr.

***Models in the Mind: The History of Human Consciousness.** Earle Wallingford. 124p. 1999. pap. 12.95 (*0-7414-0197-5*) Buy Books.

Models Manual. Arthur Elgort. 1994. 35.00 (*0-9639236-0-9*) Grand St Pr.

Models, Methods, & Analytical Procedures in Education Research. Joseph E. Hill & August Kerber. LC 66-21030. 565p. reprint ed. pap. 175.20 (*0-7837-3660-6*, 204353100009) Bks Demand.

Models, Methods, & Applications of Econometrics: Essays in Honor of A. R. Bergstrom. Ed. by Peter C. Phillips. LC 92-27177. 1992. 87.95 (*1-55786-110-2*) Blackwell Pubs.

Models Move on to Starring Roles. C. Rayban. mass mkt. 8.95 (*0-340-71428-X*, Pub. by Hodder & Stought Ltd) Trafalgar.

Models of Achievement Vol. 2: Reflections of Eminent Women in Psychology. Nancy F. Russo & Agnes N. O'Connell. 400p. (C). 1988. 79.95 (*0-8058-0083-2*); pap. text 39.95 (*0-8058-0322-X*) L Erlbaum Assocs.

Models of Action: Mechanisms for Adaptive Behavior. Ed. by Clive D. Wynne & John E. Staddon. LC 97-32852. 300p. 1997. write for info. (*0-8058-1597-X*); pap. write for info. (*0-8058-1598-8*) L Erlbaum Assocs.

Models of Adaptive Behaviour: An Approach Based on State. Alasdair I. Houston & John M. McNamara. (Illus.). 375p. (C). 1999. text 80.00 (*0-521-38480-X*); pap. text 34.95 (*0-521-65539-0*) Cambridge U Pr.

Models of Addiction. Ed. by Don C. Fowles. (Special Issue, Journal of Abnormal Psychology Ser.: Vol. 97, No. 2). 131p. 1988. pap. 16.00 (*1-55798-026-8*) Am Psychol.

Models of Adult Religious Education Practice. R. E. Wickett. LC 91-38071. 174p. (Orig.). 1992. pap. 21.95 (*0-89135-083-7*) Religious Educ.

Models of American Sailing Ships. rev. ed. Robert E. Peabody. Ed. by John Ratte. LC 94-78003. (Illus.). 116p. (Orig.). 1994. 18.00 (*1-879886-39-1*) Addison Gallery.

Models of Anaerobic Infection. Ed. by M. J. Hill. (New Perspectives in Clinical Microbiology Ser.). 1984. text 160.50 (*0-89838-688-8*) Kluwer Academic.

Models of Autonomy. Ed. by Yoram Dinstein. LC 81-11479. 303p. (C). 1982. 44.95 (*0-87855-435-1*) Transaction Pubs.

Models of Biological Pattern Formation. H. Meinhardt. 1982. text 125.00 (*0-12-488620-5*) Acad Pr.

Models of Biopolymers by Ring-Opening Polymerization. Ed. by Stanislaw Penczek. 384p. 1989. lib. bdg. 286.00 (*0-8493-5077-8*, QP801) CRC Pr.

Models of Black Theology: Issues in Class, Culture, & Gender. Julian Kunnie. LC 94-9169. 96p. (Orig.). (C). 1994. pap. 11.00 (*1-56338-088-9*) TPI PA.

Models of Bounded Rationality Vol. 3: Empirically Grounded Economic Reason. Herbert A. Simon. (Illus.). 479p. 1997. 55.00 (*0-262-19372-8*) MIT Pr.

Models of Brain Function. Ed. by Rodney M. Cotterill. (Illus.). 590p. (C). 1990. text 100.00 (*0-521-38503-2*) Cambridge U Pr.

Models of Brain Injury Rehabilitation. Ed. by Rodger L. Wood & Peter Eames. LC 88-39621. (Johns Hopkins Series in Contemporary Medicine & Public Health). (Illus.). 254p. 1989. reprint ed. pap. 78.80 (*0-608-07341-5*, 206756900009) Bks Demand.

Models of Brief Psychodynamic Therapy: A Comparative Approach. Stanley B. Messer & C. Seth Warren. LC 95-23628. 374p. 1995. lib. bdg. 39.95 (*1-57230-024-8*, 0024) Guilford Pubns.

Models of Brief Psychodynamic Therapy: A Comparative Approach. Stanley B. Messer & C. Seth Warren. 374p. 1998. pap. text 23.00 (*1-57230-340-9*) Guilford Pubns.

***Models of Capitalism: Growth & Stagnation in the Modern Era.** David Coates. LC 99-32965. 312p. 2000. text 69.95 (*0-7456-2058-2*, Pub. by Polity Pr); pap. text 29.95 (*0-7456-2059-0*, Pub. by Polity Pr) Blackwell Pubs.

***Models of Care: Case Studies in Healthcare Delivery Innovation.** Caren Heller. Ed. by E. Liza Greenberg. 188p. 1999. 195.00 (*1-930104-03-0*) U R A C.

Models of Casuality in Psychopathology: Toward Dynamic, Synthetic & Nonlinear Models of Behavior Disorders. Haynes. 1995. pap. text 30.95 (*0-205-16485-4*, H6485-0) Allyn.

Models of Change in Municipal Parks & Recreation: A Book of Innovative Case Studies. Ed. by Mark E. Havitz. LC 95-60987. 190p. (C). 1995. 24.95 (*0-910251-77-0*, MOD81) Venture Pub PA.

Models of Cities & Regions: Theoretical & Empirical Developments. Ed. by Alan G. Wilson et al. LC 77-5338. 560p. reprint ed. pap. 173.60 (*0-608-15395-8*, 202926000059) Bks Demand.

Models of Classroom Management: Principles, Applications, & Critical Perspectives. 2nd ed. Jack Martin & Jeff Sugarman. 184p. (Orig.). (C). 1993. pap. text 19.95 (*1-55059-063-4*) Temeron Bks.

***Models of Cognitive Aging.** Ed. by Timothy J. Perfect & Elizabeth A. Maylor. LC 99-15924. (Debates in Psychology Ser.). (Illus.). 320p. 2000. pap. 34.95 (*0-19-852437-4*); text 85.00 (*0-19-852438-2*) OUP.

***Models of Cognitive Development.** Ken Richardson. 288p. 1998. 59.95 (*0-86377-852-6*, Pub. by Psychol Pr); pap. 29.95 (*0-86377-853-4*, Pub. by Psychol Pr) Taylor & Francis.

Models of Collaboration. Mary S. Fishbaugh. (C). 1997. pap., teacher ed. write for info. (*0-205-26517-0*, T6517-1) Allyn.

Models of Collaboration. Mary Susan Fishbaugh. LC 96-41881. 208p. 1997. pap. text 36.00 (*0-205-18441-3*) Allyn.

Models of Collaboration: A Guide for Mental Health Professionals Working with Physicians & Health Care Practitioners. David B. Seaburn et al. 304p. 1996. 35.00 (*0-465-09580-1*, Pub. by Basic) HarpC.

Models of Computation: Exploring the Power of Computing. John E. Savage. LC 97-24307. 600p. (C). 1997. 76.00 (*0-201-89539-0*) Addison-Wesley.

Models of Computation & Formal Languages. R. Gregory Taylor. LC 96-37454. (Illus.). 688p. (C). 1997. text 79.95 (*0-19-510983-X*) OUP.

Models of Confirmation & Baptismal Affirmation: Educational & Liturgical Designs. Robert L. Browning & Roy A. Reed. 266p. (Orig.). 1995. pap. 24.95 (*0-89135-097-7*) Religious Educ.

Models of Conflict Management in Cooperative Problem Solving: Papers from the 1994 Workshop. Ed. by Mark Klein & Susan Lander. (Technical Reports). (Illus.). 130p. 1994. spiral bd. 25.00 (*0-929280-74-1*) AAAI Pr.

Models of Contextual Theology: The Struggle for Cultural Relevance. Stephen B. Bevans. LC 92-19749. (Faith & Cultures Ser.). 180p. (Orig.). 1992. pap. 20.00 (*0-88344-814-9*) Orbis Bks.

Models of Curriculum-Based Assessment. 2nd ed. Ann I. Nevin et al. LC 86-17272. (Illus.). 264p. (Orig.). (C). 1996. pap. text 34.00 (*0-89079-629-7*, 7322) PRO-ED.

Models of Curriculum-Based Assessment: A Blueprint for Learning. 3rd ed. Lorna Idol et al. LC 98-28690. 1998. 34.00 (*0-89079-787-0*) PRO-ED.

Models of Databases. Marianne Winslett. (Tracts in Theoretical Computer Science Ser.: No. 9). 221p. (C). 1990. text 49.95 (*0-521-37371-9*) Cambridge U Pr.

Models of Democracy. David Held. LC 86-62423. 334p. 1987. 45.00 (*0-8047-1358-8*); pap. 16.95 (*0-8047-1359-6*) Stanford U Pr.

Models of Democracy. 2nd ed. David Held. LC 96-69090. 392p. 1997. pap. text 16.95 (*0-8047-2861-5*) Stanford U Pr.

Models of Depressive Disorders: Psychological, Biological & Genetic Perspectives. J. J. Mann. (Depressive Illness Ser.: Vol. 2). (Illus.). 198p. (C). 1989. text 49.50 (*0-306-43277-3*, Kluwer Plenum) Kluwer Academic.

Models of Desire: Rene Girard & the Psychology of Mimesis. Paisley Livingston. LC 91-39339. 232p. 1992. reprint ed. pap. 72.00 (*0-608-06724-5*, 206692100009) Bks Demand.

Models of Development: A Comparative Study of Economic Growth in South Korea & Taiwan. rev. ed. Ed. by Lawrence J. Lau. LC 89-32765. 217p. 1990. 24.95 (*1-55815-102-8*); pap. 19.95 (*1-55815-005-6*) ICS Pr.

Models of Disequilibrium & Shortage in the Centrally Planned Economies. Ed. by Christopher Davis & Wojciech W. Charemza. 350p. (C). (gr. 13). 1989. text 215.95 (*0-412-28420-0*) Chapman & Hall.

Models of Disordered Systems. Anil A. Kumar. (C). 1994. 53.40 (*0-13-674086-3*, Macmillan Coll) P-H.

Models of Early Childhood Education. Ann S. Epstein & Lawrence J. Schweinhart. 270p. 1996. pap. 25.95 (*0-929816-95-1*, R1039) High-Scope.

Models of Economic Growth with Environmental Assets. Andrea Beltratti. LC 96-14433. (Ecology, Economy & Environment Ser.: Vol. 8). 1996. lib. bdg. 92.50 (*0-7923-4032-9*) Kluwer Academic.

Models of Election Commissions in Africa: December, 1995. Laila N. Macharia. ii, 34p. 1996. pap. text 5.00 (*1-879720-05-1*) Intl Fndt Elect.

Models of Faith: Biblical Spirituality for Our Time. Carlos G. Valles. 176p. 1990. 9.95 (*0-8294-0707-3*) Loyola Pr.

Models of Family Therapy. Williams A. Griffan. LC 98-31347. 1998. pap. text 22.95 (*0-87630-886-8*) Brunner-Mazel.

Models of Family Therapy. Vimala Pillari. (C). 2000. 55.33 (*0-205-26217-1*, Macmillan Coll) P-H.

Models of Futures Markets. Ed. by Barry Goss. LC 99-36657. (Studies in the Modern World Economy: No. 18). 256p. (C). 1999. 90.00 (*0-415-18254-9*, D6225) Routledge.

Models of God: Theology for an Ecological, Nuclear Age. Sallie McFague. LC 86-46435. 240p. 1987. pap. 17.00 (*0-8006-2051-8*, 1-2051, Fortress Pr) Augsburg Fortress.

Models of Hadron Structure Based on Quantum Chromodynamics. Ed. by R. F. Alvarez-Estrada et al. (Lecture Notes in Physics Ser.: Vol. 259). vi, 294p. 1986. 40.95 (*0-387-16795-1*) Spr-Verlag.

Models of Hysteresis. Ed. by Augusto Visintin. LC 93-9356. (Pitman Research Notes in Mathematics Ser.: Vol. 286). 221p. 1993. pap. 49.95 (*0-582-20900-5*) Wiley.

***Models of Identities in Post Communist Societies: Yugoslav Philosophical Studies.** Ed. by Zagorka Golubovic & George F. McLean. LC 99-37507. (Cultural Heritages & Contemporary Change Ser. IVA: Central & Eastern Europe: Vol. 10). 310p. 1998. pap. 17.50 (*1-56518-127-1*) Coun Res Values.

Models of Imperfect Information in Politics, Vol. 6. Randall L. Calvert. (Fundamentals of Pure & Applied Economics Ser.: Volume 6). viii, 62p. 1986. pap. text 35.00 (*3-7186-0321-7*) Gordon & Breach.

Models of Income Determination. (Studies in Income & Wealth: No. 28). 439p. 1964. reprint ed. 114.20 (*0-87014-184-8*) Natl Bur Econ Res.

Models of Industrial Democracy: Consultation, Co-Determination & Workers Management. Charles D. King & Mark Van De Vall. (New Babylon Studies in the Social Sciences: No. 29). 1978. text 106.15 (*90-279-3008-2*) Mouton.

Models of Information Processing in the Basal Ganglia. Ed. by James C. Houk et al. LC 94-14822. (Computational Neuroscience Ser.). 394p. 1994. 60.00 (*0-262-08234-9*, Bradford Bks) MIT Pr.

Models of Inpatient Group Psychotherapy. Virginia Brabender & April Fallon. (Illus.). 716p. 1993. text 59.95 (*1-55798-174-4*) Am Psychol.

Models of Intra-Urban Relocation. Frank W. Porell. (Studies in Applied Regional Science). 1982. lib. bdg. 115.50 (*0-89838-089-8*) Kluwer Academic.

Models of Jesus Revisited. John F. O'Grady. LC 94-11962. 256p. 1994. pap. 14.95 (*0-8091-3474-8*) Paulist Pr.

***Models of Language Acquisition: Inductive & Deductive Approaches.** Ed. by Peter Broeder & Jaap Murre. (Illus.). 320p. 2000. text 85.00 (*0-19-824138-0*) OUP.

Models of Learning: Tools for Teaching. Joyce et al. LC 97-11356. 1997. pap. 29.95 (*0-335-19990-9*) OpUniv Pr.

Models of Learning, Memory & Choice: Selected Papers. Ed. by William K. Estes. LC 82-9823. 395p. 1982. 65.00 (*0-275-90786-4*, C0786, Praeger Pubs) Greenwood.

Models of Literacy Instruction. Terry S. Salinger. LC 92-31881. 304p. (C). 1992. pap. text 22.60 (*0-675-21328-2*, Merrill Coll) P-H.

***Models of Local Governance: Public Opinion & Political Theory in Britain.** William Lockley Miller et al. LC 00-33293. 2000. write for info. (*0-312-23772-3*) St Martin.

Models of Love: The Parent-Child Journey. Barry Vissell & Joyce Vissell. LC 86-60823. (Illus.). 193p. (Orig.). 1986. pap. 12.95 (*0-9612720-1-5*) Ramira Pub.

Models of Lung Disease: Microscopy & Structural Methods. Joan Gil. (Lung Biology in Health & Disease Ser.: Vol. 47). (Illus.). 1032p. 1990. text 265.00 (*0-8247-8096-5*) Dekker.

Models of Man: A Phenomenological Critique of Some Paradigms in the Human Sciences. J. J. Dagenais. 173p. 1972. pap. text 57.00 (*90-247-1290-4*, Pub. by M Nijhoff) Kluwer Academic.

Models of Man: Explorations in the Western Educational Tradition. Paul Nash. LC 83-8369. 484p. 1983. reprint ed. text 53.50 (*0-89874-634-5*) Krieger.

Models of Management: Work, Authority, & Organization in a Comparative Perspective. Mauro F. Guillen. LC 94-3887. 432p. 1994. pap. text 18.95 (*0-226-31036-1*) U Ch Pr.

Models of Management: Work, Authority, & Organization in a Comparative Perspective. Mauro F. Guillen. LC 94-3887. 432p. 1996. lib. bdg. 57.50 (*0-226-31035-3*) U Ch Pr.

Models of Massive Parallelism: Analysis of Cellular Automata & Neural Networks. Max Garzon. LC 95-18962. (Texts in Theoretical Computer Science; EATCS Monographs on Theoretical Computer Science). 272p. 1995. 49.50 (*0-387-56149-8*) Spr-Verlag.

Models of Matter: Principles & Perspectives of Chemistry. Gayl H. Wiegand. LC 94-34066. 608p. (C). 1995. mass mkt. 88.95 (*0-314-04573-2*) West Pub.

Models of Mental Disorders: A New Comparative Psychiatry. W. T. McKinney. LC 88-2335. (Illus.). 212p. (C). 1988. text 55.00 (*0-306-42746-X*, Kluwer Plenum) Kluwer Academic.

Models of Metaphilosophy. Archana Banerjee. (C). 1989. 22.50 (*81-85195-21-8*, Pub. by Minerva) S Asia.

Models of Misrepresentation: On the Fiction of E. L. Doctorow. Christopher Morris. LC 91-3730. 1991. text 35.00 (*0-87805-524-X*) U Pr of Miss.

***Models of Molecular Shapes.** 5th ed. James M. Postma et al. 2000. pap. text, lab manual ed. 1.95 (*0-7167-9430-6*) W H Freeman.

Models of Monetary Economies. Ed. by John H. Kareken & Neil Wallace. 313p. (Orig.). 1980. pap. 5.00 (*0-9603936-0-9*) FRB Minneapolis.

Models of Multiparty Electoral Competition, Vol. 45. Kenneth A. Shepsle. (Fundamentals of Pure & Applied Economics Ser.). iix, 100p. 1991. pap. text 58.00 (*3-7186-5076-2*, Harwood Acad Pubs) Gordon & Breach.

Models of Music Therapy Interventions in School Settings: From Institution to Inclusion. Ed. by Brian L. Wilson. 363p. (C). 1996. 45.00 (*1-884914-04-7*) Amer Music Therapy.

Models of My Life. Herbert A. Simon. LC 96-21495. (Illus.). 445p. 1996. pap. text 22.50 (*0-262-69185-X*) MIT Pr.

Models of Narrative. David Danow. LC 96-34402. 240p. 1996. text 39.95 (*0-312-16388-6*) St Martin.

Models of Nature: Ecology, Conservation, & Cultural Revolution in Soviet Russia. Douglas R. Weiner. LC 87-45370. (Indiana-Michigan Series in Russian & East European Studies). (Illus.). 480p. 1988. 36.95 (*0-253-33837-9*) Ind U Pr.

***Models of Nature: Ecology, Conservation, & Cultural Revolution in Soviet Russia.** Douglas R. Weiner. (Pitt Ser. in Russian & East European Studies). 312p. 2000. pap. 17.95 (*0-8229-5733-7*) U of Pittsburgh Pr.

Models of Neural Networks. Ed. by J. L. Van Hemmen et al. (Physics of Neural Networks Ser.). (Illus.). xvi, 345p. (C). 1992. reprint ed. 59.00 (*0-387-51109-1*) Spr-Verlag.

Models of Neural Networks. 2nd rev. ed. Ed. by J. L. Van Hemmen et al. LC 95-31850. (Physics of Neural Networks Ser.). (Illus.). 373p. 1995. 69.95 (*3-540-59403-5*) Spr-Verlag.

Models of Neural Networks III. Ed. by J. L. Van Hemmen et al. LC 95-14288. (Physics of Neural Networks Ser.). (Illus.). 344p. 1995. 59.95 (*0-387-94368-4*) Spr-Verlag.

Models of Neural Networks II: Temporal Aspects of Coding & Information Processing in Biological Systems. J. L. Van Hemmen. Ed. by Eytan Domany et al. LC 94-28645. (Physics of Neural Networks Ser.). 316p. 1995. 64.95 (*0-387-94362-5*) Spr-Verlag.

Models of Neuropeptide Action. Ed. by Fleur L. Strand. LC 94-37116. (Annals Ser.: Vol. 739). 1994. pap. 95.00 (*0-89766-912-6*) NY Acad Sci.

Models of Noncommunicable Diseases: Health Status & Health Service Requirements. Ed. by F. Gotthard Schettler et al. LC 92-2326. (Supplement zu den Sitzungsberichten der Mathematisch-Naturwissenschaftlichen Klasse Ser.: Vol. 1992). (Illus.). 196p. 1993. 22.00 (*3-540-55217-0*); 20.95 (*0-387-55217-0*) Spr-Verlag.

Models of Nursing in Practice: A Pattern for Practical Care. Paul McGee. (Illus.). 152p. 1998. pap. 22.95 (*0-7487-3343-4*, Pub. by S Thornes Pubs) Trans-Atl Phila.

Models of Oculomotor Behavior & Control. Ed. by B. L. Zuber. 304p. 1981. 170.00 (*0-8493-5679-2*, QP477, CRC Reprint) Franklin.

Models of Organization: The Application of Organization Theory. Manning Hanline. LC 93-84212. (Illus.). 524p. (C). 1994. text 47.50 (*0-9636647-1-9*) Matrix FL.

Models of Phase Transitions. Augusto Visintin. LC 96-45299. (Progress in Nonlinear Differential Equations & Their Applications Ser.). 250p. 1996. 74.50 (*0-8176-3768-0*) Birkhauser.

Models of Phase Transitions. Augusto Visintin. LC 96-45299. (Progress in Nonlinear Differential Equations & Their Applications Ser.). 1996. write for info. (*3-7643-3768-0*) Birkhauser.

Models of Political Participation of Hispanic-Americans. Marcelino Miyares. Ed. by Carlos E. Cortes. LC 79-6216. (Hispanics in the United States Ser.). (Illus.). 1981. lib. bdg. 21.95 (*0-405-13164-X*) Ayer.

Models of Population Movements in Central California Prehistory. Gary S. Breschini. (Illus.). x, 120p. (Orig.). 1983. pap. text 14.38 (*1-55567-010-5*) Coyote Press.

Models of Power: Politics & Economics in Zola's "Rougon-Macquart" David F. Bell. LC 87-10779. 207p. 1988. reprint ed. pap. 64.20 (*0-608-02140-7*, 206280900003) Bks Demand.

Models of Psychological Space. J. Eliot. LC 87-9770. (Illus.). 200p. 1987. 128.00 (*0-387-96549-1*) Spr-Verlag.

Models of Random Processes: A Handbook for Mathematicians & Engineers. I. N. Kovalenko et al. LC 96-14022. 448p. 1996. boxed set 104.95 (*0-8493-2870-5*) CRC Pr.

Models of Reality: Shaping Thought & Action. Ed. by Jacques G. Richardson. LC 83-80819. 328p. 1984. 32.95 (*0-912338-35-0*); fiche 15.00 (*0-912338-36-9*) Lomond.

M

Models of Regional Economies in Antiquity & the Middle Ages to the 11th Century: Proceedings of the 10th International Economic History Congress, Leuven, Belgium, August 1990. Ed. by E. Aerts et al. (Studies in Social & Economic History: No. 14). 95p. (Orig.). 1990. pap. 32.50 (*90-6186-386-4*, Pub. by Leuven Univ) Coronet Bks.

Models of Revelation. Avery Dulles. LC 82-45243. 1983. 16.95 (*0-385-17975-8*) Doubleday.

Models of Revelation. 2nd ed. Avery Dulles. LC 92-25800. 365p. 1992. reprint ed. pap. 17.50 (*0-88344-842-4*) Orbis Bks.

Models of River Basin Evolution: A Hydrogeomorphic Perspective. Gary Willgoose et al. 350p. 1998. 110.00 (*0-471-96274-0*) Wiley.

Models of Scientific Development & the Case of Nuclear Magnetic Resonance. Henk Zandvoort. (Synthese Library: No. 184). 304p. 1986. text 127.50 (*90-277-2351-6*) Kluwer Academic.

***Models of Sharing Graphs: A Categorical Semantics of Let & Letrec.** M. Hasegawa. LC 99-25290. (Illus.). xii, 140p. 1999. 79.95 (*1-85233-145-3*, Pub. by Spr-Verlag) Spr-Verlag.

Models of Spatial Processes: An Approach to the Study of Point, Line & Area Patterns. Arthur Getis. LC 75-17118. (Cambridge Geographical Studies: No. 8). 214p. reprint ed. pap. 61.00 (*0-608-12512-1*, 2024462) Bks Demand.

Models of Strategic Choice in Politics. Ed. by Peter C. Ordeshook. 392p. 1989. text 57.50 (*0-472-10122-6*, 10122) U of Mich Pr.

Models of Strategic Rationality. Reinhard Selten. (C). 1988. lib. bdg. 173.50 (*90-277-2663-9*) Kluwer Academic.

Models of Sustainable Development. Ed. by Sylvie Faucheux et al. LC 96-4779. (New Horizons in Environmental Economics Ser.). (Illus.). 384p. 1996. 95.00 (*1-85898-269-3*) E Elgar.

Models of Teaching. 6th ed. (C). 1999. write for info. (*0-205-31104-0*) S&S Trade.

***Models of Teaching.** 6th ed. Bruce R. Joyce & Marsha Weil. LC 99-35737. 540p. (C). 1999. 61.33 (*0-205-31038-9*) Allyn.

Models of Teaching: Instructor's Support Package. 5th ed. Bruce R. Joyce. (C). 1996. pap., teacher ed. write for info. (*0-205-26542-1*, T6542-9) Allyn.

Models of the Atmosphere & Ionosphere: Proceedings of Workshops VIII & X of the COSPAR 25th Plenary Meeting held in Graz, Austria, 25 June-7 July 1984. Ed. by Karl Rawer et al. (Illus.). 242p. 1985. pap. 54.00 (*0-08-033196-3*, Pub. by PPL) Elsevier.

Models of the Church. Avery Dulles. LC 77-11246. 256p. 1991. reprint ed. pap. 11.95 (*0-385-13368-5*, Image Bks) Doubleday.

Models of the History of Philosophy Vol. I: From Its Origins in the Renaissance to the Historia Philosophica. Ed. by Giovanni Santinello. LC 93-16502. (Archives Internationales d'Histoire des Idees (International Archives of the History of Ideas) Ser.: Vol. 135).Tr. of Storia della Storie Generali della Filosofia. 536p. (C). 1993. lib. bdg. 264.50 (*0-7923-2200-2*, Pub. by Kluwer Academic) Kluwer Academic.

Models of the Kingdom. Howard Snyder. 1991. pap. 5.18 (*0-687-27104-5*) Abingdon.

Models of the Mind: A Psychoanalytic Theory. John E. Gedo & Arnold I. Goldberg. LC 73-77132. 236p. 1976. pap. text 16.95 (*0-226-28487-5*, P695) U Ch Pr.

Models of the Mind: Their Relationship to Clinical Work. Ed. by Arnold Rothstein. LC 85-10844. (Monograph 1 of the American Psychoanalytic Association Ser.). x, 160p. 1985. 27.50 (*0-8236-3410-8*) Intl Univs Pr.

Models of the Oil Market, Vol. 44. Jacques Cremer. (Fundamentals of Pure & Applied Economics Ser.). ix, 106p. 1991. pap. text 62.00 (*3-7186-5072-X*, Harwood Acad Pubs) Gordon & Breach.

***Models of the Self.** Shaun Gallagher. (Consciousness Studies). 1999. 38.95 (*0-907845-40-1*, Pub. by Imprint Acad) Philos Document.

***Models of the Self.** Shaun Gallagher. 544p. 2000. pap. 29.50 (*0-907845-09-6*, Pub. by Imprint Acad) Philos Document.

Models of the U. K. Economy: A Fourth Review by the ESRC Macroeconomic Modelling Bureau. Ed. by K. F. Wallis et al. 168p. 1988. 55.00 (*0-19-828633-3*) OUP.

Models of the Universe: An Anthology of the Prose Poem. Ed. by Stuart Friebert & David Young. LC 94-67564. 425p. (Orig.). 1995. pap. 25.00 (*0-932440-69-X*) Oberlin Coll Pr.

Models of the Visual Cortex. Ed. by David Rose & Vernon G. Dobson. LC 84-29143. (Illus.). 608p. 1985. reprint ed. pap. 188.50 (*0-7837-8873-8*, 204958400001) Bks Demand.

Models of Understanding Text. Ed. by Bruce K. Britton & Arthur C. Graesser. (Publication of the Cognitive Studies Group of the Institute for Behavioral Research at the University of Georgia). 376p. 1995. text 79.95 (*0-8058-1848-0*) L Erlbaum Assocs.

Models of Understanding Text. Ed. by Bruce K. Britton & Arthur C. Graesser. (Publication of the Cognitive Studies Group & the Institute for Behavioral Research at the University of Georgia). 376p. 1996. pap. 36.00 (*0-8058-1849-9*) L Erlbaum Assocs.

Models of Value: Eighteenth-Century Political Economy & the Novel. James Thompson. LC 95-600. 280p. 1996. text 49.95 (*0-8223-1711-7*); pap. text 17.95 (*0-8223-1721-4*) Duke.

Models of Vegetation Canopy Reflectance & Their Use in Estimation of Biophysical Parameters from Reflectance Data, Vol. 4. Narendra S. Goel. (Remote Sensing Reviews Ser.: Vol. 4, No. 1). 222p. 1988. pap. text 90.00 (*3-7186-4824-5*) Gordon & Breach.

Models of Visual-Spatial Cognition. Ed. by Manuel De Vega & Mark Marscharck. (Illus.). 240p. (C). 1996. text 55.00 (*0-19-510084-0*); pap. text 30.00 (*0-19-510085-9*) OUP.

Models of Working Memory: Mechanisms of Active Maintenance & Exectuive Control. Ed. by Akira Miyake & Priti Shah. LC 98-35134. (Illus.). 496p. (C). 1999. text 69.95 (*0-521-58325-X*); pap. text 29.95 (*0-521-58721-2*) Cambridge U Pr.

Models of Workplace Training: Lessons from the Employees Retraining Scheme in Hong Kong. Jackqueline T. Cheung & Kwong-Leung Tang. LC 97-29034. (Studies in Business: Vol. 9). 152p. 1997. text 69.95 (*0-7734-8544-9*) E Mellen.

Models One: Screen Kiss. C. Rayban. (Illus.). mass mkt. 7.95 (*0-340-68162-4*, Pub. by Hodder & Stought Ltd) Trafalgar.

Model's Primer. 3rd rev. ed. M. J. Wilson & Apryl Edwards. Orig. Title: A Model's Primer - Seven Steps to Get Started. 68p. 2000. spiral bd. 12.95 (*0-9659170-0-2*) Adv Multimed Designs.

Model's Primer - Seven Steps to Get Started see Model's Primer

Models That Work: Case Studies in Effective Undergraduate Mathematics Programs. Ed. by Alan C. Tucker. LC 95-81493. (MAA Notes Ser.: No. 38). 112p. (Orig.). 1995. pap. text 24.00 (*0-88385-096-6*, NTE-38) Math Assn.

Models, Theories, & Concepts. James P. Smith. LC 93-49560. (Advanced Nursing Ser.). (Illus.). 192p. 1994. pap. 24.95 (*0-632-03865-9*, Pub. by Blckwll Scitfc UK) Blackwell Sci.

Modem Handbook for the Communications Professional. Cass R. Lewart. 320p. 1987. 40.25 (*0-444-01279-6*) P-H.

Modem Love: Step-by-Step Guide to Sex on the Information Highway. Don J. Rexxxxx. 1995. pap. 12.00 (*0-8217-4921-8*, Zebra Kensgtn) Kensgtn Pub Corp.

Modem Markets: Survival of the Fastest. Market Intelligence Staff. 265p. 1992. 1495.00 (*1-56753-388-4*) Frost & Sullivan.

Modem Reference: The Complete Guide to PC Communications. 4th ed. Michael A. Banks. (C). 2000. pap. 29.95 (*0-910965-36-6*) Info Today Inc.

Modem Technical Guide. Mike Tribble. LC 98-131559. (Illus.). 638p. (Orig.). 1996. pap. 49.95 (*1-880252-29-5*) Micro Hse.

Modems & Communications on IBM PCs. W. David Schwaderer. LC 86-11101. (IBM Personal Computer Ser.). 355p. 1986. pap. 21.95 (*0-471-84459-4*) Wiley.

Modems for Dummies. Tina Rathbone. (Illus.). 400p. 1993. pap. 19.95 (*1-56884-001-2*) IDG Bks.

Modems for Dummies. 2nd ed. Tina Rathbone. LC 94-79833. 512p. 1994. pap. 19.99 (*1-56884-223-6*) IDG Bks.

Modems for Dummies. 3rd ed. Andy Rathbone & Tina Rathbone. LC 96-78141. (Illus.). 512p. 1997. pap. 19.99 (*0-7645-0069-4*) IDG Bks.

Modems, Megabytes & Me! Telecommunicating Across the Curriculum Activities for Grades K-8. Gary Garfield & Suzanne McDonough. (Illus.). 99p. (J). (gr. k-8). 1995. pap., teacher ed. 16.00 (*1-895411-78-5*) Peguis Pubs Ltd.

Modena, Biblioteca Estense e Univesitaria, MS Alpha F.9.9. Ed. by Howard Mayer Brown et al. (Renaissance Music in Facsimile Ser.). 200p. 1987. text 30.00 (*0-8240-1462-6*) Garland.

Modena Racing Memories: Italian Sports Car & Grand Prix Racing, 1957-1963. Graham Gauld. LC 99-24143. (Illus.). 148p. 1999. text 39.95 (*0-7603-0735-0*, Pub. by MBI Pubg) Motorbooks Intl.

Moderate & Formal Cohomology Associated with Constructible Sheaves. Masaki Kashiwara & Pierre Schapira. 76p. 1996. pap. 20.00 (*2-85629-050-7*) Am Math.

Moderate & Radical Islamic Fundamentalism: The Quest for Modernity, Legitimacy, & the Islamic State. Ahmad S. Moussalli. LC 98-36151. 1999. 50.00 (*0-8130-1658-4*) U Press Fla.

Moderate Drinking: The Moderation Management Guide for People Who Want to Reduce Their Drinking. Audrey Kischline. 192p. 1995. pap. 14.00 (*0-517-88656-1*) Crown Pub Group.

Moderate Inflation: The Experience of Transition Economies. Carlo Cottarelli et al. LC 98-24879. 1998. write for info. (*1-55775-699-6*) Intl Monetary.

Moderate Realism & Its Logic. D. W. Mertz. LC 95-44390. 310p. 1996. 40.00 (*0-300-06561-2*) Yale U Pr.

***Moderately Proteinuric IgA Nephropathy in the Young.** Ed. by R. Coppo & L. Peruzzi. (Biomedical & Health Research Ser.: Vol. 44). 100p. 2000. 74.00 (*1-58603-059-0*) IOS Press.

Moderates & Conservatives in West Europe. Morgan & Silv. 1982. text 72.95 (*0-435-83615-3*) Ashgate Pub Co.

Moderates & Conservatives in Western Europe. Roger Morgan & Stefano Silvestri. LC 83-5662. 288p. 1983. 37.50 (*0-8386-3201-7*) Fairleigh Dickinson.

Moderates' Dilemma: Massive Resistance to School Desegregation in Virginia. Ed. by Matthew D. Lassiter & Andrew B. Lewis. LC 98-13877. 304p. 1998. pap. 18.50 (*0-8139-1817-0*); text 49.50 (*0-8139-1816-2*) U Pr of Va.

***Moderating Focus Groups.** Thomas L. Greenbaum. LC 99-6959. 2000. write for info. (*0-7619-2044-7*) Sage.

Moderating Focus Groups. Richard A. Krueger. (Focus Group Kit Ser.: Vol. 4). 136p. 1997. pap. 17.95 (*0-7619-0821-8*) Sage.

Moderation As a Goal or Outcome of Treatment for Alcohol Problems: A Dialogue. Ed. by Mark B. Sobell & Linda C. Sobell. LC 87-7443. (Drugs & Society Ser.: Vol. 1, Nos. 2-3). 127p. 1987. text 39.95 (*0-86656-669-4*) Haworth Pr.

Moderation Diet: Cooking Great, Looking Great, Feeling Great. Renny Darling. 1990. pap. 17.95 (*0-930440-30-7*) Royal Hse.

Moderato Cantabile. Marguerite Duras. 1958. pap. 8.95 (*0-685-11399-X*) Fr & Eur.

Moderato Cantabile. Marguerite Duras. (FRE.). 112p. 1980. pap. write for info. (*0-7859-4725-6*) Fr & Eur.

Moderato Cantabile. Marguerite Duras. (FRE.). (C). pap. 13.95 (*0-8442-1975-4*, VF1975-4) NTC Contemp Pub Co.

Moderators of Competence. Ed. by Edith D. Neimark et al. (Jean Piaget Symposia Ser.). 240p. (C). 1985. text 49.95 (*0-89859-531-2*) L Erlbaum Assocs.

Modern: Masters of the 20th-Century Interior. Jonathan Glancey. (Illus.). 176p. 1999. 50.00 (*0-8478-2211-7*, Pub. by Rizzoli Intl) St Martin.

Modern - Impressionist Painting, Vol. 1. Fernando Lozano. (Illus.). 64p. 1991. 32.00 (*1-56721-009-0*) Twnty-Fifth Cent Pr.

Modern - Impressionist Painting, Vol. 2. Fernando Lozano. (Illus.). 64p. 1991. 32.00 (*1-56721-010-4*) Twnty-Fifth Cent Pr.

Modern - Impressionist Painting, Vol. 3. Fernando Lozano. (Illus.). 64p. 1991. 32.00 (*1-56721-011-2*) Twnty-Fifth Cent Pr.

Modern - Impressionist Painting, Vol. 4. Fernando Lozano. (Illus.). 64p. 1991. 32.00 (*1-56721-012-0*) Twnty-Fifth Cent Pr.

Modern - Postmodern: A Study in Twentieth-Century Arts & Ideas. Silvio Gaggi. LC 88-33786. (Pennsylvania Studies in Contemporary American Fiction). (Illus.). 218p. (Orig.). (C). 1989. pap. text 16.95 (*0-8122-1384-X*) U of Pa Pr.

Modern Abstract Algebra, 2 vols., Set. Y. Chow. 782p. 1976. text 552.00 (*0-677-03880-1*) Gordon & Breach.

Modern Academic Library: Essays in Memory of Philip Larkin. Ed. by Brian Dyson. LC 89-117023. 177p. reprint ed. pap. 54.90 (*0-608-08883-8*, 206952000004) Bks Demand.

Modern Acarology: Proceedings of the 8th International Congress of Acarology, Held in Ceske Budejovice, Czechoslovakia, 6-11 August 1990, 2 vols., Set. Ed. by F. Dusabek & V. Bukva. (Illus.). 1572p. 1991. 190.00 (*90-5103-054-1*, Pub. by SPB Acad Pub) Balogh.

Modern Accident Investigation & Analysis. 2nd ed. Ted S. Ferry. LC 87-34027. 336p. 1988. 140.00 (*0-471-62481-0*) Wiley.

Modern Accounting: Its Principles & Some of Its Problems. Henry R. Hatfield. LC 75-18472. (History of Accounting Ser.). (Illus.). 1979. 29.95 (*0-405-07554-5*) Ayer.

Modern Accounting & Auditing Checklists. rev. ed. Paul J. Wendell. 1200p. 1991. 155.00 (*0-88712-624-3*); suppl. ed. 51.50 (*0-7913-0877-4*); suppl. ed. 50.50 (*0-685-17420-4*) Warren Gorham & Lamont.

Modern Accounting 1. John Kerrigan. 1990. 65.00 (*1-872810-01-2*, Pub. by J Margers Ltd) St Mut.

Modern Accounting, Tax & Law English-Japanese-English Dictionary. 519p. 1986. 95.00 (*0-8288-0115-0*, F 81650) Fr & Eur.

Modern Accounting II. John Kerrigan. 1993. 65.00 (*1-872810-02-0*, Pub. by J Margers Ltd) St Mut.

Modern Acoustic Guitar Construction. R. J. Gluck. 100p. pap. 24.95 (*1-882731-01-8*) Cactus Pub.

Modern Acting: A Manual. Sophie Rosenstein et al. 1936. 5.00 (*0-573-69017-0*) French.

Modern Actuarial Theory & Practice. Ed. by P. H. Booth et al. LC 98-46642. 716p. 1999. 79.95 (*0-8493-0388-5*) CRC Pr.

Modern Advanced Accounting. 6th ed. E. John Larsen. LC 93-27419. (C). 1994. text 70.25 (*0-07-036595-4*) McGraw.

Modern Advanced Accounting. 7th ed. E. John Larsen. (C). 1996. pap., student ed. 31.88 (*0-07-036714-0*); text 97.75 (*0-07-036710-8*) McGraw.

***Modern Advanced Accounting.** 8th ed. Larsen. LC 98-55220. 912p. 1999. 90.31 (*0-07-029991-9*) McGraw.

Modern Advanced Accounting: Working Papers. 7th ed. E. John Larsen. (C). 1996. pap. text 32.81 (*0-07-036715-9*) McGraw.

Modern Aerodynamic Flutter Analysis. 2nd ed. Martin Hollmann. (Illus.). 168p. 1991. pap. text 39.90 (*1-893639-09-6*) Air Designs.

Modern Aesthetics see History of Aesthetics

Modern Africa. 2nd ed. Basil Risbridger Davidson. LC 82-14941. (Illus.). 289p. (C). 1989. pap. text 17.50 (*0-582-01900-1*, 78284) Longman.

Modern Africa. 3rd ed. Basil Risbridger Davidson. LC 93-3815. 320p. (C). 1995. pap. text 31.88 (*0-582-21288-X*, 76250, Pub. by Addison-Wesley) Longman.

Modern African American Writers. Matthew J. Bruccoli & Judith S. Baughman. LC 93-8643. (Essential Bibliography of American Fiction Ser.). 96p. 1994. pap. 9.95 (*0-8160-2999-7*) Facts on File.

Modern African American Writers. Ed. by Matthew J. Bruccoli & Judith S. Baughman. LC 93-8643. (Essential Bibliography of American Fiction Ser.). 112p. 1994. 19.95 (*0-8160-2998-9*) Facts on File.

Modern African History: Some Historiographical Observations. Tore L. Eriksen. (Research Report Ser.: No. 55). 27p. 1979. write for info. (*91-7106-167-3*, Pub. by Nordic Africa) Transaction Pubs.

Modern African Political Leaders. R. Kent Rasmussen. LC 97-31162. (Global Profiles Ser.). (Illus.). 130p. (J). (gr. 5-12). 1998. 19.95 (*0-8160-3277-7*) Facts on File.

Modern African Wars Vol. 2: Angola & Mocambique, 1961-74. Peter Abbott & M. R. Rodrigues. (Men-at-Arms Ser.: No. 202). (Illus.). 48p. pap. 11.95 (*0-85045-843-9*, 9135, Pub. by Ospry) Stackpole.

Modern African Wars Vol. 3: Southwest Africa. Romer Helmoed. (Men-at-Arms Ser.: No. 242). (Illus.). 48p. pap. 11.95 (*1-85532-122-X*, 9201, Pub. by Ospry) Stackpole.

Modern African Writers: Nadine Gordimer. Michael Wade. 232p. 1978. 35.00 (*0-237-49978-9*) St Mut.

Modern Age. Neil King. (Drama Ser.). 128p. 1985. pap. 13.95 (*0-7175-1236-3*) Dufour.

Modern Age: The First Twenty-Five Years: a Selection. Ed. by George A. Panichas. LC 88-8600. 914p. (C). 1988. text 17.50 (*0-86597-061-0*) Liberty Fund.

Modern Age: The First Twenty-Five Years: A Selection. Ed. by George A. Panichas. LC 88-8600. 914p. (C). 1988. pap. 8.50 (*0-86597-062-9*) Liberty Fund.

Modern Age & the Recovery of Ancient Wisdom: A Reconsideration of Historical Consciousness, 1450-1650. Stephen A. McKnight. (Illus.). 176p. 1991. text 29.95 (*0-8262-0781-2*) U of Mo Pr.

Modern Age Books: A Checklist. C. P. Stephens. 1992. pap. 4.95 (*0-89366-173-2*) Ultramarine Pub.

Modern Age, 1890 to 1960 see New Oxford History of Music

Modern Ages. Contrib. by Larry Lukas. 12p. (Orig.). 1996. pap. text 6.95 (*1-889416-04-5*, LS40005) Lukasound.

Modern Agitators. David M. Bartlett. LC 70-133146. (Black Heritage Library Collection). 1977. 28.95 (*0-8369-8702-0*) Ayer.

Modern Agriculture: Science, Finance, Production & Economics. D. Porter Price et al. (Illus.). 361p. 1989. pap., teacher ed. 27.95 (*0-9606246-7-8*); pap., student ed. 14.95 (*0-9606246-8-6*); lib. bdg. 34.50 (*0-9606246-6-X*) SWI.

Modern Agriculture & the Environment: Proceedings of an International Conference, Rehovot, Israel, October 2-6, 1994. Universi Tah Ha-Ivrit Bi-Yerushalayim Staff. Ed. by David Rosen. LC 96-36626. (Developments in Plant & Soil Sciences Ser.). 672p. (C). 1997. text 301.00 (*0-7923-4295-X*) Kluwer Academic.

***Modern Ailments, Ancient Remedies.** Gillian Kerr & Yvonne Bloomfield. LC 99-17080. 160p. 1999. 12.98 (*0-7651-1681-2*) Smithmark.

Modern Air Conditioning Practice. 3rd ed. Norman C. Harris. 464p. 1983. text 84.95 (*0-07-026833-9*) McGraw.

Modern Air Transport: Worldwide Air Transport from 1945 to the Present. Ed. by Philip Jarrett. (Putnam's History of Aircraft Ser.). 2000. 58.95 (*0-85177-877-1*, Pub. by B T B) Bks Intl VA.

Modern Aircraft Design, Vol. 1. 4th ed. Martin Hollmann. (Illus.). 236p. 1986. pap. text 69.00 (*1-893639-00-2*) Air Designs.

Modern Aircraft Design, Vol. 2. 4th ed. Martin Hollmann. (Illus.). 143p. 1987. pap. text 52.00 (*1-893639-01-0*) Air Designs.

Modern Aircraft Drafting. Martin Hollmann. (Illus.). 128p. 1992. pap. text 39.00 (*1-893639-04-5*) Air Designs.

Modern Aircraft Flight Control. M. Vukobratovic & R. Stojic. (Lecture Notes in Control & Information Sciences: Vol. 109). (Illus.). viii, 288p. 1988. 61.95 (*0-387-19119-4*) Spr-Verlag.

Modern Airliner. 2nd ed. Peter W. Brooks. (Illus.). 194p. 1982. 18.50 (*0-89745-011-6*); pap. text 12.00 (*0-89745-028-0*) Sunflower U Pr.

Modern Alchemist: A Guide to Personal Transformation. Richard Miller & Iona Miller. (Illus.). 300p. (Orig.). 1994. pap. 14.95 (*0-933999-37-2*) Phanes Pr.

Modern Alchemy: Selected Papers of Glenn T. Seaborg. Glenn Theodore Seaborg. (Twentieth Century Chemistry Ser.). 720p. 1994. text 99.00 (*981-02-1440-5*) World Scientific Pub.

Modern Algebra. Frank Ayres, Jr. (Schaum's Outline Ser.). 256p. (Orig.). (C). 1965. pap. 14.95 (*0-07-002655-6*) McGraw.

Modern Algebra. Seth Warner. (Illus.). 832p. 1990. pap. 18.95 (*0-486-66341-8*) Dover.

Modern Algebra: A Conceptual Approach. Franklin D. Pedersen. 224p. (C). 1992. text 53.75 (*0-697-11926-2*, WCB McGr Hill) McGrw-H Hghr Educ.

Modern Algebra: An Introduction. 3rd ed. John R. Durbin. LC 91-21511. 368p. (C). 1991. text 89.95 (*0-471-51001-7*) Wiley.

Modern Algebra: An Introduction. 4th ed. John R. Durbin. LC 99-13830. 328p. 1999. text 92.95 (*0-471-32147-8*) Wiley.

Modern Algebra & the Rise of Mathematical Structures. Leo Corry. LC 96-3974. (Science Networks, Historical Studies: Vol. 17). 460p. 1996. 139.00 (*0-8176-5311-2*) Birkhauser.

Modern Algebra & the Rise of Mathematical Structures, Vol. 17. Ed. by E. Hiebert & H. Wussing. 480p. 1996. 139.00 (*3-7643-5311-2*) Spr-Verlag.

Modern Algebra for Biologists. Howard M. Nahikian. LC 64-13948. 248p. reprint ed. 76.90 (*0-8357-9650-7*, 201576000097) Bks Demand.

Modern Algebra with Applications. William J. Gilbert. 368p. 1976. 150.00 (*0-471-29891-3*) Wiley.

Modern Algebra&Discr Struct 91. Anneli Lax. 384p. (C). 1997. 95.00 (*0-06-043878-9*) Addson-Wesley Educ.

Modern Algeria: A History from 1830 to the Present. Charles-Robert Ageron. LC 91-72492. 294p. 1992. 45.00 (*0-86543-266-X*); pap. 12.95 (*0-86543-267-8*) Africa World.

Modern Algeria: The Origins & Development of a Nation. John Ruedy. LC 92-4637. 320p. 1992. pap. 17.95 (*0-253-20746-0*, MB-746) Ind U Pr.

Modern Allegories of William Golding. L. L. Dickson. 160p. 1990. 49.95 (*0-8130-0971-5*) U Press Fla.

An Asterisk (*) at the beginning of an entry indicates that the title is appearing for the first time.

Modern Alphabets: 100 Complete Fonts. Dan X. Solo. 112p. 1999. pap. text 8.95 (*0-486-40710-1*) Dover.

Modern Amateur Astronomer. Patrick Moore. (Practical Astronomy Ser.). (Illus.). 176p. 1995. 24.95 (*0-387-19900-4*) Spr-Verlag.

Modern Amateur Astronomer. Ed. by Patrick Moore. (Practical Astronomy Ser.). 1995. pap. 24.95 (*3-540-19900-4*) Spr-Verlag.

Modern Amateurs Mobile Handbook. Dave Ingram. (Illus.). 155p. 1990. pap. 12.95 (*1-891237-14-4*, MFJ-33) MFJ Ent.

Modern Ambassador: The Challenge & the Search. Ed. by Martin F. Herz. LC 83-12853. 216p. (Orig.). (C). 1983. pap. text 12.00 (*0-934742-25-1*) Geo U Inst Dplmcy.

Modern America. Chris Macdonald & John Nichol. (Key History for GCSE Ser.). (Illus.). 96p. 1996. pap. 19.95 (*0-7487-2597-0*, Pub. by S Thornes Pubs) Trans-Atl Phila.

Modern America, 1914 to 1945. Ross Gregory. Ed. by Richard Balkin. (Almanacs of American Life Ser.). (Illus.). 464p. 1995. 75.00 (*0-8160-2532-0*) Facts on File.

Modern America Takes Shape see U. S. History

Modern American Capitalism: Understanding Public Attitudes & Perceptions. Robert A. Peterson et al. LC 90-42966. 144p. 1990. 55.00 (*0-89930-625-X*, PMJ/, Quorum Bks) Greenwood.

Modern American Critics, 1920-1955. Ed. by Gregory S. Jay. (Dictionary of Literary Biography Ser.: Vol. 63). 384p. 1987. text 155.00 (*0-8103-1741-9*, 006531-M99348) Gale.

Modern American Critics since 1955. Ed. by Gregory S. Jay. (Dictionary of Literary Biography Ser.: Vol. 67). 397p. 1988. text 155.00 (*0-8103-1745-1*) Gale.

Modern American Culture: An Introduction. Ed. by Mick Gidley. LC 92-28394. 448p. (C). 1993. text 83.75 (*0-582-05111-8*, 79649) Longman.

Modern American Culture: An Introduction. Ed. by Mick Gidley. LC 92-28394. 448p. (C). 1994. pap. text 29.95, (*0-582-05110-X*, 79648) Longman.

Modern American Diplomacy. rev. ed. Ed. by John M. Carroll & George C. Herring. LC 95-8681. (Illus.). 293p. 1995. pap. 17.95 (*0-8420-2555-3*); text 45.00 (*0-8420-2554-5*) Scholarly Res Inc.

Modern American Drama: The Female Canon. Ed. by June Schleuter. LC 89-45579. 312p. 1996. pap. 19.95 (*0-8386-3707-8*) Fairleigh Dickinson.

Modern American Drama: The Female Canon. Ed. by June Schlueter. LC 89-45579. 312p. 1990. 42.50 (*0-8386-3387-0*) Fairleigh Dickinson.

Modern American Drama: Williams, Miller, Albee, & Shepard. Ed. by Dorothy R. Parker. 1987. pap. 17.95 (*0-8020-3434-9*) U of Toronto Pr.

***Modern American Drama, 1945 - 2000.** C. W. E. Bigsby. 372p. 2000. write for info. (*0-521-79089-1*); pap. write for info. (*0-521-79410-2*) Cambridge U Pr.

Modern American Drama, 1945-1990. Christopher W. Bigsby. 372p. (C). 1992. pap. text 22.95 (*0-521-42667-7*) Cambridge U Pr.

Modern American Dwellings, 1897. Donald J. Berg. (Yesterday's Home Ser.). (Illus.). 96p. (Orig.). 1984. reprint ed. pap. 9.00 (*0-937214-09-4*) Antiquity Re.

Modern American English, 2 bks. Robert J. Dixson. (YA). (gr. 7-12). 1987. audio 100.00 (*0-13-543190-5*) Prentice ESL.

Modern American English, Bk. 1. Lolita Dixson. (C). 1991. pap. text, teacher ed. 24.40 (*0-13-593922-4*) P-H.

Modern American English, Bk. 1. Robert J. Dixson. 160p. (C). 1991. pap. 15.73 (*0-13-593914-3*) P-H.

Modern American English, Bk. 2. Lolita Dixson & Eugene Hall. (C). 1991. pap. text, teacher ed. 24.40 (*0-13-593963-1*) P-H.

Modern American English, Bk. 2. Robert J. Dixson. 160p. (C). 1991. pap. 15.73 (*0-13-593955-0*) P-H.

Modern American English, Bk. 2. Robert J. Dixson. (C). 1991. pap. text, student ed., wbk. ed. 10.40 (*0-13-593971-2*) P-H.

Modern American English, Bk. 3. Robert J. Dixson. 160p. (C). 1991. pap. 15.73 (*0-13-593997-6*) P-H.

Modern American English, Bk. 3. Robert J. Dixson. (C). 1991. pap. text, student ed., wbk. ed. 10.40 (*0-13-594045-1*) P-H.

Modern American English, Bk. 4. Lolita Dixson & Eugene Hall. (C). 1992. pap. text, teacher ed. 24.40 (*0-13-594078-8*) P-H.

Modern American English, Bk. 4. Robert J. Dixson. 160p. (C). 1992. pap. 15.73 (*0-13-594060-5*) P-H.

Modern American English, Bk. 5. 4th ed. Lolita Dixson & Eugene Hall. (C). 1992. pap. text, teacher ed. 24.40 (*0-13-594128-8*) P-H.

Modern American English, Bk. 5. 4th ed. Robert J. Dixson. 160p. (C). 1992. pap. 15.73 (*0-13-594110-5*) P-H.

Modern American English, Bk. 6. Lolita Dixson & Eugene Hall. (C). 1992. pap. text, teacher ed. 24.40 (*0-13-595372-3*) P-H.

Modern American English, Bk. 6. Robert J. Dixson. 160p. (C). 1992. pap. 15.73 (*0-13-595364-2*) P-H.

Modern American English, Bk. 6. Robert J. Dixson. (Illus.). 167p. (YA). (gr. 9-12). 1987. student ed. 4.25 (*0-88345-320-7*, 18731) Prentice ESL.

Modern American English, Vol. 1. Dixson. 1991. pap. text, wbk. ed. 10.40 (*0-13-593930-5*) P-H.

Modern American English, Vol. 3. Lolita Dixson & Eugene Hall. 1992. pap. text, teacher ed. 18.40 (*0-13-594029-X*) P-H.

Modern American English Grammar. Shiang-Chuan Jih. 526p. (C). 1993. pap. text 25.00 (*0-9639219-3-2*) J Shiang-Chuan.

Modern American English Skillbooks, Bk. 1. Robert J. Dixson. (Modern American English Ser.). (gr. 7 up). 1974. 1.25 (*0-88345-233-2*) Prentice ESL.

Modern American English Skillbooks, Bk. 2. Robert J. Dixson. (Modern American English Ser.). (gr. 7 up). 1974. 1.25 (*0-88345-234-0*) Prentice ESL.

Modern American English Skillbooks, Bk. 4. Robert J. Dixson. (Modern American English Ser.). (gr. 7 up). 1974. 1.25 (*0-88345-236-7*) Prentice ESL.

Modern American Family. Ed. by Donald Young. LC 72-169402. (Family in America Ser.). 232p. 1972. reprint ed. 18.95 (*0-405-03879-8*) Ayer.

Modern American Farm Tractors. Andrew Morland. (Enthusiast Color Ser.). (Illus.). 96p. 1994. pap. 13.95 (*0-87938-926-5*) MBI Pubg.

Modern American Fiction: Form & Function. fac. ed. Ed. by Thomas D. Young. LC 88-15510. 254p. 1989. reprint ed. pap. 78.80 (*0-7837-7763-9*, 204751900007) Bks Demand.

Modern American Fiction: Insights & Foreign Lights. Ed. by Wolodymyr T. Zyla & Wendell M. Aycock. (Proceedings of the Comparative Literature Symposium Ser.: Vol. V). (Illus.). 140p. 1972. pap. 9.00 (*0-89672-047-0*) Tex Tech Univ Pr.

Modern American Houses: Four Decades of Award-Winning Design in Architectural Record. Ed. by Clifford A. Pearson. LC 95-48352. (Illus.). 240p. 1996. 49.50 (*0-8109-3334-9*, Pub. by Abrams) Time Warner.

Modern American Indian Tribal Government & Politics: An Interdisciplinary Study. Howard L. Meredith. 169p. 1993. pap. 16.95 (*0-912586-76-1*) Dine College Pr.

Modern American Landscapes. Ed. by M. Gidley & R. Lawson-Peebles. LC 96-132560. (European Contributions to American Studies: Vol. 26). (Illus.). 250p. 1995. 33.00 (*90-5383-208-4*, Pub. by VU Univ Pr) Paul & Co Pubs.

Modern American Life. (Illus.). 18p. pap. text 65.00 (*1-56762-046-9*) Modern Learn Pr.

Modern American Literature see Modern American Literature

***Modern American Literature, 3 vols.** 5th ed. Incl. Modern American Literature. 5th ed. LC 98-38952. 1998. Not sold separately (*1-55862-380-9*); Modern American Literature. 5th ed. LC 98-38952. 1998. Not sold separately (*1-55862-381-7*); Modern American Literature. 5th ed. LC 98-38952. 1998. Not sold separately (*1-55862-382-5*); LC 98-38952. 1393p. 1999. 450.00 (*1-55862-379-5*) St James Pr.

Modern American Lyrics: An Anthology. Ed. by Stanton A. Coblentz. LC 76-167476. (Granger Index Reprint Ser.). 1977. reprint ed. 19.95 (*0-8369-6281-8*) Ayer.

Modern American Memoirs. Annie Dillard. 464p. 1996. pap. 16.00 (*0-06-092763-1*) HarpC.

Modern American Muse: A Complete Bibliography of American Verse, 1900-1925. Ed. by Wynot R. Irish. 1950. 45.00 (*0-89366-100-7*) Ultramarine Pub.

Modern American Music: From Charles Ives to the Minimalists. Otto Karolyi. LC 96-9213. 150p. 1996. 29.50 (*0-8386-3725-6*) Fairleigh Dickinson.

Modern American Novel. Steven G. Kellman. (Magill Bibliographies Ser.). 162p. 1991. 42.00 (*0-8108-2798-0*) Scarecrow.

Modern American Novel, 1914-1945. Linda Wagner-Martin. (Twayne's Critical History of the Novel Ser.). 184p. 1989. 23.95 (*0-8057-7851-9*, Twyne) Mac Lib Ref.

Modern American Novel, 1914-1945: A Critical History. Linda Wagner-Martin. (Twayne's Critical History of the Novel Ser.). 184p. 1991. pap. 9.95 (*0-8057-7853-5*, Twyne) Mac Lib Ref.

Modern American Novel of the Left: A Research Guide. M. Keith Booker. LC 98-55349. 424p. 1999. lib. bdg. 85.00 (*0-313-30470-X*) Greenwood.

Modern American Novel of Violence. Patrick W. Shaw. LC 99-70833. 200p. 2000. 38.50 (*0-87875-509-8*) Whitston Pub.

Modern American Novella. Ed. by A. Robert Lee. LC 89-5876. 224p. 1989. text 39.95 (*0-312-02424-X*) St Martin.

Modern American Painters. (Shorewood Art Programs for Education Ser.). 16p. 1983. teacher ed. 107.00 (*0-88185-070-5*); 143.00 (*0-685-09215-1*) Shorewood Fine Art.

***Modern American Pharmacy.** Lively. 316p. 1999. pap. text 33.00 (*0-536-02510-X*) Pearson Custom.

Modern American Pistols & Revolvers. A. C. Gould. (Library Classics). (Illus.). 244p. 1987. reprint ed. 37.00 (*0-935632-43-3*) Wolfe Pub Co.

Modern American Plays. Frederic G. Cassidy. 501p. 1977. 26.95 (*0-8369-8201-0*) Ayer.

Modern American Plays. George P. Baker. LC 73-4868. (Play Anthology Reprint Ser.). 1977. reprint ed. 31.95 (*0-8369-8247-9*) Ayer.

Modern American Poetry, 1865-1950. Fred Moramarco et al. (Critical History of Poetry Ser.). 304p. 1989. 23.95 (*0-8057-8451-9*, Twyne) Mac Lib Ref.

Modern American Poetry, 1865-1950. Alan Shucard et al. LC 89-49465. 312p. (C). 1990. reprint ed. pap. 18.95 (*0-87023-720-9*) U of Mass Pr.

Modern American Poets: Their Voices & Visions. 2nd ed. Robert DiYanni. LC 93-14414. 848p. (C). 1993. pap. 45.31 (*0-07-016957-8*) McGraw.

Modern American Popular Religion: A Critical Assessment & Annotated Bibliography, 37. Charles H. Lippy. LC 95-46009. (Bibliographies & Indexes in Religious Studies: No. 37). 264p. 1996. lib. bdg. 75.00 (*0-313-27786-9*, Greenwood Pr) Greenwood.

Modern American Profiles. Lucette R. Kenan. (Illus.). 213p. (Orig.). (C). 1975. pap. text 19.00 (*0-15-559866-X*) Harcourt Coll Pubs.

Modern American Prose. 3rd ed. John Clifford & Robert DiYanni. 640p. (C). 1993. pap., student ed. 37.50 (*0-07-011396-3*) McGraw.

Modern American Prose: A Reader for Writers. 2nd ed. John Clifford & Robert Yanni. (C). 1987. pap. text. write for info. (*0-318-57009-2*) Random.

Modern American Protestantism & Its World, Set. Ed. by Martin E. Marty. Incl. Vol. 3. Civil Religion, Church & State. 502p. 1992. lib. bdg. 120.00 (*3-598-41533-8*); Vol. 4. Theological Themes in the American Protestant World. 468p. 1992. lib. bdg. 120.00 (*3-598-41535-4*); Vol. 5. Varieties of Protestantism. 272p. 1992. lib. bdg. 120.00 (*3-598-41536-2*); Vol. 6. Protestantism & Social Christianity. 1993. lib. bdg. 120.00 (*3-598-41537-0*); Vol. 7. Protestantism & Regionalism. 248p. 1992. lib. bdg. 120.00 (*3-598-41538-9*); Vol. 8. Ethnic & Non-Protestant Themes. 311p. 1993. lib. bdg. 120.00 (*3-598-41539-7*); Vol. 9. Native American Religion & Black Protestantism. 344p. 1993. lib. bdg. 120.00 (*3-598-41540-0*); Vol. 10. Fundamentalism & Evangelicalism. 356p. 1993. lib. bdg. 120.00 (*3-598-41541-9*); Vol. 11. New & Intense Movements. 404p. 1993. lib. bdg. 120.00 (*3-598-41542-7*); Vol. 12. Women & Women's Issues. 380p. 1993. lib. bdg. 120.00 (*3-598-41543-5*); Vol. 13. Missions & Ecumenical Expressions. 222p. 1993. lib. bdg. 120.00 (*3-598-41544-3*); Vol. 14. Varieties of Religious Expression. 296p. 1993. lib. bdg. 120.00 (*3-598-41545-1*); 1993. Set lib. bdg. 1525.00 (*3-598-41530-3*) K G Saur Verlag.

Modern American Realism: The Sara Roby Foundation Collection. 2nd ed. Virginia M. Mecklenburg. LC 08-474691. (Illus.). 148p. (Orig.). 1998. pap. 21.95 (*0-87474-691-4*) Smithsonian.

Modern American Religion Vol. 1: The Irony of It All, 1893-1919. Martin E. Marty. LC 86-16524. (Illus.). 398p. (C). 1986. 29.95 (*0-226-50893-5*) U Ch Pr.

Modern American Religion Vol. 1: The Irony of It All, 1893-1919, 2 vols. Martin E. Marty. 1997. pap. text 16.95 (*0-226-50894-3*) U Ch Pr.

Modern American Religion Vol. 2: The Noise of Conflict, 1919-1941, 2 vols. Martin E. Marty. 1997. pap. text 18.95 (*0-226-50897-8*) U Ch Pr.

Modern American Religion Vol. 2: The Noise of Conflict, 1919-1941. Martin E. Marty. LC 85-16524. (Illus.). 480p. 1997. 29.95 (*0-226-50895-1*) U Ch Pr.

Modern American Religion Vol. 3: Under God Indivisible, 1941-1960. Martin E. Marty. (Modern American Religion Ser.: Vol. 5). 528p. 1996. 34.95 (*0-226-50898-6*) U Ch Pr.

Modern American Religion & the Protestant World, Vol. 2. Ed. by Martin E. Marty. 294p. 1992. lib. bdg. 120.00 (*3-598-41532-X*) K G Saur Verlag.

Modern American Remedies. 2nd ed. Douglas Laycock. LC 94-223935. 1184p. 1994. lib. bdg. 55.00 (*0-316-51759-3*) Little.

Modern American Remedies: Cases & Materials. Douglas Laycock. 1184p. 1994. teacher ed. write for info. (*0-316-51377-6*, 13776) Aspen Law.

Modern American Remedies: Cases & Materials. Douglas Laycock. LC 84-82267. (C). 1985. 46.00 (*0-316-51749-6*) Aspen Pub.

***Modern American Remedies: Cases & Materials, 1999 Supplement.** 2nd rev. ed. Douglas Laycock. 250p. 1999. pap. text, suppl. ed. 17.95 (*0-7355-0254-4*, 02544) Panel Pubs.

Modern American Short Stories. Bennett A. Cerf. (BCL1-PS American Literature Ser.). 384p. 1993. reprint ed. lib. bdg. 89.00 (*0-7812-6934-2*) Rprt Serv.

Modern American Short Story Sequences: Composite Fictions & Fictive Communities. Ed. by J. Gerald Kennedy. 239p. (C). 1995. text 69.95 (*0-521-43010-0*) Cambridge U Pr.

Modern American Urban Novel: Nature as "Interior Structure" Arnold Goldsmith. LC 90-37925. 180p. (C). 1991. text 29.95 (*0-8143-1994-7*) Wayne St U Pr.

Modern American Usage: A Guide. rev. ed. Wilson Follett. LC 98-23280. 384p. 1998. 25.00 (*0-8090-6951-2*) Hill & Wang.

Modern American Vice Presidency: The Transformation of a Political Institution. Joel K. Goldstein. LC 81-47918. 423p. 1982. reprint ed. pap. 131.20 (*0-7837-9344-8*, 206008500004) Bks Demand.

Modern American Waltz. Earl Atkinson. (Ballroom Dance Ser.). 1986. lib. bdg. 250.00 (*0-8490-3643-7*) Gordon Pr.

Modern American Women: A Documentary History. Susan Ware. LC 88-16162. xv, 468p. 1989. 30.00 (*0-256-07117-9*) Dorsey.

Modern American Women Writers. Elaine Showalter et al. LC 90-52917. 608p. 1991. 120.00 (*0-684-19057-5*, Scribners Ref) Mac Lib Ref.

Modern Analysis. 3rd ed. Kenneth Kuttler. LC 97-35735. (Studies in Advanced Mathematics). 592p. 1997. lib. bdg. 74.95 (*0-8493-7166-X*) CRC Pr.

Modern Analysis & Topology. Norman R. Howes. LC 95-3995. (Universitext Ser.). 432p. 1995. 47.95 (*0-387-97986-7*) Spr-Verlag.

Modern Analysis for Electroplating. 2nd ed. P. W. Wild. 434p. 1991. 290.00 (*0-904477-01-0*, Pub. by FMJ Intl) St Mut.

Modern Analysis of Antibiotics. Aszalos. (Drugs & the Pharmaceutical Sciences Ser.: Vol. 27). (Illus.). 568p. 1986. text 230.00 (*0-8247-7358-6*) Dekker.

Modern Analysis of Scattering Phenomena. Ed. by J. C. Dainty & Daniel Maystre. (Illus.). 208p. 1991. 137.00 (*0-7503-0156-2*) IOP Pub.

Modern Analysis of Value Theory. Y. Fujinori. (Lecture Notes in Economics & Mathematical Systems Ser.: Vol. 207). (Illus.). 165p. 1982. 31.00 (*0-387-11949-3*) Spr-Verlag.

Modern Analytic Geometry. William Wooton. 1988. text 65.12 (*0-395-43066-6*) HM.

Modern Analytic Mechanics. R. K. Cooper & C. Pellegrini. LC 99-37364. (Illus.). 290p. (C). 1998. text. write for info. (*0-306-45958-2*, Kluwer Plenum) Kluwer Academic.

Modern Analytical Auditing: Practical Guidance for Auditors & Accountants. Thomas E. McKee. LC 88-23965. 174p. 1989. 59.95 (*0-89930-354-4*, MKA/, Quorum Bks) Greenwood.

Modern Analytical Chemistry. Harvey. (Illus.). 800p. (C). (gr. 13). 2000. text 61.95 (*0-8151-4208-0*, 26564) Mosby Inc.

Modern Analytical Chemistry. W. F. Pickering. LC 77-138500. 634p. (C). reprint ed. 196.60 (*0-8357-9087-8*, 205500800007) Bks Demand.

Modern Analytical Geochemistry. Robin Gill. 1997. pap. 40.46 (*0-582-09944-7*, Pub. by Addison-Wesley) Longman.

***Modern Analytical Methodologies in Fat & Water Soluble Vitamins.** Song et al. LC 99-39542. Vol. 154. 412p. 2000. text 100.00 (*0-471-17942-6*, Wiley-Interscience) Wiley.

Modern Analytical Ultracentrifugation: Acquisition & Interpretation of Data for Biological & Synthetic Polymer Systems. Ed. by Todd M. Schuster & Thomas M. Laue. LC 94-20182. (Emerging Biochemical & Biophysical Techniques Ser). xiv, 351p. 1994. 109.50 (*0-8176-3674-9*) Birkhauser.

M

Modern & Ancient Coal-Forming Environments. Ed. by J. C. Cobb & C. B. Cecil. (Special Papers: No. 286). 1994. pap. 39.38 (*0-8137-2286-1*) Geol Soc.

Modern & Ancient Continental Shelf Anoxia. Ed. by R. V. Tyson & T. H. Pearson. (Geological Society Special Publications: No. 58). x, 470p. (C). 1991. 125.00 (*0-903317-67-2*, 260, Pub. by Geol Soc Pub Hse) AAPG.

Modern & Ancient Deep-Sea Fan Sedimentation. Carlton H. Nelson & Tor H. Nilson. LC GC0087.6.S92. (SEPM Short Course Ser.: Vol. 14). (Illus.). 411p. 1984. reprint ed. pap. 127.50 (*0-608-05677-4*, 206619300006) Bks Demand.

Modern & Ancient Geosynclinal Sedimentation: Proceedings of a Symposium Dedicated to Marshall Key & Held at Madison, Wisconsin, 1972. Ed. by Robert H. Dott & Robert H. Shaver. LC 74-175858. (Society of Economic Paleontologists & Mineralogists, Special Publication Ser.: No. 19). 389p. reprint ed. pap. 120.60 (*0-608-12952-6*, 202474200038) Bks Demand.

Modern & Ancient Shelf Clastics: A Core Workshop. SEPM Core Workshop Staff. LC TN0870.5.S46. (SEPM Core Workshop Ser.: No. 9). (Illus.). 472p. 1986. pap. 146.40 (*0-608-05188-8*, 206572500001) Bks Demand.

Modern & Antique Guitar Repair. R. J. Gluck. 60p. pap. 17.95 (*1-882731-04-2*) Cactus Pub.

Modern & Classical Essayists: Twelve Masters. Ed. by Paul Marx. LC 95-17608. xiii, 366p. 1995. pap. text 33.95 (*1-55934-451-2*, 1451) Mayfield Pub.

Modern & Contemporary Art: The Lannan Collection at the Art Institute of Chicago. Jeremy Strick. (Museum Studies: Vol. 25, No. 1). (Illus.). 104p. 1999. pap. 14.95 (*0-86559-174-1*) Art Inst Chi.

Modern & Contemporary Drama. Ed. by Carl H. Klaus et al. LC 92-62771. 896p. 1993. pap. text 55.95 (*0-312-09077-3*) St Martin.

Modern & Contemporary Spanish Women Poets. Janet Perez. 1996. 32.00 (*0-8057-4627-7*, Twyne) Mac Lib Ref.

Modern & Healthy Body Care: Recipes for Professional, Natural Skin & Hair Care Products. unabridged ed. Karin Bombeli. Ed. by Peter Ansdell. LC 97-92195. (Illus.). ix, 105p. (Orig.). 1997. pap. 19.90 (*0-9658528-0-6*, B01-97) Somerset Bks.

***Modern & Past Glacial Environments.** Menzies. 352p. 2000. pap. text 59.95 (*0-7506-4226-2*) Buttrwrth-Heinemann.

Modern & Post-Modern Mime. Thomas Leabhart. 184p. 1998. pap. 18.95 (*0-312-17451-9*) St Martin.

Modern & Postmodern Strategies: Gaming & the Question of Morality: Adorno, Rorty, Lyotard & Enzensberger. Monika Kilian. LC 97-39383. (Studies in Literary Criticism & Theory: vol. 11). X, 221p. (C). 1998. 46.95 (*0-8204-3979-7*) P Lang Pubng.

***Modern Androgyne Imagination: A Failed Sublime.** Lisa Rado. LC 00-28103. 256p. 2000. 57.50 (*0-8139-1979-7*); pap. 18.50 (*0-8139-1980-0*) U Pr of Va.

Modern Anglo Bengali Dictionary with Scientific & Technical Terms, 2 vols. Charuchandra Guha. (BEN & ENG.). 2528p. 1919. 95.00 (*0-7859-9829-2*) Fr & Eur.

Modern Anglo-Irish Verse: An Anthology Selected from the Work of Living Irish Poets. Ed. by Padric Gregory. LC 75-28816. reprint ed. 49.50 (*0-404-13809-8*) AMS Pr.

Modern Antennas. Serge Drabowitch. 656p. 1997. 109.95 (*0-7803-3473-6*) Inst Electrical.

Modern Anti-Realism & Manufactured Truth. Gerald Vision. (International Library of Philosophy). 256p. 1989. 65.00 (*0-415-00097-1*) Routledge.

***Modern Antiquarian: A Pre-Millennial Odyssey Through Megalithic Britain.** Julian Cope. 432p. 1999. pap. text 45.00 (*0-7225-3599-6*) Thorsons PA.

Modern Antiques for the Table: A Guide to Tabletop Accessories, 1890-1940. Sheila Chefetz. LC 98-216542. (Illus.). 240p. 1998. 39.95 (*0-670-87515-5*) Viking Penguin.

Modern Applications of DNA Amplification Technqiues: Problems & New Tools: Proceedings of the Augustusburg Conference of Advanced Science on Problems of Quantitation of Nucleic Acids by Amplification Techniques Held in Augustusburg, Germany, September 23-26, 1996. Ed. by Dirk Lassner et al. LC 97-41939. 152p. 1998. 75.00 (*0-306-45801-2*, Kluwer Plenum) Kluwer Academic.

Modern Applications of EPR-ESR - From Biophysics to Materials Science: The First Asia-Pacific EPR-ESR Symposium. Ed. by C. Rudowicz et al. 750p. 1998. 69.00 (981-3083-23-9, Pub. by Spr-Verlag) Spr-Verlag.

Modern Applied Biostatistical Methods: Using S-Plus. Steve Selvin. (Illus.). 480p. 1998. text 49.95 (0-19-512025-6) OUP.

***Modern Applied Energy Conservation.** J. K. Jacques et al. (Applied Science & Industrial Technology Ser.). 392p. 1988. text 73.95 (0-470-21123-7) P-H.

Modern Applied Statistics with S-Plus. W. N. Venables & Brian D. Ripley. LC 94-21589. (Statistics & Computing Ser.). (Illus.). 462p. 1996. 44.95 (0-387-94350-1) Spr-Verlag.

Modern Applied Statistics with S-Plus. 2nd ed. W. N. Venables & Brian D. Ripley. LC 97-8922. 568p. 1997. 54.95 (0-387-98214-0) Spr-Verlag.

Modern Applied Statistics with S-Plus. 3rd ed. W. N. Venables & Brian D. Ripley. LC 99-18388. (Statistics & Computing Ser.). 520p. 1999. 64.95 (0-387-98825-4) Spr-Verlag.

Modern Applied Statistics with S-Plus, Vol. XII. rev. ed. Brian D. Ripley & W. N. Venables. Ed. by D. W. Scott & S. Sheather. (Statistics & Computing Ser.). (Illus.). 462p. 1994. 44.95 incl. disk (3-540-94350-1) Spr-Verlag.

M

Modern Approach. Andrew R. Schotter. 208p. (C). 1997. pap., student ed. 30.00 (0-06-501607-6) Addson-Wesley Educ.

Modern Approach, Teacher's Manual to Accompany Civil Procedure. Richard L. Marcus et al. (American Casebook Ser.). 342p. 1989. pap. text. write for info. (0-314-54545-X) West Pub.

Modern Approach to Benign Esophageal Disease: Diagnosis & Surgical Therapy. Ed. by Cedric G. Bremner et al. LC 98-114000. (Illus.). 243p. 1995. text 65.00 (0-942219-96-1) Quality Med Pub.

Modern Approach to Business English. Annie DeCaprio. LC 73-90044. 1974. pap. text. write for info. (0-672-96102-4) Macmillan.

Modern Approach to Business Spelling. Annie DeCaprio. LC 73-86847. 1974. teacher ed. 5.00 (0-672-26105-7, Bobbs); pap. text 10.70 (0-672-96104-0, Bobbs) Macmillan.

Modern Approach to Business Spelling. 2nd ed. Annie DeCaprio. LC 78-3421. 1979. teacher ed. write for info. (0-672-97207-7); pap. text. write for info. (0-672-97206-9) Macmillan.

Modern Approach to Classical Guitar, Pt. 1. C. Duncan. 56p. 1984. pap. 7.95 (0-7935-2627-2, 00699204) H Leonard.

Modern Approach to Classical Guitar Bk. 1: With Soundsheet. C. Duncan. 1981. pap. 6.95 (0-88188-946-6, 00699200) H Leonard.

Modern Approach to Classical Guitar Bk. 2: With Soundsheet. C. Duncan. 1982. pap. 6.95 (0-7935-2712-0, 00699201) H Leonard.

Modern Approach to Classical Guitar Pt. 2: Repertoire. C. Duncan. 72p. 1985. pap. 7.95 (0-7935-3322-8, 00699208) H Leonard.

Modern Approach to Comprehensive Chemistry. G. N. Gilmore. 540p. (C). 1994. pap. 42.50 (0-85950-665-7, Pub. by S Thornes Pubs) Trans-Atl Phila.

Modern Approach to Evidence: Teacher's Manual. 2nd ed. Richard O. Lempert & Stephen A. Saltzburg. (American Casebook Ser.). 553p. (C). 1983. pap. text, teacher ed. write for info. (0-314-76113-6) West Pub.

Modern Approach to Evidence: Text, Problems, Transcripts & Cases. 2nd ed. Richard O. Lempert & Stephen A. Saltzburg. LC 82-13578. (American Casebook Ser.). 1232p. (C). 1982. reprint ed. 62.50 (0-314-67594-9) West Pub.

Modern Approach to Probability Theory. Bert Fristedt & Lawrence Gray. LC 96-5687. (Probability & Its Applications Ser.). 756p. 1996. 64.50 (0-8176-3807-5) Birkhauser.

Modern Approach to Probability Theory. Bert Fristedt & Lawrence F. Gray. LC 96-5687. (Probability & Its Applications Ser.). 1996. write for info. (3-7643-3807-5, Pub. by Birkhauser) Princeton Arch.

Modern Approach to Quantum Mechanics. John S. Townsend. 476p. (C). 1992. text 74.74 (0-07-065119-1) McGraw.

***Modern Approach to Quantum Mechanics.** John S. Townsend. LC 99-58197. 497p. 2000. reprint ed. text. write for info. (1-891389-13-0) Univ Sci Bks.

Modern Approach to the Christian Religion: The Truth. Mordecai Richler. LC 98-90022. 1998. pap. 10.95 (0-533-12685-1) Vantage.

Modern Approach to the Incidental Question. Schuz. LC 97-197061. 1997. 175.00 (90-411-0668-5) Kluwer Law Intl.

Modern Approach to the Perimenopausal Years. Ed. by Robert B. Greenblatt. (New Developments in Biosciences Ser.: No. 2). vi, 256p. (C). 1986. lib. bdg. 79.25 (3-11-010937-9) De Gruyter.

Modern Approach to the Protection of the Environment: Proceedings of a Study Week Held in the Vatican, 2-7 November 1987. Ed. by G. B. Marini-Bettolo. (Pontifical Academiae Scientiarum Scripta Ser.). (Illus.). 602p. 1990. 94.00 (0-08-040816-8, Pergamon Pr) Elsevier.

Modern Approaches in Forest Ecosystem Modelling. O. G. Chertov et al. LC 99-12155. (European Forest Institute Research Report Ser.). 130p. 1999. 59.00 (90-04-11415-7) Brill Academic Pubs.

Modern Approaches to Control System Design. Ed. by N. Munro. LC 80-479861. (IEE Control Engineering Ser.: Vol. 9). (Illus.). 431p. reprint ed. pap. 133.70 (0-608-17791-1, 203225600079) Bks Demand.

Modern Approaches to Data Assimilation in Ocean Modeling. Ed. by P. Malanotte-Rizzoli. (Oceanography Ser.: Vol. 61). 468p. 1996. pap. text 55.75 (0-444-82484-7) Elsevier.

Modern Approaches to Data Assimilation in Ocean Modeling. Ed. by P. Malanotte-Rizzoli. LC 96-3901. (Oceanography Ser.: No. 61). 468p. 1996. text 154.50 (0-444-82079-5) Elsevier.

Modern Approaches to Endometriosis. Ed. by Eric J. Thomas & John A. Rock. 304p. 1991. text 140.50 (0-7923-8901-8) Kluwer Academic.

Modern Approaches to Manufacturing Improvement: The Shingo System. Ed. by Alan Robinson. LC 89-43673. 420p. 1990. pap. 23.00 (0-915299-64-X) Productivity Inc.

Modern Approaches to School Organization. Harold S. Davis et al. 1974. pap. text 13.95 (0-8422-0368-0) Irvington.

Modern Approaches to the Dementias Pt. I: Etiology & Pathophysiology. Ed. by Clifford F. Rose. (Interdisciplinary Topics in Gerontology Ser.: Vol. 19). (Illus.). x, 230p. 1985. 155.00 (3-8055-3980-0) S Karger.

Modern Approaches to the Dementias Pt. II: Clinical & Therapeutic Aspects. Ed. by F. Clifford Rose. (Interdisciplinary Topics in Gerontology Ser.: Vol. 20). (Illus.). x, 202p. 1985. 137.50 (3-8055-3981-9) S Karger.

Modern Approaches to the Treatment of Hypertension. Ed. by Edward A. Babayan et al. 1976. 21.75 (3-8055-2400-5) S Karger.

Modern Approaches to the Treatment of Initial Stages of Breast Cancer. V. P. Letyagin et al. (Soviet Medical Reviews Ser.: Vol. 3). iv, 84p. 1989. pap. text 87.00 (3-7186-4912-8) Gordon & Breach.

Modern Approaches to Understanding & Managing Organizations. Lee G. Bolman & Terrence E. Deal. LC 83-49257. (Management Ser.). 345p. 1984. 36.45 (0-87589-592-1) Jossey-Bass.

Modern Approaches to Vaccines: Molecular & Chemical Basis of Virus Virulence & Immunogenicity. Ed. by Robert M. Chanock & Richard A. Lerner. LC 83-73176. 485p. reprint ed. pap. 150.40 (0-7837-5839-1, 204555800006) Bks Demand.

Modern Approaches to Wettability: Theory & Applications. M. E. Schrader & G. I. Loeb. (Illus.). 478p. (C). 1992. text 110.00 (0-306-43985-9, Kluwer Plenum) Kluwer Academic.

Modern Arabic. Samar Attar. (ARA.). 1988. pap., teacher ed. 5.95 (0-86685-703-6, Pub. by Librairie du Liban) Intl Bk Ctr.

Modern Arabic, Wkbk. I. Samar Attar. (ARA.). 1988. pap., student ed. 10.95 (0-86685-701-X, LDL439B, Pub. by Librairie du Liban) Intl Bk Ctr.

Modern Arabic, Wkbk. II. Samar Attar. (ARA.). pap., student ed. 10.95 (0-86685-702-8, LKL440B, Pub. by Librairie du Liban) Intl Bk Ctr.

Modern Arabic: An Introductory Course for Foreign Students, Bk. I. Samar Attar. (ARA., Illus.). 88p. 1988. pap. 11.95 (0-86685-439-8, Pub. by Librairie du Liban) Intl Bk Ctr.

Modern Arabic: Grammar in Context. Samar Attar. 24.95 (0-86685-736-2) Intl Bk Ctr.

Modern Arabic: Structures, Functions, & Varieties. Clive Holes. LC 94-19630. 1994. pap. text. write for info. (0-582-02884-1) Longman.

***Modern Arabic: The Arab-European Encounter.** Samar Attar. 939p. 1998. pap. 35.00 (0-86685-745-1) Intl Bk Ctr.

Modern Arabic Bk. 2: An Introductory Course for Foreign Students. Samar Attar. (ARA., Illus.). 263p. 1988. audio 179.95 (0-86685-544-0) Intl Bk Ctr.

Modern Arabic Bk. 2: An Introductory Course for Foreign Students, Bk. 2. Samar Attar. (ARA., Illus.). 263p. 1988. teacher ed. 6.95 (0-86685-441-X) Intl Bk Ctr.

Modern Arabic Bk. 2: An Introductory Course for Foreign Students, Bk. II. Samar Attar. (ARA., Illus.). 364p. 1988. pap. 19.95 (0-86685-440-1, Pub. by Librairie du Liban) Intl Bk Ctr.

Modern Arabic Drama: An Anthology. Ed. by Salma K. Jayyusi & Roger Allen. LC 94-49178. (Arab & Islamic Studies). 480p. 1995. text 57.50 (0-253-32897-7); pap. text 24.95 (0-253-20973-0) Ind U Pr.

Modern Arabic-English Dictionary. E. A. Elias. (ARA.). 868p. 1991. 49.95 (0-86685-287-5, EL2875, Pub. by Librairie du Liban) Intl Bk Ctr.

Modern Arabic-English Dictionary: Al-Mawrid. Rohi Ba'Albaki. 1994. 55.00 (0-86685-553-X) Intl Bk Ctr.

Modern Arabic Literary Language: Lexical & Stylistic Developments. Jaroslav Stetkevych. Ed. by William R. Polk. LC 79-123749. (Publications of the Center for Middle Eastern Studies). 1995. lib. bdg. 16.00 (0-226-77338-8) U Ch Pr.

Modern Arabic Literature. Ed. by M. M. Badawi. (History of Arabic Literature Ser.). (Illus.). 585p. (C). 1993. text 129.95 (0-521-33197-8) Cambridge U Pr.

Modern Arabic Literature: A Bibliography. Ragai N. Makar & Christen T. Bloyer. LC 98-22136. (Scarecrow Area Bibliographies Ser.: No. 17). 352p. 1998. 75.00 (0-8108-3539-8) Scarecrow.

Modern Arabic Novel: Bibliography & Critical Introduction, 1865-1995, 5 vols. Hamdi Sakkut. 3200p. 1999. pap. 150.00 (977-424-502-4, Pub. by Am Univ Cairo Pr) Col U Pr.

Modern Arabic Poetry. Ed. by Salma K. Jayyusi. 526p. 1991. pap. text 20.50 (0-231-05273-1) Col U Pr.

Modern Arboriculture. Alex L. Shigo. (Illus.). 440p. (C). 1991. 55.00 (0-943563-09-7) Shigo & Trees Assocs.

Modern Architect: A Classic Victorian Stylebook & Carpenter's Manual. unabridged ed. Edward Shaw. (Illus.). 208p. 1996. reprint ed. pap. text 12.95 (0-486-28921-4) Dover.

***Modern Architectural Dictionary & Quick Reference Guide for Architects, Interior Designers & the Construction Trades.** Robert Deitch. (Illus.). 279p. 1999. pap. 25.95 (0-9675345-6-9) Rhinoceros W Pr.

Modern Architecture. rev. ed. Vincent Scully, Jr. LC 61-13689. (Illus.). 128p. 1974. pap. 14.95 (0-8076-0334-1) Braziller.

Modern Architecture. 3rd rev. ed. Kenneth Frampton. LC 91-66733. (World of Art Ser.). (Illus.). 376p. 1992. pap. 16.95 (0-500-20257-5, Pub. by Thames Hudson) Norton.

Modern Architecture, 1. Manfredo Tafuri & Francesco D. Co. (History of World Architecture Ser.). (Illus.). 224p. 1991. pap. 29.95 (0-8478-0760-6, Pub. by Rizzoli Intl) St Martin.

Modern Architecture, 2. Manfredo Tafuri & Francesco D. Co. (History of World Architecture Ser.). (Illus.). 224p. 1987. pap. 29.95 (0-8478-0761-4) Rizzoli Intl.

Modern Architecture: A Guidebook for His Students to This Field of Art. Otto Wagner. Tr. by Harry F. Mallgrave. LC 88-24634. (Texts & Documents Ser.). (Illus.). 200p. 1989. 29.95 (0-226-86938-5); pap. 19.95 (0-226-86939-3) U Ch Pr.

Modern Architecture: Being the Kahn Lectures for 1930. Frank Lloyd Wright. LC 86-29695. (Illus.). 132p. 1987. 36.95 (0-8093-1398-7) S Ill U Pr.

Modern Architecture: International Exhibition, 1932. Henry-Russell Hitchcock, Jr. et al. LC 70-86421. (Museum of Modern Art Publications in Reprint). (Illus.). 1969. reprint ed. 24.95 (0-405-01535-6) Ayer.

Modern Architecture: Photographs by Ezra Stoller, 1939-1989. William S. Saunders. (Illus.). 228p. 1990. reprint ed. 75.00 (0-8109-3816-2, Pub. by Abrams) Time Warner.

Modern Architecture: Romanticism & Reintegration. Henry-Russell Hitchcock, Jr. (Illus.). 310p. 1993. reprint ed. pap. 16.95 (0-306-80519-7) Da Capo.

Modern Architecture & Design: An Alternative History. Bill Risebero. (Illus.). 256p. 1982. reprint ed. 32.00 (0-262-18108-8) MIT Pr.

Modern Architecture & Design: An Alternative History. Bill Risebero. (Illus.). 256p. 1985. reprint ed. pap. text 17.50 (0-262-68046-7) MIT Pr.

Modern Architecture & the Critical Present: An Architectural Design Profile. Kenneth Frampton. (Academy Architecture Ser.). (Illus.). 96p. 1982. pap. 14.95 (0-312-53631-3) St Martin.

Modern Architecture in America: Visions & Revisions. Ed. by Richard G. Wilson & Sidney K. Robinson. LC 90-34402. (Illus.). 229p. 1991. reprint ed. pap. 71.00 (0-608-06844-6, 206704200009) Bks Demand.

***Modern Architecture in Czechoslovakia & Other Writings.** Karel Tiege. Tr. by Irena Murray & David Britt. (Illus.). 384p. 2001. pap. 65.00 (0-89236-596-X) J P Getty Trust.

Modern Architecture in England. Henry-Russell Hitchcock, Jr. & Catherine K. Bauer. LC 73-86422. (Museum of Modern Art Publications in Reprint). (Illus.). 1969. reprint ed. 18.95 (0-405-01536-4) Ayer.

Modern Architecture in Germany from 1900 to 1950. Gerd Hatje Publishers Staff. 1994. 85.00 (3-7757-0452-3, Pub. by Gerd Hatje) Dist Art Pubs.

Modern Architecture in Historic Cities: Policy, Planning, & Building in Contemporary France. Sebastian Loew. LC 97-26097. (Illus.). 280p. (C). 1998. 85.00 (0-415-15492-8) Routledge.

***Modern Architecture in Israel.** Michael Levin. (Illus.). 404p. 2000. 55.00 (88-8118-523-7, Pub. by Skira IT) Abbeville Pr.

Modern Architecture, Romanticism, & Re-Integration. H. R. Hitchcock. LC 74-137241. reprint ed. 32.50 (0-404-03276-1) AMS Pr.

Modern Architecture since 1900. 3rd ed. William J. Curtis. LC 97-112837. (Illus.). 736p. 1996. 49.95 (0-7148-3524-2, Pub. by Phaidon Press) Phaidon Pr.

Modern Architecture since 1900. 3rd ed. William J. Curtis. LC 97-112837. (Illus.). 736p. 1996. pap. text 29.95 (0-7148-3356-8, Pub. by Phaidon Press) Phaidon Pr.

Modern Architecture since 1900. 3rd ed. William J. R. Curtis. LC 97-120714. 736p. (C). 1996. pap. text 70.67 (0-13-232273-0, Pub. by P-H) S&S Trade.

***Modern Architecture Through Case Studies.** Blundell-Jones. 2000. text 69.95 (0-7506-3805-2) Buttrwrth-Heinemann.

Modern Archives: Principles & Techniques. T. R. Schellenberg. LC 56-58525. (Midway Reprint Ser.). xvi, 248p. 1975. reprint ed. pap. text 13.00 (0-226-73684-9) U Ch Pr.

Modern Archives: Principles & Techniques. Theodore R. Schellenberg. LC 56-58525. (Midway Reprint Ser.). (Illus.). 264p. reprint ed. pap. 81.90 (0-608-09522-2, 205432400005) Bks Demand.

Modern Archives Reader: Basic Readings on Archival Theory & Practice. Ed. by Maygene F. Daniels & Timothy Walch. (Illus.). 357p. 1984. 25.00 (0-911333-11-8, 100017); pap. 25.00 (0-911333-12-6, 200017) National Archives & Recs.

Modern Ark: Saving Endangered Species. Daniel Cohen. LC 94-34007. (Illus.). 120p. (J). (gr. 5-9). 1995. 15.95 (0-399-22442-4, G P Putnam) Peng Put Young Read.

Modern Ark: The History of Zoos: Past, Present & Future. Vickie Croke. LC 96-48901. 272p. 1997. 25.50 (0-684-19712-X) S&S Trade.

Modern Ark: The Story of Zoos, Past, Present & Future. Vicki Croke. 272p. 1998. pap. 12.00 (0-380-73131-2, Avon Bks) Morrow Avon.

***Modern Ark: The Story of Zoos: Past, Present & Future.** Vicki Croke. (Illus.). 272p. 2000. reprint ed. pap. text 26.00 (0-7881-9169-1) DIANE Pub.

Modern Armenian Dictionary. Mardiros Koushakdjian. (ARM.). 1350p. 1986. 49.95 (0-86685-704-4, KAS1001, Pub. by Librairie du Liban) Intl Bk Ctr.

***Modern Armenian Drama: An Anthology.** Ed. by Nishan Parlakian & S. Peter Cowe. 480p. 2000. text 35.00 (0-231-11630-6) Col U Pr.

Modern Armenian-English-Armenian Dictionary. Mardiros Koushakdjian. (ARM & ENG.). 1380p. 1987. 85.00 (0-8288-1705-7, M14407) Fr & Eur.

Modern Arms & Free Men: A Discussion of the Role of Science in Preserving Democracy. Vannevar Bush. LC 85-14840. 273p. 1985. reprint ed. lib. bdg. 65.00 (0-313-24985-7, BMOA, Greenwood Pr) Greenwood.

Modern Arnis: Filipino Art of Stick Fighting. Remy A. Presas. LC 83-60128. (Specialties Ser.). (Illus.). 1983. pap. 12.95 (0-89750-089-X, 426) Ohara Pubns.

Modern Arnis: Philippine Style of Stick Fighting. Remy A. Presas. (Illus.). 176p. 1997. reprint ed. pap. 24.95 (0-9657796-0-2) Modern Arnis.

***Modern Arnis: The Filipino Art of Stick Fighting.** Remy A. Presas. 1999. pap. text 37.95 (1-58133-138-X) Black Belt Mag.

Modern Art. 5.95 (1-57717-144-6) Todtri Prods.

***Modern Art.** Christophe Domino. (Key Art/Selected Works). (Illus.). 2000. pap. 12.95 (2-86656-221-6) Scala Edit.

Modern Art. Mayfair Games Staff. 1996. 30.00 (1-56905-088-0) Mayfair Games.

Modern Art. Pauline Ridley. (Art & Artists Ser.). (Illus.). 64p. (J). (gr. 5-10). 1995. lib. bdg. 24.26 (1-56847-356-7) Raintree Steck-V.

***Modern Art.** Evelyn Toynton. LC 00-24570. (Illus.). 180p. 2000. 23.00 (1-883285-18-6) Delphinium.

Modern Art. 3rd ed. 1992. pap. 26.11 (0-8109-2494-3, Pub. by Abrams) Time Warner.

Modern Art: Impressionism to Post-Modernism. Ed. by David Britt. LC 99-70796. (Illus.). 416p. 1999. pap. 24.95 (0-500-28126-2, Pub. by Thames Hudson) Norton.

Modern Art: Painting, Sculpture, Architecture. 3rd ed. Sam Hunter & John Jacobus. (Illus.). 440p. 1992. 65.00 (0-8109-3609-7, Pub. by Abrams) Time Warner.

***Modern Art: Painting, Sculpture, Architecture.** 3rd ed. Sam Hunter et al. LC 99-35573. (Illus.). 448p. 2000. 75.00 (0-8109-4383-2, Pub. by Abrams) Time Warner.

Modern Art: The Men, the Movements, the Meaning. Thomas Craven. LC 40-7043. 1940. reprint ed. 59.00 (0-403-03081-1) Somerset Pub.

Modern Art & Man's Search for the Self. deluxe limited ed. Fritz W. Faiss. (Illus.). 30p. 1974. pap. 9.00 (0-916678-12-1) Green Hut.

Modern Art & Modernism. Ed. by Francis Frascina & Charles Harrison. LC 82-48153. (Illus.). 312p. 1983. pap. 28.00 (0-06-430124-9, IN-124, Icon Edns) HarpC.

Modern Art & Scientific Thought. John A. Richardson. LC 74-122914. (Illus.). 211p. reprint ed. pap. 65.50 (0-608-08100-0, 201489500093) Bks Demand.

***Modern Art & Society: An Anthology of Social & Multicultural Readings.** Ed. by Maurice Berger. (Illus.). 310p. 2000. reprint ed. pap. text 17.00 (0-7881-6967-X) DIANE Pub.

Modern Art & the Death of a Culture. H. R. Rookmaaker. Tr. by Robert Chang. (CHI.). 229p. 1985. pap. 8.50 (1-56582-051-7) Christ Renew Min.

Modern Art & the Death of a Culture. H. R. Rookmaaker. LC 94-16587. 256p. 1994. reprint ed. pap. 15.99 (0-89107-799-5) Crossway Bks.

Modern Art & the Modern Mind. Josef P. Hodin. LC 75-81831. (Illus.). 397p. reprint ed. pap. 123.10 (0-608-08101-9, 200214000012) Bks Demand.

***Modern Art & the Romantic Vision.** Deniz Tekiner. LC 99-49085. 136p. 1999. pap. 27.50 (0-7618-1529-5) U Pr of Amer.

***Modern Art & the Romantic Vision.** Deniz Tekiner. LC 99-49085. 136p. 1999. 49.00 (0-7618-1528-7) U Pr of Amer.

Modern Art, Being a Contribution to a New System of Aesthetics, 2 vols. Julius Meier-Graefe. LC 68-9239. (Contemporary Art Ser.). (Illus.). 1968. reprint ed. 96.95 (0-405-00719-1) Ayer.

Modern Art, Being a Contribution to a New System of Aesthetics, 2 vols., Vol. 1. Julius Meier-Graefe. LC 68-9239. (Contemporary Art Ser.). (Illus.). 1968. reprint ed. 48.95 (0-405-00826-0) Ayer.

Modern Art, Being a Contribution to a New System of Aesthetics, 2 vols., Vol. 2. Julius Meier-Graefe. LC 68-9239. (Contemporary Art Ser.). (Illus.). 1968. reprint ed. 48.95 (0-405-00827-9) Ayer.

***Modern Art Despite Modernism.** Robert Storr. (Illus.). 250p. 2000. 55.00 (0-8109-6207-1, Pub. by Abrams) Time Warner.

***Modern Art Despite Modernism.** Robert Storr. 248p. 2000. 55.00 (0-87070-031-6) Mus of Modern Art.

***Modern Art Despite Modernism.** Robert Storr. (Illus.). 248p. 2000. pap. 34.95 (0-87070-034-0) Mus of Modern Art.

***Modern Art, 1851-1929: Capitalism & Representation.** Richard Brettell. (Oxford History of Art Ser.). (Illus.). 268p. 1999. 39.95 (0-19-284273-0); pap. 16.95 (0-19-284220-X) OUP.

Modern Art from the Pacific Northwest in the Collection of the Seattle Art Museum. Barbara Johns. LC 90-52617. (Illus.). 40p. (Orig.). 1990. pap. 6.95 (0-932216-33-1) Seattle Art.

Modern Art in Britain, 1910-1919. Anna G. Robins. LC 97-181018. (Illus.). 192p. 1997. 45.00 (1-85894-032-X, Pub. by Merrell Holberton) U of Wash Pr.

Modern Art in Denver (1919-1960) Eleven Denver Artists. Elizabeth Schlosser. LC 93-17458. (Documents of Colorado Art Ser.). (Illus.). 80p. (Orig.). 1993. pap. 34.95 (0-938075-31-4) Ocean View Bks.

An Asterisk (*) at the beginning of an entry indicates that the title is appearing for the first time.

Modern Art in Eastern Europe: From the Baltic to the Balkans, CA. 1890-1939. S. A. Mansbach. LC 97-42894. (Illus.). 400p. (C). 1999. text 65.00 (*0-521-45085-3*) Cambridge U Pr.

Modern Art in Ireland. Dorothy Walker & Seamus Heaney. LC 98-102463. 240p. 1997. 49.95 (*1-874675-77-5*, Pub. by Lilliput Pr) Dufour.

Modern Art in Portugal, 1910-1940: The Artist Contemporaries of Fernando Pessoa. Joao Serra & Fernando Guimaraes. LC 98-197155. (Illus.). 335p. 1998. 75.00 (*3-908161-01-0*) Abbeville Pr.

Modern Art in Thailand in the Nineteenth & Twentieth Centuries. Apinan Poshyananda. (Illus.). 284p. (C). 1992. text 125.00 (*0-19-588562-7*) OUP.

Modern Art in the Common Culture. Thomas Crow. (Illus.). 288p. 1996. pap. 18.00 (*0-300-07649-5*) Yale U Pr.

Modern Art in the Common Culture: Essays. Thomas Crow. LC 95-17377. (Illus.). 288p. 1996. 40.00 (*0-300-06438-1*) Yale U Pr.

Modern Art in the 2000s: Andrology in the Nineties. Ed. by W. Ombelet et al. LC 98-10330. (Studies in Profertility Ser.: Vol. 8). (Illus.). 238p. 1998. 58.00 (*1-85070-043-5*) Prthnon Pub.

***Modern Art in the U. S. A.** Hills. 480p. 2000. pap. text 26.67 (*0-13-036138-0*) P-H.

Modern Art, 19th & 20th Centuries. Meyer Schapiro. LC 78-6831. (Selected Papers of Meyer Schapiro: Vol. II). (Illus.). 277p. (C). 1982. pap. 24.95 (*0-8076-1034-8*) Braziller.

Modern Art, 19th & 20th Centuries. Meyer Schapiro. LC 79-315523. (Selected Papers). xi, 277p. 1978. write for info. (*0-7011-2315-X*) Chatto & Windus.

Modern Art of Chinese Cooking: Techniques & Recipes. Barbara Tropp. 1996. pap. 17.95 (*0-688-14611-2*, Hearst) Hearst Commns.

Modern Art of Cross-Examination. Robert E. Goldman. LC 93-37856. 1993. 90.00 (*0-13-109182-4*) Aspen Law.

Modern Art of Education. 3rd ed. Rudolf Steiner. Tr. by Jesse Darrell from GER. 233p. 1981. 22.95 (*0-85440-261-6*, Pub. by R Steiner Pr) Anthroposophic.

Modern Art of Taming Wild Horses. J. S. Rarey. LC 95-36386. (Illus.). 64p. 1996. reprint ed. pap. 7.95 (*1-55709-126-9*) Applewood.

Modern Arthurian Literature: An Anthology of English & American Arthuriana from the Renaissance to the Present. Ed. by Alan Lupack. LC 91-46442. 502p. 1992. text 40.00 (*0-8153-0055-7*, H#1420) Garland.

Modern Arthurian Literature: An Anthology of English & American Arthuriana from the Renaissance to the Present. Ed. by Alan Lupack. LC 91-46442. 502p. 1992. pap. text 24.95 (*0-8153-0843-4*) Garland.

Modern Arts Criticism, Vol. 1. Ed. by Joann R. Prosyniuk. (Illus.). 575p. 1990. 115.00 (*0-8103-7689-X*) Gale.

Modern Arts Criticism, Vol. 2. Joann R. Prosyniuk. 1991. 115.00 (*0-8103-7874-4*) Gale.

Modern Arts Criticism, Vol. 3. Joann R. Prosyniuk. 1992. 115.00 (*0-8103-8310-1*) Gale.

Modern Arts Criticism, Vol. 4. Joann R. Prosyniuk. 1993. 115.00 (*0-8103-8311-X*) Gale.

***Modern Asian Art.** John Clark. (Illus.). 344p. 1998. text 56.00 (*90-5704-041-7*, Harwood Acad Pubs) Gordon & Breach.

Modern Asian Art. John Clark. LC 98-26254. (Illus.). 368p. (C). 1998. text 48.00 (*0-8248-2142-4*) UH Pr.

Modern Aspects of Ancient Acupuncture. M. Kuman. 1997. pap. 20.00 (*1-893637-05-0*) Hlth & Hap.

Modern Aspects of Colloidal Dispersions Results from the DTI Colloid Technology Programme. LC 97-42022. 320p. 1997. lib. bdg. 230.00 (*0-7923-4819-2*) Kluwer Academic.

Modern Aspects of Diffusion-Controlled Reactions: Cooperative Phenomena in Bimolecular Processes. Ed. by E. Kotomin & V. Kuzovkov. LC 96-226105. (Comprehensive Chemical Kinetics Ser.: Vol. 34). 636p. 1996. text 367.50 (*0-444-82472-3*) Elsevier.

Modern Aspects of Electrochemistry, Vol. 1. Ed. by John O. Bockris & B. E. Conway. LC 54-12732. (Modern Aspect Series of Chemistry). 354p. reprint ed. pap. 109.80 (*0-608-08102-7*, 202576500001) Bks Demand.

Modern Aspects of Electrochemistry, Vol. 2. Ed. by John O. Bockris. LC 54-12732. (Modern Aspect Series of Chemistry). 426p. reprint ed. pap. 132.10 (*0-608-08103-5*, 202576500002) Bks Demand.

Modern Aspects of Electrochemistry, Vol. 3. Ed. by John O. Bockris. LC 54-12732. 465p. reprint ed. pap. 144.20 (*0-608-08104-3*, 202576500003) Bks Demand.

Modern Aspects of Electrochemistry, Vol. 4. Ed. by John O. Bockris & B. E. Conway. LC 54-12732. (Modern Aspect Series of Chemistry). 325p. reprint ed. pap. 100.80 (*0-608-08105-1*, 202576500004) Bks Demand.

Modern Aspects of Electrochemistry, Vol. 5. Ed. by John O. Bockris & B. E. Conway. LC 54-12732. (Modern Aspect Series of Chemistry). 509p. reprint ed. pap. 157.80 (*0-608-08106-X*, 202576500005) Bks Demand.

Modern Aspects of Electrochemistry, Vol. 6. Ed. by John O. Bockris & B. E. Conway. LC 54-12732. (Modern Aspect Series of Chemistry). 395p. reprint ed. pap. 122.50 (*0-608-08107-8*, 202576500006) Bks Demand.

Modern Aspects of Electrochemistry, Vol. 7. Ed. by John O. Bockris & B. E. Conway. LC 54-12732. (Modern Aspect Series of Chemistry). 424p. reprint ed. pap. 131.50 (*0-608-08108-6*, 202576500007) Bks Demand.

Modern Aspects of Electrochemistry, Vol. 8. Ed. by John O. Bockris & B. E. Conway. LC 54-12732. (Modern Aspect Series of Chemistry). 357p. reprint ed. pap. 110.70 (*0-608-08109-4*, 202576500008) Bks Demand.

Modern Aspects of Electrochemistry, Vol. 14. Ed. by John O. Bockris et al. LC 54-12732. 678p. (C). 1982. 125.00 (*0-306-40845-7*, Plenum Trade) Perseus Pubng.

Modern Aspects of Electrochemistry, Vol. 15. Ed. by Ralph E. White et al. LC 54-12732. 376p. 1983. 95.00 (*0-306-41287-X*, Plenum Trade) Perseus Pubng.

Modern Aspects of Electrochemistry, Vol. 16. Ed. by Brian E. Conway et al. LC 54-12732. 528p. 1985. 115.00 (*0-306-42024-4*, Plenum Trade) Perseus Pubng.

Modern Aspects of Electrochemistry, Vol. 17. Ed. by John O. Bockris et al. LC 54-12732. 508p. 1986. 115.00 (*0-306-42149-6*, Plenum Trade) Perseus Pubng.

Modern Aspects of Electrochemistry, Vol. 18. Ed. by Ralph E. White et al. LC 54-12732. 376p. 1986. 95.00 (*0-306-42312-X*, Plenum Trade) Perseus Pubng.

Modern Aspects of Electrochemistry, Vol. 19. Ed. by Brian E. Conway et al. (Illus.). 414p. (C). 1989. text 132.00 (*0-306-42954-3*, Kluwer Plenum) Kluwer Academic.

Modern Aspects of Electrochemistry, Vol. 20. Ed. by John O. Bockris et al. (Illus.). 532p. (C). 1989. text 138.00 (*0-306-43127-0*, Kluwer Plenum) Kluwer Academic.

Modern Aspects of Electrochemistry, Vol. 21. R. E. White et al. LC 54-12732. (Illus.). 336p. (C). 1990. text 110.00 (*0-306-43313-3*, Kluwer Plenum) Kluwer Academic.

Modern Aspects of Electrochemistry, Vol. 22. J. O. Bockris et al. (Illus.). 566p. (C). 1992. text 138.00 (*0-306-44061-X*, Kluwer Plenum) Kluwer Academic.

Modern Aspects of Electrochemistry, Vol. 23. B. E. Conway et al. (Illus.). 432p. (C). 1992. text 110.00 (*0-306-44164-0*, Kluwer Plenum) Kluwer Academic.

Modern Aspects of Electrochemistry, Vol. 24. R. E. White et al. (Illus.). 480p. (C). 1993. text 110.00 (*0-306-44288-4*, Kluwer Plenum) Kluwer Academic.

Modern Aspects of Electrochemistry, Vol. 25. J. O. Bockris et al. (Illus.). 336p. (C). 1994. text 110.00 (*0-306-44375-9*, Kluwer Plenum) Kluwer Academic.

Modern Aspects of Electrochemistry, Vol. 26. B. E. Conway et al. (Illus.). 356p. (C). 1994. text 110.00 (*0-306-44608-1*, Kluwer Plenum) Kluwer Academic.

Modern Aspects of Electrochemistry, Vol. 27. R. E. White et al. (Illus.). 566p. (C). 1995. text 138.00 (*0-306-44930-7*, Kluwer Plenum) Kluwer Academic.

Modern Aspects of Electrochemistry, Vol. 28. B. E. Conway et al. (Illus.). 373p. (C). 1996. text 114.00 (*0-306-45146-8*, Kluwer Plenum) Kluwer Academic.

Modern Aspects of Electrochemistry, Vol. 29. J. O. Bockris et al. (Illus.). 453p. (C). 1996. text 132.00 (*0-306-45162-X*, Kluwer Plenum) Kluwer Academic.

Modern Aspects of Electrochemistry, Vol. 30. Ed. by Ralph E. White & John O. Bockris. 553p. (C). 1997. text 125.00 (*0-306-45450-5*, Kluwer Plenum) Kluwer Academic.

Modern Aspects of Electrochemistry, Vol. 31. J. O. Bockris et al. (Illus.). 364p. (C). 1998. text 132.00 (*0-306-45650-8*, Kluwer Plenum) Kluwer Academic.

***Modern Aspects of Electrochemistry, Vol. 32.** B. E. Conway et al. 420p. 1999. write for info. (*0-306-45964-7*, Kluwer Plenum) Kluwer Academic.

***Modern Aspects of Electrochemistry, Vol. 33.** B. E. Conway et al. 555p. 1999. write for info. (*0-306-45968-X*, Kluwer Plenum) Kluwer Academic.

Modern Aspects of Emulsion Science. Ed. by B. P. Binks. 450p. 1999. 165.00 (*0-85404-439-6*) Royal Soc Chem.

Modern Aspects of Gold Therapy. Ed. by M. Schattenkirchner & W. Mueller. (Rheumatology Ser.: Vol. 8). (Illus.). viii, 232p. 1983. 113.25 (*3-8055-3630-5*) S Karger.

Modern Aspects of Linear Algebra. S. K. Godunov. Tr. by Tamara Ropzhkovskaya from RUS. LC 98-13024. (Translations of Mathematical Monographs: No. 1, Godunov). 309p. (C). 1998. 119.00 (*0-8218-0888-5*, MMONO-GODUNOV1) Am Math.

Modern Aspects of Manufacturing Management: Selected Readings. Ed. by Ivan R. Vernon. LC 70-118841. (Illus.). 350p. reprint ed. pap. 108.50 (*0-8357-6488-5*, 203585900097) Bks Demand.

Modern Aspects of Mass Spectrometry: Proceedings of the NATO Advanced Study Institute on Mass Spectrometry, 2nd, 1966. NATO Advanced Study Institute Staff. Ed. by Rowland I. Reed. LC 68-16994. 401p. reprint ed. pap. 124.40 (*0-608-09938-4*, 202070300018) Bks Demand.

Modern Aspects of Medicine, Vol. 3, No. 5. H. Baum & I. Roman. (Illus.). 133p. 1980. pap. 14.50 (*0-08-027378-5*, Pergamon Pr) Elsevier.

Modern Aspects of Protein Adsorption on Biomaterials. Ed. by Y. F. Missirlis & W. Lemm. (C). 1991. text 148.50 (*0-7923-0973-1*) Kluwer Academic.

Modern Aspects of Reflectance Spectroscopy: Proceedings. American Chemical Society Symposium on Reflectance. Ed. by Wesley W. Wendlandt. LC 68-19188. (Illus.). 264p. 1968. reprint ed. pap. 81.90 (*0-608-05478-X*, 206594700006) Bks Demand.

Modern Aspects of Small-Angle Scattering: Proceedings of the NATO Advanced Study Institute on Modern Aspects of Small-Angle Scattering, Como, Italy, May 12-22, 1993. NATO Advanced Study Institute on Modern Aspects of. Ed. by H. Brumberger. LC 94-40632. (NATO ASI, Series C). 480p. (C). 1994. text 285.00 (*0-7923-3251-2*) Kluwer Academic.

Modern Aspects of Species. Ed. by Kunio Iwatsuki et al. LC 87-169282. 258p. 1986. reprint ed. pap. 80.00 (*0-608-01221-1*, 206191000001) Bks Demand.

Modern Aspects of the Laws of Naval Warfare & Maritime Neutrality. George Politakis. LC 97-50129. (Illus.). xvi, 678 p. 1997. 161.50 (*0-7103-0589-3*, Pub. by Kegan Paul Intl) Col U Pr.

Modern Assays for Plant Pathogenic Fungi: Identification, Detection & Quantification. Ed. by A. Schots et al. (CAB International Publication). (Illus.). 288p. 1994. pap. text 52.50 (*0-85198-870-9*) OUP.

***Modern Assyrians of the Middle East: Encounters with Western Christian Missions, Archaeologist & Colonial Power.** John Joseph. LC 00-22484. (Studies in Christian Mission). 320p. 2000. 94.00 (*90-04-11641-9*) Brill Academic Pubs.

Modern Astrodynamics: Fundamentals & Perturbation Methods. Victor R. Bond & Mark C. Allman. LC 95-31024. 264p. (C). 1996. text 39.50 (*0-691-04459-7*, Pub. by Princeton U Pr) Cal Prin Full Svc.

Modern Astrometry. Jean Kovalevsky. LC 94-40219. (Astronomy & Astrophysics Library). 1994. 69.95 (*0-387-57023-3*) Spr-Verlag.

Modern Astronomy see Isaac Asimov's New Library of the Universe

Modern Astronomy: An Activities Approach. rev. ed. Mary K. Hemenway & R. Robert Robbins. (Illus.). 240p. 1991. pap. 27.95 (*0-292-75133-8*) U of Tex Pr.

Modern Athens. George Horton. 1977. lib. bdg. 59.95 (*0-8490-2262-2*) Gordon Pr.

Modern Athens: or Edinburgh in the Nineteenth Century. Thomas H. Shepherd & John Britton. LC 68-29694. (Illus.). 1972. reprint ed. 15.95 (*0-405-08961-9*) Ayer.

Modern Atlantic Salmon Flies. Paul Marriner. (Illus.). 128p. 1999. pap. 34.95 (*1-57188-152-2*); spiral bd. 44.95 (*1-57188-153-0*) F Amato Pubns.

Modern Atomic & Nuclear Physics. 2nd ed. Fujia Yang & Joseph Hamilton. (Illus.). 880p. (C). 1996. 95.31 (*0-07-025881-3*) McGraw.

Modern Attitudes in Psychiatry. New York Academy of Medicine Staff. LC 70-142683. (Essay Index Reprint Ser.). 1977. 19.95 (*0-8369-2121-6*) Ayer.

***Modern Audio Science.** Johnston. 900p. 2000. write for info. (*0-471-33255-0*) Wiley.

***Modern Auditing.** Graham W. Cossetat. LC 99-40990. 1999. write for info. (*0-471-81058-4*) Wiley.

Modern Auditing. 6th ed. William C. Boynton & Walter G. Kell. LC 94-41807. 960p. 1995. text 100.95 (*0-471-59687-6*) Wiley.

***Modern Auditing.** 7th ed. William C. Boynton et al. 992p. (C). 2000. text. write for info. (*0-471-18909-X*) Wiley.

Modern Auditing & Audsamp: Statistical Sampling Templates for Lotus 1-2-3 to Accompany Modern Auditing. 6th ed. William C. Boynton & Walter G. Kell. 960p. 1997. pap. text 113.90 (*0-471-17382-7*) Wiley.

Modern Australia in Documents, 1901-1970. Ed. by F. K. Crowley. Incl. 1939-1970. 1973. 7.50 (*0-85885-033-8*); 1973. write for info. (*0-318-51605-5*) Trafalgar.

Modern Australian Furniture: Profiles of Contemporary Designer-Makers. Michael Bogle. (Illus.). 160p. 1990. text 35.00 (*0-947131-26-4*) Gordon & Breach.

Modern Austria. Ed. by Kurt Steiner et al. LC 80-53944. (Illus.). 553p. (C). 1981. 26.00 (*0-930664-03-5*) SPOSS.

Modern Austria: Empire & Republic, 1815-1986. Barbara Jelavich. (Illus.). 368p. 1987. text 74.95 (*0-521-30320-6*) Cambridge U Pr.

Modern Austria: Empire & Republic, 1815-1986. Barbara Jelavich. (Illus.). 364p. 1987. pap. text 18.95 (*0-521-31625-1*) Cambridge U Pr.

Modern Austrian Writing: A Study Guide for Austrian Literature 1945-1990. Caroline Markolin. (Austrian Culture Ser.). XII, 272p. (C). 1995. pap. text 35.95 (*0-8204-2752-7*) P Lang Pubng.

Modern Austrian Writing: Literature & Society after 1945. Ed. by Alan D. Best & Hans Wolfshutz. 307p. 1980. 44.00 (*0-389-20038-7*, 06810) B&N Imports.

Modern Authoritarianism: A Comparative Institutional Analysis. Amos Perlmutter. LC 81-3403. 208p. reprint ed. pap. 64.50 (*0-7837-3306-2*, 205770800006) Bks Demand.

Modern Automotive Technology. James E. Duffy. LC 99-10562. 2000. text 57.00 (*1-56637-610-6*) Goodheart.

Modern Aviation Electronics. 2nd ed. Albert D. Helfrick. 352p. (C). 1994. text 67.60 (*0-13-097692-X*) P-H.

Modern B-W Portrait (Selectively Tinted) (How to Triple Your Sales Without Raising Prices) 3rd ed. Helen T. Boursier. (Illus.). 87p. 1991. reprint ed. pap. 29.50 (*0-934420-11-4*, 1409) Studio Pr NE.

Modern Backpacker's Handbook. Glenn Randall. LC 93-37444. (Illus.). 288p. 1994. pap. 14.95 (*1-55821-248-5*) Lyons Pr.

Modern Ballistic Armor: Clothing, Bomb Blankets, Shields, Vehicle Protection... Everything You Need to Know. Duncan Long. (Illus.). 104p. 1986. pap. 20.00 (*0-87364-391-7*) Paladin Pr.

Modern Ballroom Dance Instructor. Phyllis Haylor et al. (Ballroom Dance Ser.). 1986. lib. bdg. 79.95 (*0-8490-3263-6*) Gordon Pr.

Modern Ballroom Dancing. Victor Silvester. (Illus.). 224p. 1993. pap. 19.95 (*0-943955-77-7*, Trafalgar Sq Pub) Trafalgar.

Modern Bank. Amos K. Fiske. Ed. by Stuart Bruchey. LC 80-1147. (Rise of Commercial Banking Ser.). (Illus.). 1981. reprint ed. lib. bdg. 35.95 (*0-405-13650-1*) Ayer.

Modern Banking Checklists, 2 vols. annuals 3rd ed. Jack Kusnet & Justine Antopol. 1991. suppl. ed. 185.00 (*0-88262-582-9*) Warren Gorham & Lamont.

Modern Banking Forms. rev. ed. Ed. by Justine Antopol & Jack Kusnet. 1992. suppl. ed. 80.75 (*0-7913-0910-X*); suppl. ed. 83.25 (*0-7913-0990-8*) Warren Gorham & Lamont.

Modern Banking Forms, 3 vols, Set. rev. ed. Ed. by Justine Antopol & Jack Kusnet. 1992. 260.00 (*0-88262-549-7*) Warren Gorham & Lamont.

Modern Banking in the Balkans & West-European Capital in the 19th & 20th Century. Konstantinos P. Kostis. LC 98-29823. (Studies in Banking History). 300p. 1999. text 86.95 (*1-84014-269-3*, Pub. by Ashgate Pub) Ashgate Pub Co.

Modern Banking in Theory & Practice. Shelagh A. Heffernan. LC 95-44830. 470p. 1996. pap. 89.00 (*0-471-96209-0*) Wiley.

Modern Banking Law. 2nd ed. E. P. Ellinger. 834p. 1995. pap. text 52.00 (*0-19-825759-7*) OUP.

Modern Banking Law. 2nd ed. E. P. Ellinger & Eva Lomnicka. 834p. 1995. text 115.00 (*0-19-825758-9*) OUP.

Modern Banks. Vickie Stulb. LC 97-119152. (Illus.). 1997. write for info. (*0-89538-084-6*) L-W Inc.

***Modern Baptists.** James Wilcox. 1998. pap. 13.00 (*0-316-19093-4*, Back Bay) Little.

Modern Baptists. James Wilcox. 1994. reprint ed. lib. bdg. 28.95 (*1-56849-521-8*) Buccaneer Bks.

Modern Baptists: A Novel. James Wilcox. 256p. 1998. pap. 13.00 (*0-316-94045-3*) Little.

Modern Bar Advocacy. Justice C. Oputa & C. A. Oputa. LC 81-85779. xix, 224p. 1982. reprint ed. 60.00 (*0-912004-19-3*) Gaunt.

Modern Basic Drafting. 2nd ed. Rip B. Weaver. LC 74-27682. 396p. reprint ed. pap. 122.80 (*0-8357-2573-1*, 204026400015) Bks Demand.

Modern Basic Drafting Workbook, 2 pts., Pt. 1. Rip B. Weaver. LC T 0353.W35. 176p. reprint ed. pap. 54.60 (*0-8357-2571-5*, 204026300001) Bks Demand.

Modern Basic Drafting Workbook, 2 pts., Pt. 2. Rip B. Weaver. LC T 0353.W35. 64p. reprint ed. pap. 30.00 (*0-8357-2572-3*, 204026300002) Bks Demand.

Modern Basic Mathematics. Hobart C. Carter. LC 63-19876. (Illus.). 1964. 32.00 (*0-89197-305-2*) Irvington.

Modern Basics of Programming. Nickerson. (C). 1992. pap. 8.33 (*0-06-501133-3*) HarpC.

Modern Basketball Team Techniques. Harry L. Harkins. LC 85-9342. 216p. (C). 1985. text 29.95 (*0-13-587908-6*) P-H.

Modern Batteries: An Introduction to Electrochemical Power Sources. Colin Angus Vincent & Bruno Scrosati. 352p. 1997. pap. 49.95 (*0-7506-7092-4*) Buttrwrth-Heinemann.

Modern Batteries: An Introduction to Electrochemical Power Sources. 2nd ed. Ed. by Colin Angus Vincent & Bruno Scrosati. LC 97-227575. write for info. (*0-340-66278-6*, Pub. by E A) Routldge.

Modern Battle Tanks & Support Vehicles. Alan K. Russell. LC 97-16371. (Greenhill Military Manuals Ser.). 1998. write for info. (*1-85367-258-0*, Pub. by Greenhill Bks) Stackpole.

Modern Belgium. Ed. by Marina Boudart et al. LC 90-61813. 592p. 1990. 45.00 (*0-930664-10-8*) SPOSS.

Modern Bengal: A Socio-Economic Survey. Ratnalakha Ray & S. P. Sen. (C). 1990. 26.00 (*81-85421-00-5*, Pub. by Naya Prokash) S Asia.

***Modern Benoni.** Andrew Kinsman. 2001. pap. 19.95 (*1-85744-222-9*, Pub. by Everyman Chess) Globe Pequot.

Modern Beretta Firearms. Gene Gangarosa, Jr. (Illus.). 288p. (Orig.). 1994. pap. 16.95 (*0-88317-174-0*) Stoeger Pub Co.

Modern Bestiary. Thomas Dugan. LC 82-14515. (Illus.). 58p. (Orig.). 1982. pap. 9.95 (*0-940170-06-X*) Station Hill Pr.

Modern Bestiary: Animals in English Fiction, 1880-1945. David B. Asker. LC 95-15704. (Studies in British Literature: Vol. 24). 212p. 1996. text 89.95 (*0-7734-8908-8*) E Mellen.

Modern Bible Translations Unmasked. Russell Standish & Celia Standish. 228p. (Orig.). 1996. pap. 10.95 (*0-923309-13-6*) Hartland Pubns.

Modern Bible Versions. David W. Cloud. (Illus.). 48p. 1994. pap. 2.50 (*1-58318-010-9*, WOL467B) Way of Life.

Modern Bioelectricity. Andrew A. Marino. (Illus.). 737p. 1988. text 295.00 (*0-8247-7788-3*) Dekker.

Modern Bioelectrochemistry. Ed. by Felix Gutmann & Hendrik Keyzer. LC 85-19337. (Illus.). 654p. (C). 1986. text 186.00 (*0-306-41981-5*, Kluwer Plenum) Kluwer Academic.

Modern Biology. Lawrence. 1996. 44.67 (*0-582-44272-9*) Addison-Wesley.

Modern Biology. Towle. 1989. pap. text, teacher ed. 99.25 (*0-03-013922-8*) Holt R&W.

Modern Biology. Towle. 1991. text, teacher ed. 64.00 (*0-03-047029-3*); pap. text, teacher ed. 108.50 (*0-03-047032-3*) Holt R&W.

Modern Biology. Towle. 1993. pap. text, teacher ed. 133.00 (*0-03-074883-6*) Holt R&W.

Modern Biology. Albert Towle. 1993. text 64.00 (*0-03-074882-8*) Holt R&W.

Modern Biology, Vol. 1. V. B. Rastogi. 508p. 1997. pap. 150.00 (*81-209-0442-7*, Pub. by Pitambar Pub) St Mut.

Modern Biology, Vol. 2. V. B. Rastogi. 782p. 1997. pap. 200.00 (*81-209-0496-6*, Pub. by Pitambar Pub) St Mut.

Modern Biology: A Play in Two Acts about Genetic Engineering. Richard Katz. 99p. (Orig.). 1987. pap. 4.95 (*0-944906-00-1*) Playwright Pr Berkeley.

Modern Biology: Section Reviews. Towle. 1989. pap. text, teacher ed. 34.50 (*0-03-013934-1*); pap. text, suppl. ed. 27.50 (*0-03-013933-3*) Holt R&W.

Modern Biology: Spanish Glossary. 1991. pap. text 12.25 (*0-03-053117-9*) Holt R&W.

Modern Biology & Its Human Implications. J. A. Butler. LC 76-27619. 119p. 1976. pap. 12.00 (*0-8448-1007-X*, Crane Russak) Taylor & Francis.

Modern Biology, 1989. Towle. 1989. 59.50 (*0-03-013919-8*) Harcourt Schl Pubs.

Modern Biology, 1991. Towle. 1989. pap. text, lab manual ed. 29.00 (*0-03-013924-4*); pap. text, lab manual ed. 25.50 (*0-03-013927-9*) Holt R&W.

Modern Bird Hunting. Bill Miller & Tony Caligiuri. LC 89-63989. (Hunter's Information Ser.). 328p. 1990. write for info. (*0-914697-27-7*) N Amer Outdoor Grp.

Modern Bistrot Cookery. Antony W. Thompson. (Illus.). 192p. 1996. pap. 27.50 (*0-7472-7883-0*, Pub. by Headline Bk Pub) Trafalgar.

M

Modern Black American Fiction Writers see Writers of English: Lives & Works

Modern Black American Poets & Dramatists see Writers of English: Lives & Works

Modern Black Nationalism: From Marcus Garvey to Louis Farrakhan. Ed. by William L. Van DeBurg. LC 96-36071. 288p. (C). 1996. text 45.00 (*0-8147-8788-6*); pap. text 19.50 (*0-8147-8789-4*) NYU Pr.

Modern Black Writers. 2nd ed. St. James Press Staff. LC 99-48501. 600p. 1999. 150.00 (*1-55862-436-8*, GML00299-200977, Pub. by St James Pr) Gale.

Modern Blackfeet: Montanans on a Reservation. Malcolm McFee. (Illus.). 134p. 1984. reprint ed. pap. text 10.50 (*0-88133-043-4*) Waveland Pr.

Modern Block Printed Textiles. Alan Powers. (Decorative Arts Library). (Illus.). 93p. 1997. 19.95 (*0-7445-1891-1*) Antique Collect.

***Modern Blood Banking & Transfusion Practices.** 4th ed. Denise M. Harmening. LC 98-54477. 672p. 1999. 52.95 (*0-8036-0419-X*) Davis Co.

Modern Blues Jam Trax. Ralph Agresta. (JamTrax Ser.). (Illus.). 1992. pap. 9.95 (*0-8256-1322-1*, AM87416) Music Sales.

Modern Blues Jam Trax for Guitar. Ralph Agresta. 28p. pap. 10.95 incl. audio compact disk (*0-8256-1604-2*, AM943096) Omnibus NY.

Modern Blues Sessions for Guitar. Ed. by Ed Lazano. 6p. 1998. pap. 12.95 (*0-8256-1625-5*, AM945153) Music Sales.

Modern Boat Maintenance: The Complete Fiberglass Boat Manual. Ed. by Bo Streiffert. (Illus.). 192p. 1994. pap. 22.50 (*0-924486-71-6*) Sheridan.

Modern Bodybuilding: The Natural Way to Health & Strength. Eddie Ferrie & Dennis Oakes. (Illus.). 160p. 1997. pap. 24.95 (*1-86126-087-3*, Pub. by Cro1wood) Trafalgar.

Modern Bodyguard: The Manual of Close Protection Training. Peter Consterdine. 1998. pap. 39.95 (*1-873475-09-8*, Pub. by Summers) Howell Pr VA.

***Modern Boeing Jetliners.** Guy Norris & Mark Wagner. LC 99-29418. (Illus.). 176p. 1999. 19.98 (*0-7603-0717-2*, Pub. by MBI Pubg) Motorbooks Intl.

Modern Book Collecting. Robert A. Wilson. 276p. 1992. pap. 16.95 (*1-55821-179-9*) Lyons Pr.

Modern Book-Keeping & Accounting. G. Mn Dar. 600p. 1992. 140.00 (*81-7041-644-2*, Pub. by Scientific Pubs) St Mut.

Modern Book of Babies' Names. Hilary Spence. 195p. 1995. pap. 5.95 (*0-572-01174-1*, Pub. by Foulsham UK) Assoc Pubs Grp.

Modern Book of Esthetics. 5th ed. Melvin Rader. 563p. (C). 1979. text 65.00 (*0-03-019331-1*, Pub. by Harcourt Coll Pubs) Harcourt.

Modern Book of Feng Shui. Steven Post. LC 97-44961. 256p. 1998. pap. 15.95 (*0-440-50768-5*, Dell Trade Pbks) Dell.

Modern Book of the Black Bass. Byron Dalrymple & Dave Precht. 288p. 1995. 19.95 (*0-8329-0510-0*, Winchester Pr) New Win Pub.

Modern Bookbinding. Alex J. Vaughan. (Illus.). 240p. 1996. pap. 25.00 (*0-7090-5820-9*, Pub. by R Hale Ltd) Antique Collect.

Modern Bookkeeping & Accounting. 2nd ed. Morris Miller & Arthur Janis. LC 72-109961. (gr. 10-12). 1973. teacher ed. 8.48 (*0-02-830820-4*) Glencoe.

Modern Bookkeeping & Accounting. 2nd ed. Morris Miller & Arthur Janis. LC 72-109961. (YA). (gr. 10-12). 1973. student ed. 48.76 (*0-02-830830-1*) Glencoe.

Modern Brazil. Ed. by Mcgraw-Hill Staff. LC 98-12374. 168p. 1998. pap. 13.75 (*0-07-289122-X*) McGraw.

Modern Brazil: Elites & Masses in Historical Perspective. Ed. by Michael L. Conniff & Frank D. McCann. LC 88-19088. (Latin American Studies). xxviii, 306p. 1989. text 50.00 (*0-8032-3131-8*) U of Nebr Pr.

Modern Brazil: New Patterns & Development. Ed. by John V. Saunders. LC 72-630255. (Illus.). 360p. reprint ed. pap. 111.60 (*0-7837-4940-6*, 204460600004) Bks Demand.

Modern Brazilian Stage. David George. LC 91-579. (Illus.). 196p. (C). 1992. text 30.00 (*0-292-75129-X*) U of Tex Pr.

Modern Breast & Pelvic Examinations: A Handbook for Health Professionals. 4th rev. ed. Lila A. Wallis. viii, 104p. 1980. pap. 15.95 (*0-9678633-0-9*) Nat Council on Womens Health.

Modern Breton Political Poet - Anjela Duval: A Biography & an Anthology. Anjela Duval. Ed. & Tr. by Lenora A. Timm. LC 89-29829. (Studies in French Literature: Vol. 5). 296p. 1990. lib. bdg. 89.95 (*0-88946-570-3*) E Mellen.

Modern Brewery Age Bluebook. 135.00 (*0-937506-11-7*) Busn Journals.

Modern Bride Guide to Etiquette: Answers to the Questions Today's Couples Really Ask. Cele G. Lalli. LC 92-42166. 240p. (Orig.). 1993. pap. 16.95 (*0-471-58299-9*) Wiley.

Modern Bride Just Married: Everything You Need to Know to Plan Your New Life Together. Stephanie H. Dahl. 239p. 1994. pap. write for info. (*0-471-59669-8*) Wiley.

Modern Bride Wedding Celebrations: The Complete Wedding Planner for Today's Bride. 2nd rev. ed. Cele G. Lalli & Stephanie H. Dahl. LC 96-6327. (Illus.). 237p. 1996. pap. 15.95 (*0-471-14111-9*) Wiley.

Modern Bridge Conventions. W. Root & Richard Pavlicek. 1995. pap. 16.00 (*0-517-88429-1*) Random.

Modern Bride 3 - Honeymoons & Weddings Away: The Complete Guide to Planning Your Most Romantic Trip Ever. Geri Bain. LC 95-1298. (Modern Bride Library). 256p. 1995. pap. 16.95 (*0-471-00722-6*) Wiley.

Modern Britain. Ed. by Boris Ford. (Cultural History of Britain Ser.). (Illus.). 362p. (C). 1992. pap. text 27.95 (*0-521-42889-0*) Cambridge U Pr.

Modern Britain. Peter Murray & Stephen Trombley. (Illus.). 192p. 1997. 14.95 (*0-7148-3133-6*, Pub. by Phaidon Press) Phaidon Pr.

Modern Britain: A Social History, 1750-1985. Edward Royle. 400p. (C). 1995. pap. text 25.00 (*0-7131-6477-8*, Pub. by E A) St Martin.

Modern Britain: An Economic & Social History. Sean Glynn & Alan Booth. LC 95-12329. 384p. (C). 1995. pap. 24.99 (*0-415-10473-4*) Routledge.

Modern Britain: An Introduction. 2nd ed. John L. Irwin. LC 93-1713. 1993. reprint ed. pap. write for info. (*0-415-09902-1*) Routledge.

Modern Britain: A Social History, 1750-1997. 2nd ed. Edward Royle. 496p. 1997. pap. text 24.95 (*0-340-57944-7*) OUP.

Modern Britain, 1700-1980: A Domestic History. Geoffrey Alderman. 256p. (C). 1986. 52.50 (*0-7099-0537-8*, Pub. by C Helm) Routldge.

***Modern Britain Since 1906: A Reader.** Keith Laybourn. 2000. pap. 24.50 (*1-86064-237-3*, Pub. by I B T); text 59.50 (*1-86064-298-5*, Pub. by I B T) St Martin.

Modern British Art: Vorticism & the Grosvenor School, 1912-1935. Judith C. Eurich. (Illus.). 28p. 1993. pap. 9.95 (*1-886091-05-6*) Hearst Art Gal.

Modern British Drama. Charles A. Carpenter. LC 76-4654. (Goldentree Bibliographies Series in Language & Literature). (C). 1979. pap. text 14.95 (*0-88295-559-4*) Harlan Davidson.

Modern British Drama, 1890-1990. Christopher D. Innes. (Illus.). 508p. (C). 1992. text 80.00 (*0-521-30536-5*); pap. text 24.95 (*0-521-31555-7*) Cambridge U Pr.

Modern British Dramatists, 1900 to 1945, 2 vols., Set. Ed. by Stanley Weintraub. (Dictionary of Literary Biography Ser.: Vol. 10). (Illus.). 664p. 1982. text 296.00 (*0-8103-0937-8*) Gale.

Modern British Economy in Historical Perspective. K. S. Reader. LC 78-423071. xii, 236 p. 1969. write for info. (*0-582-41029-0*) Longman.

Modern British Essayists. Robert L. Beum. LC 90-43746. (Dictionary of Literary Biography Ser.). 426p. 1990. text 155.00 (*0-8103-4580-3*) Gale.

Modern British Farce: A Selective Study of British Farce from Pinero to the Present Day. Leslie Smith. LC 88-29244. 224p. (C). 1989. lib. bdg. 50.50 (*0-389-20820-5*) B&N Imports.

Modern British Fiction: An Exhibit of Books, Paintings & Manuscripts. Illus. by William R. Holman. LC 73-180336. 1972. pap. 10.00 (*0-87959-033-5*) U of Tex H Ransom Ctr.

Modern British History: A Guide to Study & Research. Larry Butler & Anthony Gorst. LC 97-178046. 288p. 1997. pap. 19.95 (*1-86064-208-X*, Pub. by I B T) St Martin.

Modern British Jewry. Geoffrey Alderman. 416p. 1992. 95.00 (*0-19-820145-1*) OUP.

Modern British Jewry. Geoffrey Alderman. (Illus.). 444p. 1998. reprint ed. pap. text 35.00 (*0-19-820759-X*) OUP.

Modern British Literature. Ed. by Frank Kermode & John Hollander. (Anthology of English Literature Ser.). (Illus.). 730p. 1973. text 30.95 (*0-19-501652-1*) OUP.

Modern British Literature, 3 vols. 2nd ed. St. James Press Staff. 1800p. 1999. 350.00 (*1-55862-418-X*) St James Pr.

Modern British Lyrics: An Anthology. Ed. by Stanton A. Coblentz. LC 70-38596. (Granger Index Reprint Ser.). 1977. reprint ed. 17.95 (*0-8369-6328-8*) Ayer.

Modern British Music: The Second British Musical Renaissance - from Elgar to P. Maxwell Davies. Otto Karolyi. LC 92-55105. 1994. 31.50 (*0-8386-3532-6*) Fairleigh Dickinson.

Modern British Novel. Malcolm Bradbury. (Orig.). 1999. pap. 25.00 (*0-670-85583-9*) Viking Penguin.

Modern British Novel of the Left: A Research Guide. M. Keith Booker. LC 97-43861. 424p. 1998. lib. bdg. 89.50 (*0-313-30343-6*, Greenwood Pr) Greenwood.

Modern British Plutarch: or Lives of Men Distinguished in the Recent History of England for Their Talents, Virtues, or Achievements. William C. Taylor. LC 72-1264. (Essay Index Reprint Ser.). 1977. reprint ed. 23.95 (*0-8369-2866-0*) Ayer.

Modern British Poetry, 1900-1939. James Persoon. LC 99-29212. 207p. 1999. 29.95 (*0-8057-1681-5*, Twyne) Mac Lib Ref.

Modern British Statesmen, 1867-1945. Richard N. Kelly & John Cantrell. LC 97-14152. 224p. 1998. pap. 27.95 (*0-7190-5080-4*, Pub. by Manchester Univ Pr); text 79.95 (*0-7190-5079-0*) Manchester Univ Pr.

Modern British Utopias, 1700-1850, 8 vols. Ed. by Gregory Claeys. LC 96-23444. 4128p. 1997. 880.00 (*1-85196-319-7*, Pub. by Pickering & Chatto) Ashgate Pub Co.

Modern Buddhism & Its Followers in Orissa. Nagendra N. Vasu. 181p. (C). 1987. reprint ed. 22.00 (*81-212-0056-3*, Pub. by Usha) S Asia.

Modern Buddhist-Christian Dialogue: Two Universalistic Religions in Transformation. Paul O. Ingram. LC 87-14108. (Studies in Comparative Religion: Vol. 2). 448p. 1987. lib. bdg. 109.95 (*0-88946-490-1*) E Mellen.

Modern Budgeting. Allen Schick. LC 98-121834. 136p. 1998. pap. 30.00 (*92-64-15678-X*, 42-97-09-1, Pub. by Org for Econ) OECD.

Modern Bujutsu & Budo. Donn F. Draeger. (Martial Arts & Ways of Japan Ser.: Vol. 3). 1996. pap. text 19.95 (*0-8348-0351-8*) Weatherhill.

Modern Bulgaria: Problems & Tasks in Building an Advanced Socialist Society. Todor Zhivkov. LC 74-23868. 256p. reprint ed. pap. 79.40 (*0-608-12011-1*, 202286900030) Bks Demand.

Modern Business. Hamilton. 1994. 75.00 (*0-316-34135-5*) Little.

Modern Business Administration. R. C. Appleby. 401p. (C). 1987. 140.00 (*0-7855-5687-7*, Pub. by Inst Pur & Supply) St Mut.

Modern Business Administration. R. C. Appleby. 401p. (C). 1988. 100.00 (*0-7855-3776-7*, Pub. by Inst Pur & Supply) St Mut.

Modern Business Administration. R. C. Appleby. 401p. (C). 1989. 135.00 (*0-7855-4631-6*, Pub. by Inst Pur & Supply) St Mut.

Modern Business Administration. 6th ed. Robert C. Appleby. 512p. 1994. pap. 52.50 (*0-273-60282-9*, Pub. by Pitman Pub) Trans-Atl Phila.

Modern Business & Commercial Law Guide. 2nd ed. Kaplan. 1344p. 1992. 85.00 (*0-685-67012-0*, 04795001) CCH INC.

Modern Business Correspondence. Donna C. McComas & Marilyn L. Satterwhite. 1993. teacher ed. 21.79 (*0-02-803013-3*) Glencoe.

Modern Business Correspondence. 6th ed. Donna C. McComas & Marilyn L. Satterwhite. 320p. 1993. text, wbk. ed. 41.59 (*0-02-803012-5*) Glencoe.

Modern Business Cycle Theory. Ed. by Robert J. Barro. LC 88-28303. (Illus.). 400p. 1989. 49.95 (*0-674-57860-0*) HUP.

Modern Business English. 7th ed. M. A. Wittenberg & Price R. Voiles. 272p. 1986. text 56.95 (*0-07-071206-9*) McGraw.

Modern Business English. 8th ed. Price R. Voiles. 280p. 1992. text, wbk. ed. 42.37 (*0-02-803009-5*) Glencoe.

Modern Business English. 8th ed. Price R. Voiles. 1992. teacher ed. 21.79 (*0-02-803010-9*) Glencoe.

Modern Business English: A Text-workbook for Colleges. 6th ed. Mary A. Wittenberg & Price R. Voiles. LC 78-23855. vi, 250 p. 1979. write for info. (*0-07-071185-2*) Gregg-McGraw.

Modern Business Financing. Robert Colman. LC 85-20490. 281p. 1985. 59.95 (*0-13-589060-8*, Busn) P-H.

Modern Business Foundations. Sandomir & Boardman. 368p. 1998. pap. text, wbk. ed. 30.75 (*0-536-01431-0*) Pearson Custom.

Modern Business Law. 3rd ed. Thomas W. Dunfee et al. LC 94-40587. 1376p. (C). 1995. 90.94 (*0-07-018212-4*) McGraw.

Modern Business Law: The Regulatory Environment. 3rd ed. Thomas W. Dunfee & Frank F. Gibson. (C). 1995. pap., student ed. 31.25 (*0-07-018217-5*) McGraw.

Modern Business Statistics. George C. Canavos & Don M. Miller. LC 94-28751. 952p. 1994. pap. 110.95 (*0-534-16836-1*) Wadsworth Pub.

***Modern by Tradition: American Indian Painting in the Studio Style.** Bruce Bernstein & W. Jackson Rushing. (Illus.). 176p. 1999. pap. 29.95 (*0-89013-291-7*) Museum NM Pr.

Modern by Tradition: American Indian Painting in the Studio Style. Bruce Bernstein & W. Jackson Rushing. (Illus.). 120p. 1999. pap. 29.95 (*0-89013-286-0*, Pub. by Museum NM Pr) U of NM Pr.

***Modern Cabinetmaking.** William D. Umstattd & Davis. LC 98-44628. (Illus.). 912p. 2000. 53.28 (*1-56637-503-7*) Goodheart.

Modern Cabins: A Memoir of the Sixties. James L. Rice. LC 96-79976. 240p. (Orig.). 1997. pap. 10.95 (*0-9656250-3-6*) Mohawk Pr.

Modern Cable Television Technology: Video, Voice & Data Communication. Walter Ciciora et al. LC 98-35328. 800p. (Orig.). (C). 1998. pap. 79.95 (*1-55860-416-2*) Morgan Kaufmann.

Modern Calculus Course: From the Manuscripts of the Masters. Alexander J. Hahn. LC 97-997. 600p. 1997. 55.00 (*0-387-94606-3*) Spr-Verlag.

Modern California Business Directory & Buyers Guide 1999. 9th ed. 1546p. 1999. 175.00 (*1-57541-083-4*) Database Pub Co.

Modern California Discovery, 3 vols. 4th ed. James E. Hogan. LC 76-185900. 1993. suppl. ed. 50.00 (*0-317-03217-8*) West Group.

Modern California Discovery, 2 vols. 4th ed. James E. Hogan & Weber. LC 76-185900. Date not set. text 180.00 (*0-317-03216-X*, 68575, MICHIE) LEXIS Pub.

Modern California Politics. 4th ed. Jackson K. Putnam. Ed. by Norris Hundley, Jr. & John A. Schutz. (Golden State Ser.). (Illus.). 160p. 1990. 12.00 (*0-929651-02-2*) MTL.

Modern Calligraphy Made Easy: A New Script for Streamlined Lettering. Margaret Shepherd. (Illus.). 64p. (Orig.). 1988. pap. 9.95 (*0-399-51450-3*, Perigee Bks) Berkley Pub.

Modern Camouflage. 2nd rev. ed. Duncan Long. LC 91-73266. (Illus.). 80p. 1992. pap. text 10.00 (*0-939427-65-6*) Alpha Pubns OH.

Modern Campaigns, 15 vols. (Illus.). 1680p. (YA). (gr. 7). 1997. lib. bdg. 335.00 (*0-7172-7678-3*) Grolier Educ.

Modern Canadian Plays. 3rd ed. Ed. by Jerry Wasserman. LC 94-174204. 416p. 1994. pap. 26.95 (*0-88922-339-4*) Genl Dist Srvs.

Modern Canadian Plays, Vol. II. 3rd ed. Ed. by Jerry Wasserman. LC 94-174204. 368p. 1994. pap. 26.95 (*0-88922-340-8*) Genl Dist Srvs.

Modern Canadian Women Playrights. Cynthia Zimmerman. Ed. by Kimball King. (Studies in Modern Drama). 300p. 1997. text 45.00 (*0-8153-2090-6*) Garland.

Modern Canoe. Ted Bissland. 160p. 1994. pap. 18.95 (*0-385-25463-6*) Doubleday.

Modern Cantonese Phonology. Paul K. Benedict & Robert S. Bauer. LC 97-8574. (Trends in Linguistics Ser.). 304p. (C). 1997. lib. bdg. 117.05 (*3-11-014893-5*) Mouton.

Modern Capital Theory. Donald Dewey. LC 65-22157. (Illus.). 238p. 1965. text 57.50 (*0-231-02831-8*) Col U Pr.

Modern Capitalism: Its Growth & Transformation. John Cornwall. LC 82-5490. 240p. reprint ed. pap. 74.40 (*0-608-18123-4*, 203277600081) Bks Demand.

Modern Capitalism: Its Origin & Evolution. Henri E. See. Tr. by H. B. Vanderblue & G. Doriot. LC 67-30864. (Reprints of Economic Classics Ser.). xvi, 225p. 1968. reprint ed. 35.00 (*0-678-00388-2*) Kelley.

Modern Capitalism: Privatization, Employee Ownership, & Industrial Democracy. Nicholas V. Gianaris. LC 95-30658. 224p. 1995. 57.95 (*0-275-95241-X*, Praeger Pubs) Greenwood.

Modern Capitalism & Islamic Ideology in Iran. Ed. by Cyrus Bina & Hamid Zangeneh. LC 91-12418. 256p. 1992. text 45.00 (*0-312-04780-0*) St Martin.

Modern Capitalism & Other Essays. Paul M. Sweezy. LC 70-178716. 192p. (Orig.). 1972. pap. 10.00 (*0-85345-216-4*, Pub. by Monthly Rev) NYU Pr.

Modern Carbohydrate Chemistry. Roger W. Binkley. (Food Science & Technology Ser.: Vol. 27). (Illus.). 344p. 1987. text 175.00 (*0-8247-7789-1*) Dekker.

Modern Cardiovascular Physiology. 2nd ed. Carl R. Honig. (Illus.). 336p. 1988. 40.00 (*0-316-37213-7*, Little Brwn Med Div) Lppncott W & W.

Modern Caribbean. Ed. by Franklin W. Knight & Colin A. Palmer. LC 88-25022. xiv, 382p. (C). 1989. pap. 19.95 (*0-8078-4240-0*) U of NC Pr.

Modern Caribbean Politics. Ed. by Anthony J. Payne & Paul Sutton. LC 92-14475. 400p. 1993. pap. text 16.95 (*0-8018-4435-5*) Johns Hopkins.

Modern Caribbean Politics. Ed. by Anthony J. Payne & Paul Sutton. LC 92-14475. 400p. 1993. text 50.00 (*0-8018-4434-7*) Johns Hopkins.

Modern, Caring, Sensitive Male. Joe Soucheray. LC 94-3652. 176p. 1994. pap. 9.95 (*0-8362-8082-2*) Andrews & McMeel.

***Modern Carpentry: Building Construction Details in Easy-to-Understand Form.** Willis H. Wagner. (Illus.). 195p. 2000. pap. 11.96 (*1-56637-570-3*) Goodheart.

Modern Carpentry: Building Construction Details in Easy-to-Understand Form. Willis H. Wagner & Howard S. Smith. LC 98-53652. 795p. 2000. text 49.28 (*1-56637-569-X*) Goodheart.

Modern Catalan Literature Vol. 18: Proceedings of the 4th Catalan Symposium. Ed. by Josep M. Sola-Sole. (Catalan Studies: Translations & Criticism). 232p. (C). 1995. 48.95 (*0-8204-2779-9*) P Lang Pubng.

***Modern Catalan Plays.** John London. 2000. pap. 14.95 (*0-413-74440-X*) Methn.

Modern Catalan Poetry. Ed. by David H. Rosenthal. 93p. 1979. pap. 6.00 (*0-89823-000-4*) New Rivers Pr.

Modern Catalytic Methods for Organic Synthesis with Diazo Compounds: From Cyclopropanes to Ylides. Michael Doyle et al. LC 97-16541. 652p. 1998. 135.00 (*0-471-13556-9*) Wiley.

***Modern Catholic Dictionary.** unabridged ed. John A. Hardon. LC 99-64264. 635p. 1999. reprint ed. 26.95 (*0-9672989-1-1*); reprint ed. pap. 14.95 (*0-9672989-2-X*) Eternal Life Inc.

Modern Catholic Encyclopedia. Ed. by Monika K. Hellwig & Michael Glazier. 976p. (Orig.). 1994. 69.95 (*0-8146-5495-9*, M Glazier) Liturgical Pr.

Modern Catholic Novel. Theodore P. Fraser. LC 94-7443. (Twayne's World Authors Ser.: No. 841). 240p. 1994. 32.00 (*0-8057-4514-9*, Twyne) Mac Lib Ref.

Modern Catholic Thinkers. Ed. by Aloysius R. Caponigri. LC 78-117775. (Essay Index Reprint Ser.). 1977. 42.95 (*0-8369-1787-1*) Ayer.

Modern Catholic Thinkers: An Anthology. Aloysius R. Caponigri. (Essay Index Reprint Ser.). 650p. reprint ed. lib. bdg. 40.50 (*0-8290-0784-9*) Irvington.

Modern Cellular Automata: Theory & Applications. K. Preston, Jr. & M. J. Duff. LC 84-11672. (Advanced Applications in Pattern Recognition Ser.). (Illus.). 368p. (C). 1984. 95.00 (*0-306-41737-5*, Plenum Trade) Perseus Pubng.

Modern Ceramic Engineering: Properties, Processing, & Use in Design. 2nd ed. Ed. by D. Richerson. (Materials Engineering Ser.: Vol. 1). (Illus.). 880p. 1992. text 175.00 (*0-8247-8634-3*) Dekker.

Modern Cereal Science & Technology. Y. Pomeranz. LC 87-13364. 468p. 1987. 130.00 (*0-89573-326-9*, Wiley-VCH) Wiley.

Modern Chair: Classic Designs by Thonet, Breuer, Le Corbusier, Eames & Others. Clement Meadmore. LC 97-19699. (Illus.). 192p. 1997. pap. 13.95 (*0-486-29807-8*) Dover.

Modern Chair: Its Origins & Evolution. Richard Armstrong. LC 77-84973. (Illus.). 62p. 1977. pap. 7.00 (*0-934418-05-5*) Mus Contemp Art.

Modern Chairs. Charlotte Fiell. (SPA.). 1996. pap. 24.95 (*3-8228-0757-5*) Taschen Amer.

Modern Character of Consumer. Howells. 73.95 (*1-85521-926-3*) Ashgate Pub Co.

***Modern Characterization Methods of Surfactant Systems.** Bernard P. Binks. LC 99-22026. (Surfactant Science Ser.). (Illus.). 624p. 1999. text 195.00 (*0-8247-1978-6*) Dekker.

Modern Chartwork. rev. ed. Rev. by W. H. Squair. (C). 1987. 114.00 (*0-85174-436-2*) St Mut.

Modern Chemical Analysis & Instrumentation. Harold F. Walton & Jorge Reyes. LC 72-90967. (Undergraduate Chemistry Ser.: No. 2). (Illus.). 363p. reprint ed. pap. 112.60 (*0-7837-0765-7*, 204107900019) Bks Demand.

Modern Chemistry. H. Clark Metcalfe. 1986. text 64.50 (*0-03-001274-0*) Holt R&W.

Modern Chemistry. Tzimopoulo. 1990. text 88.25 (*0-03-014503-1*) Holt R&W.

Modern Chemistry. Nicholas D. Tzimopoulo. 1990. text 64.50 (*0-03-014502-3*) Holt R&W.

Modern Chemistry. 99th annot. ed. Ed. by HRW Staff. 1997. teacher ed. 88.25 (*0-03-051389-8*) H Holt & Co.

M

An Asterisk (*) at the beginning of an entry indicates that the title is appearing for the first time.

Modern Chemistry, 1986. Metcalfe. 1986. pap., teacher ed. 79.75 (*0-03-001277-5*) H Holt & Co.

Modern Chemistry, 1993. Tzimopoulo. 1993. text, teacher ed. 79.75 (*0-03-075961-7*); text, student ed. 58.25 (*0-03-075959-5*) H Holt & Co.

Modern Chemistry Problem Solving. 90th ed. Tzimopoulo. 1990. pap. text, student ed. 17.75 (*0-03-014508-2*) Holt R&W.

Modern Chess Brilliances. 2nd ed. Larry Evans. LC 95-119806. (Great Chess Literature Ser.). 250p. 1994. pap. 19.95 (*1-886040-11-7*) Hypermodern Pr.

Modern Chess Instructor. Wilhelm Steinitz. (Tschaturanga Ser.: Vol. 47). 310p. 1984. reprint ed. 37.70 (*3-283-00111-1*, Pub. by Edition Olms) Lubrecht & Cramer.

Modern Chess Opening Theory. A. S. Suetin. Ed. by P. H. Clarke. Tr. by D. J. Richards. (Chess Ser.). (Illus.). 336p. 1965. 21.00 (*0-08-011199-8*, Pergamon Pr); pap. 11.95 (*0-08-011198-X*, Pergamon Pr) Elsevier.

Modern Chess Openings. 13th ed. Walter Korn. 1990. 32.50 (*0-8129-1730-8*, Times Bks); pap. 23.00 (*0-8129-1785-5*, Times Bks) Crown Pub Group.

Modern Chess Openings. 14th ed. Nick De Firmian. 736p. 1999. 40.00 (*0-8129-3083-5*, Times Bks); pap. 30.00 (*0-8129-3084-3*, Times Bks) Crown Pub Group.

Modern Chess Sacrifice. Shamkovi. 1978. 9.95 (*0-679-13054-3*) McKay.

Modern Chess Self-Tutor. David Bronstein. 144p. 1996. pap. 17.95 (*1-85744-136-2*) Macmillan.

Modern Chess Strategy. Ludek Pachman. Tr. by Allen S. Russell from CZE. (Illus.). 314p. 1971. reprint ed. pap. 8.95 (*0-486-20290-9*) Dover.

Modern Chess Strategy. rev. ed. Edward Lasker. 1979. pap. 15.00 (*0-679-14022-0*, 9, Tarten) McKay.

Modern Child Custody: 1989 Supplement. Jeff Atkinson. 1989. write for info. (*0-930273-62-1*, 60214-10, MICHIE) LEXIS Pub.

Modern Child Custody Practice, 1998 Cumulative Supplement, 2 vols. Jeff Atkinson. 475p. 1998. suppl. ed. write for info. (*0-327-00352-9*, 6021715) LEXIS Pub.

Modern Child Custody Practice, 1998 Cumulative Supplement, Vol. 1. Jeff Atkinson. 475p. 1998. suppl. ed. write for info. (*0-327-00353-7*, 6021715) LEXIS Pub.

Modern Child Custody Practice, 1998 Cumulative Supplement, Vol. 2. Jeff Atkinson. 475p. 1998. suppl. ed. write for info. (*0-327-00354-5*, 6021715) LEXIS Pub.

Modern Child Custody Practices with 1991 Cumulative Supplements, 2 vols., Set. Jeff Atkinson. 1986. 170.00 (*0-930273-34-6*, 60210-10, MICHIE) LEXIS Pub.

Modern Chile: A Critical History. Mark Falcoff. 340p. (C). 1990. pap. 19.95 (*0-88738-867-1*) Transaction Pubs.

Modern Chile, 1970 to 1989: A Critical History. Mark Falcoff. 300p. 1989. 39.95 (*0-88738-257-6*) Transaction Pubs.

Modern China. McGraw-Hill Publishing Staff. LC 98-44545. 192p. 1998. pap. 13.75 (*0-07-292826-3*) McGraw.

Modern China: A History. Edwin E. Moise. (Illus.). 256p. (C). 1989. pap. text 30.80 (*0-582-49077-4*, 73474) Longman.

Modern China: A History. 2nd ed. Edwin E. Moise. LC 93-47289. (Present & Past Ser.). (C). 1995. pap. text 35.00 (*0-582-07480-0*, 76772) Addison-Wesley.

Modern China: A History (Present & the Past) Edwin E. Moise. (Illus.). 256p. (C). 1986. boxed set 26.95 (*0-582-49076-6*, 73474) Longman.

Modern China: An Encyclopedia of History, Culture, & Nationalism. Ed. by Wang Ke-wen. LC 98-31749. 442p. 1999. pap. 35.00 (*0-8153-3322-6*) Garland.

Modern China: An Encyclopedia of History, Culture & Nationalism. Ke-wen Wang & CRSN Staff. LC 97-19299. (Illus.). 480p. 1997. text 95.00 (*0-8153-0720-9*, H1519) Garland.

Modern China: An Illustrated History. J. A. Roberts. LC 98-191000. (Illus.). 320p. 1998. 39.95 (*0-86299-847-6*, Pub. by Sutton Pub Ltd) Intl Pubs Mktg.

***Modern China: An Illustrated History.** J. A. G. Roberts. 2000. reprint ed. pap. 19.95 (*0-7509-2570-1*, Pub. by Sutton Publng) Intl Pubs Mktg.

Modern China & Japan. Biggerstaff. 1988. 34.75 (*0-07-557264-8*) McGraw.

Modern China & Japan: A Brief History. Conrad Schirokauer. 358p. (C). 1982. pap. text 40.00 (*0-15-559870-8*, Pub. by Harcourt Coll Pubs) Harcourt.

Modern China in Transition: Studies in Honor of Immanuel C. Y. Hsu. Ed. by Philip Y. Leung & Edwin P. Leung. LC 95-30491. 1995. 36.95 (*0-941690-63-6*); pap. 17.95 (*0-941690-68-7*) Regina Bks.

Modern Chinese: A Basic Course. Peking University staff. LC 78-169835. 249p. 1971. reprint ed. pap. text 6.95 (*0-486-22755-3*) Dover.

Modern Chinese: A Basic Course. 16th ed. Peking University staff. LC 78-169835. 249p. 1984. reprint ed. pap. 18.95 incl. audio (*0-486-99910-6*) Dover.

Modern Chinese: A Basic Course by the Faculty of Peking University. Peking University staff. 1971. 14.95 (*0-486-98832-5*) Dover.

Modern Chinese: A Second Course. rev. ed. Peking University staff. (Illus.). 472p. (C). 1981. reprint ed. pap. 11.95 (*0-486-24155-6*) Dover.

Modern Chinese: History & Sociolinguistics. Ping Chen. LC 98-38449. (Illus.). 250p. (C). 1999. text 59.95 (*0-521-64197-7*); pap. text 21.95 (*0-521-64572-7*) Cambridge U Pr.

***Modern Chinese Art.** David Clarke. LC 99-35800. (Images of Asia Ser.). (Illus.). 96p. 2000. text 16.95 (*0-19-590606-3*) OUP.

Modern Chinese Characters. Yin Binyong & John Rohsenow. (Illus.). 397p. 1994. 16.95 (*0-8351-2474-6*) China Bks.

Modern Chinese Civilization. A. F. Legendre. Tr. by Elsie M. Jones from FRE. LC 72-7076. (Select Bibliographies Reprint Ser.). 1977. reprint ed. 23.95 (*0-8369-6946-4*) Ayer.

Modern Chinese-English Dictionary. Foreign Language Teaching & Research Press Editori. (Illus.). 1260p. 1990. 38.00 (*0-19-585189-7*) OUP.

Modern Chinese Legal & Political Philosophy. Yu-hao Tseng. 1972. lib. bdg. 250.00 (*0-87968-564-6*) Krishna Pr.

Modern Chinese Literary & Cultural Studies: Theoretical Issues. Wen-Hsin Yeh. LC 99-24300. (China Research Monograph Ser.). Date not set. pap. 15.00 (*1-55729-064-4*) IEAS.

***Modern Chinese Literary & Cultural Studies in the Age of Theory: Reimagining a Field.** Rey Chow. LC 00-29425. (Illus.). 328p. 2000. pap. write for info. (*0-8223-2597-7*) Duke.

***Modern Chinese Literary & Cultural Studies in the Age of Theory: Reimagining a Field.** Ed. by Rey Chow. LC 00-29425. (Illus.). 328p. 2000. lib. bdg. 59.95 (*0-8223-2584-5*) Duke.

Modern Chinese Literary Thought: Writings on Literature, 1893-1945. Ed. by Kirk A. Denton. LC 95-1269. 564p. 1995. 75.00 (*0-8047-2558-6*); pap. 24.95 (*0-8047-2559-4*) Stanford U Pr.

Modern Chinese Literature in the May Fourth Era: A Social Science Research Council Study. Ed. by Merle R. Goldman. (East Asian Monographs: No. 89). 448p. 1990. pap. 21.50 (*0-674-57911-9*) HUP.

Modern Chinese Medicine, 3 vols., Set. Incl. Volume 1. Ed. by Wu He-guang. 1984. lib. bdg. 186.00 (*0-85200-788-4*); Volume 3. Ed. by Lin Haifeng. 1984. text 225.00 (*0-85200-790-6*); Volume 2. Ed. by Wu He-guang. 1984. text 225.00 (*0-85200-789-2*); 1984. Set text 571.00 (*0-85200-795-7*) Kluwer Academic.

Modern Chinese Paintings: The Reyes Collection in the Ashmolean Museum. Shelagh J. Vainker. (Illus.). 96p. (Orig.). 1997. pap. 19.95 (*1-85444-079-9*, 0499, Pub. by Ashmolean Mus) A Schwartz & Co.

Modern Chinese Poetry. Harold Acton. 1972. lib. bdg. 250.00 (*0-87968-195-0*) Krishna Pr.

Modern Chinese Poetry. Ed. by Richard F. Chang. 1973. 13.95 (*0-88710-049-X*) Yale Far Eastern Pubns.

Modern Chinese Poetry: Twenty Poets from the Republic of China, 1955-1965. Tr. & Selected by Wai-lim Yip. LC 78-118721. 214p. reprint ed. pap. 66.40 (*0-7837-1629-X*, 204192200024) Bks Demand.

Modern Chinese Society: An Analytical Bibliography, 3 vols. Ed. by G. William Skinner et al. Incl. Vol. 1. Publications in Western Languages, 1644-1972. LC 70-130831. xviii, 802p. 1973. 79.50 (*0-8047-0751-0*); Vol. 2. Publications in Chinese, 1644-1969. Ed. by Winston Hsieh. LC 70-130831. lxvi, 802p. 1973. 79.50 (*0-8047-0752-9*); Vol. 3. Publications in Japanese, 1644-1971. Ed. by Shigeaki Tomita. LC 70-130831. lxx, 532p. 1973. 59.50 (*0-8047-0753-7*); LC 70-130831. 1973. write for info. (*0-318-55861-0*) Stanford U Pr.

***Modern Chinese State.** Ed. by David Shambaugh. (Cambridge Modern China Ser.). (Illus.). 228p. (C). 2000. 59.95 (*0-521-77234-6*); pap. 19.95 (*0-521-77603-1*) Cambridge U Pr.

Modern Chinese Stories & Novellas, 1919-1949. Ed. by Joseph S. Lau et al. LC 80-27572. (Modern Asian Literature Ser.). (ENG.). 608p. 1981. pap. text 32.50 (*0-231-04203-5*) Col U Pr.

Modern Chinese Women Writers: Critical Appraisals. Ed. by Michael S. Duke. LC 89-36633. 290p. (gr. 13). 1989. 74.95 (*0-87332-536-2*, East Gate Bk); pap. 38.95 (*0-87332-623-7*, East Gate Bk) M E Sharpe.

Modern Chinese Writers: Self-Portrayals. Ed. by Helmut Martin & Jeffrey C. Kinkley. LC 91-31578. (Studies on Modern China). 424p. (C). (gr. 13). 1992. 81.95 (*0-87332-816-7*, East Gate Bk); pap. 30.95 (*0-87332-817-5*, East Gate Bk) M E Sharpe.

Modern Chivalry. Hugh H. Brackenridge. Ed. by Lewis Leary. (Masterworks of Literature Ser.). 1965. pap. 14.95 (*0-8084-0221-8*, M4) NCUP.

Modern Chivalry. Hugh H. Brackenridge. 1988. reprint ed. lib. bdg. 99.00 (*0-317-90870-7*) Rprt Serv.

Modern Chivalry: Containing the Adventures of Captain John Farrago & Teague O Regan, His Servant. Hugh H. Brackenridge. (Works of Hugh Henry Brackenridge). 1989. reprint ed. lib. bdg. 79.00 (*0-7812-2047-5*) Rprt Serv.

Modern Chivalry in Early American Law: H. H. Brackenridge's Legal Thought. Madeline Sapienza. 194p. (Orig.). (C). 1991. pap. text 21.50 (*0-8191-8375-X*); lib. bdg. 42.50 (*0-8191-8374-1*) U Pr of Amer.

Modern Chlor-Alkali Technology, Vol. 7. S. Sealey. x, 246p. 1998. 140.00 (*0-85404-723-9*, Pub. by Royal Soc Chem) Spr-Verlag.

Modern Chlor-Alkali Technology, Vol. 2. Ed. by C. Jackson. LC 81-131882. 389p. 1983. text 122.00 (*0-470-27471-9*) P-H.

Modern Chlor-Alkali Technology, Vol. 3. K. Wall. (Industrial Chemistry Ser.). 1986. text 159.00 (*0-470-20317-X*) P-H.

Modern Chlor-Alkali Technology, Vol. 6. Ed. by R. W. Curry. 306p. 1995. 125.00 (*0-85404-735-2*) CRC Pr.

Modern Christian Revivals. Ed. by Edith L. Blumhofer & Randall Balmer. LC 92-31407. 256p. 1993. text 23.95 (*0-252-01990-3*) U of Ill Pr.

Modern Christian Revolutionaries. Ed. by Donald Attwater. LC 76-156608. (Essay Index Reprint Ser.). 1977. reprint ed. 25.95 (*0-8369-2304-9*) Ayer.

Modern Christian Spirituality: Methodological & Historical Essays. Ed. by Bradley C. Hanson. 278p. 1990. pap. 19.95 (*1-55540-558-4*) OUP.

Modern Christian Thought, Vol. 1. 2nd ed. James C. Livingston. 480p. (C). 1996. pap. text 61.00 (*0-02-371423-9*, Macmillan Coll) P-H.

Modern Christian Thought Vol. 2: The Twentieth Century. 2nd ed. James C. Livingston. 544p. (C). 1999. pap. text 42.00 (*0-02-371410-7*, Macmillan Coll) P-H.

***Modern Christian's Happiness Plan.** James D. Baird. LC 99-69287. 176p. 2000. pap. 11.95 (*1-57921-276-X*) WinePress Pub.

Modern Christmas in America: A Cultural History of Gift-Giving. William B. Waits. (American Social Experience Ser.). (Illus.). 267p. (C). 1994. pap. text 18.50 (*0-8147-9284-7*) NYU Pr.

Modern Chromatographic Analysis of Vitamins. 2nd ed. Ed. by Deleenheer et al. (Chromatographic Science Ser.: Vol. 60). (Illus.). 592p. 1992. text 225.00 (*0-8247-8626-2*) Dekker.

***Modern Chromatographic Analysis of Vitamins.** 3rd rev. expanded ed. A. P. De Leenheer et al. LC 00-28152. (Chromatographic Science Ser.). (Illus.). 2000. write for info. (*0-8247-0316-2*) Dekker.

***Modern Chrysler Concept Cars: The Designs That Saved the Company.** Matt DeLorenzo. (Illus.). 128p. 2000. pap. 17.95 (*0-7603-0848-9*, 130021AP, Pub. by MBI Pubg) Motorbooks Intl.

Modern Church: The Dawn of the Reformation to the Eve of the Third Millennium. Glenn T. Miller. LC 97-7866. 312p. 1996. pap. 18.95 (*0-687-00605-8*) Abingdon.

Modern Cinema of Poland. Frank Turaj. LC 87-45372. (Midland Bks.: No. MB-481). (Illus.). 223p. 1988. pap. 69.20 (*0-608-05035-0*, 205969600004) Bks Demand.

Modern Circuit & System Design. Dewhurst. (C). 2000. pap. text 50.00 (*0-13-267790-3*) P-H.

Modern Cities. Ed. by Jean-Francois Lejeune. (New City Ser.: Vol. 3). (Illus.). 160p. (Orig.). 1996. pap. 25.00 (*1-56898-058-2*) Princeton Arch.

Modern Cities & Their Religious Problems. Samuel L. Loomis. LC 73-112558. (Rise of Urban America Ser.). 1976. reprint ed. 25.95 (*0-405-02464-9*) Ayer.

Modern City: Planning in the Nineteenth Century. Francoise Choay. LC 77-90408. (Planning & Cities Ser.). (Illus.). 1969. pap. 9.95 (*0-8076-0520-4*) Braziller.

Modern City & Its Problems. Frederick C. Howe. 1982. 23.95 (*0-8434-5009-6*) McGrath NH.

Modern City & Metro Area. Levy. LC 99-32735. 302p. 1999. pap. 35.00 (*0-13-287111-4*) P-H.

***Modern City Revisited.** Thomas Deckker. LC 00-30085. (Illus.). 2000. pap. write for info. (*0-419-25640-7*, E & FN Spon) Routledge.

Modern Civic Art: or The City Made Beautiful. 4th ed. Charles M. Robinson. LC 79-112570. (Rise of Urban America Ser.). (Illus.). 1978. reprint ed. 29.95 (*0-405-02473-8*) Ayer.

Modern Civil Practice in West Virginia. 8th ed. Dale P. Olson. 697p. 1984. 55.00 (*0-614-05907-0*, MICHIE) LEXIS Pub.

Modern Civilization: A Crisis of Fragmentation. S. C. Malik. (C). 1989. 22.50 (*81-7017-255-1*, Pub. by Abhinav) S Asia.

Modern Classic Short Novels of Science Fiction. Ed. by Gardner Dozois. 672p. 1994. pap. 15.95 (*0-312-11317-X*) St Martin.

Modern Classic Writers. Matthew J. Bruccoli & Judith S. Baughman. LC 93-8641. (Essential Bibliography of American Fiction Ser.). 112p. 1993. pap. 9.95 (*0-8160-3003-0*) Facts on File.

Modern Classic Writers. Ed. by Matthew J. Bruccoli & Judith S. Bauhman. LC 93-8641. (Essential Bibliography of American Fiction Ser.). 112p. 1994. 19.95 (*0-8160-3002-2*) Facts on File.

Modern Classical Architecture & the Problem of Archaeology, Vol. 2. Ed. by Donald M. Rattner & Richard W. Cameron. (Classicist Ser.). (Illus.). 123p. (Orig.). (C). 1996. pap. text 34.95 (*1-56000-850-4*) Transaction Pubs.

Modern Classics. Taylor. 1985. pap. 14.95 (*0-684-18509-1*, Scribners Ref) Mac Lib Ref.

Modern Classics in Analytical Chemistry, Vol. 1. Ed. by Alvin L. Beilby. LC 75-125864. (ACS Reprint Collection). 1970. pap. 8.95 (*0-8412-0315-6*) Am Chemical.

Modern Classics in Analytical Chemistry, Vol. 2. Ed. by Alvin L. Beilby. LC 75-125864. (ACS Reprint Collection). 1976. pap. 10.95 (*0-8412-0332-6*) Am Chemical.

Modern Classics in Analytical Chemistry: A Collection of Articles from Analytical Chemistry Selected for Their Value As Supplementary Reading about Modern Chemical Instrumentation & Analytical Methods, Vol. 2. Ed. by Alvin L. Beilby. LC 75-125864. (ACS Reprint Collection). (Illus.). 314p. 1976. reprint ed. pap. 97.40 (*0-608-04351-6*, 206513200002) Bks Demand.

Modern Classics of Fantasy. Gardner Dozois. LC 96-32347. 688p. 1996. text 35.00 (*0-312-15173-X*) St Martin.

Modern Classics of Fantasy. Ed. by Gardner Dozois. LC 97-17821. 672p. 1997. pap. 15.95 (*0-312-16931-0*) St Martin.

Modern Classics of Science Fiction. Ed. by Gardner Dozois. LC 92-42586. 1993. pap. 17.95 (*0-312-08847-7*) St Martin.

Modern Clastic Depositional Environments, South Carolina, No. T371. Ed. by Hayes. (IGC Field Trip Guidebooks Ser.). 88p. 1989. 21.00 (*0-87590-572-2*) Am Geophysical.

Modern Clock: A Study of Time Keeping Mechanism, Its Construction, Regulation & Repair. Ward L. Goodrich. LC 98-49871. 1998. write for info. (*0-9631669-3-X*) Clockwks Pr.

Modern CMOS Circuits Manual. Ray M. Marston. (Illus.). 192p. 1999. pap. text 36.95 (*0-7506-2565-1*) Buttrwrth-Heinemann.

Modern Coating & Drying Technology. Ed. by E. Cohen & E. Guthoff. 336p. 1992. 119.00 (*0-471-18806-9*) Wiley.

Modern Coating & Drying Technology: Center for Interfacial Engineering. Ed. by Edward Cohen & Edgar B. Gutoff. (Illus.). 310p. 1992. 85.00 (*1-56081-097-1*, Wiley-VCH) Wiley.

Modern COBOL Programming. Wilson Price & Jack Olson. 480p. 1987. pap. text 32.00 (*0-317-54024-6*) Mitchell Pub.

Modern Cocktails & Appetizers. Martha Gill. LC 97-76261. (Modern Guides Ser.). (Illus.). 128p. 1998. 18.95 (*1-56352-466-X*) Longstreet.

Modern Coin Magic. J. B. Bobo. (Illus.). 358p. 1982. reprint ed. pap. 8.95 (*0-486-24258-7*) Dover.

Modern Coinage of Iran. Robert L. Clarke & Mohabat-Avin. 92p. 1974. pap. 4.00 (*1-889172-02-2*) Numismatic Intl.

Modern Collectible Dolls: Identification & Value Guide, Vol. II. Patsy Moyer. LC 97-183190. 232p. 1998. 19.95 (*1-57432-053-X*, 5050) Collector Bks.

Modern Collectible Dolls Identification & Value Guide. 3rd ed. Patsy Moyer. LC 97-183190. 224p. 1999. 24.95 (*1-57432-117-X*) Collector Bks.

***Modern Collectible Dolls Identification & Value Guide.** 4th ed. Patsy Moyer. (Illus.). 272p. 2000. 24.95 (*1-57432-174-9*) Collector Bks.

Modern Collectible Tins: Identification & Values. Linda McPherson. LC 98-153333. 1998. pap. text 19.95 (*1-57432-054-8*, 5051) Collector Bks.

Modern College Algebra & Trig. 2nd ed. Beckenbach. (Math). 1972. 13.50 (*0-534-00110-6*) Brooks-Cole.

Modern College Algebra & Trig. 3rd ed. Beckenbach. (Math). 1977. 17.75 (*0-534-00468-7*) Brooks-Cole.

Modern Coloproctology: Surgical Grand Rounds from St. Mark's Hospital. John M. Northover. 208p. 1993. text 45.00 (*0-340-55258-1*, Pub. by E A) OUP.

Modern Colposcopy: A Practical Approach. Michael Campion et al. (Illus.). 280p. (Orig.). (C). 1991. pap. text. write for info. (*0-9629655-0-2*) Educ Systems.

Modern Combat Aircraft Design: Technology & Function. Klaus Hunecke. LC 87-61280. (Illus.). 233p. 1987. 39.95 (*0-87021-426-8*) Naval Inst Pr.

Modern Combat Ammo. Duncan Long. (Illus.). 216p. 1991. 30.00 (*0-87364-628-2*) Paladin Pr.

Modern Combat Helicopters. George A. Sullivan. LC 92-31492. (Military Aircraft Ser.). (Illus.). 128p. (YA). (gr. 6-9). 1993. 19.95 (*0-8160-2353-0*) Facts on File.

Modern Combat Models: A Critique of Their Foundations. C. J. Ancker, Jr. & A. V. Gafarian. (Topics in Operations Research Ser.). x, 196p. 1992. pap. 17.00 (*1-877640-11-5*) INFORMS.

Modern Combat Uniforms. Mark Lloyd. (Illus.). 215p. 1988. pap. 19.95 (*0-89747-226-8*) Squad Sig Pubns.

Modern Combined Dictionary: English - Gujarti & Gujarti - English. S. S. Oza & R. G. Bhatt. 103p. 1992. reprint ed. 29.95 (*0-8288-8471-4*) Fr & Eur.

Modern Comedy. John Galsworthy. (Hudson River Editions Ser.). 912p. 1987. 50.00 (*0-02-542370-3*) Macmillan.

***Modern Comfort.** Katherine Sorrell. 2000. 35.00 (*1-56496-709-3*) Rockport Pubs.

***Modern Commercial Aircraft: A Revised & Updated Illustrated Directory of the World's Civil Airliners, Aircraft Technologt & Airlines.** Endres. 1998. 29.95 (*1-84065-022-2*, Pub. by Salamander) Combined Pub.

Modern Commercial Concepts in the Mahabharatam. Anjan Bhattacharyya. 1987. 15.00 (*0-8364-2317-8*, Pub. by Firma KLM) S Asia.

Modern Commercial Correspondence in English & Spanish. Wendy W Molina. (ENG & SPA.). 172p. 1991. pap. 49.95 (*0-7859-9599-4*) Fr & Eur.

Modern Commercial Drafting. A. S. Rao. (C). 1989. 200.00 (*0-7855-6694-5*) St Mut.

Modern Commercial Paper: The New Law of Negotiable Instruments (& Related Commercial Paper) Steve M. Nickles et al. LC 94-131558. (American Casebook Ser.). 767p. (C). 1993. 57.50 (*0-314-03240-1*) West Pub.

Modern Commercial Sailing Ship Fundamentals. Paul D. Priebe. LC 85-47838. 255p. 1986. reprint ed. pap. 79.10 (*0-608-02454-6*, 206309800004) Bks Demand.

Modern Commercial Wiring. Harvey N. Holzman. LC 98-44686. (Illus.). 256p. (YA). (gr. 9-12). 1999. 32.00 (*1-56637-527-4*) Goodheart.

Modern Commonwealth. William Dale. 1983. 105.00 (*0-406-17404-0*, U.K., MICHIE) LEXIS Pub.

Modern Communication Circuits. Smith. 1985. text, student ed. 34.68 (*0-07-058731-0*) McGraw.

Modern Communication Circuits. J. Smith. (Electrical Engineering Ser.). 576p. (C). 1985. text 77.74 (*0-07-058730-2*) McGraw.

Modern Communication Circuits. 2nd ed. Jack Smith. LC 97-28578. 608p. (C). 1997. 100.31 (*0-07-059283-7*) McGraw.

Modern Communication Law, Vol. 1. Harvey L. Zuckman et al. LC 98-19010. (Practitioner Ser.). 1500p. 1998. text. write for info. (*0-314-23041-6*) West Pub.

Modern Communication Law, Vol. 2. Harvey L. Zuckman et al. (Practitioner Ser.). 1500p. 1998. text. write for info. (*0-314-23315-6*) West Pub.

Modern Communication Systems. 4th ed. Ferrel G. Stremler. (C). 2001. text 95.00 (*0-201-53234-4*) Addison-Wesley.

Modern Communications. 3rd ed. Mark E. Oliver. (Illus.). 176p. (C). 1988. student ed. 21.00 (*0-317-64538-2*) P-H.

Modern Communications & Spread Spectrum. G. R. Cooper & C. D. McGillem. 544p. (C). 1985. text 83.00 (*0-07-012951-7*) McGraw.

Modern Communications Law. Donald E. Lively. LC 90-7504, 592p. 1991. 65.00 (*0-275-93735-6*, C3735, Praeger Pubs) Greenwood.

M

Modern Companion to the European Community: A Guide to Key Facts, Institutions & Terms. Andrew Cox & Paul Furlong. 336p. 1992. text 95.00 (*1-85278-516-0*) E Elgar.

Modern Competitive Analysis. 2nd ed. Sharon M. Oster. LC 93-9826. (Illus.). 424p. 1994. text 51.95 (*0-19-507579-X*) OUP.

Modern Competitive Analysis. 3rd ed. Sharon M. Oster. LC 98-38221. (Illus.). 448p. (C). 1999. text 54.00 (*0-19-511941-X*) OUP.

Modern Compiler Implementation in C. Andrew W. Appel. LC 97-31089. (Illus.). 554p. (C). 1997. text 54.95 (*0-521-58390-X*) Cambridge U Pr.

Modern Compiler Implementation in Java. Andrew W. Appel. LC 97-31090. (Illus.). 558p. (C). 1997. text 54.95 (*0-521-58388-8*) Cambridge U Pr.

Modern Compiler Implementation in ML. Andrew W. Appel. LC 97-31091. (Illus.). 548p. (C). 1997. text 54.95 (*0-521-58274-1*) Cambridge U Pr.

***Modern Compiler in Computer Science.** Dick Grune. 400p. 2000. pap. 54.99 (*0-471-97697-0*) Wiley.

Modern Compiler Optimization. Michael Wolfe. (C). 1998. text. write for info. (*0-8053-2737-1*) Addison-Wesley.

Modern Component Families Circuit Block Design. Kularatna. LC 99-31348. 384p. 2000. pap. text 49.95 (*0-7506-9992-2*) Buttrwrth-Heinemann.

Modern Composer & His World: A Report from the International Conference of Composers, Held at the Stratford Festival, Stratford, Ontario, Canada, August 1960. International Conference of Composers (1960: Strat. Ed. by John Beckwith & Udo Kasemets. LC 62-252. (Scholarly Reprint Ser.). 184p. reprint ed. pap. 57.10 (*0-608-16267-1*, 202651700050) Bks Demand.

Modern Composers. Guido Pannain. LC 76-99644. (Essay Index Reprint Ser.). 1977. 23.95 (*0-8369-1715-4*) Ayer.

Modern Compressible Flow: With Historical Perspective. 2nd ed. John D. Anderson, Jr. (Aeronautical & Aerospace Engineering Ser.). 650p. (C). 1989. 98.13 (*0-07-001673-9*) McGraw.

Modern Compressible Flow: With Historical Perspective. 2nd ed. John D. Anderson, Jr. (Aeronautical & Aerospace Engineering Ser.). 672p. (C). 1990. pap. text, teacher ed. 27.50 (*0-07-001674-7*) McGraw.

Modern Computational Mechanics. Herbert A. Koenig. LC 98-21966. (Series in Computational & Physical Processes in Mechanics & Thermal Sciences). 300p. 1998. boxed set 85.00 (*1-56032-468-6*) Hemisp Pub.

Modern Computer Algebra. Jurgen Gerhard & Joachim Von Zur Gathen. (Illus.). 750p. (C). 1999. text 59.95 (*0-521-64176-4*) Cambridge U Pr.

Modern Computer Architecture. Mohamed Rafiquzzaman. (West Engineering Ser.). 1988. pap., student ed. 9.00 (*0-534-93842-6*); text 71.95 (*0-534-93841-8*) PWS Pubs.

Modern Computer Center Operations, Procedures, & Standards. 2nd ed. Maryhelen H. Hoffman & Lanny L. Hoffman. 200p. 1995. pap. 35.00 (*1-928592-01-5*) MHP Commns.

Modern Conception of Confederation: (Proceedings, Santorini, 22-25 September, 1994) (Science & Technique of Democracy Ser.: No. 11). 1995. 18.00 (*92-871-2803-0*, Pub. by Council of Europe) Manhattan Pub Co.

Modern Concepts & Theorems of Mathematical Statistics. Edward B. Manoukian. (Series in Statistics). 175p. 1985. 62.95 (*0-387-96186-0*) Spr-Verlag.

Modern Concepts in Biochemistry. 5th ed. Bohinski. 750p. 1986. teacher ed. write for info. (*0-318-61496-0*, H88537); teacher ed. 3.00 (*0-685-17393-3*, H88545) P-H.

Modern Concepts in Gastroenterology, Vol. 1. Ed. by Alan B. Thomson et al. (Topics in Gastroenterology Ser.). (Illus.). 392p. (C). 1986. text 126.00 (*0-306-42303-0*, Kluwer Plenum) Kluwer Academic.

Modern Concepts in Gastroenterology, Vol. 2. E. Shaffer & A. B. Thomson. (Topics in Gastroenterology Ser.). (Illus.). 310p. (C). 1989. text 105.00 (*0-306-43125-4*, Kluwer Plenum) Kluwer Academic.

Modern Concepts in Gastroenterology, Vol. 3. A. B. Thomson & E. Shaffer. (Topics in Gastroenterology Ser.). (Illus.). 378p. (C). 1992. text 105.00 (*0-306-43980-8*, Kluwer Plenum) Kluwer Academic.

Modern Concepts in Macroeconomics. Ed. by Thomas M. Havrilesky. LC 84-232670. (Illus.). 528p. (C). 1985. text 23.95 (*0-88295-412-1*) Harlan Davidson.

Modern Concepts in Penicillium & Aspergillus Classification. R. A. Samson. LC 90-7008. (NATO ASI Ser.: Vol. 185). (Illus.). 488p. (C). 1990. text 135.00 (*0-306-43516-0*, Kluwer Plenum) Kluwer Academic.

Modern Concepts in the Management of Fissure Caries. R. C. Paterson et al. (Illus.). 80p. 1991. text 42.00 (*1-85097-013-0*) Quint Pub Co.

Modern Concepts of Acute & Chronic Hepatitis. G. Gitnick. LC 88-22557. (Illus.). 358p. (C). 1989. text 75.00 (*0-306-42895-4*, Kluwer Plenum) Kluwer Academic.

***Modern Concepts of Color & Appearance.** A. K. R. Choudhury. (Illus.). 340p. 2000. 75.00 (*1-57808-079-7*); pap. text 49.50 (*1-57808-078-9*) Science Pubs.

Modern Concepts of Ecology. 7th ed. H. D. Kumar. x, 377p. 1993. text 35.00 (*0-7069-6371-7*, Pub. by Vikas) S Asia.

Modern Concepts of Microbiology. H. D. Kumar & Swati Kumar. 1999. reprint ed. pap. 20.00 (*81-259-0509-X*, Pub. by Vikas) S Asia.

Modern Condition. 8th ed. Adelphi. 278p. (C). 1998. pap. text 24.75 (*0-536-01403-5*) Pearson Custom.

Modern Condition Anthology of Readings, Vol. 1. 5th ed. 278p. (C). 1994. text 34.80 (*0-536-58622-5*) Pearson Custom.

Modern Condition Anthology of Readings, Vol. 2. 282p. (C). 1993. pap. 18.80 (*0-536-58305-6*) Pearson Custom.

Modern Condition Anthology of Readings, Vol. 2. 5th ed. 326p. (C). 1994. text 30.80 (*0-536-58749-3*) Pearson Custom.

Modern Condition: Anthology of Readings, Vol. 2. 6th ed. 328p. (C). 1995. 30.80 (*0-536-59285-3*) Pearson Custom.

Modern Condition: Anthology Readings Fall 95, Vol. 1. 6th ed. 282p. (C). 1995. 34.80 (*0-536-58923-2*) Pearson Custom.

Modern Condition: Essays at Century's End. Dennis H. Wrong. LC 97-37687. 1998. 45.00 (*0-8047-3239-6*); pap. write for info. (*0-8047-3241-8*) Stanford U Pr.

Modern Conditions, Postmodern Controversies. Barry Smart. LC 91-12946. (Social Futures Ser.). 256p. (C). 1991. pap. 24.99 (*0-415-06952-1*, A6211) Routledge.

Modern Conditions, Postmodern Controversies. Barry Smart. LC 91-12946. (Social Futures Ser.). 240p. (C). (gr. 13). 1991. text 79.95 (*0-415-02902-3*, A6207) Routledge.

Modern Conductor. 6th ed. Elizabeth A. Green. LC 96-28810. 286p. 1996. 65.00 (*0-13-251481-8*) P-H.

Modern Confessional Novel. Peter M. Axthelm. LC 67-13428. (Yale College Ser.: No. 6). 201p. reprint ed. pap. 62.40 (*0-608-30112-4*, 202197600024) Bks Demand.

Modern Conformational Analysis: Elucidating Novel Exciting Molecular Structures. H. Dodziuk. (Methods in Stereochemical Analysis Ser.). 264p. 1995. 139.00 (*0-471-18611-2*, Wiley-VCH) Wiley.

Modern Conformational Analysis: Elucidating Novel Exciting Molecular Structures. Helena Dodziuk. Ed. by Alan P. Marchand. LC 95-16397. (Methods in Stereochemical Analysis Ser.). (Illus.). 288p. 1995. 99.95 (*1-56081-689-9*, Wiley-VCH) Wiley.

Modern Confucianist Theory. Y. Yu. 200p. 1996. pap. 6.00 (*1-879771-17-9*) World Scientific Pub.

Modern Constituency Electioneering: Local Campaigning in the 1992 General Election. David T. Denver & Gordon Hands. LC 97-19213. 368p. 1997. 55.00 (*0-7146-4789-6*, Pub. by F Cass Pubs); pap. 25.00 (*0-7146-4345-9*, Pub. by F Cass Pubs) Intl Spec Bk.

Modern Constitutional Law, 2 vols. Chester James Antieau. LC 69-19951. 170.00 (*0-318-11982-X*) West Group.

Modern Constitutional Law, 2 vols. Chester James Antieau. 1993. suppl. ed. 52.50 (*0-317-04342-0*) West Group.

Modern Constitutional Law. Chester James Antieau & William J. Rich. LC 97-76525. 1997. write for info. (*0-7620-0194-1*) West Group.

Modern Constitutional Law: Cases & Notes. 4th ed. Ronald D. Rotunda. LC 93-9233. (American Casebook Ser.). 1126p. 1993. text 48.50 (*0-314-01816-6*) West Pub.

Modern Constitutional Law: Cases & Notes, 1995 Supplement To. 4th ed. Ronald D. Rotunda. (American Casebook Ser.). 100p. (C). 1995. pap. text 12.50 (*0-314-06875-9*) West Pub.

Modern Constitutional Law: Cases & Notes, 1996 Supplement To. 4th ed. Ronald D. Rotunda. (American Casebook Ser.). 176p. 1996. pap. text. write for info. (*0-314-09939-5*) West Pub.

Modern Constitutional Law: Cases & Notes, 1997 Supplement To. 5th ed. Ronald D. Rotunda. (American Casebook Ser.). 150p. (C). 1997. pap. text. write for info. (*0-314-21185-3*) West Pub.

Modern Constitutional Law: Cases & Notes (5th Edition) 5th ed. Ronald D. Rotunda. LC 97-5642. (Paralegal). 1198p. (C). 1997. text 60.25 (*0-314-21140-3*) West Pub.

Modern Constitutional Theory: A Reader. 3rd ed. John H. Garvey & T. Alexander Aleinikoff. (Miscellaneous Ser.). 738p. (C). 1994. pap. text. write for info. (*0-314-03718-7*) West Pub.

***Modern Constitutional Theory: A Reader.** 4th ed. Garvey. LC 99-461937. (Paralegal Ser.). (C). 1999. pap. 21.50 (*0-314-23895-6*) West Pub.

Modern Constitutions since 1787. John A. Hawgood. xii, 539p. 1987. reprint ed. 57.50 (*0-8377-2235-7*, Rothman) W S Hein.

Modern Construction Accounting Methods & Controls. Paul D. Lucas. LC 83-22897. 252p. 1984. 39.95 (*0-13-590241-X*, Busn) P-H.

Modern Construction & Development Forms: Cumulative Supplementation. 2nd ed. James A. Douglas et al. LC 82-50345. 1612p. 1982. 160.00 (*0-88262-775-9*) Warren Gorham & Lamont.

Modern Construction & Development Forms: Cumulative Supplementation. 2nd ed. James Douglas et al. LC 82-50345. (Modern Real Estate & Mortgage Forms Ser.). 1612p. 1982. suppl. ed. 69.50 (*0-7913-1009-4*) Warren Gorham & Lamont.

Modern Construction Handbook. Andrew Watts & Tim Quick. (Illus.). 320p. 1998. 95.00 (*0-7148-3656-7*, Pub. by Phaidon Press) Phaidon Pr.

Modern Construction Management. 4th ed. Frank Harris & Ronald McCaffer. LC 94-45026. 1995. pap. 39.95 (*0-632-03897-7*) Blackwell Sci.

Modern Consumer Theory. Kelvin J. Lancaster. 256p. 1990. 95.00 (*1-85278-384-2*) E Elgar.

***Modern Contemporary: Art at MoMA since 1980.** Ed. by Kirk Varnedoe et al. 496p. 2000. pap. 35.00 (*0-87070-022-7*) Mus of Modern Art.

***Modern Contemporary: Aspects of Art at MoMA since 1980.** Ed. by Kirk Varnedoe et al. (Illus.). 496p. 2000. 65.00 (*0-8109-6214-4*, Pub. by Abrams) Time Warner.

***Modern Contemporary: Aspects of Art at MoMA since 1980.** Ed. by Kirk Varnedoe et al. (Illus.). 496p. 2000. 65.00 (*0-87070-021-9*, Pub. by Mus of Modern Art) Abrams.

Modern Contraception: Updates from the Contraception Report. David A. Grimes et al. LC 97-60969. vi, 265 p. 1997. write for info. (*0-9651745-1-4*) Emron.

Modern Contract of Guarantee. 3rd ed. John Phillips & James O'Donovan. 850p. 1996. 156.00 (*0-455-21435-2*, Pub. by LawBk Co) Gaunt.

Modern Control Engineering. 3rd ed. Ogata. 997p. (C). 1996. 100.00 (*0-13-227307-1*) P-H.

Modern Control Engineering: International Edition. Pierre Belanger. 494p. (C). 1995. pap. text 27.95 (*0-03-015247-X*) OUP.

Modern Control System: Modern Control System Analysis. 8th ed. (C). 1997. pap. text 97.00 (*0-201-36139-6*) Addison-Wesley.

Modern Control System Engineering. Zoran Gajic & Muhidin Lelic. 448p. 1996. pap. 73.00 (*0-13-134116-2*) P-H.

Modern Control System Theory. 2nd ed. M. Gopal. 688p. 1993. text 84.95 (*0-470-22157-7*) Halsted Pr.

Modern Control, System Theory & Application. 2nd ed. Stanley M. Shinners. LC 78-52497. (Electrical Engineering Ser.). 1978. text. write for info. (*0-201-07494-X*) Addison-Wesley.

Modern Control System Theory & Design. Shinners. 872p. 1993. 125.00 (*0-471-00751-X*) Wiley.

***Modern Control System Theory & Design, 1.** 2nd ed. Stanley M. Shinners. LC 97-34538. 720p. 1998. 108.00 (*0-471-24906-8*, Wiley-Interscience) Wiley.

Modern Control Systems. (C). 1991. write for info. (*0-201-55637-5*) Addison-Wesley.

Modern Control Systems. Ed. by Michael Masten et al. 500p. 1996. student ed., wbk. ed. 329.00 (*0-7803-2302-5*, HL5714) Inst Electrical.

Modern Control Systems. 4th ed. Richard C. Dorf. LC 85-7532. (Electrical Engineering Ser.). 550p. (C). 1986. text. write for info. (*0-201-05326-8*) Addison-Wesley.

Modern Control Systems. 5th ed. Richard C. Dorf. (Electrical Engineering Ser.). (Illus.). (C). 1989. text 61.25 (*0-201-14278-3*); pap. text 34.25 (*0-201-14279-1*) Addison-Wesley.

Modern Control Systems. 6th ed. Richard Dorf. (C). 1994. pap. text. write for info. (*0-201-59093-X*) Addison-Wesley.

Modern Control Systems. 6th ed. Richard C. Dorf. (C). 1991. pap. text. write for info. (*0-201-60701-8*) Addison-Wesley.

Modern Control Systems. 6th ed. Richard C. Dorf. (A-W Series in Electrical & Computer Engineering - Control Engineering). (Illus.). 603p. (C). 1992. text 69.95 (*0-201-51713-2*) Addison-Wesley.

Modern Control Systems. 7th ed. Richard C. Dorf. (C). 1995. pap. text. write for info. (*0-201-84559-8*) Addison-Wesley.

Modern Control Systems. 8th ed. Richard C. Dorf. LC 97-36632. 820p. (C). 1997. 100.00 (*0-201-30864-9*, Prentice Hall) P-H.

***Modern Control Systems.** 8th rev. ed. Richard C. Dorf & Robert H. Bishop. 1998. teacher ed. write for info. (*0-201-30866-5*) Addison-Wesley.

Modern Control Systems Analysis & Design. Walter J. Grantham & Thomas L. Vincent. 368p. 1993. text 99.95 (*0-471-81193-9*) Wiley.

Modern Control Techniques. Kilian. Date not set. pap. text, teacher ed. write for info. (*0-314-09849-6*) West Pub.

Modern Control Techniques for the Processing Industries. T. H. Tsai et al. (Chemical Industries Ser.: Vol. 23). (Illus.). 296p. 1986. text 165.00 (*0-8247-7549-X*) Dekker.

Modern Control Techniques in Textile Finishing & Making-Up. M. Bona. 1990. pap. 42.00 (*0-7855-2810-5*, Pub. by Textile Inst) St Mut.

Modern Control Technology: Components & Systems. Christopher T. Kilian. LC 95-49815. 550p. (C). 1996. pap. 89.95 (*0-314-06631-4*) West Pub.

***Modern Control Technology: Components & Systems.** 2nd ed. Kilian. (Student Material TV Ser.). (C). 2000. text 66.00 (*0-7668-2358-X*) Delmar.

Modern Control Technology Lab Manual. Christopher T. Kilian. (Electronics Technology Ser.). (C). 1996. pap., lab manual ed. 19.50 (*0-314-20150-5*) Delmar.

Modern Control Theory. 3rd ed. William L. Brogan. 736p. 1990. 105.00 (*0-13-589763-7*) P-H.

Modern Converter & Filter Circuit Encyclopedia. Rudolf F. Graf. LC 92-7498. (Illus.). 192p. 1992. pap. 12.95 (*0-8306-4158-0*, 3892) McGraw-Hill Prof.

Modern Copper Coins of the Mohammedan States. W. H. Valentine. 203p. 1977. reprint ed. 8.00 (*1-889172-06-5*) Numismatic Intl.

Modern Coral Reef Aquarium, Vol. 1. Svein A. Fossa & Alf J. Nilsen. (Illus.). 400p. 1996. 84.95 (*3-928819-29-1*, Pub. by Birgit Schmettkamp) Two Little Fish.

Modern Corporate Finance. (C). 1997. pap. text 24.00 (*0-06-501006-X*) Addison-Wesley.

Modern Corporate Finance. (C). 1997. pap. text 67.00 (*0-06-501298-4*) Addison-Wesley.

Modern Corporate Finance. (C). 1997. 24.00 (*0-06-501007-8*) Allyn.

***Modern Corporate Finance.** 2000. write for info. (*0-13-015766-X*) P-H.

Modern Corporate Finance. 2nd ed. Ed. by Donald R. Chambers. 736p. (C). 1998. 96.00 (*0-321-01447-2*) Addison-Wesley Educ.

***Modern Corporate Finance: An Interdisciplinary Approach to Value Creation.** Alan Shapiro & Balbirer. LC 99-34674. 577p. (C). 1999. 86.67 incl. cd-rom (*0-13-080098-8*) P-H.

***Modern Corporate Finance: Multidisciplinary.** 2000. write for info. (*0-13-015765-1*) P-H.

***Modern Corporate Finance: Multidisciplinary.** 224p. 2000. write for info. (*0-13-015485-7*) P-H.

Modern Corporate Finance: Theory & Practice. Donald R. Chambers & Nelson J. Lacey. LC 93-5470. 688p. (C). 1997. pap. 88.00 (*0-06-501004-3*); pap., student ed. 33.00 (*0-06-501005-1*) Addison-Wesley Educ.

Modern Corporate State: Private Governments & the American Constitution, 23. Arthur S. Miller. LC 75-35350. (Contributions in American Studies: No. 23). 269p. 1976. 49.95 (*0-8371-8589-0*, MCS/, Greenwood Pr) Greenwood.

Modern Corporation & American Political Thought. Scott R. Bowman. LC 94-45439. 424p. 1996. 60.00 (*0-271-01472-5*); pap. 19.95 (*0-271-01473-3*) Pa St U Pr.

Modern Corporation & Private Property. Adolf A. Berle & Gardiner C. Means. 426p. (C). 1991. pap. 29.95 (*0-88738-887-6*) Transaction Pubs.

Modern Corporation & Private Property. Adolf A. Berle, Jr. & Gardiner C. Means. LC 38-11139. (Business Enterprises Reprint Ser.). xiii, 396p. 1982. reprint ed. lib. bdg. 52.50 (*0-89941-183-5*, 302080) W S Hein.

Modern Corporation & Social Responsibility. Henry G. Manne & Henry C. Wallich. LC 72-91865. (Rational Debate Ser.: No. 6). 120p. reprint ed. pap. 37.20 (*0-8357-4511-2*, 203736800008) Bks Demand.

Modern Corporation Checklists. 3rd ed. James A. Douglas et al. 838p. 1990. 140.00 (*0-7913-0566-X*); suppl. ed. 56.00 (*0-7913-1188-0*) Warren Gorham & Lamont.

Modern Corporation Finance. Adams. (American Casebook Ser.). Date not set. text. write for info. (*0-314-06642-X*) West Pub.

Modern Corporation Finance. 6th ed. William Husband & James Dockeray. (C). 1966. 11.20 (*0-256-00220-7*, Irwn McGrw-H) McGrw-H Hghr Educ.

Modern Cosmological Observations & Problems. Gregory Bothun. 300p. 1997. 95.00 (*0-7484-0332-9*, Pub. by Tay Francis Ltd); pap. 34.95 (*0-7484-0645-X*, Pub. by Tay Francis Ltd) Taylor & Francis.

Modern Cosmology: A Survey in Four Lectures. P. J. Willcox. LC 82-90241. (Illus.). 96p. 1982. pap. 4.50 (*0-9608436-0-4*) P J Willcox.

Modern Cosmology & Philosophy. Ed. by John Leslie. 330p. 1998. reprint ed. pap. 19.95 (*1-57392-250-1*) Prometheus Bks.

Modern Cosmology & the Dark Matter Problem. Dennis W. Sciama. (Lecture Notes in Physics Ser.: No. 3). (Illus.). 234p. (C). 1994. pap. text 34.95 (*0-521-43848-9*) Cambridge U Pr.

Modern Cosmology in Retrospect. Ed. by Bruno Bertotti et al. (Illus.). 446p. (C). 1991. text 95.00 (*0-521-37213-5*) Cambridge U Pr.

***Modern Cost Management Analysis.** 2nd ed. Jae K. Shim & Joel G. Siegel. LC 99-86794. (Business Library). 288p. 2000. pap. 14.95 (*0-7641-1397-6*) Barron.

Modern Cost Management & Analysis. deluxe ed. Jae K. Shim & Joel G. Siegel. (Barron's Business Library). 320p. 1992. pap. text 18.95 (*0-8120-4671-4*) Barron.

Modern Countercurrent Chromatography. Ed. by Walter D. Conway & Richard J. Petroski. LC 95-7048. (Symposium Ser.: No. 593). 238p. 1995. text 75.00 (*0-8412-3167-2*, Pub. by Am Chemical) OUP.

***Modern Country: A New Approach to Country Style.** Mary Norden. (Illus.). 144p. 2000. 29.95 (*1-57076-139-6*) Trafalgar.

Modern Country Cooking. Leslie Land. 1999. pap. 13.00 (*0-14-017825-2*, Penguin Bks) Viking Penguin.

Modern County P/U/G: 22 Contemporary Country Hits. Ed. by Milton Okun. 112p. (YA). Date not set. pap. 14.95 (*1-57560-006-4*) Cherry Lane.

Modern Course for Piano. LC R418184. (John Thompson's Modern Course for Piano Ser.: Bk. 4). write for info. (*0-87718-008-3*) Willis Music Co.

Modern Course in Aeroelasticity. E. H. Dowell & H. C. Curtiss, Jr. (Mechanics: Dynamical Systems Ser.: No. 4). 479p. 1978. lib. bdg. 230.50 (*90-286-0057-4*) Kluwer Academic.

Modern Course in Aeroelasticity. E. H. Dowell & H. C. Curtiss, Jr. (Mechanics: Dynamical Systems Ser.: No. 4). 479p. 1980. pap. text 82.50 (*90-286-0737-4*) Kluwer Academic.

Modern Course in Aeroelasticity. Ed. by Earl H. Dowell et al. LC 94-9743. (Mechanics, Dynamical Systems Ser.: Vol. 11). 1995. lib. bdg. 260.00 (*0-7923-2788-8*) Kluwer Academic.

Modern Course in Aeroelasticity. enl. rev. ed. Earl H. Dowel et al. (C). 1989. pap. text 148.50 (*0-7923-0185-4*) Kluwer Academic.

Modern Course in Aeroelasticity. 2nd enl. rev. ed. Earl H. Dowel et al. (C). 1989. lib. bdg. 261.00 (*0-7923-0062-9*) Kluwer Academic.

Modern Course in Biology. M. Dearden & R. Dearden. 307p. (C). 1969. 6.64 (*0-08-013457-2*, Pergamon Pr) Elsevier.

Modern Course in English Syntax. Herman Wekker & Liliane Haegeman. 208p. (C). 1995. pap. 24.99 (*0-415-03684-4*) Routledge.

Modern Course in Statistical Physics. 2nd ed. Linda Reichl. LC 97-13550. 832p. 1998. 99.95 (*0-471-59520-9*) Wiley.

Modern Course on the Theory of Equations. 2nd ed. David Dobbs & Robert Hanks. LC 92-7178. (Illus.). 263p. (C). 1992. 25.00 (*0-936428-14-7*) Polygonal Pub.

Modern Creation Trilogy: Scripture & Creation; Science & Creation; Society & Creation, 3 vols. Henry M. Morris & John M. Morris. 1996. pap. 34.95 incl. cd-rom (*0-89051-216-7*, MCTSTP) Master Bks.

Modern Crime & Suspense Writers see Writers of English: Lives & Works

Modern Criminal Law: Cases, Comments, & Questions. 2nd ed. Wayne R. LaFave. (American Casebook Ser.). 903p. (C). 1988. reprint ed. 60.00 (*0-314-82177-5*) West Pub.

Modern Criminal Procedure: Cases, Comments & Questions. 8th ed. Yale Kamisar et al. (American Casebook Ser.). 1600p. (C). 1994. text 57.00 (*0-314-04142-7*) West Pub.

An Asterisk (*) at the beginning of an entry indicates that the title is appearing for the first time.

Modern Criminal Procedure & Basic Criminal Procedure: 1994 Supplement. Yale Kamisar et al. (American Casebook Ser.). 75p. 1994. pap. text 11.50 (*0-314-04418-3*) West Pub.

Modern Criminal Procedure & Basic Criminal Procedure & Advanced Criminal Procedure, 1995 Supplement To. 8th ed. Yale Kamisar et al. (American Casebook Ser.). 150p. (C). 1995. pap. text 12.00 (*0-314-06866-X*) West Pub.

Modern Criminal Procedure & Basic Criminal Procedure & Advanced Criminal Procedure, 1996 Supplement To. 8th ed. Yale Kamisar & Jerold H. Israel. Ed. by Wayne R. Lafave. (American Casebook Ser.). 238p. (C). 1996. pap. text. write for info. (*0-314-09926-3*) West Pub.

Modern Criminal Procedure, Basic Criminal Procedure & Advanced Criminal Procedure: 1997 Supplement. annuals 9th ed. Yale Kamesar et al. (American Casebook Ser.). 306p. (C). 1997. pap. text, suppl. ed. write for info. (*0-314-21183-7*) West Pub.

Modern Criminal Procedures. 9th ed. Kamisar. LC 99-462590. (Paralegal Ser.). (C). 1999. pap. 49.25 (*0-314-23900-6*) West Pub.

Modern Criminology: Crime, Criminal Behavior & Its Control. John L. Hagan. 320p. (C). 1984. 54.69 (*0-07-025450-8*) McGraw.

Modern Crisis. 2nd rev. ed. Murray Bookchin. 194p. 1987. write for info. (*0-920057-61-6*); pap. write for info. (*0-920057-62-4*) Black Rose.

Modern Critical Interpretations, 67 vols. Incl. Arthur Miller's Death of a Salesman. Ed. by Harold Bloom. 160p. 1988. lib. bdg. 29.95 (*1-55546-061-5*); Beowulf. Intro. by Harold Bloom. 160p. 1987. lib. bdg. 34.95 (*0-87754-904-4*); Charles Dickens' A Tale of Two Cities. Intro. by Harold Bloom. 160p. 1988. 29.95 (*0-87754-738-6*); Charlotte Bronte's Jane Eyre. Intro. by Harold Bloom. 160p. 1987. 34.95 (*0-87754-731-9*); D. H. Lawrence's The Rainbow. Intro. by Harold Bloom. 160p. 1988. lib. bdg. 29.95 (*1-55546-023-2*); Dante's The Divine Comedy. Intro. by Harold Bloom. 160p. 1987. lib. bdg. 34.95 (*0-87754-908-7*); Edgar Allan Poe's The Tales of Poe. Intro. by Harold Bloom. 160p. 1987. 34.95 (*1-55546-011-9*); Emily Bronte's Wuthering Heights. Intro. by Harold Bloom. 160p. 1986. 34.95 (*0-87754-732-7*); Ernest Hemingway's A Farewell to Arms. Ernest Hemingway. 160p. 1988. 34.95 (*1-55546-044-5*); Ernest Hemingway's The Sun Also Rises. Ernest Hemingway. 160p. 1987. 34.95 (*1-55546-045-3*); Exodus. Intro. by Harold Bloom. 160p. 1987. lib. bdg. 29.95 (*0-87754-909-5*); F. Scott Fitzgerald's The Great Gatsby. Intro. by Harold Bloom. 160p. 1986. 29.95 (*0-87754-901-X*); Franz Kafka's The Castle. Intro. by Harold Bloom. 160p. 1988. lib. bdg. 29.95 (*1-55546-069-0*); Franz Kafka's The Metamorphosis. William Golding. 160p. 1988. 29.95 (*1-55546-070-4*); Geoffrey Chaucer's the General Prologue to the Canterbury Tales. Geoffrey Chaucer. Ed. by Harold Bloom. 160p. 1988. lib. bdg. 34.95 (*0-87754-905-2*); George Bernard Shaw's Major Barbara. Intro. by Harold Bloom. 160p. 1987. 29.95 (*1-55546-027-5*); George Orwell's Nineteen Eighty-Four. Intro. by Harold Bloom. 160p. 1987. 29.95 (*1-55546-026-7*); Henry David Thoreau's Walden. Intro. by Harold Bloom. 160p. 1987. 34.95 (*1-55546-012-7*); Herman Melville's Billy Budd, Benito Cereno, Bartleby the Scrivener & Other Tales. Intro. by Harold Bloom. 160p. 1987. 34.95 (*1-55546-009-7*); Herman Melville's Moby-Dick. Intro. by Harold Bloom. 160p. 1986. 34.95 (*1-55546-010-0*); Homer's The Iliad. Intro. by Harold Bloom. 160p. 1987. 34.95 (*0-87754-912-5*); Homer's The Odyssey. Intro. by Harold Bloom. 160p. 1988. lib. bdg. 34.95 (*1-55546-043-7*); James Joyce's A Portrait of the Artist As a Young Man. Intro. by Harold Bloom. 160p. 1988. lib. bdg. 34.95 (*1-55546-020-8*); James Joyce's Dubliners. James Joyce. 160p. 1988. lib. bdg. 34.95 (*1-55546-019-4*); James Joyce's Ulysses. Intro. by Harold Bloom. 160p. 1987. 34.95 (*1-55546-021-6*); Jane Austen's Pride & Prejudice. Intro. by Harold Bloom. 160p. 1987. 34.95 (*0-87754-945-1*); John Milton's Paradise Lost. Intro. by Harold Bloom. 160p. 1987. 29.95 (*0-87754-421-2*); Jonathan Swift's Gulliver's Travels. Intro. by Harold Bloom. 160p. 1986. 34.95 (*0-87754-424-7*); Joseph Conrad's Heart of Darkness. Intro. by Harold Bloom. 160p. 1987. 34.95 (*1-55546-015-1*); Mark Twain's Adventures of Huckleberry Finn. Intro. by Harold Bloom. LC 95-13559. 160p. 1986. lib. bdg. 34.95 (*1-55546-013-5*); Mary Wollstonecraft Shelley's Frankenstein. Intro. by Harold Bloom. 160p. 1987. 34.95 (*0-87754-746-7*); Nathaniel Hawthorne's The Scarlet Letter. Intro. by Harold Bloom. 160p. 1986. 29.95 (*1-55546-005-4*); Richard Wright's Native Son. Intro. by Harold Bloom. 160p. 1988. lib. bdg. 29.95 (*1-55546-055-0*); Samuel Beckett's Endgame. Intro. by Harold Bloom. 160p. 1987. 34.95 (*1-55546-056-9*); Samuel Beckett's Waiting for Godot. Intro. by Harold Bloom. 160p. 1987. 34.95 (*1-55546-058-5*); Sophocles's Oedipus Rex. Intro. by Harold Bloom. 160p. 1987. lib. bdg. 34.95 (*0-87754-918-4*); Stephen Crane's The Red Badge of Courage. Intro. by Harold Bloom. 160p. 1987. 34.95 (*1-55546-004-6*); T. S. Eliot's Murder in the Cathedral. Intro. by Harold Bloom. 160p. 1988. 29.95 (*1-55546-037-2*); T. S. Eliot's "The Waste Land" Intro. by Harold Bloom. 160p. 1986. 34.95 (*1-55546-038-0*); Tennessee Williams' A Streetcar Named Desire. Intro. by Harold Bloom. 160p. 1987. 29.95 (*1-55546-053-4*); Tennessee Williams' The Glass Menagerie. Intro. by Harold Bloom. 160p. 1988. lib. bdg. 29.95 (*1-55546-052-6*); Thomas Hardy's Jude the Obscure. Thomas Hardy. 160p. 1987. 34.95 (*0-87754-741-6*); Thomas Hardy's Tess of the D'Urbervilles. Intro. by Harold Bloom. 160p. 1986. 29.95 (*0-87754-744-0*); Willa Cather's My Antonia. Intro. by Harold Bloom. 160p. 1987. lib. bdg. 29.95 (*1-55546-035-6*); William Faulkner's The Sound & the Fury. Intro. by Harold Bloom. 160p. 1988. 34.95 (*1-55546-042-9*); William Shakespeare's A Midsummer Night's Dream. Intro. by Harold Bloom. LC 94-12600. 160p. 1987. lib. bdg. 29.95 (*0-87754-933-8*); William Shakespeare's Antony & Cleopatra. Intro. by Harold Bloom. 160p. 1987. lib. bdg. 34.95 (*0-87754-921-4*); William Shakespeare's Hamlet. Intro. by Harold Bloom. 160p. 1986. lib. bdg. 34.95 (*0-87754-924-9*); William Shakespeare's Julius Caesar. Ed. by Harold Bloom. 160p. 1988. lib. bdg. 29.95 (*0-87754-928-1*); William Shakespeare's King Lear. Intro. by Harold Bloom. 160p. 1987. lib. bdg. 34.95 (*0-87754-929-X*); William Shakespeare's Macbeth. Intro. by Harold Bloom. 160p. 1987. lib. bdg. 34.95 (*0-87754-930-3*); William Shakespeare's Othello. Intro. by Harold Bloom. 160p. 1987. lib. bdg. 34.95 (*0-87754-935-4*); William Shakespeare's The Sonnets. Intro. by Harold Bloom. 160p. 1987. lib. bdg. 34.95 (*0-87754-938-9*); William Shakespeare's The Tempest. Ed. by Harold Bloom. 160p. 1988. lib. bdg. 34.95 (*0-87754-940-0*); Zora Neale Hurston's Their Eyes Were Watching God. Intro. by Harold Bloom. 160p. 1987. 29.95 (*1-55546-054-2*); (J). 1999. Set pap. text 2097.00 (*0-87754-900-1*) Chelsea Hse.

Modern Critical Interpretations. Ed. & Intro. by Harold Bloom. (Illus.). 144-176p. (J). 1999. 419.40 (*0-7910-5221-4*) Chelsea Hse.

Modern Critical Reception of the English Emblem. Ed. by Peter M. Daly & Mary V. Silcox. (Illus.). 353p. 1996. 90.00 (*0-7735-1576-3*, Pub. by McG-Queens Univ Pr) CUP Services.

Modern Critical Theory: A Phenomenological Introduction. Murray. 242p. 1975. pap. text 99.50 (*90-247-1697-7*, Pub. by M Nijhoff) Kluwer Academic.

Modern Critical Theory & Classical Literature. Ed. by Irene J. De Jong & J. P. Sullivan. LC 93-4053. (Mnemosyne, Bibliotheca Classica Batava Ser.: No. 130). 1993. 134.50 (*90-04-09571-3*) Brill Academic Pubs.

Modern Critical Views. Ed. by Harold Bloom. (Illus.). 144-300p. (J). 279.60 (*0-7910-5220-6*) Chelsea Hse.

Modern Critical Views Series, 78 vols. Incl. Albert Camus. Intro. by Harold Bloom. 222p. 1987. lib. bdg. 29.95 (*1-55546-313-4*); Alice Walker. Intro. by Harold Bloom. 300p. 1990. 29.95 (*1-55546-314-2*); Arthur Miller. Intro. by Harold Bloom. 222p. 1987. 29.95 (*0-87754-711-4*); Brontes. Intro. by Harold Bloom. 222p. 1987. 29.95 (*0-87754-687-8*); Carson McCullers. Intro. by Harold Bloom. 222p. 1986. 29.95 (*0-87754-630-4*); Charles Dickens. Intro. by Harold Bloom. 222p. 1987. 34.95 (*0-87754-690-8*); Contemporary Poets. Intro. by Harold Bloom. 222p. 1986. 34.95 (*0-87754-709-2*); D. H. Lawrence. Intro. by Harold Bloom. 222p. 1986. 34.95 (*0-87754-655-X*); Dante. Intro. by Harold Bloom. 222p. 1986. 34.95 (*0-87754-665-7*); Edgar Allan Poe. Intro. by Harold Bloom. 222p. 1985. 29.95 (*0-87754-602-9*); Edith Wharton. Intro. by Harold Bloom. 222p. 1986. 29.95 (*0-87754-699-1*); Emily Dickinson. Intro. by Harold Bloom. 222p. 1985. 29.95 (*0-87754-605-3*); Ernest Hemingway. Intro. by Harold Bloom. 222p. 1985. 29.95 (*0-87754-616-9*); Eudora Welty. Intro. by Harold Bloom. 222p. 1986. 29.95 (*0-87754-718-1*); Eugene O'Neill. Intro. by Harold Bloom. 222p. 1987. 34.95 (*0-87754-633-9*); F. Scott Fitzgerald. Intro. by Harold Bloom. 222p. 1986. 29.95 (*0-87754-650-9*); Flannery O'Connor. Intro. by Harold Bloom. 222p. 1986. 29.95 (*0-87754-632-0*); Franz Kafka. Intro. by Harold Bloom. 222p. 1986. 34.95 (*0-87754-724-6*); Fyodor Dostoevsky. Intro. by Harold Bloom. 222p. 1987. lib. bdg. 34.95 (*1-55546-294-4*); Gabriel Garcia Marquez. Intro. by Harold Bloom. 222p. 1989. lib. bdg. 34.95 (*1-55546-297-9*); Geoffrey Chaucer. Intro. by Harold Bloom. 222p. 1985. 29.95 (*0-87754-606-1*); George Gordon, Lord Byron. Intro. by Harold Bloom. 222p. 1986. 29.95 (*0-87754-683-5*); Henry David Thoreau. Intro. by Harold Bloom. 222p. 1987. 34.95 (*0-87754-697-5*); Henry James. Intro. by Harold Bloom. 222p. 1987. 34.95 (*0-87754-696-7*); Homer. Intro. by Harold Bloom. 222p. 1986. 29.95 (*0-87754-723-8*); Iris Murdoch. Intro. by Harold Bloom. 222p. 1986. 29.95 (*0-87754-705-X*); J. D. Salinger. Intro. by Harold Bloom. 222p. 1987. 29.95 (*0-87754-716-5*); James Baldwin. Intro. by Harold Bloom. LC 86-8238. 222p. 1986. 29.95 (*0-87754-708-4*); James Joyce. Intro. by Harold Bloom. 222p. 1986. 34.95 (*0-87754-625-8*); John Donne & the Seventeenth-Century Metaphysical Poets. Intro. by Harold Bloom. 222p. 1986. 34.95 (*0-87754-677-0*); John Steinbeck. Intro. by Harold Bloom. 222p. 1987. 29.95 (*0-87754-635-5*); John Updike. Intro. by Harold Bloom. 222p. 1987. 29.95 (*0-87754-717-3*); Joyce Carol Oates. Intro. by Harold Bloom. 222p. 1987. lib. bdg. 29.95 (*0-87754-712-2*); Kate Chopin. Intro. by Harold Bloom. 222p. 1987. 29.95 (*0-87754-693-2*); Langston Hughes. Intro. by Harold Bloom. 222p. 1990. lib. bdg. 29.95 (*1-55546-376-2*); Later Nineteenth & Early Twentieth Century English & European Novelists: Joseph Conrad. Intro. by Harold Bloom. 222p. 1986. 29.95 (*0-87754-642-8*); Lewis Carroll. Intro. by Harold Bloom. 222p. 1987. 29.95 (*0-87754-689-4*); Marianne Moore. Intro. by Harold Bloom. 222p. 1986. 29.95 (*0-87754-631-2*); Mary Wollstonecraft Shelley. Intro. by Harold Bloom. 222p. 1986. 29.95 (*0-87754-619-3*); Percy Bysshe Shelley. Intro. by Harold Bloom. 222p. 1986. 29.95 (*0-87754-609-6*); Ralph Ellison. Intro. by Harold Bloom. 222p. 1986. 29.95 (*0-87754-710-6*); Ralph Waldo Emerson. Intro. by Harold Bloom. 222p. 1985. 34.95 (*0-87754-604-5*); Richard Wright. Intro. by Harold Bloom. 222p. 1987. 34.95 (*0-87754-639-8*); Robert Browning. Intro. by Harold Bloom. 222p. 1985. 29.95 (*0-87754-614-2*); Robert Frost. Intro. by Harold Bloom. 222p. 1986. 29.95 (*0-87754-626-6*); Samuel Beckett. Intro. by Harold Bloom. 222p. 1986. 34.95 (*0-87754-651-7*); Samuel Taylor Coleridge. Intro. by Harold Bloom. 222p. 1986. 34.95 (*0-87754-684-3*); Sigmund Freud. Intro. by Harold Bloom. 222p. 1985. 29.95 (*0-87754-600-2*); Sinclair Lewis. Intro. by Harold Bloom. 222p. 1987. 29.95 (*0-87754-628-2*); Sophocles. Intro. by Harold Bloom. 222p. 1990. lib. bdg. 29.95 (*1-55546-323-1*); Sylvia Plath. Intro. by Harold Bloom. 222p. 1987. lib. bdg. 29.95 (*1-55546-280-4*); T. S. Eliot. Intro. by Harold Bloom. 222p. 1985. 29.95 (*0-87754-601-0*); Tennessee Williams. Intro. by Harold Bloom. 222p. 1987. 29.95 (*0-87754-636-3*); Thomas Hardy. Intro. by Harold Bloom. 222p. 1986. 29.95 (*0-87754-645-2*); Toni Morrison. Ed. by Harold Bloom. 222p. 1991. lib. bdg. 29.95 (*1-55546-439-4*); Willa Cather. Intro. by Harold Bloom. 222p. 1986. 34.95 (*0-87754-623-1*); William Blake. Intro. by Harold Bloom. 222p. 1985. 34.95 (*0-87754-610-X*); William Butler Yeats. Intro. by Harold Bloom. 222p. 1986. 29.95 (*0-87754-700-9*); William Faulkner. Intro. by Harold Bloom. 222p. 1986. 34.95 (*0-87754-652-5*); William Shakespeare: Comedies. Intro. by Harold Bloom. 222p. 1986. 34.95 (*0-87754-664-9*); William Shakespeare: Histories & Poems. Intro. by Harold Bloom. 222p. 1986. 34.95 (*0-87754-658-4*); William Shakespeare: Tragedies. Intro. by Harold Bloom. 222p. 1986. 34.95 (*0-87754-617-7*); William Wordsworth. Intro. by Harold Bloom. 222p. 1986. 34.95 (*0-87754-613-4*); Zora Neale Hurston. Intro. by Harold Bloom. 222p. 1986. 29.95 (*0-87754-627-4*); 1987. Set pap. text 2421.10 (*0-7910-2578-0*) Chelsea Hse.

Modern Criticism & Theory. David Lodge. 480p. (C). 1988. pap. text 39.38 (*0-582-49460-5*, 73622) Longman.

***Modern Criticism & Theory: A Reader.** 2nd ed. Ed. by David Lodge. LC 99-21398. 500p. (C). 1999. pap. 32.80 (*0-582-31287-6*) Addison-Wesley.

Modern Cruise Ships, 1965-1990: A Photographic Record. William H. Miller. (Illus.). 128p. 1992. pap. 13.95 (*0-486-26753-9*) Dover.

Modern Cruising under Sail. Don Dodds. LC 97-40749. (Illus.). 496p. 1997. pap. 33.00 (*1-55821-626-X*) Lyons Pr.

Modern Cryptography, Probabilistic Proofs & Pseudorandomness. O. Goldreich. Ed. by R. L. Graham et al. LC 98-50548. (Algorithms & Combinatorics Ser.: Vol. 17). 200p. 1999. 79.95 (*3-540-64766-X*) Spr-Verlag.

Modern Crystallography. Ed. by Boris K. Vainshtein & A. A. Chernov. Tr. by Al Peabody from RUS. (Horizons in Soviet Crystallography Ser.). (Illus.). 395p. (C). 1988. text 195.00 (*0-941743-37-3*) Nova Sci Pubs.

***Modern Crystallography, Vol. 2.** 3rd rev. ed. B. K. Vafinshtefin. LC 00-41904. 2000. pap. write for info. (*3-540-67474-8*) Spr-Verlag.

Modern Crystallography IV. Ed. by L. A. Shuvalov. (Solid-State Sciences Ser.: Vol. 37). (Illus.). xviii, 583p. 1988. 139.00 (*0-387-11517-X*) Spr-Verlag.

Modern Crystallography I. Boris K. Vainshtein. (Solid-State Sciences Ser.: Vol. 15). (Illus.). 420p. 1981. 71.00 (*0-387-10052-0*) Spr-Verlag.

Modern Crystallography I: Fundamentals of Crystals, Symmetry & Methods of Structural Crystallography. 2nd enl. ed. Ed. by Boris K. Vainshtein. LC 94-70. (Illus.). 496p. 1996. 79.00 (*0-387-56558-2*) Spr-Verlag.

Modern Crystallography II: Structure of Crystals. Boris K. Vainshtein et al. (Solid-State Sciences Ser.: Vol. 21). (Illus.). 460p. 1982. 87.00 (*0-387-10517-4*) Spr-Verlag.

Modern Crystallography II: Structure of Crystals. 2nd enl. ed. Boris K. Vainshtein et al. 536p. 1994. 86.95 (*0-387-56848-4*) Spr-Verlag.

Modern Cuisine: Fish, Shellfish, Crustaceans. Yves Thuries. 1996. text 89.95 (*0-442-01703-0*, VNR) Wiley.

Modern Cuisine: Meats, Poultry, & Game. Thuuries. 1999. text 69.95 (*0-442-01704-9*, VNR) Wiley.

Modern Culture & Critical Theory: Art, Politics, & the Legacy of the Frankfurt School. Russell A. Berman. LC 89-40249. 286p. (Orig.). (C). 1989. pap. text 18.95 (*0-299-12084-8*) U of Wis Pr.

Modern Culture from a Comparative Perspective. Wilfred C. Smith. Ed. by John W. Burbidge. LC 96-45432. 174p. (C). 1997. text 44.50 (*0-7914-3393-5*); pap. text 14.95 (*0-7914-3394-3*) State U NY Pr.

Modern Currents in Japanese Art. Charles S. Terry & Michiaki Kawakita. LC 74-76106. (Heibonsha Survey of Japanese Art Ser.: Vol. 24). (Illus.). 160p. 1974. 20.00 (*0-8348-1028-X*) Weatherhill.

Modern Custom Guns: Walnut, Steel, & Uncommon Artistry. Tom Turpin. LC 97-73035. (Illus.). 208p. 1997. 49.95 (*0-87341-499-3*, MCG01) Krause Pubns.

Modern Customs & Ancient Laws of Russia, 1891. Maxine Kovalevsky. LC 99-16487. 2000. reprint ed. 65.00 (*1-58477-017-1*) Lawbk Exchange.

Modern Cynic: To Be or Not to Be. Eugene E. Petersen. LC 94-77719. 112p. 1996. 29.95 (*0-9642614-2-1*) Knoll Pubs.

Modern Czech Grammar. William E. Harkins. LC 53-397. (Slavic Studies). (Illus.). 193p. 1952. text 52.50 (*0-231-09937-1*) Col U Pr.

***Modern Czech Theatre: Reflector & Conscience of a Nation.** Jarka M. Burian. LC 99-58328. (Studies in Theatre History & Culture). (Illus.). 280p. 2000. text 37.95 (*0-87745-711-5*); pap. text 18.95 (*0-87745-722-0*) U of Iowa Pr.

Modern Daedalus. Tom Greer. LC 74-15977. (Science Fiction Ser.). 278p. 1975. reprint ed. 25.95 (*0-405-06294-X*) Ayer.

Modern Dairy Products: Composition, Food Value, Processing, Chemistry, Bacteriology, Testing, Imitation Dairy Products. Lincoln M. Lampert. LC HD9275.L34. 425p. reprint ed. pap. 131.80 (*0-7837-1961-2*, 204224700001) Bks Demand.

***Modern Dairy Technology: Advances in Milk Processing, Vol. 1.** 2nd ed. R. K. Robinson. 504p. 1998. 160.00 (*0-8342-1357-5*) Aspen Pub.

Modern Damages, 3 vols. Melvin M. Belli, Sr. 1960. text 67.50 (*0-672-81442-0*, Bobbs) Macmillan.

Modern Damages, 3 vols. Melvin M. Belli, Sr. 1966. suppl. ed. write for info. (*0-685-99329-9*, Bobbs) Macmillan.

Modern Dance: Seven Statements of Belief. Ed. & Intro. by Selma J. Cohen. LC 66-14663. (Illus.). 112p. 1966. pap. 15.95 (*0-8195-6003-0*, Wesleyan Univ Pr) U Pr of New Eng.

Modern Dance & Ballet on Film & Video: A Catalog, Vol. 1. Dance Films Association Inc. 1986. 19.95 (*0-317-41588-3*) Dance Films.

Modern Dance Forms: In Relation to the Other Modern Arts. Louis Horst & Carroll Russell. LC 61-11421. (Illus.). 151p. 1987. reprint ed. pap. 11.95 (*0-916622-52-5*) Princeton Bk Co.

Modern Dance Fundamentals. Nona Schurman & Sharon L. Clark. (Illus.). 283p. 1972. pap. 21.95 (*0-87127-193-1*) Princeton Bk Co.

Modern Dance in a Postmodern World: An Analysis of Federal Arts Funding & Its Impact on the Field of Modern Dance. Jan Van Dyke. (Illus.). 184p. (Orig.). (C). 1992. pap. text 31.00 (*0-88314-525-1*) AAHPERD.

Modern Dance in America: The Bennington Years. Sali A. Kriegsman. (C). 1981. 60.00 (*0-8161-8528-X*, Hall Reference) Macmillan.

Modern Dance in France, 1920-1970: An Adventure. Jacqueline Robinson. (Choreography & Dance Studies). (Illus.). 478p. 1998. text 98.00 (*90-5702-015-7*, Harwood Acad Pubs); pap. text 39.00 (*90-5702-016-5*, Harwood Acad Pubs) Gordon & Breach.

M

Modern Dance in Germany & the United States: Crosscurrents & Influences. Isa Partsch-Bergsohn. (Choreography & Dance Studies: Vol. 5). 176p. 1995. text 30.00 (*3-7186-5557-8*, ECU30, Harwood Acad Pubs) Gordon & Breach.

Modern Dance in Germany & the United States: Crosscurrents & Influences, Vol. 5. Isa Partsch-Bergsohn. (Choreography & Dance Studies). 176p. 1995. pap. text 15.00 (*3-7186-5558-6*, Harwood Acad Pubs) Gordon & Breach.

Modern Dance in Germany & the United States: Crosscurrents & Influences, NTSC Video Cassette. Isa Partsch-Bergsohn. (Choreography & Dance Studies: Vol. 5). 167p. 1995. VHS 15.00 (*3-7186-5736-8*, ECU12, Harwood Acad Pubs) Gordon & Breach.

Modern Dance in Germany & the United States: Crosscurrents & Influences, PAL Video Cassette. Isa Partsch-Bergsohn. (Choreography & Dance Studies: Vol. 5). 1995. VHS 15.00 (*3-7186-5737-6*, ECU12, Harwood Acad Pubs) Gordon & Breach.

Modern Dance Reflections. Maureen Deakin & Joel Morgovsky. Ed. by Barbara Van Vliet. (Illus.). 74p. 1980. pap. 17.95 (*0-9678974-0-8*) Rigel Pr.

Modern Dance Study, Bks. 1, 2, 3. Jane Winearls. (Illus.). 1974. pap. write for info. (*0-318-54859-3*) OUP.

Modern Dance Terminology. Paul Love. (Illus.). 96p. 1997. pap. 16.95 (*0-87127-206-7*) Princeton Bk Co.

Modern Dances. Arthur Murray. (Ballroom Dance Ser.). 1986. lib. bdg. 79.95 (*0-8490-3338-1*) Gordon Pr.

Modern Dances. Arthur Murray. (Ballroom Dance Ser.). 1985. lib. bdg. 79.95 (*0-87700-695-4*) Revisionist Pr.

Modern Dancing. Vernon Castle. (Ballroom Dance Ser.). 1986. lib. bdg. 250.00 (*0-8490-3325-X*) Gordon Pr.

Modern Dancing. Vernon Castle. (Ballroom Dance Ser.). 1985. lib. bdg. 79.95 (*0-87700-758-6*) Revisionist Pr.

Modern Dancing, 1914. Vernon Castle. (Illus.). 176p. 1998. pap. 18.00 (*0-916896-99-4*, LE54) Lacis Pubns.

Modern Data Analysis: A First Course in Applied Statistics. Lawrence C. Hamilton. 704p. (C). 1990. text 66.95 (*0-534-12846-7*) Wadsworth Pub.

Modern Database Management. 4th ed. Fred R. McFadden & Jeffrey A. Hoffer. LC 93-31795. (C). 1994. text 61.95 (*0-8053-6047-6*) Benjamin-Cummings.

Modern Database Management. 5th ed. Fred R. McFadden. LC 98-4120. 656p. (C). 1998. 83.00 (*0-8053-6054-9*, Prentice Hall) P-H.

Modern Database Management: Object-Oriented & Extended Relational Database Systems. Ed. by Won Kim. LC 93-36405. 736p. (C). 1994. 55.95 (*0-201-59098-0*) Addison-Wesley.

***Modern Database Management: Oracle Edition.** 5th ed. Fred R. McFadden & Jeffrey A. Hoffer. 656p. 1999. 94.00 (*0-201-38372-1*) Addison-Wesley.

***Modern Database Management Oracle Edition.** 5th ed. 384p. (C). 1998. 24.00 (*0-201-38370-5*); 24.00 (*0-201-38371-3*) Addison-Wesley.

***Modern Database Management Oracle Edition.** 5th ed. (C). 1999. write for info. (*0-13-017486-6*) P-H.

Modern Database Management Casebook. 4th ed. Fred McFadden. 96p. (C). 1994. pap. text 19.00 (*0-8053-6048-4*) Addison-Wesley.

Modern Daughters & the Outlaw West. Melissa Kwasny. LC 90-44699. 208p. (Orig.). 1990. pap. 9.95 (*0-933216-75-0*) Spinsters Ink.

Modern Day Bounty Hunting. David Mollison. Ed. by J. Gary Parish. 124p. (C). 1997. reprint ed. pap. 19.95 (*0-918487-85-4*) Thomas Investigative.

Modern Day Legends. Intro. by Jim Murray. (Baseball Legends Ser.). (Illus.). 64p. (J). (gr. 3 up). 1994. 179.40 (*0-7910-3564-6*) Chelsea Hse.

Modern-Day Miracles: How Ordinary People Experience Supernatural Acts of God. Paul Prather. 240p. 1996. 19.95 (*0-8362-2174-5*) Andrews & McMeel.

Modern Day Miracles from the Files of President Harold B. Lee. Ed. & Compiled by L. Brent Goates. 208p. 1996. 14.95 (*1-55503-915-4*, 01112279) Covenant Comms.

Modern Day Moses? Dave Turner. Ed. by Reta Spears-Stewart. 125p. 1999. pap. 10.00 (*1-892477-11-4*, Pub. by Barnabs Pub) Hope Tomorrow.

Modern Day Poets & Authors. Ed. by L. W. Mueller. LC 77-81769. 1977. 6.50 (*0-8187-0029-7*) Harlo Press.

An Asterisk (*) at the beginning of an entry indicates that the title is appearing for the first time.

Modern Day Recipe for Duck Soup: Sleuthing & Sightseeing with 100 Poetic Slopes. Malacheck Constanza. (Self Realization Bks.: Bk. XII). (Illus.). 100p. 1986. pap. 10.00 (*0-938582-06-2*) Sensitive Man.

Modern Deeds. Robert G. Natelson. 1995. suppl. ed. 80.00 (*0-316-59933-6*, Aspen Law & Bus) Aspen Pub.

Modern Deep Sea Trawling Gear. John Garner. 1978. 40.00 (*0-7855-6940-5*) St Mut.

Modern Defence. J. Speelman. 1999. pap. text 16.95 (*0-7134-8472-1*) B T Burch.

*__Modern Defence.__ Jon Speelman & Neil McDonald. 2000. pap. 19.95 (*1-85744-281-4*, Pub. by Everyman Chess) Globe Pequot.

Modern Defensive Signals in Contract Bridge. Kit Woolsey. 64p. (Orig.). 1981. pap. 4.95 (*0-87643-032-9*) Barclay Bridge.

Modern Demonolatry. S. Connolly. 98p. 1999. 40.00 (*0-9669788-0-3*) Darkerwd Pub Gp.

Modern Density Functional Theory: A Tool for Chemistry. Ed. by J. M. Seminario & P. Politzer. LC 94-44665. (Theoretical & Computational Chemistry Ser.: Vol. 2). 418p. 1995. 261.75 (*0-444-82171-6*) Elsevier.

Modern Dental Assisting. 5th ed. Hazel O. Torres. 1995. text 67.00 (*0-7216-6161-0*, W B Saunders Co) Harcrt Hlth Sci Grp.

Modern Dental Assisting. 5th ed. Hazel O. Torres et al. (Illus.). 775p. 1995. teacher ed. write for info. (*0-7216-5054-6*, W B Saunders Co) Harcrt Hlth Sci Grp.

Modern Dental Assisting. 5th ed. Hazel O. Torres et al. (Illus.). 976p. 1995. text 52.50 (*0-7216-5053-8*, W B Saunders Co) Harcrt Hlth Sci Grp.

Modern Depositional Environments of the Texas Coast. R. A. Morton & J. H. McGowen. (Guidebook Ser.: GB 20). (Illus.). 167p. 1980. reprint ed. pap. 4.50 (*0-318-03129-9*) Bur Econ Geology.

Modern Derivatization Methods for Seperation Sciences. Toshimasa Toyo'oka. LC 98-27197. 312p. 1999. 155.00 (*0-471-98364-0*) Wiley.

Modern Dermatologic Radiation Therapy. H. L. Goldschmidt & R. G. Panizzon. xiii, 165p. 1990. 122.00 (*0-387-97328-1*) Spr-Verlag.

Modern Design, 1890-1990, in the Metropolitan Museum of Art. R. Craig Miller. (Illus.). 328p. 1990. 29.95 (*0-87099-598-7*) Metro Mus Art.

Modern Design Principles: With Reference to Aluminium in Competition with Other Materials. Ed. by K. Jakobsen. (Illus.). 258p. (Orig.). 1988. pap. 121.50 (*82-519-0858-2*) Coronet Bks.

Modern Detector Circuit Encyclopedia. Rudolf F. Graf. LC 92-10462. (Illus.). 232p. 1992. pap. 12.95 (*0-8306-4157-2*, 3891) McGraw-Hill Prof.

*__Modern Developments & Applications in Microbeam Analysis.__ Ed. by G. Love et al. (Mikrochimica Acta Supplementa Ser.: Suppl. 15). (Illus.). 400p. 1998. pap. 120.00 (*3-211-83106-1*) Spr-Verlag.

Modern Developments in Cholinergie (Muscarinic) Receptors & Drugs. Ed. by Pieter A. Van Zwieten & Eduard Schonbaum. LC 88-30087. (Progress in Pharmacology Ser.: Vol. 7, No. 1). 122p. 1989. pap. 75.00 (*0-89574-277-2*, Pub. by Gustav Fischer) Balogh.

Modern Developments in Energy, Combustion & Spectroscopy: In Honor of S. S. Penner. Ed. by M. Lapp et al. LC 93-45316. 198p. 1994. text 129.25 (*0-08-042019-2*, Pergamon Pr) Elsevier.

Modern Developments in Flow Measurement: Proceedings of the International Conference Held at Harwell, September 21-23, 1971. Ed. by Colin G. Clayton. LC 73-173002. (PPL Conference Publication Ser.: Vol. 10). (Illus.). 415p. reprint ed. pap. 128.70 (*0-608-17793-8*, 203225800079) Bks Demand.

Modern Developments in Nuclear Physics: Proceedings of the 1987 International Symposium. O. Sushkov. 832p. (C). 1988. text 141.00 (*9971-5-0391-3*) World Scientific Pub.

Modern Developments in Powder Metallurgy: Proceedings of the 1965 International Powder Metallurgy Conference, 1. Ed. by Henry H. Hausner. LC 61-65760. (Illus.). 412p. (gr. 3 up). reprint ed. pap. 127.80 (*0-608-11546-0*, 201940100001) Bks Demand.

Modern Developments in Powder Metallurgy: Proceedings of the 1965 International Powder Metallurgy Conference, 2. Ed. by Henry H. Hausner. LC 61-65760. (Illus.). 366p. (gr. 3 up). reprint ed. pap. 113.50 (*0-608-11547-9*, 201940100002) Bks Demand.

Modern Developments in Powder Metallurgy: Proceedings of the 1970 International Powder Metallurgy Conference, Vol. 4: Processes. International Powder Metallurgy Conference Staff. Ed. by Henry H. Hausner. LC 61-65760. (Progress in Powder Metallurgy Ser.: Vol. 26). (Illus.). 607p. reprint ed. pap. 188.20 (*0-7837-1557-9*, 204185000004) Bks Demand.

Modern Developments in Powder Metallurgy: Proceedings of the 1970 International Powder Metallurgy Conference, Vol. 5: Materials & Properties. International Powder Metallurgy Conference Staff. Ed. by Henry H. Hausner. LC 61-65760. (Progress in Powder Metallurgy Ser.: Vol. 26). (Illus.). 502p. reprint ed. pap. 155.70 (*0-7837-1558-7*, 204185000005) Bks Demand.

Modern Developments in Powder Metallurgy: Proceedings of the 1973 International Powder Metallurgy Conference, Vol. 6: Applications & Processes. International Powder Metallurgy Conference Staff. Ed. by Henry H. Hausner & Walter E. Smith. LC 61-65760. (Progress in Powder Metallurgy Ser.: No. 29). (Illus.). 454p. reprint ed. pap. 140.80 (*0-7837-3055-1*, 204281500006) Bks Demand.

Modern Developments in Powder Metallurgy: Proceedings of the 1973 International Powder Metallurgy Conference, Vol. 7: P-M Forging & Copper P-M. International Powder Metallurgy Conference Staff. Ed. by Henry H. Hausner & Walter E. Smith. LC 61-65760. (Progress in Powder Metallurgy Ser.: No. 29). (Illus.). 636p. reprint ed. pap. 197.20 (*0-7837-3056-X*, 204281500007) Bks Demand.

Modern Developments in Powder Metallurgy: Proceedings of the 1973 International Powder Metallurgy Conference, Vol. 8: Ferrous P-M & Special Materials. International Powder Metallurgy Conference Staff. Ed. by Henry H. Hausner & Walter E. Smith. LC 61-65760. (Progress in Powder Metallurgy Ser.: No. 29). (Illus.). 686p. reprint ed. pap. 200.00 (*0-7837-3057-8*, 204281500008) Bks Demand.

Modern Developments in Powder Metallurgy: Proceedings of the 1973 International Powder Metallurgy Conference, Vol. 10: Ferrous & Non-Ferrous P-M Materials. International Powder Metallurgy Conference Staff. Ed. by Henry H. Hausner & Walter E. Smith. LC 61-65760. (Progress in Powder Metallurgy Ser.: No. 29). (Illus.). 600p. 1977. reprint ed. pap. 186.00 (*0-7837-3058-6*, 204281600010) Bks Demand.

Modern Developments in Powder Metallurgy: Proceedings of the 1973 International Powder Metallurgy Conference, Vol. 12: Principles & Processes. International Powder Metallurgy Conference Staff. Ed. by Henry H. Hausner & Walter E. Smith. LC 61-65760. (Progress in Powder Metallurgy Ser.: No. 29). (Illus.). 943p. 1981. reprint ed. pap. 200.00 (*0-7837-3059-4*, 204281700012) Bks Demand.

Modern Developments in Powder Metallurgy Vol. 11: Proceedings of the 1976 International Powder Metallurgy Conference: P-M Special Materials & Applications. International Powder Metallurgy Conference Staff. Ed. by Henry H. Hausner & Pierre W. Taubenblat. LC 61-65760. (Progress in Powder Metallurgy Ser.: No. 32). (Illus.). 462p. reprint ed. pap. 143.30 (*0-7837-5159-1*, 204488800011) Bks Demand.

Modern Developments in Powder Metallurgy Vol. 15: Principles & Processes. E. N. Aqua & C. I. Whitman. LC 66-5483. (Illus.). 864p. 1985. 29.00 (*0-918404-64-9*) Metal Powder.

Modern Developments in Powder Metallurgy Vol. 16: Ferrous & Nonferrous Materials. Ed. by E. N. Aqua & C. I. Whitman. LC 66-5483. (Illus.). 784p. 1985. 29.00 (*0-918404-65-7*) Metal Powder.

Modern Developments in Powder Metallurgy Vol. 17: Special Materials. Ed. by E. N. Aqua & C. I. Whitman. LC 66-5483. (Illus.). 944p. 1985. 29.00 (*0-918404-66-5*) Metal Powder.

Modern Developments in Powder Metallurgy Vol. 18: International Conference Proceedings, 1988. 832p. 1988. 30.00 (*0-918404-77-0*) Metal Powder.

Modern Developments in Powder Metallurgy Vol. 19: International Conference Proceedings, 1988. 786p. 1988. 30.00 (*0-918404-78-9*) Metal Powder.

Modern Developments in Powder Metallurgy Vol. 20: International Conference Proceedings, 1988. 810p. 1988. 30.00 (*0-918404-79-7*) Metal Powder.

Modern Developments in Powder Metallurgy Vol. 21: International Conference Proceedings, 1988. 782p. 1988. 30.00 (*0-918404-80-0*) Metal Powder.

Modern Developments in Structural Interpretation, Validation & Modelling. Ed. by P. G. Buchanan & D. A. Nieuwland. (Geological Society Special Publication Ser.: No. 99). 376p. 1995. 117.00 (*1-897799-43-8*, 342, Pub. by Geol Soc Pub Hse) AAPG.

Modern Diagnostic & Surgical Arthroscopy of the Temporomandibular Joint. Glenn T. Clark et al. LC 92-11625. (Illus.). 192p. 1992. text 165.00 (*0-7216-6591-8*, W B Saunders Co) Harcrt Hlth Sci Grp.

Modern Dictators: Third World Coup Makers, Strongmen, & Populist Tyrants. Barry Rubin. 1989. 8.95 (*0-317-02814-6*) NAL.

*__Modern Dictionary.__ G. Hangin. (MON & ENG.). 1998. write for info. (*0-320-03454-2*) Fr & Eur.

Modern Dictionary Engineering Technology Vol. 1: English to French. 3rd ed. J. R. Forbes. (ENG & FRE.). 594p. 1997. 275.00 (*0-320-00428-7*) Fr & Eur.

Modern Dictionary Engineering Technology Vol. 2: French to English. 2nd ed. J. R. Forbes. (ENG & FRE.). 582p. 1997. 275.00 (*0-320-00435-X*) Fr & Eur.

Modern Dictionary for the Legal Profession. 2nd ed. Gerry W. Beyer & Kenneth R. Redden. LC 96-26480. xii,818,v, 215p. 1996. 78.00 (*1-57588-114-4*, 310770) W S Hein.

Modern Dictionary for the Legal Profession: 1997 Supplement. 2nd ed. Gerry W. Beyer & Kenneth R. Redden. LC 96-26480. 142p. 1997. 27.50 (*1-57588-406-2*, 310775) W S Hein.

*__Modern Dictionary for the Legal Profession: 1999 Supplement.__ 2nd ed. Gerry W. Beyer & Kenneth R. Redden. Ed. by Margaret Beyer. LC 96-26480. v, 215p. 1999. pap. 35.00 (*1-57588-600-6*, 310775) W S Hein.

Modern Dictionary for the Legal Profession, 1995: Supplement. Kenneth R. Redden & Gerry W. Beyer. LC 92-35678. xiii, 802p. 1993. pap., suppl. ed. 75.00 (*0-89941-829-5*, 307770) W S Hein.

Modern Dictionary for the Legal Profession, 1995: Supplement. Kenneth R. Redden & Gerry W. Beyer. LC 92-35678. 78p. 1994. suppl. ed. 25.00 (*0-89941-865-1*, 308570) W S Hein.

Modern Dictionary for the Legal Profession, 1998 Cumulative Supplement: 1998 Cumulative Supplement. 2nd ed. Gerry W. Beyer & Kenneth R. Redden. LC 96-26480. 225p. 1998. suppl. ed. 30.00 (*1-57588-454-2*, 310775) W S Hein.

Modern Dictionary of Electronics. 6th ed. Rudolf F. Graf. 1152p. 1996. pap. text 49.95 (*0-7506-9870-5*) Buttrwrth-Heinemann.

*__Modern Dictionary of Electronics.__ 7th rev. ed. Rudolf F. Graf. LC 99-17889. 1152p. 1999. pap. text 59.95 (*0-7506-9866-7*, Newnes) Buttrwrth-Heinemann.

Modern Dictionary of Engineering & Technology: English-French. 2nd ed. J. R. Forbes. (ENG & FRE.). 594p. 1993. 275.00 (*0-8288-9473-6*, F135020) Fr & Eur.

Modern Dictionary of Engineering & Technology Vol. 2: French-English. J. R. Forbes. (ENG & FRE.). 582p. 1993. 250.00 (*0-7859-8652-9*, 285206880X) Fr & Eur.

Modern Dictionary of Engineering & Technology, French-English. J. R. Forbes. (ENG & FRE.). 582p. 1997. pap. 250.00 (*0-7859-9657-5*) Fr & Eur.

Modern Dictionary of Geography. 2nd ed. John Small & Michael Witherick. 240p. 1989. 45.00 (*0-340-49317-8*, A3662, Pub. by E A); pap. 17.95 (*0-340-49318-6*, A3666, Pub. by E A) Routldge.

Modern Dictionary of Geography. 3rd ed. John Small & Michael Witherick. (Arnold Publications). (Illus.). 272p. 1994. pap. text 29.95 (*0-340-60339-9*, B4799) OUP.

Modern Dictionary Slovene-English, English-Slovene. Dasa Komac & J. Skeri. (ENG & SLV.). 787p. 1981. 29.95 (*0-7859-0816-1*, M9701) Fr & Eur.

Modern Dictionary Slovene-German-Slovene. deluxe ed. D. Debenjak. (GER & SLV.). 608p. 1981. 39.95 (*0-8288-4669-3*, M9702) Fr & Eur.

Modern Diesel Locomotives. Hans Halberstadt. LC 96-13070. (Enthusiast Color Ser.). (Illus.). 96p. 1996. pap. 13.95 (*0-7603-0199-9*) MBI Pubg.

Modern Diesel Technology. Robert N. Brady. LC 95-17079. 688p. (C). 1995. 93.33 (*0-13-288382-1*) P-H.

Modern Dietetics at a Glance. Edmond B. Szekely. (Illus.). 32p. 1997. mass mkt. 2.50 (*0-89564-047-3*) IBS Intl.

Modern Difference Engine. James Donnelly. 44p. 1992. pap. 20.00 (*1-879828-03-0*) Armstrong OR.

Modern Differential Equations. Abell. LC 95-70697. (C). 1996. text 94.50 (*0-03-098337-1*) Harcourt Coll Pubs.

Modern Differential Equations: A Theory. Abell. (C). 1995. pap. text, student ed. 26.50 (*0-03-016202-5*) Harcourt Coll Pubs.

Modern Differential Equations: A Theory. Martha L. Abell. (C). 1995. pap. text, teacher ed. 30.00 (*0-03-016199-1*) Harcourt Coll Pubs.

Modern Differential Geometry for Physicists. Ed. by C. J. Isham. (Lecture Notes in Physics Ser.: vol. 32). 192p. (C). 1989. text 53.00 (*9971-5-0956-3*); pap. text 28.00 (*9971-5-0957-1*) World Scientific Pub.

Modern Differential Geometry for Physicists. 2nd ed. C. J. Isham. LC 98-53245. (Lecture Notes in Physics Ser.). 250p. 1999. 54.00 (*981-02-3555-0*); pap. 28.00 (*981-02-3562-3*) World Scientific Pub.

Modern Differential Geometry of Curves & Surfaces. Alfred Gray. 688p. (C). 1993. boxed set 78.95 (*0-8493-7872-9*, QA) CRC Pr.

Modern Digital & Analog Communication Systems. 3rd ed. B. P. Lathi. (The Oxford Series in Electrical & Computer Engineering). (Illus.). 800p. (C). 1998. text 89.95 (*0-19-511009-9*) OUP.

Modern Digital Automatic Control Systems. Vanlanding. (C). 1996. 67.00 (*0-02-422622-X*, Macmillan Coll) P-H.

Modern Digital Control Systems. 2nd ed. Raymond G. Jacquot. (Electrical Engineering & Electronics Ser.: Vol. 89). (Illus.). 432p. 1994. text 75.00 (*0-8247-8914-8*) Dekker.

Modern Digital Design. Sandige. 1990. teacher ed. 34.68 (*0-07-054858-7*) McGraw.

Modern Digital Design: PL Designer. Richard S. Sandige. (C). 1990. 95.00 (*0-07-836407-8*) McGraw.

Modern Digital Design & Switching Theory. Eugene D. Fabricius. 496p. 1992. boxed set 94.95 (*0-8493-4212-0*, TK868) CRC Pr.

*__Modern Digital Simulation Vol. IV: Advances in Theory & Application of Distribution Fitting, Econometric Cointegrated Regression in Panel Data, System Reliability & Behrens-Fisher Problems.__ Ed. by Edward J. Dudewicz. LC 99-73665. (Series in Mathematical & Management Sciences: Vol. 40). (Illus.). 190p. 1999. 195.00 (*0-935950-44-3*) Am Sciences Pr.

Modern Digital Simulation Methodology: Input, Modeling, & Output. Ed. by Pandu R. Tadikamalla. LC 85-71230. (American Sciences Press Series in Mathematical & Management Sciences: Vol. 12). 1985. 195.00 (*0-935950-10-9*) Am Sciences Pr.

Modern Digital Simulation Methodology Vol. III: Advances in Theory, Application, & Design--Electric Power Systems, Spare Parts Inventory, Purchase Interval & Incidence Modeling, Automobile Insurance Bonus-Malus Systems, Genetic Algorithms - DNA Sequence Assembly, Education, & Water Resource Case Studies. Ed. by Edward J. Dudewicz. LC 97-71847. (American Sciences Press Series in Mathematical & Management Sciences: Vol. 39). (Illus.). 224p. 1997. 195.00 (*0-935950-43-5*) Am Sciences Pr.

Modern Digital Simulation Methodology, II: Univariate & Bivariate Distribution Fitting, Bootstrap Methods, & Applications to CensusPES & CensusPlus of the U. S. Bureau of the Census, Bootstrap Sample Size, & Biology & Environment Case Studies. Ed. by Edward J. Dudewicz. (Series in Mathematical & Management Sciences: Vol. 38). (Illus.). 240p. 1997. 195.00 (*0-935950-42-7*) Am Sciences Pr.

Modern Digital System Design. Cheung. (West Engineering Ser.). 1990. pap. 78.75 (*0-534-93872-8*); pap., student ed. 8.75 (*0-534-93871-X*) PWS Pubs.

Modern Diplomacy. R. P. Barston. Ed. by Andres MacLennan. LC 87-3943. 264p. 1988. text 36.95 (*0-582-01403-4*, 73620) Longman.

Modern Diplomacy. R. P. Barston. Ed. by Andres MacLennan. LC 87-3943. 264p. (C). 1988. pap. text 28.50 (*0-582-49441-9*, 73620) Longman.

Modern Diplomacy. 2nd ed. R. P. Barston. (C). 1997. pap. text 21.75 (*0-582-09953-6*, Pub. by Addison-Wesley) Longman.

Modern Display Alphabets. Paul E. Kennedy. LC 74-79330. 102p. (Orig.). 1974. pap. 8.95 (*0-486-23097-X*) Dover.

Modern Dogma & the Rhetoric of Assent. Wayne Booth. LC 73-89786. xviii, 254p. 1974. reprint ed. pap. text 19.00 (*0-226-06572-3*, P595) U Ch Pr.

Modern Doll Rarities. Carla M. Cross. LC 97-72121. (Illus.). 208p. 1997. pap. 24.95 (*0-930625-67-6*, Antique Trader) Krause Pubns.

Modern Drafting: An Introduction to Cad. James D. Bethune. 480p. (C). 1988. text 53.20 (*0-13-591058-7*) P-H.

Modern Drafting Practices & Standards Manual. General Electric Company Staff & Genium Publishing Staff. (Illus.). 1300p. 1994. 250.00 (*0-931690-01-3*) Genium Pub.

Modern Drafting Room Practice. G. R. Martins. (Technical Papers: Vol. P190). (Illus.). 15p. 1939. pap. text 30.00 (*1-55589-446-1*) AGMA.

Modern Dragons: A Complete Authoritative Guide. Ayden J. Young. (Illus.). 64p. 1997. 12.95 (*0-7938-0217-2*, WW-051) TFH Pubns.

Modern Drama: An Essay in Interpretation. Ludwig Lewisohn. (Collected Works of Ludwig Lewisohn). 340p. 1998. reprint ed. lib. bdg. 98.00 (*1-58201-682-8*) Classic Bks.

Modern Drama: Plays, Critics, Theatre. Bell. (C). 1994. pap. text, teacher ed. 33.75 (*0-15-502094-3*) Harcourt Coll Pubs.

Modern Drama: Selected Plays from 1879 to the Present. Levy. LC 98-4292. 985p. 1998. pap. text 55.00 (*0-13-226721-7*) P-H.

Modern Drama & the Death of God. George E. Wellwarth. LC 86-40064. 192p. 1986. text 27.95 (*0-299-10850-3*) U of Wis Pr.

Modern Drama & the Death of God. George E. Wellwarth. LC 86-40064. 189p. reprint ed. pap. 58.60 (*0-608-20483-8*, 207173500002) Bks Demand.

Modern Drama & the Rhetoric of Theater. William B. Worthen. 240p. (C). 1992. 48.00 (*0-520-07468-8*, Pub. by U CA Pr) Cal Prin Full Svc.

Modern Drama by Women, 1800-1920: An International Anthology. Ed. by Katherine E. Kelly. LC 95-31553. (Illus.). 336p. (C). 1996. 90.00 (*0-415-12493-X*); pap. 27.99 (*0-415-12494-8*) Routledge.

Modern Drama from Communist China. Ed. by Walter M. Meserve & Ruth I. Meserve. LC 77-92524. 368p. 1970. 24.95 (*0-8147-0302-X*) Boulevard.

Modern Drama in Theory & Practice, 3 vols., Set. J. L. Styan. LC 79-15947. 1983. pap. 40.00 (*0-521-27715-9*) Cambridge U Pr.

Modern Drama in Theory & Practice, 3 vols., Vol. 1. J. L. Styan. LC 79-15947. 217p. 1983. pap. text 21.95 (*0-521-29628-5*) Cambridge U Pr.

Modern Drama in Theory & Practice, 3 vols., Vol. 2. J. L. Styan. LC 79-15947. 235p. 1983. pap. text 21.95 (*0-521-29629-3*) Cambridge U Pr.

Modern Drama in Theory & Practice, 3 vols., Vol. 3. J. L. Styan. LC 79-15947. 242p. 1983. pap. text 21.95 (*0-521-29630-7*) Cambridge U Pr.

Modern Drama Scholarship & Criticism, 1981-1990: An International Bibliography. Charles A. Carpenter. LC 97-206771. 625p. 1996. text 85.00 (*0-8020-0914-X*) U of Toronto Pr.

Modern Drama Scholarship & Criticism, 1966-1980: An International Bibliography. Ed. by Charles A. Carpenter. 624p. 1986. text 80.00 (*0-8020-2549-8*) U of Toronto Pr.

Modern Dramatists. Ashley Dukes. LC 67-23210. (Essay Index Reprint Ser.). 1977. 20.95 (*0-8369-0396-X*) Ayer.

Modern Dramatists, 5 vols. Ed. by Brian Southam. (Collected Critical Heritage Ser.). 2228p. (C). 1997. 650.00 (*0-415-15955-5*) Routledge.

Modern Dramatists: A Casebook of the Major British & American Playwrights. Kimball King. (Casebooks on Modern Dramatists Ser.). 325p. 2000. text 45.00 (*0-8153-2349-2*) Garland.

Modern Dramatists: Anton Chekov. Ed. by Victor Emeljanow. (Critical Heritage Ser.). 496p. (C). 1997. 140.00 (*0-415-15951-2*) Routledge.

Modern Dramatists: Henrik Isen. Ed. by Michael Egan. (Critical Heritage Ser.). 524p. (C). 1997. 160.00 (*0-415-15950-4*) Routledge.

Modern Dramatists: Samuel Beckett. Ed. by L. Graver & Raymond Federman. (Critical Heritage Ser.). 392p. (C). 1997. 125.00 (*0-415-15954-7*) Routledge.

Modern Drills for Track & Field, 3 vols. Incl. Jumping Events. Rick Attig. 64p. (Orig.). 1987. pap. Not sold separately (*0-932741-06-1*); Sprints & Hurdles. Joe Walker. 64p. (Orig.). 1987. pap. Not sold separately (*0-932741-08-8*); Throwing Events. Jay Silvester. 64p. (Orig.). 1987. pap. Not sold separately (*0-932741-07-X*); 1987. Set pap. 21.95 (*1-56404-134-4*) Championship Bks & Vid Prodns.

Modern Drug Research: Path to Better & Safer Drugs. Kutter et al. Ed. by Yvonne Connoly Martin. (Medicinal Research Ser.: Vol. 12). (Illus.). 528p. 1989. text 215.00 (*0-8247-7902-9*) Dekker.

Modern Drug Use. Ronald D. Mann. 1984. text 242.50 (*0-85200-717-5*) Kluwer Academic.

Modern Dry-Fly Code. Vincent Marinaro. LC 97-29512. (Illus.). 288p. 1997. reprint ed. 35.00 (*1-55821-413-5*) Lyons Pr.

Modern Dunciad. Richard Nason. LC 77-92992. 114p. 1978. pap. 15.00 (*0-912292-49-0*) Smith.

Modern Earth Science. W. Ramsey. 1989. text 61.00 (*0-03-004449-9*) Holt R&W.

Modern Earth Science. 98th ed. W. Ramsey. 1998. text 62.25 (*0-03-050609-3*) Holt R&W.

Modern Echoes from Ancient Hills: Our Greek Heritage. Marvin J. Bertoch & Julia B. Bertoch. Ed. by Stan Larson. LC 96-43404. (Illus.). 224p. 1997. text 15.95 (*0-9634732-5-5*, Blue Ribbon Books) Freethinker.

M

An Asterisk (*) at the beginning of an entry indicates that the title is appearing for the first time.

Modern Eclectic Therapy: A Functional Orientation to Counseling & Psychotherapy. Joseph Hart. LC 83-11088. 408p. 1983. 75.00 (*0-306-41213-6*, Plenum Trade) Perseus Pubng.

Modern Ecology: Basic & Applied Aspects. D. G. Esser & D. Overdieck. xxx,844p. 1991. 330.50 (*0-444-89183-8*) Elsevier.

Modern Econometrics: An Introduction. Thomas Leighton. LC 97-140273. (C). 1996. pap. text 98.00 (*0-201-87694-9*) Addison-Wesley.

Modern Economic Growth: Rate, Structure & Spread. Simon Smith Kuznets. LC 66-21524. (Studies in Comparative Economics: No. 7). 547p. reprint ed. pap. 169.60 (*0-608-30116-7*, 201676600005) Bks Demand.

Modern Economic Thought. Ed. by Sidney Weintraub. LC 76-20140. 608p. (C). 1977. pap. 33.95 (*0-8122-1114-6*) U of Pa Pr.

Modern Economics. Semoon Chang. 600p. 1990. teacher ed. write for info. (*0-318-66386-4*, H22650); student ed. 18.00 (*0-685-29840-X*, H22676); write for info. (*0-318-66387-2*, H22668) P-H.

Modern Economics. Jan S. Hogendorn. 832p. 1994. text 75.00 (*0-13-103995-4*) P-H.

Modern Economics. David Moewes. 1996. pap. text, student ed. 29.60 (*0-13-150590-4*) P-H.

Modern Economics. 2nd ed. Hardwick. Date not set. pap. text. write for info. (*0-582-44706-2*, Pub. by Addison-Wesley) Longman.

Modern Economics: Principles, Goals & Trade-Offs. M. Neil Browne & Paul Haas. (Illus.). 432p. (C). 1987. pap. text 40.00 (*0-13-587940-X*) P-H.

Modern Economics of Housing: A Guide to Theory & Policy for Finance & Real Estate Professionals. Randall J. Pozdena. LC 87-32593. 224p. 1988. 62.95 (*0-89930-231-9*, Quorum Bks) Greenwood.

Modern Education: One Size Fits All. Mary E. Carreiro. LC 88-2861. (Gentle Wind Ser.: Vol. 3). (Illus.). 224p. 1988. reprint ed. pap. 14.95 (*0-89789-168-6*) Gentle Wind Proj.

Modern Education: One Size Fits All. Mary E. Carreiro. LC 88-2861. (Gentle Wind Ser.: Vol. 3). (Illus.). 224p. 1988. reprint ed. lib. bdg. 34.95 (*0-89789-169-4*) Gentle Wind Proj.

***Modern Education, Textbooks & Image of the Nation: Politics of Modernization & Nationalism in Korean Education.** Yoonmi Lee. LC 00-34725. (East Asia Ser.). 2000. write for info. (*0-8153-3874-0*) Garland.

Modern Educational Controversies. Ed. by David Tavel. LC 84-15395. 346p. (Orig.). 1985. pap. text 25.00 (*0-8191-4274-3*); lib. bdg. 55.50 (*0-8191-4273-5*) U Pr of Amer.

Modern Educational Measurement. 3rd ed. Ed. by Allyn & Bacon Incorporated Staff. 128p. (C). 1999. write for info. (*0-205-30757-4*) Allyn.

Modern Educational Measurement: A Practitioner's Perspective. 2nd rev. ed. W. James Popham. (Illus.). 464p. (C). 1989. pap. text 72.00 (*0-13-593898-8*) IOX Amnt Assocs.

***Modern Educational Measurement: Practical Guidelines for Educational Leaders.** 3rd ed. Popham. LC 99-22345. 466p. (C). 1999. 64.00 (*0-205-28770-0*, Macmillan Coll) P-H.

Modern Egypt: Studies in Politics & Society. Ed. by Elie Kedourie & Sylvia G. Haim. 136p. 1980. 35.00 (*0-7146-3168-X*, Pub. by F Cass Pubs) Intl Spec Bk.

Modern Egypt & Its Heritage. Carolyn Fluehr-Lobban. LC 89-85820. (Illus.). 48p. (Orig.). (C). 1990. pap. text 7.95 (*0-911239-13-8*) Carnegie Mus.

Modern Egypt, from 1517 to the End of the Twentieth Century: Modern Egypt, from 1517 to the End of the Twentieth Century, Vol. 2. Ed. by Martin W. Daly. (Illus.). 478p. (C). 1999. text 100.00 (*0-521-47211-3*) Cambridge U Pr.

Modern Egyptian Art: The Emergence of a National Style. Liliane Karnouk. (Illus.). 100p. 1988. pap. 20.00 (*977-424-176-2*, Pub. by Am Univ Cairo Pr) Col U Pr.

Modern Egyptian Drama: An Anthology. Ed. & Tr. by Farouk Abdel Wahab. LC 72-94939. (Studies in Middle Eastern Literatures: No. 3). 1974. 30.00 (*0-88297-005-4*) Bibliotheca.

***Modern Electrical Drives.** Bulent Ertan. LC 00-33072. (NATO ASI Ser.). 2000. write for info. (*0-7923-6376-0*) Plenum.

Modern Electrochemistry: An Introduction to an Interdisciplinary Area, Vol. 2. J. O. Bockris & A. K. Reddy. LC 68-19518. (Illus.). 810p. (C). 1970. text 47.00 (*0-306-25002-0*, Kluwer Plenum) Kluwer Academic.

Modern Electrochemistry 1: Ionics. 2nd ed. J. O. Bockris & A. K. Reddy. LC 97-24151. (Illus.). 666p. (C). 1998. 95.00 (*0-306-45554-4*, Plenum Trade) Perseus Pubng.

Modern Electrochemistry 1: Ionics. 2nd ed. John O. Bockris & Amulya K. Reddy. LC 97-24151. (Illus.). 824p. (C). 1998. pap. text 49.50 (*0-306-45555-2*, Kluwer Plenum) Kluwer Academic.

Modern Electrode Dynamics. A. C. Fisher. (Oxford Chemistry Primers Ser.). (Illus.). 90p. (C). 1996. pap. text 12.95 (*0-19-855690-X*) OUP.

Modern Electrology: Excess Hair, It's Causes & Treatment. Fino Gior. (SKIN). 1990. mass mkt. 35.95 (*0-87350-413-5*) Milady Pub.

Modern Electronic Circuits Reference Manual. John Markus. (Illus.). 1000p. 1980. 97.00 (*0-07-040446-1*) McGraw.

Modern Electronic Communication. 2nd ed. Gary M. Miller. (Illus.). 592p. (C). 1983. text 42.00 (*0-13-593152-5*) P-H.

Modern Electronic Communication. 6th ed. Gary M. Miller. LC 98-11895. 794p. 1998. pap. text 100.00 (*0-13-859828-2*) P-H.

Modern Electronic Communication. 6th ed. Oliver. 1998. pap. text, lab manual ed. 34.00 (*0-13-860917-9*) P-H.

Modern Electronic Structure Theory. David R. Yarkony. (Advanced Series in Physical Chemistry). 1600p. 1995. text 152.00 (*981-02-1959-8*) World Scientific Pub.

Modern Electronic Structure Theory. Ed. by David R. Yarkony. (Advanced Series in Physical Chemistry: Vol. 2). 768p. 1995. pap. 89.00 (*981-02-2988-7*) World Scientific Pub.

Modern Electronic Structure Theory, 2 vols., Set. David R. Yarkony. (Advanced Series in Physical Chemistry). 1600p. 1995. text 152.00 (*981-02-1960-1*) World Scientific Pub.

Modern Electronic Structure Theory, Vol. 1. Ed. by David R. Yarkony. (Advanced Series in Physical Chemistry: Vol. 2). 768p. 1995. pap. 89.00 (*981-02-2987-9*) World Scientific Pub.

Modern Electronic Structure Theory & Applications in Organic Chemistry. Ernest R. Davidson. LC 97-27046. 200p. 1997. 28.00 (*981-02-3168-7*) World Scientific Pub.

***Modern Electronic Technology Laboratory Experiments.** W. M. Gosney. 112p. (C). 1999. per. 20.95 (*0-7872-6471-7*, 41647101) Kendall-Hunt.

Modern Electronic Test & Measuring Instruments. N. Kularatna. (IEE Electrical Measurement Ser.: No. 10). 296p. 1996. pap. 45.00 (*0-85296-879-5*); boxed set 92.00 (*0-85296-813-2*) INSPEC Inc.

Modern Electronic Test Equipment. Keith Brindley. 1988. 27.00 (*0-434-90567-4*) CRC Pr.

Modern Electronic Theory, 2 vols. David R. Yarkony. (Advanced Series in Physical Chemistry). 1600p. 1994. text 234.00 (*981-02-1318-2*) World Scientific Pub.

Modern Electronics: A First Course. Victor F. Veley & John J. Dulin. (Illus.). 640p. (C). 1983. 32.95 (*0-13-481663-3*) P-H.

Modern Electronics: A Survey of the New Technology. Jefferson C. Boyce. Ed. by George Z. Zuredjian. (Illus.). 256p. (C). 1982. text 66.50 (*0-07-006915-8*) McGraw.

Modern Electronics & Integrated Circuits. B. J. Stanier. (Illus.). 160p. 1985. pap. 30.00 (*0-85274-552-4*) IOP Pub.

Modern Electronics Guidebook: A Readable Overview. Michael N. Kozicki. (Illus.). 200p. 1992. text 39.95 (*0-442-00612-8*, VNR) Wiley.

Modern Electronics Manual: A Practical Reference Manual on Electronics Technology Today. Joseph Desposito. Ed. by Elliott S. Kanter. (Illus.). 400p. 1988. ring bd. 59.95 (*0-929321-02-2*, 42000) WEKA Pub.

Modern Electroorganic Chemistry. Demetrios K. Kyriacou. LC 94-13316. (Laboratory Ser.). 1994. 79.95 (*0-387-57504-9*) Spr-Verlag.

Modern Electroplating. 3rd ed. Ed. by Frederick A. Lowenheim. (Electrochemical Society Ser.). (Illus.). 832p. 1974. 199.00 (*0-471-54968-1*) Wiley.

Modern Electrostatics: International Conference on Modern Electrostatics, October 21-25, 1988, Beijing, China. Ed. by Li Ruinian. (International Academic Publishers Ser.). xviii, 569 p. 1989. 170.00 (*0-08-037029-2*, Pergamon Pr) Elsevier.

Modern Elementary Differential Equations. 2nd rev. ed. Richard Bellman & Kenneth L. Cooke. LC 94-49360. (Illus.). 240p. 1995. pap. text 8.95 (*0-486-68643-4*) Dover.

Modern Elementary Mathematics. 4th ed. Malcolm Graham. 576p. (C). 1984. pap. text, teacher ed. 28.00 (*0-15-561044-9*) Harcourt Coll Pubs.

Modern Elementary Particle Physics: The Fundamental Particles & Forces. Gordon Kane. LC 93-16098. (C). 1993. pap. 38.00 (*0-201-62460-5*) Addison-Wesley.

Modern Elementary Probability & Statistics with Statistical Programming in SAS, Minitab, & BMDP. Edward J. Dudewicz et al. LC 89-80812. 375p. 1989. pap. text 195.00 (*0-935950-19-2*) Am Sciences Pr.

Modern Elementary School Programs & Practices, Custom Pub. Michael J. Palardy. (C). 1992. text. write for info. (*0-07-048133-4*) McGraw.

***Modern Elementary Statistics.** John E. Freund. 650p. 2000. 91.00 (*0-13-017701-6*, Prentice Hall) P-H.

Modern Elementary Statistics. 6th ed. John E. Freund. (Illus.). 576p. (C). 1984. 39.95 (*0-13-593525-3*) P-H.

Modern Elementary Statistics. 9th rev. ed. John E. Freund & Gary A. Simon. LC 96-22742. 588p. (C). 1996. pap. text 91.00 (*0-13-858291-2*) P-H.

Modern Elementary Statistics, with Theoretical Supplement & Basic Programming. Donald W. Zimmerman & Richard H. Williams. LC 86-71928. (Mathematical & Management Sciences Ser.: Vol. 16). (C). 1986. pap. text 195.00 (*0-935950-16-8*) Am Sciences Pr.

Modern Eletronics & Communications. D. E. Phillips. 132p. (C). 1986. 180.00 (*0-948691-12-3*, Pub. by Witherby & Co) St Mut.

***Modern Encyclopaedia of Educational Technology, 4 vols.** Ed. by B. D. Bhatt & Ravi Praskash. 1998. pap. 750.00 (*81-7391-026-X*, Pub. by Print Hse) St Mut.

Modern Encyclopedia Religions in Russia & Soviet Union, Vols. 1-5. Ed. by Paul D. Steeves. 1988. 177.50 (*0-87569-106-4*) Academic Intl.

Modern Encyclopedia Russia & Soviet History, Vol. 1-58. Ed. by Joseph L. Wieczynski. 1988. 43.00 (*0-87569-064-5*) Academic Intl.

Modern Encyclopedia Russia & Soviet Literatures, Vol. 9. Ed. by Peter Rollberg. 1989. 40.00 (*0-87569-038-6*) Academic Intl.

Modern Engendering: Critical Feminist Readings in Modern Western Philosophy. Ed. by Bat-Ami Bar On. LC 92-36047. (SUNY Series in Feminist Philosophy). 280p. 1993. text 64.50 (*0-7914-1641-0*); pap. text 21.95 (*0-7914-1642-9*) State U NY Pr.

Modern Engine Tuning. A. Bell. LC 97-72302. 1997. 34.95 (*0-85429-978-5*) Haynes Manuals.

Modern Engineering. Lapin. (Statistics Ser.). 1997. pap., student ed. write for info. (*0-534-50885-5*) PWS Pubs.

Modern Engineering Economy. Donovan Young. LC 92-27307. 584p. 1993. text 100.95 (*0-471-54260-1*) Wiley.

Modern Engineering for Design of Liquid-Propellant Rocket Engines. Ed. by D. K. Huzel & D. H. Huang. (PAAS Ser.: Vol. 147). 1992. 109.95 (*1-56347-013-6*) AIAA.

Modern Engineering Mathematics. 2nd ed. Glyn James & David Burley. LC 95-51351. (C). 1996. pap. text 41.95 (*0-201-87761-9*) Addison-Wesley.

Modern Engineering Statistics. Lapin. (Statistics Ser.). 1997. pap., student ed. 17.95 (*0-534-50884-7*) Wadsworth Pub.

Modern Engineering Statistics. Lawrence L. Lapin. LC 96-35230. (Statistics Ser.). (C). 1997. pap. 91.95 (*0-534-50883-9*) Wadsworth Pub.

Modern English, Vol. 1. 2nd ed. William E. Rutherford. 349p. (C). 1975. pap. text 14.00 (*0-15-561059-7*) Harcourt Coll Pubs.

Modern English: Exercises for Non Native Speakers, 2 pts. Marcella Frank. Incl. Pt. 2. Sentences & Complex Structures. 1972. 1972. Set pap. text 13.50 (*0-686-86555-3*) P-H.

Modern English: Parts of Speech, Pt. 1. 2nd ed. Marcella Frank. 224p. (C). 1986. pap. text 33.00 (*0-13-593831-7*) P-H.

Modern English: Sentences & Complex Structure, Pt. II. 2nd ed. Marcella Frank. 224p. (C). 1986. pap. text 33.00 (*0-13-593856-2*) P-H.

Modern English-Arabic Dictionary. E. A. Elias. (ARA.). 912p. 49.95 (*0-86685-288-3*, EL2883, Pub. by Librairie du Liban) Intl Bk Ctr.

Modern English-Arabic Dictionary (Al-Mawrid) Munir Ba'Albaki. (ARA., Illus.). 1118p. 1997. 55.00 (*0-86685-059-7*, DAR0597, Pub. by Librairie du Liban) Intl Bk Ctr.

Modern English-Arabic Dictionary (Al-Mawrid al-Qareb) Munir Ba'Albaki. (ARA.). 484p. 1995. pap. 6.95 (*0-86685-062-7*, DAR3251, Pub. by Librairie du Liban) Intl Bk Ctr.

Modern English-Arabic Dictionary (Mawrid al Mayassar) Munir Ba'Albaki. (ARA., Illus.). 575p. 1995. 17.95 (*0-86685-061-9*, DAR0619, Pub. by Librairie du Liban) Intl Bk Ctr.

Modern English Books of Power. George H. Fitch. LC 70-121467. (Essay Index Reprint Ser.). 1977. 21.95 (*0-8369-1706-5*) Ayer.

Modern English Essays, 5 vols. Ernest Rhys. LC 73-174316. reprint ed. 60.00 (*0-404-08070-7*) AMS Pr.

Modern English Grammar for Teachers. Julius N. Hook & Michael G. Crowell. LC 72-110550. (Illus.). 296p. reprint ed. pap. 91.80 (*0-608-30156-6*, 205513400008) Bks Demand.

Modern English-Greek Dictionary. C. N. Brown. (ENG & GRE.). 420p. 1976. 35.00 (*0-8288-5743-1*, M9592) Fr & Eur.

Modern English-Greek-English Desk Dictionary with Thumb Index. George C. Divry. (ENG & GRE.). 768p. 1979. 29.95 (*0-8288-4822-X*, M9443) Fr & Eur.

Modern English-Greek Pocket Dictionary. (ENG & GRE.). 1989. 15.95 (*0-87557-030-5*) Saphrograph.

Modern English-Gujarati Dictionary. P. G. Deshpande. (ENG & GUJ.). 820p. 1983. 39.95 (*0-8288-1147-4*, M14254) Fr & Eur.

Modern English-Gujarati Dictionary. P. G. Deshpande. (ENG & GUJ.). 806p. 1983. text 45.00 (*0-19-561140-3*) OUP.

Modern English-Hindi Dictionary. Ed. by I. N. Anand. 1136p. 1991. 57.50 (*81-215-0461-9*, Pub. by M Manoharial) Coronet Bks.

Modern English Hindi Dictionary. I. N. Anand. (C). 1996. reprint ed. 20.00 (*0-685-50024-1*, Pub. by M Manoharial) S Asia.

Modern English Nihongo Dictionary: A Comprehensive New Japanese Language Resource. Fumio Tamamura. 1997. pap. text 48.00 (*4-7700-2148-8*, Pub. by Kodansha Intl) Kodansha.

Modern English Novel. Abel Chevalley. LC 72-3283. (Studies in Fiction: No. 34). 1972. reprint ed. lib. bdg. 75.00 (*0-8383-1530-5*) M S G Haskell Hse.

Modern English Novel: An Address Before the American Academy of Arts & Letters. Wilbur L. Cross. 1977. 11.95 (*0-8369-6927-8*, 7808) Ayer.

Modern English Playwrights: Short History of English Drama from 1825. John W. Cunliffe. (BCL1-PR English Literature Ser.). 260p. 1992. reprint ed. lib. bdg. 79.00 (*0-7812-7111-8*) Rprt Serv.

Modern English-Russian Aeronautical Dictionary. A. M. Murashkevich. (ENG & RUS.). 358p. 1993. 95.00 (*0-7859-9079-8*) Fr & Eur.

Modern English-Russian Dictionary of Idioms. N. F. Kalinina & L. L. Tibkhonova. (ENG & RUS.). 70p. (C). 1992. text 60.00 (*0-569-23651-7*, Pub. by Collets) St Mut.

***Modern English Structures.** Bernard O'Dwyer. 300p. 2000. pap. 26.95 (*1-55111-273-6*) Broadview Pr.

***Modern English Structures.** Bernard O'Dwyer. 200p. 2000. pap. 17.95 (*1-55111-275-2*) Broadview Pr.

Modern English-Yiddish, Yiddish-English Dictionary. Uriel Weinreich. LC 77-76038. (ENG & YID.). 1987. reprint ed. pap. 30.00 (*0-8052-0575-6*) Schocken.

Modern English-Yiddish, Yiddish-English Dictionary. Uriel Weinreich. 790p. 1991. reprint ed. 35.00 (*0-914512-45-5*) Yivo Inst.

Modern Enlightenment & the Rule of Reason. Ed. by John C. McCarthy. LC 97-40889. (Studies in Philosophy & the History of Philosophy: Vol. 32). 308p. (C). 1998. text 59.95 (*0-8132-0904-8*) Cath U Pr.

Modern Enviromental Law & Practice. Elizabeth G. Geltman. LC 96-46480. (Paralegal). 821p. (C). 1997. text 41.50 (*0-314-20347-8*) West Pub.

Modern Environmentalism: An Introduction. David Pepper. (Illus.). 384p. (C). 1996. pap. 25.99 (*0-415-05745-0*) Routledge.

Modern Enzymology: Problems & Trends. Ed. by Boris I. Kurganov et al. LC 94-2302. (Illus.). 735p. (C). 1995. lib. bdg. 210.00 (*1-56072-167-7*) Nova Sci Pubs.

Modern Epic: The World-System from Goethe to Garcia Marquez. Franco Moretti. Tr. by Quintin Hoare from ITA. LC 95-43983. 272p. (C). 1996. 65.00 (*1-85984-934-2*, Pub. by Verso); pap. 22.00 (*1-85984-069-8*, Pub. by Verso) Norton.

Modern Epidemic: A History of Tuberculosis in Japan. William Johnston. LC 95-5509. (Harvard East Asian Monographs: No. 162). 450p. (C). 1995. text 45.00 (*0-674-57912-7*) HUP.

Modern Epidemiology. 2nd ed. Kenneth J. Rothman & Sander Greenland. LC 97-23369. 1997. write for info. (*0-7817-1049-9*) Lppncott W & W.

Modern Epidemiology. 2nd ed. Kenneth J. Rothman & Sander Greenland. LC 97-23369. 358p. 1998. text 65.00 (*0-316-75780-2*) Lppncott W & W.

Modern Epistemology: A New Introduction. Alec Fisher & Nicholas Everitt. LC 94-23289. 272p. (C). 1994. pap. 24.06 (*0-07-021214-7*) McGraw.

Modern Era Filler. Perry. Date not set. write for info. (*0-395-69111-7*) HM.

Modern Era, 1972-1989 see Forty Years of Stock Car Racing

Modern Era of Coronary Thrombolysis, 160. Ed. by Richard C. Becker. LC 94-30680. (Developments in Cardiovascular Medicine Ser.). 320p. (C). 1994. text 180.00 (*0-7923-3063-3*) Kluwer Academic.

Modern Era Shipper. Perry. Date not set. write for info. (*0-395-69109-5*) HM.

Modern Esoteric Spirituality. Ed. by Antoine Faivre et al. (World Spirituality: An Encyclopedic History of the Religious Quest Ser.: Vol. 21). 500p. 1995. reprint ed. pap. 19.95 (*0-8245-1444-0*) Crossroad NY.

Modern Essays. Incl. Civil Disobedience. Henry David Thoreau. On Going to Church. George Bernard Shaw. Religion of the Future. Charles Eliot. 1983. Set pap. 5.95 (*0-8283-1449-7*) Branden Bks.

Modern Essays. London Times Staff. LC 73-86788. (Essay Index Reprint Ser.). 1977. 23.95 (*0-8369-1630-1*) Ayer.

Modern Essays & Sketches. Ed. by James W. Marriott. LC 68-22928. (Essay Index Reprint Ser.). 1977. 18.95 (*0-8369-0679-9*) Ayer.

Modern Essays on Eighteenth-Century Literature. Ed. by Leopold Damrosch, Jr. 502p. 1988. pap. text 26.95 (*0-19-504924-1*) OUP.

Modern Essentials. Rozemarijn De Witte. LC 97-30190. (Illus.). 192p. 1997. 35.00 (*1-57959-000-4*, SOMA) BB&T Inc.

Modern Estate Planning, 7 vols. E. Fiore & M. Friedlich. 1981. ring bd. 1210.00 (*0-8205-1406-3*) Bender.

Modern Esthetics: A Scientific Source for Estheticians. Henry Gambino. (SKIN). 335p. 1992. pap. 31.95 (*1-56253-043-7*) Thomson Learn.

Modern Ethiopia: From the Accession of Menilek II to the Present, Proceedings of the International Conference of the Ethiopian Studies, Nice, 5th, 19-22 December 1977. Ed. by Joseph Tubiana. 574p. 1980. text 130.00 (*90-6191-086-2*, Pub. by A A Balkema) Ashgate Pub Co.

Modern Etiquette. Moyra Bremner. 1995. 8.98 (*0-7858-0116-2*) Bk Sales Inc.

Modern Europe. R. Peterson. (Atlas of Mankind Ser.: Vol. 3). (Illus.). 128p. 1987. 30.00 (*0-941694-31-3*) Cliveden Pr.

Modern Europe: Place, Culture & Identity. Brian Graham. LC 98-28788. (Arnold Publications). (Illus.). 336p. 1998. pap. text 24.95 (*0-340-67698-1*) OUP.

Modern Europe after Fascism, 2 vols. Stein Larsen & Bernt Hagtvet. LC 97-62081. 1900p. 1998. 250.00 (*0-88033-973-X*, Pub. by East Eur Monographs) Col U Pr.

Modern Europe after Fascism. Stein U. Larsen. (Social Science Monograph Ser.). 700p. 1996. 103.00 (*0-88033-970-5*, 414, Pub. by East Eur Monographs) Col U Pr.

Modern Europe, 1789-1989. Asa Briggs & Patricia Clavin. LC 96-10174. (History of Europe Ser.). 512p. (C). 1996. pap. text 22.50 (*0-582-49405-2*, Pub. by Addison-Wesley) Longman.

Modern Europe Since 1789. Asa Briggs & Patricia Clavin. LC 96-10174. (History of Europe Ser.). 512p. (C). 1996. 74.00 (*0-582-49406-0*) Addison-Wesley.

Modern European Art: Impressionism to Abstract Art. Alan Bowness. LC 95-60189. (World of Art Ser.). (Illus.). 224p. 1995. pap. 14.95 (*0-500-20205-2*, Pub. by Thames Hudson) Norton.

Modern European Educators & Their Work. Adolph E. Meyer. LC 73-152197. (Essay Index Reprint Ser.). 1977. reprint ed. 20.95 (*0-8369-2246-8*) Ayer.

Modern European History. John R. Barber. LC 90-56009. (Outline Ser.). (Illus.). 416p. (Orig.). (C). 1993. pap. 13.00 (*0-06-467112-7*) HarpC.

Modern European History. rev. ed. Birdsall S. Viault. 608p. (C). 1990. pap. 12.95 (*0-07-067453-1*) McGraw.

Modern European History Vol. 1: 1789 to Present, Chronological & National Courses: Selected Reading Lists & Course Outlines from American Colleges & Universities. 3rd enl. ed. Ed. by John Santore. (History Syllabi Ser.). 340p. (C). 1990. pap. 16.95 (*0-910129-94-0*) Wiener Pubs Inc.

***Modern European History 1871-2000: A Documentary Reader.** 2nd ed. David Welch. LC 99-14506. 288p. 1999. pap. 24.99 (*0-415-21582-X*) Routledge.

***Modern European History, 1871-2000: Documentary Reader.** 2nd ed. David Welch. LC 99-14506. 288p. (C). 1999. text. write for info. (*0-415-21581-1*) Routledge.

M

Modern European Intellectual History: Reappraisals & New Perspectives. Ed. by Dominick LaCapra & Steven L. Kaplan. LC 82-7418. 318p. 1982. pap. text 18.95 (*0-8014-9881-3*) Cornell U Pr.

Modern European Maritime History. Fisher & Williams. 76.95 (*1-85928-124-9*) Ashgate Pub Co.

Modern European Socialism. Lawrence Wilde. (Illus.). 228p. (C). 1994. text 72.95 (*1-85521-446-6*, Pub. by Dartmth Pub); pap. text 25.95 (*1-85521-539-X*, Pub. by Dartmth Pub) Ashgate Pub Co.

Modern Evaluation of the Mahabharata: Sharma Felicitation Volume. Ed. by Satya P. Narang. LC 95-900349. (C). 1995. 54.00 (*81-7081-291-7*, Pub. by Nag Pubs) S Asia.

Modern Evidence. Mueller. 1995. 135.00 (*0-316-59000-2*) Little.

*__Modern Exchange-Rate Regimes, Stabilisation Programmes & Co-Ordination of Macroeconomic Policies: Recent Experiences of Selected Developing Latin American Economies.__ Maria Luiza Falcao Silva. LC 99-76360. 334p. 1999. text 78.95 (*1-84014-919-1*, Pub. by Ashgate Pub) Ashgate Pub Co.

*__Modern Experimental Aircraft.__ B. Lafontaine. (Pictorial Archive Ser.). 2000. pap. 2.95 (*0-486-41037-4*) Dover.

Modern Experimental Biochemistry. 2nd ed. Rodney F. Boyer. LC 92-35064. (Series in the Life Sciences & Chemistry). 519p. (C). 1992. 60.00 (*0-8053-0545-9*) Benjamin-Cummings.

*__Modern Experimental Biochemistry.__ 3rd ed. (C). 2000. text. write for info. (*0-8053-3112-3*) Benjamin-Cummings.

Modern Experimental Biochemistry. 3rd ed. Rodney F. Boyer. 520p. (C). 2000. pap. 46.67 (*0-8053-3111-5*) Benjamin-Cummings.

Modern Exterior Ballistics: The Launch & Flight Dynamics of Symmetric Projectiles. Robert L. McCoy. (Illus.). 328p. 1999. 95.00 (*0-7643-0720-7*) Schiffer.

Modern Fables: As Told by the Old Toothsayer. Billy L. Krieg. 78p. 1999. pap. 10.95 (*0-9658898-3-1*) Holly Graduate.

Modern Factor Analysis. 3rd rev. ed. Harry H. Harman. LC 75-22267. (Illus.). 518p. 1976. lib. bdg. 42.00 (*0-226-31652-1*) U Ch Pr.

Modern Factory: Safety, Sanitation & Welfare. George M. Price. LC 74-89758. (American Labor, from Conspiracy to Collective Bargaining Ser., No. 1). 574p. 1975. reprint ed. 51.95 (*0-405-02144-5*) Ayer.

Modern Faith & Thought. Helmut Thielicke. Tr. by Geoffrey W. Bromiley. LC 90-45870. 602p. reprint ed. pap. 186.70 (*0-7837-6572-X*, 204613700011) Bks Demand.

*__Modern Faith Healing Scripturally Considered.__ William McDonald. 64p. 1999. pap. 5.99 (*0-88019-398-0*) Schmul Pub Co.

Modern Falconer: Training, Hawking & Breeding. Diana D. Walters. (Illus.). 192p. 1994. 37.95 (*1-85310-368-3*, Pub. by Swan Hill Pr) Voyageur Pr.

Modern Family see Familia Moderna

Modern Family Law: Cases & Materials. D. Kelly Weisberg & Susan F. Appleton. LC 97-35063. 1998. write for info. (*1-56706-501-5*); boxed set 60.00 (*1-56706-701-8*) Aspen Law.

Modern Fancy Dancer. C. Scott Evans & J. Rex Reddick. Ed. by Earl C. Fenner. (Illus.). 64p. 1998. pap. 15.95 (*0-9624883-2-1*, Pub. by Reddick Enterp) Book Pub Co.

*__Modern Fantastic: The Films of David Cronenberg.__ Ed. by Michael Grant. LC 00-29815. 208p. 2000. 65.00 (*0-275-97058-2*, C7058); pap. 24.95 (*0-275-97059-0*) Greenwood.

Modern Fantasy: Five Studies. Colin N. Manlove. LC 74-31798. 316p. reprint ed. pap. 90.10 (*0-608-16456-9*, 2026346) Bks Demand.

Modern Fantasy Writers see Writers of English: Lives & Works

Modern Farm Tractors. Andrew Morland. LC 97-6042. (Enthusiast Color Ser.). (Illus.). 96p. 1997. pap. 13.95 (*0-7603-0155-7*) MBI Pubg.

Modern Fascism: Liquidating the Judeo-Christian Worldview. Gene E. Veith, Jr. LC 92-41904. (Concordia Scholarship Today Ser.). 187p. 1993. pap. 17.00 (*0-570-04603-3*, 12-3189) Concordia.

Modern Fashion Drawing. Dora Shackell & W. Stuart Masters. 1978. lib. bdg. 250.00 (*0-8490-2266-5*) Gordon Pr.

Modern Fashion in Detail. Claire Wilcox & Valerie Mendes. (Illus.). 144p. 1992. 40.00 (*0-87951-450-7*, Pub. by Overlook Pr) Penguin Putnam.

Modern Fashion in Detail. Clarie Wilcox & Valerie Mendes. (Illus.). 144p. 1998. pap. 24.95 (*0-87951-869-3*, Pub. by Overlook Pr) Penguin Putnam.

Modern Federal Jury Instructions: Criminal & Civil, 4 vols. Leonard Sand. 1984. ring bd. 955.00 (*0-8205-1485-3*) Bender.

Modern Feminisms: Literary, Political, Cultural. Ed. by Maggie Humm. (Gender & Culture Ser.). 440p. (C). 1992. pap. 20.00 (*0-231-08073-5*); text 57.50 (*0-231-08072-7*) Col U Pr.

Modern Feminist Thought: From the Second Wave to "Post-Feminism" Imelda Whelehan. 288p. (C). 1995. text 45.00 (*0-8147-9299-5*); pap. text 19.00 (*0-8147-9300-2*) NYU Pr.

Modern Ferromagnetic Material for Electrical Applications. A. Goldman. (Electrical Engineering Ser.). 1993. write for info. (*0-442-00999-2*, VNR) Wiley.

Modern Fiction. Dorothy Brewster & Angus Burrell. LC 75-86732. (Essay Index Reprint Ser.). 1977. 26.95 (*0-8369-1123-7*) Ayer.

Modern Fiction & Human Time: A Study in Narrative & Belief. Wesley A. Kort. LC 85-13547. 240p. 1986. 29.95 (*0-8130-0833-6*) U Press Fla.

Modern Fiction & Human Time: A Study in Narrative & Belief. Wesley A. Kort. LC 85-13547. 237p. 1985. reprint ed. pap. 73.50 (*0-608-04482-2*, 206522700005) Bks Demand.

Modern Fiction & the Art of Subversion. Jonathan Quick. LC 98-18025. (American University Studies III: Vol. 60). 170p. 1999. text 38.95 (*0-8204-4097-3*, 40973) P Lang Pubng.

Modern Fifties & Sixties: The Spreading of Contemporary Architecture over the Netherlands. Hans Ibelings. 1997. pap. text 35.00 (*90-5662-007-X*, Pub. by NAi Uitgevers) Dist Art Pubs.

Modern Fighter Aircraft. Jeremy Flock. 1993. 19.98 (*1-55521-891-1*) Bk Sales Inc.

Modern Fighter Aircraft Technology & Tactics. Anthony Thornborough. (Illus.). 192p. 1995. 29.95 (*1-85260-426-3*, Pub. by J H Haynes & Co) Motorbooks Intl.

Modern Fighter Planes. George A. Sullivan. (Military Aircraft Ser.). 144p. (J). (gr. 6-10). 1991. lib. bdg. 19.95 (*0-8160-2352-2*) Facts on File.

Modern Fighter Planes. Nick Taylor. (J). (gr. 1-9). 1992. pap. 4.95 (*0-88388-095-4*) Bellerophon Bks.

*__Modern Fighters: The Ultimate Guide to In-Flight Tactics, Technology, Weapons & Equipment.__ Mike Spick. 144p. 1999. 19.98 (*0-7624-0526-0*) Running Pr.

*__Modern Fighting Helicopters.__ Bill Gunston. 1999. 29.95 (*0-86101-945-8*) Salamander.

*__Modern Finance.__ Eric C. Briys. 128p. 2000. pap. 18.95 (*0-471-88961-X*) Wiley.

Modern Financial Accounting, 1001-1088. Miguel A. De Capriles. 166p. 1962. reprint ed. pap. 5.00 (*0-8377-0505-3*, Rothman) W S Hein.

Modern Financial Intermediaries & Markets. Nasser Arshadi & Gordon V. Karels. LC 96-23952. 501p. (C). 1996. 98.00 (*0-13-119470-4*) P-H.

Modern Financial Managing: Continuity & Change. alternate ed. (C). 1995. teacher ed. write for info. (*0-673-55609-3*) Addson-Wesley Educ.

Modern Firearm Silencers: Great Designs, Great Designers. (Illus.). 120p. pap. 25.00 (*0-87364-269-4*) Paladin Pr.

Modern Firearm Silencers: Great Designs, Great Designers. J. David Truby. (Illus.). 120p. 1983. pap. 15.00 (*0-87364-666-5*) Paladin Pr.

Modern First Ladies: Their Documentary Legacy. Ed. by Nancy K. Smith & Mary C. Ryan. LC 88-15263. (Illus.). 192p. (C). 1989. 15.00 (*0-911333-73-8*, 100046) National Archives & Recs.

*__Modern First Ladies (to 1989) Their Documentary Legacy.__ Ed. by Nancy Kegan Smith & Mary C. Ryan. (Illus.). 184p. (C). 2000. reprint ed. text 25.00 (*0-7881-8741-4*) DIANE Pub.

Modern Fishing Encyclopedia: Worldwide Angling Guide. Ken Schultz. LC 99-33719. (Illus.). 1760p. 1999. text 60.00 (*0-02-862057-7*, Pub. by Macmillan) S&S Trade.

Modern Fluorescence Spectroscopy, 2 vols., Vol. 1. Ed. by Earl L. Wehry. LC 75-43827. (Modern Analytical Chemistry Ser.). 254p. reprint ed. pap. 78.80 (*0-608-11415-4*, 201965000001) Bks Demand.

Modern Fluorescence Spectroscopy, 2 vols., Vol. 2. Ed. by Earl L. Wehry. LC 75-43827. (Modern Analytical Chemistry Ser.). 479p. reprint ed. pap. 148.50 (*0-608-11416-2*, 201965000002) Bks Demand.

Modern Fluorescence Spectroscopy, Vol. 3. Ed. by Earl L. Wehry. LC 75-43827. (Modern Analytical Chemistry Ser.). 376p. 1981. 85.00 (*0-306-40690-X*, Plenum Trade) Perseus Pubng.

Modern Fluorescence Spectroscopy, Vol. 4. Ed. by Earl L. Wehry. LC 75-43827. (Modern Analytical Chemistry Ser.). 300p. 1981. 75.00 (*0-306-40691-8*, Plenum Trade) Perseus Pubng.

Modern Fluoropolymers: High Performance Polymers for Diverse Applications. John Scheirs. LC 96-49974. 660p. 1997. 345.00 (*0-471-97055-7*) Wiley.

Modern Fly Fishing. Jim Casada. LC 93-84838. (Complete Angler's Library). 234p. 1993. write for info. (*0-914697-56-0*) N Amer Outdoor Grp.

Modern Fly Tying Materials. Richard W. Talleur. (Illus.). 256p. 1995. 35.00 (*1-55821-344-9*) Lyons Pr.

Modern Folk Ballads. Ed. by Charles Causley. (Pocket Poet Ser.). 1968. pap. 3.95 (*0-8023-9043-9*) Dufour.

Modern Folk Guitar. Terry Kuhn & Harvey Reid. 320p. (C). 1984. pap. 43.75 (*0-07-554461-X*) McGraw.

Modern Food Gifts. Martha Gill. LC 97-71931. (Modern Guides Ser.). (Illus.). 128p. 1997. 18.95 (*1-56352-422-8*) Longstreet.

Modern Food Microbiology. James M. Jay. (Illus.). 656p. 1991. text 52.95 (*0-442-00733-7*) Chapman & Hall.

*__Modern Food Microbiology.__ 6th ed. James M. Jay. LC 99-54735. (Food Science Text Ser.). (Illus.). 720p. 2000. 65.00 (*0-8342-1671-X*, 1671X) Aspen Pub.

Modern Food Service. Charles Anderson & Derek Blakemore. 240p. 1991. pap. 34.95 (*0-7506-0057-8*) Buttrwrth-Heinemann.

*__Modern Foraminifera.__ B. K. Sen Gupta. LC 99-29610. 1999. write for info. (*0-412-82430-2*) Chapman & Hall.

Modern Forecasting. Hans Levenbach et al. 400p. boxed set. write for info. (*0-534-26268-6*, Pub. by Brooks-Cole) Thomson Learn.

Modern Forests: Statemaking & Environmental Change in Colonial Eastern India. K. C. Sivaramakrishnan. 1999. 45.00 (*0-8047-3563-8*) Stanford U Pr.

Modern Formal Logic Primer Vol. I: Sentence Logic, Vol. 1. Paul Teller. 176p. (C). 1989. pap. text 20.20 (*0-13-903170-7*) P-H.

Modern Formal Logic Primer Vol. II: Predicate Logic & Metatheory. Paul Teller. 304p. (C). 1989. pap. text 20.00 (*0-13-903196-0*) P-H.

Modern Formula One Race Car: From Concept to Competition, Design & Development of the Lola BMS-Ferrari Grand Prix Car. Nigel Macknight. (Illus.). 192p. 1993. 39.95 (*0-87938-823-4*) MBI Pubg.

Modern Fortran 77 for Scientists & Engineers. 1989. pap. 39.50 (*0-89391-156-9*) Ablx Pub.

Modern Fortran 77 for Scientists & Engineers. Peter B. Worland. (Illus.). 432p. (C). 1995. text 47.95 (*0-15-561156-9*) OUP.

Modern Fortran 77 for Scientists & Engineers. Peter B. Worland. 410p. (C). 1989. disk. write for info. (*0-318-64532-7*) SCP.

*__Modern Fortran 77-9-2000.__ Gary Bronson & Kenneth Walter. (Illus.). 757p. (C). 1999. pap. 60.65 (*1-57676-038-3*) Scott Jones Pubng.

*__Modern France: Society in Transition.__ Ed. by Malcolm Cook & Grace Davie. LC 98-21808. 279p. 1999. pap. 22.99 (*0-415-15432-4*) Routledge.

Modern France: Theories & Realities of Urban Planning. Peggy A. Phillips. LC 86-28225. (Illus.). 262p. (Orig.). 1987. pap. text 25.50 (*0-8191-6038-5*) U Pr of Amer.

Modern Frankenstein: Fiction Becomes Fact Ray Hammond. LC 86-181757. 192p. 1986. write for info. (*0-7137-1823-4*) Blandford Pr.

Modern French-Arabic Dictionary: Dictionnaire Moderne Francais-Arabe. deluxe ed. M. Elias. (ARA & FRE.). 868p. 1979. 29.95 (*0-8288-4799-1*, M9749) Fr & Eur.

Modern French CE: The Neuter Pronoun in Adjectival Predication. Samuel N. Rosenberg. (Janua Linguarum, Ser. Practica: No. 116). 1970. pap. text 90.80 (*90-279-0747-1*) Mouton.

Modern French Criticism: From Proust & Valery to Structuralism. Ed. by John K. Simon. LC 79-160840. (C). 1995. pap. text 8.00 (*0-226-75855-9*) U Ch Pr.

Modern French Grammar: A Practical Guide to Grammar & Usage. Isabelle Perez & Margaret A. Lang. LC 95-39756. (ENG & FRE.). 368p. (C). 1996. pap. 25.99 (*0-415-09852-1*) Routledge.

Modern French Grammar: A Practical Guide to Grammar & Usage. Isabelle Perez et al. LC 95-39756. (Modern Grammars Ser.). (ENG & FRE.). 368p. (C). 1996. 75.00 (*0-415-09851-3*) Routledge.

Modern French Grammar Workbook. Margaret A. Lang. Ed. by Isabelle Perez. 96p. (C). 1997. pap., wbk. ed. 12.99 (*0-415-12093-4*) Routledge.

Modern French Intermediate. H. Decker & F. Bernhard. (ENG & FRE.). 292p. 1967. lib. bdg. 9.95 (*0-8288-6972-3*, M10448) Fr & Eur.

Modern French Legal Philosophy. A. Fouilee et al. (Modern Legal Philosophy Ser.: Vol. 7). lxvi, 578p. 1998. reprint ed. 193.50 (*1-56169-386-3*) Gaunt.

Modern French Legal Philosophy. Thomas J. North et al. Tr. by Scott & Joseph P. Chamberlin. (Modern Legal Philosophy Ser.: Vol. 7). lxvi, 578p. 1969. reprint ed. 47.50 (*0-8377-2126-1*, Rothman) W S Hein.

Modern French Marxism. Michael Kelly. LC 82-47973. 246p. 1982. reprint ed. pap. 76.30 (*0-608-06725-3*, 206692200009) Bks Demand.

Modern French Music. Edward B. Hill. LC 71-87491. (Music Reprint Ser.). 1969. reprint ed. lib. bdg. 42.50 (*0-306-71497-3*) Da Capo.

Modern French Music. Edward B. Hill. 406p. 1990. reprint ed. lib. bdg. 89.00 (*0-7812-9032-5*) Rprt Serv.

Modern French Painters. Jan Gordon. LC 73-99697. (Essay Index Reprint Ser.). 1977. 20.95 (*0-8369-1573-9*) Ayer.

Modern French Painters. Maurice Raynal. LC 76-91374. (Contemporary Art Ser.). 1970. reprint ed. 23.95 (*0-405-00735-3*) Ayer.

Modern French Philosophy. Vincent Descombes. Tr. by L. Scott-Fox & J. M. Harding. 208p. 1981. pap. text 23.95 (*0-521-29672-2*) Cambridge U Pr.

Modern French Poetry: A Bilingual Anthology. Ed. by Patricia Terry & Serge Gavronsky. LC 75-17893. 255p. reprint ed. pap. 79.10 (*0-608-12598-9*, 202396800034) Bks Demand.

Modern French Poetry: A Dual Text Anthology. Ed. & Tr. by Martin Sorrell. (ENG & FRE.). 242p. (Orig.). 1991. pap. 24.00 (*1-85610-005-7*, Pub. by Forest Bks) Dufour.

Modern French Poetry: An Anthology. Ed. by Joseph T. Shipley. LC 72-8283. (Granger Index Reprint Ser.). 1977. reprint ed. 26.95 (*0-8369-6394-6*) Ayer.

Modern French Poets: Selections with Translations. unabridged ed. Ed. by Wallace Fowlie. LC 92-19215. Orig. Title: Mid-Century French Poets. 288p. 1992. reprint ed. pap. text 8.95 (*0-486-27323-7*) Dover.

Modern French Politics: Analyzing Conflict & Consensus since 1945. Nick Hewlett. LC 97-43656. 280p. 1998. 57.95 (*0-7456-1119-2*); pap. 26.95 (*0-7456-1120-6*) Blackwell Pubs.

Modern French Short Fiction. Ed. by Johnnie Gratton & Brigitte Le Juez. LC 93-27932. 1994. text 17.95 (*0-7190-4211-9*, Pub. by Manchester Univ Pr); text 69.95 (*0-7190-4210-0*, Pub. by Manchester Univ Pr) St Martin.

Modern French-Spanish, Spanish-French Dictionary: Diccionario Moderno Frances-Espanol-Frances. Ramon Garcia-Pelayo & J. Testas. (FRE & SPA.). 1816p. 1981. 59.95 (*0-8288-0737-X*, S32371) Fr & Eur.

Modern French Theatre: From Giraudoux to Genet. rev. ed. Jacques Guicharnaud & June Guicharnaud. LC 67-26198. (Yale Romanic Studies, Second Ser.: No. 7). 397p. reprint ed. pap. 123.10 (*0-8357-8226-3*, 203373600087) Bks Demand.

Modern Frenchmen: Five Biographies. Philip G. Hamerton. LC 72-4579. (Essay Index Reprint Ser.). 1977. reprint ed. 26.95 (*0-8369-2947-0*) Ayer.

Modern Freudians: Contemporary Psychoanalytic Technique. Ed. by Carolyn Ellman et al. LC 98-12097. 336p. 1998. 40.00 (*0-7657-0158-8*) Aronson.

Modern Fruit Science. rev. ed. Norman F. Childers. 1995. 59.00 (*0-938378-10-4*) N F Childers.

Modern Functional Building. Adolf Behne. Tr. by Michael Robinson from GER. LC 96-1970. (Texts & Documents Ser.). (Illus.). 280p. 1996. 40.00 (*0-89236-363-0*, Pub. by J P Getty Trust); pap. 24.95 (*0-89236-364-9*, Pub. by J P Getty Trust) OUP.

Modern Fundamentals of Golf. rev. ed. Ben Hogan. (Classics of Golf Ser.). (Illus.). 135p. 1987. 28.00 (*0-940889-18-8*) Classics Golf.

*__Modern Fungicides & Antifungal Compounds II.__ Ed. by Horst Lyr et al. (Illus.). 520p. 1999. 153.00 (*1-898298-60-2*, Pub. by Intercept UK) Spr-Verlag.

Modern Fur Flies. Petri Pajunen. (Illus.). 48p. 1998. pap. 16.95 (*952-5254-00-3*) F Amato Pubns.

Modern Furnishings for the Home. William J. Hennessey. LC 97-10737. (Twentieth Century: Vol. 7). (Illus.). 312p. 1997. reprint ed. 50.00 (*0-926494-12-0*) Acanthus Pr.

Modern Furniture Designs, 1950-1980s. Klaus-Jurgen Sembach. LC 97-80086. (Schiffer Book for Collectors Ser.). (Illus.). 320p. 1997. 59.95 (*0-7643-0382-1*) Schiffer.

Modern Furniture in Canada, 1920-1970. Virginia Wright. (Illus.). 224p. 1996. pap. 39.95 (*0-8020-7377-8*); text 75.00 (*0-8020-2873-X*) U of Toronto Pr.

Modern GaAs Processing Methods. Ralph E. Williams. (Microwave Library). 510p. 1990. text 65.00 (*0-89006-343-5*) Artech Hse.

Modern Gaelic-English Dictionary. Robert C. Owen. 139p. 1993. pap. 29.95 (*1-871901-29-4*) Colton Bk.

Modern Gaelic Poetry from Scotland & Ireland. Compiled by I Macdonald & M. Davitt. 256p. 1995. 29.95 (*0-86241-356-7*, Pub. by Canongate Books) Interlink Pub.

Modern Games with Renaissance Forms: From Leonardo & Shakespeare to Warhol & Stoppard. Peter Egri. LC 97-178864. 140p. 1996. pap. 60.00 (*963-05-7331-8*, Pub. by Akade Kiado) Intl Spec Bk.

Modern Gang Reader. Ed. by Malcolm W. Klein et al. LC 94-43283. (Illus.). 330p. (C). 1995. pap. text. write for info. (*0-935732-66-7*) Roxbury Pub Co.

*__Modern Gang Reader.__ 2nd ed. Cheryl L. Maxson & Malcolm W. Klein. Ed. by Jody A. Miller. (Illus.). 335p. (C). 2000. pap. text. write for info. (*1-891487-44-2*) Roxbury Pub Co.

*__Modern Garden.__ Jane Brown. (Illus.). 224p. 2000. 45.00 (*1-56898-238-0*) Princeton Arch.

*__Modern Garden Makers.__ Sally Court. (Illus.). 2000. 34.95 (*0-304-35325-6*) Continuum.

Modern Gardens & Landscaping. Elizabeth B. Kassler. (Illus.). 120p. 1990. pap. 17.95 (*0-8109-6053-2*) Abrams.

Modern Gas-Based Temperature & Pressure Measurements. F. Pavese & G. Molinar. (International Cryogenics Monographs). (Illus.). 544p. (C). 1992. text 130.00 (*0-306-44167-5*, Kluwer Plenum) Kluwer Academic.

Modern General Topology. 3rd rev. ed. J. Nagata. (Mathematical Library: Vol. 33). 522p. 1985. 228.00 (*0-444-87655-3*, North Holland) Elsevier.

Modern Genetic Analysis. Griffiths. 1998. 160.00 (*0-7167-3423-0*) W H Freeman.

Modern Genetic Analysis. Griffiths. 1999. write for info. incl. cd-rom (*0-7167-3347-1*) W H Freeman.

Modern Genetics: Solutions Manual. 2nd ed. Francisco J. Ayala & J. A. Kiger, Jr. 1984. pap. text, teacher ed. 10.75 (*0-8053-0317-0*) Benjamin-Cummings.

*__Modern Genetics Laboratory: Heredity & Molecular Biology.__ David Haymer. 98p. (C). 1999. per. 19.95 (*0-7872-6217-X*) Kendall-Hunt.

*__Modern Genre Theory.__ David Duff. LC 99-23077. (Critical Readers Ser.). 304p. (C). 1999. 79.95 (*0-582-36806-5*) Longman.

*__Modern Genre Theory.__ David Duff. LC 99-23077. (Critical Readers Ser.). 304p. 1999. pap. 30.73 (*0-582-36805-7*) Longman.

Modern Geographic Thought: Richard Peet. Richard Peet. LC 97-27639. 1998. 73.95 (*1-55786-206-0*); pap. 31.95 (*1-55786-378-4*) Blackwell Pubs.

Modern Geographical Trends Felicitation: Volume in Honour of Professor Enayat Ahmad. Ed. by Pradyumana Pandey. xxxvi, 616p. 1984. 89.00 (*1-55528-068-4*, Pub. by Today Tomorrow) Scholarly Pubns.

Modern Geography: An Encyclopedic Survey. Ed. by Gary S. Dunbar. LC 90-3742. 239p. 1990. text 20.00 (*0-8240-5343-5*, H1197) Garland.

Modern Geography: Survey Encyclopedia. 1991. 73.00 (*1-55862-122-9*, 00007645) St James Pr.

Modern Geography As of 1828. J. Olney. (Illus.). 200p. 1994. pap. 25.00 (*0-87556-789-4*) Saifer.

Modern Geography of the Republic of Cameroon. 2nd ed. Aaron S. Neba. LC 87-70017. (Illus.). xii, 204p. 1987. 32.50 (*0-941815-01-3*); pap. 22.50 (*0-941815-00-5*) Neba Pubs.

Modern Geometric Dimensioning & Tolerancing with Workbook Section. 2nd ed. Lowell W. Foster. 222p. 1982. teacher ed. 11.95 (*0-910399-22-0*, 5022); pap. 19.95 (*0-910399-21-2*, 5021) Natl Tool & Mach.

Modern Geometrical Optics. Richard Ditteon. (C). 1997. text. write for info. (*0-201-54836-4*) Addison-Wesley.

Modern Geometrical Optics. Richard Ditteon. LC 97-24252. 439p. 1997. 79.95 (*0-471-16922-6*, Wiley-Interscience) Wiley.

Modern Geometrical Optics. Max Herzberger. LC 77-9030. 516p. 1980. reprint ed. 46.50 (*0-88275-585-4*) Krieger.

Modern Geometries. 2nd ed. James R. Smart. Ed. by Robert J. Wisner. LC 77-15784. (Contemporary Undergraduate Mathematics Ser.). (Illus.). (C). 1978. mass mkt. 32.25 (*0-8185-0265-7*) Brooks-Cole.

Modern Geometries. 3rd ed. James R. Smart. LC 87-25048. (Math). 366p. (C). 1987. mass mkt. 48.50 (*0-534-08310-2*) Brooks-Cole.

An Asterisk (*) at the beginning of an entry indicates that the title is appearing for the first time.

Modern Geometries. 4th ed. James R. Smart. LC 93-29985. 1996. mass mkt. 53.50 (*0-534-21198-4*) Brooks-Cole.

Modern Geometries. 5th ed. James R. Smart. LC 97-41347. 445p. 1997. mass mkt. 94.95 (*0-534-35188-3*) Brooks-Cole.

Modern Geometries: An Analytic Approach. Michael G. Henle. 372p. (C). 1996. 85.33 (*0-13-193418-X*) P-H.

Modern Geometry. Thomas. (Mathematics Ser.). 2002. pap. 60.00 (*0-534-36550-7*) Brooks-Cole.

***Modern Geometry.** 2nd ed. Steven Roman. (Illus.). 51p. (C). 1999. pap. text. write for info. (*1-878015-25-7*) Innov Textbooks.

Modern Geometry - Methods & Applications Pt. I: The Geometry of Surface, Transformation Groups & Fields. B. A. Dubrovin et al. Tr. by R. G. Burns. (Graduate Texts in Mathematics Ser.: Vol. 93). (RUS., Illus.). 495p. 1984. 59.80 (*0-387-90872-2*) Spr-Verlag.

Modern Geometry - Methods & Applications Pt. 1: The Geometry of Surfaces, Transformation Groups & Fields. 2nd ed. B. A. Dubrovin et al. (Graduate Texts in Mathematics Ser.). (Illus.). xv, 468p. 1993. 65.95 (*0-387-97663-9*) Spr-Verlag.

Modern Geometry - Methods & Applications Pt. 2: The Geometry & Topology of Manifolds. B. A. Dubrovin et al. Tr. by R. G. Burns. LC 83-16851. (Graduate Texts in Mathematics Ser.: Vol. 104). (Illus.). xv, 448p. 1995. 65.95 (*0-387-96162-3*) Spr-Verlag.

Modern Geometry - Methods & Applications Pt. 3: Introduction to Homology Theory. B. A. Dubrovin et al. Ed. by J. H. Ewing et al. Tr. by R. G. Burns from RUS. (Graduate Texts in Mathematics Ser.: Vol. 124). (Illus.). 464p. 1990. 64.95 (*0-387-97271-4*) Spr-Verlag.

Modern Geometry with Applications. George Jennings. LC 93-27818. (Universitext Ser.). (Illus.). 187p. 1994. pap. 29.95 (*0-387-94222-X*) Spr-Verlag.

Modern Geophysics in Engineering Geology. Ed. by D. M. McCann et al. (Geological Society Engineering Geology Special Publication Ser.: No. 12). (Illus.). 352p. 1997. 132.00 (*1-897799-92-6*, Pub. by Geol Soc Pub Hse) AAPG.

Modern Geotechnical Methods: Instrumentation & Vibratory Hammers, 1990. (Transportation Research Record Ser.: No. 1277). 160p. 1990. 23.00 (*0-309-05057-X*) Transport Res Bd.

Modern German. 3rd ed. Van H. Vail et al. (GER.). 576p. (C). 1991. 8.00 (*0-03-054227-8*, Pub. by Harcourt Coll Pubs) Harcourt.

Modern German. 3rd ed. Van H. Vail et al. (GER.). 576p. (C). 1992. pap. text, student ed. 24.50 (*0-03-054223-5*); audio. write for info. (*0-03-066529-9*) Harcourt Coll Pubs.

Modern German. 3rd ed. Van H. Vail et al. (GER.). 576p. (C). 1992. write for info. (*0-318-69162-0*) Harcourt Coll Pubs.

Modern German Grammar: A Practical Guide. Bill Dodd et al. LC 95-35096. (GER.). 504p. (C). 1996. 75.00 (*0-415-09847-5*); pap. 25.99 (*0-415-09848-3*) Routledge.

Modern German Grammar Workbook. William Dodd & John Klapper. 112p. (C). 1996. pap., wbk. ed. 12.99 (*0-415-12094-2*) Routledge.

Modern German Historical Novel: Paradigms, Problems, Perspectives. Ed. by David Roberts & Philip Thomson. LC 89-18380. (Berg European Studies). 240p. 1991. 19.50 (*0-85496-667-6*) Berg Pubs.

Modern German Literature. 2nd ed. Benjamin W. Wells. 429p. 1977. 23.95 (*0-8369-2876-8*) Ayer.

Modern German Music: Recollections & Criticisms, 2 vols. Henry F. Chorley. LC 79-110994. (Music Reprint Ser.). 1973. reprint ed. 85.00 (*0-306-71911-8*) Da Capo.

Modern German Novel. Ed. by Keith Bullivant. LC 86-32683. 314p. 1987. 19.50 (*0-85496-522-X*) Berg Pubs.

Modern German Novel: A Series of Studies & Appreciations. Harvey W. Hewett-Thayer. LC 67-23232. (Essay Index Reprint Ser.). 1977. 20.95 (*0-8369-0537-7*) Ayer.

Modern German Painting & Sculpture. Alfred H. Barr, Jr. LC 76-169296. (Museum of Modern Art Publications in Reprint). (Illus.). 96p. 1972. reprint ed. 21.95 (*0-405-01556-9*) Ayer.

Modern German 3E. 3rd ed. Van H. Vail et al. (GER.). 576p. (C). 1992. text 76.00 (*0-03-065758-X*) Harcourt Coll Pubs.

Modern Germany. Kerbo Strasser. LC 99-21322. 176p. 1999. pap. 13.75 (*0-07-292819-0*) McGraw.

Modern Germany: An Encyclopedia of History, People, & Culture, 1871-1990, 2 vols. Ed. by Dieter K. Buse et al. LC 97-13829. (Canadian Review of Studies on Nationalism Ser.). (Illus.). 1158p. 1998. text 160.00 (*0-8153-0503-6*, H1520) Garland.

Modern Germany: Its History & Civilization. 2nd ed. Koppel S. Pinson. (Illus.). 682p. (C). 1989. reprint ed. pap. text 29.95 (*0-88133-434-0*) Waveland Pr.

Modern Germany: Politics, Society & Culture. Peter James. LC 97-37584. 256p. (C). 1998. 65.00 (*0-415-15033-7*) Routledge.

Modern Germany: Politics, Society & Culture. Peter James. LC 97-37584. (Illus.). 232p. (C). 1998. pap. 20.99 (*0-415-15034-5*) Routledge.

Modern Germany: Society, Economy & Politics in the Twentieth Century. 2nd ed. Volker R. Berghahn. (Illus.). 336p. 1987. 69.95 (*0-521-34505-7*); pap. text 19.95 (*0-521-34748-3*) Cambridge U Pr.

Modern Germany & Her Historians. Antoine Guilland. 1970. reprint ed. lib. bdg. 75.00 (*0-8371-4506-6*, GUMG, Greenwood Pr) Greenwood.

Modern Germany Reconsidered. Ed. by Gordon Martel. (Illus.). 304p. (C). 1992. 90.00 (*0-415-07811-3*); pap. 25.99 (*0-415-07812-1*) Routledge.

Modern Ghost Stories: By Eminent Women Writers. Richard Dalby. 336p. 1994. pap. 10.95 (*0-7867-0089-0*) Carroll & Graf.

Modern Girl: Girlhood & Growing Up. Lesley Johnson. LC 92-27016. 192p. 1993. 113.00 (*0-335-09999-8*); pap. 35.95 (*0-335-09998-X*) OpUniv Pr.

Modern Girls, Shining Stars, the Skies of Tokyo: Five Japanese Women. Phyllis Birnbaum. LC 98-15268. (Illus.). 240p. 1999. 26.50 (*0-231-11356-0*) Col U Pr.

***Modern Girls, Shining Stars, the Skies of Tokyo: Five Japanese Women.** Phyllis Birnbaum. 2000. pap. text 14.95 (*0-231-11357-9*) Col U Pr.

Modern Glacial Environments: Processes, Dynamics & Sediments. John Menzies. (Glacial Environments Ser.: Vol. 1). (Illus.). 392p. 1995. pap. text 85.95 (*0-7506-2351-9*) Buttrwrth-Heinemann.

Modern Glass Practice. 7th rev. ed. Samuel R. Scholes & Charles H. Green. LC 74-32219. (Illus.). 508p. (C). 1993. reprint ed. text 133.00 (*1-878907-07-7*, RAN) TechBooks.

Modern Global Cash Management Vol. 1: A Qualitative Approach. 2nd rev. ed. Steve J. Ahn. (Illus.). 402p. 1996. lib. bdg. 28.00 (*0-9650809-1-9*) GDI.

Modern Global Seismology. Thorne Lay & Terry C. Wallace. LC 94-33101. (International Geophysics Ser.: Vol. 58). (Illus.). xii, 521p. 1995. text 61.00 (*0-12-732870-X*) Acad Pr.

Modern Gnathological Concepts-Updated. Victor O. Lucia. (Illus.). 440p. 1983. text 186.00 (*0-86715-105-6*) Quint Pub Co.

Modern Gothic: A Reader. Ed. by Victor Sage & Allan L. Smith. LC 95-44012. 280p. 1997. text 24.95 (*0-7190-4208-9*, Pub. by Manchester Univ Pr) St Martin.

Modern Governance: New Government - Society Interactions. Jan Kooiman. (Illus.). 288p. (C). 1993. text 65.00 (*0-8039-8890-7*); pap. text 22.95 (*0-8039-8891-5*) Sage.

Modern Grain Sorghum Production. Ed. by William F. Bennett et al. LC 89-13470. (Illus.). 178p. (C). 1990. text 32.95 (*0-8138-1121-X*) Iowa St U Pr.

Modern Grain Sorghum Production: Student Study Guide. William F. Bennett et al. LC 89-13470. (Illus.). 56p. 1990. reprint ed. pap., student ed. 30.00 (*0-608-06885-3*, 206709300009) Bks Demand.

Modern Graph Theory. Ed. by S. Axler et al. LC 98-11960. (Graduate Texts in Mathematics Ser.: Vol. 184). 408p. 1998. 59.95 (*0-387-98491-7*); pap. 34.95 (*0-387-98488-7*) Spr-Verlag.

Modern Graphic Arts Paste-Up. Gerald A. Silver & Myrna L. Silver. (Illus.). 244p. (Orig.). (C). 1995. pap. text 45.00 (*1-880472-10-4*) Edit Enter.

Modern Graphic Arts Paste-Up: A Workshop Approach to the Graphic Arts. 3rd ed. Gerald A. Silver & Myrna L. Silver. 256p. (C). 1992. spiral bd. write for info. (*0-697-12319-7*) Bus & Educ Tech.

Modern Graphic Communication. Giesecke & Mitchell. LC 97-46927. 553p. (C). 1997. pap. text 65.00 (*0-13-863838-1*) P-H.

Modern Great Americans. Frederick H. Law. LC 72-99706. (Essay Index Reprint Ser.). 1977. 26.95 (*0-8369-1417-1*) Ayer.

***Modern Greece: A Short History.** C. M. Woodhouse. (Illus.). 384p. 2000. pap. 10.00 (*0-571-19794-9*) Faber & Faber.

Modern Greece: Facets of Underdevelopment. Nicos P. Mouzelis. LC 78-312273. 222p. (C). 1980. 39.50 (*0-8419-0357-3*) Holmes & Meier.

***Modern Greek.** 1999. 29.95 (*0-671-04400-1*) S&S Trade.

Modern Greek. Brian D. Joseph & Irene Philippaki-Warburton. (Descriptive Grammars Ser.). 304p. (C). 1986. 69.95 (*0-7099-1452-0*, Pub. by C Helm) Routldge.

Modern Greek: A Contemporary Grammar. Olga Eleftheriades. LC 85-9499. xxvi, 546p. 1985. text 27.95 (*0-87015-251-3*) Pacific Bks.

Modern Greek & American English in Contact. P. David Seaman. LC 74-170005. (Janua Linguarum, Ser. Practica: No. 132). 312p. (Orig.). 1972. pap. text 89.25 (*90-279-2148-2*) Mouton.

***Modern Greek Democracy: The End of a Long Journey?** George Stergiou Kaloudis. 136p. 1999. 49.00 (*0-7618-1531-7*); pap. 27.50 (*0-7618-1532-5*) U Pr of Amer.

Modern Greek-English, English-Greek Dictionary. Grivas. (ENG & GRE.). 715p. 45.00 (*0-7859-7498-9*) Fr & Eur.

Modern Greek for Adults, Pt. I. Theodore C. Papaloizos. (Illus.). 173p. 1978. pap. 5.00 (*0-932416-01-2*, 01) Papaloizos.

Modern Greek for Adults, Pt. II. Theodore C. Papaloizos. (Illus.). 300p. 1978. student ed. 3.00 (*0-932416-03-9*, 03); pap. 6.00 (*0-932416-02-0*, 02) Papaloizos.

Modern Greek Humor: A Collection of Jokes & Ribald Tales. Ethelyn G. Orso. LC 78-24845. 288p. reprint ed. pap. 89.30 (*0-608-13206-3*, 205604900044) Bks Demand.

Modern Greek-Hungarian Concise Dictionary. A. Mohay. 773p. (C). 1988. 45.00 (*963-05-4387-7*, Pub. by Akade Kiado) St Mut.

Modern Greek Idiom Phrase Book. Constantine N. Tsirpanlis. (GRE.). 1978. pap. 10.95 (*0-8120-0476-0*) Barron.

Modern Greek in Asia Minor. R. M. Dawkins. xii, 695p. write for info. (*0-318-70906-6*) G Olms Pubs.

Modern Greek in Asia Minor. Richard M. Dawkins. LC 78-67703. (Folktale Ser.). reprint ed. 49.50 (*0-404-16077-8*) AMS Pr.

Modern Greek Lessons: A Primer in Historical Constructivism. James D. Faubion. 340p. (C). 1993. pap. text 18.95 (*0-691-00050-6*, Pub. by Princeton U Pr) Cal Prin Full Svc.

Modern Greek Lessons: A Primer in Historical Constructivism. James Faublion. LC 93-15480. (Studies in Culture - Power - History). (Illus.). 328p. 1993. text 45.00 (*0-691-09473-X*, Pub. by Princeton U Pr) Cal Prin Full Svc.

Modern Greek Philosophers on the Human Soul: Selections from the Writings of Seven Representative Thinkers of Modern Greece - Benjamin of Lesvos, Vrailas - Armenis, Skaltsounis, St. Nectarios, Louvaris, Kontoglou, & Theodorakopoulos on the Nature & Immortality of the Soul. 2nd enl. rev. ed. Constantine Cavarnos. LC 86-83011. (Illus.). 140p. 1987. pap. 6.95 (*0-914744-77-1*) Inst Byzantine.

Modern Greek Reader, No. I. Anne Farmakides. LC 82-48913. (Yale Linguistic Ser.). 283p. 1983. pap. 25.00 (*0-300-03021-5*) Yale U Pr.

Modern Greek Society: Continuity & Change. Evan Vlachos. LC 77-87729. reprint ed. 37.50 (*0-404-16581-8*) AMS Pr.

Modern Greek Stories. Tr. by Demetra V. Brown & Aristides Phoutrides. LC 79-136414. reprint ed. 24.50 (*0-404-01134-9*) AMS Pr.

Modern Greek Thought: Three Essays Dealing with Philosophy, Critique of Science, & Views of Man's Nature & Destiny. Constantine Cavarnos. LC 71-93095. 115p. 1986. pap. 5.95 (*0-914744-11-9*) Inst Byzantine.

Modern Greeks: The War Against the Axis, the German Occupation, the Civil War. Costas Stassinopoulos. LC 97-7001. 250p. 1997. write for info. (*1-889247-01-4*) Amer Hellenic Inst.

Modern Grievance Procedure in the United States. David Lewin & Richard B. Peterson. LC 87-32612. (Illus.). 301p. 1988. 69.50 (*0-89930-149-5*, LMG/, Quorum Bks) Greenwood.

***Modern Grill & Garden.** Martha Gill. LC 99-60104. (Modern Ser.: Vol. 4). (Illus.). 106p. 1999. 18.95 (*1-56352-567-4*) Longstreet.

***Modern Grill Pan Cooking: 100 Innovative Recipes for Perfect Results.** Gina Steer. LC 00-35853. (Illus.). 2000. pap. write for info. (*0-8092-9663-2*, Contemporary Bks) NTC Contemp Pub Co.

Modern Grinding Process Technology. Stuart C. Salmon. 225p. 1992. 49.95 (*0-07-054500-6*) McGraw.

Modern Group Analysis - Advanced Analytical & Computational Methods in Mathematical Physics: Proceedings of the International Workshop Acireale, Catania, Italy, October 27-31, 1992. Ed. by N. H. Ibragimov et al. LC 93-20973. (DIVS-Diverse Ser.: Vol. 14). 380p. (C). 1993. text 214.50 (*0-7923-2480-3*) Kluwer Academic.

Modern Group Theoretical Methods in Physics: Proceedings of the Conference in Honour of Guy Rideau. Ed. by J. Bertrand et al. (Mathematical Physics Studies). 300p. (C). 1995. text 169.00 (*0-7923-3645-3*) Kluwer Academic.

Modern Guerrilla Insurgency. Anthony J. Joes. LC 91-46994. 248p. 1992. 55.00 (*0-275-94263-5*, C4263, Praeger Pubs) Greenwood.

***Modern Guide to Drink.** Paul Sargeant. (Modern Anthropologist Ser.). (Illus.). 64p. 2000. mass mkt. 5.99 (*1-903222-02-8*, Pub. by Wimbledon Publishing Co) Anthem.

Modern Guide to EDP Design & Analysis Techniques. Robert J. Walsh. LC 84-22322. 287p. 1985. 39.95 (*0-13-594920-3*, Busn) P-H.

Modern Guide to Electric Motors. Martin Clifford. 368p. (C). 1989. text 43.60 (*0-13-593336-6*) P-H.

Modern Guide to Fingerings for the Flute. James J. Pellerite. LC 72-76260. 1972. pap. text 15.00 (*0-931200-68-7*) Zalo.

Modern Guide to Fingerings for the Flute. James J. Pellerite. 64p. 1988. reprint ed. pap. text 16.50 (*0-88284-449-0*, 2887) Alfred Pub.

Modern Guide to Golf Clubmaking. 3rd ed. Jeff Jackson. (Illus.). 234p. 1994. pap. 24.95 (*0-9619413-3-2*) Dyna Golf Prods.

***Modern Guide to Hairstyles.** Paul Sargeant. (Illus.). 64p. 2000. mass mkt. 5.99 (*1-903222-00-1*, Pub. by Wimbledon Publishing Co) Anthem.

***Modern Guide to Hats.** Steve Harris. (Modern Anthropologist Ser.). (Illus.). 64p. 2000. mass mkt. 5.99 (*1-903222-01-X*, Pub. by Wimbledon Publishing Co) Anthem.

Modern Guide to Macroeconomics: An Introduction to Competing Schools of Thought. Brian Snowdon et al. LC 94-6255. (Illus.). 480p. 1995. pap. 30.00 (*1-85278-882-8*) E Elgar.

Modern Guide to Sex Etiquette, Too! Tom Carey. (Illus.). 112p. (Orig.). 1995. pap. 7.95 (*1-877590-90-8*) DE Pr IL.

***Modern Guide to Spectacles.** Paul Sargeant. (Modern Anthropologist Ser.). (Illus.). 64p. 2000. mass mkt. 5.99 (*1-903222-03-6*, Pub. by Wimbledon Publishing Co) Anthem.

Modern Guitar Chord Technique. George M. Smith. 64p. 1995. pap. 9.95 (*0-7866-0343-7*, 95422) Mel Bay.

Modern Guitar Method: Grade 1. Mel Bay & William Bay. 48p. 1948. pap. 19.95 incl. audio compact disk (*0-7866-0906-0*, 93200CDP) Mel Bay.

Modern Guitar Method: Grade 1. Bay, Mel, Publications, Inc. Staff. 48p. 1948. pap. 6.95 (*0-87166-354-6*, 93200) Mel Bay.

Modern Guitar Method: Grade 1. Bay, Mel, Publications, Inc. Staff. 1980. audio 9.98 (*0-87166-355-4*, 93200C) Mel Bay.

Modern Guitar Method: Grade 1. Bay, Mel, Publications, Inc. Staff. (SPA.). 48p. 1986. pap. 6.95 (*1-56222-011-X*, 93210SP) Mel Bay.

Modern Guitar Method: Grade 1. Bay, Mel, Publications, Inc. Staff. 1993. 14.95 incl. audio (*0-87166-356-2*, 93200P); audio compact disk 14.95 (*0-7866-0450-6*, 93200CD) Mel Bay.

Modern Guitar Method: Grade 1. Bay, Mel, Publications, Inc. Staff & William Bay. 48p. 1996. pap. 14.95 incl. audio compact disk (*0-7866-2784-0*, 93200BCD) Mel Bay.

Modern Guitar Method: Grade 2. Bay, Mel, Publications, Inc. Staff. 48p. 1949. pap. 6.95 (*0-87166-357-0*, 93201) Mel Bay.

Modern Guitar Method: Grade 2. Bay, Mel, Publications, Inc. Staff. 1989. pap. 22.95 incl. audio (*0-87166-358-9*, 93201C) Mel Bay.

Modern Guitar Method: Grade 2. Bay, Mel, Publications, Inc. Staff. 1993. 22.95 incl. audio (*0-87166-359-7*, 93201P) Mel Bay.

Modern Guitar Method: Grade 3. Bay, Mel, Publications, Inc. Staff. 48p. 1949. pap. 6.95 (*0-87166-360-0*, 93202) Mel Bay.

Modern Guitar Method: Grade 3. Bay, Mel, Publications, Inc. Staff. 1992. audio 9.98 (*0-87166-361-9*, 93202C) Mel Bay.

Modern Guitar Method: Grade 3. Bay, Mel, Publications, Inc. Staff. 1993. 14.95 incl. audio (*0-87166-362-7*, 93202P) Mel Bay.

Modern Guitar Method: Grade 4. Bay, Mel, Publications, Inc. Staff. 48p. 1950. pap. 6.95 (*0-87166-363-5*, 93203) Mel Bay.

Modern Guitar Method: Grade 5. Mel Bay. 48p. 1951. pap. 6.95 (*0-87166-364-3*, 93204) Mel Bay.

Modern Guitar Method: Grade 6. Bay, Mel, Publications, Inc. Staff. 40p. 1952. pap. 6.95 (*0-87166-365-1*, 93205) Mel Bay.

Modern Guitar Method: Grade 7. Bay, Mel, Publications, Inc. Staff. 40p. 1953. pap. 6.95 (*0-87166-366-X*, 93206) Mel Bay.

M

Modern Guitar Method Grade 2. Mel Bay & William Bay. 48p. 1949. pap. 29.95 incl. audio compact disk (*0-7866-1385-8*, 93201CDP) Mel Bay.

Modern Guns: Identification & Values. 12th ed. Russell Quertermous & Steve Quertermous. LC 98-221639. 504p. 1998. 12.95 (*1-57432-087-4*) Collector Bks.

***Modern Guns: Identification & Values.** 13th ed. Russell Quertermous & Steve Quertermous. (Illus.). 516p. 2000. pap. 14.95 (*1-57432-199-4*) Collector Bks.

Modern Gyroplane Design. Martin Hollmann. (Illus.). 134p. 1981. pap. text 52.00 (*1-893639-07-X*) Air Designs.

Modern Halakhah for Our Time. Emanuel Rackman. LC 93-35397. 1993. 29.50 (*0-88125-295-6*) Ktav.

Modern Hamlet. Ed. by Charles B. Garrigus. 60p. Date not set. pap. 4.00 (*0-614-21997-3*) Cypress Pr.

Modern Hamlets & Their Soliloquies. Mary Z. Maher. LC 92-12900. (Studies in Theatre History & Culture). (Illus.). 258p. 1992. pap. 14.95 (*0-87745-504-X*) U of Iowa Pr.

Modern Hamlets & Their Soliloquies. Mary Z. Maher. LC 92-12900. (Studies in Theatre History & Culture). (Illus.). 258p. 1992. 32.95 (*0-87745-380-2*) U of Iowa Pr.

Modern Handmade Knives. B. R. Hughes. 1982. 11.00 (*0-913150-44-4*) Pioneer Pr.

Modern Harmony in It's Theory & Practice *see* **Harmony**

Modern Harpsichord: Twentieth Century Instruments & Their Makers. Wolfgang J. Zuckermann. 255p. reprint ed. lib. bdg. 59.00 (*0-7812-0306-6*) Rprt Serv.

Modern Harpsicord Music: A Discography, 58. Compiled by Martin Elste. LC 94-37353. (Discographies Ser.: Vol. 58). 344p. 1995. lib. bdg. 85.00 (*0-313-29238-8*, Greenwood Pr) Greenwood.

Modern Hausa-English Dictionary. Ed. by Paul Newman & Roxana M. Newman. 154p. 1988. pap. text 14.95 (*0-19-575303-8*) OUP.

Modern Hawaiian History. rev. ed. Ann L. Rayson. (Illus.). 304p. (YA). (gr. 9-12). 1996. 8.95 (*1-57306-051-8*); 34.95 (*1-880188-90-2*) Bess Pr.

Modern Head & Neck Imaging. A. L. Baert et al. Ed. by S. K. Mukherji et al. LC 98-17985. (Medical Radiology Ser.). (Illus.). 300p. 1999. 189.00 (*3-540-62549-6*) Spr-Verlag.

***Modern Head & Neck Imaging.** Ed. by S. K. Mukherji & J. A. Castelijns. (Medical Radiology Ser.). (Illus.). xvi, 248p. 2000. pap. 75.00 (*3-540-66344-4*) Spr-Verlag.

Modern Health Care Administration. Richard M. Hodgetts & Dorothy M. Cascio. 496p. (C). 1982. teacher ed. write for info. (*0-15-561401-0*) SCP.

Modern Heat Transfer. Adrian Bejan & J. S. Jones. LC 92-25535. 704p. (C). 1993. text 105.95 (*0-471-50290-1*) Wiley.

Modern Heat Treating Methods & Their Application. J. Korp. (AGMA Technical Paper: Vol. P117). (Illus.). 15p. 1935. pap. text 30.00 (*1-55589-328-7*) AGMA.

Modern Heating & Ventilating Systems Design. George F. Clifford. 704p. (C). 1992. text 63.00 (*0-13-602830-6*) P-H.

Modern Hebrew: An Essential Grammar. Lewis Glinert. LC 93-12663. 196p. 1994. 50.00 (*0-415-10189-1*, B2477) Routledge.

Modern Hebrew: An Essential Grammar. Lewis Glinert. LC 93-12663. 192p. (C). (gr. 13). 1994. pap. 22.99 (*0-415-10190-5*, B2481) Routledge.

Modern Hebrew: Ivrit Hayah, Vol. 1. 3rd ed. Harry Blumberg & Mordecai H. Lewittes. 449p. 1982. pap. 13.95 (*0-88482-718-6*) Hebrew Pub.

Modern Hebrew-English Dictionary. Avraham Zilkha. 305p. 1989. 45.00 (*0-300-04647-2*); pap. 18.00 (*0-300-04648-0*) Yale U Pr.

***Modern Hebrew Fiction.** Gershon Shaked. Ed. by Emily Miller Budick. Tr. by Yael Lotan. 336p. 2000. 45.00 (*0-253-33711-9*) Ind U Pr.

***Modern Hebrew for Beginners: A Multimedia Program for Students at the Beginning & Intermediate Levels.** Esther Raizen. LC 99-58419. 224p. (C). 2000. pap. 18.95 (*0-292-77104-5*) U of Tex Pr.

Modern Hebrew Literature. Ed. by Robert Alter. LC 75-9928. (Library of Jewish Studies). 384p. 1975. pap. text 19.95 (*0-87441-235-8*) Behrman.

Modern Hebrew Poetry. Bernhard Frank. LC 80-20037. (Iowa Translations Ser.). 242p. reprint ed. pap. 75.10 (*0-7837-1623-0*, 204191600024) Bks Demand.

M

Modern Heliographic Processes. Ernst Lietze. 1974. pap. 7.95 (*0-87992-000-9*) Visual Studies.

*__Modern Hematology: Biology & Clinical Management.__ Ed. by Reinhold Munker et al. LC 99-49377. (Contemporary Hematology Ser.). 384p. 1999. 79.50 (*0-89603-687-1*) Humana.

Modern Herbal, Vol. 1. M. Grieve. Ed. by C. F. Leyel. LC 72-169784. (Illus.). 1971. reprint ed. pap. 9.95 (*0-486-22798-7*) Dover.

Modern Herbal, Vol. 2. M. Grieve. Ed. by C. F. Leyel. LC 72-169784. (Illus.). 1971. reprint ed. pap. 9.95 (*0-486-22799-5*) Dover.

*__Modern Herbal Primer: The Old Farmer's Almanac.__ Sarah Hale. 160p. 2000. pap. 12.95 (*0-7370-0083-X*) Time-Life Educ.

Modern Herbal Spellbook. Anna Riva. (Illus.). 64p. 1974. pap. 4.95 (*0-943832-03-9*) Intl Imports.

Modern Herculaneum: The New Richmond Tornado of 1899 & a Century of Tornado Documentation & Wisconsin Lore. enl. ed. Anna P. Epley. Ed. by Michael G. Corenthal. (Illus.). 278p. 1989. 15.00 (*0-9617673-2-4*) Yester Memories.

Modern Heretic & a Traditional Community: Mordecai M. Kaplan, Orthodoxy, & American Judaism. Jeffrey S. Gurock & Jacob J. Schacter. LC 96-32329. 220p. 1996. 42.00 (*0-231-10626-2*) Col U Pr.

*__Modern Heretic & a Traditional Community: Mordecai M. Kaplan, Orthodoxy, & American Judaism.__ Jeffrey Gurock & Jacob Schachter. (Illus.). 256p. 1998. pap. 17.50 (*0-231-10627-0*) Col U Pr.

Modern Hernia Repair: The Embryological & Anatomical Basis for Surgery. 2nd rev. ed. Lee J. Skandalakis et al. (Illus.). 560p. 1995. 128.00 (*1-85070-585-2*) Prthnon Pub.

Modern Heuristic Search Methods. V. Rayward-Smith. LC 97-108470. 314p. 1996. 135.00 (*0-471-96280-5*) Wiley.

Modern Hieroglyphs: Gestural Drawing & the European Vanguard, 1900-1918. Patricia G. Berman. (Illus.). 128p. 1995. pap. text 29.95 (*1-881894-06-1*) WC Davis Mus & Cult.

Modern High Temperature Science. Ed. by John L. Margrave. 484p. 1984. 115.00 (*0-89603-072-5*) Humana.

Modern Higher Algebra. Abraham A. Albert. LC 38-2937. (University of Chicago Science Ser.). 331p. reprint ed. pap. 102.70 (*0-608-30091-8*, 201699800005) Bks Demand.

Modern Higher Education: A Wholistic View. Richard Crews. 89p. (Orig.). (C). 1993. pap. text 11.95 (*0-945864-48-5*) Columbia Pacific U Pr.

Modern Hindi Poetry: An Anthology. Ed. by Vidya N. Misra. (C). 1991. 17.00 (*81-7023-299-6*, Pub. by Allied Pubs) S Asia.

Modern Hindi Short Stories. Tr. by Jai Ratan. (C). 1991. 24.00 (*81-7023-187-6*, Pub. by Allied Pubs) S Asia.

Modern Hindu Law. R. C. Nagpal. (HIN.). 815p. 1984. 225.00 (*0-7855-1365-5*) St Mut.

Modern Historians & the Study of History: Essays & Papers. Frederick M. Powicke. LC 75-25496. 256p. 1976. reprint ed. lib. bdg. 35.00 (*0-8371-8428-2*, POMH, Greenwood Pr) Greenwood.

*__Modern Historical Geographies.__ Graham. (Illus.). 296p. 1999. pap. 27.95 (*0-582-35779-9*) Longman.

Modern Historiography: An Introduction. Michael Bentley. LC 98-39603. xii, 182 p. 1999. pap. 16.99 (*0-415-20267-1*) Routledge.

Modern History of Hong Kong, 1841-1998. Steve Tsang. 288p. 1998. text 59.50 (*1-86064-184-9*, Pub. by I B T) St Martin.

Modern History of Iraq. P. Marr. Date not set. text. write for info. (*0-582-78344-5*, Pub. by Addison-Wesley) Longman.

Modern History of Iraq. 2nd ed. P. Marr. 2000. pap. 54.95 (*0-8133-8214-9*); pap. 18.95 (*0-8133-8215-7*) Westview.

Modern History of Jordan. Kamal Salibi. 304p. 1998. text 19.95 (*1-86064-331-0*) I B T.

Modern History of Jordan. Kamal S. Salibi. 305p. (C). 1993. text 55.00 (*1-85043-610-X*, Pub. by I B T) St Martin.

Modern History of Kuwait, 1750-1965. Ahmad M. Abu-Hakima. 1983. 35.00 (*0-7189-0259-9*) Intl Bk Ctr.

Modern History of Kuwait, 1750-1965. Abu H. Mustafa. 226p. 1983. 35.00 (*0-86685-698-6*, ABU02399) Intl Bk Ctr.

Modern History of Lebanon. Kamal S. Salibi. LC 77-15054. 256p. 1996. reprint ed. 35.00 (*0-88206-015-5*) Caravan Bks.

Modern History of Lebanon. Kamal S. Salibi. LC 75-14703. (Illus.). 227p. 1976. reprint ed. lib. bdg. 35.00 (*0-8371-8230-1*, SAHL, Greenwood Pr) Greenwood.

Modern History of Mongolia. Charles R. Bawden. 256p. 1989. pap. 19.95 (*0-7103-0326-2*) Routledge.

*__Modern History of New Haven & Eastern New Haven County, 2 vols.__ Everett G. Hill. (Illus.). 2000. 129.00 (*0-7404-0028-2*) Higginson Bk Co.

Modern History of New London County, Connecticut, 3 vols. in 2. Ed. by Benjamin T. Marshall. (Illus.). 1154p. 1997. reprint ed. lib. bdg. 119.00 (*0-8328-5672-X*) Higginson Bk Co.

Modern History of Punjab: Relevant Select Documents. J. C. Aggarwal. (C). 1992. 40.00 (*81-7022-431-4*, Pub. by Concept) S Asia.

Modern History of Somalia: Nation & State in the Horn of Africa. I.M. Lewis. 1980. pap. 10.95 (*0-582-64657-X*) Longman.

Modern History of Somalia: Nation & State in the Horn of Africa. rev. ed. Ioan M. Lewis. LC 79-40569. 289p. reprint ed. pap. 89.60 (*0-608-13143-1*, 202523200043) Bks Demand.

Modern History of Southeast Asia: Decolonization, Nationalism & separatism. Clive J. Christie. 288p. 1996. text 65.00 (*1-85043-997-4*, Pub. by I B T) St Martin.

Modern History of Soviet Central Asia. Geoffrey Wheeler. LC 75-14707. (Illus.). 272p. 1975. reprint ed. lib. bdg. 59.75 (*0-8371-8227-1*, WHSC, Greenwood Pr) Greenwood.

*__Modern History of the Islamic World.__ Reinhard Schulze. LC 99-53820. 2000. 35.00 (*0-8147-9776-8*) NYU Pr.

Modern History of the Kurds. David McDowall. 472p. 1996. 45.00 (*1-85043-653-3*, Pub. by I B T) St Martin.

*__Modern History of the Kurds.__ rev. ed. David McDowall. 1999. pap. 19.95 (*1-86064-535-6*, Pub. by I B T) St Martin.

Modern History Southeast Asia: Decolonization, Nationalism & Separatism. Clive J. Christie. 312p. 1998. pap. 19.95 (*1-86064-354-X*, Pub. by I B T) St Martin.

Modern Homestead Manual: What It Really Takes to Succeed Beyond Sidewalks & Power Lines. Skip Thomsen & Cat Freshwater. (Illus.). 220p. (Orig.). 1994. pap. 12.95 (*0-9625960-4-3*) Oregon Wordworks.

Modern Homestead Manual: What It Really Takes to Succeed Beyond the Sidewalks & Powerlines. 2nd rev. ed. Skip Thomsen & Cat Freshwater. (Illus.). 218p. 1998. reprint ed. pap. 14.95 (*0-9625960-7-8*) Oregon Wordworks.

Modern Homosexualities: Fragments of Lesbian & Gay Experience. Ed. by Ken Plummer. LC 92-6434. 272p. (C). 1992. pap. 24.99 (*0-415-06421-X*, A7752) Routledge.

Modern Horary Astrology. Doris C. Doane. 254p. 1994. 19.95 (*0-86690-439-5*, D3462-014) Am Fed Astrologers.

Modern Horror Film: Fifty Contemporary Classics from Curse of Frankenstein to the Lair of the White Worm. John McCarthy. (Illus.). 256p. (Orig.). (gr. 9-12). 1990. pap. 16.95 (*0-8065-1164-8*, Citadel Pr) Carol Pub Group.

Modern Horror Writers see Writers of English: Lives & Works

Modern Horse Herbal. Hilary P. Self. (Illus.). 176p. 1996. 39.95 (*1-872082-85-8*, Pub. by Kenilworth Pr) Half Halt Pr.

Modern Hotel-Motel Management Methods. Herbert K. Witzky. 25.95 (*0-8488-0670-0*) Amereon Ltd.

Modern House. John Welsh. LC 97-129185. (Illus.). 240p. (C). 1995. text 69.95 (*0-7148-2889-0*, Pub. by Phaidon Press) Phaidon Pr.

Modern House. John Welsh. 1999. pap. 29.95 (*0-7148-3837-3*) Phaidon Press.

Modern House: Designed by the World's Leading Architects. David Mackay. (Illus.). 160p. 1991. 29.95 (*0-8038-9276-4*) Archit CT.

*__Modern House 2.__ Clare Melhuish. (Illus.). 2000. 59.95 (*0-7148-3987-6*) Phaidon Pr.

Modern Housing. Catherine K. Bauer. LC 73-11908. (Metropolitan America Ser.). (Illus.). 380p. 1974. reprint ed. 25.95 (*0-405-05386-X*) Ayer.

Modern Housing for America: Policy Struggles in the New Deal Era. Gail Radford. LC 96-21155. (Illus.). 240p. 1996. pap. text 17.95 (*0-226-70223-5*, Chicago Visual Lib); lib. bdg. 45.00 (*0-226-70222-7*) U Ch Pr.

Modern Housing Prototypes. Roger Sherwood. LC 78-15508. (Illus.). 179p. 1978. pap. 42.00 (*0-674-57942-9*) HUP.

Modern Human Physiology. Cornett. 1987. text 65.25 (*0-03-005653-5*); pap. text, teacher ed. 83.00 (*0-03-005654-3*) Holt R&W.

Modern Human Relations at Work. 6th ed. Richard M. Hodgetts. (C). 1995. pap. text, teacher ed. 70.00 (*0-03-017792-8*) Harcourt Coll Pubs.

*__Modern Human Relations at Work.__ 7th ed. Hodgetts. LC 98-70998. (C). 1998. text 85.50 (*0-03-022374-1*, Pub. by Harcourt Coll Pubs) Harcourt.

Modern Humanistic Psychotherapy. Arthur Burton. LC 67-27947. (Jossey-Bass Behavioral Science Ser.). 188p. reprint ed. 58.30 (*0-8357-9335-4*, 201391500087) Bks Demand.

Modern Humanists Reconsidered. John M. Robertson. LC 72-3443. (English Literature Ser.: No. 33). 1972. reprint ed. lib. bdg. 75.00 (*0-8383-1556-9*) M S G Haskell Hse.

Modern Humanity in Search of a Myth. Donald S. Harrington. LC 87-50407. 100p. (Orig.). (C). 1987. pap. 3.00 (*0-9618233-0-5*) Zygon Jrnl of Rel.

Modern Hungarian Driving. Laszlo Toth. (Illus.). 76p. 1999. 21.00 (*963-13-2673-X*, Pub. by Corvina Bks) St Mut.

Modern Hungarian Gallery: PECS. E. Hars & F. Romvary. (Illus.). 396p. (C). 1981. text 200.00 (*0-7855-5853-5*, Pub. by Collets) St Mut.

Modern Hungarian Historiography. Steven B. Vardy. (East European Monographs: No. 16). 333p. 1976. text 61.00 (*0-914710-08-7*, Pub. by East Eur Monographs) Col U Pr.

Modern Hungarian Poetry. Ed. & Intro. by Miklos Vajda. LC 76-2453. (Illus.). 1979. pap. text 23.50 (*0-231-08370-X*) Col U Pr.

Modern Hungarian Society in the Making: The Unfinished Experience. Andras Gero. Tr. by James Patterson. (Illus.). 288p. 1995. pap. 25.95 (*1-85866-024-6*) Ctrl Europ Univ.

Modern Hungarian Society in the Making: The Unfinished Experience. Andras Gero. Tr. by James Patterson. (Central European University Press Book Ser.). (Illus.). 288p. (C). 1995. 51.95 (*1-85866-023-8*) Ctrl Europ Univ.

Modern Hungary. Jozsef Borocz. 112p. 2000. pap. 13.44 (*0-07-034429-9*) McGraw.

Modern Hydronic Heating. 2nd ed. Anita Siegenthaler. 2000. pap. text 51.50 (*0-7668-1637-0*) Delmar.

Modern Hydronic Heating for Residential & Light Commercial Buildings. John Siegenthaler. 1995. mass mkt. 79.95 (*0-8273-6595-0*) Delmar.

Modern Hypnosis. Lesley Kuhn & Salvatore Russo. 1970. pap. 5.00 (*0-87980-100-X*) Wilshire.

Modern Hypnosis: Theory & Practice. Masud Ansari. 1950. pap. 7.95 (*0-9607984-0-4*) MAS Pr.

Modern Hypnosis: Theory & Practice. Masud Ansari. (Illus.). 232p. (J). (gr. 5). 1982. pap. 6.95 (*0-685-05553-1*) MAS Pr.

Modern Ibsen: A Reconsideration. Hermann J. Weigand. LC 73-126263. (Select Bibliographies Reprint Ser.). 1977. reprint ed. 26.95 (*0-8369-5490-4*) Ayer.

Modern IC Databook: A Key Aid for Every Amateur & Professional. Charles Gagliardi. (Illus.). 1100p. 1991. ring bd. 59.95 (*0-929321-04-9*) WEKA Pub.

Modern Icelandic: An Essay. Halldor Hermannsson. LC 20-7699. (Islandica Ser.: Vol. 12). 1919. pap. 25.00 (*0-527-00342-5*) Periodicals Srv.

Modern Ideas about Children. Alfred Binet. Tr. by Suzanne Heisler from FRE. LC 86-162049. 235p. (Orig.). 1984. pap. 20.00 (*0-9617054-1-8*) S Heisler.

Modern Ideas in Chess. Richard Reti. 183p. 1960. pap. 8.95 (*0-486-20638-6*) Dover.

Modern Ideas of Evolution. J. William Dawson. 1977. pap. 8.95 (*0-88202-167-2*, Sci Hist) Watson Pub Intl.

Modern Identity Changer: How to Create & Use a New Identity for Privacy & Personal Freedom. Sheldon Charrett. LC 98-119248. (Illus.). 152p. 1997. pap. 20.00 (*0-87364-946-X*) Paladin Pr.

Modern Idolatry: Being an Analysis of Usury & the Pathology of Debt. Jeffrey P. Mark. 1980. lib. bdg. 250.00 (*0-8490-3078-1*) Gordon Pr.

Modern Imaging of the Alimentary Tube. M. Ando. Ed. by Alexander R. Margulis. LC 97-13066. (Medical Radiology Ser.). (Illus.). 350p. 1997. 159.00 (*3-540-61441-9*) Spr-Verlag.

*__Modern Imaging of the Alimentary Tube.__ Ed. by Alexander R. Margulis. (Medical Radiology Ser.). (Illus.). x, 363p. 2000. pap. 75.00 (*3-540-66345-2*) Spr-Verlag.

Modern Immigration. Christine Scriabine. 39.00 (*1-56696-118-1*) Jackdaw.

Modern Impressions. Weidauer. (College ESL Ser.). 198p. (J). 1994. mass mkt. 26.95 (*0-8384-4084-3*) Heinle & Heinle.

Modern Impressions: Writing in Our Times. 2nd ed. Marie Hutchison Weidauer. (C). 2000. 14.00 (*0-8384-0041-8*) Heinle & Heinle.

Modern Impulse of Traditional Judaism. Zvi Kurzweil. LC 84-28892. 156p. 1985. 19.95 (*0-88125-068-6*) Ktav.

*__Modern in Spain: Architecture after 1948.__ Gabriel Ruiz Cabrero. (Illus.). 200p. (C). 2000. pap. 29.95 (*0-262-53172-0*) MIT Pr.

Modern India. Joti Sekhon. LC 99-37247. 192p. 1999. pap. 13.75 (*0-07-292824-7*) McGraw.

Modern India: The Origins of an Asian Democracy. 2nd ed. Judith M. Brown. (Short Oxford History of the Modern World Ser.). (Illus.). 474p. (C). 1994. pap. text 27.95 (*0-19-873113-2*) OUP.

Modern India (1765 to 1950) Sailendra N. Sen. (C). 1993. text 10.00 (*81-224-0340-9*) S Asia.

Modern Indian Fiction. Ed. by S. Cowsjee & V. Shahane. 195p. 1981. 18.50 (*0-7069-1051-6*) Asia Bk Corp.

Modern Indian Literature: An Anthology, Vol. 2. Ed. by K. M. George. (C). 1993. 54.00 (*81-7201-506-2*, Pub. by Indian Pubs) S Asia.

Modern Indian Literature Vol. 1: An Anthology: Surveys & Poems. K. M. George. LC 92-909719. (C). 1992. text 54.00 (*81-7201-324-8*, Pub. by National Sahitya Akademi) S Asia.

Modern Indian Literature Vol. 3: Plays & Prose. Ed. by K. M. George. (C). 1994. 35.00 (*81-7201-783-9*, Pub. by Indian Pubs) S Asia.

Modern Indian Poetry in English. Bruce King. 308p. 1987. 29.95 (*0-19-561959-5*) OUP.

Modern Indian Political Thought: Chandra, Prakash. Prakash Chandra. 1998. pap. 9.00 (*81-259-0527-8*, Pub. by Vikas) S Asia.

Modern Indian Responses to Religious Pluralism. Ed. by Harold Coward. LC 87-1943. 340p. (C). 1987. pap. text 18.95 (*0-88706-572-4*) State U NY Pr.

Modern Indian Short Stories, Vol. 4. K. C. Das. 164p. 1983. 12.95 (*0-318-36918-4*) Asia Bk Corp.

Modern Indians of Alabama: Remnants of the Removal. Marie W. Cromer. (Illus.). 388p. (Orig.). 1987. pap. 12.50 (*0-685-19422-1*) Southern U Pr.

Modern Indonesia: A History since 1945. Robert Cribb & Colin Brown. LC 94-48236. (Postwar World Ser.). (C). 1995. text 44.75 (*0-582-05712-4*, Pub. by Addison-Wesley) Longman.

Modern Industrial Ceramics. Eugene C. Stafford. LC 79-14907. 1980. 23.95 (*0-672-97129-1*, Bobbs); teacher ed. 3.33 (*0-672-97127-5*, Bobbs); pap., student ed. 5.95 (*0-672-97128-3*, Bobbs) Macmillan.

Modern Industrial Electrical Motor Controls: Operation, Installation & Troubleshooting. Thomas E. Kissell. 400p. (C). 1989. text 66.00 (*0-13-596164-5*) P-H.

Modern Industrial Electronics. rev. ed. Charles A. Schuler & William L. McNamee. LC 92-33594. Orig. Title: Industrial Electronics & Robotics. 1992. 43.95 (*0-02-800862-6*) Glencoe.

Modern Industrial Electronics. 3rd ed. Timothy J. Maloney. 864p. (C). 1995. 106.00 (*0-13-457516-4*) P-H.

Modern Industrial Hygiene, Vol. 4. Perkinsj. (Occupational Health & Safety Ser.). 1998. text 59.95 (*0-442-02543-2*, VNR) Wiley.

Modern Industrial Hygiene: Recognition & Evaluation of Chemical Agents, Vol. I. Jimmy L. Perkins. LC 96-16834. (Industrial Health & Safety Ser.). (Illus.). 864p. 1997. text 49.95 (*0-442-02105-4*, VNR) Wiley.

Modern Industrial Hygiene VII, Vol. 2. Perkins. (Occupational Health & Safety Ser.). 1998. text 59.95 (*0-442-02569-6*, VNR) Wiley.

Modern Industrial Organization. 2nd ed. Dennis Carlton & Joseph K. Perloff. (C). 1994. pap. text 83.44 (*0-673-46902-6*) Addson-Wesley Educ.

*__Modern Industrial Organization.__ 3rd ed. 176p. (C). 1999. pap. text 26.00 (*0-321-03388-4*, Celebration) Addson-Wesley Educ.

*__Modern Industrial Organization.__ 3rd ed. 1999. write for info. (*0-673-98060-X*) S&S Trade.

Modern Industrial Organization. 3rd ed. Ed. by Carlton. LC 99-25713. 780p. (C). 1999. 98.00 (*0-321-01145-7*) Addson-Wesley Educ.

Modern Industrial Plastics. Terry Richardson. LC 72-92621. 1974. 24.45 (*0-672-97657-9*, Bobbs) Macmillan.

Modern Industrial Statistics. Ron Kenett & Shelemyahu Zacks. LC 97-43141. 600p. 1998. pap. 93.95 (*0-534-35370-3*) Brooks-Cole.

Modern Industrial World, 12 bks., Set. (J). (gr. 6-8). 1996. lib. bdg. 203.76 (*0-8172-4557-X*) Raintree Steck-V.

Modern Industry & the African. 2nd ed. Ed. by J. Merle Davis. 450p. 1967. reprint ed. 45.00 (*0-7146-1650-8*, BHA-01650, Pub. by F Cass Pubs) Intl Spec Bk.

Modern Industry & the African: An Enquiry into the Effect of the Copper Mines of Central Africa on Native Society & the Work of the Christian Missions. 2nd ed. International Missionary Council, Department of So. Ed. by J. Mearle Davis. LC 67-24749. xxxvi, 425p. 1968. reprint ed. 42.50 (*0-678-05042-2*) Kelley.

Modern Inertial Technology: Navigation, Guidance, & Control. Anthony Lawrence. LC 92-16602. (Instrumentation & Systems Ser.). (Illus.). 328p. 1993. 74.95 (*0-387-97868-2*) Spr-Verlag.

Modern Inertial Technology: Navigation, Guidance, & Control. 2nd ed. A. Lawrence. LC 98-13047. (Mechanical Engineering Ser.). (Illus.). 280p. 1998. 59.00 (*0-387-98507-7*) Spr-Verlag.

Modern Infectious Disease Epidemiology. Johan Giesecke. 264p. 1994. pap. text 34.50 (*0-340-59237-0*, Pub. by E A) OUP.

Modern Information Systems: Designed for Decision Support. John E. Gessford. LC 78-74684. 1980. text 28.75 (*0-201-03099-3*) Addison-Wesley.

Modern Information Systems for Managers. Hossein Bidgoli. LC 97-9582. (Illus.). 438p. 1997. text 54.95 (*0-12-095970-4*) Morgan Kaufmann.

Modern Informative Nursery Rhymes: American History, Book I. Kellet I. Min. LC 89-91719. (Illus.). 64p. (Orig.). (J). (gr. 2-5). 1992. pap. 10.95 (*0-9623411-2-6*) Rhyme & Reason.

Modern Informative Nursery Rhymes: General Science, Book I. Kellet I. Min. LC 89-91719. (Illus.). 64p. (Orig.). (J). (gr. 2-5). 1993. pap. 10.95 (*0-9623411-4-2*) Rhyme & Reason.

Modern Informative Nursery Rhymes: The Rationale. Kellet I. Min. 176p. (Orig.). 1991. pap. 10.95 (*0-9623411-1-8*) Rhyme & Reason.

Modern Informative Nursery Rhymes: Values. Kellet I. Min. LC 89-91719. (General Science, American History Ser.: Bk. I). (Illus.). 32p. (Orig.). (J). (ps-3). 1989. pap. 7.95 (*0-9623411-3-4*) Rhyme & Reason.

Modern Inhalation Anesthetics. Ed. by Maynard B. Chenoweth. LC 76-156998. (Handbook of Experimental Pharmacology Ser.: Vol. 30). (Illus.). 1972. 175.00 (*0-387-05135-X*) Spr-Verlag.

Modern Inorganic Chemicals Industry, No. 31. Royal Society of Chemistry Staff. 1989. 34.00 (*0-85186-158-X*) CRC Pr.

Modern Inorganic Chemistry. Joseph J. Lagowski. LC 72-90374. (Undergraduate Chemistry Ser.: No. 6). 824p. reprint ed. pap. 200.00 (*0-7837-3363-1*, 204332100008) Bks Demand.

Modern Inorganic Pharmaceutical Chemistry. Clarence A. Discher. LC 64-14986. 648p. reprint ed. pap. 200.00 (*0-608-30493-X*, 200634700058) Bks Demand.

Modern Inorganic Pharmaceutical Chemistry. 2nd ed. Clarence A. Discher et al. (Illus.). 631p. (C). 1985. text 43.95 (*0-88133-121-X*) Waveland Pr.

Modern Instance. William Dean Howells. (American Library). 480p. (C). 1984. pap. 12.95 (*0-14-039027-8*, Penguin Classics) Viking Penguin.

Modern Instance. large type ed. William Dean Howells. 524p. 1999. 27.95 (*1-56000-487-8*) Transaction Pubs.

Modern Instance. William Dean Howells. (Notable American Authors Ser.). 1992. reprint ed. lib. bdg. 75.00 (*0-7812-3235-X*) Rprt Serv.

Modern Instrumental Delivery. John P. O'Grady. (Illus.). 288p. 1988. 40.00 (*0-683-06632-3*) Lppncott W & W.

Modern Instrumentation: A Computer Approach. G. Silverman & H. Silver. (Illus.). 456p. 1995. 88.00 (*0-7503-0298-4*) IOP Pub.

*__Modern Instruments.__ Barrie Carson Turner. LC 99-59872. (Musical Instruments of the World Ser.). (Illus.). 32p. (J). 2000. lib. bdg. 22.60 (*1-58340-063-X*) Smart Apple.

Modern Insurance Law. 2nd ed. John Birds. (C). 1988. 250.00 (*0-7855-4076-8*, Pub. by Witherby & Co); pap. 170.00 (*0-7855-4077-6*, Pub. by Witherby & Co) St Mut.

Modern Intellectual Property. Michael A. Epstein. 650p. 1984. 85.00 (*0-15-003467-9*) Harcourt.

Modern Intellectual Property. 3rd ed. Michael A. Epstein. LC 94-47629. 1995. write for info. (*0-13-110289-3*) Aspen Law.

Modern Intellectual Property, 1. 3rd ed. Michael A. Epstein. 1014p. ring bd. 146.00 (*1-56706-150-8*, 56489) Panel Pubs.

Modern Intercity Coaches: A Review of Over-the-Road Coaches & Manufacturers Active in the United States & Canada from 1953 to 1993. Larry Plachno. LC 97-6485. 1997. 62.00 (*0-933449-27-5*) Transport Trails.

Modern Interdisciplinary University Statistics Education: Proceedings of a Symposium. Committee on Applied & Theoretical Statistics, Nat. 152p. (Orig.). (C). 1994. pap. text 29.00 (*0-309-05033-2*) Natl Acad Pr.

An Asterisk (*) at the beginning of an entry indicates that the title is appearing for the first time.

Modern Interiors: Lithographs & Confessions. Stephen Gosnell. LC 84-73436. (Illus.). 1985. pap. 12.95 (*0-933532-46-6*) BkMk.

Modern International Developments in Trust Law. David J. Hayton. LC 98-45608. 1999. 141.00 (*90-411-9706-0*) Kluwer Law Intl.

Modern International Economics. 3rd ed. Wilfred J. Ethier. (C). 1995. text, student ed. 91.00 (*0-393-96311-X*) Norton.

Modern International Economics. 3rd ed. Wilfred J. Ethier. (C). 1995. pap. text, teacher ed. write for info. (*0-393-96313-6*) Norton.

Modern International Economics. 3rd ed. Wilfrid Ethier. (C). Date not set. pap., teacher ed., suppl. ed. write for info. (*0-393-96718-2*) Norton.

Modern International Economics: Study Guide. 3rd ed. Wilfred J. Ethier. (C). 1995. pap. text, student ed. 16.50 (*0-393-96312-8*) Norton.

Modern International Law of Outer Space. Carl Q. Christol. (Policy Studies on International Politics). (Illus.). 945p. 1982. 210.00 (*0-08-029367-0*, K130, Pergamon Pr) Elsevier.

Modern International Negotiation. Arthur Lall. LC 66-17587. 404p. 1966. text 69.00 (*0-231-02935-7*) Col U Pr.

Modern Interpretation of Buddhism. H. L. Singh. 1994. pap. 40.00 (*0-7855-0415-X*, Pub. by Ratna Pustak Bhandar) St Mut.

Modern Intravenous Therapy Procedures. William J. Kurdi. Ed. by James K. Kurdi. 1995. pap. text 34.95 (*0-937142-00-X*) Med Nurs Educ.

Modern Introduction to Chemistry. D. White. 1979. pap. text 4.10 (*0-08-022620-5*, Pergamon Pr) Elsevier.

***Modern Introduction to Energy Economics.** Ferdinand E. Banks. 288p. 1999. 125.00 (*0-7923-7700-1*) Kluwer Academic.

Modern Introduction to International Law. rev. ed. Michael B. Akehurst. LC 86-28828. 1987. pap. text 24.95 (*0-04-341037-5*) Routledge.

Modern Introduction to Particle Physics. Fayyazuddin Riazuddin. 676p. 1994. text 78.00 (*981-02-1072-8*); pap. text 44.00 (*981-02-1073-6*) World Scientific Pub.

Modern Introduction to Particle Physics. 2nd ed. Fayyazuddin Riazuddin. (High Energy Physics Ser.). 700p. 1999. 86.00 (*981-02-3876-2*); pap. text 54.00 (*981-02-3877-0*) World Scientific Pub.

Modern Introduction to Philosophy. 3rd ed. Ed. by Paul Edwards & Arthur Pap. LC 65-18470. 1973. pap. 29.95 (*0-02-909200-0*) Free Pr.

Modern Introduction to the Mathematical Theory of Water Waves. R. S. Johnson. (Texts in Applied Mathematics Ser.: Vol. 19). (Illus.). 460p. (C). 1997. text 80.00 (*0-521-59172-4*); pap. text 30.95 (*0-521-59832-X*) Cambridge U Pr.

***Modern Introductory Electromagnetics.** (C). 2000. write for info. (*0-13-016571-9*); write for info. (*0-13-016550-6*) S&S Trade.

Modern Introductory Electromagnetics. Zoya B. Popovic. (C). 1999. pap. text, wbk. ed. 21.33 (*0-201-32680-9*) Addison-Wesley.

***Modern Introductory Electromagnetics.** Zoya B. Popovic. LC 99-42828. 556p. (C). 1999. 100.00 (*0-201-32678-7*, Prentice Hall) P-H.

Modern Introductory Physics. C. H. Holbrow et al. LC 98-24447. (Graduate Texts in Contemporary Physics Ser.). (Illus.). 544p. 1998. 59.95 (*0-387-98576-X*) Spr-Verlag.

Modern Investment Theory. 4th ed. Robert A. Haugen. LC 95-25279. 748p. 1996. 100.00 (*0-13-190182-6*) P-H.

***Modern Investment Theory.** 5th ed. Robert A. Haugen. LC 00-26314. 736p. 2000. 93.33 (*0-13-019170-1*) P-H.

Modern Iran. Lawrence P. Elwell-Sutton. 1976. lib. bdg. 59.95 (*0-8490-2267-3*) Gordon Pr.

Modern Iran. Grant M. Farr. LC 98-26466. (Comparative Societies Ser.). 168p. 1998. pap. 13.75 (*0-07-292825-5*) McGraw.

Modern Iran: The Dialectics of Continuity & Change. Ed. by Michael E. Bonine & Nikki R. Keddie. LC 80-19463. (Illus.). 474p. reprint ed. pap. 147.00 (*0-8357-6579-2*, 203597400097) Bks Demand.

***Modern Iran Since 1921.** 2000. write for info. (*0-582-35685-7*) Pearson Educ.

Modern Ireland. R. F. Foster. 1990. pap. 16.95 (*0-14-013250-3*, Viking) Viking Penguin.

Modern Ireland. E. G. Power. LC 87-3521. (Modern Times Ser.). 1988. write for info. (*0-582-22165-X*) Longman.

Modern Ireland: A Bibliography on Politics Planning, Research & Development. Ed. by Michael O. Shannon. LC 81-6531. 733p. 1981. lib. bdg. 79.50 (*0-313-22903-1*, SMO/, Greenwood Pr) Greenwood.

Modern Irish-American Fiction: A Reader. Ed. by Daniel J. Casey & Robert E. Rhodes. LC 88-32081. (Irish Studies). 336p. 1989. text 45.00 (*0-8156-2462-X*); pap. text 19.95 (*0-8156-0234-0*) Syracuse U Pr.

Modern Irish Drama. Ed. by John P. Harrington. (Critical Editions Ser.). 500p. (Orig.). (C). 1991. pap. text 18.25 (*0-393-96063-3*) Norton.

Modern Irish Literature: A Chronology. James M. Cahalan. LC 92-15105. (G. K. Hall Reference Ser.). 250p. 1992. 50.00 (*0-8161-7264-1*, Hall Reference) Macmillan.

Modern Irish Literature: Sources & Founders. Vivian Mercier. Ed. by Eilis Dillon. LC 93-24542. 398p. (C). 1994. text 48.00 (*0-19-812074-5*, Clarendon Pr) OUP.

Modern Irish Lives: A Dictionary of Twentieth-Century Biography. Louis McRedmond. LC 96-30676. 400p. 1996. text 35.00 (*0-312-16478-5*) St Martin.

***Modern Irish Lives: Dictionary of 20th-Century Biography.** Ed. by Louis McRedmond. LC 99-193915. xix, 328 p. 1998. write for info. (*0-7171-2786-9*, Pub. by Gill & MacMill) St Mut.

Modern Irish Poetry: An Anthology. Ed. by Patrick Crotty. 436p. 1996. pap. 19.95 (*0-85640-561-2*, Pub. by Blackstaff Pr) Dufour.

Modern Irish Short Stories. rev. ed. Ed. & Intro. by Ben Forkner. 560p. 1995. pap. 13.95 (*0-14-024699-1*, Penguin Bks) Viking Penguin.

Modern Irish Writers: A Bio-Critical Sourcebook. Alexander G. Gonzalez. LC 96-30581. 480p. 1997. lib. bdg. 95.00 (*0-313-29557-3*) Greenwood.

Modern Irish Writers & the Wars. Ed. by Kathleen Devine. LC 98-189006. 328p. 1999. text 60.00 (*0-86140-353-3*) OUP.

Modern Islam: The Search for Cultural Identity. Gustave E. Von Grunebaum. LC 83-11508. 303p. 1983. reprint ed. lib. bdg. 59.75 (*0-313-24087-6*, VGMI, Greenwood Pr) Greenwood.

Modern Islam in India. W. C. Smith. 1985. reprint ed. 18.50 (*0-8364-1338-5*, Pub. by Usha) S Asia.

Modern Islam in India: A Social Analysis. Wilfred C. Smith. LC 70-179243. reprint ed. 39.50 (*0-404-54869-5*) AMS Pr.

Modern Islamic Art: Development & Continuity. Wijdan Ali. LC 97-24325. (Illus.). 224p. 1997. 59.95 (*0-8130-1526-X*) U Press Fla.

Modern Islamic Political Thought. Hamid Enayat. 220p. 1996. pap. 12.95 (*0-614-21494-7*, 795) Kazi Pubns.

Modern Isotope Radio Mass Spectrometry. I. Platzner. LC 97-7329. (Chemical Analysis Ser.). 530p. 1997. 305.00 (*0-471-97416-1*) Wiley.

Modern Israeli Drama in Translation. Ed. by Michael Taub. LC 92-16637. 329p. (C). 1992. pap. 17.95 (*0-435-08616-2*, 08616) Heinemann.

Modern Issues in European Law: Nordic Perspectives. Ed. by Goran Melander. LC 97-19435. 233p. 1997. 93.00 (*90-411-0423-2*) Kluwer Academic.

Modern Issues in Non-Saturated Soils. Ed. by A. Gens et al. (CISM International Centre for Mechanical Sciences Ser.: No. 357). (Illus.). viii, 504p. 1996. pap. 117.00 (*3-211-82783-8*) Spr-Verlag.

Modern Italian - Spanish, Spanish - Italian Dictionary: Dizionario Moderno Italiano-Spagnuolo - Spagnuolo-Italiano. G. Frisoni. (ITA & SPA.). 748p. 1987. lib. bdg. 45.00 (*0-8288-3366-4*, F60928) Fr & Eur.

Modern Italian - Spanish, Spanish - Italian Dictionary: Dizionario Moderno Italiano-Spagnuolo: Spagnuolo-Italiano. 2nd ed. G. Frisoni. (ITA & SPA.). 1120p. 1989. lib. bdg. 45.00 (*0-8288-3365-6*, F60927) Fr & Eur.

Modern Italian Architecture: Casa Malaparte/The House in The Trees. Karl Lagerfeld. (Illus.). 112p. 1999. 54.95 (*3-88243-661-1*, Pub. by Steidl) Dist Art Pubs.

Modern Italian Cooking. Biba Caggiano. (Illus.). 336p. 1992. per. 14.00 (*0-671-75445-9*, Fireside) S&S Trade Pap.

Modern Italian Grammar. Anna Proudfoot & Francesco Cardo. LC 99-204903. 144p. (C). 1999. pap., wbk. ed. 14.99 (*0-415-12095-0*) Routledge.

***Modern Italian Grammar.** 15th ed. Frederic J. Jones. (Illus.). 392p. (C). 1998. reprint ed. pap. text 23.00 (*0-340-15637-6*, Pub. by Hodder & Stought Ltd) Lubrecht & Cramer.

Modern Italian Grammar: A Practical Guide. Anna Proudfoot & Francesco Cardo. LC 96-1193. (ENG & ITA.). 440p. (C). 1997. 75.00 (*0-415-09849-1*); pap. 25.99 (*0-415-09850-5*) Routledge.

Modern Italian History: An Annotated Bibliography, 18. Compiled by Frank J. Coppa & William C. Roberts. LC 89-78122. (Bibliographies & Indexes in World History Ser.: No. 18). 236p. 1990. lib. bdg. 65.00 (*0-313-24812-5*, CPM/, Praeger Pubs) Greenwood.

Modern Italian Poets. William Dean Howells. LC 72-6857. (Essay Index Reprint Ser.). 1977. reprint ed. 29.95 (*0-8369-7246-5*) Ayer.

Modern Italian Poets. William Dean Howells. (Notable American Authors Ser.). 1992. reprint ed. lib. bdg. 75.00 (*0-7812-3271-6*) Rprt Serv.

Modern Italian Slovene Dictionary: Italijansko-Slovenski Moderni Slovar. Anton Grad. (ITA & SLV.). 748p. 1987. 39.95 (*0-8288-1136-9*, F61040) Fr & Eur.

Modern Italian Social Theory: Ideology & Politics from Pareto to the Present. Richard Bellamy. LC 86-63257. 248p. 1987. 42.50 (*0-8047-1393-6*) Stanford U Pr.

Modern Italy: A Political History. Denis M. Smith. LC 97-19128. 522p. (C). 1997. 37.50 (*0-472-10895-6*, 10895) U of Mich Pr.

Modern Italy: Representation & Reform. Paul Furlong. LC 93-25198. (Policy Making in Liberal Democracies Ser.). 256p. (C). 1994. pap. 24.99 (*0-415-01565-0*) Routledge.

Modern Italy 1871 1982. Martin Clark. (Longman History of Italy Ser.). (Illus.). 444p. (C). 1984. pap. text 28.50 (*0-582-48362-X*, 73226) Longman.

Modern Italy 1871 1995. 2nd ed. Martin Clark. LC 95-53742. (History of Italy Ser.). 488p. (C). 1996. pap. text 28.13 (*0-582-05126-6*, Pub. by Addison-Wesley) Longman.

***Modern Japan.** Mikiso Hane. 2000. pap. 30.00 (*0-8133-3756-9*, Pub. by Westview) HarpC.

Modern Japan. Harold R. Kerbo & John A. McKinstry. LC 97-35799. 216p. 1997. pap. 14.69 (*0-07-034426-4*) McGraw.

Modern Japan. Don Nardo. (World History Ser.). (Illus.). 112p. (J). (gr. 5-9). 1995. lib. bdg. 22.45 (*1-56006-281-9*, 2819) Lucent Bks.

Modern Japan. J. E. Thomas. LC 95-51035. 304p. (C). 1996. pap. text 18.75 (*0-582-25961-4*, Pub. by Addison-Wesley) Longman.

Modern Japan. J. E. Thomas. LC 95-51035. 304p. (C). 1996. text 45.75 (*0-582-25962-2*) Addison-Wesley.

Modern Japan: A Brief History. rev. ed. Arthur E. Tiedemann. LC 80-13023. (Anvil Ser.). 192p. 1980. reprint ed. pap. text 11.50 (*0-89874-204-8*) Krieger.

Modern Japan: A Concise Survey. Hugh Cortazzi. LC 93-27056. 1993. text 45.00 (*0-312-10630-0*) St Martin.

***Modern Japan: A Concise Survey.** Hugh Cortazzi. 1999. pap. 22.95 (*0-333-54340-8*) St Martin.

Modern Japan: A Historical Survey. 2nd ed. Mikiso Hane. 488p. (C). 1992. pap. 35.00 (*0-8133-1368-6*, Pub. by Westview) HarpC.

Modern Japan: An Encyclopedia of History, Culture & Nationalism. Ed. by James L. Huffman. LC 97-21910. (Illus.). 352p. 1997. text 95.00 (*0-8153-2525-8*, H2031) Garland.

Modern Japan An Encyclopedia of History, Culture, & Nationalism. James L. Huffman. LC 98-31751. 1999. pap. write for info. (*0-8153-3321-8*) Garland.

Modern Japan: The American Nexus. John H. Boyle. LC 92-72355. 426p. (C). 1993. pap. text 41.50 (*0-15-500324-0*) Harcourt.

Modern Japan & Its Problems. 2nd ed. G. C. Allen. LC 89-18575. 180p. (C). 1990. reprint ed. text 70.00 (*0-485-11310-4*, Pub. by Athlone Pr) Humanities.

Modern Japan Through Its Weddings: Gender, Person, & Society in Ritual Portrayal. Walter Edwards. LC 88-28619. 192p. 1989. 35.00 (*0-8047-1512-2*) Stanford U Pr.

Modern Japanese. 2nd ed. Mieko S. Han. 375p. (Orig.). (C). 1983. pap. text 27.50 (*1-878463-00-4*) Inst Inter Studies Pr.

Modern Japanese. 3rd rev. ed. Mieko S. Han. (JPN., Illus.). 393p. (Orig.). 1998. pap. text 32.50 (*1-878463-09-8*) Inst Inter Studies Pr.

Modern Japanese: A Basic Reader, 2 vols., Set. 2nd ed. Howard S. Hibbett, Jr. & Gen Itasaka. LC 67-22864. 731p. (YA). (gr. 9 up). 1967. pap. 40.00 (*0-674-58000-1*) HUP.

Modern Japanese Aesthetics: A Reader. Michele Marra. LC 99-27949. 432p. 1999. 55.00 (*0-8248-2173-4*) UH Pr.

Modern Japanese Diaries: The Japanese at Home & Abroad as Revealed Through their Diaries. Donald Keene. 88p. 1995. pap. 25.00 (*0-8050-4665-8*, Owl) H Holt & Co.

Modern Japanese Diaries: The Japanese at Home & Abroad As Revealed Through Their Diaries. Donald Keene. 534p. (C). 1998. text 25.00 (*0-7881-5527-0*) DIANE Pub.

***Modern Japanese Diaries: The Japanese at Home & Abroad As Revealed Through Their Diaries.** Donald Keene. LC 98-28812. 544p. 1998. reprint ed. pap. 25.00 (*0-231-11443-5*) Col U Pr.

***Modern Japanese Diaries: The Japanese at Home & Abroad As Revealed Through Their Diaries.** Donald Keene. 534p. 2000. reprint ed. pap. text 25.00 (*0-7881-6937-8*) DIANE Pub.

Modern Japanese Drama: An Anthology. Tr. by Ted T. Takaya from JPN. LC 79-4288. 277p. 1979. text 65.00 (*0-231-04684-7*) Col U Pr.

Modern Japanese Drama: An Anthology. Tr. by Ted T. Takaya from JPN. LC 79-4288. 277p. 1980. pap. text 23.50 (*0-231-04685-5*) Col U Pr.

Modern Japanese Fiction & Its Traditions: An Introduction. J. Thomas Rimer. LC 78-51188. 327p. reprint ed. pap. 101.40 (*0-8357-4287-3*, 203708600007) Bks Demand.

Modern Japanese Haiku: An Anthology. Makoto Ueda. LC 74-75035. 273p. reprint ed. pap. 84.70 (*0-8357-4171-0*, 203694500007) Bks Demand.

Modern Japanese Leadership: Transition & Change. Conference on Nineteenth Century Japanese Elites (. Ed. by Bernard S. Silberman & H. D. Harootunian. LC 66-18532. 445p. reprint ed. pap. 138.00 (*0-608-13996-3*, 205537200017) Bks Demand.

Modern Japanese Literature: From 1868 to the Present Day. Ed. by Donald Keene. LC 56-8439. 448p. 1989. pap. 15.95 (*0-8021-5095-0*, Grove) Grove-Atltic.

Modern Japanese Novels & the West. Donald Keene. LC 61-4982. (Peters Rushton Seminars in Contemporary Prose & Poetry Ser.). 45p. reprint ed. pap. 30.00 (*0-608-30179-5*, 201614200004) Bks Demand.

Modern Japanese Organization & Decision-Making. Ed. by Ezra F. Vogel. 1975. pap. 15.95 (*0-520-05468-7*, Pub. by U CA Pr) Cal Prin Full Svc.

Modern Japanese Poets & the Nature of Literature. Makoto Ueda. LC 82-60487. 462p. 1983. 52.50 (*0-8047-1166-6*) Stanford U Pr.

Modern Japanese Prose Poem: An Anthology of Six Poets: Miyoshi Tatsuji, Anzai Fuyue, Tamura Ryuichi, Yoshioka Minoru, Tanikawa Shuntaro, Inoue Yasushi. Dennis Keene. LC 79-16809. 195p. reprint ed. pap. 60.50 (*0-8357-3709-8*, 203643100003) Bks Demand.

Modern Japanese Society, 1868-1994. Ann Waswo. (Illus.). 186p. (C). 1996. pap. text 15.95 (*0-19-289228-2*) OUP.

Modern Japanese Stories: An Anthology. Ivan Morris. LC 61-11971. (Illus.). 512p. 1977. pap. 16.95 (*0-8048-1226-8*) Tuttle Pubng.

Modern Japanese Tanka: An Anthology. Tr. & Compiled by Makoto Ueda. (Modern Asian Literature Ser.). 288p. 1996. pap. 17.50 (*0-231-10433-2*) Col U Pr.

Modern Japanese Tanka: An Anthology. Tr. & Compiled by Makoto Ueda. (Modern Asian Literature Ser.). 288p. 1996. 55.00 (*0-231-10432-4*) Col U Pr.

Modern Japanese Thought. Ed. by Bob T. Wakabayashi. 448p. (C). 1998. text 59.95 (*0-521-58218-0*); pap. text 19.95 (*0-521-58810-3*) Cambridge U Pr.

Modern Japanese Woodblock Prints: The Early Years. Helen Merritt. LC 89-27923. (Illus.). 344p. 1990. text 48.00 (*0-8248-1200-X*) UH Pr.

***Modern Japanese Writers.** Jay Rubin. (Scribner Writers Ser.). 2000. 125.00 (*0-684-80598-7*) Gale.

Modern Japanese Writers & the Nature of Literature. Makoto Ueda. LC 75-39336. 304p. reprint ed. pap. 30.00 (*0-608-20214-2*, 207146800012) Bks Demand.

Modern Jazz: A Survey of Developments since 1939. Alun Morgan & Raymond Horricks. LC 77-8002. 240p. 1977. reprint ed. lib. bdg. 59.50 (*0-8371-9674-4*, MOMO, Greenwood Pr) Greenwood.

Modern Jazz Ballett. Gunther Rebel. (GER., Illus.). 144p. (C). 1990. 50.00 (*3-8170-4003-2*, Pub. by Knstvrlag Weingrtn) Intl Bk Import.

Modern Jazz New York. Svea Becker & Laurie Winn. Ed. by Ray Cook. (Illus.). 56p. (Orig.). (C). 1982. pap. text 15.00 (*0-9602002-4-X*) Ray Cook.

Modern Jazz Piano: A Study in Harmony & Improvisation. (Illus.). 96p. pap. 17.95 (*0-7119-0841-9*, AM61953) Music Sales.

Modern Jazz Solo-ETUDE-Fakebook (For All Instruments) Garree Stephan & Karen Stephan. (Illus.). 66p. (Orig.). 1995. spiral bd. 14.95 (*1-884524-11-7*) Stephan Pubns.

Modern Jewellers Gem Profile: The First 60. David Federman. (gr. 13). 1989. text 10.50 (*0-442-00153-3*) Chapman & Hall.

***Modern Jewish Canon: A Journey Through Language & Culture.** Ruth R. Wisse. 416p. 2000. 27.50 (*0-684-83075-2*) Free Pr.

Modern Jewish Ethics, Theory & Practice. Ed. by Marvin Fox. LC 74-28395. 274p. reprint ed. pap. 85.00 (*0-608-09673-3*, 206978800006) Bks Demand.

Modern Jewish Experience, 59 vols., Set. Ed. by Moses Rischin. 1975. 1630.50 (*0-405-06690-2*) Ayer.

Modern Jewish Experience: A Reader's Guide. Ed. by Jack Wertheimer. LC 92-31668. 418p. (C). 1993. text 50.00 (*0-8147-9261-8*); pap. text 20.00 (*0-8147-9262-6*) NYU Pr.

Modern Jewish History for Everyone. David Bianco. (Illus.). 216p. 1997. pap. text 24.95 (*0-9657981-0-0*) History Everyone.

Modern Jewish Identity: A Rationalistic Approach to Judaism. Esther Reisel & Rudi Reisel. LC 98-12251. 1998. 24.95 (*965-229-163-3*) Gefen Bks.

Modern Jewish Life in Literature, 2 Vols, 1. Azriel Eisenberg. 1968. 4.50 (*0-8381-0201-8*) USCJE.

Modern Jewish Life in Literature, 2 Vols, 2. Azriel Eisenberg. 1968. 4.50 (*0-8381-0207-7*) USCJE.

Modern Jewish Morality: A Bibliographical Survey, 8. Compiled by S. Daniel Breslauer. LC 86-12145. 249p. 1986. lib. bdg. 75.00 (*0-313-24700-5*, BJM/, Greenwood Pr) Greenwood.

Modern Jewish Mythologies. Ed. by Glenda Abramson. LC 99-26975. 200p. 1999. 39.95 (*0-87820-216-1*, Pub. by Hebrew Union Coll Pr) Wayne St U Pr.

Modern Jewish Mythologies. Ed. by Glenda Abramson. 210p. Date not set. 39.95 (*0-8143-2893-8*) Wayne St U Pr.

***Modern Jewish Thinkers: An Introduction.** Alan Levenson. LC 99-41430. 300p. 2000. 25.00 (*0-7657-6121-1*) Aronson.

Modern Jewish Thought: Selected Issues, 1889-1966. LC 73-2221. (Jewish People; History, Religion, Literature Ser.). 1977. 33.95 (*0-405-05283-9*) Ayer.

Modern Jewish Writers of France. Pierre L. Horn. LC 97-10551. (Studies in French Literature: No. 27). 184p. 1997. text 89.95 (*0-7734-8693-3*) E Mellen.

Modern Journalism Workbook. Donald L. Ferguson & Jim Patten. 96p. (YA). (gr. 7-12). 1992. teacher ed. 6.60 (*0-8442-5707-9*, C5707-9, Natl Textbk Co) NTC Contemp Pub Co.

Modern Journalism Workbook. Donald L. Ferguson & Jim Patten. 176p. 1995. pap., student ed. 10.60 (*0-8442-5706-0*, Natl Textbk Co) NTC Contemp Pub Co.

Modern Judo: Techniques of East & West. Peter Seisenbacher & George Kerr. (Illus.). 192p. 1997. pap. 24.95 (*1-86126-020-2*, Pub. by Crolwood) Trafalgar.

Modern Junior High School. 3rd ed. William T. Gruhn & Harl R. Douglass. LC 78-110549. 430p. reprint ed. pap. 133.30 (*0-608-13506-2*, 201647800006) Bks Demand.

Modern Jury Trials & Advocates: Containing Condensed Cases with Sketches & Speeches of American Advocates; the Art of Winning Cases & Manner of Counsel Described, with Notes & Rules of Practice. 4th enl. rev. ed. J. W. Donovan. xxi, 720p. 1985. reprint ed. 65.00 (*0-8377-0523-1*, Rothman) W S Hein.

Modern Karate: Scientific Approach to Conditioning & Training. Milorad V. Stricevic et al. (Illus.). 216p. 1989. 40.00 (*0-9622012-0-0*) Focus Publns.

Modern Kentucky Rifle. R. H. McCrory. 1990. reprint ed. 8.95 (*0-913150-66-5*) Pioneer Pr.

Modern Kenya: Social Issues & Perspectives. Ed. by Mary Ann Watson. 408p. 2000. 67.00 (*0-7618-1633-X*) U Pr of Amer.

***Modern Kenya: Social Issues & Perspectives.** Mary Ann Watson. 408p. 2000. pap. 44.50 (*0-7618-1634-8*) U Pr of Amer.

Modern Kerala: Studies in Social & Agrarian Relations. K. K. Kurup. (C). 1988. 26.00 (*81-7099-094-7*, Pub. by Mittal Pubs Dist) S Asia.

Modern Kinematics: Developments in the Last Forty Years. Arthur G. Erdman. LC 92-26599. (Design Engineering Ser.). 608p. 1993. 140.00 (*0-471-55459-6*) Wiley.

Modern King James Version. deluxe ed. Ed. & Tr. by Jay P. Green, Sr. (Illus.). 1990. 24.95 (*1-878442-64-3*) Sovreign Grace Pubs.

Modern King James Version of the Holy Bible. Jay P. Green. 1993. 49.99 (*1-878442-70-8*) Sovreign Grace Pubs.

Modern King's Indian Attack: A Complete System for White. John Hall. 160p. 1996. pap. 16.95 (*1-880673-11-8*) Hays Pub.

Modern Knife Combat: The Training of a Knife Fighter. Greg Walker. (Illus.). 120p. 1995. pap. 34.95 (*0-87364-849-8*) Paladin Pr.

Modern Kongo Prophets: Religion in a Plural Society. Wyatt MacGaffey. LC 82-48554. (African Systems of Thought Ser.). (Illus.). 301p. reprint ed. pap. 93.40 (*0-608-18264-8*, 205672900081) Bks Demand.

***Modern Korean: An Intermediate Reader.** Nam-Kil Kim. LC 99-58188. 396p. 2000. pap. text 28.00 (*0-8248-2222-6*) UH Pr.

Modern Korean Literature: An Anthology, 1908-1965. Ed. by Chung Chong-wha. LC 94-9433. (Korean Culture Ser.). 475p. 1995. 76.50 (*0-7103-0490-0*) Routledge.

Modern Korean Poetry. Tr. by Jaihiun Kim from KOR. LC 94-18319. 320p. (Orig.). (C). 1995. pap. text 30.00 (*0-87573-057-4*) Jain Pub Co.

Modern Labor Economics. 4th ed. Ronald G. Ehrenberg & Robert S. Smith. (C). 1991. pap. text 23.66 (*0-673-46228-5*) Addson-Wesley Educ.

***Modern Labor Economics.** 7th ed. 192p. (C). 1999. pap. text 26.00 (*0-321-06478-X*, Celebration) Addson-Wesley Educ.

***Modern Labor Economics.** 7th ed. (C). 2000. write for info. (*0-321-07811-X*) Addson-Wesley Educ.

***Modern Labor Economics.** 7th ed. Ronald G. Ehrenberg. 504p. (C). 1999. pap. text, student ed. 25.00 (*0-321-06477-1*) Addson-Wesley.

Modern Labor Economics. 7th ed. Ronald G. Ehrenberg. LC 99-34536. 651p. (C). 1999. 94.00 (*0-321-05052-5*) Addson-Wesley Educ.

Modern Labor Economics with Canadian Supplement. 5th ed. Ehrenberg & Smith. (C). 1994. pap. text 69.33 (*0-673-99163-6*) Addson-Wesley Educ.

Modern Land Transactions: Environmental Cases & Materials. Elizabeth Geltman. 482p. 1994. pap. text 22.50 (*1-55834-205-2*, 11532-10, MICHIE) LEXIS Pub.

Modern Landscape Architecture: A Critical Review. Ed. by Marc Treib. LC 92-11571. (Illus.). 276p. 1993. 57.50 (*0-262-20092-9*) MIT Pr.

Modern Landscape Architecture: A Critical Review. Marc Treib. LC 92-11571. (Illus.). 306p. 1994. pap. text 32.50 (*0-262-70051-4*) MIT Pr.

Modern Landscape Architecture: Redefining the Garden. Jory Johnson. (Illus.). 240p. 1991. 55.00 (*1-55859-023-4*) Abbeville Pr.

Modern Langenscheidt French-Spanish, Spanish-French Dictionary: Diccionario Moderno Langenscheidt Frances-Espanol-Frances. 11th ed. M. Puy-Costa. (FRE & SPA.). 512p. 1981. 19.95 (*0-8288-0740-X*, S39863) Fr & Eur.

***Modern Language Journal Index, 82 vols., Set.** Ed. by Suzanne Moore & David Benseler. 1000p. 1999. 299.95 (*0-631-21827-0*) Blackwell Pubs.

Modern Language Learning: Trainers Handbook. Duncan Sidwell. (C). 1987. pap. 35.00 (*0-900559-59-4*) St Mut.

Modern Language Learning: Tutor's Handbook. Duncan Sidwell. (C). 1987. pap. 45.00 (*0-900559-58-6*) St Mut.

Modern Language of Architecture. Bruno Zevi. Tr. by Ronald Strom & William A. Packer from ITA. (Illus.). 256p. 1994. reprint ed. pap. 16.95 (*0-306-80597-9*) Da Capo.

Modern Language Teaching in Schools & Colleges. Ed. by Seymour L. Flaxman. 72p. 1961. pap. 10.95 (*0-915432-61-7*) NE Conf Teach Foreign.

***Modern Languages & Learning Strategies: In Theory & Practice.** Michael Grenfell & Vee Harris. LC 98-54121. 1999. pap. write for info. (*0-415-17868-1*) Routledge.

***Modern Languages & Learning Strategies: In Theory & Practice.** Michael Grenfell & Vee Harris. LC 98-54121. 176p. (C). 1999. text. write for info. (*0-415-21340-1*) Routledge.

Modern Languages for Musicians. Julie Yarbrough. LC 92-3451. (ENG, FRE, GER & ITA.). 250p. 1991. lib. bdg. 54.00 (*0-945193-06-8*) Pendragon NY.

Modern Languages in the Schools (UNESCO) (Education Studies & Documents: No. 6). 1974. reprint ed. pap. 25.00 (*0-8115-1330-0*) Periodicals Srv.

Modern Latin, Bk. I. J. D. Sadler. LC 72-866. 322p. 1973. pap. 22.95 (*0-8061-1046-5*) U of Okla Pr.

Modern Latin, Bk. 1. J. D. Sadler. ii, 54p. 1973. teacher ed. 5.00 (*0-8061-1168-2*) U of Okla Pr.

Modern Latin, Bk. 2. J. D. Sadler. ii, 60p. 1974. teacher ed. 5.00 (*0-8061-1276-X*) U of Okla Pr.

Modern Latin, Bk. II. J. D. Sadler. LC 73-19392. 302p. 1974. pap. text 22.95 (*0-8061-1189-5*) U of Okla Pr.

Modern Latin America. 4th ed. Thomas E. Skidmore & Peter H. Smith. (Illus.). 480p. (C). 1997. pap. text 28.95 (*0-19-510017-4*) OUP.

***Modern Latin America.** 5th ed. Thomas E. Skidmore & Peter H. Smith. LC 99-56169. (Illus.). 528p. 2000. text 59.95 (*0-19-512995-4*); pap. text 29.95 (*0-19-512996-2*) OUP.

Modern Latin America, Vol. 1. Brown. (C). 2000. pap. text 26.50 (*0-03-055387-3*, Pub. by Harcourt Coll Pubs) Harcourt.

Modern Latin American Art: A Bibliography, 3. Compiled by James A. Findlay. LC 83-10743. (Art Reference Collection Ser.: No. 3). 301p. 1983. lib. bdg. 75.00 (*0-313-23757-3*, FIN/, Greenwood Pr) Greenwood.

Modern Latin American Narratives: The Dreams of Reason. Alfred J. MacAdam. LC 76-8098. 1993. lib. bdg. 15.00 (*0-226-49993-6*) U Ch Pr.

***Modern Latin American Novel.** Raymond L. Williams. LC 98-25148. 177p. 1998. 33.00 (*0-8057-1655-6*, Twyne) Mac Lib Ref.

Modern Latin American Revolutions. 2nd ed. Eric Selbin. 248p. 1998. pap. text 24.00 (*0-8133-3563-9*, Pub. by Westview) HarpC.

Modern Law: The Law Transmission System & Equal Employment Opportunity. Alfred W. Blumrosen. LC 92-29947. 488p. (C). 1993. pap. 24.95 (*0-299-13734-1*) U of Wis Pr.

Modern Law Enforcement Weapons & Tactics. 2nd ed. Tom Ferguson. LC 86-72618. (Illus.). 256p. 1991. pap. 18.95 (*0-87349-116-5*, MLE2, DBI Bks) Krause Pubns.

Modern Law of Contracts, 2 vols., Set. Howard O. Hunter. 1987. 165.00 (*0-88712-506-9*) Warren Gorham & Lamont.

Modern Law of Contracts, 2 vols., Vol. I: Breach & Remedies. Howard O. Hunter. 1987. write for info. (*0-88712-846-7*) Warren Gorham & Lamont.

Modern Law of Copyright & Designs, 2 vols. 2nd ed. Hugh Laddie et al. 916p. 1995. text 649.00 (*0-406-61697-3*, 87607, MICHIE) LEXIS Pub.

Modern Law of Deeds to Real Property. Robert G. Natelson. 640p. 1992. 125.00 (*0-316-59876-3*, Aspen Law & Bus) Aspen Pub.

Modern Law of Diplomacy. Ludwik Dembinski. (C). 1988. lib. bdg. 74.00 (*90-247-3585-8*) Kluwer Academic.

Modern Law of Diplomacy: External Missions of States & International Organizations. 288p. 1987. 37.50 (*0-318-40153-3*, E.87.III.RR/34) UN.

Modern Law of Employment Contracts: Formation, Operation & Remedies for Breach. Charles G. Bakaly, Jr. & Joel M. Grossman. 357p. 1983. suppl. ed. 70.00 (*0-15-004288-4*, H42884) Harcourt.

Modern Law of Employment Relationships. Charles G. Bakaly, Jr. et al. 1088p. 1989. ring bd. 118.00 (*0-13-301466-5*) Aspen Law.

Modern Law of Employment Relationships. 2nd ed. Charles G. Bakaly, Jr. et al. 1100p. ring bd. 126.00 (*0-13-595315-4*, 59533) Aspen Law.

***Modern Law of Estoppel.** Elizabeth Cooke. LC 99-57718. 220p. 2000. write for info. (*0-19-826222-1*) OUP.

Modern Law of Evidence. 3rd ed. Adrian Keane. LC 94-199932. 576p. 1994. 42.00 (*0-406-01148-6*, IE, MICHIE) LEXIS Pub.

Modern Law of Evidence. 4th ed. Adrian Keane. LC 96-207441. 640p. 1996. pap. write for info. (*0-406-08185-9*, KMLE4, MICHIE) LEXIS Pub.

Modern Law of Guarantees. Richard Salter. 830p. 1994. pap. text 220.00 (*0-406-12781-6*, UK, MICHIE) LEXIS Pub.

Modern Law of Negligence. R. A. Buckley. (C). 1988. 420.00 (*0-7855-4075-X*, Pub. by Witherby & Co) St Mut.

Modern Law of Personal Property in England & Ireland. A. Bell. 1989. 105.00 (*0-406-70100-8*, U.K., MICHIE) LEXIS Pub.

Modern Law of Self-Determination. Ed. by Christian Tomuschat. LC 93-8228. (Developments in International Law Ser.). 360p. (C). 1993. lib. bdg. 117.00 (*0-7923-2351-3*) Kluwer Academic.

Modern Law of Succession in Ghana. A. K. Kludze. (Law Ser.). xxiv, 316p. (Orig.). (C). 1988. bds. 98.50 (*3-11-013312-1*) Mouton.

Modern Law of Succession in Ghana. A. K. Kludze. (Law Ser.). xxiv, 316p. (Orig.). (C). 1988. pap. 90.75 (*90-6765-406-X*) Mouton.

Modern Lebanese Coinage. Granvyl G. Hulse, Jr. 20p. 1974. pap. 1.00 (*1-889172-04-9*) Numismatic Intl.

Modern Legal Ethics. Charles W. Wolfram. LC 85-22611. (Hornbook Ser.). 1120p. (C). 1986. reprint ed. student ed. 41.00 (*0-314-92639-9*) West Pub.

Modern Legal Ethics. Charles W. Wolfram. LC 85-22611. (Hornbook Ser.). 1363p. (C). 1991. reprint ed. text. write for info. (*0-314-92638-0*) West Pub.

Modern Legal Ethics. 2nd ed. Charles W. Wolfram. (Practitioner Treatise Ser.). Date not set. text. write for info. (*0-314-06609-8*) West Pub.

Modern Legal History of England & Wales, 1750-1950. A. H. Manchester. 1980. pap. 63.00 (*0-406-62264-7*, UK, MICHIE); boxed set 76.00 (*0-406-62263-9*, UK, MICHIE) LEXIS Pub.

Modern Legal Philosophy Series, Set. reprint ed. write for info. (*1-56169-394-4*) Gaunt.

Modern Legal Research. Danner. 1996. text 26.36 (*0-256-16485-1*) McGraw.

Modern Legal Systems Cyclopedia Vols. 1 & 1A: North America, 2 vols., Set. rev. ed. Ed. by Kenneth R. Redden. LC 83-82953. 1988. ring bd. 195.00 (*0-89941-301-3*, 306250) W S Hein.

Modern Legal Systems Cyclopedia Vols. 2 & 2A: Pacific Basin, 2 vols., Set. rev. ed. Ed. by Kenneth R. Redden. LC 83-82953. 1989. ring bd. 195.00 (*0-89941-302-1*, 306260) W S Hein.

Modern Legal Systems Cyclopedia Vols. 3 & 3A: Western Europe - E. E. C. Countries, 2 vols., Set. rev. ed. Kenneth R. Redden. LC 83-82953. 1989. ring bd. 195.00 (*0-89941-303-X*, 306270) W S Hein.

Modern Legal Systems Cyclopedia Vols. 4 & 4A: Western Europe Non - E. E. C. Countries, 2 vols., Set. rev. ed. Ed. by Kenneth R. Redden. LC 83-82953. 1989. ring bd. 195.00 (*0-89941-304-8*, 306280) W S Hein.

Modern Legal Systems Cyclopedia Vols. 5 & 5A: Middle East, 2 vols., Set. rev. ed. Ed. by Kenneth R. Redden. LC 83-82953. 1990. ring bd. 195.00 (*0-89941-305-6*, 306290) W S Hein.

Modern Legal Systems Cyclopedia Vols. 6 & 6A: Africa, 2 vols., Set. rev. ed. Ed. by Kenneth R. Redden. LC 83-82953. 1990. ring bd. 195.00 (*0-89941-306-4*, 306300) W S Hein.

Modern Legal Systems Cyclopedia Vols. 7 & 7A: Central America & Caribbean, 2 vols., Set. rev. ed. Ed. by Kenneth R. Redden. LC 83-82953. 1989. ring bd. 195.00 (*0-89941-307-2*, 306310) W S Hein.

Modern Legal Systems Cyclopedia Vols. 8 & 8A: Eastern Europe, 2 vols., Set. rev. ed. Ed. by Kenneth R. Redden. LC 83-82953. 1991. ring bd. 195.00 (*0-89941-308-0*, 306320) W S Hein.

Modern Legal Systems Cyclopedia Vols. 9 & 9A: Asia, 2 vols., Set. rev. ed. Ed. by Kenneth R. Redden. LC 83-82953. 1991. ring bd. 195.00 (*0-89941-309-9*, 306330) W S Hein.

Modern Legal Systems Cyclopedia Vols. 10 & 10A: South America. rev. ed. Ed. by Kenneth R. Redden. LC 83-82953. xlvii, 1021p. 1986. ring bd. 195.00 (*0-89941-310-2*, 306340) W S Hein.

Modern Legal Systems Cyclopedia Indices. Ed. by Kenneth R. Redden. LC 83-82953. 1984. ring bd. 1995.00 (*0-89941-300-5*, 306670) W S Hein.

Modern Legal Theory: Problems & Perspectives. Ed. by Stephen C. Hicks. LC 98-31879. xx, 385p. 1998. 49.95 (*0-8377-0688-2*, 322340, Rothman); pap. 35.00 (*0-8377-0687-4*, 322340, Rothman) W S Hein.

Modern Leonardo: The Life of Joseph J. Convers. Ellsworth S. Grant. LC 98-73322. (Illus.). 102p. 1998. 35.00 (*0-9666672-0-4*) T K Hodgman.

***Modern Lexicography.** Henri Bejoint. 288p. 2000. pap. 24.95 (*0-19-829951-6*) OUP.

Modern Liberty & Its Discontents by Pierre Manent. Pierre Manent. Ed. & Tr. by Daniel J. Mahoney & Paul Seaton. LC 98-4323. 248p. 1998. 58.00 (*0-8476-9087-3*); pap. 22.95 (*0-8476-9088-1*) Rowman.

***Modern Library: The Best 200 Novels in English since 1950.** Carmen Callil & Colm Toibin. 287p. 1999. 27.50 (*0-330-34182-0*, Pub. by Picador) Trans-Atl Phila.

***Modern Library Christmas Assortment.** Modern Library Staff. 1999. write for info. (*0-676-79984-1*) Random House.

Modern Library Practice: A Manual & Textbook. Ed. by Sheila Ritchie. 1982. 70.00 (*0-9505828-5-9*, Pub. by Elm Pubns) St Mut.

***Modern Library Science Series, 10 vols.** M. Kaushal & I. M. Goswami. 3361p. 1998. pap. 2605.00 (*81-242-0038-6*, Pub. by Print Hse) St Mut.

Modern Library Technology & Reference Services. Ed. by Samuel T. Huang. LC 93-966. (Reference Librarian Ser.: No. 39). (Illus.). 139p. 1993. reprint ed. 39.95 (*1-56024-458-5*) Haworth Pr.

Modern Library Technology & Reference Services. Ed. by Samuel T. Huang. LC 93-966. (Reference Librarian Ser.: No. 39). 139p. 1995. reprint ed. pap. 14.95 (*1-56024-789-4*) Haworth Pr.

Modern Library 100 Best of Non Fiction, Bk. C. Modern Library Staff. 1999. pap. text 12.95 (*0-676-59147-7*) Hse Collectbls.

Modern Library 100 Best of Non Fiction, Bk. D. Modern Library Staff. 1999. pap. text 9.95 (*0-676-59148-5*) Hse Collectbls.

Modern Library 100 Best of Non Fiction, Bk. A. Modern Library Staff. 1999. pap. text 12.95 (*0-676-59145-0*) Hse Collectbls.

Modern Library 100 Best of Non Fiction, Bk. B. Modern Library Staff. 1999. pap. text 11.95 (*0-676-59146-9*) Hse Collectbls.

Modern Libya: A Study in Political Development. Majid Khadduri. LC 62-18509. 414p. reprint ed. pap. 128.40 (*0-608-06068-2*, 206640000008) Bks Demand.

***Modern Life & Modern Subjects: British Art in the Early Twentieth Century.** Lisa Tickner. LC 99-86310. (Illus.). 256p. 2000. 45.00 (*0-300-08350-5*) Yale U Pr.

Modern Lifestyles, Lower Energy Intake & Micronutrient Status. Ed. by K. Pietrzik. (Illus.). 212p. 1991. 40.00 (*3-540-19629-3*, 196293) Spr-Verlag.

Modern Lifestyles, Lower Energy Intake & Micronutrient Status. Ed. by K. Pietrzik & I. G. Macdonald. (ILSI Human Nutrition Reviews Ser.). (Illus.). 212p. 1991. 40.00 (*0-387-19629-3*) Spr-Verlag.

Modern Lilly. Adrienne Warren. Tr. by Sue Ward. (Illus.). 92p. (Orig.). (C). 1989. pap. 20.00 (*1-878935-07-0*) JustUs & Assocs.

Modern Linguistics & Language Teaching, Society for the Popularization of Sciences T. I. T. Federation Internationale Des Professeurs De Langues Vivantes-F.I.P.L.V. Ed. by Peter Inkey & Gyorgy Szepe. (Janua Linguarum, Ser.: No. 87). 1975. 99.25 (*90-279-3161-5*) Mouton.

Modern Linguistics, Its Development Methods & Problems. Manfred Bierwisch. (Janua Linguarum, Ser. Minor: No. 110). 103p. 1971. pap. text 24.65 (*90-279-1657-8*) Mouton.

Modern Liquid Phase Kinetics. B. G. Cox. (Oxford Chemistry Primers Ser.: Vol. 21). (Illus.). 96p. 1994. 31.95 (*0-19-855745-0*); pap. text 12.95 (*0-19-855744-2*) OUP.

Modern Literary Nepali: An Introductory Reader. Michael J. Hult. 1997. pap. 74.00 (*0-7855-7435-2*, Pub. by Ratna Pustak Bhandar) St Mut.

Modern Literary Nepali: An Introductory Reader. Michael J. Hutt. (SOAS Studies on South Asia). 304p. 2000. pap. text 7.95 (*0-19-565111-1*) OUP.

Modern Literary Perspectivism. Charles I. Glicksberg. LC 79-125979. 209p. reprint ed. pap. 64.80 (*0-8357-8958-6*, 203341900086) Bks Demand.

Modern Literary Theory. 2nd ed. A. Jeferson. 240p. 1986. 6.95 (*0-7134-5290-0*) B T Burch.

Modern Literary Theory. 3rd ed. pap. text. write for info. (*0-7131-6258-9*, Pub. by E A) Routldge.

Modern Literary Theory: A Reader. Philip Rice & Patricia Waugh. 200p. 1989. 49.50 (*0-7131-6596-0*, Pub. by E A); pap. 15.95 (*0-7131-6541-3*, Pub. by E A) Routldge.

Modern Literary Theory: A Reader. 2nd ed. Ed. by Philip Rice & Patricia Waugh. LC 92-19707. 368p. 1995. text 16.95 (*0-340-57599-9*, Pub. by E A) St Martin.

Modern Literary Theory: A Reader. 3rd ed. Philip Rice. LC 96-17312. 400p. 1996. pap. text 19.95 (*0-340-64585-7*, Pub. by E A) OUP.

Modern Literary Theory, a Comparative Introduction Ann Jefferson et al. LC 86-673512. 186 p. 1982. write for info. (*0-7134-3454-6*) U of Pa Pr.

Modern Literary Uzbek I, Vol. 161. Khayrulla Ismatulla. Ed. by Walter Feldman. LC 95-69264. 551p. 1995. 32.50 (*0-933070-36-5*) Res Inst Inner Asian Studies.

Modern Literatur und Bildung. Volker Ladenthin. ix, 405p. 1991. write for info. (*3-487-09504-1*) G Olms Pubs.

Modern Literature of the Non-Western World: Where the Waters Are Born. Compiled by Jayana Clerk & Ruth Siegel. LC 94-5832. 1504p. (C). 1997. pap. 53.00 (*0-06-501269-0*) Addson-Wesley Educ.

Modern Liturgy Answers the 101 Most-Asked Questions about Liturgy. Nick Wagner. LC 96-3639. 26p. (Orig.). 1996. pap. 14.95 (*0-89390-369-8*) Resource Pubns.

Modern Liturgy's Bulletin Inserts. Paul Turner. LC 97-40380. (Illus.). 96p. (Orig.). 1997. pap. 49.95 incl. 3.5 hd (*0-89390-414-7*) Resource Pubns.

Modern Lives: A Cultural Re-Reading of "The Lost Generation" Marc Dolan. LC 95-30211. 246p. 1996. 36.95 (*1-55753-079-3*); pap. 19.95 (*1-55753-080-7*) Purdue U Pr.

Modern Livestock & Poultry Production. 4th ed. James R. Gillespie. Orig. Title: Livestock & Poultry Production. 1990. pap., teacher ed. 12.00 (*0-8273-4088-5*) Delmar.

Modern Livestock & Poultry Production. 4th ed. James R. Gillespie. Orig. Title: Livestock & Poultry Production. 1991. text 52.95 (*0-8273-4087-7*) Delmar.

Modern Livestock & Poultry Production. 5th ed. James R. Gillespie. LC 95-15278. Orig. Title: Livestock & Poultry Production. 1040p. (C). 1995. pap. 75.95 (*0-8273-6733-3*) Delmar.

Modern Livestock & Poultry Production. 5th ed. James R. Gillespie. (Agriculture Ser.). Orig. Title: Livestock & Poultry Production. 128p. 1996. teacher ed. 16.00 (*0-8273-6734-1*) Delmar.

Modern Livestock & Poultry Production. 6th ed. Gillespie. Orig. Title: Livestock & Poultry Production. (C). 2001. pap. text 51.75 (*0-7668-1607-9*) Delmar.

Modern Livestock & Poultry Production CTB. 5th ed. James R. Gillespie. (Agriculture Ser.). 1996. 100.00 (*0-8273-7493-3*) Delmar.

Modern Local Government. John Sheldrake. 220p. 1992. 72.95 (*1-85521-254-4*, Pub. by Dartmth Pub) Ashgate Pub Co.

Modern Logic: A Text in Elementary Symbolic Logic. Graeme Forbes. 416p. (C). 1994. pap. text 33.95 (*0-19-508029-7*) OUP.

Modern Logic - A Survey: Historical, Philosophical & Mathematical Aspects of Modern Logic & Its Applications. Ed. by E. Agazzi. (Synthese Library: Vol. 149). 483p. 1980. text 206.50 (*90-277-1137-2*, D Reidel) Kluwer Academic.

Modern Logic in the Service of Law. Ilmar Tammelo. 1978. 29.95 (*0-387-81486-8*) Spr-Verlag.

Modern Logistics Management: Integrating Marketing, Manufacturing & Physical Distribution. William F. Capacino et al. LC 85-6524. (Marketing Management Ser.). 430p. 1985. 152.95 (*0-471-81261-7*) Wiley.

Modern Longman Literature: Autobiographies. Marsh. 1992. pap. text. write for info. (*0-582-08837-2*, Pub. by Addison-Wesley) Longman.

Modern Love: An Anthology of Erotic Fiction by Women. Ed. by Kerri Sharp. 256p. (Orig.). 1997. mass mkt. 9.95 (*0-352-33158-5*, Pub. by Virgin Bks) London Brdge.

***Modern Love: And Other Tall Tales.** Greg Boyd. 112p. (Orig.). 2000. pap. 11.95 (*1-888996-22-6*, Red Hen Press) Valentine CA.

Modern Love Poems. Ed. by John Smith. (Pocket Poet Ser.). 1966. pap. 3.50 (*0-8023-9050-1*) Dufour.

Modern Love Songs. (Big Note Ser.), 96p. 1996. pap. 10.95 (*0-7935-6018-7*) H Leonard.

Modern Lover. D. H. Lawrence. LC 70-38722. (Short Story Index Reprint Ser.). 1977. reprint ed. 17.95 (*0-8369-4135-7*) Ayer.

***Modern Machine-Guns.** John Walter. (Military Manuals Ser.). 2000. 22.95 (*1-85367-395-1*) Greenhill Bks.

Modern Machine Shop Practice of 1887, 2 vols. Joshua Rose. (Illus.). 1000p. 1998. reprint ed. pap. text 200.00 (*0-87556-844-0*) Saifer.

Modern Machining Technology. Richard Baril. 672p. 1987. pap., teacher ed. 14.00 (*0-8273-2579-7*); pap., student ed. 25.95 (*0-8273-2580-0*) Delmar.

Modern Macroeconomic Analysis. Paul Turner. LC 92-46192. 1993. 14.95 (*0-07-707717-2*) McGraw.

Modern Macroeconomics: A Post-Keynesian Perspective. Stanley Bober. 288p. 1987. lib. bdg. 62.50 (*0-7099-5080-2*, Pub. by C Helm) Routldge.

***Modern Macroeconomics: Study Guide.** 5th ed. 250p. 2000. pap. 31.93 (*0-13-031475-7*) P-H.

Modern Madame Butterfly: Fantasy & Reality in Japanese Cross-Cultural Relationships. Karen Ma. LC 95-60955. 286p. 1996. pap. 12.95 (*0-8048-2041-4*) Tuttle Pubng.

Modern Madame Butterfly: Fantasy & Reality in Japanese Cross-Cultural Relationships. Karen Ma. 296p. 1999. reprint ed. pap. text 14.00 (*0-7881-6263-2*) DIANE Pub.

Modern Madness. Douglas LaBier. 1986. 16.30 (*0-201-11775-4*) Addison-Wesley.

Modern Magi: A Christmas Fable. Carol L. Pearson. LC 98-18720. 96p. 1999. text 14.95 (*0-312-19300-9*) St Martin.

Modern Magic. Louisa May Alcott. Ed. & Intro. by Madeleine B. Stern. Date not set. lib. bdg. 23.95 (*0-8488-1881-4*) Amereon Ltd.

Modern Magic. Louisa May Alcott. LC 95-2830. 294p. 1995. 14.50 (*0-679-60171-6*) Modern Lib NY.

Modern Magic. Hoffman. 1987. pap. 26.00 (*0-8196-4570-2*) Biblo.

Modern Magick: Eleven Lessons in the High Magickal Arts. Donald M. Kraig. LC 87-45744. (High Magick Ser.). (Illus.). 600p. (Orig.). 1988. pap. 17.95 (*0-87542-324-8*) Llewellyn Pubns.

Modern Magnetic Materials: Principles & Applications. Robert C. O'Handley. LC 99-21372. 740p. 1999. 125.00 (*0-471-15566-7*) Wiley.

An Asterisk (*) at the beginning of an entry indicates that the title is appearing for the first time.

Modern Magnetooptics & Magnetooptical Materials. A. K. Zvezdin & V. A. Kotov. LC 97-19455. (Condensed Matter Physics Ser.). 1997. pap. write for info. (0-7503-0362-X) IOP Pub.

Modern Magyar Literature. Leslie Konnyu. LC 63-10689. 1964. pap. 4.25 (0-911862-04-8) Hungarian Rev.

Modern Maistre: The Social & Political Thought of Joseph de Maistre. Contrib. by Owen Bradley. LC 98-43636. (European Horizons Ser.). 320p. 1999. text 55.00 (0-8032-1295-X) U of Nebr Pr.

Modern Malay. Leonard R. Wheeler. LC 77-87033. reprint ed. 37.50 (0-404-16877-9) AMS Pr.

Modern Man & Religion. Thomas G. Masaryk. LC 74-107816. (Select Bibliographies Reprint Ser.). 1977. 26.95 (0-8369-5216-2) Ayer.

***Modern Man in Native America: An Abbreviated Chronology of Selected Events, People & Places.** (Illus.). 95p. 1999. spiral bd. 16.95 (0-9673750-0-2, 9707) Rock Song Pubng.

Modern Man in Search of a Soul. C. G. Jung. LC 50-4826. 282p. (C). 1955. pap. 12.00 (0-15-661206-2, Harvest Bks) Harcourt.

Modern Management. 7th ed. Certo. 1996. text. write for info. (0-13-260522-8); text. write for info. (0-13-260555-4) Allyn.

Modern Management. 7th ed. Certo. 1996. pap. text, teacher ed. write for info. (0-13-260498-1) Allyn.

Modern Management. 7th ed. Certo. 1996. text. write for info. (0-13-260514-7); pap. text, teacher ed. write for info. incl. cd-rom (0-13-260480-9); pap. text, teacher ed. write for info. (0-13-260472-8) Allyn.

Modern Management. 7th ed. Certo. 144p. (C). 1997. pap. text, student ed. 20.00 (0-13-902694-0) P-H.

***Modern Management.** 8th ed. 1999. text, teacher ed. write for info. (0-13-013650-6) P-H.

***Modern Management.** 8th ed. 208p. (C). 1999. pap. 13.33 (0-13-016168-3) P-H.

***Modern Management.** 8th ed. (C). 2000. pap. write for info. (0-13-016487-9); pap. write for info. (0-13-016488-7) P-H.

Modern Management. 8th ed. (C). 2000. text. write for info. (0-13-016993-5) S&S Trade.

***Modern Management: Diversity, Quality, Ethics & the Global Environment.** 8th ed. Samuel C. Certo. LC 99-12570. 608p. 1999. pap. 80.00 incl. disk (0-13-013307-8) P-H.

Modern Management Accounting. 2nd ed. A. Thomas Nelson & Paul B. Miller. LC 80-23023. 589p. reprint ed. pap. 182.60 (0-7837-6549-5, 204568600007) Bks Demand.

Modern Management Accounting Developments. F. Mitchell & C. Salafantinos. (Financial Times Management Briefings Ser.). 1997. pap. 94.50 (0-273-63238-8, Pub. by F T P-H) Trans-Atl Phila.

Modern Management & Information Systems for Public Administration in Developing Countries. 83p. 1985. 9.50 (92-1-123100-0, E.85.II.H.1) UN.

Modern Management Control Systems. Kenneth A. Merchant. LC 97-15527. 848p. 1997. 105.00 (0-13-554155-7) P-H.

Modern Management Methods & the Organization of Health Services. (Public Health Papers: No. 55). 1974. pap. text 10.00 (92-4-130055-8, 1110055) World Health.

Modern Management Methods for Local & Regional Authorities & the Role of Training: (Proceedings, Monte Verita, Switzerland, 28-29 November, 1994) (Congress of Local & Regional Authorities of Europe Ser.: No. 46). 1995. 18.00 (92-871-2832-4, Pub. by Council of Europe) Manhattan Pub Co.

Modern Management of Acute Myocardial Infarction in the Community Hospital. Ed. by Jeffrey Anderson. 560p. 1991. text 125.00 (0-8247-8432-4) Dekker.

***Modern Management of Cervical Spine Syndromes.** Donald R. Murphy. LC 99-35198. 747p. 1999. pap. 95.00 (0-8385-6386-4, Apple Lange Med) McGraw.

Modern Management of Myelomeningocele. Wilton H. Bunch et al. LC 75-161035. (Illus.). 320p. 1972. 22.50 (0-87527-097-2) Green.

Modern Management of Renovascular Hypertension & Renal Salvage. Ed. by Keith Calligaro et al. (Illus.). 313p. 1996. 89.00 (0-683-01357-2) Lppncott W & W.

Modern Management of Spinal Injury. S. Mahmoud Rezaian. (Illus.). 152p. 1996. pap. 50.00 (0-8059-3966-0) Dorrance.

Modern Management of the Menopause: A Perspective for the 21st Century. Ed. by Goran Berg & Mats Hammar. LC 94-1746. (International Congress, Symposium & Seminar Ser.: Vol. 8). 626p. 1994. 75.00 (1-85070-544-5) Prthnon Pub.

Modern Manners: An Etiquette Book for Rude People. P. J. O'Rourke. LC 88-31834. 300p. 1990. pap. 12.00 (0-87113-375-X, Atlntc Mnthly) Grove-Atltic.

***Modern Manners for Little Monsters.** Wilson Rogers. LC 97-62145. (Illus.). 16p. (J). (ps-3). 1998. 9.98 (0-7651-9068-0) Smithmark.

Modern Manors. Sanford M. Jacoby. 1999. pap. 16.95 (0-691-00743-8, Pub. by Princeton U Pr) Cal Prin Full Svc.

Modern Manors: Welfare Capitalism since the New Deal. Sanford M. Jacoby. LC 97-7835. 384p. 1997. text 35.00 (0-691-01570-8, Pub. by Princeton U Pr) Cal Prin Full Svc.

Modern Manual Therapy of the Vertebral Column. Ed. by Gregory P. Grieve. (Illus.). 898p. 1986. text 139.00 (0-443-03009-X) Church.

Modern Manufacturing: Information Control & Technology. Ed. by M. B. Zaremba & B. Prasad. LC 95-5939. (Advanced Manufacturing Ser.). (Illus.). 415p. 1994. 149.95 (0-387-19890-3) Spr-Verlag.

Modern Manufacturing Planning & Control. Adedeji B. Badiru & Bartholomew O. Nnaji. (C). 2000. 48.99 (0-13-095761-5, Macmillan Coll) P-H.

Modern Manufacturing Processes. James Brown. (Illus.). 256p. 1991. 24.95 (0-8311-3034-2) Indus Pr.

Modern Manufacturing Processes. David L. Goetsch. 630p. 1991. mass mkt. 59.75 (0-8273-2928-8) Delmar.

Modern Manufacturing Processes. David L. Goetsch. 630p. 1991. pap., teacher ed. 15.00 (0-8273-2929-6) Delmar.

***Modern Manuscript: Daily Handwriting Practice: K-6+** Jill Norris. Ed. by Marilyn Evans. (Daily Handwriting Practice Ser.). (Illus.). 112p. 2000. pap., teacher ed. 14.95 (1-55799-755-1, 792) Evan-Moor Edu Pubs.

Modern Manuscript Handwriting Practice. Frank Schaffer Publications, Inc. Staff. (Skill Builders Ser.). (Illus.). 128p. 1996. wbk. ed. 10.95 (0-86734-937-9, FS-32066) Schaffer Pubns.

Modern Marine Engineer's Manual, Vol. I. 3rd ed. Cynthia Lakis. Ed. by Everett C. Hunt et al. LC 99-14987. (Illus.). 1280p. 1999. text 85.00 (0-87033-496-4) Cornell Maritime.

Modern Marine Engineer's Manual, Vol. II. 2nd ed. Alan Osbourne. Ed. by Everett C. Hunt. LC 89-71201. (Illus.). 836p. 1991. text 55.00 (0-87033-307-0) Cornell Maritime.

Modern Marine Gears. Darle W. Dudley & J. J. Zrodowski. (Technical Papers: Vol. P429.03). (Illus.). 52p. 1950. pap. text 30.00 (1-55589-411-9) AGMA.

Modern Marine Salvage. William I. Milwee, Jr. LC 95-30816. (Illus.). 792p. 1996. text 65.00 (0-87033-471-9) Cornell Maritime.

Modern Marketing. 3rd ed. Frank Jefkins. 448p. 2000. pap. write for info. (0-7121-0853-X, Pub. by Pitman Pub) Trans-Atl Phila.

Modern Marriage. 24p. (Orig.). 1993. pap. 4.00 (0-9622190-3-7) Alien Bks.

Modern Marriage: How They Keep It Together. Rose S. Bell. LC 90-92119. 93p. (Orig.). 1990. pap. text, per. 10.95 (0-9614788-3-7, 333) Tivoli Pub.

Modern Marriage & Its Cost to Women: A Sociological Look at Marriage in France. Francois De Singly. Tr. by Malcolm Bailey from FRE. LC 95-42335. 248p. 1996. 38.50 (0-87413-572-9) U Delaware Pr.

Modern Marriage & the Clergy. Ed. by David R. Mace. LC 74-19593. (Special Issue of Pastoral Psychology Ser.). 84p. 1978. 16.95 (0-87705-368-5, Kluwer Acad Hman Sci) Kluwer Academic.

Modern Marriage in Sierra Leone: A Study of the Professional Group. Barbara E. Harrell-Bond. (Change & Continuity in Africa Ser.). (Illus.). 1975. pap. text 58.50 (90-279-7871-9) Mouton.

***Modern Marvels: 101 Provocative, Challenging & Mind-Blowing Questions on American Innovations, 1, 2.** History Channel Staff. (Great American History Quiz Ser.). 2000. pap. 9.95 (0-446-67685-3) Warner Bks.

Modern Maryland Civil Procedure. John A. Lynch, Jr. & Richard W. Bourne. 1,166p. 1993. 95.00 (1-55834-077-7, 64520-10, MICHIE) LEXIS Pub.

Modern Maryland Civil Procedure: 1998 Cumulative Supplement. John A. Lynch, Jr. & Richard W. Bourne. 225p. 1998. write for info. (0-327-00239-5, 64521-14) LEXIS Pub.

Modern Maryland Civil Procedure, 1999 Cumulative Supplement. John A. Lynch, Jr. & Richard W. Bourne. 250p. 1999. write for info. (0-327-01495-4, 6452115) LEXIS Pub.

Modern Mason Examines His Craft: Fact vs. Fiction. Ed. by L. C. Helms. (Illus.). x, 84p. 1981. pap. 6.95 (0-88053-065-0, M-325) Macoy Pub.

Modern Masonry. Clois E. Kicklighter. LC 96-22363. (Illus.). 384p. 1996. text 39.96 (1-56637-342-5) Goodheart.

Modern Masonry. Robert E. Putnam. 395p. (C). 1988. teacher ed. write for info. (0-15-562066-5, MASON IM); text 53.00 (0-15-562065-7, MASON, Pub. by SCP) Harcourt.

Modern Masonry: A Brief Sketch of the Craft since 1717. Joseph F. Newton. 92p. 1992. reprint ed. pap. 12.95 (1-56459-043-7) Kessinger Pub.

Modern Mass Media. 2nd ed. (C). 1997. text 24.00 (0-673-55545-3, GoodYrBooks) Addson-Wesley Educ.

Modern Mass Media. 2nd ed. John C. Merrill et al. 476p. (C). 1997. 75.00 (0-673-99025-7) Addson-Wesley Educ.

Modern Master Drawings: Forty Years of Collecting at the University of Michigan Museum of Art. Hilarie Faberman et al. (Illus.). 265p. (C). 1986. pap. 18.95 (0-912303-33-6) Michigan Mus.

Modern Masters. rev. ed. Vera Lampert. (New Grove Ser.). 1997. pap. 16.95 (0-393-31592-4) Norton.

***Modern Masters of Kyoto: The Transformation of Japanese Painting Traditions.** Michiyo Morioka & Paul Berry. LC 99-26989. (Illus.). 333p. 1999. 50.00 (0-932216-53-6) Seattle Art.

Modern Masters of Religious Education. Ed. by Marlene Mayr. LC 82-25009. 323p. (Orig.). 1983. pap. 24.95 (0-89135-033-0) Religious Educ.

Modern Masters of the Keyboard. Harriette M. Brower. LC 70-86736. (Essay Index Reprint Ser.). 1977. 21.95 (0-8369-1124-5) Ayer.

***Modern Masterworks, Vol. 1.** Ed. by Jane Magrath. 32p. 1999. pap. 7.95 (0-7390-0892-7, 18751) Alfred Pub.

Modern Material Culture: The Archaeology of the U. S. Ed. by Richard A. Gould & Michael B. Schiffer. LC 80-2332. (Studies in Archaeology). 1981. text 79.95 (0-12-293580-2) Acad Pr.

Modern Materials: Advances in Development & Applications. Ed. by Henry H. Hausner. Incl. Vol. 2. 1960. 77.00 (0-12-462202-X); Vol. 3. 1963. 77.00 (0-12-462203-8); Vol. 4. Ed. by B. W. Gonser & Henry Hausner. 1964. 77.00 (0-12-462204-6); Vol. 7. 1970. 77.00 (0-12-462207-0); write for info. (0-318-50313-1) Acad Pr.

Modern Materials & Manufacturing Processes. 2nd ed. Mileta Tomovic. Ed. by Gregg Bruce. LC 97-5993. 474p. (C). 1997. 83.00 (0-13-186859-4) P-H.

***Modern Math.** Don Fairborn. 164p. 2000. pap. 10.00 (1-886855-46-3) Tavenner Pub.

***Modern Math.** Donna A. Simms. 150p. 2000. pap. 10.00 (1-886855-35-8) Tavenner Pub.

Modern Math: An Elementary Approach. 5th ed. Wheeler. (Math). 1981. mass mkt. 25.50 (0-8185-0430-7) Brooks-Cole.

Modern Math: An Elementary Approach. 6th ed. Ruric E. Wheeler. LC 83-26163. (Math). 675p. (C). 1984. mass mkt. 34.00 (0-534-02843-8) Brooks-Cole.

Modern Math: An Elementary Approach. 7th ed. Ruric E. Wheeler. LC 87-25018. (Math). 705p. (C). 1988. mass mkt. 44.00 (0-534-08580-6) Brooks-Cole.

Modern Math, Elementary Approach. 3rd ed. Wheeler. (Math). 1973. 13.50 (0-8185-0070-0) Brooks-Cole.

Modern Math, Elementary Approach. 4th ed. Wheeler. (Math). 1977. mass mkt. 19.50 (0-8185-0213-4) Brooks-Cole.

Modern Math with Applications in Business & Social Science. 2nd ed. Wheeler. (Math). 1976. mass mkt. 18.50 (0-8185-0154-5) Brooks-Cole.

Modern Mathematical Analysis. Murray H. Protter & Charles B. Morrey, Jr. 1964. text 68.95 (0-201-05995-9) Addison-Wesley.

***Modern Mathematical, Management & Statistical Sciences I: Advances in Theory & Application.** Ed. by Edward J. Dudewicz et al. LC 99-72155. (American Series in Mathematical & Management Sciences: Vol. 41). (Illus.). 192p. 1999. pap. 195.00 (0-935950-45-1) Am Sciences Pr.

Modern Mathematical Methods for Physicists & Engineers. C. D. Cantrell. LC 98-24761. (Illus.). 700p. (C). 1999. text. write for info. (0-521-59180-5); pap. text. write for info. (0-521-59827-3) Cambridge U Pr.

Modern Mathematical Methods in Diffraction Theory & Its Applications in Engineering: Proceedings of the Sommerfeld '96 Workshop, Freudenstadt, 30 September-4 October 1996. Ed. by Erhard Meister et al. LC 97-22715. (Methoden und Verfahren der Mathematischen Physik Ser.: Bd. 42). (GER., Illus.). vi, 308p. 1997. pap. 57.95 (3-631-30874-4) P Lang Pubng.

Modern Mathematical Methods in Diffraction Theory & Its Applications in Engineering: Proceedings of the Sommerfeld '96 Workshop, Freudenstadt, 30 September-4 October 1996. Ed. by Erhard Meister et al. LC 97-22715. (Methoden und Verfahren der Mathematischen Physik Ser.: Bd. 42). (Illus.). VI, 308p. 1997. pap. 57.95 (0-8204-3230-X) P Lang Pubng.

Modern Mathematical Methods in Transport Theory. Ed. by W. Greenberg & J. Polewczak. (Operator Theory Ser.: Vol. 51). 340p. 1991. 114.00 (0-8176-2571-2) Birkhauser.

Modern Mathematical Methods of Optimization. Ed. by Karl-Heinz Elster. LC 93-27578. (Mathematical Topics Ser.: Vol. 1). 415p. 1993. text 120.75 (3-05-501452-9, Pub. by Akademie Verlag) Wiley.

Modern Mathematical Models of Time & Their Applications to Physics & Cosmology: Proceedings of the International Conference Held in Tucson, AZ, 1996. William G. Tifft & W. J. Cocke. LC 97-25568. 396p. 1997. text 214.00 (0-7923-4663-7) Kluwer Academic.

Modern Mathematical Statistics. Edward J. Dudewicz & Satya N. Mishra. LC 87-14279. (Probability & Mathematical Statistics Ser.). 864p. 1988. text 95.95 (0-471-81472-5) Wiley.

Modern Mathematicians. Harry Henderson. LC 95-18363. (Global Profiles Ser.). 128p. (YA). (gr. 5-12). 1995. lib. bdg. 19.95 (0-8160-3235-1) Facts on File.

Modern Mathematics. 8th ed. Ruric E. Wheeler. 800p. (C). 1992. text 50.95 (0-534-16602-4) Brooks-Cole.

Modern Mathematics. 10th ed. Wheeler. 600p. 1998. 49.95 (0-7872-4869-X); per. 54.95 (0-7872-5212-3) Kendall-Hunt.

Modern Mathematics: The Genesis of a School in Poland. M. Grace Kuzawa. 1968. pap. 14.95 (0-8084-0223-4) NCUP.

Modern Mathematics for Elementary School Teachers. Ruric E. Wheeler & Ed Wheeler. 896p. 1994. 49.95 (0-534-25426-8) Brooks-Cole.

Modern Mathematics for Elementary School Teachers. 9th ed. Ruric E. Wheeler & Ed R. Wheeler. 1995. text 63.95 (0-534-25326-1) Brooks-Cole.

Modern Mathematics in Secondary Schools. D. T. Marjoram. 1964. text 6.95 (0-08-010719-2, Pergamon Pr); pap. text 5.40 (0-08-010718-4, Pergamon Pr) Elsevier.

Modern Mathematics in the Light of the Fields Medal. 2nd ed. Michael Monastyrsky. LC 96-22137. 176p. (C). 1998. reprint ed. pap. 19.95 (1-56881-083-0) AK Peters.

***Modern Matrix Algebra.** Kolman. 420p. 2000. 89.00 (0-13-948852-9) P-H.

Modern Mauritius: The Politics of Decolonization. Adele Simmons. LC 81-47015. 256p. reprint ed. pap. 79.40 (0-608-18473-X, 205672000081) Bks Demand.

Modern Maya Storage Behavior: Ethnoarchaeological Case Examples from the Puuc Region of Yucatan. Michael P. Smyth. (University of Pittsburgh Memoirs in Latin American Archaeology Ser.: No. 3). (Illus.). 188p. 1990. pap. 13.50 (1-877812-04-8, M003) UPLAAP.

Modern Measuring Circuit Encyclopedia. Rudolf F. Graf. LC 92-9564. (Illus.). 240p. 1992. pap. 12.95 (0-8306-4156-4, 3890) McGraw-Hill Prof.

Modern Meatless Menus Cookbook. Lorena Bardwell. 1963. spiral bd. 4.95 (0-87511-002-9) Claitors.

Modern Mechanical Pulping: In the Pulp & Paper Industry. Ed. by Ken L. Patrick. LC 89-80421. (Illus.). 246p. (Orig.). 1989. pap. 45.00 (0-87930-218-6) Miller Freeman.

Modern Medea: A Family Story of Slavery & Child-Murder from the Old South. Steven Weisenburger. LC 98-15565. (Illus.). 288p. 1998. 25.00 (0-8090-6953-9) Hill & Wang.

***Modern Medea: A Family Story of Slavery & Child-Murder from the Old South.** Steven Weisenburger. (Illus.). 368p. 1999. pap. 14.00 (0-8090-6954-7) Hill & Wang.

Modern Media & Communication, 3 vols. M. K. Joseph. 1996. 750.00 (81-7488-169-7, Pub. by Print Hse) St Mut.

Modern Media in Foreign Language Education. Ed. by Michael D. Bush & Robert M. Terry. (ACTFL Foreign Language Education Ser.). 1998. pap. 16.90 (0-8442-9386-5, VF9386-5) NTC Contemp Pub Co.

Modern Medical Assisting. Gail A. Chester. Ed. by Adrianne Williams. LC 97-30097. (Illus.). 768p. (C). 1998. pap. text 52.00 (0-7216-4997-1, W B Saunders Co) Harcrt Hlth Sci Grp.

Modern Medical Assisting. Gail A. Chester. (C). 1998. pap. text, student ed. 16.95 (0-7216-4998-X, W B Saunders Co) Harcrt Hlth Sci Grp.

Modern Medical Chemistry. John Taylor. 500p. (C). 1994. pap. text 72.00 (0-13-590399-8) P-H.

Modern Medical Language. C. Edward Collins & Juanita J. Davies. 750p. (C). 1996. mass mkt. 63.95 (0-314-06702-7) West Pub.

Modern Medical Language Act Cards. Collins & Davies. (Medical Terminology). (C). 1996. 21.75 (0-314-08925-X) Brooks-Cole.

Modern Medical Office: A Reference. 2nd ed. Doris D. Humphrey & Kathie Sigler. 1990. text, student ed. 21.95 (0-538-70101-3) S-W Pub.

Modern Medicine: Lay Perspectives & Experiences. Williams. 288p. 1996. 65.00 (1-85728-317-1, Pub. by UCL Pr Ltd); pap. 24.95 (1-85728-318-X, Pub. by UCL Pr Ltd) Taylor & Francis.

Modern Medicine & Jewish Ethics. Fred Rosner. LC 86-2910. (C). 1986. text 29.50 (0-88125-407-X) Ktav.

Modern Medicine for the MRCP. Kevin Davies et al. 135p. 1996. pap. text 19.95 (0-7020-2112-1, Pub. by W B Saunders) Saunders.

Modern Meditations: A Buddhist Sampler. Nichiko Niwano. 152p. 1992. pap. 5.95 (4-333-01477-8, Pub. by Kosei Pub Co) Tuttle Pubng.

Modern Men: Mapping Masculinity in English & German Literature, 1880-1930. Michael Kane. LC 99-20681. 256p. 1999. pap. 24.95 (0-304-70310-9) Continuum.

***Modern Men: Mapping Masculinity in English & German Literature, 1880-1930.** Michael Kane. LC 99-20681. 256p. 1999. 69.95 (0-304-70309-5) Continuum.

Modern Mephistopheles. Louisa May Alcott. (J). Date not set. lib. bdg. 16.95 (0-8488-0412-0) Amereon Ltd.

Modern Mephistopheles. Louisa May Alcott. LC 87-8026. 437p. 1987. pap. 17.95 (0-275-92780-6, B2780, Praeger Pubs) Greenwood.

Modern Mephistopheles. Louisa May Alcott. (Works of Louisa May Alcott). 1989. reprint ed. lib. bdg. 79.00 (0-7812-1636-2) Rprt Serv.

Modern Mephistopheles: And, Taming a Tartar. Louisa May Alcott. Ed. & Intro. by Madeleine B. Stern. LC 87-8026. 437p. 1987. 59.95 (0-275-92754-7, C2754, Praeger Pubs) Greenwood.

Modern Messages from the Minor Prophets. David Pharr. 1986. pap. 6.95 (0-89137-330-6) Quality Pubns.

***Modern Metalworking.** John R. Walker. LC 99-42172. (Illus.). 600p. (YA). (gr. 9-12). 2000. text 46.64 (1-56637-710-2) Goodheart.

Modern Method for Four Mallets. Ed. by Doug Allan. 208p. (YA). 1997. pap. text 19.95 (0-7692-1228-X, 0104B) Wrner Bros.

***Modern Method for Guitar, 1&2.** William Leavitt. 432p. 1999. otabind 29.95 (0-634-01233-9) H Leonard.

Modern Method for Guitar, Vol. 1. 128p. 1995. spiral bd. 22.95 incl. audio compact disk (0-7935-4511-0) H Leonard.

Modern Method for Guitar, Vol. 1. W. Leavitt. (Berklee Ser.). 128p. 1986. otabind 14.95 (0-7935-2545-4, 50449400) H Leonard.

Modern Method for Guitar, Vol. 2. W. Leavitt. (Berklee Ser.). 128p. 1986. otabind 14.95 (0-7935-2572-1, 50449410) H Leonard.

Modern Method for Guitar, Vol. 3. W. Leavitt. (Berklee Ser.). 168p. 1987. otabind 14.95 (0-7935-2598-5, 50449420) H Leonard.

Modern Method for Keyboard, 2. James Progris. 160p. 1986. per. 14.95 (0-634-01330-0) H Leonard.

Modern Method for Keyboard, a Study Vol. 1: Supplement. J. Progris. 136p. 1986. per. 10.95 (0-7935-3901-3, 50449660) H Leonard.

Modern Method Plant Analysis. 1988. 256.95 (0-387-18819-3) Spr-Verlag.

Modern Methodism in England, 1932-1996. John M. Turner. 1997. pap. text 19.00 (0-7162-0512-2) Epworth Pr.

Modern Methods & Applications in Analysis of Explosives. Jehuda Yinon & Shmuel Zitrin. 316p. 1996. pap. 89.95 (0-471-96562-6) Wiley.

Modern Methods for Automating Finite Element Mesh Generation. Ed. by Kenneth Baldwin. (Sessions Proceedings Ser.). 84p. 1986. 14.00 (0-87262-564-8) Am Soc Civil Eng.

Modern Methods for Business Research. Ed. by George A. Marcoulides. LC 97-31706. (Methodology for Business & Management Ser.). 350p. 1998. write for info. (0-8058-2677-7); pap. 49.95 (0-8058-3093-6) L Erlbaum Assocs.

Modern Methods for Multidimensional Dynamics Computations in Chemistry. Ed. by Donald L. Thompson. LC 98-223134. 730p. 1998. 148.00 (981-02-3342-6) World Scientific Pub.

M

Modern Methods for Polymer Characteristics. Viney. text. write for info. (0-471-49070-9) Wiley.

Modern Methods for Quality Control & Improvement. 2nd ed. Harrison M. Wadsworth et al. LC 85-20285. 704p. 1986. text 99.95 (0-471-87695-X) Wiley.

Modern Methods for the Determination of Non-Metals in Non-Ferrous Metals: Applications to Particular Systems of Metallurgical Importance. C. Engleman et al. (Illus.). xiii, 410p. 1985. 153.85 (3-11-010342-7) De Gruyter.

Modern Methods for Trace Element Determination. C. Vandecasteele & C. B. Block. LC 91-10292. 344p. 1997. pap. 69.95 (0-471-97445-5) Wiley.

Modern Methods in Analytical Acoustics: Lecture Notes. D. G. Crighton et al. (Illus.). 680p. 1994. 54.95 (0-387-19737-0) Spr-Verlag.

Modern Methods in Analytical Morphology. J. Gu & G. W. Hacker. (Illus.). 458p. (C). 1994. text 135.00 (0-306-44838-6, Kluwer Plenum) Kluwer Academic.

Modern Methods in Carbohydrate Synthesis. Ed. by Shaheer H. Khan & Roger A. O'Neil. 576p. 1996. pap. text 39.00 (3-7186-5921-2, Harwood Acad Pubs) Gordon & Breach.

Modern Methods in Carbohydrate Synthesis. Ed. by Shaheer H. Khan & Roger A. O'Neill. 576p. 1996. text 102.00 (3-7186-5785-6, Harwood Acad Pubs) Gordon & Breach.

Modern Methods in Complex Analysis. Ed. by Thomas Bloom et al. LC 95-40840. (Annals of Mathematics Studies: No. 137). (Illus.). 360p. 1996. pap. text 35.00 (0-691-04428-7, Pub. by Princeton U Pr) Cal Prin Full Svc.

Modern Methods in Equilibrium Statistical Mechanics. M. G. Rasetti. (Series on Advances in Statistical Mechanics: Vol. 2). 270p. 1986. text 47.00 (9971-966-27-1); pap. text 28.00 (9971-966-29-8) World Scientific Pub.

Modern Methods in Food Mycology. Ed. by Robert A. Samson et al. LC 92-27934. (Developments in Food Science Ser.: Vol. 31). 388p. 1992. 200.00 (0-444-88939-6) Elsevier.

*__Modern Methods in Forensic Taphonomy.__ William D. Haglund & Marcella H. Sorg. 500p. 1999. 79.95 (0-8493-1189-6) CRC Pr.

Modern Methods in Kinetics. Ed. by C. H. Bamford & C. F. Tipper. (Comprehensive Chemical Kinetics Ser.: Vol. 24). xvi,528p. 1983. 424.50 (0-444-42028-2) Elsevier.

Modern Methods in Molecular Spectra. Jensen. text. write for info. (0-471-48998-0) Wiley.

Modern Methods in Protein - & Nucleic Acid Research: Review Articles. Ed. by Harald Tschesche. (Illus.). ix, 446p. (C). 1990. lib. bdg. 253.85 (3-11-012275-8) De Gruyter.

Modern Methods in Protein Chemistry: Review Articles, Vol. 1. Ed. by Harald Tschesche. LC 83-14009. x, 464p. 1983. 180.80 (3-11-009514-9) De Gruyter.

Modern Methods in Protein Chemistry: Review Articles, Vol. 2. Ed. by Harald Tschesche. (Illus.). ix, 434p. 1985. 176.95 (3-11-010180-7) De Gruyter.

Modern Methods in Protein Chemistry: Review Articles, Vol. 3. Ed. by Harald Tschesche. 385p. (C). 1988. lib. bdg. 192.35 (3-11-011216-7) De Gruyter.

Modern Methods of Analytical Mechanics & Their Applications. Ed. by V. V. Rumyantsev & A. V. Karapatyan. (CISM International Centre for Mechanical Sciences Ser.: No. 387). (Illus.). vii, 344p. 1998. pap. 78.95 (3-211-83138-X) Spr-Verlag.

Modern Methods of Aquaculture in Japan. 2nd rev. ed. Ed. by Hiromu Ikenoue & Takeichiro Kafuku. LC 92-20764. (Developments in Aquaculture & Fisheries Science Ser.: No. 24). 274p. 1992. 179.25 (0-444-98665-0) Elsevier.

Modern Methods of Clinical Investigation. Institute of Medicine, Committee on Technological. Ed. by Annetine C. Gelijns. (Medical Innovation at the Crossroads Ser.: Vol. 1). 244p. 1990. text 24.95 (0-309-04286-0) Natl Acad Pr.

Modern Methods of Data Analysis. Ed. by John Fox & J. Scott Long. (Illus.). 448p. (C). 1990. text 58.00 (0-8039-3366-5) Sage.

Modern Methods of Data Analysis. John Fox & J. Scott Long. LC 89-27842. 446p. 1990. reprint ed. pap. 138.30 (0-608-01533-4, 205957700002) Bks Demand.

Modern Methods of Finishing Gears by Shaving, Honing & Grinding. T. S. Gates & J. R. Newman. (Technical Papers: Vol. P129.16). (Illus.). 8p. 1965. pap. text 30.00 (1-55589-227-2) AGMA.

Modern Methods of Ice Fishing, 1. Tom Gruenwald. LC 99-23421. (Freshwater Angler Ser.). (Illus.). 128p. 1999. 19.95 (0-86573-071-7) Creat Pub Intl.

Modern Methods of Igneous Petrology: Understanding Magmatic Processes. Ed. by J. Nicholls & J. K. Russell. (Reviews in Mineralogy Ser.: Vol. 24). 1990. per. 24.00 (0-939950-29-4) Mineralogical Soc.

Modern Methods of Inducing Abortion. Ed. by David T. Baird et al. LC 95-14056. (Illus.). 220p. 1995. 99.95 (0-86542-819-0) Blackwell Sci.

Modern Methods of Music Analysis Using Computers. Robert M. Mason. LC 85-26142. (Illus.). viii, 299p. 1985. lib. bdg. 45.50 (0-9615669-0-6) Schoolhouse Pr.

Modern Methods of Optimization: Proceedings of the Summer School "Modern Methods of Optimization" Held at the Schlob Thurnau of the University of Bayreuth, Bayreuth, FRG, October 1-6, 1990. Ed. by W. Krabs et al. (Lecture Notes in Economics & Mathematical Systems Ser.: Vol. 378). (Illus.). viii, 348p. 1992. 71.95 (0-387-55139-5) Spr-Verlag.

Modern Methods of Particle Size Analysis. Philip J. Elving & James D. Winefordner. Ed. by Howard G. Barth. LC 84-3630. (Chemical Analysis: A Series of Monographs on Analytical Chemistry & Its Applications: No. 1-075). 320p. 1984. 199.00 (0-471-87571-6) Wiley.

Modern Methods of Pharmaceutical Analysis, 2 vols., I. 2nd ed. 416p. 1990. lib. bdg. 159.00 (0-8493-5266-5, RS189) CRC Pr.

Modern Methods of Pharmaceutical Analysis, 2 vols., II. 2nd ed. 464p. 1990. lib. bdg. 159.00 (0-8493-5267-3, RS189) CRC Pr.

Modern Methods of Pharmaceutical Analysis, Vol. I. Roger E. Schirmer. 304p. 1981. 119.95 (0-8493-5244-4, RS189, CRC Reprint) Franklin.

Modern Methods of Pharmaceutical Analysis, Vol. II. Roger E. Schirmer. 288p. 1982. 150.00 (0-8493-5245-2, RS189, CRC Reprint) Franklin.

Modern Methods of Pharmaceutical Analysis, Vol. III. Roger E. Schirmer. 256p. 1982. 81.50 (0-8493-5246-0, CRC Reprint) Franklin.

Modern Methods of Pharmaceutical Analysis: A Textbook for Pharmacy Students & Pharmaceutical Chemists. David G. Watson. LC 98-32446. 1999. write for info. (0-443-05986-1, W B Saunders Co) Harcrt Hlth Sci Grp.

Modern Methods of Pipe Fabrication. 8th rev. ed. S. D. Bowman. 1982. pap. 6.25 (0-87511-008-8) Claitors.

Modern Methods of Polymer Characterization. Ed. by Howard G. Barth & Jimmy W. Mays. LC 90-20906. (Chemical Analysis: A Series of Monographs on Analytical Chemistry & Its Applications). 574p. 1991. 185.00 (0-471-82814-9) Wiley.

Modern Methods of Protein Immobilization. William H. Scouten & Russell L. Rines. 2001. 159.00 (0-8493-7680-7) CRC Pr.

Modern Methods of Radiology in Otorhinolaryngology: Proceedings of the International Congress, 5th, Copenhagen, June, 1976. International Congress of Radiology in Oto-Rhine-L. Ed. by C. R. Pfaltz et al. (Advances in OtoRhinoLaryngology Ser.: Vol. 24). (Illus.). 1978. 115.75 (3-8055-2707-1) S Karger.

Modern Methods of Speech Processing. Ed. by Ravi P. Ramachandran & Richard J. Mammone. (International Series in Engineering & Computer Science, Natural Language Processing & Machine Translation). 488p. (C). 1995. text 145.00 (0-7923-9607-3) Kluwer Academic.

Modern Metropolis: Artists' Images of New York from the Museum of the City of New York. Ed. by Leslie Nolan. (Illus.). 48p. (Orig.). 1993. pap. 9.95 (1-56584-066-6, Pub. by New Press NY) Norton.

Modern Metropolis: Its Origins, Growth, Characteristics, & Planning - Selected Essays by Hans Blumenfeld. fac. ed. Hans Blumenfeld. Ed. by Paul D. Spreiregen. LC 67-13391. (Illus.). 395p. pap. 122.50 (0-7837-7547-4, 204692200005) Bks Demand.

Modern Metropolis: Its Origins, Growth, Characteristics, & Planning, Selected Essays. Hans Blumenfeld. Ed. by Paul D. Spreiregen. LC 76-31874. 1971. pap. text 15.50 (0-262-52028-1) MIT Pr.

Modern Mexican Art. Laurence F. Schmeckebier. LC 70-141418. (Illus.). 190p. 1971. reprint ed. lib. bdg. 59.75 (0-8371-4692-5, SCMA, Greenwood Pr) Greenwood.

Modern Mexican Artists: Critical Notes. Carlos Merida. LC 68-22931. (Essay Index Reprint Ser.). 1977. 23.95 (0-8369-0701-9) Ayer.

Modern Mexican Painters. MacKinley Helm. LC 68-22917. (Essay Index Reprint Ser.). 1977. 30.95 (0-8369-0532-6) Ayer.

Modern Mexican Painters. Ray Helm. (Illus.). 228p. 1991. pap. 11.95 (0-486-26028-3) Dover.

Modern Mexico. William L. Canak & Laura Swanson. LC 97-38941. (Comparative Societies Ser.). 240p. 1997. pap. 14.69 (0-07-034431-0) McGraw.

Modern Micro. 2nd ed. Erickson. 1996. 26.00 (0-256-23804-9) McGraw.

Modern Microbial Genetics. Ed. by Uldis N. Streips & Ronald E. Yasbin. LC 90-12718. 548p. 1991. 152.50 (0-471-56845-7) Wiley.

Modern Microbiology: Principles & Applications. Edward A. Birge. 496p. (C). 1991. text. write for info. (0-697-07628-8, WCB McGr Hill) McGrw-H Hghr Educ.

Modern Microcrystal Tests for Drugs: The Identification of Organic Compunds by Microcrystaloscopic Chemistry. Charles C. Fulton. LC 68-54599. (Illus.). 486p. reprint ed. pap. 150.70 (0-608-30291-0, 201248600096) Bks Demand.

Modern Microeconomics. David N. Hyman. 1988. 16.95 (0-8016-2845-8) Mosby Inc.

Modern Microeconomics. 3rd ed. David N. Hyman. 224p. (C). 1992. text, student ed. 22.50 (0-256-09607-4, Irwn McGrw-H) McGrw-H Hghr Educ.

Modern Microelectronics: Circuit Design, IC Applications, Fabrication Technology, 2 vols., Set. 2nd ed. Research & Education Association Staff. LC 81-50168. (Illus.). 1408p. 1986. 36.75 (0-87891-520-6) Res & Educ.

Modern Microscopies: Techniques & Applications. P. J. Duke & A. G. Michette. (Illus.). 266p. (C). 1989. text 102.00 (0-306-43288-9, Kluwer Plenum) Kluwer Academic.

Modern Microwave Technology. Victor F. Veley. (Illus.). 656p. (C). 1987. text 66.80 (0-13-595414-2) P-H.

*__Modern Middle East.__ 2000. write for info. (0-582-27318-8) Pearson Educ.

Modern Middle East. Ed. by Albert H. Hourani. 700p. 1996. pap. 20.00 (0-614-21495-5, 796) Kazi Pubns.

Modern Middle East: A Reader. Ed. by Albert H. Hourani et al. LC 93-28464. 600p. 1994. pap. 24.95 (0-520-08241-9, Pub. by U CA Pr) Cal Prin Full Svc.

*__Modern Middle East: Change & Continuity.__ Mehran Kamrava. 384p. (C). 2001. pap. text 32.95 (1-889119-49-0, Chatham House Pub) Seven Bridges.

Modern Middle East: From Imperialism to Freedom, 1880-1958. Emory C. Bogle. LC 95-15863. 528p. (C). 1995. pap. text 52.00 (0-13-206509-6) P-H.

Modern Midrash: The Retelling of Traditional Jewish Narratives by Twentieth-Century Hebrew Writers. David C. Jacobson. LC 86-1949. (SUNY Series in Modern Jewish Literature & Culture). 220p. (C). 1987. text 64.50 (0-88706-323-3); pap. text 21.95 (0-88706-325-X) State U NY Pr.

Modern Migrations in Western Africa: Studies Presented & Discussed at the 11th International African Seminar, 1972: Dakar, Senegal. International African Seminar Staff. Ed. by Samir Amin. LC HB3667.I5. 440p. reprint ed. pap. 136.40 (0-608-13683-2, 205538100017) Bks Demand.

Modern Military Cadence. Timothy P. Dunnigan. 228p. 1997. pap. 10.00 (0-9679910-0-5) Tyler Enter.

Modern Military Dictionary. Maher S. Kayyali. (ARA.). 533p. 1986. 29.95 (0-86685-426-6, AIR2743) Intl Bk Ctr.

Modern Military Dictionary: English-Arabic - Arabic-English. Maher S. Kayyali. (ARA & ENG.). 250p. 1994. reprint ed. pap. 14.95 (0-7818-0243-1) Hippocrene Bks.

Modern Military Techniques Carriers. Maritime Books Staff. (C). 1986. pap. text 30.00 (0-583-31003-6, Pub. by Maritime Bks) St Mut.

Modern Military Techniques Combined: OPS. Maritime Books Staff. (C). 1986. pap. text 40.00 (0-583-31004-4, Pub. by Maritime Bks) St Mut.

Modern Military Techniques Submarines. Maritime Books Staff. (C). 1986. pap. text 40.00 (0-583-31009-5, Pub. by Maritime Bks) St Mut.

Modern Mind. Peter Watson. 768p. 2001. 35.00 (0-06-019413-8) HarpC.

Modern Mind. Michael Roberts. LC 68-29241. (Essay Index Reprint Ser.). 1977. reprint ed. 19.95 (0-8369-0827-9) Ayer.

Modern Minstrelsy: Miquel Hernandez & Jacques Brel. Carole A. Holdsworth. (Utah Studies in Literature & Linguistics: Vol. 16). 143p. 1980. pap. 26.00 (3-261-04642-2) P Lang Pubng.

Modern Miracle Men. John D. Ratcliff. LC 79-37770. (Essay Index Reprint Ser.). 1977. reprint ed. 26.95 (0-8369-2619-6) Ayer.

Modern Missions, Their Trials & Triumphs. 2nd ed. Robert Young. LC 72-5581. (Black Heritage Library Collection). 1977. reprint ed. 35.95 (0-8369-9153-2) Ayer.

Modern Modalities. Ed. by Simo Knuuttila. 360p. (C). 1988. lib. bdg. 195.50 (90-277-2678-7, Pub. by Kluwer Academic) Kluwer Academic.

Modern Modalities for the Diagnosis of Hematologic Neoplasms. 2nd ed. Tsieh Sun et al. LC 93-33311. 1993. write for info. (0-89189-366-0) Am Soc Clinical.

Modern Modalities for the Diagnosis of Hematologic Neoplasms: Color Atlas-Text. Chin-Yang Li et al. LC 95-36945. (Illus.). 272p. 1996. 158.50 (0-89640-292-4) Igaku-Shoin.

Modern Modeling of Continuum Phenomena. Ed. by Richard O. DiPrima. LC 77-9041. (Lectures in Applied Mathematics: Vol. 16). 251p. 1977. reprint ed. pap. 70.00 (0-8218-1116-9, LAM/16) Am Math.

Modern Modified Theories of Gravitation & Cosmologies: Proceedings of International Workshop Held at Ben Gurion University Israel, June 29-30, 1997. Ed. by E. I. Guendelman. (Illus.). 385p. (C). 1998. pap. text 75.00 (1-57485-028-8) Hadronic Pr Inc.

Modern Molecular Photochemistry. Nicholas J. Turro. (Illus.). 640p. (C). 1991. reprint ed. pap. text 38.50 (0-935702-71-7) Univ Sci Bks.

Modern Monetary Theory: A Critical Survey of Recent Developments. Hans Visser. 224p. 1991. text 95.00 (1-85278-092-4) E Elgar.

Modern Monetary Theory: A Critical Survey of Recent Developments. Hans Visser. LC 93-16093. 224p. 1993. pap. 30.00 (1-85278-847-X) E Elgar.

Modern Money & Banking. 3rd ed. Roger L. Miller & David D. VanHoose. LC 92-12189. (C). 1993. text 69.00 (0-07-042335-0); text, student ed. 26.25 (0-07-042338-5) McGraw.

Modern Mongolian: A Transformational Syntax. Robert I. Binnick. LC 79-311196. (Illus.). 167p. reprint ed. pap. 51.80 (0-8357-8227-1, 203402400088) Bks Demand.

Modern Mongolian-English Dictionary. Gombojab Hangin et al. LC 86-45752. (Uralic & Altaic Ser.: Vol. 150). 900p. 1986. write for info. (0-933070-19-5) Mongolia.

Modern Monograms: Thirteen Hundred Ten Graphic Designs. Kiyoshi Takahashi. (Lettering, Calligraphy, Typography Ser.). 160p. 1985. pap. 7.95 (0-486-24788-0) Dover.

Modern Monologue: Men. Ed. by Michael Earley & Philippa Keil. 176p. 1993. pap. 11.99 (0-413-67210-7, Thtre Arts Bks) Routledge.

Modern Monologue: Men. Ed. by Michael Earley & Philippa Keil. LC 93-8441. 176p. (gr. 13). 1993. pap. 9.95 (0-87830-038-4) Routledge.

Modern Monologue: Women. Ed. by Michael Earley & Philippa Keil. LC 93-22627. 136p. (gr. 13). 1993. pap. 11.99 (0-87830-046-5, B2313) Routledge.

Modern Monologues for Modern Kids. Raf Mauro. LC 95-167520. 64p. (J). (gr. 1-3). 1994. pap. 8.95 (0-940669-29-3, D-33) Dramaline Pubns.

Modern Montessori at Home: A Creative Teaching Guide for Parents of Children Six Through Nine Years of Age. Heidi A. Spietz. LC 89-14870. 156p. 1989. pap. 14.95 (0-929487-02-8) Am Montessori Consult.

Modern Montessori at Home No. 11: A Creative Teaching Guide for Parents of Children 10 Through 12. Heidi A. Spietz. LC 90-834. 158p. 1990. pap. 14.95 (0-929487-10-9) Am Montessori Consult.

Modern Moral & Political Philosophy. Robert C. Cummins & Thomas D. Christiano. LC 98-8247. 568p. 1998. pap. text 45.95 (0-7674-0283-9, 0283-9) Mayfield Pub.

Modern Morse Code in Rehabilitation & Education. Thomas Wayne King. LC 99-25921. 308p. (C). 1999. pap. text 35.00 (0-205-28751-4) Allyn.

*__Modern Mosaic: Art & Modernism in the United States.__ Ed. by Townsend Ludington. (Illus.). 480p. 2000. 59.95 (0-8078-2578-6); pap. 29.95 (0-8078-4891-3) U of NC Pr.

*__Modern Mothers in the Heartland: Gender, Health, & Progress in Illinois, 1900-1930.__ Lynne Curry. LC 99-27611. (Women & Health Ser.). (Illus.). 224p. 1999. text 40.00 (0-8142-0830-4); pap. text 18.50 (0-8142-5032-7) Ohio St U Pr.

Modern Movement. Ed. by John Gross. (TLS Companions Ser.). 336p. (C). 1993. pap. 16.95 (0-226-30987-8); lib. bdg. 49.50 (0-226-30985-1) U Ch Pr.

Modern Movement see History of Modern Architecture

Modern Movement Heritage: A Challenge to Manage. Ed. by Allen Cunningham. LC 98-8314. (Illus.). 224p. (C). (gr. 13). 1998. pap. 39.99 (0-419-23230-3, D6229, E & FN Spon) Routledge.

Modern Movement in American Theology. Frank H. Foster. LC 76-86751. (Essay Index Reprint Ser.). 1977. 18.95 (0-8369-1131-8) Ayer.

Modern Movement in Painting. Charles Marriott. 1977. lib. bdg. 80.00 (0-8490-2269-X) Gordon Pr.

Modern Movements among Moslems. S. G. Wilson. 1977. lib. bdg. 59.95 (0-8490-2270-3) Gordon Pr.

Modern Movements in European Philosophy. 2nd ed. Richard Kearney. LC 94-26467. 384p. 1995. text 24.95 (0-7190-4248-8, Pub. by Manchester Univ Pr); text 79.95 (0-7190-4384-0, Pub. by Manchester Univ Pr) St Martin.

Modern Mule. 2nd rev. ed. Illus. by Bonnie Shields. 137p. 1978. pap. write for info. (0-9659312-4-2) Am Donkey.

Modern Multidimensional Scaling Theory & Applications. Ingwer Borg & Patrick J. Groenen. LC 96-30269. (Statistics Ser.). 471p. 1997. 54.95 (0-387-94845-7) Spr-Verlag.

Modern Multivariate Statistical Analysis: A Graduate Course & Handbook. Minoru Siotani et al. LC 82-72549. (American Sciences Press Series in Mathematical & Management Sciences: Vol. 9). (C). 1985. text 195.00 (0-935950-06-0) Am Sciences Pr.

Modern Mummies: The Preservation of the Human Body in the Twentieth Century. Christine Quigley. LC 97-43888. (Illus.). 271p. 1998. boxed set 39.95 (0-7864-0492-2) McFarland & Co.

Modern Muse: The Support & Condition of Artists. Ed. by C. Richard Swaim. LC 88-34391. (ACA Arts Research Seminar Ser.). 128p. (Orig.). 1989. pap. 9.95 (0-915400-75-8, ACA Bks) Am for the Arts.

Modern Music. 2nd rev. ed. Paul Griffiths. LC 94-60288. (World of Art Ser.). (Illus.). 216p. 1994. pap. 14.95 (0-500-20278-8, Pub. by Thames Hudson) Norton.

Modern Music, Set, Vols. 1-23. Orig. Title: League of Composers' Review. reprint ed. lib. bdg. 1095.00 (0-404-19534-2) AMS Pr.

Modern Music: A Popular Guide to Greater Musical Enjoyment. John T. Howard, Jr. & James Lyons. LC 78-60139. 202p. 1979. reprint ed. lib. bdg. 59.50 (0-313-20556-6, HOMU, Greenwood Pr) Greenwood.

Modern Music: Composers & Music of Our Time. Max Graf. Tr. by Beatrice R. Maier. LC 77-27613. 320p. 1978. reprint ed. lib. bdg. 38.50 (0-313-20185-4, GRMM, Greenwood Pr) Greenwood.

Modern Music: Composers & Music of Our Time: Music Book Index. Max Graf. 320p. 1993. reprint ed. lib. bdg. 89.00 (0-7812-9564-5) Rprt Serv.

Modern Music & After: Directions since 1945. Paul Griffiths. (Illus.). 392p. 1995. 65.00 (0-19-816578-1) OUP.

Modern Music & Musicians. New York University Society Staff. 616p. 1991. reprint ed. lib. bdg. 119.00 (0-7812-9345-6) Rprt Serv.

Modern Music from the Former U. S. S. R. Ed. by Valeria Tsenova. Tr. by Romela Kohanovskaya from RUS. 272p. 1998. text 75.00 (3-7186-5804-6, ECU60, Harwood Acad Pubs); pap. text 36.00 (3-7186-5821-6, ECU29, Harwood Acad Pubs) Gordon & Breach.

Modern Music Librarianship: Essays in Honor of Ruth Watanabe. Pref. by Alfred Mann. LC 89-30559. (Festschrift Ser.: No. 8). (Illus.). 200p. 1989. lib. bdg. 54.00 (0-918728-93-2) Pendragon NY.

Modern Muslim India & the Birth of Pakistan. S. M. Ikram. 1992. 45.50 (1-56744-143-2) Kazi Pubns.

Modern Muslim India & the Birth of Pakistan. S. M. Ikram. (C). 1991. reprint ed. 40.00 (81-85199-47-7, Pub. by Renaiss Publng Hse) S Asia.

Modern Mustangs: Twenty Years of Muscle. Jim Campisano. LC 99-17647. 1999. 14.98 (1-56799-697-3) M Friedman Pub Grp Inc.

*__Modern Muzzleloading for Today's Whitetails.__ Ian McMurchy. LC 00-102689. (Illus.). 208p. 2000. 29.95 (0-87341-951-0, MODMZ) Krause Pubns.

Modern Mycology. 3rd ed. J. W. Deacon. LC 97-3738. (Illus.). 288p. 1997. pap. text 58.00 (0-632-03077-1) Blackwell Sci.

Modern Mystery Writers see Writers of English: Lives & Works

Modern Mysticism. Francis Grierson. 1977. lib. bdg. 59.95 (0-8490-2271-1) Gordon Pr.

Modern Mysticism: Jung, Zen & the Still Good Hand of God. Michael Gellert. LC 91-8024. (Illus.). 240p. (Orig.). 1994. pap. 12.95 (0-89254-032-X) Nicolas-Hays.

Modern Mystics. Francis Younghusband. LC 67-28774. (Essay Index Reprint Ser.). 1977. 20.95 (0-8369-1015-X) Ayer.

Modern Mystics & Modern Magic. Arthur Lillie. LC 72-5680. (Essay Index Reprint Ser.). 1977. reprint ed. 20.95 (0-8369-2996-9) Ayer.

Modern Mythology. Andrew Lang. LC 68-54279. reprint ed. 40.00 (0-404-03852-2) AMS Pr.

M

An Asterisk (*) at the beginning of an entry indicates that the title is appearing for the first time.

*Modern Myths: The Art of Ronald Pennell in Glass & Bronze.** Julia Ellis. (Illus.). 128p. 2000. 39.50 (*1-85149-330-1*) Antique Collect.

Modern Myths about Satan & Spiritual Warfare. David S. Kirkwood. 168p. 1994. pap. 7.95 (*0-9629625-4-6*) Ethnos.

***Modern Myths & Wagnerian Deconstructions: Literary-Critical Approaches to Wagner's Music-Dramas, 57.** Mary A. Cicora. LC 99-31628. Vol. 57. 232p. 2000. 65.00 (*0-313-30539-0*) Greenwood.

Modern Myths, Locked Minds: Secularism & Fundamentalism in India. T. N. Madan. (Oxford India Paperbacks Ser.). 340p. 1998. reprint ed. pap. text 13.95 (*0-19-564707-6*) OUP.

Modern Naples: A Documentary History: c.1799-1999. Ed. by Pellegrino D'Acierno et al. (Documentary History of Naples Ser.: Vol. 5). (Illus.). 300p. 2001. pap. 25.00 (*0-934977-53-4*) Italica Pr.

Modern Nation. Stuart A. Kallen. Ed. by Rosemary Walner. LC 90-82629. (Building of a Nation Ser.). (Illus.). 32p. (J). (gr. 4). 1990. lib. bdg. 13.98 (*0-939179-91-1*) ABDO Pub Co.

Modern Nationalism & Religion. Salo W. Baron. LC 79-134050. (Essay Index Reprint Ser). 1977. 22.95 (*0-8369-2142-9*) Ayer.

Modern Nature. Derek Jarman. (Illus.). 314p. 1994. reprint ed. pap. 13.95 (*0-87951-549-X*, Pub. by Overlook Pr) Penguin Putnam.

Modern Navigation, Guidance, & Control Processing. Ching-Fang Lin. 560p. (C). 1991. text 63.75 (*0-13-596230-7*) P-H.

Modern Negro Art. James A. Porter. LC 92-37421. (Moorland-Spingarn Ser.). (C). 1992. 24.95 (*0-88258-163-5*) Howard U Pr.

Modern Negro Art. James A. Porter. LC 69-18593. (American Negro: His History & Literature. Series 2). 1979. reprint ed. 15.95 (*0-405-01889-4*) Ayer.

Modern Nepal: A Political History, 1769-1955, 2 vols., Set. Rishikesh Shah. 364p. (C). 1990. 924.00 (*0-89771-066-5*, Pub. by Ratna Pustak Bhandar) St Mut.

Modern Nepal: A Political History, 1769-1955, 2 vols., Set. R. Shaha. (C). 1991. text 90.00 (*0-7855-0150-9*, Pub. by Ratna Pustak Bhandar) St Mut.

Modern Nepal Vols. 1 & 2: A Political History, 1769-1955. Rishikesh Shaha. (C). 1996. reprint ed. 38.00 (*81-7304-150-4*, Pub. by Manohar) S Asia.

Modern Networking Handbook. Udo W. Pooch & Willis F. Marti. 2001. 89.95 (*0-8493-2591-9*) CRC Pr.

Modern Neuromuscular Technique. Chaitow. 1996. text 45.00 (*0-443-05298-0*, W B Saunders Co) Harcrt Hlth Sci Grp.

Modern Neuromuscular Techniques. L. Chaitow. 24p. 1997. pap. write for info. (*0-443-05977-2*) Church.

Modern Neurosurgery, Vol. I. Ed. by M. Brock. (Illus.). 400p. 1982. 79.95 (*0-387-10972-2*) Spr-Verlag.

Modern Neurosurgery of Meningiomas & Pituitary Adenomas. Ed. by R. Fahlbusch et al. (Acta Neurochirugica - Supplementum Ser.: Vol. 65). (Illus.). 150p. 1996. suppl. ed. 143.00 (*3-211-82779-X*) Spr-Verlag.

Modern New Testament: Translated from the Original Aramaic Sources. Tr. by George M. Lamsa. 560p. 1998. reprint ed. pap. 23.00 (*0-87516-716-0*) DeVorss.

Modern New York Discovery, Vol. 1. Durst et al. LC 82-84231. 1989. 115.00 (*0-317-00659-2*) West Group.

Modern New York Discovery, Vol. 1. Durst et al. 1993. suppl. ed. 65.00 (*0-317-03233-X*) West Group.

Modern Newpaper Editing. 3rd ed. Gilmore. (Mass Communication Ser.). 1983. 38.50 (*0-87835-127-2*) Wadsworth Pub.

Modern News Library: Documentation of Current Affairs in Newspaper & Broadcasting Libraries. Geoffrey Whatmore. LC 78-321303. (Illus.). 218p. reprint ed. pap. 67.60 (*0-7837-5319-5*, 204505800005) Bks Demand.

Modern Newspaper Editing. 4th ed. Gene Gilmore. LC 89-24728. (Illus.). 316p. (C). 1990. text 34.95 (*0-8138-0174-5*) Iowa St U Pr.

Modern Newspaper Practice: A Primer on the Press. 4th ed. F. W. Hodgson. LC 96-174062. 208p. 1996. pap. text 34.95 (*0-240-51459-9*, Focal) Buttrwrth-Heinemann.

Modern Nicaraguan Poetry: Dialogues with France & the United States. Steven F. White. LC 91-58938. 232p. 1993. 32.50 (*0-8387-5232-2*) Bucknell U Pr.

Modern NMR-Spectroscopy. H. Duddeck & W. Dietrich. 230p. 1989. 39.95 (*0-387-91348-3*) Spr-Verlag.

Modern NMR Spectroscopy: A Guide for Chemists. 2nd ed. Jeremy K. Sanders & Brian K. Hunter. LC 92-23518. (Illus.). 328p. 1993. pap. text 57.95 (*0-19-855567-9*) OUP.

Modern NMR Spectroscopy: A Workbook of Chemical Problems. 2nd ed. Jeremy K. Sanders et al. (Illus.). 136p. (C). 1993. pap. text 27.95 (*0-19-855812-0*) OUP.

Modern NMR Techniques & Their Application in Chemistry. A. I. Popov & K. Hallenga. (Practical Spectroscopy Ser.: Vol. 11). (Illus.). 680p. 1990. text 225.00 (*0-8247-8332-8*) Dekker.

Modern NMR Techniques for Chemical Research. A. E. Derome. (Organic Chemistry Ser.). (Illus.). 295p. 1987. text 167.00 (*0-08-032514-9*, Pergamon Pr); pap. text 50.00 (*0-08-032513-0*, Pergamon Pr) Elsevier.

Modern Non-Linear Optics. Ed. by Myron W. Evans & Stanislaw Kielich. (Advances in Chemical Physics Ser.: Vol. 85, Pt. 1). 640p. 1993. 215.00 (*0-471-57548-8*) Wiley.

Modern Nonlinear Equations. Thomas L. Saaty. 490p. (C). 1982. reprint ed. pap. 13.95 (*0-486-64232-1*) Dover.

Modern Nonlinear Optics, Vol. 1. Ed. by Myron Evans & Stanislaw Kielich. LC 58-9935. (Advances in Chemical Physics Ser.). 640p. 1996. pap. 64.95 (*0-471-17002-X*) Wiley.

Modern Nonlinear Optics, Vol. 2. Ed. by Ilya Prigogine et al. (Advances in Chemical Physics Ser.: Vol. 85B, Pt. 2). 835p. 1993. 249.00 (*0-471-57546-1*) Wiley.

Modern Nonlinear Optics, Vol. 3. Ed. by Myron Evans & Stanislaw Kielich. LC 97-118453. (Advances in Chemical Physics Ser.: Vol. 85, Pt. 3). 823p. 1993. 249.00 (*0-471-30499-9*) Wiley.

Modern Nonlinear Optics, 3 pts., Vol. 3. Ed. by Myron Evans & Stanislaw Kielich. (Advances in Chemical Physics Ser.: Vol. 85). 2298p. 1994. 599.00 (*0-471-10453-1*) Wiley.

Modern Nonlinear Optics, Vol. 3. Ed. by Myron Evans & Stanislaw Kielich. LC 58-9935. (Advances in Chemical Physics Ser.). 823p. 1996. pap. 64.95 (*0-471-16997-8*) Wiley.

Modern Nonlinear Optics, 3 vols., Vol. 3. Ed. by Myron Evans & Stanislaw Kielich. (Advances in Chemical Physics Ser.). 2298p. 1997. pap. 175.00 (*0-471-18446-2*) Wiley.

Modern Nonlinear Optics, Pt. 2, Vol. 2. Ed. by Myron Evans & Stanislaw Kielich. LC 58-9935. 835p. 1996. pap. 64.95 (*0-471-16994-3*) Wiley.

Modern Nordic Plays: Denmark. Ed. by Erik J. Friis. (Library of Scandinavian Literature). 1974. lib. bdg. 37.50 (*0-8290-1400-4*) Irvington.

Modern Nordic Plays: Denmark. Ed. by Erik J. Friis. (Library of Scandinavian Literature). 1982. pap. text 16.95 (*0-8290-1161-7*) Irvington.

Modern Nordic Plays: Finland. Ed. by Erik J. Friis. Tr. by Philip Binham et al from FIN. (Library of Scandinavian Literature). 1972. pap. text 16.95 (*0-8290-1162-5*) Irvington.

Modern Nordic Plays: Finland. Ed. by Erik J. Friis. Tr. by Philip Binham et al from FIN. (Library of Scandinavian Literature). 1973. lib. bdg. 34.50 (*0-8290-1403-9*) Irvington.

Modern Nordic Plays: Iceland. Ed. by Erik J. Friis. Tr. by Alan Boucher et al from ICE. (Library of Scandinavian Literature). 1973. lib. bdg. 37.50 (*0-8290-1401-2*) Irvington.

Modern Nordic Plays: Iceland. Ed. by Erik J. Friis. Tr. by Alan Boucher et al from ICE. (Library of Scandinavian Literature). 1982. pap. text 16.95 (*0-8290-1163-3*) Irvington.

Modern Nordic Plays: Norway. Ed. by Erik J. Friis. Tr. by Pat Shaw et al from NOR. (Library of Scandinavian Literature). 1974. lib. bdg. 37.50 (*0-8290-1402-0*) Irvington.

Modern Nordic Plays: Norway. Ed. by Erik J. Friis. Tr. by Pat Shaw et al from NOR. (Library of Scandinavian Literature). 1982. pap. text 16.95 (*0-8290-1164-1*) Irvington.

Modern Nordic Plays: Sweden. Ed. by Erik J. Friis et al. Tr. by Harry G. Carlson & Paul B. Austin from SWE. (Library of Scandinavian Literature). 1982. pap. text 16.95 (*0-8290-1165-X*) Irvington.

Modern Nordic Plays: Sweden. Ed. by Erik J. Friis et al. Tr. by Harry G. Carlson & Paul B. Austin from SWE. (Library of Scandinavian Literature). 1973. reprint ed. lib. bdg. 37.50 (*0-8290-1404-7*) Irvington.

Modern North. Ken Coates & Judith Powell. 168p. 29.95 (*1-55028-122-4*, Pub. by J Lorimer); pap. 19.95 (*1-55028-120-8*, Pub. by J Lorimer) Formac Dist Ltd.

Modern Novel Writing: Azemia, 4 vols. William Beckford. LC 74-81366. 264p. 1970. reprint ed. 50.00 (*0-8201-1063-9*) Schol Facsimiles.

Modern Nuclear Methods in Materials Science. Ed. by M. J. Fluss & Y. C. Jean. (Materials Science Forum Ser.: Vol. 2). 204p. (C). 1983. pap. text 79.00 (*0-87849-534-7*, Pub. by Trans T Pub) Enfield Pubs NH.

Modern Numerology. Morris C. Goodman. 160p. 1969. pap. 10.00 (*0-87980-102-6*) Wilshire.

Modern Nutrition in Health & Disease. 9th ed. Ed. by Maurice E. Shils et al. LC 98-38505. 2161p. 1998. 105.00 (*0-683-30769-X*) Lppncott W & W.

Modern Nutrition in Health & Disease, 2 vols., 1. 8th ed. James A. Olson et al. (Illus.). 2200p. 1993. lib. bdg. 67.50 (*0-8121-1751-4*) Lppncott W & W.

Modern Nutrition in Health & Disease, 2 vols., 2. 8th ed. James A. Olson et al. (Illus.). 3036p. 1993. lib. bdg. 67.50 (*0-8121-1752-2*) Lppncott W & W.

Modern Nutrition in Health & Disease, 2 vols., Set. 8th ed. James A. Olson et al. (Illus.). 2200p. 1993. lib. bdg. 99.50 (*0-8121-1485-X*) Lppncott W & W.

Modern Obstetric Anaesthesia. Ed. by John Urquhart et al. (Greenwich Medical Media Ser.). (Illus.). 450p. 2000. text 120.00 (*1-900151-77-4*) OUP.

Modern Obstetrics in General Practice. Ed. by G. N. Marsh. (Oxford General Practice Ser.: No. 9). (Illus.). 1986. pap. 29.95 (*0-19-261419-3*) OUP.

Modern Ocean. James Harms. LC 91-72058. (Poetry Ser.). 80p. (Orig.). 1992. pap. 11.95 (*0-88748-127-2*) Carnegie-Mellon.

Modern Odyssey. R. M. Hart. LC 97-90399. 1997. pap. 8.95 (*0-533-12382-8*) Vantage.

***Modern Odysseys: Greek American Artists of the 20th Century.** Peter Selz et al. (Illus.). 108p. 2000. pap. 25.00 (*1-929641-00-1*, Pub. by Queens Mus) Dist Art Pubs.

Modern Office Management. M. Mills & S. Standingford. 496p. (C). 1986. 130.00 (*0-7855-5684-2*, Pub. by Inst Pur & Supply) St Mut.

Modern Office Procedures. 2nd ed. Charles F. Barrett et al. LC 93-9868. 1993. mass mkt. 31.00 (*0-314-01899-9*) West Pub.

Modern Office Systems: A Simulation. 2nd ed. Lawrence Hugenberg. 206p. (C). 1998. pap. text 20.95 (*0-7872-5434-7*, 41543401) Kendall-Hunt.

***Modern Olympic Games.** Haydn Middleton. LC 99-24273. (Olympics Ser.). 1999. lib. bdg. 22.79 (*1-57572-453-7*) Heinemann Lib.

Modern Olympics. Richard Tames. LC 95-39276. (Olympic Library). (J). 1998. (*1-57572-035-3*) Heinemann Lib.

Modern Olympics: A Struggle for Revival. David C. Young. LC 96-16496. 272p. 1996. text 39.96 (*0-8018-5374-5*) Johns Hopkins.

Modern Opera Houses & Theatres, 3 vols., 1. Edwin O. Sachs & Ernest A. Woodrow. LC 67-12461. (Illus.). 1972. 38.95 (*0-405-08905-8*) Ayer.

Modern Opera Houses & Theatres, 3 vols., Set. Edwin O. Sachs & Ernest A. Woodrow. LC 67-12461. (Illus.). 1972. 118.95 (*0-405-08904-X*) Ayer.

Modern Opera Houses & Theatres, 3 vols., Vol. 2. Edwin O. Sachs & Ernest A. Woodrow. LC 67-12461. (Illus.). 1972. 38.95 (*0-405-08906-6*) Ayer.

Modern Opera Houses & Theatres, 3 vols., Vol. 3. Edwin O. Sachs & Ernest A. Woodrow. LC 67-12461. (Illus.). 1972. 41.95 (*0-405-08907-4*) Ayer.

Modern Operating Systems. Andrew S. Tanenbaum. 752p. (C). 1992. 74.00 (*0-13-588187-0*) P-H.

Modern Operations Strategy. Hayes et al. 1996. 50.00 (*0-02-874003-3*) Free Pr.

Modern Operative Techniques in Liver Surgery. Bernard Launois & Glyn G. Jamieson. LC 92-49203. 160p. 1993. text 114.00 (*0-443-04616-6*) Church.

***Modern Optical Engineering.** 3rd ed. Warren J. Smith. (Optical Engineering Ser.). (Illus.). 572p. 2000. 79.95 (*0-07-136360-2*) McGraw.

Modern Optical Engineering: The Design of Optical Systems. 2nd ed. Warren J. Smith. 524p. 1990. 69.95 (*0-07-059174-1*) McGraw.

Modern Optics. B. D. Guenther. LC 89-37809. 720p. 1990. text 103.95 (*0-471-60538-7*) Wiley.

Modern Optics. B. D. Guenther. 151p. 1990. pap. text, teacher ed. 24.50 (*0-471-51869-7*) Wiley.

Modern Optics, Electronics & High Precision Techniques in Cell Biology. Ed. by G. Isenberg. LC 97-30061. (Principles & Practice Ser.). (Illus.). 280p. 1997. 169.00 (*3-540-62673-5*) Spr-Verlag.

Modern Optimal Control: A Conference in Honor of Solomon Lefschetz & Joseph P. La Salle. Emilio D. Roxin. (Lecture Notes in Pure & Applied Mathematics Ser.: Vol. 119). (Illus.). 464p. 1989. pap. text 170.00 (*0-8247-8168-6*) Dekker.

***Modern Oral Amdo Tibetan: A Language Primer.** Kalsang Norbu et al. LC 99-47833. (Studies in Linguistics & Semiotics: Vol. 5). 324p. 2000. text 99.95 (*0-7734-7895-7*) E Mellen.

Modern Ordnance Materiel, 1943. Raritan Arsenal Staff. (Illus.). 216p. 1992. reprint ed. pap. 30.00 (*0-910667-30-6*) Victory WW Two.

Modern Organ: Including Ernest M. Skinner: Organ Builder. by T. Scott Buhrman. Ernest M. Skinner. 1978. reprint ed. pap. text 25.00 (*0-913746-11-8*) Organ Lit.

Modern Organ Building. Walter Lewis & Thomas Lewis. (Illus.). xii, 164p. 1986. reprint ed. 90.00 (*0-913746-26-6*); reprint ed. pap. 68.00 (*0-913746-27-4*) Organ Lit.

Modern Organ Course for All Organs, Bk. 1. Albert De Vito. 1964. pap. 5.95 (*0-934286-36-1*) Kenyon.

Modern Organ Course for All Organs, Bk. 2. Albert De Vito. 1964. pap. 5.95 (*0-934286-37-X*) Kenyon.

Modern Organ Course for All Organs: Primer. Albert De Vito. 1964. pap. 4.95 (*0-934286-35-3*) Kenyon.

Modern Organ Stops. Noel A. Bonavia-Hunt. (Illus.). 1974. pap. 20.00 (*0-913746-05-3*) Organ Lit.

Modern Organic Chemistry. 3rd ed. A. Atkinson. 272p. (C). 1994. pap. 25.00 (*0-85950-656-8*, Pub. by S Thornes Pubs) Trans-Atl Phila.

Modern Organic Elemental Analysis. Ma & C. Rittner. (Illus.). 512p. 1979. text 225.00 (*0-8247-6786-1*) Dekker.

Modern Organization. 2nd ed. Victor A. Thompson. LC 77-6664. 222p. 1977. pap. 68.90 (*0-608-05151-9*, 206571200005) Bks Demand.

Modern Organizations. Amitai Etzioni. (C). 1964. pap. text 21.00 (*0-13-596049-5*) P-H.

Modern Organizations: Administrative Theory in Contemporary Society. Ali Farazmand. LC 93-50072. 288p. 1994. 59.95 (*0-275-93775-5*, Praeger Pubs) Greenwood.

Modern Organizations: Organization Studies in the Postmodern World. Stewart R. Clegg. 256p. (C). 1990. 47.50 (*0-8039-8329-8*); pap. 19.95 (*0-8039-8330-1*) Sage.

Modern Organizations & Emerging Conundrums: Exploring the Post Industrial Sub-Culture of the Third Millennium. Richard A. Goodman. LC 98-38582. 656p. 1999. 70.00 (*0-7391-0001-7*) Lxngtn Bks.

Modern Organizations & Emerging Conundrums: Medium, Meaning & Method. Richard A. Goodman & Associates Staff. 384p. 1998. 38.00 (*0-7879-4125-5*) Jossey-Bass.

Modern Origami. James M. Sakoda. LC 97-22876. (Illus.). 150p. pap. 9.95 (*0-486-29843-4*) Dover.

Modern Origins, Developments, & Perspectives Against the Background of Machiavellism Bk. 1: Pre-Modern "Machiavellism" A. London Fell. LC 81-22332. (Origins of Legislative Sovereignty & the Legislative State Ser,). 432p. 1993. 79.50 (*0-275-93975-8*, Praeger Pubs) Greenwood.

Modern Orthodox Saints: St. Nikephoros of Chios, Vol. 4. 2nd rev. ed. Constantine Cavarnos. LC 86-82207. (Illus.). 124p. 1986. pap. 6.95 (*0-914744-74-7*) Inst Byzantine.

Modern Orthodox Saints Vol. 1: St. Cosmas Aitolos. enl. rev. ed. Constantine Cavarnos. LC 85-80440. (Illus.). 118p. 1995. pap. 6.95 (*0-914744-65-8*) Inst Byzantine.

Modern Orthodox Saints Vol. 2: St. Macarios of Corinth. 3rd ed. Constantine Cavarnos. LC 72-85116. (Illus.). 120p. 1993. pap. 6.95 (*0-914744-97-6*) Inst Byzantine.

Modern Orthodox Saints Vol. 3: St. Nicodemos the Hagiorite Great Theologian & Teacher of the Orthodox Church, Reviver of Hesychasm, Moralist, Canonist, Hagiologist & Writer of Liturgical Poetry, an Account of His Life, Character & Message, Together with a Comprehensive List of His Writings & Selections from Them. 2nd ed. Constantine Cavarnos. LC 78-71478. (Illus.). 167p. 1994. pap. 7.50 (*0-914744-41-0*) Inst Byzantine.

Modern Orthodox Saints Vol. 5: St. Seraphim of Sarov, Widely Beloved Mystic, Healer, Comforter, & Spiritual Guide, an Account of His Life, Character & Message, Together with a Very Edifying Conversation with His Disciple Motovilor on the Acquisition of the Grace of the Holy Spirit, & the Saint's Spiritual Counsels. Constatine Cavarnos & Mary B Zeldin. LC 80-80124. (Illus.). 167p. 1993. pap. 7.50 (*0-914744-48-8*) Inst Byzantine.

Modern Orthodox Saints Vol. 6: St. Arsenios of Paros. 2nd rev. ed. Constantine Cavarnos. LC 88-80496. (Illus.). 124p. 1988. pap. 6.95 (*0-914744-80-1*) Inst Byzantine.

Modern Orthodox Saints Vol. 7: St. Nectarios of Aegina. rev. ed. Constantine Cavarnos. LC 87-83600. (Illus.). 222p. 1995. pap. 7.95 (*0-914744-78-X*) Inst Byzantine.

Modern Orthodox Saints Vol. 8: St. Savvas the New. Constantine Cavarnos. LC 85-60117. (Illus.). 144p. 1996. pap. 6.95 (*0-914744-62-3*) Inst Byzantine.

M

Modern Orthodox Saints Vol. 9: St. Methodia of Kimolos. Constantine Cavarnos. 2nd ed. LC 86-82479. (Illus.). 123p. 1987. 15.00 (*0-914744-75-5*) Inst Byzantine.

Modern Orthodox Saints Vol. 10: Sts. Raphael, Nicholas & Irene of Lesvos. Constantine Cavarnos. LC 90-80711. (Illus.). 200p. 1994. 17.50 (*0-914744-87-9*); pap. 7.95 (*0-914744-88-7*) Inst Byzantine.

Modern Orthodox Saints Vol. 11: Blessed Elder Philotheos Zervakos. Constantine Cavarnos. LC 93-79586. (Illus.). 240p. 1993. 17.50 (*0-914744-93-3*); pap. 9.50 (*0-914744-94-1*) Inst Byzantine.

Modern Orthodox Saints Vol. 12: Blessed Hermit Philaretos of the Holy Mountain. Constantine Cavarnos. LC 96-80495. (Illus.). 109p. 1997. 15.95 (*1-884729-20-7*); pap. 7.50 (*1-884729-21-5*) Inst Byzantine.

***Modern Orthodox Saints Vol. 13: Blessed Elder Gabriel Dionysiatis (1886-1993)** Constantine Cavarnos. 238p. 1999. pap. 9.95 (*1-884729-48-7*) Inst Byzantine.

***Modern Orthodox Saints Vol. 13: Blessed Elder Gabriel Dionysiatis (1886-1993)** Constantine Cavarnos. LC 99-783339. (Illus.). 238p. 1999. 16.50 (*1-884729-47-9*) Inst Byzantine.

Modern Pacing Sire Lines. John Bradley. LC 98-36915. 1998. 39.95 (*0-929346-56-4*) R Meerdink Co Ltd.

***Modern Paint Effects: A Guide to Contemporary Paint Finishes from Inspiration to Technique.** Annie Sloan. (Illus.). 124p. 2000. 29.95 (*1-55209-490-1*) Firefly Bks Ltd.

***Modern Paint Effects: A Guide to Contemporary Paint Finishes from Inspiration to Technique.** Annie Sloan. (Illus.). 124p. 2000. pap. 19.95 (*1-55209-488-X*) Firefly Bks Ltd.

Modern Painters see Complete Works of John Ruskin

Modern Painting: The Impressions & the Avant Garde of the Twentieth Century. Ed. by Parramon's Editorial Staff. LC 98-72513. (Art Handbooks). (Illus.). 400p. 1998. 15.00 (*0-7641-5119-3*) Barron.

Modern Painting, Drawing & Sculpture: Collected by Emily & Joseph Pulitzer, Jr., Vol. 4. Angelica Z. Rudenstine. (Catalog of the Emily & Joseph Pulitzer, Jr., Collection: Vol. IV). (Illus.). 372p. (Orig.). 1988. pap. 4.95 (*0-916724-67-0*, 4670) Harvard Art Mus.

Modern Painting, Drawing & Sculpture: Collected by Louise & Joseph Pulitzer, Jr., Vol. III. Charles S. Chetham. (Catalog of the Emily & Joseph Pulitzer, Jr. Collection). (Illus.). 233p. 1971. pap. 4.95 (*0-916724-35-2*) Harvard Art Mus.

Modern Palestinian Literature & Culture. Ami Elad-Bouskila. LC 99-20736. 256p. 1999. 54.50 (*0-7146-4956-2*, Pub. by F Cass Pubs) Intl Spec Bk.

***Modern Palestinian Literature & Culture.** Ami Elad-Bouskila. LC 99-20736. (Israel Ser.). 256p. 1999. pap. write for info. (*0-7146-8015-X*, Pub. by F Cass Pubs) Intl Spec Bk.

Modern Panarion. Helena P. Blavatsky. 504p. 1981. reprint ed. 16.00 (*0-938998-22-6*) Theosophy.

***MODERN PAPACY 1789 1995.** Frank J. Coppa. LC 98-18988. (History of the Papacy Ser.). (C). 1998. 87.00 (*0-582-09629-4*) Longman.

Modern Papacy, 1798-1995. Frank J. Coppa. LC 98-18988. (History of the Papacy Ser.). 296p. (C). 1998. pap. 33.53 (*0-582-09630-8*) Addison-Wesley.

Modern Papau, New Guinea. Laura Zimmer-Tamakoshi. LC 97-50223. 424p. 1998. 40.00 (*0-943549-51-5*) Truman St Univ.

Modern Paper Finishing: New Equipment & Operations Techniques. Ed. by John C. W. Evans. (Illus.). 176p. 1988. pap. 45.00 (*0-87930-202-X*) Miller Freeman.

Modern Parables: A Collection of All-Time Favorite Venden Stories to Make Spiritual Truths Come Alive. Morris L. Venden. LC 93-35905. 1994. pap. 10.99 (*0-8163-1196-X*) Pacific Pr Pub Assn.

Modern Parasite Biology: Cellular, Immunological, & Molecular Aspects. David J. Wyler. LC 89-23317. (Illus.). 432p. (C). 1990. pap. text 70.95 (*0-7167-2038-8*) W H Freeman.

Modern Parasitology: A Textbook of Parasitology. Ed. by F. E. Cox. (Illus.). 358p. (C). 1982. pap. text 35.00 (*0-632-00612-9*) Blackwell Sci.

Modern Parliamentary Procedure. rev. ed. Ray E. Keesey. LC 94-11948. 143p. 1994. 24.95 (*1-55798-251-1*, 4311180); pap. 14.95 (*1-55798-236-8*, 4311181) Am Psychol.

Modern Particleboard & Dry-Process Fiberboard Manufacturing. Thomas M. Maloney. LC 76-47094. (Forest Industries Book). (Illus.). 688p. 1993. 59.00 (*0-87930-288-7*) Miller Freeman.

Modern Parties. Martha Gill. LC 98-66362. (Modern Ser.). (Illus.). 128p. 1998. 18.95 (*1-56352-492-9*) Longstreet.

Modern Patchwork. Ondori Publishing Company Staff. LC 81-84806. (Illus.). 108p. 1982. 12.95 (*0-87040-507-1*) Japan Pubns USA.

*__Modern Patent Litigation.__ Paul M. Janicke. LC 99-67455. 408p. 1999. boxed set 60.00 (*0-89089-810-3*) Carolina Acad Pr.

Modern Pathfinders of Christianity: The Lives & Deeds of Seven Centuries of Christian Leaders. Henry K. Rowe. LC 68-16973. (Essay Index Reprint Ser.). 1977. 19.95 (*0-8369-0839-2*) Ayer.

Modern Pathology of AIDS & Other Retroviral Infections. Ed. by A. T. Haase et al. (Illus.). viii, 230p. 1990. 167.00 (*3-8055-5079-0*) S Karger.

Modern Pavement Management. 2nd ed. Ralph C. Haas et al. LC 92-30178. 604p. (C). 1994. 89.50 (*0-89464-588-9*) Krieger.

Modern Pennsylvania Civil Practice, 2 vols. Mark A. Nordenberg et al. LC 85-71932. 775p. 1998. ring bd. 150.00 (*1-887024-36-0*) Bisel Co.

Modern Pensions. Norman Toulson. (C). 1982. 199.00 (*0-7855-4074-1*, Pub. by Witherby & Co) St Mut.

Modern Percussion Grooves. Glen Caruba. (Illus.). 48p. (Orig.). 1998. pap. 19.95 incl. audio compact disk (*1-57424-042-0*) Centerstream Pub.

Modern Perinatal Medicine. Ed. by Louis Gluck. LC 74-78364. (Illus.). 480p. reprint ed. pap. 148.80 (*0-608-15500-4*, 202973600064) Bks Demand.

Modern Persecution: or Insane Asylums Unveiled, As Demonstrated by the Report of the Investigating Committee of the Legislature of Illinois, 2 vols. Elizabeth P. Packard. LC 73-2410. (Mental Illness & Social Policy; the American Experience Ser.). 1973. reprint ed. 57.95 (*0-405-05220-0*) Ayer.

Modern Persian: Elementary Level. Gernot L. Windfuhr. (PER.). 377p. 1981. pap. 24.95 (*0-86685-443-6*) Intl Bk Ctr.

Modern Persian: Elementary Level. Gernot L. Winduhr. 377p. 1981. pap. 22.00 (*0-916798-55-0*) Intl Bk Ctr.

Modern Persian: Elementary Level Glossary. Gernot L. Windfuhr & Ann Arbor. 90p. 1981. 12.00 (*0-916798-57-7*) Intl Bk Ctr.

Modern Persian: Intermediate Level I. Gernot L. Windfuhr & Shapur Bostanbakhsh. 332p. 1980. reprint ed. 30.00 (*0-916798-54-2*) UM Dept NES.

Modern Persian: Intermediate Level II. Gernot L. Windfuhr. 322p. 1980. 20.00 (*0-916798-56-9*) UM Dept NES.

Modern Persian: Intermediate 1. Gernot L. Windfuhr. (PER.). 377p. 1981. pap. 35.00 (*0-86685-756-7*) Intl Bk Ctr.

Modern Persian: Intermediate 2. (PER.). 377p. 1981. pap. 35.00 (*0-86685-763-X*) Intl Bk Ctr.

Modern Persian Drama: An Anthology. Bahram Beyza'i et al. Ed. by Ehsan Yarshater. Tr. by Gisele Kapuscinski. (Modern Persian Literature Ser.: No. 8). 248p. (C). 1987. pap. text 24.00 (*0-8191-6579-4*) U Pr of Amer.

Modern Persian Prose Literature. Hassan Kamshad. LC 96-1869. 1996. pap. 25.00 (*0-936347-72-4*) IBEX.

Modern Persian-Urdu-English Dictionary. F. D. Razi. (ENG, PER & URD.). 250p. 1981. 29.95 (*0-8288-1454-6*, M14111) Fr & Eur.

Modern Personal Radio Systems. Ed. by Raymond C. Macario. LC 96-140440. (I. E. E. Telecommunications Ser.: No. 33). (Illus.). 336p. 1995. boxed set 92.00 (*0-85296-861-2*) INSPEC Inc.

Modern Personnel Management. Sexton Adams & Adelaide Griffin. LC 80-24173. (Illus.). 360p. (Orig.). reprint ed. pap. 111.60 (*0-608-18160-9*, 203285600081) Bks Demand.

Modern Perspectives in Inorganic Crystal Chemistry. Ed. by Erwin Parthe. LC 92-26740. 292p. (C). 1992. text 171.00 (*0-7923-1954-0*) Kluwer Academic.

Modern Perspectives in Many-Body Physics: Proceeding of the Summer School. M. P. Das & J. Mahanty. 456p. 1994. text 116.00 (*981-02-1560-6*) World Scientific Pub.

Modern Perspectives in Otology. Ed. by B. H. Colman & C. R. Pfaltz. (Advances in OtoRhinoLaryngology Ser.: Vol. 31). (Illus.). xii, 252p. 1983. 172.25 (*3-8055-3641-0*) S Karger.

Modern Perspectives in Teaching English As a Foreign Language. M. B. Willmott. 220p. (C). 1988. 130.00 (*1-85122-028-3*, Pub. by Domino Bks Ltd); pap. 90.00 (*1-85122-008-9*, Pub. by Domino Bks Ltd) St Mut.

Modern Perspectives in Western Art History: An Anthology of 20th-Century Writings on the Visual Arts. Ed. by W. Eugene Kleinbauer. 1994. reprint ed. pap. text 24.95 (*0-8020-6708-5*) U of Toronto Pr.

Modern Perspectives in World Psychiatry, Set. Ed. by John G. Howells. (Illus.). 787p. (C). 1971. text 32.00 (*0-8464-1155-5*); text 32.00 (*0-685-00726-X*) Beekman Pubs.

Modern Perspectives in World Psychiatry, Vol. 2. Ed. by John G. Howells. (Illus.). 787p. (C). 1971. 32.00 (*0-8464-1332-9*) Beekman Pubs.

Modern Perspectives in World Psychiatry, Vol. 3. Ed. by John G. Howells. (Illus.). (C). 1971. 32.00 (*0-8464-1333-7*) Beekman Pubs.

Modern Perspectives on B. F. Skinner & Contemporary Behaviorism, 28. Ed. by James T. Todd & Edward K. Morris. LC 94-42729. (Contributions in Psychology Ser.: Vol. 28). 312p. 1995. 69.50 (*0-313-29601-4*, Greenwood Pr) Greenwood.

Modern Perspectives on the Gold Standard. Ed. by Barry J. Eichengreen et al. 413p. 1997. text 64.95 (*0-521-57169-3*) Cambridge U Pr.

Modern Perspectives on Zoonoses: Proceedings of a Seminar Held on 6-7 March 1997 Celia M. Holland. LC 98-131953. xii, 175 p. 1997. pap. write for info. (*1-874045-51-8*) Royal Irish Acad.

Modern Perversity. Lewis Shiner et al. Ed. by Richard Klaw. (Omnibus Ser.). (Illus.). 48p. (Orig.). 1992. pap. 3.25 (*1-883611-05-9*) Blckbird Comics.

Modern Petroleum: A Basic Primer of the Industry. 3rd ed. Bill D. Berger & Kenneth E. Anderson. LC 92-26928. 537p. 1992. 64.95 (*0-87814-386-6*, P4481) PennWell Bks.

*__Modern Petroleum Technology, 2 vols. Set.__ 6th ed. lp. 96p. 2000. text 660.00 (*0-471-98411-6*) Wiley.

Modern Pharmaceutics, No. 72. 3rd ed. Ed. by Gilbert S. Banker & Christopher T. Rhodes. LC 95-33238. (Drugs & the Pharmaceutical Sciences Ser.: Vol. 72). (Illus.). 960p. 1995. text 195.00 (*0-8247-9371-4*) Dekker.

Modern Pharmacology. 2nd ed. Ed. by Charles R. Craig & Robert E. Stitzel. 1115p. (C). 1986. 44.50 (*0-316-15925-5*, Little Brwn Med Div) Lppncott W & W.

Modern Pharmacology. 4th ed. Ed. by Charles R. Craig & Robert E. Stitzel. LC 93-35535. 1994. 49.95 (*0-316-15932-8*, Little Brwn Med Div) Lppncott W & W.

Modern Pharmacology: International. 3rd ed. Craig. 1990. 30.00 (*0-316-15929-8*, Little Brwn Med Div) Lppncott W & W.

Modern Pharmacology with Clinical Applications. 5th ed. Craig. LC 96-23366. 848p. 1997. pap. text 51.95 (*0-316-15934-4*) Lppncott W & W.

Modern Philosophies of Human Nature: Their Emergence from Christian Thought. P. E. Langford. (Martinus Nijhoff Philosophy Library: No. 15). 272p. 1986. lib. bdg. 129.50 (*90-247-3370-7*, Pub. by M Nijhoff) Kluwer Academic.

Modern Philosophies of Human Nature: Their Emergence from Christian Thought. P. E. Langford. (Martinus Nijhoff Philosophy Library: No. 15). 272p. 1986. pap. text 59.00 (*90-247-3371-5*, Pub. by M Nijhoff) Kluwer Academic.

Modern Philosophy. Roger Scruton. 624p. 1996. pap. 15.95 (*0-14-024907-9*) Viking Penguin.

Modern Philosophy. Roger Scruton. 1999. pap. write for info. (*0-670-86312-2*) Viking Penguin.

Modern Philosophy: An Anthology of Primary Sources. Ed. by Roger Ariew & Eric Watkins. LC 98-34866. 968p. (C). 1998. pap. 29.95 (*0-87220-440-5*); lib. bdg. 49.95 (*0-87220-441-3*) Hackett Pub.

Modern Philosophy: An Introduction. A. R. Lacey. 296p. 1982. pap. 10.95 (*0-7100-0974-7*, Routledge Thoemms) Routledge.

Modern Philosophy: Empiricism, Idealism & Pragmatism in Britain & America, Vol. 8. Frederick C. Copleston. 592p. 1994. pap. 17.95 (*0-385-47045-2*) Doubleday.

Modern Philosophy: From Descartes to Leibniz, No. 4. Frederick J. Copleston. 384p. 1993. pap. 17.95 (*0-385-47041-X*) Doubleday.

Modern Philosophy: From the French Revolution to Sartre, Camus & Levi-Strauss, Vol. 9. Frederick C. Copleston. LC 92-34997. Vol. 9. 496p. 1994. pap. 17.95 (*0-385-47046-0*) Doubleday.

Modern Philosophy: From the Post-Kantian Idealists to Marx, Kierkegaard & Nietzsche, Vol. 7. Frederick C. Copleston. 512p. 1994. pap. 17.95 (*0-385-47044-4*) Doubleday.

Modern Philosophy Vol. 5: The British Philosophers from Hobbes to Hume. Frederick J. Copleston. 448p. 1993. pap. 16.95 (*0-385-47042-8*) Doubleday.

Modern Philosophy Vol. 6: From the French Enlightenment to Kant. Frederick J. Copleston. 528p. 1993. pap. 16.95 (*0-385-47043-6*) Doubleday.

Modern Philosophy of History: Its Origin & Destination. M. Murray. 137p. 1970. pap. text 57.00 (*90-247-0110-4*, Pub. by M Nijhoff) Kluwer Academic.

*__Modern Philosophy of Language.__ Maria Baghramian. LC 99-31592. 432p. 1999. text 30.00 (*1-58243-042-X*, Pub. by Counterpt DC) HarpC.

Modern Philosophy of Mind. Ed. by William Lyons. 336p. (Orig.). 1995. pap. 8.50 (*0-460-87558-2*, Everyman's Classic Lib) Tuttle Pubng.

Modern Photographic Processing, Vol. 1. Grant M. Haist. LC 78-17559. (Wiley Series on Photographic Science & Technology & the Graphic Arts). (Illus.). 793p. reprint ed. pap. 200.00 (*0-608-17413-0*, 205644300067) Bks Demand.

Modern Photomicrography. B. Bracegirdle & S. Bradbury. (Microscopy Handbooks Ser.: No. 33). 112p. 1995. pap. 42.50 (*1-85996-090-1*, Pub. by Bios Sci) Coronet Bks.

Modern Phrase Structure Grammar. Robert D. Borsley. (Textbooks in Linguistics Ser.). 300p. (C). 1996. pap. 33.95 (*0-631-18407-4*) Blackwell Pubs.

Modern Physic. Tipler. 2000. teacher ed. 21.80 (*1-57259-793-3*) Worth.

*__Modern Physical & Organic Chemistry.__ Dougherty Anslyn. (Chemistry Ser.). 2001. 77.00 (*0-534-37721-1*) Brooks-Cole.

*__Modern Physical Chemistry: A Molecular Approach.__ George H. Duffey. LC 00-35702. 2000. write for info. (*0-306-46395-4*) Plenum.

Modern Physical Geography. 4th ed. Alan H. Strahler & Arthur N. Strahler. LC 91-27551. 656p. (C). 1991. text 84.95 (*0-471-53392-0*) Wiley.

Modern Physical Geography. 4th ed. Alan H. Strahler et al. 320p. 1992. pap., student ed. 34.95 (*0-471-55103-1*) Wiley.

Modern Physical Geography. 4th ed. Alan H. Strahler et al. 976p. 1993. text, student ed. 71.00 (*0-471-31139-1*) Wiley.

Modern Physical Geology. 2nd ed. Thompson. (C). 1996. pap. text, teacher ed. 28.00 (*0-03-019167-X*); pap. text, student ed. 18.00 (*0-03-018997-7*, Pub. by Harcourt Coll Pubs) Harcourt.

Modern Physical Geology. 2nd ed. Thompson. 1996. 246.00 (*0-03-019184-X*) Harcourt Coll Pubs.

Modern Physical Geology. 2nd ed. Graham R. Thompson. (C). 1996. pap. text, teacher ed. 26.75 (*0-03-019168-8*) Harcourt.

Modern Physical Geology. 2nd ed. Graham R. Thompson. LC 96-68674. (C). 1996. pap. text 66.50 (*0-03-005222-X*, Pub. by Harcourt Coll Pubs) Harcourt.

Modern Physical Geology, Testbank. Thompson. (C). 1991. pap. text, teacher ed., suppl. ed. 40.50 (*0-03-054697-4*, Pub. by Harcourt Coll Pubs) Harcourt.

*__Modern Physical Metallurgy.__ 5th ed. R. E. Smallman & R. J. Bishop. LC 99-38178. 438p. 2000. text 54.95 (*0-7506-4564-4*) Buttrwrth-Heinemann.

Modern Physical Methods in Biochemistry, Pt. A. Ed. by A. Neuberger & L. L. Van Deenen. (New Comprehensive Biochemistry Ser.: Vol. 11). 428p. 1985. 170.75 (*0-444-80649-0*) Elsevier.

Modern Physical Science. Tropp. 1991. pap. text, teacher ed. 84.40 (*0-03-005053-7*) Harcourt.

Modern Physical Science. Tropp. 1991. text 62.25 (*0-03-005052-9*) Holt R&W.

Modern Physical Techniques in Materials Technology. Ed. by T. Mulvey & R. K. Webster. (Harwell Ser.). (Illus.). (C). 1974. text 59.00 (*0-19-851708-4*) OUP.

*__Modern Physics.__ Jeremy Bernstein & Paul M. Fishbane. LC 99-86230. 624p. 2000. 89.33 (*0-13-955311-8*) P-H.

Modern Physics. Blatt. 1992. student ed. 20.62 (*0-07-005878-4*) McGraw.

Modern Physics. Frank J. Blatt. 517p. (C). 1992. 85.63 (*0-07-005877-6*) McGraw.

Modern Physics. Jeff Sanny & William Moebs. 250p. (C). 1996. text. write for info. (*0-697-35972-7*, WCB McGr Hill) McGrw-H Hghr Educ.

Modern Physics. Thornton. (C). 1993. pap. text, student ed. 24.50 (*0-03-097975-7*, Pub. by Harcourt Coll Pubs) Harcourt.

Modern Physics. Stephen T. Thornton. (C). 1993. text 99.00 (*0-03-074966-2*, Pub. by Harcourt Coll Pubs) Harcourt.

Modern Physics. Trinklein. 1991. 97.75 (*0-03-021904-3*) Harcourt Schl Pubs.

Modern Physics. Trinklein. 1992. text 64.00 (*0-03-074317-6*) Holt R&W.

Modern Physics. Frederick E. Trinklein. 1990. text, student ed. 64.00 (*0-03-014514-7*) Holt R&W.

Modern Physics. Williams. 1984. text 64.25 (*0-03-061936-X*); pap. text, teacher ed. 88.50 (*0-03-061937-8*) Holt R&W.

Modern Physics. 2nd ed. Kenneth S. Krane. LC 95-6382. 608p. 1995. text 100.95 (*0-471-82872-6*) Wiley.

Modern Physics. 2nd ed. Hans C. Ohanian. LC 94-38687. 576p. (C). 1995. 66.00 (*0-13-124439-6*) P-H.

Modern Physics. 2nd ed. Serway. (C). 1996. 94.50 (*0-03-019682-5*) Harcourt.

Modern Physics. 2nd ed. Serway. (C). 1997. pap. text, teacher ed. 12.00 (*0-03-001548-0*) Harcourt Coll Pubs.

Modern Physics. 2nd ed. Raymond A. Serway. (C). 1996. text 92.50 (*0-03-001547-2*) Harcourt.

Modern Physics. 2nd ed. Paul A. Tipler. LC 77-58725. 502p. 1977. text 56.00 (*0-87901-088-6*) Worth.

Modern Physics. 3rd ed. Tipler. LC 98-46099. 2000. write for info. (*1-57259-164-1*) Worth.

*__Modern Physics.__ 3rd ed. Tipler & Llewellyn. 1999. pap. text, student ed. 24.95 (*1-57259-792-5*) Worth.

Modern Physics. 90th ed. Trinklein. 1990. pap. text, teacher ed. 88.50 (*0-03-014517-1*) Holt R&W.

Modern Physics: And Other Tales. Purnell Christian. 272p. 1991. 19.50 (*0-922820-16-3*) Watermark Pr.

Modern Physics: Solutions Manual. 3rd ed. Wolfson. 400p. (C). 1999. pap. text, student ed. 31.00 (*0-321-03575-5*) Addison-Wesley Educ.

Modern Physics: The Quantum Physics of Atoms, Solids, & Nuclei. 3rd ed. Robert L. Sproull & W. Andrew Phillips. 696p. (C). 1990. reprint ed. lib. bdg. 43.50 (*0-89464-420-3*) Krieger.

Modern Physics & Anti-Physics. Adolph Baker. LC 74-109506. (C). 1970. pap. text 23.16 (*0-201-00485-2*) Addison-Wesley.

Modern Physics & Its Philosophy: Selected Papers in the Logic, History & Philosophy of Physics. M. Strauss. LC 71-183369. (Synthese Library: No. 43). (Illus.). 307p. 1972. text 135.00 (*90-277-0230-6*, D Reidel) Kluwer Academic.

*__Modern Physics Expanded: Physics for Scientists & Engineers.__ 3rd ed. Wolfson. 1999. 126.56 (*0-201-39008-6*) Benjamin-Cummings.

Modern Physics for Engineers. Jasprit Singh. LC 98-48448. 400p. 1999. 84.95 (*0-471-33044-2*) Wiley.

Modern Physics for Engineers. Otto Oldenberg & Norman C. Rasmussen. (Illus.). 489p. (C). 1992. reprint ed. text 81.00 (*1-878907-47-6*) TechBooks.

Modern Physics for Science & Engineering. Marshall L. Burns. 578p. (C). 1988. teacher ed. 20.00 (*0-15-562352-4*) Harcourt Coll Pubs.

Modern Physics for Scientists & Engineers. John Taylor & Chris Zafaritos. 768p. 1991. 90.00 (*0-13-589789-0*, 530301) P-H.

Modern Physics for Scientists & Engineers. 2nd ed. Stephen T. Thornton & Andrew F. Rex. LC 99-22847. 640p. (C). 1999. text 66.00 (*0-03-006049-4*, Pub. by SCP) Harcourt.

Modern Physics from A to Z. James W. Rohlf. 664p. 1994. text 93.95 (*0-471-57270-5*) Wiley.

Modern Physics in America - A Michels-Morley Centennial Symposium. Ed. by William Fickinger & Kenneth L. Kowalski. LC 88-71348. (AIP Conference Proceedings Ser.: No. 169). 288p. 1988. lib. bdg. 55.00 (*0-88318-369-2*) Am Inst Physics.

Modern Physics, 1992. Trinklein. 1992. text, teacher ed. 86.00 (*0-03-074318-4*) Holt R&W.

Modern Physics of Soils for Students. Hillel. 300p. 1997. write for info. (*0-12-348528-2*) Acad Pr.

Modern Physics-1331. UNT, Physics Department Staff. 1996. pap. text 21.39 (*1-56870-237-X*) RonJon Pub.

Modern Physics Scientists & Engineers, Vol. II. Lawrence Lerner. (Physics Ser.). 240p. (C). 1996. pap. 33.75 (*0-86720-487-7*) Jones & Bartlett.

Modern Physics Simulations: The Consortium for Upper Level Physics Software. Douglas Brandt et al. LC 95-35661. 192p. 1995. pap. text 46.95 incl. disk (*0-471-54882-0*) Wiley.

Modern Physics with Quantum Mechanics. Bush. (C). 1999. text 81.00 (*0-03-047173-7*) Harcourt Coll Pubs.

Modern Phytochemical Methods. N. H. Fischer et al. (Recent Advances in Phytochemistry Ser.: Vol. 25). (Illus.). 418p. (C). 1991. text 120.00 (*0-306-43925-5*, Kluwer Plenum) Kluwer Academic.

Modern Pioneer: One Woman's Ministry. Violet A. Kochendoerfer. LC 97-109268. 256p. (Orig.). 1996. pap. 14.00 (*1-55896-346-4*, 5322, Skinner Hse Bks) Unitarian Univ.

Modern Pioneer in Korea: The Life Story of Henry G. Appenzeller. William E. Griffis. (Notable American Authors Ser.). 1992. reprint ed. lib. bdg. 75.00 (*0-7812-2968-5*) Rprt Serv.

Modern Pioneers of the Amargosa Valley. Robert D. McCracken. (Illus.). 112p. (Orig.). 1996. pap. 12.95 (*1-878138-58-8*) Nye Cty Pr.

Modern Placer Mining. M. J. Richardson. LC 92-90054. (Illus.). 315p. 1992. text 30.00 (*0-9665413-0-8*) Consol Placer.

Modern Planktonic Foraminifera. C. Hemieben et al. (Illus.). 370p. 1988. 214.95 (*0-387-96815-6*) Spr-Verlag.

Modern Plantation Agriculture: Corporate Wealth & Labour Squalor. Rene Loewenson. 208p. (C). 1992. text 62.50 (*0-86232-996-5*, Pub. by St Martin); text 22.50 (*0-86232-997-3*, Pub. by St Martin) St Martin.

*__Modern Plastics Handbook.__ Modern Plastics Magazine Staff. LC 99-56522. 1298p. 2000. 125.00 (*0-07-026714-6*) McGraw.

Modern Plays, Short & Long. Ed. by Frederick H. Law. (Play Anthology Reprint Ser.). 1977. reprint ed. 29.95 (*0-8369-8250-9*) Ayer.

Modern Playwrights at Work, Vol. 1. J. William Miller. 1968. 12.00 (*0-573-69018-9*) French.

Modern Plumbing. E. Keith Blankenbaker. LC 96-19156. 384p. 1997. 39.96 (*1-56637-345-X*) Goodheart.

Modern Pluralism, Vol. 1. Academy Staff. 1992. pap. 21.95 (*0-312-07539-1*) St Martin.

Modern Pocket Dictionaries: Arabic-English. Munir Ba'Albaki. 464p. 1996. pap. 6.95 (*0-86685-752-4*) Intl Bk Ctr.

Modern Poems: An Introduction to Poetry. 2nd ed. Ed. by Richard Ellmann et al. 935p. (C). 1989. pap. text 46.00 (*0-393-95907-4*) Norton.

Modern Poems from Bengal. Surabhi Banerjee. 1996. pap. 12.00 (*81-7476-089-X*, Pub. by UBS Pubs Dist) S Asia.

Modern Poems from Russia. Tr. by Gerard Shelley. LC 77-9362. (Illus.). 93p. 1977. reprint ed. lib. bdg. 49.50 (*0-8371-9708-2*, SHMP, Greenwood Pr) Greenwood.

Modern Poems on the Bible. Curzon. 1997. pap. 13.00 (*0-15-600541-7*) Harcourt.

Modern Poems on the Bible. David Curzon. 1997. pap. text 14.00 (*0-15-600526-3*, Harvest Bks) Harcourt.

Modern Poems on the Bible: An Anthology. Intro. by David Curzon. 416p. 1994. 17.50 (*0-8276-0449-1*) JPS Phila.

Modern Poetic Drama. Priscilla Thouless. LC 68-26481. (Essay Index Reprint Ser.). 1977. reprint ed. 19.95 (*0-8369-0942-9*) Ayer.

Modern Poetry. Charles F. Altieri. LC 76-4656. (Goldentree Bibliographies Series in Language & Literature). (C). 1980. pap. text 14.95 (*0-88295-550-0*) Harlan Davidson.

Modern Poetry: A Personal Essay. Louis MacNeice. LC 77-95439. (Studies in Poetry: No. 38). (C). 1969. reprint ed. lib. bdg. 75.00 (*0-8383-0992-5*) M S G Haskell Hse.

Modern Poetry: Studies in Practical Criticism. C. B. Cox & Dyson Cox. 1988. reprint ed. lib. bdg. 49.00 (*0-7812-0131-4*) Rprt Serv.

Modern Poetry: Studies in Practical Criticism. C. B. Cox & A. E. Dyson. LC 78-158904. 1971. reprint ed. 45.00 (*0-403-01306-2*) Scholarly.

Modern Poetry after Modernism. James Longenbach. LC 96-45288. 224p. 1997. text 49.95 (*0-19-510177-4*); pap. text 19.95 (*0-19-510178-2*) OUP.

Modern Poetry for Children, Bk. 8. Ed. by James J. Reynolds. LC 30-10164. (Granger Poetry Library). (J). (gr. 4). 1979. reprint ed. 20.00 (*0-89609-167-8*) Roth Pub Inc.

Modern Poets, Vol. 7. pap. 13.95 (*0-14-058744-6*, Pub. by Pnguin Bks Ltd) Trafalgar.

Modern Poets of France: With English Translations. Tr. by Louis Simpson from FRE. LC 97-16001. (ENG & FRE.). 360p. 1997. pap. 16.95 (*1-885266-44-8*) Story Line.

Modern Polargraphic Methods in Analytical Chemistry. Bond. (Monographs in Electroanalytical Chemistry & Electrochemistry: Vol.4). (Illus.). 536p. 1980. text 225.00 (*0-8247-6849-3*) Dekker.

*__Modern Pole Vaulting: Analyzing the Superior "Russian" Style & Adapting It to American Vaulting.__ Brian Ferry. (Illus.). 106p. 1998. pap. 15.00 (*0-911521-54-2*) Tafnews.

Modern Police Administration. Ed. by Donald O. Schultz. LC 78-67436. 184p. reprint ed. pap. 57.10 (*0-608-18154-4*, 203284500081) Bks Demand.

Modern Police Management. Richard N. Holden. (Illus.). 352p. 1986. text 41.60 (*0-13-596859-3*) P-H.

Modern Police Management. 2nd ed. 380p. (C). 1994. 90.00 (*0-13-089068-5*) P-H.

Modern Police Management. 2nd ed. Richard N. Holden. LC 93-31193. 380p. (C). 1993. 90.00 (*0-13-097718-7*) P-H.

Modern Police Motorcycles in Action. Robert Genat. LC 98-46893. (Enthusiast Color Ser.). (Illus.). 96p. 1999. pap. 14.95 (*0-7603-0522-6*, Pub. by MBI Pubg) Motorbooks Intl.

Modern Policing. Ed. by Michael H. Tonry & Norval Morris. (Studies in Crime & Justice: Vol. 15). 512p. 1992. lib. bdg. 46.00 (*0-226-80813-0*) U Ch Pr.

Modern Policing Vol. 15: Crime & Justice. Ed. by Michael H. Tonry & Norval Morris. (Studies in Crime & Justice: A Biannual Review of Research Ser.). 616p. (C). 1993. pap. text 27.50 (*0-226-80814-9*) U Ch Pr.

Modern Policing & the Control of Illegal Drugs: Testing New Strategies in Two American Cities. Craig D. Uchida et al. (Illus.). 61p. (Orig.). (C). 1992. pap. text 25.00 (*1-56806-091-2*) DIANE Pub.

Modern Political Analysis. 5th ed. Robert A. Dahl. 176p. (C). 1990. pap. text 34.67 (*0-13-595406-1*, Pub. by P-H) S&S Trade.

Modern Political Campaign: Mudslinging, Bombast, & the Vitality of American Politics. Richard K. Scher. LC 97-5896. 220p. (C). (gr. 13). 1997. text 57.95 (*1-56324-860-3*); pap. text 19.95 (*1-56324-861-1*) M E Sharpe.

Modern Political Economy: Old Topics, New Directions. Ed. by Jeffrey S. Banks & Eric A. Hanushek. (Political Economy of Institutions & Decisions Ser.). (Illus.). 283p. (C). 1995. text 64.95 (*0-521-47233-4*); pap. text 19.95 (*0-521-47810-3*) Cambridge U Pr.

Modern Political Economy & Latin America. Frieden & Pastor. 368p. 2000. pap. 94.50 (*0-8133-2417-3*, Pub. by Westview); pap. 35.00 (*0-8133-2418-1*, Pub. by Westview) HarpC.

Modern Political Ideologies. 2nd ed. Andrew Vincent. 352p. (C). 1995. pap. 29.95 (*0-631-19507-6*) Blackwell Pubs.

Modern Political Philosophy. Richard Hudelson. LC 98-56178. (Explorations in Philosophy Ser.). 192p. 1999. pap. text 25.95 (*0-7656-0022-6*) M E Sharpe.

***Modern Political Philosophy.** Richard Hudelson. LC 98-56178. (Explorations in Philosophy Ser.). 192p. 1999. text 59.95 (*0-7656-0021-8*) M E Sharpe.

Modern Political Systems: Europe. 7th ed. Roy C. Macridis. 528p. (C). 1990. text 48.00 (*0-13-595356-1*) P-H.

***Modern Political Theory.** S. P. Varma. 1999. pap. 10.00 (*0-7069-8682-2*, Pub. by Vikas) S Asia.

Modern Political Theory & Contemporary Feminism: A Dialectical Analysis. Jennifer Ring. LC 90-46118. (SUNY Series in Feminist Political Theory). 229p. (C). 1991. text 21.50 (*0-7914-0753-5*) State U NY Pr.

Modern Political Theory from Hobbes to Marx: Key Debates. Jack Lively & Andrew Reeve. 320p. 1989. pap. 14.95 (*0-415-01351-8*) Routledge.

Modern Political Thought: An Introduction to Political Philosophy. Raymond Plant. 352p. 1991. pap. 28.95 (*0-631-14224-X*) Blackwell Pubs.

***Modern Political Thought: Reader.** Ed. by John Gingell et al. LC 99-37892. 304p. (C). 2000. text 90.00 (*0-415-19461-X*) Routledge.

***Modern Political Thought: Reader.** John Gingell et al. LC 99-37892. 304p. 2000. pap. 27.99 (*0-415-19462-8*) Routledge.

Modern Political Thought: Readings from Machiavelli to Nietzsche. Ed. by David Wootton. LC 96-30452. 960p. (Orig.). (C). 1996. pap. text 29.95 (*0-87220-341-7*); lib. bdg. 49.95 (*0-87220-342-5*) Hackett Pub.

Modern Politics. 2nd ed. C. L. R. James. (Illus.). iv, 167p. 1973. reprint ed. pap. 12.00 (*0-935590-09-9*) Bewick Edns.

Modern Politics & Government. 5th ed. Alan R. Ball. LC 94-3063. 288p. (C). 1994. pap. text 19.95 (*1-56643-002-X*, Chatham House Pub) Seven Bridges.

Modern Politics & Government. 6th ed. Alan R. Ball & B. Guy Peters. LC 99-51531. (Illus.). 320p. (C). 2000. pap. text 27.95 (*1-889119-07-5*, Chatham House Pub) Seven Bridges.

Modern Polymer Spectroscopy. G. Zerbi. LC 99-202874. 304p. 1999. 210.00 (*3-527-29655-7*) Wiley.

Modern Portfolio & Investment Selection. 2nd ed. Levy & Sabnat. (FN - Financial Management Ser.). 2002. mass mkt. 74.95 (*0-538-86601-2*) S-W Pub.

Modern Portfolio Theory. John O'Brien & Sanjay Srivastava. 1994. write for info. (*0-538-84809-X*) S-W Pub.

Modern Portfolio Theory: Guide & Exercise. 2nd ed. O'Brien. (FD - Investments Ser.). pap. 27.95 (*0-538-87487-2*) S-W Pub.

Modern Portfolio Theory: The Principles of Investment Management. Andrew Rudd & Henry J. Clasing, Jr. 525p. 1988. pap. 50.00 (*0-9620194-0-2*) A Rudd.

Modern Portfolio Theory & Investment Analysis. Edwin J. Elton & Martin J. Gruber. 1995. pap. text 52.95 (*0-471-05576-X*) Wiley.

Modern Portfolio Theory & Investment Analysis. 3rd ed. Edwin J. Elton & Martin J. Gruber. 645p. 1987. pap. text 10.00 (*0-471-85676-2*) Wiley.

***Modern Portfolio Theory & Investment Analysis & Investment Portfolio Software.** 5th ed. Edwin J. Elton. 1998. pap. text 88.00 incl. disk (*0-471-31582-6*) Wiley.

Modern Portugal. Ed. by Antonio Costa Pinto. LC 97-45654. 332p. 1998. 39.50 (*0-930664-17-5*) SPOSS.

Modern Portuguese. Fred P. Ellison et al. (C). 1970. text 64.25 (*0-07-553561-0*) McGraw.

Modern Portuguese. Fred P. Ellison et al. LC 70-111970. (C). 1988. text 265.00 incl. audio (*0-07-553551-3*) McGraw.

Modern Postal Masterpieces. Alex Dunne. Ed. by Robert B. Long. (Illus.). 141p. 1994. pap. 16.95 (*0-938650-70-X*) Thinkers Pr.

Modern Postmodern: Off the Beaten Path of Antimodernism. Eric M. Kramer. LC 96-41392. 256p. 1997. 59.95 (*0-275-95758-6*, Praeger Pubs) Greenwood.

Modern Poverty: The Culture of Distribution & Structural Unemployment in the Foothills of Kerala. Peter Van der Werff. (C). 1992. 20.00 (*81-85425-61-2*, Pub. by Manohar) S Asia.

Modern Powder Diffraction. D. L. Bish & J. E. Post. (Reviews in Mineralogy Ser.: Vol. 20). 384p. 1989. per. 28.00 (*0-939950-24-3*) Mineralogical Soc.

Modern Power Devices. B. Jayant Baliga. LC 92-29624. 496p. (C). 1992. reprint ed. lib. bdg. 67.50 (*0-89464-799-7*) Krieger.

Modern Power Electronics: Evolution, Technology, & Applications. Ed. by B. K. Bose. LC 91-39029. (Illus.). 608p. (C). 1991. text 79.95 (*0-87942-282-3*, PC0276-6) Inst Electrical.

Modern Power Mechanics. Gary E. Grannis. LC 78-12106. 1979. write for info. (*0-672-97130-5*); teacher ed. write for info. (*0-672-97131-3*); pap., student ed. write for info. (*0-672-97132-1*) Macmillan.

Modern Power Station Practice, 8 vols. Central Electricity Generating Board Staff. Incl. Nuclear Power Generation., **8 vols.** 2nd ed. 1971. 480.00 (*0-08-016436-6*); Vol. 1. Planning & Layout. 1971. 76.00 (*0-08-006454-X*); Vol. 2. Mechanical (Boilers Fuel & Ash-Handling Plant) 1971. 68.00 (*0-08-016060-3*); Vol. 3. Mechanical (Turbines & Auxiliary Equipment) 1971. 58.00 (*0-08-006606-2*); Vol. 4. Electrical (Generator & Electrical Plant) 1971. 76.00 (*0-08-016061-1*); Vol. 5. Chemistry & Metallurgy. 1971. 76.00 (*0-08-015568-5*); Vol. 6. Instrumentation Controls & Testing. 1971. 90.00 (*0-08-006872-3*); Vol. 7. Operation & Efficiency. 1971. 90.00 (*0-08-016062-X*); Vol. 8. Nuclear Power Generation. 1971. 58.00 (*0-08-006871-5*); 1971. write for info. (*0-318-55182-9*) Elsevier.

Modern Power Station Practice, 12 vols. 3rd ed. Incl. Vol. L. System Operation. 3rd ed. Ed. by E. A. Wallis. 466p. 1993. pap. 114.25 (*0-08-042251-9*); Vol. C. Turbines, Generators & Associated Plant. 3rd ed. Ed. by P. Hambling. 594p. 1993. pap. 147.00 (*0-08-042243-8*); Vol. D. Electrical Systems & Equipment. 3rd ed. Ed. by F. Beach. 1033p. 1993. pap. 197.75 (*0-08-042244-6*); Vol. M. Index. 3rd ed. 295p. 1993. pap. 73.00 (*0-08-042252-7*); Vol. A. Station Planning & Design. 3rd ed. Ed. by P. C. Martin & I. W. Hannah. 331p. 1993. pap. 84.75 (*0-08-042241-1*); Vol. B. Boilers & Ancillary Plants. 3rd ed. Ed. by R. M. Clapp. 197p. 1993. pap. 73.00 (*0-08-042242-X*); Vol. E. Chemistry & Metallurgy. 3rd ed. Ed. by J. Brown. 589p. 1993. pap. 147.00 (*0-08-042245-4*); Vol. F. Control & Instrumentation. 3rd ed. Ed. by M. W. Jervis. 520p. 1993. pap. 137.25 (*0-08-042246-2*); Vol. G. Station Operation & Maintenance. 3rd ed. Ed. by L. C. White. 659p. 1993. pap. 157.00 (*0-08-042247-0*); Vol. H. Station Commissioning. 3rd ed. Ed. by F. Kirkby. 706p. 1993. pap. 181.50 (*0-08-042248-9*); Vol. J. Nuclear Power Generation. 3rd ed. Ed. by P. B. Myerscough. 606p. 1993. pap. 147.00 (*0-08-042249-7*); Vol. K. EHV Tranmission. 3rd ed. Ed. by M. G. Dwek. 586p. 1993. pap. 147.00 (*0-08-042250-0*); (Illus.). 6500p. 1993. Set pap. 1523.50 (*0-08-042240-3*, Pergamon Pr) Elsevier.

Modern Power Station Practice: Incorporating Modern Power System Practice, 12 vols. Ed. by British Electricity International Staff. LC 90-43748. (British Electricity International Ser.). (Illus.). 6500p. 1992. 1350.00 (*0-08-040746-3*, Pergamon Pr); 1503.50 (*0-08-040747-1*, Pergamon Pr) Elsevier.

Modern Power Station Practice: Incorporating Modern Power System Practice, 12 vols. 3rd ed. Ed. by British Electricity International Staff. LC 90-43748. (British Electricity International Ser.). (Illus.). 6500p. 1992. 2570.50 (*0-08-040510-X*, Pergamon Pr) Elsevier.

Modern Power Supply & Battery Charger Circuit Encyclopedia. Rudolf F. Graf. 144p. 1992. pap. 10.95 (*0-8306-3923-3*, 3889) McGraw-Hill Prof.

Modern Practical Ballistics. Arthur J. Pejsa. LC 88-84150. (Illus.). 200p. 1989. 19.95 (*0-9612776-1-0*) Kenwood Pub.

Modern Practical Ballistics. 2nd ed. Arthur J. Pejsa. LC 88-84150. (Illus.). 224p. (C). 1991. pap. 19.95 (*0-9612776-3-7*) Kenwood Pub.

Modern Practical Joinery. George Ellis. LC 87-22844. (Illus.). 576p. 1987. reprint ed. pap. 21.95 (*0-941936-08-2*) Linden Pub Fresno.

Modern Practical Prescriptions of Acupuncture & Moxibustion. Xiaoping Ji. Tr. by Maoxin Chen & Shuting Li. (Illus.). 297p. 1996. pap. 29.50 (*1-880132-22-2*) Sci Pr NY.

Modern Practical Stairbuilding & Handrailing. George Ellis. LC 89-14540. (Illus.). 274p. 1999. reprint ed. pap. 25.95 (*0-941936-15-5*) Linden Pub Fresno.

Modern Practice in Stress & Vibration Analysis. Ed. by J. E. Mottershead. (Proceedings of Conference, University of Liverpool, 3-5 April 1989 Ser.). 350p. 1989. pap. 40.00 (*0-08-037523-5*, Pub. by Pergamon Repr) Franklin.

Modern Practice in Stress & Vibration Analysis: Proceedings of the Third International Conference, Dublin, 3-5 September 1997. Ed. by M. D. Gilchrist. LC 99-496408. (Illus.). 598p. (C). 1997. text 162.00 (*90-5410-896-7*, Pub. by A A Balkema) Ashgate Pub Co.

Modern Practice of Adult Education: A Postmodern Critique. Derek Briton. LC 95-38597. (SUNY Series, Teacher Empowerment & School Reform). 156p. (C). 1996. text 44.50 (*0-7914-3025-1*); pap. text 16.95 (*0-7914-3026-X*) State U NY Pr.

Modern Practice of Adult Education: From Pedagogy to Andragogy. rev. ed. Malcolm S. Knowles. 400p. 1988. text 35.00 (*0-8428-2213-5*) Cambridge Bk.

Modern Practice of Community Mental Health. Ed. by Herbert C. Schulberg & Marie Killilea. LC 82-48066. 736p. reprint ed. pap. 200.00 (*0-7837-6529-0*, 204564100007) Bks Demand.

Modern Practice of Gas Chromatography. 3rd ed. Ed. by Robert L. Grob. LC 94-23516. 912p. 1995. 98.50 (*0-471-59700-7*) Wiley.

Modern Prayer Guide to St. Teresa of Avila - Interior Castle. Barbara Benjamin. LC 91-73654. 52p. 1991. pap. 4.95 (*1-880178-00-1*) Intuitive Discov.

Modern Preacher & the Ancient Text: Interpreting & Preaching Biblical Literature. Sidney Greidanus. 1989. pap. 20.00 (*0-8028-0360-1*) Eerdmans.

Modern Presenters Handbook. Jim Macnamara. 144p. (C). 1996. pap. text 14.95 (*0-13-842154-4*) P-H.

Modern Presidency. Ed. by Nelson W. Polsby. LC 81-40776. 250p. 1981. reprint ed. pap. text 24.00 (*0-8191-1822-2*) U Pr of Amer.

Modern Presidency. 2nd ed. Pfiffuer. LC 97-80009. 256p. 1997. pap. text 21.95 (*0-312-17804-2*) St Martin.

***Modern Presidency.** 3rd ed. Piffner. 1999. pap. text 21.95 (*0-312-20859-6*) St Martin.

Modern Presidency & Crisis Rhetoric. Ed. by Amos Kiewe. LC 92-37528. (Political Communication Ser.). 288p. 1993. 62.95 (*0-275-94176-0*, C4176, Praeger Pubs) Greenwood.

***Modern Presidential Electioneering: An Organizational & Comparative Approach.** Jody C. Baumgartner. LC 99-55884. 248p. 2000. 65.00 (*0-275-96760-3*, Praeger Pubs) Greenwood.

Modern Prestressed Concrete Design. G. S. Ramaswamy. (Illus.). 1976. pap. 29.95 (*0-8464-0639-X*); pap. 29.95 (*0-686-77190-7*) Beekman Pubs.

Modern Priest Looks at His Outdated Church. 25th anniversary ed. James Kavanaugh. LC 92-80924. 208p. (Orig.). 1967. reprint ed. pap. 14.95 (*1-878995-16-2*) S J Nash Pub.

Modern Priestess of Isis. Vsevolod S. Solovyoff. Tr. by Walter Leaf. LC 75-36921. (Occult Ser.). 1976. reprint ed. 29.95 (*0-405-07976-1*) Ayer.

Modern Primitive Arts of Mexico, Guatemala & the Southwest. Catharine Oglesby. LC 75-90670. (Essay Index Reprint Ser.). 1977. 18.95 (*0-8369-1215-2*) Ayer.

***Modern Primitives: Race & Language in Gertrude Stein, Ernest Hemingway & Zora Neale Hurston.** Susanna Pavloska. (Literary Criticism & Cultural Theory Ser.). 200p. 2000. 55.00 (*0-8153-3650-0*) Garland.

Modern Primitives: RE/Search #12. Ed. by Vale Vale. (RE Search Ser.: Vol. 12). (Illus.). 212p. (Orig.). 1989. pap. 17.99 (*0-9650469-3-1*) RE Search.

Modern Prince & Other Writings. Antonio Gramsci. LC 67-25646. 192p. 1959. pap. text 4.95 (*0-7178-0133-0*) Intl Pubs Co.

Modern Principles of Equity. A. K. Kludze. (Law Ser.). v, 482p. (Orig.). 1988. bds. 147.70 (*3-11-013314-8*) Mouton.

Modern Principles of Equity. A. K. Kludze. (Law Ser.). v, 482p. (Orig.). 1988. pap. 129.25 (*90-6765-147-8*) Mouton.

Modern Probability Theory & Its Applications. Emanuel Parzen. LC 91-42308. (Classics Library: No. 1826). 480p. 1992. pap. 115.00 (*0-471-57278-0*) Wiley.

Modern Probate of Wills: Containing an Analysis of the Modern Law of Probate in England & America, with Numerous References to the English & American Cases, & Copious Extracts from the Leading Cases. xx, 578p. 1994. reprint ed. 57.50 (*0-8377-2448-1*, Rothman) W S Hein.

Modern Problems - Mathematical Physics - Comp. Math. 1993. write for info. (*0-8493-7725-0*) CRC Pr.

Modern Problems-Computational Aerohydrodynamics. Anatoly A. Dorodnicyn & Pavel I. Chushkin. 1991. 110.00 (*0-8493-7533-9*, Q) CRC Pr.

Modern Problems in Gear Testing & a Proposed Testing Machine. W. Lewis. (Technical Papers: Vol. P70). (Illus.). 8p. 1923. pap. text 30.00 (*1-55589-438-0*) AGMA.

Modern Problems in Radar Target Imaging. Wolfgang M. Boerner. LC 94-8274. (Wave Phenomena Ser.: Vol. 13). 1994. 131.95 (*0-387-57791-2*) Spr-Verlag.

***Modern Problems of Electrostatics with Applications in Environment Protection.** Ion I. Inculet et al. LC 99-40890. (NATO Science Ser.: No. 2). 1999. write for info. (*0-7923-5929-1*) Kluwer Academic.

Modern Problems of Theoretical Physics. Ed. by P. I. Pronin & Yu N. Obukhov. 360p. (C). 1991. text 101.00 (*981-02-0259-8*) World Scientific Pub.

Modern Process Thought: A Brief Ideological History. James R. Gray. LC 81-43672. 272p. (C). 1982. pap. text 23.00 (*0-8191-2311-0*) U Pr of Amer.

Modern Production among Backward Peoples. Ida C. Greaves. LC 68-9759. (Reprints of Economic Classics Ser.). 229p. 1968. reprint ed. 35.00 (*0-678-00419-6*) Kelley.

Modern Production Concepts: Theory & Applications: Proceedings of an International Conference, Fernuniversitat Hagen, FRG, August 20-24, 1990. Ed. by Gunter U. Fandel & G. Zapfel. (Illus.). 756p. 1991. 196.95 (*0-387-53643-4*) Spr-Verlag.

Modern Production Management: A Japanese Experience. Eiji Ogawa. 132p. 1984. 21.70 (*92-833-1071-3*) Productivity Inc.

Modern Production-Operations Management. 8th ed. Elwood S. Buffa & Rakesh K. Sarin. (Production-Operations Management Ser.). 834p. 1987. text 83.95 (*0-471-81905-0*) Wiley.

Modern Products Liability Law. Richard A. Epstein. LC 80-11486. (Quorum Ser.). 210p. 1980. 57.95 (*0-89930-002-2*, EPL/, Quorum Bks) Greenwood.

Modern Programming: FORTRAN IV. Henry Mullish. LC 68-3217. 144p. reprint ed. pap. 44.70 (*0-608-30968-0*, 201259100082) Bks Demand.

Modern Project Management Techniques for the Environment Remediation Industry. Timothy J. Havranek. LC 99-172622. 456p. 1998. boxed set 54.95 (*1-57444-218-X*, SL218X) St Lucie Pr.

Modern Project to Rigor: Descartes to Nietzsche. Patrick Madigan. LC 85-22564. (Illus.). 224p. (Orig.). (C). 1986. lib. bdg. 49.50 (*0-8191-5080-0*) U Pr of Amer.

Modern Promethean: A Dialogue with Today's Youth. Maurice Friedman. LC 73-104050. (Orig.). 1969. pap. 1.00 (*0-87574-168-1*) Pendle Hill.

Modern Propeller & Duct Design. Martin Hollmann. (Illus.). 111p. 1993. pap. text 59.00 (*1-893639-05-3*) Air Designs.

Modern Property Law, Teacher's Manual to Accompany Cases & Materials on Modern Property Law. 3rd ed. Jon W. Bruce & James W. Ely, Jr. (American Casebook Ser.). 179p. pap. text. write for info. (*0-314-04144-3*) West Pub.

M

Modern Prophet Answers Your Key Questions about Life. Harold Klemp. LC 98-24225. (Illus.). 278p. 1998. pap. 14.00 (*1-57043-143-4*) Eckankar.

Modern Prophetic Voices: From Kierkegaard to Buchman. R. C. Mowat. (Orig.). 1994. pap. 12.95 (*0-9517695-6-1*, Pub. by New Cherwell); pap. 12.95 (*0-9517695-4-5*, Pub. by New Cherwell) Intl Spec Bk.

Modern Proportionality Law for Science, Medicine, & Engineering Applications: A Graphical Description of the Law of Nature. Ralph W. Lai et al. (Illus.). 368p. (C). 1995. text 85.00 (*0-9628526-2-7*) Toshi Co.

Modern Prose Style. 2nd ed. Bonamy Dobree. LC 77-25320. 306p. 1978. reprint ed. lib. bdg. 55.00 (*0-313-20124-2*, DOMP, Greenwood Pr) Greenwood.

Modern Proverbs. Michael G. Williams. 176p. 1990. 12.98 (*0-88290-408-6*) Horizon Utah.

Modern Proverbs & Proverbial Sayings. Bartlett J. Whiting. LC 89-31520. 752p. 1989. text 58.50 (*0-674-58053-2*) HUP.

Modern Psychic Mysteries. G. Hack. 1972. 59.95 (*0-8490-0651-1*) Gordon Pr.

Modern Psychoanalysis: New Directions & Perspectives. Ed. by Judd Marmor. LC 95-16725. 752p. 1995. pap. 44.95 (*1-56000-825-3*) Transaction Pubs.

Modern Psychoanalysis of the Schizophrenic Patient. 2nd ed. Hyman Spotnitz. LC 97-48634. 344p. 1997. pap. 50.00 (*0-7657-0157-X*) Aronson.

Modern Psychoanalytic Concepts in a General Psychology Pts. 1 & 2: Including General Concepts & Principles & Motivation. Allan Rosenblatt & James Thickstrun. LC 77-14712. (Psychological Issues Monographs: Nos. 42 & 43). 348p. 1978. text 52.50 (*0-8236-3430-2*) Intl Univs Pr.

Modern Psychology. Philip L. Harriman. (Quality Paperback Ser.: No. 20). 316p. (Orig.). 1975. reprint ed. pap. 14.00 (*0-8226-0020-X*) Littlefield.

Modern Psychometrics: The Science of Psychological Assessment. John Rust & Susan Golombok. (International Library of Psychology). 192p. 1989. 49.95 (*0-415-03058-7*) Routledge.

***Modern Psychometrics: The Science of Psychological Assessment.** 2nd ed. John Rust. LC 98-47962. (International Library of Psychology). 1999. write for info. (*0-415-20340-6*) Routledge.

Modern Psychometrics: The Science of Psychological Assessment. 2nd ed. John Rust & Susan Golombok. LC 98-47962. 1999. pap. write for info. (*0-415-20341-4*) Routledge.

Modern Psychotherapies: A Comprehensive Christian Appraisal. Stanton L. Jones & Richard E. Butman. LC 91-10470. 425p. 1991. 29.99 (*0-8308-1775-1*, 1775) InterVarsity.

Modern Public Economics. Raghbendra Jha. LC 97-21651. 576p. (C). 1998. 110.00 (*0-415-14314-4*); pap. 32.99 (*0-415-14315-2*) Routledge.

Modern Public Finance, 2 vols. Ed. by Anthony B. Atkinson. (International Library of Critical Writings in Economics: No. 15). 880p. 1991. text 360.00 (*1-85278-153-X*) E Elgar.

***Modern Public Finance.** John M. Quigley. 128p. 2000. pap. 18.95 (*0-674-00420-5*) HUP.

Modern Public Finance. Ed. by John M. Quigley & Eugene Smolensky. LC 93-23838. (Illus.). 368p. 1994. 45.95 (*0-674-58054-0*) HUP.

Modern Public Land Law in a Nutshell. Robert L. Glicksman & George C. Coggins. LC 95-16453. (Nutshell Ser.). 341p. (C). 1995. pap. 21.00 (*0-314-06338-2*) West Pub.

***Modern Public Services for Britain: Investing in Reform : Comprehensive Spending Review, New Public Spending Plans 1999-2002.** Great Britain. Treasury. LC 98-207036. (Illus.). 1998. write for info. (*0-10-140112-4*) Statnry Office.

Modern Pulsed & Continuous Wave Electron Spin Resonance. Ed. by Larry Kevan & Michael K. Bowman. LC 89-27462. 440p. 1990. 215.00 (*0-471-50274-X*) Wiley.

Modern Pure Solid Geometry. 2nd ed. Nathan A. Court. LC 64-18134. 1979. text 27.50 (*0-8284-0147-0*) Chelsea Pub.

Modern Quadrature Amplitude Modulation: Principles & Applications for Fixed & Wireless Channels. W. T. Webb & L. Hanzo. 576p. 1994. 89.95 (*0-7803-1098-5*, PC4531) Inst Electrical.

An Asterisk (*) at the beginning of an entry indicates that the title is appearing for the first time.

Modern Quantitative Analysis Experiments for Non-Chemistry Majors. George G. Guilbault. LC 73-86817. (Illus.). 255p. reprint ed. pap. 79.10 (*0-8357-6218-1*, 203453700090) Bks Demand.

Modern Quantum Chemistry: Introduction to Advanced Electronic Structure Theory. rev. unabridged ed. Attila Szabo & Neil S. Ostlund. LC 96-10775. 480p. 1996. reprint ed. pap. 13.95 (*0-486-69186-1*) Dover.

Modern Quantum Chemistry: Introduction to Advanced Structure Theory. Attila Szabo & Neil S. Ostlund. LC 81-71955. (C). 1982. 52.00 (*0-02-949710-8*) Free Pr.

Modern Quantum Field Theory II: Proceedings of the International Colloquium Tata Institute of Fundamental Research, Bombay, India 5 - 11 January 1994. Ed. by S. R. Das et al. 340p. 1995. text 86.00 (*981-02-2411-7*, PcahmMpPt-P2889) World Scientific Pub.

Modern Quantum Mechanics. J. J. Sakurai. Ed. by San-Fu Tuan. (C). 1985. text 59.25 (*0-8053-7501-5*) Addison-Wesley.

Modern Quantum Mechanics. 2nd ed. J. J. Sakurai & San F. Taun. (Illus.). 500p. (C). 1993. 109.00 (*0-201-53929-2*) Addison-Wesley.

Modern Quantum Mechanics: A Solution Manual. J. J. Sakurai. Ed. by San-Fu Tuan. (C). 1985. pap. text 5.50 (*0-8053-7502-3*) Addison-Wesley.

Modern Quantum Mechanics with Applications to Elementary Particle Physics: An Introduction to Contemporary Physical Thinking. John Eisele. LC 69-19102. 557p. (C). reprint ed. 172.70 (*0-8357-9936-0*, 205124000092) Bks Demand.

Modern Quarterly Beginnings of Aesthetic Realism, 1922-1923: The Equality of Man, The Scientific Criticism, & Other Essays (Reissue with New Introduction) 2nd ed. Eli Siegel. LC 97-7572. 52p. 1997. pap. 7.95 (*0-910492-35-2*) Definition.

Modern Quaternary Research in Southeast Asia, No. 12. Inge-Lise M. Stuyts. Ed. by Gert-Jan Bartstra & Willem A. Casparie. (Illus.). 180p. 1993. text 76.00 (*90-5410-148-2*, Pub. by A A Balkema) Ashgate Pub Co.

Modern Quaternary Research in Southeast Asia, Vol. 1. Ed. by G. J. Bartstra & W. A. Casparie. 108p. (C). 1975. text 76.00 (*90-6191-006-4*, Pub. by A A Balkema) Ashgate Pub Co.

Modern Quaternary Research in Southeast Asia, Vol. 2. Ed. by G. J. Bartstra & W. A. Casparie. 82p. (C). 1976. text 76.00 (*90-6191-013-7*, Pub. by A A Balkema) Ashgate Pub Co.

Modern Quaternary Research in Southeast Asia, Vol. 3. Ed. by G. J. Bartstra et al. 171p. (C). 1977. text 76.00 (*90-6191-016-1*, Pub. by A A Balkema) Ashgate Pub Co.

Modern Quaternary Research in Southeast Asia, Vol. 4. Ed. by G. J. Bartstra & W. A. Casparie. 80p. (C). 1978. text 76.00 (*90-6191-031-5*, Pub. by A A Balkema) Ashgate Pub Co.

Modern Quaternary Research in Southeast Asia, Vol. 5. Ed. by G. J. Bartstra & W. A. Casparie. 110p. (C). 1979. text 76.00 (*90-6191-083-8*, Pub. by A A Balkema) Ashgate Pub Co.

Modern Quaternary Research in Southeast Asia, Vol. 6. Ed. by G. J. Bartstra & W. A. Casparie. 128p. (C). 1981. text 76.00 (*90-6191-219-9*, Pub. by A A Balkema) Ashgate Pub Co.

Modern Quaternary Research in Southeast Asia, Vol. 7. Ed. by G. J. Bartstra & W. A. Casparie. 246p. (C). 1982. text 76.00 (*90-6191-200-8*, Pub. by A A Balkema) Ashgate Pub Co.

Modern Quaternary Research in Southeast Asia, Vol. 8. Ed. by G. J. Bartstra & W. A. Casparie. 188p. (C). 1984. text 76.00 (*90-6191-540-6*, Pub. by A A Balkema) Ashgate Pub Co.

Modern Quaternary Research in Southeast Asia, Vol. 11. Ed. by G. J. Bartstra & W. A. Casparie. 173p. (C). 1990. text 76.00 (*90-6191-883-9*, Pub. by A A Balkema) Ashgate Pub Co.

Modern Quaternary Research in Southeast Asia Vol. 9: Papers Read at Symposium I, 12th Congress of the Indo-Pacific Prehistory Association, Philippines, 26th Jan.-2nd Feb. 1985. Ed. by G. J. Bartstra & W. A. Casparie. 166p. (C). 1985. text 76.00 (*90-6191-605-4*, Pub. by A A Balkema) Ashgate Pub Co.

Modern Quaternary Research in Southeast Asia Vol. 10: The Kettledrums of Southeast Asia: A Bronze Age World & Its Aftermath. A. J. Kempers. Ed. by G. J. Bartstra & W. A. Casparie. 190p. (C). 1987. text 112.00 (*90-6191-541-4*, Pub. by A A Balkema) Ashgate Pub Co.

Modern Questions & Answers in Chemistry. S. Osafo Acquaah. 1986. write for info. (*0-8187-0066-1*) Harlo Press.

Modern Radar: Analysis, Evaluation & System Design. Raymond S. Berkowitz. LC 65-21446. 676p. reprint ed. pap. 200.00 (*0-608-10286-5*, 201741100007) Bks Demand.

Modern Radar System Analysis. David K. Barton. (Radar Library). 590p. 1988. text 83.00 (*0-89006-170-X*) Artech Hse.

Modern Radar System Analysis Software: Version 2.0. David K. Barton & William F. Barton. (Radar Software Library). 100p. 1992. 425.00 incl. disk (*0-89006-673-6*) Artech Hse.

Modern Radar Transmitters. (C). 2001. pap. text 90.00 (*0-13-016162-4*) P-H.

Modern Radio Production. Lewis B. O'Donnell et al. 258p. (C). 1985. pap. write for info. (*0-534-05064-6*) Wadsworth Pub.

Modern Radio Production. 2nd ed. Lewis B. O'Donnell et al. 316p. (C). 1989. pap. write for info. (*0-534-11622-1*) Wadsworth Pub.

Modern Radio Production. 3rd ed. O'Donnell & Benoit. (Radio/Tv/Film Ser.). 1993. teacher ed. 27.00 (*0-534-19081-2*) Wadsworth Pub.

Modern Radio Production. 3rd ed. Lewis B. O'Donnell et al. 347p. (C). 1993. mass mkt. 26.75 (*0-534-19080-4*) Wadsworth Pub.

Modern Radio Production. 4th ed. Carl Hausman et al. (C). 1995. pap. 35.50 (*0-534-26094-2*) Wadsworth Pub.

Modern Radio Production. 5th ed. Hausman & Benoit. LC 99-33299. (Radio/Tv/Film Ser.). 1999. pap. 55.95 (*0-534-56106-3*) Wadsworth Pub.

***Modern Radio Science 1999.** Ed. by Maria A. Stuchly. (Illus.). 352p. 1999. text 70.00 (*0-19-856570-4*) OUP.

Modern Radio Science, 1996. J. Hamelin. (Illus.). 288p. 1996. text 65.00 (*0-19-856530-5*) OUP.

Modern Radio Science, 1993. Ed. by H. Matsumoto. LC 93-22988. (Illus.). 264p. 1993. text 39.95 (*0-19-856379-5*) OUP.

Modern Reader in the Philosophy of Religion. Ed. by Willard E. Arnett. LC 66-20470. (Century Philosophy Ser.). 1966. 42.50 (*0-89197-482-2*) Irvington.

Modern Reader's Book of Psalms. Ed. by Harry Mayer. (Black & Gold Library). 1968. 6.95 (*0-87140-879-1*, Pub. by Liveright) Norton.

Modern Reader's Guide to Dante's Inferno. Rodney J. Payton. (American University Studies: Romance Languages & Literature: Ser. II, Vol. 191). 264p. 1993. pap. 31.95 (*0-8204-1827-7*) P Lang Pubng.

***Modern Reader's Guide to Dante's The Divine Comedy.** Joseph Gallagher. LC 99-20714. Orig. Title: To Hell & Back with Dante: A Modern Reader's Guide to Dante's THE DIVINE COMEDY. 256p. 1999. pap. 16.95 (*0-7648-0494-4*) Liguori Pubns.

Modern Reader's Japanese-English Character Dictionary. 2nd rev. ed. Andrew Nelson. LC 61-11973. (ENG & JPN.). 1110p. 1962. 69.95 (*0-8048-0408-7*) Tuttle Pubng.

Modern Real Analysis. Ronald F. Gariepy & William P. Ziemer. LC 94-43168. 1994. mass mkt. 111.95 (*0-534-94404-3*) PWS Pubs.

Modern Real & Complex Analysis. Bernard R. Gelbaum. LC 94-23715. 504p. 1995. 99.95 (*0-471-10715-8*) Wiley.

Modern Real Estate. 5th ed. Charles H. Wurtzebach & Mike E. Miles. 880p. 1994. text 92.95 (*0-471-30951-6*) Wiley.

Modern Real Estate Acquisition & Disposition Forms. annuals Jack Kusnet & Robert Lopatin. LC 80-52970. (Forms Ser.). 1056p. 1981. suppl. ed. 130.00 (*0-88262-523-3*) Warren Gorham & Lamont.

Modern Real Estate Acquisition & Disposition Forms. Jack Kusnet & Robert Lopatin. LC 80-52970. (Forms Ser.). 1056p. 1992. suppl. ed. 55.00 (*0-7913-1172-4*) Warren Gorham & Lamont.

Modern Real Estate & Mortgage Forms. rev. ed. Douglas. 1008p. 1986. 130.00 (*0-88712-578-6*); suppl. ed. 54.00 (*0-7913-1232-1*); suppl. ed. 68.00 (*0-685-55839-8*) Warren Gorham & Lamont.

Modern Real Estate & Mortgage Forms Checklists. annuals Alvin L. Arnold et al. 712p. 1979. ring bd., suppl. ed. 130.00 (*0-88262-280-3*) Warren Gorham & Lamont.

***Modern Real Estate Finance & Land Transfer: A Transactional Approach.** 2nd ed. Michael Madison et al. LC 99-37775. 1999. boxed set 64.00 (*0-7355-0327-3*) Panel Pubs.

Modern Real Estate Financing: A Transactional Approach. Michael T. Madison & Robert M. Zinman. 1312p. 1991. teacher ed. write for info. (*0-316-54364-0*, 43640) Aspen Law.

***Modern Real Estate Portfolio Management.** Susan Hudson-Wilson. 250p. 2000. 65.00 (*1-883249-79-1*) F J Fabozzi.

***Modern Real Estate Practice.** 15th ed. Fillmore Galaty et al. LC 99-40430. 1999. pap. 44.95 (*0-7931-3363-7*) Dearborn.

Modern Real Estate Practice, Connecticut Supplement. 7th ed. Katharine A. Pancak. LC 96-39572. 1997. pap. 16.95 (*0-7931-2267-8*, 15102707, Real Estate Ed) Dearborn.

Modern Real Estate Practice in Illinois. 2nd ed. Filmore Galaty et al. LC 97-25120. 560p. 1998. pap. text 39.95 (*0-7931-2509-X*, 1510-7002, Real Estate Ed) Dearborn.

***Modern Real Estate Practice in Illinois.** 3rd ed. Fillmore W. Galaty. LC 99-28196. 536p. 1999. pap. 43.95 (*0-7931-3307-6*) Dearborn.

Modern Real Estate Practice in New York. 6th ed. Edith Lank. LC 97-3695. 1997. pap. text 41.95 (*0-7931-2414-X*, 1510-5206) Dearborn.

***Modern Real Estate Practice in New York: For Salespersons & Brokers.** 7th ed. Edith Lank & Judith Deickler. LC 99-39630. 2000. pap. 42.95 (*0-7931-3626-1*, Real Estate Ed) Dearborn.

***Modern Real Estate Practice in North Carolina.** 4th ed. Fillmore W. Galaty et al. LC 00-28003. (Illus.). 2000. pap. 41.95 (*0-7931-3634-2*, Real Estate Ed) Dearborn.

Modern Real Estate Practice in Ohio. 4th ed. Fillmore W. Galaty et al. LC 99-10731. xii, 447p. 1999. 43.95 (*0-7931-3219-3*, Real Estate Ed) Dearborn.

Modern Real Estate Practice in Pennsylvania. 7th ed. Herbert J. Bellairs. 1996. pap. 42.95 (*0-7931-1579-5*, 1510-1707) Dearborn.

***Modern Real Estate Practice in Pennsylvania.** 8th ed. Herbert J. Bellairs et al. LC 99-45947. 2000. pap. 42.95 (*0-7931-3306-8*, Real Estate Ed) Dearborn.

Modern Real Estate Practice in Texas. 9th ed. Cheryl Nance. LC 97-32354. 528p. 1998. pap. text 44.95 (*0-7931-2689-4*, 1510-0609, Real Estate Ed) Dearborn.

***Modern Real Estate Practice in Texas.** 10th ed. Cheryl P. Nance. LC 99-53864. 2000. pap. 44.95 (*0-7931-3483-8*) Dearborn.

Modern Real Estate Practice in Texas, Keypoint Review Audio Tapes. 1995. audio 27.00 (*0-7931-1496-9*, 1518-0901, Real Estate Ed) Dearborn.

Modern Real Estate Practices. 14th ed. Fillmore W. Galaty. 1997. pap. text 39.95 (*0-7931-2677-0*, 1510-014A) Dearborn.

Modern Real Estate Practices in North Carolina. 3rd ed. Fillmore W. Galaty. LC 98-18330. 1999. pap. text 41.95 (*0-7931-3318-1*) Dearborn.

Modern Real Property, Fundamentals Of. 3rd ed. Edward H. Rabin & Roberta R. Kwall. (University Casebook Ser.). 1092p. 1992. text 45.95 (*0-88277-962-1*) Foundation Pr.

Modern Recording Techniques. 4th ed. David M. Huber. 512p. 1995. pap. 29.95 (*0-240-80308-6*, Focal) Buttrwrth-Heinemann.

Modern Redwork Designs. Betty Alderman. LC 99-40081. 96p. 1999. per. 16.95 (*1-57432-733-X*) Collector Bks.

Modern Reef Aquarium. Cliff W. Emmens. (Illus.). 160p. 1994. 35.95 (*0-7938-0063-3*, TS203) TFH Pubns.

Modern Reform Responsa. Solomon B. Freehof. LC 72-151008. 331p. reprint ed. pap. 102.70 (*0-7837-3001-2*, 204294000006) Bks Demand.

Modern Reformist Thought in the Muslim World. Mazhar-ud-Din Siddiqi. 250p. 1991. pap. 14.50 (*1-56744-144-0*) Kazi Pubns.

Modern Refrigeration & Air Conditioning. A. D. Althouse et al. LC 87-57. (Illus.). 1199p. 1996. text 55.96 (*1-56637-300-X*) Goodheart.

***Modern Refrigeration & Air Conditioning.** Andrew D. Althouse et al. LC 99-89117. 2000. write for info. (*1-56637-724-2*) Goodheart.

Modern Refrigeration & Air Conditioning, 4 vols., Set. 1993. lib. bdg. 1882.95 (*0-8490-9007-5*) Gordon Pr.

Modern Regime, Vol. 2. Hippolyte A. Taine. 1990. 16.50 (*0-8446-1436-X*) Peter Smith.

Modern Regression Methods. Thomas P. Ryan. LC 96-6368. (Series in Probability & Statistics, Applied Probability & Statistics). 515p. 1996. 84.95 (*0-471-52912-5*) Wiley.

Modern Reinsurance Law & Practice. Barry R. Ostrager & Mary K. Vyskocil. 1996. ring bd. 119.20 (*1-888075-50-3*) Glasser LegalWrks.

Modern Religion & the Destruction of Spiritual Capacity. Mary E. Carreiro. LC 87-24251. (Gentle Wind Ser.: Vol. 2). 160p. 1988. reprint ed. pap. 12.95 (*0-89789-141-4*); reprint ed. lib. bdg. 29.95 (*0-89789-140-6*) Gentle Wind Proj.

Modern Religious Cults & Movements. Gaius Atkins. LC 74-126684. reprint ed. 47.50 (*0-404-00415-6*) AMS Pr.

Modern Religious Cults & Society. Louis R. Binder. LC 77-113556. reprint ed. 34.50 (*0-404-00867-4*) AMS Pr.

Modern Religious Movements in India. J. N. Farquhar. 1977. reprint ed. 19.50 (*0-8364-2610-X*, Pub. by M Manoharial) S Asia.

Modern Religious Movements in India. J. N. Farquhar. 1998. reprint ed. 19.50 (*81-215-0273-X*, Pub. by M Manoharial) Coronet Bks.

Modern Religious Verse. Ed. by Timothy Beaumont. (Pocket Poet Ser.). 1966. pap. 3.95 (*0-8023-9039-0*) Dufour.

Modern Religious Verse & Prose: An Anthology. Ed. by Fred Merrifield. LC 79-51964. (Granger Poetry Library). 1980. reprint ed. 35.00 (*0-89609-186-4*) Roth Pub Inc.

Modern Remedies: Cases, Practical Problems & Exercises. Russell L. Weaver & Kristine Strachan. Ed. by David F. Parlett et al. LC 97-1879. (American Casebook Ser.). 898p. (C). 1997. 57.50 (*0-314-21150-0*) West Pub.

Modern Remedies: Cases, Practical Problems & Exercises, Teacher's Manual. Russell L. Weaver et al. (American Casebook Ser.). 300p. 1997. pap. text. write for info. (*0-314-22598-6*) West Pub.

Modern Renaissance in American Art: Presenting the Work & Philosophy of 54 Distinguished Artists. Ralph M. Pearson. LC 68-20329. (Essay Index Reprint Ser.). 1977. 42.95 (*0-8369-0780-9*) Ayer.

Modern Renaissance of Jewish Music. Albert Weisser. LC 82-23654. (Music Reprint Ser.). 175p. 1983. reprint ed. lib. bdg. 25.00 (*0-306-76207-2*) Da Capo.

Modern Renaissance Poetry & Philosophy. C. Antonio Provost. Ed. by William Kroll. LC 92-96848. (Illus.). 148p. (YA). (gr. 9-12). 1992. 14.00 (*0-317-05253-5*); pap. 10.00 (*0-317-05254-3*) Provost.

Modern Replication Based on the Pattern-Welded Sword of Sutton Hoo. Robert Engstrom et al. 1989. pap. 3.00 (*0-918720-29-X*) Medieval Inst.

Modern Reporter's Handbook. John P. Jones. LC 71-98233. 430p. 1970. reprint ed. lib. bdg. 75.00 (*0-8371-3964-3*, JORH, Greenwood Pr) Greenwood.

Modern Research As Illustrating the Bible. S. R. Driver. (British Academy, London, Schweich Lectures on Biblical Archaeology Series, 1930). 1974. reprint ed. pap. 25.00 (*0-8115-1250-9*) Periodicals Srv.

Modern Research Topics in Aerospace Propulsion: In Honor of Corrado Casci. Ed. by G. Angelino et al. (Illus.). 384p. 1991. 116.95 (*0-387-97417-2*) Spr-Verlag.

Modern Researcher. 5th ed. Jacques Barzun. (C). 1992. pap. text 33.50 (*0-15-562513-6*, Pub. by Harcourt Coll Pubs) Harcourt.

Modern Researcher. 5th ed. Jacques Barzun & Henry F. Graff. LC 91-74063. (Illus.). 416p. 1992. 24.95 (*0-395-64494-1*) HM.

Modern Researcher. 5th ed. Jacques Barzun & Henry F. Graff. 400p. (C). 1992. pap. text. write for info. (*0-318-69122-1*) Harcourt Coll Pubs.

Modern Researcher. 6th ed. Jacques Barzun. (C). 2002. pap. text 31.00 (*0-15-505529-1*) Harcourt Coll Pubs.

Modern Reservoir Flow & Well Transient Analysis. Wilson C. Chin. LC 92-35620. (Illus.). 400p. 1993. reprint ed. pap. 124.00 (*0-608-07945-6*, 206791800012) Bks Demand.

Modern Residential Wiring. rev. ed. Harvey N. Holzman. LC 93-21488. (Illus.). 288p. 1999. text 37.28 (*1-56637-539-8*) Goodheart.

Modern Resonance Transformer Design Theory. (Nikola Tesla Ser.). 1991. lib. bdg. 74.95 (*0-8490-4326-3*) Gordon Pr.

Modern Resonance Transformer Design Theory. 1987. 29.50 (*0-914119-17-6*) Tesla Bk Co.

Modern Restaurant Service: A Manual for Students & Practitioners. John Fuller. 296p. (C). 1999. pap. 60.00 (*0-7487-0294-6*, Pub. by S Thornes Pubs) Trans-Atl Phila.

Modern Retailing: Theory & Practice. 6th ed. Joseph B. Mason et al. LC 92-12011. 816p. (C). 1992. text 69.95 (*0-256-10257-0*, Irwn McGrw-H) McGrw-H Hghr Educ.

Modern Retelling of Chivalric Texts. Ed. by Gloria Allaire. LC 98-22085. 256p. 1999. text 69.95 (*1-84014-612-5*, PN682.C53M63, Pub. by Ashgate Pub) Ashgate Pub Co.

Modern Revival of Gnosticismin in Thomas Mann's Doctor Faustus. Kristen J. Grimstad. 2001. 55.00 (*1-57113-193-0*) Camden Hse.

Modern Revolutions: An Introduction to the Analysis of a Political Phenomenon. John Dunn. 382p. (C). 1989. pap. text 19.95 (*0-521-37814-1*) Cambridge U Pr.

Modern Rhetoric. 4th ed. Brooks. (C). 1979. pap. text, teacher ed. 4.75 (*0-15-562816-X*) Harcourt Coll Pubs.

Modern Rhetorical Criticism. Roderick Hart. LC 96-41568. 374p. 1996. pap. text 50.00 (*0-205-19665-9*) Allyn.

Modern Rhetorical Criticism. Roderick P. Hart. (C). 1996. pap. text, teacher ed. write for info. (*0-205-26586-3*, T6586-6) Allyn.

Modern Rhyming Dictionary. Gene Lees. 364p. (Orig.). (YA). (gr. 8 up). 1986. 19.95 (*0-89524-129-3*, 8649); pap. 14.95 (*0-89524-317-2*, Pub. by Cherry Lane) H Leonard.

***Modern Rhyming Dictionary.** rev. ed. Gene Lees. 2000. pap. text 14.95 (*1-57560-196-6*) Cherry Lane.

Modern Rhythmic Notation. Gardner Read. LC 77-9860. 211p. reprint ed. pap. 65.50 (*0-7837-1506-4*, 205729600024) Bks Demand.

Modern Rice Technology & Income Distribution in Asia. Ed. by Christina C. David & Keijiro Otsuka. 475p. 1994. pap. text 27.50 (*1-55587-431-2*); lib. bdg. 55.00 (*1-55587-404-5*) L Rienner.

Modern Riddles. LC 96-144907. 1995. pap. 10.95 (*0-9509797-6-7*, Pub. by Bloodaxe Bks) Dufour.

Modern Riding Techniques: Harmony in Horsemanship. Selma Brandl. (Illus.). 168p. (Orig.). (YA). 1997. pap. 32.95 (*1-85310-815-4*, Pub. by Swan Hill Pr) Voyageur Pr.

Modern Rival of Christian Faith: An Analysis of Secularism. Georgia E. Harkness. LC 77-27000. 223p. 1978. reprint ed. lib. bdg. 55.00 (*0-313-20174-9*, HAMR, Greenwood Pr) Greenwood.

Modern Rock. 110p. (YA). pap. 19.95 (*1-57560-003-X*) Cherry Lane.

Modern Rock - Piano/Vocal/Guitar. Ed. by Milton Okun. 93p. Date not set. pap. 15.95 (*1-57560-009-9*) Cherry Lane.

Modern Rock Climbing. Todd Skinner & John McMullen. LC 92-47396. (Basic Essentials Ser.). (Illus.). 196p. (Orig.). 1993. pap. 11.99 (*0-934802-90-4*) Globe Pequot.

Modern Rock Hits for Guitar - Guitar Tablature. 56p. 1997. pap. 10.95 (*0-7935-8032-3*) H Leonard.

Modern Rock Jam Trax. Ralph Agresta. (JamTrax Ser.). (Illus.). 1992. pap. 9.95 (*0-8256-1323-X*, AM87424) Music Sales.

Modern Rock Sessions for Guitar. Ed. by Ed Lazano. 5p. 1998. pap. text 12.95 (*0-8256-1626-3*, AM945164) Music Sales.

***Modern Romance.** David Levinthal. 2000. 65.00 (*0-9671744-1-4*) St Anns Pr.

Modern Romance. Luisita Torregrossa. 1996. 22.00 (*0-679-44823-3*) Random.

Modern Romances. Judy Lopatin. LC 86-7711. 256p. 1986. 15.95 (*0-932511-02-3*); pap. 7.95 (*0-932511-03-1*) Fiction Coll.

Modern Romanian Poetry: An Anthology. Nicholas Catanoy. 144p. 1989. 15.95 (*0-88962-046-6*); pap. 8.95 (*0-88962-045-8*) Mosaic.

Modern Roses. Peter Beales. 1989. write for info. (*0-8050-0963-9*) H Holt & Co.

***Modern Roses XI.** Thomas Cairns. 2000. 99.95 (*0-12-155053-2*) Acad Pr.

Modern Roses 10: The Comprehensive List of Roses of International & Botanical Importance Including All Modern International Rose Registrations. Intro. by Thomas Cairns. 760p. (C). 1993. 50.00 (*0-9636340-0-3*) Am Rose Soc.

Modern Roundabout Practice in the United States. Georges Jacquemart et al. LC 98-66468. (Synthesis of Highway Practice Ser.). 73 p. 1998. write for info. (*0-309-06120-2*) Natl Acad Pr.

Modern RPG IV Language. Robert Cozzi, Jr. LC 97-196973. (Illus.). 570p. 1996. pap. 99.00 (*1-883884-31-4*, 546) Midrange Comput.

***Modern RPG IV Language.** 2nd ed. Robert Cozzi, Jr. (Illus.). 576p. 1999. pap. 99.00 (*1-58347-002-6*) Midrange Comput.

Modern RPG IV Language Reference Summary. 2nd ed. Robert Cozzi, Jr. (Illus.). 95p. 1997. reprint ed. pap. 29.00 (*1-883884-38-1*, 545) Midrange Comput.

Modern RPG Language Reference Summary. Robert Cozzi, Jr. 60p. 1992. 24.95 (*0-9621825-3-2*) Cozzi Research.

Modern RPG Language with Structured Programming. 4th ed. Robert Cozzi, Jr. Ed. by Theresa King & Greg Veal. (Illus.). 500p. (C). 1993. pap. text 65.00 (*0-9621825-0-8*) Cozzi Research.

Modern Rugmaking & Tapestry Techniques: Speed Hook Tufting, Rya & Double-Time Latch. Susanna Cuyler. (Illus.). 120p. (Orig.). 1985. pap. 10.00 (*0-9612018-1-9*) B RUGGED.

***Modern Rules of Order: A Guide for Conducting Business Meetings.** 2nd ed. Donald A. Tortorice. LC 99-33970. 1999. write for info. (*1-57073-729-0*) Amer Bar Assn.

An Asterisk (*) at the beginning of an entry indicates that the title is appearing for the first time.

*Modern Russia. 8th ed. Titma Tuma. 2000. 45.50 (0-07-292823-9) McGraw.

Modern Russian see Modern Russian 1

Modern Russian: An Advanced Grammar Course. Derek C. Offord. 461p. 1993. pap. 31.95 (1-85399-361-1, Pub. by Brist Class Pr) Focus Pub-R Pullins.

Modern Russian Adjectives Correlative with the Past Passive Participles. Regine Dalchow Fougeres. (European University Studies: Slavonic Languages & Literatures: Ser. 16, Vol. 3). 170p. 1974. pap. 28.00 (3-261-01085-1) P Lang Pubng.

Modern Russian Classics. Incl. Father. Anton Chekhov. Her Lover. Maxim Gorki. Letter. Isaac Babel. Silence. Leonid Andreyev. White Dog. Fedor Sologub, pseud. Set pap. 4.95 (0-8283-1450-0) Branden Bks.

Modern Russian Composers. Leonid L. Sabaneev. Tr. by J. A. Joffe. LC 67-23270. (Essay Index Reprint Ser.). 1977. 20.95 (0-8369-0847-3) Ayer.

Modern Russian Composers. Leonid L. Sabaneev. 253p. 1990. reprint ed. lib. bdg. 69.00 (0-7812-9035-X) Rprt Serv.

Modern Russian Composers. Leonid Sabaneyeff. Tr. by Judah A. Joffe from RUS. LC 75-14232. (Music Reprint Ser.). 253p. 1975. reprint ed. lib. bdg. 35.00 (0-306-70673-3) Da Capo.

Modern Russian Historiography. rev. ed. Anatole G. Mazour. LC 75-16962. (Illus.). 224p. 1976. 57.95 (0-8371-8285-9, MRH/, Greenwood Pr) Greenwood.

Modern Russian Instructor's Manual see Modern Russian 1

Modern Russian Literature. Dimitry S. Mirsky. LC 74-6485. (Studies in Russian Literature & Life: No. 100). 1974. lib. bdg. 75.00 (0-8383-1941-6) M S G Haskell Hse.

Modern Russian I see Modern Russian 1

Modern Russian I, 24 cass. Clayton L. Dawson et al. 480p. pap. text 255.00 incl. audio (0-88432-044-8, AFB101) Audio-Forum.

Modern Russian 1. Incl. Modern Russian I. Clayton L. Dawson. LC 77-5837. 962p. 1977. pap. 16.95 (0-87840-169-5); Pt. 1. Modern Russian Instructor's Manual. Clayton L. Dawson. LC 77-5837. 1977. teacher ed. 7.00 (0-87840-185-7); Vol. 1. Modern Russian. 1977. 175.00 incl. audio (0-87840-182-2); LC 77-5837. 1977. reprint ed. Set pap. 16.95 (0-318-52678-6) Georgetown U Pr.

Modern Russian Reader for Intermediate Classes: Intermediate. (RUS.). (C). 22.50 (0-8442-4240-3, X4240-3) NTC Contemp Pub Co.

Modern Russian II. Clayton L. Dawson et al. 479p. pap. text 255.00 incl. audio (0-88432-056-1, AFB125) Audio-Forum.

Modern Russian 2. Clayton L. Dawson. LC 77-5837. (ENG & RUS.). 183p. 1986. reprint ed. pap., wbk. ed. 56.80 (0-608-04094-0, 206482600011) Bks Demand.

Modern Russian 2. Clayton L. Dawson & Assya Humesky. LC 77-5837. (ENG & RUS.). 493p. 1965. reprint ed. pap. 152.90 (0-608-04093-2, 206482500002) Bks Demand.

*Modern Rustic Style: Natural Ideas for a Contemporary Lifestyle. Ali Hanan. LC 00-20545. (Illus.). 144p. 2000. pap. 25.00 (0-7893-0405-8) Universe.

Modern Sacred Art & the Church of Assy. William S. Rubin. LC 61-15469. (Illus.). 245p. reprint ed. pap. 76.00 (0-608-18600-7, 205185800011) Bks Demand.

Modern Safety & Resource Control Management. Thomas D. Schneid. LC 99-29163. 336p. 1999. text 69.95 (0-471-33118-X) Wiley.

Modern Safety Management. Date not set. ring bd. write for info. (0-88061-090-5) Intl Loss Cntrl.

Modern Saints: Their Lives & Faces, 2 vols., Bk. 1. Ann Ball. LC 82-50357. (Illus.). 457p. 1994. pap. 18.00 (0-89555-222-1) TAN Bks Pubs.

Modern Saints: Their Lives & Faces, 2 vols., Bk. 2. Ann Ball. LC 82-50357. (Illus.). 457p. 1993. pap. 20.00 (0-89555-223-X) TAN Bks Pubs.

Modern Sales Management. Justus G. Frederick. Ed. by Henry Assael. LC 78-327. (Century of Marketing Ser.). 1979. reprint ed. lib. bdg. 36.95 (0-405-11185-1) Ayer.

Modern Samoa: Its Government & Changing Life. Felix M. Keesing. LC 75-30065. reprint ed. 50.00 (0-404-59536-7) AMS Pr.

Modern Satire: Four Studies. Peter Petro. (De Proprietatibus Litterarum, Ser. Minor: No. 27). 162p. 1982. 93.10 (90-279-3180-1) Mouton.

Modern Satiric Grotesque & Its Traditions. John R. Clark. LC 90-27474. 224p. 1991. text 29.95 (0-8131-1744-5) U Pr of Ky.

Modern Saturn Italian-French, French-Italian Dictionary: Dictionnaire Moderne Saturne Italien-Francais-Italien. C. Margueron. (FRE & ITA.). 1600p. 1983. 85.00 (0-8288-0370-6, M6833) Fr & Eur.

Modern Scenes for Women. Susan Pomerance. 50p. (Orig.). 1989. pap. 8.95 (0-940669-10-2, D-5) Dramaline Pubns.

Modern School Administration. Ed. by John C. Almack. LC 78-121445. (Essay Index Reprint Ser.). 1977. 23.95 (0-8369-1902-5) Ayer.

Modern School for Xylophone, Marimba & Vibraphone. M. Goldenberg. 132p. 1981. otabind 12.95 (0-7935-1938-1, 00347776) H Leonard.

Modern School Superintendent: His Principles & Practices. Robert E. Wilson. LC 77-2905. (Illus.). 1977. reprint ed. lib. bdg. 65.00 (0-8371-9575-6, WIMO, Greenwood Pr) Greenwood.

Modern Schoolman: St. Louis, 1925-1967-68, Set, Vols. 1-45. reprint ed. 1307.50 (0-404-19573-3) AMS Pr.

Modern Schuetzen Rifle. Charles E. Dell & Wayne E. Schwartz. (Illus.). xxix, 358p. 1996. 45.00 (0-9653702-0-8) Chuckan Indust.

*Modern Schuetzen Rifle. 2nd rev. ed. Charles E. Dell & Wayne E. Schwartz. 410p. 2000. 60.00 (0-9653702-1-6) Chuckan Indust.

Modern Science & an Ancient Text. Don Kopp. (Illus.). 108p. 1997. pap. write for info. (1-57579-064-5) Pine Hill Pr.

Modern Science & Anarchism. Peter Kropotkin. 1980. lib. bdg. 49.95 (0-8490-3125-7) Gordon Pr.

Modern Science & Its Philosophy. Philipp Frank. LC 74-26263. (History, Philosophy & Sociology of Science Ser.). 1975. reprint ed. 29.95 (0-405-06591-4) Ayer.

Modern Science & Modern Man. James B. Conant. LC 83-12753. 111p. 1983. reprint ed. lib. bdg. 49.75 (0-313-24119-8, CMOS, Greenwood Pr) Greenwood.

Modern Science & the Book of Genesis. James W. Skehan. (Illus.). 32p. 1986. pap. 5.00 (0-87355-046-3) Natl Sci Tchrs.

*Modern Science, Education & Reform in Qajar Iran: The Dar Al-Funun. Maryam Ekhtiar. 320p. 2000. 80.00 (0-7007-1230-5, Pub. by Curzon Pr Ltd) Paul & Co Pubs.

Modern Science Fiction: Its Meaning & Its Future. Ed. by Reginald Bretnor. LC 78-71414. 343p. 1979. 18.00 (0-911682-23-6) Advent.

Modern Science Fiction & the American Literary Community. Frederick A. Lerner. LC 85-1874. 343p. 1985. 31.00 (0-8108-1794-2) Scarecrow.

Modern Scottish Gaelic Poems: A Bilingual Anthology. Ed. by Donald MacAulay. 224p. 1995. pap. 12.95 (0-86241-494-6, Pub. by Canongate Books) Interlink Pub.

Modern Scottish Gaelic Poems-Nua-Bhardach Ghaidhlig. Ed. by Donald MacAulay et al. LC 76-21270. 220p. 1977. 16.00 (0-8112-0631-9, Pub. by New Directions) Norton.

*Modern Scottish Novel: Narrative & the National Imagination. Cairns Craig. 256p. 1998. pap. 26.00 (0-7486-0893-1, Pub. by Edinburgh U Pr) Col U Pr.

Modern Scottish Novel since 1970. Ed. by Gavin Wallace & Randall Stevenson. (Modern Scottish Writers Ser.). 282p. (C). 1993. pap. 24.50 (0-7486-0415-4, Pub. by Edinburgh U Pr) Col U Pr.

Modern Scottish Novels. I. Murray & T. Murray. 224p. 1984. 19.00 (0-685-09404-9, Pergamon Pr); pap. text 15.90 (0-08-028493-0, Pergamon Pr) Elsevier.

Modern Scottish Writers. William M. Parker. LC 68-26463. (Essay Index Reprint Ser.). 1977. reprint ed. 20.95 (0-8369-0769-8) Ayer.

Modern Scribes & Lettering Artists. Michael Gullick & Ievan Rees. 1991. pap. 19.95 (0-87923-874-7) Godine.

Modern Scriptural Approach to the Spiritual Exercises. David M. Stanley. LC 67-25219. (Original Studies Composed in English III: No. 1). xviii, 358p. 1993. reprint ed. pap. 19.95 (0-912422-07-6) Inst Jesuit.

Modern Sculpture. Herbert E. Read. (World of Art Ser.). (Illus.). 310p. 1985. pap. 14.95 (0-500-20014-9, Pub. by Thames Hudson) Norton.

Modern Sculpture. Jean Robertson. Ed. by Norma J. Roberts. LC 86-73072. (Illus.). 32p. 1986. pap. 3.50 (0-918881-17-X) Columbus Mus Art.

*Modern Sculpture at the Nelson-Atkins Museum of Art: An Anniversary Celebration. Deborah E. Scott & Martin Friedman. LC 99-27051. (Illus.). 96p. 1999. pap. 19.99 (0-942614-31-3) Nelson-Atkins.

Modern Sculpture in Denver, 1919-1960: Twelve Denver Sculptors. Elizabeth Schlesser. (Documents of Colorado Art Ser.). (Illus.). 112p. (Orig.). 1995. pap. 34.95 (0-938075-43-8) Ocean View Bks.

Modern Sea Power: An Introduction. Ed. by Geoffrey Till. (Sea Power: Naval Vessels Weapon Systems & Technology Ser.: Vol. 1). 179p. 1987. 40.00 (0-08-033623-X, Pub. by Brasseys); 25.00 (0-08-033622-1, Pub. by Brasseys) Brasseys.

Modern Seafood Cookbook. Brown. Date not set. pap. write for info. (0-517-88507-7) Crown Pub Group.

Modern Seafood Cookbook: New Tastes, New Techniques New Ease. Edward Brown & Arthur Boehm. 352p. 1995. 30.00 (0-517-70241-X) C Potter.

*Modern Seamanship. Don Dodds. 512p. 2000. 12.99 (0-517-16252-0) Random Hse Value.

Modern Seamanship: A Complete Guide for the Recreational Boater. Don Dodds. (Illus.). 512p. 1995. pap. 30.00 (1-55821-270-1) Lyons Pr.

Modern Search for the Real Jesus: An Introductory Survey of the Historical Roots of Gospels Criticism. Robert B. Strimple. 176p. (Orig.). (C). 1995. pap. 10.99 (0-87552-455-9) P & R Pubng.

Modern Securities Transfers. rev. ed. Egon Guttman & Carlos Israels. 1987. 185.00 (0-88712-514-X) Warren Gorham & Lamont.

Modern Securities Transfers. rev. ed. Egon Guttman & Carlos Israels. 1992. suppl. ed. 79.00 (0-685-55840-1) Warren Gorham & Lamont.

Modern Selective Fungicides: Properties, Applications, Mechanisms of Action. 2nd rev. ed. Horst Lyr. (Illus.). 600p. 1995. 108.00 (3-334-60455-1) Balogh.

Modern Semiconductor Device Physics. Simon Sze. LC 97-4311. 556p. 1997. 95.00 (0-471-15237-4) Wiley.

Modern Semiconductor Quantum Physics. Ming-Fu Li. (Solid State Electronics Ser.). 588p. 1995. text 84.00 (981-02-1599-1) World Scientific Pub.

Modern Senryu in English. Shuho Ohno. (Illus.). 256p. (C). 1988. 18.50 (0-9620359-0-4) Hokubei Intl.

Modern Separation of Macromolecules & Particles. Ed. by Theo Gerritsen. LC 69-14292. (Progress in Separation & Purification Ser.: Vol. 2). (Illus.). 262p. reprint ed. pap. 81.30 (0-608-30028-4, 201195800080) Bks Demand.

Modern Sequential Statistical Analysis (SSA) in Honor of Professor Herbert Robbins Vol. 1: Proceedings of the Mini-Con-SSA Conference, Syracuse University, Syracuse, New York, U. S. A., April, 1989. Ed. by Z. Govindarajulu. LC 91-74123. (American Sciences Press Series in Mathematical & Management Sciences: Vol. 29). 190p. 1991. 195.00 (0-935950-31-1) Am Sciences Pr.

Modern Sequential Statistical Analysis (SSA) in Honor of Professor Herbert Robbins Vol. 2: Proceedings of the Mini-Con-SSA Conference, Syracuse University, Syracuse, New York, U. S. A., April, 1989. Ed. by Z. Govindarajulu. LC 91-74123. (American Sciences Press Series in Mathematical & Management Sciences: Vol. 30). 200p. 1992. 195.00 (0-935950-32-X) Am Sciences Pr.

Modern Serbocroatian-Slovene Dictionary: Srpskohrvatsko-Slovenski Moderni Slovar. Janko Jurancic. (SER & SLV.). 568p. 1985. 49.95 (0-8288-1141-5, M9698) Fr & Eur.

Modern Sex. Ed. by Tani E. Barlow. (Special Issue of Positions Ser.: Vol. 2, No. 3). 275p. 1995. pap. 12.00 (0-8223-6424-7) Duke.

Modern Sex. Cloyd J. Julian. 1985. pap. text 26.00 (0-03-071899-6) Holt R&W.

Modern Sex Education. C. Julian. 1980. pap. text, teacher ed. 32.00 (0-03-049561-X) Holt R&W.

Modern Sex Magick: Lessons in Liberation. Donald M. Kraig. LC 98-19298. (Illus.). 384p. 1998. 17.95 (1-56718-394-8) Llewellyn Pubns.

Modern Sexism: Blatant, Subtle & Covert Discrimination. 2nd ed. Nijole V. Benokraitis & Joe R. Feagin. LC 94-22624. 240p. 1994. pap. text 34.67 (0-13-588617-1) P-H.

*Modern Shamanic Living: New Explorations of an Ancient Path. Evelyn C. Rysdyk. LC 99-22633. 128p. 1999. pap. 9.95 (1-57863-125-4) Weiser.

Modern Shepherd. Dave Brown & Sam Meadowcroft. (Illus.). 240p. 1989. 32.95 (0-85236-188-2, Pub. by Farming Pr) Diamond Farm Bk.

Modern Shipping Disasters, 1963-1987. Norman Hooke. 552p. 1989. 90.00 (1-85044-211-8) LLP.

Modern Ships: Elements of Their Design, Construction & Operation. 2nd ed. John H. La Dage. LC 65-21747. (Illus.). 391p. reprint ed. pap. 121.30 (0-8357-8228-X, 203396800087) Bks Demand.

Modern Short Course in Engineering Electromagnetics Accompanied by Computer Programs. S. Ratnajeevan Hoole & P. Ratnamahilan Hoole. (Oxford Engineering Science Ser.). (Illus.). 576p. (C). 1996. text 79.95 (0-19-507856-X) OUP.

Modern Short Stories. Robert J. Dixson. 96p. (C). 1987. pap. text 15.13 (0-13-597642-1) Prentice ESL.

Modern Short Stories. Martin. 160p. 1993. pap. text 21.33 (0-13-481805-9) P-H.

Modern Short Stories. 4th ed. Ed. by Arthur Mizener. 874p. (C). 1979. pap. text 37.00 (0-393-95025-5); pap. text, student ed. 3.50 (0-393-95032-8) Norton.

Modern Short Stories: A Critical Anthology. Ed. by Robert B. Heilman. LC 73-106674. 438p. 1971. reprint ed. lib. bdg. 48.50 (0-8371-3360-2, HESS, Greenwood Pr) Greenwood.

Modern Short Stories in English. Lolita Dixson. (C). 1987. 105.00 (0-13-597659-6, Macmillan Coll) P-H.

Modern Short Story in Peru. Earl M. Aldrich. LC 66-22860. 224p. 1966. reprint ed. pap. 69.50 (0-608-01901-1, 206255300003) Bks Demand.

Modern Shotguns & Loads. Charles Askins. 30.00 (0-935632-98-0) Wolfe Pub Co.

Modern Siberia. Wood. 240p. (C). Date not set. write for info. (0-415-06631-X) Routledge.

Modern Signal Processing: Proceedings of the Arab School on Science & Technology. Ed. by Thomas Kailath. LC 84-19289. (Illus.). 445p. 1986. pap. text 95.00 (0-89116-453-7) Hemisp Pub.

Modern Simulation & Modeling. Reuven Rubinstein et al. LC 97-11869. (Series in Probability & Statistics). 384p. 1998. 89.95 (0-471-17077-1) Wiley.

Modern Sioux: Social Systems & Reservation Culture. Ed. by Ethel Nurge. LC 71-88089. 368p. reprint ed. pap. 114.10 (0-608-17171-9, 202787900056) Bks Demand.

Modern Size-Exclusion Liquid Chromatography: Practice of Gel Permeation & Gel Filtration Chromatography. W. W. Yau et al. LC 79-12739. 496p. 1979. 185.00 (0-471-03387-1) Wiley.

Modern Skeletons in Postmodern Closets: A Cultural Studies Alternative. James J. Sosnoski. 256p. (C). 1995. text 45.00 (0-8139-1620-8); pap. text 19.50 (0-8139-1621-6) U Pr of Va.

Modern Slavery & the Global Economy. Ed. by Gary E. McCuen. (Ideas in Conflict Ser.). (Illus.). 176p. (YA). (gr. 7-12). 1998. lib. bdg. 15.95 (0-86596-145-X) G E M.

Modern Slaves. Claire Willows. (Illus.). 288p. 1995. 34.95 (1-897767-04-8, Pub. by Delectus Bks) Xclusiv Distrib.

Modern Slavic Literatures. Ed. by Vasa D. Mihailovich et al. Incl. Vol. 2. Bulgarian, Czechoslovak, Polish, Ukrainian, & Yugoslav Literatures. LC 64-20047. 1976. 60.00 (0-8044-3177-9); Vol. 1. LC 75-10105. (Orig.). 1972. 60.00 (0-8044-3176-0); LC 76-15658. (Library of Literary Criticism). 1972. 120.00 (0-8044-3175-2) Continuum.

Modern Sloven-French Dictionary see Dictionnaire Moderne: Slovene & Francais

Modern Small Arms. Ian Hogg. 1995. 17.98 (0-7858-0018-2) Bk Sales Inc.

Modern Small Industry in India: Problems & Prospects. Ram K. Vepa. 180p. (C). 1989. text 25.00 (0-8039-9573-3) Sage.

*Modern Snare Drummer. Ronald Spagnardi. 84p. 1999. spiral bd. 12.95 (0-634-00171-X) H Leonard.

Modern Sniper Rifles. Duncan Long. (Illus.). 120p. 1988. pap. 20.00 (0-87364-470-0) Paladin Pr.

Modern Social Conflict: An Essay on the Politics of Liberty. Ralf Dahrendorf. 1990. pap. 15.95 (0-520-06861-0, Pub. by U CA Pr) Cal Prin Full Svc.

Modern Social Movements. Savel Zimand. 1971. 300.00 (0-87700-188-X) Revisionist Pr.

Modern Social Policy. Michael Sullivan. 180p. 1995. pap. 29.95 (0-7450-1435-6) P-H.

Modern Social Theory: Key Debates & New Directions. Derek Layder. LC 97-171393. 256p. 1997. 65.00 (1-85728-385-6, Pub. by UCL Pr Ltd); pap. 19.95 (1-85728-386-4, Pub. by UCL Pr Ltd) Taylor & Francis.

Modern Social Work in Search of a Soul: Felix Biestek: in the Service of Others. Bob Mullan. LC 97-6105. (Illus.). 332p. 1997. 59.95 (1-57309-162-6, Cath Scholar Pr); pap. 34.95 (1-57309-161-8, Cath Scholar Pr) Intl Scholars.

Modern Social Work Theory: A Critical Introduction. 2nd rev. ed. Malcolm Payne. LC 96-53614. 354p. (C). 1997. pap. text 33.95 (0-925065-15-3) Lyceum IL.

Modern Society. Julia W. Howe. (Notable American Authors Ser.). 1992. reprint ed. lib. bdg. 75.00 (0-7812-3220-1) Rprt Serv.

Modern Society & Mental Disease. Carney Landis & James D. Page. Ed. by Gerald N. Grob. LC 78-22571. (Historical Issues in Mental Health Ser.). (Illus.). 1980. reprint ed. lib. bdg. 18.95 (0-405-11924-0) Ayer.

Modern Sociological Theory. Malcolm Waters. (C). 1994. text 55.00 (0-8039-8531-2); pap. text 22.95 (0-8039-8532-0) Sage.

Modern Sociological Theory. 4th rev. ed. George Ritzer. LC 95-36202. Orig. Title: Contemporary Sociological Theory, 3rd ed.. (C). 1995. pap. text 36.00 (0-07-053018-1) McGraw.

Modern Sociological Theory. 5th ed. Ritzer. LC 99-44807. 648p. 1999. pap. 50.00 (0-07-229604-6) McGraw.

Modern Sociological Theory: An Introduction. M. Francis Abraham. (Illus.). 320p. 1983. pap. text 15.95 (0-19-561384-8) OUP.

Modern Software Tools for Scientific Computing. Ed. by Erlend Arge et al. LC 97-6613. 385p. 1997. 69.95 (0-8176-3974-8) Birkhauser.

Modern Software Tools for Scientific Computing. Erlend Arge et al. LC 97-6613. 380p. 1997. write for info. (3-7643-3974-8) Birkhauser.

Modern Soil Microbiology. Ed. by J. D. Van Elsas et al. LC 97-12600. (Books in Soils, Plants & the Environment: Vol. 56). (Illus.). 688p. 1997. text 195.00 (0-8247-9436-2) Dekker.

Modern Solders & Soldering for Competitive Electronics Manufacturing. Jennie S. Hwang. (Illus.). 622p. 1996. 75.00 (0-07-031749-6) McGraw.

*Modern Solvents in Organic Synthesis. Ed. by P. Knochel. (Topics in Current Chemistry Ser.: Vol. 206). (Illus.). 226p. 1999. 146.00 (3-540-66213-8) Spr-Verlag.

*Modern Songs. Ahmad Nawaz. LC 00-133576. 89p. 2000. pap. 10.00 (1-58225-381-1) Ananta Prakashani.

Modern Sons of the Pharaohs. S. H. Leeder. LC 73-6288. (Middle East Ser.). 1973. reprint ed. 31.95 (0-405-05346-0) Ayer.

Modern Souls. Herb Ritts. 1995. 50.00 (1-881616-61-4) Dist Art Pubs.

*Modern South Africa. 2000. write for info. (0-582-38227-0) Pearson Educ.

Modern South Africa in Search of a Soul: Perspectives on the Wilderness Within. Ed. by Graham Saayman. (Illus.). 247p. 1990. 27.50 (0-938434-56-X); pap. 16.95 (0-938434-55-1) Sigo Pr.

Modern South Asia: History, Culture & Political Economy. Sugata Bose & Ayesha Jalal. LC 97-14688. 320p. (C). 1998. 75.00 (0-415-16951-8) Routledge.

Modern South Asia: History, Culture & Political Economy. Sugata Bose & Ayesha Jalal. LC 97-14688. (Illus.). 320p. (C). 1998. pap. 22.99 (0-415-16952-6) Routledge.

Modern South Wales: Essays in Economic History. Ed. by Colin Baber & L. J. Williams. xii, 324p. 1986. 70.00 (0-7083-0943-7, Pub. by Univ Wales Pr) Paul & Co Pubs.

Modern Southeast Asian Literature in Translation: A Resource for Teaching. Ed. by Grant Olson. LC 98-127912. 116p. 1997. pap. text 12.95 (1-881044-14-9) ASU Prog SE Asian.

Modern Southern Reader: Major Stories, Drama, Poetry, Essays, Interviews & Reminiscences from the Twentieth Century South. Ed. by Ben Forkner & Patrick Samway. 748p. 1986. pap. 26.95 (0-934601-08-9) Peachtree Pubs.

Modern Soviet Combat Tanks. Steven J. Zaloga. (Vanguard Ser.: No. 37). (Illus.). 48p. pap. 10.95 (0-85045-525-1, 9326, Pub. by Ospry) Stackpole.

Modern Spacecraft Dynamics & Control. Marshall H. Kaplan. 432p. 1976. text 105.95 (0-471-45703-5) Wiley.

Modern Spain, 1875-1980. Raymond Carr. (Opus Ser.). (Illus.). 256p. 1981. pap. text 18.95 (0-19-289090-5) OUP.

Modern Spanish Economy. Keith Salmon. 1991. text 49.00 (0-86187-132-4) St Martin.

Modern Spanish Economy: Transformation & Integration into Europe. Keith Salmon. LC 95-3878. 290p. 1995. 72.95 (1-85567-153-0) St Martin.

Modern Spanish Economy: Transformation & Integration into Europe. Keith Salmon. LC 95-3878. 1995. pap. 24.95 (1-85567-154-9) St Martin.

Modern Spanish Grammar. Juan Kattan-Ibarra & Christopher J. Pountain. (Routledge Grammars Ser.). (SPA.). 160p. (C). 1997. pap., wbk. ed. 14.99 (0-415-12099-3) Routledge.

Modern Spanish Grammar: A Practical Guide. Juan K. Ibarra & Christopher J. Pountain. LC 96-6874. (ENG & SPA.). 496p. (C). 1997. 75.00 (0-415-09845-9); pap. 25.99 (0-415-09846-7) Routledge.

Modern Spanish Lyric. S. Griswold Morley & E. C. Hills. 1972. 59.95 (0-8490-0652-X) Gordon Pr.

*Modern Spanish Prose: Literary Selections from Spain & Latin America. 6th ed. Gustave W. Andrian. 228p. (C). 1999. pap. text 30.80 (0-13-013052-4) P-H.

Modern Spanish Prose: With a Selection of Poetry. 5th ed. Gustave W. Andrian. 226p. 1995. pap. 37.60 (0-13-228883-4) P-H.

M

Modern Spectral Analysis with Geophysical Applications. Markus Bath. Ed. by Michael R. Cooper. (Open File Publications: No. 2). 530p. 1995. pap. 65.00 (*1-56080-031-3*, 758) Soc Expl Geophys.

Modern Spectrochemical Analysis of Metals: An Introduction for Users of Arc/Spark Instrumentation. V. B. Thomsen. LC 96-86487. 220p. 1996. 156.00 (*0-87170-578-8*, 6540) ASM.

Modern Spectroscopy. 2nd ed. John M. Hollas. LC 91-3400. (Illus.). 429p. 1992. reprint ed. pap. 133.00 (*0-608-03999-3*, 206473600011) Bks Demand.

Modern Spectroscopy. 3rd ed. J. Michael Hollas. LC 96-5964. 416p. 1996. 150.00 (*0-471-96522-7*); pap. 54.95 (*0-471-96523-5*) Wiley.

Modern Spectroscopy of Solids, Liquids, & Gases. LC 95-67218. (Nineteen Ninety-Five Technical Digest Ser.: Vol. 3). 91p. (Orig.). 1995. pap. 66.00 (*1-55752-376-2*) Optical Soc.

Modern Spectrum Analysis of Time Series. Prabhakar S. Naidu. 416p. 1995. boxed set 84.95 (*0-8493-2464-5*, 2464) CRC Pr.

Modern Spectrum Analyzer Theory & Applications. Morris Engelson. LC 84-45200. (Illus.). 269p. reprint ed. pap. 83.40 (*0-8357-4235-0*, 203702200007) Bks Demand.

Modern Speech Processing: Application to Speech Recognition & Coding. Kadambe. 400p. text (*0-471-29413-6*) Wiley.

Modern Spherical Functions. Masaru Takeuchi. Tr. by Toshinobu Nagura from JPN. LC 93-24648. (Translations of Mathematical Monographs: Vol. 135). (ENG.). 265p. 1994. text 130.00 (*0-8218-4580-2*, MMONO/135) Am Math.

Modern Spirit in Chinese Painting: Selections from the Jeannette Shambaugh Elliott Collection. Phoenix Art Museum Staff & Eden Siu-Hung Yu. Ed. by Claudia Brown & Ju-hsi Chou. LC 85-72990. (Illus.). (Orig.). 1985. pap. 15.00 (*0-910407-17-7*) Phoenix Art.

Modern Spiritual Writers: Their Legacies of Prayer. Charles J. Healey. LC 89-30504. 217p. (Orig.). 1989. pap. 10.95 (*0-8189-0550-6*) Alba.

Modern Spiritualism: Its Facts & Fanaticisms. E. W. Capron. LC 75-36833. (Occult Ser.). 1976. reprint ed. 35.95 (*0-405-07945-1*) Ayer.

Modern Spiritualities: An Inquiry. Ed. by Laurence Brown et al. LC 96-41522. (Westminster College - Oxford Ser.). 256p. 1997. 32.95 (*1-57392-112-2*) Prometheus Bks.

Modern Spirituality: An Anthology. Ed. by John Garvey. 156p. 1985. pap. 12.95 (*0-87243-162-2*) Templegate.

Modern Spirituality Series. Michael Ramsey. 96p. 1990. pap. 4.95 (*0-87243-178-9*) Templegate.

Modern Spoken Cambodian. Franklin E. Huffman. LC 71-104615. (Yale Linguistic Ser.). 465p. reprint ed. pap. 144.20 (*0-8357-8229-8*, 203376400087) Bks Demand.

Modern Spoken Cambodian. Franklin E. Huffman. 451p. 1987. reprint ed. pap. 16.00 (*0-300-01316-7*) Cornell SE Asia.

Modern Spoken Italian, Pt. B. unabridged ed. Elaine V. Baran. (Self-Instructional Language Courses). 136p. (C). pap. 185.00 incl. digital audio (*0-88432-074-X*, AFZ551) Audio-Forum.

Modern Spoken Tibetan: Lhasa Dialect. G. Goldstein & N. Norang. 1984. 85.00 (*0-7855-0318-8*, Pub. by Ratna Pustak Bhandar) St Mut.

Modern Spoken Tibetan: Lhasa Dialect. rev. ed. Ed. by Melvyn C. Goldstein & Ngawang Nornang. (C). 1984. 140.00 (*0-89771-116-5*, Pub. by Ratna Pustak Bhandar) St Mut.

Modern Sporting Guns. C. Austyn. (Illus.). 128p. 1994. 40.00 (*1-57157-025-X*) Safari Pr.

Modern Sporting Rifle Cartridges. Wayne Van Zwoll. 1999. pap. 21.95 (*0-88317-213-5*) Stoeger Pub Co.

Modern Sports Cars. Chelsea House Publishing Staff. (Concise Collection). (Illus.). 48p. (J). (gr. 3 up). 1997. 15.95 (*1-85627-733-X*) Chelsea Hse.

***Modern Sports Karate: Basics of Techniques & Tactics.** Jakhel Rudolf. 1998. pap. text 17.95 (*3-89124-428-2*) Meyer & Meyer.

Modern Sportsman's Gun & Rifle, 2. J. H. Walsh. (Library Classics). (Illus.). 536p. 1986. 55.00 (*0-935632-40-9*) Wolfe Pub Co.

Modern Sri Lankan Drama. D. C. R. A. Goonetilleke. (Sri Lanka Studies: No. 15). 228p. (C). 1991. text 18.00 (*81-7030-251-X*) S Asia.

Modern Stage & Other Worlds. Austin E. Quigley. 352p. 1986. 42.50 (*0-416-39310-1*, 9273); pap. 13.95 (*0-416-39320-9*, 9274) Routledge.

Modern Standard Arabic: Intermediate Level, 3 vols. as a set, Set. Ernest N. McCarus et al. 1971. 16.00 (*0-916798-09-7*) UM Dept NES.

Modern State. Christopher Pierson. LC 96-10759. (Key Ideas Ser.). 224p. (C). 1996. 80.00 (*0-415-14413-2*); pap. 22.99 (*0-415-07452-5*) Routledge.

Modern State: An Anarchist Analysis. Frank Harrison. 227p. 1983. 42.99 (*0-920057-01-2*, Pub. by Black Rose); pap. 13.99 (*0-920057-00-4*, Pub. by Black Rose) Consort Bk Sales.

***Modern State & Its Study: New Administrative Sciences in a Changing Europe & United States.** Ed. by Walter J. M. Kickert & Richard J. Stillman, II. LC 99-15401. 296p. 2000. 90.00 (*1-84064-138-X*) E Elgar.

Modern State Trials: With Essays & Notes, 2 vols. rev. ed. William C. Townsend. (Illus.). 1989. reprint ed. 95.00 (*0-8377-2634-4*, Rothman) W S Hein.

Modern Station: New Approaches to Railway Architecture. Brian Edwards. LC 96-71621. (Illus.). 200p. (C). 1996. 75.00 (*0-419-19680-3*, E & FN Spon) Routledge.

Modern Statistical Methods in Chronic Disease Epidemiology: Proceedings of a Conference Sponsored by SIAM Institute for Mathematics & Society & Supported by the Department of Energy. Ed. by Suresh H. Moolgavkar & Ross L. Prentice. LC 86-1597. 282p. 1986. 145.00 (*0-471-83904-3*, Wiley-Interscience) Wiley.

Modern Statistical Quality Control. Farnum. 1993. teacher ed. 29.50 (*0-534-20306-X*) Brooks-Cole.

Modern Statistical Quality Control & Management. Nicholas R. Farnum. LC 93-9510. 500p. (C). 1993. pap. 77.95 (*0-534-20304-3*) Wadsworth Pub.

Modern Statistical Selection: Proceedings of the Conference "Statistical Ranking & Selection--Three Decades of Development", University of California at Santa Barbara, December 1984, Pt. 1. Ed. by M. Haseeb Rizvi. LC 86-71924. (Mathematical & Management Sciences Ser.: Vol. 13). 1986. 195.00 (*0-935950-13-3*) Am Sciences Pr.

Modern Statistical Selection: Proceedings of the Conference "Statistical Ranking & Selection--Three Decades of Development", University of California at Santa Barbara, December 1984, Pt. II. Ed. by M. Haseeb Rizvi. LC 86-71924. (Mathematical & Management Sciences Ser.: Vol.14). 1987. 195.00 (*0-935950-14-1*) Am Sciences Pr.

***Modern Statistical System & GPSS Simulation.** 2nd ed. Zaven A. Karian & Edward J. Dudewicz. LC 98-35396. 560p. 1998. boxed set 84.95 (*0-8493-3922-7*) CRC Pr.

Modern Statistical, Systems & GPSS Simulation: The First Course. Zaven A. Karian & Edward J. Dudewicz. LC 90-2191. (Illus.). xvii, 468p. 1991. text 195.00 (*0-7167-8232-4*) Am Sciences Pr.

Modern Statistics. 2nd ed. Donald A. Berry. (Statistics Ser.). 1995. pap., student ed. 17.95 (*0-534-50481-7*) Wadsworth Pub.

Modern Statistics: Methods & Applications. Ed. by Robert V. Hogg. LC 80-16093. (Proceedings of Symposia in Applied Mathematics Ser.: Vol. 23). 110p. 1980. pap. 23.00 (*0-8218-0023-X*, PSAPM/23) Am Math.

Modern Steel House. N. Jackson. LC 96-215890. 256p. 1996. text. write for info. (*0-419-21720-7*, E & FN Spon) Routledge.

Modern Steel House. Neil Jackson. 245p. 1996. 39.95 (*0-471-28806-3*, VNR) Wiley.

Modern Steel House. Neil Jackson. (Illus.). 1996. 39.95 (*0-442-02414-2*, VNR) Wiley.

Modern Stentors: Radio Broadcasters & the Federal Government, 1920-1934, 31. Philip T. Rosen. LC 79-8952. (Contributions in Economics & Economic History Ser.: No. 31). (Illus.). 267p. 1980. 65.00 (*0-313-21231-7*, RMS/, Greenwood Pr) Greenwood.

Modern Stereotactic Neurosurgery. Ed. by L. Dade Lunsford. (C). 1988. text 309.50 (*0-89838-950-X*) Kluwer Academic.

Modern Stock Handbook, 1987. 2nd ed. 1987. 36.00 (*0-318-23501-3*) MTA Financial Servs.

Modern Stock Market Handbook. Martin Torosian. 1978. 29.00 (*0-686-24368-4*) MTA Financial Servs.

Modern Stonewall Dutch. Eric Schiller. 99p. (Orig.). 1990. pap. 6.50 (*0-931462-96-7*) Chess Ent.

Modern Stories in English. 3rd ed. New & Rosengarten. 1991. pap. text. write for info. (*0-7730-5127-9*) Addison-Wes.

Modern Stories of Ancient Patriarchs: Noah: Who Had the Best of Two Worlds, Abraham: Who Fathered Many Nations, Isaac: The Man Who Trusted Everybody, Jacob: Voted Most Likely to Fail, & Joseph: The Slave Who Made Good. Marvin L. Smith. LC 90-81709. (Illus.). 180p. (Orig.). 1990. pap. 7.00 (*0-9625115-4-4*) Campbell Rd Pr.

Modern Stranger: On Language & Membership. Lesley D. Harman. (Contributions to the Sociology of Language Ser.: No. 47). 182p. 1988. text 71.55 (*0-89925-324-5*) Mouton.

Modern Strategies for Teaching the American Revolution. Hoffer et al. 1976. 4.99 (*0-685-08163-X*) Ohio Hist Soc.

Modern Strategy. Colin S. Gray. LC 99-32729. 432p. (C). 1999. pap. text 29.95 (*0-19-878251-9*) OUP.

Modern Strategy for Preclinical Pharmaceutical R & D: Towards the Virtual Research Company. David Cavalla et al. LC 96-37234. 228p. 1997. 139.95 (*0-471-97117-0*) Wiley.

Modern Strategy for Preclinical Pharmaceutical R & D: Towards the Virtual Research Company. Colin S. Gray. LC 99-32729. 380p. (C). 2000. text 68.00 (*0-19-828030-0*) OUP.

Modern Streamers for Trophy Trout: New Techniques, Tactics, & Patterns. Bob Linsenman & Kelly Galloup. LC 99-29642. (Illus.). 224p. 1999. text 34.95 (*0-88150-466-1*, Pub. by Countryman) Norton.

Modern Street Ballads. J. Ashton. 1973. 59.95 (*0-8490-0653-8*) Gordon Pr.

Modern Street Ballads. Ed. by John Ashton. LC 68-58949. (Illus.). 1972. reprint ed. 23.95 (*0-405-08223-1*, Pub. by Blom Pubns) Ayer.

Modern Structural Analysis. (C). 1930. text. write for info. (*0-06-042403-6*) Allyn.

***Modern Structural Geology: Applications of Continuum Mechanics in Structural Geology.** John G. Ramsay & Richard J. Lisle. (Techniques of Modern Structural Geology Ser.: Vol. 3). 608p. 2000. pap. 65.00 (*0-12-576923-7*) Acad Pr.

Modern Structured Analysis. Edward Yourdon. (Yourdon Press Computing Ser.). 688p. (C). 1988. 73.00 (*0-13-598624-9*, Yourdon) P-H.

***Modern Structured Analysis.** 2nd ed. Edward Yourdon. 2000. 44.99 (*0-13-031189-8*) P-H.

Modern Structured Programming: Program Logic, Style, & Testing. R. Schneyer. 320p. 1984. pap. text 13.95 (*0-938188-19-4*) Mitchell Pub.

Modern Studies. Oliver Elton. LC 67-26739. (Essay Index Reprint Ser.). 1977. 23.95 (*0-8369-0414-1*) Ayer.

Modern Studies of Basic Quantum Concepts & Phenomena: Proceedings of Nobel Symposium No. 104 Gimo, Sweden 13 - 17 June 1997. Ed. by Erik B. Karlsson. 230p. 1998. 48.00 (*981-02-3488-0*) World Scientific Pub.

Modern Study of the Harp: L'Etude Moderne de la Harpe. L. Salzedo. Orig. Title: L'Etude Moderne de la Harpe. 1986. pap. 13.95 (*0-7935-5567-1*, 50327820) H Leonard.

Modern Style. Elinor Felcher. LC 98-5706. (Architecture & Design Library Ser.). 1998. 17.95 (*1-56799-547-0*, Friedman-Fairfax) M Friedman Pub Grp Inc.

Modern Subject: Conceptions of the Self in Classical German Philosophy. Ed. by Karl Ameriks & Dieter Sturma. LC 95-4244. (SUNY Series in Contemporary Continental Philosophy). 252p. (C). 1995. text 49.50 (*0-7914-2753-6*); pap. text 17.95 (*0-7914-2754-4*) State U NY Pr.

Modern Suburban Fire Fighting. Dick Sylvia. Ed. by Dorothy P. Ferguson. LC 83-50530. (Illus.). 386p. 1983. 20.00 (*0-912212-01-2*) Fire Eng.

Modern Sucker-Rod Pumping. Gabor Takacs. LC 92-42789. 240p. 1993. 35.00 (*0-87814-383-1*, P4489) PennWell Bks.

Modern Superabsorbent Polymer Technology. Fredric L. Buchholz & Andrew T. Graham. LC 97-12782. 304p. 1997. 105.00 (*0-471-19411-5*) Wiley.

Modern Supreme Court. Robert G. McCloskey. LC 70-173408. 388p. reprint ed. pap. 120.30 (*0-7837-6079-5*, 205912500007) Bks Demand.

Modern Surgical Care: Physiologic Foundations & Clinical Applications. 2nd ed. Thomas A. Miller. LC 97-50113. 1454p. 1998. 145.00 (*1-57626-060-7*) Quality Med Pub.

Modern Surgical Management of Endometriosis. Camran Nezhat et al. LC 94-19130. (Illus.). 288p. 1995. 129.00 (*0-387-94243-2*) Spr-Verlag.

Modern Surgical Pathology, 2 vols. Weidner. (C). 1999. text. write for info. (*0-7216-7253-1*, W B Saunders Co) Harcrt Hlth Sci Grp.

Modern Survival Retreat: A New & Vital Approach to Retreat Theory & Practice. Ragnar Benson. LC 98-209848. (Illus.). 120p. 1998. pap. 15.00 (*0-87364-980-X*) Paladin Pr.

Modern Swedish Short Stories. Anglo-Swedenish Literary Foundation, London Staff. 1977. 33.95 (*0-8369-4261-2*, 6063) Ayer.

Modern Switzerland. Aldo A. Benini. LC 98-14811. (Comparative Society Ser.). 168p. 1998. pap. 13.75 (*0-07-034427-2*) McGraw.

Modern Swordsman: Realistic Training for Serious Self-Defense. Fred Hutchinson. LC 99-188082. (Illus.). 80p. 1998. pap. 20.00 (*0-87364-995-8*) Paladin Pr.

Modern Symbolic Logic. Thomas J. McKay. 826p. (C). 1989. text 45.00 (*0-02-379286-8*, Macmillan Coll) P-H.

Modern Synthetic Methods, Vol. 5. Ed. by Rolf Scheffold. (Illus.). 310p. 1989. 75.95 (*0-387-51060-5*) Spr-Verlag.

Modern Synthetic Methods 1995. Ed. by Beat Ernst & Christian Leumann. (Illus.). 453p. 1995. 105.00 (*3-906390-12-8*, Wiley-VCH) Wiley.

Modern Synthetic Reactions. 2nd ed. Herbert O. House. LC 78-173958. (C). 1972. text 49.50 (*0-8053-4501-9*) Benjamin-Cummings.

Modern Syria: From Ottoman Rule to Pivotal Role in the Middle East. Ed. by Joseph Ginat et al. LC 99-29246. 296p. 1998. 65.00 (*1-898723-83-4*, Pub. by Sussex Acad Pr) Intl Spec Bk.

Modern Syria: From Ottoman Rule to Pivotal Role in the Middle East Moshe Ma'oz et al. LC 99-29246. 1999. write for info. (*1-902210-32-8*, Pub. by Sussex Acad Pr) Intl Spec Bk.

Modern Syrian Short Stories. Tr. by Michel G. Azrak from ARA. LC 86-51002. 131p. (Orig.). 1988. pap. 10.95 (*0-89410-441-1*, Three Contnts) L Rienner.

Modern Syrian Short Stories. rev. ed. Tr. by Michel G. Azrak from ARA. LC 86-51002. 131p. (Orig.). 1988. 25.00 (*0-89410-440-3*, Three Contnts) L Rienner.

***Modern System Analysis & Design: Grades 4-6.** 2nd ed. (C). 1999. write for info. (*0-13-017485-8*) P-H.

***Modern Systems Analysis & Design.** 2nd ed. Jeffrey A. Hoffer. LC 98-25100. 912p. (C). 1998. 90.67 (*0-201-33841-6*, Prentice Hall) P-H.

***Modern Systems Analysis & Design: Oracle Edition.** 2nd ed. Jeffrey A. Hoffer & Joey F. George. 912p. 1998. text 95.00 (*0-201-38369-1*) Addison-Wesley.

***Modern Systems Design: Oracle Edition.** 888p. (C). 1999. write for info. (*0-201-52610-7*) Addison-Wesley.

Modern Systems of Government: Exploring the Role of Bureaucrats & Politicians. Ed. by Ali Farazmand. LC 96-51224. 304p. (C). 1997. 52.00 (*0-7619-0608-8*, 06088); pap. 24.95 (*0-7619-0609-6*, 06096) Sage.

Modern Tackle Craft see Complete Book of Tackle Making

Modern Taekwondo. Gaetane Ricke. LC 98-44565. 256p. 1999. 17.95 (*0-8069-3989-3*) Sterling.

Modern Tagalog: A Functional-Structural Description. Teodoro A. Llamzon. LC 78-88212. (Janua Linguarum, Series Practica: No. 122). (Orig.). 1976. pap. text 43.10 (*90-279-3493-2*) Mouton.

Modern Tagalog: Grammatical Explanations & Exercises for Non-Native Speakers. Teresita V. Ramos & Resty M. Cena. LC 90-15577. 184p. (C). 1990. pap. text 14.00 (*0-8248-1332-4*) UH Pr.

Modern Tanks. Jane's Staff. LC 96-133382. (Jane's Gem Ser.). (Illus.). 256p. (Orig.). 1995. pap. 8.00 (*0-00-470848-2*, Perennial) HarperTrade.

Modern Tax Planning Checklists see WGL Tax Planning Checklists

Modern Technical Mathematics. Saunders. (Math). 1984. 42.50 (*0-534-02739-3*) Brooks-Cole.

Modern Technical Physics. 6th ed. Arthur Beiser. (Illus.). 860p. (C). 1991. 80.00 (*0-201-57899-9*) Addison-Wesley.

Modern Technique of the Pistol. Gregory B. Morrison. LC 91-72644. 175p. 1991. write for info. (*0-9621342-3-6*) Gunsite Trng Ctr.

Modern Techniques for Auto Restoration. Ken Wickham. LC 97-80605. (Illus.). 192p. 1998. pap. 21.95 (*0-87341-571-X*, MRTCV) Krause Pubns.

Modern Techniques for Financial Transactions & Their Effects on Currency: General & National Reports. Ed. by Michael Stathopoulos. LC 95-20729. 1995. lib. bdg. 100.50 (*90-411-0043-1*, Pub. by M Nijhoff) Kluwer Academic.

Modern Techniques for Molding & Mold Making: Technical Papers: Regional Technical Conference, Hyatt Regency Hotel, Indianapolis, Indiana, November 8-9, 1984. Society of Plastics Engineers Staff. LC TP1150.. 112p. reprint ed. pap. 34.80 (*0-608-15123-8*, 202579800046) Bks Demand.

Modern Techniques for Polymer Characterization. Pethrick. LC 98-45287. 410p. 1999. 305.00 (*0-471-96097-7*) Wiley.

Modern Techniques for Rapid Microbial Analysis. Ed. by Wilfred H. Nelson. (Illus.). xiv, 263p. 1991. 69.50 (*1-56081-001-7*, Wiley-VCH) Wiley.

Modern Techniques for Rapid Microbiological Analysis. W. Nelson. 263p. 1991. 99.95 (*0-471-18777-1*, Wiley-VCH) Wiley.

Modern Techniques in a Seventeenth-Century Writer: Anne de la Roche-Guilhen. Moses Hardin. LC 93-21152. (Contemporary Critical Concepts & Pre-Enlightenment Literature Ser.). X, 140p. 1997. 38.95 (*0-8204-2295-9*) P Lang Pubng.

Modern Techniques in Applied Molecular Spectroscopy. Francis M. Mirabella. LC 97-13437. (Techniques in Analytical Chemistry Ser.). 409p. 1998. 79.95 (*0-471-12359-5*, Wiley-Interscience) Wiley.

Modern Techniques in Computational Chemistry: MOTECC, 1989. Ed. by Enrico Clementi. 640p. (C). 1989. text 348.00 (*90-72199-05-7*, Pub. by Escom Sci Pubs) Kluwer Academic.

Modern Techniques in Computational Chemistry: MOTECC, 1990. Ed. by Enrico Clementi. 1188p. (C). 1990. text 260.00 (*90-72199-07-3*, Pub. by Escom Sci Pubs) Kluwer Academic.

Modern Techniques in Computational Chemistry: MOTECC, 1991. Ed. by Enrico Clementi. 1302p. (C). 1991. text 390.00 (*90-72199-10-3*, Pub. by Escom Sci Pubs) Kluwer Academic.

Modern Techniques in Electroanalysis. Ed. by Peter Vanysek. LC 96-8027. (Chemical Analysis Ser.: Vol. 139). 369p. 1996. 99.95 (*0-471-55514-2*) Wiley.

Modern Techniques in High Resoultion FT-NMR. N. Chandrakumar & S. Subramanian. (Illus.). 400p. 1986. 175.00 (*0-387-96327-8*) Spr-Verlag.

Modern Techniques in Meteorology. Paul L. Hewitt. 360p. 1984. 64.00 (*9971-966-45-X*); pap. 33.00 (*9971-966-47-6*) World Scientific Pub.

***Modern Techniques in Neuroscience Research, 2 vols.** Ed. by U. Windhorst & H. Johansson. LC 99-32065. (Springer Lab Manual Ser.). (Illus.). 1000p. 1999. ring bd. 189.00 incl. cd-rom (*3-540-64460-1*) Spr-Verlag.

Modern Techniques in Raman Spectroscopy. Ed. by J. J. Laserna. LC 95-46351. 446p. 1996. 265.00 (*0-471-95774-7*) Wiley.

Modern Techniques in Water & Wastewater Treatment. Ed. by L. O. Kolarik & A. J. Priestly. (Illus.). 200p. 1995. 79.95 (*0-643-05800-1*, Pub. by CSIRO) Accents Pubns.

Modern Techniques of Ion Transport. fac. ed. Ed. by Barry M. Brenner & Jay H. Stein. LC 86-20728. (Contemporary Issues in Nephrology Ser.: No. 15). (Illus.). 352p. 1987. reprint ed. pap. 109.20 (*0-7837-7887-2*, 204764300007) Bks Demand.

Modern Techniques of Supervision. 16th rev. ed. Alfred Lateiner. LC 66-4182. 1988. pap. 10.00 (*0-911722-00-9*) Lateiner.

Modern Techniques of Surface Science. 2nd ed. D. P. Woodruff & T. A. Delchar. (Cambridge Solid State Science Ser.). (Illus.). 604p. (C). 1994. pap. text 47.95 (*0-521-42498-4*) Cambridge U Pr.

Modern Techniques of Track & Field. Clarence F. Robison et al. LC 74-850. (Health Education, Physical Education, & Recreation Ser.). 357p. reprint ed. pap. 110.70 (*0-608-12689-6*, 205600700043) Bks Demand.

Modern Technology & Its Influence on Astronomy. Ed. by Alec Boksenberg & Jaspar Wall. (Illus.). 335p. 1990. text 90.00 (*0-521-34313-5*) Cambridge U Pr.

Modern Technology in the Heideggerian Perspective. William Lovitt & Harriet B. Lovitt. LC 95-1886. (Problems in Contemporary Philosophy Ser.: Vol. 17a). 1995. write for info. (*0-88946-345-X*) E Mellen.

Modern Technology in the Heideggerian Perspective. William Lovitt & Harriet B. Lovitt. LC 95-1886. (Problems in Contemporary Philosophy Ser.: Vol. 17b). 1995. write for info. (*0-88946-269-0*) E Mellen.

***Modern Technology of Radiation Oncology: A Compendium for Medical Physicists & Radiation Oncologists.** Ed. by Jacob Van Dyk. LC 99-31932. (Illus.). 1072p. 1999. pap. 145.95 (*0-944838-22-7*); text 175.95 (*0-944838-38-3*) Med Physics Pub.

Modern Telecommunications. E. B. Carne. LC 84-16103. (Applications of Communications Theory Ser.). (Illus.). 306p. (C). 1984. 69.50 (*0-306-41841-X*, Plenum Trade) Perseus Pubng.

Modern Television Practice: Principles Technology & Servicing. R. R. Gulati. 1991. write for info. (*81-224-0337-9*, Pub. by Wiley Estrn) Franklin.

Modern Temper: A Study & a Confession. Joseph Wood Krutch. LC 29-8012. 190p. (C). 1956. pap. 12.00 (*0-15-661757-9*, Harvest Bks) Harcourt.

An Asterisk (*) at the beginning of an entry indicates that the title is appearing for the first time.

Modern Temper: American Culture & Society in the 1920s. Lynn Dumenil. Ed. by Eric Foner. 352p. 1995. pap. text 13.00 (*0-8090-1566-8*) Hill & Wang.

*__Modern Templar.__ Chalmers L. Pancoast. 200p. 1999. reprint ed. pap. 14.95 (*0-7661-0771-X*) Kessinger Pub.

Modern Tendencies in Sculpture: Scammon Lectures for 1917. Lorado Taft. LC 77-105040. (Essay Index Reprint Ser.). 1977. 23.95 (*0-8369-1628-X*) Ayer.

Modern Terminal: New Approaches to Airport Architecture. Brian Edwards. LC 98-149909. (Illus.). 240p. (C). 1998. 85.00 (*0-419-21750-9*, E & FN Spon) Routledge.

Modern Tesla Coil Theory. Duane A. Bylund. (Illus.). 129p. (Orig.). 1991. 19.95 (*0-914119-09-5*) Tesla Bk Co.

Modern Tex & Its Applications. Michael Vulis. 304p. 1992. lib. bdg. 49.95 (*0-8493-4431-X*, TA) CRC Pr.

Modern Texas Discovery, 2 vols. Walter Jordan. 1991. text 178.00 (*0-327-00967-5*, 68965, MICHIE) LEXIS Pub.

Modern Texas Discovery, 2 vols. Walter E. Jordan. LC 74-78432. 1072p. Date not set. text 178.00 (*0-317-00411-5*, 68965, MICHIE) LEXIS Pub.

Modern Texas Discovery, 2 vols. Walter E. Jordan. LC 74-78432. 1072p. 1993. suppl. ed. 40.00 (*0-317-03167-8*) West Group.

Modern Texas Discovery: 1998 Supplement. 401p. 1998. suppl. ed. write for info. (*0-327-00298-0*, 6897212) LEXIS Pub.

Modern Texas Discovery: 1999 Edition, 2 Vols. Walter Jordan. 112.00 (*0-327-11244-1*) LEXIS Pub.

Modern Text-Book of Astrology. Margaret E. Hone. (Illus.). 320p. 1999. pap. 25.95 (*0-8464-4948-X*) Beekman Pubs.

Modern Textile Characterization Methods. Ed. by Mastura Raheel. (International Fiber Science & Technology Ser.: Vol. 13). (Illus.). 576p. 1996. text 225.00 (*0-8247-9473-7*) Dekker.

Modern Textile Dictionary. P. Hohenadel & V. Relton. (ENG & GER.). 375p. 1979. 125.00 (*0-8288-4823-8*, M9023) Fr & Eur.

Modern Textile Dictionary: English-German. P. Hohenadel & J. Relton. (ENG & GER.). 484p. 1977. 150.00 (*0-8288-5500-5*, M9024) Fr & Eur.

Modern Textile Dictionary, German-English. 2nd ed. Paul Hohenadel. (ENG & GER.). 437p. 1996. 195.00 (*0-7859-9527-7*) Fr & Eur.

Modern Thai Politics: From Village to Nation. Ed. by Clark D. Neher. LC 78-25917. 491p. 1979. reprint ed. pap., student ed. 152.30 (*0-608-05334-1*, 206503900012) Bks Demand.

Modern Thailand. Kerbo Skagter. LC 99-37248. 168p. 1999. pap. 13.75 (*0-07-034428-0*) McGraw.

Modern Theatre, 6 Vols, 2. Eric Bentley. 1990. 23.00 (*0-8446-1655-9*) Peter Smith.

Modern Theatre, 6 Vols, 3. Eric Bentley. 1990. 23.00 (*0-8446-1656-7*) Peter Smith.

Modern Theatre, 6 Vols, 4. Eric Bentley. 1990. 23.00 (*0-8446-1657-5*) Peter Smith.

Modern Theatre, 6 Vols, 5. Eric Bentley. 1990. 23.00 (*0-8446-1658-3*) Peter Smith.

Modern Theatre, 6 Vols, 6. Eric Bentley. 1990. 23.00 (*0-8446-1659-1*) Peter Smith.

Modern Theatre, 10 vols., 5 bks., Set. Ed. by Elizabeth S. Inchbald. LC 67-13004. 1972. reprint ed. 180.95 (*0-405-08651-2*, Pub. by Blom Pubns) Ayer.

Modern Theatre, 6 Vols, Vol. 1. Eric Bentley. 1990. 23.00 (*0-8446-1654-0*) Peter Smith.

Modern Theatre, 10 vols., 5 bks., Vol. 1. Ed. by Elizabeth S. Inchbald. LC 67-13004. 1972. reprint ed. 36.95 (*0-405-08652-0*, Pub. by Blom Pubns) Ayer.

Modern Theatre, 10 vols., 5 bks., Vol. 2. Ed. by Elizabeth S. Inchbald. LC 67-13004. 1972. reprint ed. 36.95 (*0-405-08653-9*, Pub. by Blom Pubns) Ayer.

Modern Theatre, 10 vols., 5 bks., Vol. 3. Ed. by Elizabeth S. Inchbald. LC 67-13004. 1972. reprint ed. 36.95 (*0-405-08654-7*, Pub. by Blom Pubns) Ayer.

Modern Theatre, 10 vols., 5 bks., Vol. 4. Ed. by Elizabeth S. Inchbald. LC 67-13004. 1972. reprint ed. 36.95 (*0-405-08655-5*, Pub. by Blom Pubns) Ayer.

Modern Theatre, 10 vols., 5 bks., Vol. 5. Ed. by Elizabeth S. Inchbald. LC 67-13004. 1972. reprint ed. 36.95 (*0-405-08656-3*, Pub. by Blom Pubns) Ayer.

Modern Theatre, Vols. 1-6. Eric Bentley. 1990. 138.00 (*0-8446-1653-2*) Peter Smith.

Modern Theatre: A Collection of Successful Modern Plays, 5 vols., Set. Ed. by Elizabeth S. Inchbald. (Anglistica & Americana Ser.: No. 119). 1973. reprint ed. 486.20 (*3-487-04600-8*) G Olms Pubs.

Modern Theatre & Its Background. 1950. pap. 25.00 (*0-527-01713-2*, YFS, NO. 5) Periodicals Srv.

Modern Theologians: An Introduction to Christian Theology in the Twentieth Century. 2nd ed. David Ford. LC 96-16024. 720p. (C). 1996. 77.95 (*0-631-19591-2*); pap. 34.95 (*0-631-19592-0*) Blackwell Pubs.

Modern Theologians Vol. 1: An Introduction to Christian Theology in the Twentieth Century. Ed. by David Ford. 320p. 1989. pap. text 26.95 (*0-631-15372-1*) Blackwell Pubs.

Modern Theologians Vol. 2: An Introduction to Christian Theology in the Twentieth Century, Vol. II. Ed. by David Ford. 320p. 1989. pap. text 26.95 (*0-631-16808-7*) Blackwell Pubs.

Modern Theological German: A Reader & Dictionary. Helmut W. Ziefle. LC 97-19998. 648p. (C). 1997. pap. text 29.99 (*0-8010-2144-8*, Theological Ger) Baker Bks.

Modern Theologies of Prayer. Perry D. LeFevre. LC 95-60692. 376p. 1995. text 32.95 (*0-913552-56-9*); pap. text 19.95 (*0-913552-57-7*) Exploration Pr.

Modern Theories of Art Vol. 2: From Impressionism to Kandinsky. Moshe Barasch. 384p. 1998. text 60.00 (*0-8147-1272-X*); pap. text 20.00 (*0-8147-1273-8*) NYU Pr.

Modern Theories of Art, One: From Winckelmann to Baudelaire. Moshe Barasch. 416p. (C). 1990. text 47.50 (*0-8147-1133-2*) NYU Pr.

Modern Theories of Criminality. C. Bernaldo De Quiros. Tr. by Alfonso De Salvio from SPA. (Modern Criminal Science Ser.: Vol. 1). xxvii, 249p. 1987. reprint ed. 39.00 (*0-8377-2511-9*, Rothman) W S Hein.

Modern Theories of Drama: A Selection of Writings on Drama & Theatre. George W. Brandt. LC 97-27188. 356p. 1999. text 90.00 (*0-19-871140-9*); pap. text 18.95 (*0-19-871139-5*) OUP.

Modern Theories of Exploitation. Ed. by Andrew Reeve. (Modern Politics Ser.: Vol. 14). 214p. (C). 1987. text 45.00 (*0-8039-8072-8*); pap. text 17.95 (*0-8039-8073-6*) Sage.

Modern Theories of Higher Level Predicates: Second Intentions in the Neuzeit. Larry Hickman. (Analytica Ser.). 191p. 1980. lib. bdg. 66.00 (*3-88405-000-1*) Philosophia Pr.

Modern Theories of Justice. Serge-Christophe Kolm. 448p. 1997. 46.50 (*0-262-11208-6*) MIT Pr.

Modern Theories of Language: The Empirical Challenge. Morteza Mahmoudian. LC 92-13538. (Sound & Meaning: The Roman Jakobson Series in Linguistics & Poetics). (Illus.). 256p. 1993. text 42.95 (*0-8223-1278-6*) Duke.

Modern Theories of Law. 229p. 1977. reprint ed. 70.00 (*1-56169-249-2*) Gaunt.

Modern Theories of Nuclear Moments. B. Castel & Ian S. Towner. (Oxford Studies in Nuclear Physics: No. 12). (Illus.). 282p. 1990. text 75.00 (*0-19-851728-9*) OUP.

Modern Theories of Religion. Eric S. Waterhouse. 1977. lib. bdg. 59.95 (*0-8490-2272-X*) Gordon Pr.

Modern Theories of the Universe, from Herschel to Hubble. Michael J. Crowe. (Illus.). 464p. (Orig.). 1994. pap. text 9.95 (*0-486-27880-8*) Dover.

Modern Theory & Method in Group Training. William G. Dyer. LC 80-24641. 268p. (C). 1981. reprint ed. text 23.00 (*0-89874-280-3*) Krieger.

Modern Theory of Anisotropic Elasticity & Applications. Ed. by Julian J. Wu et al. LC 91-35283. (Proceedings in Applied Mathematics Ser.: No. 57). (Illus.). x, 377p. (C). 1991. pap. 90.50 (*0-89871-289-0*) Soc Indus-Appl Math.

Modern Theory of Corporate Finance. 2nd ed. M. C. Jensen & Clifford Smith, Jr. (Finance Ser.). 695p. (C). 1990. 40.94 (*0-07-059109-1*) McGraw.

Modern Theory of Critical Phenomena. Shang-Keng Ma. LC 76-8386. (Frontiers in Physics Ser.: Vol. 46). (Illus.). (C). 1976. pap. 55.00 (*0-8053-6671-7*) Addison-Wesley.

*__Modern Theory of Critical Phenomena.__ Shang-Keng Ma. 582p. 2000. pap. text 39.00 (*0-7382-0301-7*) Perseus Pubng.

Modern Theory of Crystal Growth I. Ed. by A. A. Chernov & H. Mueller-Krumbhar. (Crystals - Growth, Properties & Applications Ser.: Vol. 9). (Illus.). 146p. 1983. 90.95 (*0-387-12161-7*) Spr-Verlag.

Modern Theory of Presidential Power: Alexander Hamilton & the Corwin Thesis, 253. Richard Loss. LC 89-27372. (Contributions in Political Science Ser.: No. 253). 192p. 1990. 52.95 (*0-313-26751-0*, LPW/, Greenwood Pr) Greenwood.

Modern Theory of Summation of Random Variable. Ed. by V. M. Zolotarev. LC 99-496368. (Modern Probability & Statistics Ser.). (Illus.). 416p. 1997. 215.00 (*90-6764-270-3*, Pub. by VSP) Coronet Bks.

Modern Thermodynamics: From Heat Engines to Dissipative Structures. D. K. Kondepudi & I. Prigogine. LC 97-48745. 508p. 1998. 89.95 (*0-471-97393-9*) Wiley.

*__Modern Thermodynamics: From Heat Engines to Dissipative Structures.__ D. K. Kondepudi & I. Prigogine. LC 97-48745. 508p. 1998. pap. 54.95 (*0-471-97394-7*) Wiley.

Modern Thin Layer Chromatography. Nelu Grinberg. (Chromatographic Science Ser.: Vol. 52). (Illus.). 504p. 1990. text 180.00 (*0-8247-8138-4*) Dekker.

Modern Thinkers: Principally upon Social Science; What They Think & Why. Van B. Denslow. LC 72-38744. (Essay Index Reprint Ser.). 1977. reprint ed. 28.95 (*0-8369-2646-3*) Ayer.

Modern Thought & Literature in France. Regis Michaud. LC 67-23248. (Essay Index Reprint Ser.). 1977. 18.95 (*0-8369-0707-8*) Ayer.

Modern Three-Hadron Physics. Ed. by A. W. Thomas. (Topics in Current Physics Ser.: Vol. 2). 1977. 45.00 (*3-540-07950-5*) Spr-Verlag.

Modern Tibet. Ram Rahul. (C). 1992. 12.00 (*0-8364-2800-5*, Pub. by M Manoharial) S Asia.

Modern Time Series Analysis in Forest Products Markets. Jens Abildtrup. LC 98-49745. (Forestry Sciences Ser.). 5p. 1999. write for info. (*0-7923-5524-5*) Kluwer Academic.

Modern Times: Life, Labor & Leisure in America, 1890-1930. Ed. by Cameron. (C). 1998. text. write for info. (*0-321-01119-8*) Addison-Wesley Educ.

Modern Times: Reflections on a Century of English Modernity. Ed. by Mica Nava & Alan O'Shea. LC 95-16372. 288p. (C). 1996. 80.00 (*0-415-06932-7*); pap. 25.99 (*0-415-06933-5*) Routledge.

Modern Times? Work, Professionalism & Citizenship in Teaching. Martin Lawn. 200p. 1996. 79.95 (*0-7507-0495-0*, Falmer Pr); pap. 27.95 (*0-7507-0496-9*, Falmer Pr) Taylor & Francis.

Modern Times - Spanish. Gloria Verges & Oriol Verges. (Journey Through History Ser.). (SPA., Illus.). 32p. (J). (gr. 2-4). 1988. pap. 6.95 (*0-8120-3393-0*) Barron.

Modern Times, Modern Places. Peter Conrad. LC 98-15888. 1999. pap. 10.01 (*0-375-70105-2*) Knopf.

Modern Times, Modern Places: A Monumental Study of the Transformation of Art & Life in the Twentieth Century. Peter Conrad. LC 98-15888. 752p. 1999. 40.00 (*0-375-40113-X*) Knopf.

*__Modern Times, 1970-99.__ Reader's Digest Association South Africa. LC 99-88341. (Eventful 20th Century Ser.). 2000. write for info. (*0-7621-0272-1*) RD Assn.

Modern Times Revised Edition: World From the Twenties to the Nineties, The. rev. ed. Paul Johnson. LC 91-55161. 880p. 1992. reprint ed. pap. 20.00 (*0-06-092283-4*, Perennial) HarperTrade.

Modern Topics in Electron Scattering. Ed. by B. Frois & I. Sick. 400p. (C). 1991. text 86.00 (*9971-5-0975-X*) World Scientific Pub.

Modern Topics in Liquid Crystals - From Neutron Scattering Ferroelectricity. Agnes Buka. 352p. 1993. text 109.00 (*981-02-1539-8*) World Scientific Pub.

Modern Topics in Micro Wave Propagation & Air-Sea Interaction: Proceedings of the NATO Advanced Study Institute, Sorrento, Italy, June, 1973. NATO Advanced Study Institute Staff. Ed. by A. Zancla. LC 73-91210. (NATO ASI Series C: No. 5). 1973. text 195.00 (*90-277-0419-8*) Kluwer Academic.

Modern Topographic Drawing. fac. ed. Robert C. Steele. LC 80-17825. (Illus.). 216p. pap. 67.00 (*0-7837-7434-6*, 204722900006) Bks Demand.

Modern Tort Law, 4 vols. rev. ed. J. D. Lee & Barry A. Lindahl. LC 88-2910. 1988. ring bd. 500.00 (*0-685-34582-3*) West Group.

Modern Towing. John S. Blank, III. LC 87-47736. (Illus.). 607p. 1989. text 45.00 (*0-87033-372-0*) Cornell Maritime.

Modern Toys, 1930-1980. Linda Baker. (Illus.). 270p. 1996. 19.95 (*0-89145-277-X*, 1540) Collector Bks.

Modern Tradition: An Anthology of Short Stories. 4th ed. Ed. by Daniel F. Howard. (C). 1997. 35.40 (*0-673-39219-8*) Addson-Wesley Educ.

Modern Tragedies & Aristotle's Theory. K. S. Misra. LC 84-672343. 252 p. 1983. write for info. (*0-391-02692-5*) Humanities.

Modern Tragedy. Raymond Williams. LC 66-19358. 208p. 1966. pap. 9.95 (*0-8047-0313-2*) Stanford U Pr.

Modern Tragicomedy & the British Tradition. Richard Dutton. LC 86-40072. 256p. 1986. pap. 14.95 (*0-8061-2025-8*) U of Okla Pr.

Modern Trains - Collector's Guide. Chris Ellis. 1995. 12.98 (*0-7858-0221-5*) Bk Sales Inc.

Modern Transfusion Medicine: A Practical Approach. Ed. by Derwood H. Pamphilon. 288p. 1995. boxed set 144.95 (*0-8493-8922-4*) CRC Pr.

Modern Transfusion Therapy, 2 vols., Vol. 1. Ed. by Janice P. Dutcher. 336p. 1989. lib. bdg. 225.00 (*0-8493-6247-4*, RM171) CRC Pr.

Modern Transfusion Therapy, 2 vols., Vol. II. Ed. by Janice P. Dutcher. 384p. 1989. lib. bdg. 216.00 (*0-8493-6248-2*, RM171) CRC Pr.

Modern Transits. Lois M. Rodden. LC 78-56415. 200p. 1978. 19.95 (*0-86690-151-5*, R1414-014) Am Fed Astrologers.

Modern Transmission Line Theory & Application. Lawrence N. Dworsky. LC 88-2753. 250p. (C). 1988. reprint ed. lib. bdg. 34.95 (*0-89464-276-6*) Krieger.

Modern Transport Geography. 2nd ed. B. S. Hoyle et al. LC 98-27242. 382p. 1999. pap. 49.95 (*0-471-97777-2*) Wiley.

Modern Trapline: Methods & Materials. Bob Gilsvik. (Illus.). 197p. 1987. reprint ed. 14.95 (*0-936622-30-X*) A R Harding Pub.

Modern Trapline: Methods & Materials. Bob Gilsvik. LC 78-14650. 213p. reprint ed. pap. 66.10 (*0-608-17205-7*, 202701800053) Bks Demand.

Modern Traveller to the Early Irish Church. Kathleen Hughes & Ann Hamill. (Illus.). 144p. (Orig.). 1997. pap. 15.00 (*1-85182-194-5*, Pub. by Four Cts Pr) Intl Spec Bk.

Modern Treasury of Great Detective & Murder Mysteries. Ed. by Ed Gorman. LC 96-36791. 416p. 1997. pap. 12.95 (*0-7867-0378-4*) Carroll & Graf.

Modern Treatise on the Law of Criminal Complicity. Keith Smith. (Oxford Monographs on Criminal Law & Justice). (Illus.). 320p. 1991. 75.00 (*0-19-825238-2*) OUP.

Modern Treatment of Severe Burns. Z. Y. Fang et al. Ed. by N. Li & S. D. Ge. (Illus.). viii, 334p. 1992. 247.00 (*0-387-54028-8*) Spr-Verlag.

*__Modern Treaty Law & Practice.__ Anthony I. Aust. 384p. (C). 2000. 90.00 (*0-521-59153-8*); pap. 39.95 (*0-521-59846-X*) Cambridge U Pr.

Modern Trends - Tracer Hydrology, Vol. I. Gaspar. 160p. 1987. 93.00 (*0-8493-4320-8*, CRC Reprint) Franklin.

Modern Trends - Tracer Hydrology, Vol. II. Gaspar. 152p. 1987. 89.00 (*0-8493-4321-6*, CRC Reprint) Franklin.

Modern Trends in Aging Research. Y. Courtois et al. (Colloque de L'INSERM Ser.). (ENG & FRE.). 620p. 1987. lib. bdg. 85.00 (*2-85598-309-6*) S M P F Inc.

Modern Trends in Biothermokinetics. S. Schuster et al. (Illus.). 512p. (C). 1994. text 135.00 (*0-306-44579-4*, Kluwer Plenum) Kluwer Academic.

Modern Trends in Cutting Tools. Ed. by George E. Kane. LC 82-61010. (Manufacturing Update Ser.). (Illus.). 279p. reprint ed. pap. 86.50 (*0-8357-6490-7*, 203586100097) Bks Demand.

Modern Trends in Ecology & Environment. R. S. Ambasht. (Illus.). viii, 362p. 1998. 125.00 (*90-73348-86-2*) Balogh.

Modern Trends in Huin Leukemia. 1976. 87.95 (*0-387-79785-8*) Spr-Verlag.

Modern Trends in Human Leukemia, No. VIII. Ed. by Rolf Neth et al. (Haematology & Blood Transfusion Ser.: Vol. 32). (Illus.). 592p. 1990. 224.00 (*0-387-50967-4*) Spr-Verlag.

Modern Trends in Human Leukemia IX: New Results in Clinical & Biological Research Including Pediatric Oncology; Organized on Behalf of the Deutsche Gesellschaft fur Hamatologie und Onkologie, Wilsede, June 17-21, 1990. Ed. by Rolf Neth et al. LC 92-2334. (Haematology & Blood Transfusion - Haematologie und Bluttransfusion Ser.: Vol. 35). (Illus.). 480p. 1992. 239.00 (*0-387-54360-0*); pap. 198.00 (*3-540-54360-0*) Spr-Verlag.

Modern Trends in Human Leukemia Three. Ed. by Rolf Neth et al. (Illus.). 1979. 100.00 (*0-387-08999-3*) Spr-Verlag.

Modern Trends in Nickel Steel & Cast Iron Gear Materials. C. M. Schwitter. (Technical Papers: Vol. P199). (Illus.). 28p. 1939. pap. text 30.00 (*1-55589-338-4*) AGMA.

Modern Trends in Sludge Management, No. 115. Ed. by J. E. McGlashan. (Water Science & Technology Ser.: Vol. 15). (Illus.). 254p. 1983. pap. 44.00 (*0-08-030416-8*, Pergamon Pr) Elsevier.

Modern Trends in the Systematics, Ecology, & Evolution of Hydroids & Hydromedusae. Ed. by Jean Bouillon et al. (Illus.). 354p. 1987. text 85.00 (*0-19-857190-9*) OUP.

Modern Trends in Tort Law: Dutch & Japanese Law Compared. Ed. by E. H. Hondius. LC 99-10523. 316p. 1999. 93.00 (*90-411-1156-5*) Kluwer Academic.

Modern Trends in Tracer Hydrology, 2 vols., Set. E. Gaspar. 1987. reprint ed. 182.00 (*0-8493-4319-4*, CRC Reprint) Franklin.

*__Modern Trends in Tunnelling & Blast Design.__ John Johansen. (Illus.). 180p. (C). 2000. text 80.00 (*90-5809-311-5*, Pub. by A A Balkema) Ashgate Pub Co.

*__Modern Trends in Tunnelling & Blast Design.__ John Johansen & C. F. Mathiesen. (Illus.). 180p. (C). 2000. pap. text 45.00 (*90-5809-312-3*, Pub. by A A Balkema) Ashgate Pub Co.

Modern Trends in World-Religions. Ed. by Albert E. Haydon. LC 68-29214. (Essay Index Reprint Ser.). 1977. 20.95 (*0-8369-0522-9*) Ayer.

Modern Trends of Colloid Science in Chemistry & Biology. Ed. by Hans-Friedrich Eicke. 394p. 1985. lib. bdg. 62.95 (*3-7643-1711-6*) Birkhauser.

Modern Trial Advocacy: Analysis & Practice. 2nd ed. Steven Lubet. LC 97-44830. 486p. 1997. 45.95 (*1-55681-539-5*) Natl Inst Trial Ad.

Modern Trial Advocacy, Canadian Edition. Steven Lubet et al. 424p. 1995. 44.95 (*1-55681-481-X*) Natl Inst Trial Ad.

*__Modern Tribal Development: Paths to Self Sufficiency & Cultural Integrity in Indian Country.__ Dean Howard Smith. (Contemporary Native American Communities Ser.: Vol. 4). 240p. 2000. pap. 23.95 (*0-7425-0410-7*); pap. 62.00 (*0-7425-0409-3*) AltaMira Pr.

Modern Trinitarian Perspectives. John R. Thompson. 176p. 1994. text 49.95 (*0-19-508898-0*); pap. text 19.95 (*0-19-508899-9*) OUP.

Modern Triple Swing. Earl Atkinson. (Ballroom Dance Ser.). 1986. lib. bdg. 250.00 (*0-8490-3645-3*) Gordon Pr.

Modern Trombone: A Definition of Its Idioms. Stuart Dempster. 1994. 29.50 (*0-918194-27-X*) Accura.

Modern Trotting Sire Lines. John Bradley. LC 97-8948. 1997. 40.00 (*0-929346-47-5*) R Meerdink Co Ltd.

Modern Trust Forms & Checklists. Robert E. Parella & Joel E. Miller. 1990. 185.00 (*0-88262-275-7*) Warren Gorham & Lamont.

Modern Trust Forms & Checklists, No. 1. Robert E. Parella & Joel E. Miller. 1992. suppl. ed. 93.00 (*0-7913-1182-1*) Warren Gorham & Lamont.

Modern Trust Forms & Checklists, No. 2. Robert E. Parella & Joel E. Miller. 1992. suppl. ed. 97.00 (*0-685-32294-7*) Warren Gorham & Lamont.

Modern Tsars & Princes: The Struggle for Hegemony in Russia. Jeremy Lester. LC 95-23359. 224p. (C). 1995. pap. 20.00 (*1-85984-039-6*, Pub. by Verso) Norton.

Modern Tsars & Princes: The Struggle for Hegemony in Russia. Jeremy Lester. LC 95-23359. 224p. (C). (gr. 13 up). 1995. 65.00 (*1-85984-914-8*, Pub. by Verso) Norton.

Modern TTL Circuits Manual. Ray M. Marston. (EDN Ser.). (Illus.). 224p. 1994. pap. text 36.95 (*0-7506-2092-7*) Buttrwrth-Heinemann.

Modern Tunisia: A Democratic Apprenticeship. Andrew Borowiec. LC 97-32948. 176p. 1998. 55.00 (*0-275-96136-2*, Praeger Pubs) Greenwood.

Modern Turkish Drama: An Anthology. Talat S. Halman. LC 73-79204. (Studies in Middle Eastern Literatures: No. 5). 1976. pap. 20.00 (*0-88297-033-X*) Bibliotheca.

Modern Twang: An Alternative Country Music Guide & Directory. David Goodman. 439p. 1999. pap. 22.00 (*1-891847-03-1*, D010000, Pub. by Dowling Pr) Music Sales.

Modern Type Setting Techniques: Electric Composition. H. W. Larken. 192p. 1984. 60.00 (*0-946095-10-8*, Pub. by Gresham Bks) St Mut.

Modern Typography: An Essay in Critical History. Robin Kinross. (Illus.). 208p. (Orig.). 1996. pap. 35.00 (*0-907259-05-7*) Princeton Arch.

Modern Tyrants: The Power & Prevalence of Evil in Our Age. Daniel Chirot. 400p. 1994. 29.95 (*0-02-905477-X*) Free Pr.

Modern Tyrants: The Power & Prevalence of Evil in Our Age. Daniel Chirot. LC 95-53117. 510p. (C). 1996. pap. text 19.95 (*0-691-02777-3*, Pub. by Princeton U Pr) Cal Prin Full Svc.

*__Modern U. S. Civil-Military Relations: Wielding the Terrible Swift Sword.__ David E. Johnson. 107p. (C). 1999. reprint ed. pap. text 25.00 (*0-7881-8389-3*) DIANE Pub.

Modern U. S. Military Vehicles. Fred Crismon. LC 98-19124. (Junior Crestline Ser.). (Illus.). 160p. 1998. pap. 21.95 (*0-7603-0526-9*) MBI Pubg.

Modern U. S. Navy Submarines - ECS. Robert Genat & Robin Genat. LC 97-8680. (Enthusiast Color Ser.). (Illus.). 96p. 1997. pap. 13.95 (*0-7603-0276-6*) MBI Pubg.

M

Modern UCC Litigation Forms, 3 vols. P. J. Betsos. 1969. 465.00 (0-8205-2118-3) Bender.

Modern Ukrainian. Assya Humesky. LC 79-94753. xvi, 438p. 1980. pap. 19.95 (0-920862-04-7) Ukrainian Acad.

***Modern Ukrainian.** 2nd ed. Assya Humesky. 435p. 1999. pap. 34.95 (1-895571-29-4, Pub. by Can Inst Ukrainian) Ukrainian Acad.

Modern Ukrainian Short Stories. rev. ed. Ed. by George S. Luckyj. 230p. 1995. lib. bdg. 27.50 (1-56308-391-4) Libs Unl.

Modern United States Civil Military Relations: Wielding the Terrible Swift Sword. David E. Johnson. 119p. 1997. per. 7.00 (0-16-061203-9) USGPO.

Modern University & Its Discontents: The Fate of Newman's Legacies in Britain & America. Sheldon Rothblatt. 475p. 1997. text 64.95 (0-521-45331-3) Cambridge U Pr.

Modern University Chemistry, Custom Pub. 2nd ed. Norbert T. Porile. (C). 1993. text 48.50 (0-07-050639-6) McGraw.

Modern UNIX. Alan Southerton. LC 92-22664. 336p. 1992. 59.99 (0-471-54928-2) Wiley.

Modern Upholstering Methods. 2nd ed. William F. Tierney. LC 96-84891. (Illus.). 160p. 1996. reprint ed. pap. 15.95 (1-56167-315-3) Am Literary Pr.

Modern Urban History in Europe, U. S. A. & Japan: A Handbook. Ed. by Christian Engeli & Horst Matzerath. LC 88-7911. 585p. 1989. 19.50 (0-85496-040-6) Berg Pubs.

M

Modern Urban Landscape: 1880 to the Present. Edward Relph. LC 87-3809. 288p. (Orig.). 1987. pap. text 16.95 (0-8018-3560-7) Johns Hopkins.

Modern Urdu Short Stories. Tr. by Jai Ratan. vi, 200p. 1987. 13.50 (0-8364-2049-7, Pub. by Allied Pubs) S Asia.

Modern Uses of Multiple-Valued Logic. Ed. by J. Michael Dunn & George Epstein. (Episteme Ser.: No. 2). 343p. 1977. text 171.00 (90-277-0747-2, D Reidel) Kluwer Academic.

Modern Utopia. H. G. Wells. LC 67-26614. xxxiv, 393p. 1967. pap. text 16.00 (0-8032-5213-7, Bison Books) U of Nebr Pr.

Modern Utopia & Other Discussions see Works of H. G. Wells

Modern Uzbeks: From the Fourteenth Century to the Present, a Cultural History. Edward A. Allworth. (Publication Series: Studies of Nationalities in the U. S. S. R.: No. 373). 410p. 1990. pap. 24.95 (0-8179-8732-0) Hoover Inst Pr.

Modern Vaccinology. Ed. by Edward Kurstak. (Illus.). 408p. (C). 1994. text 85.00 (0-306-44820-3, Kluwer Plenum) Kluwer Academic.

Modern Varieties of Judaism. Joseph L. Blau. LC 66-10732. (Lectures on the History of Religions Ser.). 217p. 1972. pap. text 20.00 (0-231-08668-7) Col U Pr.

Modern Vascular Surgery. James S. T. Yao & William H. Pearce. (Illus.). 600p. 155.00 (0-8385-6417-8) McGraw.

Modern Vascular Surgery, Vol. 5. Ed. by John B. Chang. LC 92-2307. 520p. 1992. 189.00 (0-387-97864-X); write for info. (3-540-97864-X) Spr-Verlag.

Modern Vascular Surgery, Vol. 6. Ed. by John B. Chang. 1994. write for info. (0-387-94187-8) Spr-Verlag.

Modern Vegetable Gardening. Christopher O. Bird. 192p. 1993. pap. 13.95 (1-55821-256-6) Lyons Pr.

***Modern Vegetarian Kitchen.** Peter Berley. (Illus.). 352p. 2000. 35.00 (0-06-039295-9) HarpC.

***Modern Ventilation Techniques.** W. Booth. 1998. pap. 100.00 (0-86022-493-7, Pub. by Build Servs Info Assn) St Mut.

Modern Verse Drama in English: An Annotated Bibliography, 39. Ed. by Kayla M. Wiggins. LC 93-28054. (Bibliographies & Indexes in World Literature Ser.: No. 39). 184p. 1993. lib. bdg. 65.00 (0-313-28929-8, Greenwood Pr) Greenwood.

Modern Verse from Taiwan. Ed. by Angela J. Palandri. LC 79-161994. 225p. reprint ed. pap. 69.80 (0-608-15828-3, 203131100074) Bks Demand.

Modern Versions Founded upon Apostasy. 3rd enl. rev. ed. David W. Cloud. 76p. 1997. reprint ed. pap. 5.00 (1-58318-009-5, WOL482B) Way of Life.

***Modern Vibrations Primer.** P. M. Moretti. LC 99-52988. 2000. write for info. (0-8493-2038-0) CRC Pr.

Modern Video Production: Tools, Techniques, Applications. Carl Hausman & Philip J. Palombo. 315p. (C). 1997. pap. text 53.44 (0-06-500045-5) Addson-Wesley Educ.

Modern View of Geometry. Leonard M. Blumenthal. (Illus.). 224p. (C). 1980. reprint ed. pap. text 8.95 (0-486-63962-2) Dover.

Modern View of Theodore Theodorsen. Frwd. by Earl H. Dowell. (Illus.). 372p. 1992. 30.00 (0-930403-85-1, 85-1) AIAA.

Modern Vikings: Stories of Life & Sport in the Norseland. Hjalmar H. Boyesen. 1977. 23.95 (0-8369-4266-3, 6065) Ayer.

Modern Vision: The Life of Berenice Abbott. Van Haaften. 2000. 25.00 (0-684-80978-8) Simon & Schuster.

Modern Visual Evidence. Gregory P. Joseph. 750p. 1984. 95.00 (0-318-12034-8) NY Law Pub.

***Modern Visual Poetry.** Willard Bohn. LC 99-55924. 2000. write for info. (0-87413-710-1) U Delaware Pr.

Modern Visualisation of the Endothelium. Ed. by J. M. Polak. (Endothelial Cell Research Ser.: Vol. 4). (Illus.). 252p. 1998. text 85.00 (90-5702-294-X, ECU95, Harwood Acad Pubs) Gordon & Breach.

Modern VLSI Design: A System Approach. Wayne H. Wolf. LC 93-41530. 496p. (C). 1994. text 70.00 (0-13-588377-6) Prntice Hall Bks.

Modern VLSI Design: Systems on Silicon. 2nd ed. Wayne H. Wolf. LC 98-18835. 592p. 1998. 76.00 (0-13-989690-2) P-H.

Modern Voice in American Poetry. William Doreski. LC 94-48343. 197p. 1995. 49.95 (0-8130-1362-3) U Press Fla.

Modern Voice in American Poetry. William Doreski. 197p. 1998. pap. 19.95 (0-8130-1586-3) U Press Fla.

Modern Voltammetric Methods in Analytic Chemistry. A. M. Bond. Date not set. write for info. (0-8247-9443-5) Dekker.

***Modern Voyage.** Lawhead. 2000. pap. 15.00 (0-534-56158-6) Thomson Learn.

Modern Wales: A Concise History. Gareth E. Jones. (Illus.). 395p. (C). 1994. pap. text 22.95 (0-521-46945-7) Cambridge U Pr.

Modern Wales: Politics, Places & People. Kenneth O. Morgan. 492p. 1996. 75.00 (0-7083-1317-5, Pub. by Univ Wales Pr) Paul & Co Pubs.

Modern War on Stage & Screen (Der Moderne Krief Auf der Buhne) Ed. by Wolfgang Gortschacher & Holger Klein. LC 96-51800. 604p. 1997. 129.95 (0-7734-4205-7) E Mellen.

Modern Water Control in Irrigation: Concepts, Issues, & Applications. Herve Plusquellec et al. LC 94-3821. (World Bank Technical Papers: No. 246). 116p. 1994. pap. 22.00 (0-8213-2819-0, 12819) World Bank.

Modern Water Hydraulics - Your Choice for the Future. Ed. by National Fluid Power Association Staff. 16p. 1995. pap. 3.00 (0-942220-33-1) Natl Fluid Power.

Modern Way to Die: Small Stories & Microtales. Peter Wortsman. LC 91-17416. 221p. 1993. 17.95 (0-88064-133-9); pap. 8.95 (0-88064-145-2) Fromm Intl Pub.

***Modern Weapons & Warfare: The Technology of War from 1700 to the Present Day.** Lorenz Books Staff. (Exploring History Ser.). (Illus.). 64p. (J). (gr. 3-7). 2000. 12.95 (0-7548-0453-4, Lorenz Bks) Anness Pub.

Modern Weapons Caching: A Down-to-Earth Approach to Beating the Government Gun Grab. Ragnar Benson. (Illus.). 104p. 1990. pap. 15.00 (0-87364-583-9) Paladin Pr.

Modern Welding: Complete Coverage of the Welding Field in One Easy-to-Use Volume! Andrew D. Althouse et al. LC 99-17784. 779p. 2000. 53.28 (1-56637-605-X) Goodheart.

Modern Welding Technology. 4th ed. Howard B. Cary. LC 96-40187. 780p. 1997. 88.00 (0-13-241803-7) P-H.

Modern Well Design. Bernt S. Aadnoy. (Illus.). 250p. (C). 1996. text 82.00 (90-5410-633-6, Pub. by A A Balkema) Ashgate Pub Co.

Modern Well Design. Bernt S. Aadnoy. LC 96-80206. 1997. 75.00 (0-88415-483-1, 5483) Gulf Pub.

Modern Well Test Analysis: A Computer-Aided Approach. 2nd ed. Roland N. Horne. (Illus.). 250p. (C). 1995. 36.00 (0-9626992-1-7) Petroway.

Modern Welsh: A Comprehensive Grammar. Gareth King. LC 93-22099. 340p. (C). (gr. 13). 1993. pap. 27.99 (0-415-09269-8, B2533) Routledge.

Modern Western Society: A Geographical Perspective on Work, Home & Well-Being. Peter Dicken & Peter E. Lloyd. 408p. (C). 1981. 44.00 (0-06-318048-0, Pub. by P Chapman) St Mut.

Modern Wicca: A New Approach to the Olde Religion of Witchcraft. Cerridwen Silverhorn. LC 97-92723. (Illus.). v, 122p. 1997. pap. 13.95 (1-891530-03-8) Centaur Bks.

Modern Wildlife Painting: Wildlife Art in the Twentieth Century. Nicholas Hammond. LC 98-165907. 224 p. 1998. 56.59 (1-873403-55-0) HEL1.

Modern Wildlife Painting: Wildlife Art in the Twentieth Century. Nicholas Hammond. LC 98-88106. (Illus.). 240p. 1999. 50.00 (0-300-07458-1) Yale U Pr.

Modern Winemaking. Philip Jackisch. LC 84-45803. (Illus.). 288p. 1985. text 32.50 (0-8014-1455-5) Cornell U Pr.

Modern Wiring Practice. Steward & Stubbs. 350p. pap. text. write for info. (0-7506-4648-9) Buttrwrth-Heinemann.

Modern Wiring Practice: Design & Installation. 12th ed. W. E. Steward et al. LC 94-24608. 352p. 1995. pap. text 39.95 (0-7506-2134-6) Buttrwrth-Heinemann.

Modern Witchcraft & Psychoanalysis. M. D. Faber. LC 91-58949. 192p. 1993. 32.50 (0-8386-3488-5) Fairleigh Dickinson.

Modern Witchcraft Spellbook. Anna Riva. (Illus.). 64p. (Orig.). 1973. pap. 4.95 (0-943832-02-0) Intl Imports.

Modern Witch's Book of Herbs & Healing. Sarah L. Morrison. LC 97-52341. 208p. 1998. pap. text 10.95 (0-8065-1961-4, Citadel Pr) Carol Pub Group.

Modern Witch's Book of Home Remedies. Sarah L. Morrison. 204p. 1991. pap. 8.95 (0-8065-1265-2, Citadel Pr) Carol Pub Group.

Modern Witch's Book of Symbols. Sarah L. Morrison. LC 97-218435. (Illus.). 224p. 1997. pap. text 9.95 (0-8065-1909-6, Citadel Pr) Carol Pub Group.

Modern Witch's Dreambook see New Modern Witch's Dreambook

Modern Witch's Dreambook. Sarah L. Morrison. 1990. pap. 7.95 (0-8065-1203-2, Citadel Pr) Carol Pub Group.

Modern Witch's Guide to Magic & Spells. Sarah L. Morrison. LC 97-45629. 192p. 1998. pap. 12.00 (0-8065-1963-0, Citadel Pr) Carol Pub Group.

Modern Witch's Spellbook. Sarah L. Morrison. 1994. 8.95 (0-679-50264-5) McKay.

Modern Witch's Spellbook, Bk. I. Sarah L. Morrison. LC 71-135588. 256p. 1973. reprint ed. pap. 12.00 (0-8065-0372-6) Carol Pub Group.

Modern Woman: A Stress Relief Manual Just for Women. Patricia Martin. 78p. 1995. 7.95 (1-56245-195-2) Great Quotations.

Modern Woman in Search of Soul: A Jungian Guide to the Visible & Invisible Worlds. rev. ed. June Singer. LC 97-48983. Orig. Title: Seeing Through the Visible World: Jung Gnosis & Chaos. 256p. 1998. pap. 18.95 (0-89254-041-9) Nicolas-Hays.

Modern Women. Ruth Harris. 1990. pap. 5.95 (0-685-46972-7) St Martin.

Modern Women Writers. Matthew J. Bruccoli. Ed. by Judith S. Baughman. LC 93-8642. (Essential Bibliography of American Fiction Ser.). 112p. 1994. 19.95 (0-8160-3000-6) Facts on File.

Modern Women Writers. Matthew J. Bruccoli & Judith S. Baughman. LC 93-8642. (Essential Bibliography of American Fiction Ser.). 112p. 1994. lib. bdg. 9.95 (0-8160-3001-4) Facts on File.

Modern Wood Finishing Techniques. Noel J. Leach. LC 92-37402. (Illus.). 256p. 1993. pap. 29.95 (0-941936-24-4) Linden Pub Fresno.

Modern Woodstove Cook Book No. 4: Pioneer Recipes from the Old West. rev. ed. Kriss Hammond. (Illus.). 320p. 1999. reprint ed. pap. 19.95 (0-943137-02-0) Jetsetters.

Modern Woodworking. Willis H. Wagner & Clois E. Kicklighter. LC 95-12531. 644p. 1996. text 43.96 (1-56637-220-8) Goodheart.

Modern Words: (A Thoroughly Queer International Literary Journal), Vol. 1, Issue 1. Garland R. Kyle et al. (Illus.). 106p. (Orig.). 1994. pap. 10.00 (0-9614055-3-8) modern words.

Modern Words: (A Thoroughly Queer International Literary Journal), Vol. 1, Issue 3. Garland R. Kyle et al. (Illus.). 110p. (Orig.). 1995. pap. 10.00 (0-9614055-5-4) modern words.

Modern Words: A Thoroughly Queer Literary Journal, Vol. 1, Issue 4. Ed. by Garland R. Kyle. (Illus.). 262p. (Orig.). 1996. pap. 20.00 (0-9614055-6-2) modern words.

Modern Workers Compensation, 3 vols. CBC Editorial Staff. LC 93-71460. 1993. ring bd. 395.00 (0-685-68853-4) West Group.

***Modern Working Women & the Development Debate.** Kranti Rana. 1998. 36.00 (81-7391-248-3, Pub. by Kaniska Pubs Dist) S Asia.

***Modern World.** Reg Cox. (Wonders of the World Ser.). (Illus.). (J). 2000. 16.95 (0-7910-6048-9) Chelsea Hse.

Modern World. Stephen Hoare. LC 92-2405. (Illustrated History of the World Ser.). (Illus.). 80p. (J). (gr. 4-9). 1993. 19.95 (0-8160-2792-7) Facts on File.

Modern World see Western Literature

Modern World: From the French Revolution to the Computer Age. Brian Williams. LC 94-18458. (Timelink Ser.). (Illus.). 64p. (YA). (gr. 5 up). 1994. lib. bdg. 18.95 (0-87226-312-6, 63126B, P Bedrick Books) NTC Contemp Pub Co.

Modern World Coins: An Illustrated Catalog with Valuations. 13th rev. ed. R. S. Yeoman. LC 83-72378. (Illus.). 512p. 1983. 9.95 (0-87184-713-2) Coin & Curr.

Modern World Development: A Geographical Perspective. Michael Chisholm. LC 82-11404. (Illus.). 216p. (C). 1982. text 52.00 (0-389-20320-3, N7160) B&N Imports.

Modern World Economy: Theories & Policies. Johannes Overbeek. 480p. (Orig.). (C). 1993. text 69.50 (0-8191-9131-0); pap. text 47.50 (0-8191-9132-9) U Pr of Amer.

Modern World History: Human Odyssey. Jackson J. Spielvogel. (Unknown Planning Family Ser.). 1998. student ed. 21.75 (0-538-42309-9) S-W Pub.

***Modern World History: Human Odyssey.** Jackson J. Spielvogel. 1998. 49.50 (0-538-42306-4) Thomson Learn.

Modern World History: International Relations from 1914 to the Present. Tony McAleavy. LC 96-227985. (Cambridge History Programme Ser.). (Illus.). 176p. (C). 1996. pap. 20.95 (0-521-44575-2) Cambridge U Pr.

Modern World History 1919 Onwards. Philip Sauvain. LC 85-72977. 224p. 1985. pap. 18.95 (0-7175-1312-2) Dufour.

Modern World Literature. HR&W School Division Staff. 1996. pap. text 29.75 (0-03-094635-2) Holt R&W.

***Modern World (1987) Today's Atlas for Stamp Collectors.** Kenneth A. Wood. (Illus.). 256p. 2000. reprint ed. text 25.00 (0-7881-6899-1) DIANE Pub.

Modern World, 1914-1980. Philip Sauvain. 432p. (C). 1989. pap. 28.00 (0-7487-0049-8) Dufour.

Modern World Politics. 2nd ed. Thorsten V. Kalijarvi et al. (Essay Index Reprint Ser.). 1977. reprint ed. 52.95 (0-518-10148-7) Ayer.

Modern World Rulers: A Chronology. Compiled by Alan R. Langville. LC 79-19294. 372p. 1979. 34.50 (0-8108-1251-7) Scarecrow.

Modern World since 1870. 2nd ed. L. E. Snellgrove. (Longman Secondary Histories Ser.). (Illus.). 352p. (Orig.). (YA). (gr. 9-12). 1981. teacher ed. 7.96 (0-582-36692-5); pap. text 14.56 (0-582-22299-0) Longman.

Modern World-System III: The Second Era of Great Expansion of the Capitalist World-Economy, 1730-1840. Immanuel Wallerstein. (Studies in Social Discontinuity). 595p. (C). 1988. text 72.95 (0-12-785925-X); pap. text 45.00 (0-12-785926-8) Acad Pr.

Modern World-System I. Immanuel Wallerstein. 1980. pap. text 49.95 (0-12-785919-5) Acad Pr.

Modern World-System II: Mercantilism & the Consolidation of the European World-Economy, 1600-1750. Immanuel Wallerstein. LC 73-5318. (Studies in Social Discontinuity). 1980. pap. text 45.00 (0-12-785924-1) Acad Pr.

Modern Wrestling: A Primer for Wrestlers, Parents, & Fans. Benjamin W. Niebel et al. LC 82-7478. (Illus.). 128p. (Orig.). (C). 1982. pap. text 12.50 (0-271-00328-6); lib. bdg. 25.00 (0-271-00323-5) Pa St U Pr.

Modern Wrist Watch Price Guide, 1970-1992 Bk. 1: Identification & Price Guide. Roy Ehrhardt & Joe DeMesy. (Illus.). 117p. 1992. per. 25.00 (0-913902-77-2) Heart Am Pr.

Modern Writer: Includes Homage to Sherwood Anderson. Sherwood Anderson. 212p. 15.00 (0-614-09416-X) Appel.

Modern Writer & His World. George S. Fraser. LC 75-32457. 426p. 1976. reprint ed. lib. bdg. 70.00 (0-8371-8549-1, FRMW, Greenwood Pr) Greenwood.

Modern Writers. 5th ed. Ohare & Funk. LC 99-25711. 688p. 1999. 34.00 (0-205-29899-0, Longwood Div) Allyn.

***Modern Writers.** 5th ed. Ohare & Funk. LC 99-25711. 655p. 1999. pap. text 22.00 (0-205-29900-8, Longwood Div) Allyn.

***Modern Writer's Handbook.** 5th ed. Frank O'Hare & Robert Funk. LC 99-25711. 704p. 1999. write for info. (0-205-30923-2) Allyn.

Concise Dictionary of British Literary Biography: Modern Writers, 1914-1945 see Concise Dictionary of British Literary Biography

Modern Writings on Major English Authors. Ed. by James R. Kreuzer & Lee Cogan. LC 63-12189. 686p. text 52.00 (0-8290-0189-1) Irvington.

Modern Written Arabic, Vol. I. unabridged ed. Foreign Service Institute Staff. 419p. pap. 245.00 incl. audio (0-88432-039-1, AFA269) Audio-Forum.

Modern Written Arabic, Vol. II. unabridged ed. Foreign Service Institute Staff. 385p. (C). pap. 175.00 incl. audio (0-88432-088-X, AFA320) Audio-Forum.

Modern X-Ray Analysis on Single Crystals. Peter Luger. 312p. 1980. 77.70 (3-11-006830-3) De Gruyter.

Modern Yarns for Modern Fabrics. 1992. spiral bd. 63.00 (0-7855-2833-4, Pub. by Textile Inst) St Mut.

Modern Years: Nixon to Clinton, 1969 to the Present. Rose Blue & Corinne J. Naden. LC 97-15039. (Who's That in the White House? Ser.). 96p. 1998. 28.55 (0-8172-4305-4) Raintree Steck-V.

Modern Yemen, 1918-1966. Manfred W. Wenner. LC 67-12420. (Johns Hopkins University Studies in Historical & Political Science: Series 85, No. 1). 255p. reprint ed. pap. 79.10 (0-608-06089-5, 206642100008) Bks Demand.

Modern Yiddish Culture: The Story of the Yiddish Language Movement. 2nd rev. ed. Emanuel S. Goldsmith. LC 96-45515. 321p. 1997. write for info. (0-8232-1695-0) Fordham.

Modern Yugoslav Satire. Ed. by Branko Mikasinovich. LC 79-83730. (Illus.). (Orig.). 1979. 20.00 (0-89304-029-0, CCC117); pap. 12.00 (0-89304-030-4) Cross-Cultrl NY.

Modern Zeolites: Structure & Function in Detergents & Petrochemicals. A. A. Tomlinson. (Materials Science Foundations Ser.: Vol. 3). (Illus.). 92p. (C). 48.00 (0-87849-794-3, Pub. by Trans T Pub) Enfield Pubs NH.

Moderna Enciclopedia Universal Distein. Juan Capdevila Font. (SPA.). 600p. 1974. pap. 24.95 (0-8288-6074-2, S-50448) Fr & Eur.

Moderna Museet, Stockholm: A Celebration of 40 Years. Nina Ohman. (Illus.). 160p. 1998. 40.00 (1-85759-178-X) Scala Books.

Moderna Slovencina. Mistrik. (SLO.). 294p. 1996. write for info. (80-08-01042-8, Pub. by Slov Pegagog Naklad) IBD Ltd.

Moderna Teoria de la Musica, No. 2. 76p. (Orig.). (J). 1985. pap. 6.50 (0-89898-831-4, 500130PX) Wrner Bros.

***Modernaj Robinzonoj: En la Siberia Praarbaro.** Teodoro Schwartz. (ESP.). i, 60p. 2000. pap. 6.30 (1-882251-24-5) Eldonejo Bero.

Moderne Braunschweigische Geschichte. (GER.). 306p. 1982. write for info. (3-487-07316-1) G Olms Pubs.

Moderne Dichtungen (Leseband) see Deutsch Fuer Auslaender: Oberstufe

Moderne Endoskoskopie im Kindesalter: Proceedings of Kinderchirugisches Symposium, Obergurgl, January 1977. Kinderchirurgisches Symposium Staff. Ed. by E. Bern Rossi & P. Wurnig. (Paediatrische Fortbildungskurse fuer die Praxis Ser.: Bd. 46). (Illus.). 1978. 35.75 (3-8055-2799-3) S Karger.

Moderne Man Comics. Bruce Von Alten. (Illus.). 96p. (Orig.). 1989. pap. 9.95 (0-9624218-0-4) O K Pr.

Moderne Motet Anthologies. Ed. by Richard Sherr. (Sixteenth-Century Motet Ser.: Vol. 10). 316p. 1998. text 125.00 (0-8240-7910-8) Garland.

Moderne Motet Anthologies. Ed. by Richard Sherr. (Five- & More- Voice Motets from the Motteti del Fiore Ser.: Pt. III). 328p. 1999. 135.00 (0-8240-7911-6) Garland.

Moderne Motet Anthologies. Ed. by Richard Sherr. (Sixteenth-Century Motet Ser.: Vol. 12). 288p. 1999. text 135.00 (0-8240-7912-4) Garland.

Moderne Motet Anthologies Pt. I: Four-Voice Motets from the Motteti Del Fiore Series. Ed. by Richard Sherr. (Sixteenth-Century Motet Ser.: Vol. 9). 304p. 1998. 86.00 (0-8240-7909-4) Garland.

Moderne Orientreise. August Langmesser. 178p. reprint ed. write for info. (0-318-71527-9) G Olms Pubs.

Moderne, Postmoderne - Und Nun Barock? Entwicklungslinied der Architektur des 20. Jahrhunderts. Stefan Grundmann. (Illus.). 136p. 1995. 58.00 (3-930698-63-3, Pub. by E J Wasmuth) Dist Art Pubs.

Moderne Waffen, Munition, Jagdartikel. August Stukenbrok Einbeck. (GER., Illus.). 240p. Date not set. write for info. (3-487-08404-X) G Olms Pubs.

Moderner Arbeitsschutz und Betriebsokologie - Aktulle Herausforderungen Fur Unternehmen und Interessenvertretungen. Max Geray. (Europaische Hochschulschriften Ser.: Reihe 5, Vol. 2292). 200p. 1998. pap. 39.95 (*3-631-33249-1*) P Lang Pubng.

Modernes Deutschland in Brennpunkt: A Cultural Reader. Ed. by Allen Hye. (Illus.). (C). 1978. 11.25 (*0-393-09067-1*) Norton.

Modernisation & Employment: The Coir Industry in Kerala. T. M. Isaac et al. LC 92-20727. (Indo-Dutch Studies on Development Alternatives: Vol. 10). (Illus.). 252p. (C). 1993. text 32.00 (*0-8039-9446-X*) Sage.

***Modernisation & Its Impact on Indian Women.** Vats & Mudgal. 1999. 32.00 (*81-86867-22-8*, Pub. by Om Pubns) S Asia.

***Modernisation of EC Competition Law.** Rein Wesseling. 400p. 2000. 63.00 (*1-84113-121-0*, Pub. by Hart Pub) Intl Spec Bk.

Modernisation of Medical Teaching in the Nineteenth Century Carolyn Ingram Pennington. LC 95-159417. (Quincentennial Studies). ix, 116p. 1994. write for info. (*1-85752-215-X*) Macmillan.

***Modernisation of Russia, 1676-1825.** Simon Dixon. LC 98-46739. (New Approaches to European History Ser.: No. 15). (Illus.). 256p. (C). 1999. 54.95 (*0-521-37100-7*) Cambridge U Pr.

***Modernisation of Russia, 1676-1825.** Simon Dixon. LC 98-46739. (New Approaches to European History Ser.: No. 15). (Illus.). 267p. (C). 1999. pap. 16.95 (*0-521-37961-X*) Cambridge U Pr.

Moderniser's Dilemma: Radical Politics in the Age of Blair. Ed. by Anne Coddington & Mark Perryman. 224p. 1998. pap. 19.50 (*0-85315-874-6*) Lawrence & Wishart.

Modernising Hunger: Famine, Food Surplus & Farm Policy in the EEC & Africa. Philip L. Raikes. LC 90-26661. 280p. (C). 1989. text 40.00 (*0-435-08030-X*, 08030) Heinemann.

Modernising Hunger: Famine, Food Surplus & Farm Policy in the EEC & Africa. Philip L. Raikes. LC 90-26661. 280p. (C). 1991. pap. text 27.50 (*0-435-08058-X*, 08058) Heinemann.

Modernising Lenin's Russia: Economic Reconstruction, Foreign Trade & the Railways, 1917-24. Anthony Heywood. LC 98-38611. (Russian, Soviet & Post-Soviet Studies: No. 105). (Illus.). 320p. (C). 1999. text 69.95 (*0-521-62178-X*) Cambridge U Pr.

***Modernising Parliament: Reforming the House of Lords.** (Command Papers (All) Ser.: No. 4183). 51p. 1999. pap. 18.00 (*0-10-141832-9*, HM18329, Pub. by Statnry Office) Bernan Associates.

Modernising Social Welfare. Cooper et al. 74.95 (*1-84014-387-8*) Ashgate Pub Co.

Modernising the Classics: A Study in Curriculum Development: The Origins & Early History of the Cambridge School Classics Project. Martin Forrest. LC 96-205985. 176p. 1996. text 55.00 (*0-85989-486-X*, Pub. by Univ Exeter Pr) Northwestern U Pr.

Modernising Urban India: An Essay in Environmental Sanitation. Sabir Ali. (C). 1994. 16.00 (*81-241-0116-7*, Pub. by Har-Anand Pubns) S Asia.

Modernism. Malcolm Bradbury. 688p. 1978. pap. 17.95 (*0-14-013832-3*, Viking) Viking Penguin.

***Modernism.** Peter Childs. LC 99-86582. 200p. 2000. pap. write for info. (*0-415-19648-5*) Routledge.

***Modernism.** Peter Childs. LC 99-86582. (New Critical Idiom Ser.). 200p. 2000. 50.00 (*0-415-19647-7*) Routledge.

Modernism. Peter Faulkner. (Critical Idiom Ser.). 1977. pap. 7.50 (*0-416-83710-7*, NO. 2779) Routledge.

Modernism. Charles Harrison. (Movements in Modern Art Ser.). (Illus.). 80p. (C). 1998. pap. 13.95 (*0-521-62758-3*) Cambridge U Pr.

***Modernism.** Vassiliki Kolocotroni et al. LC 99-169022. xx, 632p. 1998. write for info. (*0-7486-0973-3*) Col U Pr.

Modernism. Michelle R. Marotske & Kimberly H. Yoakum. (Illus.). 20p. (J). (gr. 1-6). 1998. pap. write for info. (*1-893397-03-3*) Painted In.

Modernism. Richard Weston. (Illus.). 240p. 1996. 75.00 (*0-7148-2879-3*, Pub. by Phaidon Press) Phaidon Pr.

Modernism: An Anthology of Sources & Documents. Ed. by Kolocotroni. (Illus.). (C). pap. text. write for info. (*0-472-06688-9*) U of Mich Pr.

Modernism: An Anthology of Sources & Documents. Ed. by Vassiliki Kolocotroni et al. LC 98-7889. 654p. 1999. pap. text 30.00 (*0-226-45074-0*); lib. bdg. 75.00 (*0-226-45073-2*) U Ch Pr.

Modernism: Challenges & Perspectives. Ed. by Monique Chefdor et al. LC 84-21932. (Illus.). 360p. 1986. text 29.95 (*0-252-01207-0*) U of Ill Pr.

Modernism: Modernist Design, 1880-1940. Alastair Duncan. (Illus.). 256p. 1998. 59.50 (*1-85149-274-7*) Antique Collect.

Modernism - Postmodernism. Ed. by Peter Brooker. (Critical Readers Ser.). 280p. (C). 1995. pap. 49.00 (*0-582-06357-4*, 79264) Longman.

Modernism & Authority: Strategies of Legitimation in Flaubert & Conrad. Mark Conroy. LC 84-21848. 204p. 1985. reprint ed. pap. 63.30 (*0-608-03647-1*, 206447300009) Bks Demand.

Modernism & Beyond: Women Artists of the Pacific Northwest. Laura Brunsman & Ruth Askey. LC 92-62399. (Regional Women Artists Ser.). (Illus.). 192p. (Orig.). 1993. pap. text 15.00 (*1-877675-13-X*) Midmarch Arts.

Modernism & Cultural Transfer: Gabriel Preil & the Tradition of Jewish Literary Bilingualism. Yael S. Feldman. LC 85-17597. (Monographs of the Hebrew Union College: Vol. 10). 236p. 1986. reprint ed. pap. 73.20 (*0-608-02085-0*, 206273800004) Bks Demand.

***Modernism & Empire 1890-1940.** Howard J. Booth. 2000. pap. 29.95 (*0-7190-5307-2*, Pub. by Manchester Univ Pr) St Martin.

***Modernism & Empire 1890-1940.** Howard J. Booth. (Illus.). 256p. 2000. text 69.95 (*0-7190-5306-4*) Manchester Univ Pr.

Modernism & Feminism: Australian Women Artists, 1900-1940. Helen Topliss. (Illus.). 272p. 1996. 65.00 (*976-641-025-9*, Pub. by IPG Chicago) Gordon & Breach.

Modernism & Hegemony: A Materialistic Critique of Aesthetic Agencies. Neil Larsen. 150p. 1990. pap. 14.95 (*0-8166-1785-6*) U of Minn Pr.

Modernism & Ideology in Persian Literature: A Return to Nature in the Poetry of Nima Yushij. Ed. by Majid Naficy. LC 97-29537. 144p. (C). 1997. 27.50 (*0-7618-0862-0*) U Pr of Amer.

Modernism & Ireland: The Poetry of the 1930's. Patricia B. Coughlan. 1995. pap. text 24.00 (*1-85918-061-2*) Intl Spec Bk.

Modernism & Its Discontents: Philosophical Problems of Twentieth-Century Literary Theory. Bruce E. Fleming. (New Studies in Aesthetics: No. 26). 168p. (C). 1995. text 42.95 (*0-8204-2740-3*) P Lang Pubng.

Modernism & Its Margins: Reinscribing Cultural Modernity from Spain & Latin America. Ed. by Anthony L. Geist & Jose B. Monleon. LC 99-15049. (Hispanic Issues Ser.: Vol. 19). 320p. 1999. 65.00 (*0-8153-3261-0*, H2133) Garland.

Modernism & Masculinity. Gerald N. Izenberg. LC 99-87470. 1997. 35.00 (*0-226-38868-9*) U Ch Pr.

***Modernism & Masculinity: Wedekind, Mann, Kandinsky Through World War I.** Gerald N. Izenberg. LC 99-87470. 2000. pap. write for info. (*0-226-38869-7*) U Ch Pr.

Modernism & Mass Politics: Joyce, Woolf, Eliot, Yeats. Michael Tratner. LC 95-10586. 356p. 1995. 45.50 (*0-8047-2516-0*) Stanford U Pr.

***Modernism & Modernization.** Helen Caslte. LC 99-203743. 128p. 1999. pap. 65.00 (*0-471-98469-8*) Wiley.

Modernism & Negritude: The Poetry & Poetics of Aime Cesaire. A. James Arnold. LC 80-29007. 329p. (C). 1981. 39.95 (*0-674-58057-5*) HUP.

Modernism & Revolution: Russian Literature in Transition. Victor Erlich. LC 93-24159. 328p. 1994. 51.95 (*0-674-58070-2*) HUP.

Modernism & Tagore. Ayyub A. Sayeed. Tr. by Amitava Ray. LC 95-902587. (C). 1995. 12.00 (*81-7201-851-7*, Pub. by Indian Pubs) S Asia.

***Modernism & the Critical Spirit.** Eugene Goodheart. LC 99-87045. 2000. 24.95 (*0-7658-0698-3*) Transaction Pubs.

Modernism & the Decorative Arts in France: Art Nouveau to le Corbusier. Nancy J. Troy. (Illus.). 336p. (C). 1991. 47.00 (*0-300-04554-9*) Yale U Pr.

Modernism & the Harlem Renaissance. Houston A. Baker, Jr. LC 87-5014. (Illus.). 144p. 1987. 19.95 (*0-226-03524-7*) U Ch Pr.

Modernism & the Harlem Renaissance. Houston A. Baker, Jr. LC 87-5014. (Illus.). 144p. 1989. pap. text 10.95 (*0-226-03525-5*) U Ch Pr.

Modernism & the Nativist Resistance: Contemporary Chinese Fiction from Taiwan. Sung-sheng Y. Chang. LC 92-41437. 256p. 1993. text 49.95 (*0-8223-1328-6*); pap. text 18.95 (*0-8223-1348-0*) Duke.

Modernism & the Other in Stevens, Frost, & Moore. Andrew M. Lakritz. 232p. 1996. 39.95 (*0-8130-1460-3*) U Press Fla.

Modernism & the Posthumanist Subject: The Architecture of Hannes Meyer & Ludwig Hilberseimer. K. Michael Hays. (Illus.). 352p. 1992. 47.50 (*0-262-08212-8*) MIT Pr.

Modernism & the Posthumanist Subject: The Architecture of Hannes Meyer & Ludwig Hilberseimer. K. Michael Hays. (Illus.). 352p. 1995. pap. text 20.00 (*0-262-58141-8*) MIT Pr.

Modernism & the Theater of Censorship. Adam Parkes. (Illus.). 256p. 1996. text 52.00 (*0-19-509702-5*) OUP.

Modernism & the Urban Imagination. Gold. (Illus.). 296p. (C). 1998. pap. 39.99 (*0-419-20740-6*, E & FN Spon) Routledge.

***Modernism & Time: The Logic of Abundance in Literature, Science & Culture, 1880-1930.** Ronald Schleifer. 264p. (C). 2000. 59.95 (*0-521-66124-2*) Cambridge U Pr.

Modernism as a Philosophical Problem: On the Dissatisfactions of European High Culture. 2nd ed. Robert B. Pippin. LC 99-17513. 320p. 1999. pap. text 26.95 (*0-631-21414-3*) Blackwell Pubs.

Modernism as a Philosophical Problem: On the Dissatisfactions of European High Culture. 2nd ed. Robert B. Pippin. LC 99-17513. 320p. (C). 1999. text 59.95 (*0-631-21413-5*) Blackwell Pubs.

Modernism at Mid-Century: The Architecture of the U. S. Air Force Academy. Ed. by Robert Bruegmann. (Illus.). 200p. 1994. 70.00 (*0-226-07693-8*) U Ch Pr.

Modernism at Mid-Century: The Architecture of the United States Air Force Academy. Ed. by Robert Bruegmann. (Illus.). 200p. 1994. pap. text 45.00 (*0-226-07694-6*) U Ch Pr.

Modernism-Dada-Postmodernism. Richard Sheppard. 496p. 1999. 89.95 (*0-8101-1492-5*) Northwestern U Pr.

***Modernism-Dada-Postmodernism.** Richard Sheppard. LC 00-8031. 496p. 1999. pap. 29.95 (*0-8101-1493-3*) Northwestern U Pr.

Modernism, Expressionism & Theories of the Avant-Garde. Richard Murphy. LC 98-8366. (Literature, Culture, Theory Ser.: No. 32). 260p. (C). 1999. text 57.95 (*0-521-63291-9*); pap. text 19.95 (*0-521-64869-6*) Cambridge U Pr.

Modernism from Right to Left: Wallace Stevens, the Thirties & Literary Radicalism. Alan Filreis. LC 93-33402. (Cambridge Studies in American Literature & Culture: No. 79). (Illus.). 396p. (C). 1994. text 64.95 (*0-521-45384-4*) Cambridge U Pr.

Modernism, Gender, & Culture: A Cultural Studies Approach. Ed. by Lisa Rado & William Cain. LC 96-46542. (Wellesley Studies in Critical Theory, Literary History & Culture: Vol. 11). (Illus.). 400p. 1997. text 95.00 (*0-8153-1786-7*) Garland.

***Modernism in Art, Design, & Architecture.** Christopher Crouch. LC 98-28318. 35p. 1999. text 65.00 (*0-312-21830-3*) St Martin.

Modernism in Art, Design & Architecture. Christopher Crouch. LC 98-28318. viii, 204 p. 1999. pap. 21.95 (*0-312-21832-X*) St Martin.

Modernism in Dispute: Art since the Forties. Jonathan Harris et al. LC 93-10674. (Illus.). 283p. (C). 1993. pap. 30.00 (*0-300-05522-6*) Yale U Pr.

Modernism in European Drama: Ibsen, Strindberg, Pirandello, Beckett: Essays from Modern Drama. Ed. by F. J. Marker & Christopher Innes. LC 99-170702. 336p. 1998. text 55.00 (*0-8020-4399-2*); pap. text 21.95 (*0-8020-8206-8*) U of Toronto Pr.

Modernism in Greece? Essays on the Critical & Literary Margins of a Movement. Ed. by Mary N. Layoun. LC 90-62251. 234p. (Orig.). 1990. pap. text 12.00 (*0-918618-43-6*) Pella Pub.

Modernism in Italian Architecture, 1890-1940. Richard A. Etlin. (Illus.). 760p. 1991. 80.00 (*0-262-05038-2*) MIT Pr.

Modernism in Poetry: Motivation, Structures & Limits. Rainer Emig. Ed. by Stan Smith. LC 95-7334. (Studies in Twentieth Century Literature Ser.). 280p. (C). 1995. pap. text 24.50 (*0-582-23920-6*, Pub. by Addison-Wesley) Longman.

Modernism in Poetry: Motivation, Structures & Limits. Rainer Emig. Ed. by Stan Smith. LC 95-7334. (Studies in Twentieth Century Literature). 280p. (C). 1996. 83.00 (*0-582-23919-2*) Longman.

Modernism in Russian Piano Music: Skriabin, Prokofiev, & Their Russian Contemporaries, 2 vols. Peter D. Roberts. LC 91-32124. (Russian Music Studies). 1993. 89.95 (*0-253-34992-3*) Ind U Pr.

Modernism in the Narrative Cinema. William C. Siska. Ed. by Garth S. Jowett. LC 79-6686. (Dissertations on Film, 1980 Ser.). 1980. lib. bdg. 15.95 (*0-405-12918-1*) Ayer.

Modernism in the Nineteen Twenties: Interpretations of Modern Art in New York from Expressionism to Constructivism. Susan N. Platt. LC 85-1070. (Studies in the Fine Arts: Criticism: No. 17). 203p. reprint ed. pap. 63.00 (*0-8357-1661-9*, 207059700004) Bks Demand.

Modernism in the Puerto Rican Lyric. Adriana R. Mimoso. (Puerto Rico Ser.). 1979. lib. bdg. 59.95 (*0-8490-2973-2*) Gordon Pr.

Modernism in the Second World War: The Later Poetry of Ezra Pound, T. S. Eliot, Basil Bunting & Hugh MacDiarmid. Keith Alldritt. 135p. (C). 1989. text 20.50 (*0-8204-0865-4*) P Lang Pubng.

Modernism, Inc. Jani Scandura. text 55.00 (*0-8147-8136-5*) NYU Pr.

Modernism, Inc. Jani Scandura. pap. text 18.50 (*0-8147-8137-3*) NYU Pr.

Modernism, Mass Culture, & Professionalism. Thomas Strychacz. LC 92-44711. (Cambridge Studies in American Literature & Culture: No. 65). 240p. (C). 1993. text 59.95 (*0-521-44079-3*) Cambridge U Pr.

***Modernism, Mass Culture & the Aesthetics of Obscenity.** Allison Pease. LC 99-56880. 2000. write for info. (*0-521-78076-4*) Cambridge U Pr.

Modernism, Medicine & William Carlos Williams. T. Hugh Crawford. LC 93-19161. (Series for Science & Culture of the Oklahoma Project for Discourse & Theory: Vol. 1). (Illus.). 208p. 1995. pap. 12.95 (*0-8061-2588-8*) U of Okla Pr.

Modernism, Modernity, & Arnold Bennett. Robert Squillace. LC 97-52827. 224p. 1997. 36.50 (*0-8387-5364-7*) Bucknell U Pr.

***Modernism, Nationalism & the Novel.** Pericles Lewis. 247p. (C). 2000. 59.95 (*0-521-66111-0*) Cambridge U Pr.

Modernism Reconsidered. Robert Kiely. (English Studies: No. 11). 272p. (C). 1983. 25.00 (*0-674-58065-6*); pap. 8.95 (*0-674-58066-4*) HUP.

***Modernism, Romance & the "Fin de Siecle" Popular Fiction & British Culture.** Nicholas Daly. LC 98-55153. 232p. (C). 2000. 59.95 (*0-521-64103-9*) Cambridge U Pr.

Modernism since Postmodernism: Essays on Intermedia. Dick Higgins. (Illus.). 252p. 1997. pap. 15.00 (*1-879691-43-4*) SDSU Press.

Modernism, Technology, & the Body: A Cultural Study. Tim Armstrong. LC 97-8815. (Illus.). 318p. (C). 1998. text 59.95 (*0-521-59004-3*); pap. text 19.95 (*0-521-59997-0*) Cambridge U Pr.

Modernism to Postmodernism: An Anthology. Ed. by Lawrence E. Cahoone. 768p. (C). 1995. pap. 34.95 (*1-55786-603-1*) Blackwell Pubs.

Modernism Without Rhetoric: The Work of Alison & Peter Smithson. Webster. 224p. 1997. 75.00 (*0-471-97759-4*) Wiley.

Modernism Without Rhetoric: The Work of Alison & Peter Smithson. Ed. by Helena Webster. (Illus.). 225p. 1997. 60.00 (*1-85490-495-7*) Academy Ed UK.

Modernism& Postmodernism. Ed. by Peter Brooker. (Critical Readers Ser.). 268p. (C). 1992. text 63.50 (*0-582-06358-2*, 79263) Longman.

Modernismo. (Arte & Arquitectura Ser.). (Illus.). 420p. 39.95 (*3-89508-546-4*, 540086) Konemann.

Modernismo. Taschen, Benedikt Staff. (SPA.). 1996. pap. 24.95 (*3-8228-0237-9*) Taschen Amer.

Modernismo en Puerto Rico: Poesia y Prosa. rev. ed. Luis Hernandez Aquino. 212p. (C). 1977. pap. 4.00 (*0-8477-0509-9*) U of PR Pr.

Modernismo en Puerto Rico: Poesia y Prosa. 2nd rev. ed. Luis Hernandez Aquino. 212p. (C). 1977. 5.00 (*0-8477-0508-0*) U of PR Pr.

Modernismo in Chilean Literature: The Second Period. John M. Fein. LC 64-25821. 177p. reprint ed. pap. 54.90 (*0-608-12720-5*, 202338000032) Bks Demand.

Modernismo, Modernity & the Development of Spanish American Literature. Cathy L. Jrade. LC 98-5890. (Texas Pan American Ser.). 208p. 1998. 30.00 (*0-292-74049-2*); pap. 15.95 (*0-292-74045-X*) U of Tex Pr.

Modernisms: A Literary Guide. Peter Nicholls. 1995. pap. 17.95 (*0-520-20103-5*, Pub. by U CA Pr) Cal Prin Full Svc.

Modernism's Body: Sex, Culture, & Joyce. Christine Froula. 320p. 1996. 45.00 (*0-231-10442-1*) Col U Pr.

Modernism's Body: Sex, Culture, & Joyce. Christine Froula. 1996. pap. 18.00 (*0-231-10443-X*) Col U Pr.

Modernism's History: A Study in Twentieth-Century Art & Ideas. Bernard Smith. LC 98-5856. 384p. 1998. 40.00 (*0-300-07392-5*) Yale U Pr.

Modernist Alchemy: Poetry & the Occult. Timothy Materer. (Illus.). 240p. 1996. text 29.95 (*0-8014-3146-8*) Cornell U Pr.

Modernist Anthropology: From Fieldwork to Text. Ed. by Marc Manganaro. 340p. (C). 1990. pap. text 17.95 (*0-691-01480-9*, Pub. by Princeton U Pr) Cal Prin Full Svc.

Modernist As Pragmatist: E. M. Forster & the Fate of Liberalism. Brian May. 240p. (C). 1996. 37.50 (*0-8262-1096-1*) U of Mo Pr.

Modernist City: An Anthropological Critique of Brasilia. James Holston. (Illus.). 384p. 1989. pap. text 33.00 (*0-226-34979-9*) U Ch Pr.

Modernist City: An Anthropological Critique of Brasilia. James Holston. (Illus.). 384p. 1998. lib. bdg. 60.00 (*0-226-34978-0*) U Ch Pr.

Modernist Culture in America. Ed. by Daniel J. Singal. 228p. (C). 1990. 19.25 (*0-534-14808-5*) Wadsworth Pub.

Modernist Debate: History of Art Discourses in U. S. 1945-1965. Foster. 1998. 85.00 (*0-7838-2033-X*) Mac Lib Ref.

***Modernist Enterprise: French Elites & The Threat of Modernity, 1900-1940.** Marjorie A Beale. LC 99-16483. 1999. 49.50 (*0-8047-3511-5*) Stanford U Pr.

Modernist Fiction. Randall Stevenson. LC 97-27972. 1997. pap. 36.95 (*0-13-837659-X*) P-H.

Modernist Fiction: An Introduction. Randall Stevenson. LC 92-24932. 256p. (C). 1992. text 34.00 (*0-8131-1814-X*); pap. text 18.00 (*0-8131-0814-4*) U Pr of Ky.

Modernist Form: Pound's Style in the Early Cantos. John S. Childs. LC 85-62781. 192p. 1986. 36.50 (*0-941664-15-5*) Susquehanna U Pr.

Modernist Garden in France. Dorothee Imbert. LC 92-30514. (Illus.). 400p. (C). 1993. 65.00 (*0-300-04716-9*) Yale U Pr.

Modernist Idea: A Critical Survey of Brazilian Writing in the Twentieth Century. Wilson Martins. Tr. by Jack E. Tomlins from POR. LC 78-24232. 345p. 1979. reprint ed. lib. bdg. 38.50 (*0-313-20811-5*, MAID, Greenwood Pr) Greenwood.

Modernist Impulse in American Protestantism. William R. Hutchison. LC 91-39184. (Illus.). 367p. 1992. text 49.95 (*0-8223-1237-9*); pap. text 18.95 (*0-8223-1248-4*) Duke.

Modernist Impulse in American Protestantism. William R. Hutchison. (Illus.). 357p. 1976. 29.95 (*0-674-58058-3*) HUP.

Modernist Impulses in the Human Sciences, 1870-1930. Ed. by Dorothy Ross. LC 93-38354. (C). 1994. 60.00 (*0-8018-4744-3*); pap. 18.95 (*0-8018-4745-1*) Johns Hopkins.

Modernist Madonna: Semiotics of the Maternal Metaphor. Jane S. Van Buren. LC 88-46013. (Illus.). 240p. 1989. 19.95 (*0-253-36203-2*); pap. 6.95 (*0-253-20544-1*, MB-544) Ind U Pr.

Modernist Montage: The Obscurity of Vision in Cinema & Literature. P. Adams Sitney. 250p. (C). 1982. pap. 20.00 (*0-231-07183-3*) Col U Pr.

Modernist Movement in the Roman Church. Alexander R. Vidler. 1976. 250.00 (*0-8490-0889-1*) Gordon Pr.

Modernist Novel, 4 vols. Ed. by Brian Southam. (Collected Critical Heritage Ser.). 1706p. (C). 1997. 485.00 (*0-415-15917-2*) Routledge.

Modernist Novel: Aldous Huxley. Ed. by Conrad Watt. (Critical Heritage Ser.). 518p. (C). 1997. 160.00 (*0-415-15915-6*) Routledge.

Modernist Patterns in Literature & the Visual Arts. Murray Roston. LC 98-45373. 1999. text 40.00 (*0-8147-7527-6*) NYU Pr.

Modernist Plated Desserts. Tish Boyle & Timothy Moriarty. 288p. 1997. 49.95 (*0-471-29251-6*, VNR) Wiley.

Modernist Poetics of History: Pound, Eliot, & the Sense of the Past. James Longenbach. LC 86-25189. 298p. reprint ed. pap. 92.40 (*0-608-06350-9*, 206671100008) Bks Demand.

Modernist Quartet. Frank Lentricchia. 319p. (C). 1994. pap. text 18.95 (*0-521-46975-9*) Cambridge U Pr.

Modernist Shakespeare: Critical Texts in a Material World. Hugh Grady. (Illus.). 272p. 1995. reprint ed. pap. text 21.00 (*0-19-818322-4*) OUP.

Modernist Still Life - Photographed. Ed. by Paul Berg. LC 89-50100. (Illus.). 72p. 1989. 20.00 (*0-9601616-6-X*) U MO-St Louis.

Modernist Themes in New Mexico: Works by Early Modernist Painters. Peters Corporation, Gerald Peters Gallery Staff. Ed. by Michael C. Rowley. LC 89-84573. (Illus.). 56p. 1989. pap. text 12.00 (*0-935037-29-2*) G Peters Gallery.

M

Modernist Tradition in American Art, 1911-1939. Marilyn S. Kushner. (Illus.). 100p. (Orig.). 1991. pap. 20.00 (*0-941680-09-6*) M&L Block.

Modernist Trend in Spanish American Poetry. Ed. by George D. Craig. 1977. lib. bdg. 59.95 (*0-8490-2273-8*) Gordon Pr.

Modernist Trend in Spanish American Poetry. George D. Craig. LC 78-131249. 347p. 1971. reprint ed. 50.00 (*0-87752-129-8*) Gordian.

Modernist View of Plated Desserts. Trish Boyle & Timothy Moriarty. LC 97-24171. (Culinary Arts Ser.). (Illus.). 304p. 1997. 49.95 (*0-442-02547-5*, VNR) Wiley.

Modernist Visions & the Contemporary American City, Vol. 5. Larwrence W. Speck & Anthony Alofsin. (Illus.). 142p. 1989. 22.00 (*0-8478-5491-4*) Ctr for Amer Archit.

Modernist Women Writers & Narrative Art. Kathleen M. Wheeler. LC 93-45749. 232p. (C). 1994. text 55.00 (*0-8147-9275-8*); pap. text 19.50 (*0-8147-9276-6*) NYU Pr.

Modernistas en Paris. Cristobal Pera. (Perspectivas Hispanicas Ser.: Tomo 8). 207p. 1997. 31.95 (*3-906757-46-3*, Pub. by P Lang) P Lang Pubng.

Modernistic Poetry. Laura Riding. reprint ed. lib. bdg. 79.00 (*0-7812-0321-X*) Rprt Serv.

Modernists, Marxists & the Nation: The Ukrainian Literary Discussion of the 1920s. Myroslav Shkandrij. LC 92-91650. xii, 265p. 24.95 (*0-920862-86-1*) Ukrainian Acad.

M

Modernitat Wider Willen: Chateaubriands Fruhwerk. Paul Geyer. (Franzosische Sprache und Literatur Ser.: Bd. 227). (GER., Illus.). 157p. 1997. 31.95 (*3-631-31718-2*) P Lang Pubng.

Modernities: A Geohistorical Interpretation. Peter J. Taylor. LC 98-45120. 1999. 47.95 (*0-8166-3395-9*) U of Minn Pr.

***Modernities: A Geohistorical Interpretation.** Peter J. Taylor. LC 98-45120. 1999. pap. text 18.95 (*0-8166-3396-7*) U of Minn Pr.

Modernities: Art-Matters in the Present. Joseph Masheck. (Illus.). 272p. 1992. 38.50 (*0-271-00808-3*) Pa St U Pr.

Modernities & Other Writings. Blaise Cendrars. Ed. & Tr. by Monique Chefdor from FRE. Tr. by Esther Allen from FRE. LC 91-43824. (French Modernist Library). xxvi, 134p. 1992. text 40.00 (*0-8032-1439-1*) U of Nebr Pr.

Modernity. Stuart Hall. (Illus.). 750p. (C). 1996. pap. text 37.95 (*1-55786-716-X*) Blackwell Pubs.

***Modernity: Christianity's Estranged Child Reconstructed.** John Thornhill. 232p. 2000. pap. 24.00 (*0-8028-4694-7*) Eerdmans.

Modernity: Critical Concepts. Malcolm Waters. LC 98-25909. 1999. write for info. (*0-415-13300-9*) Routledge.

Modernity - An Ethnographic Approach: Dualism & Mass Consumption in Trinidad. Daniel Miller. LC 93-23406. 340p. 1994. 49.50 (*0-85496-916-0*, Pub. by Berg Pubs); pap. 19.50 (*0-85496-917-9*, Pub. by Berg Pubs) NYU Pr.

Modernity, Aesthetics, & the Bounds of Art. Peter J. McCormick. LC 89-71309. (Illus.). 368p. 1990. 49.95 (*0-8014-2452-6*) Cornell U Pr.

Modernity, Aesthetics & the Bounds of Art. Peter J. McCormick. LC 89-71309. 367p. reprint ed. pap. 113.80 (*0-608-20921-X*, 207202000003) Bks Demand.

Modernity & Academic Performance: A Study of Students in a Puerto Rican High School. Ineke Cunningham. 193p. 1972. 3.50 (*0-8477-2705-X*); pap. 2.50 (*0-8477-2706-8*) U of PR Pr.

Modernity & Ambivalence. Zygmunt Bauman. LC 90-46479. 300p. 1991. text 47.50 (*0-8014-2603-0*) Cornell U Pr.

Modernity & Authenticity: A Study of the Social & Ethical Thought of Jean-Jacques Rousseau. Alessandro Ferrara. LC 91-42018. (SUNY Series in Social & Political Thought). 188p. (C). 1992. pap. text 19.95 (*0-7914-1236-9*) State U NY Pr.

Modernity & Authenticity: A Study of the Social & Ethical Thought of Jean-Jacques Rousseau. Alessandro Ferrara. LC 91-42018. (SUNY Series in Social & Political Thought). 188p. (C). 1993. text 59.50 (*0-7914-1235-0*) State U NY Pr.

Modernity & Housing. Peter G. Rowe. LC 92-45140. 420p. 1993. 52.50 (*0-262-18151-7*) MIT Pr.

Modernity & Housing. Peter G. Rowe. (Illus.). 424p. 1995. pap. text 30.00 (*0-262-68087-4*) MIT Pr.

Modernity & Identity. Ed. by Scott Lash & Jonathan Friedman. 320p. (C). 1991. pap. 29.95 (*0-631-17586-5*) Blackwell Pubs.

Modernity & Its Discontents. Ed. by James Marsh et al. LC 91-46765. xiv, 219p. 1992. 32.50 (*0-8232-1344-7*); pap. 19.95 (*0-8232-1345-5*) Fordham.

Modernity & Its Discontents: Voices from the Channel 4 Television Series. Ed. by Bill Bourne et al. 119p. 1987. 42.50 (*0-85124-472-6*, Pub. by Spkesman); pap. 24.50 (*0-85124-482-3*, Pub. by Spkesman) Coronet Bks.

Modernity & Its Malcontents: Ritual & Power in Postcolonial Africa. Ed. by Jean Comaroff & John L. Comaroff. LC 93-17. (Illus.). 272p. 1993. pap. text 17.95 (*0-226-11440-6*) U Ch Pr.

Modernity & Its Malcontents: Ritual & Power in Postcolonial Africa. Ed. by Jean Comaroff & John L. Comaroff. LC 93-17. (Illus.). 272p. 1993. lib. bdg. 46.95 (*0-226-11439-2*) U Ch Pr.

Modernity & Its Other: A Post-Script to Contemporary Architecture. Gevork Hartoonian. LC 96-38406. (Studies in Architecture & Culture: Vol. 3). (Illus.). 208p. (C). 1997. text 49.95 (*0-89096-729-6*) Tex A&M Univ Pr.

Modernity & Mass Culture. Ed. by James Naremore & Patrick Brantlinger. LC 90-41881. (Illus.). 288p. 1991. 39.95 (*0-253-33968-5*); pap. 15.95 (*0-253-20627-8*, MB-627) Ind U Pr.

Modernity & Modernism: French Painting in the Nineteenth Century. Francis Frascina et al. LC 92-35017. (Modern Art - Practices & Debates Ser.). (Illus.). 304p. (C). 1993. 60.00 (*0-300-05513-7*); pap. 30.00 (*0-300-05514-5*) Yale U Pr.

Modernity & Politics in the Work of Max Weber. Charles Turner. LC 92-289. 240p. (C). (gr. 13). 1992. 100.00 (*0-415-06490-2*, A7663) Routledge.

***Modernity & Postmodern Culture.** Jim McGuigan. LC 99-33227. 1999. write for info. (*0-03-351996-X*) Open Univ TX.

Modernity & Power: A History of the Domino Theory in the Twentieth Century. Frank A. Ninkovich. LC 94-5733. 1994. pap. text 19.95 (*0-226-58651-0*); lib. bdg. 49.95 (*0-226-58650-2*) U Ch Pr.

Modernity & Religion. Ed. by Ralph McInerny. LC 93-8804. (C). 1994. text 25.50 (*0-268-01408-6*) U of Notre Dame Pr.

Modernity & Revolution in Late Nineteenth-Century France. Ed. by Barbara T. Cooper & Mary Donaldson-Evans. LC 91-50645. (Illus.). 176p. 1992. 35.00 (*0-87413-447-1*) U Delaware Pr.

Modernity & Self-Identity: Self & Society in the Late Modern Age. Anthony Giddens. LC 91-65170. 275p. 1991. 39.50 (*0-8047-1943-8*); pap. 14.95 (*0-8047-1944-6*) Stanford U Pr.

***Modernity & Subjectivity: Body, Soul, Spirit.** Harvie Ferguson. LC 99-55551. (Richard Lectures Ser.). 240p. 2000. 49.50 (*0-8139-1965-7*); pap. 17.50 (*0-8139-1966-5*) U Pr of Va.

Modernity & the Architecture of Mexico. Ed. by Edward R. Burian. LC 96-2758. (Illus.). 240p. 1997. 40.00 (*0-292-70852-1*); pap. 19.95 (*0-292-70853-X*) U of Tex Pr.

Modernity & the Hegemony of Vision. Ed. by David M. Levin. LC 93-1523. 1993. 55.00 (*0-520-07972-8*, Pub. by U CA Pr); pap. 24.95 (*0-520-07973-6*, Pub. by U CA Pr) Cal Prin Full Svc.

Modernity & the Holocaust. Zygmunt Bauman. LC 89-7274. 250p. 1989. text 47.50 (*0-8014-2397-X*) Cornell U Pr.

Modernity & the Holocaust. Zygmunt Bauman. LC 89-7274. 280p. 1992. pap. text 17.95 (*0-8014-8032-9*) Cornell U Pr.

***Modernity & the Millennium: The Genesis of the Baha'i Faith in the Nineteenth-Century Middle East.** Juan Cole. LC 97-45661. (Illus.). 400p. 1998. 50.00 (*0-231-11080-4*) Col U Pr.

***Modernity & the Millennium: The Genesis of the Baha'i Faith in the Nineteenth-Century Middle East.** Juan Cole. LC 97-45661. (Illus.). 400p. 1998. pap. 20.50 (*0-231-11081-2*) Col U Pr.

Modernity & the State: East, West. Claus Offe. LC 96-3429. (Studies in Contemporary German Social Thought). (Illus.). 288p. 1996. 36.00 (*0-262-15046-8*); pap. text 18.00 (*0-262-65047-9*) MIT Pr.

Modernity & the Text. Ed. by Andreas Huyssen & David Bathrick. 256p. 1991. pap. text 22.00 (*0-231-06645-7*) Col U Pr.

Modernity & Tradition: Contemporary Architecture in Pakistan. Kamil K. Mumtaz. LC 99-203964. (The Jubilee Ser.). (Illus.). 150p. 1999. text 35.00 (*0-19-577853-7*) OUP.

Modernity & Tradition: The Saudi Equation. Fouad Al-Farsy. (Illus.). 360p. 1990. 77.00 (*0-7103-0395-5*, A5214) Routledge.

Modernity & War. Lawrence. LC 96-52561. 206p. 1998. text 65.00 (*0-312-17402-0*) St Martin.

Modernity at Large: Cultural Dimensions of Globalization. Arjun Appadurai. (Public Worlds Ser.: Vol. 1). 224p. (C). 1996. pap. 18.95 (*0-8166-2793-2*) U of Minn Pr.

Modernity at the Edge of Empire: State, Individual & Nation in the Northern Peruvian Andes, 1885-1935. David Nugent. LC 96-49742. 1997. write for info. (*0-8047-2782-1*); pap. write for info. (*0-8047-2958-1*) Stanford U Pr.

Modernity, Culture, & 'the Jew' Ed. by Bryan Cheyette & Laura Marcus. (Contraversions Ser.). 320p. 1998. 55.00 (*0-8047-3069-5*); pap. 18.95 (*0-8047-3070-9*) Stanford U Pr.

Modernity English Art, 1914-30. Corbett. (Illus.). 250p. 1997. pap. 29.95 (*0-7190-3733-6*, Pub. by Manchester Univ Pr) St Martin.

Modernity in Asian Art. Ed. by John Clark. (University of Sydney East Asian Ser.: No. 7). (Illus.). 210p. (C). 1993. pap. text 28.00 (*0-646-14773-0*, Pub. by Wild Peony Pty) UH Pr.

Modernity, Medicine & Health: Medical Sociology Towards 2000. Graham Scambler & Paul Higgs. LC 97-34889. 264p. (C). 1998. 80.00 (*0-415-14938-X*); pap. 24.99 (*0-415-14939-8*) Routledge.

Modernity of English Art, 1914-1930. David P. Corbett. (Illus.). 250p. 1997. 74.95 (*0-7190-3732-8*, Pub. by Manchester Univ Pr) St Martin.

Modernity of Milton: A Theological & Philosophical Interpretation. Martin A. Larson. LC 76-124764. reprint ed. 37.00 (*0-404-03880-8*) AMS Pr.

Modernity of Tradition: Political Development in India. Lloyd I. Rudolph & Susanne H. Rudolph. LC 67-25527. (Midway Reprint Ser.). x, 316p. (C). 1984. pap. text 25.00 (*0-226-73137-5*) U Ch Pr.

Modernity of Witchcraft: Politics & the Occult in Postcolonial Africa. Peter Geschiere. Tr. by Janet Roitman. LC 96-46199. 300p. 1997. text 59.50 (*0-8139-1702-6*) U Pr of Va.

Modernity Of Witchcraft: Politics & the Occult in Postcolonial Africa. Peter Geschiere. Tr. by Janet Roitman from FRE. LC 96-46199. 1997. pap. text 18.50 (*0-8139-1703-4*) U Pr of Va.

Modernity on Endless Trial. Leszek Kolakowski. Tr. by Stefan Czerniawski et al. LC 90-35966. 270p. 1990. 29.95 (*0-226-45045-7*) U Ch Pr.

Modernity on Endless Trial. Leszek Kolakowski. 267p. 1997. pap. 15.95 (*0-226-45046-5*) U Ch Pr.

Modernity, Space & Power: The American City in Discourse & Practice. Katharine Tehranian. Ed. by Gary Gumpert. LC 95-33618. (Communication Series). 176p. 1995. text 47.50 (*1-881303-82-9*); pap. text 22.95 (*1-881303-83-7*) Hampton Pr NJ.

Modernity Within Tradition: The Social History of Orthodox Jewry in Imperial Germany. Mordechai Breuer. Tr. by Elizabeth Petuchowski from GER. 514p. 1992. text 57.50 (*0-231-07470-0*) Col U Pr.

Modernity Without Restraint: The Political Religions; The New Science of Politics; & Science, Politics, & Gnosticism. Eric Voegelin. Ed. & Intro. by Manfred Henningsen. LC 99-44762. (Collected Works of Eric Voegelin: Vol. 5). 352p. 2000. 34.95 (*0-8262-1245-X*) U of Mo Pr.

Modernity's Pretenses: Making Reality Fit Reason from Candide to the Gulag. Karlis Racevskis. LC 97-43903. (Series in Postmodern Culture). 192p. (C). 1998. pap. text 18.95 (*0-7914-3954-2*) State U NY Pr.

Modernity's Pretenses: Making Reality Fit Reason from Candide to the Gulag. Karlis Racevskis. LC 97-43903. (Series in Postmodern Culture). 192p. (C). 1998. text 56.50 (*0-7914-3953-4*) State U NY Pr.

Modernity's Reluctant Exit: The Institution of Art in Postmodernity. Ales Debeljak. Ed. by Stjepan Mestrovic. LC 97-34770. (Postmodern Social Futures Ser.: No. 86). 192p. 1998. 55.00 (*0-8476-8582-9*); pap. 22.95 (*0-8476-8583-7*) Rowman.

***Modernity's Wager: Authority, the Self & Transcendence.** Adam B. Seligman. LC 00-27418. 208p. 2000. 27.95 (*0-691-05061-9*, Pub. by Princeton U Pr) Cal Prin Full Svc.

Modernizacion de las Finanzas Municipales: Un Paso Esencial para la Consolidacion Institucional. Ed. by Huascar Eguino & Fabrice Henry. (SPA.). 240p. 1999. pap. text 15.00 (*1-886938-53-9*) IADB.

Modernization: The Humanist Response to Its Promise & Problems. Ed. by Richard L. Rubenstein. LC 82-83241. 353p. (C). 1986. pap. 14.95 (*0-89226-031-9*) Paragon Hse.

Modernization & Bureaucratic-Authoritarianism: Studies in South American Politics. Guillermo O'Donnell. LC 73-620029. (Politics of Modernization Ser.: No. 9). (Illus.). xvi, 226p. 1995. pap. text 15.00 (*0-87725-209-2*) U of Cal IAS.

Modernization & Chinese Entrepreneurship, No. 3. Ambrose Y. King & Wong Siu-lun. LC 99-176654. (East Asian Institute Occasional Paper Ser.). 2p. 1998. pap. 17.50 (*981-02-3510-0*, Pub. by Sngapore Univ Pr) Coronet Bks.

Modernization & Cultural Identity: The Creation of National Space in Rural France & Colonial Space in Rural Gabon. Christopher Gray. Ed. by Victoria Cuffel. LC 93-655022. (MacArthur Scholar Series, Occasional Paper: No. 21). 91p. (Orig.). 1994. pap. 4.00 (*1-881157-22-9*) In Ctr Global.

Modernization & Foreign Policy. R. D. Tschirgi. (CISA Working Papers: No. 29). 31p. (Orig.). 1980. pap. 15.00 (*0-86682-028-0*) Ctr Intl Relations.

Modernization & Hindu Socio-Culture. Akhileshwar Jha. 151p. 1978. 10.95 (*0-318-36972-9*) Asia Bk Corp.

Modernization & Its Impact upon Korean Law. Pyong-ho Pak. LC 80-84987. (California University Center for Korean Studies.-Korea Research Monograph: No. 3). 163p. pap. 50.60 (*0-608-18567-1*, 201946900011) Bks Demand.

Modernization & Law. Kalman Kulcsar. 282p. (C). 1992. 120.00 (*963-05-6278-2*, Pub. by Akade Kiado) St Mut.

Modernization & Population Change. M. Hari. (C). 1991. 18.50 (*81-7141-157-6*) S Asia.

Modernization & Postmodernization: Cultural, Economic & Political Change in 43 Societies. Ronald Inglehart. LC 96-53839. 440p. 1997. text 60.00 (*0-691-01181-8*, Pub. by Princeton U Pr); pap. text 18.95 (*0-691-01180-X*, Pub. by Princeton U Pr) Cal Prin Full Svc.

Modernization & Revolution: Dilemmas of Progress in Late Imperial Russia. Ed. by Edward H. Judge & James Y. Simms, Jr. 400p. 1992. text 39.00 (*0-88033-233-6*, 336, Pub. by East Eur Monographs) Col U Pr.

Modernization & Revolution in China. June Grasso et al. LC 91-16481. (Studies on Modern China). 240p. (C). (gr. 13). 1991. text 64.95 (*0-87332-538-9*, East Gate Bk); pap. text 24.95 (*0-87332-539-7*, East Gate Bk) M E Sharpe.

Modernization & Revolution in China. rev. ed. June Grasso et al. LC 96-39807. 304p. (C). (gr. 13). 1997. pap. text 25.95 (*1-56324-977-4*, East Gate Bk) M E Sharpe.

Modernization & Revolution in China. rev. ed. June Grasson et al. LC 96-39807. 304p. (C). (gr. 13). 1997. text 70.95 (*1-56324-976-6*, East Gate Bk) M E Sharpe.

Modernization & Revolution in Mexico: A Comparative Approach. 162p. 35.00 (*92-808-0706-4*, 89.III.A.5) UN.

Modernization & Ritual: Identity & Social Change in Santal Society. Sitakanta Mahapatra. (Illus.). 180p. 1987. 29.95 (*0-19-561794-0*) OUP.

Modernization & Social Change. Dhirendra K. Vajpeyi. 299p. 1979. 16.95 (*0-318-36859-5*) Asia Bk Corp.

Modernization & Stagnation: Latin American Agriculture into the 1990s, 1. Ed. by Michael J. Twomey & Ann Helwege. LC 91-1. (Contributions in Latin American Studies: No. 1). 288p. 1991. 65.00 (*0-313-27449-5*, TMZ, Greenwood Pr) Greenwood.

Modernization & Status of Working Women in India. Anita Sharma. 1990. 18.00 (*81-7099-238-9*, Pub. by Mittal Pubs Dist) S Asia.

Modernization & the Structure of Societies, 2 Vols., Set. Marion Levy. 920p. 1996. pap. text 49.95 (*1-56000-897-0*) Transaction Pubs.

Modernization & the Structure of Societies: Aspects of Social Structure in Modernized & Non-Modernized Societies, 2 Vols., Vol. 1. Marion Levy. 432p. 1996. pap. text 29.95 (*1-56000-893-8*) Transaction Pubs.

Modernization & the Sturcture of Societies: The Organization Contexts of Societies, 2 Vols., Vol. 2. Marion Levy. 488p. 1996. pap. text 29.95 (*1-56000-896-2*) Transaction Pubs.

Modernization & Urbanization in India. Hans Nagpaul. 1996. 34.00 (*0-614-25276-8*, Pub. by Rawat Pubns) S Asia.

Modernization & Youth in India. R. Jayaswal. (C). 1992. 22.00 (*81-7033-162-5*, Pub. by Rawat Pubns) S Asia.

***Modernization As Ideology: American Social Science & "Nation-Building" in the Kennedy Era.** Michael E. Latham. LC 99-35517. (New Cold War History Ser.). 328p. 2000. pap. 18.95 (*0-8078-4844-1*) U of NC Pr.

***Modernization As Ideology: American Social Science & "Nation Building" in the Kennedy Era.** Michael E. Latham. LC 99-35517. (New Cold War History Ser.). 328p. 2000. lib. bdg. 45.00 (*0-8078-2533-6*) U of NC Pr.

Modernization Crisis: The Transformation of Poland. William D. Perdue. Tr. & Contrib. by Tadeusz Borkowski. Contrib. by Stanislaw Palka et al. LC 95-2491. 264p. 1995. 67.95 (*0-275-95009-3*, Praeger Pubs) Greenwood.

***Modernization, Crisis & Culture in Ireland, 1969-1992.** Conor McCarthy. 288p. 2000. 55.00 (*1-85182-475-8*, Pub. by Four Cts Pr); pap. 27.50 (*1-85182-479-0*, Pub. by Four Cts Pr) Intl Spec Bk.

Modernization, Exploitation & Dependency in Latin America. Joseph Kahl. LC 75-43190. 215p. (C). 1976. pap. text 21.95 (*0-87855-584-6*) Transaction Pubs.

Modernization in a Mexican Ejido: A Study in Economic Adaptation. Billie R. DeWalt. LC 78-3412. (Cambridge Latin American Studies: Vol. 33). 319p. reprint ed. pap. 91.00 (*0-608-16885-8*, 2027247) Bks Demand.

Modernization in East Asia: Political, Economic, & Social Perspectives. Ed. by William T. Liu et al. LC 92-9117. 200p. 1992. 57.95 (*0-275-93222-2*, C3222, Praeger Pubs) Greenwood.

Modernization in Lean Times: Modifications & Upgrades. Thomas R. Evans et al. (Illus.). 154p. (C). 1998. reprint ed. pap. text 30.00 (*0-7881-1313-5*) DIANE Pub.

Modernization in Lean Times: Modifications & Upgrades, Report of the Dsmc 1994-1995 Military Research Fellows. Thomas R. Evans. 168p. 1995. per. 11.00 (*0-16-048157-0*) USGPO.

Modernization in Nepal. Ed. by B. R. Bajracharya. (C). 1993. 22.00 (*81-7041-841-0*, Pub. by Anmol) S Asia.

Modernization in the Middle East: The Ottoman Empire & Its Afro-Asian Successors. Karl K. Barbir et al. Ed. by Cyril E. Black et al. LC 91-44788. (Illus.). 392p. 1992. 29.95 (*0-87850-085-5*); pap. 17.95 (*0-87850-084-7*) Darwin Pr.

Modernization in the Sudan. Ed. by Martin Daly. LC 85-19768. 177p. 1985. text 29.50 (*0-936508-11-6*) Barber Pr.

Modernization of Agriculture: Rural Transformation in Hungary, 1848-1975. Ed. by Joseph Held. (East European Monographs: No. 67). 508p. 1980. text 79.00 (*0-914710-60-5*, Pub. by East Eur Monographs) Col U Pr.

Modernization of Agriculture & Food Availability in India. P. D. Tiwari & C. K. Jain. 1989. 21.00 (*81-85119-56-2*, Pub. by Northern Bk Ctr) S Asia.

Modernization of Agriculture in Developing Countries: Resources, Potentials & Problems. Itzhak Arnon. LC 80-41588. (Environmental Monographs & Symposia). (Illus.). 589p. 1981. reprint ed. pap. 182.60 (*0-608-17338-X*, 202979400065) Bks Demand.

Modernization of Agriculture in Developing Countries: Resources, Potentials & Problems. 2nd fac. ed. Itzhak Arnon. LC 87-6288. (Environmental Monographs & Symposia). (Illus.). 650p. 1987. pap. 200.00 (*0-7837-7668-3*, 204742100007) Bks Demand.

Modernization of British Government. Ed. by William Thornhill. 322p. 1975. 38.00 (*0-87471-759-0*) Rowman.

Modernization of Car Fifteen: Bulletin No. 35. (Illus.). 80p. 1984. pap. 10.00 (*0-915348-03-9*, B-35) Central Electric.

Modernization of China. Ed. by Gilbert Rozman. (Illus.). 1981. 29.95 (*0-02-927480-X*) Free Pr.

Modernization of Fatherhood: A Social & Political History. Ralph LaRossa. (Illus.). 320p. 1999. lib. bdg. 55.00 (*0-226-46903-4*) U Ch Pr.

Modernization of Fatherhood: A Social & Political History. Ralph Larossa. (Illus.). 320p. 1996. pap. text 18.95 (*0-226-46904-2*) U Ch Pr.

Modernization of French Jewry: Consistory & Community in the Nineteenth Century. Phyllis C. Albert. LC 76-50680. 472p. reprint ed. pap. 146.40 (*0-7837-2995-2*, 204294600006) Bks Demand.

Modernization of Hydronic Systems. Hydronics Institute Staff. (Technical Notes Ser.: No. 13). (Illus.). 16p. (C). 1984. reprint ed. pap. 6.50 (*0-942711-10-6*) Hydronics Inst.

Modernization of Indian Tradition: A Systemic Study of Social Change. Yogendra Singh. (C). 1995. 12.50 (*81-7033-013-0*, Pub. by Rawat Pubns) S Asia.

Modernization of Inner Asia. Cyril E. Black et al. LC 90-23385. 424p. (C). (gr. 13). 1994. pap. text 38.95 (*0-87332-779-9*, East Gate Bk) M E Sharpe.

Modernization of Inner Asia. E. Endicott-West et al. LC 90-23385. 424p. (C). (gr. 13). 1991. text 88.95 (*0-87332-778-0*, East Gate Bk) M E Sharpe.

Modernization of Iran, 1921-1941. Amin Banani. LC 61-5504. (Illus.). 205p. 1961. reprint ed. pap. 30.00 (*0-608-00250-X*, 206076500006) Bks Demand.

An Asterisk (*) at the beginning of an entry indicates that the title is appearing for the first time.

Modernization of Irish Society. 2nd ed. Joseph Lee. 181p. (C). 1989. reprint ed. pap. 17.95 (*0-7171-1693-X*, Pub. by Gill & MacMill) Irish Bks Media.

Modernization of Irrigation Schemes: Past Experiences & Future Options, No. 09005686. 268p. 1998. 29.00 (*92-5-104020-6*, F40206, Pub. by FAO) Bernan Associates.

Modernization of Japanese Education, 2 vols., Set. (Japan Ser.). 1991. lib. bdg. 279.95 (*0-8490-4570-3*) Gordon Pr.

Modernization of Manchuria: An Annotated Bibliography. Ronald Suleski. LC 97-177915. 228p. 1997. pap. text 32.50 (*962-201-537-9*, Pub. by Chinese Univ) U of Mich Pr.

Modernization of Muslim Education. G. N. Saqib. 1990. 29.00 (*1-56744-145-9*) Kazi Pubns.

Modernization of North African Families in the Paris Area. Andree Michel. LC 72-184752. (New Babylon Studies in the Social Sciences: No. 16). (Illus.). 387p. (Orig.). 1974. pap. text 34.75 (*90-279-7312-1*) Mouton.

Modernization of Puerto Rico: A Political Study of Changing Values & Institutions. Henry Wells. LC 79-75435. 456p. 1969. reprint ed. pap. 141.40 (*0-7837-4133-2*, 205795600011) Bks Demand.

Modernization of Punjab Agriculture. A. S. Kahlon. 1985. 11.50 (*0-8364-1465-9*, Pub. by Ashish Pub Hse) S Asia.

Modernization of Shift Work, Police Scheduling & Resources Allocation: First National Conference. William Stenzel et al. Ed. by David Struckhoff et al. 120p. 1997. pap. 34.95 (*1-890867-03-9*) Justice Research.

Modernization of the American Stock Exchange, 1971-1989. Stuart Bruchey. LC 91-35983. 236p. 1991. text 15.00 (*0-8153-0722-5*) Garland.

Modernization of the Chinese Past. Ed. by Mabel Lee & A. D. Syrokomla-Stefanowska. (University of Sydney Asian Studies Ser.: No. 1). 195p. (C). 1993. text 20.00 (*0-86758-658-3*, Pub. by Wild Peony Pty) UH Pr.

Modernization of the Chinese Salt Administration, 1900-1920. S. A. Adshead. LC 77-120315. (East Asian Monographs: No. 53). (Illus.). 294p. 1970. 40.50 (*0-674-58060-5*) HUP.

Modernization of the Law in Arab States: An Investigation into Current Civil, Criminal & Constitutional Law in the Arab World. George N. Sfeir. LC 97-37076. 280p. 1997. pap. 75.00 (*1-57292-103-X*) Austin & Winfield.

Modernization of the Law in Arab States: An Investigation into Current Civil, Criminal, & Constitutional Law in the Arab World. George N. Sfeir. LC 97-37076. 280p. 1997. pap. 54.95 (*1-57292-102-1*) Austin & Winfield.

Modernization of Turkey: From Ataturk to the Present Day. Walter F. Weiker. LC 80-24514. 303p. 1981. 49.95 (*0-8419-0503-7*) Holmes & Meier.

***Modernization of Working Times: Flexibility & Work Sharing in Finland.** Raija Julkumen & Jouko Natti. 217p. 1999. pap. 25.00 (*951-39-0548-9*, Pub. by SoPhi Academic) Intl Spec Bk.

Modernization of Working Women in Developing Societies. Raj M. Sethi. 168p. 1976. 12.95 (*0-318-37066-2*) Asia Bk Corp.

Modernization, Political Development & Stability. Ed. by Avi Plascov. LC 80-28387. (Security in the Persian Gulf Ser.: Vol. 3). 192p. 1982. pap. text 19.50 (*0-86598-046-2*) Rowman.

Modernization Theory & Economic Development: Discontent in the Developing World. Bret L. Billet. LC 93-19115. 160p. 1993. 49.95 (*0-275-94446-8*, C4446, Praeger Pubs) Greenwood.

Modernization, Urbanization, & the Urban Crisis. Gene Somani. 257p. 1973. pap. 21.95 (*0-87855-680-X*) Transaction Pubs.

Modernization, Value Change & Fertility in the Soviet Union. Ellen Jones & Fred Grupp. (Cambridge Russian, Soviet & Post-Soviet Studies: No. 52). (Illus.). 436p. 1987. text 85.00 (*0-521-32034-8*) Cambridge U Pr.

Modernization Without Development in Africa: Patterns of Change & Community. Fuabeh Fonge. LC 97-13290. 1997. pap. text 21.95 (*0-86543-549-9*) Africa World.

Modernization Without Development in Africa: Patterns of Change & Continuity in Post-Independence Cameroonian Public Service. Fuabeh P. Fonge. LC 97-13290. 1997. write for info. (*0-86543-548-0*) Africa World.

Modernization Without Revolution: Lebanon's Experience. Elie A. Salem. LC 72-85854. (International Development Research Center, Studies in Development: No. 6). 190p. reprint ed. 58.90 (*0-608-16112-8*, 201763900007) Bks Demand.

Modernized Korea: Social, Political & Economic Changes. Ed. by Ho-Youn Kwon. 295p. (C). 1996. pap. 15.00 (*0-9643677-3-4*) North Pk Coll.

Modernizing China. Ed. by Dhirendra K. Vajpeyi. LC 94-4472. (International Studies in Sociology & Social Anthropology: Vol. 42). vi, 126p. 1994. pap. 48.50 (*90-04-10046-6*) Brill Academic Pubs.

Modernizing China's Electronics Industry: Prospects for U. S. Business. Thomas Fingar. (Special Report of the Northeast Asia-United States Forum on International Policy, Stanford University Ser.). 48p. (Orig.). 1985. pap. 8.00 (*0-935371-10-9*) CFISAC.

Modernizing Control Systems: New Management Patterns for the Retrofit Project. Edward J. Farmer. LC 83-18399. (Instrument Society of America Monographs: No. 8). 187p. reprint ed. pap. 58.00 (*0-7837-5140-0*, 204486800004) Bks Demand.

Modernizing Effects of University Education. S. L. Sharma. 1979. 11.00 (*0-8364-0543-9*) S Asia.

Modernizing Federal Classification: Operational Broad-Banding Systems Alternatives. Center for Human Resources Management Staff. (Implementing Real Change in Human Resources Management Ser.). 113p. (Orig.). 1995. pap. 15.00 (*0-9646874-9-6*) Nat Acad Public Admin.

Modernizing Financial Systems. Papadimitriou. LC 99-15311. 1999. text 79.95 (*0-312-22586-5*) St Martin.

Modernizing Foreign Assistance: Resource Management As an Instrument of Foreign Policy. American Foreign Policy Council Staff. LC 91-46992. 160p. 1992. 47.95 (*0-275-94224-4*, C4224, Praeger Pubs) Greenwood.

Modernizing Germany: Karl Bidermann's Career in the Kingdom of Saxony, 1835-1901. Richard Bazillion. LC 89-27468. (American University Studies: History: Ser. IX, Vol. 84). XXI, 450p. 1989. text 66.95 (*0-8204-1185-X*) P Lang Pubng.

Modernizing Government Regulation: The Need for Action: A Statement. Committee for Economic Development Staff. LC 97-51618. 1998. write for info. (*0-87186-127-5*) Comm Econ Dev.

Modernizing Lives: Experiments in English Biography, 1918-1939. Ruth Hoberman. LC 86-4004. 240p. 1986. text 26.95 (*0-8093-1288-3*) S Ill U Pr.

Modernizing Local Government. Committee for Economic Development. LC 66-26939. 84p. 1966. pap. 1.50 (*0-87186-023-6*) Comm Econ Dev.

Modernizing Local Government in Massachusetts: The Quest for Professionals & Reform. Edwin Gere, Jr. LC 84-13140. 208p. (Orig.). 1984. lib. bdg. 47.50 (*0-8191-4191-7*) U Pr of Amer.

Modernizing Manufacturing: New Policies to Build Industrial Extension Services. Philip Shapira. 65p. 1990. 12.00 (*0-944826-24-5*) Economic Policy Inst.

Modernizing Mexican Management Style: With Insights for U.S. Companies Working in Mexico. Eva S. Kras. LC 93-74978. (Illus.). 160p. (Orig.). 1994. pap. 14.95 (*1-884512-49-6*) Two Eagles.

Modernizing Research Libraries: The Effect of Recent Developments in University Libraries on the Research Process. Bob Erens. LC 96-38003. (British Library Research). 283p. 1996. 60.00 (*1-85739-174-8*) Bowker-Saur.

Modernizing Shakespeare's Spelling: With Three Studies in the Text of Henry V. Ed. by Stanley Wells & Gary Taylor. (Illus.). 174p. 1980. text 39.95 (*0-19-812913-0*) OUP.

Modernizing State Government. Committee for Economic Development. LC 67-27541. 85p. 1967. pap. 1.50 (*0-87186-028-7*); lib. bdg. 2.50 (*0-87186-728-1*) Comm Econ Dev.

Modernizing Super-Exploitation: Restructuring South African Agriculture. Tessa Marcus. LC 89-5835. 256p. (C). 1989. pap. 19.95 (*0-86232-845-4*, Pub. by Zed Books); text 55.00 (*0-86232-844-6*, Pub. by Zed Books) St Martin.

Modernizing the Financial System: How to Get Safer, More Competitive Banks, 2 vols., Set. 1992. lib. bdg. 555.95 (*0-8490-8855-0*) Gordon Pr.

Modernizing the Little Red Schoolhouse: The Economics of Improved Education. Edward J. Willett et al. LC 78-26604. (Illus.). 304p. 1979. 39.95 (*0-87778-133-8*) Educ Tech Pubns.

Modernizing the Mountaineer: People, Power & Planning in Appalachia. David E. Whisnant. LC 93-37800. 336p. (C). 1994. reprint ed. pap. text 18.95 (*0-87049-823-1*) U of Tenn Pr.

Modernizing the Provincial City: Toulouse, 1945-1975. Rosemary Wakeman. LC 97-23077. (Illus.). 384p. 1998. 45.00 (*0-674-58072-9*) HUP.

Modernizing the Strategic Bomber Force: Why & How. Alton H. Quanbeck & Archie L. Wood. LC 75-38890. (Studies in Defense Policy). (Illus.). 128p. reprint ed. pap. 39.70 (*0-608-30816-1*, 202256100028) Bks Demand.

Modernizing the U. S. Census. Barry Edmondston. Ed. by Charles Schultze. 480p. (Orig.). (C). 1994. pap. text 45.00 (*0-309-05182-7*) Natl Acad Pr.

Modernizing Traditional Agriculture. Marc Nerlove. 20p. 1988. pap. 9.95 (*1-55815-033-1*) ICS Pr.

Modernizing Urban Land Policy: Papers Presented at an RFF Forum Held in Washington, DC, 13-14 April 1972. Ed. by Marion Clawson. LC 72-12365. 256p. reprint ed. pap. 79.40 (*0-7837-3143-4*, 202379200034) Bks Demand.

Modernizing Women: Gender & Social Change in the Middle East. Valentine M. Moghadam. LC 92-37454. (Women & Change in the Developing World Ser.). 312p. 1993. pap. text 19.95 (*1-55587-354-5*) L Rienner.

Moderno Formulario de Hechiceria Intro. by Karen Lara. 157p. (Orig.). 1997. pap. text 11.98 (*968-409-588-0*) Edamex.

Moderns. Sheed & Ward Ltd. Staff. 1990. pap. 100.00 (*0-7220-7852-8*) St Mut.

Moderns: Essays in Literary Criticism. John Freeman. LC 67-30213. (Essay Index Reprint Ser.). 1977. 21.95 (*0-8369-0460-5*) Ayer.

***Moderns: Time, Space, & Subjectivity in Contemporary Spanish Culture.** Paul Julian Smith. (Illus.). 240p. 2000. pap. 19.95 (*0-19-816001-1*); text 65.00 (*0-19-816000-3*) OUP.

Moderns: 1955-1995, Inventory Catalogue of the Pforzheim Jewelry Museum. Fritz Falk. 1999. 75.00 (*3-925369-81-3*) Arnoldsche Art Pubs.

Moderns & Near-Moderns: Essays on Henry James, Stockton, Shaw & Others. William Chislett. LC 67-30180. (Essay Index Reprint Ser.). 1977. 18.95 (*0-8369-0302-1*) Ayer.

***ModernStarts: People, Places & Things.** John Elderfield. 360p. 1999. 55.00 (*0-8109-6203-9*, Pub. by Abrams) Time Warner.

***ModernStarts: People, Places, Things.** Ed. by John Elderfield et al. (Illus.). 248p. 1999. 55.00 (*0-87070-025-1*); pap. 29.95 (*0-87070-024-3*) Mus of Modern Art.

Modes. Albert S. Cook. LC 93-6534. 108p. 1993. pap. 24.95 (*0-7734-2788-0*) E Mellen.

Modes & Manners: From the Middle Ages to the End of the Eighteenth Century, 4 vols., 2 bks. Max Von Boehn. LC 68-56493. (Illus.). 1972. reprint ed. 55.95 (*0-405-08280-0*, Pub. by Blom Pubns) Ayer.

Modes & Manners: From the Middle Ages to the End of the Eighteenth Century, Vol. 1. Max Von Boehn. 1972. 27.95 (*0-405-19017-4*) Ayer.

Modes & Manners: From the Middle Ages to the End of the Eighteenth Century, Vol. 2. Max Von Boehn. 1972. 27.95 (*0-405-19018-2*) Ayer.

Modes & Manners of the Ninteenth Century, 4 vols., 2 bks., 2. enl. rev. ed. Max Von Boehn & Oskar Fischel. LC 68-56493. (Illus.). 1972. reprint ed. 27.95 (*0-405-08282-7*, Pub. by Blom Pubns) Ayer.

Modes & Manners of the Ninteenth Century, 4 vols., 2 bks., Set. enl. rev. ed. Max Von Boehn & Oskar Fischel. LC 68-56493. (Illus.). 747p. 1972. reprint ed. 55.95 (*0-405-08283-5*, Pub. by Blom Pubns) Ayer.

Modes & Manners of the Ninteenth Century, 4 vols., 2 bks., Vol. 1. enl. rev. ed. Max Von Boehn & Oskar Fischel. LC 68-56493. (Illus.). 1972. reprint ed. 27.95 (*0-405-08281-9*, Pub. by Blom Pubns) Ayer.

Modes & Morals. Katharine F. Gerould. LC 78-142634. (Essay Index Reprint Ser.). 1977. reprint ed. 21.95 (*0-8369-2317-0*) Ayer.

Modes & Morals of Psychotherapy. 2nd ed. Perry London. LC 84-29769. (Clinical & Community Psychology Ser.). 350p. (C). 1986. pap. 27.95 (*0-89116-350-6*); text 79.95 (*0-89116-290-9*) Hemisp Pub.

Modes et les Tons de la Musique et Specialement de la Musique Medievale. Antoine Auda. (Academie Royale De Belgique. Classe Des Beaux-Arts Collection: Vol. 3, Fasc. 1). 203p. 1979. reprint ed. lib. bdg. 40.00 (*3-487-06852-4*) G Olms Pubs.

Modes for Rock & Blues Guitar. 48p. 1996. pap. 5.95 (*0-7935-4371-1*, 00695015) H Leonard.

Modes in All Keys for Piano. Ed. by Carmela Mercuri. (Orig.). 1993. pap. 6.95 (*0-935474-22-6*) Carousel Pubns Ltd.

Modes in Denya Discourse. Samson N. Abangma. LC 87-62710. (Publications in Linguistics: No. 79). (Illus.). 140p. (Orig.). 1987. pap. 22.00 (*0-88312-007-0*) S I L Intl.

Modes of Action of GnRH & GnRH Analogs. Ed. by W. F. Crowley, Jr. & P. Michael Conn. (Serono Symposia Ser.). (Illus.). 416p. 1992. 180.00 (*0-387-97802-X*) Spr-Verlag.

Modes of Analogy in Ancient & Medieval Verse. Phillip Damon. LC 72-95296. (California Library Reprint). 81p. reprint ed. pap. 30.00 (*0-608-18497-7*, 203150300075) Bks Demand.

Modes of Argument. Monroe C. Beardsley. LC 67-18663. 1967. pap. 2.95 (*0-672-60893-6*, Bobbs) Macmillan.

Modes of Art No. 1: A Critical Work. Robert G. Cohn. (Stanford French & Italian Studies: No. 1). 217p. 1976. pap. 56.50 (*0-915838-29-X*) Anma Libri.

Modes of Construction & Their Change Through Validation & Invalidation. Harald Furst. (Studia Psychologica Upsaliensia: No. 5). 178p. (Orig.). 1979. pap. 18.75 (*91-554-0757-9*, Pub. by Uppsala Univ Acta Univ Uppsaliensis) Coronet Bks.

Modes of Historical Discourse in J. G. Herder & N. M. Karamzin. S. Mark Lewis. LC 94-18326. (Studies on the Themes & Motifs in Literature: Vol. 12). IX, 125p. (C). 1995. text 38.95 (*0-8204-2576-1*) P Lang Pubng.

Modes of Individualism & Collectivism. Ed. by John O'Niell. (Modern Revivals in Philosophy Ser.). 368p. 1993. 72.95 (*0-7512-0050-6*, Pub. by Gregg Pub) Ashgate Pub Co.

Modes of Interpretation in Old English Literature: Essays in Honour of Stanley B. Greenfield. Ed. by Phyllis R. Brown et al. 298p. 1986. text 40.00 (*0-8020-5678-4*) U of Toronto Pr.

Modes of Knowledge & the Transcendental: An Introduction to Plotinus Ennead 5.3 (49) with a Commentary & Translation. Henri Oosthout. LC 91-23974. (Bochumer Studien zur Philosophie Ser.: Vol. 17). vii, 200p. 1991. 65.00 (*90-6032-319-X*, Pub. by B R Gruner) Humanities.

Modes of Medical Instruction: A Semiotic Comparison of Textbooks of Medicine & Popular Home Medical Books. Joan Y. Kahn. LC 83-2379. (Approaches to Semiotics Ser.: No. 65). xx, 342p. 1983. 105.40 (*90-279-3070-8*) Mouton.

Modes of Modern Writing: Metaphor, Metonymy, & the Typology of Modern Literature. David Lodge. xvi, 280p. 1988. pap. text 13.95 (*0-226-48978-7*) U Ch Pr.

Modes of Operation Validation System Requirements & Procedures. Sharon Keller. 153p. 1998. per. 13.00 (*0-16-056696-7*) USGPO.

Modes of Perceiving & Processing Information. Ed. by H. L. Pick, Jr. & E. Saltzman. 240p. 1978. text 49.95 (*0-89859-354-9*) L Erlbaum Assocs.

Modes of Production in Africa: The Precolonial Era. Ed. by Donald Crummey & C. C. Stewart. LC 81-1433. (Sage Series on African Modernization & Development: No. 5). 256p. reprint ed. pap. 79.40 (*0-8357-8452-5*, 203471600091) Bks Demand.

Modes of Production of Victorian Novels. N. N. Feltes. LC 86-6927. xiv, 144p. (C). 1986. 22.95 (*0-226-24117-3*) U Ch Pr.

Modes of Production of Victorian Novels. N. N. Feltes. LC 86-6927. xiv, 144p. (C). 2000. pap. text 12.00 (*0-226-24118-1*) U Ch Pr.

Modes of Renaissance Vocal Polyphony. Bernhard Meier. Tr. by Ellen S. Beebe. (Illus.). 1988. lib. bdg. 50.00 (*0-8450-7025-8*) Broude.

Modes of Representation in Spanish Cinema. Ed. by Jenaro Talens & Santos Zunzunegui. LC 98-5971. (Hispanic Issues Ser.: Vol. 16). xxvi, 346p. 1998. pap. 21.95 (*0-8166-2975-7*); text 54.95 (*0-8166-2974-9*) U of Minn Pr.

Modes of Scepticism: Ancient Texts & Modern Interpretations. Julia Annas & Jonathan Barnes. 216p. 1985. pap. text 17.95 (*0-521-27644-6*) Cambridge U Pr.

Modes of Style in Lawrence's Fiction see D. H. Lawrence: Modes of Fictional Style

Modes of the Fantastic: Selected Essays from the Twelfth International Conference on the Fantastic in the Arts, 66. Robert A. Latham & Robert A. Collins. LC 95-4661. (Contributions to the Study of Science Fiction & Fantasy: Vol. 66). 256p. 1995. 69.50 (*0-313-29085-7*, Greenwood Pr) Greenwood.

Modes of Therapeu Action: Enhancement of Knowlwdge, Provision of Experience, & Engagement in Relationship. Martha Stark. LC RC456.S725 1999. 408p. 1999. 60.00 (*0-7657-0202-9*) Aronson.

Modes of Thinking in Young Children: A Study of the Creativity-Intelligence Distinction. Michael A. Wallach & Nathan Kogan. LC 84-15865. 357p. 1984. reprint ed. lib. bdg. 89.50 (*0-313-23249-0*, WAMT, Greenwood Pr) Greenwood.

M

Modes of Thought. Alfred North Whitehead. LC 38-33184. 1968. pap. 16.95 (*0-02-935210-X*) Free Pr.

Modes of Thought: Explorations in Culture & Cognition. Ed. by David R. Olson & Nancy Torrance. LC 97-591. (Illus.). 313p. (C). 1996. text 59.95 (*0-521-49610-1*); pap. text 21.95 (*0-521-56644-4*) Cambridge U Pr.

Modes of Transportation. Ed. by Richard J. Solomon & Joseph S. Silien. 156p. 1970. pap. 3.00 (*0-87262-021-2*) Am Soc Civil Eng.

Modes Stats Infer Causal Effect. D. Rubin. (C). (gr. 13). 1997. write for info. (*0-412-31770-2*) Chapman & Hall.

Modest Ambition of Andrew Marvell: A Study of Marvell & His Relation to Loveloace, Fairfax, Cromwell, & Milton. Patsy Griffin. LC 95-733. 216p. 1995. 35.00 (*0-87413-561-3*) U Delaware Pr.

Modest B- sWitness Second B- sMillenium.FemaleMan B- sMeets B- sOncoMouse: Feminism & Technoscience. Donna Jeanne Haraway. (Illus.). 388p. (C). 1997. pap. 19.99 (*0-415-91245-8*) Routledge.

***Modest Blackmailer.** Irene White. 160p. 2000. 18.99 (*0-7089-5771-4*) Ulverscroft.

Modest Connecticut Frame House. Robert W. Shaw. 1978. pap. 3.00 (*0-686-22869-3*) Conn Fireside.

Modest Defence of Publick Stews: or An Essay upon Whoring, As It Is Now Practis'd in These Kingdoms. Bernard Mandeville. LC 92-23890. (Augustan Reprints Ser.: No. 162). 1973. reprint ed. 14.50 (*0-404-70162-0*, HQ185) AMS Pr.

Modest Defense of Publick Stews. Bernard Mandeville. 1972. 95.95 (*0-8490-0656-2*) Gordon Pr.

Modest Fortunes: Mining in Northern Baja California. Donald Chaput et al. LC 92-8724. (Baja California Travels Ser.: Vol. 51). (ENG & SPA., Illus.). 247p. 1992. 75.00 (*0-938644-28-9*) Nat Hist Mus.

***Modest King.** Claudia Courtney. (Phonetic Bible Stories Ser.). (Illus.). 16p. (J). (ps-1). 1999. pap. text 2.59 (*0-570-07001-5*) Concordia.

Modest Livestock & Poultry Product. 3rd ed. Gillespie. (Agriculture Ser.). 1989. text, teacher ed. 12.00 (*0-8273-3278-5*) Delmar.

Modest Mennonite Home. Steve Friesen. LC 90-81732. (Illus.). 96p. 1990. pap. 9.95 (*0-934672-90-3*) Good Bks PA.

Modest Musorgsky & "Boris Godunov" Myths, Realities, & Reconsiderations. Caryl Emerson & Robert W. Oldani. LC 93-18164. (Illus.). 353p. (C). 1994. text 74.95 (*0-521-36193-1*) Cambridge U Pr.

Modest Proposal. Tr. by Richard Miller from FRE. LC 94-78232.Tr. of Y'a Bon Bamboula. 80p. (Orig.). 1994. pap. 8.95 (*0-913745-43-X*) Ubu Repertory.

Modest Proposal: Students Can Learn. John E. Roueche & John C. Pitman. LC 73-184956. (Jossey-Bass Higher Education Ser.). 160p. reprint ed. pap. 49.60 (*0-8357-9336-2*, 201386400088) Bks Demand.

Modest Proposal & Other Satire. Jonathan Swift. LC 94-24670. (Great Minds Ser.). 277p. (C). 1995. pap. 8.95 (*0-87975-919-4*) Prometheus Bks.

Modest Proposal & Other Satirical Works. unabridged ed. Jonathan Swift. (Thrift Editions Ser.). 64p. 1996. reprint ed. pap. text 1.00 (*0-486-28759-9*) Dover.

Modest Proposal & Other Stories. Jonathan Swift. 240p. 1998. 7.95 (*3-89508-688-6*) Konemann.

Modeste Mignon. Honore de Balzac. 382p. 1967. 10.95 (*0-685-58344-9*, 2070373606) Fr & Eur.

Modeste Mignon. Honore de Balzac. (FRE.). 382p. 1982. pap. 12.95 (*0-7859-3474-X*, 2070373606) Fr & Eur.

Modeste Mignon. Honore de Balzac. (Folio Ser.: No. 1360). (FRE.). 382p. 1967. pap. 9.95 (*2-07-037360-6*) Schoenhof.

Modesto: Images of Yesterday, Images of Today. Intro. by Robert Gauvreau. (Illus.). 256p. 1984. 39.95 (*0-930349-00-8*) McHenry Mus Pr.

***Modesto: Then & Now.** Colleen Stanley Bare. (Illus.). 200p. 1999. 27.50 (*0-930349-05-9*); pap. 14.95 (*0-930349-06-7*) McHenry Mus Pr.

Modesto M. Mora, M. D. La Gesta de un Medico. Octavio R. Costa. LC 96-84349. (Coleccion Cuba y sus Jueces). (SPA., Illus.). 430p. 1996. 30.00 (*0-89729-805-5*) Ediciones.

Modesto on My Mind: A Collection of Columns Published in the Modesto Bee. Dave Cummerow. LC 95-34513. 1995. write for info. (*0-930349-03-2*) McHenry Mus Pr.

Modesty. Nan M. Pamer. LC 90-30491. (Illus.). 50p. (Orig.). (YA). 1990. pap. 3.99 (*0-932581-62-5*) Word Aflame.

***Modesty: An Adornment for Life.** Pesach Eliyahu Falk. 706p. 1998. 24.95 (*0-87306-874-2*) Feldheim.

Modesty & Arrogance in Judgment: Hannah Arendt's Eichmann in Jerusalem. Barry Sharpe. LC 98-47818. 192p. 1999. 55.00 (*0-275-96403-5*, Praeger Pubs) Greenwood.

Modesty Blaise: Death in Slow Motion; The Alternative Man; Sweet Caroline. Peter O'Donnell. Ed. by Catherine Yronwode. (Comic Strip Ser.). (Illus.). 72p. (Orig.). 1986. pap. 5.95 (*0-912277-30-0*) K Pierce Bks.

Modesty Blaise: The Lady Killer; Garvin's Travels; The Scarlet Maiden. Peter O'Donnell. Ed. & Intro. by Catherine Yronwode. (Comic Strip Ser.). (Illus.). 72p. 1984. pap. 5.95 (*0-912277-25-4*) K Pierce Bks.

Modesty Blaise: The Mind of Mrs. Drake; Uncle Happy. Peter O'Donnell. Ed. by Catherine Yronwode. (Comic Strip Ser.). (Illus.). 64p. (Orig.). 1981. pap. 5.95 (*0-912277-08-4*) K Pierce Bks.

Modesty Blaise: The Moon Man; A Few Flowers for the Colonel; The Balloonatic. Peter O'Donnell. Ed. by Catherine Yronwode. (Comic Strip Ser.). (Illus.). 72p. (Orig.). 1985. pap. 5.95 (*0-912277-28-9*) K Pierce Bks.

Modesty Blaise: The Return of the Mammoth; Plato's Republic; The Sword of the Bruce. Peter O'Donnell. Ed. by Catherine Yronwode. (Comic Strip Ser.). (Illus.). 72p. (Orig.). 1986. pap. 5.95 (*0-912277-33-5*) K Pierce Bks.

M

***Modesty Supplement.** Pesach Eliyahu Falk. 1998. pap. 4.95 (*1-58330-171-2*) Feldheim.

***Modflo: A Practical Manual in Groundwater Modeling.** Philip L. Hall. 2000. ring bd. 49.95 (*1-56670-475-8*) Lewis Pubs.

Modifiability of Response to Taste Stimuli in the Preschool Child. Marguerite E. Gauger. LC 77-176799. (Columbia University. Teachers College. Contributions to Education Ser.: No. 348). reprint ed. 37.50 (*0-404-55348-6*) AMS Pr.

Modification. Michel Butor. 1957. pap. 12.95 (*0-7859-0602-9*, F89970) Fr & Eur.

Modification. Michel Butor. (FRE.). 1980. reprint ed. pap. 16.95 (*0-7859-3299-2*) Fr & Eur.

Modification & Editing of RNA. Henri Grosjean & Rob Benne. LC 97-47125. (Illus.). 600p. 1998. 99.95 (*1-55581-133-7*) ASM Pr.

Modification & Preservation of Existing Dental Restorations. Donald W. Fisher. Ed. by William W. Morgan. LC 86-9427. (Illus.). 204p. 1987. pap. text 80.00 (*0-86715-131-5*, 1315) Quint Pub Co.

Modification in Child Behavior. Garth J. Blackham. (Education Ser.). 1970. pap. 5.00 (*0-534-00005-3*) Wadsworth Pub.

Modification of Army Aircraft in the United States, 1939-1945. Virginia G. Toole & Robert W. Ackerman. (USAF Historical Studies: No. 62). 123p. 1947. pap. text 29.95 (*0-89126-130-3*) MA-AH Pub.

Modification of Cell to Cell Signals During Normal & Pathological Age. Ed. by S. Govoni & F. Battaini. (NATO ASI Series H: Vol. 9). (Illus.). xvi, 287p. 1987. 119.95 (*0-387-17886-4*) Spr-Verlag.

Modification of Inulin for Non-Food Applications. Dorine L. Verraest. (Illus.). 164p. 1997. pap. 45.00 (*90-407-1524-6*, Pub. by Delft U Pr) Coronet Bks.

Modification of Letter-Forms. Stanley Hess. LC 72-85237. (Illus.). 1972. 14.50 (*0-910158-78-9*) Art Dir.

Modification of Polymers. Ed. by Charles E. Carraher & Minoru Tsuda. LC 79-28259. (ACS Symposium Ser.: No. 121). 1980. 54.95 (*0-8412-0540-X*) Am Chemical.

Modification of Polymers. Ed. by Charles E. Carraher, Jr. & Minoru Tsuda. LC 79-28259. (ACS Symposium Ser.: Vol. 121). 511p. 1980. reprint ed. pap. 158.50 (*0-608-03059-7*, 206351200007) Bks Demand.

Modification of Proteins: Food, Nutritional & Pharmacological Aspects. Ed. by Robert E. Feeney & John R. Whitaker. LC 82-1702. (Advances in Chemistry Ser.: No. 198). 402p. 1982. lib. bdg. 65.95 (*0-8412-0610-4*) Am Chemical.

Modification of Proteins: Food, Nutritional, & Pharmacological Aspects: Based on a Symposium. Ed. by Robert E. Feeney & John R. Whitaker. LC 82-1702. (Advances in Chemistry Ser.: No. 198). (Illus.). 413p. 1982. reprint ed. pap. 128.10 (*0-608-04359-1*, 206514000001) Bks Demand.

Modification of Soil Structure. Ed. by W. W. Emerson et al. LC 77-2751. (Illus.). 458p. reprint ed. pap. 142.00 (*0-8357-3738-1*, 203646400003) Bks Demand.

Modification of Tumor Development in Rodents. Ed. by N. Ito & H. Sugano. (Progress in Experimental Tumor Research Ser.: Vol. 33). (Illus.). viii, 236p. 1991. 200.00 (*3-8055-5242-4*) S Karger.

Modifications in Indian Culture Through Inventions & Loans. Erland Nordenskiold. LC 75-46062. (Comparative Ethnographical Studies: Vol. 8). reprint ed. 55.00 (*0-404-15148-5*) AMS Pr.

Modifications of Passive Films: Papers Presented at the European Symposium on Modifications of Passive Films. Ed. by P. Marcus et al. (European Federation of Corrosion Publications Ser.: No. 12). 343p. 1994. pap. 140.00 (*0-901716-52-9*, Pub. by Inst Materials) Ashgate Pub Co.

Modifications of the Lid-Reflex by Voluntary Induced Sets. Helen Peak. (Psychology Monographs General & Applied: Vol. 42). 1974. reprint ed. pap. 55.00 (*0-8115-1441-2*) Periodicals Srv.

Modifications to Fuel Rod Material Properties & Performance Models for High-burnup Application: Frapcon-3. D. D. Lanning. 134p. 1997. per. 13.00 (*0-16-062872-5*) USGPO.

Modified Algorithm of Jacobi-Perron. L. Bernstein. LC 52-42839. (Memoirs of the American Mathematical Society Ser.: No. 67). 44p. 1966. pap. 16.00 (*0-8218-1267-X*, MEMO/1/67C) Am Math.

Modified Atmosphere food Packaging. Aaron L. Brody. (Illus.). 275p. (C). 1994. pap. 75.00 (*1-930268-11-4*) Packaging Prof.

Modified Basket Maker Sites, Ackmen-Lowry Area, Southwestern Colorado, 1938. Paul S. Martin. LC 39-30994. (Field Museum of Natural History Anthropological Ser.: Vol. 23, No. 3, June 27, 1939). (Illus.). 238p. 1939. reprint ed. pap. 73.80 (*0-608-02711-1*, 206337600004) Bks Demand.

Modified Branching Programs & Their Computational Power. C. Meinel. (Lecture Notes in Computer Science Ser.: Vol. 370). vi, 132p. 1989. 27.00 (*0-387-51340-X*) Spr-Verlag.

Modified Cages for Laying Hens. Ed. by C. M. Sherwin. 1994. pap. 72.00 (*0-900767-85-5*, Pub. by Univs Fed Animal Welfare) St Mut.

Modified Cyclodextrins: Scaffolds & Templates for Supramolecular Chemistry. Christopher J. Easton & Stephen F. Lincoln. LC 99-19665. 250p. 1999. 38.00 (*1-86094-144-3*, Pub. by Imperial College) World Scientific Pub.

Modified Differential Equations: Mathematical Laboratory Manual. Martha L. Abell. (C). 1995. pap. text, lab manual ed. write for info. (*0-03-016232-7*) Harcourt Coll Pubs.

Modified Essay Questions for the MRCGP Examination. Ed. by T. S. Murray. LC 95-34949. 204p. 1995. pap. 29.95 (*0-86542-646-5*) Blackwell Sci.

Modified Lagrangians & Monotone Maps in Optimization. E. G. Golshtein & N. V. Tretyakov. LC 95-44030. (Interscience Series in Discrete Mathematics & Optimization). 438p. 1996. 94.95 (*0-471-54821-9*) Wiley.

Modified Lipoproteins in the Pathogenesis of Atherosclerosis. Sampath Parthasarathy. (Medical Intelligence Unit Ser.). 115p. 1994. 99.00 (*1-57059-080-X*, LN9080) Landes Bioscience.

Modified Nucleosides & Cancer: Workshop, Freiburg, FRG, 1981. Ed. by G. Nass. (Recent Results in Cancer Research Ser.: Vol. 84). (Illus.). 440p. 1983. 99.00 (*0-387-12024-6*) Spr-Verlag.

Modified Pinions, Fine Pitch Spur. R. L. Thoen. (Technical Papers: Vol. P379.02). (Illus.). 6p. 1961. pap. text 30.00 (*1-55589-395-3*) AGMA.

Modified Polyester Fibres. J. Militky et al. (Textile Science & Technology Ser.: Vol. 10). 262p. 1991. 205.00 (*0-444-98735-5*) Elsevier.

Modified Radical & Other Cancer Poems. Ann Davidson. 32p. (Orig.). 1990. pap. 5.00 (*0-9627007-0-3*) Monday Pr CA.

Modified Rapture: Comedy in W. S. Gilbert's Savoy Operas. Alan Fischler. LC 91-6832. (Victorian Literature & Culture Ser.). 154p. reprint ed. pap. 47.80 (*0-608-10515-5*, 205442600009) Bks Demand.

Modified Starches: Properties & Uses. O. B. Wurzburg. 288p. 1986. lib. bdg. 239.00 (*0-8493-5964-3*, R857) CRC Pr.

Modifiers. Laurence Urdang. 216p. 1982. 95.00 (*0-8103-1195-X*) Gale.

Modifiers: Adjectives & Adverbs. Cindy Iutzi. (Illus.). 20p. (Orig.). (J). (gr. 5-8). 1996. pap. 15.95 (*1-56490-024-X*) G Grimm Assocs.

Modifiers Made Easy. Ed. by Kathy Brouch. 200p. (C). 1999. pap. 99.95 (*1-56329-536-9*) Thomson Learn.

***Modifiers Made Easy 2000.** Medicode, Med-Index Division Staff. (C). 1999. 64.00 (*1-56337-346-7*) Thomson Learn.

Modifiers on Chemical Carcinogenesis: An Approach to the Biochemical Mechanism & Cancer Prevention. Ed. by Thomas J. Slaga. LC 77-75652. (Carginogenesis: No. 5). (Illus.). 285p. 1980. reprint ed. pap. 88.40 (*0-608-00672-6*, 206125900007) Bks Demand.

Modifying & Tuning Fiat Lancia Twin Cam Engines. Guy Croft. (Illus.). 256p. 1996. 79.95 (*0-947981-98-5*, Pub. by Motor Racing) Motorbooks Intl.

Modifying & Tuning Holley Carburetors. (Best of Hot Rod Ser.: Vol. 2). (Illus.). 128p. 1998. pap. 18.95 (*1-884089-32-1*) CarTech.

Modifying Bitterness: Mechanism, Ingredients, & Applications. Ed. by Glenn Roy. LC 97-60221. 350p. 1997. text 169.95 (*1-56676-491-2*) Technomic.

Modifying Curriculum for the Special Needs Student in the Regular Classroom. Lynne Chalmers. 48p. (C). 1992. pap. text 9.95 (*1-886979-00-6*) Practicl Pr.

***Modifying Curriculum for the Special Needs Student in the Regular Classroom.** 2nd ed. Lynne Chalmers. (Illus.). 60p. (C). 2000. pap. 11.95 (*1-886979-14-6*) Practicl Pr.

Modifying Our Policy Toward the People's Republic of China. Scott Deatherage. 256p. 1995. pap. text 25.25 (*0-8442-5839-3*) NTC Contemp Pub Co.

Modifying Standard Curriculum for High-Ability Learners. 6th ed. Lois F. Roets. LC 97-150523. 96p. 1997. pap. 18.00 (*0-911943-50-1*) Leadership Pub.

Modifying the Root Environment to Reduce Crop Stress. Ed. by G. F. Arkin & H. M. Taylor. LC 81-69116. 420p. 1981. text 44.50 (*0-916150-40-2*, M1481) Am Soc Ag Eng.

Modifying the Work Environment for the Physically Disabled: An Accessibility Checklist for Employers. Margaret G. Desmond. LC 80-83500. (Illus.). 128p. 1981. 8.95 (*0-686-38822-4*) Human Res Ctr.

Modifying the Work Environment for the Physically Disabled Employee, 2 pts., Set. Incl. Pt. 1. Veronica Washam. 1981. Pt. 2. Margaret G. Desmond. 1981. (Illus.). 128p. 1981. 16.00 (*0-686-38823-2*) Human Res Ctr.

Modigliani. Tr. by Alberto Curotto from SPA. LC 97-70937. (Great Modern Masters Ser.). (Illus.). 64p. 1997. 11.98 (*0-8109-4651-3*, Pub. by Abrams) Time Warner.

Modigliani. Doris Krystof. (Basic Ser.). 1996. pap. 9.99 (*3-8228-8641-6*) Taschen Amer.

Modigliani. Carol Mann. (World of Art Ser.). 1985. 19.95 (*0-500-18176-4*, Pub. by Thames Hudson) Norton.

Modigliani. Carol Mann. LC 90-72012. (World of Art Ser.). (Illus.). 216p. 1991. pap. 14.95 (*0-500-20176-5*, Pub. by Thames Hudson) Norton.

***Modigliani.** Jack Michael. (Reveries Ser.). (Illus.). 120p. 2000. 14.95 (*1-85995-705-6*, Pub. by Parkstone Pr) Bks Intl VA.

Modigliani. Taschen Staff. 1997. 9.99 (*3-8228-8016-7*, Pub. by Benedikt Taschen) Bks Nippan.

Modigliani. Alfred Werner. (Masters of Art Ser.). (Illus.). 128p. 1986. 24.95 (*0-8109-1416-6*, Pub. by Abrams) Time Warner.

Modigliani. Douglas Hall. (Color Library Ser.). (Illus.). 128p. (C). 1994. reprint ed. pap. 14.95 (*0-7148-2758-4*, Pub. by Phaidon Press) Phaidon Pr.

Modigliani: A Study of His Sculpture. Arthur S. Pfannsteil & Bernard Schuster. (Illus.). 101p. 1986. write for info. (*0-9616170-0-4*) Mega Corp.

Modigliani: Paintings, Drawings, Sculpture. James T. Soby. LC 73-169318. (Museum of Modern Art Publications in Reprint). 1972. reprint ed. 17.95 (*0-405-01576-3*) Ayer.

Modigliani Scandal. Ken Follett. 256p. 1986. mass mkt. 6.99 (*0-451-14796-0*, Sig) NAL.

Modismos Americanos Esenciales: Essential American Idioms for Spanish Speakers. Richard A. Spears. Ed. by Deborah Skolnik. (SPA.). 1995. write for info. (*0-88427-100-5*, Natl Textbk Co) NTC Contemp Pub Co.

Modismos Americanos Esenciales: Essential American Idioms for Spanish Speakers. Richard A. Spears & Deborah Skolnik. (SPA., Illus.). 257p. 1995. pap. 9.95 (*0-8442-7100-4*) NTC Contemp Pub Co.

Modismos Inglesse Para Hisponos. Eugene Savaiano. LC 95-81412. 1996. pap. 6.95 (*0-8120-9458-1*) Barron.

Modlitby Odpustenia. 3rd rev. ed. Vladimir Uhri. 29p. 1996. pap. 1.50 (*1-56983-011-8*) New Creat WI.

Modlitby Spravodliveho. 3rd ed. Vladimir Uhri. (SLO.). 36p. (Orig.). 1996. pap. 1.70 (*1-56983-010-X*) New Creat WI.

Modo per Imparare a Sonare Di Tromba. Girolamo Fantini. Tr. by Edward H. Tarr. LC 75-17501. (Brass Research Ser.: No. 7). (Illus.). 1978. reprint ed. 30.00 (*0-914282-10-7*) Brass Pr.

Modoc: The True Story of the Greatest Elephant That Ever Lived. Ralph Helfer. LC 97-20905. (Illus.). 352p. 1998. pap. 13.00 (*0-06-092951-0*) HarpC.

Modoc County: A Geographic Time Continuum on the California Volcanic Tableland. Robert W. Pease. LC 66-63867. (University of California Publications in Social Welfare: Vol. 17). 320p. reprint ed. pap. 99.20 (*0-608-14158-5*, 202127400022) Bks Demand.

Modocs & Their War. Keith A. Murray. LC 59-7488. (Civilization of the American Indian Ser.: Vol. 52). (Illus.). 344p. 1985. pap. 16.95 (*0-8061-1331-6*) U of Okla Pr.

Modrn Const & Ground Engrg. 2nd ed. F. Harris. (C). 1994. pap. 62.95 (*0-582-23657-6*, Pub. by Addison-Wesley) Longman.

Modruvallabok: Am 132 Fol., 2 vols., Set. Andrea Van Arkel de Leeuw van Wenen. xlv, 226 , 34 mp. 1988. 169.50 (*90-04-08622-6*) Brill Academic Pubs.

Mods! Richard Barnes. 128p. 1994. per. 14.95 (*0-85965-173-8*, Pub. by Plexus) Publishers Group.

Modula-3. Samuel P. Harbison, III. 320p. 1992. pap. text 38.20 (*0-13-596396-6*) P-H.

Modula-2: A Complete Guide. K. N. King. LC 87-81177. (Computer Science Ser.). 656p. (C). Date not set. pap. 53.75 (*0-669-11091-4*) Jones & Bartlett.

Modula-2: A Second Course in Programming. John Gough & George Mohay. 352p. 1988. reprint ed. 36.00 (*0-318-37810-8*) P-H.

Modula-2: Discipline & Design. A. H. Sale. 464p. (C). 1986. pap. text 29.25 (*0-201-12921-3*) Addison-Wesley.

Modula-2 Applied. R. J. Mitchell. Ed. by F. H. Sumner. (Computer Science Ser.). (Illus.). 284p. (Orig.). (C). 1991. pap. text 35.00 (*0-333-55453-1*, Pub. by Macmillan Ed) Scholium Intl.

Modula-2 for Microcomputer Systems. Cooling. (C). 1988. mass mkt. 39.95 (*0-412-43730-9*) Chapman & Hall.

Modula-2 for Pascal Programmers. R. Gleaves. (Books on Professional Computing). (Illus.). 155p. 1985. 42.95 (*0-387-96051-1*) Spr-Verlag.

Modula-2 in Science & Engineering. M. M. Novak. 1990. write for info. (*0-07-707200-6*) Gregg-McGraw.

Modula-2 Software Component Library. Charles Lins. (Compass International Ser.). (Illus.). xix, 450p. 1989. 59.95 (*0-387-97074-6*) Spr-Verlag.

Modula-2 Software Component Library, Vol. 1. Charles Lins. (Compass International Ser.). (Illus.). xvi, 312p. 1988. 65.95 (*0-387-96867-9*) Spr-Verlag.

Modula-2 Software Component Library, Vol. 2. Charles Lins. (Compass International Ser.). (Illus.). xviii, 368p. 1989. 65.95 (*0-387-96939-X*) Spr-Verlag.

Modula-2 Software Component Library, Vol. 4. Charles Lins. Ed. by S. S. Muchnik & Peter Schnupp. (Compass International Ser.). (Illus.). xvii, 371p. 1990. 59.95 (*0-387-97255-2*) Spr-Verlag.

Modular America: Cross-Cultural Perspectives on the Emergence of an American Way, 92. John G. Blair. LC 88-3111. (Contributions in American Studies: No. 92). 196p. 1988. 49.95 (*0-313-26317-5*, BMW/, Greenwood Pr) Greenwood.

Modular & Extensible Network Storage Architecture. Sai-Lai Lo. (Distinguished Dissertations in Computer Science Ser.: No. 11). (Illus.). 152p. (C). 1995. text 49.95 (*0-521-55115-3*) Cambridge U Pr.

Modular Approach to dBASE IV: IBM Version. Charles H. Mawhinney. 96p. (C). 1992. spiral bd. write for info. (*0-697-13252-8*) Bus & Educ Tech.

Modular Approach to MS-DOS. Donald R. Chand. 80p. (C). 1991. text 15.25 (*0-697-13337-0*, Irwn McGrw-H) McGrw-H Hghr Educ.

Modular Approach to MS-DOS 6.2. Donald R. Chand. 96p. (C). 1995. text 15.00 (*0-697-22187-3*) Bus & Educ Tech.

Modular Approach to On-Board Automatic Data Collection Systems. (National Cooperative Transit Research Program Synthesis Ser.: No. 9). 123p. 1984. 10.40 (*0-309-03854-5*, NTR9) Transport Res Bd.

Modular Approaches to the Study of the Mind. Noam Chomsky. LC 82-62962. (Distinguished Graduate Research Lectures). 118p. 1984. 15.00 (*0-916304-56-6*) SDSU Press.

Modular Automation in the Batch Plant Environment. Boullart & Carlo-Stella. 1997. text. write for info. (*0-08-042021-4*, Pergamon Pr) Elsevier.

Modular Brain. Richard M. Restak. 256p. 1994. 22.00 (*0-684-19544-5*, Scribners Ref) Mac Lib Ref.

Modular Brain: How New Discoveries in Neuroscience Are Answering Age-Old Questions about Memory, Free Will, Consciousness, & Personal Identity. Richard M. Restak. 1995. pap. 14.00 (*0-684-80126-4*, Touchstone) S&S Trade Pap.

Modular C-LECT College Module User's Guide, 1996-97. rev. ed. Ed. by Nancy Kehoe & Bill Hawver. 20p. (YA). (gr. 9-12). 1996. pap. text 10.50 (*1-55631-258-X*) Chron Guide.

Modular C-LECT Counselor-Administrator's Guide & Installation Instructions, 1996-97. rev. ed. 16p. 1996. pap. text 6.50 (*1-55631-260-1*) Chron Guide.

Modular C-LECT Financial Aid Module User's Guide, 1996-97. rev. ed. Ed. by Joan Washburn. 12p. (YA). (gr. 9-12). 1996. pap. text 11.00 (*1-55631-259-8*) Chron Guide.

Modular C-LECT Occupational Modules User's Guide, 1996-97. rev. ed. Fran Brezee. 32p. (YA). (gr. 9-12). 1996. pap. text 19.00 (*1-55631-256-3*) Chron Guide.

Modular C-LECT Program, 1996-97. rev. ed. 16p. (YA). (gr. 9-12). 1996. 900.00 (*1-55631-264-4*) Chron Guide.

Modular C-LECT Vocational School Module User's Guide, 1996-97. rev. ed. Ed. by Stephen D. Thompson. 16p. (YA). (gr. 9-12). 1996. pap. text 12.00 (*1-55631-257-1*) Chron Guide.

***Modular Chapter 3 - Design of Experiments & Anova - to Accompany Weiss Introductory Statistics 5/e & Elementary Statistics 4/e.** Daniel E. Weiss. (C). 1999. ring bd. 4.00 (*0-201-43715-5*) Addison-Wesley.

Modular Chemistry: Proceedings of the NATO Advanced Research Workshop, Aspen Lodge near Estes Park, Colorado, USA, September 9-12, 1995. Ed. by Josef Michl. LC 97-33655. (NATO Advanced Science Institute Ser.: No. 499). 21p. 1997. text 314.50 (*0-7923-4730-7*) Kluwer Academic.

Modular Compiler Verification: A Refinement-Algebraic Approach Advocating Stepwise Abstraction, Vol. 128. Markus Myller-Olm. Ed. by G. Goos et al. LC 97-13428. (Lecture Notes in Computer Science Ser.: Vol. 1283). xv, 250p. 1997. pap. 49.00 (*3-540-63406-1*) Spr-Verlag.

Modular Construction & Partial Order Semantics of Petri Nets. W. Vogler. Ed. by G. Goos & J. Hartmanis. LC 92-23878. (Lecture Notes in Computer Science Ser.: Vol. 625). ix, 252p. 1992. 47.00 (*0-387-55767-9*) Spr-Verlag.

Modular Crochet: A Revolutionary New Method of Creating Custom-Design Pullovers. Judith Copeland. LC 78-3704. (Illus.). 192p. 1978. 17.50 (*0-87131-256-5*) M Evans.

Modular Curriculum. Ed. by Bob Moon. 192p. (C). 1988. 50.00 (*1-85396-008-X*, Pub. by P Chapman) St Mut.

Modular Deficits in Alzheimer-Type Dementia. Ed. by Myrna F. Schwartz. 456p. 1991. 47.50 (*0-262-19298-5*, Bradford Bks) MIT Pr.

Modular Digital Multitracks: The Power User's Guide. 2nd rev. ed. George Peterson. LC 97-73717. 176p. 1998. pap. 29.95 (*0-918371-23-6*, MixBooks) Intertec Pub.

Modular Electric Vehicle Program (MEVP) Final Technical Report (March 1994) Contrib. by Ford Motor Co. Staff et al. (Electric Vehicle Information Ser.: Vol. 25). (Illus.). 280p. 1996. pap. 135.00 (*0-89934-295-7*, BT055); lib. bdg. 185.00 (*0-89934-296-5*, BT0955) Bus Tech Bks.

Modular Fixturing Handbook. Carr Lane Mfg. Co. Staff. (Illus.). 216p. (C). 1991. pap. text 12.00 (*0-9622079-0-X*) Carr Ln.

Modular Forms. T. Miyake. (Illus.). 310p. 1989. 107.95 (*0-387-50268-8*) Spr-Verlag.

***Modular Forms & Fermat's Last Theorem.** G. Cornell et al. 587p. 2000. pap. 39.95 (*0-387-98998-6*) Spr-Verlag.

Modular Forms & Fermat's Last Theorem. Gary Cornell et al. LC 97-10930. 587p. 1997. 49.95 (*0-387-94609-8*) Spr-Verlag.

***Modular Forms & Galois Cohomology.** Haruzo Hida. (Studies in Advanced Mathematics: No. 69). (Illus.). 440p. (C). 2000. 54.95 (*0-521-77036-X*) Cambridge U Pr.

Modular Forms & Hecke Operators. A. N. Andrianov & V. G. Zhuravlev. LC 95-30915. (Translations of Mathematical Monographs: Vol. 145). 334p. 1995. text 95.00 (*0-8218-0277-1*, MMONO/145) Am Math.

Modular Forms on Half-Spaces of Quarternions. A. Krieg. (Lecture Notes in Mathematics Ser.: Vol. 1143). xiii, 203p. 1985. 37.95 (*0-387-15679-8*) Spr-Verlag.

Modular Functions & Dirichlet Series in Number Theory. 2nd ed. Tom M. Apostol. (Graduate Texts in Mathematics Ser.: Vol. 41). (Illus.). 216p. 1997. 49.95 (*0-387-97127-0*) Spr-Verlag.

Modular Functions in Analytic Number Theory. 2nd ed. Marvin I. Knopp. LC 92-73313. viii, 152p. (C). 1993. text 22.95 (*0-8284-0337-6*, 337) Chelsea Pub.

An Asterisk (*) at the beginning of an entry indicates that the title is appearing for the first time.

Modular Functions of One Variable 1: Proceedings. International Summer School, University of Antwerp. Ed. by Willem Kuyk. LC 73-77818. (Lecture Notes in Mathematics Ser.: Vol. 120). v, 195p. 1986. pap. 26.30 (*0-387-06219-X*) Spr-Verlag.

Modular Functions of One Variable 3: Proceedings. International Summer School, University of Antwerp. Ed. by Willem Kuyk & J. P. Serre. LC 73-13491. (Lecture Notes in Mathematics Ser.: Vol. 350). 1986. 54.95 (*0-387-06483-4*) Spr-Verlag.

Modular Functions of One Variable 2: Proceedings. International Summer School, University of Antwerp. Ed. by Willem Kuyk & P. Deligne. (Lecture Notes in Mathematics Ser.: Vol. 349). v, 598p. 1986. pap. 58.40 (*0-387-06558-X*) Spr-Verlag.

Modular Instruction for Independent Travel for Students Who Are Blind or Visually Impaired: Preschool Through High School. Doris M. Willoughby & Sharon L. Monthei. LC 98-9586. (Illus.). 400p. 1998. pap. 20.00 (*1-885218-09-5*) Natl Fed Blind.

Modular Interfaces: Modular Lie Algebras, Quantum Groups & Lie Superalgebras. Vyjayanthi Chari et al. LC 96-47629. (AMS-IP Studies in Advanced Mathematics: Vol. 4). 160p. 1997. pap. 35.00 (*0-8218-0748-X*, AMSIP/4) Am Math.

Modular Learning in Neural Networks: A Modularized Approach to Neural Network Classification. Tomas Hrycej. LC 92-2554. (Sixth Generation Computer Technologies Ser.). 256p. 1992. 125.00 (*0-471-57154-7*) Wiley.

Modular Lie Algebras & Their Representations. Helmut Strade & Rolf Farnsteiner. (Pure & Applied Mathematics Ser.: Vol. 116). (Illus.). 312p. 1988. text 155.00 (*0-8247-7594-5*) Dekker.

Modular Magic. Camille Remme. Ed. & Illus. by John Shimp. 80p. (Orig.). 1992. pap. 18.00 (*0-929950-07-0*) ME Pubns.

Modular Mathematics, Module C, Statistics 1. L. Bostock & S. Chandler. 352p. 1994. pap. 39.00 (*0-7855-2690-0*) St Mut.

Modular Mathematics: Module A, Pure Maths 1, Module A, Pure Maths! 2nd ed. L. Bostock & S. Chandler. 448p. 1994. pap. 39.00 (*0-7487-1777-3*, Pub. by S Thornes Pubs) Trans-Atl Phila.

Modular Mathematics: Module B, Pure Maths 2, Module B, Pure Maths 2. 2nd ed. L. Bostock & S. Chandler. 480p. 1994. pap. 32.50 (*0-7487-1775-7*, Pub. by S Thornes Pubs) Trans-Atl Phila.

Modular Mathematics: Module D, Statistics 2, Module D, Statistics 2. L. Bostock & S. Chandler. 1995. pap. 32.50 (*0-7487-1773-0*, Pub. by S Thornes Pubs) Trans-Atl Phila.

Modular Mathematics: Module E, Mechabics 1, Module E, Mechanics 1. L. Bostock & S. Chandler. (Module E, Mechanics 1 ser.). 352p. 1994. pap. 32.50 (*0-7487-1502-9*, Pub. by S Thornes Pubs) Trans-Atl Phila.

Modular Mathematics: Module F, Mechanics 2, Module F, Mechanics 2. L. Bostock & S. Chandler. 1995. pap. 32.50 (*0-7487-1774-9*, Pub. by S Thornes Pubs) Trans-Atl Phila.

Modular Multilateralism: North-South Economic Relations in the 1990s. Richard E. Feinberg & Delia M. Boylan. (Policy Essay Ser.: No. 1). 80p. (C). 1991. pap. text 13.95 (*1-56517-000-8*) Overseas Dev Council.

Modular Optical Design. O. N. Stavroudis. (Optical Sciences Ser.: Vol. 28). (Illus.). 199p. 1982. 58.95 (*0-387-10912-9*) Spr-Verlag.

Modular Origami Polyhedra. Lewis Simon & Bennett Arnstein. (Illus.). 33p. (Orig.). 1990. pap. text 7.95 (*0-9620058-1-9*) B Arnstein.

Modular Origami Polyhedra. rev. enl. ed. Lewis Simon et al. LC 99-11934. (Orig.). 1999. pap. text 5.95 (*0-486-40476-5*) Dover.

Modular Perl. Mark Schmick. 400p. 1999. 35.00 (*1-57870-033-7*, 904781Q) Macmillan Tech.

Modular Perl. Mark Schmick. 1997. 35.00 (*1-56205-807-X*) New Riders Pub.

Modular Programming Languages: Joint Modular Languages Conference, JML '97, Linz, Austria, March 19-21, 1997: Proceedings. Jeff Maynard. LC 72-180278. 100 p. 1972. write for info. (*0-408-70287-7*) Buttrwrth-Heinemann.

Modular Programming Languages: Joint Modular Languages Conference, JML '97, Linz, Austria, March 19-21, 1997: Proceedings. Ock Mossenb. LC 97-6964. (Lecture Notes in Computer Science Ser.: Vol. 120). 1997. pap. 61.00 (*3-540-62599-2*) Spr-Verlag.

Modular Remediation Testing, 001. C. H. Ward. LC 99-38600. 2000. lib. bdg. 64.95 (*1-56670-468-5*) Lewis Pubs.

Modular Representation Theory: New Trends & Methods. D. J. Benson. (Lecture Notes in Mathematics Ser.: Vol. 1081). xi, 231p. 1984. 37.95 (*0-387-13389-5*) Spr-Verlag.

Modular Subsea Production Systems. Ed. by Society for Underwater Technology Staff. (C). 1987. lib. bdg. 153.00 (*0-86010-832-5*, Pub. by Graham & Trotman) Kluwer Academic.

Modular Theory in Operator Algebras. S. V. Stratila. 492p. 1981. text 162.00 (*0-85626-190-4*) Gordon & Breach.

Modular Units. D. S. Kubert & Serge A. Lang. (Grundlehren der Mathematischen Wissenschaften Ser.: Vol. 244). 358p. 1981. 129.95 (*0-387-90517-0*) Spr-Verlag.

Modularity & Constraints in Language & Cognition: The Minnesota Symposia on Child Psychology. Ed. by Megan R. Gunnar & Michael P. Maratsos. (Minnesota Symposium on Child Psychology Ser.: Vol. 25). 256p. 1992. text 49.95 (*0-8058-1175-3*) L Erlbaum Assocs.

Modularity & the Motor Theory of Speech Perception: Proceedings of a Conference to Honor Alvin M. Liberman. Ed. by I. G. Mattingly & Michael Studdert-Kennedy. 480p. 1990. text 89.95 (*0-8058-0331-9*) L Erlbaum Assocs.

Modularity in Knowledge & Representation & Natural Language Understanding. Ed. by Jay L. Garfield. 440p. 1991. reprint ed. pap. text 17.50 (*0-262-57085-8*, Bradford Bks) MIT Pr.

Modularity in Syntax: A Study in Japanese & English. Ann K. Farmer. (Current Studies in Linguistics). 254p. 1984. 32.50 (*0-262-06087-6*) MIT Pr.

Modularity of Mind. Jerry A. Fodor. (Bradford Monograph). 216p. (C). 1983. pap. text 13.00 (*0-262-56025-9*) MIT Pr.

Modularity of Orthopedic Implants. Ed. by Donald C. Marlowe et al. LC 97-7308. (STP Ser.: No. 1301). (Illus.). 236p. 1997. text 63.00 (*0-8031-2415-5*, STP1301) ASTM.

Modulars: Poems. Albert Cook. LC 92-20742. 112p. 1992. pap. 14.95 (*0-7734-9564-9*) E Mellen.

Modulated Structure Materials. Ed. by Thomas Tsalalakos. 1984. text 278.00 (*90-247-3066-X*) Kluwer Academic.

Modulated Structures. Valery Pokrovsky et al. (Modern Condensed Matter Physics Ser.: Vol. 3). 200p. (C). 1997. text 51.00 (*981-02-0747-6*); pap. text 28.00 (*981-02-0748-4*) World Scientific Pub.

Modulated Structures - 1979. Ed. by J. M. Cowley et al. LC 79-53846. (AIP Conference Proceedings Ser.: No. 53). (Illus.). 1979. lib. bdg. 22.00 (*0-88318-152-5*) Am Inst Physics.

Modulated Structures, Polytypes & Quasicrystals. M. Farkas-Jahnke. 216p. 1993. pap. text 656.00 (*2-88124-946-9*) Gordon & Breach.

Modulated Structures, Polytypes & Quasicrystals, Pt. 1. M. Farkas-Janke & E. Pai. viii, 228p. 1993. pap. text 777.00 (*2-88124-942-6*) Gordon & Breach.

Modulated Structures, Polytypes & Quasicrystals, Vols. 43-44. M. Farkas-Jahnke. 444p. 1993. pap. text 999.00 (*2-88124-955-8*) Gordon & Breach.

Modulated Structures, Polytypes & Quasicrystals: Proceedings of the International Conference in India, December 1988: A Special Issue of the Journal Phase Transitions. Ed. by D. Pandey & V. K. Wadhawan. xii, 636p. 1989. pap. text 1396.00 (*0-677-25810-0*) Gordon & Breach.

Modulated Waves: Theory & Applications. L. A. Ostrovskii. LC 98-20381. (Series in the Mathematical Sciences). 376p. 1998. 60.00 (*0-8018-5870-4*) Johns Hopkins.

Modulating Gene Expression by Antisense Oligonucleotides to Understand Neural Functioning. Ed. by Margaret M. McCarthy. LC 98-44227. (Perspectives in Antisense Science Ser.). 172p. 1998. 99.00 (*0-7923-8242-0*) Kluwer Academic.

Modulation. Raynor Carroll. 4p. 1996. pap. 2.95 (*1-891188-08-9*) Batterie Music.

Modulation & Coding. Alister Burr. (C). 2000. pap. text. write for info. (*0-201-39857-5*) Addison-Wesley.

Modulation & Mediation of Cancer by Vitamins. Ed. by K. N. Prasad & Frank L. Meyskens. (Illus.). x, 350p. 1983. 143.50 (*3-8055-3526-0*) S Karger.

Modulation & Related Harmonic Questions. Arthur W. Foote. LC 78-98. (Illus.). 99p. 1978. reprint ed. lib. bdg. 49.50 (*0-313-20301-6*, FOMR, Greenwood Pr) Greenwood.

Modulation & Related Harmonic Questions. Arthur W. Foote. 99p. 1990. reprint ed. lib. bdg. 59.00 (*0-7812-9139-9*) Rprt Serv.

Modulation of Aging Process by Dietary Restriction. Ed. by Byung P. Yu. 304p. 1994. lib. bdg. write for info. (*0-8493-4994-X*) CRC Pr.

Modulation of Cardiac Calcium Sensitivity: A New Approach to Increasing the Strength of the Heart. Ed. by John A. Lee & David G. Allen. LC 92-43149. (Illus.). 368p. (C). 1993. text 69.50 (*0-19-262347-8*) OUP.

Modulation of Cellular Responses in Toxicity. Ed. by Corrado L. Galli et al. (NATA ASI Ser.: Vol. 93). 371p. 1995. 203.95 (*3-540-60010-8*) Spr-Verlag.

Modulation of Dopaminergic Neurotransmission by Other Neurotransmitters. Ed. by Charles R. Ashby, Jr. LC 95-43990. 240p. 1995. boxed set 159.95 (*0-8493-4780-7*) CRC Pr.

Modulation of Liver Cell Expression. Ed. by Werner Reutter et al. (Falk Ser.: No. 43). 1987. text 268.50 (*0-85200-677-2*) Kluwer Academic.

Modulation of MHC Antigen Expression & Disease. Ed. by G. Eric Blair et al. (Illus.). 480p. (C). 1995. pap. write for info. (*0-521-49921-6*) Cambridge U Pr.

Modulation of MHC Antigen Expression & Disease. Ed. by G. Eric Blair et al. (Illus.). 458p. (C). 1995. text 95.00 (*0-521-49578-4*) Cambridge U Pr.

Modulation of Neurotransmission in the Airways: An Experimental Study in Guinea Pig & Human Airways in Vitro. G. Verleden. No. 71. 150p. (Orig.). 1993. pap. 33.50 (*90-6186-578-6*, Pub. by Leuven Univ) Coronet Bks.

Modulation of Synaptic Transmission & Plasticity in Nervous Systems. Ed. by G. Hertting & H. C. Spatz. (NATO ASI Series H: Vol. 19). (Illus.). x, 457p. 1988. 205.95 (*0-387-18558-5*) Spr-Verlag.

Modulation of the Ca(2 plus) Movements in Vascular Smooth Muscle Cells by the Co-Transmitters Noradrenaline & ATP. I. DeClerck. No. 36. 135p. (Orig.). 1991. pap. 44.00 (*90-6186-431-3*, Pub. by Leuven Univ) Coronet Bks.

Modulation of the Immune Response to Vaccine Antigens: Symposium, University of Bergen, June 1996. Ed. by Fred Brown & Lars R. Haaheim. LC 98-134905. (Developments in Biological Standardization Ser.: Vol. 92, 1998). (Illus.). xii, 380p. 1998. 313.25 (*3-8055-6640-9*) S Karger.

Modulation of the Inflammatory Response in Severe Sepsis. Ed. by J. M. Tellado et al. (Progress in Surgery Ser.: Vol. 20). (Illus.). viii, 188p. 1995. 165.25 (*3-8055-6041-9*) S Karger.

Modulation of the Interaction Between Fibroblast Growth Factor-2 & Fibroblast Growth Factor Receptor-1 by Cell Surface Heparan Sulfate Proteoglycans. Robert Steinfeld. (Acta Biomedica Lovaniensia Ser.: No. 134). (Illus.). 101p. (Orig.). 1996. pap. 39.50 (*90-6186-757-6*, Pub. by Leuven Univ) Coronet Bks.

Modulation Spectroscopy of Neutrons with Diffractometry Applications. LC 97-10521. (Series on Neutron Techniques). 200p. 1997. lib. bdg. 34.00 (*981-02-2746-9*) World Scientific Pub.

Modulation Transfer Function of Screen-Film Systems. International Commission on Radiation Units & Meas. LC 86-7346. (ICRU Reports: No. 41). 40p. 1986. pap. 50.00 (*0-913394-35-1*) Intl Comm Rad Meas.

Modulation von Zelloberflaechenstrukturen. A. Raedler & Elisabeth Raedler. (Bibliotheca Anatomica Ser.: No. 25). (Illus.). vi, 82p. 1984. 41.75 (*3-8055-3755-7*) S Karger.

Modulational Interactions in Plasmas. Sergey V. Vladimirov et al. LC 95-12567. (Astrophysics & Space Science Library: Vol. 200). 1995. text 250.00 (*0-7923-3487-6*) Kluwer Academic.

Modulations: Electronic Music: Throbbing Words on Sounds. Contrib. by Peter Shapiro et al. (Illus.). 240p. 1999. 29.95 (*1-891024-06-X*) Dist Art Pubs.

Modulations: Poems. Richard Martin. 112p. 1998. pap. 12.00 (*1-878580-67-1*) Asylum Arts.

Modulators of Fish Immune Responses: Models for Environmental Toxicology-Biomarkers, Immunostimulators. Ed. by J. S. Stolen & T. C. Fletcher. LC 93-84325. (Illus.). 250p. (Orig.). (C). 1994. pap. 70.00 (*0-9625505-6-6*) SOS Pubns NJ.

Modulators of Immune Responses: The Evolutionary Trail. Ed. by J. S. Stolen et al. LC 95-67853. (Illus.). 600p. (C). 1996. pap. text 85.00 (*1-887052-00-3*) SOS Pubns NJ.

Module Curriculum Guide: Reference Works of Yosef Ben-Jochannan. E. Curtis Alexander. LC 89-81786. 35p. (Orig.). 1979. 3.95 (*0-938818-00-7*) ECA Assoc.

Module des Fibres Stables sur les Courbes Algebriques: Notes de l'Ecole Normale Superieure, Printemps 1983. Ed. by Jean-Louis Verdier & Joseph Le Poitier. (Progress in Mathematics Ser.: Vol. 54). (ENG & FRE.). (C). 1985. 42.50 (*0-8176-3286-7*) Birkhauser.

Module XI: Graphing Functions. Gary Fitts. Ed. by Leon J. Ablon. LC 76-62884. (Series in Mathematics Modules). 1977. pap. 8.95 (*0-685-42002-7*) Benjamin-Cummings.

***Module 4 Creat Continuum Of Succ For Hi Sch.** (C). 2000. text 5.00 (*0-536-61317-6*) Pearson Custom.

Module 5, Monitoring the Pharmacist's Care Plan: Advancing Pharmaceutical Care. Carla Frye. (Clinical Skills Program Ser.). 100p. (C). 1994. text 65.00 (*1-879907-49-6*) Am Soc Hlth-Syst.

Module 4: Money & Banking - Introduction to Business. Bounds. (Gb - Basic Business Ser.). 1997. pap. 2.95 (*0-538-86183-5*) S-W Pub.

Module IV, Culture, Family, & Providers: Trainer's Manual. 174p. 1995. pap. 20.00 (*0-8011-1109-9*) Calif Education.

Module I Numbers, 5 Modules, Module 1. 2nd ed. Leon J. Ablon et al. 1981. pap. text 8.95 (*0-8053-0131-3*) Addison-Wesley.

Module II Polynomials, 5 Modules, Module 2. 2nd ed. Leon J. Ablon et al. 1981. pap. text 8.95 (*0-8053-0132-1*) Addison-Wesley.

Module III Linear Equations, 5 Modules, Module 3. 2nd ed. Helen B. Siner et al. 1981. pap. text 8.95 (*0-8053-0133-X*) Addison-Wesley.

Module IV Algebric Fract, 5 Modules, Module 4. 2nd ed. Leon J. Ablon et al. 1981. pap. text 8.95 (*0-8053-0134-8*) Addison-Wesley.

***Module 1 Strats For Succss Motivatg & Accelrt.** (C). 2000. text 9.00 (*0-536-61314-1*) Pearson Custom.

Module of Curves. David Gieseker. (Tata Institute Lectures on Mathematics). 99p. 1983. 31.95 (*0-387-11953-1*) Spr-Verlag.

Module I, Social-Emotional Growth & Socialization: Trainer's Manual. Ed. by J. Ronald Lally. (Program for Infant - Toddler Caregivers Ser.). (Illus.). 164p. 1993. pap. 20.00 (*0-8011-1084-X*) Calif Education.

Module Theory: Endomorphism Rings & Direct Sum Decompositions in Some Classes of Modules. A. Facchini. (Progress in Mathematics Ser.: Vol. 167). 300p. 1998. 89.50 (*3-7643-5908-0*) Spr-Verlag.

Module Theory: Endomorphism Rings & Direct Sum Decompositions in Some Classes of Modules. Alberto Facchini. LC 98-22019. (Progress in Mathematics Ser.). 1998. 89.50 (*0-8176-5908-0*) Birkhauser.

***Module 3 Mapps Mentors Advisors & Prof Supprt.** (C). 2000. text 5.00 (*0-536-61316-8*) Pearson Custom.

Module III, Learning & Development: Trainer's Manual. 174p. 1995. pap. 20.00 (*0-8011-1108-0*) Calif Education.

***Module 2 Key Strats Devlpg Your Career Thru.** (C). 2000. text 5.00 (*0-536-61315-X*) Pearson Custom.

Module 2: Small Business - Introduction to Business. Bounds. (GB - Basic Business Ser.). 1997. pap. 2.95 (*0-538-86181-9*) S-W Pub.

Module II, Group Care: Trainer's Manual. Center for Child & Family Studies, Far West Labora. (Program for Infant - Toddler Caregivers Ser.). (Illus.). 158p. 1993. pap. 20.00 (*0-8011-1076-9*) Calif Education.

Module V Quadratic Equation, 5 Modules, Module 5. 2nd ed. Leon J. Ablon et al. 1981. pap. text 8.95 (*0-8053-0135-6*) Addison-Wesley.

Modules: Instructor's Manual. (Select Lab Series). 116p. 1998. 18.00 (*0-201-47666-5*); 18.00 (*0-201-47667-3*) Addison-Wesley.

Modules: Instructor's Manual. (Select Lab Ser.). 15.00 (*0-8053-1245-5*) Addson-Wesley Educ.

Modules & Algebras: Bimodule Structure & Group Actions on Algebra. Robert Wisbauer. (Pitman Monographs & Surveys in Pure & Applied Mathematics). 1996. 110.00 (*0-582-28981-5*) Longman.

Modules & Group Algebras. Jon F. Carlson. (Lectures in Mathematics). 1996. 26.50 (*0-8176-5389-9*); 26.50 (*3-7643-5389-9*) Birkhauser.

Modules & Rings. John Dauns. LC 93-49759. (Illus.). 460p. (C). 1994. text 80.00 (*0-521-46258-4*) Cambridge U Pr.

Modules & the Structure of Rings: A Primer. 2nd ed. Jonathan S. Golan & Tom Head. (Pure & Applied Mathematics Ser.: Vol. 147). (Illus.). 272p. 1991. text 79.75 (*0-8247-8555-X*) Dekker.

Modules for Basic Nursing Skills, Vol. 1. 6th ed. Janice R. Ellis et al. LC 95-37176. 816p. 1996. pap. text 32.95 (*0-397-55171-1*) Lppncott W & W.

Modules for Basic Nursing Skills, Vol. 2. 6th ed. Janice R. Ellis et al. LC 95-37176. 1996. pap. text 32.95 (*0-397-55170-3*) Lppncott W & W.

M

Modules for Medication Administration. Barbarito & D'Amico. 190p. (C). 1998. spiral bd. 39.95 (*0-7872-4691-3*, 41469102) Kendall-Hunt.

Modules for Training Extension Workers with Handouts. Martin L. Byram et al. (Curriculum Aid Ser.). 175p. 1986. ring bd. 15.00 (*0-932288-77-4*) Ctr Intl Ed U of MA.

Modules in Applied Mathematics: Differential Equation Models, Vol. 1. Ed. by W. F. Lucas. (Illus.). 400p. 1991. 67.95 (*0-387-90695-9*) Spr-Verlag.

Modules in Applied Mathematics Vol. 2: Political & Related Models. Ed. by W. F. Lucas. (Illus.). 396p. 1982. 67.95 (*0-387-90696-7*) Spr-Verlag.

Modules in Applied Mathematics Vol. 3: Discrete & System Models. Ed. by W. F. Lucas et al. (Illus.). 353p. 1983. 49.00 (*0-387-90724-6*) Spr-Verlag.

Modules in Applied Mathematics Vol. 4: Life Science Models. Ed. by W. F. Lucas. (Illus.). 366p. 1983. 65.95 (*0-387-90739-4*) Spr-Verlag.

Modules over Commutative Regular Rings. Richard S. Pierce. LC 52-42839. (Memoirs Ser.: No. 1/70). 112p. 1977. reprint ed. pap. 21.00 (*0-8218-1270-X*, MEMO/1/70) Am Math.

Modules over the Integral Group Ring of A Non-Abelian Group of Order Pq. L. Klinger. LC 85-27504. (Memoirs of the AMS Ser.: No. 59/341). 125p. 1986. pap. 23.00 (*0-8218-2343-4*, MEMO/59/341) Am Math.

Modules over Valuation Rings. Caszlo Fuchs & L. Salce. (Lecture Notes in Pure & Applied Mathematics Ser.: Vol. 97). (Illus.). 336p. 1985. pap. text 155.00 (*0-8247-7326-8*) Dekker.

Modules with Cores & Amalgamations of Indecomposable Modules. R. Gordon & E. L. Green. LC 77-3560. (Memoirs Ser.: No. 10/187). 145p. 1977. pap. 22.00 (*0-8218-2187-3*, MEMO/10/187) Am Math.

Moduli of Abelian Varieties, Vol. VI. Alan Adler & S. Ramanan. LC 96-39688. (Lecture Notes in Mathematics Ser.: Vol. 1644). 196p. 1996. pap. 43.00 (*3-540-62023-0*) Spr-Verlag.

Moduli of Curves. J. Harris & I. Morrison. LC 98-13036. (Universitext Ser.). 378p. 1998. 54.95 (*0-387-98438-0*) Spr-Verlag.

Moduli of Curves: A User's Guide. Joe Harris & I. Morrison. LC 98-13036. (Universitext Ser.). 378p. 1998. pap. 29.95 (*0-387-98429-1*) Spr-Verlag.

Moduli of Families of Curves & Quadratic Differentials. G. V. Kuz'mina. LC 82-8902. (Proceedings of the Steklov Institute of Mathematics Ser.: No. 139). 231p. 1982. pap. 119.00 (*0-8218-3040-6*, STEKLO/139) Am Math.

Moduli of Smoothness. Z. Ditzian & Vilmos Totik. (Computational Mathematics Ser.: Vol. 9). (Illus.). 240p. 1987. 89.95 (*0-387-96536-X*) Spr-Verlag.

Moduli of Supersingular Abelian Varieties. Frans Oort. Ed. by Ke-Zheng Li. LC 97-48780. (Lecture Notes in Mathematics Ser.: Vol. 1680). v, 116p. 1998. pap. 27.00 (*3-540-63923-3*) Spr-Verlag.

Moduli of Vector Bundles. Ed. by Masaki Maruyama. LC 96-641. (Lecture Notes in Pure & Applied Mathematics Ser.: Vol. 179). (Illus.). 336p. 1996. pap. text 145.00 (*0-8247-9738-8*) Dekker.

Moduli Space of Curves. Ed. by R. Dijkgraaf et al. LC 95-21641. (Progress in Mathematics Ser.: Vol. 129). 563p. 1995. 82.00 (*0-8176-3784-2*) Birkhauser.

Moduli Spaces of Abelian Surfaces: Compactification, Degenerations, & Theta Functions. Klaus Hulek et al. (Expositions in Mathematics Ser.: No. 12). xii, 347p. (C). 1993. lib. bdg. 99.95 (*3-11-013851-4*) De Gruyter.

Moduli Undecim Festorum. Nicolas Gombert et al. Ed. by J. Heywood Alexander. (Recent Researches in Music of the Renaissance Ser.: Vol. RRR56). (Illus.). xx, 85p. 1983. pap. 40.00 (*0-89579-186-2*, RRR56) A-R Eds.

Modulo II (Bilingue) (Module II (Bilingual)) Programa de Capacitacion para Misioneros(as) Laicos(as) y Pastores (Lay Missioner & Pastor-Mentor Training Program) National Hispanic Staff. (ENG & SPA.). 312p. 1997. pap. 16.95 (*0-88177-240-2*, DR240) Discipleship Res.

***Modulor, Modulor 2, 2 vols.** Le Corbusier Staff. LC 99-53635. (Illus.). 580p. 2000. pap. 38.00 (*3-7643-6188-3*, Pub. by Birkhauser) Princeton Arch.

***Modulor, Modulor 2, 2 vols.** Le Corbusier Staff. (FRE., Illus.). 580p. 2000. pap. 35.00 (*3-7643-6187-5*, Pub. by Birkhauser) Princeton Arch.

An Asterisk (*) at the beginning of an entry indicates that the title is appearing for the first time.

Modus Digressivus Nella "Divina Commedia" Sergio Corsi. 201p. 1990. 28.75 (*0-916379-46-9*) Scripta.

Modus Lascivus. Tibor Serly. LC 75-20646. (Illus.). 1975. 30.00 (*0-317-40591-8*); spiral bd. 12.95 (*0-317-40592-6*) Tritone Music.

Modus Novus. Lars Edlund. 111p. Date not set. pap. text 34.95 (*0-8464-4156-X*) Beekman Pubs.

Modus Operandi: A Writer's Guide to How Criminals Work. Mauro V. Corvasce & Joseph R. Paglino. LC 94-49705. (Howdunit Ser.). 224p. (Orig.). 1995. pap. 16.99 (*0-89879-649-0*, Wrtrs Digest Bks) F & W Pubns Inc.

Modus Vetus. Lars Edlund. (Illus.). 219p. Date not set. pap. text 34.95 (*0-8464-4157-8*) Beekman Pubs.

Modus Vivendi: Selected Prose. Gunnar Ekelof & Erik Thygesen. LC 96-146064. 254p. 1997. 55.00 (*1-870041-30-5*, Pub. by Norvik Pr) Dufour.

Modus Vivendi: Ulay & Marina Abramovic, 1980-85. (Illus.). 96p. 1992. pap. 20.00 (*1-56466-034-6*) Archer Fields.

Modusprobleme bei Notker: Die Modalen Werte in den Nebensaetzen. Dieter Furrer. 201p. (C). 1971. 98.50 (*3-11-001808-X*) De Gruyter.

***Moe.** Joseph A. Garduno. LC 00-90145. (Illus.). 228p. (YA). 2000. pap. 19.95 (*0-9608806-3-1*) Assoc Pubns.

Moe Berg: Athlete, Scholar, Spy. Louis Kaufman et al. Date not set. lib. bdg. 29.95 (*0-8488-1387-1*) Amereon Ltd.

Moe Berg: The Spy Behind Home Plate. Vivian Grey. LC 96-41504. (J). (gr. 3 up). 1996. pap. 9.95 (*0-8276-0620-6*) JPS Phila.

Moe Howard & the Three Stooges. Moe Howard. 1979. pap. 18.95 (*0-8065-0723-3*, Citadel Pr) Carol Pub Group.

Moe Kau a Ho'oilo: Hawaiian Mortuary Practices at Keopu, Kona, Hawaii. Tom L. Han et al. (Departmental Reports: Vol. 86-1). (Illus.). 401p. (C). 1986. pap. 23.00 (*0-930897-17-X*) Bishop Mus.

Moe, Remembrance: (March 17, 1983-February 20, 1996) Carol Lem. LC 97-204922. 36p. 1996. pap. 10.00 (*1-882868-05-6*) Peddler Pr.

Moe the Dog in Tropical Paradise. Diane Stanley. 32p. (ps-3). 1999. pap. 5.99 (*0-698-11761-1*) Putnam Pub Group.

Moebius. Bruce Andrews. 24p. (Orig.). 1993. pap. text 6.00 (*0-945112-17-3*) Generator Pr.

***Moebius Arzach.** Jean Lofficier. 272p. 2000. per. 14.00 (*0-7434-0015-1*, Pub. by ibooks) S&S Trade.

Moebius 1. Jean M. Giraud. Ed. by Archie Goodwin et al. Tr. by Jean-Marc Lofficier & Randy Lofficier. (Limited-Signed Edition Ser.: No. 12). (Illus.). 266p. 1989. 45.95 (*0-936211-10-5*) Graphitti Designs.

Moebius 3: The Incal. Alexandro Jodorowsky & Jean M. Giraud. Ed. by Archie Goodwin et al. Tr. by Jean-Marc Lofficier & Randy Lofficier. (Limited-Signed Edition Ser.: No. 14). (Illus.). 290p. 1988. 45.95 (*0-936211-12-1*) Graphitti Designs.

Moebius 2. Jean M. Giraud. Ed. by Archie Goodwin et al. Tr. by Jean-Marc Lofficier & Randy Lofficier. (Limited-Signed Edition Ser.: No. 13). (Illus.). 218p. 1988. 45.95 (*0-936211-11-3*) Graphitti Designs.

Mo'ed Katan. (ENG & HEB.). 15.00 (*0-910218-63-3*) Bennet Pub.

Moehler & Baur in Controversy, 1832-38: Romantic-Idealist Assessment of the Reformation & Counter-Reformation. Joseph Fitzer. LC 74-77619. (American Academy of Religion. Studies in Religion: No. 7). 122p. reprint ed. pap. 37.90 (*0-7837-5489-2*, 204525400005) Bks Demand.

Moen Collection of Eastern Turki (New Uighur) Popular Poetry: Edited with Translation Notes & Glossary. Gunnar Jarring. 50p. (Orig.). 1996. pap. 39.50 (*91-22-01725-9*, Pub. by Almqvist Wiksell) Coronet Bks.

Moeris Atticista: Lexicon Atticum, 2 vols., Set. Johann Pierson. 1969. reprint ed. write for info. (*0-318-72055-8*) G Olms Pubs.

Moe's Textbook of Scoliosis & Other Spinal Deformities. 3rd ed. Ed. by David S. Bradford et al. LC 94-11860. (Illus.). 672p. 1994. text. write for info. (*0-7216-5533-5*, W B Saunders Co) Harcrt Hlth Sci Grp.

Moessbauer Spectroscopy & Transition Metal Chemistry. P. Guetlich et al. (Inorganic Chemistry Concepts Ser.: Vol. 3). (Illus.). 1978. 68.00 (*0-387-08671-4*) Spr-Verlag.

Moessbauer Spectroscopy II: The Exotic Side of the Methods. Ed. by U. Gonser. (Topics in Current Physics Ser.: Vol. 25). (Illus.). 210p. 1981. 46.95 (*0-387-10519-0*) Spr-Verlag.

Moeurs et Coutumes des Fellahs. 5th ed. Henry H. Ayrout. LC 74-15009. (Illus.). reprint ed. 47.50 (*0-404-12004-0*) AMS Pr.

Moeurs et Coutumes des Khmers. Guy Poree. LC 77-87069. (Illus.). reprint ed. 42.50 (*0-404-16850-7*) AMS Pr.

Moffat: Family Histories of Moffat, Crangle, Pierson, Angel, Lichtenw. Charles Moffat & Norma Moffat. (Illus.). 168p. 1996. reprint ed. lib. bdg. 37.00 (*0-8328-5309-7*) Higginson Bk Co.

Moffat! Rio Grande - Southern Pacific - Union Pacific West of Dencer, Co. Gregory Monroe. LC 97-60870. (Illus.). 128p. 1997. 41.95 (*1-884831-05-2*) Fox Pubns.

Moffat. Family Histories of Moffat, Crangle, Pierson, Angel, Lichtenwalter, McNeelan. Charles Moffat & Norma Moffat. (Illus.). 168p. 1996. reprint ed. pap. 27.00 (*0-8328-5310-0*) Higginson Bk Co.

***Moffat Museum.** Eleanor Estes. LC 00-38845. (Illus.). (J). 2001. pap. write for info. (*0-15-202553-7*, Harcourt Child Bks) Harcourt.

Moffat the Prophet: A Word from Our Sponsor. Lavern Holdeman. (Moffat Ser.: Vol. 1). (Illus.). (Orig.). 1996. pap. 5.95 (*0-614-16019-7*) Son-Rise Pubns.

Moffats. Eleanor Estes. LC 41-51893. (Illus.). 290p. (J). (gr. 3-7). 1941. 17.00 (*0-15-255095-X*, Harcourt Child Bks) Harcourt.

***Moffats.** Eleanor Estes & Louis Slobodkin. LC 00-39726. (Illus.). 2001. write for info. (*0-15-202541-3*) Harcourt.

Moffatts: An Unauthorized Biography. Anna Louise Golden. (Illus.). 1999. mass mkt. 4.99 (*0-312-97359-4*, St Martins Paperbacks) St Martin.

***Moffatts: Backstage Pass.** Scholastic, Inc. Staff. (gr. 2-9). 1999. pap. 5.99 (*0-439-13552-4*) Scholastic Bk Fairs.

***Moffatts on the Road: All for One.** Nancy E. Krulik. (Illus.). 128p. (J). (gr. 3-9). 2000. pap. 4.99 (*0-439-13688-1*) Scholastic Inc.

***Moffit's Consolidator Guide.** 4th ed. Illus. by Laura Frank. 300p. 1999. pap. 49.95 (*0-9673088-0-1*) SFC Travel Pubns.

Mogadishu! Heroism & Tragedy. Kent DeLong. Ed. by Steven Tuckey. LC 94-31744. 144p. 1994. 24.95 (*0-275-94925-7*, DT407, Praeger Pubs) Greenwood.

Mogador. Alberto M. Ruy-Sanchez. Tr. by Mark Schafer from SPA. 124p. (Orig.). 1992. pap. 7.95 (*0-87286-271-2*) City Lights.

Mogador's Book - Fur Mogador. Robert Lax. Ed. by Paul J. Spaeth. Tr. by Alfred Kuoni from GER. 80p. (Orig.). 1992. pap. text 15.00 (*3-85842-237-1*) Franciscan Inst.

Mogana Inc. limited ed. Jean McGarry et al. (Illus.). 40p. 1992. 38.00 (*1-880392-01-1*) Flockophobic Pr.

Mogens: And Other Stories. Jens Peter Jacobsen. Tr. by Anna Grabow. LC 72-4452. (Short Story Index Reprint Ser.). 1977. reprint ed. 22.95 (*0-8369-4179-9*) Ayer.

Mogens & Other Stories. Jens Peter Jacobsen. Tr. by Tiina Nunnally from DAN. LC 94-4233. (Modern Classics Ser.: No. 5). 160p. (Orig.). 1994. pap. 12.00 (*0-940242-57-5*) Fjord Pr.

***Mogford's Winning Ways.** Ian Campbell Thomson. 288p. 2000. 31.99 (*0-7089-4222-9*) Ulverscroft.

Moggies: A Book for Owners of Non-Pedigree Cats. Marianne Mays. (Illus.). 128p. 1997. 14.95 (*1-85279-024-5*, GB-011) TFH Pubns.

Moggy the Mouser. Helen Lawton. LC 93-6571. (Voyages Ser.). (Illus.). (J). 1994. write for info. (*0-383-03702-6*) SRA McGraw.

Moghul Buffet. Cheryl Benard. LC 97-49954. 208p. 1998. 22.00 (*0-374-21179-5*) FS&G.

Moghul Buffet. Cheryl Benard. LC 99-27141. 272p. 2000. pap. 12.00 (*1-56947-179-7*) Soho Press.

Moghul Cooking: India's Courtly Cuisine. Joyce Westrip. (Illus.). 256p. 1998. pap. 19.95 (*1-897959-27-3*, Pub. by Serif) IPG Chicago.

Moghul India, 1523-1805. David Nicolle. (Men-at-Arms Ser.). (Illus.). 48p. 1993. pap. 11.95 (*1-85532-344-3*, 9234, Pub. by Ospry) Stackpole.

***Moglichkeiten und Grenzen der Ruckfuhrung Von Chronisch Psychisch Kranken in die Gemeinde - Am Beispiel Mistelbach.** Gerd Eichberger et al. (Illus.). 181p. 1999. 37.95 (*3-631-31126-5*) P Lang Pubng.

Moglichkeiten und Grenzen des Energiesparens: Eine Analyse am Beispiel der Elektrizitat. Astrid Mundt. (Europaische Hochschulschriften Ser.: Reihe 5, Vol. 2243). (Illus.). 241p. 1998. pap. 39.95 (*3-631-32295-X*) P Lang Pubng.

Mogollon Culture in the Forestdale Valley, East-Central Arizona. Emil W. Haury. LC 84-28058. (Monographs). 454p. 1985. 54.00 (*0-8165-0894-1*) U of Ariz Pr.

Mogollon Monster: Arizona's Bigfoot. Susan A. Farnsworth. (Illus.). 130p. (YA). 1996. pap. text 14.95 (*1-881260-09-7*) Southwest Pubns.

Mogollon Rim Region: East-Central Arizona. Ed. by R. H. Weber & H. W. Peirce. (Guidebook Ser.: No. 13). (Illus.). 175p. 1962. reprint ed. pap. 8.00 (*1-58546-043-5*) NMex Geol Soc.

Mogollon Slope: West-Central New Mexico & East-Central Arizona. Ed. by R. M. Chamberlin et al. (Guidebook Ser.: No. 45). (Illus.). 335p. 1994. pap. 50.00 (*1-58546-080-X*) NMex Geol Soc.

Mogreb-el-Acksa: A Journey in Morocco. R. Graham. LC 96-52696. (Marlboro Travel Ser.). 1997. 14.95 (*0-8101-6036-6*, Marlboro) Northwestern U Pr.

Mogul & Me. Peter Cumming. (Illus.). 164p. (J). (gr. 4-8). 1989. pap. 8.95 (*0-920304-82-6*, Pub. by Gynergy-Ragweed) U of Toronto Pr.

Mogul Recollected. Richard Daley Outram. LC 94-149500. (Illus.). 96p. 1993. pap. write for info. (*0-88984-174-8*, Pub. by Porcup Quill) Genl Dist Srvs.

Moguls: Hollywood's Merchants of Myth. Norman Zierold. LC 91-11426. (Illus.). 354p. 1991. reprint ed. pap. 14.95 (*1-879505-02-9*) Silman James Pr.

Moguls & Mandarins: Oil, Imperialism & the Middle East in British Foreign Policy, 1900-1940. Marian Kent. LC 92-46632. (Illus.). 192p. 1994. text 49.50 (*0-7146-4504-4*, Pub. by F Cass Pubs) Intl Spec Bk.

Mogy - An Autobiography: Father of Work Simplification. 2nd ed. Allan H. Mogensen & Rosario Rausa. Ed. by Jim Denyes. 204p. 1990. pap. text 9.95 (*0-9623050-0-6*) Idea Assocs VA.

Moha la Fou, Moha le Sage. Tahar B. Jelloun. (FRE.). 1980. pap. 11.95 (*0-7859-2679-8*) Fr & Eur.

Mohair: A Review of Its Properties, Processing & Applications. L. Hunter. 1993. 110.00 (*0-7988-3717-9*, Pub. by Textile Inst) St Mut.

Mohair Knitting. Nihon Vogue Staff. (Illus.). 80p. (Orig.). 1985. pap. 19.00 (*0-87040-610-8*) Japan Pubns USA.

Mohajir's Pakistan. M. G. Chitkara. xii, 166p. (C). 1996. 20.00 (*81-7024-746-2*, Pub. by Ashish Pub Hse) Nataraj Bks.

Mohamed Ali: Ideology & Politics. Mushirul Hasan. 1982. 18.50 (*0-8364-0878-0*, Pub. by Manohar) S Asia.

Mohammad the Prophet of Islam. B. K. Narayan. 205p. 1978. 29.95 (*0-318-37191-X*) Asia Bk Corp.

Mohammed. Essad Bey. 336p. 1984. 195.00 (*1-85077-019-0*, Pub. by Darf Pubs Ltd) St Mut.

Mohammed: The Man & His Faith. Tor Andrae. Tr. by Theophil Menzel. LC 79-160954. (Select Bibliographies Reprint Ser.). 1977. reprint ed. 25.95 (*0-8369-5821-7*) Ayer.

Mohammed & Mohammedanism. R. Bosworth Smith. 344p. 1986. 220.00 (*1-85077-081-6*, Pub. by Darf Pubs Ltd) St Mut.

Mohammed & the Rise of Islam. David S. Margoliouth. LC 73-14455. reprint ed. 45.00 (*0-404-58273-7*) AMS Pr.

Mohammed & the Rise of Islam. David S. Margoliouth. LC 73-38361. (Select Bibliographies Reprint Ser.). 1977. reprint ed. 37.95 (*0-8369-6778-X*) Ayer.

***Mohammed Ayub Khuhro: A Life of Courage in Politics.** Hamida Khuhro. LC 97-930918. (Illus.). 576p. 2000. write for info. (*969-0-01424-2*) OUP.

Mohammed, Buddha & Christ. Marcus Dods. 1986. 100.00 (*0-7855-3015-0*, Pub. by Archives Pubs) St Mut.

Mohammed, Charlemagne, & the Origins of Europe: The Pirenne Thesis in the Light of Archaeology. Richard Hodges & David Whitehouse. LC 82-34020. (Illus.). 192p. 1983. pap. text 13.95 (*0-8014-9262-9*) Cornell U Pr.

Mohammed, Sein Leben und Sein Glaube. Tor Andrae. 160p. 1977. reprint ed. 32.00 (*3-487-06302-6*) G Olms Pubs.

***Mohammed, the Man & His Faith.** Tor Andras. LC 99-57349. (Illus.). 2000. pap. 6.95 (*0-486-41136-2*) Dover.

Mohammedan Period As Described by Its Own Historians. Henry M. Elliot. LC 72-14391. (History of India Ser.: No. 5). reprint ed. 90.00 (*0-404-09005-2*) AMS Pr.

Mohammedan Theories of Finance, with an Introduction to Mohammedan Law & a Bibliography. Nicolas P. Aghnides. LC 72-82246. (Columbia University. Studies in the Social Sciences: No. 166). reprint ed. 47.50 (*0-404-51166-X*) AMS Pr.

Mohammedanism: An Historical Survey. 2nd ed. Hamilton A. Gibb. 208p. 1962. reprint ed. pap. text 10.95 (*0-19-500245-8*) OUP.

Mohan in the Jungle. Ella Grove. (Illus.). 142p. (YA). (gr. 7-10). 1991. 7.20 (*0-7399-0109-5*, 2319) Rod & Staff.

Mohandas Gandhi. John Barraclough. LC 97-19301. (Lives & Times Ser.). (J). 1998. 19.92 (*1-57572-561-4*) Heinemann Lib.

***Mohandas Gandhi.** Mike Furbee & Mary R. Furbee. (Importance of Ser.). 128p. (YA). (gr. 4-12). 2000. 18.96 (*1-56006-674-1*) Lucent Bks.

***Mohandas Gandhi.** Christopher Martin. LC 99-28431. (A & E Biography Ser.). (Illus.). 128p. (YA). (gr. 6-9). 2000. lib. bdg. 25.26 (*0-8225-4984-0*, Lerner Publctns) Lerner Pub.

Mohandas K. Gandhi. Catherine Bush. (World Leaders Past & Present Ser.). (Illus.). 120p. (YA). (gr. 5 up). 1985. lib. bdg. 19.95 (*0-87754-555-3*) Chelsea Hse.

Mohanobi Mohammad. Ahmad Nawaz. LC 98-70822. (BEN.). xiv, 98p. 1998. pap. 10.00 (*1-58225-139-8*) Ananta Prakashani.

Mohave Ethnopsychiatry & Suicide: Psychiatric Knowledge & the Psychic Disturbances of an Indian Tribe. George Devereux. (Bureau of American Ethnology Bulletins Ser.). 586p. 1995. lib. bdg. 119.00 (*0-7812-4175-8*) Rprt Serv.

Mohave Ethnopsychiatry & Suicide: The Psychiatric Knowledge & the Psychic Disturbances of an Indian Tribe. George Devereux. reprint ed. 95.00 (*0-403-03650-X*) Scholarly.

Mohave Historical Epic. fac. ed. A. L. Kroeber. Ed. by Edward W. Gifford et al. (University of California Publications: No. 11:2). 117p. (C). 1951. reprint ed. pap. 13.13 (*1-55567-125-X*) Coyote Press.

Mohave War Reminiscence, 1854-1880, Vol. 880. unabridged ed. A. L. Kroeber & Clifton B. Kroeber. LC 94-9162. (Illus.). xi, 109p. 1994. pap. text 7.95 (*0-486-28163-9*) Dover.

Mohawk see Indians of North America

Mohawk. Jill D. Duvall. LC 90-21166. (New True Books Ser.). (Illus.). 48p. (J). (gr. k-4). 1991. pap. 5.50 (*0-516-41115-2*) Childrens.

Mohawk. Jill D. Duvall. LC 90-21166. (New True Books Ser.). (Illus.). 48p. (J). (ps-3). 1991. lib. bdg. 21.00 (*0-516-01115-4*) Childrens.

Mohawk. Richard Russo. 1994. pap. 13.00 (*0-679-75382-6*) Vin Bks.

Mohawk Blood: A Native American Quest. Michael Baughman. 128p. 1995. 19.95 (*1-55821-376-7*) Lyons Pr.

Mohawk Frontier: The Dutch Community of Schenectady, New York, 1661-1710. Thomas E. Burke, Jr. LC 91-55237. 264p. 1991. text 39.95 (*0-8014-2541-7*) Cornell U Pr.

Mohawk Indians see Junior Library of American Indians

Mohawk, Let's Speak. unabridged ed. David K. Maracle. 100p. 1993. pap. text 49.95 incl. audio (*0-88432-706-X*, AFMH10) Audio-Forum.

Mohawk, One Thousand Useful Words. David K. Maracle. 158p. 1992. pap. 12.95 (*0-88432-710-8*, AFMH94) Audio-Forum.

Mohawk River Boats & Navigation Before 1820. Robert E. Hager. (Canal Society Publication Ser.: No. 1). (Illus.). 98p. Date not set. 12.95 (*0-9618172-0-8*) CSNY.

Mohawk Trail. Beth Brant. LC 85-3265. 100p. (Orig.). 1985. pap. 9.95 (*0-932379-02-8*); lib. bdg. 16.95 (*0-932379-03-6*) Firebrand Bks.

Mohawk Trail. Beth Brant. 94p. (Orig.). pap. write for info. (*0-88961-151-3*, Pub. by Womens Pr) LPC InBook.

Mohawk Valley. W. Max Reid. 455p. 1993. reprint ed. lib. bdg. 99.00 (*0-7812-5133-8*) Rprt Serv.

Mohawk Valley - Its Legends & Its History. W. Max Reid. (Illus.). 455p. 1993. reprint ed. lib. bdg. 47.50 (*0-8328-3188-3*) Higginson Bk Co.

Mohawk Valley Archaeology: The Collections. Dean R. Snow. 193p. (C). 1995. pap. text 15.00 (*0-9647913-1-5*) U Albany IAS.

Mohawk Valley Archaeology: The Sites. Dean R. Snow. 543p. (C). 1995. pap. text 30.00 (*0-9647913-0-7*) U Albany IAS.

Mohawk Woman. Barbara Riefe. 1996. mass mkt. 5.99 (*0-8125-4802-7*, Pub. by Tor Bks) St Martin.

Mohegan Fun & Learn Book. Anita Page. (Illus.). 16p. (Orig.). (J). 1997. pap. 5.00 (*0-9656933-1-7*) Lttle People.

Mohegan Indian Maps of Montville, Connecticut. Allen V. Polhemus. (Illus.). 84p. 1993. 42.95 (*1-883009-00-6*) Nutmeg Pubs.

Mohenjo-Daro & the Indus Civilization: Being an Official Account of Archaeological Excavations at Mohenjo-Daro Carried Out by the Government of India Between the Years 1922 & 1927, 3 vols., Set. John Marshall. 1996. reprint ed. 210.00 (*81-206-1179-9*, Pub. by Asian Educ Servs) S Asia.

Mohicans & Their Land, 1609-1730. 3rd ed. Shirley W. Dunn. LC 94-18080. (Illus.). 350p. 1994. pap. 24.00 (*0-935796-49-5*) Purple Mnt Pr.

Mohicans of Stockbridge. Patrick Frazier. LC 92-6494. (Illus.). xviii, 307p. 1992. pap. 12.95 (*0-8032-6882-3*, Bison Books) U of Nebr Pr.

***Moho Proviso.** J. W. Irelan. LC 00-190415. 215p. 2000. 25.00 (*0-7388-1665-5*); pap. 18.00 (*0-7388-1666-3*) Xlibris Corp.

Moho Wat: A Sheepeater Indian Boy Attempts a Rescue. Kenneth Thomasma. LC 94-4074. (Amazing Indian Children Ser.). (Illus.). 192p. (J). (gr. 4-8). 1994. pap. 5.99 (*0-8010-8919-0*) Baker Bks.

Moho Wat: A Sheepeater Indian Boy Attempts a Rescue. Kenneth Thomasma. LC 94-4074. (Amazing Indian Children Ser.). (Illus.). 192p. (YA). (gr. 7-10). 1994. 9.99 (*0-8010-8918-2*) Baker Bks.

Moho Wat: Sheepeater Boy Attempts a Rescue. Kenneth Thomasma. (Amazing Indian Children). (Illus.). 184p. (J). (gr. 3). 1994. 10.95 (*1-880114-14-3*) Grandview.

Moho Wat: Sheepeater Boy Attempts a Rescue. Kenneth Thomasma. (Amazing Indian Children Ser.). (Illus.). 184p. (J). (gr. 3-8). 1994. pap. 6.95 (*1-880114-13-5*) Grandview.

Moho Wat: Sheepeater Boy Attempts a Rescue. Kenneth Thomasma. LC 94-4074. (Amazing Indian Children Ser.). 1994. 12.05 (*0-606-10262-0*, Pub. by Turtleback) Demco.

Moholy-Nagy. Krisztina Passuth. Tr. by Theirry Heribert from HUN. (GER., Illus.). 466p. (C). 1987. 118.00 (*3-8170-2005-8*, Pub. by Knstvrlag Weingrtn) Intl Bk Import.

Moholy-Nagy. Krisztina Passuth. LC 83-50107. (Illus.). 300p. 1987. pap. 24.95 (*0-500-27449-5*, Pub. by Thames Hudson) Norton.

Moholy-Nagy. Ed. by Richard Kostelanetz. LC 70-12175. (Illus.). 1970. reprint ed. 100.00 (*0-932360-12-2*); reprint ed. pap. 75.00 (*0-932360-11-4*) Archae Edns.

Moholy-Nagy: A New Vision for Chicago. Ed. by Lloyd C. Engelbrecht & Richard Kostelanetz. (Illus.). 128p. (Orig.). 1991. 19.95 (*0-89792-127-5*) U of Ill Pr.

Moholy-Nagy: An Anthology. Laszlo Moholy-Nagy et al. (Quality Paperbacks Ser.). (Illus.). 238p. 1991. reprint ed. pap. 15.95 (*0-306-80455-7*) Da Capo.

Moholy-Nagy, Laszlo: Photography & Film. S. Starr. (C). 1990. pap. 230.00 (*0-7855-4458-5*, Pub. by Collets) St Mut.

Mohonk: Its People & Spirit: A History of One Hundred Years of Growth & Service. rev. ed. Larry E. Burgess. LC 80-15087. (Illus.). 123p. 1993. pap. 15.00 (*0-935796-42-8*) Purple Mnt Pr.

Mohop Mogande. Stanley L. Alpert. LC 98-93481. 460p. 1998. 27.00 (*1-892666-03-0*) Alperts Bookery.

MOHR Circles, Stress Paths & Geotechnics. R. H. G. Parry. LC 95-143362. (Illus.). 256p. (C). 1995. 110.00 (*0-419-19290-5*, E & FN Spon) Routledge.

***Mohr im Mor: Interkulturelles Theater in Theorie und Praxis Mit einem Vorwort von Ulf Birbaumer.** Gabriele C. Pfeiffer. (Europaische Hochschulschriften Theater-, Film- und Fernsehwissenschaften Ser.). 115p. 1999. 26.95 (*3-631-34368-X*) P Lang Pubng.

MOHR's Guide see Healthcare Safety Sourcebook

***MOHs.** Terence M. Davidson. LC 99-47753. (Self-Instructional Package Ser.). (Illus.). 121p. 1999. pap. text 25.00 (*1-56772-028-5*, 5506360) AAO-HNS.

Moh's Micrographic Surgery. Mikail. (Illus.). 432p. 1991. text 170.00 (*0-7216-3415-X*, W B Saunders Co) Harcrt Hlth Sci Grp.

MOHS Surgery: Fundamentals & Techniques. Kenneth G. Gross et al. LC 98-13759. 1998. text 139.00 (*0-323-00012-6*) Mosby Inc.

Mohun. John E. Cooke. LC 68-20008. (Americans in Fiction Ser.). (Illus.). reprint ed. pap. text 6.95 (*0-89197-856-9*); reprint ed. lib. bdg. 22.00 (*0-8398-0271-4*) Irvington.

Moi. Paul Valery. Tr. by Marthiel Mathews & Jackson Mathews. LC PQ2643.A26A2. (Collected Works of Paul Valery: Vol. 15). 434p. 1975. reprint ed. pap. 134.60 (*0-608-02896-7*, 206396000008) Bks Demand.

Moi: The Making of an African Statesman. Andrew Morton. (Illus.). 224p. 1999. 29.95 (*1-85479-253-9*, Pub. by M OMara) Trafalgar.

Moi, Claude (Moi, Claude, Empereur, I) Robert Graves. (FRE.). 448p. 1987. pap. 12.95 (*0-7859-2533-3*, 2070378136) Fr & Eur.

Moi Decapite: Le Probleme de la Personnalite dans la Litterature Francaise Contemporaine. Micheline Tison-Braun. Ed. by Mary A. Caws. (Reading Plus Ser.: Vol. 6). 440p. 1990. 70.95 (*0-8204-0997-9*) P Lang Pubng.

Moi-Je. Claude Roy. (FRE.). 497p. 1978. pap. 13.95 (*0-7859-4107-X*, 2070370666) Fr & Eur.

M

An Asterisk (*) at the beginning of an entry indicates that the title is appearing for the first time.

Moi, Laminaire. Aime Cesaire. (FRE.). 1991. pap. 10.95 (*0-7859-2724-7*) Fr & Eur.

Moi, on M'Aime. Jim Davis. (Garfield Ser.). (FRE.). (J). 1986. 18.95 (*0-8288-4587-5*, M4211) Fr & Eur.

Moi, Pierre Riviere, Ayant Egorge Ma Mere, Ma Soeur et Mon Frere . . . Michel Foucault. (Folio Ser.). (FRE.). pap. 15.95 (*2-07-032828-7*) Schoenhof.

Moi, Tituba, Sorciere . . . Maryse Conde. (Folio Ser.: No. 1929). (FRE.). 277p. 1988. pap. 9.95 (*2-07-037929-9*) Schoenhof.

Moi, Tituba Sorciere. Maryse Conde. (FRE.). 276p. 1988. pap. 11.95 (*0-7859-2087-0*, 2070379299) Fr & Eur.

Moia Zhizn' (My Life) Detstvo v Sibiri, Junost' v Shankkhaie. Nina Mokrinskaia. Ed. by Gabriel Valk. LC 90-85815. (RUS., Illus.). 224p. (Orig.). (J). 1991. pap. 16.00 (*0-911971-61-0*) Effect Pub.

Moidart among the Clanranalds. Charles MacDonald & John Watt. LC 97-130697. (Illus.). 270p. pap. 19.95 (*1-874744-65-3*, Pub. by Birlinn Ltd) Dufour.

Moina's Heaven & Earth. Moina M. Vanderveer. 262p. 2000. pap. 12.95 (*1-891929-31-3*) Four Seasons.

Moine. Antonin Artaud. (FRE.). 1975. reprint ed. pap. 13.95 (*0-7859-1808-6*, 2070366901) Fr & Eur.

Moine. unabridged ed. Gregory Lewis. (FRE.). Date not set. reprint ed. pap. 8.95 (*2-87714-358-9*, Pub. by Bookking Intl) Distribks Inc.

Mo'in's: Intermediate Persion Dictionary, 6 vols., Set. Mohammad Mo'in. (PER., Illus.). 8058p. 1994. lib. bdg. 195.00 (*1-56859-031-8*) Mazda Pubs.

Moira. Norma Cole. 1996. 9.00 (*1-882022-28-9*) O Bks.

Moira. Martin Obler. LC 92-60567. 304p. 1993. 22.95 (*0-88282-120-2*) New Horizon NJ.

Moira's Birthday see Cumpleanos de Moira

Moira's Birthday. Robert Munsch. (Illus.). 32p. (J). (gr. k-3). 1987. pap. 5.95 (*0-920303-83-8*, Pub. by Annick); lib. bdg. 15.95 (*0-920303-85-4*, Pub. by Annick) Firefly Bks Ltd.

Moira's Birthday. Robert Munsch. Ed. by Michael Martchenko. (Annikins Ser.: Vol. 14). (Illus.). (J). (ps-2). 1995. pap. 0.99 (*1-55037-389-7*, Pub. by Annick) Firefly Bks Ltd.

Moira's Birthday. Robert Munsch. (J). 1987. 11.15 (*0-606-05469-3*, Pub. by Turtleback) Demco.

*__Moira's Crossing.__ Christine Shea. 2001. pap. 12.95 (*0-7434-1057-2*, PB Trade Paper) PB.

Moise. Alfred De Vigny. Ed. by Fernande Bartfeld. (FRE.). 24p. 1967. 7.95 (*0-8288-9669-0*, F75760) Fr & Eur.

Moises Alou. Carrie Muskat. LC 98-48046. (Latinos in Baseball Ser.). (Illus.). 64p. (YA). (gr. 5 up). 1999. lib. bdg. 11.95 (*1-883845-86-6*) M Lane Pubs.

Moishe. Maurice Sendak. (J). 1994. 10.95 (*0-694-00614-9*, HarpFestival) HarpC Child Bks.

Moishe's Miracle: A Hanukkah Story. Laura Krauss Melmed. LC 99-27640. 32p. (J). 2000. 15.95 (*0-688-14682-1*, Wm Morrow); lib. bdg. 15.89 (*0-688-14683-X*, Wm Morrow) Morrow Avon.

Moisson Rouge. Dashiell Hammett. (FRE.). 256p. 1988. pap. 10.95 (*0-7859-2654-2*, 207038067X) Fr & Eur.

Moist: A Pc Program for Predicting Heat & Moisture Transfer in Building Envelopes, Release 3.0. Douglas M. Burch. 53p. 1997. pap. 5.00 (*0-16-054692-3*) USGPO.

Moist Gases: Thermodynamic Properties. V. A. Rabinovich & V. G. Beketov. 176p. 1995. 117.50 (*1-56700-033-9*) Begell Hse.

Moisture Control Handbook: Principles & Practices for Residential & Small Commercial Buildings. John Carmody & Joseph Lstiburek. LC 93-11064. (Illus.). xiv, 214 p. 1993. text 52.95 (*0-442-01432-5*, VNR) Wiley.

Moisture Control Handbook: Principles & Practices for Residential & Small Commercial Buildings. Joseph Lstiburek & John Carmody. 232p. 1996. 69.95 (*0-471-31863-9*) Wiley.

Moisture in Textiles Regain Relative Humidity. Ed. by Wira Staff. 1988. 40.00 (*0-7855-1027-3*) St Mut.

Moisture Migration in Buildings - STP 779. Ed. by M. Leiff & Heinz R. Trechsel. 291p. 1982. 39.00 (*0-8031-0605-X*, STP779) ASTM.

Moisture of the Earth: An Oral History of Mary Robinson. Fran L. Buss. (Illus.). (C). text. write for info. (*0-472-09587-0*); pap. text. write for info. (*0-472-06587-4*) U of Mich Pr.

Moisture Problems in Concrete Floors. (Illus.). 52p. 1998. pap. 11.95 (*0-924659-41-6*) Hanley.

*__Moisture Sorption: Practical Aspects of Isotherm Measurement & Use.__ 2nd rev. ed. Leonard N. Bell & Theodore P. Labuza. (Illus.). 124p. 2000. 79.00 (*1-891127-18-7*) Eagan Pr.

Moja Dusha Zhivet V Romanshke. Roman Sonynn. Ed. & Illus. by Lubov Levin. (Biblioteka Bibliofila Ser.).Tr. of My Soul Lives in a Daisy. (RUS.). 120p. 1996. pap. 30.00 (*0-914265-16-4*) New Eng Pub MA.

Moja Means One: A Swahili Counting Book. Muriel Feelings. (J). (gr. k-3). 1996. 19.50 (*0-8446-6900-8*) Peter Smith.

Moja Means One: Swahili Counting Book. Muriel L. Feelings. (J). 1971. 10.19 (*0-606-00525-0*, Pub. by Turtleback) Demco.

*__Mojac's Megan: The Legacy of a Dog, Her Masters & Memories She Left Behind.__ Jack Judge. LC 98-74714. 1999. pap. 14.95 (*1-58151-025-X*) BookPartners.

Mojave. Deborah Boe. LC 87-334. 1987. 15.00 (*0-914610-47-3*); pap. 7.00 (*0-914610-44-9*) Hanging Loose.

Mojave. Diane Siebert. LC 86-24329. (Illus.). 32p. (J). (ps up). 1988. lib. bdg. 15.89 (*0-690-04569-7*) HarpC Child Bks.

Mojave. Diane Siebert. LC 86-24329. (Trophy Picture Bk.). (Illus.). 32p. (J). (gr. k-3). 1992. pap. 5.95 (*0-06-443283-1*, HarpTrophy) HarpC Child Bks.

Mojave: A Portrait of the Definitive American Desert. David Darlington. 337p. 1995. 25.00 (*0-8050-1631-7*) H Holt & Co.

Mojave: A Portrait of the Definitive American Desert. David Darlington. 352p. 1997. pap. text 14.95 (*0-8050-5594-0*, Owl) H Holt & Co.

Mojave Crossing. Louis L'Amour. 160p. 1979. mass mkt. 4.50 (*0-553-27680-8*) Bantam.

*__Mojave Desert.__ Rose Houk. LC 00-34432. (American Deserts Handbks.). (Illus.). 2000. write for info. (*1-58369-008-5*) SW Pks Mnmts.

*__Mojave Desert.__ John D. Swisher. (Images of America Ser.). (Illus.). 128p. 1999. pap. 18.99 (*0-7385-0219-7*) Arcadia Publng.

*__Mojave Desert Trails.__ Florine Lawlor. Ed. by Andy Zdon. Orig. Title: Mojave OHV Trails. (Illus.). 80p. 2000. pap. 9.95 (*1-893343-03-0*, Pub. by Spotted Dog CA) Sunbelt Pubns.

Mojave Desert Wildflowers: A Field Guide to High Desert Wildflowers of California, Nevada, & Arizona. Jon M. Stewart. LC 97-62452. (Illus.). 216p. (C). 1998. pap. 14.95 (*0-9634909-1-5*) J Stewart Photo.

Mojave National Preserve: A Visitor's Guide, 1. Cheri Rae. 1999. pap. text 12.95 (*0-934161-18-6*) Olympus Pr.

Mojave OHV Trails see Mojave Desert Trails

Mojave Pottery. fac. ed. A. L. Kroeber & Michael Harner. Ed. by Ronald L. Olson et al. (University of California Publications: No. 16:1). (Illus.). 34p. (C). 1955. reprint ed. pap. 3.75 (*1-55567-142-X*) Coyote Press.

*__Mojave Pottery, Mojave People: The Dillingham Collection of Mojave Ceramics.__ Jill McKeever Furst. LC 99-54873. 2000. 55.00 (*0-933452-55-1*) Schol Am Res.

*__Mojave Pottery, Mojave People: The Dillirgham Collection of Mojave Ceramics.__ Jill McKeever Furst. LC 99-54873. 2000. pap. 27.50 (*0-933452-65-9*) Schol Am Res.

Mojave Road Guide. Dennis G. Casebier. (Illus.). 232p. 1983. 18.50 (*0-914224-13-1*) Tales Mojave Rd.

Mojave Wells. L. Dean James. 288p. (Orig.). 1994. mass mkt. 4.99 (*0-380-77324-4*, Avon Bks) Morrow Avon.

Moje Prvni Lasky see My First Loves

Mojo. Jez Butterworth. LC 99-462448. 1999. pap. 5.25 (*0-8222-1661-2*) Dramatists Play.

Mojo. Jez Butterworth. 96p. 1996. pap. text 14.95 (*1-85459-366-8*, Pub. by N Hern Bks) Theatre Comm.

Mojo. Keith Carter. LC 92-50335. (Illus.). 1995. pap. 29.95 (*0-89263-335-2*) Tex A&M Univ Pr.

Mojo. Dwight A. Osborne. pap. 5.95 (*0-9632817-7-1*) Osborne Bks.

Mojo: Photographs by Keith Carter. Rosellen Brown. Ed. by Kristen Gladsky. Tr. by Carlos Chimol & Haydee Watt. (SPA., Illus.). 32p. (Orig.). 1995. pap. 1.50 (*1-882603-02-8*) Mid Am Arts.

Mojo & a Filmmaker's Diary. Jez Butterworth. (Illus.). 144p. 1999. pap. 14.95 (*0-571-19218-1*) Faber & Faber.

Mojo & String. Alice Childress. 1971. pap. 5.25 (*0-8222-0768-0*) Dramatists Play.

Mojo & the Pickle Jar. Douglas Bell. 1991. pap. 3.95 (*0-8125-0880-7*, Pub. by Tor Bks) St Martin.

Mojo & the Sayso. A. Rahman. 1990. pap. 6.95 (*0-88145-086-3*) Broadway Play.

*__Mojo Hand.__ Greg Kihn. LC 99-26643. 256p. 1999. 23.95 (*0-312-87246-1*, Pub. by Forge NYC) St Martin.

Mojo Hand: An Orphic Tale. J. J. Phillips. LC 85-71335. 200p. 1985. reprint ed. pap. 6.95 (*0-933944-12-8*) City Miner Bks.

Mojo Hand: Recent Work by Richard Yarde. Richard Muhlberger. Ed. by Jeffrey Keough. (Illus.). 12p. (Orig.). 1996. pap. 15.00 (*0-9628905-5-3*) MA Collge Art.

Mojo Navigator. John Jacob. 1976. 2.00 (*0-685-88910-6*) Cats Pajamas.

MoJoe Gets a Crown. Zachary X. King & Barbara Tompkins-Brown. (MoJoe Ser.). (Illus.). 32p. (J). (gr. k-3). 1996. 14.99 (*1-886290-06-7*); pap. 6.99 (*1-886290-07-5*); lib. bdg. 21.99 (*1-886290-12-1*) J Brown Ent.

Mojor Leccion de Mi Vida. B. Bright.Tr. of Greatest Lesson I Have Learned. (SPA.). 128p. 1994. pap. 7.99 (*0-8297-1847-8*) Vida Pubs.

Mojos. Michael Shurtz. pap. 14.95 (*0-9701914-0-5*) SouthPaw.

Mojo's Drama Skits. (J). pap. 9.95 (*0-614-18232-8*) Let Us Tch Kids.

Mojo's Whole Armor of God Skits. (J). pap. 9.95 (*0-614-18222-0*, A2S1) Let Us Tch Kids.

Moki. Grace J. Penney. LC 96-34478. 176p. 1997. pap. 4.99 (*0-14-038430-8*) Viking Penguin.

Moki, a Classic Story of a Young Cheyenne Girl. Grace Jackson Penney. (J). 1997. 10.09 (*0-606-11631-1*, Pub. by Turtleback) Demco.

Moki & the Magic Surfboard: A Hawaiian Fantasy. Bruce Hale. LC 96-60743. 32p. (J). (gr. k-4). 1996. 8.95 (*0-9621280-5-8*) Wrds & Picts Pubng.

Moki Learns to Fish. Juliet R. Wichman. (J). 1981. pap. 4.75 (*0-686-86236-8*) Kauai Museum.

Moki Mongoose Finds a Friend. Deborah C. Taylor. (Illus.). 32p. (J). 1995. text 8.95 (*1-886229-08-2*) Hawaiian Resources.

Moki Serape. Joshua Baer. (Illus.). 1990. write for info. (*0-318-66829-7*) J Baer & Co.

Moki Snake Dance. Walter Hough. LC 92-862. (Illus.). 80p. 1992. reprint ed. pap. 5.95 (*0-936755-19-9*) Avanyu Pub.

Moki the Gecko's Best Christmas Ever. Bruce Hale. LC 99-215192. (Illus.). 32p. (J). (gr. 1-5). 1998. 8.95 (*0-9621280-6-6*) Wrds & Picts Pubng.

Moko: The Art & History of Maori Tattooing. H. G. Robley. (Illus.). 216p. 1999. reprint ed. text 20.00 (*0-7881-6306-X*) DIANE Pub.

*__Mokole.__ James Ray Comer. (Werewolf Ser.). (Illus.). 144p. 1999. pap. 19.95 (*1-56504-306-5*, 3081) White Wolf.

*__Mokoto Saito: The Art of the Poster.__ Jan Kubasiewicz & Elizabeth Resnick. (Illus.). 80p. 1999. pap. write for info. (*0-9628905-8-8*) MA Collge Art.

Moksha. Hal J. Daniel, III. Ed. by Michael Hathaway. Date not set. pap. 10.00 (*0-943795-34-6*) Chiron Rev.

Moksha: Aldous Huxley's Classic Writings on Psychedelics & the Visionary Experience. Aldous Huxley. Ed. by Michael Horowitz & Cynthia Palmer. LC 99-12552. 304p. 1999. 14.95 (*0-89281-758-5*) Inner Tradit.

Moksha: Writings on Psychedelics & the Visionary Experience, 1931-1963. Aldous Huxley. Ed. by Michael Horowitz & Cynthia Palmer. LC 85-672625. xxii, 280 p. 1980. write for info. (*0-7011-2319-2*) Chatto & Windus.

Mokujiki: Thirteen Tanka. Mokujiki. Tr. by Dale Pendell & Kazuaki Tanahaski from JPN. 20p. 1988. 6.00 (*1-882623-07-X*) Exiled-Am Pr.

Mokume Gane in the Small Shop: The Complete Guide to Diffusion Welded Mokume. Steve Midgett. LC 96-83701. (Illus.). 128p. (Orig.). Date not set. pap. 16.95 (*0-9651650-8-6*) Earthshine Pr.

Moku'ula: Maui's Sacred Island. P. Christiaan Klieger. LC 98-31620. 124p. 1998. 29.95 (*1-58178-002-8*) Bishop Mus.

Mola: Cuna Life, Stories, & Art. Maricel E. Presilla. LC 95-46397. (Illus.). 32p. (YA). (gr. 7 up). 1995. 16.95 (*0-8050-3801-9*, B Martin BYR) H Holt & Co.

Mola Design Book. 5th ed. Caren Caraway. (International Design Library). (Illus.). 48p. 1981. pap. 6.95 (*0-916144-71-2*, Naturencyclop) Stemmer Hse.

Mola Designs. Frederick W. Shaffer. (Illus.). 48p. 1982. pap. 4.95 (*0-486-24289-7*) Dover.

Molar Mass Determination by Freezing Point Depression in T-Butyl Alcohol. S. R. Johnson & Marcia L. Gillette. Ed. by H. Anthony Neidig. (Modular Laboratory Program in Chemistry Ser.). 16p. (C). 1988. pap. text 1.50 (*0-87540-344-1*, PROP 344-1) Chem Educ Res.

*__Molar Mass of a Gas.__ 5th ed. James M. Postma et al. 2000. pap. text, lab manual ed. 1.95 (*0-7167-9421-7*) W H Freeman.

*__Molar Volume of Dioxygen & Other Gases.__ 5th ed. James M. Postma et al. 2000. pap. text, lab manual ed. 1.95 (*0-7167-9420-9*) W H Freeman.

Molar Volume of Oxygen. Date not set. 1.50 (*0-7167-9135-8*) W H Freeman.

Molas! Patterns, Techniques, & Projects for Colorful Applique. Kate Mathews. LC 97-31249. (Illus.). 128p. 1998. 24.95 (*1-57990-020-8*, Pub. by Lark Books) Random.

Molasses Cookies. Janet Kaderli. LC 98-39607. (Illus.). 64p. (J). (gr. 4 up). 1988. 14.95 (*1-885777-05-1*) Hendrick-Long.

*__Molasses Man.__ Kathy May. LC 98-21223. (Illus.). 32p. (J). (ps-3). 2000. 16.95 (*0-8234-1438-8*) Holiday.

Molchalivaia Lubov: Collection of Stories. Eugenia Dimer. 1980. 5.00 (*0-685-44305-1*) RWCPH.

Molchalivyi Pilot. Lev Khalif. LC 83-60971. (RUS.). 171p. (Orig.). 1985. pap. 12.50 (*0-89830-070-3*) Russica Pubs.

Molchanie: The Silence of God. Catherine D. Doherty. 100p. 1991. 9.95 (*0-921440-28-6*) Madonna Hse.

*__Mold: Understanding the Problem & Recovering Safely.__ Michael Trinkley. (Illus.). 12p. 1998. pap. 2.00 (*1-58317-044-8*) Chicora Found.

Mold & Core Coatings Manual. 176p. 1982. pap. 44.00 (*0-87433-064-5*, GM8202) Am Foundrymen.

Mold & Core Test Handbook. 2nd ed. 450p. 1989. ring bd. 120.00 (*0-87433-065-3*, GM8901) Am Foundrymen.

Mold Components & Their Fabrication - Student's Manual: Working with the Mold, Module 2, Lesson 1. (Illus.). 1997. pap., student ed. write for info. (*1-58677-016-0*) Polymer Train.

Mold Compound. TEEX Staff. (Illus.). vi, 92p. 1997. spiral bd. 79.95 (*1-58257-014-0*, 8148B) TX Eng Extsn Servs.

Mold Design & Moldmaking for Plastics Products. rev. ed. Ed. by George Epstein & Seymour Schwartz. 302p. (C). 1990. reprint ed. pap. 56.00 (*0-938648-21-7*) T-C Pr CA.

Mold Design I: For Plastic Injection. Edward Allyn. (Illus.). 69p. (C). 1987. student ed. 15.00 (*0-9619068-6-3*) Allyn Air.

Mold Engineering. Herbert Rees. LC 95-2590. 644p. 1995. 129.00 (*1-56990-131-7*) Hanser-Gardner.

Mold Makers & Designers: The Future of the Plastics Industry, Amway Grand Plaza Hotel, Grand Rapids, Michigan, November 8-9, 1983. Society of Plastics Engineers Staff. LC TP1150.S63. 102p. pap. 31.70 (*0-608-13381-7*, 202251200027) Bks Demand.

Mold Making, Casting & Patina. Bruner F. Barrie. LC 91-92469. 175p. 1992. pap. text 20.00 (*0-9631867-0-1*) A B F & S.

Mold Making for Ceramics. Donald E. Frith. 240p. 1999. pap. 34.95 (*0-87341-692-9*) Krause Pubns.

Mold Making for Plastics Process. Stoecker. 1985. 85.00 (*0-02-949670-5*) Free Pr.

Mold Making for the Original Doll: The BluFrogg Method. Ralph Gonzales & Mary Gonzales. (Illus.). 192p. (C). 1994. pap. text 25.00 (*1-886204-06-3*) Pollywogg Pubns.

Mold-Making Handbook: For the Plastics Engineer. 2nd ed. Klaus Stoeckhert & Gunther Menning. LC 98-31724. 1998. 148.00 (*1-56990-261-5*) Hanser-Gardner.

Mold Making Today & Tomorrow: A Vision Toward the Future, October 26-27, 1989. Society of Plastics Engineers Staff. LC TP1150.M646. (Illus.). 181p. reprint ed. pap. 56.20 (*0-8357-3625-3*, 203632600003) Bks Demand.

Mold Operation for Quality & Productivity. LC 91-75561. 236p. 1991. 20.00 (*0-932897-67-3*) Iron & Steel.

Mold Release Agents. Business Communications Co., Inc. Staff. 133p. 1990. 2450.00 (*0-89336-777-X*, C125) BCC.

Mold Shrinkage & Warpage Handbook. Clive Maier. LC 99-63216. 400p. 1999. 285.00 (*1-884207-72-3*) William Andrew.

Mold Tryouts & Startups: A Pocket Guide to Improving Productivity in Injection Molding. William J. Tobin. (Illus.). 50p. (Orig.). 1992. pap. 3.50 (*0-936994-08-8*) W J T Assocs.

Mold Types - Student's Manual: Working with the Mold, Module Two, Lesson 5. (Illus.). 1997. pap., student ed. write for info. (*1-58677-020-9*) Polymer Train.

Moldau & Other Works for Orchestras. Bedrich Smetana. 256p. 1996. pap. 14.95 (*0-486-29252-5*) Dover.

Moldavian Art, 14th-19th Centuries. P. Balanshi & V. Druk. (Illus.). 184p. (C). 1985. text 195.00 (*0-7855-5813-6*, Pub. by Collets) St Mut.

Moldeamiento de Inyeccion Basico & Problemas Basico de Disparar, 2 vols., Set. William J. Tobin. Tr. by Martha Leguizamon & Elizabeth Sharon. Orig. Title: Basic Injection Molding & Basic Trouble Shooting. (SPA., Illus.). 128p. 1992. reprint ed. pap. 33.50 (*0-938648-12-8*) T-C Pr CA.

Molded by the Cross. rev. ed. J. C. Metcalfe. LC 97-185259. Orig. Title: In the Mould of the Cross. 144p. 1997. mass mkt. 5.99 (*0-87508-711-6*, 711) Chr Lit.

Molded-Case Circuit-Breakers & Circuit Breaker Enclosures, UL 489. 8th ed. (C). 1991. pap. text 330.00 (*1-55989-151-3*) Underwrtrs Labs.

Molded-Case Circuit Breakers, Molded-Case Switches, & Circuit-Breaker Enclosures, UL 489. 9th ed. Underwriters Laboratories Staff. (C). 1996. pap. text 330.00 (*0-7629-0091-1*) Underwrtrs Labs.

Molded-Case Switches, UL 1087. 2nd ed. (C). 1993. pap. text 290.00 (*1-55989-494-6*) Underwrtrs Labs.

Molded Image Changing Woman: Navajo Views on the Human Body & Personhood. Schwarz. LC 96-45816. 320p. 1997. pap. 21.95 (*0-8165-1627-8*) U of Ariz Pr.

Molded in the Image of Changing Woman: Navajo Views on the Human Body & Personhood. Maureen Schwarz. LC 96-45816. 320p. 1997. text 50.00 (*0-8165-1602-2*) U of Ariz Pr.

Molded Thermosets: A Handbook for Plastics Engineers, Molders, & Designers. Ralph E. Wright. 213p. 1991. 69.50 (*1-56990-112-0*) Hanser-Gardner.

Molder of Dreams, 1. Guy R. Doud. 263p. (Orig.). 1999. mass mkt. 5.99 (*1-56179-712-X*) Focus Family.

Moldes de Inyeccion Para Plasticos. Hans Gastrow. 250p. 1992. pap. write for info. (*1-56990-174-0*) Hanser-Gardner.

Molding a Legacy: A Centennial History of the Akron Porcelain & Plastics Company. Stephen H. Paschen. (Illus.). 73p. (Orig.). 1989. pap. 6.95 (*0-9621895-3-7*) Summit Cty Hist Soc.

Molding Japanese Minds: The State in Everyday Life. Sheldon Garon. 332p. 1997. pap. text 15.95 (*0-691-00191-X*, Pub. by Princeton U Pr) Cal Prin Full Svc.

Molding Japanese Minds: The State in Everyday Life. Sheldon Garon. LC 96-33488. 325p. 1997. 27.95 (*0-691-04488-0*, Pub. by Princeton U Pr) Cal Prin Full Svc.

Molding Materials. Keith Good. LC 99-36225. (Design Challenge Ser.). 32p. (J). (gr. 4-6). 1999. write for info. (*0-8225-3568-8*, Lerner Publctns) Lerner Pub.

Molding Materials & Process Troubleshooting - Student's Manual: Module Four, Lessons 1-6. (Illus.). 1997. pap., student ed. write for info. (*1-58677-033-0*) Polymer Train.

Molding Process Student's Manual: Module One, Lessons 1-6. (Illus.). 1997. pap., student ed. write for info. (*1-58677-006-3*) Polymer Train.

Molding Strategies & Process Control - Student's Manual: Working with the Machine, Module Three, Lesson 5. (Illus.). 1997. pap., student ed. write for info. (*1-58677-029-2*) Polymer Train.

*__Molding Techniques: Ceramics Class.__ Joaquim Chavarria. (Illus.). 64p. 2000. write for info. (*0-8230-0595-X*) Watsn-Guptill.

Molding the Future: A Look at the Next Century in Tooling & Design; March 3-5, 1992 at the Ramada O'Hare, Rosemont, IL. Society of Plastics Engineers Staff. LC TP1180.. 203p. reprint ed. pap. 63.00 (*0-7837-2154-4*, 204244000004) Bks Demand.

Molding the Good Citizen: The Politics of High School History Texts. Robert Lerner et al. LC 94-32922. 200p. 1995. 59.95 (*0-275-94919-2*, Praeger Pubs); pap. 20.95 (*0-275-95100-6*) Greenwood.

Molding the Hearts & Minds: Education, Communications, & Social Change in Latin America. Ed. by John A. Britton. LC 93-41937. (Jaguar Books on Latin America: No. 4). 275p. 1994. 55.00 (*0-8420-2489-1*) Scholarly Res Inc.

Molding the Hearts & Minds: Education, Communications, & Social Change in Latin America, Vol. 4. Ed. by John A. Britton. LC 93-41937. (Jaguar Books on Latin America: No. 4). 275p. 1994. pap. 18.95 (*0-8420-2490-5*) Scholarly Res Inc.

Molding the Medium: The Chinese Communist Party & the Liberation Daily. Patricia Stranahan. LC 90-8385. (Studies on Contemporary China). 184p. (C). (gr. 13). 1990. text 70.95 (*0-87332-662-8*, East Gate Bk) M E Sharpe.

Moldova Business Law Handbook, '98. Russian Information & Business Center, Inc. Staff. (World Business Law Library, '98). (Illus.). 1998. pap. 99.00 (*1-57751-694-X*) Intl Business Pubns.

Moldmaking & Die Cast Dies for Metalworking Trainees. rev. ed. John Kluz. 306p. (Orig.). 1982. teacher ed. 7.95 (*0-910399-26-3*, 5008); pap. 21.95 (*0-910399-25-5*, 5013) Natl Tool & Mach.

Moldova. Ed. by Lerner Geography Department Staff. (Then & Now Ser.). (Illus.). 64p. (YA). (gr. 6-9). 1992. lib. bdg. 23.93 (*0-8225-2809-6*, Lerner Publctns) Lerner Pub.

*Moldova, 6 vols., Set. Patricia Sheehan. LC 99-53433. (Cultures of the World Ser.: Vol. 20). 128p. (YA). (gr. 4-7). 2000. lib. bdg. 35.64 (0-7614-0997-1, Benchmark NY) Marshall Cavendish.

*Moldova: A Country Study Guide. Global Investment & Business Center, Inc. Staff. (World Country Study Guides Library: Vol. 114). (Illus.). 350p. 2000. pap. 59.00 (0-7397-2412-6) Intl Business Pubns.

Moldova: Economic Review. International Monetary Fund Staff. 91p. 1992. pap. 10.00 (1-55775-255-9) Intl Monetary.

Moldova: Moving to a Market Economy. (Country Study Ser.). 130p. 1994. pap. 22.00 (0-8213-2776-3, 12776) World Bank.

*Moldova: Poverty Assessment. LC 99-59729. (Country Study Ser.). 85p. 1999. 22.00 (0-8213-4477-3, 14477) World Bank.

Moldova - A Country Study Guide: Basic Information for Research & Pleasure. Global Investment Center, USA Staff. (World Country Study Guide Library: Vol. 114). (Illus.). 350p. 1999. pap. 59.00 (0-7397-1511-9) Intl Business Pubns.

Moldova Business & Investment Opportunities Yearbook-98: Business, Investment, Export-Import. Contrib. by Russian Information & Business Center, Inc. Staff. (Business & Investment Opportunity Library-98). (Illus.). 350p. 1998. pap. 99.00 (1-57751-948-5) Intl Business Pubns.

M

*Moldova Business Intelligence Report, 190 vols. Global Investment & Business Center, Inc. Staff. (World Business Intelligence Library: Vol. 114). (Illus.). 350p. 2000. pap. 99.95 (0-7397-2612-9) Intl Business Pubns.

*Moldova Business Law Handbook, 190 vols. Global Investment & Business Center, Inc. Staff. (Global Business Law Handbooks Library: Vol. 114). (Illus.). 350p. 2000. pap. 99.95 (0-7397-2012-0) Intl Business Pubns.

Moldova Business Law Handbook: Basic Export-Import, Investment & Business Laws. Russian Information & Business Center, Inc. Staff. (NIS Business Law Library). (Illus.). 200p. 1997. pap. 99.00 (1-57751-293-6) Intl Business Pubns.

*Moldova Business Opportunity Yearbook. Global Investment & Business Center, Inc. Staff. (Global Business Opportunity Yearbooks Library: Vol. 114). (Illus.). 2000. pap. 99.95 (0-7397-2212-3) Intl Business Pubns.

*Moldova Business Opportunity Yearbook: Export-Import, Investment & Business Opportunities. International Business Publications, U. S. A. Staff & Global Investment Center, U. S. A. Staff. (Global Business Opportunity Yearbooks Library: Vol. 114). (Illus.). 350p. 1999. pap. 99.95 (0-7397-1312-4) Intl Business Pubns.

*Moldova Country Review 2000. Robert C. Kelly et al. (Illus.). 60p. 1999. pap. 39.95 (1-58310-538-7) CountryWatch.

*Moldova Export-Import & Business Directory: Ultimate Directory for Conducting Export-Import Operations in the Country, Largest Exporters & Importers, Strategic Government & Business Contacts, Selected Export-Import Regulations & More. International Business Publications, USA Staff & Global Investment Center, USA Staff. (World Export-Import & Business Library: 22). (Illus.). 250p. 2000. pap. 99.95 (0-7397-3397-4) Intl Business Pubns.

*Moldova Foreign Policy & Government Guide. Contrib. by Global Investment & Business Center, Inc. Staff. (World Foreign Policy & Government Library: Vol. 110). (Illus.). 350p. 1999. pap. 99.00 (0-7397-3608-6) Intl Business Pubns.

*Moldova Foreign Policy & Government Guide. Global Investment & Business Center, Inc. Staff. (World Foreign Policy & Government Library: Vol. 110). (Illus.). 350p. 2000. pap. 99.95 (0-7397-3812-7) Intl Business Pubns.

*Moldova Government & business Contacts Handbook: Strategic Governemtn & business Contacts for Conducting Successful Business, Export-Import & Investment Activity, 110. International Business Publications, USA Staff & Global Investment Center, USA Staff. (World Export-Import & Business Library: 19). 250p. 2000. pap. 99.95 (0-7397-6057-2) Intl Business Pubns.

*Moldova Industrial & Business Directory. Global Investment & Business Center, Inc. Staff. (NIS Industrial & Business Directories Ser.: Vol. 11). (Illus.). 350p. 1999. pap. 99.00 (0-7397-0710-8) Intl Business Pubns.

*Moldova Investment & Business Guide. Global Investment & Business Center, Inc. Staff. (Global Investment & Business Guide Library: Vol. 114). (Illus.). 2000. pap. 99.95 (0-7397-1812-6) Intl Business Pubns.

*Moldova Investment & Business Guide: Export-Import, Investment & Business Opportunities. International Business Publications, USA Staff & Global Investment Center, USA Staff. (World Investment & Business Guide Library-99: Vol. 114). (Illus.). 350p. 1999. pap. 99.95 (0-7397-0309-9) Intl Business Pubns.

Moldova Investment & Business Guide Vol. 7: Economy, Export-Import, Business & Investment Climate, Business Contacts. Russian Information & Business Center, Inc. Staff. (Russia, NIS & Emerging Markets Investment & Business Library). (Illus.). 350p. 1998. pap. 99.00 (1-57751-571-4) Intl Business Pubns.

*Moldovans: Romania, Russia & the Politics of Culture. Charles King. LC 99-41906. (Publication Series: Vol. 471). (Illus.). 294p. 2000. 39.95 (0-8179-9791-1); pap. 24.95 (0-8179-9792-X) Hoover Inst Pr.

Molds & Man: An Introduction to the Fungi. 3rd ed. Clyde M. Christensen. LC 65-17718. 292p. reprint ed. pap. 90.60 (0-608-18632-5, 205585000039) Bks Demand.

Molds, Molecules, & Metazoe: Growing Points in Evolutionary Biology. Ed. by Peter Grant & Henry S. Horn. (Illus.). 200p. 1992. text 39.50 (0-691-08768-7, Pub. by Princeton U Pr) Cal Prin Full Svc.

Molds, Mushrooms, & Mycotoxins. Clyde M. Christensen. LC 74-21808. 276p. 1975. reprint ed. pap. 85.60 (0-7837-2971-5, 205748300006) Bks Demand.

Mole. R. David Stone. (Natural History Ser.: No. 61). (Illus.). 24p. 1989. pap. 5.25 (0-7478-0171-1, Pub. by Shire Pubns) Parkwest Pubns.

Mole: The Businessman's Guide to the Government. Eurofi Staff. 275p. (C). 1988. 395.00 (0-907304-22-2, Pub. by Eurofi) St Mut.

Mole: The True Story of the First Russian Spy to Become an American Counterspy. William Hood. (Intelligence & National Security Library). 288p. 1993. pap. 15.95 (0-02-881079-1) Brasseys.

Mole & His New Red Hat. (J). (gr. 3-7). 1974. 9.50 (0-686-23317-4) Rochester Folk Art.

Mole & Shrew All Year Through. Jackie F. Koller. LC 97-2133. (Illus.). 80p. 1997. pap. 3.99 (0-679-88666-4, Pub. by Random Bks Yng Read) Random.

Mole & Shrew All Year Through. Jackie F. Koller. LC 97-2133. (Illus.). 80p. (gr. 1-4). 1997. lib. bdg. 11.99 (0-679-98666-9, Pub. by Random Bks Yng Read) Random.

*Mole & Shrew Are Two. Jackie F. Koller. (Stepping Stone Bks.). (Illus.). (J). 2000. pap. 3.99 (0-375-80690-3) Random.

*Mole & Shrew Are Two. Jackie French Koller. LC 00-26024. (Illus.). (J). 2000. 11.99 (0-375-90690-8) Random.

*Mole & Shrew Have Jobs. Jackie French Koller. (J). 2001. 11.99 (0-375-90691-6) Random.

*Mole & Shrew Have Jobs to Do. Jackie French Koller. (J). 2001. mass mkt. 3.99 (0-375-80691-1, Pub. by Random Bks Yng Read) Random.

Mole & the Owl: A Romantic Fable about Braving the Wide World for Love. Charles Duffie. LC 98-140555. (Illus.). 104p. 1998. 18.95 (1-57174-082-1) Hampton Roads Pub Co.

*Mole Hole: A Guide for Desperate Chemistry Students on How to Do Clever Chemical Calculations the Creature-Chem Way! Marianne Flectcher. 165p. (YA). (gr. 11-13). 2000. 18.95 (0-7021-5276-5) Juta & Co.

Mole in a Hole. R.G. Geiman. LC 98-53770. (Step into Reading Ser.: A Step 1 Book). (Illus.). 32p. (J). (gr. k-3). 2000. pap. 3.99 (0-679-89037-8, Pub. by Random Bks Yng Read); lib. bdg. 11.99 (0-679-99037-2, Pub. by Random Bks Yng Read) Random.

Mole Music. David McPhail. LC 98-21318. (Illus.). 40p. (J). (gr. k-5). 1999. 15.95 (0-8050-2819-6) H Holt & Co.

Mole People: Life in the Tunnels Beneath New York City. Jennifer Toth. LC 93-23912. (Illus.). 278p. 1995. pap. 13.95 (1-55652-241-X) Chicago Review.

*Mole Sisters & the Busy Bees. Roslyn Schwartz. (Illus.). 32p. (J). (ps). 2000. lib. bdg. 12.95 (1-55037-663-2, Pub. by Annick Pr); per. 4.95 (1-55037-662-4, Pub. by Annick Pr) Firefly Bks Ltd.

Mole Sisters & the Piece of Moss. Roslyn Schwartz. (Illus.). 32p. (J). (ps-k). 1999. pap. 4.95 (1-55037-582-2, Pub. by Annick Pr) Firefly Bks Ltd.

*Mole Sisters & the Piece of Moss. Roslyn Schwartz. (Illus.). 32p. (J). (ps-k). 1999. text 14.95 (1-55037-583-0, Pub. by Annick Pr) Firefly Bks Ltd.

Mole Sisters & the Rainy Day. Roslyn Schwartz. (Illus.). 32p. (J). 1999. pap. 4.95 (1-55037-610-1, Pub. by Annick Pr) Firefly Bks Ltd.

*Mole Sisters & the Rainy Day. Roslyn Schwartz. (Illus.). 32p. (J). (ps-k). 1999. text 14.95 (1-55037-611-X, Pub. by Annick Pr) Firefly Bks Ltd.

*Mole Sisters & the Wavy Wheat. Roslyn Schwartz. (Illus.). 32p. (J). (ps). 2000. lib. bdg. 12.95 (1-55037-661-6, Pub. by Annick Pr); per. 4.95 (1-55037-660-8, Pub. by Annick Pr) Firefly Bks Ltd.

Molech: A God of Human Sacrifice in the Old Testament. John Day. (University of Cambridge Oriental Publications: No. 41). 125p. (C). 1990. text 49.95 (0-521-36474-4) Cambridge U Pr.

Molecual Modelling. Andrew R. Leach. 585p. (C). 1996. pap. 69.00 (0-582-23933-8) Addison-Wesley.

Molecuar Constants Mostly from Infared Spectroscopy: Linear Triatomic Molecules. G. Guelachvili. (Group II Ser.: Vol. 20). 415p. 1997. 2090.00 (3-540-58852-3) Spr-Verlag.

Molecular: Based Study of Fluids. Ed. by J. M. Haile & G. Ali Mansoori. LC 82-24373. (Advances in Chemistry Ser.: No. 204). 524p. 1983. lib. bdg. 76.95 (0-8412-0720-8) Am Chemical.

Molecular - Cellular Mechanisms of Immunomodulatory Drugs. Etienne C. Dupont & Cathy Walker. 1993. write for info. (0-8493-4809-9, 4809, CRC Reprint) Franklin.

Molecular Acoustics see Atomic & Molecular Physics: Group II

Molecular Acoustics. Andrew J. Matheson. LC 73-147401. (Illus.). 308p. reprint ed. pap. 95.50 (0-608-17551-X, 203053100069) Bks Demand.

Molecular Action of Insecticides on Ion Channels. Ed. by J. Marshall Clark. LC 95-6612. (ACS Symposium Ser.: No. 591). (Illus.). 356p. 1995. text 110.00 (0-8412-3165-6, Pub. by Am Chemical) OUP.

Molecular Analysis of a Chromosomal Translocation Breakpoint on the Short Arm of Chromosome 12. Jeroen Aerssens. (Acta Biomedica Lovaniensia Ser.: No. 130). (Illus.). 111p. (Orig.). 1996. pap. 39.50 (90-6186-743-6, Pub. by Leuven Univ) Coronet Bks.

*Molecular Analysis of Cancer. Ed. by Jacqueline Boultwood & Carrie Fidler. 380p. 2000. 89.50 (0-89603-622-7) Humana.

Molecular & Applied Aspects of Oxidative Drug Metabolizing Enzymes. Ed. by Emel Arinc et al. LC 98-44331. (NATO ASI Ser.: 303). (Illus.). 302p. (C). 1999. text 127.50 (0-306-46048-3) Plenum.

Molecular & Biochemical Aspects of Progesterone Function. Judith Ramaley et al. 173p. 1972. text 29.75 (0-8290-2380-1) Irvington.

Molecular & Biological Physics of Living Systems. Ed. by R. K. Mishra. (C). 1990. text 166.50 (0-7923-0470-5) Kluwer Academic.

Molecular & Biomolecular Electronics: Developed from a Symposium Sponsored by the Division of Biochemical Technology of the American Chemical Society at the 4th Annual Chemical Congress of North America (202nd National Meeting of the American Chemical Society), New York, NY, 8/25-8/30, 1991. Chemical Congress of North America Staff. Ed. by Robert R. Birge. LC 94-28455. (Advances in Chemistry Ser.: No. 240). (Illus.). 608p. 1994. text 149.00 (0-8412-2698-9, Pub. by Am Chemical) OUP.

Molecular & Cell Biological Aspects of Gastoenteropancreatic Neuroendocrine Tumor Disease. Ed. by Bertram Wiedenmann. LC 94-27923. 1994. 145.00 (0-89766-897-9) NY Acad Sci.

Molecular & Cell Biological Aspects of Gastoenteropancreatic Neuroendocrine Tumor Disease. Ed. by Bertram Wiedenmann et al. LC 94-27923. (Annals Ser.: Vol. 733). (Illus.). 535p. 1994. pap. 145.00 (0-89766-898-7) NY Acad Sci.

Molecular & Cell Biology. 2nd ed. Holly Ahern. 112p. (C). 1999. spiral bd. 104.25 (0-697-13640-X, WCB McGr Hill) McGrw-H Hghr Educ.

Molecular & Cell Biology of Liver Fibrogenesis: Proceedings of the International Falk Symposium Held in Marburg, Germany, 22-23 January 1992. Ed. by A. M. Gressner & G. Ramadori. LC 92-23629. 576p. 1992. text 268.50 (0-7923-8980-8) Kluwer Academic.

Molecular & Cell Biology of the Liver. Ed. by Albert V. LeBouton. 560p. 1993. lib. bdg. 229.00 (0-8493-8891-0, QP185) CRC Pr.

Molecular & Cell Biology of the Plant Cell Cycle: Proceedings of a Meeting Held at Lancaster University, 9-10 April 1992. Ed. by John Ormrod & Dennis Francis. LC 92-36385. 236p. (C). 1993. text 169.50 (0-7923-1767-X) Kluwer Academic.

Molecular & Cell Biology of Type 2 Diabetes & Its Complications: 5th International Diabetes Conference, Turin, April 10 - 12, 1997. Ed. by Francesco Belfiore et al. LC 98-10210. (Frontiers in Diabetes Ser.: Vol. 14). (Illus.). x, 260p. 1998. 97.50 (3-8055-6644-1) S Karger.

Molecular & Cell Biology of Yeasts. Walton & Yarranton. 1989. text 139.95 (0-442-20711-5) Chapman & Hall.

Molecular & Cellular Approaches to Neural Development. Ed. by W. Maxwell Cowan et al. LC 96-38648. (Illus.). 576p. 1998. text 68.50 (0-19-511166-4) OUP.

Molecular & Cellular Approaches to the Treatment of Neurological Disease. Ed. by Stephen G. Waxman. LC 92-49791. (Association for Research in Nervous & Mental Disease Research Publications: No. 71). (Illus.). 412p. 1993. reprint ed. pap. 127.80 (0-608-05800-9, 205976500007) Bks Demand.

Molecular & Cellular Aspects of Allergy: Proceedings of the Collegium Internationale Allergologicum Symposium, 10th, Copenhagen, 1974. Collegium Internationale Allergologicum Symposium. Ed. by B. Diamant et al. (International Archives of Allergy & Applied Immunology Ser.: Vol. 49, No. 1-2). (Illus.). 250p. 1975. pap. 88.75 (3-8055-2166-9) S Karger.

Molecular & Cellular Aspects of Calcium in Plant Development. Ed. by A. J. Trewavas. LC 85-31169. (NATO ASI Series A, Life Sciences: Vol. 104). 466p. 1986. 110.00 (0-306-42228-X, Plenum Trade) Perseus Pubng.

Molecular & Cellular Aspects of Carcinogen Screening Tests. Ed. by R. Montesano et al. (IARC Scientific Publications: No. 27). (Illus.). 372p. 1986. 43.00 (0-19-723027-X) OUP.

Molecular & Cellular Aspects of Microbial Evolution. M. J. Carlile et al. LC 80-42172. (Society for General Microbiology Symposium Ser.: No. 32). (Illus.). 378p. 1981. text 110.00 (0-521-24108-1) Cambridge U Pr.

Molecular & Cellular Aspects of Periimplanation Processes. S. K. Dey. LC 95-21136. (Serono Symposia Ser.). (Illus.). 384p. 1995. 142.00 (0-387-94569-5) Spr-Verlag.

Molecular & Cellular Aspects of Plant Reproduction. Ed. by Rod J. Scott & Anthony D. Stead. (Society for Experimental Biology Seminar Ser.: No. 55). (Illus.). 327p. (C). 1995. text 90.00 (0-521-45525-1) Cambridge U Pr.

Molecular & Cellular Aspects of Reproduction. Ed. by Dharam S. Dhindsa & Om P. Bahl. LC 86-20533. (Advances in Experimental Medicine & Biology Ser.: Vol. 205). 392p. 1986. 85.00 (0-306-42403-7, Plenum Trade) Perseus Pubng.

Molecular & Cellular Aspects of the Drug Addiction. Ed. by A. Goldstein. (Illus.). 255p. 1989. 80.00 (0-387-96827-X) Spr-Verlag.

Molecular & Cellular Aspects of Vascular Smooth Muscle in Health & Disease: Proceedings - Journal: Blood Vessels, Vol. 15, Nos. 1-3. U. S. - Japan Cooperative Symposium Staff. Ed. by D. F. Bohr & F. Takenha. (Illus.). 1978. 75.75 (3-8055-2857-4) S Karger.

Molecular & Cellular Basis of Inflammation. Charles N. Serhan & Peter A. Ward. (Current Inflammation Research Ser.). 352p. 1998. 125.00 (0-89603-595-6) Humana.

Molecular & Cellular Basis of Social Behavior in Vertebrates. Ed. by J. Balthazart. (Advances in Comparative & Environmental Physiology Ser.: Vol. 3). (Illus.). 380p. 1989. 152.95 (0-387-19429-0) Spr-Verlag.

Molecular & Cellular Basis of Visual Acuity. Ed. by S. R. Hilfer & J. B. Sheffield. (Cell & Developmental Biology of the Eye Ser.). (Illus.). 210p. 1984. 84.00 (0-387-90964-8) Spr-Verlag.

Molecular & Cellular Biochemistry see Lipid Metabolism in Normoxic & Ischemic Heart

Molecular & Cellular Biology. Stephen L. Wolfe. 1145p. (C). 1993. pap. 69.75 (0-534-12408-9) Wadsworth Pub.

Molecular & Cellular Biology. 2nd ed. Wolfe. (Biology Ser.). (C). 2002. mass mkt. 68.95 (0-534-51398-0) Wadsworth Pub.

Molecular & Cellular Biology. 3rd ed. Eversman & Johnson. 96p. (C). 1997. spiral bd. 15.00 (0-7872-4240-3) Kendall-Hunt.

*Molecular & Cellular Biology: Laboratory Observations Biology 102. 4th ed. Sharon Eversman & Carol Johnson. 84p. (C). 1999. spiral bd. 17.95 (0-7872-6321-4, 41632101) Kendall-Hunt.

Molecular & Cellular Biology of Fertilization. Ed. by Jerry L. Hedrick. LC 86-25380. (Advances in Experimental Medicine & Biology Ser.: Vol. 207). 472p. 1986. 95.00 (0-306-42478-9, Plenum Trade) Perseus Pubng.

Molecular & Cellular Biology of Insulin-Like Growth Factors. Ed. by Mohan K. Raizada & D. LeRoith. (Illus.). 524p. 1989. 120.00 (0-306-43254-4, Plenum Trade) Perseus Pubng.

Molecular & Cellular Biology of Multidrug Resistance in Tumor Cells. I. B. Roninson. (Illus.). 424p. (C). 1990. text 120.00 (0-306-43547-0, Kluwer Plenum) Kluwer Academic.

Molecular & Cellular Biology of Prostate Cancer. Ed. by James P. Karr et al. (Advances in Experimental Medicine & Biology Ser.). (Illus.). 396p. (C). 1991. text 144.00 (0-306-43884-4, 305, Kluwer Plenum) Kluwer Academic.

Molecular & Cellular Biology of the Allergic Response. Ed. by Arnold I. Levinson & Yvonne Paterson. LC 94-4449. (Clinical Allergy & Immunology Ser.: Vol. 3). (Illus.). 473p. 1994. text 185.00 (0-8247-8876-1) Dekker.

Molecular & Cellular Biology of the Potato. 2nd ed. Ed. by W. Belknap et al. LC 97-179020. (Biotechnology in Agriculture Ser.: No. 12). (Illus.). 288p. 1994. text 105.00 (0-85198-900-4) OUP.

Molecular & Cellular Biology of Wound Repair. Ed. by R. A. Clark & P. M. Henson. LC 87-37683. (Illus.). 620p. 1988. 125.00 (0-306-42716-8, Plenum Trade) Perseus Pubng.

Molecular & Cellular Biology of Wound Repair. 2nd ed. Ed. by Richard A. Clark. (Illus.). 600p. (C). 1996. text 135.00 (0-306-45159-X, Kluwer Plenum) Kluwer Academic.

Molecular & Cellular Effects of Nutrition on Disease Process. Grant M. Pierce. LC 98-3954. (Developments in Molecular & Cellular Biochemistry Ser.). 237p. 1998. write for info. (0-7923-8171-8) Kluwer Academic.

*Molecular & Cellular Endocrine Pathology. Ed. by Lucia Stefaneanu et al. (An Arnold Publication). (Illus.). 496p. 2000. text 195.00 (0-340-74197-X) E A.

Molecular & Cellular Endocrinology of the Testis. G. Verhoeven & U. F. Habenicht. (Ernst Schering Research Foundation Workshop Ser.). 1994. 62.95 (3-540-58337-8) Spr-Verlag.

Molecular & Cellular Endocrinology of the Testis. G. Verhoeven & U. F. Habenicht. LC 94-35138. (Ernst Schering Research Foundation Workshop Ser.: Supp. 1). (Illus.). xiv, 298p. 1994. text 56.00 (0-387-58337-8) Spr-Verlag.

*Molecular & Cellular Gerontology. Olivier Toussaint. LC 00-34861. 2000. write for info. (1-57331-272-X) NY Acad Sci.

*Molecular & Cellular Glycobiology. Ed. by Minoru Fukuda & Ole Hindsgual. (Frontiers in Molecular Biology Ser.: 30). (Illus.). 272p. 2000. text 115.00 (0-19-963807-1); pap. text 55.00 (0-19-963806-3) OUP.

Molecular & Cellular Mechanisms of Anesthetics. Sheldon H. Roth & Keith W. Miller. LC 85-28274. (Illus.). 502p. (C). 1986. text 150.00 (0-306-42128-3, Kluwer Plenum) Kluwer Academic.

Molecular & Cellular Mechanisms of Cardiovascular Regulation. Ed. by M. Endoh et al. 464p. 1996. 236.00 (4-431-70180-X) Spr-Verlag.

Molecular & Cellular Mechanisms of H Transport. Ed. by Barry H. Hirst. LC 94-34255. (NATO ASI Series H: Cell Biology: Vol. 89). (Illus.). x, 494p. 1994. 262.95 (3-540-58497-8) Spr-Verlag.

Molecular & Cellular Mechanisms of Neuronal Plasticity: Basic & Clinical Implications. Ed. by Y. H. Ehrlich. LC 98-31763. (Advances in Experimental Medicine & Biology Ser.: 466). (Illus.). 235p. (C). 1999. text 125.00 (0-306-46040-8, Kluwer Plenum) Kluwer Academic.

Molecular & Cellular Mechanisms of Neurotransmitter Release. Ed. by Lennart Stjarne. (Advances in Second Messenger & Phosphoprotein Research Ser.: Vol. 29). 592p. 1994. text 125.00 (0-7817-0220-8) Lppncott W & W.

Molecular & Cellular Mechanisms of Toxicity. Ed. by Francesco De Matteis & Lewis L. Smith. LC 95-16810. 240p. 1995. boxed set 199.95 (0-8493-9229-2, 9229) CRC Pr.

Molecular & Cellular Methods in Developmental Toxicology. Ed. by George P. Daston. LC 96-14296. (Methods in Toxicology Ser.). 304p. 1996. spiral bd. 94.95 (0-8493-3342-3) CRC Pr.

Molecular & Cellular Pediatric Endocrinology. Stuart Handwerger. LC 98-50918. (Contemporary Endocrinology Ser.: Vol. 10). (Illus.). 328p. 1999. 125.00 (0-89603-406-2) Humana.

*Molecular & Cellular Physiology of Neurons. Gordon L. Fan. LC 98-44886. 1999. 65.00 (0-674-58155-5) HUP.

An Asterisk (*) at the beginning of an entry indicates that the title is appearing for the first time.

Molecular & Cellular Repair Processes Johns Hopkins Medical Journal Supplement, No. 1. Ed. by Roland F. Beers, Jr. et al. LC 78-184199. (Miles International Symposia on Molecular Biology Ser.). 287p. (C). reprint ed. 89.00 (*0-8357-9278-1*, 201568500095) Bks Demand.

Molecular & Cellular Targets for Anti Epileptic Drugs. Avanzini. 272p. 114.00 (*0-86196-554-X*, Pub. by J Libbey Med) Bks Intl VA.

Molecular & Cellular View of Protein Kinase CK2. Khalil Ahmed et al. LC 98-8321. (Developments in Molecular & Cellular Biochemistry Ser.). 16p. 1998. write for info. (*0-7923-8208-0*) Kluwer Academic.

Molecular & Clinical Advances in Anticancer Drug Resistance. Ed. by Robert F. Ozols. (Cancer Treatment & Research Ser.). 320p. (C). 1991. text 204.50 (*0-7923-1212-0*) Kluwer Academic.

Molecular & Clinical Advances in Pituitary Disorders - 11993: Proceedings of the 3rd International Pituitary Congress. Ed. by Shlomo Melmed. 400p. 1993. pap. 30.00 (*0-9637943-0-2*) Endocrine Res.

Molecular & Clinical Aspects of Bacterial Vaccine Development. Ed. by Dlawer A. Ala'Aldeen & Carlos E. Hormaeche. LC 94-43839. 376p. 1995. 285.00 (*0-471-95564-7*) Wiley.

Molecular & Clinical Implications for Allergy in the 21st Century. Ed. by A. L. Sheffer & S. J. Galli. (Journal Ser.: Vol. 107, No. 1-3, 1995). (Illus.). 474p. 1995. pap. 213.25 (*3-8055-6206-3*) S Karger.

Molecular & Developmental Biology of Cartilage. Benoit De Crombrugghe & New York Academy of Medicine Staff. LC 96-1721. (Annals of the New York Academy of Sciences Ser.). 367p. 1996. pap. 110.00 (*1-57331-011-5*) NY Acad Sci.

Molecular & Diagnostic Procedures in Mycoplasmology Vol. 1: Molecular Characterization. Ed. by Shimuel Razin & Joseph G. Tully. (Illus.). 483p. 1995. text 89.95 (*0-12-583805-0*) Acad Pr.

Molecular & Diagnostic Procedures in Mycoplasmology Vol. 2: Diagnostic Procedures. Ed. by Shimuel Razin & Joseph G. Tully. LC 95-4586. (Illus.). 466p. 1996. text 89.95 (*0-12-583806-9*) Acad Pr.

Molecular & Ecological Diversity of Bacterial Adhesion. Ed. by Madilyn M. Fletcher. LC 96-15427. (Series in Ecological & Applied Microbiology). 361p. 1996. 139.95 (*0-471-02185-7*) Wiley.

Molecular & Functional Aspects of Blood Group Antigens. Ed. by Leslie E. Silberstein. (Illus.). 245p. (C). 1995. text 50.00 (*1-56395-048-0*) Am Assn Blood.

Molecular & Functional Diversity of Ion Channels & Receptors. Ed. by Bernardo Rudy & Peter Seeburg. LC 99-13744. (Annals of the New York Academy of Sciences Ser.). 1998. pap. 140.00 (*1-57331-177-4*) NY Acad Sci.

Molecular & Functional Diversity of Ion Channels & Receptors. Ed. by Bernardo Rudy & Peter Seeburg. LC 99-13744. (Annals of the New York Academy of Sciences Ser.). 1999. 140.00 (*1-57331-176-6*) NY Acad Sci.

*__Molecular & Genetic Analysis of Human Traits.__ Gustavo Maroni. LC 00-23792. (Illus.). 320p. 2000. pap. 55.95 (*0-632-04369-5*) Blackwell Sci.

Molecular & Genetic Aspects of Nitrate Assimilation. Ed. by John L. Wray & James R. Kinghorn. (Illus.). 432p. 1989. 89.00 (*0-19-857696-X*) OUP.

Molecular & Genetic Aspects of Obesity. Ed. by George A. Bray & Donna H. Ryan. LC 95-35680. (Pennington Center Nutrition Ser.: Vol. 5). (Illus.). 712p. (C). 1996. text 95.00 (*0-8071-2025-1*) La State U Pr.

Molecular & Genetic Basis of Neurological Disease. 2nd ed. Roger N. Rosenberg et al. LC 96-47652. 1430p. 1996. text 368.00 (*0-7506-9668-0*) Buttrwrth-Heinemann.

Molecular & Genetic Basis of Neurological Disease. 2nd ed. Roger N. Rosenberg et al. Ed. by Gerald M. Fenichel. 328p. 1998. pap. text 47.50 (*0-7506-7043-6*) Buttrwrth-Heinemann.

Molecular & Genetic Characterization of Selected Loci of the A2M-System. C. Hilliker. No. 81. 169p. (Orig.). 1994. pap. 42.50 (*90-6186-606-5*, Pub. by Leuven Univ) Coronet Bks.

Molecular & Immune Mechanisms of Pathogenesis of Cutaneous Leishmaniasis. Felix J. Tapia et al. LC 96-9384. (Medical Intelligence Unit Ser.). 219p. 1996. 99.00 (*1-57059-353-1*) Landes Bioscience.

Molecular & Immunological Aspects of Parasitism. Ed. by Ching Chung Wang. LC 90-27340. (AAAS Miscellaneous Publications: No. 91-01S). (Illus.). 207p. reprint ed. pap. 64.20 (*0-7837-6748-X*, 204637600011) Bks Demand.

Molecular & Ionic Recognition with Imprinted Polymers, Vol. 703. Ed. by Richard A. Bartsch & Mizuo Maeda. LC 98-6979. (ACS Symposium Ser.: No. 703). (Illus.). 352p. 1998. text 110.00 (*0-8412-3574-0*) OUP.

Molecular & Ionic Signalling of Neutrophils. Maurice B. Hallett & Darren Lloyds. LC 97-20920. (Molecular Biology Intelligence Unit Ser.). 184p. 1997. text 99.00 (*1-57059-463-5*) Landes Bioscience.

Molecular & Laser Spectroscopy. Z. G. Wang & H. R. Xia. (Chemical Physics Ser.: Vol. 50). (Illus.). 288p. 1991. 86.95 (*0-387-50829-5*) Spr-Verlag.

Molecular & Microscale Heat Transfer. Ed. by Susumu Kotake & Chang-Lin Tien. 211p. 1994. 95.00 (*1-56700-017-7*) Begell Hse.

Molecular & Quantum Pharmacology. Ed. by Ernst Bergmann & Bernard Pullman. LC 74-83002. (Jerusalem Symposia on Quantum Chemistry & Biochemistry Ser.: No. 7). 522p. 1975. text 261.50 (*90-277-0525-9*) Kluwer Academic.

Molecular & Structural Biology of Hair, Vol. 642. Ed. by Kurt S. Stenn et al. 519p. 1992. 125.00 (*0-89766-691-7*) NY Acad Sci.

Molecular & Subcellular Cardiology: Effects of Structure & Function: Proceedings of the Ninth Goldberg Workshop Held in Haifa, Israel, December 4-8, 1994. Ed. by Samuel Sideman & Rafael Beyar. LC 95-25128. (Advances in Experimental Medicine & Biology Ser.: Vol. 382). (Illus.). 372p. 1995. 110.00 (*0-306-45123-9*, Kluwer Plenum) Kluwer Academic.

Molecular & Supramolecular Chemistry of Carbohydratas: Chemical Introduction to the Glycosciences. Serge David. Tr. by Rosemary G. Beau. LC 97-18604. (Illus.). 330p. 1998. text 95.00 (*0-19-850047-5*) OUP.

Molecular & Supramolecular Chemistry of Carbohydrates: A Chemical Introduction to the Glycosciences. Serge David. Tr. by Rosemary G. Beau. LC 97-18604. (Illus.). 330p. 1998. pap. text 45.00 (*0-19-850046-7*) OUP.

Molecular Applications in Biological Anthropology. Ed. by Eric J. Devor. (Studies in Biological Anthropology: No. 10). (Illus.). 272p. (C). 1993. text 74.95 (*0-521-39109-1*) Cambridge U Pr.

*__Molecular Approach to Bscs Biology Science.__ 8th ed. BSCS Staff. 2000. pap. 2.95 (*0-538-69406-8*) Thomson Learn.

Molecular Approach to Primary Metabolism in Higher Plants. Ed. by Christine Foyer & Paul Quick. LC 97-201998. 300p. 1997. 89.00 (*0-7484-0418-X*, Pub. by Tay Francis Ltd); pap. 34.95 (*0-7484-0419-8*, Pub. by Tay Francis Ltd) Taylor & Francis.

Molecular Approach to Solids. Adrian N. Lazarev. LC 98-28915. (Vibrational Spectra & Structure Ser.). 350p. 1998. 244.00 (*0-444-50039-1*) Elsevier.

Molecular Approaches to Crop Improvement. Ed. by E. S. Dennis & D. J. Llewellyn. (Plant Gene Research Ser.). (Illus.). ix, 166p. 1991. 90.95 (*0-387-82230-5*) Spr-Verlag.

Molecular Approaches to Drug Abuse Research. 1995. lib. bdg. 251.95 (*0-8490-6809-6*) Gordon Pr.

Molecular Approaches to Ecology & Evolution. Ed. by R. DeSalle & B. Schierwater. 300p. 1998. 69.50 (*3-7643-5725-8*) Spr-Verlag.

Molecular Approaches to Ecology & Evolution. Rob DeSalle & B. Schierwater. LC 98-15347. 1998. pap. write for info. (*0-8176-5725-8*) Birkhauser.

Molecular Approaches to Food Safety: Issues Involving Toxic Microorganisms. Ed. by Mel Eklund et al. (Illus.). 532p. (C). 1995. text 110.00 (*1-880293-05-6*) Alaken.

Molecular Approaches to Fundamental & Applied Entomology. Ed. by J. Oakeshott & M. J. Whitten. (Experimental Entomology Ser.). (Illus.). 488p. 1992. 238.00 (*0-387-97814-3*) Spr-Verlag.

Molecular Approaches to Human Polygenic Diseases. CIBA Foundation Staff. LC 87-13374. (CIBA Foundation Symposium Ser.: No. 130). 284p. 1987. 128.00 (*0-471-91096-1*) Wiley.

Molecular Approaches to Parasitology. Ed. by John C. Boothroyd & Richard Komuniecki. (MBL Lectures in Biology: Vol. 12). 560p. 1995. 235.00 (*0-471-10342-X*); pap. 109.95 (*0-471-10341-1*) Wiley.

Molecular Approaches to Supracellular Phenomena. Ed. by Stephen Roth. LC 90-12412. (Developmental Biology Ser.). (Illus.). 242p. (C). 1990. reprint ed. text 45.00 (*0-8122-8251-5*) U of Pa Pr.

Molecular Approaches to the Study of Allergens. Ed. by B. A. Baldo. (Monographs in Allergy: Vol. 28). (Illus.). viii, 166p. 1990. 185.25 (*3-8055-5213-0*) S Karger.

*__Molecular Approaches to the Study of the Ocean.__ Cooksey. LC 97-75088. 568p. 1998. write for info. (*0-412-72960-1*) Kluwer Academic.

Molecular Approaches to Tumor Immunotherapy. LC 97-41654. 300p. 1997. lib. bdg. 55.00 (*981-02-2793-0*) World Scientific Pub.

Molecular Aspects of Aging: Report of the Dahlem Workshop on Molecular Aspects of Aging, Berlin, 13-18 February, 1994. Ed. by Karl Esser & G. M. Martin. LC 94-48583. (Life Sciences Research Reports: Vol. 56). 318p. 1995. 275.00 (*0-471-95689-9*) Wiley.

Molecular Aspects of Ammoniagenesis. Ed. by H. Endou et al. (Contributions to Nephrology Ser.: Vol. 92). (Illus.). x, 228p. 1991. 49.75 (*3-8055-5368-4*) S Karger.

Molecular Aspects of Anticancer Drug-DNA Interactions, Vol. 1. Ed. by Stephen Neidle & Michael J. Waring. LC 93-8201. (Topics in Molecular & Structural Biology Ser.). 1993. 110.00 (*0-8493-7770-6*) CRC Pr.

Molecular Aspects of Anticancer Drug-DNA Interactions, Vol. II. Ed. by Michael J. Waring & Stephen Neible. (Topics in Molecular & Structural Biology Ser.). 336p. 1994. 110.00 (*0-8493-7773-0*, Z7773) CRC Pr.

Molecular Aspects of Asian Medicines Vol. 1: The Orient. Ed. by A. Mori & T. Satoh. 1996. 69.95 (*0-915340-20-8*) PJD Pubns.

Molecular Aspects of Biotechnology: Computational Models & Theories: Proceedings of the NATO Advanced Research Workshop on the Role of Computational Models & Theories in Biotechnology, Sant Feliu de Guixols, Spain, 13-19 June 1991. Ed. by J. Bertran. LC 92-8531. (NATO Advanced Study Institutes Series C, Mathematical & Physical Sciences: Vol. 368). 352p. 1992. text 185.00 (*0-7923-1728-9*) Kluwer Academic.

Molecular Aspects of Cancer & Its Therapy. Ed. by Andrzej Mackiewicz & Pravinkumar B. Sehgal. LC 97-32691. (Molecular & Cell Biology Updates Ser.). (Illus.). 300p. 1997. text 118.00 (*3-7643-5724-X*) Birkhauser.

Molecular Aspects of Cancer & Its Therapy. Andrzej Mackiewicz & Pravinkumar B. Sehgal. LC 97-32691. (Molecular & Cell Biology Updates Ser.). 1998. write for info. (*0-8176-5724-X*) Birkhauser.

Molecular Aspects of Cell Biology. Garrett. LC 94-232039. (C). 1994. pap. text 23.00 (*0-03-007597-1*) Harcourt Coll Pubs.

Molecular Aspects of Chemotherapy: Proceedings of the 3rd International Symposium, Gdansk, Poland, June 19-21, 1991. Ed. by David Shugar et al. 400p. 1993. 163.00 (*0-387-54874-2*) Spr-Verlag.

Molecular Aspects of Development & Aging of the Nervous System. Ed. by Jean M. Lauder et al. LC 89-70995. (Advances in Experimental Medicine & Biology Ser.: Vol. 265). (Illus.). 335p. 1989. 89.50 (*0-306-43408-3*, Plenum Trade) Perseus Pubng.

Molecular Aspects of Hormonal Regulation of Plant Development. Ed. by M. Kutacek et al. (Illus.). viii, 253p. 1990. pap. 50.00 (*90-5103-039-8*, Pub. by SPB Acad Pub) Balogh.

Molecular Aspects of Host-Pathogen Interactions. Ed. by Malcolm A. McCrae et al. (Society for General Microbiology Symposium Ser.: Vol. 55). 372p. (C). 1997. text 115.00 (*0-521-59215-1*) Cambridge U Pr.

Molecular Aspects of Human Cytomegalovirus Diseases. Ed. by Yechiel Becker et al. LC 92-49467. (Frontiers of Virology Ser.: Vol. 2). 1993. write for info. (*3-540-55948-5*); 149.95 (*0-387-55948-5*) Spr-Verlag.

Molecular Aspects of Human Disease, Vol. 1. Ed. by John W. Gorrod et al. 1989. text 74.95 (*0-470-21298-5*) P-H.

Molecular Aspects of Human Disease, Vol. 2. Ed. by John W. Gorrod et al. 1989. text 74.95 (*0-470-21303-5*) P-H.

Molecular Aspects of Idiopathic Urolithiasis. R. Nath et al. (Illus.). 176p. 1984. pap. 59.00 (*0-08-031697-2*, Pergamon Pr) Elsevier.

Molecular Aspects of Immune Response & Infectious Diseases. Ed. by H. Kiyono et al. LC 90-8843. (Advances in Host Defense Mechanisms Ser.: Vol. 7). 224p. 1990. reprint ed. pap. 69.50 (*0-608-03423-1*, 206412200008) Bks Demand.

Molecular Aspects of Immunoglobulin Subclasses. Farouk Shakib. (Illus.). 328p. 1990. 158.25 (*0-08-037504-9*, Pergamon Pr) Elsevier.

Molecular Aspects of Inflammation: 42 Colloquium, 11-13, April 1991. Ed. by Helmut Sies et al. (Colloquium Mosbach Ser.: Vol. 42). (Illus.). ix, 288p. 1992. 172.95 (*0-387-53654-X*) Spr-Verlag.

Molecular Aspects of Insect-Plant Associations. L. B. Brattsten & S. Ahmed. LC 87-2236. (Illus.). 358p. (C). 1987. text 105.00 (*0-306-42547-5*, Kluwer Plenum) Kluwer Academic.

Molecular Aspects of Medicine, ser. vol. 2. H. Baum. (Molecular Aspects of Medicine Ser.). 1979. pap. 18.25 (*0-08-025888-3*, no. 6, Pergamon Pr) Elsevier.

Molecular Aspects of Medicine, 4 pts., Vol. 1. Ed. by H. Baum & J. Gergely. Incl. Pt. 1. Radioimmunoassay & Reproductive Endocrinology. 1977. pap. 12.75 (*0-08-021518-1*); Pt. 2. Haemoglobin Structure & Functions: Its Relevance in Biochemistry & Medicine. 1977. Pt. 3. Oedema in the Newborn. Ed. by Barnes. 1977. pap. 14.50 (*0-08-021538-6*); Pt. 4. Enzymic Regulation & Its Clinical Significance. 1977. pap. 14.50 (*0-08-022642-6*); pap. write for info. (*0-318-55183-7*) Elsevier.

Molecular Aspects of Medicine, Vol. 2. Ed. by H. Baum & J. Gergely. LC 80-40473. (Illus.). 453p. 1980. 85.00 (*0-08-026355-0*, Pergamon Pr) Elsevier.

Molecular Aspects of Medicine, Vol. 3, No. 6. 1981. pap. 14.50 (*0-08-027978-3*, Pergamon Pr) Elsevier.

Molecular Aspects of Medicine, Vol. 4. Ed. by H. Baum et al. (Illus.). 452p. 1982. 180.00 (*0-08-030007-3*, Pergamon Pr) Elsevier.

Molecular Aspects of Medicine, Vol. 5. Ed. by H. Baum et al. (Illus.). 470p. 1983. 180.00 (*0-08-030429-X*, Pergamon Pr) Elsevier.

Molecular Aspects of Medicine, Vol. 6. Ed. by H. Baum et al. (Illus.). 584p. 1984. 180.00 (*0-08-031724-3*, Pergamon Pr) Elsevier.

Molecular Aspects of Medicine, Vol. 7. Ed. by H. Baum et al. (Illus.). 554p. 1985. 205.00 (*0-08-033239-0*, H210, H125, Pub. by PPL) Elsevier.

Molecular Aspects of Medicine Vol. 1: Complete. Ed. by H. Baum & J. Gergely. 600p. 1978. 85.00 (*0-08-020277-2*, Pergamon Pr) Elsevier.

Molecular Aspects of Monooxygenases & Bioactivation of Toxic Compounds. Ed. by Emel Arinc et al. (NATO ASI Ser.: Vol. 202). (Illus.). 508p. (C). 1991. text 180.00 (*0-306-43823-2*, Kluwer Plenum) Kluwer Academic.

Molecular Aspects of Myeloid Stem Cell Development, No. 211. Ed. by L. Wolff & A. S. Perkins. (Current Topics in Microbiology & Immunology Ser.: Vol. 211). (Illus.). 298p. 1995. 152.00 (*3-540-60414-6*) Spr-Verlag.

Molecular Aspects of Oxidative Drug Metabolizing Enzymes: Their Signigicance in Environmental Toxicology, Chemical Carcinogenesis & Health. Ed. by Emel Arinc et al. LC 94-47314. (NATO ASI Series H: Cell Biology: Vol. 90). 1995. 291.95 (*3-540-58856-6*) Spr-Verlag.

Molecular Aspects of Papovaviruses. Ed. by Yosef Aloni. (Developments in Molecular Virology Ser.). (C). 1987. text 159.00 (*0-89838-971-2*) Kluwer Academic.

Molecular Aspects of Pathogenicity & Resistance: Requirement for Signa Transduction. Ed. by Dallice Mills et al. LC 96-83099. (Illus.). 312p. (C). 1996. text 59.00 (*0-89054-215-5*) Am Phytopathol Soc.

Molecular Aspects of Picornavirus Infection & Detection. Ed. by Bert L. Semler & Ellie Ehrenfeld. (Illus.). 335p. 1989. text 39.00 (*1-55581-009-8*) ASM Pr.

Molecular Aspects of Placental & Fetal Autacoids. Ed. by Gregory E. Rice & Shaun P. Brennecke. LC 92-48814. 480p. 1993. lib. bdg. 232.00 (*0-8493-6239-3*, QP281) CRC Pr.

Molecular Aspects of Primary Billiary Cirrhosis. Ed. by Owen Epstein. (Illus.). 112p. 1986. pap. 31.00 (*0-08-034275-2*, Pub. by PPL) Elsevier.

Molecular Aspects of Spermatogenesis. Dominic Poccia. 155p. 1994. 94.00 (*1-57059-204-7*, LN9204) CRC Pr.

Molecular Aspects of the Rheumatic Diseases. W. V. Williams. (Journal Ser.: Vol. 13, No. 2 - 3, 1994). (Illus.). 136p. 1995. pap. 36.75 (*3-8055-6136-9*) S Karger.

Molecular Aspects of Transport Proteins. Ed. by J. J. De Pont. LC 92-18220. (New Comprehensive Biochemistry Ser.: Vol. 21). 344p. 1992. 211.25 (*0-444-89562-0*) Elsevier.

Molecular Association in Biological & Related Systems: A Symposium Sponsored by the Division of Colloid & Surface Chemistry at the 153rd Meeting of the American Chemical Society, Miami Beach, FL, April 13-14, 1967. American Chemical Society Staff. LC 68-59079. (Advances in Chemistry Ser.: No. 84). (Illus.). 318p. 1968. reprint ed. pap. 98.60 (*0-608-06816-0*, 206701300009) Bks Demand.

Molecular Astrophysics: A Volume Honouring Alexander Dalgarno. Ed. by T. W. Hartquist. (Illus.). 500p. (C). 1990. text 100.00 (*0-521-36331-4*) Cambridge U Pr.

Molecular Astrophysics: Migration & Settlement. Andrei Rogers & Frans Willekens. 1985. lib. bdg. 162.50 (*90-277-2119-X*) Kluwer Academic.

Molecular Astrophysics: State of the Art & Future Directions. Ed. by G. H. Diercksen et al. 1985. text 318.00 (*90-277-2081-9*) Kluwer Academic.

M

Molecular Astrophysics of Stars & Galaxies. Ed. by Thomas W. Hartquist & David A. Williams. (International Series on Astronomy & Astrophysics: No. 4). (Illus.). 560p. 1999. text 140.00 (*0-19-850158-7*) OUP.

Molecular Bacteriology: Experimental & Diagnostic Applications. Ed. by Neil Woodford & Alan Johnson. (Methods in Molecular Medicine Ser.: Vol. 15). (Illus.). 675p. 1998. 69.50 (*0-89603-463-1*) Humana.

Molecular Bacteriology: Protocols & Clinical Applications. Ed. by Neil Woodford & Alan Johnson. LC 98-14185. (Methods in Molecular Medicine Ser.: Vol. 15). (Illus.). 692p. 1998. 99.50 (*0-89603-498-4*) Humana.

Molecular-Based Study of Fluids. Ed. by J. M. Haile & G. Ali Mansoori. LC 82-24373. (Advances in Chemistry Ser.: Vol. 204). 536p. 1983. reprint ed. pap. 166.20 (*0-608-03507-6*, 206422600008) Bks Demand.

Molecular Bases of Anesthesia. Eric Moody & Phil Skolnick. (Pharmacology & Toxicology Ser.). 1998. 139.95 (*0-8493-8555-5*) CRC Pr.

Molecular Bases of Axonal Growth & Pathfinding. Ed. by U. Drescher et al. LC 97-40498. (Illus.). 260p. 1997. pap. 64.95 (*3-540-63522-X*) Spr-Verlag.

Molecular Basis & Thermodynamics of Bioelectrogenesis. D. Margineanu & Ernest Schoffeniels. (C). 1990. text 104.00 (*0-7923-0975-8*) Kluwer Academic.

Molecular Basis of Aging. Ed. by Alvaro Macierira-Coelho. LC 95-15170. 576p. 1995. boxed set 199.95 (*0-8493-4786-6*, 4786) CRC Pr.

Molecular Basis of Autoimmune Hepatitis. Ian G. McFarlane. (Molecular Biology Intelligence Unit Ser.). 197p. 1996. 99.00 (*1-57059-339-6*) Landes Bioscience.

Molecular Basis of Axon Growth & Nerve Pattern Formation. Ed. by Hajime Fujisawa. LC 97-226309. (Taniguchi Symposia on Brain Sciences Ser.: Vol. 20, 1997). (Illus.). x, 280p. 1997. 259.25 (*3-8055-6587-9*) S Karger.

Molecular Basis of B-Cell Differentiation & Function. Ed. by M. Ferrerini & Benvenuto Pernis. LC 86-30596. (NATO ASI Series A, Life Sciences: Vol. 123). 182p. 1987. 65.00 (*0-306-42484-3*, Plenum Trade) Perseus Pubng.

Molecular Basis of Bacterial Metabolism. Ed. by G. Hauska & R. Thauer. (Baden Ser.: No. 41). (Illus.). 200p. 1990. 93.95 (*0-387-52996-9*) Spr-Verlag.

Molecular Basis of Bacterial Pathogenesis. Ed. by Barbara H. Iglewski & Virginia L. Clark. (Illus.). 473p. (C). 1991. pap. text 56.00 (*0-12-370390-5*) Acad Pr.

Molecular Basis of Blood Diseases. 2nd ed. George Stamatoyannopoulos et al. LC 92-48879. (Illus.). 752p. 1993. text 210.00 (*0-7216-4735-9*, W B Saunders Co) Harcrt Hlth Sci Grp.

Molecular Basis of Blood Diseases. 3rd ed. Stamatoyan. (C). 1999. text. write for info. (*0-7216-7671-5*, W B Saunders Co) Harcrt Hlth Sci Grp.

Molecular Basis of Cancer. Peter B. Farmer & John M. Walker. 358p. (Orig.). 1989. pap. 39.95 (*0-471-82755-X*) Krieger.

Molecular Basis of Cancer. John Mendelsohn et al. (Illus.). 640p. 1994. text 149.00 (*0-7216-6483-0*, W B Saunders Co) Harcrt Hlth Sci Grp.

Molecular Basis of Cancer. 2nd ed. Berk Mendelsohn et al. 700p. 1999. text. write for info. (*0-7216-7291-4*, W B Saunders Co) Harcrt Hlth Sci Grp.

Molecular Basis of Cardiology. Ed. by R. Roberts. (Molecular Basis of Clinical Medicine Ser.). (Illus.). 544p. 1992. pap. 49.95 (*0-86542-196-X*) Blackwell Sci.

Molecular Basis of Cardiovascular Disease: A Companion to Braunwald's Heart Disease. Kenneth R. Chien. Ed. by Richard Zorab. LC 98-34730. (Illus.). 592p. (C). 1998. text 135.00 (*0-7216-6401-6*, W B Saunders Co) Harcrt Hlth Sci Grp.

Molecular Basis of Cell-Cell Interaction. Ed. by Daniel Bergsma. (Alan R. Liss Ser.: Vol. 14, No. 2). 1978. 80.00 (*0-686-10131-6*) March of Dimes.

Molecular Basis of Cell Cycle & Growth Control. Ed. by Gary S. Stein et al. LC 98-27547. 389p. 1998. 89.95 (*0-471-15706-6*) Wiley.

Molecular Basis of Cellular Defence Mechanisms. Gregory R. Bock & Jamie Goode. LC 96-43728. (Ciba Foundation Symposium Ser.: Vol. 204). 260p. 1997. 128.00 (*0-471-96567-7*) Wiley.

An Asterisk (*) at the beginning of an entry indicates that the title is appearing for the first time.

Molecular Basis of Chromatographic Separation. Esther Forgacs & Tibor Cserhati. LC 97-16049. 256p. 1997. boxed set 144.95 (*0-8493-7696-3*) CRC Pr.

Molecular Basis of Cytoplasmic Male Sterility in Crop Plants. S. S. Mehetra. 196p. 1995. pap. 79.00 (*81-7089-208-2*, Pub. by Intl Bk Distr) St Mut.

Molecular Basis of Epithelial Appendage Morphogenesis. Cheng-Ming Chuong. LC 98-9174. (Molecular Biology Intelligence Unit Ser.). 444p. 1998. 99.00 (*1-57059-490-2*) Landes Bioscience.

Molecular Basis of Human Cancer. Ed. by Claudio Nicolini. (NATO ASI Ser.: Vol. 209). (Illus.). 224p. (C). 1991. text 114.00 (*0-306-44018-0*, Kluwer Plenum) Kluwer Academic.

Molecular Basis of Human Cancer: Genomic Instability & Molecular Mutation in Neoplastic Transformation. Ed. by William B. Coleman & Gregory Tsongalis. 600p. 2000. 125.00 (*0-89603-634-0*) Humana.

Molecular Basis of Human Disease: And Approaches to Its Treatment. Wallace Snipes & Neena Agarwala. LC 92-38825. (Illus.). 310p. (C). 1992. pap. text 19.95 (*0-9612798-5-0*) Woodburn Pr.

Molecular Basis of Insulin Action. Ed. by Michael P. Czech. LC 84-26423. 488p. 1985. 120.00 (*0-306-41843-6*, Plenum Trade) Perseus Pubng.

Molecular Basis of Lymphokine Action. Ed. by David R. Webb et al. LC 87-26151. (Experimental Biology & Medicine Ser.: Vol. 18). 512p. 1987. 125.00 (*0-89603-139-X*) Humana.

Molecular Basis of Medical Cell Biology. Fuller. LC 98-125598. (Illus.). 231p. (C). 1997. pap. text 32.95 (*0-8385-1384-0*, A-1384-5, Apple Lange Med) McGraw.

Molecular Basis of Medicine. Arthur M. Feldman & Daug. 700p. 1993. 49.00 (*1-55664-169-9*) Mosby Inc.

Molecular Basis of Morphogenesis. Ed. by Merton Bernfield. 276p. 1993. 199.95 (*0-471-30515-4*) Wiley.

Molecular Basis of Nerve Activity: Proceedings of the International Symposium in Memory of David Nachmansohn (1899-1983) Berlin, West Germany, October 11-13, 1984. Ed. by J. P. Changeux et al. (Illus.). xxiv, 784p. 1985. 200.00 (*3-11-010345-1*) De Gruyter.

Molecular Basis of Neuropharmacology. Steven E. Hyman. 1999. pap. 49.95 (*0-8385-6379-1*, Medical Exam) Appleton & Lange.

Molecular Basis of Neurosurgical Disease Vol. 8: Concepts in Neurosurgery. Corey Raffel & Griffith R. Harsh. (Illus.). 393p. 1997. write for info. (*0-683-18312-5*) Lppncott W & W.

Molecular Basis of NK Cell Recognition & Function. Ed. by L. Moretta. (Chemical Immunology Ser.: Vol. 64, 1996). (Illus.). xii, 184p. 1996. 172.25 (*3-8055-6332-9*) S Karger.

Molecular Basis of Oncology. Ed. by Emil J. Freireich & Sanford A. Stass. LC 94-43841. (Molecular Basis of Clinical Medicine Ser.). 300p. 1995. pap. 59.95 (*0-86542-254-0*) Blackwell Sci.

Molecular Basis of Oral Microbial Adhesion. Ed. by Stephan E. Mergenhagen & Burton Rosan. LC 84-20504. 242p. reprint ed. pap. 75.10 (*0-7837-4041-7*, 204387100011) Bks Demand.

Molecular Basis of Oxidation Damage by Leukocytes. Algirdas J. Jesaitis. 368p. 1992. boxed set 129.00 (*0-8493-6363-2*, OR185) CRC Pr.

Molecular Basis of Pain Induction. John N. Wood. LC 99-29232. 320p. 2000. text 129.95 (*0-471-34607-1*) Wiley.

Molecular Basis of Polymer Networks. Ed. by A. Baumgartner & C. E. Picot. (Proceedings in Physics Ser.: Vol. 42). (Illus.). ix, 223p. 1989. 67.95 (*0-387-51649-2*) Spr-Verlag.

Molecular Basis of Reproductive Endocrinology. Ed. by Peter C. Leung et al. LC 92-2304. (Serono Symposia Ser.). (Illus.). 312p. 1992. 130.00 (*0-387-97861-5*); write for info. (*3-540-97861-5*) Spr-Verlag.

Molecular Basis of Sex & Differentiation: A Comparative Study of Evolution, Mechanism & Control in Microorganisms. Milton H. Saier, Jr. & G. R. Jacobson. (Illus.). 225p. 1984. 105.00 (*0-387-96007-4*) Spr-Verlag.

Molecular Basis of Sex Hormone Receptor Function: New Targets for Intervention. H. Gronemeyer et al. LC 98-26256. (Ernst Schering Research Foundation Workshop Ser.). 238p. 1998. 79.00 (*3-540-64702-3*) Spr-Verlag.

Molecular Basis of Smell & Taste Transduction - Symposium No. 179. Ed. by Derek J. Chadwick et al. LC 93-28783. (CIBA Foundation Symposium Ser.: No. 179). 298p. 1993. 128.00 (*0-471-93946-3*) Wiley.

Molecular Basis of Specificity in Nucleic Acid-Drug Interactions. Ed. by Bernard Pullman & Joshua Jortner. (C). 1990. text 341.00 (*0-7923-0897-2*) Kluwer Academic.

Molecular Basis of the Action of Drugs & Toxic Substances: Proceedings International Symposium San Francisco, CA, April 23-26, 1987. Ed. by Neal Castagnoli et al. x, 318p. (C). 1988. lib. bdg. 203.85 (*3-11-011290-6*) De Gruyter.

Molecular Basis of Thrombosis & Hemostasis. Ed. by Katherine A. High & Harold R. Roberts. LC 94-43114. (Illus.). 688p. 1995. text 215.00 (*0-8247-9501-6*) Dekker.

Molecular Basis of Transitions & Relaxations, Vol. 4. D. J. Meier. (Midland Macromolecular Monographs). xii, 430p. 1978. text 428.00 (*0-677-11240-8*) Gordon & Breach.

Molecular Basis of Viral & Microbial Pathogenesis. R. Rott & W. Goebel. (Colloquium Mosbach Ser.: Vol. 38). (Illus.). 280p. 1988. 69.00 (*0-387-18606-9*) Spr-Verlag.

Molecular Basis of Viral Replication. Ed. by R. Perez Bercoff. LC 87-15226. (NATO ASI Series A, Life Sciences: Vol. 136). (Illus.). 594p. 1987. 135.00 (*0-306-42619-6*, Plenum Trade) Perseus Pubng.

Molecular Basis of Virus Evolution. Ed. by Adrian Gibbs et al. (Illus.). 623p. (C). 1995. text 105.00 (*0-521-45533-2*) Cambridge U Pr.

Molecular Beam Epitaxy. Ed. by Alfred Cho. LC 94-1433. (Key Papers in Applied Physics). 400p. 1994. 59.95 (*1-56396-132-6*) Spr-Verlag.

Molecular Beam Epitaxy. M. A. Herman & H. Sitter. (Material Science Ser.: Vol. 7). (Illus.). 382p. 1989. 89.50 (*0-387-19075-9*) Spr-Verlag.

Molecular Beam Epitaxy. Ed. by G. Minchev. 200p. 1991. text 116.00 (*0-87849-614-9*, Pub. by Trans T Pub) Enfield Pubs NH.

Molecular Beam Epitaxy. Brian R. Pamplin. (Illus.). 178p. 1980. 48.00 (*0-08-025050-5*, Pergamon Pr) Elsevier.

Molecular Beam Epitaxy: Applications to Key Materials. Ed. by Robin F. Farrow. LC 92-25244. (Illus.). 772p. 1995. 145.00 (*0-8155-1371-2*) Noyes.

Molecular Beam Epitaxy: Fundamentals & Current Status. 2nd rev. ed. M. A. Herman & H. Sitter. (Springer Series in Materials Science: Vol. 7). 456p. 1996. 69.95 (*3-540-60594-0*) Spr-Verlag.

Molecular Beam Epitaxy & Heterostructures. Ed. by Leroy L. Chang & Klaus Ploog. 1984. text 321.50 (*90-247-3118-6*) Kluwer Academic.

Molecular Beams & Low Density Gasdynamics. Ed. by Peter P. Wegener. LC 74-182243. (Gasdynamics Ser.: No. 4). (Illus.). 435p. reprint ed. pap. 134.90 (*0-7837-0767-3*, 204108100019) Bks Demand.

Molecular, Biochemical & Physiological Aspects of Plant Respiration. Ed. by H. Lambers & L. H. Van der Plas. 635p. 1992. 174.00 (*90-5103-079-7*, Pub. by SPB Acad Pub) Balogh.

Molecular Biochemistry of Human Diseases, Vol. 1. Felix A. De La Iglesia. Ed. by George Feuer. LC 84-7156. 240p. 1985. 133.00 (*0-8493-6205-9*, RC627, CRC Reprint) Franklin.

Molecular Biochemistry of Human Diseases, Vol. II. George Feuer & Felix De La Iglesia. LC 84-7156. 272p. 1986. 145.00 (*0-8493-6206-7*, RB112, CRC Reprint) Franklin.

Molecular Biochemistry of Human Diseases, Vol. 3. George Feuer & Felix De La Iglesia. LC 84-7156. 384p. 1990. 231.00 (*0-8493-6207-5*, RB112) Franklin.

Molecular Bioelectronics. LC 96-221562. 288p. 1996. lib. bdg. 41.00 (*981-02-2685-3*) World Scientific Pub.

Molecular Bioimformatics: Algorithms & Applications. Steffen Schulze-Kremer. xv, 300p. (C). 1995. lib. bdg. 79.95 (*3-11-014113-2*) De Gruyter.

Molecular Biological Clinical Medicine. Ralph C. Williams. (C). 1992. pap. text 70.00 (*0-8385-6213-2*, A6213-1, Apple Lange Med) McGraw.

Molecular Biological Methods for Bacillus. Ed. by Colin R. Harwood & Simon M. Cutting. LC 90-12415. (Modern Microbiological Methods Ser.). 618p. 1991. 434.00 (*0-471-92393-1*) Wiley.

Molecular Biology. H. D. Kumar. 1998. pap. 14.00 (*81-259-0563-4*, Pub. by Vikas) S Asia.

*__Molecular Biology.__ Robert F. Weaver. LC 98-13018. 1998. 89.72 (*0-697-14750-9*, WCB McGr Hill) McGrw-H Hghr Educ.

Molecular Biology. 2nd ed. David Freifelder. 864p. 1986. pap. text 55.00 (*0-86720-069-3*) Jones & Bartlett.

Molecular Biology. 2nd ed. Robert F. Weaver. 2002. 68.25 (*0-07-234517-9*) McGraw.

Molecular Biology, Vol. 4. Bjorn R. Olsen & Marcel E. Nimni. LC 87-20946. (Collagen Ser.: Vol. IV). 208p. 1988. 110.00 (*0-8493-4604-5*, QP552) Franklin.

Molecular Biology: A Selection of Papers. Compiled by Sydney Brenner. 622p. 1990. pap. text 52.00 (*0-12-131200-3*) Acad Pr.

Molecular Biology: Current Innovations & Future Trends, Pt. 1. Ed. by Annette M. Griffin & Hugh G. Griffin. 165p. 1995. reprint ed. 84.99 (*1-898486-13-1*, Pub. by Horizon Sci) Intl Spec Bk.

Molecular Biology: Current Innovations & Future Trends, Pt. 1. Ed. by Annette M. Griffin & Hugh G. Griffin. LC 96-139696. (Current Innovations in Molecular Biology Ser.: Vol. 1). 165p. 1995. reprint ed. pap. 32.50 (*1-898486-01-8*, Pub. by Horizon Sci) Intl Spec Bk.

Molecular Biology: Current Innovations & Future Trends, Pt. 2. Ed. by Annette M. Griffin & Hugh G. Griffin. 176p. 1995. reprint ed. 84.99 (*1-898486-14-X*, Pub. by Horizon Sci); reprint ed. pap. 32.50 (*1-898486-03-4*, Pub. by Horizon Sci) Intl Spec Bk.

*__Molecular Biology: Genes to Proteins.__ 3rd ed. Burton E. Tropp & David Freifelder. (Illus.). 896p. (C). 2001. text 75.00 (*0-7637-0916-6*) JB Pubns.

Molecular Biology: Made Simple & Fun. David Clark & Lonnie Russell. LC 96-92824. (Illus.). 480p. 1997. pap. 34.95 (*0-9627422-9-5*) Cache River Pr.

Molecular Biology & Biotechnology: A Comprehensive Desk Reference. Ed. by R. A. Meyers. 1072p. 1995. 235.00 (*0-471-18571-X*); pap. 125.00 (*0-471-18634-1*) Wiley.

Molecular Biology & Biotechnology: A Comprehensive Desk Reference. Ed. by Robert A. Meyers. LC 95-9063. (Illus.). xxxviii, 1046p. 1995. 149.95 (*1-56081-569-8*, Wiley-VCH); pap. 59.95 (*1-56081-925-1*, Wiley-VCH) Wiley.

Molecular Biology & Biotechnology of Extremophiles. Ed. by R. A. Herbert & R. J. Sharp. LC 91-25198. 1992. mass mkt. 196.50 (*0-412-03241-4*, A6490) Chapman & Hall.

Molecular Biology & Cell Regulation of the Placenta. Ed. by Richard K. Miller & Henry A. Thiede. (Trophoblast Research Ser.: Vol. 5). (Illus.). 488p. (C). 1991. 85.00 (*0-9630864-0-5*) Verav Med.

Molecular Biology & Evolution of Blood Group & MHC Antigens in Primates. A. Blancher & Jan Klein. LC 97-369. 1997. text. write for info. (*3-540-61636-5*) Spr-Verlag.

Molecular Biology & Evolution of Crystallins: Gene Recruitment & Multifunctional Proteins in the Eye Lens. Graeme Wistow. LC 95-33050. (Molecular Biology Intelligence Unit Ser.). 165p. 1995. 79.00 (*1-57059-299-3*) Landes Bioscience.

Molecular Biology & Genetic Engineering of Yeasts. Henri Heslot & Claude Gaillardin. 416p. 1991. lib. bdg. 119.00 (*0-8493-5645-8*, TP248) CRC Pr.

Molecular Biology & Human Diversity. Ed. by A. J. Boyce & C. G. Mascie-Taylor. (Society for the Study of Human Biology Symposium Ser.: No. 38). (Illus.). 318p. (C). 1996. text 69.95 (*0-521-56086-1*) Cambridge U Pr.

Molecular Biology & Immunology of Allergens. Cathy Walker et al. 352p. 1993. lib. bdg. 129.00 (*0-8493-0136-X*, QR188) CRC Pr.

Molecular Biology & Its Application to Medical Mycology. Ed. by Bruno Maresca et al. LC 92-49124. (NATO ASI Ser.: Vol. 69). 1993. write for info. (*3-540-54609-X*); 211.95 (*0-387-54609-X*) Spr-Verlag.

Molecular Biology & Pathology: A Guidebook for Quality Control. Ed. by Daniel H. Farkas. LC 92-49202. (Illus.). 326p. 1993. 53.00 (*0-12-249100-9*) Acad Pr.

Molecular Biology & Pathology of Elastic Tissues: Symposium. CIBA Foundation Symposium Staff. (CIBA Foundation Symposium Ser.: No. 192). 374p. 1995. 128.00 (*0-471-95718-6*) Wiley.

Molecular Biology & Physiology of Insulin & Insulin-Like Growth Factors. Ed. by Mohan K. Raizada & D. LeRoith. (Advances in Experimental Medicine & Biology Ser.: Vol. 293). (Illus.). 498p. (C). 1991. text 186.00 (*0-306-43928-X*, Kluwer Plenum) Kluwer Academic.

Molecular Biology Approach to the Neurosciences. Ed. by Hermona Soreq. LC 84-7341. (IBRO Handbook Series: Methods in the Neurosciences: No. 1-569). 270p. 1984. pap. 315.00 (*0-471-90437-6*) Wiley.

Molecular Biology Chromosome F. 1989. 190.00 (*0-387-96982-9*) Spr-Verlag.

Molecular Biology for Obstetricians & Gynecologists. P. R. Bennett & G. E. Moore. (Illus.). 192p. 1991. 75.00 (*0-632-02744-4*) Blackwell Sci.

Molecular Biology Frontiers. Ed. by Peter W. Hochachka & T. P. Mommsen. (Biochemistry & Molecular Biology of Fishes Ser.: Vol. 2). 484p. 1993. 269.25 (*0-444-81663-1*) Elsevier.

Molecular Biology in Cancer Medicine. Razelle Kurzrock & Moshe Talpaz. (Illus.). 456p. 1995. text 89.50 (*0-19-521173-1*) OUP.

*__Molecular Biology in Cancer Medicine.__ 2nd ed. Ed. by Razelle Kurzrock & Moshe Talpaz. 679p. 1999. 139.95 (*1-85317-676-1*) Martin Dunitz.

Molecular Biology in Critical Medicine. Reed E. Pyeritz. 1995. pap. text 30.00 (*0-07-051102-0*) McGraw.

Molecular Biology in Health Sciences: Index of Authors & Subjects. Jerry R. Krull. 180p. 1993. 47.50 (*1-55914-942-6*); pap. 44.50 (*1-55914-943-4*) ABBE Pubs Assn.

Molecular Biology in Histopathology. Ed. by John Croaker. LC 93-50921. (Molecular Medical Science Ser.). 190p. 1994. 135.00 (*0-471-94093-3*) Wiley.

Molecular Biology in Medicine. Timothy M. Cox & John Sinclair. LC 96-21997. (Illus.). 384p. 1997. pap. text 68.95 (*0-632-02785-1*) Blackwell Sci.

Molecular Biology in Medicine: A Practical Guide for the Health Care Physician. Timothy L. Reudelhuber & Christian Deschepper. Date not set. write for info. (*0-8247-9411-7*) Dekker.

Molecular Biology in Physiology. Ed. by Shu Chien. LC 87-42838. (Illus.). 179p. 1989. reprint ed. pap. 55.50 (*0-608-05785-1*, 205975000007) Bks Demand.

Molecular Biology in Reproductive Medicine. B. C. Fauser. LC 98-54925. (Illus.). 524p. 1999. 98.00 (*1-85070-994-7*) Prthnon Pub.

Molecular Biology in Toxicology. Ed. by Alvaro Puga & Kendall Wallace. LC 98-17547. 582p. 1998. text 135.00 (*1-56032-592-5*) Hemisp Pub.

Molecular Biology Labfax Vol. I: Recombinant DNA, Vol. 1. 2nd ed. Ed. by Terry A. Brown et al. LC 97-45533. (Labfax Ser.). (Illus.). 408p. (C). 1998. text 59.95 (*0-12-136055-5*) Morgan Kaufmann.

Molecular Biology Labfax Vol. 2: Gene Analysis, Vol. 2. 2nd ed. Terry Brown. (Labfax Ser.). (Illus.). 288p. 1998. 59.95 (*0-12-136110-1*) Acad Pr.

Molecular Biology of Adenoviruses. L. Philipson et al. LC 75-6658. (Virology Monographs: Vol. 14). (Illus.). iv, 115p. 1975. 47.00 (*0-387-81284-9*) Spr-Verlag.

Molecular Biology of Aging. Ed. by Avril D. Woodhead et al. LC 85-16978. (Basic Life Sciences Ser.: Vol. 35). 496p. 1985. 110.00 (*0-306-42084-8*, Plenum Trade) Perseus Pubng.

Molecular Biology of Aging: Gene Stability & Gene Expression. Ed. by R. S. Sohal et al. LC 85-19314. (Aging Ser.: No. 29). (Illus.). 367p. 1985. reprint ed. pap. 113.80 (*0-608-05779-7*, 205974400007) Bks Demand.

Molecular Biology of Alzheimer's Disease. Ed. by Caleb E. Finch & Peter Davies. (Current Communications in Molecular Biology Ser.). (Illus.). 197p. (C). 1988. pap. text 25.00 (*0-87969-319-3*) Cold Spring Harbor.

Molecular Biology of Alzheimer's Disease: Genes & Mechanisms Involved in Amyloid Generation. Christian Haass. (Illus.). 330p. 1998. text 76.00 (*90-5702-381-4*) Gordon & Breach.

Molecular Biology of Animal Viruses, 2 vols., 2. Ed. by Debi P. Nayak. LC 76-29295. (Illus.). 579p. reprint ed. pap. 179.50 (*0-8357-6220-3*, 203455600002) Bks Demand.

Molecular Biology of Animal Viruses, 2 vols., Vol. 1. Ed. by Debi P. Nayak. LC 76-29295. (Illus.). 552p. reprint ed. pap. 171.20 (*0-8357-6219-X*, 203455600001) Bks Demand.

Molecular Biology of Autoimmune Disease. Ed. by A. G. Demaine et al. (NATO ASI Series H: Vol. 38). (Illus.). 420p. 1990. 158.95 (*0-387-51771-5*) Spr-Verlag.

Molecular Biology of B-Cell & T-Cell Development. John G. Moore & Ellen Rothenberg. LC 98-12613. (Contemporary Immunology Ser.). (Illus.). 608p. 1998. 175.00 (*0-89603-536-0*) Humana.

Molecular Biology of B Cell Developments. Ed. by C. Muenster Sorg. (Cytokines Ser.: Vol. 3). (Illus.). viii, 176p. 1990. 152.25 (*3-8055-5191-6*) S Karger.

Molecular Biology of Bacteria. Ed. by V. V. Tetz & A. A. Totolian. 389p. (C). 1997. lib. bdg. 125.00 (*1-56072-245-2*) Nova Sci Pubs.

Molecular Biology of Bacterial Growth. Ed. by Moselio Schaechter et al. 384p. 1986. 75.00 (*0-86720-049-9*) Jones & Bartlett.

Molecular Biology of Bacterial Infection: Current Status & Future Perspectives. Ed. by Carlos E. Hormaeche et al. LC 92-25527. (Society for General Microbiology Symposium Ser.: No. 49). (Illus.). 343p. (C). 1992. text 115.00 (*0-521-43298-7*) Cambridge U Pr.

Molecular Biology of Bacteriophage T4. Ed. by Jim D. Karam et al. LC 94-6505. (Illus.). 600p. 1994. 120.00 (*1-55581-064-0*) ASM Pr.

Molecular Biology of Biological Control of Pests & Diseases of Plants. Ed. by Muthukumaran Gunasekaran & Darrell J. Weber. LC 95-31087. 240p. 1995. boxed set 149.95 (*0-8493-2442-4*, 2442) CRC Pr.

Molecular Biology of Brain & Endocrine Peptidergic Systems. Ed. by M. Chretien & Kenneth W. McKerns. (Biochemical Endocrinology Ser.). (Illus.). 388p. 1988. 110.00 (*0-306-42980-2*, Plenum Trade) Perseus Pubng.

Molecular Biology of Cancer. Finlay J. MacDonald & C. Ford. (Medical Perspectives Ser.). (Illus.). 160p. (Orig.). 1996. pap. text 39.95 (*1-85996-225-4*, Pub. by Bios Sci) Bks Intl VA.

Molecular Biology of Cardiac Development & Growth. Paul Barton et al. LC 95-31277. (Molecular Biology Intelligence Unit Ser.). 268p. 1995. 99.00 (*1-57059-302-7*) Landes Bioscience.

Molecular Biology of Cardiovascular Diseases. Ed. by B. Marks & Taubman. LC 96-40406. (Fundamental & Clinical Cardiology Ser.: Vol. 30). (Illus.). 560p. 1997. text 210.00 (*0-8247-9405-2*) Dekker.

Molecular Biology of Cell Determination & Cell Differentiation. L. W. Browder. LC 85-3406. (Developmental Biology Ser.). (Illus.). 460p. (C). 1988. text 105.00 (*0-306-42735-4*, Kluwer Plenum) Kluwer Academic.

Molecular Biology of Chloroplasts & Mitochondria in Chlamydomonas. J. D. Rochaix & M. Goldschmidt-Clermont. LC 98-35404. (Advances in Photosynthesis Ser.). 1998. 320.00 (*0-7923-5174-6*) Kluwer Academic.

Molecular Biology of Cyanobacteria. Ed. by Donald A. Bryant. (Advances in Photosynthesis Ser.: Vol. 1). 1995. lib. bdg. 355.00 (*0-7923-3222-9*) Kluwer Academic.

Molecular Biology of Cytokines. Tony Meager. LC 97-44184. (Molecular Medical Science Ser.). 422p. 1998. 159.95 (*0-471-98272-5*) Wiley.

Molecular Biology of Desmosomes & Hemidesosomes. David R. Garrod & Jane E. Collins. LC 94-38446. (Molecular Biology Intelligence Unit Ser.). 130p. 1994. 99.00 (*1-57059-197-0*) Landes Bioscience.

Molecular Biology of Development: Molecular Events & Problems of Regulation. A. A. Neyfakh & M. Ya. Timofeeva. Ed. by A. M. Kolchinsky. 792p. 1985. 155.00 (*0-306-41333-7*, Plenum Trade) Perseus Pubng.

Molecular Biology of Diabetes Pt. I: Autoimmunity & Genetics: Insulin Synthesis & Secretion. Ed. by Boris Draznin & Derek LeRoith. LC 94-27263. (Illus.). 424p. 1994. text 125.00 (*0-89603-286-8*) Humana.

Molecular Biology of Diabetes Pt. II: Insulin Action, Effects on Gene Expression & Regulation & Glucose Transport. Ed. by Boris Draznin & Derek Le Roith. LC 94-27263. (Illus.). 568p. 1994. 125.00 (*0-89603-287-6*) Humana.

Molecular Biology of Digestive Diseases. Ed. by Philip Quirke. 128p. 1994. pap. text 10.00 (*0-7279-0827-8*, Pub. by BMJ Pub) Login Brothers Bk Co.

Molecular Biology of DNA Methylation. R. L. Adams & R. H. Burdon. (Molecular Biology Ser.). (Illus.). xvi, 247p. 1985. 96.00 (*0-387-96161-5*) Spr-Verlag.

Molecular Biology of DNA Topolsomerases & Its Application to Chemotherapy: Proceedings of the International Symposium on DNA Topoisomerases in Chemotherapy, Nagoya, Japan, November 18-20, 1991. Ed. by Toshiwo Andoh et al. 470p. 1992. lib. bdg. 239.00 (*0-8493-4970-2*, QP616) CRC Pr.

*__Molecular Biology of Down Syndrome.__ Ed. by G. Lubec. LC 99-59530. (Journal of Neural Transmission Ser.: Suppl. 57, 1999). (Illus.). 350p. 1999. 119.00 (*3-211-83378-1*) Spr-Verlag.

Molecular Biology of Environmental Pollution. Wu. 1995. 236.00 (*0-8493-6813-8*, CRC Reprint) Franklin.

Molecular Biology of Erythropoiesis. Ed. by J. L. Ascensao et al. (Advances in Experimental Medicine & Biology Ser.: Vol. 271). (Illus.). 240p. 1989. 79.50 (*0-306-43532-2*, Plenum Trade) Perseus Pubng.

Molecular Biology of Filamentous Fungi: Proceedings of the EMBO-Workshop, Berlin, August 24-29, 1991. Ed. by U. Stahl & P. Tudzynski. LC 92-10558. 277p. 1992. 446.00 (*3-527-28481-8*, Wiley-VCH) Wiley.

Molecular Biology of Flowering. Ed. by Brian Jordan. (CAB International Publication Ser.). (Illus.). 282p. 1993. text 105.00 (*0-85198-723-0*) OUP.

Molecular Biology of Free Radical Scavenging Systems. John G. Scandalios. (Current Communications in Cell & Molecular Biology Ser.: No. 5). (Illus.). 250p. (C). 1992. pap. text 29.00 (*0-87969-409-2*) Cold Spring Harbor.

An Asterisk (*) at the beginning of an entry indicates that the title is appearing for the first time.

Molecular Biology of G-Protein-Coupled Receptors: Applications of Molecular Genetics to Pharmacology. Ed. by M. Brann. xvii, 256p. 1992. 75.50 (*0-8176-3465-7*) Birkhauser.

Molecular Biology of Gaia. G. R. Williams. LC 96-17485. (Illus.). 256p. 1996. 47.50 (*0-231-10512-6*) Col U Pr.

Molecular Biology of Hematopoiesis & Treatment of Leukemias & Lymphomas: 10th Symposium, Hamburg, Juli 1997: Abstracts. Ed. by N. G. Abraham et al. (Acta Haematologica Ser.: Vol. 98, Suppl. 1, 1997). vi, 128p. 1997. pap. 48.75 (*3-8055-6550-X*) S Karger.

Molecular Biology of Hematopoiesis & Treatment of Leukemias & Lymphomas: 10th Symposium, Hamburg, July 1997 - Proceedings. Ed. by N. G. Abraham et al. (Acta Haematologica Ser.: Vol. 90, No. 3, 1998). (Illus.). 76p. 1998. pap. 43.50 (*3-8055-6681-6*) S Karger.

***Molecular Biology of Hematopoiesis & Treatment of Myeloproliferative Diseases: 11th Symposium, Bormio, June 1998: Proceedings.** Ed. by N. G. Abraham et al. (Acta Haematologica Ser.: Vol. 101, No. 2). 50p. 1999. pap. 25.25 (*3-8055-6823-1*) S Karger.

Molecular Biology of Hematopoiesis & Treatment of Myeloproliferative Diseases: 11th Symposium, Bornio, June 1998 - Abstracts. Ed. by N. G. Abraham et al. (Acta Haematologica Ser.: Vol. 100, Suppl. 1). iv, 72p. 1998. pap. 33.25 (*3-8055-6729-4*) S Karger.

Molecular Biology of Hematopoiesis 5. Ed. by Nader G. Abraham et al. (Illus.). 737p. (C). 1996. text 179.00 (*0-306-45318-5*, Kluwer Plenum) Kluwer Academic.

Molecular Biology of Hematopoiesis Proceedings: Proceedings. Ed. by Nader G. Abraham et al. (Journal: Acta Haematologica: Vol. 95, No. 3-4, 1996). (Illus.). iv, 128p. 1996. pap. 44.00 (*3-8055-6319-1*) S Karger.

***Molecular Biology of Hematopoiesis 6.** Nader G. Abraham. LC 99-31967. 1999. write for info. (*0-306-46136-6*, Kluwer Plenum) Kluwer Academic.

Molecular Biology of Hemopoesis. Ed. by M. Tavassoli et al. LC 88-28836. (Advances in Experimental Medicine & Biology Ser.: Vol. 241). (Illus.). 350p. 1988. 89.50 (*0-306-43022-3*, Plenum Trade) Perseus Pubng.

Molecular Biology of HIV & AIDS. Ed. by A. M. Lever. LC 95-19768. (Molecular Medical Science Ser.). 232p. 1996. 137.95 (*0-471-96094-2*) Wiley.

Molecular Biology of HLA Class II Antigens. Ed. by Silver. 280p. 1990. lib. bdg. 217.00 (*0-8493-4785-8*, QR184) CRC Pr.

Molecular Biology of Homo Sapiens. LC 87-144605. (Cold Spring Harbor Symposia on Quantitative Biology Ser.: Vol. 51). 1228p. 1986. pap. 80.00 (*0-87969-053-4*) Cold Spring Harbor.

Molecular Biology of Homo Sapiens. Cold Spring Harbor Symposia on Quantitative Biolog. LC 34-8174. (Cold Spring Harbor Symposia on Quantitative Biology Ser.: No. 51, Pt. 1). 728p. reprint ed. pap. 200.00 (*0-7837-6445-6*, 204644500001) Bks Demand.

Molecular Biology of Homo Sapiens. Cold Spring Harbor Symposia on Quantitative Biolog. LC 34-8174. (Cold Spring Harbor Symposia on Quantitative Biology Ser.: No. 51, Pt. 2). 543p. reprint ed. pap. 168.40 (*0-7837-6446-4*, 204644500002) Bks Demand.

Molecular Biology of Human Hepatitis Viruses. J. Monjardino. LC 98-214266. 150p. 1997. text 24.00 (*1-86094-048-X*) World Scientific Pub.

Molecular Biology of Insect Disease Vectors: A Methods Manual. Ed. by J. M. Crampton et al. LC 96-70874. (Illus.). 416p. 1996. pap. write for info. (*0-412-73660-8*) Kluwer Academic.

Molecular Biology of Iridoviruses. Ed. by Gholamreza Daria. (Developments in Molecular Virology Ser.). 1989. text 210.50 (*0-7923-0506-X*) Kluwer Academic.

Molecular Biology of Leumocyte Chemotaxis. A. Rot. (Medical Intelligence Unit Ser.). 200p. (C). 1997. 89.95 (*0-412-11361-9*) Chapman & Hall.

Molecular Biology of Lung Disease. Ed. by Peter J. Barnes & Robert A. Stockley. LC 93-28488. (Illus.). 384p. 1994. 100.00 (*0-632-03344-4*) Blackwell Sci.

Molecular Biology of Membrane-Bound Complexes in Phototrophic Bacteria. Ed. by G. Drews & E. A. Dawes. LC 90-7068. (FEMS Symposium Ser.: No. 53). (Illus.). 500p. 1990. 135.00 (*0-306-43515-2*, Plenum Trade) Perseus Pubng.

Molecular Biology of Membrane Transport Disorders. Ed. by Stanley G. Schultz et al. LC 96-21633. (Illus.). 657p. (C). 1996. text 179.00 (*0-306-45164-6*, Kluwer Plenum) Kluwer Academic.

Molecular Biology of Membranes: Structure & Function. H. R. Petty. (Illus.). 424p. (C). 1993. text 69.50 (*0-306-44429-1*, Kluwer Plenum) Kluwer Academic.

Molecular Biology of Microbial Differentiation: Proceedings of the 9th International Spore Conference, Asilomar, CA, 3-6 September 1984. International Spore Conference Staff. Ed. by James A. Hoch & Peter Setlow. LC 85-1413. 290p. reprint ed. pap. 89.90 (*0-7837-4042-5*, 204387200011) Bks Demand.

Molecular Biology of Mitochondrial Transport Systems. Ed. by Michael Forte & Marco Colombini. LC 94-15689. (NATO ASI Ser.: Series H, Cell Biology: Vol. 83). 1994. write for info. (*0-387-57908-7*) Spr-Verlag.

Molecular Biology of Multiple Sclerosis. W. C. Russell. LC 96-9436. 320p. 1997. 175.00 (*0-471-96966-4*) Wiley.

Molecular Biology of Mutagens & Carcinogens. S. Singer & D. Grunberger. LC 83-17683. 360p. 1983. 85.00 (*0-306-41430-9*, Plenum Trade) Perseus Pubng.

Molecular Biology of Neuroreceptors & Ion Channels. Ed. by A. Maelicke. (NATO ASI Series H: Vol. 32). (Illus.). 670p. 1989. 251.95 (*0-387-50380-3*) Spr-Verlag.

Molecular Biology of Nucleases. Nawin C. Mishra. 296p. 1995. boxed set 224.95 (*0-8493-7658-0*, 7658) CRC Pr.

Molecular Biology of Paget's Disease. Paul T. Sharpe. LC 96-3238. (Medical Intelligence Unit Ser.). 214p. 1996. 99.00 (*1-57059-388-4*) Landes Bioscience.

Molecular Biology of Parasitic Protozoa. Ed. by Deborah F. Smith & Marilyn Parsons. (Frontiers in Molecular Biology Ser.: Vol. 13). (Illus.). 250p. (C). 1996. text 105.00 (*0-19-963602-8*); pap. text 55.00 (*0-19-963601-X*) OUP.

Molecular Biology of Pathogenic Fungi: A Laboratory Manual. Bruno Maresca & George S. Kobayashi. 577p. 1994. spiral bd. 95.00 (*0-914386-27-1*) Telos Pr.

Molecular Biology of Photosynthesis. Ed. by Jan A. Govindjee et al. (C). 1989. text 426.00 (*0-7923-0097-1*) Kluwer Academic.

Molecular Biology of Physarum Polycephalum. Ed. by William F. Dove et al. LC 86-4963. (NATO ASI Series A, Life Sciences: Vol. 106). 378p. 1986. 85.00 (*0-306-42267-0*, Plenum Trade) Perseus Pubng.

Molecular Biology of Plant Cells. Ed. by Harold Smith. (Botanical Monographs: Vol. 14). 1978. 70.00 (*0-520-03465-1*, Pub. by U CA Pr) Cal Prin Full Svc.

Molecular Biology of Plant Cells. Ed. by Harry Smith. LC 77-73503. (Botanical Monographs: No. 14). (Illus.). 156p. reprint ed. pap. 48.40 (*0-7837-4679-2*, 204442600003) Bks Demand.

Molecular Biology of Plant Mitochondria. Ed. by Charles S. Levings, III & Indra K. Vasil. (Advances in Cellular & Molecular Biology of Plants: Vol. 3). 676p. (C). 1995. text 368.00 (*0-7923-3224-5*) Kluwer Academic.

***Molecular Biology of Plant Viruses.** C. L. Mandahar. LC 99-28569. 1999. write for info. (*0-7923-8547-0*, Kluwer Plenum) Kluwer Academic.

Molecular Biology of Plants: A Laboratory Course Manual. Ian M. Sussex & Joachim W. Messing. LC 85-11036. 150p. (Orig.). (C). 1985. text 14.00 (*0-87969-184-0*) Cold Spring Harbor.

Molecular Biology of Plants: A Text Manual. Joe H. Cherry. LC 72-13090. (Molecular Biology Ser.). 204p. 1973. text 64.00 (*0-231-03642-6*) Col U Pr.

Molecular Biology of Poliovirus. F. Koch & G. Koch. (Illus.). 600p. 1985. 158.00 (*0-387-81763-8*) Spr-Verlag.

Molecular Biology of Positive Strand RNA Viruses. Ed. by Brian W. Mahy et al. (Fems Symposia Ser.). 334p. 1987. text 104.00 (*0-12-599930-5*) Acad Pr.

Molecular Biology of Prostate Cancer. Ed. by M. Wirth et al. 208p. 1998. 85.35 (*3-11-016159-1*) De Gruyter.

Molecular Biology of Pseudomonads. Ed. by Teruko Nakazawa et al. LC 96-18032. 526p. 1996. 98.00 (*1-55581-104-3*) ASM Pr.

Molecular Biology of Rice. Ed. by Ko Shimamoto. LC 98-33426. (Illus.). viii, 304p. 1999. 129.00 (*4-431-70215-6*) Spr-Verlag.

Molecular Biology of Seed Storage Proteins & Lectins. Ed. by Leland M. Shannon & Maarten J. Chrispeels. 252p. (C). 1986. pap. text 20.00 (*0-943088-08-9*) Am Soc of Plan.

Molecular Biology of Signal Transduction. LC 34-8174. (Cold Spring Harbor Symposia on Quantitative Biology Ser.: Vol. 53). (Illus.). 1200p. 1989. pap. text 95.00 (*0-87969-056-9*) Cold Spring Harbor.

Molecular Biology of Signal Transduction. Cold Spring Harbor Symposia on Quantitative Biolog. (Cold Spring Harbor Symposia on Quantitative Biology Ser.: Vol. 53). (Illus.). 1200p. 1989. 180.00 (*0-87969-055-0*) Cold Spring Harbor.

Molecular Biology of Steroid & Nuclear Hormone Receptors. Leonard P. Freedman. Ed. by M. Karin. LC 97-21837. (Progress in Gene Expression Ser.). (Illus.). 272p. 1997. 99.50 (*0-8176-3952-7*) Birkhauser.

Molecular Biology of Steroid & Nuclear Hormone Receptors. Leonard P. Freedman. LC 97-21837. (Progress in Gene Expression Ser.). 1997. write for info. (*3-7643-3952-7*) Birkhauser.

Molecular Biology of Symbiotic Nitrogen Fixation. Ed. by Peter M. Gresshoff. 256p. 1989. lib. bdg. 319.00 (*0-8493-6188-5*, QR89) CRC Pr.

***Molecular Biology of the Brain, Vol. 33.** S. J. Higgins. (Essays in Biochemistry Ser.). 198p. (C). 1999. pap. text 29.95 (*0-691-00952-X*, Pub. by Princeton U Pr) Cal Prin Full Svc.

Molecular Biology of the Cell. 2nd ed. Bruce Alberts et al. LC 88-38275. (Illus.). 1308p. 1989. text 63.00 (*0-8240-3695-6*) Garland.

Molecular Biology of the Cell. 3rd ed. Bruce Alberts et al. LC 93-45907. 1408p. 1994. text 73.95 (*0-8153-1619-4*) Garland.

Molecular Biology of the Cell. 3rd rev. ed. Bruce Alberts et al. LC 93-45907. (Illus.). 1408p. 1994. pap. text 63.00 (*0-8153-1620-8*) Garland.

Molecular Biology of the Cell: Final Report of the Sonderforschungsbereich, Molekularbiologie der Zelle, 1970-1988. Ed. by Walter Doerfler. LC 92-11241. (Sonderforschungsbereiche Ser.). 311p. 1992. 93.00 (*3-527-27718-8*, Wiley-VCH) Wiley.

Molecular Biology of the Cell: The Problems Book. 3rd rev. ed. John Wilson & Tim Hunt. (Illus.). 496p. 1994. pap. text 21.95 (*0-8153-1621-6*) Garland.

***Molecular Biology of the Cell & the Hypercell.** 3rd ed. Bray Alberts. (Illus.). 1999. 95.95 (*0-8153-3623-3*) Garland.

Molecular Biology of the Cytoskeleton. Ed. by Gary G. Borisy et al. LC 84-17566. 512p. 1984. 62.00 (*0-87969-174-3*) Cold Spring Harbor.

Molecular Biology of the Female Reproduction System. Ed. by J. K. Findlay. (Illus.). 457p. 1994. text 99.00 (*0-12-256365-4*) Acad Pr.

Molecular Biology of the Fission Yeast. Ed. by Anwar Nasim et al. (Cell Biology Ser.). 545p. 1989. text 157.00 (*0-12-514085-1*) Acad Pr.

Molecular Biology of the Gene, 2 vols. 4th ed. James Dewey Watson et al. (Illus.). 1163p. (C). 1987. 110.00 (*0-8053-9614-4*) Benjamin-Cummings.

Molecular Biology of the Gene. 5th ed. James Watson, Jr. 960p. (C). 2000. text 105.00 (*0-8053-1643-4*) Addison-Wesley.

Molecular Biology of the Gene, Vols. 1 & 2. 4th ed. Watson. (C). 1987. 86.25 (*0-8053-4824-7*) Benjamin-Cummings.

Molecular Biology of the Hepatitis B Virus. Alan McLachlan. (Illus.). 312p. 1991. lib. bdg. 229.00 (*0-8493-5516-8*, QR749) CRC Pr.

Molecular Biology of the Human Brain. Ed. by Edward G. Jones. 212p. (C). 1988. lib. bdg. 48.00 (*0-8451-2671-7*) Krieger.

Molecular Biology of the Islets of Langerhans. Ed. by Hiroshi Okamoto. (Illus.). 362p. (C). 1990. text 105.00 (*0-521-36204-0*) Cambridge U Pr.

Molecular Biology of the Lung, 2 vols. R. A. Stockley. LC 98-36983. (Respiratory Pharmacology & Pharmacotherapy Ser.). 650p. 1999. 299.00 (*3-7643-5969-2*, Pub. by Birkhauser) Princeton Arch.

Molecular Biology of the Lung. Robert Stockley. LC 98-36983. (Respiratory Pharmacology & Pharmacotherapy Ser.). 1998. 195.00 (*0-8176-5968-4*) Birkhauser.

Molecular Biology of the Lung Vol. 1: Emphysema & Infection. R. A. Stockley. (Respiratory Pharmacology & Pharmacotherapy Ser.). 300p. 1999. 199.00 (*3-7643-5857-2*, Pub. by Birkhauser) Princeton Arch.

Molecular Biology of the Lung Vol. II: Asthma & Cancer. R. A. Stockley. LC 98-36983. (Respiratory Pharmacology & Pharmacotherapy Ser.). 350p. 1999. 199.00 (*3-7643-5968-4*) Princeton Arch.

Molecular Biology of the Major Histocompatibility Complex of Domestic Animal Species. fac. ed. Ed. by Carol M. Warner et al. LC 88-26589. (Illus.). 201p. 1988. reprint ed. pap. 62.40 (*0-608-00952-0*, 206179800011) Bks Demand.

Molecular Biology of the Male Reproductive System. Ed. by D. M. De Kretser. (Illus.). 483p. 1993. text 99.00 (*0-12-209030-6*) Acad Pr.

Molecular Biology of the Mycobacteria. Ed. by Johnjoe McFadden. (Surrey Seminars in Molecular Microbiology Ser.). 233p. 1990. text 104.00 (*0-12-483378-0*) Acad Pr.

Molecular Biology of the Myocardium. Ed. by Michihiko Tada. 1992. 93.00 (*0-8493-7752-8*, QP) CRC Pr.

Molecular Biology of the Neuron. Ed. by R. Wayne Davies & Brian J. Morris. (The Molecular & Cellular Neurobiolgy Ser.). (Illus.). 416p. 1998. text 95.00 (*1-85996-240-8*) OUP.

Molecular Biology of the Photosynthetic Apparatus. Ed. by Katherine E. Steinback et al. LC 85-9928. 512p. 1985. 75.00 (*0-87969-188-3*) Cold Spring Harbor.

Molecular Biology of the Reproductive Systems Set. 1995. 137.00 (*0-12-481650-9*) Acad Pr.

Molecular Biology of the Skin: The Keratinocyte. Ed. by Michel Darmon & M. Blumenberg. (Illus.). 291p. 1993. text 99.00 (*0-12-203455-4*) Acad Pr.

Molecular Biology of the Staphylococci. Novick. 639p. 1990. 220.00 (*0-471-18784-4*) Wiley.

Molecular Biology of the Staphylococci. Ed. by Richard Novick. 639p. 1991. lib. bdg. 160.00 (*1-56081-032-7*, Wiley-VCH) Wiley.

Molecular Biology of the Yeast Saccharomyces: Metabolism & Gene Expression. Ed. by Jeffrey N. Strathern et al. LC 81-68203. (Monographs: No. 11B). 1985. reprint ed. text 45.00 (*0-87969-180-8*) Cold Spring Harbor.

Molecular Biology of the Yeast Saccharomyces, Life Cycle & Inheritance. Ed. by Jeffrey N. Strathern et al. LC 81-68895. (Cold Spring Harbor Monographs: Vol. 11A). 763p. 1981. reprint ed. pap. 200.00 (*0-608-01812-0*, 206246100003) Bks Demand.

Molecular Biology of Tomato: Fundamental Advances & Crop Improvement. John Yoder. LC 93-60362. 320p. 1993. 49.95 (*0-87762-992-7*) Technomic.

Molecular Biology of Tumor Cells. Ed. by Britta Wahren et al. LC 84-23786. (Progress in Cancer Research & Therapy Ser.: No. 32). (Illus.). 309p. 1985. reprint ed. pap. 95.80 (*0-7837-9516-5*, 206026500005) Bks Demand.

***Molecular Biology of Woody Plants.** S. Mohan Jain & Subhash C. Minocha. LC 99-48942. (Forestry Sciences Ser.). 1999. write for info. (*0-7923-6012-5*) Kluwer Academic.

***Molecular Biology of Woody Plants.** S. Mohan Jain & Subhash C. Minocha. 532p. 2000. 238.00 (*0-7923-6241-1*) Kluwer Academic.

Molecular Biology of Yeasts. Ed. by L. A. Grivell. LC 92-13592. 160p. (C). 1992. lib. bdg. 102.00 (*0-7923-1770-X*) Kluwer Academic.

Molecular Biology on Cell Adhesion Molecules. Ed. by Michael A. Horton. LC 96-15923. (Molecular Medical Science Ser.). 258p. 1996. 117.95 (*0-471-96677-0*) Wiley.

Molecular Biology Techniques: An Intensive Laboratory Course. Walt Ream & Katherine G. Field. (Illus.). 234p. (C). 1998. spiral bd. 39.95 (*0-12-583990-1*) Acad Pr.

***Molecular Biology Text & Lecture Outline.** Robert Frankis. 490p. (C). 1999. pap. text 90.95 (*0-7872-6389-3*, 41638901) Kendall-Hunt.

Molecular Biomethods Handbook. Ed. by Ralph Rapley & John M. Walker. (Illus.). 704p. 1998. 89.50 (*0-89603-439-9*); 89.50 (*0-89603-501-8*) Humana.

Molecular Biophysics: Structures & Dynamics. Michele DauNe. Tr. by W. J. Duffin from FRE. LC 98-36756. (Illus.). 522p. (C). 1999. pap. text 49.95 (*0-19-857782-6*) OUP.

Molecular Biophysics: Structures & Dynamics. Michael Duane. Tr. by W. D. Duffin from FRE. LC 98-36756. (Illus.). 522p. (C). 1999. text 110.00 (*0-19-857783-4*) OUP.

Molecular Biophysics of the Extracellular Matrix. Ed. by Struther Arnott et al. LC 84-6640. 189p. 1984. 89.50 (*0-89603-051-2*) Humana.

Molecular Biotechnology. 2nd ed. S. B. Primrose. (Illus.). 208p. 1991. 75.00 (*0-632-03233-2*); pap. 49.95 (*0-632-03053-4*) Blackwell Sci.

Molecular Biotechnology: Principles & Applications of Recombinant DNA. 2nd rev. ed. Bernard R. Glick & Jack J. Pasternak. LC 97-47126. (Illus.). 600p. (C). 1998. pap. text 56.95 (*1-55581-136-1*) ASM Pr.

Molecular Biotechnology: Therapeutic Applications & Strategies. Sunil Maulik & Salil Patel. LC 96-2733. 223p. 1996. pap. 59.95 (*0-471-11681-5*, Wiley-Liss) Wiley.

Molecular Biotechnology for Plant Food Production. Ed. by Octavio Paredes-Lopez. LC 98-89342. 650p. 1999. text 178.95 (*1-56676-685-0*) Technomic.

Molecular Botany: Signals & the Environment. Ed. by D. J. Bowles et al. LC 95-182887. (Biochemical Society Symposium Ser.: Vol. 60). (Illus.). 290p. (C). 1994. text 110.50 (*1-85578-050-X*, Pub. by Portland Pr Ltd) Ashgate Pub Co.

Molecular Cardiology for the Cardiologist. 2nd ed. Bernard Swynghedauw. LC 98-40587. (Developments in Cardiovascular Medicine Ser.). 301p. 1998. write for info. (*0-7923-8323-0*) Kluwer Academic.

Molecular Cardiology for the Cardiologist, No. 172. Bernard Swynghedauw. (Developments in Cardiovascular Medicine Ser.: Vol. 172). 272p. (C). 1995. text 109.00 (*0-7923-3622-4*) Kluwer Academic.

M

Molecular Cell Biology. 2nd ed. J. E. Darnell & H. Lodish. LC 89-70096. (Illus.). 1100p. (C). 1990. 160.00 (*0-7167-2164-3*) W H Freeman.

Molecular Cell Biology. 3rd ed. Lodish. 2000. 73.00 (*0-7167-3053-7*) W H Freeman.

Molecular Cell Biology. 3rd ed. H. Lodish & J. E. Darnell. (C). 1995. pap. text, teacher ed., suppl. ed. 11.95 (*0-7167-2703-X*) W H Freeman.

Molecular Cell Biology. 3rd ed. H. Lodish & J. E. Darnell. (C). 1995. pap. text, student ed. 27.95 (*0-7167-2672-6*) W H Freeman.

***Molecular Cell Biology.** 4th ed. Lodish. 1999. pap. 29.95 (*0-7167-3604-7*) W H Freeman.

***Molecular Cell Biology.** 4th ed. Harvey Lodish et al. (C). 1999. 69.00 (*0-7167-3706-X*, Pub. by W H Freeman) VHPS.

Molecular Cell Biology, Vol. 1. Harvey Lodish. 1995. 75.95 (*0-7167-3686-1*) W H Freeman.

Molecular Cell Biology: Mini Transparency Set. 3rd ed. H. Lodish. (C). 2000. 160.00 (*0-7167-2673-4*) W H Freeman.

***Molecular Cell Biology Art Notebook.** 4th ed. Lodish. 1999. pap. text. write for info. (*0-7167-4078-8*, Pub. by W H Freeman) VHPS.

***Molecular Cell Biology Preview Book.** 4th ed. Lodish. 1999. pap. text 2.95 (*0-7167-3888-0*, Pub. by W H Freeman) VHPS.

Molecular, Cellular & Clinical Aspects of Angiogenesis: Proceedings of a NATO ASI Held in Porto Carras, Halkidiki, Greece, June 16-27, 1995, Vol. A285. Ed. by Michael Maragoudakis. LC 96-21623. (NATO ASI Series A: Vol. 285). (Illus.). 302p. 1996. 126.00 (*0-306-45315-0*) Plenum.

Molecular, Cellular, & Developmental Biology of Erythropoietin & Erythropoiesis. Ed. by Ivan N. Rich & Terence R. Lappin. LC 94-10689. (Annals Ser.: Vol. 718). 376p. 1994. pap. 100.00 (*0-89766-838-3*) NY Acad Sci.

Molecular Chaperones. Ellis & Hartl. 200p. 1997. write for info. (*0-12-236540-2*); pap. write for info. (*0-12-236541-0*) Acad Pr.

***Molecular Chaperones & Folding Catalysts: Regulation, Cellular Functions & Mechanisms.** Ed. by Bernd Bukau. (Illus.). 680p. 1998. text 175.00 (*90-5702-370-9*, Harwood Acad Pubs) Gordon & Breach.

Molecular Chaperones in the Life Cycle of Proteins: Structure, Function & Mode of Action. Anthony L. Fink & Yuji Goto. LC 97-34429. (Illus.). 648p. 1997. text 210.00 (*0-8247-0100-3*) Dekker.

Molecular Characterization of the Human Pregancy Zone Protein. K. Devriendt. No. 52. 106p. (Orig.). 1992. pap. 32.00 (*90-6186-496-8*, Pub. by Leuven Univ) Coronet Bks.

Molecular Chemistry of the Transition Elements: An Introductory Course. Francois Mathey. LC 95-48041. (Inorganic Chemistry Ser.). 242p. 1996. 135.00 (*0-471-95919-7*) Wiley.

Molecular Chemistry of the Transition Elements: An Introductory Course. Francois Mathey & Alain Sevin. LC 95-48041. (Inorganic Chemistry Ser.). 242p. 1996. pap. 59.95 (*0-471-95687-2*) Wiley.

Molecular Cloning: A Laboratory Manual. T. Maniatis et al. LC 81-68891. 555p. reprint ed. pap. 172.10 (*0-7837-1892-6*, 204209600001) Bks Demand.

Molecular Cloning: A Laboratory Manual, 3 bks., Set. 2nd ed. J. Sambrook et al. (Illus.). 1659p. 1989. spiral bd. 140.00 (*0-87969-309-6*) Cold Spring Harbor.

Molecular Cloning of Hormone Genes. Ed. by Joel F. Habener. LC 86-19980. (Molecular Biology & Biophysics Ser.). (Illus.). 460p. 1987. 125.00 (*0-89603-091-1*) Humana.

Molecular Clouds. Ed. by R. A. James & T. J. Millar. (Illus.). 336p. (C). 1991. text 80.00 (*0-521-39543-7*) Cambridge U Pr.

Molecular Clouds & Star Formation: Proceedings of the 7th Guo-Shoujing Summer School on Astrophysics. Y. Chi & J. H. You. 330p. 1995. text 104.00 (*981-02-1871-0*) World Scientific Pub.

Molecular Clouds in the Milky Way & External Galaxies. Ed. by R. L. Dickman et al. (Lecture Notes in Physics Ser.: Vol. 315). xvi, 475p. 1988. 70.95 (*0-387-50438-9*) Spr-Verlag.

An Asterisk (*) at the beginning of an entry indicates that the title is appearing for the first time.

Molecular Collision Dynamics. Ed. by J. M. Bowman. (Topics in Current Physics Ser.: Vol. 33). (Illus.). 158p. 1983. 40.95 (*0-387-12014-9*) Spr-Verlag.

Molecular Collisions & Chemical Physics. Dudley R. Heurschbach. (Series on Twentieth Century Chemistry). 500p. 1998. text 112.00 (*981-02-1797-8*) World Scientific Pub.

Molecular Collisions in the Interstellar Medium. David R. Flower. (Cambridge Astrophysics Ser.: No. 17). (Illus.). 145p. (C). 1990. text 69.95 (*0-521-32032-1*) Cambridge U Pr.

Molecular Collison Theory. unabridged ed. M. S. Child. LC 96-38426. 310p. 1996. reprint ed. pap. text 9.95 (*0-486-69437-2*) Dover.

Molecular Complexes: A Lecture & Reprint Volume. Robert S. Mulliken & Willis B. Person. LC 71-84970. 516p. reprint ed. pap. 160.00 (*0-608-10196-6*, 200766600066) Bks Demand.

Molecular Complexes in Earth's, Planetary & Cometary Atmospheres. J. F. Crifo et al. LC 98-6454. 300p. 1997. text 68.00 (*981-02-3211-X*) World Scientific Pub.

Molecular Components of Hepatitis B Virus. Mark Feitelson. (Developments in Molecular Virology Ser.). 1985. text 91.00 (*0-89838-696-9*) Kluwer Academic.

Molecular Constants, Subvol. A see Atomic & Molecular Physics: Group II

M

Molecular Constants Subvolume b, Pt. 3: Linear Triatomic Molecules. Ed. by G. Guelachvili et al. (Numerical Data & Functional Relationships in Science & Technology Ser.). lxiii, 384p. 1998. 2369.00 incl. cd-rom (*3-540-63647-1*) Spr-Verlag.

Molecular Constants from Microwave-, Molecular Beam- & ESR-Spectroscopy see Atomic & Molecular Physics: Group II

Molecular Constants from Microwave Spectroscopy see Atomic & Molecular Physics: Group II

***Molecular Constants Mostly from Infrared Spectroscopy: Pt. B4: Linear Triatomic Molecules: COO+ (OCO+), CFeO (FeCO), CFeO-, (FeCO-), CNN (NCN), CNO (NCO) (CNO) (CON), CNO- (NCO-)** G. Guelachvili & K. N. Rao. Ed. by W. Martienssen. (Landolt-Boernstein Numerical Data & Functional Relationships in Science & Technology - New Series: Vol. 20). lxxi, 180p. 1999. 1800.00 (*3-540-66094-1*) Spr-Verlag.

Molecular Constants Mostly from Microwave, Molecular Beam, & Sub-Doppler Laser Spectroscopy see Atomic & Molecular Physics: Group II

***Molecular Constants Mostly from Microwave, Molecular Beam, & Sub-Doppler Laser Spectroscopy Pt. B: Rotational, Centrifugal Distortion & Related Constants of Diamagnetic Assymmetric Top Molecules.** J. Demaison et al. Ed. by W. Martienssen & W. Huettner. (Landolt-Boernstein Numerical Data & Functional Relationships in Science & Technology - New Series: Vol. 24). (Illus.). viii, 501p. 1999. 3388.00 (*3-540-65345-7*) Spr-Verlag.

Molecular Constants Mostly from Microwave, Molecular Beam, & Sub-Doppler Laser Spectroscopy, Subvol. A, Supplement to Vols. II-4, II-6 & II-14 see Atomic & Molecular Physics: Group II

Molecular Constants, Mostly from Microwaves, Molecular Beam, & Electron Resonance Spectroscopy see Atomic & Molecular Physics: Group II

Molecular Control of Blood Cells. Donald Metcalf. LC 88-605. (Illus.). 192p. 1988. 43.00 (*0-674-58157-1*) HUP.

Molecular Control of Cell Differentiation & Morphogenesis: A Systematic Theory. Gerhard D. Wassermann. LC 70-138501. (Quantitative Approach to Life Science Ser.: No. 2). (Illus.). 600p. reprint ed. pap. 186.00 (*0-8357-6221-1*, 203457500090) Bks Demand.

Molecular Control of Haemopoiesis - Symposium No. 148. CIBA Foundation Staff. LC 89-24869. (CIBA Foundation Symposium Ser.: No. 148). 242p. 1990. 128.00 (*0-471-92561-6*) Wiley.

Molecular Crystals. 2nd ed. John D. Wright. (Illus.). 235p. (C). 1995. text 74.95 (*0-521-46510-9*); pap. text 25.95 (*0-521-47730-1*) Cambridge U Pr.

Molecular Crystals & Liquid Crystals Special Topics: Proceedings of the 8th International Liquid Crystals Conference, Kyoto, Japan, June 30-July 4, 1980, 6 vols., Pts. A-F, Vols. 63, 66, 67, 68, 70 & 74. Ed. by G. J. Dienes et al. 1955p. 1981. pap. 866.00 (*0-677-40295-3*) Gordon & Breach.

Molecular Cytogenic Analysis of Adipose Tissue Tumors with Chromosome 12q13-q15 Involvement. Patrick F. Kools. (Acta Biomedica Lovaniensia Ser.: Vol. 149). (Illus.). 183p. 1997. pap. 69.50 (*90-6186-811-4*, Pub. by Leuven Univ) Coronet Bks.

Molecular Databases for Protein Sequence & Structure Studies: An Introduction. J. A. Sillince & M. Sillince. (Illus.). 288p. 1991. 84.00 (*0-387-54332-5*) Spr-Verlag.

Molecular Description of Biological Membrane Components by Computer Aided Conformational Analysis, Vol. I. Ed. by Robert Brasseur. (Illus.). 288p. 1990. lib. bdg. 202.00 (*0-8493-6375-6*) CRC Pr.

Molecular Description of Biological Membrane Components by Computer Aided Conformational Analysis, Vol. II. Ed. by Robert Brasseur. (Illus.). 224p. 1990. lib. bdg. 202.00 (*0-8493-6376-4*) CRC Pr.

***Molecular Descriptors in QSAR/QSPR.** Mati Karelson. LC 99-38911. 372p. 2000. text 195.00 (*0-471-35168-7*, Wiley-Interscience) Wiley.

Molecular Design. A. L. Horvath. (Studies in Physical & Theoretical Chemistry: Vol. 75). 1490p. 1992. 423.50 (*0-444-89217-6*) Elsevier.

Molecular Design & Bioorganic Catalysis. Ed. by Craig S. Wilcox & Andrew D. Hamilton. (NATO ASI Ser.: Series C, Vol. 478). 1996. text 161.50 (*0-7923-4024-8*) Kluwer Academic.

Molecular Design & Modeling - Concepts & Applications Pt. A: Proteins, Peptides, & Enzymes. Ed. by John N. Abelson et al. (Methods in Enzymology Ser.: Vol. 202). (Illus.). 824p. 1991. text 125.00 (*0-12-182103-X*) Acad Pr.

Molecular Design & Modeling - Concepts & Applications Pt. B: Antibodies & Antigens, Nucleic Acids, Polysaccharides, & Drugs. Ed. by John N. Abelson et al. (Methods in Enzymology Ser.: Vol. 203). (Illus.). 764p. 1991. text 136.00 (*0-12-182104-8*) Acad Pr.

Molecular Design of Life. Lubert Stryer. 1989. pap. text 13.60 (*0-7167-2050-7*) W H Freeman.

Molecular Design of Life. Lubert Stryer. (C). 1989. text 27.20 (*0-7167-2049-3*) W H Freeman.

Molecular Design of Tautomeric Compounds. V. I. Minkin et al. (C). 1987. text 221.50 (*90-277-2478-4*) Kluwer Academic.

Molecular Designing of Materials & Devices. Ed. by Arthur R. Von Hippel. 1965. 45.00 (*0-262-22006-7*) MIT Pr.

Molecular Diagnosis & Gene Therapy: Proceedings of the 88th Falk Symposium (Part III of the Basel Liver Week), Held in Basel, Switzerland, October 22-23, 1995. Ed. by H. E. Blum et al. LC 96-17381. 160p. 1996. text 88.00 (*0-7923-8702-3*) Kluwer Academic.

Molecular Diagnosis & Treatment of Melanoma. John M. Kirkwood. LC 97-52827. (Illus.). 330p. 1998. text 150.00 (*0-8247-0102-X*) Dekker.

Molecular Diagnosis of Cancer. Ed. by Finbarr Cotter. (Methods in Molecular Medicine Ser.: Vol. 6). (Illus.). 236p. 1996. 79.50 (*0-89603-341-4*) Humana.

Molecular Diagnosis of Genetic Diseases. Ed. by Rob Elles. (Methods in Molecular Medicine Ser.: Vol. 5). (Illus.). 372p. 1996. 79.50 (*0-89603-346-5*) Humana.

Molecular Diagnosis of Infectious Diseases. Ed. by Udo Reischl. LC 97-29087. (Methods in Molecular Medicine Ser.: Vol. 13). 648p. 1997. 125.00 (*0-89603-485-2*) Humana.

Molecular Diagnostic Methods for Genetic Diseases: Proposed Guideline (1997) 1997. 25.00 (*1-56238-340-X*, MM1-P) NCCLS.

Molecular Diagnostic Methods for Infectious Diseases: Approved Guideline, (1995) Contrib. by Russel K. Enns. 1995. 75.00 (*1-56238-288-8*, MM3-A) NCCLS.

Molecular Diagnostics: For the Clinical Laboratorian. Ed. by William B. Coleman & Gregory J. Tsonjalis. LC 96-37505. (Pathology & Laboratory Medicine Ser.). (Illus.). 400p. 1996. 79.50 (*0-89603-373-2*) Humana.

Molecular Diagnostics: Research Towards Application. Ed. by Ralph Rapley & Matthew R. Walker. LC 92-43669. (Illus.). 480p. 1993. 125.00 (*0-632-03528-5*) Blackwell Sci.

Molecular Diagnostics of Human Cancer. Ed. by Mark Furth & Melvyn Greaves. (Cancer Cells Ser.: No. 7). (Illus.). 414p. 1989. 95.00 (*0-87969-324-X*) Cold Spring Harbor.

Molecular Diagnostics of Infectious Diseases. Ed. by Udo Reischl. (Methods in Molecular Medicine Ser.: Vol. 13). (Illus.). 648p. 1997. spiral bd. 89.50 (*0-89603-398-8*) Humana.

Molecular Diseases. Ed. by G. Jacobasch & S. Rapoport. LC 78-41150. (Federation of European Biochemical Societies Ser.: Vol. 56). (Illus.). 102p. 1979. pap. 30.00 (*0-08-023745-2*, Pub. by Pergamon Repr) Franklin.

Molecular Dissection of Complex Traits. Andrew H. Paterson. LC 97-12278. 336p. 1997. boxed set 134.95 (*0-8493-7686-6*) CRC Pr.

Molecular Distortions in Ionic & Excited States. Ed. by Peter V. Schastnev & Lyudmila N. Schegoleva. LC 95-11948.Tr. of Strukturnye Isdazheniia Molekul V Ionnykh I Vozbuzhdennykh Sostoianiiakh. 192p. 1995. boxed set 234.95 (*0-8493-4579-0*, 4579) CRC Pr.

Molecular Diversity & Combinatorial Chemistry: Libraries & Drug Discovery. Ed. by Irwin M. Chaiken & Kim D. Janda. (ACS Conference Proceedings Ser.). (Illus.). 336p. 1996. text 115.00 (*0-8412-3450-7*, Pub. by Am Chemical) OUP.

Molecular Diversity in Drug Design. text 150.00 (*0-7923-5980-1*) Kluwer Academic.

Molecular Dosimetry & Human Cancer: Analytical, Epidemiological, & Social Considerations. John D. Groopman & Paul L. Skipper. 488p. 1991. lib. bdg. 119.00 (*0-8493-8800-7*, RC268) CRC Pr.

Molecular Dosimetry & Human Cancer: Analytical, Epidemiological & Social Considerations. Paul L. Skipper & John D. Groopman. 450p. 1990. 65.00 (*0-936923-44-X*); pap. 32.50 (*0-936923-45-8*) Telford Pr.

Molecular Dynamics. Myron W. Evans. 894p. 1986. 139.50 (*0-471-05977-3*) Krieger.

Molecular Dynamics. Julia M. Goodfellow. 1991. 99.95 (*0-8493-7119-8*, QH) CRC Pr.

Molecular Dynamics: From Classical to Quantum Methods. Perla B. Balbuena & J. M. Seminario. LC 99-22300. (Theoretical & Computational Chemistry Ser.). 970p. 1999. 421.50 (*0-444-82910-5*) Elsevier.

Molecular Dynamics & Relaxation Phenomena in Glasses. (Lecture Notes in Physics Ser.: Vol. 227). vii, 218p. 1987. 34.95 (*0-387-17801-5*) Spr-Verlag.

Molecular Dynamics & Spectroscopy by Stimulated Emission Pumping. Ed. by H. L. Dai & R. W. Field. (Advanced Series in Physical Chemistry). 1000p. 1995. text 177.00 (*981-02-1749-8*) World Scientific Pub.

Molecular Dynamics & Spectroscopy by Stimulated Emission Pumping. Ed. by H. L. Dai & R. W. Field. (Advanced Series in Physical Chemistry: Vol. 4). 1000p. 1995. pap. 95.00 (*981-02-2111-8*) World Scientific Pub.

Molecular Dynamics in Biological Membranes. Milton H. Saier, Jr. & C. D. Stiles. LC 75-12923. (Heidelberg Science Library: Vol. 22). (Illus.). 95p. (Orig.). 1975. 54.95 (*0-387-90142-6*) Spr-Verlag.

Molecular Dynamics of Additives in Polymers. A. L. Kovarski. (Illus.). 288p. 1997. 185.00 (*90-6764-259-2*, Pub. by VSP) Coronet Bks.

Molecular Dynamics of Biomembranes. Ed. by Jos A. Opden Kamp. LC 96-1972. (NATO ASI Series H: Cell Biology: No. 96). 404p. 1996. 197.00 (*3-540-60764-1*) Spr-Verlag.

Molecular Dynamics of Liquid Crystals: Proceedings of the NATO Advanced Study Institute, Il Ciocco, Barga, Italy, September 11-23, 1989. Ed. by G. R. Luckhurst & C. A. Veracini. LC 94-7985. (NATO ASI Series C: Mathematical & Physical Sciences: Vol. 431). 624p. (C). 1994. text 332.00 (*0-7923-2809-4*) Kluwer Academic.

Molecular Dynamics Simulation: Elementary Methods. J. M. Haile. LC 91-31963. (Monographs in Physical Chemistry). 489p. 1992. 99.95 (*0-471-81966-2*) Wiley.

Molecular Dynamics Simulation: Elementary Methods. J. M. Haile. LC 91-31963. 512p. 1997. pap. 69.95 (*0-471-18439-X*, Wiley-Interscience) Wiley.

Molecular Dynamics Simulations. Ed. by F. Yonezawa. (Solid-State Sciences Ser.: Vol. 103). (Illus.). 257p. 1992. 75.95 (*0-387-55099-2*) Spr-Verlag.

Molecular Dynamics Tutorial, Seattle, 1989. (American Crystallographic Association Lecture Notes Ser.: No. 10). 1991. pap. 15.00 (*0-685-51615-6*) Polycrystal Bk Serv.

Molecular Ecology & Evolution. Ed. by B. Schierwater et al. LC 94-18022. (Approaches & Applications Ser.: Vol. 69). xi, 622p. 1994. 199.00 (*0-8176-2942-4*) Birkhauser.

Molecular Ecology of Aquatic Microbes. Ed. by Joint Staff. (NATO ASI Series G: Vol. 38). (Illus.). 432p. 1995. 234.95 (*3-540-60134-1*) Spr-Verlag.

Molecular Electro-Optics, Pt. 1. Ed. by Chester T. O'Konski. LC 75-43047. (Electro-Optics Ser.: Vol. 1). 544p. 1976. reprint ed. pap. 168.70 (*0-608-03579-3*, 206440200001) Bks Demand.

Molecular Electro-Optics, Pt. 2. Ed. by Chester T. O'Konski. LC 75-43047. (Electro-Optics Ser.: Vol. 1). 351p. 1976. reprint ed. pap. 108.90 (*0-608-03580-7*, 206440200002) Bks Demand.

Molecular Electrochemistry of Inorganic, Bioinorganic & Organometallic Compounds: Proceedings of the NATO Advanced Research Workshop, Sintra, Portugal, March 25-29, 1992. Ed. by A. J. Pombeiro & J. A. McCleverty. LC 92-40897. (NATO Advanced Science Institutes Series C: Mathematical & Physical Sciences: Series C, Vol. 385). 692p. (C). 1992. text 355.00 (*0-7923-2077-8*) Kluwer Academic.

Molecular Electromagnetism. Alan Hinchliffe & Robert W. Munn. LC 85-628. 262p. reprint ed. pap. 81.30 (*0-7837-4019-0*, 204384900011) Bks Demand.

Molecular Electronic Devices. F. L. Carter. 400p. 1982. 155.00 (*0-8247-8058-2*) Dekker.

Molecular Electronic Devices, Vol. 2. Forest L. Carter. (Illus.). 560p. 1987. text 250.00 (*0-8247-7562-7*) Dekker.

Molecular Electronic Structure Theory, Vol. 1. Jorgensen. LC 99-41794. 2000. text 315.00 (*0-471-96755-6*) Wiley.

Molecular Electronics. Richard K. Miller & Terri C. Walker. LC 88-81636. (Survey on Technology & Markets Ser.: No. 45). 50p. 1989. pap. text 200.00 (*1-55865-044-X*) Future Tech Surveys.

Molecular Electronics: A Chemistry for the 21st Century Monograph. Joshua Jortner & Mark A. Ratner. LC 97-93. (IUPAC Chemical Data Ser.). (Illus.). 1997. 125.00 (*0-632-04284-2*) Blackwell Sci.

Molecular Electronics: Biosensors & Biocomputers. Ed. by F. T. Hong. LC 89-26645. (Illus.). 466p. (C). 1989. text 174.00 (*0-306-43395-8*, Kluwer Plenum) Kluwer Academic.

Molecular Electronics: Materials & Methods. Ed. by P. I. Lazarev. (C). 1991. text 191.00 (*0-7923-1196-5*) Kluwer Academic.

Molecular Electronics: Proceedings of the 4th International School on Condensed Matter Physics. Ed. by M. Borissov. 748p. 1987. text 164.00 (*9971-5-0201-1*) World Scientific Pub.

Molecular Electronics: Properties, Dynamics & Applications. Ed. by Gunter Mahler et al. (Illus.). 424p. 1996. text 175.00 (*0-8247-9526-1*) Dekker.

Molecular Electronics: Science & Technology. Ari Aviram. 372p. 1999. pap. text 22.50 (*0-8018-6302-3*) Johns Hopkins.

Molecular Electronics: Science & Technology. Ed. by Ari Aviram & Mark Ratner. LC 98-9927. (Annals of the New York Academy of Sciences Ser.: Vol. 852). 372p. 1998. 140.00 (*1-57331-155-3*); pap. 140.00 (*1-57331-156-1*) NY Acad Sci.

***Molecular Electronics Vol. 582: Materials Research Society Symposium Proceedings.** Ed. by S. T. Pantelides et al. 2000. text 90.00 (*1-55899-490-4*) Materials Res.

Molecular Electronics - Science & Technology. A. Aviram. (Conference Proceeding Ser.: No. 262). 344p. 1992. 95.00 (*1-56396-041-9*) Am Inst Physics.

Molecular Electronics & Molecular Electronic Devices, 2 vols., I. Sienicki. 272p. 1993. lib. bdg. 110.00 (*0-8493-8061-8*) CRC Pr.

Molecular Electronics & Molecular Electronic Devices, 2 vols., II. Sienicki. 288p. 1993. lib. bdg. 159.00 (*0-8493-8062-6*, TK7774) CRC Pr.

Molecular Electronics & Molecular Electronic Devices, 2 vols., Vol. III. Sienicki. 272p. 1994. lib. bdg. 119.00 (*0-8493-8063-4*) CRC Pr.

Molecular Electrostatic Potentials: Concepts & Applications. J. S. Murray & K. Sen. 1996. write for info. (*0-614-17931-9*) Elsevier.

Molecular Electrostatic Potentials: Concepts & Applications. J. S. Murray & K. D. Sen. LC 96-36531. (Theoretical & Computational Chemistry Ser.). 680p. 1996. 372.00 (*0-444-82353-0*) Elsevier.

Molecular Embryology: Methods & Protocols. Paul T. Sharpe & Ivor Mason. LC 98-23234. (Methods in Molecular Biology Ser.: Vol. 97). (Illus.). 772p. 1999. 135.00 (*0-89603-387-2*) Humana.

Molecular Embryology of Flowering Plants. V. Raghavan. LC 96-44410. (Illus.). 712p. (C). 1997. text 155.00 (*0-521-55246-X*) Cambridge U Pr.

Molecular Endocrinology. 2nd ed. Franklyn F. Bolander. LC 94-10458. (Illus.). 601p. 1994. text 74.00 (*0-12-111231-4*) Acad Pr.

Molecular Endocrinology: Basic Concepts & Clinical Correlations. Ed. by Bruce D. Weintraub. LC 94-15793. 544p. 1994. text 156.00 (*0-7817-0223-2*) Lppncott W & W.

Molecular Endocrinology: Genetic Analysis of Hormones & Their Receptors. Ed. by G. Rumsby & S. Farrow. (Human Molecular Genetics Ser.). (Illus.). 300p. 1997. 130.00 (*1-85996-235-1*, Pub. by Bios Sci) Bks Intl VA.

***Molecular Endocrinology: Genetic Analysis of Hormones & Their Receptors.** Gill Rumsby. (Illus.). 264p. 1999. 105.00 (*0-12-220440-9*) Acad Pr.

Molecular Endocrinology of Cancer. Ed. by Jonathan Waxman. (Cancer Ser.). (Illus.). 440p. (C). 1996. text 95.00 (*0-521-46067-0*) Cambridge U Pr.

Molecular Endocrinology of the Steroid Hormones. Dennis Schulster & Sumner Burstein. LC 75-31525. 337p. reprint ed. pap. 104.50 (*0-608-17585-4*, 203042500069) Bks Demand.

Molecular Engineering for Advanced Materials. Ed. by Jan Becher & Kjeld Schaumburg. LC 94-48060. (NATO ASI Ser.: Series C, Mathematical & Physical Sciences: Vol. 456). 1995. text 217.50 (*0-7923-3347-0*) Kluwer Academic.

Molecular Environmental Biology. Seymour J. Garte. 272p. 1993. lib. bdg. 95.00 (*0-87371-631-0*, L631) Lewis Pubs.

Molecular Epidemiology: Principles & Practices. Ed. by Paul A. Schulte & Frederica Perera. (Illus.). 588p. 1993. text 94.00 (*0-12-632345-3*) Acad Pr.

Molecular Epidemiology: Principles & Practices. Ed. by Paul A. Schulte & Frederica Perera. (Illus.). 588p. 1998. pap. text 49.95 (*0-12-632346-1*) Morgan Kaufmann.

***Molecular Epidemiology of Infectious Diseases.** Andrew R. C. Thompson. (Illus.). 448p. 2000. text 85.00 (*0-340-75909-7*, Pub. by E A) OUP.

Molecular Epidemiology of Tropical Diseases: Hemoparasites & Their Vectors. Ed. by Frans Jongejan et al. LC 98-13136. (Annals of the New York Academy of Sciences Ser.: Vol. 849). 503p. 1998. 140.00 (*1-57331-141-3*); pap. 140.00 (*1-57331-142-1*) NY Acad Sci.

Molecular Evolution. Wen-Hsiung Li. LC 96-38032. (Illus.). 432p. (C). 1997. text 62.95 (*0-87893-463-4*) Sinauer Assocs.

Molecular Evolution. David E. Penny et al. 450p. 1984. 62.50 (*0-86720-021-9*) Jones & Bartlett.

Molecular Evolution. S. N. Rodin et al. (Biomathematics Ser.: Vol. 24). (Illus.). 445p. 1995. 152.95 (*0-387-57083-7*) Spr-Verlag.

Molecular Evolution. 2nd ed. Vadim A. Ratner et al. LC 95-24950. (Biomathematics Ser.: Vol. 24). 1995. write for info. (*3-540-57083-7*) Spr-Verlag.

Molecular Evolution: A Phylogenic Approach. Roderic D. Page & Edward C. Holmes. LC 98-4696. (Illus.). 346p. 1998. pap. 51.95 (*0-86542-889-1*) Blackwell Sci.

Molecular Evolution: Computer Analysis of Protein & Nucleic Acid Sequences. Ed. by John N. Abelson et al. (Methods in Enzymology Ser.: Vol. 183). 736p. 1990. text 146.00 (*0-12-182084-X*) Acad Pr.

Molecular Evolution: Evidence for Monophyly of Metazoa. Ed. by Werner E. Myller et al. LC 97-27728. (Progress in Molecular & Subcellular Biology Ser.: Vol. 19). (Illus.). 198p. 1998. 119.00 (*3-540-63229-8*) Spr-Verlag.

Molecular Evolution: Producing the Biochemical Data. Ed. by John N. Abelson et al. (Methods in Enzymology Ser.: Vol. 224). (Illus.). 725p. 1993. text 104.00 (*0-12-182125-0*) Acad Pr.

Molecular Evolution: Towards the Origin of Metazoa. Ed. by W. E. Muller et al. LC 98-22469. (Progress in Molecular & Subcellular Biology Ser.: Vol. 21). (Illus.). xi, 186p. 1998. 99.00 (*3-540-64565-9*) Spr-Verlag.

Molecular Evolution & Adaptive Radiation. Ed. by Thomas J. Givnish & Kenneth J. Sytsma. (Illus.). 639p. (C). 1997. text 110.00 (*0-521-57329-7*) Cambridge U Pr.

***Molecular Evolution & Adaptive Radiation.** Ed. by Thomas J. Givnish & Kenneth J. Sytsma. (Illus.). 621p. (C). 2000. pap. 39.95 (*0-521-77929-4*) Cambridge U Pr.

***Molecular Evolution & Phylogenetics.** Masatoshi Nei & Sudhir Kumar. LC 99-39160. 336p. 2000. write for info. (*0-19-513584-9*); write for info. (*0-19-513585-7*) OUP.

Molecular Evolution & Protobiology. Ed. by Koichiro Matsuno et al. LC 83-24465. 480p. 1984. 110.00 (*0-306-41509-7*, Plenum Trade) Perseus Pubng.

Molecular Evolution & the Origin of Life. rev. ed. Sidney W. Fox & Klaus Dose. LC 77-21434. (Illus.). 392p. reprint ed. pap. 121.60 (*0-8357-6222-X*, 203453200090) Bks Demand.

Molecular Evolution of Chromosomes. Michele Calos. (Illus.). 300p. 2000. 50.00 (*0-19-509957-5*) OUP.

Molecular Evolution of Life. Ed. by Herrick Baltscheffsky et al. (Illus.). 384p. 1987. text 100.00 (*0-521-33642-2*) Cambridge U Pr.

Molecular Evolution of Physiological Processes: Proceedings: Symposium on Molecular Evolution of Physiological Process (47th: 1993: Woods Hole, Mass.) Ed. by Douglas M. Fambrough. LC 94-65642. (Society of General Physiologists Ser.: Vol. 49). 297p. 1995. pap. 50.00 (*0-87470-055-8*) Rockefeller.

An Asterisk (*) at the beginning of an entry indicates that the title is appearing for the first time.

Molecular Evolution of the Major Histocompatibility Complex. Ed. by Johannes Klein & D. Klein. (NATO ASI Series H: Cell Biology: Vol. 59). xii, 509p. 1991. 269.00 (*0-387-54608-1*) Spr-Verlag.

Molecular Evolution of Viruses - Past & Present. Ed. by Yechiel Becker. 302p. (C). 1996. text 181.50 (*0-7923-9739-8*) Kluwer Academic.

Molecular Evolutionary Genetics. R. J. MacIntyre. LC 85-19312. (Monographs in Evolutionary Biology). (Illus.). 632p. (C). 1985. text 135.00 (*0-306-42042-2*, Kluwer Plenum) Kluwer Academic.

Molecular Evolutionary Genetics. Masatoshi Nei. 448p. 1987. text 105.50 (*0-231-06320-2*) Col U Pr.

Molecular Evolutionary Genetics. Masatoshi Nei. 448p. 1989. pap. text 38.50 (*0-231-06321-0*) Col U Pr.

Molecular Fabric of Cells: Members of the BIOTOL Project. (Illus.). 1992. pap. text 44.95 (*0-7506-1499-4*) Buttrwrth-Heinemann.

Molecular Flow in Complex Vacuum Systems. G. L. Saksaganskii. xiv, 162p. 1988. text 249.00 (*2-88124-658-3*) Gordon & Breach.

Molecular Foundations of Psychiatry. Steven E. Hyman & Eric J. Nestler. LC 92-7017. 239p. 1992. text 41.95 (*0-88048-353-9*, 8353) Am Psychiatric.

***Molecular Functions of Electroactive Thin Films.** Ed. by N. Oyama & V. Birss. LC 99-62295. 274p. 1999. 46.00 (*1-56677-220-6*, PV 98-26) Electrochem Soc.

Molecular Fungal Biology. Ed. by Richard P. Oliver & Michael Schweizer. LC 99-10041. (Illus.). 320p. (C). 1999. text 80.00 (*0-521-56116-7*); pap. text 34.95 (*0-521-56784-X*) Cambridge U Pr.

Molecular Gas Dynamics & the Direct Simulation of Gas Flows. 2nd ed. G. A. Bird. (Engineering Science Ser.: Vol. 42). (Illus.). 476p. 1994. text 135.00 (*0-19-856195-4*) OUP.

Molecular Genetic Analysis. Michels. 1969. text. write for info. (*0-471-89919-4*); pap. text. write for info. (*0-471-89921-6*) Wiley.

Molecular Genetic Analysis of Populations: A Practical Approach. 2nd ed. Ed. by A. R. Hoelzel. (The Practical Approach Ser.: No. 187). (Illus.). 468p. 1998. text 115.00 (*0-19-963634-6*); pap. text 58.00 (*0-19-963635-4*) OUP.

Molecular Genetic Approaches in Conservation. Ed. by Thomas B. Smith & Robert K. Wayne. (Illus.). 504p. (C). 1996. text 85.00 (*0-19-509526-X*) OUP.

Molecular Genetic Medicine, Vol. 4. Ed. by Theodore Friedmann. (Illus.). 188p. 1994. text. write for info. (*0-12-462004-3*) Acad Pr.

Molecular Genetic Neuroscience. Ed. by Francis O. Schmitt et al. LC 82-7699. (Illus.). 512p. 1982. reprint ed. pap. 158.80 (*0-7837-9532-7*, 206028100005) Bks Demand.

***Molecular Genetics.** J. T. Hancock. LC 99-15300. (Biomedical Sciences Explained Ser.). 208p. 1999. pap. text 36.00 (*0-7506-3253-4*) Buttrwrth-Heinemann.

Molecular Genetics. Helms. 1997. 1.50 (*0-7167-9321-0*) W H Freeman.

Molecular Genetics: A Workbook. Peter Smith-Keary. LC 91-18800. 256p. (Orig.). 1991. pap. text 27.95 (*0-89862-483-5*) Guilford Pubns.

Molecular Genetics & Colorectal Neoplasia: A Primer for the Clinician. James M. Church et al. LC 96-13339. (Illus.). 128p. 1996. pap. text 39.95 (*0-89640-299-1*) Igaku-Shoin.

Molecular Genetics & Evolution of Pesticide Resistance, Vol. 645. Ed. by Thomas M. Brown. LC 96-29234. (ACS Symposium Ser.). (Illus.). 280p. 1996. text 105.00 (*0-8412-3453-1*, Pub. by Am Chemical) OUP.

Molecular Genetics & Gene Therapy of Cardiovascular Diseases. Ed. by Stephen C. Mockrin. LC 95-25992. (Fundamental & Clinical Cardiology Ser.: Vol. 26). (Illus.). 616p. 1996. text 215.00 (*0-8247-9408-7*) Dekker.

Molecular Genetics & Therapy of Leukemia. Ed. by Emil J. Freireich & Hagop Kantarjian. LC 96-4656. (Cancer Treatment & Research Ser.: Vol. 84). 352p. (C). 1996. text 278.50 (*0-7923-3912-6*) Kluwer Academic.

Molecular Genetics, Biochemistry & Clinical Aspects of Inherited Disorders of Purine & Pyrimidine Metabolism. Ed. by U. Gresser. (Illus.). 210p. 1993. write for info. (*3-540-56774-7*) Spr-Verlag.

Molecular Genetics, Biochemistry & Clinical Aspects of Inherited Disorders of Purine & Pyrimidine Metabolism. Ed. by U. Gresser. LC 93-30001. 1993. 137.00 (*0-387-56774-7*) Spr-Verlag.

***Molecular Genetics Development.** (C). 2001. text. write for info. (*0-8053-4526-4*) Benjamin-Cummings.

Molecular Genetics for the Clinician. D. J. Brock. LC 92-9574. (Illus.). 301p. (C). 1993. text 74.95 (*0-521-41179-3*); pap. text 31.95 (*0-521-42325-2*) Cambridge U Pr.

Molecular Genetics in Developmental Neurobiology. Ed. by Y. Tsukada. (Taniguchi Symposia on Brain Sciences Ser.: No. 9). 294p. 1986. lib. bdg. 115.00 (*90-6764-084-0*, Pub. by VSP) Coronet Bks.

Molecular Genetics in Diagnosis & Research. Ed. by Robert W. Allen & James P. AuBuchon. LC 95-35428. (Illus.). 161p. (C). 1995. 45.00 (*1-56395-044-8*) Am Assn Blood.

***Molecular Genetics in Early Europe: Papers in Population Prehistory.** Ed. by Colin Renfrew & Katie Boyle. 350p. (C). 2000. 80.00 (*1-902937-08-2*, Pub. by McDonald Inst) David Brown.

Molecular Genetics in Hearing Research. Ed. by Matthew C. Holley & Marcelo N. Rivolta. (Journal Ser.: Vol. 2, Nos. 1 & 2, 1997). (Illus.). iv, 112p. 1997. pap. 61.00 (*3-8055-6475-9*) S Karger.

Molecular Genetics in Surgical Oncology. J. F. Moley. (Medical Intelligence Unit Ser.). 115p. 1994. 99.00 (*1-879702-18-5*) Landes Bioscience.

***Molecular Genetics of Aging.** Ed. by Siegfried Hekimi et al. LC 99-53835. (Results & Problems in Cell Differentiation Ser.: 29). (Illus.). x, 230p. (C). 2000. 135.00 (*3-540-66663-X*) Spr-Verlag.

Molecular Genetics of Bacteria. Larry Snyder & Wendy Champness. LC 96-46770. 1997. 79.95 (*1-55581-102-7*) ASM Pr.

Molecular Genetics of Bacteria. 3rd ed. Jeremy Dale. LC 97-32243. 324p. 1998. 115.00 (*0-471-97782-9*) Wiley.

***Molecular Genetics of Bacteria.** 3rd ed. Jeremy Dale. LC 97-32243. 324p. 1998. pap. 45.00 (*0-471-97783-7*) Wiley.

Molecular Genetics of Bacterial Pathogenesis: A Tribute to Stanley Falkow. Ed. by Virginia L. Miller et al. LC 94-19193. (Illus.). 566p. (C). 1994. 79.00 (*1-55581-082-9*) ASM Pr.

Molecular Genetics of Biological Rhythms. Ed. by Michael W. Young. LC 92-29091. (Cellular Clocks Ser.: Vol. 4). (Illus.). 336p. 1992. text 165.00 (*0-8247-8774-9*) Dekker.

***Molecular Genetics of Cancer.** John K. Cowell. 245p. 1999. 105.00 (*0-12-220441-7*) Acad Pr.

Molecular Genetics of Cancer. Cold Spring Harbor Symposium on Quantitative Biolo. LC 34-8174. (Cold Spring Harbor Symposia on Quantitative Biology Ser.: No. 59). (Illus.). 767p. 1994. reprint ed. pap. 200.00 (*0-608-07906-5*, 206788700011) Bks Demand.

Molecular Genetics of Coronary Artery Disease: Candidate Genes & Processes in Atherosclerosis. Ed. by Robert S. Sparkes et al. (Monographs in Human Genetics: Vol. 14). (Illus.). xviii, 454p. 1992. 278.50 (*3-8055-5558-X*) S Karger.

Molecular Genetics of Drosophilia Oogenesis. Paul F. Lasko. (Molecular Biology Intelligence Unit Ser.). 118p. 1994. 99.00 (*1-57059-032-X*, LN9032) Landes Bioscience.

Molecular Genetics of Drug Resistance. Ed. by C. Roland Wolf & John D. Hayes. (Modern Genetics Ser.). 424p. 1997. pap. text 30.00 (*90-5702-168-4*, Harwood Acad Pubs) Gordon & Breach.

Molecular Genetics of Drug Resistance, Vol. 3. Ed. by C. Roland Wolf & John D. Hayes. (Modern Genetics Ser.). 424p. 1997. text 81.00 (*90-5702-167-6*, Harwood Acad Pubs) Gordon & Breach.

Molecular Genetics of Early Drosophila & Mouse Development. Ed. by Mario Capecchi. (Current Communications in Molecular Biology Ser.). (Illus.). 141p. 1989. pap. 24.00 (*0-87969-339-8*) Cold Spring Harbor.

***Molecular Genetics of Early Human Development.** Tom Strachan. 265p. 2000. 105.00 (*0-12-220442-5*) Acad Pr.

Molecular Genetics of Endocrine Disorders. Ed. by R. V. Thakker. LC 97-66898. (Illus.). 480p. 1997. text 99.00 (*0-412-58970-2*, Pub. by E A) OUP.

Molecular Genetics of Escherichia Coli. Peter Smith-Keary. LC 88-28453. (Molecular Cell Biology Ser.). 198p. 1989. pap. text 24.95 (*0-89862-525-4*); lib. bdg. 49.95 (*0-89862-402-9*) Guilford Pubns.

Molecular Genetics of Haemostasis & Its Inherited Disorders. Edward G. Tuddenham & David N. Cooper. (Oxford Monographs on Medical Genetics: No. 25). (Illus.). 608p. 1994. text 145.00 (*0-19-261661-7*) OUP.

Molecular Genetics of Hemophilia. G. A. Vehar. Date not set. 1.20 (*0-7167-9277-X*) W H Freeman.

Molecular Genetics of Host-Specific Toxins in Plant Diseases: Proceedings of the 3rd Tottori International Symposium on Host-Specific Toxins, Daisen, Tottori, Japan, August 24-29, 1997. Keisuke Kohmoto & Olen Yoder. LC 98-10597. (Developments in Plant Pathology Ser.). 428p. 1998. 194.00 (*0-7923-4981-4*) Kluwer Academic.

Molecular Genetics of Human Inherited Disease. Ed. by Duncan J. Shaw. LC 95-10485. (Molecular Medical Science Ser.). 260p. 1995. 147.50 (*0-471-93459-3*) Wiley.

***Molecular Genetics of Hypertension.** Dominiczak. 269p. 1999. 115.00 (*0-12-220430-1*) Acad Pr.

Molecular Genetics of Inherited Eye Disorders. Ed. by Alan F. Wright & Barrie Jay. (Modern Genetics Ser.: Vol. 2). (Illus.). xiv, 528p. 1994. text 116.00 (*3-7186-5493-8*) Gordon & Breach.

Molecular Genetics of Mammalian Cells. Ed. by Michael M. Gottesman. (Methods in Enzymology Ser.: Vol. 151). 609p. 1987. text 157.00 (*0-12-182052-1*) Acad Pr.

Molecular Genetics of Mammalian Cells. George M. Malacinski et al. 1986. text 58.50 (*0-07-039755-4*) McGraw.

Molecular Genetics of Marine Mammals: Incorporating the Proceedings of a Workshop on the Analysis of Genetic Data to Address Problems of Stock Identity As Related to Management of Marine Mammals. Workshop on the Analysis of Genetic Data to Address Problems of Stock Identity as Related to Management of Marine Mammals et al. LC 97-69395. (Special Publication / the Society for Marine Mammalogy Ser.). xi, 388 p. 1997. write for info. (*0-935868-92-5*) Allen Pr.

Molecular Genetics of Muscle Disease: Duchenne & Other Dystrophies. Ed. by A. J. Buller et al. (Illus.). 222p. 1989. text. write for info. (*0-443-04199-7*) Church.

***Molecular Genetics of Mycobacteria.** Ed. by William R. Jacobs & Graham R. Hatfull. 380p. 2000. 99.95 (*1-55581-191-4*) ASM Pr.

Molecular Genetics of Neurological & Neuromuscular Disease. Ed. by Stefano DiDonato et al. LC 87-3531. (Advances in Neurology Ser.: Vol. 48). 286p. 1988. reprint ed. pap. 88.70 (*0-608-04693-0*, 206541400004) Bks Demand.

Molecular Genetics of Ocular Disease. Ed. by Janey L. Wiggs. 256p. 1994. 149.95 (*0-471-10601-1*) Wiley.

Molecular Genetics of Parasitic Protozoa. Ed. by Mervyn Turner & David Arnot. (Current Communications in Molecular Biology Ser.). (Illus.). 204p. 1988. pap. text 25.00 (*0-87969-313-4*) Cold Spring Harbor.

Molecular Genetics of Pediatric Solid Tumors: Basic Concepts & Recent Advances. Ed. by Gian P. Tonini et al. LC 91-35383. xiv, 382p. 1992. text 132.00 (*3-7186-5080-0*) Gordon & Breach.

Molecular Genetics of Photosynthesis. Ed. by B. Anderson et al. (Frontiers in Molecular Biology Ser.: No. 14). (Illus.). 268p. 1996. text 110.00 (*0-19-963448-3*); pap. text 55.00 (*0-19-963447-5*) OUP.

Molecular Genetics of Plant Development. Stephen H. Howell. LC 97-35238. (Illus.). 384p. (C). 1998. text 85.00 (*0-521-58255-5*); pap. text 39.95 (*0-521-58784-0*) Cambridge U Pr.

Molecular Genetics of Plant-Microbe Interactions. Ed. by Desh P. Verma & N. Brisson. (Current Plant Science & Biotechnology in Agriculture Ser.). 1986. text 122.00 (*90-247-3426-6*) Kluwer Academic.

Molecular Genetics of Sex Determination. Ed. by Stephen S. Wachtel. LC 93-8302. (Illus.). 518p. 1993. text 99.00 (*0-12-728960-7*) Acad Pr.

Molecular Genetics of Type 1 Neurofibromatosis: Towards Preimplantation Genetic Diagnosis. Rina Wu. (Acta Biomedica Lovaniensia Ser.: No. 125). (Illus.). 112p. (Orig.). 1996. pap. 39.50 (*90-6186-732-0*, Pub. by Leuven Univ) Coronet Bks.

Molecular Genetics of X-Linked Alport Syndrome. Caiying Guo. (Acta Biomedica Lovaniensia Ser.: Vol. 109). (Illus.). v, 85p. (Orig.). 1995. pap. 33.50 (*90-6186-681-2*, Pub. by Leuven Univ) Coronet Bks.

Molecular Genetics of Yeast: A Practical Approach, No. 141. Ed. by John R. Johnston. (Practical Approach Ser.: Vol. 141). (Illus.). 300p. 1994. text 95.00 (*0-19-963430-0*); pap. text 55.00 (*0-19-963429-7*) OUP.

Molecular Geometry. Alison Rodger & P. Mark Rodger. (Illus.). 208p. (C). 1995. pap. text 34.95 (*0-7506-2295-4*, Prgamon Press) Buttrwrth-Heinemann.

Molecular Geometry & Bonding. Clyde Metz. Ed. by C. L. Stanitski. (Modular Laboratory Program in Chemistry Ser.). 16p. (C). 1998. pap. text 1.50 (*0-87540-409-X*, STRC 409) Chem Educ Res.

Molecular Gerontology: Research Status & Strategies. Ed. by Suresh I. Rattan & Olivier Toussaint. LC 96-37284. 224p. (C). 1997. text 69.50 (*0-306-45491-2*, Kluwer Plenum) Kluwer Academic.

Molecular Glycobiology: Frontiers in Molecular Biology. Ed. by Minoru Fukuda & Ole Hindsgaul. LC 93-41975. (Frontiers in Molecular Biology Ser.). (Illus.). 276p. (C). 1994. pap. text 50.00 (*0-19-963386-X*) OUP.

***Molecular Haematology.** Ed. by Andrew Provan & John Gribbin. LC 99-16528. (Illus.). 240p. 2000. 195.00 (*0-632-05037-3*) Blackwell Sci.

Molecular Histochemical Techniques. K. Takehiko. Ed. by T. Kojima. LC 99-52223. (Illus.). vi, 250p. 2000. pap. text 89.95 (*4-431-70231-8*) Spr-Verlag.

Molecular Hydrodynamics. Jean P. Boon & Sidney Yip. (Illus.). 432p. 1992. reprint ed. pap. 13.95 (*0-486-66949-1*) Dover.

***Molecular Hydrogen in Space.** Ed. by Francoise Combes & Guillaume Pineau des Forets. (Cambridge Contemporary Astrophysics Ser.). (Illus.). 420p. 2000. write for info. (*0-521-78224-4*) Cambridge U Pr.

Molecular Imaging in Neuroscience: A Practical Approach. Ed. by N. A. Sharif. (Practical Approach Ser.: No. 130). (Illus.). 272p. 1994. pap. text 45.00 (*0-19-963380-0*); spiral bd. 75.00 (*0-19-963381-9*) OUP.

Molecular Imaging in Oncology: PET, MRI & MRS. Edmund E. Kim & E. F. Jackson. LC 98-33852. (Illus.). 300p. 1999. 189.00 (*3-540-64101-7*) Spr-Verlag.

Molecular Immunological Considerations in Malaria Vaccine Development. Michael F. Good. 288p. 1993. lib. bdg. 179.00 (*0-8493-5258-4*, QR189) CRC Pr.

Molecular Immunology. 2nd ed. Ed. by B. David Hames & David M. Glover. (Frontiers in Molecular Biology Ser.). (Illus.). 404p. (C). 1996. text 115.00 (*0-19-963379-7*) OUP.

Molecular Immunology: A Textbook. Ed. by M. Zouhair Atassi et al. (Immunology Ser.: 22). (Illus.). 744p. 1984. text 95.00 (*0-8247-7045-5*, 7045-5) Dekker.

Molecular Immunology of Complex Carbohydrates. Ed. by A. M. Wu. LC 88-2532. (Advances in Experimental Medicine & Biology Ser.: Vol. 228). (Illus.). 882p. 1988. 165.00 (*0-306-42818-0*, Plenum Trade) Perseus Pubng.

Molecular Improvement of Cereal Crops. I. K. Vasil. LC 98-31666. 1998. write for info. (*0-7923-5471-0*) Kluwer Academic.

Molecular Industrial Mycology: Systems & Applications for Filamentous Fungi. Ed. by Sally A. Leong & Randy Berka. (Mycology Ser.: Vol. 8). (Illus.). 304p. 1990. text 145.00 (*0-8247-8392-1*) Dekker.

Molecular Insect Science. Ed. by H. H. Hagedorn et al. (Illus.). 416p. (C). 1990. text 115.00 (*0-306-43706-6*, Kluwer Plenum) Kluwer Academic.

Molecular Interactions, 3 vols., 1. Ed. by H. Ratajczak et al. LC 79-40825. (Illus.). 437p. 1980. reprint ed. pap. 135.50 (*0-608-08427-1*, 203048000001) Bks Demand.

Molecular Interactions, 3 vols., 2. Ed. by H. Ratajczak et al. LC 79-40825. (Illus.). 651p. 1981. reprint ed. pap. 200.00 (*0-608-08428-X*, 203048000002) Bks Demand.

Molecular Interactions, 3 vols., 3. Ed. by H. Ratajczak et al. LC 79-40825. (Illus.). 583p. 1982. reprint ed. pap. 180.80 (*0-608-08429-8*, 203048000003) Bks Demand.

Molecular Interactions: From Van Der Waals to Strongly Bound Complexes. Steve Scheiner. LC 96-43509. (Wiley Tutorial Series in Theoretical Chemistry). 378p. 1997. 235.00 (*0-471-97154-5*) Wiley.

Molecular Interactions & Activity in Proteins. CIBA Foundation Staff. LC 78-14500. (CIBA Foundation Symposium: New Ser.: No. 60). 287p. reprint ed. pap. 89.00 (*0-608-14299-9*, 202218400024) Bks Demand.

Molecular Interactions & Electronic Spectra. Noboru Mataga & Tanekazu Kubota. LC 71-107755. 520p. reprint ed. pap. 161.20 (*0-608-16725-8*, 202782100054) Bks Demand.

***Molecular Interactions & Time-Space Organization in Macromolecular Systems: Proceedings of the OUMS'98, Osaka, Japan, 3-6 June 1998.** Ed. by Y. Morishima et al. LC 99-34982. viii, 195p. 1999. 182.00 (*3-540-66110-7*) Spr-Verlag.

Molecular Interactions in Bioseparations. T. T. Ngo. (Illus.). 588p. (C). 1994. text 115.00 (*0-306-44435-6*, Kluwer Plenum) Kluwer Academic.

***Molecular Interactions of Actin: Actin Structure & Actin-Binding Proteins.** Cristobal G. Dos Remedios & David D. Thomas. LC 00-41288. (Results & Problems in Cell Differentiation Ser.). 2000. write for info. (*3-540-67110-2*) Spr-Verlag.

Molecular Interpretations of Sorption in Polymers, Pt. I. Ed. by L. A. Errede. (Advances in Polymer Science Ser.: Vol. 99). (Illus.). 128p. 1991. 79.00 (*0-387-53497-0*) Spr-Verlag.

Molecular Interrelations of Nutrition & Cancer: The University of Texas M. D. Anderson Hospital & Tumor Institute at Houston, 34th Annual Symposium on Fundamental Cancer Research, 1981. Symposium on Fundamental Cancer Research Staff. Ed. by Marilyn S. Arnott et al. LC 81-23408. 490p. 1982. reprint ed. pap. 151.90 (*0-608-00448-0*, 206116300007) Bks Demand.

M

Molecular Liquids: Dynamics & Interactions. Ed. by A. James Barnes et al. 1984. text 256.50 (*90-277-1817-2*) Kluwer Academic.

Molecular Liquids: New Perspectives in Physics & Chemistry. Ed. by Jose J. Teiziera-Dias. LC 92-18171. (NATO Advanced Study Institutes Series C, Mathematical & Physical Sciences: Vol. 379). 596p. (C). 1992. text 299.00 (*0-7923-1934-6*) Kluwer Academic.

Molecular Luminescence Spectroscopy: Methods & Applications. Ed. by Stephen G. Schulman. LC 84-21880. (Chemical Analysis Ser.: No. 1-075). 848p. 1985. 199.00 (*0-471-86848-5*) Wiley.

Molecular Luminescence Spectroscopy: Methods & Applications, Vol. 2. Ed. by Stephen G. Schulman. (Chemical Analysis Ser.). 526p. 1988. 199.00 (*0-471-63684-3*) Wiley.

Molecular Luminescence Spectroscopy: Methods & Applications, Vol. 3. Ed. by Stephen G. Schulman. (Chemical Analysis: A Series of Monographs on Analytical Chemistry & Its Applications). 480p. 1993. 159.00 (*0-471-51580-9*) Wiley.

Molecular Magnetism. O. Kahn. 396p. 1993. 145.00 (*0-471-18838-7*, Wiley-VCH) Wiley.

Molecular Magnetism. Olivier Kahn. LC 93-10928. 1993. 95.00 (*1-56081-566-3*, Wiley-VCH) Wiley.

Molecular Magnetism - From Molecular Assemblies to the Devices: Proceedings of the NATO Advanced Study Institute on 'Localized & Itinerany Molecular Magnetism: From Molecular Assemblies to the Devices', Puerto de la Cruz, Tenerife, Spain, April 23-May 3, 1995. Ed. by Eugenio Coronado. LC 96-26728. (NATO Advance Science Institutes Series E). 604p. (C). 1996. text 306.00 (*0-7923-4130-9*) Kluwer Academic.

Molecular Magnetochemistry. Sergey Vulfson. 472p. 1998. text 82.00 (*90-5699-535-9*) Gordon & Breach.

Molecular Manufacturing, Vol. 2. Ed. by Claudio Nicolini & Sergei Vakula. LC 96-5249. (Electronics & Biotechnology Advanced Forum Ser.: No. 2). (Illus.). 234p. (C). 1996. text 95.00 (*0-306-45284-7*, Kluwer Plenum) Kluwer Academic.

***Molecular Marine Microbiology.** Ed. by Douglas H. Bartlett. 220p. 2000. 119.99 (*1-898486-20-4*, Pub. by Horizon Sci) Intl Spec Bk.

Molecular Markers in Environmental Geochemistry. Ed. by R. P. Eganhouse. LC 97-16625. (ACS Symposium Ser.: No. 671). 436p. 1997. text 129.95 (*0-8412-3518-X*, Pub. by Am Chemical) OUP.

Molecular Markers in Plant Genome Analysis: Sponsored CRIS/ICAR Projects & Bibliography. Andrew Kalinski. 115p. (Orig.). (C). 1995. pap. text 35.00 (*0-7881-1988-5*) DIANE Pub.

Molecular Mechanics. Ulrich Burkert. 340p. 1982. pap. text 59.00 (*0-8412-0885-9*, Pub. by Am Chemical) OUP.

Molecular Mechanics. Ed. by Ulrich Burkert & Norman L. Allinger. LC 82-11442. (ACS Monograph: No. 177). 340p. 1982. text 85.00 (*0-8412-0584-1*, Pub. by Am Chemical) OUP.

Molecular Mechanics: A Symposium. Ed. by Delos F. DeTar. LC 77-14614. 1978. pap. 40.00 (*0-08-022070-3*, Pergamon Pr) Elsevier.

Molecular Mechanics Across Chemistry. Anthony K. Rappe & Carla J. Casewit. LC 96-13315. (Illus.). 444p. 1997. text 58.00 (*0-935702-77-6*) Univ Sci Bks.

Molecular Mechanics & Conformational Analysis in Drug Design. Gyorgy M. Keseru & Istvan Kolossvary. LC 98-42144. (Illus.). 1999. 99.00 (*0-632-05289-9*) Blackwell Sci.

Molecular Mechanism of Biosignal Transduction: Proceedings of the 23rd Gunma Symposium on Endocrinology, Japan, 1985. Ed. by Yasuo Kondo. 184p. 1986. lib. bdg. 110.00 (*90-6764-086-7*, Pub. by VSP) Coronet Bks.

Molecular Mechanism of Muscle Contraction. Ed. by G. H. Pollack & Haruo Sugi. LC 88-4182. (Advances in Experimental Medicine & Biology Ser.: Vol. 226). (Illus.). 756p. 1988. 145.00 (*0-306-42833-4*, Plenum Trade) Perseus Pubng.

Molecular Mechanism of Photoreception. Ed. by H. Stieve. (Dahlem Workshop Reports, Life Sciences Research Report: Vol. 34). (Illus.). xiii, 507p. 1986. 85.95 (*0-387-15363-2*) Spr-Verlag.

Molecular Mechanism of Steroid Hormone Action: Recent Advances. Ed. by Virinder K. Moudgil. (Illus.). xii, 824p. 1985. 223.10 (*3-11-010118-1*) De Gruyter.

Molecular Mechanisms in Bioenergetics. Ed. by L. Ernster. (New Comprehensive Biochemistry Ser.: Vol. 23). 542p. 1994. pap. 101.00 (*0-444-81912-6*) Elsevier.

Molecular Mechanisms in Bioorganic Processes. J. K. Bleasdale. Ed. by Bernard T. Golding. 1990. 142.00 (*0-85186-946-7*) CRC Pr.

Molecular Mechanisms in Muscular Contraction. Ed. by John M. Squire. 1990. 88.00 (*0-8493-7114-7*, QH) CRC Pr.

Molecular Mechanisms in Striated Muscle. S. V. Perry. (Lezioni Lincee Lectures). (Illus.). 176p. (C). 1996. text 59.95 (*0-521-57001-8*); pap. text 21.95 (*0-521-57916-3*) Cambridge U Pr.

Molecular Mechanisms of Adrenal Steroidogenesis & Aspects of Regulation & Application. Ed. by Klaus Ruckpaul & Horst Rein. (Frontiers in Biotransformation Ser.: Vol. 3). 251p. 1991. 90.00 (*0-7484-0025-7*, Pub. by Tay Francis Ltd) Taylor & Francis.

Molecular Mechanisms of Aging. Ed. by F. Gotthard Schettler & K. Beyreuther. (Sitzungsberichte der Heidelberger Akademie der Wissenschaften Ser., Mathematisch-Naturwissenschaftliche Klasse, Jahrgang 1991: Suppl. 2). (Illus.). vii, 206p. 1990. pap. 35.00 (*0-387-52732-X*) Spr-Verlag.

Molecular Mechanisms of Alcohol: Neurobiology & Metabolism. Ed. by Grace Y. Sun et al. LC 89-19848. (Experimental Biology & Medicine Ser.: Vol. 21). 411p. 1989. 99.50 (*0-89603-170-5*) Humana.

Molecular Mechanisms of Anesthesia. International Research Conference on Molecular Mec. LC 74-14472. (Progress in Anesthesiology Ser.: No. 1). (Illus.). 672p. reprint ed. pap. 200.00 (*0-7837-7096-0*, 204692100004) Bks Demand.

Molecular Mechanisms of Anesthesia. International Research Conference on Molecular Mec. Ed. by B. Raymond Fink. LC 79-64445. (Progress in Anesthesiology Ser.: Vol. 2). 528p. 1980. reprint ed. pap. 163.70 (*0-608-00386-7*, 206110000007) Bks Demand.

Molecular Mechanisms of Bacterial Virulence. Ed. by C. I. Kado. LC 93-11842. (Developments in Plant Pathology Ser.). 680p. (C). 1994. text 454.50 (*0-7923-1901-X*) Kluwer Academic.

Molecular Mechanisms of Cancer Predisposition. Neil F. Sullivan & Anne E. Willis. LC 94-38487. (Molecular Biology Intelligence Unit Ser.). 150p. 1994. 99.00 (*1-57059-193-8*) Landes Bioscience.

Molecular Mechanisms of Dementia. Ed. by Wilma Wasco & Rudolph Tanzi. LC 96-38858. (Contemporary Neuroscience Ser.). (Illus.). 328p. 1996. 125.00 (*0-89603-371-6*) Humana.

Molecular Mechanisms of Drug Action. 2nd ed. Christopher J. Coulson. LC 93-32329. 300p. 1993. 99.00 (*0-7484-0068-0*, Pub. by Tay Francis Ltd); pap. 39.95 (*0-7484-0078-8*, Pub. by Tay Francis Ltd) Taylor & Francis.

Molecular Mechanisms of Epithelial Cell Junctions: From Development to Disease. Ed. by Sandra Citi. (Molecular Biology Intelligence Unit Ser.). 118p. 1994. 99.00 (*1-57059-091-5*, LN9091) Landes Bioscience.

Molecular Mechanisms of Fever. Matthew J. Kluger. (Annals of the New York Academy of Science Ser.). 307p. 1999. pap. 22.50 (*0-8018-6301-5*) Johns Hopkins.

Molecular Mechanisms of Fever. Ed. by Matthew J. Kluger et al. LC 98-31202. (Annals of the New York Academy of Sciences Ser.: Vol. 856). 308p. 1998. 100.00 (*1-57331-133-2*) NY Acad Sci.

***Molecular Mechanisms of Fever.** Ed. by Matthew J. Kluger et al. LC 98-31202. (Annals of the New York Academy of Sciences Ser.: Vol. 856). xii, 308 p. 1998. pap. 100.00 (*1-57331-134-0*) NY Acad Sci.

Molecular Mechanisms of Gonadal Hormone Action. Ed. by J. A. Thomas & R. L. Singhal. LC 76-356984. (Advances in Sex Hormone Research Ser.: Vol. 1). 411p. reprint ed. pap. 127.50 (*0-608-18623-6*, 205209700033) Bks Demand.

Molecular Mechanisms of Herbicide Selectivity. D. E. Hathway. (Illus.). 224p. 1989. text 74.00 (*0-19-857642-0*) OUP.

Molecular Mechanisms of Hormone Action. U. Gehring et al. (Colloquium Mosbach Ser.: Vol. 40). (Illus.). 208p. 1990. 96.95 (*0-387-51607-7*) Spr-Verlag.

Molecular Mechanisms of Hypercoagulable States. Andrew I. Schafer. (Medical Intelligence Unit Ser.). 203p. 1997. 99.00 (*1-57059-453-8*) Landes Bioscience.

Molecular Mechanisms of Immune Regulation. Ed. by Rakesh Srivastava et al. 286p. 1991. 125.00 (*1-56081-092-0*, Wiley-VCH) Wiley.

Molecular Mechanisms of Immune Responses in Insects. Ed. by Paul T. Brey & Dan E. Hultmark. (Illus.). 256p. 1997. write for info. (*0-412-71280-6*) Kluwer Academic.

Molecular Mechanisms of Insecticide Resistance: Diversity among Insects. Ed. by Christopher A. Mullin & Jeffrey G. Scott. LC 92-28366. (Symposium Ser.: No. 505). (Illus.). 322p. 1992. text 85.00 (*0-8412-2474-9*, Pub. by Am Chemical) OUP.

Molecular Mechanisms of Membrane Fusion. Ed. by S. Okhi et al. LC 87-29163. (Illus.). 598p. 1988. 125.00 (*0-306-42773-7*, Plenum Trade) Perseus Pubng.

Molecular Mechanisms of Membrane Traffic. Ed. by D. J. Morre et al. LC 93-1200. 1993. 219.95 (*0-387-53096-7*) Spr-Verlag.

Molecular Mechanisms of Microbial Adhesion. Ed. by L. Switalski et al. 250p. 1988. 87.95 (*0-387-96892-X*) Spr-Verlag.

***Molecular Mechanisms of Neurodegenerative Diseases.** Ed. by Marie-Francoise Chesselet. (Contemporary Clinical Neuroscience Ser.). (Illus.). 411p. 2000. 125.00 (*0-89603-804-1*) Humana.

Molecular Mechanisms of Neuronal Communication. Fuxe et al. LC 96-19102. (Wenner-Gren International Ser.: Vol. 68). 344p. 1996. 175.50 (*0-08-042734-0*, Pergamon Pr) Elsevier.

Molecular Mechanisms of Neuronal Responsiveness. Ed. by Y. H. Ehrlich et al. LC 87-22074. (Advances in Experimental Medicine & Biology Ser.: Vol. 221). (Illus.). 574p. 1987. 110.00 (*0-306-42677-3*, Plenum Trade) Perseus Pubng.

Molecular Mechanisms of Pre-Eclampsia. Bradley W. Arbogast & Robert N. Taylor. LC 96-39273. (Medical Intelligence Unit Ser.). 1996. 99.00 (*1-57059-397-3*) Landes Bioscience.

Molecular Mechanisms of Resistance to Agrochemicals. Volker Sjut & J. A. Butters. LC 97-7668. (Chemistry of Plant Protection Ser.). 1997. write for info. (*3-540-62461-9*) Spr-Verlag.

***Molecular Mechanisms of Signal Transduction.** Ed. by J. L. Bos. (NATO Science Ser.: Vol. 316). 294p. 2000. 117.00 (*1-58603-016-7*) IOS Press.

Molecular Mechanisms of Signalling & Membrane Transport. Ed. by Karel W. Wirtz. LC 97-16629. (NATO ASI Series H: No. 101). (Illus.). 344p. 1997. 139.00 (*3-540-62891-6*) Spr-Verlag.

Molecular Mechanisms of Smooth Muscle Contraction. Kazuhiro Kohama. LC 98-40980. 1999. 99.00 (*1-57059-566-6*) Landes Bioscience.

***Molecular Mechanisms of the Cell.** (C). 2001. text. write for info. (*0-8053-4528-0*) Benjamin-Cummings.

Molecular Mechanisms of the Immune Response. Ed. by W. F. Bodmer & M. J. Owen. (Cancer Surveys Ser.: Vol. 22). (Illus.). 190p. (C). 1994. 56.25 (*0-87969-442-4*) Cold Spring Harbor.

Molecular Mechanisms of Water Transport. Thomas Zeuthen. (Molecular Biology Intelligence Unit Ser.). 200p. 1996. 99.00 (*1-57059-327-2*) Landes Bioscience.

Molecular Mechanisms to Regulate the Activities of Insulin-Like Growth Factors: Proceedings of the 4th International Symposium on Insulin-Like Growth Factors, Tokyo International Forum, Tokyo, Japan, 21-24 October 1997. Ed. by K. Takano et al. 408p. 1998. 189.50 (*0-444-82524-X*, Excerpta Medica) Elsevier.

Molecular Medical Bacteriology, 2 vols. Sussman. 1500p. 1998. write for info. (*0-12-677530-3*) Acad Pr.

Molecular Medical Bacteriology, Vol. 1. Sussman. 750p. 1998. write for info. (*0-12-677531-1*) Acad Pr.

Molecular Medical Bacteriology, Vol. 2. Sussman. 750p. 1998. write for info. (*0-12-677532-X*) Acad Pr.

Molecular Medicine. John Bradley et al. LC 95-8412. (Lecture Notes Ser.). 1995. 29.95 (*0-632-03851-9*) Blackwell Sci.

Molecular Medicine, Vol. 2. Ed. by Alan D. Malcolm. 140p. 1987. pap. text 45.00 (*0-947946-58-6*) OUP.

Molecular Medicine: An Introductory Text. 2nd ed. R. J. Trent. LC 96-26054. 1997. pap. text 31.95 (*0-443-05366-9*) Church.

Molecular Medicine: Clinical Implications. Benz. 1993. 55.00 (*0-397-44610-1*) Lppncott W & W.

Molecular Medicine: Novel Findings of Gene Diagnosis, Regulation of Gene Expression & Gene Therapy: Proceedings of the Second Meeting of Hirosaki International Forum of Medical Science, Hirosaki, Japan, 7 July 1998. Hirosaki International Forum of Medical Science Staff & Hashimoto. LC 99-27006. (International Congress Ser.). 222p. 1999. 139.50 (*0-444-50006-5*, Excerpta Medica) Elsevier.

Molecular Medicine of Viral Hepatitis. Tim J. Harrison & Arie J. Zuckerman. LC 96-28960. (Molecular Medical Science Ser.). 282p. 1997. 129.95 (*0-471-96996-6*) Wiley.

Molecular Methods for Virus Detection. Ed. by Danny L. Wiedbrauk & Daniel H. Farkas. (Illus.). 386p. 1995. pap. 63.00 (*0-12-748920-7*) Acad Pr.

Molecular Methods in Developmental Biology: Xenopus & Zebrafish. Ed. by Matt Guille. LC 98-50533. (Methods in Molecular Biology Ser.: No. 123). 232p. 1999. 89.50 (*0-89603-790-8*) Humana.

Molecular Methods in Ecology. (Methods in Ecology Ser.). (Illus.). 320p. 2000. pap. 49.95 (*0-632-03437-8*) Blackwell Sci.

Molecular Methods in Plant Pathology. Ed. by Uma S. Singh & Rudra P. Singh. 544p. 1995. lib. bdg. 95.00 (*0-87371-877-1*, L877) Lewis Pubs.

Molecular Microbial Ecology Manual. Ed. by A. D. Akkermans et al. LC 95-31285. 512p. (C). 1995. text 209.50 (*0-7923-3698-4*) Kluwer Academic.

Molecular Microbial Ecology Manual, Set. Ed. by A. D. Akkermans et al. LC 95-16332. 1995. write for info. (*0-7923-3411-6*) Kluwer Academic.

Molecular Microbial Ecology Manual, Vol. 1. Ed. by A. D. Akkermans et al. LC 95-16332. 1995. write for info. (*0-7923-3410-8*) Kluwer Academic.

Molecular Microbial Ecology of the Soil: Results from an FAO IAEA Co-Ordinated Research Programme, 1992-1996. G. Hardarson et al. LC 98-34654. (Developments in Plant & Soil Sciences Ser.). 1998. 117.00 (*0-7923-5252-1*) Kluwer Academic.

Molecular Microbiology. Ed. by Stephen J. Busby et al. LC 97-32739. (NATO ASI Series H: Vol. 103). viii, 334p. 1998. 129.00 (*3-540-63873-3*) Spr-Verlag.

Molecular Mimicry. Ed. by Michael B. Oldstone. (Current Topics in Microbiology & Immunology Ser.: Vol. 145). (Illus.). 145p. 1989. 84.00 (*0-387-50929-1*) Spr-Verlag.

***Molecular Mimicry, Microbes, & Autoimmunity.** Ed. by Madeleine W. Cunningham & Robert J. Fujinami. 400p. 2000. 99.95 (*1-55581-194-9*) ASM Pr.

Molecular Model Set for General Chemistry. (The Allyn & Bacon Science Ser.). 1989. pap. text 33.00 (*0-205-08281-5*, 688281) P-H.

Molecular Model Systems in the Lepidoptera. Ed. by Marian R. Goldsmith & Adam S. Wilkins. LC 93-47979. (Illus.). 556p. (C). 1995. text 125.00 (*0-521-40249-2*) Cambridge U Pr.

Molecular Modeling: Basic Principles & Applications. H. D. Hoetje & G. Folkers. LC 97-227340. 194p. 1996. 205.00 (*3-527-29384-1*, Wiley-VCH) Wiley.

Molecular Modeling: From Virtual Tools to Real Problems. American Chemical Society, Division of Agricultura. Ed. by Thomas F. Kumosinski & Michael N. Liebman. LC 94-38705. (Symposium Ser.: No. 576). (Illus.). 530p. 1994. text 125.95 (*0-8412-3042-0*, Pub. by Am Chemical) OUP.

Molecular Modeling - the Chemistry of the 21st Century. M. A. Nascimento. 172p. 1994. text 81.00 (*981-02-1620-3*) World Scientific Pub.

Molecular Modeling & Dynamics of Bioinorganic Systems. Ed. by Lucia Banci & Peter Comba. LC 97-31748. (NATO ASI Ser.). 470p. 1997. text 234.00 (*0-7923-4824-9*, D Reidel) Kluwer Academic.

***Molecular Modeling & Prediction of Bioactivity.** Klaus Gundertofte & Flemming S. Jurgensen. LC 99-44859. 1999. write for info. (*0-306-46217-6*, Kluwer Plenum) Kluwer Academic.

Molecular Modeling Annual, 1998: CD-ROM & Print Archive Edition Journal of Molecular Modeling, Vol. 4, 1998. Ed. by T. Clark. (Illus.). 435p. 1999. 280.00 incl. cd-rom (*3-540-14647-4*) Spr-Verlag.

Molecular Modeling Annual, 1995: CD-ROM & Print Archive Edition of Journal of Molecular Modeling. Ed. by T. Clark. 600p. 1996. 234.00 incl. cd-rom (*3-540-14524-9*) Spr-Verlag.

Molecular Modeling Annual 1997: CD-ROM & Print Archive Edition. Ed. by T. Clark. (Journal of Molecular Modeling Ser.). (Illus.). 490p. 1998. 189.00 incl. cd-rom (*3-540-14637-7*) Spr-Verlag.

Molecular Modeling Annual, 1996: CD-ROM & Print Archive Edition Journal of Molecular Modeling. Ed. by T. Clark. 160p. 1997. 192.00 incl. cd-rom (*3-540-14566-4*) Spr-Verlag.

Molecular Modeling Applications in Crystallization. Ed. by Allan S. Myerson. LC 98-44694. (Illus.). 300p. (C). (up). 1999. text 110.00 (*0-521-55297-4*) Cambridge U Pr.

Molecular Modeling for Chemists & Biochemists. Tamara Gund. 324p. 2000. 95.00 (*0-8493-1696-0*) CRC Pr.

Molecular Modeling of Inorganic Compounds. Peter Comba & Trevor W. Hambley. LC 95-24487. 207p. 1995. 175.00 (*3-527-29076-1*, Wiley-VCH) Wiley.

Molecular Modeling of Nucleic Acids. American Chemical Society Staff. Ed. by Neocles B. Leontis et al. LC 97-42151. (ACS Symposoium Ser.: No. 682). 450p. 1997. text 135.00 (*0-8412-3541-4*, Pub. by Am Chemical) OUP.

Molecular Modeling of Polymer Structures & Properties. Bruce R. Gelin. LC 93-48573. 256p. 1994. 89.00 (*1-56990-125-2*) Hanser-Gardner.

Molecular Modeling on the PC. Matthew F. Schlecht. 250p. 1996. 100.00 (*1-56081-535-3*, Wiley-VCH) Wiley.

Molecular Modeling on the PC. Matthew F. Schlecht. 763p. 1998. 135.00 (*0-471-18567-1*) Wiley.

Molecular Modeling Using Chem Office. David Collard & Howard Deutsch. 64p. 1998. pap. 7.50 (*0-7637-0742-2*) Jones & Bartlett.

Molecular Modeling Workbook for Organic Chemistry. Warren J. Hehre et al. (Illus.). 317p. 1998. pap. text 30.00 (*1-890661-06-6*) Wavefunction.

Molecular Modelling & Drug Design. Ed. by Andrew Vinter & Mark Gardner. LC 93-42952. (Topics in Molecular & Structural Biology Ser.). 1994. 110.00 (*0-8493-7772-2*) CRC Pr.

Molecular Modelling of High Tc Materials. C. R. Catlow. 76p. 1995. pap. text 130.00 (*2-88124-968-X*) Gordon & Breach.

Molecular Modification in Drug Design: A Symposium Sponsored by the Division of Medicinal Chemistry at the 145th Meeting of the American Chemical Society, New York, NY, Sept. 9-10, 1963. American Chemical Society Staff. LC 64-22278. (Advances in Chemistry Ser.: Vol. 45). (Illus.). 236p. 1964. reprint ed. pap. 73.20 (*0-608-06923-X*, 206713100009) Bks Demand.

Molecular Modulation of Chemical Presynaptic Neurotransmission. Nathan Moskowitz. 258p. 1985. 65.00 (*0-275-91320-1*, C1320, Praeger Pubs) Greenwood.

Molecular Motion in Polymers by ESR. Ed. by R. Boyer & S. Keinath. (MMI Press Symposium Ser.: Vol. 1). xii, 328p. 1980. text 274.00 (*3-7186-0012-9*) Gordon & Breach.

Molecular Motions of Liquids: Proceedings of the Societe de Chimie Physique, 24th, Paris Orsay, July 2-6, 1973. Societe de Chimie Physique Staff. Ed. by J. Lascombe. LC 73-91947. 1974. text 318.00 (*90-277-0431-7*) Kluwer Academic.

Molecular Motors & the Cytoskeleton. Ed. by John N. Abelson et al. (Methods in Enzymology Ser.: Vol. 196). (Illus.). 559p. 1991. text 115.00 (*0-12-182097-1*) Acad Pr.

***Molecular Mycobacteriology: Techniques & Clinical Applications.** Anne Underwood Grant & Nancy D. Connell. LC 98-50992. (Illus.). 368p. 1999. text 145.00 (*0-8247-0240-9*) Dekker.

***Molecular Nanotechnology: Current & Future Methodologies.** Edward Rietman. (Illus.). 2000. 59.95 (*0-387-98988-9*) Spr-Verlag.

Molecular Nephrology: Biochemical Aspects of Kidney Functions - Proceedings of the 8th Int'l Symposium, Dubrovnik, Yugoslavia, October 5-8. Ed. by Z. Kovacevic & W. G. Gruder. xiii, 424p. (Orig.). 1987. lib. bdg. 188.50 (*3-11-011121-7*) De Gruyter.

Molecular Nephrology: Kidney Function in Health & Disease. Ed. by Detlef Schlondorff & Joseph V. Bonventre. LC 95-23371. (Illus.). 960p. 1995. text 225.00 (*0-8247-9508-3*) Dekker.

Molecular Neuro-Oncology & Its Impact on the Clinical Management of Brain Tumours. Ed. by O. D. Wiestler et al. (Recent Results in Cancer Research Ser.). (Illus.). 208p. 1994. 105.00 (*0-387-57351-8*) Spr-Verlag.

Molecular Neurobiological Techniques. Ed. by Alan A. Boulton et al. LC 89-2053. (Neuromethods Ser.: Vol. 16). (Illus.). 310p. 1989. 84.50 (*0-89603-140-3*) Humana.

Molecular Neurobiology. Cold Spring Harbor Symposia on Quantitative Biolog. LC 34-8174. (Cold Spring Harbor Symposia on Quantitative Biology Ser.: No. 48). 943p. reprint ed. pap. 200.00 (*0-7837-6448-0*, 204644700012) Bks Demand.

Molecular Neurobiology. Gordon Guroff. LC 79-22812. (Illus.). 587p. reprint ed. pap. 182.00 (*0-7837-0854-8*, 204116300019) Bks Demand.

Molecular Neurobiology: A Practical Approach. Ed. by J. Chad & H. Wheal. (Practical Approach Ser.: 74). (Illus.). 256p. 1991. 59.00 (*0-19-963108-5*); pap. 49.95 (*0-19-963109-3*) OUP.

Molecular Neurobiology: Frontiers in Molecular Biology. Ed. by David M. Glover & B. David Hames. (Frontiers in Molecular Biology Ser.). (Illus.). 216p. 1990. 58.00 (*0-19-963042-9*); pap. text 38.00 (*0-19-963043-7*) OUP.

Molecular Neurobiology: Mechanisms Common to Brain, Skin, & Immune System: Proceedings of the International Symposium on Molecular Neurobiology Held in Tokyo, November 1992. Ed. by Gerald D. Fischbach et al. 280p. 1994. 195.00 (*0-471-05152-7*) Wiley.

Molecular Neurobiology: Proceedings of the 2nd NIMH Conference. Ed. by Steven Zalcman et al. (Illus.). 298p. (Orig.). (C). 1995. pap. text 45.00 (*0-7881-2646-6*) DIANE Pub.

Molecular Neurobiology: Recombinant DNA Approaches. S. Heinemann & J. Patrick. LC 87-2512. (Current Topics in Neurobiology Ser.). (Illus.). 316p. (C). 1987. text 89.50 (*0-306-42440-1*, Kluwer Plenum) Kluwer Academic.

Molecular Neurobiology & Brain Ischemia. K. Oki Shimoji. LC 96-26702. (Illus.). x, 166p. 1996. 70.00 (*4-431-70184-2*) Spr-Verlag.

Molecular Neurobiology in Neurology & Psychiatry. Ed. by Eric R. Kandel. LC 86-42508. (Association for Research in Nervous & Mental Disease Research Publications: No. 65). (Illus.). 221p. 1987. reprint ed. pap. 68.60 (*0-608-05778-9*, 205974300007) Bks Demand.

Molecular Neurobiology, 1987. Ed. by Nicolas G. Bazan & David C. U'Prichard. (Illus.). 416p. 1988. 95.00 (*0-89603-152-7*) Humana.

Molecular Neurobiology, 1988. Ed. by Nicolas G. Bazan & David C. U'Prichard. (Illus.). 332p. 1989. 95.00 (*0-89603-176-4*) Humana.

Molecular Neurobiology of Epilepsy. E. A. Cavalheiro et al. Ed. by J. Engel, Jr. et al. LC 92-18550. (Epilepsy Research Supplements Ser.: No. 9). xvi,412p. 1992. 289.50 (*0-444-89711-9*) Elsevier.

Molecular Neurobiology of Pain. Ed. by David Borsook. LC 97-36742. (Progress in Pain Research & Management Ser.: Vol. 9). (Illus.). 384p. 1997. 76.00 (*0-931092-19-1*) Intl Assn Study Pain.

Molecular Neurobiology of the Mammalian Brain. 2nd ed. P. L. McGeer et al. LC 86-25333. (Illus.). 800p. (C). 1987. pap. text 49.50 (*0-306-42511-4*, Kluwer Plenum) Kluwer Academic.

Molecular Neurobiology of the Mammalian Brain. 2nd ed. P. L. McGeer et al. LC 86-25333. (Illus.). 800p. (C). 1987. 95.00 (*0-306-42329-4*, Plenum Trade) Perseus Pubng.

Molecular Neurobiology of the Olfactory System: Molecular, Membranous & Cytological Studies. F. L. Margolis & T. V. Getchell. LC 88-14821. (Illus.). 398p. (C). 1988. text 115.00 (*0-306-42858-X*, Kluwer Plenum) Kluwer Academic.

Molecular Neuropathology. Ed. by Gareth W. Roberts & Julia M. Polak. (Postgraduate Medical Science Ser.: No. 4). (Illus.). 199p. (C). 1995. pap. text 47.95 (*0-521-42558-1*) Cambridge U Pr.

Molecular Neuropathology of Aging. Ed. by Peter Davies & Caleb E. Finch. LC 87-15673. (Banbury Report Ser.: No. 27). (Illus.). 484p. 1988. text 80.00 (*0-87969-227-8*) Cold Spring Harbor.

Molecular Neuroscience. P. Revest & A. Longstaff. LC 98-17627. (Illus.). 240p. 1997. pap. 34.95 (*0-387-91519-2*) Spr-Verlag.

Molecular Neuroscience. Zukin. 352p. 1997. write for info. (*0-12-782720-X*) Acad Pr.

Molecular Neuroscience: Expression of Neural Genes, Proceedings of the Fourth Galveston Neuroscience Symposium, Held at Galveston, Texas, May 8-10, 1986. Galveston Neuroscience Symposium Staff. Ed. by Fulton Wong. LC 87-16980. (Neurology & Neurobiology Ser.: No. 34). 181p. reprint ed. pap. 56.20 (*0-7837-2798-4*, 205767500006) Bks Demand.

Molecular Neurovirology: Pathogenesis of Viral CNS Infections. Ed. by Raymond P. Roos. LC 91-20851. (Illus.). 625p. 1992. 135.00 (*0-89603-222-1*) Humana.

Molecular Nonlinear Optics: Materials, Physics, & Devices. Ed. by Joseph Zyss. LC 92-42976. (Quantum Electronics - Principles & Applications Ser.). (Illus.). 478p. 1993. text 129.00 (*0-12-784450-3*) Acad Pr.

Molecular Nonostructures: Proceedings of the International Winterschool on Electronic Properties of Novel Materials Kirchberg/Tyrol, Austria 1-8 March, 1997. Ed. by Hans Kuzmany et al. LC 98-202193. 500p. 1997. 118.00 (*981-02-3261-6*) World Scientific Pub.

An Asterisk (*) at the beginning of an entry indicates that the title is appearing for the first time.

Molecular Oncology. John Michael Bishop. 1996. 71.95 (*0-89454-023-8*) Mosby Inc.

Molecular Oncology & Clinical Applications. Ed. by A. Cittadini et al. LC 93-2395. (Molecular & Cell Biology Updates Ser.). (Illus.). 448p. 1993. 119.00 (*0-8176-2915-7*) Birkhauser.

Molecular Orbital Calculations for Aminoacids & Peptides. Anne-Marie Sapse. LC 99-26375. 192p. 1999. 99.00 (*0-8176-3893-8*, Pub. by Birkhauser) Spr-Verlag.

Molecular Orbital Calculations for Biological Systems. Ed. by Anne-Marie Sapse. (Topics in Physical Chemistry Ser.). (Illus.). 256p. 1998. text 85.00 (*0-19-509873-0*) OUP.

Molecular Orbital Calculations Using Chemical Graph Theory. Jerry R. Dias. LC 92-44419. 1993. 103.95 (*0-387-56134-X*) Spr-Verlag.

Molecular Orbital Theories of Bonding in Organic Molecules. Robert L. Flurry. LC 68-13563. (Applied Quantum Chemistry Ser.). 344p. reprint ed. pap. 106.70 (*0-608-16446-1*, 202671400051) Bks Demand.

Molecular Orbitals & Their Energies, Studied by the Semiempirical HAM Method. E. Lindholm & L. Asbrink. (Lecture Notes in Chemistry Ser.: Vol. 38). x, 288p. 1985. 38.95 (*0-387-15659-3*) Spr-Verlag.

Molecular Origami: Precision Scale Models from Paper. Robert M. Hanson. LC 94-37451. (Illus.). 244p. 1995. pap. text 26.50 (*0-935702-30-X*) Univ Sci Bks.

Molecular Origins of Life: Assembling the Pieces of the Puzzle. Ed. by Andre Brack. (Illus.). 360p. (C). 1998. text 85.00 (*0-521-56412-3*); pap. text 34.95 (*0-521-56475-1*) Cambridge U Pr.

Molecular Parasitology. John E. Hyde. (Illus.). 320p. 1990. mass mkt. 69.95 (*0-442-30824-8*) Chapman & Hall.

Molecular Pathogenesis of Diabetes Mellitus. Ed. by Richard D. Leslie. LC 96-24159. (Frontiers of Hormone Research Ser.: Vol. 22, 1997). (Illus.). viii, 228p. 1997. 198.25 (*3-8055-6373-6*) S Karger.

Molecular Pathogenesis of Gastrointestinal Infections. T. Wadstrom et al. (FEMS Symposium Ser.: No. 58). (Illus.). 352p. (C). 1991. text 110.00 (*0-306-44020-2*, Kluwer Plenum) Kluwer Academic.

Molecular Pathogenesis of HTLV-1: A Current Perspective. Ed. by O. John Semmes & Marie-Louise Hammarskjold. (Illus.). 256p. 1998. 50.00 (*1-886236-19-4*) ABI Prof Pubns.

*__Molecular Pathogenesis of MODYs.__ Ed. by F. M. Matschinsky & M. A. Magnuson. (Frontiers in Diabetes Ser.: Vol. 15). (Illus.). x, 272p. 2000. 168.00 (*3-8055-6950-5*) S Karger.

*__Molecular Pathogenesis of Pancreatic Cancer.__ Ed. by T. M. Gress. (Biomedical & Health Research Ser.: Vol. 41). 116p. 2000. 69.00 (*1-58603-040-X*) IOS Press.

Molecular Pathogenesis of Periodontal Disease. Ed. by Robert Genco et al. LC 94-4855. (Illus.). 479p. reprint ed. pap. 148.50 (*0-608-08635-5*, 206915800003) Bks Demand.

Molecular Pathology. Antoni Horst. (Illus.). 440p. 1991. lib. bdg. 239.00 (*0-8493-6088-9*, RB113) CRC Pr.

Molecular Pathology. Ed. by Jonathan R. Salisbury. LC 97-201783. 168p. 1997. pap. 24.95 (*0-7484-0571-2*, Pub. by Tay Francis Ltd) Taylor & Francis.

Molecular Pathology. Wolfe. 1997. text. write for info. (*0-7216-4871-1*, W B Saunders Co) Harcrt Hlth Sci Grp.

Molecular Pathology & Genetics of Alport Syndrome. Ed. by K. Tryggvason. (Contributions to Nephrology Ser.: Vol. 117). (Illus.). viii, 204p. 1996. 184.50 (*3-8055-6193-8*) S Karger.

Molecular Pathology of Autoimmune Disease. Ed. by Constantin A. Bona et al. LC 92-49272. 795p. 1993. text 234.00 (*3-7186-0555-4*) Gordon & Breach.

Molecular Pathology of Cancer. Nicholas R. Lemoine. LC 93-246938. (Cancer Surveys Ser.: No. 16). (Illus.). 252p. 1993. pap. 78.20 (*0-608-04957-3*, 206553600004) Bks Demand.

Molecular Pathology of Connective Tissues. Ed. by Ruy Perez-Tamayo & Marcos Rojkind. LC 72-86611. (Biochemistry of Disease Ser.: No. 3). (Illus.). 416p. reprint ed. pap. 129.00 (*0-7837-0887-4*, 204119300019) Bks Demand.

Molecular Pathology of Early Cancer. Ed. by S. Srivastava. LC 97-75194. 600p. Date not set. 99.00 (*90-5199-373-0*) IOS Press.

Molecular Pathology of Nerve & Muscle: Noxious Agents & Genetic Lesions. Ed. by Antony D. Kidman et al. (Experimental & Clinical Neuroscience Ser.). 416p. 1984. 109.50 (*0-89603-057-1*) Humana.

*__Molecular Pathology Protocols.__ Ed. by Anthony A. Killeen. (Methods in Molecular Medicine Ser.: Vol. 49). 508p. 2000. 110.00 (*0-89603-681-2*) Humana.

Molecular Pharmacology. Terrence P. Kenakin. LC 96-39098. (Illus.). 300p. (Orig.). 1996. pap. text 49.95 (*0-86542-540-X*) Blackwell Sci.

Molecular Physics. T. Buyana. 300p. 1997. text 55.00 (*981-02-0830-8*); pap. text 28.00 (*981-02-0831-6*) World Scientific Pub.

Molecular Physics & Elements of Quantum Chemistry. H. Haken & H. C. Wolf. (Illus.). 430p. 1995. 49.95 (*0-387-58363-7*) Spr-Verlag.

Molecular Physics & Elements of Quantum Chemistry: Introduction to Experiments & Theory. Hermann Haken & Hans C. Wolf. LC 94-47315. 1995. write for info. (*3-540-58363-7*) Spr-Verlag.

Molecular Physics & Hypersonic Flows. Ed. by Mario Capitelli. LC 96-13182. (NATO ASI Ser.: Series C, Vol. 482). 795p. 1996. text 364.50 (*0-7923-4055-8*) Kluwer Academic.

Molecular Physiology & Pharmacology of Cardiac Ion Channels & Transporters. Ed. by M. Morad et al. LC 95-51375. (Developments in Cardiovascular Medicine Ser.: Vol. 182). 624p. (C). 1996. text 331.50 (*0-7923-3913-4*) Kluwer Academic.

Molecular Physiology of Growth. Ed. by P. T. Loughna & J. M. Pell. (Society for Experimental Biology Seminar Ser.: No. 60). (Illus.). 170p. (C). 1997. text 59.95 (*0-521-47110-9*) Cambridge U Pr.

Molecular Plant Development: From Gene to Plant. Peter Westhoff. LC 99-163559. (Illus.). 288p. (C). 1998. text 95.00 (*0-19-850204-4*) OUP.

Molecular Plant Development: From Gene to Plant. Peter Westhoff et al. Tr. by Ellen Peerenboom from GER. LC 99-163559. (Illus.). 288p. (C). 1998. pap. text 36.95 (*0-19-850203-6*) OUP.

Molecular Plant Pathology, Vols. I & II. Ed. by S. J. Gurr & D. J. Bowles. (Practical Approach Ser.: 85 & 103). (Illus.). 568p. 1993. spiral bd. 140.00 (*0-19-963354-1*) OUP.

Molecular Plant Pathology: A Practical Approach, Vol. 2. Ed. by S. J. Gurr et al. (Practical Approach Ser.: Vol. 103). (Illus.). 328p. 1992. 85.00 (*0-19-963352-5*); pap. text 49.95 (*0-19-963351-7*) OUP.

Molecular Plant Pathology Vol. 1: A Practical Approach, Vol. 1. Ed. by S. J. Gurr et al. (Illus.). 240p. 1992. pap. text 49.95 (*0-19-963102-6*) OUP.

Molecular Plant Virology: Replication & Gene Expression, Vol. II. Ed. by J. W. Davies. 240p. 1985. 138.00 (*0-8493-6291-1*, QR351, CRC Reprint) Franklin.

Molecular Plant Virology: Virus Structure & Assembly & Nucleic Acid-Protein Interactions, Vol. I. Ed. by J. W. Davies. 240p. 1985. 138.00 (*0-8493-6290-3*, QR351, CRC Reprint) Franklin.

Molecular Politics: Developing American & British Regulatory Policy for Genetic Engineering, 1972-1982. Susan Wright. LC 93-47054. (Illus.). 1994. pap. text 29.95 (*0-226-91066-0*) U Ch Pr.

Molecular Politics: Developing American & British Regulatory Policy for Genetic Engineering, 1972-1982. Susan Wright. LC 93-47054. (Illus.). 616p. 1994. lib. bdg. 75.00 (*0-226-91065-2*) U Ch Pr.

Molecular Potential Energy Functions. John N. Murrell et al. LC 84-11821. (Illus.). 205p. 1984. reprint ed. pap. 63.60 (*0-608-06822-5*, 206701900009) Bks Demand.

Molecular Probe Markets: Hoffman-La Roche Bids for Dominance. Market Intelligence Staff. 230p. (Orig.). 1992. 1895.00 (*1-56753-379-5*) Frost & Sullivan.

Molecular Probes: Technology & Medical Applications. Ed. by Alberto Albertini et al. LC 88-32473. (Illus.). 316p. 1989. reprint ed. pap. 98.00 (*0-608-00587-8*, 206117400007) Bks Demand.

Molecular Probes of the Nervous System Vol. 1: Selected Methods for Antibody & Nucleic Acid Probes. Susan Hockfield et al. (Illus.). 336p. 1993. text 21.25 (*0-87969-351-7*) Cold Spring Harbor.

Molecular Processes in Space. T. Watanabe et al. LC 89-77539. (Illus.). 272p. (C). 1990. text 89.50 (*0-306-43496-2*, Kluwer Plenum) Kluwer Academic.

Molecular Propagation Through Electron Energy Level Crossings. George A. Hagedorn. LC 94-17086. (Memoirs of the American Mathematical Society Ser.: No. 536). 130p. 1994. pap. 34.00 (*0-8218-2605-0*, MEMO/111/536) Am Math.

*__Molecular Protocols in Transfusion Medicine.__ Greg Denomme et al. 200p. 2000. 99.95 (*0-12-209370-4*) Acad Pr.

Molecular Quantum Electrodynamics: An Introduction to Radiation-Molecule Interactions. unabridged ed. D. P. Craig & T. Thirunamachandran. LC 98-12709. 324p. 1998. pap. 12.95 (*0-486-40214-2*) Dover.

Molecular Quantum Mechanics. 3rd ed. P. W. Atkins & R. S. Friedman. (Illus.). 562p. 1999. pap. text 55.00 (*0-19-855947-X*) OUP.

Molecular Quantum Mechanics: Solutions Manual. P. W. Atkins. (Illus.). 212p. 1983. pap. 25.95 (*0-19-855180-0*) OUP.

*__Molecular Quantum Similarity in QSAR & Drug Design.__ Rambon Carbbo. LC 00-41287. (Lecture Notes in Chemistry Ser.). (Illus.). 2000. pap. write for info. (*3-540-67581-7*) Spr-Verlag.

Molecular Radiations. Thomas Colson. 190p. 1996. reprint ed. spiral bd. 14.50 (*0-7873-0194-9*) Hlth Research.

Molecular Ramjet: And Other Bedtime Stories . . . Larry G. Carlson. (Illus.). 212p. (YA). (gr. 7-9). 1989. pap. 4.95 (*0-929301-01-3*) TadAlex Bks.

*__Molecular Rearrangement Reactions: Azobenzene & Benzilic Acid.__ Jerry Manion. Ed. by Joe Jeffers. (Modular Laboratory in Chemistry Ser.). 8p. (C). 1999. pap. text 1.75 (*0-87540-734-X*, REAC 734-X) Chem Educ Res.

Molecular Reasons. Tro. LC 97-45224. (Chemistry Ser.). 1998. pap. 57.00 (*0-534-35519-6*) Brooks-Cole.

Molecular Reasons. Tro. (Chemistry Ser.). 1998. pap., student ed. 18.95 (*0-534-35523-4*) Wadsworth Pub.

Molecular Recognition: Chemistry & Biochemistry Problems, No. 78. Ed. by Stanley M. Roberts. 1989. 109.00 (*0-85186-796-0*) CRC Pr.

Molecular Recognition & Inclusion: Proceedings of The Ninth International Symposium On Molecular Recognition & Inclusion Held at Lyon. International Symposium on Inclusion Phenomena & Molecular Recognition Staff & Annette W. Coleman. LC 98-37267. 1998. 268.00 (*0-7923-5330-7*) Kluwer Academic.

Molecular Recognition in Host-Parasite Interactions. T. K. Korhonen et al. (FEMS Symposium Ser.: No. 61). (Illus.). 240p. (C). 1992. text 89.50 (*0-306-44340-6*, Kluwer Plenum) Kluwer Academic.

Molecular Recognition Mechanisms. Ed. by M. Delaage. 285p. 1991. 150.00 (*0-471-18785-2*, Wiley-VCH) Wiley.

Molecular Recognition Mechanisms. Ed. by Michel Delaage. 285p. 1991. text 95.00 (*1-56081-041-6*, Wiley-VCH) Wiley.

Molecular Regulation of Arousal States. Ed. by Ralph Lydic. LC 97-21353. (Cellular & Molecular Neuropharmacology Ser.). 256p. 1997. per. 94.95 (*0-8493-3361-X*) CRC Pr.

Molecular Replacement Method, Vol. 13. M. G. Rossman. (International Science Review Ser.). 276p. 1972. text 385.00 (*0-677-13940-3*) Gordon & Breach.

Molecular Reviews in Cardiovascular Medicine. Ed. by D. Ganten & K. Lindpaintner. 212p. 1996. write for info. (*0-412-78260-X*) Kluwer Academic.

Molecular Rotation Spectra. unabridged ed. Harold W. Kroto. (Illus.). 352p. 1992. reprint ed. pap. text 10.95 (*0-486-67259-X*) Dover.

Molecular Rydberg Dynamics. Ed. by M. S. Child. 240p. 1998. 38.00 (*1-86094-094-3*, Pub. by Imperial College) World Scientific Pub.

Molecular Scattering: Physical & Chemical Applications. K. P. Lawley. LC 74-23667. (Advances in Chemical Physics Ser.: Vol. 30). 549p. reprint ed. pap. 170.20 (*0-608-18640-6*, 202401200035) Bks Demand.

Molecular Scattering of Light. Immanuil L. Fabelinskii. Tr. by Robert T. Beyer from RUS. LC 67-10534. (Illus.). 650p. 1968. reprint ed. pap. 200.00 (*0-608-05486-0*, 206595500006) Bks Demand.

Molecular Self-Assembly: Focus on Bioindustries, Vol. 2. Savage. 1995. pap. 405.00 (*0-471-34631-4*) Wiley.

Molecular Self Assembly: Key to 21st Century Manufacturing - Focus on Bioindustries. 150p. 1995. spiral bd., vinyl bd. 1625.00 (*1-56217-012-0*) Tech Insights.

Molecular Self Assembly: Key to 21st Century Manufacturing - Focus on Electronic Industries. 136p. 1995. spiral bd., vinyl bd. 1625.00 (*1-56217-013-9*) Tech Insights.

*__Molecular Self-Assembly: Organic Versus Inorganic Approaches.__ Ed. by M. Fujita et al. (Structure & Bonding Ser.: 96). x, 252p. 2000. (*3-540-66948-5*) Spr-Verlag.

Molecular Semiconductors. J. Simon & J. J. Andre. Ed. by J. M. Lehn & C. W. Rees. (Illus.). 350p. 1985. 257.95 (*0-387-13754-8*) Spr-Verlag.

Molecular Shapes: Theoretical Models of Inorganic Stereochemistry. Jeremy K. Burdett. LC 80-15463. (Wiley-Interscience Publications). 301p. reprint ed. pap. 93.40 (*0-7837-2388-1*, 204007300006) Bks Demand.

Molecular Sieve Zeolites, Vol. 1. International Conference on Molecular Sieve Zeolit. LC 77-156974. (Advances in Chemistry Ser.: Nos. 101 & 102). 536p. 1971. reprint ed. pap. 152.80 (*0-608-03273-5*, 2063792) Bks Demand.

Molecular Sieve Zeolites, Vol. 2. International Conference on Molecular Sieve Zeolit. LC 77-156974. (Advances in Chemistry Ser.: Nos. 101 & 102). 469p. 1971. reprint ed. pap. 145.40 (*0-608-03274-3*, 206379200002) Bks Demand.

Molecular Sieve Zeolites II, 2 pts., Pt. 2. Ed. by E. M. Flanigen & Leonard B. Sand. LC 77-156974. (Advances in Chemistry Ser.: No. 102). 1971. 36.95 (*0-8412-0115-3*) Am Chemical.

*__Molecular Sieves.__ 2nd ed. Rosemarie Szostak. LC 97-75353. 376p. 1998. write for info. (*0-7514-0480-2*) Kluwer Academic.

Molecular Sieves: The 3rd International Conference Co-Sponsored by the Eidgenossische Technische Hochschule & the Swiss Chemical Society at Zurich, Switzerland, Sept. 3-7, 1973. Ed. by W. M. Meier & J. B. Uytterhoeven. LC 73-83768. (Advances in Chemistry Ser.: Vol. 121). 648p. 1973. reprint ed. pap. 200.00 (*0-608-03899-7*, 206434600008) Bks Demand.

Molecular Sieves II. Ed. by James R. Katzer. LC 77-720. (ACS Symposium Ser.: No. 40). 1977. 54.95 (*0-8412-0362-8*) Am Chemical.

Molecular Sieves II: 4th International Conference. Ed. by James R. Katzer. LC 77-720. (ACS Symposium Ser.: Vol. 40). 742p. 1977. reprint ed. pap. 200.00 (*0-608-03560-2*, 206427900008) Bks Demand.

Molecular Signaling & Regulation in Glial Cells: A Key to Remyelination & Functional Repair. Ed. by G. Jeserich et al. LC 96-49970. (Illus.). 390p. 1997. 157.00 (*3-540-62076-1*) Spr-Verlag.

Molecular Signals in Plant-Microbe Communications. Desh P. Verma. (Illus.). 544p. 1991. boxed set 219.00 (*0-8493-5905-8*, QR351) CRC Pr.

Molecular Similarity & Reactivity. Ed. by Ramon Carbon. LC 94-46540. (Understanding Chemical Reactivity Ser.: Vol. 14). 1995. text 166.00 (*0-7923-3309-8*) Kluwer Academic.

Molecular Similarity I. Kali D. Sen. (Topics in Current Chemistry Ser.: Vol. 173). 144p. 1995. 133.95 (*3-540-58671-7*) Spr-Verlag.

Molecular Similarity II. Ed. by Kali D. Sen. (Topics in Current Chemistry Ser.: Vol. 174). 168p. 1995. 141.95 (*3-540-58672-5*) Spr-Verlag.

Molecular Simulation. W. V. Van Gunsteren. 323p. 1993. pap. text 700.00 (*2-88124-949-3*) Gordon & Breach.

Molecular Simulation & Industrial Applications: Methods, Examples & Prospects. Ed. by K. E. Gubbins & N. Quirke. (Current Topics in Molecular Simulation Ser.: Vol. 1). 560p. 1997. text 98.00 (*90-5699-005-5*) Gordon & Breach.

Molecular Simulation of Fluids: Theory, Algorithms & Object-Orientation. R. J. Sadus. LC 98-53172. 552p. 1999. 241.00 (*0-444-82305-0*) Elsevier.

Molecular Solid State Physics. G. G. Hall. (Illus.). 165p. 1991. 43.95 (*0-387-53792-9*) Spr-Verlag.

Molecular Specialization & Symmetry in Membrane Function. Ed. by Arthur K. Solomon & Manfred L. Karnovsky. LC 77-134. (Books in Biophysics). 406p. 1978. 49.95 (*0-674-58179-2*) HUP.

Molecular Spectra & Molecular Structure, 3 vols., Set. Gerhard Herzberg. 2108p. 1992. lib. bdg. 210.50 (*0-89464-789-X*) Krieger.

Molecular Spectra & Molecular Structure: Electronic Spectra & Electronic Structure of Polyatomic Molecules, Vol. 3. Gerhard Herzberg. LC 88-2933. (Molecular Spectra & Molecular Structure Ser.). 784p. (C). 1991. reprint ed. 94.50 (*0-89464-270-7*) Krieger.

Molecular Spectra & Molecular Structure: Infrared & Raman of Polyatomic Molecules, Vol. 2. Gerhard Herzberg. LC 88-2933. (Molecular Spectra & Molecular Structure Ser.). 650p. (C). 1990. reprint ed. lib. bdg. 72.50 (*0-89464-269-3*) Krieger.

Molecular Spectra & Molecular Structure: Spectra of Diatomic Molecules, Vol. 1. 2nd ed. Gerhard Herzberg. LC 88-2933. (Molecular Spectra & Molecular Structure Ser.). 678p. 1989. reprint ed. lib. bdg. 79.50 (*0-89464-268-5*) Krieger.

Molecular Spectra & Structure Dielectrics & Dipole Moments see Advanced Treatise on Physical Chemistry

Molecular Spectroscopy. John M. Brown. (Oxford Chemistry Primers Ser.: No. 55). (Illus.). 96p. (C). 1998. pap. text 12.95 (*0-19-855785-X*) OUP.

Molecular Spectroscopy. Jack D. Graybeal. LC 93-20566. 732p. (C). 1992. 87.81 (*0-07-024412-X*) McGraw.

Molecular Spectroscopy. Ira N. Levine. 512p. 1975. 125.00 (*0-471-53128-6*) Wiley.

Molecular Spectroscopy. Jeanne L. McHale. LC 98-4506. 463p. 1998. 91.00 (*0-13-229063-4*) P-H.

Molecular Spectroscopy, Vol. 6. Royal Society of Chemistry Staff. 1988. 126.00 (*0-85186-556-9*) CRC Pr.

Molecular Spectroscopy: Proceedings of the European Congress on Molecular Spectroscopy, 8th, Denmark, 1965. European Congress on Molecular Spectroscopy Staff. LC QC0454.M6. 327p. reprint ed. pap. 101.40 (*0-608-11834-6*, 202071300018) Bks Demand.

Molecular Spectroscopy: Proceedings of the 6th Conference on Molecular Spectroscopy, Organized by the Institute of Petroleum, Hydrocarbon Research Group, & Held at the University of Durham, 30 March-2 April, 1976. Conference on Molecular Spectroscopy (6th: 1976: U. Ed. by A. R. West. LC 78-320788. 598p. reprint ed. pap. 185.40 (*0-608-14101-1*, 202401300035) Bks Demand.

M

Molecular Spectroscopy, Electronic Structure & Intramolecular Interactions, Pt. 3. Ed. by Z. B. Maksic. (Illus.). x, 638p. 1991. 244.00 (*0-387-52252-2*) Spr-Verlag.

Molecular Spectroscopy, 1971: Proceedings, Brighton, 21-24 September, 1971. 5th ed. Ed. by Peter Hepple. LC 73-152157. 424p. reprint ed. pap. 131.50 (*0-608-13881-9*, 202369600033) Bks Demand.

Molecular Spectroscopy, 1968: Proceedings, Brighton, England, 17-19 April, 1968. LC 78-393156. 431p. reprint ed. pap. 133.70 (*0-608-13851-7*, 202369500033) Bks Demand.

Molecular Spectroscopy Workbench: Advances, Applications & Practical Advice on Modern Spectroscopic Analysis. Emil W. Ciurczak. LC 97-24060. 476p. 1998. 79.95 (*0-471-18081-5*) Wiley.

Molecular Strategies for Crop Protection: Proceedings of a DuPont - UCLA Symposium on Molecular Strategies for Crop Protection, Held in Steamboat Springs, Colorado, March 30-April 6, 1986. DuPont - UCLA Symposium on Molecular Strategies fo. Ed. by Charles J. Arntzen & Clarence Ryan. LC 86-34284. (UCLA Symposia on Molecular & Cellular Biology Ser.: Vol. 48). 465p. reprint ed. pap. 144.20 (*0-7837-2841-7*, 205763100006) Bks Demand.

Molecular Strategies in Biological Evolution. Ed. by Lynn H. Caporale. LC 99-28213. 350p. 1999. text 120.00 (*1-57331-192-8*) NY Acad Sci.

Molecular Strategies in Biological Evolution Lynne H. Caporale. LC 99-28213. (Annals of the New York Academy of Science Ser.). 1999. write for info. (*1-57331-193-6*) NY Acad Sci.

Molecular Strategies of Pathogens & Host Plants. Ed. by D. L. Mills et al. (Illus.). 264p. 1991. 79.95 (*0-387-97448-2*) Spr-Verlag.

Molecular Structure: Biological Activity of Steroids. Martin Bohl. 495p. 1992. lib. bdg. 229.00 (*0-8493-6955-X*, QP752) CRC Pr.

Molecular Structure: Its Study by Crystal Diffraction, No. 30. J. Speakman. 1989. 10.00 (*0-85186-689-1*) CRC Pr.

Molecular Structure & Bonding: The Qualitative Molecular Orbital Theory. Benjamin M. Gimarc. 1979. text 65.00 (*0-12-284150-6*) Acad Pr.

Molecular Structure & Energetics, 11 vols. Incl. Vol. 5: Advances in Boron & the Boranes: A Volume in Honor of Anton B. Burg. Ed. by Joel F. Liebman et al. LC 87-21705. 547p. 1988. lib. bdg. 95.00 (*0-89573-272-6*, Wiley-VCH); Vol. 4: Biophysical Aspects. Ed. by J. F. Liebman & A. Geenberg. 407p. 1987. 95.00 (*0-89573-336-6*, Wiley-VCH); Vol. 1: Chemical Bonding Models. Ed. by J. F. Liebman & A. Greenberg. 360p. 1986. lib. bdg. 95.00 (*0-89573-139-8*, Wiley-VCH); Vol. 10: Environmental Influences & Recognition in Enzyme Chemistry. Ed. by Joel F. Liebman & Arthur Greenberg. LC 88-19228. 349p. 1989. 95.00 (*0-89573-707-8*, Wiley-VCH); Vol. 8: Fluorine-Containing Molecules: Structure, Reactivity, Synthesis & Applications. Ed. by Arthur Greenberg & Joel F. Liebman. LC 88-19227. 346p. 1988. lib. bdg. 95.00 (*0-89573-705-1*, Wiley-VCH); Vol. 11: From Atoms to Polymers Isoelectronic Analogies. Ed. by Joel F. Liebman & Arthur Greenberg. LC 88-36684. 473p. 1989. 95.00 (*0-89573-711-6*, Wiley-VCH); Vol. 9: Mechanistic Principles of Enzyme Activity. Ed. by Arthur Greenberg & Joel F. Liebman. LC 88-19229. 404p. 1989. lib. bdg. 95.00 (*0-89573-706-X*, Wiley-VCH); Vol. 6: Modern Models of Bonding & Delocalization. Ed. by Joel F. Liebman & Arthur Greenberg. LC 88-19226. 461p. 1989. lib. bdg. 95.00 (*0-89573-714-0*, Wiley-VCH); Vol. 2: Physical Measurements. Ed. by J. F. Liebman & A. Greenberg. 388p. 1987. 95.00 (*0-89573-140-1*, Wiley-VCH); Vol. 7: Structure & Reactivity. Ed. by Joel F. Liebman & Arthur Greenberg. LC 88-19225. 385p. 1989. lib. bdg. 95.00 (*0-89573-712-4*, Wiley-VCH); 500.00 (*1-56081-842-5*, Wiley-VCH) Wiley.

Molecular Structure & Energetics, Vols. 1-11. Joel F. Liebman. 4503p. 1989. 1425.00 (*0-471-18618-X*) Wiley.

Molecular Structure & Energetics: Advances in Boron & the Boranes, Vol. 5. Ed. by J. F. Liebman & A. Greenberg. 529p. 1988. 149.00 (*0-471-18680-5*, Wiley-VCH) Wiley.

Molecular Structure & Energetics: Biophysical Aspects, 4. Ed. by J. F. Liebman & A. Greenberg. 405p. 1987. 149.00 (*0-471-18673-2*, Wiley-VCH) Wiley.

Molecular Structure & Energetics: Chemical Bonding Models, 10. Ed. by J. F. Liebman & A. Greenberg. 360p. 1986. 149.00 (*0-471-18669-4*) Wiley.

Molecular Structure & Energetics: Environmental Influences & Recognition in Enzyme Chemistry. Ed. by J. F. Liebman & A. Greenberg. 349p. 1989. 149.00 (*0-471-18713-5*, Wiley-VCH) Wiley.

Molecular Structure & Energetics: Fluorine-Containing Molecules, Vol. 8. Ed. by J. F. Liebman & A. Greenberg. 346p. 1988. 149.00 (*0-471-18711-9*, Wiley-VCH) Wiley.

Molecular Structure & Energetics: From Atoms to Polymers Isoelectronic Analogies, Vol. 11. Ed. by J. F. Liebman & A. Greenberg. 473p. 1989. 149.00 (*0-471-18721-6*, Wiley-VCH) Wiley.

Molecular Structure & Energetics: Physical Measurements, 2. Ed. by J. F. Liebman & A. Greenberg. 388p. 1987. 149.00 (*0-471-18671-6*) Wiley.

Molecular Structure & Energetics: Structure & Reactivity, Vol. 7. Ed. by J. F. Liebman & A. Greenberg. 385p. 1989. 149.00 (*0-471-18723-2*, Wiley-VCH) Wiley.

Molecular Structure & Energetics: Studies of Organic Molecules, 3. Ed. by J. F. Liebman & A. Greenberg. 385p. 1986. 149.00 (*0-471-18672-4*, Wiley-VCH) Wiley.

Molecular Structure & Energetics - Mechanistic Principles of Enzyme Activity, Vol. 9. Joel F. Liebman. 404p. 1989. 149.00 (*0-471-18712-7*) Wiley.

Molecular Structure & Energetics - Modern Models of Bonding & Delocalization, Vol. 6. Joel F. Liebman & Arthur Greenberg. 461p. 1988. 149.00 (*0-471-18722-4*) Wiley.

Molecular Structure & Life: Molecular Recognition of Nucleic Acids. Ed. by Yoshimasa Kyogoku & Yoshifumi Nishimura. 1993. 73.00 (*0-8493-7768-4*, QP552) CRC Pr.

Molecular Structure & Optical Isomerism in Carbon Compounds. Robert Silberman. Ed. by Conrad L. Stanitski. (Modular Laboratory Program in Chemistry Ser.). 12p. (C). 1996. pap. text 1.50 (*0-87540-473-1*, STRC 473-1) Chem Educ Res.

Molecular Structure & Statistical Thermodynamics. Kenneth S. Pitzer. (Twentieth Century Chemistry Ser.). 536p. 1993. text 83.00 (*981-02-1439-1*) World Scientific Pub.

Molecular Structure Description: The Electrotopological State. Lemont B. Kier. LC 98-89313. 288p. 1999. 99.95 (*0-12-406555-4*) Acad Pr.

Molecular Structure of Amino Acids: Determination by X-ray Diffraction Analysis. Galina V. Gurskaya. LC 68-18821. (Illus.). 128p. reprint ed. pap. 39.70 (*0-608-30999-0*, 202067800018) Bks Demand.

Molecular Structure of Organosilicon Compounds. E. Lukevics et al. (Organic Chemistry Ser.). 1989. text 149.00 (*0-470-21525-9*) P-H.

Molecular Structures in Biology. Ed. by R. Diamond et al. LC 92-28936. (Illus.). 352p. 1993. text 79.00 (*0-19-854771-4*) OUP.

Molecular Symmetry: Structure & Spectra. Dudley R. Huerschbach. (Series on Twentieth Century Chemistry). 500p. 1997. text 86.00 (*981-02-1774-9*) World Scientific Pub.

Molecular Symmetry & Group Theory. Robert L. Carter. LC 97-25445. 320p. 1997. pap. 53.95 (*0-471-14955-1*) Wiley.

Molecular Symmetry & Group Theory. Vincent. text. write for info. (*0-471-48938-7*); pap. text. write for info. (*0-471-48939-5*) Wiley.

Molecular Symmetry & Group Theory. Alan Vincent. 156p. 1977. pap. 64.95 (*0-471-01868-6*) Wiley.

Molecular Symmetry & Spectroscopy. 2nd ed. Philip R. Bunker & Per Jensen. 768p. 1998. 81.50 (*0-660-17519-3*) NRC Res Pr.

Molecular Symmetry Groups & Chemistry. S. C. Rakshit. 1985. 79.00 (*0-7855-0743-4*, Pub. by Current Dist) St Mut.

Molecular Systematics. 2nd rev. ed. Ed. by David M. Hillis et al. LC 95-41159. (Illus.). 655p. 1996. pap. text 64.95 (*0-87893-282-8*) Sinauer Assocs.

*__Molecular Systematics & Plant Evolution.__ P. M. Hollingsworth et al. LC 99-31705. 1999. pap. 54.95 (*0-7484-0908-4*) Tay Francis Ltd.

Molecular Systematics & Secondary Metabolites. David E. Giannasi. 1998. 189.00 (*0-8493-7687-4*) CRC Pr.

Molecular Systematics of Fishes. Ed. by Thomas D. Kocher & Carol A. Stepien. LC 96-49199. (Illus.). 314p. 1997. text 79.95 (*0-12-417540-6*) Morgan Kaufmann.

Molecular Systematics of Plants II: DNA Sequencing. Douglas E. Soltis et al. LC 97-17374. 448p. 1998. mass mkt. 59.95 (*0-412-11131-4*) Chapman & Hall.

Molecular Systematics of Plants II: DNA Sequencing. Douglas E. Soltis et al. LC 97-17374. 1998. write for info. (*0-412-11121-7*) Kluwer Academic.

Molecular Techniques in Taxonomy. Ed. by G. M. Hewitt et al. (NATO ASI Series H: Cell Biology: Vol. 57). x, 410p. 1991. 166.00 (*0-387-51764-2*) Spr-Verlag.

Molecular Theories of Cell Life & Death. Ed. by Sungchul Ji. 600p. (C). 1991. text 96.00 (*0-8135-1691-9*) Rutgers U Pr.

Molecular Theory of Evolution: Outline of a Physico-Chemical Theory of the Origin of Life. B. O. Kueppers. (Illus.). 321p. 1983. 55.00 (*0-387-12080-7*) Spr-Verlag.

Molecular Theory of Gases & Liquids. Joseph O. Hirschfelder et al. 1280p. 1964. 395.00 (*0-471-40065-3*, Wiley-Interscience) Wiley.

Molecular Theory of Radiation Biology. K. H. Chadwick & H. P. Leenhouts. (Monographs on Theoretical & Applied Genetics: Vol. 5). (Illus.). 377p. 1981. 119.95 (*0-387-10297-3*) Spr-Verlag.

*__Molecular Thermodynamcs Fluid Phase Equilib: Solutions Manual.__ 3rd ed. 1999. write for info. (*0-13-018388-1*) P-H.

Molecular Thermodynamics. Donald McQuarrie & John Simon. LC 98-48543. (Illus.). xiii, 656p. (C). 1999. text 78.00 (*1-891389-05-X*) Univ Sci Bks.

Molecular Thermodynamics: A Statistical Approach. James W. Whalen. LC 90-39767. 381p. 1991. 99.00 (*0-471-51478-0*) Wiley.

Molecular Thermodynamics: An Introduction to Statistical Mechanics for Chemists. rev. ed. John H. Knox. LC 70-147399. (Illus.). 280p. reprint ed. pap. 86.80 (*0-8357-5562-2*, 203519100093) Bks Demand.

Molecular Thermodynamics of Fluid-Phase Equilibria. 3rd ed. John M. Prausnitz. LC 98-222890. 864p. 1998. 105.00 (*0-13-977745-8*) P-H.

Molecular Toxicology. David Josephy. (Illus.). 384p. (C). 1996. text 68.00 (*0-19-509340-2*) OUP.

Molecular Transport & Reaction in Zeolites: Design & Application of Shape Selective Catalysis. N. Y. Chen et al. 328p. 1994. 159.00 (*0-471-18548-5*) Wiley.

Molecular Transport & Reaction in Zeolites: Design & Application of Shape Selective Catalysts. N. Y. Chen et al. LC 94-2231. 1994. 95.00 (*0-89573-765-5*, Wiley-VCH) Wiley.

Molecular Variability of Fungal Pathogens. P. D. Bridge et al. LC 98-14967. (CAB International Publication). 350p. 1999. text 100.00 (*0-85199-266-8*) OUP.

Molecular Vibrations: The Theory of Infrared & Raman Vibrational Spectra. E. Bright Wilson, Jr. et al. (Illus.). 388p. 1980. reprint ed. pap. text 10.95 (*0-486-63941-X*) Dover.

Molecular Virology. Yechiel Becker. 1983. text 102.00 (*90-247-2742-1*) Kluwer Academic.

Molecular Virology. D. R. Harper & C. Grose. (Medical Perspectives Ser.). 160p. 1994. pap. 47.50 (*1-872748-57-0*, Pub. by Bios Sci) Coronet Bks.

Molecular Virology. 2nd ed. D. R. Harper. (Medical Perspectives Ser.). (Illus.). 177p. 1998. pap. 38.95 (*0-387-91558-3*) Spr-Verlag.

Molecular Virology: A Practical Approach. Ed. by Andrew J. Davison & Richard M. Elliott. LC 93-7052. (Practical Approach Ser.). (Illus.). 344p. 1993. pap. text 55.00 (*0-19-963357-6*); spiral bd. 95.00 (*0-19-963358-4*) OUP.

Molecular Vision of Life: Caltech, the Rockefeller Foundation & the Rise of the New Biology. Lily E. Kay. (Illus.). 320p. 1992. text 75.00 (*0-19-505812-7*) OUP.

Molecular Vision of Life: Caltech, the Rockefeller Foundation, & the Rise of the New Biology. Lily E. Kay. (Monographs on the History & Philosophy of Biology). (Illus.). 320p. 1996. reprint ed. pap. 24.95 (*0-19-511143-5*) OUP.

Molecular Visions Organic Mode. Darling. (C). 1998. 8.50 (*0-9648837-4-0*) Darling Models.

Molecular Volumes in Chemistry & Biology: Applications Including Partitioning Toxicity. John C. McGowan & Alan Mellors. LC 86-10520. 259p. 1986. text 65.95 (*0-470-20353-6*) P-H.

Molecular Weight Determination to Pentadiene Polymers: Molecular see Encyclopedia of Polymer Science & Engineering

Molecular Zoology: Advances, Strategies & Protocols. Joan D. Ferraris & Stephen R. Palumbi. LC 96-208. 580p. 1996. pap. 63.50 (*0-471-14461-4*, Wiley-Interscience) Wiley.

Molecular Zoology: Advances, Strategies & Protocols. Ed. by Joan D. Ferraris & Stephen R. Palumbi. LC 96-208. 580p. 1996. 140.00 (*0-471-14449-5*) Wiley.

Molecularising Biology & Medicine: New Practices & Alliances, 1930s to 1970s. Soraya De Chadarevain & Harmke Kamminga. (Studies in the History of Science, Technology & Medicine Ser.: Vol. 6). 350p. 1998. text 70.00 (*3-7186-5908-5*, Harwood Acad Pubs) Gordon & Breach.

Molecularizing Biology & Medicine: New Practices & Alliances, 1930s to 1970s. Chadarevain. 292p. 1998. text 38.00 (*90-5702-293-1*) Gordon & Breach.

Molecule-Based Magnetic Materials: Theory, Techniques, & Applications, Vol. 644. Ed. by Mark M. Turnbull et al. LC 96-2923. (Symposium Ser.: No. 644). (Illus.). 352p. 1996. text 110.00 (*0-8412-3452-3*, Pub. by Am Chemical) OUP.

Molecules & Cell Movement. fac. ed. Ed. by Shinya Inoue & Raymond E. Stephens. LC 75-16666. (Society of General Physiologists Ser.: No. 30). (Illus.). 460p. pap. 142.60 (*0-7837-7528-8*, 204697600005) Bks Demand.

Molecules & Cellular Basis Cell. Hirohashi & Moses. (C). 1997. pap. text 95.00 (*0-8385-6380-5*, A8680-8, Apple Lange Med) McGraw.

Molecules & Grains in Space. Ed. by Irene Nenner et al. (AIP Conference Proceedings Ser.: No. 312). 832p. 1994. text 145.00 (*1-56396-355-8*) Am Inst Physics.

Molecules & Life: Historical Essays on the Interplay of Chemistry & Biology. Joseph S. Fruton. LC 72-3095. 589p. reprint ed. pap. 182.60 (*0-608-13615-8*, 205513500008) Bks Demand.

Molecules & Mental Illness. Samuel H. Barondes. 216p. 1999. pap. text 19.95 (*0-7167-6033-9*) W H Freeman.

Molecules & Minds: Biology & the Social Order. Steven Rose. 160p. 1991. pap. 79.95 (*0-471-93259-0*, Wiley-Liss) Wiley.

Molecules & Minds: Essays on Biology & the Social Order. Steven Rose. 160p. 1991. 260.00 (*0-471-93260-4*, Wiley-Liss) Wiley.

Molecules & Molecular Lasers for Electrical Engineers. E. B. Bradley. (Series in Electrical Engineering). 200p. 1990. 105.00 (*0-89116-788-9*) Hemisp Pub.

Molecules & Radiation: An Introduction to Modern Molecular Spectroscopy. 2nd ed. Jeffrey I. Steinfeld. (Illus.). 512p. 1985. reprint ed. 55.00 (*0-262-19231-4*) MIT Pr.

Molecules & Radicals Vol. II/20: Molecular Constants for Linear Triatomic Molecules. Ed. by G. Guelachvili. (Numerican Data & Functional Relationships in Science & Technology Ser.). lxi, 345p. 1578.00 (*3-540-62430-9*) Spr-Verlag.

Molecules & Radicals Vol. 18, Group II: Radical Reaction Rates in Liquids. R. F. Claridge & J. Dohrmann. Ed. by W. Martienssen & H. Fischer. xvi, 478p. 1997. 1931.00 (*3-540-57262-7*) Spr-Verlag.

Molecules & Their Spectroscopic Properties. S. V. Khristenko et al. LC 97-46883. (Series on Atoms & Plasmas: Vol. 21). (Illus.). ix, 212p. 1998. 109.00 (*3-540-63466-5*) Spr-Verlag.

Molecules Annual '96 Vol. 1: Organic & Natural Product CD-ROM & Print Archive Edition of Molecules - Journal of Synthic Chemistry, 1996. Ed. by S. K. Lin. 220p. 1997. 145.00 incl. cd-rom (*3-540-14572-9*) Spr-Verlag.

Molecules at an Exhibition: Intriguing Molecules in Everyday Life. John Emsley. 272p. 1997. 24.95 (*0-7167-4553-4*) W H Freeman.

Molecules at an Exhibition: Portraits of Intriguing Materials in Everyday Life. John Emsley. 272p. 1999. pap. 14.95 (*0-19-286206-5*) OUP.

Molecules, Cells & Disease. J. L. Van Lancker. LC 77-893. (Springer Study Edition Ser.). 1977. 99.00 (*0-387-90242-2*) Spr-Verlag.

Molecules, Cells, & Life: An Annotated Bibliography of Manuscript Sources on Physiology, Biochemistry, & Biophysics, 1900-1960, in the Library of the American Philosophical Society. Lily E. Kay. LC 88-82934. (American Philosophical Society Library Publication Ser.: No. 14). 103p. reprint ed. pap. 32.00 (*0-8357-3407-2*, 203966400013) Bks Demand.

Molecules, Dynamics & Life: An Introduction to Self-Organization of Matter. A. Babloyantz. LC 85-26413. (Nonequilibrium Problems in the Physical Sciences & Biology Ser.). 345p. 1986. 150.00 (*0-471-82380-5*) Wiley.

Molecules in Astrophysics: Probes & Processes. 1997. pap. text 100.50 (*0-7923-4539-8*) Kluwer Academic.

Molecules in Astrophysics - Probes & Processes: Proceedings of the 178th Symposium of the International Astronomical Union Held in Leiden, The Netherlands, July 1-5, 1996. Ewine F. Van Dishoeck. LC 97-6834. (International Astronomical Union Symposia Ser.: No. 178). 600p. 1997. lib. bdg. 210.00 (*0-7923-4538-X*) Kluwer Academic.

Molecules in Laser Fields. Ed. by Andre D. Bandrauk. LC 93-40776. (Illus.). 480p. 1993. text 225.00 (*0-8247-9175-4*) Dekker.

Molecules in Physics, Chemistry & Biology, 4 vols., Vol. 1: General Introduction to Molecular Sciences. J. Maruani. (C). 1988. lib. bdg. 162.50 (*90-277-2596-9*) Kluwer Academic.

Molecules in Physics, Chemistry & Biology, 4 vols., Vol. 2: Physical Aspects of Molecular Systems. J. Maruani. (C). 1988. lib. bdg. 342.00 (*90-277-2597-7*) Kluwer Academic.

Molecules in Physics, Chemistry & Biology, 4 vols., Vol. 3: Electronic Structure & Chemical Reactivity. J. Maruani. (C). 1988. lib. bdg. 224.50 (*90-277-2598-5*) Kluwer Academic.

Molecules in Physics, Chemistry & Biology, 4 vols., Vol. 4: Molecular Phenomena in Biological Sciences. J. Maruani. (C). 1988. lib. bdg. 197.00 (*90-277-2599-3*) Kluwer Academic.

Molecules in the Stellar Environment No. 146: Proceedings of IAU Colloquium. Ed. by U. G. Jorgensen. LC 94-8067. (Lecture Notes in Physics Ser.: Vol. 428). iv, 432p. 1994. 86.95 (*0-387-57747-5*) Spr-Verlag.

*__Molecules, Miracles & Medicine.__ Andrew Lasslo. 89p. 2000. pap. 12.99 (*0-87527-533-8*) Green.

Molecules of Death. R. H. Waring. 1998. 34.00 (*1-86094-127-3*) World Scientific Pub.

Molecules of Emotion: The Science Behind Mind-Body Medicine. Candace B. Pert. 368p. 1999. per. 14.00 (*0-684-84634-9*) S&S Trade.

Molecules of Emotion: Why You Feel the Way You Feel. Candace B. Pert. LC 97-17463. 304p. 1997. 24.50 (*0-684-83187-2*) S&S Trade.

Molecules of Life. Ed. by Felix Franks. (Water Science Reviews Ser.: No. 5). (Illus.). 299p. (C). 1991. text 135.00 (*0-521-36577-5*) Cambridge U Pr.

Molecules of the Cytoskeleton. Linda A. Amos & W. Bradshaw Amos. LC 91-16542. (Molecular Cell Biology Ser.). 247p. 1991. pap. text 27.95 (*0-89862-527-0*); lib. bdg. 52.50 (*0-89862-404-5*) Guilford Pubns.

Molecules of Transport: Carriers. Ed. by H. Murer. (Journal: Cellular Physiology & Biochemistry: Vol. 4, Nos. 5-6, 1994). (Illus.). 140p. 1994. pap. 75.75 (*3-8055-5972-0*) S Karger.

Molecules of Transport Ion Channels. Ed. by F. P. Lang. (Journal: Cellular Physiology & Biochemistry: Vol. 3, No. 5-6, 1993). (Illus.). 164p. 1993. pap. 75.75 (*3-8055-5848-1*) S Karger.

Molecules Online Annual, 1997-1998: An Advanced Forum for Innovative Research in Organic, Bio-Organic & Medicinal Chemistry. Ed. by S. Hanessian. (Illus.). 145p. 1999. 195.00 incl. cd-rom (*3-540-14573-7*) Spr-Verlag.

Molecules R2CXCR2 Including Azomethine, Carbonyl & Thiocarbonyl Ylides: Their Syntheses, Properties & Reactions. Richard M. Kellogg. 1977. pap. 14.00 (*0-08-021582-3*, Pergamon Pr) Elsevier.

Molecules to Models: Advances in Neuroscience; Papers from Sciences, 1986-1989. Ed. by Katrina L. Kelner & Daniel E. Koshland, Jr. LC 89-18042. (AAAS Miscellaneous Publications: No. 89-17S). (Illus.). 480p. reprint ed. pap. 148.80 (*0-7837-6736-6*, 204636400011) Bks Demand.

Molecules Within Us: Our Body in Health & Disease. Charles A. Pasternak. LC 98-26173. (Illus.). 350p. (C). 1998. 26.95 (*0-306-45987-6*, Plenum Trade) Perseus Pubng.

*__Moledet Solution.__ James Haddad. LC 00-105379. 204p. 2000. 19.95 (*1-892986-03-5*) Commnwlth Bks.

Molehunt. David Wise. 400p. 1994. mass mkt. 5.50 (*0-380-72127-9*, Avon Bks) Morrow Avon.

Molekular Zellbiologie. 2nd ed. David Baltimore et al. (GER., Illus.). xlii, 1448p. (C). 1996. text 94.85 (*3-11-014460-3*, 126/96) De Gruyter.

*__Molekularbiologie In der Viszeralchirurgie.__ (Chirurgische Gastroenterologie Ser.). 100p. 1999. 44.50 (*3-8055-6830-4*) S Karger.

Molekularbiologische Analyse der Pysiologischen Phaenomene des Seneszenzsyndroms Bei Dem Ascomyceten Podospora Anserina. Dirk Frese. (Bibliotheca Mycologica: Vol. 149). (GER., Illus.). x, 117p. 1993. 36.00 (*3-443-59050-0*, Pub. by Gebruder Borntraeger) Balogh.

*__Molekularbiologische Untersuchungen zur Alkaloidsynthese bei Claviceps.__ Claudia Arntz. (Bibliotheca Mycologica: Band 176). (Illus.). vi, 145p. 1999. 53.00 (*3-443-59078-0*, Pub. by Gebruder Borntraeger) Balogh.

Molekulare Analysen Zur Expression Von B-Lactam-Genen Bei Acremonium Chrysogenum. Markus Walz. (Bibliotheca Mycologica: Vol. 147). (GER., Illus.). 101p. 1992. 42.00 (*3-443-59048-9*, Pub. by Gebruder Borntraeger) Balogh.

Molekulare Entwicklungssteuerung bei Pflanzen Durch Regulierte Genexpression: Das Beispiel der rbcS Multigenfamilie bei Cruciferen. Claudia Fiebig. (Dissertationes Botanicae Ser.: Vol. 177). (GER., Illus.). 106p. 1991. pap. 36.00 (*0-685-51569-9*) Lubrecht & Cramer.

Molekulare Entwicklungssteuerung Bei Pflanzen Durch Regulierte Genexpression: Das Beispiel der rbcS Multigenfamilie Bei Cruciferen. Claudia Fiebig. (Dissertationes Botanicae Ser.: Band 177). (Illus.). x, 104p. 1991. pap. 36.00 (*3-443-64089-3*, Pub. by Gebruder Borntraeger) Balogh.

Moles. Jesus Torbado & Manuel Leguineche. Tr. by Nancy Festinger from SPA. LC 81-215226. Orig. Title: Los topos. xii, 226p. 1981. write for info. (*0-436-52600-X*) M Secker & Warburg.

Moles: Champion Excavators see Secrets of the Animal World New Releases

Moles Can Dance. Richard Edwards. LC 93-2462. (Illus.). 32p. (J). (ps up). 1994. 13.95 (*1-56402-353-2*) Candlewick Pr.

Mole's Daughter: An Adaptation of a Korean Folktale. Illus. by Julia Gukova. 24p. (J). (ps-3). 1998. pap. 6.95 (*1-55037-524-5*, Pub. by Annick); lib. bdg. 15.95 (*1-55037-525-3*, Pub. by Annick) Firefly Bks Ltd.

Mole's Hill: A Woodland Tale. Ehlert. LC 93-31151. (Illus.). 36p. (J). (ps-3). 1998. pap. 7.00 (*0-15-201890-5*) Harcourt.

Mole's Hill: A Woodland Tale. Lois Ehlert. 1998. 12.20 (*0-606-13614-2*, Pub. by Turtleback) Demco.

Mole's Hill: A Woodland Tale. abr. ed. Lois Ehlert. LC 93-31151. (Illus.). 32p. (J). (ps-3). 1994. 15.00 (*0-15-255116-6*, Harcourt Child Bks) Harcourt.

Mole's Pity. Harold Jaffe. LC 78-68129. 1979. 15.95 (*0-914590-52-9*); pap. 6.95 (*0-914590-53-7*) Fiction Coll.

Moleseide: Songs & Ballads in the Molisan Dialect. Giose Rimanelli. Ed. by Francis X. Femminella. Tr. by Luigi Bonaffini. (Studies in Southern Italian & Italian American Culture: Vol. 1). 333p. 1992. 61.95 (*0-8204-1722-X*) P Lang Pubng.

Moliere. Jacques Audiberti. (FRE.). 144p. 1973. pap. 22.95 (*0-7859-0381-X*, M1621) Fr & Eur.

Moliere. Jacques Guicharnaud. (Bibliotheque des Idees Ser.). 35.00 (*0-685-34244-1*) Fr & Eur.

Moliere. rev. ed. Hallam Walker. (Twayne's World Authors Ser.). 200p. 1990. 28.95 (*0-8057-8258-3*, TWAS 176, Twyne) Mac Lib Ref.

*__Moliere: A Theatrical Life.__ Virginia Scott. (Illus.). 323p. 2001. 54.95 (*0-521-78281-3*) Cambridge U Pr.

Moliere: An Archetypal Approach. Harold C. Knutson. LC 76-15976. (University of Toronto Romance Ser.: No. 31). 218p. reprint ed. pap. 67.60 (*0-608-18005-X*, 202643800049) Bks Demand.

Moliere: "Don Juan" David Whitton. (Plays in Production Ser.). (Illus.). 221p. (C). 1995. text 59.95 (*0-521-43296-0*); pap. text 18.95 (*0-521-47867-7*) Cambridge U Pr.

Moliere: Le Misanthrope. G. Mallinson. (French Texts Ser.). (FRE.). 168p. 1996. pap. 18.95 (*1-85399-392-1*, Pub. by Brist Class Pr) Focus Pub-R Pullins.

Moliere: L'Ecole des Femmes & la Critique de L'Ecole des Femmes. Ed. by Howarth. (Bristol French Texts Ser.). (FRE.). 177p. 1994. 18.95 (*1-85399-322-0*, Pub. by Brist Class Pr) Focus Pub-R Pullins.

Moliere: The Comedy of Unreason, Vol. 2. F. L. Lawrence. 119p. 1968. pap. 7.00 (*0-912788-01-1*) Tulane Romance Lang.

Moliere: The Theory & Practice of Comedy. Andrew Calder. LC 92-30595. 180p. (C). 1993. text 65.00 (*0-485-11427-5*, Pub. by Athlone Pr) Humanities.

An Asterisk (*) at the beginning of an entry indicates that the title is appearing for the first time.

Moliere: The Theory & Practice of Comedy. Andrew Calder. 244p. 1996. pap. 25.00 (*0-485-12127-1*, Pub. by Athlone Pr) Humanities.
***Moliere - Four Plays: The Bourgeois Gentleman, the Doctor in Spite of Himself, the Miser, the Affected Damsels.** Moliere. Ed. by Adolph Caso. Tr. by Carl Milo Pergolizzi from FRE. LC 99-18379. 368p. 1999. pap. 19.95 (*0-8283-2038-1*) Branden Bks.
Moliere a l'Ecole Republicaine: De la Critique Universitaire aux Manuels Scolaires (1870-1914) Ralph Albanese, Jr. (Stanford French & Italian Studies: No. 72). 176p. 1991. pap. 56.50 (*0-915838-88-5*) Anma Libri.
Moliere & Plurality: Decomposition on the Classicist Self. Larry W. Riggs. LC 89-31588. (Sociocriticism: Literature, Society & History Ser.: Vol. 1). 276p. (C). 1989. text 44.95 (*0-685-46923-9*) P Lang Pubng.
Moliere & the Italian Theatrical Tradition. 2nd ed. Philip A. Wadsworth. 1987. 16.95 (*0-917786-70-X*) Summa Pubns.
Moliere As Ironic Contemplator. Alvin Eustis. LC 72-94465. (De Proprietatibus Litterarum, Ser. Practica: No. 40). 231p. 1974. pap. text 50.00 (*90-279-2507-0*) Mouton.
Moliere et L'Autorite: Structures Sociales, Structures Comiques. Karolyn Waterson. LC 76-17257. (French Forum Monographs: No. 1). 150p. (Orig.). 1976. pap. 10.95 (*0-917058-00-3*) French Forum.
Moliere, ou les Metamorphoses du Comique: De la Comedie Morale au Triomphe de la Folie. Gerard Defaux. LC 79-53401. (French Forum Monographs: No. 18). (FRE.). 370p. (Orig.). 1980. pap. 17.95 (*0-917058-17-8*) French Forum.
Moliere Student's Guide to European Literature. Brian Masters. (C). 1995. pap. text 7.50 (*0-435-37570-9*, 37570) Heinemann.
Moliere Today. Michael Spingler. 88p. 1998. pap. text 14.00 (*90-5702-027-0*, Harwood Acad Pubs) Gordon & Breach.
Moliere Today 2, Vol. 2. Michael Spingler. 88p. 1998. pap. text 14.00 (*90-5702-114-5*, Harwood Acad Pubs) Gordon & Breach.
Moliere's Don Juan. Wilbur. 2000. write for info. (*0-15-100468-4*) Harcourt.
***Moliere's Don Juan.** Richard Wilbur. (Harvest Bks.). 2001. pap. 13.00 (*0-15-601310-X*) Harcourt.
Moliere's the Bungler. Tr. by Richard Wilbur. Date not set. pap. 5.95 (*0-8222-1747-3*) Dramatists Play.
Moliere's Theatrical Bounty: A New View of the Plays. Albert Bermel. LC 89-5982. (Illus.). 300p. (C). 1990. 36.95 (*0-8093-1550-5*); pap. 21.95 (*0-8093-1551-3*) S Ill U Pr.
Moline: City of Mills. David Collins et al. LC 98-85881. (Images of America Ser.). (Illus.). 128p. 1998. pap. 16.99 (*0-7524-1283-3*) Arcadia Publng.
Molineux Affair. Jane Pejsa. LC 83-82593. (Illus.). 240p. 1984. pap. 12.95 (*0-9612776-0-2*) Kenwood Pub.
Molineux Case. Ed. by Samuel Klaus. (American Trials Ser.). x, 409p. 1997. reprint ed. 126.50 (*1-56169-346-4*) Gaunt.
Molisan Poems: Selected Poems. Eugenio Cirese. Tr. by Luigi Bonaffini from ITA. (Essential Poets Ser.: Vol. 83). 154p. 2000. pap. 13.00 (*1-55071-075-3*) Guernica Editions.
Moliseide & Other Poems. Giose Rimanelli. Tr. by Luigi Bonaffini from ITA. LC 98-21632. (Italian Poetry in Translation Ser.: No. 3). 212p. 1998. pap. 20.00 (*1-881901-14-9*) LEGAS.
Molkick: Version 2.0. Ed. by Beilstein Institut fur Literatur der Organischen Chemie. 200p. 1992. student ed. 895.95 incl. disk (*0-387-14107-3*) Spr-Verlag.
Moll Cutpurse: Her True History. Ellen Galford. LC 85-3473. (Illus.). 224p. (Orig.). 1985. reprint ed. pap. 7.95 (*0-932379-04-4*); reprint ed. lib. bdg. 16.95 (*0-932379-05-2*) Firebrand Bks.
Moll Flanders. Daniel Defoe. 1976. 24.95 (*0-8488-0473-2*) Amereon Ltd.
Moll Flanders. Daniel Defoe. 272p. 1989. mass mkt. 4.95 (*0-553-21328-8*, Bantam Classics) Bantam.
Moll Flanders. Daniel Defoe. 1996. 15.95 (*0-614-97638-3*) Everymns Lib.
Moll Flanders. Daniel Defoe. 320p. 1996. 15.95 (*0-679-40548-8*) Everymns Lib.
Moll Flanders. Daniel Defoe. (FRE.). 1979. pap. 12.95 (*0-7859-1890-6*, 2070371093) Fr & Eur.
Moll Flanders, 001. Daniel Defoe. Ed. by James R. Sutherland. LC 59-16265. 1972. pap. 13.96 (*0-395-05129-0*, 3-47665, RivEd) HM.
Moll Flanders. Daniel Defoe. 240p. 1998. 7.95 (*3-89508-687-8*) Konemann.
Moll Flanders. Daniel Defoe. (C). 1950. text 6.50 (*0-07-553573-4*) McGraw.
Moll Flanders. Daniel Defoe. 1996. mass mkt. 4.95 (*0-451-52633-3*, Sig Classics) NAL.
Moll Flanders. Daniel Defoe. Ed. by Edward Kelly. LC 72-13807. (Critical Editions Ser.). 500p. (C). 1973. pap. text 14.75 (*0-393-09412-X*) Norton.
Moll Flanders. Daniel Defoe. Ed. & Intro. by G. A. Starr. LC PR3404.M6 1998. (Oxford World's Classics Ser.). 432p. 1998. pap. 7.95 (*0-19-283403-7*) OUP.
Moll Flanders. Daniel Defoe. (C). 1950. pap. text. write for info. (*0-318-57395-4*) Random.
Moll Flanders. Daniel Defoe. 384p. 1996. 15.95 (*0-676-51349-2*) Random.
Moll Flanders. Daniel Defoe. LC 96-227072. 1996. 15.50 (*0-679-60260-7*) Random.
Moll Flanders. Daniel Defoe. Ed. & Intro. by David Blewett. 464p. 1989. pap. 8.95 (*0-14-043313-9*, Penguin Classics) Viking Penguin.
Moll Flanders. Daniel Defoe. (Classics Library). 352p. 1997. pap. 3.95 (*1-85326-073-8*, 0738WW, Pub. by Wrdsworth Edits) NTC Contemp Pub Co.

Moll Flanders. Hunter. 1999. text 39.95 (*0-312-12262-4*) St Martin.
Moll Flanders. abr. ed. Daniel Defoe. 1996. 16.95 (*1-85998-593-9*) Trafalgar.
Moll Flanders. large type ed. Daniel Defoe. (Isis Clear Type Classic Ser.). (Illus.). 380p. 1992. 22.95 (*1-85089-574-0*, Pub. by ISIS Lrg Prnt) Transaction Pubs.
Moll Flanders. Daniel Defoe. 451p. 1983. reprint ed. lib. bdg. 25.95 (*0-89966-313-3*) Buccaneer Bks.
***Moll Flanders.** Daniel Defoe. (Twelve-Point Ser.). 380p. 2000. reprint ed. lib. bdg. 24.00 (*1-58287-124-8*) North Bks.
Moll Flanders. unabridged ed. Daniel Defoe. (Thrift Editions Ser.). 256p. 1998. reprint ed. pap. text 2.00 (*0-486-29093-X*) Dover.
Moll Flanders. 2nd ed. Daniel Defoe. (Critical Editions Ser.). (C). 1999. pap. write for info. (*0-393-96793-X*, Norton Paperbks) Norton.
Moll Flanders see Shakespeare Head Edition of the Novels & Selected Writings of Daniel Defoe
Moll Flanders: The Making of a Criminal Mind. Paula Backsheider. (Twayne's Masterwork Studies: No. 48). 144p. (C). 1990. 25.95 (*0-8057-9429-8*, Twyne); pap. 13.95 (*0-8057-8130-7*, Twyne) Mac Lib Ref.
Moll Flanders Companion, Vol. 1. Daniel Defoe. 2000. pap. text 9.95 (*0-312-09117-6*) St Martin.
Moll Flanders Notes. Nancy L. Arnez. (Cliffs Notes Ser.). 80p. 1969. pap. 4.95 (*0-8220-0854-8*, Cliff) IDG Bks.
Mollicute Diseases of Plants. S. P. Raychaudhuri & D. K. Mitra. 1993. text 56.00 (*1-881570-13-4*) Science Pubs.
Mollie: The Journal of Mollie Dorsey Sanford in Nebraska & Colorado Territories, 1857-1866. Mollie D. Sanford. (American Biography Ser.). 199p. 1991. reprint ed. lib. bdg. 49.00 (*0-7812-8337-X*) Rprt Serv.
Mollie: The Journal of Mollie Dorsey Sanford in Nebraska & Colorado Territories, 1857-1866. Mollie D. Sanford. LC 75-8764. (Pioneer Heritage Ser.). xii, 199p. 1959. reprint ed. pap. 8.95 (*0-8032-5826-7*, Bison Books) U of Nebr Pr.
Mollie & Company: And Gussie Too. Hazel M. Osmond. (Illus.). (J). (ps up). 1996. write for info. (*1-86106-083-1*, Pub. by Minerva Pr) Unity Dist.
Mollie & the King of Tears. Arturo Islas. LC 96-4423. 200p. (C). 1996. pap. 13.95 (*0-8263-1732-4*) U of NM Pr.
Mollie & the Last Bookworm. Michael Lancy. 52p. 1985. pap. 5.00 (*1-890298-24-7*) Centerstage Pr.
Mollie Is Three: Growing up in School. Vivian G. Paley. xvi, 160p. 1988. pap. 9.95 (*0-226-64494-4*) U Ch Pr.
Mollie Katzen's Still Life Sampler. Mollie Katzen. (Illus.). 48p. 1993. pap. 12.00 (*0-89815-573-8*) Ten Speed Pr.
Mollie Katzen's Vegetable Heaven: Over 200 Recipes for Uncommon Soups, Tasty Bites, Side-by-Side Dishes & Too Many Desserts. Mollie Katzen. LC 97-22147. (Illus.). 224p. (J). 1997. 27.00 (*0-7868-6268-8*, Pub. by Hyperion) Time Warner.
Mollie Katzen's Vegetable Heaven: Over 200 Recipes for Uncommon Soups, Tasty Bites, Side-by-Side Dishes & Too Many Desserts. Mollie Katzen. (Illus.). 448p. 2002. 30.00 (*0-7868-6269-6*, Pub. by Hyperion) Time Warner.
Mollie Katzen's Vegetable Heaven: Over 200 Recipes for Uncommon Soups, Tasty Bites, Side-by-Side Dishes, & Too Many Desserts. Mollie Katzen. (Illus.). 240p. 1997. pap. 19.95 (*0-7868-8409-6*, Pub. by Hyperion) Time Warner.
Mollie O'Leary. Mary McGowan. 117p. 1990. pap. 9.95 (*0-930061-51-9*) Interspace Bks.
Mollie O'Neill. Jean Q. Gwinne. LC 96-86811. (Illus.). 224p. 1997. 22.95 (*1-879384-31-0*) Cypress Hse.
Mollie Peer: Or the Underground Adventures of the Moosepath League. Van Reid. LC 99-17375. 336p. 1999. 24.95 (*0-670-88633-5*, Viking) Viking Penguin.
***Mollie Peer: Or the Underground Adventures of the Moosepath League.** Van Reid. 368p. 2000. pap. 12.95 (*0-14-029185-7*) Viking Penguin.
Mollies: Keeping & Breeding Them in Captivity. Spencer Glass. (Illus.). 64p. 1997. pap. 6.95 (*0-7938-0372-1*, RE-623) TFH Pubns.
***Mollie's Job: A Story of Life & Work on the Global Assembly Line.** William M. Adler. LC 99-59825. 368p. 2000. 27.00 (*0-684-83779-X*, Scb1) S&S Trade.
Mollie's Miracle. Renee Kent. LC 97-226901. (Illus.). 112p. (J). (gr. 4-6). 1997. pap. text 6.95 (*1-56309-207-7*, N977105, New Hope) Womans Mission Union.
***Mollie's Mom Died: A Child's Book of Hope Through Grief.** Margaret M. Holmes. LC 98-46213. (J). 1999. 6.95 (*1-56123-122-3*) Centering Corp.
Mollification Method & the Numerical Solution of Ill-Posed Problems. Diego A. Murio. 272p. 1993. 130.00 (*0-471-59408-3*) Wiley.
Mollifier. A. D. Michele. (Chapbook Ser.). (Illus.). 15p. 1996. pap. 10.00 (*0-9652505-1-2*) Synaesthesia.
Mollison, the Flying Scotsman: The Life of Pioneer Aviator James Allan Mollison. David Luff. (Illus.). 416p. 1996. 37.95 (*1-56098-621-2*) Smithsonian.
Molloy. Samuel Beckett. 15.95 (*0-685-37199-9*, F86060) Fr & Eur.
Molloy. Samuel Beckett. Tr. by Patrick Bowles from FRE. LC 55-5113. 256p. 1978. pap. 12.95 (*0-8021-5136-1*, Grove) Grove-Atltic.
Molloy, Malone Dies, The Unnamable: A Triology. Samuel Beckett. LC 98-119494. 1997. 20.00 (*0-375-40070-2*) Everymns Lib.
Moll's Diner: The Simple Way to Cook & Live. Mollie M. Young. (Illus.). 1989. write for info. (*0-318-66522-0*) Juniper Hill Pub Hse.
Mollusc Diseases: A Guide for Shellfish Farmers. Ralph Elston. (Illus.). 86p. 1990. pap. 9.95 (*0-295-97001-4*) U of Wash Pr.
Mollusca: Biochemistry of Mollusca Environmental Biochemistry see Mollusca: Metabolic Biochem & Molecular Biomechanics

Mollusca: Gastropoda, Rissoidea. Hans D. Boeters. (Suesswasserfauna von Mitteleuropa Ser.: Band 5, 1 & 2). (GER., Illus.). 88p. 1998. pap. 48.00 (*3-437-25528-2*) Gustav Fischer.
Mollusca: Metabolic Biochem & Molecular Biomechanics, Vol. 1. Karl M. Wilbur. Incl. Vol. 2. Mollusca: Biochemistry of Mollusca Environmental Biochemistry. 1983. text 104.00 (*0-12-751402-3*); 1983. Set text 99.00 (*0-12-751401-5*) Acad Pr.
Mollusca: Testacelldae & Zonitidae, Vol. 1. W. T. Blandford & H. N. Godwin-Austen. (Fauna of British India Ser.). xxxii, 332p. 1978. reprint ed. 30.00 (*0-685-04536-6*) Scholarly Pubns.
Mollusca: Trochomorphidae & Janellidae, Vol. 2. G. K. Gude. xii, 522p. 1978. reprint ed. 30.00 (*0-88065-091-5*) Scholarly Pubns.
Mollusca Vol. 4: Freshwater Gastropoda & Pelycypoda. H. B. Preston. (Fauna of British India Ser.). xx, 246p. 1978. reprint ed. 30.00 (*0-88065-177-6*) Scholarly Pubns.
Mollusca Vol. 5, Pt. 2: Physiology. Ed. by A. S. Saleuddin & Karl M. Wilbur. 1983. text 104.00 (*0-12-751405-8*) Acad Pr.
Mollusca Vol. 7: Reproduction. Karl M. Wilbur & C. M. Yonge. 1984. text 104.00 (*0-12-751407-4*) Acad Pr.
Mollusca Vol. 11: Form & Function. Ed. by Karl M. Wilbur et al. 504p. 1988. text 104.00 (*0-12-751411-2*) Acad Pr.
Molluscan Assemblage of the Chowan River Formation, Pt. A. Lauck W. Ward & Norman L. Gilinsky. (Illus.). 40p. 1993. pap. 18.00 (*0-9625801-7-1*) VA Mus Natl Hist.
Molluscan Biostratigraphy of the Miocene. Lauck W. Ward. 204p. 1992. 27.00 (*0-9625801-3-9*) VA Mus Natl Hist.
Molluscan Distribution in Copano Bay, Texas. T. R. Calnan. (Reports of Investigations: RI 103). (Illus.). 71p. 1980. pap. 2.50 (*0-318-03236-8*) Bur Econ Geology.
Molluscan Distribution in Florida Bay. W. Jack Turney & Bob F. Perkins. (Sedimenta Ser.: Vol. III). (Illus.). 37p. (C). 1972. pap. 6.00 (*0-932981-03-8*) Univ Miami CSL.
Molluscan Introductions & Transfers: Risks Considerations & Implications. James T. Carlton. (Illus.). 1994. pap. text 3.00 (*0-943676-58-4*) MD Sea Grant Col.
Molluscan Nerve Cells: From Biophysics to Behavior. Ed. by John Koester & John H. Byrne. LC 80-39967. (Cold Spring Harbor Reports in the Neurosciences: No. 1). 250p. reprint ed. pap. 77.50 (*0-7837-2010-6*, 204228400002) Bks Demand.
Molluscan Neuro-Endocrinology. Ed. by J. L. Lever & H. H. Boer. (Illus.). 268p. 1983. 32.00 (*0-444-85572-6*, North Holland) Elsevier.
Molluscan Neurobiology: Proceedings of the 3rd Symposium, Amsterdam, 1990. Ed. by K. S. Kits et al. (Verhandelingen der Koninklijke Nederlandse Akademie van Wetenschappen, Afd. Natuurkunde Ser.: No. 88). 360p. pap. 61.25 (*0-444-85734-6*) Elsevier.
Molluscan Shellfish Depuration. Steven Otwell & Gary E. Rodrick. (Illus.). 380p. 1991. lib. bdg. 159.00 (*0-8493-4295-3*, SH) CRC Pr.
Molluscan Systematics & Biostratigraphy, Lower Tertiary la Meseta Formation Seymour Island, Antarctic Peninsula. Ed. by J. D. Stilwell & W. J. Zinmeister. (Antarctic Research Ser.: Vol. 55). 202p. 1992. 55.00 (*0-87590-770-9*) Am Geophysical.
Mollusken. Ihre Bedeutung fuer Wissenschaft, Medizin, Handel und Kultur (Mollusks. Their Importance for Research, Medicine, Commerce & Culture) Dora Godan. (Illus.). 203p. 1996. 76.00 (*3-8263-3131-1*, Pub. by Blckwell Wissenschafts) Balogh.
Mollusks of Michigan. John B. Burch. (Illus.). (C). text. write for info. (*0-472-09650-8*); pap. text. write for info. (*0-472-06650-1*) U of Mich Pr.
Mollusks of the Arid Southwest, with an Arizona Check List. Joseph C. Bequaert & Walter B. Miller. LC 72-187825. 287p. reprint ed. pap. 89.00 (*0-608-15190-4*, 202737900055) Bks Demand.
Molly see American Girls Collection Guides
Molly. Joseph S. Bonsall. LC 97-10889. (Molly the Cat Book Ser.). (Illus.). 32p. (J). (gr. 1-4). 1997. 14.95 (*1-57102-122-1*, Ideals Child) Hambleton-Hill.
Molly: A Novel. Nancy J. Jones. LC 99-39920. 288p. 2000. 22.00 (*0-609-60462-7*, Crown) Crown Pub Group.
Molly & Me. Gertrude Berg. 22.95 (*0-88411-098-2*) Amereon Ltd.
***Molly & Monet.** Diane R. Isaacs. LC 98-68551. (Illus.). 104p. 1999. reprint ed. pap. 14.00 (*0-9674792-5-8*) Molly & Monet.
Molly & Monet: A Story about Surviving the Loss of a Loved One. Diane R. Isaacs. (Illus.). 94p. (Orig.). 1999. pap. 12.95 (*0-89716-857-7*, Peanut Btr Pubng) Elton-Wolf Pub.
Molly & Slow Teeth. Houghton Mifflin Company Staff. (Literature Experience 1993 Ser.). (J). (gr. 2). 1992. pap. 9.48 (*0-395-61775-8*) HM.
***Molly & the Magic Wishbone.** Barbara McClintock. LC 98-31789. (J). 2000. 16.00 (*0-374-34999-1*) FS&G.
***Molly & the Movie Star.** Illus. by Valerie Tripp & Nick Backes. LC 99-40580. (American Girls Collection). 56p. (YA). (gr. 2 up). 2000. 3.95 (*1-58485-036-1*) Pleasant Co.
Molly & the Phantom. Lynn Michaels. LC 97-10523. 219p. 1994. mass mkt. 2.99 (*0-373-25611-6*, 1-25611-4) Harlequin Bks.
Molly & the Snow. Judy Mullican. (HRL Little Bks.). (Illus.). 8p. (Orig.). (J). (ps). 1995. pap. text 10.95 (*1-57332-058-7*) HighReach Lrning.
Molly Bannaky. Alice McGill. LC 96-3000. (Illus.). 32p. (J). (ps-3). 1999. 16.00 (*0-395-72287-X*) HM.

Molly Blooms: A Polylogue on Penelope & Cultural Studies. Ed. by Richard Pearce. LC 93-39641. 1994. 45.00 (*0-299-14120-9*); pap. 24.95 (*0-299-14124-1*) U of Wis Pr.
Molly Boxed Set: Meet Molly; Molly Learns a Lesson; Molly's Surprise; Happy Birthday, Molly!; Molly Saves the Day; Changes for Molly. Valerie Tripp. (American Girls Collection : Bks. 1-6). (Illus.). 432p. (YA). (gr. 2 up). 1991. boxed set 74.95 (*1-56247-051-5*); boxed set 34.95 (*0-937295-78-7*) Pleasant Co.
Molly Brant: A Legacy of Her Own. Lois Huey & Bonnie Pulis. (Illus.). 144p. 1997. pap. 11.95 (*0-941967-18-2*) Old Fort Niagara Assn.
Molly Brown: Denver's Unsinkable Lady. Christine Whitacre. 1984. pap. 9.95 (*0-914248-03-0*) Hist Denver.
***Molly Brown: Sharing Her Good Fortune.** Charnan Simon. LC 99-87477. (Community Builders Ser.). 2000. 23.50 (*0-516-21606-6*) Childrens.
Molly Brown: Unraveling the Myth. Kristen Iversen. LC 98-49266. 288p. 1999. pap. 18.00 (*1-55566-237-4*) Johnson Bks.
Molly Brown's Capitol Hill Neighborhood. Leigh A. Grinstead. (Historic Denver Guides Ser.). (Illus.). 96p. 1997. pap. 8.95 (*0-914248-13-8*) Hist Denver.
Molly Collie. Stewart Cowley. (Waggy Tales Ser.: Vol. 4). (Illus.). 10p. (J). (gr. k-3). 1998. bds. 4.99 (*1-57584-246-7*, Pub. by Rdrs Digest) Random.
Molly Counts. Mireille Levert. (Molly Bear Bks.: No. 5). (Illus.). 16p. (J). (ps). 1998. bds. 4.95 (*1-55037-547-4*, Pub. by Annick Pr) Firefly Bks Ltd.
Molly Darling. Laurie Paige. 1996. per. 3.99 (*0-373-24021-X*, 1-24021-7) Silhouette.
Molly Darling. large type ed. Laurie Paige. 1998. 21.95 (*0-373-59927-7*) Silhouette.
Molly Donnelly. Jean Thesman. LC 92-10644. 192p. (J). (gr. 5-9). 1993. 13.95 (*0-395-64348-1*) HM.
Molly Donnelly. Jean Thesman. 192p. (YA). 1994. mass mkt. 4.50 (*0-380-72252-6*, Avon Bks) Morrow Avon.
Molly Donnelly. Jean Thesman. LC 92-10644. 1993. 9.60 (*0-606-06574-1*, Pub. by Turtleback) Demco.
Molly Draws. Mireille Levert. (Molly Bear Bks.: No. 6). (Illus.). 16p. (J). (ps). 1998. bds. 4.95 (*1-55037-546-6*, Pub. by Annick Pr) Firefly Bks Ltd.
***Molly for Mayor.** Judy Delton. LC 98-53926. 128p. 1999. pap. 3.99 (*0-440-41525-X*) Bantam.
Molly Fox's Step on It. Molly Fox & Deborah Broide. (Illus.). 192p. (Orig.). 1991. pap. 9.95 (*0-380-76370-2*, Avon Bks) Morrow Avon.
Molly Goes Hiking. Ruth S. Radlauer. LC 86-18761. (Illus.). 32p. (J). (ps-3). 1987. pap. 10.95 (*0-671-66860-9*) S&S Trade.
***Molly Goldberg Jewish Cookbook.** Gertrude Berg & Myra Waldo. (Illus.). 320p. 1999. pap. 12.95 (*0-9669833-0-0*) Ivyland Bks.
Molly Goldberg's Cookbook. Gertrude Berg. 1994. lib. bdg. 24.95 (*1-56849-508-0*) Buccaneer Bks.
Molly Helps Mother. Laura E. Clayton. (Illus.). 24p. (J). (ps-2). 1994. pap. 2.55 (*0-7399-0049-8*, 2538) Rod & Staff.
Molly in the Middle. Kim Morris. LC 98-34281. (Real Kids Readers Ser.). (Illus.). 48p. (J). (gr. 1-3). 1999. pap. 3.99 (*0-7613-2084-9*, Copper Beech Bks); lib. bdg. 17.90 (*0-7613-2059-8*, Copper Beech Bks) Millbrook Pr.
Molly in the Middle. Stobie Piel. 400p. (Orig.). 1997. mass mkt. 5.99 (*0-505-52193-8*) Dorchester Pub Co.
Molly Is a Good Dog. Lucinda Jacob. LC 99-174363. 32p. 1998. pap. 7.95 (*1-85371-742-8*, Pub. by Poolbeg Pr) Dufour.
Molly Is Three: Growing up in School. Vivian G. Paley. LC 85-24589. xvi, 144p. (C). 1995. 19.50 (*0-226-64493-6*) U Ch Pr.
Molly Ivins Can't Say That, Can She? Molly Ivins. LC 92-50107. 284p. 1992. pap. 12.00 (*0-679-74183-6*) Vin Bks.
Molly Learns a Lesson: A School Story. Valerie Tripp. (American Girls Collection : Bk. 2). (Illus.). 67p. (YA). (gr. 2 up). 1986. pap. 5.95 (*0-937295-16-7*) Pleasant Co.
Molly Learns a Lesson: A School Story. Valerie Tripp. Ed. by Jeanne Thieme. LC 86-60626. (American Girls Collection : Bk. 2). (Illus.). 72p. (YA). (gr. 2 up). 1986. lib. bdg. 12.95 (*0-937295-84-1*) Pleasant Co.
Molly Learns a Lesson: A School Story. Valerie Tripp. (American Girls Collection: Bk. 2). (Illus.). (YA). (gr. 2 up). 1986. 11.15 (*0-606-02824-2*, Pub. by Turtleback) Demco.
Molly Limbo. Margaret Hodges. (J). 1995. 14.95 (*0-684-19711-1*) Atheneum Yung Read.
Molly Limbo. Margaret Hodges. (J). (gr. 1-8). 1995. 14.95 (*0-689-19711-X*) S&S Childrens.
Molly Limbo. Margaret Hodges. 1996. 15.00 (*0-689-80766-X*) S&S Childrens.
Molly Limbo. Margaret Hodges. (Illus.). 40p. (J). (gr. k-3). 1996. 16.00 (*0-689-80581-0*) S&S Childrens.
***Molly Magrew & the Pencil Crew.** Sherry Fields. (Illus.). 12p. 1999. 8.95 (*1-930482-00-0*) Fields Ent.
Molly Maguire: Wide Receiver. Ann Sullivan. 112p. (Orig.). (J). 1992. pap. 2.99 (*0-380-76114-9*, Avon Bks) Morrow Avon.
Molly Maguire Riots. J. Walter Coleman. 1993. reprint ed. lib. bdg. 89.00 (*0-7812-5442-6*) Rprt Serv.
Molly Maguire Riots: Industrial Conflict in the Pennsylvania Coal Region. Walter Coleman. Ed. by Leon Stein & Philip Taft. LC 78-89726. (American Labor, from Conspiracy to Collective Bargaining Ser., No. 1). 189p. 1997. reprint ed. pap. 23.95 (*0-405-02112-7*) Ayer.
Molly Maguires. Anthony Bimba. LC 75-15046. 144p. 1970. reprint ed. pap. 4.50 (*0-7178-0273-6*) Intl Pubs Co.
Molly Maguires & the Detectives. A. Pinkerton. LC 72-2092. (American History & Americana Ser.: No. 47). 1972. lib. bdg. 75.00 (*0-8383-1289-6*) M S G Haskell Hse.

M

*Molly May on the High Seas. Rewa. LC 99-50916. (Illus.). 96p. (J). (gr. 2-5). 2000. pap. 9.95 (1-56474-340-3) Fithian Pr.

Molly, McCullough, & Tom the Rogue. Kathleen Stevens. LC 82-45584. (Illus.). 32p. (J). (gr. 2-6). 1983. 11.95 (0-690-04295-7); lib. bdg. 11.89 (0-690-04296-5) HarpC Child Bks.

Molly McLure. Barry Faber. LC 97-61040. (Aesop's Fables Running Start Ser.). (Illus.). 32p. (J). (ps-2). 1997. pap. 4.95 (1-890570-41-9) Huckleberry CT.

Molly Meets Her Match. large type ed. Val Whisenand. 251p. 1993. reprint ed. lib. bdg. 13.95 (1-56054-613-1) Thorndike Pr.

Molly Meets Mona & Friends: A Magical Day in the Museum. Gladys Walker. (Illus.). 40p. (J). 1997. 17.95 (1-880851-25-3) Greene Bark Pr.

Molly Molasses & Me: A Collection of Living Adventures. 2nd ed. Ssipsis. (Illus.). 73p. 1990. reprint ed. pap. 8.00 (0-9621498-3-7, Robin Hood) R Hood Little.

Molly Molasses & Me: A Collection of Living Adventures. 3rd ed. Ssipsis Staff. (Illus.). 73p. 1994. pap. 9.00 (1-883957-00-1) R Hood Little.

Molly Moonshine & Timothy. Kathryn Weber. (Illus.). 44p. (J). (gr. 2-4). 1990. pap. 2.95 (1-878438-01-8) Ranch House Pr.

Molly of the Shakers: A Story of Love...& Tragedy. R. H. McGaughey. 126p. Date not set. 19.95 (1-56311-087-3) Turner Pub KY.

Molly on the Outlaw Trail, Vol. 1. Stephen Overholser. LC 99-21838. 1999. pap. 22.95 (0-7838-8615-2) Thorndike Pr.

Molly Pitcher: Young Patriot. Augusta Stevenson. LC 86-10744. (Childhood of Famous Americans Ser.). (Illus.). 192p. (J). (gr. 3-7). 1986. reprint ed. mass mkt. 4.95 (0-02-042040-4) Macmillan.

Molly Pitcher, Young Patriot. Augusta Stevenson. (Childhood of Famous Americans Ser.). (J). 1986. 10.05 (0-606-03248-7, Pub. by Turtleback) Demco.

Molly Q. Lass Small. (Desire Ser.: No. 655). 1991. per. 2.75 (0-373-05655-9) Harlequin Bks.

Molly Saves the Day: A Summer Story. Valerie Tripp. Ed. by Jeanne Thieme. (American Girls Collection : Bk. 5). (Illus.). 72p. (YA). (gr. 2 up). 1988. pap. 5.95 (0-937295-43-4); lib. bdg. 12.95 (0-937295-93-0) Pleasant Co.

Molly Saves the Day: A Summer Story. Valerie Tripp. (American Girls Collection: Bk. 5). (Illus.). (YA). (gr. 2 up). 1988. 11.15 (0-606-03862-0, Pub. by Turtleback) Demco.

Molly Spotted Elk: A Penobscot in Paris. Bunny McBride. LC 95-6891. 384p. 1995. 24.95 (0-8061-2756-2) U of Okla Pr.

Molly Spotted Elk: A Penobscot in Paris. Bunny McBride. LC 95-6891. (Illus.). 384p. 1997. pap. 13.95 (0-8061-2989-1) U of Okla Pr.

Molly Sweeney. Brian Friel. 1996. pap. 5.25 (0-8222-1532-2) Dramatists Play.

Molly Sweeney. Brian Friel. LC 95-11458. 96p. 1995. pap. 10.95 (0-452-27508-3) NAL.

Molly Takes Flight see American Girls Short Stories

Molly the Brave & Me. Jane O'Connor. (Step into Reading Ser.: A Step 2 Book). (J). (gr. 1-3). 1990. 9.19 (0-606-12425-X, Pub. by Turtleback) Demco.

Molly the Brave & Me. Jane O'Connor et al. LC 89-10864. (Step into Reading Ser.: A Step 2 Book). (Illus.). 48p. (J). (ps-3). 1990. pap. 3.99 (0-394-84175-1, Pub. by Random Bks Yng Read) Random.

Molly the Hungry Mouse. large type ed. Beth Esh Smith. (HRL Big Bks.). (Illus.). 8p. (J). (ps-k). 1997. pap. text 10.95 (1-57332-101-X); pap. text 10.95 (1-57332-100-1) HighReach Lrning.

Molly the Mad Basher. Malcolm Yorke. LC 93-11407. (Teachers Secrets Ser.). (Illus.). 32p. (J). (gr. 1-4). 1994. 10.95 (1-56458-459-3) DK Pub Inc.

Molly the Perfect Houseguest. (Young Global Reader Ser.: Vol. 1). Date not set. write for info. (1-887176-07-1) Globl Age Pub.

Molly Wants More! God Gives Me What I Need. JoDee McConnaughhay. Ed. by Lise Caldwell. LC 98-61311. (Illus.). 24p. (J). (ps-2). 1999. pap. 1.99 (0-7847-0896-7, 04269) Standard Pub.

Molly Weir's Recipes. Molly Weir. 256p. (C). 1989. 45.00 (0-903065-18-5, Pub. by G Wright Pub) St Mut.

Molly y los Peregrinos (Molly's Pilgrims) Barbara Cohen. Tr. by Maria A. Fiol. (Illus.). 32p. (YA). (gr. 5 up). 1995. 12.95 (1-880507-17-X) Lectorum Pubns.

Molly y los Peregrinos (Molly's Pilgrims) Barbara Cohen. Tr. by Maria A. Fiol. (Illus.). 32p. (YA). (gr. 5 up). 1997. pap. 6.95 (1-880507-34-X) Lectorum Pubns.

Mollyhawk Poems. Michael Ventura. LC 77-20733. (Illus.). 1977. pap. 10.00 (0-930324-06-4) Wings Pr.

Molly's Bath see Charlotte Se Lave

Molly's Bath. Mireille Levert. LC 96-931194. (Molly Bear Bks.: No. 4). (Illus.). 12p. (J). (ps). 1997. bds. 4.95 (1-55037-428-1, Pub. by Annick) Firefly Bks Ltd.

Molly's Bracelet. Isabel Bissett. LC 92-34337. (Voyages Ser.). (Illus.). (J). 1993. 3.75 (0-383-03641-0) SRA McGraw.

Molly's Breakfast see Charlotte Dejeune

Molly's Breakfast. Mireille Levert. LC 96-931195. (Molly Bear Bks.: No. 1). (Illus.). 12p. (J). (ps). 1997. bds. 4.95 (1-55037-422-2, Pub. by Annick) Firefly Bks Ltd.

*Molly's Century. Roslyn Farhi. (Illus.). 32p. (J). (gr. k-4). 1999. pap. 9.95 (0-9660599-1-3) Nostalgia.

Molly's Clothes see Charlotte S'Habille

Molly's Clothes. Mireille Levert. (Molly Bear Bks.: No. 2). (Illus.). 12p. (J). (ps). 1997. bds. 4.95 (1-55037-424-9, Pub. by Annick) Firefly Bks Ltd.

Molly's Cookbook: A Peek at Dining in the Past with Meals You Can Cook Today. Polly Athan. Ed. by Jodi Evert & Jeanne Thieme. LC 94-17564. (American Girls Collection). (YA). (gr. 2 up). 1994. pap. text 5.95 (1-56247-117-1) Pleasant Co.

Molly's Cookbook: A Peek at Dining in the Past with Meals You Can Cook Today. Polly Athan. (American Girls Collection). (YA). (gr. 2 up). 1994. 11.15 (0-606-08569-6, Pub. by Turtleback) Demco.

Molly's Craft Book: A Look at Crafts from the Past with Projects You Can Make Today. Jodi Evert. (American Girls Collection). (YA). (gr. 2 up). 1994. 11.15 (0-606-08570-X, Pub. by Turtleback) Demco.

Molly's Craft Book: A Look at Crafts from the Past with Projects You Can Make Today. Jodi Evert & Rebecca Sample Bernstein. LC 94-17550. (American Girls Collection). (Illus.). (YA). (gr. 2 up). 1994. pap. text 5.95 (1-56247-118-X) Pleasant Co.

Molly's Craft Book & Kit. Illus. by Geri S. Bourget. (American Girls Collection). 44p. (YA). (gr. 2 up). 1996. text 19.95 (1-56247-146-5) Pleasant Co.

Molly's Cupboard. Roslyn Farhi. Ed. by Ralph Farhi. (Illus.). 20p. (J). (ps-3). 1997. 6.95 (0-9660599-0-5) Nostalgia.

*Molly's Delicious. Craig Wright. 80p. (C). 1998. pap. 5.60 (0-87129-884-8, MA9) Dramatic Pub.

*Molly's Fire. Janet Lee Carey. LC 99-47058. (Illus.). (YA). (gr. 5-9). 2000. 16.00 (0-689-82612-5) Atheneum Yung Read.

*Molly's Grandson. Francis X. Curry. 99p. 1999. pap. 10.95 (0-7414-0139-8) Buy Books.

Molly's Heart. Gabrielle Charbonnet. (Princess Ser.: No. 1). 128p. (J). (gr. 3-7). 1995. pap. 3.50 (0-590-22287-2) Scholastic Inc.

Molly's Heart. Gabrielle Charbonnet. (Princess Ser.). (J). 1995. 8.60 (0-606-07878-9, Pub. by Turtleback) Demco.

*Molly's Hero. Susan Amarillas. (Historical Ser.: Bk. 518). 2000. per. 4.99 (0-373-29118-3, 1-29118-6) Harlequin Bks.

Molly's in a Mess. Suzy Kline. LC 98-28817. (J). (gr. 1-4). 1999. 14.99 (0-399-23131-5) Putnam Pub Group.

Molly's Journey. Dave Sargent & Pat L. Sargent. (Animal Pride Ser.: No. 19). (Illus.). 45p. (J). (gr. 2-8). 1996. lib. bdg. 12.95 (1-56763-038-3) Ozark Pub.

Molly's Magic. Penelope C. Paine. (Key Concepts in Personal Development Ser.). (Illus.). 32p. (J). (gr. 1-4). 1995. 16.95 (1-55942-068-5, 7660) Marsh Media.

Molly's Magic Carpet Ride. Emma Fischel. (Young Puzzle Adventures Ser.). (Illus.). 32p. (J). (ps-2). 1996. pap. 5.95 (0-7460-2294-8, Usborne) EDC.

Molly's Magic Carpet Ride. Emma Fischel. (Young Puzzle Adventures Ser.). (Illus.). 32p. (J). (ps-3). 1996. lib. bdg. 13.95 (0-88110-834-0, Usborne) EDC.

Molly's New Washing Machine. Laura Geringer. LC 85-45839. (Illus.). 32p. (J). (gr. k-3). 1986. 11.95 (0-06-022150-X) HarpC Child Bks.

Molly's Paper Dolls. Pleasant Company Staff. (American Girls Collection). 24p. (YA). (gr. 2 up). 1992. pap. text 5.95 (1-56247-057-4) Pleasant Co.

Molly's Pastimes, 4 bks., Set. Ed. by Pleasant Company Staff. (American Girls Collection). (Illus.). 168p. (J). (gr. 3-7). 1995. text, boxed set 22.95 (1-56247-263-1) Pleasant Co.

Molly's Pilgrim. Prod. by Jeff Brown & Chris Pelzer. (Literature to Go Ser.). pap., teacher ed. Price not set. incl. VHS (0-7919-2685-0) Phoenix Films.

Molly's Pilgrim. Barbara Cohen. 48p. (J). (gr. 4-7). 1990. pap. 3.50 (0-440-41057-6) Dell.

Molly's Pilgrim. Barbara Cohen. (Bantam First Skylark Bks.). (J). 1990. 8.70 (0-606-04748-4, Pub. by Turtleback) Demco.

Molly's Pilgrim. Susan Kilpatrick. (Literature Unit Ser.). (Illus.). 48p. 1995. pap., teacher ed. 7.95 (1-55734-535-X) Tchr Create Mat.

Molly's Pilgrim. rev. ed. Barbara Cohen. LC 98-9227. (Illus.). 32p. (J). (gr. 1 up). 1998. mass mkt. 3.99 (0-688-16280-0, Wm Morrow) Morrow Avon.

Molly's Pilgrim. rev. ed. Barbara Cohen. LC 98-9227. (Illus.). 32p. (J). (gr. 1 up). 1998. 15.00 (0-688-16279-7, Wm Morrow) Morrow Avon.

Molly's Pilgrim: A Study Guide. Anne Spencer. Ed. by J. Friedland & R. Kessler. (Novel-Ties Ser.). 19p. (J). (gr. 1-3). 1992. pap. text 15.95 (0-88122-700-5) Lrn Links.

Molly's Rosebush. Janice Cohn. Ed. by Kathy Tucker. LC 93-50612. (Illus.). 32p. (J). (ps-2). 1994. lib. bdg. 14.95 (0-8075-5213-5) A Whitman.

Molly's Surprise: A Christmas Story. Valerie Tripp. Ed. by Jeanne Thieme. LC 86-60627. (American Girls Collection : Bk. 3). (Illus.). 72p. (YA). (gr. 2 up). 1986. pap. 5.95 (0-937295-25-6); lib. bdg. 12.95 (0-937295-87-6) Pleasant Co.

Molly's Surprise: A Christmas Story. Valerie Tripp. (American Girls Collection: Bk. 3). (Illus.). (YA). (gr. 2 up). 1986. 11.15 (0-606-02827-7, Pub. by Turtleback) Demco.

Molly's Theater Kit. Pleasant Company Staff. LC 94-234172. (American Girls Collection). (Illus.). 48p. (Orig.). (J). (gr. 3-7). 1994. pap. 5.95 (1-56247-119-8) Pleasant Co.

Molly's Toys see Charlotte Joue

Molly's Toys. Mireille Levert. (Molly Bear Bks.: No. 2). (Illus.). 12p. (J). (ps). 1997. bds. 4.95 (1-55037-426-5, Pub. by Annick) Firefly Bks Ltd.

Molna Elegy, 2 vols. Gunnar Ekelof. Tr. by Muriel Rukeyser & Leif Sjoberg. (ENG & SWE., Illus.). 124p. 1985. pap. 8.95 (0-87775-153-6) Unicorn Pr.

Molna Elegy, 2 vols., Set. Gunnar Ekelof. Tr. by Muriel Rukeyser & Leif Sjoberg. (ENG & SWE., Illus.). 124p. 1985. boxed set 35.00 (0-87775-163-3) Unicorn Pr.

Molo: The Easy Xhosa Grammar Book. Andrbe Viljoen & Antoinette Daniel. LC 98-163201. 171p. 1998. write for info. (0-7021-4541-6) Juta & Co.

Moloch Blues: The Owl Killer & Dink's Blues. Phillip H. Dean. 1996. pap. 5.25 (0-8222-1514-4) Dramatists Play.

Moloch, or, This Gentile World. Henry Miller. LC 92-10327. 288p. 1993. pap. 12.00 (0-8021-3372-X, Grove) Grove-Atltic.

Molokai. O. A. Bushnell. LC 74-31402. 540p. 1982. reprint ed. pap. 14.95 (0-8248-0287-X) UH Pr.

Molokai: The Friendly Isle. braille ed. Marlene Freedman. LC 80-109617. (Illus.). 32p. 1977. reprint ed. write for info. (0-930081-01-3) Molokai Bk Pubs.

Molokai: The Friendly Isle. Marlene Freedman. LC 80-109617. (Illus.). 32p. 1977. reprint ed. pap. text 4.50 (0-930081-00-5) Molokai Bk Pubs.

Molokai: The Story of Father Damien. Hilde Eynikel. LC 99-11593. 1999. 14.95 (0-8189-0872-6) Alba.

Molokai, an Island in Time. Richard A. Cooke, III. 196p. 1987. 75.00 (0-941831-13-2) Beyond Words Pub.

Molokai, an Island in Time. Richard A. Cooke, III. 1987. 95.00 (0-941831-06-X) Beyond Words Pub.

Molokai, an Island in Time. deluxe ed. Richard A. Cooke, III. 196p. 1987. 2250.00 (0-941831-07-8) Beyond Words Pub.

Molokai Notes Vol. 1: Meg & Todd's Portable Guide. Meg Cranston-Cuebas & Todd Cranston-Cuebas. (Illus.). 144p. (Orig.). 1996. pap. 9.95 (0-9655141-0-2) Sticky Monkey.

Molokan Oral Tradition: Legends & Memorates of an Ethnic Sect. Willard Moore. LC 72-619685. (University of California Publications, Folklore Studies: No. 28). 93p. reprint ed. pap. 30.00 (0-608-13910-6, 202120700021) Bks Demand.

Moloney up & at It. Brendan Kennelly. 1987. pap. 15.95 (0-85342-721-6) Dufour.

Molotov & Soviet Government: Sovnarkom, 1930-41. Derek Watson. LC 95-39112. 1996. pap. write for info. (0-614-09899-8) St Martin.

Molotov & Soviet Government: Sovvnarkom, 1930-41. Derek Watson. LC 95-35816. 320p. 1996. text 49.95 (0-312-15866-1) St Martin.

Molotov Remembers: Inside Kremlin Politics: Conversations with Felix Chuev. V. M. Molotov. Ed. by Felix Chuev & Albert Resis. LC 93-11253.Tr. of Sto Sorok Besed s Molotovym. 464p. 1993. text 29.95 (1-56663-027-4) I R Dee.

Molotov-Ribbentrop Pact of 1939: The Baltic Case. Izidors Vizulis. LC 89-22878. 182p. 1990. 47.95 (0-275-93456-X, C3456, Greenwood Pr) Greenwood.

Molpadiid Sea Cucumbers (Echinodermata: Holothuroidea) of the Antarctic Seas: Paper 3 in Biology of the Antarctic Seas VI. David L. Pawson. LC 77-2320. (Antarctic Research Ser.: Vol. 26). (Illus.). 28p. 1977. pap. 10.70 (0-87590-131-X) Am Geophysical.

Molt of Scrub Jays & Blue Jays in Florida. G. Thomas Bancroft & Glen E. Woolfenden. 51p. 1982. 10.00 (0-943610-29-X) Am Ornithologists.

Molten Alkali Metal Alkanoates see Solubility Data Series

Molten Carbonate Fuel Cell Technology: Proceedings of the Symposium. Symposium on Molten Carbonate Fuel Cell Technology. Ed. by J. Robert Selman & Terry D. Claar. LC 84-73016. (Electrochemical Society Proceedings Ser.: No. 84-13). 539p. reprint ed. pap. 167.10 (0-8357-2592-8, 205237200013) Bks Demand.

Molten Carbonate Fuel Cell Technology: Proceedings of the 2nd Symposium. Symposium on Molten Carbonate Fuel Cell Technology. Ed. by J. Robert Selman et al. LC 90-84347. (Electrochemical Society Proceedings Ser.: No. 90-16). (Illus.). 541p. 1990. pap. 167.80 (0-608-00802-8, 205935100011) Bks Demand.

*Molten Memoirs - Ignoring the Rational Voice: Essays, Rumros, Field Notes & Photographs from the Edge of Fury. 3rd rev. ed. Gary M. Smith. Ed. by Richard Musser & Janet M. Cinelli. (Illus.). 265p. 1999. pap. 27.50 (0-9672769-2-6, Pub. by E Village) Booksource.

Molten Salt Chemistry: An Introduction & Selected Applications. Ed. by Gleb Mamantov & Roberto Marassi. (C). 1987. text 234.00 (90-277-2483-0) Kluwer Academic.

Molten Salt Chemistry & Technology. Ed. by M. Chemla et al. 814p. 1992. text 266.00 (0-87849-600-9, Pub. by Trans T Pub) Enfield Pubs NH.

Molten Salt Chemistry & Technology 5: Proceedings of the 5th International Symposium on Molten Salt Chemistry & Technology, Dresden, Germany, August 1997. Ed. by H. Wendt. (Molten Salt Forum Ser.: Vols. 5-6). (Illus.). 656p. (C). 1998. text 198.00 (0-87849-805-2, Pub. by Trans T Pub) Enfield Pubs NH.

Molten Salt Techniques, Vol. 1. David G. Lovering. Ed. by Robert J. Gale. LC 83-9582. (Illus.). 290p. (C). 1983. text 132.00 (0-306-41307-8, Kluwer Plenum) Kluwer Academic.

Molten Salt Techniques, Vol. 2. Ed. by David G. Lovering & Robert J. Gale. LC 83-9582. (Illus.). 276p. (C). 1984. text 132.00 (0-306-41549-6, Kluwer Plenum) Kluwer Academic.

Molten Salt Techniques, Vol. 3. Ed. by David G. Lovering & Robert J. Gale. LC 83-9582. (Illus.). 368p. (C). 1987. text 132.00 (0-306-42504-1, Kluwer Plenum) Kluwer Academic.

Molten Salt Techniques, Vol. 4. R. J. Gale & D. G. Lovering. LC 83-9582. (Illus.). 296p. (C). 1990. text 110.00 (0-306-43554-3, Kluwer Plenum) Kluwer Academic.

Molten Salt Technology. Ed. by David G. Lovering. LC 82-14982. 550p. 1982. 125.00 (0-306-41076-1, Plenum Trade) Perseus Pubng.

Molten Salts: Characterization & Analysis. Ed. by Gleb Mamantov. LC 75-88481. (Illus.). 627p. reprint ed. pap. 194.40 (0-608-30544-8, 205500700007) Bks Demand.

Molten Salts: Proceedings of the International Symposium. International Symposium on Molten Salts Staff. Ed. by J. Paul Pemsler et al. LC 76-9232. (Illus.). 630p. 1981. pap. 195.30 (0-7837-9004-X, 205926900002) Bks Demand.

Molten Salts: Proceedings of the 2nd International Symposium. International Symposium on Molten Salts Staff. Ed. by Jerry Braunstein & J. Robert Selman. LC 78-74544. (Electrochemical Society Proceedings Ser.: Vol. 81-10). (Illus.). 418p. 1981. pap. 129.60 (0-7837-9005-8, 205927000002) Bks Demand.

Molten Salts: Proceedings of the 3rd International Symposium. International Symposium on Molten Salts Staff. Ed. by Gleb Mamantov et al. LC 81-69548. (Electrochemical Society Proceedings Ser.: Vol. 81-9). (Illus.). 598p. 1981. pap. 185.40 (0-7837-8991-2, 205925600002) Bks Demand.

Molten Salts: Proceedings of the 4th International Symposium Held 1983, San Francisco, CA. International Symposium on Molten Salts Staff. Ed. by Milton Blander et al. LC 84-80267. (Electrochemical Society Ser.: No. 84-2). (Illus.). 777p. 1984. reprint ed. pap. 200.00 (0-608-05729-0, 205262100007) Bks Demand.

Molten Salts: Proceedings of the 5th International Symposium Held 1985, Las Vegas, NV. International Symposium on Molten Salts Staff. Ed. by Marie-Louise Saboungi et al. LC 86-80323. (Electrochemical Society Ser.: No. 86-1). (Illus.). 620p. 1986. reprint ed. pap. 192.20 (0-608-05736-3, 205262800007) Bks Demand.

Molten Salts: 10th International Symposium. Ed. by R. T. Carlin et al. (Proceedings Ser.: Vol. 96-7). (Illus.). 568p. 1996. 92.00 (1-56677-159-5) Electrochem Soc.

Molten Salts: 11th International Symposium. Ed. by P. C. Trulove et al. (Proceedings Ser.: Vol. 98-11). (Illus.). 676p. 1998. 95.00 (1-56677-205-2) Electrochem Soc.

Molten Slags & Fluxes 3rd Intl Conf. England Proceedings of the Kew Chromosome Conference - Jodrell Laboratory. 1989. 76.00 (0-901462-54-3) Institute of Management Consultants.

Molten State of Matter: Melting & Crystal Structure. Alfred R. Ubbelohde. LC 77-28300. 470p. reprint ed. pap. 145.70 (0-608-17599-4, 203044700069) Bks Demand.

Molting Time for Antitrust: Market Realities, Economic Fallacies, & European Innovations. Dudley H. Chapman. LC 90-45199. 272p. 1991. 65.00 (0-275-93478-0, C3478, Praeger Pubs) Greenwood.

Moltke. F. E. Whitton. LC 72-7115. (Select Bibliographies Reprint Ser.). 1977. reprint ed. 23.95 (0-8369-6958-8) Ayer.

Moltke: A Biographical & Critical Study. William O. Morris. LC 68-25254. (World History Ser.: No. 48). 1969. reprint ed. lib. bdg. 75.00 (0-8383-0222-X) M S G Haskell Hse.

Moltke, Schlieffen & Prussian War Planning. Arden Bucholz. 363p. 1993. pap. 16.50 (0-85496-889-X) Berg Pubs.

Moltke's Military Correspondence. Spenser Wilkinson. (Modern Revivals in History Ser.). 134p. 1992. 48.95 (0-7512-0040-9, Pub. by Gregg Revivals) Ashgate Pub Co.

*Molto Agitato. Johanna Fiedler. 2001. 30.00 (0-385-48187-X) Doubleday.

Molts & Plumages of Flying Steamer-Ducks: Tachyeres Patachonicus. Philip S. Humphrey & Bradley C. Livezey. (Occasional Papers: No. 103). 30p. 1982. pap. 1.00 (0-317-04597-0) U KS Nat Hist Mus.

Molybdenim Enzymes. Ed. by Thomas G. Spiro. LC 85-6343. (Metal Ions in Biology Ser.). 624p. (C). 1985. text 150.00 (0-471-88542-8) Krieger.

Molybdenum. (Metals & Minerals Ser.). 1993. lib. bdg. 250.95 (0-8490-8963-8) Gordon Pr.

Molybdenum. Leslie Northcott. LC 57-228. (Metallurgy of the Rarer Metals Ser.: No. 5). 234p. reprint ed. pap. 72.60 (0-608-15059-2, 202576000046) Bks Demand.

Molybdenum, Vol. 2A. 1985. 1325.00 (0-387-93519-3) Spr-Verlag.

Molybdenum: An Outline of Its Chemistry & Uses. E. R. Braithwaite & J. Haber. LC 94-34256. (Studies in Inorganic Chemistry: Vol. 19). 680p. 1994. 349.00 (0-444-88198-0) Elsevier.

Molybdenum Pt. 9, Vol. B: Compounds with Se, Te, Po. 8th ed. Gmelin Institute For Inorganic Chemistry for the M. (Compounds with Se, Te, Po Ser.). 165p. 1994. 765.00 (0-387-93691-2) Spr-Verlag.

Molybdenum & Molybdenum Alloys: Proceedings of the Symposium Held at the 127th Annual Meeting & Exhibition of the Minerals, Metals & Materials Society in San Antonio, Texas, 16-19 February 1998 / Andrew Crowson & Metals & Materials Society. LC 98-67688. x, 245p. 1998. 94.00 (0-87339-411-9) Minerals Metals.

Molybdenum B4. 1985. 1070.00 (0-387-93518-5) Spr-Verlag.

Molybdenum Disulphide Lubrication. A. R. Lansdown. LC 99-29083. (Tribology Ser.). 406p. 1999. 175.00 (0-444-50032-4) Elsevier.

Molybdenum Enzymes, Cofactors, & Model Systems: Developed from a Symposium Sponsored by the Division of Inorganic Chemistry at the 204th National Meeting of the American Chemical Society, Washington, DC, August 23-28, 1992. Ed. by Edward I. Stiefel et al. LC 93-22876. (ACS Symposium Ser.: Vol. 535). 380p. 1993. text 105.00 (0-8412-2708-X, Pub. by Am Chemical) OUP.

Molybdenum in Agriculture. Ed. by Umesh C. Gupta. LC 96-14069. (Illus.). 286p. (C). 1997. text 80.00 (0-521-57121-9) Cambridge U Pr.

Molybdenum in the Environment: Proceedings of an International Symposium on Molybdenum in the Environment Held in Denver, Colorado, 2 vols., 2.

An Asterisk (*) at the beginning of an entry indicates that the title is appearing for the first time.

Ed. by Willard R. Chappell & Kathy K. Petersen. LC 75-40647. (Illus.). 509p. reprint ed. pap. 157.80 (*0-8357-6224-6*, 203452000002) Bks Demand.

Molybdenum in the Environment: Proceedings of an International Symposium on Molybdenum in the Environment Held in Denver, Colorado, 2 vols., Vol. 1: The Biology of Molybdenum. Ed. by Willard R. Chappell & Kathy K. Petersen. LC 75-40647. (Illus.). 327p. reprint ed. pap. 101.40 (*0-8357-6223-8*, 203452000001) Bks Demand.

Molybdenum Nutrition in Rice. Dipanker S. Das Gupta. (International Bioscience Monographs: No. 4). 74p. 1978. 8.00 (*0-88065-046-X*) Scholarly Pubns.

Molyneux: The Interior Design of Juan-Pablo Molyneux. Michael Frank & Juan-Pablo Molyneux. LC 97-18502. (Illus.). 208p. 1997. 60.00 (*0-8478-2063-7*, Pub. by Rizzoli Intl) St Martin.

Molyneux's Problem: Three Centuries of Discussion on the Perception of Forms. Marjolein Degenaar. (Archives Internationales d'Historie des Idees Ser.: Vol. 147). 160p. (C). 1996. lib. bdg. 110.50 (*0-7923-3934-7*) Kluwer Academic.

Molyneux's Question: Vision, Touch & the Philosophy of Perception. Michael J. Morgan. LC 76-54066. 222p. reprint ed. pap. 63.30 (*0-608-30648-7*, 2022463) Bks Demand.

***Molytini: (Insecta: Coleoptera: Curculionidae: Molytinae)** R. C. Craw. (Fauna of New Zealand Ser.: No. 39). 68p. 1999. pap. 29.50 (*0-478-09325-X*, Pub. by Manaaki Whenua) Balogh.

Mom: A Friendship Discovered. Emily Williams-Wheeler. (Illus.). 56p. 1995. pap. 6.95 (*1-885061-13-7*) Adventure Pubns.

***Mom: A Friendship Discovered.** Emily Williams-Wheeler. 56p. 1999. 9.95 (*1-885061-67-6*) Adventure Pubns.

Mom: A Photo Memory Album. 1997. 15.99 (*1-57977-209-9*) Havoc Pub.

Mom: A Record Book for You. 1997. 19.99 (*1-57977-106-8*) Havoc Pub.

Mom: Terroir Bassa (Cameroun) Jacques Champaud. (Atlas Des Structures Agraires Au Sud Du Sahara: No. 9). (Illus.). 1973. pap. 36.95 (*90-279-7223-0*) Mouton.

***Mom: The Best Job in the World.** Betsy L. C. Fine. 100p. 2000. 7.95 (*0-9700714-0-X*) B L C Fine.

Mom: You're the Greatest! Andrews & McMeel Staff. (Tiny Tomes Ser.). (J). 1998. 3.95 (*0-8362-3638-6*) Andrews & McMeel.

Mom . . . I Will Remember. Doreen G. Blake. (Illus.). 128p. 1998. mass mkt. 9.95 (*0-9666137-0-8*) R W Blake.

Mom - You're Incredible! Linda Weber. LC 93-39465. 150p. 1994. 16.99 (*1-56179-221-7*) Focus Family.

Mom Alphabet a Moi. Marcie Baron. (FRE., Illus.). 14p. (J). (ps up). 1996. spiral bd., bds. 12.95 (*1-55037-414-1*, Pub. by Annick) Firefly Bks Ltd.

Mom among the Liars. James Yaffe. (Worldwide Library Mysteries). 1994. mass mkt. 3.99 (*0-373-26142-X*, 1-26142-9) Harlequin Bks.

Mom & Dad Are Divorced, but I'm Not: Parenting after Divorce. Hal W. Anderson & Gail S. Anderson. LC 80-27602. 284p. 1981. text 28.95 (*0-88229-522-5*) Burnham Inc.

Mom & Dad Break Up. Joan S. Prestine. LC 97-104355. (Kids Have Feelings, Too Ser.). (Illus.). 32p. (J). (ps-3). 1996. 8.99 (*0-86653-857-7*, FE3857) Fearon Teacher Aids.

Mom & Dad Can't Live Alone Anymore: A Family Decision. Eldon Weisheit. LC 50-96. 1994. pap. 10.95 (*0-7459-2625-8*) Lion USA.

Mom & Dad Don't Live Together Anymore. Kathy Stinson. (Illus.). 32p. (J). (gr. k-3). 1984. pap. 5.95 (*0-920236-87-1*, Pub. by Annick); lib. bdg. 15.95 (*0-920236-92-8*, Pub. by Annick) Firefly Bks Ltd.

Mom & Dad Don't Live Together Anymore. Christine H. Tangvald. LC 87-34211. (Please Help Me God Ser.). 24p. (J). (ps-2). 1988. 8.99 (*1-55513-502-1*, Chariot Bks) Chariot Victor.

Mom & Dad, Please Come to the Principal's Office. Miriam M. Teaff. 1995. 14.95 (*0-533-11238-9*) Vantage.

Mom & Dad Sleep While the Children Rock in Satan's Cradle. 2nd rev. ed. David W. Cloud. 84p. 1991. pap. 2.50 (*1-58318-034-6*) Way of Life.

Mom & Dead: An Andrew Broom Mystery. large type ed. Ralph McInerny. LC 94-6062. 302p. 1994. reprint ed. lib. bdg. 21.95 (*0-7862-0211-4*) Thorndike Pr.

Mom & Her Nineteen. John E. Lawton. Ed. by Christina C. Wightman & Helen Wightman. (Illus.). 250p. 1998. pap. write for info. (*1-888911-05-0*) Benson Smythe.

Mom & Me. Karol Crosbie. (Illus.). (Orig.). (YA). (gr. 7-12). 1989. pap. 3.95 (*0-945485-13-1*) Comm Intervention.

Mom & Me. Miela Ford. LC 97-31411. (Illus.). 24p. (J). (ps-3). 1998. 15.00 (*0-688-15889-7*, Grenwillow Bks) HarpC Child Bks.

***Mom & Me.** Miela Ford. LC 97-31411. (Illus.). 24p. (J). (ps-3). 1998. 14.93 (*0-688-15890-0*, Grenwillow Bks) HarpC Child Bks.

Mom & Me. John Kaplan. LC 95-19499. (Illus.). 32p. (J). (gr. k-3). 1996. 10.95 (*0-590-47294-1*, Cartwheel) Scholastic Inc.

Mom & Me: Single Parent Activity Book. Jim Boulden & Joan Boulden. (Illus.). 32p. (J). (gr. 3-6). 1993. pap. 5.95 (*1-878076-25-6*) Boulden Pub.

Mom & Pop Stores: A Country Stores Compendium of Merchandising Tools for Display & Value Guide. Richard A. Penn. LC 98-96452. 320 p. 1998. write for info. (*0-9664576-0-9*) Pennyfield Pub.

Mom & the Kids. Ed. by Charles Boer. (Spring Journal Ser.: Vol. 63). 166p. 1998. pap. 17.50 (*1-882670-13-2*, Pub. by Spring Jrnl) Continuum.

Mom & the Lad, Level 1. Lavaun Linde & Mary Quishenberry. (Bible Stories for Early Readers Ser.: Bk. 3). (Illus.). 32p. (J). (gr. 1). 1986. pap. text 4.99 (*0-945107-02-1*) Bradshaw Pubs.

Mom, Apple Pie . . . & the Fourth of July, 3 bks. in 1. Judith Arnold et al. 1998. per. 5.99 (*0-373-20149-4*, 1-20149-0) Harlequin Bks.

***Mom, Apple Pie & Murder: A Collection of New Mysteries for Mother's Day.** Ed. by Nancy Pickard. 320p. 1999. pap. 13.00 (*0-425-16890-5*, Prime Crime) Berkley Pub.

***Mom, Apple Pie & Murder: A Collection of New Mysteries for Mother's Day.** Ed. by Nancy Pickard. 2000. mass mkt. 5.99 (*0-425-17410-7*) Berkley Pub.

Mom by Magic. Barbara Dillon. LC 89-29410. (Trophy Bk.). (Illus.). 144p. (J). (gr. 3-7). 1991. pap. 3.95 (*0-06-440388-2*, HarpTrophy) HarpC Child Bks.

Mom Can Fix Anything, Vol. 3536. Kimberlee Graves. (Emergent Reader Science Ser.). 16p. 1994. pap. 2.75 (*0-916119-46-7*, 3536) Creat Teach Pr.

Mom Can Fix Anything, Vol. 3580. Kimberlee Graves. (Emergent Reader Big Bks.). (Illus.). 16p. (J). (gr. k-2). 1995. pap. 12.98 (*1-57471-020-6*) Creat Teach Pr.

***Mom, Can I Play Football? An Introspective View of the Game for Parents & Coaches.** Stephen G. Norton. (Illus.). 180p. 1999. pap. 15.95 (*0-9673456-0-X*) Sideline Pr.

***Mom Central.** Stacy. 2001. pap. write for info. (*0-684-87146-7*, Fireside) S&S Trade Pap.

Mom Central: The Ultimate Family Organizer. Stacy Debroff & Marsha Feinberg. (Illus.). 192p. 1998. spiral bd. 22.00 (*1-56836-219-6*) Kodansha.

Mom Come Quick. Joy Crawford. (Illus.). 8p. (Orig.). (J). (ps up). 1997. pap. 4.50 (*0-9652368-3-8*) Wright Pub Co.

***Mom, Dad Are You Listening? Enhance Family Communications & Relationships While Teaching Your Children Leadership Skills.** Sonny Elliott. (Illus.). 186p. 1999. pap. 14.95 (*0-9648895-5-2*, Pub. by Elliott Ent) BookMasters.

Mom, Dad, I Want to Go to Heaven see Papa, Mama Quiero Ir Al Cielo

***Mom... Dad... This Is What I've Been Trying To Tell You: A Book for Kids to Read to Their Parents.** Peg Bayliss. (Illus.). 24p. (J). 1999. pap. 6.95 (*1-57543-078-9*) Mar Co Prods.

Mom Dictionary: All Those Terms of Endearment, Frustration & Exhaustion That Mom Uses Every Day. Shoebox Greetings Staff. (Illus.). 72p. (Orig.). 1991. pap. 5.95 (*0-87529-641-6*) Hallmark.

Mom Doesn't Work There Anymore. Mary Kalifon. (Illus.). 32p. (Orig.). (J). (ps-4). 1995. pap. 5.95 (*0-9641981-1-8*) Cedrs Sinai Hlth Sys.

Mom Factor: Dealing with the Mother You Had, Didn't Have, or Still Contend With. Henry Cloud & John Townsend. 256p. 1996. 18.99 (*0-310-20036-9*) Zondervan.

Mom Factor: Discover How To: Transform the Effects of the Past - Say "No" to Your Mom Without Feeling Guilty - Build a Healthy Relationship with Your Mom, & - Improve All Your Relationships! Henry Cloud. 256p. 1998. pap. 12.99 (*0-310-22559-0*) Zondervan.

Mom Factor Workbook: Dealing with the Mother You Had, Didn't Have, or Still Contend With. Henry Cloud & John Townsend. 176p. 1997. pap., wbk. ed. 9.99 (*0-310-21533-1*) Zondervan.

Mom for a Week. Liz Ireland. (Romance Ser.). 1995. per. 2.75 (*0-373-19058-1*, 1-19058-6) Silhouette.

Mom for Christmas. Doreen Roberts. 1996. per. 3.25 (*0-373-19195-2*, 1-19195-6) Silhouette.

Mom for Hire. Victoria Pade. 1996. per. 3.99 (*0-373-24057-0*, 1-24057-1) Silhouette.

Mom Goes to Work. Libby Gleeson. (J). 1995. pap. 4.95 (*0-590-46288-1*) Scholastic Inc.

Mom Goes to Work. Libby Gleeson. 1995. 10.15 (*0-606-09624-8*, Pub. by Turtleback) Demco.

***Mom Has a New Boyfriend, What about Me?** Vickie Aldrich. (Illus.). vi, 26p. (J). (ps-3). 2000. pap. 7.95 (*0-615-11547-0*) Aldrich Crow.

"Mom, He Hit Me!" What to Do about Sibling Rivalry. Elaine K. McEwan. 96p. 1996. pap. 6.99 (*0-87788-556-7*, H Shaw Pubs) Waterbrook Pr.

Mom, Help! It's the Holidays: Holiday Planning Book. rev. ed. KayLee Parker. (Illus.). 68p. 1995. pap. 4.95 (*1-883924-12-X*, 430) Your Moms Organizers.

Mom, How Do You Get a Meal on the Table? rev. ed. KayLee Parker. (Illus.). 106p. 1995. pap. 8.95 (*1-883924-04-9*, 200) Your Moms Organizers.

Mom, How Do You Get Organized? rev. ed. KayLee Parker. (Illus.). 110p. 1995. pap. 8.95 (*1-883924-02-2*, 400) Your Moms Organizers.

Mom, How Do You Plan a Camping Trip? rev. ed. KayLee Parker. (Illus.). 114p. 1995. pap. 8.95 (*1-883924-11-1*, 330) Your Moms Organizers.

Mom, I Broke My Arm. Angelika Wolff. LC 69-18646. (Illus.). (J). (gr. k-3). 1969. lib. bdg. 13.95 (*0-87460-121-5*) Lion Bks.

Mom, I Have a Staring Problem: A True Story of Petit Mal Seizures & the Hidden Problem It Can Cause: Learning Disability. Marian C. Buckel & Tiffany Buckel. LC 92-90113. (Illus.). 26p. 1992. pap. 4.95 (*0-317-04291-2*) M C Buckel.

***Mom, I Love You Gift Book.** Zondervan Publishing Staff. 2000. pap. 5.99 (*0-310-97815-7*) Zondervan.

Mom, I Need Glasses. Angelika Wolff. LC 74-112648. (Illus.). (J). (gr. k-3). 1971. lib. bdg. 13.95 (*0-87460-139-8*) Lion Bks.

Mom, I Need to Be a Girl. Evelyn D. Lindenmuth. LC 98-8472. (Illus.). 128p. 1998. pap. 9.95 (*0-9663272-0-9*) W Trook Pubg.

Mom, I'm All Right. 3rd ed. Kathleen Sandefer. Ed. by Mary E. Krauel. 132p. (Orig.). 1991. pap. 8.95 (*0-9626227-0-2*) K Sandefer.

Mom, I'm Pregnant: Understanding & Guiding the Teenage Mother. Teresa L. Wolff. 208p. (Orig.). 1994. pap. 11.99 (*0-945819-59-5*) Sulzburger & Graham Pub.

***Mom, I'm Telling on You.** V. Kevin Martin. 140p. 1999. pap. 8.99 (*0-7392-0455-6*, PO3760) Morris Pubng.

Mom in My Heart. Joe L. Wheeler. LC 96-37651. 159p. 1997. pap. 10.99 (*0-8423-0552-1*) Tyndale Hse.

Mom in the Making (The Baker Brood) Carla Cassidy. (Romance Ser.). 1996. per. 3.25 (*0-373-19147-2*, 1-19147-7) Silhouette.

Mom in Waiting. Maureen Child. (Desire Ser.: No. 1234). 1999. per. 3.75 (*0-373-76234-8*, 1-76234-3) Silhouette.

***Mom, Inc. Taking Your Work Skills Home.** Neale S. Godfrey. (Illus.). 240p. 2000. pap. 13.00 (*0-684-86550-5*, Fireside) S&S Trade Pap.

Mom, Inc. Taking Your Work Skills Home. Neale S. Godfrey & Tad Richards. LC 99-12861. (Illus.). 224p. 1999. 22.00 (*0-684-80793-9*) S&S Trade.

Mom Is Going to Stop It. Angela La Mann. (Foundations Ser.). 27p. (J). (gr. k). 1992. pap. text 4.50 (*1-56843-064-7*) EMG Networks.

Mom Is Going to Stop It: Big Book. Angela La Mann. (Foundations Ser.). 27p. (J). (gr. k). 1992. pap. text 23.00 (*1-56843-014-0*) EMG Networks.

***Mom Just Like You.** Vickie Farris & Jayme Farris. 2000. pap. 12.99 (*1-929125-10-0*, Pub. by Loyal Pubng) BookWorld.

Mom Made Me Go to School. Judy Delton & Noelle B. McCue. (J). 1993. pap. 2.99 (*0-440-40841-5*) Dell.

Mom Manipulatives List. 1997. write for info. (*0-201-91041-1*) Addison-Wesley.

Mom Mission Accomplished: The Life of Anna Lola Swinford. Jessie Butler. 158p. 1998. pap. write for info. (*1-57502-915-4*, PO2525) Morris Pubng.

Mom 'n Pop Apple Pie 1950's Cookbook: Over 300 Great Recipes from the Golden Age of American Home Cooking. Smithmark Staff. (Illus.). 112p. 1997. 12.98 (*0-7651-9499-6*) Smithmark.

Mom 95. Woody Leonhard & Barry Simon. 960p. 1995. pap. 39.95 incl. cd-rom (*0-201-40971-2*) Addison-Wesley.

***Mom Pie** Illus. by Lynne Jonell & Petra Mathers. LC 99-24005. (J). 2001. write for info. (*0-399-23422-5*) Putnam Pub Group.

Mom Remember When . . . Annie Pigeon. LC 97-163025. 96p. 1997. mass mkt. 5.99 (*0-7860-0381-2*, Pinncle Kensgtn) Kensgtn Pub Corp.

Mom, Share Your Life with Me . . . Kathleen Lashier. (Memory-a-Day Ser.). 366p. (Orig.). 1992. pap. 8.95 (*1-56383-039-6*, 5053) G & R Pub.

Mom Spelled Backwards Is Tired. Ann Rudy. LC 79-55442. 190p. 1980. 9.95 (*0-672-52627-1*, Bobbs) Macmillan.

***MOM Stories: Minute Meditations for Mothers.** Vickie L. Jennett. LC 99-51609. 1999. pap. 9.95 (*0-89390-474-0*) Resource Pubns.

Mom, the School Flooded. Ken Rivard. (Illus.). 32p. (J). (ps-2). 1996. pap. 4.95 (*1-55037-474-5*, Pub. by Annick); lib. bdg. 15.95 (*1-55037-475-3*, Pub. by Annick) Firefly Bks Ltd.

Mom, the Wolfman & Me. Norma Klein. 160p. 1976. pap. 3.50 (*0-380-00791-6*, Avon Bks) Morrow Avon.

Mom, There's a Lady Angel Here: Lady Angel. Marjorie E. Finn. (Illus.). 91p. 1995. per. 12.99 (*0-9644833-0-0*) M E Finn.

Mom, There's a Pig in My Bed! Francess L. Lantz. 144p. (Orig.). (J). (gr. 4). 1992. pap. 3.50 (*0-380-76112-2*, Avon Bks) Morrow Avon.

Mom to Mom: Commonsense Tips & Advice Every Mom Needs to Know. Gloria G. Adler. LC 97-32782. 144p. 1998. pap. 12.00 (*0-688-15793-9*, Wm Morrow) Morrow Avon.

Mom to Mom: Moving from Unspoken Questions to Quiet Confidence. Elisa Morgan. 112p. 1996. 12.99 (*0-310-20396-1*) Zondervan.

Mom to Mom: Moving from Unspoken Questions to Quiet Confidence. Elisa Morgan. 112p. 1998. pap. 9.99 (*0-310-22557-4*) Zondervan.

Mom to Mom, Heart to Heart. Cari Haus & Sue Murray. LC 96-138291. 112p. 1996. pap. 9.99 (*0-8280-1036-6*) Review & Herald.

Mom, What Is Peace? unabridged ed. Karl Ries. (Illus.). 200p. 1997. pap. 15.00 (*0-9659514-0-5*) K Ries Bks.

Mom, When Will It Be Halloween? Frank Fiorello. (Illus.). 36p. (J). (ps-6). 1999. 11.95 (*0-9646300-5-2*); pap. 7.95 (*0-9646300-4-4*) Fiorellos Pumpkin Patch.

Mom Who Came to Stay. Nancy Morse. 1995. per. 3.75 (*0-373-07683-5*, 1-07683-5) Silhouette.

Mom, You Don't Understand: A Daughter & Mother Share Their Views. Carol Koffinke & Julie Jordan. 240p. 1993. pap. 8.95 (*0-925190-66-7*) Fairview Press.

Mom, You're Fired! Nancy K. Robinson. 112p. (Orig.). (J). (gr. 4-6). 1992. pap. 3.50 (*0-590-44903-6*, Apple Paperbacks) Scholastic Inc.

Mom, You're Incredible! see Mama Eres Increible!

***Mom, You're Incredible! Celebrating the Power of Motherhood.** rev. ed. Linda Weber. LC 98-49505. 192p. 1999. reprint ed. 14.99 (*0-8054-1665-X*) Broadman.

***Mom... You're Not Naked, Are You? A Collection of Humor by Donna Abear.** Donna Abear. LC 00-190203. (Illus.). 256p. 2000. pap. 11.95 (*0-9677101-0-3*) Moonshadow Bks.

Mom, You're the Best! Beth M. Conny. LC 97-220798. (Charming Petites Ser.). (Illus.). 80p. 1997. 4.95 (*0-88088-813-X*) Peter Pauper.

***MoMA Highlights: 325 Works from The Museum of Modern Art, New York.** (Illus.). 356p. 1999. pap. 18.95 (*0-87070-098-7*) Mus of Modern Art.

Momaday, Vizenor, Armstrong: Conversations on American Indian Writing. Hartwig Isernhagen. LC 98-40682. (American Indian Literature & Critical Ser.). 1999. 34.95 (*0-8061-3120-9*) U of Okla Pr.

Mombasa: An African City. Harm J. De Blij. LC 68-17731. 182p. reprint ed. pap. 56.50 (*0-608-13054-0*, 201485400093) Bks Demand.

Mombasa, the Swahili, & the Making of the Mijikenda. Justin Willis. LC 92-23255. (Oxford Studies in African Affairs). (Illus.). 246p. (C). 1993. text 75.00 (*0-19-820320-9*, Clarendon Pr) OUP.

Moment. Deanna Edwards. (Illus.). 144p. 1997. 19.00 (*1-878398-19-9*) Blue Note Pubns.

Moment. William L. Fortune. LC 79-87489. 8.95 (*0-934168-00-8*) Progeny Pr.

Moment & Late Writings. Soren Kierkegaard et al. LC 97-27938. (Kierkegaard's Writings). 776p. 1998. text 65.00 (*0-691-03226-2*, Pub. by Princeton U Pr) Cal Prin Full Svc.

Moment & Other Essays. Virginia Woolf. LC 75-5004. 252p. 1974. reprint ed. pap. 12.00 (*0-15-661900-8*, Harvest Bks) Harcourt.

***Moment by Moment: A Retreat in Everyday Life.** Carol Ann Smith & Eugene F. Merz. LC 00-8684. (Illus.). 96p. 2000. pap. 10.95 (*0-87793-945-4*) Ave Maria.

Moment by Moment: The Art & Practice of Mindfulness. Jerry Braza. LC 97-4179. 112p. 1997. pap. 12.95 (*0-8048-3113-0*) Tuttle Pubng.

Moment by Moment Happiness. Roger Wendorf. 275p. 1996. pap. 12.95 (*0-9648061-1-8*) Heav on Earth.

***Moment Changes Everythjing.** Carla Eisenberg. 44p. 1998. pap. write for info. (*0-912868-02-3*) Kjellberg Inc.

Moment for Dreams. Jeanette-Marie Smith. LC 97-93692. 128p. (YA). (gr. 6 up). 1997. pap. 7.95 (*1-889440-00-0*) JMS Prods.

Moment Functions in Image Analysis - Theory & Applications. R. Mukundan. 1998. 28.00 (*981-02-3524-0*) World Scientific Pub.

Moment in Time. Eddie Kennedy. 38p. 1986. pap. 3.50 (*0-87129-705-1*, M66) Dramatic Pub.

Moment in Time. Joel Rothman. LC 72-90693. (Illus.). 32p. (J). (ps-2). 1973. 14.95 (*0-87592-034-9*) Scroll Pr.

Moment in Time. Bertrice Small. 1994. mass mkt. 5.99 (*0-345-39079-2*) Ballantine Pub Grp.

***Moment in Time.** Deb Stover. (Zebra Splendor Historical Romances Ser.). 320p. 2000. mass mkt. 4.99 (*0-8217-6620-1*, Zebra Kensgtn) Kensgtn Pub Corp.

Moment in Time. large type ed. John Bedford. (Dales Mystery Ser.). 292p. 1992. pap. 18.99 (*1-85389-318-8*, Dales) Ulverscroft.

***Moment in Time: My Life at the Dawn of the New Millennium.** Nick Beilenson. (Guided Journals). (Illus.). 128p. 1999. 11.99 (*0-88088-222-0*) Peter Pauper.

Moment Made Marvellous: A Celebration of UQP Poetry. Ed. by Tom Shapcott. LC 98-193907. 1998. 22.95 (*0-7022-3065-0*, Pub. by Univ Queensland Pr) Intl Spec Bk.

Moment Made Marvellous: A Celebration of UQP Poetry. Ed. by Tom Shapcott. LC 98-193907. 1999. pap. 19.95 (*0-7022-3012-X*, Pub. by Univ Queensland Pr) Intl Spec Bk.

Moment Mal!, Lehrbuch 1. M. Muller et al. (GER., Illus.). 128p. (C). 1996. pap. text 19.95 (*3-468-47751-1*) Langenscheidt.

Moment Mal!, Level 1. M. Muller et al. (ENG, FRE & GER., Illus.). 128p. (C). 1996. pap. text 21.95 (*3-468-96940-6*); pap. text, wbk. ed. 18.95 (*3-468-96942-2*); pap. text, wbk. ed. 39.95 incl. audio compact disk (*3-468-96943-0*) Langenscheidt.

Moment Mal!, Level 1, Arbeitsbuch 1. R. Schmidt et al. (GER.). 1996. 18.95 (*3-468-47752-X*) Langenscheidt.

Moment Mal!, Level 1, Glossary English 1. R. Schmidt et al. (GER.). 48p. 1996. 7.95 (*3-468-47760-0*) Langenscheidt.

Moment Mal!, Level 1, Glossary French 1. R. Schmidt et al. (FRE.). 48p. 1996. 7.95 (*3-468-47761-9*) Langenscheidt.

Moment Mal!, Level 1, Lehrbuch 1. R. Schmidt et al. (GER.). 1996. write for info. (*0-614-14078-1*) Langenscheidt.

Moment Mal!, Level 1, Teacher's Manual 1. R. Schmidt et al. (GER.). 1996. teacher ed. 23.50 (*3-468-47753-8*) Langenscheidt.

Moment Mal!, Level 1, Tests 1. R. Schmidt et al. 1996. 17.50 (*3-468-47755-4*) Langenscheidt.

Moment Mal!, Level 2. M. Muller et al. (ENG, FRE & GER., Illus.). 128p. (C). 1997. pap. text 21.95 (*3-468-96950-3*); pap. text, wbk. ed. 39.95 incl. audio compact disk (*3-468-96953-8*) Langenscheidt.

Moment Mal!, Level 2. R. Schmidt et al. (GER.). 160p. Date not set. teacher ed. 23.50 (*3-468-47773-2*) Langenscheidt.

Moment Mal!, Level 2, Arbeitsbuch 2. R. Schmidt et al. (GER.). 168p. Date not set. 28.95 (*3-468-47772-4*) Langenscheidt.

Moment Mal!, Level 2, Glossary English 2. R. Schmidt et al. 64p. Date not set. 9.50 (*3-468-47780-5*) Langenscheidt.

Moment Mal!, Level 2, Glossary French 2. R. Schmidt et al. (FRE.). 64p. Date not set. 9.50 (*3-468-47781-3*) Langenscheidt.

Moment Mal!, Level 2, Lehrbuch 2. R. Schmidt et al. (GER, FRE & ENG.). 144p. Date not set. 21.00 (*3-468-47771-6*) Langenscheidt.

Moment Mal!, Level 2, Tests 2. R. Schmidt et al. (GER.). 64p. Date not set. 23.50 (*3-468-47775-9*) Langenscheidt.

Moment Mal!, Level 3. R. Schmidt et al. (GER.). Date not set. teacher ed. write for info. (*3-468-47793-7*) Langenscheidt.

Moment Mal!, Level 3, Arbeitsbuch 3. R. Schmidt et al. (GER.). Date not set. 20.00 (*3-468-47792-9*) Langenscheidt.

Moment Mal!, Level 3, Glossary English 3. R. Schmidt et al. Date not set. write for info. (*3-468-47800-3*) Langenscheidt.

Moment Mal!, Level 3, Glossary French 3. R. Schmidt et al. (FRE.). Date not set. write for info. (3-468-47801-1) Langenscheidt.

Moment Mal!, Level 3, Lehrbuch 3. R. Schmidt et al. (GER.). 120p. Date not set. write for info. (3-468-47791-0) Langenscheidt.

Moment Mal!, Level 3, Tests 3. R. Schmidt et al. (GER.). Date not set. 21.95 (3-468-47795-3) Langenscheidt.

Moment Maps & Combinatorial Invariants of Hamiltonian Tn-Spaces. Victor W. Guillemin. LC 94-13894. (Progress in Mathematics Ser.: Vol. 122). vii, 150p. 1994. 43.50 (0-8176-3770-2) Birkhauser.

Moment-Moment Moments. Marlene Wills. 24p. 1978. pap. 2.00 (0-913719-29-3, High Coo Pr) Brooks Books.

Moment of Anguish: Singapore in Malaysia & the Politics of Disengagement. Albert Lau. LC 98-945733. 312p. 1998. pap. 25.00 (981-210-134-9, Pub. by Times Academic) Intl Spec Bk.

Moment of Anguish: Singapore in Malaysia & the Politics of Disengagement Albert Lau. LC 98-945733. viii, 312 p. 1998. write for info. (981-210-130-6) Times Academic.

Moment of Celebration. Tom Wright. 1998. 4.99 (0-7459-3840-X) Chariot Victor.

Moment of Change: A Systematic History in the Philosophy of Space & Time. Niko Strobach. LC 98-22288. (New Synthese Historical Library). 1998. 135.00 (0-7923-5120-7) Kluwer Academic.

Moment of Christ: The Path of Meditation. John Main. LC 62-9684. 128p. 1998. reprint ed. pap. 10.95 (0-8264-1123-1) Continuum.

Moment of Christian Witness. Hans U. Von Balthasar. LC 94-75997. 150p. (Orig.). 1994. pap. 11.95 (0-89870-516-9) Ignatius Pr.

Moment of Conquest: Meru, Kenya, 1907. Jeffrey A. Fadiman. LC 79-10870. (Papers in International Studies: Africa Ser.: No. 36). 78p. reprint ed. pap. 30.00 (0-7837-1325-8, 204147300021) Bks Demand.

Moment of Decision: Biographical Essays on American Character & Regional Identity, 156. Ed. by Randall M. Miller & John R. McKivigan. LC 93-30981. (Contributions in American History Ser.: No. 156). 256p. 1994. 65.00 (0-313-28635-3, Greenwood Pr) Greenwood.

Moment of Encounter. J. Eric Lane. LC 83-49361. (American University Studies: History: Ser. IX, Vol. 6). XXI, 163p. (Orig.). (C). 1984. pap. text 18.00 (0-8204-0090-4) P Lang Pubng.

Moment of Existence: Music, Literature & the Arts, 1990-1995. Robert Craft. LC 95-52713. 336p. 1996. 28.95 (0-8265-1276-3) Vanderbilt U Pr.

Moment of Explosion: Blake & the Illustration of Milton. Stephen C. Behrendt. LC 82-13561. (Illus.). xvi, 235p. 1983. text 60.00 (0-8032-1169-4) U of Nebr Pr.

Moment of Freedom: The Heiligenberg Manuscript. Jens Bjorneboe. LC 98-32050. 220p. 2000. pap. 15.95 (0-8023-1328-0) Dufour.

Moment of Grace: On the Catechism of the Catholic Church. John Cardinal O'Connor. LC 95-76621. 354p. 1995. pap. 16.95 (0-89870-554-1) Ignatius Pr.

Moment of Love. large type ed. Denise Robins. 432p. 1995. 27.99 (0-7089-3397-1) Ulverscroft.

Moment of Madness. Pan Pantziarka. (Crime & Passion Ser.). 256p. (Orig.). 1997. mass mkt. 5.95 (0-7535-0024-8, Pub. by Virgin Bks) London Bridge.

Moment of Movement: Dance Improvisation. Lynne A. Blom & L. Tarin Chaplin. LC 88-1332. (Illus.). 256p. (Orig.). (C). 1988. pap. 14.95 (0-8229-5405-2); text 29.95 (0-8229-3586-4) U of Pittsburgh Pr.

Moment of Peace. Tom Wright. 1998. 4.99 (0-7459-3837-X) Chariot Victor.

Moment of Peace: A Daily Devotional for Women by Women. Ed. by Rose Otis. LC 95-33463. 399p. 1995. 14.99 (0-8280-0979-1) Review & Herald.

Moment of Peace Journal. 160p. 1996. 5.99 (0-8280-1045-5) Review & Herald.

Moment of Poetry. Ed. by Don C. Allen. LC 80-17079. (Percy Graeme Turnbull Memorial Lectures on Poetry, 1958). 135p. 1980. reprint ed. lib. bdg. 49.50 (0-313-22406-4, ALMP, Greenwood Pr) Greenwood.

Moment of Prayer. Tom Wright. 1998. 4.99 (0-7459-3838-8) Chariot Victor.

Moment of Proof: Mathematical Ephiphanies. Donald C. Benson. LC 97-52139. (Illus.). 352p. 1999. 30.00 (0-19-511721-2) OUP.

*Moment of Proof: Mathematical Epiphanies. Donald C. Benson. (Illus.). 352p. 2000. pap. 17.95 (0-19-513919-4) OUP.

Moment of Quiet. Tom Wright. 1998. 4.99 (0-7459-3839-6) Chariot Victor.

Moment of Self-Portraiture in German Renaissance Art. Joseph L. Koerner. (Illus.). xx, 544p. 1996. pap. text 34.95 (0-226-44999-8) U Ch Pr.

Moment of Silence: Arlington National Cemetery. Owen Andrews. LC 93-27115. (Illus.). 64p. 1995. 14.95 (0-471-14367-7) Wiley.

Moment of Silence: Stories. Tomaslav Longinovic. 1990. 10.00 (0-936050-08-X) Burning Bks.

*Moment of Thanks Journal. Lori Wick. 80p. 2000. spiral bd. 14.99 (0-7369-0107-8) Harvest Hse.

Moment of the Magician. Alan Dean Foster. 17.00 (0-932096-33-6) Phantasia Pr.

Moment of Time. Lynn Adams. 124p. 1999. pap. 8.95 (0-7392-0166-2, PO3125) Morris Pubng.

Moment of Transition: Two Neuroscientific Articles by Sigmund Freud. Sigmund Freud. Ed. by Mark Solms & Michael Saling. 192p. 1990. reprint ed. pap. 27.50 (0-946439-92-3, Pub. by H Karnac Bks Ltd) Other Pr LLC.

Moment of Truth. Franklin W. Dixon. (Hardy Boys Casefiles Ser.: No. 109). (YA). (gr. 6 up). 1996. 9.09 (0-606-09381-8, Pub. by Turtleback) Demco.

*Moment of Truth. Lisa Scottoline. LC 99-89325. 368p. 2000. 25.00 (0-06-019609-2) HarpC.

*Moment of Truth. large type ed. Lisa Scottoline. 544p. 2000. pap. 25.00 (0-06-095611-9) HarpC.

Moment of Truth: A Guide to Effective Sermon Delivery. Wayne V. McDill. LC 99-12003. 128p. 1999. pap. 19.99 (0-8054-1827-X) Broadman.

Moment of Truth: A Novel. Jill Ammon-Wexler. LC 97-91696. 280p. (Orig.). 1997. pap. 15.00 (0-9657459-0-2) Clear Vision.

Moment of Truth for Protestant America: Interchurch Campaigns Following World War One. Eldon G. Ernst. LC 74-16567. (American Academy of Religion: Vol. 3). 209p. reprint ed. pap. 64.80 (0-608-08854-4, 206949300004) Bks Demand.

Moment of War: A Memoir of the Spanish Civil War. Laurie Lee. 192p. 1994. pap. 9.95 (1-56584-173-5, Pub. by New Press NY) Norton.

*Moment of Weakness. Karen Kingsbury. LC 99-50869. 400p. 2000. pap. 11.99 (1-57673-616-4, Pub. by Multnomah Pubs) GL Services.

Moment on the Earth: The Coming Age of Environmental Optimism. Gregg Easterbrook. 768p. 1996. pap. 16.95 (0-14-015451-5, Penguin Bks) Viking Penguin.

Moment Out of Time. Betty Cornwell. (Illus.). 82p. (Orig.). 1984. pap. 7.50 (0-918957-00-1) Pika Oregon.

Moment Resistant Connections & Simple Connections. 436p. 1988. 60.00 (0-937040-27-4, R&D1/4) P-PCI.

*Moment Resistant Connections of Steel Frames in Seismic Areas: Design & Reliability. Federico M. Mazzolani. LC 00-25172. 2000. write for info. (0-415-23577-4, Comedia) Routledge.

*Moment to Decide: The Crisis in Mainstream Presbyterianism. Lewis C. Daly. (Denominational Studies Ser.). 170p. 2000. pap. 25.00 (0-9679106-0-9) Inst for Democracy.

Moment to Moment. Barbara Delinsky. 352p. 1998. mass mkt. 6.99 (0-06-101099-5, Harp PBks) HarpC.

*Moment to Moment. Barbara Delinsky. 336p. 1999. 26.00 (0-7278-2280-2, Pub. by Severn Hse) Chivers N Amer.

Moment to Moment. Rod McKuen. 1972. pap. 5.95 (0-318-00970-6) Cheval Bks.

Moment to Moment. large type ed. Barbara Delinsky. LC 98-22070. (Large Print Book Ser.). 1998. 25.95 (1-56895-580-4) Wheeler Pub.

Moment to Moment: Poems of a Mountain Recluse. David Budbill. 132p. 1999. pap. 14.00 (1-55659-133-0, Pub. by Copper Canyon) Consort Bk Sales.

*Moment to Moment: Smith-Cameron,&J., Set. abr. ed. Barbara Delinsky. 1998. audio 18.00 (0-694-51952-9, CPN2736, Pub. by HarperAudio) Lndmrk Audiobks.

Moment to Reflect. Ed. by Diana Zeiger. 1997. 69.95 (1-57553-349-9) Nat Lib Poetry.

Moment to Shout: God's Way to Face Walls. Luis Palau. LC 98-48824. 224p. 1999. pap. 9.99 (1-57293-049-7) Discovery Hse Pubs.

Moment with Bev. Beverly W. Aach. LC 97-67140. 92p. (Orig.). 1997. pap. 10.95 (1-57197-071-1) Pentland Pr.

Moment with God. Kay Arthur. 1998. 14.99 (1-56507-995-7) Harvest Hse.

Moment with God for Caregivers: Prayers for People Who Care for Others. Bruce Fish & Becky D. Fish. LC 97-37857. 64p. 1998. pap. 5.00 (0-687-07720-6) Dimen for Liv.

Moment with God for Children: Prayers for Little Ones. Barbara Younger. LC 97-14989. (Illus.). 64p. (J). 1997. pap. 5.00 (0-687-12205-8) Dimen for Liv.

Moment with God for Fathers: Prayers for Every Dad, Every Day. Dimensions for Living Staff. LC 98-234764. (Moment with God Ser.). 1997. pap. text 5.00 (0-687-12183-3) Abingdon.

*Moment with God for Graduation: Prayers for Every Graduate. Maribeth Walker. 64p. 2000. pap. 5.00 (0-687-09003-2) Dimen for Liv.

Moment with God for Grandparents: Prayers for Every Grandparent. Kel Groseclose. LC 98-50447. 64p. 1999. pap. 5.00 (0-687-97560-3) Dimen for Liv.

*Moment with God for Men: Prayers for Every Man. Dimensions for Living Staff. LC 98-33957. 64p. 1998. pap. 5.00 (0-687-08777-5) Dimen for Liv.

Moment with God for Mothers: Prayers for Every Mother. Margaret A. Huffman. LC 97-14987. 64p. 1997. pap. 5.00 (0-687-12130-2) Dimen for Liv.

Moment with God for Single Parents: Prayers for Every Single Parent. Ramona Richards. LC 98-49919. 64p. 1999. pap. 5.00 (0-687-97550-6) Dimen for Liv.

*Moment with God for Sunday School Teachers: Prayers for Every Sunday School Teacher. Sarah McGinley. 64p. 2000. pap. 5.00 (0-687-09004-0) Dimen for Liv.

Moment with God for Teachers: Prayers for Every Teacher. Karen Cropsey et al. LC 97-47068. 64p. 1998. pap. 5.00 (0-687-07710-9) Dimen for Liv.

Moment with God for Teens: Prayers for Teens. Lisa Flinn. LC 97-14988. 64p. (J). (gr. 8-12). 1997. pap. 5.00 (0-687-12242-2) Dimen for Liv.

Moment with God for Those Who Grieve: Prayers for Those Who Grieve. Dale Clem. LC 99-42082. (Moment with God Ser.). 64p. 1999. pap. 5.00 (0-687-07304-9) Dimen for Liv.

Moment with God for Volunteers: Prayers for God's Servants. Lisa Flinn. LC 99-24683. (Moment with God Ser.). 64p. 1999. pap. 5.00 (0-687-07305-7) Dimen for Liv.

Moment with God for Women: Prayers for Every Woman. Dimensions for Living Staff. LC 98-33929. 64p. 1998. pap. 5.00 (0-687-08787-2) Dimen for Liv.

*Momentary Lapse of Reason. Vincent Boccia. LC 00-190996. 247p. 2000. 25.00 (0-7388-2185-3); pap. 18.00 (0-7388-2186-1) Xlibris Corp.

Momentary Monsters: Lucan & His Heroes. W. R. Johnson. LC 87-5442. (Cornell Studies in Classical Philology). 160p. (C). 1987. 25.00 (0-8014-2030-X) Cornell U Pr.

Momentary Monsters: Lucan & His Heroes. Walter R. Johnson. LC 87-5442. (Cornell Studies in Classical Philology: Vol. 47). 163p. reprint ed. pap. 50.60 (0-608-20907-4, 207200600003) Bks Demand.

Momentary Pleasures: Poems by Edward Wincentsen. Edward Wincentsen. (Illus.). 32p. 1997. reprint ed. mass mkt. 2.95 (0-9648133-2-7) New Thght Jour Pr.

Momentary Reflection on Movement: The Spirit of T'ai Chi. David Michaeli. (Illus.). 112p. 1998. mass mkt. 8.95 (965-494-003-5, Pub. by Astrolog Pub) Assoc Pubs Grp.

Momentary Regards. Charles Pappas. 80p. 1995. pap. 9.95 (0-916147-16-9) Regent Pr.

Momento, Souvenir, Keepsake, & Collector's Kit on the Life & Music of Elvis. Stan P. Putnam. (Illus.). 1988. reprint ed. pap. 10.00 (0-944047-08-4) Res Improvement Inst.

Momentos de Quietud para Matrimonios. Norman Wright.Tr. of Quiet Times for Couples. (SPA.). 400p. 1996. 10.99 (1-56063-973-3, 497389) Editorial Unilit.

Momentos Increibles el Salvador. K. Gire.Tr. of Incredible Moments with the Savior. (SPA.). 144p. 1992. pap. 4.99 (0-8297-0309-8) Vida Pubs.

Momentos Instructivos el Salvador. K. Gire.Tr. of Instructive Moments with the Savior. (SPA.). 160p. 1994. pap. 5.99 (0-8297-1905-9) Vida Pubs.

Momentos Intimos con el Salvad. Ken Gire.Tr. of Intimate Moments with Savior. (SPA.). 224p. 1991. pap. 5.99 (0-8297-0357-8) Vida Pubs.

Momentos Magicos: Latin American Folktales Told in English & Spanish. Olga Loya. Tr. by Carmen Lizardi-Rivera. LC 97-38582. 1997. pap. text 11.95 (0-87483-497-X) August Hse.

Momentos para Graduados: Pensamientos Positivos para Fortalecer su Espiritu. Robert Strand. LC 98-84818. (Momentos para Compartir).Tr. of Moments for Graduates. (SPA., Illus.). 80p. 1998. 6.99 (0-933657-50-1) Rainbow Studies.

Momentos para Madres: Reflexiones Profundas para Alegrar el Corazon. Robert Strand. LC 98-84817. (Momentos para Compartir).Tr. of Moments for Mothers. (SPA., Illus.). 80p. 1998. 6.99 (0-933657-48-X) Rainbow Studies.

Momentos para Padres: Pensamientos Positivos para Fortalecer su Espiritu. Robert Strand. LC 98-84807. (Momentos para Compartir).Tr. of Moments for Fathers. (SPA., Illus.). 80p. 1998. 6.99 (0-933657-49-8) Rainbow Studies.

Momentous Century: Personal & Eyewitness Accounts of the Rise of the Jewish Homeland & State, 1875-1978. Ed. by Levi Shoshuk & Azriel Eisenberg. LC 81-86164. (Illus.). 472p. 1984. 25.00 (0-8453-4748-9, Cornwall Bks) Assoc Univ Prs.

Momentous Days: An Account in Poetry & Prose of a Family in Early Walnut Creek, California. Emme I. Lorenzen. LC 90-62998. (Illus.). 64p. (Orig.). 1990. pap. text 12.00 (0-9627282-0-9) TYIL Pr.

Momentous Event. W. J. Grier. 1976. pap. 5.99 (0-85151-020-5) Banner of Truth.

*Momentous Events, Vivid Memories. David B. Pillemer. 256p. 2000. pap. 17.95 (0-674-00418-3) HUP.

Momentous Events, Vivid Memories. David H. Pillemer. LC 97-47043. (Illus.). 256p. 1998. 35.00 (0-674-58205-5) HUP.

Momentous Question: The Respective Attitudes of Labor & Capital. John Swinton. LC 77-89764. (American Labor, from Conspiracy to Collective Bargaining Ser., No. 1). 498p. 1977. reprint ed. 28.95 (0-405-02155-0) Ayer.

Moments. Ed. by Robert Drederian. (Illus.). 210p. 1998. 49.95 (1-885206-56-9) Cader Pubng.

Moments. Philip E. Duffy. LC 91-71199. x, 146p. 1991. pap. 9.95 (0-9629651-0-3) Chase Pub.

*Moments. Irene Frances. LC 98-91072. 1999. pap. 7.95 (0-533-13030-1) Vantage.

Moments. Illia Thompson. 85p. (Orig.). 1987. pap. 6.00 (0-9618553-0-4) Blackthorne.

Moments: A Collection of Acting Workshop & Audition Scenes. David W. Crawford & William-Alan Landes. LC 99-19177. 64p. 1999. pap. 10.00 (0-88734-664-2) Players Pr.

Moments: Poems. Lavlin. 80p. 1992. 10.00 (0-7069-5892-6, Pub. by Vikas) S Asia.

Moments: Roxanne Lowit Photographs. Photos by Roxanne Lowit. LC 93-11115. (Illus.). 1993. text 45.00 (0-86565-145-0) Vendome.

Moments: The Life & Career of a Texas Newsman. Chip Moody. LC 95-35286. (Illus.). 216p. 1995. 19.95 (0-87833-895-0) Taylor Pub.

*Moments: The Pulitzer Prize Photographs: a Visual Chronicle of Our Time. Hal Buell. LC 99-39193. (Illus.). 255p. 1999. 29.98 (1-57912-078-4, Pub. by Blck Dog & Leventhal) Workman Pub.

Moments Vol. 1: A Soul's Reflection. Marilyn Dale. LC 97-66263. (Orig.). 1997. pap. 10.95 (0-9656685-3-3) Soul Message.

Moments & Memories. Kathryn Grice. 160p. 1997. 15.95 (1-887750-58-4) Rutledge Bks.

Moments Beautiful Moments Bright. Brett Bartholomaus. 28p. 1993. pap. 4.95 (1-886028-09-5) Savage Pr.

*Moments Before They Come: Poems from Hollywood. Mark Dunster. 11p. 1999. pap. 5.00 (0-89642-799-4) Linden Pubs.

Moments Between. Esther C. Asmus. Ed. by Sol Squire. (Illus.). 96p. (C). 1990. text 15.95 (0-9619407-2-7) Country Messenger Inc.

Moments Between Cities. John Flynn. LC 97-13834. 64p. 1997. pap. 14.95 (0-7734-2826-7, Mellen Poetry Pr) E Mellen.

Moments Divine - Before the Blessed Sacrament. Frederick A. Reuter. 290p. 1995. pap. 8.50 (0-89555-533-6) TAN Bks Pubs.

Moments for Christmas. Robert Strand. LC 93-87690. (Moments to Give Ser.). (Illus.). 80p. 1994. 9.99 (0-89221-265-9) New Leaf.

Moments for Each Other. Robert Strand. LC 93-87689. (Moments to Give Ser.). (Illus.). 80p. 1994. 9.99 (0-89221-266-7) New Leaf.

Moments for Fathers see Momentos para Padres: Pensamientos Positivos para Fortalecer su Espiritu

Moments for Fathers. Robert Strand. LC 93-87692. (Moments to Give Ser.). (Illus.). 80p. 1994. 9.99 (0-89221-263-2) New Leaf.

Moments for Friends. Robert Strand. LC 95-69897. (Moments to Give Ser.). 80p. 1996. 9.99 (0-89221-301-9) New Leaf.

Moments for Graduates see Momentos para Graduados: Pensamientos Positivos para Fortalecer su Espiritu

Moments for Graduates. Robert Strand. LC 93-87691. (Moments to Give Ser.). (Illus.). 80p. 1994. 9.99 (0-89221-264-0) New Leaf.

Moments for Grandparents. Robert Strand. LC 94-69836. (Moments to Give Ser.). 80p. 1995. 9.99 (0-89221-281-0) New Leaf.

Moments for Mothers see Momentos para Madres: Reflexiones Profundas para Alegrar el Corazon

Moments for Mothers. Robert Strand. LC 93-87693. (Moments to Give Ser.). (Illus.). 80p. 1994. 9.99 (0-89221-262-4) New Leaf.

Moments for Pastors. Robert Strand. LC 94-73973. (Moments to Give Ser.). 80p. (YA). 1995. 9.99 (0-89221-289-6) New Leaf.

Moments for Prayer. Compiled by Daughters of St. Paul Staff. 52p. 1979. pap. 1.50 (0-8198-4753-4) Pauline Bks.

Moments for Sisters. Robert Strand. LC 95-69898. (Moments to Give Ser.). 80p. 1996. 9.99 (0-89221-302-7) New Leaf.

Moments for Teachers. Robert Strand. LC 94-69837. (Moments to Give Ser.). 80p. 1995. 9.99 (0-89221-282-9) New Leaf.

Moments for Teens. Robert Strand. LC 94-73974. (Moments to Give Ser.). 80p. (YA). 1995. 9.99 (0-89221-288-8) New Leaf.

Moments Harsh, Moments Gentle. Joan Hohl. (Men Made in America Ser.). 1994. per. 3.59 (0-373-45180-6, 1-45180-6) Silhouette.

Moments in a Singapore Life. Sin Tub Goh. LC 93-944264. ix, 78 p. 1993. write for info. (981-00-4254-X) AgBe Pub.

Moments in Eden. Richard Brown. (Illus.). 144p. 1996. pap. 22.95 (0-395-77186-2) HM.

Moments in Eden, Vol. 1. Richard Brown. 1989. 40.00 (0-316-10999-1) Little.

Moments in Jewish Life: The Folk Art of Malcah Zeldis. Yona Zeldis-Mcdonough & Malcah Zeldis. LC 96-28468. 96p. 1996. 22.50 (1-56799-368-0, Friedman-Fairfax) M Friedman Pub Grp Inc.

Moments in Light, Paintings by Billy Morrow Jackson. Howard E. Wooden. (Illus.). 48p. 1980. pap. 5.00 (0-939324-03-2) Wichita Art Mus.

Moments in Mathematics. H. Landau. LC 87-19384. (Proceedings of Symposia in Applied Mathematics Ser.: Vol. 37). 154p. 1987. pap. 33.00 (0-8218-0114-7, PSAPM/37) Am Math.

Moments in Oklahoma History: A Book of Trivia about People, Places, Things, Events. 2nd rev. ed. Bonnie S. Speer. LC 96-70454. (Illus.). x, 117p. 1997. pap. 9.95 (1-889683-01-9) Reliance Pr.

Moments in the Garden, Vol. 1. Ed. by Jef Sturm. 300p. 1998. write for info. (1-888680-26-1) Poetry Guild.

Moments in the Life of a Scientist. Bruno Rossi. (Illus.). 194p. (C). 1990. text 54.95 (0-521-36439-6) Cambridge U Pr.

*Moments in the Sun: Baseball's Briefly Famous. Mark McGuire & Michael S. Gormley. LC 99-11100. (Illus.). 247p. 1999. pap. 28.50 (0-7864-0549-X) McFarland & Co.

*Moments in Time. Laurel Danforth. 1999. pap. write for info. (1-58235-369-7) Watermrk Pr.

Moments in Time. J. P. Grady. (C). 1990. text 50.00 (0-7223-2521-5, Pub. by A H S Ltd) St Mut.

Moments in Time. Cornelia B. Hodges. 24p. 1996. 6.95 (1-885206-31-3, Iliad Pr) Cader Pubng.

Moments in Time. Mary H. Kegel. 1998. pap. write for info. (1-57553-914-4) Watermrk Pr.

Moments in Time. Mariah Stewart. Ed. by Linda Marrow. 384p. (Orig.). 1995. mass mkt. 5.99 (0-671-86854-3) PB.

Moments in Time. Ed. by Jef Sturm. 300p. 1998. 59.95 (1-888680-34-2) Poetry Guild.

Moments in Time. 2nd ed. Gilbert Saenz. Tr. by George Perazza. (Illus.). 77p. (Orig.). 1995. mass mkt. 8.00 (0-9635681-4-0) G Saenz.

*Moments in Time: On Narration & Slowness. Helmut Friedel. 2000. pap. 30.00 (3-89322-983-3) Dr Cantz sche Druckerei GmbH.

Moments in Time: One Woman's Ecumenical Journey. Margaret Flory. LC 95-6346. (Illus.). 128p. (Orig.). 1995. pap. 5.95 (0-377-00298-4) Friendship Pr.

Moments in Time Vol. 1: A Broken Field Run Through a Lifetime of Baltimore Based Sports Stories. Paul M. Bake. Ed. by Gary Adornato. LC 97-94565. (Illus.). 232p. 1997. pap. 17.95 (0-9661217-0-8) P Baker.

Moment's Indiscretion. Peggy J. Herring. LC 97-40429. 240p. (Orig.). 1998. pap. 11.95 (1-56280-194-5) Naiad Pr.

An Asterisk (*) at the beginning of an entry indicates that the title is appearing for the first time.

Moment's Liberty: The Shorter Diary. Virginia Woolf. Ed. by Anne Olivier Bell. 1990. 22.95 (*0-15-161894-1*) Harcourt.

Moment's Liberty: The Shorter Diary. Virginia Woolf. Ed. by Anne O. Bell. 1991. 14.95 (*0-685-51159-6*, Harvest Bks) Harcourt.

Moment's Liberty: The Shorter Diary. Virginia Woolf & Anne O. Bell. 528p. (C). 1992. pap. 17.95 (*0-15-661912-1*, Harvest Bks) Harcourt.

Moments Litteraires: Anthologie pour Cours Intermediaires. Bette G. Hirsch & Chantal P. Thompson. (FRE.). 235p. (C). 1992. pap. text 31.56 (*0-669-21521-X*) HM Trade Div.

Moments, Memories, Miracles: A Quarter Century with the Kansas City Royals Steve Cameron. LC 95-140490. xxv, 238 p. 1992. write for info. (*0-87833-040-2*) Taylor Pub.

Moment's Monument: Revisionary Poetics & the Nineteenth-Century English Sonnet. Jennifer A. Wagner. LC 95-21673. 256p. 1996. 38.50 (*0-8386-3630-6*) Fairleigh Dickinson.

***Moments More in Us: Poems from Hollywood.** Mark Dunster. 11p. 1999. pap. 5.00 (*0-89642-804-4*) Linden Pubs.

Moments Musicaux: Piano Solo: Centennial Edition. 5.95 (*0-7935-4364-9*, 50482381) H Leonard.

Moment's Notice. Hilton Sutton. LC 98-181843. 1999. pap. 14.99 (*1-57794-066-0*) Dake Pub.

Moment's Notice: Jazz in Poetry & Prose. Ed. by Art Lange & Nathaniel Mackey. LC 93-10151. 370p. (YA). (gr. 11-12). 1993. pap. 17.50 (*1-56689-001-2*, Pub. by Coffee Hse) SPD-Small Pr Dist.

Moment's Notice: Time Politics Across Cultures. Carol J. Greenhouse. 320p. 1996. text 52.50 (*0-8014-3061-5*); pap. text 19.95 (*0-8014-8228-3*) Cornell U Pr.

Moments of a True Romance. 95p. (Orig.). 1992. pap. write for info. (*1-881937-02-X*) Wrds Between Cov.

Moments of Being: Unpublished Autobiographical Writings. rev. ed. Virginia Woolf. Ed. by Jeanne Schulkind. 230p. 1985. pap. 11.00 (*0-15-661918-0*, Harvest Bks) Harcourt.

Moments of Decision: Political History & the Crises of Radicalism. Stephen E. Bronner. LC 91-18169. 224p. (C). 1991. pap. 21.99 (*0-415-90465-X*, A6277) Routledge.

Moments of Delhi Vols. 1-4: Lasting Splendour of the Great Mughals & Others, 4 vols. J. A. Page. 1997. 1725.00 (*81-7305-114-3*, Pub. by Print Hse) St Mut.

Moments of Doubt & Other Mountaineering Writings of David Roberts. David Roberts. LC 86-16357. 256p. (Orig.). 1986. pap. 12.95 (*0-89886-118-7*) Mountaineers.

Moments of Engagement: Intimate Psychotherapy in a Technological Age. Peter D. Kramer. (C). 1989. 24.95 (*0-393-70075-5*) Norton.

Moments of Engagement: Intimate Psychotherapy in a Technological Age. Peter D. Kramer. 272p. 1994. pap. 11.95 (*0-14-023790-9*, Penguin Bks) Viking Penguin.

***Moments of Engagement: Intimate Psychotherapy in a Technological Age.** Peter D. Kramer. 260p. 2000. reprint ed. text 25.00 (*0-7881-6450-3*) DIANE Pub.

Moments of Existence: Poems & Notes of an American: 1970-1990. Kenneth David Teel. LC 93-60555. 148p. (Orig.). 1994. pap. 11.95 (*0-913789-00-3*) Timespan Assn.

Moments of Freedom: Anthropology & Popular Culture. Johannes Fabian. LC 97-42296. (Page-Barbour Lectures Ser.). 192p. 1998. pap. 17.50 (*0-8139-1786-7*); text 45.00 (*0-8139-1785-9*) U Pr of Va.

Moments of Glory: Interviews with South Carolina's Greatest Sports Legends. John C. Griffin. (Illus.). 250p. 1998. pap. text 16.95 (*1-887714-22-7*) Summerhse Pr.

Moments of Grace. Patricia Gaines. 208p. 1998. pap. 12.00 (*0-609-80171-6*, Crown) Crown Pub Group.

***Moments of Grace: Our Time with Jason Petry Berns.** Jennifer Berns & Lauren Mittermann. 72p. 1998. pap. 7.95 (*0-9638558-1-6*) Maple Grove.

***Moments of Grace: Stories of Ordinary People & an Extraordinary God.** Nancy Sullivan-Geng. 2000. pap. 10.99 (*1-57673-698-9*) Multnomah Pubs.

Moments of Insight: Biblical & Contemporary Themes. Jeffrey M. Cohen. 216p. 1989. text 22.50 (*0-85303-233-5*, Pub. by M Vallentine & Co) Intl Spec Bk.

***Moments of Intercession.** Sandra O. Clopine. 144p. 1999. pap. 6.99 (*0-88243-727-5*, 02-0727) Gospel Pub.

Moments of Light. Fred Chappell. LC 80-81219. 166p. 1980. 12.95 (*0-917990-05-6*, New South) C & M Online.

Moments of Meaning. Charlotte Vale Allen. 230p. 1998. reprint ed. pap. 20.00 (*1-892738-00-7*) Isld Nation.

Moments of Meaning. Charlotte Vale Allen. 224p. 1998. reprint ed. 22.95 (*1-892738-15-5*, Pub. by Isld Nation) Brodart.

Moments of Memory. Troy Damron. (Illus.). 20p. (Orig.). pap. 0.99 (*1-885729-01-4*) Toccoa Falls.

Moments of Modernity? Reconstructing Britain, 1945-1964. Ed. by Becky Conekin et al. (Illus.). 304p. 1998. text 50.00 (*1-85489-104-9*); pap. text 23.00 (*1-85489-105-7*) NYU Pr.

Moments of My Life. Jacqueline S. Moore. Ed. by Ann A. Hunter. 1999. 18.50 (*1-893846-75-X*) Loft Pr.

Moments of Pride, Passion, Prejudice & Spirituality. Lattice B. McKoy. LC 97-75985. 96p. 1998. pap. 11.95 (*1-57197-103-3*) Pentland Pr.

Moments of Reflection. Ed. by Jef Sturm. 300p. 1997. 59.95 (*1-888680-06-7*, U906) Poetry Guild.

Moments of Reprieve. Primo Levi. (Twentieth-Century Classics Ser.). 176p. 1995. pap. 11.95 (*0-14-018895-9*, Penguin Classics) Viking Penguin.

Moments of Selfhood: Three Plays by Luigi Pirandello. James V. Blundo. LC 90-36613. (American University Studies: Romance Languages & Literature: Ser. II, Vol. 135). 208p. (C). 1991. text 38.95 (*0-8204-1205-8*) P Lang Pubng.

Moments of Silence see Oraciones Para Sanar

Moments of Silence. John C. Taylor. LC 93-17948. 192p. 1993. 15.00 (*1-56170-071-1*, 115) Hay House.

Moments of Silence. Albert Krassner. (Orig.). 1987. reprint ed. pap. 14.95 (*0-912061-14-6*) Veridon Edns.

Moments of Solitude. Ed. by Chris Tyler. LC 98-146540. 1998. 69.95 (*1-57553-608-0*) Watermrk Pr.

Moments of the Heart: An Inspirational Guide to Surviving a Destructive Relationship. Chuck Evans. LC 97-90028. (Illus.). 64p. (Orig.). 1997. pap. 10.95 (*0-9656577-0-1*) E A Press.

Moments of Transcendence: Inspirational Readings for Rosh Hashanah. Ed. by Dov Peretz Elkins. LC 92-9480. 336p. 1992. 40.00 (*0-87668-506-8*) Aronson.

Moments of Transcendence: Inspirational Readings for Yom Kippur. Ed. by Dov Peretz Elkins. LC 92-9303. 304p. 1992. 40.00 (*0-87668-504-1*) Aronson.

Moments of Truth. Jan Carlzon. LC 87-1070. 160p. 1987. 22.50 (*0-88730-200-9*, HarpBusn) HarpInfo.

Moments of Truth. Jan Carlzon. LC 88-45644. 160p. 1989. reprint ed. pap. 13.00 (*0-06-091580-3*, PL 1580, Perennial) HarperTrade.

Moments of Truth Vol. 1: Excerpts from the Rubaiyat of Omar Khayyam Explained. Paramhansa Yogananda. 121p. 1995. pap. 9.95 (*1-56589-721-8*) Crystal Clarity.

Moments of Truth Vol. 2: Excerpts from Autobiography of a Yogi. Paramhansa Yogananda. (Illus.). 125p. 1997. 9.95 (*1-56589-725-0*) Crystal Clarity.

***Moments of Union: The Paintings of Hal Kramer.** Hal Kramer. (Illus.). 204p. 2000. 50.00 (*0-915811-87-1*, Pub. by H J Kramer Inc) New Wrld Lib.

Moments of Unreason: The Practice of Canadian Psychiatry & the Homewood Retreat, 1883-1923. Cheryl K. Warsh. (Illus.). 304p. (C). 1989. text 65.00 (*0-7735-0701-9*, Pub. by McG-Queens Univ Pr) CUP Services.

Moments of Vision: The Poetry of Thomas Hardy. Paul Zietlow. LC 73-85184. 279p. reprint ed. pap. 86.50 (*0-7837-2348-2*, 205743600004) Bks Demand.

Moments of Vision: The Stroboscopic Revolution in Photography. Harold E. Edgerton & James R. Killian, Jr. (Illus.). 1979. pap. text 19.95 (*0-262-55010-5*) MIT Pr.

Moments of Vision Voices Verses. Joe L. Shakeenab. 50p. (Orig.). 1995. pap. 8.00 (*1-56411-135-0*) Untd Bros & Sis.

Moments on Maple Avenue: The Reality of Abortion. Louise K. Howe. 224p. 1986. mass mkt. 3.95 (*0-446-34015-4*, Pub. by Warner Bks) Little.

Moment's Peace: Words of Encouragement. rev. ed. John Paul, II, pseud. LC 95-41680. 128p. 1995. pap. 6.99 (*0-89283-966-X*, Charis) Servant.

Moments Rightly Placed: An Aleutian Memoir. Ray Hudson. Ed. by Tricia Brown. (Illus.). 224p. 1998. pap. 14.95 (*0-945397-49-6*) Epicenter Pr.

Moments Shared: A Selection of Writings on Friendship. Flavia M. Weedn. (Illus.). 90p. reprint ed. 10.00 (*0-929632-04-4*) Applause Inc.

Moments That Make Memories. Jeanne Yawney. 16p. (J). 1995. pap. 1.98 (*0-88290-526-0*, 2066) Horizon Utah.

***Moments that Matter, Vol. 1.** Dan Quayle. 144p. 1999. 12.99 (*0-8499-5529-7*) CDI.

Moments to Meander. Joseph Tootell. 88p. 1986. 35.00 (*0-7223-1956-8*, Pub. by A H S Ltd) St Mut.

Moments to Remember. Sandy Clough. 64p. 1999. spiral bd., boxed set 22.99 (*1-56507-915-9*) Harvest Hse.

Moments to Remember: The Art of Creating Scrapbook Memories. Jo Packham. LC 98-33643. 1998. 24.95 (*0-8362-5255-1*) Andrews & McMeel.

Moments to Remember: Topics & Ideas for Reminiscence Groups - A Sequel to down Memory Lane. Beckie Karras. (Illus.). 92p. 1989. spiral bd. 14.95 (*1-879633-02-7*) Eldersong.

Moments Together for Couples: Devotionals for Drawing Near to God & One Another. Dennis Rainey & Barbara Rainey. 385p. 1995. pap. 12.99 (*0-8307-1808-7*, 5422691, Regal Bks) Gospel Lght.

Moments 2+1. Edward W. Johnson. 35p. 1999. 22.00 (*1-55212-241-7*) Trafford Pub.

Moments with Angels. Robert Strand. LC 95-73135. (Moments to Give Ser.). 80p. 1996. 9.99 (*0-89221-324-8*) New Leaf.

Moments with Baha'u'llah: The Memoirs of the Hand of the Cause of God Tarazu'llah Samandari. Tarazu'llah Samandari. Tr. by Marzieh Gail & Mehdi Samandari from PEO. LC 95-43423. (Illus.). xxv, 75p. 1996. 14.95 (*0-933770-94-4*) Kalimat.

Moments with Children. Jackie Guilliams. (Illus.). 48p. 1996. pap. write for info. (*1-57579-035-1*) Pine Hill Pr.

Moments with Children in Worship. Ed. by Joseph H. Bragg, Jr. 136p. (Orig.). 1989. pap. 9.99 (*0-8272-2320-X*) Chalice Pr.

***Moments with Eugene: A Collection of Memories.** Rebecca Barrett & Carolyn Haines. LC 00-35711. 2000. write for info. (*0-9663954-1-7*) KaliOka Pr.

Moments with God. LC 97-60497. 384p. 1997. 17.99 (*0-529-10763-5*, MWG) World Pubng.

Moments with Jackie. Jean Mills. LC 99-13870. (Illus.). 120p. 1999. 19.98 (*1-56799-852-6*) M Friedman Pub Grp Inc.

***Moments with Marilyn.** Marilyn S. Murphree. 308p. 1999. pap. 12.95 (*0-7392-0313-4*, PO3456) Morris Pubng.

Moments with Mary. Mary Branson Cagle. 1998. pap. write for info. (*1-57553-858-X*) Watermrk Pr.

Moments with the Master. Georgia Adams. 156p. 1998. pap. 10.00 (*1-56469-042-3*) Harmony Hse Pub.

Moments with the Master. Stephen D. Boyd. 1987. pap. 4.75 (*0-89137-334-9*) Quality Pubns.

Moments with the Savior: A Devotional Life of Christ. Ken Gire. LC 97-43800. 416p. 1998. 17.99 (*0-310-50070-2*) Zondervan.

Moments with Thoughts & Guides. Michael Garo. 208p. 1998. pap. 6.75 (*1-57502-452-7*, PO2418) Morris Pubng.

Moments with You God. Mary Paolini. 1986. 8.95 (*0-88271-028-1*) Regina Pr.

Moments Without Self. 4th ed. Benito F. Reyes. LC 61-21760. 198p. 1970. reprint ed. 10.00 (*0-939375-36-2*) World Univ Amer.

Momentum: A Theory of Social Action. Peter Adler. LC 81-2718. (Sociological Observations Ser.: No. 11). 191p. reprint ed. pap. 59.30 (*0-8357-8465-7*, 203473300091) Bks Demand.

Momentum: On Recent South African Writing. Margaret J. Daymond et al. 336p. 1984. pap. 24.95 (*0-86980-377-8*, Pub. by Univ Natal Pr) Intl Spec Bk.

Momentum Accounting & Triple-Entry Bookkeeping. Yuji Ijiri. (Studies in Accounting Research: No. 31). 151p. 1989. 12.00 (*0-86539-071-1*) Am Accounting.

Momentum & Heat Transfer in Turbulent Gas-Solid Flows. Z. R. Gorbis & F. E. Spokoyny. LC 94-48057. 366p. 1995. 95.00 (*1-56700-022-3*) Begell Hse.

Momentum & Speed. Adrian Wisnicki. 96p. 1992. pap. text 6.95 (*0-930401-54-9*) Artex Pub.

Momentum, Direction & Divergence. William Blau. LC 94-38103. (Traders' Advantage Ser.). 160p. 1995. 55.00 (*0-471-02729-4*) Wiley.

Momentum Distributions. Ed. by R. N. Silver & P. E. Sokol. (Illus.). 424p. 1989. 120.00 (*0-306-43364-8*, Plenum Trade) Perseus Pubng.

Momentum, Heat & Mass Transfer. 3rd ed. C. O. Bennett & J. E. Myers. (Chemical Engineering Ser.). 848p. (C). 1982. 114.69 (*0-07-004671-9*) McGraw.

Momentum, Heat & Mass Transfer Fundamentals. David P. Kessler & Robert A. Greenkorn. LC 99-10432. (Illus.). 1048p. 1999. text 85.00 (*0-8247-1972-7*) Dekker.

Momentum Wave Functions: Adelaide, Australia, 1982. American Institute of Physics. Ed. by Erich Weigold. LC 82-72375. (AIP Conference Proceedings Ser.: No. 86). 345p. 1982. lib. bdg. 34.00 (*0-88318-185-1*) Am Inst Physics.

Momentum Wave Functions: Proceedings of the Workshop, Indiana Univ., Bloomington, May 31-June 4, 1976. Momentum Wave Function Determination in Atomic, Mo. Ed. by D. W. Devins. LC 77-82145. (AIP Conference Proceedings Ser.: No. 36). (Illus.). 1977. lib. bdg. 17.50 (*0-88318-135-5*) Am Inst Physics.

***Momfoolery.** Karin Vingle. 82p. 1999. pap. write for info. (*0-941147-02-9*) Charleston Gazette.

Momias de Egipto - Mummies Are Made in Egypt. Aliki. 1996. 10.95 (*84-261-2694-4*) Lectorum Pubns.

Momilies: As My Mother Used to Say. Michele B. Slung. 1985. mass mkt. 4.99 (*0-345-32289-4*) Ballantine Pub Grp.

Momma. Pat Schwiebert & Julia McCarl. 67p. 1992. pap., spiral bd. 12.50 incl. audio (*0-9615197-3-8*) Perinatal Loss.

Momma: A Start on All the Untold Stories. Alta. LC 74-79105. 77 p. (Orig.) (J). 1974. write for info. (*0-87810-528-X*) Times Change.

Momma: A Start on All the Untold Stories. Alta. LC 74-79105. (Illus.). 80p. (Orig.). 1974. pap. 4.50 (*0-87810-028-8*) Times Change.

Momma & the Meaning of Life: Tales of Psychotherapy. Irvin D. Yalom. LC 99-34831. 256p. 1999. 24.00 (*0-465-04386-0*, Pub. by Basic) HarpC.

***Momma & the Meaning of Life: Tales of Psychotherapy.** Irvin D. Yalom. 288p. 2000. pap. 14.00 (*0-06-095838-3*, Perennial) HarperTrade.

Momma Cat. Abigail M. Walsh. LC 90-823. (Illus.). 112p. (J). (gr. 2 up). 1990. 6.95 (*0-934745-16-1*) Acadia Pub Co.

***Momma Chick's Recipes: A Collection of Favorite Recipes.** 2nd ed. Helen L. Chickering. Ed. by Timothy J. Hobson. 105p. 1999. 14.95 (*1-893822-01-X*) Hobsons.

Momma Mockingbird. Sauni Wood. LC 97-48947. (Illus.). (J). 8.95 (*1-56123-105-3*) Centering Corp.

Momma Tell Me a Story. Lynn F. Wright. LC 95-19644. (Illus.). 40p. (J). (ps-2). 1995. 13.95 (*1-881519-04-X*); pap. 6.95 (*1-881519-05-8*) WorryWart.

Momma, What's It Like to Die? Myrna L. Etheridge. (YA). 1999. pap. 10.99 (*1-56043-331-0*, Treasure Hse) Destiny Image.

***Momma, Where Are You From?** Marie Bradby. LC 99-23068. (Illus.). 32p. (J). (ps-2). 2000. 16.95 (*0-531-30105-2*); 17.99 (*0-531-33105-9*) Orchard Bks Watts.

Mommakitty's Surprise: "Skyler" Saralou L. Reid. LC 88-60613. (Illus.). (J). (gr. k-3). 1997. 12.00 (*0-9620420-0-5*); ring bd. 18.00 (*0-9620420-1-3*) Surge Pub.

Mommakitty's Surprise: "Skyler" Saralou L. Reid. LC 88-60613. (Illus.). (J). (gr. k-3). 1997. lib. bdg. 35.00 (*0-9620420-3-X*) Surge Pub.

Mommakitty's Surprise: Skyler. large type ed. Sally L. Reid. (Illus.). 36p. (J). (gr. k-3). 1997. 12.00 (*0-614-30156-4*) Surge Pub.

Momma's Enchanted Supper: And Other Stories for the Long Evenings of Advent. Carol DeChant. LC 98-56192. (Illus.). 224p. 1999. 17.95 (*0-8294-1272-7*, Wild Onion) Loyola Pr.

Momma's Little Angels. Louis La Russo, II. 1979. pap. 5.25 (*0-8222-0769-9*) Dramatists Play.

Mommie Dearest. anniversary ed. Christina Crawford. (Illus.). 1997. pap. 16.95 (*0-9663369-0-9*) Seven Sprngs Pr.

***Mommie Star.** Clarine Morris. (Illus.). (J). (ps-10). 2000. pap. 3.00 (*0-9650312-3-3*) Cosmo Starr.

Mommie, What Is a Nigger? The Case of the Centuries. Mia Isaac. Ed. by Faye Chestnut. Tr. by Sandra Lemon. LC 95-80261. (Illus.). 282p. (Orig.). 1996. pap. 20.95 (*0-9630229-2-X*) IGIA.

***Mommies Are for Counting Stars: Lift-The-Flap.** Harriet Ziefert. (Illus.). 16p. (ps-1). 1999. pap. 6.99 (*0-14-056552-3*, PuffinBks) Peng Put Young Read.

Mommies at Work. Eve Merriam. (Illus.). 32p. (J). (ps-2). 1996. 3.25 (*0-689-80999-9*) Aladdin.

Mommies Don't Get Sick! Marylin Hafner. LC 94-24225. (Illus.). 32p. (J). (gr. k-3). 1995. 14.95 (*1-56402-287-0*) Candlewick Pr.

Mommies Don't Get Sick! Marylin Hafner. LC 94-24225. (Illus.). 32p. (J). (gr. k-3). 1997. reprint ed. pap. 5.99 (*0-7636-0154-3*) Candlewick Pr.

Mommy. Max A. Collins. 1996. 16.95 incl. audio (*1-882071-87-5*) B&B Audio.

Mommy. Max Allan Collins. 272p. (Orig.). 1997. mass mkt. 4.99 (*0-8439-4322-X*, Leisure Bks) Dorchester Pub Co.

Mommy . . . This Is Hard for Me: A Perspective on the Student with Special Needs Who Is Included Within the Regular Public School Classroom. Michael C. Abraham. (Illus.). 71p. 1998. pap. text 12.00 (*1-878276-60-3*) Educ Systs Assocs Inc.

Mommy - CEO (Constantly Evaluating Others) 5 Golden Rules. unabridged ed. Jodie Lynn. (Illus.). v, 120p. (Orig.). 1997. pap. 10.95 (*0-9659125-3-1*) Martin-Ola.

M

Mommy & Baby Jasmine. Patricia B. Hamilton. (Shades of Black Ser.). (Illus.). 10p. (Orig.). (J). (ps-k). 1996. pap. text 5.95 (*1-889826-05-7*) Scripts Pub.

Mommy & Daddy Are Fighting: A Book for Children about Family Violence. Susan Paris. LC 85-22193. (New Leaf Ser.). (Illus.). 24p. (Orig.). (J). (ps-4). 1986. pap. 8.95 (*0-931188-33-4*) Seal Pr WA.

***Mommy & Daddy Guide to Kindergarten: Real-Life Advice & Tips from Parents & Other Experts.** Susan Bernard & Cary O. Yager. LC 00-31411. 224p. 2000. pap. 14.95 (*0-8092-2547-6*, Contemporary Bks) NTC Contemp Pub Co.

***Mommy & Daddy Take Me to Church.** Peggy Lucinda Chumbley. LC 99-64695. (Illus.). 32p. (J). 1999. pap. 9.95 (*0-9672309-0-X*) PLC Pubng.

Mommy & Me. RGA Publishing Group Staff. (Illus.). 12p. (J). (ps up). 1997. 4.99 (*0-689-81267-1*) S&S Childrens.

Mommy & Me: A Children's Collection of Thoughts. Laura Mauk. Ed. by Patrick Caton. LC 97-71651. 168p. 1997. pap. 5.95 (*1-56245-311-4*) Great Quotations.

Mommy & Me Craft Book. Kathy Ross. 1999. write for info. (*0-7613-1418-0*, Copper Beech Bks); pap. write for info. (*0-7613-0994-2*, Copper Beech Bks) Millbrook Pr.

Mommy & the Policeman Next Door. Marie Ferrarella. 1997. per. 3.50 (*0-373-52049-2*, 1-52049-3) Silhouette.

Mommy Book. Belinda J. Bralver. 1989. pap. 5.95 (*0-8184-0503-1*) Carol Pub Group.

Mommy Book. Ann Morris. LC 95-12237. (World's Family Ser.). (Illus.). 32p. (J). (gr. k-1). 1950. lib. bdg. 22.00 (*0-382-24693-4*) Silver Burdett Pr.

Mommy Book. Ann Morris. LC 95-12237. (World's Family Ser.). (Illus.). 32p. (J). (gr. k-1). 1995. 13.95 (*0-382-24692-6*); pap. 5.95 (*0-382-24694-2*) Silver Burdett Pr.

Mommy Book. Cheryl P. Salem. LC 96-159532. 192p. (Orig.). 1995. pap. 9.99 (*0-89274-927-X*, HH-927) Harrison Hse.

Mommy Book. 2nd ed. Karen Hull. 2000. pap. 14.99 (*0-310-22814-X*) Zondervan.

Mommy Book: Advice to New Mothers from Those Who've Been There. Karen Hull. 240p. 1986. pap. 12.99 (*0-310-32241-3*, 9178P) Zondervan.

Mommy, Buy Me a China Doll. Harve Zemach. (Illus.). 32p. (J). (ps-3). 1989. pap. 4.95 (*0-374-45286-5*, Sunburst Bks) FS&G.

Mommy by Surprise. Paula D. Riggs. (Intimate Moments Ser.: No. 794). 1997. per. 3.99 (*0-373-07794-7*, 1-07794-0) Silhouette.

Mommy, Daddy, Where Do Babies Come From? Grace Ayad & Richard Panzer. LC 96-72331. (Wonderful World of True Love Ser.). (Illus.). (J). 1997. 12.95 (*1-888933-04-6*) Ctr Educ Media.

Mommy, Daddy, Where Do Babies Come From? Activity Book. Photos by Rhonda Williams. (Wonderful World of True Love Ser.). (Illus.). 16p. (J). (gr. k-4). Date not set. pap. 3.95 (*0-9675068-0-8*) Media For Life.

***Mommy Deadest: A Meg Darcy Mystery.** Jean Marcy. 224p. 2000. pap. 11.95 (*1-892281-12-0*, Pub. by New Victoria Pubs) LPC InBook.

***Mommy Diagnostics: The Naturally Healthy Family's Guide to Herbs & Whole Foods for Health.** Shonda Parker. (Illus.). 298p. 2000. pap. 14.99 (*1-929125-11-9*, Pub. by Loyal Pubng) BookWorld.

Mommy Doesn't Know My Name. Suzanne Williams. LC 89-78205. (Illus.). 48p. (J). (ps-3). 1996. pap. 5.95 (*0-395-77979-0*, Sandpiper) HM.

Mommy Doesn't Know My Name. Suzanne Williams. 1990. 11.15 (*0-606-08823-7*, Pub. by Turtleback) Demco.

Mommy Doesn't Live Here Anymore. Maureen H. Duggan. (Illus.). 48p. (Orig.). (J). (ps-7). 1987. pap. 8.95 (*0-944453-01-5*) B Brae.

Mommy, Don't Cry. Zilpha M. Booth. (Orig.). 1982. pap. 9.00 (*0-914562-11-8*) Merriam-Eddy.

Mommy Don't Cry. Zilpha M. Booth. Ed. by Jane Weinberger. LC 89-85362. (Illus.). 96p. 1989. reprint ed. pap. 5.95 (*0-932433-63-4*) Windswept Hse.

Mommy, Don't Go. 2nd rev. ed. Elizabeth Crary. LC 96-23352. (Children's Problem Solving Bk.). (Illus.). 32p. (J). (ps-3). 1996. pap. 6.95 (*1-884734-20-0*); lib. bdg. 16.95 (*1-884734-21-9*) Parenting Pr.

An Asterisk (*) at the beginning of an entry indicates that the title is appearing for the first time.

Mommy Dressing: A Love Story, after a Fashion. Lois Gould. LC 97-46573. (Illus.). 272p. 1998. 22.95 (*0-385-49053-4*, Anchor NY) Doubleday.

Mommy Dressing: A Love Story, After a Fashion. Lois Gould. 272p. 1999. pap. 12.95 (*0-385-49054-2*, Anchor NY) Doubleday.

Mommy Exchange. Amy Hest. LC 87-7539. (Illus.). 32p. (J). (ps-2). 1988. lib. bdg. 13.95 (*0-02-743650-0*, Four Winds Pr) S&S Childrens.

Mommy Exchange. Amy Hest. LC 90-40596. (Illus.). 32p. (J). (ps-2). 1991. reprint ed. pap. 3.95 (*0-689-71450-5*) Aladdin.

***Mommy Far, Mommy Near: An Adoption Story.** Carol Antoinette Peacock. (Concept Book Ser.). (Illus.). 32p. (J). (ps-2). 2000. lib. bdg. 14.95 (*0-8075-5234-8*) A Whitman.

Mommy for the Moment. Lisa K. Laurel. (Romance Ser.). 1996. per. 3.25 (*0-373-19173-1*, 1-19173-3) Silhouette.

Mommy Go Away! Lynne Jonell. LC 96-38194. (Illus.). 32p. (J). (ps-2). 1997. 12.95 (*0-399-23001-7*, G P Putnam) Peng Put Young Read.

***Mommy Go Away!** Lynne Jonell. (Illus.). 32p. (ps-1). 2000. pap. 5.99 (*0-698-11810-3*) Putnam Pub Group.

Mommy Guide. Susan Bernard. 416p. 1994. pap. 16.95 (*0-8092-3797-0*, 379700, Contemporary Bks) NTC Contemp Pub Co.

Mommy Guide for Toddlers. Bernard. 1996. pap. write for info. (*0-8092-3366-5*) NTC Contemp Pub Co.

Mommy Heiress (Accidental Dads) Linda R. Wisdom. LC 95-22330. 250p. 1995. per. 3.50 (*0-373-16608-7*) Harlequin Bks.

Mommy Hugs. Maryann Cocca-Leffler. (J). (ps-k). 1997. 5.99 (*0-614-29096-1*) Litle Simon.

Mommy, I Can't Sit Still: Coping with Hyperactive & Aggressive Children. K. Daniel O'Leary. Ed. by Joan S. Dunphy. 132p. 1989. 13.95 (*0-88282-000-1*); pap. 10.95 (*0-88282-055-9*) New Horizon NJ.

Mommy! I Have to Go Potty! A Parent's Guide to Toilet Training. Jan Faull. LC 96-68504. 140p. (Orig.). (J). (ps-1). 1996. pap. 13.95 (*0-9650477-0-9*) Raefield-Roberts.

Mommy, I Love Your Hands. Kathryn Lasky. (J). Date not set. 14.99 (*0-7868-0280-4*, Pub. by Hyperion) Little.

***Mommy, I Love Your Hands.** Kathryn Lasky. (J). 2005. lib. bdg. 15.49 (*0-7868-2225-2*, Pub. by Hyperion) Little.

Mommy I'm Bored: One Hundred & Twenty Six Fun Filled & Educational Games Your Child Can...Play Alone. Cynthia MacGregor. 160p. 1995. pap. 8.95 (*0-8065-1662-3*, Citadel Pr) Carol Pub Group.

Mommy I'm Hungry: How to Feed Your Child Nutritiously. Patricia McEntire. LC 81-68292. 168p. 1982. pap. 3.00 (*0-917982-11-8*, Cougar Books) Capitol Enquiry.

Mommy I'm Scared: How TV & Movies Frighten Children & What We Can Do to Protect Them. Joanne Cantor. LC 98-17080. 320p. (C). 1998. pap. 13.00 (*0-15-600592-1*, Harvest Bks) Harcourt.

Mommy I'm Scared: How TV & Movies Frighten Children & What We Can Do to Protect Them. Joanne Cantor. LC 98-17080. 250p. 1998. 25.00 (*0-15-100402-1*, Harvest Bks) Harcourt.

Mommy in the Sky. Leslie A. Derrig & Roxanne H. Westdyk. LC 83-73248. (Working Mommy Ser.: Vol. 2). (Illus.). 32p. (Orig.). (J). (gr. k-5). 1983. pap. 6.95 (*0-915479-68-0*) Cottage Pub Co.

Mommy Is an Histologist. Iffy Hersh. (What Does Mommy Do? Ser.). (Illus.). (Orig.). (J). (gr. k-2). pap. 10.00 (*0-936735-04-X*) Grove Educ Tech.

Mommy, Is God as Strong As Daddy? Barbara Knoll. (Mommy, Why...Ser.). (Illus.). 24p. (Orig.). (J). 1995. pap. 3.99 (*1-56043-150-4*) Destiny Image.

***Mommy, Is That You? A Move & Play Book.** Dawn Bentley. (Move & Play Bks.). (Illus.). 10p. (J). 2000. 6.95 (*1-58117-073-4*, Piggy Toes Pr) Intervisual Bks.

Mommy Isn't Sick; She's Just Dying. Ernest N. Bigelow. 157p. (Orig.). 1993. pap. 9.50 (*0-9632030-0-2*) Bigelow Pub.

Mommy Laid an Egg: or Where Do Babies Come From? Babette Cole. (Illus.). 40p. (J). (ps-3). 1993. 13.95 (*0-8118-0350-3*) Chronicle Bks.

Mommy Laid an Egg: or Where Do Babies Come From? Babette Cole. (Illus.). 40p. (J). (ps-3). 1996. pap. 6.95 (*0-8118-1319-3*) Chronicle Bks.

Mommy Love Hugs. Maryann Leffler. (Illus.). 14p. (J). (ps-k). 1997. 5.99 (*0-689-80981-6*) S&S Bks Yung.

Mommy Lovers Her Baby. Tara Jaye Centeio. 32p. (ps-1). pap. 5.95 (*0-06-443715-9*) HarpC.

Mommy Loves Her Baby. Tara Jaye Centeio. 32p. (ps-1). pap. 15.95 (*0-06-029077-3*); lib. bdg. 15.89 (*0-06-029078-1*) HarpC.

Mommy Loves Jesus. Catherine Snider. LC 93-13354. (Illus.). 24p. (Orig.). (J). (ps-6). 1993. pap. 3.95 (*0-8198-4731-3*) Pauline Bks.

***Mommy Loves Me.** Dalmatian Press Staff. (Illus.). (J). 2000. 2.99 (*1-57759-373-1*) Dalmatian Pr.

Mommy Loves Me. Donna Warren. (Baby Flaps Ser.). (Illus.). 20p. (J). (ps). 1996. bds. 2.99 (*1-56293-900-9*, McClanahan Book) Learn Horizon.

***Mommy Made & Daddy Too! Home Cooking for a Healthy Baby & Toddler.** 10th anniversary ed. Martha Kimmel et al. LC 99-86434. (Illus.). 320p. 2000. pap. 16.95 (*0-553-38090-7*, Spectra) Bantam.

Mommy Made & Daddy Too: Home Cooking for a Healthy Baby & Toddler. Martha Kimmel. 320p. 1990. pap. 15.95 (*0-553-34866-3*) Bantam.

***Mommy Magic: 450 Ways to Nurture Your Child.** Adria Manary. LC 99-96512. 221p. 2000. pap. 12.95 (*0-9665830-2-7*, Pub. by Angel Power Pr) ACCESS Pubs Network.

***Mommy Makeover.** Bonnie K. Winn. (American Romance Ser.: No. 812). 2000. per. 4.25 (*0-373-16812-8*, 1-16812-9, Harlequin) Harlequin Bks.

Mommy, May I Hug Fishes? Crystal Bowman. 2000. 6.99 (*0-310-23209-0*) HarpC.

Mommy Meals. Karen Brown. (Illus.). 107p. (Orig.). 1988. pap. 11.95 (*0-9621948-0-8*) Legacy Mktg.

Mommy Moon & the Rainbow Children. True Heitz. (Illus.). 13p. (Orig.). (J). (ps-2). 1982. pap. 3.00 (*0-686-37664-1*) True Heitz.

Mommy on Board. Muriel Jensen. LC 96-310. 248p. 1995. per. 3.50 (*0-373-16603-6*, 1-16603-2) Harlequin Bks.

Mommy, Please Don't Cry. Linda DeYmaz. (Illus.). 1996. 11.99 (*1-885305-45-1*) Multnomah Pubs.

***Mommy Poems.** Ed. by John Micklos, Jr. (Illus.). 32p. (J). 2000. 15.95 (*1-56397-849-0*); pap. 8.95 (*1-56397-908-X*, Wordsong) Boyds Mills Pr.

Mommy School. Valerie Taylor. (Rising Star Ser.). 1997. per. 3.75 (*0-373-16676-1*, 1-16676-8) Harlequin Bks.

***Mommy Tracker.** Joyce C. Frye. Ed. by Marissa Bowers. (Illus.). 176p. 1999. 13.95 (*0-9678996-0-5*) Mommy Track.

***Mommy Tracker.** rev. ed. Joyce C. Frye. Ed. by Marissa Bowers. (Illus.). 179p. 2000. 14.95 (*0-9678996-1-3*) Mommy Track.

Mommy, Was Santa Claus Born on Christmas Too? Barbara Knoll. (Mommy, Why...Ser.). (Illus.). 24p. (Orig.). (J). 1995. pap. 3.99 (*1-56043-158-X*) Destiny Image.

Mommy, What Is a Dysfunctional Family? Random Tales of Wayward Folks. Ann S. Roy. Ed. by Phillip Carmical. 150p. 1998. pap. 12.95 (*0-89896-436-9*) Larksdale.

***Mommy, When Will the Lord Be Two?** Ruth Seligman & Jonathan Mark. 1999. pap. 11.00 (*1-57566-470-4*, Knsington) Kensgtn Pub Corp.

Mommy, Where Are You? Harriet Ziefert. 1999. pap. 4.95 (*0-14-050899-6*) NAL.

Mommy, Where Are You? Joan E. Nelson. (Orig.). 1994. reprint ed. pap. 10.95 (*0-9637293-7-3*) Storm Pub.

Mommy, Who Does God Love? Mary Melcher. (J). (ps-k). 1997. 10.95 (*0-689-81036-9*) S&S Childrens.

Mommy Why Are My Eyes So Big?, No.1. Madonna B. Hanna. (Illus.). 16p. (J). (gr. 3-12). 1999. pap. 15.00 (*0-9650634-1-0*) Hanna Pubng.

Mommy, Why Are People Different Colors? Barbara Knoll. (Mommy, Why...Ser.). (Illus.). 24p. (Orig.). (J). 1995. pap. 3.99 (*1-56043-156-3*) Destiny Image.

Mommy, Why Are They Holding Hands? Deborah Phrihoda. 1998. pap. 6.99 (*0-9663380-0-6*) Cutting PA.

"Mommy Why Are They Holding Hands?" Deborah Prihoda. Ed. by Carla Tuhacek & Steve Aiken. (Illus.). (J). (gr. 3-6). 1998. pap., teacher ed. 49.95 (*0-9663380-1-4*, 222) Cutting PA.

Mommy, Why Can't Grandma Remember Me? Glenn Miller. (Illus.). 24p. (J). (gr. k-3). 1996. pap. 9.00 (*0-8059-3841-9*) Dorrance.

Mommy, Why Can't I Watch That TV Show? Dian Layton. (Mommy, Why...Ser.). (Illus.). 24p. (Orig.). (J). 1995. pap. 3.99 (*1-56043-148-2*) Destiny Image.

Mommy, Why Did Jesus Have to Die? Dian Layton. (Mommy, Why...Ser.). (Illus.). 24p. (Orig.). (J). 1995. pap. 3.99 (*1-56043-146-6*) Destiny Image.

Mommy, Why Do We Have Easter? Lou Yohe. (Mommy, Why...Ser.). (Illus.). 24p. (Orig.). (J). 1996. pap. 3.99 (*1-56043-172-5*) Destiny Image.

Mommy, Why Don't We Celebrate Halloween? Linda H. Winwood. (Mommy Why...Ser.). 24p. (Orig.). 1994. pap. 3.99 (*1-56043-823-1*) Destiny Image.

Mommy! Why Is Everyone Staring at Me? Leia A. Stinnett. (Little Angel Bks.). (Illus.). (J). (gr. k-12). 2001. pap. text, student ed. 6.95 (*1-880737-11-6*) Crystal Jrns.

***Mommy Works, Daddy Works.** Marika Pedersen & Mikele Hall. (Illus.). 32p. (J). (ps-1). 2000. lib. bdg. 17.95 (*1-55037-657-8*, Pub. by Annick Pr); per. 5.95 (*1-55037-656-X*, Pub. by Annick Pr) Firefly Bks Ltd.

Mommy, Would God Still Love Me? Laura Wallace. (Illus.). 32p. (J). 1998. 12.99 (*0-8054-1719-2*) Broadman.

Mommy, Would You Love Me If . . .? Carla Dijs. LC 96-147712. (Illus.). 14p. (J). (ps-k). 1996. 8.99 (*0-689-80813-5*) Litle Simon.

Mommy's Day. Max Allan Collins. 272p. 1998. mass mkt. 4.99 (*0-8439-4386-6*, Leisure Bks) Dorchester Pub Co.

***Mommy's Day.** Max Allan Collins. 272p. 1999. reprint ed. mass mkt. 4.99 (*0-8439-4640-7*, Pub. by Dorchester Pub Co) CMG.

Mommy's Fibromonster. Mark J. Pellegrino & Maria Pellegrino. (Illus.). 16p. (J). 1997. pap. 4.75 (*1-890018-00-7*) Anadem Pubng.

***Mommy's Hands.** Kathryn Lasky. 32p. (J). 2001. pap. 4.99 (*0-7868-1437-3*, Pub. by Hyperion) Time Warner.

Mommy's Hat. Lynette Samuel. LC 97-71217. (Illus.). 32p. (J). (gr. 2-5). Date not set. per. 15.95 (*0-9651270-4-4*) Bright Lamb.

Mommy's Hero. Audra Adams. (Intimate Moments Ser.). 1996. per. 3.99 (*0-373-07743-2*, 1-07743-7) Silhouette.

Mommy's in the Hospital Again. Carolyn S. Parkinson. (Illus.). 40p. (Orig.). (J). (gr. k-4). 1996. pap. 14.95 (*0-9630287-1-5*) Solace Pub.

Mommy's in the Hospital Having a Baby. Maxine B. Rosenberg. LC 96-12442. (Illus.). 32p. (J). (ps-1). 1997. 15.00 (*0-395-71813-9*, Clarion Bks) HM.

***Mommy's Little Helper Christmas Crafts.** Cynthia MacGregor. (Illus.). (J). 1999. 8.00 (*0-689-83071-8*, Meadowbrook Pr) S&S Childrens.

***Mommy's Little Helper Cookbook.** Karen Brown. LC 99-53515. (Illus.). 140p. (J). (ps-1). 2000. pap. 9.00 (*0-689-83072-6*) S&S Childrens.

Mommy's Monster. Irene Trimble. LC 97-80830. (Super Shape Bks.). 24p. (J). (ps-k). 1998. pap. text 3.29 (*0-307-13308-7*, 13308, Goldn Books) Gldn Bks Pub Co.

Mommy's Office. Barbara Shook Hazen. LC 91-25013. (Illus.). 32p. (J). (ps-1). 1992. 13.95 (*0-689-31601-1*) Atheneum Yung Read.

Momo. Michael Ende. 1998. pap. text 7.95 (*968-19-0255-6*) Libros Fronteras.

***Momo Cookbook.** 224p. 2000. 34.50 (*0-7432-0510-3*) Simon & Schuster.

Momotaro see Momotaro, the Peach Boy

Momotaro. Mitchell Motomora. (Real Reading Ser.). (J). (ps). 1993. pap. 4.95 (*0-8114-6714-7*) Raintree Steck-V.

***Momotaro, the Peach Boy.** large type ed. Tr. by Donna Tamaki.Tr. of Momotaro. (ENG & JPN., Illus.). 16p. (J). (ps-12). 1998. 35.00 (*1-893533-08-5*, 1) Kamish for Kids.

Momoyama Decorative Painting. Tsugiyoshi Doi. LC 76-44338. (Heibonsha Survey of Japanese Art Ser.: Vol. 14). (Illus.). 168p. 1976. 20.00 (*0-8348-1024-7*) Weatherhill.

Momoyama Genre Painting. Yuzo Yamane. Tr. by John Shields from JPN. LC 72-92099. (Heibonsha Survey of Japanese Art Ser.: Vol. 17). (Illus.). 184p. 1973. 20.00 (*0-8348-1012-3*) Weatherhill.

Mompreneurs: A Mother's Step-by-Step Guide to Work-at-Home Success. Ellen H. Parlapiano & Patricia Cobe. LC 96-3661. 288p. 1996. pap. 13.00 (*0-399-52233-6*, Perigee Bks) Berkley Pub.

Moms: A Personal Journal. Paula Hagen & Vickie L. Jennett. LC 91-45927. (Illus.). 195p. 1992. pap. 11.95 (*0-89390-224-1*) Resource Pubns.

***Moms: A Personal Journal.** rev. ed. Paula Hagen & Vickie LoPiccolo Jennett. LC 99-88887. 2000. 11.95 (*0-89390-508-9*) Resource Pubns.

Moms: Developing a Ministry. rev. ed. Paula Hagen & Patricia Hoyt. LC 92-9070. 200p. 1996. pap., teacher ed. 24.95 (*0-89390-368-X*) Resource Pubns.

Mom's All-Time Favorite Recipes. Adrienna Wehner. (Illus.). 1996. pap. 6.25 (*0-9653866-0-0*) A Wehner.

Moms & Babies: Easy Animal Reader. Shiotsu. (Illus.). 16p. (J). (ps-1). 1996. pap. 2.49 (*1-57690-055-X*) Tchr Create Mat.

Moms & Dads Bilingual Coloring Book: Mamis y Papis Libro Bilingue para Iluminar. 2nd ed. Elizabeth Reid. (ENG & SPA., Illus.). 32p. (J). (gr. k-3). 1996. pap. 1.95 (*0-9627080-5-4*) In One EAR.

Moms & Their Young Spirited Boys: An Inspirational & Lighthearted Expose of Moms' Experiences with Their Young Male Charges. Erica T. Blakeney. (Illus.). 96p. 1998. pap. 8.95 (*0-9662451-0-5*) Publish It Write.

Moms & Their Young Spirited Boys Gift Set. Erica T. Blakeney. 96p. 1999. pap. 14.95 (*0-9662451-1-3*) Publish It Write.

Mom's Appreciation Book of Wit & Wisdom. Compiled by Annette H. LaPlaca. 96p. 1996. pap. 5.99 (*0-87788-548-6*, H Shaw Pubs) Waterbrook Pr.

Moms Aren't Wimps. Barbara Johnson. (Illus.). 1999. 9.99 (*0-8499-5349-9*) Word Pub.

***Moms Best Cheap-n-Easy Recipe Book.** Wayne R. Schultz. iv, 53p. (YA). 2000. pap. 15.00 (*1-929640-11-0*) N-Mas.

Mom's Big Activity Book for Building Little Characters. Rebecca Bertolini. 175p. 1992. pap. 12.99 (*0-89693-980-4*, 6-1980, Victor Bks) Chariot Victor.

Mom's Check-Up. Dottie McDowell. 104p. 1994. pap. 14.95 (*1-57326-019-3*) Core Ministries.

Mom's Come First: Enlightened Parenting. Dvorah Adler. 180p. 1999. pap. 14.95 (*1-887472-58-4*, Pub. by Sunstar Pubng) Brodart.

Mom's Daily Book of Memories. Dean Vaughn. (Daily Memory Bks.). 392p. 1994. 12.95 (*1-885952-00-7*) Vision Mktng.

Mom's Days, Dad's Days: A Divorced Parents Guide to Child Visitation. Gary Hackney. 132p. 1995. pap. 9.95 (*0-9648500-1-X*) G R Hackney.

Mom's Diary see Diario de Mama

Moms Don't Get Sick. Pat Brack. LC 90-60228. (Illus.). 124p. (Orig.). 1990. pap. 10.95 (*0-937603-07-4*) Melius Pub.

Moms Facilitators Guide. rev. ed. Paula Hagen et al. LC 92-40032. 184p. 1997. pap., teacher ed. 19.95 (*0-89390-409-0*) Resource Pubns.

***Moms Facilitator's Guide.** 3rd ed. Paula Hagen et al. LC 00-35246. 2000. write for info. (*0-89390-509-7*) Resource Pubns.

Mom's Football Book. Robert B. Jordan. (Illus.). iv, 130p. 1997. 14.95 (*0-9657701-0-9*) Hi Mom.

Mom's Gonna Have a Baby. large type ed. Illus. by Martha Ivery. 32p. (J). (gr. 1-3). 1999. pap. 12.95 (*1-57532-144-0*) Press-Tige Pub.

Mom's Guide to Baseball. (Mom's Guide to Sports Ser.: Vol. 3). 1997. pap. 2.95 (*1-889706-02-7*) Big Wrld Media.

Mom's Guide to Basketball. (Mom's Guide to Sports Ser.: Vol. 4). 1997. pap. 2.95 (*1-889706-03-5*) Big Wrld Media.

Mom's Guide to Discipling Your Child. Vicki Poretta & Ericka Lutz. LC 97-73175. 216p. 1997. 14.95 (*0-02-861950-1*) IDG Bks.

Mom's Guide to Field Hockey. (Mom's Guide to Sports Ser.: Vol. 5). 1997. pap. 2.95 (*1-889706-04-3*) Big Wrld Media.

Mom's Guide to Football. (Mom's Guide to Sports Ser.: Vol. 2). 1997. pap. 2.95 (*1-889706-01-9*) Big Wrld Media.

Mom's Guide to Golf. (Mom's Guide to Sports Ser.: Vol. 12). 1997. pap. 2.95 (*1-889706-11-6*) Big Wrld Media.

Mom's Guide to Ice Hockey. (Mom's Guide to Sports Ser.: Vol. 6). 1997. pap. 2.95 (*1-889706-05-1*) Big Wrld Media.

Mom's Guide to Men's Lacrosse. (Mom's Guide to Sports Ser.: Vol. 9). 1997. pap. 2.95 (*1-889706-08-6*) Big Wrld Media.

Mom's Guide to Nutrition. Vicki Poretta & Marcela Kogan. LC 97-73176. 179p. 1997. 14.95 (*0-02-861968-4*) Macmillan.

Mom's Guide to Raising a Good Student. Vicki Poretta & Marian E. Borden. LC 97-73173. (Illus.). 183p. 1997. 14.95 (*0-02-861942-0*) IDG Bks.

Mom's Guide to Soccer. (Mom's Guide to Sports Ser.: Vol. 1). 1997. pap. 2.95 (*1-889706-00-0*) Big Wrld Media.

Mom's Guide to Softball. (Mom's Guide to Sports Ser.: Vol. 7). 1997. pap. 2.95 (*1-889706-06-X*) Big Wrld Media.

Mom's Guide to Sports. Vicki Poretta. LC 97-73184. 182p. 1997. 14.95 (*0-02-861966-8*) Macmillan.

Mom's Guide to Tennis. (Mom's Guide to Sports Ser.: Vol. 11). 1997. pap. 2.95 (*1-889706-10-8*) Big Wrld Media.

Mom's Guide to Volleyball. (Mom's Guide to Sports Ser.: Vol. 8). 1997. pap. 2.95 (*1-889706-07-8*) Big Wrld Media.

Mom's Guide to Women's Lacrosse. (Mom's Guide to Sports Ser.: Vol. 10). 1997. pap. 2.95 (*1-889706-09-4*) Big Wrld Media.

***Mom's Handy Book of Backyard Games.** Pete Cava. (Illus.). 192p. 2000. pap. write for info. (*1-930546-43-2*) Wish Pub.

***Mom's Helper.** Jennifer Thompson. (Picture Me Ser.). (Illus.). (J). (ps-k). 2000. mass mkt. 6.99 (*1-57151-587-9*) Picture Me Bks.

Mom's Homecookin' LC 99-189591. 84p. 1997. write for info. (*0-934474-79-6*) Cookbook Pubs.

***Mom's Homemade Jams.** Kimberly Chambers. (Illus.). 1999. pap. 5.95 (*1-56245-383-1*) Great Quotations.

Mom's Homestyle Cooking: Simply Delicious from Idaho. Lovina C. Tuttle & Tedi T. Wixom. (Illus.). 150p. (Orig.). 1996. pap. 9.95 (*1-885227-20-5*) TNT Bks.

Mom's Horseradish Cook Book: The Only Horseradish Cook Book. Dianah Hodel Wade. (Illus.). 134p. pap. 9.95 (*0-9676609-0-4*) DHW Pubng.

Mom's House, Dad's House: A Complete Guide for Parents Who Are Separated, Divorced, or Living Apart. 2nd ed. Isolina Ricci. LC 97-29867. (Illus.). 381p. 1997. per. 13.00 (*0-684-83078-7*, Fireside) S&S Trade Pap.

Moms, How Are You Doing? Carolyn Buss. 1998. pap. text 8.99 (*1-884369-94-4*, EBED Pubns) McDougal Pubng.

Moms in Touch. F. Nichols. 1996. pap. 5.00 (*0-9628244-0-2*) Moms Touch Intl.

***Mom's Kitchen: Lost & Found.** Nancy B. Fillastre. (Illus.). 212p. 1999. spiral bd. 16.00 (*0-9679328-0-7*) Memory Creat.

Mom's Life. Kathryn Grody. 128p. (Orig.). 1991. pap. 7.95 (*0-380-76361-3*, Avon Bks) Morrow Avon.

***Mom's Little Book of Displaying Children's Art.** Lisa Bearnson. (Mom's Little Book Ser.). (Illus.). 96p. 2000. 16.95 (*1-929180-16-0*, Creating Keepsakes) Porchswing Pub.

***Mom's Little Book of Photo Tips.** Lisa Bearnson & Siobhan McGowan. LC 99-39153. (Mom's Little Book of... Tips Ser.). (Illus.). 96p. 1999. 16.95 (*1-929180-12-8*, Creating Keepsakes) Porchswing Pub.

Mom's Little Instruction Book. Annie Pigeon. 96p. 1994. pap. 4.99 (*0-7860-0009-0*, Pinncle Kensgtn) Kensgtn Pub Corp.

***Mom's Marijuana: Insights about Living.** Dan Shapiro. 224p. 2000. 22.95 (*0-609-60569-0*) Harmony Bks.

***Mom's Memories: Photo Memory Album.** Havoc Publishing Staff. 1999. write for info. (*1-57977-222-6*) Havoc Pub.

***Mom's Memory Book.** Cheryl Henderson. 2000. 19.99 (*1-56245-395-5*) Great Quotations.

Mom's Metal Men. Robin L. Armie. 181p. mass mkt. 4.99 (*1-55197-367-7*) Picasso Publ.

Mom's Metric Cookbook. Sandra J. Shirk-Heath. LC 86-90378. 150p. (J). (gr. 1-6). 1986. lib. bdg. write for info. (*0-9615104-0-4*) Shirk-Heath.

Mom's New Little Instruction Book. Annie Pigeon. 96p. 1995. pap. 4.99 (*0-7860-0140-2*, Pinncle Kensgtn) Kensgtn Pub Corp.

Moms on the Move: The Complete Fitness Guide for Pregnancy & Postpartum. Susan Lawler & Katherine Graham. (Illus.). x, 225p. (Orig.). 1996. pap., mass mkt. 15.95 (*1-889152-02-1*) Logan Hse Publns.

***Moms over Miles: An Activities Handbook for Strengthening Long Distance Relationships.** Aaron B. Larson. Ed. by Elizabeth A. Larson. 28p. 1999. pap. 6.95 (*0-9673599-1-0*) A E Family.

Mom's Packing Lists. rev. ed. KayLee Parker. (Illus.). 52p. 1995. pap. 4.95 (*1-883924-10-3*, 310) Your Moms Organizers.

***Mom's Playground, Ballfield, or Anywhere Workout: 4 Months to Fitness While Your Child Plays!** Jill Quentzel Winston. (Illus.). 2000. pap. 18.95 (*0-9675478-7-3*) Pearl Power Pubng.

***Mom's Pocket Guide to Watching Football.** Linda Wong & Kailee Wong. (Illus.). 128p. 2000. pap. 12.00 (*1-57500-149-7*, Pub. by TV Bks) HarpC.

***Mom's Practical Cookery.** S. Singh. 1998. pap. 50.00 (*81-86982-34-5*, Pub. by Business Pubns) St Mut.

Mom's Pregnant. Darlene Hoffa. LC 97-187939. 32p. (J). (ps-3). 1997. 6.99 (*0-570-04968-7*, 56-1841) Concordia.

***Mom's Saving Money: Surviving & Thriving on a Shoestring Budget.** Ann Fox & Susan Fox. LC 99-41566. (Tightwad Twins Ser.). 250p. 2000. pap. 9.99 (*0-7369-0200-7*) Harvest Hse.

Moms Say the Funniest Things. Bruce Lansky. (Illus.). 112p. 1992. pap. 6.00 (*0-671-74183-7*, Pub. by Meadowbrook) S&S Trade.

Moms Say the Funniest Things: A Collection of Motherly Wit & Wisdom. Bruce Lansky. LC 90-26455. (Illus.). 110p. 1992. pap. 6.00 (*0-88166-178-3*) Meadowbrook.

M

An Asterisk (*) at the beginning of an entry indicates that the title is appearing for the first time.

Mom's Search for Sanity: A Survival Kit. Thomas Bollard & Lisa R. Turner. LC 95-70528. (Illus.). 158p. (Orig.). 1995. pap. text 9.95 (0-9644552-4-2) SunRise Pbl.

Mom's Sore Throat. Maya Nahum-Valensi. (I Love to Read Collection). (Illus.). 48p. (J). (ps-3). 1992. lib. bdg. 12.79 (0-89565-807-0) Childs World.

***Mom's the Word.** Linda A. Carson et al. 112p. 2000. pap. 15.95 (0-88922-431-5, Pub. by Talonbks) SPD-Small Pr Dist.

***Mom's the Word: 9 Months Later, Vol. 926.** Roz Denny Fox. (Superromance Ser.). 2000. mass mkt. 4.50 (0-373-70926-9, 1-70926-0) Harlequin Bks.

***Mom's Updated Recipe Box.** Donna L. Weihofen. 304p. 2000. pap. 12.95 (1-58062-251-8) Adams Media.

Moms Who Have Changed the World: What You Can Learn from Their Stories. Lindsey O'Connor. LC 98-42735. 191p. 1999. pap. 9.99 (1-56507-655-9) Harvest Hse.

***Moms with ADD: A Self-Help Manual.** Christine Adamec. 2000. pap. 14.95 (0-87833-175-1) Taylor Pub.

Mom's Year 2000 K. I. S. S. (Keep It Simple, Sister) Guide. Lawndia White. 64p. 1999. pap. 19.95 (0-9670936-0-0) L White.

Mom's Year 2000 K. I. S. S. (Keep It Simple, Sister) Cookbook. Lawndia White. 64p. 1999. pap. 19.95 incl. audio (0-9670936-1-9) L White.

***MomSense: For Clueless Parents Everywhere.** 192p. 2000. pap. 13.00 (0-9679313-0-4) Old Mesquite Pubng.

MOMStories: Instant Inspiration for Mothers. Vickie L. Jennett & Paula Hagen. LC 98-27829. 80p. 1998. pap. 9.95 (0-89390-445-7) Resource Pubns.

Momular Science Momular Songs. Alexander Galahad. 1998. pap. 14.00 (1-886467-36-6) WJM Press.

Momus: Being the Nihilistic Deeds & Opinions of an Anti-Social Criminal: a Novella in a Box. Arnold Skemer. LC 97-67310. 64p. 1997. pap. 6.00 (0-932155-05-7) Phrygian Pr.

Momus Triumphans. Gerard Langbaine. LC 74-121838. reprint ed. 37.50 (0-404-03873-5) AMS Pr.

Momus Triumphans: or The Plagiaries of the English Stage: Expos'd in a Catalogue of All the Comedies, Tragi- Comedies, Masques, Tragedies, Opera's, Pastorals, Interludes. Gerard Langbaine. LC 92-24820. (Augustan Reprints Ser.: No. 150). 1971. reprint ed. 14.50 (0-404-70150-7, PR625) AMS Pr.

Momus Truimphans: The Plagiaries of the English Stage-Expos'd in a Catalogue. Gerard Langbaine. (English Stage Ser.: Vol. 19). 1974. lib. bdg. 61.00 (0-8240-0602-X) Garland.

Mon Abecedaire. Illus. by Hella Soyka.Tr. of Schatzsuche Im Buchstabenland. (FRE.). 18p. (J). (gr. k-2). 1989. 4.95 (0-922852-05-7, E008) Another Lang Pr.

***Mon Afrique: Photographs of Sub-Saharan Africa.** Pascal Maitre. (Illus.). 176p. 2000. 50.00 (0-89381-916-6) Aperture.

Mon Ami Godefroy. Helene Vachon. (Best-Sellers Ser.).Tr. of My Friend Godefroy. (FRE.). (J). (ps-2). 2000. pap., boxed set 9.95 incl. audio (2-921997-37-1) Coffragants.

Mon Ami le Traitre. Jose Giovanni. (FRE.). 245p. 1981. pap. 10.95 (0-7859-2449-3, 2070373215) Fr & Eur.

Mon Ami Maigret. Georges Simenon. (FRE.). pap. 3.95 (0-685-11401-5) Fr & Eur.

Mon Ami Pichou. Ginette Anfousse. (Jiji et Pichou Ser.). (FRE., Illus.). 24p. (YA). (ps up). 1979. pap. 6.95 (2-89021-014-6, Pub. by La Courte Ech) Firefly Bks Ltd.

Mon Ami Valentine see Other Woman

Mon Ange Marchera Devant Toi see My Angel Will Go Before You

Mon Beau Navire. Anne Wiazemski. (FRE.). 247p. 1991. pap. 10.95 (0-7859-4527-X, 207038408X) Fr & Eur.

***Mon Canard.** Stephen Rodefer. 128p. 2000. pap. 12.50 (1-930589-03-4, Pub. by Figures) SPD-Small Pr Dist.

Mon Chat see My Cat

Mon Cher Papa: Franklin & the Ladies of Paris. Claude A. Lopez. LC 66-12507. 418p. reprint ed. pap. 129.60 (0-8357-8230-1, 203380600087) Bks Demand.

Mon Cher Papa: Franklin & the Ladies of Paris. Claude-Anne Lopez. 424p. (C). 1990. reprint ed. 50.00 (0-300-04800-9); reprint ed. pap. 20.00 (0-300-04758-4) Yale U Pr.

Mon Chien see My Dog

Mon Chien Est un Elephant (My Dog Is An Elephant) Remy Simard. (Illus.). 32p. (J). (gr. 4-7). 1994. lib. bdg. 15.95 (1-55037-987-9, Pub. by Annick) Firefly Bks Ltd.

Mon Chien Est un Elephant (My Dog Is An Elephant) Remy Simard. (FRE., Illus.). 32p. (J). (ps-2). 1994. pap. 6.95 (1-55037-978-X, Pub. by Annick); lib. bdg. 15.95 (1-55037-979-8, Pub. by Annick) Firefly Bks Ltd.

Mon Dictionnaire de Cuisine. Alexandre Dumas. (FRE.). 1998. 29.95 (0-320-00207-1) Fr & Eur.

Mon Dictionnaire Francais - Anglais-Anglais - Anglais-Francais en Couleurs. Larousse Staff. 24.95 (0-317-45756-X) Fr & Eur.

Mon Faust see Oeuvres

Mon Faust. Paul Valery. (FRE.). 1988. pap. 10.95 (0-7859-2819-7) Fr & Eur.

Mon Faust. Paul Valery. (Folio Essais Ser.: No. 114). (FRE.). pap. 8.95 (2-07-032523-7) Schoenhof.

Mon Frere Yves. Ed. by Pierre P. Loti-Viaud & Michel Desbrueres. (FRE.). 320p. 1995. pap. 69.95 (2-86808-046-4) Intl Scholars.

Mon Grand Dictionnaire Francais-Anglais. (ENG & FRE.). (J). 23.50 (0-685-11402-3) Fr & Eur.

Mon Ismenie. Eugene Labiche. 9.95 (0-686-54232-0) Fr & Eur.

Mon Monde de Mots see My World of Words

Mon Oncle Jules: Level D. Guy de Maupassant. text 8.95 (0-88436-044-X) EMC-Paradigm.

Mon Oncle Oswald. Roald Dahl. (FRE.). 315p. 1986. pap. 11.95 (0-7859-2038-2, 2070377458) Fr & Eur.

Mon Papa. Debbie Bailey & Susan Huszar.Tr. of My Dad. (FRE., Illus.). 14p. (J). (ps). 1992. bds. 4.95 (1-55037-266-1, Pub. by Annick) Firefly Bks Ltd.

Mon Papa. Jean-Marc Reiser. (FRE.). 1976. pap. 10.95 (0-7859-4067-7) Fr & Eur.

Mon Pere et Moi. Francine Ruel. (Novels in the Roman Plus Ser.). (FRE., Illus.). 160p. (YA). (gr. 8 up). 1993. pap. 8.95 (2-89021-192-4, Pub. by La Courte Ech) Firefly Bks Ltd.

Mon Plus Bel Album de Mots Illustres. Linda Hendry. (FRE., Illus.). (J). pap. 11.99 (0-590-73945-X) Scholastic Inc.

Mon Premier Dictionnaire Larousse: Francais-Anglais, English-French. Marthe Fontaneau. (ENG & FRE.). 351p. 1988. 29.95 (0-7859-7429-6, 2034010728) Fr & Eur.

Mon Premier Dictionnaire l'Attrape-Mots-Hachette. M. Politzer. (FRE.). 237p. 1980. 29.95 (0-8288-1513-5, M10420) Fr & Eur.

Mon Premier Livre des Mots (My First French Word Book) A Bilingual Word Book. Angela Wilkes. Tr. by Annie Heminway. LC 92-54499. (My First Reference Ser.). (ENG & FRE., Illus.). 48p. (J). (gr. k-4). 1993. 12.95 (1-56458-254-X) DK Pub Inc.

Mon Reve: A Visual Record of Haiti since the Departure of the Duvaliers. Alternative Museum Staff. LC 89-81813. (Illus.). (C). 1989. pap. 12.00 (0-932075-27-4) Alternative Mus.

Mon-The Japanese Family Crest. Kei Chappelear & W. M. Hawley. (Illus.). 120p. 1994. pap. 35.00 (0-910704-93-7) Hawley.

Mon Univers. Pierre Teilhard De Chardin. pap. 6.95 (0-685-36599-9) Fr & Eur.

Mona. Lawrence Block. 144p. 1994. pap. 3.95 (0-7867-0105-6) Carroll & Graf.

Mona. Lawrence Block. LC 98-31418. 1999. 21.95 (0-7862-1705-7, Five Star MI) Mac Lib Ref.

Mona & the Dry Drunk & the Amazing Mystery of the Amygdala. Howie Shannon, pseud. LC 84-90254. (Illus.). 160p. 1985. 15.00 (0-9613943-0-7) J H Strunk.

Mona Dukess: Paperworks. Brockton Art Museum Publications Staff. Ed. by Peter J Baldaia. 8p. (Orig.). 1987. pap. 4.00 (0-934358-19-2) Fuller Mus Art.

Mona Hatoum. Guy Brett. (Illus.). 160p. 1997. pap. 29.95 (0-7148-3660-5, Pub. by Phaidon Press) Phaidon Pr.

Mona Hatoum. Mona Hatoum. LC 97-16345. 1997. pap. text 19.95 (0-933856-47-4) Mus Art Chicago.

Mona Hatoum. Giorgio Verzotti. 1999. pap. text 19.95 (88-8158-228-7) Charta.

Mona in the Promised Land. Gish Jen. 1997. pap. 12.00 (0-679-77650-8) Vin Bks.

Mona Lisa Mystery. large type ed. Pat Hutchins. (Illus.). (J). 1997. 16.95 (0-7451-8926-1, Galaxy Child Lrg Print) Chivers N Amer.

***Mona Lisa of Salem Street.** Jan Marino. 155p. (J). (gr. 3-6). 1999. reprint ed. text 15.00 (0-7881-6635-2) DIANE Pub.

Mona Lisa Overdrive. William Gibson. 320p. 1997. mass mkt. 6.99 (0-553-28174-7) Bantam.

***Mona Lisa Smiled a Little.** Rachel Wyatt. 204p. 1999. text 17.95 (0-88982-180-1, Pub. by Oolichan Bks) Genl Dist Srvs.

***Mona Lisa Smiled A Little.** Rachel Wyatt. 207p. 1999. pap. 40.00 (0-88982-176-3, Pub. by Oolichan Bks) Genl Dist Srvs.

Mona Lisa Smiles: Faces of Love. Harry Barba. LC 90-93457. 252p. 1993. 19.95 (0-911906-30-4); pap. 12.95 (0-911906-31-2) Harian Creative Bks.

Mona Lisa Smiles: Faces of Love. Harry Barba. 1993. 19.95 (0-614-06134-2) Harian Creative Bks.

Mona Lisa's Escort: Andre Malraux & the Reinvention of French Culture. Herman Lebovics. LC 98-30461. 1999. 29.95 (0-8014-3565-X, ILR Press) Cornell U Pr.

Mona Minium & the Smell of the Sun. Janet Frame. 96p. (J). (gr. 4-7). 1993. 17.95 (0-8076-1334-7) Braziller.

Mona, Queen of Lost Atlantis. J. L. Dryden. 169p. 1971. reprint ed. spiral bd. 10.00 (0-7873-0298-8) Hlth Research.

Mona Queen of Lost Atlantis an Idyllic: Re-Embodiment of Long Forgotten History (1925) J. L. Dryden. 109p. 1996. reprint ed. pap. 15.95 (1-56459-918-3) Kessinger Pub.

Mona Rogers in Person: A One Woman Play. Philip-Dimitri Galas. (Illus.). 64p. (Orig.). 1993. pap. 7.95 (0-9632454-1-4) Dimitri Pubns.

Mona Winks: Self-Guided Tours of Europe's Top Museums. 4th rev. ed. Rick Steves & Gene Openshaw. LC 98-22198. (Illus.). 432p. 1998. 19.95 (1-56261-421-5, Rick Steves) Avalon Travel.

Monaca Bridge & Selected Poems. Cynthia Marshall. 70p. (Orig.). 1996. pap. 6.95 (1-57502-348-2, PO1145) Morris Pubng.

Monacan Indian Cookbook, Vol. 1. (Illus.). 144p. 1998. pap. 10.00 (1-890306-11-8) Warwick Hse.

***Monacans & Miners: Native American & Coal Mining Communities in Appalachia.** Samuel R. Cook. LC 00-36502. (Illus.). 368p. 2000. text 65.00 (0-8032-1505-3); pap. text 29.95 (0-8032-6412-7, Bison Books) U of Nebr Pr.

Monachomachia-Wojna Mnichow. Ignacy Krasicki. (Illus.). 716p. 1984. 27.50 (0-318-23355-X) Szwede Slavic.

Monaco. Grace L. Hudson. LC 92-128514. (World Bibliographical Ser.). 230p. 1991. lib. bdg. 70.00 (1-85109-117-3) ABC-CLIO.

Monaco. Norbert Michel et al. (Illus.). 440p. 1998. 39.95 (3-8290-0658-6) MBI Pubg.

***Monaco: A Country Study Guide.** Global Investment & Business Center, Inc. Staff. (World Country Study Guides Library: Vol. 115). (Illus.). 350p. 2000. pap. 59.00 (0-7397-2413-4) Intl Business Pubns.

Monaco - A Country Study Guide: Basic Information for Research & Pleasure. Global Investment Center, USA Staff. (World Country Study Guide Library: Vol. 115). (Illus.). 350p. 1999. pap. 59.00 (0-7397-1512-7) Intl Business Pubns.

***Monaco Business Intelligence Report, 190 vols.** Global Investment & Business Center, Inc. Staff. (World Business Intelligence Library: Vol. 115). (Illus.). 350p. 2000. pap. 99.95 (0-7397-2613-7) Intl Business Pubns.

***Monaco Business Law Handbook, 190 vols.** Global Investment & Business Center, Inc. Staff. (Global Business Law Handbooks Library: Vol. 115). (Illus.). 350p. 2000. pap. 99.95 (0-7397-2013-9) Intl Business Pubns.

***Monaco Business Opportunity Yearbook.** Global Investment & Business Center, Inc. Staff. (Global Business Opportunity Yearbooks Library: Vol. 115). (Illus.). 2000. pap. 99.95 (0-7397-2213-1) Intl Business Pubns.

***Monaco Business Opportunity Yearbook: Export-Import, Investment & Business Opportunities.** International Business Publications, U. S. A. Staff & Global Investment Center, U. S. A. Staff. (Global Business Opportunity Yearbooks Library: Vol. 115). (Illus.). 350p. 1999. pap. 99.95 (0-7397-1313-2) Intl Business Pubns.

Monaco City Plan. (Grafocarte Maps Ser.). 1995. 8.95 (2-7416-0025-2, 80025) Michelin.

Monaco Cool. Robert Westgate. LC 92-28027. 176p. 1993. 14.95 (0-910155-23-2, Enigma Bks) Bartleby Pr.

***Monaco Country Review 2000.** Robert C. Kelly et al. (Illus.). 60p. 1999. pap. 39.95 (1-58310-539-5) CountryWatch.

***Monaco Foreign Policy & Government Guide.** Global Investment & Business Center, Inc. Staff. (World Foreign Policy & Government Library: Vol. 111). (Illus.). 350p. 1999. pap. 99.00 (0-7397-3609-4) Intl Business Pubns.

***Monaco Foreign Policy & Government Guide.** Global Investment & Business Center, Inc. Staff. (World Foreign Policy & Government Library: Vol. 111). (Illus.). 350p. 2000. pap. 99.95 (0-7397-3813-5) Intl Business Pubns.

***Monaco Government & Business Contacts Handbook: Strategic Government & Business Contacts for Conducting Succesful Business, Export-Import & Investment Activity, 110.** International Business Publications, USA Staff & Global Investment Center, USA Staff. (World Export-Import & Business Library: 54). (Illus.). 250p. 2000. pap. 99.95 (0-7397-6093-9) Intl Business Pubns.

***Monaco Investment & Business Guide.** Global Investment & Business Center, Inc. Staff. (Global Investment & Business Guide Library: Vol. 115). (Illus.). 2000. pap. 99.95 (0-7397-1813-4) Intl Business Pubns.

***Monaco Investment & Business Guide: Export-Import, Investment & Business Opportunities.** International Business Publications, USA Staff & Global Investment Center, USA Staff. (World Investment & Business Guide Library-99: Vol. 115). (Illus.). 350p. 1999. pap. 99.95 (0-7397-0310-2) Intl Business Pubns.

Monaco Sextet. K. Dorham. 1995. pap. text 20.00 (0-7935-4827-6, 00000660) H Leonard.

Monaco Tax Guide. Lefebvre. 1991. lib. bdg. 68.50 (90-6544-595-1) Kluwer Academic.

Monad: And Other Essays on the Higher Consciousness. Charles W. Leadbeater. 1997. 10.95 (81-7059-287-9) Theos Pub Hse.

Monad & Other Essays upon the Higher Consciousness. C. W. Leadbeater. 140p. 1997. reprint ed. pap. 19.95 (0-7661-0052-9) Kessinger Pub.

***Monad & Thou: Phenomenological Ontology of Human Being.** Hiroshi Kojima. LC 99-54676. 256p. 2000. text 39.95 (0-8214-1320-1, Ohio U Ctr Intl) Ohio U Pr.

Monad to Man: The Concept of Progress in Evolutionary Biology. Michael Ruse. (Illus.). 640p. 1996. 51.95 (0-674-58220-9) HUP.

Monadnock at the Millennium. Date not set. write for info. (0-9677023-0-5) Church & Main.

Monadnock Region. Robert B. Stephenson. LC 95-163232. (Images of America Ser.). 128p. 1994. pap. 14.99 (0-7524-0073-8) Arcadia Publng.

Monadnock Revelations: A Spiritual Memoir. Tom O'Connell. LC 96-92248. 125p. (Orig.). 1999. pap. 15.00 (0-9620318-5-2) Sanctuary Unltd.

Monadnock Sightings: Birds of Dublin, N. H. (Including Gerald H. Thayer's List of 1909) Elliot Allison et al. LC 79-13478. (Illus.). (Orig.). 1979. pap. 10.00 (0-87233-051-6) Bauhan.

Monadology see Rationalists: 5 Basic Works on Rationalism

***Monahan's Gamble.** Elizabeth Bevarly. 2001. mass mkt. 3.99 (0-373-76337-9, 1-76337-4) Silhouette.

Monarch: The Big Bear of Tallac. Ernest Thompson Seton. Ed. by William R. Jones. (Illus.). 1978. reprint ed. pap. 9.95 (0-89646-040-1) Vistabooks.

Monarch Butterflies. Helen Frost. LC 98-31718. (Butterflies Ser.). 1999. write for info. (0-7368-0229-0) Capstone Pr.

Monarch Butterflies. Helen Frost. 1999. 13.25 (0-516-21811-5) Capstone Pr.

Monarch Butterflies. Emilie U. Lepthien. LC 89-456. (New True Books Ser.). (Illus.). 48p. (J). (gr. k-4). 1989. lib. bdg. 21.00 (0-516-01165-0) Childrens.

Monarch Butterflies. Charles Rotter. (Nature Books Ser.). (Illus.). 32p. (J). (gr. 2-6). 1993. lib. bdg. 22.79 (0-89565-840-2) Childs World.

Monarch Butterflies, Mysterious Travelers. Bianca Lavies. (Illus.). 32p. (J). (gr. 3-6). 1993. 15.99 (0-525-44905-1, Dutton Child) Peng Put Young Read.

Monarch Butterfly. Gail Gibbons. LC 89-1880. (Illus.). 32p. (J). (gr. k-3). 1989. lib. bdg. 16.95 (0-8234-0773-X) Holiday.

Monarch Butterfly. Jean Thurman. 1985. pap. 5.95 (0-910286-96-5) Boxwood.

Monarch Butterfly. Gail Gibbons. LC 89-1880. (Illus.). 32p. (J). (gr. k-3). 1989. reprint ed. pap. 6.95 (0-8234-0909-0) Holiday.

***Monarch Butterfly.** rev. ed. Jean Thurman & Caroline Rodgers. (Illus.). 34p. (J). 1998. pap. 5.95 (1-890625-01-9) Otter B Bks.

Monarch Butterfly, No. 3059. David M. Schwartz. Ed. by Sue Lewis & Elaine Pascoe. (Lifecycle Ser.). 16p. 1999. pap. 2.99 (1-57471-579-8) Creat Teach Pr.

Monarch Butterfly: A Fragile Tissue in the Wind. 2nd ed. David W. Bouton. (Illus.). 94p. 1995. pap. 16.95 (1-881494-06-3, MB95P) Continuum Pubs.

Monarch Butterfly: A Fragile Tissue in the Wind. 3rd ed. David W. Bouton. (Illus.). 112p. 1999. pap. 26.75 (1-881494-15-2) ADP-Hollander.

Monarch Butterfly: International Traveler. Fred A. Urquhart. LC 97-45223. 1998. pap. 20.00 (0-940473-37-2) Wm Caxton.

Monarch Butterfly of Aster Way. Elizabeth Ring. (Smithsonian's Backyard Ser.: Vol. 17). (Illus.). 32p. (J). (ps-2). 1999. 15.95 (1-56899-568-7); 19.99 incl. audio (1-56899-570-9, BC5017); 43.95 (1-56899-571-7) Soundprints.

Monarch Butterfly of Aster Way, Incl. toy. Elizabeth Ring. (Smithsonian's Backyard Ser.: Vol. 17). (Illus.). 32p. (J). (ps-2). 1999. 32.95 (1-56899-572-5); 36.95 incl. audio (1-56899-574-1) Soundprints.

Monarch Butterfly of Aster Way: Micro Book. Elizabeth Ring. LC 98-42565. (Smithsonian's Backyard Ser.: No. 17). (Illus.). 32p. (J). (ps-2). 1999. 4.95 (1-56899-569-5) Soundprints.

Monarch Butterfly of Aster Way: Micro Book, Incl. toy. Elizabeth Ring. (Smithsonian's Backyard Ser.: Vol. 17). (Illus.). 32p. (J). (ps-2). 1999. 12.95 (1-56899-573-3) Soundprints.

Monarch Butterfly of Aster Way: Micro Edition, Incl. toy. Elizabeth Ring. (Smithsonian's Backyard Ser.: Vol. 17). (Illus.). 32p. (J). (ps-2). 1999. write for info. incl. audio (1-56899-575-X) Soundprints.

Monarch Butterfly's Life. John Himmelman. LC 98-40037. (Nature Upclose Ser.). 32p. (J). (gr. k-2). 1999. 24.00 (0-516-21147-1) Childrens.

***Monarch Butterfly's Life.** John Himmelman. (Nature Upclose Ser.). (J). 2000. pap. text 6.95 (0-516-26537-7) Childrens.

Monarch Magic! Butterfly Activities & Nature Discoveries. Lynn Rosenblatt. LC 98-34421. (Good Times Ser.: Vol. 2). (Illus.). 96p. (J). (ps-7). 1998. pap. 12.95 (1-885593-23-6) Williamson Pub Co.

Monarch Moby Dick. Herman Melville. 1976. 3.95 (0-671-00623-1, Arco) Macmillan Gen Ref.

Monarch Notes: Dashiell Hammett's the Maltese Falcon, the Thin Man & Other Works. Walter J. Miller. 128p. 1988. pap. 4.50 (0-671-67128-6, Arco) Macmillan Gen Ref.

Monarch Notes: Hardy's Far from the Madding Crowd. Elizabeth R. Nelson. (C). 1994. 3.95 (0-671-00890-0, Arc) IDG Bks.

Monarch Notes: Introduction to American Minority Literature. Ann Semel. (YA). 1999. pap. 3.99 (0-671-00962-1) Macmillan Gen Ref.

Monarch Notes: Isak Dinesen's Out of Africa. Roshlind Panepinto. 128p. 1988. pap. 4.50 (0-671-67127-8, Arco) Macmillan Gen Ref.

Monarch Notes: Simone De Beauvoir's the Second Sex. Rebecca Rass. 128p. 1988. pap. 4.50 (0-671-67126-X, Arco) Macmillan Gen Ref.

Monarch Notes: Toni Morrison's Beloved, The Bluest Eye & Other Stories. Eleanor Branch. 128p. 1988. pap. 4.50 (0-671-67129-4, Arco) Macmillan Gen Ref.

Monarch Notes Grapes of Wrath. Charlotte A. Alexander. (C). 3.95 (0-671-00692-4, Arco) Macmillan Gen Ref.

Monarch Notes on Aeschylus' Plays. Robert H. Ahrens, Jr. (Orig.). (C). 3.95 (0-671-00801-3, Arco) Macmillan Gen Ref.

Monarch Notes on Aristotle's Philosophy. Barbara Jancar. (Orig.). (C). 4.95 (0-671-00506-5, Arco) Macmillan Gen Ref.

Monarch Notes on Austen's Emma & Mansfield Park. William J. Fitzpatrick. (Orig.). (C). 3.95 (0-671-00704-1, Arco) Macmillan Gen Ref.

Monarch Notes on Babbitt. Monarch Notes Staff & Sinclair Lewis. (C). 3.95 (0-671-00683-5, Arco) Macmillan Gen Ref.

Monarch Notes on Beowulf. George Quasha. (Orig.). (C). 3.95 (0-671-00550-2, Arco) Macmillan Gen Ref.

Monarch Notes on Brecht's Plays. W. P. Kenney. (Orig.). (C). 4.25 (0-671-00551-0, Arco) Macmillan Gen Ref.

Monarch Notes on Bronte's Wuthering Heights. Emily Jane Bronte. (C). 3.95 (0-671-00603-7, Arco) Macmillan Gen Ref.

Monarch Notes on Cather's My Antonia & Other Works. Joan T. Nourse. (Orig.). (C). 3.50 (0-671-00604-5, Arco) Macmillan Gen Ref.

Monarch Notes on Cervantes' Don Quixote. Gregor Roy. (Orig.). (C). 3.95 (0-671-00553-7, Arco) Macmillan Gen Ref.

Monarch Notes on Chaucer's Canterbury Tales. Joseph Grennen. (Orig.). (C). 3.95 (0-671-00511-1, Arco) Macmillan Gen Ref.

Monarch Notes on Chekhov's Plays & Stories. Jane Wexford. (Orig.). (C). 4.25 (0-671-00554-5, Arco) Macmillan Gen Ref.

Monarch Notes on Coleridge's The Rime of the Ancient Mariner & Other Poems. John Elliott. (Orig.). (C). 3.95 (0-671-00778-5, Arco) Macmillan Gen Ref.

Monarch Notes on Conrad's Heart of Darkness & the Secret Sharer. James Weiss. (Orig.). (C). 3.95 (0-671-00817-X, Arco) Macmillan Gen Ref.

M

Monarch Notes on Conrad's Lord Jim & Other Works. Barnaby Conrad. (Orig.). (C). pap. 3.95 (*0-671-00605-3*, Arco) Macmillan Gen Ref.

Monarch Notes on Cooper's Last of the Mohicans. Charles Leavitt. (C). 3.95 (*0-671-00659-2*, Arco) Macmillan Gen Ref.

Monarch Notes on Dante's The Divine Comedy. Jules Gelernt. (Orig.). (C). 3.95 (*0-671-00510-3*, Arco) Macmillan Gen Ref.

Monarch Notes on Death of a Salesman. Arthur Miller. 1976. 3.95 (*0-671-00688-6*, Arco) Macmillan Gen Ref.

Monarch Notes on Defoe's Robinson Crusoe. Thomas A. Duff. (Orig.). (C). 3.95 (*0-671-00821-8*, Arco) Macmillan Gen Ref.

Monarch Notes on Descartes' Philosophy. Leo C. Daley. (Orig.). (C). 4.25 (*0-671-00527-8*, Arco) Macmillan Gen Ref.

Monarch Notes on Dickens' Bleak House. Edward Winans. (Orig.). (C). 3.95 (*0-671-00608-8*, Arco) Macmillan Gen Ref.

Monarch Notes on Dickens' David Copperfield. Ed. by Prentice Hall General Reference & Travel Staff. (C). 3.95 (*0-671-00609-6*, Arco) Macmillan Gen Ref.

Monarch Notes on Dickens' Great Expectations. Leonard Jenkin. (Orig.). (C). 3.95 (*0-671-00610-X*, Arco) Macmillan Gen Ref.

Monarch Notes on Dickens' Hard Times. Paul M. Ochojski. (Orig.). (C). 3.95 (*0-671-00823-4*, Arco) Macmillan Gen Ref.

Monarch Notes on Donne & the Metaphysical Poets. Joseph Grennen. (Orig.). (C). 3.95 (*0-671-00731-9*, Arco) Macmillan Gen Ref.

Monarch Notes on Dostoyevsky's Crime & Punishment. Frederic Tuten. (Orig.). (C). 3.95 (*0-671-00517-0*, Arco) Macmillan Gen Ref.

Monarch Notes on Dostoyevsky's The Brothers Karamazov. H. Richmond Neuville, Jr. (Orig.). (C). 3.95 (*0-671-00556-1*, Arco) Macmillan Gen Ref.

Monarch Notes on Dreiser's Sister Carrie. Charlotte Alexander. (Orig.). (C). 3.95 (*0-671-00662-2*, Arco) Macmillan Gen Ref.

Monarch Notes on Eliot's Silas Marner. T. S. Eliot. (C). 3.95 (*0-671-00612-6*, Arco) Macmillan Gen Ref.

Monarch Notes on Emerson's Writings. Charlotte Alexander. (Orig.). (C). 3.95 (*0-671-00663-0*, Arco) Macmillan Gen Ref.

Monarch Notes on Faulkner's Absalom, Absalom. Elizabeth C. Phillips. (Orig.). (C). 3.95 (*0-671-00664-9*, Arco) Macmillan Gen Ref.

Monarch Notes on Faulkner's As I Lay Dying. Leslie A. Juhasz. (Orig.). (C). 3.95 (*0-671-00665-7*, Arco) Macmillan Gen Ref.

Monarch Notes on Faulkner's Light in August. Leslie A. Juhasz. (Orig.). (C). 3.95 (*0-671-00666-5*, Arco) Macmillan Gen Ref.

Monarch Notes on Faulkner's Sound & the Fury. Ed. by Arco Editorial Staff. 4.50 (*0-671-00613-4*, Arco) Macmillan Gen Ref.

Monarch Notes on Fielding's Joseph Andrews. Joseph Grennen. (Orig.). (C). 3.25 (*0-671-00711-4*, Arco) Macmillan Gen Ref.

Monarch Notes on Fielding's Tom Jones. Grover Cronin. (Orig.). (C). pap. 2.95 (*0-685-03404-6*, Arco) Macmillan Gen Ref.

Monarch Notes on Flaubert's Madame Bovary & Three Tales. Arthur Rozen. (Orig.). (C). 3.95 (*0-671-00560-X*, Arco) Macmillan Gen Ref.

Monarch Notes on Forster's Passage to India & Howards End. Sandra M. Gilbert. (Orig.). (C). 3.95 (*0-671-00712-2*, Arco) Macmillan Gen Ref.

Monarch Notes on Frank's Diary of a Young Girl. Anne Frank. (C). 3.95 (*0-671-00561-8*, Arco) Macmillan Gen Ref.

Monarch Notes on Frost's Poetry. John D. Sweeney & James Lindroth. (Orig.). (C). pap. 3.50 (*0-685-03405-4*, Arco) Macmillan Gen Ref.

Monarch Notes on Goethe's Faust. Paul Montgomery. (Orig.). (C). 1989. 3.95 (*0-671-00521-9*, Arco) Macmillan Gen Ref.

Monarch Notes on Golding's Lord of the Flies & Other Works. Monarch Notes Staff & William Golding. (C). 3.95 (*0-671-00616-9*, Arco) Macmillan Gen Ref.

Monarch Notes on Graham Greene's Major Novels. Gregor Roy. (Orig.). (C). 4.25 (*0-671-00838-2*, Arco) Macmillan Gen Ref.

Monarch Notes on Hardy's Mayor of Casterbridge. Monarch Notes Staff & Thomas Hardy. (C). 3.95 (*0-671-00617-7*, Arco) Macmillan Gen Ref.

Monarch Notes on Hardy's Return of the Native. Charles Leavitt. (C). 3.95 (*0-671-00618-5*, Arco) Macmillan Gen Ref.

Monarch Notes on Hardy's Tess of the D'Urbervilles. Robert Ackerman. (Orig.). (C). 3.95 (*0-671-00619-3*, Arco) Macmillan Gen Ref.

Monarch Notes on Hawthorne's House of the Seven Gables, Marble Faun. Charles Leavitt. (C). 3.95 (*0-671-00670-3*, Arco) Macmillan Gen Ref.

Monarch Notes on Hawthorne's Scarlet Letter. Charles A. Leavitt. (C). 3.95 (*0-671-00620-7*, Arco) Macmillan Gen Ref.

Catch 22. Joseph Heller. (C). 1971. 3.95 (*0-671-00905-2*, Arco) Macmillan Gen Ref.

Catch 22. abr. ed. Joseph Heller. LC 73-750578. 1973. audio 14.00 (*0-694-50253-7*, SWC 1418, Caedmon) HarperAudio.

Monarch Notes on Hemingway's For Whom the Bell Tolls. Lawrenc H. Klibbe. (Orig.). (C). 3.95 (*0-671-00672-X*, Arco) Macmillan Gen Ref.

Monarch Notes on Hemingway's Major Novels. Stanley Cooperman. (Orig.). (C). 3.95 (*0-671-00621-5*, Arco) Macmillan Gen Ref.

Monarch Notes on Hemingway's The Snows of Kilimanjaro. Austin Fowler. (Orig.). (C). 3.95 (*0-671-00839-0*, Arco) Macmillan Gen Ref.

Monarch Notes on Hemingway's The Sun Also Rises. Lawrence Klebbe. (Orig.). (C). 3.95 (*0-671-00674-6*, Arco) Macmillan Gen Ref.

Monarch Notes on Homer's Iliad. Homer. (Orig.). (C). 3.95 (*0-671-00501-4*, Arco) Macmillan Gen Ref.

Monarch Notes on Huxley's Brave New World, Point Counter Point & Other Works. Paul Gannon. (Orig.). (C). 3.95 (*0-671-00714-9*, Arco) Macmillan Gen Ref.

Monarch Notes on Ibsen's Plays. Edward Byrnes. (Orig.). (C). 3.95 (*0-671-00562-6*, Arco) Macmillan Gen Ref.

Monarch Notes on James' Portrait of a Lady. Vartkis Kinoian. (Orig.). (C). 3.95 (*0-671-00679-7*, Arco) Macmillan Gen Ref.

Monarch Notes on James' Washington Square. Ralph A. Ranald. (Orig.). (C). 3.95 (*0-671-00846-3*, Arco) Macmillan Gen Ref.

Monarch Notes on Joyce's Portrait of the Artist As a Young Man & Dubliners. George Quasha. (Orig.). (C). 3.95 (*0-671-00563-4*, Arco) Macmillan Gen Ref.

Monarch Notes on Kafka's The Trial, The Castle & Other Works. Gregor Roy. (Orig.). (C). 3.95 (*0-671-00847-1*, Arco) Macmillan Gen Ref.

Monarch Notes on Keats' Poetry. Elliot Gilbert. (Orig.). (C). 3.95 (*0-671-00785-8*, Arco) Macmillan Gen Ref.

Monarch Notes on Kesey's One Flew over the Cuckoos Nest. John Gatto. 1975. 3.95 (*0-671-00966-4*, Arco) Macmillan Gen Ref.

Monarch Notes on Lawrence's Sons & Lovers & Other Works. Sandra M. Gilbert. (Orig.). (C). 3.95 (*0-671-00716-5*, Arco) Macmillan Gen Ref.

Monarch Notes on Locke's & Hobbes' Philosophy. Sugwon Kang. (Orig.). (C). 3.95 (*0-671-00531-6*, Arco) Macmillan Gen Ref.

Monarch Notes on Machiavelli's The Prince. Robert Sobel. (Orig.). (C). 3.95 (*0-671-00565-0*, Arco) Macmillan Gen Ref.

Monarch Notes on Marlowe's Dr. Faustus & Other Writings. Peter Mullany. (Orig.). (C). 3.95 (*0-671-00717-3*, Arco) Macmillan Gen Ref.

Monarch Notes on Marxist & Utopian Socialists. Ed. by Monarch Staff. (J). (gr. 7-12). 3.95 (*0-671-00544-8*, Arco) Macmillan Gen Ref.

Monarch Notes on Miller's Crucible & View from the Bridge. Joan T. Nourse. (Orig.). (C). 3.95 (*0-671-00687-8*, Arco) Macmillan Gen Ref.

Monarch Notes on Milton's Paradise Lost. Mariam Seldin. (Orig.). (C). 3.95 (*0-671-00513-8*, Arco) Macmillan Gen Ref.

Monarch Notes on Moliere's Plays. Lawrence H. Klibbe. (Orig.). (C). 3.95 (*0-671-00568-5*, Arco) Macmillan Gen Ref.

Monarch Notes on More's Utopia. John W. Elliott. (Orig.). (C). 3.95 (*0-671-00856-0*, Arco) Macmillan Gen Ref.

Monarch Notes on Mythology. Ed. by Monarch Staff. (C). 3.95 (*0-671-00523-5*, Arco) Macmillan Gen Ref.

Monarch Notes on Of Mice & Men. John Steinbeck. 1989. 3.95 (*0-671-00693-2*, Arco) Macmillan Gen Ref.

Monarch Notes on O'Neill's Desire under the Elms. Date not set. pap. 3.25 (*0-671-00750-5*, Arco) Macmillan Gen Ref.

Monarch Notes on O'Neill's Long Day's Journey into Night. Paul Gannon. (Orig.). (C). 4.25 (*0-671-00752-1*, Arco) Macmillan Gen Ref.

Monarch Notes on O'Neill's Plays. David Rogers. (Orig.). (C). 3.95 (*0-671-00627-4*, Arco) Macmillan Gen Ref.

George Orwell's 1984. Ralph A. Ranald. (C). 3.95 (*0-671-00719-X*, Arco) Macmillan Gen Ref.

Monarch Notes on Pope's Rape of the Lock & Other Poems. Gregor Roy. (Orig.). (C). 4.25 (*0-671-00788-2*, Arco) Macmillan Gen Ref.

Monarch Notes on Remarque's All Quiet on the Western Front. John S. White. (Orig.). (C). 3.95 (*0-671-00861-7*, Arco) Macmillan Gen Ref.

Monarch Notes on Rousseau & the Eighteenth Century Political Philosophers. Edward Johnson. (Orig.). (C). 3.95 (*0-671-00536-7*, Arco) Macmillan Gen Ref.

Monarch Notes on Salinger's Franny & Zooey, Nine Stories. Charlotte Alexander. (Orig.). (C). 3.95 (*0-671-00866-8*, Arco) Macmillan Gen Ref.

Monarch Notes on Sartre's No Exit, the Flies & Other Writings. Leslie A. Juhasz. (Orig.). (C). 3.95 (*0-671-00569-3*, Arco) Macmillan Gen Ref.

Monarch Notes on Scott's Ivanhoe & Other Works. Sir Walter Scott. (C). 3.95 (*0-671-00628-2*, Arco) Macmillan Gen Ref.

Monarch Notes on Shakespeare's A Midsummer Night's Dream. Eve Leoff. (Orig.). (C). 3.95 (*0-671-00638-X*, Arco) Macmillan Gen Ref.

Monarch Notes on Shakespeare's Antony & Cleopatra. William Walsh. (Orig.). (C). 3.95 (*0-671-00630-4*, Arco) Macmillan Gen Ref.

Monarch Notes on Shakespeare's As You Like It. Pineas Rainer. (Orig.). (C). 3.95 (*0-671-00631-2*, Arco) Macmillan Gen Ref.

Monarch Notes on Shakespeare's Hamlet. William Shakespeare. (Orig.). (C). 3.95 (*0-671-00514-6*, Arco) Macmillan Gen Ref.

Monarch Notes on Shakespeare's Henry Fourth, Pt. 2. Frances Barasch. (Orig.). (C). 3.95 (*0-671-00634-7*, Arco) Macmillan Gen Ref.

Monarch Notes on Shakespeare's Henry IV, Part I (Monarch Notes), Vol. 1, Pt. 1. William Shakespeare. 3.95 (*0-671-00633-9*, Arco) Macmillan Gen Ref.

Monarch Notes on Shakespeare's King Lear. William Shakespeare. (C). 3.95 (*0-671-00515-4*, Arco) Macmillan Gen Ref.

Monarch Notes on Shakespeare's Richard Second. Mary H. Scanlan. (Orig.). (C). 3.95 (*0-671-00641-X*, Arco) Macmillan Gen Ref.

Monarch Notes on Shakespeare's Selected Comedies. Margaret L. Ranald. (Orig.). (C). 4.25 (*0-671-00629-0*, Arco) Macmillan Gen Ref.

Monarch Notes on Shakespeare's Sonnets. Unicio J. Violi. (Orig.). (C). 3.95 (*0-671-00653-3*, Arco) Macmillan Gen Ref.

Monarch Notes on Shakespeare's Taming of the Shrew. Margaret L. Ranald. (Orig.). (C). 3.95 (*0-671-00654-1*, Arco) Macmillan Gen Ref.

Monarch Notes on Shakespeare's The Tempest. Ralph A. Ranald. (Orig.). (C). 3.95 (*0-671-00644-4*, Arco) Macmillan Gen Ref.

Monarch Notes on Shakespeare's Twelfth Night. Sandra M. Gilbert. (Orig.). (C). 3.95 (*0-671-00645-2*, Arco) Macmillan Gen Ref.

Monarch Notes on Shakespeare's Winter's Tale. Margaret L. Ranald. (Orig.). (C). 3.95 (*0-671-00656-8*, Arco) Macmillan Gen Ref.

Monarch Notes on Shaw's Plays. Robert Rockman. 4.25 (*0-671-00646-0*, Arco) Macmillan Gen Ref.

Monarch Notes on Shaw's Pygmalion. Grace H. Schwartz. (Orig.). (C). 3.50 (*0-671-00724-6*, Arco) Macmillan Gen Ref.

Monarch Notes on Shaw's Saint Joan. Grace H. Schwartz. (Orig.). (C). 3.50 (*0-671-00725-4*, Arco) Macmillan Gen Ref.

Monarch Notes on Sophocles' Plays. William Walter. (Orig.). (C). 3.95 (*0-671-00507-3*, Arco) Macmillan Gen Ref.

Monarch Notes on Spenser's Faerie Queene & Other Works. William Grace. (Orig.). (C). 3.95 (*0-671-00512-X*, Arco) Macmillan Gen Ref.

Monarch Notes on Steinbeck's Major Novels. John Steinbeck. (C). 4.50 (*0-671-00647-9*, Arco) Macmillan Gen Ref.

Monarch Notes on Swift's Gulliver's Travels. Richard Feingold. (Orig.). (C). 3.95 (*0-671-00648-7*, Arco) Macmillan Gen Ref.

Monarch Notes on Tennessee Williams' Major Plays. Benjamin Nelson. (Orig.). (C). 3.95 (*0-671-00650-9*, Arco) Macmillan Gen Ref.

Monarch Notes on Thackeray's Vanity Fair & Henry Esmond. Elliot Gilbert. (Orig.). (C). 3.95 (*0-671-00727-0*, Arco) Macmillan Gen Ref.

Monarch Notes on the New Testament. Unicio J. Violi. (Orig.). (C). 4.95 (*0-671-00625-8*, Arco) Macmillan Gen Ref.

Monarch Notes on Thoreau's Walden & Other Writings. Charlotte Alexander. (Orig.). (C). 3.95 (*0-671-00695-9*, Arco) Macmillan Gen Ref.

Monarch Notes on Tolkien's Fellowship of the Ring. Louis Morrison. 1975. 3.25 (*0-671-00971-0*, Arco) Macmillan Gen Ref.

Monarch Notes on Tolstoy's Anna Karenina. Herbert Reaske. (Orig.). (C). 3.95 (*0-671-00571-5*, Arco) Macmillan Gen Ref.

Monarch Notes on Tolstoy's War & Peace. Austin Fowler. (Orig.). (C). 4.25 (*0-671-00572-3*, Arco) Macmillan Gen Ref.

Monarch Notes on Turgenev's Fathers & Sons. Jane Wexford. (Orig.). (C). 3.95 (*0-671-00877-3*, Arco) Macmillan Gen Ref.

Monarch Notes on Twain's A Connecticut Yankee in King Arthur's Court. Charles Leavitt. (Orig.). (C). 3.95 (*0-671-00879-X*, Arco) Macmillan Gen Ref.

Monarch Notes on Updike's Rabbit Run & Rabbit Redux. Samuel Beckoff. 1974. 4.25 (*0-671-00947-8*, Arco) Macmillan Gen Ref.

Monarch Notes on Virgil's Aeneid & Other Works. Julia Loomis. (Orig.). (C). 4.95 (*0-671-00509-X*, Arco) Macmillan Gen Ref.

Monarch Notes on Voltaire's Candide & Philosophies. Robert Sobel. (Orig.). (C). 4.50 (*0-671-00545-6*, Arco) Macmillan Gen Ref.

Monarch Notes on Warren's All the King's Men. George B. Gerhard. (Orig.). (C). 3.25 (*0-671-00697-5*, Arco) Macmillan Gen Ref.

Monarch Notes on Wells Invisible Man, War of the Worlds & Other Works. Randall Keenan. (C). 1969. 4.25 (*0-671-00766-1*, Arco) Macmillan Gen Ref.

Monarch Notes on Whitman's Leaves of Grass. Randall Keenan. (Orig.). (C). 3.95 (*0-671-00736-X*, Arco) Macmillan Gen Ref.

Monarch Notes on Wilde's Plays. Grace H. Schwartz. (Orig.). (C). 3.95 (*0-671-00881-1*, Arco) Macmillan Gen Ref.

Monarch Notes on Williams' Glass Menagerie. Gilbert Rathbun. (Orig.). (C). 3.95 (*0-671-00700-9*, Arco) Macmillan Gen Ref.

Monarch Notes on Williams' Street-Car Named Desire. Gilbert Rathbun. (Orig.). (C). 3.95 (*0-671-00701-7*, Arco) Macmillan Gen Ref.

Monarch Notes on Wolfe's Look Homeward Angel, Of Time & the River & Other Writings. Terence Dewsnap. (Orig.). (C). 3.95 (*0-671-00702-5*, Arco) Macmillan Gen Ref.

Monarch Notes on Woolf's Mrs. Dalloway & to the Lighthouse. Sandra M. Gilbert. (C). 3.95 (*0-671-00883-8*, Arco) Macmillan Gen Ref.

Monarch Notes on Wordsworth's Poetry. John Elliott. (Orig.). (C). 3.95 (*0-671-00729-7*, Arco) Macmillan Gen Ref.

Monarch Notes on Yeats' Poetry. Sandra M. Gilbert. (Orig.). (C). 4.50 (*0-671-00738-6*, Arco) Macmillan Gen Ref.

Monarch Notes on Zola's Germinal. Carolyn Welch. 1974. 3.50 (*0-671-00948-6*, Arco) Macmillan Gen Ref.

Monarch of All I Survey: Bechuanaland Diaries, 1929-1937. Charles Rey. Ed. by Neil Parsons & Michael Crowder. LC 87-12570. (Illus.). 282p. 1988. text 39.50 (*0-936508-22-1*) Barber Pr.

Monarch Quick & Easy Notes: "Canterbury Tales" by Chaucer. Geoffrey Chaucer. write for info. (*0-318-58791-2*) S&S Trade.

Monarch Quick & Easy Notes: "David Copperfield" by Charles Dickens. Charles Dickens. write for info. (*0-318-58792-0*) S&S Trade.

Monarch Quick & Easy Notes: "Great Expectations" by Charles Dickens. Charles Dickens. write for info. (*0-318-58793-9*) S&S Trade.

Monarch Quick & Easy Notes: "Nineteen Eighty-Four" by George Orwell. George Orwell. write for info. (*0-318-58794-7*) S&S Trade.

Monarch Quick & Easy Notes: "Wuthering Heights" by Emily Bronte. Emily Jane Bronte. write for info. (*0-318-58789-0*) S&S Trade.

Monarch the Big Bear. Ernest Thompson Seton. (Illus.). 213p. (YA). 1994. pap. 14.95 (*1-885529-01-5*) Stevens Pub.

Monarch, the Snow Goose & the Butterfly Tree. Gertrude Stonesifer. LC 98-67050. (Illus.). 32p. 1998. pap. 9.95 (*1-878044-66-4*) Mayhaven Pub.

Monarchic Principle: Studies in Jewish Self-Government in Antiquity. David Goodblatt. (Texte und Studien Zum Antiken Judentum: No. 38). 336p. 1994. 137.50 (*3-16-146176-2*, Pub. by JCB Mohr) Coronet Bks.

Monarchist. John B. Jones. (Notable American Authors Ser.). 1992. reprint ed. lib. bdg. 75.00 (*0-7812-3518-9*) Rprt Serv.

Monarchs. Photos by Christopher Knight. LC 92-33972. (Illus.). 64p. (J). (gr. 3-7). 1993. pap. 10.00 (*0-15-255297-9*, Gulliver Bks) Harcourt.

Monarchs. Kathryn Lasky. 1993. 15.20 (*0-606-12426-8*, Pub. by Turtleback) Demco.

Monarchs: A Poem Sequence. Alison H. Deming. 88p. 1997. pap. 12.95 (*0-8071-2231-9*); text 19.95 (*0-8071-2230-0*) La State U Pr.

Monarchs & Ministers: The Grand Council in Mid-Ch'ing China, 1723-1820. Beatrice S. Bartlett. (Illus.). 417p. 1990. 60.00 (*0-520-06591-3*, Pub. by U CA Pr) Cal Prin Full Svc.

Monarchs & Ministers: The Grand Council in Mid-Ch'ing China, 1723-1820. Beatrice S. Bartlett. (Illus.). 417p. (C). 1994. pap. 22.50 (*0-520-08645-7*, Pub. by U CA Pr) Cal Prin Full Svc.

Monarchs Are Flying. Marion Foster. LC 87-23160. 218p. (Orig.). 1987. pap. 8.95 (*0-932379-33-8*); lib. bdg. 18.95 (*0-932379-34-6*) Firebrand Bks.

Monarchs Are Flying. Marion Foster. 217p. (Orig.). pap. write for info. (*0-88961-120-3*, Pub. by Womens Pr) LPC InBook.

Monarch's Complete Guide to Law Schools. Arline Glotzer. (Illus.). 192p. (Orig.). 1981. 6.95 (*0-671-09192-1*, Arco) Macmillan Gen Ref.

Monarch's Feast: A World of Recipes from the Mary Munford Community. Mumford PTA Staff. (Illus.). 545p. 1997. pap. 17.95 (*0-9660007-0-6*) M Munford.

Monarchs in Conflict. Kagan. 2000. pap. text. write for info. (*0-312-20260-1*) St Martin.

Monarch's Math Review GMAT. 1987. pap. 8.95 (*0-317-56765-9*) PB.

Monarchs, Ministers, & Maps: The Emergence of Cartography As a Tool of Government in Early Modern Europe. Ed. by David Buisseret. LC 91-36088. (Kenneth Nebenzahl, Jr., Lectures in the History of Cartography). (Illus.). 202p. 1992. 49.95 (*0-226-07987-2*) U Ch Pr.

***Monarchs, Murders & Mistresses: A Book of Royal Days.** David Hilliam. 368p. 2000. 27.95 (*0-7509-2440-3*) Sutton Publng.

Monarchs of the Nile. Aidan Dodson. (Illus.). 256p. 1995. 32.50 (*0-948695-20-X*, Pub. by Rubicon Pr); pap. 24.95 (*0-948695-21-8*, Pub. by Rubicon Pr) David Brown.

***Monarchs of the Sea: The Great Ocean Liners.** Kurt Ulrich. (Illus.). 264p. 2000. 75.00 (*1-86064-373-6*, Pub. by I B T) St Martin.

Monarch's Preparation CLEP. 1987. pap. 8.95 (*0-317-56753-5*) PB.

Monarch's Preparation for the High School Competency Test in Reading & Math. 1987. pap. 6.95 (*0-317-56763-2*) PB.

Monarch's Preparation for the Real Estate Salesperson's License Examination. 1987. pap. 8.95 (*0-317-56762-4*) PB.

Monarch's Preparation GED. 1987. pap. 8.95 (*0-317-56751-9*) PB.

Monarch's Preparation GRE. 1987. pap. 8.95 (*0-317-56748-9*) PB.

Monarch's Preparation GRE: Psychology. 1987. pap. 6.95 (*0-317-56757-8*) PB.

Monarch's Preparation LSAT. 1987. pap. 8.95 (*0-685-18024-7*) PB.

Monarch's Preparation MAT. 1987. pap. 7.95 (*0-317-56760-8*) PB.

Monarch's Preparation SAT. Monarch Books Staff. pap. 8.95 (*0-317-56747-0*) PB.

Monarch's Preparation TOEFL. 1987. pap. 8.95 (*0-317-56756-X*) PB.

Monarchs, Rulers, Dynasties & Kingdoms of the World. R. F. Tapsell. LC 82-15726. 511p. reprint ed. pap. 158.50 (*0-7837-2668-6*, 204303300006) Bks Demand.

***Monarch's Son.** Valerie Parv. (Romance Ser.: Bk. 1459). 2000. mass mkt. 3.50 (*0-373-19459-5*, 1-19459-6) Silhouette.

Monarchy & Community: Politial Ideas in the Later Conciliar. 3rd ed. Anthony Black. LC 72-108101. (Cambridge Studies in Medieval Life & Thought: Vol. 2, 3rd). 201p. reprint ed. pap. 57.30 (*0-608-30062-4*, 2022436) Bks Demand.

Monarchy & Consent: The Coronation Book of Charles V of France. Carra F. O'Meara. (Illus.). 350p. 1999. text 95.00 (*1-872501-10-9*) Gordon & Breach.

An Asterisk (*) at the beginning of an entry indicates that the title is appearing for the first time.

Monarchy & Incest in Renaissance England: Literature, Culture, Kinship, & Kingship. Bruce T. Boehrer. LC 91-46228. (New Cultural Studies). 224p. (C). 1992. text 29.95 (0-8122-3134-1) U of Pa Pr.

Monarchy & Matrimony: The Courtships of Elizabeth I. Susan Doran. LC 95-9080. (Illus.). 296p. (C). 1996. 50.00 (0-415-11969-3) Routledge.

Monarchy & the Constitution. Vernon Bogdanor. LC 95-634. 344p. 1996. text 45.00 (0-19-827769-5, Clarendon Pr) OUP.

Monarchy & the Constitution. Vernon Bogdanor. 340p. 1998. reprint ed. pap. text 32.00 (0-19-829334-8) OUP.

Monarchy in Hawaii. 2nd ed. John D. Holt. 1995. reprint ed. pap. 4.95 (0-914916-00-9) Ku Paa.

Monarchy in Nepal: Tribhuvan Era. Kusum Shreshtha. 1985. 27.00 (0-8364-1376-8, Pub. by Popular Prakashan) S Asia.

Monarchy in the Emperor's Eyes: Image & Reality in the Chien-Lung Reign. Harold L. Kahn. LC 75-135546. 339p. 1971. reprint ed. pap. 105.10 (0-7837-2281-8, 205736900004) Bks Demand.

Monarchy, Magnates & Institutions in the Anglo-Norman World. Warren C. Hollister. 310p. 1986. 60.00 (0-907628-50-8) Hambledon Press.

Monarchy of Capetian France & Royal Ceremonial. Elizabeth A. Brown. (Collected Studies: No. CS 345). 350p. 1991. text 115.95 (0-86078-279-4, Pub. by Variorum) Ashgate Pub Co.

Monarchy, the Estates & the Aristocracy in Renaissance France. J. Russell Major. (Collected Studies: No. CS279). 298p. (C). 1988. reprint ed. text 101.95 (0-86078-227-1, Pub. by Variorum) Ashgate Pub Co.

Monarchy to Republic: Australian Republican Government. Ed. by George Winterton. (Illus.). 230p. 1995. pap. text 35.00 (0-19-554562-1) OUP.

Monarchy Transformed, Vol. 6. Mark Kishlansky. LC 98-100488. 400p. 1997. pap. 14.95 (0-14-014827-2) Viking Penguin.

Monash As Military Commander. P. A. Pedersen. 380p. 1992. pap. 24.95 (0-522-84504-5, Pub. by Melbourne Univ Pr) Paul & Co Pubs.

Monasteriales Indicia: The Anglo-Saxon Monastic Sign Language. Ed. & Tr. by Debby Banham. 96p. 1993. pap. 14.95 (0-9516209-4-0, Pub. by Anglo-Saxon Bks) Paul & Co Pubs.

***Monasteries & Patrons in the Groze Reform: Lotharingia C 850-1000.** John Nightingale. (Oxford Historical Monographs). (Illus.). 370p. 2000. text 95.00 (0-19-820835-9) OUP.

Monasteries in South Asia. Swami Swahananda. 1990. pap. 4.95 (0-87481-047-7) Vedanta Pr.

***Monasteries in the Landscape.** Mick Aston. (Illus.). 176p. 2000. pap. 24.99 (0-7524-1491-7, Pub. by Tempus Pubng) Arcadia Publng.

Monasteries of Gyantse, 3 vols., Set. Giuseppe Tucci. (C). 1989. 210.00 (0-8364-2490-5, Pub. by Aditya Prakashan) S Asia.

Monasteries of the Wadi 'n Natrun: Metropolitan Museum of Art Egyptian Expedition Publications, 3 vols., Set. Hugh G. White & Walter Hauser. Incl. Vol. 1. New Coptic Texts from the Monastery of Saint Macarius. LC 77-168409. (Illus.). 308p. 1973. reprint ed. 63.95 (0-405-02243-3); Vol. 3. LC 77-168409. (Illus.). 480p. 1973. reprint ed. 63.95 (0-405-02245-X); LC 77-168409. (Metropolitan Museum of Art Publications in Reprint). (Illus.). 1340p. 1973. 189.95 (0-405-02242-5) Ayer.

Monasteries of Western Europe. rev. ed. Wolfgang Braunfels. LC 91-67805. (Illus.). 264p. 1993. reprint ed. pap. 34.95 (0-500-27201-8, Pub. by Thames Hudson) Norton.

Monasterio Magico. Idries Shah. (SPA.). 1992. pap. 15.00 (84-7509-139-3) Paidos Iberica.

Monasterios de Espana. 5th ed. Palacio P. Navascues. (Illus.). 334p. 1988. 295.00 (84-239-5271-1) Elliots Bks.

Monastery. David Birt. (Resource Units: Middle Ages, 1066-1485 Ser.). (Illus.). 1974. pap. text, teacher ed. 12.95 (0-582-39380-9) Longman.

Monastery. J. N. Williamson. 352p. 1992. mass mkt. 4.99 (0-8217-3797-X, Zebra Kensgtn) Kensgtn Pub Corp.

Monastery. Charles E. Ziavras. LC 85-81279. (Illus.). 1985. 12.95 (0-915940-05-1); pap. 4.95 (0-915940-06-X) Ithaca Pr MA.

Monastery see Works of Sir Walter Scott

Monastery: A Study of Freedom, Love, & Community. George A. Hillery, Jr. LC 91-46757. 328p. 1992. 65.00 (0-275-94173-6, C4173, Praeger Pubs) Greenwood.

Monastery Nightmare. Ross H. Spencer. 240p. 1986. reprint ed. 15.45 (0-89296-233-X, Pub. by Mysterious Pr) Little.

Monastery of Epiphanius at Thebes, 2 bks., 1 vol. (Metropolitan Museum of Art Egyptian Expedition Publications: Vol. 4). 1973. reprint ed. 48.95 (0-405-02251-4) Ayer.

Monastery of Epiphanius at Thebes, 2 bks., 1 vol., Pt. 1. Incl. Archaeological Material. H. E. Winlock. 1972. Coptic Ostraca & Papyri. W. E. Crum. Greek Ostraca & Papyri. H. G. White. Literary Material. W. E. Crum. 1972. (Metropolitan Museum of Art Egyptian Expedition Publications: Vol. 3). 1973. reprint ed. 48.95 (0-405-02250-6) Ayer.

Monastery of Epiphanius at Thebes: Metropolitan Museum of Art Egyptian Expedition Publications, Vols. 3 & 4, 2 vols., Set. Herbert E. Winlock et al. LC 72-168413. (Metropolitan Museum of Art Publication in Reprint Ser.). 1973. 96.95 (0-405-02249-2) Ayer.

Monastery of Saint Catherine in Sinai. Jill Kamil. (Illus.). 96p. 1991. pap. text 12.00 (977-424-255-6, Pub. by Am Univ Cairo Pr) Col U Pr.

Monastery of the Assumption: A History. Mother Thekla. (The Library of Othodox Thinking). 30p. 1991. pap. 4.00 (0-920669-22-0, Pub. by Peregrina Pubng) Cistercian Pubns.

Monastic: An Ordained Tibetan Buddhist Speaks on Behalf of Full Ordination for Women. Mary T. Coleman. (Illus.). 117p. (Orig.). 1995. pap. write for info. (0-9646569-0-6) Dharma Inst.

Monastic & Religious Orders in Britain, 1000-1300. Janet Burton. (Cambridge Medieval Textbooks Ser.). (Illus.). 367p. (C). 1994. text 69.95 (0-521-37441-3); pap. text 22.95 (0-521-37797-8) Cambridge U Pr.

Monastic Architecture in France: From the Renaissance to the Revolution. Joan Evans. LC 64-2430. (Illus.). 649p. reprint ed. pap. 180.00 (0-608-11331-X, 2050739) Bks Demand.

***Monastic Gardens.** Mick Hales. LC 00-22478. (Illus.). 2000. 35.00 (1-55670-982-X) Stewart Tabori & Chang.

Monastic Grange in Medieval England: A Reassessment. Colin Platt. LC 74-417643. 272p. 1969. write for info. (0-333-09356-9) Macmillan.

Monastic Grange in Medieval England: A Reassessment. Colin Platt. LC 73-80106. 280p. reprint ed. pap. 86.80 (0-7837-0463-1, 204078600018) Bks Demand.

Monastic Institutes. St. John Cassiau. Tr. by Jerome Bertram. 192p. 1998. pap. 26.95 (1-901157-04-0) St Augustines Pr.

Monastic Journey to India. M. Basil Pennington. 144p. (Orig.). 1984. 9.95 (0-8164-2398-9) Harper SF.

Monastic Journey to India. 2nd rev. ed. Basil Pennington. LC 81-14422. 178p. 1999. pap. 13.95 (1-56907-009-1) Beacon Pt Pr.

Monastic Life in Medieval England. John C. Dickinson. LC 78-25804. (Illus.). 160p. 1979. reprint ed. lib. bdg. 35.00 (0-313-20774-7, DIML, Greenwood Pr) Greenwood.

Monastic Life in the Christian & Hindu Traditions: A Comparative Study. Ed. by Vasudha Narayanan & Austin B. Creel. LC 90-30951. (Studies in Comparative Religion: Vol. 3). (Illus.). 608p. 1990. lib. bdg. 129.95 (0-88946-502-9) E Mellen.

Monastic Life in the Middle Ages. Cardinal Gasquet. 1973. 59.95 (0-8490-0657-0) Gordon Pr.

Monastic Life in the Middle Ages, 1792-1806. Francis A. Gasquet. LC 76-137377. (Select Bibliographies Reprint Ser.). 1977. 18.95 (0-8369-5578-1) Ayer.

Monastic Office. Ed. by P. T. Jiyu-Kennett. Tr. by Hubert Nearman from CHI. 197p. (Orig.). 1993. pap. 10.00 (0-930066-14-6) Shasta Abbey.

Monastic Order in Yorkshire, 1069-1215. Janet Burton. LC 98-25233. (Cambridge Studies in Medieval Life & Thought: No. 40). 352p. (C). 1999. text 69.95 (0-521-55229-X) Cambridge U Pr.

Monastic Pilgrimage: Following in the Steps of Saint Benedict. Guy-Marie Oury. LC 98-6250. 184p. 1998. pap. 15.95 (1-879007-28-2, MONA) St Bedes Pubns.

Monastic Practices. Charles Cummings. pap. 8.95 (0-87907-975-4); pap. 8.95 (0-87907-875-8) Cistercian Pubns.

Monastic Quest & Interreligious Dialogue. Gilbert G. Hardy & O. Cist. X, 289p. 1991. 51.95 (0-8204-1207-4) P Lang Pubng.

Monastic Reform, Catharism, & the Crusades (900-1300) Bernard Hamilton. (Collected Studies: No. CS97). 376p. (C). 1979. reprint ed. lib. bdg. 108.95 (0-86078-042-2, Pub. by Variorum) Ashgate Pub Co.

Monastic Ritual of Fleury: Orleans, Bibliiotheque Municipale MS 123 (101) Ed. by Anselme Davril. (Henry Bradshaw Society Ser.: No. CV). (Illus.). 200p. 1990. 45.00 (0-9501009-9-4, Henry Bradshaw Soc) Boydell & Brewer.

Monastic Rule of St. Carthach: St. Mochuda the Younger. Carthach. 1990. pap. 1.50 (0-89981-059-4) Eastern Orthodox.

Monastic Rules of Ireland, 3 vols. 1992. pap. 5.95 (0-89981-060-8) Eastern Orthodox.

Monastic, Scholastic & Mystical Theologies from the Later Middle Ages. Kent Emery, Jr. LC 96-35533. (Collected Studies: Vol. CS561). 384p. 1996. 109.95 (0-86078-617-X, Pub. by Variorum) Ashgate Pub Co.

Monastic Sign Languages. Ed. by Sebeok & D. J. Umiker-Sebok. (Approaches to Semiotics Ser.: No. 76). xviii, 619p. (C). 1987. lib. bdg. 196.15 (0-89925-181-1) Mouton.

Monastic Typicon: Rule of Life. 2nd rev. ed. Monks of New Skete. viii, 59p. 1988. reprint ed. pap. 10.00 (0-935129-13-8) Monks of New Skete.

Monastic Wisdom: The Letters of Elder Joseph the Hesychast. Elder Joseph. Ed. & Tr. by Ephraim Poonen from GRE. LC 98-61485. (Illus.). 424p. 1999. 35.00 (0-9667000-0-7, Pub. by St Anthonys Greek); pap. 22.00 (0-9667000-1-5, Pub. by St Anthonys Greek) ACCESS Pubs Network.

***Monastic Year: Reflections from a Monastery.** Victor-Antoine D'Avila-Latourrette. LC 99-51380. 172p. 2000. 9.99 (1-56955-177-4, Charis) Servant.

Monastic Year: Reflections from a Monastery. Victor-Antoine D'Avila-Latourrette. (Illus.). 184p. 1996. 14.95 (0-87833-923-X) Taylor Pub.

Monasticism. 4.95 (81-7120-359-0) Vedanta Pr.

Monasticism & the Arts. Ed. by Timothy G. Verdon & John Dally. LC 83-17897. (Illus.). 367p. 1984. reprint ed. pap. 113.80 (0-608-06967-1, 206717500009) Bks Demand.

***Monasticism in North-Western Europe, 800-1200.** Nyberg. 2000. 70.95 (1-85928-212-1) Ashgate Pub Co.

Monasticism in the Orthodox Church. N. F. Robinson. LC 72-131506. reprint ed. 27.50 (0-404-05375-0) AMS Pr.

Monasticism of Egypt: Images & Stories of the Desert Fathers. Michael McClellan. 112p. 1998. 17.95 (977-424-463-X, Pub. by Am Univ Cairo Pr) Col U Pr.

Monasticon Praemonstratense, Vol. 1. 274p. 1983. 215.40 (3-11-008917-3) De Gruyter.

Monatschrift fur Theater und Musik 1855-1865, 3 vols. Ed. by H. Robert Cohen. (Repertoire International de la Presse Musicale Ser.). (GER.). 1993. lib. bdg. 430.00 (0-8357-2267-8) UMI.

Monclonal Antibodies in Diagnostic Immunohistochemistry. Ed. by Mark R. Wick & Gene P. Siegal. (Clinical & Biochemical Analysis Ser.: Vol. 24). (Illus.). 664p. 1988. text 250.00 (0-8247-7838-3) Dekker.

Moncyclic Azepines: The Syntheses & Chemical Properties of the Monocyclic Azepines, Vol. 56, Vol. 56. George R. Proctor & James Redpath. LC 95-48039. 632p. 1997. 435.00 (0-471-96372-0) Wiley.

Mondane Orte Einer Vornehmen Gesellschaft. Burkhard Fuhs. (Historische Texte und Studien: Bd. 13). (GER.). 487p. 1992. write for info. (3-487-09625-0) G Olms Pubs.

Monday after the Miracle. William Gibson. 1983. pap. 5.25 (0-8222-0770-2) Dramatists Play.

Monday Came. Catherine Jenkins. LC 93-28982. (Voyages Ser.). (Illus.). (J). 1994. 4.25 (0-383-03762-X) SRA McGraw.

Monday Connection: A Spirituality of Competence, Affirmation, & Support in the Workplace. William E. Diehl. LC 92-31436. 208p. 1992. reprint ed. pap. 14.00 (0-06-061860-4, Pub. by Harper SF) HarpC.

Monday I Love You. Constance C. Greene. LC 87-27084. 160p. (YA). (gr. 7 up). 1988. 11.95 (0-06-022183-6) HarpC Child Bks.

Monday I Was an Alligator. Susan Pearson. LC 78-23618. (Lippincott-I-Like-to-Read Bks.). (Illus.). (J). (gr. k-2). 1979. lib. bdg. 11.89 (0-397-31830-8) HarpC Child Bks.

Monday Is Meat Loaf: And Pork Chops & Burgers & Steaks & More see Everyday Cookbooks Series

Monday Man. Kristin Gabriel. 1998. per. 3.50 (0-373-44056-1, 1-44056-9) Harlequin Bks.

***Monday Memo.Com.** Daniel Wolgemuth. 2000. pap. text 14.99 (1-56292-748-5) Honor Bks OK.

Monday Monday Rise. Carol Diggory Shields. 24p. 1999. pap. 4.99 (0-14-055874-8) Viking Penguin.

***Monday Morning.** Jane Young. LC 99-65322. 64p. 2000. pap. 9.95 (1-56315-216-9, Pub. by SterlingHse) Natl Bk Netwk.

Monday Morning Guide to Comprehension. Lee Gunderson. (Pippin Teacher's Library Ser.). 128p. 1994. text 19.50 (0-88751-052-3, 00781) Heinemann.

Monday Morning Jesus. Joseph Moore. 96p. (Orig.). 1984. pap. 6.95 (0-8091-2591-9) Paulist Pr.

Monday Morning Magic. Bob Bernstein. 64p. (J). (gr. k-6). 1982. 7.99 (0-86653-080-0, GA 425) Good Apple.

Monday Morning Movie. Marilyn Zuckerman. LC 80-51924. (Illus.). 56p. (Orig.). 1980. pap. 11.00 (0-935694-04-8) St Edns.

Monday Morning Movie. limited ed. Marilyn Zuckerman. LC 80-51924. (Illus.). 56p. (Orig.). 1980. 50.00 (0-935694-03-X) St Edns.

***Monday Morning Quarterback.** Jonathan Yardley. 2000. pap. 14.95 (0-8476-9740-1) Rowman.

Monday Morning Quarterback: Notes from the 90s. Jonathan Yardley. LC 98-7243. 288p. 1998. 24.95 (0-8476-9204-3, Pub. by Rowman) Natl Bk Netwk.

***Monday Morning Word, 2000: The Best of the Monday Morning Word.** LC 99-91674. (Illus.). 110p. 1999. pap. 12.00 (0-9677133-0-7) Crawford Dienst Inst.

Monday Night. Kay Boyle. 274p. 1977. reprint ed. 15.00 (0-911858-35-0) Appel.

Monday or Tuesday: Eight Stories. unabridged ed. Virginia Woolf. LC 96-31222. (Thrift Editions Ser.). 64p. 1997. reprint ed. pap. text 1.00 (0-486-29453-6) Dover.

Monday Philosophy. J. Cole. Ed. by P. Jacquline & L. Waido. (Illus.). 76p. (Orig.). 1992. pap. 6.95 (0-9632204-0-3) J Alfieri.

Monday Rhetoric of the Love Club & Other Parables. Marvin Cohen. LC 72-93979. 128p. 1973. pap. 3.75 (0-8112-0475-8, NDP352, Pub. by New Directions) Norton.

Monday Rhetoric of the Love Club & Other Parables. Marvin Cohen. LC 72-93979. 128p. 1973. 15.00 (0-89366-250-X) Ultramarine Pub.

Monday Run-Day. Nick Sharratt. LC 91-58745. (Illus.). 24p. (J). (ps up). 1992. 5.95 (1-56402-092-4) Candlewick Pr.

Monday Tales. Alphonse Daudet. LC 78-113654. (Short Story Index Reprint Ser.). 1977. 21.95 (0-8369-3383-4) Ayer.

Monday Through Friday: Day Care Alternatives. fac. ed. Jane Merrill. LC 82-3364. 236p. 1982. reprint ed. pap. 73.20 (0-7837-8260-8, 204903800009) Bks Demand.

Monday Through Saturday. rev. ed. Joyce Landorf Heatherley. LC 84-23459. 72p. 1989. reprint ed. pap. 6.95 (0-929488-11-3) Balcony Pub Inc.

Monday-to-Friday Chicken. Michele Urvater. LC 97-52224. 288p. 1998. 22.95 (0-7611-1318-5); pap. 103.60 (0-7611-1312-6); pap. 12.95 (1-56305-931-2) Workman Pub.

Monday to Friday Cookbook. Michele Urvater. LC 90-50947. (Illus.). 368p. 1991. pap. 14.95 (1-56305-748-4, 3748) Workman Pub.

Monday-to-Friday Pasta. Michele Urvater. LC 94-22253. (Illus.). 288p. (Orig.). 1994. pap. 12.95 (1-56305-347-0, 3347) Workman Pub.

Monday-Wednesday-Friday Girl & Other Stories. Stuart Levine. 238p. 1994. pap. 10.00 (0-939391-20-1) B Woodley Pr.

***Monday's Child.** Brenda Beamon-Isabell. LC 00-190395. 2000. 25.00 (0-7388-1629-9); pap. 18.00 (0-7388-1630-2) Xlibris Corp.

Monday's Child. Josephine Carr. 416p. (Orig.). 1999. mass mkt. 6.50 (0-06-101381-1) HarpC.

***Monday's Child.** Linda Chaikin. LC 99-20926. (Day to Remember Ser.). 1999. pap. 10.99 (0-7369-0067-5) Harvest Hse.

Monday's Child. Anne Geddes. (Illus.). 28p. 1998. 12.95 (0-7683-2026-7) CEDCO Pub.

Monday's Child. Elizabeth Hathon. 1997. 2.99 (1-56293-923-8, McClanahan Book) Learn Horizon.

Monday's Child. large type ed. Mollie Hardwick. 1984. 15.95 (0-7089-1086-6) Ulverscroft.

Monday's Child: (Women Who Dare) Janice Kaiser. LC 95-13577. (Superromance Ser.). 298p. 1995. per. 3.75 (0-373-70642-1, 1-70642-3) Harlequin Bks.

***Mondays Child Poems.** 2nd ed. Louis D. Brodsky. LC 98-45900. 1998. spiral bd. 9.95 (1-56809-054-4) Time Being Bks.

Monday's Meal: Stories. Leslie H. Edgerton. LC 97-6462. 222p. (Orig.). 1997. pap. 14.95 (1-57441-026-1) UNTX Pr.

Monday's Mourning: A Retrospective of the 1915 Strike at the Nashua Manufacturing Company. 2nd rev. ed. K. A. Goddu. 100p. 1996. pap. write for info. (1-57502-175-7, PO508A) Morris Pubng.

Monday's Troll. Jack Prelutsky. LC 95-7085. (Illus.). 40p. (J). (gr. 1-4). 1996. 16.00 (0-688-09644-1, Grenwillow Bks) HarpC Child Bks.

Monday's Troll. Jack Prelutsky. LC 95-7085. (Illus.). 40p. (J). (gr. 1-4). 1996. 15.89 (0-688-14373-3, Grenwillow Bks) HarpC Child Bks.

***Monday's Troll.** Jack Prelutsky. LC 95-7085. (Illus.). 40p. (J). (ps-2). 2000. pap. 5.95 (0-688-17529-5, Wm Morrow) Morrow Avon.

Monday's Warriors. Maurice Shadbolt. 320p. 1992. 21.95 (0-87923-915-8) Godine.

Monde. Rene Descartes. Tr. by Michael S. Mahoney. LC 77-86236. (Janus Ser.).Tr. of World. 224p. 1979. lib. bdg. 35.00 (0-913870-35-8) Abaris Bks.

M

Monde a la Derive. Marie-Danielle Croteau. (Novels in the Roman Plus Ser.). (FRE., Illus.). 160p. (YA). (gr. 8 up). 1994. pap. 8.95 (2-89021-218-1, Pub. by La Courte Ech) Firefly Bks Ltd.

Monde Acadien de Ti-Jean. Oradel N. Morris. LC 81-107884. (Gens de la Louisiane - Peoples of Louisiana Ser.: Bk. 1).Tr. of Cajun World of Ti-Jean. (ENG & FRE., Illus.). 81p. (J). (gr. k-8). 1980. reprint ed. 8.95 (0-944064-01-9) Paupieres Pub.

Monde de Boris Vian et le Grotesque Litteraire. Nicole Buffard-O'Shea. (American University Studies: Romance, Languages & Literature: Ser. 2, Vol. 185). 152p. 1993. 39.95 (0-8204-1709-2) P Lang Pubng.

Monde de Felix. Sylvain Trudel. (Premier Roman Ser.). (FRE., Illus.). 64p. (J). (gr. 2 up). 1996. pap. 8.95 (2-89021-260-2, Pub. by La Courte Ech) Firefly Bks Ltd.

Monde de Vezelay. Paul Claudel. (Illus.). 200p. 27.50 (0-686-54403-X) Fr & Eur.

Monde Litteraire de la Fontaine. Collinet. 59.40 (0-685-34231-X) Fr & Eur.

Monde Minuscule Solo F Horn. D. Schnyder. 1996. pap. text 8.95 (0-7935-7449-8) H Leonard.

Monde Naturel Comme Probleme Philosophique. J. Patocka. (Phaenomenologica Ser.: No. 68). 190p. 1976. lib. bdg. 99.50 (90-247-1795-7, Pub. by M Nijhoff) Kluwer Academic.

Monde Naturel et le Mouvement de l'Existence Humaine. J. Patocka. (Phaenomenologica Ser.: Vol. 110). (FRE.). 272p. 1988. lib. bdg. 195.50 (90-247-3577-7, Pub. by M Nijhoff) Kluwer Academic.

Monde Oriental de 395 a 1081. Charles Diehl & Georges Marcais. LC 80-2356. reprint ed. 72.50 (0-404-18906-7) AMS Pr.

Monde, Plus ou Monis see World More or Less

Monde Sans Fin - World Without End: Economie, Environnement et Developpement Viable, un Resume - Economics, Environment, & Sustainable Development, a Summary. David W. Pearce & Jeremy J. Warford. (FRE.). 52p. 1994. pap. 22.00 (0-8213-2658-9, 12658) World Bank.

Mondes Imaginaires. Andre Maurois. pap. 18.50 (0-685-36949-8) Fr & Eur.

Mondesir, Edouard de Mondesir: Avec une Introd par Gilbert Chinard. Gilbert Chinard. 1979. 15.95 (0-405-10594-0) Ayer.

Mondialisation des Operations Financieres. Yusuke Kashiwagi. LC HG3881.K37. (Fondation Per Jacobsson Conference de 1990 Ser.). (FRE.). 31p. reprint ed. pap. 30.00 (0-608-08768-8, 206940700004) Bks Demand.

Mondo Bizarro. Dan Piraro. (Illus.). 104p. 1989. pap. 5.95 (0-87701-711-5) Chronicle Bks.

Mondo Desperado: A Serial Novel. Patrick McCabe. LC 99-89331. 256p. 2000. 24.00 (0-06-019461-8) HarpC.

***Mondo Desperado: A Serial Novel.** Patrick McCabe. LC 99-89331. 2000. pap. write for info. (0-06-093258-9) HarpC.

Mondo E' Troppo Piccolo: Vita Di Francesca Cabrini. Theodore Maynard. Tr. by M. Santi from ENG. (ITA.). (Orig.). (C). 1987. reprint ed. pap. text 7.00 (0-9619397-0-2) MSSH.

Mondo et Autres Histoires. J. M. Le Clezio. (FRE.). 1982. pap. 11.95 (0-8288-3704-X, M1262) Fr & Eur.

Mondo et Autres Histoires. J. M. Le Clezio. (Folio Ser.: No. 1365). (FRE.). pap. 9.95 (2-07-037365-7) Schoenhof.

Mondo Internet. Steve W. Rimmer. LC 94-27583. 1994. text 36.95 (0-07-053014-9) McGraw.

Mondo Macabro. Peter Tombs. LC 98-4658. 192p. 1998. pap. 18.95 (0-312-18748-3) St Martin.

***Mondo Materialis: Materials & Ideas for the Future.** George Beylarian & Jeffrey J. Osborne. 2000. pap. 35.00 (1-58567-087-1, Pub. by Overlook Pr) Penguin Putnam.

Mondo Materialis: Materials & Ideas for the Future. George M. Beylerian & Jeffrey J. Osborne. 1990. pap. 24.95 (0-8109-2468-4, Pub. by Abrams) Time Warner.

Mondo Utah. Trent Harris. (Illus.). 96p. (Orig.). 1996. pap. 10.95 (0-942688-11-2) Dream Garden.

Mondragon: An Economic Analysis. Henk Thomas & Chris Logan. 224p. 1983. pap. text 18.95 (0-04-334007-5) Routledge.

Mondrian. Susanne Deicher. (Illus.). 1994. pap. 9.99 (3-8228-8885-0) Taschen Amer.

An Asterisk (*) at the beginning of an entry indicates that the title is appearing for the first time.

Mondrian. Susanne Deicher. 1995. pap. 5.99 (*3-8228-9237-8*) Taschen Amer.

Mondrian. Susanne Deicher. (SPA.). 1996. pap. 9.99 (*3-8228-8831-1*) Taschen Amer.

Mondrian. Ed. by Jose M. Faerna. Tr. by Alberto Curotto from SPA. LC 96-86852. (Great Modern Masters Ser.). (Illus.). 64p. 1997. pap. 11.98 (*0-8109-4687-4*, Pub. by Abrams) Time Warner.

Mondrian. Serge Fauchereau. LC 94-66652. (Illus.). 128p. 1994. 27.50 (*0-8478-1832-2*, Pub. by Rizzoli Intl) St Martin.

Mondrian. Hans L. Jaffe. (Masters of Art Ser.). (Illus.). 128p. 1986. 24.95 (*0-8109-1413-1*, Pub. by Abrams) Time Warner.

Mondrian. rev. ed. John Milner. LC 95-202711. (Illus.). 240p. (C). 1995. pap. 29.95 (*0-7148-3167-0*, Pub. by Phaidon Press) Phaidon Pr.

Mondrian: Flowers. David Shapiro. (Illus.). 80p. 1991. 29.95 (*0-8109-3615-1*, Pub. by Abrams) Time Warner.

Mondrian: On the Humanity of Abstract Painting. Meyer Schapiro. LC 94-38797. (Illus.). 80p. 1995. pap. 12.50 (*0-8076-1370-3*) Braziller.

Mondrian Studies. Kermit S. Champa. LC 85-980. (Illus.). xviii, 150p. 1985. 35.00 (*0-226-10078-2*) U Ch Pr.

Mondrian/Reinhardt: Influence & Affinity. LC 97-76528. (Illus.). 60p. 1997. pap. write for info. (*1-878283-72-3*) PaceWildenstein.

Mondsee-Wiener Liederhandschrift. fac. ed. Intro. by H. Heger. (Codices Selecti B Ser.: Vol. XIX). (GER.). 238p. 1968. lthr. 487.00 (*3-201-00747-1*, Pub. by Akademische Druck-und) Balogh.

Mondwanderungen: Wegweiser Durch Thomas Manns Joseph-Roman. Hermann Kurzke. (GER.). 208p. 1993. pap. 18.00 (*3-596-11806-9*, Pub. by Fischer Tasch) Intl Bk Import.

M113, Pt. 2. Ed. by Francois Verlinden. (Warmachines Ser.: Vol. 9). (Illus.). 36p. 1991. 14.95 (*1-930607-01-6*, VPI 0668) Verlinden Prod.

Moneda de Oro. Alma Flor Ada.Tr. of Gold Coin. (SPA.). 1996. 11.15 (*0-606-13555-3*, Pub. by Turtleback) Demco.

Moneda de Oro (The Gold Coin) Alma F. Ada. (SPA.). 1996. 11.95 (*84-241-3338-2*); pap. text 5.95 (*84-241-3364-1*) Lectorum Pubns.

***Monedas Hispano del Tremis al Euro (411AD to Present)** J. Cayon & C. Castan. (Illus.). 1998. lib. bdg. 95.00 (*84-920980-3-1*) S J Durst.

***MONEE Report.** UNICEF Switzerland Staff. (RUS.). 184p. 1999. write for info. (*92-806-3506-9*) U N I C E.

Monerans & Protists. Alvin Silverstein et al. (Kingdoms of Life Ser.). (Illus.). 64p. (J). (gr. 5-8). 1995. lib. bdg. 21.40 (*0-8050-3521-4*) TFC Bks NY.

Monessen: Industrial Boomtown & Steel Community, 1898-1980. Ed. by Matthew S. Magda. (American Places Ser.). (Illus.). 152p. 1985. pap. text 6.95 (*0-89271-029-2*) Pa Hist & Mus.

Monet. (Illus.). 12p. 1997. 4.98 (*0-7858-0691-1*) Bk Sales Inc.

Monet. 1995. pap. 8.99 (*3-8228-9330-7*) Taschen Amer.

Monet. 1996. pap. (*3-8228-9584-9*) Taschen Amer.

Monet. 1999. 12.95 (*0-7893-0303-5*) Universe.

Monet. Compiled by Anna Barskaya. (Illus.). 50p. 1982. pap. 16.95 (*0-8109-2265-7*, 2219-3) Abrams.

Monet. Mila Boutan. (Art Activity Packs Ser.). (Illus.). 13p. (J). (ps-5). 1996. pap. 9.95 (*0-8118-1335-5*) Chronicle Bks.

Monet. DK Publishing Staff. LC 98-86756. 144p. 1999. pap. text 12.95 (*0-7894-4142-X*) DK Pub Inc.

***Monet.** DK Publishing Staff, (Eyewitness Books). 64p. (J). (gr. 4-7). 1999. 15.95 (*0-7894-4880-7*, D K Ink) DK Pub Inc.

Monet. Robert Gordon. (Illus.). 304p. 1989. pap. 34.98 (*0-8109-8091-6*, Pub. by Abrams) Time Warner.

Monet. Christoph Heinrich. 1994. pap. 9.99 (*3-8228-9317-X*) Taschen Amer.

Monet. Stephan Koja. (Illus.). 224p. 1996. 65.00 (*3-7913-1671-0*, Pub. by Prestel) te Neues.

Monet. Antony Mason. LC 94-22455. (Famous Artists Ser.). (Illus.). 32p. (YA). (gr. 5 up). 1994. 10.95 (*0-8120-6494-1*) Barron.

Monet. Antony Mason. LC 94-22455. (Famous Artists Ser.). (Illus.). 32p. (YA). (gr. 5 up). 1995. pap. 6.95 (*0-8120-9174-4*) Barron.

Monet. Antony Mason. (Famous Artists Ser.). 1995. 12.15 (*0-606-08824-5*, Pub. by Turtleback) Demco.

Monet. Frank Milner. (Illus.). 1999. pap. 19.95 (*1-57715-072-4*) Knckerbocker.

Monet. Carla Rachman. (Illus.). 352p. 1997. pap. 19.95 (*0-7148-3500-5*, Pub. by Phaidon Press) Phaidon Pr.

Monet. Random House Value Publishing Staff. 80p. 1998. 9.99 (*0-517-16055-2*) Random Hse Value.

Monet. Karin Sagner-Duchting. (Big Art Ser.). 1994. pap. 19.99 (*3-8228-0541-6*) Taschen Amer.

Monet. Karin Sagner-Duchting. (Big Art Ser.). 1998. 19.99 (*3-8228-7219-9*) Taschen Amer.

***Monet.** Karin Sagner-Duchting. 1999. 19.99 (*3-8228-6784-5*) Taschen Amer.

***Monet.** Karen Sagner. LC 99-201980. (Pegasus Library). 1999. 14.95 (*3-7913-2006-8*, Pub. by Prestel) te Neues.

Monet. William C. Seitz. (Masters of Art Ser.). (Illus.). 128p. 1983. 24.95 (*0-8109-1341-0*, Pub. by Abrams) Time Warner.

Monet. William C. Seitz. (Illus.). 160p. 1999. 19.98 (*0-8109-8197-1*, Pub. by Abrams) Time Warner.

Monet. N. Sinclair. 1992. 5.98 (*1-55521-762-1*) Bk Sales Inc.

Monet. Sandro Sproccati. 1994. 34.98 (*0-7858-0200-2*) Bk Sales Inc.

Monet. Taschen Staff. Date not set. pap. 4.99 (*3-8228-8781-1*, Pub. by Benedikt Taschen) Bks Nippan.

Monet. Mike Venezia. LC 89-25452. (Getting to Know the World's Greatest Artists Ser.). (Illus.). 32p. (J). (ps-4). 1990. pap. 6.95 (*0-516-42276-6*); lib. bdg. 21.00 (*0-516-02276-8*) Childrens.

Monet. John House. (Color Library). (Illus.). 128p. (C). 1993. reprint ed. pap. 14.95 (*0-7148-2723-1*, Pub. by Phaidon Press) Phaidon Pr.

Monet: A Postcard Book. Claude Monet. (Postcard Bks.). (Illus.). 64p. (Orig.). 1989. pap. text 8.95 (*0-89471-683-2*) Running Pr.

Monet: Artist's Garden Address. Washington Nga. 1999. 2.00 (*1-55550-947-9*) St Martin.

Monet: Catalogue Raisonne, 4 vols. Daniel Wildenstein. Ed. by Gilles Neret. (Illus.). 1600p. 1996. boxed set 169.95 (*3-8228-8559-2*) Taschen Amer.

Monet: Impressions. Daniel Wildenstein. (Rhythem & Color One Ser.). 1970. 9.95 (*0-8288-9512-0*) Fr & Eur.

Monet: Late Paintings of Giverny from the Musee Marmottan. Lynn F. Orr et al. (Illus.). 88p. 1995. pap. 14.95 (*0-8109-2610-5*, Pub. by Abrams) Time Warner.

Monet: Nature into Art. John House. LC 86-50364. 256p. 1986. 67.00 (*0-300-03785-6*) Yale U Pr.

Monet: Nature into Art. John House. (Illus.). 1988. 24.95 (*0-300-04361-9*) Yale U Pr.

Monet: Or the Triumph of Impressionism. Daniel Wildenstein. (Jumbo Ser.). (Illus.). 480p. 1999. write for info. (*3-8228-7060-9*) Taschen Amer.

Monet: The Art Institute of Chicago, Artists in Focus. 2nd ed. Andrew Forge. Ed. by Susan F. Rossen. LC 95-10039. (Artists in Focus Ser.). (Illus.). 112p. 1995. reprint ed. 19.95 (*0-8109-4290-9*) Art Inst Chi.

Monet: The Artist Speaks. Ed. by Genevieve Morgan. LC 95-38392. (Illus.). 96p. 1996. 16.95 (*0-00-225206-6*) Collins SF.

Monet: The Complete Paintings, Eighteen Ninety-Nine to Nineteen Twenty-Six. Daniel Wildenstein. (FRE., Illus.). 443p. 1988. 350.00 (*1-55660-015-1*) A Wofsy Fine Arts.

Monet: The Ultimate Impressionist. Sylvie Patin. Tr. by Anthony Roberts. (Discoveries Ser.). (Illus.). 182p. 1993. pap. 12.95 (*0-8109-2883-3*, Pub. by Abrams) Time Warner.

Monet & Bazille: A Collaboration. Kermit S. Champa et al. LC 98-31450. (Illus.). 108p. 1999. 24.95 (*0-8109-6384-1*, Pub. by Abrams) Time Warner.

Monet & Human Figure. Mary M. Gedo. 300p. (C). 1990. lib. bdg. 34.95 (*0-226-28480-8*) U Ch Pr.

Monet & Impressionism. David Spence. (Great Artists Ser.). (Illus.). 32p. 1997. pap. 5.95 (*0-7641-0291-5*) Barron.

Monet & Mediterranean. Pissarro. 1999. pap. 29.95 (*0-912804-33-5*) St Martin.

Monet & the Mediterranean. Joachim Pissarro & Kimbell Art Museum Staff. LC 96-35758. (Illus.). 92p. 1997. 45.00 (*0-8478-1783-0*, Pub. by Rizzoli Intl) St Martin.

Monet at Giverny. Karin Sagner-Duchting et al. (Pegasus Library). (Illus.). 120p. 1994. 25.00 (*3-7913-1384-3*, Pub. by Prestel) te Neues.

Monet at Vethevil: The Turning Point. Annette Dixon et al. LC 94-12045. (Illus.). 118p. 1998. pap. 29.95 (*0-912303-52-2*) Michigan Mus.

Monet by Himself. R. L. Kendall. 328p. 1996. 34.98 (*0-7858-0670-9*) Bk Sales Inc.

Monet by Himself. Richard Kendall. 1999. pap. text 39.95 (*1-57715-086-4*) Knckerbocker.

Monet, Claude: Paintings in Soviet Museums. N. Kalitina. 156p. (C). 1984. 195.00 (*0-7855-4519-0*, Pub. by Collets) St Mut.

Monet in the Nineties. Paul H. Tucker. 340p. (C). 1992. reprint ed. pap. 32.00 (*0-300-04913-7*) Yale U Pr.

Monet in the '90's: The Series Paintings. Paul H. Tucker. (Illus.). 340p. 1990. 65.00 (*0-300-04659-6*) Yale U Pr.

***Monet in the 20th Century.** Ed. by Paul H. Tucker et al. LC 98-86163. (Illus.). 300p. 2000. 55.00 (*0-300-07749-1*) Yale U Pr.

***Monet in the 20th Century.** Paul Hayes Tucker et al. (Illus.). 300p. 2000. pap. 30.00 (*0-300-07944-3*) Yale U Pr.

Monet, Narcissus, & Self-Reflection: The Modernist Myth of the Self. Steven Z. Levine. LC 94-1105. 388p. 1994. pap. text 29.95 (*0-226-47544-1*); lib. bdg. 70.00 (*0-226-47543-3*) U Ch Pr.

Monet Notes. Ed. by Helen Exley. (Artist Notebooks). (Illus.). 80p. 1996. 8.00 (*1-85015-779-0*) Exley Giftbooks.

Monet on the Normandy Coast: Tourism & Painting, 1867-1886. Robert L. Herbert. LC 94-13913. (Illus.). 220p. 1994. 55.00 (*0-300-05973-6*) Yale U Pr.

Monet on the Normandy Coast: Tourism & Painting, 1867-1886. Robert L. Herbert. (Illus.). 167p. 1996. pap. 30.00 (*0-300-06881-6*) Yale U Pr.

Monet Postcard Book, Vol. 1. Metropolitan Museum of Art Staff. (Illus.). 124p. 1994. 19.50 (*0-8212-2089-6*, Pub. by Bulfinch Pr); 9.95 (*0-8212-2088-8*, Pub. by Bulfinch Pr) Little.

Monet to Matisse: French Art in Southern California Collections. Philip Conisbee et al. (Illus.). 144p. (Orig.). 1991. pap. 29.95 (*0-87587-159-3*) LA Co Art Mus.

Monet to Moore: The Millennium Gift of Sara Lee Corporation. Richard R. Brettell & Natalie H. Lee. LC 99-24949. (Illus.). 256p. 1999. 60.00 (*0-300-08134-0*) Yale U Pr.

Monet 25 Masterworks. Seitz. (Illus.). 64p. 1995. pap. 16.95 (*0-8109-2603-2*, Pub. by Abrams) Time Warner.

Moneta Polska. Arthur J. Majewski. LC 88-92614.Tr. of Polish Coin. (Illus.). 216p. 1991. 19.50 (*0-9617557-1-7*) Maryt Pub.

Monetarism, 2 vols., Set. Ed. by K. Alec Chrystal. (Schools of Thought in Economics Ser.: Vol. 11). 964p. 1990. 360.00 (*1-85278-081-9*) E Elgar.

Monetarism: Theory & Policy. George Macesich. Ed. by J. Richard Zecher & D. Sykes Wilford. LC 82-19040. (Praeger Studies in International Monetary Economics & Finance). 269p. 1983. 55.00 (*0-275-91039-3*, C1039, Praeger Pubs) Greenwood.

Monetarism & Keynesians. Ed. by Lloyds Bank Staff. 1991. text 49.00 (*0-86187-121-9*, Pub. by P P Pubs) Cassell & Continuum.

Monetarism & Liberalization: The Chilean Experiment. Sebastian Edwards & Alejandra C. Edwards. LC 86-25959. 256p. 1987. text 34.95 (*0-88730-105-3*, HarpBusn) HarpInfo.

Monetarism & Liberalization: The Chilean Experiment. Sebastian Edwards & Alejandra C. Edwards. LC 90-20913. (Illus.). xx, 270p. 1991. pap. text 17.00 (*0-226-18489-7*) U Ch Pr.

Monetarism & the Labour Market. Derek Robinson. (Library of Political Economy). 456p. 1986. pap. 19.95 (*0-19-877192-4*) OUP.

Monetarism & the Methodology of Economics: Essays in Honour of Thomas Mayer. Ed. by Kevin D. Hoover & Steven M. Sheffrin. LC 95-5521. 288p. 1995. 95.00 (*1-85278-940-9*) E Elgar.

Monetarism, Economic Crisis & the Third World. Ed. by Karel Jansen. (Illus.). 208p. 1983. text 42.50 (*0-7146-3222-8*, Pub. by F Cass Pubs); pap. text 14.95 (*0-7146-4037-9*, Pub. by F Cass Pubs) Intl Spec Bk.

Monetarism or Prosperity? Bryan Gould et al. LC 86-673392. x, 222p. 1981. write for info. (*0-333-31973-7*) Macmillan.

Monetarist Perspectives. David E. Laidler. 232p. 1983. 37.95 (*0-674-58240-3*) HUP.

Monetary Aggregates in a Changing Environment: A Statistical Discussion Paper. Juliette Healey et al. LC HG2937.. (Bank of England - Discussion Papers: No. 47). (Illus.). 51p. 1990. reprint ed. pap. 30.00 (*0-608-03150-X*, 206360300007) Bks Demand.

Monetary & Banking Development of Singapore & Malaysia. 3rd ed. Lee Sheng-Yi. 340p. 1990. pap. 47.50 (*9971-69-146-9*, Pub. by Sngapore Univ Pr) Coronet Bks.

Monetary & Banking Policy of Chile. Benjamin Subercaseaux. 1976. lib. bdg. 69.95 (*0-8490-2274-6*) Gordon Pr.

Monetary & Banking System of Syria. Sa'id B. Himadeh. LC 77-180347. reprint ed. 47.50 (*0-404-56277-9*) AMS Pr.

Monetary & Credit Policies of the Nepal Rastra Bank & Their Impact on the Nepalese Economy. P. R. Reejal. 1986. 75.00 (*0-7855-0248-3*, Pub. by Ratna Pustak Bhandar) St Mut.

Monetary & Credit Policies of the Nepal Rastra Bank & Their Impact on the Nepalese Economy. Ed. by P. R. Reejal. 100p. (C). 1987. 220.00 (*0-89771-051-7*, Pub. by Ratna Pustak Bhandar) St Mut.

Monetary & Exchange Reforms in China: Achievements & Agenda for the Future. Hassanali Mehran et al. LC 96-34203. (Occasional Paper Ser.: 141). 1996. pap. 15.00 (*1-55775-562-0*) Intl Monetary.

Monetary & Financial Planning for a Transitory Economy: An Adaptive Control Model for India. Dipak R. Basu. 160p. 1995. 61.95 (*1-85972-021-8*, Pub. by Avebry) Ashgate Pub Co.

Monetary & Financial System. Rod Apps & David Goacher. 450p. 1990. pap. 125.00 (*0-85297-355-1*, Pub. by Chartered Bank) St Mut.

Monetary & Financial System. David Goacher. 326p. 1999. pap. 120.00 (*0-85297-338-1*, Pub. by Chartered Bank) St Mut.

Monetary & Financial System. Ed. by G. Goacher. (C). 1989. 110.00 (*0-85297-278-4*, Pub. by Chartered Bank) St Mut.

Monetary & Financial System. Geoff Lipscombe. 1997. pap. 30.00 (*0-85297-414-0*, Pub. by Chartered Bank) St Mut.

Monetary & Financial Systems. Sheffield City Poly-CIB Staff. (Bankers Workbook Ser.). (C). 1989. 110.00 (*0-85297-283-0*, Pub. by Chartered Bank) St Mut.

Monetary & Fiscal Dynamics. M. Carlberg. Ed. by Dieter Bos et al. (Studies in Contemporary Economics). (Illus.). viii, 194p. 1992. 59.95 (*0-387-91423-4*) Spr-Verlag.

Monetary & Fiscal Policy: Politics, Vol. 2. Ed. by Torsten Persson & Guido Tabellini. LC 93-35772. (Illus.). 471p. 1994. pap. text 27.50 (*0-262-66088-1*) MIT Pr.

Monetary & Fiscal Policy Vol. 1: Credibility. Ed. by Torsten Persson & Guido Tabellini. LC 93-35772. 1994. pap. text 27.50 (*0-262-66087-3*) MIT Pr.

Monetary & Fiscal Policy in an Integrated Europe. Ed. by Barry J. Eichengreen et al. LC 95-19315. (European & Transatlantic Studies). 1995. 95.00 (*3-540-59407-8*) Spr-Verlag.

Monetary & Fiscal Unification in Nineteenth-Century Germany: What Can Kohl Learn from Bismarck? Harold James. LC 97-2800. (Essays in International Finance Ser.: Vol. 202). 42p. 1997. pap. 10.00 (*0-88165-109-5*) Princeton U Int Finan Econ.

Monetary Approach to Exchange Rates: What Now Remains? James M. Boughton. LC 88-27496. (Essays in International Finance Ser.: No. 171). 28p. 1988. pap. text 10.00 (*0-88165-078-1*) Princeton U Int Finan Econ.

Monetary Approach to International Adjustment. Ed. by Bluford H. Putnam & D. Sykes Wilford. LC 78-19753. 299p. 1979. 36.95 (*0-275-90409-1*, C0409, Praeger Pubs); pap. 15.95 (*0-275-91480-1*, B1480, Praeger Pubs) Greenwood.

Monetary Approach to International Adjustment. rev. ed. Ed. by Bluford H. Putman & D. Sykes Wilford. LC 85-28314. 396p. 1986. 65.00 (*0-275-92024-0*, C2024, Praeger Pubs) Greenwood.

Monetary Approach to the Balance of Payments. Ed. by Jacob A. Frenkel & Harry G. Johnson. LC 76-376604. 388p. reprint ed. pap. 120.30 (*0-8357-8231-X*, 203401400088) Bks Demand.

Monetary Approach to the Balance of Payments: A Collection of Research Papers. International Monetary Fund Staff. x, 290p. 1977. 10.00 (*0-939934-16-7*) Intl Monetary.

Monetary Approaches to the Balance of Payments & Exchange Rates. Alan A. Rabin & Leland B. Yeager. LC 82-15587. (Essays in International Finance Ser.: No. 148). 30p. 1982. pap. text 10.00 (*0-88165-055-2*) Princeton U Int Finan Econ.

Monetary Change & Economic History in the Medieval Muslim World. Andrew S. Ehrenkreutz. Ed. by Jere L. Bacharach. (Collected Studies: No. CS371). 304p. 1992. 109.95 (*0-86078-324-3*, Pub. by Variorum) Ashgate Pub Co.

Monetary Circulation in the United Kingdom: A Statistical Study. Philip J. Welham. LC 78-92500. viii, 118p. 1969. 27.50 (*0-678-06251-X*) Kelley.

Monetary Conditions for Economic Recovery. Ed. by Klant Van Ewijk. 1985. lib. bdg. 142.00 (*90-247-3219-0*) Kluwer Academic.

Monetary Cooperation Between East & West (With an Introduction by George Garvy) Adam Zwass. LC 73-92368. 285p. reprint ed. pap. 88.40 (*0-608-14910-1*, 202613200048) Bks Demand.

Monetary Economics. P. Checkley. 1986. 100.00 (*0-946796-00-9*) St Mut.

***Monetary Economics.** Jagdish Handa. 640p. 2000. pap. 37.99 (*0-415-19926-3*); text 115.00 (*0-415-19925-5*) Routledge.

Monetary Economics. Brian Kettell. (Banking & Finance Ser.: Vol. 1). 372p. 1985. pap. text 36.00 (*0-86010-562-8*); lib. bdg. 50.00 (*0-86010-579-2*) G & T Inc.

Monetary Economics. Geoffrey E. Dennis. LC 80-40095. (Modern Economics Ser.). 328p. reprint ed. pap. 101.70 (*0-7837-1591-9*, 204188300024) Bks Demand.

Monetary Economics. 2nd ed. David G. Pierce & Peter J. Tysome. 320p. 1984. pap. 34.95 (*0-408-70953-7*) Buttrwrth-Heinemann.

Monetary Economics: Theory & Policy. Bennett T. McCallum. 352p. 1988. 34.95 (*0-02-948981-4*) Free Pr.

Monetary Economics: Theory & Practice. Bennett T. McCallum. 356p. (C). 1989. 75.00 (*0-02-378471-7*, Macmillan Coll) P-H.

Monetary Economics in Developing Countries. 2nd ed. Subrata Ghatak. LC 94-36053. 266p. 1995. text 59.95 (*0-312-12496-1*) St Martin.

Monetary Economics in 1990's, Nos. 9-17. Capie. LC 96-17556. 192p. 1997. text 69.95 (*0-312-16219-7*) St Martin.

Monetary Economics of Europe: Causes of the EMS Crisis. Christopher Johnson & Stefan Collignon. 1994. 38.50 (*0-8386-3607-1*) Fairleigh Dickinson.

Monetary Equilibrium. Gunnar Myrdal. LC 65-23216. (Reprints of Economic Classics Ser.). xi, 214p. 1965. reprint ed. 35.00 (*0-678-00092-1*) Kelley.

Monetary Errors & Deceptions of the Supreme Court. Gordon Leitch, Jr. LC 78-57901. 166p. (YA). (gr. 9-12). 1978. pap. 15.00 (*0-9605734-0-2*) Bicent Era.

Monetary Expansion in the Confederacy. John M. Godfrey. LC 77-14775. (Dissertations in American Economic History Ser.). 1978. 25.95 (*0-405-11034-0*) Ayer.

Monetary Experience of Belgium, 1914-1936. Henry L. Shephard. Ed. by Mira Wilkins. LC 78-3948. (International Finance Ser.). 1979. reprint ed. lib. bdg. 26.95 (*0-405-11248-3*) Ayer.

Monetary Experiments: Early American & Recent Scandinavian. Richard A. Lester. LC 70-75796. (Reprints of Economic Classics Ser.). (Illus.). xvii, 316p. 1970. reprint ed. 45.00 (*0-678-05547-5*) Kelley.

Monetary History of China. Xinwei Peng. Tr. by Edward H. Kaplan from CHI. (East Asian Research Aids & Translations Ser.: Vol. 5). l, 932p. (C). 1994. pap. 50.00 (*0-914584-81-2*) WWUCEAS.

Monetary History of Italy. Michele Fratianni et al. (Studies in Monetary & Financial History). 323p. 1997. text 64.95 (*0-521-44315-6*) Cambridge U Pr.

***Monetary History of the Ottoman Empire.** Sevket Pamuk. LC 98-43861. (Cambridge Studies in Islamic Civilization). (Illus.). 336p. (C). 2000. 69.95 (*0-521-44197-8*) Cambridge U Pr.

Monetary History of the United Kingdom, 1870-1982: Data, Sources, Methods, Vol. I. Forrest Capie & Alan Webber. 1985. text 100.00 (*0-04-332097-X*) Routledge.

Monetary History of the United States, 1867-1960. M. Friedman & A. J. Schwartz. (National Bureau of Economic Research Ser.: No. B.12). 888p. 1963. text 110.00 (*0-691-04147-4*, Pub. by Princeton U Pr); pap. text 42.50 (*0-691-00354-8*, Pub. by Princeton U Pr) Cal Prin Full Svc.

Monetary Incentives for Credit Union Staffs. Harry F. Krueckeberg et al. 98p. 1998. pap. 100.00 (*1-880572-23-0*, 1752-37) Filene Res.

Monetary Management in Ghana. Stephen D. Younger. (Working Papers). (C). 1991. pap. text 7.00 (*1-56401-108-9*) Cornell Food.

Monetary Model of Exchange Rates & Cointegration: Estimation, Testing & Prediction. J. Gardeazabal & M. Regulez. Ed. by Martin J. Beckmann & W. Krelle. (Lecture Notes in Economics & Mathematical Systems Ser.: Vol. 385). (Illus.). xii, 194p. 1992. 58.95 (*0-387-55635-4*) Spr-Verlag.

Monetary Nationalism & International Stability. Friedrich A. Hayek. LC 87-17244. (Reprints of Economic Classics Ser.). xiv, 94p. 1989. reprint ed. 27.50 (*0-678-00047-6*) Kelley.

Monetary Nationalism Reconsidered. Lawrence H. White. (Independent Policy Reports). 36p. 1996. pap. 6.95 (*0-945999-52-6*) Independent Inst.

Monetary Penalties in Scotland. Linda Nicholson. 96p. 1994. pap. 25.00 (*0-11-495176-4*, HM51764, Pub. by Statnry Office) Bernan Associates.

Monetary Planning for India. Suraj B. Gupta. 1980. text 19.95 (*0-19-561145-4*) OUP.

Monetary Policy. Ed. by N. Gregory Mankiw. (Illus.). 356p. 1996. lib. bdg. 50.00 (*0-226-50308-9*) U Ch Pr.

Monetary Policy, Vol. 29. Gregory Mankiw. (NBER Studies in Business Cycle). 1997. pap. text 18.00 (*0-226-50309-7*) U Ch Pr.

Monetary Policy: Finding a Place to Stand. Gerald K. Bouey. LC 86-2991. (Per Jacobsson Lecture Ser.: Vol. 1982). 36p. reprint ed. pap. 30.00 (*0-608-08757-2*, 206939600004) Bks Demand.

Monetary Policy: International Strategies. Ed. by James Swofford & Gerald Whitney. (International Review of Comparative Public Policy Ser.: Vol. 8). 197p. 1996. 78.50 (*0-7623-0190-2*) Jai Pr.

Monetary Policy, a Market Price Approach. Manuel H. Johnson & Robert E. Keleher. LC 96-3618. 336p. 1996. 75.00 (*1-56720-059-1*, Quorum Bks) Greenwood.

Monetary Policy & Inflation in Spain. Jose L. Malo de Molina et al. LC 97-38847. 256p. 1998. text 79.95 (*0-312-21295-X*) St Martin.

Monetary Policy & Interest Rates: Proceedings of a Conference Sponsored by Banca D'Italia, Centro Paolo Baffi & the Innocenzo Gasparini Institute for Economic Research (IGIER) Ignazio Angeloni & Riccardo Rovelli. LC 98-7081. xi, 295 p. 1998. write for info. (*0-333-71647-7*, Pub. by Macmillan) St Martin.

Monetary Policy & Interest Rates: Proceedings of a Conference Sponsored by Banced' Italia Centro Paolo Baffi & the Innocenzo Gasparini Institute for Economic Research (IGIER) Ed. by Ignazio Angeloni & Riccardo Rovelli. LC 98-7081. 304p. 1998. text 79.95 (*0-312-21672-6*) St Martin.

Monetary Policy & Investment Opportunities. Laura S. Nowak. LC 92-18366. 232p. 1993. 59.95 (*0-89930-611-X*, NIO, Quorum Bks) Greenwood.

Monetary Policy & Politics: Rules vs. Discretion. George Macesich. LC 92-3379. 176p. 1992. 52.95 (*0-275-94335-6*, Praeger Pubs) Greenwood.

Monetary Policy & Public Finance. Graham C. Hockley. LC 70-99928. xxv, 301p. 1970. lib. bdg. 39.50 (*0-678-06527-6*) Kelley.

Monetary Policy & Rational Expectations. George Macesich. LC 86-20538. 164p. 1987. 52.95 (*0-275-92327-4*, C2327, Praeger Pubs) Greenwood.

Monetary Policy & the Design of Financial Institutions in China, 1978-1990. Lizuo Jin. LC 94-19510. 1994. text 75.00 (*0-312-12274-8*) St Martin.

Monetary Policy & the Great Inflation in the United States: The Federal Reserve & the Failure of Macroeconomic Policy, 1965-79. Thomas Mayer. LC 98-24137. 168p. 1999. 75.00 (*1-85898-953-1*) E Elgar.

Monetary Policy & Uncertainty: Collected Papers from the 1982-1984 Konstanz Seminars. Ed. by Manfred J. Neumann. 262p. 1986. pap. 54.00 (*3-7890-1257-2*, Pub. by Nomos Verlags) Intl Bk Import.

***Monetary Policy at the European Periphery: Greek Experience & Lessons for EU Candidates.** I. A. Mourmouras & M. G. Arghyrou. Ed. by J. T. Addison et al. (European & Transatlantic Studies). xvi, 218p. 2000. (*3-540-66932-9*) Spr-Verlag.

Monetary Policy for a Changing Financial Environment. William S. Haraf & Phillip Cagan. 150p. 1990. 28.50 (*0-8447-3697-X*, AEI Pr) Am Enterprise.

Monetary Policy for a Volatile Global Economy. William S. Haraf & Thomas D. Willett. LC 89-18486. (Illus.). 100p. (C). 1990. 27.50 (*0-8447-3713-5*, AEI Pr) Am Enterprise.

Monetary Policy in a Converging Europe: Papers & Proceedings of an International Workshop Organised by De Nederlandsche Bank & the Limburg Institute of Financial Economics. Ed. by Koos Alders et al. LC 95-35840. 1996. write for info. (*0-614-08575-6*) Kluwer Academic.

Monetary Policy in a Converging Europe: Papers & Proceedings of an International Workshop Organized by the Nederlandsche Bank & the Limburg, Bank & the Limburg Institute of Financial Economics of the University of Limburg, February, 1995. Ed. by Alders Koos. (Financial & Monetary Policy Studies). 156p. (C). 1996. lib. bdg. 109.00 (*0-7923-3746-8*) Kluwer Academic.

Monetary Policy in an Integrated World Economy: Symposium, 1995. Ed. by Horst Siebert. (C). 1996. 94.50 (*0-472-10775-5*) U of Mich Pr.

Monetary Policy in an Integrated World Economy: Symposium 1995. Ed. by Horst Siebert. (Illus.). 260p. (C). 1996. text 94.50 (*3-16-146657-8*) JCB Mohr.

Monetary Policy in Developed Economies. Michele U. Fratianni. Ed. by Dominick Salvatore. (Studies in Comparative Economic Policies: Vol. 3). 576p. 1992. 140.00 (*0-444-89897-2*) Elsevier.

Monetary Policy in Developed Economies: Handbook of Comparative Economic Policies Ser., 3. Ed. by Michele U. Fratianni & Dominick Salvatore. LC 92-4886. 608p. 1992. lib. bdg. 105.00 (*0-313-26869-X*, SMZ, Greenwood Pr) Greenwood.

Monetary Policy in Dollarized Economies, 171. Tomas Balino. LC 98-43299. 1998. write for info. (*1-55775-757-7*) Intl Monetary.

Monetary Policy in Europe after Maastricht. Wilhelm Nolling. LC 93-7294. (ENG & GER.). 1993. text 45.00 (*0-312-09952-5*) St Martin.

Monetary Policy in Interdependent Economies: A Game-Theoretic Approach. Matthew Canzoneri & Dale Henderson. 192p. 1991. 30.00 (*0-262-03178-7*) MIT Pr.

Monetary Policy in Our Times. Ed. by Albert Ando et al. (Illus.). 356p. 1985. 42.00 (*0-262-01082-8*) MIT Pr.

Monetary Policy in Pacific Basin Countries. Ed. by Hang-Sheng Cheng. (C). 1988. lib. bdg. 120.00 (*0-89838-290-4*) Kluwer Academic.

Monetary Policy in the European Monetary System: A Critical Appraisal. Joao Loureiro. LC 96-1959. (European & Transatlantic Studies). (Illus.). 147p. 1996. text 79.00 (*3-540-60784-6*) Spr-Verlag.

Monetary Policy in the United States: An Intellectual & Institutional History. Richard H. Timberlake, Jr. LC 92-44937. (Illus.). 502p. (C). 1993. pap. text 28.95 (*0-226-80384-8*) U Ch Pr.

Monetary Policy in the United States: An Intellectual & Institutional History. Richard H. Timberlake, Jr. LC 92-44937. (Illus.). 528p. (C). 1995. lib. bdg. 65.00 (*0-226-80382-1*) U Ch Pr.

Monetary Policy Instruments for Developing Countries. Ed. by Gerard Caprio, Jr. & Patrick Honohan. 148p. 1991. pap. 22.00 (*0-8213-1969-8*, 11969) World Bank.

Monetary Policy Instruments for European Monetary Union. Lukas Menkhoff. LC 97-7166. 1997. write for info. (*3-540-62454-6*) Spr-Verlag.

Monetary Policy on the Seventy-Fifth Anniversary of the Federal Reserve System. Ed. by Michael T. Belongia. (C). 1990. lib. bdg. 99.00 (*0-7923-9124-1*) Kluwer Academic.

Monetary Policy Rules. John B. Taylor. LC 99-13428. (A National Bureau of Economic Research Conference Report). 456p. 1999. 70.00 (*0-226-79124-6*) U Ch Pr.

Monetary Policy, Taxation, & International Investment Strategy. Ed. by Victor A. Canto & Arthur B. Laffer. LC 90-30017. 376p. 1990. 75.00 (*0-89930-534-2*, Quorum Bks) Greenwood.

Monetary Policy Uncovered: Flying Blind: The Federal Reserve's Experiment with Unobservables. Dimitri B. Papadimitriou & L. Randall Wray. (Public Policy Brief Ser.: Vol. 15). (Illus.). 60p. (Orig.). 1994. pap. write for info. (*0-941276-03-1*) J Levy.

Monetary Policy under the International Gold Standard. Arthur I. Bloomfield. Ed. by Mira Wilkins. LC 78-3899. (International Finance Ser.). 1979. reprint ed. lib. bdg. 17.95 (*0-405-11204-1*) Ayer.

Monetary Politics: Exchange Rate Cooperation in the European Community. Thomas H. Oatley. 240p. (C). 1998. text 47.50 (*0-472-10824-7*, 10824) U of Mich Pr.

Monetary Politics: The Federal Reserve & the Politics of Monetary Policy. John T. Woolley. LC 83-21510. (Illus.). 282p. 1986. pap. text 23.95 (*0-521-31247-7*) Cambridge U Pr.

Monetary Problem: Gold & Silver. Great Britain Gold & Silver Commission. LC 72-1685. reprint ed. 55.00 (*0-404-05362-9*) AMS Pr.

Monetary Problems of an Entrepot: The Hong Kong Experience. C. F. Tom. (American University Studies: Economics: Ser. XVI, Vol. 5). XVI, 132p. (C). 1989. text 27.50 (*0-8204-0864-6*) P Lang Pubng.

Monetary Problems of an Export Economy. Henry C. Wallich. Ed. by Mira Wilkins. LC 78-3955. (International Finance Ser.). 1979. reprint ed. lib. bdg. 36.95 (*0-405-11256-4*) Ayer.

Monetary Problems of the International Economy. Ed. by Robert A. Mundell & Alexander K. Swoboda. (Midway Reprint Ser.). 1993. pap. text 19.00 (*0-226-55066-4*) U Ch Pr.

Monetary Proposals for Social Reform. Margaret Myers. LC 71-110574. 1970. reprint ed. 20.00 (*0-404-04548-0*) AMS Pr.

Monetary Reform & Cooperation Theory. George Macesich. LC 88-25883. 142p. 1989. 57.95 (*0-275-93109-9*, C3109, Praeger Pubs) Greenwood.

Monetary Reform & the Price of Gold: Alternative Approaches. Bologna Center Staff. Ed. by Randall Hinshaw. LC 67-24630. (Illus.). 192p. 1967. reprint ed. pap. 59.60 (*0-608-04029-0*, 206476500011) Bks Demand.

Monetary Reform in Former Socialist Economies. George Macesich & Dimitrije Dimitrejevic. LC 94-25042. 160p. 1994. 55.00 (*0-275-95008-5*, Praeger Pubs) Greenwood.

Monetary Regime Transformations. Ed. by Barry J. Eichengreen. (International Library of Macroeconomic & Financial History: Vol. 3). 608p. 1992. text 240.00 (*1-85278-429-6*) E Elgar.

Monetary Regimes in Transition. Michael D. Bordo & Forrest Capie. LC 92-43109. (Studies in Monetary & Financial History). (Illus.). 408p. (C). 1993. text 69.95 (*0-521-41906-9*) Cambridge U Pr.

Monetary Relations & World Development. Ed. by Fabio Basagni & Pierre Uri. LC 77-15650. 137p. 1977. 47.95 (*0-275-90254-4*, C0254, Praeger Pubs) Greenwood.

Monetary Scenarios: A Modern Approach to Financial Systems. Peter E. Earl. (Illus.). 384p. 1989. text 95.00 (*1-85278-149-1*) E Elgar.

Monetary Sovereignty: The Politics of Central Banking in Western Europe. John B. Goodman. LC 91-57897. (Cornell Studies in Political Economy). (Illus.). 248p. 1992. text 42.50 (*0-8014-2731-2*); pap. text 15.95 (*0-8014-8013-2*) Cornell U Pr.

Monetary Stability Through International Cooperation: Essays in Honour of Andre' Szasz Presented on the Occasion of His Retirement from the Governing Board. Ed. by Age Bakker. 412p. (C). 1994. lib. bdg. 106.00 (*0-7923-3004-8*) Kluwer Academic.

Monetary Standards & Exchange Rates. Maria C. Marcuzzo et al. LC 96-50052. 320p. (C). 1997. write for info. (*0-415-14297-0*) Routledge.

Monetary Standards in Peripherals. Reis Acena. LC 99-29989. 2000. text 75.00 (*0-312-22677-2*) St Martin.

Monetary Statistics of the United States: Estimates, Sources, Methods. Milton Friedman & Anna J. Schwartz. (Business Cycles Ser.: No. 20). 654p. 1970. 160.00 (*0-87014-210-0*) Natl Bur Econ Res.

Monetary Statistics of the United States: Estimates, Sources, Methods. Milton Friedman & Anna J. Schwartz. LC 78-85410. (National Bureau of Economic Research, Studies in Business Cycles: No. 20). 654p. reprint ed. pap. 200.00 (*0-8357-3245-2*, 205713900011) Bks Demand.

Monetary Structure of the Nepalese Economy: Policy Issues in Theory & Practice. Gunanidhi Sharma. 243p. 1987. 18.50 (*81-7003-076-5*, Pub. by S Asia Pubs) S Asia.

Monetary Structure of the Nepalese Economy: Policy Issues in Theory & Practice. Gunanidhi Sharma. 243p. (C). 1987. 180.00 (*0-89771-052-5*, Pub. by Ratna Pustak Bhandar) St Mut.

Monetary System in the Bengal Presidency. Debendra B. Mitra. (C). 1991. 20.00 (*81-7074-100-9*) S Asia.

Monetary Theory. Ed. by Thomas Mayer. (International Library of Critical Writings in Economics: Vol. 7). 384p. 1990. text 210.00 (*1-85278-180-7*) E Elgar.

Monetary Theory: National & International. Alvaro Cencini. LC 94-33804. 400p. (C). (gr. 13). 1995. 110.00 (*0-415-11054-8*, C0182) Routledge.

Monetary Theory: National & International. Alvaro Cencini. LC 96-40351. 400p. (C). 1997. pap. 29.99 (*0-415-11055-6*) Routledge.

Monetary Theory & Fiscal Policy. Alvin H. Hansen. LC 82-20924. 236p. (C). 1983. reprint ed. lib. bdg. 55.00 (*0-313-23736-0*, HAMT, Greenwood Pr) Greenwood.

Monetary Theory & Monetary Policy Vol. 2: The Selected Essays of Karl Brunner. Karl Brunner. Ed. by Thomas Lys. LC 96-48955. 328p. 1997. 100.00 (*1-85898-026-7*) E Elgar.

Monetary Theory & Policy. Milton H. Marquis. 400p. (C). 1996. mass mkt. 95.95 (*0-314-06923-2*) West Pub.

Monetary Theory & Policy. Carl E. Walsh. LC 98-20018. (Illus.). 504p. 1998. 55.00 (*0-262-23199-9*) MIT Pr.

Monetary Theory of Employment. Gardiner C. Means. Ed. by Warren J. Samuels & Frederic S. Lee. LC 94-26135. (Studies in Institutional Economics Ser.). 292p. (C). (gr. 13). 1994. text 81.95 (*1-56324-477-2*) M E Sharpe.

Monetary Theory of Employment. Gardiner C. Means. Ed. by Warren J. Samuels & Frederic S. Lee. LC 94-26135. (Studies in Institutional Economics). 292p. (gr. 13). 1994. pap. text 40.95 (*1-56324-478-0*) M E Sharpe.

Monetary Theory, 1601-1758, 6 vols., Set. Ed. by Antoin E. Murphy. LC 95-37515. 2200p. (C). 1997. 980.00 (*0-415-12533-2*) Routledge.

***Monetary Transmission in Europe: The Role of Financial Markets & Credit.** Jan Kakes. LC 99-87030. 168p. 2000. 75.00 (*1-84064-241-6*) E Elgar.

***Monetary Transmission Process: Recent Developments & Lessons for Europe.** Deutsche Bundesbank. LC 00-42080. (Illus.). 2000. write for info. (*0-312-23766-9*) St Martin.

Monetary Trends in the United Kingdom: Papers Presented at the Twenty-Second Meeting of the Panel of Academic Consultants on 28 October, 1983. Includes Part 2 & Appendix B to the Paper by Professor D. F. Hendry & N. R. Ericsson. Bank of England Staff. LC HG0935.. 140p. reprint ed. pap. 43.40 (*0-8357-3732-2*, 203645800003) Bks Demand.

Monetary Trends in the United States & the United Kingdom: Their Relation to Income, Prices, & Interest Rates, 1867-1975. Milton Friedman & Anna J. Schwartz. LC 81-16273. (National Bureau of Economic Research Monographs). (Illus.). xxxii, 664p. (C). 1994. reprint ed. lib. bdg. 60.00 (*0-226-26409-2*) U Ch Pr.

Monetary Trends in the United States & the United Kingdom: Their Relation to Income, Prices, & Interest Rates, 1867-1975. Milton Friedman & Anna J. Schwartz. LC 81-16273. (National Bureau of Economic Research Monographs). (Illus.). xxxii, 696p. (C). 1996. reprint ed. pap. text 30.00 (*0-226-26410-6*) U Ch Pr.

Monetary Trends in the United States & the United Kingdom, Their Relation to Income, Prices, & Interest Rates, 1867-1975. Milton Friedman. LC 81-16273. (National Bureau of Economic Research Monograph Ser.). (Illus.). 696p. reprint ed. pap. 200.00 (*0-608-09302-5*, 205417600004) Bks Demand.

***Monetary Union & Collective Bargaining in Europe.** Ed. by Philippe Pochet. (Work & Society Ser.: Vol. 22). 288p. 2000. pap. 27.95 (*0-8204-4653-X*) P Lang Pubng.

***Monetary Union & Fiscal Stability: A New Approach.** Frank Bohn. LC 99-87533. (Contributions to Economics Ser.). (Illus.). xiv, 225p. 2000. pap. 63.00 (*3-7908-1266-8*, Pub. by Physica-Verlag) Spr-Verlag.

***Monetary Union, Employment & Growth: The Impact of the Euro as a Global Currency.** Pier Carlo Padoan. LC 00-29414. 2000. write for info. (*1-84064-372-2*) E Elgar.

Monetazione di Messana: Con le Emissioni di Rhegion Dell'eta Della Tirannide. Maria C. Caltabiano. Ed. by German Archeological Institute Staff. (Antike Muenzen & Geschnittene Steine Ser.: Band XIII). (GER.). xix, 383p. (C). 1993. lib. bdg. 232.00 (*3-11-013527-2*) Mouton.

Monetry Policy Operations. Calomiris. 1993. pap. text 2.00 (*0-201-76513-6*) Addison-Wesley.

Monet's Garden at Giverny: Postcard. Photos by Richard Ross. (Illus.). 30p. 1996. pap. 10.95 (*1-55670-480-1*) Stewart Tabori & Chang.

Monet's Gardens at Giverny: A Book of Postcards. Elizabeth Murray. 1990. pap. 9.95 (*0-87654-586-X*, A556) Pomegranate Calif.

Monet's Ghost. Chelsea Quinn Yarbro. (Illus.). (YA). (gr. 7 up). 1997. 17.00 (*0-614-29093-7*) Atheneum Yung Read.

Monet's Ghost. Chelsea Quinn Yarbro. LC 96-85373. (Dragonflight Ser.: No. 12). (Illus.). 160p. (J). (gr. 7 up). 1997. 17.00 (*0-689-80732-5*) S&S Childrens.

Monet's Giverny: An Impressionist Colony. William H. Gerdts. LC 93-7379. (Illus.). 256p. 1993. 45.00 (*1-55859-386-1*) Abbeville Pr.

Monet's House. Heide Michels. Tr. by Helen Ivor from FRE. LC 97-210585. (Illus.). 144p. 1997. 35.00 (*0-517-70667-9*) C Potter.

Monet's House at Giverny: A Pop-Up Carousel. Gerald Van Der Kemp & Bob Hersey. (Illus.). 1999. pap. 19.95 (*0-7893-0268-3*, Pub. by Universe) St Martin.

***Monet's Landscapes.** Vivian Russell. (Illus.). 160p. 2000. 35.00 (*0-8212-2672-X*) Bulfinch Pr.

Monet's Passion: Ideas, Inspiration & Insights from the Painter's Gardens. Elizabeth Murray. LC 89-61640. (Illus.). 144p. 1989. 34.95 (*0-87654-443-X*) Pomegranate Calif.

Monet's Table: The Cooking Journals of Claude Monet. Claire Joyes. (Illus.). 192p. 1990. 34.50 (*0-671-69259-3*) S&S Trade.

Monet's Water Lilies, Vol. 1. Vivian Russell. LC ND553.M7A4 1998b. (Illus.). 88p. 1998. 24.95 (*0-8212-2553-7*, Pub. by Bulfinch Pr) Little.

Monet's Years at Giverny: Beyond Impressionism. Metropolitan Museum of Art Staff. LC 95-1153. (Illus.). 182p. 1995. pap. 14.98 (*0-8109-8138-6*, Pub. by Abrams) Time Warner.

Monet's Years at Giverny: Beyond Impressionism. Daniel Wildenstein. LC 78-328. (Illus.). 182p. 1978. 29.95 (*0-8109-1336-4*); pap. 16.95 (*0-8109-2183-9*, Pub. by Abrams) Time Warner.

M

Money. (Cross Training Ser.: Vol. 4). 64p. (YA). (gr. 10-12). 1995. pap. 29.95 incl. VHS (*1-57405-033-8*) CharismaLife Pub.

Money. Amy Adelstein. LC 97-6365. (Money & Me Ser.). 48p. (J). (gr. 3-8). 1998. lib. bdg. 22.60 (*0-86625-611-3*) Rourke Pubns.

Money. David Axlerod et al. 1964. pap. 7.00 (*0-8222-0771-0*) Dramatists Play.

***Money.** Victoria Benedictsson. Tr. by Sarah Death from SWE. 186p. 2000. pap. 22.95 (*1-870041-40-2*, Pub. by Norvik Pr) Dufour.

Money. Donna Burk et al. (Box It or Bag It Mathematics Ser.). (Illus.). 66p. (C). 1988. teacher ed., ring bd. 9.00 (*1-886131-08-2*, BB7) Math Lrning.

Money. Peggy Burns. (Stepping Through History Ser.). (Illus.). 32p. (J). 1994. lib. bdg. 5.00 (*1-56847-248-X*) Raintree Steck-V.

Money. Beverly Cohn & Jack Nadel. (Nit-Wits Ser.). 80p. 1997. pap. 4.95 (*0-922658-10-2*) MMS Pub.

***Money.** Joe Cribb. (Eyewitness Books). (Illus.). (J). (gr. 4-7). 2000. 19.99 (*0-7894-6567-1*) DK Pub Inc.

***Money.** Joe Cribb. (Eyewitness Books). (J). (gr. 4-7). 2000. 15.95 (*0-7894-5822-5*) DK Pub Inc.

Money. Todd Daubert & Pauline Nelson. (Activity Book for Math Ser.). (Illus.). 112p. (Orig.). 1995. pap. 14.95 (*1-57022-045-X*) ECS Lrn Systs.

***Money.** Pat Dickinson. 280p. 2000. pap. write for info. (*1-893162-79-6*) AmErica.

Money. Carolyn Englehart. (Lifesearch Ser.). 64p. 1996. pap. 4.95 (*0-687-01499-9*) Abingdon.

***Money.** Margaret Hall. LC 99-46700. (Earning, Saving, Spending Ser.). 2000. lib. bdg. write for info. (*1-57572-233-X*) Heinemann Lib.

Money. Q. High. (Orig.). 1998. pap. 2.99 (*0-7681-0029-1*, McClanahan Book) Learn Horizon.

Money. Greg Lee. LC 92-44074. (J). 1993. 9.50 (*0-685-66360-4*) Rourke Corp.

Money. Greg Lee. LC 92-44074. (Little Jokester Ser.). 24p. (J). (gr. k-4). 1993. lib. bdg. 10.95 (*0-86593-268-9*) Rourke Corp.

Money. Jo E. Moore. (Mathematics Ser.). (Illus.). 32p. (J). (gr. 2-3). 1997. pap., teacher ed. 2.95 (*1-55799-456-0*, 4058) Evan-Moor Edu Pubs.

Money. Earl Ockenga & Walt Rucker. (Elementary Mathematics Ser.). (Illus.). 16p. (J). (gr. 1). 1990. pap. text 1.25 (*1-56281-125-8*, M125) Extra Eds.

Money. Joanne F. Oppenheim. LC 94-12740. (United Nations Bookshelf Ser.). (J). 1994. text 14.95 (*0-689-31910-X*) Atheneum Yung Read.

Money. Stephen Pollan. 2000. 30.00 (*0-06-661993-9*); 18.00 (*0-06-661994-7*) HarpC.

Money. Abraham Resnick. (Lucent Overview Ser.). (Illus.). (YA). (gr. 5-8). 1995. lib. bdg. 22.45 (*1-56006-165-0*) Lucent Bks.

Money, 28 vols. Adele Richardson. LC 98-36407. (Let's Investigate Economics Ser.). (Illus.). 32p. (YA). (gr. 2 up). 1999. lib. bdg. 19.95 (*0-88682-555-5*, Creat Educ) Creative Co.

Money. Paul-Loup Sulitzer. Tr. by Susan Wald. 320p. 1985. 15.95 (*0-8184-0373-X*) Carol Pub Group.

Money. Paul-Loup Sulitzer. 1983. pap. 12.95 (*0-7859-3113-9*) Fr & Eur.

Money. Robert Young. LC 97-5287. (Household History Ser.). (J). (gr. 5 up). 1997. lib. bdg. 22.60 (*1-57505-070-6*, Carolrhoda) Lerner Pub.

Money. Robery Young. LC 98-14099. (Household History Ser.). 48p. (J). (gr. 3-6). 1999. lib. bdg. 22.60 (*1-57505-220-2*, Carolrhoda) Lerner Pub.

Money. Emile Zola. Tr. by Benjamin R. Tucker from FRE. LC 81-13515.Tr. of L'argent. 1976. lib. bdg. 250.00 (*0-8490-0658-9*) Gordon Pr.

Money. Roy F. Harrod. LC 83-22868. 355p. 1984. reprint ed. lib. bdg. 69.50 (*0-313-24373-5*, HMON, Greenwood Pr) Greenwood.

Money, 2 vols. in 1. Karl T. Helfferich. Tr. by Louis Infield. LC 67-19708. (Library of Money & Banking History). xiv, 600p. 1969. reprint ed. 57.50 (*0-678-00474-9*) Kelley.

Money. Francis A. Walker. LC 68-25641. (Reprints of Economic Classics Ser.). xv, 550p. 1968. reprint ed. 49.50 (*0-678-00395-5*) Kelley.

Money. Emile Zola. (Pocket Classics Ser.).Tr. of L'argent. 448p. 1991. reprint ed. pap. 10.95 (*0-7509-0020-2*, Pub. by Sutton Pub Ltd) Intl Pubs Mktg.

Money. 4th ed. Sri Aurobindo & Mother. Ed. by Vijay. 28p. 1997. pap. 1.00 (*81-7060-090-1*, Pub. by SAA) E-W Cultural Ctr.

Money: A History. Ed. by Jonathan Williams. (Illus.). 256p. 1998. pap. 18.95 (*0-312-21212-7*) St Martin.

Money: A Medium of Power. Roger C. Elletson. LC 96-80308. xxv, 267p. 1998. pap. 26.00 (*1-880262-05-3*) Gd Teton Univ.

Money: A One Hundred Thousand Dollar Misunderstanding. unabridged ed. C. M. Simon. 227p. 1998. pap. 16.00 (*1-892489-06-6*, 0144) Dead Trees Alive.

Money: A Study of the Theory of the Medium of Exchange. David Kinley. 415p. 1968. reprint ed. lib. bdg. 89.50 (*0-8371-0515-3*, Greenwood Pr) Greenwood.

Money: A Suicide Note. Martin Amis. (Fiction Ser.). 368p. 1986. pap. 13.95 (*0-14-008891-1*, Penguin Bks) Viking Penguin.

Money: A Thematic Unit. Jennifer Edwards. (Thematic Units Ser.). (Illus.). 80p. (J). (gr. 3-5). 1994. student ed. 9.95 (*1-55734-237-7*) Tchr Create Mat.

Money: An Owner's Manual: A Personal Guide to Financial Freedom. Dennis R. Deaton. LC 92-64320. (Illus.). 286p. (Orig.). 1992. pap. 11.95 (*1-881840-25-5*) TimeMax.

Money: Bank of the Eighties. Dimitris N. Chorafas. (Illus.). 256p. 1981. 27.50 (*0-89433-182-5*) Petrocelli.

Money: Basic Mathematics Skills. Jo Ellen Moore. (Illus.). 32p. (J). (gr. 2-3). 1995. pap., wbk. ed. 2.50 (*1-58610-078-5*, Learn on the Go) Learn Horizon.

Money: Denarius to Decimal. Compiled by Robin Grieve. 39.00 (*1-56696-127-0*) Jackdaw.

Money: Exploring the Ways We Use It. Raymond C. Clark. (Vocabureader Workbook Ser.: No. 4). (Illus.). 96p. 1989. pap. text 12.50 (*0-86647-029-8*) Pro Lingua.

Money: Gold, Silver, of Bimetalism. Melville D. Landon. (Notable American Authors Ser.). 1999. reprint ed. lib. bdg. 125.00 (*0-7812-3696-7*) Rprt Serv.

Money: How Much Is Enough. James Reapsome & Martha Reapsome. LC 93-49885. (Truthseed Ser.). 96p. 1995. pap. 4.99 (*1-56476-309-9*, 6-3309, Victor Bks) Chariot Victor.

Money: How to Get It, Keep It & Make It Grow. Tama McAleese. (Money & Power Ser.). 100p. 1997. text 19.95 (*0-7910-4471-8*) Chelsea Hse.

Money: How to Get It, Keep It, & Make It Grow. Michael Hayes. LC 78-27414. 224p. reprint ed. pap. 69.50 (*0-608-12166-5*, 202391600034) Bks Demand.

Money: How to Make It, Spend It, & Keep Lots of It. Todd Temple. LC 97-51244. (Illus.). 192p. (YA). (gr. 7-12). 1998. pap. 10.99 (*0-8054-0168-7*) Broadman.

Money: Income Taxes. Sprouse. 1995. 13.99 (*0-446-75009-3*, Pub. by Warner Bks) Little.

***Money: Its Origins, Development & Prospects.** John H. Wood. (Economic Education Bulletin Ser.: Vol. 39, No. 8). (Illus.). 109p. 1999. pap. 10.00 (*0-913610-11-9*) Am Inst Econ Res.

***Money Living Well in Retirement.** National Network Book Publishing Staff. 1999. 24.95 (*1-883013-76-3*, People Bks) Tme Inc.

Money: Lure, Lore & Literature, 55. Ed. by John L. DiGaetani. LC 93-39359. (Contributions to the Study of World Literature Ser.: No. 55). 288p. 1994. 65.00 (*0-313-29219-1*, Greenwood Pr) Greenwood.

Money: Only a By-Product. I. A. Smalis. LC 87-6439. (Key Business Ser.). 96p. 1987. 12.95 (*0-86534-100-1*) Sunstone Pr.

Money: Profitable Investing in the New Century. (Illus.). 24.95 (*1-929049-09-9*) Tme Inc.

***Money: Save It, Manage It, Spend It.** Mary Bowman-Kruhm. (Teen Issues Ser.). (Illus.). 64p. (YA). (gr. 6 up). 2000. lib. bdg. 17.95 (*0-7660-1363-4*) Enslow Pubs.

Money: The Battle for Howard Hughes's Billions. J. R. Phelan & Laura Chester. 1997. 23.00 (*0-679-44884-5*) Random.

Money: The Battle for Howard Hughes's Millions. James R. Phelan & Lewis Chester. 1997. 31.00 (*0-614-28018-4*) Random.

Money: The Financial System & Economic Policy. S. Kerry Cooper et al. (Finance Ser.). 576p. 1983. text. write for info. (*0-201-03994-X*) Addison-Wesley.

***Money: The Financial System & the Economy.** 3rd ed. Glenn Hubbard. LC 99-30554. 830p. (C). 1999. 98.00 (*0-201-47381-X*) Addison-Wesley.

Money: The Great Hoax. 1993. lib. bdg. 261.95 (*0-8490-8909-3*) Gordon Pr.

Money: Who Has How Much & Why. Andrew Hacker. LC 97-9038. 246p. 1997. 24.50 (*0-684-19646-8*) S&S Trade.

Money: Who Has How Much & Why. Andrew Hacker. 256p. 1998. per. 13.00 (*0-684-84662-4*, Touchstone) S&S Trade Pap.

Money: Ye Shall Have Honest Weights & Measures. unabridged ed. James E. Ewart. LC 98-91362. (Illus.). xxii, 325p. 1998. 59.95 (*0-9663570-0-0*) Principia Pub.

Money: Your Money - Nine "Space-Age" Investment Markets, Real Good! William West. LC 89-90129. (Illus.). 1989. 19.00 (*0-911614-30-3*) John Babish.

Money: Your Top Investing Moves for Retirement. Time-Life Books Editors. 176p. (gr. 7). 1999. 29.95 (*1-883013-18-6*) Time-Life.

Money: 127 Answers to Your Most-Asked Financial Questions: The Q & A Reference for Everything from Asset Allocation to Zero-Coupon Bonds. Steven C. Camp. Ed. by Melanie Trunkey. (Illus.). 118p. (Orig.). 1995. pap. 12.95 (*1-887620-00-1*) Trunkey Pub.

***Money: 5 Life Changing Strategies to Financial Success.** Walter Hallam. 1999. pap. write for info. (*0-9661417-1-7*) W Hallam Minist.

Money - By the Mouthful! Robert O. Nara & Steven A. Mariner. LC 79-91111. 1979. pap. write for info. (*0-933420-00-5*) Oramedics Intl.

Money - Space: Geographies of Monetary Transformation. Andrew Leyshon & Nigel Thrift. LC 96-18262. (International Library of Sociology Ser.). 424p. (C). 1997. 85.00 (*0-415-13981-3*); pap. 27.99 (*0-415-03835-9*) Routledge.

Money, Accumulation & Crisis. Duncan K. Foley. (Fundamentals of Pure & Applied Economics Ser.: Vol. 2). viii, 60p. 1986. pap. text 59.00 (*3-7186-0280-6*) Gordon & Breach.

Money Adventure: Earning, Spending, Saving, Sharing. Neale S. Godfrey. LC 94-45103. (One & Only Common Cents Ser.). (Illus.). 32p. (J). (gr. k up). 1995. 13.95 (*0-382-39113-6*) Silver Burdett Pr.

Money Adventure: Earning, Spending, Saving, Sharing. Neale S. Godfrey. (J). (gr. 4-7). 1996. lib. bdg. 15.95 (*0-382-39112-8*) Silver Burdett Pr.

Money Adventure: Earning, Spending, Saving, Sharing. Neale S. Godfrey. (Illus.). 32p. (J). (gr. 4-7). 1996. pap. text 5.95 (*0-382-39315-5*) Silver Burdett Pr.

Money Adventure: Rake It in & Squander It. Egbert Sukop. Ed. by Terry Stevens. (Illus.). 176p. 1998. pap. text 20.00 (*0-9663445-0-2*) W. Rong.

***Money Adviser 2000.** Ed. by Money Magazine Editors. (Illus.). 2000. 24.95 (*1-883013-89-5*, People Bks) Tme Inc.

***Money Affirmation Book: A 30-Day Program to Awaken the Financial Genius in You.** James L. Heath. LC 99-95687. 120p. 2000. pap. 19.95 (*0-9674223-0-2*) Road to Riches.

Money Agency Planning Guide. 8th ed. Jeffrey Brisky. 192p. 1996. pap. 25.00 (*1-56150-191-3*) Intl Wealth.

Money Agency Planning Guide. 9th ed. Jeffrey Brisky. 192p. 1998. pap. 25.00 (*1-56150-241-3*) Intl Wealth.

Money Agency Planning Guide. 10th ed. Jeffrey Brisky. 192p. 1999. pap. 25.00 (*1-56150-292-8*) Intl Wealth.

***Money Agency Planning Guide.** 11th ed. Jeffrey Brisky. 192p. 2000. pap. 25.00 (*1-56150-352-5*) Intl Wealth.

Money & Banking. Michael R. Baye. LC 94-76473. (C). Date not set. text 68.76 (*0-395-64395-3*) HM.

Money & Banking. Michael R. Baye. (C). 1995. pap., teacher ed. 11.96 (*0-395-72566-6*); pap. text, student ed. 20.36 (*0-395-72567-4*) HM.

Money & Banking. Elbert V. Bowden. Date not set. text 65.75 (*0-314-72626-8*) West Pub.

Money & Banking. Craine. (C). 1998. text 61.50 (*0-03-096959-X*) Harcourt Coll Pubs.

Money & Banking. Hein. (C). 1995. pap. text 22.00 (*0-03-012527-8*) Harcourt Coll Pubs.

Money & Banking. Herbert M. Kaufman. 508p. (C). 1992. text 72.76 (*0-669-24350-7*); teacher ed. 2.66 (*0-669-24351-5*); student ed. 23.56 (*0-669-24352-3*) HM Trade Div.

Money & Banking. Richard W. Lindholm. (Quality Paperback Ser.: No. 19). 271p. (Orig.). 1969. pap. 8.00 (*0-8226-0019-6*) Littlefield.

Money & Banking. Jack Rudman. (Dantes Subject Standardized Tests Ser.: DANTES-28). 1994. pap. 23.95 (*0-8373-6628-3*) Nat Learn.

Money & Banking. Jack Rudman. (DANTES Ser.: No. 28). 1994. 39.95 (*0-8373-6528-7*) Nat Learn.

Money & Banking. Jack Rudman. (College Level Examination (CLEP) Ser.: Vol. CLEP-25). 1994. pap. 23.95 (*0-8373-5325-4*) Nat Learn.

Money & Banking. Young. (C). 1996. text. write for info. (*0-03-096961-1*); pap. text, teacher ed. write for info. (*0-03-011747-X*) Harcourt Coll Pubs.

Money & Banking. William A. Scott. Ed. by Stuart Bruchey. LC 80-1168. (Rise of Commercial Banking Ser.). 1981. reprint ed. lib. bdg. 38.95 (*0-405-13678-1*) Ayer.

Money & Banking. 2nd ed. David H. Friedman. (Illus.). 611p. (C). 1989. text 45.00 (*0-89982-358-0*) Am Bankers.

Money & Banking. 3rd ed. David H. Friedman. (Illus.). 600p. (C). 1993. pap. text 45.00 (*0-89982-316-5*) Am Bankers.

Money & Banking. 4th ed. David H. Friedman. (Illus.). 438p. (C). 1975. 12.00 (*0-89982-016-6*) Am Bankers.

Money & Banking. 8th ed. David R. Kamerschen. (Thomson Executive Press). (C). 1984. 34.00 (*0-538-08260-7*, H26) S-W Pub.

Money & Banking: Exercise Guide. Young. (C). 1996. pap. text, suppl. ed. write for info. (*0-03-011748-8*) Harcourt Coll Pubs.

Money & Banking: Financial Institutions & Economic Policy. Marilu H. McCarty. (Economics Ser.). (Illus.). 544p. (C). 1982. text 31.25 (*0-201-05098-6*) Addison-Wesley.

Money & Banking: Financial Markets & Institutions. Garry D. Smith. (Illus.). (C). 1982. text. write for info. (*0-201-07696-9*) Addison-Wesley.

Money & Banking: Test Bank. Young. (C). 1996. pap. text, suppl. ed. write for info. (*0-03-011749-6*) Harcourt Coll Pubs.

Money & Banking: The American Experience. Ed. by George Edward Durell Foundation Staff. 390p. (C). 1994. lib. bdg. 59.50 (*0-913969-74-5*) Univ Pub Assocs.

Money & Banking: Theory & Debate (1900-1940) Riccardo Realfonzo. LC 98-27885. (ITA.). 208p. 1998. 80.00 (*1-85898-765-2*) E Elgar.

Money & Banking in Africa. J. Onoh. 1982. pap. text. write for info. (*0-582-64336-8*, Pub. by Addison-Wesley) Longman.

Money & Banking in Africa. J. K. Onoh. LC 82-15266. 224p. reprint ed. pap. 69.50 (*0-8357-2968-0*, 203923000011) Bks Demand.

Money & Banking in Britain: A History. M. Collins. 656p. 1988. lib. bdg. 99.95 (*0-7099-0760-5*, Pub. by C Helm) Routldge.

Money & Banking in Contemporary Japan: The Theoretical Setting & Its Application. Yoshio Suzuki. Tr. by John G. Greenwood. LC 79-23627. 276p. reprint ed. pap. 85.60 (*0-8357-8232-8*, 203390000087) Bks Demand.

Money & Banking in Islam. Ziauddin Ahmad et al. 299p. (Orig.). 1983. pap. 9.95 (*0-939830-27-2*, Pub. by Inst Pol Stud) New Era Publns MI.

Money & Banking in Latin America. Mario Rietti. LC 79-4157. 295p. 1979. 69.50 (*0-275-90412-1*, C0412, Praeger Pubs) Greenwood.

Money & Banking in Maryland. Stuart R. Bruchey et al. LC 96-558. 1996. 65.00 (*0-938420-52-6*) MD Hist.

Money & Banking in Medieval & Renaissance Venice, Vol. 1. Frederic C. Lane & Reinhold C. Mueller. LC 84-47947. 707p. 1985. reprint ed. pap. 200.00 (*0-608-03712-5*, 206453700001) Bks Demand.

Money & Banking in the Chinese Mainland. Katherine H. Hsiao. (Mainland China Economic Ser.: No. 1). (Illus.). 106p. 1985. pap. 30.00 (*0-295-96208-9*) U of Wash Pr.

Money & Banking Issues for the Twenty-First Century: Essays in Honour of Stephen Frowen. Ed. by Philip Arestis. LC 93-17301. 319p. 1993. text 79.95 (*0-312-09994-0*) St Martin.

Money & Banking Pakistan. 3rd ed. S. A. Meenai. 318p. 1985. pap. text 21.95 (*0-19-577327-6*) OUP.

Money & Beyond. 2nd ed. Arnold M. Patent. 226p. 1997. 16.95 (*1-885223-24-2*) Beyond Words Pub.

Money & Business Cycles Vol. 1: The Economics of F. A. Hayek. Ed. by M. Colonna & Harald Hagemann. LC 93-42575. 256p. 1994. text 100.00 (*1-85898-011-9*) E Elgar.

Money & Capital in Economic Development. Ronald I. McKinnon. LC 72-9928. 184p. 1973. pap. 14.95 (*0-8157-5613-5*) Brookings.

Money & Capital Markets. Tim S. Campbell. (C). 1988. text 67.50 (*0-673-18712-8*) Addson-Wesley Educ.

Money & Capital Markets. James. (C). 1997. pap. text, teacher ed. write for info. (*0-03-052533-0*); pap. text, student ed. write for info. (*0-03-052532-2*) Harcourt Coll Pubs.

Money & Capital Markets. Miles Livingston. 1996. pap. text 62.95 (*1-55786-884-0*) Blackwell Pubs.

Money & Capital Markets. 5th ed. Peter S. Rose. LC 93-30804. (Series in Finance). 864p. (C). 1993. text 71.75 (*0-256-12199-0*, Irwn McGrw-H) McGrw-H Hghr Educ.

Money & Capital Markets. 5th ed. Peter S. Rose. (C). 1996. text 72.58 (*0-256-18570-0*, Irwn McGrw-H) McGrw-H Hghr Educ.

Money & Capital Markets. 6th ed. Peter S. Rose. LC 96-8515. 800p. (C). 1996. text 71.75 (*0-256-15239-X*, Irwn McGrw-H) McGrw-H Hghr Educ.

Money & Capital Markets. 7th ed. Rose. LC 99-27993. 864p. 1999. 88.44 (*0-07-231002-2*) McGraw.

***Money & Capital Markets: Financial Institutions & Instruments in a Global Marketplace.** 7th ed. Peter S. Rose. LC 99-27993. (Illus.). 2000. write for info. (*0-07-116980-6*, Irwn Prfssnl) McGraw-Hill Prof.

Money & Capital Markets: Pricing, Yields & Analysis. 2nd ed. Michael Sherris. LC 97-116883. 232p. 1997. pap. text 34.95 (*1-86448-159-5*, Pub. by Allen & Unwin Pty) Paul & Co Pubs.

Money & Capital Markets: The Financial System in an Increasingly Global Economy. 4th ed. Peter S. Rose. 380p. (C). 1991. text 66.95 (*0-256-08300-2*, Irwn McGrw-H) McGrw-H Hghr Educ.

Money & Capital Markets in Postbellum America. John A. James. LC 77-85540. 311p. 1978. reprint ed. pap. 96.50 (*0-608-02879-7*, 206394300007) Bks Demand.

Money & Conquest: Allied Occupation Currencies in World War II. Vladimir Petrov. LC 66-26685. (Johns Hopkins University Studies in Historical & Political Science: Series 84: No. 2). 282p. reprint ed. pap. 87.50 (*0-608-10213-X*, 202073200018) Bks Demand.

Money & Consumer Durable Spending. rev. ed. Christopher Brown. LC 92-34573. (Financial Sector of the American Economy Ser.). 192p. 1992. text 20.00 (*0-8153-1211-3*) Garland.

Money & Credit Instruments in Their Relation to General Prices. Edwin W. Kemmerer & Oskar Morgenstern. LC 82-48192. (Gold, Money, Inflation & Deflation Ser.). 213p. 1983. lib. bdg. 30.00 (*0-8240-5245-5*) Garland.

Money & Debt: A Solution to the Global Crisis. 2nd ed. Thomas H. Greco, Jr. (Illus.). 76p. 1990. pap. 8.00 (*0-9625208-1-0*) T H Greco.

Money & Democracy. George Macesich. LC 89-26540. 184p. 1990. 52.95 (*0-275-93480-2*, C3480, Greenwood Pr) Greenwood.

Money & Economic Growth. Jac J. Sijben. 1977. lib. bdg. 77.50 (*90-207-0655-1*) Kluwer Academic.

Money & Emotional Conflicts. Edmund Bergler. LC 84-22390. xiii, 269p. 1985. 40.00 (*0-8236-3445-0*, 03445) Intl Univs Pr.

Money & European Union. Overturf. LC 99-58619. 1999. pap. 19.95 (*0-312-22460-5*) St Martin.

Money & European Union. Stephen F. Overturf. LC 96-53464. 352p. 1997. text 45.00 (*0-312-17301-6*) St Martin.

Money & Exchange in Europe & America, 1600-1775: A Handbook. John J. McCusker. (Institute of Early American History & Culture Ser.). xiii, 367p. 1992. pap. 37.50 (*0-8078-4367-9*) U of NC Pr.

***Money & Finance: Issues Institutions Policies.** Ed. by Deena Khatkhate. 1998. 30.00 (*81-250-0844-6*, Pub. by Orient Longman Ltd) S Asia.

Money & Finance: Readings in Theory, Policy & Institutions. 2nd ed. Deane Carson. LC 70-37643. (Illus.). 510p. 1972. reprint ed. pap. 158.10 (*0-7837-3508-1*, 205784100008) Bks Demand.

Money & Finance in Contemporary Yugoslavia. Dimitrije Dimitrijevic & George Macesich. LC 72-92889. (Special Studies in International Economics & Development). 1973. 42.95 (*0-275-28725-4*) Irvington.

Money & Finance in East & West. Ed. by Christopher T. Saunders. (East-West European Economic Interaction Ser.: Vol. 4). 1979. 54.95 (*0-387-81507-4*) Spr-Verlag.

Money & Finance in Economic Growth & Development: Essays in Honor of Edward S. Shaw: Proceedings of the Conference Held at Stanford University. Ed. by Ronald I. McKinnon. LC 75-21191. (Business Economics & Finance Ser.: No. 8). 351p. reprint ed. pap. 108.90 (*0-7837-0963-3*, 204126800019) Bks Demand.

Money & Finance in Hong Kong No. 2: Retrospect & Prospect. Y. C. Jao. (East Asian Institute Occasional Paper Ser.). (Illus.). 84p. 1998. pap. 20.00 (*981-02-3481-3*, Pub. by Sngapore Univ Pr) Coronet Bks.

Money & Finance in the Age of Merchant Capitalism. John Day. LC 98-25561. 240p. 1999. 59.95 (*0-631-16462-6*) Blackwell Pubs.

Money & Finance in the Transition to a Market Economy. Istvan Abel et al. LC 97-43508. 224p. 1998. 80.00 (*1-85898-228-6*) E Elgar.

Money & Finance in Yugoslavia: A Comparative Analysis. Dimitrije Dimitrijevic & George Macesich. LC 84-21162. 220p. 1983. 47.95 (*0-275-90971-9*, C0971, Praeger Pubs) Greenwood.

***Money & Financial Institutions - A Game Theoretic Approach: Selected Essays of Martin Shubik.** Martin Shubik. LC 99-22253. (Economists of the Twentieth Century Ser.: Vol. 2). 448p. 1999. 110.00 (*1-84064-190-8*) E Elgar.

Money & Foreign Exchange after 1914. Gustav Cassel. LC 72-4266. (World Affairs Ser.: National & International Viewpoints). 294p. 1972. reprint ed. 21.95 (*0-405-04563-8*) Ayer.

Money & Freedom. rev. ed. Hans F. Sennholz. 88p. (Orig.). 1985. pap. text 6.95 (*0-910884-16-1*) Libertarian Press.

Money & Freedom: The New American Game. Eric Dahlhauser. 1993. pap. 9.95 (*0-9631782-1-0*) C Y W & D Accts.

Money & Freedom: The New American Game. Eric B. Dahlhauser & Stephen J. Wolf. 127p. 1991. 24.95 (*0-9631782-0-2*) C Y W & D Accts.

Money & Friends. David Williamson. LC 98-115331. 1997. pap. 5.25 (*0-8222-1580-2*) Dramatists Play.

Money & General Equilibrium Theory: From Walras to Pareto (1870-1923) Pascal Bridel. LC 97-12052. 224p. 1997. 85.00 (*1-85898-623-0*) E Elgar.

Money & Good Intentions Are Not Enough: or Why a Liberal Democrat Thinks States Need Both Competition & Community. John E. Brandl. LC 97-45313. 177p. 1998. pap. 16.95 (*0-8157-1059-3*); text 39.95 (*0-8157-1060-7*) Brookings.

Money & Government in the Roman Empire. Richard Duncan-Jones. LC 93-31989. (Illus.). 320p. (C). 1994. text 85.00 (*0-521-44192-7*) Cambridge U Pr.

Money & Government in the Roman Empire. Richard Duncan-Jones. (Illus.). 320p. (C). 1998. pap. text 27.95 (*0-521-64829-7*) Cambridge U Pr.

***Money & Growth: Selected Papers of Allyn Abbott Young.** Allyn A. Young. 1999. 115.00 (*0-415-19155-6*) Routledge.

Money & Inflation. Frank Hahn. 128p. 1985. reprint ed. pap. text 10.50 (*0-262-58062-4*) MIT Pr.

Money & Its Laws. Henry V. Poor. LC 69-19678. 623p. 1969. reprint ed. lib. bdg. 125.00 (*0-8371-0618-4*, POML, Greenwood Pr) Greenwood.

Money & Liberty. Sally H. Frankel. LC 80-21118. (AEI Studies: No. 293). 79p. reprint ed. pap. 30.00 (*0-8357-4512-0*, 203736900008) Bks Demand.

Money & Macroeconomic Policy: Essays in Honour of Bernard Corry & Maurice Peston, Vol. 1. Ed. by Sami Daniel et al. LC 98-22389. 256p. 1999. 95.00 (*1-85898-578-1*) E Elgar.

Money & Macroeconomics: The Selected Essays of David Laidler. David E. Laidler. LC 97-14360. (Economists of the Twentieth Century Ser.). 424p. (C). 1997. 100.00 (*1-85898-596-X*) E Elgar.

Money & Magic: A Critique of the Modern Economy in the Light of Goethe's Faust. Hans P. Binswanger. Tr. by John E. Harrison from GER. LC 93-38470.Tr. of Geld und Magie. 144p. 1994. 21.50 (*0-226-05185-4*) U Ch Pr.

Money & Marco Policy. Ed. by Marc Jarsulic. 1984. lib. bdg. 97.50 (*0-89838-127-4*) Kluwer Academic.

Money & Marriage: Choices, Rights, & Responsibilities. Jennifer L. Huffman. LC 98-90239. 204p. 1998. pap. 15.95 (*0-9664232-0-8*) Torch Lake.

Money & Marriage: Making It Work Together. Steven Pybrum. LC 96-83730. 1996. pap. text 17.95 (*0-9651277-2-9*) Abundance Pub.

Money & Me: A Woman's Guide to Financial Confidence. Cynthia Yates. LC 98-51435. (Women of Confidence Ser.). 1999. pap. 11.99 (*1-56955-072-7*) Servant.

Money & Me: Healing Our Relationship with Money. Gaule R. Martinez. (Illus.). 178p. 1997. pap. 10.95 (*0-9645194-1-0*) Rose Petal.

Money & Me Workbook. 2nd rev. ed. Gayle R. Martinez. Ed. by Marilyn Twintrees & Thomas Twintrees. Tr. by Bonnie Dixon. (Illus.). 73p. 1997. pap. 9.98 (*1-892351-00-5*) Rose Petal.

***Money & Me Workbook: Revised Edition.** Gayle R. Martinez. Ed. by Jeannine Doyle. 51p. 2000. 14.95 (*1-892351-03-X*) Rose Petal.

An Asterisk (*) at the beginning of an entry indicates that the title is appearing for the first time.

Money & Mind. S. Klebanow & E. L. Lowenkopf. (Illus.). 264p. (C). 1991. text 60.00 (*0-306-43915-8*, Kluwer Plenum) Kluwer Academic.

Money & Modernity: Pound, Williams, & the Spirit of Jefferson. Alec Marsh. LC 97-45459. 264p. 1998. text 39.95 (*0-8173-0921-7*) U of Ala Pr.

Money & Modernity: State & Local Currencies in Melanesia. Ed. by David Akin & Joel Robbins. LC 98-40182. (Association of Social Anthropology in Oceania Monographs). (Illus.). 256p. 1999. pap. 19.95 (*0-8229-5689-6*); text 45.00 (*0-8229-4087-6*) U of Pittsburgh Pr.

Money & Monetary Policy in China, 1845-1895. Frank H. King. LC 65-13847. (East Asian Ser.: No. 19). (Illus.). 339p. 1965. 42.00 (*0-674-58350-7*) HUP.

Money & Monetary Policy in Early Times. Arthur R. Burns. 1976. lib. bdg. 59.95 (*0-8490-2275-4*) Gordon Pr.

Money & Monetary Policy in Interdependent Nations. Ralph C. Bryant. LC 80-19225. 584p. 1980. 44.95 (*0-8157-1130-1*); pap. 19.95 (*0-8157-1129-8*) Brookings.

Money & Monetary Policy in Less Developed Countries: A Survey of Issues & Evidence. Ed. by Warren L. Coats & Deena R. Khatkhate, Jr. LC 79-42703. (Illus.). 834p. 1980. 368.00 (*0-08-024041-0*, Pub. by Pergamon Repr) Franklin.

Money & Money Reforms: A Marxist Introduction. C. Jelset. 60p. 1947. pap. 3.50 (*0-88286-212-X*) C H Kerr.

Money & Morals in America: A History. Patricia O'Toole. LC 97-50263. 432p. 1998. 30.00 (*0-517-58693-2*) C Potter.

Money & Morals Worldwide: First Annual Report. annuals Association D'Economie Financiere Staff. 250p. (C). (gr. 13). 1996. text 81.95 (*1-56324-851-4*) M E Sharpe.

Money & Other Stories. Karel Capek. LC 73-106256. (Short Story Index Reprint Ser.). 1977. 20.95 (*0-8369-3293-5*) Ayer.

Money & Politics: Can Voters Veto Campaign Dollars? Ed. & Pref. by Bob Hall. (Southern Exposure Ser.). (Illus.). 64p. (Orig.). (C). 1992. pap. 5.00 (*0-943810-53-1*) Inst Southern Studies.

Money & Politics: Financing Our Elections Democratically. David Donnelly et al. LC 98-53710. (New Democracy Forum Ser.). 112p. 1999. pap. 11.00 (*0-8070-4315-X*) Beacon Pr.

Money & Politics: The Iranian Asset Freeze. Karin Lissakers. (Pew Case Studies in International Affairs). 50p. (C). 1995. pap. text 3.50 (*1-56927-210-7*, GU Schl Foreign) Geo U Inst Dplmcy.

Money & Politics Abroad. James K. Pollock. LC 77-37909. (Select Bibliographies Reprint Ser.). 1977. reprint ed. 24.95 (*0-8369-6747-X*) Ayer.

Money & Politics in the United States: Financing Elections in the 1980s. Ed. by Michael J. Malbin. LC 84-2900. 336p. reprint ed. pap. 104.20 (*0-8357-4828-6*, 203776500009) Bks Demand.

Money & Power: Hook or Crook. Zolo A. Azania. 56p. (Orig.). reprint ed. pap. write for info. (*1-56411-144-X*) Untd Bros & Sis.

Money & Power for Families. Tama McAleese. (Money & Power Ser.). 100p. 1997. text 14.95 (*0-7910-4468-8*) Chelsea Hse.

Money & Power for Retirement. Tama McAleese. (Money & Power Ser.). 100p. 1997. text 14.95 (*0-7910-4470-X*) Chelsea Hse.

Money & Power for Singles. Tama McAleese. (Money & Power Ser.). 100p. 1997. text 14.95 (*0-7910-4467-X*) Chelsea Hse.

Money & Power in Fifteenth-Century France. Harry A. Miskimin. LC 83-21754. (Economic History Ser.). 320p. 1984. 45.00 (*0-300-03132-7*) Yale U Pr.

***Money & Power in Provincial Thailand.** Ruth McVey. LC 99-34360. 288p. 2000. pap. text 21.95 (*0-8248-2273-0*) UH Pr.

***Money & Power in Provincial Thailand.** Ed. by Ruth McVey. LC 99-34360. 288p. 2000. 55.00 (*0-8248-2272-2*) UH Pr.

Money & Power in the New Religions. Ed. by James T. Richardson. (Studies in Religion & Society: Vol. 22). 400p. 1990. 109.95 (*0-88946-852-4*) E Mellen.

Money & Power Through Mutual Funds. Tama McAleese. (Money & Power Ser.). 100p. 1996. text 14.95 (*0-7910-4469-6*) Chelsea Hse.

***Money & Prosperity Workbook.** Diane Ronngren & Donna Stellhorn. (Illus.). 46p. 1999. wbk. ed. 5.95 (*1-930038-00-3*) E T C Pub.

Money & Recovery: An Adults-in-Recovery Workbook, 4 bks. Dennis C. Daley. 32p. 1997. pap. 11.50 (*1-55691-131-9*, 319) Learning Pubns.

Money & Risk: Creative Turmoil in Finance, Banking, & Insurance. Ed. by David F. Hoover. (ITT Key Issues Lecture). 123p. (Orig.). (C). 1986. pap. write for info. (*0-937137-00-6*) Bookscraft.

Money & Schools: A Handbook For Practitioners. David C. Thompson & Craig R. Wood. LC 97-31185. 320p. 1998. 59.95 (*1-883001-45-5*) Eye On Educ.

Money & Schools: Campaign Strategy in School Bond Elections. Alan L. Clem. 1964. 1.00 (*1-55614-065-7*) U of SD Gov Res Bur.

Money & the Christian: A Course in Biblical Economics. Caleb McAfee. 192p. pap. 14.95 (*0-9656010-0-5*) Dimensn Four.

Money & the Crocodile. Kumuda Reddy & John E. Pruitt. (Illus.). 31p. (J). (gr. 1-6). 1997. 13.67 (*1-929297-08-4*, Pub. by Samhita Prodns) ACCESS Pubs Network.

Money & the Economic Process. Sheila C. Dow. LC 93-16076. 232p. 1993. 90.00 (*1-85278-566-7*) E Elgar.

Money & the Economy: Issues in Monetary Analysis. Karl Brunner & Allan H. Meltzer. 411p. 1997. pap. text 23.95 (*0-521-59974-1*) Cambridge U Pr.

Money & the Financial System. Andrew Feltenstein. 624p. (C). 1994. 52.00 (*0-02-336892-6*, Macmillan Coll) P-H.

Money & the Global Economy. Reed. 1998. ring bd. 99.95 (*0-8493-0552-7*) CRC Pr.

Money & the Global Economy. Reed. 1998. boxed set 120.00 (*1-85573-411-7*, Pub. by Woodhead Pubng) Am Educ Systs.

***Money & the Market: Essays on Free Banking.** Kevin Dowd. LC 00-32180. (Foundations of the Market Economy Ser.). 2000. write for info. (*0-415-24212-6*) Routledge.

Money & the Market in India, 1100-1700. Ed. by Sanjay Subrahmanyam. (Oxford in India Readings: Themes in Indian History Ser.). 328p. 1994. 22.00 (*0-19-563303-2*) OUP.

Money & the Markets: An Astrological Guide. Graham Bates & Jane Bowles. 240p. 1994. pap. 16.00 (*1-85538-370-5*, Pub. by Aqrn Pr) Harper SF.

Money & the Mature Woman: How to Hold on to Your Income, Keep Your Home, Plan Your Estate. Frances Leonard. LC 92-34822. 1993. 19.95 (*0-201-60897-9*) Addison-Wesley.

Money & the Mature Woman: How to Hold on to Your Income, Keep Your Home, Plan Your Estate. Francis Leonard. (Illus.). 288p. 1994. pap. 11.95 (*0-201-62700-0*) Addison-Wesley.

Money & the Meaning of Life. Jacob Needleman. 352p. 1994. pap. 16.95 (*0-385-26242-6*) Doubleday.

Money & the Meaning of Life, Set. abr. ed. Jacob Needleman. 1997. text 17.95 incl. audio (*1-57453-213-8*) Audio Lit.

Money & the Modern Mind: George Simmel's Philosophy of Money. Gianfranco Poggi. LC 92-32231. 1993. 35.00 (*0-520-07571-4*, Pub. by U CA Pr) Cal Prin Full Svc.

Money & the Morality of Exchange. Ed. by Maurice Bloch & Jonathan P. Parry. 288p. (C). 1989. text 59.95 (*0-521-36597-X*) Cambridge U Pr.

Money & the Nation State: The Financial Revolution, Government & the World Monetary System. Ed. by Kevin Dowd & J. Richard Timberlake. LC 97-40091. 320p. (Orig.). 1997. pap. text 19.95 (*1-56000-930-6*) Transaction Pubs.

Money & the Nation State: The Financial Revolution, Government, & the World Monetary System. Ed. by Kevin Dowd & Richard H. Timberlake, Jr. LC 97-40091. (Illus.). 480p. 1997. pap. 24.95 (*1-56000-302-2*) Transaction Pubs.

***Money & the Natural Rate of Unemployment.** Finn Ostrup. LC 99-29143. 318p. (C). 2000. 74.95 (*0-521-66139-0*); pap. 27.95 (*0-521-66739-9*) Cambridge U Pr.

Money & the Power. 1985. write for info. (*0-935036-07-5*) Liberty Lobby.

Money & the Price System. C. H. Douglas. 1973. 59.95 (*0-8490-0659-7*) Gordon Pr.

Money & the Soul of the World. Robert J. Sardello & Randolph Severson. (Studies in Cultural Psychology). 64p. 1984. pap. 8.00 (*0-911005-02-1*) Dallas Inst Pubns.

***Money & the Space Economy.** R. L. Martin. LC 98-29172. 348p. 1999. 115.00 (*0-471-98346-2*); pap. 36.95 (*0-471-98347-0*) Wiley.

Money & Time Saving Household Hints. Leader-Post Carrier Foundation Inc. Staff. LC 92-73856. (Illus.). 128p. (Orig.). 1992. pap. 6.95 (*0-911493-15-8*) Blue Sky.

Money & Trade Considered: With a Proposal for Supplying the Nation with Money. John Law. LC 65-19649. (Library of Money & Banking History). 120p. 1966. reprint ed. 35.00 (*0-678-00187-1*) Kelley.

Money & Value: An Inquiry into the Means & Ends of Economic Production. Rowland Hamilton. LC 78-120326. (Reprints of Economic Classics Ser.). xxviii, 392p. 1971. reprint ed. lib. bdg. 49.50 (*0-678-00704-7*) Kelley.

Money & Votes: Constituency Campaign Spending & Election Results. R. J. Johnston. (Geography & Environment Ser.). 240p. 1987. lib. bdg. 62.50 (*0-7099-1466-0*, Pub. by C Helm) Routldge.

Money & You: A Woman's Financial Guide. Holly Nicholson. LC 97-72255. 128p. 1997. 24.95 (*1-882897-14-5*) Lost Coast.

Money Angles. Andrew Tobias. 1985. pap. 3.95 (*0-380-70036-0*, Avon Bks) Morrow Avon.

Money Around the World. Patricia Armentrout. LC 96-4564. (Money Ser.). (Illus.). (J). 1996. lib. bdg. 14.60 (*1-57103-123-5*) Rourke Pr.

Money, Astrology & You (In the Driver's Seat) Susan M. Casey-Richmond. (Illus.). 54p. 1997. pap. 10.00 (*1-885201-23-0*) Mandala CA.

Money Bait. Debby Head & Libby Pollett. (Curiosity Bait Ser.). 102p. 1997. pap., teacher ed. 32.00 (*1-885775-12-1*) BBY Pubns.

Money, Banking, & Credit. Dwight M. Jaffee. 699p. (C). 1989. text 55.95 (*0-87901-408-3*) Worth.

Money, Banking, & Credit. Dwight M. Jaffee. 211p. (C). 1989. pap. text, student ed. 13.95 (*0-87901-409-1*) Worth.

Money, Banking & Credit in Mediaeval Bruges. Raymond A. De Roover. (Medieval Academy Bks.: No. 51). 1983. reprint ed. 35.00 (*0-910956-25-1*) Medieval Acad.

Money, Banking, & Financial Intermediation. Garry D. Smith. LC 90-83500. 724p. (C). 1991. text 67.56 (*0-669-21724-7*); pap. text, teacher ed. 2.66 (*0-669-21727-1*) HM Trade Div.

Money, Banking & Financial Markets. Miller. (SWC-Finance Ser.). 2000. pap. 90.95 (*0-324-01562-3*) Thomson Learn.

***Money, Banking & Financial Markets.** Miller & Van Hoose. (SWC-General Business Ser.). (C). 2000. text 20.25 (*0-324-05891-8*) Sth-Wstrn College.

Money, Banking, & Financial Markets. Lloyd B. Thomas. (Illus.). 896p. (C). 1996. 82.50 (*0-07-064436-5*) McGraw.

Money, Banking, & Financial Markets. Lloyd B. Thomas. (C). 1997. pap., student ed. 27.50 (*0-07-064446-2*) McGraw.

Money, Banking, & Financial Markets. 2nd ed. Meir Kohn. LC 92-20845. 873p. (C). 1993. pap. text, student ed. 25.00 (*0-03-097101-2*) Dryden Pr.

Money, Banking & Inflation: Essays in the History of Monetary Thought. Thomas M. Humphrey. 464p. 1993. 100.00 (*1-85278-941-7*) E Elgar.

Money, Banking & Monetary Policy. 2nd ed. Clifton H. Kreps & Olin S. Pugh. LC 67-21678. 669p. reprint ed. pap. 200.00 (*0-608-30134-5*, 201239500081) Bks Demand.

Money, Banking, & the Economy. 6th ed. Thomas Mayer et al. LC 95-13313. (C). 1996. 85.50 (*0-393-96848-0*) Norton.

Money, Banking, & the Economy: Study Guide. 6th ed. Thomas Mayer et al. LC 96-215061. (C). 1996. pap., student ed. 16.00 (*0-393-96849-9*) Norton.

Money, Banking, & the Economy: Test Item File. 6th ed. Thomas Mayer & James Duesenberry. (C). 1996. pap. text, teacher ed., suppl. ed. write for info. (*0-393-96850-2*) Norton.

Money, Banking & Trade in Mughal India. B. S. Mallick. (C). 1991. 22.50 (*0-685-59783-0*, Pub. by Rawat Pubns) S Asia.

Money, Banking, & Usury. Vic Lockman. (Illus.). 36p. 1991. 4.00 (*0-936175-09-5*) V Lockman.

Money, Banking, International Trade & Public Finance. 4th rev. ed. M. L. Jhingan. 532p. 1993. pap. 18.95 (*81-220-0285-4*, Pub. by Konark Pubs Pvt Ltd) Advent Bks Div.

Money Before Marriage: A Financial Workbook for Engaged Couples. Larry Burkett & Michael E. Taylor. LC 96-207828. wbk. ed. 14.99 (*0-8024-6389-4*, 343) Moody.

Money Begets Money: A Guide to Personal Finance. Hancock Irving. LC 75-28508. 1975. pap. 5.00 (*0-916202-02-X*) Zimmerman.

Money Behind the Screen. F. D. Klingender & Stuart Legg. Ed. by Garth S. Jowett. LC 77-11378. (Aspects of Film Ser.). 1978. reprint ed. lib. bdg. 11.95 (*0-405-11134-7*) Ayer.

Money, Bodies & Bugs: Living in the Mundane. Karla Spitzer. (Is There Intelligent Life on Planet Earth Ser.). 309p. 1995. pap. text. write for info. (*0-9645722-0-6*) Maybe Someday Bks.

Money Bomb. James G. Stuart. 156p. 1989. 39.00 (*0-85335-256-9*, Pub. by Stuart Titles Ltd); pap. 29.00 (*0-7855-0722-1*, Pub. by Stuart Titles Ltd) St Mut.

Money, Bona Fide or Non-Bona Fide. Edward E. Popp. 1970. pap. 1.50 (*0-9600358-1-8*) CPA Bk Pub.

Money Book. J. E. Osborne. (Early Math Big Bks.). (Illus.). 16p. (J). (ps-2). Date not set. pap. 16.95 (*1-58273-141-1*) Newbridge Educ.

Money Book: A Christian Perspective. Dennis R. Maynard. LC 94-92275. 64p. (Orig.). 1994. pap. 8.00 (*1-885985-00-2*) Dionysus Pubns.

Money Book: Learn to Count & Use Money. Elise Richards. (Illus.). (J). (ps-3). 1997. pap. 6.95 (*0-8167-4296-0*) Troll Communs.

Money Book & Bank. Elaine Wyatt & Stan Hinden. (Illus.). 64p. (J). pap. 14.95 (*0-921051-47-6*) Somerville Hse.

Money Book & Hideaway Bank: A Smart Kid's Guide to Savvy Saving & Spending. Elaine Wyatt & Stan Hinden. (Illus.). 64p. (J). (gr. 1 up). 1999. pap. 14.99 (*1-58184-018-7*) Somerville Hse.

Money Book for Kids. Nancy Burgeson. LC 91-15108. (Survival Guide Ser.). (Illus.). 32p. (J). (gr. 5-9). 1991. pap. 1.95 (*0-8167-2465-2*) Troll Communs.

***Money Boot.** Ginny Russell. (First Flight Ser.). (Illus.). 64p. (J). 1999. pap. 3.95 (*1-55041-370-8*) Fitzhenry & W Ltd.

Money-Box. Robert Lynd. LC 70-84321. (Essay Index Reprint Ser.). 1977. 18.95 (*0-8369-1091-5*) Ayer.

***Money Calc Worksheet Program.** Janie Haugen. Ed. by Melissa Britt. (Illus.). 100p. 1999. ring bd. 39.95 (*1-884074-75-8*, PCI 914) PCI Educ Pubg.

Money Can't Buy You Love. 1989. write for info. (*1-877784-06-0*) T Scott Pub.

Money, Capital & Fluctuations: Early Essays. Friedrich A. Hayek. Ed. by R. K. McCloughry. LC 84-227. 196p. 1993. lib. bdg. 20.00 (*0-226-32092-8*) U Ch Pr.

Money Capital in the Theory of the Firm: A Preliminary Analysis. Douglas Vickers. (Illus.). 256p. 1987. text 80.00 (*0-521-32841-1*) Cambridge U Pr.

***Money, Capital Mobility & Trade: Essays in Honor of Robert A. Mundell.** Ed. by Guillermo A. Calvo et al. 538p. (C). 2000. 55.00 (*0-262-03282-1*) MIT Pr.

Money Captain. Will Payne. LC 68-57546. reprint ed. pap. text 8.95 (*0-8290-2381-X*); reprint ed. lib. bdg. 32.00 (*0-8398-1556-5*) Irvington.

Money Charms & Spells. Jade. Ed. by Judith Defrain & Carey Vosburg. (Illus.). 73p. (Orig.). 1984. pap. text 10.00 (*0-9619008-2-2*) Eye Cat.

Money Charms & Spells. Jade. (Illus.). 52p. (Orig.). 1997. pap. 4.95 (*0-942272-44-7*) Original Pubns.

Money Chase: Congressional Campaign Finance Reform. David B. Magleby & Candice J. Nelson. 250p. 1990. 34.95 (*0-8157-5434-5*); pap. 14.95 (*0-8157-5433-7*) Brookings.

Money, Class, & Party: An Economic Study of Civil War & Reconstruction. Robert P. Sharkey. LC 78-64232. (Johns Hopkins University. Studies in the Social Sciences. Thirtieth Ser. 1912: 2). reprint ed. 39.50 (*0-404-61337-3*) AMS Pr.

Money, Class, & Party: An Economic Study of Civil War & Reconstruction. Robert P. Sharkey. LC 59-15423. (Johns Hopkins University Studies in Historical & Political Science: Series 77, No. 2). 360p. reprint ed. pap. 111.60 (*0-608-06143-3*, 206647600008) Bks Demand.

Money Clips: 365 Tips - From the Simple to the Sophisticated - For Making, Sewing, & Investing Your Money. Lorraine Spurge. LC 99-54272. 272p. 2000. pap. 12.95 (*0-7868-8497-5*, Pub. by Hyperion) Time Warner.

Money Clips: 365 Tips that Will Pay One a Day at a Time. Lorraine Spurge. LC 98-61064. 1998. pap. 14.95 (*1-888232-44-7*) Spurge ink.

Money Clips: 365 Tips That Will Pay One Day at a Time. Lorraine Spurge. LC 97-21903. (Illus.). 250p. 1998. pap. 14.95 (*1-888232-08-0*) Spurge ink.

Money Clips (Mini) The Little Book of Big Money Ideas. Michael D. Matthews. LC 94-15351. 160p. 1994. pap. 5.99 (*0-88070-687-2*, Multnomah Bks) Multnomah Pubs.

Money Club: How We Taught Ourselves the Secret to a Secure Financial Future - And How You Can, Too. Marilyn Crockett et al. 320p. 1998. pap. 13.00 (*0-684-84605-5*) S&S Trade.

Money Club: The Park Avenue Women's Guide to Personal Finance. Marilyn Crockett et al. LC 97-23184. 288p. 1997. 24.00 (*0-684-83719-6*) S&S Trade.

***Money Clues for the Clueless: God's Word in Your World.** Compiled by Elwood Smith. (Clues for the Clueless Ser.). (Illus.). 256p. 2000. pap. 8.99 (*1-57748-739-7*) Barbour Pub.

Money Coach. Riley Moynes & Jack P. Friedman. LC 97-31312. 160p. 1998. pap. 12.95 (*0-7641-0579-5*) Barron.

Money Coach. 5th ed. Pines. 148p. (C). 1997. pap. text. write for info. (*0-201-31613-7*) Addison-Wesley.

Money Coach: Your Game Plan for Growth & Security. Riley & Moynes. 1992. pap. text. write for info. (*0-7730-5265-8*) Addison-Wes.

Money, Coins, & Commerce: Essays in the Monetary History of Asia & Europe from Antiquity to Modern Times. Ed. by E. Van Cauwenberhe. (Studies in Social & Economic History: No. 22). 554p. (Orig.). 1992. pap. 92.50 (*90-6186-485-2*, Pub. by Leuven Univ) Coronet Bks.

Money, Color & Sex in Hawai'i's Politics. Chad Blair. 208p. 1998. pap. 12.95 (*1-56647-218-0*) Mutual Pub HI.

Money Cometh. Thompson. LC 97-170316. 1996. pap. 13.95 (*0-9632584-1-9*) Ever Increase Wd Min.

Money Cometh: To the Body of Christ. Leroy Thompson. 1999. pap. text 14.99 (*1-57794-186-1*) Harrison Hse.

Money Connection: Where & How to Apply for Business Loans & Venture Capital. 2nd ed. Lawrence Flanagan. (Successful Business Library). (Illus.). 177p. 1997. pap. 24.95 (*1-55571-351-3*, Oasis Pr) PSI Resch.

***Money, Coordination & Prices.** Fieke Van der Lecq. LC 00-24527. 232p. 2000. 90.00 (*1-84064-286-6*) E Elgar.

Money Creators. Gertrude M. Coogan. 1979. 250.00 (*0-87968-317-1*) Gordon Pr.

Money, Credit, & Capital. James Tobin & Stephen S. Golub. LC 97-3766. (Advanced Series in Economics). 384p. (C). 1997. 74.69 (*0-07-065336-4*) McGraw.

Money, Credit & Commerce. Alfred Marshall. LC 90-43794. (Reprints of Economic Classics Ser.). xvi, 369p. 1991. reprint ed. lib. bdg. 45.00 (*0-678-01463-9*) Kelley.

Money, Credit & Inflation: An Historical Indictment of U. K. Monetary Policy & a Proposal for Change. Gordon T. Pepper. (IEA Research Monographs: No. 44). 80p. (Orig.). (C). 1991. pap. 19.95 (*0-255-36228-5*, Pub. by Inst Economic Affairs) Coronet Bks.

Money, Credit & Policy. Allan H. Meltzer. (Economists of the Twentieth Century Ser.). 448p. 1995. 100.00 (*1-85898-208-1*) E Elgar.

***Money, Credit & Price Stability.** Paul Dalziel. LC 00-36894. (International Studies in Money & Banking). 2000. write for info. (*0-415-24056-5*) Routledge.

Money Culture. Michael Lewis. 304p. 1992. reprint ed. pap. 13.95 (*0-14-017318-8*, Penguin Bks) Viking Penguin.

Money Demand & Monetary Policy. Douglas Fisher. (Illus.). 240p. (C). 1990. text 57.50 (*0-472-10169-2*, 10169) U of Mich Pr.

Money Demand in Europe. Ed. by H. Lutkepohl et al. LC 99-11541. (Studies in Empirical Economics). (Illus.). x, 260p. 1999. 84.95 (*3-7908-1182-3*) Spr-Verlag.

Money Demon. Diexian Chen. Tr. by Patrick Hanan from CHI. LC 98-33911. 344p. (C). 1999. text 42.00 (*0-8248-2096-7*); pap. text 19.95 (*0-8248-2103-3*) UH Pr.

Money Doctor in the Andes: U. S. Advisors, Investors, & Economic Reform in Latin America from WWI to the Great Depression. Paul W. Drake. LC 88-18045. xvi, 448p. (C). 1988. text 59.95 (*0-8223-0880-0*) Duke.

Money Doctors, Foreign Debts, & Economic Reforms in Latin America from the 1890s to the Present. Ed. by Paul W. Drake. LC 93-34563. (Jaguar Books on Latin America: No. 3). 304p. 1994. 45.00 (*0-8420-2434-4*) Scholarly Res Inc.

Money Doesn't Grow on Trees: A Parent's Guide to Raising Financially Responsible Children. Neale S. Godfrey. 176p. 1994. pap. 11.00 (*0-671-79805-7*, Fireside) S&S Trade Pap.

Money Drunk/Money Sober: 90 Days to Financial Freedom. Mark Bryan & Julia Cameron. 225p. 1999. pap. 10.00 (*0-345-43265-7*) Ball Well.

Money Economy. William Poole. LC 78-52499. (Perspectives on Economics Ser.). (Illus.). 1978. pap. text 6.95 (*0-201-08364-7*) Addison-Wesley.

***Money, Economy & Society.** John N. Smithin. 2000. text 85.00 (*0-415-19773-2*) Routledge.

***Money Economy & Society.** John N. Smithin. 240p. 2000. pap. 27.99 (*0-415-19774-0*) Routledge.

***Money (1840)** Edward Bulwer Lytton. 54p. 1999. reprint ed. pap. 7.00 (*0-7661-0807-4*) Kessinger Pub.

Money, Emotions & the Recovery Process. Mary Raphel. 96p. 1993. pap. 10.95 (*0-9639287-0-8*) M Raphel.

An Asterisk (*) at the beginning of an entry indicates that the title is appearing for the first time.

Money, Energy & Welfare: The State & the Household in India's Rural Electrification Policy. 2nd ed. Sarmila Bose. 138p. (C). 1994. text 13.95 (*0-19-563143-9*) OUP.

Money, Exchange & Production: Further Essays in the History of Economic Thought. Thomas M. Humphrey. LC 98-22236. 192p. 1998. 75.00 (*1-85898-652-4*) E Elgar.

Money, Exchange Rates, & Output. Guillermo Calvo. (Illus.). 532p. 1996. 60.00 (*0-262-03236-8*) MIT Pr.

Money, Expense, & Naval Power in Thucydides' History. Lisa Kallet-Marx. LC 92-40904. (C). 1993. 55.00 (*0-520-07820-9*, Pub. by U CA Pr) Cal Prin Full Svc.

Money Facts for the American Consumer. Jim Stachowicz. LC 88-80767. (Illus.). 144p. (Orig.). 1988. pap. 8.95 (*0-929269-00-4*) JKM Pub Co.

Money, Finance & Empire, 1790-1960. Ed. by A. N. Porter & R. F. Holland. 192p. 1985. 34.00 (*0-7146-3273-2*, Pub. by F Cass Pubs) Intl Spec Bk.

Money, Finance, & Macroeconomic Performance in Japan. Yoshio Suzuki. Tr. by Robert A. Feldman. LC 85-26375. 332p. 1986. 37.50 (*0-300-03387-7*) Yale U Pr.

Money, Financial Flows & Credit in the Soviet Union. George Garvy. LC 76-58491. (National Bureau of Economic Research. Studies in International Economic Relations: No. 7). 237p. reprint ed. pap. 73.50 (*0-608-15346-X*, 205636200061) Bks Demand.

M

Money, Financial Institutions & Macroeconomics. LC 97-7784. 1997. lib. bdg. 104.50 (*0-7923-9909-9*) Kluwer Academic.

Money Financial System Economy. 2nd ed. (C). 1997. 67.00 (*0-201-31692-7*) S&S Trade.

***Money Financial System Economy.** 3rd ed. (C). 1999. pap. text 67.00 (*0-201-65730-9*) S&S Trade.

***Money Flood: How Pension Funds Revolutionized Investing.** Michael J. Clowes. LC 99-45195. (Investments Ser.). 320p. 2000. 39.95 (*0-471-38483-6*) Wiley.

Money Folding. Florence Temko. (My Favorite Origami Ser.). (Illus.). 14p. (Orig.). 1995. pap. 5.95 (*0-89346-828-2*) Heian Intl.

Money Folding 2, Vol. 2. Florence Temko. (My Favorite Origami Ser.). (Illus.). 14p. (Orig.). (YA). (gr. 3 up). 1997. pap. 5.95 (*0-89346-842-8*) Heian Intl.

Money for a Better World. Rudolf Mees. 64p. 1991. pap. 10.95 (*1-869890-26-4*, Pub. by Hawthorn Press) Anthroposophic.

Money for Adult Students. Norman C. Tognazzini. (Illus.). 21p. 1993. pap. 3.95 (*0-9626591-2-6*) Energeia Pub.

Money for Change: Social Movement Philanthropy at the Haymarket People's Fund. Susan A. Ostrander. LC 95-12095. 256p. (C). 1995. lib. bdg. 69.95 (*1-56639-363-9*) Temple U Pr.

Money for Change: Social Movement Philanthropy at the Haymarket People's Fund. Susan A. Ostrander. LC 95-12095. 256p. (C). 1997. pap. text 22.95 (*1-56639-364-7*) Temple U Pr.

Money for College. Gail Rae. LC 97-66287. 96p. 1998. pap. 11.95 (*0-87891-072-7*) Res & Educ.

Money for College: A Guide to Financial Aid for African-American Students. Erlene Wilson. 512p. (Orig.). 1996. pap. 15.95 (*0-452-27276-9*, Plume) Dutton Plume.

Money for Entrepreneurs. 435p. Date not set. pap. 39.95 (*1-884350-69-0*) Alpha Pubng.

Money for Film & Video Artists: A Comprehensive Resource Guide. 2nd ed. Ed. by Douglas Oxenhorn. LC 93-38044. 304p. 1993. pap. 15.95 (*1-879903-09-1*) Am for the Arts.

***Money for Graduate Research & Study in the Humanities, 2000 - 2002.** Gail A. Schlachter & R. David Weber. 340p. 2000. lib. bdg. 40.00 (*0-918276-89-6*) Ref Serv Pr.

***Money for Graduate Research & Study in the Sciences, 2000 - 2002.** Gail A. Schlachter & R. David Weber. 450p. 2000. lib. bdg. 45.00 (*0-918276-90-X*) Ref Serv Pr.

***Money for Graduate Research & Study in the Social Sciences, 2000 - 2002.** Gail A. Schlachter & R. David Weber. 350p. 2000. lib. bdg. 42.50 (*0-918276-91-8*) Ref Serv Pr.

***Money for Graduate Students in the Humanities: 2001-2003.** Gail Ann Schlachter & R. David Weber. 320p. 2001. lib. bdg. 40.00 (*1-58841-008-0*) Ref Serv Pr.

***Money for Graduate Students in the Sciences: 2001-2003.** Gail Ann Schlachter & R. David Weber. 450p. 2001. lib. bdg. 45.00 (*1-58841-009-9*) Ref Serv Pr.

***Money for Graduate Students in the Social Sciences: 2001-2003.** Gail Ann Schlachter & R. David Weber. 350p. 2001. lib. bdg. 42.50 (*1-58841-010-2*) Ref Serv Pr.

Money for International Exchange in the Arts: A Comprehensive Arts Resource Guide. Ed. by Jane Gullong & Noreen Thomassi. LC 92-35492. 122p. 1992. pap. 14.95 (*1-879903-01-6*, ACA Bks) Am for the Arts.

***Money for Life: How You Can Create a Financial Plan for Life.** Stephen R. Bolt. 256p. 2000. 20.00 (*0-9677356-0-2*, 931-001, Pub. by Values Finan Net) BookWorld.

***Money For Life: The 20 Factor Plan for Accumulating Wealth While You're Young.** Robert Sheard. LC 00-38927. (Illus.). 256p. 2000. 25.00 (*0-06-662043-0*) HarpC.

Money for Love. Josephine Herbst. Ed. by Elizabeth Hardwick. LC 76-51670. (Rediscovered Fiction by American Women Ser.). 1977. reprint ed. lib. bdg. 29.95 (*0-405-10049-3*) Ayer.

Money for Nothing. P. G. Wodehouse. LC 98-117191. 240p. 1998. pap. 9.95 (*0-14-012455-1*) Viking Penguin.

Money for Nothing: Politicians, Rent Extraction, & Political Extortion. Fred S. McChesney. LC 96-47873. (Illus.). 216p. 1997. 36.50 (*0-674-58330-2*) HUP.

Money for Nothing, Tips for Free. Les Abromovitz. 168p. (Orig.). 1995. pap. 5.95 (*1-56245-185-5*) Great Quotations.

Money for Performing Artists: A Comprehensive Arts Resource Guide. Ed. by Suzanne Niemeyer. LC 91-29393. 268p. (Orig.). 1991. pap. 12.00 (*0-915400-96-0*, ACA Bks) Am for the Arts.

Money for Research & Development. Eurofi Staff. 235p. (C). 1988. pap. 300.00 (*0-907304-26-5*, Pub. by Eurofi) St Mut.

Money for Visual Artists: A Comprehensive Arts Resource Guide. 2nd ed. Ed. by Douglas Orenhorn. LC 91-13168. 317p. (Orig.). 1993. pap. 14.95 (*0-915400-91-X*, ACA Bks) Am for the Arts.

Money for Visual Artists: A Comprehensive Resource Guide. 2nd ed. Ed. by Douglas Oxenhorn. LC 93-25366. 317p. 1993. pap. 14.95 (*1-879903-05-9*) Am for the Arts.

Money for Your Campus Ministry, Church, or Other Non-Profit Organization: How to Get It. Thomas N. Emswiler. LC 81-52373. (Illus.). 152p. 1981. pap. 7.95 (*0-9606652-0-X*) Wesley Found.

Money Freedom: Finding Your Inner Source of Wealth. Patricia Remele. Ed. by Kenneth M. Skidmore. 242p. 1995. pap. 14.95 (*0-87604-333-3*, 422) ARE Pr.

Money from Antiques. Milan G. Vesely. LC 95-82417. (Illus.). 208p. 1996. pap. 12.95 (*0-87341-441-1*, MFA) Krause Pubns.

Money from Home. Damon Runyon. 19.95 (*0-89190-361-5*) Amereon Ltd.

Money from Thin Air: The Story of Craig McCaw, the Billionaire Who Invented the Cell Phone Industry & His Next Billion Dollar Idea. O. Casey Corr. LC 99-89068. (Illus.). 320p. 2000. 25.00 (*0-8129-2697-8*, Times Bks) Crown Pub Group.

Money Fund Vision. IBC Financial Data, Inc. Staff. write for info. (*0-913755-24-9*) IBC Financial.

Money Game. David Ericson. (Pacemaker Bks.). 1977. 13.85 (*0-606-02420-4*, Pub. by Turtleback) Demco.

Money Game. Adam Smith. 1976. pap. 10.00 (*0-394-72103-9*) Knopf.

Money Game. Jessee Warren. (Illus.). 71p. (Orig.). 1995. pap. 9.95 (*0-9654571-0-9*) Warren Publng.

Money Game in Old New York: Daniel Drew & His Times. Clifford Browder. LC 85-17938. 335p. reprint ed. pap. 103.90 (*0-7837-5799-9*, 204546500006) Bks Demand.

Money Games: The Business of Sports. Ann E. Weiss. LC 92-25002. 240p. (J). (gr. 5-9). 1993. 14.95 (*0-395-57444-7*) HM.

Money-Go-Rounds: The Importance of ROSCA's for Women. Ed. by Shirley Ardener et al. (Cross-Cultural Perspectives on Women Ser.). 320p. 1995. 47.50 (*0-85496-832-6*) Berg Pubs.

Money-Go-Rounds: The Importance of ROSCAs for Women. Ed. by Shirley Ardener et al. (Cross-Cultural Perspectives on Women Ser.). 320p. 1996. pap. 19.50 (*1-85973-170-8*, Pub. by Berg Pubs) NYU Pr.

Money God. Dolly Hildreth et al. (Canadiana Avant 1867 Ser.). 32p. (J). (gr. 5-12). 1972. pap. 4.95 (*0-89992-031-4*) Coun India Ed.

Money, God's Minor League. Mark Schaufler. 24p. 1995. teacher ed. 5.00 (*1-886904-16-2*); student ed. 2.00 (*1-886904-15-4*) MST Minist.

Money, Grades 1-2. Jane Crawford. (Math by All Means Ser.). (Illus.). 182p. 1996. pap. text 23.95 (*0-941355-17-9*, 00825) Math Solns Pubns.

Money, Greed & Risk: Why Financial Crises & Crashes Happen. Charles R. Morris. LC 98-32144. 297p. 1999. 25.00 (*0-8129-3173-4*, Times Business) Random.

Money, Growth & Stability. Frank Hahn. 400p. 1985. 49.50 (*0-262-08156-3*) MIT Pr.

Money Guide '92. Marshall Loeb. 1991. pap. 14.95 (*0-316-53072-7*) Little.

Money Harmony. Olivia Mellan. 246p. 1995. pap. 9.95 (*0-8027-7456-3*) Walker & Co.

Money Harmony: Resolving Money Conflicts in Your Life & Relationships. Olivia Mellan. LC 93-37876. 256p. 1994. 19.95 (*0-8027-1285-1*) Walker & Co.

Money Harvest. Ross Thomas. 256p. 1993. mass mkt. 4.99 (*0-446-40173-0*, Pub. by Warner Bks) Little.

Money, Heart & Mind: Financial Well-Being for People & Planet. William Bloom. Ed. by Philip Turner. LC 96-20594. 288p. 1996. 24.00 (*1-56836-153-X*) Kodansha.

Money, History, & International Finance: Essays in Honor of Anna J. Schwartz. Ed. by Michael D. Bordo. LC 88-39779. (National Bureau of Economic Research Conference Report Ser.). (Illus.). xii, 288p. 1989. lib. bdg. 42.00 (*0-226-06593-6*) U Ch Pr.

Money, How to Find It with Astrology. Lois M. Rodden. Ed. by Lynn Rodden. (Illus.). 275p. 1994. pap. text 20.00 (*0-9633716-1-4*) Data News Pr.

Money, How to Find It with Astrology. 2nd ed. Lois M. Rodden. (Illus.). 278p. 1994. pap. 20.00 (*0-9633716-2-2*) Data News Pr.

Money Hunt. Franklin W. Dixon. Ed. by Ann Greenberg. (Hardy Boys Mystery Stories Ser.: No. 101). 160p. (J). (gr. 3-6). 1990. pap. 3.99 (*0-671-69451-0*, Minstrel Bks) PB.

Money Hunt: 27 New Rules for Creating & Growing a Breakaway Business. Miles Spencer. LC 99-31686. 304p. 1999. 25.00 (*0-06-661995-5*) HarpC.

Money Illusion & Strategic Complementarity as Causes of Monetary Non-Neutrality. Jean-Robert Tyran. Ed. by G. Fandel & W. Trockel. LC 99-23349. (Lecture Notes in Economics & Mathematical Systems Ser.: Vol. 472). (Illus.). x, 228p. 1999. pap. 51.00 (*3-540-65871-8*) Spr-Verlag.

Money in a Maelstrom. J. W. Beyen. Ed. by Mira Wilkins. LC 73-3898. (International Finance Ser.). 1979. reprint ed. lib. bdg. 23.95 (*0-405-11203-3*) Ayer.

Money in American Elections. Frank J. Sorauf. 416p. (C). 1988. pap. text 23.53 (*0-673-39784-X*) Addson-Wesley Educ.

Money in Colonial Times. 1992. lib. bdg. 248.95 (*0-8490-5579-2*) Gordon Pr.

Money in Congressional Elections. Gary C. Jacobson. LC 79-20669. 271p. reprint ed. pap. 84.10 (*0-7837-5308-X*, 208032900005) Bks Demand.

Money in Crisis: The Federal Reserve, the Economy, & Monetary Reform. Ed. by Barry N. Siegel. LC 84-9230. (Illus.). 361p. 1984. pap. 14.95 (*0-936488-57-3*) PRIPP.

Money in Economic Systems. George Macesich & Hui-Liang Tsai. Ed. by J. Richard Zecher & D. Sykes Wilford. LC 81-20977. (Studies in International Monetary Economics & Finances). 236p. 1982. 49.95 (*0-275-90852-6*, C0852, Praeger Pubs) Greenwood.

Money in Elections. Louise Overacker. LC 73-19167. (Politics & People Ser.). (Illus.). 490p. 1974. reprint ed. 36.95 (*0-405-05889-6*) Ayer.

Money in Historical Perspective. Anna J. Schwartz. LC 87-5973. (National Bureau of Economic Research Monographs). (Illus.). 456p. (C). 1987. lib. bdg. 61.50 (*0-226-74228-8*) U Ch Pr.

Money in Industry. M. Gordon-Cumming. 1973. 59.95 (*0-8490-0660-0*) Gordon Pr.

Money in Islam: Study in Islamic Political Economy. Masudul A. Choudhury. LC 97-8285. 313p. (C). 1997. 85.00 (*0-415-16302-1*) Routledge.

***Money in Marriage: A Biblical Approach, 2 vols.** Larry Burkett. 1999. pap. 19.99 (*0-8024-4230-7*) Moody.

***Money in Marriage System: A Biblical Approach.** Larry Burkett. 1999. pap. 34.99 (*0-8024-4231-5*) Moody.

Money in Sixteenth-Century Florence. Carlo M. Cipolla. 1989. 45.00 (*0-520-06222-1*, Pub. by U CA Pr) Cal Prin Full Svc.

Money in the Bank: How Safe Is It? A. Robert Abboud. 200p. 1988. 24.00 (*1-55623-070-2*, Irwn Prfssnl) McGraw-Hill Prof.

Money in the English Tradition, 1640-1936. M. Butchart. 1973. 59.95 (*0-8490-0661-9*) Gordon Pr.

Money in the Ground: Insider's Guide to Oil & Gas Deals. 4th expanded rev. ed. John Orban, III. 416p. (Orig.). 1997. pap. 39.50 (*0-9615776-6-5*) Meridian Oklahoma.

Money in the Macroeconomy. Martin F. Prachowny. (Illus.). 352p. 1986. pap. text 34.95 (*0-521-31594-8*) Cambridge U Pr.

Money in the People's Republic of China: A Comparative Perspective. Gavin Peebles. 1992. text 45.00 (*1-86373-033-8*, Pub. by Allen & Unwin Pty) Paul & Co Pubs.

Money in Your Attic: How to Turn Your Furniture, Antiques, Silver & Collectibles into Cash. Helaine Fendelman et al. write for info. (*0-318-59676-8*) S&S Trade.

Money in Your Life: Feeling Good about Your Finances - Doing Well with Your Wealth (with Current Addenda) William E. Swailes & Heidi R. Swailes. LC 86-70148. 140p. (Orig.). 1986. pap. 12.95 (*0-932515-00-2*) APF.

Money in Your Mailbox: How to Start & Operate a Successful Mail-Order Business. 2nd ed. Perry L. Wilbur. LC 92-13550. (Small Business Editions Ser.). 256p. 1992. 39.95 (*0-471-57775-8*); pap. 16.95 (*0-471-57330-2*) Wiley.

Money, Incentives & Efficiency in the Hungarian Economic Reform. Ed. by Josef C. Brada & Istvan Dobozi. LC 89-24210. 200p. (C). (gr. 13). 1990. text 85.95 (*0-87332-566-4*) M E Sharpe.

Money, Income & Time: A Quantum Theoretical Approach. Alvaro Cencini. 232p. 1988. text 55.00 (*0-86187-943-0*) St Martin.

***Money Income in the U.S., 1998.** Ed. by Edward J. Welniak. 70p. 2000. pap. text 20.00 (*0-7567-0006-X*) DIANE Pub.

Money Income of Households, Families & Persons in the United States. (Illus.). 290p. (Orig.). (C). 1994. pap. text 50.00 (*0-7881-0240-0*) DIANE Pub.

Money Income of Households, Families & Persons in the United States. (Orig.). 1994. lib. bdg. 250.00 (*0-8490-5766-3*) Gordon Pr.

Money Income of Households, Families & Persons in the United States, 1992. (Current Population Reports Series P-60, Consumer Income: No. 162). (Illus.). 296p. 1993. pap. 19.00 (*0-16-013395-5*, 803-005-30031-5) USGPO.

Money Income Tax Handbook, 1994. Mary L. Sprouse. 672p. (Orig.). 1993. pap. 13.99 (*0-446-39426-2*, Pub. by Warner Bks) Little.

Money Income Tax Handbook, 1995. Ed. by Mary L. Sprouse. (Orig.). 1995. pap. 13.99 (*0-446-67112-6*, Pub. by Warner Bks) Little.

***Money, Inflation & Capital Formation: An Analysis of the Long Run from the Perspective of Overlapping Generations Models.** L. V. Thadden. LC HG221.T394 1999. (Lecture Notes in Economics & Mathematical Systems Ser.: Vol. 479). (Illus.). x, 193p. 2000. pap. 61.00 (*3-540-66456-4*) Spr-Verlag.

Money, Inflation & Employment: Essays in Honour of James Ball. Ed. by Sean Holly. 240p. 1994. 95.00 (*1-85278-711-2*) E Elgar.

Money, Inflation & Recession in the U. K. & U. S. A. The Fallacies of Monetarism - A Marxist View. Pantelis Ayianoglou. LC 93-23578. 280p. 1993. text 89.95 (*0-7734-9373-5*) E Mellen.

Money, Inflation & Unemployment: The Role of Money in the Economy. 2nd ed. David Gowland. LC 91-30078. 320p. 1991. text 59.95 (*0-312-07199-X*) St Martin.

Money Inflation in the United States: A Study in Social Pathology. Murray S. Wildman. 1977. lib. bdg. 69.95 (*0-8490-2276-2*) Gordon Pr.

Money Inflation in the United States: A Study in Social Pathology. Murray S. Wildman. LC 69-19689. 238p. 1970. reprint ed. lib. bdg. 35.00 (*0-8371-1408-X*, WIMI, Greenwood Pr) Greenwood.

Money, Information, & Uncertainty. 2nd ed. Charles A. Goodhart. 550p. (Orig.). 1989. 63.50 (*0-262-07122-3*) MIT Pr.

Money, Interest, & Banking in Economic Development. 2nd ed. Maxwell J. Fry. LC 94-3466. (Studies in Development). 592p. 1995. text 48.50 (*0-8018-5026-6*); pap. text 16.95 (*0-8018-5027-4*) Johns Hopkins.

Money, Interest, & Prices: An Integration of Monetary & Value Theory. 2nd ed. Don Patinkin. 576p. 1989. 65.00 (*0-262-16114-1*) MIT Pr.

Money, Interest, & Stagnation: Dynamic Theory & a Monetary Economy. Yoshiyasu Ono. (Illus.). 216p. 1994. text 49.95 (*0-19-828837-9*) OUP.

Money Interest & the Public Interest: The Development of American Monetary Thought, 1920-1970. Perry G. Mehrling. LC 97-17051. (Harvard Economic Studies: No. 162). 288p. 1998. 45.00 (*0-674-58430-9*) HUP.

Money, Interest Rates & Inflation. Frederic S. Mishkin. LC 93-2700. (Economists of the Twentieth Century Ser.). 352p. 1993. 95.00 (*1-85278-850-X*) E Elgar.

***Money is a Kid's Best Friend.** Leatherdale. 2000. pap. 22.95 (*0-13-018878-6*) P-H.

Money Is Everything: What Jesus Said about the Spiritual Power of Money. Herb Miller. LC 94-70012. 72p. 1994. pap. 8.95 (*0-88177-132-5*, DR132) Discipleship Res.

Money Is God in Action. Raymond C. Barker. 16p. pap. 3.50 (*0-87516-502-8*) DeVorss.

Money Is Honey: 501 Dollar-Wise Ways to Save Thousands & Prevent Big Losses. Tui Rose. Ed. by Jackie Roberts & Karen Love. (Illus.). 272p. 1997. pap. 9.95 (*1-885735-13-8*) Crown Jewel.

***Money Is Love: Reconnecting to the Sacred Origins of Money.** 2nd rev. ed. Barbara Wilder. 96p. 1999. pap. 9.95 (*0-9673346-0-8*) Wild Ox Pr.

Money Is My Friend. Phil Laut. LC 99-212901. 145p. 1999. pap. 5.99 (*0-345-43279-7*) Ballantine Pub Grp.

Money Is My Friend. Phil Laut. 160p. 1990. mass mkt. 5.99 (*0-8041-0534-0*) Ivy Books.

Money Is My Friend. rev. ed. Phil Laut. LC 79-51206. 150p. 1989. pap. 7.95 (*0-9610132-2-2*) Vivation Pub.

Money Is Never the Problem. Chandler H. Everett. LC 96-75844. 128p. 1996. pap. 6.75 (*1-886966-05-2*) In Print.

Money Is Not Enough. Winston Howard. LC 80-53510. 1980. 8.95 (*0-914244-05-1*) Epic Pubns.

Money Is Power: Harness It! unabridged ed. Stanford E. Andress & Irene M. Deasy. (Orig.). 1997. pap. 15.95 (*0-9656257-3-7*) S E Andress.

Money Isn't Everything--It's Nothing. Hy Rosenfeld. LC 93-7299. 149p. (Orig.). 1994. pap. 9.95 (*0-9638145-3-2*) Carillon Hse.

Money Isn't Everything but It Keeps the Kids in Touch. Stanley A. Smith. 115p. (Orig.). 1989. pap. write for info. (*0-9622315-3-3*) SXC Enterp.

Money Issues in Black Male Female Relationships. George Subira. 1996. pap. text 15.95 (*0-9605304-3-6*) VSBE.

Money Know-How. Ed. by J. Long. 64p. (Orig.). 1988. pap. text. write for info. (*0-8428-7411-9*) Cambridge Bk.

Money, Language & Thought: Literary & Philosophical Economies from the Medieval to the Modern Era. Marc Shell. LC 93-16494. (Softshell Bks.). 245p. (C). 1993. reprint ed. pap. text 15.95 (*0-8018-4693-5*) Johns Hopkins.

Money Launderers: Lessons from the Drug Wars - How Billions of Illegal Dollars Are Washed Through Banks & Businesses. Robert E. Powis. 300p. 1992. 21.95 (*1-55738-262-X*, Irwn Prfssnl) McGraw-Hill Prof.

Money Laundering. 1992. lib. bdg. 288.95 (*0-8490-8876-3*) Gordon Pr.

Money Laundering: A Framework for Understnading U. S. Efforts Overseas. (Illus.). 65p. (Orig.). 1996. pap. text 25.00 (*0-7881-3334-9*) DIANE Pub.

***Money Laundering: A Guide to Criminal Investigations.** John Madinger. LC 98-45932. 445p. 1999. boxed set 69.95 (*0-8493-0710-4*) CRC Pr.

***Money Laundering: A New International Law Enforcement Model.** Guy Stessens. LC 99-56427. 2000. write for info. (*0-521-78104-3*) Cambridge U Pr.

Money Laundering: A Practical Guide to the New Legislation. R. Bosworth-Davies & G. Saltmarsh. 320p. 1994. mass mkt. 89.95 (*0-412-57530-2*) Chapman & Hall.

Money Laundering: Asset Forfeiture & International Financial Crimes, Commentary, Analysis & Treaties, 5 vols. Fletcher N. Baldwin, Jr. & Robert J. Munro. 1993. ring bd. 600.00 (*0-379-20156-9*) Oceana.

Money Laundering: FinCEN Needs to Better Communicate Regulatory Priorities & Time Lines. Danny Burton. 54p. (C). 1999. pap. text 20.00 (*0-7881-7778-8*) DIANE Pub.

Money Laundering: Needed Improvements for Reporting Suspicious Transactions Are Planned. (Illus.). 45p. 1996. reprint ed. pap. text 20.00 (*0-7881-3274-1*) DIANE Pub.

Money Laundering: Rapid Growth of Casinos Makes Them Vulnerable. (Illus.). 51p. (Orig.). 1996. pap. text 25.00 (*0-7881-2891-4*) DIANE Pub.

Money Laundering: Reporting & Regulatory Requirements. Charles M. Carberry et al. 1993. ring bd. 85.00 (*0-317-05404-X*, 00621) NY Law Pub.

Money Laundering & Currency Smuggling: An Assessment. (Illus.). 49p. (Orig.). (C). 1994. pap. text 25.00 (*0-7881-1018-7*) DIANE Pub.

An Asterisk (*) at the beginning of an entry indicates that the title is appearing for the first time.

Money Laundering & Currency Smuggling: An Assessment. (Illus.). 49p. (Orig.). 1994. pap. text 35.00 (*1-57979-143-3*) DIANE Pub.

Money Laundering in the 21st Century: Risks & Countermeasure. Ed. by Adam Graycar & Peter Grabosky. 49p. 1999. pap. 20.00 (*0-642-24011-6*, Pub. by Aust Inst Criminology) Advent Bks Div.

Money-Lender, 3 vols., 1 bk. Catherine G. Gore. LC 79-8275. reprint ed. 44.50 (*0-404-61883-9*) AMS Pr.

Money Logic: Financial Strategies for the Smart Investor. Moshe A. Milevsky. 1999. text 28.95 (*0-7737-3171-7*, Pub. by Stoddart Publ) Genl Dist Srvs.

Money (Logo) Income Tax Handbook, 1996. Mary L. Sprouse. (Orig.). 1995. pap. write for info. (*0-446-67123-1*) Warner Bks.

***Money, Love.** Brad Barkley. 320p. 2000. 24.95 (*0-393-04929-9*) Norton.

Money Lovers. Timothy Watts. LC 92-44047. (Soho Crime Ser.). 256p. 1994. 20.00 (*1-56947-008-1*) Soho Press.

Money Lovers. Timothy Watts. LC 92-44047. (Soho Crime Ser.). 256p. 1995. pap. 10.00 (*1-56947-035-9*) Soho Press.

Money Machine. Philip Coggan. 224p. 1995. pap. 15.95 (*0-14-023399-7*, Pub. by Pnguin Bks Ltd) Trafalgar.

Money Machine: How KKR Manufactured Power & Profits. Sarah Bartlett. 368p. 1999. reprint ed. 35.95 (*0-7351-0067-5*) Replica Bks.

Money Machine: How KKR Manufactured Power & Profits. Sarah Bartlett. 1992. reprint ed. mass mkt. 12.99 (*0-446-39401-7*, Pub. by Warner Bks) Little.

Money Machine: Making Extra Income with Your Home Computer. J. L. Dolice. (Illus.). 300p. (Orig.). 1997. pap. 29.95 (*0-935901-05-1*) Dolice Graphics.

Money Machines: The Breakdown & Reform of Governmental & Party Finance in the North, 1860-1920. Clifton K. Yearley. LC 74-112605. 377p. 1970. text 18.50 (*0-87395-072-0*) State U NY Pr.

Money, Macroeconomics, & Economic Policy: Essays in Honor of James Tobin. Ed. by William Brainard et al. (Illus.). 372p. 1991. 47.50 (*0-262-02325-3*) MIT Pr.

***Money Made Easy: A Young Investors Guide to Wall Street.** Ed. by Simon & Schuster Staff. (J). (gr. 7). 2000. per. 16.00 (*0-689-83401-2*) S&S Trade.

Money Made Simple: A Computer Guide to Money. Tom Weisharr. 288p. 1987. pap. 15.95 (*0-931137-10-1*) Infobooks.

Money Madness. Gibbs Davis. (White House Ghosthunters Ser.: No. 1). (J). (gr. 3-7). 1996. per. 3.99 (*0-671-56855-8*) PB.

***Money Madness.** Ronald Kidd. (Doug Ser.). 24p. 1999. pap. 3.29 (*0-307-13257-9*) Gldn Bks Pub Co.

Money Madness: Strange Manias & Extraordinary Schemes on & off Wall Street. John M. Waggoner. 1990. 26.00 (*1-55623-290-X*, Irwn Prfssnl) McGraw-Hill Prof.

Money Madness & Financial Freedom. David G. Benner. (Life Line Ser.). 200p. (Orig.). 1996. pap. write for info. (*1-55059-138-X*) Detselig Ents.

Money Magazine: A Guide to Your Home. Money Magazine Editors. 1999. write for info. (*0-316-57835-5*) Little.

Money Magazine 401(K) Take Charge of Your Future. Eric Schurenberg. (America's Financial Advisor Ser.). 240p. (Orig.). 1996. mass mkt. 9.99 (*0-446-67163-0*, Pub. by Warner Bks) Little.

Money Magazine Income Tax Handbook, 1993. Mary L. Sprouse & Money Magazine Editors. 672p. (Orig.). 1992. pap. 13.99 (*0-446-39425-4*, Pub. by Warner Bks) Little.

Money Magic see Collected Works of Hamlin Garland

Money Magic. Hamlin Garland. (Collected Works of Hamlin Garland). 1988. reprint ed. lib. bdg. 59.00 (*0-7812-1237-5*) Rprt Serv.

Money Magic. 2nd rev. ed. Lynne Palmer. LC 96-68440. (Illus.). 124p. (Orig.). 1996. pap. 11.00 (*0-9652296-0-2*) Star Bright.

Money Magic: Incredible Low-Risk Way to Build your Fortune. Alex Green. LC 82-82535. (Illus.). 117p. (Orig.). 1983. pap. 5.95 (*0-910067-00-7*) G K Pr.

Money Magic: 11 Secrets to Success! How to Achieve Ultimate Power. Maria H. Valentin. (Illus.). 231p. (Orig.). 1997. pap. 14.95 (*0-9651657-7-9*) NWI.

***Money Magic with Annuities: Great Ideas for Creative Investors.** Richard W. Duff. 1999. 19.95 (*1-882703-03-0*) RWD Ent.

***Money Magic with Annuities: Great Ideas for Creative Investors.** Richard W. Duff. 1999. pap. 19.95 (*1-882703-01-4*) RWD Ent.

Money Magnetics. abr. ed. Roger W. Breternitz. 1985. pap. 9.95 incl. audio (*1-893417-15-8*) Vector Studios.

Money Magnetism. J. Donald Walters. 132p. 1992. pap. 7.95 (*1-878265-39-3*) Crystal Clarity.

***Money Magnetism: How to Attract What You Need When You Need It.** 2nd ed. J. Donald Walters. 176p. 2000. pap. 9.95 (*1-56589-141-4*) Crystal Clarity.

Money Magnets: Regulating International Finance & Analysing Money Flows. D. Chorafas. 1997. 170.00 (*1-85564-551-3*, Pub. by Euromoney) Am Educ Systs.

Money Makeovers. Christopher L. Hayes & Kate Kelly. 448p. 1999. pap. 14.95 (*0-385-48541-7*) Doubleday.

Money Makeovers: How Women Can Control Their Financial Destiny. Christopher L. Hayes & Kate Kelly. LC 97-12517. 448p. 1997. 24.95 (*0-385-48540-9*) Doubleday.

Money-Makers: A Social Parable. Henry F. Keenan. LC 68-57537. (Muckrakers Ser.). 343p. reprint ed. pap. text 11.75 (*0-8290-1688-0*); reprint ed. lib. bdg. 25.00 (*0-8398-1051-2*) Irvington.

Money Makers of America. Laurence J. Pino. 1991. student ed. 99.95 incl. audio (*1-56354-002-9*) Open U FL.

Money Makes the World Go. Barbara Garson. 2001. 24.95 (*0-670-86660-1*) Viking Penguin.

Money Makes Us Relatives: Women's Labor in Urban Turkey. Jenny B. White. LC 93-30881. (Illus.). 200p. (Orig.). (C). 1994. text 30.00 (*0-292-79077-5*) U of Tex Pr.

***Money Making Backyard Gardening.** Mimi Luebbermann. 256p. 2000. pap. 16.95 (*0-7615-2299-9*) Prima Pub.

Money-Making Guide to Printing Estimating. Gerald A. Silver. LC 91-92966. (Illus.). 128p. (C). 1991. pap. 42.00 (*1-880472-06-6*) Edit Enter.

Money-Making Ideas for Your Event. International Festivals & Events Assoc. Staff. Ed. by Mary Bridges. 52p. 1993. pap. 44.95 (*1-891202-03-0*) Intl Festivals.

Money Making Investments Your Broker Doesn't Tell You About. Richard J. Maturi. LC 94-152197. 200p. 1993. text 24.95 (*1-55738-537-8*) Twntyfirst Cent Pubs.

Money Making Marketing: Finding the People Who Need What You're Selling & Making Sure They Buy It. 3rd rev. ed. Jeffrey Lant. 283p. 1999. 35.00 (*0-940374-30-7*) JLA Pubns.

Money-Making 900 Numbers: How Entrepreneurs Use the Telephone to Sell Information. Carol M. Ginsburg & Robert Mastin. LC 94-74497. 336p. (Orig.). 1995. pap. 19.95 (*0-9632790-1-7*) Aegis Pub Grp.

Money Making Secrets of the Self-Made Millionaires: A Proven Plan for Structuring & Implementing a Path Toward Riches As Has Been Done by Self-Made Millionaires. Stan P. Putnam. (Illus.). (Orig.). 1987. pap. 10.00 (*0-944047-04-1*) Res Improvement Inst.

***Money Man.** Kassandra Stirling. 200p. 1999. pap. 6.99 (*1-893108-48-1*) Neighbrhd Pr Pubng.

Money Management. Ransbottom. (YA - Adult Education Ser.). 1992. pap. 9.95 (*0-538-70663-5*) S-W Pub.

Money Management: A Consumer's Guide to Savings, Spending, & Investing. M. Herbert Freeman & David K. Graf. 1980. teacher ed. write for info. (*0-672-97182-8*); pap. write for info. (*0-672-97181-X*) Macmillan.

Money Management: Choices & Decisions. Elsie Fetterman. LC 75-30240. (Illus.). 256p. (C). 1976. pap. 6.76 (*0-395-20465-8*) HM.

Money Management after Retirement--Make Your Money Last for Life. 256p. 1998. 15.95 (*0-02-862528-5*) Macmillan.

Money Management for College Students. Larry Burkett. (C). 1998. pap., wbk. ed. 11.99 (*0-8024-6347-9*) Moody.

Money Management for Lawyers & Clients. Robert W. Hamilton. 608p. 1993. pap. text 26.95 (*0-316-34131-2*, Aspen Law & Bus) Aspen Pub.

Money Management for Lawyers & Clients: Essential Concepts & Applications. Robert W. Hamilton. 608p. 1993. pap. 26.95 (*0-7355-0632-9*, 06329, Aspen Law & Bus) Aspen Pub.

Money Management for Those Who Don't Have Any. James Paris. LC 96-48957. 224p. (Orig.). 1997. pap. 9.99 (*1-56507-532-3*) Harvest Hse.

***Money Management for Women.** Sheila Freeman & Helene Richards. 144p. 1999. pap. 19.95 (*0-86840-641-4*, Pub. by New South Wales Univ Pr) Intl Spec Bk.

Money Management for Women with No Money. Patricia J. Plute. LC 95-71267. 196p. 1995. pap. 12.95 (*0-9647957-0-1*) Running Coyote Pr.

Money Management for Young Adults: A Practical Guide to Financial Independence. Charles L. Cetti. LC 92-73383. 160p. (Orig.). 1992. pap. 14.95 (*0-9633856-0-7*) Baron Pub FL.

Money Management Made Easy. (Illus.). 1997. write for info. (*1-886614-50-4*) Intl Masters Pub.

Money Management Primer: Your Guide to Successful Management. Frederick S. Earle. (Primer Guide Ser.). 1997. 29.95 (*0-9658956-1-0*) Golden Laurel.

***Money Management Series, 7 vols.** Incl. Assessing Your Organization's Finances: A Guide to Using & Understanding Financial Reports. Daryl Burrows & Bill Batko. 24p. 1999. pap. (*0-942901-59-2*, Pub. by Enterprise Fnd); Creating a Budget That Works: A Self-Guided Handbook for Nonprofit Community Development Organizations. Bill Batko & LaCharla Figgs. 60p. 1999. pap. (*0-942901-52-5*, Pub. by Enterprise Fnd); Developing Realistic Cash Flow Projections: Forecasting When Money Will Be Received & Spent at Your Nonprofit. Bill Batko & LaCharla Figgs. 1999. pap. (*0-942901-53-3*, Pub. by Enterprise Fnd); Improving Your Accounting Software: A User-Friendly Review of Automated Systems for Community Development Organizations. David Crowley. 24p. 1999. pap. (*0-942901-57-6*, Pub. by Enterprise Fnd); Sound Financial Management: An Overview of Basic Accounting & Financial Principles for Nonprofit Community Development Organizations. David Crowley & LaCharla Figgs. 32p. 1999. pap. (*0-942901-55-X*, Pub. by Enterprise Fnd); Understanding Financial Statements: Keeping Tabs on Where the Money Goes at Your Nonprofit. David Crowley & LaCharla Figgs. 56p. 1999. pap. (*0-942901-54-1*, Pub. by Enterprise Fnd); Understanding the Federal Rules for Nonprofit Fiscal Management: Complying with Federal Regulations & Maintaining Internal Control Systems. LaCharla Figgs & Bill Batko. 24p. 1999. pap. (*0-942901-58-4*, Pub. by Enterprise Fnd); 1999. pap. write for info. (*0-942901-51-7*, Pub. by Enterprise Fnd) BookMasters.

Money Management Strategies for Futures Traders. Nauzer J. Balsara. LC 91-38287. (Financial Editions Ser.). 288p. 1992. 69.95 (*0-471-52215-5*) Wiley.

Money Management Using Excel. Louise Van Osdol. Ed. by Sandra Beris. LC 94-70485. (Crisp Computer Ser.). (Illus.). 138p. (Orig.). 1994. pap. 11.95 (*1-56052-277-1*) Crisp Pubns.

Money Management Using Lotus 1-2-3. William Barth. Ed. by Toni Murray. LC 94-70484. (Crisp Computer Ser.). (Illus.). 119p. (Orig.). 1994. pap. 11.95 (*1-56052-276-3*) Crisp Pubns.

Money Management Using Quicken. L. Louise Van Osdol. Ed. by Sandra Beriss. LC 94-70483. (Crisp Computer Ser.). (Illus.). 131p. (Orig.). 1994. pap. 11.95 (*1-56052-280-1*) Crisp Pubns.

Money Management Worksheets - IBM. Nick Maffei. 1991. 24.95 (*0-8306-6621-4*) McGraw-Hill Prof.

Money Management Worksheets - IBM PC. Nick Maffei. 1991. 24.95 (*0-8306-6622-2*) McGraw-Hill Prof.

Money Managers, Mutual Funds & Their Service Providers: Dealing with Regulatory Developments. (Corporate Law & Practice Course Handbook, 1985-86 Ser.). 496p. 1994. pap. 99.00 (*0-614-17189-X*, B4-7105) PLI.

Money Mandarins: The Making of a Supranational Economic Order. 2nd rev. ed. Howard M. Wachtel. LC 90-8471. 272p. (C). (gr. 13). 1990. pap. text 39.95 (*0-87332-704-7*) M E Sharpe.

Money Manipulation & Social Order. unabridged ed. Dinis Fahey. 107p. reprint ed. pap. 10.00 (*0-945001-46-0*) GSG & Assocs.

Money, Manure & Maintenance: Ingredients for Successful Gardens of Marian Coffin, Pioneer Landscape Architect 1876-1957. Nancy Fleming. Ed. by Anne Swanson. LC 94-67963. (Illus.). 128p. (Orig.). 1995. pap. 14.95 (*0-9643003-0-3*) Country Place.

Money Market. Marco Fanno. Tr. by Cyprian P. Blamires from ITA. LC 94-35562. (Classics in the History & Development of Economics Ser.).Tr. of Banche e il Mercato Monetario. 1995. text 79.95 (*0-312-12470-8*) St Martin.

Money Market. 3rd ed. Marcia L. Stigum. 725p. 1989. text 90.00 (*1-55623-122-9*, Irwn Prfssnl) McGraw-Hill Prof.

Money Market & Money Market Calculations Package. 3rd ed. Marcia L. Stigum. 1991. text 140.00 (*1-55623-692-1*, Irwn Prfssnl) McGraw-Hill Prof.

Money Market Bond Calculations, Vol. 1. Marcia L. Stigum & Franklin L. Robinson. 432p. 1996. 65.00 (*1-55623-476-7*, Irwn Prfssnl) McGraw-Hill Prof.

Money Market Derivatives & Structured Notes. Marcia L. Stigum. 1996. 50.00 (*0-7863-0438-3*, Irwn Prfssnl) McGraw-Hill Prof.

Money Market Directory of Pension Funds & Their Investment Managers, 1997. 1997. text 975.00 (*0-685-73087-5*) Money Mkt.

Money Market Directory of Tax-Exempt Organizations, 1997. 1997. 440.00 (*0-685-65247-5*) Money Mkt.

Money Market Funds. Bernard Seligman. LC 83-13921. 110p. 1983. 47.95 (*0-275-91728-2*, C1728, Praeger Pubs) Greenwood.

***Money Markets: Interest Risk Management.** 2000. pap. 120.00 (*0-85297-441-8*, Pub. by Chartered Bank) St Mut.

Money Markets: The International Perspective. J. S. Wilson. LC 93-12620. 448p. (C). (gr. 13). 1993. pap. 130.95 (*0-415-02423-4*, A9951) Thomson Learn.

***Money Markets & Foreign Exchange.** Reuters Limited Staff. LC 99-17730. 352p. 1999. 69.95 (*0-471-83128-X*) Wiley.

Money, Markets & Method: Essays in Honor of Robert W. Clower. Ed. by Peter Howitt et al. LC 98-29677. 304p. 1999. 95.00 (*1-85898-901-9*) E Elgar.

***Money, Markets & the State: Social Democratic Economic Policies since 1918.** Ton Notermans. LC 99-24406. (Cambridge Studies in Comparative Politics). (Illus.). 328p. (C). 2000. 59.95 (*0-521-63339-7*) Cambridge U Pr.

Money, Markets, & Trade in Early Southeast Asia: The Development of Indigenous Monetary Systems to AD 1400. Robert S. Wicks. (Studies on Southeast Asia: No. 11). (Illus.). 354p. (Orig.). 1992. pap. text 20.00 (*0-87727-710-9*) Cornell SE Asia.

Money Markets of Developing East Asia. Robert F. Emery. LC 90-23784. 360p. 1991. 72.50 (*0-275-93410-1*, C3410, Praeger Pubs) Greenwood.

Money Masters. John Train. LC 78-20192. 320p. 1994. pap. 14.00 (*0-88730-638-1*, HarpBusn) HarpInfo.

Money Masters of Our Time. John Train. 208p. 2000. 23.00 (*0-88730-791-4*, HarpBusn) HarpInfo.

Money Math Series, 3 vols., Set. Janie Haugen. Ed. by Hope Doty & Susan Jacobsen. (Illus.). 300p. 1997. 134.95 (*1-884074-37-5*, PCI 519) PCI Educ Pubg.

Money Matters. Cook Communications Ministries International Staff. (Interlit Imprint Ser.: Unit 8). 40p. 1994. pap. text 6.00 (*1-884752-10-1*, 44495) Cook Min Intl.

Money Matters. J. Fane. 1996. text 27.00 (*0-09-476100-0*, Pub. by Constable & Co) Trafalgar.

Money Matters. Benjamin Piltch & Peter Smergut. (Skyview Ser.). 64p. (YA). (gr. 7-12). 1983. 6.95 (*0-934618-03-8*) Learning Well.

Money Matters. Jim Weidmann. (Family Night Tool Chest Ser.: Vol. 5). 1998. pap. 12.99 (*1-56476-736-1*, Victor Bks) Chariot Victor.

Money Matters: A Teen Guide to the Economics of Divorce see Divorce Resource Series

***Money Matters: Consequences of Campaign Finance Reform in House Elections.** Robert K. Goidel et al. LC 98-52024. (Illus.). 256p. (C). 1998. 59.00 (*0-8476-8867-4*) Rowman.

Money Matters: Consequences of Campaign Finance Reform in House Elections. Robert K. Goidel et al. LC 98-52024. (Illus.). 256p. (C). 1999. pap. 18.95 (*0-8476-8868-2*) Rowman.

Money Matters: Financial Planning & Investment Ideas for the Non Finance Professional. Charles S. Meek. 1991. text 24.95 (*1-55738-136-4*, Irwn Prfssnl) McGraw-Hill Prof.

Money Matters: Instability, Values & Social Payments in the Modern History of West African Communities. Jane I. Guyer. LC 94-11804. (Social History of Africa Ser.). 331p. 1994. pap. 22.95 (*0-435-08957-9*, 08957) Heinemann.

Money Matters: Instability, Values & Social Payments in the Modern History of West African Communities. Jane I. Guyer. LC 94-11804. (Social History of Africa Ser.). 331p. 1994. 50.00 (*0-435-08955-2*, 08955) Heinemann.

Money Matters: Personal Giving in American Churches. Michael J. Donahue et al. LC 96-22896. 240p. (Orig.). 1996. pap. 22.95 (*0-664-25687-2*) Westminster John Knox.

Money Matters: Private Finance for Sustainable Human Development. (ODS Roundtable Ser). 40p. 7.50 (*92-1-126069-8*) UN.

Money Matters: Reaching Women Microentrepreneurs with Financial Services. Gloria Almeyda.Tr. of Dinero que Cuenta - Servicios Financieros al Alcance de la Mujer Microempresaria. 190p. 1997. pap. text 15.00 (*1-886938-15-6*) IADB.

Money Matters: The Distribution of Financial Welfare. Ed. by Robert Walker, Jr. & Gillian Parker. 288p. (C). 1988. text 69.95 (*0-8039-8128-7*); pap. text 25.95 (*0-8039-8129-5*) Sage.

Money Matters: The Fee in Psychotherapy & Psychoanalysis. William G. Herron & Shelia R. Welt. LC 92-1564. 203p. 1994. pap. text 19.95 (*0-89862-305-7*, 2305) Guilford Pubns.

Money Matters: The Hassle-Free-Month-by-Month Guide to Money Management. Paul N. Strassels & William B. Mead. LC 86-10733. 288p. 1986. 16.30 (*0-201-07222-X*) Addison-Wesley.

Money Matters: What Stockbrokers Don't Always Tell You. Richard Dupuis. 1991. pap. 12.95 (*0-9623830-0-7*) Companion Bks.

Money Matters: Words You Can Bank On. Mary L. Hogenson. Ed. by Jane H. Combs. (Success Ser.). (Illus.). 37p. (Orig.). 1991. pap. text 3.25 (*0-9625440-3-5*) Longmuir Jones Pub.

Money Matters: Your IDS Guide to Financial Planning. IDS Financial Staff. 1990. mass mkt. 5.95 (*0-380-75776-1*, Avon Bks) Morrow Avon.

Money Matters - Reaching Women Microentrepreneurs with Financial Services see Dinero que Cuenta: Servicios Financieros el Alcance de la Mujer Microempresaria

Money Matters for Families. 136p. (C). 1999. text 24.95 (*0-536-01086-2*) Pearson Custom.

Money Matters for Women. Aileen Cashman. (C). 1989. 65.00 (*0-946211-75-2*) St Mut.

Money Matters in Second Marriages, Set. pap. 7.00 (*0-317-01249-5*) UWIM CCA.

Money Matters in Second Marriages Section 1: Guidelines for Financial Management in Second Marriages. write for info. (*0-318-60837-5*) UWIM CCA.

Money Matters in Second Marriages Section 2: Effect of Wisconsin's Marital Property Law on Remarrieds. write for info. (*0-318-60838-3*) UWIM CCA.

Money Matters in Second Marriages Section 3: Estate Planning by Remarrieds. write for info. (*0-318-60839-1*) UWIM CCA.

Money Matters Made Easy: The Q & A Reference on Everything from Asset Allocation to Zero-Coupon Bonds. Steven C. Camp. Ed. by Melanie Camp et al. LC 97-61406. 179p. 1997. pap. 12.95 (*1-887620-01-X*) Trunkey Pub.

Money Matters Workbook for Teens (11-14) Larry Burket & Todd Temple. (YA). 1998. pap., wbk. ed. 12.99 (*0-8024-6345-2*) Moody.

Money Matters Workbook for Teens (15-18) Larry Burkett & Todd Temple. (YA). 1998. pap., wbk. ed. 12.99 (*0-8024-6346-0*) Moody.

Money, Media & the Grass Roots: State Ballot Issues & the Electoral Process. Betty H. Zisk. LC 86-13035. (Sage Library of Social Research: No. 164). 280p. (Orig.). reprint ed. pap. 86.80 (*0-7837-4490-0*, 204426700001) Bks Demand.

Money, Medicine, & Malpractice in American Society. Iain Hay. LC 91-25188. 280p. 1992. 65.00 (*0-275-93952-9*, C3952, Praeger Pubs) Greenwood.

Money Meltdown: Restoring Order to the Global Currency System. Judy Shelton. 406p. 1994. 24.95 (*0-02-929112-7*) Free Pr.

Money Men. William Haggard. 19.95 (*0-88411-679-4*) Amereon Ltd.

***Money Men: The Real Story of Political Power in the U. S. A.** Jeffrey Birnbaum. LC 00-23463. 320p. 2000. 25.95 (*0-8129-3119-X*, Times Bks) Crown Pub Group.

Money, Method & the Market Process: Essays by Ludwig von Mises. Ludwig Von Mises. Ed. by Richard M. Ebeling. 325p. (Orig.). (C). 1990. pap. text 19.95 (*0-945466-06-4*) Ludwig von Mises.

Money, Miles, & Large Numbers: Addition & Subtraction. Karen Economopoulos et al. Ed. by Priscilla C. Samii et al. (Investigations in Number, Data, & Space Ser.). (Illus.). 103p. (Orig.). 1994. pap., teacher ed. 22.95 (*0-86651-815-0*, DS21253) Seymour Pubns.

Money, Miles, & Large Numbers: Addition & Subtraction. rev. ed. Karen Economopoulos et al. Ed. by Catherine Anderson & Beverly Cory. (Investigations in Number, Data, & Space Ser.). (Illus.). 108p. (Orig.). (YA). (gr. 4 up). 1997. pap. text 22.95 (*1-57232-749-9*, 43896) Seymour Pubns.

Money Mind at Ninety. Philip L. Carret. 248p. 1994. pap. 19.95 (*0-87034-118-9*) Fraser Pub Co.

Money Mirror: How Money Reflects Women's Dreams, Fears, & Desires. Annette Lieberman & Vicki Lindner. LC 96-83239. 232p. 1996. pap. 14.95 (*1-880559-41-2*) Allworth Pr.

M

An Asterisk (*) at the beginning of an entry indicates that the title is appearing for the first time.

Money Mischief: Episodes in Monetary History. Milton Friedman. 1992. 19.95 *(0-15-162042-3)* Harcourt.

Money Mischief: Episodes in Monetary History. Milton Friedman. LC 94-158555. 304p. (C). 1994. pap. 11.00 *(0-15-661930-X)* Harcourt.

Money Money Money. 1986. write for info. *(0-318-61718-8)* Henderikse.

***Money Money Money: A Novel of the 87th Precinct.** 224p. 2000. 24.50 *(0-7432-0269-4)* S&S Trade.

Money, Money, Money: The Meaning of the Art & Symbols on United States Paper Currency. Nancy Winslow Parker. LC 93-43534. (Illus.). 32p. (J). (gr. 2-7). 1995. 16.95 *(0-06-023411-3)*; lib. bdg. 16.89 *(0-06-023412-1)* HarpC Child Bks.

Money, Money, Money: The Search for Wealth & the Pursuit of Happiness. Michael Toms. LC 97-30584. 176p. 1998. pap. 12.95 *(1-56170-458-X)* Hay House.

Money! Money! Money! Where It Comes from & Where It Goes. Barbara Cueter. LC 94-66532. 102p. 1994. pap. 16.95 *(1-882792-03-3)* Proctor Pubns.

Money, Money, Money Student Book. Jane Vogel. 48p. (Orig.). (YA). 1993. pap. 0.60 *(1-56476-088-X*, 6-3088, Victor Bks) Chariot Victor.

***Money! Money! Money! The Hitchhiker's Guide to Laboratory Finance.** Ian Wilkinson. 68p. 1999. pap. 19.00 *(1-890883-20-4*, 202870) Am Assn Clinical Chem.

Money Moon. Jeffrey Farnol. 1975. lib. bdg. 15.30 *(0-89966-090-8)* Buccaneer Bks.

Money, Morals & Manners: The Culture of the French & the American Upper- Middle Class. Michele Lamont. LC 92-7270. (Morality & Society Ser.). (Illus.). 350p. 1992. 39.95 *(0-226-46815-1)* U Ch Pr.

Money, Morals & Manners: The Culture of the French & the American Upper-Middle Class. Michele Lamont. (Morality & Society Ser.). xxx, 350p. 1994. pap. text 15.00 *(0-226-46817-8)* U Ch Pr.

Money, Morals & Manners As Revealed in Modern Literature. H. V. Routh. 1972. 59.95 *(0-8490-0662-7)* Gordon Pr.

Money, Motivation, & Mission in the Small Church. Anthony Pappas. Ed. by Douglas A. Walrath. (Small Church in Action Ser.). 128p. (Orig.). 1989. pap. 12.00 *(0-8170-1146-3)* Judson.

Money Mountain. large type ed. Robert MacLeod. 400p. 1988. 11.50 *(0-7089-1838-7)* Ulverscroft.

Money Mountain: The Story of Cripple Creek Gold. Marshall Sprague. LC 79-13838. (Illus.). xxiv, 352p. 1979. pap. 15.95 *(0-8032-9103-5*, Bison Books) U of Nebr Pr.

Money Moves. YPI (Yockey) Staff. 228p. 1996. pap. text 24.95 *(0-7872-2106-6)* Kendall-Hunt.

***Money Mystery: The Hidden Force Affecting Your Career, Business & Investments.** 2nd ed. Richard J. Maybury. LC 99-29734. ("Uncle Eric" Book Ser.). 1999. 9.95 *(0-942617-34-7)* Blstckng Pr.

Money, 1994, Vol. 1. Frankel. 1994. suppl. ed. 43.75 *(0-316-29171-4)* Little.

Money, 1994, Vol. 2. Frankel. 1994. suppl. ed. 43.75 *(0-316-29164-1)* Little.

Money, 1994, Vol. 3. Frankel. 1994. suppl. ed. 43.75 *(0-316-29173-0)* Little.

Money, 1994, Vol. 4. Frankel. 1994. suppl. ed. 43.75 *(0-316-29175-7)* Little.

Money Now You Have It. Now You Don't. Kathleen F. Russell & Larry C. Wall. LC 95-117798. 160p. (Orig.). 1994. pap. 7.95 *(0-9635176-4-3)* Walrus Prods.

Money, Obedience & Affection: Essays on Berkeley's Moral & Political Thought. Ed. by Clark R. Stephen. (Philosophy of George Berkeley Ser.). 210p. 1989. text 10.00 *(0-8240-2445-1)* Garland.

Money of Australia. Jill B. Bruce & Jan Wade. (Illus.). 40p. (Orig.). 1993. pap. 7.95 *(0-86417-464-0*, Pub. by Kangaroo Pr) Seven Hills Bk.

Money of Pre-Federal America. Coinage of the Americas Conference Staff. LC 92-246906. (Proceedings/Coinage of the Americas Conference Ser.: No. 7). (Illus.). 266p. 1992. pap. 82.50 *(0-608-05184-5*, 206572100001) Bks Demand.

Money of Pre-Federal America. Intro. by John Kleeberg. (Coinage of the Americas Conference at the American Numismatic Society, New York Ser.: No. 7). 253p. 1992. 25.00 *(0-89722-248-2)* Am Numismatic.

Money of the American Colonies & Confederation: A Numismatic, Economic & Historical Correlation. Philip Mossman. (Numismatic Studies: No. 20). (Illus.). 312p. 1993. 100.00 *(0-89722-249-0)* Am Numismatic.

Money of the Mind: Borrowing & Lending in America from the Civil War to Michael Milken. James Grant. 544p. 1994. pap. 16.00 *(0-374-52401-7*, Noonday) FS&G.

Money on the Move: The Revolution in International Finance since 1980. Robert Solomon. LC 98-26714. 224p. 1999. 29.95 *(0-691-00444-7*, Pub. by Princeton U Pr) Cal Prin Full Svc.

Money on the Table. 2nd ed. Gary Fagg & John S. Mailho. (Illus.). 260p. (C). 1996. text 40.00 *(0-9627820-2-5)* CreditRe.

Money 101: Your Easy Step by Step Guide to Enjoying a Secure Future. Debra W. Englander. LC 97-26576. 256p. 1997. per. 14.00 *(0-7615-0012-X)* Prima Pub.

***Money Order: The Money Management Guide for Women.** Gail Shapiro. 2001. pap. write for info. *(0-684-87098-3*, Fireside) S&S Trade Pap.

Money-Order with White Genesis. Sembene Ousmane. Tr. by Clive Wake from FRE. (African Writers Ser.). 138p. (C). 1987. pap. 9.95 *(0-435-90894-4*, 90894) Heinemann.

***Money Pit Mystery.** Eric Walters. 224p. 1999. pap. 10.50 *(0-00-648151-5)* HarpC.

***Money Pitch: Baseball Free Agency & Salary Arbitration.** Roger I. Abrams. LC 99-87922. (Illus.). 224p. 2000. 27.50 *(1-56639-774-X)* Temple U Pr.

Money Players. Armen Keteyian et al. 1998. per. 6.99 *(0-671-56810-8)* PB.

Money Players: Days & Nights Inside the New NBA. Armen Keteyian. LC 97-221383. 1997. 24.00 *(0-671-56809-4)* PB.

***Money Politics: Regulation of Political Finance in Indonesia, 1999.** ii, 14p. 1999. pap. 3.00 *(1-879720-70-1)* Intl Fndt Elect.

Money, Politics, & Law: A Study of Electoral Campaign Finance Reform in Canada. Kenneth D. Ewing. (Illus.). 272p. 1992. text 65.00 *(0-19-825738-4)* OUP.

Money Politics in the New Europe: Britain, France & the Single Financial Market. Daphne Josselin. LC 97-9327. 235p. 1997. text 69.95 *(0-312-17578-7)* St Martin.

Money Power. Alpha Publishing Corporation, Staff. 1995. pap. 12.95 *(1-884350-53-4)* Alpha Pub CA.

Money, Power, & Responsibility: Common Sense for Today. Teddy Milne. LC 90-62776. 101p. 1990. pap. 9.95 *(0-938875-13-2)* Pittenbruach Pr.

Money, Power & Space. Ed. by Stuart Corbridge et al. (Illus.). 288p. (C). 1994. 65.95 *(0-631-18199-7)*; pap. 29.95 *(0-631-19201-8)* Blackwell Pubs.

***Money, Power & the Radical Right in Pennsylvania.** Ed. by Liz Hrenda-Roberts. 64p. (C). 2000. reprint ed. pap. text 20.00 *(0-7881-8700-7)* DIANE Pub.

Money, Power & the Sexes: Channeling Sexual Energy in the Workplace. Cynthia E. Darwin. LC 95-68814. 106p. (Orig.). 1995. pap. 9.57 *(0-9645975-4-3)* Cat Hill Prods.

Money, Prices & Civilization in the Mediterranean World. Carlo M. Cipolla. LC 67-18440. (Illus.). 75p. 1967. reprint ed. 20.00 *(0-87752-021-6)* Gordian.

Money, Prices & Civilization in the Mediterranean World. Carlo M. Cipolla. LC 67-18440. (Illus.). 75p. 1967. reprint ed. pap. 15.00 *(0-686-86000-4)* Gordian.

Money, Prices, & Foreign Exchange in Fourteenth Century France. Harry A. Miskimin. LC 63-7942. 1981. reprint ed. 15.00 *(0-08-022307-9*, Pergamon Pr) Elsevier.

Money, Prices & Growth: The American Experience, 1869-1896. George E. Dickey. Ed. by Stuart Bruchey. LC 76-39828. (Nineteen Seventy-Seven Dissertations Ser.). (Illus.). 1977. lib. bdg. 23.95 *(0-405-09907-X)* Ayer.

Money, Prices & Power in Poland 16th-17th Centuries: A Comparative Approach. Antoni Maczak. LC 94-43313. (Collected Studies: No. CS487). 312p. 1995. 109.95 *(0-86078-478-9*, Pub. by Variorum) Ashgate Pub Co.

Money, Prices, & the Real Economy. Geoffrey E. Wood & Institute of Economic Affairs (Great Britain). LC 98-13454. 136p. 1999. 65.00 *(1-85898-612-5)* E Elgar.

Money, Pricing, Distribution & Economic Integration. Philip Arestis. LC 96-3465. 240p. 1997. text 69.95 *(0-312-16532-3)* St Martin.

Money Problems & Pastoral Care. Paul G. Schurman. LC 81-70662. (Creative Pastoral Care & Counseling Ser.). 96p. reprint ed. pap. 30.00 *(0-608-18006-8*, 202910800058) Bks Demand.

Money Problems of the Poor: A Literature Review. Pauline Ashley. (SSRC-DHSS Studies in Deprivation & Disadvantage: No. 11). xiii, 226p. 1983. text 37.95 *(0-435-82024-9)* Ashgate Pub Co.

Money Project. Vicki Oppenheim. 1992. pap. text, teacher ed. 29.95 *(1-882247-00-0)* Dansi Pr.

Money Project. Vicki Oppenheim. (YA). (gr. 9-12). 1992. pap. text, student ed., wbk. ed. 10.95 *(1-882247-01-9)* Dansi Pr.

Money Project II. Vicki Oppenheim. 1995. pap. text, teacher ed. 31.95 *(1-882247-02-7)* Dansi Pr.

Money Project II. Vicki Oppenheim. (YA). (gr. 9-12). 1995. pap. text, student ed., wbk. ed. 10.95 *(1-882247-03-5)* Dansi Pr.

Money Puzzle. 3rd ed. Cruse & Cunni. (C). 1989. pap., student ed. 29.33 *(0-06-041454-5)* HarpC.

***Money! Questions & Answers.** Charles E. Coughlin. 192p. 1998. pap. 7.00 *(0-944379-24-9)* CPA Bk Pub.

Money Reform Scrapbook: Letters & Clippings. (Money Reform Ser.). 1994. lib. bdg. 289.88 *(0-8490-5650-0)* Gordon Pr.

***Money Rules: The New Politics of Finance in Britain & Japan.** Henry Laurence. 2000. 29.95 *(0-8014-3773-3)* Cornell U Pr.

Money-Savers Cookbook. Compiled by Jody Cameron. 256p. (Orig.). 1992. mass mkt. 4.99 *(0-380-76642-6*, Avon Bks) Morrow Avon.

Money Saving Conservation Products & Projects for the Homeowner. Stephen Kokette. LC 78-55883. 1978. 14.00 *(0-932314-07-4)* Aylmer Pr.

Money Saving Frugal Consumer Workshop Notebook. Lamp Light Press Staff. (Illus.). 93p. 1993. ring bd. 37.95 *(0-917593-15-4*, Lamp Light Pr) Prosperity & Profits.

Money-Saving Guide to Managing Your Home Remodeling. Coleman Volgenau. LC 91-45785. 208p. 1992. pap. 14.95 *(0-471-57497-X)* Wiley.

Money Saving Secrets to Buying or Leasing Your Next Car. William B. Grant. 71p. 1993. pap. 4.95 *(0-9636663-0-4)* Nuts & Bolts.

Money Savvy: Men's Health Life Improvement Guide Ser. Ed. by Stephen C. George. LC 98-28020. (Illus.). 176p. 1998. pap. 14.95 *(0-87596-505-9)* Rodale Pr Inc.

Money Secrets at the Racetrack. Barry Meadow. LC 87-51583. 148p. (Orig.). 1990. pap. 24.95 *(0-945322-02-X)* TR Pub.

Money Secrets of the Rich & Famous. Michael Reynard. LC 99-28130. 256p. 1999. 24.95 *(1-58115-032-6)* Allworth Pr.

Money Secrets the Pro's Don't Want You to Know: 365 Ways to Outsmart Your Banker, Broker, Insurance Agent, Car Dealer, Realtor, Travel Agent, Lawyer, Credit Card Company & the IRS. Stephanie Gallagher. LC 94-41741. 256p. 1995. pap. 17.95 *(0-8144-7893-X)* AMACOM.

Money Seminar. Leonard D. Orr. 1990. 20.00 *(0-945793-11-1)* Inspir Univ.

Money Sense: A Commonsense Road to Financial Security & Early Retirement. Patrick Bohan. LC 97-40892. 175p. 2000. pap. 18.95 *(1-56072-519-2*, Nova Kroshka Bks) Nova Sci Pubs.

Money Sense for Kids. Hollis P. Harman. LC 98-27099. (Illus.). 166p. (J). (gr. 4-8). 1999. pap. 9.95 *(0-7641-0681-3)* Barron.

Money Sense Overseas. David J. Schlink. 1984. reprint ed. pap. 4.50 *(0-912327-01-4)* Unicon Ent.

Money, Sex, & Power: Toward a Feminist Historical Materialism. Nancy C. Hartsock. (Northeastern Series in Feminist Theory). 320p. (C). 1983. pap. text 17.95 *(0-930350-78-2)* NE U Pr.

Money, Sex & Power: Toward a Feminist Historical Materialism. Nancy C. Hartsock. (Northeastern Series in Feminist Theory). 320p. (C). 1983. text. write for info. *(0-582-28279-9)* NE U Pr.

Money, Sex & Spiritual Power: Leader's Book. Ed. by Sharon Drury. (Illus.). 136p. 1992. teacher ed., spiral bd. 14.95 *(0-89827-104-5*, BKR81) Wesleyan Pub Hse.

Money, Sex & Spiritual Power: Student Book. Keith Drury. 128p. 1992. pap. text, student ed. 6.95 *(0-89827-103-7*, BKR82) Wesleyan Pub Hse.

Money Signs. Elbert Wade. LC 83-70272. 176p. 1982. 13.00 *(0-86690-233-3*, W2641-014) Am Fed Astrologers.

Money Signs: A Beginner's Guide. Christeen Skinner. (Beginner's Guide Ser.). (Illus.). 96p. 1998. mass mkt. 11.95 *(0-340-72083-2*, Pub. by Hodder & Stought Ltd) Trafalgar.

Money Sings: The Changing Politics of Urban Space in Post-Soviet Yaroslavl. Blair A. Ruble. (Woodrow Wilson Center Press Ser.). (Illus.). 176p. (C). 1995. text 64.95 *(0-521-48242-9)* Cambridge U Pr.

Money Skills: Learning to Manage Your Money. Janie Haugen. (Life Skills Series Educational Board Games: Series II). (Illus.). 50p. 1993. text 49.95 *(1-884074-27-8*, LSG 900) PCI Educ Pubg.

Money Skills Course. Jerry James. 70p. 1994. 9.90 *(0-9642822-0-8)* J James.

Money Smart: Secrets Women Always Wanted to Know about Money. Esther M. Berger & Connie C. Hasbun. LC 93-2694. 304p. 1993. 22.00 *(0-671-76061-0)* S&S Trade.

***Money Smart Secrets for Self Esteem.** Linda Stern. 2000. pap. write for info. *(0-375-70878-2)* Random Ref & Info.

Money Smart Secrets for the Self-Employed. Linda Stern. LC 96-41483. 1997. pap. 20.00 *(0-679-77711-3)* Random.

Money Source Book. 5th rev. ed. 200p. 1993. pap. text 24.95 *(0-9632628-1-5)* Busn Info Netwk.

Money Source Book: 1992 Texas Edition. Taylor. 1992. pap. 75.00 *(0-9632628-0-7)* Busn Info Netwk.

Money Source Directory, 1989. Sammy S. Jenkins, Sr. 425p. 1989. pap. 129.95 *(0-9620989-0-6)* All States Pub.

Money Source Workbook. 55p. 1992. pap. text 12.95 *(0-9632628-2-3)* Busn Info Netwk.

Money Sources for Small Business: How You Can Find Private, State, Federal & Corporate Financing. 2nd rev. ed. William M. Alarid. Ed. by Curt Scott. LC 96-6814. 224p. (Orig.). 1998. pap. 19.95 *(0-940673-73-8)* Puma Pub Co.

Money Stones. large type ed. Ian St. James. 512p. 1983. 11.50 *(0-7089-0923-X)* Ulverscroft.

Money Stress. David C. Rainham. (Illus.). 12p. (Orig.). 1996. pap. 3.00 *(1-884241-59-X*, EHO570) Energeia Pub.

Money Stuff: How to Increase Prosperity, Attract Riches, Experience Abundance & Have More Money! Larry Winget. 196p. 1994. pap. 11.95 *(1-881342-02-6)* Win Pubns OK.

Money Supply & Deficit Financing in Economic Development. Wassim N. Shahin. LC 92-13249. 248p. 1992. 62.95 *(0-89930-677-2*, SKI/, Quorum Bks) Greenwood.

Money Supply & the Exchange Rate. Ed. by Walter A. Eltis & P. J. Sinclair. (Illus.). (Orig.). (C). 1981. pap. text 19.95 *(0-19-877168-1)* OUP.

Money Supply in the Economic Process: A Post Keynesian Perspective, 2 Vols., set. Ed. by Marco Musella & Carlo Panico. LC 95-32857. (International Library of Critical Writings in Economics Ser.: Vol. 60). 656p. (C). 1996. text 270.00 *(1-85898-043-7)* E Elgar.

Money Supply of the American Colonies. Curtis P. Nettels. 1972. 250.00 *(0-8490-0663-5)* Gordon Pr.

Money Supply of the American Colonies Before 1720. Curtis P. Nettels. LC 64-22242. (Library of Money & Banking History). 300p. 1964. reprint ed. 45.00 *(0-678-00061-1)* Kelley.

Money Supply Process: A Comparative Analysis. Dimitrije Dimitrijevic & George Macesich. LC 90-39155. 192p. 1991. 52.95 *(0-275-93597-3*, C3597, Praeger Pubs) Greenwood.

Money Swallow. Joseph Cozzo. 287p. 1996. write for info. *(1-85863-726-0*, Pub. by Minerva Pr) Unity Dist.

Money System. Leonard D. Orr. 1990. 20.00 *(0-945793-13-8)* Inspir Univ.

Money, Systems & Growth: A New Economic Order? George Macesich. LC 98-23554. 128p. 1999. 49.95 *(0-275-96171-0*, Praeger Pubs) Greenwood.

***Money Talk: A Gay & Lesbian Guide to Financial Success.** Todd J. Rainey. 160p. 1999. pap. 18.95 *(1-891689-75-4)* Gabriel Pubns.

Money Talk: Accounting Fundamentals for Special Librarians. Madeline J. Daubert. 47p. 1995. pap. 85.00 *(0-87111-445-3)* SLA.

***Money Talk: Finance & Investment Terms for Busy People.** Edna Crew. 128p. 2000. pap. 7.95 *(1-86508-087-X*, Pub. by Allen & Unwin Pty) Paul & Co Pubs.

***Money Talk: From Alphabet Stock to the Naked Sale-The Words & Phrases That Control Your Money.** Lorraine Spurge. 2001. pap. 14.95 *(0-7868-8498-3*, Pub. by Hyperion) Time Warner.

Money Talks. large type unabridged ed. Sherry Ashworth. 416p. 1998. 26.95 *(0-7531-5857-4*, 158574) ISIS Pub.

***Money Talks: Black Finance Experts Talk to You about Money.** Juliette Fairley. 220p. 2000. pap. 14.95 *(0-471-38398-8)* Wiley.

Money Talks: How to Make a Million As a Speaker. Alan Weiss. LC 97-41226. (Illus.). 256p. 1997. pap. 14.95 *(0-07-069615-2)* McGraw.

Money Talks: How to Make a Million as a Speaker. Alan Weiss. LC 97-41226. (Illus.). 256p. 1998. 29.95 *(0-07-069614-4)* McGraw.

Money Talks: Reconstructing Old English. Fran Colman. LC 91-34452. (Trends in Linguistics, Studies & Monographs: No. 56). viii, 391p. 1991. lib. bdg. 129.25 *(3-11-012741-5)* Mouton.

Money Talks: The Complete Guide to Creating a Profitable Workshop or Seminar in Any Field. 3rd rev. ed. Jeffrey Lant. 302p. (Orig.). 1995. 35.00 *(0-940374-27-7)* JLA Pubns.

***Money Talks: The Top Black Finance Experts Talk to You about Money, 1.** Juliette Fairley. LC 97-45917. 240p. 1998. 22.95 *(0-471-24582-8)* Wiley.

Money Talks & So Can We: How Couples Can Communicate about Spending & Giving, Getting Out of Debt, Investing, Planning for Retirement, & Other Money Matters. Ron Blue & Jodie Berndt. LC 98-39128. 1999. 17.99 *(0-310-22461-6)*; pap. 12.99 *(0-310-22266-4)* Zondervan.

Money Talks, O. J. Walks. Larry Topper. 150p. (Orig.). 1997. pap. text 13.95 *(1-57532-095-9)* Press-Tige Pub.

Money, the Financial System & the Economy. Glen R. Hubbard. (C). 1994. pap. text 21.00 *(0-201-56392-4)* Addison-Wesley.

Money the Financial System & the Economy. 2nd ed. Glen R. Hubbard. 848p. (C). 1996. text. write for info. *(0-201-56870-5)* Addison-Wesley.

Money the Financial System & the Economy. 2nd ed. R. Glenn Hubbard. LC 96-46531. 848p. (C). 1997. text 76.88 *(0-201-84759-0)* Addison-Wesley.

Money, the Financial System & the Economy. 2nd ed. R. Glenn Hubbard. (C). 1997. pap. text, student ed. 23.44 *(0-201-88316-3)* Addison-Wesley.

Money, the Financial System & the Economy. 3rd ed. Glenn Hubbard. 352p. (C). 1999. pap. text, student ed. 28.00 *(0-201-65728-7)* Addison-Wesley.

***Money Therapy: Using the Eight Money Types to Create Wealth & Prosperity.** Deborah L. Price. 176p. 2000. 18.00 *(1-57731-157-4*, Pub. by New Wrld Lib) Publishers Group.

Money Thicker Than Blood. large type ed. Adam Smith. (Linford Western Library Ser.). 224p. 1997. pap. 16.99 *(0-7089-5141-4)* Ulverscroft.

Money Thoughts: The Abc of Money Management. 2nd ed. Bruce Bond. LC 94-181333. 184 p. 1990. write for info. *(0-85091-413-2)* Lothian Pub.

Money, Time, & Politics: Investment Tax Subsidies & American Democracy. Ronald F. King. LC 92-36267. 512p. (C). 1993. 52.50 *(0-300-05056-8)* Yale U Pr.

***Money to Burn.** Level 2. (C). 2000. 7.00 *(0-582-41802-X)* Addison-Wesley.

Money to Burn. Elizabeth Cadell. 1976. 21.95 *(0-88411-396-5*, Queens House) Amereon Ltd.

Money to Burn. E.M. Goldman. 1996. 9.09 *(0-606-09625-6*, Pub. by Turtleback) Demco.

Money to Burn. Michael Mewshaw. 480p. 1988. mass mkt. 4.50 *(1-55817-060-X*, Pinncle Kensgtn) Kensgtn Pub Corp.

Money to Burn. Michael Mewshaw. 1990. mass mkt. 4.95 *(1-55817-408-7*, Pinncle Kensgtn) Kensgtn Pub Corp.

Money to Burn. Katy Munger. (Casey Jones Mystery Ser.). 320p. 1999. mass mkt. 5.99 *(0-380-80063-2*, Avon Bks) Morrow Avon.

Money to Burn: Great American Foundations & Their Money. Horace Coon. 393p. (C). 1990. 49.95 *(0-88738-334-3)* Transaction Pubs.

Money to Burn? The High Costs of Energy Subsidies. Mark Kosmo. LC 87-51349. 80p. 1987. pap. 10.00 *(0-915825-26-0)* World Resources Inst.

Money to Burn: What the Great American Philanthropic Foundations Do with Money. Horace Coon. 352p. 1977. 21.95 *(0-8369-2843-1)* Ayer.

Money to Work II: Funding for Visual Artists. rev. ed. Helen M. Brunner & Don Russell. Ed. by Grant Samuelsen. 312p. 1992. pap. 15.20 *(0-685-65202-5)* Art Resources Intl.

Money Town. J. R. Roberts. (Gunsmith Ser.: No. 192). 192p. 1997. mass mkt. 4.99 *(0-515-12192-4*, Jove) Berkley Pub.

Money Tracker: A Quick & Easy Way to Keep Tabs on Your Spending. Judy M. Lawrence. 416p. 1996. 14.95 *(0-7931-1786-0*, 5680-3201) Dearborn.

Money Trade. Date not set. pap. 10.00 *(0-674-58500-3)* HUP.

Money, Trade, & Competition: Essays in Memory of Egon Sohmen. Ed. by Herbert Giersch. LC 92-20298. 320p. 1992. 107.95 *(0-387-55125-5)* Spr-Verlag.

Money, Trade & Economic Growth: Survey Lectures in Economic Theory. Harry G. Johnson. (Modern Revivals in Economics Ser.). 200p. (C). 1993. text 52.95 *(0-7512-0250-9*, Pub. by Gregg Revivals) Ashgate Pub Co.

Money Trail. William Jovanovich. 1990. 16.95 *(0-15-162050-4)* Harcourt.

An Asterisk (*) at the beginning of an entry indicates that the title is appearing for the first time.

*__Money Trail: Burmese Currencies in Crisis, 1942-1947.__ Marilyn Longmuir. (Illus.). 2000. pap. 16.95 (*1-891134-05-1*) SE Asia.

Money Trail: Confiscation of Proceeds of Crime, Money Laundering, & Cash Transaction Reporting. Ed. by Brent Fisse. 400p. 1992. 98.00 (*0-455-21064-0*, Pub. by LawBk Co) Gaunt.

Money Tree. Sam Mills. LC 98-83192. 365p. 1999. 25.00 (*0-7388-0355-3*); pap. 15.00 (*0-7388-0356-1*) Xlibris Corp.

Money Tree. Sarah Stewart. LC 89-46141. (Illus.). 32p. (J). (ps-3). 1991. 14.95 (*0-374-35014-0*) FS&G.

Money Tree. Sarah Stewart. LC 89-46141. (Illus.). 32p. (J). (gr. k-3). 1994. pap. 5.95 (*0-374-45295-4*, Sunburst Bks) FS&G.

*__Money-Tree Marketing: Innovative Secrets That Will Double Your Small-Business Profits.__ Patrick Bishop & Jennifer A. Bishop. 256p. 2000. pap. 18.95 (*0-8144-7055-6*) AMACOM.

Money Tree Myth: A Parents' Guide to Helping Kids Unravel the Mysteries of Money. Gail Vaz-Oxlade. 224p. (Orig.). 1996. pap. 12.95 (*0-7737-5817-8*) Stoddart Publ.

Money Troubles. Bill Cosby. LC 97-34106. (Little Bill Books for Beginning Readers Ser.). (Illus.). 40p. (J). (gr. k-3). 1998. 13.95 (*0-590-16402-3*); pap. 3.99 (*0-590-95623-X*) Scholastic Inc.

*__Money Troubles.__ Bill Cosby. (Little Bill Books for Beginning Readers Ser.). (J). (gr. k-3). 1998. 9.19 (*0-606-13615-0*, Pub. by Turtleback) Demco.

*__Money Troubles.__ Elisabeth McNeill. 256p. 2000. 26.00 (*0-7278-5443-7*, Pub. by Severn Hse) Chivers N Amer.

Money Troubles: Legal Strategies to Cope with Your Debts. 4th ed. Robin Leonard. LC 96-7907. 360p. 1996. 19.95 (*0-87337-341-3*) Nolo com.

Money Troubles & How to Cope with Them. 1992. lib. bdg. 79.95 (*0-8490-5287-4*) Gordon Pr.

Money Trucks. Larry E. Davis. (Illus.). 320p. (Orig.). 1987. pap. 4.95 (*0-941177-22-X*) Castle Pub.

Money under the Table: Short Stories. unabridged ed. Lewis Warsh. 115p. (Orig.). 1997. pap. 10.00 (*0-9639192-3-7*) Trip St Pr.

*__Money Unmade: Barter & the Fate of Russian Capitalism.__ David M. Woodruff. LC 99-21491. 240p. 1999. 27.50 (*0-8014-3660-5*) Cornell U Pr.

*__Money Unmade: Barter & the Fate of Russian Capitalism.__ David M. Woodruff. 2000. reprint ed. pap. 17.95 (*0-8014-8694-7*) Cornell U Pr.

Money Value of a Man. Louis I. Dublin & Alfred J. Lotka. Ed. by Barbara G. Rosenkrantz. LC 76-25659. (Public Health in America Ser.). (Illus.). 1977. reprint ed. lib. bdg. 26.95 (*0-405-09814-6*) Ayer.

*__Money Wars: The Rise & Fall of the Great Buyout Boom of the 1980s.__ Roy C. Smith. LC 00-34217. 2000. pap. write for info. (*1-893122-69-7*) Beard Bks.

Money Watchers: The Four Week Money Management Makeover. Jocelan Martell. 50p. (Orig.). 1989. pap. write for info. (*0-9623255-0-3*) Empire Pubng CO.

Money Wise & Spiritually Rich. Dennis Deaton. LC 98-71543. 1998. pap. 12.95 (*1-57008-424-6*) Bookcraft Inc.

Money Without Madness: Organize Your Budget & Stop Money Stress on Any Income. Karen Brigham. LC 98-33531. 288p. 1998. pap. text 9.95 (*1-58062-050-7*) Adams Media.

Money, Women & Guns: Crime Movies from Bonnie & Clyde to the Present. Douglas Brode. (Citadel Film Ser.). (Illus.). 256p. (Orig.). 1995. pap. 17.95 (*0-8065-1608-9*, Citadel Pr) Carol Pub Group.

Money Workbook: A 30-Day Program to Greater Abundance, Prosperity & Self-Worth. 2nd ed. Roger B. Lane. 79p. Date not set. spiral bd. 29.95 (*1-888388-24-2*) Right Lane.

Money Workbook: A 30-Day Program to Greater Abundance, Prosperity & Self-Worth. 3rd ed. Roger B. Lane. Date not set. spiral bd. 19.95 (*1-888388-12-9*) Right Lane.

Money Writes! Upton Sinclair. (BCL1-PS American Literature Ser.). 227p. 1992. reprint ed. lib. bdg. 79.00 (*0-7812-6624-6*) Rprt Serv.

Money Writes! Upton Sinclair. LC 71-115274. 1970. reprint ed. 29.00 (*0-403-00294-X*) Scholarly.

*__Money You Need It.__ Michael A. Burgess. 118p. 1999. pap. write for info. (*0-7392-0459-9*, PO3766) Morris Pubng.

*__Money Zone: Personal Finance for the Next Generation.__ Debbie Harrison. (Illus.). 256p. 2000. pap. 39.50 (*0-273-64504-8*, Pub. by F T P-H) Trans-Atl Phila.

Moneybags Must Be So Lucky: On the Literary Structure of "Capital" Robert P. Wolff. LC 87-20580. 82p. (Orig.). (C). 1988. pap. 10.95 (*0-87023-616-4*); lib. bdg. 20.00 (*0-87023-615-6*) U of Mass Pr.

Moneyblocks: How to Let Go & Get Going Financially. Faye Cameron. 150p. 1991. pap. 7.95 (*0-9630261-0-0*) Dunbar CO.

Moneychangers. large type ed. Arthur Hailey. 736p. 1983. 27.99 (*0-7089-8146-1*, Charnwood) Ulverscroft.

Moneychangers. Arthur Hailey. 1994. reprint ed. lib. bdg. 27.95 (*1-56849-566-8*) Buccaneer Bks.

*__Moneychangers.__ Upton Sinclair. (Collected Works of Upton Sinclair). 316p. 1999. reprint ed. lib. bdg. 108.00 (*1-58201-828-6*) Classic Bks.

MoneyFind BookWare: Directory of Scholarships. American Financial Directories Staff. 512p. 1994. pap. 29.95 incl. disk (*1-883609-06-2*) Am Finan.

MoneyFind BookWare: Directory of Small Business Investors. American Financial Directories Staff. 1994. pap. write for info. incl. disk (*1-883609-00-3*) Am Finan.

Moneylenders of Shahpur. large type ed. Helen Forrester. 448p. 1988. 11.50 (*0-7089-1760-7*) Ulverscroft.

Moneylove. Jerry Gillies. 208p. 1988. mass mkt. 5.99 (*0-446-35379-5*, Pub. by Warner Bks) Little.

Moneymakers. Mark Dunster. (Rin Ser.: Pt. 17). 37p. (Orig.). 1982. pap. 4.00 (*0-89642-090-6*) Linden Pubs.

Moneymakers. Duane Magnani. 1986. pap. 8.95 (*1-883858-14-3*) Witness CA.

Moneymakers: A True Story of Government-Created Inflation. Andrew D. White. 1978. reprint ed. pap. 5.00 (*0-87651-209-0*) Southern U Pr.

Moneymakers: Good Cents for Girls. Ingrid Roper. LC 98-21076. (American Girl Library Ser.). (Illus.). 110p. (J). (gr. 3-7). 1998. pap. text 7.95 (*1-56247-668-8*) Pleasant Co.

Moneymakers International. Willibald Kranister. 326p. 1990. 150.00 (*0-9514522-0-7*, Pub. by Chartered Bank) St Mut.

Moneymaking Moms: How Work at Home Can Work for You. Caroline Hull. LC 98-10383. 208p. 1998. pap. 12.00 (*0-8065-1993-2*, Citadel Pr) Carol Pub Group.

Moneys of the Bible. R. S. Yeoman. (Illus.). 1982. reprint ed. pap. 18.00 (*0-915262-77-0*) S J Durst.

Moneys Received & Paid for Secret Services of Charles II & James II from 30th March, 1679 to 25th December, 1688. Henry Guy. Ed. by John Y. Akerman. LC 77-158238. (Camden Society, London Publications, First Ser.: No. 52). reprint ed. 54.50 (*0-404-50152-4*) AMS Pr.

Moneysmart Divorce: What Women Need to Know about Money & Divorce. Esther M. Berger. 240p. 1996. 22.00 (*0-684-81165-0*) S&S Trade.

*__Moneytalk: Living Generously.__ Mark Vincent & Michele Hershberger. (Generation Why Ser.: Vol. 6:2). 42p. (YA). (gr. 9-12). 2000. pap. 12.95 (*0-87303-407-4*) Faith & Life.

Moneytown Assortment. 1997. 8.97 (*0-7849-1004-9*) SimSchuster Interact.

Moneywise. Woody Young. (Kit-Cat-Wise Ser.). (Illus.). 48p. (Orig.). (J). (gr. 1-5). 1986. pap. text 4.95 (*0-939513-30-7*) Joy Pub SJC.

Moneywise Meditations: To Be Found Faithful in God's Audit. John Rudy. LC 89-2191. (Illus.). 144p. (Orig.). 1989. pap. 7.99 (*0-8361-3486-9*) Herald Pr.

Mong Education at the Crossroads. Paoze Thao. LC 99-21902. 184p. 1999. 38.00 (*0-7618-1399-3*) U Pr of Amer.

Monge AMPERE Equation: Applications to Geometry & Optimization: NSF-CBMS Conference on the Monge AMP ERE Equation, Applications to Geometry & Optimization, July 9-13, 1997, Florida Atlantic University. Luis A. Caffarelli & Mario Milman. LC 98-38822. (Contemporary Mathematics Ser.: Vol. 226). 1998. write for info. (*0-8218-0917-2*) Am Math.

Mongol Bicgiin Zov Bicix Durmiin Xuraangui. (Mongolia Society Special Papers: Issues No. 11). 1991. pap. 5.00 (*0-910980-31-4*) Mongolia.

Mongol Conquests: A. D. 1200 - 1300 see TimeFrame Series

Mongol Conquests, (1200-1300 AD) (Time Frame Ser.). (Illus.). 176p. 1989. lib. bdg. 25.93 (*0-8094-6438-1*) Time-Life.

Mongol Elements in Manchu. William Rozycki. LC 94-65580. (Uralic & Altaic Ser.: Vol. 157). 255p. 1994. 29.90 (*0-933070-31-4*) Ind U Res Inst.

Mongol Empire. Mary Hull. LC 97-29991. (World History Ser.). (Illus.). (YA). (gr. 4-12). 1997. lib. bdg. 22.45 (*1-56006-312-2*) Lucent Bks.

Mongol Empire & Its Legacy. Reuven Amitai-Preiss. LC 98-4197. (Islamic History & Civilization Studies & Texts). 361p. 1999. 146.50 (*90-04-11048-8*) Brill Academic Pubs.

Mongol-English Practical Dictionary with English Word Reference List. Matthew Haltod et al. LC PL0406.. 691p. pap. 200.00 (*0-608-11053-1*, 201959900013) Bks Demand.

Mongol Jewelry. Martha Boyer. LC 95-60286. (Carlsberg Nomad Ser.). (Illus.). 272p. 1995. 50.00 (*0-500-01660-7*, Pub. by Thames Hudson) Norton.

Mongol Journeys. Owen Lattimore. LC 72-4436. reprint ed. 32.50 (*0-404-10633-1*) AMS Pr.

Mongol Mission. Ed. by Christopher H. Dawson. LC 78-63334. (Crusades & Military Orders Ser.: Second Series). reprint ed. 44.00 (*0-404-17008-0*) AMS Pr.

Mongol Period: A History of the Muslim World. Bertold Spuler. Tr. by F. R. Bagley from GER. (Illus.). 166p. (C). 1994. reprint ed. pap. 18.95 (*1-55876-079-2*) Wiener Pubs Inc.

Mongolia see Enchantment of the World Series

Mongolia see Festivals of the World

Mongolia. William R. Heaton. (Profiles of Asia Ser.). 1996. text 26.50 (*0-89158-911-2*) Westview.

Mongolia. Judith Nordby. LC 93-247427. (World Bibliographical Ser.). 226p. 1993. lib. bdg. 73.00 (*1-85109-129-7*) ABC-CLIO.

Mongolia. Jan Reynolds. LC 93-1351. (Vanishing Cultures Ser.). (Illus.). 32p. (J). (gr. 3-7). 1994. 16.95 (*0-15-255312-6*); pap. 8.95 (*0-15-255313-4*) Harcourt.

Mongolia. Sanders. 200p. 1987. pap. text 17.50 (*0-86187-431-5*, Pub. by P P Pubs) Cassell & Continuum.

Mongolia. Sanders. (Marxist Regimes Ser.). 200p. 1988. text 49.00 (*0-86187-430-7*) St Martin.

*__Mongolia, 6 vols., Set.__ G. Cheng-Pang. LC 98-31897. (Cultures of the World Ser.). (Illus.). 128p. (YA). (gr. 5 up). 1999. lib. bdg. 35.64 (*0-7614-0954-8*) Marshall Cavendish.

Mongolia: A Centrally Planned Economy in Transition. Asian Development Bank Staff. (Illus.). 266p. 1993. pap. text 24.95 (*0-19-585894-8*) OUP.

Mongolia: A Centrally Planned Economy in Transition. Asian Development Bank Staff. (Illus.). 266p. (C). 1993. text 49.95 (*0-19-585893-X*) OUP.

*__Mongolia: A Country Study Guide.__ Global Investment & Business Center, Inc. Staff. (World Country Study Guides Library: Vol. 116). (Illus.). 350p. 2000. pap. 59.00 (*0-7397-2414-2*) Intl Business Pubns.

Mongolia: An Assessment of the Election to the Great People's Hural. Andrew Brick et al. ii, 22p. 1992. pap. 4.00 (*1-879720-68-X*) Intl Fndt Elect.

Mongolia: Between China & the U. S. S. R. Ram Rahul. 1989. 16.00 (*0-685-37831-4*, Pub. by M Manoharial) S Asia.

Mongolia: Financing Education During Economic Transition. Kin B. Wu. LC 93-45507. (Discussion Paper Ser.: No. 226). 114p. 1994. pap. 22.00 (*0-8213-2739-9*) World Bank.

Mongolia: The Legacy of Chinggis Khan. Ed. by Therese T. Bartholomew. LC 95-60283. (Illus.). 339p. 1995. 60.00 (*0-500-23705-0*, Pub. by Thames Hudson) Norton.

Mongolia: The Legacy of Chinggis Khan. Patricia Berger & Terese T. Bartholomew. LC 95-15198. 339p. 1995. pap. 35.00 (*0-614-09404-6*) Asian Art Mus.

Mongolia: The Tangut Country & the Solitudes of Northern Tibet. N. Prejevalsky. (C). 1991. reprint ed. text 74.00 (*81-206-0680-9*, Pub. by Asian Educ Servs) S Asia.

Mongolia: Toward a Market Economy. LC 92-30609. (Country Study Ser.). 190p. 1992. pap. 22.00 (*0-8213-2247-8*) World Bank.

Mongolia - A Country Study Guide: Basic Information for Research & Pleasure. Global Investment Center, USA Staff. (World Country Study Guide Library: Vol. 116). (Illus.). 350p. 1999. pap. 59.00 (*0-7397-1513-5*) Intl Business Pubns.

Mongolia & the Mongols: Holdings at Western Washington University. Henry G. Schwarz. (East Asian Research Aids & Translations Ser.: Vol. 4). (Illus.). xviii, 905p. (C). 1993. pap. 80.00 (*0-914584-88-X*) WWUCEAS.

Mongolia Business & Investment Opportunities Yearbook-98: Business, Investment, Export-Import. Contrib. by Russian Information & Business Center, Inc. Staff. (Business & Investment Opportunity Library-98). (Illus.). 350p. 1998. pap. 99.00 (*1-57751-978-7*) Intl Business Pubns.

*__Mongolia Business Intelligence Report, 190 vols.__ Global Investment & Business Center, Inc. Staff. (World Business Intelligence Library: Vol. 116). (Illus.). 350p. 2000. pap. 99.95 (*0-7397-2614-5*) Intl Business Pubns.

*__Mongolia Business Law Handbook, 190 vols.__ Global Investment & Business Center, Inc. Staff. (Global Business Law Handbooks Library: Vol. 116). (Illus.). 350p. 2000. pap. 99.95 (*0-7397-2014-7*) Intl Business Pubns.

*__Mongolia Business Opportunity Yearbook.__ Global Investment & Business Center, Inc. Staff. (Global Business Opportunity Yearbooks Library: Vol. 116). (Illus.). 2000. pap. 99.95 (*0-7397-2214-X*) Intl Business Pubns.

*__Mongolia Business Opportunity Yearbook: Export-Import, Investment & Business Opportunities.__ International Business Publications, U. S. A. Staff & Global Investment Center, U. S. A. Staff. (Global Business Opportunity Yearbooks Library: Vol. 116). (Illus.). 350p. 1999. pap. 99.95 (*0-7397-1314-0*) Intl Business Pubns.

*__Mongolia Country Review 2000.__ Robert C. Kelly et al. (Illus.). 60p. 1999. pap. 39.95 (*1-58310-540-9*) CountryWatch.

*__Mongolia Foreign Policy & Government Guide.__ Contrib. by Global Investment & Business Center, Inc. Staff. (World Foreign Policy & Government Library: Vol. 112). (Illus.). 350p. 1999. pap. 99.00 (*0-7397-3610-8*) Intl Business Pubns.

*__Mongolia Foreign Policy & Government Guide.__ Global Investment & Business Center, Inc. Staff. (World Foreign Policy & Government Library: Vol. 112). (Illus.). 350p. 2000. pap. 99.95 (*0-7397-3814-3*) Intl Business Pubns.

*__Mongolia in the Twentieth Century.__ Ed. by Stephen Kotkin & Bruce A. Elleman. LC 99-44518. (Illus.). 336p. 1999. text 75.00 (*0-7656-0535-X*) M E Sharpe.

*__Mongolia in the Twentieth Century.__ Ed. by Stephen Kotkin & Bruce A. Elleman. (Illus.). 336p. 2000. reprint ed. pap. text 28.95 (*0-7656-0536-8*) M E Sharpe.

Mongolia in Transition: Old Patterns, New Challenges. Ed. by Ole Bruun & Ole Odgaard. (NIAS Studies in Asian Topics: No. 22). 260p. (C). 1996. text 48.00 (*0-7007-0418-3*, Pub. by Curzon Pr Ltd); pap. text 24.95 (*0-7007-0441-8*, Pub. by Curzon Pr Ltd) UH Pr.

*__Mongolia Investment & Business Guide.__ Global Investment & Business Center, Inc. Staff. (Global Investment & Business Guide Library: Vol. 116). (Illus.). 2000. pap. 99.95 (*0-7397-1814-2*) Intl Business Pubns.

*__Mongolia Investment & Business Guide: Export-Import, Investment & Business Opportunities.__ International Business Publications, USA Staff & Global Investment Center, USA Staff. (World Investment & Business Guide Library-99: Vol. 116). (Illus.). 350p. 1999. pap. 99.95 (*0-7397-0311-0*) Intl Business Pubns.

Mongolia Investment & Business Guide Vol. 12: Economy, Export-Import, Business & Investment Climate, Business Contacts. Contrib. by Russian Information & Business Center, Inc. Staff. (Russia, NIS & Emerging Markets Investment & Business Library). (Illus.). 350p. 1998. pap. 99.00 (*1-57751-598-6*) Intl Business Pubns.

Mongolia Society Bulletin, Vol. 7. 1968. write for info. (*0-910980-03-9*) Mongolia.

Mongolia Society Bulletin, Vol. 8. 1969. write for info. (*0-910980-04-7*) Mongolia.

Mongolia Society Bulletin, Vol. 9.2. 1970. write for info. (*0-910980-05-5*) Mongolia.

Mongolia Society Bulletin, Vol. 10, Nos. 1-2. 1971. write for info. (*0-910980-06-3*) Mongolia.

Mongolia Society Newsletter, New Series 13. 1993. write for info. (*0-910980-63-2*) Mongolia.

Mongolia Society Newsletter, New Series 14. 1993. write for info. (*0-910980-64-0*) Mongolia.

Mongolia Society Newsletter, No. 2. 1986. pap. 2.00 (*0-910980-91-8*) Mongolia.

Mongolia Society Newsletter, No. 3. 1987. pap. 3.00 (*0-910980-92-6*) Mongolia.

Mongolia Society Newsletter, No. 4. 1987. pap. 4.00 (*0-910980-93-4*) Mongolia.

Mongolia Society Newsletter, No. 5. 1988. pap. 5.00 (*0-910980-94-2*) Mongolia.

Mongolia Society Newsletter, No. 6. 1989. pap. 5.00 (*0-910980-95-0*) Mongolia.

Mongolia Society Newsletter, No. 7. 1989. pap. 7.00 (*0-910980-96-9*) Mongolia.

Mongolia Society Newsletter, No. 8. 1990. pap. 6.50 (*0-910980-97-7*) Mongolia.

Mongolia Society Newsletter, No. 9. 1991. pap. 7.00 (*0-910980-98-5*) Mongolia.

Mongolia Society Newsletter, No. 10. 1991. pap. 7.00 (*0-910980-99-3*) Mongolia.

Mongolia Society Newsletter, No. 15. 1994. pap. 6.00 (*0-910980-65-9*) Mongolia.

Mongolia Society Newsletter, No. 11. 1992. 3.00 (*0-910980-61-6*); 7.00 (*0-910980-62-4*) Mongolia.

Mongolia Today. Ed. by Shirin Akiner. 320p. 1991. 75.00 (*0-7103-0345-9*, A3934) Routledge.

Mongolian Arts & Crafts. N. Tsultem. (Illus.). 152p. (C). 1987. text 275.00 (*0-569-09150-0*, Pub. by Collets) St Mut.

Mongolian-English Dictionary. Charles R. Bawden. 900p. 1992. 169.95 (*0-7103-0439-0*, A9512) Routledge.

Mongolian-English Parallel Text. William Rozycki. LC 94-69716. 1995. 49.00 (*1-881265-13-7*) Dunwoody Pr.

Mongolian Epigraphical Dictionary in Reverse Listing. John G. Hangin. LC 67-63757. (Uralic & Altaic Ser.: Vol. 88). 70p. 1967. pap. text. write for info. (*0-87750-078-9*) Curzon Pr Ltd.

Mongolian Folktales. Metternich. LC 96-24687. (Illus.). 132p. 1996. pap. 19.95 (*0-937321-06-0*) Avery Pr CO.

Mongolian Heroes of the Twentieth Century. Ed. by Urgunge Onon. LC 76-23980. (Asian Studies: No. 1). (Illus.). 1976. lib. bdg. 32.50 (*0-404-15402-6*) AMS Pr.

Mongolian Jew: A Literary Study. L. S. Dembo. LC 87-40517. 208p. reprint ed. pap. 64.50 (*0-608-09904-X*, 206924200003) Bks Demand.

Mongolian Legal System. William E. Butler. 1982. lib. bdg. 452.50 (*90-247-2685-9*) Kluwer Academic.

*__Mongolian Music, Dance, & Oral Narrative; Performing Diverse Identities.__ Carole Pegg. LC 00-42308. 2001. write for info. (*0-295-98030-3*) U Pr of Amer.

Mongolian Newspaper Reader. David C. Montgomery. LC 78-627747. (Uralic & Altaic Ser.: Vol. 102). 203p. (Orig.). 1969. pap. text 13.00 (*0-87750-083-5*) Res Inst Inner Asian Studies.

*__Mongolian Nomadic Society A Reconstruction of the Medieval History of Mongolia.__ Bold Bat-Ochir. LC 99-37870. 1999. text 59.95 (*0-312-22827-9*, St Martin Griffin) St Martin.

Mongolian People's Republic, 1991: Toward a Market Economy. Elizabeth Milne et al. LC 91-4710. (Occasional Papers: No. 79). viii, 81p. (Orig.). 1991. pap. 10.00 (*1-55775-207-9*) Intl Monetary.

Mongolian Phrasebook. J. Bat-Ireedui & Alan J. Sanders. (MON., Illus.). 208p. 1995. pap. 5.95 (*0-86442-308-X*) Lonely Planet.

Mongolian Rule in China: Local Administration in the Yuan Dynasty. Elizabeth Endicott-West. LC 88-23553. (Harvard-Yenching Institute Monographs: No. 29). 300p. 1988. 30.00 (*0-674-58525-9*) HUP.

Mongolian Studies, Vol. 5. (Journal of the Mongolia Society Ser.). 1980. pap. 10.00 (*0-910980-75-6*) Mongolia.

Mongolian Studies, Vol. 8. (Journal of the Mongolia Society Ser.). 15.00 (*0-910980-78-0*) Mongolia.

Mongolian Studies in the Soviet Union: A Bibliography of Soviet Publications 1981-1986. LC 88-82554. (Uralic & Altaic Ser.: Vol. 152). (RUS.). 95p. 1988. pap. 9.90 (*0-933070-22-5*) Res Inst Inner Asian Studies.

Mongolian Studies Journal (Includes Index from Vol. 1-15), Vol. 16. 1993. pap. 20.00 (*0-910980-86-1*) Mongolia.

Mongolian Studies Journal of the Mongolia Society, Vol. 2. 1975. pap. 10.00 (*0-910980-72-1*) Mongolia.

Mongolian Studies Journal of the Mongolia Society, Vol. 3. 1976. pap. 10.00 (*0-910980-73-X*) Mongolia.

Mongolian Studies Journal of the Mongolia Society, Vol. 4. 1977. pap. 10.00 (*0-910980-74-8*) Mongolia.

Mongolia's Culture & Society. Sechin Jagchid. 1979. 52.50 (*0-89158-390-4*) Westview.

Mongols. David Morgan. 1990. pap. 31.95 (*0-631-17563-6*) Blackwell Pubs.

Mongols. Robert Nicholson. LC 94-43701. (Illus.). 32p. (J). (gr. 4-7). 1994. lib. bdg. 15.95 (*0-7910-2706-6*) Chelsea Hse.

Mongols. Robert Nicholson. LC 94-43701. (Illus.). 32p. (J). (gr. 4-7). 1994. pap. 7.95 (*0-7910-2730-9*) Chelsea Hse.

Mongols. Robert Nicholson. (Journey into Civilization Ser.). (J). 1994. 13.15 (*0-606-07879-7*) Turtleback.

Mongols. Stephen Turnbull. (Men-at-Arms Ser.: No. 105). (Illus.). 48p. pap. 11.95 (*0-85045-372-0*, 9038, Pub. by Ospry) Stackpole.

Mongols: A History. Jeremiah Curtin. (Works of Jeremiah Curtin). 1990. reprint ed. lib. bdg. 79.00 (*0-685-44782-0*) Rprt Serv.

Mongols & Mamluks: The Mamluk-Ilkhanid War, 1260-1281. Reuven Amitai-Preiss. (Studies in Islamic Civilization). (Illus.). 288p. (C). 1995. text 64.95 (*0-521-46226-6*) Cambridge U Pr.

M

Mongols & Ming China: Customs & History. Henry Serruys. Ed. by Francoise Aubin. (Collected Studies: No. CS262). 318p. (C). 1987. reprint ed. lib. bdg. 99.95 (*0-86078-210-7*, Pub. by Variorum) Ashgate Pub Co.

Mongols et la Papaute, 3 pts. in 1 vol. Paul Pelliot. LC 80-2365. reprint ed. 34.50 (*0-404-18913-X*) AMS Pr.

Mongols in Russia. Jeremiah Curtin. (Works of Jeremiah Curtin). 1990. reprint ed. lib. bdg. 79.00 (*0-685-44781-2*) Rprt Serv.

Mongols in Western American Consciousness. Kevin C. Stuart. LC 97-38815. 268p. 1997. 89.95 (*0-7734-8443-4*) E Mellen.

Mongols of the Twentieth Century. Robert A. Rupen. LC 63-64522. (Uralic & Altaic Ser.: Vol. 37-Pt. 2). (Orig.). 1964. pap. text. write for info. (*0-87750-062-2*) Mongolia.

Mongols of the West. Stephen A. Halkovic, Jr. Ed. by Larry W. Moses. LC 86-620694. (Uralic & Altaic Ser.: Vol. 148). 226p. (Orig.). (C). 1985. pap. 15.00 (*0-933070-16-0*) Res Inst Inner Asian Studies.

Mongoose & Mouse. Godfrey Nyotumba. (J). (ps-3). 1995. pap. text 4.95 (*9966-884-39-4*) Jacarada.

Mongoose Magoo. H. Montgomery. LC 68-56822. (Illus.). 64p. (J). (gr. 2-5). 1968. lib. bdg. 10.95 (*0-87783-026-6*) Oddo.

Mongoose Magoo. deluxe ed. H. Montgomery. LC 68-56822. (Illus.). 64p. (J). (gr. 2-5). 1968. pap. 3.94 (*0-87783-100-9*) Oddo.

Mongoose Man. Hoyt. LC 98-11582. 1998. text 24.95 (*0-312-86476-0*) St Martin.

***Mongoose Man.** Richard Hoyt. 352p. 2000. mass mkt. 6.99 (*0-8125-4023-9*) Tor Bks.

Mongoose R. I. P. A Blackford Oakes Novel. William F. Buckley, Jr. LC 97-47693. 376p. 1998. reprint ed. pap. 12.95 (*1-888952-72-5*) Cumberland Hse.

Mongraph of the Oxytrichidae (Ciliophore, Hypotrichia) Helmut Berger. LC 99-30413. (Monographiae Biologicae). 1999. write for info. (*0-7923-5795-7*) Kluwer Academic.

Mongrel. Justin Chin. LC 98-37185. 160p. 1998. pap. 11.95 (*0-312-19513-3*) St Martin.

Mongrel: A Story of Logan Fontanelle of the Omaha Indians. Anthony J. Barak. Ed. by James J. Reisdorff. (Illus.). 152p. (Orig.). 1988. pap. 9.95 (*0-942035-09-7*) South Platte.

Mongrelisme. Joan Retallack. (Isthmus Project Ser.). 48p. 1999. pap. 5.00 (*0-945926-54-5*) Paradigm RI.

Monhegan: Her Houses & Her People, 1780-1970. Ruth G. Faller. LC F27-M7F35 1995. (Illus.). ix, 253p. 1995. per. 15.00 (*0-9658593-1-2*) Mnstay Pub.

Monhegan, Maine, the Cradle of New England. Ida S. Proper. (Illus.). 275p. 1997. reprint ed. lib. bdg. 35.00 (*0-8328-7106-0*) Higginson Bk Co.

Monhegan, the Artists' Island. Jane Curtis et al. LC 94-48603. (Illus.). 192p. 1995. 50.00 (*0-89272-347-5*) Down East.

Moni, the Goat Boy: And Other Stories. Johanna Spyri. (Illus.). 218p. (J). 1993. pap. 5.95 (*1-883453-00-3*) Deutsche Buchhandlung.

***Moni the Goat Boy & Other Stories.** Johanna Spyri. (Illus.). 219p. (J). 2000. reprint ed. pap. 6.95 (*1-883453-09-7*) Deutsche Buchhandlung.

Monica. Arnold Klein. LC 94-78405. 80p. 1994. 12.95 (*1-56313-445-4*) BrownTrout Pubs Inc.

Monica. Saunders Lewis. LC 98-104802. 107p. 1997. pap. 17.95 (*1-85411-195-7*, Pub. by Seren Bks) Dufour.

Monica. Christine Sutherland. 1990. 21.95 (*0-374-21215-5*) FS&G.

Monica: A Prodigal's Praying Mother. George W. Rice. 48p. 1989. pap. 2.99 (*0-8341-1286-8*) Beacon Hill.

Monica & Other Stories. Paul C. Bourget. Tr. by William Marchant. LC 77-106249. (Short Story Index Reprint Ser.). 1977. 20.95 (*0-8369-3286-2*) Ayer.

Monica Castillo: Yo Es un Otro. Cuauhtemoc Medina & Justo Pastor Mellado. (ENG & SPA., Illus.). 72p. 1998. pap. 20.00 (*1-889195-23-5*) Smart Art Pr.

Monica Made Me Promise. Linda Cousins. (Illus.). 32p. (J). (gr. 5-8). 1994. pap. 3.99 (*0-912444-39-8*) DARE Bks.

Monica Poole: Wood Engraver. Anne Stevens. (Illus.). 56p. 1995. pap. 12.95 (*1-85444-048-9*, 0489, Pub. by Ashmolean Mus) A Schwartz & Co.

Monica Seles see Ovations

Monica Seles. Liza N. Burby. LC 96-30002. (Making Their Mark Ser.). (J). 1997. lib. bdg. 15.93 (*0-8239-5068-9*, PowerKids) Rosen Group.

***Monica Seles.** Suzanne J. Murdico. LC 97-16807. (Overcoming the Odds Ser.). (Illus.). 48p. (J). (gr. 4-7). 1998. pap. 7.95 (*0-8172-8001-4*) Raintree Steck-V.

Monica Seles. Suzanne J. Murdico. LC 97-16807. (Overcoming the Odds Ser.). 1998. 24.26 (*0-8172-4128-0*) Raintree Steck-V.

Monica Seles. Richard Rambeck. LC 96-14171. (Illus.). 24p. (J). (gr. 2-6). 1996. lib. bdg. 21.36 (*1-56766-312-5*) Childs World.

Monica Seles. Mark Stewart. LC 96-48806. (Sports Stars Ser.). (J). 1997. lib. bdg. 19.00 (*0-516-20489-0*) Childrens.

Monica Seles: Returning Champion. Kristin S. Fehr. LC 96-52241. (J). 1997. lib. bdg. 19.93 (*0-8225-2899-1*, Lerner Publctns) Lerner Pub.

Monica Seles: Returning Champion. Kristin S. Fehr. LC 96-52241. (Illus.). 64p. (J). 1997. pap. 5.95 (*0-8225-9773-X*, Lerner Publctns) Lerner Pub.

Monica Seles: The Comeback Kid. Mark Stewart. (Sports Stars Ser.). (J). 1998. pap. text 5.95 (*0-516-26054-5*) Childrens.

Monica's Secret. Jan L. Fausnaugh. (Little Monkey Tales Ser.). (Illus.). 24p. (Orig.). (J). (gr. k-7). 1996. pap. 4.95 (*1-889645-01-X*) Cabin Fev Pubg.

Monica's Story. Andrew Morton. LC 99-190557. (Illus.). 288p. 1999. text 24.95 (*0-312-24091-0*) St Martin.

Monica's Story. Andrew Morton. (Illus.). 385p. 1999. mass mkt. 6.99 (*0-312-97362-4*, St Martins Paperbacks) St Martin.

***Monica's Story.** ed. Andrew Morton. 2000. text. write for info. (*0-312-26365-1*) St Martin.

Monica's Story. large type ed. Andrew Morton. LC 99-33154. 1999. 28.95 (*0-7862-2051-1*) Thorndike Pr.

***Monica's Story: Van&Dyck, Jennifer.** abr. ed. Andrew Morton. 1999. audio 18.00 (*0-694-52193-0*) HarperAudio.

***Monica's Tale of Sexual Harassment.** Robert K. Landrum. 825p. 1999. pap. 39.50 (*0-9674118-0-7*) P A X Pubng.

Monika Beisner's Book of Riddles. Monika Beisner. LC 83-81529. (Sunburst Ser.). (Illus.). 32p. (gr. 2 up). 1987. pap. 3.95 (*0-374-45317-9*, Sunburst Bks) FS&G.

Monikins. James Fenimore Cooper. Ed. by James S. Hedger. (Masterworks of Literature Ser.). pap. 15.95 (*0-8084-0421-0*) NCUP.

Monikins. James Fenimore Cooper. (Works of James Fenimore Cooper). 1990. reprint ed. lib. bdg. 79.00 (*0-685-44762-6*) Rprt Serv.

Monilinia Fungi of the World: Their Ecology, Biosystematics & Control. Lekh R. Batra. (Mycologia Memoirs Ser.: No. 16). (Illus.). 500p. 1991. lib. bdg. 120.00 (*0-945345-34-8*, Pub. by Gebruder Borntraeger) Balogh.

Monino: The Russian Air Force Museum. Colin W. Prentice. 1998. pap. text 29.95 (*1-85310-898-7*) Specialty Pr.

Monique's Kindergarten. Michael Kenna. (Illus.). 112p. 45.00 (*3-923922-55-8*) Nazraeli Pr.

Monita Crece. Reba G. Gelman. 40p. (J). (ps-3). 1995. pap. 3.95 (*0-590-46940-1*) Scholastic Inc.

Monita Crece. Rita Golden Gelman. 1993. 9.15 (*0-606-08334-0*, Pub. by Turtleback) Demco.

Moniteur d'Orientation Rogerienne. fac. ed. Fernand Roussel. LC 72-366473. (FRE.). 249p. reprint ed. pap. 77.20 (*0-7837-6953-9*, 204678200003) Bks Demand.

Monitions of the Approach. Joseph Donahue. 14p. 1991. 3.00 (*0-87376-067-0*) Red Dust.

Monito Travieso Por Encima de Todo (One Tricky Monkey up on Top) Jane Belk Moncure. LC 87-11612. (Castillo Magico Ser.). (SPA., Illus.). 32p. (J). (ps-2). 1989. lib. bdg. 21.36 (*0-89565-921-2*) Childs World.

Monitor. Chief Little Summer & Warm Night Rain. (Illus.). 445p. (Orig.). 1993. 19.45 (*1-880440-06-7*) Piqua Pr.

Monitor: The Story of the Legendary Civil War Ironclad & the Man Whose Invention Changed the Course of History. James T. DeKay. 1999. pap. 11.95 (*0-345-42635-5*) Ballantine Pub Grp.

Monitor: The Story of the Legendary Civil War Ironclad & the Man Whose Invention Changed the Course of History. large type ed. James T. de Kay. LC 98-4978. 228p. 1998. 25.95 (*0-7838-8441-9*, G K Hall & Co) Mac Lib Ref.

Monitor: The Story of the Revolutionary Ship & the Men Whose Invention Changed the Course of History. James T. DeKay. LC 97-17500. (Illus.). 240p. 1997. 21.00 (*0-8027-1330-0*) Walker & Co.

Monitor America. Ed. by Richard Prelinger. (Frequency Guide Ser.: No. 8). (Illus.). 608p. 1985. 14.95 (*0-939430-07-X*) Scanner Master.

Monitor America: Frequencies, Codes, Maps & Descriptions of Public Safety. 3rd ed. Richard Barnett. (Illus.). 1000p. 1995. pap. 29.95 (*0-939430-31-2*) Scanner Master.

***Monitor Chronicles: One Sailor's Account.** Ed. by Mariners Museum Staff. LC 00-27158. (Illus.). 272p. 2000. 35.00 (*0-684-86997-7*) Simon & Schuster.

Monitor Company: The WebFeet.com Insider Guide. 2000th ed. WetFeet.com Staff. (Insider Guides Ser.). 55p. 1999. per. 25.00 (*1-58207-045-8*) WetFeet.

Monitor Lizards: Natural History, Biology & Husbandry. Daniel Bennett. (Illus.). 352p. 1997. pap. 49.95 (*3-930612-10-0*, Pub. by Edition Chimaira) Bibliomania.

Monitor, 1990 - Environmental Monitoring in Sweden. Swedish Environmental Protection Agency Staff. (Illus.). 180p. (Orig.). 1990. pap. text 48.00 (*91-620-1092-1*) Coronet Bks.

Monitor of Freemasonry. Jabez Richardson. pap. 13.00 (*0-911164-25-1*) Powner.

Monitor the World. Rickey Stein. 272p. 1995. pap. 24.95 (*0-939430-24-X*) Scanner Master.

Monitor Well Design, Installation, & Documentation at Hazardous &/or Toxic Waste Sites. United States Army Corps of Engineers Staff. LC 96-176. (Technical Engineering & Design Guides as Adapted from the U. S. Army Corps of Engineers Ser.: Vol. 17). 64p. 1996. 26.00 (*0-7844-0150-0*) Am Soc Civil Eng.

Monitored Peril: Asian Americans & the Politics of TV Representation. Darrell Y. Hamamoto. LC 93-38700. 1994. pap. 19.95 (*0-8166-2369-4*); text 49.95 (*0-8166-2368-6*) U of Minn Pr.

Monitored Retrievable Storage of High-Level Radioactive Waste: Routing Implications & Emergency Response to Transportation Accidents. (State Legislative Reports: Vol. 15, No. 18). 7p. 1990. 15.00 (*1-55516-274-6*, 7302-1518) Natl Conf State Legis.

Monitoreo y Evaluacion. 1994. write for info. (*92-806-3153-5*) U N I C E.

Monitoreo y Evaluacion de Logros en Proyectos de Ordenacion de Cuencas Hidrograficas. (SPA.). 167p. 1993. 25.00 (*92-5-303315-0*, FSP3150, Pub. by FAO) Bernan Associates.

Monitorial Instructions for the Use of Symbolic Lodges of Free & Accepted Masons (1915) William W. Perry & Jacob Dreher. 192p. 1998. reprint ed. pap. 17.95 (*0-7661-0709-4*) Kessinger Pub.

Monitoring. 1992. 51.95 (*0-387-55261-8*) Spr-Verlag.

Monitoring a Comprehensive Test Ban Treaty: Proceedings of the NATO Advanced Study Institute, Alvor, Algarve, Portugal, January 23 - February 1, 1995. Ed. by Eystein S. Husebye & Anton M. Dainty. (NATO Advanced Science Institutes Ser.: Series E). 864p. (C). 1995. text 364.50 (*0-7923-3811-1*) Kluwer Academic.

Monitoring Acid-Base Titrations with a pH Meter. John W. Alcock & M. L. Gillette. Ed. by C. L. Stanitski. (Modular Laboratory Program in Chemistry Ser.). 16p. (C). 1997. pap. text 1.50 (*0-87540-494-4*) Chem Educ Res.

Monitoring Active Volcanoes: Strategies, Procedure & Techniques. McGuire. 352p. 1994. 99.00 (*1-85728-036-9*, Pub. by UCL Pr Ltd) Taylor & Francis.

Monitoring Algal Blooms: New Techniques for Detecting Large-Scale Environmental Change. Mati Kahru & Christopher W. Brown. LC 97-17091. (Environmental Intelligence Unit Ser.). 155p. 1997. text 99.95 (*1-57059-459-7*) Landes Bioscience.

Monitoring Algal Blooms: New Techniques for Detecting Large-Scale Environmental Change. Ed. by Mati Kahru & Christopher W. Brown. LC 97-17091. (Environmental Intelligence Unit Ser.). (Illus.). 155p. 1997. 99.95 (*3-540-63188-7*) Spr-Verlag.

Monitoring & Assessing Intercollegiate Athletics. Ed. by Bruce I. Mallette & Richard P. Howard. LC 85-645339. (New Directions for Institutional Research Ser.: No. IR 74). 100p. 1992. pap. 22.00 (*1-55542-756-1*) Jossey-Bass.

Monitoring & Assessment of Adverse Drug Effects. 35p. 1987. pap. text 10.00 (*92-9036-027-5*, 1840007) World Health.

Monitoring & Compliance Vol. 4: The Political Economy of Inspection. David Hemenway. Ed. by William Breit & Kenneth G. Elzinga. LC 84-29980. (Political Economy & Public Policy Ser.: Vol. 4). 137p. 1985. 78.50 (*0-89232-477-5*) Jai Pr.

Monitoring & Controlling the International Transfer of Technology. John Pinder et al. (Illus.). 90p. 1998. pap. text 15.00 (*0-8330-2635-6*, MR-979-OSTP) Rand Corp.

Monitoring & Debugging of Distributed Real-Time Systems. Ed. by Jeffrey J. Tsai & Steve J. Yang. LC 94-77621. 440p. 1995. pap. 47.00 (*0-8186-6537-8*, BP06537) IEEE Comp Soc.

Monitoring & Evaluating Agricultural Research: A Sourcebook. D. Horton et al. (Illus.). 240p. (Orig.). 1993. pap. text 45.00 (*0-85198-860-1*) OUP.

Monitoring & Evaluating Programmes Module 5: Facilitator's Guide. Martine Hilton. (Primary Health Care Management Advancement Programme (PHC MAP) Modules Ser.). 67p. 1993. pap. text. write for info. (*1-882839-11-0*) Aga Khan Fnd.

Monitoring & Evaluating Programmes Module 5: User's Guide. Lynne M. Franco et al. (Primary Health Care Management Advancement Programme (PHC MAP) Modules Ser.). 111p. 1993. pap. text. write for info. (*1-882839-03-X*) Aga Khan Fnd.

Monitoring & Evaluating Small Business Projects: A Step by Step Guide for Private Development Organizations. Ed. by Shirley Buzzard & Elaine Edgcomb. (Illus.). 200p. (Orig.). 1987. pap. text 15.00 (*0-942127-00-5*) PACT Inc.

Monitoring & Evaluating Social Programs in Developing Countries: A Handbook for Policymakers, Managers & Researchers. Joseph Valadez & Michael Bamberger. LC 94-29582. 548p. 1995. pap. 40.00 (*0-8213-2989-8*, 12989) World Bank.

Monitoring & Evaluating the Impacts of Small-Scale Fishery Projects. Intro. by Richard B. Pollnac. 146p. 1989. pap. 4.00 (*1-882027-01-9*) URI ICMRD.

Monitoring & Evaluation: Anesthesia Services. Ed. by Robert Fromberg. LC 90-60439. 38p. 1987. pap. 25.00 (*0-86688-124-7*) Joint Comm Hlthcare.

Monitoring & Evaluation of Oral Health: Report of a WHO Expert Committee, 1987. (Technical Report Ser.: No. 782). 69p. 1989. pap. text 9.00 (*92-4-120782-5*, 1100782) World Health.

***Monitoring & Managing Microsoft Exchange 2000.** Mike Daugherty. (Illus.). 320p. 2000. pap. 32.95 (*1-55558-232-X*, Digital DEC) Buttrwrth-Heinemann.

Monitoring & Mitigation of Volcano Hazards. Roberto Scarpa & Robert I. Tilling. LC 96-8653. 1996. write for info. (*0-387-60713-7*) Spr-Verlag.

Monitoring & Mitigation of Volcano Hazards. Roberto Scarpa & Robert I. Tilling. LC 96-8653. (Illus.). 926p. 1996. 159.00 (*3-540-60713-7*) Spr-Verlag.

***Monitoring & Modelling Hydrological Fluxes in Support of Nutrient Cycling Studies in Amazonian Rain Forest Ecosystems.** Tobon Marin. (Illus.). 174p. 1999. pap. 49.00 (*90-5113-035-X*, TS 17, Pub. by Backhuys Pubs) Balogh.

Monitoring & Remediation Wells: Problem Prevention, Maintenance, & Remediation. Stuart A. Smith. 208p. 1995. lib. bdg. 85.00 (*0-87371-562-4*, L562) Lewis Pubs.

Monitoring & Targeting with a Building & Energy Management System. G. J. Levermore. 1989. pap. 320.00 (*0-86022-239-X*, Pub. by Build Servs Info Assn) St Mut.

Monitoring & Verification of Bioremediation 3(5) Ed. by Robert E. Hinchee et al. 286p. 1995. 59.95 (*1-57477-006-3*) Battelle.

Monitoring Antagonistic Fungi Deliberately Released into the Environment. Dipp. Ed. by Dan F. Jensen. LC 97-101122. (Developments in Plant Pathology Ser.). 188p. (C). 1996. text 95.50 (*0-7923-4077-9*) Kluwer Academic.

***Monitoring Bathing Waters: A Practical Guide to the Design & Implementation of Assessments & Monitoring Programmes.** Jamie Bartram & Gareth Rees. LC 99-40950. 1999. pap. text. write for info. (*0-419-24380-1*, E & FN Spon) Routledge.

***Monitoring Bathing Waters: Practical Guide to Design & Implementation of Assessments & Monitoring Programmes.** Ed. by Jamie Bartram & Gareth Rees. LC 99-40950. 352p. (C). 2000. text. write for info. (*0-419-24370-4*, E & FN Spon) Routledge.

Monitoring Bird Populations by Point Counts. Ed. by John R. Sauer et al. (Illus.). 192p. 1998. pap. 21.40 (*0-89904-652-5*, Wildlife Resrch Grp) Crumb Elbow Pub.

Monitoring Bird Populations by Point Counts. Ed. by C. John Ralph et al. (Illus.). 192p. 1998. reprint ed. 26.40 (*0-89904-651-7*, Wildlife Resrch Grp) Crumb Elbow Pub.

Monitoring Bird Populations by Point Counts. Ed. by C. John Ralph et al. (Illus.). 181p. (C). 1998. reprint ed. pap. text 35.00 (*0-7881-4344-1*) DIANE Pub.

Monitoring Building Structures. J. F. A. Moore. 150p. (C). (gr. 13). 1992. mass mkt. 102.95 (*0-442-31333-0*) Chapman & Hall.

Monitoring Butterflies for Ecology & Conservation: The British Butterfly Monitoring Scheme. E. Pollard & T. J. Yates. LC 93-12557. 288p. (gr. 13). 1993. text 88.95 (*0-412-40220-3*) Chapman & Hall.

Monitoring Child Health in the United States: Selected Issues & Policies. Ed. by Deborah K. Walker & Julius B. Richmond. (Illus.). 256p. 1984. 20.00 (*0-674-58551-8*) HUP.

Monitoring Children's Health: Key Indicators. 2nd ed. C. Arden Miller et al. 176p. 1989. 17.50 (*0-87553-162-8*) Am Pub Health.

Monitoring Children's Language Development: Holistic Assessment in Classrooms. Ed. by Elizabeth Daly. LC 90-5262. (Illus.). 169p. (C). 1991. pap. text 20.00 (*0-435-08540-9*, 08540) Heinemann.

Monitoring Children's Rights. Ed. by Eugeen Verhellen. LC 95-43186. 1996. lib. bdg. 200.00 (*90-411-0161-6*, Pub. by M Nijhoff) Kluwer Academic.

Monitoring Earth's Land, Ocean, & Atmosphere from Space: Sensors, Systems & Applications. Ed. by Abraham Schnapf. LC 85-13509. (PAAS Ser.: Vol. 97). (Illus.). 830p. 1985. 99.95 (*0-915928-98-1*) AIAA.

Monitoring Ecological Change. Ian F. Spellerberg. (Illus.). 350p. (C). 1991. pap. text 33.95 (*0-521-42407-0*) Cambridge U Pr.

Monitoring Ecological Condition at Regional Scales: Proceedings of the 3rd Symposium on the Environmental Monitoring & Assessment Program (EMAP), Albany, NY, U. S. A., April 8-11, 1997. Ed. by Shabeg Sandhu et al. LC 98-168442. 616p. 1998. reprint ed. write for info. (*0-7923-5070-7*) Kluwer Academic.

***Monitoring Ecological Condition in the Western United States: Proceedings of the 4th Symposium on the Environmental Monitoring Assessment Program (EMAP), San Francisco, CA, April 6-8, 1999.** Ed. by Shahbeg S. Sandhu. LC 00-44384. 2000. write for info. (*0-7923-6493-7*) Kluwer Academic.

Monitoring Economic Transition: The Polish Case. George Blazyca & Janusz M. Dubrowski. 192p. 1995. text 68.95 (*1-85972-068-4*, Pub. by Avebry) Ashgate Pub Co.

Monitoring Education: Indicators, Quality, & Effectiveness. Carol T. Fitz-Gibbon. LC 97-129792. (School Development Ser.). (Illus.). 256p. 1995. 90.00 (*0-304-33070-1*); pap. 35.00 (*0-304-32983-5*) Continuum.

Monitoring Educational Outcomes & Public Attitudes. Ed. by Kevin J. Gilmartin & Robert J. Rossi. LC 82-1034. (Illus.). 279p. 1982. 42.95 (*0-89885-054-1*, Kluwer Acad Hman Sci) Kluwer Academic.

Monitoring Elder Compliance & Response: A Self Learning Programme for Community Nurses. S. D. Moir. 125p. 1996. spiral bd. write for info. (*0-443-05525-4*) Church.

Monitoring Environmental Materials & Specimen Banking: Proceedings of the International Workshop, West Berlin, 1978. International Workshop on Monitoring Environmental. Ed. by Niels-Peter Luepke. (Illus.). 590p. 1980. text 234.00 (*90-247-2303-5*) Kluwer Academic.

Monitoring Environmental Progress. Ed. by John O'Connor. LC 95-30524. (Environmentally Sustainable Development Occasional Papers: No. 5). 96p. 1995. pap. 22.00 (*0-8213-3365-8*) World Bank.

Monitoring Family Planning & Reproductive Rights: A Manual for Empowerment. Anita Hardon. LC 97-28039. 192p. (C). 1997. text 55.00 (*1-85649-455-1*, Pub. by Zed Books) St Martin.

Monitoring Family Planning & Reproductive Rights: A Manual for Empowerment. Anita Hardon. LC 97-28039. 192p. (C). 1997. pap. 17.50 (*1-85649-456-X*, Pub. by Zed Books) St Martin.

Monitoring for Adverse Drug Reactions. Ed. by Stuart Walker. 1985. text 147.50 (*0-85200-876-7*) Kluwer Academic.

Monitoring for Conservation & Ecology. Ed. by Barrie Goldsmith. 288p. 1991. 67.50 (*0-412-35590-6*, A5143) Chapman & Hall.

Monitoring for Drug Safety. 2nd ed. Ed. by W. H. Inman. 1986. text 350.00 (*0-85200-721-3*) Kluwer Academic.

***Monitoring for Fine Particulate Matter.** Elisa Eiseman. LC 98-183123. 60p. 1998. pap. 7.50 (*0-8330-2618-6*, MR-974-OSTP) Rand Corp.

***Monitoring for Health Hazards at Work.** 3rd ed. Indira Ashton & F. S. Gill. LC 99-32635. 1999. pap. 49.95 (*0-632-05041-1*) Blackwell Sci.

Monitoring Genetically Manipulated Microorganisms in the Environment. Clive Edwards. LC 92-30174. (Biotechnology Ser.). 208p. 1993. 196.50 (*0-471-93795-9*) Wiley.

Monitoring Government: Inspectors General & the Search for Accountability. Paul Charles Light. 268p. (C). 1993. 16.95 (*0-8157-5255-5*); pap. 16.95 (*0-8157-5256-3*) Brookings.

Monitoring Growth Cycles in Market-Oriented Countries: Developing & Using International Economic Indicators. Philip A. Klein & Geoffrey Moore. LC 85-1297. (National Bureau of Economic Research, Studies in Business Cycles: Vol. 26). 410p. reprint ed. pap. 127.10 (*0-608-17885-3*, 205225900080) Bks Demand.

Monitoring Human Rights in Europe: Comparing International Procedures & Mechanisms. Ed. by Arie Bloed. (International Helsinki Federation for Human Rights Studies). 352p. (C). 1993. lib. bdg. 117.00 (*0-7923-2383-1*) Kluwer Academic.

Monitoring Human Rights Violations. Ed. by Alex P. Schmid. (State Violence, State Terrorism & Human Ser.). (C). 2000. pap. 49.95 (*0-8133-2525-0*) Westview.

Monitoring Human Tissues for Toxic Substances. 2nd ed. National Research Council U. S. Committee on a Nat. LC 91-61252. 223p. 1991. reprint ed. pap. 69.20 (*0-608-02444-9*, 206308700004) Bks Demand.

Monitoring Image Quality of Aperture Cared Film Image Scanners: ANSI/AIIM MS50-1994. Association for Information & Image Management Staff. 35p. 1994. 52.00 (*0-89258-285-5*, MS50) Assn Inform & Image Mgmt.

Monitoring Imports of Ozone-Depleting Substances: A Guidebook; Recommendations Based on ODS Monitoring & Control Systems in ODSONET/SEAP Countries. 78p. 1997. pap. 60.00 (*92-807-1622-0*) UN.

Monitoring in Anaesthesia & Intensive Care. Ed. by P. Hutton & C. Prys-Roberts. (Illus.). 463p. 1994. text 93.00 (*0-7020-1407-9*, Pub. by W B Saunders) Saunders.

Monitoring in Anesthesia. 3rd ed. Casey D. Blitt. 1994. text 156.00 (*0-443-08912-4*) Church.

Monitoring in Anesthesia. 3rd enl. ed. Lawrence J. Saidman & N. Ty Smith. (Illus.). 576p. 1993. text 154.00 (*0-7506-9067-4*) Buttrwrth-Heinemann.

Monitoring in Patients with Optical Tissue Sensors. 1993. 139.95 (*0-8493-4581-2*) CRC Pr.

Monitoring Industrial Emissions & Wastes. (Technical Report Ser.: No. 27). 140p. 40.00 (*92-807-1434-1*) UN.

***Monitoring Inventory: Stocking the Shelves Workbook II.** Joyce McDowell. Ed. by Debbie Woodburg & Charlotte Bosarge. LC 99-69617. (Retailing Smarts Ser.). (Illus.). 80p. 2000. pap. 7.95 (*1-56052-576-2*) Crisp Pubns.

***Monitoring, Measuring & Managing Customer Service.** Gary S. Goodman. LC 00-25368. 200p. 2000. 29.95 (*0-7879-5139-0*) Jossey-Bass.

Monitoring Medicaid Managed Care: Developing & Assessment & Evaluation Program. Melvin I. Krasner. LC 95-37658. (Special Reports). 52p. 1995. pap. 25.00 (*1-881277-25-9*) United Hosp Fund.

Monitoring Medicaid Provider Participation & Access to Care. Deborah Lewis-Idema. Ed. by Karen Glass. 42p. (Orig.). 1992. pap. text 15.00 (*1-55877-166-2*) Natl Governor.

Monitoring Methods for Toxics in the Atmosphere. Ed. by Walter L. Zielinski, Jr. & William D. Dorko. LC 89-27676. (Special Technical Publication Ser.: No. 1052). (Illus.). 225p. 1990. text 38.00 (*0-8031-1271-8*, STP1052) ASTM.

Monitoring, Modeling, & Mediating Water Quality: Proceedings of the Symposium. Symposium on Monitoring, Modeling, & Mediating Wat. Ed. by Stephan J. Nix & Peter E. Black. LC 87-70588. (American Water Resources Association Technical Publication Ser.: No. TPS-87-2). (Illus.). 724p. reprint ed. pap. 200.00 (*0-608-18113-7*, 203271600081) Bks Demand.

Monitoring NASA Communications. Anthony R. Curtis. 100p. 1992. 14.95 (*0-936653-30-2*) Tiare Pubns.

Monitoring Neuronal Activity: A Practical Approach. Ed. by J. A. Stamford. (Practical Approach Ser.). (Illus.). 320p. 1992. pap. text 45.00 (*0-19-963243-X*) OUP.

Monitoring of Cerebral Blood Flow & Metabolism in Intensive Care: Proceedings of an International Symposium, Berlin, October 1992. Ed. by A. W. Unterberg et al. LC 93-23371. 1994. 101.00 (*0-387-82484-7*) Spr-Verlag.

Monitoring of Gaseous Pollutants by Tunable Diode Lasers. Ed. by G. Schmidtke et al. (C). 1987. text 105.00 (*90-277-2603-5*) Kluwer Academic.

Monitoring of Gaseous Pollutants by Tunable Diode Lasers. M. Tacke et al. (C). 1989. text 171.00 (*0-7923-0334-2*) Kluwer Academic.

Monitoring of Gaseous Pollutants by Tunable Diode Lasers: Proceedings of the International Symposium Held in Freiburg, Germany, 17-18 October 1991. Ed. by R. Grisar et al. LC 92-17520. 388p. (C). 1992. text 226.50 (*0-7923-1826-9*) Kluwer Academic.

Monitoring of Industrial Sickness. Banarsi Misra. (C). 1990. text 30.00 (*81-7100-266-8*, Pub. by Deep & Deep Pubns) S Asia.

Monitoring of National AIDS Prevention & Control Programmes: Guiding Principles. (WHO AIDS Ser.: No. 4). (ENG, FRE, RUS & SPA.). iii, 27p. 1988. pap. text 8.00 (*92-4-121004-4*, 1870004) World Health.

Monitoring of Ongoing Research on the Health Effects of High Voltage Transmission Lines (Eighth Annual Report) Khizar Wasti. 27p. (Orig.). (C). 1993. pap. text 25.00 (*1-56806-488-8*) DIANE Pub.

Monitoring of Ongoing Research on the Health Effects on High Voltage Transmission Lines. 40p. (Orig.). (C). 1993. pap. text 20.00 (*1-56806-723-2*) DIANE Pub.

Monitoring of Radioactive Contamination on Surfaces. R. F. Clayton. (Technical Reports: No. 120). (Illus.). 8p. (Orig.). 1970. pap. 16.00 (*92-0-125570-5*, IDC120, Pub. by IAEA) Bernan Associates.

Monitoring of Radioactive Effluents from Nuclear Facilities. IAEA Staff. (Proceedings Ser.). (Illus.). 610p. 1978. pap. 135.00 (*92-0-020078-8*, ISP466, Pub. by IAEA) Bernan Associates.

Monitoring of U.S. Imports of Tomatoes. 67p. pap. text. write for info. (*0-7881-8942-5*) DIANE Pub.

Monitoring of Vital Parameters During Extracorporal Circulation. H. P. Kimmich. (Illus.). x, 334p. 1981. pap. 164.50 (*3-8055-2059-X*) S Karger.

Monitoring of Water Quality: The Contribution of Advanced Technologies. F. Colin & P. Quevauviller. LC 98-24452. 1998. 122.50 (*0-08-043340-5*); pap. 60.50 (*0-08-043203-4*) Elsevier.

Monitoring Patient Care: Are Your Patients Safe? Meridith B. Cox. (Risk Management Ser.). (Orig.). (C). 1999. pap. text 30.00 (*0-912665-23-8*) BusinessWatch.

Monitoring Performance in the Public Sector. Ed. by John Mayne & Eduardo Zapico-Goni. LC 96-43358. 172p. 1997. text 32.95 (*1-56000-292-1*) Transaction Pubs.

Monitoring Revenue Sharing. Richard P. Nathan et al. LC 74-28124. 416p. reprint ed. pap. 129.00 (*0-608-12214-9*, 202539200043) Bks Demand.

Monitoring School Achievements. Patrick Griffin. 76p. (C). 1995. pap. 30.00 (*0-7300-1334-0*, ECT338, Pub. by Deakin Univ) St Mut.

Monitoring School Performance: A Non-Technical Guide for Educational Administrators. J. Douglas Willms. 200p. 1992. pap. 34.95 (*1-85000-971-6*, Falmer Pr) Taylor & Francis.

Monitoring Social Progress in the 1990s: Data Constraints, Concerns, & Priorities. Ed. by David A. Westendorff & Dharam P. Ghai. 368p. 1994. 72.95 (*1-85628-565-0*, Pub. by Avebry) Ashgate Pub Co.

Monitoring Structural Integrity by Acoustic Emission - STP 571. 290p. 1975. 23.75 (*0-8031-0519-3*, STP571) ASTM.

***Monitoring Student Learning.** 704p. (C). 1999. pap. text 0.00 (*0-321-02333-1*) Addison-Wesley.

Monitoring Student Learning. Cangelosi. LC 99-10749. 662p. (C). 1999. 81.00 (*0-321-02332-3*) Addson-Wesley Educ.

Monitoring the Changes in Use of Medicare Posthospital Services. Andrea Steiner & C. R. Neu. LC 93-3542. 1993. pap. 9.00 (*0-8330-1361-0*, MR-153-HCFA) Rand Corp.

Monitoring the Competition: Find Out What's Really Going on over There. Leonard M. Fuld. LC 87-21607. 224p. 1988. 42.95 (*0-471-85261-9*) Wiley.

Monitoring the Effects of Recreational Use on Colorado River Beaches in Grand Canyon National Park. Barbara Phillips et al. (Bulletin Ser.: No. 55). (Illus.). 230p. (Orig.). 1986. pap. 14.95 (*0-89734-057-4*) Mus Northern Ariz.

Monitoring the Environment. Ed. by Bryan Cartledge. (Linacre Lectures). (Illus.). 224p. 1992. pap. 16.95 (*0-19-858412-1*) OUP.

Monitoring the Environmental Quality of Nordic Forests. Ed. by Lars Strand. LC 99-183975. 160p. 1997. pap. 35.00 (*92-893-0076-0*, NC0706, Pub. by Nordic Coun Minsters) Bernan Associates.

Monitoring the European Central Bank, Report No. 1. David Begg et al. 120p. 1998. pap. 14.95 (*1-898128-39-1*, Pub. by Ctr Econ Policy Res) Brookings.

Monitoring the Health of American Households: Average Monthly Estimates of Income, Labor Force Activity, Program Participation & Health Insurance. 1995. lib. bdg. 251.95 (*0-8490-6700-6*) Gordon Pr.

Monitoring the Health of Buildings. Barnes. (Illus.), 256p. 1997. text. write for info. (*0-419-20460-1*, E & FN Spon) Routledge.

Monitoring the Learning Outcomes of Education Systems. Vincent Greaney & Thomas Kellaghan. LC 96-43969. (Directions in Development Ser.). 96p. 1996. pap. 22.00 (*0-8213-3734-3*, 13734) World Bank.

Monitoring the Marine Environment. Ed. by David Nichols. LC 78-71806. 224p. 1979. 67.95 (*0-275-90401-6*, C0401, Praeger Pubs) Greenwood.

Monitoring the News: The Brilliant Launch & Sudden Collapse of the Monitor Channel. Susan Bridge. LC 98-10021. (Illus.). 264p. (YA). (gr. 13). 1998. text 38.95 (*0-7656-0315-2*) M E Sharpe.

***Monitoring the News: The Brilliant Launch & Sudden Collapse of the Monitor Channel.** Susan Bridge. (Illus.) 264p. 1999. pap. text 21.95 (*0-7656-0316-0*) M E Sharpe.

Monitoring the Outcome of Social Services, 2 vols. Annie Millar et al. Incl. Vol. 1. Preliminary Suggestions. 1977. 6.50 (*0-87766-194-4*); Vol. 2. Review of Past Research & Test Activities. 88p. 1977. 6.50 (*0-87766-200-2*); 1977. write for info. (*0-318-56305-3*) Urban Inst.

Monitoring the Outcomes of Economic Development Programs: A Manual. Harry P. Hatry et al. LC 90-12733. (Illus.). 216p. (Orig.). (C). 1990. pap. text 27.50 (*0-87766-488-9*) Urban Inst.

Monitoring the Standards of Education: Papers in Honor of John P Keeves. Albert C. Trijnman & T. Neville Postlethwaite. LC 94-15706. 284p. 1994. text 71.75 (*0-08-042386-8*, Pergamon Pr) Elsevier.

Monitoring the Work Environment: Report of 2nd European Conference. European Communities Staff. LC 94-223158. 210p. 1994. pap. 16.00 (*92-826-7315-4*, SY-82-94-254ENC, Pub. by Comm Europ Commun) Bernan Associates.

Monitoring the World Economy, 1820-1992. Angus Maddison. 255p. 1995. pap. 30.00 (*92-64-14549-4*, 41-95-09-1, Pub. by Org for Econ) OECD.

Monitoring Toxic Substances. Ed. by Dennis Schuetzle. LC 78-27490. (ACS Symposium Ser.: No. 94). 1979. 49.95 (*0-8412-0480-2*); pap. 27.95 (*0-8412-0656-2*) Am Chemical.

Monitoring Toxic Substances. Ed. by Dennis Schuetzle. LC 78-27490. (ACS Symposium Ser.: Vol. 94). 300p. 1979. reprint ed. pap. 93.00 (*0-608-03103-8*, 206355600007) Bks Demand.

Monitoring Vertebrate Populations. William L. Thompson et al. LC 98-84423. (Illus.). 365p. (C). 1998. text 69.95 (*0-12-688960-0*) Acad Pr.

Monitoring Water in the 1990's: Meeting New Challenges, STP 1102. Ed. by Jack R. Hall & Douglas G. Glysson. LC 91-34567. (Special Technical Publication Ser.). (Illus.). 625p. 1991. text 69.00 (*0-8031-1407-9*, STP1102) ASTM.

Monitoring with Indicators: Evaluating the Quality of Patient Care. Jean G. Carroll. ring bd. 170.00 (*0-8342-0264-6*) Aspen Pub.

Monitoring Your Student's Educational Progress: Module Four, 4 modules, Set. Sharon K. Johnson & Clarence D. Johnson. (FAST (Families & Schools Together) Ser.). (Illus.). 64p. 1994. pap. write for info. (*1-57035-024-8*, 56MOD) Sopris.

Monitors. Jerry L. Harlowe. (Illus.). (C). Date not set. pap. write for info. (*1-57747-056-7*) Thomas Publications.

Monitors: The Biology of Varanid Lizards. 2nd ed. Dennis King & Brian Green. LC 99-20396. 1999. pap. 22.50 (*1-57524-112-9*) Krieger.

Monitor's Guide to Aquatic Macroinvertebrates. 2nd rev. ed. Loren L. Kellogg. Ed. by Karen Firehock. (Illus.). 60p. 1994. pap. text 5.00 (*0-941675-06-8*) Izaak Walton League.

Monitors Made Simple: A No Nonsense Guide to Understanding & Repairing Computer Monitors. Tony Jomaa. LC 96-94389. (Illus.). 134p. (Orig.). 1996. reprint ed. pap. 19.95 (*0-9653029-3-8*) Pikes Peak Pr.

Monitors, Tegus, & Related Lizards: A Complete Pet Owner's Manual. Richard D. Bartlett & Patricia P. Bartlett. LC 96-19488. (Illus.). 112p. 1996. pap. 6.95 (*0-8120-9696-7*) Barron.

***Monje Que Vendio su Ferrari.** Robin S. Swaama. (SPA.). 2000. pap. 14.95 (*0-553-06115-1*) Bantam.

Monk. Laurent De Wilde. 224p. 1998. pap. 13.95 (*1-56924-776-5*) Marlowe & Co.

Monk. Matthew Lewis. 1999. pap. 5.95 (*0-451-52577-9*, Sig Classics) NAL.

Monk. Matthew Lewis. Ed. by Howard Anderson. (Oxford World's Classics Ser.). 496p. 1998. pap. 8.95 (*0-19-283394-4*) OUP.

Monk. Matthew Lewis. LC 99-236098. 384p. 1999. pap. 9.95 (*0-14-043603-0*) Viking Penguin.

Monk. Matthew G. Lewis. LC 92-38487. 368p. 1970. pap. 12.95 (*0-8021-5107-8*, Grove) Grove-Atltic.

Monk. Julian Corbett. LC 72-154148. (Select Bibliographies Reprint Ser.). 1977. reprint ed. 20.95 (*0-8369-5764-4*) Ayer.

Monk & Mason on the Tigris Frontier. Andrew N. Palmer. (University of Cambridge Oriental Publications). (Illus.). 289p. (C). 1990. text 80.00 (*0-521-36026-9*) Cambridge U Pr.

Monk & the Dancer. Arthur C. Smith. LC 73-98594. (Short Story Index Reprint Ser.). 1977. 19.95 (*0-8369-3169-6*) Ayer.

Monk & the Hangman's Daughter. Ambrose Bierce. 143p. 1976. reprint ed. lib. bdg. 19.95 (*0-89190-183-3*, Rivercity Pr) Amereon Ltd.

Monk & the Hangman's Daughter. Ambrose Bierce. 1990. reprint ed. lib. bdg. 15.95 (*0-89968-482-3*) Buccaneer Bks.

Monk & the Hangman's Daughter. Ambrose Bierce. (Principle Works of Ambrose Gwinett Bierce). 1989. reprint ed. lib. bdg. 79.00 (*0-7812-1962-0*) Rprt Serv.

***Monk & the Philosopher: A Father & Son Discuss the Meaning of Life.** Jean-Francois Revel & Matthieu Ricard. Tr. by John Canti from FRE. 2000. pap. 14.00 (*0-8052-1103-9*) Schocken.

***Monk & the Riddle: The Education of a Silicon Valley Entrepreneur.** Randy Komisar & Kent L. Lineback. LC 99-57378. 192p. 2000. 22.50 (*1-57851-140-2*, HBS Pr) Harvard Busn.

***Monk Camps Out.** Emily Arnold McCully. LC 99-23237. (Illus.). 32p. (J). (ps-4). 2000. 15.95 (*0-439-09976-5*, A A Levine) Scholastic Inc.

***Monk in the Garden: The Lost & Found Genius of Gregor Mendel, the Father of Genetics.** Robin Marantz Henig. LC 00-24341. 224p. 2000. 24.00 (*0-395-97765-7*) HM.

Monk of Fife. Andrew Lang. LC 68-59287. reprint ed. 37.50 (*0-404-03847-6*) AMS Pr.

Monk of Mount Athos: Staretz Silouan, 1866-1938. Archimandrite Sophrony. Tr. by Rosemary Edmonds from RUS. LC 61-4333. 124p. (Orig.). 1999. pap. 8.95 (*0-913836-15-X*) St Vladimirs.

Monk of Mount Athos: Staretz Silouan, 1866-1938. rev. ed. Sofronifi. LC 74-163847. 124p. 1973. write for info. (*0-264-64618-5*, Pub. by A R Mowbray) Cassell & Continuum.

Monk of Udolpho: A Romance. T. J. Curties. Ed. by Devendra P. Varma. LC 77-2037. (Gothic Novels III Ser.). 1977. lib. bdg. 101.95 (*0-405-10136-8*) Ayer.

Monk Swimming: A Memoir. Malachy McCourt. 304p. 1998. write for info. (*0-7868-6431-1*) Hyperion.

Monk Swimming: A Memoir. Malachy McCourt. LC 97-46720. (Illus.). 320p. 1998. 23.95 (*0-7868-6398-6*, Pub. by Hyperion) Time Warner.

Monk Swimming: A Memoir. large type ed. Malachy McCourt. LC 98-39410. (Large Print Book Ser.). 1998. 26.95 (*1-56895-671-1*) Wheeler Pub.

Monk Swimming: A Memoir. Malachy McCourt. 304p. 1999. reprint ed. pap. 14.00 (*0-7868-8414-2*, Pub. by Disney Pr) Time Warner.

Monk Who Dared: A Novel about Shinran. Ruth M. Tabrah. LC 95-10352. 1995. 15.95 (*0-916630-75-7*) Pr Pacifica.

Monk Who Sold His Ferrari. Robin Sharma. 1998. 19.00 (*0-06-251556-X*) Harper SF.

***Monk Who Sold His Ferrari, Set.** abr. ed. Robin S. Sharma. 1998. audio 18.00 (*0-694-52050-0*, CPN2791) HarperAudio.

Monk Who Sold His Ferrari: A Fable about Fulfilling Your Dreams & Reaching Your Destiny. Robin S. Sharma. LC 98-13247. 224p. 1999. pap. 12.00 (*0-06-251567-5*, Pub. by Harper SF) HarpC.

Monkeemania! The Story of the Monkees. 2nd ed. Glenn A. Baker. 1997. pap. text 15.95 (*0-85965-256-4*, Pub. by Plexus) Publishers Group.

***Monkeemania: The Story of the Monkees.** 3rd ed. Glenn A. Baker. (Illus.). 2000. pap. 15.95 (*0-85965-292-0*) Plexus.

Monkees - A Manufactured Image: The Ultimate Reference Guide to Monkee Memories & Memorabilia. Ed Reilly & Maggie McMannus. Ed. by Thomas Schultheiss. (Rock & Roll Reference Ser.). (Illus.). 324p. 1993. reprint ed. 39.50 (*1-56075-032-4*) Popular Culture.

Monkees Collectibles Price Guide. Marty Eck. LC 98-71067. (Illus.). 208p. 1998. pap. 21.95 (*0-930625-18-8*, Antique Trader) Krause Pubns.

***Monkees Greatest Hits.** 96p. 1999. otabind 16.95 (*0-7935-9343-3*) H Leonard.

***Monkees, Memories & the Magic.** Edward Wincentsen. (Illus.). 176p. 2000. pap. 17.95 (*0-9642808-8-4*) Wynn Pubng.

Monkees Tale. Eric Lefkowitz. 1986. pap. 9.95 (*0-86719-338-7*) Last Gasp.

Monkees Tale. rev. ed. Eric Lefcowitz. 120p. 1990. pap. 11.95 (*0-86719-378-6*) Last Gasp.

Monkey. Kwok Man-Ho. LC 93-48006. (Chinese Horoscopes Library). (Illus.). 42p. 1994. pap. 8.95 (*1-56458-604-9*) DK Pub Inc.

Monkey. Rod Moore. 78p. (Orig.). 1985. pap. 4.95 (*0-933515-04-9*) Exile Pr.

Monkey. Heidi Petach. (Little Activity Bks.). (Illus.). (J). 1995. pap. 1.00 (*0-486-26992-2*) Dover.

Monkey: A Journey to the West. David Kherdian. LC 91-50364. 184p. 1992. pap. 18.00 (*0-87773-652-9*, Pub. by Shambhala Pubns) Random.

***Monkey: A Journey to the West.** David Kherdian. (Illus.). 224p. 2000. pap. 14.95 (*1-57062-581-6*, Pub. by Shambhala Pubns) Random.

Monkey: Folk Novel of China. Arthur Waley. LC 84-22583. 320p. (Orig.). 1988. pap. 12.00 (*0-8021-3086-0*, Grove) Grove-Atltic.

Monkey - Little Lamb. Michaela Muntean. (J). 1984. pap. 69.36 (*0-8037-0104-7*, NewStar Pr) NewStar Media.

***Monkey & Mom.** David Martin. (Illus.). 8p. (J). (ps-2). 2000. pap. 4.99 (*0-7636-0771-1*) Candlewick Pr.

Monkey & the Crab. Ralph F. McCarthy. (Children's Classics Ser.). (Illus.). 48p. (J). 1994. 14.95 (*4-7700-1844-4*) Kodansha.

***Monkey & the Crab.** large type ed. Tr. by Donna Tamaki.Tr. of Saru to Kani. (ENG & JPN., Illus.). 16p. (J). (ps-12). 1998. 35.00 (*1-893533-12-3*, 15) Kamish for Kids.

Monkey & The Crocodile. Paul Galdone. LC 78-79939. (Illus.). 32p. (J). (ps-3). 1987. pap. 6.95 (*0-89919-524-5*, Clarion Bks) HM.

Monkey & the Crocodile & Other Stories. Mrudul Tata. 32p. (J). (gr. k-3). 1995. 14.99 (*0-9639913-2-9*) Tata Pubng.

Monkey & the Mango: Stories of My Granny. Eknath Easwaran. (Illus.). 32p. (J). (ps up). 1996. 14.95 (*0-915132-82-6*) Nilgiri Pr.

Monkey & the Moon. John Randall. (Illus.). 32p. (J). 1996. pap., bds. 12.95 (*0-7892-0211-5*, Abbeville Kids) Abbeville Pr.

***Monkey & the Panda.** Antonia Barber. (Illus.). (J). (ps-4). 1999. pap. text 7.99 (*0-7112-1085-3*) F Lincoln.

Monkey & the Parakeet: A Poetic Tale for Children. Bunny Z. Geller. LC 96-94784. (Illus.). 20p. (Orig.). 1996. mass mkt. 5.95 (*1-890986-01-1*) BZG-Enterprises.

Monkey & the Tetrahedron: Compelling Connections Between Mars, the UFO Dilemma & the Future of the Human Race. David M. Jinks. LC 99-60443. (Illus.). 476p. 1999. pap. 22.95 (*0-9667258-0-8*, No. 2160) Glass Mn.

Monkey & the Tiger. Robert H. Van Gulik. (J). 1980. pap. 2.95 (*0-684-16737-9*, Scribners Ref) Mac Lib Ref.

Monkey & the Tiger: Two Chinese Detective Stories. Robert H. Van Gulik. LC 92-22578. (Illus.). vii, 143p. 1992. pap. 6.95 (*0-226-84869-8*) U Ch Pr.

***Monkey & Turtle.** Mariza A. Smith. (Illus.). 18p. (J). (gr. 2-5). 1999. pap. 7.95 (*0-9674241-0-0*) IZA Pubg.

***Monkey & Turtle Philippine Folktale.** Photos by Christine Calamug & Cynthia Calamug. (Illus.). 18p. (J). 1999. pap. write for info. (*1-929416-00-8*) Magner Pubg.

***Monkey Beach.** Eden Robinson. 384p. 2000. 24.00 (*0-618-07327-2*) HM.

Monkey Beach. Eden Robinson. 1950. text. write for info. (*0-8050-4839-1*) St Martin.

Monkey Bedtime Lullaby. Kidsbooks Inc. Staff. mass mkt. 2.99 (*1-56156-341-2*) Kidsbks.

Monkey Book. Jan Pfloog. (Super Shape Bks.). (Illus.). 24p. (J). (ps-k). 1998. pap. 3.29 (*0-307-10347-1*, 10347, Goldn Books) Gldn Bks Pub Co.

Monkey Box. Art Rodriguez. LC 99-93258. 340p. 2000. pap. 12.95 (*0-9671555-1-7*, Pub. by Dream Hse Pr) Partners-West.

Monkey Brain Sushi: New Tastes in Japanese Fiction. Ed. by Elmer Luke. (Japan's Modern Writers Ser.). (Illus.). 312p. 1993. pap. 10.00 (*4-7700-1688-3*) Kodansha.

Monkey Bridge. Lan Cao. LC 96-52418. 260p. 1998. pap. 12.95 (*0-14-026361-6*) Viking Penguin.

M

Monkey Bridge. Rafe Martin. LC 96-27974. (Illus.). (J). (ps-2). 1997. 17.00 (0-679-88106-9) Random.

*__Monkey Business.__ Shirley Climo. 2001. text 16.95 (0-8050-6392-7) St Martin.

*__Monkey Business.__ John R. Erickson. (Hank the Cowdog Ser.: No. 14). (Illus.). (J). (gr. 2-5). 1999. pap. text 14.50 (0-8335-6827-2) Econo-Clad Bks.

Monkey Business. John R. Erickson. LC 99-19575. (Hank the Cowdog Ser.: No. 14). (Illus.). 144p. (J). (gr. 2-5). 1998. pap. 4.99 (0-14-130390-5, PuffinBks) Peng Put Young Read.

Monkey Business. John R. Erickson. (Hank the Cowdog Ser.: No. 14). (Illus.). (J). (gr. 2-5). 1990. 12.05 (0-606-01406-3, Pub. by Turtleback) Demco.

Monkey Business. John R. Erickson. (Hank the Cowdog Ser.: No. 14). (Illus.). 144p. (J). (gr. 2-5). 1998. 14.99 (0-670-88421-9) Viking Penguin.

Monkey Business. Johnson. 198p. 1997. pap. 29.95 (0-566-08011-7) Ashgate Pub Co.

Monkey Business. Gary Johnson. 200p. 1996. 61.95 (0-566-07620-9, Pub. by Gower) Ashgate Pub Co.

*__Monkey Business.__ David Martin. (Illus.). (J). (ps-2). 2000. pap. 5.99 (0-7636-0773-8) Candlewick Pr.

*__Monkey Business.__ David Martin & Scott Nash. LC 99-48484. (Illus.). 48p. (J). (ps-2). 2000. 10.99 (0-7636-1178-6) Candlewick Pr.

Monkey Business. Evan Skolnick. (Disney's Action Club Ser.). 1997. pap. text 4.50 (1-57840-084-8, Pub. by Acclaim Bks) Penguin Putnam.

Monkey Business. Sue Welford. LC 94-79397. (Ten-Minute Mysteries Ser.). 32p. (YA). (gr. 6-12). 1994. pap. 2.95 (0-7854-0845-2, 40766) Am Guidance.

Monkey Business: Are You Controlling Events or Are Events Controlling You? William Oncken, III. 192p. 1999. 22.95 (1-890009-24-5) Exec Excell.

*__Monkey Business: Creation vs. Evolution.__ Jeff Diedrich. (Hot Shots Ser.). 40p. 1999. pap. 10.25 (1-929784-01-5) Psitive Action.

*__Monkey Business: Swinging Through the Wall Street Jungle.__ John Rolfe & Peter Troob. LC 99-39604. 288p. 2000. 24.95 (0-446-52556-1, Pub. by Warner Bks) Little.

*__Monkey Business: The Lives & Legends of the Marx Brothers.__ Simon Louvish. (Illus.). 480p. 2000. 25.95 (0-312-25292-7) St Martin.

Monkey Business of Amusement: Multimedia Mania. Superlove Staff. LC 93-83040. 200p. (Orig.). 1998. spiral bd. 44.00 (0-9602334-3-1) Superlove.

Monkey Business Readalong. Sue Welford. LC 94-79397. (Ten-Minute Mysteries Ser.). 32p. 1994. pap. 12.95 incl. audio (0-7854-1054-6, 40768) Am Guidance.

Monkey Crosses the Equator. Paul White. (Jungle Doctor Picture Fables Ser.). (Illus.). (J). 1993. 4.99 (0-85892-048-4) O M Lit.

Monkey Day. Ruth Krauss. (Illus.). 23p. (J). (gr. k-5). 1973. reprint ed. pap. 10.00 (0-912846-05-4) Bookstore Pr.

Monkey Discovery Library, 6 bks., Set. Lynn M. Stone. (Illus.). 144p. (J). (gr. k-5). 1990. lib. bdg. 71.60 (0-86593-061-9); lib. bdg. 53.70 (0-685-36314-7) Rourke Corp.

Monkey Do. Allan Ahlberg. LC 97-36181. (Illus.). 32p. (J). (ps-k). 1998. 15.99 (0-7636-0466-6) Candlewick Pr.

*__Monkey Family Sticker Paper Dolls.__ Marjorie Sarnat. (Illus.). (J). 1999. pap. 4.95 (0-486-40579-6) Dover.

Monkey Food: The Complete "I Was Seven in '75" Collection. Ellen Forney. (Illus.). 144p. 1999. pap. 12.95 (1-56097-362-5) Fantagraph Bks.

Monkey Girl: Swinging Stories. Beth Lisick. LC 97-4728. 160p. 1997. pap. text 11.95 (0-916397-49-1) Manic D Pr.

Monkey God & Other Hindu Tales. Debjani Chatterjee. (Orig.). (C). 1993. 5.00 (81-7167-146-2, Pub. by Rupa) S Asia.

Monkey Grammarian. Octavio Paz. Tr. by Helen Lane. Orig. Title: El Mono Gramatico. 1991. pap. 9.70 (1-55970-135-8, Pub. by Arcade Pub Inc) Time Warner.

Monkey Grows Up. Rita G. Gelman. 40p. (J). (ps-3). 1991. pap. 3.95 (0-590-41510-7) Scholastic Inc.

Monkey Handlers. G. Gordon Liddy. 352p. 1991. mass mkt. 4.50 (0-312-92613-8) St Martin.

*__Monkey Hero: Official Strategy Guide.__ Christine Cain. LC 98-67307. (Secrets of the Game Ser.). (Illus.). 132p. 1998. pap. 14.99 (0-7615-1807-X) Prima Pub.

*__Monkey House.__ John Fullerton. 2000. 27.50 (0-593-04052-X, Pub. by Transworld Publishers Ltd); pap. 10.95 (0-553-50475-4, Pub. by Transworld Publishers Ltd) Trafalgar.

Monkey in a Lion's Skin. Paul White. (Jungle Doctor Picture Fables Ser.). (Illus.). (J). 1995. 4.99 (0-85892-214-2) O M Lit.

*__Monkey in a Tree.__ R. Christopherson. 180p. 2000. mass mkt. 9.95 (0-914597-07-8) Pubs West AZ.

Monkey in Art. Ptolemy Tompkins. (Illus.). 128p. 1994. 30.00 (0-614-07786-9) M T Train.

Monkey in the Middle: Writers on Growing up Biracial & Bicultural. Claudine C. O'Hearn. LC 97-49597. 224p. 1998. pap. 13.00 (0-375-70011-0) Random.

Monkey In The Mirror C. Tattersall. 2001. Price not set. (0-15-100520-6) Harcourt Coll Pubs.

*__Monkey Island.__ 2000. 9.95 (1-56137-731-7) Novel Units.

Monkey Island. Paula Fox. (American Library Association Notable Bks.). 151p. (YA). (gr. 5-9). 1993. pap. 5.50 (0-440-40770-2) Dell.

Monkey Island. Paula Fox. LC 91-7460. 160p. (YA). (gr. 5 up). 1991. 15.95 (0-531-05962-6); lib. bdg. 16.99 (0-531-08562-7) Orchard Bks Watts.

Monkey Island. Paula Fox. 1991. 10.09 (0-606-02756-4, Pub. by Turtleback) Demco.

Monkey Island . . . A Fantastic Guide to New Orleans. Hudson Marquez. 1992. pap. 8.95 (0-917905-04-0) Faust Pub Co.

Monkey Jungle. Houghton Mifflin Company Staff. (Literature Experience 1991 Ser.). (J). 1990. pap. 6.36 (0-395-53927-7) HM.

*__Monkey King.__ Adiccabandhu & Padmasri. (Illus.). 32p. (J). (ps-3). 1999. pap. 10.95 (1-899579-09-5, Pub. by Windhorse) Weatherhill.

Monkey King. Grania Davis & Nazli Gellek. LC 98-2676. (Jataka Tales Ser.). (Illus.). (J). 1998. 16.95 (0-89800-293-1) Dharma Pub.

Monkey King. Ed Young. (Illus.). 40p. (J). 2001. 15.95 (0-06-027919-2); lib. bdg. 15.89 (0-06-027950-8) HarpC Child Bks.

Monkey King. Grania Davis & Nazli Gellek. LC 98-2676. (Jataka Tales Ser.). (Illus.). 32p. (J). (gr. k-6). 1998. reprint ed. pap. 7.95 (0-89800-292-3) Dharma Pub.

Monkey King: A Novel. Patricia Chao. 320p. 1998. pap. 13.00 (0-06-092893-X) HarpC.

Monkey Link. Andrei Bitov. Tr. by Susan Brownsberger. LC 94-18864. 400p. 1994. text 30.00 (0-374-10578-2) FS&G.

Monkey Magic: Chinese Story Theatre (Playscript) Aurand Harris. 58p. (J). (ps-8). 1990. pap. 6.00 (0-87602-290-5) Anchorage.

Monkey, Monkey: Playscript. Charles Jones. 25p. (J). (gr. k-3). 1986. pap. 6.00 (0-87602-265-4) Anchorage.

Monkey-Monkey's Trick. Patricia McKissack. LC 88-3072. (Step into Reading Ser.: A Step 2 Book). (Illus.). 48p. (J). (ps-3). 1988. pap. 3.99 (0-394-89173-2, Pub. by Random Bks Yng Read) Random.

Monkey-Monkey's Trick. Patricia McKissack. (Step into Reading Ser.: A Step 2 Book). (J). (gr. 1-3). 1988. 9.19 (0-606-12428-4, Pub. by Turtleback) Demco.

Monkey Mountain Madness. Jeanne Phillips. LC 95-49114. (Living the West Ser.). 172p. (C). 1996. 14.95 (0-89301-192-4) U of Idaho Pr.

Monkey Moves. unabridged ed. Stephen Rosenholtz. LC 93-93549. (J). (ps-3). 1993. pap. 14.95 incl. audio (0-9630979-2-X) Rosewd Pubns.

Monkey of Mulberry Pass. Harley Elliott. Ed. by Thomas F. Averill. 80p. (Orig.). 1991. pap. 7.00 (0-939391-15-5) B Woodley Pr.

Monkey on a Bellrope. Gertrude Caudill. 1992. pap. 8.95 (0-9626441-1-0) Drift Creek Pr.

Monkey Painting. Thierry Lenain. (Illus.). 208p. 1997. 24.95 (1-86189-003-6, Pub. by Reaktion Bks) Consort Bk Sales.

Monkey Pop-Ups: A Book of Colors. Bernice Chardiet. (Illus.). 8p. (J). (ps-k). 1996. 6.95 (0-590-54315-6, Cartwheel) Scholastic Inc.

Monkey Pop-Ups: A Book of Opposites. Bernice Chardiet. (Illus.). 8p. (J). (ps-k). 1996. 6.95 (0-590-54314-8, Cartwheel) Scholastic Inc.

*__Monkey Puzzle.__ large type ed. Mary Cummins. 304p. 2000. 20.99 (1-84137-015-0, Pub. by Mgna Lrg Print) Ulverscroft.

Monkey Puzzle: Vacation Special. Tessa Krailing. LC 99-29278. (Petsitters Club Ser.). (Illus.). 96p. (J). (gr. 1-4). 1999. pap. 3.95 (0-7641-0737-2) Barron.

Monkey Riddles. Katy Hall & Lisa Eisenberg. LC 97-49516. (Illus.). (J). 1999. lib. bdg. 16.01 (0-8037-2238-9, Dial Yng Read); trans. 20.01 (0-8037-2237-0, Dial Yng Read) Peng Put Young Read.

Monkey Rope: A Psychotherapist's Reflections on Relationships. Jerry M. Lewis. 186p. (Orig.). 1996. pap. 17.95 (0-9641887-2-4) Bernel Bks.

Monkey Secret. Diane H. Glancy. LC 95-1716. 116p. 1995. 19.95 (0-8101-5016-6) Northwestern U Pr.

*__Monkey See, Doggie Do.__ Cartoon Network Staff. (Powerpuff Girls Ser.: Vol. 1). (Illus.). 32p. (J). (ps-3). 2000. pap. 3.50 (0-439-17305-1) Scholastic Inc.

*__Monkey See, Doggy Do.__ Laura Dower. (Powerpuff Girls Ser.). (Illus.). (J). 2000. pap. 3.50 (0-439-16013-8) Scholastic Inc.

Monkey See, Monkey Do. Geraldine M. Bennett. (Katrina Tells Ser.: Bk. 5). (J). (gr. k up). 1995. pap. 10.98 (1-882786-09-2) New Dawn NY.

Monkey See, Monkey Do. Marc Gave. LC 91-45443. (Hello Reader! Ser.). (Illus.). 32p. (J). (ps-3). 1993. pap. 3.50 (0-590-45801-9) Scholastic Inc.

Monkey See, Monkey Do. Marc Gave. (Hello, Reader! Ser.). (J). 1993. 8.70 (0-606-02757-2, Pub. by Turtleback) Demco.

*__Monkey See, Monkey Do.__ Dana Regan. (All Aboard Reading Ser.). (Illus.). 32p. (J). (ps-3). 2000. pap. 3.99 (0-448-42299-9, Planet Dexter) Peng Put Young Read.

Monkey See, Monkey Do. Linda Schwartz. LC 90-62597. (J). (ps-3). 1991. pap. 4.95 (0-88160-187-X, LW1201) Learning Wks.

Monkey See, Monkey Do! Wishing Well Staff. (Illus.). 20p. 1995. 8.99 (0-88705-652-0) Rdrs Digest.

Monkey See, Monkey Do: An Animal Exercise Book for You. Anita Holsonback. LC 97-792. (Illus.). 32p. (J). (-k). 1997. lib. bdg. 19.90 (0-7613-0260-3) Millbrook Pr.

Monkey Shines. Michael Stewart. 256p. 1983. 15.95 (0-88191-001-5) Freundlich.

Monkey Sonatas. Orson Scott Card. (Maps in a Mirror Ser.: No. 4). 320p. 1993. mass mkt. 4.99 (0-8125-2367-9, Pub. by Tor Bks) St Martin.

Monkey Stickers. Heidi Petach. (Illus.). (J). (gr. k-3). 1993. pap. 1.00 (0-486-27493-4) Dover.

Monkey Suit: And Other Short Fiction on African Americans & Justice. David Dante Troutt. LC 97-23023. 320p. 1998. 24.00 (1-56584-326-6, Pub. by New Press NY) Norton.

Monkey Suit: And Other Short Fiction on African Americans & Justice. David Dante Troutt. 317p. 1999. pap. 14.95 (1-56584-524-2, Pub. by New Press NY) Norton.

Monkey Sunday: Story from a Village in Zaire. Sanna Stanley. LC 97-18529. (Illus.). 32p. (J). (gr. k-3). 1998. 16.00 (0-374-35018-3) FS&G.

Monkey Tag. Pete Fromm. LC 93-34593. 352p. (J). (gr. 4-7). 1994. 14.95 (0-590-46525-2) Scholastic Inc.

Monkey Tales. Illus. by Vlasta van Kampen. 40p. (J). (ps-3). 1998. pap. 6.95 (1-55037-530-X, Pub. by Annick Pr); lib. bdg. 18.95 (1-55037-531-8, Pub. by Annick Pr) Firefly Bks Ltd.

Monkey Thief. Aileen K. Henderson. LC 97-11402. (Illus.). 157p. (J). (gr. 3-8). 1997. 14.95 (1-57131-612-4); pap. 6.95 (1-57131-613-2) Milkweed Ed.

Monkey Thieves. Rebecca E. Snavely. LC 99-176493. 1998. 12.95 (0-9667004-0-6) Nurun Gardens Pubg.

Monkey Tree. Janet S. Anderson. LC 98-24315. (Illus.). 176p. (J). (gr. 7-9). 1998. 15.99 (0-525-46032-2, Dutton Child) Peng Put Young Read.

Monkey Tricks. Camilla Ashforth. LC 92-53013. (Illus.). 32p. (J). (ps up). 1993. 15.95 (1-56402-170-X) Candlewick Pr.

*__Monkey Trouble.__ David Martin & Scott Nash. (Illus.). (J). 2000. pap. 10.99 (0-7636-1179-4) Candlewick Pr.

Monkey Trouble. John A. Rowe. LC 99-17364. (Illus.). 32p. (J). (gr. k-3). 1999. lib. bdg. 15.88 (0-7358-1034-6, Pub. by North-South Bks NYC) Chronicle Bks.

*__Monkey Trouble.__ John A. Rowe. LC 99-17364. (Illus.). 32p. (J). (gr. k-3). 1999. 15.95 (0-7358-1033-8, Pub. by North-South Bks NYC) Chronicle Bks.

*__Monkey vs. Robot.__ unabridged ed. James Kochalka. (Illus.). 160p. 2000. pap. 14.95 (1-891830-15-5, Pub. by Top Shelf Prodns) LPC InBook.

Monkey Wars. Deborah Blum. (Illus.). 334p. 1995. pap. 14.95 (0-19-510109-X) OUP.

Monkey Wrench. Nancy Martin. (Tyler Ser.: No. 4). 1992. per. 3.99 (0-373-82504-8, 0-82504-2) Harlequin Bks.

Monkey Wrench Gang. Edward Abbey. 22.95 (0-8488-0902-5) Amereon Ltd.

Monkey Wrench Gang. Edward Abbey. LC 75-831. 387p. 1976. mass mkt. 6.99 (0-380-00741-X, Avon Bks) Morrow Avon.

*__Monkey Wrench Gang.__ Edward Abbey & Douglas Brinkley. 368p. 2000. pap. 13.00 (0-06-095644-5, Perennial) HarperTrade.

Monkey Wrench Gang. Edward Abbey. 1991. reprint ed. lib. bdg. 37.95 (1-56849-083-6) Buccaneer Bks.

Monkey Wrench Gang. rev. ed. Edward Abbey. LC 75-831. (Illus.). 368p. 1999. reprint ed. 24.95 (0-942688-18-X) Dream Garden.

Monkey Wrench Gang T. Edward Abbey. 368p. 1992. pap. 12.50 (0-380-71339-X, Avon Bks) Morrow Avon.

Monkeypuzzle. Rita Wong. 104p. 1998. pap. 10.95 (0-88974-088-7, Pub. by Press Gang Pubs) LPC InBook.

*__Monkeys.__ Sarah Albee. LC 98-47463. (Very First Things to Know about Ser.). (Illus.). 32p. (J). (ps-2). 1999. bds. 8.95 (0-7611-1134-4) Workman Pub.

Monkeys. Pamela Chanko & Susan Canizares. LC 97-34203. (Science Emergent Readers Ser.). (J). 1997. pap. 2.50 (0-590-76964-2) Scholastic Inc.

Monkeys. Susan Minot. 176p. 1989. pap. 12.00 (0-671-70361-7, WSP) PB.

*__Monkeys.__ Susan Minot. (Contemporaries Ser.). 176p. 2000. pap. 11.00 (0-375-70836-7) Vin Bks.

Monkeys & Apes. Sy Barlowe. (Learning about Ser.). pap. 1.00 (0-486-40018-2) Dover.

*__Monkeys & Apes.__ Gallimard Jeunesse. LC 98-18848. (First Discovery Book). (Illus.). 24p. (J). (ps-2). 1999. 12.95 (0-590-87610-4) Scholastic Inc.

Monkeys & Apes. K. W. Lumley. LC 82-12779. (New True Books Ser.). (Illus.). 48p. (J). (gr. k-4). 1982. pap. 5.50 (0-516-41633-2) Childrens.

Monkeys & Apes. Joanne Mattern. LC 92-28080. (Illus.). 24p. (J). (gr. 4-7). 1992. pap. text 1.95 (0-8167-2962-X) Troll Communs.

Monkeys & Apes A Portrait of the Animal World, 1. Paul Sterry. 1998. pap. text 10.98 (1-880908-24-7) Todtri Prods.

Monkeys & Apes of the World. Rita Goldman Gelman. LC 88-34550. (Illus.). 32p. (J). (gr. 5-8). 1990. lib. bdg. 24.00 (0-531-10749-3) Watts.

Monkeys & the Mango Tree: Teaching Stories of the Saints & Sadhus of India. Harish Johari. LC 97-38921. (Illus.). 144p. 1997. pap. 12.95 (0-89281-564-7) Inner Tradit.

Monkeys, Apes & Other Primates. Tr. by Vicki Bogard from FRE. LC 89-5378. (Young Discovery Library). (Illus.). 38p. (J). (ps-3). 1989. 5.95 (0-944589-26-X, 026) Young Discovery Lib.

Monkeys, Apes & Other Primates. Lynn Bromley. (Illus.). 64p. 1981. pap. 3.95 (0-88388-069-5) Bellerophon Bks.

Monkeys Are a Lot Like Us. Allan Fowler et al. LC 95-5564. (Rookie Read-About Science Ser.). (Illus.). 32p. (J). (ps-3). 1995. lib. bdg. 18.50 (0-516-06040-6) Childrens.

Monkeys Are a Lot Like Us. Allan Fowler. (Rookie Read-About Science Ser.). (Illus.). 32p. (J). (ps-2). 1996. reprint ed. pap. 4.95 (0-516-46040-4) Childrens.

Monkey's Bridge: Mysteries of Evolution in Central America. David R. Wallace. 277p. 1999. pap. 14.00 (1-57805-018-9, Pub. by Sierra) Random.

Monkey's Constitution. Duncan Brown. LC 97-68483. (Illus.). 88p. (J). (gr. 4-8). 1997. pap. 7.95 (1-57960-030-1) Disc Enter Ltd.

Monkey's Face. Penny Harter. 36p. 1987. pap. 3.00 (0-89120-031-2) From Here.

Monkeys from Asia & Africa. Patricia A. Martin. LC 99-17064. (Illus.). 48p. (gr. 3-5). 2000. 21.50 (0-516-21573-6) Childrens.

Monkeys from Central & South America Patricia A. Martin. LC 99-17063. (Illus.). 48p. (gr. 3-5). 2000. 21.50 (0-516-21574-4) Childrens.

Monkey's Haircut: And Other Stories Told by the Maya. Ed. by John Bierhorst. LC 85-28471. (Illus.). 160p. (J). (gr. 5 up). 1986. 16.00 (0-688-04269-4, Wm Morrow) Morrow Avon.

Monkey's Mask. Dorothy Porter. (Mask Noir Title Ser.). 256p. 1997. pap. text 14.99 (1-85242-549-0) Serpents Tail.

Monkey's Mask: An Erotic Murder Mystery by Dorothy Porter. Dorothy Porter. LC 95-17755. 272p. 1995. 19.45 (1-55970-304-0, Pub. by Arcade Pub Inc) Time Warner.

Monkeys of Arashiyama: 35 Years of Research in Japan & the West. Ed. by Linda M. Fedigan & Pamela J. Asquith. LC 90-9918. 353p. (C). 1991. pap. text 24.95 (0-7914-0553-2) State U NY Pr.

*__Monkeys of Asia & Africa.__ Patricia A. Fink Martin. (True Bks.). (Illus.). 48p. (J). (gr. 3-5). 2000. pap. 6.95 (0-516-27016-8) Childrens.

*__Monkeys of Central & South America.__ Patricia A. Fink Martin. (True Bks.). (Illus.). 48p. (J). (gr. 3-5). 2000. pap. 6.95 (0-516-27017-6) Childrens.

Monkeys of the Mesquite: The Social Life of the American Snow Monkey. Mary McDonald-Pavelka. 128p. (C). 1995. pap. text, per. 14.95 (0-8403-8986-8) Kendall-Hunt.

Monkey's Paw. W. W. Jacobs. (Classic Frights Ser.). 1997. 11.05 (0-606-13616-9, Pub. by Turtleback) Demco.

Monkey's Paw. W. W. Jacobs. (J). 1999. 6.20 (0-606-12427-6) Turtleback.

Monkey's Paw. W. W. Jacobs. (Classic Frights Ser.). (Illus.). 64p. (J). (gr. 3 up). 1997. reprint ed. pap. 5.95 (0-929605-65-9) Books of Wonder.

Monkey's Paw. rev. ed. W. W. Jacobs. (Read-Along Radio Dramas Ser.). (J). (gr. 6-10). 1983. reprint ed. ring bd. 38.00 (1-878298-02-X) Balance Pub.

Monkey's Paw: A Facsimile & Transcript of the Original Manuscript. W. W. Jacobs. Ed. by John Jascoll. LC 98-70029. (Illus.). 151p. 1998. write for info. (0-9643012-8-8) Hazelwood Pr.

Monkey's Paw: New Chronicles from Peru. Robin Kirk. LC 97-16068. (Illus.). 232p. 1997. 45.00 (1-55849-108-2); pap. 16.95 (1-55849-109-0) U of Mass Pr.

Monkey's Paw & Other Great Ghost Stories, Boxed Set. Ed. by John Grafton. (Illus.). (J). 1997. pap. text, boxed set 6.95 incl. audio (0-486-29618-0, 29618-0) Dover.

Monkey's Raincoat. Robert Crais. 201p. 1992. reprint ed. mass mkt. 6.50 (0-553-27585-2) Bantam.

Monkey's Raincoat (Sarumino) Linked Poetry of the Basho School with Haiku Selections. Matsu Basho et al. Tr. by Lenore Mayhew from JPN. LC 85-51629. (Illus.). 151p. 1985. 9.95 (0-8048-1500-3) Tuttle Pubng.

Monkey's Trick. Houghton Mifflin Company Staff. (Literature Experience 1991 Ser.). (J). (gr. 2). 1990. pap. 9.48 (0-395-55144-7) HM.

Monkey's Trick. Houghton Mifflin Company Staff. (Literature Experience 1993 Ser.). (J). (gr. 2). 1992. pap. 9.48 (0-395-61771-5) HM.

Monkey's Wrench. Primo Levi. Tr. by Ruth Feldman. (Twentieth-Century Classics Ser.). 176p. 1995. pap. 12.95 (0-14-018892-4, Penguin Classics) Viking Penguin.

Monkeyshines Goes Buggy: The Study of Entomology. Phyllis B. Goldman. (Illus.). (J). 1992. pap. 18.95 (0-9620900-3-4) Monkeyshines.

Monkeyshines on Ancient Cultures. Ed. by Phyllis Goldman. (Illus.). 160p. (J). 2000. 30.95 (1-888325-12-7) Monkeyshines.

Monkeyshines on Art & Great Artists. 1996. 26.95 (1-888325-00-3) Monkeyshines.

Monkeyshines on Canada, the Great White North Culture, History, Facts. Ed. by Phyllis B. Goldman. (Illus.). 144p. (Orig.). 1994. pap. 26.95 (0-9620900-5-0) Monkeyshines.

Monkeyshines on Central & South America. 1995. 26.95 (0-9620900-9-3) Monkeyshines.

Monkeyshines on Customs & Cultures from Around the World. (Illus.). 160p. (J). (gr. 4 up). 1997. pap. 26.95 (1-888325-03-8) Monkeyshines.

Monkeyshines on Europe. Phylis Goldman. (Illus.). 225p. (J). (gr. 5-8). 1998. pap. 32.95 (1-888325-08-9) Monkeyshines.

Monkeyshines on Fossils... Mysteries of the Past. Phyllis B. Goldman. (Illus.). 1999. pap. 26.95 (1-888325-05-4) Monkeyshines.

Monkeyshines on Great American Authors. 1997. 28.95 (1-888325-02-X) Monkeyshines.

Monkeyshines on Great Inventors. 1997. 26.95 (1-888325-04-6) Monkeyshines.

Monkeyshines on How Are Things with You. Phyllis B. Goldman. (Illus.). (J). 1995. pap. 12.95 (0-9620900-8-5) Monkeyshines.

Monkeyshines on How Are Things with You. Phyllis B. Goldman. (Illus.). (J). 1995. pap. 16.95 incl. cd-rom (1-888325-16-X) Monkeyshines.

Monkeyshines on How the Fifty States Were Named. Ed. by Phyllis B. Goldman. (Illus.). 118p. (Orig.). (YA). 1993. pap. 18.95 (0-9620900-4-2) Monkeyshines.

Monkeyshines on Mexico - Land of Legends. Ed. by Phyllis B. Goldman. (Illus.). 138p. (Orig.). 1995. pap. 26.95 (0-9620900-7-7) Monkeyshines.

Monkeyshines on Music & Great Musicians. 1996. 26.95 (1-888325-01-1) Monkeyshines.

*__Monkeyshines on Rocks & Minerals.__ (Illus.). 115p. (J). (ps-7). 2000. pap. 26.95 (1-888325-14-3) Monkeyshines.

Monkeyshines on Strange & Wonderful Facts. Phyllis B. Goldman. (Illus.). 116p. (Orig.). (J). (ps-8). 1991. pap. 18.95 (0-9620900-2-6) Monkeyshines.

Monkeyshines on the Primates: The Study of Primatology. Phyllis B. Goldman. (Illus.). (J). 1995. pap. 18.95 (0-9620900-6-9) Monkeyshines.

Monkeyshines on the U. S. A. in Spanish & English. (ENG., Illus.). (J). (gr. 4 up). 1997. pap. 26.95 (1-888325-06-2) Monkeyshines.

Monkeyshines on the United States Government. (Illus.). 112p. (J). (gr. 4 up). 1997. pap. 26.95 (1-888325-07-0) Monkeyshines.

An Asterisk (*) at the beginning of an entry indicates that the title is appearing for the first time.

Monkeyshines on the United States Presidents: Games, Puzzles, & Trivia. Ed. by Phyllis B. Goldman. (Illus.). 97p. (J). (gr. 4 up). 1990. pap. 18.95 (*0-9620900-1-8*) Monkeyshines.

Monkeyshines on World Holidays & Festivals. Phyllis Goldman. (Illus.). 135p. (J). 1998. pap. 26.95 (*1-888325-09-7*) Monkeyshines.

Monkeytalia: Monkeying Around with the ABCs. Marilyn Bollinger. (Magic Touch Talking Bks.). (Illus.). 22p. (J). (ps-2). 1996. 19.99 (*1-888208-05-8*) Hasbro.

Monkfish Moon. Romesh Gunesekera. LC 92-50841. 144p. 1993. 16.95 (*1-56584-077-1*, Pub. by New Press NY) Norton.

Monkfish Moon. Romesh Guneskara. LC 95-47305. 144p. 1996. pap. 11.00 (*1-57322-550-9*, Riverhd Trade) Berkley Pub.

Monkfish Moon: Short Stories. Romesh Gunesekera. 144p. 1995. pap. 10.00 (*1-56584-078-X*, Pub. by New Press NY) Norton.

Monki et el Grand Oiseau Blanc. Serena Romanelli. (FRE., Illus.). (J). (gr. k-3). pap. 15.95 (*3-314-21087-6*, Pub. by North-South Bks NYC) Chronicle Bks.

Monklands: An Illustrated Architectural Guide. Allan Peden. (Illus.). 88p. (C). 1992. pap. 40.00 (*1-873190-05-0*, Pub. by Rutland Pr) St Mut.

Monks & Laymen in Byzantium, 843-1118. Rosemary Morris. (Illus.). 252p. (C). 1995. text 69.95 (*0-521-26558-4*) Cambridge U Pr.

Monks & Magicians: Religious Biographies in Asia. Ed. by Phyllis Granoff & Koichi Shinohara. 268p. 1996. 29.95 (*0-88962-413-5*); pap. 14.95 (*0-88962-412-7*) Mosaic.

Monks & Monasteries of the Egyptian Deserts. rev. ed. Otto F. Meinardus. 200p. 1989. pap. 20.00 (*977-424-188-6*, Pub. by Am Univ Cairo Pr) Col U Pr.

***Monks & Nuns, Saints & Outcasts: Religion in Medieval Society: Essays in Honor of Lester K. Little.** Lester K. Little et al. LC 99-56454. 2000. pap. 21.95 (*0-8014-8656-4*) Cornell U Pr.

Monks, Bards & Thieves. TSR Hobbies STaff. 1983. 10.00 (*0-394-53614-2*) Random.

Monk's Confession: The Memoirs of Guibert of Nogent. Paul J. Archambault. LC 95-11479.Tr. of De Vita Sua. 248p. 1995. pap. 14.95 (*0-271-01482-2*) Pa St U Pr.

Monk's Confession: The Memoirs of Guibert of Nogent. Paul J. Archambault & Guibert of Nogent. LC 95-11479.Tr. of De Vita Sua. 248p. 1995. 40.00 (*0-271-01481-4*) Pa St U Pr.

Monk's Dream. James Harpur. LC 97-154768. 62p. 1997. pap. 15.95 (*0-85646-278-0*, Pub. by Anvil Press) Dufour.

Monk's Fans: A Unique Religious Art Form. Natthapatra Chandauij. (Illus.). 312p. 1996. 65.00 (*974-8225-13-5*, Pub. by River Books) Weatherhill.

Monks, Hermits & Crusaders in Medieval Europe. Giles Constable. (Collected Studies: No. CS273). 346p. (C). 1988. reprint ed. lib. bdg. 108.95 (*0-86078-221-2*, Pub. by Variorum) Ashgate Pub Co.

Monk's Hollow. large type ed. John Marsh. (Dales Large Print Ser.). 293p. 1997. pap. 18.99 (*1-85389-782-5*, Dales) Ulverscroft.

Monk's Hood. Ellis Peters. 224p. 1992. mass mkt. 5.99 (*0-446-40300-8*, Pub. by Warner Bks) Little.

Monk's Hood: The Third Chronicle of Brother Cadfael. large type ed. Ellis Peters. LC 97-1199. 1997. pap. 23.95 (*0-7862-1073-7*) Thorndike Pr.

Monks in the Modern World: The Monks of Mount Angel Abbey. Joachim McCann. (Illus.). 105p. (Orig.). 1993. pap. 15.95 (*1-884563-00-7*) Canyon Creat.

Monk's Magic. Alexander De Comeau. Ed. by R. Reginald & Douglas Melville. LC 77-84213. (Lost Race & Adult Fantasy Ser.). 1978. reprint ed. lib. bdg. 24.95 (*0-405-10968-7*) Ayer.

Monks, Nuns, & Friars in Medieval Society, No. 4. Edward B. King. Ed. by Jacqueline T. Schaefer & William B. Wadley. LC 82-50575. (Illus.). 188p. (Orig.). 1989. pap. 20.00 (*0-918769-23-X*) Univ South Pr.

Monks of Kublai Khan, Emperor of China. E. A. Wallis Budge. LC 71-38051. reprint ed. 55.00 (*0-404-56905-6*) AMS Pr.

Monks of Redon: Gesta Sanctorum Rotonensium & Vita Conuuoionis. Ed. by Caroline Brett. (Studies in Celtic History: No. X). (ENG & LAT.). 270p. 1989. 75.00 (*0-85115-504-9*) Boydell & Brewer.

Monks of the West from St. Benedict to St. Bernard, 6 vols., Set. Charles Montalembert, pseud. LC 03-11386. reprint ed. 410.00 (*0-404-04410-7*) AMS Pr.

Monks of War: The Military Religious Orders. Desmond Seward. 400p. 1996. pap. 13.95 (*0-14-019501-7*, Arkana) Viking Penguin.

Monks Pond: Thomas Merton's Little Magazine. Ed. by Thomas Merton. LC 89-8918. (Illus.). 368p. 1989. 40.00 (*0-8131-1694-5*) U Pr of Ky.

Monk's Reflections: A View From the Dome. Edward A. Malloy. LC 99-21803. 256p. 1999. 19.95 (*0-7407-0116-9*) Andrews & McMeel.

Monks, Spies & a Soldier of Fortune: The Japanese in Tibet. Scott Berry. LC 94-28744. 352p. 1995. text 59.95 (*0-312-12398-1*) St Martin.

Monk's Tale: A Biography of Godfrey Diekmann, O.S.B. Kathleen Hughes. 408p. (Orig.). 1991. pap. 18.95 (*0-8146-1984-3*) Liturgical Pr.

Monkshood. large type ed. Anne Mather. 283p. 1994. 27.99 (*0-7505-0602-4*, Pub. by Mgna Lrg Print) Ulverscroft.

Monmouth Beach & Sea Bright. Randall Gabrielan. (Images of America Ser.). (Illus.). 128p. 1998. pap. 16.99 (*0-7524-0813-5*) Arcadia Pubng.

Monmouth Cemeteries, 2 vols. in 1. A. M. Whiting. (Illus.). 66p. 1997. reprint ed. pap. 7.00 (*0-8328-5876-5*) Higginson Bk Co.

Monmouth County see Hagstrom Atlases

Monmouth County. Randall Gabrielan. (Images of America Ser.). (Illus.). 128p. 1998. pap. 16.99 (*0-7524-0995-6*) Arcadia Pubng.

Monmouth County, New Jersey: Families of Color in 1880. Compiled by Ellen Morris. (New Jersey, 1880: Afro-Americans & Native Americans Ser.). (Illus.). 134p. 1992. pap. 20.00 (*0-317-04688-8*) Morris Genealog Lib.

***Monmouth County New Jersey Deeds: Books A,B,C & D.** Richard S. Hutchinson. 162p. 2000. pap. 26.88 (*0-7884-1479-8*, 1479) Heritage Bk.

Monmouth County the Sharkriver District, Monmouth County & Genealogies of Chambers, Corlies, Drummond, Morris, Potter, Shafto, Webley & White. George C. Martin. (Illus.). 99p. 1997. reprint ed. pap. 16.00 (*0-8328-6058-1*) Higginson Bk Co.

Monmouth Court: Boston. Doris Pritchard. LC 81-3589. (Illus.). 1981. 15.00 (*0-87233-064-8*) Bauhan.

Monmouth Dine-a-Mate Book. 288p. 1996. pap. text 30.00 (*1-57393-056-3*) Dine-A-Mate.

Monmouth, NJ Dine-a-Mate. Ed. by Andrea Paradis & Margo Wiper. (Illus.). 272p. 1994. pap. 25.00 (*0-614-03521-X*) Dine-A-Mate.

Monna Vanna. Maurice Maeterlinck. (FRE.). 186p. 1967. reprint ed. pap. write for info. (*0-7859-4686-1*) Fr & Eur.

Monna Vanna: A Play in Three Acts. Maurice Maeterlinck. Tr. by Alexis I. Coleman from FRE. LC 93-10174. 102p. 1993. reprint ed. pap. 11.95 (*1-56114-166-6*) Second Renaissance.

Monnaie et Finances a Byzance: Analyses, Techniques. Cecile Morrisson. (Collected Studies: CS 461). 352p. 1994. 115.95 (*0-86078-401-0*, Pub. by Variorum) Ashgate Pub Co.

Monnaies Francaises, 1991. Victor Gadoury. (FRE.). 320p. 1992. 75.00 (*0-8288-7232-5*, 290660206X) Fr & Eur.

Monnaies Grecques. Friedrich Imhoof-Blumer. 518p. reprint ed. write for info. (*0-318-71358-6*) G Olms Pubs.

Monnaies Grecques Antiques et Imperiales Romaines. R. Jameson. (FRE.). 1007p. 1980. reprint ed. 295.00 (*0-916710-65-3*) Obol Intl.

Monnaies Royales de France Sous la Race Carolingienne, 2 vols., Set. Ernest Gariel. 526p. 1974. reprint ed. write for info. (*3-487-05228-8*) G Olms Pubs.

Monne, Outrages et Defis. Ahmaadou Kourouma. (FRE.). 1992. pap. 14.95 (*0-7859-2728-X*, 2020146290) Fr & Eur.

Monnet & the Americans: The Father of a United Europe & His U. S. Supporters. rev. ed. Ed. by Clifford P. Hackett. LC 94-48830. 288p. (C). 1995. 34.95 (*0-9642541-0-7*); pap. 17.95 (*0-9642541-1-5*) Am Coun J Monnet.

Monnew. Ahmadou Kourouma. Tr. by Nidra Poller. LC 92-11224. 272p. 1993. 25.00 (*1-56279-027-7*) Mercury Hse Inc.

Monnew. Ahmadou Kourouma. Tr. by Nidra Poller. LC 93-40234. 272p. 1994. reprint ed. pap. 13.95 (*1-56279-058-7*) Mercury Hse Inc.

Mono: A Collection of Dark Fiction. unabridged ed. Len Rely. 198p. 1998. pap. 14.95 (*1-892896-22-2*) Buy Books.

Mono-Alu Folklore: Bougainville Strait, Western Solomon Islands. G. C. Wheeler. LC 70-174374. 1977. reprint ed. 30.95 (*0-405-09065-X*) Ayer.

Mono Basin Geology. Timothy Tierney. (Field Guide Ser.). (Illus.). 56p. 1995. pap. text 3.95 (*0-939716-08-9*) Mono Lake Comm.

Mono Diggings. Frank S. Wedertz. LC 78-1839. 1978. pap. 12.95 (*0-912494-28-X*) Commun Print.

Mono Gramatico see Monkey Grammarian

Mono Lake: Mirror of Imagination. Mark A. Schlenz. (Illus.). 96p. 1996. 29.95 (*0-944197-45-0*); pap. 16.95 (*0-944197-44-2*) Companion CA.

Mono Lake: Stories. Martha C. Cummings. LC 95-68710. 172p. 1995. pap. 8.95 (*0-9646201-2-X*) Rowbarge Pr.

Mono Lake: Twenty Postcards. Dennis Flaherty. (Illus.). 48p. (Orig.). 1995. pap. 8.95 (*0-944197-38-8*) Companion CA.

Mono Lake Guidebook. 4th ed. David Gaines. LC 89-60858. (Illus.). 104p. (Orig.). 1989. pap. 8.95 (*0-939716-01-1*) Mono Lake Comm.

Mono Lake Viewpoint. David Carle. (Illus.). 136p. (Orig.). 1993. pap. 5.00 (*0-932347-06-1*) Artemisia Pr.

Mono-Olefins: Chemistry & Technology. H. Asinger. 1968. 513.00 (*0-08-011547-0*, Pub. by Pergamon Repr) Franklin.

Monoamine Oxidase: Basic & Clinical Aspects. Ed. by H. Yasuhara et al. 256p. 1993. 137.50 (*90-6764-146-4*) Coronet Bks.

Monoamine Oxidase & Its Inhibition. CIBA Foundation Staff. LC 76-10396. (CIBA Foundation Symposium: New Ser.: No. 39). 427p. reprint ed. pap. 132.40 (*0-608-14595-5*, 202216700024) Bks Demand.

Monoamine Oxidase & Its Selective Inhibitors. Ed. by H. Beckmann & P. Riederer. (Modern Problems of Pharmacopsychiatry Ser.: Vol. 19). (Illus.). x, 354p. 1983. 172.25 (*3-8055-3595-3*) S Karger.

Monoamine Oxidase Inhibitors: Proceedings of the Collegium Internationale Neuro-Psychopharnacologicum,12th Congress, Gothenberg, 1980. Collegium Internationale Neuro-Psychopharmacologic. Ed. by M. B. Youdim & E. S. Paykel. LC 80-41258. (Wiley-Interscience Publications). 232p. reprint ed. pap. 72.00 (*0-608-13105-9*, 205210100033) Bks Demand.

Monoamine Oxidase Inhibitors in Neurological Diseases. Ed. by Lieberman et al. (Neurological Disease & Therapy Ser.: Vol. 21). (Illus.). 400p. 1994. text 165.00 (*0-8247-9082-0*) Dekker.

Monoamine Oxidases - New Vistas. fac. ed. Ed. by E. Costa & M. Sandler. LC 72-192861. (Advances in Biochemical Psychopharmacology Ser.: No. 5). (Illus.). 464p. pap. 143.90 (*0-7837-7537-7*, 204696700005) Bks Demand.

Monobenzine Hydrocarbons Derivatives with Functional Groups see Rodd's Chemistry of Carbon Compounds

Monocacy. Alfred S. Roe. Ed. by Jerry L. Harlowe. Orig. Title: Monocacy: A Sketch of the Battle of Monocacy, Maryland. 64p. 1996. pap. 9.95 (*0-9612670-5-4*) Toomey Pr.

Monocacy: The Battle That Saved Washington. B. Franklin Cooling. LC 97-6135. (Illus.). 333p. 1997. 34.95 (*1-57249-032-2*) White Mane Pub.

***Monocacy: The Battle That Saved Washington.** B. Franklin Cooling. (Illus.). 335p. 2000. pap. 19.95 (*1-57249-229-5*) White Mane Pub.

Monocacy: A Sketch of the Battle of Monocacy, Maryland see Monocacy

Monocacy Cemetery Beallsville Maryland. Elizabeth R. Frain. 337p. 1997. pap. 30.00 (*1-888265-22-1*) Willow Bend.

Monocarbocyclic Compounds to & Including Five Ring Atoms see Rodd's Chemistry of Carbon Compounds

Monocarbonyl Derivatives of Aliphatic Hydrocarbons, Analogues & Derivatives see Rodd's Chemistry of Carbon Compounds

***Monochord: Versuchsinstrument zur quantitativen Erklarung von Tonsystemen.** Franz Naf. 1999. 29.95 (*3-906763-30-7*, Pub. by P Lang) P Lang Pubng.

Monochrome: The Readercon Anthology. Bryan Cholfin. LC 95-176810. 157 p. 1990. pap. write for info. (*0-9623824-3-4*) Broken Mirrors Pr.

Monochrome: The Readercon Anthology. Ed. by Bryan Cholfin. 160p. 1990. 25.00 (*0-9623824-2-6*); pap. 9.95 (*0-685-50105-1*) Broken Mirrors Pr.

Monochrome Porcelain of the Ch'ing Dynasty. (Collections of the National Palace Museum, Taipei). (CHI & ENG., Illus.). 164p. 1994. boxed set 45.00 (*957-562-088-7*) Heian Intl.

***Monochrome Porcelains.** (Illus.). 1999. 99.95 (*962-07-5230-9*, Pub. by Commercial Pr) Cheng & Tsui.

Monoclonal Antibodies. Ed. by Peter Allen. 300p. 1988. pap. 1795.00 (*0-941285-26-X*) FIND-SVP.

Monoclonal Antibodies. Ed. by Peter C. Beverley. LC 85-19512. (Illus.). 352p. 1986. 132.00 (*0-443-02990-3*) Church.

***Monoclonal Antibodies.** H. Zoladek. (Basics Ser.). (Illus.). 168p. 1999. pap. 34.95 (*0-387-91590-7*) Spr-Verlag.

Monoclonal Antibodies: A Manual of Techniques. Heddy Zola. 232p. 1987. boxed set 239.00 (*0-8493-6476-0*) CRC Pr.

***Monoclonal Antibodies: A Practical Approach.** Ed. by Phil S. Shepherd & Chris Dean. LC 99-59426. No. 227. (Illus.). 512p. 2000. text 160.00 (*0-19-963723-7*); pap. text 90.00 (*0-19-963722-9*) OUP.

Monoclonal Antibodies: A Practical Guide. Ed. by J. H. Peters & H. Baumgarten. LC 92-30163. (Laboratory Ser.). (Illus.). 480p. 1992. 74.95 (*0-387-50843-0*) Spr-Verlag.

Monoclonal Antibodies: Principles & Applications. Ed. by J. R. Birch & E. S. Lennox. 344p. 1995. 110.00 (*0-471-05147-0*) Wiley.

Monoclonal Antibodies: Principles & Practice. 3rd ed. James W. Goding. (Illus.). 512p. 1996. text 49.95 (*0-12-287023-9*) Acad Pr.

Monoclonal Antibodies: Production, Engineering & Clinical Application. Ed. by Mary A. Ritter & Heather M. Ladyman. (Postgraduate Medical Science Ser.: No. 2). (Illus.). 496p. (C). 1995. pap. text 47.95 (*0-521-42503-4*) Cambridge U Pr.

Monoclonal Antibodies: Standardization of Their Characteristization & Use. Ed. by W. Hennessen. (Developments in Biological Standardization Ser.: Vol. 57). (Illus.). xii, 430p. 1985. pap. 61.00 (*3-8055-3971-1*) S Karger.

Monoclonal Antibodies: The Second Generation. Heddy Zola. (Illus.). 250p. 1994. 137.50 (*1-872748-78-3*, Pub. by Bios Sci) Coronet Bks.

Monoclonal Antibodies & Breast Cancer. Ed. by Roberto L. Ceriani. (Developments in Oncology Ser.). 1985. text 127.00 (*0-89838-739-6*) Kluwer Academic.

Monoclonal Antibodies & Functional Cell Lines: Progress & Applications. Ed. by Roger H. Kennett et al. LC 84-4877. 444p. 1984. 95.00 (*0-306-41567-4*, Plenum Trade) Perseus Pubng.

Monoclonal Antibodies & T Cell Products. David H. Katz. LC 81-21604. 184p. 1982. 110.00 (*0-8493-6580-5*, QR186) Franklin.

Monoclonal Antibodies, Cytokines & Arthritis: Mediators of Inflammation & Therapy. Ed. by Thomas Kresina. (Inflammatory Disease & Therapy Ser.: Vol. 7). (Illus.). 512p. 1991. text 225.00 (*0-8247-8116-3*) Dekker.

Monoclonal Antibodies for Therapy, Prevention & in Vivo Diagnosis of Human Disease. Ed. by H. Van de Donk & W. Hennessen. (Developments in Biological Standardization Ser.: Vol. 71). (Illus.). xiv, 248p. 1990. pap. 61.00 (*3-8055-5115-0*) S Karger.

Monoclonal Antibodies in Biotechnology: Theoretical & Practical Aspects. Kenneth C. McCullough. Ed. by Raymond E. Spier. (Cambridge Studies in Biotechnology: No. 8). (Illus.). 399p. (C). 1990. text 115.00 (*0-521-25890-1*) Cambridge U Pr.

Monoclonal Antibodies in Cancer. Ed. by Stewart Sell & Ralph A. Reisfeld. LC 85-4735. (Contemporary Biomedicine Ser.: Vol. 6). 428p. 1985. 99.50 (*0-89603-068-7*) Humana.

Monoclonal Antibodies in Cardiovascular Diseases. Ban A. Khaw et al. LC 93-8769. (Illus.). 325p. 1993. text 115.00 (*0-8121-1611-9*) Lppncott W & W.

Monoclonal Antibodies in Clinical Medicine. Ed. by A. McMichael & J. Fabre. 1982. text 157.00 (*0-12-485580-6*) Acad Pr.

Monoclonal Antibodies in Drug Development. Ed. by J. Thomas August. (Illus.). 237p. (Orig.). 1982. 24.00 (*0-9609094-0-0*) Am Phar & Ex.

Monoclonal Antibodies in Endocrine Research. Ed. by Robert E. Fellows & George S. Eisenbarth. LC 81-15854. (Illus.). 212p. 1981. pap. 65.80 (*0-608-00636-X*, 206122400007) Bks Demand.

Monoclonal Antibodies in Immunoscintigraphy. Jean-Francois Chantal. (Illus.). 440p. 1989. boxed set 259.00 (*0-8493-4716-5*, RC78) CRC Pr.

Monoclonal Antibodies in Transplantation. Lucienne Chatenoud. LC 95-24139. (Medical Intelligence Unit Ser.). 181p. 1995. 89.00 (*1-57059-269-1*) Landes Bioscience.

Monoclonal Antibodies in Tumor Therapy: Present Stage, Chances & Limitations. Ed. by Louis A. Kuhlmann et al. (Contributions to Oncology Ser.: Vol. 32). (Illus.). x, 178p. 1988. 51.50 (*3-8055-4763-3*) S Karger.

Monoclonal Antibodies Markets. (Market Research Reports: No. 570). 111p. 1995. 995.00 (*0-614-14197-4*) Theta Corp.

Monoclonal Antibodies Therapy. Ed. by H. Waldmann. (Progress in Allergy Ser.: Vol. 45). (Illus.). x, 174p. 1988. 120.00 (*3-8055-4803-6*) S Karger.

Monoclonal Antibodies to Neural Antigens. Ed. by Ronald McKay et al. LC 81-10185. (Cold Spring Harbor Reports in the Neurosciences: No. 2). 300p. reprint ed. pap. 93.00 (*0-7837-2085-8*, 204235900004) Bks Demand.

Monoclonal Antibodies to Receptors: Probes for Receptor Structure & Function. Ed. by M. Greaves. (Receptors & Recognition Series B: Vol. 17). 250p. (C). 1984. text 75.00 (*0-412-25330-5*, 9015) Chapman & Hall.

Monoclonal Antibody & Immunosensor Technology. A. M. Campbell. (Laboratory Techniques in Biochemistry & Molecular Biology Ser.: Vol. 23). xvii,428p. 1991. 213.00 (*0-444-81413-2*); pap. 76.50 (*0-444-81412-4*) Elsevier.

Monoclonal Antibody-Based Therapy of Cancer. Ed. by Michael L. Grossbard. LC 98-29118. (Illus.). 464p. 1998. text 185.00 (*0-8247-0196-8*) Dekker.

Monoclonal Antibody Markets. Market Intelligence Staff. 320p. 1994. 2295.00 (*0-7889-0057-9*) Frost & Sullivan.

Monoclonal Antibody Markets: Enormous Potential in Diagnostic & Therapeutic Products, Cancer Leads the Way. Market Intelligence Staff. 267p. (Orig.). 1992. 1995.00 (*1-56753-048-6*) Frost & Sullivan.

Monoclonal Antibody Production. Ed. by Shelley Minden. (Biomedical Library). 225p. 1996. pap. 795.00 (*1-57936-007-6*) IBC USA.

***Monoclonal Antibody Production.** National Research Council Staff. 74p. 1999. pap. 18.00 (*0-309-06447-3*) Natl Acad Pr.

Monoclonal Antibody Production Techniques & Applications. Ed. by Lawrence B. Schook. LC 86-29090. (Immunology Ser.: Vol. 33). 336p. 1987. reprint ed. pap. 104.20 (*0-608-04565-9*, 206530400001) Bks Demand.

Monoclonal Antibody Protocols. Ed. by William C. Davis. LC 95-13504. (Methods in Molecular Biology Ser.: Vol. 45). (Illus.). 274p. 1995. 79.50 (*0-89603-308-2*) Humana.

Monoclonal Antibody Purification. Ed. by Shelley Minden. (Biomedical Library). 1996. pap. 795.00 (*1-57936-020-3*) IBC USA.

Monoclonal Antibody Therapy of Human Cancer. Ed. by Kenneth F. Foon & Alton C. Morgan, Jr. (Development in Oncology Ser.). 1985. text 97.50 (*0-89838-754-X*) Kluwer Academic.

Monoclonal Hybridoma Antibodies: Techniques & Applications. Ed. by John G. Hurrell. 240p. 1982. 139.00 (*0-8493-6511-2*, QR186, CRC Reprint) Franklin.

Monoclonals & DNA Probes in Diagnostic & Preventive Medicine. Ed. by Robert C. Gallo et al. LC 85-31635. 256p. 1987. reprint ed. pap. 79.40 (*0-608-00325-5*, 206104200007) Bks Demand.

Monocotyledon: A Comparative Study. R. M. Dahlgren & H. T. Clifford. LC 81-67906. (Botanical Systematics Ser.: No. 2). 1982. text 209.00 (*0-12-200680-1*) Acad Pr.

Monocotyledoneae: Cat-Tails to Orchids. E. Lucy Braun. LC 66-25170. (Vascular Flora of Ohio Ser.: Vol. 1). (Illus.). 464p. 1967. text 60.00 (*0-8142-0028-1*) Ohio St U Pr.

Monocotyledons: A Morphological Study. Agnes Arber. (Illus.). 1961. reprint ed. 64.00 (*3-7682-0074-4*) Lubrecht & Cramer.

Monocotyledons: Systematics & Evolution, 2 vols. Ed. by P. J. Rudall et al. Incl. Vol. 1. xxii, 750p. 1995. (*0-947643-83-4*, Pub. by Royal Botnic Grdns); Vol. 2. xxii, 750p. 1995. (*0-947643-84-2*, Pub. by Royal Botnic Grdns); 1995. Set pap. 90.00 (*0-947643-85-0*, Pub. by Royal Botnic Grdns) Balogh.

Monocrotophos Health & Safety Guide. (Health & Safety Guides Ser.: No. 80). 36p. 1993. pap. text 5.00 (*92-4-151080-3*, 1860080) World Health.

Monoculture of the Mind: Perspectives on Biodiversity & Biotechnology. Vandana Shiva. 160p. (C). 1993. text 15.00 (*1-85649-218-4*, Pub. by Zed Books) St Martin.

Monodispersed Particles. T. Sugimoto. 1999. write for info. (*0-444-89569-8*) Elsevier.

Monodrama, Attitudes & Tableaux Vivants: Studies on Some Trends of Theatrical Fashion 1770-1815. Kirsten Gram-Holstrom. (Stockholm Studies in Theatrical History: No. 1). 278p. (Orig.). 1978. pap. 31.00 (*0-317-65803-4*) Coronet Bks.

Monodromy Groups of Isolated Singularities of Complete Intersections. W. Ebeling. (Lecture Notes in Mathematics Ser.: Vol. 1293). 153p. 1987. 35.95 (*0-387-18686-7*) Spr-Verlag.

Monofluorophosphate Perspectives. Ed. by P. Gron & Y. Ericsson. (Journal: Caries Research: Vol. 17, Suppl. 1). (Illus.). iv, 140p. 1983. pap. 38.50 (*3-8055-3793-X*) S Karger.

Monogamist. Christopher Kyle. 1996. pap. 5.25 (*0-8222-1525-X*) Dramatists Play.

Monogamy. Adam Phillips. LC 96-27857. 1997. 1.99 (*0-679-44264-2*) Pantheon.

Monogamy. Adam Phillips. 1999. pap. 11.00 (*0-679-77617-6*) Vin Bks.

Monogamy Myth: Your Personal Handbook for Recovering from Affairs. rev. ed. Peggy Vaughan. 224p. 1998. pap. 14.95 (*1-55704-353-1*, Pub. by Newmarket) Norton.

***Monogram Checklist: The Films of Monogram Pictures Corporation, 1931-1952.** Ted Okuda. LC 86-43089. (Illus.). 399p. 1999. per. 25.00 (*0-7864-0750-6*, McFarland Cls) McFarland & Co.

Monogram Checklist: The Films of Monogram Pictures Corporation, 1931-1958. Ted Okuda. LC 86-43089. (Illus.). 399p. 1987. lib. bdg. 29.95 (*0-89950-286-5*) McFarland & Co.

Monogramm Lexikon: Internationales Verzeichnis der Monogramme Bidlend. Goldstein. (GER.). 931p. 1964. 895.00 (*0-7859-8265-5*, 3110008734) Fr & Eur.

Monogramme Entworfen & Ausgef Uhrt see Two Thousand One Hundred Victorian Monograms

Monogrammlexikon 1. Franz Goldstein.Tr. of Dictionary of Monograms 1. 248p. 1998. 399.00 (*3-11-014453-0*) De Gruyter.

Monogrammlexikon 2 - Dictionary of Monograms 2: Internationales Verzeichnis der Monogramme Bildender Kuenstler des 19. und 20. Jahrhunderts/ International List of Monograms in the Visual Arts of the 19th & 20th Centuries. Ed. by Paul Pfisterer. (ENG & GER.). xx, 1067p. (C). 1998. lib. bdg. 425.35 (*3-11-014300-3*) De Gruyter.

Monograms & Alphabetic Devices. Hayward Cirker & Blanche Cirker. (Illus.). 226p. (Orig.). 1970. pap. 10.95 (*0-486-22330-2*) Dover.

Monograms & Ciphers. A. A. Turbayne. LC 68-55285. (Illus.). 136p. 1968. reprint ed. pap. 6.95 (*0-486-22182-2*) Dover.

Monograms & Decorations from the Art Nouveau Period. Ed. by Wilhelm Diebener. 1983. 16.50 (*0-8446-6007-8*) Peter Smith.

Monograms & Decorations from the Art Nouveau Period. Wilhelm Diebener. (Pictorial Archive Ser.). (Illus.). 144p. 1982. reprint ed. pap. 9.95 (*0-486-24347-8*) Dover.

Monograph. Gottfried Bechtold. (Illus.). 447p. 1997. 95.00 (*3-908162-58-0*) Dist Art Pubs.

Monograph - Shock Testing on Shakers by Using Digital Control. David O. Smallwood. 28p. 1986. pap. 50.00 (*0-915414-92-9*) IEST.

Monograph & Iconograph of the Characeae, 2 vols., Set. R. D. Wood & K. Imahori. 1965. 180.00 (*3-7682-0245-3*) Lubrecht & Cramer.

Monograph of Azaleas. Ernest Wilson & Alfred Rehder. LC 77-23265. (Illus.). 1977. reprint ed. 12.50 (*0-913728-22-5*) Theophrastus.

Monograph of Crocicreas: Ascomycetes, Helotiales, Helotiaceae. Steven E. Carpenter. LC 81-4025. (Memoirs Ser.: Vol. 33). (Illus.). 290p. 1981. pap. 26.50 (*0-89327-230-2*) NY Botanical.

Monograph of Desmanthus (Leguminosae-Mimosoideae) Melissa Luckow. Ed. by Christiane Anderson. (Systematic Botany Monographs: Vol. 38). (Illus.). 166p. 1993. pap. 20.00 (*0-912861-38-X*) Am Soc Plant.

Monograph of Favolaschia. R. Singer. 1974. 48.00 (*3-7682-5450-X*) Lubrecht & Cramer.

Monograph of Herknessia & Mastigospoella with Notes on Associated Teleomorphs. Raj T. Nag & F. DiCosmo. (Bibliotheca Mycologica Ser.: Vol. 80). (Illus.). 160p. 1981. text 40.00 (*3-7682-1300-5*) Lubrecht & Cramer.

Monograph of Kadsura (Schisandraceae) Richard M. Saunders. Ed. by Christiane Anderson. (Systematic Botany Monographs: Vol. 54). (Illus.). 106p. 1998. pap. 14.00 (*0-912861-54-1*) Am Soc Plant.

Monograph of Leochilus (Orchidaceae) Mark W. Chase. Ed. by Christiane Anderson. LC 86-22258. (Systematic Botany Monographs: Vol. 14). (Illus.). 97p. (Orig.). 1986. pap. 12.00 (*0-912861-14-2*) Am Soc Plant.

***Monograph of Leucaena (Leguminosae-Mimosoideae)** Colin Hughes. Ed. by Christiane Anderson. (Systematic Botany Monographs: Vol. 55). (Illus.). 244p. 1998. 32.00 (*0-912861-55-X*) Am Soc Plant.

Monograph of Living Chitons Vol. 4: Mollusca: Polyplacophora, Ischnochitonidae: Ischnochitoninad (Continued) Piet Kaas & Richard A. Van Belle. LC 88-1108. (Illus.). 298p. 1990. lib. bdg. 67.00 (*90-04-09259-5*) Brill Academic Pubs.

Monograph of Mecranium (Melastomataceae-Miconieae) James D. Skean, Jr. Ed. by Christiane Anderson. (Systematic Botany Monographs: Vol. 39). (Illus.). 116p. 1993. pap. 15.00 (*0-912861-39-8*) Am Soc Plant.

Monograph of Nymphaea Subgenus Hydrocallis (Nymphaeaceae) John H. Wiersema. Ed. by Christiane Anderson. (Systematic Botany Monographs: Vol. 16). (Illus.). 112p. (Orig.). 1987. pap. 13.50 (*0-912861-16-9*) Am Soc Plant.

***Monograph of Pictetia (Leguminosae-Papilionoideae) & Review of the Aeschynomeneae.** Angela Beyra M. & Matt Lavin. Ed. by Christiane Anderson. (Systematic Botany Monographs: Vol. 56). (Illus.). 93p. 1999. pap. 13.00 (*0-912861-56-8*) Am Soc Plant.

Monograph of Stigmaphyllon (Malpighiaceae) Christiane Anderson. Ed. by Thomas F. Daniel. (Systematic Botany Monographs: Vol. 51). (Illus.). 313p. 1997. 40.00 (*0-912861-51-7*) Am Soc Plant.

Monograph of the Birdwing Butterflies: The Systematics of Ornithoptera, Troides & Related Genera, Vol. 1: Ornithoptera. J. Haugum & A. M. Low. (Illus.). 308p. 1979. pap. 150.00 (*87-87491-18-4*) Lubrecht & Cramer.

Monograph of the Birdwing Butterflies Vol. 2: The Genera Trogonoptera, Ripponia & Troides, 3 pts. J. Haugum & A. M. Low. (Illus.). 356p. 1985. pap. 150.00 (*90-04-07761-8*) Lubrecht & Cramer.

Monograph of the British Lichens, 1918-1926, 2 vols., Set. 2nd ed. A. L. Smith. (Illus.). 1970. 110.00 (*90-6123-140-X*) Lubrecht & Cramer.

Monograph of the Choanephoraceae. Ed. by P. M. Kirk. (Mycological Papers: No. 152). 61p. (C). 1984. pap. text 22.00 (*0-00-000079-5*) C A B Intl.

Monograph of the Descent of the Family of Beebe. Clarence Beebe. (Illus.). 127p. 1988. reprint ed. pap. 25.00 (*0-8328-0225-5*); reprint ed. lib. bdg. 33.00 (*0-8328-0224-7*) Higginson Bk Co.

Monograph of the Eremolepidaceae. Job Kuijt. Ed. by Christiane Anderson. (Systematic Botany Monographs: Vol.18). (Illus.). (Orig.). 1988. pap. 8.00 (*0-912861-18-5*) Am Soc Plant.

Monograph of the Erysiphales (Powdery Mildews) Uwe Braun. (Nova Hedwigia, Beihefte/Supplementary Issues Ser.: Beih 89). (Illus.). 700p. 1987. pap. 199.00 (*3-443-51011-6*, Pub. by Gebruder Borntraeger) Balogh.

Monograph of the Fern Genus Platycerium (Polypodiaceae) E. Hennipman & M. C. Roos. (Verhandelingen der Koninklijke Nederlandse Akademie van Wetenschappen, Afd. Natuurkunde Ser.: No. 80). 126p. pap. 47.00 (*0-444-85569-6*) Elsevier.

Monograph of the Fern Genus Microsorum (Polypodiaceae) M. T. Bosman. (Leiden Botanical Ser.: Vol. 14). (Illus.). 161p. 1991. pap. 36.00 (*90-71236-09-9*, Pub. by Rijksherbarium) Balogh.

Monograph of the Fern Genus Pyrrosia. P. H. Hovenkamp. (Leiden Botanical Ser.: No. 9). (Illus.). 310p. 1986. pap. 31.00 (*90-04-08065-1*, Pub. by Rijksherbarium) Balogh.

Monograph of the Genera Dicranolejeunea & Acanthocoleus. R. C. Kruijt. Ed. by S. R. Gradstein. (Bryophytorum Bibliotheca: Vol. 36). (GER., Illus.). 136p. 1988. pap. 36.00 (*3-443-62008-6*, Pub. by Gebruder Borntraeger) Balogh.

Monograph of the Genus Alaria. K. Yendo. (Illus.). 1919. 48.00 (*3-7682-1066-9*) Lubrecht & Cramer.

Monograph of the Genus Anaptychia. S. Kurokawa. 1962. pap. 32.00 (*3-7682-5406-2*) Lubrecht & Cramer.

Monograph of the Genus Aponogeton: Aponogetonaceae. H. W. Van Bruggen. (Bibliotheca Botanica: Vol. 137). (GER., Illus.). viii, 76p. 1985. pap. 99.00 (*3-510-48008-2*, Pub. by E Schweizerbartsche) Balogh.

Monograph of the Genus Cerithium Bruguiere in the Indo-Pacific: Cerithiidae: Prosobranchia. Richard S. Houbrick. LC 91-11552. (Smithsonian Contributions to Zoology Ser.: No. 510). (Illus.). 215p. reprint ed. pap. 66.70 (*0-7837-3868-4*, 204369000010) Bks Demand.

Monograph of the Genus Gongora Ruiz & Pavon. Rudolf Jenny. (Illus.). 136p. 1993. reprint ed. 150.00 (*3-87429-332-7*, Pub. by Koeltz Sci Bks) Lubrecht & Cramer.

Monograph of the Genus Jubula Dumortier. W. R. Guerke. (Bryophytorum Bibliotheca Ser.: No. 17). (Illus.). 1979. pap. 40.00 (*3-7682-1213-0*) Lubrecht & Cramer.

Monograph of the Genus Lilaeopsis (Umbelliferae) James M. Affolter. Ed. by Christiane Anderson. LC 85-1291. (Systematic Botany Monographs: Vol. 6). (Illus.). 140p. (Orig.). 1985. pap. 18.00 (*0-912861-06-1*) Am Soc Plant.

Monograph of the Genus Saprolegnia. R. Seymour. (Illus.). 1970. 32.00 (*3-7682-0657-2*) Lubrecht & Cramer.

Monograph of the Ithomiidae Napeogenini (Lepidoptera), Pt. 4. R. M. Fox & H. G. Real. (Memoir Ser.: No. 15). (Illus.). 368p. 1971. 45.00 (*1-56665-013-5*) Assoc Pubs FL.

Monograph of the Lichen Family Megalospraceae. H. J. Sipman. (Bibliotheca Lichenologica Ser.: No. 18). (Illus.). 268p. 1983. text 80.00 (*3-7682-1354-4*) Lubrecht & Cramer.

Monograph of the Lichen Genus Dirinaria. D. D. Awasthi. 1975. 32.00 (*3-7682-0957-1*) Lubrecht & Cramer.

Monograph of the Marine Triclads. R. Sluys. (Illus.). 475p. (C). 1989. text 226.00 (*90-6191-872-3*, Pub. by A A Balkema) Ashgate Pub Co.

Monograph of the Maurandyinae (Scrophulariaceae-Antirrhinae) Wayne J. Elisens. Ed. by Christiane Anderson. LC 85-1266. (Systematic Botany Monographs: Vol. 5). (Illus.). 97p. (Orig.). 1985. pap. 12.00 (*0-912861-05-3*) Am Soc Plant.

Monograph of the Mexican & Central American Species of Trixis (Compositae) C. Anderson. (Memoirs Ser.: Vol. 22 (3)). (Illus.). 68p. 1972. pap. 8.00 (*0-89327-076-8*) NY Botanical.

Monograph of the Pheasants, Vol. 1. William Beebe. 1990. 50.00 (*0-486-26579-X*) Dover.

Monograph of the Pheasants, Vol. 2. William Beebe. 1990. 50.00 (*0-486-26580-3*) Dover.

Monograph of the Pyrenulaceae (Excluding Anthracothecium & Pyrenula) & the Requienellaceae, with Notes on the Pleomassariaceae, the Trypetheliaceae & Mycomicrothelia (Lichenized & Non-Lichenized Ascomycetes) Andre Aptroot. Ed. by Volkmar Wirth et al. (Bibliotheca Lichenologica: Vol. 44). (GER., Illus.). 178p. 1991. pap. 53.00 (*3-443-58023-8*, Pub. by Gebruder Borntraeger) Balogh.

Monograph of the Saxicolous Lecideoid Lichens of Australia: Excl. Tasmania. Gerhard Rambold. Ed. by Volkmar Wirth et al. (Bibliotheca Lichenologica: Vol. 34). (GER., Illus.). 345p. 1989. pap. 77.00 (*3-443-58013-0*, Pub. by Gebruder Borntraeger) Balogh.

Monograph of the Stipitate Steroid Fungi. Derek A. Reid. (Illus.). 1965. pap. 145.00 (*3-7682-5418-6*) Lubrecht & Cramer.

Monograph of the Tettigoniidae of Australia Vol. 1: The Tettigoniidae, with an Appendix by D. H. Colles. D. C. Rentz. (Illus.). 384p. 1985. lib. bdg. 70.00 (*0-685-25035-0*) Lubrecht & Cramer.

Monograph of the Work of McKim, Mead & White, 1879-1915. Intro. by Allan Greenberg & Michael George. (Illus.). 160p. 1991. pap., student ed. 14.95 (*0-8038-6775-1*) Archit CT.

Monograph of the Work of McKim, Mead & White, 1879-1915. McKim et al. LC 75-152624. 1972. 55.95 (*0-405-08770-5*, Pub. by Blom Pubns) Ayer.

Monograph of the Work of Mellor, Meigs & Howe. Owen Wister. 2000. 65.95 (*0-942655-11-7*, Pub. by Archit CT) Natl Bk Netwk.

Monograph of the Works of McKim, Mead & White, 1879-1915. Intro. by Paul Goldberger. (Quality Paperbacks Ser.). (Illus.). 405p. 1985. reprint ed. pap. 24.50 (*0-306-80240-6*) Da Capo.

Monograph of the World Species of Hypoxylon. Julian H. Miller. LC 61-15571. 250p. reprint ed. pap. 77.50 (*0-608-15797-X*, 203104600073) Bks Demand.

Monograph on Bamboo. D. N. Tawari. 510p. (C). 1992. pap. 450.00 (*81-7089-176-0*, Pub. by Intl Bk Distr) St Mut.

Monograph on Chir Pine (Pinus Roxburghil Sarg.) Ed. by D. N. Tewari. 311p. 1994. pap. 225.00 (*81-7089-205-8*, Pub. by Intl Bk Distr) St Mut.

Monograph on Dalbergia Sissoo. D. N. Tewari. 316p. 1994. pap. 213.00 (*81-7089-171-X*, Pub. by Intl Bk Distr) St Mut.

Monograph on Dengue-Dengue Haemorrhagic Fever. Compiled by P. Thongcharoen. (WHO Regional Publications: No. 22). ix, 163p. 1994. pap. text 15.00 (*92-9022-124-0*, 1560022) World Health.

Monograph on Deodar (Cedrus Deodara Roxb. G. Dan) D. N. Tewari. 200p. 1994. pap. 214.00 (*81-7089-210-4*, Pub. by Intl Bk Distr) St Mut.

Monograph on J. Steuart Curry. write for info. (*0-87413-235-5*) U Delaware Pr.

Monograph on Khair, Acacia Catechu, Wield. D. N. Tewari. 127p. 1994. pap. 150.00 (*81-7089-218-X*, Pub. by Intl Bk Distr) St Mut.

Monograph on Neem. D. N. Tewari. 287p. 1992. pap. 270.00 (*81-7089-175-2*, Pub. by Intl Bk Distr) St Mut.

Monograph on Plectognath Fishes of the Superfamily Triacanthoidea. James C. Tyler. (Monograph: No. 16). (Illus.). 364p. 1968. lib. bdg. 15.00 (*0-910006-24-5*) Acad Nat Sci Phila.

Monograph on Polyporaceae of India. Anjali Roy. LC 96-904929. 1996. pap. 163.00 (*81-7089-213-9*, Pub. by Intl Bk Distr) St Mut.

Monograph on Rosewood. D. N. Tewari. LC 97-905421. 1995. pap. 85.00 (*81-7089-230-9*, Pub. by Intl Bk Distr) St Mut.

Monograph on Sal (Shorea Robusta Gaertn. F.) D. N. Tewari. 276p. 1995. pap. 190.00 (*81-7089-217-1*, Pub. by Intl Bk Distr) St Mut.

***Monograph on Silver Oak (Grevillea Robusta)** Ed. by P. Devaraj. 167p. 1999. pap. 325.00 (*81-7089-267-8*, Pub. by Intl Bk Distr) St Mut.

Monograph on Sissoo. D. N. Tewari. 316p. 1993. pap. 425.00 (*0-7855-2735-4*, Pub. by Intl Bk Distr) St Mut.

Monograph on Spent Nuclear Fuel Storage Technologies. Ed. by E. R. Johnson & P. M. Saverot. LC 97-70726. (Illus.). 270p. 1997. write for info. (*1-890468-00-2*) Inst of Nuclear Mtrls.

Monograph on Teak: Tectona Grandis Linn. D. N. Tweari. 490p. 1992. pap. 500.00 (*81-7089-181-7*, Pub. by Intl Bk Distr) St Mut.

Monograph on the Complications of Unsafe Abortion in Africa. Stephen N. Kinoti et al. LC 97-950106. (Orig.). 1995. pap. text. write for info. (*0-929817-38-9*) JHPIEGO.

Monograph on the Epidemic of Poliomyelitis (Infantile Paralysis) in New York City in 1946. Haven Emerson. Ed. by Barbara G. Rosenkrantz. LC 76-25662. (Public Health in America Ser.). (Illus.). 1977. reprint ed. lib. bdg. 41.95 (*0-405-09817-0*) Ayer.

Monograph on the Erosion of Materials by Solid Particle Impact. Ian M. Hutchings. LC TA0418.74.C3. (MTI Publication Ser.: No. 10). (Illus.). 109p. 1993. reprint ed. pap. 33.80 (*0-608-06732-6*, 206692900009) Bks Demand.

Monograph on the Genus Microcoella (Orchidaceae) Lars Jonsson. (Illus.). 152p. (Orig.). 1981. pap. text 26.00 (*91-554-1213-0*) Coronet Bks.

Monograph on the Geysers Geothermal Field. (Special Reports: No. 17). (Illus.). 350p. 1992. 25.00 (*0-934412-17-0*) Geothermal.

Monographia Hymenomycetum Sueciae, 1857-62, 2 vols. in 1. Elias M. Fries. 1963. 65.00 (*90-6123-067-5*) Lubrecht & Cramer.

Monographia Uredinearum: Seu Specierum Omnium As Hunc Usque Diem Cognitarum Descripto & Adumbratio Systematica, Vols. 1-4. Hans Sydow & Paul Sydow. 1971. reprint ed. pap. 150.00 (*3-7682-0730-7*) Lubrecht & Cramer.

Monographic Dictionary of Medicine & Health see Diccionario Monografico de Medicina y Salud

Monographic Dictionary of the Animal Kingdom see Diccionario Monografico del Reino Animal

Monographic Revision of the Helothripinae of the World (Thysanoptera) Thomas H. Wilson. (Memoir Ser.: No. 23). (Illus.). 354p. 1975. 45.00 (*1-56665-021-6*) Assoc Pubs FL.

Monographic Studies in Cassia (Leguminosae-Caesalpinioideae) One: Section Xerocalyx. Howard S. Irwin. (Memoirs Ser.: Vol. 12 (1)). (Illus.). 114p. 1964. 10.00 (*0-89327-045-8*) NY Botanical.

Monographic Study of the Fern Genus Woodsia. D. F. Brown. (Illus.). 1964. 48.00 (*3-7682-5416-X*) Lubrecht & Cramer.

Monographic Study of the Hawaiian Species of the Tribe Lobelioideae, Family Campanulaceae. J. F. Rock. (BMB Ser.). (Orig.). 1919. 128.00 (*0-527-01651-9*) Periodicals Srv.

Monographie & Iconographie der Oedogoniaceen. K. E. Hirn. (Illus.). 1960. reprint ed. pap. 130.00 (*3-7682-7056-4*) Lubrecht & Cramer.

Monographie der Athelieae (Corticaceae, Basidiomycetes) W. Juelich. (Willdenowia. Ser.: Suppl. 7). (GER., Illus.). 284p. 1972. pap. text 36.00 (*3-7682-0919-9*) Lubrecht & Cramer.

Monographie der Flechtengattung Thelenella. Helmut Mayrhofer. Ed. by Volkmar Wirth et al. (Bibliotheca Lichenologica: Vol. 26). (GER., Illus.). 116p. 1987. 36.00 (*3-443-58005-X*, Pub. by Gebruder Borntraeger) Balogh.

Monographie des Oscillariees, 1892-93, 2 parts in 1 vol. M. Gomont. (Illus.). 1962. 52.00 (*3-7682-0038-8*) Lubrecht & Cramer.

Monographie und Iconographie der Orchideen Europas und des Mittelmeergebietes, 1930-1940 Band 2: Keller: Kritische Monographie Enthaltend die Beschreibung der Arten und Unterarten, Rassen, Varietaeten, Formen und Bastarde. Gottfried Keller & Richard R. Schlechter. (Feddes Repertorium Ser.: Vol. A.2). (Illus.). 472p. 1972. reprint ed. 185.00 (*3-87429-032-8*, Pub. by Koeltz Sci Bks) Lubrecht & Cramer.

Monographien Zur Russischen Musik, 2 bande. Oskar Von Riesemann. xxxiv, 1044p. 1975. reprint ed. write for info. (*3-487-05627-5*) G Olms Pubs.

Monographische Bearbeitung Von Paepalanthus Subgenus Platycaulon. Mara L. Tissot-Squalli Houssaini. (Dissertationes Botanicae Ser.: Band 280). (Illus.). 242p. 1997. pap. 71.00 (*3-443-64192-X*, Pub. by Gebruder Borntraeger) Balogh.

Monographs in Classical Studies, 32 vols., Set. Ed. by W. R. Connor et al. 1981. lib. bdg. 1055.00 (*0-405-14025-8*) Ayer.

Monographs in Sci-Tech Libraries. Ed. by Ellis Mount. LC 82-23435. (Science & Technology Libraries: Vol. 3, No. 3). 101p. 1983. text 29.95 (*0-86656-218-4*) Haworth Pr.

Monographs on Fragrance Raw Materials. Ed. by D. L. Opdyke. (Illus.). 1979. 323.00 (*0-08-023775-4*, Pub. by Pergamon Repr) Franklin.

Monographs on Galactic Intelligence. unabridged ed. Charles L. Spiegel. LC 96-61497. (Illus.). 84p. (Orig.). 1997. pap. 12.00 (*0-935097-36-8*) Unarius Acad Sci.

Monographs on Infancy: An Original Anthology. Judith K. Gardner & Howard Gardner. LC 74-21702. 316p. 1975. reprint ed. 25.95 (*0-405-06472-1*) Ayer.

Monographs on Invertebrate Taxonomy 2: Click Beetles. Genera of the Australian Elateriade (Coleoptera) A. A. Calder. LC 97-123634. (Illus.). 142p. 1996. 130.00 (*0-643-05671-8*, Pub. by CSIRO) Accents Pubns.

Monographs on Varieties of United States Large Cents, 1795-1803. Ed. by Denis W. Loring. LC 75-39497. (Illus.). 248p. 1976. 40.00 (*0-88000-075-9*) Quarterman.

Monohydric Alcohols: Manufacture, Applications, & Chemistry. Ed. by Edward J. Wickson. LC 81-5950. (ACS Symposium Ser.: No. 159). 1981. 37.95 (*0-8412-0637-6*) Am Chemical.

Monohydric Alcohols: Manufacture, Applications, & Chemistry Based on a Symposium. Ed. by Edward J. Wickson. LC 81-5950. (ACS Symposium Ser.: Vol. 159). 232p. 1981. reprint ed. pap. 72.00 (*0-608-03038-4*, 206349100007) Bks Demand.

Monohydric Alcohols, Their Ethers & Esters see Rodd's Chemistry of Carbon Compounds

***Monoids, Acts & Categories with Applications to Wreath Products & Graphs.** M. Kilpatrick et al. LC 99-45793. (Expositions in Mathematics Ser.). 1999. write for info. (*3-11-015248-7*) De Gruyter.

Monoids & Semigroups Theory with Applications. Ed. by J. Rhodes. 548p. (C). 1991. text 113.00 (*981-02-0117-6*) World Scientific Pub.

Monolayers: A Memorial Symposium to N. K. Adam, Sponsored by the Division of Colloid & Surface Chemistry at the 168th Meeting of the American Chemical Society, Atlantic City, NJ, September 11-13, 1974. Ed. by E. D. Goddard. LC 75-25757. (Advances in Chemistry Ser.: No. 144). (Illus.). 384p. 1975. reprint ed. pap. 119.10 (*0-608-06741-5*, 206693800009) Bks Demand.

Monolingualism & Bilingualism: Lessons from Canada & Spain. Ed. by Sue Wright. LC 96-11906. 108p. 1996. 54.95 (*1-85359-354-0*, Pub. by Multilingual Matters) Taylor & Francis.

Monolingualism of the Other: or The Prosthesis of Origin. Jacques Derrida. Tr. by Patrick Mensah. (Cultural Memory in the Present Ser.). 108p. 1998. pap. 12.95 (*0-8047-3289-2*) Stanford U Pr.

Monolingualism of the Other: or The Prosthesis of Origin. Jacques Derrida. Tr. by Patrick Mensah from ENG. LC 98-4454. (Cultural Memory in the Present Ser.). 108p. 1998. 39.50 (*0-8047-3288-4*) Stanford U Pr.

Monolith. rev. ed. Adams. 1997. 30.00 (*0-8212-2412-3*, Pub. by Bulfinch Pr) Little.

Monolithic Architecture. Rodolfo Machado & Rodolphe El-Khoury. (Illus.). 173p. 1995. 60.00 (*3-7913-1609-5*, Pub. by Prestel) te Neues.

Monolithic Diode-Laser Arrays. Nils W. Carlson. LC 94-11598. (Electronics & Photonics Ser.: Vol. 33). 1994. 75.95 (*0-387-57910-9*) Spr-Verlag.

Monolithic Jinas. Jose Pereira. 1977. 8.50 (*0-8426-1027-8*, Pub. by Motilal Bnarsidass) S Asia.

Monolithic Jinas: The Iconography of the Jain Temples of Ellora. Jose Pereira. (C). 1977. 11.00 (*0-8364-2632-0*, Pub. by Motilal Bnarsidass) S Asia.

An Asterisk (*) at the beginning of an entry indicates that the title is appearing for the first time.

Monolithic Microwave Integrated Circuits: Technology & Design. Goyal Ravender. (Microwave Library). (Illus.). 842p. 1989. text. write for info. (0-89006-309-5) Artech Hse.

Monolithic Microwave Intergrated Circuits: Technology & Design. Ed. by Ravender Goyal. LC 89-327. (Artech House Microwave Library). (Illus.). 862p. 1989. reprint ed. pap. 200.00 (0-7837-9769-9, 206049700005) Bks Demand.

Monolithic Phase-Locked Loops & Clock Recovery Circuits: Theory & Design. Behzag B. Razavi. LC 96-6102. 508p. 1996. 89.95 (0-7803-1149-3, PC5620) Inst Electrical.

Monolithic Refractories. American Concrete Institute Staff. Ed. by David R. Lankard. LC 82-72101. (ACI Publication: No. SP-74). (Illus.). 162p. reprint ed. pap. 50.30 (0-7837-5222-9, 204495400005) Bks Demand.

Monolithic Refractories: A Comprehensive Handbook. Subrata Banerjee. LC 98-19043. (Illus.). 350p. 1998. 68.00 (981-02-3120-2, G046) World Scientific Pub.

Monologhi: Fatti e Fantasie di Donne Detti Spudoretamente. Enid Dame. Tr. by Nina Scammacca. (Monologues Ser.: Women of Fact & Fancy Speak Their Minds). (ENG & ITA., Illus.). 95p. 1989. 25.00 (0-89304-069-X); pap. 10.00 (0-89304-070-3) Cross-Cultrl NY.

Monologion & Proslogion: With the Replies of Gaunilo & Anselm. Anselm, Saint of Canterbury. Tr. by Thomas Williams from LAT. LC 95-47275. (Hackett Classics Ser.). 192p. (Orig.). (C). 1996. pap. text 7.95 (0-87220-297-6); lib. bdg. 34.95 (0-87220-298-4) Hackett Pub.

Monologo con Yolanda: Novela Sobre las Sombras de Una Isla. Alberto Muller. (Coleccion Caniqui). (SPA.). 126p. (Orig.). 1995. pap. 9.99 (0-89729-782-2) Ediciones.

Monologue: Anantaram. A Film. Adoor Gopalakrishnan. (C). 1991. pap. text 8.00 (81-7046-054-9, Pub. by Seagull Bks) S Asia.

Monologue from a Doomed Fetus in Utero & Other Works. J. A. Jacques Desrosiers. LC 97-90183. 69p. 1998. pap. 8.95 (0-533-12316-X) Vantage.

Monologue with God: In Remembrance of the Holocaust. R. C. Peet. LC 95-95112. (Illus.). 20p. (Orig.). 1996. write for info. (0-9649871-0-4) Remembrnce Hse.

Monologue Workshop: From Search to Discovery in Audition & Performance. Jack Poggi. (Acting Ser.). 272p. 1990. pap. 12.95 (1-55783-031-2) Applause Theatre Bk Pubs.

Monologues: Includes: Another Story, Night Just Before the Forest, The Sifter, All It Takes Is Something Small, Madame Bertin's Testimony, Anatomy Lesson. Martine Drai et al. Ed. by Francoise Kourilsky. Tr. by Judith G. Miller et al from FRE. 246p. (Orig.). 1995. pap. 15.95 (0-913745-44-8) Ubu Repertory.

Monologues & Novelties. Ed. by B. C. Griffith et al. LC 70-38599. (Granger Index Reprint Ser.). 1977. reprint ed. 21.95 (0-8369-6331-8) Ayer.

Monologues & Scenes for Lesbian Actors. Carolyn Gage. LC 99-61570. 224p. 1999. pap. 15.95 (1-887237-10-0) Odd Girls Pr.

*__Monologues & Scenes for Lesbian Actors.__ Carolyn Gage. 224p. (C). 1999. 39.95 (1-887237-07-0) Odd Girls Pr.

Monologues & Scenes for Middle School Actors. Mary H. Surface. LC 99-52457. (Young Actors Ser.). 256p. (YA). (gr. 7-12). 1999. pap. 11.95 (1-57525-179-5) Smith & Kraus.

Monologues & Scenes from World Theatre Vol. 4: English. Ed. by William-Alan Landes. 1993. pap. 8.00 (0-88734-128-4) Players Pr.

Monologues & Scenes from World Theatre - American. William-Alan Landes. LC 93-16180. (World Theatre Ser.: Vol. 5). 62p. (Orig.). 1993. pap. 8.00 (0-88734-129-2) Players Pr.

Monologues & Scenes from World Theatre - Ancient Greek & Roman, Vol. 1. William-Alan Landes. LC 93-16180. 100p. (Orig.). 1999. pap. 8.00 (0-88734-125-X) Players Pr.

Monologues & Scenes from World Theatre - Belgian, Austrian, Scandinavian, Irish, Vol. 3. William-Alan Landes. LC 93-16180. 100p. (Orig.). 1993. pap. 8.00 (0-88734-127-6) Players Pr.

Monologues & Scenes from World Theatre - German, French, Spanish, Italian, Russian, Vol. 2. William-Alan Landes. 100p. (Orig.). 1993. pap. 8.00 (0-88734-126-8) Players Pr.

Monologues for Actors of Color: Men. Roberta Uno. LC 99-14179. 1999. 60.00 (0-87830-070-8); pap. 11.99 (0-87830-071-6) Routledge.

Monologues for Actors of Color: Women. Roberta Uno. LC 99-14171. 160p. 1999. 60.00 (0-87830-068-6) Routledge.

Monologues for Actors of Color Women. Roberto Uno. LC 99-14171. 1999. pap. 11.99 (0-87830-069-4) Routledge.

Monologues for Competition & Performance: Exploring God, Man, & the Christian Experience, Vol. I. unabridged ed. Ed. by Travis Tyre. 52p. (Orig.). (YA). (gr. 9-12). 1994. pap. 12.50 (1-887710-25-6, ArtCan Drama) Promise Prodns.

Monologues for Kids. Ruth M. Roddy. 64p. (Orig.). (J). (gr. 1-3). 1987. pap. 8.95 (0-940669-02-1, D-7) Dramaline Pubns.

Monologues for Teenage Girls. Susan Pomerance. LC 98-21314. 64p. 1998. pap. 9.95 (0-940669-39-0, D-45) Dramaline Pubns.

Monologues for Teenagers. Roger Karshner. 64p. (YA). (gr. 7-12). 1986. pap. 9.95 (0-9611792-8-7, D-10) Dramaline Pubns.

*__Monologues for Teens.__ unabridged ed. Vernon Howard. Ed. by William-Allan Landes. (Illus.). 128p. 2000. pap. text 15.00 (0-88734-666-9) Players Pr.

Monologues for Women, by Women. Ed. by Tori Haring-Smith. LC 94-1259. 144p. 1994. pap. 9.95 (0-435-08630-8, 08630) Heinemann.

Monologues for Young Act. Ed. by Lorraine Cohen. 192p. 1994. mass mkt. 5.99 (0-380-76187-4, Avon Bks) Morrow Avon.

Monologues from Chekhov. Anton Chekhov. Tr. & Intro. by Mason W. Cartwright. LC 95-25799. 64p. (Orig.). 1987. pap. 8.95 (0-940669-03-X, D-18) Dramaline Pubns.

Monologues from Classic Plays, 468 B. C. - 1960 A. D. Ed. by Jocelyn A. Beard. LC 92-36194. (Monologue Audition Ser.). 236p. 1992. pap. 11.95 (1-880399-09-1) Smith & Kraus.

Monologues from Contemporary Literature, Vol. I. Ed. by Eric Kraus. 100p. 1992. pap. 8.95 (1-880399-04-0) Smith & Kraus.

Monologues from George Bernard Shaw. George Bernard Shaw. Ed. by Ian Michaels. 64p. (Orig.). 1988. pap. 7.95 (0-940669-05-6, D-21) Dramaline Pubns.

Monologues from Literature: A Sourcebook for Actors. Marisa Smith. 1990. 16.10 (0-606-01227-3, Pub. by Turtleback) Demco.

Monologues from Literature: A Sourcebook for Actors. Ed. by Marisa Smith & Kristin Graham. 384p. 1990. pap. 11.00 (0-449-90535-7, Columbine) Fawcett.

Monologues from Moliere. Moliere. Ed. & Tr. by Dick Dotterer from FRE. 80p. (Orig.). 1991. pap. 9.95 (0-940669-11-0, D-22) Dramaline Pubns.

Monologues from Oscar Wilde. 3rd ed. Oscar Wilde. Ed. by Ian Michaels. 58p. 1988. pap. 7.95 (0-940669-04-8, D-20) Dramaline Pubns.

Monologues from the Classics. Ed. by Roger Karshner. 64p. 1986. pap. 8.95 (0-9611792-7-9, D-17) Dramaline Pubns.

Monologues from the Road. Ed. by Lavonne Mueller. LC 99-28940. (Orig.). 1999. pap. 12.95 (0-325-00124-3) Heinemann.

*__Monologues Galore: 57 More Monologues for Women by Women.__ Ed. by Tori Haring-Smith. 2000. pap. 14.95 (0-325-00247-9) Heinemann.

Monologues on Black Life. Gus Edwards. LC 96-49296. 1997. pap. 10.95 (0-435-07035-5) Heinemann.

Monologues They Haven't Heard. Roger Karshner. LC 93-45432. 64p. 1983. pap. 9.95 (0-9611792-0-1, D-1) Dramaline Pubns.

Monomotapa, Great Zimbabwe, Zululand, Lesotho: Southern Africa. Kenny Mann. LC 95-45536. (African Kingdoms of the Past Ser.). (Illus.). 128p. (J). (gr. 5 up). 1996. pap. 7.95 (0-382-39300-7) Silver Burdett Pr.

Monomotapa, Great Zimbabwe, Zululand, Lesotho: Southern Africa. Kenny Mann. LC 95-45536. (African Kingdoms of the Past Ser.). (Illus.). 128p. (YA). (gr. 5 up). 1996. lib. bdg. 15.95 (0-87518-659-9, Dillon Silver Burdett) Silver Burdett Pr.

Monon Route. George W. Hilton. (Illus.). 324p. 1996. 49.95 (0-911581-41-3) Heimburger Hse Pub.

Monona Terrace Vol. 1: Frank Lloyd Wright's Vision on the Lake. Ed. by Margo O. Hokanson & Deborah Kades. LC 97-61051. (Illus.). 64p. 1997. pap. 10.95 (1-878569-43-0) WI State Journal.

Mononeuropathies. Staal. (C). 1999. text 59.00 (0-7020-1779-5, Pub. by W B Saunders) Saunders.

Monongahela: River of Dreams, River of Sweat. Arthur C. Parker. LC 99-14652. (Illus.). 200p. 1999. 35.00 (0-271-01875-5) Pa St U Pr.

*__Monongalia Co. (West) Virginia Records of the District, Superior & County Courts, 1815-1819, Vol. 10.__ Melba P. Zinn. 379p. 1999. pap. 33.00 (0-7884-1201-9, Z364) Heritage Bk.

Monongalia County, West Virginia Vol. 8: Records of the District, Superior & County Courts, 1811-1812 & 1814-1820. Melba P. Zinn. viii, 420p. (Orig.). 1996. pap. 24.00 (0-7884-0538-1, Z362) Heritage Bk.

Monongalia County, (West) Virginia, Records of the District, Superior & County Courts, 1813-1817, Vol. 9. Melba P. Zinn. 421p. 1998. pap. 34.00 (0-7884-0941-7, 2363) Heritage Bk.

Monongalia Story: Prelude, Vol. 1. Earl L. Core. 484p. 1974. 35.00 (0-87012-169-3) McClain.
Probably the most voluminous of all the West Virginia county histories is THE MONONGALIA STORY. The first volume (subtitled Prelude) contains a general description of the county, including its geology, flora, fauna, & an account of the aborigines, followed by a record of more than 1,000 early settlers. Volume II (The Pioneers) presents the history from the establishment of the county, in 1776, up to 1826.
Probably the most voluminous of all the West Virginia country histories is THE MONONGALIA STORY. The first volume (subtitled Prelude) contains a general description of the county, including its geology, flora, fauna & an account of the aborigines, followed by a record of more than 1,000 early settlers. Volume II (The Pioneers) presents the history from the establishment of the county in 1776, up to 1826. VOLUMES III, IV & V are currently out-of-print. Will be available in 2001. ***Publisher Paid Annotation.***

Monongalia Story Vol. II: The Pioneers. Earl L. Core. 595p. 1977. 35.00 (0-87012-245-2) McClain.

Monongalia, (West) Virginia, Records of the District, Superior, & County Courts, Vol. 7: 1808-1814. Melba P. Zinn. 443p. (Orig.). 1994. pap. text 30.00 (0-7884-0138-6) Heritage Bk.

Mononitrates: International Symposium, Held at the Royal Society of Medicine, London , June 1986. Ed. by M. Weiss et al. (Journal: Cardiology: Vol. 74, Suppl. 1, 1987). (Illus.). viii, 80p. 1987. pap. 28.00 (3-8055-4626-2) S Karger.

Mononuclear Phagocyte Biology. Ed. by Alvin Volkman. LC 84-17460. (Immunology Ser.: No. 26). (Illus.). 524p. reprint ed. pap. 162.50 (0-7837-4304-1, 204399500012) Bks Demand.

Mononuclear Phagocytes. Ed. by Ralph Van Furth. 1985. text 642.00 (0-89838-732-9) Kluwer Academic.

Mononuclear Phagocytes: Biology of Monocytes & Macrophages. Ed. by Ralph Van Furth. LC 92-19773. 1992. text 426.00 (0-7923-1843-9) Kluwer Academic.

Mononuclear Phagocytes in Cell Biology. Ed. by Gabriel Lopez-Berestein & Jim Klostergaard. 256p. 1992. lib. bdg. 189.00 (0-8493-4706-8, QR185) CRC Pr.

Mononucleic Hydrocarbons & Their Halogen Derivatives see Rodd's Chemistry of Carbon Compounds

*__Mononucleosis.__ Mark Gustav Gedatus. (Perspectives on Disease & Illness Ser.). (Illus.). 64p. (YA). 1999. 22.60 (0-7368-0284-3) Capstone Pr.

Mononucleosis. Alvin Silverstein et al. LC 93-48721. (Diseases & People Ser.). (Illus.). 112p. (YA). (gr. 6 up). 1994. lib. bdg. 20.95 (0-89490-466-3) Enslow Pubs.

*__Mononucleosis & Other Infectious Diseases.__ Laurel Shader. LC 99-47867. (Illus.). 128p. 1999. 24.95 (0-7910-5520-5) Chelsea Hse.

Mononucleosis & Other Infectious Diseases. Laurel Shader & Jon Zonderman. (Encyclopedia of Health Ser.). (Illus.). 116p. (YA). (gr. 7 up). 1989. lib. bdg. 19.95 (0-7910-0069-9) Chelsea Hse.

Monophasic Action Potentials: Basics & Clinical Application. Ed. by M. R. Franz et al. LC 97-4382. (Illus.). 288p. 109.00 (3-540-63152-6) Spr-Verlag.

Monophasic Action Potentials: Bridging Cell & Bedside. Ed. by Michael R. Franz. LC 99-25522. (Illus.). 920p. 1999. 159.00 (0-87993-430-1) Futura Pub.

Monophonic Lauda & the Lay Religious Confraternities of Tuscany & Umbria in the Late Middle Ages. Cyrilla Barr. (Early Drama, Art & Music Monograph: No. 10). 1988. pap. 15.95 (0-918720-90-7); boxed set 25.95 (0-918720-89-3) Medieval Inst.

Monophonic Songs in the ROMAN de FAUVEL. Samuel N. Rosenberg & Hans Tischler. LC 90-751897. (Illus.). x, 171p. 1991. text 60.00 (0-8032-3898-3) U of Nebr Pr.

Monophyly & Phylogenetic Diagnosis of the Family Cetopsidae, with Synonymization of the Helogenidae (Teleostei: Siluriformes) Mario C. Pinna & Richard P. Vari. LC 94-48553. (Smithsonian Contributions to Zoology Ser.: Vol. 571). 30p. 1995. reprint ed. pap. 30.00 (0-608-00509-6, 206132900008) Bks Demand.

Monophysisme Severien: Etude Historique, Litteraire et Theologique sur la Resistance Monophysite au Concile de Chalcedoine Jusqu'a la Constitution de l'Eglise Jacobite. Joseph Lebon. LC 77-84704. reprint ed. 72.50 (0-404-16111-1) AMS Pr.

Monopoles in Quantum Field Theory: Proceedings of the Monopole Meeting, Trieste, Italy, Dec. 11-15, 1981. Ed. by N. S. Craigie et al. 461p. 1982. 78.00 (9971-950-28-6); pap. 33.00 (9971-950-29-4) World Scientific Pub.

Monopolies Act, Doctrinaire Quantification & Industrial Growth in India. Har Govind. 198p. 1986. text 22.50 (81-7027-097-9, Pub. by Radiant Pubs) S Asia.

Monopolies & Patents: A Study of the History & Future of the Patent Monopoly. Harold G. Fox. LC 47-28708. (University of Toronto Legal Ser.: Extra vol.). 424p. reprint ed. pap. 131.50 (0-608-13071-0, 201421000094) Bks Demand.

Monopolies & Trust. Richard T. Ely. LC 73-2505. (Big Business; Economic Power in a Free Society Ser.). 1973. reprint ed. 20.95 (0-405-05087-9) Ayer.

Monopolies in America: Empire Builders & Their Enemies from Jay Gould to Bill Gates. Charles R. Geisst. LC 99-14340. (Illus.). 368p. 2000. 30.00 (0-19-512301-8) OUP.

Monopolistic & Unfair Trade Practices, 2 vols. U. S. House of Representatives Select Committee on. Ed. by Stuart Bruchey & Vincent P. Carosso. LC 78-18986. (Small Business Enterprise in America Ser.). (Illus.). 1979. reprint ed. lib. bdg. 106.95 (0-405-11487-7) Ayer.

Monopolistic Competition & Effective Demand. Hukukane Nikaido. LC 74-25623. (Princeton Studies in Mathematical Economics: No. 6). 158p. reprint ed. pap. 49.00 (0-8357-6225-4, 203464800090) Bks Demand.

Monopolistic Competition & International Trade. Ed. by Henryk Kierzkowski. (Illus.). 266p. 1989. reprint ed. pap. text 39.95 (0-19-828726-7) OUP.

Monopolistic Competition & Macroeconomic Theory. Robert M. Solow. LC 99-191733. (Federico Caffe Lectures: No. 2). (Illus.). 104p. (C). 1999. text 39.95 (0-521-62338-3); pap. text 11.95 (0-521-62616-1) Cambridge U Pr.

Monopolistic Competition, Technical Progress & Income Distribution. J. G. Hilhorst. xii, 154p. 1970. pap. text 129.00 (0-677-61545-0) Gordon & Breach.

Monopolistic Competition Theory: Origins, Results, & Implications. Jan Keppler. LC 93-48382. 1994. text 37.50 (0-8018-4813-X) Johns Hopkins.

Monopolists & Freebooters. Spate. (Australian National University Press Ser.). 1996. write for info. (0-08-032996-9, Pergamon Pr) Elsevier.

Monopolization of International Criminal Law in the United Nations: A Jurisprudential Approach. 2nd ed. Farhad Malekian. 240p. (Orig.). 1995. pap. 122.50 (91-630-3196-5) Coronet Bks.

*__Monopoly.__ Paul Buchanan & Rod Randall. LC 98-7206. (Misadventures of Willie Plummet Ser.). 128p. (J). (gr. 3-7). 1998. 5.99 (0-570-05089-8) Concordia.

Monopoly & Competition: A Study in English Industrial Organisation. Hermann Levy. Ed. by Mira Wilkins. LC 76-29993. (European Business Ser.). 1977. reprint ed. lib. bdg. 31.95 (0-405-09751-4) Ayer.

Monopoly & Competition in Banking. David A. Alhadeff. Ed. by Stuart Bruchey. LC 80-1129. (Rise of Commerical Banking Ser.). (Illus.). 1981. reprint ed. lib. bdg. 25.95 (0-405-13629-3) Ayer.

Monopoly & Competition in British Telecommunications: The Past, the Present & the Future. J. M. Harper. LC 96-34968. 256p. 1997. 89.50 (1-85567-455-6) Bks Intl VA.

Monopoly & Competition Policy, 2 vols. Ed. by F. M. Scherer. (International Library of Critical Writings in Economics: Vol. 30). 1248p. 1993. 470.00 (1-85278-753-8) E Elgar.

Monopoly Capital: An Essay on the American Economic & Social Order. Paul A. Baran & Paul M. Sweezy. LC 65-15269. 416p. 1968. reprint ed. pap. 18.00 (0-85345-073-0, Pub. by Monthly Rev) NYU Pr.

Monopoly Capital Theory: Hilferding & Twentieth-Century Capitalism, 115. Jonas Zoninsein. LC 90-37844. (Contributions in Economics & Economic History Ser.: No. 115). 152p. 1990. 49.95 (0-313-27402-9, ZMC/, Greenwood Pr) Greenwood.

Monopoly Companion. 2nd ed. Philip Orbanes. LC 99-16930. 216p. 1999. pap. 7.95 (1-58062-175-9) Adams Media.

M

Monopoly Economics of Juvenile Custody: Could Private Competition Keep Costs Down? Rex Reed & David W. Holm. 10p. 1988. pap. text 8.00 (1-57655-107-5) Independ Inst.

*__Monopoly Gift Pack.__ (Illus.). 200p. 1999. pap. write for info. (1-891056-23-9) Winning Moves.

Monopoly in Economics & Law. Donald Dewey. LC 76-5436. (Illus.). 328p. 1976. reprint ed. lib. bdg. 35.00 (0-8371-8811-3, DEME, Greenwood Pr) Greenwood.

Monopoly Issue & Antitrust, 1900-1917. Intro. by Robert F. Himmelberg. LC 93-44788. (Business & Government in America since 1870 Ser.: Vol. 2). 408p. 1994. text 88.00 (0-8153-1404-3) Garland.

Monopoly Law & Market: Studies of EC Competition Law with U. S. American Antitrust Law As a Frame of Reference & Supported by Basic Market Economics. Jens Fejo. 434p. 1990. 122.00 (90-6544-435-1) Kluwer Law Intl.

Monopoly, M. D. James Gettins. 227p. (Orig.). 1997. pap. 11.95 (1-57901-014-8) Intl Promotions.

Monopoly Mail: Privatizing the United States Postal Service. Douglas K. Adie. 280p. (Orig.). 1988. 39.95 (0-88738-203-7); pap. 24.95 (0-88738-747-0) Transaction Pubs.

Monopoly of Credit. C. H. Douglas. 1972. 59.95 (0-8490-0664-3) Gordon Pr.

Monopoly Policy in the U. K. Assessing the Evidence. Roger Clarke et al. LC 97-50054. 224p. 1998. 80.00 (1-85898-585-4) E Elgar.

Monopoly Politics. James C. Miller, III. LC 99-23021. (Publication Ser.: Vol. 457). 152p. 1999. pap. 17.95 (0-8179-9652-4) Hoover Inst Pr.

Monopoly Power: How It Is Measured & How It Has Changed. Garry K. Ottosen. LC 89-81840. 125p. 1990. pap. 9.95 (0-9624038-1-4) Crossroads Rsch.

Monopoly Practice Set. Knechel. (C). 1992. 29.50 (0-15-500304-6) Harcourt Coll Pubs.

Monopoly Problems in Regulated Industries: Hearings Before the House Committee on the Judiciary, 84th Congress, Serial No. 14, 8 vols., Set. Ed. by Bernard D. Reams, Jr. LC 91-72268. (Illus.). 8378p. 1991. reprint ed. lib. bdg. 675.00 (0-89941-766-3, 307180) W S Hein.

Monopoly Problems in Regulated Industries: Hearings Before the House Committee on the Judiciary, 84th Congress, Serial No. 22, 8 vols., Set. Ed. by Bernard D. Reams, Jr. LC 91-72318. (Illus.). 6656p. 1991. lib. bdg. 750.00 (0-89941-765-5, 307190) W S Hein.

Monopoly Problems in Regulated Industries: Hearings Before the House Committee on the Judiciary, 87th Congress, Serial No. 10, 2 vols., Set. Ed. by Bernard D. Reams, Jr. LC 91-72670. (Illus.). 2004p. 1991. reprint ed. lib. bdg. 195.00 (0-89941-764-7, 307150) W S Hein.

Monopoly Rent. King. (Progress in Planning Ser.). 1988. pap. 28.00 (0-08-036874-3, Pergamon Pr) Elsevier.

Monopoly's Moment: The Organization & Regulation of Canadian Utilities 1830-1930. Christopher Armstrong & H. V. Nelles. 408p. (C). 1988. pap. 19.95 (0-8020-6709-3); text 47.50 (0-8020-2671-0) U of Toronto Pr.

Monopsony: Antitrust Law & Economics. Roger D. Blair & Jeffrey L. Harrison. (Illus.). 193p. 1993. text 45.00 (0-691-04309-4, Pub. by Princeton U Pr) Cal Prin Full Svc.

Monopulse Principles & Techniques. Samuel M. Sherman. LC 84-70221. 381p. reprint ed. pap. 118.20 (0-7837-3015-2, 204292500006) Bks Demand.

Monopulse Radar. David K. Barton. LC 74-82597. (Radars Ser.: Vol. 1). 343p. reprint ed. pap. 106.40 (0-608-13080-X, 202505900041) Bks Demand.

Monosaccharide Sugars: Chemical Synthesis by Chain Elongation, Degradation, & Epimerization. Ed. by Zoltan Gyordydeak & Istvan Pelyas. LC 97-23437. (Illus.). 508p. 1997. text 89.95 (0-12-550360-1) Morgan Kaufmann.

Monosaccharides: Their Chemistry & Their Roles in Natural Products. Peter M. Collins & Robert J. Ferrier. LC 94-26989. 594p. 1995. pap. 69.95 (0-471-95343-1) Wiley.

Monosyllabic Nouns in Modern Standard Bulgarian Roger Gyllin. LC 98-119887. 87 p. 1997. write for info. (91-506-1241-7) Uppsala Universitet.

Monoterpenoid Indole Alkaloids Pt. 4: Supplement Volume. J. Edwin Saxton. LC 94-4941. 860p. 1994. 675.00 (0-471-95112-9) Wiley.

An Asterisk (*) at the beginning of an entry indicates that the title is appearing for the first time.

Monotheism: A Philosophic Inquiry into the Foundations of Theology & Ethics. Lenn E. Goodman. LC 79-24818. (Publications of the Oxford Centre for Postgraduate Hebrew Study). 228p. 1981. 48.00 (0-86598-068-3) Rowman.

Monotheism & the Prophetic Minority: An Essay in Biblical History & Sociology. Bernhard Lang. (Social World of Biblical Antiquity Ser.: No. 1). 191p. 1983. pap. 15.95 (0-907459-31-5, Pub. by Sheffield Acad) CUP Services.

Monotheism, Power, - Justice: Collected Old Testament Essays. Millard C. Lind. (Text-Reader Ser.: No. 3). 273p. 1990. pap. text 10.00 (0-936273-16-X) Inst Mennonite.

***Monotheism, the Trinity & Mysticism: A Semiotic Approach to Jewish-Christian Encounter.** Antti Laato. 159p. 1999. pap. 31.95 (3-631-34531-3) P Lang Pubng.

***Monotheism, the Trinity & Mysticism: A Semiotic Approach to Jewish-Christian Encounter.** Antti Laato. 159p. (C). 1999. pap. 31.95 (0-8204-4312-3) P Lang Pubng.

Monotheismus Im Alten Israel und Seiner Umwelt. Ed. by Othmar Keel. (Orig.). 1980. pap. text 25.00 (3-7203-0014-5) Eisenbrauns.

Monotone Dynamical Systems: An Introduction to the Theory of Competitive & Cooperative Systems. Hal L. Smith. LC 94-48032. (Mathematical Surveys & Monographs: No. 41). 174p. 1995. text 49.00 (0-8218-0393-X, SURV/41) Am Math.

Monotone Iterative Techniques for Discontinuous Nonlinear Differential Equations. Seppo Heikkila & V. Lakshmikantham. LC 94-2465. (Pure & Applied Mathematics Ser.: Vol. 181). (Illus.). 536p. 1994. text 179.50 (0-8247-9224-6) Dekker.

Monotone Matrix Functions & Analytic Continuation. Ed. by W. F. Donoghue, Jr. LC 73-15293. (Grundlehren der Mathematischen Wissenschaften Ser.: Vol. 207). 210p. 1974. 54.00 (0-387-06543-1) Spr-Verlag.

Monotone Operators in Banach Space & Nonlinear Partial Differential Equations. R. E. Showalter. LC 96-43343. (Mathematical Surveys & Monographs: Vol. 49). 278p. 1996. text 75.00 (0-8218-0500-2) Am Math.

Monotone Potentialoperatoren in Theorie & Anwendung. A. Langenbach. (GER.). 1977. 37.80 (3-540-08071-6) Spr-Verlag.

Monotone Processes of Convex & Concave Type. R. Tyrrell Rockafellar. LC 52-42839. (Memoirs Ser.: No. 1/77). 74p. 1967. pap. 16.00 (0-8218-1277-7, MEMO 1/77) Am Math.

Monotone Structure in Discrete-Event Systems. Ed. by Paul Glasserman & David D. Yao. (Series in Probability & Mathematical Statistics). 297p. 1994. 89.95 (0-471-58041-4, Wiley-Interscience) Wiley.

Monotype: Mediums & Methods for Painterly Printmaking. Julia Ayres. (Illus.). 144p. 1991. 29.95 (0-8230-3129-2) Watsn-Guptill.

***Monotype: Mediums & Methods for Painterly Printmaking.** Julia Ayres. (Illus.). 144p. 2000. pap. 19.95 (0-8230-3128-4) Watsn-Guptill.

Monotype-Monoprint: History & Techniques. Kurt Wisneski. Ed. by John M. Kingsbury. LC 95-10733. (Illus.). iv, 168p. 1995. pap. 35.00 (0-9612610-4-8) Bullbrier Pr.

Monotypes. Frank Howell. (Frank Howell Ser.). (Illus.). 40p. (Orig.). 1987. pap. 18.50 (0-944082-00-9) Santa Fe Fine Art.

Monotypes of Sam Francis. Hulten Pontus. (Illus.). 350p. 1994. 500.00 (3-87135-013-3, Pub. by Daco-Verlag) U of Wash Pr.

Monovalent Cations in Biological Systems. Ed. by Charles A. Pasternak. 408p. 1990. lib. bdg. 268.00 (0-8493-4775-0, QP531) CRC Pr.

Monovasia & the Women of Monemvasia. Yannis Ritsos. Tr. by Kimon Friar & Kostas Myrsiades from GRE. LC 87-62280. 67p. 1988. 20.00 (0-932963-04-8) Nostos Bks.

Monovassia, 1976. Eleni Fourtouni. (Greek Women Poets Ser.). (Illus.). 110p. (Orig.). 1979. pap. text 11.95 (0-915017-01-6) Thelpini Pr.

Monro, His Expedition with the Worthy Scots Regiment Called Mac-Keys. Ed. by William S. Brockington, Jr. LC 98-33578. (Praeger Series in War Studies). 480p. 1999. 75.00 (0-275-96267-9, Praeger Pubs) Greenwood.

Monrobey Report: An Economic Detective Story Solving the Mysteries of Inflations & Recessions. Hank Monrobey. LC 89-174366. (Illus.). 362p. 1989. 42.50 (0-9623564-2-5); pap. 29.90 (0-9623564-0-9) H Monrobey & Assocs.

Monroe. Margaret Tranzillo. (Images of America Ser.). 1998. pap. 16.99 (0-7524-0958-1) Arcadia Publng.

***Monroe: Character in Time: The U. S. Presidents.** Lorraine Ash. Ed. by R. David Cox & Brian Kuhens. 44p. 1999. 5.95 (1-929403-12-7) History Proj.

Monroe - West Monroe. San Antonio Cartographers Staff. 1995. 2.95 (0-671-56290-8) Macmillan.

Monroe & Conecuh Counties, Alabama, Marriages, 1833-1880. Robert E. Colson & Lucy W. Colson. 172p. 1983. 20.00 (0-89308-335-6) Southern Hist Pr.

Monroe County, Tennessee, Records, 1820-1870, Vol. 1. Reba B. Boyer. 198p. 1983. reprint ed. pap. 25.00 (0-89308-329-1) Southern Hist Pr.

Monroe County Tennessee, Records, 1820-1870, Vol. 2. Reba B. Boyer. 198p. 1983. reprint ed. pap. 25.00 (0-89308-327-5) Southern Hist Pr.

Monroe County, (West) Virginia Marriages: Compiled 1799-1850. Norma P. Evans. LC 84-73368. (Orig.). 1985. pap. 15.00 (0-937418-12-9) N P Evans.

Monroe County (W)Virginia Abstracts: Deeds (1799-1817) Wills (1799-1829) Sim's Land Grant Index (1780-1829) Larry G. Shuck. 187p. 1996. per. 19.95 (1-55856-223-0, 029) Closson Pr.

Monroe-Crook House Presents Crokett Cooks. 250p. 1984. 14.95 (0-317-39615-3) Pubns Devl Co.

Monroe Doctrine see Teaching American Diplomacy Using Primary Sources

Monroe Doctrine. Ed. by Armin Rappaport. LC 64-25181. 128p. 1976. reprint ed. pap. 10.50 (0-03-048705-6) Krieger.

Monroe Doctrine Clause of the League of Nations Covenant. S. M. Kennedy. (Graduate Studies: No. 20). 60p. (Orig.). 1979. pap. 5.00 (0-89672-073-X) Tex Tech Univ Pr.

Monroe Mission to France, 1794-1796. Beverley W. Bond. LC 78-63920. (Johns Hopkins University. Studies in the Social Sciences. Thirtieth Ser. 1912: 2-3). reprint ed. 42.50 (0-404-61171-0) AMS Pr.

Monroe Pinckey, My Father. Claudette Pinckey-Harris. 135p. (Orig.). 1995. pap. 12.95 (0-910671-14-1) Path Pr Chicago.

Monroe's Ghosts. David W. Dent. LC 98-15326. 432p. 1999. 59.95 (0-313-30109-3, Greenwood Pr) Greenwood.

Monroeville: Literary Capital of Alabama. Kathy McCoy. LC 98-87570. (Images of America Ser.). (Illus.). 128p. 1998. pap. 18.99 (0-7524-1212-4) Arcadia Publng.

***Monroeville: The Search of Harper Lee's Maycomb.** Monroe County Heritage Museum Staff. (Images of America Ser.). 128p. 1999. pap. 18.99 (0-7385-0204-9) Arcadia Publng.

***Mons - 1914.** Nigel Cave. (Battleground Europe Ser.). 1999. pap. write for info. (0-85052-677-9) Pen & Sword Bks Ltd.

Mons Graupius. Robert Clifton-Wallace. Ed. by Rena Kincade-Clifton. (Illus.). 600p. 1993. 24.00 (0-9634992-1-1) Pretani.

Mons Graupius. rev. ed. Robert C. Wallace. (Illus.). 578p. 1996. pap. text 12.00 (0-9634992-9-7) Pretani.

Mons, 1914. David Lomas. (Campaign Ser.: No. 46). (Illus.). 96p. 1996. pap. 15.95 (1-85532-551-9, Pub. by Ospry) Stackpole.

Mons Perfectionis. John Alcock. LC 74-28823. (English Experience Ser.: No. 706). 1974. reprint ed. 20.00 (90-221-0706-X) Walter J Johnson.

Monsanto Company: A Report on the Company's Environmental Policies & Practices. (Illus.). 47p. (C). 1994. reprint ed. pap. text 40.00 (0-7881-0924-3, Coun on Econ) DIANE Pub.

Monshin: Hearing Faith. Seikan Fukuma. LC 83-60645. 150p. 1983. 7.95 (0-912624-02-7) Nembutsu Pr.

Monsieur Barnett: Suivi de l'Orchestre. Jean Anouilh. (FRE.). 160p. 1982. pap. 10.95 (0-7859-1965-1, 2070374262) Fr & Eur.

Monsieur Beaucaire. Booth Tarkington. reprint ed. lib. bdg. 18.95 (0-88411-703-0) Amereon Ltd.

***Monsieur Beaucaire.** Booth Tarkington. (Works of Booth Tarkington). 127p. 1999. reprint ed. lib. bdg. 88.00 (1-58201-863-4) Classic Bks.

Monsieur Beaucaire. Booth Tarkington. (BCL1-PS American Literature Ser.). 127p. 1992. reprint ed. lib. bdg. 69.00 (0-7812-6875-3) Rprt Serv.

Monsieur Beaucaire & the Beautiful Lady. Booth Tarkington. (YA). (gr. 6 up). 1968. mass mkt. 0.95 (0-8049-0158-9) Airmont.

Monsieur Bergeret a Paris. Anatole France, pseud. (FRE.). 1966. pap. 10.95 (0-8288-9761-1, F101291) Fr & Eur.

Monsieur Bergeret a Paris see Romans et Contes

Monsieur Croche, Antidilettante. Claude Debussy. 212p. 1977. 18.95 (0-8369-2897-0) Ayer.

Monsieur Croche, the Dilettante Hater. Claude Debussy. 212p. 1990. lib. bdg. 69.00 (0-7812-9059-7) Rprt Serv.

Monsieur De Brillancourt. large type ed. Clare Harkness. 1996. pap. 19.95 (0-7862-0730-2) Thorndike Pr.

Monsieur de Charette. Michel De Saint Pierre. (FRE.). 1982. pap. 15.95 (0-7859-4175-4) Fr & Eur.

***Monsieur de Chauvelin's Will.** Alexandre Dumas. 252p. 2000. pap. 9.95 (0-594-01561-8) Eightn Hundrd.

Monsieur de Phocas. 2nd ed. Jean Lorrain. Ed. & Tr. by Francis Amery. LC 94-100376. (Decadence Ser.). 272p. 1999. reprint ed. pap. 14.95 (1-873982-15-1, Pub. by Dedalus) Hippocrene Bks.

Monsieur Gallet, Decede, le Pendu De Saint-Pholien, le Charretier De la Providence. Georges Simenon. (FRE.). 924p. 1991. 49.95 (0-7859-0485-9, 2258032458) Fr & Eur.

***Monsieur Iletaitunefois.** Remy Simard. (J). (ps-3). 1998. pap. 6.95 (1-55037-544-X, Pub. by Annick); lib. bdg. 16.95 (1-55037-545-8, Pub. by Annick) Firefly Bks Ltd.

Monsieur Jadis Ou l'Ecole du Soir. Antoine Blondin. (FRE.). 1972. pap. 10.95 (0-7859-1688-1, 2070360296) Fr & Eur.

Monsieur Lambert. Goscinny Sempe. (FRE.). 1990. pap. 10.95 (0-8288-3787-2, F42176) Fr & Eur.

Monsieur l'Arbre et la Petite Fille. European Language Institute Staff. (Raconte et Chante Ser.). (FRE., Illus.). 27p. (J). (gr. k-2). 1992. pap. 19.95 (88-85148-68-9, Pub. by Europ Lang Inst) Midwest European Pubns.

Monsieur le Trouhadec Saisi par la Debauche. Jules Romains, pseud. (FRE.). 160p. 1975. pap. 10.95 (0-7859-1371-8, 2070366510) Fr & Eur.

Monsieur Motte. Grace E. King. LC 79-98582. (Short Story Index Reprint Ser.). 1977. 21.95 (0-8369-3156-4) Ayer.

Monsieur Nicholas, Vol. 2. Nicholas E. Restif De La Bretonne. Ed. by Jean-Yves Testud. (FRE.). 1989. lib. bdg. 170.00 (0-7859-3888-5) Fr & Eur.

Monsieur Nicolas, Vol. 1. A. Retif de la Bretonne. (FRE.). 1989. lib. bdg. 150.00 (0-8288-3531-4, F26670) Fr & Eur.

Monsieur Nomme Piquet Qui Adorait les Animaux. Raymond Plante. (Il Etait une Fois... Ser.: Vol. 4). (FRE., Illus.). 24p. (J). 1996. pap. write for info. (2-89021-271-8, Pub. by La Courte Ech) Firefly Bks Ltd.

Monsieur Ou le Prince des Tenebres. Lawrence Durrell. (FRE.). 338p. 1976. pap. 29.95 (0-7859-2193-1, 207029515X) Fr & Eur.

Monsieur Ouine. Georges Bernanos. 1960. 8.95 (0-7859-0923-0, F87790) Fr & Eur.

Monsieur Ouine. Georges Bernanos. Tr. & Intro. by William S. Bush. LC 99-39572. 256p. 2000. pap. 20.00 (0-8032-6161-6, Bison Books) U of Nebr Pr.

***Monsieur Ouine.** Georges Bernanos. Tr. & Intro. by William S. Bush. LC 99-39572. 256p. 2000. 40.00 (0-8032-1304-2, Bison Books) U of Nebr Pr.

Monsieur Pamplemousse. large type ed. Michael Bond. (Nightingale Series Large Print Bks.). 240p. 1991. pap. 14.95 (0-8161-5111-3, G K Hall Lrg Type) Mac Lib Ref.

***Monsieur Pamplemousse Afloat.** Michael Bond. 1999. pap. 9.95 (0-7490-0347-2) Allison & Busby.

Monsieur Pamplemousse & the Secret Mission: A Gastronomic Mystery. large type ed. Michael Bond. (Nightingale Ser.). 280p. 1991. pap. 14.95 (0-8161-5110-5, G K Hall Lrg Type) Mac Lib Ref.

***Monsieur Pamplemousse Omnibus, Vol. 2.** Michael Bond. 1999. pap. text 9.95 (0-7490-0410-X) Allison & Busby.

***Monsieur Pamplemousse Omnibus, Vol. 3.** Michael Bond. 1999. pap. 9.95 (0-7490-0442-8) Allison & Busby.

***Monsieur Pamplemousse on Probation.** Michael Bond. 2000. pap. 9.95 (0-7490-0463-0, Pub. by Allison & Busby) Intl Pubs Mktg.

Monsieur Pamplemousse Rests His Case. Michael Bond. 1993. mass mkt. 4.50 (0-449-22045-1) Fawcett.

Monsieur Pamplemousse Stands Firm. Michael Bond. 1994. mass mkt. 4.99 (0-449-22201-2) Fawcett.

Monsieur Pamplemousse Takes the Cure. large type ed. Michael Bond. (Nightingale Ser.). 288p. 1990. pap. 14.95 (0-8161-4893-7, G K Hall Lrg Type) Mac Lib Ref.

Monsieur Parent. Guy de Maupassant. (Folio Ser.: No. 1913). (FRE.). 248p. 1988. pap. 9.95 (2-07-037913-2) Schoenhof.

Monsieur Qui a Brule une Dame. Eugene Labiche. 9.95 (0-686-54233-9) Fr & Eur.

Monsieur Qui Prend la Mouche. Eugene Labiche. 9.95 (0-686-54234-7) Fr & Eur.

Monsieur Qui Se Prenait pour l'Hiver. Sylvain Trudel. (Novels in the Premier Roman Ser.). (FRE., Illus.). 64p. (J). (gr. 2-5). 1995. pap. 8.95 (2-89021-241-6, Pub. by La Courte Ech) Firefly Bks Ltd.

***Monsieur Rene.** Peter Ustinov. LC 99-34220. 320p. 1999. 24.95 (1-57392-740-6) Prometheus Bks.

Monsieur Ripois et la Nemesis. L. Hemon. (FRE.). 1986. pap. 19.95 (0-7859-3046-9) Fr & Eur.

Monsieur Shoushana's lemon Trees. Patricia Duncker. LC 97-31152. 1998. 22.95 (0-88001-604-3) HarpC.

Monsieur Songe. Robert Pinget. Tr. by Barbara Wright. LC 88-61955. (French Ser.). 200p. 1989. 10.95 (0-87376-060-3) Red Dust.

Monsieur Tac. Pascal Bruckner. (FRE.). 310p. 1986. pap. 12.95 (0-7859-2055-2, 2070377873) Fr & Eur.

Monsieur Teste see Oeuvres

Monsieur Teste. Paul Valery. (Imaginaire Ser.). pap. 9.95 (2-07-027913-8) Schoenhof.

Monsieur Thermidor: A Fantastic Fishy Tale. Richard Kidd. LC 97-36379. (Illus.). 32p. (J). (gr. k-3). 1998. 16.95 (1-56711-800-3, Blackbirch Picturebk) Blackbirch.

Monsieur Thogo-gnini. Bernard B. Dadie. pap. 8.95 (0-685-33976-9) Fr & Eur.

Monsieur Thogo-Gnini. Bernard B. Dadie. Tr. by Townsend T. Brewster from FRE. 104p. (Orig.). 1986. pap. text 8.95 (0-913745-16-2) Ubu Repertory.

Monsieur Vautrin. Honore de Balzac & A. Charpak. (FRE.). 46p. 1963. pap. 14.95 (0-8288-9058-7, FA530) Fr & Eur.

Monsieur Venus. 2nd ed. Rachilde. Ed. by Mavora Barres & Madeleine Johnston. Tr. by Liz Heron from FRE. LC 96-120963. (Decadence Ser.). 149p. 1999. reprint ed. pap. 10.95 (1-873982-20-8, Pub. by Dedalus) Hippocrene Bks.

Monsieur Vernet see Oeuvres

Monsieur Vous Oubliez Votre Cadavre. Pascal Laine. (Folio Ser.: No. 2186). (FRE.). 1970. pap. 9.95 (2-07-038276-1) Schoenhof.

Monsignor Escriva: A Short Biography of the Founder of the Opus Dei. William Keenan. 1989. pap. 22.00 (1-85390-136-9, Pub. by Veritas Pubns) St Mut.

Monsoon. William Hart. (Illus.). 35p. (Orig.). (C). 1991. pap. 7.50 (0-944048-03-X) Timberline Missouri.

***Monsoon.** MOTOI ICHIHARA. 1999. 60.00 (3-908163-03-X) Abbeville Pr.

Monsoon. Wilbur Smith. LC 99-24554. 544p. 1999. text 26.95 (0-312-20339-X) St Martin.

***Monsoon.** Wilbur Smith. 864p. 2000. mass mkt. 7.99 (0-312-97154-0, St Martins Paperbacks) St Martin.

Monsoon: A Novel to End World Hunger. John Ballard. Ed. by Prema Ghose. LC 84-62121. (MacBurnie King Adventure Ser.). (Illus.). 242p. 1985. 14.95 (0-932279-00-7, New Horiz CA); pap. 9.95 (0-932279-01-5, New Horiz CA) World Citizens.

Monsoon: A Novel to End World Hunger. John Ballard. LC 84-62121. (MacBurnie King Adventure Ser.). (Illus.). 240p. (YA). (gr. 7 up). 1986. pap. text 29.95 (0-932279-02-3, Clsrm Classics) World Citizens.

Monsoon Breezes. Kirpal. 1990. 150.00 (81-209-0156-8, Pub. by Pitambar Pub) St Mut.

Monsoon Molly. Annie Kubler. 1999. pap. text 9.99 (0-85953-612-2) Childs Play.

Monsoon Season. William Q. Wu. LC 96-60262. 1996. 10.00 (1-885854-01-3) UniStar Pubng.

Monsoon Surgeon. large type ed. Margaret Barker. (Magna Large Print Ser.). 264p. 1996. 27.99 (0-7505-0998-8, Pub. by Mgna Lrg Print) Ulverscroft.

Monsoonal Australia: Landscape, Ecology & Man. Ed. by C. M. Haynes et al. (Illus.). 270p. (C). 1991. text 123.00 (90-6191-638-0, Pub. by A A Balkema) Ashgate Pub Co.

Monsoons: A Collection of Writing. Laraine Herring. 208p. 1999. pap. write for info. (1-892579-06-5) Duality Pr.

Monsoons over China. Yihui Ding. LC 92-12017. (Atmospheric Sciences Library). 432p. (C). 1994. text 264.50 (0-7923-1757-2) Kluwer Academic.

Monster. Illus. by Toni Goffe. LC 93-21862. 24p. (J). (ps-3). 1993. 4.99 (0-85953-406-5) Childs Play.

Monster. Diane Hoh. (Nightmare Hall Ser.: No. 13). 176p. (YA). (gr. 7-9). 1994. pap. 3.50 (0-590-48321-8) Scholastic Inc.

Monster. Steve Jackson. LC 99-169771. 384p. 1998. mass mkt. 5.99 (0-7860-0586-6, Pinncle Kensgtn) Kensgtn Pub Corp.

***Monster.** Jonathan Kellerman. (Alex Delaware Novel Ser.). 416p. 2000. mass mkt. 7.99 (0-345-41387-3, Ballantine) Ballantine Pub Grp.

Monster. Walter Dean Myers. LC 98-40958. (Illus.). 288p. (J). (gr. 7-12). 1999. 15.95 (0-06-028077-8) HarpC Child Bks.

Monster. Walter Dean Myers. LC 98-40958. (Illus.). 288p. (YA). (gr. 7 up). 1999. lib. bdg. 15.89 (0-06-028078-6) HarpC Child Bks.

***Monster.** Walter Dean Myers & Christopher A. Myers. LC 98-40958. (Illus.). 288p. (YA). (gr. 7 up). 1999. 5.95 (0-06-440731-4) HarpC Child Bks.

Monster. Christopher Pike, pseud. Ed. by Pat MacDonald. 256p. (YA). (gr. 9 up). 1992. mass mkt. 3.99 (0-671-74507-7, Archway) PB.

Monster. Christopher Pike, pseud. (J). 1992. 9.09 (0-606-02203-1, Pub. by Turtleback) Demco.

Monster. Mick Stewart. 320p. 1997. mass mkt. 5.99 (0-7860-0391-X, Pinncle Kensgtn) Kensgtn Pub Corp.

***Monster.** large type ed. Jonathan Kellerman. 2000. pap. 14.95 (0-375-72794-9) Random.

Monster. Edgar E. Saltus. LC 70-113266. reprint ed. 37.50 (0-404-05541-9) AMS Pr.

***Monster: A Novel.** Jonathan Kellerman. LC 99-20098. 396p. 1999. 25.95 (0-679-45960-X) Random.

***Monster: A Novel.** large type ed. Jonathan Kellerman. LC 99-36463. 1999. 25.95 (0-375-40868-1) Random Hse Lrg Prnt.

Monster: Living off the Big Screen. John G. Dunne. 1998. pap. 12.00 (0-375-75024-X) Vin Bks.

Monster: The Autobiography of an LA Gang Member. Monster K. Scott, pseud. 400p. (C). 1998. pap. 12.95 (0-14-023225-7) Addson-Wesley Educ.

Monster Activity & Game Book. Elvira Gamiello. (Illus.). (Orig.). (J). (gr. 4-6). 1988. pap. 1.95 (0-942025-28-8) Kidsbks.

Monster & Lie Algebras: Proceedings of a Special Research Quarter Held at the Ohio State University, Spring 1996. J. Ferrar & Koichiro Harada. LC 98-29397. (Ohio State University Mathematical Research Institute Publications). 252p. 1998. 99.95 (3-11-016184-2) De Gruyter.

Monster & Magic Umbrella. Blance & Cook. Date not set. pap. text. write for info. (0-582-18593-9, Pub. by Addison-Wesley) Longman.

Monster & Other Stories. Stephen Crane. (Works of Stephen Crane). 1990. reprint ed. lib. bdg. 79.00 (0-685-44792-8) Rprt Serv.

Monster & Surprise Cookie. Blance & Cook. Date not set. pap. text. write for info. (0-582-19308-7, Pub. by Addison-Wesley) Longman.

Monster & the Mural. Blance & Cook. Date not set. pap. text. write for info. (0-582-19301-X, Pub. by Addison-Wesley) Longman.

Monster & the Teddy Bear. David McKee. (Illus.). 32p. (J). (ps-1). 1998. pap. 9.95 (0-86264-762-2, Pub. by Andersen Pr) Trafalgar.

Monster at Christmas. Thomas Canty. (Illus.). 1986. 30.00 (0-937986-67-4) D M Grant.

Monster at School. Blance & Cook. Date not set. pap. text. write for info. (0-582-18597-1, Pub. by Addison-Wesley) Longman.

***Monster at the End of This Book.** Jon Stone. 1999. 2.99 (0-375-80401-3) Random.

***Monster at the End of This Book.** Jon Stone. (Big Bird's Favorites Board Bks.). (Illus.). 24p. (J). (ps). 2000. 4.99 (0-375-80561-3, Pub. by Random Bks Yng Read) Random.

Monster Bash. Jane King. (Ghoul School Ser.: No. 3). (J). (gr. 2-4). 1996. pap. 3.50 (0-671-51025-8) PB.

Monster Bed. Jeanne Willis. LC 86-10366. (Illus.). 32p. (J). (ps-2). 1987. 15.00 (0-688-06804-9); lib. bdg. 14.93 (0-688-06805-7) Lothrop.

***Monster Bed.** Jeanne Willis & Susan Varley. LC 99-200797. 32p. (J). 1999. mass mkt. 5.95 (0-688-16707-1, Wm Morrow) Morrow Avon.

Monster Birds: A Navajo Folktale. Vee Browne. LC 92-82139. (Illus.). 32p. (J). 1993. lib. bdg. 14.95 (0-87358-558-5, Rising Moon Bks) Northland AZ.

Monster Blood see Sangre de Monstruo

Monster Blood. R. L. Stine, pseud. (Goosebumps Ser.: No. 3). 160p. (J). (gr. 3-7). 1992. pap. 3.99 (0-590-45367-X, 061, Apple Paperbacks) Scholastic Inc.

Monster Blood. R. L. Stine, pseud. (Goosebumps Ser.: No. 3). (J). 1992. 9.09 (0-606-01910-3, Pub. by Turtleback) Demco.

Monster Blood. Adapted by Elizabeth Winfrey. (Goosebumps Presents Ser.: No. 15). (Illus.). 64p. (J). (gr. 2-5). 1997. pap. text 3.99 (0-590-30547-6, Apple Paperbacks) Scholastic Inc.

Monster Blood. Adapted by Elizabeth Winfrey. (Goosebumps Presents Ser.: No. 15). 1997. 9.19 (0-606-11409-2, Pub. by Turtleback) Demco.

Monster Blood see Goosebumps

M

An Asterisk (*) at the beginning of an entry indicates that the title is appearing for the first time.

Monster Blood IV. R. L. Stine, pseud. (Goosebumps Ser.: No. 62). (YA). 1997. pap. text 3.99 (*0-590-39987-X*, Little Apple) Scholastic Inc.

Monster Blood IV. R. L. Stine, pseud. (Goosebumps Ser.: No. 62). (J). 1997. 9.09 (*0-606-12993-6*, Pub. by Turtleback) Demco.

Monster Blood II see Sangre de Monstruo II

Monster Blood III; It Came from Beneath the Sink; Night of the Living Dummy 2; The Barking Ghost, Bks. 29-32. R. L. Stine, pseud. (Goosebumps Ser.: 8). (J). (gr. 3-7). 1995. pap. text 15.96 (*0-590-53557-9*) Scholastic Inc.

Monster Blood III. R. L. Stine, pseud. (Goosebumps Ser.: No. 29). 160p. (J). (gr. 4-6). 1995. pap. 3.99 (*0-590-48347-1*) Scholastic Inc.

Monster Blood III. R. L. Stine, pseud. (Goosebumps Ser.: No. 29). (J). 1995. 9.09 (*0-606-07880-0*, Pub. by Turtleback) Demco.

Monster Blood II. R. L. Stine, pseud. (Goosebumps Ser.: No. 18). 160p. (J). (gr. 3-7). 1994. pap. 3.99 (*0-590-47740-4*) Scholastic Inc.

Monster Blood II. R. L. Stine, pseud. (Goosebumps Ser.: No. 18). 1994. 9.09 (*0-606-06575-X*, Pub. by Turtleback) Demco.

***Monster Book.** Christopher Golden et al. (Illus.). 352p. (J). 2000. pap. 16.95 (*0-671-04259-9*, PB Trade Paper) PB.

Monster Book of ABC Sounds. Alan Snow. LC 90-39384. (J). 1991. 10.19 (*0-606-06576-8*, Pub. by Turtleback) Demco.

Monster Boy. Christine M. Winn & David Walsh. LC 95-43558. (Illus.). 32p. (J). (gr. k-4). 1996. 14.95 (*0-925190-87-X*) Fairview Press.

Monster Brigade 3000. Ed. by Martin H. Greenberg & Charles Waugh. 224p. (Orig.). 1996. mass mkt. 5.99 (*0-441-00323-0*) Ace Bks.

Monster Brother. Mary J. Auch. LC 93-41746. (Illus.). 32p. (J). (gr. k-3). 1994. lib. bdg. 15.95 (*0-8234-1095-1*) Holiday.

Monster Bucks, How to Take: Secrets to Finding Trophy Deer. John E. Phillips. LC 94-72944. 160p. (Orig.). 1995. pap. 11.95 (*0-936513-46-2*) Larsens Outdoor.

Monster Bugs. Lucille R. Penner. LC 95-347. (Step into Reading Ser.: A Step 2 Book). (Illus.). 48p. (J). (ps-3). 1996. pap. 3.99 (*0-679-86974-3*) Random.

Monster Bugs. Lucille R. Penner. LC 95-347. (Step into Reading Ser.: A Step 2 Book). (Illus.). (J). (ps-3). 1996. lib. bdg. 11.99 (*0-679-96974-8*) Random.

Monster Bugs. Lucille R. Penner. LC 95-347. (Step into Reading Ser.: A Step 2 Book). (J). (gr. 1-3). 1996. 9.19 (*0-606-09626-4*, Pub. by Turtleback) Demco.

Monster Buys a Pet. Blance & Cook. Date not set. pap. text. write for info. (*0-582-19311-7*, Pub. by Addison-Wesley) Longman.

Monster C++ An Introduction to Object-Oriented Programming Using C++ & the Unified Modeling Language (UML) Michael S. Sandberg. (Illus.). 432p. (C). 1998. pap. text 59.95 (*0-9665116-0-3*) Neon Lizard.

***Monster Cake.** Rebecca Dickinson. LC 00-21112. (Illus.). 32p. (J). (ps-3). 2000. 4.99 (*0-439-06752-9*) Scholastic Inc.

Monster Channel. M. T. Coffin. (Spinetinglers Ser.). 1997. 8.60 (*0-606-10880-7*, Pub. by Turtleback) Demco.

Monster Channel, Vol. 17. M. T. Coffin. (Spinetinglers Ser.). (J). 1997. pap. 3.50 (*0-380-78610-9*, Avon Bks) Morrow Avon.

Monster Cheese. Steve Wolfson. (Illus.). 32p. 1985. reprint ed. pap. 5.95 (*0-919926-43-6*, Pub. by Coteau) Genl Dist Srvs.

Monster Christmas. Antonio Jocson. (Muddy Tom's Wacky Adventure Ser.). (J). 1998. 14.95 (*1-890963-05-4*) Lib Bell.

Monster Cleans His House. Blance & Cook. Date not set. pap. text. write for info. (*0-582-18590-4*, Pub. by Addison-Wesley) Longman.

Monster Club Handbook. JTG of Nashville Staff. (J). (ps-3). 1994. pap. 12.95 (*1-884832-04-0*) JTG Nashville.

Monster Comes to the City. Blance & Cook. Date not set. pap. text. write for info. (*0-582-18588-2*, Pub. by Addison-Wesley) Longman.

Monster Crossword Omnibus. Stanley Newman. 1998. pap. 17.50 (*0-8129-3059-2*, Times Bks) Crown Pub Group.

Monster Den: or Look What Happened at My House - And to It. John Ciardi. LC 90-85904. (Illus.). 64p. (J). (gr. k up). 1991. reprint ed. 13.95 (*1-878093-35-5*, Wordsong) Boyds Mills Pr.

Monster Dinosaur. Daniel Cohen. LC 82-48460. 192p. (J). (gr. 3-6). 1983. 11.95 (*0-397-31953-3*) HarpC Child Bks.

Monster Dog. R. L. Stine, pseud. (Ghosts of Fear Street Ser.: No. 24). (J). (gr. 4-7). 1997. per. 3.99 (*0-671-00853-6*) PB.

Monster Dog. R. L. Stine, pseud. (Ghosts of Fear Street Ser.: No. 24). (J). (gr. 4-7). 1997. 9.09 (*0-606-12711-9*, Pub. by Turtleback) Demco.

Monster Dots: Connect the Dots & Color. Rick Tynes & Diane Whittemore. LC 96-3459. (Illus.). 80p. (J). (gr. 1-6). 1993. pap. 5.95 (*0-8069-8642-5*) Sterling.

Monster Encyclopedia. Dave Branson. LC 98-71906. (Illus.). 40p. (J). (gr. k-3). 1998. 16.95 (*1-880851-35-0*) Greene Bark Pr.

Monster Faces. (J). (gr. 3-7). 19.95 (*0-614-19299-4*) DK Pub Inc.

Monster Faces. Sesame Street Staff. (Illus.). (J). 1996. pap. 3.99 (*0-679-87761-4*, Pub. by Random Bks Yng Read) Random.

Monster Faces Stickers. Bob Censoni. (Illus.). (J). (gr. k-3). 1998. pap. 1.00 (*0-486-27751-8*) Dover.

Monster Factory. Richard Rainey. LC 92-26191. (Illus.). 128p. (YA). (gr. 6 up). 1993. lib. bdg. 19.00 (*0-02-775663-7*, Mac Bks Young Read) S&S Childrens.

Monster for Hire. Trevor Wilson. LC 94-28976. (Illus.). 32p. (Orig.). (J). (gr. k-5). 1994. pap. 4.95 (*1-879531-61-5*) Mondo Pubng.

Monster from the Middle Class & Other Books. rev. ed. Charles A. Kimball. LC 84-90366. 295p. 1984. pap. 7.95 (*0-9613507-0-9*) C Kimball.

Monster from the Sea see Bank Street Ready-to-Read Books: Levels 1, 2 & 3

Monster from the Swamp: Native Legends about Demons, Monsters & Other Creatures. Illus. & Retold by C. J. Taylor. LC 95-60980. 32p. (J). (gr. 3-6). 1995. 17.95 (*0-88776-361-8*) Tundra Bks.

Monster Gang. Felicity Everett. (Reading for Beginners Ser.). (Illus.). 24p. (J). (gr. k-4). 1995. text 4.95 (*0-7460-1460-0*, Usborne) EDC.

Monster Gang. Felicity Everett. (Reading for Beginners Ser.). (Illus.). 24p. (J). (gr. k-4). 1995. lib. bdg. 12.95 (*0-88110-728-X*, Usborne) EDC.

Monster Garden. Vivien Alcock. LC 88-6900. 160p. (J). (gr. 5-9). 1988. 13.95 (*0-440-50053-2*) Delacorte.

Monster Gets a Job. Blance & Cook. Date not set. pap. text. write for info. (*0-582-19307-9*, Pub. by Addison-Wesley) Longman.

Monster Goes Around Town. Blance & Cook. Date not set. pap. text. write for info. (*0-582-19309-5*, Pub. by Addison-Wesley) Longman.

Monster Goes to Circus. Blance & Cook. Date not set. pap. text. write for info. (*0-582-19304-4*, Pub. by Addison-Wesley) Longman.

Monster Goes to School. Blance & Cook. Date not set. pap. text. write for info. (*0-582-18596-3*, Pub. by Addison-Wesley) Longman.

Monster Goes to School. Virginia Mueller. (Illus.). 24p. (J). (ps-1). 1997. reprint ed. pap. 4.95 (*0-8075-5265-8*) A Whitman.

Monster Goes to the Beach. Blance & Cook. Date not set. pap. text. write for info. (*0-582-19306-0*, Pub. by Addison-Wesley) Longman.

Monster Goes to the Hospital. Blance & Cook. Date not set. pap. text. write for info. (*0-582-19305-2*, Pub. by Addison-Wesley) Longman.

Monster Goes to the Zoo. Blance & Cook. Date not set. pap. text. write for info. (*0-582-18599-8*, Pub. by Addison-Wesley) Longman.

Monster Hunt Activity Book. Jeffrey Nelson. (Orig.). (YA). 1994. pap. 2.99 (*0-8125-9434-7*, Pub. by Tor Bks) St Martin.

Monster Hunters. Joyce Milton. (J). 1998. pap. 3.99 (*0-679-88575-7*); lib. bdg. 11.99 (*0-679-98575-1*, Pub. by Random Bks Yng Read) Random.

Monster Hunters Case, No. 4. Nancy Garden. LC 94-152911. (J). 1994. pap. 2.99 (*0-671-76008-4*, Minstrel Bks) PB.

***Monster Hunter's Guide.** Golden Books Staff. (Illus.). (J). 2000. pap. 3.99 (*0-307-10476-1*, Goldn Books) Gldn Bks Pub Co.

Monster in a Box. Spalding Gray. 1992. pap. 13.00 (*0-679-73739-1*) Vin Bks.

Monster in a Box: Television Violence, the First Amendment, & the Case for Government Regulation. Terry Rakolta et al. (Law & Violence Ser.: No. 2). 160p. (Orig.). 1996. pap. 14.00 (*1-880831-15-5*) Aletheia Pr.

Monster in Creeps Head Bay. Mel Gilden. (Fifth Grade Monsters Ser.: No. 9). 96p. (J). 1990. pap. 2.75 (*0-380-75905-5*, Avon Bks) Morrow Avon.

Monster in Harry's Backyard. Karen Gray-Ruelle. LC 98-17471. (Holiday House Reader Ser.). (Illus.). (J). (ps-3). 1999. 14.95 (*0-8234-1417-5*) Holiday.

Monster in Our Midst: Will You Be Spared by the Monster. Elie Robinson. 184p. 1997. pap. 15.00 (*0-8059-4229-7*) Dorrance.

Monster in Room 202. Justine Korman. LC 93-2215. (Illus.). 32p. (J). (gr. 2-4). 1997. pap. 2.95 (*0-8167-3183-7*) Troll Communs.

Monster in Room 202. Justine Korman. 1994. 8.70 (*0-606-06577-6*, Pub. by Turtleback) Demco.

Monster in the Cereal see Monstruo en los Cereales

Monster in the House. Elisa Kleven. LC 98-5250. (Illus.). 32p. (J). (ps-2). 1998. 15.99 (*0-525-45973-1*, Dutton Child) Peng Put Young Read.

Monster in the Lake. Franklin W. Dixon. (Hardy Boys Are: The Clues Brothers Ser.: Vol. 11). (Illus.). 80p. (J). (ps-3). 1999. pap. 3.99 (*0-671-02662-3*) PB.

***Monster in the Machine: Magic, Medicine, & the Marvelous in the Time of the Scientific Revolution.** Zakiya Hanafi. (Illus.). 312p. 2000. pap. 20.95 (*0-8223-2568-3*); lib. bdg. 59.95 (*0-8223-2536-5*) Duke.

***Monster in the Maze: The Story of the Minotaur.** Stephanie Spinner. (All Aboard Reading Ser.). (Illus.). 48p. (J). (gr. 1-3). 2000. 13.89 (*0-448-42287-5*, Planet Dexter) Peng Put Young Read.

***Monster in the Maze: The Story of the Minotaur.** Stephanie Spinner. (All Aboard Reading Ser.). (Illus.). 48p. (J). (ps-3). 2000. pap. 3.99 (*0-448-42183-6*, Planet Dexter) Peng Put Young Read.

Monster in the Media see Pedophiles on Parade

Monster in the Mirror: Gender & the Sentimental - Gothic Myth in Frankenstein. Mary K. Thornburg. LC 87-5560. (Studies in Speculative Fiction: No. 14). 164p. reprint ed. pap. 50.90 (*0-8357-1798-4*, 207063800011) Bks Demand.

Monster in the Mirror: Studies in Nineteenth-Century Realism. Ed. by D. Z. Williams. (C). 1978. 38.00 (*0-19-713433-5*) OUP.

***Monster in the Shadows.** Julia Van Nutt. (Cobtown Stories Ser.). (Illus.). 32p. (J). (ps up). 2000. 15.95 (*0-385-32565-7*) Doubleday.

Monster in the Third Dresser Drawer. Janice L. Smith. LC 81-47109. (Illus.). 96p. (J). (ps-3). 1981. lib. bdg. 15.89 (*0-06-025739-3*) HarpC Child Bks.

Monster in the Third Dresser Drawer: A Study Guide. Laurie Diamond. (Novel-Ties Ser.). (J). (gr. 1-3). 1989. pap. text, teacher ed., student ed. 15.95 (*0-88122-041-8*) Lrn Links.

Monster in the Third Dresser Drawer: And Other Stories about Adam Joshua. Janice L. Smith. LC 81-47109. (Trophy Chapter Bk.: No. 1). (Illus.). 96p. (J). (ps-3). 1988. pap. 4.25 (*0-06-440223-1*, HarpTrophy) HarpC Child Bks.

Monster in the Third Dresser Drawer & Otherstories about Adam Joshua. Janice Lee Smith. (J). 1981. 9.05 (*0-606-03863-9*, Pub. by Turtleback) Demco.

***Monster is Hiding, 1vol.** Bianca Cowan. (Illus.). (J). 1999. pap. text 7.95 (*0-9669645-3-5*) OHollow.

Monster Jam. Kieran Flynn. (Screammates Ser.: Vol. 3). (J). 1998. pap. text 3.99 (*0-590-09896-9*, Little Apple) Scholastic Inc.

Monster Jam. Hank Herman. (Super Hoops Ser.: No. 4). (J). (gr. 4-6). 1996. pap. 4.75 (*0-553-54251-6*) BDD Bks Young Read.

Monster Jam. Hank Herman. (Super Hoops Ser.: No. 4). (J). (gr. 4-6). 1996. 8.60 (*0-606-09915-8*, Pub. by Turtleback) Demco.

Monster Java: An Introduction to Object-Oriented Programming & the Unified Modeling Language (UML) Michael S. Sandberg. (Illus.). 400p. (C). 2000. pap. text. write for info. (*0-9665116-1-1*) Neon Lizard.

Monster Joke Book. Gordon Hill. 165p. 1995. pap. 4.95 (*0-572-01561-5*, Pub. by Foulsham UK) Assoc Pubs Grp.

Monster Jokes & Riddles. Jeffrey S. Nelson. (Illus.). 24p. (J). (gr. 3 up). 1988. pap. 1.95 (*1-56288-342-9*) Checkerboard.

Monster Knock Knocks. William Cole. (Orig.). (J). (gr. 3-6). 1990. mass mkt. 2.75 (*0-671-70653-5*) PB.

Monster Looks for a House. Blance & Cook. Date not set. pap. text. write for info. (*0-582-18589-0*, Pub. by Addison-Wesley) Longman.

Monster Looks for Friend. Blance & Cook. Date not set. pap. text. write for info. (*0-582-18591-2*, Pub. by Addison-Wesley) Longman.

Monster Love. Scott Deschaine. (Illus.). 36p. (J). 1993. pap. 2.50 (*1-878181-05-X*) Discovery Comics.

Monster Machines. DK Editors. LC 97-39624. (Illus.). 32p. (J). (gr. 1 up). 1998. 14.95 (*0-7894-2796-6*) DK Pub Inc.

Monster Mad Libs, No. 4. Roger Price & Leonard Stern. (Mad Libs Ser.). (Illus.). 48p. (Orig.). (J). (gr. 4-7). 1974. pap. 3.99 (*0-8431-0058-3*, Price Stern) Peng Put Young Read.

Monster Madness Sticker Pad. Illus. by M.J. Studios Staff. 32p. (J). (gr. k-6). 1993. pap. 2.95 (*1-879424-56-8*) Nickel Pr.

Monster Magic. Cecily Matthews. LC 97-122010. 96p. (J). 1996. pap. 10.95 (*0-7022-2796-X*, Pub. by Univ Queensland Pr) Intl Spec Bk.

***Monster Magnet: Powertrip.** 96p. 1999. otabind 19.95 (*0-634-00800-5*) H Leonard.

Monster Maker. Nate Evans. (Illus.). 8p. (J). (ps-3). 1994. pap. 2.95 (*0-590-48393-5*, Cartwheel) Scholastic Inc.

Monster Mama. Liz Rosenberg. LC 91-46825. (Illus.). 32p. (J). (ps-3). 1993. 15.95 (*0-399-21989-7*, Philomel) Peng Put Young Read.

Monster Mama. Liz Rosenberg. LC 91-46825. (J). 1997. 11.15 (*0-606-11633-8*, Pub. by Turtleback) Demco.

Monster Man. Frank Mundus. 1976. 22.95 (*0-8488-0407-4*); pap. 14.95 (*0-8488-0408-2*) Amereon Ltd.

Monster Mania. 1997. pap. 1.50 (*0-8167-0684-0*) Troll Communs.

Monster Mania Paint Box. Golden Books Staff. 1999. pap. text 3.99 (*0-307-09242-9*) Golden Bks Pub.

Monster Manners. Joanna Cole. (Hello Reader! Ser.). (Illus.). 56p. (J). (gr. 1-2). 1995. pap. 3.50 (*0-590-53951-5*, Cartwheel) Scholastic Inc.

Monster Manners. Joanna Cole. (Hello, Reader! Ser.). (J). 1995. 9.19 (*0-606-07881-9*, Pub. by Turtleback) Demco.

Monster Manners. Bethany Roberts. LC 94-23219. (Illus.). 32p. (J). (ps-3). 1997. pap. 5.95 (*0-395-86622-7*, Clarion Bks) HM.

Monster Manners: A Guide to Monster Etiquette. Bethany Roberts. LC 94-23219. (Illus.). 32p. (J). (ps-3). 1996. 15.00 (*0-395-69850-2*, Clarion Bks) HM.

***Monster Manual.** Skip Williams. 224p. 2000. 19.95 (*0-7869-1552-8*) Wizards Coast.

Monster Manual: A Complete Guide to Your Favorite Creatures. Erich Ballinger. LC 93-34219. (Late-Night Library). (Illus.). 144p. (YA). (gr. 5 up). 1994. lib. bdg. 19.93 (*0-8225-0722-6*, Lerner Publctns) Lerner Pub.

Monster Manual: A Complete Guide to Your Favorite Creatures. Erich Ballinger. (Illus.). 144p. (J). (gr. 5-9). 1997. reprint ed. pap. text 8.95 (*0-8225-9771-3*) Lerner Pub.

Monster MASH. Mimi Maxwell. 1998. pap. text 6.99 (*0-9680678-8-3*) Tumbleweed Pr.

Monster Mashers. Mel Gilden. (Fifth Grade Monsters Ser.: No. 6). 96p. (Orig.). (J). (gr. 5 up). 1989. pap. 2.75 (*0-380-75785-0*, Avon Bks) Morrow Avon.

Monster Math. 1998. 24.72 (*0-395-83427-9*) HM.

Monster Math. Grace Maccarone. LC 95-12133. (Hello Math Reader Level 1 Ser.). (Illus.). 32p. (J). (ps-3). 1995. pap. 3.50 (*0-590-22712-2*, Cartwheel) Scholastic Inc.

Monster Math. Grace Maccarone. (J). 1995. 8.70 (*0-606-07882-7*, Pub. by Turtleback) Demco.

***Monster Math.** Anne Miranda. LC 98-12933. 32p. (J). (ps-3). 1999. 16.00 (*0-15-201835-2*, Harcourt Child Bks) Harcourt.

Monster Math Bk. 2: Puzzles & Games Workbook. Oksana Hlodan. (Illus.). 64p. (J). (gr. 1-3). 1999. pap., wbk. ed. 4.95 (*0-7373-0147-3*, 01473W) NTC Contemp Pub Co.

Monster Math Multiplication Workbook. Oksana Hlodan. (Monster Math Ser.). (Illus.). 64p. (J). (gr. 1-3). 1998. pap., wbk. ed. 4.95 (*1-56565-678-4*, 06784W, Pub. by Lowell Hse Juvenile) NTC Contemp Pub Co.

***Monster Math Picnic.** Grace Maccarone. 1998. 8.70 (*0-606-13617-7*, Pub. by Turtleback) Demco.

Monster Math Picnic. Grace MacCarone et al. LC 97-12854. (Hello Math Reader Ser.). (Illus.). (J). (ps-4). 1998. 3.50 (*0-590-37127-4*) Scholastic Inc.

Monster Math School Time. Grace Maccarone. (Hello Math Reader Ser.). (J). 1997. 8.70 (*0-606-11634-6*, Pub. by Turtleback) Demco.

Monster Math School Time. Grace MacCarone & Marilyn Burns. LC 97-5035. (Hello Math Reader Ser.). (Illus.). 32p. (J). (ps-1). 1997. 3.50 (*0-590-30859-9*) Scholastic Inc.

Monster Math Super Edition for Ages 4-6. Oksana Hlodan. (Monster Math Super Editions Ser.). (Illus.). 256p. (J). (ps-1). 2000. pap. 14.95 (*0-7373-0214-3*, 02143W) NTC Contemp Pub Co.

Monster Math Super Edition for Ages 6-8. Mary Cron et al. (Monster Math Super Editions Ser.). (Illus.). 256p. (J). (gr. 1-3). 2000. pap. 14.95 (*0-7373-0216-X*, 0216XW) NTC Contemp Pub Co.

Monster Math Workbook, Bk. 1. Mary Cron & Martha C. Cheney. 64p. (J). 1995. pap., wbk. ed. 4.95 (*1-56565-307-6*, 03076W, Pub. by Lowell Hse) NTC Contemp Pub Co.

Monster Math Workbook, Bk. 2. Martha C. Cheney. 64p. (J). 1995. pap., wbk. ed. 4.95 (*1-56565-309-2*, 03092W, Pub. by Lowell Hse) NTC Contemp Pub Co.

Monster Math Workbook for Ages 4-6. Oksana Hlodan. (Monster Math Ser.). 64p. (J). (ps-1). Date not set. pap., wbk. ed. 4.95 (*1-56565-576-1*, 05761W, Pub. by Lowell Hse Juvenile) NTC Contemp Pub Co.

Monster Math Workbook for Ages 4-6, Bk. 2. Oksana Hlodan. (Monster Math Ser.). (Illus.). 64p. (J). (ps-1). 1997. pap., wbk. ed. 4.95 (*1-56565-762-4*, 07624W, Pub. by Lowell Hse Juvenile) NTC Contemp Pub Co.

Monster Mayhem. (J). 1996. 6.98 (*1-57082-393-6*, Pub. by Mouse Works) Time Warner.

Monster Mazes. Kim Blundell & Jenny Tyler. (Maze Fun Ser.). (Illus.). 24p. (J). (gr. k-2). 1994. pap. 4.50 (*0-7460-1325-6*, Usborne) EDC.

Monster Mazes. Patrick Merrell. (Illus.). 32p. 1997. pap. text 3.95 (*0-8167-4400-9*) Troll Communs.

Monster Mazes. Myron M. Morris. 1997. pap. 1.25 (*0-89375-072-7*) NAL.

Monster Mazes. Dave Phillips. 48p. 1989. pap. 2.95 (*0-486-26005-4*) Dover.

Monster Meets Lady Monster. Blance & Cook. Date not set. pap. text. write for info. (*0-582-18592-0*, Pub. by Addison-Wesley) Longman.

Monster Men. Edgar Rice Burroughs. LC 62-8707. (Illus.). (J). 1962. 25.00 (*0-940724-06-5*) P Hunt.

Monster Metal Ballads. 1991. 19.95 (*0-7935-0357-4*, 00660229) H Leonard.

Monster Mischief. June. LC 96-15106. (J). 2000. 16.00 (*0-689-80471-7*) S&S Childrens.

Monster Mix-Up. Ed. by Ruth Ashby. (Nintendo Bk.: No. III). 128p. (Orig.). (J). 1991. mass mkt. 3.50 (*0-671-74201-9*, Archway) PB.

***Monster Money.** Grace MacCarone. (Hello Math Reader Ser.). (J). (ps-1). 1998. 8.70 (*0-606-13618-5*, Pub. by Turtleback) Demco.

***Monster Money.** Grace Maccarone & Marilyn Burns. LC 97-43658. (Hello Reader! Math Ser.: Level 1). (Illus.). 32p. (J). (ps-3). 1998. pap. 3.50 (*0-590-12007-7*) Scholastic Inc.

Monster Money Book. Loreen Leedy. LC 91-18168. (Illus.). 32p. (J). (gr. k-3). 1992. lib. bdg. 16.95 (*0-8234-0922-8*) Holiday.

***Monster Money Book.** Loreen Leedy. (Illus.). 2000. pap. 6.95 (*0-8234-1558-9*) Holiday.

Monster! Monster! Betty S. Garner. 192p. 1995. pap. 12.95 (*0-88839-357-1*) Hancock House.

Monster Motel. Douglas Florian. LC 92-7309. (Illus.). 32p. (J). 1996. pap. 5.00 (*0-15-201386-5*) Harcourt.

Monster Motel. abr. ed. Douglas Florian. LC 92-7309. (Illus.). 32p. (J). (ps-3). 1993. 13.95 (*0-15-255320-7*) Harcourt.

Monster Motel, Poems & Paintings. Douglas Florian. LC 92-7309. 1996. 10.20 (*0-606-11632-X*, Pub. by Turtleback) Demco.

Monster Mother. Deanna R. LuBin. Tr. by Tom Fosten. (Illus.). (J). (ps-9). 1991. lib. bdg. write for info. (*0-318-67146-8*); audio. write for info. (*0-318-67147-6*) Lubin Pr.

Monster Mouse Mystery. Laura Lee Hope. Ed. by Ann Greenberg. (New Bobbsey Twins Ser.: No. 23). (Illus.). 96p. (J). (gr. 3-5). 1991. pap. 2.95 (*0-671-69295-X*, Minstrel Bks) PB.

Monster Munchies. Laura Numeroff. LC 97-48559. (J). 1998. lib. bdg. 11.99 (*0-679-99163-8*, Pub. by Random Bks Yng Read) Random.

Monster Munchies. Laura Numeroff. LC 97-48559. 48p. (J). (gr. k-3). 1998. 7.99 (*0-679-89163-3*, Pub. by Random Bks Yng Read) Random.

Monster Museum. Marilyn Singer. 32p. (J). Date not set. pap. 4.99 (*0-7868-1436-5*, Pub. by Hyperion) Time Warner.

Monster Museum. Marilyn Singer. 32p. Date not set. 14.99 (*0-7868-0520-X*, Pub. by Hyprn Ppbks) Little.

***Monster Musical Chairs.** Stuart J. Murphy. LC 99-27902. (MathStart Ser.: Vol. 28). 40p. (J). 2000. lib. bdg. 15.89 (*0-06-028021-2*) HarpC Child Bks.

***Monster Musical Chairs.** Stuart J. Murphy. LC 99-27902. (Illus.). 40p. (J). 2000. pap. 4.95 (*0-06-446730-9*, HarpTrophy) HarpC Child Bks.

***Monster Musical Chairs.** 28th ed. Stuart J. Murphy. LC 99-27902. (MathStart Ser.). (Illus.). 40p. (J). 2000. 15.95 (*0-06-028020-4*) HarpC Child Bks.

Monster Mysteries. John Grant. 1992. 12.98 (*1-55521-789-3*) Bk Sales Inc.

Monster Mythology. 15.00 (*1-56076-362-0*) TSR Inc.

Monster of a Hampster. Elizabeth Hawkins. (Illus.). 96p. (J). pap. 7.95 (*0-14-038124-4*, Pub. by Pnguin Bks Ltd) Trafalgar.

Monster of Minnesota. Mark Summer. 208p. 1997. mass mkt. 5.99 (*0-441-00459-8*) Ace Bks.

***Monster of St. Marylebone.** Wayne Worcester. (Journals of Dr. Watson). 272p. (J). 1999. mass mkt. 5.99 (*0-451-19871-9*, Sig) NAL.

Monster of the Month. Dian Curtis Regan. (J). 1997. mass mkt. 3.99 (*0-590-62391-5*) Scholastic Inc.

Monster of the Month Club. Dian Curtis Regan. 1997. 9.09 (*0-606-11635-4*, Pub. by Turtleback) Demco.

***Monster of the Month Club, Class Set.** unabridged ed. Dian C. Regan. (J). (gr. 4). 1998. 89.70 incl. audio (*0-7887-2544-0*, 46714) Recorded Bks.

***Monster of the Month Club, Homework Set.** unabridged ed. Dian C. Regan. (J). 1998. 38.24 incl. audio (*0-7887-2239-5*, 40723) Recorded Bks.

Monster of the Year. Bruce Coville. (J). (gr. 3-6). 1990. pap. 3.50 (*0-671-73147-5*, Minstrel Bks) PB.

Monster of the Year. Bruce Coville. (J). 1989. 9.09 (*0-606-01968-5*, Pub. by Turtleback) Demco.

Monster on the Bus. Blance & Cook. Date not set. pap. text. write for info. (*0-582-18595-5*, Pub. by Addison-Wesley) Longman.

Monster on the Loch. Alanna Knight. LC 99-475372. (Thumbprint Mysteries Ser.). 128p. (J). 1999. pap. 5.95 (*0-8092-0688-9*, 068890) NTC Contemp Pub Co.

Monster Party. Patricia A. Jensen. LC 93-220275. (Giant First-Start Reader Ser.). (Illus.). 32p. (J). (gr. k-2). 1993. lib. bdg. 17.25 (*0-8167-3184-5*) Troll Communs.

Monster Party. Patricia A. Jensen. (Giant First-Start Reader Ser.). (Illus.). 32p. (J). (gr. k-2). 1997. pap. 3.95 (*0-8167-3185-3*) Troll Communs.

Monster Phonics: Consonants for Grades K-1. Vicky Shiotsu. (Illus.). 48p. (J). (gr. k-1). 1999. pap. 5.95 (*0-7373-0141-4*, 01414W) NTC Contemp Pub Co.

Monster Phonics: Monster Town. Judith B. Stamper. (Hello, Reader! Ser.). (J). (gr. 1-2). 1998. 8.70 (*0-606-13619-3*, Pub. by Turtleback) Demco.

Monster Phonics: Short Vowels for Grades K-1. Vicky Shiotsu. (Illus.). 48p. (J). (gr. k-1). 1999. pap. 5.95 (*0-7373-0143-0*, 01430W) NTC Contemp Pub Co.

***Monster Phonics: Special Vowels for Grades 1-2.** Vicky Shiotsu. (Illus.). 48p. (J). (gr. 1-2). 2000. pap. 5.95 (*0-7373-0334-4*, 03344W, Pub. by Lowell Hse Juvenile) NTC Contemp Pub Co.

Monster Places. Sesame Street Staff. LC 95-71641. (Illus.). (J). 1996. pap. 3.99 (*0-679-87760-6*, Pub. by Random Bks Yng Read) Random.

Monster Poems. Illus. & Compiled by Korky Paul. 32p. (J). (gr. k up). 1997. pap. 7.95 (*0-19-276147-1*) OUP.

Monster Poems. Ed. by Daisy Wallace. LC 75-17680. (Illus.). 32p. (J). (gr. k-3). 1976. reprint ed. lib. bdg. 14.95 (*0-8234-0268-1*) Holiday.

Monster Pop-Up. (Pop-Up Bks.). (J). (ps-3). 1997. pap. 9.95 (*0-8167-1445-2*) Troll Communs.

Monster Rabbit Runs. Patricia Reilly Giff. (Kops Ser.: No. 15). 80p. (J). (gr. 4-7). 1991. pap. 3.99 (*0-440-40424-X*) Dell.

Monster Rabbit Runs Amuck! Patricia Reilly Giff. (Kids of the Polk Street School Ser.). (J). 1991. 9.19 (*0-606-04978-9*, Pub. by Turtleback) Demco.

Monster Riddles. Louis Phillips. LC 96-47722. (Viking Easy-To-Read Ser.). (Illus.). 32p. (J). (gr. 1-4). 1998. pap. 3.99 (*0-14-038790-0*) Viking Penguin.

Monster Riddles. Viki Woodworth. (Funny Side Up Ser.). (Illus.). 32p. (J). (gr. 1-4). 1993. lib. bdg. 19.93 (*0-89565-863-1*) Childs World.

***Monster Road.** David Lubar. (Illus.). 128p. (gr. 2-5). 1999. pap. 3.99 (*0-590-28168-2*) Scholastic Inc.

Monster Rolling Skull & Other Native American Tales. Anita Gustafson & Marilyn Kriney. LC 79-7890. (Illus.). (J). (gr. 4-6). 1980. lib. bdg. 8.89 (*0-690-04020-2*) HarpC Child Bks.

Monster Scales & Modes. Dave Celentano. 48p. 1992. pap. 7.95 (*0-931759-59-5*) Centerstream Pub.

***Monster Shoes.** Emma Laybourn. (J). 2000. pap. 6.95 (*0-552-54634-8*, Pub. by Transworld Publishers Ltd) Trafalgar.

Monster Songs. Deborah Eaton. LC 98-34283. (Real Kids Readers Ser.). (Illus.). 32p. (J). (gr. k-2). 1999. 16.90 (*0-7613-2054-7*, Copper Beech Bks); pap. 3.99 (*0-7613-2079-2*, Copper Beech Bks) Millbrook Pr.

Monster Soup. Dilys Evans. (Illus.). 40p. (J). (ps). 1992. 14.95 (*0-590-45208-8*, 001, Scholastic Hardcover) Scholastic Inc.

Monster Soup: And Other Spooky Poems. Dilys Evans. 40p. (J). (ps-7). 1995. pap. 4.95 (*0-590-45209-6*, Cartwheel) Scholastic Inc.

Monster Soup & Other Spooky Poems. Jacqueline Rogers. (J). 1992. 10.15 (*0-606-07883-5*, Pub. by Turtleback) Demco.

Monster Spray. Brandy Gardner. Ed. & Illus. by Greg Gardner. 20p. (J). (ps-2). 1998. pap. 4.95 (*0-9667770-0-X*) New Horizons VA.

Monster Stew. Date not set. pap. 4.95 (*0-89868-370-X*) ARO Pub.

Monster Stew. Mitra Modarressi. LC 97-39418. 48p. (J). (gr. 3-6). 1998. 15.95 (*0-7894-2517-3*) DK Pub Inc.

Monster Stew. Janie Spaht-Gill. (Illus.). (J). 5.95 (*0-89868-307-6*); lib. bdg. 10.95 (*0-89868-306-8*) ARO Pub.

Monster Stew, Vol. 4474. Marcia S. Gresko. Ed. by Joel Kupperstein. (Learn to Read Math Ser.). (Illus.). 16p. (J). 1998. pap. 2.75 (*1-57471-381-7*, 4474) Creat Teach Pr.

Monster Stick & Other Appalachian Tall Tales. Paul Lepp & Bil Lepp. LC PS3562.E6132M66 1999. 160p. (YA). (gr. 10 up). 1999. pap. 9.95 (*0-87483-577-1*) August Hse.

Monster Stories for under 5s. Joan Stimson. (Series 922). (Illus.). 44p. (J). (ps). 1992. pap. 3.50 (*0-7214-1505-9*, Ladybrd) Penguin Putnam.

Monster Stories for under Fives. Joan Stimson. (Illus.). 44p. (J). 1994. text 3.50 (*0-7214-1639-X*, Ladybrd) Penguin Putnam.

Monster Storm. Jeanne Willis. LC 94-73774. (Illus.). 32p. (J). (ps up). 1995. 14.00 (*0-688-13785-7*) Lothrop.

***Monster Story-Teller.** Wilson. (J). 2000. pap. 6.95 (*0-552-54529-5*, Pub. by Transworld Publishers Ltd) Trafalgar.

Monster Talk. YES! Entertainment Corporation Staff. (Interactive Books - Listen to This Ser.). 12p. (J). (ps-2). 1994. write for info. (*1-57234-042-8*) YES Ent.

Monster Tayles. Carl Hoffman. LC 83-62046. (Illus.). 114p. 1983. pap. 6.00 (*0-9612014-0-1*) Porkyspine.

Monster Theory: Reading Culture. Ed. by Jeffrey J. Cohen. 288p. (C). 1996. pap. 21.95 (*0-8166-2855-6*); text 54.95 (*0-8166-2854-8*) U of Minn Pr.

Monster Tots: Opening Day at Loretta's Day Care Center. Kirk Muzzy. LC 98-68212. (Illus.). (J). (ps-5). 1999. 14.95 (*1-880015-31-5*) Petra Pub.

Monster Town, Level 1. Judith B. Stamper & Wiley Blevins. LC 97-14516. (Hello Reader! Ser.). (Illus.). 32p. (J). 1997. 3.50 (*0-590-76265-6*) Scholastic Inc.

***Monster Town Fair.** Judith Bauer Stamper & Wiley Blevins. LC 97-23399. (Hello Reader! Ser.). (Illus.). 32p. (J). (gr. 1-2). 1998. pap. 3.50 (*0-590-76268-0*, Pub. by Scholastic Inc) Penguin Putnam.

Monster Tracks. Houghton Mifflin Company Staff. (Literature Experience 1991 Ser.). (J). (gr. 1). 1990. pap. 8.72 (*0-395-55138-2*) HM.

Monster Tracks. Houghton Mifflin Company Staff. (Literature Experience 1993 Ser.). (J). (gr. 1). 1992. pap. 8.72 (*0-395-61759-6*) HM.

***Monster Train.** Michael Ratnett. (Illus.). 12p. (J). (gr. k-1). 2000. 15.95 (*0-531-30293-8*) Orchard Bks Watts.

Monster Truck. Kindersley Publishing Dorling. 1999. 4.95 (*0-7894-4734-7*) DK Pub Inc.

Monster Truck Drag Racing see Drag Racing

Monster Truck Drag Racing. Martin Hintz & Kate Hintz. (Drag Racing Ser.). (Illus.). 48p. (J). (gr. 3-7). 1996. lib. bdg. 19.00 (*0-516-20242-1*) Childrens.

Monster Truck Racing see MotorSports

Monster Truck Racing. Scott Johnston. (Motorsports Ser.). (Illus.). 48p. (J). (gr. 3-6). 1994. 19.00 (*0-516-35204-0*) Childrens.

Monster Truck Wars see MotorSports

Monster Truck Wars. Jeff Savage. (Motorsports Ser.). (Illus.). 48p. (J). (gr. 3-6). 1995. 19.00 (*0-516-35258-X*) Childrens.

Monster Trucks see Rollin'

Monster Trucks. James Koons. (Rollin' Ser.). (Illus.). 48p. (J). (gr. 3-7). 1996. 19.00 (*0-516-20094-1*) Childrens.

***Monster Trucks.** Jeff Savage. LC 00-30912. (Action Events Ser.). (Illus.). 2000. write for info. (*0-7660-1712-5*) Enslow Pubs.

Monster Trucks. Jeff Savage. LC 95-35531. (Action Events Ser.). (J). 1996. lib. bdg. 14.95 (*0-89686-889-3*, Crstwood Hse) Silver Burdett Pr.

Monster Trucks. Jeff Savage. LC 95-35531. (Action Events Ser.). (Illus.). 48p. (J). 1996. pap. 4.95 (*0-382-39295-7*) Silver Burdett Pr.

***Monster Trucks & Tractors.** Sue Mead. LC 98-8216. (Race Car Legends Ser.). (Illus.). 64p. (YA). (gr. 3 up). 1999. lib. bdg. 16.95 (*0-7910-5021-1*) Chelsea Hse.

Monster under My Bed. Suzanne Gruber. LC 84-45687. (Illus.). 32p. (J). (gr. k-2). 1997. pap. 3.95 (*0-8167-0457-0*) Troll Communs.

Monster under the Bed. Stan Davis. 192p. 1995. per. 11.00 (*0-684-80438-7*, Touchstone) S&S Trade Pap.

Monster under the Bed. R. U. Scary. LC 95-71384. (Illus.). (J). 1996. 8.99 (*0-679-87415-1*) Random.

Monster Vehicles see Cruisin'

Monster Vision. Ellen W. Leroe. LC 95-45994. (F(r)iendly Corners Ser.: Vol. 1). (Illus.). 128p. (J). (gr. 4-7). 1996. pap. 3.95 (*0-7868-1095-5*, Pub. by Hyprn Ppbks) Little.

Monster with a Thousand Faces: Guises of the Vampire in Myth & Literature. Brian J. Frost. LC 89-61747. 148p. (C). 1989. 27.95 (*0-87972-459-5*) Bowling Green Univ Popular Press.

Monster Within. Darryl Bristen. Ed. by JoAnne Cramberg. 48p. 1998. pap. 6.00 (*0-9657706-7-2*) Phos Pub.

Monster Within: Overcoming Eating Disorders. Cynthia Rowland McClure. 192p. 1998. mass mkt. 5.99 (*0-8007-8652-1*, Spire) Revell.

Monster Wrecks of Loch Ness & Lake Champlain. Joseph W. Zarzynski. LC 86-90418. 111p. 1986. pap. text 8.95 (*0-937559-00-8*) M-Z Info.

***Monster/Beauty: Building the Body of Love.** Joanna Frueh. LC 00-21024. (Illus.). 383p. 2000. 55.00 (*0-520-22113-3*); pap. 22.50 (*0-520-22114-1*, Pub. by U CA Pr) Cal Prin Full Svc.

Monstered Self: Narratives of Death & Performance in Latin American Fiction. Eduardo Gonzalez. LC 91-27927. 295p. 1992. text 42.95 (*0-8223-1209-3*) Duke.

Monstergrams: Twelve Spooky Pop-Up Greeting Cards to Make Yourself. Sandra McCabe. (Illus.). 24p. (J). (gr. k-5). 1999. pap. 5.95 (*0-8037-1647-8*, Dial Yng Read) Peng Put Young Read.

Monsterous Civilizations of Delos. Ben R. Ezzell & Mary M. Ezzell. (Illus.). 115p. 1986. pap. 11.95 (*0-940918-49-8*, STK 82-012) Dragon Tree.

Monsters. (J). 1992. mass mkt. 24.95 (*1-85227-283-X*) Carol Pub Group.

Monsters. Melvin Berger. (Stranger Than Fiction Ser.). 128p. (J). 1991. pap. 2.95 (*0-380-76053-3*, Avon Bks) Morrow Avon.

***Monsters.** Jonathan Clements. (Unexplained Ser.). 32p. (YA). (gr. 5 up). 1999. pap. 5.95 (*0-7641-1064-0*) Barron.

Monsters. Dan Dramer. (Illus.). 160p. (YA). (gr. 6 up). 1985. pap. text 12.64 (*0-89061-451-2*, Jamestwn Pub) NTC Contemp Pub Co.

Monsters. Linda Jennings. (Spooky Pop-Ups Ser.). 1999. 4.95 (*1-899607-19-6*) Levinson Bks.

Monsters. Miller. (World of the Unknown Ser.). (Illus.). 32p. (J). (gr. k-6). 1977. text 6.95 (*0-86020-146-5*) EDC.

Monsters. Marge Murphy. 11p. (J). (gr. 1). 1989. pap. text 2.50 (*1-882225-07-4*) Tott Pubns.

Monsters, 9 bks. Janet Perry & Victor Gentle. Incl. Aliens. LC 99-14720. (Illus.). 24p. (YA). (gr. 2 up). 1999. lib. bdg. 18.60 (*0-8368-2435-0*); Dragons & Dinosaurs. LC 99-25566. (Illus.). 24p. (YA). (gr. 2 up). 1999. lib. bdg. 18.60 (*0-8368-2436-9*); Giants & Wild Hairy Monsters. LC 99-14719. (Illus.). 24p. (YA). (gr. 2 up). 1999. lib. bdg. 18.60 (*0-8368-2437-7*); Mad Scientists. LC 99-25418. (Illus.). 24p. (YA). (gr. 2 up). 1999. lib. bdg. 18.60 (*0-8368-2438-5*); Manmade Monsters. LC 99-14713. (Illus.). 24p. (YA). (gr. 2 up). 1999. lib. bdg. 18.60 (*0-8368-2439-3*); Monsters of the Deep. LC 99-22864. (Illus.). 24p. (YA). (gr. 2 up). 1999. lib. bdg. 18.60 (*0-8368-2440-7*); Morph Monsters. LC 99-14714. (Illus.). 24p. (YA). (gr. 2 up). 1999. lib. bdg. 18.60 (*0-8368-2441-5*); Vampires. LC 99-22509. (YA). (gr. 2 up). 1999. lib. bdg. 18.60 (*0-8368-2442-3*); Zombies. LC 99-22510. (Illus.). 24p. (YA). (gr. 2 up). 1999. lib. bdg. 18.60 (*0-8368-2443-1*); (Illus.). (J). (gr. 2 up). Set lib. bdg. 167.40 (*0-8368-2434-2*) Gareth Stevens Inc.

Monsters. Kenneth Robeson. 144p. Date not set. 18.95 (*0-8488-2621-3*) Amereon Ltd.

Monsters, Bk. 6. Regents. (J). 1996. pap. text 7.80 (*0-13-349879-4*) P-H.

Monsters: And Creatures of the Night. Sue Burztynski. 96p. (J). (gr. 3-8). 1996. pap. text 6.95 (*1-86448-245-1*) IPG Chicago.

Monsters: Pop-Up. (Illus.). (J). (ps-3). 1993. 4.95 (*0-8167-2926-3*) Troll Communs.

***Monsters: The World's Most Incredible Animals.** Beatrice Fontanel. LC 99-58414. (Illus.). 92p. (J). (gr. 3-7). 2000. 19.95 (*0-87226-605-2*, 66052B, P Bedrick Books) NTC Contemp Pub Co.

Monster's Alphabet see Sesame Street Little Library

Monsters among Us see Monstruos Entre Nosotros: Teenage Mutant Ninja Turtles

Monsters among Us see I Mostri Sono Tra Noi: Teenage Mutant Ninja Turtles

Monsters among Us: Teenage Mutant Hero Turtles. Stephen Murphy. (Comes to Life Bks.). 16p. (J). (ps-2). 1994. write for info. (*1-883366-76-3*) YES Ent.

Monsters among Us: Teenage Mutant Ninja Turtles. Stephen Murphy. (Comes to Life Bks.). 16p. (J). (ps-2). 1993. write for info. (*1-883366-09-7*) YES Ent.

Monsters & Aliens from George Lucas. Bob Carrau. (Illus.). 64p. 1996. reprint ed. pap. 9.98 (*0-8109-8139-4*, Pub. by Abrams) Time Warner.

Monsters & Animals. rev. ed. Kevin Siembieda & Matthew Balent. Ed. by Alex Marciniszyn et al. LC 97-161436. (RPG Reference Ser.: Vol. 1). (Illus.). 240p. (Orig.). (YA). (gr. 8 up). 1996. pap. 20.95 (*0-916211-12-6*, 454) Palladium Bks.

Monsters & Extraterrestrials see Draw, Model & Paint

Monsters & Madonnas. William Mortensen. LC 72-9220. (Literature of Photography Ser.). 1977. reprint ed. 18.95 (*0-405-04927-7*) Ayer.

Monsters & Madonnas: The Roots of Christian Anti-Semitism. rev. ed. Judith Taylor Gold. LC 99-20632. 304p. 1999. pap. text 19.95 (*0-8156-0583-8*) Syracuse U Pr.

Monsters & Magic: Myths of North & South America. Stewart Ross. LC 97-52739. (Best Tales Ever Told Ser.). (Illus.). 44p. (YA). (gr. 5 up). 1998. lib. bdg. 23.90 (*0-7613-0707-9*, Copper Beech Bks) Millbrook Pr.

Monsters & Magical Sticks: There's No Such Thing As Hypnosis? 2nd ed. Steven Heller & Terry Steele. LC 87-80595. 160p. 1991. pap. 12.95 (*1-56184-026-2*) New Falcon Pubns.

Monsters & My One True Love. Dian Curtis Regan. LC 97-50411. (Illus.). 198p. (J). (gr. 4-6). 1995. 15.95 (*0-8050-4676-3*) H Holt & Co.

Monsters & Other Lovers. Lisa Glatt. 96p. (Orig.). 1996. pap. 11.95 (*1-888219-00-9*) Pearl Edit.

Monsters & Revolutionaries: Colonial Family Romance & Metissage. Francoise Verges. LC 98-39781. 1999. write for info. (*0-8223-2262-5*); pap. 21.95 (*0-8223-2294-3*) Duke.

***Monsters & Wildflowers.** Kristina Marshae. 1999. pap. 6.95 (*0-9673675-0-6*) In Flight.

Monsters Are Attacking Tokyo: The Incredible World of Japanese Fantasy Films. Stuart Galbraith. 1997. pap. 16.95 (*0-922915-47-4*) Feral Hse.

Monster's Birthday Hiccups. Virginia Mueller. Ed. by Abby Levine. LC 91-2118. (Illus.). 24p. (J). (ps-1). 1991. lib. bdg. 13.95 (*0-8075-5267-4*) A Whitman.

Monster's Birthday Hiccups. Virginia Mueller. (Illus.). 24p. (J). (ps-1). 1997. reprint ed. pap. 4.95 (*0-8075-5268-2*) A Whitman.

Monsters, Dinosaurs & Beasts. Stuart A. Kallen. LC 91-73061. (Ghastly Ghost Stories Ser.). (Illus.). 202p. (J). (gr. 3-8). 1991. lib. bdg. 13.98 (*1-56239-040-6*) ABDO Pub Co.

Monsters Don't Scuba Dive. Debbie Dadey & Marcia Thornton Jones. (Adventures of the Bailey School Kids Ser.: No. 14). (FRE., Illus.). 80p. (J). (gr. 2-4). pap. 5.99 (*0-590-24550-3*) Scholastic Inc.

Monsters Don't Scuba Dive. Debbie Dadey & Marcia Thornton Jones. LC 00-5206. (Adventures of the Bailey School Kids Ser.: No. 14). (Illus.). 96p. (J). (gr. 2-5). 1995. pap. 2.99 (*0-590-22635-5*) Scholastic Inc.

Monsters Don't Scuba Dive. Debbie Dadey & Marcia Thornton Jones. (Adventures of the Bailey School Kids Ser.: No. 14). (J). (gr. 2-4). 1995. 8.70 (*0-606-07884-3*, Pub. by Turtleback) Demco.

***Monsters from the Id: The Rise of Horror in Fiction & Film.** E. Michael Jones. LC 99-49602. xii, 336p. 2000. 24.95 (*1-890626-06-6*) Spence Pub.

Monsters from the Movies. Thomas G. Aylesworth. LC 72-1995. (Illus.). 160p. (J). (gr. 5-9). 1972. 12.95 (*0-397-31590-2*) HarpC Child Bks.

***Monsters Get Scared Too.** rev. ed. Sharon Shi. (Illus.). 24p. (J). 2000. mass mkt. 4.99 (*0-9678636-8-6*, B009, Tattootles Bks) Tattoo Manuf.

Monster's Handsome Face: Patty Cannon in Fiction & Fact. Hal Roth. LC 98-65707. (Illus.). 243p. 1998. boxed set 19.95 (*0-9647694-2-5*) Nanticoke Bks.

Monsters, He Mumbled. Sean O. Huigin. (Illus.). 28p. (J). (ps-7). 1989. pap. 4.95 (*0-88753-187-3*) Black Moss.

Monsters in Cyberspace. Dian Curtis Regan. LC 96-37559. (J). 1995. 14.95 (*0-8050-4677-1*) H Holt & Co.

***Monsters in My Closet.** Patricia Searby. Ed. by Noreen Wise. (Book-a-Day Collection). (Illus.). 32p. 2000. pap. 5.95 (*1-58584-364-4*) Huckleberry CT.

Monsters in My Mailbox. Ellen B. Jackson. LC 95-4157. (Illus.). 32p. (J). (ps-3). 1905. pap. 3.50 (*0-8167-3580-8*, Whistlstop) Troll Communs.

Monsters in My Mailbox. Ellen B. Jackson. (J). 1995. 8.15 (*0-606-07885-1*, Pub. by Turtleback) Demco.

***Monsters in My Tummy.** Roman Dirge. (Illus.). 48p. 1999. pap. 5.95 (*0-943151-23-6*) Slave Labor Bks.

***Monsters in Our Midst.** Ed. by Robert Bloch. 304p. 2000. pap. 13.95 (*0-312-86943-6*, Pub. by Tor Bks) St Martin.

Monsters in Our Mist. Ed. by Robert Bloch. 1995. pap. 4.99 (*0-8125-0344-9*, Pub. by Tor Bks) St Martin.

Monsters in the Attic. Dian Curtis Regan. LC 95-16174. (Illus.). 178p. (J). (gr. 4-7). 1995. 14.95 (*0-8050-3709-8*) H Holt & Co.

Monsters in the Attic. Dian Curtis Regan. (J). 1998. pap. 4.50 (*0-590-84473-3*) Scholastic Inc.

Monsters in the Attic. Dian Curtis Regan. 1998. 9.60 (*0-606-13620-7*, Pub. by Turtleback) Demco.

***Monsters in the Attic.** Dian Curtis Regan. (Illus.). 178p. (J). (gr. 4-6). 1999. reprint ed. text 15.00 (*0-7881-6676-X*) DIANE Pub.

Monsters in the Closet: Homosexuality & the Horror Film. Harry M. Benshoff. (Illus.). 304p. 1997. pap. 18.95 (*0-7190-4473-1*) St Martin.

***Monsters in the Italian Literary Imagination.** Ed. by Keala J. Jewell. (Illus.). 463p. 2001. 34.95 (*0-8143-2838-5*) Wayne St U Pr.

Monsters in the M. A. C. Monster's Athletic Club. Wendy Brotherlin. (Illus.). 31p. (J). 1996. pap. 15.95 (*0-9655704-0-1*) Three Dog Prods.

Monsters in the Sky. Paolo Maffei. (Illus.). 1980. 35.00 (*0-262-13153-6*) MIT Pr.

Monsters in Your Bed . . . Monsters in Your Head. Rainey L. Friedman. (Illus.). 32p. (J). 1999. 15.95 (*0-9666199-1-9*) DreamDog Press.

Monsters! Just Imagine. Rob Morrison & James Morrison. LC 93-26927. (Voyages Ser.). (Illus.). (J). 1994. 4.25 (*0-383-03763-8*) SRA McGraw.

Monster's Legacy. Andre Norton. LC 95-80677. (Dragonflight Ser.: No. 11). (Illus.). 160p. (YA). (gr. 7 up). 1996. 17.00 (*0-689-80731-7*) Atheneum Yung Read.

Monster's Lunchbox. Marc Tolon Brown. LC 94-26103. 8p. (J). (gr. k-3). 1995. 14.95 (*0-316-11313-1*) Little.

Monsters, Magic & Make-Believe. Vowery D. Carlile. (J). Date not set. teacher ed. 12.95 (*1-56644-956-1*, 956-1AP) Educ Impress.

Monsters, Magic & Sorcery. Unicorn Game Pubs. Staff. Ed. by Vince Garcia. (Illus.). 80p. (Orig.). 1991. pap. text 15.00 (*0-9628003-1-7*) Unicorn Game Pubns.

Monsters Myth & Legend 3. Mayfair Games Staff. 1992. 10.00 (*0-923763-56-2*) Mayfair Games.

Monsters Myth Game. Mayfair Games Staff. Date not set. pap. 10.00 (*0-912771-29-1*) Mayfair Games.

Monsters Next Door. Marcia Thornton Jones & Debbie Dadey. (Bailey City Monsters Ser.: No. 1). (Illus.). 71p. (J). (gr. 2-5). 1998. pap. 3.50 (*0-590-10787-9*, Pub. by Scholastic Inc) Penguin Putnam.

Monsters of Affection: Dickens, Eliot, & Bronte on Fatherhood. Dianne F. Sadoff. LC 82-15378. 205p. 1982. reprint ed. pap. 63.60 (*0-608-03706-0*, 206453100009) Bks Demand.

Monsters of Architecture: Anthropomorphism in Architectural Theory. Marco Frascari. (Illus.). 176p. (C). 1990. lib. bdg. 39.50 (*0-8476-7648-X*) Rowman.

Monsters of Marble Avenue. Linda Gondosch. (Illus.). (J). (gr. 2-4). 1988. 10.95 (*0-316-31991-0*) Little.

Monsters of Mythology, 20 vols. (Illus.). 2600p. 1987. lib. bdg. 399.00 (*1-55546-235-9*) Chelsea Hse.

Monsters of the Deep see Monsters

Monsters of the Deep. Saviour Pirotta. (Remarkable World Ser.). (Illus.). 48p. (YA). (gr. 3-8). 1995. lib. bdg. 24.26 (*1-56847-367-2*) Raintree Steck-V.

Monsters of the Deep. Stewart Ross. LC 97-10081. (Fact or Fiction Ser.). (Illus.). 1997. pap. 7.95 (*0-7613-0595-5*, Copper Beech Bks) Millbrook Pr.

Monsters of the Deep. Stewart Ross. LC 97-10081. (Fact or Fiction Ser.). (Illus.). 48p. (YA). (gr. 6 up). 1997. lib. bdg. 24.90 (*0-7613-0548-3*, Copper Beech Bks) Millbrook Pr.

Monsters of the Northwoods. Paul Bartholomew et al. LC 92-23460. 1992. pap. 12.95 (*0-925168-00-9*) North Country.

Monsters of the Sea. Richard Ellis. LC 93-48180. (Illus.). 400p. 1994. 35.00 (*0-679-40639-5*) Knopf.

Monsters of the Sea: The History, Natural History, & Mythology of the Oceans' Most Fantastic Creatures. Richard Ellis. 1996. pap. text 12.95 (*0-07-021732-7*) McGraw.

Monsters of the Sea: The History, Natural History, & Mythology of the Oceans' Most Fantastic Creatures. Richard Ellis. 432p. 1996. pap. 12.95 (*0-385-48233-7*, Main St Bks) Doubleday.

An Asterisk (*) at the beginning of an entry indicates that the title is appearing for the first time.

Monsters on the Loose. Michael D. Chesworth. LC 96-205412. (Illus.). 32p. (Orig.). (J). (ps-3). 1996. pap. 2.95 (*0-8167-4122-0*, Whistlstop) Troll Communs.
Monsters Press-Out. (J). 1997. pap. 6.95 (*0-8167-3151-9*) Troll Communs.
Monster's Progress. Jim Barsness. 48p. 1999. pap. text 19.95 (*1-889097-31-4*, Pub. by Hard Pr MA) Consort Bk Sales.
Monster's Ring. Bruce Coville. (Magic Shop Bks.). (J). (gr. 3-6). 1989. mass mkt. 3.99 (*0-671-69389-1*, Minstrel Bks) PB.
Monster's Ring. Bruce Coville. (J). 1982. 9.09 (*0-606-03620-2*, Pub. by Turtleback) Demco.
Monsters, Strange Dreams, & UFO's. Phyllis R. Emert. (Strange Unsolved Mysteries Ser.: No. 2). 128p. (YA). 1990. pap. 2.50 (*0-8125-9425-8*, Pub. by Tor Bks) St Martin.
Monsters, Strange Dreams, & UFO's, 2. Phyllis Raybin-Emert. (Strange Unsolved Mysteries Ser.). (J). 1994. 7.60 (*0-606-11926-4*, Pub. by Turtleback) Demco.
Monsters' Tea Party, Vol. 4353. Will Barber. Ed. by Kimberlee Graves. (Fun & Fantasy Ser.). (Illus.). 16p. (J). (ps-1). 1997. pap. 2.75 (*1-57471-250-0*, 4353) Creat Teach Pr.
Monsters' Test. Brian J. Heinz. LC 95-45477. (Illus.). 32p. (J). (ps-3). 1996. 14.95 (*0-7613-0095-3*) Millbrook Pr.
Monsters' Test. Brian J. Heinz. LC 95-45477. (Illus.). 32p. (J). (gr. k-3). 1996. lib. bdg. 23.90 (*0-7613-0050-3*) Millbrook Pr.
*__Monsters 3-D Journal.__ (Illus.). 128p. (gr. 3 up). 2000. 14.95 (*0-7624-0464-7*) Running Pr.
Monsters to Playful Penquins. Christopher Carrie. (Crayola Encyclopedia of Coloring Fun Bks.). (Illus.). 40p. (Orig.). (J). (gr. k up). 1989. pap. 1.49 (*0-86696-227-1*) Binney & Smith.
Monsters, Tricksters & Sacred Cows: Animal Tales & American Identities. Ed. by A. James Arnold. (New World Studies). 1996. pap. text 18.50 (*0-8139-1646-1*) U Pr of Va.
Monsters, Tricksters & Sacred Cows: Animal Tales & American Identities. Ed. by A. James Arnold. (New World Studies). 291p. (C). 1996. text 45.00 (*0-8139-1645-3*) U Pr of Va.
Monsters under the Bed. Dominic Garramone. 1998. pap. 3.50 (*0-87129-794-9*, M71) Dramatic Pub.
Monsters, Vampires & Werewolves Dingbats Book. Carole Marsh. (Carole Marsh Dingbats Bks.). (Illus.). (J). (gr. 3-12). 1994. pap. 19.95 (*0-7933-5393-9*); lib. bdg. 29.95 (*0-7933-5392-0*); disk 29.95 (*0-7933-5394-7*) Gallopade Intl.
Monsters You've Never Heard of & Never Will Unless You Read This Book. Daniel C. Jackson & Kate Summers-Dawes. (J). (gr. 1-5). 1991. pap. 5.95 (*1-880722-00-3*) S L Jackson.
Monster.Tools.Net. Que Development Group Staff. (Illus.). 1200p. (Orig.). 1996. 49.99 (*0-7897-0361-0*) Que.
Monsterville. R. A. Noonan. LC 95-25850. (Monsterville USA Ser.: Vol. 6). (Illus.). 144p. (J). (gr. 3-7). 1996. pap. 3.99 (*0-689-71868-3*) Aladdin.
Monsterville U. S. A., Vol 7. R. A. Noonan. LC 95-52865. (J). 1996. pap. 3.99 (*0-689-71869-1*) Aladdin.
Monstre dans les Cereales. Marie-Francine Hebert. (Novels in the Premier Roman Ser.). (FRE.). 64p. (J). (gr. 2-5). 1988. pap. 8.95 (*2-89021-084-7*, Pub. by La Courte Ech) Firefly Bks Ltd.
Monstre Gai. Wyndham Lewis. (Orig.). 1981. pap. 9.95 (*0-7145-0386-X*) Riverrun NY.
*__Monstress Activities.__ (Illus.). 2000. 30.00 (*1-893125-12-2*) Womens Studio Wrkshop.
Monstrico (Little Monster) Raquel Coelho. Tr. by Stella Matrangelo. (SPA., Illus.). (J). (gr. 2). 1994. pap. 5.99 (*968-16-4573-1*, Pub. by Fondo) Continental Bk.
*__Monstrous & the Marvelous.__ Rikki Ducornet. LC 99-19319. 180p. 1999. pap. 12.95 (*0-87286-354-9*) City Lights.
Monstrous & the Unspeakable: The Bible As Fantastic Literature. Ed. by George Aichele & Tina Pippin. (Playing the Texts Ser.: Vol. 1). 246p. 1997. 74.00 (*1-85075-692-9*, Pub. by Sheffield Acad); pap. 24.50 (*1-85075-821-2*, Pub. by Sheffield Acad) CUP Services.
Monstrous Compendium: Mystara, Vol. 19. John Nephew. LC 94-215338. (Advanced Dungeons & Dragons, 2nd Edition Ser.: MC19). 1994. 18.00 (*1-56076-875-4*) TSR Inc.
Monstrous Compendium: Planescape. Allen Varney. LC 94-227803. (Advanced Dungeons & Dragons, 2nd Edition Ser.). 1994. 19.95 (*1-56076-862-2*, Pub. by TSR Inc) Random.
Monstrous Compendium: Ravenloft, Vol. 2. TSR Inc. Staff. (Advanced Dungeons & Dragons, Second Edition; Al-Qadim Ser.). (Illus.). 1993. 10.95 (*1-56076-586-0*, Pub. by TSR Inc) Random.
Monstrous Compendium - Planescape: Appendix II. TSR Inc. Staff. (Advanced Dungeons & Dragons, 2nd Edition: Planescape Adventures Ser.). 1995. 18.00 (*0-7869-0173-X*, Pub. by TSR Inc) Random.
Monstrous Compendium Annual: Volume 4, Vol. 4. 1998. 20.00 (*0-7869-0783-5*) TSR Inc.
Monstrous Compendium, 1994, Vol. 2. Jeff Easley. (Advanced Dungeons & Dragons, 2nd Edition Ser.). (Illus.). 1995. 19.95 (*1-56076-838-X*, Pub. by TSR Inc) Random.
Monstrous Compendium Annual: Volume 4, Vol. 4. TSR Incorporated Staff. 1998. 19.95 (*0-7869-1212-X*, Pub. by TSR Inc) Random.
Monstrous Feminine: Film, Feminism, Psychoanalysis. Barbara Creed. LC 93-445. (Popular Fiction Ser.). 192p. (C). (gr. 13). 1993. pap. 22.99 (*0-415-05259-9*, B2278) Routledge.
Monstrous Imagination. Marie-Helene Huet. LC 92-29384. (Illus.). 344p. 1993. 57.00 (*0-674-58651-4*); pap. 22.95 (*0-674-58649-2*) HUP.
Monstrous Opera: Rameau & the Tragic Tradition. Charles William. Dill. LC 97-31073. 240p. 1998. text 39.95 (*0-691-04443-0*, Pub. by Princeton U Pr) Cal Prin Full Svc.
Monstrous Possibility: An Invitation to Literary Politics. Curtis White. LC 97-51439. 160p. 1998. pap. 12.50 (*1-56478-190-9*) Dalkey Arch.
*__Monstrous Races in Medieval Art & Thought.__ John Block Friedman. LC 99-47066. (Medieval Studies). (Illus.). 288p. 2000. pap. 29.95 (*0-8156-2826-9*) Syracuse U Pr.
Monstrous Races in Medieval Art & Thought. John B. Friedman. LC 80-23181. 284p. reprint ed. pap. 88.10 (*0-7837-2262-1*, 205735000004) Bks Demand.
*__Monstrous Regiment.__ John Newton Chance. 240p. 2000. 18.99 (*0-7089-5737-4*) Ulverscroft.
Monstrous Regiment of Women. Laurie R. King. LC 95-21088. (Mary Russell Ser.: No. 2). 368p. 1996. mass mkt. 6.50 (*0-553-57456-6*, Crimeline) Bantam.
Monstrous Regiment of Women. Laurie R. King. LC 95-21088. viii, 326p. 1995. text 22.95 (*0-312-13565-3*) St Martin.
Monstrous Regiment Women. Jansen. 1999. text 45.00 (*0-312-21341-7*) St Martin.
Monstrous Trick Kenneth McDonald. 1998. write for info. (*0-9695634-2-6*) A1PEC.
Monstrum. Donald James. 1999. mass mkt. write for info. (*0-449-00431-7*, Crest) Fawcett.
Monstrum. Donald James. 1999. mass mkt. 6.99 (*0-8041-1891-4*) Ivy Books.
*__Monstrum.__ Donald James. 1999. 32.95 (*84-08-02903-7*) Planeta.
Monstruo, 12 bks., Set. Blance & Cook. Incl. Monstruo Compre un Animalito. 1.98 (*0-8372-3482-4*); Monstruo Encuentra Trabajo. 1.98 (*0-8372-3485-9*); Monstruo, la Senorita Monstruo y el Paseo en Bicicleta. 1.98 (*0-8372-3488-3*); Monstruo Recorre la Ciudad. 1.98 (*0-8372-3490-5*); Monstruo Va a la Playa. 1.98 (*0-8372-3479-4*); Monstruo Va Al Circo. 1.98 (*0-8372-3483-2*); Monstruo Va Al Hospital. 1.98 (*0-8372-3489-1*); Monstruo y el Muro. 1.98 (*0-8372-3487-5*); Monstruo y la Galleta de Sorpresa. 1.98 (*0-8372-3486-7*); Monstruo y la Liquidacion de Juguetes. 1.98 (*0-8372-3480-8*); Plan de la Senorita Monstruo. 1.98 (*0-8372-3481-6*); Senorita Monstruo Ayuda. 1.98 (*0-8372-3484-0*); (gr. k-4). Set pap. 215.00 (*0-8372-3493-X*) Bowmar-Noble.
Monstruo Compre un Animalito see Monstruo
Monstruo en los Cereales. Marie-Francine Hebert. (Primeros Lectores Ser.).Tr. of Monster in the Cereal. (SPA., Illus.). 60p. (J). (gr. 2 up). 1994. pap. 5.95 (*958-07-0072-9*) Firefly Bks Ltd.
Monstruo Encuentra Trabajo see Monstruo
Monstruo, la Senorita Monstruo y el Paseo en Bicicleta see Monstruo
Monstruo Recorre la Ciudad see Monstruo
Monstruo Va a la Playa see Monstruo
Monstruo Va Al Circo see Monstruo
Monstruo Va Al Hospital see Monstruo
Monstruo y el Muro see Monstruo
Monstruo y la Galleta de Sorpresa see Monstruo
Monstruo y la Liquidacion de Juguetes see Monstruo
Monstruo y Milagro. Thomas Henry. 1946. pap. 3.00 (*0-87535-060-7*) Hispanic Soc.
Monstruos Entre Nosotros: Teenage Mutant Ninja Turtles. Stephen Murphy. Tr. by DigiPro Staff from ENG. (Comes to Life Bks.).Tr. of Monsters among Us. (SPA.). 16p. (J). (ps-2). 1994. write for info. (*1-57234-009-6*) YES Ent.
Mont Analogue. Rene Daumal. (Imaginaire Ser.). (FRE.). 175p. 1981. pap. 11.95 (*2-07-022877-0*) Schoenhof.
Mont Blanc. Robert Kelly. (Illus.). 51p. 1994. pap. 7.00 (*0-9626046-1-5*) OtherWind Pr.
Mont Blanc: Discovery & Conquest of the Giant of the Alps. Stefano Ardito. Tr. by A. B. Milan from ITA. LC 97-223132. (Illus.). 228p. 1997. 48.00 (*0-89886-519-0*) Mountaineers.
Mont Blanc Massif: The 100 Finest Routes. Gaston Rebuffat. 240p. 1996. 39.95 (*0-89886-477-1*) Mountaineers.
Mont-de-Marsan/Pau/Toulouse Map. 1997. 6.95 (*2-06-700082-9*, 82) Michelin.
Mont-Dragon. Robert Margerit. (FRE.). 1973. pap. 10.95 (*0-7859-4018-9*) Fr & Eur.
Mont-Oriol. Guy de Maupassant. (Folio Ser.: No. 811). (FRE.). (Orig.). pap. 9.95 (*2-07-036811-4*) Schoenhof.
Mont Oriol. Guy de Maupassant. (FRE.). 1976. pap. 12.95 (*0-7859-2886-3*) Fr & Eur.
Mont-Oriol. unabridged ed. Guy de Maupassant. (FRE.). (Orig.). 1996. pap. 5.95 (*2-87714-337-6*, Pub. by Bookking Intl) Distribks Inc.
Mont Reid Surgical Handbook. 4th ed. Scott Berry. LC 97-4039. (Illus.). 920p. (C). (gr. 13). 1997. pap. text 35.95 (*0-8151-1007-3*, 29155) Mosby Inc.
Mont Royal - Ville Marie: Early Plans & Views of Montreal. Conrad Graham & Shahin Farzaneh. (Illus.). 160p. 1991. pap. 49.95 (*0-7735-0969-0*, Pub. by McG-Queens Univ Pr) CUP Services.
Mont Saint-Michel. Rene-Jacques. (Panorama Bks.). (FRE.). 62p. 3.95 (*0-685-23348-0*) Fr & Eur.
Mont-Saint-Michel & Chartres. Henry (Brooks) Adams. 1974. 250.00 (*0-87968-178-0*) Gordon Pr.
Mont Saint Michel & Chartres. Henry (Brooks) Adams. (Classics Ser.). 398p. 1986. pap. 14.95 (*0-14-039054-5*, Penguin Classics) Viking Penguin.
Mont-Saint Michel & Chartres. Henry (Brooks) Adams. (Works of Henry Adams). 1989. reprint ed. lib. bdg. 79.00 (*0-7812-1442-4*) Rprt Serv.
Montage. Ed. by Montage Staff. (Illus.). 72p. (Orig.). 1989. pap. 5.95 (*0-9623452-1-0*) Oregon Coast Cmnty Col.
Montage. 2nd ed. Lucia F. Baker et al. (C). 1991. text 39.25 (*0-07-003469-9*) McGraw.
Montage. 3rd ed. Baker. 1996. audio 28.13 (*0-07-913240-5*) McGraw.
Montage: Grammaire, Literature, Culture, Activities. Carmen Grace et al. 1988. write for info. (*0-07-556100-X*) McGraw.
Montage, Deuxieme Niveau. 3rd ed. Lucia F. Baker et al. (C). 1996. pap., wbk. ed., lab manual ed. 31.25 (*0-07-006029-0*) McGraw.
Montage, Deuxieme Niveau. 3rd ed. Lucia F. Baker et al. 528p. (C). 1997. pap. 50.31 (*0-07-006020-7*) McGraw.
Montage Eisenstein. Jacques Aumont. Tr. by Lee Hildreth et al from FRE. LC 85-45074. (Theories of Representation & Difference Ser.). (Illus.). 256p. (C). 1987. 41.95 (*0-253-33874-3*) Ind U Pr.
Montage Eisenstein. Jacques Aumont. Tr. by Lee Hildreth et al. LC 85-45074. (Theories of Representation & Difference Ser.). (Illus.). 253p. Date not set. reprint ed. pap. 78.50 (*0-608-20579-6*, 205449400002) Bks Demand.
Montage, 1990: Anthology of Oregon Coast Community College. OCCC Press Staff, Students & Friends. Ed. by OCCC Montage Staff. 56p. (Orig.). 1990. pap. 6.00 (*0-9623452-5-3*) Oregon Coast Cmnty Col.
Montage of Life. Ed. by Diana Zeiger. 1997. 69.95 (*1-57553-607-2*) Watermrk Pr.
Montagnards du Tonkin. Edouard J. Diguet. LC 77-87484. (Illus.). 176p. reprint ed. 39.50 (*0-404-16811-6*) AMS Pr.
Montagne Noire. Chrystine Brouillet. (Novels in the Roman Jeunesse Ser.). (FRE.). 96p. (J). (gr. 4-7). 1988. pap. 8.95 (*2-89021-080-4*, Pub. by La Courte Ech) Firefly Bks Ltd.
Montague County Texas Marriage Book D, 1888-1892. fac. ed. Navena H. Troxel. 68p. 1982. pap. 20.00 (*0-944619-29-0*) Gregath Pub Co.
Montague County Texas Marriage Book E, 1892-1895. fac. ed. Navena H. Troxel. 70p. 1982. pap. 20.00 (*0-944619-30-4*) Gregath Pub Co.
Montague County Texas Marriage Book F, 1895-1899. fac. ed. Navena H. Troxel. 93p. 1982. pap. 20.00 (*0-944619-31-2*) Gregath Pub Co.
Montague County Texas Marriage Books B&C, 1879-1888. fac. ed. Navena H. Troxel. ii, 105p. 1982. pap. 20.00 (*0-944619-28-2*) Gregath Pub Co.
Montague. Cowdray: The History of a Great English House (Seat of the Montagues, with Some Genealogy) Juie A. Roundell. (Illus.). 178p. 1997. reprint ed. pap. 25.00 (*0-8328-9473-7*); reprint ed. lib. bdg. 35.00 (*0-8328-9472-9*) Higginson Bk Co.
Montague Rods. 48p. 1992. pap. 9.95 (*1-882418-03-4*) Centenn Pubns.
Montague Summers: A Bibliographical Portrait. Frederick S. Frank. LC 88-10048. (Great Bibliographers Ser.: No. 7). 298p. 1988. 31.00 (*0-8108-2136-2*) Scarecrow.
Montaigne. Peter Burke. (Past Masters Ser.). 90p. 1983. pap. text 6.95 (*0-19-287522-1*) OUP.
Montaigne. Hugo Friedrich. Tr. by Dawn Eng. LC 90-47726. 433p. 1991. 65.00 (*0-520-06581-6*, Pub. by U CA Pr); pap. 19.95 (*0-520-07253-7*, Pub. by U CA Pr) Cal Prin Full Svc.
Montaigne. Marcel Tetel. (Twayne's World Authors Ser.: No. 317). 168p. 1990. 32.00 (*0-8057-8259-1*, Twyne) Mac Lib Ref.
Montaigne: And Other Essays, Chiefly Biographical. Thomas Carlyle. LC 72-13208. (Essay Index Reprint Ser.). 1977. reprint ed. 25.95 (*0-8369-8149-9*) Ayer.
Montaigne: Essays. Michel de Montaigne. 1993. pap. 12.95 (*0-14-017897-X*, Penguin Classics) Viking Penguin.
Montaigne: Essays in Memory of Richard Sayce. I. D. McFarlane & Ian Maclean. (Illus.). 1982. 55.00 (*0-19-815769-X*) OUP.
Montaigne among the Moderns: Receptions of the Essais. Dudley M. Marchi. LC 94-29461. 352p. (C). 1994. text 59.95 (*1-57181-007-2*) Berghahn Bks.
Montaigne & Bayle: Variations on the Theme of Skepticism. C. B. Brush. (International Archives of the History of Ideas Ser.: No. 14). 361p. 1966. lib. bdg. 99.50 (*90-247-0190-2*, Pub. by M Nijhoff) Kluwer Academic.
Montaigne & Melancholy. M. A. Screech. LC 83-24143. 208p. 1984. 32.50 (*0-941664-08-2*) Susquehanna U Pr.
Montaigne & Shakespeare & Other Essays on Cognate Questions. John M. Robertson. LC 68-24914. (Studies in Comparative Literature: No. 35). 1969. reprint ed. lib. bdg. 75.00 (*0-8383-0234-3*) M S G Haskell Hse.
Montaigne & Shakespeare & Other Essays on Cognate Questions. John M. Robertson. (BCL1-PR English Literature Ser.). 358p. 1992. reprint ed. lib. bdg. 89.00 (*0-7812-7291-2*) Rprt Serv.
*__Montaigne & the Ethics of Compassion.__ Max Gauna. LC 00-32447. (Studies in the History of Philosophy: Vol. 55). 352p. 2000. 99.95 (*0-7734-7706-3*) E Mellen.
Montaigne & the Quality of Mercy: Ethical & Political Themes in the Essais. David Quint. LC 97-36185. 200p. 1998. text 35.00 (*0-691-04836-3*, Pub. by Princeton U Pr) Cal Prin Full Svc.
Montaigne, Gentilhomme et Essayiste. Boon. 18.40 (*0-685-34192-5*) Fr & Eur.
Montaigne in Dialogue: Censorship & Defensive Writing, Architecture & Friendship, The Self & the Other. Patrick Henry. (Stanford French & Italian Studies: No. 57). 140p. 1988. pap. 56.50 (*0-915838-73-7*) Anma Libri.
Montaigne in Motion. Jean Starobinski. Tr. by Arthur Goldhammer from FRE. LC 85-1026. xii, 360p. 1985. lib. bdg. 36.00 (*0-226-77129-6*) U Ch Pr.
Montaigne in Motion. Jean Starobinski. Tr. by Arthur Goldhammer from FRE. LC 85-1026. xii, 348p. 1993. pap. text 14.95 (*0-226-77131-8*) U Ch Pr.
Montaigne: or The Anguished Soul. Pierre Leschmelle. Tr. by William J. Beck from FRE. LC 93-46833. (Currents in Comparative Romance Languages & Literatures Ser.: Vol. 29). XVII, 222p. (C). 1994. text 51.95 (*0-8204-2476-5*) P Lang Pubng.
Montaigne, Rabelais, & Marot as Readers of Erasmus. Edmund J. Campion. LC 95-1894. 1995. write for info. (*0-7734-9029-9*) E Mellen.
Montaigne Studies: An Interdisciplinary Forum. Ed. by Philippe Desan. (Illus.). 187p. 1989. 11.95 (*1-878417-01-0*) Hestia Pr.
Montaigne's: Message & Method, 5 vols., Set. Ed. by Dikka Berven. LC 94-41683. 433p. 1995. 380.00 (*0-8153-1838-3*) Garland.
Montaigne's Career. George Hoffman. LC 98-22112. (Illus.). 202p. 1999. text 75.00 (*0-19-815962-5*) OUP.
Montaigne's Discovery of Man. Donald M. Frame. LC 55-7926. 210p. reprint ed. 65.10 (*0-8357-9068-1*, 200720200062) Bks Demand.
Montaigne's Discovery of Man: The Humanization of a Humanist. Donald M. Frame. LC 83-12716. 202p. 1983. reprint ed. lib. bdg. 55.00 (*0-313-24120-1*, FRM0, Greenwood Pr) Greenwood.
Montaigne's Essais. Dorothy Coleman. (Unwin Critical Library). 192p. (C). 1987. text 49.95 (*0-04-800072-8*) Routledge.
Montaigne's Essays & Selected Writings. Michel de Montaigne. Ed. by Donald M. Frame. (ENG & FRE.). 496p. (Orig.). 1969. pap. 23.95 (*0-312-54635-1*) St Martin.
Montaigne's Message & Method: A Collection of Essays: An Anthology of Scholarly Articles, 5 vols. Ed. by Dikka Berven. LC 94-41683. (Montaigne Ser.: Vol. 1). (ENG & FRE.). 456p. 1995. text 85.00 (*0-8153-1839-1*) Garland.
Montaigne's Rhetoric: Composing Myself for Others. Ed. by Dikka Berven. LC 94-41683. (Montaigne Ser.: Vol. 3). 408p. 1995. reprint ed. text 75.00 (*0-8153-1841-3*) Garland.
Montaigne's Self-Portrait & Its Influence in France, 1580-1630. Ian J. Winter. LC 76-17259. (French Forum Monographs: No. 3). 128p. (Orig.). 1976. pap. 9.95 (*0-917058-02-X*) French Forum.
Montaigne's Unruly Brood: Textual Engendering & the Challenge to Paternal Authority. Richard L. Regosin. LC 95-6077. 255p. (C). 1996. 48.00 (*0-520-20194-9*, Pub. by U CA Pr) Cal Prin Full Svc.
Montaillou. Ladurie. 376p. 1978. 69.95 (*0-85967-403-7*) Ashgate Pub Co.
Montaillou: The Promised Land of Error. Emmanuel L. Ladurie. Tr. by Barbara Bray from FRE. (Illus.). 1979. pap. 11.96 (*0-394-72964-1*) Vin Bks.
Montaillou, Village Occitan de 1294 a 1324. Emmanuel Le Roy-Ladurie. (Folio-Histoire Ser.: No. 9). (FRE.). 640p. 1982. pap. 14.95 (*2-07-032328-5*) Schoenhof.
Montalbert. Charlotte Smith. LC 88-38441. 232p. 1989. 50.00 (*0-8201-1437-5*) Schol Facsimiles.
Montale & Dante. Arshi Pipa. LC 68-31650. (Minnesota Monographs in the Humanities: Vol. 4). 227p. reprint ed. pap. 70.40 (*0-608-15975-1*, 203328300084) Bks Demand.
Montale & the Occasions of Poetry. Claire C. Huffman. LC 82-21522. 312p. 1983. reprint ed. pap. 96.80 (*0-7837-9351-0*, 206009300004) Bks Demand.
Montale, Debussy & Modernism. Gian-Paolo Biasin. LC 89-10516. (Princeton Essays on the Arts Ser.). (Illus.). 171p. 1989. reprint ed. pap. 53.10 (*0-608-02560-7*, 206320500004) Bks Demand.
Montale's "Mestiere Vile" The Elective Translations from English in the 1930s & 1940s. George Talbot. LC 96-117144. 272p. 1995. 39.50 (*0-7165-2526-7*, Pub. by Irish Acad Pr) Intl Spec Bk.
Montalvo en Su Epistolario. Juan Montalvo. LC 78-9810. (Illus.). 456p. 1982. pap. 10.00 (*0-8477-0856-X*) U of PR Pr.
Montalvo y Rodo. Gonzalo Zaldumbide. (SPA.). 85p. 2.25 (*0-318-14292-9*) Hispanic Inst.
Montana see From Sea to Shining Sea
Montana see Atlas of Historical County Boundaries
Montana see One Nation Series
*__Montana.__ (Switched on Schoolhouse Ser.). (Illus.). (J). 2000. pap. 24.95 (*0-7403-0278-7*) Alpha AZ.
*__Montana.__ Ann Bell. 464p. 2000. pap. 4.97 (*1-57748-794-X*) Barbour Pub.
*__Montana.__ Clayton Bennett. (Celebrate the States Ser.). (Illus.). (J). 2001. 35.64 (*0-7614-1068-6*, Benchmark NY) Marshall Cavendish.
Montana. Capstone Press, Geography Department Staff. (One Nation Ser.). (Illus.). 48p. (J). (gr. 3-7). 1997. lib. bdg. 19.00 (*0-516-20929-9*) Childrens.
Montana. Dennis B. Fradin. LC 91-37958. (From Sea to Shining Sea Ser.). (Illus.). 64p. (J). (gr. 3-5). 1992. pap. 7.95 (*0-516-43826-3*) Childrens.
Montana. Paul Joseph. LC 97-15206. (United States Ser.). (Illus.). 32p. (J). 1998. lib. bdg. 19.93 (*1-56239-864-4*, Checkerboard Library) ABDO Pub Co.
Montana. Rita Ladoux. (Hello U. S. A. Ser.). (Illus.). 72p. (J). (gr. 3-6). 1997. pap. text 5.95 (*0-8225-9782-9*) Lerner Pub.
Montana. Rita C. LaDoux. (Hello U. S. A. Ser.). (Illus.). 72p. (J). (gr. 3-6). 1992. lib. bdg. 19.93 (*0-8225-2714-6*, Lerner Publctns) Lerner Pub.
Montana. Debbie Macomber. LC 97-17245. 299p. 1997. pap. 21.95 (*1-55166-316-3*, 1-66316-0, Mira Bks) Harlequin Bks.
Montana. Debbie Macomber. (Mira Bks.). 1998. per. 6.99 (*1-55166-434-8*, 1-66434-1, Mira Bks) Harlequin Bks.
Montana. Joe Montana & Dick Schaap. (Illus.). 144p. 1999. pap. text 25.00 (*0-7881-6009-5*) DIANE Pub.
Montana. Genevieve Rowles. (Adventure Guide Ser.). (Illus.). 550p. 1999. pap. 17.95 (*1-55650-856-5*) Hunter NJ.

M

An Asterisk (*) at the beginning of an entry indicates that the title is appearing for the first time.

M

Montana. Isidro Sanchez & Carme Peris. (World of Sports Ser.). (SPA., Illus.). 32p. (J). (ps-1). 1992. pap. 6.95 (*0-8120-4872-5*) Barron.

Montana. Bob Schaller. (Arlingtons Ser.). (Illus.). 128p. (J). (gr. 4-7). 1998. pap. text 7.95 (*1-887002-78-2*) Cross Trng.

Montana. Kathleen Thompson. LC 87-26465. (Portrait of America Library). 48p. (YA). (gr. 4-8). 1996. pap. 5.95 (*0-8114-7452-6*) Raintree Steck-V.

Montana. Kathleen Thompson. LC 87-26465. (Portrait of America Library). (Illus.). 48p. (YA). (gr. 3-6). 1996. lib. bdg. 22.83 (*0-8114-7346-5*) Raintree Steck-V.

Montana. rev. ed. Ann Heinrichs. LC 90-21035. (America the Beautiful Ser.). (Illus.). 144p. (J). (gr. 4 up). 1991. lib. bdg. 28.00 (*0-516-00472-7*) Childrens.

Montana. 4th ed. Ed. by Compass America Staff. LC 99-217843. (Compass American Guides Ser.). 320p. 1999. pap. 19.95 (*0-679-00281-2*) Fodors Travel.

Montana: A Contemporary Profile. Michael P. Malone. 200p. 1996. pap. 14.95 (*1-56037-109-9*) Am Wrld Geog.

Montana! A Photographic Celebration, Vol. 2. Rick Graetz. (Illus.). 104p. (Orig.). 1989. 19.95 (*0-938314-80-7*); pap. 13.95 (*0-938314-81-5*) Am Wrld Geog.

Montana! A Photographic Celebration, Vol. 3. Rick Graetz. (Illus.). 104p. (Orig.). 1991. pap. 13.95 (*1-56037-007-6*) Am Wrld Geog.

Montana! A Photographic Celebration, Vol. I, Vol. I. Rick Graetz. (Illus.). 104p. (Orig.). 1988. pap. 13.95 (*0-938314-60-2*) Am Wrld Geog.

Montana: A State Guide Book. Federal Writers' Project Staff. (American Guidebook Ser.). 430p. 1939. reprint ed. 79.00 (*0-403-02176-6*) Somerset Pub.

Montana: A State Guide Book. Federal Writers' Project Staff & Writers Program-WPA Staff. (American Guide Ser.). 1989. reprint ed. lib. bdg. 69.00 (*0-7812-1025-9*, 1025) Rprt Serv.

Montana: An Uncommon Land. K. Ross Toole. LC 59-7489. (Illus.). 320p. 1984. reprint ed. pap. 14.95 (*0-8061-1890-3*) U of Okla Pr.

Montana: High, Wide & Handsome. Joseph K. Howard. LC 59-9606. (Illus.). 359p. reprint ed. pap. 111.30 (*0-8357-8233-6*, 203376000087) Bks Demand.

Montana: High, Wide & Handsome. Joseph K. Howard. LC 82-17667. xiv, 349p. 1983. reprint ed. pap. 14.95 (*0-8032-7214-6*, Bison Books) U of Nebr Pr.

Montana: History of 2 Centuries. rev. ed. Malone et al. LC 91-21742. (Illus.). 480p. 1991. pap. 22.50 (*0-295-97129-0*) U of Wash Pr.

Montana: Its Story & Biography: History of Aboriginal & Territorial Montana, & Three Decades of Statehood, 3 vols. Ed. by Tom Stout. (Illus.). 2343p. 1997. reprint ed. lib. bdg. 215.00 (*0-8328-6861-2*) Higginson Bk Co.

Montana: Land of Giant Rams. Duncan B. Gilchrist. (Illus.). 208p. (Orig.). 1990. pap. 19.95 (*0-9622796-4-1*) Outdoor Expeditions.

Montana: Off the Beaten Path: A Guide to Unique Places. 3rd ed. Michael McCoy. LC 98-33899. (Illus.). 160p. 1998. pap. 12.95 (*0-7627-0271-0*) Globe Pequot.

***Montana: The Best Cross-Country Ski & Snowshoe Trails.** Jean Arthur. (Winter Trails Ser.). (Illus.). 2000. pap. 14.95 (*0-7627-0730-5*) Globe Pequot.

Montana: The Last Best Place. Ed. by Chris Cauble. LC 92-72803. (Illus.). 120p. 1992. 29.95 (*1-56044-151-8*) Falcon Pub Inc.

Montana: The Magazine of Western History Comprehensive Index, 1951-1990. Compiled by Douglas J. Easton. 377p. 1994. 20.00 (*0-917298-30-6*) MT Hist Soc.

Montana - A Postcard Book. Michael S. Sample. 1993. pap. text 7.95 (*1-56044-195-X*) Falcon Pub Inc.

Montana - Collected Works of Federal Writers Project, 2 vols. Federal Writers' Project Staff. 1991. reprint ed. lib. bdg. 98.00 (*0-7812-5646-1*) Rprt Serv.

Montana - Land of Giant Rams II, Vol. II. Duncan Gilchrist. (Illus.). 208p. 1992. pap. 19.95 (*0-9622796-8-4*, B110) Outdoor Expeditions.

***Montana - Off the Beaten Path: A Guide to Unique Places.** 4th ed. Michael McCoy. (Illus.). 2000. pap. 12.95 (*0-7627-0760-7*) Globe Pequot.

Montana - The Gold Frontier. Dan Cushman. LC 73-83492. 1973. 21.95 (*0-911436-03-0*) Stay Away.

Montana Adventure: The Recollections of Frank B. Linderman. Frank B. Linderman. Ed. by Harold G. Merriam. LC 85-1051. 236p. reprint ed. pap. 67.30 (*0-7837-4277-0*, 2043969) Bks Demand.

Montana Almanac. Andrea Merrill & Judy Jacobson. LC 97-13198. (Illus.). 500p. (Orig.). 1997. pap. 18.95 (*1-56044-493-2*) Falcon Pub Inc.

Montana & Idaho's Continental Divide Trail: The Official Guide. Lynna Howard. LC 98-49511. (Illus.). 312p. 2000. pap. 27.95 (*1-56579-330-7*) Westcliffe Pubs.

Montana & Other State Greats (Biographies) Carole Marsh. (Carole Marsh Montana Bks.). (Illus.). (J). (gr. 3 up). 1994. pap. 19.95 (*1-55609-773-5*); lib. bdg. 29.95 (*1-55609-772-7*); disk 29.95 (*1-55609-774-3*) Gallopade Intl.

Montana Angel. Kathleen Harrington. 384p. (Orig.). 1994. mass mkt. 4.50 (*0-380-77059-8*, Avon Bks) Morrow Avon.

Montana Angel. Theresa Scott. 400p. 1998. mass mkt. 5.99 (*0-8439-4392-0*, Leisure Bks) Dorchester Pub Co.

Montana Angling Guide. Chuck Fothergill & Bob Sterling. (Illus.). 303p. 1988. spiral bd. 29.95 (*0-9614704-2-9*) Stream Stalker.

Montana As It Is. Granville Stuart. LC 72-9469. (Far Western Frontier Ser.). 180p. 1980. reprint ed. 20.95 (*0-405-04996-X*) Ayer.

***Montana Atlas & Gazetteer.** 3rd ed. DeLorme Mapping Company Staff. LC 99-462933. (Orig.). 1999. pap. 16.95 (*0-89933-226-9*) DeLorme Map.

Montana Bandits, Bushwackers, Outlaws, Crooks, Devils, Ghosts, Desperadoes & Other Assorted & Sundry Characters! Carole Marsh. (Carole Marsh Montana Bks.). (Illus.). (J). (gr. 3 up). 1994. pap. 19.95 (*0-7933-0696-5*); lib. bdg. 29.95 (*0-7933-0697-3*); disk 29.95 (*0-7933-0698-1*) Gallopade Intl.

***Montana Bed & Breakfast Guide & Cookbook.** 2nd rev. ed. Janet Ollila Colberg. (Illus.). 288p. 2001. pap. 14.95 (*0-9653647-3-9*) Summer Kitchen Press.

***Montana Behind the Scenes.** Durrae Johanek. LC 99-86332. (Illus.). 2000. pap. text 12.95 (*1-56044-791-5*) Falcon Pub Inc.

Montana "BIO" Bingo! 24 Must Know State People for Kids to Learn about While Having Fun! Carole Marsh. (Bingo! Ser.). (Illus.). (J). (gr. 2-8). 1998. pap. 14.95 (*0-7933-8600-4*) Gallopade Intl.

Montana Birds. James Kavanagh. (Pocket Naturalist Ser.). (Illus.). 12p. 1998. 5.95 (*1-889903-67-1*, Pub. by Waterford WA) Falcon Pub Inc.

***Montana Blue-Ribbon Fly Fishing Guide.** Steve Probasco. (Illus.). 96p. 2001. pap. 24.95 (*1-57188-165-4*) F Amato Pubns.

Montana Bookstore Book: A Surprising Guide to Our State's Bookstores & Their Specialties for Students, Teachers, Writers & Publishers. Carole Marsh. (Carole Marsh Montana Bks.). (Illus.). 1994. pap. 19.95 (*0-7933-2934-5*); lib. bdg. 29.95 (*0-7933-2933-7*); disk 29.95 (*0-7933-2935-3*) Gallopade Intl.

***Montana Born & Bred.** Alexis Harrington. 2000. pap. 5.99 (*0-312-97587-2*, St Martins Paperbacks) St Martin.

Montana Bound: An Activity Approach to Teaching Montana History. Bruce Whitehead & Charlotte Whitehead. (Illus.). 200p. 1978. pap. 10.95 (*0-929521-10-2*) Pictorial Hist.

Montana Bride. Catherine Lanigan. 1998. per. 3.75 (*0-373-76151-1*, 1-76151-9) Silhouette.

***Montana Business Directory, 1999-2000.** rev. ed. American Business Directories Staff. 624p. 1999. boxed set 375.00 incl. cd-rom (*0-7687-0151-1*) Am Busn Direct.

Montana Campfire Tales: Fourteen Historical Narratives. Dave Walter. LC 97-19135. (Illus.). 226p. (Orig.). 1997. pap. 16.95 (*1-56044-539-4*, Two Dot) Falcon Pub Inc.

Montana Celebrity Cookbook. Compiled by Susie B. Graetz. (Illus.). 208p. (Orig.). 1992. pap. 9.95 (*1-56037-022-X*) Am Wrld Geog.

Montana Census Index, 1880 Mortality Schedule (Every Name) (Illus.). lib. bdg. 30.00 (*0-89593-414-0*, Accel Indexing) Genealogical Srvcs.

Montana Census Index, 1890 Union Vets. (Illus.). 1984. lib. bdg. 49.00 (*0-89593-415-9*, Accel Indexing) Genealogical Srvcs.

Montana Census Index, 1870 Mortality Schedule. (Illus.). lib. bdg. 30.00 (*0-89593-412-4*, Accel Indexing) Genealogical Srvcs.

***Montana Century: 100 Years in Pictures & Words.** Michael P. Malone. LC 99-27502. 307p. 1999. 50.00 (*1-56044-827-X*, Two Dot) Falcon Pub Inc.

Montana Christmas. Jackie Merritt. 1996. per. 3.50 (*0-373-76039-6*, 1-76039-6) Silhouette.

Montana Christmas. Lynn Russell. (Stolen Moments Ser.). 1993. pap. 1.99 (*0-373-83288-5*, 1-83288-0) Harlequin Bks.

Montana Classic Christmas Trivia. Carole Marsh. (Carole Marsh Montana Bks.). (J). (gr. 3 up). 1994. pap. 19.95 (*0-7933-0699-X*); lib. bdg. 29.95 (*0-7933-0700-7*); disk 29.95 (*0-7933-0701-5*) Gallopade Intl.

Montana Coastales. Carole Marsh. (Carole Marsh Montana Bks.). (J). 1994. lib. bdg. 29.95 (*0-7933-7291-7*) Gallopade Intl.

Montana Coastales. Carole Marsh. (Carole Marsh Montana Bks.). (Illus.). (J). (gr. 3 up). 1994. pap. 19.95 (*1-55609-767-0*); lib. bdg. 29.95 (*1-55609-766-2*); disk 29.95 (*1-55609-768-9*) Gallopade Intl.

Montana Cookbook. Falcon Press Staff. LC 95-61746. (Illus.). 352p. 1995. 22.95 (*1-56044-413-4*) Falcon Pub Inc.

***Montana Cowboy.** 2nd ed. Patrick Dawson. (Illus.). 276p. 1999. text 60.00 (*0-922029-67-9*, Pub. by Stoecklein Pub) Gr Arts Ctr Pub.

Montana Cowboy: My Life Around the World. Edward R. Rebich & Sally Garrett. 498p. (Orig.). 1996. pap. 25.00 (*1-885916-01-9*) Unconvntl Pr.

Montana Cree: A Study in Religious Persistence. Verne Dusenberry. LC 97-43208. (Illus.). 296p. (Orig.). 1998. pap. 15.95 (*0-8061-3025-3*) U of Okla Pr.

***Montana Crime in Perspective 2000.** Ed. by Kathleen O'Leary Morgan & Scott E. Morgan. 22p. 2000. spiral bd. 19.00 (*0-7401-0325-3*) Morgan Quitno Corp.

Montana Crime Perspective, 1998. Ed. by Kathleen O'Leary Morgan & Scott E. Morgan. 20p. 1998. pap. 19.00 (*1-56692-925-3*) Morgan Quitno Corp.

Montana Crime Perspectives,1999. Kathleen O'Leary Morgan. 22p. 1999. spiral bd. 19.00 (*0-7401-0125-0*) Morgan Quitno Corp.

Montana "Crinkum-Crankum" A Funny Word Book about Our State. Carole Marsh. (Carole Marsh Montana Bks.). (Illus.). (J). 1994. pap. 19.95 (*0-7933-4887-0*); lib. bdg. 29.95 (*0-7933-4886-2*); disk 29.95 (*0-7933-4888-9*) Gallopade Intl.

Montana de Fuego. Thomas P. Lewis. 1997. 10.15 (*0-606-10858-0*, Pub. by Turtleback) Demco.

Montana Dingbats! Bk. 1: A Fun Book of Games, Stories, Activities & More about Our State That's All in Code! for You to Decipher. Carole Marsh. (Carole Marsh Montana Bks.). (Illus.). (J). (gr. 3-12). 1994. pap. 19.95 (*0-7933-3852-2*); lib. bdg. 29.95 (*0-7933-3851-4*); disk 29.95 (*0-7933-3853-0*) Gallopade Intl.

Montana East of the Mountains. Rick Graetz & Susie Graetz. 96p. 1998. pap. 14.95 (*1-891152-01-7*) Nth Rock Pub.

Montana, 1889: The Centennial News Melange. O. J. Taylor. (Illus.). 176p. (Orig.). 1989. 23.95 (*0-685-28034-9*); pap. 14.95 (*0-685-28035-7*) O J Taylor Pub.

Montana Entrepreneur's Guide: How to Start & Manage a Business in Montana. 2nd ed. Paul Larson. 368p. 1995. pap. 19.95 incl. disk (*0-9624819-4-7*) University MT.

***Montana Entrepreneurs Guide How to Start & Manage a Business in Montana.** 3rd ed. Paul Larsen. 1999. pap. 19.95 (*0-9624819-6-3*) University MT.

Montana Environmental Law Handbook. 2nd ed. Crowley, Haughy, Hanson, Toole & Dietrich Staff. LC 96-217034. 391p. 1996. pap. text 89.00 (*0-86587-531-6*) Gov Insts.

Montana Facts & Factivities. Carole Marsh. (Carole Marsh State Bks.). (Illus.). (J). (gr. 4-7). 1996. pap., teacher ed. 19.95 (*0-7933-7899-0*, C Marsh) Gallopade Intl.

Montana Facts & Symbols. Emily McAuliffe. 1999. 15.00 (*0-531-12004-X*) Watts.

***Montana Facts & Symbols.** Shelley Swanson Sateren. LC 99-31826. (States & Their Symbols Ser.). 1999. 14.60 (*0-7368-0378-5*) Capstone Pr.

Montana Family Outdoor Guide: Featuring Montana State Parks. Vicky Soderberg. (Illus.). 224p. (Orig.). 1995. pap. 9.95 (*1-56037-071-8*) Am Wrld Geog.

Montana Farm & Ranch Life. Daniel N. Vichorek. LC 92-11558. (Montana Geographic Ser.: No. 18). (Illus.). 104p. (Orig.). 1992. pap. 9.95 (*1-56037-016-5*) Am Wrld Geog.

Montana Feathers. Penny Hayes. 256p. 1990. pap. 9.95 (*0-941483-61-4*) Naiad Pr.

Montana Federal Census Index, 1880 (Every Name) (Illus.). 1985. lib. bdg. 100.00 (*0-89593-413-2*, Accel Indexing) Genealogical Srvcs.

Montana Federal Census Index, 1870. (Illus.). lib. bdg. 55.00 (*0-89593-411-6*, Accel Indexing) Genealogical Srvcs.

Montana Festival Fun for Kids! Carole Marsh. (Carole Marsh Montana Bks.). (Illus.). (J). (gr. 3-12). 1994. pap. 19.95 (*0-7933-4005-5*); lib. bdg. 29.95 (*0-7933-4004-7*) Gallopade Intl.

Montana Festival Fun for Kids! Carole Marsh. (Carole Marsh Montana Bks.). (Illus.). (YA). (gr. 3-12). 1994. disk 29.95 (*0-7933-4006-3*) Gallopade Intl.

Montana Fever. Jackie Merritt. (Desire Ser.: No. 1014). 1996. per. 3.50 (*0-373-76014-0*, 1-76014-9) Silhouette.

Montana Fishing. 2nd rev. ed. Dale A. Burk. LC 82-99817. (Illus.). 152p. 1983. pap. 5.95 (*0-912299-08-8*) Stoneydale Pr Pub.

Montana Fishing & Camping Guide - Glacier to Yellowstone. (Illus.). 176p. (Orig.). 1999. pap. 16.00 (*0-9670806-0-6*) glaciertoyellow.

Montana Fly Fishing Guide Vol. 1: West of the Continental Divide. John Holt. LC 95-225. (Illus.). 304p. 1995. per., otabind 29.95 (*0-9626663-2-7*) Greycliff Pub.

Montana Fly Fishing Guide Vol. 2: East of the Continental Divide. John Holt. LC 96-20424. (Illus.). 288p. (Orig.). 1996. per., otabind 29.95 (*0-9626663-3-5*) Greycliff Pub.

Montana Fly Line, 1993. Jeffrey Herman & Greg Thomas. Ed. by Bradley Hurd & Mike McInally. (Illus.). 98p. 1998. 5.95 (*1-890375-01-2*) Missoulian.

Montana from the Big Sky. Larry Mayer. (Illus.). 144p. 1990. 29.95 (*0-9627618-1-8*) Billings Gazette.

Montana "GEO" Bingo! 38 Must Know State Geography Facts for Kids to Learn While Having Fun! Carole Marsh. (Bingo! Ser.). (Illus.). (J). (gr. 2-8). 1998. pap. 14.95 (*0-7933-8601-2*) Gallopade Intl.

Montana Ghost Dance: Essays on Land & Life. John B. Wright. LC 97-33741. 224p. 1998. 35.00 (*0-292-79121-6*, WRIMON) U of Tex Pr.

Montana Ghost Dance: Essays on Land & Life. John B. Wright. LC 97-33741. (Illus.). 224p. 1998. pap. 17.95 (*0-292-79120-8*, WRIMOP) U of Tex Pr.

Montana Gold Rush Diary of Kate Dunlap. limited ed. Ed. by S. Lyman Tyler. 1969. 25.00 (*0-912094-14-1*) Old West.

Montana Gothic. Dirck Van Sickle. LC 98-89775. 209p. 2000. reprint ed. pap. 16.00 (*1-892323-14-1*) Vivisphere.

Montana Government! The Cornerstone of Everyday Life in Our State! Carole Marsh. (Carole Marsh Montana Bks.). (Illus.). (J). (gr. 3-12). 1996. pap. 19.95 (*0-7933-6260-1*); lib. bdg. 29.95 (*0-7933-6259-8*); disk 29.95 (*0-7933-6261-X*) Gallopade Intl.

***Montana Grizzlies: Odyssey to a National Championship - Illustrated 100 Year History of University of Montana Football.** Dave Guffey & Mick Holien. Ed. by Jeff Herman. LC 98-68879. (Illus.). 192p. 1998. pap. 25.00 (*1-57510-056-8*) Pictorial Hist.

Montana Grizzly Tales. Dick Dontigny. (Illus.). 64p. 1986. pap. 5.00 (*0-918292-05-0*) Griggs Print.

***Montana Gunsmoke.** large type ed. Carter West. 240p. 2000. pap. 18.99 (*0-7089-5627-0*, Linford) Ulverscroft.

***Montana Health Care in Perspective 2000.** Ed. by Kathleen O'Leary Morgan & Scott E. Morgan. 21p. 2000. spiral bd. 19.00 (*0-7401-0225-7*) Morgan Quitno Corp.

Montana Health Care Perspective, 1998. Ed. by Kathleen O'Leary Morgan & Scott E. Morgan. 20p. 1998. pap. 19.00 (*1-56692-825-7*) Morgan Quitno Corp.

Montana Health Care Perspective, 1999. Ed. by Kathleen O'Leary Morgan. 21p. 1999. spiral bd. 19.00 (*0-7401-0075-0*) Morgan Quitno Corp.

Montana, Here I Be! large type ed. Dan Cushman. (Sagebrush Large Print Westerns Ser.). 196p. 1995. lib. bdg. 17.95 (*1-57490-008-0*) T T Beeler.

Montana Heritage: An Anthology of Historical Essays. Robert R. Swartout, Jr. & Harry W. Fritz. LC 91-44516. (Illus.). 314p. 1992. pap. 15.95 (*0-917298-25-X*) MT Hist Soc.

Montana High-Potassium Igneous Province. Ed. by Hearn. (IGC Field Trip Guidebooks Ser.). 96p. 1989. 21.00 (*0-87590-638-9*, T346) Am Geophysical.

Montana "HISTO" Bingo! 42 Must Know State History Facts for Kids to Learn While Having Fun! Carole Marsh. (Bingo! Ser.). (Illus.). (J). (gr. 2-8). 1998. pap. 14.95 (*0-7933-8602-0*) Gallopade Intl.

Montana Historical Society Contributions, 10 vols., Set. 1966. reprint ed. 295.00 (*0-910324-12-3*) Da Capo.

Montana History! Surprising Secrets about Our State's Founding Mothers, Fathers & Kids! Carole Marsh. (Carole Marsh Montana Bks.). (Illus.). (J). (gr. 3-12). 1996. pap. 19.95 (*0-7933-6107-9*); lib. bdg. 29.95 (*0-7933-6106-0*); disk 29.95 (*0-7933-6108-7*) Gallopade Intl.

Montana History Calendar. Bruce Baxter. (Illus.). (Orig.). 1993. pap. 6.95 (*0-9625849-1-6*) Montana Hist.

Montana Hit. large type ed. Charles L. Hayes. (Linford Western Library). 240p. 1996. pap. 16.99 (*0-7089-7826-6*, Linford) Ulverscroft.

Montana Hitch. Richard S. Wheeler. 1992. mass mkt. 3.99 (*0-8125-1299-5*, Pub. by Tor Bks) St Martin.

Montana Horseman No. 1. John S. McCord. 256p. (Orig.). 1995. mass mkt. 4.99 (*0-515-11532-0*, Jove) Berkley Pub.

Montana Hot Air Balloon Mystery. Carole Marsh. (Carole Marsh Montana Bks.). (Illus.). (J). (gr. 2-9). 1994. 29.95 (*0-7933-2552-8*); pap. 19.95 (*0-7933-2553-6*); disk 29.95 (*0-7933-2554-4*) Gallopade Intl.

Montana Hot Zones! Viruses, Disease, & Epidemics in Our State's History. Carole Marsh. (Hot Zones! Ser.). (Illus.). (J). (gr. 3-12). 1998. pap. 19.95 (*0-7933-8907-0*); lib. bdg. 29.95 (*0-7933-8906-2*) Gallopade Intl.

Montana Hunting Almanac. Mark Henckel. Ed. by Mike McInally. (Illus.). 175p. 1998. 9.95 (*1-890375-00-4*) Missoulian.

Montana Hunting Guide. exp. rev. ed. Dale A. Burk. LC 83-60660. (Illus.). 188p. 1985. pap. 13.95 (*0-912299-16-9*) Stoneydale Pr Pub.

Montana Hunting Guide. 3rd exp. rev. ed. Dale A. Burk. LC 83-60660. (Illus.). 188p. 1985. 18.95 (*0-912299-19-3*) Stoneydale Pr Pub.

Montana in Perspective, 1998. Ed. by Kathleen O'Leary Morgan & Scott E. Morgan. 24p. 1998. pap. 19.00 (*1-56692-875-3*) Morgan Quitno Corp.

Montana in Perspective, 1999. Ed. by Kathleen O'Leary Morgan. 26p. 1999. spiral bd. 19.00 (*1-56692-975-X*) Morgan Quitno Corp.

***Montana in Perspective 2000.** Ed. by Kathleen O'Leary Morgan & Scott E. Morgan. 26p. 2000. spiral bd. 19.00 (*0-7401-0275-3*) Morgan Quitno Corp.

Montana Indian Dictionary for Kids! Carole Marsh. (Carole Marsh State Bks.). (J). (gr. 2-9). 1996. 29.95 (*0-7933-7722-6*, C Marsh); pap. 19.95 (*0-7933-7723-4*, C Marsh) Gallopade Intl.

***Montana Investment & Business Guide: Business, Investment, Export-Import Opportunities, 50 vols., Vol. 26.** Global Investment Center, USA Staff. (U. S. Regional Investment & Business Library-99: Vol. 26). (Illus.). 350p. (Orig.). 1999. pap. 59.95 (*0-7397-1125-3*) Intl Business Pubns.

Montana Is.... M. Logan. 1995. 24.95 (*1-56044-355-3*) Falcon Pub Inc.

Montana Is . . . Montana in Verse & Photography. rev. ed. Mike Logan. LC 89-91009. (Illus.). 96p. 1989. pap. 13.95 (*0-937959-82-0*) Falcon Pub Inc.

Montana Jeopardy! Answers & Questions about Our State! Carole Marsh. (Carole Marsh Montana Bks.). (Illus.). (J). (gr. 3-12). 1994. pap. 19.95 (*0-7933-4158-2*); lib. bdg. 29.95 (*0-7933-4157-4*); disk 29.95 (*0-7933-4159-0*) Gallopade Intl.

Montana "Jography" A Fun Run Thru Our State. Carole Marsh. (Carole Marsh Montana Bks.). (Illus.). (J). (gr. 3 up). 1994. pap. 19.95 (*1-55609-755-7*); lib. bdg. 29.95 (*1-55609-754-9*); disk 29.95 (*1-55609-756-5*) Gallopade Intl.

Montana Kid's Cookbook: Recipes, How-To, History, Lore & More. Carole Marsh. (Carole Marsh Montana Bks.). (Illus.). (J). (gr. 3 up). 1994. pap. 19.95 (*0-7933-0708-2*); lib. bdg. 29.95 (*0-7933-0709-0*); disk 29.95 (*0-7933-0710-4*) Gallopade Intl.

Montana Land of Giant Rams, Vol. III. (Illus.). 224p. 1999. pap. 19.95 (*1-885924-05-4*) Outdoor Expeditions.

***Montana Legacy.** Roxanne Rustand. (Superromance Ser.: Vol. 895). 2000. mass mkt. 4.50 (*0-373-70895-5*) Harlequin Bks.

Montana Library Book: A Surprising Guide to the Unusual Special Collections in Libraries Across Our State for Students, Teachers, Writers & Publishers - Includes Reproducible Mailing Labels Plus Activities for Young People! Carole Marsh. (Carole Marsh Montana Bks.). (Illus.). 1994. pap. 19.95 (*0-7933-3084-X*); lib. bdg. 29.95 (*0-7933-3083-1*); disk 29.95 (*0-7933-3085-8*) Gallopade Intl.

Montana Lovers. Jackie Merritt. 1996. per. 3.99 (*0-373-24065-1*, 1-24065-4) Silhouette.

***Montana Magazine Photography, Vol. 1.** Rick Graetz. 1998. write for info. (*1-891152-00-9*) Nth Rock Pub.

Montana Magica. Thomas Mann. 1998. pap. 10.95 (*84-01-42611-1*) Lectorum Pubns.

Montana Man. Barbara Delinsky. LC 95-22355. 248p. 1995. per. 4.99 (*1-55166-077-6*, 1-66077-8, Mira Bks) Harlequin Bks.

Montana Man. Jackie Merritt. (Desire Ser.). 1998. per. 3.75 (*0-373-76159-7*, 1-76159-2) Silhouette.

Montana Manufacturers Register 1999. Ed. by Frances C. Carlson. 373p. 1999. 61.00 (*1-55600-686-1*) Harris InfoSource.

Montana Margins: A State Anthology. Ed. by Joseph K. Howard. LC 73-38747. (Essay Index Reprint Ser.). 1977. reprint ed. 30.95 (*0-8369-2652-8*) Ayer.

An Asterisk (*) at the beginning of an entry indicates that the title is appearing for the first time.

Montana Math! How It All Adds up in Our State. Carole Marsh. (Carole Marsh Montana Bks.). (Illus.). (YA). (gr. 3-12). 1996. pap. 19.95 (0-7933-6566-X); lib. bdg. 29.95 (0-7933-6565-1) Gallopade Intl.

***Montana Mavericks: Big Sky Brides.** Christine Rimmer et al. 2000. per. 5.99 (0-373-48381-3) Harlequin Bks.

***Montana Mavericks Christmas: Married in Whitehorn; Born in Whitehorn, No. 128.** Susan Mallery & Karen Hughes. 1999. mass mkt. 4.25 (0-373-24286-7) Silhouette.

Montana Mavericks Weddings: The Bride Who Was Stolen in the Night; Bride, Baby & All; Cowgirl Bride, 3 bks. in 1. Diana Palmer et al. (Silhouette Promo Ser.). 1998. per. 5.99 (0-373-48357-0, 1-48357-7) Harlequin Bks.

Montana Media Book: A Surprising Guide to the Amazing Print, Broadcast & Online Media of Our State for Students, Teachers, Writers & Publishers - Includes Reproducible Mailing Labels Plus Activities for Young People! Carole Marsh. (Carole Marsh Montana Bks.). (Illus.). 1994. pap. 19.95 (0-7933-3240-0); lib. bdg. 29.95 (0-7933-3239-7); disk 29.95 (0-7933-3241-9) Gallopade Intl.

Montana Mirage. J. T. Flynn. Ed. by Lynn Arensmeyer. 300p. 1998. pap. 16.00 (0-9667930-0-5) Mtn Vally Pubg.

Montana Mistress. Cort Martin. (Bolt Ser.: No. 13). 1984. mass mkt. 2.25 (0-8217-1316-7, Zebra Kensgtn) Kensgtn Pub Corp.

Montana Molly & the Peppermint Kid: Musical. Monica L. Ross. (J). 1990. 6.00 (0-87602-285-9) Anchorage.

***Montana Moon Lady.** Gina Beth Clark. LC 99-91962. 2000. 25.00 (0-7388-1420-2); pap. 18.00 (0-7388-1421-0) Xlibris Corp.

Montana (Mountains) Maria Rius & Josep M. Parramon. (Let's Discover Ser.). (SPA., Illus.). 32p. (J). (ps-1). 1986. pap. 6.95 (0-8120-3752-9) Barron.

Montana Mystery Van Takes Off! Bk. 1: Handicapped Montana Kids Sneak off on a Big Adventure. Carole Marsh. (Carole Marsh Montana Bks.). (Illus.). (J). (gr. 3-12). 1994. 29.95 (0-7933-5039-5); pap. 19.95 (0-7933-5040-9); disk 29.95 (0-7933-5041-7) Gallopade Intl.

Montana Native Plants & Early Peoples. Jeff Hart. LC 92-20345. (Illus.). 168p. 1996. reprint ed. pap. 9.95 (0-917298-29-2) MT Hist Soc.

Montana, 1948. Larry Watson. LC 93-25962. 186p. 1993. 17.95 (0-915943-13-1) Milkweed Ed.

Montana, 1948. Larry Watson. Ed. by Jane Rosenman. 182p. 1995. per. 12.00 (0-671-50703-6, WSP) PB.

Montana, 1948. large type ed. Larry Watson. 256p. 31.50 (0-7089-3693-8) Ulverscroft.

Montana on My Mind. Photos by Michael S. Sample & Larry Mayer. (America on My Mind Ser.). (Illus.). 120p. 1987. 29.95 (0-937959-26-X) Falcon Pub Inc.

Montana Passion. Jackie Merritt. (Special Edition Ser.). 1996. per. 3.99 (0-373-24051-1, 1-24051-4) Silhouette.

Montana Pay Dirt: A Guide to the Mining Camps of the Treasure State. Muriel S. Wolle. LC 63-14650. 1963. pap. 24.95 (0-8040-0722-5) Swallow.

***Montana Places: Exploring Big Sky Country.** Jack Wright. (Illus.). 160p. 2000. pap. 15.95 (0-8166-3705-9) U of Minn Pr.

***Montana Places: Exploring Big Sky Country.** John B. Wright. (Illus.). 160p. 2000. 39.95 (0-8166-3704-0) U of Minn Pr.

Montana Portrait: The Land & Its People. John A. Alwin. LC 93-9396. (Montana Geographic Ser.: No. 17). (Illus.). 160p. (Orig.). 1993. pap. 9.95 (1-56037-008-4) Am Wrld Geog.

Montana Primer. David Dale. (Illus.). 46p. (Orig.). 1996. pap. 8.95 (0-9622429-5-0) Big Mtn.

Montana Quiz Bowl Crash Course! Carole Marsh. (Carole Marsh Montana Bks.). (Illus.). (J). (gr. 3 up). 1994. pap. 19.95 (1-55609-770-0); lib. bdg. 29.95 (1-55609-769-7); disk 29.95 (1-55609-771-9) Gallopade Intl.

Montana Rail Link: Mainstreet of Southern Montana. Wesley Fox. (Illus.). 96p. 1997. 37.95 (1-884831-04-4) Fox Pubns.

Montana Related Laws to the Insurance Laws. Montana & NILS Publishing Company. LC 97-75434. 1997. write for info. (0-89246-488-7) NILS Pub.

***Montana Rescue.** large type ed. Billy Hall. 256p. 1999. pap. 18.99 (0-7089-5572-X, Linford) Ulverscroft.

Montana Retirement & Relocation Guide. large type ed. Gene Thornberg & Donna Thornberg. (Retirement & Relocation Guides Ser.). (Illus.). 300p. Date not set. pap. 24.95 (1-56559-122-4) HGI-Over Fifty.

Montana Rides. Max Brand. 300p. Date not set. reprint ed. lib. bdg. 20.95 (0-89190-203-1, Am Repr) Amereon Ltd.

Montana Rides Again. Max Brand. 253p. Date not set. reprint ed. lib. bdg. 22.95 (0-89190-204-X, Am Repr) Amereon Ltd.

Montana Roadside Directory & Trip Planner. Michael Dougherty. Ed. by Corinne Gaffner & Jennifer Williams. (Illus.). 304p. 1999. pap. 24.95 (1-888550-06-6, Kirke Ministries) Champions Pubng.

Montana Rogue. Jessica Douglass. 1995. per. 3.75 (0-373-07665-7) Harlequin Bks.

Montana Rollercoasters! Carole Marsh. (Carole Marsh Montana Bks.). (Illus.). (J). (gr. 3-12). 1994. pap. 19.95 (0-7933-5303-3); lib. bdg. 29.95 (0-7933-5302-5) Gallopade Intl.

Montana Rollercoasters! Carole Marsh. (Carole Marsh Montana Bks.). (Illus.). (YA). (gr. 3-12). 1994. disk 29.95 (0-7933-5304-1) Gallopade Intl.

Montana School Trivia: An Amazing & Fascinating Look at Our State's Teachers, Schools & Students! Carole Marsh. (Carole Marsh Montana Bks.). (Illus.). (J). (gr. 3 up). 1994. pap. 19.95 (0-7933-0705-8); lib. bdg. 29.95 (0-7933-0706-6); disk 29.95 (0-7933-0707-4) Gallopade Intl.

Montana Science & Technology Action Agenda. (Illus.). 67p. (Orig.). (C). 1993. pap. text 30.00 (1-56806-764-X) DIANE Pub.

Montana Silly Basketball Sportsmysteries, Vol. I. Carole Marsh. (Carole Marsh Montana Bks.). (Illus.). (J). (gr. 3 up). 1994. pap. 19.95 (0-7933-0702-3); lib. bdg. 29.95 (0-7933-0703-1); disk 29.95 (0-7933-0704-X) Gallopade Intl.

Montana Silly Basketball Sportsmysteries, Vol. II. Carole Marsh. (Carole Marsh Montana Bks.). (Illus.). (J). (gr. 3 up). 1994. pap. 19.95 (0-7933-1750-9); lib. bdg. 29.95 (0-7933-1749-5); disk 29.95 (0-7933-1751-7) Gallopade Intl.

Montana Silly Football Sportsmysteries, Vol. I. Carole Marsh. (Carole Marsh Montana Bks.). (Illus.). (J). (gr. 3 up). 1994. pap. 19.95 (1-55609-761-1); lib. bdg. 29.95 (1-55609-760-3); disk 29.95 (1-55609-762-X) Gallopade Intl.

Montana Silly Football Sportsmysteries, Vol. II. Carole Marsh. (Carole Marsh Montana Bks.). (Illus.). (J). (gr. 3 up). 1994. pap. 19.95 (1-55609-764-6); lib. bdg. 29.95 (1-55609-763-8); disk 29.95 (1-55609-765-4) Gallopade Intl.

Montana Silly Trivia! Carole Marsh. (Carole Marsh Montana Bks.). (Illus.). (J). (gr. 3 up). 1994. pap. 19.95 (1-55609-752-2); lib. bdg. 29.95 (1-55609-751-4); disk 29.95 (1-55609-753-0) Gallopade Intl.

Montana Sky. Jackie Merritt. (Desire Ser.). 1993. per. 2.99 (0-373-05790-3, 5-05790-6) Silhouette.

Montana Sky. Nora Roberts. 467p. 1997. mass mkt. 7.99 (0-515-12061-8, Jove) Berkley Pub.

Montana Sky. large type ed. Nora Roberts. 707p. 1996. 26.95 (0-7862-0672-1) Thorndike Pr.

***Montana Small Business Start-Up Kit.** large type ed. Klarryse L. Murphy. 79p. 1999. 34.95 (0-9635844-2-1, Pub. by Lilly & Blair) Sapphire Enter.

Montana Spaces: Essays in Celebration of Montana. Ed. by William Kittredge. 208p. 1996. pap. text 16.95 (1-55821-520-4) Lyons Pr.

Montana Spelling Bee! Score Big by Correctly Spelling Our State's Unique Names. Carole Marsh. (Carole Marsh Montana Bks.). (Illus.). (YA). (gr. 3-12). 1996. pap. 19.95 (0-7933-6719-0); lib. bdg. 29.95 (0-7933-6718-2) Gallopade Intl.

***Montana State Constitution: A Reference Guide.** Larry M. Elison & Fritz Snyder. (Reference Guides to the State Constitutions of the United States: Vol. 31). 264p. 2000. lib. bdg. 79.00 (0-313-27346-4, EMS) Greenwood.

Montana Stories of Frank B. Linderman: The Authorized Edition. Frank B. Linderman. LC 97-17727. viii, 214p. 1997. pap. 9.95 (0-8032-7970-1, Bison Books) U of Nebr Pr.

Montana Sunrise. Charlene Bowen. LC 96-95279. 192p. 1997. 17.95 (0-8034-9189-1, Avalon Bks) Bouregy.

Montana Tech: Eighteen Ninety-Three to Nineteen Eighty-Four. Terrence D. McGlynn. (Illus.). 112p. 1984. 14.95 (0-930609-00-X) Montana Tech.

Montana Territorial (Note: Part of Washington Territory) Census Index, 1860. (Illus.). 1982. lib. bdg. 49.00 (0-89593-410-8, Accel Indexing) Genealogical Srvcs.

Montana Time: The Seasons of a Trout Fisherman. John Barsness. 144p. 1996. pap. text 14.95 (1-55821-492-5) Lyons Pr.

Montana Timeline: A Chronology of Montana History, Mystery, Trivia, Legend, Lore & More. Carole Marsh. (Carole Marsh Montana Bks.). (Illus.). (J). (gr. 3-12). 1994. pap. 19.95 (0-7933-5954-6); lib. bdg. 29.95 (0-7933-5953-8); disk 29.95 (0-7933-5955-4) Gallopade Intl.

Montana Tribute. DeWayne A. Williams. LC 90-82465. (Heirloom Edition Ser.). (Illus.). 128p. (C). 1990. lib. bdg. 100.00 (0-9626877-9-0) Artistwork.

Montana 2000! Coming Soon to a Calendar Near You - The 21st Century! - Complete Set of AL 2000 Items. Carole Marsh. (Two Thousand! Ser.). (Illus.). (J). (gr. 3-12). 1998. pap. 75.00 (0-7933-9361-2); lib. bdg. 85.00 (0-7933-9362-0) Gallopade Intl.

Montana 2000! Coming Soon to a Calendar near You--The 21st Century! Carole Marsh. (Two Thousand! Ser.). (Illus.). (J). (gr. 3-12). 1998. pap. 19.95 (0-7933-8754-X); lib. bdg. 29.95 (0-7933-8753-1) Gallopade Intl.

Montana U. S. Marshal: A Fictional Novel about the Escapades of a U. S. Marshal in & about Jacksonhole, Wyoming, Circa 1870. Gary Twesten. 1988. write for info. (0-9602428-7-2) G Twesten.

Montana UFO's & Extraterrestrials! A Look at the Sightings & Science in Our State. Carole Marsh. (Carole Marsh Montana Bks.). (Illus.). (J). (gr. 3-12). 1997. pap. 19.95 (0-7933-6413-2); lib. bdg. 29.95 (0-7933-6412-4) Gallopade Intl.

Montana Vistas: Selected Historical Essays. Ed. by Robert R. Swartout, Jr. LC 81-40522. 292p. (Orig.). 1982. pap. text 24.00 (0-8191-2047-2) U Pr of Amer.

***Montana Wild & Beautiful.** Photos by Chuck Haney & John Reddy. (Illus.). 120p. 1999. 29.95 (1-56037-144-7) Am Wrld Geog.

Montana Wilderness: Discovering the Heritage. Steve Woodruff & Don Schwennesen. (Illus.). 128p. 1984. 25.00 (0-913504-88-2) Lowell Pr.

Montana Wildflowers. Beverly Magley. LC 91-58876. (Interpreting the Great Outdoors Ser.). (Illus.). 32p. 1992. pap. 6.95 (1-56044-118-6) Falcon Pub Inc.

Montana Wildlife. James Kavanagh. (Pocket Naturalist Ser.). (Illus.). 1998. 5.95 (1-889903-66-3, Pub. by Waterford WA) Falcon Pub Inc.

Montana Wildlife. Jan L. Wassink & R. C. Gildart. (Montana Geographic Ser.: No. 3). (Illus.). 128p. (Orig.). 1982. pap. 9.95 (0-938314-04-1) Am Wrld Geog.

Montana Wildlife: A Children's Field Guide to the State's Most Remarkable Animals. Gayle C. Shirley. LC 92-55081. (Interpreting the Great Outdoors Ser.). (Illus.). 48p. (Orig.). (J). 1993. pap. 7.95 (1-56044-154-2) Falcon Pub Inc.

Montana Wildlife Viewing Guide. Hank Fischer & Carol Fischer. LC 95-10265. (Watchable Wildlife Ser.). (Illus.). 112p. (Orig.). 1990. pap. 9.95 (1-56044-348-0) Falcon Pub Inc.

Montana Women. Toni Volk. LC 91-18737. 310p. 1992. 19.95 (0-939149-60-5) Soho Press.

Montana Women. Toni Volk. LC 91-18737. 310p. 1993. pap. 12.00 (0-939149-89-3) Soho Press.

Montana Writers' Daybook. Ed. & Photos by Gennie Nord. (Illus.). 172p. (Orig.). 1995. pap. 12.95 (1-889367-03-6) Up the Creek.

Montanans' Fishing Guide Vol. 1: Montana Waters West of the Continental Divide. 5th rev. ed. Dick Konizeski. Ed. by Gwen McKenna. LC 97-51573. (Illus.). 416p. 1998. pap. 18.00 (0-87842-371-0) Mountain Pr.

Montana's Agony: Years of War & Hysteria, 1917-1921. Arnon Gutfeld. LC 78-31495. (University of Florida Monographs: Social Sciences: No. 64). 184p. reprint ed. pap. 57.10 (0-7837-5103-6, 204480200004) Bks Demand.

***Montana's Bitterroot Valley.** Russell Lawrence. LC 99-75625. 158p. 1999. pap. 19.95 (0-912299-89-4) Stoneydale Pr Pub.

***Montana's Bitterroot Valley.** Russell Lawrence. LC 99-75625. (Illus.). 158p. 1999. 29.95 (0-912299-88-6) Stoneydale Pr Pub.

Montana's Bob Marshall Wilderness. Roland Cheek. (Illus.). 80p. 1982. 15.95 (0-918981-00-X); pap. 10.95 (0-918981-01-8) Skyline Pub.

Montana's Brand of Western Humor. Albert Erickson. (Orig.). 1990. pap. 3.95 (0-938314-95-5) Am Wrld Geog.

Montana's Cowboys: Living the Heritage. Daniel N. Vichorek. LC 94-18971. (Montana Geographic Ser.: No. 20). (Illus.). 104p. (Orig.). 1994. pap. 9.95 (1-56037-066-1) Am Wrld Geog.

Montanas Escalar. Richard M. Wainwright. LC 90-13990.Tr. of Mountains to Climb. (SPA., Illus.). 64p. (J). 1991. 18.00 (0-9619566-5-8) Family Life.

***Montana's Feisty Cowgirl.** Carolyn Zane. 2001. mass mkt. 3.50 (0-373-19488-9) Silhouette.

***Montana's Flathead.** Rick Graetz. (Illus.). 1999. 22.95 (1-891152-03-3); pap. 14.95 (1-891152-02-5) Nth Rock Pub.

Montana's Fur Trade Era. Lee Graves. LC 94-11761. (Illus.). 64p. (Orig.). 1994. pap. 4.95 (1-56037-054-8) Am Wrld Geog.

Montana's Gallatin Canyon: A Gem in the Treasure State. Janet Cronin & Dorothy Vick. LC 92-36887. 259p. 1993. 12.00 (0-87842-277-3) Mountain Pr.

Montana's Historical Highway Markers. 3rd rev. expanded ed. Robert H. Fletcher. Ed. by Glenda C. Bradshaw & John Axline. LC 99-18372. (Illus.). 208p. 1999. pap. 10.95 (0-917298-60-8) MT Hist Soc.

Montana's Home Front During WWII: America's First Hero of WW II. Gary Glynn. LC 94-67868. (Illus.). 224p. (Orig.). 1994. pap. 14.95 (0-929521-93-5) Pictorial Hist.

Montana's Indians: Yesterday & Today. 2nd ed. William L. Bryan. (Illus.). 144p. (Orig.). 1996. pap. 24.95 (1-56037-064-5) Am Wrld Geog.

Montana's Last Desperado: The Life & Death of Joe Reagin. limited ed. Don L. Weibert. LC 92-96939. (Illus.). 248p. 1992. 35.00 (0-9631762-9-3) D L Weibert.

Montana's Mineral County in Retrospect. Margie E. Hahn. (Montana Legacy Ser.: No. 2). (Illus.). 160p. 1998. pap. 12.95 (0-912299-70-3) Stoneydale Pr Pub.

Montana's Missouri River. Robert C. Gildart. (Montana Geographic Ser.: No. 8). (Illus.). 104p. (Orig.). 1984. pap. 9.95 (0-938314-10-6) Am Wrld Geog.

Montana's (Most Devastating!) Disasters & (Most Calamitous!) Catastrophies! Carole Marsh. (Carole Marsh Montana Bks.). (Illus.). (J). (gr. 3 up). 1994. pap. 19.95 (0-7933-0692-2); lib. bdg. 29.95 (0-7933-0694-9); disk 29.95 (0-7933-0695-7) Gallopade Intl.

Montana's Righteous Hangmen: The Vigilantes in Action. Lew L. Callaway, Jr. Ed. & Frwd. by Merrill G. Burlingame. LC 81-40282. (Illus.). 256p. 1997. pap. 12.95 (0-8061-2912-3) U of Okla Pr.

Montana's Righteous Hangmen: The Vigilantes in Action. Lew L. Callaway. Ed. by Lew L. Callaway, Jr. LC 81-40282. (Illus.). 240p. 1982. 21.95 (0-8061-1728-1) U of Okla Pr.

Montana's Unsolved Mysteries (& Their "Solutions") Includes Scientific Information & Other Activities for Students. Carole Marsh. (Carole Marsh Montana Bks.). (Illus.). (J). (gr. 3-12). 1994. pap. 19.95 (0-7933-5801-9); lib. bdg. 29.95 (0-7933-5800-0); disk 29.95 (0-7933-5802-7) Gallopade Intl.

Montane Foragers: Asana & the South-Central Andean Archaic. Mark S. Aldenderfer. LC 97-40225. (Illus.). 344p. 1998. text 39.95 (0-87745-621-6) U of Iowa Pr.

Montangeologisches Woerterbuch Fuer den Westharz: Mit Stichwoertern aus der Geologie, Palaeontologie, Petrographie, Mineralogie, Lagerstaettenkunde und dem Bergbau von A-Z. K. Mohr. iii, 182p. 1989. 23.00 (3-510-65142-1, Pub. by E Schweizerbartsche) Balogh.

Montanism: Gender, Authority & the New Prophecy. Christine Trevett. (Illus.). 313p. (C). 1996. text 64.95 (0-521-41182-3) Cambridge U Pr.

Montanist Inscriptions & Testimonia: Epigraphic Sources. William Tabbernee. LC 97-21911. (Patristic Monograph: Vol. 16). 712p. 1996. text 45.00 (0-86554-521-9, MUP/H403) Mercer Univ Pr.

Montanye: or The Slavers of Old New York: A Historical Romance. William O. Stoddard. LC 72-2928. (Black Heritage Library Collection). 1977. reprint ed. 31.95 (0-8369-9081-1) Ayer.

Montargis/Auxerre/Dijon Map. 1997. 6.95 (2-06-700065-9, 65) Michelin.

Montasticism in the Orthodox Churches. N. F. Robinson. 175p. 1998. reprint ed. pap. 15.95 (1-886412-25-1) Preserv Press.

***Montauban: Somme.** Graham Maddocks. (Battleground Europe Ser.). 1998. pap. text 16.95 (0-85052-579-9, Pub. by Leo Cooper) Trans-Atl Phila.

Montauk. Max Frisch. Tr. by Geoffrey Skelton. LC 77-16016. (Helen & Kurt Wolff Bk.). 143p. 1978. pap. 4.95 (0-15-661990-3, Harvest Bks) Harcourt.

Montauk: The Alien Connection. Stewart Swerdlow. Ed. by Peter Moon. LC 97-62051. (Montauk Ser.). 266p. 1998. pap. 19.95 (0-9631889-8-4) Sky Bks NY.

Montauk Files: Unearthing the Phoenix Conspiracy. K. B. Wells, Jr. LC 97-75755. (Illus.). 192p. 1998. pap. 14.95 (1-56184-134-X) New Falcon Pubns.

***Montauk Mystery.** Diane Sawyer. LC 99-91312. 192p. 2000. 18.95 (0-8034-9399-1, Avalon Bks) Bouregy.

Montauk Point, Long Island: An 1871 Visit. Charles Parsons. (Illus.). 15p. (Orig.). 1990. reprint ed. pap. 2.95 (0-89646-082-7) Vistabooks.

Montauk Project: Experiments in Time. Preston B. Nichols & Peter Moon. LC 91-91514. (Illus.). 160p. (Orig.). 1992. pap. 15.95 (0-9631889-0-9) Sky Bks NY.

Montauk Revisited: Adventures in Synchronicity. Preston B. Nichols & Peter Moon. LC 93-84992. (Illus.). 224p. 1994. pap. 19.95 (0-9631889-1-7) Sky Bks NY.

Montcalm & Wolfe. Francis Parkman. Ed. by Caleb Carr. LC 98-48972. (Modern Library War Ser.). 522p. 1999. pap. 16.95 (0-375-75420-2) Modern Lib NY.

***Montcalm & Wolfe.** Francis Parkman. (Notable American Authors Ser.). 1999. reprint ed. lib. bdg. 125.00 (0-7812-4736-5) Rprt Serv.

Montcalm & Wolfe: The French & Indian War. Francis Parkman. (Illus.). 674p. 1995. reprint ed. pap. 18.95 (0-306-80621-5) Da Capo.

Montclair. Sara Mitchell. LC 97-4712. (Portraits Ser.). 256p. 1997. pap. 8.99 (1-55661-963-4) Bethany Hse.

Montclair: A Postcard Guide to Its Past. Philip Jaeger. (Images of America Ser.). 1998. pap. 16.99 (0-7524-1224-8) Arcadia Publng.

Montclair: Evolution of a Surburban Town. Edwin B. Goodell. (Illus.). 303p. 1997. reprint ed. lib. bdg. 38.00 (0-8328-6879-5) Higginson Bk Co.

Montclair Brides. Jane Peart. Date not set. 19.99 (0-310-23043-8) Zondervan.

Montclair Brides, Vol. 2. 2nd ed. Jane Peart. Date not set. 19.99 (0-310-23044-6) HarpC.

***Montclair Homecoming.** Jane Peart. LC 99-88527. (Brides of Montclair Ser.). 2000. 9.99 (0-310-67161-2) Zondervan.

***Montclair Neighborhood.** Thomas J. Noel & William J. Hansen. (Illus.). 112p. 1999. pap. 9.95 (0-914248-24-3) Hist Denver.

Monte Alban: Estudios Recientes. Ed. by Marcus Winter. (SPA.). 128p. 1994. pap. 20.00 (1-877812-72-2, UC003) UPLAAP.

Monte Alban's Hinterland: The Prehispanic Settlement Patterns of the Central & Southern Parts of the Valley of Oaxaca, Mexico, Pt. 1. Richard E. Blanton et al. (Memoirs Series, Prehistory & Human Ecology of the Valley of Oaxaca: No. 15, Vol. 7). 1982. pap. 20.00 (0-932206-91-3) U Mich Mus Anthro.

Monte Alban's Hinterland Pt. II: Prehispanic Settlement Patterns in Tlacolula, Etla, & Ocotlan, the Valley of Oaxaca, Mexico, 2 vols., Pt. II. Stephan A. Kowalewski. LC F 1219.1.O11. (Memoirs of the Museum of Anthropology, University of Michigan Ser.: No. 23). (Illus.). 540p. (Orig.). reprint ed. pap. 167.40 (0-7837-1214-6, 204174600001); reprint ed. pap. 190.10 (0-7837-1215-4, 204174600002) Bks Demand.

Monte Burch's Black Bass Basics: Techniques for Largemouth, Smallmouth, Kentuckies. Monte Burch. LC 94-69861. (Illus.). 192p. 1994. pap. 12.95 (1-879206-20-X) Outdoor World Pr.

Monte Burch's Pole Building Projects: Over 25 Low-Cost Plans. Monte Burch. LC 92-56148. (Illus.). 208p. 1993. 27.95 (0-88266-860-9, Garden Way Pub); pap. 18.95 (0-88266-859-5, Garden Way Pub) Storey Bks.

Monte Carlo: Concepts, Algorithms & Applications. George S. Fishman. LC 95-17144. (Operations Research Ser.). 712p. 1997. 69.95 (0-387-94527-X) Spr-Verlag.

Monte Carlo & Molecular Dynamics Simulations in Polymer Science. Ed. by Kurt Binder. (Topics in Polymer Science Ser.). (Illus.). 608p. 1995. text 110.00 (0-19-509438-7) OUP.

Monte Carlo & Quasi-Monte Carlo Methods in Scientific Computing: Proceedings of a Conference at the University of Nevada, Las Vegas, Nevada, USA, June 23-25, 1994. Ed. by Harald Niederreiter & Peter J. Shieu. LC 95-37688. (Lecture Notes in Statistics Ser.: Vol. 106). 1995. 54.95 (0-387-94577-6) Spr-Verlag.

Monte Carlo & Quasi-Monte Carlo Methods, 1996. Ed. by Harald Niederreiter et al. LC 97-34133. (Lecture Notes in Statistics Ser.: Vol. 127). 464p. 1997. pap. 44.95 (0-387-98335-X) Spr-Verlag.

***Monte Carlo & Quasi-Monte Carlo Methods 1998: Proceedings of a Conference at the Claremont Graduate University, Claremont, California, USA, June 22-26, 1998.** Ed. by Harald Niederreiter & Jerome Spanier. LC 99-47502. xvi, 472p. 1999. pap. 99.95 (3-540-66176-X) Spr-Verlag.

Monte Carlo Approach to Biopolymers & Protein Folding: Hlrz, Forschungszentrum Julich, Germany 3 - 5 December 1997. Ed. by Peter Grassberger et al. 300p. 78.00 (981-02-3658-1) World Scientific Pub.

M

M

Monte Carlo Calculations in Nuclear Medicine: Applications in Diagnostic Imaging. Ed. by M. Ljungberg & M. A. King. LC 98-11380. (Medical Science Ser.). (Illus.). 256p. 1998. 99.00 (*0-7503-0479-0*) IOP Pub.

Monte Carlo Device Simulation: Full Band & Beyond. Ed. by Karl Hess. (C). 1991. text 122.00 (*0-7923-9172-1*) Kluwer Academic.

Monte Carlo Girls. Christine Vincent. 448p. 1995. pap. 8.95 (*0-450-59649-4*, Pub. by Hodder & Stought Ltd) Trafalgar.

Monte Carlo Method. 2nd ed. I. M. Sobol. Tr. by Peter Fortini et al from RUS. LC 73-98791. (Popular Lectures in Mathematics). (Illus.). 76p. (C). 1975. pap. text 4.50 (*0-226-76749-3*) U Ch Pr.

Monte Carlo Method: The Method of Statistical Trials. E. Shreider & Ian N. Sneddon. LC 64-8052. (International Series of Monographs on Pure & Applied Mathematics: Vol. 87). 1966. 171.00 (*0-08-011088-6*, Pub. by Pergamon Repr) Franklin.

Monte Carlo Method for Semiconductor Device Simulation. C. Jacobini & P. Lugli. (Computational Microelectronics Ser.). (Illus.). 360p. 1989. 137.95 (*0-387-82110-4*) Spr-Verlag.

***Monte Carlo Method for Solving Inverse Problems of Radiation Transfer.** V. S. Antyufeev. (Illus.). 202p. 2000. 132.50 (*90-6764-320-3*, Pub. by Uppsala Universitet) Coronet Bks.

Monte-Carlo Method in Condensed Matter Physics. Ed. by Kurt Binder. (Topics in Applied Physics Ser.: Vol. 71). (Illus.). 392p. 1992. 67.00 (*0-387-54369-4*) Spr-Verlag.

Monte Carlo Method in Condensed Matter Physics, Vol. 71. Ed. by Kurt Binder. LC 95-33224. (Topics in Applied Physics Ser.). 430p. 1995. 59.95 (*3-540-60174-0*) Spr-Verlag.

Monte Carlo Methods. J. M. Hammersley & D. C. Handscomb. (Monographs on Statistics & Applied Probability). 1964. 27.50 (*0-412-15870-1*, NO. 6140) Chapman & Hall.

***Monte Carlo Methods.** Neal Noah Madras. LC 00-39810. (Fields Institute Communications Ser.: Vol. 26). 228p. 2000. 69.00 (*0-8218-1992-5*) Am Math.

Monte Carlo Methods: Basics, Vol. 1, Basics. 99th ed. Malvin H. Kalos & Paula A. Whitlock. LC 86-11009. 208p. 1986. 115.00 (*0-471-89839-2*) Wiley.

Monte Carlo Methods: In Boundary Value Problems. K. K. Sabelfeld. (Illus.). xii, 283p. 1991. 102.95 (*0-387-53001-0*) Spr-Verlag.

Monte-Carlo Methods & Applications in Neutronics, Photonics & Statistical Physics. R. Alcouffe et al. (Lecture Notes in Physics Ser.: Vol. 240). viii, 483p. 1985. 53.95 (*0-387-16070-1*) Spr-Verlag.

Monte Carlo Methods & Parallel Algorithms: International Youth Workshop, Primosko, Bulgaria, 24-30, Sept. 1989. B. L. Sendov & Ivan T. Dimov. 144p. (C). 1991. text 67.00 (*981-02-0293-8*) World Scientific Pub.

Monte Carlo Methods for Applied Scientists. Ivan T. Dimov & Dean McKee. 240p. 1998. text 48.00 (*981-02-2329-3*) World Scientific Pub.

Monte Carlo Methods in Atmospheric Optics. Gurii I. Marchuk et al. (Optical Sciences Ser.: Vol. 12). (Illus.). 1980. 44.95 (*0-387-09402-4*) Spr-Verlag.

***Monte Carlo Methods in Bayesian Computation.** Ming-Hui Chen et al. Ed. by P. Bickel et al. LC 99-46366. (Series in Statistics). (Illus.). 400p. 2000. 79.95 (*0-387-98935-8*) Spr-Verlag.

Monte Carlo Methods in Quantum Problems. Ed. by Malvin H. Kalos. 1984. text 147.50 (*90-277-1755-9*) Kluwer Academic.

Monte Carlo Methods in Statistical Physics. Mark Newman & G. T. Barkema. LC 99-213405. (Illus.). 490p. 1999. pap. text 45.00 (*0-19-851797-1*) OUP.

***Monte Carlo Methods in Statistical Physics.** Mark Newman & G. T. Barkema. LC 99-213405. (Illus.). 490p. 1999. text 98.00 (*0-19-851796-3*) OUP.

Monte Carlo Modelling for Electron Microscopy & Microanalysis, No. 9. David C. Joy. (Illus.). 224p. 1995. text 70.00 (*0-19-508874-3*) OUP.

Monte Carlo Optimization, Simulation & Sensitivity of Queueing Networks. Reuven Y. Rubinstein. LC 92-13121. 272p. (C). 1992. reprint ed. lib. bdg. 54.00 (*0-89464-764-4*) Krieger.

Monte Carlo Particle Transport Methods: Neutron & Photon Calculations. Ivan Lux & Laszlo Koblinger. 448p. 1991. lib. bdg. 119.95 (*0-8493-6074-9*, QC793) CRC Pr.

Monte Carlo Simulation. Christopher Z. Mooney. LC 96-45873. (Quantitative Applications in the Social Sciences Ser.: Vol. 116). 96p. 1997. pap. 10.95 (*0-8039-5943-5*) Sage.

Monte Carlo Simulation in High Energy & Nuclear Physics: Proceedings of the 93 International Conference. S. L. Linn et al. 400p. 1994. text 112.00 (*981-02-1621-1*) World Scientific Pub.

Monte Carlo Simulation in Statistical Physics: An Introduction. Kurt Binder & D. W. Heermann. (Solid-State Sciences Ser.: Vol. 80). (Illus.). 135p. 1988. 37.00 (*0-387-19107-0*) Spr-Verlag.

Monte Carlo Simulation in Statistical Physics: An Introduction. 2nd ed. Kurt Binder & D. W. Heermann. (Illus.). 135p. 1992. 31.95 (*0-387-55729-6*) Spr-Verlag.

Monte Carlo Simulation in Statistical Physics: An Introduction. 3rd ed. K. Binder & Dieter W. Heermann. LC 97-28559. (Series in Solid-State Sciences: Vol. 80). (Illus.). x, 130p. 1997. pap. 24.95 (*3-540-63265-4*) Spr-Verlag.

Monte Carlo Simulation in the Radiological Sciences. Ed. by Richard L. Morin. LC 88-10478. 240p. 1988. 141.00 (*0-8493-5559-1*, R905, CRC Reprint) Franklin.

Monte Carlo Simulations of Disordered Systems. S. Jain. 150p. 1992. text 36.00 (*9971-5-0660-2*) World Scientific Pub.

Monte Carlo Statistical Methods. Christian P. Robert & George Casella. LC 98-55413. (Texts in Statistics Ser.). 528p. 1999. 79.95 (*0-387-98707-X*) Spr-Verlag.

Monte Carlo Transport of Electrons & Photons. T. M. Jenkins et al. (Ettore Majorana International Science Ser., Life Sciences: Vol. 38). (Illus.). 656p. (C). 1988. text 149.50 (*0-306-43099-1*, Kluwer Plenum) Kluwer Academic.

Monte Carmelo: An Italian-American Community in the Bronx, Vol. 9. A. L. LaRuffa. (Library of Anthropology). 192p. 1988. text 69.00 (*2-88124-253-7*) Gordon & Breach.

Monte Cassino in the Middle Ages, 3 vols. Herbert Bloch. LC 80-39809. (Illus.). 1576p. 1988. 228.95 (*0-674-58655-7*) HUP.

Monte Cristo. Philip R. Woodhouse. LC 78-71665. (Illus.). 312p. 1996. pap. 16.95 (*0-89886-071-7*) Mountaineers.

Monte Foreman's Horse-Training Science. Monte Foreman & Patrick Wyse. LC 82-40450. (Illus.). 156p. 1983. 32.95 (*0-8061-1583-1*) U of Okla Pr.

***Monte Homes: A History of the Melbourne Jewish Philanthropic Society & the Montefiore Homes.** Judith R. Buckrich. 224p. 1999. pap. (*0-522-84845-1*, Pub. by Melbourne Univ Pr) Paul & Co Pubs.

Monte Rushmore. Lynda Sorensen. LC 94-20739. (Simbolos Americanos Ser.).Tr. of Mount Rushmore. (ENG & SPA.). 24p. (J). (gr. k-4). 1994. lib. bdg. 17.27 (*1-55916-068-3*) Rourke Bk Co.

Monte Verde: A Late Pleistocene Settlement in Chile: A Paleoenvironment & Site Context, Vol. 1. Tom D. Dillehay. LC 88-23947. (Series in Archaeological Inquiry). (Illus.). 336p. 1989. text 60.00 (*0-87474-350-8*) Smithsonian.

Monte Verde: A Late Pleistocene Settlement in Chile: The Archaeological Context & Interpretation, Vol. 2. Tom D. Dillehay. (Smithsonian Series in Archaeological Inquiry). (Illus.). 1080p. 1996. text 155.00 (*1-56098-680-8*) Smithsonian.

Monte Walsh. Jack Schaefer. LC 80-25036. ix, 442p. 1981. pap. 15.95 (*0-8032-9121-3*, Bison Books) U of Nebr Pr.

Monte Walsh. Jack Schaefer. 42p. 1993. reprint ed. lib. bdg. 31.95 (*0-89968-321-5*, Lghtyr Pr) Buccaneer Bks.

Montecito & Santa Barbara, Vol. 2. David F. Myrick. LC 87-30188. (Illus.). 320p. (YA). (gr. 11). 1991. 54.95 (*0-87046-100-1*) Pentrex Media.

Montee du Soir. Michel Deon. (FRE.). 151p. 1989. pap. 10.95 (*0-7859-2115-X*, 2070381269) Fr & Eur.

Montelimar, Nicaragua: Ulysses Due South Guide. Carol Wood. (Illus.). 120p. 1994. pap. 5.95 (*2-921444-90-9*) Ulysses Travel.

Montelimar/Avignon/Digne Map. 1997. 6.95 (*2-06-700081-0*, 81) Michelin.

Montemayor's Diana, Music, & the Visual Arts. Bruno M. Damiani. vi, 118p. 1983. 11.00 (*0-942260-28-7*) Hispanic Seminary.

Montenegrin Social Organization & Values. C. Boehm. (Studies in Anthropology: No. 1). 1983. 29.50 (*0-404-62601-7*) AMS Pr.

Montenegrin Social Organization & Values: Political Ethnography of a Refuge Area Tribal Adaptation. Christopher Boehm. LC 77-87156. (Studies in Anthropology: No. 1). 1983. 29.50 (*0-404-16895-7*) AMS Pr.

Montenegro. Milovan Djilas. Tr. by Kenneth Johnstone. LC 63-8090. 367p. 1963. 9.95 (*0-15-162102-0*) Harcourt.

Montenegro. Starling Lawrence. LC 96-52424. 320p. 1997. 23.00 (*0-374-21407-7*) FS&G.

Montenegro. Marko Spadijer. (Illus.). 208p. (C). 1980. 115.00 (*0-7855-5158-1*, Pub. by Collets) St Mut.

Montenegro. Starling Lawrence. 350p. 1998. reprint ed. mass mkt. 6.99 (*0-425-16446-2*) Berkley Pub.

Montenegro: Its People & Their History. William Denton. LC 77-87162. x, 292p. 1977. reprint ed. 54.00 (*0-404-16896-5*) AMS Pr.

Monteregian Treasures: The Minerals of Mont Saint-Hilaire, Quebec. Joseph A. Mandarino & Violet Anderson. (Illus.). 302p. 1989. text 110.00 (*0-521-32632-X*) Cambridge U Pr.

Monterey: A View from Garlic Hill. Peter J. Cutino. LC 95-44754. (Illus.). 213p. (Orig.). 1995. pap. 14.95 (*0-940168-37-5*) Boxwood.

***Monterey: Furnishings of California's Spanish Revival.** Ed. & Photos by Douglas Congdon-Martin. LC 99-59827. (Illus.). 176p. 2000. 49.95 (*0-7643-1067-4*) Schiffer.

Monterey & Pacific Grove Street Car Era. Erle C. Hanson. LC 90-37133. (Illus.). 80p. pap. 16.95 (*0-916374-91-2*) Pentrex Media.

Monterey Bay: The Ultimate Guide. Lucinda Jaconette. LC 98-43451. (Illus.). 336p. 1999. pap. 14.95 (*0-8118-1925-6*) Chronicle Bks.

Monterey Bay Area: Natural History & Cultural Imprints. 3rd rev. ed. Burton L. Gordon. LC 95-25409. (Illus.). 375p. 1996. pap. 19.95 (*0-940168-38-3*) Otter B Bks.

Monterey Bay, Big Sur & Gold Coast Wine Country Book: A Complete Guide. 2nd ed. Christina Waters & Buz Bezore. LC 98-22303. (Great Destinations Ser.). (Illus.). 320p. 1998. pap. 17.95 (*0-936399-99-6*, Pub. by Berkshire Hse) Natl Bk Netwk.

Monterey Bay C. A. R. D. Cycle America Resource Directory. Martin Krieg. (Illus.). 64p. 1989. pap. 2.95 (*0-9611490-0-0*) Cycle Amer.

Monterey Bay Shoreline Guide. Jerry Emory. LC 98-36120. (Monterey Bay Aquarium Series in Marine Conservation: No. 1). (Illus.). 320p. 1999. pap. 16.95 (*0-520-21712-8*, Pub. by U CA Pr) Cal Prin Full Svc.

Monterey Bay Shoreline Guide. Jerry Emory. LC 98-36120. (Monterey Bay Aquarium Series in Marine Conservation: Vol. 1). (Illus.). 302p. 1999. 35.00 (*0-520-21153-7*, Pub. by U CA Pr) Cal Prin Full Svc.

Monterey Bay Sports Directory, Summer 1990. 1990. write for info. (*0-9625106-0-2*) World Sports.

Monterey Bay Sports Directory, Winter 1990. 1990. write for info. (*0-9625106-1-0*) World Sports.

Monterey Bay Yesterday: A Nostalgic Era in Postcards. Betty Lewis. (Illus.). 124p. (Orig.). 1987. reprint ed. pap. 4.98 (*0-9617681-1-8*) Otter B Bks.

Monterey County: The Dramatic Story of Its Past. Augusta Fink. LC 72-76931. 254p. 1978. pap. 12.95 (*0-913548-62-6*) Good Life.

***Monterey County Guide: Including Free & Fun Things to See & Do.** 2nd rev. ed. Patricia A. Hamilton. (Illus.). 304p. 2000. 15.95 (*1-877809-44-6*) Park Pl Pubns.

Monterey County Place Names: A Geographical Dictionary. Donald T. Clark. LC 91-32260. 800p. 1991. 29.95 (*1-880478-01-3*); pap. 21.95 (*1-880478-00-5*) Kestrel Pr.

Monterey Formation & Associated Coarse Clastic Rocks, Central San Joaquin Basin, California. Ed. by L. A. Williams & S. A. Graham. (Illus.), 95p. (Orig.). 1982. pap. 4.00 (*1-878861-47-6*) Pac Section SEPM.

Monterey Jazz Festival: 40 Legendary Years. William Minor & Bill Wishner. LC 97-4908. (Illus.). 176p. 1997. 40.00 (*1-883318-40-8*) Angel City Pr.

Monterey Peninsula. 64p. 9.95 (*88-8029-094-0*, Pub. by Bonechi) Eiron.

Monterey Peninsula. Vicki Leon. (Illus.). 56p. (Orig.). 1985. pap. 7.95 (*0-918303-03-6*) Blake Pub.

Monterey Peninsula. Writers Program, California Staff. LC 73-3599. (American Guide Ser.). reprint ed. 49.50 (*0-404-57903-5*) AMS Pr.

Monterey Peninsula: A Photographic Guide to the Big Sur Coastline, Monterey Peninsula & Santa Cruz. (Illus.). 32p. (Orig.). 1988. pap. 2.50 (*1-878395-02-5*) Smith-Western.

***Monterey Peninsula Entertainment, 2000.** (Illus.). 550p. 1999. pap. 35.00 (*1-880248-42-5*, 00U3) Enter Pubns.

Monterey Peninsula Exploring: Big Sur, Carmel, Monterey, Pacific Grove. 2nd rev. ed. Nancy M. Evans & Neil A. Evans. LC 97-61974. Orig. Title: Exploring the Monterey Peninsula. (Illus.). 208p. 1998. pap. 14.95 (*0-9632143-3-0*) Wrldview Assocs.

Monterey Peninsula Sketches. Carl Duerksen. (Illus.). 96p. (Orig.). 1997. mass mkt. 14.95 (*0-9657579-0-0*) C Duerksen.

Monterey Symposium: Monterey Formation & Related Siliceous Rocks of California. Ed. by Robert Garrison & Robert G. Douglas. (Illus.). 327p. (Orig.). 1981. pap. 9.00 (*1-878861-54-9*) Pac Section SEPM.

Monterey's Cookin' Pisto Style: From Sicily to Monterey. John Pisto. (Illus.). 110p. (Orig.). 1994. pap. 12.95 (*0-9640828-0-2*) Pistos Kitchen.

Monterey's Cooking Secrets: Whispered Recipes & Guide to Restaurants, Inns & Wineries of the Monterey Peninsula. 6th rev. ed. Kathleen D. Fish. (Illus.). 288p. 1996. pap. text 13.95 (*0-9620472-6-0*) Bon Vivant Pr.

Monterey's Mother Lode. Randall A. Reinstedt. LC 79-110351. Orig. Title: Gold in the Santa Lucias. (Illus.). 104p. 1977. pap. 7.95 (*0-933818-01-7*) Ghost Town.

Monterrey Is Ours: The Mexican War Letters of Lt. Dana, 1845-1847. Napoleon J. Dana. Ed. by Robert H. Ferrell. LC 88-29351. (Illus.). 248p. 1990. text 29.95 (*0-8131-1703-8*) U Pr of Ky.

Montes the Matador & Other Stories. Frank Harris. LC 72-104476. reprint ed. pap. text 8.95 (*0-8290-2382-8*); reprint ed. lib. bdg. 22.00 (*0-8398-0761-9*) Irvington.

Montesquieu. Allain Glykos. (Maison D'Ecrivain Collection). (FRE., Illus.). 1995. pap. 54.95 (*2-86808-082-0*) Intl Scholars.

Montesquieu & His Reader: A Study of the Esprit des Lois. Diane K. Monticone. LC 89-38370. (Illus.). 168p. (C). 1989. lib. bdg. 41.00 (*0-8191-7596-X*) U Pr of Amer.

Montesquieu & Machiavelli. E. Levi-Malvano. Ed. & Comment by Anthony J. Pansini. 90p. (Orig.). (C). 1991. pap. 15.00 (*0-911876-05-7*) Greenvale.

Montesquieu & the Philosophy of Natural Law. M. H. Waddicor. (International Archives of the History of Ideas Ser.: No. 37). 225p. 1970. lib. bdg. 85.50 (*90-247-5039-3*) Kluwer Academic.

Montesquieu e la Scienza Della Societa. Sergio Cotta. Ed. by J. P. Mayer. LC 78-67343. (European Political Thought Ser.). (ITA.). 1979. reprint ed. lib. bdg. 53.95 (*0-405-11688-8*) Ayer.

Montesquieu Revisited. Peter V. Conroy, Jr. LC 92-18575. (Twayne's World Authors Ser.). 170p. 1992. 32.00 (*0-8057-8273-7*, Twyne) Mac Lib Ref.

Montesquieu-Rezeption in Deutschland Im 18 und Beginnenden 19 Jahrhundert. Frank Herdmann. (Philosophische Texte und Studien: Vol. 25). (GER.). xvi, 314p. 1990. write for info. (*3-487-09270-0*) G Olms Pubs.

Montesquieu's Philosophy of Liberalism: A Commentary on "The Spirit of the Laws" Thomas L. Pangle. 1994. lib. bdg. 25.00 (*0-226-64543-6*) U Ch Pr.

Montesquieu's Philosophy of Liberalism: A Commentary on the Spirit of the Laws. Thomas L. Pangle. LC 73-77139. (Illus.). x, 346p. 1989. pap. text 18.00 (*0-226-64545-2*) U Ch Pr.

Montesquieu's Vision of Uncertainty & Modernity in Political Philosophy. Christopher Sparks. LC 99-24680. (Studies in Social & Political Theory: Vol. 21). 292p. 1999. text 89.95 (*0-7734-7976-7*) E Mellen.

Montessori: A Modern Approach. Paula P. Lillard. LC 78-163334. (Illus.). 192p. (C). 1988. pap. 12.00 (*0-8052-0920-4*) Schocken.

Montessori at Home: A Complete Guide to Teaching Your Preschooler at Home Using the Montessori Method. rev. ed. Heidi A. Spietz. LC 91-18212. 120p. 1991. pap. 11.95 (*0-929487-37-0*) Am Montessori Consult.

***Montessori Based Activities for Persons with Dementia, Vol. 1.** Illus. by Cameron J. Camp. 76p. 1999. pap. 46.50 (*0-9676343-1-8*) Myers Resear Inst.

Montessori Class Management. Franco Albanesi. LC 90-83194. 172p. (C). 1990. pap. 23.00 (*0-9628008-0-5*) Albanesi Educ Ctr.

Montessori Controversy. John Chattin-McNichols. 224p. (C). 1991. mass mkt. 26.25 (*0-8273-4517-8*) Delmar.

Montessori for the Millenium: Pratical Guidance on the Teaching & Education of Children of All Ages, Based on a Rediscovery of the True Principles & Vision of Maria Montessori. Roland A. Wentworth. LC 98-21723. 144p. 1999. 32.50 (*0-8058-3136-3*) L Erlbaum Assocs.

Montessori in Contemporary American Culture. Ed. by Margaret Loeffler. LC 92-523. 298p. (C). 1992. pap. text 26.00 (*0-435-08709-6*, 08709) Heinemann.

Montessori in the Classroom: A Teacher's Account of How Children Really Learn. Paula P. Lillard. LC 97-3290. 1997. pap. 14.00 (*0-8052-1087-3*) Schocken.

Montessori Method. 1990. write for info. (*81-900106-9-7*, Pub. by Kalakshetra Pubns) N Montessori.

Montessori Method. Maria Montessori. LC 64-24014. 416p. (C). 1988. pap. 14.00 (*0-8052-0922-0*) Schocken.

Montessori Method. Maria Montessori. 1976. 26.95 (*0-8488-0303-5*) Amereon Ltd.

Montessori Method & the American School. Florence E. Ward. LC 70-165744. (American Education Ser, No. 2). (Illus.). 1974. reprint ed. 20.95 (*0-405-03722-8*) Ayer.

Montessori Play & Learn: A Practical Guide for Parents & Children. Lesley Britton. (Illus.). 144p. (J). 1992. pap. 19.95 (*0-517-59182-0*, Crown) Crown Pub Group.

Montessori Read & Write: A Parents Guide for Teaching at Home. Lynne Lawrence. LC 98-26639. (Illus.). 160p. 1998. pap. 19.95 (*0-609-80335-2*, Crown) Crown Pub Group.

Montessori Resources: A Complete Guide to Finding Montessori Materials for Parents & Teachers. Heidi A. Spietz. Ed. by Frances Henderson. (Illus.). 87p. 1999. pap. 11.95 (*0-929487-99-0*, Pub. by Am Montessori Consult) Baker & Taylor.

Montessori System Examined. William H. Kilpatrick. LC 70-165739. (American Education Ser, No. 2). 1971. reprint ed. 8.00 (*0-405-03609-4*) Ayer.

Montessori Today: A Comprehensive Approach to Education from Birth to Adulthood. Paula P. Lillard. (Illus.). 240p. 1996. pap. 12.00 (*0-8052-1061-X*) Schocken.

Montessori's Concept of Personality. Michael J. Gross. 152p. (Orig.). (C). 1986. pap. text 20.00 (*0-8191-5075-4*); lib. bdg. 40.50 (*0-8191-5074-6*) U Pr of Amer.

Monteverde: Ecology & Conservation of a Tropical Cloud Forest. Ed. by Nalini M. Nadkarni & Nathaniel T. Wheelwright. LC 98-26919. (Illus.). 608p. 2000. pap. 75.00 (*0-19-513310-2*) OUP.

Monteverde: Ecology & Conservation of a Tropical Cloud Forest. Ed. by Nalini M. Nadkarni & Nathaniel T. Wheelwright. LC 98-26919. (Illus.). 608p. 2000. text 130.00 (*0-19-509560-X*) OUP.

Monteverde: Science & Scientists in a Costa Rican Cloud Forest. Sneed B. Collard, III. LC 96-49515. (Venture Books-Science). 144p. (J). 1997. lib. bdg. 24.00 (*0-531-11369-8*) Watts.

Monteverde: Science & Scientists in a Costa Rican Cloud Forest. Sneed B. Collard, III. (Venture Books-Science). (Illus.). (YA). (gr. 7 up). 1998. pap. 9.95 (*0-531-15901-9*) Watts.

Monteverdi. (Dent Master Musicians Ser.). (Illus.). (C). pap. write for info. (*0-614-07880-6*) OUP.

***Monteverdi.** Arnold. 256p. 2000. pap. 17.95 (*0-19-816465-3*) OUP.

Monteverdi. Paolo Fabbri. Tr. by Tim Carter. (Illus.). 366p. (C). 1994. text 69.95 (*0-521-35133-2*) Cambridge U Pr.

Monteverdi: His Life & Work. Henry Prunieres. Tr. by Marie D. MacKie. LC 70-100830. (Illus.). 293p. 1973. reprint ed. lib. bdg. 55.00 (*0-8371-3996-1*, PRMO, Greenwood Pr) Greenwood.

Monteverdi: His Life & Work. Henry Prunieres. 293p. 1990. reprint ed. lib. bdg. 69.00 (*0-7812-9075-9*) Rprt Serv.

Monteverdi: Sacred, Secular & Occasional Music. Denis Stevens. 147p. 1978. 28.50 (*0-8386-1937-1*) Fairleigh Dickinson.

Monteverdi & the End of the Renaissance. Gary Tomlinson. 292p. 1986. pap. 19.95 (*0-520-06980-3*, Pub. by U CA Pr) Cal Prin Full Svc.

Monteverdi, Creator of Modern Music. Leo Schrade. LC 79-12292. (Music Reprint Ser.). 1979. reprint ed. lib. bdg. 42.50 (*0-306-79565-5*) Da Capo.

***Monteverdi in Venice.** Denis Stevens. LC 00-34766. 2001. write for info. (*0-8386-3879-1*) Fairleigh Dickinson.

Monteverdi Vespers of 1610: Music, Context & Performance. Jeffrey Kurtzman. LC 98-15026. (Illus.). 624p. 2000. text 90.00 (*0-19-816409-2*) OUP.

Monteverdi's Tonal Language. Eric Chafe. 442p. 1992. 55.00 (*0-02-870495-9*, Schirmer Books) Mac Lib Ref.

Montevideo-Maybank: Some Memoirs of a Southern Christian. Robert Q. Mallard. 1977. text 21.95 (*0-8369-9230-X*, 9084) Ayer.

Montezuma Amish Mennonite Cookbook. Ruth Yoder. 1988. pap. 13.95 (*0-9630704-0-1*) Yoders Cater.

Montezuma Amish Mennonite Cookbook II. Wimmer Books Plus Publishing Staff. 352p. 1998. pap. 17.95 (*0-9630704-1-X*) Yoders Cater.

Montezuma & the Aztecs. Heily. 1996. 0.85 (*0-8050-5286-0*) H Holt & Co.

An Asterisk (*) at the beginning of an entry indicates that the title is appearing for the first time.

Montezuma & the Aztecs. Mathilde Heily. LC 96-26389. (W5 Who, What, Where, When, & Why Ser.). (Illus.). 96p. (YA). (gr. 6 up). 1996. 19.95 (*0-8050-5060-4*) H Holt & Co.

***Montezuma & the Fall of the Aztecs.** Eric A. Kimmel. LC 99-37134. (Illus.). 32p. (J). 2000. 16.95 (*0-8234-1452-3*) Holiday.

Montezuma Castle National Monument. Susan Lamb. Ed. by Ronald J. Foreman & T. J. Priehs. LC 92-62157. (Illus.). 16p. (Orig.). 1992. pap. 3.95 (*1-877856-19-3*) SW Pks Mnmts.

Montezuma Castle National Monument, Arizona. 1995. lib. bdg. 250.00 (*0-8490-6547-X*) Gordon Pr.

***Montezuma's Daughter.** H. Rider Haggard. 252p. 2000. pap. 9.95 (*0-594-01720-3*) Eightn Hundrd.

Montezuma's Daughter. H. Rider Haggard. 1976. reprint ed. lib. bdg. 24.95 (*0-89190-704-1*, Rivercity Pr) Amereon Ltd.

***Montezuma's Ferrari: And Other Adventures.** Burt Levy. LC 99-93834. (Last Open Road Ser.). 416p. 1999. 30.00 (*0-9642107-1-1*) Think Fast Ink.

Montezuma's Man. Jerome Charyn. 288p. 1993. 18.95 (*0-89296-461-8*) Mysterious Pr.

Montezuma's Man. Jerome Charyn. 272p. 1994. mass mkt. 5.99 (*0-446-40047-5*, Pub. by Warner Bks) Little.

Montezuma's Pearl. David L. Jones. 256p. (Orig.). 1995. mass mkt. 4.99 (*0-380-77383-X*, Avon Bks) Morrow Avon.

Montezuma's Revenge. Cari Best. LC 99-11716. (Illus.). 32p. (J). (ps-2). 1999. 15.95 (*0-531-30198-2*); lib. bdg. 16.99 (*0-531-33198-9*) Orchard Bks Watts.

Montezuma's Serpent: And Other True Supernatural Tales of the Southwest. Brad Steiger & Sherry Hansen-Steiger. 205p. 1994. 22.95 (*1-56924-918-0*) Marlowe & Co.

Montgolfier Brothers & the Invention of Aviation, 1783-1784: With a Word on the Importance of Ballooning for the Science of Heat & the Art of Building Railroads. Charles C. Gillispie. LC 82-61363. (Illus.). 231p. reprint ed. pap. 71.70 (*0-7837-6761-7*, 204659100003) Bks Demand.

Montgomery. Ronald Lewin. (Military Commanders Ser.). 1998. pap. 18.95 (*0-938289-17-9*, 289179) Combined Pub.

***Montgomery.** Robert L. Williams. (Images of America Ser.). 128p. 1999. pap. 18.99 (*0-7385-0096-8*) Arcadia Publng.

Montgomery: A Genealogy History of the Montgomerys & Their Descendants. D. B. Montgomery. (Illus.). 436p. 1991. reprint ed. pap. 67.50 (*0-8328-1712-0*); reprint ed. lib. bdg. 77.50 (*0-8328-1711-2*) Higginson Bk Co.

Montgomery: At the Forefront of a New Century. Wendi L. Lewis. 384p. 1996. 39.00 (*1-885352-36-0*) Community Comm.

Montgomery: Capital City Corners. Mary Ann Neeley. (Images of America Ser.). 1997. pap. 16.99 (*0-7524-0553-5*) Arcadia Publng.

Montgomery: Launching the Civil Rights Movement. Linda R. Wade. LC 90-8974. (Doors to America's Past Ser.). 48p. (J). (gr. 3-6). 1991. lib. bdg. 22.60 (*0-86592-465-1*) Rourke Enter.

Montgomery - Biography of a City. Wayne Greenhaw. Ed. by Allen Phillips. (Illus.). 124p. 1993. 24.95 (*1-882616-03-0*) Advertiser.

***Montgomery & "colossal Cracks" The 21st Army Group in Northwest Europe, 1944-45.** S. Hart. LC 99-46306. (Praeger Series in War Studies). 240p. 2000. 59.95 (*0-275-96162-1*, Praeger Pubs) Greenwood.

Montgomery & Guderian. Ed. by R. K. Bhonsle. 356p. 1986. pap. 35.00 (*81-7002-019-0*, Pub. by Himalayan Bks) St Mut.

Montgomery & the Portsmouth. Fred B. Rogers. LC 90-20215. (Portsmouth Marine Society Ser.: Vol. 17). (Illus.). 176p. 1990. reprint ed. 25.00 (*0-915819-16-3*, 17) Portsmouth Marine Soc.

Montgomery Bus Boycott. Richard C. Stein. LC 93-16854. (Cornerstones to Freedom Ser.). (Illus.). 32p. (J). (gr. 3-6). 1993. pap. 5.95 (*0-516-46671-2*) Childrens.

Montgomery Bus Boycott. Richard C. Stein. LC 93-16854. (Cornerstones to Freedom Ser.). (Illus.). 32p. (J). (gr. 4-7). 1993. lib. bdg. 19.50 (*0-516-06671-4*) Childrens.

Montgomery Bus Boycott & the Women Who Started It. Jo A. Robinson. Ed. by David J. Garrow. LC 86-14684. (Illus.). 208p. 1987. pap. 16.50 (*0-87049-527-5*) U of Tenn Pr.

Montgomery Bus Boycott & the Women Who Started It. JoAnn G. Robinson. Ed. by David J. Garrow. LC 86-14684. (Illus.). 208p. 1987. text 36.00 (*0-87049-524-0*) U of Tenn Pr.

***Montgomery Circuit Records, 1788-1988: Methodist Episcopal, Methodist Episcopal South & United Methodist.** Dona Lou Cuttler. 278p. 2000. pap. 34.00 (*0-7884-1427-5*, 1427) Heritage Bk.

Montgomery City Business Profiles: Montgomery, AL. Mary Ellis. 1996. pap. text 19.95 (*1-885352-37-9*) Community Comm.

Montgomery Clift: A Bio-Bibliography, 52. Mary C. Kalfatovic. LC 94-3034. (Bio-Bibliographies in the Performing Arts Ser.). 320p. 1994. lib. bdg. 59.95 (*0-313-28603-5*, Greenwood Pr) Greenwood.

Montgomery Clift: A Biography. Patricia Bosworth. LC 89-49725. (Illus.). 438p. 1990. reprint ed. pap. 18.00 (*0-87910-135-0*) Limelight Edns.

Montgomery County. Jane C. Sween & William Offutt. (Illus.). 256p. 1999. 32.95 (*1-892724-05-7*) Am Historical Pr.

Montgomery County: A History, 3 vols. in 2. Clifton S. Hunsicker. (Illus.). 1133p. 1997. reprint ed. lib. bdg. 120.00 (*0-8328-6434-X*) Higginson Bk Co.

Montgomery County: Picture of a Dream Coming True. Margaret Simpson & Heritage Museum of Montgomery County (Conroe, Tex. LC 97-10442. 1997. write for info. (*0-89865-997-3*) Donning Co.

Montgomery County & the Beltway Street Guide & Directory: 1999 Edition. Thomas Bros. Maps Staff. (Illus.). 280p. 1998. pap. 14.95 (*1-58174-028-X*) Thomas Bros Maps.

Montgomery County, Arkansas, Loose Probate Records, 1842-1930. Marion S. Craig. Ed. by Desmond W. Allen. 65p. (Orig.). 1996. pap. 15.00 (*1-56546-098-7*) Arkansas Res.

Montgomery County Carry Out. Ed. by Ann H. Waigand. 96p. (Orig.). 1988. pap. 4.95 (*0-942231-01-5*) Educ Traveler.

Montgomery County, 1890 Texas Census Uniquely Reconstructed & Annotated. Mary C. Moody. LC 93-74229. 211p. (Orig.). 1993. pap. 34.50 (*1-884130-00-3*) Blackstone Pub.

***Montgomery County Ghost Stories.** (Illus.). 192p. 2000. pap. 11.95 (*1-880683-14-8*) Exeter Hse.

***Montgomery County, Maryland - 1880 Census.** William N. Hurler, Jr. 680p. 1999. 92.00 (*0-7884-1319-8*, H855) Heritage Bk.

Montgomery County, Maryland - 1860 Census. William N. Hurley. 374p. 1999. 53.00 Heritage.

Montgomery County, Maryland 1850 Census. William N. Hurley, Jr. LC 99-160891. 1998. 53.00 (*0-7884-1032-6*, H862) Heritage Bk.

Montgomery County Maryland 1870 Census. William N. Hurley, Jr. 556p. 1999. 80.00 (*0-7884-1142-X*, H860) Heritage Bk.

Montgomery County, Maryland Land Records, 1777-1781. 178p. 1999. spiral bd. 20.00 (*1-57445-051-4*) TLC Genealogy.

Montgomery County, Mississippi Cemetery Records. Evelyn B. Crouch & Christie C. Genola. 407p. (Orig.). 1996. pap. 42.50 (*1-885480-09-1*) Pioneer Pubng.

Montgomery County, New York Marriage Records, Performed by Reverend Elijah Herrick, 1795-1844; Also Record of Reverend Calvin Herricl, 1834-1876; Reverend John Calvin Toll, 1803-1844. Compiled by Melvin W. Lethbridge. (Illus.). 38p. 1997. reprint ed. pap. 8.00 (*0-8328-7145-1*) Higginson Bk Co.

Montgomery County, Ohio Vol. II: 5-Generation Pedigree Charts. Montgomery County Chapter, O. G. S. Staff. LC 95-78197. 235p. 1995. pap. 15.00 (*1-887665-09-9*) MCC OGS.

Montgomery County, Ohio, Cemetery Inscriptions Vol. V: Book A - Dayton National Cemetery. Karen J. Duhart. Ed. by Montgomery County Chapter OGS Staff. LC 82-222963. (Illus.). 706p. 1998. pap. 35.00 (*1-887665-10-2*) MCC OGS.

***Montgomery County, Ohio, Cemetery Inscriptions Vol. VI, Bk. A: All Except Hillgrove Cemetery.** Ed. by Anne Walker Johnson & Robert Eugene Johnson. Tr. by Mary Lou Lubinski. LC 82-222963. (Illus.). 430p. 2000. pap. 25.00 (*1-887665-15-3*) MCC OGS.

***Montgomery County, Ohio, German Church Records: First Reformed Church of Miamisburg (Trinity UB Church of Christ)** Anne Walker-Johnson & Robert E. Johnson. LC 98-87627. (Illus.). 275p. 1999. pap. 20.00 (*1-887665-14-5*) MCC OGS.

Montgomery County, Ohio German Church Records Vol. I: Emmanuel's & Salem's Evangelcal Lutheran & Slifer's Reformed Churches. Anne W. Johnson & Robert E. Johnson. LC 98-87627. 340p. 1998. pap. 20.00 (*1-887665-13-7*) MCC OGS.

Montgomery County, PA Court Rules. Ed. by Thomas Davies. 272p. (Orig.). 1996. per. 52.50 (*1-57786-037-3*) Legal Communs.

Montgomery County Short Term Traffic Alleviation Policy. (Illus.). 109p. (Orig.). (C). 1993. pap. text 30.00 (*1-56806-817-4*) DIANE Pub.

***Montgomery County Story 1776 - 1957.** Charles W. Crush. (Illus.). 216p. 2000. 15.00 (*0-9701648-0-7*) Mont Mus.

***Montgomery County Street Guide & Directory: 2000 Edition.** (Illus.). 184p. 2000. pap. 10.95 (*1-58174-135-9*) Thomas Bros Maps.

Montgomery County, Virginia: Circa 1790. Netti Schreiner-Yantis. LC 72-86678. 124p. 1972. 17.50 (*0-89157-011-X*); pap. 15.00 (*0-89157-012-8*) GBIP.

***Montgomery Family Magazine: Genealogical, Historical & Biographical.** fac. ed. Illus. by Wm. M. Clemens. 128p. 1999. reprint ed. 31.00 (*0-8328-9944-5*); reprint ed. pap. 21.00 (*0-8328-9945-3*) Higginson Bk Co.

Montgomery Hall. Doris H. Masi. LC 94-69573. 74p. 1994. pap. 8.95 (*0-9628208-9-X*) Canal Side Pubs.

Montgomery, Hampden Co., Massachusetts Families from the Early Times to about 1900: From the Manuscript Notes of George McKenzie Roberts. George M. Roberts & Jayne P. Lovelace. LC 98-183806. 270p. 1997. pap. 40.00 (*1-878545-24-8*) ACETO Bookmen.

***Montgomery in the Good War: Portrait of a Southern City, 1939-1946.** Wesley Phillips Newton. 368p. 2000. text 34.95 (*0-8173-1043-6*) U of Ala Pr.

Montgomery Museum of Fine Arts: A Handbook to the Collection. C. Reynolds Brown. LC 80-80053. (Illus.). 68p. (J). (ps-12). 1980. pap. 3.00 (*0-89280-014-3*) Montgomery Mus.

Montgomery White Sulphur Springs: A History of the Resort, Hospital, Cemeteries, Markers, & Monument. Dorothy H. Bodell. LC 93-5005. (Illus.). 98p. (Orig.). 1993. pap. 7.95 (*0-936015-43-8*) Pocahontas Pr.

Montgomery's Auditing. 2nd ed. Vincent M. O'Reilly et al. 1344p. 1998. 175.00 (*0-471-14063-5*) Wiley.

Montgomery's Auditing: College Version. 3rd rev. ed. Philip L. Defliese et al. LC 90-33826. 912p. 1990. text 106.95 (*0-471-50706-7*) Wiley.

Montgomery's Auditing Continuing Professional Education. Vincent M. O'Reilly et al. 694p. 1999. 85.00 (*0-471-34605-5*) Wiley.

Montgomery's Children. Richard Perry. LC 98-233109. 282p. 1998. pap. 14.95 (*1-885478-25-9*, Pub. by Genesis Press) BookWorld.

Month & a Day: A Detention Diary. Ken Saro-Wiwa. LC 96-118233. 1996. pap. 11.95 (*0-14-025914-7*) Viking Penguin.

Month Arts: December-February. Compiled by Marcia Schonzeit. (gr. 1-6). 1991. pap. 9.95 (*0-590-49124-5*) Scholastic Inc.

Month Arts: March-May. Ed. by Marcia Schonzeit. (gr. 1-6). 1991. pap. 9.95 (*0-590-49125-3*) Scholastic Inc.

Month-Brothers. Samuel Marshak. Tr. by Thomas P. Whitney from RUS. LC 82-7927. (Illus.). 32p. (J). (gr. k up). 1983. 15.93 (*0-688-01510-7*, Wm Morrow) Morrow Avon.

Month by Month: Language Enrichment Activities for Early Learning. Noah's Ark Staff. (Illus.). 299p. 1989. pap. text 59.00 (*0-7616-7582-5*) Commun Skill.

Month by Month, a Year Goes Round. Carol Diggory Shields. LC 98-216042. (Illus.). 24p. (J). (ps-1). 1998. 7.99 (*0-525-45458-6*, Dutton Child) Peng Put Young Read.

***Month-By-Month Artic Carry-Over Fun.** Chrissy Hailsip & Nancy Fulton. (Illus.). 165p. (J). (ps-6). 1999. spiral bd. 31.95 (*1-58650-079-1*, BK-277) Super Duper.

Month by Month Arts & Crafts. Marcia Schonzeit. 1991. pap. 9.95 (*0-590-49123-7*) Scholastic Inc.

Month-by-Month Arts & Crafts, 3 bks., Set. Marcia Schonzeit. 1996. pap. text 29.85 (*0-590-56093-X*) Scholastic Inc.

Month by Month Arts & Crafts: March, April, May. Marcia Schonzeit. (Illus.). 64p. 1998. pap. 9.95 (*0-590-37903-8*) Scholastic Inc.

***Month-by-Month Collaborative Books for Young Learners.** Mary Beth Spann. (Month by Month Ser.). (Illus.). 72p. (J). 2000. pap. 10.95 (*0-439-04882-6*) Scholastic Inc.

***Month-by-Month Gardening in Florida.** Tom MacCubbin. LC 99-51669. 1999. 19.95 (*1-888608-24-2*) Cool Springs Pr.

***Month by Month Gardening in Georgia.** Walter Reeves & Erica Glasener. (Illus.). 320p. 2000. pap. 18.95 (*1-888608-27-7*) Cool Springs Pr.

Month by Month Gardening in Illinois. James A. Fizzell. (Illus.). 332p. 1999. pap. 18.95 (*1-888608-18-8*) Cool Springs Pr.

Month by Month Gardening in Indiana. James A. Fizzell. (Illus.). 332p. 1999. pap. 18.95 (*1-888608-20-X*) Cool Springs Pr.

Month by Month Gardening in Louisiana. Dan Gill. LC 99-50397. (Illus.). 320p. 1999. pap. 18.95 (*1-888608-22-6*) Cool Springs Pr.

Month by Month Gardening in Michigan. James A. Fizzell. (Illus.). 332p. 1999. pap. 18.95 (*1-888608-19-6*) Cool Springs Pr.

***Month by Month Gardening in Missouri.** Mike Miller. (Illus.). 320p. 2000. pap. 18.95 (*1-888608-25-0*) Cool Springs Pr.

Month by Month Gardening in Texas. Dale Groom. (Illus.). 332p. 2000. pap. 18.95 (*1-888608-21-8*) Cool Springs Pr.

***Month by Month Gardening in the Carolinas.** Bob Polomski. (Illus.). 320p. 2000. pap. 18.95 (*1-888608-23-4*) Cool Springs Pr.

***Month by Month Gardening in Wisconsin.** Melinda Myers. (Illus.). 320p. 2000. pap. 18.95 (*1-888608-26-9*) Cool Springs Pr.

Month by Month Guide to Entertaining Angels: Meeting God's Messengers in Scripture & in Our Lives. Mark G. Boyer. LC 95-78803. 192p. 1995. pap. 11.95 (*0-87946-121-7*) ACTA Pubns.

Month by Month in a Waterwise Garden. Kevin Connelly. (Illus.). 80p. (Orig.). 1991. pap. 5.00 (*0-914421-01-8*) Hist Soc So CA.

Month by Month in a Waterwise Garden. Kevin Connelly. LC 93-61036. (Illus.). 68p. (Orig.). 1993. pap. 12.95 (*0-914421-11-5*) Hist Soc So CA.

Month-by-Month Masterpieces: Exploration of 10 Great Works with Step-by-Step Art Projects. Bobbi Chertok et al. 1996. pap. text 18.95 (*0-590-25101-5*) Scholastic Inc.

Month-by-Month Phonics for First Grade. Patricia M. Cunningham & Dorothy P. Hall. Ed. by Chris McIntyre. (Professional Resources Ser.). (Illus.). 128p. 1997. pap. text 17.99 (*0-88724-397-5*, CD-2402) Carson-Dellos.

Month-by-Month Phonics for Second Grade. Dorothy P. Hall & Patricia M. Cunningham. (Professional Resources Ser.). (Illus.). 157p. 1997. pap. 17.99 (*0-88724-492-0*, CD-2403) Carson-Dellos.

Month-by-Month Phonics for Third Grade. Patricia M. Cunningham & Dorothy P. Hall. (Professional Resources Ser.). (Illus.). 174p. 1997. pap. 17.99 (*0-88724-493-9*, CD-2404) Carson-Dellos.

***Month-by-Month Phonics for Upper Grades.** Patricia Cunningham & Dorothy Hall. Ed. by Lynn Ruppard & Louise Vaughn. (Professional Resources Ser.). (Illus.). 158p. 1998. pap. text 19.99 (*0-88724-473-4*, CD-2405) Carson-Dellos.

***Month-By-Month Poetry: December, January & February.** Compiled by Marian Reiner. 1999. pap. text 9.95 (*0-590-37900-3*) Scholastic Inc.

***Month-by-Month Poetry: September, October & November.** Professional Books Staff. 1999. pap. 9.95 (*0-590-37898-8*) Scholastic Inc.

Month-by-Month Reading & Writing for Kindergarten. Dorothy P. Hall & Patricia M. Cunningham. Ed. by Tracy Soles. (Professional Resources Ser.). (Illus.). 124p. 1997. pap. text 17.99 (*0-88724-398-3*, CD-2401) Carson-Dellos.

Month by Month Treasure Box. Sally Patrick et al. LC 86-82599. (Illus.). 80p. (Orig.). (J). (ps-1). 1988. 9.95 (*0-86530-124-7*, IP 130-1) Incentive Pubns.

***Month-by-Month Write & Read Books: 15 Reproducible Predictable Books That Your Students Help Write.** Veronica Robillard. (Illus.). 96p. 1999. pap. 12.95 (*0-590-98360-1*) Scholastic Inc.

Month by the Lake & Other Stories. H. E. Bates. LC 87-5680. (New Directions Classics Ser.). 224p. 1987. 17.95 (*0-8112-1035-9*, Pub. by New Directions); pap. 9.95 (*0-8112-1036-7*, NDP645, Pub. by New Directions) Norton.

***Month in the Country.** J. L. Carr. (Classics). 152p. 2000. pap. 12.95 (*0-940322-47-1*, Pub. by NY Rev Bks) Midpt Trade.

Month in the Country. Ivan Sergeevich Turgenev. Tr. by Ariadne Nicolaeff. 1980. pap. 5.25 (*0-8222-0772-9*) Dramatists Play.

Month in the Country. Ivan Sergeevich Turgenev. 93p. (YA). (gr. 7). 1987. pap. 6.95 (*0-435-20966-3*, 20966) Heinemann.

Month in the Country. Ivan Sergeevich Turgenev. Ed. & Tr. by Richard Freeborn. (World's Classics Ser.). 160p. 1991. pap. 7.95 (*0-19-282622-0*) OUP.

Month in the Country. Ivan Sergeevich Turgenev. Tr. & Intro. by Isaiah Berlin. (Classics Ser.). 128p. 1983. pap. 8.95 (*0-14-044436-X*, Penguin Classics) Viking Penguin.

Month in the Country: After Turgenev. Ivan Sergeevich Turgenev. Tr. by Brian Friel. 1993. pap. 5.25 (*0-8222-1342-7*) Dramatists Play.

Month in the School of the Sacred Heart of Jesus. Henry De Osso. Tr. by Grace Chamorro. LC 96-69118. (Illus.). 166p. 1997. pap. 7.95 (*0-9638041-3-8*) Soc St Teresa.

Month of Birth, Creativity, & the "Two Classes of Men" Vol. 1: A Prenatal Influence of the Sum's Radiation on the Left-Right "Configuration" of the Brain. Giovanni Marzullo. LC 96-92663. 304p. 1996. 24.95 (*0-9652322-9-8*, 223) Per Aspera.

Month of Fundays: A Whole Year of Games & Activities. Dawn DiPrince. 220p. (J). (gr. 5-12). 1996. pap. text 23.95 (*1-877673-29-3*, Fun) Cottonwood Pr.

Month of Gladness. large type ed. Eileen Barry. (Linford Romance Library). 304p. 1985. pap. 16.99 (*0-7089-6061-8*, Linford) Ulverscroft.

Month of Meals see Classic Cooking

Month of Meals: One Day to a Freezerful of Entrees. Kelly Machel. Ed. by Judith A. Engstrom & Ron Engstrom. LC 97-92239. 140p. 1997. ring bd. 21.95 (*0-9659528-0-0*) KRM.

Month of Meals 3 see Meals on the Go: Meals in Minutes

Month of Meals 5 see Vegetarian Pleasures: Vegetarian Pleasures

Month of Not Speaking. Michelle C. Berry. 94p. 1997. mass mkt. 12.95 (*0-9660466-9-2*) A&R Assocs.

Month of Summers. Ian Scott. 140p. 1990. 27.00 (*0-86138-104-1*, Pub. by T Dalton) St Mut.

Month of Sundays. Kent Biffle. LC 93-7882. 261p. 1993. pap. 12.95 (*0-929398-56-4*) UNTX Pr.

Month of Sundays. Hal D. Stewart. Ed. by William-Alan Landes. LC 96-37385. 72p. 1997. pap. 6.00 (*0-88734-716-9*) Players Pr.

Month of Sundays. John Updike. 1996. pap. 12.00 (*0-449-91220-5*) Fawcett.

Month of Sundays. John Updike. 1975. 16.95 (*0-394-49551-9*) Knopf.

Month of Sundays: A Comedy Bob Larbey. LC 88-142128. 99 p. 1988. write for info. (*0-573-61870-4*) S French Trade.

Month of Sundays: The Best of Rick O'Shay & Hipshot. 2nd ed. Stan Lynde. LC 92-72285. (Illus.). 64p. (Orig.). 1993. reprint ed. pap. 15.00 (*0-9626999-8-5*, BK60) Cttnwd Pub.

Month of the Freezing Moon: The Sand Creek Massacre, November 1864. Duane Schultz. LC 89-77673. (Illus.). 229p. 1990. 19.95 (*0-685-39943-5*) St Martin.

Month of the Freezing Moon: The Sand Creek Massacre, November 1864. Duane Schultz. LC 91-20724. (Illus.). 240p. 1991. pap. 12.95 (*0-312-06417-9*) St Martin.

***Month-to-Month Gardening, Colorado: Tips for Designing, Growing & Maintaining Your Colorado.** 2nd rev. ed. Kelli Dolecek. (Month-to-Month Gardening Ser.). (Illus.). 156p. 1999. 22.95 (*0-9663566-0-8*) Four Sisters Pubg.

***Month-to-Month Gardening, New Mexico: Tips for Desiging, Growing & Maintaining Your New Mexico Garden.** Kelli Dolecek. (Month-to-Month Gardening Ser.). (Illus.). 156p. 1999. 22.95 (*0-9663566-2-4*) Four Sisters Pubg.

***Month-to-Month Gardening, Utah: Tips for Designing, Growing & Maintaining Your Utah Garden.** Kelli Dolecek. (Month-to-Month Gardening Ser.). (Illus.). 156p. 1999. 22.95 (*0-9663566-1-6*) Four Sisters Pubg.

Montherlant et la Parole: Etude d'un Langage Dramatique. Pierre J. Lapaire. LC 93-83301. (FRE.). 149p. 1993. lib. bdg. 33.95 (*0-917786-94-7*) Summa Pubns.

Monthly & Annual Mean Heights of Sea-Level: 1937-1948, & Unpublished Data for Earlier Years. (Publications Scientifiques). 82p. 1950. write for info. (*0-318-14513-8*) Intl Assoc Phys Sci Ocean.

Monthly & Annual Mean Heights of Sea Level: 1947-1951, & Unpublished Data for Earlier Years. (Publications Scientifiques). 61p. 1953. write for info. (*0-318-14514-6*) Intl Assoc Phys Sci Ocean.

Monthly & Annual Mean Heights of Sea Level: 1959-1961, & Unpublished Data for Earlier Years. (Publications Scientifiques). 59p. 1963. write for info. (*0-318-14515-4*) Intl Assoc Phys Sci Ocean.

Monthly & Annual Mean Heights of Sea Level: 1962-1964, & Unpublished Data for Earlier Years. (Publications Scientifiques). 109p. 1967. write for info. (*0-318-14516-2*) Intl Assoc Phys Sci Ocean.

M

Monthly & Annual Mean Heights of Sea-Level for the Period of the International Geophysical Year (1957-1958) & Unpublished Data for Earlier Years. S. F. Grace. (Publications Scientifiques: No. 20). write for info. (*0-614-17808-8*) Intl Assoc Phys Sci Ocean.

Monthly & Annual Mean Heights of Sea-Level, up to & Including the Year 1936. S. F. Grace. (Publications Scientifiques: No. 5). write for info. (*0-614-17801-0*) Intl Assoc Phys Sci Ocean.

Monthly & Annual Mean Heights of Sea-Level, 1951 to 1956, & Unpublished Data for Earlier Years. S. F. Grace. (Publications Scientifiques: No. 19). write for info. (*0-614-17807-X*) Intl Assoc Phys Sci Ocean.

Monthly Calendars. William R. Johnson. Ed. by Pauline Johnson. (BLIP Production Reference Board Bks.). (Illus.). 48p. (J). (gr. k-4). 1989. write for info. (*0-936917-04-0*, B607) Blip Prods.

Monthly Chronicles - April. Paul W. Bates. (Illus.). 24p. (Orig.). 1992. pap. 4.95 (*1-56046-004-0*) Interact Pubs.

Monthly Chronicles - August. Paul W. Bates. (Illus.). 24p. (Orig.). 1992. pap. 4.95 (*1-56046-008-3*) Interact Pubs.

Monthly Chronicles - December. Paul W. Bates. (Illus.). 24p. (Orig.). 1992. pap. 4.95 (*1-56046-012-1*) Interact Pubs.

Monthly Chronicles - February. Paul W. Bates. (Illus.). 24p. (Orig.). 1992. pap. 4.95 (*1-56046-002-4*) Interact Pubs.

Monthly Chronicles - January. Paul W. Bates. (Illus.). 24p. (Orig.). 1992. pap. 4.95 (*1-56046-001-6*) Interact Pubs.

Monthly Chronicles - July. Paul W. Bates. (Illus.). 24p. (Orig.). 1992. pap. 4.95 (*1-56046-007-5*) Interact Pubs.

Monthly Chronicles - June. Paul W. Bates. (Illus.). 24p. (Orig.). 1992. pap. 4.95 (*1-56046-006-7*) Interact Pubs.

Monthly Chronicles - March. Paul W. Bates. (Illus.). 24p. (Orig.). 1992. pap. 4.95 (*1-56046-003-2*) Interact Pubs.

Monthly Chronicles - May. Paul W. Bates. (Illus.). 24p. (Orig.). 1992. pap. 4.95 (*1-56046-005-9*) Interact Pubs.

Monthly Chronicles - November. Paul W. Bates. (Illus.). 24p. (Orig.). 1992. pap. 4.95 (*1-56046-011-3*) Interact Pubs.

Monthly Chronicles - October. Paul W. Bates. (Illus.). 24p. (Orig.). 1992. pap. 4.95 (*1-56046-010-5*) Interact Pubs.

Monthly Chronicles - September. Paul W. Bates. (Illus.). 24p. (Orig.). 1992. pap. 4.95 (*1-56046-009-1*) Interact Pubs.

Monthly Citizen Slips. Lee Canter. (Illus.). 80p. 1991. student ed. 6.95 (*0-939007-41-X*) Canter & Assocs.

Monthly Date Book. annuals Financial Publishing Co. Staff. 48p. 1997. pap. 15.00 (*0-87600-501-6*) Finan Pub.

Monthly Energy Review. Government Printing Office Staff. pap. text 85.00 (*0-16-012575-8*) USGPO.

Monthly Income & Expense Log. (Believer's Life System Women's Edition Ser.). 1998. ring bd. 2.50 (*0-8024-6971-X*) Moody.

Monthly Interest Amortization Tables. Contemporary Books Staff. 283p. 1994. pap. 6.95 (*0-8092-3564-1*) NTC Contemp Pub Co.

Monthly Labor Review. Government Printing Office Staff. 1989. per. 27.00 (*0-16-011454-3*) USGPO.

Monthly Mortgage Payment Handbook. 5th ed. Financial Publishing Co. Staff. 928p. 1979. pap. 40.00 (*0-87600-158-4*) Finan Pub.

Monthly Mortgage Payment Tables, 3 to 30 percent. Financial Publishing Co. Staff. 192p. 1984. pap. 15.00 (*0-87600-589-X*) Finan Pub.

Monthly Murders: A Checklist & Chronological Listing of Fiction in the Digest-size Mystery Magazines in the United States & England. Ed. by Michael L. Cook. LC 81-6986. 1147p. 1982. lib. bdg. 69.50 (*0-313-23126-5*, CMM/, Greenwood Pr) Greenwood.

Monthly Nutrition Companion: Up-to-Date Tips from the World's Foremost Nutrition Experts. American Dietetic Association Staff. LC 98-231231. 224p. 1997. pap. 6.95 (*1-56561-099-7*) Wiley.

Monthly Nutrition Companion: Up-to-Date Tips from the World's Foremost Nutrition Experts. American Dietetic Association Staff. 208p. 1997. pap. 10.95 (*0-471-34688-8*) Wiley.

Monthly Payment Direct Reduction Loan Schedules. 13th ed. 2080p. 75.00 (*0-87600-185-1*) Finan Pub.

Monthly Payment Direct Reduction Loan Schedules: Supplement. rev. ed. Ed. by Financial Publishing Co. Staff. 300p. 1987. pap. 30.00 (*0-87600-186-X*) Finan Pub.

Monthly Payment Table for 1000 Dollars. Financial Publishing Co. Staff. 256p. 1980. pap. 30.00 (*0-87600-198-3*) Finan Pub.

Monthly Planner for Florida Gardeners, 1989. Don Zimmet. (Illus.). 33p. (Orig.). 1988. pap. 4.95 (*0-944590-01-2*) D Zimmet.

***Monthly Sky Guide.** 5th ed. Ian Ridpath & Wil Tirion. LC 99-21390. (Illus.). 64p. 1999. pap. 16.95 (*0-521-66771-2*) Cambridge U Pr.

Monthly Statement of the Public Debt of the United States. Government Printing Office Staff. 1985. pap. 25.00 (*0-16-011788-7*) USGPO.

Monthly Tax Service, 1986. J. K. Lasser. 1985. pap. 12.00 (*0-671-31059-3*) PB.

Monthly Terrors: An Index to the Weird Fantasy Magazines Published in the United States & Great Britain, 4. Ed. by Mike Ashley. LC 84-19225. (Bibliographies & Indexes in World Literature Ser.: No. 4). 602p. 1985. lib. bdg. 89.50 (*0-313-23989-4*, PMO/) Greenwood.

Monthly Treasury Statement of Receipts & Outlays of the United States Government. Government Printing Office Staff. 1985. pap. 38.00 (*0-16-011793-3*) USGPO.

Months & Seasons. Alexander Harvey. 20p. 1980. 8.00 (*0-936198-00-1*); pap. 4.00 (*0-936198-01-X*) Hollow Spring Pr.

Months of the Sun. Ian Nyschens. (Illus.). 420p. 1998. 100.00 (*1-57157-045-4*) Safari Pr.

Months of the Year, Days of the Week Poster Set. Broadman & Holman. 1998. 3.99 (*0-8054-0420-1*) Broadman.

Months of the Year Quiet Book. Deni Newey. (Illus.). 45p. 1990. pap. 10.98 (*0-88290-363-2*) Horizon Utah.

Monticello. Leonard Everett Fisher. LC 87-25219. (Illus.). 64p. (J). (gr. 4-6). 1988. lib. bdg. 18.95 (*0-8234-0688-1*) Holiday.

Monticello. Catherine Reef. LC 91-15850. (Places in American History Ser.). (Illus.). 72p. (J). (gr. 4-6). 1991. lib. bdg. 14.95 (*0-87518-472-3*, Dillon Silver Burdett) Silver Burdett Pr.

Monticello. Norman Richards. LC 94-35654. (Cornerstones to Freedom Ser.). (Illus.). 32p. (J). (gr. 3-6). 1995. lib. bdg. 19.50 (*0-516-06695-1*) Childrens.

Monticello. Norman Richards. (Cornerstones to Freedom Ser.). (Illus.). 32p. (J). 1995. pap. 5.95 (*0-516-46695-X*) Childrens.

Monticello. Frederick D. Nichols & James A. Bear, Jr. LC 67-5861. 86p. reprint ed. pap. 30.00 (*0-7837-2022-X*, 204229700002) Bks Demand.

Monticello, Vol. IV. Ann O. Rust. LC 91-72853. (Floridians Ser.). 250p. 1991. 17.50 (*0-9620556-6-2*); pap. 12.95 (*0-9620556-5-4*) Amaro Bks.

Monticello: A Family Story. Elizabeth Langhorne. (Illus.). 328p. 1987. 24.95 (*0-912697-58-X*) Algonquin Bks.

Monticello: A Guidebook. Susan R. Stein et al. LC 99-236855. 144p. (Orig.). 1997. pap. 9.95 (*1-882886-04-6*) T J Mem Fnd.

Monticello Cook Book. University of Virginia Hospital Circle Staff. 1950. spiral bd. 7.95 (*0-87517-005-6*) Dietz.

Montie Montana: Not Without My Horse! Montie Montana, Jr. (Illus.). 350p. 1993. pap. 19.95 (*1-883472-55-5*) Double M CA.

Montjoie: Studies in Crusade History. Rudolf Hiestand et al. LC 96-39878. 296p. 1997. text 83.95 (*0-86078-646-3*, Pub. by Variorum) Ashgate Pub Co.

Monthly Tax Service, 1988. J. K. Lasser. 1987. pap. 24.00 (*0-13-600800-3*) P-H.

Montmartre Murders. large type ed. Richard Grayson. (Linford Mystery Library). 352p. 1987. pap. 16.99 (*0-7089-6359-5*, Linford) Ulverscroft.

Monton de Bebes (Too Many Babies) La Camada Mas Grande Del Mundo. Rose Impey. Tr. by Ernestina Loyo. (SPA.). 56p. (J). (gr. 3-4). 1994. pap. 5.99 (*968-16-4496-4*, Pub. by Fondo) Continental Bk.

Montour Railroad. Ed. by Dale W. Woodland. (Illus.). 144p. (Orig.). 1996. pap. 29.95 (*0-9640425-2-5*) Silver Brook Junct.

Montoya's Heart. Bonnie Gardner. 1998. per. 4.25 (*0-373-07846-3*, 1-07846-8) Silhouette.

Montpellier City Plan. (Grafocarte Maps Ser.). 1995. 8.95 (*2-7416-0026-0*, 80026) Michelin.

Montpellier Codex. Ed. by Hans Tischler. Tr. by Susan Stakel & Joel C. Relihan. (Recent Researches in Music of the Middle Ages & Early Renaissance Ser.: Vol. RRM8). (Illus.). xxii, 118p. 1978. pap. 45.00 (*0-89579-084-X*) A-R Eds.

Montpellier Codex, Pt. I. Ed. by Hans Tischler. Tr. by Susan Stakel & Joel C. Relihan. (Recent Researches in Music of the Middle Ages & Early Renaissance Ser.: Vol. RRM2-3). (Illus.). lxxi, 72p. 1978. pap. 50.00 (*0-89579-081-5*) A-R Eds.

Montpellier Codex, Pt. II. Ed. by Hans Tischler. Tr. by Susan Stakel & Joel C. Relihan. (Recent Researches in Music of the Middle Ages & Early Renaissance Ser.: Vol. RRM4-5). (Illus.). xi, 198p. 1978. pap. 65.00 (*0-89579-082-3*) A-R Eds.

Montpellier Codex, Pt. III. Ed. by Hans Tischler. Tr. by Susan Stakel & Joel C. Relihan. (Recent Researches in Music of the Middle Ages & Early Renaissance Ser.: Vol. RRM6-7). (Illus.). xi, 231p. 1978. pap. 75.00 (*0-89579-083-1*) A-R Eds.

Montreal. Fodors Travel Publications, Inc. Staff. LC 98-103939. (Citypacks Ser.). 96p. 1997. pap. 12.00 (*0-679-03167-7*) Fodors Travel.

Montreal. Tanya Lloyd. (America Ser.). (Illus.). 96p. 1999. text 14.95 (*1-55110-753-8*) Whitecap Bks.

Montreal. Francois Remillard et al. Ed. by Ulysses Travel Guide Staff. (Ulysses Travel Guide Ser.). (Illus.). 416p. 1999. pap. 14.95 (*2-89464-190-7*) Ulysses Travel.

***Montreal** Stillman Rogers. LC 99-33908. (Cities of the World Ser.). (J). 2000. 26.00 (*0-516-21637-6*) Childrens.

Montreal. Ed. by Jean-Hugues Roy & Brendan Weston. LC 90-81637. 250p. 1996. 43.99 (*0-921689-71-3*, Pub. by Black Rose); pap. 14.99 (*0-921689-70-5*, Pub. by Black Rose) Consort Bk Sales.

***Montreal.** D. Rogers Stillman. (Cities of the World Ser.). (Illus.). 64p. (J). (gr. 4-7). 2000. pap. text 9.95 (*0-516-27038-9*) Childrens.

Montreal. 2nd ed. Fodors Travel Publications, Inc. Staff. 2000. pap. 12.00 (*0-679-00250-2*) Crown.

Montreal. 2nd ed. Insight Guides Staff. (Insight Guides Staff). 1998. pap. text 21.95 (*0-88729-714-5*); pap. text 12.95 (*0-88729-915-6*) Langenscheidt.

Montreal. 2nd rev. ed. Benoit Prieur et al. Ed. by Ulysses Travel Guide Staff. (Illus.). 400p. 1996. pap. text 13.95 (*2-921444-80-1*) Ulysses Travel.

Montreal: La Joie de Vivre. Peggy Curran et al. (Urban Tapestry Ser.). (Illus.). 1998. write for info. (*1-881096-47-5*) Towery Pub.

Montreal after Drapeau. Jean-François Leonard & Jacques Leveillee. Tr. & Intro. by Dimitrios I. Roussopoulos. (FRE.). 134p. 1986. write for info. (*0-920057-89-6*); pap. write for info. (*0-920057-88-8*) Black Rose.

Montreal & Quebec City. 2nd ed. Ed. by Paul Waters. (Colour Guides Ser.). (Illus.). 208p. 1999. pap. 16.95 (*0-88780-474-8*, Pub. by Formac Publ Co) Seven Hills Bk.

Montreal & Quebec City Access. Access Guides Staff. (Access Travel Guides Ser.). 160p. 1996. pap. 148.00 (*0-06-273136-X*, Access Trvl) HarpInfo.

Montreal & Quebec City 2000. Fodors Travel Publications, Inc. Staff. (Illus.). 2000. pap. 14.00 (*0-679-00364-9*) Fodors Travel.

Montreal & the Casino: The Gaming Guide to Montreal. Zack Lewis & Jacques Levesque. (Illus.). 192p. (Orig.). 1994. pap. 12.95 (*0-930016-21-1*) Pass Pr Trvl Line.

Montreal by Night. Robert Hatch et al. (Vampire Ser.). (Illus.). 128p. (Orig.). 1997. pap. 15.00 (*1-56504-224-7*, 2216) White Wolf.

Montreal Canadians: Stanley Cup Champions, 1959-1960, Vol. 3. Hockey Information Service Staff. 1997. pap. write for info. (*1-894014-02-2*) Hockey Info.

Montreal Canadiens see NHL Today

Montreal Canadiens. Jim Stevens. LC 98-21921. (Inside the NHL Ser.). (J). 1999. 16.45 (*1-57765-056-5*) ABDO Pub Co.

Montreal Canadiens Hockey Team. David Aretha. LC 97-21308. (Great Sports Teams Ser.). (Illus.). 48p. (J). (gr. 4-10). 1998. lib. bdg. 18.95 (*0-7660-1022-8*) Enslow Pubs.

Montreal Cats. Lois Braun. 226p. 1997. pap. 14.95 (*0-88801-199-7*, Pub. by Turnstone Pr) Genl Dist Srvs.

Montreal Chinese Property Ownership & Occupational Change, 1881-1981. Rebecca B. Aiken. LC 87-45785. (Immigrant Communities & Ethnic Minorities in the U. S. & Canada Ser.: No. 20). 1988. 55.00 (*0-404-19430-3*) AMS Pr.

Montreal de Mon Enfance. Illus. by Antonio De Thomasis. (FRE.). 40p. (J). 1996. 15.99 (*0-88776-343-X*) Tundra Bks.

***Montreal et Environs Entertainment, 2000.** (Illus.). 854p. 1999. pap. 25.00 (*1-880248-43-3*, 0089) Enter Pubns.

Montreal Expos. Chris W. Sehnert. LC 96-25684. (America's Game Ser.). (J). 1997. lib. bdg. 15.95 (*1-56239-675-7*) ABDO Pub Co.

Montreal Forties: Modernist Poetry in Transition. Brian Trehearne. 416p. 1999. text 60.00 (*0-8020-4452-2*) U of Toronto Pr.

Montreal in Evolution: Historical Analysis of the Development of Montreal's Architecture & Urban Environment. Jean-Claude Marsan. (Illus.). 456p. (C). 1990. reprint ed. pap. text 22.95 (*0-7735-0798-1*, Pub. by McG-Queens Univ Pr) CUP Services.

Montreal Inside Out: A New View of the City. John Sobol. (Canadian Urban Studies: No. 1). (Illus.). 100p. (C). 1992. pap. text 14.95 (*1-55022-159-0*, Pub. by ECW) Genl Dist Srvs.

Montreal Massacre. Ed. by Chalouh & Louise Malette. 184p. 1994. pap. 12.95 (*0-921881-14-2*, Pub. by Gynergy-Ragweed) U of Toronto Pr.

Montreal Metropole, 1880-1930. Ed. by France Vanlaethem & Isabelle Gournay. 208p. 1998. pap. 39.95 (*0-7737-5974-3*) Stoddart Publ.

Montreal Museum of Fine Arts, Formerly Art Association of Montreal: Spring Exhibition, 1880-1970. Evelyn D. McMann. 418p. 1988. text 125.00 (*0-8020-2650-8*) U of Toronto Pr.

Montreal, 1979: Tournament of Stars. M. Tal et al. Tr. by Kenneth P. Neat. LC 80-40715. (Illus.). 204p. 1980. 29.90 (*0-08-024132-8*, Pergamon Pr); pap. 17.90 (*0-08-024131-X*, Pergamon Pr) Elsevier.

Montreal of My Childhood. Illus. by Antonio De Thomasis. LC 95-109227. 40p. (J). (gr. 3 up). 1994. 15.95 (*0-88776-342-1*) Tundra Bks.

Montreal Pocket Guide. rev. ed. Berlitz Staff. (Berlitz Pocket Guide Ser.). 1998. pap. 8.95 (*2-8315-6981-8*) Berlitz.

Montreal Protocol on Substances That Deplete the Ozone Layer: Report of the Aerosols Sterilants, Miscellaneous Uses & Carbon Tetrachloride - Technical Options Committee. LC 96-980507. 101p. pap. 10.00 (*92-807-1451-1*) UN.

Montreal Protocol on Substances That Deplete the Ozone Layer: Report of the Economics Option Committee 1995 Assessment. LC 96-981089. 198p. 1994. pap. 15.00 (*92-807-1452-X*) UN.

Montreal Protocol on Substances That Deplete the Ozone Layer: Report of the Flexible & Rigid Foams - Technical Options Committee 1995 Assessment. LC 96-981090. 150p. pap. 10.00 (*92-807-1453-8*) UN.

Montreal Protocol on Substances That Deplete the Ozone Layer: Report of the Halon Fire Extinguishing Agents - Technical Options Committee. 174p. pap. 15.00 (*92-1-127020-0*) UN.

Montreal Protocol on Substances That Deplete the Ozone Layer: Report of the Methyl Bromide Technical Options Committee 1995 Assessment. LC 96-981353. 260p. 30.00 (*92-807-1448-1*) UN.

Montreal Protocol on Substances That Deplete the Ozone Layer: Report of the Refrigeration, Airconditioning & Heat Pumps - Technnical Options Committee 1995 Assessment. LC 95-980476. 301p. 25.00 (*92-807-1455-4*) UN.

Montreal Protocol on Substances That Deplete the Ozone Layer: Report of the Technology & Economics Assessment Panel 1995 Assessment. LC 95-980479. 176p. pap. 15.00 (*92-807-1450-3*) UN.

Montreal Protocol on Substances That Deplete the Ozone Layer: Scientific Assessment of Ozone Depletion. 425p. 45.00 (*92-807-1449-X*) UN.

Montreal Protocol on Substances That Deplete the Ozone Layer: 1994 Report of the Aerosols Sterilants, Miscellaneous Uses & Carbon Tetrachloride: Technical Options Committee: October 1994 Edition. 101p. 1995. 10.00 (*92-1-127019-7*) UN.

Montreal Protocol on Substances That Deplete the Ozone Layer: 1994 Report of the Economics Option Committee: 1995 Assessment. 198p. 1995. 15.00 (*92-1-127023-5*) UN.

Montreal Protocol on Substances That Deplete the Ozone Layer: 1994 Report of the Flexible & Rigid Foams Technical Options Committee: 1995 Assessment. 150p. 1995. 10.00 (*92-1-127025-1*) UN.

Montreal Protocol on Substances That Deplete the Ozone Layer: 1994 Report of the Methyl Bromide Technical Option Committee: 1995 Assessment. 260p. 1995. 30.00 (*92-1-127024-3*) UN.

Montreal Protocol on Substances That Deplete the Ozone Layer: 1994 Report of the Refrigeration, Air Conditioning & Heat Pumps Technical Options Committee: 1995 Assessment. 301p. 1995. 25.00 (*92-1-127029-4*) UN.

Montreal Protocol on Substances That Deplete the Ozone Layer: 1994 Report of the Technology & Economics Assessment Panel: 1995 Assessment. 176p. 1995. 15.00 (*92-1-127028-6*) UN.

Montreal Protocol on Substances That Deplete the Ozone Layer: 1994 Scientific Assessment of Ozone Depletion. 425p. 1995. 45.00 (*92-1-127022-7*) UN.

Montreal Protocol on Substances That Deplete the Ozone Layer: 1995 Assessment. 410p. 1995. 35.00 (*92-1-127027-8*) UN.

***Montreal's Best Restaurants.** Byron Ayanoglu. (Illus.). 172p. 2000. pap. 14.95 (*1-55065-130-7*) Vehicule Pr.

Montrose. C. V. Wedgwood. (History Paperback Ser.). (Illus.). 192p. 1998. pap. 21.95 (*0-7509-1753-9*, Pub. by Sutton Pub Ltd) Intl Pubs Mktg.

Montrose: For Covenant & King. Edward J. Cowan. 326p. 1998. pap. 14.95 (*0-86241-556-X*) Interlink Pub.

Montrose Omnibus: The Young Montrose & Montrose, the Captain General. Nigel Tranter. mass mkt. 16.95 (*0-340-40763-8*, Pub. by Hodder & Stought Ltd) Trafalgar.

Montse, a Fun Loving Teenager. Jose M. Cejas. 256p. 1998. pap. 9.95 (*0-906138-46-9*) Scepter Pubs.

Montserrat. R. Berleant. LC 92-146793. (World Bibliographical Ser.). 131p. 1991. lib. bdg. 55.00 (*1-85109-154-8*) ABC-CLIO.

***Montserrat: A Country Study Guide, 110 vols.** International Business Publications, USA Staff & Global Investment Center, USA Staff. (World Country Study Guides Library Ser.: Vol. 213). (Illus.). 350p. 2000. pap. 69.95 (*0-7397-1036-2*) Intl Business Pubns.

Montserrat Caballe: Casta Diva. Robert Pullen & Stephen Taylor. LC 94-36295. 1995. text 29.95 (*1-55553-228-4*) NE U Pr.

Montserrat Gudiol: Reality & Symbol. Jose Corredor-Matheos. (Great Monographs). (Illus.). 332p. 1993. 250.00 (*84-343-0637-9*) Elliots Bks.

Montuoro Collection - New Jersey Realist: More Than Meets the Eye: A Century of Realism in New Jersey, 1900-1994. Robert J. Koenig. 28p. 1994. pap. 5.00 (*0-9613046-9-3*) Morris Mus.

Monty. James Stevenson. (SPA., Illus.). 32p. (J). (ps-3). 13.95 (*980-257-171-7*, Pub. by Ediciones Ekare) Kane-Miller Bk.

***Monty Alexander Collection.** 104p. 1998. otabind 19.95 (*0-7935-6045-4*) H Leonard.

Monty Python & the Holy Grail. Monty Python. 1977. pap. 9.95 (*0-458-92970-0*) NAL.

Monty Python & the Holy Grail. Monty Python. 1977. pap. 17.95 (*0-416-00341-9*) Routledge.

Monty Python Encyclopedia. Robert Ross. LC 99-237219. 1998. pap. text 24.95 (*0-7134-8279-6*, Pub. by B T B) Branford.

Monty Python Encyclopedia. Robert Ross. 1999. 22.00 (*1-57500-036-9*, Pub. by TV Bks) HarpC.

Monty Python Speaks! David Morgan. LC 99-20146. (Masters in Film Ser.: Vol. 1). (Illus.). 352p. 1999. pap. 13.50 (*0-380-80479-4*, Avon Bks) Morrow Avon.

Monty Python's Complete Waste of Time: An Official Compendium of Answers to Ruddy Questions... Rusel De Maria. LC 95-69171. 1995. pap. text 14.95 (*0-7615-0139-8*) Prima Pub.

Monty Python's Flying Circus, Vol. 1. Monty Python. 1989. pap. 15.00 (*0-679-72647-0*) Fodors Travel.

Monty Python's Flying Circus, Vol. 2. Monty Python. 1989. pap. 16.00 (*0-679-72648-9*) Fodors Travel.

***Monty's Folly: Operation Market Garden.** Frederick Dustin Worthen. Ed. by Carroll A. Berner. (Illus.). 170p. 1999. pap. 15.95 (*0-914379-05-4*) CalAero.

Monty's Highlanders: 51st Highland Division at War. Patrick Delaforce. 224p. 1997. pap. (*1-871085-42-X*) Donovan Pub.

Monty's Iron Sides: From the Normandy Beaches to Bremen with the 3rd Division. Patrick Delaforce. (British Army Divisional History Ser.). (Illus.). 224p. 1996. pap. 19.95 (*0-7509-0781-9*, Pub. by Sutton Pub Ltd) Intl Pubs Mktg.

Monty's Leap. large type ed. Derek Tangye. (Illus.). 240p. 1996. 27.99 (*0-7089-8879-2*, Charnwood) Ulverscroft.

Monty's Marauders: Black Rat & Red Fox: 4th & 8th Independent Armoured Brigades in WW2. Patrick Delaforce. 224p. 1997. pap. (*1-871085-41-1*) Donovan Pub.

Monty's Men: The British Soldier & the D-Day Campaign. Julianna Humphreys. 1997. pap. 23.00 (*0-901721-30-1*, Pub. by Natl Army Mus) St Mut.

Monty's Pal. Howard I. Small. LC 78-73621. (Illus.). viii, 120p. (J). (gr. 3-8). 1979. 6.95 (*0-931474-08-6*) TBW Bks.

Monty's Private Pictures: Thirty Postcards from a Class Apart. James Gardiner. 31p. 1995. pap. 99.90 (*1-85242-026-X*) Serpents Tail.

Monty's Private Pictures: Thirty Postcards from a Class Apart. James Gardiner. (Illus.). 31p. 1995. pap. 9.99 (*1-85242-393-5*) Serpents Tail.

Monument. William Eakin. 64p. 1997. 15.00 (*0-9683181-0-X*, Pub. by W Eakin) RAM Publications.

Monument. Gary Paulsen. 160p. (J). 1991. 15.00 (*0-385-30518-4*) Delacorte.

An Asterisk (*) at the beginning of an entry indicates that the title is appearing for the first time.

Monument. Gary Paulsen. 160p. (YA). 1993. pap. 4.99 *(0-440-40782-6)* Dell.

Monument. Gary Paulsen. (J). 1991. 9.60 *(0-606-05471-5,* Pub. by Turtleback) Demco.

Monument. Colleen Wagner. LC 97-124272. 88p. 1997. pap. text 11.95 *(0-88754-507-6)* Theatre Comm.

Monument Builders. Robert Wernick. (Emergence of Man Ser.). (Illus.). 160p. (gr. 11). 1999. pap. 19.90 *(0-8094-1312-4)* Time-Life.

Monument Builders: Modern Architecture & Death, Academy Edition. Edwin Heathcote. LC 99-190859. (Illus.). 224p. 1999. 90.00 *(0-471-98368-3)* Wiley.

Monument for a City: Philip Johnson's Design for the Amon Carter Museum. George S. Wright & Philip Johnson. LC 97-73957. (Illus.). 40p. 1997. pap. 15.95 *(0-88360-088-9)* Amon Carter.

Monument in a Summer Hat: (Poems) James Armstrong. (New Issues Press Poetry Ser.). 64p. 1999. 22.00 *(0-932826-77-6,* Pub. by WMU Poetry & Prose) Partners Pubs Grp.

***Monument in a Summer Hat: (Poems)** James Armstrong. (New Issues Press Poetry Ser.). 64p. 1999. pap. 12.00 *(0-932826-78-4,* Pub. by WMU Poetry & Prose) Partners Pubs Grp.

Monument in the Storm: A Town Spawned from the Violence of New Mexico History. John A. Truett. LC 97-24802. 288p. (Orig.). 1997. pap. 12.95 *(0-86534-266-0)* Sunstone Pr.

Monument or Tombe-Stone: A Sermon Preached at the Funeral of Mrs. Elizabeth Juxon (1620) Stephen Denison. LC 96-21877. (History of Psychology Ser.). 96p. 1996. 50.00 *(0-8201-1498-7)* Schol Facsimiles.

Monument Rock. large type ed. Louis L'Amour. LC 98-30790. 1998. 27.95 *(0-7862-1645-X)* Thorndike Pr.

Monument Rock. large type ed. Louis L'Amour. LC 98-30790. 1999. pap. 25.95 *(0-7862-1646-8)* Thorndike Pr.

Monument Rock. Louis L'Amour. 244p. 1999. reprint ed. mass mkt. 4.99 *(0-553-58082-5)* Bantam.

Monument School of the People: A Sesquicentennial History of St. Mary's College of Maryland, 1840-1990. J. Frederick Fausz. LC 90-60400. (Illus.). 159p. (C). 1990. text 25.00 *(0-9625867-0-6)* St Marys Coll MD.

Monument to an Era: The Life & Art of Ben Hampton. Patsy H. Wichmann. (Illus.). 135p. 1988. 50.00 *(0-9622298-1-4)*; pap. 27.50 *(0-9622298-0-6)* Hamptn Hse Studios.

***Monument to Good Intentions: The Story of the Maryland Penitentiary.** Wallace Shugg. 1999. 30.00 *(0-938420-66-6)* MD Hist.

Monument to Magic. J. Dunninger. 1974. 14.95 *(0-8184-0160-5)* Carol Pub Group.

Monument to the Memory of George Eliot: Edith J. Simcox's "Autobiography of a Shirtmaker" Ed. by Constance M. Fulmer et al. LC 97-38310. (Literature & Society in Victorian Britain Ser.: Vol. 4). 312p. 1997. text 70.00 *(0-8153-2782-X,* H2054) Garland.

Monument und Nation: Das Bild vom Nationalstaat im Medium Denkmal-zum Verhaeltnis Nation und Staat im Deutschen Kaiserreich 1871-1918. Reinhard Alings. (Beitraege zur Kommunikationsgeschichte Ser.: Vol. 4). (GER., Illus.). xvi, 642p. (C). 1996. lib. bdg. 220.75 *(3-11-014985-0)* De Gruyter.

Monument Valley: Arizona, Utah & New Mexico. Ed. by H. L. James. (Guidebook Ser.: No. 24). (Illus.). 232p. 1973. 9.00 *(1-58546-054-0)* NMex Geol Soc.

Monument Valley: Navajo Tribal Park. Anne Markward. (Illus.). 64p. 1992. 24.95 *(0-944197-22-1)*; pap. 14.95 *(0-944197-20-5)* Companion CA.

Monument Valley: The Story Behind the Scenery. K. C. Den Dooven. LC 92-70430. (Illus.). 48p. (Orig.). 1992. pap. 7.95 *(0-88714-062-9)* KC Pubns.

Monument Valley: The Story Behind the Scenery. K. C. Den Dooven. Tr. by Brigitte Morales. (GER., Illus.). 48p. (Orig.). 1992. pap. 8.95 *(0-88714-737-2)* KC Pubns.

Monument Valley: The Story Behind the Scenery. K. C. Den Dooven. Tr. by Yvon Le Bras. (FRE., Illus.). 48p. (Orig.). 1992. pap. 8.95 *(0-88714-738-0)* KC Pubns.

Monument Valley: The Story Behind the Scenery. K. C. Den Dooven. Tr. by Saori Petzinger. (JPN., Illus.). 48p. (Orig.). 1993. pap. 8.95 *(0-88714-739-9)* KC Pubns.

Monument Valley Navajo Tribal Park. Stewart Aitchison & Susie Yazzie. Ed. by Nicky Leach. (Visual Interpretation Ser.). (Illus.). 48p. 1994. pap. 7.95 *(0-939365-38-3)* Panorama Intl.

Monument Valley Navajo Tribal Park. Ed. by Jeff Nicholas. (Wish You Were Here Postcard Book Ser.). (Illus.). 32p. 1993. pap. 4.95 *(0-939365-27-8)* Panorama Intl.

Monument Valley Park. Donald L. Baars. (Geology of National Parks & Monuments Ser.: Vol. 4). (Illus.). 16p. 1998. pap. 3.25 *(0-9616591-9-X)* Canon Pubs.

Monumenta Britannica. John Aubrey. Ed. by John Fowles. 1982. 125.00 *(0-316-05908-0)*; 250.00 *(0-316-05907-2)* Little.

Monumenta Bulgarica: A Bilingual Anthology of Bulgarian Texts from the 9th to the 19th Century. Thomas Butler. LC 96-25043. (Michigan Slavic Materials Ser.: No. 41). 1998. 36.00 *(0-930042-80-8)* Mich Slavic Pubns.

Monumenta Franciscana, 2 vols. Ed. by J. S. Brewer & Richard Howlett. (Rolls Ser.: No. 4). 1974. reprint ed. 140.00 *(0-8115-1004-2)* Periodicals Srv.

Monumenta Polonica. Bogdana Carpenter. (Michigan Slavic Materials Ser.: No. 31). 1990. 27.50 *(0-930042-68-9)* Mich Slavic Pubns.

Monumenta Zrinyiana, 1635-1720 Vol. 2: Insula Murakoz. Ed. by I. N. Kiss & Gy. Kenez. 1991. pap. 350.00 *(963-05-5547-6,* Pub. by Akade Kiado) St Mut.

Monumenta Zrinyiana, 1627-1685: Bona Maritima. V. Zimanyi. 1991. pap. 235.00 *(963-05-4582-9,* Pub. by Akade Kiado) St Mut.

Monumental Accusations: The 'Monuments aux Morts' As Expressions of Popular Resentment. Marilene P. Henry. (Francophone Cultures & Literatures Ser.: Vol. 13). (Illus.). XIII, 242p. (C). 1996. text 58.95 *(0-8204-2807-8)* P Lang Pubng.

Monumental Anxieties: Homoerotic Desire & Feminine Influence in 19th-Century U. S. Literature. Scott S. Derrick. LC 97-17699. (Illus.). 256p. 1997. 50.00 *(0-8135-2471-7)*; pap. 20.00 *(0-8135-2472-5)* Rutgers U Pr.

Monumental Bali: Introduction to Balinese Archaeology & Guide to the Monuments. A. J. Kempers. (Illus.). 204p. 1992. 29.95 *(0-945971-16-8)* Periplus.

Monumental Brasses As Art & History. Ed. by Jerome Bertram. LC 96-35981. (Illus.). 256p. 1996. 51.95 *(0-7509-1051-8,* Pub. by Sutton Pub Ltd) Intl Pubs Mktg.

Monumental Christianity: The Art & Symbolism of the Primitive Church. John P. Lundy. 1977. lib. bdg. 59.95 *(0-8490-2278-9)* Gordon Pr.

Monumental Christianity, or The Art & Symbolism of the Primitive Church. John P. Lundy. (Illus.). 453p. 1998. reprint ed. pap. 39.95 *(1-55818-460-0)* Holmes Pub.

Monumental Cities. Incl. Vol. 1. Potosi, St. Augustin & Ouro Preto. pap. 1.00 *(0-8270-4275-2)*; Vol. 1. Potosi, St. Augustin & Ouro Preto. pap. 1.00 *(0-8270-4280-9)*; Vol. 2. Antigua. pap. 1.00 *(0-8270-4405-4)*; Vol. 2. Antigua. pap. 1.00 *(0-8270-4525-5)*; Vol. 3. Quito. pap. 1.00 *(0-8270-4290-6)*; Vol. 3. Quito. (SPA.). pap. 1.00 *(0-8270-4295-7)*; (ENG & SPA.). pap. write for info. *(0-318-54737-6)* OAS.

Monumental Cities, Vol. 1, Potosi, St. Augustine, Ouro Preto see Americas: Supplement Series.

Monumental Coins: Building & Structures on Ancient Coinage. Marvin Tameanko. LC 98-87366. (Illus.). 248p. 1999. 39.95 *(0-87341-713-5)* Krause Pubns.

Monumental Drawing. Charlotta Kotik. (Illus.). 62p. 1986. pap. 7.95 *(0-87273-106-5)* Bklyn Mus.

Monumental Gateway for a Temple of King Sety I. Alexander Badawy. (Wilbur Monographs). (Illus.). 26p. 1985. reprint ed. pap. 2.50 *(0-913696-20-X)* Bklyn Mus.

Monumental Ghosts: Legends. Alice Bullock. LC 85-8164. 48p. (Orig.). 1987. pap. 5.95 *(0-86534-029-3)* Sunstone Pr.

***Monumental Impulse: Architecture's Biological Roots.** George Hersey. LC 98-45657. (Illus.). 327p. 1999. 40.00 *(0-262-08274-8)* MIT Pr.

Monumental Inscriptions from Early Islamic Iran & Transoxiana. S. S. Blair. LC 90-29890. (Muqarnas Supplements Ser.: No. 5). (Illus.). xvi, 307p. 1991. 129.50 *(90-04-09367-2)* Brill Academic Pubs.

Monumental Inscriptions from Wappaquian Burial Ground in Pomfret, Copied in 1862. Marian C. Holt. Ed. by Henry S. Mathewson. (Illus.). 150p. 1997. reprint ed. pap. 19.50 *(0-8328-5681-9)* Higginson Bk Co.

Monumental Intolerance: Jean Baffier, A Nationalist Sculptor in Fin-de-Siaecle France. Neil McWilliam. LC 99-17642. 2000. write for info. *(0-271-01965-4)* Pa St U Pr.

Monumental Islamic Calligraphy from India. W. E. Begley. LC 84-29717. (Illus.). 144p. 1985. 17.95 *(0-932815-00-6)*; pap. 10.95 *(0-932815-01-4)* Islamic Found.

Monumental Java. J. F. Scheltema. (C). 1985. reprint ed. 21.00 *(0-8364-2413-1,* Pub. by Asian Educ Servs) S Asia.

Monumental Manifestation of the Shi'ite Faith in Late Twelfth-Century Iran: The Case of the Gunbad-i 'Alawiyan, Hamadan. Raya Shani. (Oxford Studies in Islamic Art: Vol. 11). (Illus.). 172p. 1996. text 65.00 *(0-19-728021-8)* OUP.

Monumental Mazes. Richard Burnie. LC 98-49317. (Illus.). 32p. 1999. 14.95 *(0-375-80155-3)* Knopf.

Monumental Minatures: Souvenir Buildings from the Collection of Ace Architects. David Weingarten & Margaret Majua. (Illus.). 192p. 1999. pap. 28.95 *(0-930625-17-X)* Krause Pubns.

Monumental Minnesota: A Guide to Outdoor Sculpture. Moira F. Harris. LC 91-50931. (Illus.). 146p. (Orig.). 1992. pap. 15.95 *(0-9617767-9-X)* Pogo Pr.

Monumental Propaganda. Andrei Bitov & Remo Guidieri. Ed. by Dore Ashton. 96p. 1995. pap. 20.00 *(0-916365-42-5)* Ind Curators.

Monumental Remains of the Dutch East India Company in the Presidency of Madras Alexander Rea. LC 98-905013. 79 p. 1998. write for info. *(81-206-1316-3)* Asian Educ Servs.

Monumental Tombs of the Hellenistic Age: A Study of Selected Tombs from the Pre-Classical to the Early Imperial Era. Janos Fedak. (Phoenix Supplementary Volumes Ser.). 480p. 1990. text 95.00 *(0-8020-2694-X)* U of Toronto Pr.

Monumental Vision: The Sculpture of Henry Moore. John Hedgecoe & Henry Moore. LC 97-34152. (Illus.). 256p. 1998. 55.00 *(1-55670-683-9)* Stewart Tabori & Chang.

Monumental Writing: Aspects of Rhetoric in Wordsworth's Poetry. J. Douglas Kneale. LC 87-38069. 245p. 1988. reprint ed. pap. 76.00 *(0-608-02046-X,* 206269900003) Bks Demand.

Monumentale Hollendarstellungen Im Trecento in der Toskana. Marion Opitz. (Europaische Hochschulschriften Ser.: Reihe 28, Vol. 320320). (Illus.). 273p. 1998. pap. 51.95 *(3-631-32997-0)* P Lang Pubng.

Monumentality in Early Chinese Art & Architecture. Wu Hung. LC 94-18434. (Illus.). 396p. 1995. 75.00 *(0-8047-2428-8)* Stanford U Pr.

Monumentality in Early Chinese Art & Architecture. Wu Hung. LC 94-18434. (Illus.). 396p. 1997. pap. 29.95 *(0-8047-2626-4)* Stanford U Pr.

***Monuments.** Laura Brooks. 1998. pap. 10.98 *(1-57717-033-4)* Todtri Prods.

Monuments. Ed. by Amrita Kumar. (C). 1993. 7.50 *(0-614-06174-1,* Pub. by Rupa) S Asia.

***Monuments.** Clay Reynolds. LC 99-89489. 400p. 2000. 29.95 *(0-89672-433-6)* Tex Tech Univ Pr.

Monuments. Paul Sebillot. (FRE.). 300p. 1985. pap. 39.95 *(0-7859-1572-9,* 2902702280) Fr & Eur.

Monuments & Inscriptions of Caracol, Belize. Carl P. Beetz & Linton Satterthwaite, Jr. (University Museum Monographs: No. 45). (Illus.). xiv, 188p. 1981. text 40.00 *(0-934718-41-5)* U Museum Pubns.

***Monuments & Maidens: The Allegory of the Female Form.** Marina Warner. (Illus.). 440p. 2000. pap. 18.95 *(0-520-22733-6)* U CA Pr.

Monuments & Main Streets: Messages from Architecture. Harris Stone. LC 83-42528. (Illus.). 256p. 1983. 22.50 *(0-85345-638-0,* Pub. by Monthly Rev); pap. 12.00 *(0-85345-639-9,* Pub. by Monthly Rev) NYU Pr.

Monuments & Masterpieces: Histories & Views of Public Sculpture in New York City. Donald M. Reynolds. LC 96-61457. (Illus.). 496p. 1997. pap. 19.95 *(0-500-01774-3,* Pub. by Thames Hudson) Norton.

Monuments de la Musique Francaise au Temps de la Renaissance, 10 vols, Set. Ed. by Henry Expert. Incl. Octonaires de la Vanite et Inconstance du Monde (IX-XII) Pseaumes, Dialogue. Claude LeJeune. 1953. reprint ed. pap. 37.50 *(0-8450-1238-X)*; Vol. I. Octonaires de la Vanite et Inconstance du Monde (I-VIII) Claude LeJeune. (Illus.). 1953. reprint ed. pap. 37.50 *(0-8450-1231-2)*; Vol. II. Messes a Quatre Voix. Pierre Certon. 1953. reprint ed. pap. 37.50 *(0-8450-1232-0)*; Vol. III. Airs de plusiers musiciens reduits a quatre parties. Didier Le Blanc. (Illus.). 1953. reprint ed. pap. 37.50 *(0-8450-1233-9)*; Vol. IV. Premier Livre des Amours de Pierre de Ronsard, (I-XIX) Anthoine De Bertrand. 1953. reprint ed. pap. 37.50 *(0-8450-1234-7)*; Vol. V. Premier livre des Amours de Pierre de Ronsard, (XX-XXXV) Anthoine De Bertrand. 1953. reprint ed. pap. 37.50 *(0-8450-1235-5)*; Vol. VI. Second Livre des Amours de Pierre de Ronsard. Antoine De Bertrand. 1953. reprint ed. pap. 37.50 *(0-8450-1236-3)*; Vol. VII. Troisieme Livre de Chansons. Anthoine De Bertrand. 1953. reprint ed. pap. 37.50 *(0-8450-1237-1)*; Vol. IX. Messes a Quatre Voix. Claude Goudimel. 1953. reprint ed. pap. 37.50 *(0-8450-1239-8)*; Vol. X. Premier livre des Octonaires de la vanite du Monde. Paschal De l'Estocart. 1953. reprint ed. pap. 37.50 *(0-8450-1240-1)*; (Illus.). 1953. reprint ed. Set pap. 300.00 *(0-8450-1230-4)* Broude.

Monuments de l'Notation Ekphonetique et Hagiopolite de l'Eglise Grecque. Jean-Baptiste Thibaut. xvi, 159p. 1976. reprint ed. write for info. *(3-487-05835-9)* G Olms Pubs.

Monuments de l'Notation Ekphonetique et Neumatique de l'Eglise Latine. Jean-Baptiste Thibaut. xvii, 104p. 1984. reprint ed. write for info. *(3-487-07508-3)* G Olms Pubs.

Monuments des Croises dans le Royaume de Jerusalem, 4 vols., Set. Camille Enlart. LC 78-63336. (Crusades & Military Orders Ser.: Second Series). reprint ed. 495.00 *(0-404-17050-1)* AMS Pr.

Monuments for Intimate Use, Pt. I. Coco Gordon. (Intimate Ser.: No. 2). (Illus.). 97p. (Orig.). 1987. 50.00 *(0-943375-01-0)* W Space.

Monuments for Intimate Use, Pt. II. Coco Gordon. (Intimate Ser.: No. 2). (Illus.). 117p. (Orig.). 1987. 50.00 *(0-943375-02-9)* W Space.

***Monuments Help Us Remember.** Lee Sullivan Hill. LC 99-50606. (Building Block Book Ser.). (Illus.). 32p. (J). (gr. 4-7). 2000. lib. bdg. 21.27 *(1-57505-475-2,* Carolrhoda) Lerner Pub.

Monuments Illustrating New Comedy. 3rd ed. T. B. L. Webster et al. LC 99-225944. (Illus.). 1995. write for info. *(0-900587-73-3)*; write for info. *(0-900587-74-1)*; write for info. *(0-900587-76-8)* St Mut.

Monuments in the Past: Photographs, 1870-1936. Compiled by John Scarry. (Illus.). ix, 82p. 1996. 20.00 *(0-7076-0193-2,* Pub. by SO Dublin) Balogh.

Monuments of Central Asia: A Guide to the Archaeology Art & Architecture. Edgar Knobloch. pap. 25.00 *(1-86064-590-9,* Pub. by I B T) St Martin.

Monuments of Egypt. Ed. by Charles C. Gillispie. (Illus.). 640p. 1987. reprint ed. 125.00 *(0-910413-21-5)* Princeton Arch.

Monuments of Egypt. Francis L. Hawks. (Notable American Authors Ser.). 1992. reprint ed. lib. bdg. 75.00 *(0-7812-3032-2)* Rprt Serv.

Monuments of Endlesse Labours: English Canonists & Their Work, 1300-1900. John H. Baker. LC 97-45674. 1998. 45.00 *(1-85285-167-8)* Hambledon Press.

Monuments of Manda. A. P. Singh. (C). 1992. 41.00 *(0-8364-2816-1,* Pub. by Agam) S Asia.

Monuments of Mars: A City on the Edge of Forever. 2nd rev. ed. Richard C. Hoagland. 420p. 1991. pap. 16.95 *(1-55643-118-X)* North Atlantic.

Monuments of Mars: A City on the Edge of Forever. 4th rev. ed. Richard C. Hoagland. LC 96-39041. (Illus.). 526p. (C). 1996. pap. 25.00 *(1-883319-30-7)* Frog Ltd CA.

Monuments of Medieval Art. Robert G. Calkins. 1985. pap. text 18.95 *(0-8014-9306-4)* Cornell U Pr.

Monuments of Romanesque Art. Hanns Swarzenski. LC 55-937. (Illus.). 342p. 1974. reprint ed. pap. 10.95 *(0-226-78606-4,* P587) U Ch Pr.

Monuments of Russian Architecture & Monumental Art. Collet's Holdings, Ltd. Staff. 280p. 1983. 45.00 *(0-7855-7572-3)* St Mut.

Monuments of Senenmut: Problems in Historical Methodology. Peter F. Dorman. (Studies in Egyptology). 344p. (C). 1988. lib. bdg. 89.95 *(0-7103-0317-3)* Routledge.

Monuments of South Arabia. Brian Doe. 284p. (C). 1990. 150.00 *(0-7855-7019-5,* Pub. by IMMEL Pubng) St Mut.

Monuments of Syria: A Historical Guide. Ross Burns. (Illus.). 320p. 1999. pap. 24.50 *(1-86064-244-6,* Pub. by I B T) St Martin.

Monuments of Syria: A Historical Guide. Ross Burns. LC 92-25220. (Illus.). 297p. (C). 1992. text 110.00 *(0-8147-1200-2)* NYU Pr.

Monuments of Syria: A Historical Guide. Ross Burns. (Illus.). 297p. (C). 1997. pap. text 25.00 *(0-8147-1287-8)* NYU Pr.

Monuments of Unaging Intellect: Historic Postcards of Byzantine Istanbul. Robert G. Ousterhout & Nezih Basgelen. (Illus.). 136p. (C). 1995. pap. text 29.95 *(0-252-06473-9)* U of Ill Pr.

Monuments to the Industrial Revolution. Charles Agel. (Illus.). 64p. 1998. pap. 20.00 *(0-89822-122-6)* Visual Studies.

Monza. large type ed. Bob Judd. 400p. 1993. 27.99 *(0-7505-0533-8,* Pub. by Mgna Lrg Print) Ulverscroft.

Monzano Trails: A Hiker's Guide to Appreciate the Nature of the Sandia-Monzano Mountains. Steve Plumb. Ed. by David Wilde. (Sun Also Sets Ser.). (Illus.). 50p. (Orig.). 1992. pap. 13.95 *(0-9625472-7-1)* Wilde Pub.

Moo. Sally Clark. LC 90-175646. 132p. 1997. pap. text 11.95 *(0-88754-476-2)* Theatre Comm.

Moo. Jane Smiley. 432p. 1996. pap. 12.00 *(0-449-91023-7,* Columbine) Fawcett.

Moo. Jane Smiley. 1998. mass mkt. 7.99 *(0-8041-1768-3)* Ivy Books.

Moo. large type ed. Jane Smiley. LC 95-23552. (Large Print Bks.). 25.95 *(1-56895-242-2,* Compass) Wheeler Pub.

Moo Baa Baa Quack: Seven Farmyard Stories. Francesca Simon. LC 97-75135. (Illus.). 80p. (J). (ps-2). 1998. 18.00 *(0-689-82004-6)* Atheneum Yung Read.

Moo Baa La La La. Sandra Boynton. Ed. by Kate Klimo. LC 95-142201. (Boynton Board Bks.). (Illus.). 14p. (J). (ps). 1982. 4.99 *(0-671-44901-X)* Litle Simon.

Moo Duk Kwan History. H. C. Hwang & Tom Wasylyk. (Illus.). 100p. (Orig.). 1995. vinyl bd. write for info. *(0-9631358-7-2)* H Kee.

Moo Duk Kwan Tae Kwon Do, Vol. 2. Richard Chun. (Illus.). 256p. (YA). 1983. reprint ed. pap. 19.95 *(0-89750-085-7,* 422) Ohara Pubns.

Moo Duk Kwan Tae Kwon Do, Korean Art of Self-Defense. Richard Chun. Ed. by Gilbert Johnson et al. LC 75-3784. (Korean Arts Ser.). (Illus.). 1975. pap. text 19.95 *(0-89750-015-6,* 120) Ohara Pubns.

Moo-Ha! Bernard Most. LC 96-10591. (Illus.). 20p. (J). 1997. pap. 5.95 *(0-15-201248-6)* Harcourt.

Moo in the Morning. Barbara Maitland. LC 97-17354. (Illus.). 32p. (J). 2000. 15.00 *(0-374-35038-8)* FS&G.

Moo Magnet: Cow Magnet Activity Kit. Amanda Behrens et al. (Illus.). 16p. (Orig.). (J). (gr. k-12). 1995. pap. text 7.95 *(1-887105-00-X)* Master Magnet.

Moo Moo, Brown Cow. J. Wood. LC 90-23121. (Illus.). 28p. (J). (ps-1). 1992. 14.00 *(0-15-200533-1,* Gulliver Bks) Harcourt.

Moo Moo, Brown Cow. Jakki Wood. LC 96-219577. (Illus.). 24p. (J). 1996. pap. 5.95 *(0-15-200998-1)* Harcourt Coll Pubs.

***Moo Moo Cow.** Tony Potter. 1998. 7.95 *(1-902553-08-X)* Grimond.

Moo, Moo Peekaboo. Jane Dyer. LC 85-61530. (Illus.). (J). (ps). 1986. 4.99 *(0-394-87883-3,* Pub. by Random Bks Yng Read) Random.

Moobli. large type ed. Mike Tomkies. (Non-Fiction Ser.). (Illus.). 512p. 1992. 11.50 *(0-7089-2703-3)* Ulverscroft.

Mooch & Me. Gilles Gauthier. (First Novels Ser.). (Illus.). 60p. (J). (gr. 1-4). 1995. mass mkt. 3.99 *(0-88780-096-3,* Pub. by Formac Publ Co); bds. 14.95 *(0-88780-097-1,* Pub. by Formac Publ Co) Formac Dist Ltd.

Mooch Forever. Gilles Gauthier. (First Novels Ser.). (Illus.). 60p. (J). (gr. 1-4). 1995. mass mkt. 3.99 *(0-88780-308-3,* Pub. by Formac Publ Co); bds. 14.95 *(0-88780-309-1,* Pub. by Formac Publ Co) Formac Dist Ltd.

Mooch Gets Jealous. Gilles Gauthier. (First Novels Ser.). (Illus.). 59p. (J). (gr. 1-4). 1995. mass mkt. 3.99 *(0-88780-217-6,* Pub. by Formac Publ Co); bds. 14.95 *(0-88780-218-4,* Pub. by Formac Publ Co) Formac Dist Ltd.

Mooching Sub: The Salmon Fisherman's Bible. David Nuttall. (Illus.). 180p. 1980. pap. 16.95 *(0-88839-097-1)* Hancock House.

Mood. W. N. Morris. (Social Psychology Ser.). (Illus.). 248p. 1989. 96.95 *(0-387-96978-0)* Spr-Verlag.

Mood & Anxiety Disorders. Ed. by A. John Rush. 379p. 1997. pap. 49.95 *(0-683-30516-6)* Lppncott W & W.

Mood & Memory: Theory, Research, & Applications. Ed. by Don Kuiken. (Illus.). 192p. 1991. 31.50 *(0-8039-4093-9)*; pap. 15.50 *(0-8039-4094-7)* Sage.

Mood & Memory: Theory, Research, & Applications. Ed. by Don Kuiken. LC 90-23792. 212p. 1991. reprint ed. pap. 65.80 *(0-608-04316-8,* 206509500012) Bks Demand.

Mood & Modality. F. R. Palmer. (Cambridge Textbooks in Linguistics Ser.). (Illus.). 256p. 1986. pap. text 20.95 *(0-521-31930-7)* Cambridge U Pr.

***Mood & Temperament.** David Watson. LC 99-54213. (Emotions & Social Behavior Ser.). 340p. 2000. lib. bdg. 40.00 *(1-57230-526-6,* C0526) Guilford Pubns.

Mood Apart: Depression, Mania & Other Afflictions of the Self. Peter C. Whybrow. 288p. 1998. pap. 13.00 *(0-465-04726-2)* Basic.

Mood Apart: The Thinker's Guide to Emotion & Its Disorders. Peter C. Whybrow. 384p. 1998. pap. 15.00 *(0-06-097740-X,* Perennial) HarperTrade.

Mood Changes. Zulma Gonzalez-Parker. Ed. by G. Scott Henderson. 1989. reprint ed. pap. 5.00 *(1-878255-01-0)* Heartfelt Pr.

M

*Mood Disorders. Susan D. Gold. LC 98-48582. 1999. 17.95 (0-382-42096-9) Silver Burdett Pr.
Mood Disorders: Systematic Medication Management. Ed. by A. John Rush. LC 97-21357. (Modern Problems of Pharmacopsychiatry Ser.: Vol. 25, 1996). (Illus.). viii, 262p. 1997. 224.50 (3-8055-6223-3) S Karger.
Mood Disorders: Toward a New Psychobiology. P. C. Whybrow et al. LC 84-3339. (Critical Issues in Psychiatry Ser.). (Illus.). 244p. (C). 1984. text 42.50 (0-306-41568-2, Kluwer Plenum) Kluwer Academic.
Mood Disorders Throughout the Lifespan. Ed. by Kenneth I. Shulman et al. LC 96-15350. 464p. 1996. 98.95 (0-471-10477-9, Wiley-Liss) Wiley.
Mood, Family Album: An Account of the Moods of Charleston, S.C. & Connected Families. T. M. Stubbs. 246p. 1993. reprint ed. pap. 39.50 (0-8328-3720-2); reprint ed. lib. bdg. 49.50 (0-8328-3719-9) Higginson Bk Co.
*Mood Food. H. Ellis. LC 99-224114. 1998. text 29.95 (0-7472-2164-2, Pub. by Headline Bk Pub) Trafalgar.
*Mood Food: Recipes to Reflect Your Mood. Photos by Phil White. (Illus.). 2000. 24.95 (0-600-60186-2, Pub. by Hamlyn Publishing Group Ltd) Sterling.
Mood Foods: The Psycho-Nutrition Guide. William Vayda. Ed. by Ray Riegert & Leslie Henriques. LC 94-61103. (Illus.). 192p. 1995. pap. 11.95 (1-56975-023-8) Ulysses Pr.
Mood Genes: Hunting for Origins of Mania & Depression. Samuel H. Barondes. LC 99-11427. (Illus.). 256p. 1999. pap. 14.95 (0-19-513106-1) OUP.
Mood Genes: Hunting for Origins of Mania & Depression. Samuel H. Barondes. LC 98-4678. 237p. 1998. pap. text 24.95 (0-7167-2943-1) W H Freeman.
Mood Indigo. Charlotte Vale Allen. 288p. 1997. 23.95 (0-9657437-1-3) Isld Nation.
*Mood Indigo. Sally Stewart. 224p. 1999. 25.00 (0-7278-5452-6, Pub. by Severn Hse) Chivers N Amer.
*Mood Indigo. large type ed. Charlotte Vale Allen. 426p. 2000. lib. bdg. 27.95 (1-58547-038-4) Ctr Point Pubg.
Mood Interest Theory of American Foreign Policy. Jack E. Holmes. LC 84-25679. 256p. 1985. 29.95 (0-8131-1533-7) U Pr of Ky.
Mood Medicine: Consciousness & the Healing of Mind & Body by the Brain, 3 vols., Set. (Alternative Medicine Ser.). 1992. lib. bdg. 555.95 (0-8490-5340-4) Gordon Pr.
Mood of Christmas. Howard Thurman. LC 85-16018. 127p. 1985. reprint ed. pap. 11.00 (0-913408-90-5) Friends United.
Mood Shifts. 4th rev. ed. Dan Weiss. 168p. 1998. pap. 15.00 (0-9611236-1-3) Black Plankton.
*Mood Spa Weight-Loss Plan: You Can Now Control Your Weight, Stress & Moods. Paula McClure. (Mood Spa System Ser.). 132p. 2000. pap. 19.95 (0-9677527-0-1) Mood Spa.
Mood-Swings. Enid Vien. 62p. (Orig.). 1997. pap. 12.95 (0-9648330-2-6) Dynamism Pubns.
Mood-Swings. 2nd large type rev. ed. Enid Vien. 110p. (Orig.). 1998. pap. 12.95 (0-9648330-9-3) Dynamism Pubns.
Mood Swings Slam Book. Havoc Publishing Staff. 1999. write for info. (1-57977-019-3) Havoc Pub.
*Mood Swings to Murder: A Bel Barrett Mystery. Jane Isenberg. 224p. 2000. mass mkt. 5.99 (0-380-80282-1) Morrow Avon.
*Mood to Murder. Joyce Christmas. 1999. 5.99 (0-449-15012-7) Fawcett.
*Moodles. Beverley C. Berman. 176p. 2000. pap. 14.95 (1-58244-074-3) Rutledge Bks.
Moods. Louisa May Alcott. Ed. by Sarah Elbert. LC 90-48069. (American Women Writers Ser.). 284p. (C). 1991. pap. text 16.00 (0-8135-1670-6) Rutgers U Pr.
Moods. Louisa May Alcott. (Works of Louisa May Alcott). 1989. reprint ed. lib. bdg. 79.00 (0-7812-1626-5) Rprt Serv.
Moods: A Prevailing Persuasion of the Holy Spirit. Carolyn J. Wright. 80p. 1999. pap. 12.95 (0-7392-0139-5, PO3061) Morris Pubng.
Moods in Brass & Glass Vol. II: A Supplemental Guide to the Fine Art of Wire Wrapping. Ellsworth E. Sinclair. LC 95-96251. 102p. (Orig.). (YA). (gr. 9-12). 1996. pap., spiral bd. 24.95 (0-9640483-1-0) Orig Ellsworth.
*Moods in the Landscape. A. E. Bye. 1999. text 49.95 (1-888931-18-3) Spacemkr Pr.
*Moods in Wire: A Comprehensive Guide to the Fine Art of Wirewrapping. 2nd ed. Ellsworth E. Sinclair. Ed. by Barbara Teel. 192p. 2000. pap. 29.95 (0-9640483-3-7) Rodgers & Nelsen.
Moods in Wire Vol. I: A Comprehensive Guide to the Fine Art of Wirewrapping. Ellsworth E. Sinclair. LC 94-94275. 112p. (YA). (gr. 9-12). 1994. pap. text 24.95 (0-9640483-0-2) Orig Ellsworth.
Moods of a Mountain. Marie M. Higdon. (Illus.). 24p. 1988. 11.00 (0-9619148-0-7); pap. 7.00 (0-9619148-1-5) M M Higdon.
Moods of LaVerne. LaVerne Abel. 1998. pap. write for info. (1-57553-834-2) Watermrk Pr.
Moods of Life. Charles M. West. LC 98-88434. 64p. 1998. pap. 9.95 (1-56315-117-0, Pub. by SterlingHse) Natl Bk Netwk.
Moods of the Ohio Moons: An Outdoorsman's Almanac. Merrill C. Gilfillan. LC 90-46805. (Illus.). 152p. 1991. 22.00 (0-87338-436-9); pap. 11.50 (0-87338-437-7) Kent St U Pr.
Moods of the Prairie. Ed Eakin. (Illus.). 64p. 1985. 8.95 (0-89015-537-2) Sunbelt Media.
*Moods Reflected in Poetry & Stories. Angeline Lopatka. 112p. 1999. (1-58244-050-6) Rutledge Bks.
Moods, Tears & Music. 96p. 1973. 11.95 (0-685-19259-8) Shepherd-Moore Ed Foun.
Moodswing. rev. ed. Ronald R. Fieve. LC 97-197479. 336p. 1989. mass mkt. 6.99 (0-553-27983-1) Bantam.
Moodus: Poems by Robert H. Neal. Robert H. Neal. (Illus.). 1988. pap. 9.00 (0-917764-03-X) Hog Hill Pr.
Moody: A Biography. 2nd anniversary ed. John Pollock. 320p. 1997. pap. 12.99 (0-8010-5786-8) Baker Bks.
Moody: Descendants of Levi Moody & Rebecca Wages, born 1801, Darlington County, SC & born 1811, SC. Dan Franklin. (Illus.). 247p. 1994. reprint ed. pap. 41.00 (0-8328-3885-3); reprint ed. lib. bdg. 51.00 (0-8328-3884-5) Higginson Bk Co.
Moody: Special Anniversary Edition. John Pollock. LC 97-202436. 1997. pap. 11.99 (1-85792-270-0, Pub. by Christian Focus) Spring Arbor Dist.
Moody Atlas of Bible Lands. Barry Beitzel. 42.99 (0-8024-0438-3, 218) Moody.
Moody Bible Atlas. 1985. 42.99 (0-88469-169-1) BMH Bks.
*Moody Blues, Across the Threshold: Thirty Years of Music & Retrospection. Mark Murley & Moody Blues. (Illus.). 112p. 2000. 27.95 (1-886110-99-9, Pub. by Addax Pubng) Midpt Trade.
Moody Blues Song Book. 80p. 1985. per. 14.95 (0-7935-3542-5, 00120023) H Leonard.
Moody Forever. Steve Oliver. LC 98-21446. 272p. 1998. text 22.95 (0-312-19301-7) St Martin.
Moody Forever. Steve Oliver. 272p. 1999. pap. 5.99 (0-312-96923-6, St Martins Paperbacks) St Martin.
Moody Gets the Blues. Steve Oliver. (Illus.). 256p. 1996. 21.95 (0-9644138-7-6) OffByOne.
Moody Gets the Blues, Vol. 1. Steve Oliver. 1998. 5.99 (0-312-96502-8, Pub. by Tor Bks) St Martin.
Moody Handbook of Theology. Paul P. Enns. 32.99 (0-8024-3428-2, 219) Moody.
Moody Millenium. Stanley Majors. 1998. pap. write for info. (1-58235-091-4) Watermrk Pr.
Moody Without Sankey. John Pollock. 1995. 11.99 (1-85792-167-4, Pub. by Christian Focus) Spring Arbor Dist.
Moodys & Related Families. Mary C. Moody & Virgil B. Moody. LC 79-90278. 184p. 1979. 35.00 (0-9615836-0-6) Blackstone Pub.
Moody's Child Stories. Dwight Lyman Moody. LC 94-70941. (Illus.). 237p. 1994. reprint ed. 19.95 (1-880045-12-5) Back Home Indust.
Moody's Handbook of Dividend Achievement. 1995. pap. text 19.95 (1-56429-008-5) F I S.
Moody's Handbook of Dividend Achievers, 1992. Moody's Investors Service Staff. 400p. 1992. pap. 19.95 (1-56429-003-4) F I S.
Moody's Handbook of Dividend Achievers, 1994. Moodys Investor Service Staff. 1994. pap. 19.95 (1-56429-007-7) F I S.
Moody's Handbook of Dividend Archievers. 1993. pap. 19.95 (1-56429-006-9) F I S.
*Moody's Skidrow Beanery. Patrick J. O'Connor. (Illus.). 1999. pap. 9.00 (1-929731-02-7) Rowfant.
Mooga Mega Mekki. Jahn Wahl. LC 73-16818. (Lead-off Bks.). (Illus.). 48p. (J). (gr. 2-4). 1974. 7.95 (0-87955-111-9) O'Hara.
*Moogie the Messy Beastie. (Beastie Buddies Ser.). (Illus.). 32p. (J). (gr. k-3). 2000. pap. 3.95 (1-891100-26-2, Pub. by Smart Kids Publ) Penton Overseas.
Moogie the Messy Beastie: A Beastie Book about Being Neat. Ron Berry et al. (Good Behavior Builders Ser.). (Illus.). 161p. (J). (ps-1). 1993. 5.95 (1-883761-05-0) Fmly Life Prods.
Mook Jong Construction Manual: Building Modern & Traditional Wooden Dummies on a Budget. Michael D. Janich. (Illus.). 72p. pap. 20.00 (1-58160-077-1) Paladin Pr.
*Mookie: A Girl in Maximsubornia. Joseph N. Chomiak & Matt Swanson. (Illus.). 48p. (J). 2000. 17.95 (0-9676688-0-8) Tremiak Pubng.
Mooki's Secret. Kari S. Gibson & Gary Smalley. LC 97-45003. (Forest Tales Ser.). (Illus.). 22p. (J). (ps-3). 1998. 12.99 (1-57673-266-5, Gold n Honey) Zondervan.
Mookster's Mitzvah Mishaps. Chana Nestlebaum. LC 91-75362. (Illus.). 32p. (J). (gr. k-4). 1991. 12.95 (0-910818-26-6); pap. 9.95 (0-910818-27-4) Judaica Pr.
*Moolie Kajoolie's Star: By Cecilia Soprano. Cecilia Soprano. (Illus.). 24p. 1999. pap. 8.00 (0-9674603-1-X) Ceres.
Mooly's Slow Teeth. Houghton Mifflin Company Staff. (Literature Experience 1991 Ser.). (J). (gr. 2). 1990. pap. 9.48 (0-395-55147-1) HM.
Moominland Midwinter. Tove Jansson. 176p. (J). (gr. 4-7). 1992. 14.00 (0-374-35041-8); pap. 4.95 (0-374-45303-9) FS&G.
Moominpappa at Sea. Tove Jansson. Tr. by Kingsley Hart from FIN. LC 93-1434. 240p. (J). (gr. 4-7). 1993. 17.00 (0-374-35044-2); pap. 5.95 (0-374-45306-3) FS&G.
Moominpappa's Memoirs. Tove Jansson. 176p. (J). (ps-3). 1994. pap. 4.95 (0-374-45307-1, Sunburst Bks) FS&G.
Moominpappa's Memoirs. Tove Jansson. Tr. by Thomas Warburton. LC 94-50954. 176p. (J). 1994. 16.00 (0-374-35045-0) FS&G.
Moominsummer Madness. Tove Jansson. 176p. (J). (gr. 4-7). 1991. 13.95 (0-374-35039-6) FS&G.
Moominsummer Madness. Tove Jansson. Tr. by Thomas Warburton. (Illus.). 144p. (J). (ps-3). 1992. pap. 5.95 (0-374-45310-1, Sunburst Bks) FS&G.
Moon see Images
Moon see Eye on the Universe Series
*Moon. (Handstitched Zen Ser.). 128p. 2000. 15.95 (1-55156-140-9) Paperblank.
Moon. Ariel Books Staff. LC 97-164372. 128p. 1996. 3.95 (0-8362-1002-6, Arie Bks) Andrews & McMeel.
Moon. Carmen Bredeson. LC 96-40226. (First Bk.). 64p. (J). (gr. 4-6). 1998. 22.00 (0-531-20308-5) Watts.
Moon. Carmen Bredeson. (First Books--The Solar System). (Illus.). 64p. (J). (gr. 4 up). 1998. pap. 6.95 (0-531-15911-6) Watts.
Moon. Mark Dunster. 10p. (Orig.). (J). 1993. pap. 4.00 (0-89642-220-8) Linden Pubs.
*Moon. Tim Furniss. LC 00-20759. (Spinning Through Space Ser.). (Illus.). (J). 2000. 25.69 (0-7398-2738-3) Raintree Steck-V.
*Moon. Tim Furniss. (Spinning Through Space Ser.). (Illus.). (J). 2000. pap. 8.95 (0-7398-3090-2) Raintree Steck-V.
Moon. Michael George. LC 96-46675. (Our Universe Ser.). (Illus.). 32p. (J). (gr. 2-6). 1997. lib. bdg. 22.79 (1-56766-386-9) Childs World.
Moon. Robin Kerrod. LC 98-34703. (Planet Library Ser.). (Illus.). 32p. (J). (gr. 4-7). 2000. 22.60 (0-8225-3900-4, Lerner Publctns) Lerner Pub.
Moon. Lorella Rizzatti. 1999. 5.95 (0-8109-5636-5) Abrams.
Moon. Lorella Rizzatti. (Illus.). 12p. 1999. bds. 5.95 (0-8109-5637-3, Pub. by Abrams) Time Warner.
Moon. David Romtvedt. LC 82-22812. (Illus.). 1984. 195.00 (0-931460-14-X) Bieler.
Moon. Maryam Sachs. LC 98-17962. (Illus.). 208p. 1998. 19.95 (0-7892-0341-3) Abbeville Pr.
Moon. Simon & Schuster Staff. 1984. 10.95 (0-590-07883-6) Scholastic Inc.
Moon. Seymour Simon. LC 84-28753. (Illus.). 32p. (J). (gr. k-3). 1984. lib. bdg. 16.00 (0-02-782840-9, Four Winds Pr) S&S Childrens.
Moon. Lesley Sims. 32p. (J). (gr. 1-4). 1995. pap. text 4.95 (0-8114-4924-6) Raintree Steck-V.
Moon. Lynda Sorensen. LC 93-14875. (Solar System Discovery Library). 24p. (J). (gr. k-4). 1993. lib. bdg. 10.95 (0-86593-273-5) Rourke Corp.
Moon. Lynda Sorensen. LC 93-14875. (Solar System Ser.). (J). (ps-6). 1993. 9.50 (0-685-66589-5) Rourke Corp.
Moon. Jenny Tesar. LC 97-25176. (Space Observer Ser.). 1998. 19.92 (1-57572-579-7) Heinemann Lib.
Moon. Illus. by Gerald Witcomb. (Butterfly Bks.). 32p. (J). (gr. 3-5). 1985. 9.95 (0-86685-448-7) Intl Bk Ctr.
*Moon. limited ed. Prod. by Benjamin Britton. (Illus.). 12p. 1999. write for info. incl. cd-rom (0-9677388-1-4) Britton & Assocs.
Moon. Henry David Thoreau. LC 80-2521. (Thoreau Ser.). 80p. 1985. reprint ed. 27.50 (0-404-19069-3) AMS Pr.
Moon see Isaac Asimov's New Library of the Universe
Moon. rev. ed. George Gamow & Harry G. Stubbs. (gr. 5 up). 1971. 9.57i (0-200-71761-8) Macmillan.
Moon. unabridged ed. Paulette Bourgeois. (Starting with Space Ser.). (Illus.). 40p. (J). (gr. 2-6). 1997. 14.95 (1-55074-157-8, Pub. by Kids Can Pr) Genl Dist Srvs.
Moon. unabridged ed. Paulette Bourgeois. (Starting with Space Ser.). (Illus.). 40p. (J). (gr. 2-6). 1999. pap. 6.95 (1-55074-332-5, Pub. by Kids Can Pr) Genl Dist Srvs.
Moon: An Outline of Astronomy & Physics of Our Satellite on the Eve of the Apollo Era. Zdenek Kopal. (Illus.). 525p. 1969. text 155.50 (90-277-0124-5) Kluwer Academic.
Moon: Its Creation, Form & Significance. John C. Whitcomb & Donald B. DeYoung. 7.95 (0-88469-102-0) BMH Bks.
Moon: Proceedings of the International Astronomical Union, 47th Symposium, Newcastle-Upon-Tyne, 1971. International Astronomical Union Staff. Ed. by H. C. Urey & S. K. Runcorn. LC 73-188005. (I.A.U. Symposia Ser.: No. 47). 480p. 1972. lib. bdg. 146.00 (90-277-0149-0) Kluwer Academic.
Moon: The Life & Death of a Rock Legend. Tony Fletcher. LC 98-39872. (Illus.). 608p. 1999. 30.00 (0-380-97337-5, Avon Bks) Morrow Avon.
*Moon: The Life & Death of a Rock Legend. Tony Fletcher. (Illus.). 624p. 2000. pap. 16.00 (0-380-78827-6, HarpEntertain) Morrow Avon.
*Moon - Blank. (Handstitched Zen of Nothingness Ser.). 128p. 2000. 15.95 (1-55156-164-6) Paperblank.
Moon above, Earth Below. Thomas-Cocran. (What a Wonderful World Intro Ser.). 1993. pap. text. write for info. (0-582-91092-7, Pub. by Addison-Wesley) Longman.
*Moon Adventure. Tom Van Steenhoven. (Billy Bks.). (Illus.). (J). 1999. 15.99 (0-9672652-0-7) Nation of Imagi.
Moon & Bai Insiang & Other Stories. Gracianus R. Reyes. 108p. (Orig.). (C). 1990. pap. 10.75 (971-10-0276-0, Pub. by New Day Pub) Cellar.
Moon & Flowers: A Woman's Path to Enlightenment. Ed. by Kalyanavaca. 304p. 1998. pap. 23.95 (0-904766-89-6) Windhorse Pubns.
Moon & I. Betsy C. Byars. LC 95-53100. (Illus.). 112p. (YA). (gr. 7 up). 1996. mass mkt. 4.95 (0-688-13704-0, Wm Morrow) Morrow Avon.
Moon & I. Betsy C. Byars. 1996. 10.05 (0-606-11636-2, Pub. by Turtleback) Demco.
Moon & I. large type ed. Betsy C. Byars. 1994. 29.00 (0-614-09808-4, L-34134-00) Am Printing Hse.
Moon & I: Personal Journal, 1995. Deborah Garrison. (Illus.). 408p. (Orig.). 1994. pap. 14.95 (1-886185-23-9) Mosley Pubng.
Moon & Mercury. Elisabeth Murawski. LC 90-11915. 72p. (Orig.). 1990. pap. 8.00 (0-931846-37-4) Wash Writers Pub.
*Moon & Other Failures. F. D. Reeve. (Illus.). 150p. 1999. pap. 17.95 (0-87013-514-7) Mich St U Pr.
Moon & Otter & Frog. Illus. by Clifford Brycelea. LC 93-39879. 32p. (J). (gr. 1-4). 1995. lib. bdg. 14.89 (0-7868-2022-5, Pub. by Hyprn Child) Little.
Moon & Otter & Frog. Illus. by Clifford Brycelea. LC 93-39879. 32p. (J). (ps-3). 1995. 14.95 (0-7868-0027-5, Pub. by Hyprn Child) Time Warner.
Moon & Riddles Diner & Synnysi. Willard. LC 99-50834. 2001. write for info. (0-15-201941-3) Harcourt Coll Pubs.
Moon & Sixpence. W. Somerset Maugham. 22.95 (0-8488-2653-1) Amereon Ltd.
Moon & Sixpence. W. Somerset Maugham. 224p. 1993. pap. 9.95 (0-14-018597-6) Viking Penguin.
Moon & Sixpence. W. Somerset Maugham. (Ghosts of Fear Street Ser.). (gr. 3-6). 1984. per. 1.50 (0-671-00851-X, Minstrel Bks) PB.
*Moon & Sixpence. W. Somerset Maugham. LC 99-57094. (International Ser.). 160p. 2000. pap. 11.00 (0-375-72456-7) Vin Bks.
Moon & Sixpence. large type ed. W. Somerset Maugham. 384p. 1995. lib. bdg. 24.00 (0-939495-78-3) North Bks.
Moon & Sixpence. large type ed. W. Somerset Maugham. LC 98-52327. 327p. 1999. 27.95 (1-56000-483-5) Transaction Pubs.
Moon & Sixpence. W. Somerset Maugham. LC 75-25357. (Works of W. Somerset Maugham). 1977. reprint ed. 23.95 (0-405-07816-1) Ayer.
Moon & Sixpence. W. Somerset Maugham. 242p. 1998. reprint ed. lib. bdg. 24.00 (1-58287-050-0) North Bks.
Moon & Sixpence. unabridged ed. W. Somerset Maugham. 156p. 1997. reprint ed. pap. 14.95 (1-57002-016-7) Univ Publng Hse.
Moon & Sixpence. unabridged ed. W. Somerset Maugham. LC 95-34752. (Thrift Editions Ser.). 176p. 1995. reprint ed. pap. text 2.00 (0-486-28731-9) Dover.
Moon & the Island: Poems by Laura Stortoni. Laura Stortoni. 1997. pap. 13.00 (0-9641003-3-9) Hesperia Pr.
Moon & the Mistypips. Joseph Volpe & Tracey Volpe. (Hopewell Stories Ser.). (Illus.). 32p. (J). (ps-4). 1991. teacher ed. write for info. (0-9631215-2-9); pap. write for info. (0-9631215-1-0) Hopewell Stories.
Moon & the Planets. Ed. by William R. Corliss. LC 85-61380. (Catalog of Astronomical Anomalies Ser.). (Illus.). 380p. 1985. 18.95 (0-915554-19-4) Sourcebook.
Moon & the Sun. Vonda N. McIntyre. LC 97-3232. 432p. 1997. 23.00 (0-671-56765-9, PB Hardcover) PB.
Moon & the Sun. Vonda N. McIntyre. 1998. mass mkt. 6.99 (0-671-56766-7) PB.
Moon & the Sun. large type ed. Vonda N. McIntyre. LC 98-28867. 1998. 30.00 (0-7862-1591-7) Thorndike Pr.
Moon & the Thorn. Teresa Edgerton. 336p. (Orig.). 1995. mass mkt. 5.99 (0-441-00188-2) Ace Bks.
Moon & the Western Imagination. Scott L. Montgomery. LC 99-6090. 1999. pap. write for info. (0-8165-1989-7) U of Ariz Pr.
Moon & the Western Imagination. Scott L. Montgomery. LC 99-6090. (Illus.). 264p. 1999. 35.00 (0-8165-1711-8) U of Ariz Pr.
Moon & the Zither: The Story of the Western Wing. Wang Shifu. Ed. by Stephen H. West & Wilt L. Idema. LC 89-20232. (Illus.). 300p. 1990. 48.00 (0-520-06807-6, Pub. by U CA Pr) Cal Prin Full Svc.
*Moon & You. Edwin C. Krupp. LC 99-42813. (Illus.). 32p. (YA). (gr. k-3). 2000. pap. 5.95 (0-688-17818-9, Wm Morrow) Morrow Avon.
Moon & You. Edwin C. Krupp. LC 92-16231. (Illus.). 48p. (J). (gr. k-4). 1993. lib. bdg. 15.00 (0-02-751142-1, Mac Bks Young Read) S&S Childrens.
Moon & You for Beginners. Teresa Vidgen-Moorey. (Illus.). 96p. 1996. pap. 11.95 (0-340-64836-8, Pub. by Hodder & Stought Ltd) Trafalgar.
Moon Base: First Colony in Space. Michael D. Cole. LC 98-13126. (Countdown to Space Ser.). 48p. (J). (gr. 4-10). 1999. lib. bdg. 18.95 (0-7660-1118-6) Enslow Pubs.
Moon Basket see Cesta de Luna
Moon Belongs to Everyone: Making Theatre with 7:84. Elizabeth Maclennan. 214p. (Orig.). (C). 1990. pap. write for info. (0-413-64150-3, A0478, Methuen Drama) Methn.
Moon Below. Barbara Bickmore. 624p. 1994. mass mkt. 5.99 (0-8217-4454-2, Zebra Kensgtn) Kensgtn Pub Corp.
*Moon Blessings Pack: Let the Creative Energies of the Moon Enhance Your Life & Illuminate Your Soul with Book & Cards & Other. Lori Reid. 2000. pap. 24.95 (1-85868-857-4, Pub. by Carlton Bks Ltd) Natl Bk Netwk.
Moon Book. Gail Gibbons. LC 96-36826. (Illus.). 32p. (J). (gr. k-3). 1997. lib. bdg. 16.95 (0-8234-1297-0) Holiday.
Moon Book. Gail Gibbons. (Illus.). (J). (gr. k-3). 1997. pap. 6.95 (0-8234-1364-0) Holiday.
*Moon Book: A Pictorial Journal of a Year of Painting the Full Moon. Emily Eve Weinstein. LC 99-62140. (Illus.). 96p. 1999. 14.95 (0-9667246-1-5) Discovery WV.
Moon Book: Fascinating Facts about the Magnificent, Mysterious Moon. 2nd rev. ed. Kim Long. LC 98-26266. (Illus.). 160p. 1998. pap. 12.50 (1-55566-230-7) Johnson Bks.
Moon Box: Legends, Mystery, & Lore from Luna, 4 vols. Ed. by John Miller & Tim Smith. (Illus.). 160p. 1995. pap. 29.95 (0-8118-1060-7) Chronicle Bks.
Moon Boy. Barbara A. Brenner. 32p. (J). 1990. pap. 4.50 (0-553-34851-5) Bantam.
Moon Bridge. Marcia Savin. 231p. (YA). (gr. 6-9). 1995. pap. 3.50 (0-590-43765-8) Scholastic Inc.
Moon Bridge. Marcia Savin. (J). 1995. 8.60 (0-606-08571-8, Pub. by Turtleback) Demco.
Moon by Night. Madeleine L'Engle. 256p. (YA). (gr. 6 up). 1981. mass mkt. 4.99 (0-440-95776-1, LE) Dell.
Moon by Night. Madeleine L'Engle. LC 63-9072. 224p. (J). (gr. 5-9). 1963. 16.00 (0-374-35049-3) FS&G.
Moon by Night. Madeleine L'Engle. (Austin Family Ser.). (J). 1963. 9.60 (0-606-02181-7, Pub. by Turtleback) Demco.
Moon by Whalelight: And Other Adventures among Bats, Penguins, Crocodilians, & Whales. Diane Ackerman. LC 92-50004. 1992. pap. 12.00 (0-679-74226-3) Vin Bks.
Moon Cakes. Andrea Louie. LC 94-48115. 1995. 341.10 (0-345-39622-7) Ballantine Pub Grp.

An Asterisk (*) at the beginning of an entry indicates that the title is appearing for the first time.

Moon Cakes in Gold Mountain: From China to the Canadian Plains. J. Brian Dawson. (Illus.). 256p. (Orig.). 1991. pap. 19.95 (*1-55059-026-X*) Temeron Bks.
Moon Cakes to Maize: Delicious World Folk Tales. Ed. by Norma J. Livo. LC 98-33373. 181p. (J). (gr. 3-8). 1999. pap. 16.95 (*1-55591-973-1*) Fulcrum Pub.
Moon-Calf: or Accurate Reflections on the Consolidator. Joseph Browne. LC 93-36533. (Augustan Reprints Ser.: No. 269 (1991)). 1993. reprint ed. 14.50 (*0-404-70269-4*) AMS Pr.
Moon Called. Andre Norton. (Illus.). (Orig.). 1991. mass mkt. 3.99 (*0-8125-1533-1*, Pub. by Tor Bks) St Martin.
Moon Changes Shape. 95th ed. HB Staff. (J). (gr. 1). 1998. pap. text 7.00 (*0-15-303633-8*) Harcourt Coll Pubs.
Moon Cloud. F. Asch. (J). 1998. 10.95 (*0-13-600552-7*) P-H.
Moon Crossing Bridge. Tess Gallagher. 128p. 1992. 17.00 (*1-55597-156-3*); pap. 14.00 (*1-55597-175-X*) Graywolf.
Moon Cycle. Effie Mihopoulos. (Offset Offshoot Ser.: No. 14). 8.00 (*0-941240-17-7*) Ommation Pr.
Moon Dance. S. P. Somtow. 1991. mass mkt. 4.95 (*0-8125-1127-1*, Pub. by Tor Bks) St Martin.
Moon Dance. Mariah Stewart. 1998. per. 6.50 (*0-671-02624-0*) PB.
Moon Dancer. Judith E. French. 1992. mass mkt. 4.50 (*0-380-76105-X*, Avon Bks) Morrow Avon.
Moon Dancer. Margaret I. Rostkowski. LC 94-39553. 224p. (YA). (gr. 7 up). 1995. pap. 5.00 (*0-15-200194-8*, Harcourt Child Bks) Harcourt.
Moon Dancer. Margaret I. Rostkowski. LC 94-39553. (J). 1995. 10.10 (*0-606-09627-2*, Pub. by Turtleback) Demco.
Moon Dancing: Poems. William J. Middleton. LC 98-96000. (Illus.). 60p. 1998. pap. 5.50 (*1-886467-30-7*) WJM Press.
Moon Dash Warrior: The Story of an American Indian in Vietnam, a Marine from the Land of the Lumbee. unabridged ed. Delano Cummings. Ed. by Marian Novak & David Novak. (Illus.). 266p. 1998. 22.00 (*0-9651858-3-4*) Signal Tree.
***Moon Days: Creative Writings About Menstruation.** Ed. by Cassie P. Steele. LC 99-17878. 175p. 1999. 21.95 (*1-887714-41-3*) Summerhse Pr.
***Moon Days: Creative Writings about Menstruation.** Ed. by Cassie P. Steele. LC 99-17878. 173p. 1999. pap. 12.95 (*1-887714-40-5*) Summerhse Pr.
Moon Deluxe: Stories. Frederick Barthelme. LC 95-22804. 240p. 1995. pap. 12.00 (*0-8021-3437-8*, Grove) Grove-Atltic.
Moon Dies. Godfrey Turton. (Illus.). 1984. 110.00 (*0-904920-06-2*) St Mut.
Moon-Earth's Neighbor. Robin Kerrod. LC 98-34703. (J). 1999. write for info. (*1-57505-362-4*, Carolrhoda) Lerner Pub.
Moon Equipped: 60 Years of Hot Rod Photo Memories. David Fetherston. LC 95-90286. (Hot Rod History Ser.). (Illus.). 128p. 1995. pap. 19.95 (*0-9646175-0-1*) Fetherston Pub.
Moon Exploration Sticker Picture Book. J. Petruccio. (J). 1995. pap. 3.95 (*0-486-28722-X*) Dover.
Moon-Face, & Other Stories. Jack London. LC 71-140334. (Short Story Index Reprint Ser.). 1977. 15.95 (*0-8369-3726-0*) Ayer.
***Moon-Face & Other Stories.** Jack London. (Collected Works of Jack London). 273p. 1998. reprint ed. lib. bdg. 88.00 (*1-58201-728-X*) Classic Bks.
Moon Fate. James Axler. (Deathlands Ser.: No. 16). 1992. per. 4.99 (*0-373-62516-2*, 1-62516-9) Harlequin Bks.
Moon Fate. James Axler. (Deathlands Ser.: Bk. 16). 1999. per. 5.99 (*0-373-62554-5*, 1-62554-0, Wrldwide Lib) Harlequin Bks.
Moon Festival. Ching Y. Russell. LC 97-70583. (Illus.). 32p. (J). (ps-4). 1997. 15.95 (*1-56397-596-3*) Boyds Mills Pr.
Moon Fire. 52p. (Orig.). 1996. pap. 6.95 (*0-9639931-4-3*) Dawnstar Runelore.
Moon Flower. Shirl Henke. 432p. (Orig.). 1989. mass mkt. 3.95 (*0-446-34644-6*, Pub. by Warner Bks) Little.
***Moon Flower.** Wendy J. Pierre. LC 99-94918. 2000. pap. 7.95 (*0-533-13220-7*) Vantage.
Moon for a Candle, No. 25. Mary Langer. (Serenade Saga Ser.). 1985. pap. 2.50 (*0-310-47052-8*, 15558P) Zondervan.
Moon for Lavinia. Betty A. Neels. (Promo Ser.). 1999. per. 3.99 (*0-373-63104-9*, 1-63104-3) Harlequin Bks.
Moon for Seasons. Ann Turner. LC 92-36857. (Illus.). 40p. (J). (gr. 1-5). 1994. mass mkt. 14.95 (*0-02-789513-0*, Mac Bks Young Read) S&S Childrens.
Moon for the Misbegotten see Best American Plays: Fourth Series, 1952-1957
Moon for the Misbegotten, Eugene O'Neill. LC 74-5218. 115p. 1974. pap. 8.00 (*0-394-71236-6*) Vin Bks.
Moon Frog: Animal Poems for Young Children. Richard Edwards. LC 92-53014. (Illus.). 48p. (J). (ps up). 1993. 16.95 (*1-56402-116-5*) Candlewick Pr.
Moon Gaffney. Harry Sylvester. LC 76-6367. (Irish Americans Ser.). 1976. reprint ed. 26.95 (*0-405-09359-4*) Ayer.
Moon Gate. Calvin L. Criner. 72p. 1999. pap. 8.00 (*0-8059-4579-2*) Dorrance.
Moon Gate Dreams: A Quest for Romance & Adventure Beyond the Moon Gate. George A. Barker, Jr. LC 97-93223. (Illus.). 204p. (Orig.). 1997. pap. 11.95 (*0-9657414-0-0*) Apple Tree Bks.
***Moon Gazing: A Journal.** Laurie Wagner. (Illus.). 2000. pap. 17.95 (*0-8118-2437-3*) Chronicle Bks.
Moon Go Away, I Don't Love You No More: Poems. Jim Simmerman. LC 94-14637. (Poetry Ser.). 88p. (C). 1994. 15.95 (*1-881163-08-3*); pap. 9.95 (*1-881163-09-1*) Miami Univ Pr.
Moon Goddess: The Queen of Sheba. Janice L. Dennie. (Romance Ser.). 245p. 1999. pap. 7.99 (*0-9643349-1-7*) Kente Pubns.
Moon Goes Fishing. Dana Simson. (Legend Bks.). (Illus.). 32p. (J). 1996. 14.95 (*0-8362-1022-0*) Andrews & McMeel.
Moon Goes Fishing. Dana Simson. (Legend Bks.). (Illus.). 32p. (J). (ps-4). 1994. 17.95 (*0-9642943-0-3*) Sourdough Pr.
Moon Gold. Carolyn Sibr. LC 91-38350. (Poets Ser.). 96p. 1991. 12.50 (*0-940473-24-0*) Wm Caxton.
Moon Handbooks: Alaska-Yukon. 6th ed. Don Pitcher & Deke Castleman. (Illus.). 540p. 1997. pap. 17.95 (*1-56691-089-7*, Moon Handbks) Avalon Travel.
***Moon Handbooks: Alberta & the Northwest Territories: Including Banff, Jasper & the Canadian Rockies.** 3rd rev. ed. Andrew Hempstead. Vol. 3. (Illus.). 530p. 1999. pap. 18.95 (*1-56691-144-3*, Moon Handbks) Avalon Travel.
Moon Handbooks: Archaeological Mexico: A Traveler's Guide to Ancient Cities & Sacred Sites. Andrew Coe. LC 99-113368. (Illus.). 420p. 1998. pap. 19.95 (*1-56691-105-2*, Moon Handbks) Avalon Travel.
Moon Handbooks: Arizona: Including Grand Canyon National Park. 7th ed. Bill Weir. Vol. 7. (Illus.). 650p. 1999. pap. 18.95 (*1-56691-143-5*, Moon Handbks) Avalon Travel.
Moon Handbooks: Atlantic Canada: New Brunswick, Nova Scotia, Prince Edward Island, Newfoundland & Labrador. 2nd rev. ed. Mark Morris. Vol. 2. (Illus.). 490p. 1999. pap. 18.95 (*1-56691-114-1*, Moon Handbks) Avalon Travel.
***Moon Handbooks: Australia.** 2nd ed. Moon Travel Handbooks Editors. Vol. 2. (Illus.). 940p. 2000. 21.95 (*1-56691-158-3*, Moon Handbks) Avalon Travel.
Moon Handbooks: Baja: Tijuana to Cabo San Lucas. 3rd rev. ed. Joe Cummings. LC 98-657868. (Illus.). 540p. 1998. pap. 16.95 (*1-56691-120-6*, Moon Handbks) Avalon Travel.
Moon Handbooks: Bali. 2nd rev. ed. Bill Dalton. (Illus.). 750p. 1997. pap. 19.95 (*1-56691-073-0*, Moon Handbks) Avalon Travel.
***Moon Handbooks: Bangkok.** 3rd rev. ed. Carl Parkes. Vol. 3. (Illus.). 330p. 2000. pap. 15.95 (*1-56691-159-1*, Pub. by Avalon Travel) Publishers Group.
Moon Handbooks: Belize. 4th rev. ed. Chicki Mallan & Patti Lange. (Illus.). 360p. 1998. pap. 15.95 (*1-56691-137-0*, Moon Handbks) Avalon Travel.
Moon Handbooks: Big Island of Hawaii: Including Hawaii Volcanoes National Park, the Kona Coast & Waipio Valley. 3rd rev. ed. Joe D. Bisignani & Robert Nilsen. Vol. 3. (Illus.). 390p. 1998. pap. 15.95 (*1-56691-100-1*, Moon Handbks) Avalon Travel.
Moon Handbooks: Boston. Jeff Perk. (Illus.). 250p. 1999. pap. 13.95 (*1-56691-136-2*, Moon Handbks) Avalon Travel.
Moon Handbooks: Cabo: La Paz to Cabo San Lucas. 2nd rev. ed. Joe Cummings. (Illus.). 270p. 1998. pap. 14.95 (*1-56691-119-2*, Moon Handbks) Avalon Travel.
Moon Handbooks: Canadian Rockies: Including Banff & Jasper National Parks. Andrew Hempstead. (Illus.). 260p. 1999. pap. 14.95 (*1-56691-151-6*, Moon Handbks) Avalon Travel.
Moon Handbooks: Cancun: Mexico's Caribbean Coast. 5th rev. ed. Chicki Mallan. (Illus.). 240p. 1998. pap. 14.95 (*1-56691-121-4*, Moon Handbks) Avalon Travel.
Moon Handbooks: Caribbean Vacations: How to Create Your Own Tropical Adventure. Karl Luntta. (Illus.). 910p. 1998. pap. 18.95 (*1-56691-125-7*, Moon Handbks) Avalon Travel.
***Moon Handbooks: Coastal California.** Kim Weir. (Illus.). 500p. 2000. pap. 17.95 (*1-56691-178-8*, Moon Handbks) Avalon Travel.
Moon Handbooks: Colonial Mexico: A Traveler's Guide to Distinctive Lodging, Dining & Shopping in Historic Districts & Artisans' Communities Throughout Mexico. Chicki Mallan & Oz Mallan. (Illus.). 400p. 1998. pap. 18.95 (*1-56691-109-5*, Moon Handbks) Avalon Travel.
Moon Handbooks: Colorado: Including Denver, Aspen, Mesa Verde & Rocky Mountain National Parks. 4th rev. ed. Stephen Metzger. Vol. 4. (Illus.). 480p. 1999. pap. 17.95 (*1-56691-145-1*, Moon Handbks) Avalon Travel.
***Moon Handbooks: Connecticut.** Andrew Collins. (Illus.). 400p. 2000. pap. 17.95 (*1-56691-181-8*, Moon Handbks) Avalon Travel.
Moon Handbooks: Costa Rica. 3rd expanded ed. Christopher P. Baker. Vol. 3. (Illus.). 820p. 1999. pap. 19.95 (*1-56691-124-9*, Moon Handbks) Avalon Travel.
Moon Handbooks: Cuba. Christopher P. Baker. 750p. 1997. pap. 19.95 (*1-56691-095-1*, Moon Handbks) Avalon Travel.
Moon Handbooks: Dominican Republic. Gaylord Dold. (Illus.). 420p. 1997. pap. 15.95 (*1-56691-090-0*, Moon Handbks) Avalon Travel.
Moon Handbooks: Ecuador: Including the Galapagos Islands. Julian Smith. LC 98-149247. (Illus.). 460p. 1998. pap. 16.95 (*1-56691-107-9*, Moon Handbks) Avalon Travel.
***Moon Handbooks: Fiji.** 5th rev. ed. David Stanley. (Illus.). 350p. 1999. pap. 14.95 (*1-56691-139-7*, Moon Handbks) Avalon Travel.
Moon Handbooks: Georgia: Including Atlanta, Savannah & the Blue Ridge Mountains. 3rd rev. ed. Kap Stann. LC 94-905. Vol. 3. (Illus.). 410p. 1999. pap. 17.95 (*1-56691-150-8*, Moon Handbks) Avalon Travel.
Moon Handbooks: Grand Canyon: Including Arizona's Indian Country. Bill Weir. (Illus.). 250p. 1999. pap. 14.95 (*1-56691-152-4*, Moon Handbks) Avalon Travel.
***Moon Handbooks: Havana.** Christopher P. Baker. (Illus.). 370p. 2000. pap. 16.95 (*1-56691-182-6*, Moon Handbks) Avalon Travel.
***Moon Handbooks: Hawaii: The All-Island Guide.** 5th rev. ed. Joe D. Bisignani. (Illus.). 1030p. 1999. pap. 19.95 (*1-56691-160-5*, Moon Handbks) Avalon Travel.
Moon Handbooks: Honduras: Including the Bay Islands & Copan. Chris Humphrey. 330p. 1997. pap. 15.95 (*1-56691-099-4*, Moon Handbks) Avalon Travel.
Moon Handbooks: Hong Kong: Including Macau & Guangzhou. 2nd rev. ed. Kerry Moran. LC 96-648119. (Illus.). 380p. 1998. pap. 16.95 (*1-56691-108-7*, Moon Handbks) Avalon Travel.
***Moon Handbooks: Honolulu-Waikiki: The Island of Oahu.** 3rd rev. ed. Joe D. Bisignani. Vol. 3. (Illus.). 360p. 1999. pap. 14.95 (*1-56691-128-1*, Moon Handbks) Avalon Travel.
Moon Handbooks: Idaho. 3rd ed. Don Root. (Illus.). 610p. 1997. pap. 18.95 (*1-56691-088-9*, Moon Handbks) Avalon Travel.
Moon Handbooks: Indonesia. 6th ed. Bill Dalton. LC 95-222255. (Illus.). 1380p. 1995. pap. 25.00 (*1-56691-062-5*, Moon Handbks) Avalon Travel.
***Moon Handbooks: Jamaica.** 4th rev. ed. Karl Luntta. Vol. 4. (Illus.). 340p. 2000. 15.95 (*1-56691-161-3*, Moon Handbks) Avalon Travel.
Moon Handbooks: Kauai: Including the Island of Niihau. 3rd ed. Joe D. Bisignani. (Illus.). 320p. 1997. pap. text 15.95 (*1-56691-091-9*, Moon Handbks) Avalon Travel.
Moon Handbooks: Los Angeles. Kim Weir. (Illus.). 380p. 1999. pap. 16.95 (*1-56691-155-9*, Moon Handbks) Avalon Travel.
Moon Handbooks: Maine. Kathleen M. Brandes. (Illus.). 690p. 1998. pap. 18.95 (*1-56691-094-3*, Moon Handbks) Avalon Travel.
***Moon Handbooks: Massachusetts: Including Boston, the Berkshires & Cape Cod.** Jeff Perk. (Illus.). 490p. 1998. pap. 18.95 (*1-56691-083-8*, Moon Handbks) Avalon Travel.
***Moon Handbooks: Maui: Including Molokai & Lanai.** 5th rev. ed. Joe D. Bisignani. (Illus.). 450p. 1999. pap. 15.95 (*1-56691-138-9*, Moon Handbks) Avalon Travel.
Moon Handbooks: Mexico. 2nd rev. ed. Joe Cummings & Chicki Mallan. LC 97-649746. (Illus.). 1220p. 1999. pap. 21.95 (*1-56691-123-0*, Moon Handbks) Avalon Travel.
***Moon Handbooks: Mexico City.** Joe Cummings & Chris Humphrey. (Illus.). 250p. 2000. pap. 14.95 (*1-56691-186-9*, Moon Handbks) Avalon Travel.
***Moon Handbooks: Michigan: Featuring the Great Lakes & the Upper Peninsula.** Tina Lassen. LC 98-767. (Illus.). 360p. 1999. pap. 15.95 (*1-56691-134-6*, Moon Handbks) Avalon Travel.
***Moon Handbooks: Micronesia.** 5th rev. ed. Neil M. Levy. Vol. 5. (Illus.). 340p. 2000. pap. 16.95 (*1-56691-162-1*, Moon Handbks) Avalon Travel.
Moon Handbooks: Montana: Including Glacier National Park. 4th rev. ed. W. C. McRae & Judy Jewell. Vol. 4. (Illus.). 490p. 1999. pap. 17.95 (*1-56691-142-7*, Moon Handbks) Avalon Travel.
***Moon Handbooks: Moon: A 21st-Century Travel Guide.** 2nd rev. ed. Carl Koppeschaar. Tr. by Susan Massotty from DUT. (Illus.). 160p. 2000. pap. 10.00 (*1-56691-200-8*, Moon Handbks) Avalon Travel.
***Moon Handbooks: Nepal.** 3rd rev. ed. Kerry Moran. (Illus.). 500p. 2000. pap. 18.95 (*1-56691-164-8*, Moon Handbks) Avalon Travel.
Moon Handbooks: Nevada. 5th rev. ed. Deke Castleman. (Illus.). 560p. 1998. pap. 18.95 (*1-56691-116-8*, Moon Handbks) Avalon Travel.
Moon Handbooks: New Hampshire: Including Portsmouth, the Lakes Region, the Upper Valley & the White Mountains. Steve Lantos. (Illus.). 480p. 1998. pap. 18.95 (*1-56691-111-7*, Moon Handbks) Avalon Travel.
***Moon Handbooks: New Mexico: Santa Fe, Taos, Roswell & the Rio Grande.** 5th rev. ed. Steve Metzger. (Illus.). 370p. 2000. pap. 15.95 (*1-56691-203-2*, Moon Handbks) Avalon Travel.
***Moon Handbooks: New York City.** 2nd rev. ed. Christiane Bird. (Illus.). 300p. 2000. pap. 13.95 (*1-56691-202-4*, Moon Handbks) Avalon Travel.
***Moon Handbooks: New York State.** 2nd rev. ed. Christiane Bird. (Illus.). 780p. 2000. pap. 19.95 (*1-56691-201-6*, Moon Handbks) Avalon Travel.
***Moon Handbooks: New Zealand.** 5th rev. ed. Jane King. Vol. 5. (Illus.). 540p. 1999. pap. 18.95 (*1-56691-165-6*, Moon Handbks) Avalon Travel.
***Moon Handbooks: North Carolina: From the Great Smoky Mountains to the Outer Banks.** Rob Hirtz et al. (Illus.). 320p. 1999. pap. 14.95 (*1-56691-130-3*, Moon Handbks) Avalon Travel.
***Moon Handbooks: Northern California: Including San Francisco, Big Sur, Yosemite, Wine Country & the Redwood Coast.** 3rd rev. ed. Kim Weir. Vol. 3. (Illus.). 800p. 2000. pap. 19.95 (*1-56691-084-6*, Pub. by Avalon Travel) Publishers Group.
Moon Handbooks: Northern Mexico: Including the Copper Canyon. 2nd rev. ed. Joe Cummings. Vol. 2. (Illus.). 610p. 1998. pap. 17.95 (*1-56691-118-4*, Moon Handbks) Avalon Travel.
***Moon Handbooks: Oaxaca: Mountain Craft Regions, Archaeological Sites & Coastal Resorts.** Bruce Whipperman. (Illus.). 410p. 2000. pap. 16.95 (*1-56691-166-4*, Moon Handbks) Avalon Travel.
Moon Handbooks: Ohio: Including Cleveland, Cincinnati, Columbus, Amish Country & the Ohio River Valley. David Wright. (Illus.). 340p. 1999. pap. 15.95 (*1-56691-154-0*, Moon Handbks) Avalon Travel.
Moon Handbooks: Oregon. 4th rev. ed. Stuart Warren & Ted L. Ishikawa. (Illus.). 590p. 1998. pap. 17.95 (*1-56691-113-3*, Moon Handbks) Avalon Travel.
Moon Handbooks: Outback Australia: Including the Red Centre, Kakadu National Park & the Kimberley. 2nd ed. Marael Johnson. (Illus.). 450p. 1996. pap. 18.95 (*1-56691-047-1*, Moon Handbks) Avalon Travel.
***Moon Handbooks: Pacific Mexico: Including Acapulco, Puerto Vallarta, Oaxaca, Guadalajara & Mazatlan.** 4th rev. ed. Bruce Whipperman. Vol. 4. (Illus.). 610p. 2000. pap. 18.95 (*1-56691-167-2*, Moon Handbks) Avalon Travel.
Moon Handbooks: Pakistan. 2nd rev. ed. Isobel Shaw. Vol. 2. (Illus.). 660p. 1999. pap. 24.95 (*1-56691-069-2*, Pub. by Avalon Travel) Publishers Group.
Moon Handbooks: Pennsylvania: Including Pittsburgh, the Poconos, Philadelphia, Gettysburg & the Dutch Country. Joanne Miller. (Illus.). 450p. 1998. pap. 18.95 (*1-56691-110-9*, Moon Handbks) Avalon Travel.
***Moon Handbooks: Philippines.** 3rd rev. ed. Carl Parkes. Vol. 3. (Illus.). 580p. 1999. pap. 18.95 (*1-56691-168-0*, Moon Handbks) Avalon Travel.
***Moon Handbooks: Puerto Vallarta: Including 300 Miles of Coastal Coverage & Sidetrips to Guaderlajara & Lake Chapala.** 3rd rev. ed. Bruce Whipperman. Vol. 3. (Illus.). 340p. 1999. pap. 15.95 (*1-56691-169-9*, Moon Handbks) Avalon Travel.
Moon Handbooks: Santa Fe-Taos: Including Albuquerque. Stephen Metzger. (Illus.). 180p. 1998. pap. 13.95 (*1-56691-135-4*, Moon Handbks) Avalon Travel.
***Moon Handbooks: Silicon Valley: Including San Jose, Sunnyvale, Palo Alto & South Valley.** Martin Cheek. (Illus.). 250p. 2000. pap. 15.95 (*1-56691-196-6*, Moon Handbks) Avalon Travel.
Moon Handbooks: Singapore. Carl Parkes. (Illus.). 360p. 1997. pap. 15.95 (*1-56691-078-1*, Moon Handbks) Avalon Travel.
Moon Handbooks: South Carolina: Including Charleston, Hilton Head, the Blue Ridge & Hell Hole Swamp. Mike Sigalas. (Illus.). 400p. 1999. pap. 16.95 (*1-56691-153-2*, Moon Handbks) Avalon Travel.
Moon Handbooks: South Korea. 2nd ed. Robert Nilsen. (Illus.). 820p. 1997. pap. 19.95 (*1-56691-074-9*, Moon Handbks) Avalon Travel.
Moon Handbooks: Southeast Asia. 3rd rev. ed. Carl Parkes. Vol. 3. (Illus.). 1080p. 1998. pap. 21.95 (*1-56691-127-3*, Moon Handbks) Avalon Travel.
Moon Handbooks: Southern California: Including Greater Los Angeles, Disneyland, San Diego, Death Valley & Other Desert Parks. Kim Weir. 710p. 1998. pap. 19.95 (*1-56691-102-8*, Moon Handbks) Avalon Travel.
***Moon Handbooks: Staying Healthy in Asia, Africa & Latin America: Your Complete Health Guide to Traveling & Living in Less-Developed Regions of the World.** 5th rev. ed. Dirk G. Schroeder. Vol. 5. (Illus.). 230p. 2000. pap. 11.95 (*1-56691-133-8*, Moon Handbks) Avalon Travel.
***Moon Handbooks: Tahiti: Including Easter Island & the Cooks.** 4th rev. ed. David Stanley. (Illus.). 450p. 1999. pap. 15.95 (*1-56691-140-0*, Moon Handbks) Avalon Travel.
***Moon Handbooks: Tennessee: Including Nashville, Memphis, the Great Smoky Mountains & Nutbush.** 2nd rev. ed. Jeff Bradley. Vol. 2. (Illus.). 540p. 1999. pap. 17.95 (*1-56691-147-8*, Moon Handbks) Avalon Travel.
Moon Handbooks: Texas. 4th rev. ed. Joe Cummings. (Illus.). 690p. 1998. pap. 18.95 (*1-56691-112-5*, Moon Handbks) Avalon Travel.
***Moon Handbooks: Toaga Samoa.** David Stanley. (Illus.). 310p. 1999. pap. 15.95 (*1-56691-174-5*, Moon Handbks) Avalon Travel.
Moon Handbooks: Utah. 5th ed. Bill Weir & W. C. McRae. (Illus.). 480p. 1997. pap. 17.95 (*1-56691-087-0*, Moon Handbks) Avalon Travel.
***Moon Handbooks: Vancouver: Including Victoria & Vancouver Island.** Andrew Hempstead. (Illus.). 250p. 2000. pap. 14.95 (*1-56691-198-2*, Moon Handbks) Avalon Travel.
Moon Handbooks: Vietnam, Cambodia & Laos. 2nd rev. ed. Michael Buckley. Vol. 2. (Illus.). 760p. 1998. pap. 18.95 (*1-56691-131-1*, Moon Handbks) Avalon Travel.
Moon Handbooks: Virgin Islands. Karl Luntta. (Illus.). 220p. 1997. pap. 13.95 (*1-56691-093-5*, Moon Handbks) Avalon Travel.
***Moon Handbooks: Virginia: Including Chesapeake Bay, Shenandoah Valley, Blue Ridge Mountains & Washington D. C.** Julian Smith. (Illus.). 410p. 1999. pap. 15.95 (*1-56691-141-9*, Moon Handbks) Avalon Travel.
Moon Handbooks: Washington: Including Seattle, Mount Rainier & Olympic National Park. 6th rev. ed. Don Pitcher. Vol. 6. (Illus.). 840p. 1999. pap. 19.95 (*1-56691-148-6*, Moon Handbks) Avalon Travel.
Moon Handbooks: Wisconsin: Including Door County. Thomas Huhti. (Illus.). 600p. 1997. pap. 18.95 (*1-56691-092-7*, Moon Handbks) Avalon Travel.
***Moon Handbooks: Wyoming: Including Yellowstone & Grand Teton National Parks.** 4th rev. ed. Don Pitcher. (Illus.). 620p. 2000. pap. 17.95 (*1-56691-204-0*, Moon Handbks) Avalon Travel.
***Moon Handbooks: Yellowstone - Grand Teton.** Don Pitcher. (Illus.). 240p. 2000. pap. 14.95 (*1-56691-199-0*, Moon Handbks) Avalon Travel.
Moon Handbooks: Yucatan Peninsula: Including Yucatan, Campeche, Chiapas, Tabasco, Quintana Roo. 6th rev. ed. Chicki Mallan. LC 98-657779. Vol. 6. (Illus.). 400p. 1998. pap. 16.95 (*1-56691-122-2*, Moon Handbks) Avalon Travel.
***Moon Handbooks - Baja: Tijuana to Cabo San Lucas.** 4th rev. ed. Joe Cummings. (Moon Handbks.). (Illus.). 540p. 2000. pap. 17.95 (*1-56691-208-3*, Pub. by Avalon Travel) Publishers Group.

M

An Asterisk (*) at the beginning of an entry indicates that the title is appearing for the first time.

***Moon Handbooks - Cabo: La Paz to Cabo San Lucas.** 3rd rev. ed. Joe Cummings. (Moon Handbks.). (Illus.). 270p. 2000. pap. 14.95 (*1-56691-207-5*, Pub. by Avalon Travel) Publishers Group.

***Moon Handbooks - Cuba.** 2nd rev. ed. Christopher P. Baker. (Moon Handbks.). (Illus.). 790p. 2000. pap. 19.95 (*1-56691-209-1*, Pub. by Avalon Travel) Publishers Group.

***Moon Handbooks - Honduras: Including the Bay Islands & Copan.** 2nd rev. ed. Chris Humphrey. (Moon Handbks.). (Illus.). 330p. 2000. pap. 17.95 (*1-56691-210-5*, Pub. by Avalon Travel) Publishers Group.

***Moon Handbooks - Tahoe: Including Reno & Carson Valley.** 3rd rev. ed. Ken Castle. (Moon Handbks.). (Illus.). 680p. 2000. pap. 19.95 (*1-56691-211-3*, Pub. by Avalon Travel) Publishers Group.

Moon Horns-Razor Door. Gene Detro. LC 81-6493. 72p. 1981. pap. 7.95 (*0-914974-31-9*) Holmgangers.

***Moon Hunter.** Deanna Mascle. (Zebra Splendor Historical Romances Ser.). 288p. 2000. mass mkt. 4.99 (*0-8217-6619-8*, Zebra Kensgtn) Kensgtn Pub Corp.

Moon Illusion. Ed. by Maurice Hershenson. 472p. (C). 1989. text 89.95 (*0-8058-0121-9*) L Erlbaum Assocs.

Moon Illustrated Weekly: Black America's First Weekly Magazine. Paul G. Partington. 1986. pap. 10.00 (*0-9602538-2-3*) P G Partington.

M

Moon in a Baad House, 1 Vol. Willard Gellis. 73p. 1984. pap. 6.00 (*0-917455-00-2*) Big Foot NY.

Moon in a Dewdrop: Writings of Zen Master Dogen. Eihei Dogen. Ed. by Kazuaki Tanahashi. 356p. 1995. 16.00 (*0-374-47186-X*) FS&G.

Moon in a Dewdrop: Writings of Zen Master Dogen. Eihei Dogen. Ed. by Kazuaki Tanahashi. LC 84-62309. 356p. 1995. pap. 16.00 (*0-86547-186-X*) N Point Pr.

Moon in a Mason Jar & What My Father Believed. Robert Wrigley. LC 97-22182. 152p. 1998. 16.95 (*0-252-06672-3*) U of Ill Pr.

Moon in Bear's Eyes. Stephen Swinburne. 32p. (J). (gr. k-3). 1999. pap. write for info. (*0-7613-0991-8*, Copper Beech Bks) Millbrook Pr.

Moon in Bear's Eyes. Stephen R. Swinburne. LC 97-16038. (Illus.). 32p. (J). (gr. 2-4). 1998. 20.40 (*0-7613-0059-7*) Millbrook Pr.

Moon in Each Eye. Charles B. Dickson. (Illus.). 80p. (Orig.). 1993. pap. 7.00 (*0-944676-95-2*) AHA Bks.

Moon in Hand: Journeys into Feminist Mysticism. Eclipse. LC 90-85390. (Illus.). 160p. (Orig.). 1991. pap. 12.95 (*0-9624626-1-6*) Astarte Shell Pr.

Moon in Here Is Brighter Than My Country. Quach Hung. 100p. 1996. pap. text 6.00 (*1-888065-10-9*) New Wrld Poetry.

Moon in My Teacup. Anita Riggio. LC 91-77622. (Illus.). 32p. (J). (ps-3). 1993. lib. bdg. 14.95 (*1-56397-008-2*) Boyds Mills Pr.

Moon in Pisces. large type ed. Catherine Darby. (Ulverscroft Large Print Ser.). 272p. 1998. 29.99 (*0-7089-3937-6*) Ulverscroft.

Moon in the Cloud. Rosemary Harris. (J). (gr. 3-6). 1990. 20.25 (*0-8446-6429-4*) Peter Smith.

***Moon in the Gutter.** David Goodis. (Midnight Classics Ser.). 183p. 1999. pap. 11.95 (*1-85242-449-4*) Serpents Tail.

***Moon in the Pines: Zen Haiku Poetry.** Jonathan Clements. 2000. 19.95 (*0-670-89229-7*, Viking) Viking Penguin.

Moon in the Post-Apollo Era. Zdenek Kopal. LC 74-26877. (Geophysics & Astrophysics Monographs: No.7). 224p. 1974. pap. text 88.00 (*90-277-0278-0*); lib. bdg. 100.50 (*90-277-0277-2*) Kluwer Academic.

Moon in the Water: Understanding Tanizaki, Kawabata, & Mishima. Gwenn B. Petersen. LC 79-14994. 380p. (C). 1992. reprint ed. pap. text 20.00 (*0-8248-1476-2*) UH Pr.

Moon in the Well: And Other Macedonian Folk Tales. Tr. by Danica Cvetanovska et al. (Illus.). 84p. 1990. 7.95 (*0-912678-74-7*) Greenfld Rev Lit.

Moon in Your Life. Arlene Robertson. LC 84-71623. 245p. 1986. 19.95 (*0-86690-283-X*, R2604-014) Am Fed Astrologers.

Moon in Your Life: Being a Lunar Type in a Solar World. Donna Cunningham. LC 95-52002. Orig. Title: Being a Lunar Type in a Solar World. (Illus.). 384p. 1996. reprint ed. pap. 15.95 (*0-87728-837-2*) Weiser.

Moon in Your Lunch Box. Michael Spooner. (Illus.). 64p. (J). (gr. 2-6). 1995. pap. 4.95 (*0-8050-3545-1*) H Holt & Co.

***Moon Inside.** Ruth Daigon. (Contemporary Poetry Ser.: Vol. 1). 96p. 1999. pap. 11.95 (*0-9667228-3-3*) Newtons Baby.

Moon Is a Harsh Mistress. Robert A. Heinlein. 384p. 1997. pap. 14.95 (*0-312-86355-1*) St Martin.

Moon Is Always Female. Marge Piercy. LC 79-21866. 133p. 1980. pap. 15.00 (*0-394-73859-4*) Knopf.

Moon Is Blue see Best American Plays: Third Series, 1945-51

Moon Is Blue. F. Hugh Herbert. 1953. pap. 5.25 (*0-8222-0773-7*) Dramatists Play.

***Moon Is Bread.** Naomi Samuel. LC 96-35366. Orig. Title: Hajarach Hu Lechem. (Illus.). 150p. 1999. 14.95 (*965-229-212-5*) Gefen Bks.

Moon Is Broken. Eleanor Craig. 1999. pap. 9.00 (*0-452-26990-3*, Plume) Dutton Plume.

Moon Is Dead! Give Us Our Money! The Cultural Origins of an African Work Ethic, Natal, South Africa, 1843-1900. Keletso E. Atkins. LC 92-41611. 190p. (C). 1994. pap. 22.95 (*0-435-08078-4*, 08078) Heinemann.

Moon Is Down. John Steinbeck. 1942. pap. 5.25 (*0-8222-1599-3*) Dramatists Play.

Moon is Down. John Steinbeck. LC 95-14803. (Penguin Great Books of the 20th Century Ser.). 112p. 1995. pap. 10.95 (*0-14-018746-4*, Penguin Bks) Viking Penguin.

***Moon Is Down.** large type ed. John Steinbeck. (G. K. Hall Perennial Bestsellers Ser.). 2000. 28.95 (*0-7838-8965-8*, G K Hall Lrg Type) Mac Lib Ref.

Moon Is Hell! John W. Campbell, Jr. 256p. 1990. mass mkt. 3.95 (*0-88184-674-0*) Carroll & Graf.

Moon Is My Confessor. George H. Clowers. ii, 70p. 1999. pap. 9.40 (*0-9669871-0-1*) Clowers.

Moon Is Red. Sax Rohmer, pseud. 1976. 12.50 (*0-685-80029-6*) Bookfinger.

Moon Is Shining Bright As Day. Ed. by Ogden Nash. LC 53-7143. (Illus.). 192p. (YA). (gr. 7 up). 1953. 12.95 (*0-397-30244-4*) HarpC Child Bks.

Moon Island. large type ed. Kay Winchester. 1991. 27.99 (*0-7089-2399-2*) Ulverscroft.

Moon Journals: Writing, Art & Inquiry Through Focused Nature Study. Joni Chancer & Gina Rester-Zodrow. LC 96-50400. 211p. 1997. pap. text 32.50 (*0-435-07221-8*, 07221) Heinemann.

Moon Jumpers. Janice M. Udry. (Illus.). 32p. (J). (gr. k-2). 1959. 15.00 (*0-06-026145-5*) HarpC Child Bks.

Moon Jumpers. Janice M. Udry. (Illus.). 32p. (J). (ps-1). 1999. lib. bdg. 14.89 (*0-06-028461-7*) HarpC Child Bks.

Moon Jumpers. Janice M. Udry. (J). Date not set. write for info. (*0-06-443583-0*) HarpC Child Bks.

Moon Jumpers. Janice M. Udry. (Illus.). 32p. (J). (ps-1). 2000. 14.95 (*0-06-028460-9*) HarpC Child Bks.

Moon-Kissed Promises. Sylvie F. Sommerfield. 480p. 1993. mass mkt. 4.99 (*1-55817-709-4*, Pinncle Kensgtn) Kensgtn Pub Corp.

Moon Lady. Amy Tan. LC 91-22321. (Illus.). 32p. (J). (gr. 1 up). 1995. mass mkt. 5.95 (*0-689-80616-7*) Aladdin.

Moon Lady. Amy Tan. (J). 1998. pap. 5.95 (*0-87628-573-6*) Ctr Appl Res.

Moon Lady. Amy Tan. LC 91-22321. (Illus.). 32p. (J). (gr. 1 up). 1992. lib. bdg. 16.95 (*0-02-788830-4*, Mac Bks Young Read) S&S Childrens.

Moon Lady. Amy Tan. 1995. 11.15 (*0-606-07886-X*) Turtleback.

Moon Lady's Lover. Vanessa Grant. (Romance Ser.: Vol. 398). 1998. mass mkt. 3.50 (*0-373-17398-9*, 1-17398-8) Harlequin Bks.

Moon Lake see Pierres de Lune

Moon Lake see Pietra di Luna

Moon Lake. Ivan Gantschev. (J). (ps-3). 1991. pap. 14.95 (*0-907234-08-9*, Picture Book Studio) S&S Childrens.

Moon Lake. Tony Muskas. (Illus.). 115p. (Orig.). 1994. pap. 4.75 (*1-884295-05-3*) Ananta Prnting.

Moon Lake. Ivan Gantschev. (Illus.). 28p. (J). (gr. k-3). 1993. reprint ed. pap. 4.95 (*0-88708-304-8*, Picture Book Studio) S&S Childrens.

***Moon Landing.** Kindersley Publishing Dorling. 1999. pap. 6.95 (*0-7894-4876-9*) DK Pub Inc.

Moon Landings. DK Publishing Staff. LC 99-11937. (DK Discoveries Series). 1999. 14.95 (*0-7894-3958-1*) DK Pub Inc.

Moon Life 2069. Nancy Henderson. 90p. (Orig.). (YA). (gr. 7-11). 1999. pap. 6.99 (*1-57532-126-2*) Press-Tige Pub.

Moon-Light of Logic: Studies in Laugaksi Bhaskara's Tarka-Kaumudi. P. I. Gradinarov. (C). 1991. text 8.75 (*81-202-0276-7*, Pub. by Ajanta) S Asia.

Moon Looked Down & Laughed. M. Coney & Paul Holden. pap. 9.95 (*1-56097-263-7*, Pub. by Fantagraph Bks) Seven Hills Bk.

Moon Lord. Terri Lynn Wilhelm. 1999. mass mkt. 3.99 (*0-451-19896-4*) Signet.

***Moon Lore: Kabbalistic Writings on the Fall & Rise of Shekhina.** Susan Schneider. 2001. write for info. (*0-7657-6148-3*) Aronson.

Moon Lore: Myths & Folklore from Around the World. Gwydion O'Hara. LC 95-51456. (Illus.). 216p. 1999. pap. 9.95 (*1-56718-342-5*) Llewellyn Pubns.

Moon Lore & Moon Magic. Al G. Manning. 1980. 14.95 (*0-13-600668-X*) Pan Ishtar.

Moon Madness & Other Effects of the Full Moon. Paul Katzeff. 1988. pap. 7.95 (*0-8065-1089-7*, Citadel Pr) Carol Pub Group.

Moon Magic. Dion Fortune. (Orig.). 1990. pap. 8.95 (*0-85030-814-3*, Pub. by Aqrn Pr) Harper SF.

Moon Magic. Dion Fortune. LC 83-185917. 241p. (Orig.). 1979. reprint ed. pap. 12.95 (*0-87728-423-7*, Pub. by Weiser) ACCESS Pubs Network.

Moon Magic: Stories from Asia. Katherine Davison. LC 92-44504. (Middle-Grade Fiction Ser.). (Illus.). 48p. (J). (gr. 2-5). 1993. lib. bdg. 19.95 (*0-87614-751-1*, Carolrhoda) Lerner Pub.

Moon Magic Journal: Blank Journal with Lunar Dates & Explanations. 172p. (Orig.). 1996. pap. 8.95 (*0-9632970-5-8*) Doorway.

Moon Magick: Myth & Magic, Crafts & Recipes, Rituals & Spells. D. J. Conway. LC 95-18474. (Illus.). 320p. 1995. pap. 16.95 (*1-56718-167-8*) Llewellyn Pubns.

Moon Maid & Other Fantastic Adventures. R. Garcia y Robertson. LC 97-73940. 275p. 1998. 22.95 (*0-9655901-8-6*) Golden Gryphon.

Moon Maiden & Other Asian Folktales. Hua Long. (Illus.). 32p. (J). 1993. 12.95 (*0-8351-2494-0*); pap. 8.95 (*0-8351-2493-2*) China Bks.

Moon Man. Gerda M. Scheidl. Tr. by J. Alison James. LC 93-39759. (Illus.). 32p. (J). (gr. k-3). 1997. pap. 6.95 (*1-55858-695-4*, Pub. by North-South Bks NYC) Chronicle Bks.

Moon Man. Tomi Ungerer. LC 97-48697. (Illus.). 40p. (J). 1998. pap. text 6.95 (*1-57098-207-4*) Roberts Rinehart.

***Moon Man & Other Stories.** Tomi Ungerer. (gr. k). 1999. 9.95 (*1-57098-293-7*, TomiCo) Roberts Rinehart.

Moon Man (El Hombre de la Luna) Tomi Ungerer. (SPA.). (J). 7.95 (*84-204-3746-8*) Santillana.

Moon Mansions. Mohan Kopakar. (Illus.). 128p. 1974. pap. 6.95 (*0-918922-01-1*) Mohan Ents.

Moon Marked & Touched by Sun: Plays by African-American Women. Intro. by Sydne Mahone. LC 93-11831. 448p. 1994. reprint ed. pap. 15.95 (*1-55936-065-8*) Theatre Comm.

Moon, Meteorites & Comets. Ed. by Gerard P. Kuiper & Barbara M. Middlehurst. LC 62-18117. (Solar System Ser.: Vol. 4). 1993. lib. bdg. 60.00 (*0-226-45928-4*) U Ch Pr.

Moon Mirror. Ed. by Andre Norton. 1989. pap. 4.99 (*0-8125-0303-1*, Pub. by Tor Bks) St Martin.

Moon Missions: Mankind's First Voyages to Another World. William F. Mellberg. LC 98-114035. (Illus.). 198p. (Orig.). 1997. pap. 19.95 (*1-882663-12-8*) Plymouth VT.

Moon-Months & Sun-Days. Miriam Schlein. pap. 5.00 (*0-201-09292-1*) Addison-Wesley.

Moon, Moon, Tell Me True. Ellen Tifft. LC 96-24858. (Illus.). 212p. 1996. pap. 13.00 (*1-879378-25-6*) Xenos Riverside.

Moon Morphology: Interpretations Based on Lunar Orbiter Photography. Peter H. Schultz. LC 74-22176. (Illus.). 644p. 1976. 75.00 (*0-292-75036-6*) U of Tex Pr.

Moon Music. Faye Kellerman. 512p. 1999. mass mkt. 7.50 (*0-380-72626-2*, Avon Bks) Morrow Avon.

Moon Music. large type ed. Faye Kellerman. LC 98-39409. (Large Print Bks.). 621p. 1998. 26.95 (*1-56895-672-X*) Wheeler Pub.

Moon Mysteries. Jan Brodie. (Orig.). 1997. pap. 21.95 (*1-898307-81-4*, Pub. by Capall Bann Pubng) Holmes Pub.

Moon-Node Astrology. Bruno Huber & Louise Huber. LC 95-4320. (Illus.). 256p. (Orig.). 1995. pap. 14.95 (*0-87728-784-8*) Weiser.

Moon of Cobre. William R. Cox. 224p. 1989. pap. 2.95 (*0-380-70832-9*, Avon Bks) Morrow Avon.

Moon of Desire. Sophie Danson. (Black Lace Ser.). 1995. mass mkt. 5.95 (*0-352-32911-4*, Pub. by Virgin Bks) London Brdge.

Moon of Gomrath: A Tale of Alderley. Alan Garner. LC 97-32518. 208p. (J). (gr. 4-7). 1998. pap. 6.00 (*0-15-201796-8*) Harcourt.

Moon of Hunger. Ian McCulloch. 48p. 1982. 5.95 (*0-920806-33-3*, Pub. by Penumbra Pr) U of Toronto Pr.

Moon of Ice. Brad Linaweaver. 288p. 1993. mass mkt. 4.99 (*0-8125-2020-3*) Tor Bks.

Moon of Isis. Jack Little. LC 76-8728. (J). (gr. 5 up). 1976. pap. 5.00 (*0-934768-00-5*) Altair Pr.

Moon of Popping Trees. Rex A. Smith. LC 80-24863. (Illus.). xviii, 219p. 1981. pap. 9.95 (*0-8032-9120-5*, Bison Books) U of Nebr Pr.

***Moon of Reflection.** Adams. 88p. 2000. pap. 12.95 (*1-882897-43-9*) Lost Coast.

Moon of the Big-Dog. Jay Leech & Zane Spencer. LC 79-7893. (Illus.). 64p. (J). (gr. 2-6). 1980. 6.95 (*0-690-04001-6*) HarpC Child Bks.

Moon of the Caribbees see Famous American Plays of the Nineteen Twenties

Moon of the Falling Leaves. Virginia B. Weddle. LC 93-94333. 125p. 1994. per. write for info. (*0-9640352-0-0*) V B Weddle.

Moon of the Gray Wolves. Jean Craighead George. LC 90-38166. (Thirteen Moons Ser.). (Illus.). 48p. (J). (gr. 3-7). 1991. 15.00 (*0-06-022442-8*) HarpC Child Bks.

Moon of the Monarch Butterflies. Jean Craighead George. LC 91-33152. (Thirteen Moons Ser.). (Illus.). 48p. (J). (gr. 3-7). 1993. 15.00 (*0-06-020816-3*); lib. bdg. 14.89 (*0-06-020817-1*) HarpC Child Bks.

Moon of the Owls. Jean Craighead George. LC 91-2735. (Thirteen Moons Ser.). (Illus.). 48p. (J). (gr. 3-7). 1993. 15.00 (*0-06-020192-4*); lib. bdg. 14.89 (*0-06-020193-2*) HarpC Child Bks.

Moon of the Salamanders. Jean Craighead George. LC 90-25591. (Thirteen Moons Ser.). (Illus.). 48p. (J). (gr. 3-7). 1992. lib. bdg. 14.89 (*0-06-022694-3*) HarpC Child Bks.

Moon of the 2 Dark Horses. Sally M. Keehn. 224p. (J). (gr. 5-12). 1997. pap. 3.99 (*0-440-41287-0*) Dell.

Moon of Thunder. Don Coldsmith. LC 84-13516. 1985. 11.95 (*0-385-18923-0*) Doubleday.

Moon of 2 Dark Horses. Sally Keehn. LC 94-33951. 224p. (J). (gr. 5-9). 1995. 16.95 (*0-399-22783-0*, Philomel) Peng Put Young Read.

Moon of Two Dark Horses. Sally M. Keehn. (YA). 1997. 9.09 (*0-606-11637-0*, Pub. by Turtleback) Demco.

Moon of Wintertime: Missionaries & Indians of Canada in Encounter since 1534. John W. Grant. 384p. 1984. pap. text 19.95 (*0-8020-6541-4*) U of Toronto Pr.

Moon of Wintertime: Missionaries & the Indians of Canada in Encounter since 1534. John W. Grant. LC 84-217823. (Illus.). 335p. reprint ed. pap. 103.90 (*0-8357-8234-4*, 203402800088) Bks Demand.

***Moon Oracle.** Smith. (Illus.). 128p. 2000. pap. 24.95 (*0-312-24172-0*) St Martin.

Moon over Broadway. Mark Hellinger. LC 71-37271. (Short Story Index Reprint Ser.). 1977. reprint ed. 19.95 (*0-8369-4082-2*) Ayer.

Moon over Crete. Jyotsna Sreenivasan. (Illus.). 128p. (Orig.). (J). (gr. 3-7). 1996. reprint ed. pap. 6.95 (*0-9619401-6-6*) Smooth Stone Pr.

Moon over Minneapolis. Fay Weldon. 1999. pap. 19.95 (*0-670-83646-X*) Viking Penguin.

Moon over Mitosis: E=Tc Squared. Matt Pollard. (Illus.). 80p. 1999. 4.95 (*1-893859-08-8*) Thumb Cinema.

Moon over Moonachie. rev. ed. Timothy Fernandez, Sr. 48p. 1994. pap. 4.95 (*0-685-72004-7*) Evanston Pub.

Moon over Tennessee: A Boy's Civil War Journal. Craig Crist-Evans. LC 98-11912. (Illus.). 64p. (YA). (gr. 3 up). 1999. 15.00 (*0-395-91208-3*) HM.

Moon over the Brewery. Bruce Graham. 1990. pap. 5.25 (*0-8222-0774-5*) Dramatists Play.

Moon over Water. Debbie Macomber. (Mira Bks.). 1998. 21.95 (*1-55166-319-8*, 1-66319-4, Mira Bks) Harlequin Bks.

***Moon over Water.** Debbie Macomber. 378p. 1999. mass mkt. 6.99 (*1-55166-533-6*, 1-66533-0, Mira Bks) Harlequin Bks.

Moon Palace. Paul Auster. 320p. 1990. pap. 12.95 (*0-14-011585-4*, Penguin Bks) Viking Penguin.

***Moon Pearl.** Ruthanne Lum McCunn. LC 00-8738. 336p. 2000. 24.00 (*0-8070-8348-8*) Beacon Pr.

***Moon People.** Melinda Lilly & Charles Reasoner. LC 99-12099. 1999. write for info. (*1-57103-265-7*) Rourke Pr.

Moon People. Sondra Shulman. LC 93-48954. 353p. 1994. 20.00 (*1-880909-18-9*) Baskerville.

Moon Phases: A Symbolic Key to Self Discovery. Martin Goldsmith. Ed. by Skye Alexander. LC 88-50421. (Illus.). 252p. 1988. pap. 16.95 (*0-914918-83-4*, Whitford) Schiffer.

Moon Pie at Britton Hill. Harriet Ziefert. 1924. write for info. (*0-688-17424-8*, Wm Morrow) Morrow Avon.

***Moon Pool.** A. Merritt. (Bison Frontiers of Imagination Ser.). 254p. 2001. pap. 10.95 (*0-8032-8268-0*, Bison Books) U of Nebr Pr.

Moon Pool. Abraham Merritt. 448p. 1993. pap. 4.95 (*0-88184-891-3*) Carroll & Graf.

Moon Pool. A. Merrit. 1993. reprint ed. lib. bdg. 18.95 (*0-89968-408-4*, Lghtyr Pr) Buccaneer Bks.

Moon Power Starguide, 1999. Nancy Mepton. (Moon Power Ser.: Vol. 5). 314p. 1999. pap. 19.95 (*0-9667312-0-4*) Startheme Pubns.

Moon Princess. Ralph F. McCarthy. LC 93-18300. (Children's Classics Ser.: Vol. 2). (Illus.). 48p. (J). 1993. 19.95 (*4-7700-1756-1*) Kodansha.

***Moon Princess.** Ralph F. McCarthy. 2000. 10.00 (*4-7700-2099-6*) Kodansha Intl.

Moon Quest. Anson Montgomery. (Choose Your Own Adventure Ser.: No. 167). (Illus.). 128p. (J). (gr. 4-7). 1995. pap. 3.50 (*0-553-56621-0*, Choose) BDD Bks Young Read.

Moon Quest. Anson Montgomery. (Choose Your Own Adventure Ser.: No. 167). (J). (gr. 4-8). 1996. 8.60 (*0-606-08572-6*, Pub. by Turtleback) Demco.

***Moon Quilt.** Sunny Warner. LC 00-32007. (Illus.). (J). 2001. write for info. (*0-618-05583-5*) HM.

Moon Rabbit Review Vol. 1, No. 2: Asian Pacific American Voices. Ed. by Mary Lee & Eileen Tabios. (Illus.). v, 144p. 1996. pap. write for info. (*1-889572-00-4*) MoonRabbit Review.

Moon Reflected Fire. Doug Anderson. LC 94-26156. 80p. 1994. pap. 9.95 (*1-882295-03-X*) Alice James Bks.

Moon, Resources, Future Development & Colonization. David G. Schrunk et al. LC 97-14895. (Wiley-Praxis Series in Space Science & Technology). 466p. 1999. 64.95 (*0-471-97635-0*) Wiley.

***Moon Ride.** Harriet Ziefert. LC 99-13458. (Illus.). 32p. (J). (ps-3). 2000. 15.00 (*0-618-00229-4*) HM.

Moon Robber. Dean Morrissey. mass mkt. 5.95 (*0-06-442113-9*) HarpC.

Moon Robber. Dean Morrissey. Date not set. lib. bdg. 15.89 (*0-06-028582-6*) HarpC Child Bks.

Moon Robber. Dean Morrissey. (J). Date not set. 15.95 (*0-06-028581-8*) HarpC Child Bks.

Moon Rock Heist. Betty Harman & Nancy Meador. LC 88-16274. 112p. (J). (gr. 6-7). 1988. 9.95 (*0-89015-667-0*) Sunbelt Media.

***Moon Rocks & Dinosaur Bones.** Nancy I. Sanders. (Parables in Action Ser.: Vol. 4). (Illus.). 48p. (J). (ps-2). 2000. pap. text 4.99 (*0-570-07015-5*) Concordia.

Moon Rope. Lois Ehlert. (J). 1996. 14.95 (*0-15-201616-3*, Harcourt Child Bks) Harcourt.

Moon Rope: Un Lazo a la Luna. abr. ed. Lois Ehlert. LC 91-36438. (SPA., Illus.). 32p. (J). (ps-3). 1992. 17.00 (*0-15-255343-6*, Harcourt Child Bks) Harcourt.

Moon Sandwich Mom. Jennifer R. Jacobson. LC 98-36352. (Illus.). 24p. (J). (ps-1). 1999. lib. bdg. 14.95 (*0-8075-4071-4*) A Whitman.

Moon Seems to Change. rev. ed. Franklyn M. Branley. LC 86-27097. (Trophy Let's-Read-&-Find-Out Bk.). (Illus.). 32p. (J). (ps-3). 1987. pap. 4.95 (*0-06-445065-1*, HarpTrophy) HarpC Child Bks.

Moon Shadow. Joe Barfield. 220p. Date not set. pap. 9.95 (*1-884797-02-4*) Moran Pub.

Moon Shadow. Julia Wild. 400p. 1999. text 19.95 (*1-85487-549-3*, Pub. by Scarlet Bks) London Brdge.

Moon Shadows. Nann Edler. 26p. (Orig.). 1993. text. write for info. (*0-9635547-0-0*) Patturns.

Moon Shining the Millennium. Kerry S. Keys. 36p. 1997. pap. 10.00 (*0-930502-33-7*) Pine Pr.

Moon Shots. Ed. by Peter Crowther. 320p. 1999. mass mkt. 6.99 (*0-88677-848-4*, Pub. by DAW Bks) Penguin Putnam.

***Moon Signs: Picking the Right Time for Everything You Want to Do.** Sabine Heideweg. LC 99-20315. 160p. 1999. pap. text 12.95 (*0-8069-1897-7*) Sterling.

Moon Signs: The Key to Your Inner Life. Donna Cunningham. 1989. mass mkt. 0.05 (*0-345-34724-2*) Ballantine Pub Grp.

Moon Sisters, Krishna Mothers, Rajneesh Lovers: Women's Roles in New Religions. Susan J. Palmer. LC 94-17364. (Women & Gender in North American Religion Ser.). (Illus.). 208p. 1994. 45.00 (*0-8156-0297-9*) Syracuse U Pr.

Moon Sisters, Krishna Mothers, Rajneesh Lovers: Women's Roles in New Religions. Susan J. Palmer. (Women & Gender in North American Religions Ser.). (Illus.). 264p. (C). 1996. pap. 19.95 (*0-8156-0382-7*, PAMSP) Syracuse U Pr.

Moon Song. Byrd Baylor. LC 81-18427. (Illus.). 24p. (J). (gr. 3-6). 1982. lib. bdg. 13.95 (*0-684-17463-4*) Scribner.

Moon Soup. Lisa Desimini. LC 92-55041. (Illus.). 32p. (J). (ps-3). 1993. 14.95 (*1-56282-463-5*, Pub. by Hyprn Child); lib. bdg. 14.89 (*1-56282-464-3*, Pub. by Hyprn Child) Little.

Moon Struck: Hunting Strategies That Revolve Around the Moon. Jeff Murray. 174p. 1996. pap. text 14.95 (*0-9646823-0-3*) Fool Moon Pr.

Moon, Sun & Witches: Gender Ideologies & Class in Inca & Colonial Peru. Irene Silverblatt. (Illus.). 305p. 1987. pap. text 17.95 (*0-691-02258-5*, Pub. by Princeton U Pr) Cal Prin Full Svc.

Moon, the Grass & Us. Joe DiMattio. LC 94-66847. 64p. 1994. pap. text 12.00 (*0-9641891-0-0*) Chelsea Lit.

Moon Tides of Brewster. Robert W. Sproul. 56p. 1993. pap. 9.00 (*0-9639642-0-8*) R W Sproul.

Moon Tiger. Penelope Lively. 224p. 1997. pap. 12.00 (*0-8021-3533-1*, Grove) Grove-Atltic.

Moon Tiger. Phyllis Root. LC 85-7572. (Illus.). 32p. (J). (ps-2). 1995. 14.95 (*0-8050-0896-9*, Bks Young Read); pap. 4.95 (*0-8050-0803-9*, Bks Young Read) H Holt & Co.

Moon Time: The Art of Harmony with Nature & Lunar Cycles. Johanna Paungger & Thomas Poppe. (Illus.). 187p. 1995. pap. 19.95 (*0-85207-284-8*, Pub. by C W Daniel) Natl Bk Netwk.

Moon Time: The Art of Harmony with Nature & Lunar Cycles. Johanna Paunnger. pap. 23.95 (*0-8464-4881-5*) Beekman Pubs.

Moon to Sun: An Adding Book. Sheila W. Samton. LC 90-85729. (Illus.). 24p. (J). (ps-1). 1991. 9.95 (*1-878093-13-4*) Boyds Mills Pr.

Moon Trouble. M. C. Helldorfer. LC 92-22233. (Illus.). 40p. (J). 1994. mass mkt. 15.95 (*0-02-743517-2*, Mac Bks Young Read) S&S Childrens.

Moon under Her Feet. Clysta Kinstler. LC 88-45670. 336p. 1991. reprint ed. pap. 14.00 (*0-06-250497-5*, Pub. by Harper SF) HarpC.

Moon ups & the Sun Downs. J. Davis Mannino. (Illus.). 150p. (C). 1995. 20.00 (*0-9647388-0-5*) Teddy-Bear Pub.

Moon Veils Vulcan & the Sun Veils Neptune. Kurt Abraham. LC 89-84728. 114p. (Orig.). 1989. pap. 10.50 (*0-9609002-4-1*) Lampus Pr.

Moon-Wales & Other Moon Poems. Ted Hughes. LC 76-6168. (Illus.). 86p. 1976. 15.00 (*0-670-48864-X*) Ultramarine Pub.

Moon Walk, 1835: Was Neil Armstrong Really the First Man on the Moon? 5th ed. Richard A. Locke. Ed. by Calvert W. Tazewell. LC 90-81467. (Illus.). 80p. 1990. pap. 10.00 (*1-878515-34-9*) W S Dawson.

Moon Was at a Fiesta see Luna se Fue de Fiesta

Moon Was at a Fiesta. rev. ed. Matthew Gollub. Tr. by Martin L. Guzman. LC 97-90856. (Illus.). 32p. (J). (gr. k-6). 1997. 15.95 (*1-889910-11-2*) Tortuga Pr.

Moon Was the Best. Charlotte Zolotow. LC 91-47748. (Illus.). 32p. (J). (ps-3). 1993. 15.00 (*0-688-09940-8*, Grenwillow Bks) HarpC Child Bks.

Moon Watch. Vickie York. 1994. mass mkt. 2.99 (*0-373-22279-3*, 1-22279-3) Harlequin Bks.

Moon Wife. Windling. 2000. text 22.95 (*0-312-85989-9*) St Martin.

Moon Wife. Windling. 1996. mass mkt. write for info. (*0-8125-4930-9*) Tor Bks.

Moon Will Forever Be a Distant Love. Luis H. Crosthwaite. Tr. by Debbie Nathan & Willivaldo Delgadillo. LC 97-26920.Tr. of La Luna Siempre Sera Un Dificil Amor. 160p. 1997. pap. 12.95 (*0-938317-31-8*) Cinco Puntos.

Moon Window. Jane L. Curry. LC 95-52558. 170p. (J). (gr. 4-7). 1996. 16.00 (*0-689-80945-X*) S&S Bks Yung.

***Moon Wisdom: A Guide For Life.** Sally Morningstar. 64p. 2000. pap. 6.95 (*1-84215-125-8*) Anness Pub.

***Moon Wise: Astrology, Self Understanding & Lunar Energies.** Daniel Pharr. 2000. pap. 12.95 (*1-56718-521-5*) Llewellyn Pubns.

Moon Worship: Ancient & Modern. Gerald Massey. 1990. pap. 6.95 (*1-55818-136-9*) Holmes Pub.

Moonball. Jane Yolen. LC 96-44368. 40p. (J). (gr. 2-6). 1999. 16.00 (*0-689-81095-4*) S&S Childrens.

Moonbase One. Raymond F. Jones. LC 71-160108. 144 p. (J). 1971. write for info. (*0-200-71853-3*) Criterion Bks.

Moonbather. large type ed. Roy Clarke. 307p. 1989. 27.99 (*0-7089-1926-X*) Ulverscroft.

***Moonbathers.** D. Lawrenson. 330p. 1998. 27.00 (*0-434-00462-6*, Pub. by Random) Trafalgar.

***Moonbathers.** D. Lawrenson. 330p. 1998. pap. 11.95 (*0-7493-2434-1*, Pub. by Random) Trafalgar.

Moonbay: Short Stories by Ty Pak. Ty Pak. LC 98-94005. 214p. 1999. pap. 12.00 (*0-9667458-1-7*) Woodhouse.

Moonbeam: A Book of Meditations for Children. Maureen Garth. 112p. 1993. pap. 12.00 (*1-86371-142-2*, Pub. by Harper SF) HarpC.

***Moonbeam Cow.** Sharma Krauskopf. (Books for Young Learners). (Illus.). 16p. (J). (gr. k-2). 1999. pap. text 5.00 (*1-57274-271-2*, A2756) R Owen Pubs.

Moonbeam on a Cat's Ear. unabridged ed. Marie-Louise Gay. (Illus.). 32p. (J). (gr. k up). 1986. 11.95 (*0-7737-2053-7*) STDK.

Moonbeam on a Cat's Ear. 2nd unabridged ed. Marie-Louise Gay. (Illus.). 32p. (J). (gr. k up). 1986. pap. 5.95 (*0-7736-7365-2*) STDK.

***Moonbeams: A Hadassah Rosh Hodesh Guide.** Ed. by Carol Diament. 2000. pap. 20.00 (*1-58023-099-7*) Jewish Lights.

***Moonbeams: A Hadassah Rosh Hodesh Guide.** Leora Tanenbaum et al. Ed. by Carol Diament. 2000. pap., student ed. 20.00 (*1-889525-09-X*) WZO.

Moonbeams & Magic. Janelle Taylor. 1995. mass mkt. 5.99 (*0-7860-0184-4*, Pinncle Kensgtn) Kensgtn Pub Corp.

Moonbeams & Mutton. Edna Giles-Tolley. (Orig.). 1997. pap. write for info. (*1-57553-533-5*) Watermrk Pr.

Moonbeams & Starlight. Patricia E. Duncan. 1990. write for info. (*0-9626313-0-2*) Leprechauns Unltd.

Moonbeams Aplenty. Mary L. Baxter. LC 96-533. (Western Lovers Ser.). 248p. 1995. per. 3.99 (*0-373-88519-9*, 1-88519-3) Harlequin Bks.

***Moonbeam's Big Splash.** Jill Dow. (Windy Edge Farm Ser.). (Illus.). 32p. (J). 1999. pap. text 7.99 (*0-7112-1028-4*) F Lincoln.

Moonbeams Come at Dark Times: Turning 50 in the '90s. Susan White-Bowden. LC 92-73517. 250p. (Orig.). 1992. pap. 9.95 (*0-9633762-0-9*) White-Bowden Assocs.

***Moonbeam's Courage: Includes Toy.** Skye von Zennenfels. (Pixie Tales of the Mystical Forest Ser.). (Illus.). v, 23p. (J). (ps-6). 2000. pap. 14.99 (*0-9678580-2-X*, MY9004, IPI Toys) Interstellar Prod.

***Moonbeams on Water.** Anne Demarest. 1999. mass mkt. 2.50 (*0-7390-0306-2*, 18540) Alfred Pub.

Moonbear Book & Bear. Frank Asch. (Moonbear Ser.). (Illus.). (J). (ps-k). 1994. 16.95 (*0-671-89555-9*) Litle Simon.

***Moonbear's Bargain.** Frank Asch. (Moonbear Ser.). (J). (gr. k-3). 2000. per. 5.99 (*0-689-83516-7*) Aladdin.

Moonbear's Books. Frank Asch. (Moonbear Ser.). (Illus.). 14p. (J). (ps-k). 1993. 3.95 (*0-671-86744-X*) Litle Simon.

Moonbear's Canoe. Frank Asch. LC 94-160067. (Moonbear Ser.). (Illus.). 14p. (J). (ps-k). 1993. pap. 3.95 (*0-671-86745-8*) Litle Simon.

Moonbear's Dream. Frank Asch. LC 98-24133. (Moonbear Ser.). (Illus.). 32p. (J). (ps-k). 1999. per. 15.00 (*0-689-82244-8*) S&S Bks Yung.

Moonbear's Friend. Frank Asch. LC 94-127052. (Moonbear Ser.). (Illus.). 14p. (J). (ps-k). 1993. pap. 3.95 (*0-671-86746-6*) Litle Simon.

***Moonbear's Pet.** Frank Asch. (Moonbear Ser.). (J). (gr. k-3). 2000. per. 5.99 (*0-689-83580-9*) Aladdin.

Moonbear's Pet. Frank Asch. (Moonbear Ser.). (J). (ps-k). 1997. 15.00 (*0-614-29069-4*) S&S Childrens.

Moonbear's Pet. Frank Asch. LC 95-30011. (Moonbear Ser.). (Illus.). 32p. (J). (ps-k). 1997. 15.00 (*0-689-80794-5*) S&S Childrens.

Moonbear's Pet. Frank Asch. LC 95-30011. (Moonbear Ser.). (Illus.). 32p. (J). (ps-1). 2000. per. 4.99 (*0-689-82094-1*) S&S Childrens.

***Moonbear's Shadow.** Frank Asch. (Moonbear Ser.). (J). (ps-k). 2000. per. 5.99 (*0-689-83519-1*) Aladdin.

***Moonbear's Skyfire.** Frank Asch. (Moonbear Ser.). (J). (ps-k). 2000. per. 5.99 (*0-689-83545-0*) Aladdin.

Moonbird. Robin Stewart. (Storybridge Ser.). (Illus.). 80p. (J). (gr. 3-7). 1995. pap. 9.95 (*0-7022-2695-5*, Pub. by Univ Queensland Pr) Intl Spec Bk.

Moonblight & Six Feet of Romance. Daniel C. Beard. LC 74-22767. (Labor Movement in Fiction & Non-Fiction Ser.). (Illus.). 1976. reprint ed. 41.50 (*0-404-58405-5*) AMS Pr.

Moonbog. Rick Hautala. 1982. mass mkt. 2.95 (*0-8217-1087-7*, Zebra Kensgtn) Kensgtn Pub Corp.

Moonbog. Rick Hautala. 1986. pap. 4.95 (*0-8217-3356-7*) NAL.

Moonboy. Carolyn Garcia. LC 98-41584. (Illus.). 32p. (J). (gr. 1-4). 1999. 15.95 (*1-885223-81-1*) Beyond Words Pub.

Moonburnt. Roy Williamson. 79p. (Orig.). 1994. pap. 10.00 (*0-9641853-0-X*) Handshake Edits.

***Mooncake.** Frank Asch. (Moonbear Ser.). (J). (gr. k-3). 2000. per. 5.99 (*0-689-83517-5*) Aladdin.

Mooncake. Frank Asch. (Moonbear Ser.). (Illus.). 32p. (J). (ps-k). 1986. pap. 4.95 (*0-671-66451-4*) S&S Trade.

Mooncake. Frank Asch. (Moonbear Ser.). (J). (ps-k). 1983. 10.15 (*0-606-02840-4*, Pub. by Turtleback) Demco.

Mooncakes & Hungry Ghosts: Festivals of China. Carol Stepanchuk & Charles Wong. LC 91-73127. (Illus.). 176p. 1992. pap. 14.95 (*0-8351-2481-9*) China Bks.

Mooncaller. Patricia Chandler. (Superromance Ser.). 1994. mass mkt. 3.50 (*0-373-70582-4*, 1-70582-1) Harlequin Bks.

***Moonchasers & Other Stories.** Gorman. 1998. mass mkt. 5.99 (*0-8125-4939-2*) Tor Bks.

Moonchasers & Other Stories. Ed Gorman. 384p. 1995. 24.95 (*0-312-86010-2*, Pub. by Forge NYC) St Martin.

***Moonchasers & Other Stories.** Ed Gorman. 2000. pap. 14.95 (*0-312-87718-8*) St Martin.

Moonchild. Aleister Crowley. 1995. reprint ed. lib. bdg. 28.95 (*1-56849-670-2*) Buccaneer Bks.

Moonchild. Aleister Crowley. LC 72-142496. 336p. 1970. reprint ed. pap. 12.95 (*0-87728-147-5*) Weiser.

Moonchild from Wolfe Creek. Jesse Stuart. 19.95 (*0-89190-892-7*) Amereon Ltd.

Mooncranker's Gift: A Novel. Barry Unsworth. 1996. pap. 11.00 (*0-393-31478-2*, Norton Paperbks) Norton.

Mooncusser. H. P. Dunne. 368p. 1994. 23.00 (*1-885173-03-2*) Write Way.

***Moondance.** Frank Asch. (Moonbear Ser.). (Illus.). (J). (ps-k). 1999. pap. 12.25 (*0-7857-3558-5*) Econo-Clad Bks.

Moondance. Frank Asch. LC 92-12358. (Moonbear Ser.). (Illus.). 32p. (J). (ps-k). 1993. 12.95 (*0-590-45487-0*) Scholastic Inc.

Moondance. Frank Asch. LC 92-12358. (Moonbear Ser.). (J). (ps-3). 1994. pap. 3.95 (*0-590-45488-9*) Scholastic Inc.

Moondance. Frank Asch. LC 92-12358. (Moonbear Ser.). (J). (ps-k). 1993. 9.15 (*0-606-06578-4*, Pub. by Turtleback) Demco.

Moondance. Donald Verger. LC 95-70054. 64p. 1995. pap. 6.95 (*1-887716-03-3*) Designs Disc.

Moondog. Jean Hollander. (QRL Poetry Bks.: Vol. XXXV). 1996. 20.00 (*0-614-15859-1*) Quarterly Rev.

Moondogs. Daniel Kirk. LC 98-15521. (Illus.). 32p. (J). (ps-3). 1999. 15.99 (*0-399-23128-5*) Putnam Pub Group.

Moondom, Vol. 1. rev. ed. Adams. 1997. 30.00 (*0-8212-2413-1*, Pub. by Bulfinch Pr) Little.

Moondust & Madness. Janelle Taylor. 416p. (Orig.). 1992. mass mkt. 5.99 (*1-55817-659-4*, Pinncle Kensgtn) Kensgtn Pub Corp.

Mooneshine Logs. Francis Stokes. (Illus.). 250p. 1994. 23.95 (*0-924486-67-8*) Sheridan.

Mooney History. write for info. (*0-9702281-8-X*) T Mooney.

Mooneyed Hound. 2nd ed. Billy C. Clark. Ed. by James M. Gifford & Patricia A. Hall. LC 95-7143. (Illus.). 128p. (J). (gr. 4 up). 1995. pap. 8.50 (*0-945084-49-8*) J Stuart Found.

Moonfall. Jack McDevitt. LC 98-147774. 480p. 1998. 24.00 (*0-06-105036-9*, HarperPrism) HarpC.

Moonfall. Jack McDevitt. 560p. 1999. mass mkt. 6.50 (*0-06-105112-8*, HarperPrism) HarpC.

Moonfall. Tamara Thorne. 384p. 1996. mass mkt. 4.99 (*0-8217-5315-0*) Kensgtn Pub Corp.

***Moonfall.** Tamara Thorne. 2000. mass mkt. 5.99 (*0-7860-1132-7*, Pinncle Kensgtn) Kensgtn Pub Corp.

Moonfeather. Judith E. French. 384p. (Orig.). 1990. pap. 3.95 (*0-380-76103-3*, Avon Bks) Morrow Avon.

Moonfire. Linda Lael Miller. Ed. by Linda Marrow. 384p. 1991. mass mkt. 5.99 (*0-671-73770-8*) PB.

Moonfleet. (Nelson Readers Ser.). (J). Date not set. pap. text. write for info. (*0-17-557052-3*) Addison-Wesley.

Moonfleet. Falkner. (York Notes Ser.). 1992. pap. text. write for info. (*0-582-79211-8*, Pub. by Addison-Wesley) Longman.

Moonfleet. J. Meade Falkner. 1990. reprint ed. lib. bdg. 21.95 (*0-89966-698-1*) Buccaneer Bks.

Moonflower. Peter Loewer. LC 96-35976. (Illus.). 32p. (J). (gr. 4-7). 1997. 15.95 (*1-56145-138-5*) Peachtree Pubs.

Moonflower. Beverley Nichols. LC 74-171256. 224 p. (J). 1973. write for info. (*0-491-01111-3*) Virgin Bks.

Moonflower: Erotic Dreaming with the Goddess. Sirona Knight. LC 95-42623. (Illus.). 320p. 1996. pap. 19.95 (*1-56718-385-9*) Llewellyn Pubns.

Moonflower Madness. large type ed. Margaret A. Pemberton. 386p. 1994. 27.99 (*0-7505-0588-5*, Pub. by Mgna Lrg Print) Ulverscroft.

Moonflower Vine. Jetta Carleton. (J). 1995. reprint ed. lib. bdg. 24.95 (*1-56849-617-6*) Buccaneer Bks.

Moonflowers. Alexis K. Rotella. (Illus.). 20p. (Orig.). 1987. pap. 7.00 (*0-916133-05-2*) Jade Mtn.

Moonflowers at Dusk. Anna R. Baehr. (Illus.). 1996. pap. 10.00 (*1-878173-15-4*) Birnham Wood.

Moonflute. Audrey Wood. LC 86-4666. (Illus.). 32p. (J). (ps-3). 1986. 14.95 (*0-15-255337-1*) Harcourt.

Moonfolk. Jane G. Austin. (Works of Jane (Goodin) Austin). 1989. reprint ed. lib. bdg. 79.00 (*0-7812-1826-8*) Rprt Serv.

***Moongame.** Frank Asch. (Moonbear Ser.). (J). (ps-k). 2000. per. 5.99 (*0-689-83518-3*) Aladdin.

***Moongame.** Frank Asch. (Moonbear Ser.). (Illus.). (J). (ps-k). 1999. pap. 12.20 (*0-8085-9171-1*) Econo-Clad Bks.

Moongame. Frank Asch. (Moonbear Ser.). (Illus.). 32p. (J). (ps-k). 1987. pap. 4.95 (*0-671-66453-0*) S&S Bks Yung.

Moongame. Frank Asch. (Moonbear Ser.). (J). (ps-k). 1992. 19.95 (*0-590-72624-2*) Scholastic Inc.

Moongate: Suppressed Findings of the U. S. Space Program: The NASA-Military Cover-Up. William L. Brian, II. LC 81-69211. (Illus.). 119p. (C). 1982. spiral bd. 49.95 (*0-941292-00-2*) Future Sci Res.

Moongate Wish. large type ed. Nancy John. 358p. 1992. 27.99 (*0-7505-0425-0*) Ulverscroft.

Moongift. Mandy Higa. Ed. by Jane Weinberger. LC 93-61194. (Illus.). 40p. (J). (ps-4). 1994. pap. 7.95 (*0-932433-69-3*) Windswept Hse.

Moongirl. Craig Sodaro. 89p. (YA). 1987. pap. 5.50 (*0-87129-688-8*, M50) Dramatic Pub.

Moonglow. Judy Baer. 224p. (Orig.). 1986. pap. 5.70 (*0-310-47681-X*) Zondervan.

Moonglow. Peggy Darty. LC 97-12382. 286p. 1997. pap. 9.99 (*1-57673-112-X*, Palisades OR) Multnomah Pubs.

Moonglow. Katherine Sutcliffe et al. 336p. 1998. pap. 5.99 (*0-425-16571-X*) Berkley Pub.

Moonglow Roll-O-Rama. Dav Pilkey. LC 94-24846. (Illus.). 32p. (J). (ps-3). 1995. 15.95 (*0-531-06876-5*); lib. bdg. 16.99 (*0-531-08726-3*) Orchard Bks Watts.

Moonheart. Charles De Lint. 496p. 1994. pap. 13.95 (*0-312-89004-4*) Orb NYC.

Moonheart. Charles De Lint. 1992. mass mkt. write for info. (*0-8125-1622-2*) Tor Bks.

Moonhorse. Mary Pope Osborne. (Dragonfly Bks.). (Illus.). 40p. (J). (ps-2). 1994. pap. 6.99 (*0-679-86709-0*, Pub. by Knopf Bks Yng Read) Random.

Moonhorse. Mary Pope Osborne. 1994. 12.19 (*0-606-06579-2*, Pub. by Turtleback) Demco.

Moonie-Buddhist-Catholic: A Spiritual Odyssey. Thomas W. Case. LC 95-90655. 240p. (Orig.). 1995. pap. 12.95 (*0-9648310-0-7*, 8310-0-7) Whte Hrse Pr.

Moonies in America: Cult, Church, & Crusade. David G. Bromley & Anson D. Shupe. LC 79-16456. (Sage Library of Social Research: No. 92). 269p. reprint ed. pap. 83.40 (*0-8357-4771-9*, 203770800009) Bks Demand.

Mooniversity. Haynes & Holmevik. LC 99-50344. 170p. 1999. pap. text 29.00 (*0-205-27114-6*) Allyn.

Moonkey. Mike Thaler. LC 76-58716. (Illus.). 32p. (J). (ps-3). 1981. 10.95 (*0-06-026124-2*) HarpC Child Bks.

Moonkid & Liberty. Paul Kropp. (J). (gr. 3-6). 1990. 13.95 (*0-316-50485-8*, Joy St Bks) Little.

Moonkid & Liberty. unabridged ed. Paul Kropp. 160p. (YA). (gr. 8-12). 1994. mass mkt. 4.95 (*0-7736-7442-X*) Stoddart Publ.

Moonkid & Prometheus. unabridged ed. Paul Kropp. 304p. (J). (gr. 6-9). 1998. pap. 5.95 (*0-7736-7465-9*) Stoddart Publ.

Moonlanding Historical Account & Cachet Catalog. 2nd ed. Monte Eiserman & Harry Anderson. 85p. 1992. pap. text 10.95 (*1-879390-08-6*) AFDCS.

Moonless Night. large type ed. B. A. James. (Large Print Ser.). 528p. 1996. 27.99 (*0-7089-3573-7*) Ulverscroft.

Moonlight see Yok-Yok

Moonlight see Clair de Lune: For the Piano

Moonlight. Jarrett. 1999. mass mkt. 6.50 (*0-671-03261-5*) PB.

Moonlight. Robert F. Mainone. (Haiku Series: Vol. 8). (Illus.). 52p. 1979. pap. 7.00 (*1-888693-08-8*) Wnderlnd MI.

Moonlight. Harold Pinter. 1995. pap. 5.25 (*0-8222-1481-4*) Dramatists Play.

Moonlight. rev. ed. Joyce Cary. (Everyman Paperback Classics Ser.). 320p. (C). 1995. pap. 6.95 (*0-460-87585-X*, Everyman's Classic Lib) Tuttle Pubng.

Moonlight: A Play. Harold Pinter. LC 94-76461. 112p. 1994. pap. 12.00 (*0-8021-3393-2*, Grove) Grove-Atltic.

***Moonlight: Abraham Lincoln & the Almanac Trial.** John Evangelist Walsh. LC 99-59606. 176p. 2000. 22.95 (*0-312-22922-4*) St Martin.

Moonlight & Lace. Linda Turner. (Family Continuity Program Ser.: No. 2). 1999. mass mkt. 4.50 (*0-373-82150-6*, 1-82150-3) Harlequin Bks.

Moonlight & Lovesongs. Lilian Harry. 360p. 1998. pap. 17.95 (*0-7528-0499-5*, Pub. by Orion Pubng Grp) Trafalgar.

Moonlight & Magic. Rainy Kirkland. 416p. 1994. pap. 4.50 (*0-8217-4729-0*) NAL.

Moonlight & Magic. Rebecca Paisley. 1990. pap. 3.95 (*0-380-76020-7*, Avon Bks) Morrow Avon.

Moonlight & March Roses. large type ed. D. Y. Cameron. 1990. 27.99 (*0-7089-2280-5*) Ulverscroft.

Moonlight & Mill Whistles. Terry W. Tucker. LC 98-36360. 210p. 1998. 15.00 (*1-887714-32-4*) Summerhse Pr.

Moonlight & Music: The Enchanted World of Gayleen Aiken. Gayleen Aiken & Rachel Klein. LC 97-3656. (Illus.). 32p. 1997. 14.95 (*0-8109-4299-2*, Pub. by Abrams) Time Warner.

***Moonlight & Vines.** Charles De Lint. 480p. 1999. mass mkt. 6.99 (*0-8125-6549-5*, Pub. by Tor Bks) St Martin.

Moonlight & Vines: A Newford Collection. Charles De Lint. LC 98-44610. 384p. 1999. 24.95 (*0-312-86518-X*, Pub. by Tor Bks) St Martin.

Moonlight Becomes You. Mary Higgins Clark. 339p. 1997. per. 7.99 (*0-671-86711-3*) PB.

Moonlight Becomes You. large type ed. Mary Higgins Clark. 320p. 1996. pap. 24.00 (*0-684-83127-9*) Simon & Schuster.

Moonlight Becomes You: A Novel. Mary Higgins Clark. 336p. 1996. 24.00 (*0-684-81038-7*) Simon & Schuster.

Moonlight Becomes You, a Novel. Mary Higgins Clark. LC 96-11529. 1996. 13.09 (*0-606-11638-9*, Pub. by Turtleback) Demco.

Moonlight Blues: An Artist's Art Criticism. Peter Plagens. LC 86-11335. (Contemporary American Art Critics Ser.: No. 9). 355p. reprint ed. pap. 110.10 (*0-8357-1753-4*, 207061200005) Bks Demand.

Moonlight Boy see Collected Works of E. W. Howe

Moonlight Boy. E. W. Howe. (Collected Works of E. W. Howe). (YA). 1988. reprint ed. lib. bdg. 59.00 (*0-7812-1288-X*) Rprt Serv.

Moonlight Bride. Buchi Emecheta. LC 82-17816. 77p. (J). (gr. 6-10). 1983. pap. 8.95 (*0-8076-1063-1*) Braziller.

***Moonlight Chronicles: A Wandering Artist's Journal.** Dan Price. LC 99-58200. (Illus.). 160p. 2000. pap. 12.95 (*1-58008-171-1*) Ten Speed Pr.

Moonlight Dream. Noelle B. McCue. (Desire Ser.). 1993. per. 2.99 (*0-373-05815-2*, 5-05815-1) Silhouette.

***Moonlight Fire.** Connie Crow. 2000. 4.50 (*1-928670-85-7*) Awe Struck E Bks.

Moonlight for Maggie. Alexis Hart. 196p. 1999. pap. 6.99 (*1-893108-09-0*) Neighbrhd Pr Pubng.

Moonlight for Maggie. enl. limited num. ed. Alexis Hart. 1998. pap. 8.00 (*0-9655340-9-X*) Neighbrhd Pr Pubng.

Moonlight Hide-&-Seek Club in the Pollution Solution. Rosamund Elwin & Michele Paulse. (Illus.). 24p. (J). pap. 4.95 (*0-88961-173-4*, Pub. by Womens Pr) LPC InBook.

Moonlight in Duneland: The Illustrated Story of the Chicago South Shore & South Bend Railroad. Chicago, South Shore & South Bend Railroad Staff et al. Ed. by Ronald D. Cohen & Stephen G. McShane. LC 98-16812. (Illus.). 160p. 1998. 39.95 (*0-253-33418-7*) Ind U Pr.

Moonlight in Jungleland. Lesley A. Crosten. 132p. 1996. pap. 9.95 (*1-888345-03-9*) Paper Jam.

Moonlight in the Dark Night. Hua-Ching Ni. LC 90-60708. 168p. (Orig.). 1992. pap. 12.95 (*0-937064-44-0*) SevenStar Comm.

Moonlight Investing: A Simple Four Phase Program for Starting Small, Making Smart Choices, Insuring a Stress-Free Financial Future, Becoming You Own Savvy Money Manager. J. W. Dicks. 256p. 1998. 17.95 (*1-886284-28-8*, Pub. by Chandler Hse) Natl Bk Netwk.

Moonlight Kite. Helen E. Buckley. LC 91-34285. (Illus.). 32p. (J). (ps up). 1997. 16.00 (*0-688-10931-4*); lib. bdg. 15.93 (*0-688-10932-2*) Lothrop.

Moonlight Lady. Barbara Faith. (Intimate Moments Ser.). 1995. per. 3.75 (*0-373-07623-1*, 1-07623-1) Silhouette.

Moonlight Madness. John R. Erickson. LC 94-14263. (Hank the Cowdog Audio Ser.: No. 23). (Illus.). (J). (gr. 2-5). 1994. audio 16.95 (*0-87719-253-7*, 9253) Gulf Pub.

Moonlight Madness. John R. Erickson. LC 99-19579. (Hank the Cowdog Ser.: No. 23). (Illus.). 144p. (J). (gr. 2-5). 1998. pap. 4.99 (*0-14-130399-9*, PuffinBks) Peng Put Young Read.

Moonlight Madness. John R. Erickson. (Hank the Cowdog Ser.: No. 23). (Illus.). (J). (gr. 2-5). 1994. 12.05 (*0-606-08766-4*, Pub. by Turtleback) Demco.

Moonlight Madness. Penny Williams & Skip Williams. 1998. 11.95 (*0-7869-1151-4*, Pub. by TSR Inc) Random.

M

An Asterisk (*) at the beginning of an entry indicates that the title is appearing for the first time.

Moonlight Madness, 23. John R. Erickson. (Hank the Cowdog Ser.). (Illus.). (J). 1998. 14.99 (*0-670-88430-8*, PuffinBks) Peng Put Young Read.

Moonlight, Magnolias, & Madness: Insanity in South Carolina from the Colonial to the Progressive Eras. Peter McCandless. LC 95-16641. (Illus.). 432p. (C). 1996. pap. text 19.95 (*0-8078-4558-2*); lib. bdg. 55.00 (*0-8078-2251-5*) U of NC Pr.

Moonlight Man. Paula Fox. LC 85-26907. 192p. (YA). (gr. 7 up). 1986. lib. bdg. 14.95 (*0-02-735480-6*, Bradbury S&S) S&S Childrens.

Moonlight Man. Paula Fox. (J). 1986. 9.09 (*0-606-03864-7*, Pub. by Turtleback) Demco.

***Moonlight Man.** Betty R. Wright. LC 99-27016. (Illus.). 176p. (J). (gr. 3-7). 2000. 15.95 (*0-590-25237-2*, Scholastic Ref) Scholastic Inc.

Moonlight Man. Paula Fox. 192p. (YA). (gr. 6-12). 1988. reprint ed. mass mkt. 4.50 (*0-440-20079-2*, LLL BDD) BDD Bks Young Read.

Moonlight Masquerade. Joyce Adams. 416p. 1994. mass mkt. 4.50 (*0-8217-4669-3*, Zebra Kensgtn) Kensgtn Pub Corp.

Moonlight Meeting. large type ed. Peggy Gaddis. (Linford Romance Library). 224p. 1997. pap. 16.99 (*0-7089-5035-3*) Ulverscroft.

Moonlight Miracle. Noelle B. McCue. (Desire Ser.: No. 694). 1992. per. 2.79 (*0-373-05694-X*, 5-05694-0) Harlequin Bks.

Moonlight Mistress. Patricia Rice. 1999. mass mkt. 5.99 (*0-8217-6175-7*, Zebra Kensgtn) Kensgtn Pub Corp.

Moonlight Mustangs: Haiku. Lia La Mer. (Illus.). v, 87p. 1998. 14.00 (*1-58486-000-6*) LyricLine Pr.

Moonlight on the Avenue of Faith. Gina Barkhordar-Nahai. LC 98-33767. 384p. 1999. 24.00 (*0-15-100388-2*) Harcourt.

***Moonlight on the Avenue of Faith.** Gina Barkhordar-Nahai. 400p. 2000. reprint ed. per. 13.95 (*0-671-04283-1*, WSP) PB.

Moonlight on the Himalayas. Krishna Skukla. 1983. 30.00 (*0-946270-01-5*, Pub. by Pentland Pr) St Mut.

Moonlight on the Lake. large type ed. Ivy Preston. (Linford Romance Library). 1990. pap. 16.99 (*0-7089-6886-4*, Linford) Ulverscroft.

Moonlight on the Mersey. Anne Baker. 512p. 1997. pap. 11.95 (*0-7472-5319-6*, Pub. by Headline Bk Pub) Trafalgar.

Moonlight on the River. Deborah Kovacs. LC 92-28377. (J). 1996. 11.19 (*0-606-09628-0*, Pub. by Turtleback) Demco.

Moonlight on the Sphinx. large type ed. Barbara Cartland. (Magna Large Print Ser.). 304p. 1998. 29.99 (*0-7505-1239-3*, Pub. by Mgna Lrg Print) Ulverscroft.

Moonlight on the Wabash: Still More Poems about Indiana & Hoosiers. L. D. Gilley. 48p. 1996. pap. 7.50 (*0-9643707-2-7*) L D Gilley.

Moonlight Run Till Daylight Catch It. Judy Parris. 1998. pap. 10.95 (*1-874509-56-5*) X Pr.

Moonlight Shadows. large type ed. Natalie Daniels. 203p. 1995. pap. 18.99 (*1-85389-564-4*, Dales) Ulverscroft.

Moonlight Snow. Thomas H. Knight. LC 96-79603. (Illus.). ix, 146p. 1997. 10.00 (*1-890399-11-6*, 022) Blck Moon.

Moonlight Sonata & 29 PS: Piano. 95p. pap. 10.95 (*0-7692-1173-9*, PF0389) Wrner Bros.

Moonlight Standing in As Cordelia. William Lane. 1980. pap. 4.00 (*0-914610-20-1*) Hanging Loose.

Moonlight Stars Candles Wine Roses Romance. Gypsy A. Coolidge. 1990. write for info. (*0-318-66958-7*) Celestial Gems.

***Moonlight Through the Pines: Tales of the Georgia Evenings.** Jimmy Jacobs. (Illus.). 118p. (YA). (gr. 7-12). 2000. pap. 11.95 (*0-9637477-3-8*) Franklin-Sarrett Pubs.

Moonlight Unicorn. Gale Albury. LC 94-90363. (Illus.). 14p. (Orig.). (J). (ps-8). 1994. pap. 4.00 (*0-9642344-0-8*) TEA Printers & Pubs.

Moonlight War. large type ed. Clifton Adams. (Linford Western Library). 320p. 1992. pap. 16.99 (*0-7089-7249-7*, Linford) Ulverscroft.

Moonlight War. large type ed. Terence O'Brien. (Non-Fiction Ser.). 1990. 11.50 (*0-7089-2176-0*) Ulverscroft.

***Moonlight Wish.** Janice Bennett. (Zebra Regency Romance Ser.). 224p. 2000. mass mkt. 4.99 (*0-8217-6627-9*, Zebra Kensgtn) Kensgtn Pub Corp.

Moonlighters. large type ed. Ray Hogan. (Sagebrush Large Print Westerns Ser.). 164p. 1995. lib. bdg. 18.95 (*1-57490-003-X*) T T Beeler.

Moonlighters: A Fictionalized Account of Central Oregon's Vigilant Years 1882-1884. Martel Scroggin. LC 92-71415. (Illus.). 200p. (Orig.). 1992. pap. 9.95 (*0-8323-0496-4*) Binford Mort.

Moonlighter's Manual. John Swantek. (Illus.). 208p. (Orig.). 1982. pap. 14.95 (*0-941818-00-4*) Moonlght Pr.

Moonlighting. Ruth J. Dale. (Love & Laughter Ser.). 1997. per. 3.50 (*0-373-44015-4*, 1-44015-5) Harlequin Bks.

Moonlighting: Earn a Second Income at Home. Jo Frohbieter-Mueller. LC 97-40968. 209p. 1997. pap. 15.95 (*1-55571-406-4*, Oasis Pr) PSI Resch.

***Moonlighting: Sweet Talkin' Guys.** Heather MacAllister. (Temptation Ser.: Bk. 785). 2000. per. 3.99 (*0-373-25885-2*, 1-25885-4) Harlequin Bks.

Moonlighting: 148 Great Ways to Make Money on the Side. Carl Hausman & Philip Lief Group Inc. Staff. 320p. (Orig.). 1989. pap. 8.95 (*0-380-75485-1*, Avon Bks) Morrow Avon.

Moonlighting for Fun & Profit: How to Keep Your Day Job While Earning Extra Income. Robert E. Mitchell. LC 98-4972. 160p. 1998. pap. text 9.95 (*0-8065-1987-8*, Citadel Pr) Carol Pub Group.

***Moonlighting in the Arts.** Gregory Wassall. 104p. 2000. pap. 11.95 (*0-929765-85-0*) Seven Locks Pr.

Moonlit: Short Stories by Antonio Lupez Ortega. Antonia L. Ortega. Tr. by Nathon Budoff from SPA. LC 98-33715.Tr. of Lunar. 208p. (Orig.). 1998. pap. 15.95 (*1-57129-057-5*, Lumen Eds) Brookline Bks.

Moonlit Door. large type ed. Anne Maybury. 448p. 1995. 27.99 (*0-7089-3222-3*) Ulverscroft.

Moonlit Garden. Scott Ogden. LC 98-10604. 152p. 1998. 16.95 (*0-87833-893-4*) Taylor Pub.

Moonlit Pond: Korean Classical Poems in Chinese. Tr. by Sung Il Lee. 252p. 1997. pap. text 17.00 (*1-55659-076-8*) Copper Canyon.

***Moonlit Road & Other Ghost & Horror Stories.** Ambrose Bierce. Ed. by John Grafton. LC 98-2677. (Dover Thrift Editions Ser.). 96p. 1998. pap. 1.00 (*0-486-40056-5*) Dover.

Moonlit Upper Deckerina. Naomi Lazard. LC 76-57519. 77p. 1977. pap. 12.95 (*0-8180-1540-3*, Pub. by Sheep Meadow) U Pr of New Eng.

***Moonpearl.** large type ed. Irene Roberts. 368p. 1999. pap. 20.99 (*1-85389-882-1*) Ulverscroft.

Moonpenny. Bill Meek. 145p. pap. 11.95 (*0-946005-30-3*, OS 10181, Pub. by Ossian) Music Sales.

***Moonpie & Ivy.** Barbara O'Connor. 2001. text. write for info. (*0-374-35059-0*) FS&G.

Moonpies & Lullabies, & Other Bedtime Poems. Young. (Let's Read Aloud Ser.). 20p. Date not set. 7.95 (*0-694-00718-8*, HarpFestival) HarpC Child Bks.

Moonraker. Ian Fleming. (James Bond Ser.). 224p. 1994. 9.98 (*1-56731-050-5*, MJF Bks) Fine Comms.

Moonrise. Ben Bova. 592p. 1998. mass mkt. 6.99 (*0-380-78697-4*, Avon Bks) Morrow Avon.

Moonrise. Roberta Gayle. 1996. pap. 4.99 (*0-7860-0268-9*) Kensgtn Pub Corp.

Moonrise. Ana Seymour. LC 96-527. 296p. 1995. per. 4.50 (*0-373-28890-5*, 1-28890-1) Harlequin Bks.

Moonrise. large type ed. Anne Stuart. LC 97-7605. 1997. lib. bdg. 23.95 (*1-57490-082-X*, Beeler LP Bks) T T Beeler.

Moonrise. rev. ed. Adams. 1997. 30.00 (*0-8212-2414-X*, Pub. by Bulfinch Pr) Little.

Moonrise: Apollo Plus 20. (Illus.). 76p. (Orig.). pap. text 7.95 (*0-936447-01-X*) Main Stage.

Moonrise over the Landfill. Ferne F. Schmidtchen. 174p. (Orig.). 1993. pap. 9.95 (*0-9637648-0-2*) Aries Pubng.

Moonrise, Sunset. Gopal Baratham. (Mask Noir Ser.). 256p. (Orig.). 1996. pap. 12.99 (*1-85242-501-6*) Serpents Tail.

Moons. Anne Welsbacher. LC 96-26775. (The Universe Ser.). 24p. (J). (ps-4). 1997. lib. bdg. 13.95 (*1-56239-721-4*) ABDO Pub Co.

Moon's Acceleration & Its Physical Origins Vol. 1: As Deduced from Solar Eclipses. Robert R. Newton. LC 78-20529. 602p. reprint ed. pap. 186.70 (*0-608-06176-X*, 206650900001) Bks Demand.

Moon's Acceleration & Its Physical Origins Vol. 2: As Deduced from General Lunar Observations. Robert R. Newton. LC 78-20529. 333p. reprint ed. pap. 103.30 (*0-608-06177-8*, 206650900002) Bks Demand.

Moons & Planets. Hartmann. (Astronomy Ser.). 1972. pap. 21.50 (*0-534-00321-4*) Wadsworth Pub.

Moons & Planets. 2nd ed. William K. Hartmann. 509p. (C). 1983. 41.00 (*0-534-00719-8*) Wadsworth Pub.

Moons & Planets. 3rd ed. William K. Hartmann. 510p. (C). 1992. pap. 64.95 (*0-534-18894-X*) Wadsworth Pub.

Moons & Planets. 3rd ed. William K. Hartmann. (Astronomy Ser.). (C). 1997. pap. 57.00 (*0-534-18898-2*) Wadsworth Pub.

Moons & Planets. 4th ed. William K. Hartmann. LC 98-22660. (Astronomy Ser.). 1998. pap. 89.95 (*0-534-54630-7*) Wadsworth Pub.

Moons & Rings. Time-Life Books Editors. (Voyage Through the Universe Ser.). 144p. 1991. lib. bdg. write for info. (*0-8094-8451-X*) Time-Life.

Moons & Rings. Time-Life Books Editors. (Voyage Through the Universe Ser.). (Illus.). 144p. 1991. write for info. (*0-8094-8450-1*) Time-Life.

Moons & Rings: Companions to the Planets. Jeanne Bendick. (Early Bird Astronomy Ser.). (Illus.). 32p. (J). (gr. k-2). 1991. pap. 4.95 (*1-878841-54-8*); lib. bdg. 19.90 (*1-56294-000-7*) Millbrook Pr.

Moon's Choice. John W. Stewig. (J). (ps-6). 1993. pap. 15.00 (*0-671-76962-6*) S&S Bks Yung.

Moon's Dominion: Narrative Dichotomy & Female Dominance in the First Five Novels of D. H. Lawrence. Gavriel Ben-Ephraim. LC 78-75172. 256p. 1981. 35.00 (*0-8386-2266-6*) Fairleigh Dickinson.

Moon's Nodes & Their Importance. G. White. 80p. 1989. 13.00 (*0-86690-171-X*, W1517-014) Am Fed Astrologers.

Moon's Nodes & Their Importance in Natal Astrology. George White. (Illus.). 76p. 1998. reprint ed. pap. 12.95 (*0-7661-0442-7*) Kessinger Pub.

Moons of Jupiter. Debra Sutter et al. Ed. by Lincoln Bergman et al. (Great Explorations in Math & Science (GEMS) Ser.). (Illus.). 112p. (J). (gr. 4-9). 1993. pap. 42.00 (*0-912511-84-2*, GEMS) Lawrence Science.

Moons of Jupiter: Stories. Alice Munro. 233p. 1991. pap. 12.00 (*0-679-73270-5*) Villard Books.

Moons of Palmares. Zainab Amadahy. LC 98-154430. 224p. 1998. pap. write for info. (*1-896705-22-7*) Sister Vis Pr.

Moons of the Solar System: An Illustrated Encyclopedia. John Stewart. LC 91-52641. (Illus.). 260p. 1991. lib. bdg. 49.95 (*0-89950-568-6*) McFarland & Co.

Moon's Our Home. Faith Baldwin. 1976. reprint ed. lib. bdg. 24.95 (*0-88411-602-6*) Amereon Ltd.

Moon's Party. Helena C. Pittman. LC 92-40866. (J). 1994. 15.95 (*0-399-22541-2*, G P Putnam) Peng Put Young Read.

Moons That Come & Go. Ed. by R. D. Schmidt et al. 40p. (Orig.). (C). 1996. pap. 3.00 (*1-882294-08-4*) Green Gate.

***Moonscapes: A Celebration of Lunar Astronomy, Magic, Legend & More.** Rosemary Ellen Guiley. (Illus.). 192p. 2000. reprint ed. text 18.00 (*0-7881-9149-7*) DIANE Pub.

***Moonseed.** Stephen Baxter. 672p. 1999. mass mkt. 6.99 (*0-06-105903-X*) HarpC.

Moonshadow. Susan Wiggs. 384p. (Orig.). 1989. pap. 3.95 (*0-380-75639-0*, Avon Bks) Morrow Avon.

Moonshadow. large type ed. Patricia Burns. 480p. 1996. 27.99 (*0-7089-3625-3*) Ulverscroft.

Moonshadow, No. 18. deluxe limited ed. J. M. DeMatteis. Ed. by Margaret Clark. (Illus.). 396p. 1989. 39.95 (*0-936211-16-4*) Graphitti Designs.

Moonshadow: Bedtime Storybook & Coloring Book. Jasmine Sabu. (Illus.). 46p. (J). (ps-2). 1997. 4.99 (*0-9655666-1-7*) UBASFILM.

Moonshadow: The Adventures of the Thief of Bagdad. Jasmine Sabu. 278p. (Orig.). (J). (gr. 8-12). 1997. pap. 5.25 (*0-9655666-0-9*) UBASFILM.

Moonshadow Man. large type ed. Jessica Hart. 1995. 23.99 (*0-263-14153-5*, Pub. by Mills & Boon) Ulverscroft.

Moonshadows: Fantasies of Love & Magick. Ed. by S. G. Johnson. 32p. 1995. pap. 5.00 (*1-887666-04-4*) Obelesk Bks.

Moonshell. large type ed. L. Bergstrom. (Orig.). 1990. pap. 16.99 (*0-7089-6914-3*, Linford) Ulverscroft.

Moonshine. Gary L. Blackwood. LC 99-10756. 144p. (J). (gr. 3-7). 1999. 14.95 (*0-7614-5056-4*, Cav Child Bks) Marshall Cavendish.

Moonshine. Jim Nolan. 86p. 1992. pap. 12.95 (*1-85235-096-2*) Dufour.

Moonshine: A Life in Pursuit of White Liquor. Alec Wilkinson. LC 98-73186. 153p. 1998. reprint ed. pap. 12.95 (*1-886913-24-2*) Ruminator Bks.

Moonshine: A Story of the Reconstruction Period. Frederic A. Tupper. LC 72-2067. (Black Heritage Library Collection). 1977. reprint ed. 20.95 (*0-8369-9071-4*) Ayer.

Moonshine, the Monster, & Related Topics: Proceedings, AMS-IMS-SIAM Summer Research Conference on Moonshine, the Monster, & Related Topics, Mount Holyoke College, 1994. Ed. by Chongying Dong & Geoffrey Mason. LC 95-40534. (Contemporary Mathematics Ser.: No. 193). 368p. 1995. pap. 70.00 (*0-8218-0385-9*, CONM/193) Am Math.

Moonshine War. Elmore Leonard. 224p. 1985. mass mkt. 6.99 (*0-440-15807-9*) Dell.

Moonshiner. large type ed. Lucy Walker. 1988. 15.95 (*0-7089-1795-X*) Ulverscroft.

Moonshiner's Son. Carolyn Reeder. 208p. (J). (gr. 4-7). 1995. mass mkt. 4.50 (*0-380-72251-8*, Avon Bks) Morrow Avon.

Moonshiner's Son. Carolyn Reeder. LC 92-39570. 208p. (J). (gr. 3-7). 1993. lib. bdg. 14.95 (*0-02-775805-2*, Mac Bks Young Read) S&S Childrens.

Moonshiner's Son. Carolyn Reeder. (J). 1995. 9.85 (*0-606-07887-8*) Turtleback.

Moonshot. Paul Kupperberg. 1989. pap. 9.00 (*0-912771-50-X*) Mayfair Games.

Moonshot Tape & a Poster of the Cosmos: 2 One Act Plays in Monologue. Lanford Wilson. 1991. pap. 3.25 (*0-8222-0912-8*) Dramatists Play.

Moonsigns for Lovers: An Astrological Guide to Perfect Relationships. Carole Golder. LC 92-20096. 224p. (Orig.). 1995. pap. 8.95 (*0-8050-2121-3*, Owl) H Holt & Co.

Moonsilver. Linda Hilton. Ed. by Carolyn Tolley. 416p. (Orig.). 1995. mass mkt. 5.50 (*0-671-89809-4*) PB.

Moonsnacks & Assorted Nuts. Mary G. Dembeck. LC 94-75986. (Illus.). 40p. 1994. 15.95 (*1-880851-11-3*) Greene Bark Pr.

***Moonspeaker.** K. D. Wentworth. 2000. pap. 14.95 (*0-9673131-6-3*) HAWK Pubng Grp.

Moonspell. Regan Forest. (Harlequin Dreamscape Ser.: No. 3). 1990. per. 3.25 (*0-373-79003-1*) Harlequin Bks.

Moonspell. Linda Ladd. 368p. 1985. pap. 3.95 (*0-380-89639-7*, Avon Bks) Morrow Avon.

Moonspun Magic. Catherine Coulter. 1999. mass mkt. 7.50 (*0-451-40884-5*, Topaz) NAL.

***Moonspun Magic.** large type ed. Catherine Coulter. LC 99-56260. 2000. 28.95 (*0-7862-2348-0*) Thorndike Pr.

Moonstick: The Seasons of the Sioux. Eve Bunting. LC 95-44865. (Joanna Cotler Bks.). (Illus.). 32p. (J). (gr. k-4). 1997. 15.95 (*0-06-024804-1*) HarpC.

***Moonstick: The Seasons of the Sioux.** Eve Bunting. LC 95-44865. (Illus.). 32p. (J). (gr. k-4). 2000. pap. 5.95 (*0-06-443619-5*) HarpC Child Bks.

Moonstick: The Seasons of the Sioux, Class Set. unabridged ed. Eve Bunting. (J). 1997. boxed set 167.80 incl. audio (*0-7887-3927-1*, 46348) Recorded Bks.

Moonstick: The Seasons of the Sioux, Homework. unabridged ed. Eve Bunting. (J). 1997. boxed set 31.70 incl. audio (*0-7887-1832-0*, 40612) Recorded Bks.

***Moonstone.** Wilkie Collins. Ed. by Steve Farmer. 720p. 1999. pap. 9.95 (*1-55111-243-4*) Broadview Pr.

Moonstone. Wilkie Collins. LC 92-52918. 480p. 1992. 17.00 (*0-679-41722-2*) Everymns Lib.

Moonstone. Wilkie Collins. 496p. 1984. mass mkt. 6.95 (*0-451-52394-6*, Sig Classics) NAL.

Moonstone. Wilkie Collins. LC 99-461888. (Oxford World's Classics Hardcovers Ser.). 576p. 1999. 16.50 (*0-19-210028-9*) OUP.

Moonstone. Wilkie Collins. 576p. 1999. pap. 6.95 (*0-14-043408-9*, PuffinBks) Peng Put Young Read.

Moonstone. Wilkie Collins. 1984. 12.05 (*0-606-01905-7*, Pub. by Turtleback) Demco.

Moonstone. Wilkie Collins. (Classics Library). 1997. pap. 3.95 (*1-85326-044-4*, 0444WW, Pub. by Wrdsworth Edits) NTC Contemp Pub Co.

Moonstone. large type ed. Wilkie Collins. (Isis Clear Type Classic Ser.). 605p. 1992. 25.95 (*1-85089-543-0*, Pub. by ISIS Lrg Prnt) Transaction Pubs.

Moonstone. Wilkie Collins. 1976. reprint ed. lib. bdg. 29.95 (*0-89190-241-4*, Rivercity Pr) Amereon Ltd.

Moonstone. Wilkie Collins. 1976. reprint ed. lib. bdg. 25.95 (*0-89968-498-X*) Buccaneer Bks.

Moonstone. Wilkie Collins. 570p. 1998. reprint ed. lib. bdg. 25.00 (*1-58287-094-2*) North Bks.

Moonstone. 2nd ed. Wilkie Collins. Ed. by John Sutherland. (Oxford World's Classics Ser.). 560p. 2000. pap. 6.95 (*0-19-283338-3*) OUP.

Moonstone see Works of Wilkie Collins

Moonstone, Vol. 1. Claire Cross. (Time Passages Ser.). 1999. mass mkt. 5.99 (*0-515-12654-3*, Jove) Berkley Pub.

Moonstone: Masters of Literature. Wilkie Collins. 1996. pap. 5.00 (*81-207-1887-9*, Pub. by Sterling Pubs) S Asia.

Moonstone: New Edition. 2nd ed. Ed. by D. H. Howe. (Illus.). 110p. 1993. pap. text 5.95 (*0-19-585462-4*) OUP.

Moonstone, Pt. 2, Incl. The New Magdalen see Works of Wilkie Collins

Moonstone Castle Mystery. Carolyn Keene. LC 63-1033. (Nancy Drew Mystery Stories Ser.: No. 40). (Illus.). 180p. (J). (gr. 4-7). 1962. 5.99 (*0-448-09540-8*, G & D) Peng Put Young Read.

Moonstone Woman: Selected Prose & Poems. Tada Chimako. Ed. by Thomas Fitzsimmons. Tr. by Robert Brady et al from JPN. (Asian Poetry in Translation Ser.: No. 11). 64p. 1990. text 20.00 (*0-942668-21-9*) Katydid Bks.

Moonstone Woman: Selected Prose & Poems. Tada Chimako. Ed. by Thomas Fitzsimmons. Tr. by Robert Brady et al from JPN. (Asian Poetry in Translation Ser.: No. 11). 64p. 1990. pap. 15.00 (*0-942668-22-7*) Katydid Bks.

Moonstones. Jean Thesman. LC 97-52307. 166p. (YA). (gr. 8-10). 1998. 15.99 (*0-670-87959-2*) Viking Penguin.

***Moonstones.** Jean Thesman. (Illus.). 208p. (YA). (gr. 5-9). 2000. pap. 5.99 (*0-14-130809-5*, PuffinBks) Peng Put Young Read.

Moonstruck: The True Story of the Cow That Jumped over the Moon. Gennifer Choldenko. LC 95-14846. (Illus.). 32p. (ps-3). 1999. 5.99 (*0-7868-1394-6*, Pub. by Hyperion) Time Warner.

Moonstruck: The True Story of the Cow That Jumped over the Moon. Gennifer Choldenko. LC 95-14846. (Illus.). 32p. (J). (ps-3). 1997. 14.95 (*0-7868-0158-1*, Pub. by Hyprn Child); lib. bdg. 14.89 (*0-7868-2130-2*, Pub. by Hyprn Child) Little.

Moonstruck in Manhattan. Wendy L. Nentwig. (Unmistakably Cooper Ellis Ser.). 16p. 1998. pap. 5.99 (*0-7642-2066-7*) Bethany Hse.

Moonstruck, Joe vs. the Volcano, & 5 Corners. John P. Shanley. 352p. (Orig.). 1996. pap. 13.00 (*0-8021-3471-8*, Grove) Grove-Atltic.

Moonstruck Mongrel. Pandora Pollen. 1997. 16.95 (*0-7188-2788-0*, Lutterworth-Parkwest) Parkwest Pubns.

Moontan. Don Rodgers. 72p. 1996. pap. 14.95 (*1-85411-154-X*, Pub. by Seren Bks) Dufour.

Moontellers: Myths of the Moon from Around the World. Lynn Moroney. LC 95-2418. (Illus.). 32p. (J). (ps-3). 1995. lib. bdg. 14.95 (*0-87358-601-8*, Rising Moon Bks) Northland AZ.

Moontide. Stella Cameron. (Mira Bks.). 1998. per. 5.50 (*1-55166-463-1*, 1-66463-0, Mira Bks) Harlequin Bks.

***Moontide.** E. V. Thompson. 512p. 1998. pap. 10.95 (*0-7472-4824-9*, Pub. by Headline Bk Pub) Trafalgar.

Moontide. large type ed. E. V. Thompson. (Charnwood Large Print Ser.). 656p. 1997. 27.99 (*0-7089-8976-4*) Ulverscroft.

Moontide Embrace. Constance O'Banyon. 1987. mass mkt. 3.95 (*0-8217-2182-8*, Zebra Kensgtn) Kensgtn Pub Corp.

Moontime Anthology: Mensis, a Call to Power, a Return to the Sacred. Ed. by Shinan N. Barclay. (Illus.). 250p. (Orig.). 1991. pap. 13.95 (*0-945086-89-X*) Sunlight Prodns.

***Moontime Stories.** large type ed. Jesse Centeno. Ed. by Patricia A. Flanagan. 14p. 1999. pap. 5.00 (*0-923242-84-8*) Sparrowgrass Poetry.

Moonwalk: The First Trip to the Moon. Judy Donnelly. LC 88-23668. (Step into Reading Ser.: A Step 4 Book). (Illus.). 48p. (J). (gr. 2-5). 1989. pap. 3.99 (*0-394-82457-1*, Pub. by Random Bks Yng Read) Random.

Moonwalk: The First Trip to the Moon. Judy Donnelly. (Step into Reading Ser.: A Step 4 Book). (J). (gr. 2-4). 1989. 9.19 (*0-606-12429-2*, Pub. by Turtleback) Demco.

Moonwalker. Rick Hautala. 1989. mass mkt. 4.50 (*0-8217-2598-X*, Zebra Kensgtn) Kensgtn Pub Corp.

***Moonwar.** Ben Bova. LC 97-18177. 400p. 1998. mass mkt. 23.00 (*0-380-97303-0*, Avon Bks) Morrow Avon.

Moonwar. Ben Bova. 512p. 1998. mass mkt. 6.99 (*0-380-78698-2*, Eos) Morrow Avon.

Moonwind. Louise Lawrence. LC 85-45507. 192p. (YA). (gr. 7 up). 1986. 12.95 (*0-06-023733-3*) HarpC Child Bks.

Moonwind. Susannah Leigh. 512p. 1988. pap. 3.95 (*0-317-66162-0*, Sig) NAL.

Moonwitch. Nicole Jordan. (Harlequin Historical Ser.: No. 62). 1991. mass mkt. 3.25 (*0-373-28662-7*) Harlequin Bks.

Moor: A Mary Russell novel. Laurie R. King. LC 97-31886. 400p. (YA). (gr. 5 up). 1999. mass mkt. 6.50 (*0-553-57952-5*) Bantam.

Moor: A Mary Russell novel. Laurie R. King. LC 97-31886. (Illus.). 307p. 1997. text 23.95 (*0-312-16934-5*) St Martin.

An Asterisk (*) at the beginning of an entry indicates that the title is appearing for the first time.

Moor: A Mary Russell novel. large type ed. Laurie R. King. LC 98-15548. (Large Print Bks., Mystery Ser.). 419p. 1998. 27.95 (*0-7838-0162-9*, G K Hall & Co) Mac Lib Ref.

Moor: The Descendants of Ensign John Moor of Canterbury, N.H., born 1696 - died 1786. H. P. Moore. (Illus.). 370p. 1992. reprint ed. pap. 57.00 (*0-8328-2691-X*); reprint ed. lib. bdg. 67.00 (*0-8328-2690-1*) Higginson Bk Co.

Moor- und Torfkunde (Moors & Peat Bogs) 3rd ed. Ed. by Karlhans Gottlich. (GER., Illus.). xvi, 520p. 1990. 52.00 (*3-510-65139-1*, Pub. by E Schweizerbartsche) Balogh.

Moor in English Renaissance Drama. Jack D'Amico. 288p. (C). 1991. lib. bdg. 49.95 (*0-8130-1068-3*) U Press Fla.

Moor of Venice: Cinthio's Tale & Shakspeare's Tragedy. John E. Taylor. LC 73-144694. reprint ed. 32.50 (*0-404-06355-1*) AMS Pr.

Moorarji Desai: The Man & His Ideas. S. R. Bakshi. (Indian Freedom Fighters Ser.: No. 23). (C). 1992. 27.00 (*81-7041-494-6*, Pub. by Anmol) S Asia.

Moorchild. Eloise McGraw. LC 95-34107. 240p. (J). (gr. 4-7). 1996. lib. bdg. 16.00 (*0-689-80654-X*) McElderry Bks.

Moorchild. Eloise McGraw. 256p. (J). (gr. 4-7). 1998. per. 4.50 (*0-689-82033-X*) S&S Childrens.

***Moorchild.** Eloise McGraw. 1998. 9.60 (*0-606-13621-5*, Pub. by Turtleback) Demco.

Moorcroft: A Guide to Moorcroft Pottery, 1897-1993. Paul Atterbury. 1996. 85.00 (*0-903685-33-7*, Pub. by R Dennis) Antique Collect.

Moore: Ancestors & Descendants of Andrew Moore, 1612-1897. J. A. Passmore. (Illus.). 1599p. 1991. reprint ed. pap. 179.00 (*0-8328-1800-3*); reprint ed. lib. bdg. 189.00 (*0-8328-1799-6*) Higginson Bk Co.

Moore: Ancestry of Sharpless & Rachel (Roberts) Moore. B. M. Haines. (Illus.). 214p. 1991. reprint ed. pap. 33.50 (*0-8328-2161-6*); reprint ed. lib. bdg. 43.50 (*0-8328-2160-8*) Higginson Bk Co.

Moore: Genealogy of the Moore Family of Londonderry, N.H. & Peterborough, N.H. 1648-1924. George W. Moore. (Illus.). 109p. 1995. reprint ed. pap. 18.00 (*0-8328-4928-6*); reprint ed. lib. bdg. 28.00 (*0-8328-4927-8*) Higginson Bk Co.

Moore about Revelation. Charles Moore. 184p. 1997. 12.00 (*0-8059-4205-X*) Dorrance.

Moore & Wittgenstein on Certainty. Avrum Stroll. 208p. 1994. text 49.95 (*0-19-508488-8*) OUP.

Moore County, North Carolina. Richard J. Schoegl. LC 97-210258. (Images of America Ser.). (Illus.). 128p. 1997. pap. 16.99 (*0-7524-0526-8*) Arcadia Publng.

Moore Family History, 1599-1962. A. L. Moore. 42p. 1994. reprint ed. pap. 8.50 (*0-8328-4127-7*) Higginson Bk Co.

Moore Hollow Group of Central Texas. V. E. Barnes & W. C. Bell. (Reports of Investigations: RI 88). (Illus.). 169p. 1977. pap. 5.00 (*0-318-03228-7*) Bur Econ Geology.

Moore House: The Site of Surrender-Yorktown; A National Park Service Historic Structures Report. Charles E. Peterson. 116p. 1981. 8.45 (*0-940091-08-9*); pap. 4.20 (*0-940091-07-0*) Natl Parks & Cons.

Moore in the Bagatelle Gardens, Paris. Text by David Cohen. (Illus.). 128p. 1994. 60.00 (*0-87951-526-0*, Pub. by Overlook Pr) Penguin Putnam.

Moore Kids: A Look Back. Iola Pair. 152p. (YA). (gr. 3 up). 1997. pap. 12.95 (*0-9651775-2-1*) I Pair.

Moore McGuffey Readers, 1836-43: First Reader for Young Children. William H. McGuffey. Ed. by Raymond S. Moore et al. (Illus.). 167p. (J). (gr. 1-3). 1984. text 16.95 (*0-913717-01-0*) Moore Fnd.

Moore on Right & Wrong: The Normative Ethics of G. E. Moore. William H. Shaw. (Philosophical Studies). 216p. (C). 1995. lib. bdg. 110.50 (*0-7923-3223-7*, Pub. by Kluwer Academic) Kluwer Academic.

Moore, Ruble & Yudell: Houses & Housing. Oscar Ojeda. 1994. pap. 29.99 (*1-56496-279-2*) Rockport Pubs.

Moore Ruble Yudell: Campus & Community. Oscar R. Ojeda & Lucas H. Guerra. (Illus.). 192p. 1997. 39.99 (*1-56496-230-X*) Rockport Pubs.

Moore Ruble Yudell: Houses & Housing. LC 94-230305. 192p. 1993. 39.99 (*1-56496-100-1*) Rockport Pubs.

Moore School Lectures. Ed. by Martin Campbell-Kelly & M. R. Williams. (Charles Babbage Institute Reprint Series for the History of Computing). (Illus.). 616p. 1985. 65.00 (*0-262-03109-4*) MIT Pr.

Moorea French Polynesia: Managing the Balance Between Development & Conservation. 42p. 1990. pap. 35.00 (*1-882866-50-9*) Pac Asia Trvl.

Moored to the Mast: The U. S. Navy's Lighter-Than-Air Program at Lakehurst, New Jersey. Thomas A. Williams. (Illus.). 76p. (Orig.). 1996. pap. 13.00 (*0-941965-09-0*) Ocean Cnty Hist.

***Mooreland, Indiana: A Memoir.** Haven Kimmel. LC 00-27922. (Illus.). 2001. write for info. (*0-385-49982-5*) Doubleday.

Moore's Federal Practice, 26 vols. 3rd ed. James W. Moore. LC 97-137086. 1948. ring bd. 3820.00 (*0-8205-1410-1*) Bender.

Moore's Federal Practice, Admiralty, Vol. 29. 3rd ed. text 160.00 (*0-8205-2999-0*) Bender.

Moore's Federal Rules Pamphlet, 3 vols. J. W. Moore. 1961. ring bd. write for info. (*0-8205-2800-5*) Bender.

Moore's Historical Guide to the Battle of Bentonville. 2nd ed. Mark A. Moore. (Illus.). 104p. 1997. pap. 14.95 (*1-882810-15-5*, 15-5) Savas Pub.

Moore's Historical Guide to the Wilmington Campaign & the Battles for Fort Fisher. Mark A. Moore. (Illus.). 240p. (Orig.). 1999. pap. 15.95 (*1-882810-19-8*) Savas Pub.

Moore's Imaging Dictionary. 2nd ed. Andy Moore. 19.95 (*0-936648-74-0*) Telecom Bks.

Moore's Irish Melodies (Selections From) With Music of Turlough O'Carolan, Slow Aires, Dance Tunes, & Harmonized Vocal Arrangements. abr. ed. John Stevenson et al. (Illus.). 55p. 1996. reprint ed. pap. 15.95 (*0-931877-27-X*) Captain Fiddle Pubns.

Moore's Irish Melodies with Symphonies & Accompaniments. Thomas Moore. LC 81-81465. 261p. 1981. 65.00 (*0-89453-259-6*) Scholarly Res Inc.

Moore's Manual: Federal Practice & Procedure, 3 vols. James W. Moore. 1962. ring bd. 780.00 (*0-8205-1411-X*) Bender.

Moore's Manual: Federal Practice Forms, 7 vols. James W. Moore & Louis R. Frumer. 1965. ring bd. 1100.00 (*0-8205-1413-6*) Bender.

Moores Rowland's Orange Tax Guide 1997-98. Ed. by John Jeffrey-Cook. 1997. pap. write for info. (*0-406-99544-3*, MROT1997, MICHIE) LEXIS Pub.

Moores Rowland's Yellow & Orange Tax Guides, 1994-1995 see Moores Rowland'S Yellow & Orange Tax Guides 1994-95: Orange

Moores Rowland'S Yellow & Orange Tax Guides 1994-95: Orange, 2 pts. Moores Rowland Staff. Incl. Moores Rowland's Yellow & Orange Tax Guides, 1994-1995. 1995. pap. 31.95 (*0-406-03648-9*, MICHIE); 31.95 (*0-406-03647-0*, MICHIE) LEXIS Pub.

Moores Rowland's Yellow Tax Guide 1997-98. Ed. by John Jeffrey-Cook. 1997. pap. write for info. (*0-406-99594-X*, MRYT1997, MICHIE) LEXIS Pub.

Moorhaven. large type ed. Daoma Winston. (Ulverscroft). 720p. 1994. 27.99 (*0-7089-3033-6*) Ulverscroft.

Moorhaven Fair. Richard Novak. 16p. (Orig.). 1994. pap. 3.00 (*0-9640168-0-X*) Pirate Writings.

Moorhen: Poems. William Logan. 1984. 22.50 (*0-317-40770-8*) Abattoir.

***Mooring Against the Tide: Writing Fiction & Poetry.** Jeffrey Knott & Tim Schell. LC 99-89266. 320p. 2000. pap. 32.00 (*0-13-026011-8*) P-H.

Mooring Equipment Guidelines. OCIMF Staff. 125p. (C). 1992. 195.00 (*1-85609-018-3*, Pub. by Witherby & Co) St Mut.

Mooring Equipment Guidelines. OCIMF Staff. 1997. pap. 180.00 (*1-85609-088-4*, Pub. by Witherby & Co) St Mut.

Mooring Of Starting Out. John Ashbery. LC 96-36982. 400p. 1997. 25.00 (*0-88001-527-6*) HarpC.

Mooring Of Starting Out. John Ashbery. LC 96-36982. 392p. 1998. pap. 18.00 (*0-88001-547-0*) HarpC.

Moorings & Metaphors: Figures of Culture & Gender in Black Women's Literature. Karla F. Holloway. LC 91-16803. 225p. (C). 1992. text 40.00 (*0-8135-1745-1*); pap. text 16.00 (*0-8135-1746-X*) Rutgers U Pr.

Mooring's Book of Prayers. Mary Batchelor. 1996. 24.99 (*0-345-40520-X*) Ballantine Pub Grp.

Moorish Architecture: In Andalusia. Marianne Barrucand & Achim Bednorz. LC 00-500243. (Architecture & Design Ser.). (Illus.). 250p. 1999. reprint ed. 24.99 (*3-8228-7634-8*) Taschen Amer.

Moorish Spain. Richard Fletcher. LC 92-11289. 208p. 1995. 25.00 (*0-8050-2395-X*) H Holt & Co.

Moorish Spain. Richard Fletcher. 189p. 1996. pap. 15.95 (*0-614-21160-3*, 801) Kazi Pubns.

Moorish Spain. Richard Fletcher. LC 93-11117. 1993. pap. 16.95 (*0-520-08496-9*, Pub. by U CA Pr) Cal Prin Full Svc.

Moorish Style. Miles Danby. 240p. 1999. pap. 29.95 (*0-7148-3861-6*) Phaidon Pr.

Moorish Style. Miles Danby. LC 96-147153. (Illus.). 240p. (C). 1995. 59.95 (*0-7148-2951-X*, Pub. by Phaidon Press) Phaidon Pr.

Moorland Hanging. Michael Jecks. 384p. 1998. pap. 9.95 (*0-7472-5071-5*, Pub. by Headline Bk Pub) Trafalgar.

Moors in Spain. Stanley Lane-Poole. 212p. 1924. pap. text 22.00 (*0-916157-31-8*) African Islam Miss Pubns.

Moors in Spain. Stanley Lane-Poole. 304p. 1984. 190.00 (*1-85077-042-5*, Pub. by Darf Pubs Ltd) St Mut.

Moors in Spain. Stanley L. Poole. (African Heritage Classical Research Studies). 290p. reprint ed. 16.00 (*0-938818-65-1*) ECA Assoc.

Moor's Last Sigh. Salman Rushdie. LC 95-24392. 448p. 1996. 25.00 (*0-679-42049-5*) Pantheon.

Moor's Last Sigh. Salman Rushdie. 1997. pap. 14.00 (*0-679-74466-5*) Pantheon.

Moor's Last Sigh. Salman Rushdie. Date not set. pap. 13.00 (*0-614-26587-8*) Vin Bks.

Moorvegetation der Zentralen Hochvogesen. Hans Bick. (Dissertationes Botanicae Ser.: Band 91). (GER., Illus.). 288p. 1985. pap. 53.00 (*3-443-64001-X*, Pub. by Gebruder Borntraeger) Balogh.

Moose. Alan Carey & Sandy Carey. (Illus.). 80p. Date not set. 10.98 (*0-7858-0827-2*) Bk Sales Inc.

Moose. Jason Cooper. LC 96-52094. (Giants Among Us Discovery Library). 24p. (J). (gr. k-4). 1997. lib. bdg. 15.93 (*1-55916-184-1*) Rourke Bk Co.

Moose. Lesley A. Dutemple. LC 97-24685. (Early Bird Nature Books Ser.). (Illus.). (J). 1997. lib. bdg. 19.93 (*0-8225-3031-7*) Lerner Pub.

***Moose.** Anthony Frederick. (Our Wild World Ser.). (Illus.). 48p. (J). (gr. 3-7). 2000. pap. 8.95 (*1-55971-744-0*, NorthWord Pr) Creat Pub Intl.

Moose. Hemstock. LC 98-3625. (Wildlife of North America Ser.). (Illus.). 48p. (J). 1998. 19.00 (*0-7368-0030-1*) Capstone Pr.

Moose. Jenny Markert. LC 98-34032. (Illus.). 32p. (J). 1999. lib. bdg. 22.79 (*1-56766-583-7*) Childs World.

Moose. David Petersen. LC 94-10948. (New True Books Ser.). (Illus.). 48p. (J). (gr. k-4). 1994. pap. 5.50 (*0-516-41069-5*); lib. bdg. 21.00 (*0-516-01069-7*) Childrens.

***Moose.** Text by Daniel Wood. (Illus.). 120p. 1999. 24.95 (*1-55110-950-6*) Whitecap Bks.

***Moose.** Scott Wrobel. LC 99-29936. (Northern Trek Ser.). (Illus.). 24p. (J). (gr. 2-7). 2000. lib. bdg. 21.30 (*1-58340-034-6*) Smart Apple.

Moose, 9. Annie Hemstock. (Wildlife of North America Ser.). (J). 1998. 19.00 (*0-516-21482-9*) Childrens.

Moose: Behavior, Ecology, Conservation. Valerius Geist. LC 99-24769. (Illus.). 160p. 1999. 35.00 (*0-89658-422-4*) Voyageur Pr.

Moose: Giants of the Northern Forest. Bill Silliker. 144p. 1998. pap. 19.95 (*1-55209-255-0*) Firefly Bks Ltd.

Moose: The Story of a Very Special Person. 2nd ed. Scott MacDonald & Chester W. Oden, Jr. 200p. (Orig.). (YA). (gr. 8 up). 1978. pap. 10.95 (*0-03-043936-1*) Brookline Bks.

Moose Als Bioindikatoren Von Schwermetall-Immissionen. Joachim Maschke. (Bryophytorum Bibliotheca Ser.: No. 22). (GER., Illus.). 492p. 1981. lib. bdg. 120.00 (*3-7682-1320-X*) Lubrecht & Cramer.

Moose & Caribou from Alaska. Cecilia Nibeck. (Illus.). 182p. 1992. spiral bd. 12.95 (*0-9622117-3-7*) AK Anchorage.

Moose & Friends. Jim Latimer. LC 91-14047. (Illus.). 32p. (J). (gr. 1-3). 1993. 14.95 (*0-684-19335-3*) Scribner.

Moose, Bruce & the Goose. 2nd rev. ed. Robert S. McKinnon. LC 96-94057. (Illus.). 165p. (J). (gr. 4-5). 1996. pap. 12.00 (*0-9651943-0-2*) R S McKinnon.

Moose, Caribou, & Muskox. Alaska Geographic Society Staff. Ed. by Penny Rennick. LC 72-92087. (Alaska Geographic Ser.: Vol. 23-4). (Illus.). (Orig.). 1997. pap. 19.95 (*1-56661-033-8*) Alaska Geog Soc.

Moose Country: A Saga of the Woodland Moose. Michael W. Runtz. 112p. 1996. pap. 24.95 (*0-7737-5766-X*) Stoddart Publ.

Moose Country: Saga of the Woodland Moose. Michael Runtz. (Illus.). 112p. 1999. 39.95 (*0-7737-2469-9*) Genl Dist Srvs.

Moose Creek Charlie & the Quick Freeze: A Tall, Tall Tale by Bernie Rinear. Bernie Rinear. (Illus.). 14p. (Orig.). 1982. pap. 2.00 (*1-878654-49-7*) Lit Coun AK.

Moose des Kaisergebirges-Tirol. Hans Smettan. (Bryophytorum Bibliotheca Ser.: Vol. 23). 127p. 1982. pap. text 40.00 (*3-7682-1331-5*) Lubrecht & Cramer.

Moose Don't Fly! Illus. by Mel Sundby. 220p. 1997. pap. 12.95 (*0-9649775-2-4*) Planet Books.

Moose Don't Fly! Essays by Dave Carlson. Dave Carlson. (Illus.). 220p. 1995. pap. 12.95 (*0-9649775-0-8*) Planet Books.

***Moose Droppings & Other Crimes Against Nature: Funny Stories from Alaska.** Tom Brennan. (Illus.). 128p. 2000. pap. 12.95 (*0-945397-84-4*) Epicenter Pr.

Moose for Jessica. Pat A. Wakefield & Larry Carrara. (Illus.). 64p. (J). (ps up). 1992. pap. 5.99 (*0-14-036134-0*, PuffinBks) Peng Put Young Read.

Moose for Kids. Jeff Fair. (Wildlife for Kids Ser.). (Illus.). 48p. (J). (gr. k-8). 1993. pap. 6.95 (*1-55971-211-2*, NorthWord Pr) Creat Pub Intl.

Moose in the Garden. Nancy W. Carlstrom. LC 89-29407. (Illus.). 32p. (J). (ps-2). 1990. 13.95 (*0-06-021015-X*) HarpC Child Bks.

***Moose in the Pot Cookbook.** (Illus.). 75p. 1999. pap. text 13.00 (*1-57833-086-6*) Todd Commns.

Moose Magic for Kids see Animal Magic for Kids

Moose Mating. David Grae. LC 98-178106. 1996. pap. 5.25 (*0-8222-1543-8*) Dramatists Play.

Moose Meat & Wild Rice see Ojibway Tales

Moose, of Course! Lynn Plourde. LC 99-27492. (Illus.). 24p. (J). (ps-1). 1999. 14.95 (*0-89272-454-4*); pap. 9.95 (*0-89272-473-0*) Down East.

Moose on the Loose. Ann Hassett & John Hassett. LC 88-105943. (Illus.). 48p. (Orig.). (J). (gr. k-3). 1987. pap. 9.95 (*0-89272-245-2*) Down East.

Moose on the Loose. Pamela Jane. (Illus.). 64p. (Orig.). (J). 1996. pap. 3.99 (*0-380-78263-4*, Avon Bks) Morrow Avon.

Moose Racks, Bear Tracks & Other Alaska Kidsnacks: Cooking with Kids Has Never Been So Easy! Alice Bugni. LC 99-14003. (Illus.). 32p. (J). (gr. k-5). 1999. pap. 8.95 (*1-57061-214-5*) Sasquatch Bks.

Moose Sticker Book. Laura Joffe Numeroff. (Illus.). (J). 7.95 (*0-694-01425-7*) HarpC.

Moose Stroller Songs. Laura Joffe Numeroff. (Illus.). (J). 9.95 (*0-694-01424-9*) HarpC.

Moose Tales. Nancy Van Laan. LC 97-41273. (Illus.). 48p. (J). (gr. k-2). 1999. 15.00 (*0-395-90863-9*) HM.

***Moose That Roared: The Story of Jay Ward, Bill Scott, a Flying Squirrel, & a Talking Moose.** Keith Scott. LC 00-25478. (Illus.). 480p. 2000. text 27.95 (*0-312-19922-8*) St Martin.

Moose Tracks. Mary Casanova. LC 94-19907. (Illus.). 128p. (J). (gr. 4-7). 1995. 14.95 (*0-7868-0042-9*, Pub. by Hyprn Child); lib. bdg. 14.89 (*0-7868-2035-7*, Pub. by Hyprn Child) Little.

Moose Tracks. Mary Casanova. (J). 1997. 10.05 (*0-606-13082-9*, Pub. by Turtleback) Demco.

***Moose Tracks.** Karma Wilson. LC 00-28374. (Illus.). (J). 2002. write for info. (*0-689-83437-3*) McElderry Bks.

Moose Tracks. Mary Casanova. LC 94-19907. 128p. (J). (gr. 4-7). 1997. reprint ed. pap. 4.95 (*0-7868-1137-4*, Pub. by Hyprn Ppbks) Little.

Moosehead Lake Region. Nathan D. Hamilton. (Images of America Ser.). 1995. pap. 16.99 (*0-7524-0224-2*) Arcadia Publng.

Moosehead Reflections. Everett L. Parker. (Illus.). 94p. (Orig.). 1996. pap. 8.95 (*0-9646054-4-9*) Moosehead Communs.

***Mooseltoe.** Margie Palatini. LC 99-86322. (Illus.). 32p. (J). (gr. k-4). 2000. 16.49 (*0-7868-2492-1*) Hyprn Child.

***Moosemilk.** Ed. by Grant Loewen & Patti Sonntag. (Moosehead Anthology Ser.: No. 7). 114p. 1999. 14.95 (*0-919688-52-7*, Pub. by DC Books) Genl Dist Srvs.

Mooses Come Walking. Arlo Guthrie. LC 95-15441. (Illus.). 32p. (J). (ps-1). 1995. 11.95 (*0-8118-1051-8*) Chronicle Bks.

Moosetache. Margie Palatini. LC 96-26256. (Illus.). 32p. (J). (ps-2). 1997. 15.95 (*0-7868-0306-1*, Pub. by Hyprn Child); lib. bdg. 15.89 (*0-7868-2246-5*, Pub. by Hyprn Child) Little.

Moosetache. Margie Palatini. (Illus.). 32p. (J). (ps-2). 1999. pap. 5.99 (*0-7868-1170-6*, Pub. by Hyprn Child) Time Warner.

Moosewhopper: A Juicy, Moosey Min-Min-Minnesota Burger Tale. 3rd ed. Al Blair. LC 83-61092. (Illus.). 32p. (J). (gr. 3). 1983. pap. 3.95 (*0-930366-04-2*) Northcountry Pub.

Moosewood Cookbook. Mollie Katzen. LC 99-54408. (Illus.). 256p. 2000. 27.95 (*1-58008-135-5*) Ten Speed Pr.

Moosewood Cookbook. rev. ed. Mollie Katzen. LC 99-54408. (Illus.). 256p. 2000. pap. text 19.95 (*1-58008-130-4*) Ten Speed Pr.

Moosewood Restaurant Big Book. Moosewood College Staff. 2001. 40.00 (*0-609-60165-2*); pap. 27.50 (*0-609-80241-0*) C Potter.

Moosewood Restaurant Book of Desserts. Moosewood Collective Staff. LC 97-1234. 416p. 1997. 32.50 (*0-517-70209-6*); pap. 22.00 (*0-517-88493-3*) C Potter.

Moosewood Restaurant Cooks at Home: Fast & Easy Recipes for Any Day. Moosewood Collective Staff. LC 93-39126. (Illus.). 416p. 1994. per. 16.00 (*0-671-67992-9*, Fireside) S&S Trade Pap.

Moosewood Restaurant Cooks for a Crowd: Recipes with a Vegetarian Emphasis for 24 or More. Moosewood Collective Staff. LC 95-41512. 500p. 1996. 34.95 (*0-471-12017-0*) Wiley.

Moosewood Restaurant Cooks for a Crowd: Recipes with Vegetarian Emphasis for 24 or More. Moosewood Restaurant Staff. (Illus.). 520p. 1997. pap. 24.95 (*0-471-23877-5*) Wiley.

***Moosewood Restaurant Daily Special: More Than 275 Recipes for Soups, Stews, Salads & Extras.** Moosewood Collective Staff. 384p. 1999. 35.00 (*0-609-60166-0*) Crown Pub Group.

***Moosewood Restaurant Daily Special: More Than 275 Recipes for Soups, Stews, Salads & Extras.** Ed. by Moosewood Collective Staff. LC 99-13543. 384p. 1999. pap. 24.00 (*0-609-80242-9*, Crown) Crown Pub Group.

Moosewood Restaurant Kitchen Garden: Creative Gardening for the Adventurous Cook. David Hirsch. (Illus.). 256p. (Orig.). 1992. 28.00 (*0-671-69239-9*, Fireside); pap. 15.00 (*0-671-75597-8*, Fireside) S&S Trade Pap.

***Moosey Moose.** Chris Raschka. LC 99-39078. (Illus.). 24p. (J). (ps-1). 2000. 3.99 (*0-7868-0581-1*, Pub. by Disney Pr) Time Warner.

Moosflora (Mosses) 3rd rev. ed. J. Frahm. (GER., Illus.). 528p. 1992. 40.00 (*3-8001-2594-3*) Balogh.

Moosflora und -Vegetation in Regenwaeldern No-Perus: Ergebnisse der Bryotrop-Expedition Nach Peru, 1982. Wolfgang Frey. (Nova Hedwigia, Beihefte/Supplementary Issues Ser.: Beih 88). (Illus.). 159p. 1987. pap. 77.00 (*3-443-51010-8*, Pub. by Gebruder Borntraeger) Balogh.

Moosilaukee Reader, Vol. I. Robert W. Averill. Ed. by Jack Noon. LC 98-44413. (Illus.). 300p. 1999. pap. 20.00 (*0-9642213-7-3*) Moose Cntry.

Moosilaukee Reader, Vol. II. Robert W. Averill. Ed. by Jack Noon. LC 98-44413. (Illus.). 300p. 1999. pap. 20.00 (*0-9642213-8-1*) Moose Cntry.

Moostletoe. Margie Palatini. LC 99-86322. (Illus.). 32p. (J). (gr. k-4). 2000. 15.99 (*0-7868-0567-6*) Little.

Moosvegetation des Noerdlichen Bodenseegebietes. Matthias Ahrens. (Dissertationes Botanicae Ser.: Band 190). (GER., Illus.). vi, 681p. 1992. pap. 106.00 (*3-443-64102-4*, Pub. by Gebruder Borntraeger) Balogh.

Moot Corporation. Mansur. 332p. 1996. pap. text, per. 34.95 (*0-7872-2761-7*) Kendall-Hunt.

Moot Court Book, 1994. 3rd ed. Gaubatz & Mattis. 307p. 1994. pap. text 25.00 (*1-55834-195-1*, 11526-11, MICHIE) LEXIS Pub.

Moot Plays of Corneille. Tr. by Lacy Lockert. LC 59-15968. 486p. 1959. 29.95 (*0-8265-1053-1*) Vanderbilt U Pr.

Mooting Manual. T. Gygar. LC 98-105304. (Butterworths Skills Ser.). 160p. 1996. pap. write for info. (*0-409-30826-9*, MICHIE) LEXIS Pub.

Moozie's Cow Wisdom for Grabbing Life by the Horns, Vol. 2. Ted Dreier. LC 99-90040. (Illus.). 96p. 1999. 4.95 (*0-9662268-2-8*, CWII) Best Frnds Bks.

Moozie's Cow Wisdom for Life's Little Beefs. Ted Dreier. (Illus.). 96p. 1998. 4.95 (*0-9662268-0-1*, CW1) Best Frnds Bks.

***Moozie's Kind Adventure.** deluxe ed. Jane Morton & Ted Dreier. LC 99-90526. (Moozie Adventures Ser.). (Illus.). 28p. (J). (gr. k-2). 1999. 14.95 (*0-9662268-1-X*) Best Frnds Bks.

Mop for Pop. Gina C. Erickson. (Get Ready...Get Set...Read! Ser.). (Illus.). 24p. (J). (ps-2). 1991. pap. 3.50 (*0-8120-4680-3*) Barron.

Mop for Pop. Kelli C. Foster. (Get Ready - Get Set - Read! Ser.). (J). 1991. 8.70 (*0-606-01641-4*, Pub. by Turtleback) Demco.

Mop for Pop. Kelli C. Foster & Gina C. Erickson. (Get Ready...Get Set...Read! Ser.: Set 1). (Illus.). (J). 1996. lib. bdg. 11.95 (*1-56674-136-X*) Forest Hse.

Mop, Moondance, & the Nagasaki Knights. Walter Dean Myers. (J). (gr. 6). 1995. 9.28 (*0-395-73269-7*) HM.

Mop, Moondance, & the Nagasaki Knights. large type ed. Walter Dean Myers. 174p. 43.50 (*0-614-20605-7*, L-38204-00 APHB) Am Printing Hse.

Mop to the Rescue. Martine Schaap. LC 98-87421. (Illus.). 33p. (J). (gr. k-2). 1998. 15.95 (*0-8126-0167-X*, Pub. by Front St-Cricket Bks) Publishers Group.

M

An Asterisk (*) at the beginning of an entry indicates that the title is appearing for the first time.

Mop Top. Don Freeman. (Picture Puffin Ser.). 1978. pap. 5.99 (*0-14-050326-9*, PuffinBks) Peng Put Young Read.

Mop Top. Don Freeman. (J). 1955. 10.19 (*0-606-02182-5*, Pub. by Turtleback) Demco.

Mop Top. unabridged ed. Don Freeman. (Illus.). (J). (gr. k-3). 1982. pap. 15.95 incl. audio (*0-941078-12-4*) Live Oak Media.

Mop Top, 4 bks., Set. unabridged ed. Don Freeman. (Illus.). (J). (gr. k-3). 1982. pap., teacher ed. 33.95 incl. audio (*0-941078-13-2*) Live Oak Media.

Mopan: Culture & Ethnicity in a Changing Belizean Community. J. R. Gregory. (Illus.). vi, 152p. 10.00 (*0-913134-74-0*) Mus Anthro MO.

***Mopar Parts Locating Guide.** David Gimbal. (Parts Locating Guides Ser.). 2000. pap. 21.95 (*1-891752-31-6*) Jalopy Joe.

Mopar Parts Locating Guide. David R. Gimbel & Adam Gimbel. (Illus.). 210p. 1999. reprint ed. pap. 19.95 (*1-891752-15-4*) Jalopy Joe.

Moppets & Their Manners. Agnes M. Koch. (Illus.). 20p. (Orig.). (J). (gr. 1-6). 1996. 5.95 (*0-9655587-0-3*) A M Koch.

***Mop's Treasure Hunt.** Martine Schaap & Alex de Wolf. LC 00-9696. (Illus.). 2001. write for info. (*1-57768-891-0*) MG-Hill OH.

Mopwater Files. John R. Erickson. (Hank the Cowdog Audio Ser.: No. 28). (Illus.). (J). (gr. 2-5). 1997. 16.95 incl. audio (*0-87719-315-0*, 9315) Gulf Pub.

Mopwater Files. John R. Erickson. LC 99-38427. (Hank the Cowdog Ser.: o. 28). (Illus.). 144p. (J). (gr. 2-5). 1998. pap. 4.99 (*0-14-130404-9*, PuffinBks) Peng Put Young Read.

Mopwater Files. John R. Erickson. (Hank the Cowdog Ser.: No. 28). (Illus.). (J). (gr. 2-7). 1997. 12.05 (*0-606-12716-X*, Pub. by Turtleback) Demco.

Mopwater Files, 28. John R. Erickson. (Hank the Cowdog Ser.: No. 28). (Illus.). (J). (gr. 3-7). 1998. 14.99 (*0-670-88435-9*, PuffinBks) Peng Put Young Read.

Mor-Ling: Catalyst for Survival. Ben Paliferro. (Illus.). 192p. 1997. pap. 14.00 (*0-8059-4098-7*) Dorrance.

Mora Books Gift Set. Jo Mora. 1995. 60.00 (*0-922029-21-0*) Stoecklein Pub.

Moraceae, Olmedieae, Brosimeae. Cees C. Berg. LC 70-130519. (Flora Neotropica Monographs: No. 7). (Illus.). 228p. 1985. reprint ed. pap. 18.00 (*0-89327-264-7*) NY Botanical.

Moraeas of Southern Africa. P. Goldblatt. (Annals of Kirstenbosch Botanic Gardens Ser.: Vol. 14). (Illus.). 224p. 1986. 15.00 (*0-620-09974-7*, Pub. by Natl Botanical Inst) Balogh.

Morag - Myself or Mother Hen? Ed. by Moira Walker. (In Search of a Therapist Ser.). 160p. 1995. pap. 30.95 (*0-335-19224-6*) Taylor & Francis.

Moraines & Varves: Origin, Genesis, Classification: Proceedings of an INQUA Symposium on Genesis & Lithology of Quaternary Deposits, Zurich, 10-20 September 1978. Ed. by C. Schluchter. 455p. (C). 1979. text 188.00 (*90-6191-039-0*, Pub. by A A Balkema) Ashgate Pub Co.

Moral Absolute: An Essay on the Nature & Rationale of Morality. Nicholas Rescher. (Studies in Moral Philosophy: Vol. 2). X, 115p. (C). 1989. text 29.00 (*0-8204-0797-6*) P Lang Pubng.

Moral Absolutes: Tradition, Revision & Truth. John Finnis. LC 90-26434. 113p. 1991. pap. 10.95 (*0-8132-0745-2*); text 24.95 (*0-8132-0744-4*) Cath U Pr.

Moral Absolutes, Catholic Traditions, Current Trends & the Truth. William E. May. LC 88-44163. (Pere Marquette Lectures). 1989. text 15.00 (*0-87462-544-0*, PM-20) Marquette.

Moral Acquaintances: Methodology in Bioethics. Kevin Wildes. 248p. 2000. 35.00 (*0-268-03450-8*, Pub. by U of Notre Dame Pr) Chicago Distribution Ctr.

***Moral Acquaintances: Methodology on Bioethics.** Kevin William Wildes. 248p. 2000. reprint ed. pap. 20.00 (*0-268-03452-4*, Pub. by U of Notre Dame Pr) Chicago Distribution Ctr.

Moral Action & Christian Ethics. Jean Porter. (New Studies in Christian Ethics: No. 5). 252p. (C). 1999. pap. text 19.95 (*0-521-65710-5*) Cambridge U Pr.

Moral Action in Young Adulthood. John M. Whiteley & Norma Yokota. 280p. (C). 1999. pap. 40.00 (*1-889271-26-8*) Nat Res Ctr.

Moral Agendas for Children's Welfare. Michael King. LC 98-27632. 1999. 85.00 (*0-415-18012-0*); pap. 27.99 (*0-415-18013-9*) Routledge.

Moral Agoraphobia Vol. 25: The Challenge of Egoism, Vol. 25. Kim-Chong Chong. (Revisioning Philosophy Ser.). 104p. (C). 1996. text 34.95 (*0-8204-2839-6*) P Lang Pubng.

Moral Analysis: Foundations, Guides, & Applications. Louis G. Lombardi. LC 87-12469. (SUNY Series in Philosophy). 185p. (C). 1988. pap. text 21.95 (*0-88706-666-6*) State U NY Pr.

Moral Anatomy. Ed. by Christopher Maurer. 1995. write for info. (*0-614-16413-3*) Doubleday.

Moral Anatomy & Moral Reasoning. Robert V. Hannaford. LC 93-18648. 208p. 1993. 29.95 (*0-7006-0607-6*) U Pr of KS.

Moral & Political Discourse: Theory & Practice in International Relations. Kenneth W. Thompson. LC 87-8192. (Exxon Education Foundation Series on Rhetoric & Political Discourse: Vol. 12). 120p. (Orig.). 1987. pap. text 14.00 (*0-8191-6347-3*, Pub. by White Miller Center) U Pr of Amer.

Moral & Political Essays. Lucius Annaeus Seneca. Ed. by John M. Cooper & J. F. Procope. (Cambridge Texts in the History of Political Thought Ser.). 366p. (C). 1995. pap. text 19.95 (*0-521-34818-8*) Cambridge U Pr.

Moral & Political Naturalism of Baron Kato Kiroyuki. Winston Davis. LC 96-13847. (Japan Research Monographs: Vol. 13). 1996. pap. 15.00 (*1-55729-052-0*) IEAS.

Moral & Political Philosophy. David Hume. Ed. by Henry D. Aiken. (Library of Classics: No. 3). 448p. 1970. pap. 14.95 (*0-02-846170-3*) Hafner.

Moral & Political Philosophy of David Hume. John B. Stewart. LC 72-6406. 422p. 1973. reprint ed. lib. bdg. 55.00 (*0-8371-6488-5*, STDH, Greenwood Pr) Greenwood.

Moral & Political Thought of Mahatma Gandi. Raghavan N. Iyer. (Pythagorean Sangha Ser.). (Illus.). 465p. (C). 1983. reprint ed. pap. 21.75 (*0-88695-002-3*) Concord Grove.

Moral & Political Writings of Mahatma Gandhi Vol. I: Civilization, Politics & Religion. Mahatma Gandhi. Ed. by Raghavan N. Iyer. (Illus.). 500p. 1986. 125.00 (*0-19-824754-0*) OUP.

Moral & Practical Issues of Cloning. (Illus.). 60p. (Orig.). 1997. pap. 9.95 (*0-9647446-8-6*) Great Albany.

Moral & Spiritual Crisis in Education: A Curriculum for Justice & Compassion in Education. David E. Purpel. LC 88-16602. (Critical Studies in Education). 192p. (Orig.). 1988. 55.00 (*0-89789-153-8*, H153, Bergin & Garvey); pap. 18.95 (*0-89789-152-X*, G152, Bergin & Garvey) Greenwood.

Moral & Spiritual Cultivation in Japanese Neo-Confucianism: The Life & Thought of Kaibara Ekken. Ed. by Mary E. Tucker. LC 88-15381. (SUNY Series in Philosophy). 451p. 1989. text 24.50 (*0-88706-889-8*) State U NY Pr.

Moral Animal. Robert Wright. 480p. 1995. pap. 15.00 (*0-679-76399-6*) Random.

Moral Animal: Evolutionary Psychology & Everyday Life. Robert Wright. 1995. 25.50 (*0-8446-6927-X*) Peter Smith.

Moral Animus of David Hume. Donald T. Siebert. LC 88-40581. 248p. 1990. 36.50 (*0-685-32621-7*) Bucknell U Pr.

Moral Animus of David Hume. Donald T. Siebert. LC 88-40581. 248p. 1990. 39.50 (*0-87413-367-X*) U Delaware Pr.

Moral Apostasy in Russian Literature. George J. Gutsche. LC 86-8513. 1987. 30.00 (*0-87580-118-8*) N Ill U Pr.

Moral Appraisability: Puzzles, Proposals & Perplexities. Ishtiyaque Haji. 288p. (C). 1998. text 49.95 (*0-19-511474-4*) OUP.

***Moral Architecture of World Peace: Nobel Laureates Discuss Our Global Future.** Helena Cobban. LC 99-56608. (Illus.). 288p. 2000. 24.95 (*0-8139-1987-8*) U Pr of Va.

Moral Argument & Social Vision in the Courts: A Study of Tort Accident Law. Henry J. Steiner. LC 86-28121. 243p. 1987. reprint ed. pap. 75.40 (*0-608-01962-3*, 206261700003) Bks Demand.

Moral Art: Grammar, Society, & Culture in Trecento Florence. Paul F. Gehl. LC 92-47067. (Illus.). 320p. (C). 1993. text 45.00 (*0-8014-2836-X*) Cornell U Pr.

Moral Art of Dickens. 2nd ed. Barbara Hardy. LC 84-18554. 164p. (C). 1970. pap. 9.95 (*0-485-12049-6*, Pub. by Athlone Pr) Humanities.

Moral Art of Philip Massinger. Ira Clark. LC 91-58964. 320p. 1993. 42.50 (*0-8387-5225-X*) Bucknell U Pr.

Moral Aspects of Economic Growth, & Other Essays. Barrington Moore, Jr. LC 97-45210. (Wilder House Series in Politics, History, & Culture). 240p. 1998. 29.95 (*0-8014-3376-2*) Cornell U Pr.

Moral Aspects of Legal Theory: Essays on Law, Justice, & Political Responsibility. David Lyons. LC 92-28985. 233p. (C). 1993. text 64.95 (*0-521-43244-8*) Cambridge U Pr.

Moral Authority, Ideology & the Future of American Social Welfare. Andrew W. Dobelstein. LC 98-29480. 304p. 1998. text 79.00 (*0-8133-3311-3*, Pub. by Westview); pap. text 29.00 (*0-8133-3312-1*, Pub. by Westview) HarpC.

***Moral Authority of Government: Essays to Commemorate the Centennial of the National Institute of Social Sciences.** Moorhead Kennedy et al. LC 99-46674. 2000. write for info. (*0-7658-0024-1*) Transaction Pubs.

Moral Base for Teacher Professionalism. Hugh Sockett. LC 92-34913. (Professional Ethics in Education Ser.). 208p. (C). 1993. text 29.00 (*0-8077-3238-9*) Tchrs Coll.

Moral Basis for Liberty. Robert A. Sirico. (IEA Health & Welfare Unit Ser.: No. 2). 40p. 1994. pap. 14.50 (*0-255-36354-0*, Pub. by Inst Economic Affairs) Coronet Bks.

Moral Basis for Liberty. 2nd rev. ed. Robert A. Sirico. LC 96-61910. 67p. 1996. pap. 2.95 (*1-57246-059-8*) Foun Econ Ed.

Moral Basis of a Backward Society. Edward C. Banfield & L. F. Banfield. LC 58-9398. 1967. pap. 14.95 (*0-02-901510-3*) Free Pr.

Moral Basis of a Free Society. H. Verlan Andersen. Ed. by Hans V. Andersen, Jr. LC 96-70759. 204p. 1996. pap. 12.95 (*1-57636-027-X*) SunRise Pbl.

Moral Basis of Faith. Tom Wells. 28p. (Orig.). 1986. pap. 1.45 (*0-85151-469-3*) Banner of Truth.

Moral Behavior in Chinese Society. Ed. by Richard W. Wilson et al. LC 81-4581. 199p. 1981. 52.95 (*0-275-90744-9*, C0744, Praeger Pubs) Greenwood.

Moral Bond of Community: Justice & Discourse in Christian Morality. Bernard V. Brady. LC 98-5663. 192p. 1998. 49.95 (*0-87840-690-5*); pap. 16.95 (*0-87840-691-3*) Georgetown U Pr.

Moral Boundaries: A Political Argument for an Ethic of Care. Joan Tronto. LC 93-10700. 256p. (C). (gr. 13). 1993. pap. 20.99 (*0-415-90642-3*, A7579) Routledge.

Moral Calculations: Game Theory, Logic, & Human Frailty. Laszlo Mero. LC 98-17443. 300p. 1998. 27.00 (*0-387-98419-4*) Spr-Verlag.

Moral Case Against Religious Belief. R. A. Sharpe. 1997. pap. 15.00 (*0-334-02680-6*) TPI PA.

Moral Case for the Free Market Economy: A Philosophical Argument. Tibor R. Machan. LC 88-37917. (Problems in Contemporary Philosophy Ser.: Vol. 15). 140p. 1989. lib. bdg. 69.95 (*0-88946-343-3*) E Mellen.

Moral Challenge of Alzheimer Disease. Stephen G. Post. LC 95-13505. 160p. 1995. text 29.95 (*0-8018-5174-2*) Johns Hopkins.

***Moral Challenge of Alzheimer Disease: Ethical Issues from Diagnosis to Dying.** 2nd ed. Stephen G. Post. LC 99-50625. 192p. 2000. pap. 18.95 (*0-8018-6410-0*) Johns Hopkins.

Moral Challenges of Health Care Management. John R. Griffith. LC 92-48699. 153p. 1992. text 40.00 (*0-910701-93-8*, 0928) Health Admin Pr.

Moral, Character, & Civic Education in the Elementary School. Ed. by Jacques Benninga. 304p. (C). 1991. text 49.00 (*0-8077-3056-4*) Tchrs Coll.

Moral, Character & Civic Education in the Elementary School. Ed. by Jacques Benninga. 304p. (C). 1991. pap. text 24.95 (*0-8077-3055-6*) Tchrs Coll.

Moral Characters of Theophrastus. Theophrastus of Eresus. Tr. by Eustace Budgell. LC 73-158308. (Augustan Translators Ser.). reprint ed. 49.50 (*0-404-54147-X*) AMS Pr.

Moral Child: Nurturing Children's Natural Moral Growth. William Damon. 224p. 1988. text 29.95 (*0-02-906932-7*) Free Pr.

Moral Child: Nurturing Children's Natural Moral Growth. William Damon. 192p. 1990. per. 14.95 (*0-02-906933-5*) Free Pr.

Moral Choice. Daniel C. Maguire. 1984. reprint ed. 12.95 (*0-86683-771-X*, AY8112) Harper SF.

Moral Choices. Joseph Grcic. 1989. 39.75 (*0-314-47163-4*) West Pub.

Moral Choices: An Introduction to Ethics. Scott B. Rae. 320p. 1995. 24.99 (*0-310-20013-X*) Zondervan.

Moral Choices: An Introduction to Ethics. 2nd ed. Scott B. Rae. 2000. 27.99 (*0-310-23015-2*) Zondervan.

Moral Choices Series 1: The Moral Theology of Saint Alphonsus. Theodule Rey-Meret. Tr. by Paul Laverdure from FRE. LC 98-12012. 208p. 1998. reprint ed. pap. 14.95 (*0-7648-0233-X*) Liguori Pubns.

Moral Claims in World Affairs. Pettman. (Australian National University Press Ser.). 1996. write for info. (*0-08-033016-9*, Pergamon Pr) Elsevier.

Moral Classrooms, Moral Children: Creating a Constructivist Atmosphere in Early Education. Rheta DeVries & Betty Zan. LC 93-44317. (Early Childhood Education Ser.). 320p. (C). 1994. text 48.00 (*0-8077-3342-3*); pap. text 21.95 (*0-8077-3341-5*) Tchrs Coll.

Moral Codes & Social Structure in Ancient Greece: A Sociology of Greek Ethics from Homer to the Epicureans & Stoics. Joseph M. Bryant. LC 95-40573. (SUNY Series in the Sociology of Culture). 592p. (C). 1996. text 81.50 (*0-7914-3041-3*); pap. text 27.95 (*0-7914-3042-1*) State U NY Pr.

Moral Collapse of Communism: Poland As a Cautionary Tale. John Clark & Aaron Wildavsky. 400p. 1990. 24.95 (*1-55815-121-4*) ICS Pr.

Moral Collapse of the University: Professionalism, Purity, & Alienation. Bruce Wilshire. LC 89-4455. (SUNY Series, the Philosophy of Education). 287p. (C). 1990. pap. text 19.95 (*0-7914-0197-9*) State U NY Pr.

Moral Combat. Heidi M. Hurd. LC 98-36590. (Cambridge Studies in Philosophy & Law). 400p. (C). 1999. text 59.95 (*0-521-64224-8*) Cambridge U Pr.

Moral Commonwealth: Social Theory & the Promise of Community. Philip Selznick. LC 94-97082. 1994. pap. 22.50 (*0-520-08934-0*, Pub. by U CA Pr) Cal Prin Full Svc.

Moral Communities. Robyn Gill. 95p. 1992. pap. text 17.95 (*0-85989-391-X*, Pub. by Univ Exeter Pr) Northwestern U Pr.

Moral Communities: The Culture of Class Relations in the Russian Printing Industry, 1867-1907. Mark D. Steinberg. (Studies on the History of Society & Culture: No. 14). (C). 1992. 48.00 (*0-520-07572-2*, Pub. by U CA Pr) Cal Prin Full Svc.

Moral Compass. William J. Bennett. 825p. 1996. per. 16.00 (*0-684-83578-9*) S&S Trade.

Moral Compass: Seventeenth & Eighteenth Century Painting in the Netherlands. Arthur K. Wheelock, Jr. et al. LC 98-71838. (Illus.). 120p. 1999. 40.00 (*0-942159-23-3*, Pub. by Rizzoli Intl) St Martin.

Moral Compass: Stories for a Life's Journey. Ed. by William J. Bennett. 824p. 1999. text 30.00 (*0-7881-6168-7*) DIANE Pub.

Moral Compass: Stories for a Life's Journey. Ed. & Comment by William J. Bennett. LC 95-4783. 608p. 1995. 29.50 (*0-684-80313-5*) S&S Trade.

***Moral Compass of the American Lawyer: Truth, Justice, Power & Greed.** R. Zitrin & C. M. Langford. 288p. 2000. pap. 14.00 (*0-449-00671-9*, Ballantine) Ballantine Pub Grp.

Moral Compass of the American Lawyer: Truth, Justice, Power, & Greed. Richard A. Zitrin & Carol M. Langford. LC 98-47753. 288p. 1999. 24.95 (*0-345-43314-9*) Ballantine Pub Grp.

Moral Competence: An Application of Model Logic to Nationalistic Psychology. Moshe Kroy. (Studies in Philosophy: No. 28). 356p. (Orig.). 1975. pap. text 76.95 (*90-279-3301-4*) Mouton.

Moral Competence: An Integrated Approach to the Study of Ethics. Liszka. LC 98-41837. 410p. 1998. pap. text 35.40 (*0-13-974403-7*) P-H.

Moral Concepts. Ed. by Peter A. French et al. LC 95-16519. (Midwest Studies in Philosophy: Vol. 20). (C). 1996. text 52.95 (*0-268-01419-1*); text 26.95 (*0-268-01420-5*) U of Notre Dame Pr.

Moral Concerns. Kai Nelson. 240p. Date not set. 16.95 (*1-55111-013-X*) Broadview Pr.

Moral Conflict: When Social Worlds Collide. W. Barnett Pearce & Stephen W. Littlejohn. LC 96-51308. 320p. 1997. 48.00 (*0-7619-0052-7*); pap. 22.95 (*0-7619-0053-5*) Sage.

***Moral Conflict & Legal Reasoning.** Scott Veitch. (European Academy of Legal Theory Monograph Ser.). 224p. 1999. 45.00 (*1-84113-108-3*, Pub. by Hart Pub) Intl Spec Bk.

Moral Consciousness & Communicative Action. Jurgen Habermas. Tr. by Shierry W. Nicholsen from GER. (Studies in Contemporary German Social Thought). 200p. 1990. 34.00 (*0-262-08192-X*) MIT Pr.

Moral Consciousness & Communicative Action. Jurgen Habermas. Tr. by Christian Lenhardt & Shierry W. Nicholsen. (Studies in Contemporary German Social Thought). (Illus.). 244p. 1992. reprint ed. pap. text 14.95 (*0-262-58118-3*) MIT Pr.

Moral Construction of Poverty & Welfare Reform. Joel F. Handler & Yeheskel Hasenfeld. (Illus.). 300p. 1991. text 55.00 (*0-8039-4197-8*); pap. text 24.50 (*0-8039-4198-6*) Sage.

Moral Controversies. 2nd ed. Gold. (Philosophy Ser.). 1994. pap. 18.95 (*0-534-21692-7*) Wadsworth Pub.

***Moral Controversies in American Politics: Cases in Social Regulatory Policy.** expanded rev. ed. Ed. by Raymond Tatlovich & Byron W. Daynes. LC 97-35839. 320p. (C). (gr. 13). 1998. pap. text 30.95 (*1-56324-994-4*) M E Sharpe.

Moral Controversies in American Politics: Cases in Social Regulatory Policy. rev. ed. Ed. by Raymond Tatlovich & Byron W. Daynes. LC 97-35839. 320p. (C). (gr. 13). 1998. text 74.95 (*1-56324-993-6*) M E Sharpe.

***Moral Conundrum of Success: Searching for Values in an Age of Prosperity & Technology.** Dinesh D'Souza. 2000. 26.00 (*0-684-86814-8*) Free Pr.

Moral Core of Judaism & Christianity: Reclaiming the Revolution. Daniel C. Maguire. LC 92-39136. 256p. 1993. pap. 18.00 (*0-8006-2689-3*, 1-2689) Augsburg Fortress.

Moral Crisis in the Schools: What Parents & Teachers Need to Know. Donald J. Reitz. LC 98-23768. 174p. 1998. pap. 18.00 (*1-885938-09-8*) Cathdrl Fndtn Pr.

Moral Culture. Keith Tester. LC 96-72301. 192p. (C). 1997. 69.95 (*0-8039-7486-8*, 74868); pap. 23.95 (*0-8039-7487-6*, 74876) Sage.

Moral Dealing: Contracts, Ethics, & Reason. David Gauthier. LC 89-45975. (Illus.). 376p. 1990. 49.95 (*0-8014-2431-3*) Cornell U Pr.

Moral Decision. Edmond Cahn. xii, 342p. 1993. reprint ed. 42.50 (*0-8377-2050-8*, Rothman) W S Hein.

Moral Demands & Personal Obligations. Josef Fuchs. Tr. by Brian McNeil from GER. LC 93-3804. 232p. 1993. 37.50 (*0-87840-537-2*); pap. 19.95 (*0-87840-543-7*) Georgetown U Pr.

***Moral Demands in Nonideal Theory.** Liam B. Murphy. (Oxford Ethics Ser.). 192p. 2000. text 35.00 (*0-19-507976-0*) OUP.

Moral Desperado: A Life of Thomas Carlyle. Simon Heffer. 420p. 1996. 29.95 (*0-297-81564-4*, Pub. by Orion Pubng Grp) Trafalgar.

Moral Development: A Compendium, 7 Vols., Set. Ed. by Bill Puka. LC 94-462. 2784p. 1995. 454.00 (*0-8153-1547-3*) Garland.

Moral Development: Advances in Research & Theory. James R. Rest. LC 86-21708. 241p. 1986. 55.00 (*0-275-92254-5*, C2254, Praeger Pubs) Greenwood.

Moral Development: An Introduction. Ed. by William M. Kurtines & Jacob L. Gewirtz. LC 94-32899. 495p. 1995. 86.00 (*0-205-15519-7*) Allyn.

Moral Development: Current Theory & Research. David J. DePalma & Jeanne M. Foley. LC 75-14211. (Child Psychology Ser.). 206p. 1975. text 39.95 (*0-89859-116-3*) L Erlbaum Assocs.

Moral Development & Character Education: A Dialogue. Ed. by Larry P. Nucci. LC 88-63921. (National Society for the Study of Education Publication Ser.). 200p. 1989. 31.75 (*0-8211-1308-9*) McCutchan.

Moral Development & Politics. Ed. by Richard W. Wilson & Gordon J. Schochet. LC 79-15922. 338p. 1980. 55.00 (*0-275-90568-3*, C0568, Praeger Pubs) Greenwood.

Moral Development & Social Environment: Studies in the Philosophy & Psychology of Moral Judgement & Education. Georg Lind et al. Ed. by Roland Wakenhut & Hans Hartman. 314p. 1985. 39.95 (*0-913750-27-1*) Transaction Pubs.

Moral Development in the Professions: Psychology & Applied Ethics. Ed. by James R. Rest & Darcia F. Narvaez. 248p. 1994. pap. 27.50 (*0-8058-1539-2*); text 39.95 (*0-8058-1538-4*) L Erlbaum Assocs.

Moral Development, Moral Education, & Kohlberg. Ed. by Brenda Munsey. LC 80-50. 457p. (Orig.). 1980. pap. 24.95 (*0-89135-020-9*) Religious Educ.

Moral Development Theories - Secular & Religious: A Comparative Study, 68. R. Murray Thomas. LC 96-33070. (Contributions to the Study of Education Ser.). 328p. 1997. 65.00 (*0-313-30236-7*) Greenwood.

Moral Differences: Truth, Justice & Conscience in a World of Conflict. Richard W. Miller. 416p. 1992. pap. text 19.95 (*0-691-02092-2*, Pub. by Princeton U Pr) Cal Prin Full Svc.

Moral Dilemma of the Scientist in Modern Drama. Allen E. Hye. LC 95-48784. (Symposium Ser.: Vol. 38). 1996. write for info. (*0-7734-8869-3*) E Mellen.

An Asterisk (*) at the beginning of an entry indicates that the title is appearing for the first time.

Moral Dilemmas: Biblical Perspectives on Contemporary Ethical Issues. J. Kerby Anderson. Ed. by Charles R. Swindoll. LC 98-15087. (Swindoll Christian Leadership Library). 262p. 1998. 24.99 (*0-8499-1446-9*) Word Pub.

Moral Dilemmas: Philosophical & Psychological Issues in the Development of Moral Reasoning. Ed. by Carol Harding. 304p. 1986. 32.95 (*0-913750-35-2*) Precednt Pub.

Moral Dilemmas Supersaver ed. Biblical Perspectives on Contemporary Ethical Issues. J. Kerby Anderson. Ed. by Charles R. Swindoll. (Swindoll Leadership Library). 1998. 19.97 (*0-8499-1565-1*) Word Pub.

Moral Dilemmas & Moral Theory. Ed. by H. E. Mason. 256p. 1996. text 52.00 (*0-19-509681-9*) OUP.

Moral Dilemmas in the Mahabharata. Ed. by Bimal K. Matilal. (C). 1989. 18.00 (*81-208-0603-4*, Pub. by Motilal Bnarsidass) S Asia.

Moral Dilemmas of Feminism: Prostitution, Adultery, & Abortion. Laurie Shrage. LC 93-48107. (Thinking Gender Ser.). 256p. (C). (gr. 13). 1994. pap. 23.99 (*0-415-90551-6*) Routledge.

Moral Dimension: Toward a New Economics. Amitai Etzioni. 336p. 1990. pap. 17.95 (*0-02-909901-3*) Free Pr.

Moral Dimension in State Policy: Why Economics Is Not Enough & Washington Is Too Much. Donald P. Hodel. (Issue Papers: No. 9-92). 8p. 1992. pap. text 8.00 (*1-57655-047-8*) Independ Inst.

Moral Dimension of Man in the Age of Computers. Adam Drozdek. 162p. (Orig.). (C). 1995. pap. text 28.50 (*0-8191-9984-2*); lib. bdg. 47.00 (*0-8191-9983-4*) U Pr of Amer.

Moral Dimensions of Academic Administration. Rudolph H. Weingartner. LC 98-39054. (Issues in Academic Ethics Ser.: No. 41). 240p. 1998. 58.00 (*0-8476-9096-2*); pap. 22.95 (*0-8476-9097-0*) Rowman.

Moral Dimensions of American Foreign Policy. Ed. by Kenneth W. Thompson. LC 93-48827. 370p. (C). 1994. pap. 24.95 (*1-56000-742-7*) Transaction Pubs.

Moral Dimensions of Marriage & Family Therapy. August G. Lageman. LC 92-33573. 138p. (Orig.). (C). 1993. pap. text 21.50 (*0-8191-8966-9*); lib. bdg. 42.50 (*0-8191-8965-0*) U Pr of Amer.

Moral Dimensions of Public Policy Choice: Beyond the Market Paradigm. Ed. by John M. Gillroy & Maurice Wade. LC 91-27052. (Political Science Ser.). 656p. 1992. pap. 22.50 (*0-8229-5463-X*) U of Pittsburgh Pr.

Moral Dimensions of Teaching. Ed. by John I. Goodlad et al. LC 89-28755. (Education-Higher Education Ser.). 368p. 1993. reprint ed. pap. 19.95 (*1-55542-637-9*) Jossey-Bass.

Moral Dimensions of the International Conduct: The Jesuit Community Lectures, 1982. Ed. by James A. Devereux. LC 83-11660. 118p. reprint ed. pap. 36.60 (*0-7837-6317-4*, 204603200010) Bks Demand.

***Moral Disagreements: Classic & Contemporary Readings.** Christopher W. Gowans. LC 99-46278. 264p. 2000. pap. write for info. (*0-415-21712-1*) Routledge.

Moral Discernment. Richard M. Gula. LC 97-25298. 128p. (Orig.). 1997. pap. 9.95 (*0-8091-3734-8*, 3734-8) Paulist Pr.

Moral Discourse & Practice: Some Philosophic Approaches. Ed. by Stephen Darwall et al. 432p. (C). 1996. text 58.00 (*0-19-510749-7*); pap. text 36.95 (*0-19-509669-X*) OUP.

Moral Disputes: A Reader in Meta, Normative & Applied Ethics. Feiser. LC 99-47192. (Philosophy Ser.). 1999. pap. 57.95 (*0-534-57384-3*) Wadsworth Pub.

Moral Divorce & Other Stories. Jacinto O. Pincon. Tr. by Robert M. Fedorchek. LC 94-28807. 1995. 35.00 (*0-8387-5299-3*) Bucknell U Pr.

Moral Domain: Essays in the Ongoing Discussion Between Philosophy & the Social Science. Ed. by Thomas E. Wren. (Studies in Contemporary German Social Thought). 440p. 1990. 44.00 (*0-262-23147-6*) MIT Pr.

Moral Duty & Legal Responsibility: A Philosophical-Legal Casebook. 2nd ed. Ed. by Philip E. Davis. (Orig.). write for info. (*0-8290-0681-8*) Irvington.

Moral Economy. John P. Powelson. (Illus.). 296p. (C). pap. text 21.95 (*0-472-08672-3*, 08672) U of Mich Pr.

Moral Economy. John P. Powelson. LC 98-8146. 296p. 1998. text 32.50 (*0-472-10925-1*, 10925) U of Mich Pr.

Moral Economy & American Realistic Novels. Da Zheng. (Modern American Literature: Vol. 2). 141p. (C). 1997. text 38.95 (*0-8204-2773-X*) P Lang Pubng.

***Moral Economy & Popular Protest.** Adrian Randall & Andrew Charlesworth. LC 99-15312. 1999. text 69.95 (*0-312-22592-X*) St Martin.

Moral Economy of Labor: Aristotelian Themes in Economic Theory. James B. Murphy. LC 92-45689. 256p. 1993. 30.00 (*0-300-05406-8*) Yale U Pr.

Moral Economy of the Peasant: Rebellion & Subsistence in Southeast Asia. James C. Scott. LC 75-43334. 1976. pap. 16.00 (*0-300-02190-9*) Yale U Pr.

Moral Economy of the State: Conservation, Community Development & State-Making in Zimbabwe. William A. Munro. LC 97-46465. (Monographs in International Studies, Africa: Vol. 68). xxxix, 461p. (C). 1998. pap. text 26.00 (*0-89680-202-7*) Ohio U Pr.

Moral Education. Ed. by Joel H. Rosenthal. 82p. (Orig.). 1992. pap. write for info. (*0-87641-119-7*) Carnegie Ethics & Intl Affairs.

Moral Education. Ed. by Barry I. Chazan & Jonas F. Soltis. LC 72-89127. 204p. reprint ed. 63.30 (*0-8357-9603-5*, 201776400008) Bks Demand.

Moral Education, Vol. 4. Ed. by Joel H. Rosenthal. 131p. (Orig.). 1995. pap. write for info. (*0-87641-143-X*) Carnegie Ethics & Intl Affairs.

Moral Education, Vol. 5. Ed. by Joel H. Rosenthal. 89p. (Orig.). 1995. pap. write for info. (*0-87641-144-8*) Carnegie Ethics & Intl Affairs.

Moral Education: A First Generation of Research & Development. Ed. by Ralph Mosher. LC 80-18607. 412p. 1980. 42.95 (*0-275-90528-4*, C0528, Praeger Pubs) Greenwood.

Moral Education: A Study in the Theory & Application of the Sociology of Education. Emile Durkheim. Tr. by Everett K. Wilson. LC 59-6815. 288p. 1973. pap. 17.95 (*0-02-908320-6*) Free Pr.

Moral Education: Secular & Religious. John L. Elias. LC 87-29715. 228p. (C). 1989. lib. bdg. 26.50 (*0-89464-260-X*) Krieger.

Moral Education: Theory & Applications. Ed. by Marvin W. Berkowitz & Fritz K. Oser. 472p. (C). 1985. text 89.95 (*0-89859-557-6*) L Erlbaum Assocs.

Moral Education among the North American Indians. Claude A. Nichols. LC 75-177112. (Columbia University. Teachers College. Contributions to Education Ser.: No. 427). reprint ed. 37.50 (*0-404-55427-X*) AMS Pr.

***Moral Education & Pluralism** Mal Leicester et al. LC 99-36828. (Education, Culture & Values Ser.). 1999. write for info. (*0-7507-1005-5*) Taylor & Francis.

Moral Education & the Liberal Arts, 50. Ed. by Michael H. Mitias. LC 91-22369. (Contributions to the Study of Education Ser.: No. 50). 192p. 1992. 55.00 (*0-313-27236-0*, MMB, Greenwood Pr) Greenwood.

Moral Education for Americans. Robert D. Heslep. LC 95-3327. 224p. 1995. 65.00 (*0-275-95073-5*, Praeger Pubs); pap. 18.95 (*0-275-95197-9*, Praeger Pubs) Greenwood.

Moral Education in America: Schools & the Shaping of Character from Colonial Times to the Present. B. Edward McClellan. LC 99-13652. 2. 160p. 1999. pap. 21.95 (*0-8077-3820-4*); text 46.00 (*0-8077-3821-2*) Tchrs Coll.

Moral Education in Aristotle. Gerard Verbeke. LC 89-38380. 243p. 1990. 39.95 (*0-8132-0717-7*) Cath U Pr.

Moral Education Through English 11-16. Ros McCulloch & Margaret Mathieson. 144p. 1995. pap. 24.95 (*1-85346-276-4*, Pub. by David Fulton) Taylor & Francis.

Moral Emergency: Breaking the Cycle of Child Sexual Abuse. Jade C. Angelica. LC 93-939. 192p. (Orig.). 1993. pap. 10.95 (*1-55612-617-4*) Sheed & Ward WI.

Moral en la Educacion. Ramon M. Parsons. LC 83-10594. (SPA.). 90p. 1983. 6.00 (*0-8477-2746-7*) U of PR Pr.

Moral Equivalent of War? A Study of Non-Military Service in 9 Nations, 6. Ed. by Donald J. Eberly & Michael W. Sherraden. LC 90-2745. (Contributions to the Study of Childhood & Youth Ser.: No. 6). 240p. 1990. 59.95 (*0-313-25756-6*, EYS/, Greenwood Pr) Greenwood.

Moral Essays. Giacomo Leopardi. Tr. by Patrick Creagh from ITA. LC 82-23473. Orig. Title: Operette Morali. 265p. 1985. pap. text 21.00 (*0-231-05707-5*) Col U Pr.

Moral Essays, 3 vols., 1. Lucius Annaeus Seneca. (Loeb Classical Library: No. 214, 254, 310). 470p. 1928. text 19.95 (*0-674-99236-9*) HUP.

Moral Essays, 3 vols., 2. Lucius Annaeus Seneca. (Loeb Classical Library: No. 214, 254, 310). 508p. 1932. text 19.95 (*0-674-99280-6*) HUP.

Moral Essays, 3 vols., 3. Lucius Annaeus Seneca. (Loeb Classical Library: No. 214, 254, 310). 540p. 1935. text 19.95 (*0-674-99343-8*) HUP.

Moral Essays: Operette Morali. Giacomo Leopardi. Tr. by Patrick Creagh from ITA. LC 82-23473. 265p. 1985. text 49.00 (*0-231-05706-7*) Col U Pr.

Moral Essays: Operette Morali. Giacomo Leopardi. Tr. by Patrick Creagh from ITA. LC 82-23473. (Works of Giacomo Leopardi: Vol. 1). 265p. reprint ed. pap. 82.20 (*0-7837-0429-1*, 204075200018) Bks Demand.

Moral Evaluation of Contraception & Sterilization: A Dialogical Study. Gary M. Atkinson & Albert S. Moraczewski. LC 79-90971. viii, 115p. (Orig.). 1979. pap. 4.95 (*0-935372-05-9*) NCBC.

Moral Fable-Talk. limited ed. Arthur Golding. (Illus.). 356p. 1987. 315.00 (*0-910457-15-8*) Arion Pr.

Moral Fables. Giovanni Meli. Ed. by Leonard G. Sbrocchi. Tr. & Intro. by Gaetano Cipolla. (Biblioteca di Quaderni d'Italianistica Ser.: Vol. 6). (Illus.). 146p. (Orig.). 1988. pap. 20.00 (*0-9691979-5-0*, Pub. by Can Soc Ital Stu) Speedimpex.

Moral Fables & Other Poems Vol. III: A Bilingual Anthology (Sicillian - English) Giovanni Meli. Ed. & Tr. by Gaetano Cipolla from ENG. LC 94-47001. (Pueti D'arba Sicula - Poets of ARBA Sicula: Vol. 3). (ITA., Illus.). 216p. (Orig.). 1995. pap. 16.00 (*1-881901-07-6*) LEGAS.

Moral Fables of Aesop. Robert Henryson. 240p. 1989. pap. 21.00 (*0-7073-0505-5*, Pub. by Mercat Pr Bks) St Mut.

Moral Fables of Aesop. Robert Henryson. Ed. by George D. Gopen. LC 85-41012. 240p. 1987. text 26.50 (*0-268-01361-6*) U of Notre Dame Pr.

Moral Fables of Robert Henryson. Robert Henryson. Ed. by Andrew W. Hart. LC 72-144423. (Maitland Club, Glasgow. Publications: No. 15). reprint ed. 37.50 (*0-404-52950-X*) AMS Pr.

Moral Fiction in Milton & Spenser. John M. Steadman. LC 95-12810. 216p. (C). 1995. 29.95 (*0-8262-1017-1*) U of Mo Pr.

Moral Formation in the Parish: With Your Whole Heart Turn to God. Anthony J. Ciorra & James Keating. LC 98-5365. 200p. 1998. pap. 12.95 (*0-8189-0815-7*) Alba.

Moral Foundation of Democracy. John H. Hallowell. LC 54-11938. (Midway Reprint Ser.). 144p. 1997. reprint ed. pap. text 12.00 (*0-226-31413-8*) U Ch Pr.

Moral Foundation of the Islamic Movement. S. Abul Ala Maududi. Tr. by Mohamed Amin. 56p. (Orig.). 1988. pap. 3.00 (*1-56744-336-2*) Kazi Pubns.

Moral Foundations of Business Practice. James B. Wilbur, III. 138p. (Orig.). (C). 1992. pap. text 19.50 (*0-8191-8651-1*) U Pr of Amer.

Moral Foundations of Business Practice. James B. Wilbur, III. 138p. (Orig.). (C). 1992. lib. bdg. 43.50 (*0-8191-8650-3*) U Pr of Amer.

Moral Foundations of Canadian Federalism: Paradoxes, Achievements & Tragedies of Nationhood. Samuel V. LaSelva. LC 97-117934. 280p. (C). 1996. 65.00 (*0-7735-1405-8*); pap. 22.95 (*0-7735-1422-8*, JL65, Pub. by McG-Queens Univ Pr) CUP Services.

Moral Foundations of Civil Rights. Ed. by Robert K. Fullinwider & Claudia Mills. 1986. pap. 19.00 (*0-8476-7511-4*) IPPP.

Moral Foundations of Civil Rights. Ed. by Robert K. Fullinwider & Claudia Mills. (Maryland Studies in Public Philosophy). 216p. (C). 1986. 61.50 (*0-8476-7523-8*); pap. 25.50 (*0-8476-7524-6*) Rowman.

Moral Foundations of Civil Society. Wilhelm Roepke. 250p. (C). 1995. pap. text 24.95 (*1-56000-852-0*) Transaction Pubs.

Moral Foundations of Constitutional Thought: Current Problems, Augustinian Prospects. Graham Walker. (Illus.). 200p. (C). 1990. text 35.00 (*0-691-07823-8*, Pub. by Princeton U Pr) Cal Prin Full Svc.

Moral Foundations of Professional Ethics. Alan H. Goldman. LC 80-11696. (Philosophy & Society Ser.). 305p. 1980. pap. 25.50 (*0-8476-6285-3*) Rowman.

Moral Foundations of the American Republic. 3rd ed. Ed. by Robert H. Horwitz. LC 85-17772. (Kenyon Public Affairs Conference Center Ser.). 1986. pap. text 16.00 (*0-8139-1082-X*) U Pr of Va.

Moral Fragments & Moral Community: A Proposal for Church in Society. Larry L. Rasmussen. LC 93-18155. (Fry Lectureship Ser.). 176p. 1993. pap. 17.00 (*0-8006-2757-1*, 1-2757, Fortress Pr) Augsburg Fortress.

Moral Freedom. Jeffrey Olen. LC 88-15916. 149p. (C). 1988. 27.95 (*0-87722-578-8*) Temple U Pr.

Moral Gap: Kantian Ethics, Human Limits, & God's Assistance. John E. Hare. LC 95-41862. (Oxford Studies in Theological Ethics). 302p. 1996. text 45.00 (*0-19-826381-3*) OUP.

Moral Gap: Kantian Ethics, Human Limits, & God's Assistance. John E. Hare. (Oxford Studies in Theological Ethics). 302p. 1997. reprint ed. pap. text 19.95 (*0-19-826957-9*) OUP.

***Moral Geographies: Ethics in a World of Difference.** David M. Smith. 272p. 2000. text 75.00 (*0-7486-1278-5*); pap. text 25.00 (*0-7486-1279-3*) Col U Pr.

Moral Glory of the Lord Jesus Christ. J. G. Bellett. pap. 2.95 (*0-88172-176-X*) Believers Bkshelf.

***Moral Government of God.** Gordon C. Olson. (Illus.). 48p. 1999. reprint ed. pap. 1.00 (*0-9664597-2-5*) Rev Theol Prom.

Moral Grandeur & Spiritual Audacity: Essays. Abraham Joshua Heschel. Ed. by Susannah Heschel. 320p. 1996. 27.50 (*0-374-19980-9*) FS&G.

Moral Grandeur & Spiritual Audacity: Essays. Abraham Joshua Heschel. 1997. pap. text 15.00 (*0-374-52495-5*, Noonday) FS&G.

***Moral Guide for the Teenagers of the Next Millennium.** T. Nagendran. 35p. 1999. pap. 9.95 (*0-7414-0116-9*) Buy Books.

Moral Healer's Handbook: The Psychology of Spiritual Chivalry. Laleh Bakhtiar. (God's Will Be Done Ser.: Vol. 2). 320p. (C). 1994. pap. 19.95 (*1-871031-39-7*) Kazi Pubns.

Moral Healing. Ibn Miskawah. 234p. 1996. pap. 19.95 (*0-614-21555-2*, 1465) Kazi Pubns.

Moral Healing Through the Most Beautiful Names: The Practice of Spiritual Chivalry. Laleh Bakhtiar. (God's Will Be Done Ser.: Vol. 3). 276p. (C). 1994. pap. 19.95 (*1-871031-40-0*) Kazi Pubns.

Moral Idea of the Main Dogmas of the Faith. Antony Khrapovitsky. Tr. by Varlaam Novakshonoff & Lazar Puhalo from RUS. 170p. (Orig.). 1984. pap. text 8.00 (*0-911523-01-4*) Synaxis Pr.

Moral Idealists, Bureaucracy, & Catherine the Great. Walter J. Gleason. LC 80-18658. 264p. reprint ed. pap. 81.90 (*0-8357-7946-7*, 205701900002) Bks Demand.

Moral Ideals of Our Civilization. Radoslav A. Tsanoff. 1977. lib. bdg. write for info. (*0-8490-2279-7*) Gordon Pr.

Moral Ideals of Our Civilization. Radoslav A. Tsanoff. LC 70-38738. (Essay Index Reprint Ser.). 1977. reprint ed. 40.95 (*0-8369-2675-7*) Ayer.

Moral Ideas for America. Ed. by Larry P. Arnn & Douglas A. Jeffrey. 149p. (Orig.). (C). pap. text 6.95 (*0-930783-21-2*) Claremont Inst.

Moral Ideas of the Main Dogmas of Faith. Antony Krapovitsky. 147p. Date not set. pap. 8.00 (*1-879038-69-2*, 9039) Synaxis Pr.

Moral Imagination. Edward Tivnan. 1995. 24.00 (*0-671-74708-8*) S&S Trade.

Moral Imagination: Essays on Literature & Ethics. Christopher Clausen. LC 86-11282. 208p. (C). 1986. text 25.95 (*0-87745-151-6*) U of Iowa Pr.

Moral Imagination: How Literature & Films Can Stimulate Ethical Reflection in the Business World. Oliver F. Williams. LC 97-46844. (John Houck Notre Dame Series in Business Ethics). 232p. 1998. 28.00 (*0-268-01432-9*); pap. 15.00 (*0-268-01434-5*) U of Notre Dame Pr.

Moral Imagination: Implications of Cognitive Science for Ethics. Mark Johnson. xiv, 302p. 1994. pap. 16.95 (*0-226-40169-3*) U Ch Pr.

Moral Imagination: Implications of Cognitive Science for Ethics. Mark Johnson. LC 92-29896. 300p. (C). 1996. 32.95 (*0-226-40168-5*) U Ch Pr.

Moral Imagination & Management Decision Making. Patricia H. Werhane. LC 98-17928. (Ruffin Series in Business Ethics). 160p. 1999. text 35.00 (*0-19-512569-X*) OUP.

Moral Imagination & Public Life: Raising the Ethical Question. Thomas E. McCollough. LC 91-6821. (Chatham House Studies in Political Thinking). 192p. (C). 1991. pap. text 19.95 (*0-934540-85-3*, Chatham House Pub) Seven Bridges.

Moral Imagination in Kaguru Modes of Thought. Thomas O. Beidelman. 240p. (C). 1993. pap. text 16.95 (*1-56098-236-5*) Smithsonian.

Moral Imperative: New Essays on the Ethics of Resistance in National Socialist Germany, 1933-1945. Ed. by Andrew Chandler. LC 98-18430. 124p. (C). 1998. pap. 65.00 (*0-8133-3466-7*, Pub. by Westview) HarpC.

Moral Imperium: Afro-Caribbeans & the Transformation of British Rule, 1776-1838, 22. Ronald K. Richardson. LC 86-3154. (Contributions in Comparative Colonial Studies: No. 22). 219p. 1987. 57.95 (*0-313-24724-2*, RMI/, Greenwood Pr) Greenwood.

Moral Inquiries on the Situation of Man & of Brutes: On the Crime of Committing Cruelty on Brutes, & of Sacrificing Them to the Purposes of Man. Lewis Gompertz. Ed. by Charles Magel. LC 97-2376. (Animal Rights Library: Vol. 4). 204p. 1997. text 89.95 (*0-7734-8722-0*) E Mellen.

Moral Intelligence of Children: How to Raise a Moral Child. Robert Coles. LC 97-41475. 240p. (C). 1998. pap. 12.95 (*0-452-27937-2*) Dutton Plume.

Moral Interpretation of Religion. Peter Byrne. LC 98-28239. 1998. pap. 26.00 (*0-8028-4554-1*) Eerdmans.

Moral Intuition & the Principle of Self-Realization. C. A. Campbell. 1970. reprint ed. pap. 39.95 (*0-8383-0114-2*) M S G Haskell Hse.

Moral Intuitions. James Q. Wilson. LC 99-13424. 72p. 1999. pap. 12.95 (*0-7658-0631-2*) Transaction Pubs.

Moral Issues. Ed. by Jan Narveson. 462p. 1983. pap. text 28.95 (*0-19-540426-2*) OUP.

Moral Issues: Philosophical & Religious Perspectives. Compiled by Gabriel Palmer-Fernandez. LC 95-35640. 527p. 1995. pap. text 54.00 (*0-13-819145-X*) P-H.

Moral Issues & Christian Response. 6th ed. Jersild. LC 97-75099. 2001. pap. 45.00 (*0-03-018062-7*, Pub. by Harcourt Coll Pubs) Harcourt.

Moral Issues in Business. Barry. (Philosophy Ser.). 1979. pap. 16.00 (*0-534-00709-0*) Wadsworth Pub.

Moral Issues in Business. 3rd ed. Vincent E. Barry. 502p. (C). 1985. pap. write for info. (*0-534-05484-6*) Wadsworth Pub.

Moral Issues in Business. 4th ed. William H. Shaw & Vincent E. Barry. 542p. (C). 1988. pap. write for info. (*0-534-09786-3*) Wadsworth Pub.

Moral Issues in Business. 5th ed. William H. Shaw & Vincent Barry. 588p. (C). 1991. pap. 31.25 (*0-534-16704-7*) Wadsworth Pub.

Moral Issues in Business. 6th ed. William H. Shaw & Vincent Barry. LC 94-12355. 588p. 1994. mass mkt. 46.95 (*0-534-21702-8*) Wadsworth Pub.

Moral Issues in Business. 7th ed. William H. Shaw & Vincent Barry. LC 97-15858. (Philosophy Ser.). (C). 1997. pap. 58.95 (*0-534-52452-4*) Wadsworth Pub.

Moral Issues in Business. 8th ed. Shaw. (Philosophy Ser.). 2000. pap. 42.00 (*0-534-53595-X*) Wadsworth Pub.

Moral Issues in Global Perspective. Ed. by Christine M. Koggell. 600p. 1998. pap. 34.95 (*1-55111-186-1*) Broadview Pr.

Moral Issues in Health Care. 2nd ed. Terrence McConnell. LC 96-19413. (Philosophy Ser.). 320p. (C). 1996. 31.95 (*0-534-24744-X*) Wadsworth Pub.

Moral Issues in International Affairs: Problems of European Integration William McSweeney. LC 97-40513. viii, 265 p. 1998. 5.25 hd. write for info. (*0-333-69848-7*) Macmillan.

Moral Issues in Mental Retardation. Ed. by Ronald S. Laura & Adrian F. Ashman. LC 84-29329. 224p. 1985. 35.00 (*0-7099-1692-2*, Pub. by C Helm) Routldge.

Moral Issues in Military Decision Making. Anthony E. Hartle. LC 88-33918. viii, 180p. 1989. 25.00 (*0-7006-0397-2*); pap. 14.95 (*0-7006-0463-4*) U Pr of KS.

Moral Issues in Police Work. Ed. by Frederick Elliston & Michael Feldberg. LC 84-22259. (Illus.). 316p. (C). 1985. pap. 25.00 (*0-8476-7192-5*) Rowman.

Moral Issues in Psychology: Personalist Contributions to Selected Problems. Ed. by James M. DuBois. LC 96-36306. 182p. 1996. pap. text 28.50 (*0-7618-0543-5*); lib. bdg. 46.00 (*0-7618-0542-7*) U Pr of Amer.

Moral Issues Internat Affairs. McSweeney. LC 97-40513. 265p. 1998. text 65.00 (*0-312-21128-7*) St Martin.

Moral Judgment: Does the Abuse Excuse Threaten Our Legal System? James Q. Wilson. 1997. 18.00 (*0-614-28007-9*) Basic.

Moral Judgment: Does the Abuse Excuse Threaten Our Legal System? James Q. Wilson. 128p. 1998. pap. 10.00 (*0-465-04733-5*, Pub. by Basic) HarpC.

Moral Judgment of the Child. Jean Piaget. Tr. by Marjorie Gabain. 416p. 1965. pap. 17.95 (*0-02-925240-7*) Free Pr.

Moral Judgment of the Child. Jean Piaget. 416p. 1997. per. 15.00 (*0-684-83330-1*) Free Pr.

Moral Knowing in a Hindu Sacred City: An Exploration of Mind, Emotion, & Self. Steven M. Parish. LC 94-366. 1994. pap. 22.00 (*0-231-08439-0*) Col U Pr.

Moral Knowing in a Hindu Sacred City: An Exploration of Mind, Emotion, & Self. Steven M. Parish. LC 94-366. 1994. 57.50 (*0-231-08438-2*) Col U Pr.

Moral Knowledge. Alan H. Goldman. 240p. 1989. 35.00 (*0-415-01310-0*) Routledge.

Moral Knowledge? New Readings in Moral Epistemology. Ed. by Walter Sinnott-Armstrong & Mark Timmons. 352p. (C). 1996. text 57.00 (*0-19-508988-X*); pap. text 29.95 (*0-19-508989-8*) OUP.

Moral Knowledge & Ethical Character. Robert Audi. LC 96-36703. 320p. 1997. pap. 19.95 (*0-19-511469-8*); text 60.00 (*0-19-511468-X*) OUP.

Moral Landscapes: French Art & Politics Between the 2 World Wars. Romy Golan. LC 95-15989. 1995. 50.00 (*0-300-06350-4*) Yale U Pr.

Moral Language. Mary G. Forrester. 240p. 1982. 28.00 (*0-299-08630-5*) U of Wis Pr.

Moral Leadership. Eloy Annelo & Joan B. Hernandez. 166p. 1998. pap. 16.95 (*0-9659945-1-1*) Global Classrm.

Moral Leadership: Getting to the Heart of School Improvement. Thomas J. Sergiovanni. LC 91-31187. (Education-Higher Education Ser.). 195p. 1992. text 32.95 (*1-55542-400-7*) Jossey-Bass.

Moral Leadership: Getting to the Heart of School Improvement. Thomas J. Sergiovanni. LC 91-31187. 195p. 1996. pap. 18.95 (*0-7879-0259-4*) Jossey-Bass.

Moral Leadership in a Postmodern Age. Robin Gill. 192p. 1997. pap. 24.95 (*0-567-08550-3*, Pub. by T & T Clark) Bks Intl VA.

Moral Leadership in Business. LaRue T. Hosmer. LC 93-5058. 320p. (C). 1993. text 27.25 (*0-256-14325-0*, Irwn McGrw-H) McGrw-H Hghr Educ.

Moral Legislation: A Legal-Political Model for Indirect Consequentialist Reasoning. Conrad D. Johnson. (Cambridge Studies in Philosophy). 244p. (C). 1991. text 69.95 (*0-521-39224-1*) Cambridge U Pr.

Moral Lessons of Yesterday. A. L. Byers. Ed. by Richard Wheeler & Noelle Wheeler. (Illus.). 168p. (C). 1995. 15.00 (*1-889128-30-9*) Mantle Ministries.

Moral Letters, 3 vols., 1. Lucius Annaeus Seneca. (Loeb Classical Library: No. 75-77). 484p. 1917. text 19.95 (*0-674-99084-6*) HUP.

Moral Letters, 3 vols., 2. Lucius Annaeus Seneca. (Loeb Classical Library: No. 75-77). 486p. 1920. text 19.95 (*0-674-99085-4*) HUP.

Moral Letters, 3 vols., 3. Lucius Annaeus Seneca. (Loeb Classical Library: No. 75-77). 470p. 1925. text 19.95 (*0-674-99086-2*) HUP.

Moral Life. Steven Luper-Foy & Curtis Brown. 480p. (C). 1992. pap. text 51.50 (*0-03-033969-3*) Harcourt Coll Pubs.

Moral Life. Hugo L. Odhner. 142p. 1985. reprint ed. 3.75 (*0-910557-08-X*) Acad New Church.

Moral Life. 2nd ed. Steven Luper & Curtis Brown. 168p. (C). 1998. pap. text 51.50 (*0-15-505547-X*, Pub. by Harcourt Coll Pubs) Harcourt.

Moral Life: An Introduction Reader in Ethics & Literature. Ed. by Louis P. Pojman. LC 98-46486. 960p. (C). 1999. pap. text 38.00 (*0-19-512844-3*) OUP.

Moral Life & the Ethical Life. Eliseo Vivas. 320p. (C). 1984. reprint ed. pap. text 24.00 (*0-8191-3308-6*) U Pr of Amer.

Moral Life of Children. Robert Cole. (Illus.). 324p. 1991. pap. 14.00 (*0-395-59921-0*) HM.

***Moral Life of Children.** Robert Coles. 320p. 2000. pap. 13.50 (*0-87113-770-4*, Atlntc Mnthly) Grove-Atltic.

Moral Life of Schools. Philip W. Jackson. 1998. pap. text 21.95 (*0-7879-4066-6*) Jossey-Bass.

Moral Life of Schools. Philip W. Jackson et al. LC 93-22370. (Education-Higher Education Ser.). 241p. 1993. text 34.45 (*1-55542-577-1*) Jossey-Bass.

Moral Limitations of Capitalism. Irving S. Michelman. (Avebury Series in Philosophy). 184p. 1994. 72.95 (*1-85628-877-3*, Pub. by Avebry) Ashgate Pub Co.

Moral Literacy: or How to Do the Right Thing. Colin McGinn. 110p. (C). 1993. pap. text 8.95 (*0-87220-196-1*); lib. bdg. 29.95 (*0-87220-197-X*) Hackett Pub.

Moral Love Songs & Laments. Susanna G. Fein. LC 97-49951. (Middle English Texts Ser.). 1998. pap. 20.00 (*1-879288-97-4*) Medieval Inst.

Moral Luck: Philosophical Essays, 1973-80. Bernard Williams. LC 81-10152. 192p. 1982. pap. text 19.95 (*0-521-28691-3*) Cambridge U Pr.

Moral Majority & Fundamentalism: Plausability & Dissonance. Sharon Georgianna. LC 89-36103. (Studies in Religion & Society: Vol. 23). 179p. 1989. lib. bdg. 79.95 (*0-88946-851-6*) E Mellen.

Moral Management: Integrating Ethics. Andrew F. Sikula, Sr. 176p. (C). 1995. text 22.00 (*0-256-20368-7*, Irwn Prfssnl) McGraw-Hill Prof.

Moral Manager. Clarence C. Walton. 304p. 1988. 24.95 (*0-88730-309-9*, HarpBusn) HarpInfo.

Moral Manager. Clarence C. Walton. 1990. pap. 16.00 (*0-88730-447-8*, HarpBusn) HarpInfo.

***Moral Mandate to Vote.** Kenneth M. Wilson. LC 00-103970. 240p. 2000. pap. 12.99 (*1-56384-177-0*) Huntington Hse.

Moral Matters. Jan Narveson. 256p. 1993. pap. 16.95 (*1-55111-011-3*) Broadview Pr.

Moral Matters. 2nd ed. Jan Narveson. 300p. 1999. pap. 19.95 (*1-55111-212-4*) Broadview Pr.

Moral Maturity: Measuring the Development of Sociomoral Reflection. John C. Gibbs et al. 232p. (C). 1992. text 49.95 (*0-8058-0425-0*) L Erlbaum Assocs.

Moral Maze. Joan Greco. 256p. 1998. pap. 14.00 (*0-465-04763-7*) Basic.

Moral Mazes: The World of Corporate Managers. Robert Jackall. 272p. 1989. pap. text 14.95 (*0-19-506080-6*) OUP.

Moral Meaning of Revolution. Jon P. Gunnemann. LC 79-10219. 289p. reprint ed. pap. 89.60 (*0-8357-8235-2*, 203373700087) Bks Demand.

Moral Measure of Literature. Keith F. McKean. LC 73-2339. 137p. 1973. reprint ed. lib. bdg. 55.00 (*0-8371-6842-2*, MCMM, Greenwood Pr) Greenwood.

***Moral Measures: An Introduction to Ethics West & East.** J. E. Tiles. LC 99-53170. 328p. 2000. pap. 25.99 (*0-415-22496-9*) Routledge.

***Moral Measures: Introduction to Ethics West & East.** J. E. Tiles. LC 99-53170. 328p. (C). 2000. text. write for info. (*0-415-22495-0*) Routledge.

***Moral Meltdown.** unabridged ed. Sally Ann Kates. Ed. by Lana Wegeng. (Illus.). 1999. pap. 12.95 (*1-892651-23-8*) Columbia Pubns.

Moral Meltdown: The Core of Globalism. Hilmar Von Campe. LC 95-72814. 224p. (Orig.). 1996. pap. 10.99 (*0-933451-35-0*) Prescott Pr.

Moral Metafiction: The Novels of Timothy Findley. Donna Pennee. 140p. (C). 1991. pap. 20.00 (*1-55022-138-8*, Pub. by ECW) Genl Dist Srvs.

Moral Military. Sidney Axinn. LC 88-29294. 264p. (C). 1989. 37.95 (*0-87722-615-6*) Temple U Pr.

Moral Military. Sidney Axinn. 264p. 1990. pap. 22.95 (*0-87722-780-2*) Temple U Pr.

Moral Monopoly: The Rise & Fall of the Catholic Church in Ireland. 2nd ed. Tom Inglis. 312p. pap. 25.95 (*1-900621-12-6*, Pub. by Univ Coll Dublin Pr) Dufour.

Moral Nation: Humanitarianism & U. S. Foreign Policy Today. Ed. by Bruce Nichols & Gilburt D. Loescher. LC 88-40323. (C). 1990. pap. text 18.50 (*0-268-01398-5*) U of Notre Dame Pr.

Moral Nexus: Ethics of Christian Identity & Community. 25th anniversary ed. James B. Nelson. LC 96-22894. 264p. 1996. pap. 24.95 (*0-664-25678-3*) Westminster John Knox.

Moral Norms & Moral Order: The Philosophy of Human Affairs. William A. Banner. LC 80-24206. 126p. reprint ed. pap. 39.10 (*0-7837-5032-3*, 204470100004) Bks Demand.

Moral Objectives, Rules & the Forms of Social Change. David Braybrooke. LC 98-167106. (Toronto Studies in Philosophy). 384p. 1998. text 55.00 (*0-8020-4169-8*); pap. text 21.95 (*0-8020-8031-6*) U of Toronto Pr.

***Moral Obligation to Be Intelligent: Selected Essays.** Lionel Trilling. Ed. by Leon Wieseltier. LC 99-87875. 576p. 2000. 35.00 (*0-374-25794-9*) FS&G.

Moral Obligation to Be Intelligent & Other Essays. John Erskine. LC 70-93337. (Essay Index Reprint Ser.). 1977. 19.95 (*0-8369-1291-8*) Ayer.

Moral of Molliston Madison Clark. Joseph R. Washington, Jr. LC 90-6446. (Studies in American History: Vol. 6). 170p. 1990. lib. bdg. 79.95 (*0-88946-083-3*) E Mellen.

***Moral of the Story: An Introduciton to Ethics.** 3rd ed. Nina Rosenstand. LC 99-17115. xi, 564p. 1999. pap. text 44.95 (*0-7674-0595-1*, 0595-1) Mayfield Pub.

***Moral of the Story: Folktales for Character Development.** Bobby Norfolk & Sherry Norfolk. LC 99-13190. 175p. 1999. pap. 14.95 (*0-87483-555-0*) August Hse.

Moral of the Story: Folktales for Character Development. Bobby Norfolk & Sherry Norfolk. LC 99-13190. 175p. 1999. 24.95 (*0-87483-542-9*) August Hse.

***Moral of the Story: Literature & Public Ethics.** Ed. by Henry T. Edmondson, III. 272p. 2000. 75.00 (*0-7391-0148-X*); pap. 24.95 (*0-7391-0149-8*) Lxngtn Bks.

Moral of the Story: Literature, Values & American Education. Susan R. Parr. 236p. (C). 1982. pap. text 17.95 (*0-8077-2716-4*) Tchrs Coll.

***Moral of the Story: Timeless Tales To Cherish & Share.** Jerry Newcombe. (Illus.). 1999. 21.99 (*0-8054-2009-6*) Broadman.

Moral of the Story & the Last Hero. Jerry Patterson. 50p. pap., per. 7.95 (*0-89697-311-5*) Intl Univ Pr.

Moral Ontology of Human Fetuses: A Metaphysical Investigation of Personhood. Jens Saugstad. (Studien und Materialien Zur Geschichte der Philosophie). 350p. 1997. write for info. (*3-487-10270-6*) G Olms Pubs.

Moral Opposition to Authoritarian Rule in Chile, 1973-1990. Pamela Lowden. LC 95-36938. (St. Antony's Ser.). 224p. 1996. text 65.00 (*0-312-15870-X*) St Martin.

Moral or Less: An Adventure in Addition & Subtraction. Maxine Nodel. (Arithmetic Math Ser.). (Illus.). 32p. (J). (ps-3). 1990. 8.95 (*0-922613-25-7*); pap. 6.95 (*0-922613-26-5*); pap., student ed. 4.95 (*0-922613-27-3*) Hachai Pubng.

Moral Order: An Introduction to the Human Situation. Raoul Naroll. LC 82-19204. 498p. reprint ed. pap. 154.40 (*0-7837-1129-8*, 204165900022) Bks Demand.

Moral Order & Social Disorder: The American Search for Civil Society. Frank Hearn. LC 97-18771. (Sociological Imagination & Structural Change Ser.). 221p. 1997. pap. text 22.95 (*0-202-30604-6*); lib. bdg. 47.95 (*0-202-30603-8*) Aldine de Gruyter.

Moral Order of a Suburb. M. P. Baumgartner. 192p. 1989. text 60.00 (*0-19-505413-X*) OUP.

Moral Order of a Suburb. M. P. Baumgartner. 192p. (C). 1991. reprint ed. pap. text 20.95 (*0-19-506995-1*, 5317) OUP.

Moral Order of the World in Ancient & Modern Thought. Alexander B. Bruce. LC 77-527224. (Gifford Lectures: 1898). reprint ed. 49.50 (*0-404-60456-0*) AMS Pr.

Moral Order of the World in Ancient & Modern Thought (1899) Alexander B. Bruce. 425p. 1998. reprint ed. pap. 29.95 (*0-7661-0165-7*) Kessinger Pub.

***Moral Outrage in Education.** David E. Purpel. LC 98-37877. (Counterpoints Ser.: Vol. 102). viii, 258p. (C). 1999. pap. text 29.95 (*0-8204-4169-4*) P Lang Pubng.

Moral Panic: Changing Concepts of the Child Molester in Modern America. Philip Jenkins. LC 98-14890. 320p. 1998. 30.00 (*0-300-07387-9*) Yale U Pr.

Moral Panic: Exposing the Religious Right's Agenda on Sexuality. Terry Murray & Michael McClure. 64p. 1995. pap. 5.95 (*0-304-33327-1*) Bks Intl VA.

Moral Panics. Kenneth Thompson. LC 97-28401. 176p. (C). 1998. 65.00 (*0-415-11976-6*); pap. 17.99 (*0-415-11977-4*) Routledge.

Moral Panics: The Social Construction of Deviance. Erich Goode & Nachman Ben-Yehuda. LC 93-48397. 288p. 1994. pap. 29.95 (*0-631-18905-X*) Blackwell Pubs.

Moral Parameters of Good Talk: A Feminist Analysis. Maryann N. Ayim. 265p. 1997. 45.00 (*0-88920-282-6*) W Laurier U Pr.

Moral Partners: Building Moral Character for Business. Edward J. Conry. 750p. (C). 1995. text. write for info. (*1-887959-00-9*) Sage CO.

Moral Partners: Building Moral Character for Business. abr. ed. Edward J. Conry. 265p. (C). 1995. write for info. (*1-887959-01-7*) Sage CO.

Moral Passages: Notes Toward a Collectivist Ethics. Kathryn P. Addelson. LC 94-20583. 272p. (C). 1994. pap. 19.99 (*0-415-91021-8*, B3836) Routledge.

Moral Passages: Notes Toward a Collectivist Ethics. Kathryn P. Addelson. LC 94-20583. 256p. (C). (gr. 13). 1994. 70.00 (*0-415-91020-X*, B3832) Routledge.

Moral Passion of Bruce Springsteen. Patrick D. Primeaux. (ISP Ser.). (Illus.). 142p. 1996. 54.95 (*1-57309-037-9*); pap. 32.95 (*1-57309-036-0*) Intl Scholars.

Moral Perception & Particularity. Lawrence A. Blum. 285p. (C). 1994. text 69.95 (*0-521-43028-3*) Cambridge U Pr.

Moral Personhood: An Essay in the Philosophy of Moral Psychology. G. E. Scott. LC 89-39221. (SUNY Series in Ethical Theory). 202p. (C). 1990. pap. text 21.95 (*0-7914-0322-X*) State U NY Pr.

Moral Perspectives. Ed. by Chong K. Chong. 150p. (Orig.). 1992. pap. 34.95 (*9971-69-162-0*, Pub. by Sngapore Univ Pr) Coronet Bks.

Moral Perspectives on U. S. Security Policy: Views from the LDS Community. Ed. by Kennedy, David M., Center for International Studie et al. LC 95-1875. 192p. (Orig.). (C). 1995. pap. text 24.00 (*0-912575-14-X*, BYU DMK Ctr Intl) Brigham.

Moral Philosophers: An Introduction to Ethics. 2nd ed. Richard Norman. 240p. (C). 1998. text 44.00 (*0-19-875217-2*); pap. text 21.95 (*0-19-875216-4*) OUP.

Moral Philosophers in Britain: From Bradley to Wittgenstein. Cahal Daly. 220p. 1996. 45.00 (*1-85182-227-5*, Pub. by Four Cts Pr) Intl Spec Bk.

Moral Philosophies in Shakespeare's Plays. Ben Kimpel. LC 87-5757. (Studies in Art & Religious Interpretation: Vol. 7). 262p. 1987. lib. bdg. 89.95 (*0-88946-558-4*) E Mellen.

Moral Philosophy. Ed. by William C. Starr & Richard C. Taylor. LC 88-63249. 200p. 1988. pap. text 15.00 (*0-87462-476-2*) Marquette.

Moral Philosophy. 2nd ed. D. D. Raphael. LC 93-3919. 160p. (Orig.). 1994. pap. text 16.95 (*0-19-289246-0*) OUP.

Moral Philosophy: A Comprehensive Introduction. Brooke N. Moore & Robert M. Stewart. LC 93-11106. xii, 660p. (C). 1993. 57.95 (*1-55934-037-1*, 1037) Mayfield Pub.

Moral Philosophy: A Reader. 2nd rev. ed. Ed. by Louis P. Pojman. LC 98-7956. 320p. (C). 1998. pap. 16.95 (*0-87220-408-1*); lib. bdg. 34.95 (*0-87220-409-X*) Hackett Pub.

Moral Philosophy: Selected Readings. 2nd ed. Sher. (C). 1995. text 53.00 (*0-15-501755-1*, Pub. by Harcourt Coll Pubs) Harcourt.

Moral Philosophy: Theory & Issues. Barcalow. (Philosophy Ser.). 1993. teacher ed. 25.25 (*0-534-21037-6*) Wadsworth Pub.

Moral Philosophy: Theory & Issues. Emmett Barcalow. 378p. 1993. mass mkt. 30.25 (*0-534-21036-8*) Wadsworth Pub.

Moral Philosophy: Theory & Issues. 2nd ed. Emmett Barcalow. LC 97-28869. (C). 1997. 51.95 (*0-534-52645-4*) Wadsworth Pub.

Moral Philosophy & Development: The Human Condition in Africa. Tedros Kiros. LC 92-9546. (Monographs in International Studies, Africa: No. 61). 199p. (Orig.). (C). 1992. pap. text 20.00 (*0-89680-171-3*) Ohio U Pr.

Moral Philosophy at 17th-Century Harvard: A Discipline in Transition. Norman Fiering. LC 80-18282. (Institute of Early American History & Culture Ser.). xiii, 323p. 1981. 37.50 (*0-8078-1459-8*) U of NC Pr.

Moral Philosophy for Modern Life. Anthony Falikowski. LC 99-182861. 465p. 1997. pap. text 51.00 (*0-13-598046-1*) P-H.

Moral Philosophy from Montaigne to Kant: An Anthology, Vol. I. Ed. by Jerome B. Schneewind. 364p. (C). 1990. pap. text 21.95 (*0-521-35875-2*) Cambridge U Pr.

Moral Philosophy from Montaigne to Kant: An Anthology, Vol. II. Ed. by Jerome B. Schneewind. 319p. (C). 1990. pap. text 22.95 (*0-521-35876-0*) Cambridge U Pr.

Moral Philosophy of G. E. Moore. Robert P. Sylvester. Ed. by Ray Perkins, Jr. & R. W. Sleeper. 240p. 1990. 44.95 (*0-87722-645-8*) Temple U Pr.

Moral Philosophy of Gandhi. Jaladhar Pal. 345p. 1998. 30.00 (*81-212-0524-7*, Pub. by Gyan Publishing Hse) Nataraj Bks.

Moral Philosophy of George Berkeley. Paul J. Olscamp. (International Archives of the History of Ideas Ser.: No. 33). 251p. 1970. lib. bdg. 88.00 (*90-247-0303-4*) Kluwer Academic.

Moral Philosophy of John Stuart Mill: Toward Modifications of Contemporary Utilitarianism. Mark P. Strasser. LC 91-15218. 1991. text 35.00 (*0-89341-681-9*, Longwood Academic) Hollowbrook.

Moral Philosophy of Josiah Royce. Peter L. Fuss. LC 65-11590. 288p. reprint ed. pap. 89.30 (*0-608-10110-9*, 200296500016) Bks Demand.

Moral Philosophy of Management: From Quesnay to Keynes. Pierre G. De Monthoux. LC 93-16576. (Studies in Socio-Economics). 328p. (C). (gr. 13). 1993. pap. text 40.95 (*1-56324-377-6*) M E Sharpe.

Moral Philosophy of Management: From Quesnay to Keynes. Pierre Guillet de Monthoux. LC 93-16576. (Studies in Socio-Economics Ser.). 328p. (C). (gr. 13). 1993. text 81.95 (*1-56324-081-5*) M E Sharpe.

Moral Philosophy of R. M. Hare: A Vindication of Utilitarianism? Patrick A. Adu-Amankwah. LC 94-41395. (American University Studies V: Vol. 172). XXXV, 603p. (C). 1998. text 72.95 (*0-8204-2703-9*) P Lang Pubng.

Moral Philosophy of T. H. Green. Geoffrey Thomas. 422p. 1988. text 90.00 (*0-19-824788-5*) OUP.

***Moral Philosophy Through the Ages.** James Fieser. LC 00-28443. 2000. write for info. (*0-7674-1298-2*) Mayfield Pub.

Moral Picturesque: Studies in Hawthorne's Fiction. Darrel Abel. LC 87-26843. 336p. 1988. 28.95 (*0-911198-91-1*) Purdue U Pr.

Moral Pluralism & Legal Neutrality. Wojciech Sadurski. 229p. (C). 1990. lib. bdg. 148.50 (*0-7923-0565-5*, Pub. by Kluwer Academic) Kluwer Academic.

Moral Politics: What Conservatives Know That Liberals Don't. George Lakoff. LC 95-47690. 432p. 1996. 24.95 (*0-226-46796-1*) U Ch Pr.

Moral Politics: What Conservatives Know That Liberals Don't. George Lakoff. xii, 414p. 1997. pap. 14.95 (*0-226-46805-4*) U Ch Pr.

Moral Powers: Normative Necessity in Language & History. Anthony Holiday. 224p. 1988. lib. bdg. 65.00 (*0-415-00304-0*) Routledge.

Moral Predicament: Morley Callaghan's More Joy in Heaven. George Woodcock. (Canadian Fiction Studies: No. 14). 71p. (C). 1993. pap. 14.95 (*1-55022-134-5*, Pub. by ECW) Genl Dist Srvs.

Moral Prejudices: Essays on Ethics. Annette C. Baier. LC 93-2442. 368p. 1994. text 49.95 (*0-674-58715-4*) HUP.

Moral Prejudices: Essays on Ethics. Annette C. Baier. 384p. 1995. pap. text 19.50 (*0-674-58716-2*, BAIMOX) HUP.

Moral Principles & Nuclear Weapons. Douglas P. Lackey. LC 84-11540. (Philosophy & Society Ser.). (Illus.). 284p. (C). 1984. 56.50 (*0-8476-7116-X*) Rowman.

Moral Principles & Nuclear Weapons. Douglas P. Lackey. 288p. 1986. pap. 22.50 (*0-8476-7515-7*) Rowman.

Moral Principles & Policy Priorities for Welfare Reform. Administrative Board, U.S. Catholic Conference Sta. 12p. 1995. pap. text 1.25 (*1-57455-011-X*) US Catholic.

Moral Principles & Political Obligations. Alan J. Simmons. LC 79-2505. 248p. reprint ed. pap. 76.90 (*0-8357-8959-4*, 205227900085) Bks Demand.

Moral Principles in Education. John Dewey. LC 74-18472. (Arcturus Books Paperbacks). 79p. 1975. reprint ed. pap. 12.95 (*0-8093-0715-4*) S Ill U Pr.

Moral Problem. Michael A. Smith. LC 94-6156. (Philosophical Theory Ser.). 240p. 1994. pap. 28.95 (*0-631-19246-8*) Blackwell Pubs.

Moral Problems & Mental Health. Richard Egenter & Paul Matussek. 190p. (Orig.). 1967. pap. 4.95 (*0-8189-0095-4*) Alba.

Moral Problems in American Life: New Perspectives on Cultural History. Ed. by Karen Halttunen & Lewis Perry. LC 98-8356. (Illus.). 352p. 1998. 50.95 (*0-8014-3270-7*) Cornell U Pr.

Moral Problems in American Life: New Perspectives on Cultural History. Ed. by Karen Halttunen & Lewis Perry. LC 98-8356. (Illus.). 352p. 1999. pap. 19.95 (*0-8014-8350-6*) Cornell U Pr.

Moral Problems in Medicine: A Practical Coursebook. Michael Palmer. LC 99-206718. 224p. 1999. text 19.95 (*0-8020-8257-2*) U of Toronto Pr.

Moral Progress: A Process Critique of Mac Intyre. Lisa Bellantoni. LC 99-30969. (C). 2000. pap. text 15.95 (*0-7914-4444-9*) State U NY Pr.

***Moral Progress: A Process Critique of Mac Intyre.** Lisa Bellantoni. LC 99-30969. (C). 2000. text 47.50 (*0-7914-4443-0*) State U NY Pr.

Moral Proverbs of Santob de Carrion: Jewish Wisdom in Christian Spain. Santob De Carrion De Los Condes. LC 87-45532. 208p. 1987. reprint ed. pap. 64.50 (*0-608-07158-7*, 206738300009) Bks Demand.

Moral Psychology. Daniel K. Lapsley. (Developmental Psychology Ser.). (C). 1996. pap. 25.00 (*0-8133-3033-5*, Pub. by Westview) HarpC.

***Moral Purity & Persecution in History.** Barrington Moore, Jr. LC BJ1533.P97M66 2000. 149p. 2000. 24.95 (*0-691-04920-3*, Pub. by Princeton U Pr) Cal Prin Full Svc.

Moral Purity Imperative. Aaron Shank. (Cornerstone Ser.). 122p. 1990. pap. 4.40 (*0-7399-0194-X*, 2336) Rod & Staff.

Moral Purpose of the State: Culture, Social Identity & Institutional Rationality in International Relations. Christian Reus-Smit. LC 98-33162. (Princeton Studies in International History & Politics). 208p. 1999. 35.00 (*0-691-02735-8*, Pub. by Princeton U Pr) Cal Prin Full Svc.

Moral Quest: Foundations of Christian Ethics. Stanley J. Grenz. LC 97-28853. 240p. 1997. 22.99 (*0-8308-1549-X*, 1549) InterVarsity.

***Moral Quest: Foundations of Christian Ethics.** Stanley J. Grenz. 2000. pap. 19.99 (*0-8308-1568-6*) InterVarsity.

Moral Question of Abortion. Stephen Schwarz. 304p. 1990. pap. 9.95 (*0-8294-0623-9*) Sophia Inst Pr.

Moral Questions: An Introduction to Ethics. Jon Nuttall. LC 92-19117. 240p. 1993. 58.95 (*0-7456-1039-0*); pap. 22.95 (*0-7456-1040-4*) Blackwell Pubs.

***Moral Questions by Rush Rhees.** Rush Rhees. LC 99-17493. 1999. text 65.00 (*0-312-22355-2*) St Martin.

Moral Re-Armament: A Factor in World Affairs. Michael Henderson. 1989. 0.75 (*0-913342-35-1*) Grosvenor USA.

Moral Realism. Torbjorn Tannsjo. 146p. (C). 1990. lib. bdg. 50.00 (*0-8476-7618-8*) B&N Imports.

Moral Realism & the Foundations of Ethics. David O. Brink. (Cambridge Studies in Philosophy). 352p. (C). 1989. text 80.00 (*0-521-35080-8*); pap. text 25.95 (*0-521-35937-6*) Cambridge U Pr.

Moral Reasoning. Fox. 1996. 40.50 (*0-15-504383-8*, Pub. by Harcourt Coll Pubs) Harcourt.

Moral Reasoning. 2nd ed. Fox. (C). 1999. pap. text 31.00 (*0-15-505520-8*, Pub. by Harcourt Coll Pubs) Harcourt.

Moral Reasoning: A Philosophic Approach to Applied Ethics. Richard M. Fox & Joseph P. DeMarco. 480p. (C). 1990. pap. text 26.00 (*0-03-026594-0*) Harcourt Coll Pubs.

Moral Reasoning: A Psychological-Philosophical Integration. fac. ed. William D. Boyce & Larry C. Jensen. LC 78-5935. 303p. 1978. reprint ed. pap. 94.00 (*0-7837-8102-4*, 204790600008) Bks Demand.

Moral Reasoning & Statecraft: Essays Presented to Kenneth W. Thompson. Ed. by Reed M. Davis. (Illus.). 208p. (Orig.). (C). 1988. pap. text 21.00 (*0-8191-7019-4*, Pub. by White Miller Center); lib. bdg. 45.00 (*0-8191-7018-6*, Pub. by White Miller Center) U Pr of Amer.

Moral Reasoning for Journalists: Cases & Commentary. Steven R. Knowlton. LC 96-37734. 240p. 1997. 59.95 (*0-275-94871-4*, Praeger Pubs) Greenwood.

Moral Reasoning for Journalists: Cases & Commentary. Steven R. Knowlton. LC 96-37734. 240p. 1997. pap. 19.95 (*0-275-94872-2*, Praeger Pubs) Greenwood.

Moral Reasons. Jonathan Dancy. LC 92-21888. 256p. 1997. pap. 29.95 (*0-631-18792-8*) Blackwell Pubs.

Moral Reflections & Epistles. Ludvig Holberg. Tr. & Intro. by P. M. Mitchell. (Norvik Press Series A: No. 8). 197p. (Orig.). 1991. pap. 35.00 (*1-870041-16-X*, Pub. by Norvik Pr) Dufour.

Moral Rejection of Nuclear Deterrence: The Contemporary Peace Witness of Churches in... Europe with Insights for U. S. Churches. Ed. by James E. Will. 1985. pap. 8.95 (*0-377-00163-5*) Friendship Pr.

***Moral Relativism: A Reader.** Ed. by Paul K. Moser & Thomas L. Carson. LC 99-55853. 320p. 2000. text 45.00 (*0-19-513129-0*); pap. text 24.95 (*0-19-513130-4*) OUP.

Moral Relativism & Moral Objectivity. Gilbert Harman & Judith L. Thomson. (Great Debates in Philosophy Ser.). 1995. pap. 27.95 (*0-631-19211-5*) Blackwell Pubs.

Moral Relevance & Moral Conflict. James D. Wallace. LC 87-47961. 168p. 1988. text 32.50 (*0-8014-2096-2*) Cornell U Pr.

***Moral Responsibility & Ontology.** A. Van den Beld. LC 00-25766. (Library of Ethics & Applied Philosophy). 2000. write for info. (*0-7923-6255-1*) Kluwer Academic.

Moral Responsibility & Persons. Eugene S. Schlossberger. (C). 1992. 54.95 (*0-87722-879-5*) Temple U Pr.

Moral Responsibility & the Boundaries of Community: Power & Accountability from a Pragmatic Point of View. Marion Smiley. LC 91-37468. 296p. 1992. pap. text 19.95 (*0-226-76327-7*) U Ch Pr.

Moral Responsibility & the Boundaries of Community: Power & Accountability from a Pragmatic Point of View. Marion Smiley. LC 91-37468. 296p. 1992. lib. bdg. 51.00 (*0-226-76326-9*) U Ch Pr.

Moral Responsibility & the Professions. Bernard Baumrin & Benjamin Freedman. LC 83-83296. (Professional Ethics Ser.). 400p. (Orig.). 1983. pap. text 20.50 (*0-930586-10-7*) Haven Pubns.

Moral Responsibility in Conflicts: Essays on Nonviolence, War, & Conscience. James F. Childress. LC 82-15197. xvi, 224p. (C). 1982. text 35.00 (*0-8071-1019-1*) La State U Pr.

Moral Responsibility in the Holocaust: A Study in the Ethics of Character. David H. Jones. LC 98-48271. 272p. 1999. 55.95 (*0-8476-9266-3*) Rowman.

***Moral Responsibility in the Holocaust: A Study in the Ethics of Character.** David H. Jones. LC 98-48271. 272p. 1999. pap. 15.95 (*0-8476-9267-1*) Rowman.

Moral Review of the Revolutionary War: Or Some of the Evils of That Event Considered. Sylvester Judd. LC 74-137548. (Peace Movement in America Ser.). 49p. 1972. reprint ed. lib. bdg. 22.95 (*0-89198-076-8*) Ozer.

Moral Revolution & Economic Science: The Demise of Laissez-Faire in Nineteenth Century British Political Economy, 23. Ellen F. Paul. LC 78-73797. (Contributions in Economics & Economic History Ser.: No. 23). 309p. 1979. 65.00 (*0-313-21055-1*, PMR/) Greenwood.

Moral Rightness. David W. Haslett. 1975. pap. text 64.50 (*90-247-1627-6*, Pub. by M Nijhoff) Kluwer Academic.

Moral Rights: Reports Presented at the Meeting of the International Association of Entertainment Lawyers MIDEM 1995, Cannes. Ed. by Cees Van Rij. 287p. 1995. pap. 156.00 (*90-6715-013-4*, Pub. by Maklu Uitgev) Gaunt.

Moral Rights & Political Freedom. Tara Smith. 234p. (C). 1995. pap. text 24.95 (*0-8476-8027-4*); lib. bdg. 60.50 (*0-8476-8026-6*) Rowman.

Moral Rights in the Workplace. Ed. by Gertrude Ezorsky. LC 86-6949. 312p. (C). 1972. pap. text 16.95 (*0-88706-363-2*) State U NY Pr.

Moral Rights in the Workplace. Ed. by Gertrude Ezorsky. LC 86-6949. 312p. (C). 1986. text 54.50 (*0-88706-362-4*) State U NY Pr.

***Moral Science & Moral Order.** James M. Buchanan. LC 99-42627. (Collected Works of James M. Buchanan : Vol. 17). 2000. pap. 12.00 (*0-86597-246-X*) Liberty Fund.

***Moral Science & Moral Order.** James M. Buchanan. LC 99-42627. (Collected Works of James M. Buchanan : Vol. 17). 2001. 20.00 (*0-86597-245-1*) Liberty Fund.

Moral Search: Humanitarian Intervention in Internal Conflicts. Ed. by Jonathan Moore. LC 98-19157. 336p. 1998. pap. 24.95 (*0-8476-9031-8*); text 65.00 (*0-8476-9030-X*) Rowman.

Moral Self. Pauline Chazan. LC 97-40021. 252p. (C). 1998. 75.00 (*0-415-16861-9*); pap. 24.99 (*0-415-16862-7*) Routledge.

Moral Self: Building a Better Paradigm. Ed. by Gil G. Noam & Thomas E. Wren. LC 92-21501. (Illus.). 412p. (C). 1993. 46.50 (*0-262-14052-7*) MIT Pr.

Moral Sense. James Q. Wilson. LC 93-18520. 316p. 1993. 22.95 (*0-02-935405-6*) Free Pr.

Moral Sense. James Q. Wilson. 316p. 1995. pap. 13.00 (*0-02-935406-4*) Free Pr.

Moral Sense. James Q. Wilson. LC 97-26459. 336p. 1997. per. 13.00 (*0-684-83332-8*) Free Pr.

Moral Sense: 1930 Edition. James Bonar. 300p. 1996. reprint ed. 64.00 (*1-85506-148-1*) Bks Intl VA.

Moral Sense & Its Foundational Significance: Self, Person, Historicity, Community: Phenomenological Praxeology & Psychiatry. Ed. by Anna-Teresa Tymieniecka. 464p. (C). 1990. lib. bdg. 221.50 (*0-7923-0678-3*, Pub. by Kluwer Academic) Kluwer Academic.

Moral Sense in the Communal Significance of Life. Ed. by Anna-Teresa Tymieniecka. 424p. 1986. text 206.50 (*90-277-2085-1*, D Reidel) Kluwer Academic.

Moral Sex: Woman's Nature in the French Enlightenment. Lieselotte Steinbrugge. Tr. by Pamela Selwyn. 168p. 1995. pap. 19.95 (*0-19-509493-X*) OUP.

Moral Situations. N. Fotion. LC 68-31034. 136p. reprint ed. pap. 42.20 (*0-7837-6151-1*, 204587300009) Bks Demand.

Moral, Social & Professional Duties of Attorneys & Solicitors. Samuel Warren. 304p. 1991. reprint ed. 42.50 (*0-8377-2724-3*, Rothman) W S Hein.

Moral Society. John D. Garcia. LC 75-137086. (Illus.). 325p. 1974. 8.95 (*0-87426-033-7*) Whitmore.

Moral Standards: An Introduction to Ethics. 2nd ed. Charles H. Patterson. LC 57-6801. 545p. reprint ed. pap. 169.00 (*0-608-30263-5*, 201252300081) Bks Demand.

Moral Status: Obligations to Persons & Other Living Things. Mary A. Warren. LC 97-7803. (Issues in Biomedical Ethics Ser.). 274p. (C). 1998. text 39.95 (*0-19-823668-9*) OUP.

***Moral Status: Obligations to Persons & Other Living Things.** Mary Anne Warren. (Issues in Biomedical Ethics Ser.). 2000. pap. 19.95 (*0-19-825040-1*) OUP.

Moral Status of Children: Essays on the Rights of the Child. Michael Freeman. LC 97-34181. 420p. 1997. pap. 71.00 (*90-411-0377-5*, Pub. by M Nijhoff) Kluwer Academic.

Moral Strangers, Moral Acquaintance, & Moral Friends: Connectedness & Its Conditions. Erich H. Loewy. LC 96-2444. 251p. (C). 1996. text 57.50 (*0-7914-3131-2*); pap. text 18.95 (*0-7914-3132-0*) State U NY Pr.

Moral Tale: Children's Fiction & American Culture, 1820-1860. Anne S. MacLeod. LC 75-12533. 196p. (Orig.). (C). 1975. lib. bdg. 30.00 (*0-208-01552-3*, Archon Bks) Shoe String.

Moral Tale: Children's Fiction & American Culture, 1820-1860. Anne S. MacLeod. LC 75-12533. 196p. (Orig.). (C). 1990. reprint ed. pap. text 21.50 (*0-208-02292-9*, Archon Bks) Shoe String.

Moral Tales. Ed. by Leopoldo (Clarin) Alas. Tr. by Kenneth A. Stackhouse from SPA. 218p. (Orig.). (C). 1988. lib. bdg. 47.00 (*0-913969-12-5*) Univ Pub Assocs.

Moral Tales. Jules Laforgue. Tr. by William J. Smith from FRE. LC 84-25498. (Illus.). 224p. 1985. 9.95 (*0-8112-0942-3*, Pub. by New Directions) Norton.

Moral Tales. Lawrence P. Spingarn. LC 82-6216. (Illus.). 70p. 1983. pap. 7.95 (*0-912288-19-1*) Perivale Pr.

Moral Teachings of Paul: Selected Issues. rev. ed. Victor P. Furnish. 1985. pap. 14.95 (*0-687-27181-9*) Abingdon.

Moral Textures: Feminist Narratives in the Public Sphere. Maria Pia Lara. LC 99-200368. 280p. 1999. 45.00 (*0-520-21776-4*, Pub. by U CA Pr); pap. 19.95 (*0-520-21777-2*, Pub. by U CA Pr) Cal Prin Full Svc.

Moral Theology. Heribert Jone. Tr. by Urban Adelman. LC 92-60957. 610p. 1993. reprint ed. pap. 16.50 (*0-89555-472-0*) TAN Bks Pubs.

Moral Theology: A Continuing Journey. Charles Curran. LC 81-23160. 238p. 1982. text 26.50 (*0-268-01350-0*) U of Notre Dame Pr.

Moral Theology: Dead Ends & Alternatives. Antonio Moser & Bernardino Leers. Tr. by Paul Burns from POR. LC 90-187473. (Theology & Liberation Ser.).Tr. of Teologia Moral: Impasses e Alternativas. 256p. reprint ed. pap. 79.40 (*0-608-20245-2*, 207150400012) Bks Demand.

Moral Theology: Dead Ends & Ways Forward. Antonio Moser & Bernardino Leers. 256p. 1994. pap. 30.00 (*0-86012-171-2*, Pub. by Srch Pr) St Mut.

Moral Theology & Suffering. Sebastian K. MacDonald. LC 93-41341. (AUS VII: Vol. 171). XIV, 185p. (C). 1995. text 39.95 (*0-8204-2371-8*) P Lang Pubng.

Moral Theology Today: Certitudes & Doubts. Ed. by Donald G. McCarthy. LC 84-11714. 355p. (Orig.). 1984. pap. 17.95 (*0-935372-14-8*) NCBC.

Moral Theory. Joseph P. Demarco. (Philosophy). (C). 1995. 37.95 (*0-534-54247-6*) Wadsworth Pub.

***Moral Theory: A Non-Consequentialist Approach.** David S. Oderberg. LC 99-45661. 224p. 2000. text 59.95 (*0-631-21902-1*); pap. text 27.95 (*0-631-21903-X*) Blackwell Pubs.

Moral Theory & Anomaly. Tom Sorell. LC 99-16128. (Aristotelian Society Monographs: Vol. 18). 288p. 1999. text 64.95 (*0-631-21833-5*) Blackwell Pubs.

***Moral Theory & Anomaly.** Tom Sorell. LC 99-16128. (Aristotelian Society Monographs: Vol. 18). 288p. 1999. pap. text 29.95 (*0-631-21834-3*) Blackwell Pubs.

Moral Theory & Legal Reasoning. Ed. by Scott Brewer & Robert Nozick. LC 98-5171. (Philosophy of Legal Reasoning Ser.: No. 3). 408p. 1998. reprint ed. text 75.00 (*0-8153-2657-2*) Garland.

Moral Theory & Moral Judgments in Medical Ethics. Ed. by Baruch A. Brody. (Philosophy & Medicine Ser.: No. 32). 238p. 1988. text 120.00 (*1-55608-060-3*) Kluwer Academic.

Moral Theory for Public Education. Philip G. Smith. (DeGarmo Lectures: No. 8). 1983. 10.00 (*0-933669-32-1*) Soc Profs Ed.

Moral Theory of Poststructuralism. Todd May. LC 94-45435. 152p. 1995. 35.00 (*0-271-01468-7*); pap. 16.95 (*0-271-01469-5*) Pa St U Pr.

Moral Thinking: Its Levels, Methods, & Point. Richard M. Hare. 250p. 1982. pap. text 23.00 (*0-19-824660-9*) OUP.

Moral Threats & Dangerous Desires: AIDS in the News Media. Deborah Lupton. (Social Aspects of AIDS Ser.). 208p. 1994. 75.00 (*0-7484-0179-2*, Pub. by Tay Francis Ltd); pap. 27.00 (*0-7484-0180-6*, Pub. by Tay Francis Ltd) Taylor & Francis.

Moral Tone of Jacobean & Caroline Drama. J. A. Bastiaenen. LC 68-951. (Studies in Drama: No. 39). 1969. reprint ed. lib. bdg. 75.00 (*0-8383-0507-5*) M S G Haskell Hse.

Moral Tradition in English Fiction, 1785-1850. Samuel Pickering. LC 74-12540. 194p. reprint ed. pap. 60.20 (*0-7837-0380-5*, 204070000018) Bks Demand.

Moral Tradition of American Constitutionalism: A Theological Interpretation. H. Jefferson Powell. LC 92-42290. 309p. 1993. text 42.95 (*0-8223-1314-6*) Duke.

Moral Treatment of Returning Warriors in Early Medieval & Modern Times. Bernard J. Verkamp. LC 92-85212. 200p. 1993. 35.00 (*0-940866-22-6*) U Scranton Pr.

Moral Truth & Moral Tradition: Essays in Honour of Peter Geach & Elizabeth Anscombe. Ed. by Luke Gormally. 320p. 1994. 45.00 (*1-85182-158-9*, Pub. by Four Cts Pr) Intl Spec Bk.

Moral Uncertainty & its Consequences. Ted Lockhart. LC 99-17331. (Illus.). 232p. 2000. text 45.00 (*0-19-512610-6*) OUP.

Moral Understandings: Feminist Study in Ethics. Margaret U. Walker. LC 97-24499. 272p. (C). 1997. pap. 19.99 (*0-415-91421-3*) Routledge.

Moral Understandings: Feminist Study in Ethics. Margaret U. Walker. LC 97-24499. 272p. (C). 1997. 75.00 (*0-415-91420-5*) Routledge.

Moral Universe: A Preface to Christian Living. Fulton J. Sheen. LC 67-28766. (Essay Index Reprint Ser.). 1977. 18.95 (*0-8369-0873-2*) Ayer.

Moral Universe of Shakespeare's Problem Plays. Vivian Thomas. 256p. (C). 1991. pap. text 15.95 (*0-415-04226-7*, Pub. by Tavistock) Routldge.

Moral Values & Higher Education. Ed. by Dennis L. Thompson. LC 90-19857. 171p. (C). 1991. text 29.50 (*0-7914-0793-4*) State U NY Pr.

Moral Values & the Human Zoo: The Novellen of Stefan Zweig. David Turner. 353p. 1989. 45.00 (*0-85958-476-3*) Denali Press.

Moral Values & the Idea of God. William R. Sorley. LC 77-27215. (Gifford Lectures: 1914-15). 1978. reprint ed. 37.50 (*0-404-60465-X*) AMS Pr.

Moral Values in Ancient Egypt. Miriam Lichtheim. LC 98-101349. 1997. text 26.75 (*3-7278-1138-2*, 155, Pub. by Presses Univ Fribourg) Eisenbrauns.

Moral Values in Liberalism & Conservatism. Andrew R. Cecil et al. Ed. by Lawson Taitte. LC 95-60717. (Andrew R. Cecil Lectures on Moral Values in a Free Society: Vol. 16). 1995. text 16.50 (*0-292-78139-3*) U of Tex Pr.

Moral Values in the Ancient World. John Ferguson. Ed. by Gregory Vlastos. LC 78-19348. (Morals & Law in Ancient Greece Ser.). 1979. reprint ed. lib. bdg. 31.95 (*0-405-11542-3*) Ayer.

Moral Values the Challenge of the Twenty-First Century. Andrew R. Cecil. LC 96-60491. 253p. 1996. 16.50 (*0-292-71192-1*) U of Tex Pr.

Moral Views of Commerce, Society & Politics in 12 Discourses. Orville Dewey. LC 68-27851. (Reprints of Economic Classics Ser.). 300p. 1969. reprint ed. 45.00 (*0-678-00527-3*) Kelley.

Moral Virtue or Mental Health? Mark Pestana. LC 96-38658. (San Francisco State University Series in Philosophy: Vol. 10). XVI, 152p. (C). 1998. text 39.95 (*0-8204-3687-9*) P Lang Pubng.

Moral Virtues & Theological Ethics. Romanus Cessario. LC 90-70854. (C). 1992. pap. text 13.00 (*0-268-01389-6*) U of Notre Dame Pr.

Moral Vision: An Introduction to Ethics. David McNaughton. 288p. 1988. pap. text 28.95 (*0-631-15945-2*) Blackwell Pubs.

Moral Vision & Professional Decisions: The Changing Values of Women & Men Lawyers. Rand Jack & Dana C. Jack. (Illus.). 240p. (C). 1989. text 19.95 (*0-521-37161-9*) Cambridge U Pr.

Moral Vision & Tradition: Essays in Chinese Ethics. A. S. Cua. LC 96-53933. (Studies in Philosophy & the History of Philosophy). 357p. 1998. text 66.95 (*0-8132-0890-4*) Cath U Pr.

Moral Vision for America. Joseph Louis Bernardin. Ed. by John P. Langan. LC 97-37973. 176p. 1998. 45.00 (*0-87840-675-1*) Georgetown U Pr.

Moral Vision in International Politics: The Foreign Aid Regime, 1949-1989. David H. Lumsdaine. LC 92-18508. (Illus.). 416p. (C). 1993. text 60.00 (*0-691-07887-4*, Pub. by Princeton U Pr); pap. text 19.95 (*0-691-02767-6*, Pub. by Princeton U Pr) Cal Prin Full Svc.

Moral Vision in the History of Polybius. Arthur M. Eckstein. LC 94-10638. (Hellenistic Culture & Society Ser.: Vol. 16). 1994. 55.00 (*0-520-08520-5*, Pub. by U CA Pr) Cal Prin Full Svc.

Moral Vision of Dorothy Day: A Feminist Perspective. June E. O'Connor. 200p. 1991. 16.95 (*0-8245-1080-1*) Crossroad NY.

Moral Vision of Jacobean Tragedy. Robert E. Ornstein. LC 74-25893. 299p. 1975. reprint ed. lib. bdg. 45.00 (*0-8371-7864-9*, ORJT, Greenwood Pr) Greenwood.

Moral Vision of Oscar Wilde. Philip K. Cohen. LC 76-50283. (Illus.). 287p. 1978. 38.50 (*0-8386-2052-3*) Fairleigh Dickinson.

Moral Vision of the New Testament: A Contemporary Introduction to New Testament Ethics. Richard Hays. LC 96-11845. 528p. 1996. 26.00 (*0-06-063796-X*, Pub. by Harper SF) HarpC.

Moral Voices, Moral Selves: Carol Gilligan & Feminist Moral Theory. Susan J. Hekman. LC 95-5634. 210p. 1995. 50.00 (*0-271-01483-0*); pap. 18.95 (*0-271-01484-9*) Pa St U Pr.

Moral Voyages of Stephen King. Anthony S. Magistrale. LC 88-1076. (Starmont Studies in Literary Criticism: No. 25). iv, vi, 157p. 1989. pap. 21.00 (*1-55742-070-X*) Millefleurs.

Moral Wisdom & Good Lives. John Kekes. LC 96-44864. 272p. 1996. pap. 16.95 (*0-8014-8278-X*) Cornell U Pr.

Moral Wisdom & Good Lives. John Kekes. LC 96-44864. 272p. 1997. text 35.00 (*0-8014-3171-9*) Cornell U Pr.

Moral Wisdom in the Allocation of Economic Resources. Ed. & Pref. by Paul C. Goelz. 136p. 1988. 16.95 (*0-945632-00-2*) St Marys Univ Pr.

Moral World of the First Christians. Wayne A. Meeks. LC 86-5504. (Library of Early Christianity: Vol. 6). 180p. (C). 1986. reprint ed. pap. 24.95 (*0-664-25014-9*) Westminster John Knox.

***Moral World of the Law.** Ed. by Peter Coss. (Past & Present Publications). (Illus.). 270p. (C). 2000. 59.95 (*0-521-64059-8*) Cambridge U Pr.

Moral Writings of John Dewey. rev. ed. Ed. by James Gouinlock. LC 94-4482. (Great Books in Philosophy). 338p. (C). 1994. pap. 11.95 (*0-87975-882-1*) Prometheus Bks.

Moraldo in the City & a Journey with Anita. Federico Fellini. Ed. & Tr. by John C. Stubbs. LC 82-17526. (Illus.). 178p. 1983. text 19.95 (*0-252-01023-X*) U of Ill Pr.

Morale see Oeuvres Completes, Tome IV, Emile Education, Morale, Botanique

Morale see Oeuvres Completes

Morale, Culture & Character: Assessing Schools of Hope. Douglas H. Heath. LC 98-94949. 320p. 1999. 30.00 (*0-9641727-2-0*); pap. 24.00 (*0-9641727-3-9*) Conrow Pubng.

Morale de la Foi, No. Betl 119. E. Peters. 1998. 93.95 (*90-6831-665-6*, Pub. by Peeters Pub) Bks Intl VA.

Morale Elementaire. Raymond Queneau. (FRE.). 152p. 1975. pap. 17.95 (*0-7859-1345-9*, 2070293505) Fr & Eur.

Morale in the Civil Service: A Study of the Desk Worker. Nigel Walker. LC 76-49867. (Illus.). 1977. reprint ed. lib. bdg. 59.50 (*0-8371-9397-4*, WAMCS, Greenwood Pr) Greenwood.

Morale of the American Revolutionary Army. Allen Bowman. (History - United States Ser.). 160p. 1993. reprint ed. lib. bdg. 69.00 (*0-7812-4874-4*) Rprt Serv.

Morale Proberbes of Christyne. Christine Du Castel. LC 73-25783. (English Experience Ser.: No. 241). 8p. 1970. reprint ed. 20.00 (*90-221-0241-6*) Walter J Johnson.

Morales du Grand Siecle. Paul Benichou. (Folio Essais Ser.: No. 99). (FRE.). 383p. 1948. pap. 11.95 (*2-07-032473-7*) Schoenhof.

Moralia see Selected Essays & Dialogues

Moralia. Plutarch. Incl. Vol. 1. 19.95 (*0-674-99217-2*); Vol. 2. 19.95 (*0-674-99245-8*); Vol. 3. 19.95 (*0-674-99270-9*); Vol. 4. 19.95 (*0-674-99336-5*); Vol. 5. 19.95 (*0-674-99337-3*); Vol. 6. 19.95 (*0-674-99371-3*); Vol. 7. 19.95 (*0-674-99446-9*); Vol. 8. 19.95 (*0-674-99466-3*); Vol. 9. 19.95 (*0-674-99467-1*); Vol. 10. 19.95 (*0-674-99354-3*); Vol. 11. 19.95 (*0-674-99469-8*); Vol. 12. 19.95 (*0-674-99447-7*); Vol. 14. 19.95 (*0-674-99472-8*); Vol. 15. 19.95 (*0-674-99473-6*); write for info. (*0-318-53118-6*) HUP.

***Moralische im Politischen: Hannah Arendts Theorie des Handelns im Horizont der Theologischen Ethik.** Christa Schnabl. (Forum Interdisziplinare Ethik Ser.). XIII, 399p. 1999. 52.95 (*3-631-34066-4*) P Lang Pubng.

***Moralisierung im Kriegsdiskurs: Eine Analyse von Printmedienbeitragen Zum Golfkrieg und Zum Vietnamkrieg.** Stefan Schallenberger. (Theorie und Vermittlung der Sprache Ser.). 280p. 1999. 45.95 (*3-631-35124-0*) P Lang Pubng.

Moralism & Christianity: or Man's Experience & Destiny in 3 Lectures. Henry James, Sr. LC 72-917. (Selected Works of Henry James, Sr.: Vol. 4). 1983. reprint ed. 35.00 (*0-404-10084-8*) AMS Pr.

Moralism & the Model Home: Domestic Architecture & Cultural Conflict in Chicago 1873-1913. Gwendolyn Wright. LC 79-25584. (Illus.). viii, 382p. 1980. 17.50 (*0-226-90835-6*) U Ch Pr.

Moralism & the Model Home: Domestic Architecture & Cultural Conflict in Chicago 1873-1913. Gwendolyn Wright. LC 79-25584. (Illus.). viii, 382p. 1985. pap. 13.95 (*0-226-90837-2*) U Ch Pr.

M

An Asterisk (*) at the beginning of an entry indicates that the title is appearing for the first time.

Moralism & the Model Home: Domestic Architecture & Cultural Conflict in Chicago, 1873-1913. Gwendolyn Wright. LC 79-25584. (Illus.). 390p. reprint ed. pap. 120.90 (*0-608-09560-5*, 205436200005) Bks Demand.

Moralist. Walter A. Roberts. LC 73-18601. reprint ed. 42.50 (*0-404-11411-3*) AMS Pr.

Moralist in & Out of Parliament: John Stuart Mill at Westminster, 1865-1868. Bruce L. Kinzer et al. 336p. 1992. text 65.00 (*0-8020-5949-X*) U of Toronto Pr.

Moralistes des Seizieme et Dix-Septieme Siecles. Alexandre R. Vinet. Ed. by J. P. Mayer. LC 78-67394. (European Political Thought Ser.). (FRE.). 1980. reprint ed. lib. bdg. 33.95 (*0-405-11747-7*) Ayer.

Moralists & Modernizers: America's Pre-Civil War Reformers. Steven Mintz. LC 94-43690. (American Moment Ser.). 208p. 1995. text 38.95 (*0-8018-5080-0*); pap. text 14.95 (*0-8018-5081-9*) Johns Hopkins.

Moralites Legendaires. Jules Laforgue. (Folio Ser.: No. 855). (FRE.). 243p. 1977. pap. 8.95 (*2-07-036855-6*) Schoenhof.

Moralities on the Gospels: A New Source of Ancrene Wisse. E. J. Dobson. 192p. 1975. text 26.50 (*0-19-812056-7*) OUP.

Morality. Bernard Williams. (Canto Book Ser.). 120p. (C). 1993. pap. 9.95 (*0-521-45729-7*) Cambridge U Pr.

Morality: A Course on Catholic Living: Keystone Parish Edition. Paul J. Wadell. (Faith & Witness Program Ser.). (Illus.). 128p. (J). (gr. 7-9). 1999. pap. text 7.50 (*0-8215-5654-1*) Sadlier.

Morality: A Course on Catholic Living, Parish Annotated Guide: Keystone Parish Edition. Marcella P. Syracuse & Paul J. Wadell. (Faith & Witness Program Ser.). (Illus.). 208p. (J). (gr. 7-9). 1999. pap. 15.00 (*0-8215-5664-9*) Sadlier.

Morality: Its Nature & Justification. Bernard Gert. 424p. 1998. pap. 19.95 (*0-19-512256-9*) OUP.

Morality - A Course on Catholic Living: Keystone School Edition. Paul J. Wadell. (Faith & Witness Program Ser.). (Illus.). 272p. (YA). (gr. 7-9). 1998. pap. text 11.40 (*0-8215-5603-7*) Sadlier.

Morality - A Course on Catholic Living, Journal: Keystone Edition. Helen Hemmer. (Faith & Witness Program Ser.). (Illus.). 64p. (J). (gr. 7-9). 1998. pap., student ed. 4.50 (*0-8215-5633-9*) Sadlier.

Morality - A Course on Catholic Living, Parish Guide: Keystone Edition. Marcella P. Syracuse & Paul J. Wadell. (Faith & Witness Program Ser.). (Illus.). 208p. (J). (gr. 7-9). 1998. pap. 10.89 (*0-8215-5623-1*) Sadlier.

Morality - A Course on Catholic Living, School Guide: Keystone School Edition. annot. ed. Marcella P. Syracuse & Paul J. Wadell. (Faith & Witness Program Ser.). (Illus.). 272p. 1998. pap., teacher ed. 21.90 (*0-8215-5613-4*) Sadlier.

Morality after Auschwitz: The Radical Challenge of the Nazi Ethic. Peter J. Haas. LC 87-45891. 272p. 1992. pap. 21.00 (*0-8006-2581-1*, 1-2581, Fortress Pr) Augsburg Fortress.

Morality among Nations: An Evolutionary View. Mary Maxwell. LC 89-27881. (SUNY Series in Bio-politics). 198p. (C). 1990. pap. text 19.95 (*0-7914-0350-5*) State U NY Pr.

Morality & Action. Warren Quinn. LC 93-2769. (Studies in Philosophy). 271p. (C). 1994. text 69.95 (*0-521-44164-1*); pap. text 21.95 (*0-521-44696-1*) Cambridge U Pr.

Morality & American Foreign Policy: The Role of Ethics in International Affairs. Robert W. McElroy. (Illus.). 244p. 1992. pap. text 16.95 (*0-691-00078-6*, Pub. by Princeton U Pr) Cal Prin Full Svc.

Morality & Architecture: The Development of a Theme in Architectural History & Theory from the Gothic Revival to the Modern Movement. David Watkin. LC 84-8587. x, 136p. 1984. pap. text 12.50 (*0-226-87487-7*) U Ch Pr.

Morality & Beyond. Paul Johannes Tillich. (Library of Theological Ethics). 104p. 1995. pap. 13.00 (*0-664-25564-7*) Westminster John Knox.

Morality & Citizenship. John Beck. LC 98-221244. 1998. pap. 24.95 (*0-304-70187-4*) Continuum.

Morality & Conflict. Stuart Hampshire. LC 83-12693. 192p. 1984. 28.50 (*0-674-58728-6*) HUP.

Morality & Conflict. Stuart Hampshire. 192p. 1987. pap. 16.50 (*0-674-58732-4*) HUP.

Morality & Contemporary Warfare. James Turner Johnson. LC 98-54952. 256p. 1999. 25.00 (*0-300-07837-4*) Yale U Pr.

***Morality & Cultural Differences.** John W. Cook. LC 98-27685. 224p. 1999. 29.95 (*0-19-512679-3*) OUP.

Morality & Economics: De Moribus Est Disputandum. Viktor Vanberg. 64p. 1987. pap. 10.95 (*0-912051-19-1*) Soc Phil Pol.

***Morality & Ethics in Public Life.** Ravindra Kumar. 1999. 27.00 (*81-7099-715-1*, Pub. by Mittal Pubns) S Asia.

Morality & Expediency in International & Corporate Relations CLXIII. Ed. by W. Lawson Taitte. LC 92-81688. (Andrew R. Cecil Lectures on Moral Values in a Free Society). 326p. 1992. text 16.50 (*0-292-78125-3*) U of Tex Pr.

Morality & Foreign Policy. Kenneth W. Thompson. LC 79-23211. xvi, 197p. 1980. pap. text 15.95 (*0-8071-1007-8*) La State U Pr.

Morality & Foreign Policy: Realpolitik Revisited. Ed. by Kenneth M. Jensen & Elizabeth Faulkner. LC 90-25576. (C). 1992. pap. text 8.95 (*1-878379-09-7*) US Inst Peace.

Morality & Good Life: An Introduction to Ethics Through Classical Sources. 2nd ed. Robert C. Solomon. 448p. (C). 1991. text. write for info. (*0-07-059672-7*) McGraw.

Morality & Health. Ed. by Paul Rozin. LC 96-52813. 432p. (C). 1997. 80.00 (*0-415-91581-3*); pap. 25.99 (*0-415-91582-1*) Routledge.

Morality & Human Nature: A New Route to Ethical Theory. Robert J. McShea. 240p. 1990. 49.95 (*0-87722-735-7*) Temple U Pr.

Morality & Imagination: Paradoxes of Progress. Yi-Fu Tuan. LC 88-40445. 232p. (C). 1989. pap. text 16.95 (*0-299-12064-3*) U of Wis Pr.

Morality & International Relations: Concepts & Issues. Ed. by Moorhead Wright. LC 95-83734. (Avebury Series in Philosophy). 213p. 1996. 67.95 (*1-85972-156-7*, Pub. by Avebry) Ashgate Pub Co.

Morality & Its Beyond. Dick Westley. LC 83-51512. 336p. (Orig.). (C). 1984. pap. 8.95 (*0-89622-207-1*) Twenty-Third.

***Morality & Law.** 2nd ed. J. Muraskin. 400p. 2000. pap. 43.00 (*0-13-916958-X*) P-H.

Morality & Machines: Computer Ethics. Stacey L. Edgar. LC 96-22261. (Philosophy Ser.). 464p. 1996. pap. 32.50 (*0-7637-0184-X*) Jones & Bartlett.

Morality & Modernity. Ross Poole. 224p. (C). 1991. pap. 20.99 (*0-415-03601-1*, A5263) Routledge.

Morality & Moral Controver. 5th ed. Arthur. LC 98-33679. (C). 1998. pap. text 39.80 (*0-13-914128-6*) S&S Trade.

Morality & Moral Theory: A Reappraisal & Reaffirmation. Robert B. Louden. 256p. 1992. text 70.00 (*0-19-507145-X*); pap. text 26.00 (*0-19-507292-8*) OUP.

Morality & Objectivity: A Tribute to John Mackie. Ed. by Ted Honderich. (International Library of Philosophy). 256p. 1985. 42.50 (*0-7100-9991-6*, Routledge Thoemms) Routledge.

Morality & Politics in Modern Europe: The Harvard Lectures, 1958. Michael Oakeshott. Ed. by Shirley R. Letwin. LC 93-24981. 192p. 1993. 32.00 (*0-300-05644-3*) Yale U Pr.

Morality & Politics in Nigeria: Moral Integration in Nigerian Politics As a Way Out. James-Michael Okpalaonwuka. (European University Studies: Ser. 23). xii, 306p. 1997. 57.95 (*3-631-31532-5*) P Lang Pubng.

Morality & Politics in Nigeria: Moral Integration in Nigerian Politics As a Way Out. James-Michael Okpalaonwuka. (European University Studies, Seris 23: No. 599). XII, 306p. 1997. 57.95 (*0-8204-3268-7*) P Lang Pubng.

Morality & Population Policy. Michael D. Bayles. LC 79-23965. 158p. 1980. pap. 49.00 (*0-608-05127-6*, 206568600005) Bks Demand.

Morality & Power: Contemporary Jewish Views. Ed. by Daniel J. Elazar. LC 89-39021. 156p. (Orig.). (C). 1990. lib. bdg. 40.00 (*0-8191-7608-7*) U Pr of Amer.

Morality & Power: The U. S. Colonial Experience in Puerto Rico from 1898 to 1948, Vol. XIX. Maria Del Pilar Arguelles. (American Values Projected Abroad Ser.: Vol. 19). 256p. (C). 1995. pap. text 28.50 (*0-7618-0109-X*); lib. bdg. 57.50 (*0-7618-0108-1*) U Pr of Amer.

Morality & Public Life in a Time of Change No. 1: Bulgarian Philosophical Studies. Ed. by Vasil Prodanov & Maria Stoyanova. LC 93-11927. (Cultural Heritage & Contemporary Change Series IVA: Vol. 6). 200p. (Orig.). 1994. pap. 17.50 (*1-56518-055-0*) Coun Res Values.

Morality & Public Life in a Time of Change No. 1: Bulgarian Philosophical Studies. Ed. by Vasil Prodanov & Maria Stoyanova. LC 93-11927. (Cultural Heritage & Contemporary Change Series VI: Foundations of Moral Education,: Vol. IVA,6). 200p. (Orig.). 1994. 45.00 (*1-56518-054-2*) Coun Res Values.

Morality & Rational Choice. Jonathan Baron. LC 93-10276. (Theory & Decision Library, Series A, Philosophy & Methodology of the Social Sciences: Vol. 18). 216p. 1993. text 120.50 (*0-7923-2276-2*) Kluwer Academic.

Morality & Religion in Liberal Democratic Societies. Intro. by Gordon L. Anderson & Morton A. Kaplan. LC 91-11309. 368p. (C). 1992. 24.95 (*0-943852-96-X*); pap. text 14.95 (*0-943852-97-8*) Prof World Peace.

Morality & Social Class in 18th Century French Literature & Painting. Warren Roberts. LC 74-187951. (Toronto University Romance Ser.: No. 25). (Illus.). 204p. reprint ed. pap. 63.30 (*0-608-11322-0*, 202051400018) Bks Demand.

Morality & Social Justice: Point - Counterpoint. Carol C. Gould et al. 320p. 1994. pap. text 27.95 (*0-8476-7978-0*) Rowman.

Morality & Social Justice: Point - Counterpoint. Carol C. Gould et al. 320p. 1994. lib. bdg. 71.50 (*0-8476-7977-2*) Rowman.

Morality & Social Order in Television Crime Drama. John Sumser. LC 95-40178. 204p. 1996. lib. bdg. 34.50 (*0-7864-0125-7*) McFarland & Co.

Morality & the Adolescent: A Pastoral Psychology Approach. Charles M. Shelton. 1991. pap. 12.95 (*0-8245-1134-4*) Crossroad NY.

Morality & the Good Life. Ed. by Thomas L. Carson & Paul K. Moser. LC 96-44810. 528p. (C). 1997. text 58.00 (*0-19-510537-0*); pap. text 35.95 (*0-19-510538-9*) OUP.

Morality & the Good Life. 3rd ed. Solomon. LC 98-12394. 504p. 1998. pap. 33.13 (*0-07-289911-5*) McGraw.

Morality & the Law. Robert M. Baird & Stuart E. Rosenbaum. LC 88-18650. (Contemporary Issues Ser.). 148p. (C). 1988. pap. 16.95 (*0-87975-474-5*) Prometheus Bks.

Morality & the Law. Samuel E. Stumpf. LC 66-15286. 261p. reprint ed. pap. 81.00 (*0-8357-3264-9*, 203948500013) Bks Demand.

Morality & The Market. Heath. 2001. 34.74 (*0-07-234508-X*) McGraw.

Morality & the Market in Victorian Britain. G. R. Searle. 314p. 1998. text 85.00 (*0-19-820698-4*) OUP.

Morality & the Meaning of Life: An Introduction to Ethical Theory. Joseph Ellin. LC 94-76131. 340p. (C). 1994. pap. text 41.50 (*0-15-501308-4*) Harcourt.

Morality & the New Genetics. Bernard Gert. (Philosophy Ser.). (C). 1996. 22.50 (*0-534-54248-4*) Wadsworth Pub.

Morality & the Perfect Life. Henry James, Sr. LC 72-918. (Selected Works of Henry James, Sr.: Vol. 5). 1983. reprint ed. 35.00 (*0-404-10085-6*) AMS Pr.

***Morality & the Prof Life.** Brincat & Wike. LC 98-56099. 434p. 1999. pap. text 31.00 (*0-13-915729-8*) P-H.

Morality & the Professional Life: Values at Work. (C). 2000. pap. write for info. (*0-13-016299-X*) P-H.

Morality & Universality. Ed. by Nelson Potter & Mark Timmons. 348p. 1985. text 167.00 (*90-277-1909-8*, D Reidel) Kluwer Academic.

Morality & Utility. Jan Narveson. LC 66-29908. 313p. reprint ed. pap. 97.10 (*0-608-10130-3*, 200388900037) Bks Demand.

Morality & Utility in American Antislavery Reform. Louis S. Gerteis. LC 86-19217. xvi, 264p. 1987. 45.00 (*0-8078-1722-8*) U of NC Pr.

***Morality & Work.** Tibor R. Machan. LC 00-21785. 2000. write for info. (*0-8179-9852-7*) Hoover Inst Pr.

Morality & Youth: Fostering Christian Identity. James DiGiacomo. LC 93-938. 160p. (Orig.). 1993. pap. 8.95 (*1-55612-652-2*) Sheed & Ward WI.

***Morality As the End of Philosophy: The Teleological Dialectic of the Good in J. N. Findlay's Philosophy of Religion.** Bockja Kim. LC 99-38759. 176p. 1999. 42.00 (*0-7618-1490-6*) U Pr of Amer.

Morality, Culture & History: Essays on German Philosophy. Raymond Geuss. LC 98-8083. 216p. (C). 1999. text 49.95 (*0-521-63202-1*); pap. text 14.95 (*0-521-63568-3*) Cambridge U Pr.

Morality, Decisions, & Social Organization Toward a Logic of Ethics. Karl Menger. Ed. by Henk L. Mulder. Tr. by E. Van Der Schalie from GER. LC 74-81941. (Vienna Circle Collection: No. 6). 124p. 1974. pap. text 73.50 (*90-277-0319-1*, D Reidel); lib. bdg. 78.00 (*90-277-0318-3*, D Reidel) Kluwer Academic.

Morality, Halakha & the Jewish Tradition. Shubert Spero. 1983. pap. 19.95 (*0-87068-727-1*) Ktav.

Morality, Harm & the Law. Ed. by Gerald Dworkin. 208p. (C). 1994. pap. 24.00 (*0-8133-8711-6*, Pub. by Westview) HarpC.

***Morality Imposed: The Rehnquist Court & the State of Liberty in America.** Stephen E. Gottlieb. 2000. text 40.00 (*0-8147-3128-7*) NYU Pr.

Morality in Accounting. Ahmed Riahi-Belkaoui. LC 92-7485. 224p. 1992. 57.95 (*0-89930-729-9*, BUN, Quorum Bks) Greenwood.

Morality in Classical European Sociology: The Denial of Social Plurality. Steven J. Thiele. LC 96-41012. (Studies in Sociology: Vol. 12). 172p. 1997. text 79.95 (*0-7734-8757-3*) E Mellen.

Morality in Criminal Justice: An Introduction to Ethics. Daryl Close & Nicholas Meier. LC 94-25650. 604p. 1994. 52.95 (*0-534-22116-5*) Wadsworth Pub.

Morality in Discourse: A Special Double Issue of Research on Language & Social Interaction. Ed. by Jorg R. Bergmann & Per Linell. 200p. 1999. pap. 39.50 (*0-8058-9811-5*) L Erlbaum Assocs.

Morality in Everyday Life: Developmental Perspectives. Ed. by Melanie Killen & Daniel Hart. (Studies in Social & Emotional Development). (Illus.). 439p. (C). 1995. text 59.95 (*0-521-45478-6*) Cambridge U Pr.

***Morality in Everyday Life: Developmental Perspectives.** Ed. by Melanie Killen & Daniel Hart. (Studies in Social & Emotional Development). (Illus.). 360p. (C). 1999. pap. 24.95 (*0-521-66586-8*) Cambridge U Pr.

Morality in Practice. James P. Sterba. 334p. (C). 1984. pap. write for info. (*0-534-02745-8*) Wadsworth Pub.

Morality in Practice. 2nd ed. Ed. by James P. Sterba. 458p. (C). 1987. pap. write for info. (*0-534-08616-0*) Wadsworth Pub.

Morality in Practice. 3rd ed. Ed. by James P. Sterba. 560p. (C). 1990. pap. 31.95 (*0-534-14592-2*) Wadsworth Pub.

Morality in Practice. 4th ed. James P. Sterba. 558p. 1993. mass mkt. 31.25 (*0-534-21277-8*) Wadsworth Pub.

Morality in Practice. 5th ed. James P. Sterba. LC 96-20524. (Philosophy Ser.). (C). 1996. 56.95 (*0-534-50655-0*) Wadsworth Pub.

Morality in Practice. 6th ed. Sterba. (Philosophy Ser.). 2000. pap. 40.50 (*0-534-52111-8*) Wadsworth Pub.

Morality in the Making: Thought, Action & the Social Context. Ed. by Helen Weinreich-Haste & Don Locke. LC 82-2749. (Wiley Series in Developmental Psychology & Its Applications). 271p. reprint ed. pap. 84.10 (*0-8357-4629-1*, 203755800008) Bks Demand.

Morality, Kindred, & Ethnic Boundary: A Study of the Oregon Old Believers. Michael A. Colfer. LC 83-45351. (Immigrant Communities & Ethnic Minorities in the U. S. & Canada Ser.: No. 3). (Illus.). 1985. 37.50 (*0-404-19404-4*) AMS Pr.

Morality Lives for Knowledge Hunters: Journal & Calendar Set. Katherine E. Anderson. (Illus.). (Orig.). 1996. pap., spiral bd. 21.95 (*1-57876-696-6*) Triple U Enterprises.

Morality Lives for Promise Keepers: Journal & Calendar Set. Katherine E. Anderson. (Illus.). (Orig.). 1996. pap., spiral bd. 21.95 (*1-57876-695-8*) Triple U Enterprises.

Morality Lives for the Integrity Seekers: Journal & Calendar Set. Katherine E. Anderson. (Illus.). (Orig.). 1996. pap., spiral bd. 21.95 (*1-57876-697-4*) Triple U Enterprises.

Morality Lives for the Rich & Famous: Journal & Calendar Set. Katherine E. Anderson. (Illus.). (Orig.). 1996. pap., spiral bd. 21.95 (*1-57876-699-0*) Triple U Enterprises.

Morality Lives for the Young & Restless: Journal & Calendar Set. Katherine E. Anderson. (Illus.). (Orig.). 1996. pap., spiral bd. 21.95 (*1-57876-698-2*) Triple U Enterprises.

Morality Lives for Truth Seekers: Journal & Calendar Set. Katherine E. Anderson. (Illus.). (Orig.). 1996. pap., spiral bd. 21.95 (*1-57876-694-X*) Triple U Enterprises.

Morality Lives Journal for Integrity Seekers. Katherine E. Anderson. (Illus.). 150p. (Orig.). 1994. pap. 15.95 (*1-57876-603-6*) Triple U Enterprises.

Morality Lives Journal for Knowledge Hunters. Katherine E. Anderson. (Illus.). 150p. (Orig.). 1994. pap., spiral bd. 15.95 (*1-57876-602-8*) Triple U Enterprises.

Morality Lives Journal for Promise Keepers. Katherine E. Anderson. (Illus.). 150p. (Orig.). 1994. pap. 15.95 (*1-57876-601-X*) Triple U Enterprises.

Morality Lives Journal for the Rich & Famous. Katherine E. Anderson. (Illus.). 150p. (Orig.). 1994. pap., spiral bd. 15.95 (*1-57876-605-2*) Triple U Enterprises.

Morality Lives Journal for the Young & Restless. Katherine E. Anderson. (Illus.). 150p. (Orig.). 1994. pap., spiral bd. 15.95 (*1-57876-604-4*) Triple U Enterprises.

Morality Lives Journal for Truth Seekers. Katherine E. Anderson. (Illus.). 150p. (Orig.). 1994. pap., spiral bd. 15.95 (*1-57876-600-1*) Triple U Enterprises.

Morality Maze: An Introduction to Moral Ecology. Neil M. Daniels. LC 91-18489. 227p. 1991. 27.95 (*0-87975-697-7*) Prometheus Bks.

Morality, Metaphysics, & Chinese Culture. Ed. by Vincent Shen & Tran Van Doan. LC 92-28170. (Cultural Heritage & Contemporary Change Series III: Vol. 4). 1992. 45.00 (*1-56518-026-7*); pap. 17.50 (*1-56518-027-5*) Coun Res Values.

Morality, Mortality: Death & Whom to Save from It. Frances M. Kamm. (Oxford Ethics Ser.: Vol. I). (Illus.). 352p. 1993. text 60.00 (*0-19-507789-X*) OUP.

Morality, Mortality: Death & Whom to Save from It, Vol. 1. F. M. Kamm. (Oxford Ethics Ser.). (Illus.). 352p. 1998. reprint ed. pap. 19.95 (*0-19-511911-8*) OUP.

Morality, Mortality: Rights, Duties & Status, Vol. 2. F. M. Kamm. (Oxford Ethics Ser.). 400p. 1996. text 60.00 (*0-19-508459-4*) OUP.

Morality, Normativity & Society. David Copp. 280p. 1995. text 49.95 (*0-19-507879-9*) OUP.

Morality of Abortion: Legal & Historical Perspectives. Ed. by John T. Noonan et al. LC 70-129118. 296p. reprint ed. pap. 91.80 (*0-7837-2305-9*, 205739300004) Bks Demand.

Morality of Business Enterprise. Norman P. Barry. (David Hume Papers: No. 13). 120p. (C). 1991. pap. text 11.85 (*0-08-037964-8*, Pub. by Aberdeen U Pr) Macmillan.

Morality of Capitalism. 2nd rev. ed. Ed. by Mark W. Hendrickson. LC 96-85563. (The Freeman Classics Ser.). 213p. 1996. pap. 12.95 (*1-57246-055-5*) Foun Econ Ed.

Morality of Consent. Alexander M. Bickel. LC 75-10988. 176p. 1977. pap. 14.00 (*0-300-02119-4*) Yale U Pr.

Morality of Democratic Citizenship: Goals for Civic Education in the Republics Third Century. R. Freeman Butts. 233p. (Orig.). 1988. pap. 14.95 (*0-89818-132-1*) Ctr for Civic Educ.

Morality of Freedom. Joseph Raz. 448p. 1988. pap. text 32.00 (*0-19-824807-5*) OUP.

Morality of Groups: Collective Responsibility, Group-Based Harm & Corporate Rights. Larry May. LC 87-40350. (Soundings: A Series in Ethics, Economics & Business: Vol. 1). 216p. (C). 1989. pap. text 13.00 (*0-268-01378-0*) U of Notre Dame Pr.

Morality of Happiness. Julia Annas. 512p. 1995. pap. text 22.00 (*0-19-509652-5*) OUP.

Morality of Law. rev. ed. Lon L. Fuller. (Storrs Lectures). 262p. 1965. pap. 14.00 (*0-300-01070-2*, Y152) Yale U Pr.

Morality of Nationalism. Ed. by Robert McKim & Jeff McMahan. LC 96-21168. 384p. 1997. pap. 19.95 (*0-19-510392-0*) OUP.

Morality of Pluralism. John Kekes. LC 92-40492. 256p. 1993. text 42.50 (*0-691-03230-0*, Pub. by Princeton U. Pr) Cal Prin Full Svc.

Morality of Proust. Malcolm Bowie. 28p. 1994. pap. text 8.95 (*0-19-952265-0*) OUP.

Morality of Punishment. Alfred C. Ewing. LC 70-108233. (Criminology, Law Enforcement, & Social Problems Ser.: No. 116). 1970. reprint ed. 30.00 (*0-87585-116-9*) Patterson Smith.

Morality of Scarcity: Limited Resources & Social Policy. Ed. by William M. Finnin, Jr. & Gerald A. Smith. LC 78-21514. 150p. 1979. pap. 46.50 (*0-7837-8466-X*, 204927100010) Bks Demand.

Morality of Shakespeare's Drama Illustrated. Elizabeth Griffith. LC 70-96358. (Eighteenth Century Shakespeare Ser.: No. 14). xvi, 528p. 1971. reprint ed. lib. bdg. 35.00 (*0-678-05125-9*) Kelley.

Morality of Spending: Attitudes Toward the Consumer Society in America, 1875-1940. Daniel Horowitz. LC 84-27851. (New Studies in American Intellectual & Cultural History). 288p. reprint ed. pap. 89.30 (*0-7837-0049-0*, 204029600016) Bks Demand.

Morality of Spending: Attitudes Toward the Consumer Society in America, 1875-1940. Daniel Horowitz. 288p. 1992. reprint ed. pap. text 12.95 (*0-929587-77-4*, Elephant Paperbacks) I R Dee.

Morality of Terrorism, Vol. 4. Haig Khatchadourian. LC 97-8540. (Conflict & Consciousness). XV, 180p. (C). 1998. pap. text 32.95 (*0-8204-3790-5*) P Lang Pubng.

Morality of Terrorism: Religious & Secular Justifications. Ed. by David C. Rapoport & Jonah Alexander. (Morningside Bk.). 377p. 1989. text 87.50 (*0-231-06752-6*) Col U Pr.

Morality of Terrorism: Religious Origins & Ethical Implications. Ed. by David C. Rapoport & Yonah Alexander. (Policy Studies on International Politics). 280p. 1982. 47.00 (*0-08-026347-X*, Pergamon Pr) Elsevier.

An Asterisk (*) at the beginning of an entry indicates that the title is appearing for the first time.

Morality of the Heart: A Psychology for the Christian Moral Life. Charles M. Shelton. 156p. 1997. pap. 18.95 (0-8245-1603-6, Herdr & Herdr) Crossroad NY.

Morality of the Mass Media. Ed. by W. Lawson Taitte. (Andrew R. Cecil Lectures on Moral Values in a Free Society: Vol. XIV). 258p. 1994. text 16.50 (0-292-71160-3) U of Tex Pr.

Morality of the School: The Theory & Practice of Values in Education. Mike Bottery. 192p. 1989. pap. text 37.95 (0-304-31830-2) Continuum.

Morality-Patterned Comedy of the Renaissance. Sylvia D. Feldman. (De Proprietatibus Litterarum, Ser. Practica: No. 12). (Orig.). (C). 1970. pap. text 25.40 (90-279-1547-4) Mouton.

Morality, Philosophy & Practice: Historical & Contemporary Readings & Studies. Abraham Edel et al. 656p. (C). 1988. text 50.74 (0-07-554364-8) McGraw.

Morality Play. Barry Unsworth. 208p. 1996. pap. 13.00 (0-393-31560-6) Norton.

Morality Play. Gordon Weaver. LC 85-22408. 122p. (Orig.). 1985. pap. 15.00 (0-933428-05-7) Chariton Review.

Morality Play. large type ed. Barry Unsworth. 1996. 23.95 (1-56895-297-X) Wheeler Pub.

Morality Plays for Modern Man. Michael Whalen. 290p. (Orig.). 1990. pap. 8.00 (0-9624992-0-X) Padua Pr.

Morality, Politics & Law. Michael J. Perry. 336p. 1990. reprint ed. pap. text 21.00 (0-19-506456-9) OUP.

Morality, Prudence & Nuclear Weapons. Steven P. Lee. LC 92-30904. (Cambridge Studies in Philosophy & Public Policy). 432p. (C). 1993. text 80.00 (0-521-38272-6) Cambridge U Pr.

Morality, Prudence & Nuclear Weapons. Steven P. Lee. (Cambridge Studies in Philosophy & Public Policy). 432p. 1996. pap. text 25.95 (0-521-56772-6) Cambridge U Pr.

Morality, Rationality, & Efficiency: New Perspectives on Socio-Economics. Ed. by Richard M. Coughlin. LC 90-19137. (Studies in Socio-Economics). 432p. (gr. 13). 1991. pap. text 42.95 (0-87332-822-1) M E Sharpe.

Morality, Rationality, & Efficiency: New Perspectives on Socio-Economics. Ed. by Richard M. Coughlin. LC 90-19137. (Studies in Socio-Economics). 432p. (C). (gr. 13). 1991. text 87.95 (0-87332-821-3) M E Sharpe.

Morality, Responsibility, & the University: Studies in Academic Ethics. Steven M. Cahn. 1992. pap. 24.95 (0-87722-959-7) Temple U Pr.

Morality, Self-interest, & the Cities. Simon D. Perry & John Deaver Drinko Academy for American Political Institutions. LC 98-216556. 106 p. 1997. write for info. (1-891607-01-4) Drinko Acad.

Morality, Sex & the Constitution: A Christian Perspective on the Power of Government to Regulate Private Sexual Conduct Between Consenting Adults. G. Sidney Buchanan. LC 85-3249. 242p. (Orig.). 1985. pap. text 22.50 (0-8191-4603-X); lib. bdg. 50.00 (0-8191-4602-1) U Pr of Amer.

Morality U. S. A. Ellen Friedman. LC 98-2999. 1998. 49.95 (0-8166-2748-7); pap. 19.95 (0-8166-2749-5) U of Minn Pr.

Morality, Utilitarianism, & Rights. Richard B. Brandt. 403p. (C). 1992. text 74.95 (0-521-41507-1); pap. text 24.95 (0-521-42527-1) Cambridge U Pr.

Morality Within the Life - And Social World: Interdisciplinary Phenomenology of the Authentic Life in the "Moral Sense" Ed. by Anna-Teresa Tymieniecka. 608p. (C). 1987. text 272.50 (90-277-2411-3, D Reidel) Kluwer Academic.

Morality Within the Limits of Reason. Russell Hardin. 254p. 1990. pap. text 17.95 (0-226-31620-3) U Ch Pr.

Morality Within the Limits of Reason. Russell Hardin. 248p. 1993. 27.50 (0-226-31618-1) U Ch Pr.

Morality Without Foundations: A Defense of Ethical Contextualism. Mark Timmons. (Illus.). 280p. 1998. text 49.95 (0-19-511731-X) OUP.

Moralized Song: The Character of Augustan Lyricism. Richard Feingold. LC 88-23861. 250p. (C). 1989. text 45.00 (0-8135-1390-1) Rutgers U Pr.

Moralizing Cultures. Vytautas Kavolis. 164p. (Orig.). (C). 1992. lib. bdg. 44.00 (0-8191-8640-6) U Pr of Amer.

Moralizing Prints of Cornelis Anthonisz. Christine M. Armstrong. LC 88-34199. (Illus.). 321p. reprint ed. pap. 99.60 (0-608-06414-9, 206662700008) Bks Demand.

Moralizing States & the Ethnography of the Present. Ed. by Sally F. Moore. LC 93-33898. (American Ethnological Society Monograph Ser.: Vol. 5). 1993. write for info. (0-913167-60-6) Am Anthro Assn.

Moralizing the Environment: Countryside Change, Farming & Pollution. Philip Lowe et al. 224p. 1998. 69.95 (1-85728-839-4, Pub. by UCL Pr Ltd); pap. 22.95 (1-85728-840-8, Pub. by UCL Pr Ltd) Taylor & Francis.

Morall Fabillis of Esope in Scottis Meter Be Maister Henrisone. Aesop. LC 79-25964. (English Experience Ser.: No. 282). 104p. 1970. reprint ed. 25.00 (90-221-0282-3) Walter J Johnson.

Morally Deep World: An Essay on Moral Significance & Environmental Ethics. Lawrence E. Johnson. 311p. (C). 1993. pap. text 23.95 (0-521-44706-2) Cambridge U Pr.

Morally Good Politician: Why Our Politicians Are So Bad & How to Create Ones That Will Respect & Protect Our Rights. Lorenz F. Kraus. LC 96-114652. 228p. (C). 1995. 21.95 (0-9647446-1-9) Great Albany.

Morals & Dogma of the Ancient & Accepted Scottish Rite of Freemasonry. Albert Pike. (Illus.). 878p. 1992. reprint ed. pap. 45.00 (1-56459-275-8) Kessinger Pub.

Morals & Dogma of the Ancient & Accepted Scottish Rite of Freemasonry. Albert Pike. (Notable American Authors Ser.). 1999. reprint ed. lib. bdg. 125.00 (0-7812-8749-9) Rprt Serv.

Morals & Issues: Index of Modern Information. rev. ed. Larry C. Overstreet. 145p. 1994. 47.50 (0-7883-0466-6); pap. 44.50 (0-7883-0467-4) ABBE Pubs Assn.

Morals & Law. Max Hamburger. LC 65-15244. 1965. 30.00 (0-8196-0151-9) Biblo.

Morals & Law in Ancient Greece Series, 57 bks., Set. Ed. by Gregory Vlastos. 1979. lib. bdg. 1353.00 (0-405-11529-6) Ayer.

Morals & Markets: The Development of Life Insurance in the United States. Viviana A. Zelizer. LC 83-684. 210p. 1983. reprint ed. pap. text 24.95 (0-87855-929-9) Transaction Pubs.

***Morals & Markets: 7th Annual IEA Hayek Memorial Lecture.** Jonathan Sacks et al. (Occasional Paper Ser.: No. 8). 57p. 1999. pap. 17.95 (0-255-36424-5, Pub. by Inst Economic Affairs) Coronet Bks.

Morals & Medicine: The Moral Problems of the Patient's Right to Know the Truth, Contraception, Artificial Insemination, Sterilization, Euthanasia. Joseph F. Fletcher. LC 54-9019. 267p. reprint ed. pap. 82.80 (0-8357-4198-2, 203697600006) Bks Demand.

Morals & Might: Ethics & the Use of Force in Modern International Affairs. Ed. by George A. Lopez. 288p. (C). 1997. pap. 55.00 (0-8133-8726-4) Westview.

Morals & Politics of Psychology: Psychological Discourse & the Status Quo. Isaac Prilleltensky. LC 93-37494. (SUNY Series, Alternatives in Psychology). 283p. (C). 1994. pap. text 21.95 (0-7914-2038-8) State U NY Pr.

Morals & Politics of Psychology: Psychological Discourse & the Status Quo. Isaac Prilleltensky. LC 93-37494. (SUNY Series, Alternatives in Psychology). 283p. (C). 1994. text 64.50 (0-7914-2037-X) State U NY Pr.

Morals & Society in Asian Philosophy. Ed. by Brian Carr. (Curzon Studies in Asian Philosophy). 260p. (C). 1996. text 42.00 (0-7007-0345-4, Pub. by Curzon Pr Ltd) UH Pr.

Morals & Stories. Tobin Siebers. 236p. 1992. text 34.50 (0-231-07846-3) Col U Pr.

Morals & the Evolution of Man. Max Nordau. 1976. lib. bdg. 250.00 (0-8490-2280-0) Gordon Pr.

Morals & the Media: Information, Entertainment, & Manipulation. John J. Stuhr. (Autzen Lectures in Humanities & Professions). 1990. pap. 5.00 (0-87114-226-0) U of Oreg Bks.

Morals & Values in Ancient Greece. John Ferguson. (Classical World Ser.). (Illus.). 111p. (C). 1989. pap. 18.95 (1-85399-118-X, Pub. by Brist Class Pr) Focus Pub-R Pullins.

Morals Based on Needs. Ragnar Ohlsson. 164p. (C). 1995. lib. bdg. 38.00 (0-8191-9853-6) U Pr of Amer.

Morals by Agreement. David Gauthier. 384p. 1987. pap. text 29.95 (0-19-824992-6) OUP.

Morals for the Heart. Nizam A. Awliya. Tr. by Bruce B. Lawrence. 404p. 1996. 19.95 (0-614-21314-2, 804) Kazi Pubns.

***Morals in Idealistic & Naturalistic Thought.** Nicholas Churchich. LC 99-96746. 2000. 26.95 (0-533-13347-5) Vantage.

Morals in Review. Arthur K. Rogers. LC 72-126697. reprint ed. 34.50 (0-404-05379-3) AMS Pr.

Morals in World History. Archibald T. Robertson. LC 74-6354. (World History Ser.: No. 48). (C). 1974. lib. bdg. 75.00 (0-8383-1918-1) M S G Haskell Hse.

Morals, Marriage & Parenthood: An Introduction to Family Ethics. Laurence D. Houlgate. LC 98-28477. 1998. mass mkt. 49.95 (0-534-55157-2) Wadsworth Pub.

Morals, Motivation, & Convention: Hume's Influential Doctrines. Francis Snare. (Studies in Philosophy). 336p. (C). 1991. text 80.00 (0-521-39261-6) Cambridge U Pr.

Morals of Abou Ben Adhem. David R. Locke. LC 76-91086. (American Humorists Ser.). reprint ed. lib. bdg. 25.50 (0-8398-1164-0) Irvington.

Morals of History. Tzvetan Todorov. Tr. by Alyson Waters. LC 94-28977. Orig. Title: Les Morales de L'Histoire. 1995. pap. 37.95 (0-8166-2298-1); text 47.95 (0-8166-2297-3) U of Minn Pr.

Morals of Knowledge: Between Mathematics & Ethics. J. Fang. 230p. 1996. pap. 19.50 (0-912490-22-5) PAIDEIA & PM.

Morals of Markets & Related Essays. H. B. Acton. Ed. by David Gordon & Jeremy Shearmur. LC 92-42151. 284p. 1993. 20.00 (0-86597-106-4); pap. 7.50 (0-86597-107-2) Liberty Fund.

Morals of Modernity. Charles E. Larmore. (Modern European Philosophy Ser.). 236p. (C). 1996. pap. text 20.95 (0-521-49772-8) Cambridge U Pr.

Morals of the Movie. Ellis P. Oberholtzer. LC 74-160244. (Moving Pictures Ser.). 251p. 1971. reprint ed. lib. bdg. 28.95 (0-89198-045-8) Ozer.

Morals, Reason & Animals. Steven F. Sapontzis. LC 86-30221. 332p. 1987. 59.95 (0-87722-493-5) Temple U Pr.

Morals, Reason & Animals. Steven F. Sapontzis. 1992. pap. 24.95 (0-87722-961-9) Temple U Pr.

***Morals under the Gun: The Cardinal Virtues, Military Ethics & American Society.** James H. Toner. LC 99-89730. 256p. 2000. 29.95 (0-8131-2159-0) U Pr of Ky.

Moramona: The Mormons in Hawaii. R. Lanier Britsch. LC 89-37402. (Mormons in the Pacific Ser.). (Illus.). 256p. (Orig.). 1989. pap. 12.95 (0-939154-46-3) Inst Polynesian.

Moran: Descendants of Franklin Peirce Moran & Mary Adelaide Snyder Moran, with Family Tree of Early Moran Ancestors (From Hezekia of Montgomery Co., Md.) Evelyn W. Brown et al. (Illus.). 373p. 1993. pap. 59.00 (0-8328-2823-8); lib. bdg. 69.00 (0-8328-2822-X) Higginson Bk Co.

Moran Family: Two Hundred Years in Detroit. J. B. Moran. (Illus.). 152p. 1991. reprint ed. pap. 28.00 (0-8328-2036-9); reprint ed. lib. bdg. 38.00 (0-8328-2035-0) Higginson Bk Co.

Moran Family Pts. I & II: Descendants of Hezekiah, Robert Milton, Franklin Pierce Moran & Alice Grace Moran Wright; Services of George Brinton Mcclellan for the Preservation of the Union. Evelyn W. Brown & Alice G. Wright. (Illus.). 369p. 1997. pap. 45.00 (0-8328-9475-3); lib. bdg. 55.00 (0-8328-9474-5) Higginson Bk Co.

Moran Family Legacy. Katherine Cameron & Henry Korn. 1997. pap. 20.00 (0-933793-45-6) Guild Hall.

Moran of Kathmandu Priest, Educator & Ham Radio Voice of the Himalayas. D. A. Messerschmidt. 1997. pap. 87.00 (0-7855-7438-7, Pub. by Ratna Pustak Bhandar) St Mut.

Moran of the Lady Letty: A Story of Adventure off the California Coast. Frank Norris. LC 70-104533. 297p. 1979. reprint ed. lib. bdg. 11.50 (0-8398-1351-1) Irvington.

Moran of the Lady Letty: A Story of Adventure off the California Coast. Frank Norris. (BCL1-PS American Literature Ser.). 293p. 1992. reprint ed. pap. text 59.00 (0-685-51393-9); reprint ed. lib. bdg. 79.00 (0-7812-6811-7) Rprt Serv.

Moran of the Lady Letty, a Story of Adventure off the California Coast. Frank Norris. LC 75-144665. 293p. 1971. reprint ed. 29.50 (0-404-04790-4) AMS Pr.

Moranilini: Insecta: Hymenoptera see Fauna of New Zealand Series

Moratin: El Si de las Ninas. Ed. by P. Deacon. (SPA.). 1995. pap. 18.95 (1-85399-417-0, Pub. by Brist Class Pr) Focus Pub-R Pullins.

Morava K-theories & Localisation Mark Hovey & Neil P. Strickland. LC 99-19210. (Memoirs of the Society Ser.). 1999. write for info. (0-8218-1079-0) Am Math.

Moravagine. Blaise Cendrars. Tr. by Alan Brown from FRE. 250p. 1990. pap. 9.95 (0-922233-04-7) Blast Bks.

Moravagine. Blaise Cendrars. (Illus.). 236p. 1968. 24.00 (0-7206-5202-2, Pub. by P Owen Ltd) Dufour.

Moravian Architecture & Town Planning: Bethlehem, Pennsylvania, & Other Eighteenth-Century American Settlements. William J. Murtagh. LC 97-43397. (Illus.). 160p. (C). 1997. pap. 19.95 (0-8122-1637-7) U of Pa Pr.

Moravian Book of Worship. LC 94-79796. 960p. 1995. 18.00 (1-878422-15-4) Moravian Ch in Amer.

Moravian Book of Worship. deluxe ed. LC 94-79796. 960p. 1995. lthr. 28.00 (1-878422-16-2) Moravian Ch in Amer.

Moravian Book of Worship. limited large type ed. 848p. 1995. 18.00 (1-878422-17-0) Moravian Ch in Amer.

Moravian Book of Worship Manual for Worship Planners. Ed. by Robert T. Burcaw. 146p. 1995. pap., student ed. 6.00 (1-878422-19-7) Moravian Ch in Amer.

Moravian Church in England, 1728-1760. Colin Podmore. (Oxford Historical Monographs). (Illus.). 352p. 1998. text 85.00 (0-19-820725-5) OUP.

Moravian Church Through the Ages. John R. Weinlick & Albert H. Frank. LC 89-62195. 128p. 1989. reprint ed. pap. 8.00 (1-878422-27-8) Moravian Ch in Amer.

Moravian Families of Carroll's Manor, Frederick County, Maryland. 2nd ed. George E. Russell. (Illus.). 150p. (Orig.). 1996. pap. 19.00 (0-914385-07-0) Catoctin Pr.

Moravian Journals Relating to Central New York. William M. Beauchamp. LC 72-8246. (Communal Societies in America Ser). reprint ed. 41.50 (0-404-11000-2) AMS Pr.

***Moravian Journals Relating to Central New York, 1745-1766.** William M. Beauchamp. 211p. 1999. reprint ed. pap. 22.50 (0-7884-1311-2, B112) Heritage Bk.

Moravian Potters in North Carolina. John Bivins. LC 70-172396. (Illus.). 315p. reprint ed. pap. 97.70 (0-7837-5234-2, 204496800005) Bks Demand.

Moravian Tales: Legends & Myths. rev. ed. Karla Bufkova-Wankelova. (Illus.). 209p. (J). 1992. pap. 19.50 (0-685-71137-4) Kabel Pubs.

Moravian Tales: Legends & Myths. 3rd rev. ed. Karla Butkova et al. (Illus.). 209p. (YA). 1992. text 34.50 (0-930329-51-1) Kabel Pubs.

Moravian Women's Memoirs: Their Related Lives , 1750-1820. Ed. & Tr. by Katherine M. Faull. LC 96-21261. (Women & Gender in North American Religions Ser.). (Illus.). xl, 166p. 1997. pap. 17.95 (0-8156-0397-5, FAMWP) Syracuse U Pr.

Moravians in Jamaica. J. H. Buchner. LC 77-178470. (Black Heritage Library Collection). 1977. reprint ed. 24.95 (0-8369-8918-X) Ayer.

Moravians, the Miskitu & the Sandinistas on Nicaragua's Atlantic Coast, 1979-90. C. alton Robertson. LC 98-65183. 96p. 1998. pap. 16.00 (1-878422-37-5) Moravian Ch in Amer.

Moravigne. Blaise Cendrars. (FRE.). 1983. pap. 19.95 (0-7859-3044-2) Fr & Eur.

Moray & Badenoch: A Historical Guide. Richard Oram. (Illus.). 190p. pap. 15.95 (1-874744-46-7, Pub. by Birlinn Ltd) Dufour.

Moray Coast Railways: Exploring the Remains & Environs of the Great North of Scotland & Highland Railways in Morayshire & Banffshire. Rosemary Burgess & Robert Kinghorn. (Illus.). 140p. 1990. pap. text 17.75 (0-08-037970-2, Pergamon Pr) Elsevier.

Moray Coast Speyside & the Cairngorms. Jimmie Macgregor. (Illus.). 88p. 1991. pap. 7.95 (0-563-20560-1, Pub. by BBC) Parkwest Pubns.

Moray Eels. Don Rothaus. LC 95-12144. (Nature Books Ser.). (Illus.). 32p. (J). (gr. 2-6). 1995. lib. bdg. 22.79 (1-56766-187-4) Childs World.

Moray Firth Ships & Trade in the 19th Century. Ian Hustwick. 180p. 1990. pap. 27.00 (1-898218-05-6) St Mut.

Morbid Craving for Morphia: Die Morphiumsucht. Edward Levinstein. Ed. by Gerald N. Grob. Tr. by Charles Harrer. LC 80-1259. (Addiction in America Ser.). 1981. reprint ed. lib. bdg. 15.95 (0-405-13602-1) Ayer.

Morbid Fascination: White Prose & Politics in Apartheid South Africa, 78. Richard Peck. LC 96-27387. (Contributions to the Study of World Literature Ser.). 216p. 1997. 59.95 (0-313-30091-7) Greenwood.

Morbid Kitchen. large type ed. Jennie Melville. LC 95-53281. 1996. pap. 21.95 (0-7862-0642-X) Thorndike Pr.

Morbid Taste for Bones. Ellis Peters. 208p. 1994. mass mkt. 6.50 (0-446-40015-7, Pub. by Warner Bks) Little.

Morbidity & Mortality of Dialysis. 1994. lib. bdg. 250.00 (0-8490-8404-0) Gordon Pr.

Morbidity & Mortality Weekly Report. Government Printing Office Staff. 1983. pap. 133.00 (0-16-010482-3) USGPO.

Morbidity Statistics: Twelfth Report of the WHO Expert Committee on Health Statistics. (Technical Report Ser.). 29p. 1968. pap. text 3.00 (92-4-120389-7, 1100389) World Health.

Morbus Crohn Aus Psychosomatischer Sicht. Hermann Federschmidt. (Illus.). 218p. 1993. 39.95 (3-631-45659-X) P Lang Pubng.

Morbus Kitahara. Christoph Ransmayr. 1999. 24.95 (3-596-13782-9) Fischer Taschen.

Morbus Kitahara. Christoph Ransmayr. (GER.). 448p. 1995. 39.75 (3-10-062908-6, Pub. by S Fischer) Intl Bk Import.

Morceaux Choisis: Poesie. Charles Peguy. pap. 6.95 (0-685-37014-3) Fr & Eur.

Morcom: A Guide to the Trade Marks Act 1994. Christopher Morcom. (Butterworths Annotated Legislation Service Ser.). 1994. pap. write for info. (0-406-04581-X, AMGT1994, MICHIE) LEXIS Pub.

Morcom: The Modern Law of Trade Marks & Service Marks. Christopher Morcom. 1997. ring bd. write for info. (0-406-06552-7, MMLTSUB, MICHIE) LEXIS Pub.

Mord - Selbstmord - Unfall. Ed. by W. Duerwald. (Limited Volume Series: Gerichtliche Medizin im 19. Jahrhundert: Vol. 2). xvi, 338p. 1991. 71.50 (3-8055-4779-X) S Karger.

Mord & Mordmotiv: Ein Gerichtsmedizinischer Pitaval Zusammengestellt aus Fachzeitschriften des 19. Jahrhunderts. Ed. by W. Duerwald. (Gerichtliche Medizin im 19. Jahrhundert Ser.: Vol. 1). xx, 290p. 1987. 71.50 (3-8055-4777-3) S Karger.

Mord Auf Dem Golfplatz. (Easy Reader Ser.: Level 1). (GER.). 40p. 1995. 5.95 (3-468-49690-7) Langenscheidt.

Mordant's Wish. Valerie Coursen. LC 96-44210. (Illus.). 32p. (J). (ps-2). 1995. 15.95 (0-8050-4374-8) H Holt & Co.

***Mordecai: The Defender of the Jews.** John G. Butler. 273p. 1999. 16.50 (1-889773-19-0) LBC Publns.

Mordecai - The Man & His Message: The Story of Mordecai Wyatt Johnson. Richard I. McKinney & Mordecai W. Johnson. LC 96-47507. 1997. write for info. (0-88258-197-X) Howard U Pr.

Mordecai - The Man & His Message: The Story of Mordecai Wyatt Johnson. Richard I. McKinney & Mordecai W. Johnson. LC 96-47507. (Illus.). 354p. (C). 1997. pap. text 21.95 (0-88258-193-7, MCMMP) Howard U Pr.

Mordecai M. Kaplan & the Development of Reconstructionism. Richard Libowitz. LC 83-923. (Studies in American Religion: Vol. 9). (Illus.). 266p. 1983. lib. bdg. 89.95 (0-88946-651-3) E Mellen.

Mordecai Manuel Noah: First American Jew. Abraham J. Karp. (Illus.). 80p. 1988. pap. write for info. (0-945447-02-7) Yesh Mus.

Mordecai of Monterey. Keith Abbott. LC 84-72513. (Illus.). 224p. 1985. 13.95 (0-933944-10-1); pap. 8.95 (0-933944-11-X) City Miner Bks.

Mordecai of Monterey. deluxe ed. Keith Abbott. LC 84-72513. (Illus.). 224p. 1985. 25.00 (0-933944-21-7) City Miner Bks.

Mordecai Richler: An Annotated Bibliography. Michael Darling. 211p. (C). 1979. pap. 9.00 (0-920763-62-6, Pub. by ECW) Genl Dist Srvs.

Mordecai Sheftall: Jewish Revolutionary Patriot. B. H. Levy. LC 99-73260. (Illus.). 150p. 1999. 15.00 (1-881682-07-2) GA Hist Soc.

Mordechai. Perry Haalman. (Illus.). 36p. (J). (gr. 4 up). 1990. pap. 8.00 (0-9624155-2-9) Cottage Wordsmiths.

Mordechai Gebirtig: His Poetic & Musical Legacy. Ed. by Gertrude Schneider. 224p. 2000. 65.00 (0-275-96657-7, Praeger Pubs) Greenwood.

Mordechai Schamz. Marc Cholodenko. Tr. by Dominic Di Bernardi from FRE. LC 88-25050. 128p. 1989. 19.95 (0-916583-31-7) Dalkey Arch.

***Mordechai Schamz.** Marc Cholodenko. Tr. by Dominic Di Bernardi from FRE. LC 88-25050. 121p. 2000. pap. 10.95 (1-56478-246-8, Pub. by Dalkey Arch) Chicago Distribution Ctr.

Mordovia Republic: Economy, Industry, Government, Business. 2nd rev. ed. Russian Information & Business Center, Inc. Staff. (Russian Regional Business Directories Ser.). (Illus.). 200p. 1997. pap. 99.00 (1-57751-365-7) Intl Business Pubns.

***Mordovian Republic Regional Investment & Business Guide.** Global Investment & Business Center, Inc. Staff. (Russian Regional Investment & Business Guides Ser.: Vol. 46). (Illus.). 350p. 1999. pap. 99.00 (0-7397-0817-1) Intl Business Pubns.

***Mordovian Republic Regional Investment & Business Guide.** Contrib. by Global Investment & Business Center, Inc. Staff. (Russian Regional Investment & Business Guides Ser.). (Illus.). 350p. 2000. pap. 99.95 (0-7397-2994-2) Intl Business Pubns.

Mordred's Curse. Ian McDowell. 304p. (Orig.). 1996. mass mkt. 5.99 (0-380-78195-6, Avon Bks) Morrow Avon.

More. Max Beerbohm. LC 67-28730. (Essay Index Reprint Ser.). 1977. 19.95 (0-8369-0181-9) Ayer.

M

An Asterisk (*) at the beginning of an entry indicates that the title is appearing for the first time.

More! Emma Chichester Clark. LC 98-45497. (Illus.). 32p. (J). 1999. 15.95 (*0-385-32630-0*) BDD Bks Young Read.
***More!** Sheilagh Noble. (Illus.). 24p. (J). 2000. 9.95 (*1-84089-127-0*, Pub. by Zero to Ten) IPG Chicago.
More. Ted Washington. LC 94-69131. 77p. 1994. pap. write for info. (*0-9644366-0-4*) Puna Pr.
More: Chronicles of the More Family. Ed. by Grace V. More. (Illus.). 424p. 1993. reprint ed. pap. 63.50 (*0-8328-3376-2*); reprint ed. lib. bdg. 73.50 (*0-8328-3375-4*) Higginson Bk Co.
More: History of the More Family, & an Account of Their Reunion in 1890, with a Genealogical Record. David F. More. (Illus.). 409p. 1992. reprint ed. pap. 63.00 (*0-8328-2429-1*); reprint ed. lib. bdg. 73.00 (*0-8328-2428-3*) Higginson Bk Co.
More: In-Depth Discussion of the Reasoning Activities in "Teaching Fractions & Ratios for Understanding" Susan J. Lamon. LC 99-193054. 192p. 1999. pap. 24.50 (*0-8058-3299-8*) L Erlbaum Assocs.
***More: The Politics of Economic Growth in Postwar America.** Robert M. Collins. LC 99-22524. 304p. 2000. 35.00 (*0-19-504646-3*) OUP.
More . . . Occupation & Hobby Patterns for Cake Decorating. Roland A. Winbeckler. (Illus.). 24p. (Orig.). 1987. pap. 5.95 (*0-930113-07-1*) Winbeckler.
More . . . The Merrier: A Collection of 54 Original Old-Timey Style Fiddle Tunes. Edmond P. Cormier. LC 98-96742. (Illus.). 84p. 1998. pap. 12.00 (*0-9668020-0-4*) Abundance Ltd.

M

***More about... APL: A Help File for the APL Text: Preparing the Portfolio for an Assessment of Prior Learning.** Roslyn Snow. 39p. 1999. pap. text 25.00 (*0-9679093-1-7*, WebSpeed) Easy Guides.
More about Carpinteria As It Was, Vol 2. LC 79-83931. (Illus.). (YA). (gr. 11 up). 1982. 9.95 (*0-9608826-1-8*) Papillon Pr.
More about Dinosaurs. David Cutts. LC 81-11432. (Now I Know Ser.). (Illus.). 32p. (J). (gr. k-2). 1982. lib. bdg. 17.25 (*0-89375-668-7*) Troll Communs.
More about Dinosaurs. David Cutts. LC 81-11432. (Now I Know Ser.). (Illus.). 32p. (J). (gr. k-2). 1997. pap. 3.50 (*0-89375-669-5*) Troll Communs.
More about Flip 'n' Flop. Tony Hickey. 96p. (J). 1994. pap. 6.95 (*0-947962-73-5*) Dufour.
More about Justifying Violence: Methodological Studies of Attitudes. Monica D. Blumenthal et al. LC 74-620136. 413p. reprint ed. pap. 128.10 (*0-7837-5261-X*, 204499900005) Bks Demand.
More about Life in the World Unseen. Anthony Borgia. Ed. by Mike Rigby. 168p. 1993. pap. 10.00 (*0-9636435-2-5*) M A P.
More about Masonry. 3rd ed. H. L. Haywood. xxviii, 220p. 1993. pap. 7.50 (*0-88053-031-6*, M081) Macoy Pub.
More about Me: Another Keepsake Journal for Kids. Linda Kranz. (Keepsakes Ser.). 128p. (J). (gr. 3-6). 1998. pap. 12.95 (*0-87358-716-2*, Rising Moon Bks) Northland AZ.
More about Paddington see Hilarious Adventures of Paddington
More about Paddington, Michael Bond. (Paddington Ser.). (Illus.). 144p. (J). (gr. 2-5). 1979. 15.00 (*0-395-06640-9*) HM.
More about Ramakrishna. Swami Prabhananda. 276p. (Orig.). 1994. pap. 5.95 (*0-87481-242-9*, Pub. by Advaita Ashrama) Vedanta Pr.
***More about the Fickle Mrs. Whiskers & Other Cat Tales.** Gloria Williams Hearn. LC 98-91080. (Illus.). 60p. (J). 2000. pap. 7.95 (*0-533-13037-9*) Vantage.
More about the Mob. John Fairbairn. (Storybridge Ser.). 96p. (J). (gr. 4-7). 1995. pap. 9.95 (*0-7022-2790-0*, Pub. by Univ Queensland Pr) Intl Spec Bk.
More about the U. S. A. Milada Broukal & Janet Milhomme. LC 95-24398. 1995. pap. text 17.59 (*0-201-87679-5*) Longman.
More about this Business of Music. 5th enl. rev. ed. M. William Krasilovsky & Sidney Shemel. LC 94-27593. 224p. 1994. 18.95 (*0-8230-7642-3*, Billboard Bks) Watsn-Guptill.
More Activities for Girls: For 8-11 Year-Old Girls. Doris Grossnickle & Glorianne Muggli. (Illus.). 100p. (Orig.). (J). (gr. 3-6). 1996. pap. 6.95 (*1-57665-021-9*) Muggli Graphics.
***More Activities That Teach.** Tom Jackson. 341p. 1999. pap. 18.95 (*0-9664633-2-3*) Red Rock Pubg.
More Adventures. Goodman. (Goodman's Five-Star Stories Ser.). (YA). (gr. 6-12). 1998. 13.00 (*0-89061-825-9*, R0825-9E, Jamestwn Pub) NTC Contemp Pub Co.
More Adventures in Jazz. Willie Myette. (Adventures in Jazz Ser.). (Illus.). 36p. (J). (gr. k-12). 1997. pap. text 10.00 (*1-891679-02-3*, MAJ) Jazzkids.
More Adventures of Gilly, the Guitar, Bk. 3. Cathy Ellis. (Illus.). 48p. (J). (ps-2). 1993. audio 17.95 (*1-879542-09-9*) Ellis Family Mus.
More Adventures of Minnie. Jan S. Hart. (Illus.). 115p. (J). (gr. 3-6). 1995. 12.95 (*0-9644559-0-0*) Hart Publ.
More Adventures of the Black Hole Modulator. Ellen S. Decklon. (Black Hole Modulator Trilogy Ser.: Vol. 2). (Illus.). 300p. 1998. 19.95 (*1-884939-39-2*); pap. 10.95 (*1-884939-40-6*) Antoine Versailles.
More Adventures of the Great Brain. John D. Fitzgerald. 160p. (J). (gr. k-6). 1971. pap. 3.99 (*0-440-45822-6*, YB BDD) BDD Bks Young Read.
More Adventures of the Great Brain. John D. Fitzgerald. (Dell Yearling Bks.). (J). 1969. 9.09 (*0-606-02183-3*, Pub. by Turtleback) Demco.
***More Adventures of the Great Brain.** John D. Fitzgerald & Mercer Mayer. (Illus.). (J). 2000. 6.99 (*0-8037-2591-4*, Dial Yng Read) Peng Put Young Read.
More Adventures of the Plant That Ate Dirty Socks. Nancy McArthur. (Plant That Ate Dirty Socks Ser.: No. 5). 128p. (J). (gr. 2-5). 1994. pap. 3.99 (*0-380-77663-4*, Avon Bks) Morrow Avon.
More Adventures of the Plant That Ate Dirty Socks. Nancy McArthur. LC 94-94095. (Plant That Ate Dirty Socks Ser.: Bk. 5). (J). (gr. 2-5). 1994. 9.09 (*0-606-06580-6*, Pub. by Turtleback) Demco.
More Adventures with Basie, the Electric Bass Guitar. Cathy Ellis. (Complete Guide for the Guitar Ser.: Bk. 2). (Illus.). 48p. (J). (ps-2). 1993. wbk. ed. 16.95 (*1-879542-31-5*, EFM BS2) Ellis Family Mus.
More Adventures with Basie, the Electric Bass Guitar. Cathy Ellis. (Complete Guide for the Guitar Ser.: Bk. 3). (Illus.). 50p. (J). (ps-2). 1993. wbk. ed. 17.95 (*1-879542-32-3*, EFM BS3) Ellis Family Mus.
***More Adventures with Britannia.** William R. Louis. LC 98-61464. x, 388 p. 1998. write for info. (*1-86064-293-4*) I B T.
More Adventures with Britannia: Personalities, Politics, & Culture in Britain. Ed. by William R. Louis. LC 98-61464. (Illus.). 384p. 1999. 40.00 (*0-292-74708-X*); pap. 19.95 (*0-292-74709-8*) U of Tex Pr.
More Adventures with Gilly, the Guitar, Bk. 2. Cathy Ellis. (Illus.). 48p. (J). (ps-2). 1992. student ed., spiral bd., wbk. ed. 16.95 (*1-879542-08-0*); audio 17.95 (*1-879542-14-5*) Ellis Family Mus.
More Adventures with LOGO, Teacher's Edition: MIT Version. Joyce Tobias & Carolyn Markuson. Ed. by Nola J. Hague. 240p. (Orig.). 1985. pap. text 20.12 (*0-07-064973-1*) McGraw.
More Ah Mo. Trenholme J. Griffin. 64p. 1993. pap. 7.95 (*0-88839-303-2*) Hancock House.
More Algebra by Design. Russell F. Jacobs. Ed. by Erika Jacobs. 50p. (YA). (gr. 8-10). 1994. pap. text, wbk. ed. 17.95 (*0-918272-24-6*, 162) Jacobs.
More Alike Than Different: An Inspiring Message for Anyone Coping with Life's Difficulties. Lee Bussard. 136p. 1997. 19.95 (*1-890009-02-4*) Exec Excell.
More Alike Than Different: Treating Severely Dissociative Trauma Survivors. Margo Rivera. 304p. 1996. text 50.00 (*0-8020-0450-4*); pap. text 24.95 (*0-8020-7238-0*) U of Toronto Pr.
More All-of-a-Kind Family. Sydney Taylor. (All-of-a-Kind Family Ser.). (Illus.). 160p. (J). (gr. 3-6). 1988. reprint ed. 11.95 (*0-929093-02-X*, Pub. by GRM Assocs) IPG Chicago.
More! All Star Poet: New & Selected Poems. Stephen Scriver. (Illus.). 152p. 1989. mass mkt. 4.95 (*1-55050-001-5*, Pub. by Coteau) Genl Dist Srvs.
More All-Time Christmas Favorites. 80p. 1981. per. 10.95 (*0-7935-0935-1*, 00360489) H Leonard.
More All-Time Christmas Favorites. 64p. 1983. pap. 6.95 (*0-7935-0941-6*, 00218819) H Leonard.
More All-Time Hockey Lists. Stan Fischler & Shirley Fischler. (Illus.). 117p. 1998. pap. text 14.00 (*0-7881-5390-0*) DIANE Pub.
More Altitude, Quick! Scott E. Sutton. (Wizard Tells a Story Ser.: Bk. 4). (Illus.). 51p. (J). (gr. 2-4). 1988. 13.95 (*0-9617199-4-X*) Action Publng.
More Amazing Achievement Days. Beth Lefgren & Jennifer Jackson. LC 97-74878. 1997. pap. 9.95 (*1-57008-334-7*) Bookcraft Inc.
More Amazing but True Mormon Stories. Joan Oviatt. 176p. (Orig.). 1996. pap. 13.98 (*0-88290-578-3*, 1043) Horizon Utah.
More Amazing Dinosaurs Maze Book. John Cartwright. 32p. (J). 1989. pap. 1.50 (*0-8167-1221-2*) Troll Communs.
More Amazing Sports Photos: More Funny, Famous, & Fantastic Photographs from the World of Sports. rev. ed. Sherie Holder. 32p. (J). Date not set. pap. 3.95 (*1-886749-13-2*) SI For Kids.
***More Amazing Stories.** Ed. by Kim Mohan. 2000. pap. 14.95 (*0-312-87437-5*) St Martin.
More American Dolls: From the Post War Era 1945-1965. Cynthia Gaskill. (Illus.). 96p. 1993. pap. 33.00 (*0-912823-43-7*, BT-138, Pub. by Gold Horse) Dollmasters.
More Analysts at Work. Joseph Reppen. LC 96-13800. 268p. 1997. pap. 50.00 (*1-56821-857-5*) Aronson.
More & Better Jobs for Women: An Action Guide. Lin L. Lim. LC 97-103824. xii, 193p. 1996. pap. 22.50 (*92-2-109459-6*) Intl Labour Office.
***More & Less.** Ed. by Sylvere Lotringer. 261p. 1999. pap. 14.00 (*1-57027-091-0*, Pub. by Autonomedia) SPD-Small Pr Dist.
More & More. Stella Cameron. 408p. 1999. mass mkt. 6.99 (*0-446-60613-8*, Pub. by Warner Bks) Little.
***More & More.** large type ed. Stella Cameron. LC 99-43302. (Thorndike Basic Ser.). 600p. 1999. 28.95 (*0-7862-2212-3*) Thorndike Pr.
More & More: Poems from Hollywood. Mark Dunster. 11p. 1998. pap. 5.00 (*0-89642-613-0*) Linden Pubs.
More & More & More Tales to Give You Goosebumps: Book & Holiday Stocking Set. R. L. Stine, pseud. (Goosebumps Special Edition Ser.: No. 6). (J). 1997. pap. text 9.95 (*0-590-36682-3*, Apple Paperbacks) Scholastic Inc.
More & More Tales to Give You Goosebumps. R. L. Stine, pseud. (Goosebumps Special Edition Ser.: No. 5). (J). (gr. 3-7). 1997. pap. 14.95 (*0-614-29022-8*, Apple Classics) Scholastic Inc.
More & More Tales to Give You Goosebumps: Book & Cap Pack. R. L. Stine, pseud. (Goosebumps Special Edition Ser.: No. 5). (J). 1997. 11.95 (*0-590-23795-0*) Scholastic Inc.
More & Still More: A Passion for All God Offers. Joe Engelkemier. Ed. by Kenneth R. Wade. LC 98-37475. 143p. 1998. pap. 9.99 (*0-8163-1710-0*) Pacific Pr Pub Assn.
More Anguished English. Richard Lederer. 208p. 1994. mass mkt. 6.50 (*0-440-21577-3*) Dell.
More Animals in My Life. Kendall Grant. 224p. 1998. 22.95 (*0-87605-368-1*) Howell Bks.
More Animals in My Life: Stories of a Country Vet. Grant Kendall. LC 98-17342. 1998. 22.95 (*0-87605-168-9*) Howell Bks.
More Annie Stories: Therapeutic Storytelling Techniques. Doris Brett. LC 91-46084. 224p. 1992. 16.95 (*0-945354-47-9*) Am Psychol.
More Annotated H. P. Lovecraft. H. P. Lovecraft. Ed. by S. T. Joshi & Peter Cannon. LC 99-23457. (Illus.). 320p. 1999. pap. 13.95 (*0-440-50875-4*, Dell Trade Pbks) Dell.
More Answers from the Mother. 448p. 1987. 15.00 (*81-7058-237-7*, Pub. by SAA) E-W Cultural Ctr.

***More Ardent Fire: From Everyday Love to Love of God.** Eknath Easwaran. 192p. 1999. 22.00 (*1-888314-03-6*, Pub. by Nilgiri Pr); pap. 12.95 (*1-888314-02-8*, Pub. by Nilgiri Pr) Publishers Group.
More Australian Tales of Ghost & Fantasy. Dorothy Michell. 207p. (C). 1990. 50.00 (*0-947333-00-2*, Pub. by Pascoe Pub) St Mut.
More Authors & I. Charles L. Hind. LC 69-17576. (Essay Index Reprint Ser.). 1977. 20.95 (*0-8369-0078-2*) Ayer.
More Authors & Illustrators Through the Year: Ready-to-Use Literature Activities for Grades K-3. David J. Fiday. 272p. 1992. pap. text 27.95 (*0-87628-576-0*) Ctr Appl Res.
More Awesome Good Clean Jokes for Kids. Bob Phillips. LC 94-29224. (J). 1995. mass mkt. 3.99 (*1-56507-270-7*) Harvest Hse.
More Awesome Truth. Eddie Eddings. (Awesome Truth Ser.: Vol. 2). (Illus.). 1997. pap. 2.97 (*1-57748-075-9*) Barbour Pub.
More Baby Animals. Debby Slier. (Baby Animal Padded Photo Board Bks.). (Illus.). 18p. (J). (ps). 1992. bds. 4.50 (*1-56288-308-9*) Checkerboard.
More Baby Animals: A Sierra Club Postcard Book for Kids. Sierra Club Staff. (Illus.). 40p. (J). (ps up). 1992. 8.95 (*0-87156-595-1*) Sierra Club Childrens.
More Back of the Box Gourmet. Michael McLaughlin. LC 93-25840. 1994. 15.00 (*0-671-86721-0*) S&S Trade.
More Back Roads of the Central Coast. Ron Stob. (Illus.). 152p. (Orig.). 1989. pap. 7.95 (*0-939919-26-5*) Bear Flag Bks.
More Bad Dates: Tales from the Dark Side of Love. Carole Markin. LC 98-14773. 224p. 1998. pap. 10.95 (*1-58063-016-2*) Renaissance.
More Bad Housekeeping. Sue Limb. 176p. 1995. pap. 13.95 (*1-85702-151-7*) Trafalgar.
More Balloon Animals. Aaron Hsu-Flanders. (Illus.). 144p. 1990. pap. 15.95 (*0-8092-4183-8*, 418380, Contemporary Bks) NTC Contemp Pub Co.
More Ballpoint Bananas. Illus. by Leonard Shortall. LC 77-5356. (J). (gr. 1-3). 1980. 7.95 (*0-13-600767-8*) Simon & Schuster.
More Balls Than Strikes: 120 Years of Baseball in New York's Hudson Valley. Charles Tiano. LC 95-81296. (Illus.). 136p. (Orig.). 1995. pap. 11.95 (*0-910746-14-1*) Hope Farm.
More Basic Chess Openings. Gabor Kallai. 1997. pap. 19.95 (*1-85744-206-7*) S&S Trade.
More Basic Course, Set. unabridged ed. Foreign Service Institute Staff. 339p. 1994. pap. text 255.00 incl. audio (*0-88432-379-X*, AFMR10) Audio-Forum.
More BAX Seat: New Logs of a Pasture Pilot. Gordon Baxter. 196p. 1988. 17.95 (*0-8306-9029-8*, 2429H); pap. 11.95 (*0-8306-9429-3*) McGraw-Hill Prof.
More Bazaar Bestsellers. (Illus.). 28p. (Orig.). 1987. pap. 5.95 (*0-933491-22-0*) Hot off Pr.
More Beautiful Lighthouses. 3rd ed. John Spatuzzi. (Beautiful Lighthouses Ser.: No. 2). (Illus.). 64p. 1998. pap. 7.95 (*1-881254-33-X*) Horizon Images.
More Beautiful Purses. Evelyn M. Haertig. (Illus.). 576p. 1990. 125.00 (*0-943294-01-0*) Gallery Graphics.
More Bell Lore. Dorothy M. Anthony. (World of Bells Ser.). (Illus.). 1993. ring bd. 11.95 (*0-9607944-7-6*) World of Bells.
More Bench-Tested Circuits: Innovative Designs for Surveillance & Countersurveillance Technicians. Tom Larsen. LC 99-160374. (Illus.). 72p. 1998. pap. 21.00 (*1-58160-007-0*) Paladin Pr.
More Berried Treasures & Other Good Pickin's. Elaine K. Jauman. (Illus.). 128p. 1983. pap. 4.95 (*0-9609282-2-7*) Kitchen Treas.
More Best-Loved Stories Told at the National Storytelling Festival. Ed. by National Association for Preservation & Perpetuati. 224p. 1992. 24.95 (*1-879991-09-8*); pap. 14.95 (*1-879991-08-X*) Natl Storytlng Network.
More Best Paper Aircraft. Campbell Morris. (Illus.). 32p. 1988. pap. 6.95 (*0-399-51446-5*, Perigee Bks) Berkley Pub.
More Better Than Mom's. Janet E. Talbert. Ed. by Lisa J. Talbert. (Better Than Mom's Ser.). 1995. write for info. (*0-9638345-1-7*) J Talbert.
More Bible Activities. Ken Save. (Young Reader's Christian Library). (Illus.). 192p. (J). (gr. 3-7). 1999. pap. 1.39 (*1-57748-597-1*) Barbour Pub.
More Bible Activities You Can Do. Nellie De Vries & Mary Currier. (Repro Bks Ser.). (Illus.). 160p. (J). (gr. k-7). 1999. pap. 6.99 (*0-8010-4416-2*) Baker Bks.
More Bible Word Searches. William C. Gordon. (Quiz & Puzzle Bks.). 96p. (Orig.). (gr. 5). 1997. pap. 7.99 (*0-8010-5751-5*) Baker Bks.
More Big Book of Questions & Answers. (Illus.). 192p. (J). 1990. 14.98 (*1-56173-412-8*) Pubns Intl Ltd.
More Big Sky Cooking. Greg Patent. (Big Sky Cooking Ser.: No. 2). (Illus.). 151p. (Orig.). 1980. pap. 9.50 (*0-686-29281-2*) Eagle Comm.
***More Binscombe Tales: Sinister Sutangli Stories.** John Whitbourn. xvi, 232p. 1999. 40.00 (*1-899562-72-9*) Ash-Tree.
More Biology in the Laboratory. Helms. 1989. pap. text 29.95 (*0-87901-396-6*) Worth.
More Biology in the Laboratory, Pt. I, Labs 1-17. Helms. 1990. pap. 16.95 (*0-87901-461-X*) Worth.
More-Bits: A Coaching Plan Book. Susan F. Tierno. (Illus.). 96p. 1998. pap. text, teacher ed. 25.95 (*1-58237-028-1*) Creat Think.
More Black American Playwrights: A Bibliography. Esther S. Arata. LC 78-15231. 335p. 1978. lib. bdg. 31.50 (*0-8108-1158-8*) Scarecrow.
More Black Collectibles: A Handbook & Price Guide. Jan Lindenberger. LC 94-37616. (Illus.). 160p. (Orig.). 1995. pap. 16.95 (*0-88740-733-1*) Schiffer.
More Black Magic. Anonymous. 752p. 1997. mass mkt. 7.95 (*0-7867-0548-5*) Carroll & Graf.
More Black Memorabilia: A Handbook & Price Guide. 2nd rev. ed. Jan Lindenberger. LC 99-61081. (Illus.). 160p. 1999. pap. 16.95 (*0-7643-0849-1*) Schiffer.
More Blacks in Toms Drawings. 1997. pap. 12.95 (*1-879055-46-5*) Tom Finland.
More Blessed to Give. Theda Hagan. (ENG & SPA.). 156p. 1999. pap. 9.99 (*0-7392-0300-2*, PO3421) T Hagan.
More Blessed to Give: A Pentecostal Mission to Bolivia in Anthropological Perspective. Goran Johansson. (Stockholm Studies in Social Anthropology: No. 30). 254p. (Orig.). 1992. pap. 49.50 (*91-7153-016-9*) Coronet Bks.
More Blues Jam Trax for Guitar. Ralph Agresta. (Illus.). 1993. pap. 9.95 (*0-8256-1364-7*, AM91303) Music Sales.
More Blues Jam Trax for Guitar. Ralph Agresta. 28p. pap. 10.95 incl. audio compact disk (*0-8256-1602-6*) Omnibus NY.
***More Board Games.** Desi Scarpone. (Illus.). 176p. 2000. pap. 29.95 (*0-7643-1161-1*) Schiffer.
More Bob Books for Young Readers, 8 bks. Bobby L. Maslen. (Bob Books Ser.: Set 2). (Illus.). 144p. (J). (ps-3). 1994. pap. 14.95 (*0-590-20374-6*) Scholastic Inc.
More Book. Norma J. Stodden & Linda McCormick. Ed. by Gail Levy. (Baby Sign Bks.). (Illus.). 18p. (J). (ps). 1988. bds. 3.95 (*0-943693-03-9*) TRI Pubns.
More Books Alive. Vincent Starrett. (Vincent Starrett Memorial Library: Vol. 5). 223p. 1995. text 24.00 (*1-896032-76-1*) Battered Silicon.
More Books Appeal: Keep Young Teens in the Library. Karen C. Gomberg. LC 89-43619. 176p. 1990. pap. 25.00 (*0-89950-476-0*) McFarland & Co.
More Books from the Library of the Byrds of Westover. Edwin Wolf, 2nd. 1978. pap. 3.00 (*0-912296-46-1*) Am Antiquarian.
More Books Kids Will Sit Still For. Judy Freeman. (Illus.). 869p. 1995. 49.95 (*0-8352-3520-3*) Bowker.
More Books Kids Will Sit Still For, 1990-1994. Ed. by Bowker Staff. 867p. 1995. pap. 29.95 (*0-8352-3731-1*) Bowker.
More Books on the Table. Edmund W. Gosse. LC 71-93340. (Essay Index Reprint Ser.). 1977. 26.95 (*0-8369-1410-4*) Ayer.
More Boys' Toys of the Fifties & Sixties: Toy Pages from the Great Montgomery Ward Christmas Catalogs, 1950-1969, Vol. 2. Ed. by Thomas W. Holland. (Illus.). 192p. 1998. pap. 19.95 (*1-887790-05-5*) Windmill Group.
More Brazilian Music Acoustic Guitar. Carlos Barbosa-Lima. 1993. 18.95 incl. audio (*0-7866-1194-4*, 95073P); pap. 8.95 (*1-56222-892-7*, 95073) Mel Bay.
More Brazilian Music Acoustic Guitar. Carlos Barbosa-Lima. 1993. audio 10.98 (*1-56222-901-X*, 95073C) Mel Bay.
More Brazilian Music for Acoustic Guitar. Carlos Barbosa-Lima. 64p. 1993. pap. 23.95 incl. audio compact disk (*0-7866-1193-6*, 95073CDP) Mel Bay.
More Bread Machine Bounty. Better Homes & Gardens. LC 93-86597. (Better Homes & Gardens Ser.). 144p. 1994. 14.95 (*0-696-00072-5*) Meredith Bks.
More Bread Machine Magic. Linda Rehberg & Lois Conway. LC 97-20540. (Illus.). 224p. 1997. pap. 11.95 (*0-312-16935-3*, St Martin Griffin) St Martin.
***More Bread or I'll Appear.** Emer Martin. LC 99-56406. 288p. 2000. pap. 12.00 (*0-385-72009-2*, Anchor NY) Doubleday.
More Bread or I'll Appear. Emer Martin. LC 98-49676. 256p. 1999. 23.00 (*0-395-91871-5*) HM.
More Brer Rabbit & His Tricks. Ennis Rees. (J). 1990. pap. 5.95 (*0-929077-11-3*) WaterMark Inc.
More Brief Prayers for Bread & Cup. Russell F. Harrison. LC 86-6076. 80p. (Orig.). 1986. pap. 5.99 (*0-8272-2319-6*) Chalice Pr.
More Bright & Bold Bulletin Boards. Christine Menard. (Illus.). 64p. 1995. pap. 12.95 (*0-917846-61-3*, 34009, Alleyside) Highsmith Pr.
More Brilliant Than the Sun: Adventures in Sonic Fiction. Kodwo Eshun. LC 98-164279. 1999. pap. 15.00 (*0-7043-8025-0*, Pub. by Quartet) Interlink Pub.
More Brochures. Rockport Publishers Staff. (Design Library Ser.). (Illus.). 80p. 1998. pap. text 14.99 (*1-56496-437-X*) Rockport Pubs.
More Bugs in a Box. Simon & Schuster Staff. 1996. pap. 14.77 (*0-671-52024-5*) Simon & Schuster.
More Bugs in Boxes. David A. Carter. (Illus.). 20p. (J). (ps-1). 1990. 13.95 (*0-671-69577-0*) S&S Trade.
More Bulletin Boards for Every Month. Jeanne Cheyney. (Illus.). 128p. 1998. pap. text 11.95 (*0-673-36385-6*) Addson-Wesley Educ.

An Asterisk (*) at the beginning of an entry indicates that the title is appearing for the first time.

More Bunny Trouble. Hans Wilhelm. 32p. (J). (ps-3). 1990. pap. 4.99 (*0-590-41590-5*) Scholastic Inc.

More Burs under the Saddle: Books & Histories of the West. Ramon F. Adams. LC 77-18606. 200p. 1989. pap. 14.95 (*0-8061-2171-8*) U of Okla Pr.

More Business Cards. Rockport Publishers Staff. (Design Library Ser.). (Illus.). 80p. 1998. pap. text 14.99 (*1-56496-438-8*) Rockport Pubs.

More C Tools for Scientists & Engineers. Louis Baker. (Computing That Works Ser.). 304p. 1991. pap. 34.95 (*0-07-003358-7*) McGraw.

More Cajun Humor. Justin Wilson & Howard Jacobs. LC 84-7087. 132p. 1984. pap. 10.95 (*0-88289-454-4*) Pelican.

More Calf Fries to Caviar. Janel Franklin. 1991. spiral bd. 16.95 (*0-9610956-1-X*) JAN-SU Pubns.

***More Canada Firsts: Another Collection of Canadian Firsts & Foremosts in the World.** Duff Conacher. 224p. 2000. pap. 19.99 (*0-7710-2244-1*) McClelland & Stewart.

More Can't Wait to Communicate! Fun Activities That Shape Nonverbal Communication. Robbie Wise. Ed. by Cindy Drolet & Suzanne Schafer. (Illus.). 129p. 1997. spiral bd. 36.00 (*1-883315-28-X*, 8508) Imaginart Intl.

More Captain Whopper Tales. Albert G. Miller. (Illus.). (J). (gr. 3-7). 1968. 10.95 (*0-8392-3060-5*) Astor-Honor.

More Card Manipulations: Series One to Four. Jean Hugard. LC 74-75264. (Orig.). 1974. pap. 6.95 (*0-486-23060-0*) Dover.

More Cargoes. William W. Jacobs. LC 71-75780. (Short Story Index Reprint Ser.). 1977. 18.95 (*0-8369-3005-3*) Ayer.

More Carl Sandburg Reads: Sandburg,&Carl, Set. abr. ed. Carl Sandburg. 1993. audio 19.00 (*1-55994-846-9*, DCN 2400) HarperAudio.

***More Case Presentations in Paediatric & Intensive Care.** N. S. Morton. 160p. 2000. pap. text 28.50 (*0-7506-4215-7*) Buttrwrth-Heinemann.

More Casino Gambling Made Easier: (More Winning Strategies, Casino Selections & Intelligent Gambling with Worldwide Casino Travelogoe) Gayle Mitchell. (Illus.). 120p. 1998. pap. 19.95 (*0-9656118-6-8*) Webster Res-Info Servs.

More Celtic Fairy Tales. Ed. by Joseph Jacobs. 22.95 (*0-89190-079-9*) Amereon Ltd.

More Celtic Fairy Tales. Joseph Jacobs. 1972. 59.95 (*0-8490-0670-8*) Gordon Pr.

More Celtic Fairy Tales. Ed. by Joseph Jacobs. LC 67-24224. (Illus.). 234p. (J). (ps-6). 1968. reprint ed. pap. 6.95 (*0-486-21827-9*) Dover.

More Celtic Greats. Hugh Keevins. 180p. (C). 1989. pap. text 21.00 (*0-85976-308-0*, Pub. by J Donald) St Mut.

More Changes, More Chances. Henry W. Nevinson. 1973. 69.95 (*0-8490-0671-6*) Gordon Pr.

More Chapel Messages. L. C. Johnson. 1983. pap. 6.95 (*0-89265-087-7*) Randall Hse.

***More Charlotte Mason Education: A Homeschooling How to Manual.** Catherine Levison. 2000. pap. 13.95 (*1-891400-17-7*) Champion Pr.

***More Chatup Lines & Put Downs.** Stewart Ferris. 1999. pap. 6.95 (*1-84024-046-6*) Seven Hills Bk.

More Cheerful Americans. Charles B. Loomis. LC 72-101817. (Short Story Index Reprint Ser.). 1977. 20.95 (*0-8369-3205-6*) Ayer.

More Cheers & Chants. rev. ed. Lynda Haller. (Orig.). (J). (gr. 3-12). 1988. reprint ed. audio 9.95 (*0-9614174-5-5*) Cheertime USA.

More Cheers & Chants. rev. ed. Lynda Haller. (Illus.). 39p. (Orig.). (J). (gr. 3-12). 1988. reprint ed. pap. text 10.95 (*0-685-22930-0*) Cheertime USA.

More Chemistry & Crime: From Marsh Arsenic Test to DNA Profile. Samuel M. Gerber & Richard Saferstein. LC 97-29913. 256p. 1997. text 29.95 (*0-8412-3406-X*, Pub. by Am Chemical) OUP.

More Chess Openings: Traps & Zaps 2. Bruce Pandolfini. 256p. 1993. per. 11.00 (*0-671-79499-X*) S&S Trade Pap.

More Chessercizes: Checkmate: Three Hundred Strategies for Players of All Levels. Bruce Pandolfini. (Illus.). 208p. 1991. per. 11.00 (*0-671-70185-1*) S&S Trade Pap.

More Chicken Breasts: 91 New & Classic Recipes for the Fairest Part of the Fowl. Diane Rozas. (Illus.). 128p. 1996. pap. 10.00 (*0-517-88706-1*, Crown) Crown Pub Group.

***More Chicken Soup & Other Folk Remedies.** Joan Wilen. 320p. 2000. pap. 14.00 (*0-345-44062-5*, Ballantine) Ballantine Pub Grp.

***More Chicken Soup for the Christian Family Soul: 101 Stories to Open the Heart & Rekindle the Spirit.** Jack Canfield et al. (Chicken Soup for the Soul Ser.). 350p. 2000. 24.00 (*1-55874-715-X*) Health Comm.

More Children's Sermons. Bucky Dann. 96p. (Orig.). 1993. pap. 9.95 (*0-664-25307-5*) Westminster John Knox.

More Chiller Thriller. A. Bates. (J). 1992. pap., boxed set 12.70 (*0-590-66251-1*) Scholastic Inc.

More Chills. (Illus.). (J). (gr. 1-7). 12.66 (*0-614-20165-9*) NTC Contemp Pub Co.

More Chills: 12 More Chilling Tales & Exciting Adventures. Goodman. (Goodman's Five-Star Stories Ser.). (YA). (gr. 6-12). 1998. 13.00 (*0-89061-859-3*, R0859-3E, Jamestwn Pub) NTC Contemp Pub Co.

More Chinese Brain Twisters: 57 Fast, Fun Puzzles That Help Children Develop Quick Minds. Baifang. LC 99-12224. 118p. 1999. pap. 14.95 (*0-471-24613-1*) Wiley.

More Chips from the Mathematical Log. Ed. by Josephine P. Andree. 1978. pap. 1.25 (*0-686-00324-1*) Mu Alpha Theta.

***More Chocolate Less Stress: A Penny & Wade Assortment.** Ruben Gerard. (Penny & Wade Ser.: No. 1). (Illus.). 100p. 1999. pap. 12.95 (*1-893316-00-9*) Inkwell Bks.

More Choices: A Strategic Planning Guide for Mixing Career & Family. Mindy Bingham & Sandy Stryker. Ed. by Penelope C. Paine & Barbara Greene. LC 87-11494. (Illus.). 240p. (Orig.). 1993. pap. 19.95 (*0-911655-28-X*) Advocacy Pr.

More Choices for a Healthy Low-Fat You: Tasty Meals in 30 Minutes or Less. Cheryl D. Peters & James A. Peters. LC 97-13418. 144p. 1997. ring bd. 12.99 (*0-8280-1306-3*) Review Pr.

More Choices Workbook: A Strategic Planning Guide for Mixing Career & Family. rev. ed. Mindy Bingham & Sandy Stryker. Ed. by Barbara Greene et al. LC 87-11494. (Illus.). 104p. (Orig.). 1992. pap. 6.95 (*0-911655-29-8*) Advocacy Pr.

More Choir Prayers. Jeanne Hunt. 96p. 1990. pap. 7.95 (*0-912405-67-8*, Pastoral Press) OR Catholic.

More Christian Assemblies for Primary Schools. Sharon Swain. 160p. 1998. 21.95 (*0-281-05150-X*) Intl Pubs Mktg.

More Christian Than African American: An Autobiography of Spiritual Growth. Kimberly Cash Tate. LC 99-19754. x, 197p. 1999. text 19.95 (*0-87596-548-2*) Rodale Pr Inc.

More Christmas Classics. Glenda Austin. 16p. (J). 1996. pap. 3.95 (*0-87718-101-2*, 12070E) Willis Music Co.

More Christmas Eve Services: Celebrating Christ with Creative, Evangelistic Worship. Robert L. Kintigh. Ed. by Cindy G. Spear. 114p. 1998. ring bd. 54.95 (*1-57052-096-8*) Chrch Grwth VA.

***More Christmas Ornaments Kids Can Make.** Kathy Ross. LC 00-20376. (Illus.). (J). 2000. lib. bdg. 8.95 (*0-7613-1396-6*) Millbrook Pr.

***More Chuck Wagon Recipes & Others, Vol. 2.** Sue Cunningham & Jean Cates. (Illus.). 1999. pap. 15.00 (*0-9645414-1-6*) Chuck Wagon.

More Church Chuckles. Dick Hafer. LC 95-71122. 128p. 1995. pap. 8.95 (*0-89221-305-1*) New Leaf.

More Civil War Curiosities: Fascinating Tales, Infamous Characters, & Strange Coincidences. Webb Garrison. LC 95-33602. (Illus.). 256p. (Orig.). 1995. pap. 9.95 (*1-55853-366-4*) Rutledge Hill Pr.

More Class Notes. Arthur Corey. 1962. pap. 4.00 (*0-87516-016-6*) DeVorss.

***More Classic American Railroads.** Mike Schafer. (Illus.). 160p. 2000. 29.95 (*0-7603-0758-X*, 130133AP, Pub. by MBI Pubg) Motorbooks Intl.

More Classics of the Horror Film. William K. Everson. (Illus.). 1990. pap. 14.95 (*0-8065-1179-6*, Citadel Pr) Carol Pub Group.

More Classics Revisited. Kenneth Rexroth. Ed. by Bradford Morrow. LC 88-22789. (Revived Modern Classics Ser.). 160p. 1989. pap. 10.95 (*0-8112-1083-9*, NDP668, Pub. by New Directions) Norton.

More Classics-Romantics-Moderns. Paul Sheftel. (Carl Fischer's "All Time Favorites" Music Ser.). 160p. (Orig.). 1984. pap. 12.95 (*0-8258-0345-4*, ATF103) Fischer Inc NY.

More Classics to Read Aloud to Your Children. William F. Russell. 272p. 1994. pap. 10.00 (*0-517-88227-2*, Crown) Crown Pub Group.

More Classroom Clangers. John G. Muir. (Illus.). 64p. (C). 1989. 30.00 (*0-903065-54-1*, Pub. by G Wright Pub) St Mut.

***More Clean Jokes for Kids.** Dan Harmon & Tamela H. Murray. (Young Reader's Christian Library: Vol. 2). 192p. (J). (gr. 3-7). 1999. pap. 1.39 (*1-57748-600-5*) Barbour Pub.

More Climbing Anchors. John Long & Bob Gaines. (How to Rock Climb Ser.). (Illus.). 84p. (Orig.). 1996. pap. 9.95 (*1-57540-000-6*) Falcon Pub Inc.

More Clinician's Choice: Favorite Activities. (Illus.). 117p. 1990. pap. 25.00 (*0-7616-7640-6*) Commun Skill.

More Clip Art for the Liturgical Year. Placid Stuckenschneider. (Illus.). 128p. 1990. pap. 15.95 (*0-8146-1959-2*) Liturgical Pr.

More Coffee Shop Theology. Frank Moore. LC 98-25705. 1998. 13.99 (*0-8341-1746-0*) Nazarene.

More Collected Adventures of Captain Jack: Spacemen, Farmers, & Other Presidential Candidates. Mike Kazaleh. (Illus.). 110p. 1996. pap. 12.95 (*1-883847-22-2*) MU Press.

More Collectible Bells: Classic to Contemporay. Donna S. Baker. LC 99-17656. (Illus.). 192p. 1999. 39.95 (*0-7643-0865-3*) Schiffer.

More Comics & Conversation: Using Humor to Elicit Conversation & Develop Vocabulary. Joan Ashkenas. (Illus.). 30p. 1991. pap. 12.95 (*0-943327-06-7*) JAG Pubns.

More Communication Keys in Your Marriage see Claves para una Mejor Comunicacion en el Matrimonio

More Complete Audio Writing, Vol. I. Richard Kostelanetz. 360p. 1992. pap. 125.00 (*0-932360-89-0*) Archae Edns.

More Complete Audio Writing, Vol. II. Richard Kostelanetz. 360p. 1992. pap. 125.00 (*0-932360-86-6*) Archae Edns.

More Complete Audio Writing, Vol. III. Richard Kostelanetz. 360p. 1992. pap. 125.00 (*0-932360-87-4*) Archae Edns.

More Complete Audio Writing, Vol. IV. Richard Kostelanetz. 360p. 1992. pap. 125.00 (*0-932360-88-2*) Archae Edns.

More Complete Audio Writing, Vol. V. Richard Kostelanetz. 360p. 1992. pap. 125.00 (*0-932360-94-7*) Archae Edns.

More Complete Audio Writing (Nineteen Eighty-Seven) Richard Kostelanetz. 424p. 500.00 incl. audio (*0-932360-84-X*) Archae Edns.

More Concoctions from the Beer Engineer. James F. Willenbecher. 200p. 1995. pap. text 13.95 (*0-9632514-1-4*) Crossfire Eng.

More Confederate Faces: Photographs of Confederates. William A. Albaugh, III. (William Albaugh Collection). (Illus.). 233p. 1993. reprint ed. 45.00 (*1-56837-259-0*) Broadfoot.

More Confederate Imprints, 2 vols., Vol. 1. Richard B. Harwell. LC 57-9084. (Virginia State Library Richmond Publications: Nos. 4-5). 194p. 1957. reprint ed. pap. 60.20 (*0-608-08431-X*, 201478700092) Bks Demand.

More Confederate Imprints, 2 vols., Vol. 2. Richard B. Harwell. LC 57-9084. (Virginia State Library Richmond Publications: Nos. 4-5). 194p. reprint ed. pap. 60.20 (*0-608-11356-5*, 201478700093) Bks Demand.

More Conference Activities. Sherry Nedreberg. (Gospel Games Ser.). (Illus.). 60p. 1997. pap. 5.95 (*1-57665-039-1*) Muggli Graphics.

More Conflicts. Burton Goodman. 160p. (J). (gr. 8). 1993. pap. 13.23 (*0-89061-718-X*, Jamestwn Pub) NTC Contemp Pub Co.

More Conservations with Walker Percy. Ed. by Lewis A. Lawson & Victor A. Kramer. LC 92-44968. (Literary Conversations Ser.). 288p. 1993. pap. 16.95 (*0-87805-624-6*); text 39.50 (*0-87805-623-8*) U Pr of Miss.

More Contemporary Americans. Percy H. Boynton. LC 67-26718. (Essay Index Reprint Ser.). 1977. 20.95 (*0-8369-0239-4*) Ayer.

More Contemporary Americans. Percy H. Boynton. (BCL1-PS American Literature Ser.). 230p. 1992. reprint ed. lib. bdg. 79.00 (*0-7812-6618-1*) Rprt Serv.

More Contemporary Americans. Percy H. Boynton. LC 75-131642. 1970. reprint ed. 16.00 (*0-403-00529-9*) Scholarly.

***More Contemporary Cinematographers on Their Art.** Pauline B. Rogers. 224p. 2000. pap. 19.95 (*0-240-80368-X*, Focal) Buttrwrth-Heinemann.

More Conversations with Eudora Welty. Ed. by Peggy W. Prenshaw. LC 95-25720. (Literary Conversations Ser.). 328p. 1996. 39.50 (*0-87805-864-8*); pap. 16.95 (*0-87805-865-6*) U Pr of Miss.

More Conversations with the Awakener. Bal Natu. 100p. (Orig.). 1993. pap. 10.00 (*1-880619-07-5*) Sheriar Found.

More Cooking Secrets of the CIA: The Companion Book to the Public Television Series. Photos by Joyce O. Pool. LC 97-33978. (Illus.). 1998. pap. text 14.95 (*0-8118-1863-2*) Chronicle Bks.

More Cooking with Old Bay. McCormick Spice Staff. (Collector's Ser.). (Illus.). 64p. 1996. per. 3.95 (*0-942320-58-1*) Am Cooking.

More Cosmic Encounters. Mayfair Games Staff. 1994. 35.00 (*0-923763-58-9*) Mayfair Games.

More Costumes for the Stage. Sheila Jackson. LC 98-13427. (Illus.). 144p. 1994. pap. 14.95 (*1-871569-54-0*, NAB); pap. 14.95 (*1-56131-066-2*, NAB) I R Dee.

More Country Chaff. Jerry Easterling. 144p. 1992. 7.95 (*0-9635833-0-1*) Twin Pines OR.

More Country Things. Bob Artley. LC 95-22049. (Illus.). 152p. (Orig.). 1995. pap. 12.95 (*0-8138-2451-6*) Iowa St U Pr.

More Cowboy Movie Posters. Ed. by Bruce Hershenson & Richard Allen. (Illustrated History of Movies Through Posters Ser.: Vol. 6). (Illus.). 80p. 1998. 50.00 (*1-887893-24-5*); pap. 20.00 (*1-887893-23-7*) B Hershenson.

More Cowboy Shooting Stars. rev. ed. John A. Rutherford & Richard B. Smith, 3rd. LC 92-74737. (Illus.). 214p. 1992. 18.00 (*0-944019-11-0*) Empire NC.

More Cowpokes. 14th ed. Ace Reid. (Illus.). 60p. 1960. reprint ed. pap. 6.00 (*0-917207-01-7*) Cowpokes.

***More C++ Gems.** Robert Martin. (SIGS Reference Library: No. 17). 525p. 2000. pap. 44.95 (*0-521-78618-5*) Cambridge U Pr.

More Craftsman Homes: Floor Plans & Illustrations for 78 Mission Style Dwellings. Gustav Stickley. (Illus.). 208p. 1982. reprint ed. pap. 10.95 (*0-486-24252-8*) Dover.

More Creative Connections: Literature & the Reading Program, Grades 4-6. Mary L. Olsen. (Illus.). xvii, 319p. 1993. pap. text 25.00 (*1-56308-027-3*) Teacher Ideas Pr.

More Creative Sewing Ideas. Cy DeCosse Incorporated Staff. LC 92-9272. (Singer Sewing Reference Library). (Illus.). 128p. 1992. 18.95 (*0-86573-276-0*); pap. 16.95 (*0-86573-277-9*) Creat Pub Intl.

More Creative Uses of Children's Literature, Vol. 1 Vol. 1: Introducing Books in All Kinds of Ways. Mary A. Paulin. LC 92-8916. xvii, 619p. (C). 1992. pap. text 35.00 (*0-208-02203-1*, Lib Prof Pubns); lib. bdg. 57.50 (*0-208-02202-3*, Lib Prof Pubns) Shoe String.

More Creative Window Treatments. Home Decorating Institute Staff. LC 95-17089. (Arts & Crafts for Home Decorating Ser.). (Illus.). 128p. 1996. 18.95 (*0-86573-380-5*); pap. 16.95 (*0-86573-381-3*) Creat Pub Intl.

More Creeks I Have Been Up. Sue Spencer. LC 98-89497. 375p. 1998. text 25.00 (*0-7388-0253-0*); pap. text 15.00 (*0-7388-0254-9*) Xlibris Corp.

More Cross-Training Bk. 2: Build a Better Athlete with Dressage. Jane Savoie. LC 98-27214. (Illus.). 208p. 1998. 26.00 (*1-57076-090-X*, Trafalgar Sq Pub) Trafalgar.

***More Cunning Than Man, 1.** Robert Hendrikson. 288p. 1999. pap. 13.00 (*1-57566-393-7*) Kensgtn Pub Corp.

More Cupid's Coupons. Don Byrd. 1998. pap. text 5.95 (*1-56352-549-6*) Longstreet.

***More Customers: A Practical, Affordable Marketing Approach for the Service Business.** Frederick M. Houston. (Illus.). 288p. 1998. pap. 39.95 (*1-892690-00-4*) NTC Enter.

More Daily Prayers for Busy People. William J. O'Malley. 192p. 1999. spiral bd. 10.95 (*0-88489-634-X*); per. 8.95 (*0-88489-618-8*) St Marys.

More Dark Secrets of the Turf: Over 40 Betting Strategies. John White. 1998. pap. text 18.95 (*0-7134-8395-4*, Pub. by B T B) Branford.

More Data on "Pastor Russell" Charles C. Cook. 30p. 1988. reprint ed. pap. 1.95 (*1-883858-38-0*) Witness CA.

More Dead Dicks. Linda S. Amstutz. (Illus.). 112p. (Orig.). 1996. pap. 6.95 (*1-887652-26-4*) Off Color Pr.

More Dead Than Alive. Anthony Hill. Ed. by Henry Anderson. (Orig.). 1995. pap. text 10.00 (*1-887333-02-9*) Touch Down Prodns.

More DEAFinitions!, Set. Kenneth P. Glickman. LC 89-50119. (Illus.). 128p. (Orig.). 1989. pap. 15.95 (*0-9617583-1-7*) DEAFinitely Yours.

More Deaths Than One. large type ed. Bruno Fischer. 400p. 1992. 27.99 (*0-7089-2586-3*) Ulverscroft.

More Decisive Than Bastogne, Hitler's "Bulge" Dream for Dunkirk II Exploded Green GI's & Vets on Elsenborn Ridge & N. Shoulder Did It! Green GI's & Vets on Elsenborn Ridge & N. Shoulder Did It! Walt Malinowski. (Illus.). 42p. (Orig.). (C). pap. write for info. (*0-935648-47-X*) Halldin Pub.

More Decorating with Flowers. Ronaldo Maia & Denise Otis. (Illus.). 208p. 1991. 60.00 (*0-8109-3622-4*) Abrams.

More Decorative Napkin Folding. Lillian Oppenheimer & Natalie Epstein. (Cookery, Wine, Nutrition Ser.). 48p. 1984. pap. 2.95 (*0-486-24673-6*) Dover.

More Dematiaceous Hyphomycetes. M. B. Ellis. (Illus.). 512p. (Orig.). 1976. pap. text 90.00 (*0-85198-365-0*) OUP.

More Designer Sweatshirts. Mary Mulari. (Illus.). 60p. (Orig.). 1986. pap. 8.95 (*0-9613569-4-4*) Mary Prodns.

More Diabetic Meals in 30 Minutes - Or Less! More Than 150 Brand-New, Lightning-Quick Recipes. Robyn Webb. LC 99-42702. 178p. 1999. pap. 16.95 (*1-58040-029-9*, 00299Q, Pub. by Am Diabetes) NTC Contemp Pub Co.

More Dialing, More Dollars: Twelve Steps to Successful Telemarketing. Michael E. Blimes & Ron Sproat. LC 85-30682. (Illus.). 93p. (Orig.). 1986. pap. 9.95 (*0-915400-47-2*, ACA Bks) Am for the Arts.

More Dialogues in Swing: Intimate Conversations with the Stars of the Big Band Era. Fred Hall. Ed. by Eugene D. Wheeler. LC 91-11466. (Illus.). 240p. (Orig.). 1991. 14.95 (*0-934793-31-X*); pap. 9.95 (*0-934793-32-8*) Pathfinder CA.

More Die of Heartbreak. Saul Bellow. 336p. 1997. pap. 11.95 (*0-385-31877-4*) Doubleday.

More Dinosaurs! And Other Prehistoric Beasts. Michael Emberley. (Illus.). 64p. (J). (ps-3). 1992. mass mkt. 5.95 (*0-316-23441-9*) Little.

More Disputed Questions in the Liturgy. John M. Huels. LC 96-46520. 200p. 1996. pap. 10.00 (*1-56854-171-6*, MOREDQ) Liturgy Tr Pubns.

More Diversity Icebreakers: A Trainer's Guide. Selma Myers & Jonamay Lambert. 77p. 1996. 55.00 (*1-883998-18-2*) Amherst Educ.

More Dog Tales for the Heart: Stories of Hope, Love & Wisdom. Sue A. Hershkowitz. 220p. 1999. pap. 9.95 (*0-9648464-2-X*) High Impct.

More Dogs on Main Street. 160p. 1998. pap. 12.00 (*0-9668829-0-3*) Giardia Springs.

More Dolls, The Early Years. Florence Theriault. (Illus.). 111p. 1992. 68.00 (*0-912823-21-6*, BT-118, Pub. by Gold Horse) Dollmasters.

More DOS for Dummies. Dan Gookin. (More...for Dummies Ser.). (Illus.). 420p. 1994. pap. 19.95 (*1-56884-046-2*) IDG Bks.

More Doubloons & Other Buried Treasure. Thomas P. Terry. (Illus.). 126p. (Orig.). 1970. pap. 5.95 (*0-939850-03-6*) Spec Pub.

More Drawings of Delacroix. Stephen Longstreet. (Master Draughtsman Ser.). (Illus.). 48p. (Orig.). 1970. pap. 4.95 (*0-87505-208-8*) Borden.

More Drawings of Rembrandt. Stephen Longstreet. (Master Draughtsman Ser.). 48p. 1970. pap. 4.95 (*0-87505-207-X*) Borden.

More Dreams Alive: Prayers by Teenagers. Ed. by Carl Koch. 112p. (YA). (gr. 7-12). 1995. pap. 4.95 (*0-88489-321-9*) St Marys.

More Dribble Drabble: Process-Oriented Art. Deya Brashears & Lea Brashears. (Illus.). 120p. (Orig.). 1992. pap. text 14.95 (*0-9614717-2-7*) Deya Brashears.

More Dubliners Songs. Intro. by Mary Hardy. (Illus.). 48p. 1979. pap. 11.95 (*0-86001-581-5*, AM23078) Music Sales.

More Dumb, Dumber, Dumbest: True News of the World's Least Competent People. John Kohut. LC 97-34063. 240p. 1998. pap. 11.95 (*0-452-27891-0*, Plume) Dutton Plume.

More Dusty Trails. Glorianne Weigand. (Illus.). 211p. (Orig.). 1996. pap. 14.95 (*0-9644141-1-2*) One-Hund-One Ranch.

More Dykes to Watch Out For. Alison Bechdel. LC 88-6892. (Illus.). 112p. (Orig.). 1988. pap. 10.95 (*0-932379-45-1*); lib. bdg. 20.95 (*0-932379-46-X*) Firebrand Bks.

More Dylan Thomas Reads: Thomas,& Dylan, Set. abr. ed. Dylan Thomas. 1993. audio 19.00 (*1-55994-844-2*, DCN2398) HarperAudio.

More E. K. Means. Eldred K. Means. LC 72-4738. (Black Heritage Library Collection). (Illus.). 1977. reprint ed. 32.95 (*0-8369-9112-5*) Ayer.

***More E-Mail from God for Teens.** Claire Cloninger. (YA). 2000. pap. 12.99 (*1-56292-931-3*) Honor Bks.

M

An Asterisk (*) at the beginning of an entry indicates that the title is appearing for the first time.

More E-Prime: To Be or Not II. Ed. by Paul D. Johnston et al. LC 94-16584. 368p. (Orig.). 1994. pap. write for info. (*0-918970-40-7*) Intl Gen Semantics.
More Early Massachusetts Broadsides. (Picture Bks.). 24p. 1981. pap. 4.00 (*0-934909-64-4*) Mass Hist Soc.
More Early Records of Trinity Episcopal Church, Pottsville, Schuylkill County, Pennsylvania. Schuylkill Roots Staff & Phillip A. Rice. 131p. 1993. per. 14.50 (*1-55856-112-9*, 051) Closson Pr.
More Easy Beans. Trish Ross & Jacquie Trafford. 120p. 1997. pap. 10.95 (*0-9698162-1-9*, Pub. by B Bean Pubng) Midpt Trade.
More Easy Classics to Moderns (MFM 27) Artie Traum & Artie Funaro. (Classics to Moderns Ser.). 160p. 1997. pap. 11.95 (*0-8256-4027-X*, AM 41542, Oak) Music Sales.
More Easy Crossword Puzzles for People Learning English. Walter P. Allen. 1970. pap. 2.50 (*0-87789-031-5*) ELS Educ Servs.
More Easy Jazz Standards - Piano Solo. 48p. 1985. pap. 7.95 (*0-7935-7260-6*) H Leonard.
More Easy Piano Classics. E. Danes. (Learn to Play Ser.). (Illus.). 64p. (J). (gr. 1 up). 1994. text 9.95 (*0-7460-1698-0*, Usborne); lib. bdg. 17.95 (*0-88110-703-4*, Usborne) EDC.
More Easy Piano Tunes. Anya Suschitzy. (Tunebooks Ser.). (Illus.). 32p. (J). (gr. 1-4). 1993. text 10.95 (*0-7460-1390-6*, Usborne) EDC.
More Easy Pop Melodies. 24p. 1984. pap. 12.95 (*0-7935-3151-9*) H Leonard.
More Easy Pop Melodies. 24p. 1993. pap. 14.95 (*0-7935-2184-X*, 00697269) H Leonard.
More Easy Pop Melodies. 24p. 1997. pap. 5.95 (*0-7935-7384-X*) H Leonard.
More Easy Windows 98. Joe Kraynak. LC 98-85583. 1998. pap. 19.99 (*0-7897-1740-9*) Que.
*__More Edible Art: 75 Fresh Ideas for Garnishing.__ 2nd ed. David Paul Larousse. LC 99-49568. (Illus.). 168p. 2000. 40.00 (*0-471-17639-7*) Wiley.
More Effective C++ Thirty-Five New Ways to Improve Your Programs & Designs. Scott Meyers. 336p. (C). 1995. pap. text 39.95 (*0-201-63371-X*) Addison-Wesley.
*__More Effective Communication: A Manual for Professionals__ John V. Vilanilam. LC 99-16513. 1999. write for info. (*0-7619-9363-0*) Sage.
More Effective Learning Experiences for Direct Care Staff in Social Service Agencies Serving Persons with Developmental Disabilities. Amy Tabor. 1996. pap. 27.50 (*1-57654-010-3*, Creative Core) Creat Core.
More Electric Bread. Suzan Nightingale & I.C.E. Inc. Staff. (Illus.). 120p. 1995. 29.95 (*0-9629831-6-0*) Innov Cook Enter.
More Elmore. Annie's Attic Inc. Staff & William E. Elmore. 1994. 9.95 (*0-9641505-0-6*) Annies Attic Pr.
More Enchanting Friends: Storybook Characters, Toys & Keepsakes. Dee Hockenberry. LC 97-43826. 224p. 1998. write for info. (*0-7643-0513-1*) Schiffer.
More Encounters. Burton Goodman et al. (Critical Reading Ser.). 136p. 1995. pap. text 12.97 (*0-89061-769-4*, 778, Jamestwn Pub) NTC Contemp Pub Co.
More Energizers & Icebreakers: For All Ages & Stages, Bk. II. Elizabeth S. Foster-Harrison. Ed. by Don L. Sorenson. LC 94-70342. (Illus.). 160p. 2000. teacher ed. 9.95 (*0-932796-64-8*) Ed Media Corp.
More Engineering Projects for Young Scientists. Peter H. Goodwin. (Projects for Young Scientists Ser.). (Illus.). 144p. (YA). (gr. 9-12). 1994. lib. bdg. 24.00 (*0-531-11193-8*) Watts.
More English Fairy Tales. Ed. by Joseph Jacobs. 22.95 (*0-89190-077-2*) Amereon Ltd.
More English Than the English. Terry Reksten. (Illus.). 192p. 1986. pap. 12.95 (*0-920501-03-6*) Orca Bk Pubs.
More English That We Need. Helen R. Prevo. 64p. 1984. teacher ed. 1.25 (*0-88323-237-5*, 261); pap. 4.50 (*0-88323-198-0*, 155) Pendergrass Pub.
More English with a Smile. Barbara Zaffran & David Krulik. (English with a Smile Ser.: Bk. 3). 152p. 1994. pap. 10.60 (*0-8442-0585-0*, Natl Textbk Co) NTC Contemp Pub Co.
More English with a Smile. Barbara Zaffran & David Krulik. (English with a Smile Ser.: Bk. 3). 160p. 1995. audio 20.00 (*0-8442-0576-1*, Natl Textbk Co) NTC Contemp Pub Co.
More Englishes: New Studies in Varieties of English, 1988-1994. Manfred Gorlach. LC 95-35084. (Varieties of English Around the World General Ser.: No. 13). 276p. 1995. 49.00 (*1-55619-444-7*) J Benjamins Pubng Co.
More Equal Than Others: Women & Men in Dual-Career Marriages. Rosanna Hertz. 220p. (C). 1986. 45.00 (*0-520-05804-6*, Pub. by U CA Pr); pap. 15.95 (*0-520-06337-6*, Pub. by U CA Pr) Cal Prin Full Svc.
*__More Equine Law & Horse Sense.__ Julie I. Fershtman. 200p. 2000. pap. 23.95 (*0-9648430-1-3*) Horses & The Law.
More Erotica from Penthouse. Penthouse Magazine Editors. 224p. (Orig.). 1992. mass mkt. 7.50 (*0-446-36297-2*, Pub. by Warner Bks) Little.
More Erte Fashion Paper Dolls in Full Color, Vol. 181. Tom Tierney. (J). 1984. pap. 4.95 (*0-486-24630-2*) Dover.
More Essays from the World of Music. Ernest Newman. 1986. 14.95 (*0-7145-3549-4*) Riverrun NY.
More Essays on Books. Arthur Clutton-Brock. LC 68-57313. (Essay Index Reprint Ser.). 1977. 18.95 (*0-8369-0315-3*) Ayer.
More Essays on Religion, Pt. 2. Arthur Clutton-Brock. LC 76-156632. (Essay Index Reprint Ser.). 1977. reprint ed. 20.95 (*0-8369-2349-9*) Ayer.
More Everyday Circle Times. Liz Wilmes & Dick Wilmes. (Illus.). 224p. (Orig.). 1992. pap. 16.95 (*0-943452-14-7*) Building Blocks.
More Everyday Legal Forms. Margaret C. Jasper. (Legal Almanac Ser.). 146p. 1996. text 22.50 (*0-379-11228-0*) Oceana.
More Excel 97 for Windows for Dummies. 2nd ed. Greg Harvey. LC 97-72419. 432p. 1997. pap. 22.99 (*0-7645-0138-0*) IDG Bks.
*__More Excellent HTML with an Introduction to JavaScript.__ Timothy T. Gottleber & Timothy N. Trainor. LC 99-15468. 2000. write for info. (*0-07-233745-1*) McGrw-H Hghr Educ.
*__More Excellent HTML with an Introduction to Javascript with Student CD-ROM.__ Timothy T. Gottleber & Timothy N. Trainor. (C). 1999. pap., student ed. 45.31 (*0-07-233839-3*) McGrw-H Hghr Educ.
More Excellent Ministry. Kelley Varner. 280p. (Orig.). 1988. pap. text 10.99 (*0-914903-60-8*) Destiny Image.
*__More Excellent Way: A Teaching on the Spiritual Roots of Disease.__ Henry W. Wright. xvi,296p. 2000. pap. text 24.95 (*0-9678059-0-2*) Pleasant Vally GA.
More Exciting Easy Classics for Piano. Charles Bateman. (Illus.). 144p. 1996. pap. text 14.95 (*1-56922-162-6*, 07-2054) Creat Cncpts.
More Exciting, Funny, Scary, Short, Different, & Sad Books Kids Like about Animals, Science, Sports, Families, Songs, & Other Things. Frances L. Carroll & Mary Meacham. LC 92-11588. 180p. 1992. pap. text 22.00 (*0-8389-0585-4*) ALA.
More Exciting, Funny, Scary, Short, Different, & Sad Books Kids Like about Animals, Science, Sports, Families, Songs, & Other Things. Ed. by Frances L. Carroll & Mary Meacham. LC 92-11588. 209p. 1992. reprint ed. pap. 64.80 (*0-608-02737-5*, 206340200004) Bks Demand.
More Excuses to Kill Things: Adventures for Macho Women with Guns. Greg Porter et al. (Illus.). 48p. 1995. pap. text 9.95 (*0-943891-31-0*) Blacksburg Tactical.
More Exercises in Fetal Monitoring. Barry S. Schifrin. (Illus.). 208p. (C). (gr. 13). 1993. pap. text 43.00 (*0-8151-7566-3*, 22102) Mosby Inc.
More Expeditious Conveyance. Bevan Rider. 160p. 1990. 50.00 (*0-85131-394-9*, Pub. by J A Allen) St Mut.
*__More Experiments upon the Word.__ Susan Luke. LC 99-183453. 1998. pap. 7.95 (*1-57734-314-X*, 01113577) Covenant Comms.
*__More Eyedentical Twins.__ (Illus.). 112p. 2000. pap. 10.99 (*1-895837-51-0*) Insomniac.
*__More Faith-Building with Preschoolers: Teachers & Parents Together.__ Linda Prenzlow & Ilene Allinger Candreva. 112p. 1999. pap., teacher ed. 12.99 (*0-570-05366-8*, 12-3417GJ) Concordia.
*__More Faith Facts for Young Catholics Vol. 2: Fun Ways To Teach the Basics of Our Faith.__ Kieran Sawyer. LC 00-8682. (Illus.). 128p. 2000. teacher ed., spiral bd. 17.95 (*0-87793-947-0*) Ave Maria.
More Faith Than Fear: The Los Angeles Stake Story. Chad M. Orton. 1987. 12.95 (*0-88494-646-0*) Bookcraft Inc.
More Fantastic Fundraisers for Sport & Recreation. William F. Stier, Jr. LC 96-48717. (Illus.). 232p. 1997. pap. text 17.00 (*0-88011-525-4*, BSTI0525) Human Kinetics.
More Fantastic TV & Movie Songs: Piano. 80p. 1987. pap. 9.95 (*0-7692-1174-7*, PF0464) Wrner Bros.
More Far-Out Facts. LC 80-8798. (Books for World Explorers Series 3: No. 4). (Illus.). 104p. (J). (gr. 3-8). 1982. 8.95 (*0-87044-384-4*); lib. bdg. 12.50 (*0-87044-389-5*) Natl Geog.
More Fascinating Conversion Stories. Samuel Fisk. 192p. 1994. pap. 10.99 (*0-8254-2640-5*) Kregel.
More Fast Ideas for Busy Teachers: One Hundred Productive Activities for Teachers, Substitutes, & Parents. Greta B. Lipson. (Illus.). 144p. 1994. 13.99 (*0-86653-821-6*, GA1513) Good Apple.
More Fat Burning Foods. Porter Shimer. Ed. by Betty Bianconi. LC 99-12083. 192p. 1998. pap. 12.95 (*0-8092-2599-9*, 259990, Contemporary Bks) NTC Contemp Pub Co.
More Fat Free & Ultra Lowfat Recipes from Doris' Kitchen. Doris Cross. (Cookbook Ser.). 215p. 1993. pap. 12.95 (*0-9631490-1-6*) Doris Diet.
More Favorite Fairy Tales. Ed. by Andrew Lang. 1976. 22.95 (*0-8488-0822-3*) Amereon Ltd.
More Favorite Tales. Sholem Aleichem. 1988. 25.95 (*0-8488-0413-9*) Amereon Ltd.
More Favourite Poems We Learned in School. Ed. by Tom Walsh. 160p. 1997. pap. 9.95 (*1-85635-087-8*, Pub. by Mercier Pr) Irish Amer Bk.
More Festive Strings for String Quartet or String Orchestra: Cello. Joanne Martin. 16p. 1998. pap. text 4.95 (*0-87487-997-3*) Summy-Birchard.
More Festive Strings for String Quartet or String Orchestra: Score. Joanne Martin. 36p. 1998. pap. text 7.95 (*0-87487-971-X*) Summy-Birchard.
More Festive Strings for String Quartet or String Orchestra: String Bass. Joanne Martin. 16p. 1998. pap. text 4.95 (*0-87487-998-1*) Summy-Birchard.
More Festive Strings for String Quartet or String Orchestra: Viola. Joanne Martin. 16p. 1998. pap. text 4.95 (*0-87487-995-7*) Summy-Birchard.
More Festive Strings for String Quartet or String Orchestra: 1st Violin. Joanne Martin. 16p. 1998. pap. text 4.95 (*0-87487-972-8*) Summy-Birchard.
More Festive Strings for String Quartet or String Orchestra: 2nd Violin. Joanne Martin. 16p. 1998. pap. text 4.95 (*0-87487-987-6*) Summy-Birchard.
More Festive Strings for String Quartet or String Orchestra: 3rd Violin. Joanne Martin. 16p. 1998. pap. text 4.95 (*0-87487-994-9*) Summy-Birchard.
More, Fewer, Less. Tana Hoban. LC 97-36665. (Illus.). 32p. (J). (ps-3). 1998. 15.00 (*0-688-15693-2*, Grenwillow Bks) HarpC Child Bks.
*__More, Fewer, Less.__ Tana Hoban. LC 97-36665. (Illus.). 32p. (J). (ps-3). 1998. 14.89 (*0-688-15694-0*, Grenwillow Bks) HarpC Child Bks.
More Fifth Grade Magic. Beatrice Gormley. 112p. (J). 1990. pap. 3.50 (*0-380-70883-3*, Avon Bks) Morrow Avon.
More Films of the Thirties. Jerry Vermilye. (Citadel Film Ser.). 1989. pap. 16.95 (*0-8065-1148-6*, Citadel Pr) Carol Pub Group.
More Firefighting Lore: Forty More Strange but True Stories from Firefighting History. W. Fred Conway. LC 98-220582. (Illus.). 176p. 1998. pap. 9.95 (*0-925165-23-9*) Fire Buff Hse.
More First Nights. James Agate. LC 74-86886. 359p. 1972. reprint ed. 24.95 (*0-405-08190-1*, Pub. by Blom Pubns) Ayer.
More First Words. Tony Tallarico. Date not set. pap. 3.95 (*0-448-40432-X*) Putnam Pub Group.
More Fishing - Less Fussing: Paul H. Young Catalog. 64p. 1994. pap. 10.00 (*1-882418-10-7*) Centenn Pubns.
More 5-Minute Challenges: Mini-Problem Solving Activities. Frances M. Thompson. (Illus.). 60p. (Orig.). (YA). (gr. 8-12). 1992. pap. text 8.50 (*0-918932-98-X*, A-2224) Activity Resources.
More Five Minute Mysteries. Ken Weber. (Illus.). 214p. 1991. pap. 7.95 (*1-56138-058-X*) Running Pr.
More Florida Stories. Ed. by Kevin McCarthy. LC 96-14366. 326p. 1996. 29.95 (*0-8130-1468-9*) U Press Fla.
More Florida Stories. Kevin McCarthy. LC 96-14366. 326p. 1996. pap. 17.95 (*0-8130-1485-9*) U Press Fla.
*__More Flowers.__ Jane O'Connor. 64p. 1999. pap. text 4.99 (*0-448-41993-9*, G & D) Peng Put Young Read.
More Food! A Reading Program. Jeffrey E. Stewart. (Illus.). 116p. (Orig.). (J). (gr. 4 up). 1988. pap. 32.50 (*1-877866-01-6*) J E Stewart.
More Food from Your Garden see Mittleider Grow-Box Gardens
More Food of My Friends: Their Favorite Recipes. Judith Shepard. LC 82-84010. 176p. (Orig.). 1983. pap. 16.00 (*0-932966-29-2*) Permanent Pr.
More Food That Really Schmecks. Edna Staebler. (Illus.). 320p. 1998. pap. text 13.95 (*0-7710-8258-4*) McCland & Stewart.
More Foot-Loose in Tokyo: The Curious Traveler's Guide to Shitamachi & Narita. Jean Pearce. LC 83-51221. (Exploring Japan Ser.). (Illus.). 148p. 1984. pap. 11.95 (*0-8348-0190-6*) Weatherhill.
More for Eagle Eyes. (J). (gr. 4-7). 1992. pap. 3.95 (*0-8167-2614-0*) Troll Communs.
More for Me. Sydnie M. Kleinhenz et al. LC 97-5283. (Hello Math Reader Ser.). (Illus.). (J). (gr. k-2). 1997. 3.99 (*0-590-30877-7*) Scholastic Inc.
More for Me. Sydnie Meltzer-Kleinhenz. (Hello Reader! Level 1 Ser.). (J). 1997. 8.70 (*0-606-12994-4*, Pub. by Turtleback) Demco.
More Forgotten Towns of Southern New Jersey. Henry C. Beck. 1984. reprint ed. pap. 14.95 (*0-8135-0432-5*) Rutgers U Pr.
More Frequent Error Pairs. Margaret J. Martin & Carolyn Weiner. 96p. (Orig.). 1982. pap. text 49.00 (*0-7616-3127-5*) Commun Skill.
More from an Englishman in the Midi. John P. Harris. (Illus.). 127p. 1994. pap. 7.95 (*0-563-36493-9*, BBC-Parkwest) Parkwest Pubns.
More from Love's Little Instruction. Annie Pigeon. 1995. mass mkt. 4.99 (*0-7860-0107-0*, Pinncle Kensgtn) Kensgtn Pub Corp.
More from Love's Little Instruction Book. Annie Pigeon. 96p. 1999. mass mkt. 5.99 (*0-7860-0623-4*) Kensgtn Pub Corp.
More From Malinda Graham. Malinda Graham. 104p. 1993. 9.95 (*0-942407-25-3*) Father & Son.
More from the Gluten-Free Gourmet: Delicious Dining Without Wheat. Bette Hagman. LC 92-30281. 1995. pap. 14.95 (*0-8050-2323-2*) H Holt & Co.
*__More from the Gluten-Free Gourmet: Delicious Dining Without Wheat.__ Bette Hagman. (Illus.). 2000. pap. 18.00 (*0-8050-6524-5*, Owl) H Holt & Co.
More from the Molesons. Burny Bos. LC 94-40892. (Illus.). 48p. (J). (gr. 1-4). 1997. pap. 5.95 (*1-55858-778-0*, Pub. by North-South Bks NYC) Chronicle Bks.
*__More from the Sensitive Gourmet: Cakes, Cookies, Desserts & Breads Without Dairy, Wheat or Gluten.__ Antoinette Savill. 2000. pap. 19.95 (*0-7225-3848-0*) Thorsons PA.
More Fun & Games with Dogs. Roy Hunter. (Illus.). 1997. spiral bd. 24.95 (*1-888994-05-3*) Howln Moon.
More Fun Around the World. Jackie Faughn. 48p. (J). (ps). 1998. pap. text 6.95 (*1-56309-260-3*, N987103, New Hope) Womans Mission Union.
More Fun in Biology: The Manual. 2nd ed. Sandy Winter. 168p. (C). 1997. spiral bd. 23.95 (*0-7872-4468-6*, 41446801) Kendall-Hunt.
More Fun on the Go. Andrea Posner. 48p. 1999. 4.99 (*0-307-25201-9*) Gldn Bks Pub Co.
More Fun Things to Do with Stickers: 30 Crafts, Games, & Activities. Karen Brewer & Donna Rushing. Ed. by Lise Caldwell. (Illus.). 48p. (J). (gr. 1-6). 1998. pap. 3.99 (*0-7847-0692-1*, 14-03382) Standard Pub.
More Fun to Find Word Search. Elvira Gamiello. (Illus.). 64p. (Orig.). (J). 1991. pap. 1.95 (*1-56156-000-6*) Kidsbks.
More Fun with Bible Facts. Ruby Peterson. 1977. pap. 3.00 (*0-89137-617-8*) Quality Pubns.
More Fun with Math-E-Magic. Donald W. McCarthy. LC 94-61919. (Illus.). 83p. (J). (gr. 5-8). 1995. pap. 7.33 (*0-914127-45-4*, M005) Univ Class.
*__More Fun with Pup! Activity Book.__ J. R. Rose. (Illus.). 64p. (J). (gr. k-3). 1998. pap. text 4.95 (*1-56554-368-8*) Pelican.
More Fun with Science: Practice at Home. Derek Dwyer & Jill Corby. (Illus.). 24p. (Orig.). (J). (gr. 3-5). 1992. pap., student ed. 2.95 (*0-7214-3240-9*, S9115-3, Ladybrd) Penguin Putnam.
More Fun with Science Magic. Donald W. McCarthy. LC 91-75095. (Illus.). 80p. (Orig.). (J). 1991. pap. 6.63 (*0-914127-12-8*) Univ Class.
More Fun with the Clarinet. William Bay. (Fun Bks.). 32p. 1976. pap. 5.95 (*0-87166-476-3*, 93385) Mel Bay.
More Fun with the Elves of Bellaire Drive. James S. Janssen. (Illus.). 66p. (J). (gr. 2-10). 1992. pap. text 5.95 (*0-9619160-2-8*) W S Nelson & Co.
More Fun with the Flute. William Bay. (Fun Bks.). 32p. 1976. pap. 5.95 (*0-87166-477-1*, 93386) Mel Bay.
More Fun with the Saxophone. William Bay. (Fun Bks.). 32p. 1981. 5.95 (*0-87166-478-X*, 93493) Mel Bay.
More Fun with the Trombone. William Bay. (Fun Bks.). 32p. 1976. pap. 5.95 (*0-87166-479-8*, 93387) Mel Bay.
More Fun with the Trumpet. William Bay. (Fun Bks.). 32p. 1976. pap. 5.95 (*0-87166-480-1*, 93384) Mel Bay.
More Fun with the Violin. William Bay. (Fun Bks.). 32p. 1976. pap. 5.95 (*0-87166-481-X*, 93388) Mel Bay.
More Funny Faces Tracing Fun. Anita Sperling. 32p. (J). (gr. 4-7). 1990. pap. 1.99 (*0-590-43489-6*) Scholastic Inc.
More Games & Giggles: Wild about Animals. Jeanette Wall. (J). (gr. 3 up). 1998. pap. text 5.95 (*1-56247-664-5*) Pleasant Co.
*__More Games Teams Play: Activities & Games for Powering up Your Team's Potential.__ Leslie Bendaly. 400p. 2000. pap. 34.95 (*0-07-560939-8*, Schaums Outlne) McGraw-Hill Prof.
*__More Games Teams Play: Activities & Games for Powering up Your Team's Potential.__ Leslie Bendaly. (Illus.). 400p. 2000. 99.95 (*0-07-560931-2*, Schaums Outlne) McGraw-Hill Prof.
More Games to Play with Toddlers. Jackie Silberg. LC 98-15002. (Illus.). 271p. (Orig.). 1996. pap. 14.95 (*0-87659-178-0*) Gryphon Hse.
More Games Trainers Play. Edward E. Scannell & John W. Newstrom. 1983. pap. 24.95 (*0-07-055045-X*) McGraw.
More Gardening in New Orleans. Ed. by Louise C. Coleman. (Orig.). 1989. pap. write for info. (*0-944681-03-4*) Celestial Pub.
More Gems of Japanized English. Miranda Kenrick. (JPN., Illus.). 136p. 1992. pap. 8.95 (*0-8048-1854-1*) Tuttle Pubng.
More Gene Manipulations in Fungi. Ed. by J. W. Bennett & Linda L. Lasure. (Illus.). 470p. (C). 1991. text 100.00 (*0-12-088642-1*) Acad Pr.
More Generals in Gray. Bruce S. Allardice. LC 94-43870. (Illus.). 317p. 1995. 29.95 (*0-8071-1967-9*) La State U Pr.
More Geometrics. Illus. by Ruth Heller. (Ruth Heller's Designs for Coloring Ser.). Orig. Title: Designs for Coloring. 64p. 1991. pap. 4.99 (*0-448-40121-5*, G & D) Peng Put Young Read.
*__More Geometrics.__ Ruth Heller. Orig. Title: Designs for Coloring. (Illus.). 32p. (J). (ps-3). 2000. pap. 5.99 (*0-448-42199-2*, G & D) Peng Put Young Read.
More Ghost Stories of Alberta. Barbara J. Smith. LC 97-148631. 1996. pap. 11.95 (*1-55105-083-8*) Lone Pine.
More Ghost Stories of an Antiquary. Montague R. James. LC 72-163031. (Short Story Index Reprint Ser.). 1977. reprint ed. 24.95 (*0-8369-3945-X*) Ayer.
More Ghost Stories of the Estes Valley. Celeste Lasky. 53p. 1999. pap. 4.99 (*0-9643331-4-7*) Write On Pubns.
*__More Ghostly Tales from Minnesota.__ Ruth Hein. LC 99-39773. 1999. write for info. (*0-87839-134-7*) North Star.
More Ghosts of Georgetown. Elizabeth R. Huntsinger. LC 97-46354. 1998. pap. 9.95 (*0-89587-209-9*) Blair.
More Ghosts of Gettysburg: Spirits, Apparitions & Haunted Places of the Battlefield. Mark V. Nesbitt. (Illus.). 100p. (C). 1992. pap. text 5.95 (*0-939631-51-2*) Thomas Publications.
More Gift Boxes. Gerald Jenkins & Anne Wild. (Illus.). 32p. (Orig.). 1993. pap. 6.95 (*0-906212-87-1*, Pub. by Tarquin Pubns) Parkwest Pubns.
More Give to Live: How Giving Can Change Your Life. rev. expanded ed. Douglas M. Lawson. 304p. 1998. pap. 16.95 (*1-883051-22-3*, Pub. by ALTI Pub) Natl Bk Netwk.
More Gleanings from Alta California. MaryDean Alsworth. LC 82-72383. 146p. (Orig.). 1982. pap. 22.00 (*0-939052-01-6*) Dean Pubns.
More Gleanings from "South of the Mountains" 1971. pap. 1.00 (*0-911183-12-4*) Rockland County Hist.
*__More God, More Power: Filled & Transformed by the Holy Spirit.__ Wesley Duewel. LC 99-58136. 2000. pap. 10.99 (*0-310-23085-3*) Zondervan.
More God's Abundance: Joyful Devotions for Every Season. Ed. by Kathy Collard Miller. (God's Abundance Ser.). 320p. 1999. 19.95 (*1-892016-13-3*, Pub. by Starburst) Natl Bk Netwk.
More Gold in Your Piano Bench: Collectible Sheet Music: Inventions, Wars, & Disasters. Marion Short. LC 97-5156. (Illus.). 176p. 1997. pap. 29.95 (*0-7643-0012-1*) Schiffer.
More Gold Than Gold. Ruthe T. Spinnanger. 381p. (Orig.). 1992. pap. 12.95 (*0-943167-19-1*) Faith & Fellowship Pr.
More Golden Apples: A Further Celebration of Women & Sport. Ed. by Sandra H. Martz. 64p. (Orig.). 1986. pap. 5.95 (*0-918949-01-7*) Martz.
More Golden Oak. Velma S. Warren. LC 98-86444. (Illus.). 192p. (Orig.). 1999. pap. 29.95 (*0-7643-0645-6*) Schiffer.
More Good Old Maine: 101 Past & Present Pop Delights. Will Anderson. LC 95-75481. (Illus.). 140p. (Orig.). 1995. pap. 17.95 (*0-9601056-7-0*) Anderson & Sons.

An Asterisk (*) at the beginning of an entry indicates that the title is appearing for the first time.

More Goodies & Guess-Whats: A Treasured Recipe Collection. Helen Christiansen. 192p. 1989. ring bd. 13.00 (*0-9621419-1-7*) H Christiansen.

More Goodly Country. rev. ed. John B. Sanford. LC 74-28317. 286p. 1975. 10.00 (*0-87685-578-8*) Black Sparrow.

More Goops & How Not to Be Them: A Manual of Manners for Impolite Infants. Gelett Burgess. LC 68-55531. (Illus.). 88p. (J). (ps-4). 1968. reprint ed. pap. 3.95 (*0-486-22234-9*) Dover.

More Gospel Truth. 1997. 6.99 (*0-8341-9537-2*, MB-746) Lillenas.

More Grammar Games: Cognitive, Affective & Movement Activities for EFL Students. Paul Davis & Mario Rinvolucri. (Illus.). 193p. (C). 1995. pap. text 19.95 (*0-521-46630-X*) Cambridge U Pr.

More Grammar Plus. Daphne Mackey. 224p. 1996. pap. text, student ed. 13.23 (*0-201-89884-5*) Addison-Wesley.

More Grammar Plus. Daphne Mackey. 224p. 1996. pap. text, wbk. ed. 15.44 (*0-201-87677-9*) Addison-Wesley.

More Grammar Plus. Daphne Mackey & Anita J. Sokmen. Ed. by Sharon Hilles. LC 95-24396. 1996. pap. text, student ed. 26.46 (*0-201-87675-2*) Addison-Wesley.

More Grammar Plus, Bk. A. Daphne Mackey. 1996. pap. text, student ed. 13.23 (*0-201-89883-7*) Addison-Wesley.

More Grammar Plus, Bk. A. Daphne Mackey. 112p. 1996. pap. text, wbk. ed. 8.13 (*0-201-89885-3*) Addison-Wesley.

More Grammar Plus, Bk. B. Daphne Mackey. 112p. 1996. pap. text, wbk. ed. 8.13 (*0-201-89886-1*) Addison-Wesley.

More Graphics for Sundays & Feast Days. Susan Daily. 1991. 29.95 (*0-85924-921-2*) Harper SF.

More Great Design Using, 1, 2, & 3 Colors. Ed. by Supon Design Group Staff. (Illus.). 192p. 1994. 39.95 (*3-910052-52-5*) Madison Square.

More Great Fundraising Ideas for Youth Ministry: Over 150 More Easy-to-Use Money-Makers That Really Work. David Lynn & Kathy Lynn. LC 95-41234. 144p. 1996. pap. 12.99 (*0-310-20780-0*) Zondervan.

More Great Popular Music BN. 79p. 1985. pap. 8.95 (*0-7692-1175-5*, PF0392) Wrner Bros.

More Great Railway Journeys. Bonington Allen & Henry Louis Gates, Jr. 224p. 1996. 29.95 (*0-563-38717-3*) MBI Pubg.

***More Great Railway Journeys.** Benedict Allen. (Illus.). 224p. 2000. reprint ed. 27.00 (*0-7881-9411-9*) DIANE Pub.

More Great Southern Mysteries. E. Randall Floyd. 224p. 1991. 16.95 (*0-87483-160-1*) August Hse.

More Great Tales of Crime & Detection. Peter Haining. 1994. 10.98 (*0-7858-0043-3*) Bk Sales Inc.

More Great Teachings of Edgar Cayce. Mark A. Thurston. LC 97-27335. (ARE Membership Ser.). 1998. pap. 7.95 (*0-87604-396-1*) ARE Pr.

More Greek Folktales. Ed. & Tr. by Richard M. Dawkins from GRE. LC 74-9218. 178p. 1974. reprint ed. lib. bdg. 35.00 (*0-8371-7631-X*, DAMGF, Greenwood Pr) Greenwood.

More Grounded Theory Methodology. Barney G. Glaser. LC 94-167614. 1994. pap. 30.00 (*1-884156-07-X*) Sociology Pr.

***More Guitar Chords & Accompaniment: Take a Step up in Your Chord Vocabulary & Accompaniment Skills!** Yoichi Arakawa. (Illus.). 89p. 1999. pap. 14.95 (*1-891370-01-4*, SSM00761, Pub. by Six Strings) Music Sales.

***More Guitar Workshop.** Jim Kelly. 64p. 1999. pap. 14.95 incl. audio compact disk (*0-7935-9454-5*) H Leonard.

More Gulf Oil Collectibles: An Unauthorized Guide. Charles Whitworth. LC 99-60136. (Illus.). 144p. 1999. pap. 29.95 (*0-7643-0803-3*) Schiffer.

More Guns! Weapon Compendium for Any Role-Playing Game. Greg Porter. (Illus.). 232p. 1993. pap. text 19.95 (*0-943891-26-4*, 4002) Blacksburg Tactical.

More Guns, Less Crime: Understanding Crime & Gun Control Laws. John R. Lott, Jr. LC 97-51481. (Illus.). 232p. 1998. 23.00 (*0-226-49363-6*) U Ch Pr.

***More Guns, Less Crime: Understanding Crime & Gun Control Laws.** 2nd ed. John R. Lott, Jr. LC 00-20724. (Studies in Law & Economics). (Illus.). 280p. 1999. pap. 12.00 (*0-226-49364-4*) U Ch Pr.

More Halloween Collectibles: Anthropomorphic Vegetables & Fruits of Halloween. Pamela E. Apkarian-Russe. LC 98-86161. 160p. 1998. pap. 29.95 (*0-7643-0658-8*) Schiffer.

More han Ola og han Per. Peter J. Rosendahl. Ed. by Einar Haugen & Joan N. Buckley. LC 87-30208. (Bur Oak Bk.). (Illus.). 195p. (Orig.). 1988. pap. 25.95 (*0-87745-192-3*) U of Iowa Pr.

More Hands-On Reading. Jane Kelly & T. Friend. (Illus.). 400p. (J). 1995. spiral bd. 34.00 (*1-884135-22-6*) Mayer-Johnson.

More Hard Sayings of the New Testament. Peter H. Davids. LC 91-22655. (Hard Sayings Ser.). 300p. (Orig.). 1991. pap. 12.99 (*0-8308-1747-6*, 1747) InterVarsity.

More Harm Than Help: The Ramifications for Rape Survivors of Mandatory HIV Testing of Rapists. Lisa Bowleg & Kathleen D. Stoll. (Violence Against Women Ser.). (Orig.). (C). 1991. pap. 10.00 (*1-877966-08-8*) Ctr Women Policy.

More Hats off to Microwave Cooking. Hat Stevens. LC 85-90479. 208p. (Orig.). 1985. pap. 9.95 (*0-9605690-1-4*) Hat Stevens.

More Haunted House Stories. Eve Marar. (Illus.). 96p. (Orig.). (J). 1988. pap. 1.95 (*0-942025-64-4*) Kidsbks.

More Haunted Houses. Delores Riccero & Joan Bingham. Ed. by Sally Peters. 336p. (Orig.). 1991. pap. 9.00 (*0-671-69585-1*) PB.

***More Haunted Tennessee.** Charles Edwin Price. (Illus.). 143p. 1999. pap. 12.95 (*1-57072-089-4*) Overmountain Pr.

More Hawaiian Folk Tales: A Collection of Native Legends & Traditions. Thomas G. Thrum. LC 75-35212. reprint ed. 41.50 (*0-404-14235-4*) AMS Pr.

More Headlines. Jay Leno. 1990. mass mkt. 6.95 (*0-446-39236-7*, Pub. by Warner Bks) Little.

***More Healthy Homestyle Cooking: 200 Family Favorites You'll Make Again & Again.** Evelyn Tribole. (Illus.). 384p. 2000. 29.95 (*1-57954-117-8*) Rodale Pr Inc.

More Hearsay: Interactive Listening & Speaking. 256th ed. D. Griffer. 104p. (YA). 1992. pap. 16.91 (*0-201-50969-5*) Addison-Wesley.

More Heat Than Light: Economics as Social Physics, Physics as Nature's Economics. Philip Mirowski. (Historical Perspectives on Modern Economics Ser.). (Illus.). 462p. (C). 1991. pap. text 25.95 (*0-521-42689-8*) Cambridge U Pr.

More Help! Nancy Holyoke. 1996. 10.15 (*0-606-10881-5*, Pub. by Turtleback) Demco.

More Help! Another Absolutely Indispensable Guide to Life for Girls. Ed. by Nancy Holyoke. LC 96-11550. (American Girl Library Ser.). (Illus.). 90p. (Orig.). (J). (gr. 3-7). 1996. pap. text 4.95 (*1-56247-481-2*) Pleasant Co.

More Herbs You Can Master: Twelve Wondrous Plants for Extra Nutrition, Improved Health, Natural Beauty. Carol R. Peterson. Ed. by Connie Chaplin & Bob Lilly. LC 99-90021. (Illus.). 255p. 1999. pap. 17.95 (*0-9639620-1-9*) Mtn Garden.

More Heroes & Heroines in Music. Wendy-Ann Ensor. (Illus.). 1982. audio 18.00 (*0-685-06585-5*) OUP.

More Heroes of Modern Adventure. Thomas C. Bridges & Hubert H. Tiltman. LC 76-86735. (Essay Index Reprint Ser.). 1977. 23.95 (*0-8369-1343-4*) Ayer.

More High School Talksheets: Fifty All-New Creative Discussions for High School Youth Groups. David Lynn. 112p. (YA). 1992. pap. 12.99 (*0-310-57491-9*) Zondervan.

More Historic Homes of Brisbane. Ray Sumner. 120p. (C). 1990. 42.00 (*0-908009-16-X*, Pub. by Boolarong Pubns) St Mut.

More Historical Tales of Old Reynoldsburg, Vol. II. Cornelia M. Parkinson. (Illus.). 168p. (Orig.). 1985. pap. 5.00 (*0-938404-04-0*, MORE HT) Hist Tales.

More Hold'em Excellence: A Winner for Life. Louis C. Krieger. 160p. 1999. pap. 19.95 (*1-886070-13-X*) ConJelCo.

More Holiness in Everyday Life. George Lyons. LC 97-3826. 120p. (Orig.). 1997. pap. 8.99 (*0-8341-1661-8*) Beacon Hill.

More Hollywood Characters. Dave Schreiner & P. S. Mueller. (Illus.). 36p. 1993. ring bd. 9.95 (*0-87816-180-5*) Kitchen Sink.

More Holmes for the Holidays. Ed. by Martin H. Greenberg et al. LC 99-27229. 1999. 21.95 (*0-425-17033-0*, Prime Crime) Berkley Pub.

***More Holy Hilarity: Inspirational Wit & Cartoons.** Cal Samra & Rose Samra. LC 99-33694. (Holy Humor Ser.: Vol. 4). 224p. 1999. pap. 11.95 (*1-57856-282-1*) Waterbrook Pr.

***More Holy Humor: Inspirational Wit & Cartoons.** Cal Samra & Rose Samra. (Holy Humor Ser.: Vol. 2). (Illus.). 208p. 1999. pap. 11.95 (*1-57856-280-5*) Waterbrook Pr.

More Home Cooking. Laurie Colwin. 240p. 1995. pap. 12.00 (*0-06-092578-7*) HarperTrade.

***More Home Cooking: A Writer Returns to the Kitchen.** Laurie Colwin. (Illus.). 240p. 2000. pap. 12.00 (*0-06-095531-7*, Perennial) HarperTrade.

More Homebrew Favorites: More Than 260 New Brews! Karl F. Lutzen & Mark Stevens. LC 97-6490. 1997. pap. 14.95 (*0-88266-968-0*) Storey Bks.

More Homemaking Blueprints. Diane B. Orton & Renee B. Malouf. LC 97-74881. 1997. pap. 9.95 (*1-57008-333-9*) Bookcraft Inc.

More Hoosier Cooking. Elaine Lumbra. LC 82-47959. 256p. 1994. pap. 13.95 (*0-253-20917-X*) Ind U Pr.

More Horse Stories. Christine Pullein-Thompson. 1999. pap. 7.95 (*0-7534-5169-7*, Kingfisher) LKC.

***More Hot Chocolate for the Mystical Soul: 101 True Stories of Angels, Miracles & Healings.** Arielle Ford. LC 98-54932. 352p. 1999. pap. 12.95 (*0-452-28069-9*, Plume) Dutton Plume.

More Hot Illustrations for Youth Talks: 100 More Attention-Getting Stories, Parables, & Anecdotes. Wayne Rice. LC 95-35691. 112p. 1996. pap. 14.99 (*0-310-20768-1*) Zondervan.

More Hours in My Day. rev. ed. Emilie Barnes. LC 94-6866. (Orig.). 1994. pap. 9.99 (*1-56507-233-2*) Harvest Hse.

More House Specialties. Deanna House. 270p. 1986. 14.95 (*0-9610752-1-X*) Deanna Hse.

More How Do They Do That. Caroline Sutton. 1994. pap. 9.95 (*0-688-13221-9*, Quil) HarperTrade.

More How to Hook & Cookbook. Michael R. Sakamoto. LC 94-77958. (Illus.). 160p. (Orig.). 1994. pap. 14.95 (*1-880188-78-3*) Bess Pr.

More How to Speak Southern. Steve Mitchell. 64p. (Orig.). 1983. mass mkt. 4.99 (*0-553-27392-2*) Bantam.

More How to Use Windows 95. 1995. 21.95 (*1-56276-323-7*, Ziff-Davis Pr) Que.

More HTML for Dummies. Tittel. 416p. 1996. pap. 22.99 (*1-56884-996-6*) IDG Bks.

More Hugs! Dave Ross. LC 83-46167. (Illus.). 32p. (J). (ps up). 1984. lib. bdg. 11.89 (*0-690-04407-0*) HarpC Child Bks.

More Human Face. Donna Brook. 1999. 21.00 (*1-882413-59-8*); pap. 13.00 (*1-882413-58-X*) Hanging Loose.

More I Could Not Ask: Finding Christ in the Margins: A Priest's Story. James Peterson. 192p. 1998. pap. 12.95 (*0-8245-1772-5*, Crsrd) Crossroad NY.

More I Learned about Flying From That Flying Magazine. 1984. 17.95 (*0-02-579350-0*) Macmillan.

More I Learned about Flying from That Flying Magazine. Flying Magazine Staff. 196p. 1989. pap. 16.95 (*0-07-155418-1*) McGraw.

More I Learned about Flying from That Flying Magazine. Ed. by Flying Magazine Staff. (Illus.). 196p. 1989. pap. 12.95 (*0-8306-3317-0*) McGraw-Hill Prof.

More I See You. Lynn Kurland. 1999. mass mkt. 6.99 (*0-425-17107-8*) Berkley Pub.

More Ideas for Science Projects. rev. ed. Richard C. Adams & Robert Gardner. LC 97-5792. (Experimental Science Series Book). (Illus.). 160p. (J). (gr. 9 up). 1997. 24.00 (*0-531-11380-9*) Watts.

***More Improper Limericks: Thirty Dirty Ditties.** Robert William Birch. 57p. 1998. spiral bd. 3.00 (*1-57074-414-9*) PEC.

More in Common Than You Think: The Bridge Between Islam & Christianity. William W. Baker. LC 99-164157. (Illus.). vii, 136p. (Orig.). 1998. pap. 15.00 (*0-910650-01-6*) Defenders Pubns.

More Incidents along the Way: Continuing the Fascinating Tales of a Kansas City Story-Teller. Rosemary F. Kidd. LC 97-76076. 323p. 1999. 14.95 (*1-890622-58-3*) Leathers Pub.

More Incredible Answers to Prayer. Roger J. Morneau. LC 93-18276. 1993. pap. 7.99 (*0-8280-0719-5*) Review & Herald.

More Incredible Hawaii. Terence Barrow & Ray Lanterman. LC 85-5112. (Illus.). 120p. (Orig.). 1986. pap. 6.95 (*0-8048-1427-9*) Tuttle Pubng.

More Incredibly Awesome Crafts for Kids. Ed. by Carol F. Dahlstrom. LC 97-71328. (Illus.). 144p. 1997. pap. 16.95 (*0-696-20691-9*) Meredith Bks.

More Index Card Games & Activities for English. Raymond C. Clark. (Supplementary Materials Handbook Ser.: No. 9). (Illus.). 104p. (Orig.). 1993. pap. text 12.50 (*0-86647-075-1*) Pro Lingua.

***More Innocent Times.** Parker. 2000. pap. 10.95 (*0-552-14498-3*, Pub. by Transworld Publishers Ltd) Trafalgar.

More Innovative Games. Brenda Lichtman. LC 98-39169. (Illus.). 200p. 1999. pap. 18.00 (*0-88011-712-5*, BLIC0712) Human Kinetics.

More Instant Teaching Tools for Health Care Educators. Michele L. Deck. LC 99-178835. 272p. 1998. pap. text 36.95 (*0-323-00085-1*) Mosby Inc.

More Instructions from the Centre: Top Secret Files on KGB Global Operations, 1975-1985. Ed. by Christopher Andrew & Oleg Gordievsky. 130p. 1992. text 35.00 (*0-7146-3475-1*, Pub. by F Cass Pubs) Intl Spec Bk.

More Instruments & Broader Goals : Moving Toward the Post Washington Consensus. Joseph E. Stiglitz. LC 99-172064. (Wider Annual Lectures). 40p. 1998. write for info. (*952-9520-70-0*) UN.

More International Recipes: Europe, Vol. VII, Bk. 11. Vicki Corona. (Celebrate the Cultures Ser.). (Illus.). 50p. 1989. pap. 16.95 (*1-58513-057-5*) Dance Fantasy.

More Internet for Dummies. Margaret L. Young & John Levine. LC 94-77183. 356p. 1994. pap. 19.95 (*1-56884-164-7*) IDG Bks.

More Internet for Dummies. 4th ed. John R. Levine. LC TK5105.875.I57L483. 420p. 1998. pap. 22.99 (*0-7645-0369-3*) IDG Bks.

More Internet Troubleshooter: New Help for the Logged on & Lost. Nancy R. John & Edward J. Valauskas. 192p. 1998. pap. 36.00 (*0-8389-0718-0*) ALA.

More Inventions & Discoveries. John A. Hurst. LC 87-2289. (And so the Story Goes...Ser.: No. 4). 80p. (Orig.). 1987. pap. 7.95 (*0-89196-135-6*, 31715) Quality Bks IL.

More Irish Families. Edward MacLysaght. LC 96-216061. (Illus.). 254p. 1996. pap. 19.95 (*0-7165-2604-2*, Pub. by Irish Acad Pr) Intl Spec Bk.

More Irish Short Stories. John B. Keane. 116p. 1991. pap. 10.95 (*0-85342-818-2*) Dufour.

More Irish Stories for Christmas. John B. Keane. 160p. 1996. 19.95 (*1-57098-069-1*) Roberts Rinehart.

More Irons by Irons. (Illus.). 160p. 1997. pap. 45.00 (*0-9641710-1-5*) D Irons Antiques.

More Is Caught Than Taught. Federation of Child Care Centers of Alabama Staff. (Illus.). 1997. 24.95 (*0-9658522-0-2*) Fed Child Care.

More Is Not Enough. Pieter Greeff. 64p. 1998. 18.50 (*0-9630797-7-8*) Loft Pr.

More Island Adventures: An Outdoors Guide to Vancouver Island. Richard K. Blier. (Illus.). 176p. (Orig.). 1993. pap. 14.95 (*0-920501-91-5*) Orca Bk Pubs.

More Issues at Hand. William Atheling, Jr. LC 72-115400. 160p. 1970. 15.00 (*0-911682-10-4*) Advent.

More Issues at Hand. William Atheling, Jr. LC 72-115400. 160p. 1972. pap. 8.00 (*0-911682-18-X*) Advent.

***More Java Gems.** Ed. by Dwight Deugo. (SIGS Reference Library Ser.: No. 16). 450p. 2000. pap. 40.00 (*0-521-77477-2*) Cambridge U Pr.

More Jazz from Judy Murrah: New Shapes & Great Ideas for Wonderful Wearable Art. Judy Murrah. LC 95-49842. (Illus.). 128p. 1996. pap. 24.95 (*1-56477-135-0*, B252) Martingale & Co.

***More Jesus, Less Religion: Moving from Rules to Relationship.** Stephen Arterburn & Jack Felton. LC 99-55258. 224p. 2000. pap. 12.95 (*1-57856-250-3*) Waterbrook Pr.

More Jewish, Less Jewish: Reconciling Differences over Judaism in Your Marriage. Azriela L. Jaffe. LC 99-40519. 1999. 19.95 (*1-55972-528-1*, Birch Ln Pr) Carol Pub Group.

***More Jobs per Drop: Targeting Irrigation to Poor Women & Men** B. C. Van Koppen. LC 99-204434. (ENG & DUT.). 187 p. 1998. write for info. (*90-6832-124-2*, Pub. by Royal Tropical) Eiron.

More Jokes! David Lewman. (Rugrats Ser.). (Illus.). 48p. (J). (ps-3). 1999. pap. 2.99 (*0-689-82538-2*) S&S Childrens.

More Joking Off. Johnny Lyons. 128p. 1999. mass mkt. 4.99 (*0-8217-6117-X*) Kensgtn Pub Corp.

More Jonathan Papers. Elizabeth Morris. LC 68-8484. (Essay Index Reprint Ser.). 1977. 19.95 (*0-8369-0722-1*) Ayer.

More Joy... An Advanced Guide to Solo Sex. Harold Litten. (Illus.). 200p. 1996. pap. 12.95 (*0-9626531-8-7*, Pub. by Factor Pr) BookWorld.

More Joy in Heaven. Morley Callaghan. 200p. 1996. pap. text 6.95 (*0-7710-9956-8*) McCland & Stewart.

More Joy in Heaven! Confession, the Sacrament of Reconciliation. Kevin Doran. 112p. 1989. pap. 22.00 (*0-7855-6978-2*, Pub. by Veritas Pubns) St Mut.

More Joy of Airbrushing . . . Plus. Carole Faxon. (Illus.). 44p. 1993. pap. write for info. (*0-9623426-2-9*) Carousel Enterprises.

More Joy of Law. 2nd ed. Halamka. LC 97-173897. 1996. mass mkt. 16.00 (*0-314-20900-X*) West Pub.

More Joy of Mathematics. Theoni Pappas. LC 91-11295. (Illus.). 304p. (Orig.). 1991. pap. 10.95 (*0-933174-73-X*) Wide World-Tetra.

More Joy of Painting with Bob Ross: America's Favorite Art Instructor. Annette Kowalski. 1995. pap. 17.00 (*0-688-14355-5*, Hearst) Hearst Commns.

More Joy of Photography: Advanced Techniques for More Creative Photographs. rev. ed. Eastman Kodak Company Staff. write for info. (*0-318-62953-4*) Addison-Wesley.

More Joy of Sex. rev. ed. Alex Comfort. 1991. pap. 20.00 (*0-671-74076-8*) PB.

More Jumping JavaScript. 2nd ed. Janice Winsor & Brian Freeman. LC 99-462628. 512p. (C). 1998. pap. text 44.99 (*0-13-922832-2*, Macmillan Coll) P-H.

More Junior Authors. Ed. by Muriel Fuller. LC 63-11816. (Illus.). 235p. 1963. 35.00 (*0-8242-0036-5*) Wilson.

More Junior High Game Nights. Keith Betts & Dan McCollam. 96p. 1992. pap. 12.99 (*0-310-54101-8*) Zondervan.

More Junior High Talksheets: Fifty All-New Creative Discussions for Junior High Youth Groups. David Lynn. 112p. (YA). 1992. pap. 12.99 (*0-310-57481-1*) Zondervan.

More Kaua'i Tales. Frederick B. Wichman. (Bamboo Ridge Ser.: Vol. 70). (Illus.). 144p. 1997. pap. 15.00 (*0-910043-49-3*) Bamboo Ridge Pr.

More Kennywood Memories. Charles J. Jacques. LC 98-70119. 1998. pap. text 29.95 (*0-9614392-4-6*) Amuse Pk Journ.

More Kentucky Ghost Stories. Michael P. Henson. 192p. (Orig.). 1996. pap. 14.95 (*1-57072-044-4*) Overmountain Pr.

More Kicks Than Pence: A Life in Irish Journalism. Michael O'Toole. 200p. 1992. pap. 17.95 (*1-85371-143-8*, Pub. by Poolbeg Pr) Dufour.

More Kids Speak. Compiled by Chaim Walder. LC 95-20337.Tr. of Yeladim Mesaprim al Atsmam 2. 208p. (J). 1995. 19.95 (*0-87306-720-7*) Feldheim.

More Killing Defense at Bridge. Hugh Kelsey. (Illus.). 192p. 1993. pap. 15.95 (*0-575-04941-3*, Pub. by V Gollancz) Trafalgar.

More Kitchen Keepsakes. Bonnie Welch. (Illus.). 283p. 1987. 14.95 (*0-9612258-1-5*) Kitch Keepsakes.

More Kites for Everyone. Margaret Greger. LC 90-92944. (Illus.). 64p. (Orig.). 1990. pap. 10.00 (*0-685-45910-1*) M Greger.

More Knitting with Leftover Yarn. Ruth E. Braatz. (Illus.). 47p. (Orig.). 1990. pap. 7.95 (*0-9622959-1-4*) Frugal Knitting.

***More Lab Reports: For Grades 3-6.** Kimberley Nash. (Illus.). 58p. (J). (gr. 3-6). 1999. spiral bd., wbk. ed. 6.95 (*0-9653723-4-0*) Resurrection Res.

***More Lab Reports: For Grades 7-12.** Kimberley Nash. (Illus.). 89p. (YA). (gr. 7-12). 1999. spiral bd., wbk. ed. 8.95 (*0-9653723-5-9*) Resurrection Res.

More Lake District Walks. (Ordnance Survey Pathfinder Guides Ser.). (Illus.). 80p. (Orig.). 1995. pap. 14.95 (*0-7117-0817-7*, Pub. by JARR UK) Seven Hills Bk.

***More Landscape Projects.** Erin Hynes. (Time Life How to Ser.). (Illus.). 144p. 2001. pap. 16.95 (*0-7370-0625-0*) Time-Life Educ.

***More Language of Letting Go: 366 New Meditations by Melody Beattie.** Melody Beattie. 400p. 2000. 15.00 (*1-56838-558-7*) Hazelden.

More Lap Quilting with Georgia Bonesteel. Georgia Bonesteel. LC 84-60287. (Illus.). 132p. 1985. 19.95 (*0-8487-0634-X*) Oxmoor Hse.

More Larry Hatteberg's Kansas People. Larry Hatteberg. LC 94-61197. 1996. pap. text 17.95 (*1-880652-37-4*) Wichita Eagle.

More Lasting Than Bronze. Andrew J. Galambos & Suzanne J. Galambos. 1991. 175.00 (*0-88078-000-2*) Univ Sci Publns.

***More Lasting Unions: Christianity, the Family & Society.** Stephen G. Post. LC 99-86147. (Religion, Marriage & the Family Ser.). 208p. 2000. pap. 15.00 (*0-8028-4707-2*) Eerdmans.

More Latin for the Illiterati: A Guide to Everyday Medical, Legal & Religious Latin. Jon R. Stone. LC 98-43820. 1999. 60.00 (*0-415-92210-0*); pap. 16.99 (*0-415-92211-9*) Routledge.

More Latin Lyrics: From Virgil to Milton. Tr. by Helen Waddell. 392p. 1985. reprint ed. pap. 9.95 (*0-393-30232-6*) Norton.

More Latin Readings. Ed. by Gertrude Drake. 112p. 1984. pap. 13.00 (*0-86516-046-5*); pap., teacher ed. 8.00 (*0-86516-045-7*) Bolchazy-Carducci.

M

An Asterisk (*) at the beginning of an entry indicates that the title is appearing for the first time.

More Laughing & Loving with Autism. R. Wayne Gilpin. 108p. 1994. pap. 9.95 (*1-885477-12-0*) Fut Horizons.

More Laughter in Appalachia: Southern Mountain Humor. Loyal Jones & Billy E. Wheeler. (American Storytelling Ser.). (Illus.). 224p. 1995. pap. 11.95 (*0-87483-411-2*) August Hse.

More Leadership Lessons of Jesus: A Timeless Model for Todays Leaders. Bob Briner & Ray Pritchard. LC 98-24153. 176p. 1998. 14.99 (*0-8054-1687-0*) Broadman.

More Lean & Luscious. Bobbie Hinman & Millie Snyder. (Lean & Luscious Ser.: Vol. II). (Illus.). 480p. (Orig.). 1988. pap. 16.95 (*0-914629-49-2*) Prima Pub.

More Learning in Less Time: A Guide for Students, Professionals, Career-Changers, & Lifelong Learners. 5th rev. ed. Norma B. Kahn. LC 98-60706. (Illus.). xi, 157p. 1998. pap. 11.95 (*0-9664353-0-3*) Ways-to Bks.

More Learning Is Fun: Grades K-1. (Illus.). 144p. (Orig.). (J). (gr. k-2). 1994. pap. 3.95 (*1-56144-440-5*, Honey Bear Bks) Modern Pub NYC.

More Learning Is Fun: Preschool. (Illus.). 144p. (Orig.). (J). (gr. k-2). 1994. pap. 3.95 (*1-56144-439-1*, Honey Bear Bks) Modern Pub NYC.

More Leaves from the Copper Beeches. William H. Miller et al. Ed. by H. W. Starr et al. LC 76-244. (Illus.). 222p. 1976. 15.00 (*0-915010-16-X*) Sutter House.

***More Leaves from the Inn of the Last Home.** Ed. by Margaret Weis & Tracy Hickman. 256p. 1999. pap. text 19.95 (*0-7869-1516-1*) TSR Inc.

More Led Zeppelin Hits/Guitar Superstar: Guitar Personality Book. 108p. (Orig.). 1988. pap. 16.95 (*0-7692-0553-4*, GF0341) Wrner Bros.

***More Lefton China.** Ruth McCarthy. (Illus.). 176p. 1999. pap. 29.95 (*0-7643-1028-3*) Schiffer.

More Legal Fictions: A Series of Cases from Shakespeare. Alfred L. Polak. LC 73-153344. reprint ed. 27.50 (*0-404-05068-9*) AMS Pr.

More Legal Fictions: A Series of Cases from Shakespeare. Illus. by Diana Pullinger. 134p. 1995. reprint ed. 42.00 (*1-56169-107-0*) Gaunt.

More Legendary Voices: With Recommended Recordings on CD. Nigel Douglas. (Illus.). 342p. 1995. 35.00 (*0-87910-193-8*) Limelight Edns.

More Legends & Stories of the Finger Lakes Region: The Heart of New York State. Emerson Klees. LC 96-84782. (Illus.). 184p. 1997. pap. 17.00 (*0-9635990-7-0*) Frnds Finger Lks.

More Lessons from the Spelling Doctor: Ten New Essays on the Way Words Work, Pt. 2. Raymond E. Laurita. 117p. 1998. spiral bd. 12.95 (*0-914051-38-5*) Leonardo Pr.

More Let's Articulate. Bonita L. Martin & Greta C. Momeir. 286p. 1987. 33.50 (*0-7616-7341-5*) Commun Skill.

More Letters from a Nut. Ted L. Nancy. (Illus.). 208p. 1998. 18.00 (*0-553-10958-8*) Bantam.

More Letters from Penthouse. Penthouse Magazine Editors. 224p. (Orig.). 1989. mass mkt. 7.50 (*0-446-34515-6*, Pub. by Warner Bks) Little.

More Letters from the American Farmer: An Edition of the Essays in English Left Unpublished by Crevecoeur. J. Hector De Crevecoeur. Ed. by Dennis D. Moore. LC 93-23005. 736p. (C). 1995. text 75.00 (*0-8203-1599-0*) U of Ga Pr.

More Letters to Rollins. Compiled by R. K. Overton. 180p. 2000. pap. 12.00 (*1-880985-68-3*) Two Thirteen Sixty-one.

***More Letters to Uncle Mike.** Michael Burgess. 200p. 2000. pap. 14.00 (*0-9657638-6-2*) Saddle Mtn.

More Liberty Means Less Government: Our Founders Knew This Well. Walter E. Williams. LC 98-49950. (Publication Ser.: Vol. 453). 264p. 1999. pap. 18.95 (*0-8179-9612-5*) Hoover Inst Pr.

***More Life Vol. 1: Principles & Practices for Purposeful Living.** Douette Cunningham. Ed. by Africa Gordon & Derek Nichols. 128p. 1999. pap. 16.99 (*0-9674320-0-6*) DOC Commns.

More Life in Poetry. Donald R. Siegel & Jeanne R. Siegel. LC 96-92070. 66p. (Orig.). 1996. pap. 12.95 (*0-9644769-1-6*) D R Siegel.

More Life's Little Frustration Book. G. Gaynor Mctigue. 1997. mass mkt. 6.99 (*0-312-96098-0*) St Martin.

More Lifeways: Sharing Parenting & Family Paths. Ed. by Patti Smith & Signe E. Schaefer. (Lifeways Ser.). 224p. (Orig.). 1997. pap. 19.95 (*1-869890-86-8*, Pub. by Hawthorn Press) Anthroposophic.

***More Light.** Bryony Lavery. (Connections Ser.). (Illus.). 112p. 2000. pap. 17.95 (*0-7487-4287-5*, Pub. by S Thornes Pubs) Trans-Atl Phila.

More Light. rev. ed. 200p. 1992. 10.00 (*0-88053-076-6*, M402) Macoy Pub.

More Light: Father & Daughter Poems - A Twentieth-Century American Selection. Ed. by Jason Shinder. LC 93-16198. 192p. 1993. pap. 9.95 (*0-15-662142-8*) Harcourt.

More Light for the Day. Ed. by C. E. Andrew et al. 370p. 1991. spiral bd. 6.50 (*0-9624991-1-0*) NWestern Prods.

More Light in Masonry see Masonic Lifeline: Leadership

More Light, Larger Vision. Geraldine C. Little. (Orig.). 1992. pap. 9.00 (*0-944676-38-3*) AHA Bks.

More Light, Less Heat: How Dialogue Can Transform Christian Conflict into Growth. Joseph Phelps. LC 98-25321. 176p. 1998. 22.00 (*0-7879-4286-3*) Jossey-Bass.

More Light on the Path: Daily Scripture Readings in Hebrew & Greek. David Baker et al. LC 98-40712. 384p. (C). 1999. pap. 21.99 (*0-8010-2165-0*) Baker Bks.

More Lights on Yoga. Sri Aurobindo. 1979. pap. 2.95 (*0-89744-950-9*) Auromere.

More Lights on Yoga. 4th ed. Sri Aurobindo. 86p. 1995. pap. 2.50 (*81-7058-277-6*, Pub. by SAA) E-W Cultural Ctr.

More Like the Master: A Christian Musician's Reader. Glenn Kaiser et al. LC 96-22948. 140p. 1996. pap. 9.95 (*0-940895-25-0*) Cornerstone IL.

***More Litanies for All Occasions.** Garth House. LC 99-57317. 112p. 2000. pap. 12.00 (*0-8170-1354-7*) Judson.

More Literary Recreations. Edward T. Cook. LC 76-105005. (Essay Index Reprint Ser.). 1977. 29.95 (*0-8369-1457-0*) Ayer.

More Little Books to Make & Read. Kathy Dunlavy & Jeri A. Carroll. 176p. 1995. teacher ed. 13.99 (*1-56417-720-3*, GA1539) Good Apple.

More Little Missionaries. Mary R. Zook. (Illus.). 132p. (J). (gr. 3-6). 1982. 7.10 (*0-7399-0088-9*, 2337') Rod & Staff.

More Little Notes: On Management, Motivation & . . . Living. Frank A. Little. (Illus.). 140p. (Orig.). 1996. pap. 5.95 (*0-9641206-5-8*) E W Franklin.

More Little Stories for Little Children: A Worship Resource, 2 vols. Donna McKee Rhodes. LC 96-32340. 128p. (J). 1997. pap. 7.99 (*0-8361-9059-9*) Herald Pr.

More Little Talks for Little People. Susan Luke. (J). 1996. pap. 7.95 (*1-55503-833-6*, 01112031) Covenant Comms.

More Little Visits with God see Little Visits for Families

More Little Visits with God. Allan H. Jahsmann & Martin P. Simon. (Illus.). 228p. 1968. pap. 9.99 (*0-570-03033-1*, 6-1159) Concordia.

More Liturgies of the Word for Children. Alison Travers. 76p. (C). 1988. 30.00 (*0-85597-426-5*, Pub. by McCrimmon Pub) St Mut.

More Lively Ghosts. Susan Crites. 48p. 1992. pap. 5.00 (*1-881562-01-8*) Butternut Pubns.

***More Lives Than One: A Biography of Hans Fallada.** Jenny Williams. LC 98-150827. (Illus.). 300p. 1999. 45.00 (*1-870352-38-6*, Pub. by Libris) Paul & Co Pubs.

More Lives Than One (1917) Claude Bragdon. 374p. 1998. reprint ed. pap. 24.95 (*0-7661-0263-7*) Kessinger Pub.

More Logos & Letterheads. Rockport Publishers Staff. (Design Library Ser.). (Illus.). 80p. 1998. pap. text 14.99 (*1-56496-439-6*) Rockport Pubs.

***More Looking at Cooking.** Mildred Swift. 2000. pap. 16.95 (*1-56554-825-6*) Pelican.

More Lovable Critters. Sherry Gunter. (Illus.). 1991. pap. 7.50 (*0-941284-89-1*, 89) J Shaw Studio.

More Love: Tender Moments. Stuart Wilde. 309p. pap. Price not set. incl. audio (*0-930603-45-1*) White Dove NM.

More Love Tactics: How to Win that Special Someone. Thomas W. McKnight & Robert H. Phillips. LC 92-2729. 192p. 1993. pap. 8.95 (*0-89529-531-8*, Avery) Penguin Putnam.

More Love Tactics: How to Win That Special Someone. Thomas W. McKnight & Robert H. Phillips. 1996. 16.95 incl. audio (*1-882071-85-9*) B&B Audio.

More Love to Thee: The Life & Letters of Elizabeth Prentiss. George L. Prentiss. 605p. (Orig.). 1994. pap. 18.95 (*1-879737-14-0*) Calvary Press.

More Low Fat & Loving It, No. 2. Ruth A. Spear. 336p. (Orig.). 1998. pap. 12.99 (*0-446-67128-2*) Warner Bks.

More Lyrics from the Song-Books of the Elizabethan Age see Collections of Lyrics & Poems: Sixteenth & Seventeenth Centuries

More "M&M's" Brand Chocolate Candies Math. Barbara B. McGrath. LC 97-29345. (Illus.). 32p. (J). (gr. 3-7). 1998. 15.95 (*0-88106-993-0*) Charlesbridge Pub.

More "M&M's" Brand Chocolate Candies Math. Barbara B. McGrath. LC 97-29345. (Illus.). 32p. (J). (gr. 3 up). 1998. pap. 6.95 (*0-88106-994-9*) Charlesbridge Pub.

More Mac Programming Techniques. Dan P. Sydow. LC 95-4233. 1995. pap. 39.95 incl. disk (*1-55851-405-8*, M&T Bks) IDG Bks.

More MacGregor's Mixture. Forbes Macgregor. 144p. (C). 1989. 40.00 (*0-903065-42-8*, Pub. by G Wright Pub) St Mut.

More Macs for Dummies. David Pogue. LC 94-75910. 432p. 1994. pap. 19.95 (*1-56884-087-X*) IDG Bks.

More Mad Marginals. Sergio Aragones. 192p. 1988. mass mkt. 3.50 (*0-446-35245-4*, Pub. by Warner Bks) Little.

More Magic. Houghton Mifflin Company Staff. (J). (gr. 3). 1990. pap. 9.48 (*0-395-55155-2*) HM.

More Magic Kits: More Meaningful Activities for the Gifted in the Classroom Through Knowledge, Interest, Training & Stimulation. Janet Heuer et al. (Illus.). 56p. 1982. pap. 14.95 (*0-936386-18-5*) Creative Learning.

More Magic Methods in Oil with Lynne Pittard: Thirteen New Paintings Illustrated in Four Stages, in Full Color. Lynne Pittard. (Illus.). 72p. (Orig.). 1984. pap. 14.95 (*0-943295-05-X*) Graphics Plus FL.

More Magic of Magic: A How-To Guide for Using Magic in Affective Education. Rich Campbell. (Illus.). 160p. 1992. pap., spiral bd. 26.95 (*0-9633284-3-3*); ring bd. 29.95 (*0-9633284-2-5*) Brougham Pr.

More Magic of the Minimum Dose. Shepherd. 1996. 17.95 (*0-85207-299-6*, Pub. by C W Daniel) Natl Bk Netwk.

More Magic of the Minimum Dose. Dorothy Shepherd. 1974. 17.95 (*0-85032-056-9*) Formur Intl.

More Magic Secrets . . . All the Secrets of Magic Revealed. Herbert L. Becker. (Illus.). 1997. pap. 29.99 incl. cd-rom (*1-890167-26-6*) MagicWeb.

More Magic Secrets . . . All the Secrets of Magic Revealed. rev. ed. Herbert L. Becker. (Illus.). 190p. (YA). 1997. pap. 19.99 (*1-890167-25-8*) MagicWeb.

***More Magical Science: Magic Tricks for Young Scientists.** Eric Ladizinsky. (Illus.). (J). 2000. pap. 6.95 (*0-7373-0513-4*) Lowell Hse Juvenile.

More Make-a-Games. Milian France. 1997. 15.00 (*1-57128-069-3*, 8069-3) High Noon Bks.

More Make Your Own Groceries. Daphne M. Hartwig. LC 83-3806. (Illus.). 224p. 1983. pap. write for info. (*0-672-52774-X*) Macmillan.

More Makers of American Machinist Tools. unabridged ed. Kenneth L. Cope. (Illus.). 165p. 1998. pap. 19.95 (*1-879335-83-2*) Astragal Pr.

More Making Out in Japanese. Todd Geers & Erika Geers. 104p. (Orig.). 1989. pap. 6.95 (*4-900737-10-0*) Tuttle Pubng.

More Man-Eaters of Kumaon. Jim Corbett, pseud. 210p. 1991. lib. bdg. 23.95 (*0-89966-797-X*) Buccaneer Bks.

More Management for Results: A "How to" Workbook for Improving the Management of Your Veterinary Practice. Michael H. Riegger. 300p. 1995. pap. 59.95 (*0-929870-32-8*) Advanstar Commns.

More Management Ideas That Work!, No. 2. Zweig White & Associates Staff. 262p. 1994. pap. text 39.00 (*1-885002-05-X*) Zweig White.

More Maple Hill Stories. Roderick Turnbull. LC 74-15147. (Illus.). 312p. 1974. 9.95 (*0-913504-17-3*) Lowell Pr.

More Marine & Drawings in the Peabody Museum. limited ed. Philip C. Smith. (Illus.). 192p. 1979. 35.00 (*0-87577-058-4*, PEMP143, Peabody Museum) Peabody Essex Mus.

More Marketing Without Money for Small Businesses! 246 Free & Cheap Ways to Increase Your Sales! Nicholas E. Bade. LC 94-79474. 164p. (Orig.). 1995. pap. text 16.95 (*1-882923-15-4*) Halle Hse Pub.

More Mathematical Challenges: Problems for the U. K. Junior Mathematical Olympiad. Tony Gardiner. LC 97-184218. 144p. (C). 1997. pap. 14.95 (*0-521-58568-6*) Cambridge U Pr.

More Mathematical Morsels. Ross Honsberger. (Dolciani Mathematical Expositions Ser.). 315p. 1990. pap. text 27.50 (*0-88385-314-0*, DOL-10) Math Assn.

More Mathematical People: Contemporary Conversations. Ed. by Donald J. Albers et al. LC 94-21956. 375p. 1994. pap. text 45.00 (*0-12-048251-7*) Acad Pr.

More Mathematical Puzzles of Sam Loyd. Sam Loyd. 1960. pap. 5.95 (*0-486-20709-9*) Dover.

***More Matter: Essays & Criticism.** John Updike. 856p. 2000. pap. 19.95 (*0-449-00628-X*, Ballantine) Ballantine Pub Grp.

More Matter: Essays & Criticism. John Updike. LC 98-43124. (Illus.). 928p. 1999. 35.00 (*0-375-40630-1*) Knopf.

More Max Danger: The Continuing Adventures of an Expat in Tokyo. Robert J. Collins. LC 88-51066. 180p. 1988. pap. 9.95 (*0-8048-1570-4*) Tuttle Pubng.

More Maya Missions: Exploring Colonial Chiapas. Richard D. Perry. LC 93-72945. (Illus.). 128p. (Orig.). (C). 1994. pap. 12.95 (*0-9620811-2-4*) Espadana Pr.

***More Meanderings from Doc's Diary.** Charles Lamb. Ed. by Christina Case Wightman. 125p. 2000. pap. write for info. (*1-888911-18-2*) Benson Smythe.

More Meditations on the New Testament & Psalms. George H. Morrison. LC 96-85657. (Walk in the Word Ser.). 652p. 1996. 24.99 (*0-89957-215-4*) AMG Pubs.

More Meditations to Make You Smile. Martha J. Beckman. 112p. 1997. pap. 8.00 (*0-687-00952-9*) Dimen for Liv.

More Memories. large type ed. Ralph Emery & Tom Carter. 380p. 1994. lib. bdg. 23.95 (*0-8161-5928-9*, G K Hall Lrg Type) Mac Lib Ref.

More Memories of a Magistrate: Including Twenty-Five Years on the South African Bench. Napier Devitt. 263p. 1999. reprint ed. 80.00 (*1-56169-302-2*) Gaunt.

More Metrics. Ron Marson. LC 81-90448. (Science with Simple Things Ser.: No. 36). (Illus.). 80p. 1985. teacher ed. 15.00 (*0-941008-36-3*) Tops Learning.

More Michigan Cooking . . . & Other Things, Vol. 2. Carole Eberly. (Illus.). 112p. (Orig.). 1981. pap. 5.95 (*0-932296-07-6*) Eberly Pr.

***More Microsoft: Office 2000 for Dummies.** Wang. (More...for Dummies Ser.). 408p. 1999. pap. 22.99 (*0-7645-0605-6*) IDG Bks.

More Microsoft Office 97 for Windows for Dummies. Wallace Wang. LC 97-70734. 416p. 1997. pap. 22.99 (*0-7645-0136-4*) IDG Bks.

More Microsoft Windows 95 Step by Step. Catapult, Inc., Staff. (Step by Step Ser.). 304p. 1996. 29.95 incl. disk (*1-55615-888-2*) Microsoft.

***More Microsoft's Windows Millennium Edition for Dummies.** Andy Rathbone. (For Dummies Ser.). (Illus.). 384p. 2000. pap. 22.99 (*0-7645-0734-6*) IDG Bks.

***More Milly-Molly-Mandy.** Joyce Lakester Brisley. (Milly-Molly-Mandy Ser.). 224p. (J). (gr. k-3). 1999. 13.95 (*0-7534-0200-9*) LKC.

More Mind-Bending Lateral Thinking Puzzles, Vol. 2. Lagoon Bks Staff. (Mind-Bending Puzzle Bks.). (Illus.). 96p. 1996. 6.95 (*1-899712-19-4*, Pub. by Lagoon Bks) Midpt Trade.

More Minds. Carol Matas. (J). 1998. pap. text 4.50 (*0-590-39469-X*) Scholastic Inc.

***More Minds.** Carol Matas. 1998. 9.60 (*0-606-13622-3*, Pub. by Turtleback) Demco.

More Minds. Carol Matas & Perry Nodelman. 192p. (J). (gr. 5-9). 1996. per. 16.00 (*0-689-80388-5*) S&S Bks Yung.

More Miniature Perfume Bottles. Glinda Bowman. (Illus.). 176p. 1996. pap. 29.95 (*0-88740-999-7*) Schiffer.

More Miniature Sweater Designs, Bk. 2. Betty Lampen. (Knitting Books Ser.: Vol. 5, Bk. III). (Illus.). 16p. 1994. pap. 7.00 (*0-9634890-3-8*, MS3) B Lampen Knit.

***More Minstrel Banjo: Frank Converse Banjo Instructor 1865.** Joe Wiedlich. (Illus.). 48p. 1999. pap. 12.95 (*1-57424-075-7*) Centerstream Pub.

***More Missouri Ghosts: Fact, Fiction & Folklore.** Joan Gilbert. LC 00-92004. (Illus.). 250p. 2000. pap. 14.95 (*0-615-11888-7*) MoGho Bks.

***More Moab Country Day Hikes: Forty More One-Day Hikes in the Moab Vicinity.** Fran Barnes & Terby Barnes. (Canyon Country Ser.: Vol. 59). (Illus.). 48p. 1999. pap. 6.00 (*0-925685-40-2*) Canyon Country Pubns.

More Modems & On-Line Services for Dummies. Tina Rathbone. 416p. 1996. pap. 22.99 (*1-56884-365-8*) IDG Bks.

More Modern American Poets. James G. Southworth. LC 68-54371. (Essay Index Reprint Ser.). 1977. 18.95 (*0-8369-0889-9*) Ayer.

More Momilies: As My Mother Used to Say. Michele B. Slung. 96p. 1986. mass mkt. 4.99 (*0-345-33493-0*) Ballantine Pub Grp.

More Money for More Opportunity: Financial Support of Community College Systems. James L. Wattenbarger & Bob N. Cage. LC 74-3608. (Jossey-Bass Higher Education Ser.). 126p. reprint ed. 39.10 (*0-8357-9337-0*, 201375700087) Bks Demand.

More Money from Antiques! Milan Vesely. LC 98-84443. (Illus.). 160p. 1998. pap. 12.95 (*0-87341-621-X*, MFAII) Krause Pubns.

More Money Is No Mystery: 3 Key Questions to Grow Your Business. Gene M. Romagna. (Illus.). 120p. 1997. pap. 14.95 (*0-9664389-0-6*) Learn Group.

***More Money, More Ministry: Money & Evangelicals in Recent North American History.** Ed. by Larry Eskridge & Mark A. Noll. 2000. 20.00 (*0-8028-4777-3*) Eerdmans.

More Money, New Money, Big Money: Creative Strategies for Funding Today's Church. Wayne C. Barrett. LC 92-76039. 168p. 1993. pap. 14.95 (*0-88177-120-1*, DR120) Discipleship Res.

More Monologues for Kids. Ruth M. Roddy. 64p. (Orig.). (J). (gr. 1-3). 1992. pap. 8.95 (*0-940669-18-8*, D-8) Dramaline Pubns.

***More Monologues for Teenager.** Roger Karshner. LC 99-32513. 64p. (YA). (gr. 8-12). 1999. pap. 9.95 (*0-940669-44-7*, 0-49) Dramaline Pubns.

More Monologues for Women, by Women. Ed. by Tori Haring-Smith. LC 96-5549. 176p. 1996. pap. 13.95 (*0-435-07022-3*) Heinemann.

***More Monologues on Black Life.** Gus Edwards. 224p. 2000. pap. 15.95 (*0-325-00289-4*) Heinemann.

More Monologues They Haven't Heard. Roger Karshner. 64p. 1984. pap. 9.95 (*0-9611792-2-8*, D-2) Dramaline Pubns.

More Monsters in School. Martyn Godfrey. (Illus.). 1999. pap. text 3.95 (*1-55041-506-9*) Fitzhenry & W Ltd.

More Montana: Tall Tales, Damn Lies & Otherwise. Dick Hoskins. 204p. 1995. pap. 10.95 (*0-9639816-1-7*) Polecat Pr.

***More Montignac Menus.** Michel Montignac. 32p. 1999. pap. 4.95 (*1-893162-07-9*) Erica Hse.

More More More Said the Baby. Vera B. Williams. LC 89-2023. (Illus.). 34p. 1997. pap. 6.95 (*0-688-15634-7*, Hearst) Hearst Commns.

"More More More," Said the Baby. Vera B. Williams. LC 89-2023. (Illus.). 32p. (J). (ps-3). 1990. 15.95 (*0-688-09173-3*, Grenwillow Bks) HarpC Child Bks.

"More More More," Said the Baby. Vera B. Williams. LC 89-2023. (Illus.). 32p. (J). (ps up). 1990. 15.89 (*0-688-09174-1*, Grenwillow Bks) HarpC Child Bks.

"More More More," Said the Baby. Vera B. Williams. LC 89-2023. 40p. (J). 1996. mass mkt. 5.95 (*0-688-14736-4*, Wm Morrow) Morrow Avon.

More More More Said the Baby: 3 Love Stories. Vera B. Williams. 1996. 10.15 (*0-606-08825-3*, Pub. by Turtleback) Demco.

More Motor Racing: The Postwar Years. Rivers Fletcher. (Illus.). 224p. 1991. 49.95 (*0-85429-687-5*) Haynes Manuals.

More Motorcycle Collectibles. Leila Dunbar. (Schiffer Book for Collectors Ser.). (Illus.). 192p. 1997. pap. 29.95 (*0-7643-0333-3*) Schiffer.

More Mountain People, Places & Ways: Another Southern Applachian Sampler. Michael Joslin & Ruth Joslin. (Illus.). 288p. 1992. pap. 12.95 (*0-932807-83-6*) Overmountain Pr.

More Mountain Spirits: The Continuing Chronicle of Moonshine Life. Joseph E. Dabney. LC 85-10932. (Illus.). 208p. 1985. reprint ed. pap. 8.95 (*0-914875-03-5*) Bright Mtn Bks.

***More Mouse Tales: A Closer Peek Backstage at Disneyland.** David Koenig. 1999. 24.95 (*0-9640605-7-4*) Bonaventure.

More MRCP, Pt. 1. N. I. Johnson & C. Bunker. 100p. 1989. 15.95 (*0-387-19507-6*) Spr-Verlag.

More Ms. Murder: More of the Best Mysteries Featuring Women Detectives, by the Top Women Writers. Ed. by Marie Smith. 272p. 1991. 16.95 (*0-8065-1267-9*, Citadel Pr); pap. 10.95 (*0-8065-1274-1*, Citadel Pr) Carol Pub Group.

More Mudpies: 101 Alternatives to Television. Nancy Blakey. LC 94-11709. (Illus.). 144p. (J). (ps-7). 1994. pap. 8.95 (*1-883672-11-2*) Tricycle Pr.

More Mudpies to Magnets: Science for Young Children. Robert Williams et al. Ed. by Kathy Charner. (Illus.). 204p. 1990. pap. 14.95 (*0-87659-150-0*) Gryphon Hse.

More Muffins: 76 Recipes for Moist, Delicious, Fresh-Baked Muffins. Barbara Albright & Leslie Weiner. LC 99-34013. (Illus.). 128p. 1999. pap. 8.95 (*0-312-24313-8*) St Martin.

More Murder, They Wrote. Elizabeth Foxwell. 1999. mass mkt. 6.99 (*0-425-16990-1*) Blvd Books.

More Muscle. Ken Sprague. LC 96-2482. (Illus.). 216p. (Orig.). 1996. pap. 17.95 (*0-87322-899-5*, PSPR0899) Human Kinetics.

More Musical Reflections of Ireland. John Loesburg. 1997. pap. text 10.95 (*0-946005-37-0*) Dufour.

More Musical Reflections of Scotland. John Loesberg. 1994. 10.95 (*0-946005-83-4*, OS00098) Omnibus NY.

More Mysteries. Library of Congress National Library Service for the Blind & Physically Handicapped Staff. LC 92-30160. 1992. write for info. (*0-8444-0763-1*) Lib Congress.

An Asterisk (*) at the beginning of an entry indicates that the title is appearing for the first time.

More Mysteries of Astrology. Mary Elsnau. 59p. 1996. reprint ed. spiral bd. 12.00 (*0-7873-0312-7*) Hlth Research.

More Mysteries of Science: Research Activities for Investigating Scientific Fact & Fiction. Thomas Christie. (Illus.). 64p. (J). (gr. 4-8). 1994. 8.99 (*0-86653-820-8*, GA1512) Good Apple.

More Myths about Lee's Surrender. 3rd rev. ed. Patrick A. Schroeder. (Illus.). 32p. (YA). (gr. 7 up). 1998. pap. 4.00 (*1-889246-01-8*) P A Schroeder.

More Names & Naming: An Annotated Bibliography, 9. Compiled by Edwin D. Lawson. LC 95-31626. (Bibliographies & Indexes in Anthropology Ser.: No. 9). 320p. 1995. lib. bdg. 75.00 (*0-313-28582-9*, Greenwood Pr) Greenwood.

More Natural Remedies: What to Do to Prevent & Treat Disease...Naturally. Phylis Austin et al. 123p. 1985. pap. 6.95 (*1-878726-18-8*) Fam Hlth Pubns.

More Nature in Your Backyard. Susan Lang. LC 97-32181. (Illus.). 48p. (J). (gr. 2-5). 1998. lib. bdg. 22.90 (*0-7613-0308-1*) Millbrook Pr.

More Nature, Nuture, Nostalgia: Gleaned fro "Black River Journal" Louis Mihalyi. 1990. pap. 9.95 (*0-932052-79-7*) North Country.

More Nature Walks in Eastern Massachusetts: Discover 45 New Walks Including Scenic Cape Cod. Michael Tougias. LC 98-28882. (Illus.). 192p. 1998. pap. 12.95 (*1-878239-67-8*) AMC Books.

More NetSpy: How You Can Access the Facts & Cover Your Tracks Using the Internet & Online Services. Wolff New Media Staff. 200p. 1997. pap. 14.95 (*1-889670-27-8*) Wolff New Media.

More New Business for Ad Agencies. Edward Buxton & Susan Fulton. 358p. 1991. pap. 35.00 (*0-917168-13-5*) Executive Comm.

More News of the Weird. Chuck Shepherd et al. 1990. pap. 10.95 (*0-452-26545-2*, Plume) Dutton Plume.

More! 1944-1996: The Companion Volume to Henry Miller : a Book of Tributes, 1931-1994. Craig P. Standish. LC 97-171425. xxxv, 743 p. 1997. write for info. (*0-9641415-6-6*) Standish Bks.

More! 1944-1996: The Companion Volume to Henry Miller: A Book of Tributes, 1931-1994. Craig P. Standish. LC 97-171425. (Illus.). 781p. (C). 1997. 65.00 incl. audio (*0-9641415-3-1*) Standish Bks.

More! 1944-1996: The Companion Volume to Henry Miller: A Book of Tributes, 1931-1994, Incl. poster. aut. deluxe num. ed. Craig P. Standish. (Illus.). 781p. (C). 1997. per. 100.00 (*0-9641415-4-X*) Standish Bks.

***More Nitty-Gritty Grammar: Another Not-So-Serious Guide to Clear Communication.** Edith Fine & Judith Josephson. 112p. 2001. pap. 8.95 (*1-58008-228-9*) Ten Speed Pr.

More Noise, Please! 2nd ed. Steven J. Bernstein. LC 95-81515. (Illus.). 192p. (Orig.). 1996. pap. 8.00 (*0-939306-09-3*) Left Bank.

More Notices from Methodist Papers, 1830-1857. Donald A. McKenzie. 424p. 1986. lib. bdg. 25.00 (*0-912606-29-0*) Hunterdon Hse.

***More Novels & Plays: Teaching Guides for Grades Six Through Twelve.** Janet E. Worthington & Albert B. Somers. 250p. 2000. pap. 27.00 (*1-56308-691-3*) Libs Unl.

More Nutritional Chinese Cooking with Christine Liu. 3rd ed. Christine Liu. LC 81-90263. (Illus.). 452p. 1996. 27.95 (*0-9610566-5-7*) Graphique Pubs.

More Obiter Dicta. Augustine Birrell. LC 68-57304. (Essay Index Reprint Ser.). 1977. 19.95 (*0-8369-0062-6*) Ayer.

More Obiter Dicta. Augustine Birrell. (BCL1-PR English Literature Ser.). 212p. 1992. reprint ed. lib. bdg. 79.00 (*0-7812-7439-7*) Rprt Serv.

More Object Lessons from Nature. Joanne De Jonge. (Objects Lesson Ser.). 160p. (Orig.). (gr. 10). 1991. pap. 7.99 (*0-8010-3004-8*) Baker Bks.

***More of America's Best Bread Machine Baking Recipes.** Donna Washburn & Heather Butt. (Illus.). 192p. 2000. pap. 18.95 (*0-7788-0021-0*, Pub. by R Rose Inc) Firefly Bks Ltd.

More of Andrew Lloyd Webber. (Easy Piano Ser.). 10.95 (*0-7935-2841-0*, 00308209) H Leonard.

More of Brer Rabbit's Tricks. Ennis Rees. LC 93-32676. (Illus.). 48p. (J). (gr. k-5). 1994. reprint ed. pap. 5.95 (*1-56282-578-X*, Pub. by Hyprn Child) Little.

More of Don Munson's WJBC Sesquicentennial Stories: Glimpses of McLean County's 150 Years. Don Munson. (Illus.). 81p. 1981. 1.50 (*0-943788-13-7*) McLean County.

More of Duffy. Brian Duffy. (Illus.). 152p. 1995. pap. 14.95 (*0-8138-2666-7*) Iowa St U Pr.

More of Everything Else: Saratoga - Lexington Thoroughbred. David A. Siegenthaler. LC 98-86350. (Illus.). 150p. 1998. pap. 15.95 (*1-891181-00-9*) Good Times.

More of God. Patti G. Mansfield. 220p. 1990. pap. 3.75 (*0-940535-32-7*, UP132) Franciscan U Pr.

***More of God's Seasons Inside: Spring & Summer Bulletin Board Designs.** 1999. pap. text. write for info. (*0-570-05223-8*) Concordia.

More of Grandfather's Stories. Donna Roland. (Grandfather's Stories Ser.). (Illus.). 25p. (Orig.). (J). (gr. k-3). 1995. teacher ed. 6.50 (*0-941996-13-1*) Open My World.

More of Grandfather's Stories. Donna Roland. (Grandfather's Stories Ser.). (Illus.). 25p. (Orig.). (J). (gr. k-3). 1997. pap. 5.95 (*0-941996-02-6*) Open My World.

More of Grandfather's Stories from Cambodia. Donna Roland. (J). (gr. k-3). 1984. teacher ed. 6.50 (*0-941996-14-X*); pap. 5.95 (*0-941996-06-9*) Open My World.

More of Grandfather's Stories from Germany. Donna Roland. (J). (gr. k-3). 1984. pap. 5.95 (*0-941996-04-2*) Open My World.

More of Grandfather's Stories from Mexico. Donna Roland. (J). (gr. k-3). 1986. pap. 5.95 (*0-941996-10-7*) Open My World.

More of Grandfather's Stories from the Philippines. Donna Roland. (J). (gr. k-3). 1985. teacher ed. 6.50 (*0-941996-17-4*); pap. 5.95 (*0-941996-08-5*) Open My World.

More of Grandfather's Stories from Vietnam. Donna Roland. (J). (gr. k-3). 1985. pap. 5.95 (*0-941996-12-3*) Open My World.

More of Him, Less of Me: A Daybook of My Personal Insights, Inspirations, & Meditations on the Weigh down Diet. Jan Christiansen. 384p. 1999. 17.95 (*1-892016-00-1*, Pub. by Starburst) Natl Bk Netwk.

More of Jesus, Less of Me. Joan Cavanaugh & Pat Forseth. LC 76-23361. 144p. 1976. pap. 6.99 (*0-88270-174-6*) Bridge-Logos.

***More of Lifes Imponderables: Even More Answers to Civiliations Most Perplexing Questions.** David Feldman. (Illus.). 880p. 2000. 12.99 (*1-57866-096-3*) Galahad Bks.

More of Love's Little Instruction Book. Annie Pigeon. 96p. 1995. mass mkt. 4.99 (*0-8217-0107-X*, Zebra Kensgtn) Kensgtn Pub Corp.

More of Microbiology. (C). 1991. write for info. (*0-8087-9250-4*) Pearson Custom.

More of Neil Zurcher's One Tank Trips: Travels in Ohio & over the Edge. Neil Zurcher. LC 97-21158. (Illus.). 224p. (Orig.). 1997. pap. 13.95 (*1-886228-17-5*) Gray & Co Pubs.

More of Paul Harvey's the Rest of the Story. Paul Aurandt. 208p. 1984. mass mkt. 6.50 (*0-553-26074-X*) Bantam.

More of the Best from New Mexico Kitchens. NM Magazine Staff & Sheila M. Cameron. Ed. by Scottie King. LC 82-62076. (Illus.). 164p. 1983. pap. 9.95 (*0-937206-02-4*) New Mexico Mag.

More of the Best of Bits & Pieces. Ed. by Rob Gilbert. LC 97-60808. 288p. 1997. 29.95 (*0-910187-11-8*) Economics Pr.

More of the Best of Milton Berle's Private Joke File. Milton Berle. 553p. 1996. 12.98 (*0-7858-0719-5*) Castle Bks.

More of the Best of Milton Berle's Private Joke File. Milton Berle. Ed. by Milt Rosen. 560p. 1994. reprint ed. pap. 15.00 (*0-380-71953-3*, Avon Bks) Morrow Avon.

More of the Best Romantic Escapes in Florida: A Lover's Guide to Exceptionally Romantic Inns, Resorts, Restaurants, Activities, & Experiences. Pamela Acheson & Richard B. Myers. LC 98-48766. 128p. 1999. pap. 13.95 (*0-9639905-0-0*) Two Thous-Three Assocs.

More of the Four Ingredient Cookbook. Linda Coffee & Emily Cale. 121p. 1994. pap. 9.95 (*0-9628550-1-4*) Coffee & Cale.

More of the Salem Story . . . with Photographs. Dale E. Shaffer. (Illus.). 324p. (Orig.). 1992. pap. 20.00 (*0-915060-28-0*) D E Shaffer.

More of the Songs We Sing. Ed. by Harry Coopersmith. (ENG & HEB., Illus.). 288p. (J). (gr. 4-10). 1970. 9.50 (*0-8381-0217-4*) USCJE.

More of the World's Best Dirty Jokes. 136p. 1997. 5.98 (*0-89009-390-3*) Bk Sales Inc.

More of the World's Best Dirty Jokes by Mr. "J" (Illus.). 1979. 8.95 (*0-8065-0689-X*, Citadel Pr) Carol Pub Group.

More of the World's Dirty Jokes. Mr. J. 1980. pap. 5.95 (*0-8065-0710-1*, Citadel Pr) Carol Pub Group.

More of the World's Greatest Stamp Collectors. Stanley M. Bierman. (Illus.). 224p. 1990. 30.00 (*0-940403-28-5*); pap. 14.95 (*0-940403-27-7*) Linns Stamp News.

More of What You Thought You Knew about Judaism: 354 Common Misconceptions about Jewish Life. Reuven P. Bulka. LC 92-44591. 464p. 1996. pap. 35.00 (*1-56821-015-9*) Aronson.

More of What's Cooking. Veronica C. Coronado & Patty Kirk. 214p. (Orig.). 1995. 14.95 (*0-9649658-0-1*) Its Cooking.

More of Yesterday's Tucson Today Bk. 2: Your Guide to Walking the Historic Towns of the Santa Cruz Valley. Harry Cuming & Mary Cuming. (Illus.). 138p. 1996. per. 16.95 (*0-9653649-2-5*) Thirteenth Bomb Sqndrn.

More Ole & Lena Jokes. E. C. Stangland. 1987. pap. 2.50 (*0-9613274-3-X*) Norse Pr.

More Olympic Fun. (U. S. Olympic Committee's Activity Book). (Illus.). 16p. (J). (gr. k-3). 1996. pap. 2.95 (*1-882180-61-5*) Griffin CA.

More on Interest-Free Loans. rev. ed. Harry G. Gordon. 123p. (Orig.). (C). 1982. reprint ed. pap. 19.95 (*0-9612184-1-X*) H G Gordon.

More on the 64. H. C. Wagner. 148p. 9.95 (*3-88963-183-5*) Blue Cat.

More Once Told Tales of Worcester County. Albert B. Southwick. LC 94-71906. (Illus.). 180p. (Orig.). 1994. pap. 14.99 (*0-9636277-5-9*) Chandler Hse.

More Once upon a Time Saints. Ethel Pochocki. LC 97-77144. (Golden Key Bks.). (Illus.). 96p. (J). (ps up). 1998. pap. 9.95 (*1-883937-34-5*, 34-5) Bethlehem ND.

More 101 Home-Based Businesses for Women. Priscilla Huff. LC 97-43994. 448p. 1998. pap. 14.95 (*0-7615-1269-1*) Prima Pub.

More One Minute Nonsense. Anthony De Mello. LC 92-35241. 161p. 1993. pap. 10.95 (*0-8294-0749-9*) Loyola Pr.

More One-Story Homes: 475 Superb Plans from 800 to 5,000 Square Feet. Home Planners Editors. LC 98-72349. (Illus.). 448p. 1998. pap. 9.95 (*1-881955-48-6*) Home Planners.

More 1-2-3 for DOS for Dummies. John Weingarten. 368p. 1995. pap. 19.99 (*1-56884-224-4*) IDG Bks.

More Opera Scenes for Class & Stage from 100 Selected Operas. Mary E. Wallace & Robert Wallace. LC 89-10048. 256p. (C). 1990. text 31.95 (*0-8093-1429-0*) S Ill U Pr.

More Opposites. Richard Wilbur. LC 91-14411. 48p. (J). (gr. 1-5). 1991. 12.95 (*0-15-170072-9*) Harcourt.

More or Less? Judy Nayer. Ed. by Stephanie Pliakas. (Early Math Big Bks.). (Illus.). 16p. (J). (ps-2). 1997. pap. 16.95 (*1-56784-954-7*) Newbridge Educ.

More or Less a Mess! Sheila Keenan. LC 96-20477. (Hello Math Reader Ser.). (Illus.). (J). 1997. 3.50 (*0-590-60248-9*) Scholastic Inc.

More or Less a Mess! Sheila Keenan. (Hello Math Reader Ser.). 1997. 8.70 (*0-606-11639-7*, Pub. by Turtleback) Demco.

More or Less Urgent. Nina Zivancevic. 68p. 1988. pap. 2.50 (*0-89823-100-0*) New Rivers Pr.

More Oral Sadism & the Vegetarian Personality. Glenn C. Ellenbogen. LC 96-783. 192p. 1996. pap. 13.95 (*0-87630-795-0*, 7950) Brunner-Mazel.

More Oriental Stories for Young & Old. Leon Comber. (Illus.). 128p. 1988. reprint ed. pap. 5.95 (*9971-4-9088-9*) Heian Intl.

More Out Than In. Ed. by Rachel Kaplan & Keith Hennessy. (Illus.). (Orig.). (C). 1995. pap. text 8.00 (*1-881430-51-0*) AFP.

More Outbound Journeys in Pennsylvania: A Guide to Natural Places for Individual & Group Outings. Marcia Bonta. LC 94-23946. (Illus.). 176p. 1995. 32.50 (*0-271-01444-X*); pap. 14.50 (*0-271-01445-8*) Pa St U Pr.

More over the Top with Jim Stories. Hugh Lunn. (Fred & Olive's Blessed Lino Collection). 184p. 1995. pap. 14.95 (*0-7022-2863-X*, Pub. by Univ Queensland Pr) Intl Spec Bk.

More! Overhead Projector Games. Ed Dunlop. Ed. by Karen Brewer. (Illus.). 48p. (J). (gr. 1-6). 1996. teacher ed. 10.99 (*0-7847-0507-0*, 03510) Standard Pub.

***More Pages off the Doctor's Pad.** Harold C. Klein. Ed. by Miriam S. Klein. 104p. 1999. pap. 9.95 (*1-879653-20-6*) Lakeside Pr.

More Painted Ladies: Modern Military Aircraft Nose-Art & Unusual Markings. Randy Walker. LC 93-84796. (Illus.). 144p. (Orig.). 1994. pap. 24.95 (*0-88740-514-2*) Schiffer.

More Palatine Families: Some Immigrants to the Middle Colonies 1717-1776 & Their European Origins, Plus New Discoveries on German Families Who Arrived in Colonial New York in 1710. Henry Z. Jones, Jr. LC 91-90811. (Illus.). 625p. 1991. 65.00 (*0-9613888-3-8*, 1161) Picton Pr.

More Palomino, Please, More Fuchsia. Marilyn Kaysl. pap. 4.00 (*0-317-01118-9*) League Bks.

More Palomino, Please, More Fuchsia. Marilyn Krysl. LC 80-65889. (CSU Poetry Ser.: No. VIII). 65p. 1980. pap. 4.00 (*0-914946-20-X*) Cleveland St Univ Poetry Ctr.

More Paper Airplane Power. (Illus.). 32p. (J). 1993. pap. 12.95 (*1-56173-237-0*) Pubns Intl Ltd.

More Paper Piecing Patterns. Shirley Liby. (Illus.). 76p. 1994. spiral bd. 14.95 (*1-890952-09-5*) S Liby Pubns.

More Parables & Fables. Peter Ribes. 144p. 1996. pap. 39.95 (*0-85439-431-1*, Pub. by St Paul Pubns) St Mut.

More Parables in Depth. George E. Drew. 1988. pap. 7.95 (*0-940754-52-5*, 6348) Ed Ministries.

More Paragraphs on Translation. Peter Newmark. LC 97-51150. 226p. 1998. 59.00 (*1-85359-403-2*); pap. 19.95 (*1-85359-402-4*) Multilingual.

More Parkside Pranks & Sunset Stunts. Mary A. Williams & George Stanton. Ed. by Kali Sichen. LC 90-63655. (Illus.). 142p. 1990. pap. 8.95 (*0-916299-13-9*) North Scale Co.

***More Parsha Parables.** Mordechai Kamenetsky. 1998. 17.95 (*0-9657697-1-2*, Pub. by Bentsh Pr) Feldheim.

***More Parts of the Puzzle; You Name it.** R. Pease. 346p. 2000. per. 16.95 (*1-889455-06-7*) Flagg Mtn Pr.

More Passages: A New History of Amherst County VA. Sherrie S. McLeroy & William McLeroy. (Illus.). 189p. (Orig.). 1995. pap. 17.00 (*0-7884-0331-1*, M149) Heritage Bk.

More Passion for Lending, Vol. 2. A. Rex Johnson. 90p. (Orig.). 1994. pap. write for info. (*1-889265-00-4*) Callahan & Assocs.

More Pasta Light. Norman Kolpas. LC 95-22525. (Illus.). 144p. 1995. pap. 11.95 (*0-8092-3725-3*, 372530, Contemporary Bks) NTC Contemp Pub Co.

More Peanuts Gang Collectibles. Jan Lindenberger & Cher Porges. LC 98-88435. (Illus.). 160p. (Orig.). 1999. pap. 29.95 (*0-7643-0747-9*) Schiffer.

More People, Less Erosion: Enviornmental Recovery in Kenya. Mary Tiffen et al. LC 93-2192. 326p. 1994. pap. 80.00 (*0-471-94143-3*) Wiley.

More Perfect Legacy: A Portrait of Brother Ephrem O'Dwyer, C. S. C., 1888-1978. Philip Armstrong. LC 94-15933. (C). 1995. text 34.50 (*0-268-01414-0*) U of Notre Dame Pr.

More Perfect Union. Ed. by Virginia Hartman & Barbara Esstman. LC 98-158118. 272p. 1998. text 23.95 (*0-312-18526-X*) St Martin.

More Perfect Union. J. A. Jance. LC 88-91575. (J.P. Beaumont Ser.). 224p. 1988. mass mkt. 6.99 (*0-380-75413-4*, Avon Bks) Morrow Avon.

More Perfect Union. Harold Weiss. 20p. 1945. pap. 3.50 (*1-58342-004-5*, M33) Dramatic Pub.

***More Perfect Union.** 21st ed. Beverly J. Armento. LC 98-234526. (Social Studies). xvii, 767 p. 1999. write for info. (*0-395-93072-3*) HM.

More Perfect Union: Parenting by Just & Holy Principles. Mollie H. Sorensen. (Illus.). xi, 217p. 1990. pap. 10.95 (*0-9659261-1-7*) Sun W Publ.

More Perfect Union: Poems & Stories about the Modern Wedding. Ed. by Virginia Hartman & Barbara Esstman. 1999. pap. 12.95 (*0-312-20480-9*, St Martin Griffin) St Martin.

More Perfect Union: The Story of Alexander Hamilton. Nancy Whitelaw. LC 97-11703. (Notable Americans Ser.). (Illus.). 112p. (YA). (gr. 5 up). 1997. lib. bdg. 18.95 (*1-883846-20-X*) M Reynolds.

More Perfect Union: The Story of Our Constitution. Betsy Maestro. (J). 1987. 13.15 (*0-606-04750-6*, Pub. by Turtleback) Demco.

More Perfect Union: The Story of Our Constitution. Betsy C. Maestro. LC 87-4083. (Illus.). 48p. (J). (gr. 1-5). 1987. lib. bdg. 15.93 (*0-688-06840-5*) Lothrop.

More Perfect Union: The Story of Our Constitution. Betsy C. Maestro & Giulio Maestro. LC 87-4083. (Illus.). 48p. (J). (ps-3). 1990. mass mkt. 7.95 (*0-688-10192-5*, Wm Morrow) Morrow Avon.

More Perfect Union: Vermont Becomes a State, 1777-1816. Ed. by Michael Sherman. 238p. 1991. pap. 14.95 (*0-934720-33-9*) VT Hist Soc.

More Perfect Union: Why Straight America Must Stand up for Gay Rights. Richard D. Mohr. 144p. 1995. pap. 9.00 (*0-8070-7933-2*) Beacon Pr.

More Perfect Union - The Creation of the U. S. Constitution. (Milestone Documents in the National Archives Ser.). (Illus.). 34p. 1986. pap. 3.50 (*0-911333-24-X*, 200105) National Archives & Recs.

More Period Details: The House Renovator's Bible. Judith Miller. 1999. 40.00 (*0-609-60410-4*) Random Hse Value.

More Pet Bugs: A Kid's Guide to Catching & Keeping Insects & Other Small Creatures. Sally Stenhouse Kneidel. LC 98-51625. (Illus.). 118p. (J). (gr. 3-7). 1999. pap. text 12.95 (*0-471-25489-4*) Wiley.

More Pez. 2nd expanded rev. ed. Richard Geary. (Illus.). 80p. 1998. pap. 14.95 (*0-7643-0453-4*) Schiffer.

***More Pez for Collectors.** 3rd ed. Richard Geary. (Illus.). 2000. 14.95 (*0-7643-0994-3*) Schiffer.

More Phil King. Phil King. LC 91-90729. 1992. pap. 5.00 (*0-9601900-8-2*) Phil King.

More Philosophy & Opinions of Marcus Garvey: Previously Published Papers, Vol. 3. Ed. by E. U. Essien-Udom & Amy Garvey. (Illus.). 248p. 1977. 37.50 (*0-7146-1751-2*, Pub. by F Cass Pubs); pap. 22.00 (*0-7146-4027-1*, Pub. by F Cass Pubs) Intl Spec Bk.

More Phobias: Phobias II. Wendy Webb. 1995. mass mkt. 5.99 (*0-671-89547-8*) PB.

More Phonics Through Poetry: Teaching Phonemic Awareness Using Poetry. Babs Bell Hajdusiewicz. LC 99-179663. 1998. pap. 15.95 (*0-673-36346-5*) Addison-Wesley.

More Picture Stories: Language & Problem-Posing Activities for Beginners. Fred Ligon et al. 128p. 1991. pap. text 16.55 (*0-8013-0839-9*, 78905) Longman.

More Piggyback Songs: New Songs Sung to the Tunes of Childhood Favorites. Illus. by Marion H. Ekberg. LC 84-90020. (Piggyback Songs Ser.). 96p. (Orig.). (J). (ps-1). 1984. pap. 8.95 (*0-911019-02-2*, WPH 0202) Totline Pubns.

More Piggyback Songs for School. Ed. by Elizabeth McKinnon. LC 95-60006. (Piggyback Songs Ser.). (Illus.). 80p. (Orig.). (J). (ps-1). 1995. pap. 8.95 (*1-57029-067-9*, WPH 0211) Totline Pubns.

More Plastics for Collectors: A Handbook & Price Guide. Jan Lindenberger & Jean Rosenthal. (Illus.). 160p. (YA). (gr. 10-13). 1996. pap. 19.95 (*0-88740-967-9*) Schiffer.

More Plays by Rivals of Corneille & Racine. Tr. by Lacy Lockert. LC 68-17282. 694p. 1968. 29.95 (*0-8265-1110-4*) Vanderbilt U Pr.

More Plays of William Dunlap. Intro. by Julian Mates. LC 95-38126. 336p. 1995. 50.00 (*0-8201-1495-2*) Schol Facsimiles.

More Poems for My Family. Philip R. Overly. 120p. 1998. pap. write for info. (*1-57502-873-5*, PO2376) Morris Pubng.

More Poems for People. Milton Acorn. 116p. 1978. text 9.95 (*0-919600-10-7*, Pub. by NC Ltd) U of Toronto Pr.

More Poems from a Dog's Point of View: Another Collection of Some Down-to-Earth (And Some Not-So-Down-to-Earth) Canine Poetry by Summerset's Toby. Jeanne M. Hess. (Illus.). 64p. 1998. pap. 5.00 (*0-9629745-1-X*) Summerset Ent.

More Poetic Thoughts: By Love Pain Hope Poet, Barbara-Marie Green & Others. Barbara-Marie Green et al. 70p. (Orig.). 1990. pap. 4.95 (*1-883414-01-6*) Bar JaMae.

More Poetic Truths. Mia Sillanpaa. LC 94-90834. (Illus.). 60p. (Orig.). pap. 9.95 (*0-9643761-1-3*) M Sillanpaa.

More Poetical Whims of Wilson: Another Walk with Me. Archie W. Wilson. 100p. 1998. pap. 6.00 (*0-9658785-1-1*) A W Wilson.

More Poetry Hunter. Ed. by Richard A. Spiegel & Barbara Fisher. (Illus.). 92p. (Orig.). (J). (gr. 3 up). 1981. pap. 2.00 (*0-934830-23-1*) Ten Penny.

More Poetry Please. BBC Radio 4 Staff. (Everyman's Poetry Ser.). 128p. 1998. 3.50 (*0-460-87899-9*, Everyman's Classic Lib) Tuttle Pubng.

More Points of View. Archbishop of York et al. LC 69-18933. (Essay Index Reprint Ser.). 1977. 17.95 (*0-8369-0048-0*) Ayer.

***More Points Schmoints.** Marty Bergen. 224p. 1999. 19.95 (*0-9637533-5-5*) Bergen Bks.

More Polarfleece Adventures: Exciting New Fleece Techniques from the Best-Selling Author of Adventures. Nancy Cornwell. LC 99-61442. 160p. 1999. pap. 19.95 (*0-87341-791-7*) Krause Pubns.

More Police on Patrol. Linda Kleinschmidt. Ed. by Deena A. Quilty. (Illus.). 140p. (Orig.). 1998. per. 14.95 (*0-9652255-2-6*) A J Pubng.

More Political Babble: The Dumbest Things Politicians Ever Said. David Olive. LC 95-37784. 244p. 1996. 16.95 (*0-471-13548-8*) Wiley.

M

An Asterisk (*) at the beginning of an entry indicates that the title is appearing for the first time.

More Porcelain Enamel Advertising. Michael Bruner. LC 97-19062. 160p. 1997. pap. 29.95 (*0-7643-0373-2*) Schiffer.

More Portfolio Theory & Investment Analysis. 5th ed. Edwin J. Elton & Martin J. Gruber. (Portfolio Management Ser.). 736p. 1995. text 95.95 (*0-471-00743-9*) Wiley.

More Postcards from Paradise Vol. 2: Romancing Key West. June Keith. LC 98-66398. (Illus.). 256p. 1998. pap. 19.95 (*0-9643434-0-1*) Palm Island.

More Power to the People: Young Fabian Essays on Democracy in Britain. Brian Lapping & Giles Radice. 1968. pap. 49.50 (*0-614-01798-X*) Elliots Bks.

More Power to You. Merlin R. Carothers. 143p. (Orig.). 1982. pap. 6.95 (*0-943026-00-8*) Carothers.

More Power to You! Charles Roth. LC 82-50122. 158p. 1982. 3.98 (*0-87159-093-X*) Unity Bks.

More Power to You! A Proven Path to Electric Energy Independence. 2nd ed. H. Skip Thomsen. (Illus.). 92p. (Orig.). 1993. 9.95 (*0-9625960-5-1*) Oregon Wordworks.

More Power to You! How Women Can Communicate Their Way to Success. Connie B. Glaser & Barbara S. Smalley. 192p. 1995. reprint ed. mass mkt. 11.95 (*0-446-67070-7*, Pub. by Warner Bks) Little.

More Power Tools for Teaching. Beth Lefgren & Jennifer Jackson. 1991. pap. 6.95 (*0-88494-780-7*) Bookcraft Inc.

**More Practice in Mathematics, Bk. 1.* J. W. Adams & R. P. Beaumont. Ed. by T. R. Goddard. (J). (gr. 2-7). 1999. pap. 19.00 (*0-7217-2346-2*, Pub. by Schofield) St Mut.

***More Practice in Mathematics, Bk. 2.** J. W. Adams & R. P. Beaumont. Ed. by T. R. Goddard. (J). (gr. 2-7). 1999. pap. 19.00 (*0-7217-2347-0*, Pub. by Schofield) St Mut.

***More Practice in Mathematics, Bk. 3.** J. W. Adams & R. P. Beaumont. Ed. by T. R. Goddard. (J). (gr. 2-7). 1999. pap. 19.00 (*0-7217-2348-9*, Pub. by Schofield) St Mut.

***More Practice in Mathematics, Bk. 4.** J. W. Adams & R. P. Beaumont. Ed. by T. R. Goddard. (J). (gr. 2-7). 1999. pap. 19.00 (*0-7217-2349-7*, Pub. by Schofield) St Mut.

***More Practice in Mathematics, Bk. 5.** J. W. Adams & R. P. Beaumont. Ed. by T. R. Goddard. 1999. pap. 19.00 (*0-7217-2350-0*, Pub. by Schofield) St Mut.

***More Practice in Mathematics: Answer Book, Bk. 1.** J. W. Adams & R. P. Beaumont. Ed. by T. R. Goddard. 1999. pap. 19.00 (*0-7217-2351-9*, Pub. by Schofield) St Mut.

***More Practice in Mathematics: Answer Book, Bk. 2.** J. W. Adams & R. P. Beaumont. Ed. by T. R. Goddard. 1999. pap. 19.00 (*0-7217-2352-7*, Pub. by Schofield) St Mut.

***More Practice in Mathematics: Answer Book, Bk. 3.** J. W. Adams & R. P. Beaumont. Ed. by T. R. Goddard. 1999. pap. 19.00 (*0-7217-2353-5*, Pub. by Schofield) St Mut.

***More Practice in Mathematics: Answer Book, Bk. 4.** J. W. Adams & R. P. Beaumont. Ed. by T. R. Goddard. 1999. pap. 19.00 (*0-7217-2354-3*, Pub. by Schofield) St Mut.

***More Practice in Mathematics: Answer Book, Bk. 5.** J. W. Adams & R. P. Beaumont. Ed. by T. R. Goddard. 1999. pap. 19.00 (*0-7217-2355-1*, Pub. by Schofield) St Mut.

More Practice Questions for the Registered Professional Reporter Exam. Ed. by Marianne Cammarota. 16p. 1998. pap. 19.95 (*1-881859-24-X*) Natl Ct Report.

More Pray to Love - Love to Pray: Good Thoughts from Good People - Prayers, Reflections & Life Stories of 15 Great Pray-ers. Carol A. Graser. 76p. 1998. pap. 5.95 (*0-937997-43-9*) Hi-Time Pflaum.

More Prayers. Tasha Tudor. LC 72-366095. 39 p. 1968. write for info. (*0-7188-1364-2*, Lutterworth-Parkwest) Parkwest Pubns.

***More Prayers.** Tasha Tudor. (Illus.). 32p. (J). 2000. 6.99 (*0-375-80326-2*, Pub. by Random Bks Yng Read) Random.

More Prayers for Plain People. William Barclay. (Abingdon Classics Ser.). 160p. (Orig.). 1993. pap. 5.95 (*0-687-27187-8*) Abingdon.

***More Prayers on My Pillow.** Celia Straus. 2000. 18.50 (*0-345-44195-8*) Ballantine Pub Grp.

More Prayers That Prevail. Clift Richards. LC 96-228293. (Believer's Manual of Prayers Ser.). 1995. pap. 8.99 (*0-932081-46-0*) Victory Hse.

More Precious. 1997. pap. 1.30 (*0-8341-9673-5*) Lillenas.

More Precious Than: How Dialogue Can Transform Relationships & Build Community. Margaret Van Den Brink. (Social Ecology Ser.). 160p. (Orig.). 1996. pap. 16.95 (*1-869890-83-3*, Pub. by Hawthorn Press) Anthroposophic.

***More Precious Than Diamonds.** Lisa J. Peck. 2000. pap. 10.95 (*1-55517-450-7*) CFI Dist.

More Precious Than Gold see **Deseables Mas Que Oro**

More Precious Than Gold: Psalm 19. Ed. by San Francisco Harper Staff. 48p. 1985. 8.20 (*0-86683-845-7*) Harper SF.

More Precious Than Gold: Psalms of Praise & Hope. Crossway Books. LC 97-38478. 32p. 1998. 7.99 (*0-89107-988-2*) Crossway Bks.

More Precious Than Gold: Quiet Times with God. William A. Lauterbach. LC 93-84930. 133p. (Orig.). 1993. pap. 8.99 (*0-8100-0500-X*, 06N0702) Northwest Pub.

More Precious Than Gold: The Fiery Trial of a Family's Faith. John Vaughan & Brenda Vaughan. LC 93-37584. 232p. 1994. pap. 11.99 (*0-8007-5519-7*) Revell.

More Precious Than Pearls: Selected Insights into the Qualities of the Ideal Woman; Based on Eshes Chayil. Tziporah Heller. LC 94-4129. 1994. 14.95 (*0-87306-661-8*) Feldheim.

More Precious than Silver: 366 Daily Devotional Readings. Joni Eareckson Tada. LC 98-28366. 416p. 1998. 16.99 (*0-310-21627-3*) Zondervan.

More Prejudice. Arthur B. Walkley. LC 79-84345. (Essay Index Reprint Ser.). 1977. 20.95 (*0-8369-1237-3*) Ayer.

More Pricks Than Kicks. Samuel Beckett. LC 72-119923. 191p. 1972. pap. 11.00 (*0-8021-5137-X*, Grove) Grove-Atltic.

More Pricks Than Kicks. Samuel Beckett. 1995. pap. 11.95 (*0-7145-0705-9*) Riverrun NY.

More Pricks Than Kicks. large type ed. Samuel Beckett. 254p. 1990. 22.95 (*1-85290-015-6*, Pub. by ISIS Lrg Prnt) Transaction Pubs.

More Prime Time Activities with Kids. Donna Erickson. LC 91-43933. (Illus.). 128p. (Orig.). 1992. pap. 14.99 (*0-8066-2606-2*, 9-2606, Augsburg) Augsburg Fortress.

More Process Patterns: Delivering Large-Scale Systems Using Object Technology. Scott W. Ambler. LC 98-45451. (Managing Object Technology Ser.: No. 19). 416p. (C). 1999. 44.95 (*0-521-65262-6*) Cambridge U Pr.

More Profit from Your PC: How to Turn Your PC into a Share Investment Powerhouse. David Linton. 1998. pap. text 21.95 (*0-7134-8388-1*, Pub. by B T B) Branford.

More Profound Alleluia. Charles Pottie. 1984. 5.95 (*0-912405-12-0*, Pastoral Press) OR Catholic.

More Programming Pearls: Confessions of a Coder. Jon L. Bentley. (Illus.). 224p. (C). 1988. pap. text 20.95 (*0-201-11889-0*) Addison-Wesley.

More Prophecies for the Coming Millennium. Shawn Robbins & Edward Susman. 224p. (Orig.). 1996. mass mkt. 5.99 (*0-380-78455-6*, Avon Bks) Morrow Avon.

More Psychic Roots: Further Adventures in Serendipity & Intuition in Genealogy. Henry Z. Jones, Jr. LC 96-78239. xiii, 261p. 1999. reprint ed. pap. 16.95 (*0-8063-1524-5*) Genealog Pub.

More Punctuation see **Learn Writing & Grammar Quickly**

More Puzzlegrams: A Colorful, Beguiling Collection of 148 More Classic Puzzles Designed by Pentagram. Pentagram Partnership Staff. (Illus.). 160p. 1994. per. 18.00 (*0-671-51059-2*) S&S Trade Pap.

More Puzzles, Paradoxes & Brain Teasers. Stan Gibilisco. (Illus.). 140p. 1989. 14.95 (*0-8306-9095-6*); pap. 8.95 (*0-8306-3295-6*) McGraw-Hill Prof.

More Puzzles, Riddles & Muddles. (J). (gr. 4-7). 1992. pap. 3.95 (*0-8167-2699-X*) Troll Communs.

More Quaker Laughter. William H. Sessions. 1999. pap. 21.00 (*0-900657-31-6*, Pub. by W Sessions) St Mut.

More Queries & Responses on UCP 500 - 1997: Opinions of the ICC Banking Commission 1997. International Chamber of Commerce Staff. Ed. by Gary Collyer. (Letters of Credit Ser.). 92p. 1998. pap. 49.95 (*92-842-1253-7*, 596) ICC Pub.

More Questions & Answers. Bailey Kennedy. LC 98-100007. (Gifted & Talented Ser.). (Illus.). 64p. (J). (gr. 1-3). Date not set. pap. 5.95 (*1-56565-564-8*, 05648W, Pub. by Lowell Hse Juvenile) NTC Contemp Pub Co.

More Questions & Answers: Ages 4-6. Bailey Kennedy. LC 96-27297. (Gifted & Talented Ser.). (Illus.). 64p. (J). (ps-1). 1996. pap., wbk. ed. 5.95 (*1-56565-504-4*, 05044W, Pub. by Lowell Hse Juvenile) NTC Contemp Pub Co.

More Questions & Answers on the ISO 9000 Standards Series & Related Issues. 165p. (Orig.). (C). 1994. pap. text 40.00 (*0-7881-0409-8*) DIANE Pub.

More Quick Country Quilting: Over Sixty New Fast & Fun Projects from the Author of Quick Country Quilting. Debbie Mumm. (Illus.). 256p. 1996. pap. 14.95 (*0-87596-757-4*) Rodale Pr Inc.

More Quick Hits: Successful Strategies by Award-Winning Teachers. Ed. by S. Holly Stocking et al. LC 98-20679. 144p. 1998. pap. 9.95 (*0-253-21238-3*) Ind U Pr.

More Quick Rotary-Cutter Quilts. Pam Bono. LC 95-72637. 160p. 1996. pap. 19.95 (*0-8487-1514-4*) Oxmoor Hse.

More Quickie Comebacks. Lisa Eisneberg. 96p. (J). (gr. 4-7). 1994. pap. 1.95 (*0-590-47296-8*) Scholastic Inc.

More Quilts for Baby: Easy as ABC. Sally Schneider. Ed. by Ursula G. Reikes. LC 97-1246. (Illus.). 80p. 1997. pap. 16.95 (*1-56477-187-3*, B301) Martingale & Co.

More Quizzles. Wayne Williams. 1997. pap. text 11.25 (*0-86651-208-X*) Seymour Pubns.

***More Radical Hermeneutics: On Not Knowing Who We Are.** John D. Caputo. LC 99-88428. (Studies in Continental Thought). 336p. 2000. pap. 19.95 (*0-253-21387-8*); lib. bdg. 44.95 (*0-253-33747-X*) Ind U Pr.

More Rail Fences, Rolling Pins & Rainbows. Lois Costomiris. 1995. 20.00 (*1-878208-72-1*) Guild Pr IN.

More Random Acts of Kindness. Conari Press Editors. (Practice of Kindness Ser.). (Illus.). 180p. 1996. pap. 8.95 (*0-943233-82-8*) Conari Press.

***More Random Acts of Kindness.** Ed. by Conari Press Editors. 192p. 1998. 6.98 (*1-56731-277-2*, MJF Bks) Fine Comms.

More Random Walks in Science. R. L. Weber. (Illus.). 208p. 1982. 38.00 (*0-85498-040-7*) IOP Pub.

More Rapid Math Tricks & Tips: 30 Days to Number Mastery. Edward H. Julius. LC 95-35581. 240p. 1996. pap. 14.95 (*0-471-12238-6*) Wiley.

***More Read & Understand Stories & Activities, Grade 1.** Jill Norris. Ed. by Marilyn Evans. (Read & Understand Ser.: Vol. 5). (Illus.). 144p. 1999. pap., teacher ed. 12.95 (*1-55799-737-3*, 745) Evan-Moor Edu Pubs.

***More Read & Understand Stories & Activities, Grade 2.** Jo Ellen Moore. Ed. by Marilyn Evans. (Read & Understand Ser.: Vol. 6). (Illus.). 144p. 1999. pap., teacher ed. 12.95 (*1-55799-736-5*, 746) Evan-Moor Edu Pubs.

***More Read & Understand Stories & Activities, Grade 3.** Jo Ellen Moore. Ed. by Marilyn Evans. (Read & Understand Ser.: Vol. 7). (Illus.). 144p. 1999. pap., teacher ed. 12.95 (*1-55799-738-1*, 747) Evan-Moor Edu Pubs.

***More Reading Connections: Bringing Parents, Teachers, & Librarians Together.** Elizabeth Knowles & Martha Smith. 175p. 1999. pap. 26.50 (*1-56308-723-5*) Libs Unl.

More Reading Power. Jeffries & Bea Mikulecky. 304p. 1995. pap. text 23.52 (*0-201-60970-3*) Addison-Wesley.

More Ready to Sing. Mauldin. 1992. pap. 6.95 (*1-55897-395-8*) Brentwood Music.

***More Ready-to-Tell Tales: From Around the World.** David Holt & Bill Mooney. 256p. 2000. 24.95 (*0-87483-592-5*); pap. 14.95 (*0-87483-583-6*) August Hse.

More Real Characters. J. Vernon Mcgee. LC 96-50886. 240p. 1997. 14.99 (*0-7852-7172-4*) Nelson.

More Real Than Reality: The Fantastic in Irish Literature & the Arts, 45. Ed. by Donald E. Morse & Bertha Csilla. LC 90-47537. (Contributions to the Study of Science Fiction & Fantasy Ser.: No. 45). 288p. 1991. 59.95 (*0-313-26612-3*, MFM/, Greenwood Pr) Greenwood.

More Reasons for Reading. Carrie S. Dobbs. 304p. (C). 1992. pap. text 30.47 (*0-13-594433-3*) P-H.

More Recipes for Tired Teachers. Christopher Sion. 128p. 1991. pap. text 27.20 (*0-201-52318-3*) Addison-Wesley.

More Recipes for Your Heart's Delight: The Stanford Guide to Healthy Cooking. Christopher Gardener & Karla Oliveira. (Illus.). 68p. 1997. pap. 4.95 (*1-879552-07-8*) SCRDP.

More Recipes from a Kitchen Garden. Renee Shepherd & Fran Raboff. LC 94-47272. (Illus.). 164p. (Orig.). 1995. pap. 11.95 (*0-89815-730-7*) Ten Speed Pr.

More Recitations for Church Occasions. LC 98-115044. 1996. 7.99 (*0-8341-9499-6*, MP-505) Lillenas.

More Red Meat. Max Cannon. LC 98-36215. 112p. 1998. pap. 9.95 (*0-312-19514-1*) St Martin.

More Reflections for Managers: A New Collection of Wisdom & Inspiration. Bruce N. Hyland & Merle J. Yost. LC 95-33419. 145p. 1995. 14.95 (*0-07-031785-2*) McGraw.

More Reflections of a Prairie Daughter. Intro. by H. M. Briggs. (Illus.). 200p. 1993. pap. 10.00 (*0-9623066-1-4*) Prairie Daughter.

More Reflections of a Prairie Daughter. Elizabeth E. Williams. 198p. 1996. per. 13.00 (*0-614-24801-9*) Tesseract SD.

More Results Oriented Job Descriptions. Roger J. Plachy & Sandra J. Plachy. LC 97-35903. 320p. 1997. spiral bd. 65.00 (*0-8144-7961-8*) AMACOM.

More Retail Details Mother Forgot to Mention. T. J. Reid. (Illus.). 128p. 1999. pap. 34.95 (*1-880522-25-X*) Retail Res.

More Return Tickets. L. Grace Dibble. 373p. (C). 1991. 35.00 (*0-7223-1320-9*, Pub. by A H S Ltd) St Mut.

More Ribbon Embroidery by Machine. Marie Duncan & Betty Farrell. LC 97-73026. (Illus.). 96p. (Orig.). 1997. pap. 21.95 (*0-8019-9047-5*, BCUR) Krause Pubns.

More Rip-Roaring Reads for Reluctant Teen Readers. Betty D. Ammon & Gale W. Sherman. 161p. 1998. pap. 26.50 (*1-56308-571-2*) Teacher Ideas Pr.

***More Roads Around Britain.** Gary Rhodes. 2000. 26.95 (*1-884656-15-3*) W One Hund Seventy Five.

More Rock Family Trees. Pete Frame. (Illus.). 32p. 1998. pap. 21.95 (*0-7119-6879-9*, OP48064) Omnibus NY.

More Roman Than Rome: English Catholicism in the Nineteenth Century. J. Derek Holmes. LC 77-92886. (Illus.). 278p. 1978. 21.95 (*0-915762-05-6*) Patmos Pr.

More Root Beer Advertising & Collectibles. Tom Morrison. LC 97-68111. (Schiffer Book for Collectors Ser.). (Illus.). 160p. 1997. pap. 29.95 (*0-7643-0042-3*) Schiffer.

More Royal Ruby. Philip Hopper. (Illus.). 128p. 1999. pap. 24.95 (*0-7643-0870-X*) Schiffer.

More Roycroft Art Metal. Kevin McConnell. LC 95-69727. (Illus.). 160p. (Orig.). 1995. pap. 19.95 (*0-88740-848-6*) Schiffer.

More Rules of Neighborhood Poker According to Hoyle. Stewart Wolpin. 2000. pap. text 6.95 (*0-942257-36-7*) New Chapter Pr.

More San Francisco Memoirs, 1852-1899: The Ripening Years. Compiled & Intro. by Malcolm E. Barker. (Illus.). 320p. (Orig.). 1996. pap. 16.95 (*0-930235-05-3*) Londonborn Pubns.

More Santa Carving with Tom Wolfe. Tom James Wolfe. LC 98-85792. 64p. 1998. pap. 14.95 (*0-7643-0626-X*) Schiffer.

More Saskatchewan Gold. Ed. by Geoffrey Ursell. 425p. 1984. mass mkt. 5.95 (*0-919926-38-X*, Pub. by Coteau) Genl Dist Srvs.

More Scary Stories to Tell in the Dark. Illus. by Stephen Gammell. LC 83-49494. (Trophy Bk.). 112p. (J). (gr. 4-7). 1986. pap. 4.95 (*0-06-440177-4*, HarpTrophy) HarpC Child Bks.

More Scary Stories to Tell in the Dark. Illus. by Stephen Gammell. 80p. (J). (gr. 4-6). pap. 4.95 (*0-8072-1424-8*) Listening Lib.

More Scary Stories to Tell in the Dark. Alvin Schwartz. (J). 1986. 10.15 (*0-606-03252-5*, Pub. by Turtleback) Demco.

More Scary Stories to Tell in the Dark: Collected & Retold from Folklore. Alvin Schwartz. LC 83-49494. (Illus.). 112p. (J). (gr. 4-7). 1984. 14.95 (*0-397-32081-7*); lib. bdg. 14.89 (*0-397-32082-5*) HarpC Child Bks.

More Scary Stories to Tell in the Dark Audio. abr. ed. Alvin Schwartz & Stephen Gammell. (J). (gr. 3-7). 1990. audio 11.95 (*1-55994-284-3*, CPN 1869) HarperAudio.

More Scary Story Starters: Write Your Own Scary Stories! Julie Koerner. (Scary Story Starters Ser.). 64p. (J). 1997. pap. 5.95 (*1-56565-766-7*, 07667W, Pub. by Lowell Hse) NTC Contemp Pub Co.

***More Scenes from Shakespeare: Twenty Cuttings for Acting & Directing Practice.** William Shakespeare. LC 98-55478. 144p. 1999. pap. 12.95 (*1-56608-050-9*) Meriwether Pub.

More Scenes That Happen: Real-Life Snapshots of Teenage Lives. Mary Krell-Oishi. Ed. by Theodore O. Zapel. LC 93-40926. 208p. (Orig.). (YA). (gr. 9-12). 1994. pap. text 12.95 (*1-56608-000-2*, B112) Meriwether Pub.

More Science Activities. Megan Stine et al. Ed. by Cheryl Solimini. (Science Activity Book Ser.). (Illus.). 100p. (J). (gr. 2-6). 1988. pap. text 8.95 (*0-939456-16-8*) Galison.

More Science Experiments on File. Ed. by Facts on File Staff. (Illus.). 288p. (J). (gr. 4-12). 1990. ring bd. 165.00 (*0-8160-2196-1*) Facts on File.

More Science Experiments You Can Eat. Vicki Cobb. LC 78-12732. (Trophy Nonfiction Bk.). (Illus.). 128p. (J). (gr. 5-9). 1984. pap. 4.95 (*0-06-446003-7*, HarpTrophy) HarpC Child Bks.

More Science Experiments You Can Eat. Vicki Cobb. 1979. 10.05 (*0-606-07040-0*, Pub. by Turtleback) Demco.

More Science for You: One Hundred Twelve Illustrated Experiments. Bob Brown. (Illus.). 128p. (J). (ps-8). 1988. 12.95 (*0-8306-9125-1*, 3125); pap. 7.95 (*0-8306-3125-9*, 3125) McGraw-Hill Prof.

More Science Surprises from Dr. Zed. Gordon Penrose. (Illus.). 32p. (J). (gr. 3-9). 1996. pap. 8.95 (*0-920775-70-5*, Pub. by Greey dePencier) Firefly Bks Ltd.

More Science Teasers. Dilip M. Salwi. (Illus.). xiv, 122p. 1989. text 17.95 (*81-220-0141-6*, Pub. by Konark Pubs Pvt Ltd) Advent Bks Div.

More Science Through Children's Literature: An Integrated Approach. Carol M. Butzow & John W. Butzow. LC 98-2734. (Illus.). 250p. (J). (gr. k-3). 1998. pap. 26.00 (*1-56308-266-7*) Libs Unl.

More Scott Operas: Further Analysis of Operas Based on the Works of Sir Walter Scott. Jerome Mitchell. 348p. (C). 1996. lib. bdg. 44.00 (*0-7618-0260-6*) U Pr of Amer.

More Scrimshaw Artists. Stuart M. Frank. (Illus.). xiii, 189p. 1998. 45.00 (*0-913372-82-X*) Mystic Seaport.

More Scrimshaw Artists. deluxe ed. Stuart M. Frank. (Illus.). 1998. 125.00 (*0-937854-07-7*) Kendall Whaling.

More Second Thoughts. John W. Hartman. LC 95-60252. 1995. pap. 9.95 (*1-885884-01-X*, M Wheeler Pr) Cormorant Pr.

More Secrets: More Inside Information. Boardroom's Experts & Editors Staff. 352p. 1994. 59.00 (*0-88723-087-3*) Boardroom.

More Secrets of America's Best Bass Pros, Vol. II. Tim Tucker & Bill Dance. 1992. pap. 12.95 (*0-937866-26-1*) Atlantic Pub Co.

More Secrets of Happy Children. Steve Biddulph. 1999. pap. 11.95 (*0-207-18941-2*) HarpC.

More Secrets of Hebrew Words: Holy Days & Happy Days. Benjamin Blech. LC 93-14636. 232p. 1993. 30.00 (*0-87668-223-9*) Aronson.

More Secrets of Small Business Success. rev. ed. Malcolm Newell. 126p. 1995. pap. 14.95 (*0-949142-01-8*, Pub. by Stirling Pr) Intl Spec Bk.

More Secrets of the Flute: More of the Physics, Math, & Design of Non-Mechanical Folk Flutes. Lew P. Price. (Illus.). 66p. (C). 1997. pap. 15.00 (*0-917578-17-1*) L Paxton Price.

***More Seeing Is Believing: Dramatic Evidence of a Creator-God.** Mark Finley & Steven R. Mosley. LC 99-55542. 1999. pap. 1.99 (*0-8163-1770-4*) Pacific Pr Pub Assn.

More Selected Verse of Robert Service. Robert W. Service. 22.95 (*0-89190-927-3*) Amereon Ltd.

More Self-Working Card Tricks: 88 Fool-Proof Card Miracles for the Amateur Magician. Karl Fulves. (Magic, Legerdemain Ser.). (Illus.). 96p. (Orig.). (YA). (gr. 6 up). 1984. pap. 5.95 (*0-486-24580-2*) Dover.

More Semantically Speaking. Krassowski. 1992. 59.00 (*0-7616-7767-4*) Commun Skill.

More Sermon Outlines for Special Occasions. Al Bryant. LC 95-7832. (Sermon Outlines Ser.). 64p. 1995. pap. 4.99 (*0-8254-2268-X*) Kregel.

More Sermon Outlines on Prayer. Al Bryant. (Sermon Outline Ser.). 64p. 1995. pap. 4.99 (*0-8254-2190-X*) Kregel.

More Sermon Outlines on Special Days & Occasions. Charles R. Wood. LC 90-38561. (Easy-to-Use Sermon Outline Ser.). 64p. 1990. pap. 4.99 (*0-8254-3987-6*) Kregel.

More Sermons That Work: Prize Winning Sermons 1992 with Addresses & Sermons from a Conference for Preachers. Pref. by Roger Alling, Jr. 142p. (Orig.). 1992. pap. 4.00 (*0-88028-135-9*, 1186) Forward Movement.

More Sewing for the Home, Vol. 9. Cy DeCosse Incorporated Staff. LC 87-24556. (Singer Sewing Reference Library). (Illus.). 128p. 1987. 18.95 (*0-86573-235-3*); pap. 16.95 (*0-86573-236-1*) Creat Pub Intl.

More Sewing Machine Fun. Lynda S. Milligan & Nancy J. Smith. Ed. by Sharon Holmes. (I'll Teach Myself Ser.). (Illus.). 72p. (J). (gr. 2-8). 1993. spiral bd. 15.95 (*1-880972-05-0*) Pssblts Denver.

More Shapes Than One. Fred Chappell. 208p. 1992. pap. 8.95 (*0-312-08265-7*) St Martin.

More Short & Shivery. Robert D. San Souci. (J). 1995. 17.95 (*0-385-30986-4*) Doubleday.

An Asterisk (*) at the beginning of an entry indicates that the title is appearing for the first time.

More Short & Shivery: Thirty Terrifying Tales. Robert D. San Souci. (Illus.). 176p. (J). (gr. 3-7). 1996. pap. 10.95 (*0-385-32250-X*, Delacorte Pr Bks) BDD Bks Young Read.

More "Short Sixes" Henry C. Bunner. 1972. reprint ed. lib. bdg. 21.50 (*0-8422-8015-4*) Irvington.

More Short Stories for Long Rainy Days: Simple Tales of Life & Love. Katherine Anne Douglas. 224p. 1999. 12.99 (*1-57748-572-6*) Barbour Pub.

More Short Trips. British Broadcasting Company Staff. 1999. mass mkt. 5.95 (*0-563-55565-3*, Pub. by BBC Bks) Genl Dist Srvs.

More Short Vowel Syllables: Brown Sequence Level 11. Ellis Richardson & Barbara DiBenedetto. (Linguistic Pattern Ser.). (Illus.). 64p. (J). 1997. pap. text 90.00 (*1-56775-083-4*) ISM Teach Systs.

More Shotguns & Shooting. Michael McIntosh. LC 98-43589. (Illus.). 272p. 1998. 30.00 (*0-924357-75-4*) Countrysport Pr.

***More Shotguns & Shooting.** limited ed. Michael McIntosh. (Illus.). 272p. 1999. write for info. (*0-924357-76-2*) Countrysport Pr.

More Sideways Arithmetic from Wayside School. Louis Sachar. 112p. (J). (gr. 4-7). 1994. pap. 3.50 (*0-590-47762-5*) Scholastic Inc.

More Sideways Arithmetic from Wayside School. Louis Sachar. 1994. 9.09 (*0-606-06581-4*, Pub. by Turtleback) Demco.

More Sidrah Sparks: Weekly Torah Lessons & Questions. Dov P. Elkins. 112p. 1999. pap. 45.00 (*0-918834-18-X*) Growth Assoc.

More Silhouettes: Eight Hundred Sixty-Eight Copyright-Free Copy Illustrations for Artists & Craftsmen. Ed. by Carol B. Grafton. (Illus.). 112p. (C). 1982. pap. 6.95 (*0-486-24256-0*) Dover.

***More Silly Songs: Twenty More Simply Super Singable Silly Songs.** Prod. by Walt Disney Records Staff. (J). 1998. pap. 12.98 incl. audio compact disk (*0-7634-0437-3*) W Disney Records.

More Silver Wings, Pinks & Greens: An Expanded Study of USAS, USAAC, & USAAF Uniforms, Wings & Insignia, 1913-1945 Including Civilian Auxiliaries. Jon A. Maguire. LC 96-67626. (Illus.). 392p. 1996. 79.95 (*0-7643-0091-1*) Schiffer.

More Simple Dishes. Rochester Folk Art Guild Staff. 1977. 4.50 (*0-686-21777-2*) Rochester Folk Art.

More Simple Signs. Cindy Wheeler. LC 97-26797. (Illus.). 32p. (J). 1998. 14.99 (*0-670-87477-9*) Viking Penguin.

More Simplified Magic: Pathworking & the Tree of Life. rev. ed. Ted Andrews. Ed. by Pagyn Alexander-Harding. LC 96-71460. Orig. Title: Imagick - Qabalistic Pathworking for Imaginative Magicians. (Illus.). 450p. 1997. pap. 14.95 (*1-888767-28-6*) Dragonhawk Pubg.

More Single Shot Rifles. James L. Grant. (Illus.). 35.00 (*0-88227-006-0*) Gun Room.

***More Sketches: Carmel to Orcas Island.** Barbara M. Meyer. 100p. 1999. pap. 24.95 (*1-888345-17-9*) Paper Jam.

More Skits That Win. Ruth Vaughn. 1977. pap. 3.25 (*0-310-33671-6*, 10942P) Zondervan.

More Slices of Orange. Ed. by Nancy B. Rayl. 89p. 1996. pap. 14.00 (*1-888574-01-1*) Lightning.

More Smart Choices for Preteen Kids: 20 No Miss Lessons on Family, Friends & School. Ed. by Jim Hawley. LC 98-33173. (Illus.). 112p. (J). 1998. per. 16.99 (*0-7644-2110-7*, Vital Ministry) Group Pub.

More Smurf Collectibles: An Unauthorized Handbook & Price Guide. Jan Lindenberger. LC 97-80131. (Illus.). 144p. 1998. pap. 19.95 (*0-7643-0408-9*) Schiffer.

***More Snippet Sensations.** Cindy Walter. LC 99-69494. (Illus.). 112p. 2000. pap. 19.95 (*0-87341-915-4*, SNIP2) Krause Pubns.

More Snoopy Collectibles: An Unauthorized Guide with Values. Jan Lindenberger & Cher Porges. LC 97-65475. (Schiffer Book for Collectors Ser.). (Illus.). 176p. 1997. pap. 29.95 (*0-7643-0283-3*) Schiffer.

***More Snoopy Collectibles, An Unauthorized Guide with Values.** 2nd rev. ed. Jan Lindenberger & Cher Porges. (Illus.). 176p. 1999. pap. 29.95 (*0-7643-0881-5*) Schiffer.

More So Fat, Low Fat, No Fat: Recipes for Family & Friends that Cut the Fat but Not the Flavor! Betty Rohde. 256p. 1996. per. 12.00 (*0-684-81574-5*, Fireside) S&S Trade Pap.

More Social Skills Stories. Anne M. Johnson. (Illus.). 352p. (J). (gr. 3-12). 1996. spiral bd. 29.00 (*1-884135-30-7*) Mayer-Johnson.

***More Social Studies Through Children's Literature: Integrated Approach.** Anthony D. Fredericks. LC 99-41002. 275p. (J). 2000. pap. 27.50 (*1-56308-761-8*) Libs Unl.

More Solder Magic: In Your Wildest Imagination. Kay B. Weiner. (Illus.). 64p. 1992. pap. text 15.95 (*0-9625663-4-9*) Eastman Pub.

More Soldiers of Colonial America. Ed. by Alan Quincannon. (Learning & Coloring Bks.). (Illus.). 24p. (YA). (gr. k up). 1992. pap. 3.95 (*1-878452-12-6*, Tory Corner) Quincannon.

***More Solid Learning: New Perspectives on Alexander Pope's Dunciad.** Catherine Ingrassia & Claudia N. Thomas. LC 99-59167. 256p. 2000. 42.50 (*0-8387-5443-0*) Bucknell U Pr.

More Solo Readings. Sonya Fogle & Marjorie Seligman. 1944. pap. 5.25 (*0-8222-0775-3*) Dramatists Play.

More Songs about Food Vats. (Paranoia Ser.). 6.00 (*0-87431-151-9*, 12013) West End Games.

More Songs & Ballads of Ireland. Ed. & Selected by John Loesberg. pap. 7.95 (*0-946005-54-0*, OS 00077, Pub. by Ossian) Music Sales.

More Songs for Harmonica. William Bay. 32p. 1990. pap. 5.95 (*1-56222-000-4*, 94426) Mel Bay.

More Songs from the Plains. Elizabeth B. Lewis. 26p. 1990. pap. 3.50 (*0-614-24769-1*) Tesseract SD.

More Songs of the 80's, No. 373. (Decade Ser.). 192p. 1994. otabind 12.95 (*0-7935-3104-7*, 00102298) H Leonard.

More Songs of the Eighties: Piano, Vocal, Guitar. (Decade Ser.). 224p. (Orig.). 1994. per. 14.95 (*0-7935-3097-0*, HL00311653) H Leonard.

More Songs of the Fifties, No. 370. (Decade Ser.). 144p. 1994. per. 12.95 (*0-7935-3101-2*, 00102295) H Leonard.

More Songs of The 50's: Piano, Vocal, Guitar. (Decade Ser.). 192p. (Orig.). (YA). 1994. per. 20.95 (*0-7935-3094-6*, 00311650) H Leonard.

More Songs of the 40's, No. 369. (Decade Ser.). 160p. 1994. per. 12.95 (*0-7935-3100-4*, 00102294) H Leonard.

More Songs of the Forties: Piano, Vocal, Guitar. (Decade Ser.). 224p. (Orig.). 1994. per. 14.95 (*0-7935-3093-8*, HL00311649) H Leonard.

***More Songs of the Nineties: 295.** 200p. 1998. otabind 14.95 (*0-7935-9802-8*) H Leonard.

More Songs of the Seventies. (The Decade Ser.). 224p. 1994. per. 14.95 (*0-7935-3096-2*, HL00311652) H Leonard.

More Songs of the Seventies, No. 372. (Decade Ser.). 192p. 1994. otabind 12.95 (*0-7935-3103-9*, 00102297) H Leonard.

More Songs of the 60's, No. 371. (Decade Ser.). 192p. 1994. per. 12.95 (*0-7935-3102-0*, 00102296) H Leonard.

More Songs of the Sixties: Piano, Vocal, Guitar. (Decade Ser.). 224p. (Orig.). 1994. otabind 14.95 (*0-7935-3095-4*, HL00311651) H Leonard.

More Songs of the 30's, No. 368. (Decade Ser.). 152p. 1994. per. 12.95 (*0-7935-3099-7*, 00102293) H Leonard.

More Songs of the Thirties: Piano, Vocal, Guitar. (Decade Ser.). 224p. (Orig.). 1994. per. 14.95 (*0-7935-3092-X*, HL00311648) H Leonard.

More Songs of the 20's, No. 367. (Decade Ser.). 144p. 1994. per. 12.95 (*0-7935-3098-9*, 00102292) H Leonard.

More Songs of the Twenties: Piano, Vocal, Guitar. (Decade Ser.). 192p. (Orig.). 1994. per. 14.95 (*0-7935-3091-1*, HL00311647) H Leonard.

More Songs of Vagabondia (with Bliss Carman) Richard Hovey. (Notable American Authors Ser.). 1992. reprint ed. lib. bdg. 75.00 (*0-7812-3193-0*) Rprt Serv.

More Songs to Grow On. 1984. 12.50 (*0-88188-309-3*, 00008632) H Leonard.

More Songwriting & Composing Techniques: Making Something Out of Nothing. Peter L. Alexander. (Illus.). 147p. (C). 1988. pap. text 19.95 (*0-939067-80-3*) Alexander Pub.

More Sonnets by Oldknow see Cow-in-a-Green-Field Charm

More Sounds to Say. (Key Words Readers Ser.: Series S705, No. 5). (Illus.). (J). (ps-5). student ed. 1.95 (*0-317-04020-0*, Ladybrd) Penguin Putnam.

More Sounds to Say. W. Murray. (Key Words Readers Ser.: C Series, No. 641-5c). (Illus.). (J). (ps-5). pap. 3.50 (*0-7214-0029-9*, Ladybrd) Penguin Putnam.

More Southern Oregon Cross Country Ski Trails. John W. Lund. (Illus.). 138p. (Orig.). (C). 1990. pap. 8.95 (*0-9619389-2-7*) J W Lund.

More Sower's Seeds: Second Planting. rev. ed. Ed. by Brian Cavanaugh. LC 92-12675. 128p. 1992. pap. 7.95 (*0-8091-3324-5*) Paulist Pr.

***More Soy of Cooking: Healthful Renditions of Classic Traditional Meals.** Marie Oser. 304p. 2000. pap. 16.95 (*0-471-37761-9*) Wiley.

More Space: PKZip & Other Compression Utilities for Your PC. Thomas M. Gardner. 272p. 1997. pap. 15.95 incl. disk (*0-646-27536-4*) Helion Audio.

More Spaghetti, I Say! Rita G. Gelman. (J). 1993. 8.15 (*0-606-03621-0*, Pub. by Turtleback) Demco.

More Spaghetti, I Say! Rita Golden Gelman. LC 91-43181. (Hello Reader! Ser.). (Illus.). 30p. (J). (gr. k-2). 1993. pap. 2.95 (*0-590-45783-7*) Scholastic Inc.

More Spaghetti, I Say. large type ed. Rita G. Gelman. 32p. (J). (ps-3). 1989. 19.95 (*0-590-71439-2*) Scholastic Inc.

More Speech: Dialogue Rights & Modern Liberty. Paul Chevigny. LC 87-10075. (C). 1987. 32.95 (*0-87722-514-1*) Temple U Pr.

More Speech Improvement. Phyllis R. Weiss. 32p. 1990. pap. text 39.50 (*0-88432-268-8*, 523725) Audio-Forum.

More Speech, Not Less: Communications Law in the Information Age. Mark Sableman. LC 96-53449. 272p. 1997. pap. 19.95 (*0-8093-2135-1*) S Ill U Pr.

More Speech Sound Trivia: Articulation Practice for -ch-, -j-, -l-, -r-, & -sh- Karen D. Vargo & Susan A. Dorsch. 41p. 1990. 54.50 (*0-7616-7611-2*) Commun Skill.

More Speedwell Families. Joyce E. Davis. (Illus.). 616p. 1988. 37.50 (*0-89308-630-4*, TN 112) Southern Hist Pr.

***More Spice Than Sugar: Poems about Feisty Females.** Lillian Morrison & Ann Boyajian. LC 00-31947. 2001. write for info. (*0-618-06892-9*) HM.

More Splash Than Cash Decorating Ideas. Donna Babylon. (Illus.). 222p. 1999. pap. 15.95 (*0-9668227-0-6*) Windsor Oak Pubg.

More Stage Dialects. Jerry Blunt. 140p. 1996. pap. 19.95 (*0-87129-603-9*, M92) Dramatic Pub.

More Stage Favorites of the 18th Century. Lewis S. Benjamin. (Essay Index Reprint Ser.). 1977. 19.95 (*0-8369-0194-0*) Ayer.

More Star Tales. Gretchen W. Mayo. (North American Indian Tales Ser.). (J). 1990. 11.15 (*0-606-04751-4*, Pub. by Turtleback) Demco.

More Stately Mansions. abr. ed. Eugene O'Neill. Ed. by Donald Gallup. (Illus.). (Orig.). 1964. pap. 11.00 (*0-300-00177-0*, Y101) Yale U Pr.

More Steamboat Simmers. 6.50 (*0-943768-07-1*) C Coleman.

More Steps to Heaven. Bernice Lum. (Illus.). 28p. 1993. 6.00 (*1-872819-06-0*, Pub. by Tuppy Owens) AK Pr Dist.

More Steve Allen on the Bible, Religion & Morality, Bk. II. Steve Allen. LC 92-41364. 452p. 1993. 27.95 (*0-87975-736-1*) Prometheus Bks.

More Stitches for Effects. Suzanne Howren & Beth Robertson. (Illus.). 79p. 1997. pap. 28.00 (*0-9663024-1-9*) Shear Creat.

***More Stories & Songs of Jesus Activity Book.** 2nd ed. Paule Freeburg. (Illus.). 54p. 1999. pap. 1.50 (*1-57992-068-3*) OR Catholic.

More Stories for Around the Campfire. Ray Harriot. (J). (gr. 3-10). 1998. pap. text 7.95 (*0-9617653-1-3*) Campfire Pub.

***More Stories for Our Children.** Byron Douglas. LC 98-40578. 1998. write for info. (*0-910683-36-0*) Townsnd-Pr.

More Stories for the Heart: Over 100 Stories to Warm Your Heart. Compiled by Alice Gray. LC 97-3234. (Stories for the Heart Ser.). 300p. 1997. pap. 11.99 (*1-57673-142-1*, Multnomah Bks) Multnomah Pubs.

***More Stories from Grandma's Attic.** Arleta Richardson. (Grandma's Attic Ser.). (Illus.). (J). 1999. pap. 5.99 (*0-7814-3269-3*) Chariot Victor.

More Stories from Grandpa's Rocking Chair. Sarah Kaetler. (Illus.). 73p. (J). (gr. 3-6). 1991. pap. 4.95 (*0-919797-75-X*) Kindred Prods.

More Stories from Guideposts. Guideposts Staff & Robert T. Teske. 320p. 1991. pap. 9.99 (*0-8423-4560-4*) Tyndale Hse.

More Stories from Magnolia Street. Angela Johnson. (J). 1999. lib. bdg. 17.99 (*0-679-99077-1*, Pub. by Random Bks Yng Read) Random.

***More Stories from Magnolia Street.** Angela Johnson. (J). 1999. 16.00 (*0-679-89077-7*, Pub. by Random Bks Yng Read) Random.

***More Stories from My Father's Court.** Isaac Bashevis Singer. Tr. by Curt Leviant from YID. 240p. 2000. 23.00 (*0-374-21343-7*) FS&G.

More Stories from the Great Irish Writers John McCarthy. LC 96-151875. 160p. 1994. write for info. (*1-85635-085-1*) I B T.

More Stories from Westport's Past. Joanna Foster. (Illus.). 40p. (Orig.). 1986. pap. 8.95 (*0-9615410-1-6*) Stories Westports Past.

More Stories Huey Tells. Ann Cameron. LC 96-18420. (Illus.). 128p. (J). (gr. 3-5). 1997. 13.00 (*0-374-35065-5*) FS&G.

More Stories Huey Tells. Ann Cameron. LC 98-26989. (J). 1999. pap. 4.99 (*0-679-88363-0*) Knopf.

More Stories Huey Tells. Ann Cameron. (J). 1998. pap. 4.99 (*0-679-88576-5*, Pub. by Knopf Bks Yng Read) Random.

More Stories Julian Tells. Ann Cameron. (J). 1986. 10.09 (*0-606-04278-4*, Pub. by Turtleback) Demco.

More Stories Julian Tells. Ann Cameron. LC 84-10095. (Illus.). 96p. (J). (gr. k-3). 1989. reprint ed. pap. 4.99 (*0-394-82454-7*, Pub. by Knopf Bks Yng Read) Random.

More Stories of Composers for Young Musicians. large type ed. Catherine W. Kendall. LC 83-103936. (Illus.). 340p. (Orig.). (J). (gr. 1-12). 1988. pap. 16.25 (*0-9610878-1-1*) Toadwood Pubs.

More Stories of Lake George: Fact & Fancy. Thomas R. Lord. 218p. 1994. pap. 21.75 (*0-9640267-0-8*) Pinelands Pr.

More Stories of Married Life. Mary S. Cutting. LC 75-37264. (Short Story Index Reprint Ser.). 1977. reprint ed. 19.95 (*0-8369-4075-X*) Ayer.

More Stories of the Old Duck Hunters, Vol. 2. Gordon M. Quarrie. Ed. by Zack Taylor. (Illus.). 198p. 1994. 19.50 (*1-57223-004-5*, 1509) Willow Creek Pr.

More Stories of the Old Duck Hunters Audio, Vol. 2. abr. ed. Gordon MacQuarrie. (Gordon MacQuarrie Trilogy Ser.). 1994. 16.95 incl. audio (*1-57223-015-0*, 0150) Willow Creek Pr.

More Stories to Solve. George Shannon. (J). 1994. pap. 4.95 (*0-380-73261-0*) Morrow Avon.

More Stories to Solve: Fifteen Folktales from Around the World. George Shannon. LC 93-11719. 1994. 10.85 (*0-606-06582-2*, Pub. by Turtleback) Demco.

More Stories to Solve: Fifteen Folktales from Around the World. George Shannon. LC 93-11719. (Illus.). 64p. (J). (gr. 4 up). 1994. reprint ed. mass mkt. 4.95 (*0-688-12947-1*, Wm Morrow) Morrow Avon.

More Stories Worth Reading. Evelyn Witter et al. No. II. (Illus.). (J). 1989. write for info. (*0-318-64958-6*) Printemps Bks.

More Stories Worth Reading. Evelyn Witter et al. (Illus.). 192p. 1990. pap. 7.00 (*0-9621844-1-1*) Printemps Bks.

More Story Stretchers. Shirley C. Raines. 254p. 1991. pap. 19.95 (*0-87659-153-5*) Gryphon Hse.

More Strange Tales from China. P. Sungling. 1998. reprint ed. pap. 9.95 (*981-218-028-1*, Pub. by Select Bks) Weatherhill.

***More Strange Tales from Old Quabbin.** J. R. Greene. (Illus.). 126p. 1999. pap. 11.95 (*1-884132-05-7*) J R Greene.

***More Strawberry Shortcake: An Unauthorized Handbook & Price Guide.** Jan Lindenberger & Jennifer Bowles. LC 98-88721. (Books for Collectors Ser.). 160 p. 1999. write for info. (*0-7643-0762-2*) Schiffer.

More Strip-Pieced Watercolor Magic: New Designs & Techniques for 30 Watercolor Quilts. Deanna Spingola. Ed. by Sally Schneider. LC 96-37091. (Illus.). 108p. (Orig.). 1997. pap. 24.95 (*1-56477-181-4*, B295) Martingale & Co.

More Strong-Minded Women: Iowa Feminists Tell Their Stories. Ed. by Louise R. Noun. LC 92-23124. (Illus.). 317p. reprint ed. pap. 98.30 (*0-608-08904-4*, 206953900004) Bks Demand.

More Structured Workshops for Customer Care. Cook. 264p. 1993. ring bd. 262.95 (*1-85904-005-5*) Ashgate Pub Co.

More Stuff. Patrick McDonnell. LC 98-85338. (Mutts Ser.: Vol. III). (Illus.). 128p. 1998. pap. 9.95 (*0-8362-6823-7*) Andrews & McMeel.

More Stupid Jokes for Kids. Michael Kilgariff. 224p. (Orig.). 1991. mass mkt. 4.50 (*0-345-37061-9*) Ballantine Pub Grp.

More Stupid Jokes for Kids. Michael Kilgarriff. (J). 1991. 9.60 (*0-606-01290-7*, Pub. by Turtleback) Demco.

***More Sublime Chant.** Richard Proulx. 1999. 15.95 (*5-550-71988-6*); pap. 10.95 (*5-550-71992-4*) Nairi.

More Sunshine on the Soapsuds. Beneth P. Jones. 110p. (Orig.). 1983. pap. 5.95 (*0-89084-192-6*, 020636) Bob Jones Univ.

More Surprises. Burton Goodman. 144p. (J). (gr. 4). 1990. pap. 11.97 (*0-89061-676-0*, Jamestwn Pub) NTC Contemp Pub Co.

More Surprises. Ed. by Lee B. Hopkins. LC 86-45335. (I Can Read Bks.). (Illus.). 64p. (J). (ps-3). 1987. lib. bdg. 13.89 (*0-06-022605-6*) HarpC Child Bks.

More Surprises in Theoretical Physics. Rudolph Peierls. (Physics Ser.). 115p. 1991. text 39.50 (*0-691-08576-5*, Pub. by Princeton U Pr) Cal Prin Full Svc.

More Surrey Tales. Matthew Alexander. 96p. 1987. 40.00 (*0-905392-61-2*) St Mut.

More Swahili Proverbs from East Africa. Leonard Kalugila & Abdulaztz Y. Lodhi. 107p. 1980. write for info. (*91-7106-172-X*, Pub. by Nordic Africa) Transaction Pubs.

***More Swamp Cookin' with the River People.** Dana Holyfield. (Illus.). 128p. 2000. pap. 17.95 (*1-58008-203-3*) Ten Speed Pr.

More Sweaters: A Riot of Color, Pattern & Form. Lise Kolstad & Tone Takle. (Illus.). 144p. 1994. pap. 19.95 (*0-934026-99-8*) Interweave.

More Sweatshirts with Style. Mary Mulari. LC 96-20440. (Illus.). 160p. 1996. pap. 19.95 (*0-8019-8759-8*) Krause Pubns.

More Tales Alive in Turkey. Walker & Ahmet E. Uysal. x, 326p. (C). 1992. pap. 17.50 (*0-89672-286-4*) Tex Tech Univ Pr.

More Tales for the Midnight Hour. Judith B. Stamper. (J). (gr. 5-7). 1987. pap. 2.75 (*0-590-43998-7*) Scholastic Inc.

More Tales for the Midnight Hour. Judith B. Stamper. 128p. (J). (gr. 7-9). 1992. pap. 2.95 (*0-590-45344-0*, Point) Scholastic Inc.

More Tales for the Midnight Hour: 13 Stories of Horror. J. B. Stamper. (Point Ser.). (J). 1987. 8.05 (*0-606-03622-9*, Pub. by Turtleback) Demco.

***More Tales from Shakespeare.** Lv. 5. (C). 2000. 7.00 (*0-582-41934-4*) Addison-Wesley.

More Tales from Shakespeare. Longman Publishing Group, Staff. 1997. pap. write for info. (*0-582-27510-5*) Addison-Wesley.

More Tales from Slim Ellison. Glenn R. Ellison. LC 80-27498. (Illus.). 205p. 1981. reprint ed. pap. 63.60 (*0-7837-9232-8*, 204998300004) Bks Demand.

More Tales from the Ark. Arril Rowlands. (Illus.). 160p. (Orig.). (J). (gr. 3-5). 1995. pap. 4.99 (*0-7459-3035-2*) Lion USA.

More Tales of a Low-Rent Birder. Pete Dunne. LC 93-47657. (Illus.). 125p. (C). 1994. 18.95 (*0-292-71572-2*) U of Tex Pr.

More Tales of Amanda Pig. Jean Van Leeuwen. (Illus.). (J). (gr. k-3). 1995. pap. 3.99 (*0-14-037603-8*, PuffinBks) Peng Put Young Read.

More Tales of Amanda Pig. Jean Van Leeuwen. (Puffin Easy-To-Read. Level 2 Ser.). (J). 1995. 8.70 (*0-606-07888-6*, Pub. by Turtleback) Demco.

More Tales of Oliver Pig. Jean Van Leeuwen. LC 80-23289. (Easy-to-Read Bks.). (Illus.). (J). (ps-3). 1993. pap. 3.99 (*0-14-036554-0*, PuffinBks) Peng Put Young Read.

More Tales of the City. Armistead Maupin. LC 92-52596. (Tales of the City Ser.). 320p. 1992. 11.00 (*0-685-60778-X*, Perennial) HarperTrade.

More Tales of the City TV Tie In. Armistead Maupin. LC 79-1710. Vol. 2. (Illus.). 352p. 1998. pap. 13.00 (*0-06-092938-3*, Perennial) HarperTrade.

More Tales of the Defective Detective. Ed. by Gary Hoppenstand et al. LC 85-73561. 172p. 1986. 20.95 (*0-87972-335-1*); pap. 10.95 (*0-87972-336-X*) Bowling Green Univ Popular Press.

More Tales of the South Carolina Low Country. Nancy Rhyne. LC 84-21710. 121p. 1984. pap. 6.95 (*0-89587-042-8*) Blair.

More Tales of Uncle Remus: Further Adventures of Brer Rabbit, His Friends, Enemies & Others. Illus. by Jerry Pinkney. LC 86-32890. 160p. (J). (gr. 2 up). 1988. 18.99 (*0-8037-0419-4*, Dial Yng Read) Peng Put Young Read.

More Tales to Give You Goosebumps. R. L. Stine, pseud. LC 49-251310. (Goosebumps Special Edition Ser.: No. 2). (Illus.). 144p. (J). (gr. 3-7). 1997. pap. text 3.99 (*0-590-26602-0*) Scholastic Inc.

More Tales to Give You Goosebumps. R. L. Stine, pseud. (Goosebumps Special Edition Ser.: No. 2). 1995. 9.09 (*0-606-11640-0*, Pub. by Turtleback) Demco.

More Tales to Give You Goosebumps: Book & Light Set. R. L. Stine, pseud. (Goosebumps Special Edition Ser.: No. 2). 144p. (J). (gr. 4-6). 1995. pap. 11.95 (*0-590-26603-9*) Scholastic Inc.

More Talking of Shakespeare. Ed. by John Garrett. LC 73-128887. (Select Bibliographies Reprint Ser.). 1977. 18.95 (*0-8369-5507-2*) Ayer.

More Talks for Children. Compiled by Ian MacLeod. 128p. (C). 1992. pap. 39.00 (*0-7855-6836-0*, Pub. by St Andrew) St Mut.

More Talks for Children. Compiled by Ian MacLeod. 128p. 1993. pap. 24.00 (0-7152-0657-5, Pub. by St Andrew) St Mut.

***More Taste Berries for Teens: Inspirational Short Stories & Encouragement on Life, Love, Friends.** Bettie B. Youngs. (YA). 2000. pap. 12.95 (1-55874-813-X) Health Comm.

More Taste Than Time. Annie Bell. 192p. 1997. pap. 22.95 (0-09-180677-1, Pub. by Ebury Pr) Trafalgar.

More Tastes & Tales from Texas. Peg Hein. 1987. pap. 12.95 (0-9613881-1-0) Hein & Assocs.

More Tea at Miss Cranston's. Anna Blair. (Illus.). 240p. 1985. pap. 8.95 (0-85683-127-1, Pub. by Shepheard-Walwyn Pubs) Paul & Co Pubs.

More Teachers' Favorite Books for Kids: Teachers' Choices, 1994-1996. IRA Staff. LC 97-217433. (Illus.). 104p. (J). 1997. pap. 10.95 (0-87207-179-0, 179) Intl Reading.

More Teachers' Favorite Books for Kids: Teachers', Choices, 1994-1996. International Reading Association Staff. LC 97-217433. (Illus.). 92p. Date not set. reprint ed. pap. 30.00 (0-608-20631-8, 207206700003) Bks Demand.

More Teaching Kids to Love the Earth. Marina Lachecki & James Kasperson. (Illus.). 192p. (Orig.). (YA). 1994. pap. 14.95 (1-57025-040-5) Pfeifer-Hamilton.

M

More Team Building Challenges. Daniel W. Midura & Donald R. Glover. LC 95-8965. (Illus.). 120p. (Orig.). 1995. pap. text 14.95 (0-87322-785-9, BMID0785) Human Kinetics.

More Team Games for Trainers. Carolyn Nilson. LC 97-41224. (Illus.). 283p. 1997. pap. 27.95 (0-07-046590-8) McGraw.

More Techniques of Beading Earrings. Deon DeLange. Ed. by Monte Smith. LC 83-82121. (Illus.). 68p. 1985. pap., per. 9.95 (0-943604-12-5, BOO/04) Eagles View.

More Techno Sex. Ed. by Cecilia Tan. (Illus.). 192p. 2000. pap. 14.95 (1-885865-20-1) Circlet Pr.

More Tell & Draw Stories. Margaret J. Oldfield. (Illus.). (J). (ps-3). 1969. pap. 6.95 (0-934876-02-9); lib. bdg. 11.95 (0-934876-06-1) Creative Storytime.

More Telling Stories, Compelling Stories. William J. Bausch. LC 92-60889. 200p. (Orig.). 1993. pap. 9.95 (0-89622-534-8) Twenty-Third.

More 10-Minute Devotions for Youth Groups: 52 Quick New Devotions to Involve Teenagers. (Illus.). 96p. 1992. pap. 14.99 (1-55945-068-1) Group Pub.

More Terrible Than Victory: North Carolina's Bloody Bethel Regiment, 1861-1865. Craig S. Chapman. LC 97-27207. (Illus.). 368p. 1998. 25.95 (1-57488-129-9) Brasseys.

***More Terrible Than Victory: North Carolina's Bloody Bethel Regiment, 1861-1865.** Craig S. Chapman. (Illus.). 288p. 1999. pap. 16.95 (1-57488-219-8) Brasseys.

More Terrific Tablecloths. Loretta Smith Fehling. (Illus.). 160p. 1999. pap. 29.95 (0-7643-0975-7) Schiffer.

More Test Examples for Nonlinear Programming Codes. K. Schittkowski. (Lecture Notes in Economics & Mathematical Systems Ser.: Vol. 282). v, 261p. 1986. 41.70 (0-387-17182-7) Spr-Verlag.

More Texas Sayings. Anne Dingus. LC 96-16538. (Illus.). 128p. 1996. pap. 9.95 (0-87719-292-8, 9292) Gulf Pub.

More Texture with Textiles. Linda F. McGehee. 52p. 1993. pap. text 14.95 (0-9637160-0-X) Ghees.

More Than a Ball Game: An Inside Look at Minor League Baseball. Sam Lazzaro. LC 97-18355. (Illus.). (Orig.). 1997. pap. 18.95 (0-936015-71-3) Pocahontas Pr.

More Than a Carpenter see Mas Que un Carpintero

More Than a Carpenter see Bien Plus Qu'un Charpentier

More Than a Carpenter. Josh McDowell. 128p. 1977. mass mkt. 4.99 (0-8423-4552-3) Tyndale Hse.

More Than a Carpenter - Evangelism Pack. 1996. pap. 15.97 (0-8423-4548-5) Tyndale Hse.

More Than a Champion: The Style of Muhammad Ali. Jan Philipp Reemtsa. Tr. by John E. Woods. (Vintage Ser.). 192p. 1999. pap. 11.00 (0-375-70005-6) Vin Bks.

More Than a Champion: The Style of Muhammad Ali. Jan P. Reemtsma. Tr. by John E. Woods from GER. LC 97-36675. 172p. 1998. 3.99 (0-375-40030-3) Knopf.

More Than a Conqueror. Grace Livingston Hill. 256p. reprint ed. lib. bdg. 22.95 (0-89190-053-5, Rivercity Pr) Amereon Ltd.

More Than a Conqueror: Winning in the Face of Adversity. Howard Bell. LC 98-133724. 176p. 1997. pap. 10.99 (1-56043-302-7, Treasure Hse) Destiny Image.

More Than a Constructive Hobby: The Paintings of Frank Freed. William A. Camfield & Museum of Fine Arts Staff. LC 96-19437. (Illus.). 108p. (C). 1997. pap. 19.95 (0-89090-073-6) Tex A&M Univ Pr.

More Than a Cookbook. Nelson T. Offutt. LC 79-93281. 192p. 1981. pap., spiral bd. 6.95 (0-89709-019-5) Liberty Pub.

***More... Than a Cookbook.** 3rd rev. ed. Kathleen Botta & Claire Mendonca. 328p. 1998. 24.95 (0-9701111-0-X) More Than A Cookbk.

More Than a Dream. Emma Richmond. (Presents Ser.). 1994. per. 2.99 (0-373-11669-1, 1-11669-8) Harlequin Bks.

More Than a Dream: Eighty-Five Years at the College of St. Catherine. Rosalie Ryan & John C. Wolkerstorfer. LC 92-72011. 168p. 1992. 24.95 (0-9633553-0-9) Coll St Catherine.

More Than a Father: Breaking down the Barriers to Intimacy. Duane Rawlins. 132p. (Orig.). 1993. pap. 7.99 (1-883002-00-1) Emerald WA.

***More Than a Feeling: Worship That Pleases God.** Jimmy Jividen. 142p. (J). (gr. 1-5). 1999. pap. 8.99 (0-89225-381-9) Gospel Advocate.

More Than a Fig Leaf: A Guide for Christian Clothing, Clarification of Women's Clothing, Men's Clothing & the Distinction Between the Two. Edna Nation. 128p. (Orig.). 1986. pap. 5.95 (0-9614669-2-8) Edna Nation.

More Than a Foot in the Door: The Sales Professional's Guide to Winning New Accounts. Dartnell Editors. (Professional Selling Ser.: Vol. 1). 164p. 1995. pap. 13.95 (0-85013-239-8) Dartnell Corp.

More Than a Friend. Elizabeth Winfrey. (Love Stories Ser.). 192p. (Orig.). (YA). (gr. 7-12). 1995. mass mkt. 4.50 (0-553-56666-0) BDD Bks Young Read.

More Than a Game. Mike Gaherty. LC 97-97112. 192p. 1998. 18.95 (0-8034-9273-1, Avalon Bks) Bouregy.

More Than a Game: A New Focus on Senior Activity Services. Brenda Corbett. LC 97-80848. (Illus.). 210p. 1998. 25.95 (0-910251-94-0, MTG99) Venture Pub PA.

More Than a Game: Sports & Politics, 217. Martin B. Vinokur. LC 88-155. (Contributions in Political Science Ser.: No. 217). 169p. 1988. 57.95 (0-313-25353-6, VMT/, Greenwood Pr) Greenwood.

***More Than a Hero: Muhammad Ali's Life Lessons Presented Through His Daughter's Eyes.** Hana Ali. LC 00-27422. (Illus.). 128p. 2000. 15.95 (0-671-04236-X, PB Hardcover) PB.

***More Than a Historian: The Political & Economic Thought of Charles A. Beard.** Clyde W. Barrow. LC 00-37391. 378p. 2000. 39.95 (0-7658-0027-6) Transaction Pubs.

More Than a Horse. C. S. Adler. LC 96-42175. 192p. (J). (gr. 5-9). 1997. 15.00 (0-395-79769-1, Clarion Bks) HM.

More Than a Job: A Curriculum on Work & Society, Reading Level 3 & Above. 1993. 10.00 (0-88336-859-5); teacher ed. 11.95 (0-88336-860-9); 29.95 (0-88336-861-7); audio 16.95 (0-88336-862-5) New Readers.

More Than a Job: Securing Satisfying Careers for People with Disabilities. Paul Wehman & John Kregel. LC 97-53075. 1998. 34.95 (1-55766-328-9) P H Brookes.

More Than a Labour of Love: Three Generations of Women's Work in the Home. Meg Luxton. 260p. pap. 14.95 (0-88961-062-2, Pub. by Womens Pr) LPC InBook.

More Than a Lifetime: Far Away from Home. Sterling McNeil. LC 96-92547. 240p. (Orig.). 1997. pap. 14.95 (0-9654195-0-9) Open Shadow.

More Than a Matter of Trust: Managing the Risks of Mentoring. Leslie T. White et al. LC 99-192524. 59p. 1998. pap. 15.00 (0-9637120-9-8) Nonprof Risk Mgmt Ctr.

More Than a Memory: A Tribute to John Denver. Ann L. Ramsey. (Illus.). 24p. 1997. pap. write for info. (0-9645663-2-X) Crown Peak Pubns.

More Than a Million Menus. Linda Doeser. 1994. 19.98 (0-7858-0134-0) Bk Sales Inc.

More Than a Million Quick & Light Menus. Kerstein Wachtmeister. 1995. 19.98 (0-7858-0455-2) Bk Sales Inc.

More Than a Mirror: How Clients Influence Therapists' Lives. Ed. by Marcia Hill. LC 97-6349. (Women & Therapy Monograph Ser.: Vol. 20, No. 1). 145p. (C). 1997. 24.95 (1-56023-099-1, Harrington Park) Haworth Pr.

***More Than a Mistress.** Mary Balogh. LC 99-462117. 352p. 2000. 16.95 (0-385-33531-8) Delacorte.

***More Than a Mistress.** large type ed. Sandra Marton. 288p. 2000. 25.99 (0-263-16312-1, Pub. by Mills & Boon) Ulverscroft.

More Than a Mistress: The Barons. Sandra Marton. 1999. per. 3.75 (0-373-12045-1, 1-12045-0) Harlequin Bks.

More Than a Momentary Nightmare: The Yokohama Incident & Wartime Japan. Janice Matsumura. LC 99-179200. (Cornell East Asia Ser.: Vol. 92). 172p. (C). 1998. 18.70 (1-885445-52-0); pap. 11.90 (1-885445-92-X) Cornell East Asia Pgm.

More Than a Mother. Curtiss A. Matlock. 1992. per. 4.99 (0-373-48239-6, 5-48239-3) Harlequin Bks.

***More Than a Motorcycle: The Leadership Journey at Harley-Davidson.** Rich Teerlink & Lee Ozley. LC 00-25209. 2000. 24.95 (0-87584-950-4) Harvard Busn.

***More Than a Movie: Ethnical Decision Making in the Entertainment Industry.** Miguel Valenti. 256p. 2000. pap. 25.00 (0-8133-9075-3) Westview.

More Than a Muckraker: Ida Tarbell's Lifetime in Journalism. Ed. & Intro. by Robert C. Kochersberger. (Illus.). 296p. 1996. pap. 19.50 (0-87049-934-3) U of Tenn Pr.

More Than a Mutt. Roger Watson. LC 99-70098. (Illus.). 112p. 1999. pap. 11.95 (1-57197-160-2) Pentland Pr.

***More Than a Name.** Candice F. Ransom. 115p. (J). (gr. 2-5). 1999. reprint ed. text 14.00 (0-7881-6609-3) DIANE Pub.

More Than a Native Speaker. Don Snow. LC 96-60035. 321p. 1996. pap. 29.95 (0-939791-64-1) Tchrs Eng Spkrs.

More Than a Number Book. Selma Hooge. (Illus.). 32p. (J). (ps). 1990. pap. 7.95 (0-919797-95-4) Kindred Prods.

More Than a Pastime: An Oral History of Baseball Fans. William Freedman. LC 98-10297. 263p. 1998. lib. bdg. 29.95 (0-7864-0510-4) McFarland & Co.

More Than a Pastor's Wife: Setting Boundaries, Coping with Frustrations, Defining You Own Role. Lorna Dobson. 176p. 1995. pap. 9.99 (0-310-48551-7) Zondervan.

More Than a Recycling Directory for More Than Atlanta. Wendy Crager. 44p. 1991. pap. text 2.75 (0-9629951-0-X) Atlanta Sierra.

More Than a Report - Celebrations. Despard & Supancich. (More Than a Report Ser.). (Illus.). 80p. (J). (gr. 3-6). 1996. pap., teacher ed. 9.95 (1-55799-574-5, 560) Evan-Moor Edu Pubs.

More Than a Report - Science. Despard & Supancich. (More Than a Report Ser.). (Illus.). 80p. (J). (gr. 3-6). 1996. pap., teacher ed. 9.95 (1-55799-573-7, 559) Evan-Moor Edu Pubs.

More Than a Report - Social Studies. Despard & Supancich. (More Than a Report Ser.). (Illus.). 80p. (J). (gr. 3-6). 1996. pap., teacher ed. 9.95 (1-55799-572-9, 558) Evan-Moor Edu Pubs.

More Than a Savior: When Jesus Calls You Friend. Robert Crosby. LC 99-21883. 230p. 1999. 16.99 (1-57673-497-8) Multnomah Pubs.

More Than a Secretary. Betsy Rossen Elliot. LC 98-53389. 1999. pap. text 5.99 (0-87788-530-3, H Shaw Pubs) Waterbrook Pr.

More Than a Sentimental Bloke. John Derum. (Illus.). 152p. 1990. pap. 19.95 (0-86840-116-1, Pub. by New South Wales Univ Pr) Intl Spec Bk.

More Than a Shadow. Harry Forse. 190p. mass mkt. 4.99 (1-896329-90-X) Picasso Publ.

***More Than a Shining Star: Behind the Scenes with the Characters of Christmas.** S. Warren Way. 84p. 1999. 9.99 (1-929097-04-2) Windmill Pubns.

More Than a Soldier's War: Pacification in Vietnam. Edward P. Metzner. LC 95-18482. (Texas A&M University Military History Ser.: No. 47). (Illus.). 224p. (C). 1995. 29.95 (0-89096-666-4) Tex A&M Univ Pr.

More Than a Song. 1983. pap. 1.30 (0-8341-9562-3, AN-2552) Lillenas.

More Than a Sparrow. Belle Buckley. 1997. pap. write for info. (1-57553-633-1) Watermrk Pr.

More Than a Story: A Daily Touch of the Savior's Love. Scott Krippayne. LC 98-9700. (Artists Devotional Ser.). (Illus.). 192p. 1998. 14.99 (1-878990-83-7) Howard Pub LA.

More Than a Summer's Love, No. 23. Yvonne Lehman. (Serenade Serenata Ser.). 1985. pap. 2.50 (0-310-47042-0, 15557P) Zondervan.

More Than a Thousand Words: Graphics for Clinical Practice. Mark A. Mattaini. LC 93-6591. (Illus.). 297p. (C). 1993. 28.95 (0-87101-224-3); disk 60.95 (0-87101-227-8); disk 60.95 (0-87101-229-4) Natl Assn Soc Wkrs.

More Than a Tradition: Mexican Naciementos in Los Angeles. Michael Heisley & Mary M. Villareal. (Illus.). 47p. 1991. pap. 10.95 (0-916561-70-4) Southwest Mus.

More Than a Uniform: A Navy Woman in a Navy Man's World. Winifred Q. Collins & Herbert M. Levine. LC 96-29497. (Illus.). 224p. (Orig.). 1997. pap. 16.95 (1-57441-022-9) UNTX Pr.

More Than a Vision: Real Improvement in Urban Education. 47p. 1990. 6.00 (0-317-05343-4) NASBE.

More Than Allies. Sandra J. Scofield. LC 92-34342. 176p. 1993. 22.00 (1-877946-32-X) Permanent Pr.

More Than Altruism: The Politics of Private Foreign Aid. Brian H. Smith. LC 91-9366. 363p. 1990. text 52.50 (0-691-07845-9, Pub. by Princeton U Pr) Cal Prin Full Svc.

More Than Amazing Grace. E. Lonnie Melashenko & David B. Smith. Ed. by B. Russell Holt. 48p. 1995. pap. 1.49 (0-8163-1268-0) Pacific Pr Pub Assn.

More Than an Academic Question: Universities, Government & Public Policy in Canada. David M. Cameron. 471p. 1991. pap. 35.95 (0-88645-134-5, Pub. by Inst Res Pub) Ashgate Pub Co.

More Than an Average Guy. Janet Kastner. LC 89-1447. (Illus.). 224p. 1989. pap. 8.95 (0-938736-25-6) Life Enrich.

More Than Anything Else. Marie Bradby. LC 94-48804. (Illus.). 32p. (J). (gr. k-3). 1996. 15.95 (0-531-09464-2); lib. bdg. 16.99 (0-531-08764-6) Orchard Bks Watts.

More Than Bake Sales: The Resource Guide to Family Involvement in Education. James Vopat. LC 98-24867. (Illus.). 160p. 1998. pap. text 19.50 (1-57110-083-0) Stenhse Pubs.

More Than Beans & Cornbread: Traditional West Virginia Cooking. Barbara McCallum. LC 93-86404. (Illus.). 200p. 1993. pap. text 12.95 (0-929521-81-1) Pictorial Hist.

More Than Beautiful: The Story of Esther. Marilyn Lashbrook. (Me Too! Bks.). (J). (gr. k-5). 1998. 5.95 (0-933657-87-0, 30001056) Rainbow Studies.

More Than Blarney: The Irish Influence in Appalachia. Eileen McCullough. LC 96-61512. (Illus.). 179p. 1997. pap. 14.95 (1-888715-00-6) Wolfhnd Pr.

More Than Boxes see Homeplay: Joyful Learning for Children & Adults, Series I

More Than Bricks & Mortar: A History of the Atlanta Athletic Club. Atlanta Athletic Club Staff & Nancy Neill. LC 87-51024. (Illus.). 200p. (C). 1988. text. write for info. (0-9613474-2-2) Wolfe Pubng.

More Than Chains & Toil: A Christian Work Ethic of Enslaved Women. Joan M. Martin. LC 99-86475. 220p. 2000. pap. 24.95 (0-664-25800-X, Pub. by Westminster John Knox) Presbyterian Pub.

More Than Chattel: Black Women & Slavery in the Americas. Ed. by David B Gaspar & Darlene Clark Hine. LC 95-36096. (Blacks in the Diaspora Ser.). 384p. 1996. pap. text 18.95 (0-253-21043-7) Ind U Pr.

More Than Chattel: Black Women & Slavery in the Americas. abr. ed. Ed. by David B Gaspar & Darlene Clark Hine. LC 95-36096. (Blacks in the Diaspora Ser.). 384p. 1996. 39.95 (0-253-33017-3) Ind U Pr.

More Than Chicken Cookbook. Sara Pitzer. LC 83-48975. (Illus.). 160p. (Orig.). 1984. pap. 9.95 (0-88266-368-2, Garden Way Pub) Storey Bks.

More Than Class: Studying Power in U. S. Workplaces. Ed. by Ann E. Kingsolver. LC 97-19762. (SUNY Series in the Anthropology of Work). 288p. (C). 1998. text 65.50 (0-7914-3719-1); pap. text 21.95 (0-7914-3720-5) State U NY Pr.

More Than Coincidence? 1979. 5.50 (0-7152-0445-9) Grosvenor USA.

More Than Complete NetWare Command Reference. 2nd ed. Dorothy L. Cady. 688p. 1995. 35.00 (1-56205-451-1) New Riders Pub.

***More Than Conquerors.** Stuart E. Abrams. 2000. pap. 13.95 (1-878647-58-X) APU Pub Grp.

More Than Conquerors. Kenneth K. Foreman & Rosmarie Foreman. (Family of God Ser.). 112p. 1985. student ed. 2.95 (1-882449-14-2) Messenger Pub.

More Than Conquerors. Ariadne Gilbert. LC 68-58791. (Essay Index Reprint Ser.). 1977. 26.95 (0-8369-1036-2) Ayer.

More Than Conquerors. Gary Houston. (Orig.). 1989. pap. 5.25 (1-55673-099-3, 9810) CSS OH.

More Than Conquerors. Terry Mize. pap. 7.99 (0-89274-930-X, HH-930) Harrison Hse.

More Than Conquerors. Edward A. Thibault. LC 99-189829. 44 p. 1998. write for info. (0-932085-16-4) Word Among Us.

More Than Conquerors: A History of the Officers' Christian Fellowship of the U. S. A. Robert W. Spoede. LC 93-86791. 200p. 1993. 19.95 (0-913991-02-3) Officers Chris.

More Than Conquerors: An Interpretation of the Book of Revelation. William Hendriksen. 224p. 1998. reprint ed. pap. 12.99 (0-8010-5792-2) Baker Bks.

More Than Conquerors: Portraits of Believers from All Walks of Life. John D. Woodbridge. 29.99 (0-8024-9054-9, 220) Moody.

More Than Conquerors: The History of Oakville Baptist Church. 108p. 1986. pap. 7.50 (0-317-69452-9) Iris Dunn.

***More Than Conquerors: The Ultimate Christian Lifestyle.** Archie L. Baglery, Jr. 185p. 2000. pap. 13.95 (0-7414-0373-0) Buy Books.

More Than Cool Reason: A Field Guide to Poetic Metaphor. George Lakoff & Mark Turner. LC 88-29306. 242p. 1989. pap. text 13.00 (0-226-46812-7) U Ch Pr.

More Than Cool Reason: A Field Guide to Poetic Metaphor. George Lakoff & Mark Turner. LC 88-29306. 240p. 1998. lib. bdg. 29.95 (0-226-46811-9) U Ch Pr.

More Than Counting: Whole Math Activities for Preschool & Kindergarten. Sally Moomaw & Brenda Hieronymus. LC 95-13460. (Illus.). 244p. (Orig.). 1995. pap. 24.95 (1-884834-03-5, 3019) Redleaf Pr.

More Than Dancing: Essays on Afro-American Music & Musicians, 83. Ed. & Intro. by Irene V. Jackson. LC 84-8990. (Contributions in Afro-American & African Studies: No. 83). (Illus.). 281p. 1985. 55.00 (0-313-24554-1, JMD/) Greenwood.

More Than Delicious. Erie Art Museum Staff. (Illus.). 188p. 1993. 16.98 (0-9616623-5-2) Erie Art Mus.

More Than Dreams & Visions. Wanda Kellems. 200p. 1997. 19.95 (0-9659951-9-4) W Kellems Pub.

More Than Drumming: Essays on African & Afro-Latin American Music & Musicians, 80. Ed. by Irene V. Jackson. LC 84-8956. (Contributions in Afro-American & African Studies: No. 80). (Illus.). 204p. 1985. 55.00 (0-313-23093-5, JBM/) Greenwood.

More Than Empty Dreams: Stories of Friends (Quakers) Who did More Then Just Dream of Doing Good. Betty M. Hockett. LC 88-71327. (Illus.). 140p. (J). (gr. 3-8). 1988. pap. 7.50 (0-913342-65-3) Barclay Pr.

More Than Enough. C. C. Gibb. 83p. pap. 4.95 (0-88172-071-2) Believers Bkshelf.

More Than Enough: Proven Keys to Building Your Family & Financial Peace. Dave Ramsey. LC 98-31590. 330p. 1999. 22.95 (0-670-88253-4) Viking Penguin.

More Than Equals: Racial Healing for the Sake of the Gospel. Chris Rice & Spencer Perkins. LC 93-7442. (Illus.). 244p. (Orig.). 1993. pap. 12.99 (0-8308-1318-7, 1318) InterVarsity.

***More Than Equals: Racial Healing for the Sake of the Gospel.** 2nd rev. enl. ed. Spencer Perkins & Chris Rice. LC 99-86863. 2000. pap. 14.99 (0-8308-2256-9) InterVarsity.

More Than 15,000 Chords for Guitar. Ed. by Aaron Stang. 324p. (Orig.). (C). 1987. pap. text 24.95 (0-7692-1338-3, GF0428) Wrner Bros.

More Than Fifty Recipes for Very Low Fat Beef: There Is a Healthy Choice. Shirley Hawkins & Al Hawkins. 30p. 1993. pap. 7.95 (0-9640056-0-3) Arrowhd Pubng.

More Than 50 Ways to Build Team Consensus. R. Bruce Williams. LC 93-78420. (Illus.). 242p. 1993. pap. 24.95 (0-932935-48-6) SkyLght.

More Than 50 Ways to Learner-Centered Literacy. Laura Lipton & Deborah Hubble. LC 96-80016. 224p. (Orig.). 1997. pap. 21.95 (1-57517-069-8, 1445) SkyLght.

More Than Fine Writing: The Life & Calligraphy of Irene Wellington. Heather Child et al. LC 86-62197. (Illus.). 140p. 1999. 35.00 (0-87951-269-5, Pub. by Overlook Pr) Penguin Putnam.

More Than Fire. Philip Jose Farmer. 320p. 1995. mass mkt. 5.99 (0-8125-1959-0, Pub. by Tor Bks) St Martin.

More than Food, Clothing, & Shelter: Stories of Lizzie Grey & Minnie Chandler. Lizzie G. Chandler & Wynolia C. Apple. LC 98-91716. xxvi, 179 p. 1998. pap. 13.95 (0-9666073-0-9) Moon Lodge.

More Than Four: A Guide for Multiple Harness Weavers. Mary E. Laughlin. 1992. pap. 16.50 (1-56659-048-5) Robin & Russ.

More Than Friends see Mas Que Amigos: Courtship in Granite Ridge

More Than Friends. Judy Baer. (Cedar River Daydreams Ser.: No. 18). 128p. (J). (gr. 7-10). 1992. mass mkt. 4.99 (1-55661-298-2) Bethany Hse.

More Than Friends. Barbara Delinsky. 496p. 1993. mass mkt. 6.99 (0-06-104199-8, Harp PBks) HarpC.

More Than Friends. Melissa Lowell. (J). 1996. pap. 4.75 (0-553-54277-X) BDD Bks Young Read.

An Asterisk (*) at the beginning of an entry indicates that the title is appearing for the first time.

More Than Friends. Susan Mallery. (Men at Work Ser.: Vol. 28). 1998. mass mkt. 4.50 (*0-373-81040-7*, 1-81040-7) Harlequin Bks.

More Than Friends. Susan Mallery. 1993. mass mkt. 3.39 (*0-373-09802-2*, 5-09802-5) Silhouette.

More Than Glue & Glitter: Classroom Guide for Volunteer Teachers. Debbie T. O'Neal. LC 91-47157. 96p. 1992. pap. 11.99 (*0-8066-2561-9*, 9-2561) Augsburg Fortress.

***More Than Gold.** Shirley Hailstock. (Arabesque Ser.). 320p. 2000. mass mkt. 5.99 (*1-58314-120-0*) BET Bks.

More Than Gold. Evelyn Hege. (Illus.). 204p. 1994. 8.45 (*0-7399-0149-4*, 2565) Rod & Staff.

More Than Gold. Nora Jean Perkins. 1999. pap. write for info. (*1-893108-20-1*) Neighbrhd Pr Pubng.

More Than Graphs. Jim Specht. 228p. (J). (gr. 6-10). 1995. text 24.95 (*1-55953-147-9*) Key Curr Pr.

More Than He Bargained For: That Special Woman! Carole Halston. (Special Edition Ser.). 1993. mass mkt. 3.50 (*0-373-09829-4*, 5-09829-4) Silhouette.

More Than Health Insurance: State Initiatives to Improve Infant & Child Health. Charles Bruner & James M. Perrin. (Illus.). 44p. (Orig.). 1995. pap. write for info. (*1-887748-00-8*) Milbank Memorial.

More Than Honor. Ed. by David Weber. 1998. per. 5.99 (*0-671-87857-3*) Baen Bks.

***More Than Houses.** Millard Fuller. LC 99-24425. 224p. 1999. pap. 12.99 (*0-8499-3762-0*) Word Pub.

More Than Housing: Lifeboats for Women & Children. Joan F. Sprague. (Illus.). 248p. 1991. pap. text 42.95 (*0-7506-9146-8*, Butterwrth Archit) Buttrwrth-Heinemann.

More Than Human. Theodore Sturgeon. 192p. 1992. pap. 3.95 (*0-88184-918-9*) Carroll & Graf.

More Than Human. Theodore Sturgeon. LC 98-40420. 1999. pap. 11.00 (*0-375-70371-3*) Vin Bks.

More Than Human. large type ed. Theodore Sturgeon. LC 92-35760. 346p. 1993. reprint ed. lib. bdg. 21.95 (*1-56054-588-7*) Thorndike Pr.

More Than Human. Theodore Sturgeon. 1993. reprint ed. lib. bdg. 18.95 (*0-89968-371-1*, Lghtyr Pr) Buccaneer Bks.

More Than "I Do" Devotions for the Engaged Couple. Harold I. Smith. 56p. (Orig.). 1983. pap. 4.99 (*0-8341-0805-4*) Beacon Hill.

More Than "I Do" Pastor's Resource Book for Premarital Counseling. Harold I. Smith. 88p. (Orig.). 1983. pap. 6.99 (*0-8341-0865-8*) Beacon Hill.

More Than Information: The Role of the Library Media Center in the Multimedia Classroom. Lesley S. Farmer. 1998. pap. 34.95 (*0-938865-71-4*) Linworth Pub.

More Than Intelligence Goes to School. Jim Grant. 40p. (Orig.). 1992. pap. text 6.00 (*0-935493-90-5*) Modern Learn Pr.

More Than Just a . . . Series, 2 vols., Set. Dwight Kuhn. (Illus.). 80p. (J). (gr. 2 up). 1990. 15.90 (*0-671-94439-8*) Silver Burdett Pr.

More Than Just a Flower Garden. Dwight Kuhn. Ed. by Bonnie Brook. (More Than Just a Ser.). (Illus.). 40p. (J). (gr. 2 up). 1990. 7.95 (*0-671-69644-0*) Silver Burdett Pr.

***More Than Just a Game: The Military Nature of Greek Athletic Contests.** Nancy B. Reed. (Illus.). 82p. 1999. pap. 15.00 (*0-89005-572-6*) Ares.

More Than Just a Numbers Game? U. S. Policy on Global Population. Nancy W. Gallagher & Elizabeth A. Shakman. (Pew Case Studies in International Affairs). 50p. (C). 1996. pap. text 3.50 (*1-56927-215-8*, GU Schl Foreign) Geo U Inst Dplmcy.

***More Than Just a Pet.** Illus. by Maggie Raynor. (Pony Guides Ser.: No. 1). 16p. (J). (gr. 1-5). 1999. pap. 5.95 (*1-900667-00-2*, Pub. by Compass Equestrian Ltd) Trafalgar.

More Than Just a Room Vol. 1: The Story of Immanuel House & Its Predecessor. Robert L. Edwards. (Illus.). 128p. 1996. 15.00 (*0-9653670-0-2*) Immanuel Chur.

More Than Just a Vegetable Garden. Dwight Kuhn. Ed. by Bonnie Brook. (More Than Just a Ser.). (Illus.). 40p. (J). (gr. 2 up). 1990. 7.95 (*0-671-69645-9*) Silver Burdett Pr.

More Than Just Hot Air Vol. 1: Comman Sense Counter-Top Convection Oven Cookbook. Donovan J. Fandre. Ed. by Janet Casados. (Illus.). 160p. (Orig.). 1994. pap. text 14.99 (*0-9603168-3-3*) D Fandre.

More Than Just Minstrel Shows: The Rise of Black Musical Theatre at the Turn of the Century. Thomas L. Riis. LC 92-72055. (I.S.A.M. Monographs: No. 33). (Illus.). 72p. (Orig.). (C). 1992. pap. 15.00 (*0-914678-36-1*) Inst Am Music.

More Than Just Sex: A Committed Couple's Guide to Keeping Relationships Lively, Intimate & Gratifying. Daniel Beaver. LC 91-42286. 240p. (Orig.). 1992. pap. 12.95 (*0-944031-35-8*) Aslan Pub.

More Than Just Surviving Handbook: ESL for Every Classroom Teacher. Barbara Law & Mary Eckes. (Illus.). 209p. (Orig.). (gr. k-12). 1990. pap., teacher ed. 19.00 (*0-920541-98-4*) Peguis Pubs Ltd.

***More Than Just Veggies: Healthful, Conscious Eating in the 21st Century.** Amy Erez. 238p. 1999. pap. 14.95 (*0-7392-0478-5*, PO3815) Morris Pubng.

More Than Kindness: A Compassionate Approach to Crisis Childbearing. Marvin N. Olasky & Susan Olasky. LC 90-80625. 224p. 1990. pap. 14.99 (*0-89107-584-4*) Crossway Bks.

More Than Kisses. Glenda Sanders. (Orig.). 1994. mass mkt. 4.50 (*0-380-77588-3*, Avon Bks) Morrow Avon.

More Than Legend. Daryl N. Patterson. 238p. 1995. pap. 9.95 (*0-9646761-0-9*) Cabin Bks.

More Than LIP Service: A Lifetime Investment Plan. Alvin H. Danenberg. LC 96-47762. (Illus.). 350p. 1996. 49.95 (*0-87814-655-5*) PennWell Bks.

More Than Lovers. large type ed. Natalie Fox. 1995. 18.95 (*0-263-14037-7*) Thorndike Pr.

More Than Magic. Olga Bicos. 544p. 1994. mass mkt. 4.99 (*0-7860-0049-X*, Pinncle Kensgtn) Kensgtn Pub Corp.

More Than Magic. Kathleen Nance. 400p. 1999. mass mkt. 5.99 (*0-505-52299-3*) Dorchester Pub Co.

More Than Magnets: Exploring the Wonders of Science in Preschool & Kindergarten. Sally Moomaw & Brenda Hieronymus. LC 97-23247. (Illus.). (Orig.). 1997. pap. 24.95 (*1-884834-33-7*, 4024) Redleaf Pr.

More Than Magnifiers. rev. ed. Cary I. Sneider & Alan Gould. Ed. by Lincoln Bergman & Kay Fairwell. (Great Explorations in Math & Science (GEMS) Ser.). (Illus.). 68p. (YA). (gr. 6-8). 1991. reprint ed. pap. 10.50 (*0-912511-62-1*, GEMS) Lawrence Science.

***More Than Married! The Keys to Intimacy for a Lasting Marriage.** David Ferguson. 2000. pap. 12.99 (*0-8499-5503-3*) J Countryman.

More Than Me: Confessions, Perceptions & Inspirations of a Modern-Day Mystic. Isana M. Dhyana. LC 92-97500. 151p. (Orig.). 1993. pap. 10.95 (*0-9635218-0-2*) Dhyana Pr.

More Than Meat Joy: Performance Art & Selected Writings. 2nd rev. ed. Carolee Schneemann. LC 96-50384. (Illus.). 296p. 1997. pap. 35.00 (*0-929701-54-2*) McPherson & Co.

More Than Meets the Eye. Michael Cassin. (National Gallery Publications). (Illus.). 1990. pap. 16.00 (*0-300-06161-7*) Yale U Pr.

***More Than Meets the Eye.** Richard A. Swenson. 2000. pap. 12.00 (*1-57683-069-1*) NavPress.

More Than Meets the Eye: A Candid Journal of Two Eye Surgeons. 2nd rev. ed. Rudi Binder. 210p. (YA). 1999. reprint ed. per. 11.95 (*1-893309-00-2*, 1) Red Maple Pubg.

More Than Meets the Eye: A Young Man's Introduction to Women. Linda Bairstow. LC 89-91247. 1989. 8.95 (*0-87212-228-X*) Libra.

More Than Meets the Eye: An Introduction to Media Studies. Graeme Burton. 192p. 1995. text 16.95 (*0-340-50409-9*, A4810, Pub. by E A) St Martin.

More Than Meets the Eye: An Introduction to Media Studies. 2nd ed. Graeme Burton. LC 97-961. 256p. 1997. pap. text 19.95 (*0-340-67663-9*, Pub. by E A) OUP.

***More Than Meets the Eye: Energy.** Judith Poole. (Illus.). 153p. 1999. spiral bd. 17.95 (*0-9674257-1-9*) Pooled Res.

***More Than Meets the Eye: Finding God in the Creases & Folds of Family Life.** Mary Jo Pedersen et al. 160p. (YA). 2000. pap. 14.95 (*0-88489-594-7*) St Marys.

***More Than Meets the Eye: How Relationships Enhance Literacy Learning.** Donna Skolnick. 2000. pap. text 17.50 (*0-325-00249-5*) Heinemann.

More Than Meets the Eye: Watching Television Watching Us. John J. Pungente & Martin O'Malley. 272p. 1999. 24.95 (*0-7710-7100-0*) McCland & Stewart.

More Than Meets the Eye: Wyoming along Interstate 80. Mary A. Trevathan. LC 93-4245. (Illus.). 224p. 1993. pap. 11.95 (*0-931271-20-7*) Hi Plains Pr.

More Than Meets the I. John Hemming. 1999. pap. 21.00 (*1-85072-068-1*, Pub. by W Sessions) St Mut.

More than Memories: The Complete Guide for Preserving Your Family History. Julie Stephani. LC 98-85815. (Illus.). 128p. 1998. pap. 14.95 (*0-87341-689-9*) Krause Pubns.

More Than Memories Vol. II: Beyond the Basics. Ed. by Julie Stephani. LC 98-85815. (Illus.). 128p. 1999. pap. 16.95 (*0-87341-739-9*, MTMB) Krause Pubns.

***More Than Memories III: Mastering the Techniques.** Ed. by Julie Stephani. LC 99-67508. (Illus.). 128p. 2000. pap. 16.95 (*0-87341-875-1*, MTM3) Krause Pubns.

***More Than Memory.** Dorothy Garlock. 2001. mass mkt. 6.99 (*0-446-60814-9*) Warner Bks.

More Than Mere Words. Ed. by Faye Short. 46p. 1996. pap. 6.95 (*1-885224-07-9*) Bristol Hse.

More Than Merkle: A History of the Best & Most Exciting Baseball Season in Human History. David W. Anderson. LC 99-35024. (Illus.). 304p. 2000. 29.95 (*0-8032-1056-6*) U of Nebr Pr.

More Than Metaphors: Strategies for Teaching Process Writing. Stephen Smuin. 1992. pap. 18.75 (*0-201-45501-3*) Addison-Wesley.

More Than Milk: Exposing the Occult. Nita Scoggan. (Illus.). 128p. (Orig.). 1994. pap. text 7.95 (*0-910487-27-8*) Royalty Pub.

More Than Moccasins: A Kid's Activity Guide to Traditional North American Indian Life. Laurie Carlson. LC 93-39922. (Illus.). 200p. (J). (gr. k-6). 1994. pap. 12.95 (*1-55652-213-4*) Chicago Review.

More Than Moonshine: Appalachian Recipes & Recollections. Sidney S. Farr. LC 82-13524. 232p. 1983. pap. 15.95 (*0-8229-5347-1*); text 29.95 (*0-8229-3475-2*) U of Pittsburgh Pr.

More Than Mortal? Contrasting Concepts & Enigmatic Evidence about Life after Death. 64p. 1991. pap. 18.00 (*0-9607532-4-9*) Squantum Pr.

More Than Mountains: One Leg, Fifty Mountains, an Unconquerable Faith: the Todd Huston Story. Todd Huston & Kay D. Rizzo. LC 94-48724. (Illus.). 190p. 1995. 4.97 (*0-8163-1250-8*) Pacific Pr Pub Assn.

More than Movement for Fit to Frail Older Adults: Creative Activities for the Body, Mind, & Spirit. Pauline P. Fisher. LC 94-41602. 256p. 1995. pap. 24.00 (*1-878812-21-1*) Hlth Prof Pr.

More Than Mud Pies: Bible Learning Crafts & Games for Preschoolers. Ed. by Susan Lingo & Beth Wolf. LC 97-37795. 112p. 1998. per. 15.99 (*0-7644-2044-5*) Group Pub.

More Than Munitions. Wightman. (C). 1999. pap. 45.00 (*0-582-41435-0*) Addison-Wesley.

***More Than Muscle: A Fitness Program for Corrections & Law Enforcement, the Variable Cyclic Phase System.** Jerry Pearson. LC 99-88643. (Illus.). 2000. pap. write for info. (*1-56991-118-5*) Am Correctional.

More Than Music. Ann E. Weeks. (Illus.). 8p. (Orig.). 1995. pap. 1.50 (*1-886036-04-7*) Passages Pbg.

More Than My Job's Worth. J. Muir. 6.99 (*1-85792-018-X*, Pub. by Christian Focus) Spring Arbor Dist.

More Than News: Media Power in Public Affairs. Michael B. MacKuen & Steven L. Coombs. LC 81-183. (People & Communication Ser.: No. 12). (Illus.). 231p. reprint ed. pap. 71.70 (*0-8357-4767-0*, 203770400009) Bks Demand.

More Than Night: Film Noir in Its Contexts. James Naremore. LC 97-33090. 342p. 1998. 45.00 (*0-520-21293-2*, Pub. by U CA Pr); pap. 19.95 (*0-520-21294-0*, Pub. by U CA Pr) Cal Prin Full Svc.

More Than Numbers see **Mucho Mas Que Numeros**

More Than Numbers. David Y. Cho & R. Whitney Manzano. 172p. 1983. mass mkt. 5.99 (*1-85030-000-3*) Bridge-Logos.

More Than Numbers: Mathematical Thinking in the Early Years. Ed. by Dennie P. Wolf & Bonnie Neugebauer. (Illus.). 64p. (Orig.). 1996. pap. 14.00 (*0-942702-19-0*) Child Care.

More Than Numbers: The Ways Churches Grow. Loren B. Mead. LC 92-75724. 1993. pap. 11.25 (*1-56699-109-9*, AL141) Alban Inst.

More Than One. Miriam Schlein. LC 95-38136. (Illus.). 24p. (J). (ps-3). 1996. 15.00 (*0-688-14102-1*, Grenwillow Bks) HarpC Child Bks.

More Than One. Miriam Schlein. LC 95-38136. (Illus.). 24p. (J). (ps-3). 1996. 14.93 (*0-688-14103-X*, Grenwillow Bks) HarpC Child Bks.

***More Than One Angel.** Billie Hughes Locke. LC 99-64804. 266p. 2000. pap. 15.99 (*1-57921-244-1*, Pub. by WinePress Pub) BookWorld.

***More Than One Enemy.** 260p. 1999. pap. 14.95 (*0-9674381-0-1*) Diva Pubng.

More Than 100 Furniture Repairs You Can Do Yourself: A Practical Handbook for Anyone Who Buys, Sells, or Owns Furniture. Donna S. Morris. LC 98-91678. (Illus.). xv, 272p. 1998. pap. 24.95 (*0-9665673-3-1*) Phoenix Pr Ltd.

More Than One Journey. Charles Jackson, Sr. (Illus.). 80p. (Orig.). 1989. pap. 3.45 (*0-9622128-0-6*) C Jackson.

More Than One Life. Miloslava Holubova. Tr. by Alex Zucker et al from CZE. LC 99-13058. 104p. 1999. 22.95 (*0-8101-1705-3*, Hydra Bks) Northwestern U Pr.

More Than One Mystery: Explorations in Quantum Interference. Mark P. Silverman. LC 94-21442. 240p. 1994. 59.95 (*0-387-94340-4*) Spr-Verlag.

More Than One Mystery: Explorations in Quantum Interference. M. P. Silvermann. (Illus.). 212p. 1994. 29.95 (*0-387-94376-5*) Spr-Verlag.

More Than Opium: An Anthropological Approach to Latin American & Caribbean Pentecostal Praxis. Ed. by Barbara Boudewijnse et al. LC 97-30704. (Studies in Evangelicalism: No. 14). 336p. 1998. 55.00 (*0-8108-3390-5*) Scarecrow.

***More Than Painting: Exploring the Wonders of Art for Preschool & Kindergarten.** Sally Moomaw & Brenda Hieronymus. LC 99-35321. (More Than... Ser.). (Illus.). 320p. 1999. pap. 24.95 (*1-884834-67-1*, 406401, Pub. by Redleaf Pr) Gryphon Hse.

***More Than Petticoats: North Carolina.** Scotti Kent. LC 99-44216. 2000. pap. 12.95 (*1-56044-900-4*) Falcon Pub Inc.

***More Than Petticoats: Remarkable California Women.** Erin H. Turner. LC 99-27234. 1999. pap. 9.95 (*1-56044-859-8*, Two Dot) Falcon Pub Inc.

More Than Petticoats: Remarkable Montana Women. Gayle C. Shirley. LC 95-32881. (Illus.). 144p. 1995. pap. 8.95 (*1-56044-363-4*) Falcon Pub Inc.

More Than Petticoats: Remarkable Washington Women. L. E. Bragg. LC 98-7356. (Illus.). 208p. 1998. pap. 9.95 (*1-56044-667-6*) Falcon Pub Inc.

More Than Pink & Blue: How Gender Can Shape Your Curriculum. Linda Karges-Bone. Ed. by Judy Mitchell. (Illus.). 144p. (J). (ps-3). 1998. pap., teacher ed. 13.95 (*1-57310-113-3*) Teachng & Lrning Co.

More Than Pumpkins in October: Visual Literacy in the 21st Century. (Illus.). 56p. 1992. pap. 12.00 incl. VHS (*0-89236-237-5*, Pub. by Edizioni Quasar) J P Getty Trust.

***More Than Puppy Love Gift Book: Expressions of Affection.** Compiled by Garborg's Inc. Staff. (Illus.). 64p. 1999. 9.99 (*1-58375-465-2*) Garborgs.

***More Than Recipes.** deluxe ed. Kathy Heerensperger & Leonard Heerensperger. (Illus.). 594p. (C). 1998. 62.95 (*0-9661614-0-8*) Menu Cookbook.

More Than Riches. large type ed. Josephine Cox. 544p. 1997. 27.99 (*0-7089-8865-2*) Ulverscroft.

***More Than Rubies: Becoming a Woman of Godly Influence.** Debra White Smith. LC 99-57993. 152p. 2000. pap. 12.99 (*0-8341-1813-0*) Beacon Hill.

More Than Screen Deep: Toward Every-Citizen Interfaces to the Nation's Information Infrastructure. National Research Council Staff. LC 97-21211. 275p. 1997. pap. 29.95 (*0-309-06357-4*) Natl Acad Pr.

More Than 7 Watchmen. Helen Norris. 144p. 1985. 3.95 (*0-310-45470-0*, 9359) Zondervan.

More Than 70 Native American Art Projects. Susan Major-Tingey. LC 95-223049. 1995. pap. 18.95 (*0-590-25635-1*) Scholastic Inc.

More Than Seventy Summers: Notes on Rural Life. large type ed. Tony Harman & Ruth Boyd. (Reminiscence Ser.). 24.95 (*1-85695-046-8*, Pub. by ISIS Lrg Prnt) Transaction Pubs.

***More Than Sex: Reinventing the Black Male Image.** George E. Smith. 256p. 2000. 23.00 (*1-57566-498-4*) Kensgtn Pub Corp.

More Than Singing. Lotte Lehmann. Tr. by Frances Holden from GRE. LC 75-8688. 192p. 1975. reprint ed. lib. bdg. 55.00 (*0-8371-8116-X*, LEMT, Greenwood Pr) Greenwood.

More Than Singing: Discovering Music in Preschool & Kindergarten. Sally Moomaw. LC 97-19869. (Illus.). xii, 257 p. (Orig.). 1997. pap. 29.95 incl. audio (*1-884834-34-5*, 3050) Redleaf Pr.

More Than Singing: The Interpretation of Songs. Lotte Lehmann. (Music Bks.). 192p. 1985. reprint ed. pap. 5.95 (*0-486-24831-3*) Dover.

More Than Singing, the Interpretation of Songs: Music Book Index. Lotte Lehmann. 192p. 1993. reprint ed. lib. bdg. 69.00 (*0-7812-9675-7*) Rprt Serv.

***More Than 60 Ways to Make Your Life Amazing: A Complete Guide for Women.** Lynda Field. (Illus.). 160p. 2000. pap. 9.95 (*1-86204-835-5*) Element MA.

More Than Skin Deep. Margaret Armitage. 1988. pap. 4.95 (*9971-972-67-0*) OMF Bks.

More Than Soup - Bean Bookbook. Anna Aughenbaugh. LC 90-91471. 128p. 1995. spiral bd. 7.95 (*0-9625869-2-7*) Starlite CO.

More Than Stories: The Range of Children's Writing. Thomas Newkirk. LC 88-26067. (Illus.). 228p. (Orig.). (C). 1989. pap. 29.50 (*0-435-08490-9*, 08490) Heinemann.

More Than Subsistence: Minimum Wages for the Working Poor. Sar A. Levitan & Richard S. Belous. LC 79-11688. (Policy Studies in Employment & Welfare: Vol. 34). 193p. 1979. reprint ed. pap. 59.90 (*0-608-03720-6*, 206454500009) Bks Demand.

More Than Survival: Access to Higher Education for Low Income Women. Erika Kates. 30p. 1991. 8.00 (*1-877966-06-1*) Ctr Women Policy.

More Than Survival: One Man's Plan to Move Mississippi Forward. Robert M. Berman. LC 88-90829. 256p. (Orig.). 1988. pap. 9.95 (*0-937552-25-9*, QRP Bks) Quail Ridge.

More Than Survival: Prospects for Higher Education in a Period of Uncertainty: A Commentary with Recommendations. Carnegie Foundation for the Advancement of Teachin. LC 75-4481. (Carnegie Council Ser.). 182p. reprint ed. pap. 56.50 (*0-608-17069-0*, 202774800056) Bks Demand.

More Than Surviving: Caring for Yourself While You Grieve. Kelly Osmont. (Illus.). 52p. (Orig.). 1990. pap. 3.75 (*1-56123-004-9*) Centering Corp.

More Than Survivors: Conversations with Multiple Personality Clients. James G. Friesen. 224p. (Orig.). 1997. pap. 18.00 (*1-57910-063-5*) Wipf & Stock.

***More Than Talk: Communication Studies & The Christian Faith.** Bill Strom. LC 99-164227. 352p. (C). 1998. per. 24.94 (*0-7872-4858-4*) Kendall-Hunt.

More Than the ABCs: The Early Stages of Reading & Writing. Judith A. Schickedanz. LC 85-63122. 147p. pap. 6.00 (*0-912674-95-4*, NAEYC #204) Natl Assn Child Ed.

More Than the Facts: The Research Division of the National Education Association, 1922-1997. Wayne J. Urban. LC 97-36952. 176p. (C). 1997. 40.50 (*0-7618-0930-9*) U Pr of Amer.

***More Than the Sum of His Parts: Arnold Krekel.** Joan M. Juern. (Missouri Research Roundtable Papers: No. 2). (Illus.). 24p. 1999. pap. 4.00 (*0-931227-50-X*) Mallinckrodt Comm.

More Than the Truth: Teaching Nonfiction Writing Through Journalism. Dennie Wolf et al. LC 96-28738. (Moving Middle Schools Ser.). 1996. pap. text 19.50 (*0-435-07216-1*, 07216) Heinemann.

***More Than They Promised: The Studebaker Story.** Thomas E. Bonsall. 376p. 1999. 45.00 (*0-8047-3586-7*) Stanford U Pr.

More Than This. Laura Peyton Roberts. (Clearwater Crossing Ser.). 224p. (YA). (gr. 5-8). 1999. mass mkt. 3.99 (*0-553-49296-9*) Bantam.

More Than 25 Million Acres? DOD As a Federal, Natural & Cultural Resource Manager. David Rubenson et al. LC 96-17909. 130p. 1996. pap. text 15.00 (*0-8330-2363-2*, MR-715-OSD) Rand Corp.

More than Two Aspirin see **Hope for Your Headache Problem,**

More Than Victims. Downs. 1998. pap. text 17.00 (*0-226-16160-9*) U Ch Pr.

More Than Victims: Battered Women, the Syndrome Society & the Law. Donald A. Downs. LC 96-16427. 320p. 1996. 27.50 (*0-226-16159-5*) U Ch Pr.

***More Than We Imagined: Parables of the Kingdom of God.** Prentice A. Meador, Jr. LC 00-105861. 150p. 2000. pap. 9.95 (*0-89112-446-2*, Hill Crest Pubg) Abilene Christ U.

More Than Welcome: Learning to Embrace Gay, Lesbian, Bisexual, & Transgendered Persons in the Church. Maurine C. Waun. LC 98-43562. 160p. 1999. pap. 15.99 (*0-8272-2325-0*) Chalice Pr.

More Than Winners see **Mas Que Vencedores**

More Than Winners: An Athlete's Study Guide Through the Epistles. Elliot Johnson. 160p. 1992. pap. 6.99 (*0-9634057-2-1*, TX3461-307) Full Court MI.

More Than Words. Mario Cuomo. LC 94-18982. 1994. pap. 13.95 (*0-312-11385-4*) St Martin.

More Than Words. Edward Horrell. 1995. write for info. (*0-9644788-0-3*) Ctr Spoken Commun.

More Than Words, Bk. 1. rev. ed. Harmer. Date not set. pap. text. write for info. (*0-582-09481-X*, Pub. by Addison-Wesley) Longman.

More Than Words: An Introduction to Communication. Richard Dimbleby & Graeme Burton. (Illus.). (C). 1985. pap. 10.95 (*0-416-38070-0*, 9574) Routledge.

More Than Words: An Introduction to Communication. 3rd ed. Richard Dimbleby. (Illus.). 296p. (C). 1998. pap. 21.99 (*0-415-17007-9*) Routledge.

M

More Than Words: Introduction to Communication. 3rd ed. Richard Dimbleby & Graeme Burton. LC 97-38903. (Illus.). 296p. (C). 1998. 75.00 (*0-415-17006-0*) Routledge.

More Than Words: Prayer As a Way of Life. Leonard J. Vander Zee. (Illus.). 52p. 1995. pap., teacher ed. 23.45 (*1-56212-121-9*, 1360-0330) CRC Pubns.

More Than Words: The Speeches of Mario Cuomo. limited ed. Mario Cuomo. 320p. 1993. text 150.00 (*0-312-10005-1*) St Martin.

More Than Words Can Say: The Ink Spots & Their Music. Marv Goldberg. LC 98-35748. (Illus.). 336p. 1998. 39.50 (*0-8108-3568-1*) Scarecrow.

More Than You & Me: Touching Others Through the Strength of Your Marriage. Kevin Miller & Karen Miller. LC 94-1740. 270p. 1994. pap. 9.99 (*1-56179-217-9*) Focus Family.

More Than You Dare to Ask: The First Year of Living with Cancer. Mac N. Turnage & Anne S. Turnage. 120p. 1992. reprint ed. pap. 10.00 (*0-89896-143-2*) Larksdale.

More Than You Dreamed. Kathleen G. Seidel. Ed. by Claire Zion. 352p. (Orig.). 1991. mass mkt. 5.99 (*0-671-66217-1*, Pocket Star Bks) PB.

*__More Than You Know.__ Jo Goodman. 2000. mass mkt. 5.99 (*0-8217-6569-8*, Zebra Kensgtn) Kensgtn Pub Corp.

More Than You Know. Phyllis Halldorson. (Romance Ser.). 1993. per. 2.75 (*0-373-08948-1*, 5-08948-7) Silhouette.

More Than You Know. Judith Kelman. 336p. 1996. mass mkt. 6.50 (*0-553-56270-3*) Bantam.

More Than You Know. Helen R. Myers. (Mira Bks.). 400p. 1999. mass mkt. 5.99 (*1-55166-504-2*, Mira Bks) Harlequin Bks.

*__More Than You Know: A Novel.__ Beth Gutcheon. LC 99-45936. 288p. 2000. 24.00 (*0-688-17403-5*, Wm Morrow) Morrow Avon.

*__More Than You Know Reading.__ Beth Gutcheon. 2000. write for info. (*0-688-17816-2*, Wm Morrow) Morrow Avon.

*__More Than 100 Tools for Literacy in Today's Classroom__ Joan F. Groeber & Judy Plazyk. LC 98-61507. xii, 241 p. 1999. write for info. (*1-57517-143-0*) SkyLght.

*__More the Merrier.__ Lenora Mattingly Weber. (Beany Malone Ser.). 246p. (J). 1999. reprint ed. pap. 12.95 (*1-930009-00-3*) Image Cascade.

More Theatre: Stage to Screen to Television, 2 vols. Alvin H. Marill. LC 93-4687. 1648p. 1993. 160.00 (*0-8108-2717-4*) Scarecrow.

More Thematic Learning Centers. Vaude Putte. 208p. (J). (gr. 5-8). 1997. pap. 15.95 (*1-57690-064-9*) Tchr Create Mat.

More Thematic Units for Creating the Integrated Curriculum. Liz Rothlein et al. 200p. (J). (gr. k-6). 1996. pap. 27.95 (*0-926842-53-6*) CG Pubs Inc.

More They Told Barron. Clarence W. Barron. Ed. by Arthur Pound & Samuel T. Moore. LC 73-1991. (Big Business; Economic Power in a Free Society Ser.). 1973. reprint ed. 23.95 (*0-405-05075-5*) Ayer.

More Things Change... Kent J. Quirk. 252p. 1998. pap. text 20.00 (*0-9641681-1-1*) Polestar CT.

More Things in Heaven & Earth: A Celebration of Physics at the Millennium. Ed. by Benjamin Bederson. LC 98-53116. (Illus.). 600p. 1999. 75.00 (*0-387-98662-6*) Spr-Verlag.

More Things Than Are Dreamt Of: Masterpieces of Supernatural Horror - from Mary Shelley to Stephen King - Transformed on Film. Alain Silver & James Ursini. LC 94-1655. (Illus.). 224p. (Orig.). 1994. pap. 20.00 (*0-87910-177-6*) Limelight Edns.

More Things That Matter. George A. Riddell. LC 79-128299. (Essay Index Reprint Ser.). 1977. 21.95 (*0-8369-1843-6*) Ayer.

More Things They Didn't Teach Me in Worship Leading School. Tom Kraeuter. 1998. pap. 9.99 (*1-883002-67-2*) Emerald WA.

More Things to Do with Toddlers & Twos. Karen Miller. LC 90-70984. (Illus.). 212p. (Orig.). (C). 1990. pap. 14.95 (*0-910287-08-2*) TelShare Pub Co.

More Things You Can Do to Defend Your Gun Rights. Alan M. Gottlieb. 180p. 1995. pap. text 9.95 (*0-936783-13-3*) Merril Pr.

More Things You Can Do with a Useless Man. Scott Wilson. Ed. by Cliff Carle. 64p. 1996. pap. 5.95 (*0-918259-89-4*) CCC Pubns.

More Thought Provokers. Doug Rohrer. (YA). (gr. 9-12). 1994. 9.95 (*1-55953-070-7*) Key Curr Pr.

More Thoughts on Restoring a Marriage: A Guide Allowing God to Heal Your Marriage. Robert E. Steinkamp & Charlyne A. Steinkamp. 135p. 1997. mass mkt. 9.95 (*1-892230-01-1*) Rejoice Ministries.

More Tic-Tac-Toe Math. Dave Clark. Ed. by Joan Gideon. (Tic-Tac-Toe Math Ser.). (Illus.). 121p. (Orig.). 1995. teacher ed. 11.95 (*0-86651-948-3*, DS21405) Seymour Pubns.

*__More Time, Less Stress.__ Martin Scott. 1998. pap. 24.95 (*0-7126-7991-X*, Pub. by Random) Trafalgar.

More Timely Rhymes. Henry Fischer. 72p. 1996. pap. 6.50 (*1-880286-47-5*) Singular Speech Pr.

More Tish. Mary Roberts Rinehart. reprint ed. lib. bdg. 23.95 (*0-89190-328-3*, Rivercity Pr) Amereon Ltd.

More to Be Desired Than Gold: True Stories Told by Christy Wilson. J. Christy Wilson, Jr. LC 92-75930. 180p. 1994. pap. 5.95 (*0-9640910-0-3*) Gordon-Conwell.

More to Come: The First 100 Years. George Brand. (Illus.). 181p. 1989. 39.95 (*0-685-24280-3*) CA News Pubs Assn.

More Toddlers Together: The Complete Planning Guide for a Toddler Curriculum, Vol. II. Cynthia Catlin. LC 96-26582. (Illus.). 272p. (Orig.). 1996. pap. 24.95 (*0-87659-179-9*) Gryphon Hse.

More Top Secret Recipes: More Kitchen Clones of America's Favorite Brand-Name Foods. Todd Wilbur. LC 94-14369. (Illus.). 144p. 1994. pap. 9.95 (*0-452-27299-8*, Plume) Dutton Plume.

More Torah Therapy: Further Reflections on the Weekly Sedra & Special Occasions. Reuven P. Bulka. LC 93-13931. 1993. 20.00 (*0-88125-464-9*) Ktav.

More Tracks: 78 Years of Mountains, People & Happiness. Howard Copenhaver. (Illus.). 1991. pap. 13.95 (*0-912299-50-9*) Stoneydale Pr Pub.

More Tracks: 78 Years of Mountains, People & Happiness. Howard Copenhaver. (Illus.). 1992. 18.95 (*0-912299-49-5*) Stoneydale Pr Pub.

More Traditional Foods Vol. 2: Processing for Profit. Sue Azam-Ali et al. (Illus.). 224p. 1998. pap. 47.50 (*1-85339-429-7*, Pub. by Intermed Tech) Stylus Pub VA.

More Trails: In Pikes Peak Country. Zoltan Malocsay. (Illus.). 1994. pap. 9.99 (*0-9629250-2-0*) Squeezy Pr.

More Tramps Abroad. Mark Twain, pseud. (Works of Samuel Clemens). 1989. reprint ed. lib. bdg. 79.00 (*0-685-28370-4*) Rprt Serv.

More Travel Games. K. D. Kuch. LC 94-31230. (Fifty Nifty Ser.). 64p. (J). (gr. 4-7). 1995. pap. 5.95 (*1-56565-222-3*, 02223W, Pub. by Lowell Hse Juvenile) NTC Contemp Pub Co.

*__More Travellers' Tales from Heaven & Hell.__ Ed. by Dan Hiscocks. (Illus.). 256p. 2000. pap. 14.95 (*1-903070-02-3*, Pub. by Travellerseye Ltd) Midpt Trade.

More Treasured Mennonite Recipes II: Food, Fun & Fellowship from the Mennonite Relief Sales. Mennonite Central Committee Kenya. (Illus.). 224p. 1995. pap. 12.95 (*1-56523-028-0*) Fox Chapel Pub.

More Treasured Poems That Touch the Heart. Compiled by Mary S. Laurence. 256p. 1997. 14.00 (*0-88486-171-6*, Bristol Park Bks) Arrowood Pr.

More Tree Talk: The People, Politics & Economics of Timber. LC 93-48896. 1994. text 47.00 (*1-55963-253-4*); pap. text 24.95 (*1-55963-254-2*) Island Pr.

More Tricks of the Game Programming Gurus. (Illus.). 608p. (Orig.). 1995. 49.99 (*0-672-30697-2*) Sams.

More Trouble with the Obvious: Poems. Michael Van Walleghen. LC 80-24215. 72p. (C). 1981. 9.95 (*0-252-00865-0*); text 14.95 (*0-252-00864-2*) U of Ill Pr.

More True Blue Tales. Leo G. Frangipane, Jr. & Rita E. Miller. (Illus.). 250p. (Orig.). 1996. pap. write for info. (*0-9647313-1-2*) L G Frangipane.

*__More True Lies.__ George Shannon. LC 99-52860. (J). 2001. write for info. (*0-688-17643-7*, Grenwillow Bks); lib. bdg. write for info. (*0-06-029188-5*, Grenwillow Bks) HarpC Child Bks.

More True Stories: A Beginning Reader. 2nd ed. Sandra Heyer. LC 96-50334. 96p. (C). 1997. pap. text 17.59 (*0-201-69516-2*) Longman.

More True Tales of Old St. Helena. Jarvis Finger. (C). 1990. pap. 21.00 (*0-86439-024-6*, Pub. by Boolarong Pubns) St Mut.

More True Tales of Old-Time Kansas. David Dary. LC 87-6152. (Illus.). x, 268p. 1987. 19.95 (*0-7006-0331-X*); pap. 9.95 (*0-7006-0329-8*) U Pr of KS.

More Truly Stupid Sports Quotes. Jeff Parietti. LC 98-51521. (Illus.). 208p. 1999. pap. 10.95 (*0-06-273647-7*) HarpC.

More Truth Than Poetry. Fran Landesman. LC 80-85345. 64p. (Orig.). 1981. pap. 16.00 (*0-932966-13-6*) Permanent Pr.

More T.S. Eliot Reads: Eliot,& T.S. abr. ed. T. S. Eliot. 1993. audio 12.00 (*1-55994-835-3*, DCN 1045) HarperAudio.

More Turmoil in the Marianas, 1679-1683 see History of Micronesia: A Collection of Source Documents

More Twig Mosaic Furniture. L. J. Hawkins. LC 97-81407. 64p. 1998. pap. 14.95 (*0-7643-0499-2*) Schiffer.

More Twists. Burton Goodman. 120p. (J). (gr. 6). 1993. pap. text 12.64 (*0-89061-502-0*, Jamestwn Pub) NTC Contemp Pub Co.

More UFF Da Jokes, Vol. II. E. C. Stangland. 1984. 2.50 (*0-9613274-0-5*) Norse Pr.

More Ukulele Solos. Hideo Kimura. pap. 10.95 (*0-917822-29-3*) Heedays.

More Ukulele Solos by "Ear," Hawaiian Style. rev. ed. Hideo M. Kimura. 56p. 1986. pap. 10.95 (*0-917822-14-5*) Heedays.

More Uncommon Cats! John R. Guevin. LC 96-95305. (Illus.). 240p. 1997. 35.00 (*0-9637240-6-1*); pap. 16.95 (*0-9637240-5-3*) Biograph Pub.

More Unfinished Business. W. Gunther Plaut. LC 98-106746. (Illus.). 376p. 1997. text 35.00 (*0-8020-0888-7*) U of Toronto Pr.

More Unforgettable: Enjoyable Reading for the Intellect. Sidney S. Clarkson. 104p. 1996. pap. text, per. 13.95 (*0-7872-2299-2*) Kendall-Hunt.

More Unholy Writ: Jewish Verses & Vices. Mollee Kruger. 100p. 1973. pap. 2.25 (*0-913184-02-0*) Maryben Bks.

*__More Universe at Your Fingertips: Astronomy, Activities & Resources.__ Ed. by Andrew Fraknoi & Dennis Schatz. (Illus.). 356p. 2000. pap. 24.95 (*1-886733-98-8*, BO 123) Astron Soc Pacific.

More Urgent Than Usual: The Final Homilies of Mark Hollenhorst. Ed. by William Graham. 160p. (Orig.). 1995. pap. 11.95 (*0-8146-2356-5*, Liturg Pr Bks) Liturgical Pr.

More Vegetables, Please: Delicious Vegetable Side Dishes for Everyday Meals. Janet K. Fletcher. LC 92-15605. (Illus.). 228p. 1992. pap. 16.95 (*0-9627345-3-5*) Harlow & Ratner.

*__More Veggiecational Fun.__ Phil Vischer. LC 99-32496. (Illus.). 64p. (J). (ps-2). 1999. 10.99 (*0-8499-7531-X*) Tommy Nelson.

More Vignettes of Old Hawaii. David Free. pap. 12.95 (*0-9637946-1-2*) Free Advice.

More Virginia Broadsides Before 1877. Ray O. Hummel, Jr. ix, 106p. 1975. pap. text 9.95 (*0-88490-065-7*) Library of VA.

More Virtual Field Trips. 2nd ed. Gail Cooper Markunas & Garry Cooper. LC 99-19355. 200p. 1999. pap. 25.50 (*1-56308-770-7*) Libs Unl.

More Visual Basic 4 for Windows for Dummies. Wallace Wang. LC 95-77594. 432p. 1996. pap. 29.99 (*1-56884-326-7*) IDG Bks.

More Vocabulary Expanders. Mary Ellen Pierce. 1987. 4.95 (*1-55708-371-1*, MCR360) McDonald Pub Co.

More Voices from the Land. Ed. by Robert Wolf. (Folk Literature Ser.). 60p. (Orig.). 1993. pap. 5.95 (*1-878781-10-3*) Free River Pr.

More Voices in My Ear. large type ed. Doris Stokes. 312p. 1990. 22.95 (*0-7451-1149-1*, G K Hall Lrg Type) Mac Lib Ref.

More Walks & Rambles in Rhode Island. Ken Weber. LC 91-39176. (Walks & Rambles Ser.). (Illus.). 176p. (Orig.). 1992. pap. 14.00 (*0-88150-224-3*, Pub. by Countryman) Norton.

More Wandering Stars: An Anthology of Outstanding Stories of Jewish Fantasy & Science Fiction. Ed. by Jack Dann. LC 99-45347. 192p. 1999. pap. 16.95 (*1-58023-063-6*) Jewish Lights.

More Watery Still. Patricia Young. 85p. (Orig.). 1993. pap. 13.95 (*0-88784-541-X*, Pub. by Hse of Anansi Pr) Genl Dist Srvs.

More Ways Than One: Fostering Creativity in the Classroom. Arthur J. Cropley. LC 92-13362. (Creativity Research Ser.). 144p. 1992. pap. 24.50 (*0-89391-939-X*); text 73.25 (*0-89391-789-3*) Ablx Pub.

More Ways to Drive Your Man Wild in Bed. Graham Masterton. 1985. mass mkt. 6.99 (*0-451-16174-2*, Sig) NAL.

More We Find in Each Other: Meditations for Couples. Mavis Fossum & Merle Fossum. 154p. pap. 9.00 (*0-89486-793-8*, 5087A) Hazelden.

More We Get Together Big Book: Black & White Nellie Edge I Can Read & Sing Big Book. Adapted by Nellie Edge. (Illus.). (J). (ps-2). 1994. pap. text 20.00 (*0-922053-32-4*) N Edge Res.

More We Than Me: On Being One with Self & Others. rev. ed. Eva Thayer. (Illus.). 88p. 1986. vinyl bd. 8.95 (*0-9616432-0-X*) Tes Pub.

More Wealth Through Beating the Money Traps. Austin Donnelly. 195p. (C). 1990. pap. 60.00 (*0-86439-124-2*, Pub. by Boolarong Pubns) St Mut.

More Wealth Without Risk. Charles J. Givens. Ed. by Tom Miller. 624p. 1995. pap. 16.00 (*0-671-69403-0*) PB.

More Weekends for Two in Northern California: Fifty Romantic Getaways. Bill Gleeson. LC 94-10308. (Illus.). 132p. 1995. pap. 14.95 (*0-8118-0511-5*) Chronicle Bks.

*__More Weekends for Two in Northern California: 50 Great Romantic Getaways.__ rev. ed. Bill Gleeson. (Illus.). 132p. 2000. pap. 16.95 (*0-8118-2626-0*) Chronicle Bks.

More Welcome Speeches: Responses for All Occasions. Abingdon Press Staff. LC 97-190845. 64p. 1997. 6.95 (*0-687-05298-X*) Abingdon.

More West Highland Tales, 2 vols., Set. John F. Campbell. Ed. by W. J. Watson et al. Tr. by John G. McKay. LC 78-67695. (Folktale Ser.). reprint ed. 90.00 (*0-404-16070-0*) AMS Pr.

More West Highland Tales, Vol. 1. J. F. Campbell. 562p. pap. 25.95 (*1-874744-22-X*, Pub. by Birlinn Ltd) Dufour.

More West Highland Tales, Vol. 2. J. F. Campbell. 400p. pap. 25.95 (*1-874744-23-8*, Pub. by Birlinn Ltd) Dufour.

More What Canadians Believe But Shouldn't about Their Economy. Luciani. 1997. pap. text. write for info. (*0-201-89286-3*) Addison-Wesley.

More, Where Have You Been? Delma Morton. (Illus.). (J). (gr. k-3). 1989. 12.50 (*1-57842-114-4*) Delmas Creat.

More Whirligigs see Making Animated Whirligigs

*__More Wicked Words.__ Kerri Sharp. 2000. mass mkt. 6.95 (*0-352-33487-8*) BLA4.

More Wild Camp Tales. Mike Blakely. 208p. 1995. pap. 12.95 (*1-55622-392-7*, Rep of TX Pr) Wordware Pub.

More Wild Critters. Tim Jones. LC 94-75555. (Illus.). 48p. 1994. 15.95 (*1-55868-192-2*) Gr Arts Ctr Pub.

More Wildlife Painting: Techniques of Modern Masters. Susan Rayfield. LC 96-2887. (Illus.). 144p. 1996. 29.95 (*0-8230-5747-X*) Watsn-Guptill.

*__More Wildlife Painting: Techniques of Modern Masters.__ Susan Rayfield. (Illus.). 144p. 2000. pap. 19.95 (*0-8230-5745-3*) Watsn-Guptill.

*__More Windows 98: Simplified.__ Ruth Maran. LC 98-75156. 224p. 1998. pap. 24.99 (*0-7645-6037-9*) IDG Bks.

More Windows 98 for Dummies. Andy Rathbone. 384p. 1998. pap. 22.99 (*0-7645-0234-4*) IDG Bks.

*__More Windows 98 Secrets.__ Brian Livingston. LC 99-28102. (Secrets Ser.). 816p. 1999. pap. 34.99 (*0-7645-3360-6*) IDG Bks.

More Windows 95 for Dummies. Andy Rathbone. 360p. 1996. pap. 22.99 (*1-56884-607-X*) IDG Bks.

More Windows 95 Simplified. Maran Graphics Staff. 224p. 1996. pap. 19.99 (*1-56884-689-4*) IDG Bks.

More Windows 3.1 Secrets. Brian Livingston. 700p. 1993. pap. 39.95 (*1-56884-019-5*) IDG Bks.

More Windows to the World. Nancy Everix. (Illus.). 128p. (J). (gr. 2-8). 1985. student ed. 12.99 (*0-86653-316-8*, GA 640) Good Apple.

More Wings. C. David Hay. LC 92-97118. (Illus.). 1992. 8.00 (*0-9634527-0-3*) C D Hay.

More Winning One Acts. Ed. by Neil Johnson. 188p. pap. 24.95 (*1-56861-019-X*) Swift Lrn Res.

More Winning One Acts for Women. Ed. by Neil Johnson. 127p. pap. 19.95 (*1-56861-024-6*) Swift Lrn Res.

More Wisconsin Crimes of the Century. Marv Balousek. Ed. by Barbara Snell. (Illus.). 174p. (Orig.). 1993. pap. 12.95 (*1-878569-11-2*, Waubesa Pr) Badger Bks Inc.

More Wise Men of Helm: And Their Merry Tales. Solomon Simon. LC 65-14594. (Illus.). (Orig.). (J). (gr. 4-7). 1979. reprint ed. pap. 10.95 (*0-87441-470-9*) Behrman.

More with Less: Work Reorganization in the Canadian Mining Industry. Bob Russell. (Studies in Comparative Political Economy & Public Policy Ser.). (Illus.). 352p. 1998. text 55.00 (*0-8020-4354-2*); pap. text 21.95 (*0-8020-8178-9*) U of Toronto Pr.

More-with-Less Cookbook. Doris Longacre. LC 75-23563. 320p. 1976. spiral bd. 17.99 (*0-8361-1786-7*) Herald Pr.

*__More-with-Less Cookbook.__ 25th anniversary rev. ed. Doris Janzen Longacre. 332p. 2000. spiral bd. 20.99 (*0-8361-9103-X*) Herald Pr.

More Wonderful Yard-Long Prints: An Illustrated Value Guide for the Old Lithographs. William D. Keagy et al. (Illus.). 128p. 1992. 14.95 (*0-9633922-1-2*) W D Keagy.

More Word for Windows 97 for Dummies. Doug Lowe. LC 97-70744. 416p. 1997. pap. 22.99 (*0-7645-0137-2*) IDG Bks.

More Word Works. Alana Trisler & Patrice Cardiel. 64p. (Orig.). 1997. pap., wbk. ed. write for info. (*1-56762-068-X*) Modern Learn Pr.

More WordPerfect 6 for DOS for Dummies. Wallace Wang. LC 93-81200. 416p. 1994. pap. 19.95 (*1-56884-047-0*) IDG Bks.

More WordPerfect 6 for Windows for Dummies. Margaret L. Young & David C. Kay. LC 94-78908. 432p. 1994. pap. 19.95 (*1-56884-206-6*) IDG Bks.

*__More Words.__ Stephen Hearst. 127p. 1999. reprint ed. text 15.00 (*0-7881-6739-1*) DIANE Pub.

More Words, Ancient & Modern. Ernest Weekley. LC 70-164633. (Select Bibliographies Reprint Ser.). 1977. reprint ed. 20.95 (*0-8369-5917-5*) Ayer.

More Words I Use When I Write: For Grades Three to Four. Alana Trisler & Patrice H. Cardiel. 88p. (Orig.). 1990. pap., student ed. 2.75 (*0-935493-38-7*) Modern Learn Pr.

More Words, More Arrows: A Further Saying of Yiddi. Shirley Kumove. LC 98-10851. 1999. text 34.95 (*0-8143-2740-0*) Wayne St U Pr.

More Words You Should Know: Fifteen Hundred More Words Every Educated Person Should Be Able to Use & Define. Michelle Bevilacqua. LC 93-47470. 276p. 1994. pap. 8.95 (*1-55850-293-9*) Adams Media.

More Work! A Reading Program. Jeffrey E. Stewart. (Illus.). 116p. (Orig.). 1989. pap. 32.50 (*1-877866-03-2*) J E Stewart.

More Work for Mother: The Ironies of Household Technology from the Open Hearth to the Microwave. Ruth S. Cowan. LC 83-70759. 272p. 1985. pap. 17.00 (*0-465-04732-7*, Pub. by Basic) HarpC.

More Work for the Undertaker. Margery Allingham. 272p. 1989. pap. 3.95 (*0-380-70573-7*, Avon Bks) Morrow Avon.

More Work for the Undertaker. Margery Allingham. 253p. 1998. lib. bdg. 22.95 (*1-56723-013-X*) Yestermorrow.

More Workbench Silencers. George M. Hollenback. LC 98-234674. 43 p. 1998. write for info. (*0-87364-994-X*) Paladin Pr.

More Works of George F. Brown, Sr., Vol. 2. George F. Brown, Sr. 34p. 1995. lib. bdg. 10.00 (*0-9645242-1-X*) OceanFront IA.

More World War II Aircraft in Combat: 47 Famous Warplanes Depicted in Raging Conflict. Glenn B. Bavousett. LC 80-12082. (Illus.). 15.00 (*0-668-04550-7*, ARCO) Macmillan.

More Writing about Pictures: Using Pictures to Develop Language & Writing Skills. A. J. Evans & Marilyn Palmer. (J). (gr. 1-3). 1982. teacher ed. 2.95 (*0-8077-6040-4*) Tchrs Coll.

More Writing about Pictures: Using Pictures to Develop Language & Writing Skills, Bk. 1: Familiar Places. A. J. Evans & Marilyn Palmer. (J). (gr. 1-3). 1982. pap. 3.95 (*0-8077-6037-4*) Tchrs Coll.

More Writing about Pictures: Using Pictures to Develop Language & Writing Skills, Bk. 2: Action & Activity. A. J. Evans & Marilyn Palmer. (J). (gr. 1-3). 1982. pap. 3.95 (*0-8077-6038-2*) Tchrs Coll.

More Writing about Pictures: Using Pictures to Develop Language & Writing Skills, Bk. 3: Supplement-Fables. A. J. Evans & Marilyn Palmer. (J). (gr. 1-3). 1982. pap. 3.95 (*0-8077-6039-0*) Tchrs Coll.

More Writing Wizardry. Nancy B. Culberson. 64p. 1992. 10.95 (*0-8403-8143-3*) Kendall-Hunt.

More Years on the Tractor Seat. Arthur Battelle. (Illus.). 145p. 1995. pap. 12.95 (*0-85236-315-X*, Pub. by Farming Pr) Diamond Farm Bk.

More Yes & Know. (J). (gr. 3 up). 1991. pap. 2.47 (*1-56297-009-7*, YK-08); pap. 2.47 (*1-56297-010-0*, YK-09) Lee Pubns KY.

More You Love: Poetry by Jose Angel Vera. Jose A. Vera. 32p. 1998. pap. 2.95 (*1-887480-78-1*) Wrds Lght Intl.

More You Watch, the Less You Know: News Wars - (Sub)Merged Hopes - Media Adventures. Danny Schechter. (Illus.). 512p. 1999. pap. 17.95 (*1-888363-80-0*) Seven Stories.

More You Watch, the Less You Know: News Wars: Sub Merged Hopes/Media Adventures. Danny Schechter. LC 97-502. (Illus.). 512p. 1997. 26.95 (*1-888363-40-1*) Seven Stories.

More Youth Retreats: Creating Sacred Space for Young People. Aileen A. Doyle. 124p. 1989. spiral bd. 12.95 (*0-88489-223-9*) St Marys.

More Youthwalk: Faith, Dating, Friendship, & Other Topics for Teen Survival. Walk Thru the Bible Staff. (Youthwalk Ser.). 272p. (YA). 1992. pap. 12.99 (*0-310-54591-9*) Zondervan.

M

An Asterisk (*) at the beginning of an entry indicates that the title is appearing for the first time.

Moreau Factor. Jack L. Chalker. 2000. mass mkt. 6.99 (0-345-40296-0, Del Rey) Ballantine Pub Grp.

***Morecambe & Wise.** McCann. 2000. pap. 17.95 (1-85702-911-9, Pub. by Fourth Estate) Trafalgar.

***Morecambe & Wise.** Graham McCann. (Illus.). 416p. 2000. 35.00 (1-85702-735-3, Pub. by Fourth Estate) Trafalgar.

Morehead Family Day Book. Ed. by Michelle T. Puzio. (Illus.). (Orig.). 1996. pap. 6.25 (0-9647647-1-7) Preserv Greensboro.

Morehouse College - Then & Now. Photos by Jim Robinson. (First Edition Ser.). (Illus.). 112p. 1992. 39.95 (0-916509-86-9) Harmony Hse Pub.

Morei Ha'Umah. Yisroel Shurin. (HEB.). 214p. (YA). 1992. text 8.00 (1-878895-02-8, D451) Torah Umesorah.

Morei Ha'Umah, Vol. 2. Israel Shurin. (Illus.). 1997. pap. 5.00 (0-914131-46-X, D450) Torah Umesorah.

Morel: A Lifetime Pursuit. V. V. Thompson. (Illus.). (Orig.). 1995. pap. 3.95 (0-9645079-0-0) MO Micol Soc.

Morel Hunter's Companion. Nancy S. Weber. 208p. 1988. pap. 14.95 (0-941912-10-8) Mich Nat Res.

Morel Hunter's Companion: Guide to True & False Morels. Nancy S. Weber. (Illus.). 209p. 1995. reprint ed. pap. 19.95 (1-882376-16-1) Thunder Bay Pr.

Morel Mushrooms of the Wood River Valley. Doreen Marsh-Dorward. (Illus.). 8p. (Orig.). 1996. pap. 4.75 (0-9615729-3-0) Dorward Photo.

Morel Tales: The Culture of Mushrooming. Gary A. Fine. LC 97-37201. 336p. 1999. 35.00 (0-674-08935-9) HUP.

Morelling: The Joys of Hunting & Preparing Morel Mushrooms. Nettie L. Samuels & Margaret M. Evans. LC 87-15623. (Illus.). 96p. (Orig.). 1988. pap. 8.95 (0-936784-40-7) J Daniel.

Morelos of Mexico - Man with a Future: A Novel. Starr Jenkins. LC 96-94330. (Illus.). 204p. (Orig.). (C). 1996. pap. 15.00 (1-886659-18-4) M Starr Bks.

Morels: True or False: The Essential Field Guide & More. Larry Lonik. Ed. by Stephanie Reed & James Utley. (Illus.). 80p. 1999. pap. 11.95 (0-931715-04-0) R K T Pub.

Morels & More: Wild Mushrooms & Gourmet Recipes, Tales & Tips. Larry Lonik. Ed. by Stephanie Reed. (Illus.). 160p. 1999. pap. 14.95 (0-931715-02-4) R K T Pub.

Moremi Africa Calling, 1. Photos by Giacomo Medici del Vascello. 1998. 75.00 (88-422-0624-5) Dist Art Pubs.

Morenita. Virgilio P. Elizondo. (Illus.). 150p. 1980. 6.95 (0-614-04870-2) Mex Am Cult.

Morenita. Virgilio P. Elizondo. (SPA., Illus.). 146p. 1981. 6.95 (0-614-04869-9) Mex Am Cult.

Morenita: The Story of Lupe Cordoba. Guadalupe Cordoba. 104p. 1998. pap. 10.00 (0-8059-4452-4) Dorrance.

Morepartitions. Richard Kostelanetz. 28p. (Orig.). 1994. pap. 3.00 (0-926935-97-6) Runaway Spoon.

More's Utopia. Dominic Baker-Smith. 224p. 1991. 69.95 (0-04-800078-7, A8191) Routledge.

More's Utopia: Ideal & Illusion. Robbin S. Johnson. LC 75-81421. (Yale College Ser.: No. 9). 178p. reprint ed. pap. 55.20 (0-8357-8236-0, 203377200087) Bks Demand.

More's Utopia: The Biography of an Idea, No. 5--5. Jack H. Hexter. LC 76-15177. (History of Ideas Ser.: No. 5). 171p. 1976. reprint ed. lib. bdg. 49.75 (0-8371-8947-0, HEMU, Greenwood Pr) Greenwood.

More's Utopia & Utopian Inheritance. Ed. by A. D. Cousins & Damian Grace. LC 95-7779. 159p. 1995. lib. bdg. 37.50 (0-8191-9915-X) U Pr of Amer.

Moreshet Moshe Vol. 1: Torah Thoughts. Dayan M. Swift & Bereishith-Shemoth. 416p. 1989. 20.95 (0-87306-506-9) Feldheim.

Moreshet Moshe Vol. 2: Torah Thoughts. Vayikra-Devarim. 1989. 20.95 (0-87306-583-2) Feldheim.

Moreshet Sephard: The Sephardi Legacy, Vol. 1. Haim Beinart. 492p. 1992. 45.00 (965-223-793-0) Gefen Bks.

Moreshet Sephard: The Sephardi Legacy, Vol. 2. Haim Beinart. 478p. 1992. 45.00 (965-223-822-8) Gefen Bks.

Moreta, Dragonlady of Pern. Anne McCaffrey. 384p. 1984. mass mkt. 6.99 (0-345-29873-X, Del Rey) Ballantine Pub Grp.

Moreta, Dragonlady of Pern. Anne McCaffrey. 1983. 12.09 (0-606-03412-9, Pub. by Turtleback) Demco.

Moreta, Dragonlady of Pern. Anne McCaffrey. LC 83-4630. 286p. 1983. 25.00 (0-89366-251-8) Ultramarine Pub.

Morfologia del Ojo: Histologia y Estructura Microscopica, Cornea, y Esclera. G. K. Smelser et al. Tr. by Norma Boschetti. LC 78-15614. (Illus.). 380p. 1980. 18.00 (0-8477-2322-4) U of PR Pr.

Morfologia Flexional del Espanol. Ricardo A. Narvaez. Ed. by Leon O. Narvaez. LC 85-1208. (Illus.). 184p. (Orig.). (C). 1985. pap. text 13.95 (0-930795-00-8) Editorial AI.

***Morgaine Saga: Gate of Ivrel, Well of Shiuan, Fires of Azeroth.** C. J. Cherryh. (Morgaine Ser.). 2000. mass mkt. 7.99 (0-88677-877-8, Pub. by DAW Bks) Penguin Putnam.

Morgan. A. M. Bjornstad. 320p. mass mkt. 5.99 (1-896329-10-1) Picasso Publ.

Morgan. Chris Harvey. (Classic Car Ser.: No. 14). 256p. (Orig.). 1987. 41.95 (0-946609-28-4, P128, Pub. by Oxford Ill Pr) Haynes Manuals.

Morgan. Ken Hill. (Illus.). 160p. 1997. pap. 15.95 (0-7509-1368-1, Pub. by A Sutton) Motorbooks Intl.

Morgan. Ken Hill. (Album Ser.: No. 327). (Illus.). 32p. 1997. pap. 4.75 (0-7478-0328-5, Pub. by Shire Pubns) Parkwest Pubns.

Morgan: A History of That Branch of the Morgan Family Beginning with James of New London & Continued Through Line of Col. Samuel & Sybil Huntington Morgan of Weathersfield, VT to 1911. C. W. Morgan. 100p. 1991. reprint ed. pap. 15.00 (0-8328-1756-2) Higginson Bk Co.

Morgan: A History of the Descendants of Henry Oscar Morgan & Ellen Jane Mandigo. James K. Raywalt. (Illus.). 203p. 1992. reprint ed. pap. 29.00 (0-8328-2411-9); reprint ed. lib. bdg. 39.00 (0-8328-2410-0) Higginson Bk Co.

***Morgan: American Financier.** Jean Strouse. LC 99-87598. (Illus.). 816p. 2000. pap. 18.00 (0-06-095589-9, Perennial) HarperTrade.

Morgan: American Financier. Jean Strouse. LC 98-35028. (Illus.). 796p. 1999. 34.95 (0-375-50166-5) Random.

Morgan: Art of Selling a Unique Sports Car. Ken Hill. LC 97-3910. (Illus.). 168p. 1996. 29.95 (0-7603-0353-3) MBI Pubg.

***Morgan: The Buckhorn Brothers, Vol. 790.** Lori Foster. (Temptation Ser.). 2000. mass mkt. 3.99 (0-373-25890-9, 1-25890-4) Harlequin Bks.

Morgan Affair & Anti-Masonry. John C. Palmer. 117p. 1992. reprint ed. pap. 12.95 (1-56459-052-6) Kessinger Pub.

Morgan & Me. Stephen Cosgrove. LC 78-101413. (Serendipity Bks.). (Illus.). 32p. (J). (ps-3). 1978. pap. 4.99 (0-8431-0560-7, Price Stern) Peng Put Young Read.

Morgan & Me. Stephen Cosgrove. (Serendipity Ser.). 1985. 9.15 (0-606-02418-2, Pub. by Turtleback) Demco.

Morgan & the Money. Ted Staunton. (First Novels Ser.). (Illus.). 64p. (J). (gr. 1-4). 1999. text 3.99 (0-88780-456-X, Pub. by Formac Publ Co) Orca Bk Pubs.

***Morgan & the Money.** Ted Staunton. (First Novels). (Illus.). 64p. (J). 1998. bds. write for info. (0-88780-457-8, Pub. by J Lorimer) Formac Dist Ltd.

Morgan & Yew. Stephen Cosgrove. (Serendipity Bks.). (Illus.). 32p. (Orig.). (J). (gr. 1-4). 1982. pap. 4.99 (0-8431-0589-5, Price Stern) Peng Put Young Read.

Morgan Bay Mysteries: Low Vocabulary, High Interest Level. large type ed. Rambeau. Incl. Mystery of the Midnight Visitor. (gr. 3-10). (0-89064-084-X); Mystery of the Morgan Castle. (gr. 2-9). (0-89064-083-1); (J). reprint ed. write for info. (0-318-66044-X) NAVH.

Morgan-Collins-Teeples Book: Idaho Pioneers. Peg Morgan & George Morgan. 82p. 1992. pap. 20.00 (0-9634328-0-X) Knit-Toons.

Morgan County. S. Bzdell. (Images of America Ser.). Date not set. pap. 18.99 (0-7385-0011-9) Arcadia Publng.

Morgan County, Missouri, Marriage Records, 1833-1893. Sherida K. Eddlemon. 138p. (Orig.). 1990. pap. 12.00 (1-55613-305-7) Heritage Bk.

Morgan Dollars, 1878-1891, Vol. 1. 1978. 26.95 (0-307-09128-7) St Martin.

Morgan Dollars 1892, Vol. II. 1984. 23.95 (0-307-09129-5) St Martin.

Morgan Family Vol. 1: Thomas Warren & Lue Ella & Their Descendants, 1866-1998. Wanda B. Carter. (Illus.). 276p. 1998. pap. 30.00 (0-9625488-1-2) June Pubns.

***Morgan Freeman.** Gina DeAngelis. LC 99-18478. (Black Americans of Achievement Ser.). (Illus.). 88p. (YA). (gr. 7 up). 1999. 19.95 (0-7910-4963-9) Chelsea Hse.

***Morgan Freeman - Actor.** Gina DeAngelis. (Black Americans of Achievement Ser.). (Illus.). 144p. (YA). (gr. 5 up). 1999. pap. 9.95 (0-7910-4964-7) Chelsea Hse.

Morgan-Greer Tarot. Bill F. Greer. (Illus.). 1979. pap. 15.00 (0-913866-91-1, MG78) US Games Syst.

Morgan-Greer Tarot Deck-Book Set. Bill F. Greer & Susan Gerulskis-Estes. (Illus.). 96p. 1981. pap. 26.00 (0-88079-593-X) US Games Syst.

Morgan Grenfell, 1838 to 1988: The Biography of a Merchant Bank. Kathleen Burk. (Illus.). 364p. 1990. text 42.00 (0-19-828306-7) OUP.

Morgan Horse see Learning about Horses Series

Morgan Horse. (Learning about Horses Ser.). (Illus.). 48p. (J). (gr. 3-7). 1996. 19.00 (0-516-20082-8) Childrens.

***Morgan Horse.** Clint O'Conner. 272p. 2000. 18.99 (0-7089-5710-2) Ulverscroft.

Morgan Horse. Sally Spencer. 160p. 1994. 60.00 (0-85131-599-2, Pub. by J A Allen) Trafalgar.

***Morgan Library: An American Masterpiece.** (Illus.). 176p. 2000. 40.00 (1-85759-217-4, Pub. by Scala Books) Antique Collect.

Morgan Library Ghost Stories. Ed. by Inge Dupont & Hope Mayo. LC 90-82150. (Illus.). 107p. 1990. 24.95 (0-8232-1283-1) Fordham.

Morgan Makes Magic. Ted Staunton. LC 96-950186. (First Novels). (Illus.). 64p. (J). 1997. bds. 4.95 (0-88780-391-1, Pub. by Formac Publ Co) Formac Dist Ltd.

Morgan Makes Magic. Ted Staunton. LC 96-950187. (First Novels). (Illus.). 64p. (J). (gr. 1 up). 1999. mass mkt. 3.99 (0-88780-390-3, Pub. by Formac Publ Co) Formac Dist Ltd.

Morgan Morning. Stephen Cosgrove. (Serendipity Bks.). (Illus.). 32p. (Orig.). (J). (ps-3). 1996. pap. 3.95 (0-8431-3923-4, Price Stern) Peng Put Young Read.

Morgan-OCL. Rowan Isaacs. (Color Library). (Illus.). 128p. 1994. pap. 15.95 (1-85532-465-2, Pub. by Ospry) Motorbooks Intl.

Morgan Plays Soccer. Anne Rockwell. LC 99-39894. (Illus.). 32p. (J). (ps-1). 5.95 (0-06-446739-2) HarpC.

***Morgan Plays Soccer.** Anne Rockwell. LC 99-39894. (Illus.). 32p. (J). (ps-1). 2000. 14.89 (0-06-028444-7) HarpC.

***Morgan Plays Soccer.** Anne Rockwell. LC 99-39894. (Illus.). 32p. (J). (ps-1). 2000. 14.95 (0-06-028440-4) HarpC Child Bks.

Morgan Raid in Indiana & Ohio, 1863. rev. ed. Arville L. Funk. (Illus.). 68p. 1978. pap. 7.95 (0-9623292-3-1) Nugget IN.

Morgan Robbins' Tarot. Morgan Robbins. 1983. pap. 12.00 (0-88079-028-8, MG88) US Games Syst.

Morgan Spirit. Audrey Pavia. (Spirit of the Horse Ser.: No. 1). (Illus.). 64p. 2001. pap. 16.95 (1-889540-19-6) Bowtie Press.

Morgan Sportscar: The Early Years. Ed. by George Aichele & Tina Pippin. 1997. write for info. (1-85075-680-5, Pub. by Sheffield Acad) CUP Services.

Morgan Stanley Dean Witter Guide to Personal Investing, Revised ed. Robert Gardiner. 1999. pap. 12.95 (0-452-28121-0, Plume) Dutton Plume.

Morgan State. Sealy. 1998. pap. text, student ed. 15.00 (0-471-48042-8) Wiley.

***Morgan Takes a Hand.** large type ed. Al Joyson. 232p. 1999. pap. 18.99 (0-7089-5618-1, Linford) Ulverscroft.

Morgan Trail: A Story of Hashknife Hartley. Wilbur C. Tuttle. 1976. lib. bdg. 14.75 (0-89968-127-1, Lghtyr Pr) Buccaneer Bks.

Morgana: Two Stories from 'The Golden Apples' Eudora Welty. LC 88-20552. (Author & Artist Ser.). (Illus.). 160p. 1988. 25.00 (0-87805-400-6) U Pr of Miss.

Morgans see Great American Horses

Morgans: Private International Bankers, 1854-1913. Vincent P. Carosso. LC 86-14829. (Harvard Studies in Business History: No. 38). (Illus.). 904p. 1987. 69.95 (0-674-58729-4) HUP.

***Morgan's Child.** large type ed. Anne Mather. (Harlequin Romance Ser.). 2000. 22.95 (0-263-16409-8) Mills & Boon.

Morgan's Child: (Millenium Celebration) Anne Mather. (Presents Ser.: No. 2000). 1998. per. 3.75 (0-373-12000-1, 1-12000-5) Harlequin Bks.

Morgan's Coming Again: Civil War Books. Richard J. Reid. (Morgan's Comin' Agin! Ser.). (Illus.). 160p. 1999. 10.00 (1-877713-09-0) R J Reid.

Morgans Dream. Marilyn Singer. (Illus.). 88p. (J). (gr. 1-6). 1995. 15.95 (0-8050-3004-2, Bks Young Read) H Holt & Co.

Morgans Dream, Vol. 1. Singer. (J). 1995. 15.95 (0-8050-4354-3) H Holt & Co.

Morgan's Freemasonry Exposed & Explained. William Morgan. 131p. 1998. reprint ed. pap. 14.50 (0-7873-0623-1) Hlth Research.

Morgan's Guide: Lake Accesses in Washington. Bill Hanson. (Orig.). 1991. pap. text 12.95 (0-9629860-4-6) Sound Pub WA.

Morgan's Guide: Launches & Ramps on the Columbia River. Bill Hanson. (Orig.). 1991. pap. text 12.95 (0-9629860-3-8) Sound Pub WA.

Morgan's Guide: Ramps & Launches on Puget Sound. Bill Hanson. (Illus.). 250p. 1991. 12.95 (0-9629860-1-1) Sound Pub WA.

Morgan's Marriage. Lindsay McKenna. 1996. per. 3.75 (0-373-24005-8, 1-24005-0) Silhouette.

Morgan's Men: A Narrative of Personal Experiences. Henry L. Stone. 36p. 1992. reprint ed. pap. 5.00 (0-9623292-2-3) Nugget IN.

Morgan's Mercenaries: Heart of the Jaguar. Lindsay McKenna. 1999. pap. 5.99 (0-373-48371-6, 1-48371-8) Silhouette.

***Morgan's Mercenaries: Heart of the Warrior.** Lindsay McKenna. (Silhouette Ser.). 2000. mass mkt. 5.99 (0-373-48416-X, 1-48416-1) Harlequin Bks.

Morgan's Park. Katherine R. Chandler & Roy F. Chandler. (Illus.). 300p. (YA). 1997. lib. bdg. 35.00 (1-885633-10-6) Iron Brigade.

Morgan's Passing. Anne Tyler. LC 96-96708. 346p. 1996. pap. 12.00 (0-449-91172-1) Fawcett.

Morgan's Rescue. Lindsay McKenna. 1995. per. 3.75 (0-373-23998-X, 1-23998-7) Silhouette.

***Morgan's Run: A Novel.** Colleen McCullough. 608p. 2000. 28.00 (0-684-85329-9) S&S Trade.

Morgan's Son: Morgan's Mercenaries: Love & Danger. Lindsay McKenna. 1995. mass mkt. 3.75 (0-373-09992-4, 1-09992-8) Silhouette.

Morgan's Summit. Kathy Alba. 186p. mass mkt. 5.99 (1-55197-415-0) Picasso Publ.

Morgans to 1997: A Collectors Guide. Roger Bell. (Illus.). 128p. 1997. 27.95 (1-899870-20-2, Pub. by Motor Racing) Motorbooks Intl.

Morgan's Voice - Poems & Voices. Morgan Segal. 128p. 1997. pap. 15.00 (0-9662027-0-8) R Segal.

Morgan's Wife. Lindsay McKenna. 1995. per. 3.75 (0-373-09986-X, 1-09986-0) Silhouette.

***Morgan's Woman.** Judith E. French. 1999. mass mkt. 5.99 (0-345-40875-6) Ballantine Pub Grp.

Morgan's Zoo. James Howe. (Illus.). 192p. (J). (gr. 3-7). 1996. per. 4.50 (0-689-80833-X) Aladdin.

Morgan's Zoo. James Howe. LC 84-6325. (Illus.). 192p. (J). (gr. 3-6). 1984. 16.00 (0-689-31046-3) Atheneum Yung Read.

Morgan's Zoo. James Howe. (Illus.). 192p. (J). (gr. 3-7). 1986. pap. 3.99 (0-380-69994-X, Avon Bks) Morrow Avon.

Morgan's Zoo. James Howe. LC 84-6325. (J). 1996. 9.60 (0-606-09630-2, Pub. by Turtleback) Demco.

Morgante: The Epic Adventures of Orlando & His Giant Friend Morgante. Luigi Pulci. Tr. by Joseph Tusiani. LC 97-44991. (Indiana Masterpiece Editions Ser.). 975p. 1998. 49.95 (0-253-33399-7) Ind U Pr.

Morgantina, No. 3. Chatrio Di. 264p. (C). 1991. text 80.00 (0-691-04014-1, Pub. by Princeton U Pr) Cal Prin Full Svc.

Morgantina, Vol. 6. Princeton University Staff. (Morgantina Studies: No. 6). 1998. 85.00 (0-691-04017-6, Pub. by Princeton U Pr) Cal Prin Full Svc.

Morgantina, Vol. 7. Princeton University Staff. (Morgantina Studies: No. 7). 1999. 85.00 (0-691-04018-4, Pub. by Princeton U Pr) Cal Prin Full Svc.

Morgantown Glass. Jeffrey B. Snyder. LC 97-48420. 224p. 1998. write for info. (0-7643-0504-2) Schiffer.

***Morgen-Glantz.** 1999. 31.95 (3-906763-23-4, Pub. by P Lang) P Lang Pubng.

Morgen-Glantz: Zeitschrift der Christian Knorr von Rosenroth Gesellschaft. Sulzbach-Rosenberg. 396p. 1997. 40.95 (3-906757-92-7, Pub. by P Lang) P Lang Pubng.

Morgenlandisches Kleeblatt & Duftkorner, Aus Persischen Dichtern Gesammelt. Joseph F. Von Hammer-Purgstall. write for info. (0-318-71515-5) G Olms Pubs.

Morgentaler: The Doctor Who Couldn't Turn Away. 2nd ed. Eleanor W. Pelrine. 222p. 1975. mass mkt. 4.95 (0-88780-119-6, Pub. by Formac Publ Co) Formac Dist Ltd.

Morgenthau Diaries. Henry Morgenthau et al. LC 99-30853. (Research Collections in American Politics). 1995. write for info. incl. mic. film (1-55655-563-6) U Pubns Amer.

Morgenthau Diary (China) Proceedings of the U. S. Senate Committee on the Judiciary, 89th Congress, 1st Session, 2 vols. in 1. U. S. Senate Committee on the Judiciary. LC 70-167844. (FDR & the Era of the New Deal Ser.). 1693p. 1974. reprint ed. lib. bdg. 165.00 (0-306-70332-7) Da Capo.

Morgenthau Era Letters. Austin J. App. 1986. 250.00 (0-87700-878-7) Revisionist Pr.

Morgenthau, The New Deal & Silver. Allan S. Everest. LC 72-2368. (FDR & the Era of the New Deal Ser.). 209p. 1973. reprint ed. lib. bdg. 32.50 (0-306-70469-2) Da Capo.

Morgesons. Elizabeth Stoddard. Ed. by Lawrence Buell & Sandra Zagarell. LC 97-21263. 2XXIII, 64p. 1997. pap. 11.95 (0-14-043651-0) Viking Penguin.

Morgoth's Ring Pt. 1: The Later Silmarillion: The History of Middle-Earth, Vol. 10. J. R. R. Tolkien. 488p. 1993. 29.95 (0-395-68092-1) HM.

Morgy Makes His Move. Maggie Lewis. LC 98-43245. (Illus.). 80p. (J). (gr. 1-4). 1999. 15.00 (0-395-92284-4) HM.

Morhpophonemic Variability, Productivity & Change: The Case of Rusyn. Marta Harasowska. LC 98-20333. (Trends in Linguistics Ser.: No. 110). 288p. 1998. 124.00 (3-11-015761-6) De Gruyter.

Mori Arinori. Ivan P. Hall. LC 78-188348. (East Asian Monographs: No. 68). (Illus.). 547p. 1973. 47.95 (0-674-58730-8) HUP.

Mori, El Hebreo sin Maestro, Vol. 1. L. I. Riklis. (SPA.). 1987. pap. 11.00 (965-09-0129-9, 73895, Pub. by R Mass Ltd) Lambda Pubs.

Mori, El Hebreo sin Maestro, Vol. 2. L. I. Riklis. (SPA.). 1987. pap. 11.00 (965-09-0130-2, 73896, Pub. by R Mass Ltd) Lambda Pubs.

Mori, Moi Ucitel, 2 vols. L. I. Riklis. Incl. Vol. 1. Mori, Moi Ucitel. (RUS.). 1987. pap. 10.00 (965-09-0131-0, 73897, Pub. by R Mass Ltd); Vol. 2. Mori, Moi Ucitel. (RUS.). 1987. pap. 10.00 (965-09-0132-9, 73898, Pub. by R Mass Ltd); (RUS.). 1987. Set pap. 20.00 Lambda Pubs.

Mori, Moi Ucitel see Mori, Moi Ucitel

Mori, My Teacher: Hebrew Self-Taught, 2 vols. L. I. Riklis. Incl. Vol. 1. Mori, My Teacher: Hebrew Self-Taught. 1987. pap. 11.00 (965-09-0127-2, 73893, Pub. by R Mass Ltd); Vol. 2. Mori, My Teacher: Hebrew Self-Taught. 1987. pap. 11.00 (965-09-0128-0, 73894, Pub. by R Mass Ltd); 1987. Set pap. 22.00 Lambda Pubs.

Mori, My Teacher: Hebrew Self-Taught see Mori, My Teacher: Hebrew Self-Taught

Mori Ogwai: Great Short Stories from Around the World I. Illus. by James Balkovek. LC 94-75345. (Classic Short Stories Ser.). 80p. 1994. pap. 5.95 (0-7854-0653-0, 40066) Am Guidance.

Mori-Xwanzig Theory in Statistical Mechanics: Fundamentals & Applications. Ed. by Pozhar Liudmila. LC 94-37468. (Series in Contemporary Chemical Physics). 184p. 1995. text 53.00 (981-02-1750-1) World Scientific Pub.

Moriah's Magic. large type ed. Anne Ladley. LC 93-15497. 1993. pap. 13.95 (1-56054-749-9) Thorndike Pr.

Moriah's Mourning & Other Half Hour Sketches. Ruth M. Stuart. LC 71-198600. (Short Story Index Reprint Ser.). 1977. 18.95 (0-8369-3175-0) Ayer.

Moriah's Mourning & Other Half Hour Sketches. Ruth M. Stuart. LC 70-104573. (Illus.). reprint ed. pap. text 6.95 (0-89197-859-3); reprint ed. lib. bdg. 18.50 (0-8398-1878-5) Irvington.

Moriah's Pond. Ethel F. Smothers. LC 94-6490. (Illus.). 128p. (J). 1995. 16.00 (0-679-84504-6, Pub. by Knopf Bks Yng Read) Random.

***Moriarity's Greatest Con.** Jack. 2000. pap. 25.00 (0-7382-0345-9, Pub. by Perseus Pubng) HarpC.

Moriarty Principle: An Irregular Look at Sherlock Holmes. Rolf J. Canton. LC 96-40346. (Illus.). 272p. 1997. pap. 19.95 (1-880090-46-5) Galde Pr.

Moribundo. Michael G. Michaud. LC 92-96944. (Illus.). 32p. (Orig.). (C). 1992. pap. 9.95 (0-9620574-9-5) MGM Pr.

Moribundo. deluxe limited ed. Michael G. Michaud. LC 92-96944. (Illus.). 32p. (Orig.). (C). 1992. pap. 50.00 (0-9620574-8-7) MGM Pr.

Moriculture: Science of Mulberry Cultivation. Kichisaburo Minamizawa. (Illus.). 440p. 1997. text 120.00 (90-5410-287-X, Pub. by A A Balkema) Ashgate Pub Co.

Morien: A Metrical Romance Rendered into English Prose from the Mediaeval Dutch. Jessie L. Weston. LC 79-141786. (Arthurian Romances Unrepresented in Malory's "Morte DArthur" Ser.: Vol. 5). reprint ed. 22.50 (0-404-00475-X) AMS Pr.

Morigu: The Desecration. Mark C. Perry. 336p. (Orig.). 1986. mass mkt. 3.50 (0-445-20300-5, Pub. by Warner Bks) Little.

Morike: Poems. Eduard Morike. Ed. by Lionel Thomas. (Bristol German Texts Ser.). (GER.). 152p. 1960. 14.95 (0-631-01660-0) Blackwell Pubs.

M

Morike's Muses: Critical Essays on Eduard Morike. Ed. by Jeffrey Adams. LC 89-48764. (GERM Ser.: Vol. 49). (Illus.). 250p. 1990. 45.00 (0-938100-75-0) Camden Hse.

Morinus System of Interpretation. J. B. Morin. 116p. 1974. 10.00 (0-86690-132-9, M1348-014) Am Fed Astrologers.

Morir en Berlin see To Die in Berlin

Morir en la Habana: Novel. Antonio Villa. LC 95-76309. (Novels Ser.). (SPA.). 210p. (Orig.). 1995. pap. 14.95 (0-940788-04-7) Modern Guides.

Moriras Lejos. Jose E. Pacheco. (SPA.). 154p. 1980. pap. 8.00 (84-85859-00-6, 2011) Ediciones Norte.

Moris Havivel Melamid La-uf see Flying Lessons

Mori's Story: A Book about a Boy with Autism. Zachary M. Gartenberg. LC 97-33495. (Illus.). (J). 1998. lib. bdg. 21.27 (0-8225-2585-2) Lerner Pub.

Moriscos of Spain: Their Conversion & Expulsion. Henry Lea. LC 68-26358. (Studies in Spanish Literature: No. 36). 1969. reprint ed. lib. bdg. 75.00 (0-8383-0266-1) M S G Haskell Hse.

Moriscos of Spain: Their Conversion & Expulsion. Henry C. Lea. LC 68-19286. 463p. 1968. reprint ed. lib. bdg. 75.00 (0-8371-0141-7, LEMS, Greenwood Pr) Greenwood.

Morisot: Enchantment. (Rhythm & Color One Ser.). 1970. 9.95 (0-8288-9509-0) Fr & Eur.

Morisot Diary. Berthe Morisot. 64p. pap. 1.00 (0-486-27642-2) Dover.

Morita Equivalence & Continuous-Trace C*-Algebras. Iain Raeburn & Dana P. William. LC 98-25838. (Mathematical Surveys & Monographs: Vol. 60). 327p. 1998. 65.00 (0-8218-0860-5) Am Math.

Morita Therapy & the True Nature of Anxiety-Based Disorders (Shinkeishitsu) Shoma Morita. Ed. by Peg LeVine. Tr. by Akihisa Kondo. LC 97-35187. (Illus.). 160p. (C). 1998. text 52.50 (0-7914-3765-5); pap. text 17.95 (0-7914-3766-3) State U NY Pr.

Moritz Hauptmann of Leipzig. Dale A. Jorgenson. LC 86-23902. (Studies in the History & Interpretation of Music: Vol. 2). 248p. 1986. lib. bdg. 89.95 (0-88946-427-8) E Mellen.

Moritz Schlick. Ed. by Brian F. McGuinness. 156p. 1985. text 88.00 (90-277-2096-7, D Reidel) Kluwer Academic.

Moritz Schlick: Philosophical Papers, Vol. 2. Ed. by Henk L. Mulder & Barbara Van de Velde-Schlick. (Vienna Circle Collection: No. 11). 572p. 1980. pap. text 115.00 (90-277-0942-4, D Reidel) Kluwer Academic.

Moritz Schlick: Philosophical Papers, Vol. 2, 1925-1936. Ed. by Henk L. Mulder & Barbara Van de Velde-Schlick. (Vienna Circle Collection: No. 11). 572p. 1980. lib. bdg. 182.50 (90-277-0941-6, D Reidel) Kluwer Academic.

Moritz Schlick: Philosophical Papers, Vol. 1, 1909-1922, Vol. 1. Ed. by Henk L. Mulder & Barbara Van De Velde-Schlick. (Vienna Circle Collection: No. 11). 414p. 1978. pap. text 78.50 (90-277-0315-9, D Reidel); lib. bdg. 158.50 (90-277-0314-0, D Reidel) Kluwer Academic.

***Moriz von Craun.** Tr. by Albrecht Classen. 176p. 2000. pap. 9.95 (1-57766-152-4) Waveland Pr.

Moriz Von Craun. Ed. & Tr. by Stephanie C. Van D'Elden. LC 90-31444. (Library of Medieval Literature). 160p. 1990. text 15.00 (0-8240-4968-3, GLML 69A) Garland.

***Morkinskinna: The Earliest Icelandic Chronicle of the Norwegian Kings.** Theodore M. Andersson & Kari E. Gade. LC 99-43299. (Islandica Ser.). 2000. 75.00 (0-8014-3694-X) Cornell U Pr.

Morkmon: A Quarterly Model of the Netherlands Economy for Macro-Economic Policy Analysis. Ed. by M. M. G. Fase et al. 1985. pap. text 61.50 (90-247-3158-5) Kluwer Academic.

Morley: The Intimate Story of Virginia's Governor & Mrs. Westmoreland Davis. annot. ed. Carolyn Green. Ed. & Illus. by John T. Phillips, II. 128p. 1998. per. 19.95 (0-9656758-5-8) Goose Creek.

Morley Callaghan: Literary Anarchist. Gary Boire. LC 95-138552. (Illus.). 130p. 1994. pap. 9.95 (1-55022-185-X, Pub. by ECW) LPC InBook.

Morley Callaghan & His Works. Gary Boire. (Canadian Author Studies). 70p. (C). 1990. pap. text 9.95 (1-55022-029-2, Pub. by ECW) Genl Dist Srvs.

Morley's Canzonets for Two Voices. John E. Uhler. LC 54-62976. (Louisiana State University Studies, Humanities Ser.: No. 4). 81p. reprint ed. pap. 30.00 (0-608-10804-9, 200340000021) Bks Demand.

Mormans. Charles F. Browne. (Works of Charles Farrar Browne). 1989. reprint ed. lib. bdg. 79.00 (0-7812-2094-7) Rprt Serv.

Mormon America: The Power & the Promise. Richard N. Ostling & Joan K. Ostling. LC 99-28516. (Illus.). 480p. 1999. 26.00 (0-06-066371-5) HarpC.

***Mormon America: The Power & the Promise.** Richard N. Ostling & Joan K. Ostling. LC 99-28516. 480p. 2000. reprint ed. pap. 17.00 (0-06-066372-3) HarpC.

Mormon Americana: A Guide to Sources & Collections in the United States. Ed. by David J. Whittaker. LC 94-29931. (Studies Monographs). 1994. 29.95 (0-8425-2315-4, BYU Studies) Brigham.

Mormon Arts: Featuring Articles & Art Work by Mormon Artists & Authors. Mormon Festival of Arts Staff et al. LC 72-93467. 1972. write for info. (0-8425-0094-4, BYU Press) Brigham.

Mormon Basic Beliefs: On Christianity, with Questions, Answers, Verses, Illustrations & Index. 2nd rev. ed. Virgil B. Smith. LC 89-82076. (Illus.). 140p. (C). 1990. pap. 5.95 (1-878507-00-1, 42B) Human Grwth Services.

Mormon Battalion: United States Army of the West, 1846-1848. Norma B. Ricketts. LC 96-35706. (Illus.). 400p. 1996. pap. 22.95 (0-87421-215-4) Utah St U Pr.

Mormon Battalion, the Lord's Faithful. 2nd rev. ed. Robert O. Day. (Illus.). 364p. 1998. pap. 19.95 (1-890905-09-7) Day to Day.

Mormon Bibliography. 1992. lib. bdg. 300.95 (0-8490-5403-6) Gordon Pr.

Mormon Church see Hechos Acerca de los Mormones

Mormon Church. Roger Thompson. Ed. by James Haskins. (Religions of the World Ser.). 210p. 1993. 14.95 (0-7818-0126-5) Hippocrene Bks.

Mormon Church: A Basic History. Dean Hughes. LC 86-13566. 230p. 1990. reprint ed. pap. 7.95 (0-87579-343-6) Deseret Bk.

Mormon Concept of God: A Philosophical Analysis. Francis J. Beckwith & Stephen E. Parrish. LC 91-15131. (Studies in American Religion: Vol. 55). 156p. 1991. lib. bdg. 69.95 (0-7734-9787-0) E Mellen.

Mormon Controversies: A Balanced Approach. Joseph T. Carrieres. LC 88-90810. (Illus.). 156p. 1988. pap. 8.95 (0-929251-00-8) Sideris Pr.

Mormon Country. Wallace Stegner. LC 81-3410. x, 362p. 1981. pap. 15.00 (0-8032-9125-6, Bison Books) U of Nebr Pr.

***Mormon Culture of Salvation: Force, Grace & Glory.** 290p. 2000. 84.95 (0-7546-1328-3, Pub. by Ashgate Pub) Ashgate Pub Co.

***Mormon Culture of Salvation: Force, Grace & Glory.** Douglas James Davies. LC 00-29310. 2000. pap. write for info. (0-7546-1330-5) Ashgate Pub Co.

Mormon Democrat: The Religious & Political Memoirs of James Henry Moyle. limited ed. James H. Moyle. Ed. by Gene A. Sessions. LC 94-40560. (Significant Mormon Diaries Ser.: No. 8). (Illus.). 407p. 1998. 85.00 (1-56085-023-X) Signature Bks.

Mormon Doctrine. Bruce R. McConkie. 1958. 25.95 (0-88494-062-4) Bookcraft Inc.

Mormon Doctrine. Bruce R. McConkie. 1979. pap. 9.95 (0-88494-446-8) Bookcraft Inc.

Mormon Doctrine of Deity: The Roberts-Van der Donckt Discussion. Brigham H. Roberts. 296p. 1975. 17.98 (0-88290-058-7) Horizon Utah.

Mormon Doctrine of Deity: The Roberts-Van der Donckt Discussion. B. H. Roberts. LC 98-4089. (Mormon Classics: No. 3). 328p. 1998. reprint ed. pap. 14.95 (1-56085-111-2) Signature Bks.

Mormon Enigma: Emma Hale Smith. 2nd ed. Linda K. Newell & Valeen T. Avery. LC 93-32626. (Illus.). 432p. 1994. 16.95 (0-252-06291-4) U of Ill Pr.

Mormon Experience: A History of the Latter-Day Saints. 2nd ed. Leonard J. Arrington & Davis Bitton. (Illus.). 456p. 1992. 16.95 (0-252-06236-1) U of Ill Pr.

Mormon Girls Bk. 1: Something Lost, Something Gained. Susan Evans McCloud. 1995. pap. 6.95 (0-88494-993-1) Bookcraft Inc.

Mormon Girls Bk. 2: The Giving Heart. Susan Evans McCloud. 1995. pap. 5.95 (0-88494-994-X) Bookcraft Inc.

Mormon Girls Bk. 3: The Angels Sing. Susan Evans McCloud. 1995. pap. 5.95 (0-88494-995-8) Bookcraft Inc.

Mormon Girls Bk. 4: New Friends. Susan Evans McCloud. 1996. pap. 5.95 (1-57008-282-0) Bookcraft Inc.

Mormon Girls Bk. 5: A Lesson Learned. Susan Evans McCloud. 1996. pap. 5.95 (1-57008-283-9) Bookcraft Inc.

Mormon Girls Bk. 6: The Little Stranger. Susan Evans McCloud. 1996. pap. 5.95 (1-57008-284-7) Bookcraft Inc.

Mormon Graphic Image, 1834-1914: Cartoons, Caricatures, & Illustrations. Gary L. Bunker & Davis Bitton. LC 83-1305. (University of Utah Publications in the American West: No. 16). 164p. reprint ed. pap. 50.90 (0-8357-3274-6, 203949500013) Bks Demand.

Mormon Hierarchy: Extensions of Power. D. Michael Quinn. LC 95-7798. Vol. 2. (Illus.). 960p. 1997. 44.95 (1-56085-060-4) Signature Bks.

Mormon Hierarchy: Origins of Power, No. 1. D. Michael Quinn. LC 94-14854. Vol. 1. (Illus.). 720p. 1994. 29.95 (1-56085-056-6) Signature Bks.

***Mormon History.** Ronald W. Walker et al. LC 00-9378. 2001. write for info. (0-252-02619-5) U of Ill Pr.

Mormon Identities in Transition. Ed. by Douglas J. Davies. LC 96-1635. (Religious Studies). 256p. 1996. text 55.00 (0-304-33686-6) Continuum.

Mormon Illusion: What the Bible Says about the Latter-Day Saints. rev. ed. Floyd C. McElveen. LC 96-3420. 224p. 1997. pap. 10.99 (0-8254-3192-1) Kregel.

Mormon Landscape: Existence, Creation & Perception of a Unique Image in the American West. Richard V. Francaviglia. LC 77-83791. (Studies in Social History: No. 2). (Illus.). 42.50 (0-404-16020-4) AMS Pr.

Mormon Lives: A Year in the Elkton Ward. Susan B. Taber. LC 92-15573. (Illus.). 392p. (C). 1993. text 27.50 (0-252-01966-0) U of Ill Pr.

***Mormon Mafia Gestapo: America's K. G. B.** John Schlitz. 1999. pap. 24.00 (0-9646897-2-3) J Schlitz.

Mormon Mailables: Peculiar Postcards for a Peculiar People. Val Bagley. pap. 5.95 (1-57734-187-2, 01113259) Covenant Comms.

Mormon Mailables for Sister Missionaries: Peculiar Postcards for a Peculiar People. Val Bagley. pap. 5.95 (1-57734-291-7, 01113453) Covenant Comms.

Mormon Mazes: Twenty-Four Mazes Based on Familiar Church Events. Brett R. Bartlett. 26p. 1985. 4.98 (0-88290-301-2, 1340) Horizon Utah.

***Mormon Midwife: The 1846-1888 Diaries of Patty Bartlett Sessions.** Donna T. Smart. (Life Writings of Frontier Women: Vol. 2). 1999. pap. 19.95 (0-87421-274-X) Utah St U Pr.

Mormon Missionaries: An Inside Look at Their Real Message. Janis Hutchinson. 272p. 1996. pap. 12.99 (0-8254-2886-6) Kregel.

Mormon Mother: An Autobiography by Annie Clark Tanner. 3rd ed. Annie C. Tanner. Ed. by Obert C. Tanner. (Utah, the Mormons, & the West Ser.: No. 1). 382p. 1983. pap. 14.95 (0-941214-31-1, Tanner Trust) Signature Bks.

Mormon Odyssey: The Story of Ida Hunt Udall, Plural Wife. Ed. by Maria S. Ellsworth. (Illus.). 312p. 1992. text 29.95 (0-252-01875-3) U of Ill Pr.

Mormon Origins: An Eyewitness Account. John A. Clark. 1991. reprint ed. pap. 12.50 (0-89979-058-5) British Am Bks.

Mormon Passage: A Missionary Chronicle. Gary Shepherd & Gordon Shepherd. LC 97-4789. 472p. 1998. 24.95 (0-252-06662-6); text 49.95 (0-252-02356-0) U of Ill Pr.

Mormon Pioneer Trail: Mormon Trail Association 1997 Official Guide. Stanley B. Kimball. (Illus.). 46p. 1997. pap. 6.00 (0-87905-263-5) Gibbs Smith Pub.

Mormon Polygamy: A History. 2nd ed. Richard S. Van Wagoner. LC 89-6222. 268p. 1989. pap. 14.95 (0-941214-79-6) Signature Bks.

Mormon Presence in Canada. Ed. by Brigham Y. Card et al. LC 90-34484. (Illus.). 408p. reprint ed. pap. 126.50 (0-608-08566-9, 206908900002) Bks Demand.

Mormon Question in Its Economic Aspects. Dyer D. Lum. 1973. lib. bdg. 59.95 (0-8490-0672-4) Gordon Pr.

Mormon Rebel: The Life & Travels of Frederick Gardiner. Frederick Gardiner. Ed. by Hugh C. Garner. (Utah, the Mormons, & the West Ser.: No. 13). (Illus.). 184p. 1993. 21.95 (0-941214-51-6, Tanner Trust) Signature Bks.

Mormon Redress Petitions Vol. 16: Documents of the 1833-1838 Missouri Conflict. Clark Johnson. 1992. 24.95 (0-88494-850-1) Bookcraft Inc.

Mormon Settlement in Arizona. James McClintock. LC 78-134397. reprint ed. 54.00 (0-404-08439-7) AMS Pr.

Mormon Sisters: Women in Early Utah. Ed. by Claudia L. Bushman. LC 97-13396. (Illus.). 336p. 1997. pap. 17.95 (0-87421-233-2) Utah St U Pr.

Mormon Songs from the Rocky Mountains: A Compilation of Mormon Folksong. Ed. by Thomas E. Cheney. LC 68-63018. (Publications of the American Folklore Society, Bibliographical & Special Ser.: No. 53). 239p. reprint ed. pap. 74.10 (0-7837-5531-7, 204530400005) Bks Demand.

Mormon Tabernacle Organ. Barbara Owen. 19.95 (1-55517-054-4) CFI Dist.

Mormon Temple Square: The Story Behind the Scenery. Susan E. Black. Tr. by Saori Petzinger. (JPN., Illus.). 48p. (Orig.). 1993. pap. 8.95 (0-88714-760-7) KC Pubns.

Mormon Temple Square: The Story Behind the Scenery. Susan E. Black. LC 93-77026. (Illus.). 48p. (Orig.). 1993. pap. 7.95 (0-88714-076-9) KC Pubns.

Mormon Temple Square: The Story Behind the Scenery. Susan E. Black. Tr. by Brigitte Morales. (GER., Illus.). 48p. (Orig.). 1993. pap. 8.95 (0-88714-758-5) KC Pubns.

Mormon Temple Square: The Story Behind the Scenery. Susan E. Black. Tr. by Yvon Le Bras. (FRE., Illus.). 48p. (Orig.). 1993. pap. 8.95 (0-88714-759-3) KC Pubns.

Mormon Temple Square: The Story Behind the Scenery. Susan E. Black. Tr. by Carlos Marapodi. (SPA., Illus.). 48p. (Orig.). 1993. pap. 8.95 (0-88714-761-5) KC Pubns.

Mormon Thunder: A Documentary History of Jedediah Morgan Grant. Gene A. Sessions. LC 81-16075. (Illus.). 432p. 1982. text 24.95 (0-252-00944-4) U of Ill Pr.

Mormon Towns in the Region of the Colorado. Leland H. Creer. Incl. Activities of Jacob Hamblin in the Region of the Colorado. (Glen Canyon Ser.: Nos. 3-4). reprint ed. 20.00 (0-404-60633-4) AMS Pr.

Mormon Trail: Voyage of Discovery. Stanley B. Kimball & Violet T. Kimball. LC 95-75095. (Illus.). 64p. (Orig.). 1995. pap. 7.95 (0-88714-092-0) KC Pubns.

Mormon Trail: Voyage of Discovery. Stanley B. Kimball & Violet T. Kimball. Tr. by Brigitte Morales. (GER., Illus.). 48p. (Orig.). 1995. pap. 8.95 (0-88714-803-4) KC Pubns.

Mormon Trail: Yesterday & Today. William E. Hill. (Illus.). 240p. 1996. pap. 19.95 (0-87421-202-2) Utah St U Pr.

Mormon Trail & the Latter-Day Saints in American History. Carol Rust Nash. LC 98-35588. (In American History Ser.). 128p. (YA). (gr. 5 up). 1999. lib. bdg. 20.95 (0-89490-988-6) Enslow Pubs.

Mormon Trail Cookbook: Endeavors, Struggles & Cooking Traditions of the Mormon Pioneers. Morris Publishing Company Staff. Ed. by Dawn Feely et al. (Illus.). 194p. 1997. 10.95 (1-57502-476-4, Cookbks by Morris) Morris Pubng.

Mormon Village: A Study in Social Origins. Lowry Nelson. 1972. 250.00 (0-8490-0673-2) Gordon Pr.

Mormonism see Mormonismo

Mormonism. Alan W. Gomes. Ed. by Patti Picardi & Mike Carter. (Zondervan Guide to Cults & Religious Movements Ser.). 64p. 1995. pap. 5.99 (0-310-70401-4) Zondervan.

Mormonism. Salem Kirban. (Doctrines of Deception Ser.). 61p. 1971. pap. 4.99 (0-912582-13-8) Second Comng Inc.

Mormonism. Walter Martin. 32p. 1968. pap. 3.99 (0-87123-367-3) Bethany Hse.

Mormonism: Its Rise, Progress & Present Condition. N. W. Green. LC 79-134401. reprint ed. 71.00 (0-404-08445-1) AMS Pr.

Mormonism: Or Life Among the Mormons. Emily Austin. LC 74-134388. 1972. reprint ed. 44.50 (0-404-08480-X) AMS Pr.

Mormonism: Outline Study. Homer Hailey. 78p. 1992. pap. 5.95 (0-940999-77-3, C2183) Star Bible.

Mormonism: The Prophet, the Book & the Cult. Peter Bartley. 102p. (Orig.). 1989. pap. 8.95 (1-85390-063-X, Pub. by Veritas Pubns) St Mut.

Mormonism: The Prophet, the Book & the Cult: A Critique of Mormonism from the Origins to the Present Day. Ed. by Peter Bartley. 130p. 1989. pap. 22.00 (0-7855-6977-4, Pub. by Veritas Pubns) St Mut.

Mormonism: The Story of a New Religious Tradition. Jan Shipps. LC 84-2672. (Illus.). 232p. 1987. 13.95 (0-252-01417-0) U of Ill Pr.

Mormonism: What You Need to Know: Quick Reference Guide. Ron D. Rhodes & Decker. (Quick Reference Guide Ser.). 10p. (Orig.). 1997. pap. 1.99 (1-56507-511-0) Harvest Hse.

Mormonism Al Descubierto. Fernando Saravi. 416p. 1997. pap. 12.99 (0-8254-1670-1) Kregel.

Mormonism & Early Christianity. Hugh Nibley. LC 87-25291. (Collected Works of Hugh Nibley: Vol. 4). 446p. 1987. 25.95 (0-87579-127-1) Deseret Bk.

Mormonism & Masonry. S. H. Goodwin. 106p. 1992. reprint ed. pap. 12.95 (1-56459-051-8) Kessinger Pub.

Mormonism & Music: A History. Michael Hicks. LC 88-37886. (Music in American Life Ser.). (Illus.). 280p. 1989. text 24.95 (0-252-01618-1) U of Ill Pr.

Mormonism & the American Experience. Klaus J. Hansen. LC 80-19312. (Chicago History of American Religion Ser.). xx, 258p. 1994. pap. text 8.50 (0-226-31553-3) U Ch Pr.

Mormonism & the Mormons. Daniel P. Kidder. 1972. 59.95 (0-8490-0674-0) Gordon Pr.

***Mormonism & the Nature of God: A Theological Evolution, 1830-1915.** Kurt Widmer. LC 00-25624. 215p. 2000. 38.50 (0-7864-0776-X) McFarland & Co.

***Mormonism... Eternal Life or Eternal Death.** Jean Aardahl. Ed. by Pamela Sue Thurston. 40p. 2000. mass mkt. 5.99 (0-9675264-1-8) A A Pubs.

Mormonism in Conflict: The Nauvoo Years. Annette P. Hampshire. LC 84-27263. (Studies in Religion & Society: Vol. II). 350p. 1985. lib. bdg. 99.95 (0-88946-874-5) E Mellen.

Mormonism in Transition: A History of the Latter-Day Saints, 1890-1930. Thomas G. Alexander. LC 96-4170. 396p. (C). 1996. pap. text 16.95 (0-252-06578-6) U of Ill Pr.

Mormonism in Transition: A History of the Latter-day Saints, 1890-1930. Thomas G. Alexander. LC 84-22164. (Illus.). 396p. 1986. text 24.95 (0-252-01185-6) U of Ill Pr.

Mormonism, Mama & Me. Thelma Geer. pap. 9.99 (0-8024-5633-2, 221) Moody.

Mormonism, Mama & Me. 3rd rev. ed. Thelma Geer. LC 81-146846. (Illus.). 228p. 1983. pap. 3.95 (0-912375-00-0) Calvary Miss Pr.

Mormonism, Mama & Me. 4th ed. Ed. by Thelma Geer. (Illus.). 252p. 1984. pap. 4.95 (0-912375-01-9) Calvary Miss Pr.

Mormonism, Masonry, & Godhood: Can Angels Be Trusted? Cathy Burns. LC 98-170233. (Illus.). 132p. (Orig.). 1997. pap. 6.95 (1-891117-01-7) Sharing.

***Mormonism 101: Examining the Religion of the Latter-Day Saints.** Bill McKeever. LC 99-89663. 304p. 2000. pap. 15.99 (0-8010-1192-2) Baker Bks.

Mormonism Unmasked: Confronting the Contradictions Between Mormonism Beliefs & True Christianity. R. Philip Roberts. LC 98-12749. 120p. 1998. pap. 8.99 (0-8054-1652-8) Broadman.

Mormonism Unvailed: or A Faithful Account of That Singular Imposition & Delusion, from Its Rise to the Present Time. Eber D. Howe. LC 72-2967. reprint ed. 46.50 (0-404-10730-3) AMS Pr.

Mormonismo. Antonio A. Hoekema. (SPA.). 93p. 5.95 (1-55883-023-5, 6704-5030C) Libros Desafio.

Mormonismo. Walter Martin.Tr. of Mormonism. 112p. 1988. 7.99 (0-88113-208-X) Caribe Betania.

Mormonism's Negro Policy: Social & Historical Origins. Stephen G. Taggart. LC 77-116760. 88p. reprint ed. pap. 30.00 (0-8357-4384-5, 203721600007) Bks Demand.

Mormons. H. Berry. 1988. pap. text 1.35 (0-8474-0820-5) Back to Bible.

Mormons. Jean Kinney Williams. LC 96-33829. (American Religious Experience Ser.). 112p. (J). 1996. lib. bdg. 21.50 (0-531-11276-4) Watts.

Mormons. Thomas F. O'Dea. LC 57-6984. 1996. pap. text 13.50 (0-226-61744-0, P162) U Ch Pr.

Mormons. Thomas F. O'Dea. LC 57-6984. 301p. reprint ed. pap. 93.40 (0-608-09028-X, 206966300005) Bks Demand.

Mormons: How to Witness to Them. John R. Farkas & David A. Reed. LC 97-1616. 208p. (gr. 11). 1997. pap. 12.99 (0-8010-5739-6) Baker Bks.

Mormons: Or, Latter-Day Saints, in the Valley of the Great Salt Lake; a History of Their Rise & Progress, Peculiar Doctrines, Present Condition & Prospects, Derived from Personal Observation During a Residence Among Them. John W. Gunnison. LC 70-38355. (Select Bibliographies Reprint Ser.). 1977. reprint ed. write for info. (0-8369-6772-0) Ayer.

Mormons Against the Mob. Gary Roe. 200p. (Orig.). 1996. pap. 12.95 (1-888106-23-9) Agreka Bks.

Mormons & Mormonism, 15 vols. Edgar R. Snow et al. 1973. lib. bdg. 50.00 (0-8490-0675-9) Gordon Pr.

***Mormons & Mormonism: An Introduction to an American World Religion.** Eric A. Eliason. LC 00-8707. 2001. write for info. (0-252-06912-9) U of Ill Pr.

Mormons & the Bible: The Place of the Latter-Day Saints in American Religion. Philip L. Barlow. (Religion in America). (Illus.). 296p. 1997. reprint ed. pap. 18.95 (0-19-510971-6) OUP.

Mormons Answered Verse by Verse. David A. Reed & John R. Farkas. 160p. (Orig.). (gr. 11). 1992. pap. 9.99 (0-8010-7761-3) Baker Bks.

An Asterisk (*) at the beginning of an entry indicates that the title is appearing for the first time.

Mormons at Home. B. G. Ferris. LC 70-134395. reprint ed. 47.50 (0-404-08437-0) AMS Pr.

Mormons in America. Claudia L. Bushman & Richard L. Bushman. (Religion in America Ser.). (Illus.). 144p. (J). 1999. text 22.00 (0-19-510677-6) OUP.

Mormons in Iowa. Hazel Jensen. (History of Iowa Ser.). (Illus.). 51p. (Orig.). (YA). (gr. 5 up). 1988. pap. text 1.50 (0-924702-10-9) Grn Valley Area.

Mormons in Mexico: The Dynamics of Faith & Culture. F. LaMond Tullis. LC 87-14782. 286p. reprint ed. pap. 88.70 (0-7837-7064-2, 204687600004) Bks Demand.

Mormons in the Major Leagues: Career Histories of 44 LDS Baseball Players. James L. Ison. 304p. (Orig.). 1991. pap. 16.95 (0-9630122-0-7) Action Spts.

Mormons in the Pacific: A Bibliography. Compiled by Russell T. Clement. 239p. (C). 1981. text 12.95 (0-939154-17-X); pap. text 7.95 (0-939154-18-8) Inst Polynesian.

Mormons, Murders & AIDS. Darr Anderson. 450p. 1988. text 21.95 (0-9620810-0-0) B Devildog & Co.

Mormons on the Internet. Laura M. Gold. LC 97-39987. 368p. 1997. per. 18.00 (0-7615-1148-2) Prima Pub.

***Mormons on the Internet 2000-2.** Laura Gold. LC 99-41660. 368p. 1999. pap. 18.00 (0-7615-1568-2) Prima Pub.

Mormons: or Latter Day Saints. Henry Mayhew. LC 71-134398. reprint ed. 45.00 (0-404-08440-0) AMS Pr.

Mormons: or Latter-Day Saints, in the Valley of the Great Salt Lake: Their Rise & Progress, Peculiar Doctrines, Present Condition, & Prospects. John W. Gunnison. LC 92-25912. 175p. (C). 1992. reprint ed. text 20.00 (0-912111-37-2) Paradigm Publns.

Mormons, Scripture, & the Ancient World: Studies in Honor of John L. Sorenson. John L. Sorenson & Davis Bitton. LC 98-9753. 1998. write for info. (0-934893-31-4, F A R M S) Brigham.

Mormor's Immigrant Cookbook. 2nd ed. (ENG & SWE., Illus.). 404p. 1991. reprint ed. pap. 14.95 (0-944996-07-8) Carlsons.

Morn of Mystery. Betty K. Schultz. Ed. by Betty A. Kott. LC 98-68345. (Illus.). 112p. (Orig.). (J). (gr. 6-8). 2000. pap. write for info. (0-929568-02-8) Raspberry IL.

Morne-Paysan: A Peasant Village in Martinique. Michael M. Horowitz. 120p. 1983. reprint ed. pap. text 6.95 (0-8290-0712-1) Irvington.

Morne-Paysan: Peasant Village in Martinique. rev. ed. Michael M. Horowitz. (Illus.). 128p. (C). 1992. reprint ed. pap. text 10.50 (0-88133-683-1) Waveland Pr.

Mornin' Star Risin' Jean E. Holmes. LC 91-29460. (Weldon Oaks Ser.: No. 1). 160p. 1992. pap. 4.97 (0-8163-1064-5) Pacific Pr Pub Assn.

Morning. Nancy Thayer. 256p. 1990. mass mkt. 4.95 (0-380-70683-0, Avon Bks) Morrow Avon.

Morning: Two Poems. Joan Baranow. (Tanbark Ser.). 16p. (Orig.). 1997. pap. 6.00 (1-887853-14-6) Radiolarian.

***Morning After.** Suzanne Forster. 352p. 2000. mass mkt. 6.99 (0-515-12800-7, Jove) Berkley Pub.

Morning After. Created by Francine Pascal. (Sweet Valley High Ser.: No. 95). 224p. (YA). (gr. 7-12). 1993. mass mkt. 3.50 (0-553-29852-6) Bantam.

Morning After. Michelle Reid. 1997. per. 3.50 (0-373-11859-7, 1-11859-5) Silhouette.

Morning After. Kate William. (Sweet Valley High Ser.: No. 95). (YA). (gr. 7 up). 1993. 8.60 (0-606-05636-X, Pub. by Turtleback) Demco.

Morning After. large type ed. Michelle Reid. (Harlequin Ser.). 1996. 20.95 (0-263-14752-5) Thorndike Pr.

Morning After: American Successes & Excesses, 1981-1986. George F. Will. 1986. 27.95 (0-02-934430-1) Free Pr.

***Morning After: Making Corporate Mergers Work after the Deal is Sealed.** Stephen J. Wall & Shannon Rye Wall. 288p. 2000. text 25.00 (0-7382-0371-8, Pub. by Perseus Pubng) HarpC.

Morning After: Poems by Judith Hawk. Judith Hawk. 27p. 1999. pap. 5.00 (1-893068-03-X) P & Q Pr.

Morning After: Sex, Fear, & Feminism, Vol. 1. Katie Roiphe. 200p. 1994. pap. 8.95 (0-316-75432-3) Little.

Morning After: Sexual Politics at the End of the Cold War. Cynthia Enloe. LC 92-43416. 293p. 1993. 50.00 (0-520-08335-0, Pub. by U CA Pr); pap. 17.95 (0-520-08336-9, Pub. by U CA Pr) Cal Prin Full Svc.

***Morning After: Surviving Your Year 2000 Solution. Strategies to Keep Pace with the Technological Evolution.** large type ed. J. Keith Baker & Pamela Smith Baker. LC 99-70370. 128p. 1999. 22.95 (0-9668049-2-9, 1-2-9) Electec Pr.

Morning after Death. L. D. Johnson. 176p. 1995. 13.00 (1-57312-029-4) Smyth & Helwys.

Morning after Earth Day: Today's Practical Environmental Politics. Mary Graham. LC 98-58141. 1999. 36.95 (0-8157-3236-8); pap. 14.95 (0-8157-3235-X) Brookings.

Morning after Mourning. Vickee Martin. 58p. 1999. write for info. (0-7541-0825-2, Pub. by Minerva Pr) Unity Dist.

Morning after the First Night. George J. Nathan. LC 75-120099. 282p. 1975. 25.00 (0-8386-7779-7) Fairleigh Dickinson.

***Morning & Evening.** Charles H. Spurgeon. (Christian Classics). 528p. 2000. 4.97 (1-57748-789-3) Barbour Pub.

Morning & Evening. Charles H. Spurgeon. 1997. pap. 19.99 (1-85792-300-6, Pub. by Christian Focus) Spring Arbor Dist.

Morning & Evening. Charles H. Spurgeon. 762p. 1991. 14.95 (0-943575-53-2) Hendrickson MA.

Morning & Evening. Charles H. Spurgeon. LC 97-18623. 735p. 1997. pap. 17.99 (0-88368-410-1) Whitaker Hse.

Morning & Evening. Charles H. Spurgeon. 736p. 1980. reprint ed. 17.95 (0-310-32940-X, 10873) Zondervan.

***Morning & Evening.** unabridged ed. Charles H. Spurgeon. (Essential Christian Library Ser.). 540p. 1998. reprint ed. 9.97 (1-57748-347-2) Barbour Pub.

Morning & Evening, I & II. Charles H. Spurgeon. (Fifty Greatest Christian Classics Ser.). 740p. 1989. 24.95 (0-685-30022-6) Sovreign Grace Pubs.

Morning & Evening: A Parish Celebration. Joyce A. Zimmerman. 88p. 1996. pap. 10.00 (1-56854-117-1, MEPCEL) Liturgy Tr Pubns.

Morning & Evening: An Updated Ed. of the Classic Devotional in Today's Language. Charles H. Spurgeon. Ed. by Roy H. Clarke. 752p. 1994. 14.99 (0-7852-8239-4) Nelson.

Morning & Evening: Black. Charles H. Spurgeon. 1995. 19.99 (1-85792-125-9, Pub. by Christian Focus) Spring Arbor Dist.

Morning & Evening: Blue. Charles H. Spurgeon. 1995. 19.99 (1-85792-104-6, Pub. by Christian Focus) Spring Arbor Dist.

Morning & Evening: Burgundy. Charles H. Spurgeon. 1995. 19.99 (1-85792-126-7, Pub. by Christian Focus) Spring Arbor Dist.

Morning & Evening: Green. Charles H. Spurgeon. Date not set. 19.99 (1-85792-127-5, Pub. by Christian Focus) Spring Arbor Dist.

Morning & Evening: NIV Edition. Charles H. Spurgeon. 746p. 1995. 16.95 (1-56563-173-0) Hendrickson MA.

Morning & Evening Prayer. 1980. pap. 9.90 (0-88271-068-0) Regina Pr.

Morning & Evening Thoughts. James Allen. 71p. 1983. pap. 7.00 (0-89540-137-1, SB-137) Sun Pub.

Morning & Evening with the Spiritual Classics. Bernard Bangley. 90p. 1999. pap. 2.99 (0-87788-534-6, H Shaw Pubs) Waterbrook Pr.

Morning & the Evening. Joan Williams. LC 61-6381. (Voices of the South Ser.). 248p. 1994. pap. 11.95 (0-8071-1955-5) La State U Pr.

Morning at Pride Rock. Teddy Slater. (Disney Miniatures Ser.). (Illus.). 32p. (J). (gr. 3-7). 2001. pap. 16.99 (0-7868-4223-7, Pub. by Disney Pr) Time Warner.

Morning at Willoughby Run: July 1, 1863. Richard S. Shue. LC 98-84434. (Illus.). 336p. (C). 1995. text 24.95 (0-939631-79-2); pap. text 19.95 (0-939631-74-1) Thomas Publications.

***Morning Bakes.** Linda Collister. LC 99-40075. 64p. (J). (gr. 11). 2000. write for info. (0-7370-2033-4) Time-Life Educ.

Morning Before the Journey. Julian Schutting. Tr. by Barbara Z. Schoenberg. LC 98-48745. (Studies in Austrian Literature, Culture & Thought; Translation Ser.).Tr. of Am Morgen vor der Reise. 120p. 1999. pap. 14.50 (1-57241-071-X) Ariadne CA.

Morning Breaks: Stories of Conversion & Faith in the Former Soviet Union. Howard L. Biddulph. LC 96-13912. 188p. 1996. 15.95 (1-57345-152-5) Deseret Bk.

Morning Breaks: The Trial of Angela Davis. 2nd ed. Bettina Aptheker. LC 98-52220. 1999. pap. 16.95 (0-8014-8597-5) Cornell U Pr.

Morning by Morning. Charles H. Spurgeon. 368p. 1984. mass mkt. 6.99 (0-88368-156-0) Whitaker Hse.

***Morning by Morning, Vol. 8.** Charles H. Spurgeon. (Royal Classics Ser.). 2000. 9.97 (0-7852-4265-1) W1CL.

Morning by Morning: A Contemporary Version of a Devotional Classic Based on the King James Versi. Charles H. Spurgeon. 382p. 1998. 9.95 (1-56563-111-0) Hendrickson MA.

Morning Calm. Gerald A. Winter. Ed. by Caroline A. Winter et al. Tr. by Ruth Lucero. (Jeremy Stark Ser.). 304p. 1990. 19.95 (0-9626139-0-8) Dolph-Ann Pr.

Morning Calm: A Journey Through the Korean Countryside. 2nd ed. Robert Kowalczyk. (Asian Photos Ser.). (Illus.). 60p. 1983. pap. 14.95 (0-933704-47-X) Dawn Pr.

Morning Chair. Barbara M. Joosse. LC 93-4870. (Illus.). 32p. (J). (gr. k-3). 1995. 14.95 (0-395-62337-5, Clarion Bks) HM.

Morning Cometh: Forty-Five Years with Anatolia College. Carl C. Compton. Ed. by John O. Iatrides & William R. Compton. xxii, 116p. 1986. lib. bdg. 25.00 (0-89241-422-7) Caratzas.

Morning Contemplations. Osho. 1999. pap. 16.95 (0-312-24505-X) St Martin.

***Morning Dance.** Todd Hannert. LC 00-8943. (J). 2001. pap. write for info. (0-8118-2812-3) Chronicle Bks.

Morning Devotional. Compiled by Dwight Lyman Moody. 249p. 1999. mass mkt. 5.99 (0-88368-580-9) Whitaker Hse.

Morning Dew. large type ed. Elizabeth S. Ames. (Illus.). 24p. (Orig.). (J). (gr. 3-5). 1997. pap. write for info. (0-9647244-3-X, 46141) Cortland NY.

Morning Dew: Contemplations. Ron Puhalo, Jr. 48p. Date not set. pap. 5.00 (1-879038-52-8, 9021) Synaxis Pr.

Morning Dew & Roses: Nuance, Metaphor & Meaning in Folksongs. Barre Toelken. LC 94-13608. 208p. 1995. text 32.95 (0-252-02134-7) U of Ill Pr.

Morning Dewdrops of the Mind: Teachings of a Contemporary Zen Master. Shodo H. Roshi. Tr. by Daichi-Priscilla Storandt. LC 93-8465. 90p. (Orig.). 1993. pap. 9.95 (1-883319-10-2) Frog Ltd CA.

***Morning Drive to Midnight.** Renee P. Killingsworth. LC 99-74254. 290p. 1999. pap. 12.50 (1-882792-80-7) Proctor Pubns.

Morning Exercises. Judy McGorray. 113p. 1993. pap. text 10.00 (1-888200-00-6) JayMac Commun.

Morning Face. Gene S. Porter. 20.95 (0-8488-0872-X) Amereon Ltd.

Morning Faces. John Brown. (American Autobiography Ser.). 187p. 1995. reprint ed. lib. bdg. 69.00 (0-7812-8466-X) Rprt Serv.

Morning Faces: A Book of Children & Parents. John M. Brown. LC 78-167317. (Essay Index Reprint Ser.). (Illus.). 1977. reprint ed. 20.95 (0-8369-2755-9) Ayer.

Morning Food: From Cafe Beaujolais. Margaret Fox. (Illus.). 208p. (Orig.). 1994. pap. 19.95 (0-89815-308-5) Ten Speed Pr.

***Morning for Flamingos.** James Lee Burke. 1999. pap. 9.98 (0-671-04408-7) PB.

Morning for Flamingos. large type ed. James Lee Burke. LC 98-26235. 1998. 24.95 (1-57490-155-9, Beeler LP Bks) T T Beeler.

Morning for Flamingos. James Lee Burke. 336p. 1991. reprint ed. mass mkt. 6.99 (0-380-71360-8, Avon Bks) Morrow Avon.

***Morning for Mr. Prothero.** Jane Oliver. LC 99-80172. 320p. 2000. write for info. (1-893766-18-7) Aeon Pub Co.

Morning Gift. large type ed. Eva Ibbotson. 1994. 27.99 (0-7089-3167-7) Ulverscroft.

Morning Gift. large type ed. Diana Norman. 544p. 1987. 11.50 (0-7089-1629-5) Ulverscroft.

Morning Girl see Tainos

Morning Girl. Michael Dorris. 80p. (J). (gr. 4-7). 1999. pap. text 4.99 (0-7868-1372-5, Pub. by Hyperion) Time Warner.

Morning Girl. Michael Dorris. LC 92-52989. 80p. (YA). (gr. 4-7). 1994. pap. 4.95 (1-56282-661-1, Pub. by Hyprn Child) Little.

Morning Girl. Michael Dorris. LC 92-52989. (J). 1994. 9.15 (0-606-06583-0, Pub. by Turtleback) Demco.

Morning Girl. rev. ed. Michael Dorris. LC 92-52989. 80p. (J). (gr. 4-7). 1999. pap. 4.99 (0-7868-1358-X, Pub. by Hyperion) Time Warner.

Morning Glass: The Adventures of Legendary Waterman Mike Doyle. Mike Doyle & Steve Sorensen. LC 93-78947. (Illus.). 272p. (Orig.). 1993. pap. 14.95 (0-9629418-2-4) Fuyu Pr.

Morning Glories. Amy Bridges. (Princeton Studies in American Politics). 264p. 1999. pap. 19.95 (0-691-01009-9, Pub. by Princeton U Pr) Cal Prin Full Svc.

Morning Glories. Sylvia A. Johnson. (Lerner Natural Science Bks.). (Illus.). 48p. (J). (gr. 4-6). 1985. lib. bdg. 22.60 (0-8225-1462-1, Lerner Publctns) Lerner Pub.

Morning Glories. Jeanette Lockerbie. (Quiet Time Books for Women). (Orig.). pap. 4.99 (0-8024-6861-6, 413) Moody.

***Morning Glories: Breakfast, Brunch, & Light Fare from an Herb Garden.** Sharon Kebschull Barrett. LC 00-23030. (Illus.). 156p. 2000. text 24.95 (0-312-25224-2) St Martin.

Morning Glories: Municipal Reform in the Southwest. Amy Bridges. LC 96-45262. 258p. 1997. text 35.00 (0-691-02780-3, Pub. by Princeton U Pr) Cal Prin Full Svc.

Morning Glories: Recipes for Breakfast, Brunch & Beyond from an American Country Inn. Donna Leahy & Louis Wallach. LC 95-49832. (Illus.). 208p. 1996. 30.00 (0-8478-1923-X, Pub. by Rizzoli Intl) St Martin.

Morning Glories among the Peas: A Vietnam Veteran's Story. James D. Seddon. LC 90-43477. (Illus.). 155p. 1990. reprint ed. pap. 48.10 (0-608-00125-2, 206089000006) Bks Demand.

Morning Glories & Sapphires. Michael B. Devlin. 1999. pap. write for info. (1-58235-045-0) Watermrk Pr.

Morning Glories Out of Stone. Lisl Auf der Heide. LC 90-42896. 64p. (Orig.). 1990. pap. 7.50 (0-931832-55-1) Fithian Pr.

Morning Glory. Composed by Oasis. 96p. 1996. otabind 19.95 (0-7935-6288-0) H Leonard.

Morning Glory. LaVyrle Spencer. 448p. 1990. mass mkt. 7.50 (0-515-10263-6, Jove) Berkley Pub.

***Morning Glory: A Biography of Mary Lou Williams.** Linda Dahl. LC 99-34970. 480p. 2000. 30.00 (0-375-40899-1) Pantheon.

***Morning Glory Afternoon.** large type ed. Irene Bennett Brown. (Thorndike Romance Ser.). (J). 1999. 24.95 (0-7862-2253-0) Thorndike Pr.

***Morning Glory Devotional.** Juanita Bynum. (Illus.). 1999. pap. 15.99 (1-56229-150-5) Pneuma Life Pub.

Morning Glory, Evening Shadow: Yamato Ichihashi & His Internment Writings, 1942-1945. Ed. & Anno. by Gordon H. Chang. LC 96-7339. 1996. 45.00 (0-8047-2733-3) Stanford U Pr.

Morning Glory, Evening Shadow: Yamato Ichihashi & His Internment Writings, 1942-1945. Gordon H. Chang. (Asian America Ser.). 1999. pap. text 24.95 (0-8047-3653-7) Stanford U Pr.

Morning Glory Mother. Carol L. Pearson. LC 97-912. 101p. 1997. text 13.95 (0-312-15592-1) St Martin.

Morning Glory Mother. Carol L. Pearson. 1997. 13.95 (0-614-27909-7) St Martin.

Morning Glory Mother, Vol. 1. Pearson. 1998. write for info. (0-312-96508-7) Tor Bks.

Morning Glory Prayer Journal. Juanita Bynum. 1999. 19.99 (1-56229-156-4) Pneuma Life Pub.

Morning Glory-Quote Book. Juanita Bynum. 1998. pap. 6.99 (1-56229-151-3) Pneuma Life Pub.

Morning Has Broken. Eleanor Farjeon. LC 96-935. (Illus.). 32p. (J). 1996. 15.00 (0-8028-5127-4, Eerdmans Bks); pap. 7.50 (0-8028-5132-0, Eerdmans Bks) Eerdmans.

Morning Has Broken. Lynda Ward. (Superromance Ser.: No. 491). 1992. per. 3.39 (0-373-70491-7, 1-70491-5) Harlequin Bks.

Morning Has Broken: Stories & Poems for Easter. Pat Alexander. (Lion Book). 192p. (J). 1997. 15.99 (0-7459-3742-X, Lion) Chariot Victor.

Morning Hill Cookbook: A Whole Foods Vegetarian Cookbook. Jennifer S. Barker. LC 94-96617. 192p. 1995. pap. 11.95 (0-9642977-0-1) Morning Hill Assocs.

Morning Hill Solar Cookery Book. Jennifer S. Barker. LC 99-70204. (Illus.). x, 102p. 1999. pap. 14.95 (0-9642977-1-X) Morning Hill Assocs.

Morning in My Heart. Harold G. MacKay. (Illus.). 120p. (Orig.). 1993. pap. 5.95 (1-882701-04-6) Uplook Min.

Morning in the Burned House. Margaret Atwood. 127p. 1996. pap. 14.00 (0-395-82521-0) HM.

Morning Is a Little Child. Joan W. Anglund. LC 69-11592. (Illus.). (J). (gr. 4-6). 1969. 7.95 (0-15-255652-4, Harcourt Child Bks) Harcourt.

Morning Is a Long Time Coming. Bette Greene. 272p. (YA). 1993. mass mkt. 4.99 (0-440-21893-4) Dell.

Morning Is a Long Time Coming. Bette Greene. 1978. 9.60 (0-606-05928-8, Pub. by Turtleback) Demco.

***Morning Is a Long Time Coming.** Bette Greene. 1999. reprint ed. pap. 5.99 (0-14-130635-1, PuffinBks) Peng Put Young Read.

Morning Is Breaking. large type ed. Lesley Denny. 1990. 27.99 (0-7089-2297-X) Ulverscroft.

Morning Is for Joy. Ruth L. Hill. 1976. reprint ed. lib. bdg. 22.95 (0-89190-254-6, Rivercity Pr) Amereon Ltd.

***Morning Light.** 88p. 1999. otabind 14.95 (0-634-00908-7) H Leonard.

Morning Light. Lenora Boneck. (Illus.). 270p. (Orig.). 1986. pap. 12.95 (0-940415-00-3) B&K Pub Hse.

***Morning Light.** Steve Green. 256p. 2000. pap. 10.99 (0-7369-0384-4) Harvest Hse.

***Morning Light.** George Hammond. LC 99-91963. 2000. 25.00 (0-7388-1422-9); pap. 18.00 (0-7388-1423-7) Xlibris Corp.

Morning Light. Lee Harwood. 72p. 1998. pap. 13.95 (1-871033-41-1) Slow Dancer.

Morning Light. Curt Johnson. LC 76-50958. (Illus.). (Orig.). 1977. pap. 12.50 (0-914140-02-7) Carpenter Pr.

Morning Light. White Eagle. 64p. 1957. 6.95 (0-85487-018-0) White Eagle.

Morning Light: An Educational Storybook for Children & Caregivers about AIDS & Saying Goodbye. unabridged ed. Margaret Merrifield. (Illus.). 30p. (J). (ps-2). 1996. pap. 6.99 (0-7737-5704-X) STDK.

Morning Light: Choral Expressions of a Living Faith. Arranged by Mosie Lister. 108p. 1991. pap. 6.99 (0-8341-9800-2) Lillenas.

Morning Light: The Spiritual Journal of Jean Sulivan. Jean Sulivan. Tr. by Joseph Cuneen & Patrick Gormally. 192p. 1988. pap. 12.95 (0-8091-2985-X) Paulist Pr.

Morning Manna. Morris L. Venden. (Discovery Ser.). 31p. 1987. pap. 0.99 (0-8163-0731-8) Pacific Pr Pub Assn.

Morning Meditations. (In Classical Mood Ser.: Vol. 27). (Illus.). 1998. write for info. incl. cd-rom (1-886614-53-9) Intl Masters Pub.

Morning Meditations: Daily Meditations for Spiritual Humanists. Barbara Kopitz. 40p. 1999. spiral bd. 16.00 (0-9673259-0-0) Intl Inst for Secular.

Morning Meeting Book. Roxann Kriete. LC 98-68612. (Strategies for Teachers Ser.: No. 1). (Illus.). 140p. (Orig.). 1999. pap. 14.95 (1-892989-00-X) NE Found Child.

Morning Mist: Through the Seasons with Matsuo Basho & Henry David Thoreau. Ed. by Mary Kullberg. (Illus.). 132p. 1993. pap. 7.95 (0-8348-0277-5, Inklings Edits) Weatherhill.

Morning Moon. large type ed. Paula Reibel. 608p. 1987. 27.99 (0-7089-8399-5, Charnwood) Ulverscroft.

Morning Morning True: A Novel of Intrigue in New Guinea. Ernest Herndon. 240p. 1990. pap. 9.99 (0-310-27271-8) Zondervan.

Morning Mosh: Morning Radio Show Prep. Sunny Quinn. 216p. 1998. pap. 29.95 (0-9660531-1-7) Airwave Pub.

Morning, Noon, & Night. Jean Craighead George. LC 97-28796. (Illus.). 32p. (J). (ps-3). 1999. 15.95 (0-06-023628-0); lib. bdg. 15.89 (0-06-023629-9) HarpC Child Bks.

Morning, Noon & Night. Spalding Gray. LC 99-25630. 112p. 1999. 18.00 (0-374-29985-4) FS&G.

***Morning, Noon & Night.** Spalding Gray. 160p. 2000. pap. 12.00 (0-374-52721-0) FS&G.

Morning, Noon & Night. Sidney Sheldon. 398p. 1995. 24.00 (0-688-08492-3, Wm Morrow) Morrow Avon.

Morning, Noon & Night. Sidney Sheldon. 1996. pap. 7.50 (0-614-19493-8) Warner Bks.

Morning, Noon & Night. Sidney Sheldon. 388p. 1996. reprint ed. mass mkt. 7.50 (0-446-60221-3, Pub. by Warner Bks) Little.

Morning, Noon & Night: Poems to Fill Your Day. Illus. by Nancy Doniger. LC 95-25527. 24p. (J). (ps-2). 1996. 14.95 (1-57255-128-3) Mondo Pubng.

Morning of a Coup: The Dictatorship of Nigeria's Ibrahim B. Babamgida. Oladimeji Adeoye. 192p. (Orig.). 1995. pap. 19.95 (1-886094-14-4) Chicago Spectrum.

Morning of a Machine Gun: Including Surrealist Documents, 1966-68. Franklin Rosemont. (Illus.). 1968. pap. 12.00 (0-941194-00-0) Black Swan Pr.

Morning of the Fourth Day. 2nd rev. ed. Wiley E. Bean. LC 94-94263. 363p. 1992. 18.00 (0-9637650-0-0) W E Bean.

Morning of the World. Bob Hartman. (What Was It Like Ser.). (Illus.). 24p. (J). (ps-2). 1993. 8.99 (1-56476-040-5, 6-3040, Victor Bks) Chariot Victor.

Morning of the World. Bob Hartman & Michael McGuire. (J). (ps-3). 1994. 11.99 incl. audio (7-900882-45-6, 3-1212, Chariot Bks) Chariot Victor.

Morning of the World: Creation. Bob Hartman. (J). 1993. 11.99 incl. audio Chariot Victor.

Morning on the Lake. Jan Bourdeau Waboose. (J). 1997. pap. 5.95 (1-55074-588-3) Kids Can Pr.

Morning on the Lake. unabridged ed. Jan B. Waboose. (Illus.). 32p. (J). (gr. k-4). 1998. pap. 15.95 (1-55074-373-2, Pub. by Kids Can Pr) Genl Dist Srvs.

M

Morning Passage. deluxe ed. Janine P. Vega. Ed. by Maureen Owen. LC 76-19056. 1977. pap. 10.00 (*0-916382-15-X*) Telephone Bks.

Morning Poems. Robert Bly. LC 97-1502. 128p. 1997. 23.00 (*0-06-018251-2*) HarpC.

Morning Poems. Robert Bly. 128p. 1998. pap. 12.00 (*0-06-092873-5*) HarpC.

Morning Post, 1772 to 1937: Portrait of a Newspaper. Wilfrid Hindle. LC 73-16946. (Illus.). 260p. (C). 1974. reprint ed. lib. bdg. 35.00 (*0-8371-7243-8*, HIMP, Greenwood Pr) Greenwood.

Morning Prayer, Evening Praise. Ed. by Douglas Fisher & Brett Hoover. LC 96-37743. (Spiritual Samplers Ser.). 96p. (Orig.). 1997. pap. 1.95 (*0-8091-3720-8*) Paulist Pr.

Morning Prayer Evening Prayer: Chants, Songs & Prayers. Composed by Gregory Norbet. (Illus.). 70p. 1996. pap. 8.95 (*0-915531-53-4*, 10118) OR Catholic.

***Morning Prayer Evening Prayer Vol. 2: Chants, Songs & Prayers.** Gregory Norbet. (Illus.). 69p. 1998. pap. 8.95 incl. audio (*0-915531-91-7*, 10637) OR Catholic.

Morning, Rabbit, Morning. Mary Caldwell. LC 81-47724. (Illus.). 32p. (J). (ps-1). 1982. 10.95 (*0-06-020939-9*) HarpC Child Bks.

Morning, Rabbit, Morning. Mary Caldwell. LC 81-47724. (Trophy Picture Bk.). (Illus.). 32p. (J). (ps-1). 1987. pap. 2.95 (*0-06-443131-2*, HarpTrophy) HarpC Child Bks.

***Morning Reflections: A Collection of Inspirational Poetry.** Karen Jean Hood. (Illus.). 96p. 2000. write for info. (*0-9679368-4-5*) Whsprng Pine.

Morning Rendezvous: Praise & Worship in Poetry. Lena Cross. 48p. (Orig.). 1996. pap. 7.95 (*0-9637112-4-5*) Greater Success.

Morning Report: Internal Medicine. Thomas P. Archer et al. LC 99-33659. (Illus.). 240p. 1999. pap. text 42.50 (*0-07-006692-2*) McGraw-Hill HPD.

Morning Riser. Ed. by Penny E. Wheeler. 384p. (J). (gr. 3-6). 1988. 10.99 (*0-8280-0457-9*) Review & Herald.

Morning River. W. Michael Gear. 1997. mass mkt. 6.99 (*0-8125-5153-2*, Pub. by Forge NYC) St Martin.

Morning River: The Man from Boston. W. Michael Gear. 384p. 1996. 24.95 (*0-312-89039-7*) Forge NYC.

Morning Shows the Day. Ev Miller. LC 93-48187. 60p. (Orig.). 1994. pap. 6.00 (*0-88734-246-9*) Players Pr.

Morning Side of Dawn. Justine Davis. 1995. per. 3.75 (*0-373-07674-6*, 1-07674-4) Silhouette.

Morning Side of Dawn. large type ed. Justine Davis. (Silhouette Romance Ser.). 1997. 20.95 (*0-373-59819-X*) Mac Lib Ref.

Morning Song. Kimberly Cates. 1997. per. 5.99 (*0-671-56873-6*) PB.

Morning Song. Ed. by Rick Schaub. Date not set. 69.95 (*1-57553-160-7*) Watermrk Pr.

***Morning Song.** Mary Mckenna Siddals. 2001. text 15.95 (*0-8050-6369-2*) St Martin.

Morning Song. large type ed. Karen Robards. LC 97-13853. (Americana Series). 584p. 1997. 25.95 (*0-7862-1133-4*) Thorndike Pr.

Morning Song. Karen Robards. 400p. 1990. reprint ed. mass mkt. 5.99 (*0-380-75888-1*, Avon Bks) Morrow Avon.

Morning Song, No. 7. Linda Herring. (Serenade Serenata Ser.). 1984. pap. 1.49 (*0-310-46502-8*, 15510P) Zondervan.

Morning Song-Mourning Song: Narcissa: Her Story, Bk. II. Marje Blood. 285p. 1987. write for info. (*0-318-61951-2*); pap. 10.95 (*0-9615233-5-2*) Image Imprints.

Morning Star. Sigmund Brouwer. LC 94-7591. (Ghost Rider Ser.). 312p. (Orig.). 1994. pap. 9.99 (*1-56476-340-4*, 6-3340, Victor Bks) Chariot Victor.

Morning Star. Eleanor Burns. LC 88-92069. (Illus.). 64p. (Orig.). 1988. pap. text 8.95 (*0-922705-12-7*) Quilt Day.

Morning Star. Margaret Holley. LC 92-2577. 63p. (Orig.). 1992. pap. 9.95 (*0-914278-58-4*) Copper Beech.

Morning Star. Sylvia Regan. pap. 5.95 (*0-8222-1729-5*) Dramatists Play.

Morning Star. Marian Wells. LC 86-14781. (Starlight Trilogy Ser.: No. 3). 34p. (Orig.). 1986. pap. 8.99 (*0-87123-651-6*) Bethany Hse.

Morning Star. H. Rider Haggard. reprint ed. lib. bdg. 24.95 (*0-89190-710-6*) Amereon Ltd.

Morning Star: A Tribute to the American Dream. Noreen Wise. 496p. 1997. 24.00 (*0-9653035-8-6*); pap. 16.00 (*0-9653035-9-4*) Huckleberry CT.

Morning Star: The Life & Works of Francis Florentine Hagen. James Boeringer. LC 84-62100. (Illus.). 176p. 1986. 29.50 (*0-941642-01-1*) Morav Music Found.

Morning Star Journal, Vol. 1, No. 1. Ed. by Rick Joyner & Francis Frangipane. 64p. 1990. pap. 2.95 (*1-878327-07-0*) Morning NC.

Morning Star Journal, Vol. 1, No. 2. Ed. by Rick Joyner & Francis Frangipane. 64p. 1991. pap. 2.95 (*1-878327-08-9*) Morning NC.

Morning Star Journal, Vol. 1, No. 3. Ed. by Rick Joyner & Francis Frangipane. 64p. 1991. pap. 2.95 (*1-878327-11-9*) Morning NC.

Morning Star Journal, Vol. 1, No. 4. Ed. by Rick Joyner & Francis Frangipane. 64p. 1991. pap. 2.95 (*1-878327-12-7*) Morning NC.

Morning Star Journal, Vol. 1, No. 5. Ed. by Rick Joyner. 64p. 1991. pap. 2.95 (*1-878327-13-5*) Morning NC.

Morning Star Journal, Vol. 1, No. 6. Ed. by Rick Joyner. 64p. 1991. pap. 2.95 (*1-878327-14-3*) Morning NC.

Morning Star Journal, Vol. 2, No. 1. Ed. by Rick Joyner. 96p. (C). 1991. pap. 3.95 (*1-878327-15-1*) Morning NC.

Morning Star Journal, Vol. 2, No. 2. Ed. by Rick Joyner. 96p. (C). 1992. pap. 3.95 (*1-878327-16-X*) Morning NC.

Morning Star Journal, Vol. 2, No. 3. Ed. by Rick Joyner. 96p. (C). 1992. pap. 3.95 (*1-878327-18-6*) Morning NC.

Morning Star Journal, Vol. 2, No. 4. Ed. by Rick Joyner. 96p. 1992. pap. 3.95 (*1-878327-20-8*) Morning NC.

Morning Star Journal, Vol. 3, No. 1. Ed. by Rick Joyner. 96p. 1992. pap. 4.00 (*1-878327-24-0*, MSJ3-001) Morning NC.

Morning Star Journal, Vol. 3, No. 2. Ed. by Rick Joyner. 96p. 1993. pap. 4.00 (*1-878327-26-7*, MSJ3-002) Morning NC.

Morning Star Journal, Vol. 3, No. 3. Ed. by Rick Joyner. 96p. 1993. pap. 4.00 (*1-878327-28-3*, MSJ3-003) Morning NC.

Morning Star Journal, Vol. 3, No. 4. Ed. by Rick Joyner. 96p. 1993. pap. 4.00 (*1-878327-29-1*, MSJ3-004) Morning NC.

Morning Star Journal, Vol. 4, No. 1. Ed. by Rick Joyner. 96p. 1993. pap. 4.00 (*1-878327-32-1*, MSJ4-001) Morning NC.

Morning Star Journal, Vol. 4, No. 2. Ed. by Rick Joyner. 96p. 1994. pap. 4.00 (*1-878327-34-8*, MSJ4-002) Morning NC.

Morning Star Journal, Vol. 4, No. 3. Ed. by Rick Joyner. 96p. 1994. pap. 4.00 (*1-878327-35-6*, MSJ4-003) Morning NC.

Morning Star Journal, Vol. 4, No. 4. Ed. by Rick Joyner. 96p. 1994. pap. 4.00 (*1-878327-38-0*, MSJ4-004) Morning NC.

Morning Star Journal, Vol. 5, No. 1. Ed. by Rick Joyner. 96p. 1994. pap. 4.00 (*1-878327-39-9*, MSJ5-001) Morning NC.

Morning Star Journal, Vol. 5, No. 2. Ed. by Rick Joyner. 96p. 1995. pap. 4.00 (*1-878327-42-9*, MSJ5-002) Morning NC.

Morning Star Journal, Vol. 5, No. 3. Ed. by Rick Joyner. 96p. 1995. pap. 4.00 (*1-878327-43-7*, MSJ5-003) Morning NC.

Morning Star Journal, Vol. 5, No. 4. Ed. by Rick Joyner. 96p. 1995. pap. 4.00 (*1-878327-48-8*, MSJ5-004) Morning NC.

Morning Star Journal, Vol. 6, No. 1. Ed. by Rick Joyner. 96p. 1995. pap. 4.00 (*1-878327-49-6*, MSJ6-001) Morning NC.

Morning Star Journal, Vol. 6, No. 2. Ed. by Rick Joyner. 96p. 1996. pap. 4.00 (*1-878327-51-8*, MSJ6-002) Morning NC.

Morning Star Journal, Vol. 6, No. 3. Ed. by Rick Joyner. 96p. 1996. pap. 4.00 (*1-878327-53-4*, MSJ6-003) Morning NC.

Morning Star Journal, Vol. 6, No. 4. Ed. by Rick Joyner. 96p. 1996. pap. 4.00 (*1-878327-54-2*, MSJ6-004) Morning NC.

Morning Star Journal, Vol. 7, No. 1. Ed. by Rick Joyner. 96p. 1996. pap. 4.00 (*1-878327-56-9*, MSJ7-001) Morning NC.

Morning Star Journal, Vol. 7, No. 2. Ed. by Rick Joyner. 96p. 1997. pap. 4.00 (*1-878327-57-7*, MSJ7-002) Morning NC.

Morning Star Journal, Vol. 7, No. 3. Ed. by Rick Joyner. 96p. 1997. pap. 4.00 (*1-878327-64-X*, MSJ7-003) Morning NC.

Morning Star Journal, Vol. 7, No. 4. Ed. by Rick Joyner. 96p. 1997. pap. 4.00 (*1-878327-68-2*, MSJ7-004) Morning NC.

Morning Star Journal, Vol. 8, No. 1. Ed. by Rick Joyner. 96p. 1997. pap. 4.00 (*1-878327-73-9*, MSJ8-001) Morning NC.

Morning Star Journal, Vol. 8, No. 2. Ed. by Rick Joyner. 96p. 1998. pap. 4.00 (*1-878327-71-2*, MSJ8-002) Morning NC.

Morning Star Journal, Vol. 8, No. 3. Ed. by Rick Joyner. 96p. 1998. pap. 4.00 (*1-878327-80-1*, MSJ8-003) Morning NC.

Morning Star Journal, Vol. 8, No. 4. Ed. by Rick Joyner. 96p. 1998. pap. 4.00 (*1-878327-81-X*, MSJ8-004) Morning NC.

***Morning Star Journal, Vol. 9, No. 1.** Ed. by Rick Joyner. 96p. 1998. pap. 4.00 (*1-878327-85-2*, MSJ9-001) Morning NC.

***Morning Star Journal, Vol. 9, No. 2.** Ed. by Rick Joyner. 96p. 1999. pap. 4.00 (*1-878327-88-7*, MSJ9-002) Morning NC.

***Morning Star Journal, Vol. 9, No. 3.** Ed. by Rick Joyner. 96p. 1999. pap. 4.00 (*1-878327-89-5*, MSJ9-003) Morning NC.

***Morning Star Journal, Vol. 9, No. 4.** Ed. by Rick Joyner. 96p. 1999. pap. 4.00 (*1-878327-98-4*, MSJ9-004) Morning NC.

***Morning Star Journal, Vol. 10, No. 1.** Ed. by Rick Joyner. 96p. 1999. pap. 4.00 (*1-878327-92-5*, MSJ10-001) Morning NC.

Morning Star of the Reformation. Andy Thompson. 134p. (YA). 1988. pap. 6.49 (*0-89084-453-4*, 034637) Bob Jones Univ.

Morning Star Quilts. Florence Pulford. (Illus.). 80p. 1989. 34.95 (*0-942786-00-9*); pap. 24.95 (*0-942786-28-9*) Eddies Q Bee.

Morning Star Quilts: A Presentation of the Work & Lives of Northern Plains Indian Women. Florence Pulford. (Illus.). 80p. 1996. text 9.95 (*0-486-29466-8*) Dover.

***Morning Star Youth Journal: The Message, Vol. 1, No. 1.** Ed. by Rick Joyner. 48p. 1999. pap. 3.00 (*1-878327-86-0*, TM9901) Morning NC.

***Morning Star Youth Journal: The Message, Vol. 1, No. 2.** Ed. by Rick Joyner. 54p. 1999. pap. 3.00 (*1-878327-87-9*, TM9902) Morning NC.

***Morning Star Youth Journal: The Message, Vol. 1, No. 3.** Ed. by Rick Joyner. 48p. 1999. pap. 3.00 (*1-878327-99-2*, TM9903) Morning NC.

***Morning Star Youth Journal: The Message, Vol. 1, No. 4.** Ed. by Rick Joyner. 48p. 1999. pap. 3.00 (*1-878327-91-7*, TM9904) Morning NC.

Morning Streets: Reading Level 1-3 & Above. Ruth Radin. LC 92-42220. (Illus.). 1993. 4.75 (*0-88336-040-3*) New Readers.

Morning Sun: Interviews with Chinese Writers of the Lost Generation. Laifong Leung. LC 92-33902. (Studies on Contemporary China). 440p. (C). (gr. 13). 1994. text 85.95 (*1-56324-093-9*, East Gate Bk) M E Sharpe.

Morning Sun: Interviews with Chinese Writers of the Lost Generation. Laifong Leung. LC 92-33902. (Studies on Contemporary China). 440p. (C). (gr. 13). 1994. pap. text 39.95 (*1-56324-130-7*, East Gate Bk) M E Sharpe.

Morning Sun on a White Piano. Robin R. Meyers. LC 97-23082. (Illus.). 144p. 1998. 16.95 (*0-385-48954-4*) Doubleday.

***Morning Sun on a White Piano: Simple Pleasures & the Sacramental Life.** Robin R. Meyers. 144p. 2000. pap. 9.95 (*0-385-49869-1*) Doubleday.

Morning Talks. 3rd ed. Kirpal Singh. (Illus.). 260p. (C). 1988. reprint ed. pap. 8.25 (*0-942735-16-1*) Ruhani Satsang.

Morning Talks. 4th ed. Kirpal Singh. LC 81-51514. (Illus.). 260p. 1982. reprint ed. pap. 10.00 (*0-918224-15-2*) S K Pubns.

Morning the Sun Went Down. Darryl B. Wilson. LC 99-162310. 190p. 1998. pap. 13.95 (*0-930588-81-9*) Heyday Bks.

Morning the Sun Went Down. Darryl B. Wilson. LC 99-162310. 192p. 1998. 22.50 (*0-930588-97-5*) Heyday Bks.

Morning Tide. large type ed. Neil M. Gunn. LC 93-611. 335p. 1993. lib. bdg. 17.95 (*1-56054-717-0*) Thorndike Pr.

Morning to Polish & Keep. Julie Lawson. (Illus.). 32p. (J). (ps-3). 1998. pap. 7.95 (*0-88995-179-9*, Pub. by Red Deer) Genl Dist Srvs.

***Morning Train.** Gerald Dawe. 52p. 2000. 25.95 (*1-85235-260-4*, Pub. by Gallery Pr); pap. 13.95 (*1-85235-259-0*, Pub. by Gallery Pr) Dufour.

Morning Walk. Emma Moffett. 52p. 1998. pap. 9.95 (*1-885206-62-3*) Cader Pubng.

Morning Window. Laura J. Coats. LC 94-14515. (J). 1995. text. write for info. (*0-02-719055-2*) Macmillan.

Morning Wounds in the Warehouse. Dennis Paddie. (Illus.). 64p. (Orig.). 1993. pap. 12.00 (*0-9631569-1-8*) Backyard Pr.

Morningland Astrology, Bk. 2. (Astrology Ser.). 1979. pap. 4.95 (*0-935146-06-7*) Morningland.

Morningland Astrology, Bk. 3. Patricia. Ed. by Morningland Publications, Inc. Staff. (Astrology Ser.). (Illus.). 301p. (Orig.). 1980. pap. 7.95 (*0-935146-07-5*) Morningland.

Morningland Astrology Chart Construction. Morningland Publications, Inc. Staff. (Illus.). 100p. (Orig.). 1980. pap., spiral bd. 3.50 (*0-935146-10-5*) Morningland.

Morningland Color Book. Gopi Gyan. 1979. pap. 7.95 (*0-935146-09-1*) Morningland.

Morningquest. large type ed. Joan Aiken. 544p. 1994. 27.99 (*0-7089-3125-1*) Ulverscroft.

Mornings. Eleanor A. McQuilkin. 80p. (Orig.). 1986. 13.95 (*0-9608824-2-1*); pap. 8.95 (*0-9608824-3-X*) Stereopticon Pr.

Morning's Gate. Ann V. Roberts. 640p. 1993. reprint ed. mass mkt. 5.99 (*0-380-70992-9*, Avon Bks) Morrow Avon.

Mornings in Florence. John Ruskin. 1994. lib. bdg. 21.95 (*1-56849-424-6*) Buccaneer Bks.

Mornings in Florence: Being Simple Studies of Christian Art for English Travellers. John Ruskin. LC 71-11568. 271p. 1972. reprint ed. 69.00 (*0-403-00306-7*) Scholarly.

Mornings Inn Style: A Cookbook & Travel Guide from the Wisconsin Bed & Breakfast Assn. Member Inns of the Wisconsin Bed & Breakfast Association Staff. LC 98-86310. (Illus.). 176p. 1999. pap. 15.95 (*0-942495-83-7*) Palmer Pubns Inc.

Morning's Intelligence. Rosmarie Waldrop. (Illus.). 20p. (Orig.). 1986. 4.00 (*0-938535-77-3*) Salt-Works Pr.

Mornings Like This: Found Poems. Annie Dillard. 96p. 1996. pap. 11.00 (*0-06-092725-9*) HarpC.

Mornings on Horseback. David McCullough. 1994. 28.00 (*0-8446-6732-3*) Peter Smith.

Mornings on Horseback. David McCullough. 446p. 1982. pap. 15.00 (*0-671-44754-8*, Touchstone) S&S Trade Pap.

Mornings with Fulton Sheen: 120 Holy Hour Readings. Fulton J. Sheen & Beverly Coney Heirich. LC 97-45754. 1998. 15.99 (*1-56955-040-9*, Charis) Servant.

Mornings with Henri Nouwen: 120 Daily Readings. Evelyn Bence. LC 97-36041. 1997. 14.99 (*1-56955-057-3*) Servant.

Mornings with Mary: 120 Daily Readings. Ed. & Selected by Servant Publications Staff. LC 97-13523. (Illus.). 143p. 1997. 14.99 (*0-89283-995-3*, Charis) Servant.

Mornings with Therese of Lisieux: 120 Daily Readings. Patricia Treece. LC 97-20512. 150p. 1997. 14.99 (*1-56955-059-X*, Charis) Servant.

Mornings with Thomas Merton: 120 Daily Readings. Thomas Merton. LC 97-45998. 1998. 15.99 (*1-56955-009-3*) Servant.

Morning's Work: Photographs from the Burns Archive. Stanley Burns. (Illus.). 248p. 1998. 60.00 (*0-944092-45-4*) Twin Palms Pub.

Morningside. Charles J. Smith. 290p. (C). 1996. pap. 33.00 (*0-85976-354-4*, Pub. by J Donald) St Mut.

Morningside Heights: A History of Its Architecture & Development. Andrew Dolkart. LC 97-44482. (History of Urban Life Ser.). (Illus.). 471p. 1998. 50.00 (*0-231-07850-1*) Col U Pr.

Morningside Years. Peter Gzowski. (Illus.). 344p. 1998. 27.95 (*0-7710-3706-6*) McCland & Stewart.

Morningsong. Patricia H. Rushford. LC 97-33860. (Portraits Ser.). 256p. 1998. pap. 8.99 (*1-55661-993-6*) Bethany Hse.

Morningstar. David Gemmell. (Orig.). 1993. mass mkt. 5.50 (*0-345-37909-8*) Ballantine Pub Grp.

MorningStar: Thirty-Six Songs of Christ, The Redeemer. Arranged by Tom Fettke & Doug Holck. 119p. 1981. pap. 6.99 (*0-8341-9416-3*) Lillenas.

Morningstar Closed-End Fund 250: 1996 Edition. 2nd ed. Morningstar Inc. Staff. 1996. 35.00 (*0-7863-0538-X*, Irwn Prfssnl) McGraw-Hill Prof.

Morningstar Conspiracy. William C. Kern. 201p. (Orig.). 1988. pap. 6.95 (*0-9621518-0-7*) Kerson Pub.

***Morningstar 500: 2000-2001 Edition.** Morningstar Inc. Staff. 600p. 2000. pap. 39.95 (*0-07-135774-2*) McGraw.

Morningstar Mutual Fund 500: An In-Depth Look at 500 Select Mutual Funds from the Leading Authority in Mutual-Fund Analysis, 1996 Edition. 4th ed. Morningstar Inc. Staff. 525p. 1996. 35.00 (*0-7863-0539-8*, Irwn Prfssnl) McGraw-Hill Prof.

Morningstar Mutual Fund 500: 1998 Edition. Morningstar Staff. 626p. 1998. pap. 35.00 (*0-07-043431-X*) McGraw.

Morningstar Mutual Fund 500: 1999-2000 Edition. Morningstar Inc. Staff. 1999. pap. text 35.00 (*0-07-134948-0*) McGraw.

Morningstar Papers. Bradd Hopkins. 1999. write for info. (*1-891954-50-4*) Russell Dean.

MorningStar Program Resources. 1981. 6.99 (*0-685-68657-4*, MB-502A) Lillenas.

Morningtown Ride. Malvina Reynolds. (Illus.). 32p. (J). (ps-12). 1996. 14.95 (*0-89594-763-3*) Crossing Pr.

Morningtown Ride. Malvina Reynolds. (Illus.). 20p. (J). (ps-4). 1984. pap. 4.95 (*0-931793-00-9*) Turn-the-Page.

Moro: Ellis Heywood's Dialogue in Memory of Thomas More. Ellis Heywood. Tr. by Roger L. Deakins. LC 75-184107. 158p. 1978. 22.95 (*0-674-58735-9*) HUP.

Moro de Oro: Un Romance Historico. (SPA.). 25p. (Orig.). 1997. pap. 4.99 (*1-878382-08-X*) Book Gallery.

Moro Morality Play: Terrorism As Social Drama. Robin E. Wagner-Pacifici. LC 86-11317. xiv, 374p. (C). 1986. pap. text 17.95 (*0-226-86984-9*) U Ch Pr.

***Moro Morality Play: Terrorism as Social Drama.** Robin E. Wagner-Pacifici. LC 86-11317. xiv, 374p. (C). 1998. lib. bdg. 54.00 (*0-226-86983-0*) U Ch Pr.

Morobullia: Seventy-Five Years of Winston-Salem Rotary. Douglas M. Young. Ed. by Jane Kelly. (Illus.). xii, 404p. 1992. 35.00 (*0-9621194-5-8*) Stratford NC.

***Moroccan.** Ed. by Lorenz Books Staff. 2000. pap. 9.95 (*0-7548-0044-X*, Lorenz Bks) Anness Pub.

Moroccan Arabic Phrasebook. Dan Bacon. (ARA., Illus.). 176p. 1991. pap. 3.95 (*0-86442-071-4*) Lonely Planet.

Moroccan Arabic Phrasebook. 2nd ed. Dan Bacon. (Lonely Planet Phrasebooks). 180p. 1999. pap. text 5.95 (*0-86442-586-4*) Lonely Planet.

Moroccan Carpets. Brooke Pickering et al. (Illus.). 160p. 1998. 75.00 (*1-85669-146-2*) L King Pubng.

Moroccan Collection: Traditional Flavors from Northern Africa. Hilaire Walden. LC 98-6192. (Illus.). 144p. 1998. 25.00 (*1-57959-017-9*, SOMA) BB&T Inc.

***Moroccan Cookbook.** Irene Frances Day. LC 99-26996. (Illus.). 160p. 1999. pap. 12.95 (*1-56554-700-4*) Pelican.

***Moroccan Cooking.** Rebekah Hassan. 96p. 1999. pap. 12.95 (*0-7548-0556-5*) Anness Pub.

Moroccan Cuisine see Al Maghribi

Moroccan Dialogues: Anthropology in Question. Kevin Dwyer. LC 82-15167. 327p. 1982. reprint ed. pap. 101.40 (*0-608-03727-3*, 206455200009) Bks Demand.

Moroccan Dialogues: Anthropology in Question. Kevin Dwyer. (Illus.). 297p. (C). 1987. reprint ed. pap. text 13.95 (*0-88133-293-3*) Waveland Pr.

***Moroccan Foods & Culture.** Jennifer Ferro. LC 99-21049. (Festive Foods & Celebrations Ser.). (Illus.). 48p. (J). (gr. 3-4). 1999. lib. bdg. 19.45 (*1-57103-304-1*) Rourke Pr.

Moroccan Goums: Tribal Warriors in a Modern War, 177. L. Bimberg. LC 98-52989. (Contributions in Military Studies Ser.: Vol. 177). 176p. 1999. 55.00 (*0-313-30913-2*) Greenwood.

Moroccan Interiors. Lisa Lovatt-Smith. (Jumbo Ser.). 1998. 39.99 (*3-8228-8177-5*) Taschen Amer.

Moroccan Mirages: Agrarian Dreams & Deceptions, 1912-1986. Will D. Swearingen. LC 87-6981. (Illus.). 236p. 1987. reprint ed. pap. 73.20 (*0-608-07498-5*, 206772100009) Bks Demand.

Moroccan Silk Designs in Full Color. Ed. by Lucien Vogel. LC 96-9379. (Illus.). 48p. 1996. pap. 10.95 (*0-486-29255-X*) Dover.

***Moroccan Style.** Alexandra Bonfante-Warren. LC 99-57931. (Architecture & Design Library Ser.). (Illus.). 96p. 2000. 17.95 (*1-56799-956-5*, Friedman-Fairfax) M Friedman Pub Grp Inc.

Morocco see Cultures of the World - Group 10

Morocco. 1998. 7.95 (*0-88729-155-4*) Langenscheidt.

Morocco. Ettagale Blauer & Jason Laure. LC 98-17644. (Enchantment of the World Ser.). 144p. (YA). (gr. 5-9). 1999. 32.00 (*0-516-20961-2*) Childrens.

Morocco. Photos by Bruno Brukoff. LC 93-20181. (Illus.). 128p. 1993. 49.50 (*0-8109-3631-3*) Abrams.

Morocco. Hugues Demende. 1998. 19.99 (*3-8228-7757-3*) Taschen Amer.

Morocco. Ed. by Anne M. Findlay et al. (World Bibliographical Ser.: No. 47). 311p. 1984. lib. bdg. 65.00 (*0-903450-84-4*) ABC-CLIO.

***Morocco.** Ed. by Fodors Travel Publications, Inc. Staff. 320p. 1999. pap. 19.00 (*0-679-00393-2*, Pub. by Random Bks Yng Read) Random.

Morocco. Shirley Kay. (Illus.). 160p. 1981. 30.00 (*0-7043-2224-2*, Pub. by Quartet) Charles River Bks.

Morocco. Jim Keeble. LC 94-68183. (Illustrated Travel Guides from Thomas Cook Ser.). (Illus.). 192p. (Orig.). 1994. pap. 12.95 (*0-8442-9079-3*, Passprt Bks) NTC Contemp Pub Co.

***Morocco.** Patrick Merrick. LC 99-40504. (J). 2000. lib. bdg. write for info. (*1-56766-737-6*) Childs World.

An Asterisk (*) at the beginning of an entry indicates that the title is appearing for the first time.

Morocco. NTC Publishing Group Staff. (Passport Essential Guide Ser.). 128p. 1998. pap. 8.95 (*0-8442-0128-6*, 01286, Passprt Bks) NTC Contemp Pub Co.
Morocco. Hans Seligo. (Panorama Bks.). (Illus.). 1966. 3.50 (*0-685-11405-8*) Fr & Eur.
***Morocco.** Annette Solyst. LC 00-37569. (Timeless Places Ser.). (Illus.). 2000. pap. write for info. (*1-56799-990-5*, Friedman-Fairfax) M Friedman Pub Grp Inc.
***Morocco.** Taschen Staff. 1999. 19.99 (*3-8228-8033-7*) Taschen Amer.
Morocco. rev. ed. Compiled by Nelles Verlag. (Nelles Guides Ser.). (Illus.). 256p. 1992. pap. 14.95 (*3-88618-385-8*, Pub. by Nelles Verlag) Seven Hills Bk.
Morocco. 2nd ed. Insight Guides Staff. (Insight Guides). 1998. pap. text 12.95 (*0-88729-916-4*) Langenscheidt.
Morocco. 2nd ed. Annabelle Barker. 1997. reprint ed. mass mkt. 6.50 (*1-56333-541-7*, Rosebud) Masquerade.
Morocco. 2nd rev. ed. Anne M. Findlay. LC 96-192658. (World Bibliographical Ser.). 212p. 1991. lib. bdg. 61.00 (*1-85109-216-1*) ABC-CLIO.
Morocco. 2nd rev. ed. Nelles Verlag Staff. (Nelles Guides Ser.). (Illus.). 256p. 1999. pap. 15.95 (*3-88618-113-8*) Hunter NJ.
Morocco. 3rd ed. Barnaby Rogerson. (Cadogan Country Guides Ser.). (Illus.). 576p. 1997. pap. text 19.95 (*1-86011-043-6*, Pub. by Cadgn Bks) Macmillan.
Morocco. 5th ed. Insight Guides Staff. (Insight Guides). 1998. pap. text 22.95 (*0-88729-715-3*) Langenscheidt.
Morocco: A Country Study. Ed. by Harold D. Nelson. LC 85-600265. (DA Pam Area Handbook Ser.: No. 550-49). (Illus.). 476p. (YA). (gr. 9-12). 1986. 20.00 (*0-16-001640-1*, S/N 008-020-01072-3) USGPO.
***Morocco: A Country Study Guide.** Global Investment & Business Center, Inc. Staff. (World Country Study Guides Library: Vol. 117). (Illus.). 350p. 2000. pap. 59.00 (*0-7397-2415-0*) Intl Business Pubns.
Morocco: Casablanca to Marrakesh. Lisl Dennis. LC 98-43875. 1999. pap. 25.00 (*0-609-80465-0*) Crown Pub Group.
Morocco: Its People & Places. E. De Amicis. 396p. 1984. 220.00 (*1-85077-055-7*, Pub. by Darf Pubs Ltd) St Mut.
***Morocco: Jews & Art in a Muslim Land.** Vivian B. Mann et al. (Illus.). 192p. 2000. 50.00 (*1-85894-110-5*, Pub. by Merrell Holberton) Rizzoli Intl.
Morocco: Major World Nations. Chelsea House Publishing Staff. (Major World Nations Ser.). (Illus.). 144p. 1999. 19.95 (*0-7910-5389-X*) Chelsea Hse.
***Morocco: Marrakesh, Fez, Rabat.** Barnaby Rogerson. (City Guides Ser.). (Illus.). 2000. pap. 17.95 (*1-86011-973-5*) Cadgn Bks.
Morocco: Sahara to the Sea. Tahar Ben Jelloun. LC 95-1266. (Illus.). 240p. 1995. 60.00 (*0-7892-0030-9*) Abbeville Pr.
Morocco: The Travel Notebook. Pascale Loiseau. 104p. 1997. 14.95 (*2-911141-07-5*, Pub. by Les Edtns Pascale) Assoc Pubs Grp.
Morocco: Trial in Rabat Arising Out of Disturbances on 20 & 21 June 1981: Report to the International Commission of Jurists on a Mission in July 1981 to Morocco. Andre Tremblay. LC 84-172848. 32p. reprint ed. pap. 30.00 (*0-608-18112-9*, 203271100081) Bks Demand.
Morocco - A Country Study Guide: Basic Information for Research & Pleasure. Global Investment Center, USA Staff. (World Country Study Guide Library: Vol. 117). (Illus.). 350p. 1999. pap. 59.00 (*0-7397-1514-3*) Intl Business Pubns.
Morocco, a Pattern of Political Imprisonment, "Disappearances" & Torture. 76p. 1991. 6.00 (*0-939994-65-8*) Amnesty Intl USA.
Morocco & the Moors. A. Leard. 416p. 1985. 280.00 (*1-85077-026-3*, Pub. by Darf Pubs Ltd) St Mut.
Morocco & Tunisia Handbook: With Algeria, Libya & Mauritania. Ed. by Anne McLachlan & Keith McLachlan. (Illus.). 624p. 1995. 21.95 (*0-8442-8889-6*, Passprt Bks) NTC Contemp Pub Co.
Morocco & Western Sahara: Torture in Morocco. 1986. 3.00 (*0-685-23315-4*) Amnesty Intl USA.
Morocco Business & Investment Opportunities Yearbook, 1998: Business, Investment, Export-Import. Russian Information & Business Center, Inc. Staff. (Business & Investment Opportunities Library, '98). (Illus.). 1998. pap. 99.00 (*1-57751-994-9*) Intl Business Pubns.
***Morocco Business Intelligence Report, 190 vols.** Global Investment & Business Center, Inc. Staff. (World Business Intelligence Library: Vol. 117). (Illus.). 350p. 2000. pap. 99.95 (*0-7397-2615-3*) Intl Business Pubns.
***Morocco Business Law Handbook, 190 vols.** Global Investment & Business Center, Inc. Staff. (Global Business Law Handbooks Library: Vol. 117). (Illus.). 350p. 2000. pap. 99.95 (*0-7397-2015-5*) Intl Business Pubns.
***Morocco Business Opportunity Yearbook.** Global Investment & Business Center, Inc. Staff. (Global Business Opportunity Yearbooks Library: Vol. 117). (Illus.). 2000. pap. 99.95 (*0-7397-2215-8*) Intl Business Pubns.
***Morocco Business Opportunity Yearbook: Export-Import, Investment & Business Opportunities.** International Business Publications, U. S. A. Staff & Global Investment Center, U. S. A. Staff. (Global Business Opportunity Yearbooks Library: Vol. 117). (Illus.). 350p. 1999. pap. 99.95 (*0-7397-1315-9*) Intl Business Pubns.
***Morocco Country Review 2000.** Robert C. Kelly et al. (Illus.). 60p. 1999. pap. 39.95 (*1-58310-541-7*) CountryWatch.
Morocco, "Disappearances" of People of Western Saharan Origin & a Summary of Amnesty International's Concerns: Submission to the United Nations Human Rights Committee. 42p. 1990. 4.00 (*0-685-50861-7*, MDE 29-17-90) Amnesty Intl USA.
***Morocco Foreign Policy & Government Guide.** Contrib. by Global Investment & Business Center, Inc. Staff. (World Foreign Policy & Government Library). (Illus.). 350p. 1999. pap. 99.00 (*0-7397-3611-6*) Intl Business Pubns.
***Morocco Foreign Policy & Government Guide.** Global Investment & Business Center, Inc. Staff. (World Foreign Policy & Government Library: Vol. 113). (Illus.). 350p. 2000. pap. 99.95 (*0-7397-3815-1*) Intl Business Pubns.
Morocco from the Air. Photos by Yann A. Bertrand. LC 94-16536. (Illus.). 156p. 1994. text 45.00 (*0-86565-955-9*) Vendome.
Morocco Handbook with Mautitania. Anne McLachlan. (Illus.). 450p. 1997. 17.95 (*0-8442-4866-5*) NTC Contemp Pub Co.
Morocco in Pictures. rev. ed. Ed. by Lerner Publications, Department of Geography Staff. (Visual Geography Ser.). (Illus.). 64p. (YA). (gr. 6-9). 1996. lib. bdg. 19.93 (*0-8225-1843-0*, Lerner Publctns) Lerner Pub.
Morocco in Your Pocket Guide. (In Your Pocket Guide Ser.). 1997. per. 9.95 (*2-06-651401-2*, 6514) Michelin.
***Morocco Investment & Business Guide.** Global Investment & Business Center, Inc. Staff. (Global Investment & Business Guide Library: Vol. 117). (Illus.). 2000. pap. 99.95 (*0-7397-1815-0*) Intl Business Pubns.
Morocco Investment & Business Guide: Economy, Export-Import, Business & Investment Climate, Business Contacts. Contrib. by Russian Information & Business Center, Inc. Staff. (Russia, NIS & Emerging Markets Investment & Business Library-98). (Illus.). 350p. 1998. pap. 99.00 (*1-57751-916-7*) Intl Business Pubns.
***Morocco Investment & Business Guide: Export-Import, Investment & Business Opportunities.** International Business Publications, USA Staff & Global Investment Center, USA Staff. (World Investment & Business Guide Library-99: Vol. 117). (Illus.). 350p. 1999. pap. 99.95 (*0-7397-0312-9*) Intl Business Pubns.
Morocco Journal. Richard Harteis. LC 81-69798. 1981. pap. 11.95 (*0-915604-63-9*) Carnegie-Mellon.
Morocco Map. Michelin Staff. 1997. 10.95 (*2-06-700959-1*, 959) Michelin.
Morocco Modern. Herbert Ypma. (Illus.). 160p. 1996. pap. 27.50 (*1-55670-501-8*) Stewart Tabori & Chang.
Morocco of Today. E. Aubin. 1977. lib. bdg. 59.95 (*0-8490-2283-5*) Gordon Pr.
***Morocco Pocket Guide.** Berlitz Publishing Staff. (Berlitz Pocket Guide Ser.). 144p. 1999. pap. 8.95 (*2-8315-7222-3*) Berlitz.
Morocco Since 1830: A History. C. R. Pennell. 1999. pap. text 20.00 (*0-8147-6677-3*) NYU Pr.
***Morocco Since 1830: A History.** C. R. Pennell. LC 99-33567. 1999. text 60.00 (*0-8147-6676-5*) NYU Pr.
Morocco That Was. Walter B. Harris. LC 75-106838. 333p. 1970. reprint ed. lib. bdg. 35.00 (*0-8371-3460-9*, HMW&) Greenwood.
Morocco-Tunisia: Politics & Planning. Douglas E. Ashford. LC 65-25988. 85p. reprint ed. pap. 30.00 (*0-608-13888-6*, 202039500017) Bks Demand.
Morocco under Colonial Rule: French Administration of Tribal Areas, 1912-1956. Robin L. Bidwell. 349p. 1973. 52.50 (*0-7146-2877-8*, Pub. by F Cass Pubs) Intl Spec Bk.
Moroney's Surgery for Nurses. 16th ed. Ed. by Malcolm R. Colmer. LC 85-26938. (Illus.). 624p. 1987. text 39.95 (*0-443-03355-2*) Church.
Moroni Smith: In the Land of Zarahemla. Thom Duncan. 167p. 1991. pap. 10.98 (*0-88290-415-9*) Horizon Utah.
Moroni vs. St. Michael: A Dialogue with the Mormons. Luke Gehring. 16p. (Orig.). 1988. pap. 1.00 (*0-912927-30-5*, X030) St John Kronstadt.
Moronic Inferno: And Other Visits to America. Martin Amis. 1991. pap. 12.95 (*0-14-012719-4*, Viking) Viking Penguin.
Moroni's Camp: Where Snakes Lurk. Boyd Richardson. (Illus.). 174p. 1998. pap. 9.95 (*1-890828-08-4*, 08-4, Pub. by Camden Ct) Origin Bk Sales.
Morons & Madmen: A Mac Fontana Mystery. Earl Emerson. 256p. 1994. reprint ed. mass mkt. 4.99 (*0-380-72075-2*, Avon Bks) Morrow Avon.
Morons of Blackjack & Other Monsters. King Seobe. 128p. 1992. pap. 16.95 (*1-882173-02-3*) Paone Pr.
Moros y Cristianos in Zacatecas: Text of a Mexican Folk Play. Michael J. Doudoroff. LC 81-1558. 66p. (Orig.). 1981. pap. text 5.00 (*0-939448-00-9*) Amadeo Concha.
Moroscos of Spain: Their Conversion & Expulsion. Henry C. Lea. (Notable American Authors Ser.). 1999. reprint ed. lib. bdg. 125.00 (*0-7812-3781-5*) Rprt Serv.
***Morot Boating: A Motor Boat & Yachting Book.** McMullen. (Illus.). 92p. 2000. pap. 16.95 (*0-906754-89-5*, Pub. by Fernhurst Bks) Motorbooks Intl.
Morotai: A Memoir of War. 2nd rev. ed. John S. Boeman. (Illus.). 284p. 1989. pap. 14.95 (*0-89745-124-4*) Sunflower U Pr.
Morountodun & Other Plays. Fremir Orsrofisan. LC 85-840264. 138 p. 1982. write for info. (*0-582-78575-8*) Longman.
Morph-Aid: A Source of Roots, Prefixes & Suffixes. 2nd ed. Marilyn M. Toomey. (Illus.). 124p. 1989. pap. 15.95 (*0-923573-03-8*) Circuit Pubns.
Morph Monsters see Monsters
Morphed: New Life in Romans. Ryan Ahlgrim. (Generation Why Ser.). 35p. 1998. pap. 12.95 (*0-87303-277-2*) Faith & Life.
Morpheme-Ant. E. Peters. 1998. 50.00 (*90-6831-924-8*, Pub. by Peeters Pub) Bks Intl VA.
Morpheme Concordance of the Book of Chilam Balam of Chumayel. Victoria R. Bricker. LC 89-9359. (Publications: No. 59). viii, 638p. 1991. 45.00 (*0-939238-90-X*) Tulane MARI.
Morpheme Concordance of the Book of Chilam Balam of Tizimin. Victoria R. Bricker. LC 89-9360. (Publications: No. 58). viii, 483p. 1991. 35.00 (*0-939238-89-6*) Tulane MARI.
***Morpheme Order & Semantic Scope: Word Formation in the Athapaskan Verb.** Keren Rice. LC 99-20442. (Cambridge Studies in Linguistics: No. 90). 288p. (C). 2000. 64.95 (*0-521-58354-3*) Cambridge U Pr.
Morphemic & Semantic Analysis of the Word Families: Finnish ETE- & Hungarian El- 'Fore' Kalman Keresztes. LC 64-64194. (Uralic & Altaic Ser.: Vol. 41). (Orig.). 1964. pap. text 11.00 (*0-87750-010-X*) Res Inst Inner Asian Studies.
Morpheus Conspiracy. Douglas A. Volk. 350p. 1998. pap. 12.99 (*0-9662181-0-8*) Danjon Pr.
Morphinism & Narcomanias from Other Drugs: Their Etiology, Treatment, & Medicolegal Relations. T. D. Crothers. Ed. by Gerald N. Grob. LC 80-1220. (Addiction in America Ser.). 1981. reprint ed. lib. bdg. 31.95 (*0-405-13577-7*) Ayer.
Morphisms & Categories: Comparing & Transforming. Jean Piaget et al. Tr. by Terrance Brown from FRE. 248p. 1992. text 49.95 (*0-8058-0300-9*) L Erlbaum Assocs.
Morpho-Syntactic Erosion Between Two Generational Groups of Spanish Speakers in the United States. Elizabeth A. Martinez. LC 92-14656. (Theoretical Studies in Second Language Acquisition: Vol. 4). XIII, 136p. (C). 1994. text 45.95 (*0-8204-1944-3*) P Lang Pubng.
Morphodynamics of the Inner Continental Shelf. L. Donelson Wright. 256p. 1995. boxed set 139.95 (*0-8493-8043-X*) CRC Pr.
Morphodynamics of the Wadden Sea. Jurgen Ehlers. 320p. (C). 1988. text 188.00 (*90-6191-679-8*, Pub. by A A Balkema) Ashgate Pub Co.
Morphogene des Humanpathogenen Pilzes Candida Albicans: Isolierung und Charakterisierung der Gene EFG1 und RFG1. Volker R. Stoldt. (Bibliotheca Mycologica: Vol. 162). (GER., Illus.). iii, 86p. 1995. 36.00 (*3-443-59064-0*, Pub. by Gebruder Borntraeger) Balogh.
Morphogenesis: An Analysis of the Development of Biological Form. Ed. by Edward F. Rossomando & Stephen Alexander. LC 92-3820. (Illus.). 448p. 1992. text 199.00 (*0-8247-8667-X*) Dekker.
Morphogenesis: Cellular Interactions. Ed. by Raul Fleischmajer et al. LC 98-41670. (Annals of the New York Academy of Sciences Ser.: Vol. 857). 288p. 1998. 100.00 (*1-57331-131-6*); pap. write for info. (*1-57331-132-4*) NY Acad Sci.
Morphogenesis: The Cellular & Molecular Processes of Developmental Anatomy. Jonathan B. Bard. (Developmental & Cell Biology Monographs: No. 23). (Illus.). 315p. (C). 1990. text 95.00 (*0-521-36196-6*) Cambridge U Pr.
Morphogenesis: The Cellular & Molecular Processes of Developmental Anatomy. Jonathan B. Bard. (Developmental & Cell Biology Monographs: No. 23). (Illus.). 325p. (C). 1992. pap. text 42.95 (*0-521-43612-5*) Cambridge U Pr.
Morphogenesis & Malformation of Face & Brain. Ed. by Daniel Bergsma. LC 75-24570. (Alan R. Liss Ser.: Vol. 11, No. 7). 1976. 43.00 (*0-686-14575-5*) March of Dimes.
Morphogenesis & Malformation of the Genital System, Vol. 13, No. 2. Ed. by Daniel Bergsma. LC 77-535. (Alan R. Liss Ser.). 1977. 25.00 (*0-686-20483-2*) March of Dimes.
Morphogenesis & Malformation of the Limb, Vol. 13, No. 1. Ed. by Daniel Bergsma. LC 76-55004. (Alan R. Liss Ser.). 1977. 49.00 (*0-686-20484-0*) March of Dimes.
Morphogenesis & Malinformation of the Cardiovascular System. Ed. by Glenn C. Rosenquist & Daniel Bergsma. LC 78-14527. (Alan R. Liss Ser.: Vol. 14, No. 7). 1978. 64.00 (*0-685-03292-2*) March of Dimes.
Morphogenesis & Maturation of Retroviruses. Ed. by M. Potter et al. (Current Topics in Microbiology & Immunology Ser.: Vol. 214). 360p. 1996. 159.00 (*3-540-60928-8*) Spr-Verlag.
Morphogenesis & Microscopic Cytochemistry of Marine Pyrenomycete Ascospores. P. W. Kirk. (Illus.). 1966. pap. 32.00 (*3-7682-5422-4*) Lubrecht & Cramer.
Morphogenesis & Pattern Formation. fac. ed. Ed. by Thomas G. Connelly et al. LC 80-5538. (Illus.). 312p. pap. 96.80 (*0-7837-7358-7*, 204716700005) Bks Demand.
Morphogenesis in Plant Tissue Cultures. Woong Y. Soh & S. S. Bhojwani. LC 99-21108. 1999. 252.00 (*0-7923-5682-9*) Kluwer Academic.
Morphogenesis in Plants: Molecular Approaches, Vol. 253. K. A. Roubelakis-Angelakis & K. Tran Thanh Van. LC 93-20954. (NATO ASI Ser.: Vol. 256). (Illus.). 292p. (C). 1993. text 110.00 (*0-306-44597-2*, Kluwer Plenum) Kluwer Academic.
Morphogenesis of Lung Cancer, Vol. I. Ed. by Yukio Shimosato et al. 184p. 1982. 108.00 (*0-8493-6526-0*, RC280, CRC Reprint) Franklin.
Morphogenesis of Lung Cancer, Vol. II. Ed. by Yukio Shimosato et al. 224p. 1983. 129.00 (*0-8493-6527-9*, RC280, CRC Reprint) Franklin.
Morphogenesis of T-Even Bacteriophages. B. F. Poglazov. (Monographs in Developmental Biology: Vol. 7). 1973. 47.00 (*3-8055-1645-2*) S Karger.
Morphogenesis of the Arteries of the Pelvic Extremity. C. Funke & H. J. Kuhn. Ed. by F. Beck et al. LC 98-29669. (Advances in Anatomy, Embryology & Cell Biology Ser.: Vol. 144). (Illus.). v, 122p. 1998. pap. 95.00 (*3-540-64706-6*) Spr-Verlag.
Morphogenesis of the Behaviour of the Domestic Cat. J. M. Baerends-Van Roon & G. P. Baerends. (Verhandelingen der Koninklijke Nederlandse Akademie van Wetenschappen, Afd. Natuurkunde Ser.: No. 72). 116p. 1979. pap. text 43.75 (*0-7204-8480-4*) Elsevier.
Morphogenetic Hormones of Arthropods, Pt. 1. Ed. by Ayodhya P. Gupta. (Recent Advances in Comparative Arthropod Morphology, Physiology, & Development Ser.). 568p. (C). 1990. 125.00 (*0-8135-1414-2*) Rutgers U Pr.
Morphogenetic Hormones of Arthropods, Pt. 2. Ed. by Ayodhya P. Gupta. (Recent Advances in Comparative Arthropod Morphology, Physiology, & Development Ser.). 550p. (C). 1990. 125.00 (*0-8135-1415-0*) Rutgers U Pr.
Morphogenetic Hormones of Arthropods, Pt. 3. Ed. by Ayodhya P. Gupta. (Recent Advances in Comparative Arthropod Morphology, Physiology, & Development Ser.). 600p. (C). 1990. 125.00 (*0-8135-1416-9*) Rutgers U Pr.
Morphogenetic Hormones of Arthropods, Set. Ed. by Ayodhya P. Gupta. (Recent Advances in Comparative Arthropod Morphology, Physiology, & Development Ser.). (C). 1990. 325.00 (*0-8135-1479-7*) Rutgers U Pr.
Morphogenetic Re-Evaluation of Haplomitrium Nees (Hepatophyta) Sharon E. Bartholomew-Began. Ed. by S. R. Gradstein. (Bryophytorum Bibliotheca: Vol. 41). (GER., Illus.). 484p. 1991. pap. 130.00 (*3-443-62013-2*, Pub. by Gebruder Borntraeger) Balogh.

M

Morpholine. (Health & Safety Guides Ser.: No. 92). 28p. (C). 1995. pap. text 5.00 (*92-4-151092-7*, 1860092) World Health.
Morpholine. rev. ed. (Environmental Health Criteria Ser.: Vol. 179). (FRE & SPA.). 163p. (C). 1996. pap. 36.00 (*92-4-157179-9*, 1160179) World Health.
Morphologic & Functional MR of the Kidneys & Adrenal Glands. Gabriel Krestin. 1990. 115.00 (*0-938607-40-5*) Field & Wood Inc Medical.
Morphologic & Systematic Relationships of Some Middle Ordovician Ostracoda. John C. Kraft. LC 63-1127. (Geological Society of America, Memoir Ser.: No. 86). 137p. reprint ed. pap. 42.50 (*0-608-15638-8*, 203179100077) Bks Demand.
Morphological Analysis see Particle Characterization in Technology
***Morphological Analysis in Comparison.** Ed. by Wolfgang U. Dressler et al. LC 00-24553. (Current Issues in Linguistic Theory Ser.: Vol. 201). 250p. 2000. 65.00 (*1-55619-979-1*) J Benjamins Pubng Co.
***Morphological & Compositional Evolution of Heteroepitaxial Semiconductor Thin Films: Materials Research Society Symposium Proceedings, Vol. 618.** Ed. by J. M. Millunchick et al. 2000. text 82.00 (*1-55899-526-9*) Materials Res.
Morphological & Functional Aspects of Placental Dysfunction. Ed. by Hiroaki Soma. (Contributions to Gynecology & Obstetrics Ser.: Vol. 9). (Illus.). viii, 180p. 1982. pap. 111.50 (*3-8055-3510-4*) S Karger.
Morphological & Morphometric Analysis of the "Sorex Vagrans Species Complex" in the Pacific Coast Region. Ed. by Leslie N. Carraway. (C). 1990. pap. 14.00 (*0-89672-176-0*) Tex Tech Univ Pr.
Morphological & Phonological Component of the Arabic Verb. M. Hassan Bakalla. (ARA.). 70p. 1979. 30.00 (*0-86685-054-6*, Pub. by Librairie du Liban) Intl Bk Ctr.
Morphological & Physical Classification of Galaxies: Proceedings of the Fifth International Workshop of the Osservatorio Astronomico di Capodimonte, Held in Sant'Agata Sui Due Golfi, Italy, September 3-7, 1990. Ed. by Giovanni Busarello et al. LC 92-1502. (Astrophysics & Space Science Library: Vol. 178). 490p. (C). 1992. text 226.50 (*0-7923-1712-2*) Kluwer Academic.
Morphological Aspects of Language Processing. Ed. by Laurie B. Feldman. 432p. 1995. 79.95 (*0-8058-1358-6*) L Erlbaum Assocs.
Morphological Atlas of Insect Larvae. H. Steinmann & L. Zombori. 404p. (C). 1984. 140.00 (*963-05-3417-7*, Pub. by Akade Kiado) St Mut.
Morphological Bases of the Systematics & Phylogeny of the Notothenioid Fishes. A. V. Balushkin. Tr. by I. Kohli. (Russian Translation Ser.: No. 73). 160p. (C). 1990. text 91.00 (*90-6191-960-6*, Pub. by A A Balkema) Ashgate Pub Co.
Morphological Bases of the Systematics & Phylogeny of the Notothenoid. A. V. Baluhkin. (C). 1989. 28.00 (*81-7087-048-8*) S Asia.
Morphological Basis of Human Reproductive Function. G. Spera & D. M. DeKretser. LC 87-42790. (Illus.). 264p. (C). 1987. text 89.50 (*0-306-42738-9*, Kluwer Plenum) Kluwer Academic.
Morphological Change in Quaternary Mammals of North America. Ed. by Robert A. Martin & Anthony D. Barnosky. (Illus.). 427p. (C). 1993. text 74.95 (*0-521-40450-9*) Cambridge U Pr.
Morphological Control in Multiphase Polymer Mixtures. Ed. by R. M. Briber et al. LC 97-6800. (Materials Research Society Symposium Proceedings Ser.: No. 461). 241p. 1997. text 75.00 (*1-55899-365-7*) Materials Res.
Morphological Cosmology. Ed. by P. Flin & H. W. Duerbeck. (Lecture Notes in Physics Ser.: Vol. 332). vii, 438p. 1989. 64.95 (*0-387-51223-3*) Spr-Verlag.
Morphological Diagnosis of Skin Disease: A Study of the Living Gross Pathology of the Skin. Robert Jackson. (Illus.). 496p. 1998. 79.00 (*1-896918-02-6*) Manticore Pubs.
Morphological Dictionary of Classical Nahuatl: A Morpheme Index to the Vocabulario en Lengua Mexicana y Castellana of Fray Alonso de Molinas. R. Joe Campbell. xxiv, 488p. 1985. 50.00 (*0-942260-52-X*) Hispanic Seminary.

*Morphological Image Analysis: Principles & Applications. Pierre Soille. LC 99-25205. 315p. 1999. 95.00 (3-540-65671-5) Spr-Verlag.

Morphological Image Processing: Architecture & VLSI Design. P. P. Jonker. 296p. (C). 1993. pap. text 134.00 (90-201-2766-7) Kluwer Academic.

Morphological Integration. Everett C. Olson. LC 99-24323. 1999. pap. text 19.00 (0-226-62905-8) U Ch Pr.

Morphological Investigations of Single Neurons in Vitro. Ed. by Gloria E. Meredith & Gordon W. Arbuthnott. LC 93-10269. (IBRO Handbook Series: Methods in the Neurosciences: No. 16). 210p. 1993. pap. 230.00 (0-471-93928-5) Wiley.

Morphological Organizations in Epitaxial Growth & Removal. Zhenyu Zheng. 1998. 88.00 (981-02-3471-6) World Scientific Pub.

Morphological Productivity: Structural Constraints in English Derivation. Ingo Plag. LC 98-51325. 240p. 1999. 124.00 (3-11-015833-7) De Gruyter.

*Morphological, Semantic & Functional aspects of English Lexical Borrowings in Norwegian. Anne Line Graedler. 390p. 1998. pap. 48.00 (82-00-12944-6) Scandnvan Univ Pr.

Morphological Signal Processing. Ronald W. Schafer & Petros Maragos. (C). 2001. 62.67 (0-13-588435-7, Macmillan Coll) P-H.

Morphological Stability, Convection, Graphite, & Integrated Optics. Ed. by William R. Wilcox. LC 78-24426. (Preparation & Properties of Solid State Materials Ser.: No. 4). (Illus.). 219p. reprint ed. pap. 67.90 (0-7837-4295-9, 20439870012) Bks Demand.

Morphological Studies of the Marine Brown Alga Taonia Lennebackerae Farlow Ex. J. Agardh L. A. C. Mathieson. (Illus.). 1966. pap. 12.00 (3-7682-0439-1) Lubrecht & Cramer.

Morphological Study of Egyptian Colloquial Arabic. Hilmi M. Aboul-Fetouh. (Janua Linguarum, Ser. Practica: No. 33). 1969. pap. text 75.40 (90-279-0691-2) Mouton.

Morphological Theory: An Introduction to Word Structure in Generative Grammar. Andrew Spencer. 448p. 1991. pap. 38.95 (0-631-16144-9) Blackwell Pubs.

Morphological Tumor Markets. Ed. by G. Seifert. (Current Topics in Pathology Ser.: Vol. 77). (Illus.). 415p. 1987. 214.00 (0-387-16733-1) Spr-Verlag.

*Morphologie, Okologie und Phylogenie Aquatischer Oomyceten. A. Riethmuller. (Bibliotheca Mycologica Ser.: Band 185). viii, 344p. 2000. 90.00 (3-443-59087-X, Pub. by Gebruder Borntraeger) Balogh.

Morphologie und Chemie der Epikutikularwachse Von Picea Abies (L.) Karsten Unter Dem Einfluss Von Klima und Immissionen. Thomas Euteneuer-Macher. (Dissertationes Botanicae Ser.: Band 150). (GER., Illus.). xxx, 158p. (C). 1990. pap. 53.00 (3-443-64062-1, Pub. by Gebruder Borntraeger) Balogh.

Morphologies of Meaning: Dynamic Semiotics & Cognitive Linguistics. Aage Brandt. LC 96-128784. 272p. (C). 1995. pap. 27.00 (87-7288-514-9, Pub. by Aarhus Univ Pr) David Brown.

Morphologisch und Entwicklungsgeschichtliche Untersuchungen an Blueten und Bluetenstaenden Von Solannaceen und Von Nolana Paradoxa Lindl: Nolanaceae. K. A. Huber. (Dissertationes Botanicae Ser.: No. 55). (GER., Illus.). 486p. 1980. pap. text 60.00 (3-7682-1268-8) Lubrecht & Cramer.

Morphologische, Embryologische und Systematische IUntersuchungen an Triuridaceae. Traudel Rubsamen-Weustenfeld. (Bibliotheca Botanica: Vol. 140). (GER., Illus.). iv, 113p. 1991. 105.00 (3-510-48011-2, Pub. by E Schweizerbartsche) Balogh.

Morphologische, Embryologische und Systematische Untersuchungen An Burmanniaceae und Corsiaceae. Traudel Rubsamen. (Dissertationes Botanicae Ser.: Band 92). (GER., Illus.). 512p. 1986. pap. 95.00 (3-443-64004-4, Pub. by Gebruder Borntraeger) Balogh.

Morphologische, Phytochemische und Botranische Untersuchungen Zur Selektion Hypericin-, Pseudohypericin- und Flavonoidreicher Hypericum Perforatum L. Staemme. Heide Schutt. (Dissertationes Botanicae Ser.: Band 263). (Illus.). 184p. 1996. pap. 53.00 (3-443-64175-X, Pub. by Gebruder Borntraeger) Balogh.

Morphologische Untersuchungen Auf Dem Gebiete der Indogermanischen Sprachen, 3 vols., Set. Hermann Osthoff & Karl Brugman. (Documenta Semiotica, Ser. Linguistica). lxxx, 1810p. 1974. reprint ed. write for info. (3-487-05079-X) G Olms Pubs.

Morphology. Favis. 330p. 2000. write for info. (0-471-33128-7) Wiley.

Morphology. 2nd ed. P. H. Matthews. (Cambridge Textbooks in Linguistics Ser.). 263p. (C). 1991. text 59.95 (0-521-41043-6); pap. text 19.95 (0-521-42256-6) Cambridge U Pr.

Morphology: A Study of the Relation Between Meaning & Form. Joan L. Bybee. LC 85-9021. (Typological Studies in Language Ser.: No. 9). xii, 235p. 1985. pap. 24.95 (0-915027-38-0) J Benjamins Pubng Co.

Morphology: Algorithms & Applications. 500p. 1999. text 79.95 (0-521-41516-0) Cambridge U Pr.

Morphology: Word Structure in Generative Grammar. John T. Jensen. LC 89-18170. (Current Issues in Linguistic Theory Ser.: Vol. 70). x, 210p. 1990. 53.00 (1-55619-125-1); pap. 19.95 (1-55619-126-X) J Benjamins Pubng Co.

Morphology, Anatomy, & Systematics of the Cinctiporidae, New Family, Bryozoa, Stenolaemata. Richard S. Boardman et al. LC 91-38765. (Smithsonian Contributions to Paleobiology Ser.: No. 70). 85p. reprint ed. pap. 30.00 (0-7837-3160-4, 204282200006) Bks Demand.

Morphology & Anatomy of Aneurophyton: A Progymnosperm from the Late Devonian of New York see Palaeontographica Americana: Vol. 8

Morphology & Computation. Richard Sproat. (ACL Series in Natural Language Processing). (Illus.). 320p. 1992. 44.00 (0-262-19314-0, Bradford Bks) MIT Pr.

Morphology & Development of Branches in the Leafy Hepaticae. B. J. Crandall. (Illus.). 1970. 80.00 (3-7682-5430-5) Lubrecht & Cramer.

*Morphology & Dynamics of Crystal Surfaces in Complex Molecular Systems: Materials Research Society Symposium Proceedings, Vol. 620. Ed. by J. DeYoreo et al. 2000. text 77.00 (1-55899-528-5) Materials Res.

Morphology & Function in MRI of the Cardiovascular & Renal Systems. G. K. Von Schulthess. (Illus.). 160p. 1988. 158.00 (0-387-19061-9) Spr-Verlag.

Morphology & Its Interfaces in Second-Language Knowledge. Ed. by Maria-Luise Beck. LC 98-44714. (Language Acquisition & Language Disorders Ser.: Vol. 19). x, 387p. 1998. 75.00 (1-55619-784-5) J Benjamins Pubng Co.

Morphology & Its Relation to Phonology & Syntax. Ed. by Steven G. Lapointe et al. LC 97-39330. 512p. (C). 1998. pap. 27.95 (1-57586-112-7); text 69.95 (1-57586-113-5) CSLI.

Morphology & Modularity. Martin Everaert et al. Ed. by Mieke Trommelen. (Publications in Language Sciences: No. 29). x, 438p. 1988. pap. 107.70 (90-6765-395-0) Mouton.

Morphology & Pathology see Nephrology: Proceedings of the International Congress, 5th, Mexico, 1972

Morphology & Stratigraphic Ranges of Selected Mesozoic-Cenozoic Dinoflagellate Taxa in the Northern Hemisphere. Graham L. Williams. (GSC Paper Ser.: No. 92-10). 137p. (Orig.). 1993. pap. 27.95 (0-660-14553-7, Pub. by Canadian Govt Pub) Accents Pubns.

*Morphology & Syntax, Pt. 2. Graham Shorrocks. (Illus.). xxvii, 282p. 1999. pap. 51.95 (3-631-34661-1) P Lang Pubng.

Morphology & Systematics of Paepalanthus Subgenus Xeractis (Eriocaulaceae) Nancy Hensold. Ed. by Christiane Anderson. (Systematic Botany Monographs: Vol. 23). (Illus.). 150p. (Orig.). 1988. pap. 18.00 (0-912861-23-1) Am Soc Plant.

Morphology & Taxonomy of Aneilema R. Brown (Commelinaceae) Robert B. Faden. LC 90-9629. (Smithsonian Contributions to Botany Ser.: No. 76). 172p. reprint ed. pap. 53.40 (0-7837-0154-3, 204044400017) Bks Demand.

Morphology & Taxonomy of Species of the Diatom Genus Asteromphalus Ehr. David U. Hernandez-Becerril. (Bibliotheca Diatomologica Ser.: Band 23). (Illus.). iv, 90p. 1991. pap. text 42.00 (3-443-57014-3, Pub. by Gebruder Borntraeger) Balogh.

Morphology by Itself: Items & Inflectional Classes. Mark Aronoff. LC 93-20543. (Linguistic Inquiry Monographs: Vol. 22). (Illus.). 275p. 1993. 40.00 (0-262-01136-0); pap. text 20.00 (0-262-51072-3) MIT Pr.

Morphology, Development, & Systematic Relevance of Pollen & Spores. Ed. by M. Hesse & F. Ehrendorfer. (Plant Systematics & Evolution Ser.: Suppl. 5). (Illus.). 120p. 1990. 111.95 (0-387-82182-1) Spr-Verlag.

Morphology-Driven Syntax: A Theory of V to I Raising & Pro- Drop. Bernhard W. Rohrbacher. LC 99-19817. (Linguistik Aktuell/Linguistics Today Ser.: Vol. 15). viii, 296p. 1999. 75.00 (1-55619-234-7) J Benjamins Pubng Co.

Morphology in Lung Transplantation: Proceedings of the Congress of Experimental Surgery Symposium, 7th, Amsterdam, April 1972. Congress of Experimental Surgery Symposium Staff. Ed. by R. H. Wildevuur. (Illus.). 1973. 85.25 (3-8055-1441-7) S Karger.

Morphology in the Reader's Mental Lexicon. Sandra Dominiek. LC 94-33477. (Illus.). II, 144p. 1994. write for info. (3-631-44251-3) P Lang Pubng.

Morphology Now. Ed. by Mark Aronoff. LC 90-22725. (SUNY Series in Linguistics). 227p. (C). 1992. text 67.50 (0-7914-0815-9) State U NY Pr.

Morphology of Aspect in Seventeenth-Century Russian: Based on Texts of the Smutnoe Vremja. Peter J. Mayo. xi, 234p. (Orig.). 1985. pap. 22.95 (0-89357-145-8) Slavica.

*Morphology of Chinese: A Linguistic & Cognitive Approach. Jerome L. Packard. 300p. (C). 2000. 59.95 (0-521-77112-9) Cambridge U Pr.

Morphology of Crystals, 3 vols. 1987. text 405.00 (90-277-2510-1) Kluwer Academic.

Morphology of Crystals, 3 pts., Pt. C. Ed. by Ichiro Sunagawa. (C). 1995. lib. bdg. 78.00 (90-277-2509-8) Kluwer Academic.

Morphology of Crystals, 3 pts., Set. Ed. by Ichiro Sunagawa. (C). 1988. 249.00 (0-317-59608-X) Kluwer Academic.

Morphology of Crystals Pt. C: The Geometry of Crystal Growth, Pt. C. J. Van Suchtelen. Ed. by Ichiro Sunagawa. LC 87-9571. (Materials Science of Minerals & Rocks Ser.). 419p. (Orig.). (C). 1995. lib. bdg. 228.00 (0-7923-3592-9) Kluwer Academic.

Morphology of Experimental Respiratory Carcinogenesis: Proceedings. Ed. by Paul Nettesheim et al. LC 73-609398. (AEC Symposium Ser.). 500p. 1970. pap. 20.50 (0-87079-277-6, CONF-700501); fiche 9.00 (0-87079-278-4, CONF-700501) DOE.

Morphology of Luvarus Imperialis (Luvaridae), with a Phylogenetic Analysis of the Acanthuroidei (Pisces) James C. Tyler et al. LC 89-600070. (Smithsonian Contributions to Zoology Ser.: No. 485). 84p. reprint ed. pap. 30.00 (0-8357-6413-3, 203577400096) Bks Demand.

Morphology of New Testament Greek: A Review & Reference Grammar. James A. Brooks & Carlton L. Winbery. LC 94-1376. 478p. (Orig.). 1994. pap. text 39.50 (0-8191-9491-3); lib. bdg. 65.00 (0-8191-9490-5) U Pr of Amer.

Morphology of Pits in Hardwood Fibres: (1) Nomenclature of Axial Xylary Elements: A Morphological & Physiological Approach, (2) Bordered Pits & Funnel Pits: Further Evidence of Convergent Evolution. J. F. C. Magendans & W. L. H. Van Veenendaal. (Wageningen Agricultural University Papers). (Illus.). 100p. 1999. pap. 39.00 (90-5782-036-6, Pub. by Backhuys Pubs) Balogh.

Morphology of Plants & Fungi. 5th ed. Harold C. Bold et al. 928p. (C). 1997. pap. 126.00 (0-06-040839-1) Addson-Wesley Educ.

Morphology of Polymers: Proceedings of the 17th Europhysics Conference on Macromolecular Physics, Prague, Czechoslovakia July 15-18, 1985. Ed. by Blahoslav Sedlacek. (Illus.). xiv, 794p. 1986. lib. bdg. 273.10 (3-11-010519-5) De Gruyter.

Morphology of Russian Mentality: A Philosophical Inquiry into Conservatism & Pragmatism. Vladimir A. Zviglyanich. LC 93-19208. 336p. 1993. text 99.95 (0-7734-9863-X) E Mellen.

Morphology of Seed Plants. M. Guedes. (Plant Science Ser.: No. 2). (Illus.). 1979. lib. bdg. 35.00 (3-7682-1195-9) Lubrecht & Cramer.

Morphology of Solo Man. Franz Weidenreich. LC 76-44799. (American Museum of Natural History Anthropological Papers: Vol. 43, Pt. 3). 128p. reprint ed. 47.50 (0-404-15979-6) AMS Pr.

Morphology of the Angiosperms. Arthur J. Eames. LC 76-57780. 532p. 1977. reprint ed. 29.50 (0-88275-527-7) Krieger.

Morphology of the Blood. Giuseppe D'Onofrio & Gina Zini. Tr. by Barbara J. Bain. LC 97-51175. 384p. 1998. text 195.00 (0-7506-4055-3) Buttrwrth-Heinemann.

Morphology of the Bony Stapes (Columella) in the Passeriformes & Related Groups: Evolutionary Implications. Alan Feduccia. (Miscellaneous Publications: No. 63). 34p. 1975. pap. 2.00 (0-317-04586-5) U KS Nat Hist Mus.

Morphology of the Folktale. 2nd ed. Vladimir Propp. Ed. by Louis A. Wagner. Tr. by Laurence Scott from RUS. (American Folklore Society Bibliographical & Special Ser.: No. 9). 184p. 1968. pap. 9.95 (0-292-78376-0) U of Tex Pr.

Morphology of the Hupa Language. fac. ed. Pliny E. Goddard. Ed. by Frederic W. Putnam. (University of California Publications in American Archaeology & Ethnology: Vol. 3). 344p. (C). 1905. reprint ed. pap. text 36.25 (1-55567-162-4) Coyote Press.

Morphology of the Hupa Language. P. E. Goddard. (CU PAAE Ser.: Vol. 3). 1974. reprint ed. 75.00 (0-527-01359-5) Periodicals Srv.

Morphology of the Modern French Verb. Michael H. Gertner. (Janua Linguarum, Series Practica: No. 204). 1973. pap. 44.65 (90-279-2504-6) Mouton.

Morphology of the Rat Brain Ventricles, Ependyma & Periventricular Structures. A. Mitro & M. Palkovits. (Bibliotheca Anatomica Ser.: No. 21). (Illus.). x, 110p. 1981. pap. 85.25 (3-8055-2546-X) S Karger.

Morphology of the Rocky Members of the Solar System. E. Uchupi & K. O. Emery. LC 93-30159. 1994. 118.95 (0-387-56234-6) Spr-Verlag.

Morphology of the Sirenia. H. E. Kaiser. (Illus.). 1973. 21.00 (3-8055-1609-6) S Karger.

Morphology, Phonology & Aphasia. Ed. by J. L. Nespoulous & P. Villiard. (Neuropsychology Ser.). (Illus.). 304p. 1990. 89.95 (0-387-97183-1) Spr-Verlag.

Morphology, Physiology & Behavioural Biology of Ticks. John R. Sauer & J. A. Hair. (Acarology Ser.). 510p. 1986. text 89.95 (0-470-20327-7) P-H.

Morphology, Taxonomy & Interrelationships of the Ribbed Araphid Diatoms from the Genera Diatoma & Meridion: Diatomaceae, Bacillariophyta. D. M. Williams. (Bibliotheca Diatomologica Ser.: No. 8). (Illus.). 256p. 1985. lib. bdg. 52.00 (3-7682-1431-1) Lubrecht & Cramer.

*Morphology/Morphologie, 2 vols. Ed. by Herausgegeben von Geert Booij et al. 1999. 441.00 (3-11-011128-4) De Gruyter.

Morphometric Studies of Subhumid & Semiarid Drainage Basins, Texas Panhandle & Northeastern New Mexico. R. W. Baumgardner, Jr. (Reports of Investigations: RI 163). (Illus.). 68p. 1987. pap. 3.00 (0-318-23672-9) Bur Econ Geology.

Morphometric Tools for Landmark Data: Geometry & Biology. Fred L. Bookstein. 455p. (C). 1992. text 100.00 (0-521-38385-4) Cambridge U Pr.

Morphometric Tools for Landmark Data: Geometry & Biology. Fred L. Bookstein. 455p. 1997. pap. text 36.95 (0-521-58598-8) Cambridge U Pr.

Morphometrics & Phylogenetic Systematics: Stochastic Methods, Chaos & Fractals. Zelditch et al. 224p. 1998. write for info. (0-12-778350-4) Acad Pr.

Morphometrics for the Life Sciences. Pete E. Lestrel. (Recent Advances in Human Biology Ser.). 1999. 38.00 (981-02-3610-7) World Scientific Pub.

Morphometry. William A. Aherne. LC 82-185020. 1982. 49.50 (0-7131-4403-3) St Martin.

Morphometry. Ed. by Piero Tosi & G. Mariuzzi. (Journal: Applied Pathology: Vol. 4, No. 1-2, 1986). (Illus.). 112p. 1987. pap. 62.75 (3-8055-4563-0) S Karger.

Morphopragmatics: Diminutives & Intensifiers in Italian, German & Other Languages. Wolfgang U. Dressler & Lavinia M. Barbaresi. LC 94-28594. (GER & ITA.). 690p. (C). 1994. 213.85 (3-11-014041-1, 169-94) Mouton.

Morphopragmatics: Diminutives & Intensifiers in Italian, German, & Other Languages. Wolfgang U. Dressler & Lavinia M. Barbaresi. (GER & ITA.). 690p. (C). 1994. lib. bdg. 191.75 (0-614-00665-1, 169-94) Mouton.

Morphosis. Peter Cook. 1995. boxed set. write for info. (0-8478-1948-5) Rizzoli Intl.

Morphosis, Vol. 2. Richard Weinstein. (Illus.). 288p. 1994. 40.00 (0-8478-1663-X, Pub. by Rizzoli Intl) St Martin.

Morphosis: A Decade of Architectural Confrontation. 40p. 1989. pap. write for info. (0-910524-10-6) Eastern Wash.

Morphosis: Architectural Projects. John Perkins. Ed. by Carolyn Krause. (Illus.). 7p. 1989. pap. 2.50 (0-917562-53-4) Contemp Arts.

Morphosis: Buildings & Projects. Ed. by Peter Cook. LC 88-43453. (Illus.). 240p. 1990. 60.00 (0-8478-1030-5, Pub. by Rizzoli Intl); pap. 40.00 (0-8478-1031-3, Pub. by Rizzoli Intl) St Martin.

Morphosis: Buildings & Projects, Vol. 2. Richard Weinstein. (Illus.). 288p. 1994. pap. 40.00 (0-8478-1664-8, Pub. by Rizzoli Intl) St Martin.

Morphosis: The Crawford House. Photos by Kim Zwarts. LC 97-16400. (Illus.). 96p. 1998. pap. 35.00 (0-8478-2082-3, Pub. by Rizzoli Intl) St Martin.

Morphosis Buildings & Projects, Vol. 3. Contrib. by Thom Mayne & Tony Robins. (Illus.). 320p. 1999. 55.00 (0-8478-2074-2, Pub. by Rizzoli Intl) St Martin.

Morphosis Connected Isolation. Thom Mayne. (Architectural Monographs: No. 23). 1993. 55.00 (1-85490-150-8) Academy Ed UK.

*Morphosis/Diamond Ranch High School: Source Books in Architecture. Thom Mayne. 272p. 2000. pap. 40.00 (1-58093-079-4, Pub. by Monacelli Pr) Penguin Putnam.

Morphosyntax of Detransitive Suffixes -p- & -n- in Gothic: A Synchronic & Diachronic Study. Seiichi Suzuki. (Studies in Old Germanic Languages & Literatures). XVIII, 307p. (C). 1989. text 47.95 (0-8204-1032-2) P Lang Pubng.

Morphosyntax of Verb Movement: A Minimalist Approach to the Syntax of Dutch. C. J. Zwart. (Studies in Natural Language & Linguistic Theory). 328p. (C). 1996. pap. text 54.00 (0-7923-4264-X) Kluwer Academic.

Morphosyntax of Verb Movement: A Minimalist Approach to the Syntax of Dutch. C. Jan Zwart. LC 96-41309. (Studies in Natural Language & Linguistic Theory). 328p. (C). 1996. lib. bdg. 124.00 (0-7923-4263-1) Kluwer Academic.

Morphy's Games of Chess. Philip W. Sergeant. 352p. 1957. pap. 8.95 (0-486-20386-7) Dover.

Morrell Future of Dollar Worldres. Sys. Louis Morrell. 160p. 1981. pap. 34.95 (0-408-10675-1) Buttrwrth-Heinemann.

Morrells of Oxford: The Family & Their Brewery, 1743-1993. Brigid Allen. (Illus.). 192p. 1994. pap. 17.95 (0-7509-0634-0, Pub. by Sutton Pub Ltd) Intl Pubs Mktg.

*Morrimac Valley & Vicinity Street Atlas: Area Includes Strafford, Nottingham, & Raymond Through Concord, Hooksett, Manchester & Nashua. DeLorme US Staff. (Illus.). 64p. 1999. 9.95 (0-89933-403-2) DeLorme Map.

Morris: The Life & Works of Don H. Morris. Owen Cosgrove. (Illus.). 155p. (Orig.). 1993. pap. 11.95 (0-940999-89-7, C2247) Star Bible.

Morris & Boris at the Circus. Bernard Wiseman. LC 87-45682. (I Can Read Bks.). (Illus.). 64p. (J). (ps-3). 1988. lib. bdg. 15.89 (0-06-026478-0) HarpC Child Bks.

Morris & Boris at the Circus. Bernard Wiseman. LC 87-45682. (I Can Read Bks.). (Illus.). 64p. (J). (ps-3). 1990. pap. 3.95 (0-06-444143-1, HarpTrophy) HarpC Child Bks.

Morris & Boris at the Circus. Bernard Wiseman. (I Can Read Bks.). (J). (ps-1). 1988. 8.95 (0-606-04752-2, Pub. by Turtleback) Demco.

*Morris & Chan on Fly Fishing Trout Lakes. Skip Morris & Brian Chan. (Illus.). 96p. 1999. 39.95 (1-57188-182-4); pap. 24.95 (1-57188-181-6) F Amato Pubns.

Morris & the Kingdom of Knoll. T. L. Hill. LC 95-39556. (Illus.). 36p. (J). (gr. k-6). 1996. 16.95 (0-89236-341-X, Pub. by J P Getty Trust) OUP.

Morris, Arnold & Related Families. Louis A. Morris. (Illus.). 288p. 1985. 25.00 (0-89308-550-2) Southern Hist Pr.

*Morris Canal, Across New Jersey by Water & Rail. Bob Goller. (Images of America Ser.). (Illus.). 128p. 1999. pap. 18.99 (0-7385-0076-3) Arcadia Publng.

Morris County Golf Club, 1894-1994. William L. Quirin. LC 94-24079. 1995. write for info. (0-89865-928-0) Donning Co.

Morris Cox & the Gogmagog Press. David Chambers et al. 184p. 1991. 90.00 (0-900002-25-5, Pub. by Priv Lib Assn) Oak Knoll.

*Morris Design for Bird. (William Morris Lined Ser.). 160p. 1999. 12.95 (1-55156-084-4, Pub. by Paperblank) Andrews & McMeel.

*Morris Design for Honeysuckle. William Morris. (William Morris Lined Ser.). 160p. 1999. 12.95 (1-55156-086-0, Pub. by Paperblank) Andrews & McMeel.

*Morris Design for Iris Journal. William Morris. 160p. 1999. 12.95 (1-55156-085-2, Pub. by Paperblank) Andrews & McMeel.

*Morris Design for Windrush. William Morris. (William Morris Lined Ser.). 160p. 1999. 12.95 (1-55156-087-9, Pub. by Paperblank) Andrews & McMeel.

Morris Dictionary of Word & Phrase Origins. 2nd ed. William Morris & Mary Morris. LC 87-45651. 688p. 1988. 38.00 (0-06-015862-X) HarperTrade.

An Asterisk (*) at the beginning of an entry indicates that the title is appearing for the first time.

Morris E. Fine Symposium, October 8-11, 1990, Detroit, MI: TMS Fall Meeting. Morris E. Fine Symposium Staff. Ed. by Peter K. Liaw et al. LC 90-64027. (Illus.). 522p. 1991. reprint ed. pap. 161.90 (*0-608-02493-7*, 206313700004) Bks Demand.

Morris Goes to School. Bernard Wiseman. (I Can Read Bks.). (Illus.). (J). (ps-1). 1970. 6.93 (*0-06-026547-7*, 958266) HarpC.

Morris Goes to School. Bernard Wiseman. (I Can Read Bks.). (Illus.). 64p. (J). (ps-1). 1970. lib. bdg. 15.89 (*0-06-026548-5*) HarpC Child Bks.

Morris Goes to School. Bernard Wiseman. (I Can Read Bks.). (Illus.). 64p. (J). (ps-1). 1983. pap. 3.95 (*0-06-444045-1*, HarpTrophy) HarpC Child Bks.

Morris Goes to School. Bernard Wiseman. (I Can Read Bks.). (J). (ps-1). 1983. 8.95 (*0-606-09631-0*, Pub. by Turtleback) Demco.

Morris Goes to School. unabridged ed. B. Wiseman. (I Can Read Bks.). (Illus.). 64p. (J). (ps-3). 1991. audio 8.95 (*1-55994-495-1*, TBC 4951) HarperAudio.

Morris Graves: The Early Works. Theodore F. Wolff. LC 97-75835. (Illus.). 72p. 1999. pap. 19.95 (*0-295-97763-9*) U of Wash Pr.

Morris Graves: Vision of the Inner Eye. Ray Kass. LC 83-2606. (Illus.). 176p. (Orig.). 1983. pap. 20.00 (*0-8076-1069-0*) Braziller.

Morris Graves Flower Paintings: Flower Paintings. Theo Wolff. LC 94-11125. (Illus.). 144p. 1994. 39.95 (*0-295-97379-X*) U of Wash Pr.

Morris H. Kushner on Specialty Foods. Morris H. Kushner. LC 96-80531. (Illus.). 208p. (Orig.). 1996. pap. 19.00 (*0-9634299-3-0*) Cumberland Ent.

Morris Has a Cold. Bernard Wiseman. (J). Date not set. 11.95 (*0-399-21906-4*) Putnam Pub Group.

Morris High School & the Creation of the New York City Public High School System. Gary D. Hermalyn. LC 93-22083. 232p. 1995. 32.00 (*0-941980-31-6*) Bronx County.

Morris Hillquit: A Political History of an American Jewish Socialist, 20. Norma F. Pratt. LC 78-55349. (Illus.). 272p. 1979. 59.95 (*0-313-20526-4*, PMH/, Greenwood Pr) Greenwood.

Morris Hillquit Papers: Guide to a Microfilm Edition. Ed. by F. Gerald Ham & Carole Sue Warmbrodt. LC 74-632298. (Guides to Historical Resources Ser.). 116p. 1969. pap. 2.00 (*0-87020-109-3*) State Hist Soc Wis.

Morris Hillquit Papers, 1886-1944: Guide to a Microfilm Edition. Ed. by F. Gerald Ham. 116p. 1969. pap. write for info. (*0-89887-180-8*) Chadwyck-Healey.

Morris Louis: The Complete Paintings, A Catalogue Raisonne. Diane Upright. LC 85-1256. (Illus.). 264p. 1985. 135.00 (*0-8109-1280-5*, Pub. by Abrams) Time Warner.

Morris Louis in the Museum of Fine Arts, Boston. Kenworth W. Moffett. LC 79-6360. (Illus.). 40p. 1979. pap. 4.95 (*0-87846-135-3*) Mus Fine Arts Boston.

Morris Machine Works Catalogue of 1885: Boilers & Engines. Morris Machine Works Company Staff. (Illus.). 20p. 1998. reprint ed. pap. 25.00 (*0-87556-866-1*) Saifer.

Morris Migration: A Saga of Forebears & Descendants. Anne M. Mertz. (Illus.). xvi, 476p. (Orig.). 1996. 40.00 (*0-7884-0516-0*, MERT) Heritage Bk.

Morris Migration: A Saga of Forebears & Descendants. Anne M. Mertz. (Illus.). xii, 472p. (Orig.). 1996. pap. 30.00 (*0-7884-0550-0*, M167) Heritage Bk.

Morris Minor. Ray Newell. (Album Ser.: No. 277). (Illus.). 32p. 1998. pap. 6.25 (*0-7478-0149-5*, Pub. by Shire Pubns) Parkwest Pubns.

Morris Minor. Ray Newell. (Illus.). 192p. 1998. 35.95 (*1-86126-133-0*, Pub. by Cro1wood) Motorbooks Intl.

Morris Minor: A Collector's Guide. Guy Saddlestone. (Illus.). 128p. 1997. 27.95 (*1-899870-17-2*, Pub. by Motor Racing) Motorbooks Intl.

Morris Minor: Exploring the Legend Jon Pressnell. LC 98-70519. 168p. 1998. write for info. (*1-85960-429-3*) Haynes Manuals.

***Morris Minor Light Commercials.** Russell Harvey. (Illus.). 128p. 2000. pap. 18.99 (*0-7524-1735-5*, Pub. by Tempus Pubng) Arcadia Publng.

Morris Minor Restoration. Jim Tyler. (Illus.). 240p. 1995. pap. 39.95 (*1-85532-471-7*, Pub. by J H Haynes & Co) Motorbooks Intl.

Morris Minor Workshop Manual: All Models, 1956-1971. British Leyland Motors. (Illus.). 460p. (Orig.). 50.00 (*0-8376-0520-2*) Bentley Pubs.

Morris. My No. Carolina Heritage Vol. 4: Zebedee William Morris of Montgomery Co., N.C.: The Ancestry & Descendants of a Civil War Veteran, a Genealogy of the N.C. Cos. Buncombe, Haywood, Madison McDowell & Montgomery, 1805-1995 (Including Primary Families of Lamb & Styles) Marshall L. Styles. (Illus.). 385p. 1996. reprint ed. pap. 59.00 (*0-8328-5416-6*) Higginson Bk Co.

Morris. My No. Carolina Heritage Vol. 4: Zebedee William Morris of Montgomery Co., N.C.: The Ancestry & Descendants of a Civil War Veteran, a Genealogy of the N.C. Cos. Buncombe, Haywood, Madison McDowell & Montgomery, 1805-1995 (Including Primary Families of Lamb & Styles) 2nd ed. Marshall L. Styles. (Illus.). 385p. 1996. reprint ed. lib. bdg. 69.00 (*0-8328-5415-8*) Higginson Bk Co.

Morris on Torts. 2nd ed. Clarence R. Morris & C. Robert Morris. LC 80-170. (University Textbook Ser.). 443p. 1980. text 25.95 (*0-88277-002-0*) Foundation Pr.

Morris, Orange & King William Artillery. Gregory J. Macaluso. (Virginia Regimental Histories Ser.). (Illus.). 122p. 1991. 19.95 (*1-56190-011-7*) H E Howard.

***Morris Rumpel & the Wings of Icarus.** Betty Waterton. (Illus.). (J). 2000. pap. 3.95 (*0-88899-409-5*) Grndwd Bks.

Morris-Somerset Counties see Hagstrom Atlases

Morris the Moose. Bernard Wiseman. LC 87-33485. (I Can Read Bks.). (Illus.). 64p. (J). (ps-3). 1996. pap. 8.95 incl. audio (*0-694-70005-3*) HarpC.

Morris the Moose. Bernard Wiseman. (I Can Read Bks.). (J). (ps-1). 1991. 8.95 (*0-606-04979-7*, Pub. by Turtleback) Demco.

Morris the Moose. rev. ed. Bernard Wiseman. (I Can Read Bks.). (Illus.). 32p. (J). (ps-1). 1989. 14.00 (*0-06-026475-6*); lib. bdg. 15.89 (*0-06-026476-4*) HarpC Child Bks.

Morris the Moose. rev. ed. Bernard Wiseman. LC 87-33485. (I Can Read Bks.). (Illus.). 32p. (J). (ps-3). 1991. pap. 3.95 (*0-06-444146-6*, HarpTrophy) HarpC Child Bks.

Morris Township, New Jersey: A Glimpse into the Past. Barbara Hoskins. (Illus.). x, 140p. (Orig.). 1987. reprint ed. pap. 10.00 (*0-940631-03-2*) JFP Lib Morristown.

Morrisey on Planning Vol. 1: A Guide to Strategic Thinking: Building Your Planning Foundation. George L. Morrisey. 143p. 1995. 24.50 (*0-7879-0168-7*) Jossey-Bass.

Morrisey on Planning Vol. 2: Guide to Long-Range Planning: Creating Your Strategic Journey, Vol. II. George L. Morrisey. (Management Ser.). 135p. 1995. 24.50 (*0-7879-0169-5*) Jossey-Bass.

Morrisey on Planning Vol. 3: Guide to Tactical Planning: Producing Your Short-Term Results, Vol. #III. George L. Morrisey. 158p. 1995. 24.95 (*0-7879-0170-9*) Jossey-Bass.

Morrisey on Planning Series, 3 vols., Set. George L. Morrisey. 1995. 59.00 (*0-7879-0115-6*) Jossey-Bass.

Morrison: Genealogy of the Descendants of John Morrison & Prudence Gwyn. G. H. Morrison. 31p. 1994. reprint ed. pap. 6.00 (*0-8328-4163-3*) Higginson Bk Co.

Morrison Era: Reform Politics in New Orleans. Joseph B. Parker. LC 74-7142. 172p. 1974. pap. 25.00 (*1-56554-550-8*) Pelican.

Morrison Foundation Lectures. LC 71-156698. (Essay Index Reprint Ser.). 1977. reprint ed. 23.95 (*0-8369-2419-3*) Ayer.

***Morrison Symposium Proceedings.** Nick Fraser. 1072p. 1998. pap. text 404.00 (*90-5699-183-3*, Harwood Acad Pubs) Gordon & Breach.

Morrisons: They Came to the Land That Hudgin Drains. Glenn H. Morrison. LC 93-81022. (Orig.). 1994. pap. 15.95 (*0-9640081-0-6*) G H Morrison.

Morrison's Essential Recruitment & Selection Guide: For a Post-ADA Environment. Don A. Morrison & Jenifer Gilliland. (Illus.). 270p. 1993. ring bd. 7.00 (*0-927160-08-0*) Sound Resc Mgmt.

***Morrison's Sound-It-Out Speller: A Phonic Key to English.** rev. ed. Marvin L. Morrison. Ed. by Penelope Kister McRann. xiv, 1069p. (YA). (gr. 5 up). 2000. 39.95 (*0-9678068-0-1*) Stone Cloud.

Morris's Disappearing Bag. Rosemary Wells. (J). 1992. pap. 5.99 (*0-14-054664-2*, PuffinBks) Peng Put Young Read.

Morrissey: Landscapes of the Mind. David Bret. LC 95-10371. (Illus.). 208p. 1995. pap. 9.95 (*0-7867-0218-4*) Carroll & Graf.

Morrissey & Marr: The Severed Alliance. Johnny Rogan. (Illus.). 392p. pap. 17.95 (*0-7119-3000-7*, OP46804) Omnibus NY.

Morrissey Shot. Linder Sterling. LC 94-1747. (Illus.). 144p. (YA). 1994. pap. 14.45 (*1-56282-773-1*, Pub. by Hyperion) Time Warner.

Morristown. Joan M. Williams. (Images of America Ser.). 128p. 1996. pap. 16.99 (*0-7524-0207-2*) Arcadia Publng.

Morristown: A History & Guide, Morristown National Historical Park, New Jersey. George F. Scheer, III. 111p. 1984. pap. 72.00 (*0-16-003457-4*) USGPO.

Morristown: A History & Guide, Morristown National Historical Park, New Jersey. Russell F. Weigley. 111p. 1985. pap. 12.00 (*0-16-003489-2*) USGPO.

Morristown Courthouse Atrocity, Vol. 1. Thomas P. Coffey. (Studies in Judicial Perversion). 96p. 1995. pap. 6.95 (*0-87193-300-4*) Dimension Bks.

Morristown Courthouse Atrocity, Vol. 2. Thomas P. Coffey. (Studies in Judicial Perversion). 1995. pap. 4.95 (*0-87193-301-2*) Dimension Bks.

Morristown Courthouse Atrocity, Vol. 3. Thomas P. Coffey. (Studies in Judicial Perversion). 96p. (J). 1997. pap. 4.95 (*0-87193-302-0*) Dimension Bks.

Morristown Courthouse Atrocity, Vol. 4. Thomas P. Coffey. (Studies in Judicial Perversion). 1997. pap. 4.95 (*0-87193-303-9*) Dimension Bks.

Morristown Manuscript Collection: A Guide to the Microfilm Edition of the Manuscript Collection Morristown National Historical. Bruce W. Stewart & Hans Mayer. v, 190p. reprint ed. 45.00 (*0-8357-0896-9*) Univ Microfilms.

Morristown National Historical Park. Russell F. Weigley. LC 83-600130. (Official National Park Handbook Ser.: No. 120). (Illus.). 112p. 1984. pap. 12.00 (*0-912627-21-2*) Natl Park Serv.

Morristown Two Times: History of Morristown, Vermont & More About Morristown, 1935-1980. Anna L. Mower & Robert L. Hagerman. LC 81-84221. (Illus.). 575p. 1982. 16.95 (*0-9607288-0-5*) Morristown Hist Soc.

Morrisville. James Murray. (Images of America Ser.). 1997. pap. 16.99 (*0-7524-0926-3*) Arcadia Publng.

Morro: Derrota y Muerte de Piratas: De Ingleses, Holandeses y Franceses. Jose Morales. (SPA.). 160p. 1998. pap. 6.00 (*0-938693-14-X*) Maya Pubns.

Morro Bay Meanderings. 2nd ed. Harold Wieman. LC 72-2793. (Illus.). 112p. 1984. pap. 5.95 (*0-914598-22-8*) Bear Flag Bks.

Morrocan Cooking. (Mini Cook Bks.). (Illus.). 64p. 1999. pap. 1.95 (*3-8290-1612-3*) Konemann.

Morrow Anthology of Younger American Poets. Ed. by Dave Smith & David Bottoms. LC 84-18044. (Illus.). 472p. 1985. pap. 17.95 (*0-688-03450-0*, Quil) HarperTrade.

Morrow Guide to Knot. Maria Bigon et al. Ed. by Kennie Lyman. Tr. by Maria Piotrowska from ITA. LC 82-6308. (Illus.). 258p. 1982. pap. 13.95 (*0-688-01226-4*, Wm Morrow) Morrow Avon.

Morrow's Ants. Edward Hyams. LC 76-366418. 188 p. (J). 1975. 3.95 (*0-7139-0676-6*) Viking Penguin.

Mors et Vita, Service Inutile. Henry De Montherlant. pap. 9.50 (*0-685-36984-6*) Fr & Eur.

Morsas. Sarah Palmer. (Mamifero Marino Ser.).Tr. of Walruses. 24p. (J). (gr. k-4). 1991. lib. bdg. 14.60 (*0-86592-689-1*) Rourke Enter.

***Morse Code.** Mary Packard. Ed. by Cathy Nichols. (Illus.). 16p. (YA). 2000. write for info. (*1-884270-14-X*) Nancy Hall.

Morse Code: Breaking the Barrier. Dave Finley. (Illus.). 88p. 1998. pap. 14.95 (*1-891237-19-5*) MFJ Ent.

Morse Code: The Essential Language. Carron. 1991. pap. 8.00 (*0-87259-035-6*) Am Radio.

Morse Genealogy, Being a Revision of the Memorial of the Morse Publication by Abner Morse in 1850, 2 vols. in 1. J. H. Morse & Emily W. Leavitt. 596p. 1989. reprint ed. pap. 90.00 (*0-8328-0885-7*); reprint ed. lib. bdg. 98.00 (*0-8328-0884-9*) Higginson Bk Co.

Morse Homology. Matthias Schwarz. LC 93-20738. (Progress in Mathematics Ser.: Vol. 111). 235p. 1993. 49.50 (*0-8176-2904-1*) Birkhauser.

Morse Theory. John W. Milnor. (Annals of Mathematics Studies: No. 51). 160p. (Orig.). 1963. pap. text 37.50 (*0-691-08008-9*, Pub. by Princeton U Pr) Cal Prin Full Svc.

Morse Theory & Its Applications. Ed. by G. M. Rassias. 400p. (C). 1994. text 58.00 (*9971-5-0977-6*) World Scientific Pub.

Morsels. John Repar. 150p. 1998. pap. 5.00 (*0-9661910-1-3*) J Repar.

***Morsels from the Better Mousetrap: Tips, Tricks & Tales about Corporate Communications for Small Businesses.** Nancy Parsons & Dick Amsterdam. LC 00-190419. 227p. 2000. 25.00 (*0-7388-1673-6*); pap. 18.00 (*0-7388-1674-4*) Xlibris Corp.

Morsels of Manna. Mike W. Blottenberger. LC 95-3922. 68p. 1996. pap. 14.95 (*0-7734-2721-X*, Mellen Poetry Pr) E Mellen.

Morse's Greatest Mystery & Other Stories. Colin Dexter. 1996. mass mkt. 5.99 (*0-8041-1309-2*) Ivy Books.

Morson's English Guide for Court Reporters. Lillian I. Morson. 400p. 1997. pap. text. write for info. (*0-9657932-0-6*); pap. text, teacher ed. write for info. (*0-9657932-1-4*) Morson Guide.

Morsure de L'Ange. Yvette Cathiard. 200p. 59.95 (*2-86808-091-X*) Intl Scholars.

Mort. Terry Pratchett. 272p. 1989. mass mkt. 6.99 (*0-552-13106-7*) Bantam.

***Mort.** Terry Pratchett. 2000. pap. 8.95 (*0-552-14429-0*, Pub. by Transworld Publishers Ltd) Trafalgar.

Mort a Credit. Louis-Ferdinand Celine. (FRE.). pap. 17.95 (*0-8288-3673-6*, F92033) Fr & Eur.

Mort a Credit. Louis-Ferdinand Celine. (Folio Ser.: No. 1692). (FRE.). 1972. pap. 14.95 (*2-07-037692-3*) Schoenhof.

Mort Artu: An Old French Prose Romance of the Thirteenth Century. Ed. by J. Douglas Bruce. LC 75-178546. reprint ed. 54.50 (*0-404-56649-9*) AMS Pr.

Mort Crim's Second Thoughts: One Hundred Upbeat Messages for Beat up Americans. unabridged ed. Mort Crim. 1997. audio 14.95 (*1-55874-570-X*) Health Comm.

Mort d'Aggrippine. De Bergerac. Ed. by Gossip. (Exeter French Texts Ser.: Vol. 44). (FRE.). 113p. Date not set. pap. text 19.95 (*0-85989-182-8*, Pub. by Univ Exeter Pr) Northwestern U Pr.

Mort dans l'Ame. Jean-Paul Sartre. (Chemins de Liberte Ser.: Bk. 3). (FRE.). 1972. pap. 11.95 (*0-8288-3748-1*, F125281) Fr & Eur.

Mort dans l'Ame. Jean-Paul Sartre. (Folio Ser.: No. 58). (FRE.). 1972. pap. 9.95 (*2-07-036058-X*) Schoenhof.

Mort dans l'Ame see Chemins de la liberte

Mort d'Artemio Cruz. Carlos Fuentes. (FRE.). 401p. 1976. pap. 11.95 (*0-7859-2378-0*, 2070368564) Fr & Eur.

Mort de Belle, le Revolver de Maigret, les Freres Rico, Maigret et l'Homme Du Banc, Antoine et Julie, Maigret a Peur, l'Escalier De Fer, Feux Rouges. Georges Simenon. (FRE.). 1989. 49.95 (*0-7859-0481-6*, 2258027098) Fr & Eur.

Mort de Quelqu'un. Jules Romains, pseud. (Folio Ser.: No. 1882). (FRE.). 160p. 1970. pap. 6.95 (*2-07-037882-9*) Schoenhof.

Mort de Solon: Piece Attribuee a Corneille Par Elisabeth M. Fraser. Pierre Corneille. (FRE.). 136p. 1949. 10.95 (*0-7859-5375-2*) Fr & Eur.

Mort de Venise. Maurice Barres. Ed. & Pref. by Marie-Odile Germain. (FRE., Illus.). 160p. 1995. pap. 64.95 (*2-86808-045-6*) Intl Scholars.

Mort des Enfans D'Herodes. La Calprenede. Ed. by Smith. (Exeter French Texts Ser.: Vol. 69). (FRE.). 116p. Date not set. pap. text 19.95 (*0-85989-259-X*, Pub. by Univ Exeter Pr) Northwestern U Pr.

Mort du Petit Cheval. Herve Bazin. (FRE.). 1955. pap. 10.95 (*0-7859-3073-6*) Fr & Eur.

Mort d'un Personnage. Jean Giono. (FRE.). 256p. 1949. 10.95 (*0-7859-0096-9*, M3494) Fr & Eur.

Mort Est Mon Metier. Robert Merle. (FRE.). 1976. pap. 11.95 (*0-7859-4058-8*) Fr & Eur.

Mort Heureuse. Albert Camus. (Cahiers Albert Camus Ser.). 34.95 (*0-685-37268-5*, F90660) Fr & Eur.

Mort Irreguliere. Beatrix Beck. (FRE.). 1981. pap. 10.95 (*0-685-66710-3*, 2070372782) Fr & Eur.

Mort Kunstler's Civil War: The North. Mort Kunstler. LC 97-9408. (Illus.). 192p. 1997. 12.95 (*1-55853-477-6*) Rutledge Hill Pr.

Mort Kunstler's Civil War: The South. Mort Kunstler. LC 97-9407. (Illus.). 192p. 1997. 12.95 (*1-55853-478-4*) Rutledge Hill Pr.

Mort Kunstler's Old West: Indians. Mort Kunstler. LC 98-15248. (Illus.). 192p. 1998. 12.95 (*1-55853-589-6*) Rutledge Hill Pr.

Mort Kunstler's Old West Cowboys: Cowboys. Mort Kunstler. LC 98-16102. (Illus.). 192p. 1998. 12.95 (*1-55853-588-8*) Rutledge Hill Pr.

Mort Qui Fait le Trottoir: Don Juan. Henry De Montherlant. (FRE.). 1991. pap. 10.95 (*0-8288-3724-4*, F115760) Fr & Eur.

MORT Safety Assurance Systems. W. Johnson. (Occupational Safety & Health Ser.: Vol. 4). (Illus.). 544p. 1980. text 140.00 (*0-8247-6897-3*) Dekker.

Mort Safety Assurance Systems. 2nd ed. D. Riffe. (Occupational Safety & Health Ser.). Date not set. write for info. (*0-8247-9936-4*) Dekker.

Mort Saisit le Vif. Henri Troyat. (FRE.). 1988. pap. 11.95 (*0-7859-3432-4*) Fr & Eur.

***Mort the Sport.** Robert Kraus. LC 99-28574. (Illus.). 32p. (J). (ps-2). 2000. 15.95 (*0-531-30247-4*); lib. bdg. 16.99 (*0-531-33247-0*) Orchard Bks Watts.

Mort Tres Douce. Simone de Beauvoir. (FRE.). 160p. 1972. pap. 10.95 (*0-8288-3654-X*) Fr & Eur.

Mort Tres Douce. Simone de Beauvoir. (Folio Ser.: No. 137). (FRE.). 160p. 1972. pap. 6.95 (*2-07-036137-3*) Schoenhof.

***Mort Walker's Private Scrapbook: A Celebration of 50 Years of Comic Excellence.** Mort Walker. (Illus.). 312p. 2000. pap. 19.95 (*0-7407-1126-1*) Andrews & McMeel.

Mortadello: or the Angel of Venice. Aleister Crowley. 144p. 1993. reprint ed. pap. 37.50 (*1-872736-17-3*, Pub. by Mandrake Pr) Holmes Pub.

Mortage Kit. 4th ed. Thomas Steinmetz. LC 98-9541. 282p. 1998. pap. text 19.95 (*0-7931-2852-8*) Dearborn.

Mortal. Judas Riley Martinez. 25p. 1999. pap. 6.00 (*0-9670994-1-2*) Longleaf Meth Coll.

***Mortal Affair.** large type ed. Stella Allan. 352p. 1999. 31.99 (*0-7089-4081-1*) Ulverscroft.

Mortal & Immortals: Life under the Last Three Czars. Julius I. Block. (Illus.). 257p. (Orig.). 1994. pap. 34.50 (*0-930329-57-0*) Kabel Pubs.

Mortal Antipathy. Oliver W. Holmes. LC 70-96887. 317p. reprint ed. pap. text 9.50 (*0-8290-1690-2*); reprint ed. lib. bdg. 22.00 (*0-8398-0788-0*) Irvington.

Mortal Antipathy. Oliver W. Holmes. (Notable American Authors Ser.). 1992. reprint ed. lib. bdg. 75.00 (*0-7812-3168-X*) Rprt Serv.

Mortal Bane. Roberta Gellis. LC 99-38761. 304p. 1999. 23.95 (*0-312-87000-0*, Pub. by Forge NYC) St Martin.

Mortal Beings. Carl Lombard. 224p. 1994. pap. 17.95 (*1-85702-103-7*) Fourth Estate.

Mortal Causes. Ian Rankin. 1995. 21.50 (*1-883402-75-1*) S&S Trade.

Mortal Causes. 3rd ed. Ian Rankin. (Dead Letter Mysteries Ser.). 288p. 1997. mass mkt. 5.99 (*0-312-96094-8*) St Martin.

Mortal City: Storefront Books. Ed. by Peter J. Lang. LC 95-867. (Illus.). 112p. (Orig.). 1995. pap. 12.95 (*1-56898-046-9*) Princeton Arch.

Mortal City One-Hundred Epigrams from Martial. William Matthews. 128p. (Orig.). 1995. pap. 15.00 (*0-942148-17-7*) Ohio Review.

Mortal Coils. John H. Crowe, 3rd et al. (Illus.). 190p. 1998. pap. 19.95 (*1-887797-11-4*, PAG 1007, Pagan Pubng) Tynes Cowan.

Mortal Combat Jr. Novel Vol. 1: Reptile's World. Dean Anderson. (Mortal Kombat Ser.). 1996. mass mkt. 4.50 (*1-57297-131-2*) Blvd Books.

Mortal Companions. Charles Fishman. (Illus.). 1977. 7.00 (*0-918870-02-X*); pap. 3.50 (*0-918870-01-1*) Pleasure Dome.

Mortal Consequences. Clayton Emery. (Arcane Age Campaign Ser.). 1998. pap. 5.99 (*0-7869-0683-9*, Pub. by TSR Inc) Random.

***Mortal Education.** Joyce Peseroff. LC 99-72502. (Poetry Ser.). 80p. 2000. pap. 12.95 (*0-88748-326-7*, Pub. by Carnegie-Mellon) CUP Services.

Mortal Enemies: Sentinels. Don Mappin. 150p. (YA). (gr. 10 up). 1999. pap. 15.00 (*0-9641722-2-4*) Black Gate.

Mortal Enemy, My Beloved. Rita Zamora. 240p. 1999. pap. 12.95 (*1-880710-45-5*) Monterey Pacific.

Mortal Engines. Stanislaw Lem. 256p. 1992. pap. 8.95 (*0-15-662161-4*, Harvest Bks) Harcourt.

Mortal Fear. Robin Cook. 1989. mass mkt. 7.99 (*0-425-11388-4*) Berkley Pub.

Mortal Fear. Robin Cook. 1989. 12.60 (*0-606-00930-2*, Pub. by Turtleback) Demco.

Mortal Friends: A Novel. James Carroll. LC 91-41137. 608p. 1992. pap. 17.00 (*0-8070-6339-8*) Beacon Pr.

***Mortal Friends, Best Enemies: German-Russian Cooperation After the Cold War.** Celeste A. Wallander. LC 98-47907. 240p. 1999. pap. text 19.95 (*0-8014-8608-4*) Cornell U Pr.

***Mortal Friends, Best Enemies: German-Russian Cooperation After the Cold War.** Celeste A. Wallander. (Cornell Studies in Security Affairs). 1999. write for info. (*0-8014-3581-1*) Cornell U Pr.

Mortal Fusion. B. Charles Tatum. 314p. 1997. pap. 10.00 (*0-938711-49-0*) Tecolote Pubns.

Mortal Hero: An Introduction to Homer's Iliad. Seth L. Schein. LC 83-5096. 275p. (C). 1984. pap. 16.95 (*0-520-05626-4*, Pub. by U CA Pr) Cal Prin Full Svc.

Mortal Immortal: The Complete Supernatural Short Fiction of Mary Shelley. Mary Wollstonecraft Shelley. xviii, 58p. 1996. pap. 10.00 (*1-892391-01-5*) Tachyon Pubns.

M

Mortal Judgments. John A. Peak. LC 98-43846. 352p. 1999. 23.95 (0-312-19837-X, Thomas Dunne) St Martin.

Mortal Kombat. Martin Delrio. 1995. pap. 3.99 (0-8125-4453-6, Pub. by Tor Bks); pap., mass mkt. 5.99 (0-8125-4452-8, Pub. by Tor Bks) St Martin.

Mortal Kombat. Jeff Rovin. (Orig.). 1995. mass mkt. 4.99 (1-57297-059-6) Blvd Books.

***Mortal Kombat: Mythologies: Special.** Prima Publishing Staff. 96p. 2000. pap. 14.99 (0-7615-2326-X) Prima Pub.

Mortal Kombat: Shango's Thunder. C. Dean Andersson. 1996. mass mkt. 4.50 (1-57297-149-5) Blvd Books.

Mortal Kombat: The Movie: Behind the Scenes. Michael Goldman. (Illus.). 96p. 1995. pap. text 14.95 (0-7615-0082-0) Prima Pub.

Mortal Kombat IV: Official Arcade Game Secrets. Prima Creative Services Staff. LC 96-72647. 96p. 1997. per. 12.99 (0-7615-1076-1) Prima Pub.

Mortal Kombat IV: Official Game Secrets. Prima Publishing Staff. LC 96-72648. (Secrets of the Game Ser.). 96p. 1998. per. 12.99 (0-7615-1077-X) Prima Pub.

***Mortal Kombat Gold: Official Strategy Guide.** Prima Pub Staff. LC 99-65216. (Illus.). 95p. 1999. pap. 12.99 (0-7615-2329-4) Prima Pub.

Mortal Kombat II: Official Fighters Kompanion. Brady Games Staff. (Illus.). 157p. (Orig.). 1994. 9.95 (1-56686-198-5) Brady Pub.

Mortal Kombat Mythologies Official Guide. Brady Games Staff. (Illus.). 112p. (J). 1997. 11.99 (1-56686-722-3) Brady Pub.

Mortal Kombat Mythology: Official Game Secrets. Prima Publishing Staff. LC 97-69326. (Secrets of the Game Ser.). 96p. 1997. per. 12.99 (0-7615-1215-2) Prima Pub.

***Mortal Kombat Special Forces Official Strategy Guide.** 128p. 1999. 12.99 (1-56686-914-5) Brady Pub.

Mortal Kombat III: Official Arcade Secrets. Simon Hill. 1995. pap. text 9.95 (0-7615-0204-1) Prima Pub.

Mortal Kombat III: Player's Guide. J. Douglas Arnold & Zach Meston. (Gaming Mastery Ser.). (Illus.). 128p. (Orig.). 1995. pap. 12.95 (1-884364-14-4) Sandwich Islands.

Mortal Kombat Trilogy: Official Game Secrets. LC 96-67983. 96p. 1996. pap., per. 9.99 (0-7615-0732-9) Prima Pub.

Mortal Kombat 2: Custom Power Play Guide. Prima Publishing Staff. 1995. 9.95 (1-55958-839-X) Prima Pub.

Mortal Kombat 4 Ultimate Arcade Strategy Guide: Official. Sybex, Inc. Staff. 1997. pap. text 9.99 (0-7821-2239-6) Sybex.

Mortal Lessons: Notes on the Art of Surgery. Richard Selzer. (Illus.). 224p. (C). 1996. pap. 13.00 (0-15-600400-3, Harvest Bks) Harcourt.

Mortal Love: Selected Poems, 1971-1998. Franklin Abbott. 162p. 1999. pap. 14.00 (0-9627616-3-X, Pub. by RFD Pr) Bookazine Co Inc.

Mortal Memory. Thomas Cook. 320p. 1994. mass mkt. 5.99 (0-553-56532-X) Bantam.

Mortal Memory. large type ed. Thomas H. Cook. LC 93-1388. (Cloak & Dagger Ser.). 431p. 1993. lib. bdg. 22.95 (1-56054-707-3) Thorndike Pr.

Mortal Men: Living with Asymptomatic HIV. Richard MacIntyre. LC 98-8501. 256p. (C). 1999. 26.00 (0-8135-2596-9) Rutgers U Pr.

Mortal Messiah: From Bethlehem to Calvary, Bk. 2. Bruce R. McConkie. LC 79-19606. (Messiah Ser.). 424p. 1990. reprint ed. pap. 9.95 (0-87579-404-1) Deseret Bk.

Mortal Messiah: From Bethlehem to Calvary, Bk. 3. Bruce R. McConkie. LC 79-19606. (Messiah Ser.). 486p. 1990. reprint ed. pap. 10.95 (0-87579-405-X) Deseret Bk.

Mortal Midnight. Danny Daniels. 224p. (Orig.). 1996. pap. 11.99 (1-883893-64-X) WinePress Pub.

Mortal, Muse, Mystic. Stan Howse. 200p. Date not set. pap. 10.00 (1-887150-03-X) Millennia Bks.

Mortal Nuts. Pete Hautman. 1997. per. 5.99 (0-671-00304-6) PB.

Mortal on the Mend: A Passage to Healing. Vincent Marquis. 107p. 1997. pap. write for info. (1-57502-587-6, PO1680) Morris Pubng.

Mortal Pages, Literary Lives: Studies in the Nineteenth-Century Autobiography. Ed. by Vincent Newey & Philip Shaw. (Nineteenth Century Ser.). 250p. 1996. text 78.95 (1-85928-206-7, Pub. by Scolar Pr) Ashgate Pub Co.

Mortal Peril: Our Inalienable Right to Health Care? Richard A. Epstein. LC 96-46024. 528p. 1997. 27.50 (0-201-13647-3) Perseus Pubng.

***Mortal Peril: Our Inalienable Right to Healthcare?** Richard A. Epstein. 528p. 2000. pap. text 18.00 (0-7382-0189-8, Pub. by Perseus Pubng) HarpC.

***Mortal Poetry.** Anthony DiGiacomo. 20p. 1999. pap. 6.00 (1-58265-010-1, 00030) Orphan Press.

Mortal Presidency: Illness & Anguish in the White House. 2nd ed. Robert E. Gilbert. LC 97-50051. xix, 353p. 1998. pap. 18.95 (0-8232-1837-6) Fordham.

Mortal Presidency: Illness & Anguish in the White House. 2nd rev. ed. Robert E. Gilbert. LC 97-50051. xxix, 353p. 1998. 39.00 (0-8232-1836-8) Fordham.

Mortal Pursuit. Brian Harper. 458p. 1997. mass mkt. 5.99 (0-451-18200-6, Sig) NAL.

Mortal Questions. Thomas Nagel. (Canto Book Ser.). (Illus.). 229p. (C). 1991. pap. 12.95 (0-521-40676-5) Cambridge U Pr.

Mortal Refrains: The Complete Collected Poetry, Prose & Songs of Julia A. Moore, the Sweet Singer of Michigan. Julia A. Moore. Ed. by Thomas J. Riedlinger. LC 98-10566. (Illus.). 256p. 1998. pap. 24.95 (0-87013-449-3) Mich St U Pr.

Mortal Remains. Rick Hanson. 1996. mass mkt. 4.99 (0-7860-0284-0, Pinncle Kensgtn) Kensgtn Pub Corp.

Mortal Remains. large type ed. Margaret Yorke. 1990. 18.95 (0-7089-2163-9) Ulverscroft.

Mortal Remains. 2nd ed. Patrick Lane. (Picas Ser.: No. 17). 92p. reprint ed. pap. 7.00 (1-55096-541-7, Pub. by Exile Edns) Paul & Co Pubs.

Mortal Sin. Paul Levine. 352p. 1995. mass mkt. 5.50 (0-380-72161-9, Avon Bks) Morrow Avon.

Mortal Sins. Maya. Ed. by Robert E. Duncan. (Illus.). 175p. 2000. mass mkt. 15.95 (1-888347-28-7, Enigma) Donnchad.

Mortal Sins. Penn Williamson. LC 99-52357. 432p. 2000. 23.95 (0-446-52154-X, Pub. by Warner Bks) Little.

Mortal Souls: A Neo-Aristotelian Theory of the Human Psyche. Leonard S. Carrier. LC 95-53028. (San Francisco State University Series in Philosophy: Vol. 9). 1997. pap. write for info. (0-8204-3111-7) P Lang Pubng.

Mortal Stakes. Robert B. Parker. 336p. 1987. mass mkt. 6.99 (0-440-15758-7) Dell.

Mortal Stakes. Robert B. Parker. LC 95-15248. 1995. Not sold separately (0-614-32323-1) Random.

Mortal Stakes. large type ed. Robert B. Parker. LC 92-23911. 290p. 1992. reprint ed. lib. bdg. 20.95 (1-56054-314-0) Thorndike Pr.

Mortal Stakes. Robert B. Parker. 1994. reprint ed. lib. bdg. 32.95 (1-56849-316-9) Buccaneer Bks.

***Mortal Storm: A Novel.** Phyllis Bottome. LC 98-24701. xxv, 357p. 1998. pap. text 18.95 (0-8101-1471-2) Northwestern U Pr.

Mortal Term. Penn. 1985. 12.95 (0-684-18317-X, Scribners Ref) Mac Lib Ref.

Mortal Term. large type ed. John Penn. (Mystery Ser.). 352p. 1988. 27.99 (0-7089-1822-0) Ulverscroft.

Mortal Words Birds Politically-Incorrect Scientifically-Unsupported Treasonous Government-Bashing Libertarian Cartoon Book. John Bryant. (Illus.). 126p. (Orig.). 1997. pap. 12.95 (1-886739-36-6) Socratic Pr.

Mortal Words of J. B. R. Yant & Other Irritations. John Bryant. (Illus.). 1987. 16.95 (0-9617444-0-5); pap. 12.95 (0-9617444-1-3) Socratic Pr.

Mortal World: Poems. Deborah Pope. LC 95-10354. (C). 1995. pap. 9.95 (0-8071-1984-9); text 17.95 (0-8071-1983-0) La State U Pr.

***Mortalis.** R. A. Salvatore. 464p. 2000. 25.95 (0-345-43039-5, Del Rey) Ballantine Pub Grp.

Mortality & Health Policy. 1984. 30.00 (92-1-151098-8, E 84.XIII.4) UN.

Mortality & Migration in the Modern World. Ralph Shlomowitz. (Collected Studies: No. CS543). 336p. 1996. 109.95 (0-86078-596-3, Pub. by Variorum) Ashgate Pub Co.

Mortality & Morality: A Search for the Good after Auschwitz. Hans Jonas. Ed. by Lawrence Vogel. (Studies in Phenomenology & Existential Philosophy). 224p. 1996. text 79.95 (0-8101-1285-X); pap. text 22.50 (0-8101-1286-8) Northwestern U Pr.

Mortality & Morbidity in the United States. Ed. by Carl L. Erhardt & Joyce E. Berlin. LC 74-83140. (Vital & Health Statistics Monographs). 315p. reprint ed. pap. 97.70 (0-7837-4476-5, 204418400001) Bks Demand.

Mortality & Society in Sub-Saharan Africa. Ed. by Etienne Van de Walle et al. (International Studies in Demography). (Illus.). 470p. 1992. text 95.00 (0-19-828372-5) OUP.

Mortality Costs of Regulatory Expenditures. Ed. by W. Kip Viscusi. 108p. (C). 1994. lib. bdg. 127.00 (0-7923-9445-3) Kluwer Academic.

***Mortality Crisis in Transitional Economies.** Ed. by Giovanni Andrea Cornia & Renato Paniccia. (Wider Studies in Development Economics). (Illus.). 528p. 2000. text 99.00 (0-19-829741-6) OUP.

Mortality Decline & Its Demographic Effects in Latin America. Eduardo E. Arriaga. LC 76-4852. (Population Monograph: No. 6). (Illus.). 1976. reprint ed. lib. bdg. 55.00 (0-685-02004-5, ARLT, Greenwood Pr) Greenwood.

Mortality from Malignant Neoplasms, 1955-1965, 2 vols. (World Health Statistics Ser.). (ENG & FRE.). 1147p. 1970. pap. text 110.00 (92-4-056008-4, 1151107) World Health.

Mortality Immortality? The Legacy of 20th-Century Art. Ed. by Miguel A. Corzo. LC 98-38695. (Illus.). 212p. 1999. pap. 39.95 (0-89236-528-5, Pub. by J P Getty Trust) OUP.

Mortality, Immortality, & Other Life Strategies. Zygmunt Bauman. iv, 215p. (C). 1992. 42.50 (0-8047-2163-7); pap. 15.95 (0-8047-2164-5) Stanford U Pr.

Mortality Models for Countries with Deficient Data. Maged Ishak. LC 92-34126. 203p. 1992. write for info. (3-631-45436-8) P Lang Pubng.

Mortality Mortgage: Pricing Practices & Reform in the Life Insurance Industry. A. R. Barnes, Jr. LC 95-19464. 216p. 1995. 57.95 (1-56720-003-6, Quorum Bks) Greenwood.

Mortality of Children under Age 5: World Estimates & Projections, 1950-2025. (Population Studies: No. 105). 50p. 1988. 9.50 (92-1-151169-0, E.88.XIII.4) UN.

Mortality of Hispanic Populations: Mexicans, Puerto Ricans, & Cubans in the United States & in the Home Country, 6. Ed. by Ira Rosenwaike. LC 91-2. (Studies in Population & Urban Demography: No. 6). 240p. 1991. 59.95 (0-313-27500-9, RMY, Greenwood Pr) Greenwood.

Mortality of Indigenous Australians. Phil Anderson et al. LC 98-119419. (Occasional Papers.). v, 76 p. 1996. write for info. (0-642-23190-7) Aust Inst Criminology.

Mortality of Veteran Participants in the Crossroads Nuclear Test. Institute of Medicine Staff. 160p. (Orig.). 1996. pap. text 29.00 (0-309-05596-2, Joseph Henry Pr) Natl Acad Pr.

Mortality Patterns & Trends in the United States, 7. Paul E. Zopf, Jr. LC 92-15488. (Studies in Population & Urban Demography: No. 7). 301p. 1992. 69.50 (0-313-26769-3, ZMP, Greenwood Pr) Greenwood.

***Mortality Records of the Town of Watertown, Connecticut.** Ed. by Charles D. Townsend. 121p. 2000. reprint ed. pap. 25.00 (1-878545-51-5) ACETO Bookmen.

***Mortality Schedule 1850-1880-1850 Census for Northampton Co., VA.** Frances Bibbins Latimer. 1999. 20.00 (1-886706-12-3) Hickory Hse.

Mortality Schedule for State of Michigan, 1850. Ed. by Joan Pate. 150p. (Orig.). 1996. pap. 10.00 (1-879766-24-8) OCG Society.

Mortality Schedules for Arkansas, 1850. Bobbie J. McLane & Capitola Glazner. 64p. (Orig.). 1968. pap. 15.00 (0-929604-10-5) Arkansas Ancestors.

Mortality Schedules for Arkansas, 1860. Bobbie J. McLane & Capitola Glazner. 108p. (Orig.). 1969. pap. 15.00 (0-929604-12-1) Arkansas Ancestors.

Mortality Schedules for Arkansas, 1870. Bobbie J. McLane & Capitola Glazner. 93p. (Orig.). 1971. pap. 15.00 (0-929604-13-X) Arkansas Ancestors.

Mortality Schedules for Arkansas, 1880. Bobbie J. McLane & Capitola Glazner. 261p. (Orig.). 1975. pap. 28.00 (0-929604-14-8) Arkansas Ancestors.

Mortality Statistics: Cause (OPCS Series DH2) 1996. TSO Staff. (OPCS Reference Ser.: Series 81020274, No. 23). 107p. 1998. pap. 80.00 (0-11-621025-7, HM210257, Pub. by Statnry Office) Bernan Associates.

***Mortality Statistics: Review of the Registrar General on Deaths by Cause, Sex & Age, in England & Wales, 1998.** Office for National Statistics Staff. (Series DH2, 25). (Illus.). xxxii, 250p. 1999. 70.00 (0-11-621257-8, Pub. by Statnry Office) Balogh.

Mortality Statistics - Cause. TSO Staff. (OPCS Series DH2: No. 22, 1995). 107p. 1997. pap. 75.00 (0-11-620913-5, HM09135, Pub. by Statnry Office) Bernan Associates.

Mortality Statistics - Cause. rev. ed. HMSO Staff. (OPCS Series DH2, 1993 & 1994: Vol. 21). 107p. 1996. pap. 55.00 (0-11-691682-6, HM16826, Pub. by Statnry Office) Bernan Associates.

***Mortality Statistics - Cause 1997.** TSO Staff. (OPCS Series DH2: No. 24). 107p. 1998. pap. 80.00 (0-11-621095-8, HM210958) Statnry Office.

Mortality Statistics - Child, Infant & Perinatal. (OPCS Series, 1996: No. 29). 81p. 1998. pap. 75.00 (0-11-621048-6, HM10486, Pub. by Statnry Office) Bernan Associates.

Mortality Statistics - Child, Infant & Perinatal No. 30: 1997. (OPCS Ser.: No. DH3). 81p. 1999. pap. 75.00 (0-11-621165-2, HM211652, Pub. by Statnry Office) Bernan Associates.

***Mortality Statistics - Child, Infant & Perinatal, 1998.** (OPCS Series DH3: No. 31). 81p. 2000. pap. 75.00 (0-11-621363-9, HM13639, Pub. by Statnry Office) Bernan Associates.

***Mortality Statistics - General 1996.** (OPCS Series DH1: No. 29). 41p. 1998. pap. 55.00 (0-11-621094-X, HM1094X) Statnry Office.

Mortality Statistics - Injuries & Poisoning. OPCS Staff. (OPCS Series DH4: No. 19). 50p. 1997. pap. 60.00 (0-11-691698-2, HM16982, Pub. by Statnry Office) Bernan Associates.

Mortality Surveillance System: Models from the First Year. LC 92-48958. (Vital & Health Statistics Ser.: Series 20, No. 21). 1992. write for info. (0-8406-0468-8) Natl Ctr Health Stats.

Mortality Surveillance System: Models from the Second Year. National Center for Health Statistics Staff. LC 94-1859. (Vital & Health Statistics Ser.: Series 20, No. 22). 82p. 5.50 (0-614-02919-8, 017-022-01273-1) Natl Ctr Health Stats.

Mortality Trends for Alzheimer's Disease. 1996. lib. bdg. 250.75 (0-8490-6058-3) Gordon Pr.

Mortality Trends for Alzheimer's Disease, 1979-91. Donna L. Hoyert. LC 95-50806. (Vital & Health Statistics Ser.: Series 20, No. 28). 1995. write for info. (0-8406-0511-0) Natl Ctr Health Stats.

***"Mortalium Animos" On Fostering True Religious Unity.** Pius XII, pseud. 16p. 1998. reprint ed. pap. 1.95 (0-935952-46-2) Angelus Pr.

Mortally Wounded: Stories of Soul Pain, Death & Healing. Michael Kearney. 1996. 21.50 (0-614-20430-5, Scribners Ref) Mac Lib Ref.

Mortally Wounded: Stories of Soul Pain, Death & Healing. Michael Kearney. 192p. 1996. 21.50 (0-684-83220-8) S&S Trade.

Mortally Wounded: Stories of Soul Pain, Death & Healing. Michael Kearney. (Illus.). 192p. 1997. per. 11.00 (0-684-83537-1, Touchstone) S&S Trade Pap.

Mortals & Others: American Essays, 1931-1935. 2nd ed. Bertrand Russell. Ed. by Harry Ruja. 192p. (C). 1996. pap. 20.99 (0-415-12585-5) Routledge.

Mortals & Others: American Essays 1931-1935, Vol. 2. Bertrand Russell. Ed. by Harry Ruja. 192p. (C). 1998. 65.00 (0-415-17866-5) Routledge.

Mortals & Others Vol. II: American Essays, 1931-1935, Vol. II. Bertrand Russell. 192p. (C). 1998. pap. 20.99 (0-415-17867-3) Routledge.

Mortals in the Immortal Profession: An Oral History of Teaching. Alice D. Rinehart. LC 82-17200. 410p. 1983. pap. text 22.95 (0-8290-1049-1) Irvington.

Mortar: How to Specify & Use Masonry Mortar. (Illus.). 56p. 1990. pap. 14.00 (0-924659-44-0, 4500) Hanley.

Morte Accidentale Di un Anarchico. Lorch. 192p. 1997. pap. 19.95 (0-7190-3848-0) St Martin.

Morte Amoureuse & Avatar et Autre Recits Fantastiques. Theophile Gautier. (FRE.). 512p. 1981. pap. 11.95 (0-7859-2447-7, 2070373169) Fr & Eur.

Morte Amoureuse & Avatar et Autres Recits Fantastiques. Theophile Gautier. (Folio Ser.: No. 1316). (FRE.). pap. 10.95 (2-07-037316-9) Schoenhof.

Morte Arthur: A Critical Edition. P. F. Hissiger. (Studies in English Literature: No. 96). 184p. 1975. pap. text 52.35 (90-279-3386-3) Mouton.

Morte Arthur, a Romance in Stanzas of Eight Lines. Ed. by J. Douglas Bruce. LC 75-41201. reprint ed. 21.50 (0-404-14793-3) AMS Pr.

Morte Arthure. (EETS, OS Ser.: Vol. 8). 1974. reprint ed. 20.00 (0-8115-3343-3) Periodicals Srv.

Morte Arthure: An Alliterative Poem of the Fourteenth Century. From the Thornton. Ed. by Mary M. Banks. LC 71-178545. reprint ed. 37.50 (0-404-56648-0) AMS Pr.

Morte Arthure (Alliterative Version from Thornton MS.) Ed. by E. Brock. (EETS Original Ser.: No. 8). 228p. 1963. reprint ed. text 20.00 (0-19-722008-8, Pub. by EETS) Boydell & Brewer.

Morte d' Arthur: The Winchester Manuscript. Thomas Malory. Ed. & Intro. by Helen Cooper. (The World's Classics Ser.). 610p. 1998. pap. 16.95 (0-19-282420-1) OUP.

Morte D'Arthur. Thomas Malory. 432p. 28.95 (0-8488-2616-7) Amereon Ltd.

Morte D'Arthur. Thomas Malory. 976p. 1994. 22.00 (0-679-60099-X) Modern Lib NY.

Morte D'Arthur. Thomas Malory. LC 98-31432. 976p. 1999. pap. 12.95 (0-375-75322-2) Modern Lib NY.

Morte D'Arthur. Thomas Malory. 1962. mass mkt. 7.99 (0-451-62567-6, Ment) NAL.

Morte D'Arthur. Thomas Malory. Ed. by Derek S. Brewer. LC 68-22420. (York Medieval Texts Ser.). 166p. (C). 1968. pap. 17.95 (0-8101-0031-2) Northwestern U Pr.

Morte D'Arthur. Thomas Malory. (Classics of World Literature Ser.). 1997. pap. 5.95 (1-85326-463-6, 4636WW, Pub. by Wrdsworth Edits) NTC Contemp Pub Co.

Morte D'Arthur. Scudder. 1970. lib. bdg. 75.00 (0-8383-0619-5) M S G Haskell Hse.

Morte D'Arthur. abr. ed. Thomas Malory. Ed. by C. R. Sanders & C. E. Ward. 1979. reprint ed. pap. text 13.95 (0-89197-308-7) Irvington.

Morte D'Arthur. Ed. by J. Douglas Bruce. (EETS, ES Ser.: No. 88). 1974. reprint ed. 40.00 (0-527-00293-3) Periodicals Srv.

Morte D'Arthur, 3 vols. in 2. Thomas Malory. Ed. by H. Oskar Sommer. LC 78-172839. reprint ed. 185.00 (0-404-04175-2) AMS Pr.

Morte D'Arthur. Thomas Malory. (BCL1-PR English Literature Ser.). 148p. 1992. reprint ed. lib. bdg. 69.00 (0-7812-7189-4) Rprt Serv.

Morte D'Arthur, 2 vols., 2. Thomas Malory. Ed. by Janet Cowen. (English Library). 554p. 1970. pap. 11.95 (0-14-043044-X, Penguin Classics) Viking Penguin.

Morte D'Arthur, 2 vols., Vol. 1. Thomas Malory. Ed. by Janet Cowen. (English Library). 494p. 1970. pap. 10.95 (0-14-043043-1, Penguin Classics) Viking Penguin.

Morte D'Arthur: Curriculum Unit. Thomas Malory & Center for Learning Network Staff. (Novel Ser.). 89p. (YA). (gr. 9-12). 1995. spiral bd. 18.95 (1-56077-341-3) Ctr Learning.

Morte D'Arthur Notes. John Gardner. (Cliffs Notes Ser.). 80p. (Orig.). 1967. pap. 4.95 (0-8220-0726-6, Cliff) IDG Bks.

Morte d'August. Georges Simenon. (FRE.). 1991. pap. 11.95 (0-7859-3249-6, 2266045911) Fr & Eur.

Morte d'un Poete. Michel Del Castillo. (FRE.). 367p. 1991. pap. 11.95 (0-7859-2164-8, 2070383784) Fr & Eur.

***Morte d'Urban.** J. F. Powers. LC 99-45446. 336p. 2000. 12.95 (0-940322-23-4) NY Rev Bks.

Mortelle Randonnee. Marc Behm. (FRE.). 247p. 1987. pap. 10.95 (0-7859-2070-6, 2070378594) Fr & Eur.

Mortgage - Credit Workbook. large type ed. Ronni Jenkins. 62p. 1996. pap., wbk. ed. 19.95 (0-9653549-0-3, 2512) KIMRON Pub.

Mortgage Administrator. Jack Rudman. (Career Examination Ser.: C-2311). 1994. reprint ed. pap. 29.95 (0-8373-2311-8) Nat Learn.

Mortgage Analysis Programs. Arefaine G. Yohannes. 35p. (C). 1994. pap. text 7.00 (1-57074-227-8) Greyden Pr.

Mortgage Analyst. Jack Rudman. (Career Examination Ser.: C-2653). 1994. pap. 29.95 (0-8373-2653-2) Nat Learn.

Mortgage & Consumer Loan Disclosure Handbook, 1994-95. Kenneth F. Hall. (Real Property - Zoning Ser.). 1992. pap. 125.00 (0-87632-881-8) West Group.

Mortgage & Foreclosure Workouts. 515p. 1995. pap. 30.00 (0-614-26712-9, 1066); pap. 92.00 incl. audio (0-614-26713-7, 20661) NYS Bar.

Mortgage & Loan Payment Guide: A Valuable Reference Book for Anyone Who Borrows Money. Michael E. Dugan. (Illus.). 250p. 1998. 17.00 (0-7881-5389-7) DIANE Pub.

Mortgage Arrears & Possessions: Perspectives from Borrowers, Lenders & the Courts. H. M. S. O. Staff. 146p. 1995. pap. 55.00 (0-11-753107-3, HM31073, Pub. by Statnry Office) Bernan Associates.

Mortgage-Backed Securities: Investment Analysis & Advanced Valuation Techniques. Andrew S. Davidson & Michael D. Herskovitz. 300p. 1993. text 65.00 (1-55738-440-1, Irwn Prfssnl) McGraw-Hill Prof.

Mortgage-Backed Securities: Products, Analysis, Training. William W. Bartlett. 1988. 49.95 (0-317-03944-X) NY Inst Finance.

Mortgage-Backed Securities Workbook: Hands-on Analysis, Valuation, & Strategies For Investment Decision Making. Andrew S. Davidson & Michael D. Herskovitz. 224p. 1996. pap. 50.00 (1-55738-915-2, Irwn Prfssnl) McGraw-Hill Prof.

An Asterisk (*) at the beginning of an entry indicates that the title is appearing for the first time.

*Mortgage Banker's Guide to Regulatory Compliance. 2nd ed. RSM McGladrey Inc. Staff & Negroni & Winston PLLC Staff. (C). 1999. ring bd. 400.00 (1-57599-061-X, PB2-110112-SO-P, Real Est Fin Pr) Mortgage Bankers.

Mortgage Banking & Title Insurance. American Land Title Association Staff. 60p. (C). 1996. pap. 45.00 (1-57599-009-1, PB2-110108-BK-P, Real Est Fin Pr) Mortgage Bankers.

*Mortgage Banking Sourcebook. 5th ed. 120p. (C). 2000. pap. 40.00 (1-57599-067-9, PB2-110103-BK-P, Real Est Fin Pr) Mortgage Bankers.

Mortgage Banking Terms see Terminos de Banca Hipotecaria: Glosaria de Trabajo

Mortgage Banking Terms: A Working Glossary. 8th ed. 158p. (C). 1995. pap. 12.00 (0-945359-98-5) Mortgage Bankers.

Mortgage Bond Indenture Form. (American Bar Foundation Publications). 188p. 1979. 52.50 (1-57588-334-1, 304730); pap. 35.00 (1-57588-335-X, 304730) W S Hein.

Mortgage Check. 56p. 1997. pap. 15.00 incl. disk (0-931032-34-2) Edison Electric.

Mortgage Foreclosure & Alternatives. Timothy D. Haines et al. LC 95-61272. (Florida Bar's Fastrain Ser). xi, 121p. 1995. write for info. (0-945979-73-8) FL Bar Legal Ed.

Mortgage Foreclosure & Alternatives. 2nd ed. Timothy D. Haines et al. LC 98-71697. (Fastrain Ser.). xi, 123p. 1998. write for info. (1-57976-014-7) FL Bar Legal Ed.

Mortgage Fraud. Michael Clarke. LC 91-26319. (Illus.). 64p. (Orig.). (C). (gr. 13). 1992. pap. text 114.00 (0-412-45620-6, Chap & Hall NY) Chapman & Hall.

Mortgage Fraud. Caroline Osborn. 314p. 1995. pap. 60.00 (1-85811-025-4, Pub. by CLT Prof) Gaunt.

Mortgage-Free! Radical Strategies for Home Ownership. Robert L. Roy. LC 98-10080. (Real Goods Solar Living Book Ser.). (Illus.). 280p. 1998. pap. 24.95 (0-930031-98-9) Chelsea Green Pub.

Mortgage Handbook. William K. Brunette. LC 96-41436. 1997. pap. 12.95 (0-452-27710-8, Plume) Dutton Plume.

Mortgage Industry Directory, 1998 Edition: The Blue Book of the U. S. Mortgage Industry. Paul Muolo. 1997. 395.00 (1-57987-021-X, Natl Mortgage News) Faulkner & Gray.

Mortgage Law see Ley Hipotecaria y del Registro de la Propiedad: Con Su Reglamento, Legislaci/aon y Otros Reglamentos Relacionados al Registro de la Propiedad

*Mortgage Lenders' Guide to Loss Mitigation. 3rd ed. Dennis A. Jankowski. 198p. (C). 1999. pap. 45.00 (1-57599-058-X, PB2-110105-BK-P, Real Est Fin Pr) Mortgage Bankers.

Mortgage Lending - "From the Streets", Vol. 1. Joseph Adamaitis & Mary Scott. (Illus.). 150p. 1994. 149.00 (1-885462-01-8) New Eng Mortgage.

Mortgage Lending & Race: Conceptual & Analytical Perspectives of the Urban Financing Dilemma. David Listokin & Stephen Casey. LC 79-12209. 225p. 1980. text 1.00 (0-88285-060-1) Ctr Urban Pol Res.

Mortgage Lending Experience in Agriculture. Lawrence A. Jones & David Durand. (Financial Research Program VI: Studies in Agricultural Financing: No. 1). 259p. 1954. reprint ed. 67.40 (0-87014-149-X) Natl Bur Econ Res.

Mortgage Lending Inside the FHA & VA, Vol. 2. Joseph Adamaitis & Mary Scott. (Illus.). 150p. 149.00 (1-885462-02-6) New Eng Mortage.

Mortgage Lending, Racial Discrimination, & Federal Policy. Ed. by John M. Goering & Ron Wienk. LC 96-15612. 725p. 1996. 73.00 (0-87766-656-3) Urban Inst.

Mortgage Liens in New York. Robert H. Bowmar. LC 89-63829. 1989. 115.00 (0-317-03792-7) West Group.

Mortgage Liens in New York. Robert H. Bowmar. LC 89-63829. 1993. suppl. ed. 65.00 (0-317-03793-5) West Group.

Mortgage-Lifter & Other Stories. Olive Lockhart. 145p. (C). 1995. pap. 16.95 (1-875560-54-8) Intl Spec Bk.

Mortgage Loan Origination Correspondence Course: Keys to Success in the Mortgage Banking Industry. rev. ed. Mortgage Bankers Association of America Staff. 260p. (C). 1998. pap. 270.00 (1-57599-029-6) Mortgage Bankers.

Mortgage Loan Underwriting Correspondence Course. rev. ed. Mortgage Bankers Association of America Staff. 280p. (C). 1998. pap. 270.00 (1-57599-030-X) Mortgage Bankers.

Mortgage Loans: What's Right for You? 4th ed. James E. Bridges. LC 96-54243. 144p. 1997. pap. 14.99 (1-55870-434-5, Betrwy Bks) F & W Pubns Inc.

Mortgage Payment Handbook: Monthly Payment Tables & Annual Amortization Schedules for Fixed-ra. Peter Hay. LC 94-176991. 1992. pap. 5.95 (0-88029-970-3) Dorset Pr MA.

Mortgage Payment Table. rev. ed. Financial Publishing Co. Staff. 128p. 1983. pap. 15.00 (0-87600-593-8) Finan Pub.

Mortgage Payments. 2nd ed. Stephen S. Solomon et al. LC 92-16587. (Barron's Financial Tables for Better Money Management Ser.). 322p. 1992. pap. 6.95 (0-8120-1386-7) Barron.

Mortgage Revenue Bonds: Housing Markets, Home Buyers & Public Policy. Ed. by Danny W. Durning. 288p. (C). 1991. lib. bdg. 102.00 (0-7923-9180-2) Kluwer Academic.

Mortgage Securities: The High-Yield Alternative to CDs - The Low Risk Alternative to Stocks. Daniel R. Amerman. 300p. 1993. text 32.50 (1-55738-477-0, Irwn Prfssnl) McGraw-Hill Prof.

Mortgage Securitisation. Eilis Ferran. 248p. 1992. 165.00 (0-406-10940-0, MICHIE) LEXIS Pub.

Mortgage Tax Clerk. Jack Rudman. (Career Examination Ser.: C-929). 1994. pap. 23.95 (0-8373-0929-8) Nat Learn.

Mortgage Techniques. 4th ed. Albert Santi. 1989. pap. 10.95 (0-9615886-5-9) Mortgage Tech.

Mortgage Tips & Payment Tables: Your Guide to Getting the Right Kind of Mortgage, the Best Rate, & Saving Money at Closing. Bruce N. Hahn. (Illus.). 64p. (Orig.). 1997. pap. 7.95 (0-940313-13-8) Am Home Found.

Mortgage Trap: How to Avoid the Twelve Biggest Mistakes When Purchasing or Refinancing Your Home. Peggy Hofemann. Ed. by Anna Peerbolt. LC 97-61084. 68p. 1997. pap. write for info. (0-9658755-0-4) High Flying.

Mortgage Yield & Amortization Tables. Financial Publishing Co. Staff. 640p. 1983. pap. 50.00 (0-87600-659-4) Finan Pub.

Mortgage Your Heart. Sophus K. Winther. Ed. by Franklyn D. Scott. LC 78-15857. (Scandinavians in America Ser.). 1979. reprint ed. lib. bdg. 29.95 (0-405-11665-9) Ayer.

Mortgage Your Way to Wealth: How Your Mortgage Lender, Realtor & Stock Broker Can Help You. Matthew T. Mckean. 1998. pap. 21.95 (1-890586-41-2) Pipeline Pr.

Mortgagee's Power of Sale. C. E. Croft. 200p. 1980. 65.00 (0-409-44850-8, AT, MICHIE) LEXIS Pub.

Mortgages & Foreclosure: Know Your Rights. 7th rev. ed. David M. Goldenberg. (Legal Ser.). 136p. (Orig.). 1993. pap. 8.95 (0-88908-763-6) Self-Counsel Pr.

*Mortgages & Investment Planning. Keith Popplewell. 260p. 1999. pap. 60.00 (0-85297-548-1, Pub. by Chartered Bank) St Mut.

Mortgages & Mortgage-Backed Securities Markets. Frank J. Fabozzi & Franco Modigliani. LC 91-40849. 352p. 1992. 35.00 (0-87584-322-0) Harvard Busn.

Mortgages & Mortgage-Backed Securities Markets. Harvard Business Review Staff. 300p. 1992. 45.00 (0-07-103372-6) McGraw.

Mortgages & Securities. 3rd ed. E. A. Francis & K. Thomas. 1986. 109.00 (0-409-49169-1, AT, MICHIE) LEXIS Pub.

*Mortgages for Dummies. Eric Tyson & Ray Brown. LC 99-61335. 250p. 1999. pap. 16.99 (0-7645-5147-7) IDG Bks.

Mortgages Law in Australia. 2nd ed. W. D. Duncan & Lindy Willmott. 432p. 1996. pap. 50.00 (1-86287-193-0, Pub. by Federation Pr) Gaunt.

Mortgaging a Home Vol. 1: Simple Guide to Financing a Home in Basic Terms - What to Do...What Not to Do...& Why. Linda M. Rose. Ed. by Marisa Di Ianni. 200p. (Orig.). 1994. pap. 14.95 (1-885878-00-1) Essent Finan.

Mortgaging the Earth: The World Bank, Environmental Impoverishment, & the Crisis of Development. Bruce Rich. LC 93-3848. 384p. 1995. pap. 16.00 (0-8070-4707-4) Beacon Pr.

Mortgaging Women's Lives: Feminist Critiques of Structural Adjustment. Ed. by Pamela Sparr. 256p. (C). 1994. text 22.50 (1-85649-101-3, Pub. by Zed Books) St Martin.

*Mortification del Pecado: Lo Que Cada Creyente Deberia Saber Acerca de la Mortificacion del Pecado. John Owen. Ed. by Andrew Swanson. Tr. by Thomas Montgomery & Omar Ibanez Negrete. Orig. Title: What Every Christian Needs to Know about Temptation & Putting Sin to Death. (SPA.). 80p. 1999. pap. 1.80 (1-928980-09-0) Pub Faro.

Mortification of Sin. Henry Scougal. 1996. 6.99 (1-85792-107-0, Pub. by Christian Focus) Spring Arbor Dist.

Mortification of the American Woman: The Hidden Story of Her Subjugation. Ed Hibler. Ed. by Ernest Weckbaugh. 382p. (Orig.). (C). 1995. pap. 16.95 (1-881474-00-3) Socratic Pr Calif.

Mortified Christian. rev. ed. Christopher Love. Ed. by Don Kistler. 150p. 1998. 16.95 (1-57358-078-3) Soli Deo Gloria.

Mortim Frog Level 2: HBJ Reading 1987. Early. (J). 1987. pap., teacher ed. 60.25 (0-15-330517-7) Harcourt Schl Pubs.

Mortimer. Robert Munsch. (Illus.). 24p. (J). (gr. k-3). 1985. lib. bdg. 15.95 (0-920303-12-9, Pub. by Annick) Firefly Bks Ltd.

Mortimer. Robert Munsch. (Illus.). 24p. (J). (gr. k-3). 1985. pap. 5.95 (0-920303-11-0, Pub. by Annick) Firefly Bks Ltd.

Mortimer. Robert Munsch. (Annikins Ser.: Vol. 3). (Illus.). 24p. (J). (ps-1). 1986. pap. 0.99 (0-920236-68-5, Pub. by Annick) Firefly Bks Ltd.

Mortimer. Robert Munsch. (Munsch for Kids Ser.). (J). 1985. 11.15 (0-606-02845-5, Pub. by Turtleback) Demco.

Mortimer: The Very Rich Mouse. 2nd rev. ed. Dixon DeVore, II. (Illus.). 32p. (J). (gr. k-5). 1987. pap. Price not set. incl. audio (0-9614998-1-8, CP3109-A) Cricket Power.

Mortimer Meets Melody. Helen Forelle. (Illus.). 32p. (J). (gr. 1-3). 1982. pap. 2.00 (1-877649-02-3) Tesseract SD.

Mortimer Mooner Makes Lunch. Frank Edwards. (Illus.). 24p. (J). (gr. k-3). 1995. lib. bdg. 14.95 (0-921285-37-X, Pub. by Bungalo Books) Firefly Bks Ltd.

Mortimer Mooner Makes Lunch. Frank B. Edwards. (Illus.). 24p. (J). (gr. k-3). 1995. pap. 4.95 (0-921285-36-1, Pub. by Bungalo Books) Firefly Bks Ltd.

Mortimer Mooner Stopped Taking A Bath see Luis Luna Dejo de Banarse

Mortimer Mooner Stopped Taking a Bath. Frank B. Edwards. (Illus.). 24p. (J). (ps-2). 1990. lib. bdg. 16.95 (0-921285-21-3, Pub. by Bungalo Books) Firefly Bks Ltd.

Mortimer Plays I-Spy see Mortimer's Fun with Words

Mortimer's ABC's see Mortimer's Fun with Words

Mortimer's Cross. Joan Aiken. LC 83-49475. (Charlotte Zolotow Bk.). (Illus.). 160p. (J). (gr. 3-6). 1984. 12.95 (0-06-020032-4) HarpC Child Bks.

*Mortimer's Fun with Words, 6 bks. Karen Bryant-Mole. Incl. Beginning Letters. Illus. by Zul Mukhida. 24p. (J). (ps up). 2000. lib. bdg. 19.93 (0-8368-2746-5); Ending Letters. Photos by Zul Mukhida. (Illus.). 24p. (J). (ps up). 2000. lib. bdg. 19.93 (0-8368-2747-3); Letters Make Words. Photos by Zul Mukhida. (Illus.). 24p. (J). (ps up). 2000. lib. bdg. 19.93 (0-8368-2748-1); Mortimer Plays I-Spy. Illus. by Zul Mukhida. 24p. (J). (ps up). 2000. lib. bdg. 19.93 (0-8368-2749-X); Mortimer's ABC's. Illus. by Zul Mukhida. 24p. (J). (ps up). 2000. lib. bdg. 19.93 (0-8368-2750-3); Rhyming Words. Illus. by Zul Mukhida. 24p. (J). (ps up). 2000. lib. bdg. 19.93 (0-8368-2751-1); 24p. (J). (ps up). 2000. Set lib. bdg. 119.58 (0-8368-2745-7) Gareth Stevens Inc.

Mortimer's Magic Machine. 1991. pap. 3.95 (0-8167-2428-8) Troll Communs.

*Mortimer's Math, 6 bks. Karen Bryant-Mole. Incl. Counting. LC 99-54603. (Illus.). 24p. (J). (ps up). 1999. lib. bdg. 19.93 (0-8368-2617-5); Patterns. LC 99-56188. (Illus.). 24p. (J). (ps up). 1999. lib. bdg. 19.93 (0-8368-2618-3); Shapes. LC 99-55987. (Illus.). 24p. (J). (ps up). 1999. lib. bdg. 19.93 (0-8368-2619-1); Size. LC 99-55989. (Illus.). 24p. (J). (ps up). 1999. lib. bdg. 19.93 (0-8368-2620-5); Sorting. LC 99-55988. (Illus.). 24p. (J). (ps up). 1999. lib. bdg. 19.93 (0-8368-2621-3); Where Is Mortimer? LC 99-54602. (Illus.). 24p. (J). (ps up). 1999. lib. bdg. 19.93 (0-8368-2622-1); (Illus.). (J). (ps up). 1999. Set lib. bdg. 119.58 (0-8368-2616-7) Gareth Stevens Inc.

Mortised Cuts. Cirker. 1998. pap. 1.00 (0-486-27918-9) Dover.

Mortmere Stories. Christopher Isherwood & Edward Upward. LC 95-167631. (Illus.). 206p. 1995. pap. 15.95 (1-870612-69-8, Pub. by Enitha Pr) Dufour.

Morton Allan Directory of European Passenger Steamship Arrivals for the Years 1890 to 1930 at the Port of New York, & for the Years 1904 to 1926 at the Ports of New York, Philadelphia, Boston & Baltimore. Morton Allan. LC 78-65163. 268p. 1998. reprint ed. 20.00 (0-8063-0830-3) Genealog Pub.

Morton D. Barker Paperweight Collection. Ellen S. Penwell & George N. Kulles. (Handbook of Collections: No. 5). (Illus.). 72p. 1985. pap. 15.00 (0-89792-106-2) Ill St Museum.

Morton Family Tree: Chauncy Morton & Betsy Pike; Their Ancestry & Descent. John N. Morton. (Illus.). 125p. 1995. reprint ed. pap. 33.00 (0-8328-4930-8); reprint ed. lib. bdg. 23.00 (0-8328-4929-4) Higginson Bk Co.

Morton Friedman. Morton Friedman. (American Composer Ser.). 1998. pap. 28.00 (0-02-864897-8) Mac Lib Ref.

*Morton Gould: American Salute. Peter W. Goodman. LC 99-59948. (Illus.). 391p. 2000. 29.95 (1-57467-055-7, Amadeus Pr) Timber.

*Morton Hollinger: Paintings. Ed. by Steve Hollinger. LC 98-66610. (Illus.). 140p. 1999. write for info. (0-9661969-0-2) S H Pierce.

Morton Livingston Schamberg. Text by William Agee. (Illus.). 42p. 25.00 (1-58821-066-9) Salander OReilly.

Morton Potteries: 99 Years. Doris Hall & Burdell Hall. (Orig.). 1995. pap. 24.95 (0-89538-028-5) L-W Inc.

Morton: The Mortons & Their Kin: A Genealogy & a Source Book. D. Morton. 899p. 1992. reprint ed. pap. 119.00 (0-8328-2298-1); reprint ed. lib. bdg. 129.00 (0-8328-2297-3) Higginson Bk Co.

Morton, the Stem of Morton: Collection of Genealogical Notes Respecting the Family of Morton, Chiefly Seated in the Wapentake of Strafford-cum-Tickhill, S. Yorkshire. W. Morton. 311p. 1995. lib. bdg. 57.50 (0-8328-4450-0) Higginson Bk Co.

Morton, the Stem of Morton: Collection of Genealogical Notes Respecting the Family of Morton, Chiefly Seated in the Wapentake of Strafford-cum-Tickhill, S. Yorkshire. W. Morton. 311p. 1995. reprint ed. pap. 47.50 (0-8328-4451-9) Higginson Bk Co.

Morton's Medical Bibliography. 5th ed. Ed. by Jeremy M. Norman. 1046p. 1991. text 159.95 (0-85967-897-0, Pub. by Scolar Pr) Ashgate Pub Co.

MORTPAK & MORTPAK-Lite Upgrades. (Population Studies: No. 117). 82p. 1990. 25.00 (92-1-151191-7, E.90.XIII.7) UN.

MORTPAK-Lite: The United Nations Software Package for Mortality Measurement. (Population Studies: No. 104). 126p. 1988. 17.00 (92-1-151167-4, E.88.XIII.2) UN.

Morts Ont Tous la Meme Peau. Boris Vian. (FRE.). 185p. 1977. pap. 12.95 (0-7859-1475-7, 2264001151) Fr & Eur.

Morts Sans Sepulture see Putain Respectueuse

Mortuaries. 157p. 1996. pap. 16.00 (0-16-061965-3) USGPO.

Mortuaries: Audit Technique Guides. (IRS Tax Audit Information Ser.). 152p. 1994. pap. 41.00 (1-57402-103-6) Athena Info Mgt.

Mortuary Caretaker. Jack Rudman. (Career Examination Ser.: C-500). 1994. pap. 23.95 (0-8373-0500-4) Nat Learn.

Mortuary Customs of the Shawnee & Other Eastern Tribes. Erminie W. Voegelin. LC 76-43885. (Indiana Historical Society Prehistory Research Ser.: Vol. 2, No. 4). reprint ed. 49.50 (0-404-15742-4) AMS Pr.

*Mortuary Feasting on New Ireland: The Activation of Matriliny among the Sursurunga. Alexander H. Bolyanatz. LC 99-59735. 208p. 2000. 59.95 (0-89789-721-8, Bergin & Garvey) Greenwood.

Mortuary Law. 9th ed. Thomas F. Stueve. 200p. (C). 1994. pap. text 25.00 (1-883031-01-X) CF Mortuary.

Mortuary Monuments in Ancient & Medieval India. Ratan L. Mishra. 1991. 18.00 (81-7018-622-6, Pub. by BR Pub) S Asia.

Mortuary Posts of the Giryama. J. Newton Hill. (Illus.). 23p. 1978. 10.00 (0-685-70729-6) Gal Assn NY.

Mortuary Practices & Skeletal Remains at Teotihuacan. Martha L. Sempowski & Michael W. Spence. Ed. by Rene Millon. LC 93-6395. (Urbanization at Teotihuacan, Mexico Ser.: Vol. 3). (Illus.). 464p. (C). 1994. text 50.00 (0-87480-413-2) U of Utah Pr.

Mortuary Practices & Social Differentiation at Casas Grandes, Chihuahua, Mexico. John C. Ravesloot. LC 88-15385. (Anthropological Papers). 113p. 1988. pap. 27.95 (0-8165-1048-2) U of Ariz Pr.

Mortuary Records with Genealogical Notes: Town of Spafford Onondaga New York. Ed. by Charles D. Townsend. LC 98-222119. 372p. 1997. reprint ed. pap. 40.00 (1-878545-26-4) ACETO Bookmen.

Mortuary Science. Frederick C. Gale. (Illus.). 238p. 1960. 42.95 (0-398-04166-0) C C Thomas.

Mortuary Science: A Sourcebook. John F. Szabo. LC 93-28803. 206p. 1993. 32.00 (0-8108-2719-0) Scarecrow.

Mortuary Technician. Jack Rudman. (Career Examination Ser.: C-514). 1994. pap. 23.95 (0-8373-0514-4) Nat Learn.

Morty Mouse's Number Search. Fiona Conboy. (Illus.). 5p. (J). 1997. pap. 9.99 (1-58048-000-4) Sandvik Pub.

Morvern Callar. Alan Warner. LC 96-23398. 256p. (Orig.). 1997. pap. 12.95 (0-385-48741-X, Anchor NY) Doubleday.

Morvern Transformed: A Highland Parish in the Nineteenth Century. Philip Gaskell. LC 67-24944. 289p. reprint ed. pap. 82.40 (0-608-16849-1, 2027235) Bks Demand.

Morwyn: Or, The Vengeance of God. John Cowper Powys. Ed. by R. Reginald & Douglas A. Menville. LC 75-46301. (Supernatural & Occult Fiction Ser.). 1976. reprint ed. lib. bdg. 26.95 (0-405-08161-8) Ayer.

MOS Digital Electronics. S. S. Cheng. 224p. (C). 1987. text 54.00 (9971-5-0372-7) World Scientific Pub.

Mos Eisley Starter Set. (Star Wars Ser.). 1997. boxed set 35.00 (0-87431-295-7, 40212) West End Games.

MOS Integrated Circuits: Theory, Fabrication, Design & Systems Applications. American Micro Systems Staff. Ed. by William M. Penny & Lillian Lau. LC 79-1039. 494p. 1979. reprint ed. 49.50 (0-88275-897-7) Krieger.

MOS (Metal Oxide Semiconductor) Physics & Technology. Edward H. Nicollian & John R. Brews. LC 81-7607. 928p. 1982. 250.00 (0-471-08500-6) Wiley.

MOS Switched-Capacitor & Continuous-Time Integrated Circuits & Systems. R. Ubehauen & A. Cichocki. (Communications & Control Engineering Ser.). (Illus.). xiii, 631p. 1989. 181.95 (0-387-50599-7) Spr-Verlag.

MOS Switched-Capacitor Filters: Analysis & Design. Ed. by G. M. S. Moschytz. LC 84-9055. 512p. 1986. 79.95 (0-87942-177-0, PC01701) Inst Electrical.

Mosaic. Gayle Lynds. 1999. per. 6.99 (0-671-02406-X) PB.

Mosaic. Gayle Lynds. 480p. 1998. 24.00 (0-671-02405-1) S&S Trade.

*Mosaic. John R. Maxim. LC 98-46869. 384p. 1999. 24.00 (0-380-97544-0, Avon Bks) Morrow Avon.

*Mosaic. John R. Maxim. LC 98-46869. 448p. 2000. mass mkt. 6.99 (0-380-79354-7, Avon Bks) Morrow Avon.

Mosaic. Jeri Taylor. (Star Trek). 1997. per. 5.99 (0-671-56312-2, Pocket Books) PB.

Mosaic. Jeri Taylor. (Star Trek Voyager Ser.). 1996. audio 18.00 (0-671-57400-0) S&S Audio.

*Mosaic: A Chronicle of Five Generations. Diane Armstrong. LC 99-487959. 1998. write for info. (0-09-183713-8) Trafalgar.

Mosaic: A Step by Step Cut & Paste Drawing Book. Ed Emberley. (Illus.). (J). 1995. write for info. (0-316-23398-6) Little.

Mosaic: Jewish Life in Florida. Henry A. Green & Marcia K. Zerivitz. (Illus.). 80p. 1992. pap. 22.95 (1-879438-00-3) Mosaic FL.

*Mosaic: New Writings from British & Indian Award-Winning Writers. Great Britain Staff. LC 99-931906. xi, 210 p. 1998. 16.00 (0-14-028301-3) Penguin Putnam.

*Mosaic Vol. I: Hell City Ripper. Kyle Hotz. (Illus.). 144p. 2000. pap. 14.95 (1-57989-033-4) Sirius Ent.

Mosaic Afghans: The Easy Way to Colorful Crochet. Lily Chin. (Illus.). 144p. 1999. pap. 14.95 (0-8487-1903-4) Oxmoor Hse.

Mosaic & Tessellated Patterns: How to Create Them, with 32 Plates to Color. John Willson. (Illus.). 64p. (Orig.). 1983. pap. 5.95 (0-486-24379-6) Dover.

Mosaic Big Band. Date not set. 40.00 (0-7935-4832-2, 00000794) H Leonard.

Mosaic Book: Ideas, Projects & Techniques. Goodrick-Clarke & Vance. 1998. 29.95 (1-85029-658-8) Trafalgar.

Mosaic Book: Ideas, Projects & Techniques. Peggy Vance & Celia Goodrich-Clarke. (Illus.). 128p. 1996. pap. 19.95 (1-57076-060-8) Trafalgar.

*Mosaic Christmas. Dione Roberts. 1999. pap. 14.95 (0-935133-78-X, 2013378X) CKE Pubns.

Mosaic-Cycle Concept of Ecosystems. Ed. by Hermann Remmert et al. (Ecological Studies: Vol. 85). (Illus.). 200p. 1991. 136.95 (0-387-52502-5) Spr-Verlag.

Mosaic Decoration of San Marco, Venice. Otto Demus. Ed. by Herbert L. Kessler. (Illus.). 278p. 1988. 72.00 (0-226-14291-4); pap. 30.00 (0-226-14292-2) U Ch Pr.

Mosaic Evolution of Subterranean Mammals: Regression, Progression & Global Convergence. Eviatar Nevo. LC 99-10301. (Illus.). 512p. 2000. text 175.00 (0-19-857572-6) OUP.

Mosaic for Dummies. 2nd ed. David F. Angell. LC 96-75411. 384p. 1996. pap. 29.99 (1-56884-852-8) IDG Bks.

M

Mosaic for Dummies: Windows Edition. Brent Heslop & David Angell. LC 94-72742. 336p. 1994. pap. 19.99 (*1-56884-242-2*) IDG Bks.

Mosaic for Windows: A Hands-on Configuration & Set-up Guide to Popular Web Browsers. Richard Raucci. LC 95-11636. (Illus.). 192p. 1995. 21.95 (*0-387-97996-4*) Spr-Verlag.

Mosaic Funbook. Scott Sullivan. (Troubador Ser.). (Illus.). 32p. (J). (ps up). 1997. reprint ed. pap. 3.50 (*0-8431-8228-8*, Price Stern) Peng Put Young Read.

***Mosaic II: Grammar/Writing.** 4th ed. Patricia K. Werner et al. 2000. 23.00 (*0-07-232963-7*) McGraw.

Mosaic Knitting. Barbara G. Walker. (Illus.). 259p. 1997. reprint ed. 31.00 (*0-942018-15-X*) Schoolhouse WI.

Mosaic Madness: Pluralism Without a Cause. Reginald W. Bibby. 224p. 1990. pap. 15.95 (*0-7737-5399-0*) Genl Dist Srvs.

***Mosaic Magic: Afghans Made Easy.** Lily M. Chin. LC 99-75769. (Illus.). 144p. 1999. pap. 14.95 (*0-8487-1902-6*) Oxmoor Hse.

Mosaic Man. Ronald Sukenick. LC 98-53043. 260p. 1999. pap. 23.00 (*1-57366-079-5*, Pub. by Fiction Coll) Northwestern U Pr.

Mosaic Memoirs. Lincoln Kirstein. (Illus.). 270p. 1994. pap. 23.00 (*0-374-52643-5*) FS&G.

Mosaic Mind: Empowering the Tormented Selves of Child Abuse Survivors. Regina A. Goulding & Richard C. Schwartz. 304p. 1995. 35.00 (*0-393-70178-6*) Norton.

***Mosaic Mirrors, Platters & More.** Chris Stewart. (Illus.). 36p. 1999. pap. 15.95 (*0-935133-75-5*) CKE Pubns.

***Mosaic Modernism: Anarchism, Pragmatism, Culture.** David Kadlec. LC 00-8135. (New Studies in American Intellectual & Cultural History). 312p. 2000. 42.50 (*0-8018-6438-0*) Johns Hopkins.

Mosaic Navigator TM: The Essential Guide to the Internet Interface. Paul A. Gilster. (Illus.). 243p. 1995. pap. 16.95 (*0-471-11336-0*) Wiley.

Mosaic of Care: Frail Elderly & Their Families in the Real World. Jaber F. Gubrium. 192p. 1990. 31.95 (*0-8261-7570-8*) Springer Pub.

Mosaic of Contemporary Psychiatry Perspectives. Ed. by A. Kales & M. Greenblatt. (Illus.). xvi, 448p. 1992. 99.00 (*0-387-97760-0*) Spr-Verlag.

Mosaic of Despair: Human Breakdowns in Prison. rev. ed. Hans Toch. LC 92-17878. Orig. Title: Men in Crisis. 452p. 1992. text 19.95 (*1-55798-177-9*) Am Psychol.

Mosaic of Economic Growth. Ed. by Ralph Landau et al. LC 95-22572. 512p. 1996. 55.00 (*0-8047-2599-3*); pap. 18.95 (*0-8047-2604-3*) Stanford U Pr.

***Mosaic of Fear: Poland & East Germany Before 1989.** Helena Flam. 360p. 1998. text 50.00 (*0-88033-406-1*, 508, Pub. by East Eur Monographs) Col U Pr.

Mosaic of Learning Styles: Participant. Stephen G. Barkley. (Illus.). 60p. 1995. pap., wbk. ed. 9.95 (*1-892334-05-4*) Perf Lrn Systs.

Mosaic of the Air: A Setting to Words of Music by Berlioz. Michael Wright. 1997. pap. 12.95 (*3-7052-0965-5*, Pub. by Poetry Salzburg) Intl Spec Bk.

Mosaic of the Hundred Days: Personalities, Politics, & Ideas of 1898. Luke S. Kwong. (East Asian Monographs: No. 112). 376p. 1984. 26.00 (*0-674-58742-1*) HUP.

***Mosaic of the Ineffable.** Astara Leopold. 144p. 2001. pap. 13.95 (*1-885226-27-6*) StarLineage.

Mosaic of Thought: Teaching Comprehension in a Reader's Workshop. Ellin O. Keene & Susan Zimmermann. LC 96-53181. 1997. pap. text 27.50 (*0-435-07237-4*) Heinemann.

***Mosaic of Thoughts: Poems.** Joyce P. Nightingale-Holder. LC 99-96758. 2000. 13.95 (*0-533-13342-4*) Vantage.

Mosaic of Victims: Non-Jews Persecuted & Murdered by the Nazis. Michael Berenbaum. 320p. (Orig.). (C). 1990. text 45.00 (*0-8147-1131-6*) NYU Pr.

Mosaic of Victims: Non-Jews Persecuted & Murdered by the Nazis. Michael Berenbaum. 244p. (Orig.). (C). 1992. pap. text 18.50 (*0-8147-1175-8*) NYU Pr.

Mosaic 1. A. Seligson. 1991. pap., student ed. write for info. (*0-17-555929-5*, Pub. by ITP Nelson) Thomson Learn.

Mosaic I: A Communicative Grammar, Vol. 1. 3rd ed. Patricia Warner. LC 96-75306. 430p. (C). 1996. pap. 28.13 (*0-07-069576-8*) McGraw.

Mosaic I: A Content-Based Reading Book, Vol. 2. 3rd ed. Brenda Wegmann & Miki P. Knezevic. 272p. (C). 1995. pap. 23.13 (*0-07-068997-0*) McGraw.

Mosaic I: A Writing Process Book, Vol. 1. 3rd ed. Laure Lass & Meredith Pike-Baky. 430p. (C). 1995. pap. 23.13 (*0-07-005849-0*) McGraw.

Mosaic I: Video Activities Manual, Vol. 5. Emily Thrush. (C). 1997. pap. 10.31 (*0-07-050331-1*) McGraw.

Mosaic Sourcebook: Projects, Designs, Motifs. Paul Siggins & Paul Cooper. LC 97-60188. (Illus.). 96p. 1997. pap. 22.95 (*1-57076-098-5*, Trafalgar Sq Pub) Trafalgar.

Mosaic 3. A. Seligson. 1991. pap., student ed. write for info. (*0-17-555955-4*, Pub. by ITP Nelson); pap., student ed. write for info. (*0-17-555957-0*, Pub. by ITP Nelson) Thomson Learn.

Mosaic Tile Designs. Susan Johnston. (Illus.). 48p. 1981. pap. 5.95 (*0-486-24080-0*) Dover.

Mosaic 2. A. Seligson. 1991. pap. write for info. (*0-17-555951-1*, Pub. by ITP Nelson); pap., student ed. write for info. (*0-17-555953-8*, Pub. by ITP Nelson) Thomson Learn.

Mosaic II: A Communicative Grammar, Vol. 1. 3rd ed. Patricia K. Werner & John P. Nelson. LC 96-75178. 448p. (C). 1996. pap. 29.38 (*0-07-069581-4*) McGraw.

Mosaic Two: A Content-Based Writing Book. 3rd ed. Laurie Blass & Meredith Pike-Baky. LC 95-82405. xix, 242 p. 1996. write for info. (*0-07-114513-3*) McGraw.

Mosaic II: A Reading Skills Book, Vol. 2. 3rd ed. Brenda Wegmann & Miki P. Knezevic. LC 95-82407. 320p. (C). 1996. pap. 24.38 (*0-07-068998-9*) McGraw.

Mosaic II: A Writting Process Book, Vol. 3. 3rd ed. Laurie Laurie & Meredith Pike-Bakey. LC 95-82405. 254p. (C). 1996. pap. 24.38 (*0-07-005932-2*) McGraw.

***Mosaic II: Poems of an Ancient Order.** Lester Hirsh. 78p. 1999. pap. 10.00 (*0-9658903-9-2*, Minimal Pr) Writers Pubg Coop.

Mosaic II: Video Activities Manual, Vol. 5. Emily Thrush. 50p. (C). 1997. pap. 10.31 (*0-07-050452-0*) McGraw.

Mosaic User's Guide. Bryan Pfaffenberger. LC 94-37780. 1994. pap. 24.95 incl. disk (*1-55828-409-5*, MIS Pr) IDG Bks.

Mosaic User's Guides: Microsoft Windows, Macintosh, & X-Windows. LC 94-40176. 1994. 15.95 (*0-929306-21-X*) Silicon Pr.

Mosaic Workshop: A Guide to Designing & Creating Mosaics. Emma Biggs & Tessa Hunkin. 1999. 24.95 (*1-57076-149-3*, Trafalgar Sq Pub) Trafalgar.

Mosaic 1: Listening. 3rd ed. Ferrer. 176p. 1996. pap. 21.88 (*0-07-020634-1*) McGraw.

Mosaic 2: Listening. 3rd ed. Ferrer. 208p. 1996. pap., student ed. 22.50 (*0-07-020636-8*) McGraw.

Mosaicarum et Romanarum Legum Collatio. M. Hyamson. LC 95-80915. ii,lvi,300p. 1997. reprint ed. text 65.00 (*1-57588-000-8*, 309010) W S Hein.

Mosaicos. 2nd ed. Castells. 280p. (C). 1997. pap. text, wbk. ed. 14.67 (*0-13-915893-6*) P-H.

Mosaicos. 2nd ed. Castells. 168p. (C). 1998. pap. text, lab manual ed. 14.67 (*0-13-915885-5*) P-H.

Mosaicos. 2nd ed. Suzanne De Castell et al. 465p. 1997. 66.67 (*0-13-237587-7*) P-H.

Mosaicos: Spanish As a World Language. Matilda O. De Castells et al. LC 93-27189. 576p. 1993. text 72.00 (*0-13-064700-4*) P-H.

Mosaics. Helen Baird. (New Crafts Ser.). (Illus.). 96p. 1997. 15.95 (*1-85967-382-1*, Lorenz Bks) Anness Pub.

Mosaics. Jackie Mallis. (Pathways to Poetry Ser.). 95p. 1984. pap. 17.95 (*0-86617-030-8*) Multi Media TX.

Mosaics: Design Sourcebook. Martin Cheek. LC 97-80886. (Design Sourcebooks Ser.). (Illus.). 128p. 1998. 24.95 (*1-57076-111-6*, Trafalgar Sq Pub) Trafalgar.

Mosaics: Essential Techniques & Classic Projects. Fran Soler. (Illus.). 127p. 1998. 24.95 (*0-8069-6305-0*) Sterling.

Mosaics: Focus on the Sentence. Kim Flachmann. LC 96-45503. 395p. 1997. pap. text 44.00 (*0-13-102179-6*) P-H.

Mosaics: Focusing on Essays. Kim Flachmann et al. LC 97-12338. 505p. 1997. pap. text 44.00 (*0-13-272907-5*) P-H.

Mosaics: Focusing on Paragraphs in Contex. National Center for Construction Education & Reseach Staff. LC 96-45504. 460p. 1997. pap. text 44.00 (*0-13-272899-0*) P-H.

Mosaics: Focusing on Sentences in Context. Magee. (C). 1997. wbk. ed. 6.67 (*0-13-919481-9*, Macmillan Coll) P-H.

***Mosaics: Inspiration & Original Projects for Interiors & Exteriors.** Kaffe Fassett & Candace Bahouth. 160p. 1999. text 35.00 (*1-56158-373-1*) Taunton.

Mosaics - New Age Piano: Easy Piano. Prod. by Zobeida Perez. 20p. (Orig.). (YA). 1989. pap. 5.95 (*0-89898-653-2*, F2981P2X) Wrner Bros.

Mosaics & Wallpaintings in Roman Churches. John Osborne & Amanda Claridge. (Paper Museum of Cassiano Dal Pozzo Ser.: Ser. A, Pt. II, Vol. 1). (Illus.). 388p. 1996. text 150.00 (*1-872501-62-1*) Gordon & Breach.

Mosaics for Four Viols & Optional Recorder Quartet. Martha Bishop. (Contemporary Consort Ser.: No. 12). i, 22p. 1990. 12.00 (*1-56571-014-2*) PRB Prods.

Mosaics in a Weekend see Weekend Crafter - Mosaics: Inspirational Ideas & Practical Projects to Make in a Weekend

Mosaics in an Afternoon: Quick & Easy Techniques for Creating Mixed Media Mosaics. Connie Sheerin. LC 98-50986. 1999. 21.95 (*0-8069-5775-1*) Sterling.

Mosaics in the Holy Land: Christian, Moslem & Jewish. Yoel Rappel & Meir Ben-Dov. Tr. by Shmuel Himmelstein from HEB. (Illus.). 148p. 1987. 15.95 (*0-915361-54-X*) Lambda Pubs.

Mosaics in the Holy Land: Christian, Moslem & Jewish. Yoel Rappel & Meir Ben-Dov. (Illus.). 148p. (J). (ps up). 1987. 15.95 (*0-915351-54-4*) Lambda Pubs.

Mosaics of a Life. Tibor Gerstl. LC 98-85309. (Illus.). 192p. 1999. pap. 12.95 (*1-56315-108-1*, Pub. by SterlingHse) Natl Bk Netwk.

Mosaics of Hagia Sophia, Istanbul: The Fossati Restoration & the Work of the Byzantine Institute. Natalia B. Teteriatnikov. LC 98-3393. (Illus.). 1998. pap. 15.00 (*0-88402-264-1*) Dumbarton Oaks.

Mosaics of Learning Styles: Facilitator Guide. Stephen G. Barkley. (Illus.). 133p. 1995. pap. 99.50 (*1-892334-04-6*) Perf Lrn Systs.

Mosaics of Meaning: Enhancing the Intellectual Life of Young Adults Through Story. Ed. by Kay E. Vandergrift. LC 95-51386. 1996. 42.00 (*0-8108-3110-4*) Scarecrow.

Mosaics of Norman Sicily. Otto Demus. LC 86-81973. (Illus.). xx, 478p. 1988. reprint ed. lib. bdg. 95.00 (*0-87817-310-2*) Hacker.

Mosaics of St. Mary's of the Admiral in Palermo. Ernst Kitzinger. (Dumbarton Oaks Studies: No. 27). (Illus.). 480p. 1991. 85.00 (*0-88402-179-3*, KIMO) Dumbarton Oaks.

Mosaics of San Marco in Venice: Part I: Eleventh & Twelfth Centuries; Part II: The Thirteenth Century, 4 vols. Otto Demus. LC 82-2787. (Illus.). 360p. 1984. lib. bdg. 420.00 (*0-226-14289-2*) U Ch Pr.

Mosaics of San Marco in Venice: Part I: Eleventh & Twelfth Centuries; Part II: The Thirteenth Century, 4 vols. Otto Demus. LC 82-2787. (Illus.). 80p. 1986. lib. bdg. 600.00 (*0-226-68975-1*) U Ch Pr.

***Mosaics of the Greek & Roman World.** Katherine Dunbabin. LC 98-38082. (Illus.). 384p. (C). 1999. write for info. (*0-521-46143-X*) Cambridge U Pr.

Mosaics, Paintings, Sarcophagi & Small Objects, Vol. 2. John Osborne et al. (Paper Museum of Cassiano Dal Pozzo Ser.: Ser. A, Pt. II, Vol. 2). (Illus.). 304p. 1997. text 150.00 (*1-872501-67-2*) Gordon & Breach.

Mosaik. 3rd ed. Barrack. 1992. teacher ed. 29.37 (*0-07-004048-6*) McGraw.

Mosaik: Deutsche Grammatik. 3rd ed. Charles M. Barrack & Horst M. Rabura. 416p. (C). 1992. pap. 49.69 (*0-07-003964-X*) McGraw.

Mosaik: Deutsche Grammatik. 3rd ed. Charles M. Barrack & Horst M. Rabura. (C). 1992. pap. text 22.18 (*0-07-004049-4*) McGraw.

Mosaik: Deutsche Kultur und Literatur. 3rd ed. Horst M. Rabura et al. 312p. (C). 1992. pap. 41.25 (*0-07-003963-1*) McGraw.

Mosaique. Prosper Merimee & Maurice Levaillant. (FRE.). 530p. 1933. pap. 105.00 (*0-7859-0026-8*, F68008) Fr & Eur.

Mosaique Biotech. Ed. by Ernst & Young Staff. 88p. 1991. pap. 107.00 (*2-906077-20-8*) Elsevier.

***Mosaiques Cahier Dintroduction a l'Analuse Culturelle.** 2nd ed. Gilles Bousquet & Andrew Irving. 100p. 1999. per. 20.95 (*0-7872-6264-1*, 41626401) Kendall-Hunt.

Mosaiques de la Grande Mosquee de Cordoue. Henri Stern. (Madrider Forschungen Ser.: Vol. 11). (Illus.). 55p. (C). 1976. 123.10 (*3-11-002126-9*) De Gruyter.

Mosan Art: An Annotated Bibliography. Gretel Chapman. 1988. 65.00 (*0-8161-8329-5*, Hall Reference) Macmillan.

MOSA4 - Advances in Model-Oriented Data Analysis: Proceedings of the 4th International Workshop in Spetses, Greece, June 5-9, 1995. Ed. by C. P. Kitsos & W. G. Muller. (Contributions to Statistics Ser.). (Illus.). xiv, 297p. 1995. 85.95 (*3-7908-0864-4*) Spr-Verlag.

Mosby & His Men. J. Marshall Crawford. 375p. 1987. reprint ed. 30.00 (*0-942211-02-2*) Olde Soldier Bks.

Mosby & His Men: A Record of the Adventures of That Renowned Partisan Ranger, John S. Mosby (Colonel C. S. A.) Mary L. Selph. (Illus.). 209p. 1998. pap. 13.00 (*1-883228-22-0*) Invictus MI.

Mosby Buyer's Guide to Ten Essential Herbs. Mosby Editorial Staff. 96p. 1997. pap. text 10.00 (*1-57857-004-2*) Mosby Consmer Hlth.

Mosby Handbook of Diseases. 2nd ed. Langford. 2000. pap. text 26.95 (*0-323-00895-X*) Mosby Inc.

Mosby Medical Encyclopedia. rev. ed. Walter D. Glanze. (Illus.). 1024p. (Orig.). 1992. pap. 19.95 (*0-452-26672-6*, Plume) Dutton Plume.

Mosby Nursing Boards Review - International: Mosby Year Book Staff. 10th ed. Ajn. (Illus.). 624p. 1996. pap. text 30.95 (*0-8151-2782-0*, 31113) Mosby Inc.

Mosby Patient Teaching Guides. Mosby Staff. (C). (gr. 13). 1996. 160.00 incl. disk (*0-8151-8557-X*, 28720) Mosby Inc.

Mosby Patient Teaching Guides for Health Promotion. Mosby Staff. 32p. (C). (gr. 13). 1997. pap. text 24.95 (*0-8151-2574-7*, 31313) Mosby Inc.

Mosby Pharmacy. 21st ed. McKenry. 2000. text 56.00 (*0-323-01005-9*) Mosby Inc.

Mosby Textbook for Nursing Assistants. Relda Kelly & Sheila A. Sorrentino. 1996. wbk. ed. 41.00 (*0-8151-8599-5*, 28309) Mosby Inc.

***Mosby Textbook for Nursing Assistants.** 5th ed. Gilbert Sorrentino. 1999. text 36.95 (*0-323-00923-9*) Harcourt.

Mosby, the Kennedy Center Cat: A True Story Made Legend. 2nd ed. Beppie Noyes. (Illus.). 130p. (J). (gr. 5-9). 1998. reprint ed. 14.95 (*0-9637688-8-3*) Vacation Spot.

Mosby's ABCs of Test Taking for Nurses: Anchor Your Anxiety, Build Your Basic. Rollant. LC 99-10465. (Illus.). 240p. (C). (gr. 13). 1999. pap. text 21.95 (*0-8151-3858-X*, 31669) Mosby Inc.

Mosby's Ace the Boards: General Clinical Sciences. Mosby Year Books Staff. LC 98-51164. 336p. (C). (gr. 13). 1999. pap. text 28.95 (*0-8151-3715-X*, 31410) Mosby Inc.

Mosby's Anatomy & Physiology Lab Manual. Kathleen B. Sloan. (Illus.). 312p. (C). (gr. 13). 1990. pap. text 18.95 (*0-8016-5986-8*, 05986) Mosby Inc.

***Mosby's Assesstest: A Practice Exam for RN Licensure.** Dolores F. Saxton. 80p. 1999. write for info. (*0-323-00539-X*) Mosby Inc.

Mosby's Assesstest: 1999 Secured Version. Dolores F. Saxton et al. 86p. 1998. write for info. (*0-323-00290-0*) Mosby Inc.

***Mosby's Assesstest: 1999 Unsecured Version.** Dolores F. Saxton et al. 72p. 1998. write for info. (*0-323-00291-9*) Mosby Inc.

Mosby's Assisting with Patient Care. Sheila A. Sorrentino. (Illus.). 912p. (C). (gr. 13). 1998. pap. text 35.00 (*0-8151-2033-8*, 31707) Mosby Inc.

***Mosby's Assisting with Patient Care: Includes Testbank.** Sheila A. Sorrentino. (Illus.). 1999. teacher ed. write for info. (*0-8151-2034-6*) Mosby Inc.

Mosby's Basic Science for Soft Tissue & Movement Therapies. Sandy Fritz et al. LC 98-14479. 1998. pap. text 36.00 (*0-323-00284-6*) Mosby Inc.

Mosby's Biomedical Science Series: Understanding Immunology. Roth Coe-Clough. LC 97-9892. (Illus.). 240p. (gr. 13). 1997. pap. text 23.00 (*0-8151-8582-0*, 28791) Mosby Inc.

Mosby's Clinical Nursing. 4th ed. June Thompson. 1848p. 1997. text 49.95 (*0-8151-2573-9*, 31312) Mosby Inc.

***Mosby's Clinical Nursing.** 5th ed. Thompson. 2001. text. write for info. (*0-323-01195-0*) Mosby Inc.

***Mosby's Clinical Skills for Medical Assistants.** 4th ed. Sharron M. Zakus. (Illus.). 752p. 1999. text 38.95 (*0-323-00766-X*) Mosby Inc.

***Mosby's Complementary & Alternative Therapies.** Lyn Freeman. (Illus.). 2000. 49.00 (*0-323-00697-3*) Mosby Inc.

Mosby's Comprehensive Bookmarks to Internet Resources. Mosby Staff. (gr. 13). 1996. write for info. (*0-8151-4816-X*, 30462) Mosby Inc.

Mosby's Comprehensive Dental Assisting: Includes Testbank. Betty L. Finkbeiner & Claudia S. Johnson. 1995. teacher ed. write for info. (*0-8151-3352-9*) Mosby Inc.

Mosby's Comprehensive Review of Dental Hygiene. 4th ed. Michele L. Darby. LC 97-34800. (Illus.). 912p. (C). (gr. 13). 1997. pap. text 45.95 (*0-8151-2267-5*, 29189) Mosby Inc.

Mosbys Comprehensive Review of Nursing. 16th ed. Saxton. LC 99-184202. 1998. pap. text 29.95 (*0-323-00286-2*) Mosby Inc.

Mosby's Comprehensive Review of Practical Nursing. Mary O. Eyles. 1999. 39.95 (*0-323-00313-3*) Mosby Inc.

Mosby's Comprehensive Review of Practical Nursing for NCLEX-PN. 12th ed. Ed. by Mary O. Eyles. LC 97-17859. (Illus.). 648p. (C). (gr. 13). 1997. pap. text 27.95 incl. disk (*0-8151-2388-4*, 31041) Mosby Inc.

Mosby's Comprehensive Review of Radiography. 2nd ed. William J. Callaway. LC 97-41998. (Illus.). 336p. (C). (gr. 13). 1998. pap. text 32.95 (*0-8151-2900-9*, 31811) Mosby Inc.

Mosby's Computerized NCLEX Review: Student Version. Delores F. Saxton. (C). (gr. 13). 1994. pap. text 32.00 incl. 3.5 hd (*0-8151-8148-5*, 24915) Mosby Inc.

Mosby's Conventional Medicine, Alternative Medicine. Green. 1998. pap. text 12.95 (*0-916363-17-1*) Beechwood Hlthbks.

***Mosby's CPG Mentor - Patient Cases in Respiratory Care Series, 8 Units.** Lonny J. Ashworth. 1998. write for info. (*0-8151-2276-4*) Mosby Inc.

***Mosby's Crash Course: Internal Medicine.** Ed. by Daniel A. Horton-Szar. 1998. write for info. (*0-7234-3114-0*) Mosby Inc.

Mosby's Critical Care Nursing Consultant. Pamela L. Swearingen & Janet H. Keen. LC 97-6318. 1997. write for info. (*0-08-151378-X*) Elsevier.

Mosby's Critical Care Nursing Reference. 2nd ed. Susan B. Stillwell. (Illus.). 816p. (C). (gr. 13). 1996. text 34.95 (*0-8151-8241-4*, 26898) Mosby Inc.

Mosby's Dental Dictionary. Thomas J. Zwemer. LC 97-41342. (Illus.). 704p. (C). (gr. 13). 1998. text 39.95 (*0-8151-9888-4*, 29172) Mosby Inc.

Mosby's Dental Drug Reference. 4th ed. Mosby Year Book Publishing Staff. 1998. pap. 33.95 (*0-323-00501-2*) Mosby Inc.

Mosby's Desktop Primary Care Consultant: Rapid Access to Current Diagnosis Treatments. Fred F. Ferri. LC 98-3837. (Illus.). 1216p. (C). (gr. 13). 1998. text 54.95 (*0-8151-0317-4*, 30998) Mosby Inc.

Mosbys Diagnostic & Laboratory Test, 1900-2000. 4th ed. Kathleen D. Pagana. LC 98-27246. 1998. 27.95 (*0-323-00288-9*) Mosby Inc.

***Mosby's Drug Guide for Nurses.** 3rd ed. Linda Skidmore. (C). 1999. text 29.95 (*0-323-01130-6*) Mosby Inc.

***Mosby's Drug Guide for Nurses.** 3rd ed. Linda Skidmore-Roth. 1998. write for info. (*0-323-00500-4*) Mosby Inc.

Mosby's Drug Guide for Nurses. 3rd ed. Linda Skidmore-Roth. LC 98-23778. (Illus.). 1568p. 1998. 29.95 (*0-323-00308-7*) Mosby Inc.

***Mosby's Drug Guide for Nurses.** 4th ed. Linda Skidmore. 2000. pap. text 34.95 (*0-323-01174-8*) Mosby Inc.

Mosby's Drug Reference: British Edition. Linda Skidmore-Roth. 1991. write for info. (*0-8016-4586-7*) Mosby Inc.

Mosby's Emergency & Flight Nursing Review. 2nd ed. Renee S. Holleran. LC 95-21393. (Illus.). 536p. (C). (gr. 13). 1995. pap. text 34.95 (*0-8151-4226-9*, 24711) Mosby Inc.

Mosby's Emergency Department Patient Teaching Guides. Jean A. Proehl & Linell M. Jones. LC 97-15759. (Illus.). 128p. (C). (gr. 13). 1997. text 69.95 (*0-8151-3829-6*, 30305) Mosby Inc.

***Mosby's Emergency Department Patient Teaching Guides.** Jean A. Proehl & Linell M. Jones. (Illus.). 168p. 1998. write for info. (*1-55664-564-3*) Mosby Inc.

Mosby's Emergency Dictionary: Quick Reference. 2nd ed. William Garcia. LC 97-34822. (Illus.). 512p. (C). (gr. 13). 1997. pap. text 33.95 (*0-8016-7941-9*, 07941) Mosby Inc.

Mosby's Emergency Nursing Reference. Pamela S. Kidd. Ed. by Patty Sturt. (Illus.). 896p. (C). (gr. 13). 1995. text 35.95 (*0-8151-5226-4*, 24497) Mosby Inc.

***Mosby's Emergency Nursing Reference.** 2nd ed. Pamela S. Kidd. (Illus.). 2000. pap. text 35.95 (*0-323-01108-X*) Mosby Inc.

Mosby's EMT - Basic Textbook. Walt A. Stoy. (Illus.). 616p. (C). (gr. 13). 1995. spiral bd. 35.95 (*0-8151-8055-1*, 27238) Mosby Inc.

Mosby's EMT - Basic Textbook. Walt A. Stoy & Center for Emergency Medicine Staff. LC 95-24140. (Illus.). 704p. (C). (gr. 13). 1995. text 37.95 (*0-8151-7958-8*, 25207) Mosby Inc.

Mosby's EMT-Basic Hardcover. Walt Stoy. 1996. teacher ed. write for info. (*0-8151-7960-X*); pap., wbk. ed. write for info. (*0-8151-9653-9*); text, wbk. ed. write for info. (*0-8151-9654-7*) Mosby Inc.

Mosby's EMT-Basic Textbook. Walt Stoy. 1996. wbk. ed. write for info. (*0-8151-7959-6*) Mosby Inc.

Mosby's Essentials for Nursing Assistants. Sheila Sorrentino. (Illus.). 1997. teacher ed. write for info. (*0-8151-5258-2*) Mosby Inc.

Mosby's Essentials for Nursing Assistants Pocket Guide. Sheila A. Sorrentino. (Illus.). 88p. 1997. write for info. (*0-8151-1565-2*) Mosby Inc.

An Asterisk (*) at the beginning of an entry indicates that the title is appearing for the first time.

Mosby's Family Practice Sourcebook, 2000. Kenneth G. Marshall. (Illus.). 512p. (C). 1999. text 59.00 (*1-55664-468-X*) Mosby Inc.
Mosby's First Responder Textbook. Walt A. Stoy. LC 96-79893. (Illus.). 352p. (C). (gr. 13). 1997. pap. text 29.95 (*0-8151-8279-1*, 28070) Mosby Inc.
***Mosby's Front Office Skills for the Medical Assistant: Study Guide.** De A. Eggers & Anne Conway. 1999. student ed. write for info. (*0-8151-2205-5*) Mosby Inc.
Mosby's Fundamentals of Medical Assistants. 2nd ed. Eggars & Sharron M. Zakus. (Illus.). 736p. (gr. 13). 1990. text 39.95 (*0-8016-4280-9*, 04280); pap. text, student ed. 16.95 (*0-8016-5293-6*, 05293) Mosby Inc.
Mosby's Fundamentals of Medical Assisting. 2nd ed. Sharron M. Zakus et al. 1990. teacher ed. write for info. (*0-8151-2702-2*) Mosby Inc.
Mosby's Fundamentals of Therapeutic Massage. Sandra Fritz. 1995. teacher ed. write for info. (*0-8151-3253-0*); wbk. ed. write for info. (*0-8151-3301-4*) Mosby Inc.
Mosby's Fundamentals of Therapeutic Massage, Set. Sandra Fritz. (C). 1995. text, wbk. ed. write for info. (*0-8151-3323-5*) Mosby Inc.
***Mosby's Fundamentals of Therapeutic Message.** 2nd ed. Fritz. LC 99-14180. 1999. text 46.95 (*0-323-00677-9*) Harcourt.
Mosby's GenRx: 1999 Edition. Genrx. (Mosby's Physicians GenRx Ser.). 1998. 72.95 (*0-323-00625-6*) Mosby Inc.
Mosby's Genrx Retail Direct Mail 1998. Mosby Yearbook, Inc. Staff. (C). 1997. text 69.95 (*0-8151-4418-0*, 30812) Mosby Inc.
Mosby's Guide to Physical Examination. Henry M. Seidel. 816p. (gr. 13). 1991. text 175.00 (*0-8016-6520-5*) Mosby Inc.
Mosby's Guide to Physical Examination. 3rd ed. Henry M. Seidel et al. (Illus.). 1995. teacher ed. write for info. (*0-8151-6136-0*) Mosby Inc.
Mosby's Guide to Physical Examination. 4th ed. Henry M. Seidel. LC 98-27245. 1008p. 1998. text 58.00 (*0-323-00178-5*) Mosby Inc.
***Mosby's Guide to Physical Examination.** 4th ed. Henry M. Seidel. (Illus.). 1008p. 1998. student ed. write for info. (*0-323-00451-2*) Mosby Inc.
Mosby's Handbook of Diseases. Rae Langford & June M. Thompson. LC 95-52142. 624p. (C). (gr. 13). 1996. text 26.95 (*0-8151-8771-8*, 25183) Mosby Inc.
***Mosby's Handbook of Herbs & Natural Supplement.** Skidmore. 2001. text. write for info. (*0-323-01208-6*) Mosby Inc.
Mosby's Handbook of Patient Teaching. Mary M. Canobbio. LC 96-15637. (Illus.). 752p. (C). (gr. 13). 1996. text 26.95 (*0-8151-1537-7*, 24917) Mosby Inc.
Mosby's Home Care & Hospice Drug Handbook. Tina M. Marrelli. (Illus.). 816p. (C). (gr. 13). 1999. text 26.95 (*0-8151-1226-2*, 31777) Mosby Inc.
Mosby's Home Health Client. Karen Martin. (Illus.). 96p. 2000. text, teacher ed. 24.95 (*0-8151-8589-8*, 28841) Mosby Inc.
Mosby's Home Health Client Teaching. Karen Martin. (Illus.). 416p. (C). (gr. 13). 1997. text 114.00 (*0-8151-2296-9*, 29975) Mosby Inc.
Mosby's Home Health Client Teaching Guides: RX for Teaching. 3rd rev. ed. (Illus.). 96p. 1999. text 24.95 (*0-8151-8590-1*, 28842) Mosby Inc.
Mosby's Home Health Nursing Pocket Consultant. C. V. Mosby. LC 95-136742. (Illus.). 352p. (C). (gr. 13). 1994. spiral bd. 29.95 (*0-8151-6125-5*, 25341) Mosby Inc.
Mosby's Manual of Diagnostic & Laboratory Tests. Kathleen D. Pagana & Timothy Pagana. LC 97-40589. (Illus.). 960p. (C). (gr. 13). 1998. pap. text 29.95 (*0-8151-5586-7*, 29626) Mosby Inc.
***Mosby's Maternal-Newborn Patient Teaching Guides.** Carol Schlef. LC 99-12448. (Illus.). 200p. 1999. write for info. (*0-323-00465-2*) Mosby Inc.
***Mosby's Medical Assisting Examination Review.** Joanna Bligh. (Illus.). 320p. (C). 1999. text. write for info. (*0-323-00349-4*) Mosby Inc.
Mosby's Medical Drug Reference, 1999. Allan J. Ellsworth et al. (Illus.). 1072p. (C). (gr. 13). 1998. pap. text 29.95 (*0-8151-3656-0*, 31227) Mosby Inc.
***Mosby's Medical Drug Reference 2000.** (Illus.). 1152p. 2000. text 31.95 (*0-8151-3657-9*, 31228) Mosby Inc.
Mosby's Medical Drug Reference, 2003-2004. Ellsworth et al. 1184p. 2002. pap. text 32.95 (*0-8151-3658-7*, 31229) Mosby Inc.
Mosby's Medical, Nursing & Allied Health Dictionary. 4th ed. Kenneth N. Anderson & C. V. Mosby. (Illus.). 2208p. (C). (gr. 13). 1993. text 32.95 (*0-8016-7225-2*, 07225) Mosby Inc.
Mosby's Medical, Nursing & Allied Health Dictionary. 5th ed. Kenneth Anderson et al. LC 97-33687. (Illus.). 2112p. (C). (gr. 13). 1997. text 32.95 (*0-8151-4800-3*, 29948) Mosby Inc.
Mosby's Medical, Nursing & Allied Health Dictionary. 5th ed. Kenneth Anderson et al. LC 97-33687. 1998. write for info. (*1-55664-566-X*) Mosby Inc.
Mosby's Medical Surfari: A Guide to Exploring the Internet. Scott R. Gibbs et al. LC 97-119657. (Illus.). 220p. (C). (gr. 13). 1996. pap. text 24.95 incl. disk (*0-8151-4817-8*, 30461) Mosby Inc.
Mosby's Medical Surfari: Guide to Exploring Internet & Discover. 2nd ed. Gibbs. 2000. 24.95 incl. cd-rom (*1-55664-558-9*) Mosby Inc.
Mosby's Medical Terminology Instructor's Resource Library. Mosby Year Book Staff. (Illus.). 281p. 1994. pap. text. write for info. (*0-8151-5887-4*, 24525) Mosby Inc.
Mosby's Memoirs. John S. Mosby. LC 94-69016. 1995. pap. 14.95 (*1-879941-27-9*) J S Sanders.
Mosby's Memoirs & Other Stories. Saul Bellow. 1996. pap. 11.95 (*0-14-018945-9*) Viking Penguin.
Mosby's Men. John H. Alexander. 180p. 1987. reprint ed. 22.50 (*0-942211-15-4*) Olde Soldier Bks.
Mosby's 1999 Nursing Drug Reference & Review Cards. 9th ed. Joseph A. Albanese & Patricia A. Nutz. 300p. (C). (gr. 13). 1998. text 29.95 (*0-8151-2056-7*, 27777) Mosby Inc.
***Mosby's Nursing Drug Database, 1999.** Mosby. 1998. pap. 39.95 (*0-323-00659-0*) Mosby Inc.
Mosby's Nursing Drug Reference. Linda Skidmore-Roth. (Mosby's Nursing Drug Reference Ser.). 1185p. 1998. pap. 29.95 (*0-323-00307-9*) Harcrt Hlth Sci Grp.
***Mosby's Nursing Drug Reference 2001.** Linda Skidmore-Roth. (Illus.). 1280p. 2000. pap. text 31.95 (*0-323-00981-6*) Mosby Inc.
Mosby's OTC Drugs: A Resource for Health Professionals. Richard P. Donjon & Bryon J. Goeckner. LC 98-39429. (Illus.). 464p. (C). (gr. 13). 1998. text 29.95 (*0-8151-8395-X*, 31695) Mosby Inc.
Mosby's Outdoor Emergency Medical Guide. David H. Manhoff. 1996. spiral bd. 12.95 (*0-916363-14-7*) Mosby Inc.
Mosby's Paramedic Text. Mick J. Sanders & McKenna. (C). (gr. 13). 1996. reprint ed. text, wbk. ed. 59.95 (*0-8151-2470-8*, 31259) Mosby Inc.
Mosby's Paramedic Textbook. Mick J. Sanders. 1994. teacher ed. write for info. (*0-8151-7506-X*) Mosby Inc.
Mosby's Paramedic Textbook. Mick J. Sanders. 1008p. (gr. 13). 1995. text 51.95 (*0-8016-4315-5*, 28181) Mosby Inc.
***Mosby's Patient Carelink.** Mosby Staff. 160p. 1998. write for info. (*0-8151-4457-1*) Mosby Inc.
Mosby's Patient Teaching Guides. (Illus.). 226p. 1996. 72.95 (*0-8151-3315-4*) Mosby Inc.
Mosby's Patient Teaching Guides. Mosby Staff. (C). (gr. 13). 1994. spiral bd. 52.95 (*0-8151-5862-9*, 25114) Mosby Inc.
***Mosby's Patient Teaching Guides: Update 3, Update 3.** Mosby Staff. (Illus.). 40p. 1998. write for info. (*0-323-00073-8*) Mosby Inc.
***Mosby's Patient Teaching Guides with Updates 2 & 3.** Mosby Staff. 1998. write for info. (*0-323-00227-7*) Mosby Inc.
***Mosby's Patient Teaching Guides with Updates 2 & 3: Tips.** Mosby Staff. 1998. write for info. (*0-8151-6196-4*) Mosby Inc.
Mosby's Pediatric Nursing Reference. 3rd ed. Ed. by Cecily L. Betz & Linda A. Sowden. LC 95-26736. (Illus.). 672p. (C). (gr. 13). 1996. pap. text 33.95 (*0-8151-0599-1*, 26571) Mosby Inc.
***Mosby's Pediatric Nursing Reference.** 4th ed. Betz. 1999. text 34.95 (*0-323-00935-2*) Mosby Inc.
Mosby's Pediatric Patient Teaching Guides. Jane W. Ball. LC 97-37998. (Illus.). 224p. (C). (gr. 13). 1998. text 74.95 (*0-8151-1558-X*, 29994) Mosby Inc.
Mosby's Pediatric Patient Teaching Guides on CD-Rom. Jane W. Ball. LC 97-37607. (Illus.). 225p. (C). (gr. 13). 1998. text 129.00 (*0-8151-2577-1*) Mosby Inc.
Mosby's Perfect Pregnancy. Thompson. 1998. pap. text 12.95 (*0-916363-15-5*) Beechwood Hlthbks.
Mosby's Pharmacology in Nursing. Leda M. McKenry. (Nursing Texts Ser.). 96p. (C). (gr. 13). 1998. pap. text, student ed. 14.95 (*0-8151-4516-0*, 30650) Mosby Inc.
Mosby's Pharmacology in Nursing, Vol. 20. 20th ed. Leda M. McKenry & Evelyn Salerno. LC 98-220129. (Nursing Texts Ser.). (Illus.). 1200p. (C). (gr. 13). 1997. text 56.00 (*0-8151-4515-2*, 30649) Mosby Inc.
Mosby's Pharmacology in Nursing: Includes Testbank. 20th ed. Leda M. McKenry & Evelyn Salerno. 1998. teacher ed. write for info. (*0-8151-2132-6*) Mosby Inc.
Mosby's Pharmacology in Nursing Package. 20th ed. Leda M. McKenry. 1392p. (C). (gr. 13). 1998. text 63.00 (*0-8151-4517-9*, 30651) Mosby Inc.
Mosbys Physical Examination Handbook. 2nd ed. Seidel. LC 98-27273. 1998. pap. text 25.95 (*0-323-00179-3*) Mosby Inc.
Mosby's PN Assesstest. 3rd ed. Mary O. Eyles. 48p. (C). (gr. 13). 1995. pap. text 29.95 (*0-8151-9775-6*, 25329) Mosby Inc.
Mosby's Pocket Dictionary of Medicine, Nursing & Allied Health, Vol. 3. 3rd ed. Kenneth N. Anderson & Lois E. Anderson. LC 98-3311. 1312p. (C). (gr. 13). 1998. text 25.95 (*0-8151-3166-6*, 28931) Mosby Inc.
Mosby's Primary Care Patient Teaching Guides. 2nd rev. ed. Mosby Staff. Date not set. ring bd. 39.95 (*0-8151-8399-2*) Mosby Inc.
Mosby's Psychiatric Nursing Study Guide: Instructor's Resource Manual. Mosby Staff. (C). (gr. 13). 1997. text. write for info. (*0-8151-2131-8*, 30751) Mosby Inc.
***Mosby's Questions & Answers for NCLEX-PN.** 2nd ed. Mary O. Eyles. LC 99-181156. 320p. (C). 1998. text 25.95 (*0-323-00151-3*) Mosby Inc.
Mosby's Quick Review: Neuroscience. Mosby. 350p. 1999. text. write for info. incl. cd-rom (*0-323-00836-4*) Mosby Inc.
Mosby's Rangers. Jeffrey D. Wert. (Illus.). 384p. 1991. pap. 13.00 (*0-671-74745-2*, Touchstone) S&S Trade Pap.
Mosby's Rangers. James J. Williamson. 1996. 25.00 (*0-8094-4227-2*) Time-Life.
***Mosby's Rapid Reference to Diagnostic & Laboratory Tests.** Kathleen D. Pagana & Timothy J. Pagana. 350p. 1999. text 17.95 (*1-55664-515-5*) Mosby Inc.
Mosby's Resource Guide to Children with Disabilities & Chronic Illness. Ed. by Helen M. Wallace et al. LC 96-10609. (Illus.). 528p. (C). (gr. 13). 1996. text 59.00 (*0-8151-9051-4*, 28151) Mosby Inc.
Mosby's Respiratory Care Workbook Series: Comprehensive. Karen Milikowski. (Illus.). 272p. (C). (gr. 13). 1995. pap. text 46.00 (*0-8151-6313-4*, 26030) Mosby Inc.
Mosby's Respiratory Care Workbook Series: Introduction to Respiratory Care. Karen Milikowski. 24p. (gr. 13). 1995. text 8.95 (*0-8151-6303-7*, 26022) Mosby Inc.
Mosby's Review Cards: Marternity Women Health Nursing. Multi-Resources Incorporation et al. 273p. 1997. text 22.95 (*0-8151-7382-2*, 28138) Mosby Inc.
Mosby's Review Cards: Mental Health Nursing. Multi-Resources Incorporation & Paulette D. Rollant. 232p. 1997. text 22.95 (*0-8151-7378-4*, 28137) Mosby Inc.
Mosby's Review Cards: Pediatric Nursing. Multi-Resources Incorporation Staff et al. 190p. 1997. text 22.95 (*0-8151-7377-6*, 28136) Mosby Inc.
Mosby's Review for Long-Term Care Certification for Practical & Vocational Nurses. Mary O. Eyles. 224p. (C). (gr. 13). 1996. pap. text 25.95 (*0-8151-3170-4*, 29307) Mosby Inc.
Mosby's Review for the Clinical Competency Test: Large Animal Medicine & Surgery. Corrine R. Sweeney. 264p. (C). (gr. 13). 1997. pap. text 39.95 (*0-8151-4443-1*, 30740) Mosby Inc.
Mosby's Review for the Clinical Competency Test: Small Animal Medicine & Surgery. Ellen Miller. LC 98-231811. 264p. (C). (gr. 13). 1997. pap. text 39.95 (*0-8151-4379-6*, 31125) Mosby Inc.
Mosby's Review Questions for NCLEX-RN. 3rd ed. Delores F. Saxton. LC 97-1041. 736p. (C). (gr. 13). 1997. pap. text 28.95 (*0-8151-2836-3*, 30965) Mosby Inc.
Mosby's Rounds: Interactive Case Studies in Internal Medicine, Windows. Timothy Rice. 32p. 1995. write for info. incl. disk (*0-8151-6478-5*) Mosby Inc.
Mosby's Spanish/English-English/Spanish Medical Dictionary. Ed. by Mosby Editorial Staff. (ENG & SPA.). 1996. 275.00 (*0-7859-9704-0*) Fr & Eur.
Mosby's Sports Therapy: Taping Guide. Robert Kennedy. LC 95-165980. 144p. 1995. spiral bd. 16.95 (*0-8151-5198-5*, 26955) Mosby Inc.
Mosby's Success in Medicine: Anatomy (Ibm) Mosby Staff. (Illus.). 480p. (C). (gr. 13). 1996. pap. text 29.95 incl. 3.5 hd (*0-8151-8974-5*, 29056) Mosby Inc.
Mosby's Success in Medicine: Biochemistry (Ibm) Mosby Staff. 400p. (C). (gr. 13). 1996. pap. text 29.95 (*0-8151-8985-0*, 29062) Mosby Inc.
Mosby's Success in Medicine: Physiology (IBM) Mosby Staff. (Illus.). 304p. (C). (gr. 13). 1996. pap. text 29.95 (*0-8151-8914-1*, 29046) Mosby Inc.
Mosby's Survival Guide to Medical Abbreviations, Acronyms, Symbols, Prefixes & Suffixes. June M. Campbell. LC 95-119665. 608p. (C). (gr. 13). 1994. text 24.95 (*0-8151-1398-6*, 25635) Mosby Inc.
Mosby's Textbook & Workbook for Nursing Assistants. 4th ed. Sheila A. Sorrentino. 1p. (gr. 13). 1995. pap. text 40.00 (*0-8151-8028-4*, 25742) Mosby Inc.
Mosby's Textbook for Long Term Care Assistants. 2nd ed. Sheila Sorrentino & Jean Hogan. (Illus.). 1994. teacher ed. write for info. (*0-8151-7945-6*); teacher ed. write for info. (*0-8151-7946-4*) Mosby Inc.
***Mosby's Textbook for Long-Term Care Assistants.** 3rd ed. Sheila Sorrentino. LC 99-461782. 724p. 1999. text 34.00 (*0-323-00709-0*) Mosby Inc.
Mosby's Textbook for Long Term Care Assistants: LTC Textbook & Workbook Package. 2nd ed. Sheila A. Sorrentino & Jean Hogan. (Illus.). 1994. wbk. ed. write for info. (*0-8151-7887-5*) Mosby Inc.
Mosby's Textbook for Nursing Assistants. 3rd ed. Sheila A. Sorrentino. (Illus.). 528p. (gr. 13). 1991. text 28.95 (*0-8016-6589-2*, 06589) Mosby Inc.
Mosby's Textbook for Nursing Assistants. 4th ed. Sheila A. Sorrentino. teacher ed. write for info. (*0-8151-8027-6*) Mosby Inc.
Mosby's Textbook for Nursing Assistants. 4th ed. Sheila A. Sorrentino. LC 95-43198. (Illus.). 800p. (C). (gr. 13). 1995. pap. text 32.00 (*0-8151-8026-8*, 25739) Mosby Inc.
Mosby's Textbook for Nursing Assistants. 4th ed. Sheila A. Sorrentino. (Illus.). 1996. teacher ed. write for info. (*0-8016-6273-7*) Mosby Inc.
***Mosbys Textbook for Nursing Assistants.** 5th ed. Shelia A. Sorentino. 1999. pap. text 34.95 (*0-323-00924-7*) Mosby Inc.
Mosby's Textbook for Nursing Assistants: Text & Seed Package. 4th ed. Sheila A. Sorrentino. (Illus.). 1996. write for info. (*0-8151-8239-2*) Mosby Inc.
Mosby's Textbook for the Home Care Aide. Joan M. Birchenall & Mary E. Streight. teacher ed. write for info. (*0-8151-0728-5*) Mosby Inc.
Mosby's Textbook for the Home Care Aide. Joan M. Birchenall & Mary E. Streight. 1997. pap. text, wbk. ed. 16.00 (*0-8151-0727-7*) Mosby Inc.
Mosby's Textbook for the Home Care Aide: Instructor's Resource Kit. Joan Birchenall. (Illus.). 1997. teacher ed. write for info. (*0-8151-0730-7*) Mosby Inc.
Mosby's Tour Guide to Alternative Medicine. Marilyn Freedman. (C). (gr. 13). 1997. pap. text 10.00 (*0-8151-2198-9*, 30952) Mosby Inc.
Mosby's Tour Guide to Alternative Medicine. Mosby Editorial Staff. 160p. 1997. pap. text 10.00 (*1-57857-003-4*) Mosby Consmer Hlth.
Mosby's Tour Guide to Nursing School: A Student's Road Survival Guide. 3rd ed. Melodie Chenevert. LC 94-32030. (Illus.). 216p. (C). (gr. 13). 1994. pap. text 21.95 (*0-8151-1539-3*, 24868) Mosby Inc.
Mosby's Trade Dictionary. 5th ed. Kenneth Anderson. LC 97-33687. (Illus.). 2128p. (C). (gr. 13). 1997. text 28.95 (*0-8151-4631-0*, 29951) Mosby Inc.
***Mosby's 2000 Nursing Drug Reference & Review Cards.** 10th ed. Joseph A. Albanese & Patricia A. Nutz. 448p. (C). 1999. text. write for info. (*0-323-00795-3*) Mosby Inc.
Mosby's USMLE Step 1 Reviews: Pathology. John Wurzel et al. LC 96-44703. (Ace the Boards Ser.). (Illus.). 624p. (C). (gr. 13). 1997. pap., pap. text 29.95 incl. disk, 3.5 hd (*0-8151-9276-2*, 28895) Mosby Inc.
Mosby's USMLE Step 1 Reviews: Anatomy. N. Anthony Moore. LC 96-2738. (Ace the Boards Ser.). (Illus.). 480p. (C). (gr. 13). 1996. pap. text 29.95 incl. 3.5 hd (*0-8151-6905-1*, 27051) Mosby Inc.
Mosby's USMLE Step 1 Reviews: Histology & Cell Biology. E. Robert Burns & M. Donald Cave. LC 95-52478. (Ace the Boards Ser.). (Illus.). 272p. (C). (gr. 13). 1996. pap. text 30.00 incl. audio compact disk (*0-8151-1338-2*, 27045) Mosby Inc.
Mosby's USMLE Step 1 Reviews: Microbiology & Immunology. Ken S. Rosenthal & James S. Tan. LC 95-52095. (Ace the Boards Ser.). (Illus.). 344p. (C). (gr. 13). 1996. pap. text 30.00 incl. 3.5 hd (*0-8151-7349-0*, 27042) Mosby Inc.
Mosby's USMLE Step 1 Reviews: Neuroscience. Anthony J. Castro. LC 96-22065. (Ace the Boards Ser.). (Illus.). 496p. (C). (gr. 13). 1996. pap. text 30.00 (*0-8151-1479-6*, 27046); pap. text 30.00 (*0-8151-1480-X*, 28956) Mosby Inc.
Mosby's USMLE Step 1 Reviews: Pharmacology. Sam J. Enna et al. (Illus.). 416p. (C). (gr. 13). 1996. pap. text 30.00 incl. 3.5 hd (*0-8151-3112-7*, 27049) Mosby Inc.
Mosby's USMLE Step 3 Reviews: Specialty Clinical Sciences. Joseph L. Donnelly & Randolph B. Lipscher. (Ace the Boards Ser.). (Illus.). 504p. (C). (gr. 13). 1996. pap. text 38.00 incl. disk (*0-8151-2734-0*, 27047) Mosby Inc.
Mosby's USMLE Step 2 Reviews: General Clinical Sciences. Alfred J. Bollet. LC 96-4742. (Ace the Boards Ser.). (Illus.). 552p. (C). (gr. 13). 1996. pap. text 37.00 (*0-8151-0723-4*, 27048) Mosby Inc.
Mosby's USMLE Step 2 Reviews: Surgery. Koutlas. (Ace the Boards Ser.). (Illus.). 480p. (C). (gr. 13). 1999. text 29.95 (*0-8151-3703-6*, 31407) Mosby Inc.
Mosby's Visual Guide to Massage Essentials. Sandra Fritz. 128p. 1997. pap. text 16.00 (*1-57857-002-6*) Mosby Consmer Hlth.
Mosby's Visual Guide to Massage Essentials. Sandra Fritz. LC 96-29696. (C). (gr. 13). 1997. 15.00 (*0-8151-3968-3*) Mosby Inc.
Mosby's War Reminiscences. John S. Mosby. 264p. 1997. pap. text 12.95 (*1-887269-09-6*) J Culler & Sons.
Mosca: A Factual Fiction. unabridged ed. Richard Miller. LC 97-91845. (Illus.). iv, 237p. 1997. pap. 16.00 (*0-9658423-0-4*, DFI Bks) Dada Found.
Moschino. (Made in Italy Ser.: No. 3). (Illus.). 128p. 1997. 19.95 (*3-927258-48-2*) Gingko Press.
Moschus et Bion - Index Verborum in Moschum et Bionem. Ed. by Malcolm Campbell. (Alpha-Omega, Reihe A Ser.: Bd. LXXXIX). (GER.). vi, 96p. 1987. 50.00 (*3-487-07851-1*) G Olms Pubs.
Moschus Europa. Moschus. (Altertumswissenschaftliche Texte und Studien: Vol. 19). (GER.). xii, 144p. 1991. pap. text 20.00 (*3-487-09432-0*) G Olms Pubs.
Moscovia of Antonio Possevino, S. J. Antonio Possevino. Tr. & Intro. by Hugh F. Graham. LC 77-12648. (UCIS Series in Russian & East European Studies: No. 1). 214p. 1977. pap. 66.40 (*0-7837-8539-9*, 204935400011) Bks Demand.
Moscoviana: The Life & Art of Ivan Shmelyov. Olga Sorokin. (Illus.). 380p. (Orig.). 1987. pap. 19.95 (*0-936041-02-1*) Barbary Coast Bks.
Moscow see World Cities
Moscow. 136p. text 14.95 (*88-7009-775-7*, Pub. by Bonechi) Eiron.
Moscow. (New Essential Guides Ser.). 1996. pap. 7.95 (*0-614-97912-9*) NTC Contemp Pub Co.
Moscow. Huri Aleksandrov. 358p. 1984. 39.00 (*0-7855-0925-9*) St Mut.
Moscow. Allan Fowler. LC 98-37341. (Rookie Read-About Geography Ser.). 32p. (J). (gr. 1-2). 1999. 19.00 (*0-516-21558-2*) Childrens.
***Moscow.** Allan Fowler. (Rookie Read-About Geography Ser.). (J). 2000. pap. text 5.95 (*0-516-26557-1*) Childrens.
Moscow. Christine Hatt. LC 98-55586. 1999. lib. bdg. write for info. (*0-382-42192-2*) Silver Burdett Pr.
Moscow. Burton Holmes. Ed. by Fred L. Israel & Arthur Meier Schlesinger, Jr. LC 97-29395. (World 100 Years Ago Ser.). (Illus.). 132p. (YA). (gr. 5 up). 1998. pap. 19.95 (*0-7910-4659-1*) Chelsea Hse.
Moscow. Burton Holmes. Ed. by Arthur Meier Schlesinger, Jr. & Fred L. Isreal. LC 97-29395. (World 100 Years Ago Ser.). (Illus.). 144p. (YA). (gr. 5 up). 1999. 29.95 (*0-7910-4658-3*) Chelsea Hse.
Moscow. Insight Guides Staff. (Insight Guides). 1998. pap. text 7.95 (*0-88729-547-9*) Langenscheidt.
***Moscow** Deborah Kent. LC 99-33909. (Cities of the World Ser.). (J). 2000. 26.00 (*0-516-21193-5*) Childrens.
Moscow. Jonathan Moberly. (Architecture Guides Ser.). (Illus.). 320p. 1998. pap. 5.95 (*3-8290-0474-5*, 520211) Konemann.
Moscow. Marsha Nordby. (Soviet Guides Ser.). (Illus.). 256p. 1991. pap. 15.95 (*0-8442-9675-9*, Passprt Bks) NTC Contemp Pub Co.
Moscow. Olga Pirumova. (Great Cities Ser.). (Illus.). 96p. 1996. 20.00 (*1-85995-194-5*) Parkstone Pr.
***Moscow.** Lesley Pitman. 1999. lib. bdg. 63.00 (*1-85109-270-6*) ABC-CLIO.
Moscow. Contrib. by Christopher Rice & Melanie Rice. LC 98-7232. 256p. 1998. 22.95 (*0-7894-3529-2*) DK Pub Inc.
Moscow. 2nd ed. Dan Richardson. (Rough Guide Ser.). (Illus.). 416p. 1998. pap. text 16.95 (*1-85828-322-1*) Rough Guides.
Moscow. 3rd ed. Insight Guides Staff. (Insight Guides). 1998. pap. text 21.95 (*0-88729-716-1*) Langenscheidt.
Moscow: An Architectural History. Kathleen Berton. (Illus.). 255p. 1991. 41.00 (*0-685-38703-8*, Pub. by I B T) St Martin.
Moscow: An Architectural History. L. Berton. (C). 1990. 180.00 (*0-7855-4488-7*, Pub. by Collets) St Mut.

M

An Asterisk (*) at the beginning of an entry indicates that the title is appearing for the first time.

Moscow: Economy, Industry, Government, Business. 2nd rev. ed. Russian Information & Business Center, Inc. Staff. (Russian Regional Business Directories Ser.), (Illus.). 200p. 1997. pap. 99.00 (*1-57751-371-1*) Intl Business Pubns.
Moscow: Governing the Socialist Metropolis. Timothy J. Colton. LC 95-14662. (Russian Research Center Studies: Vol. 88). (Illus.). 896p. (C). 1996. 45.00 (*0-674-58741-3*) Belknap Pr.
Moscow: Governing the Socialist Metropolis. Timothy J. Colton. (Russian Research Center Studies). (Illus.). 960p. 1998. pap. 24.95 (*0-674-58749-9*) HUP.
Moscow: The Turning Point? Klaus Reinhardt. 495p. 1992. 47.50 (*0-85496-695-1*) Berg Pubs.
Moscow: Treasures & Traditions. W. Bruce Lincoln et al. LC 90-30271. (Illus.). 320p. 1990. 50.00 (*0-295-96994-6*) U of Wash Pr.
Moscow - St. Petersburg. 2nd rev. ed. Nelles Verlag Staff. (Nelles Guides Ser.). (Illus.). 256p. 1999. pap. 15.95 (*3-88618-904-X*) Hunter NJ.
Moscow & Beyond, 1986-1989. Andrei D. Sakharov. Tr. by Antonina W. Bouis. 158p. 1991. 19.95 (*0-685-39961-3*) Knopf.
Moscow & Chinese Communists. 2nd ed. Robert C. North. viii, 310p. 1963. pap. 15.95 (*0-8047-0454-6*) Stanford U Pr.
Moscow & Greek Communism, 1944-1949. Peter J. Stavrakis. LC 88-47767. 288p. 1989. text 39.95 (*0-8014-2125-X*) Cornell U Pr.
Moscow & Leningrad. large type ed. Marsha Nordby. (Guidebook Ser.). (Illus.). 1991. pap. 9.95 (*962-217-117-6*) L A Michaux.
Moscow & Leningrad. 2nd ed. Evan Mawdsley. 1991. pap. 22.50 (*0-393-30773-5*) Norton.
Moscow & St. Petersburg. Rose Baring. LC 93-47109. (Cadogan City Guides Ser.). (Illus.). 608p. (Orig.). 1995. pap. 17.95 (*1-56440-274-6*) Globe Pequot.
Moscow & St. Petersburg. Christopher Booth. (Passport's Illustrated Travel Guides Ser.). (Illus.). 192p. 1996. pap. 14.95 (*0-8442-4826-6*, 48266, Passprt Bks) NTC Contemp Pub Co.
***Moscow & St. Petersburg.** Ed. by Fodors Travel Publications, Inc. Staff. 2001. pap. 19.00 (*0-679-00616-8*, Pub. by Random Bks Yng Read) Random.
Moscow & St. Petersburg. Masha Nordbye. (Odyssey Passport Ser.). (Illus.). 592p. 1999. pap. 24.95 (*962-217-611-9*) Norton.
Moscow & St. Petersburg: Pocket Guide. Text by Neil Wilson. LC 99-222938. 1999. pap. text 8.95 (*2-8315-6328-3*) Berlitz.
Moscow & St. Petersburg Guide. 1999. pap. 14.95 (*0-14-027314-X*) Viking Penguin.
Moscow & the Communist Party of India: A Study in the Post War Evolution of International Communist Strategy. John H. Kautsky. LC 82-11859. 220p. 1982. reprint ed. lib. bdg. 59.50 (*0-313-23568-6*, KAMO, Greenwood Pr) Greenwood.
Moscow & the Global Left in the Gorbachev Era. Ed. by Joan B. Urban. LC 91-57898. 224p. 1992. pap. 14.95 (*0-8014-8008-6*) Cornell U Pr.
Moscow & the Global Left in the Gorbachev Era. Ed. by Joan B. Urban. LC 91-57898. 219p. reprint ed. pap. 67.90 (*0-608-20955-4*, 207205400003) Bks Demand.
Moscow & the Golden Ring. 2nd ed. Photos by Patricia Lanza. LC 93-87281. (Illustrated Travel Guides from Thomas Cook Ser.). (Illus.). 272p. 1995. pap. 16.95 (*0-8442-9959-6*, Passprt Bks) NTC Contemp Pub Co.
Moscow & the Italian Communist Party: From Togliatti to Berlinguer. Joan B. Urban. 368p. 1986. 49.95 (*0-8014-1832-1*); pap. text 19.95 (*0-8014-9342-0*) Cornell U Pr.
Moscow Art Nouveau. Kathleen B. Murrell. (Illus.). 160p. 1997. 65.00 (*0-85667-488-5*, Pub. by P Wilson) Antique Collect.
Moscow Art Theatre. Nick Worrall. LC 95-45724. 256p. (C). 1996. 90.00 (*0-415-05598-9*) Routledge.
Moscow Art Theatre Letters. Ed. & Tr. by Jean Benedetti. LC 91-19730. (Illus.). 320p. (C). (gr. 13). 1991. 45.00 (*0-87830-084-8*, A6381, Thtre Arts Bks) Routledge.
Moscow Boy. Morris. (J). 1995. 14.95 (*0-689-31657-7*) Atheneum Yung Read.
Moscow Business Elite, 1840-1905: A Social & Cultural Portrait of Two Generations. Jo Ann Ruckman. LC 83-23732. 275p. 1984. 32.00 (*0-87580-096-3*) N Ill U Pr.
Moscow Circles. Benedict Erofeev. Tr. by J. R. Dorell. (RUS.). 188p. 1982. 12.95 (*0-906495-26-1*); pap. 7.95 (*0-685-42453-7*) Writers & Readers.
Moscow Circles. Benedict Erofeev. 192p. 1984. pap. 7.95 (*0-906495-74-1*) Writers & Readers.
Moscow Conceptualism. Natalia Tamruchi. (Illus.). 120p. 1995. text 26.00 (*976-8097-86-8*) Gordon & Breach.
Moscow Connection. Robin Moore. 500p. 1994. 20.00 (*1-879915-11-1*) Affil Writers America.
Moscow Days: Life & Hard Times in the New Russia. Galina Dutkina. Tr. by Catherine A. Fitzpatrick. 208p. 1996. 23.00 (*1-56836-066-5*) Kodansha.
Moscow Diary. Walter Benjamin. Ed. by Gary Smith. Tr. by Richard Sieburth. LC 86-9964. (Illus.). 160p. 1986. pap. text 9.95 (*0-674-58744-8*) HUP.
Moscow DMZ: The Story of the Internatinal Effort to Convert Russian Weapons. Glenn E. Schweitzer. LC 95-42353. 302p. (C). (gr. 13). 1996. 69.95 (*1-56324-625-2*) M E Sharpe.
Moscow DMZ: The Story of the International Effort to Convert Russian Weapons Science to Peaceful Purposes. Glenn E. Schweitzer. LC 95-42353. 302p. (C). (gr. 13). 1996. pap. 32.95 (*1-56324-626-0*) M E Sharpe.
Moscow Does Not Believe in Tears: Reflections of Moscow's Mayor. Y. M. Luzhkov. Ed. by Gary Esterman. Tr. by M. Davidov from RUS.Tr. of Nash dom- Moskva. (RUS., Illus.). 7300p. 1996. 20.00 (*0-9653464-0-4*) J M Martin.
Moscow Dossier of President Clinton. Yury Yugarev. Ed. by L. Eliseeva. (RUS., Illus.). 805p. Date not set. 29.99 (*1-887869-01-8*) ASOFSPP.
Moscow, Germany, & the West from Khruschev to Gorbachev. Michael J. Sodaro. 456p. 1991. pap. text 19.95 (*0-8014-9762-0*) Cornell U Pr.
***Moscow Guide.** 2nd ed. Yves Gerem. 624p. 2000. pap. text 16.95 (*1-892975-29-7*) Open Rd Pub.
Moscow Hotel Restaurant Guide. John E. Felber. (Illus.). 32p. 1991. 6.95 (*0-910794-09-X*) Intl Intertrade.
Moscow Icons. C. Smimova. (C). 1990. 500.00 (*0-7855-4430-5*, Pub. by Collets) St Mut.
Moscow in Prints of the 19th & 20th Centuries. V. Sannikova. (C). 1989. 550.00 (*0-7855-4518-2*, Pub. by Collets) St Mut.
Moscow in Prints of the 19th & 20th Centuries. V. Sannikova. (Illus.). (C). 1989. text 550.00 (*0-7855-5828-4*, Pub. by Collets) St Mut.
Moscow International Chess Tournament, 1936. Gregory Levenfish. Tr. by Jimmy Adams from RUS. (Tournament Bk.). (Illus.). 245p. 1988. 34.00 (*0-939433-08-7*) Caissa Edit.
Moscow Kremlin in Watercolour: A Tribute to Eternal Russia. Irina Bagetskaya. (Illus.). 200p. 1994. 85.00 (*2-909838-05-6*) Antique Collect.
Moscow Lectures on Psychoanalysis. Ed. by Arnold Rothstein. LC 91-30974. 186p. (C). 1991. 30.00 (*0-8236-3435-3*) Intl Univs Pr.
Moscow Literary Memoir: Among the Great Artists of Russia from 1946 to 1980. Robert A. Ford. Ed. by Carole Jerome. (Illus.). 304p. 1995. text 34.95 (*0-8020-0615-9*) U of Toronto Pr.
Moscow, Livonia & the Hanseatic League, 1487-1550. Erik Tiberg. LC 96-121614. (Studia Baltica Stockholmiensia: No. 15). 290p. (Orig.). 1995. pap. 49.50 (*91-22-01697-X*) Coronet Bks.
Moscow Madness: Crime, Corruption, & One Man's Pursuit of Profit in the New Russia. Timothy Harper. LC 99-11347. 256p. 1999. 24.95 (*0-07-026700-6*) McGraw.
Moscow Meets Madison Avenue: The Adventures of the First American Adman in the U. S. S. R. Gary Burandt & Nancy Giges. LC 92-52609. (Illus.). 208p. 1992. 22.50 (*0-88730-570-9*, HarpBusn) HarpInfo.
Moscow Metro: Photoguide. V. Berezin. (Illus.). 234p. (C). 1989. 100.00 (*0-569-08961-1*, Pub. by Collets) St Mut.
Moscow Mule. James Young. 232p. 1997. 35.00 (*0-7126-6005-4*, Pub. by CEN3) Trafalgar.
Moscow Mutterings: The Collected Wit & Wisdom of the Former Soviet Leadership. Craig Cartier. LC 97-68962. 190p. (Orig.). 1997. pap. write for info. (*1-57502-564-7*, PO1633) Morris Pubng.
***Moscow Nights.** Arthur E. Adams. LC 99-96648. 2000. 23.95 (*0-533-13299-1*) Vantage.
Moscow, 1911-1933. Allan Monkhouse. LC 76-115566. (Russia Observed Ser., No. 1). 1970. reprint ed. 23.95 (*0-405-03051-7*) Ayer.
Moscow 1935 International Chess Tournament. Tr. by Jimmy Adams & Sarah Murst. (Great Tournaments Ser.: Vol. 8). (Illus.). 356p. 1998. 45.00 (*0-939433-52-4*) Caissa Edit.
Moscow Notebooks. Osip Mandelshtam. Tr. by Richard McKane & Elizabeth McKane from RUS. 80p. (Orig.). 1991. pap. 14.95 (*1-85224-126-8*, Pub. by Bloodaxe Bks) Dufour.
Moscow Oblast: Economy, Industry, Government, Business. 2nd rev. ed. Russian Information & Business Center, Inc. Staff. (Russian Regional Business Directories Ser.). (Illus.). 200p. 1997. pap. 99.00 (*1-57751-398-3*) Intl Business Pubns.
***Moscow Oblast Regional Investment & Business Guide.** Global Investment & Business Center, Inc. Staff. (Russian Regional Investment & Business Guides Ser.: Vol. 47). (Illus.). 350p. 1999. pap. 99.00 (*0-7397-0849-X*) Intl Business Pubns.
***Moscow Oblast Regional Investment & Business Guide.** Contrib. by Global Investment & Business Center, Inc. Staff. (Russian Regional Investment & Business Guides Ser.: Vol. 8). (Illus.). 350p. 2000. pap. 99.95 (*0-7397-2995-0*) Intl Business Pubns.
Moscow Performances: The New Russian Theater, 1991-1996. John Freedman. (Russian Theatre Archive Ser.). (Illus.). 280p. 1998. pap. text 38.00 (*90-5702-181-1*, Harwood Acad Pubs) Gordon & Breach.
***Moscow Performances: The New Russian Theater 1991-1996.** John Freedman. (Russian Theatre Archive Ser.: Vol. 12). (Illus.). 280p. 1998. text 83.00 (*90-5702-180-3*, Harwood Acad Pubs) Gordon & Breach.
***Moscow Performances II: The 1996-1997 Season.** John Freedman. (Russian Theatre Archive Ser.: Vol. 20). (Illus.). 140p. 1998. text 40.00 (*90-5755-083-0*, Harwood Acad Pubs); pap. text 22.50 (*90-5755-084-9*, Harwood Acad Pubs) Gordon & Breach.
Moscow Puzzles. Boris A. Kordemsky. 1992. pap. 8.95 (*0-486-27078-5*) Dover.
Moscow Racetrack. Anatoly Gladilin. 1992. pap. 12.00 (*0-679-74261-1*) Vin Bks.
***Moscow Regional Investment & Business Guide.** Global Investment & Business Center, Inc. Staff. (Russian Regional Investment & Business Guides Ser.: Vol. 48). (Illus.). 350p. 1999. pap. 99.00 (*0-7397-0800-7*) Intl Business Pubns.
***Moscow Regional Investment & Business Guide.** Contrib. by Global Investment & Business Center, Inc. Staff. (Russian Regional Investment & Business Guides Ser.: Vol. 29). (Illus.). 350p. 2000. pap. 99.95 (*0-7397-2996-9*) Intl Business Pubns.
Moscow Revealed. Kathleen Berton. (Illus.). 222p. 1991. 29.98 (*1-55859-215-6*) Abbeville Pr.
Moscow, Russia Autosolitons: A New Approach to Problems of Self-Organization & Turbulence. B. S. Kerner. 688p. (C). 1994. text 390.50 (*0-7923-2816-7*) Kluwer Academic.
Moscow, St. Petersburg. Nelles Verlag. (Nelles Guides Ser.). 1994. pap. 14.95 (*3-88618-397-1*, Pub. by Nelles Verlag) Seven Hills Bk.
***Moscow Seminar in Mathematical Physics.** Ed. by A. Yu Morozov & M. A. Olshanetsky. LC 91-640741. (Translations Ser.: Ser. 2, Vol. 191, No. 43). 299p. 1999. 110.00 (*0-8218-1388-9*) Am Math.
Moscow, St. Petersburg. 4th ed. Fodors Staff. 1999. pap. 19.00 (*0-679-00094-1*) Fodors Travel.
***Moscow State Yiddish Theater: Jewish Culture on the Soviet Stage.** Jeffrey Veidlinger. LC 00-35004. 2000. write for info. (*0-253-33784-4*) Ind U Pr.
Moscow Station. Ronald Kessler. 368p. 1990. mass mkt. 5.99 (*0-671-69338-7*) PB.
Moscow Stations. Venedikt Yerofeev. 54p. 1997. pap. 12.95 (*1-870259-47-5*) Theatre Comm.
Moscow Symposium on the Law of the Sea: Proceedings. Thomas A. Clingan, Jr. & Anatoly Kolodkin. (Law of the Sea Institute Workshop Ser.: W10). 394p. (C). 1992. text 51.00 (*0-911189-24-6*) Law Sea Inst.
Moscow, the Kremlin, the Supreme Soviet of the U. S. S. R. Aleksandr Zharkov & Iuril S. Korolev. (RUS.). 1982. 110.00 (*0-7855-1581-X*) St Mut.
Moscow, the Third Rome. 2nd ed. Nicholas Zernov. LC 76-149664. reprint ed. 32.50 (*0-404-07075-2*) AMS Pr.
Moscow to Stalingrad: Decision in the East. LC 86-600063. (Army Historical Series, Center for Military History Publication: No. 30-12). (Illus.). 574p. 1996. boxed set 31.00 (*0-16-001942-7*, 008-029-00140-3) USGPO.
Moscow to the End of the Line. Erofeev Venedikt. Tr. by H. William Tjalsma from RUS. 194p. 1994. pap. 12.95 (*0-8101-1200-0*) Northwestern U Pr.
Moscow Trials. Francis Heisler. 1976. lib. bdg. 59.95 (*0-8490-2284-3*) Gordon Pr.
Moscow Twilight. William E. Holland. Ed. by Bill Grosse. 352p. 1993. mass mkt. 5.50 (*0-671-74644-8*) PB.
Moscow Twilight. large type ed. William Holland. LC 92-33706. 622p. 1993. reprint ed. lib. bdg. 18.95 (*1-56054-584-4*) Thorndike Pr.
Moscow Uprising of December, 1905: A Background Study. Joseph L. Sanders. (Modern European History Ser.). 896p. 1987. text 20.00 (*0-8240-8062-9*) Garland.
Moscow Was My Parish. Georges Bissonnette. LC 78-16489. 272p. 1978. reprint ed. lib. bdg. 65.00 (*0-313-20594-9*, BIMM, Greenwood Pr) Greenwood.
Moscow Yankee. Myra Page. LC 95-2992. (Radical Novel Reconsidered Ser.). 320p. 1995. 15.95 (*0-252-06499-2*) U of Ill Pr.
Moscow's Afghan War: Soviet Motives & Western Interests. Radek Sikorski. (C). 1990. 50.00 (*0-907967-85-X*, Pub. by Inst Euro Def & Strat) St Mut.
Moscow's Challenge to U. S. Vital Interests in Southern Africa. Howard Phillips. 204p. (Orig.). 1987. pap. 5.95 (*0-940355-01-9*) Policy Analysis.
Moscow's City Government. Emanuel S. Savas & J. A. Kaiser. LC 84-26308. 240p. 1985. 55.00 (*0-275-90159-9*, C0159, Praeger Pubs) Greenwood.
Moscow's Lost Empire. Michael Rywkin. LC 93-29308. (Illus.). 230p. (C). (gr. 13). 1994. text 74.95 (*1-56324-236-2*) M E Sharpe.
Moscow's Lost Empire. Michael Rywkin. LC 93-29308. (Illus.). 230p. (C). (gr. 13). 1994. pap. text 35.95 (*1-56324-237-0*) M E Sharpe.
Moscow's Muslim Challenge: Soviet Central Asia. rev. ed. Michael Rywkin. LC 89-29825. 202p. (gr. 13). 1990. text 66.95 (*0-87332-613-X*) M E Sharpe.
Moscow's Muslim Challenge: Soviet Central Asia. rev. ed. Michael Rywkin. LC 89-29825. 202p. (gr. 13). 1990. pap. text 42.95 (*0-87332-614-8*) M E Sharpe.
Moscow's Road to Nuremberg: The Soviet Background to the Trial. George Ginsburgs. 164p. 1996. 80.00 (*90-411-0182-9*) MNP-G&T.
Mose. Loren Graham. LC 94-15412. (Wesleyan Poetry Ser.). 60p. 1994. pap. 12.95 (*0-8195-1220-6*, Wesleyan Univ Pr); text 25.00 (*0-8195-2215-5*, Wesleyan Univ Pr) U Pr of New Eng.
Mose in Den Chronikbuechern: Garant Theokratischer Zukunftserwartung. Ernst M. Doerrfuss. (Beiheft zur Zeitschrift fuer die Alttestamentliche Wissenschaft Ser.: Vol. 219). (GER.). xii, 302p. (C). 1994. lib. bdg. 113.85 (*3-11-014017-9*) De Gruyter.
Mose Ou le Lezard Qui Pleurait. Ines Cagnati. (FRE.). 256p. 1984. pap. 11.95 (*0-7859-2227-X*, 207037582X) Fr & Eur.
Mose the Fireman. Eric Metaxas & Everett Peck. LC 95-36725. (Illus.). 48p. (J). (ps up). 1996. pap. 19.95 (*0-689-80227-7*) Aladdin.
Mose und Israel Im Konflikt: Eine Redaktionsgeschichtliche Studie Zu Den Wustenerzahlungen. Aaron Schart. (Orbis Biblicus et Orientalis Ser.: Vol. 98). (GER.). 296p. 1990. text 53.25 (*3-7278-0672-9*, Pub. by Presses Univ Fribourg) Eisenbrauns.
***Mosel Legacy.** rev. ed. David Peretz. 272p. 1999. pap. 15.95 (*1-58444-098-8*) DiscUs Bks.
Moselgedichte. Decimus M. Ausonius & Venantus Fortunatus. (GER.). 126p. 1981. reprint ed. 20.00 (*0-318-70578-6*) G Olms Pubs.
Moselle: River & Canal from the Roman Empire to the European Economic Community. Jean Cermakian. LC 75-22132. (University of Toronto, Department of Geography Research Publications: No. 14). 176p. reprint ed. pap. 54.60 (*0-608-17027-5*, 202642900049) Bks Demand.
Mosemans' Illustrated Catalog of Horse Furnishing Goods: An Unabridged Republication of the Fifth Edition. Moseman, C. M. & Brother Staff. (Illus.). 320p. 1987. reprint ed. pap. 19.95 (*0-486-25381-3*) Dover.
Mosen Millan. Ramon J. Sender. Ed. by R. M. Duncan. (SPA.). 111p. (C). 1964. pap. text 28.76 (*0-669-32631-3*) HM Trade Div.
Moser Artistic Glass. Gary D. Baldwin. LC 98-105107. (Illus.). 192p. 1997. 44.95 (*1-57080-038-3*) Antique Pubns.
Moser Artistic Glass. 2nd rev. ed. Gary D. Baldwin. LC 98-105107. (Illus.). 192p. 1997. pap. 34.95 (*1-57080-037-5*) Antique Pubns.
Moser Farmstead, Independent but Not Isolated: The Archeology of a Late Nineteenth Century Ozark Farmstead. Leslie C. Stewart-Abernathy. (Illus.). 183p. 1986. pap. 6.00 (*1-56349-051-X*, RS26) AR Archaeol.
Moser Untitled Bow A. Barry Moser. (J). Date not set. write for info. (*0-688-16764-0*) Morrow Avon.
Moser Untitled Bow B. Barry Moser. (J). Date not set. write for info. (*0-688-16765-9*) Morrow Avon.
Moses. (Now You Can Read Bible Stories Ser.). 32p. (J). 1994. 3.98 (*0-86112-783-8*) Brimax Bks.
Moses. (Bible Big Bks.). 2000. 14.99 (*1-55945-578-0*) Group Pub.
Moses. (J). write for info. (*0-614-30323-0*) Random.
Moses. (Very Easy Coloring Bks.). (Illus.). 16p. (J). (ps). 1995. pap. 1.49 (*0-7847-0374-4*, 22004) Standard Pub.
Moses. Katy K. Arnsteen. LC 96-37085. (KidScripts Ser.). (Illus.). 24p. (Orig.). (J). (gr. 2-5). 1997. pap. 3.95 (*0-8198-4793-3*) Pauline Bks.
Moses. Greg Asimakoupoulos. (Fisherman Bible Studyguide Ser.). 80p. 1998. pap. 4.99 (*0-87788-519-2*, H Shaw Pubs) Waterbrook Pr.
***Moses.** Chariot Victor Publishing Staff. (Shadowbox Bks.). (J). 2000. write for info. (*0-7814-3421-1*) Chariot Victor.
Moses. Anne De Graaf. (Little Children's Bible Books Ser.). (Illus.). 38p. (J). (gr. k-1). 1999. 5.99 (*0-8054-1900-4*) Broadman.
Moses. Illus. & Retold by Leonard Everett Fisher. LC 94-12131. 32p. (J). (gr. k-3). 1995. lib. bdg. 15.95 (*0-8234-1149-4*) Holiday.
Moses. Sam E. Gato. (Beginners Bible Play-A-Sound Bks.). (Illus.). 16p. (J). (ps). 1997. bds. 10.99 (*0-7847-0610-7*) Standard Pub.
Moses. Margaret Hodges. LC 97-5099. (Illus.). 2001. 17.00 (*0-15-200946-9*) Harcourt.
***Moses.** Peter Jones. 196p. 1999. pap. 17.95 (*0-7541-0728-0*, Pub. by Minerva Pr) Unity Dist.
Moses. Ladybird Books Staff. (Bible Stories Ser.: No. S846-3). (Illus.). (J). (ps-2). 1990. pap. 3.00 (*0-7214-5066-0*, Ladybrd) Penguin Putnam.
Moses. James Shott. (Young Reader's Christian Library). 224p. (J). (gr. 3-7). 1998. pap. text 1.39 (*1-57748-176-3*) Barbour Pub.
Moses. Lou E. Smith. (Illus.). (J). (gr. 1-8). 1996. 8.00 (*1-888535-04-0*) Firefly Prods.
Moses. R. Woodman. Date not set. pap. 1.75 (*0-906731-58-5*, Pub. by Christian Focus) Spring Arbor Dist.
***Moses.** Marilyn J. Woody. (Splish-Splash Devotions Ser.). (J). 2000. pap. text 4.99 (*0-7814-3418-1*) Chariot Victor.
Moses: A Life. Jonathan Kirsch. LC 98-25299. 415p. 1998. 27.50 (*0-345-41269-9*) Ballantine Pub Grp.
Moses: A Life. Jonathan Kirsch. 1999. pap. 14.95 (*0-345-41270-2*) Ballantine Pub Grp.
***Moses: A Man of Selfless Dedication.** Charles R. Swindoll. 191p. 1998. pap., student ed. 5.95 (*1-57972-097-8*) Insight Living.
Moses: A Man of Selfless Dedication. Charles R. Swindoll. LC 99-17106. (Great Lives from God's Word Ser.). 1999. 19.99 (*0-8499-1385-3*) Word Pub.
Moses: A Psychodynamic Study. Ed. by Dorothy F. Zeligs. 460p. 1986. 45.95 (*0-89885-236-6*, Kluwer Acad Hman Sci) Kluwer Academic.
Moses: Becoming a Light in the Darkness. Woodrow Kroll. 1999. pap. text 3.99 (*0-8474-0676-8*) Back to Bible.
***Moses: C.E.O.** Robert L. Dilenschneider. 1999. text 19.95 (*1-893224-02-3*) New Millenn Enter.
Moses: Founder of Preventive Medicine. P. Wood. 1976. lib. bdg. 59.95 (*0-8490-2285-1*) Gordon Pr.
Moses: Freeing Yourself to Know God. Gene A. Getz. LC 97-22584. (Men of Character Ser.). 192p. 1997. pap. 10.99 (*0-8054-6169-8*, 4261-69) Broadman.
Moses: From the Mysteries of Egypt to the Judges of Israel. Emil Bock. 224p. 1990. pap. 12.95 (*0-89281-117-X*, 1162, Pub. by Floris Bks) Anthroposophic.
Moses: Heroic Man, Man of God. George W. Coats. (Journal for the Study of the Old Testament Supplement Ser.: Vol. 57). 248p. 1988. 50.00 (*1-85075-096-3*, Pub. by Sheffield Acad); pap. 23.75 (*1-85075-095-5*, Pub. by Sheffield Acad) CUP Services.
Moses: His Mission. Luis A. Schokel & Guillermo Gutierrez. 144p. (C). 1996. pap. 39.95 (*0-85439-345-5*, Pub. by St Paul Pubns) St Mut.
Moses: Living in the Valley. Woodrow Kroll. 1999. pap. text 3.99 (*0-8474-0677-6*) Back to Bible.
Moses: Portrait of God. Bennie Goodwin. 96p. (Orig.). 1994. pap. text 4.95 (*0-940955-28-8*) Urban Ministries.
Moses: Preparing to Serve Just as You Are. Woodrow Kroll. 1999. pap. text 3.99 (*0-8474-0675-X*) Back to Bible.
***Moses: Prince of Egypt.** Howard Fast. 310p. 2000. per. 14.00 (*0-671-03911-3*, Pub. by ibooks) S&S Trade.

M

An Asterisk (*) at the beginning of an entry indicates that the title is appearing for the first time.

***Moses: Take Two Tablets & Call Me in the Morning.** Mike Thaler. LC 99-33100. (Heaven & Mirth Ser.). (Illus.). 32p. 1999. 12.99 (*0-7814-3262-6*) Chariot Victor.

Moses: The Emancipator of Israel. John G. Butler. 810p. 1996. 29.50 (*1-889773-12-3*) LBC Publns.

Moses: The Lawgiver. Gordon Lindsay. (Old Testament Ser.: Vol. 11). 1964. pap. 1.95 (*0-89985-959-3*) Christ for the Nations.

***Moses: The Lost Book of the Bible.** Les Whitten. 1999. 22.95 (*1-893224-03-1*, New Millenn Pr) New Millenn Enter.

Moses: The Man of God. G. Andre. 78p. (Orig.). 1988. pap. 2.50 (*0-88172-134-4*) Believers Bkshelf.

Moses: The Practice of God's Presence. Woodrow Kroll. 1999. pap. text 3.99 (*0-8474-0678-4*) Back to Bible.

Moses: The Revelation & the Covenant. Martin Buber. LC 87-26169. 232p. (C). 1988. reprint ed. pap. 17.50 (*0-391-03547-9*) Humanities.

Moses - The Prince, the Prophet: His Life, Legend & Message for Our Lives. Levi Meier. LC 98-35473. 224p. 1998. 23.95 (*1-58023-013-X*) Jewish Lights.

Moses - The Prince, the Prophet: His Life, Legend & Message for Our Lives. Levi Meier. 224p. 1999. pap. 16.95 (*1-58023-069-5*) Jewish Lights.

Moses--the Making of a leader. Thom Cleland. LC 99-29559. (Victor Bible Character Ser.). 208p. 1999. 7.99 (*1-56476-716-7*, Victor Bks) Chariot Victor.

Moses, Aaron & Joshua. Norman L. Heap. 345p. 1990. text 16.00 (*0-945905-05-X*) Family Hstory Pubns.

Moses & Civilization: The Meaning Behind Freud's Myth. Robert A. Paul. LC 95-23585. 268p. 1996. 37.00 (*0-300-06428-4*) Yale U Pr.

Moses & His Contemporaries. Gordon Lindsay. (Old Testament Ser.: Vol. 13). 1965. 1.95 (*0-89985-133-9*) Christ for the Nations.

Moses & Monotheism. Sigmund Freud. Ed. by Katherine Jones. 1955. pap. 9.00 (*0-394-70014-7*, V14) Knopf.

Moses & Paul. Cornelius R. Stam. 81p. 1956. 9.50 (*1-893874-09-5*) Berean Bibl Soc.

Moses & Pharaoh: Dominion Religion vs. Power Religion. Gary North. 426p. (C). 1985. pap. text 12.50 (*0-930464-05-2*) Inst Christian.

Moses & the Angel of Death. Rella Kushelevsky. LC 93-6957. (Studies on Themes & Motifs in Literature: Vol. 4). XXII, 325p. (C). 1995. text 57.95 (*0-8204-2147-2*) P Lang Pubng.

Moses & the Angels. Ileene Smith Sobel. LC 98-5125. (Illus.). 80p. (J). 1999. 16.95 (*0-385-32612-2*) BDD Bks Young Read.

Moses & the Burning Bush: A Story about Faith & Obedience. Mary Manz Simon. LC 98-38569. (Prince of Egypt Ser.). 32p. (J). (ps-3). 1998. 8.99 (*0-8499-5853-9*) Tommy Nelson.

Moses & the Church in the Wilderness. Gordon Lindsay. (Old Testament Ser.: Vol. 12). 1964. 1.95 (*0-89985-132-0*) Christ for the Nations.

Moses & the Deuteronomist: A Literary Study of the Deuteronomic History. Robert M. Polzin. 224p. 1984. 17.95 (*0-8164-0456-9*); 8.95 (*0-8164-2284-2*) Harper SF.

Moses & the Gods of Egypt: Studies in Exodus. rev. ed. John J. Davis. (Illus.). 1985. pap. 14.99 (*0-88469-177-2*) BMH Bks.

Moses & the Great Escape. Terry Whalin. (Sticker Story Adventures Ser.). (Illus.). 16p. (J). (gr. 2 up). 1998. pap. 5.99 (*0-8054-1670-6*) Broadman.

Moses & the Law. Kristy L. Christian & Kathryn L. Merrill. (Illus.). (Orig.). (J). (gr. 3 up). 1996. spiral bd. 19.95 (*0-9626535-0-0*) Infinite Discovery.

Moses & the Pharaoh. Alice J. Davidson. LC 98-182174. (My Bible Friends Board Bks.). (Illus.). 12p. (J). 1998. 3.99 (*0-310-97456-9*, Zondervan Gifts) Zondervan.

Moses & the Ten Commandments Activity Book. (J). 1992. pap. text 1.49 (*0-88271-231-4*) Regina Pr.

Moses & the Ten Plagues: Exodus 1:6 - 12:36. Hodges. (Arch Bks.). 24p. (Orig.). (J). (gr. k-4). 1985. pap. 1.99 (*0-570-06190-3*, 59-1291) Concordia.

Moses Ascending. Samuel Selvon. (Caribbean Writers Ser.). 141p. (C). 1991. reprint ed. pap. 9.95 (*0-435-98952-9*, 98952) Heinemann.

Moses Austin: His Life. David B. Gracy, II. (Illus.). 324p. 1987. 24.95 (*0-292-75120-6*) U of Tex Pr.

Moses Austin & Stephen F. Austin: A Gone to Texas Dual Biography. Betsy Warren. LC 95-13875. (Illus.). 64p. (J). (gr. 4 up). 1996. 16.95 (*0-937460-96-6*) Hendrick-Long.

***Moses Baby in the Bulrushes.** Dalmatian Press Staff. (Illus.). (J). 2000. pap. text 4.97 (*1-888567-36-8*) Dalmatian Pr.

Moses Brown: Reluctant Reformer. Mack Thompson. LC 62-52443. (Illus.). 325p. reprint ed. pap. 100.80 (*0-8357-3915-5*, 203664900004) Bks Demand.

Moses Code: Modeling the Experimentally Organized Economy, Technical Documentation. James W. Albrecht et al. (Industrial Institute for Economic & Social Research Report Ser.: No. 36). (Illus.). 354p. (Orig.). 1989. pap. 84.00 (*91-7204-322-9*) Coronet Bks.

Moses Cordovero's Introduction to Kabbalah: An Annotated Translation of His Or Neerav. Ira Robinson. LC 93-45501. 1993. 35.00 (*0-88125-439-8*) Ktav.

Moses Crosses the Red Sea: A Story of Faith & Courage. Mary Manz Simon. LC 98-38568. (Prince of Egypt Ser.). 32p. (J). (ps-3). 1998. 8.99 (*0-8499-5852-0*) Tommy Nelson.

MOSES Database. Industrial Institute for Economic & Social Researc. Ed. by James W. Albrecht et al. (Illus.). 361p. (Orig.). 1992. pap. 83.00 (*91-7204-381-4*) Coronet Bks.

Moses' Dry Feet. Illus. by Ron Wheeler. LC 98-227940. 16p. (gr. k-4). 1998. pap. 1.99 (*0-570-07545-9*) Concordia.

Moses, Exodus & Covenant. 1996. pap. 6.99 (*1-85078-208-3*) CUP Services.

Moses Goes to a Concert. Isaac Millman. (Illus.). 40p. (J). (gr. k-3). 1998. 16.00 (*0-374-35067-1*) FS&G.

***Moses Goes to School.** Isaac Millman. LC 99-40582. 2000. text 16.00 (*0-374-35069-8*) FS&G.

Moses Goodleaf Learns to Walk: A Short Tale of Discovery. Michael Bridge. (Illus.). 32p. (J). 2000. pap. 16.95 (*0-944963-19-6*); pap. 7.95 incl. audio (*0-944963-33-1*); lib. bdg. 22.95 (*0-944963-18-8*) Glastonbury CA.

MOSES Handbook: Model for Stimulating the Economy of Sweden. Fredrik Bergholm. (Industrial Institute for Economic & Social Research Report Ser.: No. 35). 213p. (Orig.). 1989. pap. 85.00 (*91-7204-319-9*) Coronet Bks.

Moses Hazen & the Canadian Refugees in the American Revolution. Allan S. Everest. LC 76-54260. (New York State Study Ser.). 232p. 1976. reprint ed. pap. 72.00 (*0-608-06968-X*, 206717600009) Bks Demand.

Moses in Egypt. Brad Kessler & Sounds of Blackness. LC 95-12493. (Rabbit Ears Ser.). (Illus.). 40p. (J). (gr. k-3). 1997. pap. 22.00 incl. audio (*0-689-80226-9*) Aladdin.

Moses in Egypt: A Novel. Lynne Reid Banks. (Prince of Egypt Ser.). (J). (gr. 2-5). 1998. pap. text 4.99 (*0-8499-5898-9*) Tommy Nelson.

Moses in Greco-Roman Paganism. John G. Gager. LC 73-173954. (Society of Biblical Literature, Ser.: No. 16). 173p. reprint ed. pap. 53.70 (*0-7837-5397-7*, 204516100005) Bks Demand.

***Moses in Sinai.** Simone Zelitch. 300p. 2001. 23.95 (*0-930773-59-4*, Pub. by Black Heron Pr) Midpt Trade.

Moses in the Bulrushes. Heather Amery. Ed. by Jenny Tyler. (Bible Tales Ser.). (Illus.). 16p. (Orig.). (J). (ps-k). 1997. pap. 4.50 (*0-7460-2743-5*, Usborne) EDC.

Moses in the Bulrushes. Heather Amery. Ed. by Jenny Tyler. (Bible Tales Ser.). (Illus.). 16p. (Orig.). (J). (ps up). 1997. lib. bdg. 12.95 (*0-88110-936-3*, Usborne) EDC.

Moses in the Bulrushes. Mary Auld. LC 98-33203. 31p. (J). (ps-3). 1999. 20.25 (*0-531-14516-6*) Watts.

Moses in the Bulrushes. Mary Auld & Diana Mayo. LC 98-33203. (Bible Stories Ser.). 31 p. (ps-3). 1999. lib. bdg. 7.95 (*0-531-15387-8*) Watts.

Moses in the Bulrushes. Melody Carlson. (Story Pockets Ser.). 1997. 4.99 (*1-57673-168-5*, Gold n Honey) Zondervan.

Moses in the Bulrushes. Illus. by Kate Davies. (Bible Pop-Ins Ser.). 10p. (J). 1997. bds. 4.99 (*1-884628-29-X*, Flyng Frog) Allied Pub MD.

Moses in the Bulrushes. Ed. by Henrietta Gambill. (Picture Window Bks.). (Illus.). 10p. (J). (ps). 1995. pap. 7.99 (*0-7847-0341-8*, 03707) Standard Pub.

Moses in the Bulrushes. Ronne Randall. (Illus.). 32p. (J). 1996. pap. 3.99 (*1-884628-26-5*, Flyng Frog) Allied Pub MD.

Moses in the Bulrushes. Illus. & Retold by Warwick Hutton. LC 91-13971. 32p. (J). (gr. k-3). 1992. reprint ed. pap. 4.95 (*0-689-71553-6*) Aladdin.

Moses in the Letter to the Hebrews. Mary R. D'Angelo. LC 78-12917. (Society of Biblical Literature. Dissertation Ser.: No. 42). 280p. reprint ed. pap. 86.80 (*0-7837-5431-0*, 204519600005) Bks Demand.

Moses in the Twentieth Century: A Universal Primer. Susan Roth. 1994. 24.95 (*0-9638861-0-X*) S J R Assocs.

Moses' Law for Modern Government: The Intellectual & Sociological Origins of the Christian Reconstructionist Movement. J. Ligon Duncan. 40p. 1996. pap. text 7.95 (*1-884416-18-7*) A Press.

Moses Leads His People. Chariot Victor Publishing Staff. (J). 1999. pap. text 3.99 (*0-7814-3328-2*) Chariot Victor.

Moses Maimonides. Oliver Leaman. 212p. 1997. pap. 29.95 (*0-7007-0676-3*, Pub. by Curzon Pr Ltd) Paul & Co Pubs.

Moses Maimonides: Physician, Scientist, & Philosopher. Ed. by Fred Rosner & Samuel S. Kottek. LC 92-41882. 304p. 1993. pap. 30.00 (*0-87668-470-3*) Aronson.

Moses Maimonides & His Time. Ed. by Eric L. Ormsby. LC 88-18910. (Studies in Philosophy & the History of Philosophy: No. 19). 188p. 1989. reprint ed. pap. 58.30 (*0-7837-9105-4*, 204990700004) Bks Demand.

Moses Maimonides' Treatise on Resurrection. Tr. by Fred Rosner. LC 96-42496. 138p. 1997. pap. 30.00 (*0-7657-5954-3*) Aronson.

Moses, Man of the Mountain. Zora Neale Hurston. LC 90-55502. 320p. 1994. reprint ed. pap. 14.00 (*0-06-091994-9*, Perennial) HarperTrade.

Moses Meets Israel: The Origins of One God. unabridged ed. Joseph Winsten. 1999. 27.95 (*0-9663406-0-4*) Rumford Pr.

Moses Mendelssohn: A Biographical Study. Alexander Altmann. (Illus.). 914p. 1998. pap. 34.95 (*1-874774-53-6*, Pub. by Littman Lib) Intl Spec Bk.

Moses Mendelssohn: Critic & Philosopher. H. Walter. LC 73-2230. (Jewish People; History, Religion, Literature Ser.). 1973. reprint ed. 23.95 (*0-405-05291-X*) Ayer.

Moses Mendelssohn: Philosophical Writings. Tr. by Daniel O. Dahlstrom. LC 97-16141. (Cambridge Texts in the History of Philosophy Ser.). 361p. 1997. text 64.95 (*0-521-57383-1*); pap. text 21.95 (*0-521-57477-3*) Cambridge U Pr.

Moses Mendelssohn & the Enlightenment. Allan Arkush. LC 93-39401. (SUNY Series in Judaica: Hermeneutics, Mysticism, & Religion). 304p. (C). 1994. text 64.50 (*0-7914-2071-X*); pap. text 21.95 (*0-7914-2072-8*) State U NY Pr.

Moses Mendelssohn & the Religious Enlightenment. David Sorkin. LC 95-23910. 214p. (C). 1996. 45.00 (*0-520-20261-9*, Pub. by U CA Pr) Cal Prin Full Svc.

Moses Mystery: The African Origins of the Jewish People. Gary Greenberg. 336p. 1996. 24.95 (*1-55972-371-8*, Birch Ln Pr) Carol Pub Group.

Moses on Leadership: How to Lead People With Purpose. Richard Koch. 1998. pap. 17.95 (*1-900961-60-1*) Capstone Pub NH.

***Moses on Management: 50 Leadership Lessons from the Greatest Manager of All Time.** David Baron & Lynette Padwa. LC 99-26708. 272p. 1999. 23.00 (*0-671-03259-3*) PB.

Moses on Management: 50 Leadership Lessons from the Greatest Manager of All Time. David Baron & Lynette Padwa. 320p. 2000. per. 12.95 (*0-671-03260-7*) PB.

MOSES on PC: Manual, Initialization & Calibration. Erol Taymaz. (Industrial Institute for Economic & Social Research Report Ser.). (Illus.). 273p. (Orig.). 1991. pap. 65.00 (*91-7204-369-5*) Coronet Bks.

***Moses on the Mountain.** James R. Short. LC 00-191026. 2000. 25.00 (*0-7388-2204-3*); pap. 18.00 (*0-7388-2205-1*) Xlibris Corp.

***Moses Parts the Sea.** Theresa Morin. (Little Bible Bks.). (Illus.). 24p. (J). (ps-1). 2000. 1.99 (*1-57748-686-2*) Barbour Pub.

Moses, Prince of Egypt: Storyteller's Edition. Madeleine L'Engle. 48p. 1998. 15.99 (*0-525-46051-9*, PuffinBks) Peng Put Young Read.

Moses' Rock. Frank O'Connor & Hugh Hunt. Ed. by Ruth Sherry. LC 82-23478. (Irish Dramatic Texts Ser.). 110p. 1983. 15.95 (*0-8132-0584-0*); pap. 7.95 (*0-8132-0585-9*) Cath U Pr.

Moses Rose. William Reinbolt, III. Ed. by Richard S. Danbury. 220p. (Orig.). 1996. pap. text 10.95 (*0-89754-125-1*, 12077354-0998) Dan River Pr.

Moses Supposes. Ellen Currie. 1994. 20.00 (*0-671-65673-2*) S&S Trade.

Moses Supposes. Dan Greenburg. LC 96-51914. 128p. 1997. pap. 8.95 (*1-56980-100-2*) Barricade Bks.

Moses Supposes: Stories. Ellen Currie. 224p. 1995. pap. 10.00 (*0-684-80421-2*) S&S Trade.

Moses Supposes: 5-Copy Reader's Guide. Ellen Currie. (Reading Group Guides Ser.). 1995. pap. text. write for info. (*0-684-00048-2*, Touchstone) S&S Trade Pap.

Moses Supposes His Toeses Are Roses: And 7 Other Silly Old Rhymes. Nancy Patz. LC 82-3099. (Illus.). 32p. (J). (ps-3). 1989. pap. 6.00 (*0-15-255691-5*) Harcourt.

Moses, the Deliverer. Gordon Lindsay. (Old Testament Ser.: Vol. 10). 1964. 1.95 (*0-89985-131-2*) Christ for the Nations.

Moses the Egyptian: The Memory of Egypt in Western Monotheism. Jan Assmann. LC 96-51600. (Illus.). 288p. 1997. 29.95 (*0-674-58738-3*) HUP.

Moses the Egyptian: The Memory of Egypt in Western Monotheism. Jan Assmann. (Illus.). 288p. 1998. pap. 18.95 (*0-674-58739-1*) HUP.

***Moses the Kitten.** James Herriot. (Illus.). (J). 1999. pap. text 14.50 (*0-7857-9664-9*) Econo-Clad Bks.

Moses the Kitten. James Herriot. (Illus.). (J). 1991. pap. 6.95 (*0-312-06419-5*) St Martin.

Moses the Kitten. James Herriot. (J). 1984. 12.15 (*0-606-05474-X*, Pub. by Turtleback) Demco.

Moses the Lawgiver. Rabbit. LC 95-12494. 1999. per. 10.95 (*0-689-80228-5*) Aladdin.

Moses the Leader. Elrose Hunter. (Jigsaw Bks.). (Illus.). 10p. (J). (ps). 1992. 1.79 (*0-687-27246-7*) Abingdon.

Moses, the Man of God - Gideon, Samson (Combination) G. Andre. pap. 2.75 (*0-88172-133-6*) Believers Bkshelf.

Moses, the Servant of Yahweh. Dewey M. Beegle. LC 79-84558. 368p. 1972. reprint ed. pap. text 8.95 (*0-933462-03-4*) Pryor Pettengill.

Moses Tradition. George W. Coats. (Journal for the Study of the Old Testament Supplement Ser.: Vol. 161). 203p. 1993. 57.50 (*1-85075-410-1*, Pub. by Sheffield Acad) CUP Services.

Moses Unchained. Marilyn F. Moriarty. LC 97-40787. 192p. 1998. 22.95 (*0-8203-1985-6*) U of Ga Pr.

Moses Washington. Robert L. Merriam. (Illus.). 31p. 1978. pap. 2.00 (*0-686-32489-7*) R L Merriam.

Moses Whitepapers. Ed. by UniForum Staff. 92p. (Orig.). (C). 1994. pap. text 25.00 (*0-936593-29-6*) UniForum.

***Moses Wrote about Me.** Contrib. by Alice Livingston. 1999. pap. 7.95 (*1-56794-184-2*) Star Bible.

Mosesegen Im Deuteronomium: Eine Text-, Kompositions- und Formkritische Studie Zu Deuteronomium 33. Stefan Beyerle. (Beihefte zur Zeitschrift fuer die Alttestamentliche Wissenschaft Ser.: Vol. 250). (GER.). x, 345p. (C). 1997. lib. bdg. 127.15 (*3-11-015062-X*) De Gruyter.

***MOSFET Modeling & BSIM 3 User's Guide.** Yuhua Cheng & Chenming Hu. LC 99-37157. 1999. write for info. (*0-7923-8575-6*) Kluwer Academic.

MOSFET Modeling with Spice. Daniel P. Foty. LC 96-49414. 653p. (C). 1996. 92.00 (*0-13-227935-5*) P-H.

***MOSFET Models for SPICE Simulation Including BSIM3v3 & BSIM4.** William Liu. 544p. 2001. 98.00 (*0-471-39697-4*) Wiley.

MOSFET Models for VLSI Circuit Simulation: Theory & Practice. N. Arora. (Computational Microelectronics Ser.). (Illus.). 632p. 1993. 238.95 (*0-387-82395-6*) Spr-Verlag.

MOSFET Theory & Design. R. M. Warner & B. L. Grung. LC 98-13184. (Illus.). 272p. (C). 1999. pap. text 29.95 (*0-19-511642-9*) OUP.

Moshe Dayan: Story of My Life. Moshe Dayan. (Illus.). 640p. 1992. reprint ed. pap. 17.95 (*0-306-80497-2*) Da Capo.

Moshe Kupferman: Between Oblivion & Remembrance. John W. Coffey, II. LC 91-62645. (Illus.). 64p. (Orig.). 1991. pap. 19.95 (*0-88259-963-1*) NCMA.

Moshe Kupferman: Paintings, Works on Paper, Scrolls. Allan Schwartzman & Benjamin Harshav. Ed. by Elsa Longhauser. LC 98-70724. (Illus.). 20p. 1998. pap. 20.00 (*1-58442-027-8*) Galleries at Moore.

Moshe Mendel the Mitzva Maven & His Amazing Mitzva Quest. Shiffy Apelbaum. LC 94-4118. (J). 1994. 13.95 (*0-87306-662-6*) Feldheim.

Moshe Safdie. Wendy Kohn. (Illus.). 321p. 1996. 85.00 (*1-85490-453-1*, Pub. by Wiley) Wiley.

Moshe Safdie: Buildings & Projects, 1967-1992. Ed. by Irene Z. Murray. LC 96-181072. (Illus.). 332p. 1996. pap. 65.00 incl. cd-rom (*0-7735-1510-0*, Pub. by McG-Queens Univ Pr) CUP Services.

Moshe Sharett: Biography of a Political Moderate. Gabriel Sheffer. 1,082p. 1996. text 125.00 (*0-19-827994-9*) OUP.

Mosher Survey. Clelia D. Mosher. Ed. by James MaHood & Kristine Wanburg. LC 79-48014. 490p. 1980. lib. bdg. 30.95 (*0-405-13090-2*) Ayer.

Moshe's Adventures in Brachaland. I. Marcus. (YA). 1990. 8.99 (*0-89906-990-8*) Mesorah Pubns.

Moshi Moshi. Jonathan London. LC 97-10612. (Illus.). 32p. (J). (gr. 1-3). 1998. lib. bdg. 21.40 (*0-7613-0110-0*) Millbrook Pr.

***Moshino's Works for Girl Studio.** 160p. 1999. 35.00 (*4-309-90280-4*) Dist Art Pubs.

Mosiacs: Inspirations. Lorenz Pub. (Illus.). 96p. 1998. 12.95 (*1-85967-751-7*) Anness Pub.

Mosin-Nagant Rifle. Terence W. Lapin. (For Collectors Only Ser.). (Illus.). 200p. 1998. pap. 19.95 (*1-882391-21-7*) N Cape Pubns.

MOSIX Distributed Operation System: Load Balancing for UNIX. Amnon Barak et al. LC 93-3663. (Lecture Notes in Computer Science Ser.: Vol. 672). 1993. 39.95 (*0-387-56663-5*) Spr-Verlag.

***Moskovisea Saga.** 6th ed. A.I. Aksonov. 1999. 19.95 (*5-87113-066-6*) Distribks Inc.

***Moskovskie Slova I Slovechki: Proiskhozhdenie Moskovskikh Poslovits, Pogovorok, Rechenii & Pesen.** 8th ed. Vassily Aksyonov. 1999. pap. 9.95 (*5-87113-022-4*) Distribks Inc.

Moskva 2042. Vladimir Voinovich. (RUS.). 1987. pap. 13.50 (*0-87501-031-8*) Ardis Pubs.

Moskva Zlatoglavaya - Moscow Gold-Coupoled: A Novel - Memoirs. David Shrayer-Petrov. Ed. by Boris Kalyuzhny. LC 93-60851. (RUS., Illus.). 312p. (Orig.). 1994. pap. 12.00 (*1-885563-00-0*) VIA Press MD.

Moslem Egypt & Christian Abyssinia. William M. Dye. LC 78-97365. 500p. 1969. reprint ed. lib. bdg. 49.75 (*0-8371-2432-8*, DYM&) Greenwood.

Moslem Rebellion in Northwest China, 1862-1878. Wen-Djang Chu. (Central Asiatic Studies: No. 5). 1966. pap. text 60.00 (*90-279-0017-5*) Mouton.

Moslem Schisms & Sects: Being the History of the Various Philosophic Systems Developed in Islam. Abd-Al-Kahir Ibn-Tahir ibn-Mahammad. Tr. by Kate C. Seelye. LC 75-158216. (Columbia University. Oriental Studies: No. 15). 1920. 20.00 (*0-404-50505-8*) AMS Pr.

Moslem Wife & Other Stories. Mavis Gallant. 6.95p. 1996. pap. text 6.95 (*0-7710-9891-X*) McCland & Stewart.

Moslem Women Enter a New World. Ruth F. Woodsmall. LC 75-180309. reprint ed. 31.50 (*0-404-56334-1*) AMS Pr.

Moslems in Spain. R. Dozy. 816p. 1988. 350.00 (*1-85077-180-4*, Pub. by Darf Pubs Ltd) St Mut.

Moslems of Rural Bengal. Ranjit K. Bhattacharya. (C). 1991. 20.00 (*0-8364-2761-0*, Pub. by Usha) S Asia.

Mosman: A History. Gavin Souter. LC 95-112729. (Illus.). 304p. 1994. 39.95 (*0-522-84591-6*, Pub. by Melbourne Univ Pr) Paul & Co Pubs.

Mospower Applications Handbook. Ed. by Rudy Severns & Jack Armijos. LC 84-14140. (Illus.). 512p. 1985. 20.00 (*0-930519-00-0*) Siliconix Inc.

***Mosque Architecture: Principals & Design.** Osamah El Gohary. 300p. 2000. text 212.50 (*0-7103-0683-0*) Col U Pr.

Mosque in Early Ottoman Architecture. Aptullah Kuran. LC 68-16701. (Publications of the Center for Middle Eastern Studies). (Illus.). 1968. lib. bdg. 25.00 (*0-226-46293-5*) U Ch Pr.

Mosque Libraries: An Historical Study. M. Sibai. 184p. 1987. text 90.00 (*0-7201-1896-4*) Continuum.

Mosquita: A Guide to the Land of Savannas, Rain Forests & Turtle Hunters. Derek A. Parent. (Illus.). 74p. (Orig.). 1995. pap. 14.95 (*1-896677-00-2*) Intrepid Travel.

***Mosquito.** Jill Bailey. LC 98-10596. (Bug Bks.). (Illus.). 32p. (J). (gr. 1-3). 1998. 13.95 (*1-57572-663-7*) Heinemann Lib.

Mosquito. Jennifer Coldrey & George Bernard. LC 96-22648. (Stopwatch Ser.). (J). 1997. pap. 4.95 (*0-382-39763-0*); lib. bdg. 11.95 (*0-382-39758-4*) Silver Burdett Pr.

Mosquito. Gayl Jones. Ed. by Helene Atwan. LC 98-27644. 632p. 1999. 28.50 (*0-8070-8346-1*, Pub. by Beacon Pr) Ballantine Pub Grp.

Mosquito. Gayl Jones. LC 98-27644. (Bluestreak Ser.). 624p. 2000. pap. 18.00 (*0-8070-8347-X*) Beacon Pr.

Mosquito: The Illustrated History. Philip J. Birtles. LC 99-187988. (Illus.). 192p. 1998. 39.95 (*0-7509-1495-5*, Pub. by Sutton Pub Ltd) Intl Pubs Mktg.

***Mosquito: The Illustrated History.** Philip J. Birtles. (Illus.). 256p. 1999. pap. 22.95 (*0-7509-2327-X*) Sutton Pub Ltd.

Mosquito & Ant. Kimiko Hahn. LC 98-41003. 80p. 1999. 21.00 (*0-393-04732-6*) Norton.

***Mosquito & Ant.** Kimiko Hahn. (Illus.). 104p. 2000. pap. 12.00 (*0-393-32062-6*) Norton.

Mosquito Bomber Units. Martin Bowman. LC 98-181178. (Combat Ser.). (Illus.). 96p. 1997. pap. 17.95 (*1-85532-690-6*, Pub. by Ospry) Stackpole.

Mosquito Book. Scott Anderson & Tony Dierkins. LC 98-92515. (Illus.). 128p. 1998. pap. 6.95 (*0-9644521-1-1*) DENNOCH.

***Mosquito Coast.** Level 4. (C). 2000. 7.00 (*0-582-41814-3*) Addison-Wesley.

Mosquito Coast. Paul Theroux. 384p. 1983. mass mkt. 5.95 (*0-380-61945-8*, Avon Bks) Morrow Avon.

Mosquito Coast. Paul Theroux. 384p. 1996. pap. 12.95 (*0-14-006089-8*, Penguin Bks) Viking Penguin.

M

Mosquito Coast. large type ed. Paul Theroux. 575p. 1982. 11.50 (*0-7089-8064-3*, Charnwood) Ulverscroft.

Mosquito Coast. Paul Theroux. 1994. reprint ed. lib. bdg. 32.95 (*1-56849-348-7*) Buccaneer Bks.

Mosquito Control Inspector. Jack Rudman. (Career Examination Ser.: C-2912). 1994. pap. 29.95 (*0-8373-2912-4*) Nat Learn.

Mosquito Control Pesticides: Ecological Impacts & Management Alternatives: Proceedings of a Conference Held on Jan. 18, 1991 at the University of Florida, Gainesville, Florida. Ed. by Thomas C. Emmel & J. C. Tucker. 112p. 1991. pap. 8.95 (*0-945417-22-5*) Sci Pubs.

Mosquito Ecology: Report of a WHO Scientific Group, 1967. (Technical Report Ser.: No. 368). 22p. 1967. pap. text 3.00 (*92-4-120368-4*, 1100368) World Health.

Mosquito Ecology Field Sampling Methods. 2nd ed. Chapman & Hall Staff. (C). text 286.50 (*0-412-54080-0*) Chapman & Hall.

Mosquito Fighter Squadrons of World War II. Martin Bowman. (Combat Aircraft Ser.: No. 9). (Illus.). 96p. 1998. pap. 16.95 (*1-85532-731-7*, Pub. by Ospry) Motorbooks Intl.

Mosquito Games. Dana A. Jennings. 224p. 1989. 17.95 (*0-89919-694-2*) Ticknor & Fields.

Mosquito Girl. Sally Gwin. 108p. (YA). (gr. 7 up). 1997. pap. 9.99 (*0-88092-267-2*) Royal Fireworks.

***Mosquito Island: Grade 6+ Life Science.** McGraw-Hill Staff. 1999. pap. 14.95 (*1-57768-002-2*) MG-Hill OH.

Mosquito Park Secrets: How to Live Outrageously Happy & Healthy. D. Dean Benton. 96p. 1998. pap. 9.95 (*0-9664821-0-7*) Spring Daisy.

Mosquito Photo-Reconnaissance Units of World War II, Vol.13. Martin W. Bowman. 1999. pap. text 17.95 (*1-85532-891-7*) Ospry.

Mosquito Point. Christopher Barry. (Joe Bass Ser.). (Illus.). 115p. (YA). (gr. 8 up). 1996. pap. 9.99 (*0-88092-318-0*) Royal Fireworks.

Mosquito Test. Richard Kent. Ed. by Jane Weinberger. LC 93-61634. 250p. (Orig.). (YA). (gr. 8-12). 1994. pap. 8.95 (*1-883650-03-8*) Windswept Hse.

***Mosquito Thunder: No. 105 Squadron RAF at War 1942-45.** Stuart R. Scott. (Illus.). 224p. 1999. 36.00 (*0-7509-1800-4*, Pub. by Sutton Pub Ltd) Bks Intl VA.

Mosquito Walk Around. Ron Mackay. LC 99-189609. (Walk Around Ser.: Vol. 15). (Illus.). 80p. 1998. pap. 14.95 (*0-89747-396-5*, 5515) Squad Sig Pubns.

***Mosquito Zumbador: (The Buzzing Mosquito)** Veronica Uribe. (SPA., Illus.). (J). (gr. 1-4). 2000. 6.95 (*980-257-232-2*, Pub. by Ediciones Ekare) Kane-Miller Bk.

Mosquitobush: Yankee Stories. Francis Tolman. (Illus.). 1963. 15.00 (*0-87233-859-2*) Bauhan.

Mosquitoes see New Creepy Crawly Collection

Mosquitoes. Cheryl Coughlan. 1999. 13.25 (*0-516-21831-X*) Capstone Pr.

***Mosquitoes.** Mary Ann McDonald. LC 98-49135. (Illus.). 32p. (J). 1999. lib. bdg. write for info. (*1-56766-635-3*) Childs World.

Mosquitoes: A Facsimile & Transcription of the University of Virginia Holograph Manuscript. William Faulkner. Ed. by Thomas McHaney & David Vander Meulen. LC 98-206074. (Illus.). xx, 99p. 1997. 75.00 (*1-883631-05-X*) Biblgraph Soc.

Mosquitoes: A Handbook for Survival. Ken Kaplan & Ted Krueger. LC 93-8894. (Pamphlet Architecture Ser.: No. 14). (Illus.). 80p. (Orig.). 1993. pap. 12.95 (*1-878271-83-0*) Princeton Arch.

Mosquitoes: A Novel. William Faulkner. 304p. 1996. reprint ed. pap. 13.00 (*0-87140-167-3*, Pub. by Liveright) Norton.

Mosquitoes in the Classroom. Univ. of Wisconsin-Madison Medical Staff. 144p. 1995. pap. text, spiral bd. 14.95 (*0-7872-0730-6*) Kendall-Hunt.

Mosquitoes of California. 3rd ed. R. M. Bohart & R. K. Washino. LC 77-84551. 164p. 1978. pap. 6.00 (*0-931876-15-X*, 4084) ANR Pubns CA.

Mosquitoes to Wolves: The Evolution of the Airborne Forward Air Controller. Gary Robert Lester. LC 97-18377. (Illus.). 294p. 1987. pap. 18.00 (*1-58566-033-7*) Air Univ.

Mosquitos, 1927. William Faulkner. Ed. by J. Blotner. (William Faulkner Manuscripts). 504p. 1987. text 80.00 (*0-8240-6804-1*) Garland.

Moss & Adams' Heart Disease in Infants, Children & Adolescents: Including the Fetus & Young Adult. 6th ed. Hugh D. Allen et al. Orig. Title: Adams' Heart Disease in Infants, Children, & Adolescents. 1,472p. text 259.00 (*0-683-30742-8*) Lppncott W & W.

Moss & Adams' Heart Disease in Infants, Children & Adolescents: Including the Fetus & Young Adult, 2 vols., Set. 5th ed. Ed. by George C. Emmanouilides et al. Orig. Title: Adams' Heart Disease in Infants, Children, & Adolescents. (Illus.). 2016p. 1994. 249.00 (*0-683-02999-1*) Lppncott W & W.

Moss Burning: Poems. Marianne Boruch. LC 93-85658. (Field Poetry Ser.: No. 2). 90p. 1993. 22.95 (*0-932440-64-9*); pap. 12.95 (*0-932440-63-0*) Oberlin Coll Pr.

Moss Flora of Central America Pt. 1: Sphagnaceae-Calymperaceae. Bruce Allen. (Monographs in Systematic Botany from the Missouri Botanical Garden: No. 49). (Illus.). 242p. 1994. 27.95 (*0-915279-26-6*) Miss Botan.

***Moss Flora of Central America Pt. 2: Pottiaceae-Orthotrichaceae.** Ed. by Bruce Allen. (Illus.). 2000. write for info. (*0-915279-87-8*) Miss Botan.

***Moss Flora of China Vol. 1: Sphagnaceae Through Leucobryaceae.** Ed. by Gao Chien et al. (Moss Flora of China Ser.). (Illus.). viii, 288p. 1999. 75.00 (*0-915279-68-1*) Miss Botan.

***Moss Flora of China Vol. 2: Fissidentaceae Through Ptychomitriaceae.** Ed. by Gao Chien et al. (Illus.). 2000. 75.00 (*0-915279-89-4*) Miss Botan.

Moss Flora of Mexico. Ed. by Aaron J. Sharp et al. (Memoirs Ser.: No. 69). (Illus.). 809p. 1993. 195.00 (*0-89327-379-1*) NY Botanical.

Moss Gardening: Including Lichens, Liverworts, & Other Miniatures. George H. Schenk. LC 96-9357. (Illus.). 262p. 1997. 34.95 (*0-88192-370-2*) Timber.

Moss Gown. William H. Hooks. (J). 1987. 12.15 (*0-606-04753-0*, Pub. by Turtleback) Demco.

Moss Gown. William H. Hooks. (Illus.). 48p. (J). (ps-3). 1990. reprint ed. pap. 6.95 (*0-395-54793-8*, Clarion Bks) HM.

Moss Haggadah. 2nd ed. write for info. (*0-9624473-4-X*) Bet Alpha Editions.

Moss' Heart Disease in Infants, Children & Adolescents, 2 vols., Set. 4th ed. Ed. by Forrest Adams. 1085p. 1989. text 172.00 (*0-683-00052-7*) Lppncott W & W.

***Moss Lamps, Lighting the 50's.** Donald Brian-Johnson & Leslie Pina. (Illus.). 192p. 1999. 49.95 (*0-7643-1002-X*) Schiffer.

***Moss Landing Hill Site: A Technical Report on Archaeological Studies at CA-MNT-234.** Randall Milliken et al. 432p. 1999. pap. text 45.00 (*1-55567-926-9*) Coyote Press.

Moss, Mallards & Mules: And Other Hunting & Fishing Stories. Bob Brister. LC 98-45553. (Illus.). 216p. 1998. reprint ed. 30.00 (*0-924357-73-8*) Countrysport Pr.

Moss Moon: New Work from the Institute of American Indian Arts. Ed. by Jody Barnes et al. 192p. (C). 1998. pap. text 8.00 (*1-881396-14-2*) IOA Indian Arts.

Moss Pillows. Rosemary Wells. LC 91-41600. (Voyage to the Bunny Planet Ser.). (Illus.). 32p. (J). (ps-3). 1992. 12.89 (*0-8037-1177-8*, Dial Yng Read) Peng Put Young Read.

Moss' Radiation Oncology: Rationale, Technique & Results. 7th ed. James D. Cox. LC 93-34732. (Illus.). 1040p. (C). (gr. 13). 1993. text 155.00 (*0-8016-6940-5*, 06940) Mosby Inc.

Moss' Radiation Oncology: Rationale, Technique & Results. 7th rev. ed. Ed. by James D. Cox. LC 93-34732. 1992. 40.00 (*0-8016-6906-5*) Mosby Inc.

Moss Side Massive. Karline Smith. 304p. 1996. pap. 9.95 (*1-874509-09-3*) LPC InBook.

Moss That Rides on the Back of the Rock. Kenneth Fifer. LC 93-19687. 64p. 1993. pap. 14.95 (*0-7734-2765-1*, Mellen Poetry Pr) E Mellen.

Mossa. Frank Dituri. (Illus.). 70p. (Orig.). 1985. pap. text. write for info. (*0-318-68760-7*) Edit Heliodor.

Mossadegh Era: Roots of the Iranian Revolution. Sepehr Zabih. LC 81-80670. 1982. 35.00 (*0-941702-00-6*); pap. 12.95 (*0-941702-01-4*) Lake View Pr.

Mossbauer Effect & Its Application in Chemistry: A Symposium Organized by Carl W. Seidel for Nuclear Science & Engineering Corp., Pittsburgh, PA. Held in New York, NY, September 12, 1966. American Chemical Society Staff. LC 67-31407. (Advances in Chemistry Ser.: No. 68). (Illus.). 188p. 1967. reprint ed. pap. 58.30 (*0-608-06794-6*, 206699100009) Bks Demand.

Mossbauer Effect Methodology, Vol. 1. Symposium on Mossbauer Effect Methodology Staff. Ed. by Irwin J. Gruverman. LC 65-21188. 208p. 1965. reprint ed. pap. 64.50 (*0-608-05503-4*, 206597200001) Bks Demand.

Mossbauer Effect Methodology, Vol. 2. Symposium on Mossbauer Effect Methodology Staff. Ed. by Irwin J. Gruverman. LC 65-21188. (Illus.). 199p. 1965. reprint ed. pap. 61.70 (*0-608-05504-2*, 206597200002) Bks Demand.

Mossbauer Spectroscopy. Ed. by D. P. Dickson & F. J. Berry. (Illus.). 286p. 1987. text 69.95 (*0-521-26101-5*) Cambridge U Pr.

Mossbauer Spectroscopy. A. Vertes et al. 1979. pap. 180.00 (*963-05-1670-5*, Pub. by Akade Kiado) St Mut.

Mossbauer Spectroscopy: Principles & Applications of the Techniques. Alfred G. Maddock. 250p. 1998. 89.00 (*1-898563-16-0*, Pub. by Horwood Pub) Paul & Co Pubs.

Mossbauer Spectroscopy & Its Applications. (Panel Proceedings Ser.). (Illus.). 424p. (Orig.). 1972. pap. 70.00 (*92-0-131072-2*, ISP304, Pub. by IAEA) Bernan Associates.

Mossbauer Spectroscopy & Its Chemical Applications. Ed. by John Stevens & Gopal K. Shenoy. LC 81-17540. (Advances in Chemistry Ser.: No. 194). 1981. 76.95 (*0-8412-0593-0*) Am Chemical.

Mossbauer Spectroscopy & Its Chemical Applications. Ed. by John G. Stevens & Gopal K. Shenoy. LC 81-17540. (Advances in Chemistry Ser.: Vol. 194). 655p. 1981. reprint ed. pap. 200.00 (*0-608-03500-9*, 206421900008) Bks Demand.

Mossbauer Spectroscopy Applied to Inorganic Chemistry, Vol. 1. Ed. by Gary J. Long. LC 84-13417. (Modern Inorganic Chemistry Ser.). (Illus.). 686p. (C). 1984. text 174.00 (*0-306-41647-6*, Kluwer Plenum) Kluwer Academic.

Mossbauer Spectroscopy Applied to Inorganic Chemistry, Vol. 2. G. J. Long. LC 84-13417. (Modern Inorganic Chemistry Ser.). (Illus.). 642p. (C). 1987. text 145.00 (*0-306-42507-6*, Kluwer Plenum) Kluwer Academic.

Mossbauer Spectroscopy Applied to Inorganic Chemistry, Vol. 3. G. J. Long & F. Grandjean. (Modern Inorganic Chemistry Ser.). (Illus.). 660p. (C). 1989. text 145.00 (*0-306-43073-8*, Kluwer Plenum) Kluwer Academic.

Mossbauer Spectroscopy Applied to Magnetism & Materials Science, Vol. 1. G. J. Long & F. Grandjean. LC 93-14059. (Modern Inorganic Chemistry Ser.). (Illus.). 496p. (C). 1993. text 110.00 (*0-306-44447-X*, Kluwer Plenum) Kluwer Academic.

Mossbauer Spectroscopy Applied to Magnetism & Materials Science, Vol. 2. Ed. by Gary J. Long & Fernande Grandjean. (Modern Inorganic Chemistry Ser.). (Illus.). 330p. (C). 1996. text 107.00 (*0-306-45398-3*, Kluwer Plenum) Kluwer Academic.

Mossbauer Spectroscopy in Materials Science. Marcel Miglierini & Dimitris Petridis. LC 99-13873. (Nato Science Ser.). 1999. write for info. (*0-7923-5640-3*) Kluwer Academic.

Mossbauer Spectroscopy of Sophisticated Oxides. Zoltan Homonnay et al. 400p. 1996. 75.00 (*963-05-6953-1*, Pub. by Akade Kiado) Intl Spec Bk.

Mossberg Guide to Modern Slug Shooting . . . & More. 2nd rev. ed. R. W. Zwirz & Edward A. Matunas. (Illus.). 128p. 1997. pap. 9.95 (*0-9624421-1-9*) O F Mossberg & Sons.

***Mosser - Musser Family.** Anita L. Mott. 227p. 1999. pap. 24.00 (*0-7884-1187-X*, M577) Heritage Bk.

Mosses: Utah & the West. Seville Flowers. Ed. by Arthur Holmgren. LC 72-96422. (Illus.). xii, 567p. (C). 1973. 7.95 (*0-8425-1524-0*, Friends of the Library) Brigham.

Mosses & Liverworts. 2nd ed. Louisa S. Conard. (Pictured Key Nature Ser.). 316p. (C). 1979. text. write for info. (*0-697-04768-7*, WCB McGr Hill) McGrw-H Hghr Educ.

Mosses & Liverworts of Rainforest in Tasmania & South-Eastern Australia. S. J. Jarman & B. A. Fuhrer. LC 96-133470. (Illus.). 134p. 1995. pap. 24.95 (*0-643-05685-8*, Pub. by CSIRO) Accents Pubns.

***Mosses & Other Bryophytes: An Illustrated Glossary.** Bill Malcolm & Nancy Malcolm. (Illus.). 226p. 2000. 39.95 (*0-473-06730-7*) Timber.

Mosses from an Old Manse. Nathaniel Hawthorne. 402p. Date not set. 27.95 (*0-8488-2289-7*) Amereon Ltd.

Mosses from an Old Manse. Nathaniel Hawthorne. LC 79-122717. (Short Story Index Reprint Ser.). 1980. 39.95 (*0-8369-3550-0*) Ayer.

Mosses from an Old Manse. Nathaniel Hawthorne. Ed. by William Charvat et al. LC 73-5364. (Centenary Edition of the Works of Nathaniel Hawthorne: Vol. 10). 664p. 1974. text 80.00 (*0-8142-0203-9*) Ohio St U Pr.

Mosses from an Old Manse. Nathaniel Hawthorne. (Notable American Authors Ser.). 1992. reprint ed. lib. bdg. 75.00 (*0-7812-3043-8*) Rprt Serv.

Mosses, Lichens & Ferns of Northwest North America. Dale H. Vitt et al. 1988. pap. 24.95 (*0-919433-41-3*) Lone Pine.

Mosses of Amazonian Ecuador. Steven P. Churchill. Ed. by Henrik Balslev. (AAU Reports: No. 35). (Illus.). 211p. (C). 1995. pap. text 12.95 (*87-87600-62-5*, Pub. by Aarhus Univ Pr) David Brown.

Mosses of Arctic Alaska. William C. Steere. (Bryophytorum Bibliotheca Ser.: No. 14). (Illus.). 1978. lib. bdg. 144.00 (*3-7682-1181-9*) Lubrecht & Cramer.

Mosses of Eastern North America, 2 vols. Howard A. Crum & Lewis E. Anderson. LC 79-24789. (Illus.). 576p. 1981. text 274.00 (*0-231-04516-6*) Col U Pr.

Mosses of Indiana. W. Welch. 1957. 25.00 (*1-883362-08-3*) IN Acad Sci.

Mosses of New Zealand. Jessica Beever et al. 1996. 79.95 (*0-908569-52-1*, Pub. by Univ Otago Pr) Intl Spec Bk.

Mosses of North America. Ed. by Ronald J. Taylor & Alan E. Leviton. 170p. (Orig.). 1980. 11.95 (*0-934394-02-4*) AAASPD.

Mosses of the Gulf South: From the Rio Grande to the Apalachicola. William Dean Reese. LC 83-889. (Illus.). xvi, 252p. 1984. text 35.00 (*0-8071-1110-4*) La State U Pr.

Mosses of the Society Islands. Henry O. Whittier. LC 75-23309. (Illus.). 420p. reprint ed. pap. 130.20 (*0-7837-5013-7*, 204468000004) Bks Demand.

Mossflower. Brian Jacques. (Redwall Ser.). 384p. (Orig.). (J). (gr. 4-8). 1990. mass mkt. 5.99 (*0-380-70828-0*, Avon Bks) Morrow Avon.

Mossflower. Brian Jacques. (Redwall Ser.). (Illus.). 432p. (Orig.). (J). (gr. 4-8). 1988. 21.99 (*0-399-21549-2*, Philomel) Peng Put Young Read.

Mossflower. Brian Jacques. (Redwall Ser.). (Illus.). 373p. (Orig.). (J). (gr. 4-7). 1998. reprint ed. mass mkt. 5.99 (*0-441-00576-4*) Ace Bks.

Mossi. Kibibi V. Mack-Williams. LC 95-20839. (Heritage Library of African Peoples: Set 2). (Illus.). 64p. (YA). (gr. 7-12). 1996. lib. bdg. 16.95 (*0-8239-1984-6*) Rosen Group.

Mossy Cape: 3 Act Drama. Rosemary Poole-Carter. (Illus.). 27p. 1994. pap. 4.00 (*0-88680-396-9*) I E Clark.

***Most Amazing Chess Moves of all Time.** John Emms. (Illus.). 160p. 2000. pap. 19.95 (*1-901983-29-3*, Pub. by Gambit) BHB Intl.

Most Amazing Dinosaur. James Stevenson. LC 99-25347. (Illus.). 32p. (J). (gr. k-3). 2000. 15.95 (*0-688-16432-3*, Grenwillow Bks); lib. bdg. 15.89 (*0-688-16433-1*, Grenwillow Bks) HarpC Child Bks.

***Most Amazing Man Who Ever Lived.** Robert Rankin. 2000. pap. 10.95 (*0-552-14211-5*, Pub. by Transworld Publishers Ltd) Trafalgar.

Most Ancient Egypt. William C. Hayes. Ed. by Keith C. Seele. LC DT0060.H4. (Midway Reprint Ser.). (Illus.). 180p. reprint ed. pap. 55.80 (*0-608-18228-1*, 205663600078) Bks Demand.

Most Approved & Long Experienced Water-Works. Rowland Vaughan. LC 77-7437. (English Experience Ser.: No. 898). 1977. reprint ed. lib. bdg. 35.00 (*90-221-0898-8*) Walter J Johnson.

Most Art Sucks: Five Years of Coagula. Mat Gleason & Walter Robinson. Ed. by Tom Patchett. (Illus.). 200p. 1998. pap. 19.95 (*1-889195-16-2*, Pub. by Smart Art Pr) Dist Art Pubs.

Most Asked Questions about Architecture & Building, Vol. 1. William P. Dirr. 258p. 1994. pap. 34.95 (*0-9638666-0-5*) Archi-Tech Pr.

Most Asked Questions about the Society of Saint Pius X: A Handbook Explaining Their Positions on the Pope, the New Mass, the New Code of Canon Law. Fathers of Holy Cross Seminary Staff. LC 98-118851. 130p. 1997. pap. 6.95 (*0-935952-43-8*) Angelus Pr.

Most Baffling, Mrs. Hudson: An Emma Hudson Mystery. Sydney Hosier. 256p. 1998. mass mkt. 5.50 (*0-380-79216-8*, Avon Bks) Morrow Avon.

Most Beautiful & Handy Name: Wisconsin Place Names in the St. Croix Valley. Timothy L. Ericson. 120p. (Orig.). 1997. pap. 14.95 (*1-878619-24-1*) U Wisc-River Falls Pr.

Most Beautiful Girl. Jei D. Lewis. 250p. 1998. pap. 12.95 (*0-9639917-4-4*) Writers Unltd.

Most Beautiful Girl in the World: Beauty Pageants & National Identity. Sarah Banet-Weiser. LC 99-19922. 280p. 1999. 48.00 (*0-520-21789-6*, Pub. by U CA Pr) Cal Prin Full Svc.

Most Beautiful Girls in the World: Beauty Pageants & National Identity. Sarah Banet-Weiser. LC 99-19922. 290p. 1999. 17.95 (*0-520-21791-8*, Pub. by U CA Pr) Cal Prin Full Svc.

Most Beautiful House in the World. Witold Rybczynski. (Illus.). 240p. 1990. pap. 12.95 (*0-14-010566-2*, Penguin Bks) Viking Penguin.

Most Beautiful Kid in the World. Jennifer A. Ericsson. LC 95-53063. (Illus.). 32p. (J). 1996. 16.00 (*0-688-13941-8*, Wm Morrow); lib. bdg. 15.93 (*0-688-13942-6*, Wm Morrow) Morrow Avon.

Most Beautiful Man in Existence: The Scandalous Life of Alexander Lesassier. Lisa Rosner. LC 98-48567. (Illus.). 304p. 1999. 29.95 (*0-8122-3486-3*) U of Pa Pr.

Most Beautiful Mathematical Formulas. Lionel Salem et al. LC 00-41. 141p. 1992. 24.95 (*0-471-55276-3*) Wiley.

Most Beautiful Mathematical Formulas. Lionel Salem et al. LC 91-31959. (Illus.). 141p. 1997. pap. 14.95 (*0-471-17662-1*) Wiley.

Most Beautiful Molecule: The Discovery of the Buckyball. Hugh Aldersey-Williams. LC 95-12422. 340p. 1995. 24.95 (*0-471-10938-X*) Wiley.

Most Beautiful Molecule: The Discovery of the Buckyball. Hugh Aldersey-Williams. (Illus.). 340p. 1997. pap. 16.95 (*0-471-19333-X*) Wiley.

Most Beautiful Names. Sheikh T. Al-Halveti. 100p. 1996. pap. 13.00 (*0-614-21184-0*, 805); pap. 13.00 (*0-614-21315-0*, 805) Kazi Pubns.

Most Beautiful Names. Sheikh Tosun Bayrak al-Jerrahi al Halveti. LC 84-50951. (Illus.). 192p. 1985. pap. 14.00 (*0-939660-10-5*) Threshold CA.

Most Beautiful Place in the World. Ann Cameron. (J). 1993. 9.19 (*0-606-05475-8*, Pub. by Turtleback) Demco.

Most Beautiful Place in the World: A Study Guide. Laurie Diamond. Ed. by J. Friedland & R. Kessler. (Novel-Ties Ser.). (J). (gr. 2-4). 1994. pap. text, student ed. 15.95 (*1-56982-056-2*) Lrn Links.

Most Beautiful Roof: Exploring the Rainforest Canopy. Kathryn Lasky. LC 95-48193. (Illus.). 48p. 1997. pap. 8.00 (*0-15-200897-7*) Harcourt.

Most Beautiful Roof in the World. Kathryn Lasky. LC 95-48193. (Illus.). 48p. (J). 1997. 18.00 (*0-15-200893-4*) Harcourt.

Most Beautiful Story: Our Lady of Fatima Coloring Book. 64p. 1987. 3.00 (*0-911988-33-5*, 35969) AMI Pr.

Most Beautiful Tree in the Forest. Joy Jackson McHugh. Ed. by Pamela J. Reid. LC 96-77926. (Illus.). 32p. (J). (ps-6). 1997. 14.95 (*0-9654485-0-9*) Kinder Hse.

***Most Beautiful Villages & Towns of the South.** Photos by Dennis O'Kain. LC 99-96559. (Most Beautiful Villages of... Ser.). (Illus.). 208p. 2000. 40.00 (*0-500-01999-1*, Pub. by Thames Hudson) Norton.

Most Beautiful Villages of Brittany. James Bentley. LC 98-61828. (Illus.). 208p. 1999. 40.00 (*0-500-01935-5*, Pub. by Thames Hudson) Norton.

Most Beautiful Villages of Burgundy. James Bentley. LC 98-60038. (Illus.). 224p. 1998. 40.00 (*0-500-01862-6*, Pub. by Thames Hudson) Norton.

Most Beautiful Villages of England. James Bentley. LC 98-61184. (Most Beautiful Villages Ser.). (Illus.). 208p. 1999. 40.00 (*0-500-01905-3*, Pub. by Thames Hudson) Norton.

Most Beautiful Villages of France. Photos by Dominique Reperant. LC 90-70389. (Illus.). 220p. 1990. 45.00 (*0-500-54162-0*, Pub. by Thames Hudson) Norton.

Most Beautiful Villages of Greece. Mark Ottaway. LC 97-61611. (Illus.). 224p. 1998. 40.00 (*0-500-01834-0*, Pub. by Thames Hudson) Norton.

***Most Beautiful Villages of Ireland.** Photos by Hugh Palmer. LC 99-69558. (Illus.). 208p. 2000. 40.00 (*0-500-01998-3*, Pub. by Thames Hudson) Norton.

Most Beautiful Villages of New England. Len Rubenstein. 1998. pap. 12.95 (*0-500-95049-0*, Pub. by Thames Hudson) Norton.

Most Beautiful Villages of New England. Tom Schachtman. LC 97-60272. (Illus.). 208p. 1997. 40.00 (*0-500-01800-6*, Pub. by Thames Hudson) Norton.

Most Beautiful Villages of Provence. Michael Jacobs. LC 94-60276. (Illus.). 224p. 1994. 40.00 (*0-500-54187-6*, Pub. by Thames Hudson) Norton.

Most Beautiful Villages of the Dordogne: France's Hidden Treasure. James Bentley. LC 96-60055. (Illus.). 224p. 1996. 40.00 (*0-500-54201-5*, Pub. by Thames Hudson) Norton.

Most Beautiful Villages of Tuscany. Photos by Hugh Palmer. LC 95-60274. (Illus.). 224p. 1995. 40.00 (*0-500-01664-X*, Pub. by Thames Hudson) Norton.

Most Beautiful Villages of Tuscany. Hugh Palmer. 1998. pap. 12.95 (*0-500-95050-4*, Pub. by Thames Hudson) Norton.

Most Beautiful Villas of Provence. Hugh Palmer. 1998. pap. 12.95 (*0-500-95048-2*, Pub. by Thames Hudson) Norton.

***Most Beautiful Way to Live.** Ken Bible. 64p. 1999. pap. write for info. (*1-892078-08-2*) Liv the Natural.

An Asterisk (*) at the beginning of an entry indicates that the title is appearing for the first time.

Most Beautiful Woman in Shanghai. Scott Shaw. 89p. (Orig.). 1990. pap. 10.95 (*1-877792-24-1*) Buddha Rose.

***Most Beautiful Woman in the World: The Obsessions, Passions & Courage of Elizabeth Taylor.** Ellis Amburn. 304p. 2000. 25.00 (*0-06-019376-X*, Cliff Street) HarperTrade.

***Most Beautiful Woman in the World: The Obsessions, Passions & Courage of Elizabeth Taylor.** large type ed. Ellis Amburn. (Illus.). 656p. 2000. pap. 25.00 (*0-06-019719-6*) HarpC.

Most Beautiful Woman in Town. Charles Bukowski. 1983. reprint ed. pap. 12.95 (*0-87286-156-2*) City Lights.

Most Beautiful Woman on the Screen: The Fabrication of the Star Greta Garbo. Michaela Krutzen. LC 92-36301. (Studien zum Theater, Film & Fernsehen Ser.: Bd. 19). (Illus.). VIII, 149p. 1992. 33.00 (*3-631-42412-4*) P Lang Pubng.

Most Beloved Bible Passages. Ideals Publications Editors. (Illus.). 160p. 1996. 24.95 (*0-8249-4077-6*, Ideals TN) Ideals.

Most Brilliant Thoughts of All Time: (in Two Lines or Less) John M. Shanahan. Date not set. pap. 13.00 (*0-06-093232-5*) HarpC.

Most Brilliant Thoughts of All Time (In Two Lines or Less) Ed. by John M. Shanahan. LC 99-13454. 336p. 1999. 22.95 incl. cd-rom (*0-06-019411-1*) HarpC.

Most Caring Adults in America. W. Halamandariss. (Profiles in Caring Ser.). 128p. 1997. pap. text 15.00 (*0-9628363-6-2*) Caring Pub.

Most Chimneys Are Crooked. Harry D. Hewitt. Ed. by Elizabeth R. Hewitt. 60p. (Orig.). 1993. pap. text 10.00 (*0-9627244-2-4*) Penn Sounds.

Most Cited Articles from the Yale Law Journal. Ed. by Fred R. Shapiro. LC 91-70588. iv, 1146p. 1987. 65.00 (*0-89941-758-2*, 307170) W S Hein.

Most-Cited Law Review Articles. Fred R. Shapiro. LC 87-81960. iv, 1146p. 1987. lib. bdg. 65.00 (*0-89941-578-4*, 305310) W S Hein.

Most Cited U. S. Courts of Appeals Cases from 1932 until the Late 1980s. Ed. by Robert Schriek. LC 93-80514. xx, 454p. 1994. 65.00 (*0-89941-861-9*, 307380) W S Hein.

Most Common Manual for Medical Students. 2nd ed. Steven M. Grosso. (Orig.). 1997. pap. 14.95 (*1-883205-29-8*) Intl Med Pub.

Most Common Mistakes in English Usage. T. E. Berry. 146p. (C). 1971. reprint ed. pap. 7.95 (*0-07-005053-8*) McGraw.

Most Commonly Asked Questions about "A Course in Miracles" Gloria Wapnick & Kenneth Wapnick. LC 95-2113. 144p. 1995. pap. 8.00 (*0-933291-21-3*) Foun Miracles.

Most Commons in Medicine. Edward F. Goljan. 635p. Date not set. text. write for info. (*0-7216-8759-8*, W B Saunders Co) Harcrt Hlth Sci Grp.

Most Commons in Pathology & Laboratory Medicine. Edward F. Goljan. Ed. by William Schmitt. LC 98-38024. 365p. (C). 1999. pap. text. write for info. (*0-7216-7992-7*, W B Saunders Co) Harcrt Hlth Sci Grp.

Most Complete & Reliable Source of State Information Is Now Also the Most Current & Up to Date: Rankings Across America. 3rd ed. 406p. 1999. 79.95 (*1-56802-447-9*); pap. 44.95 (*1-56802-446-0*) Congr Quarterly.

Most Complete Book Published Canine Lexicon. Andrew DePrisco & James B. Johnson. (Illus.). 896p. 1993. text 89.95 (*0-86622-198-0*, TS175) TFH Pubns.

Most Complete Food Counter. Annette Natow & Jo-Ann Heslin. LC 99-17169. 448p. 1999. per. 16.00 (*0-671-02561-9*, PB Trade Paper) PB.

Most Complex Machine: A Survey of Computers & Computing. David J. Eck. LC 95-32935. (Illus.). 464p. (C). 1995. text 54.00 (*1-56881-054-7*) AK Peters.

***Most Complex Machine: A Survey of Computers & Computing.** David J. Eck. (Illus.). 464p. 2000. pap. 30.00 (*1-56881-128-4*) AK Peters.

Most Convincing Witness. Randall K. Mehew. (Personal Enrichment Ser.). 41p. (Orig.). 1991. pap. write for info. (*0-929985-63-X*) Jackman Pubng.

Most Cunning Workmen. Roy Lewis. LC 85-25244. (Atlantic Ser.). 274 p. 1986. write for info. (*0-89340-966-9*) Chivers N Amer.

Most Cunning Workmen. Roy Lewis. LC 84-23738. 182 p. 1985. 10.95 (*0-312-54907-5*) St Martin.

Most Dangerous Area in the World: John F. Kennedy Confronts Communist Revolution in Latin America. Stephen G. Rabe. LC 98-23112. 272p. 1999. pap. 17.95 (*0-8078-4764-X*); lib. bdg. 39.95 (*0-8078-2461-5*) U of NC Pr.

Most Dangerous Decade: World Militarism & the New Non-Aligned Peace Movement. Ken Coates. (Illus.). 211p. 1984. 42.50 (*0-85124-405-X*, Pub. by Spkesman); pap. 24.00 (*0-85124-406-8*, Pub. by Spkesman) Coronet Bks.

Most Dangerous Game see Creative Short Stories

Most Dangerous Game. Mary Wibberley. (Scarlet Ser.). 1998. mass mkt. 3.99 (*1-85487-873-5*, Pub. by Scarlet Bks) London Brdge.

Most Dangerous Game: Advanced Mantrapping Techniques. Ragnar Benson. (Illus.). 120p. 1986. pap. 16.00 (*0-87364-356-9*) Paladin Pr.

Most Dangerous Jobs in the U. S. A. June A. English. LC 97-26642. (Illus.). 40p. (J). (gr. 1-5). 1998. pap. 4.99 (*0-590-89751-9*) Scholastic Inc.

Most Dangerous Jobs in the U. S. A. June A. English. 1998. 10.09 (*0-606-13623-1*, Pub. by Turtleback) Demco.

Most Dangerous Journal. Roger A. Caras. 1999. pap. 4.99 (*0-14-038227-5*) Viking Penguin.

Most Dangerous Man in America? Pat Robertson & the Rise of the Christian Coalition. Robert Boston. LC 96-4169. 248p. 1996. pap. text 17.95 (*1-57392-053-3*) Prometheus Bks.

Most Dangerous Method: The Story of Jung, Freud & Sabina Spielrein. John Kerr. 624p. 1994. pap. 16.00 (*0-679-73580-1*) Vin Bks.

Most Dangerous Money Book Ever Written. Bruce G. Gould. 444p. (Orig.). 1983. pap. 100.00 (*0-918706-13-0*) B Gould Pubns.

Most Deadly Hate. Sara Woods. 240p. 1987. pap. 3.50 (*0-380-70477-3*, Avon Bks) Morrow Avon.

Most Deadly Retirement. John Miles. 1997. per. 4.99 (*0-373-26252-3*, 1-26252-6, Wrldwide Lib) Harlequin Bks.

Most Deadly Retirement: A Laura Michaels Mystery. John Miles. 246p. 1995. 22.95 (*0-8027-3258-5*) Walker & Co.

Most Defiant Act. Ginny Knight & Hazel Clayton. LC 85-81611. 60p. (Orig.). 1985. pap. 4.50 (*0-940248-25-5*) Guild Pr.

Most Delectable & Pleasant History of Clitiphon & Leucippe. Tatius Achilles. Tr. by W. Burton. LC 77-6841. (English Experience Ser.: No. 837). 1977. reprint ed. lib. bdg. 30.00 (*90-221-0837-6*) Walter J Johnson.

Most Delicious Camping Trip Ever. Alice Bach. LC 76-2956. (Illus.). 48p. (J). (gr. k-3). 1976. 10.95 (*0-06-020338-2*) HarpC Child Bks.

Most Delightful Station: The British Army on the Curragh of Kildare, Ireland. Con Costello. LC 96-170733. 432p. 1996. 59.95 (*1-898256-08-X*) Dufour.

***Most Delightful Station: The British Army on the Curragh of Kildore, Ireland, 1855-1922.** Con Costello. (Illus.). 432p. 1999. pap. 27.95 (*1-898256-73-X*, Pub. by Collins Press) Irish Bks Media.

Most Democratic Sport: Basketball & Culture in the Central Piedmont, 1893-1994. Pamela Grundy. (Illus.). 50p. (Orig.). 1994. pap. 10.95 (*0-9640482-3-X*) Museum N South.

***Most Desperate Situation 1854-1864: Frontier Adventures of a Young Scout.** Walter Cooper. 328p. 2000. 29.95 (*1-56044-891-1*, Falcon) Falcon Pub Inc.

Most Detestable Crime: New Philosophical Essays on Rape. Ed. by Keith Burgess-Jackson. LC 98-26835. 328p. 1999. text 45.00 (*0-19-512075-2*) OUP.

Most Diplomatic General: The Life of Lord Robertson of Oakridge. David G. Williamson. LC 97-108341. 1997. 32.95 (*1-85753-180-9*, Pub. by Brasseys) Brasseys.

Most Distinguished Characters on the American Frontier, Robert Looney (B. 1692-1702, D. 1770) of Augusta (Now Botetourt) County, Virginia, & Some of His Descendants, with Histories of the Great Road, Looney's Ferry, Crow's Ferry, Anderson's Ferry, Boyd's Ferry, & Beale's Bridge. Madge L. Crane & Phillip L. Crane. LC 98-72164. (Illus.). 442p. 1998. 40.00 (*0-9664321-1-8*) P L Crane.

***Most Eligible . . . Daddy: Sexy Single Dads.** Tina Leonard. 1999. per. 3.99 (*0-373-16771-7*, 1-16771-7, Harlequin) Harlequin Bks.

Most Eligible Bachelor. Jessica Steele. (Romance Ser.: No. 448). 1999. mass mkt. 3.50 (*0-373-17448-9*, 1-17448-1) Harlequin Bks.

Most Eligible Bachelor. large type ed. 1999. 21.95 (*0-263-15938-8*) Chivers N Amer.

Most Eligible Dad. Karen R. Smith. (Romance Ser.). 1996. per. 3.25 (*0-373-19174-X*, 1-19174-1) Silhouette.

Most Eligible M. D. The Bachelor Bet. Joan Elliott Pickart. (Special Edition Ser.). 1999. per. 4.25 (*0-373-24262-X*, 1-24262-7) Silhouette.

Most Embarrassing Mother in the World. Peter Filichia. 192p. (J). 1991. pap. 3.50 (*0-380-76084-3*, Avon Bks) Morrow Avon.

Most Excellent & Lamentable Tragedie of Romeo & Juliet: A Critical Edition. William Shakespeare. Ed. by George W. Williams. LC 64-10526. xviii, 170p. 1964. text 32.95 (*0-8223-0187-3*) Duke.

Most Excellent Book of Dress Up. Moe Casey. LC 96-48290. (Most Excellent Book of...Ser.). (Illus.). 32p. (J). (gr. 4-6). 1997. lib. bdg. 19.90 (*0-7613-0550-5*, Copper Beech Bks) Millbrook Pr.

Most Excellent Book of Dress Up. Moe Casey. (Most Excellent Book of...Ser.). (Illus.). 32p. (J). (gr. 4-6). 1997. pap. 6.95 (*0-7613-0575-0*, Copper Beech Bks) Millbrook Pr.

Most Excellent Book of Face Painting. Margaret Lincoln. LC 96-48466. (Illus.). 32p. (J). (gr. 4-6). 1997. lib. bdg. 19.90 (*0-7613-0551-3*, Copper Beech Bks) Millbrook Pr.

Most Excellent Book of Face Painting. Margaret Lincoln. LC 96-48466. (Most Excellent Book...Ser.). (Illus.). 32p. (J). (gr. 4-6). 1997. pap. 6.95 (*0-7613-0576-9*, Copper Beech Bks) Millbrook Pr.

Most Excellent Book of How to Be a Cheerleader. Bob Kiralfy. LC 97-8011. (Most Excellent Book of...Ser.). (J). 1997. lib. bdg. 19.90 (*0-7613-0617-X*, Copper Beech Bks) Millbrook Pr.

Most Excellent Book of How to Be a Cheerleader. Bob Kiralfy. LC 97-8011. (Most Excellent Book of . . . Ser.). (Illus.). 32p. (J). (gr. 4-6). 1997. pap. 5.95 (*0-7613-0631-5*, Copper Beech Bks) Millbrook Pr.

Most Excellent Book of How to Be a Clown. Catherine Perkins. (Illus.). 32p. (J). (gr. 4-6). 1996. pap. 6.95 (*0-7613-0499-1*, Copper Beech Bks); lib. bdg. 19.90 (*0-7613-0486-X*, Copper Beech Bks) Millbrook Pr.

Most Excellent Book of How to Be a Juggler. Mitch Mitchelson. LC 97-8012. (Most Excellent Book of Ser.). (Illus.). 32p. (J). (gr. 4-6). 1997. pap. 6.95 (*0-7613-0632-3*, Copper Beech Bks); lib. bdg. 19.90 (*0-7613-0618-8*, Copper Beech Bks) Millbrook Pr.

Most Excellent Book of How to Be a Magician. Peter Eldin. (Illus.). 32p. (J). (gr. 4-6). 1996. pap. 6.95 (*0-7613-0473-8*, Copper Beech Bks); lib. bdg. 19.90 (*0-7613-0458-4*, Copper Beech Bks) Millbrook Pr.

Most Excellent Book of How to Be a Puppeteer. Roger Lade. LC 96-12641. (Illus.). 32p. (J). (gr. 4-6). 1996. 5.95 (*0-7613-0505-X*, Copper Beech Bks); lib. bdg. 19.90 (*0-7613-0526-2*, Copper Beech Bks) Millbrook Pr.

Most Excellent Book of How to Do Card Tricks. Peter Eldin. LC 96-7973. (Illus.). 32p. (J). (gr. 4-6). 1996. pap. 5.95 (*0-7613-0504-1*, Copper Beech Bks); lib. bdg. 19.90 (*0-7613-0525-4*, Copper Beech Bks) Millbrook Pr.

Most Excellent Differences: Essays on Using Type Theory in the Composition Classroom. Thomas C. Thompson. LC 96-43373. (Illus.). 200p. (Orig.). 1997. pap. text 17.00 (*0-935652-29-9*) Ctr Applications Psych.

Most Excellent Homish Apothecarye, No. 43. Von Brunveig Hieronymus. LC 68-54620. 1968. reprint ed. 30.00 (*90-221-0043-X*) Walter J Johnson.

Most Excellent Instruction for Keeping Merchants Bookes of Accounts. John Carpenter. LC 76-57368. (English Experience Ser.: No. 786). 1977. reprint ed. lib. bdg. 30.00 (*90-221-0786-8*) Walter J Johnson.

Most Excellent Majesty, a History of Mt. Greylock. Deborah E. Burns & Lauren R. Stevens. Ed. by George Wislocki. (Illus.). 112p. (Orig.). 1988. pap. 12.95 (*0-9620959-0-7*) Berkshire Natural.

Most Excellent Sir: Letters Received by Sam Houston, President of the Republic of Texas Columbia 1836-1837. Ed. by James L. Haley. (Illus.). 96p. 1987. 48.00 (*0-9616212-2-2*); 125.00 (*0-9616212-3-0*) Duncan & Gladstone.

Most Excellent Treaties of the Three Kings of Coleyne. LC 74-80169. (English Experience Ser.: No. 648). (Illus.). 91p. 1974. reprint ed. 25.00 (*90-221-0648-9*) Walter J Johnson.

Most Excellent Way: Overcoming Chronic Issues That Divide the Church. Eldred Echols. LC 93-86981. (Faith Focus Adult Studies). 1994. pap. 9.95 (*0-8344-0233-5*) Sweet Pub.

Most Excellent Works of Chirurgerye Made M. T. Vignon. Johannes De Vigo. Tr. by B. Traheron. LC 68-54639. (English Experience Ser.: No. 67). 540p. 1968. reprint ed. 83.00 (*90-221-0067-7*) Walter J Johnson.

***Most Exceptional Quest.** Sarah Westleigh. (Readers Choice Ser.). 2000. mass mkt. 4.50 (*0-373-51114-0*, 1-51114-6, Harlequin) Harlequin Bks.

Most Fabulous Story Ever Told. Paul Rudnick. pap. 5.95 (*0-8222-1720-1*) Dramatists Play.

***Most Fabulous Story Ever Told: And Mr. Charles, Currently of Palm Beach.** Paul Rudnick. 2000. pap. 12.95 (*1-58567-052-9*, Pub. by Overlook Pr) Penguin Putnam.

Most Famous Soldier in America: Nelson A. Miles, 1839-1925. Arthur J. Amchan. (Illus.). 214p. 1989. pap. 14.95 (*0-9617132-1-6*) Amchan Pubns.

Most Fantastic Fakebook in the World. rev. ed. 752p. (YA). 1997. pap. 49.95 (*0-7692-1620-X*) Wrner Bros.

Most Favored Nation: The Republican Revisionists & U. S. Tariff Policy, 1897-1912. Paul Wolman. LC 91-50792. xxviii, 328p. (C). 1992. 22.50 (*0-8078-2022-9*) U of NC Pr.

Most Fortunate Ship: A Narrative History of Old Ironsides. rev. ed. Tyrone G. Martin. LC 96-39863. (Illus.). 440p. 1997. 35.00 (*1-55750-588-8*) Naval Inst Pr.

Most Frequent Diagnoses & Procedures for DRGs, by Insurance Status. Ed. by Cassandra Swartz. (Illus.). 132p. 1998. reprint ed. pap. text 30.00 (*0-7881-4246-1*) DIANE Pub.

Most Frequent Value: Introduction to a Modern Conception of Statistics. Ferenc Steiner. 315p. (C). 1991. 117.00 (*963-05-5687-1*, Pub. by Akade Kiado) St Mut.

***Most Frequently Used Standards for Behavioral Health Care Services for Tailored or Extension Surveys.** Joint Commission on Accreditation of Healthcare Organizations. 190p. 1998. pap. 30.00 (*0-86688-615-X*, BHCT-99) Joint Comm Hlthcare.

Most Frightful Deception: The Today's English Version & Translator Robert Bratcher. 2nd rev. ed. David W. Cloud. 27p. 1986. pap. 2.00 (*1-58318-008-7*, WOLO3113) Way of Life.

Most Fundamental Legal Right: Habeas Corpus in the Commonwealth. David Clark & Gerard McCoy. LC 99-88625. 380p. 2000. text 90.00 (*0-19-826584-0*) OUP.

Most German of the Arts: Musicology & Society from the Weimar Republic to the End of Hitler's Reich. Pamela M. Potter. LC 97-50585. 364p. 1998. 40.00 (*0-300-07228-7*) Yale U Pr.

Most Happy Clip Art of the Thirties, Forties & Fifties. Ed. by Jerry Jankowski. LC 92-74313. 120p. 1992. text 15.95 (*0-88108-109-4*) Art Dir.

Most Happy Clip Art of the Thirties, Forties & Fifties, Set. Ed. by Jerry Jankowski. LC 92-74313. 120p. 1992. disk 89.95 (*0-685-63093-5*) Art Dir.

Most Happy Fella. (Vocal Score Ser.). 272p. 1983. per. 45.00 (*0-88188-472-3*, 00448248) H Leonard.

Most Happy Fella: Vocal Selections. (Illus.). 32p. 1983. pap. 8.95 (*0-88188-205-4*, 00446746) H Leonard.

Most High. Maurice Blanchot. Tr. & Intro. by Allan Stoekl. LC 95-31873. (French Modernist Library). xxxii, 258p. 1996. text 40.00 (*0-8032-1240-2*) U of Nebr Pr.

Most High: Seeing the Almighty. Lester Sumrall. 117p. (C). 1985. pap. text 12.00 (*0-937580-88-0*) Sumrall Pubng.

Most High God. Renald E. Showers. LC 82-90990. 1982. pap. 9.95 (*0-915540-30-4*) Frnds Israel.

Most High Illuminations. William Hutton. LC 88-2443. (Illus.). 62p. 1988. pap. text 4.00 (*0-943123-05-4*) Arjuna Lib Pr.

Most Holy Place. (Spurgeon Collection). 1996. 27.99 (*1-85792-195-X*, Pub. by Christian Focus) Spring Arbor Dist.

Most Holy Tablet. Baha'u'llah. Tr. by Shoghi Effendi & Habib Taherzadeh. (Illus.). 72p. 1995. 19.95 (*1-870989-39-2*); pap. 13.95 (*1-870989-40-6*) Bahai.

Most Holy Theotokos: Contemplations. Lazar Puhalo. 57p. Date not set. pap. 6.00 (*1-879038-51-X*, 9020) Synaxis Pr.

***Most Holy Trinosophia: The New Revelation of the Divine Feminine.** Robert Powell & Daniel Andreev. 144p. 2000. pap. 16.95 (*0-88010-480-5*) Anthroposophic.

Most Holy Trinosophia of the Comte de St. Germain. Comte de St. Germain. (Illus.). 221p. 1985. 16.95 (*0-89314-417-7*) Philos Res.

Most Honest People. Bill Lufburrow. LC 80-69253. (Illus.). (Orig.). 1980. pap. 4.95 (*0-918464-23-4*) D Armstrong.

Most Humble Servants: The Advisory Role of Early Judges. Stewart Jay. LC 97-8983. 288p. 1997. 35.00 (*0-300-07018-7*) Yale U Pr.

Most Illustrious Order: The Order of St. Patrick & Its Knights. Peter Galloway. 320p. 1999. 90.00 (*0-906290-23-6*) Boydell & Brewer.

Most Important Building in Town. Garry Hurle. (Illus.). 54p. (J). (gr. 1-6). 1994. 12.95 (*0-85572-210-X*, Pub. by Hill Content Pubng) Seven Hills Bk.

Most Important Christmas. James H. Nelesen. 32p. (J). (gr. 5-9). 1985. 8.99 (*0-570-04110-4*, 56-1521) Concordia.

Most Important Decision see Decision Mas Importante Nunca Antes Hecha

Most Important Decision You'll Ever Make. Joyce Meyer. 80p. (Orig.). 1996. mass mkt. 4.99 (*0-89274-940-7*, HH-940) Harrison Hse.

Most Important Decision You'll Ever Make. Joyce Meyer. (Orig.). pap. 3.00 (*0-944834-02-7*) Life Word-Meyer Ministries.

Most Important Lessons in Life. Rachel Chandler. 1998. 10.95 (*1-86204-421-X*, Pub. by Element MA) Penguin Putnam.

Most Important Lessons in Life: Letters to a Young Girl. Rachel Chandler. LC 98-24918. (Illus.). 128p. 1998. 10.95 (*1-86204-420-1*, Pub. by Element MA) Penguin Putnam.

Most Important Picture: A Very Tender Manual for Taking Pictures of Stillborn Babies & Infants Who Die. Joy Johnson & Marvin Johnson. 1985. 10.00 (*1-56123-014-6*) Centering Corp.

Most Important Questions a Surety Can Ask about Bad Faith Claims. LC 93-71307. 104p. 1993. pap. 24.95 (*0-89707-879-9*, 519-0222, ABA Tort) Amer Bar Assn.

Most Important Questions a Surety Can Ask about Performance Bonds. Steven J. Strawbridge & Lawrence Lerner. LC 97-74089. x, 224p. 1997. write for info. (*1-57073-509-3*) Amer Bar Assn.

Most Important Questions a Surety Can Ask about the Surety's Environmental Risk. Ed. by Donald G. Gavin & Robert M. Wright. LC 96-92998. 136p. 1997. pap. 39.95 (*1-57073-442-9*, 519-0270, ABA Tort) Amer Bar Assn.

Most Important Rule of All. unabridged ed. Pam Church. (Illus.). 48p. (Orig.). (J). (ps-6). 1997. pap. 9.95 (*0-9657000-0-3*) Prevent & Motivat.

Most Important Thing & Other Stories. Graham Chaffee. 64p. 1995. pap. 7.95 (*1-56097-193-2*) Fantagraph Bks.

Most Important Thing I Know. Adrain. 192p. 1999. 6.98 (*1-56731-353-1*, MJF Bks) Fine Comms.

Most Important Thing I Know: Life Lessons from Colin Powell, Stephen Covey, Maya Angelou & More Than 100 Other Individuals. gif. ed. Ed. by Lorne Adrain. LC 97-5890. 192p. 1997. 12.95 (*0-8362-2771-9*, Cader Bks) Andrews & McMeel.

***Most Important Thing I Know About Love: Inspiring Messages From Eminent Writers, Poets, Musicians, Thinkers, And Others.** Lorne A. Adrain. LC 99-47934. (Most Important Thing I Know Ser.). 160p. 2000. 13.00 (*0-688-16401-3*, Wm Morrow) Morrow Avon.

***Most Important Thing I Know About the Spirit of Sport: 101 Inspiring Messages From Athletes, Coaches, Sportswriters, And Commentators.** Lorne Adrain. LC 98-51011. 176p. 1999. 12.95 (*0-688-16400-5*, Wm Morrow) Morrow Avon.

Most Important Thing I've Learned in Life. Beau Bauman. 192p. 1994. pap. 7.95 (*0-671-89228-2*, Fireside) S&S Trade Pap.

***Most Incredible Cardboard Toys in the Whole Wide World.** Stefan Czernecki & Michael Haijtink. (Illus.). 112p. 1999. pap. 19.95 (*1-57990-161-1*) Lark Books.

Most Incredible Cardboard Toys in the Whole Wide World. Stefan Czernecki & Michael Haijtink. Ed. by Laura Dover Doran. LC 99-33603. (Illus.). 112p. 1999. pap. 19.95 (*1-57990-137-9*, Pub. by Lark Books) Random.

Most Incredible, Outrageous, Packed-to-the Gills, Bulging-at-the-Seams Sticker Book You've Ever Seen. Ed. by Klutz Press Editors. (Illus.). 30p. (J). (ps-3). 1997. pap. 10.95 (*1-57054-117-5*) Klutz.

Most Incredible Poems Ever Told. Santy Salernitano. 1997. pap. write for info. (*1-57553-661-7*) Watermrk Pr.

Most Incredible Prison Escape of the Civil War. W. Fred Conway. (True Adventure Stories from the Civil War Ser.). (Illus.). 120p. (Orig.). 1991. pap. 9.95 (*0-925165-04-2*) Fire Buff Hse.

Most Indispensable Art: Native Fiber Industries from Eastern North America. Ed. by James B. Peterson. LC 95-4405. (Illus.). 232p. 1996. text 45.00 (*0-87049-915-7*) U of Tenn Pr.

Most Influential Women in Film: A View from Both Sides of the Camera. Dawn B. Sova. LC 95-19787. (Illus.). 256p. 1995. pap. 18.95 (*0-8065-1708-5*, Citadel Pr) Carol Pub Group.

Most Instructive Games of Chess Ever Played: Sixty-Two Masterpieces of Chess Strategy. unabridged ed. Irving Chernev. LC 92-25679. (Illus.). 81p. 1992. reprint ed. pap. text 7.95 (*0-486-27302-4*) Dover.

***Most Interesting Empire.** Walter A. McDougall. 2000. 35.00 (*0-06-019789-7*); pap. 18.00 (*0-06-095755-7*) HarpC.

M

An Asterisk (*) at the beginning of an entry indicates that the title is appearing for the first time.

Most Lamentable & Tragicall Historie, Conteyning the Tyrannie Which Violenta Executed Upon Her Lover Didaco. Thomas Acheley. LC 77-6840. (English Experience Ser.: No. 836). 1977. reprint ed. lib. bdg. 20.00 (*0-90-221-0836-8*) Walter J Johnson.

*__Most Learned of the Shi'a: The Institution of the Marja'i Taqlid.__ Ed. by Linda S. Walbridge. 304p. 2000. text 45.00 (*0-19-513799-X*) OUP.

Most Likely to Decieve. Jennifer Baker. (Class Secrets Ser.: No. 01). 188p. (YA). (gr. 7 up). 1995. mass mkt. 3.99 (*0-671-51033-9*, Archway) PB.

Most Likely to Die. Jaqueline Girdner. LC 95-22449. 288p. 1996. pap. 21.95 (*0-425-15145-X*, Prime Crime); pap. 10.00 (*0-425-15146-8*) Berkley Pub.

Most Likely to Die. Jaqueline Girdner. 288p. 1997. reprint ed. mass mkt. 5.99 (*0-425-15721-0*, Prime Crime) Berkley Pub.

Most Mannerly Cow & the Rude Cowbird. Grace R. Hicks. (Illus.). 64p. (J). 1992. 11.95 (*0-89015-882-7*) Sunbelt Media.

Most Marvellous Summer. Betty A. Neels. (Romance Ser.: No. 185). 1992. pap. 2.89 (*0-373-03185-8*, 1-03185-5) Harlequin Bks.

Most Memorable Birthday. Welleran Poltarnees. (J). 1993. 15.00 (*0-671-77862-5*, Green Tiger S&S) S&S Childrens.

Most Necessary Luxuries: The Mercers' Company of Coventry, 1550-1680. Ronald M. Berger. (Illus.). 328p. (C). 1993. 60.00 (*0-271-00867-9*) Pa St U Pr.

Most Noble Diet: Food Selection & Ethics. 4th rev. ed. George L. Eisman et al. LC 94-94442. (Illus.). 118p. 1994. pap. 9.95 (*0-9614435-1-0*) Diet-Ethics.

Most Noble of Professions: Poe & the Poverty of Authorship. Bruce I. Weiner. 1987. pap. 3.95 (*0-910556-27-X*) Enoch Pratt.

Most Notable Antiquity of Great Britain Vulgarly Called Stonehenge, 1655. Inigo Jones & John Webb. LC 73-178414. 110p. 1972. reprint ed. write for info. (*0-85417-826-0*) Scolar Pr.

Most of All. Loure Busey. 288p. 1997. mass mkt. 4.99 (*0-7860-0456-8*, Pinncle Kensgtn) Kensgtn Pub Corp.

Most of Andy Rooney. Andy Rooney. 784p. 1990. 14.98 (*0-88365-765-1*) Galahad Bks.

*__Most of Lewis Grizzard.__ Lewis Grizzard. 992p. 1999. 16.99 (*0-88365-885-2*) Galahad Bks.

*__Most of P. G. Wodehouse.__ 704p. 2000. per. 16.00 (*0-7432-1130-8*) S&S Trade.

Most of P. G. Wodehouse. P. G. Wodehouse. 666p. 1969. pap. 12.95 (*0-671-20349-5*, Fireside) S&S Trade Pap.

*__Most of P. G. Wodehouse.__ P. G. Wodehouse. 2000. pap. 16.00 (*0-7432-0358-5*, Scribner Pap Fic) S&S Trade Pap.

Most of the Good Stuff: Memories of Richard Feynman. Ed. by Laurie M. Brown & John S. Rigden. LC 92-46471. 181p. 1993. text 39.95 (*0-88318-870-8*, AIP Pr) Spr-Verlag.

*__Most of the Most of S. J. Perelman.__ S. J. Perelman. LC 99-462419. 544p. 2000. pap. 15.95 (*0-679-64037-1*) Modern Lib NY.

Most of What We Take Is Given. Stephen Smith. 64p. (Orig.). 1991. pap. 8.00 (*1-880286-05-X*) Singular Speech Pr.

Most Offending Soul Alive: Tom Harrisson & His Remarkable Life. Judith M. Heimann. LC 99-23535. (Illus.). 480p. 1999. text 54.00 (*0-8248-2149-1*); pap. text 26.95 (*0-8248-2199-8*) UH Pr.

Most Paradoxist Mathematician of the World. Charles T. Le. LC PC0840.29.M2. 58p. reprint ed. pap. 30.00 (*0-608-20021-2*, 207114300010) Bks Demand.

*__Most Passionate Revenge.__ Jacqueline Baird. (Presents Ser.: Bk. 2137). 2000. mass mkt. 3.99 (*0-373-12137-7*, 1-12137-5) Harlequin Bks.

Most Perfectly Safe: The Convict Shipwreck Disasters of 1833-42. Granville A. Mawer. LC 97-147977. (Illus.). 208p. 1997. pap. 24.95 (*1-86448-186-2*, Pub. by Allen & Unwin Pty) Paul & Co Pubs.

Most Popular Easy Duets for Piano, Vol. 6. 127p. 1968. pap. 7.95 (*1-892586-06-1*) Cent Mus Pub.

Most Popular Music from the Masters to the Minors, Vol. 5A. 96p. 1967. pap. 7.95 (*1-892586-05-3*) Cent Mus Pub.

Most Popular 93 Short Classics, Vol. 7. 128p. 1971. pap. 7.95 (*1-892586-07-X*) Cent Mus Pub.

Most Popular 107 Easy to Play Hymns, Vol. 9. 128p. 1973. pap. 7.95 (*1-892586-09-6*) Cent Mus Pub.

Most Popular Piano Music of the Great Masters, Vol. 13. 144p. 1988. pap. 7.95 (*1-892586-13-4*) Cent Mus Pub.

Most Popular Piano Pieces. 128p. 1964. pap. 7.95 (*1-892586-00-2*) Cent Mus Pub.

Most Popular Plays of the American Theatre. Stanley Richards. LC 79-65112. (Illus.). 1979. 24.95 (*0-8128-2682-5*, Scrbrough Hse) Madison Bks UPA.

Most Popular Web Sites. 2nd ed. Lycos Development Group Staff. 1997. 39.99 (*0-7897-1246-6*) Macmillan.

Most Popular Web Sites: The Best of the Net from A2Z. Lycos Press Staff. 1272p. 1996. 49.99 (*0-7897-0792-6*) Que.

Most Popular Web Sites: The/Best of the Net from A to Z. 2nd ed. Lycos Press Staff. LC 97-69185. 1128p. 1997. 39.99 (*0-7897-1348-9*) Que.

Most Powerful Golf Swing on Earth! Ronald A. Tutt. (Illus.). 70p. 1998. pap. 29.95 (*0-9669541-0-6*) Master Golf.

Most Powerful Idea Ever Discovered. John Bryant. 1987. pap. 7.95 (*0-9617444-5-6*) Socratic Pr.

*__Most Precious Gift.__ Lawrence Liebling. LC 99-54867. (Illus.). 240p. 2000. 19.95 (*0-9642874-2-0*, Silent River Pr) Liebling Press.

Most Probable World. Stuart Chase. LC 81-2307. 239p. 1981. reprint ed. lib. bdg. 65.00 (*0-313-22971-6*, CHMP, Greenwood Pr) Greenwood.

Most Profitable Science of Surveying. Valentine Leigh. LC 72-171772. (English Experience Ser.: No. 397). 128p. 1971. reprint ed. 45.00 (*90-221-0397-8*) Walter J Johnson.

Most Promising Weed: A History of Tobacco Farming & Labor in Colonial Zimbabwe, 1890-1945. Steven C. Rubert. LC 98-19136. (Monographs in International Studies, Africa). xvi, 255p. 1998. pap. text 26.00 (*0-89680-203-5*) Ohio U Pr.

Most Promising Young Officer: A Life of Ranald Slidell Mackenzie. Michael D. Pierce. LC 92-32281. 1993. 24.95 (*0-8061-2494-6*) U of Okla Pr.

*__Most Qualified: A Nurse Reservist's Experience in the Persian Gulf War.__ Denise Figueroa. LC 00-90508. 2000. 24.95 (*0-533-13527-3*) Vantage.

Most Radical Gesture: The Situationist International in the Postmodern Age. Sadie Plant. LC 91-32553. 240p. (Orig.). (C). 1992. pap. 22.99 (*0-415-06222-5*, A6857) Routledge.

Most Reckless Lady. Sandy Hingston. 416p. 1998. mass mkt. 5.99 (*0-440-22368-7*) Dell.

Most Remarkable Bear. Peter Elwell. LC 97-6128. (Illus.). 32p. (J). (gr. k-3). Date not set. 15.95 (*0-7614-5008-4*, Benchmark NY) Marshall Cavendish.

Most Remarkable Enterprise: Maritime Commerce & Culture on the Northwest Coast. William Sturgis. Ed. by Mary Malloy. (Illus.). 192p. 1998. 65.00 (*0-940160-69-2*, Pinnacle Prss) Parnassus Imprints.

*__Most Remarkable Fella: Frank Loesser & the Guys & Dolls in His Life.__ Susan Loesser. (Illus.). 2000. pap. 14.95 (*0-634-00927-3*, Berklee Pr) H Leonard.

Most Requested Classical Themes for Piano. 96p. (Orig.). 1993. pap. 10.95 (*0-89724-105-3*, PF0882) Wrner Bros.

Most Requested Standards. (Most Requested...Ser.). 160p. (Orig.). (YA). 1993. pap. 49.95 (*0-89724-065-0*, VF1990) Wrner Bros.

Most Requested Superstar Hit. 160p. (Orig.). (YA). 1992. pap. 14.95 (*0-7692-1050-3*, VF1884) Wrner Bros.

*__Most Riveting Read Alouds of All Time! Build Comprehension, Listening & Higher-Order Thinking.__ Patrick Allen Daley. 1999. pap. 14.95 (*0-439-04759-5*) Scholastic.

Most Rugged All-Terrain Vehicles (ATVs) see Wheels

Most Satisfactory Man: The Story of Theodore Brevard Hayne, Last Martyr of Yellow Fever. Charles S. Bryan. LC 95-50693. (Illus.). 220p. 1996. text 19.95 (*1-57003-123-1*) U of SC Pr.

Most Scenic Drives in America. Reader's Digest Editors. LC 95-47306. (Illus.). 400p. 1997. 30.00 (*0-89577-862-9*, Pub. by RD Assn) Penguin Putnam.

Most Secret. John Dickson Carr. 235p. 1989. pap. 3.95 (*0-88184-542-6*) Carroll & Graf.

Most Secret. Nevil Shute. 24.95 (*0-88411-319-1*) Amereon Ltd.

*__Most Secret & Confidential: Intelligence in the Age of Nelson.__ Steven E. Maffeo. LC 99-48837. (Illus.). 368p. 2000. 32.95 (*1-55750-545-4*) Naval Inst Pr.

Most Secret Science. Archibald E. Roberts. LC 84-70100. (Illus.). 200p. 1984. pap. 12.00 (*0-934120-08-0*) Betsy Ross Pr.

Most Secret Science. Archibald E. Roberts. 1984. pap. write for info. (*0-318-61784-6*) Comm Restore Const.

*__Most Secret War.__ Jones, 3rd. 1998. pap. 12.99 (*1-85326-699-X*, Pub. by Wrdsworth Edits) Combined Pub.

Most Singular Adventures of Eddie Vernon Eleanor Berry. LC 99-182302. 278p. 1998. write for info. (*0-7223-3232-7*, Pub. by A H S Ltd) St Mut.

Most Singular Country: A History of Occupation in the Big Bend. Arthur R. Gomez. (Monographs in Western History: No. 18). (Illus.). 252p. 1990. pap. 10.95 (*1-56085-000-0*, C Redd Ctr Wstrn Studies) Signature Bks.

Most Solitary of Afflictions: Madness & Society in Britain, 1700-1900. Andrew T. Scull. LC 92-48395. (Illus.). 448p. (C). 1993. 50.00 (*0-300-05051-8*) Yale U Pr.

Most Southern Place on Earth: The Mississippi Delta & the Roots of Regional Identity. James C. Cobb. (Illus.). 416p. 1994. reprint ed. pap. 16.95 (*0-19-508913-8*) OUP.

Most Special Person. (Illus.). 24p. (J). (gr. k-6). 1999. 12.95 (*1-893672-00-X*) M J Presents.

Most Splendid Failure: Faulkner's, The Sound & the Fury. Andre Bleikasten. LC 75-22638. 286p. reprint ed. pap. 88.70 (*0-608-17132-8*, 205621700056) Bks Demand.

Most Superior Land: Life in the Upper Peninsula of Michigan. 2nd ed. Ed. by Susan Newhof Pyle. LC 83-620003. (Michigan Heritage Bks.: Vol. 4). (Illus.). 192p. 1987. 24.95 (*0-941912-03-5*) TwoPeninsula Pr.

Most Surprising Song: Exploring the Mystical Experience. Louann Stahl. LC 91-65820. 194p. 1992. pap. 5.98 (*0-87159-106-5*) Unity Bks.

Most True Relation of the Affairs of Cleve & Gulick, with the Articles of Peace Propounded at Santen. Henry Peacham. LC 72-6024. (English Experience Ser.: No. 549). (Illus.). 44p. 1973. reprint ed. 35.00 (*90-221-0549-0*) Walter J Johnson.

Most Trusted Man in America. G. Gates. 356p. 1995. 24.95 (*0-471-55526-6*) Wiley.

Most Unique Machine: The Michigan Origins of the American Automobile Industry. George S. May. LC 74-19230. (Illus.). 406p. reprint ed. pap. 125.90 (*0-608-10735-2*, 201273600083) Bks Demand.

*__Most Unlikely Collection.__ Elaine Stuart. 2000. pap. write for info. (*1-58235-418-9*) Watermrk Pr.

Most Unlikely God: A Philosophical Enquiry. Barry Miller. LC 95-50518. 224p. (C). 1996. text 27.00 (*0-268-01422-1*) U of Notre Dame Pr.

Most Unsordid Act: Lend-Lease, 1939-1941. Warren F. Kimball. LC 69-14712. 292p. 1969. reprint ed. pap. 90.60 (*0-7837-2651-1*, 204300500006) Bks Demand.

Most Unusual Christmas Eve: The Story of a Boy Named David. Ernest Knowles. (Illus.). 20p. 1994. reprint ed. 4.20 (*0-9645277-0-7*) E Knowles.

Most Unusual Dog. Tohby Riddle. LC 93-38724. (Illus.). 32p. (J). (gr. 1 up). 1994. lib. bdg. 21.27 (*0-8368-1088-0*) Gareth Stevens Inc.

Most Unusual Lady. Janet Grace. (Regency Romance Ser.: No. 171). 1992. mass mkt. 2.99 (*0-373-31171-0*, 1-31171-1) Harlequin Bks.

Most Unusual Lunch. Robert Bender. 1999. pap. 4.99 (*0-14-055670-2*) Viking Penguin.

Most Unusual Marriage. large type ed. Barbara Best. (Linford Romance Library). 288p. 1997. pap. 16.99 (*0-7089-5076-0*, Linford) Ulverscroft.

Most Used Words & Phases. John R. Gregg et al. 1963. text 10.96 (*0-07-024592-4*) McGraw.

Most Useful Sentence Patterns in Mandarin Chinese: Shih yung Chung Ying wen Chu hsing. Matthew Laszewski & Marina H. Sung. LC 98-154964. 1998. write for info. (*0-9630354-2-8*) Brave New Wrld.

*__Most Valuable Asset of The Reich: A History of The German National Railway 1920-1932, Vol. 1.__ Alfred C. Mierzejewski. LC 98-53440. (Illus.). 656p. 1999. 85.00 (*0-8078-2496-8*) U of NC Pr.

*__Most Valuable Asset of the Reich: A History of the German National Railway Vol. 2: 1933-1945.__ Alfred C. Mierzejewski. (Illus.). 368p. 2000. 45.00 (*0-8078-2574-3*) U of NC Pr.

Most Valuable Book Ever Published. 2nd rev. ed. American Publishing Editors. 244p. 1997. pap. 16.95 (*0-9638596-5-X*) Amer Pubng.

Most Valuable Business Legal Forms You'll Ever Need. 2nd ed. James C. Ray. LC 98-3338. (Legal Survival Guides Ser.). 140p. 1998. pap. 19.95 (*1-57071-345-6*) Sourcebks.

Most Valuable Corporate Forms You'll Ever Need. 2nd ed. James C. Ray. LC 98-6006. (Legal Survival Guides Ser.). 220p. 1998. pap. 24.95 (*1-57071-346-4*) Sourcebks.

*__Most Valuable Legal Forms You'll Ever Need.__ Mark Warda. 2000. pap. 19.95 (*1-57248-130-7*, Sphinx Pubng) Sourcebks.

Most Valuable Personal Legal Forms You'll Ever Need. Mark Warda & Sourcebooks Staff. (Legal Survival Guides Ser.). 144p. 1998. pap. 14.95 (*1-57071-347-2*) Sourcebks.

Most Valuable Player & Four Other All-Star Plays for Middle & High School Audiences. Mary Hall Surface. LC 99-30018. 256p. (YA). (gr. 9 up). 1999. pap. 16.95 (*1-57525-178-7*) Smith & Kraus.

Most Valuable Prayer: Larry Brown Manuscript. Michael D. Evans. (Larry Brown Super Bowl XXX Ser.). 211p. 1996. pap. 15.00 (*0-935199-10-1*) Bedfrd Books.

Most Vehement Flame. Bill Panko & Margaret Panko. 300p. (Orig.). Date not set. pap. 19.95 (*1-885342-12-8*) Creative Ways.

Most Wanted. Jordan Cray. LC 97-52648. (Danger.com Ser.: No. 7). 208p. (YA). (gr. 6 up). 1998. mass mkt. 3.99 (*0-689-82040-2*) Aladdin.

Most Wanted. Ed. by Laura Foreman. LC 93-24031. (True Crime Ser.). (Illus.). 192p. 1993. lib. bdg. 17.45 (*0-7835-0021-1*) Time-Life.

*__Most Wanted.__ Diana Palmer. 434p. 2000. per. 12.95 (*1-55166-612-X*, Mira Bks) Harlequin Bks.

Most Wanted. Margret Pierce. 1996. mass mkt. 5.50 (*0-312-95759-9*, Pub. by Tor Bks) St Martin.

*__Most Wanted.__ Peter Sagal. 71p. 1999. pap. 5.60 (*0-87129-931-3*, MA7) Dramatic Pub.

Most Wanted. large type ed. Jacquelyn Mitchard. LC 98-22083. (Compass Press Large Print Book Ser.). 407p. 1998. 34.99 (*1-56895-605-3*, Compass) Wheeler Pub.

Most Wanted. Jacquelyn Mitchard. 392p. 1999. reprint ed. mass mkt. 7.99 (*0-451-19685-6*, Sig) NAL.

Most Wanted, 7. Jordan Cray. (Danger.com Ser.: No. 7). (YA). (gr. 6 up). 1998. 9.09 (*0-606-13311-9*, Pub. by Turtleback) Demco.

Most Wanted, Vol. 3. Clancy. (J). Date not set. pap. write for info. (*0-671-03288-7*) PB.

Most Wanted: Men in Blue. Maggie Price. (Intimate Moments Ser.: Vol. 948). 1999. per. 4.25 (*0-373-07948-6*, 1-07948-2) Silhouette.

*__Most Wanted Bachelor.__ Susan K. Law. 384p. 2000. mass mkt. 5.99 (*0-380-80497-2*) Morrow Avon.

Most Wanted Dad (Fabulous Father) Arlene James. (Romance Ser.). 1996. per. 3.25 (*0-373-19144-8*, 1-19144-4) Silhouette.

Most Wanted Holiday Hunks, Vol. 1. Ed. by Archway Paperbacks Editorial Staff. (J). 1998. mass mkt. 7.99 (*0-671-02665-8*) S&S Trade.

Most Wanted Words: A New Approach to Spelling, Writing & Thinking. Carla Crutsinger & Debra Moore. (Illus.). 156p. (Orig.). (J). (gr. 2-6). 1995. pap. text 29.95 (*0-944662-04-8*) Brainworks Inc.

*__Most Way Home.__ Kevin Young. LC 99-89812. 112p. 2000. pap. 12.00 (*1-58195-021-7*) Zoland Bks.

*__Most Wise & Valiant Ladies.__ Andrea Hopkins. (Illus.). 160p. 1999. pap. 16.95 (*1-56649-073-1*) Welcome Rain.

Most Wonderful Books: Writers on Discovering the Pleasures of Reading. Ed. by Michael Dorris & Emilie Buchwald. LC 96-29624. 320p. (Orig.). 1997. pap. 14.95 (*1-57131-216-1*) Milkweed Ed.

Most Wonderful Doll in the World. Phyllis McGinley. 64p. (J). (gr. 2-5). 1990. 10.95 (*0-590-43476-4*) Scholastic Inc.

Most Wonderful Doll in the World. Phyllis McGinley. 64p. (J). (ps-3). 1992. 3.95 (*0-590-43477-2*, Blue Ribbon Bks) Scholastic Inc.

Most Wonderful Doll in the World. Phyllis McGinley. (Blue Ribbon Bks.). (J). 1978. 9.15 (*0-606-02762-9*, Pub. by Turtleback) Demco.

Most Wonderful Machine: Mechanization & Social Change in Berkshire Paper Making, 1801-1885. Judith A. McGaw. (Illus.). 457p. 1987. pap. text 19.95 (*0-691-00625-3*, Pub. by Princeton U Pr) Cal Prin Full Svc.

Most Wonderful One. Michael Walker, Jr. (Amazing English Ser.: Little Bks., Level A). (J). 1995. pap. text 17.64 (*0-201-85342-6*) Addison-Wesley.

Most Wonderful One in the World Little Book, Level A. Walker. 16p. (J). 1995. ring bd. 4.78 (*0-201-85336-1*) Addison-Wesley.

Most Wonderful Work: Our Constitution Interpreted. Thomas E. Baker. 706p. 1996. 26.95 (*0-314-20339-7*) West Pub.

*__Most Wonderful Writing Lessons Ever: Everything You Need to Know to Teach the Essential Elements.__ Barbara Mariconda. (Illus.). 128p. 1999. pap. 14.95 (*0-590-87304-0*) Scholastic Inc.

Most Wondrous Babble: American Art Composers, Their Music, & The American Scene, 1950-1985, 9. Nicholas E. Tawa. LC 86-22728. (Contributions to the Study of Music & Dance Ser.: No. 9). 297p. 1987. 59.95 (*0-313-25692-6*, TMW/, Greenwood Pr) Greenwood.

Most Work Measurement Systems. 2nd expanded rev. ed. K. Zandin. (Industrial Engineering Ser.: Vol. 17). (Illus.). 432p. 1990. text 55.00 (*0-8247-7604-6*) Dekker.

*__Most World Records.__ Annie Auerbach. Vol. 8. (Illus.). 64p. (gr. 2-5). 2000. 3.99 (*0-689-83465-9*) S&S Trade.

Mostert: Famous & Well-Known Marks. Frederick Mostert. 1996. write for info. (*0-406-99734-9*, MFWKM, MICHIE) LEXIS Pub.

Mosteshar on Telecommunications: Regulation in the European Community. Sai'd Mosteshar. (European Business Law & Practice Ser.). 448p. (C). 1993. lib. bdg. 145.00 (*1-85333-756-0*, Pub. by Graham & Trotman) Kluwer Academic.

Mostly about Dogs. Tom McNally. (Illus.). 254p. 1972. pap. 4.95 (*0-87955-403-7*) O'Hara.

Mostly about Writing. Nancy Martin. LC 83-9972. 168p. (Orig.). (C). 1983. pap. text 18.50 (*0-86709-069-3*, 0069, Pub. by Boynton Cook Pubs) Heinemann.

Mostly Amusing, Always Amazingly True Memories: North Dakota Seniors Tell Their Stories. Ed. by Everett C. Albers. LC 96-70617. (Illus.). 178p. (Orig.). 1996. pap. 10.00 (*0-9654579-0-7*) N Dakota Hum.

Mostly BASIC: Applications for Your IBM-PC, 2 Vols., Bk. 1. Howard Berenbon. 1983. write for info. (*0-672-22076-8*, 22093) Macmillan.

Mostly BASIC: Applications for Your IBM-PC, 2 Vols., Bk. 2. Howard Berenbon. 1983. write for info. (*0-672-22093-8*) Macmillan.

Mostly Canallers. Walter D. Edmonds. (New York State Bks.). 470p. 1987. reprint ed. pap. text 16.95 (*0-8156-0214-6*) Syracuse U Pr.

Mostly Finite Geometries: In Celebration of T. G. Ostrom's 80th Birthday. T. G. Ostrom & Normal L. Johnson. LC 97-10208. (Lecture Notes in Pure & Applied Mathematics Ser.). (Illus.). 456p. 1997. pap. text 175.00 (*0-8247-0035-X*) Dekker.

Mostly Ghostly: Eight Spooky Tales to Chill Your Bones. Steven Zorn. (Children's Illustrated Classics Ser.). (Illus.). 56p. (J). (gr. 2-7). 1998. 9.98 (*0-7624-0406-X*, Courage) Running Pr.

Mostly Golf: A Bernard Darwin Anthology. rev. ed. Ed. by Peter Ryde. (Illus.). 206p. 1989. 28.00 (*0-940889-12-9*) Classics Golf.

Mostly Good & Competent Men: The Illinois Governors. 2nd rev. ed. Robert P. Howard et al. LC 98-50866. (Illus.). 420p. 1998. pap. 19.95 (*0-938943-15-4*) U IL Spgfld Pub Affrs.

Mostly Happy Clip Art of the Thirties, Forties & Fifties, Vol. 2. Ed. by Jerry Jankowski. LC 94-73087. 120p. 1995. pap. text 15.95 (*0-88108-151-5*) Art Dir.

Mostly Harmless. Douglas Adams. 288p. 1993. pap. 12.00 (*0-345-37933-0*) Ballantine Pub Grp.

Mostly Harmless. Douglas Adams. 2000. mass mkt. 6.99 (*0-345-41877-8*) Ballantine Pub Grp.

Mostly Harmless. large type ed. Douglas Adams. 272p. 1996. 24.95 (*1-85695-333-5*, Pub. by ISIS Lrg Prnt) Transaction Pubs.

Mostly Huntin' Bill Jordan. (Illus.). 128p. 1989. 21.95 (*0-944419-00-3*) Police Bkshelf.

Mostly in the Line of Duty: Thirty Years with Books. Herman Liebaers. 1980. lib. bdg. 85.50 (*90-247-2228-4*) Kluwer Academic.

Mostly Love. Robert A. Julius. (Illus.). 42p. (Orig.). 1995. pap. 14.95 (*0-9645730-0-8*) R Julius Photo.

Mostly Macro: A Guide to Healthy Cuisine for the Discriminating Palate. Lisa Turner. LC 94-48512. (Illus.). 192p. 1995. pap. 16.95 (*0-89281-534-5*) Inner Tradit.

Mostly Magnets. Evalyn Hoover et al. (Magnetism & Electricity Ser.). (J). (gr. 2-8). 1991. 16.95 (*1-881431-29-0*, 1210) AIMS Educ Fnd.

Mostly Mazes. 1997. pap. 1.95 (*0-8167-1679-X*) Troll Communs.

Mostly Michael. Robert K. Smith. LC 86-19618. 192p. (J). (gr. 4-7). 1988. pap. 4.50 (*0-440-40097-X*, YB BDD) BDD Bks Young Read.

Mostly Michael. Robert K. Smith. (J). 1987. 9.09 (*0-606-04102-8*, Pub. by Turtleback) Demco.

Mostly Microwave. Janice Martin. Ed. by Kitty Toney. (Illus.). 130p. 1984. spiral bd. 6.50 (*0-9614072-0-4*) Mostly Micro.

Mostly Mine. rev. ed. 1986. 3.95 (*0-913748-05-6*) Orovan Bks.

*__Mostly Miniatures: An Introduction to Persian Painting.__ Oleg Grabar. LC 00-35961. (Illus.). 184p. 2000. 49.50 (*0-691-04941-6*) Princeton U Pr.

An Asterisk (*) at the beginning of an entry indicates that the title is appearing for the first time.

Mostly Mittens: Traditional Knitting Patterns from Russia's Komi People. Charlene Schurch. LC 98-4632. (Illus.). 112p. 1998. 21.95 (*1-57990-059-3*, Pub. by Lark Books) Random.

***Mostly Monsters: Eight Terrifying Tales to Tingle Your Spine.** Steven Zorn. (Children's Illustrated Classics Ser.). (Illus.). 56p. (J). (gr. 4-7). 1998. 9.98 (*0-7624-0407-8*, Courage) Running Pr.

Mostly Movement: Accent on Autumn, Bk. 2. Edith Wax & Sydell Roth. 1982. 12.95 (*0-934848-02-5*) Mostly Movement.

Mostly Movement Bk. 1: First Steps. Edith Wax & Sydell Roth. 1979. 12.95 (*0-934848-00-9*) Mostly Movement.

Mostly Muffins. Barbara Albright & Leslie Weiner. (Illus.). 104p. 1984. pap. 6.95 (*0-312-54916-4*) St Martin.

Mostly Mullet Cookbook: A Culinary Celebration of the South's Favorite Fish (& other great Southern seafood) George Griffin. LC 97-45021. (Illus.). 112p. 1998. pap. 7.95 (*1-56164-147-2*) Pineapple Pr.

Mostly on Foot. Ben Yandell & Janet Nippell. 80p. (Orig.). 1989. pap. 8.00 (*0-912449-30-6*) Floating Island.

Mostly on the Edge: Karl Hess, an Autobiography. Ed. by Karl Hess, Jr. LC 98-55751. (Illus.). 410p. 1999. 28.95 (*1-57392-687-6*) Prometheus Bks.

Mostly Puppies. (Illus.). 30p. 1995. pap. 7.95 (*1-55859-924-X*) Abbeville Pr.

Mostly Santa Barbara. Lynn Richardson. (Illus.). 224p. 1998. 35.00 (*1-56474-301-2*) Fithian Pr.

Mostly Scary. Jay O'Callahan. (J). (gr. 2 up). 1987. 10.00 incl. audio (*1-877954-12-8*) Artana Prodns.

Mostly Shaker from the New Yankee Workshop. Norm Abram. 1992. 35.00 (*0-316-00473-1*); pap. 22.00 (*0-316-00475-8*) Little.

Mostly Tailfeathers. Gene Hill. LC 82-62599. 192p. 1975. 17.95 (*0-8329-1670-6*, Winchester Pr) New Win Pub.

***Mostly Theatre: A History of the Theatre Department of Muskingum College.** Ed. by Donald Hill. (Illus.). 2000. write for info. (*1-887932-76-3*) Equine Graph Pubng.

Mostly True: Collected Stories & Drawings. Brian Andreas. 80p. 1993. pap. 20.00 (*0-9642660-0-8*) StoryPeople.

Mostly True Life Adventures of Dr. Leisure, Vol. II. George R. Harker. LC 98-35927. 345p. 1998. 32.95 (*1-887471-08-1*) Dr Leisure.

Mostly Unfabulous Social Life of Ethan Green. Eric Orner. (Illus.). 128p. 1992. pap. 8.95 (*0-312-07635-5*) St Martin.

Mostraci, Signore, Il Tuo Volto - E Compiremo Meraviglie see Show Us Your Face Lord, & We Shall Work Wonders

Mosul before Iraq: Like Bees Making Five-Sided Cells. Sarah D. Shields. LC 00-22855. (C). 2000. text 68.50 (*0-7914-4487-2*); pap. text 22.95 (*0-7914-4488-0*) State U NY Pr.

Moszkowski/15 Virtuosic Etudes, Opus 27: For the Piano. Ed. by Maurice Hinson. (Masterwork Edition Ser.). 72p. 1992. pap. 8.95 (*0-7390-0539-1*, 4859) Alfred Pub.

Mot d'Esprit et Sa Relation a L'Inconscient. Sigmund Freud. (FRE.). 1992. pap. 14.95 (*0-7859-2830-8*) Fr & Eur.

Mot Juste: A Dictionary of Classical & Foreign Words & Phrases. Kogan Page, Ltd. Staff. LC 91-50029. 176p. 1991. pap. 11.00 (*0-679-73455-4*) Vin Bks.

Mot Juste: A Dictionary of Classical & Foreign Words & Phrases. Compiled by Kogan Page, Ltd. Staff & John Buchanan-Brown. LC 80-6122. 176p. 1981. pap. 4.95 (*0-394-74690-2*, V-690) Vin Bks.

Mot pour Mot: French Vocabulary Organizer. William Aaron. (Efficient Language Ser.). (FRE., Illus.). 68p. (Orig.). 1994. pap. 39.95 incl. disk (*1-884677-00-2*) Salix.

Motaky Do Usi Peny - Prison Notes Smuggled into the Wars of Seafoam. Bronislava Volkova. LC 98-42365. 158p. 1999. text 29.95 (*0-7734-3100-4*) E Mellen.

Mote in God's Eye. Larry Niven & Jerry Pournelle. Ed. by Dave Stern. 592p. 1991. per. 6.99 (*0-671-74192-6*) PB.

Motel Chronicles. Sam Shepard. 144p. (Orig.). 1982. pap. 10.95 (*0-87286-143-0*) City Lights.

Motel Clerk. Ad Wittemann. LC 88-30756. 15p. (Orig.). (C). 1988. pap. 25.00 (*0-938481-48-7*) Camelot Consult.

Motel in America. John A. Jakle et al. LC 96-14762. (Road & American Culture Ser.). (Illus.). 296p. 1996. 32.95 (*0-8018-5383-4*) Johns Hopkins.

Motel Moods. John M. Bennett. 1980. pap. 2.50 (*0-935350-03-9*) Luna Bisonte.

Motel Moods. limited ed. John M. Bennett. 1980. pap. 6.00 (*0-935350-82-9*) Luna Bisonte.

Motel Nirvana. Melanie McGrath. 1996. 22.00 (*0-614-96868-2*, Picador USA) St Martin.

Motel of the Mysteries, 001. David Macaulay. 96p. 1979. pap. 13.00 (*0-395-28425-2*) HM.

Moteris. Algimantas Kezys. LC 97-71772.Tr. of Woman. (LIT., Illus.). 224p. (Orig.). 1997. pap. 40.00 (*1-886060-08-8*) Galerija.

Motes et les Choses: Une Archaeologie des Sciences Humaines. Michel Foucault. (FRE.). 1990. pap. 24.95 (*0-7859-2746-8*) Fr & Eur.

Motes for Three Voices. Ed. by Anthony Petti. (Chester's Books of Motets: Bk. 7). pap. 9.95 (*0-685-69096-2*, CH55222) Shawnee Pr.

Motet, "Ave Regina Coelorum" for Twelve Voices or Voices & Instruments. Giovanni Bassano. Ed. by Richard Charteris. (Baroque Ser.: No. 11). i, 30p. 1994. pap. text 10.00 (*1-56571-110-6*) PRB Prods.

Motet Books of Andrea Antico. Ed. by Martin Picker. LC 85-754400. (Monuments of Renaissance Music Ser.: Vol. III). (Illus.). 456p. (C). 1987. lib. bdg. 120.00 (*0-226-66796-0*) U Ch Pr.

Motet, "In Ecclesiis" for Four Solo Voices, SATB Choir, Six Instruments. Giovanni Gabrieli. Ed. by Richard Charteris. (Baroque Ser.: No. 6). iii, 56p. 1994. pap. text. write for info. (*1-56571-096-7*) PRB Prods.

Motet in England in the Fourteenth Century. Peter Lefferts. LC 86-6900. (Studies in Musicology: No. 94). (Illus.). 391p. reprint ed. pap. 121.30 (*0-8357-1722-4*, 207059400004) Bks Demand.

***Motet in the Age of Du Fay: Subgenres, Transformation & Interpretation.** Julie E. Cumming. LC 98-44114. (Illus.). 403p. (C). 1999. 69.95 (*0-521-47377-2*) Cambridge U Pr.

Motet, "Jubilate Deo" for Twelve Voices-Instruments. Hans L. Hassler. Ed. by Richard Charteris. (Baroque Ser.: No. 13). 1995. pap. text 8.00 (*1-56571-116-5*) PRB Prods.

Motet, "O Gloriosa Virgo" for Twelve Voices or Voices & Instruments. Giovanni Gabrieli. Ed. by Richard Charteris. (Baroque Ser.: No. 10). ii, 37p. 1994. pap. text 15.00 (*1-56571-109-2*) PRB Prods.

Motet, "Regina Coeli" for Twelve Voices or Instruments. Giovanni Gabrieli. Ed. by Richard Charteris. (Baroque Ser.: No. 7). 1995. pap. text 5.00 (*1-56571-097-5*) PRB Prods.

Motet, "Sancta et Immaculata Virginitas" for Eight Voices. Giovanni Gabrieli. Ed. by Richard Charteris. (Baroque Ser.: No. 9). i, 10p. 1994. pap. text 2.00 (*1-56571-108-4*) PRB Prods.

Motet,"O Sacrum Convivium" for Eight Voices. Hans L. Hassler. Ed. by Richard Charteris. (Baroque Ser.: No. 12). 1995. pap. text 5.00 (*1-56571-115-7*) PRB Prods.

***Motets: Poems from Hollywood.** Mark Dunster. 11p. 1999. pap. 5.00 (*0-89642-778-1*) Linden Pubs.

Motets of Jacob Praetorius II. Jacob Praetorius, II. Ed. by Frederick K. Gable. (Recent Researches in Music of the Baroque Era Ser.: Vol. RRB73). (Illus.). xxiv, 102p. 1994. pap. 40.00 (*0-89579-308-3*) A-R Eds.

Motets, I ,1664, Tome 1, Miserere Mei Deus see Oeuvres Completes de Jean-Baptiste Lully

Motets, (Premiere Serie) see Oeuvres Completes de Jean-Philippe Rameau

Motets, (Seconde Serie) see Oeuvres Completes de Jean-Philippe Rameau

Motets, 1600-1650: Alessandro Grandi, Works from 1610-1616. Elizabeth Roche. Ed. by Anne Schnoebelen. (Seventeenth-Century Italian Sacred Music: Vol. 21). 280p. 1996. text 99.00 (*0-8153-2361-1*) Garland.

Motets, 1600-1650: Alessandro Grandi, Works from 1619-1630. Elizabeth Roche. Ed. by Anne Schnoebelen. (Seventeenth-Century Italian Sacred Music Ser.: Vol. 22). 280p. 1996. text 99.00 (*0-8153-2362-X*) Garland.

Motets, 1668-1677, Tome 2, Plaude, Laetare, Gallia; Te Deum Laudamus; Dies Irae; Dies Illa see Oeuvres Completes de Jean-Baptiste Lully

Motetti a Numero Trentatre: Selections from Motetti Numero Trentare (Venice, 1502) Ed. by Richard Sherr. LC 90-754886. (Sixteenth-Century Motet Ser.: Vol. 1). 112p. 1991. text 83.00 (*0-8240-7901-9*) Garland.

Motettum "O Bone Jesu," Tripartitum see Complete Works of Philippe De Monte

Moth. Catherine Cookson. 432p. 1987. mass mkt. 7.99 (*0-552-12524-5*) Bantam.

***Moth.** Catherine Cookson. 2000. pap. 10.95 (*0-552-14545-9*) Transworld Publishers Ltd.

Moth. Louise F. Underhill. 46p. (Orig.). 1978. pap. 5.00 (*0-9616734-1-9*) Underhill Ent.

Moth. Barrie Watts. (Stopwatch Ser.). (Illus.). 25p. (J). (gr. k-4). 1991. pap. 3.95 (*0-382-24241-6*); lib. bdg. 9.95 (*0-382-24218-1*, Silver Pr NJ) Silver Burdett Pr.

Moth. large type ed. Catherine Cookson. 480p. 1987. 18.95 (*0-7089-8386-3*, Charnwood) Ulverscroft.

Moth & Other Stories. (Bridge Ser.). (Illus.). 128p. (YA). 1991. pap. text 5.95 (*0-582-53018-0*) Longman.

Moth & Rust & Other Stories. Mary Cholmondeley. LC 71-101794. (Short Story Index Reprint Ser.). 1977. 20.95 (*0-8369-3182-3*) Ayer.

***Moth & the Flame.** Dylan Bolduc. LC 99-56241. (Publish-a-Book Ser.). (Illus.). 24p. (ps-3). 2000. pap. text 8.50 (*0-7398-2369-8*) Raintree Steck-V.

Moth Comes to the Flame: Conversations Between Seekers & Sage. John Roberts. Ed. by Carol Lyons. LC 98-92078. 368p. 1998. pap. 20.00 (*1-878682-03-2*) Roaring Lion Pub.

Moth Comes to the Flame Vol. 2: Conversations Between Seeker & Sage. John Roberts. Ed. by Carol Lyons. LC 98-92155. 488p. 1998. pap. 25.00 (*1-878682-04-0*) Roaring Lion Pub.

Moth or Phoenix? J. R. Thomas. 197p. (C). 1980. pap. 30.00 (*0-85088-503-5*, Pub. by Gomer Pr) St Mut.

***Moth Smoke.** Mohsin Hamid. LC 99-45753. 246p. 2000. text 24.00 (*0-374-21354-2*) FS&G.

Moth-Wings: Poems. deluxe ed. Mark McMorris. (Burning Deck Poetry Chapbooks Ser.). 40p. 1996. pap. 20.00 (*1-886224-11-0*) Burning Deck.

Mothballing Historic Buildings. Sharon C. Park. 14p. 1993. pap. 1.50 (*0-16-061659-X*) USGPO.

Mother. Sri Aurobindo. LC 94-72971. 62p. (Orig.). 1995. pap. 2.95 (*0-941524-79-5*) Lotus Pr.

Mother. Sibylle Birkhauser-Oeri. 176p. 1995. pap. 18.00 (*0-919123-33-3*, Pub. by Inner City Bks) BookWorld.

Mother. Bertolt Brecht. Tr. by Lee Baxandall from GER. LC 65-14211. 160p. 1989. pap. 7.95 (*0-8021-3160-3*, Grove) Grove-Atltic.

Mother. Mary Higgins Clark et al. Ed. by Claudia O'Keefe. 1996. pap. 12.00 (*0-614-97652-9*, Pocket Books) PB.

***Mother.** Ed. by Great Quotations Publishing Staff. (My Memories Ser.). 2000. 12.99 (*1-56245-456-0*) Great Quotations.

Mother. Joyce B. Griffin. (Illus.). 16p. (Orig.). pap. write for info. (*0-935996-02-8*) Wibat Pubns.

***Mother.** Havoc Publishing Staff. 1999. pap. 5.00 (*0-7416-1101-5*); pap. 5.00 (*0-7416-1118-X*) Havoc Pub.

Mother. Kathleen T. Norris. 176p. 1995. pap. 9.95 (*1-887548-01-7*) St Michael NC.

***Mother.** Judy Olausen. 96p. 2000. pap. 15.95 (*0-14-029084-2*, Viking); pap. 15.95 (*0-14-026362-4*) Viking Penguin.

Mother, 1. Lauren White. (Orig.). 1999. 9.95 (*0-8362-9275-8*) Andrews & McMeel.

Mother. Sholem Asch. Tr. by Nathan Ausubel. LC 73-114047. (BCL Ser.: No. 1). reprint ed. 35.00 (*0-404-00408-3*) AMS Pr.

Mother. Pearl Synderstricker Buck. (Good Earth Trilogy Ser.: Vol. 3). 302p. (Orig.). 1993. reprint ed. pap. 8.95 (*1-55921-091-5*) Moyer Bell.

Mother. Kathleen Norris. reprint ed. lib. bdg. 17.95 (*0-89190-308-9*, Rivercity Pr) Amereon Ltd.

Mother. unabridged ed. Sri Aurobindo. 62p. 1980. reprint ed. 12.95 (*0-89744-914-2*, Pub. by Sri Aurob Ashram Trust) Acrpls Bks CO.

Mother. 14th ed. Sri Aurobindo. 63p. (Orig.). 1996. pap. 1.25 (*81-7058-484-1*, Pub. by SAA) E-W Cultural Ctr.

Mother: A Collective Portrait. Mary M. Kalergis. (Illus.). 133p. 1997. 19.95 (*0-9659646-3-9*, 00297); pap. 12.95 (*0-9659646-4-7*, 00297) Sugarday Bks.

Mother: A Novel of the Revolution. Pamela Millward. LC 76-78045. (Writing Ser.: No. 26). 64p. (Orig.). 1970. pap. 2.00 (*0-87704-015-X*) Four Seasons Foun.

Mother A Son's Remembrance. Henrik Stangerup. 1999. pap. text 14.95 (*0-7145-3029-8*) M Boyars Pubs.

Mother: A Story. Kathleen Norris. (Collected Works of Kathleen Norris). 172p. 1999. reprint ed. lib. bdg. 88.00 (*1-58201-797-2*) Classic Bks.

Mother: A Suburban Horror Story. R. R. Rullman & S. S. Rullman. 290p. (Orig.). 1993. pap. text 8.95 (*0-9615938-5-7*) Banner Bks.

Mother: Miniature Size. unabridged ed. Sri Aurobindo. 62p. 1980. reprint ed. pap. 0.75 (*0-89744-148-6*, Pub. by Sri Aurob Ashram Trust) Acrpls Bks CO.

Mother! The Frank Zappa Story. Michael Gray. 224p. 1994. per. 14.95 (*0-85965-217-3*, Pub. by Plexus) Publishers Group.

Mother: The Great Revolutionary Novel. Maxim Gorky. Tr. by Isadore Schneider from RUS. 416p. 1992. pap. 10.95 (*0-8065-0890-6*, Citadel Pr) Carol Pub Group.

Mother: The Heart of the Home. (Little Treasures Ser.). (Illus.). 88p. 1995. 4.99 (*1-57051-067-9*) Brownlow Pub Co.

Mother: Twenty Famous Writers Celebrate Mother with a Treasury of Short Stories, Essays, Poems. Ed. by Claudia O'Keefe. 256p. 1996. pap. 12.00 (*0-671-52998-6*, PB Trade Paper) PB.

Mother: With Letters on the Mother. Sri Aurobindo. 496p. 1997. pap. 10.95 (*81-7058-010-2*, Pub. by SAA) E-W Cultural Ctr.

Mother: With Letters on the Mother. Sri Aurobindo. 496p. 1997. 16.50 (*81-7058-373-X*, Pub. by SAA) E-W Cultural Ctr.

Mother: With Sri Aurobindo's Handwriting. unabridged ed. Sri Aurobindo. 62p. 1980. reprint ed. pap. 2.50 (*0-89744-915-0*, Pub. by Sri Aurob Ashram Trust) Acrpls Bks CO.

Mother: With the Mother's Comments. Sri Aurobindo & Mother. 177p. (Orig.). 1988. pap. 4.95 (*0-317-99970-2*, Pub. by Sri Aurob Ashram Trust) Acrpls Bks CO.

Mother - A Short Biography. Wilfried Huchzermeyer. 104p. 1997. pap. 4.95 (*81-7060-015-4*, Pub. by SAA) E-W Cultural Ctr.

Mother - Son Talk. Gail Rebhan. (Artists' Books Ser.). (Illus.). 36p. (Orig.). 1996. pap. 18.00 (*0-89822-117-X*) Visual Studies.

Mother - Through the Eyes of Children. 1988. pap. 0.50 (*0-88494-653-3*) Bookcraft Inc.

Mother, a Story. Kathleen Norris. LC 70-137319. reprint ed. 27.50 (*0-404-04792-0*) AMS Pr.

Mother Always Told Me . . . Karen Dean. LC 95-50685. 56p. (Orig.). 1996. pap. 2.99 (*0-8341-1622-7*) Beacon Hill.

Mother & Baby Exercise: An Easy Fitness Program to Take You Through Pregnancy. Emma Scattergood. (Illus.). 128p. 1995. pap. 16.95 (*0-7063-7392-8*, Pub. by WrLock) Sterling.

Mother & Baby Homes: A Survey of Homes for Unmarried Mothers. Jill Nicholson. 1968. 45.00 (*0-7855-0584-9*, Pub. by Natl Inst Soc Work) St Mut.

Mother & Baby Zoo Animals. Caroline Arnold. LC 98-15749. (Zoo Animals Ser.). (Illus.). 32p. (J). (gr. k-2). 1999. 21.27 (*1-57505-285-7*, Carolrhoda) Lerner Pub.

***Mother & Baby Zoo Animals.** Caroline Arnold. LC 98-15749. (Zoo Animals Ser.). 32p. (J). (gr. k-2). 1999. 9.95 (*1-57505-390-X*, Carolrhoda) Lerner Pub.

***Mother & Child.** Sanduik Bokforlag. 120p. 1998. pap. 11.95 (*1-58048-051-9*) Sandvik Pub.

***Mother & Child: Reflections of Our First Year Together.** April R. Rogers. 144p. 1999. 17.95 (*0-9643763-7-7*, Pub. by U-Talk Pubns) Partners Pubs Grp.

Mother & Child: Visions of Parenting from Indigenous Cultures. Jan Reynolds. LC 96-32597. (Illus.). 112p. 1996. pap. 19.95 (*0-89281-637-6*, Inner Trad) Inner Tradit.

Mother & Child Vol. I: Inspirations for a New Mother's First Year. 2nd rev. ed. Sue E. Willett. (Family Ser.). 374p. 1995. pap. text 9.95 (*1-56383-050-7*, 9200) G & R Pub.

Mother & Child Health: Delivering the Services. 3rd ed. Cicely D. Williams et al. LC 93-16378. (Illus.). 416p. 1994. text 59.95 (*0-19-508148-X*); pap. text 35.00 (*0-19-508149-8*) OUP.

***Mother & Daughter.** Havoc Publishing Staff. 1999. 8.00 (*0-7416-1710-2*); pap. 5.00 (*0-7416-1120-1*); pap. 8.00 (*0-7416-1108-2*) Havoc Pub.

***Mother & Daughter.** Ed. by Havoc Publishing Staff. 1999. 20.00 (*1-57977-156-4*) Havoc Pub.

***Mother & Daughter.** Havoc Publishing Staff. 1999. 8.00 (*1-57977-611-6*) Havoc Pub.

Mother & Daughter: The Letters of Eleanor & Anna Roosevelt. Ed. by Bernard Asbell. LC 88-16572. 366p. 1988. pap. 9.95 (*0-88064-108-8*) Fromm Intl Pub.

Mother & Daughter Jewish Cooking: Two Generations Of Jewish Women Share Traditional And Contemporary Recipes. Evelyn Rose & Judi Rose. LC 99-38247. (Illus.). 304p. 2000. 26.00 (*0-688-16451-X*, Wm Morrow) Morrow Avon.

Mother & Daughter Record Memory Book: A Gift of Memories. Linda Spivey. 1997. 20.00 (*1-57977-111-4*) Havoc Pub.

***Mother & Daughter Reflections.** Pat Ross. LC 99-55090. 2000. 14.95 (*0-7407-0499-0*) Andrews & McMeel.

Mother & Daughter Tales. Illus. by Helen Cann. LC 97-146158. (Abbeville Anthology Ser.). 80p. (J). (ps-3). 1996. 19.95 (*0-7892-0281-6*, Abbeville Kids) Abbeville Pr.

Mother & Disciple: A Devout Discourse on the Blessed Virgin Mary. Charles E. Miller. LC 89-32761. 108p. (Orig.). 1989. pap. 4.95 (*0-8189-0548-4*) Alba.

Mother & Fetus: Changing Notions of Maternal Responsibility, 36. Robert H. Blank. LC 91-38029. (Contributions in Medical Studies: No. 36). 224p. 1992. 55.00 (*0-313-27639-0*, BOF/, Greenwood Pr) Greenwood.

Mother & Me. large type ed. Nancy L. Spinelle. (Illus.). 12p. (J). (gr. k-1). 1998. text 4.95 (*1-57874-000-2*, Kaeden) Kaeden Corp.

Mother & Narrative Politics in Modern China. Sally T. Lieberman. LC 97-30291. (Feminist Issues Ser.). 300p. 1998. text 39.50 (*0-8139-1790-5*) U Pr of Va.

Mother & Other Unsavory Plays. Stanislaw I. Witkiewicz. Ed. by Daniel Gerould. 128p. 1992. pap. 10.95 (*1-55783-139-4*) Applause Theatre Bk Pubs.

***Mother & Son.** Havoc Publishing Staff. 1999. pap. text 20.00 (*1-57977-153-X*) Havoc Pub.

Mother & Son: Tales of a Shtetle, 1908-1923. Abrasha Wilcher. 128p. 1993. 18.00 (*0-9635307-0-4*) First Prsn Pr.

Mother & the Father: Poetry. William Dean Howells. (Notable American Authors Ser.). 1992. reprint ed. lib. bdg. 75.00 (*0-7812-3280-5*) Rprt Serv.

Mother & Two Daughters. Gail Godwin. 608p. 1983. mass mkt. 4.95 (*0-380-61598-3*, Avon Bks) Morrow Avon.

Mother & Two Daughters. Gail Godwin. 512p. 1994. reprint ed. pap. 12.00 (*0-345-38923-9*) Ballantine Pub Grp.

Mother Angelica's Answers, Not Promises. Mother Angelica. 1991. per. 6.50 (*0-671-74673-1*) PB.

Mother Angelica's Answers, Not Promises. Mother M. Angelica. LC 96-77717. 275p. 1996. 15.95 (*0-89870-606-8*) Ignatius Pr.

Mother Angelica's Answers, Not Promises. large type ed. Mary Angelica. 464p. 1987. pap. 16.95 (*0-8027-2595-3*) Walker & Co.

Mother Ann Lee, Morning Star of the Shakers. Nardi R. Campion. LC 90-50305. (Illus.). 205p. (YA). (gr. 9-10). 1990. reprint ed. pap. 15.95 (*0-87451-527-0*) U Pr of New Eng.

Mother As I Saw Her. Swami Saradeshananda. Tr. by J. N. Dey from BEN. 237p. 1985. pap. 4.95 (*0-87481-530-4*, Pub. by Ramakrishna Math) Vedanta Pr.

***Mother at Heart.** Carlyne Aarsen. 2000. per. 4.50 (*0-373-87100-7*) Harlequin Bks.

Mother at Heart. Robin Elliott. (Special Edition Ser.). 1995. per. 3.75 (*0-373-09968-1*, 1-09968-8) Silhouette.

Mother at Heart. large type ed. Robin Elliott. (Silhouette Romance Ser.). 1997. 20.95 (*0-373-59767-3*) Thorndike Pr.

Mother at Home. John Abbott. 1998. pap. 7.49 (*0-87377-128-1*) GAM Pubns.

Mother at Home: or The Principles of Maternal Duty. John S. Abbott. LC 72-169366. (Family in America Ser.). (Illus.). 198p. 1976. reprint ed. 17.95 (*0-405-03841-0*) Ayer.

Mother-Baby Package: Implementing Safe Motherhood in Countries. (Illus.). 89p. 1994. pap. 13.50 (*0-614-32416-5*, 1930070) World Health.

Mother-Baby Pocket Coder, 1999. rev. ed. Ed. by Jerry Gill. 91p. 1998. 10.00 (*1-889823-05-8*) GLB Worldwide.

Mother Bear's Christmas Dilemma. 2nd ed. Annette M. Nardi. LC 97-226312. (Illus.). 24p. (Orig.). (J). (ps-3). 1996. per. 7.95 (*0-9648150-0-1*) TRI-CAR Pubns.

Mother Beluga Whales & Their Babies. Sarah S. Craft. LC 98-18931. (Zoo Life Book Ser.). 24p. (J). (gr. k-4). 1999. 17.27 (*0-8239-5315-7*, PowerKids) Rosen Group.

Mother Branch & Her Leaf Children: A Story about Assertiveness. (Excellence in Character Series Storybks.). (Illus.). 30p. (J). (gr. k-8). 1998. pap. 6.00 (*1-58259-015-X*) Global Classrm.

Mother Cabrini: Italian Immigrant of the Century. Mary L. Sullivan. LC 86-32721. 318p. 1992. 19.50 (*0-934733-06-6*); pap. 14.50 (*0-934733-71-6*) CMS.

Mother Cabrini: Missionary to the World. Frances P. Keyes. LC 97-70811. 1997. pap. text 9.95 (*0-89870-599-1*) Ignatius Pr.

Mother Camp: Female Impersonators in America. Esther Newton. LC 76-37634. 158p. 1979. pap. 15.95 (*0-226-57760-0*, P807) U Ch Pr.

Mother Carey's Chickens. Kate D. Wiggin. LC 92-239441. (Illus.). 366p. (J). (gr. 4-8). 1991. reprint ed. pap. 15.00 (*0-912498-10-2*) F A C E.

***Mother Cat.** large type ed. Kyoko Watambe. Tr. by Donna Tamaki.Tr. of Neko No Okasan. (ENG & JPN., Illus.). 12p. (J). (ps-3). 1998. 35.00 (*1-893533-09-3*, 18) Kamish for Kids.

***Mother Caught a Flea.** Jessica Souhami. (Silly Rhymes Ser.). (Illus.). (J). 1999. 7.99 (*0-7112-1243-0*) F Lincoln.

Mother-Child Dyad-Nutritional Aspects. Ed. by Leif Hambraeus & Stig Sjolin. (Illus.). 159p. (Orig.). 1979. pap. text 40.00 (*0-685-13806-2*) Coronet Bks.

M

Mother Church: Ecclesiology & Ecumenism. Carl E. Braaten. LC 98-11785. 1998. pap. 18.00 (0-8006-3082-3, Fortress Pr) Augsburg Fortress.

Mother Church: What the Experience of Women Is Teaching Her. Sally Cunneen. 1991. pap. 11.95 (0-8091-3265-6) Paulist Pr.

Mother Comes of Age. Driss Chraibi. Tr. by Hugh A. Harter from FRE. LC 81-51655.Tr. of La Civilisation, Ma Mere!. 121p. 1984. reprint ed. pap. 12.00 (0-89410-323-7, Three Contnts) L Rienner.

Mother Country. Marilynne Robinson. 1989. 18.95 (0-374-21361-5) FS&G.

Mother Country. Elisabeth Russell-Taylor et al. 167p. 1993. 32.00 (0-7206-0848-1, Pub. by P Owen Ltd) Dufour.

Mother Courage. Ellis Amburn. 2000. mass mkt. 6.99 (0-06-101408-7) HarpC.

Mother Courage & Her Children. Bertolt Brecht. Ed. by Ralph Manheim. Ed. & Tr. by John Willett from GER. LC 93-25408. 176p. 1994. pap. 8.70 (1-55970-234-6, Pub. by Arcade Pub Inc) Time Warner.

Mother Courage & Her Children. Bertolt Brecht. 112p. 1996. pap. 10.45 (1-55970-361-X, Pub. by Arcade Pub Inc) Time Warner.

Mother Courage & Her Children. Bertolt Brecht. Tr. & Adapted by Eric Bentley. LC 91-761. 128p. 1987. pap. 6.95 (0-8021-3082-8, Grove) Grove-Atltic.

Mother Courage & Her Children. Bertolt Brecht. 1999. text 10.95 (0-312-54923-7) St Martin.

M

Mother Crocodile. Rosa Guy. (J). 1996. mass mkt. 6.50 (0-440-91104-4) BDD Bks Young Read.

Mother Crocodile: "Maman-Caiman" Guy. 1981. 10.42 (0-440-06406-6) Delacorte.

Mother Dance: How Children Change Your Life. Harriet G. Lerner. LC 97-51852. 336p. 1998. 25.00 (0-06-018768-9) HarpC.

Mother Dance: How Children Change Your Life. Harriet G. Lerner. LC 97-51852. 336p. 1999. pap. 14.00 (0-06-093025-X) HarpC.

***Mother Dance: How Children Change Your Life, Set.** abr. ed. Harriet G. Lerner. 1998. audio 18.00 (0-694-51974-X, AF07R) HarperAudio.

Mother-Daughter Book Club: How 10 Busy Mothers & Their Daughters Came Together to Talk, Laugh, Learn, andShare Through Their Love of Reading. Shireen Dodson. LC 97-3702. 304p. 1997. pap. 14.00 (0-06-095242-3) HarpC.

Mother-Daughter Choices: A Handbook for the Coordinator. Mindy Bingham et al. Ed. by Barbara Greene & Sandy Stryker. (Illus.). 150p. 1988. pap. 14.95 (0-911655-44-1) Advocacy Pr.

***Mother Daughter Connection.** Susie Shellenberger. LC 99-86517. 180p. 2000. pap. 12.99 (0-8499-3769-8) Word Pub.

***Mother-Daughter Literary Social Event Kit.** (J). 2000. pap. write for info. (0-06-449276-1, HarpTrophy) HarpC Child Bks.

Mother-Daughter Relationship: Echoes Through Time. Ed. by Gerd H. Fenchel. LC 97-14588. 1997. text 50.00 (0-7657-0101-4) Aronson.

Mother Daughter Revolution: From Betrayal to Power. Elizabeth Debold et al. (Illus.). 1993. 22.95 (0-201-63277-2) Addison-Wesley.

Mother Daughter Revolution: From Good Girls to Great Women. Elizabeth Debold. 400p. 1994. pap. 12.95 (0-553-37418-4) Bantam.

Mother, Daughter, Sister: Journeys of the Spirit. T. P. David. LC 98-75061. 125p. 1998. 18.95 (1-57860-069-3) Guild Pr IN.

Mother-Daughter Switch. Created by Francine Pascal. (Sweet Valley Twins Ser.: No. 87). 144p. (J). (gr. 3-7). 1995. pap. 3.50 (0-553-48117-7) Bantam.

Mother-Daughter Switch. Jamie Suzanne. (Sweet Valley Twins Ser.: No. 86). (J). (gr. 3-7). 1995. 8.60 (0-606-08242-5, Pub. by Turtleback) Demco.

Mother Ditch: How Water Came to a New Mexico Town. Oliver LaFarge. Tr. by Pedro R. Ortego. LC 82-10712. (ENG & SPA., Illus.). 64p. 1983. pap. 8.95 (0-86534-009-9) Sunstone Pr.

Mother Doesn't Know about Kissing. Corinne Templeman. LC 96-223461. 128p. (C). 1995. pap. 16.95 (1-875560-67-X) Intl Spec Bk.

Mother Donit Fore the Best: Correspondence of a Nineteenth-Century Orphan Asylum. Judith A. Dulberger. (Illus.). 272p. (C). 1996. pap. 17.95 (0-8156-0341-X, DUMDP) Syracuse U Pr.

Mother Earth. Luenn. (J). 1998. pap. 4.95 (0-87628-942-1) Ctr Appl Res.

Mother Earth. Nancy Luenn. (Illus.). 32p. (J). (ps-3). 1995. mass mkt. 5.99 (0-689-80164-5) Aladdin.

Mother Earth. Nancy Luenn. LC 90-19134. (Illus.). 32p. (J). (ps-3). 1992. 15.00 (0-689-31668-2) Atheneum Yung Read.

Mother Earth. Nancy Luenn. (J). 1995. 10.15 (0-606-07890-8) Turtleback.

Mother Earth. Cynthia Todd & Debbie Ziemann. (Sing Me a Song Ser.). (Illus.). 24p. (J). 1998. pap. 15.95 (1-879056-03-8) Alpenhorn Pr.

Mother Earth: An American Story. Sam D. Gill. LC 86-30711. x, 196p. 1987. 24.95 (0-226-29371-8) U Ch Pr.

Mother Earth: An American Story. Sam D. Gill. 206p. 1991. pap. 13.95 (0-226-29372-6) U Ch Pr.

Mother Earth: Land Grants in Virginia, 1607-1699. W. Stitt Robinson, Jr. (Illus.). 77p. 1957. pap. text 5.95 (0-8139-0136-7) U Pr of Va.

Mother Earth & Father Time. Richard M. Sherman & Robert B. Sherman. (Illus.). 24p. (J). 1995. 14.95 (1-885297-52-1); lib. bdg. 14.95 (1-885297-54-8) Paradon Pubng.

***Mother Earth & Her Relations.** Elke Poths. 2000. write for info. (1-58235-527-4) Watermrk Pr.

Mother Earth Father Sky. Sue Harrison. 400p. 1991. mass mkt. 6.99 (0-380-71592-9, Avon Bks) Morrow Avon.

Mother Earth Father Sky. large type ed. Sue Harrison. LC 90-25536. 561p. 1991. reprint ed. lib. bdg. 21.95 (1-56054-093-1) Thorndike Pr.

Mother Earth, Father Sky: Ancient Chants by Pueblo & Navajo Indians of the Southwest. Marcia Keegan. LC 73-7091. 112p. 1988. 29.95 (0-940666-05-7) Clear Light.

Mother Earth, Father Sky: Native American Myth. Time-Life Books Editors. (Myth & Mankind Ser.). (Illus.). 144p. (J). (gr. 7). 1999. 29.95 (0-7054-3523-7) T-L Custom Pub.

***Mother Earth, Father Sky: Native American Wisdom.** Ariel. LC 99-60617. (Illus.). 80p. 1999. 4.95 (0-7407-0073-1) Andrews & McMeel.

Mother Earth, Father Sky: Poems of Our Planet. Jane Yolen. LC 95-60724. (Illus.). 64p. (J). (gr. 4 up). 1995. 15.95 (1-56397-414-2, Wordsong) Boyds Mills Pr.

Mother Earth, Father Sky: The Pueblo Indians of the American Southwest. David Lavender. LC 97-38119. (Illus.). 96p. (J). (gr. 4-7). 1998. 16.95 (0-8234-1365-9) Holiday.

Mother Earth Messages: For Twenty-First Century Parenting. Jennifer R. Doster. LC 92-90271. 80p. 1992. pap. 7.95 (0-9633152-0-X) Doster Pub.

Mother Earth Muse. Lia La Mer. (Illus.). 140p. 1997. 14.00 (1-58486-009-X) LyricLine Pr.

Mother Earth News Alcohol Fuel Handbook. Ed. by Mother Earth News Editors & Michael R. Kerley. (Illus.). 120p. (Orig.). 1980. pap. 12.95 (0-938432-00-1) Mother Earth.

***Mother Earth Reader.** Glassgold. 2000. 24.00 (1-58243-040-3, Pub. by Counterpt DC) HarpC.

Mother Earth Spanish. Nancy Luenn. (Illus.). (J). 1999. pap. 15.00 (0-689-80000-2) Atheneum Yung Read.

Mother Earth Spirituality: Native American Paths to Healing Ourselves & Our World. Ed McGaa. LC 89-46149. (Illus.). 256p. (Orig.). 1990. pap. 17.00 (0-06-250596-3, Pub. by Harper SF) HarpC.

Mother Earth Talks to the Sun, Wind & Rain: A Story about Kindness. (Excellence in Character Series Storybks.). (Illus.). 30p. (J). (gr. k-8). 1998. pap. 6.00 (1-58259-021-4) Global Classrm.

Mother Earth's Mercantile: Plants of the Four Corners Area & Their Uses Through Time. Elizabeth M. Wheeler. LC 94-71580. (Illus.). 40p. (Orig.). 1994. pap. 9.95 (0-9624640-4-X) Crow Canyon Archaeol.

Mother, Father, Big Sopha & Me. Mark Kogan. Ed. by Olga Chotianovsky. (Illus.). 104p. (Orig.). (YA). 1991. pap. text 6.00 (0-9624922-2-1) Hazar NY.

Mother Father Deaf: Living Between Sound & Silence. Paul Preston. LC 93-44895. 296p. (C). 1994. text 24.95 (0-674-58747-2) HUP.

Mother Father Deaf: Living Between Sound & Silence. Paul Preston. 288p. (C). 1995. pap. 15.95 (0-674-58748-0) HUP.

***Mother Flies Hurricanes.** E. M. Singer. ix, 864p. 1999. pap. 22.95 (0-9674677-0-5, Pub. by Avidia Cascade) BookMasters.

***Mother for Amanda.** Anna Schmidt. (Love Inspired Ser.). 2000. mass mkt. 4.50 (0-373-87115-5, 1-87115-1, Steeple Hill) Harlequin Bks.

Mother for Choco. Keiko Kasza. (Illus.). 32p. (J). (ps-1). 1992. lib. bdg. 15.95 (0-399-21841-6, G P Putnam) Peng Put Young Read.

Mother for Choco. Keiko Kasza. LC 91-12361. (Illus.). 32p. (J). (ps-3). 1996. pap. 5.99 (0-698-11364-0, PapStar) Peng Put Young Read.

Mother for Choco. Keiko Kasza. LC 91-12361. (J). 1996. 10.15 (0-606-09632-9, Pub. by Turtleback) Demco.

Mother for Hire. Marie Ferrarella. (Family Continuity Program Ser.: No. 8). 1999. per. 4.50 (0-373-82156-5, 1-82156-0) Harlequin Bks.

Mother for Jeffrey. Trisha Alexander. 1998. mass mkt. 4.25 (0-373-24211-5, 1-24211-4) Silhouette.

***Mother for Mollie.** Barbara McMahon. (Romance Ser.). 2000. mass mkt. 3.50 (0-373-03616-7, 1-03616-9) Harlequin Bks.

***Mother for Mollie, Vol. 462.** large type ed. Barbara McMahon. (Large Print Ser.: Vol. 462). 2000. mass mkt. 3.50 (0-373-15862-9) Harlequin Bks.

Mother Gave a Shout: Poems by Women & Girls. Ed. by Susanna Steele & Morag Styles. LC 90-12938. (Illus.). 128p. (J). (gr. 3-8). 1991. 14.95 (0-912078-90-1) Volcano Pr.

Mother Giraffes & Their Babies. Sarah S. Craft. LC 98-23985. (Zoo Life Book Ser.). 24p. (J). (gr. k-4). 1999. 18.60 (0-8239-5316-5, PowerKids) Rosen Group.

***Mother Goddess: A Global Perspective.** Gupta. 1999. 15.00 (81-202-0525-1, Pub. by Indus Pub) S Asia.

Mother Goddess & Other Goddesses. Ed. by V. Subramaniam. (C). 1993. text 22.00 (81-202-0392-5, Pub. by Ajanta) S Asia.

Mother Goddess Candi: (Its Socio Ritual Impact on the Folk Life) Sibendu Manna. 1993. 36.00 (81-85094-60-8, Pub. by Punthi Pus) S Asia.

Mother Goddess Durga. Pranab Bandyopadhyay. 1987. 13.00 (0-8364-2065-9) S Asia.

Mother Goddess Vaishno Devi. N. Tiwari. (C). 1988. 17.50 (81-7062-046-5, Pub. by Lancer India) S Asia.

Mother Goddesses in Early Indian Religion. Savitri Dhawan. LC 97-901637. 1997. 30.00 (81-86803-07-6, Pub. by Natl Pub Hse) S Asia.

Mother Gone Bad: The Hidden Confession of JonBenet's Killer. Andrew G. Hodges. (Illus.). 240p. 1998. pap. 12.95 (0-9617255-1-6) Village Hse Pubs.

Mother Goose. write for info. (0-528-87081-5) Checkerboard.

Mother Goose. (Pictureback Ser.). 1978. pap. write for info. (0-318-55417-8) Random Bks Yng Read.

Mother Goose. Ed. by Aurelius Battaglia. (J). (ps-1). 1973. pap. 3.25 (0-394-82661-2, Pub. by Random Bks Yng Read) Random.

Mother Goose. William Joyce. (Illus.). 1995. 4.99 (0-679-86655-8) Random.

Mother Goose. Illus. by Carl Morton. (J). (gr. k-1). 1992. 10.00 (1-57842-092-X) Delmas Creat.

***Mother Goose.** Willy Pogany. (Books of Wonder Ser.). (Illus.). (J). 2000. 19.95 (1-58717-026-4) SeaStar.

Mother Goose. Arthur Rackham. (Children's Library). 176p. (J). 1998. pap. 3.95 (1-85326-146-7, 1467WW, Pub. by Wrdsworth Edits) NTC Contemp Pub Co.

Mother Goose. Illus. by Frederick Richardson. LC 72-161577. 160p. (J). (ps-4). 1915. 12.95 (1-56288-254-6) Checkerboard.

Mother Goose. Brian Wildsmith. (J). 1987. 17.15 (0-606-03865-5, Pub. by Turtleback) Demco.

Mother Goose. Eloise Wilkin. (Little Golden Treasures Ser.). 26p. (J). 1998. 5.99 (0-307-20310-7, 20310, Goldn Books) Gldn Bks Pub Co.

Mother Goose: A Collection of Classic Nursery Rhymes. Illus. by Michael Hague. LC 83-22559. 80p. (J). (ps-2). 1995. 15.95 (0-8050-0214-6, Bks Young Read) H Holt & Co.

Mother Goose: A Sampler. Frwd. by Celia Barker Lottridge. 64p. (J). (gr. k-1). 1996. 18.95 (0-88899-260-2) Publishers Group.

Mother Goose: Designs for Applique & Embroidery Based on Traditional Nursery Rhymes. Martha Parker. (Illus.). 48p. (Orig.). 1983. pap. 8.00 (0-932946-10-0) Burdett CA.

Mother Goose: Level Two, Yellow. Illus. by Michael Foreman. LC 98-88074. (Reading Together Ser.). (J). 1999. pap. write for info. (0-7636-0855-6) Candlewick Pr.

Mother Goose: Nursery Rhymes. Brian Wildsmith. (Illus.). 80p. (J). (ps-3). 1987. reprint ed. pap. 11.95 (0-19-272180-1) OUP.

Mother Goose: The Original Volland Edition. Illus. by Frederick Richardson. 128p. (J). (gr. k up). 1988. 9.99 (0-517-43619-1) Random Hse Value.

Mother Goose - Deluxe: Blue, Vol. IV. Illus. by Blanche F. Wright. 24p. (J). (ps-2). 1988. pap. 7.98 incl. audio (1-55886-015-0) Smarty Pants.

Mother Goose - Deluxe: Green, Vol. III. Illus. by Blanche F. Wright. 24p. (J). (ps-2). 1988. pap. 7.98 incl. audio (1-55886-014-2, DC 7003) Smarty Pants.

Mother Goose - Deluxe: Red, Vol. I. Illus. by Blanche F. Wright. 24p. (J). (ps-2). 1988. pap. 7.98 incl. audio (1-55886-012-6, DC7001) Smarty Pants.

Mother Goose - Deluxe: Yellow, Vol. II. Illus. by Blanche F. Wright. 24p. (J). (ps-2). 1988. pap. 7.98 incl. audio (1-55886-013-4, DC 7002) Smarty Pants.

Mother Goose & Friends: A Number Activity Book. Becky Daniel. Ed. by Judy Mitchell. (Illus.). 352p. (Orig.). (J). (ps-3). 1995. pap. 24.95 (1-57310-011-0) Teachng & Lrning Co.

Mother Goose & Friends: An Alphabet Activity Book. Becky Daniel. Ed. by Judy Mitchell. (Illus.). 352p. (J). (ps-3). 1994. pap., teacher ed. 24.95 (1-57310-000-5) Teachng & Lrning Co.

Mother Goose & Grimm, No. 3. Mike Peters. LC 96-44783. 128p. 1997. pap. 10.95 (0-312-86069-2, Pub. by Tor Bks) St Martin.

Mother Goose & Grimm: Bone in the U. S. A. Mike Peters. (Illus.). 128p. 1992. pap. 3.50 (0-8125-1526-9, Pub. by Tor Bks) St Martin.

Mother Goose & Grimm: Grimmy-Best in Show. Mike Peters. 1990. pap. 3.50 (0-8125-0712-6, Pub. by Tor Bks) St Martin.

Mother Goose & Grimm: On the Move. Mike Peters. 1992. pap. 3.50 (0-8125-1527-7, Pub. by Tor Bks) St Martin.

Mother Goose & Grimm: Pick of the Litter. Mike Peters. 1990. pap. 2.95 (0-8125-1080-1, Pub. by Tor Bks) St Martin.

Mother Goose & Grimm: Top Dog. Mike Peters. (Illus.). 128p. (Orig.). 1991. pap. 3.50 (0-8125-1511-0, Pub. by Tor Bks) St Martin.

***Mother Goose & Her Animal Friends: Big Book, Theme 2.** large type ed. Lee Bennett Hopkins. (Mother Goose Ser.). (Illus.). 16p. (J). 1999. pap. text 28.95 (0-8215-0472-X) Sadlier.

***Mother Goose & Her Children: Big Book, Theme 1.** large type ed. Lee Bennett Hopkins. (Mother Goose Ser.). (Illus.). 16p. (J). (ps-1). 1999. pap. text 28.95 (0-8215-0462-2) Sadlier.

Mother Goose & Her Nursery-Rhyme Friends. (Look & Find Ser.). (Illus.). 24p. (J). 1993. 7.98 (1-56173-418-7) Pubns Intl Ltd.

Mother Goose & Her Nursery-Rhyme Friends. Illus. by Bob Terrio. (Look & Find Ser.). 24p. (J). (gr. k-6). 1995. lib. bdg. 14.95 (1-56674-096-7, HTS Bks) Forest Hse.

Mother Goose & More: Classic Nursery Rhymes with Added Lines. Dr. Hickey. (Illus.). 48p. (J). (ps-3). 1990. 7.77 (0-9623940-0-9); teacher ed. 9.00 (0-685-45372-3); text 12.95 (0-685-45371-5); lib. bdg. 7.00 (0-685-45370-7) Additions Pr.

***Mother Goose & Nursery Rhymes.** (J). 1998. 9.95 incl. audio (1-887120-08-4, Pub. by Prodn Assocs) Penton Overseas.

Mother Goose & Other Nursery Songs, Set. Illus. by Walter Crane & Randolph Caldecott. 46p. (J). (ps up). 1997. 16.95 incl. audio (0-930647-03-3) Lancaster Prodns.

Mother Goose & Others in Wall Street. Bond Mann. LC 68-21700. 1968. reprint ed. pap. 5.00 (0-87034-032-8) Fraser Pub Co.

***Mother Goose Around the World: Big Book, Theme 4.** large type ed. Lee Bennett Hopkins. (Mother Goose Ser.). (Illus.). 20p. (J). 1999. pap. text 28.95 (0-8215-0492-4) Sadlier.

Mother Goose Audio Gift Pack, 4 bks., Set. Illus. by Blanche F. Wright. 96p. (J). (ps-2). 1990. pap. 19.98 incl. audio (1-55886-018-5, AGP 4-201) Smarty Pants.

Mother Goose Book. Joan W. Anglund. Ed. by Liz Van Doren. LC 90-4466. (Illus.). 32p. (J). (ps up). 1991. 7.95 (0-15-200529-3, Gulliver Bks) Harcourt.

Mother Goose Caboose. Marilynn G. Barr. 256p. (J). (ps-2). 1991. 14.99 (0-86653-618-3, GA1337) Good Apple.

Mother Goose Charted Designs. Kathleen Thorne-Thomsen. (Illus.). 48p. (Orig.). 1987. reprint ed. pap. 3.50 (0-486-25483-6) Dover.

Mother Goose-Coloring Book. (J). 1985. pap. 4.95 (0-88388-012-1) Bellerophon Bks.

Mother Goose Coloring Book. Kate Greenaway. (Illus.). (J). (gr. k-3). 1976. pap. 2.95 (0-486-22883-5) Dover.

Mother Goose Comedy Revue. Patricia B. Rumble. 30p. (Orig.). (J). (gr. k-6). 1994. pap. 3.00 (1-57514-222-8, 1101) Encore Perform Pub.

Mother Goose Cookbook: Rhymes & Recipes for the Very Young. Marianna Mayer. LC 97-5942. (Illus.). 37p. (J). (ps-3). 1998. 11.95 (0-688-15242-2, Wm Morrow) Morrow Avon.

Mother Goose Favorite Lullabies. Margaret A. Hughes. (Talking Mother Goose Ser.). (Illus.). 26p. (J). (ps). 1987. 9.95 (0-934323-51-8); audio. write for info. (0-318-61877-X) Alchemy Comms.

Mother Goose Favorites: With Matching Foam Play Pieces. Illus. by Bob Pepper. 8p. (J). 1999. 9.99 (1-58476-002-8) Innovative Kids.

Mother Goose Feast: Rhymes & Recipes. Ed. by Michele Palmer. LC 79-65819. (Illus.). (J). (ps-12). 1979. pap. 1.95 (0-932306-01-2) Rocking Horse.

Mother Goose Gospel, Vol. 1. (J). write for info. incl. audio (1-55897-574-8, CSBK5075) Brentwood Music.

Mother Goose in Hieroglyphics. Mother Goose Staff. Ed. by Everett F. Bleiler. 64p. 1973. pap. 4.95 (0-486-20745-5) Dover.

Mother Goose in Prose. L. Frank Baum. (J). (gr. k up). 1986. 4.98 (0-685-16878-6, 519046) Random Hse Value.

Mother Goose in Sign. S. Harold Collins. (Beginning Sign Language Ser.). (Illus.). 15p. (J). (ps). 1994. pap. 3.95 (0-931993-66-0, GP-066) Garlic Pr OR.

Mother Goose Jazz Chants: Student Book. Carolyn Graham. (Illus.). 1994. pap. text, student ed. 13.95 (0-19-434001-5) OUP.

Mother Goose Math. Illus. by Emily Bolam. LC 96-61716. 32p. (J). 1997. 14.99 (0-670-87569-4) Viking Penguin.

Mother Goose Math. Emily Bolam. 32p. 1999. pap. 5.99 (0-14-056393-8, PuffinBks) Peng Put Young Read.

Mother Goose Mazes. Dave Phillips. LC 92-17679. (J). 1992. pap. 2.95 (0-486-27319-9) Dover.

Mother Goose Meets a Woman Called Wisdom: A Short Course in the Art of Self-Determination. Linda H. Hollies. LC 99-41005. 192p. 1999. pap. 21.95 (0-8298-1348-9) Pilgrim OH.

Mother Goose Melodies. Notes by Everett F. Bleiler. (Illus.). 128p. (J). (ps up). 1970. reprint ed. pap. 3.95 (0-486-22577-1) Dover.

***Mother Goose News.** Claire Janosik Griffin. LC 00-22244. (Rollicking Rhymes Ser.). (Illus.). (J). 2000. write for info. (1-56822-976-3) Instruct Fair.

Mother Goose Nursery Rhymes: Super Chubby Books. Mother Goose. LC 84-72862. (Illus.). 32p. (J). (ps). 1984. 4.99 (0-671-49878-9) S&S Trade.

Mother Goose on the Rio Grande. Frances Alexander. (Illus.). 96p. (J). (gr. 4 up). 1994. pap. 6.95 (0-8442-7641-3, Natl Textbk Co) NTC Contemp Pub Co.

Mother Goose on the Rio Grande. Frances Alexander. LC 97-33333. (ENG & SPA., Illus.). 96p. 1997. pap. 7.95 (0-8442-7642-1, 76421) NTC Contemp Pub Co.

Mother Goose PaperCrafts. Jerome C. Brown. (PaperCrafts & Literature Ser.). (J). (gr. k-5). 1989. pap. 7.99 (0-8224-3154-8) Fearon Teacher Aids.

***Mother Goose Phonics: Learning to Read Fun with Adorable Activities, Games & Manipulatives.** Deborah Schecter. (Illus.). 64p. 1999. pap. 10.95 (0-439-12927-3) Scholastic Inc.

Mother Goose Picture Book. Margot Zemach. LC 94-75640. (Michael di Capua Bks.). (Illus.). (J). 2000. 14.95 (0-06-205046-X); lib. bdg. 14.89 (0-06-205047-8) HarpC Child Bks.

Mother Goose Pop-Up. Illus. & Read by Joan Walsh Anglund. 16p. (J). (ps up). 1995. 11.95 (0-671-87079-3) Litle Simon.

***Mother Goose Remembers.** Clare Beaton. (Illus.). 64p. (J). (ps-2). 2000. 16.99 (1-84148-073-8) Barefoot Bks NY.

Mother Goose Revisited: German Shepherd Puppies Reenacting Nursery Rhymes. Photos by G. A. Bradley. (Illus.). (J). (gr. 2-4). 1994. 29.95 (1-886123-04-7) Geyers Garten.

Mother Goose Revisited: Rottweiler Puppies Reenacting Nursery Rhymes. Photos by G. A. Bradley. (Illus.). 32p. (J). (gr. 2-4). 1994. 29.95 (1-886123-01-2) Geyers Garten.

Mother Goose Rhymes. Berthe Amoss. (Illus.). 10p. (J). (ps-7). 1989. pap. 2.95 (0-922589-02-X) More Than a Card.

Mother Goose Rhymes. Jill Dublin. (Itty Bitties Ser.). (Illus.). 20p. (J). (ps). 1991. bds. 3.50 (0-8120-6267-1) Barron.

Mother Goose Rhymes. McClanahan Book Company Staff. (I-See-You-Bks.). (Illus.). 8p. (J). 1997. 3.50 (1-56293-983-1, McClanahan Book) Learn Horizon.

Mother Goose Rhymes for Jewish Children. Sara G. Levy. (Illus.). (J). (ps-2). 1979. reprint ed. pap. 8.95 (0-8197-0254-4) Bloch.

Mother Goose Rhymes-Versos Infantiles-Vers D'Enfance. Laurie M. Rollings. 64p. 1988. 19.95 incl. audio (0-945206-00-3) Matterplay.

Mother Goose Songbook. Carol Barratt. (J). (gr. k up). 1986. 4.98 (0-685-16882-4, 615754) Random Hse Value.

An Asterisk (*) at the beginning of an entry indicates that the title is appearing for the first time.

Mother Goose Songs. (Play - a - Sound Ser.). (Illus.). 24p. (J). 1993. 12.98 (*0-7853-0053-8*) Pubns Intl Ltd.

Mother Goose Songs Jerry Tiritilli. LC 98-234946. (Illus.). 1997. write for info. (*0-7853-2639-1*) Pubns Intl Ltd.

Mother Goose Stickers & Seals: 40 Full-Color Pressure-Sensitive Designs. Carolyn Bracken. (Illus.). (J). 1992. pap. 3.50 (*0-486-27031-9*) Dover.

Mother Goose Suite Piano. 7.95 (*0-7935-3535-2*, 50482200) H Leonard.

Mother Goose Sweeps History. Stella K. Abbey. LC 13-275. (Illus.). 1967. 2.99 (*0-686-00888-X*) S K Abbey.

Mother Goose Teaches the Ten Commandments. Phyllis Meulendyk. 23p. 1989. pap. text 10.00 (*1-58302-051-9*, BPS-02) One Way St.

Mother Goose, the Old Nursery Rhymes. Illus. by Arthur Rackham. (J). (ps-6). 1978. reprint ed. lib. bdg. 13.00 (*0-932106-02-1*, Pub. by Marathon Press) S J Durst.

Mother Goose III. Illus. by Carl Morton. (J). (gr. k-1). 1992. 10.00 (*1-57842-094-6*) Delmas Creat.

***Mother Goose Through the Seasons: Big Book, Theme 3.** large type ed. Lee Bennett Hopkins. (Mother Goose Ser.). (Illus.). 16p. (J). 1999. pap. text 28.95 (*0-8215-0482-7*) Sadlier.

Mother Goose Time: Library Programs for Babies & Their Caregivers. Jane Marino & Dorothy F. Houlihan. 172p. 1992. 30.00 (*0-8242-0850-1*) Wilson.

Mother Goose II. Illus. by Carl Morton. (J). (gr. k-1). 1992. 10.00 (*1-57842-093-8*) Delmas Creat.

Mother Goose's Animal Farm. (Read-A-Rhyme Ser.). (Illus.). 24p. (J). (gr. 1-4). 1996. pap. write for info. (*1-56144-717-X*, Honey Bear Bks) Modern Pub NYC.

Mother Goose's Animals. Nancy Polette. (Illus.). 128p. 1992. pap. 12.95 (*1-879287-13-7*, BL023) Pieces of Lrning.

***Mother Goose's Basket Full of Ryhmes: Board Book & Cassette.** Carly Simon & Public Domain Research Staff. (Illus.). 12p. (J). (ps-k). 2000. 11.95 (*0-689-83117-X*) Litle Simon.

Mother Goose's Bedtime Rhymes. (Read-A-Rhyme Ser.). (Illus.). 24p. (J). (gr. 1-4). 1996. pap. write for info. (*1-56144-715-3*, Honey Bear Bks) Modern Pub NYC.

Mother Goose's House. Peter Lippman. (Mini House Bks.). (Illus.). 20p. (J). (ps-1). 1996. bds. 9.95 (*0-7611-0536-0*, 10536) Workman Pub.

Mother Goose's Kitchen. (Read-A-Rhyme Ser.). (Illus.). 24p. (J). (gr. 1-4). 1996. pap. write for info. (*1-56144-714-5*, Honey Bear Bks) Modern Pub NYC.

Mother Goose's Nursery Rhymes. Ariel Books Staff. (Illus.). 80p. (J). 1992. 4.95 (*0-8362-3024-8*) Andrews & McMeel.

Mother Goose's Nursery Rhymes. Illus. by Robyn Officer. (Children's Classics Ser.). 32p. (J). (ps-3). 1992. 6.95 (*0-8362-4907-0*) Andrews & McMeel.

Mother Goose's Nursery Rhymes. Ed. by Walter Jerrold. LC 93-22604. (Children's Classics Ser.). Orig. Title: The Big Book of Nursery Rhymes. (J). 1993. reprint ed. 13.95 (*0-679-42815-1*) Everymns Lib.

Mother Gorillas & Their Babies. Sarah S. Craft. LC 98-23986. (Zoo Life Book Ser.). 24p. (J). (gr. k-4). 1999. 18.60 (*0-8239-5313-0*, PowerKids) Rosen Group.

Mother-Headed Families & Why They Have Increased. Ailsa Burns & Cath Scott. 232p. 1994. text 49.95 (*0-8058-1440-X*) L Erlbaum Assocs.

Mother, Help. Lurlene McDaniel. (One Last Wish Ser.: No. 3). (J). 1997. mass mkt. 4.99 (*0-553-54280-X*) BDD Bks Young Read.

Mother, Help Me Live. Lurlene McDaniel. (One Last Wish Ser.). 1992. 9.09 (*0-606-00704-0*, Pub. by Turtleback) Demco.

Mother, Help Me Live: One Last Wish. Lurlene McDaniel. 176p. (YA). 1992. mass mkt. 4.50 (*0-553-29811-9*) Bantam.

Mother Hicks: Playscript. Suzan L. Zeder. 68p. (J). (gr. k-3). 1986. pap. 7.00 (*0-87602-263-8*) Anchorage.

Mother Holle. Charlotte Dorn & Peter Becker. (Illus.). 24p. (J). Date not set. 12.95 (*1-55082-042-7*, Pub. by Quarry Pr) LPC InBook.

Mother Holle. Charlotte Dorn & Peter Becker. (Illus.). 24p. 1993. per. 8.95 (*1-55082-043-5*, Pub. by Quarry Pr) LPC InBook.

Mother Hubbard's Christmas. John O'Brien. LC 95-83169. (Illus.). 32p. (J). (ps-1). 1996. 14.95 (*1-56397-139-9*) Boyds Mills Pr.

Mother Hubbard's Christmas. John O'Brien. 32p. (J). (ps-2). 1998. pap. 6.99 (*0-440-41450-4*) Dell.

Mother I Always. Schutz. 1992. 6.95 (*0-446-77632-7*) Warner Bks.

Mother I Carry: A Memoir of Healing from Emotional Abuse. Louise M. Wisechild. LC 93-25030. 280p. (Orig.). 1993. pap. 12.95 (*1-878067-38-9*) Seal Pr WA.

Mother, I Love You. Roy Honegger. Ed. by Patrick Caton. LC 96-78978. 168p. 1997. pap. 5.95 (*1-56245-278-9*) Great Quotations.

***Mother, I Love You.** Helen Steiner Rice. 2001. 8.99 (*0-517-16284-9*) Crown Pub Group.

Mother, I Love You. Helen Steiner Rice & Virginia J. Ruehlmann. LC 98-41203. (Illus.). 80p. 1999. 14.99 (*0-8007-1764-3*) Revell.

Mother, I Love You Forever. Ed. by Susan Polis Schutz. 64p. 1994. mass mkt. 7.99 (*0-446-67018-9*, Pub. by Warner Bks) Little.

Mother I Will. Schutz. 1993. 6.95 (*0-446-77804-4*) Warner Bks.

Mother, I Will Always Love You. Ed. by Susan Polis Schutz. 64p. 1990. mass mkt. 7.99 (*0-446-39143-3*, Pub. by Warner Bks) Little.

***Mother Imagery in the Novels of Afro-Caribbean Women.** Simone A. James Alexander. 224p. 2001. 32.50 (*0-8262-1309-X*) U of Mo Pr.

***Mother in a Moment.** Alison Leigh. 2001. mass mkt. 4.50 (*0-373-24367-7*, 1-24367-4) Silhouette.

Mother in Israel. Compiled by Christeen L. Anderson & David L. Keyston. (Illus.). 120p. 1998. pap. 14.95 (*0-9645803-6-5*, PB-M1) Healing Unltd.

Mother in Israel: The Story of Deborah. Bert Polman. (Scripture Alive Ser.). 25p. 1998. pap. text 14.95 (*1-56212-329-7*, 2280-0050) CRC Pubns.

Mother-in-Law Diaries. Carol Dawson. LC 98-27774. 294p. 1999. 19.95 (*1-56512-127-9*) Algonquin Bks.

***Mother-in-Law Diaries.** Carol Dawson. LC 99-52912. 288p. 2000. reprint ed. per. 12.95 (*0-671-04085-5*, WSP) PB.

Mother in the Making (Home on the Ranch) Ellen James. (Superromance Ser.). 1996. per. 3.99 (*0-373-70685-5*, 1-70685-2) Harlequin Bks.

Mother in the Work & Life of Peter Weiss. Asa Eldh. LC 89-8186. (American University Studies: Germanic Languages & Literature: Ser. I, Vol. 84). 238p. (C). 1990. 46.50 (*0-8204-0983-9*) P Lang Pubng.

***Mother India.** Katherine Mayo. Ed. by Mrinalini Sinha. LC 99-58162. 308p. 2000. text 49.50 (*0-472-09715-6*, 09715); pap. text 19.95 (*0-472-06715-X*, 06715) U of Mich Pr.

Mother India. Katherine Mayo. LC 76-88906. 440p. 1970. reprint ed. lib. bdg. 75.00 (*0-8371-2309-7*, MAMO, Greenwood Pr) Greenwood.

Mother Indian Rhinos & Their Babies. Sarah S. Craft. LC 98-7668. (Zoo Life Book Ser.). 24p. (J). (gr. k-4). 1999. 18.60 (*0-8239-5318-1*, PowerKids) Rosen Group.

Mother-Infant Bonding: A Scientific Fiction. Diane E. Eyer. LC 92-17292. 256p. (C). 1993. 32.50 (*0-300-05682-6*) Yale U Pr.

Mother-Infant Bonding: A Scientific Fiction. Diane E. Eyer. 256p. 1994. pap. 16.00 (*0-300-06051-3*) Yale U Pr.

***Mother Ireland.** Edna O'Brien. LC 98-40435. 112p. 1999. pap. 11.95 (*0-452-28050-8*) NAL.

Mother Ireland. Maria Valentin. 120p. 1998. pap. 12.00 (*0-9651657-4-4*) NWI.

Mother is a Freshman. Raphael David Blay & Christopher Sergel. 78p. 1949. pap. 5.50 (*0-87129-633-0*, M34) Dramatic Pub.

Mother Is a Special Person. Lois L. Kaufman. LC 99-222838. (Keepsakes Ser.). (Illus.). 1998. 7.99 (*0-88088-864-4*) Peter Pauper.

Mother Is Blessed: A Sermon & Order of Service for Mother's Day. Robert J. Campbell. 1992. pap. 3.95 (*1-55673-602-9*, 9322) CSS OH.

Mother Is Born: Preparing for Motherhood During Pregnancy. Merete Leonhardt-Lupa. LC 94-29716. 176p. 1995. 16.95 (*0-89789-353-0*, Bergin & Garvey) Greenwood.

Mother Jackson Murders the Moon. Gloria Escoffery. LC 99-185284. 60p. 1998. pap. 12.95 (*1-900715-24-4*, Pub. by Peepal Tree Pr) Paul & Co Pubs.

Mother Jones. Joan C. Hawxhurst. LC 92-22191. (American Troublemakers Ser.). (Illus.). 128p. (J). (gr. 7-10). 1992. lib. bdg. 27.11 (*0-8114-2327-1*) Raintree Steck-V.

Mother Jones. Madelyn Horton. LC 95-2860. (Importance of . . . Ser.). 112p. (J). (gr. 6-9). 1996. lib. bdg. 22.45 (*1-56006-057-3*) Lucent Bks.

***Mother Jones: An American Life.** Elliott J. Gorn. (Illus.). 352p. 2001. 27.00 (*0-8090-7093-6*) Hill & Wang.

Mother Jones: Mini-Play. (Women's Studies). (J). (gr. 5). 1975. 6.50 (*0-89550-367-0*) Stevens & Shea.

Mother Jones: One Woman's Fight for Labor. Betsy H. Kraft. LC 94-19715. (Illus.). 128p. 1995. 16.95 (*0-395-67163-9*) HM.

Mother Jones: The Worker's Champion. Judith Pinkerton Josephson. (YA). 1996. lib. bdg. 23.93 (*0-8225-4924-7*, Lerner Publctns) Lerner Pub.

Mother Jones & Her Sisters. Robert Cook & Roberts. 290p. (C). 1999. per. 33.95 (*0-7872-5809-1*, 41580902) Kendall-Hunt.

Mother Jones Speaks: Speeches & Writings of a Working-Class Fighter. Mary H. Jones. Ed. by Philip S. Foner. LC 83-60486. 724p. 1983. reprint ed. lib. bdg. 70.00 (*0-913460-88-5*) Pathfinder NY.

Mother Jones Speaks: Speeches & Writings of a Working-Class Fighter. Mary H. Jones. Ed. by Philip S. Foner. LC 83-60486. 724p. 1983. reprint ed. pap. 28.95 (*0-87348-810-5*) Pathfinder NY.

Mother Jones, the Miners' Angel: A Portrait. Dale Fetherling. LC 73-12444. (Illus.). 280p. 1974. 26.95 (*0-8093-0643-3*) S Ill U Pr.

Mother Jones, the Miners' Angel: A Portrait. Dale Fetherling. LC 78-16328. (Arcturus Books Paperbacks). (Illus.). 279p. 1979. reprint ed. pap. 9.95 (*0-8093-0896-7*) S Ill U Pr.

Mother Journeys: Feminists Write about Mothering. Ed. by Maureen T. Reddy et al. LC 94-18338. 300p. 1994. 29.95 (*1-883523-04-4*) Spinsters Ink.

Mother Journeys: Feminists Write about Mothering. Ed. by Martha Roth et al. LC 94-18338. (Illus.). 352p. (C). 1994. pap. 15.95 (*1-883523-03-6*) Spinsters Ink.

***Mother Julian & the Gentle Vampire.** Jack Pantaleo. (New Voices in American Fiction Ser.). 230p. 2000. pap. 14.95 (*1-883938-66-X*) Dry Bones Pr.

Mother Knew Best: Wit & Wisdom from the Moms of Celebrities. Elsa Hornfischer. 1999. pap. text 22.95 (*0-7838-8562-8*, G K Hall & Co) Mac Lib Ref.

Mother Knot. Jane Lazarre. LC 97-13516. 176p. 1997. pap. 14.95 (*0-8223-2039-8*) Duke.

Mother Knows Best. Barbara Bretton. (Family Continuity Program Ser.: No. 3). 1999. mass mkt. 4.50 (*0-373-82151-4*, 1-82151-1) Harlequin Bks.

Mother Knows Best. Edna Ferber. LC 77-110187. (Short Story Index Reprint Ser.). 1977. 19.95 (*0-8369-3338-9*) Ayer.

Mother Knows Best: How to Live Through & Love Your Child's First Four Years! Karen Javitch & Amy Friedman. (Illus.). 208p. 1982. pap. 6.95 (*0-89709-032-2*) Liberty Pub.

Mother Knows Best: How to Live Through & Love Your Child's First Four Years! Karen Javitch & Amy Friedman. (Illus.). 201p. 1998. reprint ed. pap. text 7.00 (*0-7881-5215-7*) DIANE Pub.

Mother Knows Best: The Natural Way to Train Your Dog. Carol Lea Benjamin. LC 84-27871. (Illus.). 256p. 1985. 22.95 (*0-87605-666-4*) Howell Bks.

Mother Knows Best? The Truth about Mom's Well Meaning (but Not Always Accurate) Advice. Sue Castle. (Illus.). 160p. 1995. pap. 8.95 (*0-8065-1631-3*, Citadel Pr) Carol Pub Group.

Mother Knows Just What to Do. Michel & Company Staff. (Illus.). 32p. 1995. 6.95 (*0-8362-4738-8*) Andrews & McMeel.

Mother Left Baby with Voodoo Priest. 220p. 1995. pap. 15.95 (*0-9660301-0-9*) Fitzgerald Prodns.

Mother-Light. David C. Phillips. (Collected Works of David G. Phillips). 1988. reprint ed. lib. bdg. 59.00 (*0-7812-1327-4*) Rprt Serv.

Mother-Light. David G. Phillips. (American Author Ser.). 1981. reprint ed. lib. bdg. 69.00 (*0-686-71935-2*) Scholarly.

Mother Link: Stories of Psychic Bonds Between Mother & Child. Cassandra Eason. 192p. 1999. pap. text 12.95 (*1-56975-167-6*) Ulysses Pr.

Mother Load. V. Penn. 1999. pap. text 5.95 (*1-56245-356-4*) Great Quotations.

Mother Lode: A Celebration of California's Gold Country. rev. ed. Photos by Charles Moore. LC 98-47519. (Illus.). 132p. 1999. pap. 18.95 (*0-8118-2357-1*) Chronicle Bks.

Mother Lode: Montana Poems & Narratives. Joe Beardsley. LC 96-90781. (Illus.). ix, 104p. 1997. pap. 9.95 (*0-9654056-0-5*) Tobacco Root.

Mother Lode Guide Map AAA. Auto Club, Southern California Editors. (Illus.). 1997. 3.95 (*1-56413-367-2*) Auto Club.

Mother Lode's Children. Ray Taylor. (Illus.). 186p. (Orig.). 1989. pap. 8.95 (*0-9624364-0-2*) R Taylor.

Mother Looks at the Gay Child. Jesse Davis. LC 97-65810. 176p. (Orig.). 1997. pap. 14.95 (*1-56184-126-9*) New Falcon Pubns.

Mother Loss Workbook: Healing Exercises for Daughters. Diane Hambrook et al. LC 97-219221. (Illus.). 352p. 1997. pap. 15.00 (*0-06-095222-9*, Perennial) HarperTrade.

Mother Love. Elizabeth Badinter. 1981. 13.95 (*0-02-504610-1*) Macmillan.

Mother Love. Rita Dove. 88p. 1995. 17.95 (*0-393-03808-4*) Norton.

Mother Love. Rita Dove. 78p. 1996. pap. 10.00 (*0-393-31444-8*, Norton Paperbks) Norton.

Mother Love. large type ed. Judith H. Wall. 528p. 31.50 (*0-7089-3712-8*) Ulverscroft.

Mother Love: A Karl Alberg Mystery with Cassandra Mitchell. Laurali R. Wright. 264p. 1996. pap. 7.99 (*0-7704-2716-2*) Bantam.

Mother Love, Deadly Love: The Texas Cheerleader Murder Plot. Anne M. Maier. (Illus.). 256p. 1992. 18.95 (*1-55972-137-5*, Birch Ln Pr) Carol Pub Group.

Mother, Love Me: Playscript. Martha Monigle. LC 87-61308. (Orig.). 1986. pap. 5.00 (*0-88734-313-9*) Players Pr.

Mother Love, Mother Earth. Chantal Chawaf. Tr. by Monique F. Nagem from FRE. LC 90-3034. (Library of World Literature in Translation: Vol. 20). 150p. 1992. text 15.00 (*0-8240-4399-5*) Garland.

Mother, Madonna, Whore: The Idealization & Denigration of Motherhood. Estela Weldon. 179p. 1998. reprint ed. 52.00 (*1-892746-12-3*, 46123); reprint ed. pap. 18.95 (*1-892746-11-5*, 46115) Other Pr LLC.

Mother Mary's Final Message. Ralph White. LC 97-90666. 208p. 1998. pap. 14.95 (*0-9651085-1-1*) White Lght NC.

Mother Mary's Teachings for the New World. Ileah Van Hubbard & Mother Mary. (Illus.). 112p. 1997. pap. 22.95 (*0-9659740-0-6*) EloHim Pub.

Mother Mason. large type ed. Bess S. Aldrich. LC 93-17772. 219p. 1993. lib. bdg. 20.95 (*1-56054-502-X*) Thorndike Pr.

Mother Mason. Bess S. Aldrich. 268p. 1975. reprint ed. lib. bdg. 22.95 (*0-88411-257-8*) Amereon Ltd.

Mother Mason. Bess S. Aldrich. LC 86-25111. v, 269p. 1987. reprint ed. pap. 11.95 (*0-8032-5913-1*, Bison Books) U of Nebr Pr.

Mother May I: A Sydney Sloane Mystery. Randye Lordon. 320p. 1998. mass mkt. 5.99 (*0-380-79166-8*, Avon Bks) Morrow Avon.

Mother, May I Sleep with Danger? Claire R. Jacobs. LC 97-12905. 320p. 1997. 23.95 (*1-55611-515-6*, Pub. by D I Fine) Penguin Putnam.

Mother Midnight: Birth, Sex & Fate in the Eighteenth-Century Novel: Defoe, Richardson, & Sterne. Robert A. Erickson. LC 85-48001. (Studies in the Eighteenth Century: No. 10). 1986. 39.50 (*0-404-61476-0*) AMS Pr.

Mother Moose & Her Whole Caboose. Betty Bakay. (Illus.). 32p. (J). (gr. k-2). 1998. pap. 12.95 (*0-8059-4358-7*) Dorrance.

Mother Mother I Feel Sick Send for the Doctor Quick Quick Quick. Remy Charlip & Burton Supree. (Illus.). (J). 1993. reprint ed. pap. 14.95 (*1-56849-172-7*) Buccaneer Bks.

Mother Mountain & Father Sea: Living Musical Traditions of Vietnam. Phong Nguyen & Terry Miller. LC 98-6300. (Performance in World Music Ser.: No. 13). 1999. pap. 19.95 (*0-941677-93-1*, Pub. by White Cliffs Media) Words Distrib.

Mother Murphy. Colleen O. McKenna. 160p. (J). (gr. 4-6). 1993. pap. 2.95 (*0-590-44856-0*, Scholastic Hardcover) Scholastic Inc.

Mother Murphy's Law. Bruce Lansky. LC 86-5240. 96p. 1986. pap. 5.00 (*0-88166-080-9*) Meadowbrook.

Mother Murphy's Law. Bruce Lansky. 108p. 1986. per. 4.50 (*0-671-62274-9*) S&S Trade.

Mother Mysteries. Maren T. Hansen. LC 97-13517. 360p. 1997. pap. 15.00 (*1-57062-252-3*, Pub. by Shambhala Pubns) Random.

Mother Nature: A History of Mothers, Infants & Natural Selection. Sarah Blaffer Hrdy. LC 99-13092. 752p. 1999. 35.00 (*0-679-44265-0*) Pantheon.

Mother Nature: Animal Parents & Their Young. Candace Savage. LC 97-7181. 1997. 27.50 (*0-87156-983-3*, Pub. by Sierra) Random.

***Mother Nature: Maternal Instincts & How They Shape the Human Species.** Sarah Blaffer Hrdy. 752p. 2000. pap. 18.95 (*0-345-40893-4*, Ballantine) Ballantine Pub Grp.

Mother Nature, Father Time: Tales of Medicine. Robert A. Norman. 190p. 1998. pap. 14.95 (*1-891576-05-4*) North Shore Pr.

Mother Nature Nursery Rhymes. Bingham & Sandy Stryker. Ed. by Paine. (Illus.). 32p. (J). (ps up). 1990. 14.95 (*0-911655-01-8*) Advocacy Pr.

Mother Nature's Greatest Hits: The Top 40 Wonders of the Animal World. Bartleby Nash. (Illus.). 132p. (Orig.). (J). 1991. pap. 5.95 (*0-9626072-7-4*) Living Planet Pr.

Mother Nature's Guide to Vibrant Beauty & Health. Myra Cameron. 1990. pap. 9.95 (*0-685-33309-4*) P-H.

Mother Nature's Guide to Vibrant Beauty & Health. Myra Cameron. 251p. (C). 1990. text 24.95 (*0-13-603119-6*) P-H.

Mother Nature's Guide to Vibrant Beauty & Health. 2nd ed. Myra Cameron & Theresa DiGeronimo. LC 96-52951. 288p. (C). 1997. text 24.95 (*0-13-845314-4*) P-H.

Mother Nature's Guide to Vibrant Beauty & Health. 2nd rev. expanded ed. Myra Cameron & Theresa DiGeronimo. LC 96-52951. 288p. (C). 1997. pap. text 13.95 (*0-13-845018-8*) P-H.

***Mother Nature's Herbal.** Judy Griffin. LC 00-37144. (Illus.). 384p. 2000. 10.99 (*0-517-16228-8*) Random Hse Value.

Mother Nature's Herbal: Herbs for Healthy Living. Judy Griffin. LC 96-43893. (Whole Life Ser.). (Illus.). 400p. 1997. pap. 19.95 (*1-56718-340-9*, K-340-9) Llewellyn Pubns.

Mother Nature's Hidden Agenda. Kate Freiman. 1997. per. 3.99 (*0-373-24120-8*, 1-24120-7) Silhouette.

Mother Nature's Kitchen: Growing & Using Herbs. Judy Griffin. 96p. 1993. pap. 14.95 (*1-884335-50-0*) HerbalEssence.

Mother Nature's Pharmacy: Potent Medicines from Plants. J. S. Kidd & Renee A. Kidd. LC 97-37925. (Science & Society Ser.). (Illus.). 134p. (YA). (gr. 7-12). 1998. 19.95 (*0-8160-3584-9*) Facts on File.

Mother Nature's Shopping List: A Buying Guide for Environmentally Concerned Consumers. Michael D. Shook. LC 94-45491. (Illus.). 192p. 1995. pap. 9.95 (*0-8065-1633-X*, Citadel Pr) Carol Pub Group.

***Mother Nature's Two Laws: Ringmasters for Circus Earth, Lessons on Entropy, Energy, the Practice of Science & Critical Thinking.** A. D. Kirwan. 100p. 2000. 28.00 (*981-02-4314-6*) World Scientific Pub.

***Mother Night.** Kurt Vonnegut, Jr. 288p. 1999. pap. 11.95 (*0-385-33414-1*) Dell.

Mother O' Mine. Mary Engelbreit. (Illus.). 80p. 1993. 4.95 (*0-8362-4606-3*) Andrews & McMeel.

***Mother Octopus.** R. Hugh Rice. (Books for Young Learners). (Illus.). 12p. (J). (gr. k-2). 1999. pap. text 5.00 (*1-57274-272-0*, A2472) R Owen Pubs.

Mother of a Family: The Life of Mme Gabrielle Lefebvre, 1880-1938. Reverend Le Crom.Tr. of Une Mere de Famille. 35p. 1994. pap. 3.25 (*0-935952-55-1*) Angelus Pr.

Mother of Agni Yoga. 1977. reprint ed. pap. 3.00 (*0-933574-18-5*) Agni Yoga Soc.

Mother of All: A Revelation of the Motherhood of God in the Life & Teachings of the Jillellamudhi Mother. Richard Schiffman. 364p. 2000. pap. 16.95 (*1-884997-28-7*) Blue Dove Pr.

Mother of All Car Books: How to Get More Fun & Profit Buying, Showing & Selling Vintage & Classic Cars. Rod Reprogle et al. LC 91-58795. 270p. 1995. pap. 14.95 (*0-911663-78-9*) Duncliffs Intl.

Mother of All Departments: The History of the Department of Internal Affairs. Michael Bassett. LC 97-221697. (Illus.). 256p. 1997. pap. 29.95 (*1-86940-175-1*, Pub. by Auckland Univ) Paul & Co Pubs.

Mother of All Hooks: The Story of the U. S. Navy's Tailhook Scandal. William H. McMichael. LC 96-49046. 342p. 1997. text 32.95 (*1-56000-293-X*) Transaction Pubs.

***Mother of All Life.** Judith Pearl. LC 98-72538. 212 p. 1998. write for info. (*0-9665792-8-3*) Chalet Magnificat.

Mother of all Lists. 2nd ed. Barbara Holesinsky. (Illus.). 24p. 1997. spiral bd. 19.95 (*1-891687-00-X*) Mother List.

Mother of All Lists: Goin' Traveling Activity Book for Kids Ages 4-8. Barbara Holesinsky. (Illus.). 20p. (J). (ps-3). 1998. spiral bd. 9.95 (*1-891687-50-6*) Mother List.

Mother of All Lists: Goin' Traveling Activity Book for Kids Ages 9-12. Barbara Holesinsky. (Illus.). 20p. (J). (gr. 4-7). 1998. spiral bd. 9.95 (*1-891687-51-4*) Mother List.

Mother of All Lists: Mini-Mother Goin' Abroad. Barbara Holesinsky. (Illus.). 10p. 1997. spiral bd. 9.95 (*1-891687-05-0*) Mother List.

Mother of All Lists: Mini-Mother Goin' Camping. Barbara Holesinsky. (Illus.). 16p. 1997. spiral bd. 14.95 (*1-891687-03-4*) Mother List.

M

An Asterisk (*) at the beginning of an entry indicates that the title is appearing for the first time.

M

Mother of All Lists: Mini-Mother Goin' Hunting. Barbara Holesinsky. (Illus.). 18p. 1997. spiral bd. 15.95 (*1-891687-01-8*) Mother List.

Mother of All Lists: Mini-Mother Goin' Mountaineering. Barbara Holesinsky. (Illus.). 8p. 1997. spiral bd. 9.95 (*1-891687-04-2*) Mother List.

Mother of All Lists: Mini-Mother Goin' Paddling. Barbara Holesinsky. (Illus.). 18p. 1997. spiral bd. 9.95 (*1-891687-06-9*) Mother List.

Mother of All Lists: Quick Load Goin' Archery Hunting. Barbara Holesinsky. (Illus.). 2p. 1997. spiral bd. 1.95 (*1-891687-23-9*) Mother List.

Mother of All Lists: Quick Load Goin' Babysitting. Barbara Holesinsky. (Illus.). 2p. 1998. spiral bd. 1.95 (*1-891687-38-7*) Mother List.

Mother of All Lists: Quick Load Goin' Back Packing. Barbara Holesinsky. (Illus.). 2p. 1997. spiral bd. 1.95 (*1-891687-18-2*) Mother List.

Mother of All Lists: Quick Load Goin' Black Powder Hunting. Barbara Holesinsky. (Illus.). 2p. 1997. spiral bd. 1.95 (*1-891687-24-7*) Mother List.

Mother of All Lists: Quick Load Goin' Boating. Barbara Holesinsky. (Illus.). 2p. 1997. spiral bd. 1.95 (*1-891687-11-5*) Mother List.

Mother of All Lists: Quick Load Goin' Canoeing. Barbara Holesinsky. (Illus.). 2p. 1997. spiral bd. 1.95 (*1-891687-14-X*) Mother List.

Mother of All Lists: Quick Load Goin' Cross Country Skiing. Barbara Holesinsky. (Illus.). 2p. 1997. spiral bd. 1.95 (*1-891687-33-6*) Mother List.

Mother of All Lists: Quick Load Goin' Cycling. Barbara Holesinsky. (Illus.). 2p. 1997. spiral bd. 1.95 (*1-891687-28-X*) Mother List.

Mother of All Lists: Quick Load Goin' Fishing. Barbara Holesinsky. (Illus.). 2p. 1997. spiral bd. 1.95 (*1-891687-09-3*) Mother List.

Mother of All Lists: Quick Load Goin' Float Tube Fishing. Barbara Holesinsky. (Illus.). 2p. 1997. spiral bd. 1.95 (*1-891687-07-7*) Mother List.

Mother of All Lists: Quick Load Goin' Fly Fishing. Barbara Holesinsky. (Illus.). 2p. 1997. spiral bd. 1.95 (*1-891687-08-5*) Mother List.

Mother of All Lists: Quick Load Goin' Flying. Barbara Holesinsky. (Illus.). 2p. 1998. spiral bd. 1.95 (*1-891687-47-6*) Mother List.

Mother of All Lists: Quick Load Goin' Gold Panning. Barbara Holesinsky. (Illus.). 2p. 1998. spiral bd. 1.95 (*1-891687-45-X*) Mother List.

Mother of All Lists: Quick Load Goin' Grocery Shopping. Barbara Holesinsky. (Illus.). 2p. 1998. spiral bd. 1.95 (*1-891687-37-9*) Mother List.

Mother of All Lists: Quick Load Goin' Hiking. Barbara Holesinsky. (Illus.). 2p. 1997. spiral bd. 1.95 (*1-891687-19-0*) Mother List.

Mother of All Lists: Quick Load Goin' Horseback. Barbara Holesinsky. (Illus.). 2p. 1997. spiral bd. 1.95 (*1-891687-36-0*) Mother List.

Mother of All Lists: Quick Load Goin' Hunting Horseback. Barbara Holesinsky. (Illus.). 2p. 1997. spiral bd. 1.95 (*1-891687-25-5*) Mother List.

Mother of All Lists: Quick Load Goin' Hustling. Barbara Holesinsky. (Illus.). 2p. 1998. spiral bd. 1.95 (*1-891687-48-4*) Mother List.

Mother of All Lists: Quick Load Goin' Ice Fishing. Barbara Holesinsky. (Illus.). 2p. 1997. spiral bd. 1.95 (*1-891687-10-7*) Mother List.

Mother of All Lists: Quick Load Goin' Jet Skiing. Barbara Holesinsky. (Illus.). 2p. 1998. spiral bd. 1.95 (*1-891687-43-3*) Mother List.

Mother of All Lists: Quick Load Goin' Kayaking. Barbara Holesinsky. (Illus.). 2p. 1997. spiral bd. 1.95 (*1-891687-13-1*) Mother List.

Mother of All Lists: Quick Load Goin' Motorbiking. Barbara Holesinsky. (Illus.). 2p. 1997. spiral bd. 1.95 (*1-891687-26-3*) Mother List.

Mother of All Lists: Quick Load Goin' Mountain Biking. Barbara Holesinsky. (Illus.). 2p. 1997. spiral bd. 1.95 (*1-891687-29-8*) Mother List.

Mother of All Lists: Quick Load Goin' on a Sunday Drive. Barbara Holesinsky. (Illus.). 2p. 1997. spiral bd. 1.95 (*1-891687-30-1*) Mother List.

Mother of All Lists: Quick Load Goin' Picnicking. Barbara Holesinsky. (Illus.). 2p. 1998. spiral bd. 1.95 (*1-891687-46-8*) Mother List.

Mother of All Lists: Quick Load Goin' Rafting. Barbara Holesinsky. (Illus.). 2p. 1997. spiral bd. 1.95 (*1-891687-15-8*) Mother List.

Mother of All Lists: Quick Load Goin' Rifle Hunting. Barbara Holesinsky. (Illus.). 2p. 1997. spiral bd. 1.95 (*1-891687-20-4*) Mother List.

Mother of All Lists: Quick Load Goin' Rock Climbing. Barbara Holesinsky. (Illus.). 2p. 1997. spiral bd. 1.95 (*1-891687-17-4*) Mother List.

Mother of All Lists: Quick Load Goin' Rock Hounding. Barbara Holesinsky. (Illus.). 2p. 1998. spiral bd. 1.95 (*1-891687-44-1*) Mother List.

Mother of All Lists: Quick Load Goin' Sailing. Barbara Holesinsky. (Illus.). 2p. 1998. spiral bd. 1.95 (*1-891687-40-9*) Mother List.

Mother of All Lists: Quick Load Goin' Scuba Diving. Barbara Holesinsky. (Illus.). 2p. 1997. spiral bd. 1.95 (*1-891687-16-6*) Mother List.

Mother of All Lists: Quick Load Goin' Skiing. Barbara Holesinsky. (Illus.). 2p. 1997. spiral bd. 1.95 (*1-891687-31-X*) Mother List.

Mother of All Lists: Quick Load Goin' Snowboarding. Barbara Holesinsky. (Illus.). 2p. 1997. spiral bd. 1.95 (*1-891687-34-4*) Mother List.

Mother of All Lists: Quick Load Goin' Snowmobiling. Barbara Holesinsky. (Illus.). 2p. 1997. spiral bd. 1.95 (*1-891687-32-8*) Mother List.

Mother of All Lists: Quick Load Goin' Snowshoeing. Barbara Holesinsky. (Illus.). 2p. 1997. spiral bd. 1.95 (*1-891687-35-2*) Mother List.

Mother of All Lists: Quick Load Goin' Surfing. Barbara Holesinsky. (Illus.). 2p. 1998. spiral bd. 1.95 (*1-891687-39-5*) Mother List.

Mother of All Lists: Quick Load Goin' Traveling. Barbara Holesinsky. (Illus.). 2p. 1998. spiral bd. 1.95 (*1-891687-41-7*) Mother List.

Mother of All Lists: Quick Load Goin' Upland Game Hunting. Barbara Holesinsky. (Illus.). 2p. 1997. spiral bd. 1.95 (*1-891687-21-2*) Mother List.

Mother of All Lists: Quick Load Goin' Water Skiing. Barbara Holesinsky. (Illus.). 2p. 1997. spiral bd. 1.95 (*1-891687-12-3*) Mother List.

Mother of All Lists: Quick Load Goin' Waterfowl Hunting. Barbara Holesinsky. (Illus.). 2p. 1997. spiral bd. 1.95 (*1-891687-22-0*) Mother List.

Mother of All Lists: Quick Load Goin' Wind Surfing. Barbara Holesinsky. (Illus.). 2p. 1998. spiral bd. 1.95 (*1-891687-42-5*) Mother List.

Mother of All Lists: Quick Load Goin' 4-Wheeling. Barbara Holesinsky. (Illus.). 2p. 1997. spiral bd. 1.95 (*1-891687-27-1*) Mother List.

Mother of All Lists: Quick Load My Party Friends. Barbara Holesinsky. (Illus.). 2p. 1998. spiral bd. 1.95 (*1-891687-49-2*) Mother List.

Mother of All Loves. John Wheatcroft. LC 93-29022. 1994. 18.95 (*0-8453-4849-3*, Cornwall Bks) Assoc Univ Prs.

Mother of All the Behans: The Autobiography of Kathleen Behan. Brian Behan. 138p. 1995. pap. 12.95 (*1-85371-337-6*, Pub. by Poolbeg Pr) Dufour.

Mother of All Windows Books, Set. Woody Leonhard. 1072p. 1993. 39.95 incl. disk (*0-201-62475-3*) Addison-Wesley.

Mother of All Windows CD Rom Swap for 62475. Woody Leonhard. (C). 1994. cd-rom 10.00 (*0-201-40693-4*) Addison-Wesley.

Mother of All Windows 98 Books. (C). 1993. write for info. (*0-201-96450-3*); write for info. (*0-201-96453-8*) Addison-Wesley.

Mother of All Windows 98 Books. Woody Leonhard & Barry Simon. LC 98-39309. 864p. (C). 1998. pap. 39.95 (*0-201-43312-5*) Addison-Wesley.

*__Mother of America.__ 3rd expanded rev. ed. Robert Feeney. Orig. Title: Mother of the Americas. (Illus.). 130p. 1999. pap. 9.95 (*0-9622347-5-3*) Aquinas Pr.

Mother of Battles: Saddam's Folly. N. C. Menon. (Illus.). 181p. 1992. text 25.00 (*81-220-0254-4*, Pub. by Konark Pubs Pvt Ltd) Advent Bks Div.

Mother of Bliss: Anandamayi Ma (1896-1982) Lisa L. Hallstrom. LC 97-42456. (Illus.). 328p. 1999. 35.00 (*0-19-511647-X*) OUP.

*__Mother of Bliss: Anandamayi Ma (1896-1982)__ Lisa Lassell Hallstrom. LC 97-42456. (Illus.). 1999. write for info. (*0-19-511648-8*) OUP.

Mother of Christ. C. Houselander. 1990. pap. 24.00 (*0-7220-7813-7*) St Mut.

*__Mother of Christ, Mother of the Church: Documents on the Blessed Virgin Mary.__ M. Jean Frisk. 500p. 2000. pap. 22.95 (*0-8198-4808-5*) Pauline Bks.

Mother of Demons. Eric Flint. 384p. 2000. per. 5.99 (*0-671-87800-X*) Baen Bks.

Mother of Detective Fiction: The Life & Works of Anna Katharine Green. Patricia D. Maida. 120p. 1989. 24.95 (*0-87972-445-5*) Bowling Green Univ Popular Press.

Mother of Dreams & Other Short Stories: Portrayals of Women in Modern Japanese Fiction. Ed. by Makoto Ueda et al. Tr. by John Bester. 280p. 1993. pap. 12.00 (*0-87011-926-5*) Kodansha.

Mother of Eve - As a First Language Teacher. Ernst L. Moerk. Ed. by Lewis P. Lipsitt. LC 82-16358. (Monographs on Infancy: Vol. 3). 160p. 1984. text 73.25 (*0-89391-162-3*) Ablx Pub.

Mother of God. Luna Tarlo. (Illus.). 1997. 14.95 (*1-57027-043-0*) Autonomedia.

Mother of God. large type ed. David Ambrose. 496p. 1997. 34.50 (*0-7089-8936-5*) Ulverscroft.

Mother of God & Her Glorious Feasts. H. O'Laverty. LC 87-50580. (Illus.). 200p. 1987. pap. 10.00 (*0-89555-317-1*) TAN Bks Pubs.

Mother of God Coloring Book: Famous Images of Our Lady to Color. 2nd rev. ed. Illus. by Katherine Sotnik. iii, 70p. 1999. pap. 6.95 (*1-893883-00-0*, 10133) Catholic Color.

Mother of Good Counsel of Genazzano. Joao C. Dias. LC 91-68343. (Illus.). 244p. (Orig.). 1992. 23.95 (*0-685-70864-0*); pap. 19.95 (*1-881008-03-7*) Am Soc Defense TFP.

Mother of His Child. Ann H. White. (Special Edition Ser.). 1995. mass mkt. 3.75 (*0-373-09948-7*, 1-09948-0) Silhouette.

*__Mother of His Child.__ large type ed. Sandra Field. 288p. 1999. 25.99 (*0-263-16242-7*, Pub. by Mills & Boon) Ulverscroft.

Mother of His Child (Conveniently Wed) Laurey Bright. (Intimate Moments Ser.: No. 918). 1999. per. 4.25 (*0-373-07918-4*, 1-07918-5) Harlequin Bks.

Mother of His Son. Janis R. Hudson. 1997. per. 3.99 (*0-373-24095-3*, 1-24095-1) Silhouette.

*__Mother of Inventions.__ Mark Atwell. 242p. 1999. pap. 8.95 (*0-9670583-0-9*) Lindsay Pr.

Mother of Jesus: Present with Us. Paul Hinnebusch. LC 79-93231. 170p. 1980. pap. 7.95 (*0-913382-32-9*, 101-27) Marytown Pr.

Mother of Jesus Was There. Quentin Hakenewerth. (Illus.). 49p. 1984. pap. 2.00 (*0-9608124-6-6*) Marianist Com Ctr.

Mother of Knowledge: The Enlightenment of Ye-shes Mtsho-Rgyal. Namkhay Nyingpo. Tr. by Tarthang Tulku. LC 83-23208. (Translation Ser.: Vol. 12). Orig. Title: Tibetan. (Illus.). 250p. 1983. 35.00 (*0-913546-90-9*); pap. 19.95 (*0-913546-91-7*) Dharma Pub.

Mother of Mercy & Love. Therese M. Green. LC 97-61752. 96p. 1998. pap. 7.99 (*1-57921-058-9*) WinePress Pub.

Mother of My Child. Beverly Barton. (Desire Ser.). 1994. per. 2.99 (*0-373-05831-4*, 5-05831-8) Silhouette.

*__Mother of My Heart, Daughter of My Dreams: Kali & Uma in the Devotional Poetry of Bengal.__ Rachel Fell McDermott. LC 99-89433. (Illus.). 432p. 2001. text 60.00 (*0-19-513435-4*) OUP.

Mother of My Mother: The Intricate Bond Between Generations. Hope Edelman. LC 98-52330. 288p. 1999. 23.95 (*0-385-31796-4*) Dell.

*__Mother of My Mother: The Intricate Bond Between Generations.__ Hope Edelman. 288p. 2000. pap. 12.95 (*0-385-31799-9*, Delta Trade) Dell.

*__Mother of My Mother: The Intricate Bond Between Generations.__ large type ed. Hope Edelman. LC 00-22629. (Nonfiction Ser.). 315p. 2000. 29.95 (*0-7838-9029-X*, G K Hall Lrg Type) Mac Lib Ref.

Mother of Nations: Visions of Mary. Joan Ashton. 228p. 1989. pap. 22.00 (*1-85390-057-5*, Pub. by Veritas Pubns) St Mut.

Mother of Pearl. Anatole France, pseud. Tr. by Frederic Chapman. LC 70-142262. (Short Story Index Reprint Ser.). 1977. 20.95 (*0-8369-3746-5*) Ayer.

Mother of Pearl. Melinda Haynes. LC 98-47014. 445p. 1999. 23.95 (*0-7868-6485-0*, Pub. by Hyperion) Time Warner.

*__Mother of Pearl.__ Melinda Haynes. 496p. 2000. reprint ed. per. 13.95 (*0-671-77467-0*, WSP) PB.

*__Mother of Pearl: A Novel.__ Melinda Haynes. LC 98-47014. 448p. 1999. 23.95 (*0-7868-6627-6*, Pub. by Hyperion) Time Warner.

*__Mother of Pearl: A Novel.__ large type ed. Melinda Haynes. LC 99-40566. 730p. 1999. 30.95 (*0-7862-2181-X*) Thorndike Pr.

Mother of Pearl, Lp. 1950. 30.00 (*0-7862-2182-8*) Mac Lib Ref.

Mother of Plenty. Colin Greenland. 480p. 1998. mass mkt. 5.99 (*0-380-78776-8*, Eos) Morrow Avon.

Mother of Royalty. Yehoshua Bachrach. Tr. by Leonard Oschry. 1995. 9.95 (*0-87306-727-4*) Feldheim.

Mother of Sri Aurobindo Ashram. Prema Nandakumar. (National Biography Ser.). 1979. pap. 2.25 (*0-89744-198-2*) Auromere.

Mother of Storms. John Barnes. 576p. 1995. mass mkt. 5.99 (*0-8125-3345-3*, Pub. by Tor Bks); mass mkt. write for info. (*0-8125-3343-7*) Tor Bks.

Mother of 1084: Mahasweta Devi. Tr. by Samik Bandyopadhyay from BEN. LC 97-901803. (C). 1997. pap. 14.00 (*81-7046-139-1*, Pub. by Seagull Bks) S Asia.

Mother of the Americas *see* **Mother of America**

Mother of the Americas. Robert Feeney. LC 89-83441. (Illus.). 80p. (Orig.). 1989. pap. 5.95 (*0-9622347-0-2*) Aquinas Pr.

Mother of the Americas. 2nd ed. Robert Feeney. (Illus.). 99p. (Orig.). 1993. pap. text 6.95 (*0-9622347-2-9*) Aquinas Pr.

Mother of the Blues: A Study of Ma Rainey. Sandra R. Lieb. LC 81-1168. (Illus.). 256p. 1983. pap. 17.95 (*0-87023-394-7*) U of Mass Pr.

Mother of the Bride. Carole Mortimer. (Presents Plus Ser.). 1993. per. 2.99 (*0-373-11607-1*, 1-11607-8) Harlequin Bks.

Mother of the Bride. Patricia T. Westfall. (WWL Mystery Ser.: No. 312). 1999. per. 4.99 (*0-373-26312-0*, 1-26312-8, Wrldwide Lib) Harlequin Bks.

Mother of the Bride. large type ed. Carole Mortimer. (Harlequin Ser.). 1993. reprint ed. lib. bdg. 18.95 (*0-263-13266-8*) Mac Lib Ref.

Mother of the Bride, Vol. 1. Patricia T. Westfall. LC 98-10205. 224p. 1998. text 21.95 (*0-312-18631-2*) St Martin.

*__Mother of the Bride: The Dream, the Reality, the Search for a Perfect Dress.__ Ilene Beckerman. 2000. 17.95 (*1-56512-288-7*) Algonquin Bks.

*__Mother of the Bride: The Dream, the Reality, the Search for a Perfect Dress.__ Ilene Beckerman. LC 99-88845. (Illus.). 192p. 2000. 17.95 (*1-56512-259-3*, 72259) Algonquin Bks.

Mother-of-the-Bride Book: Giving Your Daughter A Wonderful Wedding. Sharon Naylor. LC 99-28530. 1999. 14.95 (*1-55972-531-1*, Birch Ln Pr) Carol Pub Group.

Mother of the Buddhas: Meditation on the Prajnaparamita Sutra. Lex Hixon. LC 92-56485. 266p. 1993. pap. 16.00 (*0-8356-0689-9*, Quest) Theos Pub Hse.

Mother of the Graduate. Cynthia P. Seton. LC 70-116111. 1970. 4.95 (*0-393-08612-7*) Norton.

Mother of the Grass. Jovette Marchessault. Tr. by Klein. 176p. 1989. pap. 13.95 (*0-88922-267-3*, Pub. by Talonbks) Genl Dist Srvs.

Mother of the Groom. Trisha Alexander. 1993. mass mkt. 3.39 (*0-373-09801-4*, 5-09801-7) Silhouette.

Mother of the Groom, Vol. 1. Eileen Posner. 256p. 1996. pap. 12.95 (*0-9654749-0-9*) P M G Publns.

Mother of the Groom: A Collection of Women's Voices. Ed. by Eileen Posner. LC 95-11281. 256p. 1995. pap. 12.95 (*0-942963-64-4*) Distinctive Pub.

Mother of the Messiah in Judaism: The Book of Ruth. Jacob Neusner. LC 93-31398. (Bible of Judaism Library). 160p. 1993. pap. 12.00 (*1-56338-061-7*) Sigler Pr.

*__Mother of the Pound: Memoirs on the Life & History of the Iraqi Jews.__ David Kazzaz. LC 99-32299. (Illus.). 496p. 1999. 30.00 (*0-87203-154-3*) Hermon.

Mother of the Redeemer: Redemptoris Mater. John Paul, II, pseud. 79p. pap. 3.50 (*0-8198-4744-5*) Pauline Bks.

Mother of the Redeemer: Redemptoris Mater. John Paul, II, pseud. 120p. 1987. pap. 5.95 (*1-55586-159-8*) US Catholic.

Mother of the Saviour - & Our Interior Life. Reginald Garrigou-Lagrange. Tr. by Bernard J. Kelley. LC 93-61564. 290p. 1994. pap. 13.50 (*0-89555-499-2*) TAN Bks Pubs.

Mother of the Secret. Thomas W. Petrisko. LC 97-68889. 328p. (Orig.). 1997. pap. text 9.95 (*1-57918-003-5*, 3453) Queenship Pub.

Mother of the Universe: Visions of the Goddess & Tantric Hymns of Enlightenment. Lex Hixon. 237p. 1994. pap. 16.00 (*0-8356-0702-X*, Quest) Theos Pub Hse.

Mother of the Wire Fence: Inside & Outside the Holocaust. Karl Plank. 192p. (Orig.). 1994. pap. 19.95 (*0-664-25219-2*) Westminster John Knox.

Mother of the World. 1977. reprint ed. pap. 3.00 (*0-933574-17-7*) Agni Yoga Soc.

*__Mother of the Year.__ Lori Handeland. (Superromance Ser.: Bk. 922). 2000. per. 4.50 (*0-373-70922-6*, 1-70922-9) Harlequin Bks.

Mother of Tribes. Joan A. Geier. Ed. by Doris Reich. LC 86-91532. 76p. (Orig.). 1987. pap. 12.95 (*0-938739-00-X*) Four Circles Pr.

Mother of Us All: A History of Queen Nanny, Leader of the Windward Jamaican Maroons. Karla Gottlieb. LC 97-47259. 138p. 1997. pap. text 14.95 (*0-86543-565-0*) Africa World.

Mother of Us All: A History of Queen Nanny, Leader of the Windward Jamaican Maroons. Karla Gottlieb. LC 97-47259. 138p. 1998. 45.95 (*0-86543-564-2*) Africa World.

Mother of Vietnam Country *see* **Me Que Huong Vietnam**

Mother of Vietnam Country D. V. D. *see* **Me Que Huong Viet Nam D. V. D.**

Mother of Winter. Barbara Hambly. 1997. mass mkt. 5.99 (*0-345-39723-1*, Del Rey) Ballantine Pub Grp.

Mother of World Peace: The Life of Muriel Lester. Jill Wallis. 1993. 22.95 (*1-874312-15-X*, Pub. by Hisarlik Pr) Intl Spec Bk.

Mother of Writing: The Origin & Development of a Hmong Messianic Script. William A. Smalley et al. Tr. by Mitt Moua. (Illus.). 234p. 1990. pap. text 19.50 (*0-226-76287-4*); lib. bdg. 48.00 (*0-226-76286-6*) U Ch Pr.

*__Mother on Herself.__ 2nd ed. Mother. 46p. 1998. pap. 2.50 (*81-7058-172-9*, Pub. by SAA) E-W Cultural Ctr.

Mother on the Other Side of the World. James B. Hall. LC 98-48470. (Illus.). 72p. 1999. 20.95 (*1-889330-30-2*, Pub. by Sarabande Bks); pap. 12.95 (*1-889330-31-0*, Pub. by Sarabande Bks) Consort Bk Sales.

Mother on the Wing: Baby's Choice. Marie Ferrarella. (Silhouette Romance Ser.). 1994. per. 2.75 (*0-373-19026-3*, 1-19026-3) Harlequin Bks.

Mother Opossum & Her Babies. Jean C. Echols et al. Ed. by Lincoln Bergman et al. (Illus.). 100p. (J). (ps-1). 1999. pap. 16.00 (*0-924886-21-8*, Pub. by Lawrence Science) Consort Bk Sales.

Mother: or The Divine Materialism. Satprem Staff. Tr. by Luc Venet from FRE. LC 82-27467.Tr. of Mere ou le Materialisme Divin. 408p. 1987. pap. 9.95 (*0-938710-22-2*) Inst Evolutionary.

Mother: or The Mutation of Death. Satprem Staff. Tr. by Luc Venet from FRE.Tr. of Mere ou la Mutation de la Mort. 300p. (Orig.). 1987. pap. 9.95 (*0-938710-17-6*) Inst Evolutionary.

Mother: or The New Species. SATPREM Staff. Tr. by Luc Venet from FRE. LC 83-4370. Orig. Title: Mere Ou L'espece Nouvelle. 530p. 1983. pap. 9.95 (*0-938710-03-6*) Inst Evolutionary.

Mother Osmond's Favorite Recipes, Vol. I. Olive D. Osmond. 150p. 1990. pap. text. write for info. (*0-929786-01-7*) Know Unltd UT.

Mother Pig's Big Black Cooking Pot. Sue Inman. (Illus.). 24p. (J). (ps-3). 1997. 3.98 (*1-85854-582-X*) Brimax Bks.

Mother Plane. Elijah Muhammad. 64p. 1995. pap. text 6.95 (*1-884855-08-3*) Secretarius.

Mother Plays with Dolls: And Finds an Important Key to Unlocking Creativity. Elinor P. Bailey. LC 90-3210. (Illus.). 96p. 1990. pap. 22.95 (*0-939009-39-0*, EPM) Howell Pr VA.

Mother Pletsch's Painless Sewing. rev. ed. Pati Palmer & Susan Pletsch. (Illus.). 128p. 1996. pap. 8.95 (*0-935278-44-3*) Palmer-Pletsch.

Mother Puzzle: Daughters & Mothers in Contemporary American Literature, 110. Ed. by Mickey Pearlman. LC 89-11725. (Contributions in Women's Studies: No. 110). 210p. 1989. 55.00 (*0-313-26414-7*, PMC/, Greenwood Pr) Greenwood.

Mother Quotations. Ed. by Helen Exley. (Quotations Bks.). (Illus.). 60p. 1993. 8.00 (*1-85015-362-0*) Exley Giftbooks.

Mother Rabbit's Son Tom. Dick Gackenbach. LC 76-18399. (I Can Read Bks.). (Illus.). 32p. (J). (ps-3). 1977. 9.95 (*0-06-021947-5*) HarpC Child Bks.

Mother Rites. Gilbert. 1990. lib. bdg. 34.95 (*0-226-29315-7*) U Ch Pr.

Mother Rocket: Stories. Rita Ciresi. LC 92-22666. (Flannery O'Connor Award for Short Fiction Ser.). 160p. 1993. 19.95 (*0-8203-1508-7*) U of Ga Pr.

*__Mother Russia.__ 2000. write for info. (*0-582-23415-8*) Pearson Educ.

Mother Russia: The Feminine Myth in Russian Culture. Joanna Hubbs. LC 87-46086. (Illus.). 320p. 1993. pap. 13.95 (*0-253-20842-4*) Ind U Pr.

Mother Ruth's Rhymes. Ruth I. Dowell. (Illus.). 104p. (J). (ps-6). 1996. pap. 12.95 (*0-945842-13-9*) Pollyanna Prodns.

An Asterisk (*) at the beginning of an entry indicates that the title is appearing for the first time.

Mother Said. Hal Sirowitz. Date not set. pap. write for info. (*0-517-88848-3*, Crown) Crown Pub Group.

Mother Said. Hal Sirowitz. 128p. 1996. 15.00 (*0-517-70497-8*, Crown) Crown Pub Group.

Mother Santa Claus Stories. William F. O'Donnell. 1998. lib. bdg. 18.95 (*1-56723-079-2*) Yestermorrow.

Mother Santa Claus's Stories. William F. O'Donnell. (J). 1976. 18.95 (*0-8488-1116-X*) Amereon Ltd.

Mother Sawtooth's Nome: A Novel of Alaskan History. James A. Von der Heydt. LC 90-7323. (Illus.). 136p. (Orig.). 1990. pap. 7.95 (*0-88196-003-9*) Oak Woods Media.

Mother Scorpion Country: Read Along Set. Dorminster Newton Wilson. (YA). (gr. 1 up). 1989. 22.95 incl. audio (*0-89239-037-9*) Childrens Book Pr.

Mother Scorpion Country (La Tierra de la Madre Escorpion) Harriet Rohmer & Dorminster Wilson. LC 86-32649. (ENG & SPA., Illus.). 32p. (YA). (gr. 4-7). 1987. 14.95 (*0-89239-032-8*) Childrens Book Pr.

Mother Seton. Regina Press Staff. 1994. pap. 25.00 (*0-88271-448-1*) Regina Pr.

Mother Seton: Saint Elizabeth of New York. Leonard Feeney. LC 75-23224. 212p. 1991. reprint ed. 13.95 (*0-911218-05-X*); reprint ed. pap. 7.95 (*0-911218-06-8*) Ravengate Pr.

***Mother Seton & the Sisters of Charity.** Alma Powers-Water. 168p. 2000. pap. 9.95 (*0-89870-766-8*, Pub. by Ignatius Pr) Midpt Trade.

Mother Shadow. large type ed. Melodie J. Howe. LC 90-42940. 452p. 1990. reprint ed. lib. bdg. 18.95 (*1-56054-045-1*) Thorndike Pr.

Mother Snow Leopards & Their Babies. Sarah S. Craft. LC 98-23987. (Zoo Life Book Ser.). 24p. (J). (gr. k-4). 1999. 18.60 (*0-8239-5317-3*, PowerKids) Rosen Group.

Mother So Dear. Alda Ellis. LC 97-40135. (Illus.). 48p. 1998. 10.99 (*1-56507-820-9*) Harvest Hse.

Mother Son & Other Plays. Raymond J. Barry. (Illus.). 276p. (Orig.). 1997. pap. 13.95 (*0-9657588-0-X*) R J Barry.

Mother-Son Incest: The Unthinkable Broken Taboo: An Overview of Findings. Hani Miletski. Ed. by Euan Bear et al. LC HV6570.7.M5 1997. 46p. 1995. pap. 10.00 (*1-884444-31-8*) Safer Soc.

Mother Spring. Driss Chraibi. Tr. by Hugh A. Harter from FRE. LC 83-50206. 118p. 1990. 18.00 (*0-89410-401-2*, Three Contnts); pap. 12.00 (*0-89410-402-0*, Three Contnts) L Rienner.

Mother Sun. Graham Willoughby. (Illus.). 40p. 1991. pap. 17.50 (*0-89822-070-X*) Visual Studies.

Mother Sun & Her Planet Children. Sigrid Rahmas. (Illus.). 32p. (Orig.). (J). (ps-3). 1991. 6.25 (*0-87157-099-8*); pap. 2.95 (*0-87157-599-X*) Story Hse Corp.

Mother Syndrome in the Russian Folk Imagination. Adele M. Barker. (Illus.). 180p. (Orig.). 1986. pap. 19.95 (*0-89357-160-1*) Slavica.

Mother T. The Biography of Irene Blyden Taylor. Ann E. Gunn. (Family Missionary Ser.). (Illus.). 64p. (Orig.). (J). (gr. 4-7). 1987. pap. 5.99 (*0-89827-037-5*, BKD62) Wesleyan Pub Hse.

***Mother Teresa.** (On My Own Biographies Ser.). (Illus.). 32p. (J). (ps-3). 2000. 19.93 (*1-57505-441-8*, Carolrhoda) Lerner Pub.

Mother Teresa. John Barraclough. LC 97-16133. (Lives & Times Ser.). (J). 1998. 19.92 (*1-57572-562-2*) Heinemann Lib.

Mother Teresa. M. G. Chitkara. LC 98-908788. 1998. 42.00 (*81-7024-968-6*, Pub. by Ashish Pub Hse) S Asia.

Mother Teresa. Charlotte Gray. LC 88-2226. (People Who Have Helped the World Ser.). (Illus.). 68p. (J). (gr. 5-6). 1990. 7.95 (*0-8192-1523-6*) Morehouse Pub.

Mother Teresa. Caroline Lazo. LC 92-23765. (Peacemakers Ser.). (Illus.). 64p. (J). (gr. 4 up). 1993. lib. bdg. 13.95 (*0-87518-559-2*, Dillon Silver Burdett) Silver Burdett Pr.

***Mother Teresa.** Haydn Middleton. LC 99-89881. 2000. lib. bdg. write for info. (*1-57572-227-5*) Heinemann Lib.

Mother Teresa. Mother Teresa of Calcutta. LC 97-38584. 128p. 1997. 5.99 (*0-517-20169-0*) Random Hse Value.

Mother Teresa. Tanya Rice. LC 97-26030. (Life & Times of...Ser.). (Illus.). 48p. (YA). (gr. 5 up). 1999. lib. bdg. 15.95 (*0-7910-4637-0*) Chelsea Hse.

Mother Teresa. Amy Ruth. LC 98-23315. (A&E Biography Ser.). 112p. (YA). (gr. 6-9). 1999. 25.26 (*0-8225-4943-3*) Lerner Pub.

***Mother Teresa.** Rafael Tilton. LC 99-35395. (Importance of...Ser.). (Illus.). 128p. (YA). (gr. 6-9). 2000. lib. bdg. 23.70 (*1-56006-565-6*) Lucent Bks.

Mother Teresa. Jill C. Wheeler. LC 98-8335. (Women of the World Ser.). (J). 2002. lib. bdg. 21.35 (*1-57765-315-7*) ABDO Pub Co.

Mother Teresa: A Complete Authorized Biography. Kathryn Spink. LC 97-41349. (Illus.). 336p. 1998. pap. 15.00 (*0-06-251553-5*) HarpC.

Mother Teresa: A Life of Charity see Junior World Biographies

***Mother Teresa: A Life of Love.** Elaine Murray Stone. LC 98-32042. 128p. (YA). (gr. 4-9). 1999. pap. 6.95 (*0-8091-6651-8*) Paulist Pr.

Mother Teresa: A Life of Pictures. Roger Royle & Gary Woods. LC 92-52654. 160p. (Orig.). 1995. pap. 14.95 (*0-89870-584-3*) Ignatius Pr.

Mother Teresa: Beyond the Image. Anne Sebba. (Illus.). 320p. 1998. pap. 12.95 (*0-385-49356-8*) Doubleday.

Mother Teresa: Caring for All God's Children. Betsy Lee. LC 80-20286. 1985. 8.95 (*0-87518-205-4*, Dillon Silver Burdett) Silver Burdett Pr.

***Mother Teresa: God's Slumlord.** Eugene Palumbo. 80p. 2000. pap. 5.95 (*1-878718-59-2*, Resurrection Pr) Catholic Bk Pub.

Mother Teresa: Helping the Poor. William J. Jacobs. (Gateway Biographies Ser.). (Illus.). 48p. (J). (gr. 2-4). 1991. lib. bdg. 20.90 (*1-56294-020-1*) Millbrook Pr.

Mother Teresa: Helping the Poor. William J. Jacobs. (Gateway Biographies Ser.). 48p. (J). (gr. 2-4). 1992. pap. 4.80 (*1-878841-57-2*) Millbrook Pr.

Mother Teresa: Her Life, Her Work, Her Message. rev. ed. Jose L. Gonzalez-Balado. LC 96-47383. (Illus.). 192p. (Orig.). 1997. pap. 8.00 (*0-89243-809-6*) Liguori Pubns.

Mother Teresa: Her Life, Her Works. 7th ed. Lush Gjergji. Tr. by Richard Arnandez from ITA. 160p. 1991. 8.95 (*0-911782-88-5*) New City.

Mother Teresa: In My Own Words. Mother Teresa of Calcutta. LC 97-38338. (Illus.). 128p. 1997. pap. 8.00 (*0-7648-0200-3*) Liguori Pubns.

***Mother Teresa: Living in Love: A Compilation of Mother Teresa's Teaching on Love.** Glenna Hammer Moulthrop. LC 99-88406. 112p. 2000. 12.95 (*0-9668774-1-1*) TowleHse Pubg.

Mother Teresa: Love Stays. Christian Feldman. Tr. by Peter Heinegg. LC 97-45766. 160p. 1998. 12.95 (*0-8245-1738-5*) Crossroad NY.

Mother Teresa: Missionary of Charity. Sam Wellman. LC 98-184965. (Heroes of the Faith Ser.). 1997. pap. 3.97 (*1-57748-105-4*) Barbour Pub.

Mother Teresa: Missionary of Charity. Sam Wellman. LC 98-7057. (Heroes of the Faith Ser.). 208p. (YA). (gr. 6 up). 1999. lib. bdg. 17.95 (*0-7910-5033-5*) Chelsea Hse.

***Mother Teresa: No Greater Love.** Mother Teresa of Calcutta. 224p. 2000. 6.98 (*1-56731-401-5*, MJF Bks) Fine Comms.

Mother Teresa: Protector of the Sick. Linda C. Johnson. LC 90-47213. (Library of Famous Women). 64 p. 1991. 14.95 (*0-8239-1203-5*) Rosen Group.

***Mother Teresa: Protector of the Sick.** rev. ed. Linda C. Johnson. LC 90-47213. (Library of Famous Women). (Illus.). 64p. (J). (gr. 4-7). 1998. lib. bdg. 17.95 (*1-56711-034-7*) Blackbirch.

Mother Teresa: Saint of the Poor. Nina Morgan. 1998. pap. 7.95 (*0-8172-7848-6*) Raintree Steck-V.

Mother Teresa: Saint of the Poor. Richard Wood. LC 97-45165. (J). (ps-4). 1997. 25.69 (*0-8172-3997-9*) Raintree Steck-V.

Mother Teresa: Sister to the Poor. Patricia Reilly Giff. (Illus.). (J). (gr. 2-6). 1987. pap. 4.99 (*0-14-032225-6*, PuffinBks) Peng Put Young Read.

Mother Teresa: The Authorized Biography. Navin Chawla. LC 97-45124. (Illus.). 256p. 1996. pap. 24.95 (*1-85230-911-3*, Pub. by Element MA) Penguin Putnam.

Mother Teresa: The Authorized Biography. Navin Chawla. LC 97-45124. (Illus.). 256p. 1998. pap. 16.95 (*1-86204-222-5*, Pub. by Element MA) Penguin Putnam.

Mother Teresa: The Woman Who Served God with Her Hands. Ben Alex. (Heroes of Faith & Courage Ser.). (Illus.). 42p. (J). (gr. 4-9). 1995. 11.99 (*1-56476-477-X*, 6-3477, Victor Bks) Chariot Victor.

Mother Teresa: To Live, to Love, to Witness: Her Spiritual Way. Lush Gjergji. Tr. by Jordan Aumann from ITA. (Illus.). 152p. 1998. 24.95 (*1-56548-109-7*) New City.

Mother Teresa & Damien Of Molokai: Caring for those who Suffer. Joan Guntzelman. 128p. 1999. pap. text 8.95 (*0-86716-311-9*) St Anthony Mess Pr.

Mother Teresa & India. B. Srinivasa Murthy. LC 82-80522. (Illus.). 144p. (Orig.). 1982. pap. 6.95 (*0-941910-00-8*) Long Beach Pubns.

***Mother Teresa, Called to Love.** Maryanne Raphael. 200p. 2000. pap. 14.95 (*0-9679865-0-8*) Writers World.

Mother Teresa, 1910-1997: A Pictorial Biography. Joanna Hurley. (Illus.). 120p. 1999. reprint ed. text 25.00 (*0-7881-6409-0*) DIANE Pub.

Mother Teresa of Calcutta: Her Call, Her Example, Her Life Story. Sunita Kumar. 1998. 24.95 (*0-89870-729-3*) Ignatius Pr.

Mother Teresa, Sister to the Poor. Patricia Reilly Giff. (Women of Our Time Ser.). (J). 1987. 10.19 (*0-606-02859-5*, Pub. by Turtleback) Demco.

Mother Teresa Treasury: Mother Teresa of Calcutta, 3 vols. Mother Teresa of Calcutta. Incl. Vol. 1. Gift for God. LC 85-42786. 96p. Vol. 2. Love of Christ. LC 85-42786. 128p. 1985. Vol. 3. Life in the Spirit. LC 85-42786. 96p. 1985. LC 85-42786. 1985. 32.95 (*0-06-068228-0*) Harper SF.

Mother Teresa's Little Instruction Book. Honor Books Staff. 1998. per. 5.99 (*1-57757-004-9*) Trade Life.

Mother, Thank You for All Your Love see Mama, te Agradezco por Tu Gran Amor: Anthology

Mother, the Son, & the Socialite: The True Story of a Mother-Son Crime Spree. Adrian Havill. LC 99-205936. (St. Martin's True Crime Library). 280p. 1999. mass mkt. 6.50 (*0-312-97069-2*) St Martin.

Mother Theodore Guerin: A Woman for Our Time. Penny B. Mitchell. (Illus.). Date not set. pap. 10.00 (*1-893789-06-3*) Sists Prov.

***Mother Theresa.** Tracy Dils. (Women of Achievement Ser.). 2000. 19.95 (*0-7910-5887-5*) Chelsea Hse.

***Mother Theresa.** Tracy Dils. (Women of Achievement Ser.). (Illus.). 2001. pap. 9.95 (*0-7910-5888-3*) Chelsea Hse.

***Mother Time: Women, Aging & Ethics.** Ed. by Margaret U. Walker. LC 98-45361. 272p. 1999. 26.95 (*0-8476-9260-4*) Rowman.

***Mother Time: Women, Aging & Ethics.** Margaret U. Walker. (Illus.). 304p. 2000. pap. 18.95 (*0-8476-9261-2*) Rowman.

Mother to Be. Cheryl Reavis. (Family Blessings Ser.). 1997. per. 3.99 (*0-373-24102-X*, 1-24102-5) Silhouette.

Mother to Be: A Guide to Pregnancy & Birth for Women with Disabilities. Judith Rogers & Molleen Matsumura. 424p. 1991. pap. 39.95 (*0-939957-30-2*) Demos Medical.

***Mother-to-Be's Dream Book: Understanding the Dreams of Pregnancy.** Raina M. Paris. LC 99-49032. 304p. 2000. mass mkt. 12.95 (*0-446-67524-5*) Warner Bks.

Mother to Daughter, Daughter to Mother: A Daybook & Reader. Ed. & Afterword by Tillie Olsen. LC 84-21038. 312p. 1984. 19.95 (*1-55861-008-1*, Pub. by Feminist Pr); pap. 10.95 (*0-935312-37-4*) Feminist Pr.

***Mother to Mother.** Sindiwe Magona. LC 99-26023. 216p. 1999. 20.00 (*0-8070-0948-2*) Beacon Pr.

***Mother to Mother.** Sindiwe Magona. 224p. 2000. pap. 14.00 (*0-8070-0949-0*) Beacon Pr.

Mother to Mother: A Companion Study Book. Linda F. Lein. 70p. 1999. spiral bd., wbk. ed. 4.95 (*0-9670516-1-4*) Annika Pubns.

Mother to Mother: Letters about Being a Mom. Linda F. Lein. LC 99-94690. 60p. 1999. pap. 7.95 (*0-9670516-0-6*) Annika Pubns.

Mother-to-Mother Baby Care Book. Barbara Wilcox Sills & Jeannie Henry. LC 79-15708. 1980. 14.95 (*0-913290-18-1*); pap. write for info. (*0-318-51263-7*) Camaro Pub.

Mother to Mother on Breastfeeding. Miriam Biehn. LC 99-185764. 1998. pap. 6.50 (*1-884377-06-8*) Green Psturs Pr.

Mother Tongue. Rebeccca M. Devet. LC 86-16100. (University of Central Florida Contemporary Poetry Ser.). 79p. 1987. 17.95 (*0-8130-0858-1*) U Press Fla.

Mother Tongue. Demetria Martinez. 1997. pap. 10.00 (*0-345-41656-2*) Ballantine Pub Grp.

Mother Tongue. Bill Bryson. LC 89-77521. 272p. 1991. reprint ed. pap. 13.50 (*0-380-71543-0*, Avon Bks) Morrow Avon.

Mother Tongue: An American Life in Italy. Wallis Wilde-Menozzi. LC 96-41229. 300p. 1997. 25.00 (*0-86547-501-6*) N Point Pr.

Mother Tongue: How Humans Create Language. Joel Davis. 320p. 1993. 21.95 (*1-55972-206-1*, Birch Ln Pr) Carol Pub Group.

Mother Tongue: On the Origins of Human Language. Vitaly Shevoroshkin. 1992. write for info. (*0-201-19980-7*) Addison-Wesley.

Mother Tongue, Father Time: A Decade of Linguistic Revolt. Alette O. Hill. LC 85-45582. 180p. (C). 1986. pap. 10.95 (*0-253-20389-9*, MB-389) Ind U Pr.

Mother Town: Civic Ritual, Symbols, & Experience in the Borders of Scotland. Gwen K. Neville. (Illus.). 176p. 1994. pap. 24.95 (*0-19-509032-2*) OUP.

Mother Town: Civic Ritual, Symbols & Experience in the Borders of Scotland. Gwen K. Neville. (Illus.). 176p. 1994. text 60.00 (*0-19-508837-9*) OUP.

***Mother Trip: Hip Mama's Guide to Staying Sane in the Chaos of Motherhood.** Ariel Gore. LC 00-25423. (Illus.). 2000. pap. 14.95 (*1-58005-029-8*) Seal Pr WA.

Mother Troubles: Rethinking Contemporary Maternal Dilemmas. Ed. by Julia E. Hanigsberg et al. LC 99-12363. 384p. 1999. pap. 26.00 (*0-8070-6787-3*) Beacon Pr.

Mother Voices: Real Women Write about Growing into Motherhood. Ed. by Traci Dyer. 256p. 1999. pap. 12.95 (*1-887166-45-9*) Sourcebks.

Mother Wallabies & Their Babies. Sarah S. Craft. LC 98-23982. (Zoo Life Book Ser.). 24p. (J). (gr. k-4). 1999. 18.60 (*0-8239-5314-9*, PowerKids) Rosen Group.

Mother Was a Gunner's Mate: World War II in the Waves. Josette D. Wingo. LC 94-10440. (Illus.). 246p. 1994. 27.95 (*1-55750-924-7*) Naval Inst Pr.

Mother Was a Lady, 12. R. Gordon Kelly. LC 72-5451. (Illus.). 233p. 1974. 49.95 (*0-8371-6451-6*, KEM/, Greenwood Pr) Greenwood.

Mother Was a Minister: Evangelizing the World - Beginning at Home. John W. Neal. 64p. 1994. pap. 9.95 (*1-881576-32-9*) Providence Hse.

Mother Was Not a Person. Ed. by Margret Andersen. 274p. 1972. 36.99 (*0-919618-12-X*, Pub. by Black Rose); pap. 7.99 (*0-919618-00-6*, Pub. by Black Rose) Consort Bk Sales.

Mother West Wind's Children. Thornton W. Burgess. (Nature-Story Bks.). (Illus.). 156p. (J). (gr. k-3). 1985. pap. 12.95 (*0-316-11657-2*) Little.

Mother West Wind's Neighbors. Thornton W. Burgess. LC 68-21862. (Nature-Story Bks.). (Illus.). 148p. (J). (gr. k-3). 1985. pap. 12.95 (*0-316-11656-4*) Little.

Mother West Wind's Neighbors. Thornton W. Burgess. (Illus.). 160p. (J). 1992. reprint ed. lib. bdg. 14.95 (*0-89966-901-8*) Buccaneer Bks.

Mother Wit: The Ex-Slave Narratives of the Louisiana Writers' Project. Ronnie W. Clayton. (University of Kansas Humanistic Studies). (Illus.). 263p. (C). 1990. text 59.95 (*0-8204-1240-6*) P Lang Pubng.

Mother Wit: 365 Meditations for African American Women. Andrea Bishop. 336p. 1996. pap. 12.95 (*0-687-04794-3*) Abingdon.

Mother Wit from the Laughing Barrel: Readings in the Interpretation of Afro-American Folklore. rev. ed. Ed. by Alan Dundes. LC 90-40867. 640p. (C). 1991. reprint ed. pap. text 23.00 (*0-87805-478-2*) U Pr of Miss.

Mother with Child: Transformation Through Children. Kathryn A. Rabuzzi. LC 92-45765. 192p. 1994. 31.95 (*0-253-34769-6*) Ind U Pr.

Mother with Child Inspirational for Expectant Mothers. Annette Evans. (Illus.). 280p. 1997. boxed set 10.95 (*0-9660250-0-8*) Marian & Co.

Mother, with Letters on the Mother & Translations of Prayers & Meditations. Sri Aurobindo. 500p. 1982. 16.00 (*0-89071-311-1*, Pub. by SAA); pap. 13.00 (*0-89071-310-3*, Pub. by SAA) Acrpls Bks CO.

***Mother, with Love.** Susan Diamond. 2000. 4.99 (*1-56245-401-3*) Great Quotations.

Mother Without a Mask: A Westerner's Story of Her Arab Family. Patricia Holton. 278p. 1996. reprint ed. pap. 16.95 (*1-85626-288-X*, Pub. by Cathie Kyle) Trafalgar.

Mother Without Child: Contemporary Fiction & the Crisis of Motherhood. Elaine T. Hansen. LC 96-13716. 273p. 1997. pap. 17.95 (*0-520-20578-2*, Pub. by U CA Pr) Cal Prin Full Svc.

Mother Wore Combat Boots & Chased Troop Trains: A Young Woman's Adventure Story As an Army Nurse in World War II. unabridged ed. Merdith M. Matthews. LC 98-93842. (Illus.). xxi, 180p. 1998. pap. 14.95 (*0-9667358-0-3*, 080798) Grapevine OH.

Mother-Work: Women, Child Welfare, & the State, 1890-1930. Molly Ladd-Taylor. LC 93-9926. (Women in American History Ser.). 232p. 1994. 39.95 (*0-252-02044-8*) U of Ill Pr.

Mother-Work: Women, Child Welfare, & the State, 1890-1930. Molly Ladd-Taylor. 224p. (C). 1995. pap. text 14.95 (*0-252-06482-8*) U of Ill Pr.

Mother Worship: Theme & Variations. Ed. by James J. Preston. LC 81-3336. (Studies in Religion). (Illus.). 384p. 1982. pap. 119.10 (*0-608-05209-4*, 206574600001) Bks Demand.

Mother Wove the Morning: A One-Woman Play. Carol L. Pearson. LC 92-31236. 1992. write for info. (*1-56236-307-7*, Pub. by Aspen Bks) Origin Bk Sales.

Mother Zone. Marni Jackson. 1995. pap. write for info. (*0-8050-3207-X*) H Holt & Co.

Mother Zone: Love, Sex, & Laundry in the Modern Family. Marni Jackson. 224p. 1995. 19.95 (*0-8050-1709-7*) H Holt & Co.

M

Motherboard Companion. Phil Croucher. (Companion Ser.). 427p. 1999. pap. 49.95 (*1-889671-24-X*) Advice Pr.

Mothercare Guide to Child Health: Keeping Children Healthy, A-Z of Illnesses, Coping with Emergencies. Penny Stanway. 1989. 17.95 (*0-318-41491-0*) P-H.

***Mothercare New Guide to Pregnancy & Child Care: An Illustrated Guide to Caring for Your Child from Pregnancy Through Age Five.** rev. ed. Ed. by Penny Stanway. LC 99-87127. (Illus.). 320p. 2000. per. 22.00 (*0-7432-0103-5*) S&S Trade.

Mothercare's New Guide to Pregnancy & Childcare: An Illustrated Guide to Caring for Your Child from Pregnancy Through Age Five. Ed. by Penny Stanway. LC 94-1161. (Illus.). 304p. 1994. per. 20.00 (*0-671-50095-3*) S&S Trade Pap.

Motherfuckers: The Auschwitz of Oz. David Birtton. Ed. by Michael Butterworth. 250p. 1996. 30.95 (*0-86130-098-X*, Pub. by Savoy Bks) AK Pr Dist.

Motherhood. Pierce Maassen. 1959. pap. 0.70 (*0-686-23476-6*) Rose Pub MI.

Motherhood. Regina Pagoulatou. LC 85-62595. 87p. 1985. pap. 8.00 (*0-918618-25-8*) Pella Pub.

Motherhood. Jane Price. 1989. pap. 10.95 (*0-86358-211-7*, Pub. by Pandora) Harper SF.

Motherhood. Elizabeth Sirimarco. LC 91-11169. (Women Today Ser.). 64p. (YA). (gr. 6-12). 1991. lib. bdg. 17.95 (*0-86593-121-6*); lib. bdg. 17.27 (*0-685-59204-9*) Rourke Corp.

***Motherhood.** Photos by Sulamith Wulfing. (Illus.). 58p. 2000. 9.95 (*1-885394-44-6*) Bluestar Communs.

Motherhood see Psychology of Women

Motherhood: A Celebration of Blessings & Blunders. Nancy Moser. LC 97-157265. 1997. pap. text 5.99 (*0-87788-564-8*, H Shaw Pubs) Waterbrook Pr.

Motherhood: A Feminist Perspective. Ed. by Jane P. Knowles. LC 90-37913. (Women & Therapy Ser.: Vol. 10, Nos. 1-2). 234p. 1993. text 39.95 (*1-56024-044-X*) Haworth Pr.

Motherhood: A Gift of Love: Miniature Edition. (Illus.). 112p. 1999. 4.95 (*0-7624-0513-9*) Running Press Min.

Motherhood: A Spiritual Journey. Ellyn Sanna. LC 97-17924. 160p. 1997. 14.95 (*0-8091-0494-6*, 0494-6) Paulist Pr.

Motherhood: Meanings, Practices, & Ideologies. Ed. by Ann Phoenix et al. (Gender & Psychology Ser.). (Illus.). 256p. 1991. 45.00 (*0-8039-8313-1*); pap. 14.99 (*0-8039-8314-X*) Sage.

Motherhood: The Second Oldest Profession. Erma Bombeck. 192p. 1987. mass mkt. 5.99 (*0-440-15901-6*) Dell.

Motherhood - Journey into Love: An Anthology of Poetry from Welcome Home. Ed. by Edwina P. Cross. LC 97-8268. (Illus.). 102p. 1997. 12.00 (*0-9631188-2-X*) Mothers at Home.

Motherhood, a Celebration. Bill Adler, Jr. LC 87-739. ix, 116 p. 1987. write for info. (*0-88184-307-5*) Carroll & Graf.

Motherhood after Miscarriage. Kathleen Diamond. 252p. 1991. pap. 10.95 (*1-55850-043-X*) Adams Media.

Motherhood after 35: Choices, Decisions, Options. Maggie Jones. LC 98-12305. 224p. 1998. pap. 12.95 (*1-55561-149-4*) Fisher Bks.

Motherhood & Child. Cathy Luchetti. Date not set. pap. write for info. (*0-517-88450-X*, Crown) Crown Pub Group.

Motherhood & Mental Health. Ian Brockington. (Illus.). 640p. 1996. pap. text 59.00 (*0-19-262935-2*) OUP.

Motherhood & Mental Health. Ian F. Brockington. (Illus.). 632p. 1996. 102.50 (*0-19-262126-2*) OUP.

Motherhood & Modernity: An Investigation into the Rational Dimension of Mothering. Christine Everingham. LC 93-51489. 176p. 1994. pap. 32.95 (*0-335-19195-9*) OpUniv Pr.

***Motherhood & Mothering in Anglo-Saxon England.** Mary Dockray-Miller. LC 99-39680. 1999. text 39.95 (*0-312-22721-3*) St Martin.

Motherhood & Mourning: Perinatal Death. Larry G. Peppers & Ronald J. Knapp. LC 80-286. 165p. 1980. 49.95 (*0-275-91760-6*, C1760, Praeger Pubs) Greenwood.

Motherhood & Representation. E. Ann Kaplan. LC 91-45539. (Illus.). 256p. (C). 1992. pap. 24.99 (*0-415-01127-2*, 9851) Routledge.

An Asterisk (*) at the beginning of an entry indicates that the title is appearing for the first time.

***Motherhood & Sexuality.** Marie Langer. LC 00-27427. 2000. 30.00 (*1-892746-64-6*) Other Pr LLC.

Motherhood & Sexuality. Marie Langer. Tr. by Nancy C. Hollander from SPA. 305p. 1998. reprint ed. 42.00 (*1-892746-06-9*, 46069) Other Pr LLC.

Motherhood by Choice: Pioneers in Women's Health & Family Planning. Perdita Huston. LC 91-44239. (Illus.). 192p. 1992. 35.00 (*1-55861-068-5*); pap. 14.95 (*1-55861-069-3*) Feminist Pr.

Motherhood Career Connection. Ann Bradshaw. 155p. 1993. write for info. (*0-9637505-1-8*) Anthea Pr.

Motherhood Constellation: A Unified View of Parent Infant Psychotherapy. Daniel N. Stern. LC 94-24388. 288p. 1995. pap. 45.00 (*0-465-02602-8*, Pub. by Basic) HarpC.

***Motherhood Deferred: A Woman's Journey.** Anne Taylor Fleming. 256p. 1999. reprint ed. text 24.00 (*0-7881-6558-5*) DIANE Pub.

***Motherhood in Black & White: Race & Sex in American Liberalism, 1930-1965.** Ruth Feldstein. 2000. pap. write for info. (*0-8014-8438-3*) Cornell U Pr.

Motherhood in Human & Nonhuman Primates: Biological & Social Determinants. R. D. Martin et al. (Illus.). x, 176p. 1995. 82.75 (*3-8055-6109-1*) S Karger.

Motherhood in Islam. 2nd ed. Aliah Schleifer. 105p. 1996. reprint ed. pap. 15.95 (*1-887752-01-3*) Fons Vitae.

Motherhood in the Old South: Pregnancy, Childbirth, & Infant Rearing. Sally G. McMillen. 256p. 1997. pap. 12.95 (*0-8071-2166-5*) La State U Pr.

Motherhood Is a Contact Sport. Susan Reimer. LC 98-70956. 212p. (Orig.). 1998. pap. 11.95 (*0-9649819-6-3*) Baltimore Sun.

Motherhood Is Not for Wimps. Catherine Burr et al. 160p. (Orig.). 1996. pap. 7.95 (*0-9635176-7-8*) Walrus Prods.

Motherhood Is Stranger Than Fiction. Mary Chambers. (Illus.). 104p. 1995. pap. 6.99 (*0-8308-1603-8*, 1603) InterVarsity.

***Motherhood Made a Man Out of Me.** Karen Karbo. 288p. 2000. 23.95 (*1-58234-083-8*) Bloomsbury Pubg.

Motherhood of God, Report of the Woman's Guild/Panel on Doctrine Study Group. Ed. by Alan E. Lewis. 80p. 1984. pap. 2.95 (*0-7152-0577-3*) Outlook.

Motherhood of the Church. Henri De Lubac. Tr. by Sergia Englund from FRE. LC 81-83857.Tr. of Les/Eglises particulieres & La maternite de l'eglise. 363p. (Orig.). 1983. pap. 14.95 (*0-89870-014-0*) Ignatius Pr.

Motherhood on the Wisconsin Frontier. Lillian Krueger. (Wisconsin Stories Ser.). 28p. pap. 1.75 (*0-87020-199-9*) State Hist Soc Wis.

Motherhood 101: Inspiration & Wisdom to Help You Become a Great Mom. Cheri Fuller. 160p. 1997. pap. 6.99 (*1-56292-269-6*) Honor Bks OK.

Motherhood Optional: A Psychological Journey. Phyllis Z. Tobin & Barbara Aria. LC 97-29367. 376p. 1998. 23.95 (*0-7657-0127-8*) Aronson.

Motherhood Reconceived: Feminism & the Legacies of the Sixties. Lauri Umansky. 257p. (C). 1996. text 45.00 (*0-8147-8561-1*); pap. text 18.50 (*0-8147-8562-X*) NYU Pr.

MotherHoot. Margaret Bigger. LC 98-71924. (Illus.). 128p. 1999. pap. 9.95 (*0-9640606-8-X*) A Borough Bks.

Mothering. Judith Kerman. LC 77-21471. 1977. 8.00 (*0-931588-04-9*); pap. 3.50 (*0-931588-03-0*) Allegany Mtn Pr.

Mothering. Rudolph Schaffer. (Developing Child Ser.). (Illus.). 128p. 1977. 23.50 (*0-674-58745-6*); pap. text 8.95 (*0-674-58746-4*) HUP.

Mothering: A Practical Guide for Moms. Grace Ketterman. LC 98-20671. 112p. 1998. 8.99 (*0-8341-1745-2*) Nazarene.

Mothering: And Dream of Rain. Judith Kerman. 82p. (Orig.). 1996. pap. text 12.00 (*1-56439-062-4*) Ridgeway.

Mothering: Ideology, Experience, & Agency. Ed. by Evelyn N. Glenn et al. (Perspectives on Gender Ser.). 288p. (C). (gr. 13). 1993. pap. 19.99 (*0-415-90776-4*, B0564) Routledge.

Mothering: Toward a New Psychoanalytic Construction. Silvia Vegetti-Finzi. Tr. by Kathrine Jason. LC 95-38876. (Feminism & Psychoanalysis Ser.). 196p. 1995. lib. bdg. 30.00 (*0-89862-334-0*, C2334) Guilford Pubns.

Mothering Against the Odds: Diverse Voices of Contemporary Mothers. Ed. by Cynthia Garcia-Coll et al. LC 97-47699. 288p. 1998. pap. text 18.95 (*1-57230-339-5*, C0339); lib. bdg. 38.95 (*1-57230-330-1*, C0330) Guilford Pubns.

Mothering & Ambivalence. Ed. by Wendy Hollway & Brid Featherstone. LC 97-224465. 216p. (C). 1997. 80.00 (*0-415-13910-4*); pap. 25.99 (*0-415-13911-2*) Routledge.

Mothering & Fathering: The Gender Differences in Child Rearing. Tine Thevenin. LC 93-13760. 288p. 1993. pap. 9.95 (*0-89529-569-5*, Avery) Penguin Putnam.

Mothering As a Spiritual Journey: Learning to Let God Nurture Your Children & You along with Them. Ann T. Linthorst. 140p. (Orig.). 1993. pap. 12.95 (*0-8245-1250-2*) Crossroad NY.

Mothering by the Heart: Celebrating Moments That Last Forever. Robin J. Gunn. 80p. 1996. 16.99 (*0-88070-888-3*, Multnomah Bks) Multnomah Pubs.

Mothering, Education, & Ethnicity: The Transformation of Japanese American Culture. Susan M. Adler. LC 98-8583. (Asian Americans). 203p. 1998. 53.00 (*0-8153-3159-2*) Garland.

***Mothering from the Inside: Parenting in a Women's Prison.** Sandra Enos. (C). 2001. pap. text 15.95 (*0-7914-4850-9*) State U NY Pr.

***Mothering from the Inside: Parenting in a Women's Prison.** Sandra Enos. (C). 2001. text 47.50 (*0-7914-4849-5*) State U NY Pr.

Mothering Heights. Sonia Taitz. 224p. 1994. reprint ed. pap. 8.00 (*0-425-14236-1*) Berkley Pub.

***Mothering Inner-City Children: The Early School Years.** Katherine Brown Rosier. LC 99-55855. 256p. 2000. pap. 22.00 (*0-8135-2797-X*); text 52.00 (*0-8135-2796-1*) Rutgers U Pr.

Mothering Modernity: Feminism, Modernism, & the Maternal Muse. Marylu Hill. LC 98-40425. (Origins of Modernism Ser.: No. 10). 250p. 1998. 65.00 (*0-8153-2431-6*, H2004) Garland.

Mothering Multiples: Breastfeeding & Caring for Twins or More! 3rd rev. ed. Karen Gromada. (Illus.). 354p. 1999. pap. 14.95 (*0-912500-51-4*) La Leche.

Mothering Ourselves: Help & Healing for Adult Daughters. Evelyn S. Bassoff. 240p. 1992. reprint ed. pap. 12.95 (*0-452-26788-9*, Plume) Dutton Plume.

Mothering Teens: Understanding the Adolescent Years. Ed. by Miriam Kaufman. 320p. 1997. pap. 16.95 (*0-921881-46-0*, Pub. by Gynergy-Ragweed) U of Toronto Pr.

Mothering the Mind: Twelve Studies of Writers & Their Silent Partners. Ed. by Ruth Perry & Martine Watson Brownley. LC 83-10849. (Illus.). 261p. (C). 1984. 39.95 (*0-8419-0892-3*); pap. 19.95 (*0-8419-0893-1*) Holmes & Meier.

Mothering the Mother: How a Doula Can Help You Have a Shorter, Easier, Healthier Birth. Marshall H. Klaus. 1993. 19.95 (*0-201-56797-0*); pap. 16.50 (*0-201-63272-1*) Addison-Wesley.

Mothering the New Mother - Women's Feelings & Needs after Childbirth: A Support & Resource Guide. 2nd rev. ed. Sally Placksin. LC 98-9194. 420p. 2000. pap. 16.95 (*1-55704-317-5*) Newmarket.

Mothering Twins: From Hearing the News to Beyond the Terrible Twos. Linda Albi et al. 416p. (Orig.). 1993. per. 14.00 (*0-671-72357-X*) S&S Trade Pap.

Mothering with Soul: Raising Children As Special Work. Joan Salter. (Illus.). 144p. 1998. pap. write for info. (*1-869890-84-1*, Pub. by Hawthorn Press) Anthroposophic.

***Mothering Without a Compass: White Mother's Love, Black Son's Courage.** Becky Thompson. 2000. 22.95 (*0-8166-3635-4*) U of Minn Pr.

***Mothering Without a Compass: White Mother's Love, Black Son's Courage.** Becky W. Thompson. LC 00-9339. 2000. write for info. (*0-8166-3636-2*) U of Minn Pr.

Mothering Your Nursing Toddler. 2nd rev. ed. Norma J. Bumgarner. (Illus.). 308p. 1999. pap. 12.95 (*0-912500-52-2*) La Leche.

The handbook for mothers who breastfeed their children past infancy has been revised & updated. Norma Jane Bumgarner puts the experience of nursing an older baby or child in perspective, within the context of the entire mother-child relationship. She cites biological, cultural & historical evidence in support of extended breastfeeding & shares stories gleaned from thousands of families in which nursing & natural weaning have been the norm. *Publisher Paid Annotation.*

***MotherKind: A Novel.** Jayne Anne Phillips. LC 99-49256. 295p. 2000. 24.00 (*0-375-40194-6*) Knopf.

***Motherland.** Vineeta Vijayaraghavan. 2001. 23.00 (*1-56947-217-3*) Soho Press.

***Motherland: A Daughter's Journey to Reclaim the Past.** Fern Schumer Chapman. LC 99-23796. 190p. 2000. 23.95 (*0-670-88105-8*, Viking) Viking Penguin.

***Motherland: Writings by Irish American Women about Mothers & Daughters.** Caledonia Kearns. 272p. 2000. pap. 13.00 (*0-688-17586-4*, Quil) HarperTrade.

***Motherland: Writings by Irish American Women about Mothers & Mothering.** Ed. by Caledonia Kearns. LC 98-33901. 272p. 1999. 22.00 (*0-688-16565-6*, Wm Morrow) Morrow Avon.

Motherland of Humanity: A Handbook of Africa. Charles K. Aka. 48p. 1999. pap. 8.00 (*0-8059-4806-6*) Dorrance.

Motherlands: Black Women's Writings from Africa, the Caribbean, & South Asia. Ed. by Susheila Nasta. LC 91-30110. 365p. 1992. text 45.00 (*0-8135-1781-8*); pap. text 17.95 (*0-8135-1782-6*) Rutgers U Pr.

Motherless Brooklyn. Jonathan Lethem. LC 99-18194. 320p. 1999. 23.95 (*0-385-49183-2*) Doubleday.

***Motherless Brooklyn.** Jonathan Lethem. 2000. pap. 13.00 (*0-375-72483-4*) Knopf.

***Motherless Brooklyn.** Jonathan Lethem. LC 00-33759. 2000. write for info. (*0-7862-2695-1*) Thorndike Pr.

***Motherless Child Long Way from Home.** Raissa Silver. Ed. by Valeriya Popova. (RUS., Illus.). 210p. 2000. pap. 7.00 (*1-893552-06-3*) Mir Collection.

Motherless Children, Fatherless Waifs: Modern Fictional Protagonists & the Artist's Search for the Real Self. Leo Schneiderman. LC 95-5021. (Evans Studies in the Philosophy & Criticism of Literature: No. 12). 232p. 1996. pap. 25.00 (*0-89370-406-7*) Millefleurs.

Motherless Daughters: The Legacy of Loss. Hope Edelman. LC 93-45048. 1994. 23.00 (*0-201-63288-8*) Addison-Wesley.

Motherless Daughters: The Legacy of Loss. Hope Edelman. LC 93-45048. 352p. 1995. pap. 14.95 (*0-385-31438-8*, Delta Trade) Dell.

Motherload: When Your Life's on Spin Cycle & You Just Can't Get the Lid up! Caryl Kristensen. (Illus.). 256p. 1999. pap. 12.95 (*0-06-092928-6*) HarpC.

***Motherloss.** Lynn Davidman. LC 99-53072. 293p. 2000. 24.95 (*0-520-22319-5*, Pub. by U CA Pr) Cal Prin Full Svc.

Motherlove. Virginia L. Kroll. (Illus.). 36p. (J). (ps-3). 1998. 16.95 (*1-883220-81-5*); pap. 7.95 (*1-883220-80-7*) Dawn CA.

***Motherlove: Reinventing a Good & Blessed Future for Our Children.** Esther Davis-Thompson. LC 99-11524. 160p. (Orig.). 1999. pap. 12.00 (*1-880913-38-0*) Innisfree Pr.

Motherlove 2: More Stories about Births, Babies & Beyond. Debra Adelaide. LC 97-156315. 1997. write for info. (*0-09-183512-7*) Trafalgar.

Motherly Advice from Cathy's Mom. Anne Guisewite. (Illus.). 128p. (Orig.). 1987. pap. 8.95 (*0-8362-2091-9*) Andrews & McMeel.

Motherly & Fatherly Roles in Education. Erich Gabert. Tr. by William N. Weaver, Jr. from GER.Tr. of Das/Muetterliche & das Vaeterliche Element in der Erziehung. 56p. (Orig.). 1988. pap. 6.95 (*0-88010-199-7*) Anthroposophic.

Mothermassage. Elaine Stillerman. (Illus.). 192p. 1992. pap. 13.95 (*0-440-50702-2*) Dell.

Mothernation: Poems from 1984 to 1987. Lasana M. Sekou. LC 91-72367. (Illus.). 109p. (Orig.). 1991. pap. text 10.00 (*0-913441-13-9*) Hse of Nehesi.

Motherpeace: A Way to the Goddess Through Myth, Art & Tarot. Vicki Noble. LC 82-47752. (Illus.). 288p. 1994. reprint ed. pap. 19.00 (*0-06-251085-1*, Pub. by Harper SF) HarpC.

Motherpeace Tarot Deck & Book Set. Karen Vogel. (Illus.). 127p. 1997. pap. 30.00 (*1-57281-031-9*, MMPS99) US Games Syst.

Motherpeace Tarot Playbook. Vicki Noble & Jonathan Tenney. LC 86-1510. (Illus.). 207p. 1986. pap. 21.00 (*0-914728-53-9*) Wingbow Pr.

Motherpiece Tarot Guidebook. Karen Vogel. (Illus.). 128p. 1997. pap. 9.95 (*0-88079-747-9*, BK139) US Games Syst.

Mothers. Ariel Books Staff. (Illus.). 80p. 1992. 4.95 (*0-8362-3008-6*, Arie Bks) Andrews & McMeel.

Mothers. Reva Y. Bignall. (Illus.). xii, 204p. 1998. 19.95 (*1-891403-00-1*); pap. 11.95 (*1-891403-01-X*) Bookage Press.

Mothers. Claire Bretecher. (Illus.). 70p. (C). 1992. pap. write for info. (*0-413-58850-5*, A0663, Methuen Drama) Methn.

Mothers. Ed. by Helen Exley. (Miniature Square Bks.). (Illus.). 64p. 1996. 6.00 (*1-85015-695-6*) Exley Giftbooks.

Mothers. Vardis Fisher. 287p. 1943. 15.95 (*0-614-22016-5*, Idaho Center for the Bk); pap. 10.95 (*0-614-22017-3*, Idaho Center for the Bk) Heming W Studies.

Mothers. Gloria Goldreich. 1989. 18.95 (*0-316-31936-8*) Little.

Mothers. Jax P. Lowell. 336p. 1996. pap. 13.95 (*0-312-14373-7*) St Martin.

Mothers. Lavonne Mueller. LC 97-28472. 72p. 1997. write for info. (*1-55783-328-1*) Applause Theatre Bk Pubs.

Mothers. Lola M. Schaefer. 1999. 13.25 (*0-516-21812-3*) Capstone Pr.

Mothers. Lola N. Schaefer. LC 98-31600. 1999. write for info. (*0-7368-0259-2*) Capstone PC.

Mothers. Vardis Fisher. 1976. reprint ed. lib. bdg. 25.95 (*0-89190-831-5*, Rivercity Pr) Amereon Ltd.

Mothers: A Celebration. Alexandra Stoddard. 1996. 22.00 (*0-614-97009-1*, Wm Morrow) Morrow Avon.

Mothers: A Celebration. Alexandra Stoddard. 288p. 1997. pap. 12.00 (*0-380-72619-X*, Avon Bks) Morrow Avon.

Mothers: A Loving Celebration. Courage Books Staff. LC 96-71607. (Illus.). 128p. 1997. 19.98 (*0-7624-0050-1*, Courage) Running Pr.

Mothers: A Pop-Up Book. Ariel Books Staff. LC 99-163151. (Tiny Tomes Ser.). 12p. 1997. 3.95 (*0-8362-2958-4*, Arie Bks) Andrews & McMeel.

***Mothers: Memories from Famous Daughters & Sons.** Niamh Malone. LC 99-490355. 160p. 1999. write for info. (*0-86278-605-3*, Pub. by OBrien Pr) Irish Amer Bk.

Mothers: Praising the Daughters of God. Susan Evans McCloud. 24p. 1996. pap. 3.95 (*1-55503-912-X*, 01112244) Covenant Comms.

Mothers: The Matriarchal Theory of Social Origins. Robert Briffault. LC 90-34114. 451p. 1993. reprint ed. lib. bdg. 45.00 (*0-86527-398-7*) Fertig.

Mothers: Twenty Stories of Contemporary Motherhood. Ed. by Katrina Kenison & Kathleen Hirsch. LC 96-35329. 356p. 1997. pap. 14.00 (*0-86547-511-3*) N Point Pr.

Mothers: Twenty Stories of Contemporary Motherhood. Ed. by Katrina Kenison & Kathleen Hirsh. 352p. 1996. 22.00 (*0-86547-498-2*) N Point Pr.

***Mothers: Twenty Stories of Contemporary Motherhood.** Ed. by Katrina Kenison & Kathleen Hirsch. 343p. 2000. reprint ed. text 22.00 (*0-7881-6928-9*) DIANE Pub.

Mothers Address Book. Ed. by Helen Exley. (Mini Address Bks.). (Illus.). 64p. 1994. 7.00 (*1-85015-540-2*) Exley Giftbooks.

Mother's Agenda, Vol. 2, 1961. Satprem Staff & Mother. LC 80-472990.Tr. of L'Agenda de Mere. 500p. (Orig.). 1981. pap. 12.50 (*0-938710-01-X*) Inst Evolutionary.

Mother's Agenda, Vol. 3, 1962. Satprem Staff & Mother. LC 80-472990.Tr. of L'Agenda de Mere. 540p. (Orig.). 1982. pap. text 12.50 (*0-938710-02-8*) Inst Evolutionary.

Mother's Agenda, 1971, Vol. 12. Satprem Staff. LC 80-472990. (Mother's Agenda Ser.). Orig. Title: L'Agenda De Mere. 400p. (Orig.). 1983. pap. text 12.50 (*0-938710-05-2*) Inst Evolutionary.

Mother's Agenda, 1972-73, Vol. 13. Satprem Staff & Mother. LC 80-472990. 460p. (Orig.). 1984. pap. text 12.50 (*0-938710-07-9*) Inst Evolutionary.

Mother's Agenda, 1965, Vol. 6. Satprem Staff. Tr. by Team Staff from FRE. LC 80-472990. 384p. 1990. pap. text 12.50 (*0-938710-12-5*) Inst Evolutionary.

Mother's Agenda, 1964, Vol. 5. Satprem Staff & Mother.Tr. of L'Agenda de Mere, 1964, Vol. 5. 450p. (Orig.). 1988. pap. text 12.50 (*0-938710-10-9*) Inst Evolutionary.

Mother's Agenda, 1966, Vol. 7. Mother & Satprem. LC 80-472990. 340p. 1991. pap. 12.50 (*0-938710-13-3*) Inst Evolutionary.

Mother's Agenda, 1963, Vol. 4. Satprem Staff & Mother. LC 80-472990. (Works of Satprem-Institute for Evolutionary Research).Tr. of L'Agenda de Mere 1963. 485p. (Orig.). 1987. pap. 12.50 (*0-938710-09-5*) Inst Evolutionary.

Mother's Album. BHB International Staff. 1997. 14.95 (*1-85833-599-X*, Pub. by CLib Bks) Whitecap Bks.

Mother's Almanac. rev. ed. Marguerite Kelly. 416p. 1975. pap. 18.95 (*0-385-46877-6*) Doubleday.

Mother's Almanac Goes to School: Your Child from Six to Twelve. rev. ed. Marguerite Kelly. Orig. Title: Mother's Almanac II. (Illus.). 416p. 1989. pap. 17.95 (*0-385-13155-0*) Doubleday.

Mother's Almanac II see Mother's Almanac Goes to School: Your Child from Six to Twelve

Mothers Alone: Strategies for a Time of Change. Sheila B. Kamerman & Alfred J. Kahn. LC 88-6195. 255p. 1988. 49.95 (*0-86569-183-5*, Auburn Hse) Greenwood.

Mothers & Babies. Ed. by Mac Anderson. 78p. (Orig.). 1988. pap. 7.95 (*1-56245-012-3*) Great Quotations.

***Mothers & Babies.** MQP Creative Staff. LC 99-87688. (Illus.). 112p. 2000. 10.00 (*0-688-17701-8*, Hearst) Hearst Commns.

Mothers & Children. Ellen Lewin. Ed. by Carlos E. Cortes. LC 79-6215. (Hispanics in the United States Ser.). (Illus.). 1981. lib. bdg. 23.95 (*0-405-13163-1*) Ayer.

Mothers & Children. Roxana Marcoci. LC 94-32474. (Celebrations in Art Ser.). (Illus.). 72p. 1995. 12.98 (*1-56799-162-9*, MetroBooks) M Friedman Pub Grp Inc.

***Mothers & Children: Feminist Analyses & Personal Narratives.** Susan E. Chase & Mary F. Rogers. LC 00-39032. 384p. (C). 2001. text 55.00 (*0-8135-2875-5*); pap. text 25.00 (*0-8135-2876-3*) Rutgers U Pr.

Mothers & Children Facing Divorce. Tracy B. Grossman. LC 86-11336. (Research in Clinical Psychology Ser.: No. 15). 220p. reprint ed. pap. 68.20 (*0-8357-1767-4*, 207038400088) Bks Demand.

Mothers & Daughters. Marie Chapian. LC 88-4199. 224p. (Orig.). 1988. pap. 9.99 (*1-55661-007-6*) Bethany Hse.

Mothers & Daughters. Alison Gray. 231p. 1996. pap. 16.95 (*0-908912-37-4*) Paul & Co Pubs.

Mothers & Daughters. Carolyn J. Griffin. (Lyrics on Matters Relating to Ser.). 10p. 1985. 8.00 (*1-929388-08-X*) Griffin Pubg Co Inc.

Mothers & Daughters. Madeleine L'Engle. LC 96-50117. 112p. 1997. 17.99 (*0-87788-561-3*, H Shaw Pubs) Waterbrook Pr.

Mothers & Daughters. Jill Morgan. 1999. mass mkt. 5.99 (*0-451-19786-0*) NAL.

Mothers & Daughters. Carol Saline & Sharon J. Wohlmuth. LC 96-39529. (Illus.). 144p. 1997. 24.95 (*0-385-48125-X*) Doubleday.

Mothers & Daughters: A Giftbook with Envelope. Nancy C. Akmon. (Illus.). 49p. 1998. 6.95 (*1-884807-25-9*, EC706) Blushing Rose.

Mothers & Daughters: A Lasting Bond. Andrews & McMeel Staff. (Tiny Tomes Ser.). 1998. 3.95 (*0-8362-5245-4*) Andrews & McMeel.

***Mothers & Daughters: A Record Book.** Jerianne Van Dijk. 1999. 20.00 (*1-57977-130-0*) Havoc Pub.

***Mothers & Daughters: A Record Book about Us.** Havoc Publishing Staff. (Illus.). 1999. 20.00 (*1-57977-161-0*) Havoc Pub.

Mothers & Daughters: An Anthology. Alberto Manguel. LC 97-32273. 352p. 1998. 15.95 (*0-8118-1629-X*) Chronicle Bks.

Mothers & Daughters: An Exploration in Photographs. Estelle Jussim & Julie O. Edwards. (Illus.). 112p. 1989. reprint ed. pap. 37.95 (*0-89381-379-6*) Aperture.

Mothers & Daughters: Celebrating the Gift of Love in Twelve New Stories. Ed. by Jill M. Morgan. LC 97-32519. 256p. 1998. mass mkt. 14.95 (*0-451-19383-0*, Sig) NAL.

***Mothers & Daughters: Connection, Empowerment & Transformation.** Ed. by Andrea O'Reilly & Sharon Abbey. LC 99-45590. 336p. 2000. pap. 25.95 (*0-8476-9487-9*); text 65.00 (*0-8476-9486-0*) Rowman.

Mothers & Daughters: Loving & Letting Go. Evelyn S. Bassoff. 306p. 1989. pap. 13.95 (*0-452-26319-0*, Dutt) Dutton Plume.

Mothers & Daughters: Searching for New Connections. Ann F. Caron. LC 97-52977. 288p. 1998. 25.00 (*0-8050-5149-X*) H Holt & Co.

Mothers & Daughters: That Special Bond. Suzanne Beilenson. LC 98-232376. (Pocket Gift Editions Ser.). 1998. 4.95 (*0-88088-072-4*) Peter Pauper.

Mothers & Daughters: The Distortion of a Relationship. Vivien E. Nice. 1996. 35.00 (*0-333-52528-0*, Pub. by Macmillan) St Martin.

***Mothers & Daughters at Home: 35 Projects to Make Together.** Charlotte Lyons. LC 99-54522. (Illus.). 160p. 2000. 24.00 (*0-684-86273-5*) Simon & Schuster.

Mothers & Daughter's Gift Book. Zondervan Publishing Staff. 2000. 12.99 (*0-310-97754-1*) Zondervan.

Mothers & Daughters in American Short Fiction: An Annotated Bibliography of Twentieth-Century Women's Literature, 19. Compiled by Susanne Carter. LC 93-10822. 160p. 1993. lib. bdg. 59.95 (*0-313-28511-X*, Greenwood Pr) Greenwood.

Mothers & Daughters in Medieval German Literature. Ann M. Rasmussen. LC 96-19775. 304p. 1996. text 45.00 (*0-8156-2709-2*, RAMD); pap. text 17.95 (*0-8156-0389-4*, RAMDP) Syracuse U Pr.

Mothers & Daughters in Nineteenth-Century America: The Biosocial Construction of Femininity. rev. ed. Nancy Theriot. LC 95-14672. 240p. (C). 1995. pap. 17.00 (*0-8131-0858-6*) U Pr of Ky.

An Asterisk (*) at the beginning of an entry indicates that the title is appearing for the first time.

*Mothers & Daughters in the 20th Century: A Literary Anthology.** Ed. by Columbia University Press Staff. 2000. 19.95 (*0-7486-1175-4*, Pub. by Edinburgh U Pr) Col U Pr.

Mothers & Daughters of Invention: Notes for a Revised History of Technology. Autumn Stanley. 700p. 1995. pap. text 30.00 (*0-8135-2197-1*) Rutgers U Pr.

Mothers & Daughters of Invention: Notes for a Revised History of Technology. Autumn Stanley. LC 92-42054. 1165p. 1993. 110.50 (*0-8108-2586-4*) Scarecrow.

Mothers & Daughters Photo Memory Album: A Gift of Memories. Linda Spivey. 1998. write for info. (*1-57977-229-3*) Havoc Pub.

*Mothers & Daughters Together.** Compiled by Lil Copan & Helen Copan Neubacher. LC 98-33140. (Shaw Greetings Ser.). 96p. 1999. pap. 5.99 (*0-87788-186-3*, H Shaw Pubs) Waterbrook Pr.

Mothers & Divorce: Legal, Economic, & Social Dilemmas. Terry Arendell. 320p. (C). 1986. pap. 15.95 (*0-520-06215-9*, Pub. by U CA Pr) Cal Prin Full Svc.

Mothers & Education, Inside Out? Exploring Family-Education Policy & Experience. Miriam David et al. LC 93-15. 256p. 1993. text 39.95 (*0-312-09596-1*) St Martin.

Mothers & Fathers. Elizabeth Wentzel. Date not set. pap. 11.50 (*0-8488-0894-0*) Amereon Ltd.

*Mothers & Fathers: Health & Financial Advice to Share with Your Parents.** Louis Sapi & Peter Zawadzki. 256p. 2000. pap. 24.95 (*0-13-018181-1*) P-H.

Mothers & Illicit Drugs: Transcending the Myths. Susan C. Boyd. (Illus.). 272p. 1999. text 50.00 (*0-8020-4331-3*); pap. text 19.95 (*0-8020-8151-7*) U of Toronto Pr.

Mothers & Medicine: A Social History of Infant Feeding, 1890-1950. Rima D. Apple. LC 87-40137. (Wisconsin Publications in the History of Science & Medicine). (Illus.). 280p. 1987. pap. text 18.95 (*0-299-11484-8*) U of Wis Pr.

Mothers & Midwives: A History of Traditional Childbirth. Janet I. Ashford. (Illus.). 21p. (Orig.). (C). 1988. pap. 7.95 (*0-9619968-1-1*) J I Ashford.

Mothers & More: American Women in the 1950s. Eugenia Kaledin. (American Women in the Twentieth Century Ser.). 280p. 1984. 24.95 (*0-8057-9904-4*, Twyne) Mac Lib Ref.

Mothers & More: American Women in the 1950s. Eugenia Kaledin. (American Women in the Twentieth Century Ser.). 280p. 1985. pap. 14.95 (*0-8057-9907-9*, Twyne) Mac Lib Ref.

Mothers & Motherhood: Readings in American History. Ed. by Rima D. Apple & Janet L. Golden. LC 97-15670. (Women & Health Ser.). 605p. 1997. text 60.00 (*0-8142-0738-3*) Ohio St U Pr.

Mothers & Motherhood: Readings in American History. Ed. by Rima Apple & Janet L. Golden. LC 97-15670. (Women & Health Ser.). 1997. pap. text 21.95 (*0-8142-0739-1*) Ohio St U Pr.

Mothers & Others Be Aware. Donna Miller. 228p. 1986. pap. 12.95 (*0-934263-13-2*) Res Bks.

Mothers & Others for a Livable Planet: Guide to Natural Baby Care. Mindy Pennybacker & Aisha Ikramuddin. LC 98-31591. 320p. 1999. pap. 16.95 (*0-471-29333-4*) Wiley.

Mothers & Shadows. rev. ed. Marta Traba. Tr. by Jo Labanyi from SPA. (Readers International Ser.). (Illus.). 180p. 1989. pap. 12.95 (*0-930523-16-4*) Readers Intl.

Mothers & Sons. Madeleine L'Engle. LC 98-55387. (Illus.). 105p. 1999. 17.99 (*0-87788-567-2*, H Shaw Pubs) Waterbrook Pr.

*Mothers & Sons.** Ed. by Jill Morgan. 2000. pap. 14.95 (*0-451-20009-8*, Sig) NAL.

Mothers & Sons: In Their Own Words. Photos by Mariana Cook. LC 95-30152. (Illus.). 132p. 1996. 40.00 (*0-8118-1194-8*); pap. 22.95 (*0-8118-1170-0*) Chronicle Bks.

Mothers & Sons: Raising Boys to Be Men. Jean Lush & Pamela Vredevelt. LC 88-18210. 230p. 1994. pap. 9.99 (*0-8007-5503-0*) Revell.

Mothers & Sons: The Truth about Mother-Son Relationships. 2nd rev. ed. Babette Smith. 248p. 1997. pap. 12.95 (*1-86448-222-2*, Pub. by Allen & Unwin Pty) IPG Chicago.

Mothers & Sons in Chinese Buddhism. R. Alan Cole. LC 97-46028. x, 303p. 1998. 39.50 (*0-8047-3152-7*) Stanford U Pr.

Mothers & the Mexican Antinuclear Power Movement. Velma Garcia-Gorena. LC 98-25504. (Society, Environment & Place Ser.). 1999. 45.00 (*0-8165-1874-2*) U of Ariz Pr.

*Mothers & the Mexican Antinuclear Power Movement.** Velma Garcia-Gorena. LC 98-25504. (Society, Environment & Place Ser.). xii, 187p. 1999. pap. 19.95 (*0-8165-1875-0*) U of Ariz Pr.

Mothers & Their Children: A Feminist Sociology of Childrearing. Jane Ribbens. 240p. 1995. 69.95 (*0-8039-8834-6*); pap. 22.95 (*0-8039-8835-4*) Sage.

Mothers & Wives: Gusii Women of East Africa. Sarah LeVine et al. LC 78-21573. 1994. lib. bdg. 26.00 (*0-226-47548-4*) U Ch Pr.

Mothers & Wives: Gusii Women of East Africa. Sarah Levine. LC 78-21573. 391p. reprint ed. pap. 121.30 (*0-608-09464-1*, 205426400005) Bks Demand.

Mothers & Work in Popular American Magazines, 139. Kathryn Keller. LC 93-37508. (Contributions in Women's Studies: No. 139). 208p. 1994. 49.95 (*0-313-28864-X*) Greenwood.

Mothers Apple Pie: A Collection of Treasured Words & Recipes. Marsha K. Castello. Ed. by Herbert A. Enos. (Illus.). 140p. (Orig.). 1997. pap. 10.95 (*1-57502-536-1*, P01576) Morris Pubng.

Mothers Are Always Special. rev. ed. Celestine Sibley. (Illus.). 96p. 1985. 12.95 (*0-931948-73-8*) Peachtree Pubs.

Mothers Are Forever. Criswell Freeman. 1998. pap. text 6.95 (*1-887655-76-X*) Walnut Gr Pr.

Mothers Are Like Miracles: They Make Everything Possible. Janet Lanese. LC 97-46849. 128p. 1998. per. 10.00 (*0-684-84251-3*, Fireside) S&S Trade Pap.

*Mothers Are Like That.** Carol Carrick. LC 99-16587. (Illus.). 32p. (J). (ps-1). 2000. 15.00 (*0-395-88351-2*, Clarion Bks) HM.

*Mothers Are Special.** Lucy Mead. LC 99-43266. 2000. 5.99 (*0-517-20955-1*) Random Hse Value.

Mothers Around the Manger. J. Timothy Allen. LC 98-17456. 128p. 1998. pap. 12.00 (*1-57312-186-X*) Smyth & Helwys.

*Mothers at Work: Effects on Children's Well-Being.** Lois W. Hoffman & Lise M. Youngblade. LC 98-49508. (Studies in Social & Emotional Development). (Illus.). 392p. 1999. 54.95 (*0-521-57289-4*) Cambridge U Pr.

*Mothers at Work: Effects on Children's Well-Being.** Lois W. Hoffman & Lise M. Youngblade. LC 98-49508. (Studies in Social & Emotional Development). (Illus.). 338p. 1999. pap. 19.95 (*0-521-66896-4*) Cambridge U Pr.

Mothers, Babies, & Cocaine: The Role of Toxins in Development. Ed. by Michael Lewis et al. 408p. 1995. pap. 37.50 (*0-8058-1584-8*); text 79.95 (*0-8058-1583-X*) L Erlbaum Assocs.

Mothers, Babies & Health in Later Life. 2nd ed. D. J. Barker. LC 98-14947. ix, 217p. 1998. write for info. (*0-443-06165-3*) Church.

Mother's Beloved: Stories from Laos. Othine Bounyavong et al. LC 98-17631. 118p. 1998. pap. 14.95 (*0-295-97736-1*) U of Wash Pr.

Mothers Bereaved by Stillbirth, Neonatal Death or Sudden Infant Death Syndrome: Patterns of Distress & Recovery. Frances M. Boyle. LC 97-70894. (Illus.). 160p. 1997. text 55.95 (*1-85972-149-4*, Pub. by Ashgate Pub) Ashgate Pub Co.

*Mother's Blood.** Liz Lesiak. LC 99-67406. 112p. 1999. pap. 16.00 (*1-892323-18-4*) Vivisphere.

Mother's Book. Lydia Maria Child. LC 92-17577. 169p. 1989. 12.95 (*1-55709-124-2*) Applewood.

Mother's Book. Lydia Maria Child. LC 73-169377. (Family in America Ser.). 184p. 1976. reprint ed. 15.95 (*0-405-03854-2*) Ayer.

Mother's Book: Practical Ideas for Preschool Parenting. Patricia Van Nes & Lenora Andres. (Illus.). 218p. (Orig.). 1988. pap. 12.95 (*0-919797-56-3*) Kindred Prods.

Mother's Book of Home Medical Tests for Infants & Children. Herbert Haessler & Raymond Harris. LC 98-10365. (Illus.). 240p. 1998. pap. 14.95 (*0-8092-3037-2*, 303720, Contemporary Bks) NTC Contemp Pub Co.

Mother's Book of Poems. Compiled by Christine Benton. LC 94-29325. 160p. 1994. 12.00 (*0-8092-3525-0*) NTC Contemp Pub Co.

Mother's Book of Prayers. Julie Mitchell Marra. 1999. 8.95 (*0-88271-648-4*) Regina Pr.

Mother's Book of Prayers. Mayhew. 1996. 5.95 (*0-88271-494-5*) Regina Pr.

*Mothers Change the World... One Child at a Time.** Mary Carlisle Beasley & Criswell Freeman. 128p. 2000. pap. 4.95 (*1-58334-058-0*, Pub. by Walnut Gr Pr) Midpt Trade.

Mother's Choice. Elizabeth Mansfield. 208p. (Orig.). 1994. mass mkt. 3.99 (*0-515-11386-7*, Jove) Berkley Pub.

*Mother's Cry.** Arlenda Vieger. 40p. 1999. pap. 9.95 (*1-883866-17-0*) Clarion Pub.

*Mothers, Daughters & Traditions.** Marlowe. 2001. write for info. (*0-684-87264-1*, Fireside) S&S Trade Pap.

Mother's Day see Dia de las Madres

Mother's Day. Kate Cavanaugh. (Illus.). 228p. (Orig.). 1989. pap. 9.95 (*0-9622353-0-X*) KAC.

Mother's Day. Dennis McDougal. 1995. mass mkt. 5.99 (*0-449-14930-7*) Fawcett.

Mother's Day. Shelly Nielsen. (Illus.). 32p. (J). (ps-4). 1996. lib. bdg. 13.98 (*1-56239-704-4*) ABDO Pub Co.

Mother's Day: From Surviving to Thriving. H. Dee Callahan. LC 97-7358. (Illus.). 144p. (Orig.). 1997. pap. 11.95 (*1-56474-220-2*) Fithian Pr.

Mothers' Day: Its History, Origin, Celebration, Spirit & Significance As Related in Prose & Verse. Ed. by Robert H. Schauffler. LC 89-43371. 363p. 1990. reprint ed. lib. bdg. 42.00 (*1-55888-864-0*) Omnigraphics Inc.

Mother's Day: Voices from the Heart. William J. Crockett. 15p. 1985. pap. 3.00 (*0-934383-33-2*) Pride Prods.

Mother's Day Activities. (Illus.). 16p. 1995. pap. text, wbk. ed. 2.95 (*1-55734-782-4*) Tchr Create Mat.

Mother's Day & Father's Day Program Builder, No. 6. Compiled by Evelyn Stenbock. 37p. 1979. 4.99 (*0-8341-9172-5*, MP-306) Lillenas.

Mother's Day & Father's Day Program Builder, No. 7. Compiled by Paul M. Miller. 55p. 1985. pap. 4.50 (*0-8341-9405-8*, MP-307) Nazarene.

Mother's Day & Father's Day Program Builder, No. 8. Compiled by Diane K. Cunningham. 37p. 1988. 4.50 (*0-8341-9061-3*, MP-308) Lillenas.

Mother's Day & Father's Day Program Builder, No. 9. Compiled by Paul M. Miller. Vol. 9. 23p. 1934. pap. 4.50 (*0-8341-9493-7*, MP-309) Nazarene.

Mother's Day Classics from Modern Library. Modern Library. LC 98-14562. 208p. 1998. pap. 12.00 (*0-375-75153-X*) Modern Lib NY.

Mother's Day Crafts. Jean Eick. LC 98-3249. (Illus.). 24p. (J). 1998. lib. bdg. 21.36 (*1-56766-538-1*) Childs World.

Mother's Day, Holiday, Pet Birthday, Secretaries Day Etc. Promise, Favor Letters with Suggestions in Poetry. Greetings Etc. by Alfreda Staff. 1984. ring bd. 25.95 (*0-318-04373-4*) Prosperity & Profits.

Mother's Day Mice. Eve Bunting. LC 85-13991. (Illus.). 32p. (J). (ps-3). 1986. 15.00 (*0-89919-387-0*, Clarion Bks) HM.

Mother's Day Mice. Eve Bunting. LC 85-13991. (Illus.). 32p. (J). (ps-3). 1988. pap. 5.95 (*0-89919-702-7*, Clarion Bks) HM.

Mother's Day Mice. Eve Bunting. LC 85-13991. (Carry-Along Book & Cassette Favorites Ser.). (Illus.). (J). (ps-3). 1989. pap. 9.95 incl. audio (*0-89919-895-3*, 111302, Clarion Bks) Ticknor & Flds Bks Yng Read.

Mother's Day Mice. Eve Bunting. (J). 1986. 11.15 (*0-606-04130-3*, Pub. by Turtleback) Demco.

Mother's Day Miniature Editions Gift Set: Motherhood: A Gift of Love; Mom; & Quotable Women. gif. ed. (Illus.). 1999. 17.95 (*0-7624-0537-6*) Running Press Min.

*Mother's Day Miracle.** Lois Richer. (Love Inspired Ser.: Vol. 101). 2000. per. 4.50 (*0-373-87107-4*) Harlequin Bks.

*Mother's Day Murder.** Wensley Clarkson. (Illus.). 232p. 2000. mass mkt. 6.50 (*0-312-97411-6*) St Martin.

*Mother's Day Murder.** Lee Harris. LC 00-190071. Vol. 12. 257p. 2000. mass mkt. 6.50 (*0-449-00442-2*) Fawcett.

Mother's Day Out: How to Start a Business That Gives Mothers the Day Off. Shirley Eichenberger. LC 82-42762. (Illus.). 1983. 12.95 (*0-911391-25-8*) Oak Hill UT.

Mother's Delight. Ed. by Jennifer Sawyer. 320p. 1995. mass mkt. 3.99 (*0-8217-4910-2*, Zebra Kensgtn) Kensgtn Pub Corp.

Mother's Dilemma. Wendy Lyon. 123p. 1993. 8.95 (*1-878526-44-8*) Pineapple MI.

Mother's Energy Efficiency Book: Heat, Light, Power. Mother Earth News Editors & William C. Davis. (Illus.). 250p. 1983. 17.95 (*0-938432-22-2*) Mother Earth.

Mother's Eye View. Lemlem Tsegaw. LC 98-164865. 80p. (Orig.). per. write for info. (*0-9657719-0-3*) A Memorial Pr.

Mothers, Fathers, Sons & Daughters. 32p. (Orig.). 1996. 2.50 (*0-916872-13-0*) Delafield Pr.

Mother's Favorite Quotes: Wisdom for Life & Motherhood. LC 99-175741. 40 p. 1998. 1.99 (*1-57748-326-X*) Barbour Pub.

Mother's First-Born Daughters: Early Shaker Writings on Women & Religion. Ed. by Jean M. Humez. LC 92-20920. (Religion in North America Ser.). 336p. (C). 1993. 41.95 (*0-253-32870-5*); pap. 18.95 (*0-253-20744-4*) Ind U Pr.

Mother's First Year. Copeland C. Lewis. 1992. pap. 5.50 (*0-425-13488-1*) Berkley Pub.

Mother's First Year: A Realistic Guide to the Changes & Challenges of Motherhood. Cynthia C. Lewis. 384p. 1997. reprint ed. pap. 12.00 (*0-425-15677-X*) Berkley Pub.

Mother's First Year Journal. 128p. 1994. 15.00 (*0-687-00315-6*) Dimen for Liv.

Mother's Footprints of Faith: Stories of Hope & Encouragement. Carol Kuykendall. LC 96-51523. 192p. 1997. 12.99 (*0-310-21083-6*) Zondervan.

Mother's Footprints of Faith: Stories of Hope & Encouragement. Carol Kuykendall. 1999. pap. text 9.99 (*0-310-22562-0*) Zondervan.

*Mother's Garden of Prayer: Cultivating a Lifestyle of Praying for Your Children.** Sarah O. Maddox & Patricia F. Webb. LC 98-31067. 128p. 1999. pap. 13.99 (*0-8054-1768-0*) Broadman.

Mother's Gift: Waiting for Mom; Nobody's Child; Mother's Day Baby, 3 bks. in 1. Kathleen Eagle et al. (Silhouette Promo Ser.). 1998. per. 5.99 (*0-373-48358-9*, 1-48358-5) Harlequin Bks.

*Mother's Gifts to Me.** Dianna Daniels Booher. 1999. 12.99 (*0-8499-5509-2*) J Countryman.

Mother's Goose's Seasons. (Read-A-Rhyme Ser.). (Illus.). 24p. (J). (gr. 1-4). 1996. pap. write for info. (*1-56144-716-1*, Honey Bear Bks) Modern Pub NYC.

Mother's Grief Observed. Rebecca Faber. LC 96-47555. 1997. pap. 9.99 (*0-8423-3995-7*) Tyndale Hse.

Mother's Guide to a Healthier Pregnancy & Easier Birth. Jeanine L. LaBaw & Mary M. Lepley. (Illus.). 1991. 24.95 incl. audio (*0-9627583-0-2*) Lifesounds.

Mother's Guide to Computers. Norma Leonardi Leone. Ed. by Jean Koenemann. LC 85-46037. (Illus.). 102p. (Orig.). 1986. pap. 5.95 (*0-936635-03-7*) Lion Pr & Vid.

Mother's Guide to Raising Healthy Children Naturally. Sue E. Frederick. LC 99-42973. 256p. 1999. pap. 14.95 (*0-87983-926-0*, 39260K, Keats Publng) NTC Contemp Pub Co.

Mother's Handbook Bk. 1: An Easy-to-Read Guide for Mothers. Beverly J. Crump. (Illus.). 192p. (Orig.). 1991. pap. 13.95 (*1-879520-09-5*) Cntry Ln Bks.

Mothers Have Angel Wings: A Tribute to the Tears & Triumphs of Being a Mom. Carol Kent. LC 96-51870. 176p. (Orig.). 1997. pap. 12.00 (*1-57683-001-2*) NavPress.

Mother's Heart. Veronica Ashley et al. 352p. 1998. pap. 5.99 (*0-8217-5896-9*, Zebra Kensgtn) Kensgtn Pub Corp.

Mother's Heart. Barbour Publishing, Inc. Editors & Ellyn Sanna. LC 99-215454. 94p. 1999. pap. 0.99 (*1-57748-431-2*) Barbour Pub.

Mother's Heart: A Look at Values, Vision & Character for the Christian Mother. Jean M. Fleming. (NavClassics Ser.). 1996. pap. 9.00 (*0-89109-944-1*) NavPress.

Mother's Heart, a Father's Hurt & a Sister's Love. Bob Fisher et al. 93p. pap. text. write for info. (*0-9642444-0-3*) Betach Minist.

Mother's Heartsong. Carolyn Larsen. LC 96-61532. (Illus.). 32p. 1997. 11.99 (*0-529-10727-9*) World Publng.

Mother's Helper. A. Bates. 176p. (YA). (gr. 7-9). 1991. 3.25 (*0-590-44582-0*, Point) Scholastic Inc.

Mother's Helpmate Complete Child Care Planner. Cora H. Thomas. (Illus.). 225p. 1997. pap. text 30.00 (*0-9642214-1-1*) Mothers Helpmates.

Mother's Helpmates Guide to Child Care, Nannies & Companions. Cora H. Thomas. Ed. by Jeff Corydon, III. LC 94-76905. (Illus.). 160p. (Orig.). 1994. pap. 16.95 (*0-9642214-0-3*) Mothers Helpmates.

*Mother's Herbal: Caring for Yourself & Your Family with Natural Remedies.** Anne McIntyre. 2000. pap. 24.95 (*1-86204-744-8*, Pub. by Element MA) Penguin Putnam.

Mother's Homebuilding & Shelter Guide. Mother Earth News Editors. Ed. by Robert Miner. (Illus.). 200p. 1983. pap. text 15.95 (*0-938432-15-X*) Mother Earth.

Mothers in Faust: The Myth of Time & Creativity. Harold S. Jantz. LC 68-31017. 102p. reprint ed. pap. 31.70 (*0-7837-2198-6*, 204253600004) Bks Demand.

Mothers in Industry: Wage-Earning by Mothers in Philadelphia. Gwendolyn S. Hughes. Ed. by Leon Stein. LC 77-70507. (Illus.). 1977. reprint ed. lib. bdg. 29.95 (*0-405-10177-5*) Ayer.

Mothers in Law: Feminist Theory & the Legal Regulation of Motherhood. Ed. by Martha A. Fineman & Isabelle Karpin. LC 94-47019. (Gender & Culture Ser.). 384p. 1995. pap. 19.50 (*0-231-09681-X*) Col U Pr.

Mothers-in-Law & Daughters-in-Law Tell It Like It Is. Joyce W. Williams & Frances J. Wagner. LC 96-94150. (Illus.). 128p. (Orig.). 1996. pap. 10.00 (*0-9651894-0-6*) Joy Bks Tampa.

Mothers in Mourning: With the Essay of Amnesty & Its Opposite. Nicole Loraux. Tr. by Corinne Pache. LC 97-29264. (Myth & Poetics Ser.). 136p. 1998. pap. 11.95 (*0-8014-8242-9*); text 29.95 (*0-8014-3090-9*) Cornell U Pr.

Mothers in Prison. 2nd ed. Phyllis J. Baunach. 150p. (C). 1985. pap. 21.95 (*0-88738-741-1*) Transaction Pubs.

Mothers in the English Novel: From Stereotype & Archetype. Marjorie J. McCormick. LC 91-249241. (Gender & Genre in Literature Ser.: Vol. 1). 232p. 1991. text 15.00 (*0-8240-7131-X*, H1302) Garland.

Mother's Intuition: Choosing Secondary Schools. Miriam David et al. LC 94-17289. 174p. 1994. 85.00 (*0-7507-0286-9*, Falmer Pr) Taylor & Francis.

Mother's Job: The History of Day Care, 1890-1960. Elizabeth Rose. (Illus.). 296p. 1999. text 45.00 (*0-19-511112-5*) OUP.

Mother's Journal. Tracy Porter. 1999. 10.95 (*0-8362-7830-5*) Andrews & McMeel.

Mother's Journal: A Book of Days. Museum of Fine Arts Staff. (Illus.). 128p. 1991. 16.95 (*0-8212-1886-7*, Pub. by Bulfinch Pr) Little.

Mother's Journal: A Collection of Family Memories. Mary Engelbreit. (Illus.). 112p. 1993. 12.95 (*0-8362-4619-5*) Andrews & McMeel.

Mother's Journal: A Keepsake Book for Thoughts & Dreams. (Illus.). 96p. (Orig.). 1985. pap. 5.95 (*0-89471-333-7*) Running Pr.

Mother's Journal on the Go. Mary Engelbreit. (Illus.). 80p. 1995. 6.95 (*0-8362-4630-6*) Andrews & McMeel.

Mother's Journey. Linda Dillow. 48p. 1998. 14.95 (*1-57856-041-1*); 119.60 (*1-57856-061-6*) Waterbrook Pr.

Mother's Kiss. Anita K. Nobles. 144p. 1993. pap. 4.95 (*1-882626-13-3*) Impress Ink.

*Mothers Kisses.** Bruce Jay Friedman. 2000. pap. 14.00 (*0-226-26416-5*) U Ch Pr.

Mothers, Leadership, & Success. Guy R. Odom. LC 89-23027. 358p. 1990. 22.50 (*0-9624006-0-2*) Polybius Pr.

Mother's Legacy: Encouragement from Mothers in the Bible. Jeanne Hendricks. 110p. 1988. pap. 7.00 (*0-89109-253-6*) NavPress.

*Mother's Legacy: Wisdom from Mothers to Daughters.** Compiled by Barbara Rainey & Ashley Escue. LC 99-85984. 144p. 2000. 12.99 (*0-7852-7007-8*) Nelson.

Mother's Letters. Hampsten. LC 92-40901. 175p. 1993. pap. 17.95 (*0-8165-1373-2*) U of Ariz Pr.

Mother's Little Helper: 12 Heart to Heart Talks. 1996. pap. 4.45 (*0-935952-98-5*) Angelus Pr.

Mother's Little Helper Cookbook. Mary Jane Boll. (Illus.). 42p. (J). 1996. pap. 4.40 (*0-7399-0246-6*, 2357) Rod & Staff.

Mother's Little Instruction Book. Jasmine Birtles. 128p. (Orig.). 1997. pap. 10.95 (*0-7522-1104-8*, Pub. by Boxtree) Trans-Atl Phila.

Mother's Love. Lisa T. Bergren et al. LC 97-480. 286p. 1997. pap. 9.99 (*1-57673-106-5*, Palisades OR) Multnomah Pubs.

Mother's Love. Kitty De Ruyter. LC 98-157402. 1998. pap. 3.95 (*1-57734-225-9*, 01113364) Covenant Comms.

Mother's Love. Guideposts Magazine Editors. LC 93-23324. 112p. 1994. 3.00 (*0-687-27256-4*) Dimen for Liv.

Mother's Love. Violet Hamilton et al. 288p. 1997. mass mkt. 4.99 (*0-8217-5623-0*, Zebra Kensgtn) Kensgtn Pub Corp.

Mother's Love. Monica Harris. 1996. pap. 4.99 (*0-7860-0269-7*) Kensgtn Pub Corp.

Mothers Love. Deborah Kerr. (Illus.). 60p. 1998. pap. 10.50 (*1-56770-435-2*) S Scheewe Pubns.

Mother's Love. Lighten-Up Staff. (Small Wonders Ser.). 120p. 1994. spiral bd. 4.99 (*1-879127-47-4*) Lighten Up Enter.

Mother's Love. Cheryl Wolverton. (Love Inspired Ser.: Bk. 63). 1999. per. 4.50 (*0-373-87063-9*, 1-87063-3, Harlequin) Harlequin Bks.

*Mother's Love: A Treasury of Love & Inspiration.** Ron Dicianni. 2000. 12.99 (*0-8054-2370-2*) Broadman.

Mother's Love: A Tribute to Mothers. Lisa Guest. LC 97-44463. (Illus.). 64p. 1998. 19.99 (*1-56507-814-4*) Harvest Hse.

Mother's Love: Classic Poems Celebrating the Maternal Heart. Kathleen Blease. LC 98-51979. 144p. 1999. pap. 10.00 (*0-449-00545-3*) Fawcett.

Mother's Love: Defiled by Incest. J. Marilyn Van Wingerden. LC 97-9478. 195p. 1999. pap. 13.99 (*0-9661782-1-1*) Fam Life Today.

Mother's Love: In Praise of African-American Mothers. Illus. by Synthia St. James. (Charming Petites Ser.). 80p. 1996. 4.95 (*0-88088-736-2*) Peter Pauper.

***Mother's Love Vocal Solo (Low)** Composed by Paul Sjoland. 1998. pap. 3.50 (*0-634-00348-8*) H Leonard.

Mother's Love (Women Who Dare) Janice Kaiser. LC 95-21535. 299p. 1995. per. 3.75 (*0-373-70669-3*) Harlequin Bks.

Mothers, Madams, & "Lady-Like" Men: Proust & the Maternal. Elizabeth R. Viti. LC 94-69024. (Marcel Proust Studies: Vol. 4). 120p. 1995. lib. bdg. 32.95 (*1-883479-01-0*) Summa Pubns.

Mother's Maiden Name: Identity Fraud's Missing Link. LC 95-81306. (Illus.). 160p. (Orig.). 1997. pap. 29.50 (*1-56866-098-7*) Index Pub Grp.

***Mothers' Manual.** A. Francis Coomes. (Illus.). 2000. pap. 3.95 (*1-929198-18-3*) W J Hirten.

Mothers Manual. William J. Hirten. 1994. 11.95 (*0-00-506482-1*) HarpC.

Mother's Manual for Holiday Survival. Kathy Peel & Judie Byrd. (Orig.). 1991. pap. 9.99 (*1-56179-040-0*) Focus Family.

Mother's Manual for Summer Survival. 1988. pap. 5.95 (*0-9620657-0-6*) Crtv Alternatives.

Mother's Manual for Summer Survival. Kathy Peel & Joy Mahaffey. LC 89-1348. (Illus.). 72p. 1989. reprint ed. pap. 9.99 (*0-929608-31-3*) Focus Family.

Mothers' Memories: Padded Cover with Photo Frame Onlay, Inspirational Verse on Each Page. Broadman & Holman. 1998. 7.99 (*0-8054-0358-2*) Broadman.

***Mother's Memories to Her Child.** Thomas Kinkade. 96p. 2000. 12.99 (*0-8499-7571-9*) Tommy Nelson.

Mothers' Miracles: Magical True Stories of Maternal Love & Courage. Jamie C. Miller et al. LC 98-43268. (Illus.). 192p. 1999. 16.00 (*0-688-16622-9*, Wm Morrow) Morrow Avon.

Mother's Mission: The Sue Molhan Story. Suzanne P. Molhan & Jack Kavanagh. (Illus.). 195p. 1996. 22.95 (*0-912083-86-7*) Diamond Communications.

Mother's, Mother's Day. Lorna Balian. (Illus.). 32p. (J). (ps-3). 1987. reprint ed. 12.95 (*0-687-37097-3*) Humbug Bks.

Mother's Nature: Timeless Wisdom for the Journey into Motherhood. Andrea Gosline et al. LC 98-54823. (Illus.). 320p. 1999. 17.95 (*1-57324-152-0*) Conari Press.

Mother's Nightmare - Incest: A Practical Legal Guide for Parents & Professionals. John E. Myers. LC 97-4759. 256p. 1997. 49.95 (*0-7619-1057-3*); pap. 22.95 (*0-7619-1058-1*) Sage.

Mother's Notebook: An Illustrated Journal. Illus. by Cheryl A. Benner. (Blank Notebook Ser.). 96p. (Orig.). 1990. pap. 5.95 (*0-934672-91-1*) Good Bks PA.

Mothers of a New World: Maternalist Politics & the Origins of Welfare States. Ed. by Seth Koven & Sonya Michel. 416p. (C). 1993. pap. 19.99 (*0-415-90314-9*, A4800) Routledge.

Mothers of All Children: Women Reformers & the Rise of Juvenile Courts in Progressive Era America. Elizabeth J. Clapp. LC 97-49129. 256p. 1998. 55.00 (*0-271-01777-5*); pap. 18.95 (*0-271-01778-3*) Pa St U Pr.

Mothers of Feminism: The Story of Quaker Women in America. 2nd ed. Margaret H. Bacon. (Illus.). 273p. 1995. reprint ed. pap. 12.95 (*0-9620912-9-4*) Friends Genl Conf.

Mothers of Incest Survivors: Another Side of the Story. Janis T. Johnson. LC 91-46253. 176p. 1992. 21.95 (*0-253-33096-3*); pap. 10.95 (*0-253-20737-1*, MB-737) Ind U Pr.

Mothers of Invention. Drew G. Faust. LC 97-6670. 1997. pap. 15.00 (*0-679-78104-8*) Vin Bks.

Mothers of Invention: Women, Italian Fascism, & Culture. Ed. by Robin Pickering-Iazzi. 280p. 1995. pap. 19.95 (*0-8166-2651-0*); text 49.95 (*0-8166-2650-2*) U of Minn Pr.

Mothers of Invention: Women of the Slaveholding South in the American Civil War. Drew G. Faust. LC 95-8896. (Fred W. Morrison Series in Southern Studies). (Illus.). 326p. (C). 1996. 37.50 (*0-8078-2255-8*) U of NC Pr.

Mothers of Jesus: From Matthew's Genealogy. Elaine N. Davis. LC 94-75436. 40p. (Orig.). 1994. pap. 12.95 (*1-884289-05-3*) Grandmother Erth.

Mothers of Plaza de Mayo: The Story of Renee Epelbaum, 1976-1985. Marjorie Agosin. Tr. by Janice Molloy from SPA. LC 89-63626. (Illus.). 125p. (C). 1990. 29.95 (*0-932415-51-2*); pap. 9.95 (*0-932415-52-0*) Red Sea Pr.

Mothers of Priests: True Stories of the "Other Marys" Behind the "Other Christs" Robert Quardt. Ed. by Angelus Press Editors. Tr. by Marc S. Fisher. LC 98-181102. (GER.). 57p. (Orig.). 1995. pap. 4.25 (*0-935952-56-X*) Angelus Pr.

Mothers of Psychoanalysis: Helene Deutsch, Karen Horney, Anna Freud, & Melanie Klein. Janet Sayers. 336p. 1993. pap. 12.95 (*0-393-30942-8*) Norton.

Mothers of Sons: Toward an Understanding of Responsibility. Linda R. Forcey. LC 86-30331. 176p. 1987. 49.95 (*0-275-92323-1*, C2323, Praeger Pubs); pap. 14.95 (*0-275-92658-3*, B2658, Praeger Pubs) Greenwood.

Mothers of Steel: The Women of Um Gargur, an Eritrean Refugee Settlement in the Sudan. Nancee O. Bright. 330p. 1997. 79.95 (*1-56902-063-9*) Red Sea Pr.

Mothers of Steel: The Women of Um Gargur, an Eritrean Refugee Settlement in the Sudan. Nancee O. Bright. (Illus.). 330p. 1997. pap. 21.95 (*1-56902-064-7*) Red Sea Pr.

Mothers of the Bible: A Worship Service for Mother's Day or Other Special Occasions. Lynda Pujado. 52p. (Orig.). 1995. pap. 6.95 (*0-7880-0370-4*) CSS OH.

Mothers of the Disappeared. Jo Fisher. LC 89-11583. 168p. (Orig.). (C). 1989. 35.00 (*0-89608-371-3*); pap. 13.00 (*0-89608-370-5*) South End Pr.

***Mothers of the Nation: Women's Political Writing in England, 1780-1830.** Anne Mellor. LC 99-47328. (Illus.). 208p. 2000. 39.95 (*0-253-33713-5*) Ind U Pr.

Mothers of the NBA Cookbook. Mothers of NBA. 1998. pap. write for info. (*0-375-75098-3*) Villard Books.

Mothers of the Novel. Dale Spender. 1987. pap. 8.95 (*0-86358-251-6*, Pub. by Pandora) Harper SF.

Mothers of the Revolution: The War Experiences of Thirty Zimbabwean Women. Compiled by Irene Staunton. LC 91-9980. (Illus.). 320p. 1991. 36.95 (*0-253-35450-1*) Ind U Pr.

Mothers of the South: Portraiture of the White Tenant Farm Woman. Margaret J. Hagood. LC 70-169384. (Family in America Ser.). 264p. 1972. reprint ed. 20.95 (*0-405-03862-3*) Ayer.

Mothers of the South: Portraiture of the White Tenant Farm Woman. Margaret J. Hagood. LC 74-90521. 252p. 1969. reprint ed. lib. bdg. 59.50 (*0-8371-2141-8*, HAMS, Greenwood Pr) Greenwood.

Mothers of the South: Portraiture of the White Tenant Farm Woman. Margaret J. Hagood. LC 96-24324. (Illus.). 262p. 1996. reprint ed. pap. text 16.50 (*0-8139-1696-8*) U Pr of Va.

Mothers of Thyme: Customs & Rituals of Infertility & Miscarriage. Janet L. Sha. LC 89-92778. (Illus.). 144p. (Orig.). 1990. pap. 9.95 (*0-9625957-5-6*) Lida Rose Press.

Mothers on the Job: Maternity Policy in the U. S. Workplace. Lise Vogel. LC 92-21874. 200p. (C). 1993. pap. 16.00 (*0-8135-1919-5*) Rutgers U Pr.

Mothers on Welfare. Gail B. Stewart. LC 97-43223. (Other America Ser.). (Illus.). 112p. (YA). (gr. 8 up). 1997. lib. bdg. 22.45 (*1-56006-576-1*) Lucent Bks.

Mother's One Hundred & One Workshop Projects. Mother Earth News Editors. (Illus.). 208p. 1984. pap. 14.95 (*0-938432-06-0*) Mother Earth.

Mother's Picture Alphabet. Ed. by Peter Stockham. (Illus.). 54p. (J). (ps-3). 1974. reprint ed. pap. 4.95 (*0-486-23089-9*) Dover.

Mother's Place: Taking the Debate about Working Mothers Beyond Guilt & Blame. Susan Chira. LC 97-44916. 336p. 1998. 25.00 (*0-06-017327-0*) HarpC.

Mother's Place: Taking the Debate about Working Mothers Beyond Guilt & Blame. Susan Chira. LC 97-44916. 336p. 1999. pap. 13.00 (*0-06-093024-1*) HarpC.

Mothers' Plays Vol. 13: Complete Plays 13: The Chronicle of Soledad. . .; Ira Evans. Manuel P. Garcia. 82p. 1998. 4.95 (*1-885901-63-1*, Liberts) Presbyters Peartree.

Mother's Prayer. Jean D. Crowther. 14p. 1978. pap. 1.98 (*0-88290-099-4*) Horizon Utah.

Mother's Prayer. unabridged ed. (Children's Heritage Ser.). (Illus.). 32p. (J). (gr. 4-6). 1996. pap. 3.75 (*1-58339-111-8*, D11) Triangle Press.

Mother's Quotation Book: A Literary Companion. Elspeth McIntosh. (Illus.). 1997. 12.95 (*0-7090-5427-0*) Parkwest Pubns.

Mother's Recipes Seasoned with Memories. Edith Robinson-Mitzel. (Seasoned with Memories Ser.: Vol. 1). (Illus.). 120p. 1991. 12.50 (*0-9628852-0-7*) Twinberry.

Mother's Recompense. Edith Wharton. 342p. 1986. pap. 12.00 (*0-684-18737-X*, Scribners Ref) Mac Lib Ref.

Mother's Recompense. Edith Wharton. LC 96-24304. 288p. 1996. per. 12.00 (*0-684-82531-7*) S&S Trade.

Mother's Recompense. Edith Wharton. (Collected Works of Edith Wharton). 341p. 1998. reprint ed. lib. bdg. 98.00 (*1-58201-988-6*) Classic Bks.

Mother's Secret. Carolyn Haddad. 512p. 1988. 19.95 (*0-15-162666-9*) Harcourt.

***Mother's Secrets.** Joanna Wayne. (Intrigue Ser.). 2000. mass mkt. 4.25 (*0-373-22577-6*, 1-22577-0) Harlequin Bks.

Mother's Shoah. Susan Kaszas. Ed. by Steven Kingsley. (Illus.). 1998. 45.00 (*1-893798-00-3*) Ail New.

Mother's Shoah. Susan Kaszas. Ed. & Tr. by Steven Kingsley. (HUN., Illus.). 1998. 12.50 (*1-893798-02-X*, NMP BK/SW/CD-1); cd-rom 15.00 (*1-893798-01-1*) Ail New.

Mothers, Shoes & Other Mortal Songs. Mario Susko. LC 95-61663. 120p. (Orig.). 1995. pap. 11.95 (*0-938999-07-9*) Yuganta Pr.

Mothers, Sisters, Resisters: Oral Histories of Women Who Survived the Holocaust. Ed. by Brana Gurewitsch. LC 98-19753. (Judaic Studies). 432p. 1998. pap. 22.95 (*0-8173-0952-7*); text 49.95 (*0-8173-0931-4*) U of Ala Pr.

Mother's Son: Another Look at the Abortion Issue. Gerald N. Wright. 54p. (Orig.). 1993. pap. 2.95 (*1-56794-044-7*, C-2324) Star Bible.

Mother's Songs: Images of God the Mother. Meinrad Craighead. LC 85-50408. 96p. (Orig.). 1985. pap. 17.95 (*0-8091-2716-4*) Paulist Pr.

Mother's Songs, Games & Stores: Froebel's Mutter-und Rose-Lieder Rendered in English. Friedrich Froebel. LC 75-35068. (Studies in Play & Games). (Illus.). 1976. reprint ed. 30.95 (*0-405-07919-2*) Ayer.

Mothers, Sons & Lovers: How a Man's Relationship with His Mother Affects the Rest of His Life. Michael Gurian. LC 93-23926. 232p. (Orig.). 1993. pap. 18.00 (*0-87773-945-5*, Pub. by Shambhala Pubns) Random.

Mothers, Sons & Wives: Understanding a Mother's Impact on Her Son & How It Affects His Marriage. 2nd rev. ed. Norman Wright. LC 93-44832. 240p. 1996. pap. 11.99 (*0-8307-1806-0*, 5422652, Regal Bks) Gospel Lght.

Mother's Sorrow. Kathy Brewer. 130p. 1999. pap. write for info. (*0-7392-0107-7*, PO3002) Morris Pub.

***"Mother's Sorrow"** Kathy Brewer. 1999. pap. text. write for info. (*0-9676288-0-6*) T Wideman.

***Mother's Spirit: The First 100 Days.** Frank Kuhnert. LC 99-73022. 82p. 1999. pap. 9.95 (*1-890622-86-9*) Leathers Pub.

Mother's Story. Gloria Vanderbilt. LC 96-29870. (Illus.). 160p. 1997. pap. 10.95 (*0-452-27822-8*, Plume) Dutton Plume.

Mother's Story. Mary Beth Whitehead & Loretta Schwartz-Nobel. 1990. pap. 4.95 (*0-685-30875-8*) St Martin.

Mother's Story. large type ed. Gloria Vanderbilt. LC 96-30427. 170p. 1996. lib. bdg. 23.95 (*0-7838-1886-6*, G K Hall Lrg Type) Mac Lib Ref.

***Mother's Story: My Battle to Free David Milgaard.** Joyce Milgaard & Peter Edwards. 288p. 1999. 24.95 (*0-385-25807-0*) BDD Bks Young Read.

Mother's Survival Guide to Recovery: All about Alcohol, Drugs & Babies. Laurie Tanner. LC 96-67937. 160p. (Orig.). 1996. pap. 12.95 (*1-57224-049-0*) New Harbinger.

Mother's Table, Father's Chair: Cultural Narratives of Basque American Women. Jacqueline S. Thursby. LC 98-58072. (Illus.). 152p. 1999. 29.95 (*0-87421-265-0*); pap. 16.95 (*0-87421-264-2*) Utah St U Pr.

Mother's Tapestry: Stories, Verse, Music & a Bit of Everything Else for Those Who've Ever Felt Her Loving Touch. Ed. by Janet K. Hoffmann & Janelle B. Hyatt. LC 94-12045. (Illus.). 128p. (Orig.). 1997. pap. 7.95 (*0-9655157-2-9*) Three Pines Pub.

Mother's Taxi: Sport & the Incorporation of Women's Labor. Shona M. Thompson. LC 98-16743. (SUNY Series on Sport, Culture, & Social Relations). (Illus.). 317p. (C). 1999. text 73.50 (*0-7914-4059-1*); pap. text 24.95 (*0-7914-4060-5*) State U NY Pr.

Mother's Tears: Understanding the Mood Swings That Follow Childbirth. Arlene Huysman. LC 97-52079. 192p. 1998. 23.95 (*1-888363-70-3*) Seven Stories.

Mother's Things to Do Organizer: Balancing It All. abr. ed. Tamra W. Lewis. write for info. (*0-9633508-0-3*); audio 10.95 (*0-9633508-1-1*) TRB & Assocs.

Mothers to Daughters: Searching for New Connections. Ann F. Caron. 288p. 1999. pap. 13.00 (*0-8050-5150-3*) St Martin.

Mothers Together. Ruth Bell Graham & Gigi G. Tchividjian. LC 98-12089. (Illus.). 144p. 1998. 19.99 (*0-8010-1166-3*) Baker Bks.

Mother's Touch. 1973. write for info. (*0-88207-128-9*, Victor Bks) Chariot Victor.

Mother's Touch. Claudia L. Boyfen. (God's Little Wonders Ser.). 120p. 1998. spiral bd. 4.50 (*1-879127-81-4*) Lighten Up Enter.

***Mother's Touch: The Difference a Mom Makes.** Ed. by Elisa Morgan. (Illus.). 155p. 1999. pap. text 30.00 (*0-7881-6808-8*) DIANE Pub.

Mother's Tragedy & Other Poems. Aleister Crowley. 1993. reprint ed. pap. 37.50 (*1-872736-19-X*, Pub. by Mandrake Pr) Holmes Pub.

***Mother's Treasury.** Tyndale Publishers Staff. 2000. 15.99 (*0-8423-3703-2*) Tyndale Hse.

***Mother's Treasury: Expectations: Best Kept Secrets Every New Mother Should Know: The Little Baby Book.** Mcmeel Andrews. 2000. pap. 19.95 (*0-7407-1181-4*) Andrews & McMeel.

Mother's Victory. Robin M. Potts. LC 98-90732. 1999. pap. 8.95 (*0-533-12896-X*) Vantage.

Mother's Voice: Diverse Voices of Contemporary Mothers. Kathy Weingarten. LC 97-24756. 241p. 1997. pap. text 16.95 (*1-57230-259-3*, C0259) Guilford Pubns.

Mother's Voice: Strengthening Intimacy in Families. Kathy Weingarten. LC 93-41929. 1994. 22.95 (*0-15-162680-4*) Harcourt.

Mother's War. Fey Von Hassell. Ed. by David Forbes-Watt. 384p. (Orig.). 1995. 21.95 (*1-85695-076-X*, Pub. by ISIS Lrg Prnt) Transaction Pubs.

Mother's Way to the Cross. 32p. 1990. pap. text 1.95 (*0-89622-447-3*) Twenty-Third.

Mothers Who Drive Their Daughters Crazy: The 10 Types of "Impossible" Moms & How to Deal with Them. Susan Cohen & Ed Cohen. LC 97-19769. 240p. 1997. boxed set 20.00 (*0-7615-0985-2*) Prima Pub.

Mothers Who Leave: Behind the Myth of Women Without Their Children. Rosie Jackson. 340p. 1994. pap. text 14.00 (*0-04-440899-4*) NYU Pr.

Mothers Who Think: Tales of Real Life Parenthood. Ed. by Kate Moss & Camille Peri. LC 98-48168. 282p. 1999. 22.95 (*0-375-50269-6*) Villard Books.

***Mothers Who Think: Tales of Real Life Parenthood.** Ed. by Camille Peri & Kate Moses. 304p. 2000. reprint ed. pap. 12.95 (*0-671-77468-9*, WSP) PB.

Mother's Will. A. Wilson. Date not set. write for info. (*0-393-03560-3*) Norton.

Mother's Wisdom. R. D. Ramsey. 288p. 1995. 12.00 (*0-8092-3433-5*, 343350, Contemporary Bks) NTC Contemp Pub Co.

Mother's World: Journeys of the Heart. Ed. by Pamela Michael & Marybeth Bond. 233p. 1998. pap. 14.95 (*1-885211-26-0*, 26-0) Trvlers Tale.

Mothers, Your Best Is Good Enough. Lucile Johnson. 1996. pap. 2.95 (*1-55503-554-X*, 01111590) Covenant Comms.

MotherSong. J. Michael Ross. 32p. 1995. 19.95 (*0-9643748-0-3*) Side Door.

MotherSongs: Poems for, by & about Mothers. Ed. by Sandra M. Gilbert et al. LC 94-42757. (Illus.). 26p. 1995. 22.50 (*0-393-03771-1*) Norton.

MotherSongs: Poems for, by & about Mothers. Sandra M. Gilbert & Susan Gubar. 1996. 25.00 (*0-393-04039-9*) Norton.

***Mothertalk: Life Stories of Mary Kiyoshi Kiyooka.** Roy Kiyooka. (Illus.). 192p. 1998. pap. 16.95 (*1-896300-24-3*) NeWest Pubs.

Motherteacher: The Feminization of American Education. Redding S. Sugg & Redding S. Sugg. LC 78-2675. 294p. reprint ed. pap. 91.20 (*0-7837-4363-7*, 204407300012) Bks Demand.

Motherwell & Orbiston: The First Owenite Attempts at Cooperative Communities, 1822-1825. LC 72-2534. (British Labour Struggles Before 1850 Ser.). 1974. 23.95 (*0-405-04427-5*) Ayer.

***Motherwell at the Columbus Museum.** Tom Butler & Les Reker. (Illus.). 16p. 2000. pap. write for info. (*1-882650-10-7*) Colmbs Mus GA.

Motherwise! 101 Tips for a New Mother. Alice Bolster. LC 97-73188. (Illus.). 120p. 1997. pap. 7.50 (*0-912500-23-9*) La Leche.

Motherwise! 101 Tips for a New Mother. Alice Bolster. Tr. by Cecilia Vallejo from ENG. LC 99-63633. (SPA., Illus.). 127p. 1999. pap. 7.50 (*0-912500-57-3*) La Leche.

MotherWit: A Guide to Healing & Psychic Development. rev. ed. Diane Mariechild. (Illus.). 192p. 1989. pap. 14.95 (*0-89594-358-1*) Crossing Pr.

Motherwriter: Poems. Judith W. Steinbergh. 104p. (Orig.). 1983. per. 9.95 (*0-931694-27-2*, 83-50726) Talking Stone Pr.

***Mothjer's Guide to Sex.** Anne Semans. 2000. write for info. (*0-8129-3273-0*, Times Bks) Random.

***Moths.** Helen Frost. LC 00-9677. (Insects Ser.). (Illus.). (J). 2001. write for info. (*0-7368-0852-3*, Pebble Bks) Capstone Pr.

Moths. Adele Richardson. LC 98-14619. (Bugs Ser.). (Illus.). 32p. (J). 1998. lib. bdg. 21.30 (*1-887068-36-8*) Smart Apple.

Moths. Lynn M. Stone. LC 93-15695. (Nighttime Animals Discovery Library). 24p. (J). (gr. k-4). 1993. lib. bdg. 10.95 (*0-86593-297-2*) Rourke Corp.

Moths. Lynn M. Stone. LC 93-15695. (Nighttime Animals Ser.). (J). (gr. 4 up). 1993. 9.50 (*0-685-66590-9*) Rourke Corp.

Moths & Butterflies. Dave Beaty. LC 92-29741. (Nature Books Ser.). (Illus.). 32p. (J). (gr. 2-6). 1994. lib. bdg. 22.79 (*1-56766-001-0*) Childs World.

Moths & Butterflies of Great Britain & Ireland, Vol. 1. Ed. by John Heath. (Illus.). 343p. (Orig.). 1976. text 39.95 (*0-632-00331-6*) Entomological Repr.

Moths & Mothers, Feathers & Fathers: A Story about a Tiny Owl Named Squib, Vol. 1. 2nd ed. Larry Shles. Ed. by Bradley L. Winch. LC 89-83467. (Creative Parenting & Adventures of Squib Ser.). (Illus.). 72p. (J). (gr. k-8). 1989. reprint ed. pap. 9.95 (*0-915190-57-5*, JP9057-5) Jalmar Pr.

Moths & Other Stories. 2nd ed. Helena M. Viramontes. LC 84-72308. 200p. (C). 1995. pap. 11.95 (*1-55885-138-0*) Arte Publico.

Moths, Butterflies, Insects, & Spiders: Science in Art, Song & Play. Rhonda Vansant & Barbara L. Dondiego. LC 94-45011. (Illus.). 1994. 12.95 (*0-07-017906-9*) McGraw-Hill Prof.

***Moths in the Machine: Power & Perils of Programming.** Daniel Kohanski. (Illus.). 256p. 2000. pap. 13.95 (*0-312-25406-7*) St Martin.

Moths Lepidoptera, Vol. 1. G. F. Hampson. vii, 527p. 25.00 (*0-88065-099-0*) Scholarly Pubns.

Moths Lepidoptera, Vol. 2. G. F. Hampson. iv, 609p. 30.00 (*0-88065-100-8*) Scholarly Pubns.

Moths Lepidoptera, Vol. 4. (Fauna of British India Ser.). xxviii, 594p. 1976. 30.00 (*0-88065-102-4*) Scholarly Pubns.

Moths Lepidoptera: Sphingidae, Vol. 5. R. D. Bell & F. B. Scott. (Fauna of British India Ser.). (Illus.). xviii, 537p. 1976. reprint ed. 40.00 (*0-88065-056-7*) Scholarly Pubns.

Moths Lepidoptera: Subfam. Focillinae, Deltoidinae, Vol. 3. G. F. Hampson. xxxiii, 546p. 1976. 25.00 (*0-88065-101-6*) Scholarly Pubns.

Moths of America North of Mexico: Fascicle 13.1A-Pyraloidea - Scopariinae, Nymphulinae. Eugene Munroe. Ed. by Dominick et al. LC 78-149292. (Illus.). 134p. (Orig.). (C). 1972. pap. text 22.00 (*0-900848-53-7*) Wedge Entomological.

Moths of America North of Mexico: Fascicle 13.1B-Pyraloidea, Pyralidae: Odontiinae, Glaphyriinae. Eugene Munroe. LC 78-149292. (Illus.). 250p. (Orig.). (C). 1972. pap. text 22.00 (*0-900848-54-5*) Wedge Entomological.

Moths of America North of Mexico: Fascicle 13.1C-Pyraloidea, Pyralidae: Evergestinae. Eugene Munroe. LC 78-149292. (Illus.). 304p. (Orig.). (C). 1974. pap. text 44.00 (*0-900848-63-4*) Wedge Entomological.

Moths of America North of Mexico: Fascicle 13.2A-Pyraloidea, Pyralidae: Pyraustinae, Pyraustini (Part) Eugene Munroe. LC 78-149292. (Illus.). viii, 78p. (C). 1976. pap. text 38.00 (*0-900848-79-0*) Wedge Entomological.

Moths of America North of Mexico: Fascicle 13.2B-Pyraloidea, Pyralidae: Pyraustinae, Pyraustini (Conclusion) Eugene Munroe. LC 78-149292. (Illus.). xviii, 150p. (C). 1976. pap. text 38.00 (*0-900848-96-0*) Wedge Entomological.

Moths of America North of Mexico: Fascicle 15.2 Pyraloidea, Pyralidae: Phycitinae: Acrobasis & Allies. H. H. Neunzig. Ed. by Ronald W. Hodges et al. LC 85-51913. (Illus.). xii, 113p. (Orig.). 1986. pap. text 45.00 (*0-933003-01-3*) Wedge Entomological.

Moths of America North of Mexico: Fascicle 15.3-Pyraloidea, Pyralidae Phycitinae (Part) H. H. Neunzig. Ed. by Ronald W. Hodges et al. LC 90-70020. (Illus.). 165p. (C). 1990. pap. text 55.00 (*0-933003-05-6*) Wedge Entomological.

An Asterisk (*) at the beginning of an entry indicates that the title is appearing for the first time.

Moths of America North of Mexico: Fascicle 18.1 Geometroidea, Geometridae (part) Douglas C. Ferguson. Ed. by Ronald W. Hodges et al. LC 84-52866. (Illus.). xxii, 131p. (Orig.). 1986. pap. text 55.00 (*0-933003-00-5*) Wedge Entomological.

Moths of America North of Mexico: Fascicle 20.1-Mimallonoidea, Mimallonidae Bombycoidea: Apatelodidae, Bombycidae, Lasiocampidae. John G. Franclemont. Ed. by R. B. Dominick et al. LC 78-149292. (Illus.). vii, 86p. (C). 1973. pap. text 33.00 (*0-900848-52-9*) Wedge Entomological.

Moths of America North of Mexico: Fascicle 20.2A-Bombycoidea, Saturniidae: Citheroniinae, Hemileucinae (Part) Douglas C. Ferguson. Ed. by R. B. Dominick et al. LC 78-149292. (Illus.). x, 153p. (C). 1971. pap. text 38.00 (*0-900848-50-2*) Wedge Entomological.

Moths of America North of Mexico: Fascicle 20.2B-Bombycoidea, Saturniidae: Hemileucinae (Concl.), Saturniinae. Douglas C. Ferguson. Ed. by R. B. Dominick et al. LC 78-149292. (Illus.). xxi, 275p. (C). 1972. pap. text 38.00 (*0-900848-51-0*) Wedge Entomological.

Moths of America North of Mexico: Fascicle 21-Sphingoidea, Sphingidae. Ronald W. Hodges. Ed. by Richard B. Dominick et al. Intro. by Charles R. Edwards. LC 78-149292. (Illus.). xii, 158p. (C). 1971. pap. text 50.00 (*0-900848-35-9*) Wedge Entomological.

Moths of America North of Mexico: Fascicle 22.2-Noctuoidea, Lymantriidae. Douglas C. Ferguson. Ed. by Richard B. Dominick et al. LC 78-149292. (Illus.). x, 110p. (C). 1978. pap. text 48.00 (*0-900848-65-0*) Wedge Entomological.

Moths of America North of Mexico: Fascicle 27.2-Noctuoidea, Noctuidae: Noctuinae (Part-Euxoa) J. Donald Lafontaine. Ed. by R. W. Hodges et al. LC 87-50657. (Illus.). 235p. (C). 1987. pap. text 75.00 (*0-933003-03-X*) Wedge Entomological.

Moths of America North of Mexico: Fascicle 5.1-Sesioidea, Sesiidae. Thomas D. Eichlin & W. Donald Duckworth. Ed. by Ronald W. Hodges. LC 88-51015. (Illus.). 176p. (Orig.). (C). 1989. pap. text 65.00 (*0-933003-04-8*) Wedge Entomological.

Moths of America North of Mexico: Fascicle 6.1-Gelechioidea, Cosmopterigidae. Ronald W. Hodges. Ed. by Richard B. Dominick et al. LC 78-149292. (Illus.). x, 166p. (Orig.). (C). 1978. pap. text 48.00 (*0-900848-31-6*) Wedge Entomological.

Moths of America North of Mexico: Fascicle 6.2-Gelechioidea, Oecophoridae. Ronald W. Hodges. Ed. by R. B. Dominick et al. LC 78-149292. (Illus.). x, 142p. (Orig.). (C). 1974. pap. text 59.00 (*0-900848-64-2*) Wedge Entomological.

Moths of America North of Mexico: Fascicle 7.1-Gelechioidea, Gelechiidae. Ronald W. Hodges. LC 86-62334. (Illus.). xii, 195p. (Orig.). 1986. pap. 70.00 (*0-933003-02-1*) Wedge Entomological.

***Moths of America North of Mexico: Gelechioidea, Gelechiidae, Gelechiinae (Part Chionodes)** Ronald W. Hodges. (Illus.). 339p. 1999. pap. 115.00 (*0-933003-10-2*) Wedge Entomological.

Moths of America North of Mexico: Noctuoidea - Noctuidae. J. Donald Lafontaine. (Illus.). 349p. 1998. pap. 115.00 (*0-933003-09-9*) Wedge Entomological.

Moths of America North of Mexico: Noctuoidea, Noctuidae (Part), Cucullii. Robert W. Poole. Ed. by Ronald W. Hodges. LC 94-61667. (Illus.). 249p. (Orig.). 1995. pap. text 70.00 (*0-933003-07-2*) Wedge Entomological.

Moths of America North of Mexico: Pyralidae, Odontiinae & Glaphryiinae, Fasc. 13. 1b. Ronald W. Hodges. (Illus.). 1984. 125.00 (*0-7855-0661-6*) St Mut.

Moths of America North of Mexico: Pyraloidea, Pyralidae, Phycitinae (Part) H. H. Neunzig. Ed. by Ronald W. Hodges. LC 74-169990. (Illus.). 157p. (Orig.). 1997. pap. text 60.00 (*0-933003-08-0*) Wedge Entomological.

Moths of America North of Mexico: Saturniidae, Pt. 1. Ronald W. Hodges. 1984. 125.00 (*0-7855-0662-4*) St Mut.

Moths of America North of Mexico: Saturniidae, Pt. 2. Ronald W. Hodges. 1984. 135.00 (*0-7855-0663-2*) St Mut.

Moths of America North of Mexico: Sphigoidea, Fasc. 21. Ronald W. Hodges. 1984. 95.00 (*0-7855-0664-0*) St Mut.

Moths of America North of Mexico: Walshiidae & Cosmopterigidae, Fasc. 6. 1. Ronald W. Hodges. 1984. 95.00 (*0-7855-0665-9*) St Mut.

Moths of America North of Mexico, Fascicle 25.1: Noctuoidea, Noctuidae (Part), Plusiinae. J. Donald Lafontaine & Robert W. Poole. Ed. by R. W. Hodges et al. LC 91-65196. (Illus.). 182p. (C). 1991. pap. text 70.00 (*0-933003-06-4*) Wedge Entomological.

Moths of Australia. Bernard Abrera. 96p. 1984. 37.00 (*0-7855-0666-7*) St Mut.

Moths of Australia. I. F. Common. (Illus.). 535p. 1990. 236.00 (*90-04-09227-7*) Brill Academic Pubs.

Moths of Australia. Ian Common. 544p. 1990. reprint ed. 150.00 (*0-522-84326-3*, Pub. by Melbourne Univ Pr) Paul & Co Pubs.

Moths of Southern Africa. E. C. Pinhey. (Illus.). 347p. 1993. 140.00 (*90-6191-078-1*, Pub. by A A Balkema) Ashgate Pub Co.

Moths of the Limberlost. Gene S. Porter. 42.95 (*0-8488-0699-9*) Amereon Ltd.

Moths of the Limberlost. Gene Stratton Porter. 1986. reprint ed. lib. bdg. 25.95 (*0-89966-512-8*) Buccaneer Bks.

Moths of the Limberlost. Gene Stratton-Porter. 1980. reprint ed. lib. bdg. 25.95 (*0-89967-042-3*, Harmony Rain) Buccaneer Bks.

Moths Round the Flame. Geoffrey F. Hall. LC 72-93343. (Essay Index Reprint Ser.). 1977. 35.95 (*0-8369-1413-9*) Ayer.

Moths to the Flame: The Seductions of Computer Technology. Gregory J. Rawlins. LC 96-4729. (Illus.). x, 184p. 1996. 25.00 (*0-262-18176-2*, Bradford Bks) MIT Pr.

Moths to the Flame: The Seductions of Computer Technology. Gregory J. Rawlins. (Illus.). 194p. 1997. reprint ed. pap. text 12.50 (*0-262-68097-1*, Bradford Bks) MIT Pr.

***Motiba's Tattoos: A Grandaughter's Journey into Her Indian Family's Past.** Mira Kamdar. (Illus.). 2000. 24.00 (*1-891620-58-4*) PublicAffairs NY.

Motif & Meaning. Lisa Melas-Kyriazi. LC 87-71912. (Illus.). 30p. (Orig.). 1987. pap. 4.00 (*0-934358-18-4*) Fuller Mus Art.

***Motif Complete!** 2000. pap. 149.95 incl. cd-rom (*0-9670172-0-3*) Metro Link.

Motif Index for Lost Mines & Treasures Applied to Redaction of Arizona Legends, & to Lost Mine & Treasure Legends Exterior to Arizona. Byrd H. Granger. LC 77-27331. (FF Communications Ser.: No. 218). 277p. reprint ed. pap. 85.90 (*0-8357-8590-4*, 203496200091) Bks Demand.

Motif-Index of Folk-Literature: A Classification of Narrative Elements in Folk Tales, Ballads, Myths, Fables, Mediaeval Romances, Exempla, Fabliaux, Jest-Books, & Local Legends, 6 vols. Stith Thompson. Incl. Vol. I. LC 55-8055. 560p. 1958. 400.00 (*0-253-33881-6*); Vol. II. LC 55-8055. 520p. 1958. 65.00 (*0-253-33882-4*); Vol. III. LC 55-8055. 520p. 1958. 65.00 (*0-253-33883-2*); Vol. IV. LC 55-8055. 500p. 1958. 65.00 (*0-253-33884-0*); Vol. V. LC 55-8055. 568p. 1958. 65.00 (*0-253-33885-9*); Vol. VI. LC 55-8055. 896p. 1958. 75.00 (*0-253-33886-7*); LC 55-8055. 1958. 320.00 (*0-253-33887-5*) Ind U Pr.

***Motif-Index of Folk Narratives in the Pan. Hispanic Romancero.** Ed. by Harriet Goldberg. (Medieval & Renaissance Texts & Studies: Vol. 206). 2000. write for info. (*0-86698-248-5*, MR206) MRTS.

Motif-Index of Medieval Catalan Folktales. Ed. by Edward Neugaard. LC 92-16905. (Medieval & Renaissance Texts & Studies: Vol. 96). 160p. 1993. 22.00 (*0-86698-110-1*, MR96) MRTS.

Motif-Index of Medieval Spanish Folk Narratives. Harriet Goldberg. LC 97-31019. (Medieval & Renaissance Texts & Studies: Vol. 162). 320p. 1997. 32.00 (*0-86698-203-5*, MR162) MRTS.

Motif-Index of Polynesian, Melanesian & Micronesian Narratives. Bacil F. Kirtley. Ed. by Richard M. Dorson. LC 80-729. (Folklore of the World Ser.). 1981. lib. bdg. 70.95 (*0-405-13316-2*) Ayer.

Motif Index of the Child Corpus: The English & Scottish Popular Ballad. Natascha Wuerzbach & Simone M. Salz. LC 95-1137. Orig. Title: Motif-Index zum Child Corpus. xiv, 249p. (C). 1995. lib. bdg. 121.55 (*3-11-014290-2*) De Gruyter.

Motif-Index of the Cuentos of Juan Timoneda. J. Wesley Childers. Ed. by Richard M. Dorson. LC 80-791. (Folklore of the World Ser.). 1981. reprint ed. lib. bdg. 17.95 (*0-405-13330-8*) Ayer.

Motif-Index of the Italian Novella in Prose. D. P. Rotunda. LC 72-6778. (Studies in Italian Literature: No. 46). 1972. reprint ed. lib. bdg. 75.00 (*0-8383-1653-0*) M S G Haskell Hse.

Motif-Index zum Child Corpus see Motif Index of the Child Corpus: The English & Scottish Popular Ballad

Motif of Adultery in Elizabethan, Jacobean & Caroline Tragedy. Ilse Born-Lechleitner. LC 95-5397. (Salzburger Studien Ser.). 428p. 1995. text 109.95 (*0-7734-1284-0*) E Mellen.

Motif of the Journey in Nineteenth-Century Italian Literature. Ed. by Bruno Magliocchetti & Anthony Verna. LC 94-8388. 210p. 1994. 49.95 (*0-8130-1291-0*) U Press Fla.

Motif of Wonder in the Gospel of Mark. Timothy Dwyer. LC 96-147332. (JSNT Supplement Ser.: No. 128). 243p. 1996. 70.00 (*1-85075-603-1*, Pub. by Sheffield Acad) CUP Services.

Motif Programming: The Essentials . . . & More. Brian Marshall. (X & MOTIF Programming Ser.). (Illus.). 600p. 1992. pap. 39.95 (*1-55558-089-0*, EY-J816E-DP) DEC.

Motif Programming Tips & Tricks. Don Clayton. (C). 2001. pap., pap. text 39.95 incl. cd-rom (*0-13-588212-5*) P-H.

Motif Reference Manual, Vol. 6A. 2nd ed. Dan Heller et al. (Computer Science). 1016p. 1994. pap. 49.95 (*1-56592-016-3*) Thomson Learn.

Motif Reference Manual, Vol. 6B. 2nd ed. Antony Fountain. Ed. by Paula Ferguson. (Illus.). 1000p. 1999. pap. 44.95 (*1-56592-654-4*) OReilly & Assocs.

Motif Symbolism in the Disciples of Mallarme. John A. Frey. LC 73-94193. (Catholic University of America. Studies in Romance Languages & Literatures: No. 55). reprint ed. 37.50 (*0-404-50355-1*) AMS Pr.

Motif Tools: Streamlined GUI Design & Programming with the Xmt Library. David Flanagan. Ed. by Tim O'Reilly. (Illus.). 1024p. (Orig.). 1995. pap. 54.95 (*1-56592-044-9*) Thomson Learn.

Motif User's Guide. Osf Motif Series Staff. (C). 1990. pap. text 27.00 (*0-13-640509-6*) P-H.

Motifs. Mary Engelbreit. 1995. pap. 9.95 (*0-8362-0077-2*) Andrews & McMeel.

Motifs. Jansma. (C). 1996. 77.50 (*0-15-503421-9*) Harcourt.

Motifs. Kassen. (C). 1996. text 71.00 (*0-15-500593-6*) Harcourt Coll Pubs.

Motifs: Testing Program. Kassen. (C). 1997. pap. text, teacher ed. 33.50 (*0-03-049023-5*, Pub. by Harcourt Coll Pubs) Harcourt.

Motifs from Genesis 1-11 in the Genuine Hymns of Ephrem the Syrian. Tryggve Kronholm. (Coniectanea Biblica. Old Testament Ser.: No. 11). (Orig.). 1978. pap. 46.50 (*91-40-04639-7*) Coronet Bks.

Motifs of Franciscan Mission Theory in Sixteenth Century New Spain. Edwin E. Sylvest, Jr. (Monograph Ser.). 1975. 30.00 (*0-88382-061-7*) AAFH.

Motigraphics: Measuring Human Motivation. Richard C. Maddock. LC 99-27546. 320p. 2000. 69.50 (*1-56720-284-5*, Quorum Bks) Greenwood.

Motilal Nehru: The Man & His Ideology. S. R. Bakshi. 1990. 42.00 (*81-7041-257-9*, Pub. by Anmol) S Asia.

Motile Muscle & Cell Models. Nikola'i I. Arronet. LC 72-88884. (Studies in Soviet Science). 202p. reprint ed. pap. 62.70 (*0-608-13734-0*, 202068500018) Bks Demand.

Motilin Receptor: Localization & Modulation by Inflammation. Gert Van Assche. (Acta Biomedica Lovaniensia Ser.). (Illus.). 157p. 1998. pap. 45.00 (*90-6186-877-7*, Pub. by Leuven Univ) Coronet Bks.

Motility & Taxis in Prokaryotes. A. N. Glagolev. (Physicochemical Biology Reviews Supplement Ser.: Soviet Scientific Reviews, Sect. B, Vol. 4). x, 280p. 1984. text 473.00 (*3-7186-0160-5*) Gordon & Breach.

Motility Disorders of the Gastrointestinal Tract: Principles & Practice. Ed. by Sinn Anuras. LC 92-14367. (Illus.). 479p. 1992. reprint ed. pap. 148.50 (*0-608-07229-X*, 206745400009) Bks Demand.

Motility of the Digestive Tract. International Symposium on Gastrointestinal Motili. Ed. by Martin Wienbeck. LC 81-40741. 637p. 1982. reprint ed. pap. 197.50 (*0-608-00413-8*, 206112700007) Bks Demand.

Motility of Vertebrate Cells in Culture & in the Organism. G. Haemmerli & P. Strauli. (Experimental Biology & Medicine Ser.: Vol. 10). (Illus.). x, 266p. 1985. 121.00 (*3-8055-4135-X*) S Karger.

Motion. Ron Marson. (Task Cards Ser.: No. 21). (Illus.). 88p. 1990. teacher ed. 16.00 (*0-941008-98-3*) Tops Learning.

Motion. Philip Sauvain. LC 91-24480. (Way It Works Ser.). (Illus.). 48p. (YA). (gr. 6 up). 1992. lib. bdg. 22.00 (*0-02-781077-1*, Mac Bks Young Read) S&S Childrens.

Motion Aftereffect: A Modern Perspective. George Mather et al. LC 97-52191. (Illus.). 232p. 1998. 27.50 (*0-262-13343-1*, Bradford Bks) MIT Pr.

Motion Analysis & Image Sequence Processing. Ed. by Ibrahim Sezan & Reginald L. Lagendijk. LC 92-46330. (International Series in Engineering & Computer Science, VLSI, Computer Architecture, & Digital Screen Processing). 512p. (C). 1993. text 164.50 (*0-7923-9329-5*) Kluwer Academic.

Motion Analysis for Image Sequence Coding. G. Tziritas & C. Labit. LC 94-27697. 392p. 1994. 178.50 (*0-444-89297-4*) Elsevier.

Motion Analysis of Living Cells. Ed. by David Soll & Deborah Wessels. LC 97-41848. (Techniques in Modern Biomedical Microscopy Ser.). 312p. 1997. 185.00 (*0-471-15915-8*, Wiley-Liss) Wiley.

Motion & Design Student Activity Book. National Science Resources Center Staff. (Science & Technology for Children Ser.). (Illus.). 69p. (J). (gr. 4). 1997. pap. text, student ed. write for info. (*0-89278-677-9*, 97-3003) Carolina Biological.

Motion & Design Teacher's Guide. National Science Resources Center Staff. (Science & Technology for Children Ser.). (Illus.). 205p. 1997. pap. text, teacher ed. write for info. (*0-89278-676-0*, 97-3002) Carolina Biological.

Motion & Motion's God: Thematic Variations in Aristotle, Cicero, Newton, & Hegel. Michael J. Buckley. LC 73-132234. 295p. reprint ed. pap. 91.50 (*0-8357-3307-6*, 203953000013) Bks Demand.

Motion & Relativity. Leopold Infeld & J. Plebanski. LC 60-14864. (Polish Academy of Sciences Physical Monographs). 1960. 104.00 (*0-08-009436-8*, Pub. by Pergamon Repr) Franklin.

Motion & Space Sickness. Ed. by George H. Crampton. 496p. 1990. lib. bdg. 219.00 (*0-8493-4703-3*, RC103) CRC Pr.

Motion & Speed. John Marshall. LC 95-17283. (Read All about Energy & Action Ser.). 24p. (J). (gr. 1-4). 1995. lib. bdg. 18.60 (*1-55916-154-X*) Rourke Bk Co.

Motion & Structure from Image Sequences. Juyang Weng et al. LC 92-28268. (Information Sciences Ser.: Vol. 29). 1992. 75.95 (*0-387-55672-9*) Spr-Verlag.

Motion & Time Study. 9th ed. Benjamin W. Niebel. LC 92-15051. 880p. (C). 1992. text 74.95 (*0-256-09248-6*, Irwn McGrw-H) McGrw-H Hghr Educ.

Motion & Time Study. 10th ed. Benjamin Niebel. 727p. 1998. 97.25 (*0-256-19507-2*) McGraw.

Motion & Time Study: Design & Measurement of Work. 7th ed. Ralph M. Barnes. LC 80-173. 704p. 1980. text 103.95 (*0-471-05905-6*) Wiley.

Motion & Time Study: Improving Productivity. 7th ed. Marvin E. Mundel & David L. Danner. LC 93-23108. (C). 1994. text 68.20 (*0-13-588369-5*) Prntice Hall Bks.

Motion & Time Study: Improving Work Methods & Management. 2nd ed. Fred E. Meyers. LC 97-52133. 334p. (C). 1998. 77.00 (*0-13-897455-1*) P-H.

Motion-Based Recognition. Mubarak Shah & Ramesh Jain. LC 97-20565. (Computational Imaging & Vision Ser.). 1997. text 197.50 (*0-7923-4618-1*) Kluwer Academic.

Motion by Mean Curvature & Related Topics: Proceedings of the International Conference Held at Trento, July 20-24, 1992. Ed. by Giuseppe Buttazzo & Augusto Visintin. LC 94-680. viii, 219p. (C). 1994. lib. bdg. 104.95 (*3-11-013881-6*) De Gruyter.

Motion Capture. Moon Jung. 350p. (C). 2000. 59.00 (*1-56881-086-5*) AK Peters.

Motion Characteristics of Silent Chains. H. A. McAninch. (Technical Papers: Vol. P215). (Illus.). 11p. 1940. pap. text 30.00 (*1-55589-453-4*) AGMA.

Motion Control. D. Georges & O. Sename. LC 99-36744. (International Proceedings Volumes Ser.). 400p. 1999. pap. 93.50 (*0-08-043044-9*, Pergamon Pr) Elsevier.

Motion Control for Intelligent Automation: Preprints of the IFAC Workshop, Perugia, Italy, 27-29 October 1992. Ed. by A. De Carli & E. Masada. LC 92-41311. (IFAC Pre-Print Ser.). 434p. 1993. pap. 118.50 (*0-08-042058-3*, Pergamon Pr) Elsevier.

Motion Control of a Water Stage: A Design Approach for Speeding up IC Production. Dick De Roover. (Illus.). 290p. 1997. pap. 59.50 (*90-407-1562-9*, Pub. by Delft U Pr) Coronet Bks.

***Motion Devices & Transformers.** Hi-Dong Chai. LC 97-44407. 384p. 1998. 83.00 (*0-13-263419-8*) P-H.

Motion Estimation Algorithms for Video Compression. Borko Furht et al. LC 96-41138. (Kluwer International Series in Engineering & Computer Science). 176p. (C). 1996. text 106.00 (*0-7923-9793-2*) Kluwer Academic.

Motion, Evolution of Orbits & Origins of Comets: Proceedings of the I. A. U. Symposium, No. 45, Leningrad, U. S. S. R., Aug. 4-11, 1970. International Astronomical Union Staff. Ed. by V. P. Chebotarev. LC 73-179895. (I.A.U. Symposia Ser.). 521p. 1972. lib. bdg. 165.00 (*90-277-0207-1*) Kluwer Academic.

Motion, Forces & Energy. 2nd ed. PH Inc. Staff. 1994. text, student ed. 10.97 (*0-13-402041-3*) P-H.

Motion Game Offenses for Men's & Women's Basketball. Harry L. Harkins & Jerry Krause. LC 97-67162. 1997. pap. 16.95 (*1-57167-136-6*) Coaches Choice.

***Motion Graphics: Graphic Design for Broadcast & Film.** Steven Curran. 2000. 45.00 (*1-56496-646-1*) Rockport Pubs.

Motion in Molecules: Calculation of Crystal Packing & Non-Bonded Forces. American Crystallographic Association Staff. (American Crystallographic Association Program & Abstracts Ser. 2: Vol.12, No. 1). 58p. 1984. pap. 10.00 (*0-317-05920-3*) Polycrystal Bk Serv.

Motion Is a Fall. Rick London. 1985. pap. 5.00 (*0-917588-11-8*) Trike.

Motion Lamps: Identification & Values. Sam Samuelian. (Collector's Guide to Ser.). 1998. pap. text 19.95 (*1-57432-055-6*, 5052) Collector Bks.

Motion Moves Machines. Thomas-Cochran. (What a Wonderful World 2 Ser.). 1992. pap. text. write for info. (*0-582-90970-8*, Drumbeat) Longman.

Motion of Allochthonous Terranes Across the North Pacific Basin. Michel G. Debiche et al. LC 86-33721. (Geological Society of America Ser.: Vol. 207). (Illus.). 56p. 1987. reprint ed. pap. 30.00 (*0-608-07735-6*, 206782300010) Bks Demand.

Motion of Light in Water: Sex & Science Fiction Writing in the East Village, 1960-1965. Samuel R. Delany. 1993. reprint ed. pap. 12.95 (*1-56333-133-0*, R Kasak Bks) Masquerade.

Motion of the Cypher. Ray DiPalma. 99p. (Orig.). 1995. pap. 10.95 (*0-937804-61-4*) Segue NYC.

Motion of the Moon. Alan Cook. (Illus.). 236p. 1988. 137.00 (*0-85274-348-3*) IOP Pub.

Motion of Water & Other Fluids: Being a Treatise of Hydrostaticks. Edme Mariotte. Ed. by Claude C. Albritton. Tr. by J. T. Desaguliers. (History of Geology Ser.). (Illus.). 1978. reprint ed. lib. bdg. 30.95 (*0-405-10449-9*) Ayer.

Motion Palpation & Chiropractic Technic: Principles Dynamic Chiropractic. R. C. Schafer & Leonard J. Faye. LC 88-93050. (Illus.). 500p. (C). 1989. text 59.00 (*0-924889-00-4*) Motion Palpat Inst.

Motion Picture & Video Lighting. rev. ed. Blain Brown. (Illus.). 226p. 1995. pap. 37.95 (*0-240-80249-7*, Focal) Buttrwrth-Heinemann.

Motion Picture Biographies: The Hollywood Spin on Historical Figures. John W. Cones. (Hollywood Ser.). 283p. 1996. pap. 23.95 (*1-890341-04-5*) Rivas Canyon.

Motion Picture Camera & Lighting Equipment. 2nd ed. David W. Samuelson. LC 86-14300. (Media Manuals Ser.). 240p. 1987. pap. 29.95 (*0-240-51261-8*, Focal) Buttrwrth-Heinemann.

***Motion Picture Camera Data.** 2nd ed. W. Bolton. 352p. 2001. pap. 49.95 (*0-240-51598-6*, Focal) Buttrwrth-Heinemann.

Motion Picture Camera Techniques. 2nd ed. David W. Samuelson. LC 84-6151. (Media Manuals Ser.). 200p. 1984. pap. 29.95 (*0-240-51247-2*, Focal) Buttrwrth-Heinemann.

Motion-Picture Cameraman. Edwin G. Lutz. LC 76-169332. (Literature of Cinema, Ser. 2). (Illus.). 264p. 1978. reprint ed. 18.95 (*0-405-03899-2*) Ayer.

Motion Picture Commission. U. S. House of Representatives Committee on Educat & U. S. House of Representatives Committee on Bankin. Ed. by Garth S. Jowett. LC 77-11386. (Aspects of Film Ser.). 1978. reprint ed. lib. bdg. 24.95 (*0-405-11136-3*) Ayer.

Motion Picture Exhibition in Washington, D. C. An Ilustrated History of Parlors, Palaces & Multiplexes in the Metropolitan Area, 1894-1997. Robert K. Headley. LC 98-31204. (Illus.). 408p. 1999. lib. bdg. 55.00 (*0-7864-0544-9*) McFarland & Co.

Motion Picture Film Editor. Rene L. Ash. LC 74-4072. 193p. 1974. 29.00 (*0-8108-0718-1*) Scarecrow.

Motion Picture Goes to War: The U. S. Government Film Effort During World War I. Larry W. Ward. Ed. by Diane Kirkpatrick. LC 85-14034. (Studies in Cinema: No. 37). 192p. 1985. reprint ed. pap. 59.60 (*0-8357-1683-X*, 207047600095) Bks Demand.

Motion Picture Guide, 12 vols., Set. Jay R. Nash & Stanley R. Ross. LC 85-71145. (Complete Film Resource Center Ser.). 1987. 600.00 (*0-933997-00-0*) CineBooks.

Motion Picture Guide: Annual 1990. The Films of 1989. Ed. by Jay R. Nash et al. 700p. 1990. write for info. (*3-598-10934-2*) K G Saur Verlag.

M

Motion Picture Guide: Annual 1991 - The Films of 1990. Ed. by Jay R. Nash et al. 720p. 1991. write for info. (*3-598-11067-7*) K G Saur Verlag.

Motion Picture Guide: Annual 1993 - The Films of 1992. Ed. by Jay R. Nash et al. ix, 635p. 1993. write for info. (*3-598-11168-1*) K G Saur Verlag.

Motion Picture Guide: Annual 1995 - The Films of 1994. Ed. by Jay R. Nash et al. 650p. 1995. write for info. (*3-598-11268-8*) K G Saur Verlag.

Motion Picture Guide: Annual 1996 - The Films of 1995. Ed. by Jay R. Nash et al. 600p. 1996. write for info. (*3-598-11330-7*) K G Saur Verlag.

Motion Picture Guide: Annual 1997 - The Films of 1996. Ed. by Jay R. Nash et al. 600p. 1997. write for info. (*3-598-11354-4*) K G Saur Verlag.

Motion Picture Guide Vol. 1: 1927-1984, Films A-B. 1997. 99.50 (*0-933997-01-9*) CineBks.

Motion Picture Guide Vol. 2: 1927-1984, Films C-D. 1997. 99.50 (*0-933997-02-7*) CineBks.

Motion Picture Guide Vol. 3: 1987-1984, Films E-G. 1997. 99.50 (*0-933997-03-5*) CineBks.

Motion Picture Guide Vol. 4: 1927-1984, Films H-K. 1997. 99.50 (*0-933997-04-3*) CineBks.

Motion Picture Guide Vol. 5: 1927-1984, Films L-M. 1997. 99.50 (*0-933997-05-1*) CineBks.

Motion Picture Guide Vol. 6: 1927-1984, Films N-R. 1997. 99.50 (*0-933997-06-X*) CineBks.

Motion Picture Guide Vol. 7: 1927-1984, Films S. 1997. 99.50 (*0-933997-07-8*) CineBks.

Motion Picture Guide Vol. 8: 1927-1984, Films T-V. 1997. 99.50 (*0-933997-08-6*) CineBks.

Motion Picture Guide Vol. 9: 1927-1984, Films W-Z. 1997. 99.50 (*0-933997-09-4*) CineBks.

Motion Picture Guide Vol. 10: Silent Films A-Z. 1997. 100.00 (*0-933997-10-8*) CineBks.

Motion Picture Guide Annual, 1999. Ed. by Jay R. Nash et al. 600p. 1999. 179.95 (*0-933997-43-4*, Pub. by CineBks) Whitehurst & Clark.

Motion Picture Guide Index, 2 vols. Jay R. Nash & Stanley R. Ross. LC 85-71145. 3170p. 1987. 100.00 (*0-933997-11-6*) CineBks.

Motion Picture Guide Index Vol. 11: A-J. 1997. 99.50 (*0-933997-12-4*) CineBks.

Motion Picture Guide Index Vol. 12: K-Z. 1997. 99.50 (*0-933997-13-2*) CineBks.

Motion Picture Guide 1988 Annual: The Films of 1987. Ed. by Jay R. Nash & Stanley R. Ross. (Illus.). 799p. 1997. 99.50 (*0-933997-16-7*) CineBks.

Motion Picture Guide 1989 Annual: The Films of 1988. Ed. by Jay R. Nash & Stanley R. Ross. (Films of 1988 Ser.). (Illus.). 665p. 1997. 99.50 (*0-933997-20-5*) CineBks.

Motion Picture Guide 1987 Annual: The Films of 1986. Ed. by Jay R. Nash & Stanley R. Ross. (Illus.). 726p. 1997. 99.50 (*0-933997-15-9*) CineBks.

Motion Picture Guide 1986 Annual: The Films of 1985. Ed. by Jay R. Nash & Stanley R. Ross. (Illus.). 450p. 1997. 99.50 (*0-933997-14-0*) CineBks.

Motion Picture Guide 1990 Annual: The Films of 1989. Ed. by Jay R. Nash & Stanley R. Ross. (Illus.). 480p. 1997. 99.50 (*0-933997-29-9*) CineBks.

Motion Picture Guide, 1998 Annual: The Films of 1997. CineBooks Staff. 1998. 179.95 (*0-933997-41-8*) CineBks.

Motion Picture Guide 1995 Annual: The Films of 1994. Ed. by James Pallot. 600p. 1997. 99.50 (*0-933997-35-3*) CineBks.

Motion Picture Guide, 1994 Annual: THe Films of 1993. Cine Books Staff. 600p. 1994. 99.50 (*0-933997-33-7*) CineBks.

Motion Picture Guide, 1991 Annual: The Films of 1990. Ed. by Cine Books Staff. 460p. 1991. 99.50 (*0-918432-92-8*) CineBks.

Motion Picture Guide, 1997 Annual: The Films of 1996. CineBooks Staff. 1997. 99.50 (*0-933997-39-6*) CineBks.

Motion Picture Guide 1996 Annual: The Films of 1995. Ed. by CineBooks Staff. 1997. 99.50 (*0-933997-37-X*) CineBks.

Motion Picture Guide, 1993 Annual: The Films of 1992. Ed. by James Pallot. 635p. 1993. 99.50 (*0-918432-95-2*) CineBks.

Motion Picture Guide 1992 Annual: The Films of 1991. Ed. by James Pallot. (Illus.). 593p. 1992. 99.50 (*0-918432-93-6*) CineBks.

Motion Picture Guide, Vol. 10 see Silents: Silent Feature Films, 1910-36

Motion Picture Guide 1998: The Films of 1997. annuals Ed. by Jay R. Nash et al. 600p. 1998. 180.00 (*3-598-11386-2*) K G Saur Verlag.

Motion Picture Guide 1999: The Films of 1998. annuals Ed. by Stanley R. Ross et al. 1998. 180.00 (*3-598-11415-X*) K G Saur Verlag.

***Motion Picture Image: From Film to Digital.** Steven Barclay. LC 99-45476. 224p. 1999. pap. 34.95 (*0-240-80390-6*, Focal) Buttrwrth-Heinemann.

Motion Picture in the Soviet Union, 1918-1952: A Sociological Analysis. John Rimberg. LC 72-559. (Dissertations on Film Ser.). 238p. 1974. reprint ed. 19.95 (*0-405-04102-0*) Ayer.

Motion Picture Industry. Ed. by Peter Allen. 200p. 1982. pap. 985.00 (*0-931634-24-5*) FIND-SVP.

Motion Picture Industry Reform. John W. Cones. (Hollywood Ser.). 208p. 1996. pap. 22.50 (*1-890341-09-6*) Rivas Canyon.

Motion Picture Mega-Industry. Barry R. Litman. LC 97-22703. 336p. 1998. pap. text 34.67 (*0-205-20026-5*) Allyn.

Motion Picture Moods for Pianists & Organists, a Rapid Reference Collection of Selected Pieces. Erno Rapee. LC 70-124035. (Literature of Cinema, Ser. 1). 1979. reprint ed. 48.95 (*0-405-01635-2*) Ayer.

Motion Picture Operator. Jack Rudman. (Career Examination Ser.: C-501). 1994. pap. 23.95 (*0-8373-0501-2*) Nat Learn.

Motion Picture Players' Credits: Worldwide Performers of 1967 Through 1980 with Filmographies of Their Entire Careers, 1905-1983. Jeffrey Oliviero. LC 89-13644. 1023p. 1991. lib. bdg. 145.00 (*0-89950-315-2*) McFarland & Co.

Motion Picture Prescription: Watch This Movie & Call Me in the Morning. Gary Solomon. LC 95-237. 256p. (Orig.). 1995. pap. 12.95 (*0-944031-27-7*) Aslan Pub.

Motion Picture Problems. William M. Seabury. Ed. by Garth S. Jowett. LC 77-11383. (Aspects of Film Ser.). 1978. reprint ed. lib. bdg. 27.95 (*0-405-11143-6*) Ayer.

Motion Picture Projection & Theatre Presentation Manual. Frwd. by Don V. Kloepfel. (Illus.). 166p. 1982. reprint ed. 20.00 (*0-940690-01-2*) Soc Motion Pic & TV Engrs.

Motion Picture Restoration: Digital Algorithms for Artifact Suppression in Degraded Motion Pictures. A. C. Kokaram. LC 98-4855. (Illus.). xvi, 336p. 1998. 99.00 (*3-540-76040-7*) Spr-Verlag.

Motion Picture Scripts: A Union List. 2nd ed. Ed. by Gregory Walsh & Lucia Schultz. 801p. 1998. pap. 70.00 (*0-942102-29-0*) Acad Motion Pic.

Motion Picture Serial: An Annotated Bibliography. Wayne Schutz. LC 91-41833. 397p. 1992. 49.50 (*0-8108-2484-1*) Scarecrow.

Motion Picture Stunt Pilots & Hollywood's Classic Aviation Movies. H. Hugh Wynne. LC 87-60073. (Illus.). 176p. 1987. pap. 9.95 (*0-933126-85-9*) Pictorial Hist.

Motion-Picture Work. David Hulfish. LC 71-124011. (Literature of Cinema, Ser. 1). 1978. reprint ed. 42.95 (*0-405-01617-4*) Ayer.

Motion Pictures. LaMond F. Beatty. Ed. by James E. Duane. LC 80-21340. (Instructional Media Library: Vol. 8). (Illus.). 112p. 1981. 27.95 (*0-87778-168-0*) Educ Tech Pubns.

Motion Pictures: A Study in Social Legislation. Donald R. Young. LC 79-160248. (Moving Pictures Ser.). vi, 109p. 1971. reprint ed. lib. bdg. 18.95 (*0-89198-049-0*) Ozer.

Motion Pictures Bk. I: 1973 & 1974 Supplement: Forms. Joseph Taubman. LC 74-189328. 60.00 (*0-685-08141-9*) Law Arts.

Motion Pictures & Film Strips, Pt. 2, Subject Index see National Union Catalog: A Cumulative Author List, 1958-62

Motion Pictures & Film Strips, Pt. 2, Titles see National Union Catalog: A Cumulative Author List, 1958-62

Motion Pictures & Standards of Morality. Charles C. Peters. LC 72-124030. (Literature of Cinema Ser.). 1970. reprint ed. 15.95 (*0-405-01648-4*) Ayer.

Motion Pictures & the Social Attitudes of Children. Ruth C. Peterson & Louis L. Thurstone. LC 76-124031. (Literature of Cinema: Payne Fund Studies of Motion Pictures & Social Values). 1970. reprint ed. 15.95 (*0-405-01630-1*) Ayer.

Motion Pictures & Youth: A Summary. W. W. Charters. LC 73-124025. (Literature of Cinema Ser.: Payne Fund Studies of Motion Pictures & Social Values). reprint ed. 11.95 (*0-405-01642-5*) Ayer.

Motion Pictures from the Library of Congress Paper Print Collection 1894-1912. Kemp Niver. 424p. 1997. 200.00 (*0-913616-34-6*) Hollywd Film Arch.

Motion Pictures in Education: A Summary of the Literature. Edgar Dale et al. LC 71-124003. (Literature of Cinema, Ser. 1). 1970. reprint ed. 31.95 (*0-405-01609-3*) Ayer.

Motion Planning in Dynamic Environments. K. Fujimura. Ed. by Toshiyasu L. Kunii. (Computer Science Workbench Ser.). (Illus.). xiii, 178p. 1992. 96.95 (*0-387-70083-8*) Spr-Verlag.

Motion Practice. David E. Herr et al. 688p. 1985. 85.00 (*0-685-27094-7*, Aspen Law & Bus) Aspen Pub.

Motion Practice. David E. Herr et al. 688p. 1988. suppl. ed. 22.50 (*0-685-27096-3*, Aspen Law & Bus) Aspen Pub.

Motion Practice. David E. Herr et al. 688p. 1989. suppl. ed. 35.00 (*0-685-27095-5*, Aspen Law & Bus) Aspen Pub.

Motion Practice. 2nd ed. H. Herr. 1990. 155.00 (*0-316-35174-1*) Aspen Pub.

Motion Practice. 3rd ed. David F. Herr et al. LC 98-19268. 1998. ring bd. 160.00 (*0-7355-0128-9*) Aspen Law.

Motion-Resistant Twisted-Pair Conductor Guide: CRN Project 97-10. Ulteig Engineers, Inc. Staff & National Rural Electric Cooperative Association Staff. LC 98-39454. 1998. write for info. (*0-917599-22-5*) Natl Rural.

Motion Set. 2nd ed. Herr. 1991. 155.00 (*0-316-35195-4*, Aspen Law & Bus) Aspen Pub.

***Motion Sickness.** Terry O'Neal. Ed. by Andrea Burrise. 103p. 2000. pap. 7.95 (*0-9679446-0-0*) Motion Pubns.

Motion Sickness. Lynne Tillman. LC 90-19843. 208p. 1992. reprint ed. pap. 11.99 (*1-85242-219-X*) Serpents Tail.

***Motion Sickness: A Memoir.** David Layton. (Illus.). 240p. 2000. 21.95 (*1-55199-039-3*) MW&R.

Motion to Dismiss. Jonnie Jacobs. 304p. 1999. text 22.00 (*1-57566-395-3*) Kensgtn Pub Corp.

***Motion to Dismiss.** Jonnie Jacobs. (Kali O'Brien Mystery Ser.). 400p. 2000. mass mkt. 5.99 (*1-57566-543-3*) Kensgtn Pub Corp.

Motion to Reconsider: Education Governance at a Crossroads. 2nd ed. NASBE Study Group on Education Governance Staff. 56p. 1996. pap. 12.00 (*1-58434-022-3*) NASBE.

Motion to Suppress. Perri O'Shaughnessy. 480p. 1996. mass mkt. 6.99 (*0-440-22068-8*, Island Bks) Dell.

Motion to Suppress. Perri O'Shaughnessy. LC 99-31988. 1999. write for info. (*1-56895-755-6*) Wheeler Pub.

Motion Toward Perfection: The Achievement of Joseph Priestley, 1733-1804. Ed. by John G. McEvoy & A. Truman Schwartz. (Orig.). 1990. pap. 7.00 (*1-55896-010-4*, Skinner Hse Bks) Unitarian Univ.

Motion Understanding: Robot & Human Vision. Ed. by Worthy N. Martin & J. K. Aggarwal. LC 88-7. 1988. text 246.00 (*0-89838-258-0*) Kluwer Academic.

Motion Will Be Denied see Chicago Conspiracy Trial

Motional Electric Fields Associated with Relative Moving Charge. (Nikola Tesla Ser.). 1991. lib. bdg. 79.75 (*0-8490-4325-5*) Gordon Pr.

Motions in Federal Court. 3rd ed. 1800p. 1996. text. write for info. (*0-7620-0100-3*) West Group.

***Motions in the Solar Atmosphere: Proceedings of the Summerschool & Workshop Held at the Solar Observatory Kanzelhhohe Kharnten, Austria, September 1-12, 1997.** Arnold Hanslmeier & Mauro Messerotti. LC 98-49071. (Astrophysics & Space Science Library). 14p. 1999. write for info. (*0-7923-5507-5*) Kluwer Academic.

Motions of Love: Woolman As Mystic & Activist. Sterling Olmsted. LC 93-85961. (Orig.). 1993. pap. 4.00 (*0-87574-312-9*) Pendle Hill.

Motions Practice Before the Merit Systems Protection Board & the Equal Employment Opportunity Commission. Ernest C. Hadley & Sarah S. Tuck. 285p. 1998. pap. 65.00 (*1-878810-48-0*) Dewey Pubns.

Motivando a Nuestra Gente. J. Ramon.Tr. of Motivating Our People. (SPA.). 1995. pap. 6.99 (*0-8297-1863-X*) Vida Pubs.

Motivando la Lectura: Actividades de Razonamiento en Torno a la Literatura. Sandra M. Simons & Anne Maley. (ENG & SPA., Illus.). 125p. (Orig.). (J). (gr. 1-3). 1993. pap. text 16.65 (*0-9627689-3-6*) Spring St OR.

Motivated Brain: A Neurophysiological Analysis of Human Behavior. P. V. Simonov. (Monographs in Psychobiology). vii, 280p. 1991. text 160.00 (*2-88124-444-0*) Gordon & Breach.

Motivated Irrationality. David Pears. LC 97-37665. 268p. 1997. reprint ed. 40.00 (*1-890318-41-8*) St Augustines Pr.

Motivated Salon. Mark Foley. LC 96-15099. (Salon Business Ser.). 256p. 1997. pap. 26.95 (*1-56253-320-7*) Thomson Learn.

Motivated Women. Stacia Pierce. 15p. 1994. student ed. 10.00 (*1-886880-03-4*) Life Changers.

Motivating: Helping Staff Achieve Peak Performance. Ida M. Halasz. (Illus.). 110p. 1999. pap. 17.95 (*1-56991-100-2*) Am Correctional.

***Motivating & Inspiring Teachers: The Educational Leader's Guide for Building Staff Morale.** Todd Whitaker et al. LC 00-24911. 2000. write for info. (*1-883001-99-4*) Eye On Educ.

Motivating & Managing Computer Personnel. Daniel J. Couger & Robert A. Zawacki. 232p. 1980. 25.95 (*0-318-17053-1*); 27.95 (*0-318-17054-X*) AITP.

Motivating & Managing Computer Personnel. J. Daniel Couger & Robert A. Zawacki. 213p. 1980. 101.95 (*0-471-08485-9*) Wiley.

Motivating & Managing Today's Volunteers: How to Build & Lead a Terrific Team. Flora MacLeod. (Reference Ser.). 192p. 1993. pap. 11.95 (*0-88908-275-8*) Self-Counsel Pr.

Motivating & Preparing Black Youth to Work. Jawanza Kunjufu. (Illus.). 74p. 1986. pap. text 6.95 (*0-913543-02-0*) African Am Imag.

Motivating & Rewarding Employees: New & Better Ways to Inspire Your People. Alexander Hiam. LC 98-49361. (Illus.). 319p. 1999. pap. 17.95 (*1-58062-130-9*) Adams Media.

Motivating At-Risk Students. Mary R. Karlsson. (Professional's Guide Ser.). 80p. 1997. pap. 9.95 (*1-55734-890-1*) Tchr Create Mat.

Motivating at Work: Empowering Employees to Give Their Best. rev. ed. Twyla Dell. Ed. by Michael G. Crisp. LC 87-72484. (Fifty-Minute Ser.). (Illus.). 80p. (Orig.). 1993. pap. 10.95 (*1-56052-201-1*) Crisp Pubns.

Motivating Behavior Change among Illicit-Drug Abusers: Research on Contingency Management Interventions. Ed. by Stephen T. Higgins & Kenneth Silverman. LC 98-47471. 399p. 1999. 39.95 (*1-55798-570-7*, 431-8860) Am Psychol.

Motivating Blood Donors in Today's World: Recruitment & Retention. Ed. by Merlyn H. Sayers. 1998. pap. text. write for info. (*1-56395-095-2*) Am Assn Blood.

Motivating Classroom Discipline. William J. Gnagey. LC 89-28616. 160p. (C). 1990. reprint ed. pap. text 19.50 (*0-8191-7663-X*) U Pr of Amer.

Motivating Clients in Therapy: Values Love & the Real Relationship. Richard Rappaport. LC 97-205912. 352p. (C). 1997. 75.00 (*0-415-91265-2*); pap. 20.99 (*0-415-91266-0*) Routledge.

Motivating Correctional Staff Course, 3 bks., Set. Lucien Leduc. Ed. by Diane Geiman et al. 1992. pap. 70.00 (*0-929310-67-5*, 174) Am Correctional.

Motivating Customer Service Employees. Leslie Hansen Harps. 41p. 1993. pap. 36.95 (*0-915910-36-5*) Customer Srv Grp.

Motivating Donors in Today's World: Recruitment & Retention. Lorraine Kohr & Marilyn Sayers. LC 98-173369. xviii, 318 p. 1998. write for info. (*1-56395-075-8*, AABB Pr) Am Assn Blood.

Motivating Employees. Anne Bruce & James S. Pepitone. LC 98-41554. (Briefcase Books Ser.). (Illus.). 192p. 1998. pap. 14.95 (*0-07-071868-7*) McGraw.

Motivating for Change: Coaching & Motivating Your Team. Nicola Phillips. (Institute of Management Ser.). 250p. 1995. pap. 48.50 (*0-273-61176-3*, Pub. by Pitman Pub) Trans-Atl Phila.

Motivating Hard to Reach Students. Barbara L. McCombs & James E. Pope. LC 94-8336. (Psychology in the Classroom Ser.). 123p. (Orig.). 1994. pap. text 17.95 (*1-55798-220-1*) Am Psychol.

Motivating Health Behavior. John P. Elder et al. LC 93-12430. 388p. (C). 1993. mass mkt. 44.25 (*0-8273-4963-7*) Delmar.

Motivating High Level Learners. David Cranmer. (Pilgrims Longman Resource Bks.). 1996. pap. 21.32 (*0-582-20976-5*) Addison-Wesley.

Motivating Human Service Staff: Supervisory Strategies for Maximizing Work Effort & Work Enjoyment. Dennis H. Reid & Marsha B. Parsons. LC 95-79661. 218p. 1995. pap. 27.00 (*0-9645562-0-0*, Pub. by Habilit Mgt Consult) Quality Bks IL.

Motivating Humans: Goals, Emotions, & Personal Agency Beliefs. Martin E. Ford. (Illus.). 336p. (C). 1992. 52.00 (*0-8039-4528-0*) Sage.

Motivating Ideas for Teachers, Parents & Students. rev. ed. Mary L. Oakes & Mary L. Harris-Oakes. (Illus.). 20p. 1976. pap. 3.50 (*0-9622843-0-0*) Oakes & Assocs.

Motivating Kids. J. Zink. (Champions in the Making Ser.). 125p. (Orig.). 1983. pap. 14.95 (*0-942490-02-9*) J Zink.

Motivating Language Learners. Gary N. Chambers. LC 99-22423. (Modern Languages in Practice Ser.). 1999. 27.95 (*1-85359-448-2*) Taylor & Francis.

Motivating Low-Achieving Students: A Special Focus on Unmotivated & Underachieving African American Students. Gary L. Reglin. 190p. 1993. pap. 33.95 (*0-398-06341-9*); text 48.95 (*0-398-05852-0*) C C Thomas.

Motivating Minority Students: Strategies That Work. Simon O. Johnson & Verna J. Johnson. (Illus.). 114p. 1988. pap. 20.95 (*0-398-06186-6*) C C Thomas.

Motivating Minority Students: Strategies That Work. Simon O. Johnson & Verna J. Johnson. (Illus.). 114p. (C). 1988. text 30.95 (*0-398-05406-1*) C C Thomas.

Motivating Others: A Teacher's Guide to Nurturing Innermotivational Resources. John M. Reeve. 256p. 1995. pap. text 46.00 (*0-205-16969-4*) Allyn.

Motivating Others: Creating the Conditions. David P. Thompson. LC 96-5825. (School Leadership Library). (Illus.). 160p. 1996. 29.95 (*1-883001-25-0*) Eye On Educ.

Motivating Our People see Motivando a Nuestra Gente

Motivating People. 80p. pap. text. write for info. (*0-7506-3314-X*) Buttrwrth-Heinemann.

***Motivating People.** Alpha Development Group Staff. 368p. 1999. pap. text 16.95 (*0-02-863200-1*, Pub. by Macmillan) S&S Trade.

Motivating People. Robert Heller & Tim Hindle. LC 98-15313. (Essential Managers Handbks.). (Illus.). 72p. 1999. pap. 6.95 (*0-7894-2896-2*) DK Pub Inc.

***Motivating People.** Iain Maitland. 96p. 2000. pap. 17.95 (*0-8464-5121-2*) Beekman Pubs.

Motivating People. 2nd ed. (Open Learning Super Ser.). 1991. pap. text 26.00 (*0-08-041531-8*, Pergamon Pr) Elsevier.

Motivating People. 2nd ed. Dayle M. Smith. LC 97-25981. 96p. 1997. pap. text 6.95 (*0-8120-9898-6*) Barron.

Motivating People: How to Motivate Others to Do What You Want & Thank You for the Opportunity. Kurt Hanks. LC 90-84074. (Quick Read Ser.). 135p. (Orig.). 1991. pap. 13.95 (*1-56052-085-X*) Crisp Pubns.

Motivating People in Lean Organizations. Linda Holbeche. LC 98-139497. 320p. 1997. pap. text 35.95 (*0-7506-3375-1*) Buttrwrth-Heinemann.

Motivating People to Care. rev. ed. Bernard H. Petrina. Ed. by James W. Ickes. 140p. 1989. pap. text 49.00 (*0-940799-01-4*) Exec Mgmt Renew Prog.

Motivating Quotes for Motivated People. Susanne Stark. Ed. by Patrick Caton. 168p. (Orig.). 1996. pap. 5.95 (*1-56245-241-X*) Great Quotations.

Motivating Reluctant Readers. International Reading Association Staff. Ed. by Alfred J. Ciani. LC 80-25199. (Illus.). 112p. reprint ed. pap. 34.80 (*0-8357-4306-3*, 203710300007) Bks Demand.

Motivating Safety in the Workplace. Insurance Research Council, Inc. Staff & National Federation of Independent Business Staff. 42p. 1995. pap. 10.00 (*1-56594-004-0*) Ins Res Coun.

Motivating Soldiers: Morale or Mutiny. Ed. by Peter Karsten. LC 98-42477. (Military & Society Ser.: Vol. 3). 368p. 1998. reprint ed. 85.00 (*0-8153-2977-6*) Garland.

Motivating Strategies for Performance & Productivity: A Guide to Human Resource Development. Paul J. Champagne & R. Bruce McAfee. LC 88-18261. 233p. 1989. 65.00 (*0-89930-312-9*, CEG/, Quorum Bks) Greenwood.

Motivating Students. Ed. by Gail Thompson et al. 192p. 1998. pap. 29.95 (*0-7494-2494-X*, Kogan Pg Educ) Stylus Pub VA.

Motivating Students to Learn. Jere E. Brophy. LC 97-1283. 320p. 1997. pap. 30.00 (*0-07-008198-0*) McGraw.

Motivating Students to Learn: Overcoming Barriers to High Achievement. Ed. by Tommy M. Tomlinson. LC 92-81780. (NSSE Series on Contemporary Educational Issues). 270p. 1993. 38.75 (*0-8211-1909-5*) McCutchan.

Motivating Teaching in Higher Education: A Manual for Faculty Development. Edwin G. Ralph. (Illus.). 236p. (C). 1998. pap. 20.95 (*0-913507-96-2*) New Forums.

Motivating Team Leader. Lewis E. Losoncy. LC 94-46380. 256p. 1995. per. 29.95 (*1-884015-82-4*) St Lucie Pr.

***Motivating the Difficult to Teach.** Galloway. 162p. (C). 1998. pap. text 21.75 (*0-582-23155-8*) Longman.

Motivating the Uncooperative Student: A Guidebook for School Counselors. John F. Taylor. (Illus.). 44p. 1990. 10.95 (*1-884063-86-1*) Mar Co Prods.

Motivating the Unmotivated. Dick Hartman. LC 87-50744. (Illus.). (Orig.). 1987. pap. 8.95 (*0-9619238-0-6*) Valley Hill Pub.

An Asterisk (*) at the beginning of an entry indicates that the title is appearing for the first time.

Motivating Today's Work Force: When the Carrot Can't Always Be Cash. Lin Grensing. (Business Ser.). 216p. (Orig.). 1991. pap. 8.95 (*0-88908-955-8*) Self-Counsel Pr.

Motivating Underachievers. Carolyn Coil. 1992. pap. 11.95 (*1-880505-04-5*, CLC0195) Pieces of Lrning.

Motivating Volunteers in the Local Church. Leslie Parrott. 144p. 1991. pap. 9.99 (*0-8341-1415-1*) Beacon Hill.

Motivating with Love: A Memoir. Mary D. Nelson. LC 89-10021. (Illus.). xxii, 327p. 1989. pap. 17.50 (*0-8425-2372-3*, BYU DMK Ctr Intl) Brigham.

Motivating with Sales Contests: The Complete Guide to Motivating Your Telephone Professionals with Contests That Produce Record-Breaking Results. David L. Worman. 270p. (Orig.). 1992. pap. 29.00 (*1-881081-02-8*) Busn By Phone.

***Motivating Without Money: Cashless Ways to Stimulate Maximum Results, Raise Morale & Lower Turnover with Your Telephone Sale & Service Professionals.** Dave Worman. 224p. 1999. pap. 29.95 (*1-881081-10-9*) Busn By Phone.

Motivating Writing in Middle School. LC 95-49421. (Standards Consensus Ser.: No. 3). 114p. 1996. pap. 12.95 (*0-8141-5287-2*) NCTE.

Motivating Your Audience: Speaking from the Heart. McCarty. 164p. (C). 1998. pap. text 14.95 (*0-205-26894-3*) P-H.

Motivating Your Child to Success. Barbara S. Fritz. (For Parents Only Ser.). 16p. 1994. 1.95 (*1-56688-190-0*) Bur For At-Risk.

Motivating Your Organization: Achieving Business Success Through Reward & Recognition. Colin Pitts. LC 95-1427. (Quality in Action Ser.). 1995. 22.95 (*0-07-707967-1*) McGraw.

Motivating Your Parish to Change: Concrete Leadership Strategies for Pastors, Administrators, & Lay Leaders. David Heney. LC 98-5005. 128p. 1998. pap. 16.95 (*0-89390-433-3*) Resource Pubns.

Motivating Your Sales Force. John Lidstone. 144p. 1978. text 46.95 (*0-566-02082-3*) Ashgate Pub Co.

Motivating Your Sales Force. John Lidstone. 144p. 1995. pap. 26.95 (*0-566-07617-9*, Pub. by Gower) Ashgate Pub Co.

Motivating Your Student. Barbara Gruber. (Instant Idea Bks.). (Illus.). 64p. 1987. 7.95 (*0-86734-072-X*, FS-8310) Schaffer Pubns.

Motivating Your Student, Module 2. Sharon K. Johnson & Clarence D. Johnson. (FAST (Families & Schools Together) Ser.). (Illus.). 66p. 1994. pap. write for info. (*1-57035-025-6*, 56MOD) Sopris.

Motivating Youth at Risk. 1991. 8.00 (*0-911365-31-1*, A261-08478) Family & Consumer Sci Educ.

Motivation. Harvard Business School Press Staff. 100p. 1991. pap. 1995.00 (*0-07-103323-8*) McGraw.

***Motivation.** 2nd ed. 314p. (C). 1999. text 32.00 (*0-536-60339-1*) Pearson Custom.

***Motivation: A Biobehavioural Approach.** Roderick Wong. (Illus.). 296p. 2000. 85.00 (*0-521-56175-2*); pap. 29.95 (*0-521-56727-0*) Cambridge U Pr.

Motivation: A Biosocial & Cognitive Integration of Motivation & Emotion. Eva Dreikurs Ferguson. LC 99-25805. (Illus.). 416p. (C). 2000. text 59.95 (*0-19-506866-1*) OUP.

Motivation: A Systematic Reinterpretation. Dalbir Bindra. LC 59-6101. (Illus.). 371p. reprint ed. pap. 115.10 (*0-608-11275-5*, 201255900081) Bks Demand.

Motivation: How to Be a Positive Force in a Negative World. L. Michael Hall. (Illus.). 209p. (Orig.). 1987. pap. 10.00 (*1-890001-01-5*) Empowerment Tech.

Motivation: Strategy, Theory & Practice. Ed. by Ivan T. Robertson et al. 200p. (C). 1992. pap. 75.00 (*0-85292-488-7*, Pub. by IPM Hse) St Mut.

Motivation: The Organization of Action. 2nd ed. Douglas G. Mook. LC 95-32839. (C). 1995. text 75.00 (*0-393-96717-4*) Norton.

Motivation: Theories & Principles. 4th ed. Robert C. Beck. LC 99-12289. 477p. (C). 1999. 73.00 (*0-13-011292-5*) P-H.

Motivation: Theory & Research. Ed. by Michael Drillings & Harold F. O'Neil. 328p. 1994. pap. 29.95 (*0-8058-1287-3*); text 69.95 (*0-8058-1286-5*) L Erlbaum Assocs.

Motivation: Theory & Research. Petri. (Psychology Ser.). 1981. mass mkt. 30.50 (*0-534-00936-0*) Brooks-Cole.

Motivation: Theory & Research. 2nd ed. Petri. (Psychology Ser.). 1986. text. write for info. (*0-534-05383-1*) Brooks-Cole.

Motivation: Theory & Research. 2nd ed. Herbert L. Petri. 432p. (C). 1985. mass mkt. 40.50 (*0-534-05382-3*) Brooks-Cole.

Motivation: Theory, Research & Applications. Petri. (Adaptable Courseware Ser.). 1996. reprint ed. 15.50 (*0-534-49772-1*) Brooks-Cole.

Motivation: Theory, Research & Applications. 3rd ed. Herbert L. Petri. 434p. (C). 1991. text 46.20 (*0-534-14364-4*) Brooks-Cole.

Motivation: Theory, Research & Applications. 4th ed. Herbert L. Petri. LC 95-22770. 440p. 1995. pap. 87.95 (*0-534-20460-0*) Wadsworth Pub.

Motivation: Theory, Research, & Applications, Test Items. 4th ed. Herbert L. Petri. 1995. mass mkt. write for info. (*0-534-20461-9*) Brooks-Cole.

Motivation, Achievement & Testing. Ed. by Edward Miller & Roberta Tovey. (Focus Ser.: No. 2). 24p. 1996. pap. 9.95 (*1-883433-03-7*) Harv Educ Letter.

Motivation & Achievement. John W. Atkinson et al. LC 73-21754. (Illus.). 491p. reprint ed. pap. 152.30 (*0-608-11144-9*, 205070700082) Bks Demand.

Motivation & Action. Heinz Heckhausen. (Illus.). 528p. 1991. 70.95 (*0-387-54204-3*) Spr-Verlag.

Motivation & Compensation. Stephen Riddell. 200p. 1994. write for info. (*0-936840-14-5*) Tech Marketing.

Motivation & Concentration. rev. ed. Herman Ohme. Ed. by Jean Ohme. (Illus.). 48p. 1989. pap. 5.00 (*0-936047-01-1*) CA Educ Plan.

Motivation & Culture. Donald Munro et al. LC 96-51882. 256p. (C). 1997. pap. 23.99 (*0-415-91510-4*) Routledge.

Motivation & Culture. Donald Munro et al. LC 96-51882. 256p. (C). 1997. 75.00 (*0-415-91509-0*) Routledge.

Motivation & Emotion. Decatanzaro. LC 98-7523. 352p. 1998. 66.00 (*0-13-849159-3*) P-H.

Motivation & Emotion. Deckers. 448p. (C). 2000. 72.00 (*0-205-27115-4*) Allyn.

Motivation & Emotion. Phil Evans. 160p. 1989. 39.50 (*0-415-01475-1*); pap. 13.95 (*0-415-01476-X*) Routledge.

Motivation & Emotion. Phil Evans. LC 88-26356. 179p. reprint ed. pap. 55.50 (*0-608-20337-8*, 207159000002) Bks Demand.

Motivation & Emotion: Evolutionary, Physiological, Cognitive, & Social Influences. David C. Edwards. LC 98-19717. (Advanced Psychology Texts Ser.). 467p. 1998. write for info. (*0-7619-0832-3*) Sage.

Motivation & Emotion in Sport Reversal Theory. John H. Kerr. LC 97-202989. (Illus.). xiv, 223p. 1997. 54.95 (*0-86377-499-7*) Psychol Pr.

Motivation & Explanation: An Essay on Freud's Philosophy of Science. Nigel Mackay. (Psychological Issues Monographs: No. 56). 260p. 1989. 37.50 (*0-8236-3474-4*) Intl Univs Pr.

Motivation & Goal Setting: A Quick & Hardy Guide for Any Manager or Business Owner. 2nd ed. Ed. by Career Press Staff. (Business Desk Reference Ser.). 128p. 1993. pap. 8.95 (*1-56414-111-X*) Career Pr Inc.

Motivation & Goal Setting: How to Set & Achieve Goals & Inspire Others. Jim Cairo. LC 98-10412. 128p. 1998. pap. 10.99 (*1-56414-364-3*) Career Pr Inc.

Motivation & Indian Bureaucracy. P. K. Agrawal. LC 94-906774. 119p. 1995. pap. 88.00 (*81-85880-66-2*, Pub. by Print Hse) St Mut.

Motivation & Job Design: Theory, Research & Practice. Ivan T. Robertson & Mike Smith. 176p. (C). 1985. 70.00 (*0-85292-346-5*) St Mut.

Motivation & Job Satisfaction. K. Koteswara Rao. (Dynamic Organisational Behaviour Ser.). (C). 1991. 38.00 (*81-7141-153-3*) S Asia.

Motivation & Leadership at Work. 6th ed. Richard M. Steers et al. 704p. (C). 1996. 77.50 (*0-07-061031-2*) McGraw.

Motivation & Learning: A Teachers Guide to Building Excitement for Learning & Igniting the Drive for Quality. Spence Rogers et al. LC 96-72327. (Illus.). 286p. 1997. pap. 24.95 (*1-889852-30-9*) Peak Lrning Systs.

Motivation & Learning: Applying Contingency Management Techniques. Ed. by Mark L. Berman. LC 70-160894. 222p. 1972. pap. 24.95 (*0-87778-023-4*) Educ Tech Pubns.

***Motivation & Learning Strategies for College Success.** Myron H. Dembo. LC 99-48735. (C). 2000. pap. write for info. (*0-8058-3214-9*) L Erlbaum Assocs.

Motivation & Market Behavior. Ed. by Robert Ferber. LC 75-39244. (Getting & Spending: The Consumer's Dilemma Ser.). (Illus.). 1976. reprint ed. 36.95 (*0-405-08018-2*) Ayer.

Motivation & Personality: Handbook of Thematic Content Analysis. Ed. by Charles P. Smith. (Illus.). 726p. (C). 1992. text 74.95 (*0-521-40052-X*) Cambridge U Pr.

Motivation & Political Technique in the California Constitutional Convention of 1878-1879. Carl B. Swisher. LC 69-16843. (Law, Politics & History Ser.). 1969. reprint ed. lib. bdg. 22.50 (*0-306-71248-2*) Da Capo.

Motivation & Productivity in Public Sector Human Service Organizations. William T. Martin. LC 88-3099. 161p. 1988. 55.00 (*0-89930-314-5*, MMV/, Quorum Bks) Greenwood.

Motivation & Productivity in the Construction Industry. Robert Warren. (Illus.). 304p. (gr. 13). 1989. text 58.95 (*0-442-23351-5*) Chapman & Hall.

Motivation & Self-Regulation Across the Life-Span. Ed. by Jutta Heckhausen & Carol S. Dweck. LC 97-32110. (Illus.). 400p. (C). 1998. 64.95 (*0-521-59176-7*) Cambridge U Pr.

Motivation & Society. Ed. by Abigail J. Stewart. LC 81-48666. (Jossey-Bass Social & Behavioral Science Ser.). 415p. reprint ed. pap. 128.70 (*0-8357-4923-1*, 203785300009) Bks Demand.

Motivation & Teaching: A Practical Guide. Raymond J. Wlodkowski. 224p. 1986. pap. 16.95 (*0-8106-0751-4*) NEA.

Motivation & the Moral Sense in Francis Hutcheson's Ethical Theory. H. Jensen. (International Archives of the History of Ideas Ser.: No. 46). 133p. 1971. lib. bdg. 81.00 (*90-247-1187-8*) Kluwer Academic.

Motivation & the Neural & Neurohumoral Factors in Regulation of Behaviour: Recent Development of Neurobiology in Hungary, Vol. 10. Ed. by K. Lissak & P. Molnar. (Recent Developments of Neurobiology in Hungary Ser.: No. 10). 331p. (C). 1982. 145.00 (*963-05-2993-9*, Pub. by Akade Kiado) St Mut.

Motivation Assessment Scale: Administration Guide & Set of 25 Forms. unabridged ed. V. Mark Durand & Daniel B. Crimmins. 90p. 1992. spiral bd. 55.00 (*1-882322-29-0*, 2003) Monaco & Assocs.

Motivation Assessment Scale (MAS) Administration Guide. V. Mark Durand & Daniel B. Crimmins. 64p. (Orig.). (C). 1992. pap. text 49.00 (*1-882322-00-2*) Monaco & Assocs.

Motivation at Work. Jane R. Miskell & Vincent Miskell. LC 93-18112. 96p. 1993. pap. 10.95 (*1-55623-868-1*, Irwn Prfssnl) McGraw-Hill Prof.

***Motivation at Work: A Critical Reappraisal.** Steen Scheuer. 230p. 2000. Price not set. (*87-16-13498-2*, Pub. by Copenhagen Busn Schl) Bks Intl VA.

Motivation, Behavior, & Emotional Health: An Everyman's Interpretation. Donald M. Wonderly. 576p. (Orig.). (C). 1991. pap. text 44.00 (*0-8191-8384-9*); lib. bdg. 69.00 (*0-8191-8383-0*) U Pr of Amer.

Motivation, Beliefs & Organizational Transformation. Thad B. Green & Raymond T. Butkus. LC 98-51660. 224p. 1999. 59.95 (*1-56720-282-9*, Quorum Bks) Greenwood.

Motivation Books: Same & Different, What Is It, How Many, Letters & Words, 4 bks., Set. John Presland & Pam Adams. 1995. 14.99 (*0-85953-130-9*) Childs Play.

Motivation, Career Striving & Aging. Joel O. Raynor & Elliot E. Entin. 1981. text 24.95 (*0-07-051274-4*) McGraw.

Motivation Counts. David Johnson. 1997. pap. text 8.95 (*0-86651-740-5*) Seymour Pubns.

Motivation, Emotion, & Goal Direction in Neural Networks. Ed. by Daniel S. Levine & Samuel J. Leven. 472p. (C). 1992. text 99.95 (*0-8058-0447-1*) L Erlbaum Assocs.

Motivation, Emotions & Leadership: The Silent Side of Management. Richard C. Maddock & Richard L. Fulton. LC 98-6021. 224p. 1998. 59.95 (*1-56720-151-2*, Quorum Bks) Greenwood.

Motivation for Achievement: Possibilities for Teaching & Learning. Kay Alderman. 304p. 1999. pap. 29.95 (*0-8058-3077-4*) L Erlbaum Assocs.

Motivation for Greatness. C. Edd Caudle. Ed. by Velda Brotherton. LC 96-161560. 1969. 4.50 (*0-9652493-0-1*) E C Publishing.

Motivation for Ministry. Nathan R. Pope. 1993. pap. 10.99 (*0-8100-0417-8*, 15N0546) Northwest Pub.

Motivation for Reading: Individual, Home, Textual & Classroom Perspectives. Ed. by Allan Wigfield & John T. Guthrie. 78p. 1997. pap. write for info. (*0-8058-9872-7*) L Erlbaum Assocs.

Motivation in Education. Paul R. Pintrich & Dale H. Schunk. 434p. 1995. pap. text, student ed. 48.00 (*0-02-395621-6*, Macmillan Coll) P-H.

Motivation in Education Management: Issues & Strategies. B. Mukhopadhyay. (C). 1995. write for info. (*81-207-1621-3*) Sterling Pubs.

Motivation in Functional Systems. Ed. by K. V. Sudakov et al. (Systems Research in Physiology Ser.: Vol. 1). xvi, 364p. 1987. text 376.00 (*2-88124-193-X*) Gordon & Breach.

Motivation in Mathematics. Ed. by Martha Carr. LC 95-39941. 208p. (C). 1996. text 45.00 (*1-57273-026-9*); pap. text 20.95 (*1-57273-027-7*) Hampton Pr NJ.

Motivation in Sport & Exercise. Ed. by Glyn C. Roberts. LC 91-22864. (Illus.). 288p. (Orig.). 1995. reprint ed. pap. text 25.00 (*0-87322-876-6*, BROB0876) Human Kinetics.

Motivation in the Classroom. Cheryl Spaulding. (C). 1991. text 26.74 (*0-07-059927-0*) McGraw.

Motivation in the Workplace: Inspiring Your Employees. Lydia Banks. Ed. by Karen M. Miller. LC 97-70993. (How-to Book Ser.). 110p. (Orig.). 1997. pap. 12.95 (*1-884926-46-0*, MOTIV) Amer Media.

Motivation in the Workplace: Practical Techniques for Motivating Workers to Peak Performance & Productivity. Barbara Fielder. Ed. by Kelly Scanlon. LC 96-68884. 73p. (Orig.). 1996. pap. 12.95 (*1-878542-83-4*, 12-0016) SkillPath Pubns.

Motivation in Work Organizations. Edward E. Lawler, 3rd. LC 93-50161. (Management Ser.). 336p. 1994. pap. 27.00 (*1-55542-661-1*) Jossey-Bass.

Motivation, Intention, & Volition. Ed. by F. Halisch & Julius Kuhl. (Illus.). 430p. 1987. 122.95 (*0-387-16191-0*) Spr-Verlag.

Motivation Lombardi Style. Compiled by Successories, Inc. Staff. (Power of One Ser.). 48p. 1998. pap. 5.95 (*1-880461-45-5*) Successories Inc.

***Motivation Management.** Sheila Ritchie & Peter Martin. LC 98-40509. xviii, 293 p. 1999. 96.95 (*0-566-08102-4*) Ashgate Pub Co.

***Motivation Management: Fueling Performance by Discovering What People Believe about Themselves & Their Organizations.** Thad Green. LC 99-86822. 280p. 2000. 29.95 (*0-89106-143-6*, Davies-Black Pub) Consulting Psychol.

Motivation Manual. Gisela Hagemann. 200p. 1992. 65.95 (*0-566-07295-5*, Pub. by Gower) Ashgate Pub Co.

Motivation of Personnel. Ed. by A. Dale Timpe. LC 86-2099. (Art & Science of Business Management Ser.). 383p. reprint ed. pap. 118.80 (*0-7837-6691-2*, 204630800011) Bks Demand.

Motivation of Politicians. James L. Payne et al. LC 83-26853. 216p. 1984. pap. text 24.95 (*0-88229-824-0*) Burnham Inc.

Motivation of the Under-Privileged Worker. Allison Davis. (Reprint Series in Social Sciences). (C). 1993. reprint ed. pap. text 1.90 (*0-8290-2672-X*, S-62) Irvington.

Motivation, Planning & Action: A Relational Theory of Behavior Dynamics. J. M. Nuttin. 259p. (Orig.). 1984. pap. 52.50 (*90-6186-154-3*, Pub. by Leuven Univ) Coronet Bks.

Motivation, Planning & Action: A Relational Theory of Behavior Dynamics. Joseph R. Nuttin et al. 264p. 1984. text 49.95 (*0-89859-332-8*) L Erlbaum Assocs.

Motivation Plus. Elizabeth Clay. LC 83-62405. 1983. student ed., ring bd. 49.95 (*0-914607-01-4*) Master Tchr.

***Motivation Pocketbook.** 2000. pap. 8.95 (*1-870471-60-1*) Stylus Pub VA.

***Motivation Pocketbook.** Max Eggert. (Management Pocketbks.). 112p. 2000. pap. 8.95 (*1-57922-008-8*) Stylus Pub VA.

Motivation Research in Advertising & Marketing. George H. Smith. LC 70-100175. (Illus.). 242p. 1971. reprint ed. lib. bdg. 65.00 (*0-8371-4023-4*, SMMO, Greenwood Pr) Greenwood.

Motivation Theory for Teachers. Madeline C. Hunter. LC 95-11689. 56p. 1967. pap. 14.95 (*0-8039-6321-1*) Corwin Pr.

Motivation, Thought, & Action. Julius Kuhl & John W. Atkinson. LC 85-16739. (Illus.). 407p. 1986. 65.00 (*0-275-92096-8*, C2096, Praeger Pubs) Greenwood.

Motivation to Excellence: A Coach's Collection of Illustrations. Elliot Johnson. 120p. 1998. pap. text 9.95 (*1-887002-20-0*) Cross Trng.

Motivation to Last a Lifetime. Ted W. Engstrom. 96p. 1984. pap. 5.99 (*0-310-24251-7*, 9570P) Zondervan.

Motivation to Last a Lifetime. Ted W. Engstrom. 96p. 1984. 9.95 (*0-310-24250-9*, 9570Z) Zondervan.

Motivation to Learn: From Theory to Practice. 3rd ed. Deborah J. Stipek. LC 97-77132. 301p. 1997. pap. text 45.00 (*0-205-27777-2*) P-H.

Motivation to Manage: A Ten Year Update on the "Studies in Management Education" Research. John B. Miner. (Illus.). 1977. text 25.00 (*0-917926-00-5*) Organizat Meas.

Motivation to Work. Frederick Herzberg et al. LC 92-16067. 180p. (C). 1993. pap. 19.95 (*1-56000-634-X*) Transaction Pubs.

Motivation to Work. 2nd ed. Frederick Herzberg et al. LC 59-14119. 173p. reprint ed. pap. 53.70 (*0-608-13339-6*, 205571700032) Bks Demand.

Motivation Towards Adult Education. Ram L. Kanwal. 78p. 1987. 19.95 (*0-318-36825-0*) Asia Bk Corp.

Motivational Classics: Acres of Diamonds; As a Man Thinketh; Kingship of Self Control. Ed. by Charles E. Jones. 143p. 1996. pap. 10.00 (*0-937539-07-4*) Executive Bks.

Motivational English for At-Risk Students: A Language Arts Course That Works. Marge Christensen. LC 98-160771. 95p. (Orig.). 1992. pap. 18.95 (*1-879639-19-X*) Natl Educ Serv.

Motivational Enhancement Therapy Manual: A Clinical Research Guide for Therapists Treating Individuals with Alcohol Abuse & Dependence. William R. Miller et al. 121p. (Orig.). (C). 1994. pap. text 35.00 (*0-7881-1476-X*) DIANE Pub.

Motivational Interviewing: Preparing People to Change Addictive Behavior. William R. Miller & Stephen Rollnick. LC 91-16597. 348p. 1991. lib. bdg. 39.95 (*0-89862-566-1*) Guilford Pubns.

Motivational Interviewing: Preparing People to Change Addictive Behavior. William R. Miller & Stephen Rollnick. LC 91-16597. 348p. 1992. reprint ed. pap. text 23.00 (*0-89862-469-X*) Guilford Pubns.

Motivational Interviewing with Dr Bill Miller. (C). 2000. VHS 95.00 (*0-205-31575-5*) Allyn.

Motivational Lessons My Dog Skipper Taught Me! It's a Dog-Gone Wonderful Life. Don Vieweg. (Illus.). 105p. (Orig.). 1998. per. write for info. (*1-884487-06-8*) Bellman Pubng.

Motivational Magic. Linda Diebert. (Illus.). 128p. (J). (ps-2). 1990. 7.99 (*0-86653-535-7*, GA1137) Good Apple.

Motivational Minutes: Insightful Ideas for Improving the Quality of Your Life. Don Essig. LC 96-39983. (Successories Ser.). 144p. 1997. 13.00 (*1-56414-290-6*) Career Pr Inc.

Motivational Sayings. Angela M. Aschbrenner. (Successful Ideas Ser.). 60p. 1990. pap. 10.00 (*1-880662-04-3*) A M Aschbrenner.

***Motivational Science: Social & Personality Perspectives.** E. Tory Higgins & Arie W. Kruglanski. LC 00-25430. (Key Readings in Social Psychology Ser.). 2000. pap. write for info. (*0-86377-697-3*, Pub. by Psychol Pr) Taylor & Francis.

Motivational Units for Fall. Georgeann Grewe & Susanne Glover. 144p. 1990. 10.99 (*0-86653-543-8*, GA1146) Good Apple.

Motivational Units for Spring. Georgeann Grewe & Susanne Glover. (Illus.). 144p. (J). (gr. 2-6). 1990. 10.99 (*0-86653-524-1*, GA1145) Good Apple.

Motivative Skills see Productive Supervisor: A Program of Practical Managerial Skills

Motive. large type ed. Harry Carmichael. 320p. 1983. 27.99 (*0-7089-0954-X*) Ulverscroft.

***Motive, America.** Gordon Hammond. 64p. 2000. pap. 8.00 (*0-9676758-4-7*) W L F Pubng.

Motive & Intention: An Essay in the Appreciation of Action. Roy Lawrence. LC 72-186548. (Publications in Analytical Philosophy). 146p. reprint ed. 45.30 (*0-8357-9465-2*, 201530100094) Bks Demand.

Motive Clauses in Hebrew Law: Biblical Forms & near Eastern Parallels. Rifat Sonsino. LC 79-15024. (Society of Biblical Literature. Dissertation Ser.: No. 45). 356p. reprint ed. pap. 110.40 (*0-7837-5444-2*, 204520900005) Bks Demand.

Motive for Marriage. Linda Markowiak. (Superromance Ser.: No. 755). 1997. per. 3.99 (*0-373-70755-X*, 1-70755-3) Harlequin Bks.

Motive for Marriage. large type ed. Lee Wilkinson. 1996. 11.50 (*0-7505-0854-X*, Pub. by Mgna Lrg Print) Ulverscroft.

***Motive for Marriage: Sweet Promise, Cristen's Choice, If There Be Love.** Ginna Gray. 2000. mass mkt. 6.99 (*0-373-20176-1*, 1-20176-3) Harlequin Bks.

Motive for Mayhem. Abigail Child. 96p. (Orig.). 1989. pap. 8.50 (*0-937013-26-9*) Potes Poets.

Motive, Means . . . & Marriage? Women to Watch. Hilary Byrnes. (Intimate Moments Ser.). 1998. per. 4.25 (*0-373-07888-9*, 1-07888-0) Harlequin Bks.

Motive on Record. Dell Shannon. 1990. mass mkt. 3.50 (*0-373-26049-0*) Harlequin Bks.

An Asterisk (*) at the beginning of an entry indicates that the title is appearing for the first time.

Motivemos a Su Hijos (A) para Que Triunte en la Escuela (Motivating Your Child for School Success) Paquete para Los Instructores (Leader's Kit) Dale Baker & Thomas Baker. (SPA.). 1998. ring bd. 150.00 (1-885903-06-5) ParentingKids.

Motives, Pt. 1. Ed. by U. Jannsen et al. LC 93-38970. (Proceedings of Symposia in Pure Mathematics Ser.: Vol. 55). 747p. 1994. text 140.00 (0-8218-1636-5, PSPUM/55.1) Am Math.

Motives, Pt. 2. Ed. by U. Jannsen et al. LC 93-38970. (Proceedings of Symposia in Pure Mathematics Ser.: Vol. 55). 676p. 1994. text 129.00 (0-8218-1637-3, PSPUM/55.2) Am Math.

Motives, Set. Ed. by U. Jannsen et al. LC 93-38970. (Proceedings of Symposia in Pure Mathematics Ser.: Vol. 55). 1423p. 1994. text 250.00 (0-8218-1635-7, PSPUM/55) Am Math.

***Motives: Stories That Tell Why.** Antione Duie. 180p. 2000. pap. 18.00 (0-7388-2197-7) Xlibris Corp.

Motives & Goals in Groups. Alvin Zander. LC 95-48943. 212p. 1996. pap. text 24.95 (1-56000-883-0) Transaction Pubs.

Motives & Mechanisms: An Introduction to the Psychology of Action. Rom Harre et al. 192p. 1985. 35.00 (0-416-36230-3, 9467); pap. 12.95 (0-416-36240-0, 9468) Routledge.

Motives & Thoughts: Psychoanalytic Essays in Honor of David Rapaport. Ed. by Robert R. Holt. LC 67-20615. (Psychological Issues Monographs: No. 18-19, Vol. 5, Nos. 2-3). 214p. (Orig.). 1967. 60.00 (0-8236-3480-9); pap. 42.50 (0-8236-3460-4) Intl Univs Pr.

Motives for Creative Work. LC 96-51718. (Perspectives on Creativity Ser.). 288p. 1997. 59.50 (1-881303-92-6) Hampton Pr NJ.

Motives for Creative Work. Jock Abra. LC 96-51718. (Perspectives on Creativity Ser.). 288p. 1997. pap. 24.95 (1-881303-93-4) Hampton Pr NJ.

Motives for Fiction. Robert Alter. LC 83-10829. 248p. 1984. 35.95 (0-674-58762-6) HUP.

Motives for Linguistic Change in the Formation of the Spanish Object Pronouns. Joel Rini. (Estudios Linguisticos Ser.). 152p. 1992. pap. 12.00 (0-936388-52-8) Juan de la Cuesta.

Motives for Metaphor: Literacy, Curriculum Reform & the Teaching of English. James E. Seitz. LC 99-6118. (Pittsburgh Series in Composition, Literacy, & Culture). 224p. 1999. pap. 19.95 (0-8229-5692-6); text 45.00 (0-8229-4093-0) U of Pittsburgh Pr.

Motives for Murder. Patricia Gebhard. LC 99-61765. 282p. 2000. pap. 14.95 (0-88739-268-7) Creat Arts Bk.

***Motives for Writing.** 3rd ed. Robert K. Miller. LC 98-48744. 695p. 1999. pap. text 31.95 (1-55934-924-7, 924-7) Mayfield Pub.

Motives of Men. George A. Coe. LC 75-3112. reprint ed. 32.50 (0-404-59108-6) AMS Pr.

Motives of My Life see Motivi Moijej Zhizni

Motives of Proteus. Jose E. Rodo. 1973. lib. bdg. 250.00 (0-87968-384-8) Gordon Pr.

Motives of Woe: Shakespeare & "Female Complaint" - A Critical Anthology. Ed. by John Kerrigan. (Illus.). 324p. (C). 1991. text 85.00 (0-19-811770-1) OUP.

Motives, Personality & Society. David C. McClelland. LC 84-2033. (Centennial Psychology Ser.). 502p. 1984. 65.00 (0-275-91224-8, C1224, Praeger Pubs) Greenwood.

Motivgeschichte und Ikonologie. Katrin Seidel. (Studien Zur Kunstgeschichte Ser.: Bd. 103). (GER., Illus.). 350p. 1996. write for info. (3-487-10193-9) G Olms Pubs.

Motivi Moijej Zhizni. Archbishop Vitaly Maximenko.Tr. of Motives of My Life. 205p. 1955. pap. 7.00 (0-317-29054-1) Holy Trinity.

Motivo de Una Flor. Ruth Heller. 1990. 14.15 (0-606-10487-9, Pub. by Turtleback) Demco.

Motivos de Conversacion. 4th ed. Nicholas. 1997. audio 26.88 (0-07-913102-6) McGraw.

***Motivos de Conversacion.** 5th ed. Robert L. Nicholas & Maria Canteli Dominicis. (SPA & ENG.). 288p. (C). 1999. pap. 27.81 (0-07-230918-0) McGrw-H Hghr Educ.

Motivos de Conversacion: Essentials of Spanish. 3rd ed. Robert L. Nicholas et al. 1991. text 43.00 (0-07-046708-0) McGraw.

Motivos de Conversacion: Essentials of Spanish. 3rd ed. Robert L. Nicholas et al. (C). 1992. pap. text, wbk. ed., lab manual ed. 21.00 (0-07-046714-5) McGraw.

Motivos de Conversacion: Essentials of Spanish. 4th ed. Robert L. Nicholas & Maria C. Dominicis. LC 96-37557. (SPA.). 1997. write for info. (0-07-047089-8) McGraw.

Motivos de Conversacion: Essentials of Spanish. 4th ed. Robert L. Nicholas & Maria C. Dominicis. LC 96-37557. 448p. (C). 1997. 59.38 (0-07-047088-X) McGraw.

Motivos de Conversacion: Essentials of Spanish. 4th ed. Robert L. Nicholas & Maria C. Dominicis. (C). 1997. pap., wbk. ed., lab manual ed. 26.88 (0-07-047090-1) McGraw.

Motivos de Conversacion: Essentials of Spanish. 5th ed. Robert L. Nicholas & Marbia Canteli Dominicis. LC 99-23951. 1999. write for info. (0-07-230923-7) McGraw.

***Motivos De Conversacion: Essentials of Spanish.** 5th ed. Robert L. Nicholas & Maria Canteli Dominicis. LC 99-23951. 1999. write for info. (0-07-230984-9) McGrw-H Hghr Educ.

Motivos Equivocados: Mistaken Reasons. Kelly Jamison. (Deseo Ser.: Vol. 123).Tr. of Mistaken Reasons. 1998. per. 3.50 (0-373-35253-0, 1-35253-3) Harlequin Bks.

***Motivos Para Creer.** Jorge Loring. 1999. 17.95 (84-08-02021-8) Planeta Edit.

Motley. Susannah Amoore. LC 97-61324. (Illus.). 32p. (J). (ps-4). 1998. 14.99 (0-670-87730-1) Viking Penguin.

Motley. John Galsworthy. 1988. reprint ed. lib. bdg. 49.00 (0-7812-0045-8) Rprt Serv.

Motley. John Galsworthy. 1971. reprint ed. 59.00 (0-403-00978-2) Scholarly.

Motley: Poems from Hollywood. Mark Dunster. 11p. 1999. pap. 5.00 (0-89642-699-8) Linden Pubs.

Motley Crue. (Rock Legends Ser.). 128p. (Orig.). 1994. pap. 18.95 (0-89724-175-4, GF0640) Wrner Bros.

Motley Crue. 44p. (Orig.). 1994. pap. 22.95 (0-89724-315-3, VF2143) Wrner Bros.

Motley Crue - Selections from Two Albums. Ed. by Carol Cuellar. 60p. (Orig.). (C). 1984. pap. text 12.95 (0-7692-0766-9, VF1114) Wrner Bros.

Motley Crue - Selections from Two Albums: Guitar Personality Book. 100p. (Orig.). 1992. pap. 24.95 (0-7692-0585-2, GF0515) Wrner Bros.

Motley Crue Guitar Superstar Series: Guitar Personality Book. 76p. (Orig.). 1986. pap. 14.95 (0-7692-0586-0, GF0286) Wrner Bros.

Motley Fool Investment Guide: How the Fool Beats Wall Street's Wise Men & How You Can Too. David Gardner & Thomas Gardner. 224p. 1996. 24.50 (0-684-81594-X) S&S Trade.

Motley Fool Investment Guide: How the Fool Beats Wall Street's Wise Men & How You Can Too. David Gardner & Tom Gardner. 304p. 1997. per. 13.00 (0-684-82703-4) S&S Trade.

***Motley Fool Investment Guide: How the Fool Beats Wall Street's Wise Men & How You Can Too.** David Gardner & Tom Gardner. 2001. pap. 14.00 (0-7432-0173-6, Fireside) S&S Trade Pap.

Motley Fool Investment Workbook. David Gardner & Tom Gardner. LC 97-43602. 224p. 1998. per. 12.00 (0-684-84401-X) S&S Trade.

***Motley Fool's Industry Focus 2000: 16 Investment Ideas from 16 Industries for the Year Ahead.** Ed. by Jeff Fischer. (Illus.). 140p. 1999. pap. 35.00 (1-892547-10-4, Pub. by Motley Fool) Publishers Group.

***Motley Fool's Investing Without a Silver Spoon: How Anyone Can Build Wealth Through Direct Investing.** unabridged ed. Jeff Fischer & David Gardner. (Illus.). 450p. 1999. pap. 15.00 (1-892547-04-X, Pub. by Motley Fool) Publishers Group.

Motley Fool's Investment Tax Guide, 2000: Smart Tax Strategies for Investors. unabridged ed. Selena Maranjian & Roy A. Lewis. 384p. 1999. pap. 15.00 (1-892547-05-8) Motley Fool.

***Motley Fools Rule Breakers Rule Makers: The Foolish Guide to Picking Stocks.** 2000. 23.50 (0-7435-0654-5) SimSchuster Interact.

***Motley Fool's Rule Breakers, Rule Makers: The Foolish Guide to Picking Stocks.** David Gardner & Tom Gardner. 336p. 2000. per. 13.00 (0-684-85717-0) Free Pr.

Motley Fool's Rule Breakers, Rule Makers: The Foolish Guide to Picking Stocks. David Gardner & Tom Gardner. LC 98-54919. (Illus.). 288p. 1999. 24.50 (0-684-84400-1) Simon & Schuster.

Motley Tales & a Play. deluxe ed. Anton Chekhov et al. LC 97-40220. (New York Public Library Collector's Edition Ser.). 432p. 1998. 18.50 (0-385-48730-4) Doubleday.

Moto Cross. David Armentrout. LC 97-12420. (Sports Challenge Ser.). 24p. (J). (gr. 3-7). 1997. lib. bdg. 18.60 (1-55916-218-X) Rourke Bk Co.

Moto Europa: The Complete Guide to European Motoring. 3rd ed. Eric Bredesen. LC 95-70769. (Illus.). 306p. (Orig.). 1996. pap. 15.95 (0-9641488-3-8) Seren Pubng.

Moto Guzzi. David G. Styles. 2000. pap. text 19.95 (0-7509-2041-6) Sutton Pub Ltd.

Moto Guzzi. Mick Walker. (Illus.). 128p. 1997. pap. 10.95 (1-85532-720-1, Pub. by Ospry) Stackpole.

Moto Guzzi Story. Ian Falloon. LC 98-75403. (Illus.). 192p. 1999. 39.95 (1-85960-414-5, Pub. by J H Haynes & Co) Motorbooks Intl.

Moto Guzzi Twins Restoration. Mick Walker. (Illus.). 240p. 1999. pap. 39.95 (1-85532-679-5, 126611AE, Pub. by Ospry) Motorbooks Intl.

Moto Guzzi V-Twins - The Complete Story. Mick Walker. (Illus.). 192p. 1999. 35.95 (1-86126-180-2, Pub. by Cro1wood) Motorbooks Intl.

Moto MV Agusta. Mario Colombo & Roberto Patrignani. (Illus.). 248p. 1991. 60.00 (88-7911-060-8, Pub. by Giorgio Nada Editore) Howell Pr VA.

***Moto MV Agusta.** Mario Colombo & Roberto Patrignani. (Illus.). 278p. 2000. 44.95 (88-7911-180-9, 117733AE, Pub. by Giorgio Nada Editore) Motorbooks Intl.

Moto Perpetuo for Violin & Piano, Op. 11. Nicolo Paganini. Ed. by P. Mittell. (Carl Fischer Music Library: No. 88). 1968. pap. 6.00 (0-8258-0014-5, L88) Fischer Inc NY.

***Moto Raid.** Keith Thye. Ed. by Laurel Strand. LC 99-72751. (Illus.). 240p. 1999. pap. 12.95 (0-944958-48-6) Elfin Cove Pr.

Motocicletas. Jason Cooper. (Maquinas de Viaje Ser.).Tr. of Motorcycles. 24p. (J). (gr. k-4). 1991. lib. bdg. 14.60 (0-86592-508-9) Rourke Enter.

***Motocourse, 1999-2000.** Mike Scott. (Illus.). 200p. 2000. 54.95 (1-874557-39-X, Pub. by Hazelton Publishing) Motorbooks Intl.

Motocourse Official History: 50 Years of the FIM Road Racing World Championships. Ed. by Motocourse Editors. (Illus.). 208p. 1999. 59.95 (1-874557-83-7) Hazelton Publishing.

***Motocourse, 2000-2001.** Michael Scott. (Illus.). 216p. 2000. 54.95 (1-874557-84-5, 130754AE, Pub. by Hazelton Publishing) Motorbooks Intl.

Motocross & Trials. Jeremy Evans. LC 93-9385. (Adventurers Ser.). (Illus.). 48p. (J). (gr. 5-6). 1994. lib. bdg. 13.95 (0-89686-821-4, Crstwood Hse) Silver Burdett Pr.

Motocross Cycles see Cruisin'

Motocross Cycles see Rollin'

Motocross Mania. Raymond A. Montgomery. (Choose Your Own Adventure Ser.: No. 139). (J). (gr. 4-8). 1993. 8.60 (0-606-05478-2, Pub. by Turtleback) Demco.

Motocross Racing see MotorSports

Motocycle Poems by the Biker Poet. Frazier. (Illus.). 200p. 1995. pap. 24.95 (0-935151-44-3) Arrowstar Pub.

Motocyclette. Andre Pieyre de Mandiargue. (FRE.). 1973. pap. 10.95 (0-7859-4008-1) Fr & Eur.

Motograph Moving Picture Book see Magic Moving Picture Book

Motoguzzi Big Twins. Greg Field. LC 98-23731. (Motorcycle Color History Ser.). (Illus.). 128p. 1998. pap. 21.95 (0-7603-0363-0) Motorbooks Intl.

Motoharu Goushi: Calcite. Motoharu Goushi. (JPN., Illus.). 114p. 1993. 29.95 (4-8457-0734-9) RAM Publications.

Motoori Norinaga, 1730-1801. Shigeru Matsumoto. LC 77-95928. (Harvard East Asian Ser.: No. 44). 275p. reprint ed. pap. 85.30 (0-608-10090-0, 200549700054) Bks Demand.

Motor Accident Claims. S. Sengupta. (C). 1990. 130.00 (0-89771-169-6) St Mut.

Motor Accidents Law NSW. Malcolm M. Britts. LC 94-191207. 1994. pap. 35.00 (0-455-21268-6, Pub. by LawBk Co) Gaunt.

Motor Activity & Movement Disorders: Research Issues & Applications. Ed. by Klaus-Peter Ossenkopp et al. LC 95-40459. (Contemporary Neuroscience Ser.). (Illus.): 392p. 1995. 119.50 (0-89603-327-9, RC376) Humana.

Motor Activity & the Education of Retardates. Bryant J. Cratty. LC 73-23008. (Lea & Febiger Health, Physical Education & Recreation Ser.). (Illus.). 312p. reprint ed. 96.80 (0-8357-9411-3, 201453700093) Bks Demand.

***Motor Air Bag Manual.** John Lypen. (Illus.). 1999. 76.00 (1-58251-020-2) Motor Info Sys.

Motor & Cognitive Functions of the Prefrontal Cortex. Ed. by A. M. Thierry et al. LC 93-37169. (Research & Perspectives in Neurosciences Ser.). 1994. 59.00 (0-387-57128-0) Spr-Verlag.

Motor & Generator Industry. M. Linger. 235p. 2000. 1350.00 (0-318-00533-6) Busn Trend.

Motor & Sensory Processes of Language. Ed. by Eric Keller & Myrna Gopnik. (Whitaker-Neuropsychology & Neurolinguistics Ser.). 312p. 1987. text 59.95 (0-89859-631-9) L Erlbaum Assocs.

Motor Assessment of the Developing Infant. Martha C. Piper & Johanna Darrah. LC 93-24914. (Illus.). 224p. 1994. text 46.00 (0-7216-4307-8, W B Saunders Co) Harcrt Hlth Sci Grp.

Motor Auto Body Repair. Scharff. (Automotive Technology Ser.). 1988. pap., teacher ed. 16.00 (0-8273-3090-1) Delmar.

Motor Auto Body Repair. Robert Scharff. LC 87-15719. 1988. text 48.95 (0-8273-3089-8) Delmar.

Motor Auto Body Repair. 2nd ed. Robert Scharff. 1992. text 56.00 (0-8273-4667-0) Delmar.

Motor Auto Body Repair. 3rd ed. James E. Duffy. LC 96-47077. (Automotive Technology Ser.). 1997. mass mkt. 101.95 (0-8273-6858-5) Delmar.

Motor Auto Body Repair - IG. 3rd ed. Duffy. (Automotive Technology Ser.). 96p. 1998. teacher ed. 16.00 (0-8273-6859-3) Delmar.

Motor Auto Body Repair, Instructors Guide. 2nd ed. Robert Scharff. 1992. pap. 18.00 (0-8273-4668-9) Delmar.

Motor Auto Body Repair, Technical Manual. 2nd ed. Scharff Associates, Ltd. Staff. 1992. pap. 20.95 (0-8273-4661-1) Delmar.

Motor Auto Tech. 3rd ed. Schwaller. 576p. 1997. pap., wbk. ed. 19.95 (0-8273-8377-0) Delmar.

Motor Auto Tech. 3rd ed. Schwaller. 160p. 1998. pap. text, teacher ed. 30.95 (0-8273-8355-X) Delmar.

Motor Auto Tech. 3rd ed. Schwaller. 100p. 1998. teacher ed. 153.95 (0-8273-8356-8) Delmar.

Motor Autobody Repair. 3rd ed. James E. Duffy. (Automotive Repair Ser.). 1997. mass mkt., student ed. 20.50 (0-8273-6786-4) Delmar.

Motor Automotive Mechanics. Anthony E. Schwaller. (Automotive Technology Ser.). 1988. text 14.00 (0-8273-2539-8) Delmar.

Motor Automotive Mechanics. Anthony E. Schwaller. (Automotive Technology Ser.). 1988. pap., wbk. ed. 17.50 (0-8273-2544-4) Delmar.

Motor Automotive Mechanics - Transmission Master. Anthony E. Schwaller. (Automotive Technology Ser.). 1988. text 16.50 (0-8273-2545-2) Delmar.

Motor Automotive Technology. 2nd ed. Anthony E. Schwaller. LC 87-32956. 864p. 1992. text 44.50 (0-8273-5100-3) Delmar.

Motor Automotive Technology. 3rd ed. Schwaller. LC 97-45609. 1042p. 1998. mass mkt. 79.95 (0-8273-8354-1) Delmar.

Motor Automotive Technology: Instructor's Guide. 2nd ed. Anthony E. Schwaller & Barry Hollembeak. 1993. 19.50 (0-8273-5101-1); text 22.95 (0-8273-5983-7) Delmar.

Motor Automotive Technology: Reference Manual. 2nd ed. Anthony E. Schwaller. 42p. 1993. 14.95 (0-8273-5986-1) Delmar.

Motor Automotive Technology CTB Apple. 2nd ed. Anthony E. Schwaller. (Tech & Industrial Education Ser.). 1993. 99.00 (0-8273-5982-9) Delmar.

Motor Automotive Technology CTB IBM. 2nd ed. Anthony E. Schwaller. (Tech & Industrial Education Ser.). 1993. 69.95 (0-8273-5738-9) Delmar.

Motor Automotive Technology Workbook. 2nd ed. Anthony E. Schwaller. 408p. 1993. student ed. 18.95 (0-8273-5574-2) Delmar.

Motor Behavior & Human Skill: A Multidisciplinary Approach. Jan P. Piek. LC 97-40755. (Illus.). 448p. 1998. text 49.00 (0-88011-675-7, BPIE0675) Human Kinetics.

Motor Bill & the Lovely Caroline. Jenny Wagner. LC 94-20241. (Illus.). 32p. (J). 1995. 14.95 (0-395-71547-4) Ticknor & Flds Bks Yng Read.

***Motor Boat & Yachting Logbook for Cruising under Power.** Bartlett & Willis. 96p. 2000. pap. 14.95 (1-898660-36-0, Pub. by Fernhurst Bks) Motorbooks Intl.

Motor Boating for Beginners. G. Prout. (C). 1987. 25.00 (0-85174-142-8) St Mut.

Motor Boys in Ottawa. 6th ed. Hugh Hood. 304p. 1986. pap. 14.95 (0-7737-5080-0) Genl Dist Srvs.

Motor Buses in Wales, 1898-1932. D. E. Brewster. 52p. (C). 1985. 50.00 (0-7855-3367-2) St Mut.

Motor Camps & Maine Guides: Two Studies. Mia Boynton & Nathan Lowrey. Ed. by Edward D. Ives. (Northeast Folklore Ser.: Vol. XXVIII). (Illus.). 110p. (Orig.). 1991. pap. 10.00 (0-943197-20-1) ME Folklife Ctr.

Motor Car. (ARA., Illus.). (J). (gr. 5-12). 1980. 4.95 (0-86685-209-3) Intl Bk Ctr.

Motor Car Mascots & Badges. Peter W. Card. 1989. pap. 30.00 (0-7478-0117-7, Pub. by Shire Pubns) St Mut.

***Motor Carrier Annual Report.** American Trucking Association, Trucking Informatio. (Financial & Operating Statistics Ser.). 548p. 1999. pap. text 400.00 (0-88711-376-1) Am Trucking Assns.

Motor Carrier Coverage Form Analysis. Diana Kowatch. 86p. 1996. 19.95 (1-56461-177-9) Rough Notes.

Motor Carrier Credit & Collection Practices Manual. rev. ed. American Trucking Association, National Accounting & American Trucking Association, National Freight Cl. 400p. 1992. pap. 155.00 (0-88711-143-2) Am Trucking Assns.

Motor Carrier Entry Regulation in Texas. Jared E. Hazleton. (Policy Research Project Report Ser.: No. 24). 28p. 1978. pap. 3.00 (0-89940-617-3) LBJ Sch Pub Aff.

***Motor Carrier Industry Bar Code Implementation Guide.** (Illus.). 1999. pap. 175.00 (0-88711-397-4) Am Trucking Assns.

Motor Carrier Industry Guide to EDI Implementation & Conventions. 1200p. 1994. pap. 330.00 (0-88711-274-9) Am Trucking Assns.

Motor Carrier Industry in Transition. Transportation Technical Services Staff. (Illus.). 100p. 1999. student ed., ring bd. 95.00 (1-880701-04-9) Trans Tech Srvs.

Motor Carrier Investigator. Jack Rudman. (Career Examination Ser.: C-523). 1994. pap. 27.95 (0-8373-0523-3) Nat Learn.

Motor Carrier Rate Structure: The Need for Basic Revision. Grant M. Davis & Eugene H. Shephard. LC 78-24194. 132p. 1979. 55.00 (0-275-90345-1, C0345, Praeger Pubs) Greenwood.

Motor Carrier Road Atlas 97. 9th ed. pap. 269.55 (0-528-81526-1) Rand McNally.

***Motor Carrier Road Atlas 2000.** Rand McNally Staff. 1999. pap. 19.95 (0-528-84129-7) Rand McNally.

***Motor Carrier Safety: A Guide to Regulatory Compliance.** E. Scott Dunlap. LC 99-51410. (Occupational Safety & Health Guide Ser.). 313p. 2000. 89.95 (1-56670-356-5) Lewis Pubs.

Motor Carrier Safety Regulations. 1982. 1.40 (0-686-31451-4) Private Carrier.

***Motor Carrier Safety Regulations: Management Edition.** Ed. by Tracie Ross. 389p. 2000. pap. 9.95 (0-940394-83-9) Labelmaster.

***Motor Carrier Safety Regulations: Management Edition.** Ed. by Tracie Ross. 389p. 2000. pap. 9.95 (0-940394-85-5) Labelmaster.

***Motor Carrier Safety Regulations: Management Edition.** rev. ed. Ed. by Tracie Ross. 400p. 1999. pap. 7.65 (0-940394-80-4) Labelmaster.

Motor Carrier Safety Standards: Canadian Compliance Manual. Keller, J. J., & Associates, Inc. Staff. LC 90-62525. 500p. 2000. ring bd. 145.00 (0-934674-88-4, 41-M) J J Keller.

***Motor Carrier Technology Directory.** American Trucking Association Staff. 88p. 1999. pap. text 45.00 (0-88711-398-2) Am Trucking Assns.

Motor Carriers Road Atlas. Rand McNally Staff. 1998. pap. 19.95 (0-528-84028-2) Rand McNally.

Motor Carrier's Road Atlas, 1997. deluxe ed. (Illus.). 1996. pap. text 79.95 (0-528-81528-8) Rand McNally.

Motor Carrier's Road Atlas, 1997. rev. ed. Rand McNally Staff. (Illus.). 216p. 1996. pap. text 19.95 (0-528-81525-3) Rand McNally.

Motor Cars & Serv-Us Stations. William D. Jones. LC 98-73202. (Illus.). 160p. 1998. pap. text 30.00 (0-9666342-0-9) Jones Photo.

***Motor City Blue: An Amos Walker Mystery.** Loren D. Estleman. 248p. 2000. reprint ed. pap. 14.00 (0-671-03898-2) ibooks.

Motor City Marquees: A Comprehensive, Illustrated Reference to Motion Picture Theaters in the Detroit Area, 1906-1922. Stuart Galbraith, IV. LC 94-27564. (Illus.). 189p. 1994. lib. bdg. 34.50 (0-89950-915-0) McFarland & Co.

***Motor City Memoirs.** Ed. by Jennifer Thomas Vanadia. (Illus.). 180p. 2000. 39.95 (0-9701305-0-3); pap. 29.95 (0-9701305-1-1) Lorien Studio.

Motor City Muscle: Gordie Howe, Terry Sawchuk & the Championship Detroit Red Wings. Stanley I. Fischler. LC 96-117629. (Illus.). 160p. 1995. pap. 18.95 (1-895629-48-9) Warwick Publ.

Motor City Muscle: High-Powered History of the American Muscle Car. Michael Mueller. LC 97-10100. (Illus.). 192p. 1997. 29.95 (0-7603-0196-4) MBI Pubg.

Motor Coach Permit Guide. Keller, J. J., & Associates, Inc. Staff. LC 92-81286. 550p. 2000. ring bd. 189.00 (1-877798-09-6, 41-G) J J Keller.

An Asterisk (*) at the beginning of an entry indicates that the title is appearing for the first time.

Motor Coaching Bible: A Complete Dogma for the RV Enthusiast. Dave Galey. LC 99-90077. (Illus.). 408p. 1999. pap. 24.95 (*1-890461-14-8*) Winlock Publng Co.
Motor Control. Ed. by G. N. Gantchev et al. LC 87-2326. 232p. 1987. 65.00 (*0-306-42560-2*, Plenum Trade) Perseus Pubng.
Motor Control. International Symposium on Motor Control Staff. Ed. by Alexander A. Gydikov et al. LC 73-19722. (Illus.). 271p. 1973. reprint ed. pap. 84.10 (*0-608-05469-0*, 206593800006) Bks Demand.
Motor Control: Concepts & Issues. Ed. by D. R. Humphrey & H. J. Freund. LC 90-13046. (Dahlem Workshop Reports - Life Sciences). 518p. 1991. 343.95 (*0-471-92919-0*) Wiley.
Motor Control: Theory & Practical Applications. Anne Shumway-Cook & Marjorie H. Woollacott. (Illus.). 496p. 1995. 43.00 (*0-683-07757-0*) Lppncott W & W.
Motor Control: Theory & Practical Applications. 2nd ed. Anne Shumway-Cook & Marjorie H. Wollacott. 552p. 49.95 (*0-683-30643-X*) Lppncott W & W.
Motor Control & Accessories Market (U. S.) Market Intelligence Staff. 284p. 1992. 2400.00 (*1-56753-868-1*, A2494) Frost & Sullivan.
Motor Control & Learning: A Behavioral Emphasis. 3rd ed. Richard A. Schmidt & Timothy D. Lee. LC 98-15263. (Illus.). 512p. 1998. 59.00 (*0-88011-484-3*, BSCH0484) Human Kinetics.
Motor Control & Motor Learning in Rehabilitation. Carolyn Crutchfield & Marylou R. Barnes. (Illus.). 520p. (C). 1993. text 50.00 (*0-936030-06-2*) Stokesville Pub.
Motor Control & Physical Therapy: Theoretical Framework & Practical Applications. Ed. by Patricia C. Montgomery & Barbara Connolly. (Illus.). 240p. (Orig.). (C). 1991. pap. text 34.95 (*1-879971-00-3*) Chattanga Grp.
Motor Control & Sensory Motor Integration: Issues & Directions. Ed. by Denis J. Glencross & Jan P. Piek. LC 95-41895. (Advances in Psychology Ser.: Vol. 111). 462p. 1995. 145.00 (*0-444-81921-5*, QP454) Elsevier.
Motor Control Centers, UL 845. 4th ed. (C). 1995. pap. text 215.00 (*1-55989-713-9*) Underwrtrs Labs.
Motor Control Electronic Handbook. Richard Valentine. LC 98-5074. 700p. 1998. 79.50 (*0-07-066810-8*) McGraw.
Motor Control, Feedback Elements & Variable Speed Drive Markets: Technology Advancements & Production Methods Transform Industry. Market Intelligence Staff. 306p. 1993. 2400.00 (*1-56753-483-X*) Frost & Sullivan.
*__Motor Controls.__ David R. Carpenter. LC 99-32122. (Electricians Technical Reference Ser.). 352p. 1999. 39.95 (*0-8273-8514-5*) Delmar.
*__Motor Coordination Disorders in Children.__ David Sugden & Helen Wright. LC 98-19704. (Developmental Clinical Psychology & Psychiatry Ser.). 136p. 1998. 19.99 (*0-7619-0999-0*) Sage.
Motor Cortex. Hiroshi Asanuma. LC 88-43160. 202p. 1989. reprint ed. pap. 62.70 (*0-608-04671-X*, 206539200004) Bks Demand.
Motor Development & Sport Skills Clinic. Duane G. Millslagle. LC 97-41227. 172p. 1997. pap. 59.95 (*0-7734-8425-6*) E Mellen.
Motor Development in Children. Ed. by Ermellina Fedrizzi et al. (Mariani Foundation Paediatric Neurology Ser.: Vol. 2). (Illus.). 192p. 1994. 68.00 (*0-86196-448-9*, Pub. by J Libbey Med) Bks Intl VA.
Motor Development in Children: Aspects of Coordination & Control. Ed. by M. G. Wade & H. T. Whiting. 1986. lib. bdg. 278.50 (*90-247-3389-8*) Kluwer Academic.
Motor Development in Early & Later Childhood: Longitudinal Approaches. Ed. by Alex F. Kalverboer et al. (Illus.). 403p. (C). 1993. text 99.95 (*0-521-40101-1*) Cambridge U Pr.
Motor Development of Children with Down Syndrome: Birth to Six Years. rev. ed. Ron French & Jack Share. (Illus.). 125p. 1993. reprint ed. teacher ed. 35.00 (*1-878276-46-8*) Educ Systs Assocs Inc.
Motor Equipment Maintenance Foreman. Jack Rudman. (Career Examination Ser.: C-2084). 1994. reprint ed. pap. 29.95 (*0-8373-2084-4*) Nat Learn.
Motor Equipment Maintenance Supervisor. Jack Rudman. (Career Examination Ser.: C-3298). 1994. pap. 29.95 (*0-8373-3298-2*) Nat Learn.
Motor Equipment Manager. Jack Rudman. (Career Examination Ser.: C-359). 1994. pap. 34.95 (*0-8373-0359-1*) Nat Learn.
Motor Equipment Mechanic. Jack Rudman. (Career Examination Ser.: C-459). 1994. pap. 23.95 (*0-8373-0459-8*) Nat Learn.
Motor Equipment Partsman. Jack Rudman. (Career Examination Ser.: C-1790). 1994. pap. 23.95 (*0-8373-1790-8*) Nat Learn.
Motor Equipment Records Assistant. Jack Rudman. (Career Examination Ser.: C-3206). 1994. pap. 27.95 (*0-8373-3206-0*) Nat Learn.
Motor Equipment Repairman. Jack Rudman. (Career Examination Ser.: C-524). 1994. pap. 23.95 (*0-8373-0524-1*) Nat Learn.
Motor Equipment Specialist. Jack Rudman. (Career Examination Ser.: C-3299). 1994. pap. 27.95 (*0-8373-3299-0*) Nat Learn.
Motor Fleet Safety Manual. 4th rev. ed. Ed. by John E. Brodbeck. LC 95-33267. 207p. 1995. 48.95 (*0-87912-188-2*, 22133-0000) Natl Safety Coun.
*__Motor Fleet Safety Supervision: Principals & Practices.__ North American Transportation Management Institute Staff. 1998. pap. 25.00 (*0-88711-390-7*) Am Trucking Assns.
Motor Fleet Safety Supervisor: Principles & Practices. (Illus.). 165p. 1987. pap. text 25.00 (*0-88711-241-2*) Am Trucking Assns.
Motor Flight Through France. Edith Wharton. LC 90-25675. (Illus.). 210p. 1991. reprint ed. pap. text 16.00 (*0-87580-553-1*); reprint ed. lib. bdg. 28.00 (*0-87580-163-3*) N Ill U Pr.
Motor-Flight Through France. Edith Wharton. (Collected Works of Edith Wharton). 201p. 1998. reprint ed. lib. bdg. 88.00 (*1-58201-989-4*) Classic Bks.
Motor-Free Visual Perception Test (MVPT-R) rev. ed. Ronald P. Colarusso & Donald D. Hammill. Ed. by Nancy Martin. 32p. 1995. pap. 27.00 (*0-87879-042-X*, 042-1-A) Acad Therapy.
*__Motor Fuel Tax Laws of North Carolina: 1999 Edition.__ 202p. 2000. pap. 18.00 (*0-327-10454-6*, 3054513) LEXIS Pub.
Motor Fuels: Issues Related to Reformulated Gasoline, Oxygenated Fuels, & Biofuels. (Illus.). 64p. (Orig.). (C). 1996. pap. text 25.00 (*0-7881-3453-1*) DIANE Pub.
Motor Gasoline. Ed. by Keith Owen & E. L. Marshall. 282p. 1995. 156.00 (*0-85404-409-4*, TJ751) CRC Pr.
Motor Gasoline Assessment: Spring 1997. (Illus.). 69p. (C). 1998. pap. text 25.00 (*0-7881-4831-1*) DIANE Pub.
Motor Gasoline Assessment, 1997, Spring. 75p. 1997. pap. 7.50 (*0-16-063488-1*) USGPO.
*__Motor Gasoline Industry: Past, Present & Future.__ Robert Schmer. (Illus.). 56p. (C). 2000. reprint ed. pap. text 20.00 (*0-7881-8736-8*) DIANE Pub.
Motor Goods Distributors. Ed. by ICC Information Group Staff. 1987. 720.00 (*1-85319-042-X*, Pub. by ICC Info Group Ltd) St Mut.
Motor Grader Operator. Jack Rudman. (Career Examination Ser.: C-502). 1994. pap. 27.95 (*0-8373-0502-0*) Nat Learn.
Motor Graders. Jean Eick. (Big Yellow Machines Ser.). (J). (gr. k-3). 1997. pap. text 4.95 (*1-56239-736-2*) ABDO Pub Co.
Motor Graders. Jean Eick. (Big Yellow Machines Ser.). (Illus.). 32p. (J). (gr. k-3). 1997. pap. 5.95 (*0-8172-7239-9*) Raintree Steck-V.
Motor Graders: What in the World Can You Do with a Motor Grader. Jean Eick. (Big Yellow Bk.). (Illus.). 32p. (J). (ps-6). 1996. lib. bdg. 14.99 (*1-888637-05-6*) Venture MN.
Motor Growth & Development. 1980. 6.00 (*0-939418-20-7*) Ferguson-Florissant.
Motor Home Rental Guide. William L. Galloway. (Illus.). 110p. 1980. spiral bd. 7.95 (*0-9604230-0-1*) B&G Assoc.
Motor Industries of South America & Mexico. South AmeriCar Staff. LC 99-172465. (Research Reports: Bo. R344). 314 p. 1997. 945.00 (*0-85058-923-1*, R344) Economist Intell.
Motor Industries of South America & Mexico No. R325: Poised for Growth. 1994. 770.00 (*0-85058-815-4*) Economist Intell.
Motor Installation, Clustering & Staging. Jerry Irvine & Korey Kline. (Advanced Information Reports: Nos. 1-3). 12p. 1984. 1.99 (*0-912468-01-7*, AIR-3) CA Rocketry.
Motor Insurance. Michael G. Collins. 120p. (C). 1989. 75.00 (*0-948691-74-3*, Pub. by Witherby & Co) St Mut.
Motor Insurance Theory & Practice. Kenneth Cannar. 410p. (C). 1979. 150.00 (*0-900886-24-2*, Pub. by Witherby & Co) St Mut.
Motor Insurance Theory & Practice. Kenneth Cannar. 450p. (C). 1995. 120.00 (*1-85609-065-5*, Pub. by Witherby & Co) St Mut.
Motor Law, Vol. 1. W. E. Cooper. 740p. 1982. 50.00 (*0-7021-1253-4*, Pub. by Juta & Co) Gaunt.
Motor Law, Vol. 2. W. E. Cooper. 507p. 1987. 68.00 (*0-7021-1906-7*, Pub. by Juta & Co) Gaunt.
Motor Learning. 5th ed. Magill. 1997. lab manual ed. write for info. (*0-697-38953-7*) McGrw-H Hghr Educ.
*__Motor Learning: A Practical Guide.__ 2nd ed. Douglas E. Young & William S. Husak. 118p. (C). 2000. pap. text 36.95 (*1-57879-004-2*) E Bowers Pub.
Motor Learning: An Experiential Guide for Teachers. E. Doris McKinney. 1985p. pap. 24.95 (*0-932392-25-3*) Mouvement Pubns.
Motor Learning: Concepts & Application. 4th ed. Richard A. Magill. 480p. (C). 1996. text. write for info. (*0-697-38984-7*, WCB McGr Hill) McGrw-H Hghr Educ.
Motor Learning: Concepts & Application. 5th ed. Richard A. Magill. LC 97-16623. 352p. (C). 1997. text. write for info. (*0-697-24652-3*, WCB McGr Hill) McGrw-H Hghr Educ.
*__Motor Learning: Concepts & Application.__ 6th ed. Richard A. Magill. (Illus.). 384p. 2001. Price not set. (*0-07-232936-X*) McGraw.
Motor Learning: Concepts & Applications. 4th ed. Richard A. Magill. 480p. (C). 1992. text. write for info. (*0-697-12643-9*) Brown & Benchmark.
Motor Learning & Control. Charles H. Shea et al. 368p. (C). 1993. 80.00 (*0-13-605684-9*) P-H.
Motor Learning & Performance. 2nd fac. ed. Richard A. Schmidt & Craig A. Wrisberg. LC 99-28368. (Illus.). 352p. (C). 1999. text 45.00 (*0-88011-500-9*, BSCH0500) Human Kinetics.
Motor Learning & Synaptic Plasticity in the Cerebellum. Ed. by Paul J. Cordo et al. LC 97-1229. (Illus.). 206p. (C). 1997. text 80.00 (*0-521-59286-0*); pap. text 34.95 (*0-521-59705-6*) Cambridge U Pr.
Motor Learning Applied to Sports. 4th ed. Marilyn Colby. (Illus.). 208p. (C). 2000. pap. text 27.95 (*0-89641-290-3*) American Pr.
Motor Learning Concepts & Appl. 4th ed. Magill. 1992. 63.75 (*0-697-12645-5*) McGraw.
Motor Learning in Childhood Education: Curricular, Compensatory, Cognitive. James H. Humphrey. 206p. 1992. pap. 31.95 (*0-398-06165-3*) C C Thomas.
Motor Learning in Childhood Education: Curricular, Compensatory, Cognitive. James H. Humphrey. 206p. (C). 1992. text 44.95 (*0-398-05795-8*) C C Thomas.
Motor Learning Laboratory Manual. 2nd ed. Larry Hall. 186p. (C). 1998. spiral bd. 19.95 (*0-7872-3271-8*, 41327101) Kendall-Hunt.
Motor Learning Lecture Notes. Larry Hall. 532p. (C). 1996. pap. text, spiral bd. 33.95 (*0-7872-2872-9*) Kendall-Hunt.
Motor Learning Lecture Notes. 2nd ed. Larry Hall. 540p. (C). 1998. spiral bd. 41.95 (*0-7872-3270-X*, 41327001) Kendall-Hunt.
Motor Neuron Disease. 1995. text 145.00 (*3-540-19685-4*) Spr-Verlag.
Motor Neuron Disease. Ed. by P. N. Leigh & Michael Swash. LC 94-14875. (Illus.). 486p. 1995. 135.00 (*0-387-19685-4*) Spr-Verlag.
Motor Neurone Disease. Ed. by Gourie Devi. (C). 1987. 50.00 (*81-204-0195-6*, Pub. by Oxford IBH) S Asia.
Motor Neurone Disease. Ian Robinson & Margaret Hunter. LC 97-32221. 160p. (C). 1998. pap. 22.99 (*0-415-09711-8*) Routledge.
Motor Neurone Disease (Amyotrophic Lateral Sclerosis) S. Beresford. 196p. 1995. pap. 41.50 (*1-56593-318-4*, 0648) Singular Publishing.
Motor-Operated Air Compressors, Vacuum Pumps, & Painting Equipment, UL 1450. 2nd ed. (C). 1993. pap. text 230.00 (*1-55989-371-0*) Underwrtrs Labs.
Motor-Operated Appliances, UL 73. 8th ed. (C). 1993. pap. text 95.00 (*1-55989-273-0*) Underwrtrs Labs.
Motor-Operated Commercial Food Preparing Machines, UL 763. 2nd ed. (C). 1993. pap. text 95.00 (*1-55989-490-3*) Underwrtrs Labs.
Motor-Operated Household Food Preparing Machines, UL 982. 4th ed. (C). 1995. pap. text 95.00 (*1-55989-799-6*) Underwrtrs Labs.
Motor-Operated Massage & Exercise Machines, UL 1647. 3rd ed. (C). 1997. pap. text 215.00 (*1-55989-188-2*) Underwrtrs Labs.
Motor-Operated Valve (MOV) Actuator Motor & Gearbox Testing. K. DeWall. 52p. 1997. pap. 5.00 (*0-16-054688-5*) USGPO.
Motor Operated Water Pumps, UL 778. 3rd ed. (C). 1996. pap. text 135.00 (*1-55989-992-1*) Underwrtrs Labs.
Motor Performance in Adolescence. Anna Espenschade. (SRCD Ser.: Vol. 5, No. 1). 1940. 25.00 (*0-527-01513-X*) Periodicals Srv.
Motor Problem Resolution & Avoidance. Stanley Consultants Staff & National Rural Electric Cooperative Association St. LC 98-8184. 1998. write for info. (*0-917599-21-7*) Natl Rural.
*__Motor Racing.__ Konemann Inc. Staff. (Illus.). 350p. 2000. pap. 9.95 (*3-8290-3625-6*) Konemann.
Motor Relearning Programme for Stroke. 2nd ed. Janet H. Carr & Roberta B. Shepherd. 198p. (C). 1987. 54.00 (*0-87189-312-6*) Aspen Pub.
Motor Repairers. (Survive & Prosper Ser.). 78p. 1994. 17.95 (*0-644-32432-5*, Pub. by Aust Gov Pub) Accents Pubns.
Motor Skills - Grades PK-K: Preparing to Read & Write. Jo Ellen Moore. (Illus.). 32p. (J). (ps-k). 1995. pap., wbk. ed. 2.50 (*1-58610-023-8*, Learn on the Go) Learn Horizon.
Motor Skills Acquisition in the First Year: An Illustrated Guide to Normal Development. Lois Bly. (Illus.). 1998. pap. text 67.00 (*0-12-784552-6*) Acad Pr.
Motor Speech Disorders. Frederick L. Darley et al. LC 74-25475. (Illus.). 304p. 1975. text 68.00 (*0-7216-2878-8*, W B Saunders Co) Harcrt Hlth Sci Grp.
Motor Speech Disorders. James Paul Dworkin. 351p. (C). (gr. 13). 1991. text 49.95 (*1-55664-223-7*) Mosby Inc.
Motor Speech Disorders: Substrates & Differential. Joseph R. Duffy. (Illus.). 480p. (gr. 13). 1995. text 54.00 (*0-8016-6944-8*, 06944) Mosby Inc.
Motor Speech Disorders in Children. Caruso. LC 99-17630. (Illus.). 384p. 1999. 45.00 (*0-86577-762-4*) Thieme Med Pubs.
Motor Sports. (Illus.). 768p. 304.00 (*0-7368-0127-8*) Capstone Pr.
Motor Sports in the Twenties. A. B. Demaus. 120p. 1989. 24.95 (*0-86299-599-X*, 3-AQ-0063) Auto Quarterly.
Motor Thalamus. Ed. by P. L. Gildenberg et al. (Journal Ser.: Vol. 60, Nos. 1-3, 1993). (Illus.). 156p. 1993. pap. 109.75 (*3-8055-5756-6*) S Karger.
Motor Trade, 2 bks. in 1 Norm Foster. LC 94-153458. 216p. (Orig.). 1997. pap. 14.95 (*0-88754-491-6*) Theatre Comm.
Motor Transport. Margaret Walsh. LC 97-32125. (Studies in Transport History Ser.). 236p. 1997. text 61.95 (*1-85928-345-4*) Ashgate Pub Co.
Motor Truck Engineering Handbook. 4th ed. James W. Fitch. LC 93-35469. 452p. 1993. 39.00 (*1-56091-378-9*, R-125) Soc Auto Engineers.
Motor Unit, Neuromuscular Disorders, Electromyographic Kinesiology see New Developments in Electromyography & Clinical Neurophysiology
Motor Unit Types, Recruitment & Plasticity in Health & Disease. Ed. by J. E. Desmedt. (Progress in Clinical Neurophysiology Ser.: Vol. 9). (Illus.). x, 418p. 1981. 128.75 (*3-8055-1929-X*) S Karger.
Motor Vehicle. 9th ed. K. Newton et al. 1972. 26.50 (*0-592-00070-2*) Transatl Arts.
Motor Vehicle. 11th ed. K. Newton & W. Steeds. 880p. 1989. text 79.95 (*0-7506-0407-7*) Buttrwrth-Heinemann.
Motor Vehicle. 12th ed. K. Newton et al. (Illus.). 1016p. 2000. pap. text 74.95 (*0-7506-3763-3*) Buttrwrth-Heinemann.
Motor Vehicle. 12th ed. K. Newton et al. 976p. 1996. 85.00 (*1-56091-898-5*, R-172) Soc Auto Engineers.
Motor Vehicle Accident Reconstruction: Review & Update. 196p. 1989. 39.00 (*0-89883-434-1*, SP777) Soc Auto Engineers.
Motor Vehicle Accident Reconstruction & Cause Analysis. 3rd ed. Rudolph Limpert. (Illus.). 843p. 1989. boxed set 110.00 (*0-87473-462-2*, MICHIE) LEXIS Pub.
Motor Vehicle Accident Reconstruction & Cause Analysis. 4th ed. Rudolf Limpert. LC 94-79932. 876p. 1994. 85.00 (*1-55834-207-9*, 64362-11, MICHIE) LEXIS Pub.
Motor Vehicle Accident Reconstruction & Cause Analysis. 4th ed. Rudolf Limpert. 1995. suppl. ed. 20.00 (*0-614-25249-0*, 64363, MICHIE) LEXIS Pub.
*__Motor Vehicle Accident Reconstruction & Cause Analysis.__ 5th ed. Rudolf Limpert. 1000p. 1999. write for info. (*0-327-04974-X*, 6436212) LEXIS Pub.
Motor Vehicle Accident Reconstruction & Cause Analysis, 1998 Supplement. 4th ed. Rudolf Limpert. (Illus.). 100p. 1998. write for info. (*0-327-00846-6*, 6436311) LEXIS Pub.
Motor Vehicle Air Conditioning Certification Manual & Exam: Federal Clean Air Act Section 609. 3rd rev. ed. (Section 609 MVA Certification Exam Ser.). (Illus.). 11p. 1997. pap. 20.00 (*1-930044-05-4*) East Lake Pubg.
Motor Vehicle Batteries in Italy: A Strategic Entry Report, 1995. Compiled by Icon Group International Staff. (Illus.). 125p. 1999. ring bd. 1250.00 incl. audio compact disk (*0-7418-0689-4*) Icon Grp.
Motor Vehicle Bureau Supervisor. Jack Rudman. (Career Examination Ser.: C-3574). 1994. pap. 34.95 (*0-8373-3574-4*) Nat Learn.
Motor Vehicle Cashier. Jack Rudman. (Career Examination Ser.: C-1722). 1994. pap. 19.95 (*0-8373-1722-3*) Nat Learn.
Motor Vehicle Collision Injuries: Mechanisms, Diagnosis & Management. Lawrence Nordhoff. 391p. 1995. 72.00 (*0-8342-0727-3*) Aspen Pub.
Motor Vehicle Dispatcher. Jack Rudman. (Career Examination Ser.: C-503). 1994. pap. 23.95 (*0-8373-0503-9*) Nat Learn.
Motor Vehicle Dynamics: Modelling & Simulation. LC 96-51020. 500p. 1997. lib. bdg. 59.00 (*981-02-2911-9*) World Scientific Pub.
Motor Vehicle Foreman. Jack Rudman. (Career Examination Ser.: C-1781). 1994. pap. 29.95 (*0-8373-1781-9*) Nat Learn.
Motor Vehicle Fuel Economy. Richard Stone. (Illus.). 234p. (C). 1989. pap. text 32.50 (*0-333-43820-5*) Scholium Intl.
Motor-Vehicle Inspection & Maintenance in California. Buzz Breadlove. 42p. 1993. pap. write for info. (*1-58703-013-6*, CRB-93-007) CA St Libry.
Motor Vehicle Inspector. Jack Rudman. (Career Examination Ser.: C-2384). 1994. pap. 27.95 (*0-8373-2384-3*) Nat Learn.
Motor Vehicle Investigator. Jack Rudman. (Career Examination Ser.: C-504). 1994. pap. 27.95 (*0-8373-0504-7*) Nat Learn.
Motor Vehicle Law. Margaret C. Jasper. LC 99-167937. (Legal Almanac Ser.). 130p. 1998. text 22.50 (*0-379-11329-5*, 4582403) Oceana.
Motor Vehicle Law & Practice & Related Topics with Forms. 3rd ed. Raymond J. Kenney. LC 98-60564. (Massachusetts Practice Ser.). 1998. write for info. (*0-314-23574-4*) West Pub.
*__Motor Vehicle Law & the Law of Impaired Driving in North Carolina.__ Ben F. Loeb, Jr. & James C. Drennan. (C). 2000. pap. 16.50 (*1-56011-360-X*) Institute Government.
*__Motor Vehicle Law & the Law of Impaired Driving in North Carolina.__ Ben F. Loeb, Jr. & James C. Drennan. (C). 2000. cd-rom. write for info. (*1-56011-383-9*) Institute Government.
Motor Vehicle Law of North Carolina, 1993 Edition. 1993. 25.00 (*0-614-05908-9*, MICHIE) LEXIS Pub.
*__Motor Vehicle Laws of North Carolina Legislative Service: 1999 Edition.__ 224p. 1999. pap. write for info. (*0-327-09869-4*, 3031810) LEXIS Pub.
Motor Vehicle Laws of North Carolina with Cd-rom: 1999 Edition. Publisher's Editorial Staff. 1083p. pap. 34.00 (*0-327-10153-9*) LEXIS Pub.
Motor Vehicle Laws of North Carolina, 1998 Supplement. 141p. 1999. pap. write for info. (*0-327-07736-0*, 3051812) LEXIS Pub.
Motor Vehicle Laws of Vermont: 1998 Edition. Lexis Law Publishing Staff. 550p. 1998. write for info. (*0-327-06578-8*) LEXIS Pub.
*__Motor Vehicle Laws of Vermont, 1999 Edition.__ 580p. 1999. 40.00 (*0-327-09961-5*, 3410515) LEXIS Pub.
Motor Vehicle License Clerk. Jack Rudman. (Career Examination Ser.: C-505). 1994. pap. 23.95 (*0-8373-0505-5*) Nat Learn.
Motor Vehicle License Examiner. Jack Rudman. (Career Examination Ser.: C-506). 1994. pap. 23.95 (*0-8373-0506-3*) Nat Learn.
Motor Vehicle License Examiner 1. Jack Rudman. (Career Examination Ser.: C-1937). 1994. pap. 27.95 (*0-8373-1937-4*) Nat Learn.
Motor Vehicle Licensing Supervisor. Jack Rudman. (Career Examination Ser.: C-2809). 1994. pap. 29.95 (*0-8373-2809-8*) Nat Learn.
Motor Vehicle Lighting. Ed. by George J. Gaudaen. 536p. 1996. 89.00 (*1-56091-753-9*, PT-60) Soc Auto Engineers.
Motor Vehicle Occupant Protection Program. Mark M. Moran. (OSHA Written Compliance Programs Ser.: No. 20). (Illus.). 20p. 1992. ring bd. 169.00 (*1-890966-14-2*) Moran Assocs.
Motor Vehicle Officer. Jack Rudman. (Career Examination Ser.: C-2031). 1994. pap. 27.95 (*0-8373-2031-3*) Nat Learn.
Motor Vehicle Operator. Jack Rudman. (Career Examination Ser.: C-507). 1994. pap. 23.95 (*0-8373-0507-1*) Nat Learn.
Motor Vehicle Operator (U. S. P. S.) Jack Rudman. (Career Examination Ser.: C-508). 1994. pap. 23.95 (*0-8373-0508-X*) Nat Learn.

M

Motor Vehicle Parts Aftermarket: An Analysis of Current Markets & Prospects for Future Growth. R. Ebbin. 647p. 1999. 1495.00 (*0-317-55195-7*) Busn Trend.

Motor Vehicle Pollution: Reduction Strategies Beyond 2010. 133p. (Orig.). 1995. pap. 29.00 (*92-64-14312-2*, Pub. by Org for Econ) OECD.

Motor Vehicle Program Manager. Jack Rudman. (Career Examination Ser.: C-311). 1994. pap. 34.95 (*0-8373-0311-7*) Nat Learn.

Motor Vehicle Referee. Jack Rudman. (Career Examination Ser.: C-2330). 1994. pap. 34.95 (*0-8373-2330-4*) Nat Learn.

Motor Vehicle Representative. Jack Rudman. (Career Examination Ser.: C-3258). 1994. pap. 23.95 (*0-8373-3258-3*) Nat Learn.

Motor Vehicle Safety: Comprehensive State Programs Offers Best Opportunities for Increasing Use of Safety Belts. (Illus.). 49p. (Orig.). (C). 1996. pap. text 20.00 (*0-7881-3112-5*) DIANE Pub.

Motor Vehicle Safety Design Innovations. 1997. 99.00 (*1-56091-938-8*, SP-1226) Soc Auto Engineers.

Motor Vehicle Safety Pocket Guide. John V. Conforti. (Illus.). 63p. (Orig.). 1992. pap. 41.80 (*0-931690-48-X*) Genium Pub.

Motor Vehicle Size & Weight Regulations, Enforcement, & Permit Operations. (National Cooperative Highway Research Program Report Ser.: No. 68). 45p. 1980. 6.00 (*0-309-03019-6*) Transport Res Bd.

Motor Vehicle Supervisor. Jack Rudman. (Career Examination Ser.: C-3544-2). 1994. pap. 29.95 (*0-8373-3544-2*) Nat Learn.

Motor Vehicles see Rhode Island General Laws, 1998 Cumulative Supplement

Motor Vehicles see Burns Indiana Statutes Annotated 1999 Cumulative Supplement Set: Pocket Part

Motor Vehicles, Connecticut: Condensed Guide. 2000. spiral bd. 5.95 (*0-930137-68-X*) Looseleaf Law.

Motor Vehicles Field Manual for Law Enforcement Officers, Connecticut "The Blue Book" Ronald T. Sullivan. 100p. 2000. ring bd. 8.95 (*0-930137-76-0*) Looseleaf Law.

***Motor viehicle.** 3rd ed. Garrett. 2000. 125.00 (*0-7506-4449-4*) Buttrwrth-Heinemann.

Motorbikes. Philip Raby & Simon Nix. LC 98-48685. (Need for Speed Ser.). 32p. (J). (gr. 3-9). 1999. 18.60 (*0-8225-2486-4*, Lerner Publctns) Lerner Pub.

Motorbikes. Philip Raby & Simon Nix. (Need for Speed Ser.). 32p. (YA). (gr. 5-10). 1999. pap. 23.93 (*0-8225-9854-X*, LernerSports) Lerner Pub.

Motorboat & Yachting Log Book for Cruising under Power. Tom Willis & Tim Bartlett. 96p. (C). 1990. text 59.00 (*0-906754-61-5*, Pub. by Fernhurst Bks) St Mut.

Motorboater's Guide to Lake Winnipesaukee: Exploring the Lake by Boat. J. E. Clay. Ed. by Heidi Perlman & Carl Lichenstein. LC 97-97173. (Illus.). 64p. 1998. pap. 8.95 (*0-9661870-0-8*) Oceanview.

Motorboating. Boy Scouts of America. (Illus.). 64p. (YA). (gr. 6-12). 1996. pap. 2.90 (*0-8395-3345-4*, 33345) BSA.

Motorboating: A Complete Guide. Bill Pike. LC 95-12176. 176p. 1995. pap. 17.95 (*1-56799-206-4*, Friedman-Fairfax) M Friedman Pub Grp Inc.

Motorcourse, 1995-1996. annuals Mike Scott. (Illus.). 208p. 1995. 49.95 (*1-874557-41-1*, Pub. by Hazelton) Motorbooks Intl.

Motorcourse, 1997-1998. Michael Scott. (Illus.). 192p. 1997. 54.95 (*1-874557-52-7*, Pub. by Hazelton) Motorbooks Intl.

***Motorcross & Off-Road Motorcycle Performance Handbook.** 2nd ed. Eric Gorr. (Cyclepro Ser.). (Illus.). 224p. 2000. pap. 21.95 (*0-7603-0660-5*, 129997AP, Pub. by MBI Pubg) Motorbooks Intl.

Motorcross Cycles. S. X. Carser. (Cruisin' Ser.). (Illus.). 48p. (J). (gr. 3-6). 1992. 19.00 (*0-516-35069-2*) Childrens.

Motorcycle. Deni Bown. (Ultimate Sticker Books Ser.). (Illus.). 20p. (J). (ps-3). 1995. pap. 6.95 (*0-7894-0010-3*) DK Pub Inc.

***Motorcycle.** Kindersley Publishing Dorling. 10p. (J). (gr. k-2). 1999. 4.95 (*0-7894-4733-9*) DK Pub Inc.

Motorcycle. André Pieyre de Mandiargues. Tr. by Richard Howard from FRE. LC 76-40432. 187p. 1977. reprint ed. lib. bdg. 55.00 (*0-8371-9061-4*, MAMC, Greenwood Pr) Greenwood.

Motorcycle: Cross-Country Racing. Gene Tardy & Al Jackson. (Sports Action Ser.). (Illus.). (J). (gr. 3-7). 1974. lib. bdg. 9.89 (*0-914844-00-8*) J Alden.

Motorcycle: Grand Prix Racing. Gene Tardy & Al Jackson. (Sports Action Ser.). (Illus.). (J). (gr. 3-7). 1974. lib. bdg. 9.89 (*0-914844-01-6*) J Alden.

Motorcycle Accessories in France: A Strategic Entry Report, 1997. Compiled by Icon Group International Staff. (Illus.). 118p. 1999. ring bd. 1180.00 incl. audio compact disk (*0-7418-0770-X*) Icon Grp.

Motorcycle Accident Investigation. 2nd ed. Albert T. Baxter. 261p. (C). 1997. pap. text 44.50 (*1-884566-09-X*) Inst Police Tech.

Motorcycle Accident Investigation. 2nd rev. ed. Albert T. Baxter. LC 97-183937. (Illus.). 348p. 1997. pap. text 44.50 (*1-884566-21-9*) Inst Police Tech.

Motorcycle Accident Reconstruction & Litigation. 2nd ed. Kenneth S. Obenski & Paul F. Hill. LC 96-32923. 1133p. 1997. 110.00 (*0-913875-97-X*, 5031-N) Lawyers & Judges.

Motorcycle Arizona! A Guide to Touring Arizona by Motorcycle. Frank Del Monte. LC 94-38135. (Illus.). 160p. (Orig.). 1994. pap. 9.95 (*0-914846-99-X*) Golden West Pub.

Motorcycle Collectibles. Leila Dunbar. LC 96-644. (Illus.). 216p. (YA). (gr. 10-13). 1996. pap. write for info. (*0-88740-947-4*) Schiffer.

***Motorcycle Cruiser Performance & Customizing Guide.** Tim Remus. (Illus.). 144p. 2000. pap. 24.95 (*1-929133-02-2*, 130731AE, Pub. by Wolfgang Pubns) Motorbooks Intl.

***Motorcycle Design & Technology.** Gaetano Cocco. (Illus.). 272p. 2000. 44.95 (*88-7911-189-2*, 129466AE, Pub. by Giorgio Nada Editore) Motorbooks Intl.

Motorcycle Diaries: A Journey Around South America. Ernesto Guevara. 1996. pap. 15.00 (*1-85984-066-3*, Pub. by Verso) Norton.

Motorcycle Diaries: A Journey Around South America. Ernesto-Che Guevara. LC 95-15530. (Illus.). 160p. 1995. 25.00 (*1-85984-971-7*, B4967, Pub. by Verso) Norton.

Motorcycle Drag Racing see Drag Racing

Motorcycle Drag Racing. Martin Hintz & Kate Hintz. (Drag Racing Ser.). (Illus.). 48p. (J). (gr. 3-7). 1996. 19.00 (*0-516-20239-1*) Childrens.

Motorcycle Electrical Manual 3rd ed. A. Tranter. LC 98-71630. (Tech Bks.). 1998. 23.95 (*1-85960-471-4*) Haynes Manuals.

Motorcycle Electrics Without Pain. Mike Arman. (Illus.). 1980. pap. 11.00 (*0-933078-03-X*) M Arman.

***Motorcycle Enlightenment.** Charles H. Sides. 2000. pap. 12.95 (*1-57174-172-0*) N D Walsch.

***Motorcycle Fuel Systems TechBook.** John Robinson. (Illus.). 256p. 2000. 23.95 (*1-85960-514-1*, 130364AM, Pub. by Haynes Manuals) Motorbooks Intl.

***Motorcycle Guide to Route 66: Complete Information for Touring Historic Route 66 on Two Wheels.** (Illus.). 148p. 2000. pap. 19.95 (*1-929954-06-9*) H H J M Inc.

Motorcycle Guide to the Golden Triangle. David Unkovich. 208p. 1998. pap. 10.00 (*974-7100-36-3*) U of Wash Pr.

***Motorcycle Handbook.** Chilton Automotive Editorial Staff. (New Total Service Ser.). (C). 1998. pap. text 22.95 (*0-8019-9099-8*) Thomson Learn.

Motorcycle Identification. Lee S. Cole. 159p. (Orig.). 1986. pap. 9.00 (*0-939818-11-6*) Lee Bks.

***Motorcycle Jackets: A Century of Leather Design.** Rin Tanaka. (Illus.). 272p. 2000. 69.95 (*0-7643-1150-6*) Schiffer.

***Motorcycle Journeys Through California.** Clement Salvadori. (Motorcycle Journeys Ser.). (Illus.). 320p. 2000. pap. 24.95 (*1-884313-18-3*, MJCA) Whitehorse NH.

Motorcycle Journeys Through New England: You Don't Have to Get Lost to Find the Good Roads. 2nd ed. Martin C. Berke. (Motorcycle Journeys Ser.). (Illus.). 224p. 1994. pap., per. 19.95 (*0-9621834-8-2*) Whitehorse NH.

***Motorcycle Journeys Through Northern Mexico.** Neal Davis. (Motorcycle Journeys Ser.). (Illus.). 221p. 1999. pap. 19.95 (*1-884313-20-5*, MJNM) Whitehorse NH.

Motorcycle Journeys Through the Alps & Corsica. 2nd rev. ed. John Hermann. (Motorcycle Journeys Ser.). (Illus.). 303p. 1998. pap. 19.95 (*1-884313-12-4*) Whitehorse NH.

Motorcycle Journeys Through the Appalachians. Dale Coyner. (Motorcycle Journeys Ser.). (Illus.). 320p. 1995. pap. 19.95 (*1-884313-02-7*) Whitehorse NH.

Motorcycle Journeys Through the Baja. Clement Salvadori. (Motorcycle Journeys Ser.). (Illus.). 239p. (Orig.). 1997. pap. 19.95 (*1-884313-08-6*) Whitehorse NH.

Motorcycle Journeys Through the Southwest. Martin C. Berke. LC 95-229145. (Motorcycle Journeys Ser.). (Illus.). 432p. 1994. pap. 19.95 (*0-9621834-9-0*) Whitehorse NH.

Motorcycle Legends: Harley Davidson. Roy Bacon. (Illus.). 1995. 19.95 (*0-7858-0253-3*) Bk Sales Inc.

Motorcycle Mania: Harley-Davidson: The Power, the Glory, the Legend Lives. Graham Scott. (Illus.). 80p. 1995. pap. 14.95 (*0-312-13334-0*) St Martin.

Motorcycle Mania: The Biker Book. Ed. by Matthew Drutt. 128p. 1998. 27.50 (*0-7893-0132-6*, Pub. by Universe) St Martin.

Motorcycle Marines: An Illustrated History. Jack Sands. 32p. 1985. pap. 12.95 (*0-938242-12-1*) Portrayal.

Motorcycle Memories. Nona K. Carver. 18p. (Orig.). 1994. pap. 5.00 (*0-9641195-7-9*) Carver Cntry.

Motorcycle Milestones, Vol. 1. Richard Renstrom. LC 80-66669. (Illus.). 112p. 1980. 20.00 (*0-936660-00-7*) Classics Unltd.

Motorcycle Owner's Manual. Hugo Wilson. LC 96-35925. 112p. 1997. spiral bd. 9.95 (*0-7894-1615-8*) DK Pub Inc.

Motorcycle Police. Michael Green. 1999. 19.00 (*0-531-11810-X*) Capstone Pr.

***Motorcycle Police.** Michael Green. LC 98-31540. 1999. write for info. (*0-7368-0187-1*) Capstone Pr.

Motorcycle Racing see MotorSports

Motorcycle Racing. Bill Holden. 1994. 15.98 (*0-7858-0021-2*) Bk Sales Inc.

Motorcycle Racing in America: A Definitive Look at the Sport. Jim Spence & Gar Brown. LC 74-6144. (Illus.). 144p. 1977. pap. 6.95 (*0-87955-418-5*) O'Hara.

Motorcycle Restores Workshop Manual. Geoff Purnell. (Illus.). 160p. 1992. 32.95 (*1-85260-393-3*) Haynes Manuals.

***Motorcycle Roadcraft: The Police Rider's Handbook to Better Motorcycling.** Philip Coyne. 178p. 2000. pap. 24.00 (*0-11-341143-X*, Pub. by Statnry Office) Balogh.

Motorcycle Sex: or Freud Would Never Understand the Relationship Between Me & My Motorcycle. 2nd ed. Gregory W. Frazier. LC 94-202752. (Illus.). 150p. (Orig.). (C). 1999. pap. 22.95 (*0-935151-19-2*) Arrowstar Pub.

Motorcycle Song. Diane Siebert. (Illus.). 32p. (J). (ps-3). 15.95 (*0-06-028732-2*); 15.89 (*0-06-028733-0*); 5.95 (*0-06-443632-2*) HarpC.

Motorcycle Touring: An International Directory - 1991-92. Ed. by Susie De Ville. (Illus.). 360p. 1991. pap., per. 19.95 (*0-9621834-3-1*) Whitehorse NH.

Motorcycle Touring: An International Directory - 1993-94 Supplement. Ed. by Daniel W. Kennedy. (Illus.). 224p. 1993. pap., per. 9.95 (*0-9621834-7-4*) Whitehorse NH.

Motorcycle Toys: Antique & Contemporary. Christine Gentry. (Illus.). 296p. 1995. pap. 18.95 (*0-89145-618-X*, 3888) Collector Bks.

Motorcycle Tuning: Chassis. John Robinson. (Illus.). 259p. 1994. pap. text 36.95 (*0-7506-1840-X*) Buttrwrth-Heinemann.

Motorcycle Tuning: Four-Stroke. 2nd ed. John Robinson. 160p. 1994. pap. text 36.95 (*0-7506-1805-1*) Buttrwrth-Heinemann.

Motorcycle Tuning: Two-Stroke. 2nd ed. John Robinson. 144p. 2000. pap. text 36.95 (*0-7506-1806-X*) Buttrwrth-Heinemann.

Motorcycle Turbocharging, Supercharging & Nitrous Oxide: A Complete Guide to Forced Induction & Its Use on Modern Motorcycle Engines. Joe Haile. (Tech Ser.). (Illus.). 198p. (Orig.). 1997. pap. 19.95 (*1-884313-07-8*) Whitehorse NH.

Motorcycle Vagabonding in Japan. Guy de La Rupelle. (Motorcycle Journey Ser.). (Illus.). 255p. 1999. pap. 19.95 (*1-884313-16-7*, GUY) Whitehorse NH.

Motorcycles see Cruisin'

Motorcycles see Rollin'

Motorcycles see Transportation Series

Motorcycles see Motocicletas

Motorcycles. Mark Dunster. LC 77-155954. (Rin Ser.: Pt. 7). 1978. pap. 4.00 (*0-89642-006-X*) Linden Pubs.

Motorcycles. Don Emde. (The Confident Collector Ser.). 1995. pap. 14.00 (*0-380-77217-5*, Avon Bks) Morrow Avon.

Motorcycles. Ian Graham. LC 97-51302. (Built for Speed Ser.). (Illus.). 32p. (J). (gr. 3-7). 1998. pap. 7.95 (*0-8172-8074-X*) Raintree Steck-V.

Motorcycles. Ian Graham. LC 97-51302. (Built for Speed Ser.). (J). (gr. 3-7). 1999. 22.83 (*0-8172-4223-6*) Raintree Steck-V.

Motorcycles. Ian Graham. LC 97-5963. (Worldwise Ser.). 40p. (J). (gr. 2 up). 1998. 23.00 (*0-531-14464-X*) Watts.

Motorcycles. Ian Graham. (Worldwise Ser.). (Illus.). 40p. (J). (gr. 3-7). 1998. pap. 7.00 (*0-531-15321-5*) Watts.

Motorcycles. Dee Ready. (Early-Reader Science Transportation Ser.). 24p. (J). (gr. k-3). 1997. lib. bdg. 14.00 (*0-516-20904-3*) Childrens.

Motorcycles. Jeff Savage. LC 97-8679. (Race Car Legends Ser.). (Illus.). 64p. (J). (gr. 3 up). 1997. 15.95 (*0-7910-4433-5*) Chelsea Hse.

Motorcycles, 4 bks. Jesse Young. Incl. Dirt Bikes. LC 94-22827. (Illus.). 48p. (J). (gr. 3-4). 1994. lib. bdg. 19.00 (*1-56065-226-8*, Cpstone High Low); Harley-Davidson Motorcycles. LC 94-26767. (Illus.). 48p. (J). (gr. 3-4). 1994. lib. bdg. 19.00 (*1-56065-224-1*, Cpstone High Low); Sidecar Motorcycles. LC 94-29979. (Illus.). 48p. (J). (gr. 3-4). 1994. lib. bdg. 19.00 (*1-56065-225-X*, Cpstone High Low); Street Bikes. LC 94-22828. (Illus.). 48p. (J). (gr. 4-7). 1994. lib. bdg. 19.00 (*1-56065-227-6*, Cpstone High Low); 76.00 (*1-56065-651-4*, Cpstone High Low) Capstone Pr.

Motorcycles. Jesse Young et al. (Illus.). 48p. 159.60 (*0-7368-0551-6*) Capstone Pr.

Motorcycles: Fundamentals, Service & Repair. Bruce A. Johns et al. LC 98-23297. 1998. text 44.60 (*1-56637-479-0*) Goodheart.

Motorcycles: Index of New Information with Authors, Subjects & References. Fred L. Widmer. 150p. 1996. 47.50 (*0-7883-1258-8*); pap. 44.50 (*0-7883-1259-6*) ABBE Pubs Assn.

Motorcycles from Around the World. Paul Trautwein. 1991. pap. 5.00 (*0-932526-77-2*) Nexus Pr.

Motorcycling: A Beginner's Manual. Jerry Matthews. 64p. (C). 1990. text 65.00 (*0-906754-53-4*, Pub. by Fernhurst Bks) St Mut.

Motorcycling Excellence: The Motorcycle Safety Foundation's Guide to Skills, Knowledge, & Strategies for Riding Right. Motorcycle Safety Foundation Staff. (Illus.). 176p. 1995. pap. 24.95 (*1-884313-01-9*) Whitehorse NH.

***Motorcycling Manual.** Stationery Office Staff. 300p. 1999. pap. 25.00 (*0-11-552193-3*, Pub. by Statnry Office) Balogh.

Motorcycling Touring & Travel. 2nd rev. ed. Bill Stermer. LC 99-222634. (Illus.). 160p. 1999. pap. 19.95 (*1-884313-15-9*) Whitehorse NH.

Motorcyclists: Image & Reality. Ed. by J. Peter Rothe & P. J. Cooper. 222p. 1989. pap. 21.95 (*0-88738-784-5*) Transaction Pubs.

Motores. Dale McCreedy. (National Science Partnership para Girl Scouts y Museos de Ciencia Ser.). Orig. Title: Movers. (ENG & SPA., Illus.). 33p. 1997. pap. 8.00 (*1-889939-03-X*) Franklin PA.

Motorgraders. Jean Eich. LC 96-14127. (Big Yellow Machines Ser.). (Illus.). 32p. (J). (ps-3). 1997. lib. bdg. 14.95 (*1-56239-732-X*) ABDO Pub Co.

Motorin' Along. Reiman Publications Staff. Ed. by Mike Martin. LC 97-76274. 164p. 1998. 16.95 (*0-89821-232-4*) Reiman Pubns.

Motoring Atlas France. 10th ed. Michelin Staff. 192p. 1996. 39.95 (*0-7859-9747-4*) Fr & Eur.

Motoring Costume. Andrew Lane. (Album Ser.: No. 197). (Illus.). 32p. 1989. pap. 6.25 (*0-85263-872-8*, Pub. by Shire Pubns) Parkwest Pubns.

Motoring for Money: How to Earn a Cash Profit Buying & Selling Motor Vehicles. A. Vincent. Ed. by D. Saunders. (Illus.). 62p. (Orig.). 1995. pap. 9.95 (*0-9650898-0-0*) Anthonys Auto.

Motoring Jokes. Bill Stott. Ed. by Helen Exley & Samantha Armstrong. (Joke Bks.). (Illus.). 60p. 1993. 7.00 (*1-85015-402-3*) Exley Giftbooks.

Motoring Mascots of the World. William C. Williams. 1993. pap. text 60.00 (*0-87938-036-5*) Gr Arts Ctr Pub.

Motoring Mascots of the World. 2nd ed. William C. Williams. LC 79-4529. (Illus.). 228p. 1979. 60.00 (*1-55868-043-8*) Gr Arts Ctr Pub.

Motoring Specials. Ian Dussek. (Album Ser.: no. 266). (Illus.). 32p. 1989. pap. 6.25 (*0-7478-0118-5*, Pub. by Shire Pubns) Parkwest Pubns.

Motoring to Nalut. Philip Ward & Angelo Pesce. (Libya Past & Present Ser.: Vol. 8). (Illus.). 1968. pap. 5.95 (*0-902675-03-6*) Oleander Pr.

Motoring to Yellowstone in Slim's Model T, 1927. Charles R. Monroe. (Illus.). 64p. (Orig.). 1994. pap. 9.95 (*0-9615125-1-2*) Merryleaf.

Motoring with Mohammed: Journeys to Yemen & the Red Sea. Eric Hansen. 1992. pap. 13.00 (*0-679-73855-X*) Vin Bks.

Motorist's Guide to the Law. Jane Benjamin. 124p. 1993. 40.00 (*1-85190-189-2*, Pub. by Tolley Pubng) St Mut.

Motorist's Guide to the Law. James Mathers. 90p. 1986. 100.00 (*0-906840-95-3*, Pub. by Fourmat Pub) St Mut.

Motorization Myth. Ed. by W. Victor Madeja. LC 84-8625. (Illus.). 176p. 1984. 14.00 (*0-941052-57-5*); pap. 14.00 (*0-941052-20-6*) Valor Pub.

Motorization of American Cities. David J. St. Clair. LC 86-523. 201p. 1986. 49.95 (*0-275-92126-3*, C2126, Praeger Pubs) Greenwood.

Motorized Fire Apparatus of the West, 1900-1960. Wayne Sorensen & Donald F. Wood. (Illus.). 232p. 1992. pap. 43.00 (*0-933449-11-9*) Transport Trails.

Motorized Mail. James H. Bruns & Krause Publications Staff. LC 97-73776. (Illus.). 272p. 1997. pap. 19.95 (*0-87341-485-3*, MOTM) Krause Pubns.

Motorman. Jack Rudman. (Career Examination Ser.: C-509). 1994. pap. 23.95 (*0-8373-0509-8*) Nat Learn.

Motorman Instructor. Jack Rudman. (Career Examination Ser.: C-510). 1994. pap. 27.95 (*0-8373-0510-1*) Nat Learn.

Motormaniacs. Lloyd Osbourne. LC 70-85692. (Short Story Index Reprint Ser.). 1977. 19.95 (*0-8369-3035-5*) Ayer.

Motorola: A Journey Through Time & Technology. Motorola Museum of Electronics Staff. (Illus.). 96p. 1994. 50.00 (*1-56946-005-1*); 35.00 (*1-56946-008-6*); pap. 25.00 (*1-56946-011-6*) Motorola Univ.

Motorola: A Journey Through Time & Technology. Motorola Museum of Electronics Staff. (SPA., Illus.). 96p. (C). 1994. pap. 25.00 (*1-56946-012-4*); pap. text 25.00 (*1-56946-013-2*) Motorola Univ.

Motorola: A Journey Through Time & Technology. Motorola Museum of Electronics Staff. (CHI., Illus.). 96p. (YA). 1994. 35.00 (*1-56946-006-X*); pap. text 25.00 (*1-56946-010-8*) Motorola Univ.

Motorola MC68000 Microprocessor Family: Assembly Language, Interface Design & System System. Thomas L. Harman & Barbara Lawson. (Illus.). 592p. 1950. text 22.60 (*0-13-603986-3*) P-H.

Motorola MC68000 Microprocessor Family: The Assembly Language Interface Design & System Design. 2nd ed. Thomas L. Harman & David T. Hein. LC 95-9116. 633p. 1995. 72.00 (*0-13-158742-0*) P-H.

Motorola MC68332 Microcontroller: Product Design, Assembly Language Programming & Interfacing. Thomas L. Harman. 512p. 1991. text 41.25 (*0-13-603127-7*, 330206) P-H.

Motorola 68, Vol. 11. Haupa. Date not set. teacher ed. write for info. (*0-314-06974-7*) West Pub.

Motorola University & the Learning Organization. Michael Ryan et al. (Pew Case Studies in International Affairs). 50p. (C). 1995. pap. text 3.50 (*1-56927-714-1*, GU Schl Foreign) Geo U Inst Dplmcy.

Motors & Generators. (Illus.). 96p. (Orig.). 1981. pap. text 10.00 (*0-86657-003-9*) Lab-Volt.

Motors As Generators for Micro-Hydro Power. Nigel Smith. 84p. (Orig.). 1994. pap. 12.00 (*1-85339-286-3*, Pub. by Intermed Tech) Stylus Pub VA.

Motors, Generators & Robotics. Temes. (C). 1994. text 57.00 (*0-03-028382-5*) Harcourt Coll Pubs.

Motors, Generators & Transformers. Multi-Amp Institute Staff. LC 94-20840. 512p. 1995. pap. 39.25 (*0-8273-4920-3*) Delmar.

Motors, Generators & Transformers. Multi-Amp Institute Staff. LC 94-20840. 160p. 1995. text, teacher ed. 23.50 (*0-8273-4921-1*) Delmar.

***Motorspeech & Related Oropharyngeal Disorders in Children.** Sheppard. 2001. 44.00 (*1-56593-699-X*) Thomson Learn.

***Motorsphere to the Max.** Michael Teitelbaum. (gr. 1-5). 2000. 7.95 (*0-06-107193-5*, HarpEntertain) Morrow Avon.

Motorsport America: The Men & Machines of American Motorsports, 1997-98. Autosport International Staff. 1998. 29.90 (*0-929323-16-5*) Autosport Intl.

***Motorsport Art of Juan Carlos Ferrigno.** Christopher Hilton. (Illus.). 96p. 2000. 69.95 (*1-85960-665-2*, 130422AE, Pub. by Haynes Manuals) Motorbooks Intl.

Motorsport Art of Michael Turner. Michael Turner. (Illus.). 96p. 1996. 49.95 (*1-85260-545-6*, Pub. by J H Haynes & Co) Motorbooks Intl.

MotorSports, 12 bks. Incl. Demolition Derby. Jeff Savage. (Illus.). 48p. (J). (gr. 3-4). 1995. lib. bdg. 19.00 (*1-56065-259-4*, Cpstone High Low); Drag Racing. Jay H. Smith. LC 94-22625. (Illus.). 48p. (J). (gr. 3-4). 1994. lib. bdg. 19.00 (*1-56065-230-6*, Cpstone High Low); Indianapolis 500. Michael Dregni. LC 93-44567. (Illus.). 48p. (J). (gr. 3-4). 1994. lib. bdg. 19.00 (*1-56065-205-5*, Cpstone High Low); Kart Racing. Jay H. Smith. LC 94-29510. (Illus.). 48p. (J). (gr. 3-4). 1994. lib. bdg. 19.00 (*1-56065-229-2*, Cpstone High Low); Monster Truck Racing. Scott Johnston. LC 93-44566. (Illus.). 48p. (J). (gr. 4-7). 1994. lib. bdg. 19.00 (*1-56065-204-7*, Cpstone High Low); Monster Truck Wars. Jeff Savage. (Illus.). 48p. (J). (gr. 3-4). 1995. lib. bdg. 19.00

M

An Asterisk (*) at the beginning of an entry indicates that the title is appearing for the first time.

(*1-56065-258-6*, Cpstone High Low); Motocross Racing. Jesse Young. LC 94-26939. (Illus.). 48p. (J). (gr. 3-4). 1994. lib. bdg. 19.00 (*1-56065-228-4*, Cpstone High Low); Motorcycle Racing. Michael Dregni. LC 93-44569. (Illus.). 48p. (J). (gr. 3-4). 1994. lib. bdg. 19.00 (*1-56065-207-1*, Cpstone High Low); Mud Racing. Jeff Savage. LC 95-7127. (Illus.). 48p. (J). (gr. 4-7). 1995. lib. bdg. 19.00 (*1-56065-257-8*, Cpstone High Low); Powerboat Racing. Jay H. Smith. LC 94-22626. (Illus.). 48p. (J). (gr. 3-4). 1994. lib. bdg. 19.00 (*1-56065-231-4*, Cpstone High Low); Stock Car Racing. Michael Dregni. LC 93-44568. (Illus.). 48p. (J). (gr. 3-4). 1994. lib. bdg. 19.00 (*1-56065-206-3*, Cpstone High Low); Truck & Tractor Pulling. Jeff Savage. (Illus.). 48p. (J). (gr. 3-4). 1995. lib. bdg. 19.00 (*1-56065-260-8*, Cpstone High Low); 228.00 (*1-56065-653-0*, Cpstone High Low) Capstone Pr.

***Motorsports.** Bill McAuliffe. 1999. 59.79 (*0-516-29624-8*) Capstone Pr.

***Motorsports America: The Men & Machines of American Motorsport.** Autosport International Staff. (Illus.). 196p. 2000. 29.90 (*0-929323-18-1*, 130140AE, Pub. by Autosport Intl) Motorbooks Intl.

Motorsports America: The Men & Machines of American Motorsport, 1995-96. Autosport International Staff. (Illus.). 192p. 1996. 29.90 (*0-929323-14-9*) Autosport Intl.

Motorsports America: The Men & Machines of American Motorsport, 1998-1999. Autosport International Editorial Staff. (Illus.). 196p. 1999. 29.90 (*0-929323-17-3*, Pub. by Autosport Intl) Motorbooks Intl.

Motorsports America: The Men & Machines of Motorsports, 1994-95. Autosport International, Inc. Staff. (Illus.). 192p. 1995. 29.90 (*0-929323-13-0*) Autosport Intl.

Motorsports America, 1996-97: The Men & Machines of American Motorsport, 3 vols. David Phillips & Benny Phillips. (Annual Ser.). (Illus.). 192p. 1997. 29.90 (*0-929323-15-7*) Autosport Intl.

Motorsports Medicine: Race Faster! Longer! Safer! Harlen C. Hunter & Rick Stoff. LC 92-39754. (Illus.). 250p. 1992. pap. 19.95 (*0-9634819-0-8*) Lake Hill Pr.

Motortherapy. Bill Schermbrucker. 176p. 1993. pap. 13.95 (*0-88922-330-0*, Pub. by Talonbks) Genl Dist Srvs.

Motorway Traffic Analysis: New Methodologies & Recent Empirical Findings. Piet H. Bovy. (Illus.). 326p. 1998. pap. 57.50 (*90-407-1651-X*, Pub. by Delft U Pr) Coronet Bks.

Motown & Didi: A Love Story. Walter Dean Myers. 176p. (YA). (gr. k-12). 1987. mass mkt. 4.99 (*0-440-95762-1*, LLL BDD) BDD Bks Young Read.

Motown & Didi: A Love Story. Walter Dean Myers. (Laurel-Leaf Contemporary Fiction Ser.). (J). 1987. 9.60 (*0-606-03623-7*, Pub. by Turtleback) Demco.

Motown Anthology. Leonard, Hal, Corporation Staff. 312p. 1998. otabind 19.95 (*0-7935-9201-1*) H Leonard.

***Motown Bass Classics.** 112p. 1998. otabind 14.95 (*0-7935-8837-5*) H Leonard.

Motown Greatest Hits, No. 109. 160p. 1992. otabind 12.95 (*0-7935-1449-5*, 00102232) H Leonard.

***Motown Guitar Classics.** 80p. 1999. otabind 14.95 (*0-7935-8836-7*) H Leonard.

Motown Hits. Leonard, Hal, Corporation Staff. 256p. 1999. per. 6.95 (*0-7935-9823-0*) H Leonard.

Mots. Jean-Paul Sartre. (FRE.). 1977. pap. 10.95 (*0-8288-3749-X*, F125431) Fr & Eur.

Mots. Jean-Paul Sartre. (FRE.). (C). 1964. pap. 9.95 (*0-8442-1944-4*, VF1944-4) NTC Contemp Pub Co.

Mots. Jean-Paul Sartre. (Folio Ser.: No. 607). (FRE.). 210p. 1972. pap. 8.95 (*2-07-036607-3*) Schoenhof.

Mots Croises Faciles see Easy French Crossword Puzzles

Mots Dans le Peinture. Michel Butor. (Coll. Les Sentiers de la Creation). 14.50 (*0-685-37255-3*, F89980) Fr & Eur.

Mots de la Maison: English, French, German Vocabulary of Home Buying, Construction, Restoration. A. Brochen. (ENG, FRE & GER.). 339p. 1995. pap. 79.95 (*0-7859-9636-2*) Fr & Eur.

Mots de la Micro: Petit Dictionnaire Micro-Informatique Pour Tous. Maithe De Vos. (FRE.). 224p. 1992. pap. 38.95 (*0-7859-7729-5*) Fr & Eur.

Mots de l'Histoire: Dictionnaire Historique Universel des Mots, des Moeurs et des Mentalites. Jacques Boudet. (FRE.). 1374p. 1990. pap. 155.00 (*0-7859-7801-1*, 2221052528) Fr & Eur.

Mots en Liberte Futuristes. Filippo Tommaso Marinetti. 1956. pap. 20.00 (*0-87556-216-7*) Saifer.

Mots et les Choses: Une Archeologie des Scieces Humaines. Michel Foucault. (Tel Ser.). (FRE.). pap. 19.95 (*2-07-029335-1*) Schoenhof.

Mots et Phrases Usuels de la Vie Quotidienne, Chinois-Frances: Chinese-French Words & Phrases from Everyday Life. T. Yon-Sun. (CHI & FRE.). 535p. 1979. pap. 14.95 (*0-8288-4824-6*, M9249) Fr & Eur.

Mots Francais. Henri Mitterand. 128p. 1968. 9.95 (*0-8288-7461-1*) Fr & Eur.

Mots pour le Dire. Marie Cardinal. (FRE.). 1977. pap. 10.95 (*0-7859-3093-0*) Fr & Eur.

Mots Preferes de Bertrand see Clifford's Work Book

Mots sous les Mots: Les Anagrammes de Ferdinand de Saussure. Jean Starbinski. (Gallimard Ser.). (FRE.). pap. 25.95 (*2-07-028069-1*) Schoenhof.

Mots-Vendeurs: Francais-Anglais. Alain Arnaud. (ENG & FRE.). 122p. 1989. pap. 59.95 (*0-7859-3915-6*, 2856080324) Fr & Eur.

Mott Metal-Insulator Transition: Models & Methods. Florian Gebbhard. LC 96-29969. (Springer Tracts in Modern Physics Ser.: Vol. 137). (Illus.). 290p. 1997. 199.00 (*3-540-61481-8*) Spr-Verlag.

Motta: Upward. Christopher L. Clutter. (Illus.). 125p. (Orig.). 1995. mass mkt. 13.30 (*0-9644321-3-7*) Camel Dung Writ.

Mottke the Thief. Sholem Asch. LC 73-98807. 314p. 1970. reprint ed. lib. bdg. 65.00 (*0-8371-2953-2*, ASMO, Greenwood Pr) Greenwood.

Mottla's Proof of Cases in Massachusetts. 3rd ed. Marc G. Perlin. LC 92-74614. 1992. 230.00 (*0-317-05377-9*) West Group.

Mottled Duck: Its Life History, Ecology & Management. Charles D. Stutzenbaker. (Illus.). 230p. 1998. 16.95 (*1-885696-25-6*, STUMOT) U of Tex Pr.

Mottled Screen: Reading Proust Visually. Mieke Bal. LC 96-49839. 272p. 1997. 45.00 (*0-8047-2807-0*); pap. 17.95 (*0-8047-2808-9*) Stanford U Pr.

Motto, Context, Essay: The Classical Background of Samuel Johnson's "Rambler" & "Adventurer" Essays. Robert C. Olson. 398p. (Orig.). 1985. pap. text 32.00 (*0-8191-4236-0*) U Pr of Amer.

Motton: Plays Three. Gregory Motton. 204p. 1999. pap. 18.95 (*1-84002-021-0*, Pub. by Theatre Comm) Consort Bk Sales.

Motton: Plays 2. Gregory Motton. (Oberon Bks.). 256p. 1998. pap. 18.95 (*1-84002-020-2*) Theatre Comm.

Mottos for Many Moods: Humorous Slogans to Brighten Your Day (Cross-Stitch) Annette Bradshaw & Gwyn Franson. 1983. 5.98 (*0-88290-225-3*) Horizon Utah.

Mottos of the Heart. 123p. 1999. pap. 5.95 (*1-883368-02-2*) Ramsey Pr.

Mottos to Live By see Lemas para Vivir

Mottos to Live By: A Collection of Poems. Ed. by Susan Polis Schutz. LC 93-30909. (Illus.). 64p. 1993. pap. 8.95 (*0-88396-370-1*) Blue Mtn Art.

Mott's Illustrated Catalog of Victorian Plumbing Fixtures for Bathrooms & Kitchens. Mott Iron Works Staff. (Illus.). 288p. 1988. reprint ed. pap. 15.95 (*0-486-25526-3*) Dover.

Mott's Miniature Furniture Workshop Manual: Techniques & Patterns for 144 Miniature Masterpieces. 2nd rev. ed. Barbara Mott & Elizabeth Mott. (Illus.). 216p. 1995. pap. 19.95 (*1-56523-052-3*) Fox Chapel Pub.

Motu Tapu: Short Stories of the South Pacific. Graeme Lay. 172p. (C). 1991. pap. text 20.00 (*0-908597-06-1*) UH Pr.

Mouches. Jean-Paul Sartre. (FRE.). 121p. 1947. 9.95 (*0-7859-9251-0*) Fr & Eur.

***Moufang Loops of Order Less Than 64.** Edgar G. Goodaire et al. 248p. 1999. 85.00 (*1-56072-659-8*) Nova Sci Pubs.

Moufang Loops of Small Order. Orin Chein. LC 77-25155. (Memoirs Ser.: No. 13/197). 131p. 1978. pap. 22.00 (*0-8218-2197-0*, MEMO/13/197) Am Math.

Moujam al Buldan, 5 vols. Yakut Al-Rumi. 1967. 95.00 (*0-86685-497-5*) Intl Bk Ctr.

Moukabilat Arabia. Sonia Beiruti. Ed. by Ramzi Kaliffe. (Silsilat Daliluki Sayidati (Woman's Guide) Ser.: No. 5).Tr. of Arab Appetizer. (ARA., Illus.). 40p. 1990. pap. 8.50 (*1-58311-028-3*) Eastern Corp.

Mould Allergy. Ed. by Yousef Al-Doory & Joanne F. Domson. LC 83-14951. (Illus.). 299p. reprint ed. pap. 92.70 (*0-8357-7639-5*, 205696200096) Bks Demand.

***Mould Making.** John Colclough. (Illus.). 128p. 1999. text. write for info. (*90-5703-891-9*, Pub. by Craftsman House) Gordon & Breach.

Moulders of Legal Thought. Bernard L. Shientag. LC 90-56335. 264p. 1991. reprint ed. 75.00 (*0-912004-87-8*) Gaunt.

Moulding Political Opinion. Robert James Waller. 128p. 1987. lib. bdg. 49.95 (*0-7099-5230-9*, Pub. by C Helm) Routldge.

Mouldings Recipe Book: Recipes, Ideas, Instructions, Hints & Other Stuff. Tammy McBride. 20p. 1993. pap. write for info. (*0-9639921-0-4*) Mouldings.

Mouldings Recipe Book: Recipes, Ideas, Instructions, Hints & Other Stuff, Bk. 2. 2nd ed. Tammy McBride. (Illus.). 32p. pap. 1.50 (*0-9639921-1-2*) Mouldings.

Moulds: Their Isolation, Cultivation & Identification. David Malloch. LC 81-195429. (Illus.). 107p. reprint ed. pap. 33.20 (*0-8357-3996-1*, 203669600005) Bks Demand.

Mould's Medical Anecdotes: Omnibus Edition. Richard F. Mould. LC 96-9553. (Illus.). 496p. 1996. pap. 35.00 (*0-7503-0390-5*) IOP Pub.

Moulds of Understanding: A Pattern of Natural Philosophy. Joseph Needham. (Modern Revivals in Philosophy Ser.). 320p. 1993. 72.95 (*0-7512-0209-6*, Pub. by Gregg Revivals) Ashgate Pub Co.

Moulds, Toxins & Food. Claude Moreau. Tr. by Maurice Moss. LC 78-8715. (Illus.). 491p. reprint ed. pap. 152.30 (*0-608-17604-4*, 203045400069) Bks Demand.

Mouldy Mummies. Mary Dobson. LC 99-170346. (Smelly Old History Ser.). (Illus.). 32p. (J). 1998. pap. 7.95 (*0-19-910495-6*) OUP.

Mouldylocks. Bernard Lodge. LC 97-51183. 32p. (J). (ps-2). 1998. 15.00 (*0-395-90945-7*) HM.

Moulids of Egypt: Egyptian Saints-Days. Joseph W. McPherson. LC 77-87654. reprint ed. 28.50 (*0-404-16408-0*) AMS Pr.

Moulin de la Sourdine. Marcel Ayme. (FRE.). 1973. pap. 10.95 (*0-7859-2200-8*, 207036321X) Fr & Eur.

Moulin de Pologne. Jean Giono. (FRE.). 1972. pap. 10.95 (*0-7859-2293-8*, 2070362744) Fr & Eur.

Moulin de Pologne. Jean Giono. (Folio Ser.: No. 274). (FRE.). 1972. pap. 6.95 (*2-07-036274-4*) Schoenhof.

Moulin et l'Hospice. Jules Romains, pseud. (FRE.). 240p. 1950. pap. 10.95 (*0-7859-1596-6*, 208050617X) Fr & Eur.

Moulin Rouge Hotel History Book. Richard B. Taylor. 100p. (Orig.). 1994. pap. 12.00 (*0-9616633-8-3*) Beehive NV.

Moulin Short History of Breast. 1983. text 106.00 (*0-89838-562-8*) Kluwer Academic.

Moulins see Encyclopedic Poetique: Anthologie Thematique de la Poesie Francaise Contemporaine

Moult & Ageing of European Passerines. Lukas Jenni & Raffael Winkler. (Illus.). 224p. 1994. text 63.00 (*0-12-384150-X*) Acad Pr.

Moulton Annals. H. W. Moulton. Ed. by C. Moulton. (Illus.). 454p. 1989. reprint ed. pap. 68.00 (*0-8328-0889-X*); reprint ed. lib. bdg. 76.00 (*0-8328-0888-1*) Higginson Bk Co.

Moulton's Analytical Greek Lexicon Revised. rev. ed. Ed. by Harold K. Moulton. (GRE.). 1967. 25.95 (*0-310-20280-9*, 6257) Zondervan.

Moun Espelido see Memoirs of Frederic Mistral

Mound Builders. Lanford Wilson. 1996. pap. 5.25 (*0-8222-1509-8*) Dramatists Play.

Mound Builders. Henry C. Shetrone. 1993. reprint ed. lib. bdg. 89.00 (*0-7812-5400-0*) Rprt Serv.

Mound Builders. Robert Silverberg. LC 85-25953. 276p. (YA). 1986. reprint ed. pap. 9.95 (*0-8214-0839-9*) Ohio U Pr.

Mound Builders. Eric Waddell. LC 84-45543. (American Ethnological Society Monographs: No. 53). 1988. reprint ed. 35.00 (*0-404-62951-2*) AMS Pr.

Mound Builders & Cliff Dwellers see Lost Civilizations Series

Mound Builders & Cliff Dwellers. Time-Life Books Editors. Ed. by Dale Brown. LC 92-18534. (Lost Civilizations Ser.). (Illus.). 144p. 1993. lib. bdg. 25.93 (*0-8094-9859-6*) Time-Life.

Mound City Chronicles. William Stage. (Illus.). (Orig.). pap. write for info. (*0-9629124-0-9*) Hartmann MO.

Mound Excavations near Stockton. fac. ed. Philip M. Jones. (University of California Publications in American Archaeology & Ethnology: Vol. 20: 7). 10p. (C). 1923. reprint ed. pap. text 1.56 (*1-55567-243-4*) Coyote Press.

Mound People: An Earth Parable. limited ed. Mark James. Ed. by Cindy Lambert & Elaine Kozar. (Green Legend Ser.). (Illus.). 80p. (Orig.). (J). (gr. 5-12). 1985. pap. 7.95 (*0-943806-03-8*) Neahtawanta Pr.

Mound Stand: Lord's Cricket Ground London 1987 Michael Hopkins & Partners. David Jenkins. (Architecture in Detail Ser.). (Illus.). 60p. (Orig.). 1997. pap. 29.95 (*1-85454-558-2*) Chronicle Bks.

Mound Stand Lord's Cricket Ground: Architecture in Detail. David Jenkins. (Architecture in Detail Ser.). 1991. pap. 44.95 (*0-471-29071-8*, VNR) Wiley.

Moundbuilders of the Amazon: Geophysical Archaeology on Marajo Island, Brazil. Anna C. Roosevelt. 495p. 1991. text 110.00 (*0-12-595348-8*) Acad Pr.

Mounds, Embankments, & Ceremonialism in the Midsouth. Ed. by Robert C. Mainfort & Richard Walling. LC 96-38731. (Arkansas Archaeological Survey Research Ser.). (Illus.). 98p. (Orig.). 1996. pap. 15.00 (*1-56349-077-3*, RS46) AR Archaeol.

Mounds for the Dead. Don W. Dragoo. (Annals of C.M.N.H. Ser.: Vol. 37). (Illus.). 315p. 1963. pap. 13.95 (*0-911239-09-X*) Carnegie Mus.

Mounds of Earth & Shell. Bonnie Shemie. (Native Sites, the Southeast Ser.). 1993. 12.15 (*0-606-08826-1*, Pub. by Turtleback) Demco.

Mounds of Earth & Shell: Native Sites: The Southeast. Bonnie Shemie. LC 93-60335. (Native Dwellings Ser.). (Illus.). 24p. (J). (gr. 3 up). 1993. 13.95 (*0-88776-318-9*) Tundra Bks.

Mounds of Earth & Shell: The Southeast. Bonnie Shemie. (Native Sites Ser.). (Illus.). 24p. 1996. pap. 6.95 (*0-88776-352-9*) Tundra Bks.

Mounds of Koshkonong & Rock River: A History of Ancient Indian Earthworks in Wisconsin. Hugh Highsmith. LC 96-94953. (Illus.). 1997. 19.95 (*0-917846-96-6*) Highsmith Pr.

Mounds of Sacred Earth: Burial Mounds of Ontario. Walter A. Kenyon. (Illus.). 144p. pap. 24.57 (*0-88854-303-4*) Brill Academic Pubs.

***Mounds of Sounds.** Peter Baroth. iv, 52p. 2000. pap. write for info. (*0-9674900-8-1*) Wordrunner.

Moundville Expeditions of Clarence Bloomfield Moore. Ed. & Intro. by Vernon J. Knight, Jr. LC 95-26455. (Classics in Southeastern Archaeology Ser.). 232p. (C). 1996. pap. text 29.95 (*0-8173-0840-7*) U of Ala Pr.

Moundville's Economy. Paul D. Welch. LC 90-34220. 248p. 1991. pap. text 29.95 (*0-8173-0512-2*) U of Ala Pr.

Mount: History & Genealogy Record of the Mount & Flippin Families. J. A. Mount. 120p. 1991. reprint ed. pap. 21.00 (*0-8328-1821-6*); reprint ed. lib. bdg. 31.00 (*0-8328-1820-8*) Higginson Bk Co.

Mount: Home of Edith Wharton. Scott Marshall & John G. Waite. (Illus.). 256p. 1997. pap. 25.00 (*0-9665004-0-7*) E Wharton.

***Mount Airy.** Mt. Airy Regional Museum Staff. (Images of America Ser.). 128p. 1999. pap. 18.99 (*0-7385-0105-0*) Arcadia Publng.

Mount Allegro: A Memoir of Italian American Life. Jerre G. Mangione. LC 97-50547. (New York Classics Ser.). 1998. pap. 19.95 (*0-8156-0429-7*) Syracuse U Pr.

Mount Allison University: A History, to 1963, Vol. 1. John G. Reid. LC 84-175462. (Illus.). 441p. 1984. reprint ed. pap. 136.80 (*0-8357-3663-6*, 203639000001) Bks Demand.

Mount Allison University: A History, to 1963, Vol. 2: 1914-1963. John G. Reid. LC 84-175462. (Illus.). 544p. 1984. reprint ed. pap. 168.70 (*0-8357-3664-4*, 203639000002) Bks Demand.

Mt. Angel Abbey: A Centennial History of the Benedictine Community & Its Library, 1882-1982. Compiled by Lawrence J. McCrank. LC 83-10536. 224p. 1983. pap. 20.00 (*0-8420-2212-0*) Scholarly Res Inc.

Mount Athos: A Guide for Pilgrims. J. Demakis. 1991. pap. 7.95 (*0-937032-78-6*) Light&Life Pub Co MN.

Mount Athos & Byzantine Monasticism: Papers from the 28th Spring Symposium of Byzantine Studies, University of Birmingham, March 1994. Ed. by Anthony Bryer & Mary Cunningham. LC 96-902. (Society for the Promotion of Byzantine Studies: Vol. 4). 304p. 1996. 78.95 (*0-86078-551-3*, Pub. by Variorum) Ashgate Pub Co.

Mount Athos & Russia. Igor Smolich. Tr. by Bessarion Agioantonioes from FRE. 1988. pap. text. write for info. (*0-936649-16-X*) St Anthony Orthodox.

***Mt. Baker: Stories, Legends & Exploration.** Ed. by Charles Finley Easton et al. (Illus.). 1999. cd-rom 29.95 (*0-938506-06-4*) Whatcom.

Mount Batten, Plymouth: A Prehistoric & Roman Port. Barry Cunliffe. (Illus.). 108p. 1988. pap. 32.50 (*0-947816-26-7*, Pub. by Oxford Univ Comm Arch) David Brown.

Mt. Carmel & Summerside, Ohio, from 1788 to Modern Times. Alma A. Smith. (Illus.). 101p. 1983. pap. 10.00 (*0-9614863-2-5*) Alma Smith.

Mount Carmel Cemetery: Mt. Carmel, Northumberland Co., Pa. Jean Dellock & Philip A. Rice. 145p. 1989. per. 16.00 (*1-55856-034-3*, 059) Closson Pr.

***Mt. Charleston Resort History Book, Vol. IV.** Richard B. Taylor. (Illus.). 286p. 2000. 25.00 (*0-9678530-5-2*) Beehive NV.

***Mt. Charleston Resort History Book, Vol. V.** Ed. by Richard B. Taylor. (Illus.). 300p. 2000. pap. 25.00 (*0-9678530-6-0*) Beehive NV.

Mount Desert: A History. George E. Street. Ed. by Samuel A. Eliot. (Illus.). 386p. 1988. reprint ed. lib. bdg. 42.00 (*0-8328-0025-2*, ME0024) Higginson Bk Co.

Mount Desert, 1872. George W. Nichols. Ed. by William R. Jones. (Illus.). 24p. 1995. reprint ed. pap. 2.95 (*0-89646-029-0*) Vistabooks.

Mount Desert Island & Acadia National Park: An Informal History. Sargent F. Collier. Ed. by G. W. Helfrich. (Illus.). 146p. 1978. pap. 12.95 (*0-89272-044-1*) Down East.

***Mount Diablo Guide: Mount Diablo Interpretive Association.** Mount Diablo Interpretive Association Staff. (Illus.). 160p. 2000. pap. write for info. (*1-893163-07-5*, Pub. by Berkeley Hills) Publishers Group.

***Mount Dora.** Lynn M. Homan & Thomas Reilly. (Images of America Ser.). (Illus.). 128p. 2000. pap. 18.99 (*0-7385-0568-4*) Arcadia Publng.

***Mount Dorans: African American History Notes of a Florida Town.** Vivian W. Owens. LC 99-93878. (Illus.). 248p. 2000. 18.95 (*0-9623839-8-8*, Pub. by Eschar Pubns) Baker & Taylor.

Mount Dragon. Douglas J. Preston & Lincoln Child. LC 95-41323. 349p. (J). 1996. 22.95 (*0-312-86042-0*) Forge NYC.

Mount Dragon. Douglas J. Preston & Lincoln Child. LC 95-41323. (J). mass mkt. 6.99 (*0-8125-6437-5*, Pub. by Tor Bks) St Martin.

Mount Dragon. Douglas J. Preston & Lincoln Child. (J). 1997. mass mkt. 6.99 (*0-614-20533-6*) Tor Bks.

Mount Eagle. John Montague. LC 88-40663. 75p. 1989. pap. 6.95 (*0-916390-33-0*) Wake Forest.

Mt. Edgecube High School Case Study Report. Susan Hubbard & Scott Menzel. (Cross Case Report & Case Studies). 50p. 1995. text, teacher ed. 20.00 (*0-614-24544-3*); pap. text, teacher ed. 10.00 (*0-614-24545-1*) Natl Inst Work.

Mt. Equinox: Past & Present. 2nd rev. ed. Ed. & Intro. by Susan Grant. (Illus.). 32p. 1994. pap. text 2.95 (*0-9641092-0-4*) Wrds In Motion.

Mount Etna: The Anatomy of a Volcano. David K. Chester. (C). text 189.50 (*0-412-23890-X*) Chapman & Hall.

Mount Everest: Its Spiritual Attainment (1933) George S. Arundale. 198p. 1998. reprint ed. pap. 17.95 (*0-7661-0237-8*) Kessinger Pub.

***Mount Everest: The Highest Mountain.** Aileen Weintraub. LC 00-36712. (Great Record Breakers in Nature Ser.). (Illus.). (J). 2000. write for info. (*0-8239-5636-9*, PowerKids) Rosen Group.

Mount Everest National Park: Sagarmatha Mother of the Universe. Margaret Jefferies. (Illus.). 192p. 1991. pap. 18.95 (*0-89886-267-1*) Mountaineers.

Mount Forest in 1871: Census & Assessment Roll for Mount Forest, Ontario. Jeff Stewart & Sherilyn Bell. LC 98-224030. v, 72 p. 1997. write for info. (*0-9681980-1-5*) Win5 Pub.

Mount Fui & Mount Sinai - A Pilgramage in Theology see Mount Fuji & Mount Sinai: A Critique of Idols

Mt. Fuji: Selected Poems, 1943-1986. Shimpei Kusano. Ed. by Thomas Fitzsimmons. Tr. by Leith Morton from JPN. (Asian Poetry in Translation: Japan Ser.: No. 13). 1991. pap. 20.00 (*0-942668-29-4*); text 30.00 (*0-942668-30-8*) Katydid Bks.

Mount Fuji & Mount Sinai: A Critique of Idols. Kosuke Koyama. LC 84-16556. Orig. Title: Mount Fui & Mount Sinai - A Pilgramage in Theology. 288p. (Orig.). 1985. reprint ed. pap. 89.30 (*0-608-02147-4*, 206281600003) Bks Demand.

Mount Hood. Writers Program, Work Projects Administration Staf. (Illus.). 168p. 1996. 25.00 (*0-89904-304-6*); pap. 20.00 (*0-89904-305-4*) Crumb Elbow Pub.

Mt. Hope Cemetery: Afton, OK. Ed. by Hildred Hughes Ables. 81p. 1988. pap. 10.00 (*1-892744-01-5*, A-101) Maloy.

Mount Horeb. Russell Birdwell. LC 77-187991. (Illus.). 104p. 1972. 12.00 (*0-8315-0122-7*) Speller.

***Mt. Kilauea: Home of the Hawaiian Goddess of Fire.** Kathy Furgang. LC 00-20880. (Volcanoes of the World Ser.). (Illus.). (J). 2000. write for info. (*0-8239-5659-8*) Rosen Group.

***Mt. Krakatoa: History's Loudest Volcano.** Kathy Furgang. LC 00-28594. (Volcanoes of the World Ser.). (Illus.). 2000. write for info. (*0-8239-5662-8*, PowerKids) Rosen Group.

M

Mount Laurel II & the Fair Housing Act. Jeffrey Surenian. (Illus.). 667p. 1986. ring bd. 65.00 (0-685-14647-2) NJ Inst CLE.

Mount Lebanon: A Ten Years' Residence, from 1842 to 1852, 3 vols., Set. Charles H. Churchill. LC 77-87615. reprint ed. 155.00 (0-404-16440-4) AMS Pr.

Mount Lu Revisited: Buddhism in the Life & Writings of Su Shih. Beata Grant. LC 94-9955. 260p. (C). 1994. text 36.00 (0-8248-1625-0) UH Pr.

Mount McKinley: Icy Crown of North America. Fred Beckey. (Illus.). 320p. 1993. 29.95 (0-89886-362-7) Mountaineers.

Mount McKinley: Icy Crown of North America. Fred Beckey. 320p. 1999. pap. 19.95 (0-89886-646-4) Mountaineers.

*Mount McKinley: The Conquest of Denali. (Illus.). 208p. 2000. 27.98 (0-8109-8194-7, Pub. by Abrams) Time Warner.

Mount McKinley: The Conquest of Denali. Bradford Washburn & David Roberts. (Illus.). 208p. 1991. 60.00 (0-8109-3611-9, Pub. by Abrams) Time Warner.

Mount McKinley & Wonderlake Denali National Park,Alaska 1947. Ansel Adams. 1997. write for info. (0-8212-2415-8) Little.

Mount McKinley Climber's Handbook. Glenn Randall. (Illus.). 120p. (Orig.). 1992. pap. 18.00 (0-934641-55-2) Falcon Pub Inc.

Mount Misery. Samuel Shem. 1998. mass mkt. 6.99 (0-8041-1555-9) Ivy Books.

Mount Mitchell: Its Railroad & Toll Road. Jeff Lovelace. (Illus.). 96p. 1994. pap. 9.95 (0-932807-84-4) Overmountain Pr.

Mount Morgan. 38p. 1994. pap. 35.00 (1-882866-42-8) Pac Asia Trvl.

Mount Moriah Studies. Harald Wyndham. 120p. 1989. pap. 13.00 (0-937179-03-5) Blue Scarab.

Mount Morris: Past & Present, Illustrated History of the Village of Mt. Morris, Ogle County, Illinois. H. G. Kable. (Illus.). 464p. 1998. reprint ed. lib. bdg. 48.00 (0-8328-9739-6) Higginson Bk Co.

*Mount Nimro. Bill Coffin & Kevin Siembieda. Ed. by Alex Marciniszyn et al. (Palladium Sourcebook Ser.: Vol. 10). (Illus.). 160p. (YA). (gr. 8 up). 1999. pap. 16.95 (1-57457-028-5, 464) Palladium Bks.

Mount-Orgueil. William Prynne. LC 83-20361. 232p. 1984. reprint ed. 50.00 (0-8201-1392-1) Schol Facsimiles.

*Mt. Pelbee: The Biggest Volcano Eruption of the 20th Century. Kathy Furgang. LC 00-28591. (Volcanoes of the World Ser.). (Illus.). 2000. write for info. (0-8239-5663-6, PowerKids) Rosen Group.

Mt. Pelee Redemption: A Metalphysical Mystery. Stephen H. Martin. LC 98-71586. 224p. 1998. pap. 12.95 (1-57174-116-X) Hampton Roads Pub Co.

Mount People. Jane Mason. (C). 1989. 70.00 (1-85022-057-3, Pub. by Dyllansow Truran) St Mut.

Mount Pinatubo Eruption: Effects on the Atmosphere & Climate. Giorgio Fiocco et al. LC 96-21643. (NATO ASI Series: Global Environmental Change). 310p. 1996. 139.50 (3-540-61281-5) Spr-Verlag.

Mount Pleasant, Dorset: Excavations, 1970-1971. G. J. Wainwright. (Illus.). 266p. 1979. 19.98 (0-85431-220-X, Pub. by Soc Antiquaries) David Brown.

Mount Pleasant, South Carolina: A Victorian Village. Mary Julia C. Royall. (Images of America Ser.). (Illus.). 128p. 1996. pap. 16.99 (0-7524-0531-4) Arcadia Publng.

*Mount Rainier. Jeff Nicholas. 1998. pap. (0-939365-83-9) Panorama Intl.

*Mount Rainier: A Climbing Guide. Mike Gauthier. (Illus.). 1999. pap. 16.95 (0-89886-655-3) Mountaineers.

*Mount Rainier: A Visitor's Companion. George Wuerthner. LC 99-46094. (Illus.). 240p. 2000. pap. 19.95 (0-8117-2856-0) Stackpole.

Mount Rainier: Active Cascade Volcano. National Research Council, U. S. Geodynamics Commi. 128p. (Orig.). (C). 1994. pap. text 29.00 (0-309-05083-9) Natl Acad Pr.

Mount Rainier: The Story Behind the Scenery. Ray S. Snow. LC 83-80764. (Illus.). 48p. (Orig.). 1984. pap. 7.95 (0-916122-83-2) KC Pubns.

Mount Rainier National Park. Sharlene Nelson & Ted Nelson. Ed. by Sarah DeCapua. (True Bks.). (Illus.). 48p. (J). 1998. pap. 6.95 (0-516-26381-1) Childrens.

Mount Rainier National Park. Sharlene P. Nelson & Ted W. Nelson. LC 97-8233. (True Bks.). (Illus.). 48p. (J). (gr. 2-4). 1998. 21.00 (0-516-20624-9) Childrens.

Mount Rainier National Park. Ron Warfield. Ed. by Jeff Nicholas & Nicky Leach. (Pocket Portfolio Ser.: Vol. 11). (Illus.). 32p. 1998. pap. 5.95 (0-939365-66-9) Panorama Intl.

Mount Rainier National Park: America's Mountain Glacier Wonderland. (Illus.). 24p. (Orig.). 1987. pap. 2.50 (1-878395-01-7) Smith-Western.

Mount Rainier National Park: Tales, Trails, & Auto Tours. Jerry Rohde & Gisela Rohde. LC 96-75512. (Illus.). 320p. (Orig.). 1996. pap. 17.95 (0-9640261-1-2) MtnHome Bks.

Mount Rainier National Park Paradise. Jeff Smoot. (Twelve Short Hikes Ser.). (Illus.). 32p. (Orig.). 1997. pap. 4.95 (1-57540-017-0) Falcon Pub Inc.

Mount Rainier National Park Sunrise. Jeff Smoot. (Twelve Short Hikes Ser.). (Illus.). 32p. (Orig.). 1997. pap. 4.95 (1-57540-016-2) Falcon Pub Inc.

Mount Rainier National Park, WA. rev. ed. Ed. by Trails Illustrated Staff. (Illus.). 1997. 8.99 (0-925873-17-9) Trails Illustrated.

Mount Rushmore see Monte Rushmore

Mount Rushmore. Craig A. Doherty & Katherine M. Doherty. Ed. by Bruce Glassman. LC 94-24757. (Building America Ser.). (Illus.). 48p. (J). (gr. 5-7). 1995. lib. bdg. 17.95 (1-56711-108-4) Blackbirch.

Mount Rushmore. Thomas S. Owens. LC 97-11539. (Library of American Landmarks). (Illus.). 24p. (J). (gr. k-4). 1997. lib. bdg. 15.93 (0-8239-5017-4, PowerKids) Rosen Group.

*Mount Rushmore. Judith J. Presnall. LC 99-31390. (Building History Ser.). (Illus.). 128p. (YA). (gr. 6-9). 2000. lib. bdg. 23.70 (1-56006-529-X) Lucent Bks.

Mount Rushmore. Andrew Santella. (Cornerstones to Freedom Ser.). 32p. (gr. 4-6). 1999. lib. bdg. 5.95 (0-516-26459-1) Childrens.

Mount Rushmore. Andrew Santella. LC 98-3494. (Cornerstones to Freedom Ser.). (Illus.). 32p. (J). (gr. 4-6). 1999. 20.00 (0-516-21140-4) Childrens.

Mount Rushmore. Lynda Sorensen. LC 94-7053. (American Symbols Discovery Library). 24p. (J). (gr. k-4). 1994. lib. bdg. 15.93 (1-55916-047-0) Rourke Bk Co.

Mount Rushmore: Monument to America's Democracy. Dorothy K. Hilburn & Steven L. Walker. LC 97-66358. 48 p. 1997. pap. write for info. (1-879924-31-5) Camelback Design.

Mount Rushmore: The Story Behind the Scenery. Lincoln Borglum. Tr. by Brigitte Morales. (GER., Illus.). 48p. 1994. pap. 8.95 (0-88714-782-8) KC Pubns.

Mount Rushmore: The Story Behind the Scenery. Lincoln Borglum. Tr. by Saori Petzinger. (JPN., Illus.). 48p. 1994. pap. 8.95 (0-88714-783-6) KC Pubns.

Mount Rushmore: The Story Behind the Scenery. Lincoln Borglum. Tr. by Yvon Le Bras. (FRE., Illus.). 48p. 1997. pap. 8.95 (0-88714-817-4) KC Pubns.

Mount Rushmore: The Story Behind the Scenery. rev. ed. Lincoln Borglum. LC 93-77025. (Illus.). 48p. 1993. pap. 7.95 (0-88714-074-2) KC Pubns.

Mount Rushmore - In Pictures. (Illus.). (Orig.). Date not set. pap. text. write for info. (1-56944-114-6) Terrell Missouri.

Mount Rushmore Souvenir Book. (Orig.). pap. text. write for info. (1-56944-010-7) Terrell Missouri.

Mount St. Elias by the Sea. Jonathan Waterman. LC 97-8314. 288p. 1995. 25.00 (0-8050-4453-1); pap. 12.00 (0-8050-4454-X) H Holt & Co.

Mount St. Helena & R. L. Stevenson State Park: A History & Guide. Ken Stanton. Ed. by Gene Dekovic. LC 93-79308. (Illus.). 256p. (Orig.). 1994. pap. 15.95 (0-937088-20-X) Illum Pr.

Mt. St. Helena & Robert Louis Stevenson State Park: A History & Guide. 3rd rev. ed. Photos by Gene DeKovic. LC 93-79308. (Illus.). 256p. 1993. pap. 17.95 (0-9661209-0-6) Bonnie View Bks.

Mount St. Helens: Five Years Later. Ed. by S. A. Keller. 441p. (Orig.). 1987. pap. 27.95 (0-910055-09-2) East Wash Univ.

Mount St. Helens: One Year Later. Ed. by S. A. Keller. 243p. (Orig.). 1982. pap. 20.00 (0-910055-00-9) East Wash Univ.

Mount St. Helens: The Eruption & Recovery of a Volcano. Rob Carlson. LC 90-31009. (Illus.). 160p. 1990. pap. 19.95 (0-912365-32-3) Sasquatch Bks.

*Mount St. Helens: The Eruption & Recovery of a Volcano. 20th anniversary ed. Rob Carson. (Illus.). 160p. 2000. pap. 19.95 (1-57061-248-X) Sasquatch Bks.

*Mt. St. Helens: The Smoking Mountain. Kathy Furgang. LC 00-28585. (Volcanoes of the World Ser.). (Illus.). 2000. write for info. (0-8239-5660-1, PowerKids) Rosen Group.

Mount St. Helens: The Story Behind the Scenery. Thom Corcoran. LC 85-50108. (Illus.). 48p. (Orig.). 1985. pap. 7.95 (0-88714-000-9) KC Pubns.

Mt. St. Helens & the Toutle Valley: The Early Years. Dale Hoy. Ed. by Susan Keegan. 177p. 1993. pap. 12.95 (0-9636954-0-1) Art Farm WA.

Mount St. Helens Ash Potpourri: Yakima's Story. Mary McConville Stensrud. 341p. 1985. 15.00 (0-614-30201-3) Mary M Stensrud.

Mount St. Helens Eruption. Sue Hamilton. Ed. by John Hamilton. LC 88-71721. (Day of Disaster Ser.). (Illus.). 32p. (J). (gr. 4). 1989. lib. bdg. 12.98 (0-939179-41-5) ABDO Pub Co.

Mount St. Helens Is My Home. Gina Garlie. (Illus.). 40p. (J). (gr. k-3). 1993. pap. 3.95 (0-9637878-0-2, 574180) Lupine Pr.

Mount St. Helens National Volcanic Monument Trail Guide. (Illus.). 144p. (Orig.). 1994. pap. text 12.95 (0-914019-35-X, 5382) NW Interpretive.

Mount St. Helens National Volcanic Monument. Barbara Decker & Robert Decker. (Pocket Portfolio Ser.: Vol. 3). (Illus.). 32p. (Orig.). 1997. pap. 5.95 (0-939365-54-5); pap. 6.95 (0-939365-80-4); pap. 6.95 (0-939365-79-0); pap. 6.95 (0-939365-77-4); pap. 6.95 (0-939365-78-2) Panorama Intl.

Mount St. Helens National Volcanic Monument. Sharlene Nelson. (True Bks.). (J). 1998. pap. text 6.95 (0-516-26269-6) Childrens.

Mount St. Helens National Volcanic Monument. Sharlene P. Nelson & Ted W. Nelson. LC 96-46738. (True Bk.). (J). 1997. lib. bdg. 21.00 (0-516-20444-0) Childrens.

Mount St. Helens National Volcanic Monument. Ed. by Jeff Nicholas. (Wish You Were Here Postcard Book Ser.). (Illus.). 32p. 1998. pap. 4.95 (0-939365-88-X) Panorama Intl.

Mount St. Helens, Pathways to Discovery: The Complete Visitor Guide to America's Favorite Volcano. David H. Seesholtz. LC 93-90139. (Illus.). 224p. (Orig.). 1993. pap. 14.95 (0-9636168-0-3) A Plus Images.

Mount St. Helens Volcano. William Bankier. Ed. by Liz Parker. (Take Ten Bks.). (YA). (gr. 6-12). 1993. pap. text 3.95 (1-56254-098-X) Saddleback Pubns.

*Mount St. Helens Volcano. rev. ed. William Bankier. (Take Ten Ser.). (Illus.). 45p. (YA). (gr. 4-12). 1999. pap. 3.95 (1-58659-023-5) Artesian.

*Mount St. Helens Volcano: Violent Eruption. Carmen Bredeson. LC 00-9199. (American Disasters Ser.). (Illus.). 2001. write for info. (0-7660-1552-1) Enslow Pubs.

*Mount Saint Vincent University: A Vision Unfolding, 1873-1988. Theresa Corcoran. LC 99-36526. (Illus.). 384p. 1999. 57.00 (0-7618-1473-6) U Pr of Amer.

*Mount San Antonio College Chemistry 2a. 4th ed. 292p. (C). 1999. lab manual ed. 25.50 (0-536-60247-6) Pearson Custom.

Mount Shasta: History, Legends, & Lore. Michael Zanger. LC 92-24720. 144p. 1995. pap. 19.95 (0-89087-674-6) Celestial Arts.

Mount Shasta: Where Heaven & Earth Meet. Jane English. LC 95-90740. 120p. 1996. 35.00 (0-934747-07-5); pap. text 19.95 (0-934747-06-7) Earth Heart.

Mount Shasta Home of the Ancients. Bruce Walton. (Illus.). 132p. 1997. reprint ed. pap. 21.00 (0-7873-1301-7) Hlth Research.

Mount Sinai. Joseph J. Hobbs. LC 94-31952. (Illus.). 376p. 1995. pap. 19.95 (0-292-73094-2); text 50.00 (0-292-73091-8) U of Tex Pr.

Mt. Sinai Arabic Version, No. AR 48. E. Peters. 1998. 50.00 (90-6831-838-1, Pub. by Peeters Pub) Bks Intl VA.

Mt. Sinai Arabic Version, No. AR49. E. Peters. 1998. 50.00 (90-6831-839-X, Pub. by Peeters Pub) Bks Intl VA.

Mt. Sinai Clinical Handbook of Surgery: A Case-Oriented Approach. Joel J. Bauer & Mount Sinai Hospital (New York, N. Y.) Staff. LC 98-6114. 706p. 1998. spiral bd. 33.95 (0-683-18001-0) Lppncott W & W.

Mount Sinai Manual of Rehab Nursing. Schmerzler. 1997. spiral bd. write for info. (0-316-77452-9) Lppncott W & W.

Mount Soledad. Harry Polkinhorn. (Illus.). 112p. (Orig.). 1996. pap. 9.00 (1-880516-19-5) Left Hand Bks.

Mount St Helens National Volcanic Monument Completion Act: Hearing Before the Subcommittee on National Parks, Historic Preservation & Recreation of the Committee on Energy & Natural Resources, United States Senate, One Hundred Fifth Congress, First Session, On S. 638 . . . October 29, 1997. USGPO Staff. LC 98-161367. (S. Hrg. Ser.). iii, 31 p. 1998. write for info. (0-16-056266-X) USGPO.

Mount Tamalpais: A History. Lincoln Fairley. Ed. by James Heig. (Illus.). 212p. 1987. pap. 18.00 (0-942087-01-1) Scottwall Assocs.

Mount to the Sky Like Eagles. Bernard Perner & Majorie Perner. (Heritage Ser.: Vol. 9). 1986. 10.95 (0-911802-64-9); pap. 8.95 (7-100-07622-6) Free Church Pubns.

Mount up on Wounded Wings: For Women from Hurtful Home Backgrounds. Beneth P. Jones. LC 94-28759. 105p. 1994. pap. 8.25 (0-89084-772-X, 081430) Bob Jones Univ.

*Mount up! We're Moving Out! A World War II Memoir of D Troop, 94th Cavalry Reconnaissance Squadron (Mechanized) of the 14th Armored Division. Vernon H. Brown, Jr. (World War II Memoir Ser.: Vol. 59). (Illus.). 98p. 1999. 34.95 (1-57638-180-3, M59-H); pap. 19.95 (1-57638-179-X, M59-S) Merriam Pr.

Mount up with Wings: A Book of Inspirational Verse. deluxe ed. Eleanor Eastep. (Illus.). 53p. 1998. pap. 8.95 (0-9661590-0-4) Balm Gilead.

Mount up with Wings A View from the Peaks. Evaline Echols. 1999. pap. text 10.99 (0-87148-604-0) Pathway Pr.

Mount Vernon. Mary Collins. LC 97-26584. (Cornerstones to Freedom Ser.). (Illus.). 32p. (J). (gr. 4-6). 1998. 19.50 (0-516-20939-6) Childrens.

Mount Vernon. Mary Collins. (Cornerstones to Freedom Ser.). (Illus.). 32p. (J). (gr. 4-6). 1999. pap. text 5.95 (0-516-26343-9) Childrens.

Mount Vernon. Jason Cooper. LC 99-27475. (American Landmarks Ser.). (Illus.). 24p. 1999. lib. bdg. write for info. (0-86593-548-3) Rourke Corp.

Mount Vernon. Catherine Reef. LC 91-33494. (Places in American History Ser.). (Illus.). 72p. (J). (gr. 4 up). 1992. lib. bdg. 14.95 (0-87518-474-X, Dillon Silver Burdett) Silver Burdett Pr.

Mount Vernon: A Handbook. (Illus.). 114p. 1.91 (0-931917-02-6) Mt Vernon Ladies.

Mount Vernon: The Civil War Years. Dorothy T. Muir. 1993. pap. 10.95 (0-931917-26-3) Mt Vernon Ladies.

Mount Vernon: The Legacy. Elswyth Thane. 1976. reprint ed. lib. bdg. 24.95 (0-88411-959-9) Amereon Ltd.

Mount Vernon: The Story of a Shrine. 2nd ed. Gerald W. Johnson. (Illus.). 130p. 1989. pap. write for info. (0-931917-17-4) Mt Vernon Ladies.

Mount Vernon Coloring Book. (Illus.). pap. 2.00 (0-931917-12-3) Mt Vernon Ladies.

Mount Vernon Cookbook. (Illus.). 1987. reprint ed. 15.95 (0-931917-13-1) Mt Vernon Ladies.

Mount Washington: Baltimore Suburb. Mark Miller. (Illus.). 84p. (Orig.). pap. 8.95 (0-939928-00-0) GBS Pubs.

*Mt. Washington Art Glass: Identification & Value Guide. Betty Sisk. (Illus.). 224p. 2000. 29.95 (1-57432-200-1) Collector Bks.

Mount Washington in Winter, 1870-1871. Mount. (Illus.). 363p. 1993. reprint ed. pap. text 21.00 (1-55613-891-1) Heritage Bk.

Mount Whitney Guide: For Hikers & Climbers. Paul Hellweg & Scott McDonald. LC 90-62176. (Illus.). 144p. (Orig.). 1990. pap. 7.95 (0-942568-22-2) Canyon Pub Co.

Mount Zion: The Mystery of God. Joseph O. Obiaya. LC 93-93712. (Illus.). 198p. (C). 1993. lib. bdg. 25.00 (0-9638850-0-6) J O Obiaya.

Mount Zion Cemetary, Aldie, Virginia. Wynne Saffer. 102p. 1997. pap. 12.00 (1-888265-26-4) Willow Bend.

Mount Zion Field. J. Thomas O'Connell. 101p. 1990. 24.50 (0-916379-39-6) Scripta.

Mountain. Ab Hugh Dafydd. (Swept Away Ser.). 1996. 9.60 (0-606-10338-4, Pub. by Turtleback) Demco.

Mountain. Dafydd Hugh. (YA). (gr. 7 up). 1996. pap. 4.50 (0-614-15655-6, Harp PBks) HarpC.

*Mountain. Elvi Rhodes. 2000. 27.95 (0-593-03932-7, Pub. by Transworld Publishers Ltd); pap. 10.95 (0-552-14400-2, Pub. by Transworld Publishers Ltd) Trafalgar.

Mountain. A. Alexander Volenski. LC 94-96809. 50p. (Orig.). 1995. pap. 12.95 (0-9644554-0-4) Alexnder Pub.

Mountain. John H. Wills. Ed. by Qual-Tech Staff & Cor Van den Heuvel. (Illus.). 152p. (Orig.). 1991. pap. 11.95 (0-685-51963-5) Qual-Tech.

Mountain: Four Seasons. John Wills. 152p. 1991. pap. text 11.95 (1-880354-00-4) Qual-Tech.

Mountain: Renewed Studies in Impressions & Appearances. John C. Van Dyke. LC 91-51096. 268p. (C). 1992. reprint ed. pap. 14.95 (0-87480-387-X) U of Utah Pr.

Mountain: The Journey of Justice Douglas. Douglas Scott. 1990. pap. 5.25 (0-8222-0776-1) Dramatists Play.

Mountain, a Pickax, a College: A History of Pacific Union College. Walter C. Utt. Ed. by J. Paul Stauffer. (Illus.). 192p. 1996. 39.00 (0-9650789-0-6) Pacific Union.

Mountain Adventure. W. Murray. (Key Words Readers Ser.: B Series, No. 641-12b). (Illus.). (J). (ps-5). pap. 3.50 (0-7214-0024-8, Ladybrd) Penguin Putnam.

Mountain Adventure: Exploring the Appalachian Trail. Ron Fisher. Ed. by Donald J. Crump. (Special Publications Series 23: No. 3). (Illus.). (YA). 1988. 12.95 (0-87044-668-1) Natl Geog.

Mountain Agriculture & Crop Genetics Resources. N. Mateo. (C). 1989. 44.00 (81-204-0472-6) S Asia.

Mountain Alphabet. Margriet Ruurs. LC 96-60349. (Illus.). 32p. (J). (gr. 3 up). 1996. 19.95 (0-88776-374-X) Tundra Bks.

Mountain Alphabet. Margriet Ruurs. LC 96-931266. (Illus.). 32p. (J). (gr. 3 up). 1996. pap. 8.95 (0-88776-384-7) Tundra Bks.

Mountain & Other Stories. St. John G. Ervine. LC 72-101809. (Short Story Index Reprint Ser.). 1977. 19.95 (0-8369-3197-1) Ayer.

*Mountain & Plain: From the Lycian Coast to the Phrygian Plateau in the Late Roman & Early By. Martin Harrison. 230p. 1999. text 42.50 (0-472-11084-5, 11084) U of Mich Pr.

Mountain & Sorrel Land Tales. Jack Rushing. 40p. Date not set. pap. 5.00 (1-891538-01-2) River Dragon.

Mountain & the Migration: A Guide to Hawk Mountain. James J. Brett. LC 91-14929. (Illus.). 112p. (Orig.). 1991. pap. 15.95 (0-8014-9613-6) Cornell U Pr.

Mountain & the Valley. Ernest Buckler. 304p. 1996. pap. 7.95 (0-7710-9952-5) McCland & Stewart.

Mountain Animals in Danger. Gary Turbak. LC 94-26302. (Illus.). 32p. (J). (gr. 1-3). 1994. lib. bdg. 14.95 (0-87358-573-9, Rising Moon Bks) Northland AZ.

Mountain Arbiters: The Changing Life of a Philippine Hill People. Edward P. Dozier. LC 66-18530. (Illus.). 319p. reprint ed. pap. 98.90 (0-608-11659-9, 205537300017) Bks Demand.

Mountain Artisans - Appalachia. Daniel Robbins & Eleanor Fayerweather. (Illus.). 1970. pap. 3.00 (0-911517-28-6) Mus of Art RI.

Mountain Ash & Penrhiwceiber Remembered in Pictures. Bernard Baldwin. 80p. (C). 1989. 65.00 (0-905928-50-4, Pub. by D Brown & Sons Ltd) St Mut.

Mountain Bears. Wayne Lynch. 1999. pap. text 14.95 (1-894004-28-0) Fifth Hse Publ.

Mountain Behind the Mountain: Aspects of the Celtic Tradition. Noel D. O'Donoghue. 1993. text 37.95 (0-567-09652-1, Pub. by T & T Clark) Bks Intl VA.

Mountain Bicycling in the San Gabriels. Robert Immler. LC 87-40203. (Illus.). 128p. 1987. pap. 10.95 (0-89997-078-8) Wilderness Pr.

Mountain Bike! Northern California. Linda G. Austin. (Illus.). 416p. 1999. pap. 15.95 (0-89732-288-6) Menasha Ridge.

Mountain Bike! Oregon. Laurie Leman & Chris Leman. LC 98-30987. (Mountain Bike! Ser.). (Illus.). 400p. 1998. pap. 15.95 (0-89732-281-9) Menasha Ridge.

Mountain Bike: Repair & Maintenance. W. Lindorf. (Illus.). 72p. 1995. pap. 14.95 (0-7063-7420-7, Pub. by WrLock) Sterling.

Mountain Bike! Southern California. 2nd rev. ed. David Story et al. LC 98-27165. (Mountain Bike! Ser.). (Illus.). 400p. 1998. pap. 15.95 (0-89732-283-5) Menasha Ridge.

Mountain Bike! The Midwest. 2nd rev. ed. Richard Ries & Dave Shepard. (America by Mountain Bike Ser.). (Illus.). 1999. pap. write for info. (0-89732-306-8) Menasha Ridge.

Mountain Bike! The Midwest. 2nd rev. ed. Richard Ries & Dave Shepard. (America by Mountain Bike Ser.). 400p. 1999. pap. 15.95 (0-89732-282-7) Menasha Ridge.

Mountain Bike! The Southern Appalachian & Smoky Mountains. Steve Jones. LC 99-13586. (Mountain Bike! Ser.). 416p. 1998. pap. 15.95 (0-89732-270-3) Menasha Ridge.

Mountain Bike! Washington. Alan Bennett et al. (Mountain Bike! Ser.). (Illus.). 400p. 1998. pap. 15.95 (0-89732-280-0) Menasha Ridge.

Mountain Bike! A Manual of Beginning to Advanced Technique. William Nealy. LC 91-40292. (Illus.). 172p. 1992. pap. 14.95 (0-89732-114-6) Menasha Ridge.

Mountain Bike Adventure Guide: For the Sun Valley Area. John Zilly & Eloise Christensen. 60p. 1995. pap. 8.95 (1-881583-00-7) Advent Pr WA.

Mountain Bike Adventures in Southwest British Columbia: 50 Rides. Greg Maurer. LC 99-6060. (Mountain Bike Adventures Ser.). 224p. 1999. pap. 16.95 (0-89886-628-6) Mountaineers.

An Asterisk (*) at the beginning of an entry indicates that the title is appearing for the first time.

Mountain Bike Adventures in the Four Corners Region. Michael McCoy. LC 90-40743. (Illus.). 224p. (Orig.). 1990. pap. 12.95 (*0-89886-251-5*) Mountaineers.

Mountain Bike Adventures in the Northern Rockies. Michael McCoy. LC 89-3007. (Illus.). 224p. (Orig.). 1989. pap. 10.95 (*0-89886-190-X*) Mountaineers.

Mountain Bike Adventures in Washington's North Cascades & Olympics. 2nd ed. Tom Kirkendall. LC 96-12027. (Illus.). 224p. (Orig.). 1996. pap. 14.95 (*0-89886-413-5*) Mountaineers.

Mountain Bike Adventures in Washington's South Cascades & Puget Sound. 2nd ed. Tom Kirkendall. (Illus.). 224p. 1996. pap. 14.95 (*0-89886-414-3*) Mountaineers.

Mountain Bike America: Oregon: An Atlas of Oregon's Greatest Off-Road Bicycle Rides. Lizann Dunegan. Ed. by Scott E. Adams. (Illus.). 224p. 2000. pap. 15.95 (*1-882997-10-7*, Pub. by Beachway Pr) Globe Pequot.

Mountain Bike America: Vermont: An Atlas of Vermont's Greatest Off-Road Bicycle Rides. Jen Mynter. (Illus.). 192p. 2000. pap. 14.95 (*1-882997-07-7*, Pub. by Beachway Pr) Globe Pequot.

Mountain Bike America: Washington: An Atlas of Washington's Greatest Off-Road Bicycle Rides. Amy Poffenbarger & Mark Poffenbarger. Ed. by Ryan Croxton. (Illus.). 224p. 2000. pap. 15.95 (*1-882997-09-3*, Pub. by Beachway Pr) Globe Pequot.

***Mountain Bike! Atlantic Canada.** Sarah L. Hale & Jodi Bishop. Ed. by Dennis Coello. LC 99-29364. (North America by Mountain Bike Ser.). (Illus.). 400p. 1999. pap. 15.95 (*1-55068-096-X*, Pub. by Vanwell Publ) Howell Pr VA.

***Mountain Bike! Atlantic Canada: A Guide to the Classic Trails** Sarah L. Hale & Jodi Bishop. LC 99-29364. (America by Mountain Bike Ser.). 1999. write for info. (*0-89732-286-X*) Menasha Ridge.

Mountain Bike Book. David Leslie. (Illus.). 144p. 1996. 21.95 (*0-7063-7373-1*, Pub. by WrLock) Sterling.

Mountain Bike Book. David Leslie. (Illus.). 144p. 1997. pap. 16.95 (*0-7063-7524-6*, Pub. by WrLock) Sterling.

Mountain Bike Emergency Repair. Tim Toyoshima. LC 94-44409. (Illus.). 128p. 1995. pap. 7.95 (*0-89886-422-4*) Mountaineers.

Mountain Bike! Florida: A Guide to the Classic Trails. Steve Jones. Ed. by Dennis Coello. LC 97-9250. (Mountain Bike Ser.). (Illus.). 350p. (Orig.). 1997. pap. 14.95 (*0-89732-231-2*) Menasha Ridge.

Mountain Bike! Great Lake States. Philip Van Valkenberg & Jack McHugh. LC 98-23032. (America by Mountain Bike Ser.). (Illus.). 256p. 1995. pap. 14.95 (*0-89732-253-3*) Menasha Ridge.

Mountain Bike Here: Ontario & Central & Western New York. Sue Lebrecht. (Illus.). 168p. 1999. pap. 13.95 (*1-55046-292-X*, Pub. by Boston Mills) Genl Dist Srvs.

***Mountain Bike Like a Champion: Master All the Skills to Tackle the Toughest Terrain.** Ned Overend & Ed Pavelka. LC 99-28633. (Illus.). 240p. 1999. pap. 16.95 (*1-57954-081-3*) Rodale Pr Inc.

Mountain Bike Log. Kenneth G. Hukari & Scott Griebel. 62p. 1995. 14.95 (*1-884751-03-2*) Wy East LogBk.

Mountain Bike Madness in Central PA: An Atlas of Central Pennsylvania's Greatest Mountain Bike Rides. Scott E. Adams. (Illus.). 142p. (Orig.). 1993. pap. 10.95 (*1-882997-02-6*) Beachway Pr.

Mountain Bike Magazine's Complete Guide to Mountain Biking Skills: Expert Tips on Conquering Curves, Corners, Dips, Descents, Hills, Water Hazards, & Other All-Terrain Challenges. Mountain Bike Magazine Editors & Bicycling Magazine Editors. (Illus.). 224p. 1996. pap. 14.95 (*0-87596-300-5*) Rodale Pr Inc.

Mountain Bike Magic: The Complete Full-Color Book on Mountain Biking. Rob Van der Plas. (Illus.). 127p. 1998. pap. text 15.00 (*0-7881-5403-6*) DIANE Pub.

Mountain Bike! Maine. Sarah Hale & David Gibbs. LC 98-11035. (North America by Mountain Bike Ser.). 320p. 1998. pap. 15.95 (*0-89732-266-5*) Menasha Ridge.

Mountain Bike Maintenance: Repairing & Maintaining the Off-Road Bicycle. 3rd ed. Rob Vanderplas. LC 95-47611. (Illus.). 128p. 1996. pap. 14.95 (*0-933201-65-6*) MBI Pubg.

Mountain Bike Mania. Matt Christopher. LC 98-24050. 160p. (J). (gr. 2-7). 1998. 15.95 (*0-316-14355-3*) Little.

Mountain Bike Mania. Matt Christopher. LC 98-24050. 160p. (J). (gr. 3-7). 1998. pap. 3.95 (*0-316-14292-1*) Little.

Mountain Bike! New Hampshire. Jeff Faust. (North America by Mountain Bike Ser.). 320p. 1998. pap. 15.95 (*0-89732-268-1*) Menasha Ridge.

Mountain Bike! Northwest Washington: A Guide to Trails & Adventure. John Zilly. LC 98-16759. (Illus.). 224p. 1998. pap. 15.95 (*1-57061-138-6*) Sasquatch Bks.

Mountain Bike Nova Scotia: A Guide to Off-Road Cycling in Nova Scotia. Geoff Brown & Kemit DeGooysr. (Illus.). 96p. (Orig.). 1996. pap. 9.95 (*1-55109-155-0*) Nimbus Publ.

Mountain Bike Owner's Manual. Velo News Technical Editors. (Illus.). 96p. 1998. pap. 9.95 (*1-884737-52-8*) VeloPress.

Mountain Bike Performance Handbook. Leonard Zinn. LC 98-23791. (Illus.). 160p. 1998. pap. 19.95 (*0-933201-95-8*) Motorbooks Intl.

Mountain Bike Repair. Ken Gronseth. (Nuts-N-Bolts Ser.). (Illus.). 32p. (Orig.). 1997. pap. 4.95 (*0-89732-238-X*) Menasha Ridge.

Mountain Bike Repair Handbook. Dennis Coello. (Illus.). 176p. 1990. pap. 12.95 (*1-55821-064-4*) Lyons Pr.

Mountain Bike Ride Guide, Lane County, Oregon. 3rd ed. Ed. by Dan Geiger & Keith Nelson. (Illus.). 144p. 1992. reprint ed. pap. 11.95 (*0-87114-078-0*) U of Oreg Bks.

Mountain Bike Southern New England: An Atlas of Southern New Englands' Greatest Off-Road Bicycle Rides. Jeff Cutler. (Mountain Bike America Ser.). 256p. 1998. pap. 15.95 (*1-882997-15-8*) Beachway Pr.

***Mountain Bike! Southern Utah: A Guide to the Classic Trails.** Michael McCoy. LC 00-39444. (Illus.). 2000. pap. 15.95 (*0-89732-314-9*) Menasha Ridge.

Mountain Bike! Southwest Washington: A Guide to Trails & Adventure. John Zilly. (Illus.). 224p. 1998. pap. 15.95 (*1-57061-137-8*) Sasquatch Bks.

***Mountain Bike! Southwestern British Columbia.** Ward Cameron. Ed. by Dennis Coello. LC 99-29363. (North America by Mountain Bike Ser.). (Illus.). 400p. 1999. pap. 15.95 (*1-55068-094-3*, Pub. by Vanwell Publ) Howell Pr VA.

Mountain Bike Technique. Steve Jones. (Nuts-N-Bolts Guides Ser.). (Illus.). 32p. (Orig.). 1997. pap. 4.95 (*0-89732-239-8*) Menasha Ridge.

Mountain Bike! Texas & Oklahoma. Chuck Cypert. (Mountain Bike Ser.). 384p. 1998. pap. text 14.95 (*0-89732-258-4*) Menasha Ridge.

Mountain Bike! The Canadian Rockies. Ward Cameron. LC 98-1235. (Illus.). 250p. 1997. pap. text 14.95 (*0-89732-250-9*) Menasha Ridge.

Mountain Bike! The Deep South. Steve Jones. (Mountain Bike Ser.). (Illus.). 350p. 1998. pap. text 14.95 (*0-89732-252-5*) Menasha Ridge.

Mountain Bike! The Great Plains States. Andy Knapp. (Mountain Bike Ser.). 256p. 1998. pap. text 14.95 (*0-89732-254-1*) Menasha Ridge.

Mountain Bike! The Mid-Atlantic States: Charleston, SC to Washington, DC. Joe Surkiewicz. LC 98-7062. (North America by Mountain Bike Ser.). 320p. 1998. pap. 15.95 (*0-89732-271-1*) Menasha Ridge.

Mountain Bike! The Mid-Atlantic States: Maryland to New Jersey. Joe Surkiewicz. Ed. by Dennis Coello. LC 99-38556. (Illus.). 352p. 1999. pap. 15.95 (*0-89732-305-X*) Menasha Ridge.

Mountain Bike! The Ozarks. Steve Henry. (Mountain Bike Ser.). 270p. 1998. pap. text 14.95 (*0-89732-260-6*) Menasha Ridge.

***Mountain Bike! The Ozarks.** 2nd rev. ed. Steve Henry. Ed. by Dennis Coello. (North America by Mountain Bike Ser.). (Illus.). 288p. 2000. pap. 15.95 (*0-89732-325-4*) Menasha Ridge.

Mountain Bike! The Southeast. Lori Finley. (Mountain Bike Ser.). 262p. 1998. pap. text 14.95 (*0-89732-257-6*) Menasha Ridge.

Mountain Bike Trails of Wisconsin. Ray Hoven. (Illus.). 128p. Date not set. 14.95 (*1-57430-025-3*) Am Bike Trails.

Mountain Bike Utah: An Atlas of Southern Utah's Greatest Off-Road Bicycle Rides. Lee Bridgers. (Mountain Bike America Ser.). 224p. 1998. pap. 15.95 (*1-882997-13-1*) Beachway Pr.

Mountain Bike! Vermont. Kate Carter. LC 98-6082. (North America by Mountain Bike Ser.). 320p. 1998. pap. 15.95 (*0-89732-267-3*) Menasha Ridge.

Mountain Bike! Virginia. Randy Porter. LC 97-49133. (Mountain Bike! Ser.). 352p. 1997. pap. 14.95 (*0-89732-248-7*) Menasha Ridge.

Mountain Bike Virginia: An Atlas of Virginia's Greatest Off-Road Bicycle Rides. 2nd ed. Scott E. Adams. (Mountain Bike America Ser.). (Illus.). 224p. (YA). 1998. pap. 15.95 (*1-882997-11-5*) Beachway Pr.

Mountain Bike Virginia: An Atlas of Virginia's Greatest Off-Road Bike Rides. Scott E. Adams. (Mountain Bike America Ser.). (Illus.). 256p. (Orig.). 1995. pap. 12.95 (*1-882997-04-2*) Beachway Pr.

Mountain Bike Way of Knowledge. William Nealy. LC 89-27655. (Illus.). 128p. 1989. pap. 7.95 (*0-89732-097-2*) Menasha Ridge.

Mountain Bike! Wisconsin. Phil Van Valkenberg. LC 98-27166. (North America by Mountain Bike Ser.). 352p. 1998. pap. 15.95 (*0-89732-269-X*) Menasha Ridge.

Mountain Biker. Edward Packard. (Choose Your Own Adventure Ser.: No. 172). (Illus.). 128p. (J). (gr. 4-8). 1996. pap. 3.50 (*0-553-56625-3*, Choose) BDD Bks Young Read.

Mountain Biker. Edward Packard. (Choose Your Own Adventure Ser.: No. 172). (J). (gr. 4-8). 1996. 8.60 (*0-606-09633-7*, Pub. by Turtleback) Demco.

Mountain Bikers Almanac. Grant Wolf, Inc., Editors. LC 95-78725. (Premier Issue Ser.). (Illus.). 256p. 1995. pap. 19.95 (*0-9647601-0-X*) Grant Wolf.

Mountain Biker's Guide to New Mexico. Sarah L. Bennett. LC 93-46387. (Mountain Bike Ser.). 245p. (Orig.). 1994. pap. 14.95 (*1-56044-219-0*) Falcon Pub Inc.

Mountain Biker's Guide to O'ahu: Mauka Trails of Hawai'i. John Alford. Ed. by John Clark. (Illus.). 112p. (Orig.). 1995. pap. 12.95 (*0-9649843-0-X*) Ohana Pubng.

Mountain Biker's Guide to Ski Resorts: Where to Ride Downhill in New York, New England, & Northeastern Canada. Robert M. Immler. LC 97-43218. (Illus.). 176p. 1998. pap. 14.95 (*0-88150-371-1*, Pub. by Countryman) Norton.

***Mountain Biker's Training Bible.** Joe Friel. (Illus.). 368p. 2000. pap. 19.95 (*1-884737-71-4*) VeloPress.

Mountain Bikes. J. Cook. (Superskills Ser.). (Illus.). xp. (YA). (gr. 6-10). 1990. pap. 5.95 (*0-7460-0520-2*, Usborne) EDC.

Mountain Bikes. J. Cook. (Superskills Ser.). (Illus.). 48p. (YA). (gr. 6-10). 1999. lib. bdg. 13.95 (*0-88110-426-4*, Usborne) EDC.

Mountain Bikes: Maintaining, Repairing & Upgrading. Herman Seidl. LC 92-18773. (Illus.). 128p. (J). (gr. 4 up). 1992. 16.95 (*0-8069-8764-2*) Sterling.

Mountain Bikes: Maintaining, Repairing & Upgrading. Herman Seidl. (Illus.). 128p. (YA). (gr. 10-12). 1993. pap. 12.95 (*0-8069-8765-0*) Sterling.

Mountain Biking see Action Sports

Mountain Biking. Steve Behr. LC 98-3983. (Extreme Sports Ser.). (Illus.). 32p. (J). (gr. 5-9). 1998. pap. 6.95 (*0-7641-0796-8*) Barron.

***Mountain Biking.** Kirk Bizley. LC 99-24038. (Radical Sports Ser.). 1999. lib. bdg. write for info. (*1-57572-944-X*) Heinemann Lib.

Mountain Biking. Larry D. Brimner. (First Bks.). 64p. (J). 1997. pap. 6.95 (*0-531-15814-4*); lib. bdg. 22.00 (*0-531-20243-7*) Watts.

Mountain Biking. Don Davis & David Carter. LC 93-24692. (Outdoor Pursuits Ser.). (Illus.). 144p. 1993. pap. 12.95 (*0-87322-452-3*, PDAV0452) Human Kinetics.

Mountain Biking. Football Association Staff & Carolyn B. Mitchell. LC 97-22049. (Know the Sport Ser.). (Illus.). 48p. 1997. pap. 5.95 (*0-8117-2840-4*) Stackpole.

Mountain Biking. Keith Mills. 128p. 1989. pap. 18.95 (*0-8117-2315-1*) Stackpole.

Mountain Biking. unabridged ed. Mark Langton. LC 98-102784. (Outdoor Action Guides Ser.). 1997. pap. 6.95 (*0-307-24600-0*, Whitman Coin) St Martin.

***Mountain Biking.** 2nd ed. Michael A. Strassman. (Basic Essentials Ser.). (Illus.). 80p. 2000. pap. 7.95 (*0-7627-0663-5*) Globe Pequot.

Mountain Biking!: Get on the Trail see Extreme Sports Collection

Mountain Biking: Moab. David Crowell. LC 97-199910. (Illus.). 160p. (Orig.). 1997. pap. 10.95 (*1-56044-530-0*) Falcon Pub Inc.

Mountain Biking . . . to the Extreme - Cliff Dive. Sigmund Brouwer. LC 96-34928. (Short Cuts Sports Mysteries Ser.: Vol. 2). 64p. (J). (gr. 5-9). 1996. mass mkt. 3.99 (*0-8499-3952-6*) Tommy Nelson.

Mountain Biking - Over the Edge. Bill Strickland. LC 98-3014. (Illus.). 128p. 1998. pap. 15.95 (*0-07-038703-6*) Intl Marine.

***Mountain Biking Albuquerque.** Nicole Blouin. LC 99-22407. (Illus.). 120p. 1999. pap. 10.95 (*1-56044-746-X*) Falcon Pub Inc.

Mountain Biking Arizona. Sarah L. Bennett. LC 97-1713. (America by Mountain Bike Ser.). (Illus.). 229p. 1996. pap. 12.95 (*1-56044-431-2*) Falcon Pub Inc.

Mountain Biking Bend. Scott Rapp. LC 97-50137. (Illus.). 1998. pap. 10.95 (*1-56044-593-9*) Falcon Pub Inc.

Mountain Biking Boise. Martin Potucek. LC 97-44038. (Illus.). 1998. pap. 10.95 (*1-56044-599-8*) Falcon Pub Inc.

Mountain Biking British Columbia: The Trail Guide & Inspirational Resource Book. Darrin Polischuk. 1996. pap. 24.95 (*0-9680342-1-7*) Ok1anagan Mtn.

Mountain Biking California's Central Coast Best 100 Trails: Big Sur to Point Mugu. Delanie Fragnoli. LC 98-46441. (Illus.). 272p. 1999. per. 18.95 (*0-938665-59-6*) Fine Edge Prods.

***Mountain Biking Central Texas.** 4th ed. Becky Youman & Rick Youman. 1999. pap. write for info. (*0-9671018-0-8*) Ragged Edge TX.

Mountain Biking Chequamegon. Steve Johnson. LC 97-53249. (Illus.). 1998. pap. 10.95 (*1-56044-598-X*) Falcon Pub Inc.

***Mountain Biking Chico.** Mark M. Menard. LC 98-49085. (Illus.). 160p. 1999. pap. 10.95 (*1-56044-804-0*) Falcon Pub Inc.

Mountain Biking Colorado. Gregg Bromka. 1998. pap. 14.95 (*1-56044-840-7*) Falcon Pub Inc.

Mountain Biking Colorado Springs. David Crowell. (Illus.). 158p. 1998. pap. text 9.95 (*1-56044-822-9*) Falcon Pub Inc.

Mountain Biking Colorado's Front Range: Great Rides in & Around Fort Collins, Denver & Boulder. Derek Ryter & Jarral Ryter. LC 98-23659. (Illus.). 197p. 1998. pap. 16.95 (*0-87108-890-8*) Pruett.

Mountain Biking Colorado's Historic Mining Districts. Laura Rossetter. LC 90-85222. (Illus.). 176p. (Orig.). 1991. pap. 10.95 (*1-55591-090-4*) Fulcrum Pub.

Mountain Biking Colorado's la Platas: Great Rides Between Durango & Telluride. Derek Ryter. LC 95-3520. (Illus.). 129p. 1995. pap. 16.95 (*0-87108-860-6*) Pruett.

***Mountain Biking Colorado's Western Slope.** Phillip Benningfield. LC 00-131518. (Illus.). 112p. 2000. pap. 9.95 (*1-892540-11-8*) Sharp End.

***Mountain Biking Connecticut: A Guide to the Best 25 Places to Ride.** Stuart A. Johnstone. (Illus.). 185p. 2000. pap. (*0-9627990-8-4*) Active Pubns.

Mountain Biking Denver-Boulder. Bob D'Antonio. LC 97-13318. (Illus.). 136p. (Orig.). 1997. pap. 10.95 (*1-56044-532-7*) Falcon Pub Inc.

Mountain Biking Durango. John Peel. LC 97-50138. (Illus.). 1998. pap. 10.95 (*1-56044-531-9*) Falcon Pub Inc.

***Mountain Biking Flagstaff & Sedona.** Bruce Grubbs. LC 98-50418. (Illus.). 160p. 1999. pap. 10.95 (*1-56044-801-6*) Falcon Pub Inc.

Mountain Biking for Women. Robin Stewart & Cathy Jensen. LC 94-27396. 176p. 1994. pap. 15.00 (*0-937921-54-8*) Acorn Pub.

Mountain Biking Georgia. Alex Nutt. LC 98-40717. (Illus.). 256p. 1998. pap. 12.95 (*1-56044-647-1*) Falcon Pub Inc.

***Mountain Biking Grand Junction & Fruita.** Bob D'Antonio. (Illus.). 128p. 2000. pap. 9.95 (*1-56044-945-4*) Falcon Pub Inc.

Mountain Biking Guide to Vail, Colorado. Michael J. Murphy. Ed. & Illus. by Mary E. Giuiland. Illus. by Dannette Peterson. 72p. (Orig.). 1990. pap. text 8.95 (*0-9626114-0-9*) M Murphy & Assocs.

Mountain Biking Helena. Will Harmon. LC 97-50156. (Illus.). 1998. pap. 10.95 (*1-56044-597-1*) Falcon Pub Inc.

***Mountain Biking Idaho.** Stephen Stuebner. LC 98-52472. (Illus.). 345p. 1999. pap. 15.95 (*1-56044-744-3*) Falcon Pub Inc.

Mountain Biking in Boise. Stephen Stuebner. (Illus.). 110p. 1997. pap. text 12.95 (*0-9644343-3-4*) Boise Front.

Mountain Biking in Canyon Rims Recreation Area. Peggy Utesch & Bob Utesch. LC 91-75556. (Canyon Country Ser.: No. 27). (Illus.). 88p. (Orig.). 1991. pap. 6.00 (*0-925685-02-X*) Canyon Country Pubns.

Mountain Biking in Kentucky. Stuart Ulferts & Bruce Montana. LC 95-68798. 119p. 1995. pap. 12.95 (*1-887187-04-9*) RSH Media.

***Mountain Biking in New Jersey: 37 Off-Road Rides in the Garden State.** Christopher Mackinnon. (Illus.). 2000. pap. 13.95 (*0-9652733-5-0*) Freewheeling.

Mountain Biking in Northern New Mexico: Historical & Natural History Rides. Craig Martin. LC 93-49530. (Coyote Book Ser.). (Illus.). 205p. (Orig.). 1994. reprint ed. pap. 63.60 (*0-608-07277-X*, 206750500009) Bks Demand.

Mountain Biking in South-Central Colorado. P. S. Lee. LC 95-90662. (Illus.). 140p. (Orig.). 1995. pap. 12.00 (*0-9648169-0-3*) Wherever Guidebks.

Mountain Biking in the High Country of Steamboat Springs, Colorado. Thomas R. Litteral. 104p. 1993. pap. 10.95 (*1-883966-00-0*) Am Kestrel Pr.

Mountain Biking in West Virginia. Frank Hutchins. (Illus.). 208p. (Orig.). 1995. pap. 12.95 (*0-9646197-1-7*) Quarrier Pr.

Mountain Biking L. A. County: Southern Section. Donald G. Brundige & Sharron L. Brundige. LC 95-94085. (Illus.). 218p. 1996. pap. 11.95 (*0-9619151-7-X*) BD Enterprises.

Mountain Biking Marin: 40 Great Rides in Marin County. Theresa Martin & Brian Simon. 112p. 1998. pap. 10.95 (*0-9617044-7-0*) Martin Press.

Mountain Biking Michigan: Best Trails in Southern Michigan. Dwain Abramowski & Sandra Davison. (Illus.). 272p. 1997. pap. 13.95 (*1-882376-20-X*) Thunder Bay Pr.

Mountain Biking Michigan: The Best Trails in Northern Lower Michigan. Mike Terrell. (Illus.). 224p. 1996. pap. 13.95 (*1-882376-21-8*) Thunder Bay Pr.

Mountain Biking Michigan: The Best Trails in the Upper Peninsula. Mike McLelland. (Illus.). 284p. 1998. pap. 14.95 (*1-882376-57-9*) Thunder Bay Pr.

Mountain Biking near Boston: A Guide to the Best 35 Places to Ride. 5th rev. ed. Stuart A. Johnstone. LC 90-85109. (Illus.). 245p. 1999. pap. text 14.95 (*0-9627990-5-X*) Active Pubns.

Mountain Biking New Hampshire: A Guide to the Best 30 Places to Ride. 2nd rev. ed. Stuart A. Johnstone. LC 92-74375. (Illus.). 186p. 1995. pap. 12.95 (*0-9627990-0-9*) Active Pubns.

Mountain Biking New Hampshire's State Parks & Forests. Linda J. Chestney. LC 95-50711. (Illus.). 176p. (Orig.). 1996. pap. 14.95 (*0-9637077-3-6*) Nicolin Flds.

Mountain Biking New York. Michael Margulis. LC 97-593. (America by Mountain Bike Ser.). (Illus.). 256p. (Orig.). 1997. pap. 14.95 (*1-56044-534-3*) Falcon Pub Inc.

Mountain Biking North America's Best 100 Ski Resorts. Delaine Fragnoli. LC 96-15086. (Illus.). 304p. (Orig.). 1996. pap. 16.95 (*0-938665-46-4*) Fine Edge Prods.

***Mountain Biking North Carolina.** Timm Muth. LC 99-55393. (Illus.). 262p. 2000. pap. 16.95 (*1-56044-809-1*) Falcon Pub Inc.

Mountain Biking North Lake Tahoe's Best Trails. Carol Bonser & R. W. Miskimins. LC 97-15307. (Illus.). 140p. (Orig.). 1997. pap. 14.95 (*0-938665-40-5*) Fine Edge Prods.

***Mountain Biking Northern California's Best 100 Trails.** 2nd ed. Delaine Fragnoli & Robin Stuart. LC 00-25433. (Illus.). 352p. 2000. 18.95 (*0-938665-73-1*) Fine Edge Prods.

Mountain Biking Northern New England. Paul Angiolillo. LC 98-30950. (America by Mountain Bike Ser.). (Illus.). 208p. 1996. pap. 12.95 (*1-56044-432-0*) Falcon Pub Inc.

Mountain Biking Ohio: A Guide to Singletrack Trails in the Buckeye State. James Buratti. LC 97-91767. (Illus.). 56p. (Orig.). 1997. pap. 10.95 (*0-9657566-0-2*) Single Track Pr.

Mountain Biking Ohio: A Guide to Singletrack Trails in the Buckeye State. 2nd rev. ed. James Buratti. (Illus.). 96p. (Orig.). 1999. pap. 11.95 (*0-9657566-1-0*) Single Track Pr.

Mountain Biking Orange County. Randy Vogel & Larry Kuechlin, Jr. (Illus.). 150p. (Orig.). 1996. pap. 14.95 (*1-57540-011-1*) Falcon Pub Inc.

Mountain Biking Oregon. Mark Wigg. LC 98-29617. (Illus.). 224p. 1998. pap. 12.95 (*1-56044-671-4*) Falcon Pub Inc.

***Mountain Biking Pennsylvania.** Rob Ginieczki. (Guide Ser.). (Illus.). 288p. 2000. pap. 16.95 (*1-56044-861-X*) Falcon Pub Inc.

***Mountain Biking Phoenix.** Bruce Grubbs. LC 99-462041. (Guides Mountain Biking Ser.). 133p. 2000. pap. 10.95 (*1-56044-745-1*) Falcon Pub Inc.

Mountain Biking South Carolina. Nicole Blovin. LC 98-11814. (Illus.). 128p. 1998. pap. 12.95 (*1-56044-684-6*) Falcon Pub Inc.

Mountain Biking South Lake Tahoe's Best Trails. Carol Bonser & R. W. Miskimins. LC 97-46182. (Illus.). 144p. 1998. pap. 14.95 (*0-938665-52-9*, Mtn Biking Pr) Fine Edge Prods.

***Mountain Biking Southern California.** Mark A. Ross & Brad L. Fine. LC 99-12361. (Illus.). 352p. 1999. pap. 14.95 (*1-56044-807-5*) Falcon Pub Inc.

Mountain Biking Southern California's Best 100 Trails. 2nd ed. Ed. by Delaine Fragnoli. LC 97-37592. (Illus.). 352p. 1998. pap. 16.95 (*0-938665-53-7*) Fine Edge Prods.

Mountain Biking Southern New England. Paul Angiolillo. LC 98-49647. (Illus.). 256p. 1999. pap. 12.95 (*1-56044-748-6*) Falcon Pub Inc.

Mountain Biking Spokane-Coeur D'Alene. Martin Potucek. LC 99-11652. (Illus.). 120p. 1999. pap. 10.95 (*1-56044-815-6*) Falcon Pub Inc.

Mountain Biking the Appalachians: Brevard, Asheville, The Pisgah Forest. 2nd ed. Lori Finley. LC 95-30396. 144p. 1995. 9.95 (*0-89587-136-X*) Blair.

Mountain Biking the Appalachians: Northwest North Carolina - Southwest Virginia. 2nd ed. Lori Finley & Tom Horsch. LC 98-5099. (Illus.). (Orig.). 1998. pap. 10.95 (*0-89587-205-6*) Blair.

Mountain Biking the Coast Range Guide 11: Orange County & Cleveland National Forest. 2nd ed. Robert Rasmussen. 1995. pap. 11.95 (*0-938665-37-5*) Fine Edge Prods.

Mountain Biking the Eastern Sierra's Best 100 Trails. Reanne Hemingway-Douglass et al. Ed. by Cindy Kamler. LC 97-2342. (Illus.). 260p. (Orig.). 1997. pap. 18.95 (*0-938665-42-1*) Fine Edge Prods.

Mountain Biking the Hawaiian Islands: Mauka to Makai. large type ed. John Alford. LC 97-91699. (Illus.). 264p. (Orig.). 1997. pap. 15.95 (*0-9649843-1-8*) Ohana Pubng.

***Mountain Biking the Hawaiian Islands: Mauka to Makai.** 2nd ed. John Alford. Ed. by John Clark. LC 00-91396. (Illus.). 264p. (Orig.). 2000. pap. 15.95 (*0-9649843-2-6*) Ohana Pubng.

Mountain Biking the Houston Area. Bill Pellerin & Ralph Neidhardt. 72p. (Orig.). 1993. pap. text. write for info. (*1-882358-03-1*) TX Bicycle Map.

Mountain Biking the National Parks: Off-Road Cycling Adventures in America's National Parks. Jim Clark. LC 95-76297. (Active Travel Ser.). (Illus.). 208p. (Orig.). 1996. pap. 12.95 (*0-933201-69-9*) MBI Pubg.

***Mountain Biking the Reno/Carson Area's Best Trails.** Ray W. Miskimins. (Illus.). 160p. 2000. 14.95 (*0-938665-66-9*) Fine Edge Prods.

Mountain Biking the Roaring Fork Valley: A Guidebook for Mountain Bikers Featuring Maps, Descriptions & Photographs for 65 Rides in the Mountains near Aspen, Colorado. Richard Compton. Ed. by Warren H. Ohlrich. LC 96-60373. (Illus.). 128p. (Orig.). 1996. pap. 14.95 (*1-882426-04-5*) W H O Pr.

Mountain Biking the San Bernardino Mountains, Guide 10. Robert Shipley & Allen Thibault. Ed. by Reanne Douglass. LC 93-5705. 1993. pap. 10.95 (*0-938665-16-2*) Fine Edge Prods.

Mountain Biking the San Gabriel Mountain's Best Trails: With Angeles National Forest to Mt. Pinos. Mike Troy & Kevin Woten. Ed. by Delaine Fragnoli. LC 97-776. (Illus.). 140p. (Orig.). 1997. pap. 14.95 (*0-938665-43-X*) Fine Edge Prods.

Mountain Biking the Santa Monica Mountain's Best Trails. Jim Hasenauer & Mark Langton. Ed. by Delaine Fragnoli. LC 98-23023. (Illus.). 130p. 1998. pap. 14.95 (*0-938665-55-3*, Mtn Biking Pr) Fine Edge Prods.

Mountain Biking the White Mountains (West) J. Richard Durnan. LC 98-6249. (Illus.). 160p. 1998. pap. 10.95 (*1-56044-663-3*) Falcon Pub Inc.

Mountain Biking to Natural Arches. Virginia Allen. Ed. by Chris Moore & Frank Anderson. (Illus.). 70p. 2001. mass mkt. 7.95 (*1-891858-07-6*, 4011) Arch Hunter Bks.

Mountain Biking Utah. Gregg Bromka. (Illus.). 450p. 1999. pap. 19.95 (*1-56044-824-5*) Falcon Pub Inc.

Mountain Biking Utah's Brian Head - Bryce Country. Gregg Bromka. LC 98-67191. (Illus.). 224p. 1998. pap. 14.95 (*0-9624374-3-3*) Off-Road Pubns.

***Mountain Biking Utah's St. George & Cedar City Area.** Bruce Grubbs. LC 98-48431. (Illus.). 176p. 1999. pap. 10.95 (*1-56044-803-2*) Falcon Pub Inc.

Mountain Biking Utah's Wasatch & Uinta Mountains. Gregg Bromka. (Illus.). 364p. 1996. pap. 18.95 (*0-9624374-2-5*) Off-Road Pubns.

Mountain Biking Washington. Gordon Black. LC 99-25894. (Illus.). 256p. 1999. pap. 14.95 (*1-56044-806-7*) Falcon Pub Inc.

Mountain Biking Whiskeytown: A Guide to Backcountry Trail Riding in the Whiskeytown Recreation Area. John W. Shuman, 4th. 137p. 1995. pap. 11.95 (*0-9649648-0-5*) J W Shuman.

***Mountain Biking Wisconsin.** Colby T. Waller. LC 98-16773. (Illus.). 224p. 1998. pap. 14.95 (*1-56044-666-8*) Falcon Pub Inc.

***Mountain Biking Wyoming.** Amber Travsky. LC 98-50260. (Illus.). 256p. 1999. pap. 14.95 (*1-56044-805-9*) Falcon Pub Inc.

Mountain Blood. Joseph Hergesheimer. (Collected Works of Joseph Hergesheimer). 312p. 1998. reprint ed. lib. bdg. 98.00 (*1-58201-655-0*) Classic Bks.

Mountain Born. Elizabeth Yates. LC 93-25967. (Illus.). 106p. (J). 1993. pap. 6.49 (*0-89084-706-1*, 072108) Bob Jones Univ.

Mountain Born. Elizabeth Yates. LC 92-40545. (Newbery Honor Roll Ser.). (Illus.). 128p. (J). (gr. 3-7). 1993. reprint ed. pap. 6.95 (*0-8027-7402-4*) Walker & Co.

Mountain Boyhood. Joe Mills. LC 87-30202. (Illus.). lvi, 311p. 1988. pap. 9.95 (*0-8032-8154-4*, Bison Books) U of Nebr Pr.

Mountain Boys Are Free: Portrait of Ned Guthrie, the Musicians' Abraham Lincoln. Jim Lowe. (Illus.). 160p. (Orig.). 1993. pap. write for info. (*0-9635197-0-0*) J G Lowe.

Mountain Breezes: The Collected Poems of Amy Carmichael. Amy Carmichael. 470p. 1999. 29.95 (*0-87508-790-6*, 790) Chr Lit.

Mountain Breezes: The Collected Poems of Amy Carmichael. Amy Carmichael. 470p. 1999. pap. 15.95 (*0-87508-789-2*, 789) Chr Lit.

Mountain Bride. Susan Sawyer. 352p. 1997. mass mkt. 5.99 (*0-380-78479-3*, Avon Bks) Morrow Avon.

Mountain Brook Jokebook. Elizabeth Price. 96p. (Orig.). 1996. pap. 5.95 (*1-878561-53-7*) Seacoast AL.

Mountain Carriboo: And Other Gold Camps in Idaho. 2nd ed. Ellen Carney & Elaine S. Johnson. (Illus.). 238p. 1994. pap. write for info. (*0-9636479-2-X*) Traildust Pub.

Mountain Cattle & Frontier People. 2nd ed. Genevra S. Snedden. (Illus.). 160p. (J). (gr. 6). 1989. reprint ed. pap. 17.50 (*0-932400-04-3*) Intervale Pub Co.

Mountain Chant: A Navajo Ceremony. Washington Matthews. LC 97-25249. 120p. 1997. pap. 14.95 (*0-87480-542-2*) U of Utah Pr.

Mountain Charley: or The Adventures of Mrs. E. J. Guerin. E. J. Guerin. LC 68-15671. 128p. (Orig.). 1985. pap. 9.95 (*0-8061-1964-0*) U of Okla Pr.

***Mountain City.** Gregory Martin. LC 99-56160. 224p. 2000. 23.00 (*0-86547-594-6*) N Point Pr.

Mountain City. large type ed. Frank Fields. (Linford Western Large Print Ser.). 256p. 1996. pap. 16.99 (*0-7089-7947-5*, Linford) Ulverscroft.

***Mountain Climbing.** Jean Craighead George. 32p. (J). 2001. 15.99 (*0-7868-0556-0*, Pub. by Hyperion) Time Warner.

Mountain Climbing for Beginners. Mike Banks. 1978. 8.95 (*0-8128-2448-2*, Scrbrough Hse) Madison Bks UPA.

Mountain Cookbook: Recipes from the Cooking Corner. 2nd ed. Patricia J. Hicks. LC 91-72542. (Illus.). 128p. 1991. spiral bd. 10.50 (*0-9626392-2-2*) I Collect Facts.

Mountain Cookin' 2.95 (*0-936672-32-3*) Aerial Photo.

Mountain Country Cooking. Mark F. Sohn. LC 96-20436. (Illus.). 352p. 1996. text 26.95 (*0-312-14682-5*) St Martin.

***Mountain Courage.** Judson Gray. (Mountain Man Ser.). 320p. 1999. mass mkt. 5.99 (*0-451-19870-0*, Sig) NAL.

Mountain Dance: And Other Stories. Denis Ledoux. 55p. 1990. pap. 7.95 (*0-9626857-0-4*) Maine Writers.

***Mountain Dance: And Other Stories.** Locker. 2001. write for info. (*0-15-202622-3*) Harcourt.

Mountain Days & Bothy Nights. Dave Brown & Ian Mitchell. LC 99-185040. (Illus.). 192p. 1999. pap. 12.95 (*0-946487-15-4*, Pub. by Luath Pr Ltd) Midpt Trade.

***Mountain Demon, Vol. 8.** Doug Hawkins. 176p. 1999. mass mkt. 3.99 (*0-8439-4619-9*, Leisure Bks) Dorchester Pub Co.

Mountain Devil. David Thompson. (Wilderness Ser.: No. 9). 176p. 1993. mass mkt. 3.50 (*0-8439-3515-4*) Dorchester Pub Co.

Mountain Devil - Blackfoot Massacre, 2 vols. in 1. David Thompson. (Wilderness Ser.: Nos. 9 & 10). 352p. 1997. mass mkt. 4.99 (*0-8439-4327-0*, Leisure Bks) Dorchester Pub Co.

***Mountain Dialogues.** Frank Waters. LC 99-32518. 248p. 1999. reprint ed. pap. 16.95 (*0-8040-1018-8*) Ohio U Pr.

***Mountain Dimensions: An Altitude Geographic Analysis of the Environment & Development of the Himalayas.** Ram Kumar Panday. 1999. pap. 94.00 (*0-7855-7610-X*) St Mut.

Mountain Directory East for Truckers, RV, & Motorhome Drivers. Richard W. Miller. (Illus.). 85p. (Orig.). 1997. pap. 12.95 (*0-9646805-2-1*) R&R Pub.

Mountain Directory East for Truckers, RV & Motorhome Drivers. 2nd rev. ed. Richard W. Miller. (Illus.). 92p. 1999. pap. 12.95 (*0-9646805-5-6*) R&R Pub.

Mountain Directory for Truckers, RV, & Motorhome Drivers. 3rd rev. ed. Richard W. Miller. (Illus.). 119p. 1996. pap. 12.95 (*0-9646805-1-3*) R&R Pub.

***Mountain Directory West for Truckers, RV & Motorhome Drivers.** 4th rev. ed. Richard Wilson Miller. (Illus.). 152p. 2000. pap. 14.95 (*0-9646805-6-4*) R&R Pub.

***Mountain Dog Rescue.** Coleen Hubbard. (Dog Tales Ser.: No. 3). (Illus.). 160p. (J). (gr. 3-7). 2000. pap. 5.50 (*0-590-18977-8*, Apple Paperbacks) Scholastic Inc.

Mountain Dreamer. Pat Werner. 320p. 1998. pap. 4.99 (*0-8217-5928-0*) Kensgtn Pub Corp.

Mountain Dreamers: Visionaries of Sierra Nevada Skiing. Robert Frohlich. Ed. by Laurel H. Lippert. LC 97-66550. (Illus.). 160p. 1997. 50.00 (*0-9633056-5-4*); pap. 29.95 (*0-9633056-6-2*) Coldstream Pr.

Mountain Dreams. Gail Kennedy. LC 98-41734. 312p. 1998. pap. 12.50 (*0-9659701-0-8*) Laughing Owl.

Mountain Drive: Santa Barbaras Pioneer Bohemian Community. Ed. & Pref. by Elias Chiacos. (Illus.). 133p. (Orig.). 1995. pap. 12.95 (*1-885375-00-X*, Shore Line Pr) Pacific Books.

***Mountain Dulcimer.** Mark Biggs. 80p. 1998. pap. 17.95 (*0-7866-3444-8*, 93859BCD) Mel Bay.

Mountain Dulcimer. Patricia Brown. LC 85-71923. (Illus.). 130p. 1985. pap. 12.95 (*0-9614939-3-3*) Backyard Music.

Mountain Dulcimer: How to Make It & Play It - After a Fashion. Howard W. Mitchell. 50p. 1965. pap. 4.95 (*0-938702-01-7*, FSI-29) Folk-Legacy.

Mountain Ecology in the Australian Region. Ed. by P. W. Purdie & I. R. Noble. 178p. (C). 1983. text 75.00 (*0-909436-05-3*, Pub. by Surrey Beatty & Sons) St Mut.

Mountain Elegance. Junior League of Ashville. 1991. pap. 14.95 (*0-9608444-0-6*) Jr League Asheville.

Mountain Elegance. Asheville Junior League Staff. (Illus.). 320p. 1991. reprint ed. otabind 14.95 (*0-914875-17-5*) Bright Mtn Bks.

Mountain Elegance Cookbook. Junior League of Asheville Staff. 340p. 1982. 11.95 (*0-686-97705-X*) Jr League Asheville.

Mountain Environment: Understanding the Change. A. A. Pirazizy. (Illus.). x, 194p. 1993. 25.00 (*81-7024-563-X*, Pub. by Ashish Pub Hse) Nataraj Bks.

Mountain Environments: An Examination of the Physical Geography of Mountain. A. John Gerrard. 326p. 1990. 34.50 (*0-262-07128-2*) MIT Pr.

Mountain Environments & GIS. Ed. by Martin Price & Ian Heywood. 300p. 1994. 99.00 (*0-7484-0088-5*, Pub. by Tay Francis Ltd) Taylor & Francis.

Mountain Environments in Changing Climates. Ed. by Martin Beniston. LC 93-45308. (Illus.). 464p. (C). 1994. 150.00 (*0-415-10224-3*, B3824) Routledge.

Mountain-Ese. Aubrey Garber. LC 76-3278. 105p. 1976. 4.95 (*0-89227-004-7*); pap. 2.95 (*0-89227-038-1*) Commonwealth Pr.

Mountain Experience: The Psychology & Sociology of Adventure. Richard G. Mitchell, Jr. LC 83-6454. xvi, 272p. 1985. pap. 10.95 (*0-226-53225-9*) U Ch Pr.

Mountain Experience: The Psychology & Sociology of Adventure. Richard G. Mitchell, Jr. LC 83-6454. xvi, 272p. 1995. lib. bdg. 18.00 (*0-226-53224-0*) U Ch Pr.

Mountain Farmers: Moral Economies of Land & Development in Arusha & Meru. Thomas Spear. LC 96-37622. (Illus.). 288p. 1997. 48.00 (*0-520-20618-5*, Pub. by U CA Pr); pap. 18.95 (*0-520-20619-3*, Pub. by U CA Pr) Cal Prin Full Svc.

Mountain Fever. Tom Alexander. Ed. by Jane Alexander. LC 94-23589. (Illus.). 176p. 1995. 29.95 (*0-914875-26-4*) Bright Mtn Bks.

***Mountain Fever: Historic Conquests of Rainier.** Aubrey L. Haines. LC 99-37124. (Illus.). 278p. 1999. pap. text 18.95 (*0-295-97847-3*) U of Wash Pr.

Mountain, Field & Family: The Economy & Human Ecology of an Andean Valley. Stephen B. Brush. LC 77-24364. 223p. reprint ed. pap. 69.20 (*0-8357-3320-3*, 203954400013) Bks Demand.

Mountain Fires: The Red Army's Three-Year War in South China, 1934-1938. Gregor Benton. (Philip E. Lilienthal Bks.). (C). 1992. 85.00 (*0-520-04158-5*, Pub. by U CA Pr) Cal Prin Full Svc.

Mountain Flora of Greece. Ed. by Arne Strid. (Illus.). 1991. text 165.00 (*0-7486-0207-0*, Pub. by Edinburgh U Pr) Col U Pr.

Mountain Flowers of the Cascades & Olympics. Ira Spring & Harvey Manning. LC 79-9284. (Illus.). 96p. 1990. pap. 7.95 (*0-916890-92-9*) Mountaineers.

Mountain Flying. 3rd rev. ed. Sparky Imeson. (Illus.). 259p. pap. 7.50 (*0-934754-02-0*) Airguide Pubns.

Mountain Folk, Mountain Food: Down-Home Wisdom, Plain Tales & Recipe Secrets from Appalachia. Betsy T. White. 1997. pap. text 13.95 (*0-9615995-3-7*) Recover Comns.

Mountain Folks: Of Old Smoky. unabridged ed. Veta W. King. LC 97-92864. (Illus.). 120p. 1997. pap. 11.50 (*0-9662017-0-1*) Mountain Folks.

Mountain Footfalls: A Calendar of the Scottish Hills. Ian Mitchell. 136p. 1996. pap. 36.00 (*1-873644-53-1*, Pub. by Mercat Pr Bks) St Mut.

Mountain for Luenda. large type ed. Essie Summers. 1984. 15.95 (*0-7089-1165-X*) Ulverscroft.

***Mountain Fury.** Taylor Brady. LC 99-55333. (Kincaids Ser.). 2000. 26.95 (*0-7862-2336-7*) Five Star.

Mountain Geography: A Critique & Field Study. Roderick Peattie. LC 70-88918. 1970. lib. bdg. 75.00 (*0-8371-2243-0*, PEMG, Greenwood Pr) Greenwood.

Mountain, Get Out of My Way: Life Lessons & Learned Truths. large type ed. Montel Williams. 266p. 1996. lib. bdg. 24.95 (*0-7862-0822-8*) Thorndike Pr.

Mountain Getaways: Anniversary. Rusty Hoffland. 1994. pap. text 7.95 (*0-9616316-2-7*) On the Road Pub.

Mountain Getaways in Georgia, North Carolina, & Tennessee. 5th rev. ed. Rusty Hoffland. (Illus.). 208p. 1990. pap. 5.95 (*0-9616316-1-9*) On the Road Pub.

Mountain Ghost Stories & Curious Tales of Western North Carolina. Randy Russell & Janet Barnett. LC 88-19380. 109p. 1988. 11.95 (*0-89587-064-9*) Blair.

Mountain Giants. Charles Wood. 96p. 1996. pap. 12.95 (*0-948230-62-2*, Pub. by Absolute Classics) Theatre Comm.

Mountain Gloom & Mountain Glory: The Development of the Aesthetics of the Infinite. Marjorie Hope Nicolson. LC 96-49189. (Weyerhaeuser Environmental Classics Ser.). 432p. 1997. pap. 17.95 (*0-295-97577-6*) U of Wash Pr.

Mountain Goat. J. W. Arbuckle & Alan C. Shook. (Illus.). 135p. 1992. pap. 12.95 (*0-932807-64-X*) Overmountain Pr.

Mountain Goats. Frank Staub. LC 93-32491. (Early Bird Nature Bks.). (Illus.). 48p. (J). (gr. 2-3). 1994. lib. bdg. 19.93 (*0-8225-3000-7*, Lerner Publctns) Lerner Pub.

Mountain Goddess: Gender & Politics in a Himalayan Pilgrimage. William S. Sax. (Illus.). 256p. 1991. pap. text 22.95 (*0-19-506979-X*) OUP.

Mountain Golf: Top Mountain Resort Courses in U. S. A. & Canada. Diane Scholfield et al. 360p. Date not set. pap. 19.95 (*0-915009-65-X*) World Leis Corp.

Mountain Gorilla. George B. Schaller. 2000. lib. bdg. 27.50 (*0-226-73635-0*) U Ch Pr.

***Mountain Gorilla.** Rod Theodorou. LC 00-24324. (Illus.). (J). 2000. lib. bdg. write for info. (*1-57572-266-6*) Heinemann Lib.

Mountain Gorilla: Ecology & Behavior. George B. Schaller. LC 77-151373. (Illus.). 479p. reprint ed. pap. 148.50 (*0-608-09521-4*, 205432300005) Bks Demand.

***Mountain Gorillas.** Karen Kane. (Early Bird Nature Ser.). (Illus.). 48p. (J). (ps-3). 2000. 22.60 (*0-8225-3040-6*, Lerner Publctns) Lerner Pub.

Mountain Gorrilla: Ecology & Behavior. George B. Schaller. (Illus.). 484p. 1996. pap. text 26.50 (*0-226-73649-0*, Midway Reprint) U Ch Pr.

Mountain Grizzly, Vol. 1. Michael S. Quinton. (Illus.). 64p. (YA). (gr. 3 up). 1999. pap. text 12.95 (*0-88839-417-9*) Hancock House.

Mountain Guide: The White Mountains of New Hampshire & Maine. Ed Frost & Roon Frost. 195p. 1988. pap. 9.95 (*0-9618806-1-9*) Glove Compart Bks.

***Mountain Hands: A Portrait of Southern Appalachia.** Sam Venable. LC 00-8227. (Illus.). 232p. 2000. 55.00 (*1-57233-089-9*, Pub. by U of Tenn Pr); pap. 25.00 (*1-57233-090-2*, Pub. by U of Tenn Pr) U Ch Pr.

Mountain Heritage. Ed. by B. B. Maurer. (Illus.). 352p. 1975. reprint ed. pap. 14.60 (*0-87012-279-7*) McClain. The most complete one volume work available on the Appalachian Cultural Heritage of West Virginians. Written by a group of West Virginia's finest scholars. The twelve chapters cover Man & the Appalachian Wilderness, Culture, Arts & Crafts, Language, Folklore & Literature, Family & Home, Music, Religion, Black Culture, The Mountain State, Songs, & Dances. Scholarly yet easily readable, the book is a ready resource for home, school, office & community. Seventh Edition, 1996. ***Publisher Paid Annotation.***

Mountain High, Mountain Rescue. Peggy Parr. LC 86-25773. 202p. 1986. 15.95 (*1-55591-005-X*) Fulcrum Pub.

Mountain High, White Avalanche: Cocaine & Power in the Andean States & Panama, 137. Scott B. MacDonald. LC 88-39214. (Washington Papers: No. 137). (Illus.). 166p. 1989. 49.95 (*0-275-93234-6*, C3234, Praeger Pubs); pap. 13.95 (*0-275-93235-4*, B3235, Praeger Pubs) Greenwood.

***Mountain Hike.** Steck-Vaughn Company Staff. (Read All about It Ser.). (Illus.). (J). 2000. pap. 4.95 (*0-8114-3793-0*) Raintree Steck-V.

Mountain Home. Rosemary Whitlock. LC 87-6940. (Illus.). 242p. (Orig.). 1987. 13.95 (*0-931807-10-7*) Makin Do Ent.

Mountain Homespun. Frances L. Goodrich. LC 89-33843. (Illus.). 192p. 1989. 26.00 (*0-87049-620-4*) U of Tenn Pr.

***Mountain Houses.** Aurora Cuito. (Illus.). 2000. pap. 35.00 (*0-8230-7392-0*) Watsn-Guptill.

Mountain in the Clouds: A Search for the Wild Salmon. Bruce C. Brown. LC 95-13392. (Illus.). 240p. (C). 1995. reprint ed. pap. 12.95 (*0-295-97475-3*) U of Wash Pr.

Mountain in the Sunlight: Studies in Conflict & Unity. Alick West. LC 79-16755. 208p. 1980. reprint ed. lib. bdg. 59.50 (*0-313-22013-1*, WEMO, Greenwood Pr) Greenwood.

Mountain Interval see Road Not Taken & Other Poems

Mountain Interval. fac. ed. Robert Frost. (Library of American Poets). 99p. 1995. reprint ed. 25.00 (*1-56515-012-0*) Collect Reprints.

Mountain Interval: And New Hampshire: Poems. Robert Frost. LC 98-7905. 160p. 1999. mass mkt. 4.95 (*0-451-52718-6*, Sig Classics) NAL.

Mountain Is High Unless Elevator. Smith. (Freshman Orientation/College Success Ser.). 1992. pap., teacher ed. write for info. (*0-534-13177-8*) Wadsworth Pub.

Mountain Is High Unless You Take the Elevator: Success Strategies for Adult Learners. Laurence N. Smith & Timothy L. Walter. 177p. (C). 1992. pap. 17.95 (*0-534-13176-X*) Wadsworth Pub.

Mountain Is Moving: Japanese Women's Lives. Patricia A. Morley. LC 98-53302. 240p. 1999. text 28.50 (*0-8147-5626-3*) NYU Pr.

Mountain Is to Climb. Tord Bijou Le. (Illus.). 40p. 5.95 (*0-06-443591-1*) HarpC.

Mountain Is to Climb. Bijou Le Tord. 40p. (J). 2001. 15.95 (*0-06-028514-1*) HarpC Child Bks.

Mountain Island in Owen County, KY: The Settlers & Their Churches. James C. Bryant. 488p. (Orig.). (C). 1986. pap. text 19.00 (*0-9617100-0-4*) Owen Cnty Hist.

Mountain Islands & Desert Seas: A Natural History of the U. S.-Mexican Borderlands. Frederick R. Gehlbach. LC 81-40402. (Louise Lindsey Merrick Natural Environment Ser.: No. 15). (Illus.). 340p. 1993. pap. 15.95 (*0-89096-566-8*) Tex A&M Univ Pr.

Mountain Jack Pike No. 10: Bull's Eye Blood. Joseph Meek. 1992. mass mkt. 3.50 (*1-55817-617-9*, Pinncle Kensgtn) Kensgtn Pub Corp.

Mountain Jack Pike No. 11: Deep Canyon Kill. Joseph Meek. 256p. 1992. mass mkt. 3.50 (*1-55817-657-8*, Pinncle Kensgtn) Kensgtn Pub Corp.

Mountain Jack Pike No. 14: Trail Heat. Joseph Meek. 1993. mass mkt. 3.50 (*1-55817-733-7*, Pinncle Kensgtn) Kensgtn Pub Corp.

Mountain Jake & the Reporter. Flora Joy. (Educational Comic Book Ser.). (Illus.). 12p. (J). (gr. 3-12). 1996. pap. 2.00 (*1-884624-07-3*) Storytelling Wrld Pr.

Mountain Journeys: Stories of Climbers & Their Climbs. Ed. by James P. Vermeulen. 272p. 1989. 19.95 (*0-87951-357-8*, Pub. by Overlook Pr) Penguin Putnam.

Mountain Journeys: Stories of Climbers & Their Climbs. Ed. by James P. Vermeulen. 272p. 1990. pap. 9.95 (*0-87951-366-7*, Pub. by Overlook Pr) Penguin Putnam.

Mountain King. Rick Hautala. 276p. 1996. 50.00 (*1-881475-16-6*) Cemetery Dance.

Mountain Kingdom: Portraits of Nepal & the Gurkhas. Bruce M. Niven. (Illus.). 96p. (Orig.). 1991. pap. 18.95 (*0-911977-07-4*) Seven Hills Bk.

***Mountain Lake & It's Bird Life.** David Johnston. (Illus.). 100p. 2000. pap. 14.95 (*1-884549-14-4*) VA Mus Natl Hist.

Mountain Lake Diving: California-Nevada. Keith B. Namestka & Philip D. Moyer. (Illus.). 1998. pap. text 14.95 (*0-9666143-0-5*) Enviro-tech Dist.

Mountain Lake Remembered: In Memory of the Late Mary Moody Northern & Our Friend the Late Molly Malloy Brooks. Virginia F. Roberts. LC 97-25366. 1997. write for info. (*1-57168-901-X*, Eakin Pr) Sunbelt Media.

Mountain Lake Resort, 1751-1900. Patricia G. Johnson. LC 87-51181. (Illus.). 90p. 1987. 15.00 (*0-9614765-8-3*) Walpa Pub.

An Asterisk (*) at the beginning of an entry indicates that the title is appearing for the first time.

Mountain Lake Workshop: Artists in Locale. Howard Risatti. (Illus.). (Orig.). 1996. pap. write for info. (*0-935519-21-1*) Anderson Gal.

Mountain Language. Harold Pinter. 1988. pap. 5.25 (*0-8222-0777-X*) Dramatists Play.

Mountain Language. Harold Pinter. LC 88-35782. 48p. 1989. pap. 7.95 (*0-8021-3168-9*, Grove) Grove-Atltic.

Mountain Laurel. abr. ed. Jude Deveraux. 1990. 14.95 incl. audio (*0-671-70872-4*, Audioworks) S&S Trade.

Mountain Laurel. large type ed. Jude Deveraux. (General Ser.). 405p. 1991. lib. bdg. 21.95 (*0-8161-5124-5*, G K Hall Lrg Type) Mac Lib Ref.

Mountain Laurel. Jude Deveraux. Ed. by Linda Marrow. 320p. 1991. reprint ed. per. 6.99 (*0-671-68976-2*) PB.

Mountain Legacy: A Story of Rabun Gap - Nacoochee School with Emphasis on the Junior College Years. Frances P. Statham. LC 99-28257. (Illus.). 384p. 1999. 40.00 (*0-87797-282-6*) Cherokee.

Mountain Light. 1987. pap. 30.00 (*0-87156-724-5*, Pub. by Sierra) Random.

Mountain Light. Laurence Yep. 1997. 11.05 (*0-606-11642-7*, Pub. by Turtleback) Demco.

Mountain Light: Golden Mountain Chronicles:1855. Laurence Yep. LC 85-42643. 288p. (YA). (gr. 7 up). 1997. pap. 6.95 (*0-06-440667-9*, HarpTrophy) HarpC Child Bks.

Mountain Light: In Search of the Dynamic Landscape. anniversary ed. Galen A. Rowell. (Illus.). 240p. 1995. pap. 25.00 (*0-87156-367-3*, Pub. by Sierra) Random.

Mountain Lion. Daniel J. Cox. LC 98-3760. (Illus.). 120p. 1999. pap. 18.95 (*0-8118-1930-2*) Chronicle Bks.

Mountain Lion. Sabrina Crewe. LC 96-53251. (Life Cycles Bks.). (Illus.). 32p. (J). (ps-4). 1998. lib. bdg. 21.40 (*0-8172-4378-X*) Raintree Steck-V.

Mountain Lion. Jean Stafford. LC 91-28409. 245p. 1992. reprint ed. pap. 11.95 (*0-292-75136-2*) U of Tex Pr.

Mountain Lion: An Unnatural History of Pumas & People. Chris Bolgiano. LC 95-10063. (Illus.). 224p. 1995. 19.95 (*0-8117-1044-0*) Stackpole.

Mountain Lion: Puma, Panther, Painter, Cougar. Sandra C. Robinson. (Wonder Ser.). (Illus.). 64p. (J). (gr. 4-6). 1991. pap. 7.95 (*1-879373-00-9*) Roberts Rinehart.

Mountain Lion Alert: Safety for Pets, Landowners, & Outdoor Adventurers. Steve Torres. LC 97-17551. (Illus.). 128p. 1997. pap. 6.95 (*1-56044-583-1*) Falcon Pub Inc.

Mountain Lions. Maura M. Gouck. LC 93-16250. (Nature Books Ser.). (Illus.). 32p. (J). (gr. 2-6). 1994. lib. bdg. 22.79 (*1-56766-057-6*) Childs World.

Mountain Lions. David Petersen. LC 94-36353. (New True Books Ser.). 48p. (J). (gr. k-4). 1995. lib. bdg. 21.00 (*0-516-01077-8*) Childrens.

Mountain Lions. David Petersen. (New True Books Ser.). (Illus.). 48p. (J). 1995. pap. 5.50 (*0-516-41077-6*) Childrens.

Mountain Lions. Scott Wrobel. LC 98-51601. (Northern Trek Ser.). 24p. 2000. lib. bdg. 21.30 (*1-58340-035-4*) Smart Apple.

Mountain Lions & California State Parks. Kenneth W. Umbach. 12p. 1994. pap. write for info. (*1-58703-020-9*, CRB-94-002) CA St Libry.

Mountain Lovers. William Sharp. LC 79-8164. reprint ed. 44.50 (*0-404-62013-2*) AMS Pr.

Mountain Madness. David Thompson. (Wilderness Ser.: Vol. 24). 176p. 1998. mass mkt. 3.99 (*0-8439-4399-8*, Leisure Bks) Dorchester Pub Co.

Mountain Madness. adapted ed. Adapted by C. Archer. LC 96-38918. (Christy Fiction Ser.: Vol. 9). 128p. (Orig.). (J). (gr. 5-9). 1997. mass mkt. 4.99 (*0-8499-3960-7*) Tommy Nelson.

Mountain Madness: A Deadly Night, a Bloody Secret, a True Story. Jimmy D. Taylor & Donald G. Bross. LC 96-68930. 312p. 1996. 23.95 (*0-88282-148-2*) New Horizon NJ.

Mountain Madness: A Handful of Lakeland Lunacies. Richard Clough. LC 74-181699. 32 p.p. 1974. write for info. (*0-85983-026-8*) Graham Publishing Co.

***Mountain Magic.** Susan Hardy. 1999. mass mkt. 3.99 (*0-8217-6315-6*) Kensgtn Pub Corp.

Mountain Magic. Alice B. Lentz. LC 98-11050. (Illus.). (J). 1998. 12.99 (*0-8499-5841-5*) Tommy Nelson.

Mountain Magic. large type ed. Ivy Preston. (Romance Ser.). 288p. 1992. 27.99 (*0-7089-2683-5*) Ulverscroft.

Mountain Magic: Fairy Tales That Are Almost True. Jeanette M. Harris. 74p. (J). (gr. 3 up). 1994. pap. 10.00 (*0-9632303-1-X*) Butternut Bks.

Mountain Magic Cuisine: Secret Recipes of the Dude & Guest Ranches of Colorado. unabridged ed. Colorado Dude & Guest Ranch Association Staff et al. LC 98-65071. (Illus.). 420p. 1998. pap. 23.95 (*1-889120-11-1*) StarsEnd Creations.

Mountain Magick: Folk Wisdom from the Heart of Appalachia. Edain McCoy. LC 97-17470. (Illus.). 240p. 1997. reprint ed. pap. 14.95 (*1-56718-671-8*) Llewellyn Pubns.

***Mountain Maid Best Made: A Complete Guide to Haitian Cooking, 5.** Ed. by Amy K. Wolfe. (Illus.). vi, 155p. 1998. pap. 9.95 (*0-9679937-0-9*, 14808, Pub. by Bapt Haiti) Mountain Maid.

Mountain Majesties. LC 96-92792. 366p. 1996. 30.00 (*0-9654746-0-7*) C A Strange.

Mountain Mama: Courageous Backwoods Mistress. Dora Axsom & Erra Pelham. (Illus.). 210p. (Orig.). 1988. reprint ed. pap. 7.00 (*0-317-92291-2*) Lil Red Hen OK.

Mountain Mama: Courageous Backwoods Mistress. 3rd rev. ed. Dora Axsom & Erra Pelham. (Orig.). (YA). 1990. pap. 10.00 (*0-9621669-1-X*) Lil Red Hen OK.

Mountain Mammals. Elaine Landau. LC 96-3893. (True Bk.). (Illus.). 48p. (J). 1996. lib. bdg. 21.00 (*0-516-20040-2*) Childrens.

Mountain Mammals. Elaine Landau. (True Bks.). 48p. (J). 1997. pap. 6.95 (*0-516-26109-6*) Childrens.

Mountain Man. Vardis Fisher. pap. text 19.95 (*0-685-62672-5*) ISBN Agency.

Mountain Man. Vardis Fisher. 320p. (gr. 10 up). 1990. mass mkt. 4.95 (*0-671-73907-7*) PB.

Mountain Man. James Magorian. LC 88-71606. 40p. 1989. pap. 6.00 (*0-930674-31-6*) Black Oak.

Mountain Man. Doris Rangel. (Special Edition Ser.: No. 1140). 1997. per. 3.99 (*0-373-24140-2*, 1-24140-5) Silhouette.

Mountain Man. Vardis Fisher. 1976. reprint ed. lib. bdg. 24.95 (*0-89190-832-3*, Rivercity Pr) Amereon Ltd.

Mountain Man. Vardis Fisher. 1993. reprint ed. lib. bdg. 27.95 (*1-56849-196-4*) Buccaneer Bks.

Mountain Man & the President. David Weitzman. LC 92-23040. (Stories of America Ser.). (Illus.). 40p. (J). (gr. 2-5). 1992. pap. 4.95 (*0-8114-8064-X*); lib. bdg. 24.26 (*0-8114-7224-8*) Raintree Steck-V.

Mountain Man Cookbook: Venison & Other Recipes. 2nd ed. Thomas L. Canino. (Illus.). 100p. (Orig.). 1989. spiral bd. 8.95 (*0-9614922-1-X*) TLC Enterprises.

Mountain Man Crafts & Skills: An Illustrated Guide to Clothing, Shelter, Equipment & Wilderness Living. David Montgomery. LC 80-82706. (Illus.). 1981. 17.98 (*0-88290-156-7*, 4024) Horizon Utah.

Mountain Man's Blood. Jess McCreede. 1990. mass mkt. 2.95 (*1-55817-326-9*, Pinncle Kensgtn) Kensgtn Pub Corp.

Mountain Man's Fury. Ralph Hayes. 256p. 1992. mass mkt. 3.50 (*1-55817-623-3*, Pinncle Kensgtn) Kensgtn Pub Corp.

Mountain Man's Gold. Ralph Hayes. 256p. (J). (gr. k). 1993. mass mkt. 3.99 (*1-55817-779-5*, Pinncle Kensgtn) Kensgtn Pub Corp.

Mountain Man's Vengeance. Robert Lake. 1991. mass mkt. 3.50 (*0-8217-3619-1*, Zebra Kensgtn) Kensgtn Pub Corp.

Mountain Marauders. Doyle Trent. 256p. 1995. mass mkt. 3.99 (*0-8217-4942-0*, Pinncle Kensgtn) Kensgtn Pub Corp.

Mountain Mary: An Historical Tale of Early Pennsylvania. Ludwig A. Wollenweber. Tr. & Intro. by John J. Stoudt. LC 73-5412. (Liberty Cap Bks.). Orig. Title: Die Berg-Maria: eine Geschichtliche Erzalung aus Pennsylvanien. (Illus.). 80p. (Orig.). 1974. pap. 10.00 (*0-87387-058-1*) Shumway.

Mountain Massacre, 1 vol. Jason Manning. 320p. 1999. mass mkt. 5.99 (*0-451-19689-9*) NAL.

Mountain Massacres: A Bomber Hanson Mystery. David Champion. LC 95-9702. 161p. 1995. 14.95 (*0-9627297-4-4*) A A Knoll Pubs.

Mountain Massacres & Other Stories of Appalachia. Ralph V. Cutlip. (Illus.). 167p. (Orig.). (J). (gr. 8 up). 1986. pap. 6.50 (*0-317-47675-0*) B Cutlip.

Mountain Masters: Slavery & the Sectional Crisis in Western North Carolina. John C. Inscoe. (Illus.). 368p. 1996. pap. text 17.00 (*0-87049-933-5*) U of Tenn Pr.

Mountain Mazes. Roger Moreau. (Illus.). 64p. 1996. pap. 5.95 (*0-8069-6110-4*) Sterling.

Mountain Meadow 123. Caroline Stutson. LC 95-69282. (Illus.). 32p. (J). (gr. k-2). 1995. 14.95 (*1-57098-022-5*) Roberts Rinehart.

Mountain Meadows Massacre. Juanita Brooks. LC 62-18053. (Illus.). 352p. 1991. pap. 17.95 (*0-8061-2318-4*) U of Okla Pr.

Mountain Meadows Witness: The Life & Times of Bishop Philip Klingensmith. Anna J. Backus. LC 95-37173. (Western Frontiersmen Ser.: Vol. XXV). (Illus.). 315p. 1995. 32.50 (*0-87062-229-3*) A H Clark.

Mountain Measure: A Southern Appalachian Verse Notebook. Francis P. Hulme. LC 84-70294. (Illus.). 88p. 1984. pap. 10.95 (*0-913239-12-7*) Appalach Consortium.

Mountain Measures. Junior League of Charleston, Inc. Staff. LC 75-316544. 394p. 1974. 9.95 (*0-9606232-0-5*) Jr League Charleston.

Mountain Measures: A Second Serving. Junior League of Charleston, Inc. Staff. 385p. 1984. 11.95 (*0-9606232-1-3*) Jr League Charleston.

Mountain Medicine. A. B. Guthrie. 5.95 (*0-89174-057-0*) Comstock Edns.

Mountain Melody. large type ed. Peggy Gaddis. (Linford Romance Library). 256p. 1995. pap. 16.99 (*0-7089-7793-6*, Linford) Ulverscroft.

Mountain Memories, No. 1. 5th ed. 128p. (C). reprint ed. pap. 6.95 (*0-934750-30-0*) Mntn Memories Bks.

Mountain Memories, No. 4. 3rd ed. J. Dennis Deitz. Ed. by Kathleen Browning. 170p. (C). reprint ed. pap. 6.95 (*0-934750-37-8*) Mntn Memories Bks.

Mountain Memories: Folk Tales of the Adirondacks. 3rd ed. Helen E. Tyler. (Illus.). 120p. 1993. reprint ed. pap. 6.95 (*1-892404-02-8*) Tyler-John Assocs.

Mountain Memories V. Deitz. 1995. pap. 6.95 (*0-938985-07-8*) Mntn Memories Bks.

Mountain Memories III. Dennis J. Deitz. 180p. reprint ed. pap. text 6.95 (*0-938985-00-0*) Mntn Memories Bks.

Mountain Memories II. Dennis J. Deitz. (Illus.). 144p. 1983. pap. 6.95 (*0-934750-18-1*) Mntn Memories Bks.

Mountain Memory. Romulus Linney. LC 98-178025. 1996. pap. 5.25 (*0-8222-1538-1*) Dramatists Play.

Mountain Men. Walter S. Campbell. LC 77-99620. (Essay Index Reprint Ser.). 1977. 27.95 (*0-8369-1397-3*) Ayer.

Mountain Men. Jim Collins. LC 95-49301. (First Bks.). (Illus.). 64p. (J). (gr. 5-8). 1996. lib. bdg. 22.00 (*0-531-20229-1*) Watts.

Mountain Men. Charles L. Convis. (True Tales of the Old West Ser.: Vol. 4). (Illus.). 62p. 1997. pap. 7.95 (*0-9651954-4-9*) Pioneer Pr NV.

Mountain Men. George Laycock. (Illus.). 288p. 1996. pap. 16.95 (*1-55821-454-2*, 14542) Lyons Pr.

Mountain Men. Robert Miller. (Reflections of a Black Cowboy Ser.). (Illus.). 104p. (J). (gr. 4-7). 1991. pap. 4.95 (*0-382-24087-1*) Silver Burdett Pr.

Mountain Men. Rick Steber. (Tales of the Wild West Ser.: Vol. 8). (Illus.). 60p. 1990. pap. 4.95 (*0-945134-08-8*); lib. bdg. 14.95 (*0-945134-86-X*) Bonanza Pub.

Mountain Men. John G. Neihardt. LC 70-134770. (Cycle of the West Ser.: Vol. 1). (Illus.). xvi, 369p. 1971. reprint ed. pap. text 20.00 (*0-8032-5733-3*, Bison Books) U of Nebr Pr.

Mountain Men, Bk. 4. Robert Miller. (Reflections of a Black Cowboy Ser.). (Illus.). 104p. (J). (gr. 4-7). 1991. lib. bdg. 12.95 (*0-382-24082-0*) Silver Burdett Pr.

Mountain Men & Fur Traders of the Far West: Eighteen Biographical Sketches. Ed. by LeRoy R. Hafen. LC 81-21803. (Illus.). xviii, 401p. 1982. reprint ed. pap. 14.95 (*0-8032-7210-3*, Bison Books) U of Nebr Pr.

Mountain Men & the Fur Trade. James A. Crutchfield. 39.00 (*1-56696-148-3*) Jackdaw.

***Mountain Men in California.** Adam D. Parker. (California Biography Ser.). (Illus.). 64p. (J). (gr. 4-8). 1999. pap. text 14.95 (*1-884925-80-4*) Toucan Valley.

Mountain Men of the American West. James A. Crutchfield. (Illus.). 200p. (Orig.). 1997. pap. 17.95 (*1-886609-07-1*) Tamarack Bks.

Mountain Men of the Frontier. Charles W. Sundling. LC 98-10144. (Frontier Land Ser.). (Illus.). 32p. (J). 2000. lib. bdg. 19.93 (*1-57765-043-3*, ABDO & Dghtrs) ABDO Pub Co.

Mountain Men on the Santa Fe Trail. Jess McCreede. 1992. mass mkt. 3.99 (*1-55817-594-6*, Pinncle Kensgtn) Kensgtn Pub Corp.

***Mountain Meteorology: Fundamentals & Applications.** C. D. Whiteman. LC 99-24940. 368p. 2000. 39.95 (*0-19-513271-8*) OUP.

Mountain Miracle. T. L. Tedorw. LC 92-19927. (Days of Laura Ingalls Wilder Ser.: Bk. 6). (J). 1992. 4.99 (*0-8407-7733-7*) Nelson.

Mountain Miracle. T. L. Tedrow. (Days of Laura Ingalls Wilder Ser.). (J). 1992. 10.09 (*0-606-12431-4*, Pub. by Turtleback) Demco.

Mountain Miss. Leroy B. Inman. (Illus.). 160p. 1998. pap. 12.95 (*0-9655076-1-0*) South Fork Pr.

Mountain Mist Blue Book of Quilts. Linda Pumphrey et al. (Illus.). 56p. (Orig.). 1996. pap. 8.95 (*0-9652122-0-3*) Stearns Tech.

Mountain Mist Quilt Favorites. Oxmoor House Staff. LC 97-75544. (Illus.). 160p. 1998. pap. 19.95 (*0-8487-1669-8*) Oxmoor Hse.

Mountain Mists: A Story of the Virungas. Evelyn Lee. LC 99-19981. (Habitat Ser.: No. 14). (Illus.). 36p. (J). (gr. 1-4). 1999. 19.95 incl. audio (*1-56899-787-6*, BC7014) Soundprints.

Mountain Mists: A Story of the Virungas. Evelyn Lee. (Habitat Ser.: No. 14). (Illus.). 36p. (J). (gr. 1-4). 1999. 26.95 (*1-56899-789-2*); pap. 5.95 (*1-56899-786-8*); pap. 16.95 (*1-56899-790-6*) Soundprints.

Mountain Mists: A Story of the Virungas. Evelyn Lee. LC 99-19981. (Habitat Ser.: No. 14). (Illus.). 36p. (J). (ps-3). 1999. 15.95 (*1-56899-785-X*) Soundprints.

Mountain Monarchs: Wild Sheep & Goats of the Himalaya. George B. Schaller. LC 77-1336. (Wildlife Behavior & Ecology Ser.). 1983. pap. text 12.50 (*0-226-73642-3*) U Ch Pr.

Mountain Monarchs: Wild Sheep & Goats of the Himalaya. George B. Schaller. (Illus.). 476p. 1998. pap. text 23.00 (*0-226-73651-2*, Midway Reprint) U Ch Pr.

***Mountain Moonlight.** Jane Anderson. 1999. mass mkt. 3.99 (*0-8217-6440-3*) Kensgtn Pub Corp.

Mountain Moonlight. Elizabeth Leigh. 352p. 1997. mass mkt. 4.99 (*0-8217-5632-X*, Zebra Kensgtn) Kensgtn Pub Corp.

Mountain Moonshine to Delta Gumbo. Wilson Ferguson. 1991. 15.95 (*1-879034-00-X*) MS River Pub.

Mountain Mornings: Breakfasts & Other Recipes from the Inn at 410 B&B. Sally Krueger. LC 96-60994. (Illus.). 128p. (Orig.). 1996. pap. 10.95 (*1-883651-04-2*) Winters IN.

Mountain Moving Faith. Kenneth E. Hagin. 184p. 1993. pap. 7.95 (*0-89276-522-4*) Faith Lib Pubns.

Mountain Mysteries. 2nd ed. P. David Smith & Marvin Gregory. (Illus.). 224p. 1984. pap. 12.95 (*0-9608764-1-3*) Wayfinder Pr.

Mountain Never Cries: A Mother's Diary. Ann Holaday. LC 96-79711. 234p. 1999. pap. 14.95 (*1-885221-63-0*) BookPartners.

***Mountain Nightmare.** David Thompson. (Wilderness Ser.: Vol. 29). 176p. (Orig.). 1999. mass mkt. 3.99 (*0-8439-4656-3*, Leisure Bks) Dorchester Pub Co.

Mountain of Black Glass. Tad Williams. (Otherland Ser.: Vol. 3). 689p. 1999. 24.95 (*0-88677-849-2*, Pub. by DAW Bks) Penguin Putnam.

***Mountain of Black Glass.** Tad Williams. (Otherland Ser.: Vol. 3). 2000. mass mkt. 7.99 (*0-88677-906-5*, Pub. by DAW Bks) Penguin Putnam.

Mountain Of Blintzes C. Goldin. 2001. Price not set. (*0-15-201902-2*) Harcourt Coll Pubs.

Mountain of Death. Clarice H. Rainey. LC 97-92202. 238p. 1998. pap. 12.95 (*0-9659622-0-2*) C H Rainey.

Mountain of Fame: Portraits in Chinese History. John E. Willis, Jr. LC 93-46773. 416p. 1994. text 47.50 (*0-691-05542-4*, Pub. by Princeton U Pr) Cal Prin Full Svc.

Mountain of Fame: Portraits in Chinese History. John E. Wills. 424p. 1994. pap. text 16.95 (*0-691-02674-2*, Pub. by Princeton U Pr) Cal Prin Full Svc.

Mountain of Fear. Rona Randall. 1989. 18.00 (*0-7278-1760-4*) Severn Hse.

Mountain of Fear. large type ed. Rona Randall. 1995. 27.99 (*0-7089-3381-5*) Ulverscroft.

***Mountain of God: Community in Spirit.** Richard Vestnys. 124p. 1999. pap. write for info. (*0-7392-0266-9*, PO3345) Morris Pubng.

Mountain of Green Tea & Other Stories. Yahya Taher Abdullah. Tr. by Denys Johnson-Davies. 125p. 1992. pap. 10.00 (*977-424-267-X*, Pub. by Am Univ Cairo Pr) Col U Pr.

Mountain of Lovers. Paul H. Hayne. (Notable American Authors Ser.). 1992. reprint ed. lib. bdg. 75.00 (*0-7812-3062-4*) Rprt Serv.

Mountain of Names: A History of the Human Family. Alex Shoumatoff. Ed. by Philip Turner. (Kodansha Globe Trade Paperback Ser.). 336p. 1995. pap. 15.00 (*1-56836-071-1*, Kodansha Globe) Kodansha.

Mountain of Shiva: A Novel. Karan Singh. (C). 1994. write for info. (*81-207-1589-6*) Sterling Pubs.

Mountain of the Condor: Metaphor & Ritual in an Andean Ayllu. Joseph W. Bastien. (Illus.). 227p. (C). 1985. reprint ed. pap. text 12.50 (*0-88133-143-0*) Waveland Pr.

Mountain of the Lion: The Great Revival in Sierra Leone, West Africa. Donald H. O'Keefe. LC 96-20617. 172p. (Orig.). 1996. pap. 8.99 (*1-56722-192-0*) Word Aflame.

Mountain of the Lord. Universal House of Justice Staff. 16p. 1993. pap. 3.50 (*1-870989-44-9*) Bahai.

Mountain of Truth: The Counterculture Begins, Ascona, 1900-1920. Martin B. Green. LC 85-26363. 313p. 1986. reprint ed. pap. 97.10 (*0-608-02310-8*, 206295100004) Bks Demand.

Mountain Operations. 1995. lib. bdg. 251.99 (*0-8490-6676-X*) Gordon Pr.

Mountain Papuans: Historical & Comparative Perspectives from New Guinea Fringe Highlands Societies. Ed. by James F. Weiner. 240p. (C). 1988. pap. text 18.95 (*0-472-06377-4*, 06377) U of Mich Pr.

Mountain Partisans: Guerrilla Warfare in the Southern Appalachians, 1861-1865. Sean Michael O'Brien. LC 98-56073. 264p. 1999. 35.00 (*0-275-96430-2*, C6430, Praeger Pubs) Greenwood.

Mountain Passage: The Life of a Mountain Man/The Story of America. Jason Manning. 1998. mass mkt. 5.99 (*0-451-19569-8*, Sig) NAL.

Mountain Passage & Other Stories. Garry Barker. LC 86-82567. 250p. (Orig.). 1986. pap. 9.95 (*0-935680-33-0*) Kentucke Imprints.

***Mountain Patterns: The Survival of Nuosu Culture in China.** Stevan Harrell et al. LC 99-50681. (Illus.). 88p. 2000. pap. 20.00 (*0-295-97937-2*) U of Wash Pr.

Mountain Peaks. unabridged ed. Bud Robinson. 121p. 1994. reprint ed. pap. 7.99 (*0-88019-330-1*) Schmul Pub Co.

Mountain People. Ed. by Michael Tobias. LC 86-40085. (Illus.). 256p. 1987. 34.95 (*0-8061-1976-4*) U of Okla Pr.

Mountain People. Colin M. Turnbull. 320p. 1987. pap. 12.00 (*0-671-64098-4*, Touchstone) S&S Trade Pap.

Mountain People in a Flat Land: A Popular History of Appalachian Migration to Northeast Ohio, 1940-1965. Carl E. Feather. LC 97-46493. (Illus.). 200p. 1998. pap. 19.95 (*0-8214-1230-2*); text 39.95 (*0-8214-1229-9*) Ohio U Pr.

Mountain People of Kentucky: Account of the Present (1906) Conditions with the Attitude of the People Toward Improvement. William H. Haney. (Illus.). 196p. 1997. reprint ed. lib. bdg. 25.00 (*0-8328-6727-6*) Higginson Bk Co.

Mountain People, Places & Ways: A Southern Appalachian Sampler. Michael Joslin & Ruth Joslin. (Illus.). 288p. 1991. pap. 12.95 (*0-932807-65-8*) Overmountain Pr.

Mountain Pierces the Blue Sky: Second Collection of Poems, 1960-1993. Peter Z. Bangjiu. Ed. by Jim Moeller et al. LC 94-12045. (Illus.). 240p. Date not set. write for info. (*1-881614-02-6*) Serenity CA.

Mountain Pierces the Blue Sky: Second Collection of Poems, 1960-1993. Peter Z. Bangjiu. Ed. by Jim Moeller et al. LC 94-12045. (Illus.). 1995. pap. 11.95 (*1-881614-01-8*) Serenity CA.

Mountain Plants of the Pacific Northwest: A Field Guide to Washington, Western British Columbia, & Southeastern Alaska. Ronald J. Taylor & George Douglas. Ed. by Kathleen Ort. LC 95-14240. (Illus.). 442p. (Orig.). 1995. pap. 25.00 (*0-87842-314-1*) Mountain Pr.

***Mountain Pose.** Nancy Hope Wilson. 2000. text (*0-374-35078-7*) FS&G.

Mountain Preacher, Vol. 1. R. Paul Caudill. LC 84-71992. 1984. pap. 2.98 (*0-938980-02-5*) Blue Ridge.

Mountain Preacher, Vol. 2. R. Paul Caudill. LC 84-71992. (Illus.). 165p. 1985. pap. 3.00 (*0-938980-03-3*) Blue Ridge.

Mountain Preacher, Vol. 3. R. Paul Caudill. LC 84-71992. (Illus.). 165p. 1986. pap. 3.00 (*0-938980-05-X*) Blue Ridge.

Mountain Preacher Stories: Laughter among the Trumpets. Ben C. Fisher. LC 89-39225. 76p. (Orig.). 1990. pap. 5.95 (*0-913239-64-X*) Appalach Consortium.

Mountain Pygmy-Possum of the Australian Alps. Ian Mansergh & Linda Broome. (Natural History Ser.). (Illus.). 116p. 1996. reprint ed. pap. 21.95 (*0-86840-085-8*, Pub. by New South Wales Univ Pr) Intl Spec Bk.

Mountain Rain: A Biography of James O. Fraser, Pioneer Missionary to China. Eileen F. Crossman. LC 93-47631. (Illus.). 256p. 1994. mass mkt. 5.99 (*0-87788-551-6*) OMF Bks.

Mountain Range: A Dictionary of Expressions from Appalachia to the Ozarks. Robert Hendrickson. LC 96-48660. (Dictionary of American Regional Expressions Ser.). 176p. 1997. 24.95 (*0-8160-2113-9*); pap. 14.95 (*0-8160-3692-6*) Facts on File.

Mountain Ranges. Neil Morris. LC 96-4091. (World's Top Ten Ser.). (Illus.). 32p. (J). 1997. lib. bdg. 22.83 (*0-8172-4339-9*) Raintree Steck-V.

Mountain Reader. Carol Kimmons. (Illus.). 308p. 1984. spiral bd. write for info. (*0-930739-00-0*) Sequatchie.

M

Mountain Reader. Carol Kimmons. 260p. 1995. pap. text. write for info. (0-930739-02-7) Sequatchie.

***Mountain Reader: A Nature Conservancy Book.** Ed. by John A. Murray. 320p. 2000. 30.00 (1-58574-022-5); pap. 17.95 (1-58574-065-9) Lyons Pr.

Mountain Real Estate. Kent Gunnufson Gunnufson. (Illus.). 192p. (Orig.). 1999. pap. 9.95 (0-9605366-2-0) Snowstorm.

Mountain Rebels: East Tennessee Confederates & the Civil War, 1860-1870. W. Todd Groce. LC 99-6207. (Illus.). 240p. 1999. 28.00 (1-57233-057-0, Pub. by U of Tenn Pr) U Ch Pr.

Mountain Recipe Collection. 2nd ed. Valeria S. Ison. Ed. by Gail Deaton. (Illus.). 318p. 1981. spiral bd. 16.00 (0-9617605-0-8) Ison Collect.

Mountain Research in Europe: An Overview of MAB Research from the Pyreness to Siberia. Price. LC 94-27565. (Man & the Biosphere Ser.: Vol. 14). 254p. 1995. 65.00 (1-85070-570-4) Prthnon Pub.

***Mountain Riders.** Max Brand. 158p. 1999. pap. 19.00 (0-7540-8062-5) Chivers N Amer.

Mountain Rising: A Novel. Judy Merritt. LC 95-33615. 250p. (Orig.). 1996. pap. write for info. (1-887786-09-0) Sky & Sage Bks.

Mountain River: Vietnamese Poetry from the Wars, 1948-1993. Ed. by Kevin Bowen et al. Tr. by Nguyen Ba Chung et al. LC 98-12598. (ENG & VIE.). 296p. (Orig.). 1998. 40.00 (1-55849-140-6); pap. 17.95 (1-55849-141-4) U of Mass Pr.

***Mountain Rivers.** Ellen E. Wohl. LC 00-30617. (Water Resources Monograph Ser.). (Illus.). 2000. write for info. (0-87590-318-5) Am Geophysical.

Mountain Roads & Quiet Places: A Complete Guide to the Roads of Great Smoky Mountains National Park. Jerry Delaughter. (Illus.). 96p. (Orig.). 1986. pap. 8.95 (0-937207-00-4) GSMNH.

Mountain Rose. Jessica Wulf. 432p. 1996. pap. 2.99 (0-8217-5486-6) Kensgtn Pub Corp.

Mountain Sage - The Life Story of Carl Sharsmith, Yosemite Ranger - Naturalist. 2nd ed. Elizabeth S. O'Neill. (Illus.). 220p. (Orig.). 1988. pap. 14.95 (0-939666-47-2) Albicaulis Pr.

Mountain School Teacher. Melville D. Post. 196p. 1980. reprint ed. lib. bdg. 12.75 (0-89968-199-9, Lghtyr Pr) Buccaneer Bks.

Mountain Science. Carol Kimmons. (Illus.). 289p. 1986. spiral bd. write for info. (0-930739-01-9) Sequatchie.

Mountain Science. Carol Kimmons. 260p. 1995. pap. text. write for info. (0-930739-03-5) Sequatchie.

***Mountain Scouting: A Hand-Book for Officers & Soldiers on the Frontiers.** Edward S. Farrow. LC 99-55162. 284p. 2000. 12.95 (0-8061-3209-4) U of Okla Pr.

Mountain Search for the Lost Victim. Dennis Kelley. 283p. 1973. 39.00 (0-9603392-1-3) Search & Rescue.

Mountain Sheep of North America. Ed. by Raul Valdez & Paul R. Krausman. LC 98-25333. (Illus.). 353 p. 1999. write for info. (0-8165-1839-4) U of Ariz Pr.

Mountain Sheriff No. 3: The Canyon Mountain War. Earl P. Murray. 256p. 1988. mass mkt. 2.95 (0-8217-2413-4, Zebra Kensgtn) Kensgtn Pub Corp.

Mountain Sickness: Prevention Recognition & Treatment. 2nd ed. Peter Hackett. (Illus.). 80p. 1997. reprint ed. pap. 8.50 (0-930410-10-6) Amer Alpine Club.

Mountain Signs/Mountain Life. Gerald Cox. (Illus.). 96p. 1990. 5.95 (0-935576-35-5) Kesend Pub Ltd.

Mountain Singer: The Life & the Legacy of Byron Herbert Reece. Raymond A. Cook. LC 80-8067. (Illus.). 368p. 1980. pap. 14.95 (0-87797-246-X) Cherokee.

Mountain Sojourns. Ronald H. Smith. 136p. 1994. pap. 11.95 (0-9640308-2-9) Castle R Pubng.

Mountain Song. unabridged ed. Dave Fullen. (Illus.). 20p. (Orig.). (J). (gr. 1-6). 1992. pap. 14.95 incl. audio (1-881650-00-6) Mntn Bks.

Mountain Songs. Edith Schaeffer. 80p. 1988. 12.95 (0-310-54640-0, 12917) Zondervan.

Mountain Speaks. Kanawati. 1988. pap. 35.00 (0-85668-570-4, Pub. by Aris & Phillips) David Brown.

Mountain Spirit. Ed. by Michael C. Tobias & Harold Drasdo. LC 77-20740. 264p. 1979. reprint ed. 25.00 (0-87951-073-0, Pub. by Overlook Pr) Penguin Putnam.

Mountain Spirit. Ed. by Michael C. Tobias & Harold Drasdo. LC 77-20740. 264p. 1983. reprint ed. pap. 14.95 (0-87951-168-0, Pub. by Overlook Pr) Penguin Putnam.

Mountain Spirits: A Chronicle of Corn Whiskey. Joseph E. Dabney. LC 84-17442. (Illus.). 288p. 1984. reprint ed. pap. 10.95 (0-914875-02-7) Bright Mtn Bks.

***Mountain Stands There.** A. Robert Hill. 352p. 2000. pap. 16.95 (0-595-00214-5, Writers Club Pr) iUniversecom.

Mountain State: An Introduction to West Virginia. Otis K. Rice & Stephen W. Brown. Ed. by James W. Rowley. LC 97-60861. (Illus.). (J). (gr. 8). 1997. 30.00 (0-914498-14-2) WV Hist Ed Found.

Mountain State Mammals: A Guide to Mammals of the Rocky Mountain Region. Ron Russo. (Illus.). 136p. 1991. pap. 5.25 (0-912550-21-X) Nature Study.

Mountain State Stories of the People: Celebrating West Virginia. Ed. by Amy A. Stevenson & Rae J. Sielen. LC 97-65941. (Illus.). 186p. (Orig.). 1997. pap. 18.00 (0-9652699-1-4) Populore Pub.

Mountain States of America: People, Politics & Power in the Eight Rocky Mountain States. Neal R. Pierce. (Illus.). 320p. 1971. 15.95 (0-393-05255-9) Norton.

Mountain Storm, Pine Breeze: Folk Song in Japan. Patia R. Isaku. LC 81-706. 138p. 1981. pap. 42.80 (0-608-05621-9, 206607700006) Bks Demand.

Mountain Stream. Paul Fleisher. LC 97-48279. (Webs of Life Ser.). (Illus.). (J). (gr. 2-4). 1998. lib. bdg. 22.79 (0-7614-0838-X, Benchmark NY) Marshall Cavendish.

Mountain Summer. William H. Mashburn. LC 88-11782. (Appalachian Connection Ser.). (Illus.). 128p. (Orig.). 1990. reprint ed. pap. 8.95 (0-936015-14-4) Pocahontas Pr.

Mountain Summers: Tales of Hiking & Exploration in the White Mountains from 1878 to 1886 As Seen Through the Eyes of Women. Peter Rowan & June H. Rowan. (Illus.). 273p. 1995. pap. 16.95 (0-9648801-0-5) Gulfside Pr.

Mountain Tasting: Zen Haiku. Santoka Taneda & John Stevens. LC 80-97. 112p. 1980. pap. 12.50 (0-8348-0151-5) Weatherhill.

Mountain Tavern, & Other Stories. Liam O'Flaherty. LC 73-178453. (Short Story Index Reprint Ser.). 1980. reprint ed. 18.95 (0-8369-4054-7) Ayer.

Mountain That Burns Within. Tad Hardy. LC 97-205368. Vol. 1. 216p. (J). (gr. 3-7). 1997. write for info. (0-7814-3001-1, Chariot Bks) Chariot Victor.

Mountain That Loved a Bird. Alice McLerran. (Illus.). 28p. (J). (gr. k-3). 2000. per. 5.99 (0-689-83319-9) Aladdin.

Mountain That Loved a Bird. Alice McLerran. LC 85-9391. (Illus.). 28p. (J). (ps up). 1991. 16.00 (0-88708-000-6, Picture Book Studio) S&S Childrens.

Mountain, the Miner & the Lord, & Other Tales from a Country Law Office. Harry M. Caudill. LC 80-51012. 192p. 1980. pap. 16.00 (0-8131-0195-6) U Pr of Ky.

Mountain, the Stone. Kathleen Kranidas. 100p. 1975. pap. 3.50 (0-913006-07-6) Puckerbrush.

***Mountain Time.** Ivan Doig. LC 99-14324. 320p. 1999. 24.50 (0-684-83295-X) Scribner.

***Mountain Time.** large type ed. Ivan Doig. LC 99-45075. (Thorndike Americana Ser.). 1999. 28.95 (0-7862-2216-6) Thorndike Pr.

***Mountain Time: A Novel.** Ivan Doig. 2000. pap. 13.00 (0-684-86569-6) Scribner.

Mountain Time: A Yellowstone Memoir. 3rd ed. Paul D. Schullery. 236p. 1995. pap. text 13.95 (1-57098-037-3) Roberts Rinehart.

Mountain to Stand Strong, No. 8. Peggy Darty. (Serenade Serenata Ser.). 1984. pap. 1.49 (0-310-46532-X, 15513P) Zondervan.

***Mountain Too Far: A Father's Search for Meaning in the Climbing Death of His Son.** Karl H. Purnell. LC 00-132565. 304p. 2001. 24.95 (0-88282-204-7, Pub. by New Horizon NJ) Natl Bk Netwk.

Mountain Top Mystery. Gertrude Chandler Warner. LC 64-7722. (Boxcar Children Ser.: No. 9). (Illus.). 128p. (J). (gr. 2-5). 1964. pap. 5.95 (0-8075-5293-3); lib. bdg. 19.95 (0-8075-5292-5) A Whitman.

Mountain Top Mystery. Gertrude Chandler Warner. (Boxcar Children Ser.: No. 9). (J). (gr. 2-5). 1964. 9.05 (0-606-04481-7, Pub. by Turtleback) Demco.

Mountain Torrent of the Tien Shan: An Ecology-Faunistic Essay. K. A. Brodsky. (Monographiae Biologicae: No. 39). (Illus.). 311p. 1980. text 211.50 (90-6193-091-X) Kluwer Academic.

***Mountain Town.** Bonnie Geisert & Arthur Geisert. LC 99-29856. 32p. (J). 2000. 16.00 (0-395-95390-1) HM.

Mountain Township. Walter R. Hard. LC 62-22261. xx, 267p. 1985. reprint ed. pap. 8.95 (0-911570-21-7) Vermont Bks.

Mountain Trail. Jerry Haggard. 202p. (Orig.). 1996. pap. 12.95 (1-57502-261-3, P0944) Morris Pubng.

Mountain Trail & Its Message. 2nd expanded ed. Albert W. Palmer. Ed. & Photos by Charles P. Fisk. LC 97-66260. (Illus.). 96p. 1997. pap. 12.00 (0-9641404-7-0) Sixth St Pr.

Mountain Treasures. Jane V. Barker & Sybil Downing. (Colorado Heritage Ser.). (Illus.). 44p. (J). (gr. k-6). reprint ed. pap. 7.95 (1-878611-01-1) Silver Rim Pr.

Mountain Trivia Challenge. Ralph Storer. LC 95-9143. 128p. 1995. pap. 5.95 (0-89886-444-5) Mountaineers.

Mountain Troops of the Waffen-SS, 1941-1945. Roland Kaltenegger. Tr. by Edward Force from GER. LC 95-68641. (Illus.). 160p. 1995. 24.95 (0-88740-813-3) Schiffer.

Mountain Troubadour. Charles Carson. 1951. 5.95 (0-87505-127-8) Borden.

Mountain Valley War. Louis L'Amour. 208p. 1997. mass mkt. 4.50 (0-553-25090-6) Bantam.

Mountain Valley War. large type ed. Louis L'Amour. LC 96-36268. (Westerm Ser.). 281p. 1998. 25.95 (0-7838-1953-6, G K Hall Lrg Type) Mac Lib Ref.

Mountain Valor. Gloria M. Houston. LC 92-26218. (Illus.). 240p. (YA). (gr. 8 up). 1994. 15.95 (0-399-22519-6, Philomel) Peng Put Young Read.

Mountain Valor. Gloria M. Houston. LC 92-26218. (Illus.). 248p. (J). (gr. 4-7). 1996. pap. 5.99 (0-698-11383-7, PapStar) Peng Put Young Read.

Mountain Valor. Gloria M. Houston. LC 92-26218. (J). 1996. 11.05 (0-606-09634-5, Pub. by Turtleback) Demco.

Mountain View Ranch, 1915-1945. Merideth A. Hmura. LC 96-94280. (Illus.). 320p. (Orig.). 1996. pap. 23.95 (0-9652070-1-3) Leaning Pine.

Mountain Villages: Historic Sites in New Mexico. 3rd ed. Alice Bullock. LC 81-5687. (Illus.). 1991. pap. 8.95 (0-913270-13-X) Sunstone Pr.

Mountain Voices. 2nd ed. Warren Moore. (Illus.). 288p. 1997. 35.95 (0-9654911-0-2); pap. 25.95 (0-9654911-1-0) Blair.

Mountain Walking in Africa: Kenya. David Else. (Illus.). 180p. (Orig.). 1991. pap. 19.95 (1-85365-205-9, Pub. by McCarta) Seven Hills Bk.

Mountain Walks in Gran Canaria. Javier M. Garcia. (Illus.). 88p. 1999. pap. 14.95 (1-85182-349-2, Pub. by Four Cts Pr) Intl Spec Bk.

Mountain Warriors: The Pre-Colonial Meru of Mt. Kenya. Jeffrey A. Fadiman. LC 75-620140. (Papers in International Studies: Africa Ser.: No. 27). 83p. reprint ed. pap. 30.00 (0-7837-1324-X, 204147200021) Bks Demand.

Mountain Water: The Way of the High Country Angler. Craig Martin. LC 99-37861. (Illus.). 174p. 2000. pap. 18.95 (0-87108-896-7) Pruett.

Mountain Weather: A Guide for Skiers & Hillwalkers. William S. Burroughs. (Illus.). 111p. 1996. pap. 24.95 (1-85223-877-1, Pub. by Crolwood) Trafalgar.

Mountain Weather & Climate. Roger G. Barry. LC 80-42348. (Illus.). 313p. 1981. 57.50 (0-416-73730-7, NO. 3464) Routledge.

Mountain Weather & Climate. 2nd ed. Roger G. Barry. (Physical Environment Ser.). (Illus.). 432p. (C). 1992. pap. 34.99 (0-415-07113-5, A6547) Routledge.

Mountain Wedding. Faye Gibbons. LC 95-18197. (Illus.). 40p. (J). (ps up). 1996. 16.00 (0-688-11348-6, Wm Morrow) Morrow Avon.

Mountain Wedding. Faye Gibbons. LC 95-18197. (Illus.). 40p. (J). (ps up). 1996. 15.93 (0-688-11349-4, Wm Morrow) Morrow Avon.

Mountain West: Interpreting the Folk Landscape. Terry G. Jordan et al. LC 96-15912. (Creating the North American Landscape Ser.). (Illus.). 192p. 1996. text 35.95 (0-8018-5431-8) Johns Hopkins.

Mountain Wilderness: An Illustrated History of the Wrangell-St. Elias National Park & Preserve, Alaska. William R. Hunt. LC 96-24564. 1996. pap. write for info. (0-89865-971-X) Donning Co.

Mountain Wildflowers Date Book. D. M. Dorward. (Illus.). 52p. (Orig.). pap. 5.50 (0-9615729-1-4) Dorward Photo.

Mountain Wildlife. A. Claybourne & A. Cunningham. (World Wildlife Ser.). (Illus.). 32p. (J). (gr. 3-7). 1994. lib. bdg. 14.95 (0-88110-683-6, Usborne) EDC.

Mountain Wildlife. A. Claybourne & Antonia Cunningham. (World Wildlife Ser.). (Illus.). 32p. (J). (gr. 3-7). 1994. pap. 6.95 (0-7460-1660-3, Usborne) EDC.

Mountain Wildlife. Marjorie Dunmire. (Illus.). 48p. (Orig.). (J). (gr. 2 up). 1986. pap. 4.95 (0-942559-03-7) Pegasus Graphics.

Mountain Windsong: A Novel of the Trail of Tears. Robert J. Conley. LC 92-54150. 224p. 1995. pap. 11.95 (0-8061-2746-5) U of Okla Pr.

Mountain Winter & Other Poems. Alan Rickard. (Australian Collection). 1984. pap. 7.00 (0-936128-12-7) De Young Pr.

Mountain Wolf Woman, 1884-1960: A Resource Guide. Jocelyn Riley. 114p. (YA). (gr. 5 up). 1995. 45.00 incl. VHS (1-877933-12-0) Her Own Words.

Mountain Wolf Woman, Sister of Crashing Thunder: The Autobiography of a Winnebago Indian. rev. ed. Ed. by Nancy O. Lurie. (Ann Arbor Paperbacks Ser.). (Illus.). 176p. 1961. pap. 15.95 (0-472-06109-7, 06109, Ann Arbor Bks) U of Mich Pr.

Mountain Woman. Elia W. Peattie. LC 79-98590. (Short Story Index Reprint Ser.). 1977. 20.95 (0-8369-3164-5) Ayer.

***Mountain Woman Tales & the Bird Journal.** 2nd rev. ed. Jane Wodening. (Illus.). 120p. 2000. reprint ed. pap. 12.00 (1-887997-17-2, Pub. by Baksun Bks) SPD-Small Pr Dist.

***Mountain World: A Literary Journal.** Ed. by Gregory McNamee. LC 99-46907. (Illus.). 320p. 2000. 25.00 (0-87156-898-5, Pub. by Sierra) Random.

Mountain Worlds. Ed. by Margaret Sedeen. 320p. 1988. 33.95 (0-87044-653-3); lib. bdg. 23.95 (0-87044-652-5) Natl Geog.

Mountain Wreath. Petar Petrovic Njegos. Ed. & Tr. by Vasa D. Mihailovich. LC 86-21998. xix, 220p. 1986. pap. 22.50 (1-884445-18-7) C Schlacks Pub.

Mountain Wreath of P. P. Nyegosh, Prince Bishop of Montenegro. Prince Petar, 2nd. Tr. by James W. Wiles. LC 71-109820. 250p. 1970. reprint ed. lib. bdg. 47.50 (0-8371-4311-X, PEMW, Greenwood Pr) Greenwood.

Mountain Yarns: Home-Spun Stories Woven from the Threads of Life. John Kincaid. 169p. (Orig.). 1996. pap. 8.95 (0-9651707-0-5) Kincaid Kountry.

Mountain Year. Barbara G. Hallowell. LC 98-21685. (Illus.). 1998. pap. 18.95 (0-89587-222-6) Blair.

Mountain Year. Michael J. Murphy. 73p. 1987. pap. 5.95 (0-685-25951-X, Pub. by Blackstaff Pr) Dufour.

Mountain Year. Michael J. Murphy. 73p. 1987. pap. 8.95 (0-85640-382-2, Pub. by Blackstaff Pr) Dufour.

Mountain Year: Life on the Slopes of Slieve Gullion. Michael J. Murphy. LC 64-25512. 1964. 12.95 (0-8023-1079-6) Dufour.

Mountaineer. G. Turner Howard, Jr. LC 97-91121. 102p. 1998. 15.95 (0-533-12562-6) Vantage.

Mountaineer, Vol. 1, No. 1. Ed. by Michael P. Jones & Jeanine Boldt. (Illus.). 42p. (J). 1984. pap. text 4.00 (0-89904-017-9) Crumb Elbow Pub.

Mountaineer, Vol. 2, No. 1. Welches School, Jeanine Boldt's English Class. (Illus.). 58p. (J). 1984. pap. 7.00 (0-89904-018-7) Crumb Elbow Pub.

Mountaineer: Thirty Years of Climbing on the World's Great Peaks. Chris Bonington. LC 89-38267. (Sierra Club Guides to the Natural Areas Ser.). 1990. 29.95 (0-87156-618-4, Pub. by Sierra) Random.

Mountaineer: Thirty Years of Climbing on the World's Great Peaks. Chris Bonington. (Illus.). 192p. 1996. pap. 30.00 (0-87156-905-1, Pub. by Sierra) Random.

Mountaineer Battlewagon: U. S. S. West Virginia (BB-18) Myron J. Smith, Jr. 48p. (Orig.). 1982. pap. 7.95 (0-933126-16-6) Pictorial Hist.

Mountaineer Jamboree: Country Music in West Virginia. Ivan M. Tribe. (Illus.). 288p. 1996. pap. 18.00 (0-8131-0880-9) U Pr of Ky.

Mountaineer Jamboree: Country Music in West Virginia. fac. ed. Ivan M. Tribe. LC 84-7467. (Illus.). 271p. 1984. pap. 84.10 (0-7837-7603-9, 204735600007) Bks Demand.

Mountaineer Sabres: A Pictorial History 167th Fighter Squadron West Va. Air National Guard, 1955-1961. Jack A. Smith. LC 88-90958. (Illus.). 56p. 1988. pap. text 7.95 (0-929521-02-1) Pictorial Hist.

Mountaineering: A Woman's Guide. Andrea Gabbard. LC 98-41573. (Illus.). 126p. 1998. pap. 14.95 (0-07-103402-1) McGraw.

Mountaineering: The Freedom of the Hills. 6th ed. Don Graydon & Mountaineers Staff. Ed. by Kurt Hanson. LC 97-11920. 528p. 1997. reprint ed. pap. 24.95 (0-89886-427-5) Mountaineers.

Mountaineering: The Freedom of the Hills. 6th ed. Don Graydon & Mountaineers Staff. LC 97-11920. (Illus.). 544p. 1997. reprint ed. 35.00 (0-89886-426-7) Mountaineers.

***Mountaineering Adventures.** Matt Doeden. (Dangerous Adventures Ser.). 48p. (YA). (gr. 5 up). 2000. lib. bdg. 21.26 (0-7368-0575-3, Capstone Bks) Capstone Pr.

Mountaineering Dictionary: English, French, German, Italian. Rudolf Weiss. (ENG, FRE, GER & ITA.). 452p. 1989. 85.00 (0-7859-9965-5) Fr & Eur.

Mountaineering Essays. John Muir. Ed. by Richard Fleck. LC 98-6137. 200p. 1997. pap. text 10.95 (0-87480-544-9) U of Utah Pr.

Mountaineering First Aid: A Guide to Accident Response & First Aid Care. 4th ed. Jan D. Carline et al. LC 96-15825. (Illus.). 144p. 1996. pap. 10.95 (0-89886-478-X) Mountaineers.

Mountaineering in Patagonia. Alan Kearney. (Illus.). 144p. 1993. 22.95 (0-938567-30-6) Mountaineers.

Mountaineering in the Andes. Ed. by Jill Neate. (C). 1993. 60.00 (0-907649-64-5, Pub. by Expedit Advisory Ctr) St Mut.

Mountaineering in the Kings River Country. Clerence King. Ed. by William R. Jones. (Illus.). 48p. 1978. reprint ed. pap. 3.95 (0-89646-042-8) Vistabooks.

Mountaineering in the Sierra Nevada. Clarence King. Ed. & Pref. by Francis P. Farquhar. LC 96-47072. (Illus.). 320p. 1997. pap. 12.00 (0-8032-7783-0, Bison Books) U of Nebr Pr.

Mountaineering in the Sierra Nevada. Clarence King. LC 97-29750. (High Sierra Classics Ser.). 1997. 9.95 (0-939666-86-3) Yosemite Assn.

Mountaineering in the Sierra Nevada. Clarence King. (Notable American Authors Ser.). 1999. reprint ed. lib. bdg. 125.00 (0-7812-3678-9) Rprt Serv.

Mountaineering in the Tetons: The Pioneer Period, 1898-1940. 2nd ed. Fritiof Fryvell. Ed. by Phil D. Smith. Date not set. pap. 8.95 (0-931895-50-2) Grand Teton NHA.

Mountaineering Literature: A Bibliography of Material Published in English. 2nd enl. rev. ed. Jill Neate. 296p. 1987. pap. 29.95 (0-938567-04-7) Mountaineers.

Mountaineering Medicine. 14th rev. ed. Fred Darvill, Jr. LC 98-9968. (Illus.). 116p. 1998. pap. 7.95 (0-89997-207-1) Wilderness Pr.

Mountaineering on the Pacific in 1868. Edmund T. Coleman. Ed. by William R. Jones. (Illus.). 24p. 1977. reprint ed. pap. 2.00 (0-89646-014-2) Vistabooks.

***Mountaineering 2000.** Mountaineers Books Staff. 1999. 11.99 (0-89886-634-0) Mountaineers.

Mountaineering Women: Stories by Early Climbers. Ed. by David Mazel. LC 94-11260. (Illus.). 200p. 1994. pap. 14.95 (0-89096-617-6) Tex A&M Univ Pr.

Mountaineering Women: Stories by Early Climbers. Ed. by David Mazel. LC 94-11260. (Illus.). 200p. 1994. 27.50 (0-89096-616-8) Tex A&M Univ Pr.

Mountaineers: A History. Jim Kjeldsen. Ed. by Ken Lans. LC 98-7795. (Illus.). 224p. 1998. 30.00 (0-89886-615-4); pap. 19.95 (0-89886-599-9) Mountaineers.

Mountaineers Are Always Free! Paul Metcalf. 100p. 1991. pap. 9.50 (0-917453-21-2) Bamberger.

Mountaineers to Main Streets: The Old Dominion As Seen Through the Farm Security Administration Photographs. Brooks Johnson. LC 85-71481. 176p. (Orig.). reprint ed. pap. 54.60 (0-7837-2413-6, 204236200006) Bks Demand.

Mountainhouse: A Novella. Patt C. McDermid. LC 81-83724. 137p. (Orig.). 1981. pap. 9.95 (0-912288-17-5) Perivale Pr.

***Mountainman Crafts & Skills: A Fully Illustrated Guide to Wilderness Living & Survival.** David R. Montgomery. LC 00-21623. (Illus.). 2000. pap. 14.95 (1-58574-066-7) Lyons Pr.

Mountainous West: Explorations in Historical Geography. Ed. by William Wyckoff & Lary M. Dilsaver. LC 94-31183. (Illus.). vii, 422p. 1995. pap. text 35.00 (0-8032-9759-9, Bison Books) U of Nebr Pr.

Mountains see Images

Mountains see Wonders of Our World Series

Mountains see Read-&-Discover Science Series

Mountains. (Butterfly Bks.). (Illus.). 32p. (J). (gr. 3-5). 1985. 9.95 (0-86685-455-X) Intl Bk Ctr.

***Mountains.** (Japanese Screens & Scrolls Lined Ser.). 160p. 1999. 14.95 (1-55156-014-3, Pub. by Paperblank) Andrews & McMeel.

Mountains. (Play & Discover Ser.). (Illus.). 32p. (J). (ps-2). 1997. pap. 3.95 (0-8069-4235-5) Sterling.

Mountains. Norman S. Barrett. (Picture Library). 32p. 1990. lib. bdg. 20.00 (0-531-10838-4) Watts.

***Mountains.** BHB International Staff. (Here We Go Round Ser.). (J). 1998. 5.95 (2-215-06180-4) CE75.

***Mountains.** Larry Dane Brimner. LC 99-58039. (True Bks.). (Illus.). (J). 2000. 22.00 (0-516-21568-X) Childrens.

***Mountains.** Catherine Chambers. LC 99-46852. (Mapping Earthforms Ser.). 2000. lib. bdg. write for info. (1-57572-525-8) Heinemann Lib.

Mountains. Allan Collinson. LC 91-34171. (Ecology Watch Ser.). (Illus.). 48p. (YA). (gr. 5 up). 1992. lib. bdg. 13.95 (0-87518-493-6, Dillon Silver Burdett) Silver Burdett Pr.

Mountains. David Cumming. (Habitats Ser.). (Illus.). 48p. (J). (gr. 4-6). 1995. lib. bdg. 24.26 (1-56847-388-5) Raintree Steck-V.

***Mountains.** David Cumming. (Habitats Ser.). (gr. 4-9). 1999. 24.26 (0-8172-5239-8) Raintree Steck-V.

M

An Asterisk (*) at the beginning of an entry indicates that the title is appearing for the first time.

Mountains. Carroll L. Fenton & Mildred A. Fenton. LC 70-84305. (Essay Index Reprint Ser.). 1977. 24.95 (*0-8369-1129-6*) Ayer.

***Mountains.** Susan H. Gray. (First Reports). (Illus.). 48p. (J). (gr. 2-3). 2000. write for info. (*0-7565-0021-4*) Compass Point.

***Mountains.** Cally Hall. LC 99-23422. (Closer Look at Ser.). (Illus.). 32p. (J). 1999. 20.90 (*0-7613-0902-0*, Copper Beech Bks) Millbrook Pr.

Mountains. Mel Higginson. LC 94-10721. (This Earth of Ours Discovery Library). 24p. (J). (gr. k-4). 1994. lib. bdg. 10.95 (*0-86593-383-9*) Rourke Corp.

Mountains. Ed. by Jack D. Ives. LC 93-34439. (Illustrated Library of the Earth Ser.). 1994. 35.00 (*0-87596-633-0*) Rodale Pr Inc.

Mountains. Terry Jennings. LC 97-10937. (Restless Earth Ser.). (J). 1998. write for info. (*0-382-39941-2*); pap. write for info. (*0-382-39942-0*) Silver Burdett Pr.

Mountains. Keith Lye. (What about Ser.). 32p. (J). (gr. 1-4). 1996. pap. text 4.95 (*0-8114-9659-7*) Raintree Steck-V.

Mountains. Keith Lye. (Our World Ser.). (Illus.). 48p. (J). (gr. 5-8). 1987. lib. bdg. 12.95 (*0-382-09498-0*) Silver Burdett Pr.

Mountains. Peter Murray. (Biomes of Nature Ser.). (Illus.). 32p. (J). (gr. 2-6). 1996. lib. bdg. 22.79 (*1-56766-279-X*) Childs World.

Mountains. Anna O'Mara. (Read-&-Discover Bks.). (Illus.). 24p. (J). (gr. k-3). 1996. 14.00 (*0-516-20127-1*) Childrens.

Mountains. Andy Owen & Miranda Ashwell. LC 97-34420. (Geography Starts Ser.). (J). 1998. (*1-57572-607-6*) Heinemann.

Mountains. Graham Percy. (Press & Lift Bks.). (Illus.). 16p. (J). (gr. 1-5). 1989. 6.50 (*1-881469-11-5*) Safari Ltd.

Mountains. Seymour Simon. LC 93-11398. (Illus.). 40p. (J). (gr. k up). 1994. 15.00 (*0-688-11040-1*, Wm Morrow) Morrow Avon.

Mountains. Seymour Simon. LC 93-11398. (Illus.). 40p. (J). (gr. k up). 1994. lib. bdg. 14.93 (*0-688-11041-X*, Wm Morrow) Morrow Avon.

Mountains. Seymour Simon. LC 93-11398. (Illus.). 32p. (J). 1997. mass mkt. 5.95 (*0-688-15477-8*, Wm Morrow) Morrow Avon.

Mountains. Seymour Simon. 1997. 11.15 (*0-606-11643-5*, Pub. by Turtleback) Demco.

Mountains. Philip Steele. LC 90-20741. (Pocket Facts Ser.). (Illus.). 32p. (J). (gr. 5-6). 1991. lib. bdg. 11.95 (*0-89686-587-8*, Crstwood Hse) Silver Burdett Pr.

Mountains. Lynn M. Stone. LC 83-7276. (New True Books Ser.). (Illus.). 48p. (J). (gr. k-4). 1983. lib. bdg. 21.00 (*0-516-01698-9*) Childrens.

Mountains. Lynn M. Stone. (Ecozones Ser.). (Illus.). 48p. (J). (gr. 4-8). 1989. 11.95 (*0-685-67721-4*) Rourke Corp.

Mountains. Lynn M. Stone. (Ecozones Ser.). (Illus.). 48p. (J). (gr. 4-8). 1988. lib. bdg. 22.60 (*0-86592-448-1*) Rourke Enter.

Mountains. Neil Stronach. (Endangered People & Places Ser.). (J). 1996. lib. bdg. 22.60 (*0-8225-2777-4*, Lerner Publctns) Lerner Pub.

Mountains. Zuza Vrbova. LC 89-20299. (Our Planet Ser.). (Illus.). 32p. (J). (gr. 4-6). 1990. pap. 4.95 (*0-8167-1974-8*) Troll Communs.

Mountains. Zuza Vrbova. LC 89-20299. (Our Planet Ser.). (Illus.). 32p. (J). (gr. 4-6). 1997. lib. bdg. 17.25 (*0-8167-1973-X*) Troll Communs.

Mountains. A. Wilkes. (Explainers Ser.). 24p. (J). (gr. 2-4). 1980. pap. 4.95 (*0-7460-0755-8*, Usborne); lib. bdg. 12.95 (*0-88110-682-8*, Usborne) EDC.

Mountains. S. E. White. (Illus.). 328p. 1987. reprint ed. 25.00 (*0-935632-50-6*) Wolfe Pub Co.

Mountains Against the Sun. Perry Holmes. LC 97-27719. 243p. 1997. lib. bdg. 17.95 (*0-7862-0754-X*) Five Star.

Mountains Against the Sun. large type ed. Holmes. LC 98-30796. 1999. 30.00 (*0-7862-0778-7*) Thorndike Pr.

Mountains & Canyons. William Russell. LC 94-505. (From This Earth Discovery Library). 24p. (J). (gr. k-4). 1994. lib. bdg. 10.95 (*0-86593-360-X*) Rourke Corp.

Mountains & Canyons: A Photographic Description of the Rocky Mountain Region. Ed. by Lawrence J. Goldman & Mark W. Longman. LC 95-71213. (Illus.). 100p. 1995. write for info. (*0-933979-18-5*) Rocky Mtn Assoc Geol.

Mountains & Constancy. Maggie A. Smith. (Paper Moon Bks.). (Orig.). 1992. pap. 6.95 (*1-884438-01-6*) Epiphany AR.

Mountains & Hills of Britain: A Guide to the Uplands of England, Scotland, & Wales. Michael Marriott. LC 82-194503. 176p. 1982. write for info. (*0-00-218028-6*) Collins.

Mountains & Memories. Wilhemina Edwards. 68p. (C). 1989. text 70.00 (*1-872795-70-6*, Pub. by Pentland Pr) St Mut.

Mountains & Mesas: The Northern Rockies & the Colorado Plateau. Pete Bengeyfield. LC 95-48042. (Western Horizons Bks.). (Illus.). 160p. (Orig.). 1996. pap. 17.95 (*0-87358-608-5*) Northland AZ.

Mountains & Pioneers of Lake County. 2nd ed. Henry Mauldin. Ed. by Carolyn W. Greenlee. 56p. 1998. pap. 6.95 (*1-887400-22-2*, EUB-1010) Earthen Vessel Prodns.

Mountains & Plains: The Ecology of Wyoming Landscapes. Dennis H. Knight. LC 93-37673. (Illus.). 352p. 1994. 50.00 (*0-300-05545-5*) Yale U Pr.

Mountains & Plains: The Ecology of Wyoming Landscapes. Dennis H. Knight. (Illus.). 352p. 1996. pap. 19.00 (*0-300-06856-5*) Yale U Pr.

Mountains & Rainbows: Modern Pioneers--How Alaska Changed Their Lives. Ardyce Czuchna-Curl. LC 89-3079. (Illus.). 220p. (Orig.). 1989. 16.95 (*0-88196-002-0*); pap. 9.95 (*0-88196-001-2*) Oak Woods Media.

Mountains & Rivers Without End. Gary Snyder. 176p. 1997. pap. 13.50 (*1-887178-57-0*, Pub. by Counterpt DC) HarpC.

Mountains & the City: The Tuscan Appennines in the Early Middle Ages. C. J. Wickham. (Illus.). 448p. 1988. 85.00 (*0-19-821966-0*) OUP.

Mountains & the Sky. Lorne E. Render. LC 75-27295. (Illus.). 224p. 1976. 35.00 (*0-295-95462-0*) U of Wash Pr.

Mountains & Valleys, 6 vols. unabridged ed. Text by Steve Parker & Jane Parker. LC 96-5010. (Changing World Ser.). (Illus.). 80p. (J). (gr. 3-7). 1996. 12.95 (*1-57145-026-2*, Silver Dolph) Advantage Pubs.

Mountains & Volcanoes. Eileen Curran. LC 84-8638. (Illus.). 32p. (J). (gr. k-2). 1996. pap. 3.50 (*0-8167-0348-5*) Troll Communs.

Mountains & Volcanoes. Rose Pipes. LC 97-5986. (World Habitats Ser.). (J). 1998. lib. bdg. 22.78 (*0-8172-5006-9*) Raintree Steck-V.

Mountains & Volcanoes. Barbara Taylor. LC 92-23374. (Young Discoverers Ser.). (Illus.). 32p. (J). (gr. 1-4). 1993. pap. 7.95 (*1-85697-938-5*, Kingfisher) LKC.

Mountains & Volcanoes. Barbara Taylor. (Young Discoverers Ser.). (J). 1993. 12.15 (*0-606-05306-9*, Pub. by Turtleback) Demco.

Mountains Are Mountains & Rivers Are Rivers: Applying Eastern Techniques to Everyday Life. Ilana Rabinowitz. LC 98-56644. 336p. 1999. 22.95 (*0-7868-6476-1*, Pub. by Hyperion) Time Warner.

***Mountains Are Mountains & Rivers Are Rivers: Applying Eastern Techniques to Everyday Life.** Ilana Rabinowitz. 304p. 2000. pap. 12.95 (*0-7868-8544-0*, Pub. by Hyperion) Time Warner.

Mountains at Risk: Current Issues in Environmental Studies. Ed. by Nigel J. Allan. (C). 1995. 38.00 (*81-7304-133-4*, Pub. by Manohar) S Asia.

Mountains Crack Up! Jasper Tomkins. (Illus.). 60p. (J). (gr. k-6). 1991. pap. 5.95 (*0-671-75273-1*, Green Tiger S&S) S&S Childrens.

Mountains Forgotten by God: The Story of a Moroccan Berber Family. Brick Oussaid. Tr. by Ann Woollcombe from FRE. 129p. 1989. 10.95 (*0-89410-481-0*, Three Contnts) L Rienner.

Mountains Gush Lava & Ash: And Other Amazing Facts about Volcanoes. Clare Oliver. LC 98-18033. (I Didn't Know That... Ser.). (Illus.). 32p. (J). (gr. 1-3). 1998. 8.95 (*0-7613-0739-7*, Copper Beech Bks); lib. bdg. 20.90 (*0-7613-0820-2*, Copper Beech Bks) Millbrook Pr.

Mountains Have a Secret. Arthur W. Upfield. 20.95 (*0-8488-0653-0*) Amereon Ltd.

Mountains Have Come Closer. Jim W. Miller. LC 80-80456. 1980. pap. 9.95 (*0-913239-19-4*) Appalach Consortium.

Mountains I Raise: A Garnering in Prose & Verse. Terry Marotta. LC 96-45289. 115p. 1997. pap. 12.00 (*0-9638603-1-3*) Ravenscroft.

Mountains in Berlin: Selected Poems. Elke Erb. Tr. by Rosmarie Waldrop from GER. (Dichten=Ser.: No. 2). 96p. (Orig.). 1995. pap. 8.00 (*1-886224-06-4*) Burning Deck.

Mountains in the Mist. Frank W. Boreham. (Illus.). 288p. 1995. pap. 12.99 (*0-8254-2163-2*, 95-008) Kregel.

Mountains in the Mist: Impressions of the Great Smokies. Roger Bansemer. LC 93-19261. 184p. 1993. 26.95 (*0-87833-839-X*) Taylor Pub.

Mountains into Goldmines: Robert Schuller & the Gospel of Success. Dennis Voskuil. LC 83-1729. 188p. reprint ed. pap. 58.30 (*0-608-14515-7*, 202534700043) Bks Demand.

Mountains Look Down: A History of Chichester, a Company Town in the Catskills. Reginald Bennett. Ed. by Howard Frank Mosher. LC 99-12854. (Illus.). 151p. 1999. pap. 15.00 (*0-916346-69-2*) Purple Mnt Pr.

Mountains, Meadows & Moonbeams: A Child's Spiritual Reader. Mary S. Rain. (Illus.). 240p. 1992. pap. 11.95 (*1-878901-39-7*) Hampton Roads Pub Co.

Mountains, Meadows & Mushrooms: A Guide to Cooking with Wild Mushrooms. Brenda Davidson-Shaddox. (Illus.). 107p. 1992. pap. 10.95 (*0-9631719-1-7*) C R Shaddox.

Mountains near Florida: Georgia High Country. Joan L. Scalpone. (Illus.). (Orig.). 1988. pap. 4.95 (*0-929198-05-0*) Mini DayTrip Bks.

Mountains Next Door. Janice E. Bowers. LC 91-11824. (Illus.). 147p. 1991. 15.95 (*0-8165-1243-4*) U of Ariz Pr.

Mountains of California. John Muir. LC 88-23938. (John Muir Library). (Illus.). 304p. 1989. pap. 10.00 (*0-87156-663-X*, Pub. by Sierra) Random.

Mountains of California. John Muir. LC 92-43496. 264p. 1993. pap. 9.95 (*0-14-026661-5*) Viking Penguin.

Mountains of California. John Muir. LC 90-47833. (Illus.). 406p. 1990. reprint ed. 34.95 (*0-87797-191-9*) Cherokee.

Mountains of California. John Muir. 1992. reprint ed. lib. bdg. 75.00 (*0-7812-5067-6*) Rprt Serv.

***Mountains of Colorado.** Richard D. Lamm. LC 99-25301. 1999. 35.00 (*1-55868-470-0*) Gr Arts Ctr Pub.

Mountains of Fire: San Luis Obispo County's Famous Nine Sisters - A Chain of Ancient Volcanic Peaks. Sharon L. Dickerson. (Illus.). 128p. (Orig.). 1990. pap. 8.95 (*0-945092-14-8*) EZ Nature.

Mountains of Fire, Lands That Shake: Earthquakes & Volcanic Eruptions in the Historic Past of Central America (1505-1899) Lawrence H. Feldman. LC 92-76101. (ENG & SPA., Illus.). 300p. (C). 1993. pap. text 44.00 (*0-911437-20-7*) Labyrinthos.

Mountains of Giants: A Racial & Cultural Study of the North Albanian Mountain Ghegs. Carleton S. Coon. (HU PMP Ser.: Vol. 23, No. 3). 1974. reprint ed. 25.00 (*0-527-01258-0*) Periodicals Srv.

Mountains of Glemts. George L. Eisberg & Nelson A. Ossorio. (Orig.). 1995. pap. 12.95 (*1-56721-121-6*) Twnty-Fifth Cent Pr.

***Mountains of Madness: A Scientist's Odyssey in Antartica.** John Long. 2000. 24.95 (*0-309-07077-5*, Joseph Henry Pr) Natl Acad Pr.

Mountains of Majipoor. large type ed. Robert Silverberg. (Large Print Ser.). 304p. 1996. 27.99 (*0-7089-3580-X*) Ulverscroft.

Mountains of Music: West Virginia Traditional Music from Goldenseal. John Lilly. LC 99-6043. 224p. 1999. 49.95 (*0-252-02499-0*) U of Ill Pr.

Mountains of Music: West Virginia Traditional Music from Goldenseal. Ed. by John Lilly. LC 99-6043. (Music in American Life Ser.). (Illus.). 224p. 1999. pap. 21.95 (*0-252-06815-7*) U of Ill Pr.

***Mountains of My Life.** Walter Bonatti. (Exploration Ser.). 2000. pap. 14.95 (*0-375-75640-X*) Modern Lib NY.

Mountains of North America. Fred Beckey. LC 82-3315. (Illus.). 288p. 1982. 35.00 (*0-87156-320-7*, Pub. by Sierra) Random.

Mountains of Northeastern Tasmania: A Study of Alpine Geomorphology. Nel Caine. 208p. (C). 1983. text 110.00 (*90-6191-289-X*, Pub. by A A Balkema) Ashgate Pub Co.

Mountains of Paradise. Edith R. Tjepkema. (Northwest Paradise Ser.: Vol. 6). 120p. (Orig.). (YA). (gr. 8-12). 1993. pap. 4.95 (*0-9620280-5-3*) Northland Pr.

Mountains of Quilt. Nancy Willard. LC 86-19577. (Illus.). 40p. (J). (ps-3). 1987. 12.95 (*0-15-256010-6*, Harcourt Child Bks) Harcourt.

Mountains of Quilt. Nancy Willard. LC 86-19577. (Illus.). 32p. (J). 1997. pap. 6.00 (*0-15-201480-2*) Harcourt.

Mountains of Quilt. Nancy Willard. 1997. 11.20 (*0-606-11644-3*, Pub. by Turtleback) Demco.

***Mountains of Silver: Life in Colorado's Red Mountain Mining District.** P. David Smith. LC 94-4318. (Illus.). 236p. 2000. reprint ed. pap. 16.95 (*1-890437-36-0*) Western Reflections.

Mountains of Spices. Hannah Hurnard. 250p. 1983. mass mkt. 5.99 (*0-8423-4611-2*) Tyndale Hse.

Mountains of the Blue Stone: A Novel. Dorothy Cave. LC 98-7915. Orig. Title: Go Find the Mountain. 304p. 1998. 26.95 (*0-86534-272-5*) Sunstone Pr.

***Mountains of the Coast: Travels to Remote Corners of the Pacific Ranges.** John Baldwin. (Illus.). 112p. 1999. 36.95 (*1-55017-213-1*) Harbour Pub Co.

Mountains of the Great Blue Dream. Robert L. Reid. LC 97-37793. 208p. 1998. reprint ed. pap. 16.95 (*0-8263-1923-8*) U of NM Pr.

***Mountains of the Heart: A Natural History of the Appalachians.** Scott Weidensaul. (Illus.). 288p. 2000. pap. 17.95 (*1-55591-139-0*) Fulcrum Pub.

Mountains of the Middle Kingdom: Exploring the High Peaks of China & Tibet. Galen A. Rowell. LC 82-19508. (Illus.). 208p. 1984. pap. 24.95 (*0-87156-829-2*, Pub. by Sierra) Random.

***Mountains of the Moon: Stories about Social Justice.** Ed. by Stephanie W. Hanson. 168p. (YA). (gr. 7-12). 1999. pap. 6.95 (*0-88489-542-4*) St Marys.

Mountains of the Moon: Stories about Social Justice. Ed. by Stephanie Weller Hanson. 32p. 1999. pap., teacher ed. 5.00 (*0-88489-543-2*) St Marys.

Mountains of the World: A Global Priority. Bruno Messerli & Jack D. Ives. LC 97-7699. (Illus.). 510p. 1997. 75.00 (*1-85070-781-2*) Prthnon Pub.

Mountains of Thunder. Howard L. Norskog. 35p. (Orig.). 1994. pap. 6.00 (*0-685-71206-0*) H L Norskog.

Mountains of Tibet. Mordicai Gerstein. LC 85-45684. (Trophy Picture Bk.). (Illus.). 32p. (J). (gr. 4-7). 1989. pap. 6.95 (*0-06-443211-4*, HarpTrophy) HarpC Child Bks.

Mountains of Wales: An Anthology in Verse & Prose. Ed. & Intro. by Ioan B. Rees. xvii, 299p. 1995. reprint ed. pap. write for info. (*0-7083-1163-6*, Pub. by Univ Wales Pr) Paul & Co Pubs.

Mountains Out of Molehills. Terence P. O'Halloran. 250p. (C). 1993. 110.00 (*1-85609-048-5*, Pub. by Witherby & Co) St Mut.

Mountains Round About. Ori Z. Soltes. (Illus.). (Orig.). 1992. pap. text. write for info. (*1-881456-04-8*) B B K Natl Jew Mus.

Mountains to Climb see **Montanas Escalar**

Mountains to Climb. 3rd ed. Richard M. Wainwright. (Illus.). 64p. (J). 1997. 18.00 (*0-9619566-3-1*) Family Life.

Mountains to Desert: Selected Inyo Readings. Ed. by Friends of the Eastern California Museum Staff. (Illus.). 250p. (Orig.). 1988. pap. 12.95 (*0-9620913-0-8*) Frnds E Calif Mus.

Mountains to Motown: A Brief Anthology. Ed Sanders et al. Ed. by James M. Burdine. (Illus.). 68p. (Orig.). 1997. pap. text 12.00 (*1-56439-067-5*) Ridgeway.

Mountains to Ocean: A Guide to the Santa Monica Mountains National Recreation Area. Randolph Jorgen. Ed. by Sandra Scott & Susan Tasaki. LC 94-67914. (Illus.). 112p. 1995. pap. 12.95 (*1-877856-52-5*) SW Pks Mnmts.

Mountains-to-Sea Trail: Western North Carolina's Majestic Rival to the Appalachian Trail. Donald E. Dossey & John I. Hillyer. LC 97-40303. (Illus.). 240p. (Orig.). pap. 15.95 (*0-925640-09-3*) Outcomes Unltd.

Mountains Touched with Fire: Chattanooga Besieged, 1863. Wiley Sword. LC 94-47255. 1995. 27.50 (*0-312-11859-7*) St Martin.

Mountains Touched with Fire: Chattanooga Besieged, 1863. Wiley Sword. 1997. pap. 17.95 (*0-312-15593-X*, St Martin Griffin) St Martin.

Mountains We Have Crossed: Diaries & Letters of the Oregon Mission, 1838. Intro. by Clifford M. Drury & Bonnie Sue Lewis. LC 99-23583. (Illus.). 336p. 1999. pap. 15.00 (*0-8032-6621-9*, Bison Books) U of Nebr Pr.

***Mountains Were Not Found.** Wayne S. Ramsden. LC 98-91118. 1999. pap. 7.95 (*0-533-13050-6*) Vantage.

Mountains Without Handrails: Reflections on the National Parks. Joseph L. Sax. 160p. 1980. pap. 17.95 (*0-472-06324-3*, 06324) U of Mich Pr.

***Mountains Won't Remember Us: And Other Stories.** Robert Morgan. 2000. pap. 12.00 (*0-7432-0421-2*, Scribner Pap Fic) S&S Trade Pap.

Mountains Won't Remember Us & Other Stories. Robert Morgan. 256p. 1992. 15.95 (*1-56145-049-9*) Peachtree Pubs.

Mountaintop. Barbour Publishing Staff. 1997. pap. text 1.66 (*1-57748-246-8*) Barbour Pub.

Mountaintop & Valley: Greene County Folk Arts Today. Field Horne. (Illus.). 48p. (Orig.). 1991. pap. 10.00 (*0-9628523-1-7*) Blk Dome Pr.

Mountaintop Blues. Wanda Olugbala. pap. 6.00 (*0-9657107-0-X*) Olugbalas Way.

***Mountaintop U. S. A.** William Graney. LC 00-190673. 2000. 25.00 (*0-7388-1713-9*); pap. 18.00 (*0-7388-1714-7*) Xlibris Corp.

Mountainwild. Emery George. LC 74-75962. 64p. (Orig.). 1974. pap. 1.95 (*0-914408-00-3*) Kylix Pr.

Mountainy Singer by Seosamh MacCathmhaoil. Joseph Campbell. LC 74-64007. (Des Imagistes: Literature of the Imagist Movement Ser.). 88p. reprint ed. 29.50 (*0-404-17078-1*) AMS Pr.

Mountebanks. Ben Jonson. (Classic Plays Ser.). 46p. (Orig.). 1996. pap. 3.50 (*1-57514-223-6*, 1123) Encore Perform Pub.

Mounted Archers: The Beginnings of Central Asian History. Laszlo Torday. LC 98-102022. (Illus.). 464p. 1997. 35.00 (*1-900838-03-6*, Pub. by Durham Acad Pr) U of Wash Pr.

Mounted Cops Are Ten Feet Tall. Bill Walsh & Ralph Reynolds. 112p. 1995. pap. 8.95 (*0-9650278-0-5*) LBR Pubng.

Mounted Games. Toni Weber. (Threshold Picture Guides Ser.). (Illus.). 24p. 1994. pap. 12.00 (*1-872082-60-2*, Pub. by Kenilworth Pr) Half Halt Pr.

Mounted in the City by the Bay. Richard Blanchard. 1998. pap. 10.00 (*0-9663942-2-4*) Forever Fine Art.

Mounted Oriental Porcelain: In the J. Paul Getty Museum. J. Paul Getty Museum Staff & Gillian Wilson. LC 99-25298. 128p. 1999. 75.00 (*0-89236-562-5*, Pub. by J P Getty Trust) OUP.

Mounted Oriental Porcelain in the J. Paul Getty Museum. F. J. Watson et al. LC 82-81308. (Illus.). 104p. 1983. 49.95 (*0-89236-034-8*, Pub. by J P Getty Trust) OUP.

Mounted Police. Michael Green. LC 97-40393. (Law Enforcement Ser.). (J). 1998. lib. bdg. write for info. (*1-56065-757-X*) Capstone Pr.

Mounted Police. Michael Green. (Law Enforcement Ser.). 48p. (J). 1998. lib. bdg. 19.00 (*0-531-11560-7*) Watts.

Mountian Air: The Life of Gordon Stuart, Mountain Man of the North Cascades. Sandy N. Bryant. 1991. pap. 15.95 (*1-879992-02-7*) Directed Media.

Mountian Biking in McCall. Stephen Stuebner & Roger Phillips. (Illus.). 96p. 1997. pap. 12.95 (*0-9644343-2-6*) Boise Front.

Mountie Makers: Putting the Canadian in RCMP. Robert G. Teather. LC 98-174184. (Illus.). 160p. 1997. pap. 14.95 (*1-895811-41-4*) Heritage Hse.

Mounties, Moose, & Moonshine: The Patterns & Context of Outport Crime. Norman Okihiro. LC 97-139115. (Illus.). 224p. 1997. text 45.00 (*0-8020-0891-7*); pap. text 19.95 (*0-8020-7874-5*) U of Toronto Pr.

Mountifort Longfield: Ireland's First Professor of Political Economy. Laurence S. Moss. LC 75-34003. 240p. 1976. 14.95 (*0-916054-02-0*) Jameson Bks.

Mounting a Prenatal Care Campaign in Your Community. Dana Hughes. Ed. by Children's Defense Fund Staff. 44p. (Orig.). 1986. pap. 3.00 (*0-938008-56-0*) Childrens Defense.

Mounting & Laminating Handbook. Chris A. Paschke. LC 97-91792. (Illus.). xx, 160p. 1997. pap. 19.95 (*0-9657625-0-5*) Designs Ink.

Mounting & Preserving Pictorial Materials: A Programmed Primer. (Illus.). 1976. 2.95 (*0-9601006-1-X*) G T Yeamans.

Mounting Biking. David Armentrout. LC 97-12419. (Sports Challenge Ser.). 24p. (J). (gr. 3-7). 1997. lib. bdg. 18.60 (*1-55916-219-8*) Rourke Bk Co.

Mounting Biking the Twin Cities. Steve Johnson. LC 98-54385. (Illus.). 120p. 1999. pap. 9.95 (*1-56044-743-5*) Falcon Pub Inc.

Mounting Lenses in Optical Instruments. Paul R. Yoder, Jr. (Tutorial Texts in Optical Engineering Ser.: Vol. TT 21). 1995. pap. 42.00 (*0-8194-1941-9*) SPIE.

Mounting Methods Vol. 5: Library of Professional Picture Framing. Vivian Kistler. LC 86-72676. (Illus.). 96p. 1998. pap. 19.00 (*0-938655-04-3*, B043) Columba Pub.

Mounting Prisms & Small Mirrors in Optical Instruments. Paul R. Yoder. LC 98-19947. (Tutorial Texts in Optical Engineering Ser.). 1998. pap. 42.00 (*0-8194-2940-6*) SPIE.

Mounting Threat of Home Intruders: Weighing the Moral Option of Armed Self-Defense. Brendan F. Furnish & Dwight H. Small. 274p. 1993. pap. 39.95 (*0-398-06139-4*) C C Thomas.

Mounting Threat of Home Intruders: Weighing the Moral Option of Armed Self-Defense. Brendan F. Furnish & Dwight H. Small. 274p. (C). 1993. text 59.95 (*0-398-05828-8*) C C Thomas.

***Mountjoy: The Story of a Prison.** Timothy Carey. 2000. pap. 22.95 (*1-898256-89-6*, Pub. by Collins Press) Dufour.

Mountmellick Embroidery. Ed. by Jules Kliot & Kaethe Kliot. (Illus.). 96p. 1998. pap. 18.00 (*0-916896-94-3*, LE44) Lacis Pubns.

Mountmellick Work: Irish White Embroidery. 2nd ed. Jane H. Almqvist. 80p. 1996. pap. 15.95 (*0-85105-512-5*, Pub. by Smyth) Dufour.

M

***Mountolive.** large type ed. Lawrence Durrell. LC 99-47952. 2000. 25.95 (*0-7838-8820-1*, G K Hall & Co) Mac Lib Ref.

Mountolive. Lawrence Durrell. 1991. reprint ed. pap. 12.95 (*0-14-015320-9*, Penguin Bks) Viking Penguin.

Moura Lympany: Her Autobiography. Moura Lympany & Margot Strickland. (Illus.). 186p. 1991. 40.00 (*0-7206-0824-4*, Pub. by P Owen Ltd) Dufour.

Mourir Sur Fond Blanc. Guy Lavigne. (Novels in the Roman Plus Ser.). (FRE.). 160p. (YA). (gr. 8 up). 1994. pap. 8.95 (*2-89021-209-2*, Pub. by La Courte Ech) Firefly Bks Ltd.

Mourjou: Life & Food. Peter Graham. (Illus.). 256p. pap. 14.95 (*0-14-046860-9*, Pub. by Pnguin Bks Ltd) Trafalgar.

Mourn Not Your Dead. Deborah Crombie. 304p. 1997. reprint ed. mass mkt. 5.99 (*0-425-15778-4*, Prime Crime) Berkley Pub.

Mourn Not Your Dead: A Duncan Kincaid/Gemma James Crime Novel. large type ed. Deborah Crombie. LC 96-3011. 1996. 24.95 (*1-56895-367-4*, Compass) Wheeler Pub.

***Mourn the Living.** Max A. Collins. LC 99-45469. 157p. 1999. 20.95 (*0-7862-2211-5*) Five Star.

Mourned One. Stanlake Samkange. (African Writers Ser.). 150p. (C). 1975. pap. 9.95 (*0-435-90169-9*, 90169) Heinemann.

Mourner. Donald E. Westlake. 144p. 1984. pap. 2.50 (*0-380-68668-6*, Avon Bks) Morrow Avon.

Mourner at the Door. 3rd ed. Gordon Lish. LC 96-51153. 220p. 1997. reprint ed. pap. 12.95 (*1-56858-084-3*) FWEW.

Mourners Below. James Purdy. 295p. 1984. 28.00 (*0-7206-0621-7*, Pub. by P Owen Ltd) Dufour.

Mourners' Bench: A Novel. Susan Dodd. LC 97-52564. 288p. 1998. 24.00 (*0-688-15799-8*, Wm Morrow) Morrow Avon.

Mourners' Bench: A Novel. Susan Dodd. LC 98-46989. 1999. 25.95 (*1-56895-599-5*) Wheeler Pub.

***Mourners' Bench: A Novel.** Susan Dodd. 288p. 1999. reprint ed. pap. 13.00 (*0-688-16973-2*, Wm Morrow) Morrow Avon.

Mournful Demeanour of Lieutenant Boruvka: Detective Tales. Josef Skvorecky. 1991. pap. 8.95 (*0-393-30786-7*) Norton.

Mourning: The Journey from Grief to Healing. Ed. by Patrick M. DelZoppo. LC 95-15288. 46p. (Orig.). 1995. pap. 3.95 (*0-8189-0737-1*) Alba.

Mourning: The Prelude to Laughter. Bonnie Bruno. (Beatitudes Ser.). 1993. mass mkt. 5.99 (*0-310-59613-0*) Zondervan.

Mourning after Suicide. Lois A. Bloom. (Looking up Ser.). 24p. 1986. pap. 1.95 (*0-8298-0588-5*) Pilgrim OH.

Mourning & Dancing: A Memoir of Grief & Recovery. Sally D. Miller. LC 99-10952. 215p. 1999. pap. 10.95 (*1-55874-671-4*) Health Comm.

***Mourning & Dancing for Schools: A Grief & Recovery Sourcebook for Students, Teachers & Parents.** Sally Downham Miller. 200p. 2000. pap. 10.95 (*1-55874-775-3*) Health Comm.

Mourning & Mitzvah: A Guided Journal for Walking the Mourner's Path through Grief to Healing. Anne Brener. LC 93-16920. 288p. (Orig.). 1993. pap. 19.95 (*1-879045-23-0*) Jewish Lights.

Mourning & Panegyric: The Poetics of Pastoral Ceremony. Celeste M. Schenck. LC 88-1588. 240p. 1989. lib. bdg. 35.00 (*0-271-00641-2*) Pa St U Pr.

Mourning & Psychic Transformation: Facing the Demon-Lover Within. Susan Kavaler-Adler. LC RC455.4.L67K39 1999. 9376p. 1999. 50.00 (*0-7657-0222-3*) Aronson.

Mourning & Remembrance in Halachah & Jewish Tradition. Aaron Felder. LC 92-70694. 200p. 1992. 15.95 (*1-56062-121-4*) CIS Comm.

Mourning Becomes the Law: Philosophy & Representation. Gillian Rose. 170p. (C). 1996. text 54.95 (*0-521-57045-X*); pap. text 17.95 (*0-521-57849-3*) Cambridge U Pr.

Mourning Breaks. Jan Hindman. 325p. (Orig.). (C). 1991. pap. 34.95 (*0-9611034-5-0*) AlexAndria OR.

Mourning Bride, Poems, & Miscellanies. William Congreve. (BCL1-PR English Literature Ser.). 540p. 1992. reprint ed. lib. bdg. 99.00 (*0-7812-7335-8*) Rprt Serv.

Mourning Crazy Horse. Harold Jaffe. LC 81-71645. 211p. (Orig.). 1982. 15.95 (*0-914590-72-3*); pap. 7.95 (*0-914590-73-1*) Fiction Coll.

Mourning Cry & Woe Oracle. Waldemar Janzen. (Beiheft zur Zeitschrift fuer die Alttestamentliche Wissenschaft Ser.: No. 125). 120p. (C). 1972. 63.10 (*3-11-003848-X*) De Gruyter.

***Mourning Diana.** Ed. by Adrian Kear & Deborah Lynn Steinberg. LC 99-25590. 240p. (C). 1999. text. write for info. (*0-415-19392-3*) Routledge.

***Mourning Diana: Nation Culture & Performing of Grief.** Adrian Kear & Deborah Lynn Steinberg. LC 99-25590. 1999. pap. 22.99 (*0-415-19393-1*) Routledge.

Mourning Dove. Heyday Books Staff. 1993. pap. 5.00 (*0-930588-63-0*) Heyday Bks.

Mourning Dove: A Salishan Autobiography. Ed. by Jay Miller. LC 89-14780. (American Indian Lives Ser.). (Illus.). xl, 267p. 1990. pap. 12.95 (*0-8032-8207-9*, Bison Books) U of Nebr Pr.

Mourning Dove: A Salishan Autobiography. Mourning Dove. Ed. by Jay Miller. LC 89-14780. (American Indian Lives Ser.). (Illus.). xl, 267p. 1990. text 45.00 (*0-8032-3119-9*) U of Nebr Pr.

Mourning Dove: A Story of Love. Larry Barkdull. 96p. 1996. pap. write for info. (*1-889025-00-3*, KenningHse) HomeStar Corp.

Mourning Dove's Stories. Ed. by Clifford E. Trafzer & Richard E. Scheuerman. 118p. 1991. pap. 10.95 (*0-934931-05-4*) SDSU Press.

Mourning for Diana. Ed. by Tony Walter. (Illus.). 256p. 1999. 65.00 (*1-85973-233-X*, Pub. by Berg Pubs); pap. 19.50 (*1-85973-238-0*, Pub. by Berg Pubs) NYU Pr.

Mourning for My Father: A Primer for Mourners. Seymour Freedman. 128p. 1992. 8.95 (*965-229-048-3*, Pub. by Gefen Pub Hse) Gefen Bks.

Mourning Gloria. Joyce Christmas. 232p. 1996. mass mkt. 4.99 (*0-449-14704-5*) Fawcett.

Mourning Glory: The Making of a Marine. David J. Regan. 1980. 9.95 (*0-8159-6218-5*) Devin.

Mourning Glory: The Story of the Lowell Cemetery. Catherine L. Goodwin. 50p. 1992. pap. 5.95 (*0-9631604-1-9*) Lowell Hist Soc.

Mourning Glory: The Will of the French Revolution. Marie-Helene Huet. LC 97-2936. (Critical Authors & Issues Ser.). (C). (gr. 13). 1997. text 37.50 (*0-8122-3414-6*) U of Pa Pr.

Mourning Glory: The Will of the French Revolution. Marie-Helene Huet. (Critical Authors & Issues Ser.). (Illus.). 232p. (C). (gr. 13). 1997. pap. 17.50 (*0-8122-1617-2*) U of Pa Pr.

Mourning Handbook: A Complete Guide for the Bereaved. Helen Fitzgerald. 320p. 1994. 22.00 (*0-671-86972-8*) S&S Trade.

Mourning Handbook: A Complete Guide for the Bereaved. Helen Fitzgerald. 320p. 1995. per. 12.00 (*0-684-80161-2*) S&S Trade.

Mourning in Bethlehem: Impact of the Gulf War on Palestinian Society. Reginald E. White. 244p. 1992. pap. 12.95 (*0-85244-174-6*, 950, Pub. by Gra1cewing) Morehouse Pub.

Mourning in Halacha. C. B. Goldberg. Ed. by Meir Zlotowitz. (ArtScroll Halachah Ser.). 1991. 24.99 (*0-89906-171-0*); pap. 19.99 (*0-89906-172-9*) Mesorah Pubns.

Mourning in Late Imperial China: Filial Piety & the State. Norman Kutcher. LC 98-36386. (Cambridge Studies in Chinese History, Literature & Institutions). (Illus.). 256p. 1999. text 64.95 (*0-521-62439-8*) Cambridge U Pr.

***Mourning in the Ancient Near East & the Hebrew Bible.** Xuan Huong Thi Pham. (Journal for the Study of the Old Testament Supplement Ser.: No. 302). 224p. 2000. 57.50 (*1-84127-029-6*, Pub. by Sheffield Acad) CUP Services.

Mourning into Joy: Music, Raphael, & Saint Cecilia. Thomas Connolly. LC 94-5325. 1995. 40.00 (*0-300-05901-9*) Yale U Pr.

Mourning-Liberation Process, 2 vols., Vol. I. George H. Pollock. 315p. 1989. 60.00 (*0-8236-3485-X*) Intl Univs Pr.

Mourning-Liberation Process, 2 vols., Vol. II. George H. Pollock. 325p. 1989. 47.50 (*0-8236-3486-8*) Intl Univs Pr.

Mourning of John Lennon. Anthony Elliott. LC 98-3637. 274p. 1998. 45.00 (*0-520-21548-6*, Pub. by U CA Pr); 17.95 (*0-520-21549-4*, Pub. by U CA Pr) Cal Prin Full Svc.

Mourning on the Pejepscot. Teresa M. Flanagan. 132p. (C). 1992. lib. bdg. 36.00 (*0-8191-8695-3*) U Pr of Amer.

Mourning Our Mothers: Poems about Loss. Carole A. Stasiowski. LC 98-17598. 1998. pap. write for info. (*0-916897-33-8*) Andrew Mtn Pr.

Mourning Sex: Performing Public Memories. Peggy Phelan. LC 96-9345. 208p. (C). 1997. pap. 20.99 (*0-415-14759-X*) Routledge.

Mourning Sex: Performing Public Memories. Peggy Phelan. LC 96-9345. (Illus.). 208p. (C). 1997. 85.00 (*0-415-14758-1*) Routledge.

Mourning Shift: A Tory Bauer Mystery. Kathleen Taylor. (Tory Bauer Mystery Ser.: No. 4). 288p. 1998. mass mkt. 5.99 (*0-380-79943-X*, Avon Bks) Morrow Avon.

Mourning Sickness: Poems, Paintings, Stories & Dreams. Keith Smith. (Illus.). 75p. (Orig.). 1993. pap. 16.00 (*0-9639908-0-2*) Rainbow Press.

Mourning Song. Lurlene McDaniel. (One Last Wish Ser.). 1992. 9.09 (*0-606-00496-3*, Pub. by Turtleback) Demco.

Mourning Song. 2nd expanded rev. ed. Joyce Landorf Heatherley. LC 74-9938. 240p. (gr. 11). 1994. pap. 8.99 (*0-8007-5547-2*) Revell.

Mourning Song, No. 2. Lurlene McDaniel. 192p. (YA). 1992. mass mkt. 4.50 (*0-553-29810-0*) Bantam.

***Mourning the Living: Families Coping with the Losses of Substance Abuse.** rev. ed. Ed. by Florence Selder et al. 2000. reprint ed. pap. 17.95i (*0-930194-85-3*) Ctr Thanatology.

Mourning to Morning. Michael S. Piazza. 80p. 1996. pap. 9.95 (*1-887129-01-4*) Sources of Hope.

Mourt's Relation. William Bradford. 96p. 1922. pap. 9.95 (*0-918222-84-2*) Applewood.

Mourt's Relation: A Journal of the Pilgrims of Plymouth. Ed. by Jordan D. Fiore. (Illus.). 100p. 1985. 15.95 (*0-942516-07-9*) Plymouth Rock Found.

***MOUS Access 2000 Exam Prep.** Lisa Friedrichsen. (Exam Prep Ser.). 2000. pap. text. write for info. (*1-57610-479-6*) Coriolis Grp.

***Mous Essentials Excel 2000.** Fox & Metzelaar. 477p. 2000. pap. 45.33 (*0-13-019104-3*, Prentice Hall) P-H.

***Mous Essentials Excel 97 Expert.** annot. ed. Dawn Wood. (Illus.). 498p. 1999. pap., teacher ed. 0.00 (*1-58076-072-4*) Que Educ & Trng.

MOUS Essentials Excel 97 Proficient. Jane Calabria. LC 98-66766. 350p. (C). 1998. pap. text 31.00 incl. audio compact disk (*1-58076-054-6*) Que Educ & Trng.

***Mous Essentials Powerpoint 2000.** 2nd ed. Linda Bird. 350p. 2000. pap. 42.67 (*0-13-019105-1*) P-H.

***Mous Essentials Powerpoint 97.** annot. ed. Jean S. Insinga. (Mouse Essentials Ser.). (Illus.). 524p. 1999. pap., teacher ed. 0.00 (*1-58076-062-7*) Que Educ & Trng.

***Mous Essentials Word 2000.** 2nd ed. Keith Mulbery. 550p. 2000. pap. 45.33 (*0-13-019106-X*) P-H.

***Mous Excel 2000 Exam Prep.** Elizabeth Eisner Reding & Tara Lynn O'Keefe. LC 00-26971. 2000. write for info. (*1-57610-480-X*) Coriolis Grp.

***MOUS PowerPoint 2000 Exam Prep: The Most Comprehensive, Interactive & Visual Microsoft Certification Study Guide on Microsoft PowerPoint 2000.** David W. Beskeen. (Exam Prep Ser.). (Illus.). 2000. pap. write for info. incl. cd-rom (*1-57610-579-2*) Coriolis Grp.

***Mous Test Preparation Guide for Access 2000.** Emily Ketcham. 300p. 2000. pap. 37.33 (*0-13-027743-6*) P-H.

***Mous Test Preparation Guide for Excel 2000.** Emily Ketcham. 300p. 2000. pap. 37.33 (*0-13-027744-4*) P-H.

***Mous Test Preparation Guide for Powerpoint 2000.** Emily Ketcham. 350p. 2000. pap. 37.33 (*0-13-027742-8*) P-H.

***Mous Test Preparation Guide for Word 2000.** Emily Ketcham. 448p. 2000. pap. 37.33 (*0-13-027745-2*) P-H.

***MOUS Word 2000 Exam Prep.** Carol M. Cram. (Exam Prep Ser.). 2000. pap. text 29.99 (*1-57610-481-8*) Coriolis Grp.

***Mouse.** Anne V. Gleason. (Illus.). 40p. (J). (ps-k). 1999. mass mkt. 19.95 (*0-9673900-0-1*) A V Gleason.

***Mouse.** Stephen N. Shulman. LC 99-37567. 128p. 1999. 12.95 (*1-58245-006-4*) Howell Bks.

***Mouse.** Bradley Viner. (All about Your Pet Ser.). (Illus.). 32p. 1999. pap. 3.50 (*0-7641-1009-8*) Barron.

***Mouse.** Spasa Voynovich. LC 99-93979. 2000. pap. 21.95 (*0-533-13214-2*) Vantage.

Mouse & Elephant, Measuring Growth: Middle Grades Mathematics Projects. Glenda Lappan. 1986. text 18.95 (*0-201-21474-1*) Addison-Wesley.

***Mouse & His Child.** Russell Hoban. LC 00-38453. (Illus.). (J). 2001. write for info. (*0-439-09826-2*, A A Levine) Scholastic Inc.

Mouse & Lion Little Play-a-Sound. (J). 1995. write for info. (*0-7853-1041-X*) Pubns Intl Ltd.

***Mouse & Mole.** Dunbar. (J). 2000. 15.95 (*0-385-40198-1*, Pub. by Transworld Publishers Ltd) Trafalgar.

***Mouse & Mole Have a Party.** Joyce Dunbar. (J). 2000. pap. 6.95 (*0-552-54557-0*, Pub. by Transworld Publishers Ltd) Trafalgar.

Mouse & Motorcycle. Houghton Mifflin Company Staff. (Literature Experience 1991 Ser.). (J). (gr. 5). 1990. pap. 10.24 (*0-395-55168-4*) HM.

Mouse & Motorcycle. Houghton Mifflin Company Staff. (Literature Experience 1993 Ser.). (J). (gr. 5). 1992. pap. 10.24 (*0-395-61823-1*) HM.

Mouse & Owl. Joan Hoffman. (Start to Read! Ser.). (Illus.). 32p. (J). (ps-3). 1993. student ed. 3.99 (*0-88743-419-3*, 06071) Sch Zone Pub Co.

Mouse & Owl. Joan Hoffman & Barbara Gregorich. (Start to Read! Ser.). (Illus.). 16p. (J). (gr. k-2). 1991. student ed. 2.29 (*0-88743-025-2*, 06025) Sch Zone Pub Co.

Mouse & the Lion. Gyorgy Varnai. LC 92-43693. (Classic Tales from Around the World Ser.). (Illus.). (J). (gr. 1-5). 1997. 22.79 (*1-56766-091-6*) Childs World.

Mouse & the Mill & the Bottle Babies. Alma S. Coon. (Illus.). 44p. (J). (ps-1). 1982. 6.95 (*0-87935-061-X*) Colonial Williamsburg.

Mouse & the Motorcycle. 158p. (J). (gr. 3-5). pap. 4.95 (*0-8072-1475-2*) Listening Lib.

***Mouse & the Motorcycle.** 1999. 9.95 (*1-56137-274-9*) Novel Units.

***Mouse & the Motorcycle.** 1999. 11.95 (*1-56137-706-6*) Novel Units.

Mouse & the Motorcycle. Beverly Cleary. 160p. (J). (gr. k-6). 1980. pap. 3.25 (*0-440-46075-1*, YB BDD) BDD Bks Young Read.

Mouse & the Motorcycle. Beverly Cleary. (Illus.). (J). (gr. 5). 1995. 9.32 (*0-395-73250-6*) HM.

Mouse & the Motorcycle. Beverly Cleary. LC 65-20956. (Illus.). (J). (gr. 4-7). 1965. 15.95 (*0-688-21698-6*, Wm Morrow) Morrow Avon.

Mouse & the Motorcycle. Beverly Cleary. LC 65-20956. (Illus.). 160p. (J). (gr. 4-7). 1965. 15.89 (*0-688-31698-0*, Wm Morrow) Morrow Avon.

Mouse & the Motorcycle. Beverly Cleary. (J). 1996. mass mkt. 4.50 (*0-380-72799-4*, Avon Bks) Morrow Avon.

Mouse & the Motorcycle. Beverly Cleary. (J). 1956. 9.60 (*0-606-04754-9*, Pub. by Turtleback) Demco.

Mouse & the Motorcycle. Beverly Cleary. (J). 1996. 8.60 (*0-606-09635-3*, Pub. by Turtleback) Demco.

Mouse & the Motorcycle. Deborah Hayes. (Literature Unit Ser.). (Illus.). 48p. 1996. pap., teacher ed. 7.95 (*1-55734-529-5*, TCM529) Tchr Create Mat.

Mouse & the Motorcycle. large type ed. Beverly Cleary. (Illus.). 182p. (J). (gr. 5). 45.50 (*0-614-20606-5*, L-38189-00 APHB) Am Printing Hse.

Mouse & the Motorcycle. Beverly Cleary. 160p. (J). (gr. 2-6). 1990. reprint ed. pap. 4.99 (*0-380-70924-4*, Wm Morrow) Morrow Avon.

Mouse & the Motorcycle, Set. Beverly Cleary. (Illus.). (J). 1996. boxed set 15.96 (*0-380-72402-2*, Avon Bks) Morrow Avon.

Mouse & the Motorcycle: A Study Guide. Anne Spencer. Ed. by J. Friedland & R. Kessler. (Novel-Ties Ser.). (J). (gr. 2-4). 1994. pap. text, student ed. 15.95 (*1-56982-057-0*) Lrn Links.

Mouse & the Potato. Thomas Berger. Tr. by Polly Lawson. (DUT., Illus.). 32p. (J). (ps-2). 1990. reprint ed. 14.95 (*0-86315-103-5*, Pub. by Floris Bks) Gryphon Hse.

Mouse Around. Pat Schories. LC 90-56156. 40p. (J). (ps-3). 1991. bds. 13.00 (*0-374-35080-9*) FS&G.

Mouse Around. Pat Schories. 40p. (J). (ps-3). 1993. pap. 4.95 (*0-374-45414-0*, Sunburst Bks) FS&G.

Mouse Around. Pat Schories. (J). 1993. 10.15 (*0-606-05480-4*, Pub. by Turtleback) Demco.

***Mouse at Night.** Nancy Christensen Hall. LC 99-27779. (Illus.). 32p. (J). (ps-1). 2000. 14.95 (*0-531-30260-1*) Orchard Bks Watts.

Mouse Brain in Stereotaxic Coordinates. Keith B. Franklin & George T. Paxinos. LC 96-35307. (Illus.). 216p. 1996. pap. text 143.00 (*0-12-266070-6*) Morgan Kaufmann.

Mouse Bride. Illus. by David Christiana. LC 94-32409. 32p. (J). (ps-2). 1995. 13.95 (*0-590-47503-7*, Scholastic Hardcover) Scholastic Inc.

Mouse Bride: La Novia Raton. Monica Chang & Lesley Liu. Tr. by Beatriz Zeller from CHI. (ENG & SPA., Illus.). 32p. (J). (gr. 2-4). 1994. 16.95 (*957-32-2150-0*) Pan Asian Pubns.

Mouse Called Wolf. Dick King-Smith. LC 97-1526. (Illus.). 108p. (J). (gr. 2-5). 1997. lib. bdg. 17.99 (*0-517-70974-0*) C Potter.

Mouse Called Wolf. Dick King-Smith. LC 97-1526. (Illus.). 108p. (J). (gr. 2-5). 1997. 16.00 (*0-517-70973-2*) Crown Pub Group.

Mouse Called Wolf. Dick King-Smith. (Illus.). 98p. (J). (gr. k-5). 1999. pap. 4.99 (*0-375-80066-2*) Knopf.

***Mouse Cleaning.** Rose-Marie Provencher. 2001. text 15.95 (*0-8050-6240-8*) St Martin.

Mouse Cookies: 10 Easy-to-Make Cookie Recipes. Laura J. Numeroff. LC 95-238087. (Illus.). 32p. (J). (gr. 2-4). 1995. spiral bd., boxed set 13.95 (*0-694-00633-5*, HarpFestival) HarpC Child Bks.

Mouse Count see Cuenta Ratones

Mouse Count. Walsh. 1995. pap. 5.00 (*0-15-201050-5*) Harcourt.

Mouse Count. Ellen S. Walsh. Ed. by Diane D'Andrade. LC 90-35915. (Illus.). 32p. (J). (ps-1). 1991. 13.00 (*0-15-256023-8*) Harcourt.

Mouse Count. Ellen S. Walsh. LC 90-35915. (Illus.). 32p. (J). (ps-1). 1995. pap. 5.50 (*0-15-200223-5*, Voyager Bks) Harcourt.

Mouse Count. Ellen S. Walsh. LC 90-35915. (Illus.). 32p. (J). (ps). 1995. pap. 5.95 (*0-15-200266-9*, Red Wagon Bks) Harcourt.

Mouse Count. Ellen Stoll Walsh. (J). 1991. 10.95 (*0-606-07891-6*) Turtleback.

Mouse Droppings Book of Macintosh Hints: What Apple Didn't Tell You about Your Macintosh Computer. Philip Russell. 100p. 1986. spiral bd. 8.95 (*0-318-22782-7*) Macintosh Users Group.

Mouse Droppings Second Book of Macintosh Hints. Philip Russell. 116p. 1988. spiral bd. 8.95 (*0-318-32989-1*) Macintosh Users Group.

***Mouse Essentials Access 97 Expert.** (C). 1999. write for info. (*0-13-018049-1*); pap. 29.33 (*0-13-018048-3*) P-H.

***Mouse Essentials Access 97 Expert.** Robert Ferrett et al. 350p. (C). 1999. pap. text 29.33 incl. audio compact disk (*1-58076-057-0*) Que Educ & Trng.

***Mouse Essentials Excel 97 Expert.** (C). 1999. write for info. (*0-13-018051-3*) P-H.

***Mouse Essentials Excel 97 Proficient.** (C). 1999. write for info. (*0-13-018054-8*) P-H.

***Mouse Essentials Excel 97 Proficient.** Jane Calabria. (C). 1999. pap. 29.33 (*0-13-018053-X*) P-H.

***Mouse Essentials Excel 97 Expert.** Jane Calabria. 350p. (C). 1999. pap. 29.33 (*0-13-018040-8*) P-H.

***Mouse Essentials Excel 97 Expert.** Jane Calabria & Dorothy Burke. 350p. (C). 1998. pap. text 29.33 incl. audio compact disk (*1-58076-055-4*) Que Educ & Trng.

***Mouse Essentials Powerpoint 97 Expert.** (C). 1999. write for info. (*0-13-018056-4*); pap. 29.33 (*0-13-018055-6*) P-H.

***Mouse Essentials Powerpoint 97 Expert.** Jane Calabria et al. 350p. (C). 1998. pap. text 29.33 incl. audio compact disk (*1-58076-056-2*) Que Educ & Trng.

***Mouse Essentials Word 97 Expert.** (C). 1999. write for info. (*0-13-018058-0*); pap. 29.33 (*0-13-018057-2*) P-H.

***Mouse Essentials Word 97 Proficient.** (C). 1999. write for info. (*0-13-018050-5*); pap. 29.33 (*0-13-018059-9*) P-H.

***Mouse Essentials Word 97 Expert.** Jane Calabria et al. 350p. (C). 1998. pap. text 29.33 incl. audio compact disk (*1-58076-053-8*) Que Educ & Trng.

***Mouse Essentials Word 97 Expert.** annot. ed. Laura J. Goforth & Donna M. Matherly. (Mouse Essentials Ser.). (Illus.). 594p. 1999. pap. 0.00 incl. cd-rom (*1-58076-061-9*) Que Educ & Trng.

Mouse Family's Christmas. Anna L. Carlson. (Illus.). 24p. (Orig.). (J). (gr. k-4). 1983. pap. 1.95 (*0-939938-04-9*) Karwyn Ent.

***Mouse Finds a House.** School Zone Publishing Staff. (Start to Read Board Bks.). (Illus.). (J). 2000. bds. 4.99 (*0-88743-807-5*) Sch Zone Pub Co.

Mouse Flute. Andrew Matthews. (Blue Bananas Ser.). (Illus.). (J). 1997. pap. 4.99 (*0-7497-2634-2*) Dell.

Mouse Food. large type ed. Lillian Slim. (Illus.). 12p. (J). (gr. k-3). 1999. pap. text 17.00 (*1-58084-068-X*) Lower Kuskokwim.

Mouse Genetics: Concepts & Applications. Lee M. Silver. (Illus.). 376p. 1995. text 65.00 (*0-19-507554-4*) OUP.

***Mouse Genetics & Transgenics: A Practical Approach.** Ed. by Ian J. Jackson & Cathy Abbott. LC 99-37591. No. 217. (Illus.). 320p. 2000. text 110.00 (*0-19-963709-1*); pap. text 55.00 (*0-19-963708-3*) OUP.

Mouse Histopathology. Ed. by J. M. Faccini et al. xii,226p. 1990. 165.00 (*0-444-81345-4*) Elsevier.

Mouse House. Jim Becker & Andy Mayer. LC 95-183060. (Illus.). 44p. (Orig.). 1995. pap. 9.95 (*0-14-024441-7*, Penguin Bks) Viking Penguin.

Mouse House Sticker Book. Laura Joffe Numeroff. (J). 7.95 (*0-694-01422-2*) HarpC.

An Asterisk (*) at the beginning of an entry indicates that the title is appearing for the first time.

growing up as the youngest of eleven children on a farm in Marion County, West Virginia. It captures the simple pleasures in life in a simpler time such as picking greens, cracking hickory nuts & making apple butter in October. THE MOUSE HUNTER shares remembrances of the author as a newly-graduated school teacher who faces tragedy & a love & marriage that has lasted over fifty-eight years. *Publisher Paid Annotation.*

Mouse in Biomedical Research Vol. 4: Experimental Biology & Oncology. Ed. by Henry L. Foster et al. 545p. 1982. text 188.00 (*0-12-262504-8*) Acad Pr.

***Mouse in Love.** Robert Kraus. LC 99-58611. (Illus.). 32p. (J). (gr. k-2). 2000. 16.99 (*0-531-33297-7*); 15.95 (*0-531-30297-0*) Orchard Bks Watts.

Mouse in My House! Nancy Van Laan. LC 95-52236. (Illus.). 32p. (J). (ps-1). 1996. pap. 4.95 (*0-7868-1094-7*, Pub. by Hyprn Ppbks) Little.

Mouse in My House. Nancy Van Laan. LC 95-52236. (J). 1996. 10.15 (*0-606-09636-1*, Pub. by Turtleback) Demco.

Mouse in My House: Book Fair Edition, Vol. 1. Nancy Van Laan. (J). 1996. pap. 4.95 (*0-7868-1199-4*, Pub. by Hyprn Ppbks) Little.

Mouse in Our Jewish House. Florence Zeldin. LC 89-40362. (Illus.). 32p. (J). (ps). 1990. 11.95 (*0-933873-43-3*) Torah Aura.

Mouse in Solomon's House. Mack Thomas. (Illus.). 120p. (J). (ps up). 1995. 9.99 (*0-88070-771-2*) Zondervan.

***Mouse in the Corner: A Consultant's View of the Business World.** 2nd ed. Ian G. Greig. (Illus.). 133p. 1998. pap. 24.95 (*0-9609052-6-X*) Natl Trade.

Mouse in the House. Patricia Baehr. LC 93-4068. (Illus.). 32p. (J). (ps-3). 1994. lib. bdg. 15.95 (*0-8234-1102-8*) Holiday.

Mouse in the House! Gerda Wagener. Tr. by Rosemary Lanning. LC 95-8453. (Illus.). 47p. (J). (gr. 2-4). 1995. 13.95 (*1-55858-506-0*, Pub. by North-South Bks NYC) Chronicle Bks.

Mouse in the House! Gerda Wagener. LC 95-8453. (Illus.). 48p. (J). (gr. 2-4). 1996. pap. 5.95 (*1-55858-621-0*, Pub. by North-South Bks NYC) Chronicle Bks.

Mouse in the Kitchen. Helmut Spanner. LC 94-79628. (Illus.). 12p. (J). (ps). 1995. bds. 3.95 (*1-56397-474-6*) Boyds Mills Pr.

Mouse Letters: A Very First Alphabet Book. Jim Arnosky. (Illus.). 48p. 1999. teacher ed. 4.95 (*0-395-55386-5*, Clarion Bks) HM.

Mouse Liver Carcinogenesis: Mechanisms & Species Comparisons. Ed. by Donald E. Stevenson et al. LC 89-14012. (Progress in Clinical & Biological Research Ser.). 464p. 1990. 345.00 (*0-471-56695-0*) Wiley.

Mouse, Look Out! Judy Waite. LC 98-5249. 32p. (J). (gr. k-2). 1998. 15.99 (*0-525-42031-2*, Dutton Child) Peng Put Young Read.

***Mouse Magic.** Lucy Daniels. (Animal Ark Pets Ser.: No. 5). (Illus.). 128p. (J). (gr. 3-5). 1999. pap. 3.99 (*0-439-05162-2*) Scholastic Inc.

***Mouse Magic.** Ellen Stoll Walsh. LC 98-51129. (Illus.). 32p. (J). (ps-3). 2000. 14.00 (*0-15-200326-6*, Harcourt Child Bks) Harcourt.

Mouse Match. Ed Young. LC 96-20889. (Illus.). 26p. (J). 1997. 20.00 (*0-15-201453-5*) Harcourt.

Mouse Mess. Linnea A. Riley. LC 96-49499. (Illus.). 32p. (J). (ps-2). 1997. 15.95 (*0-590-10048-3*) Scholastic Inc.

Mouse Mills Catalogue for Spring. Tasha Tudor. Tr. by Timothy D. Mouse. LC 89-50061. (Illus.). 40p. (J). (gr. k up). 1989. pap. text 6.95 (*0-9621753-2-3*) Jenny Wren Pr.

Mouse Models in the Study of Genetic Neurological Disorders. Ed. by Brian Popko. LC 98-55684. (Advances in Neurochemistry Ser.: Vol. 9). (Illus.). 366p. (C). 1999. text 149.00 (*0-306-45965-5*, Kluwer Plenum) Kluwer Academic.

Mouse Numbers: A Very First Counting Book. Jim Arnosky. (Illus.). 1999. teacher ed. 4.95 (*0-395-55006-8*) HM.

Mouse of Amherst: A Tale of Young Readers. Elizabeth Spires. LC 98-17758. (Illus.). 64p. (J). (gr. 3 up). 1999. 15.00 (*0-374-35083-3*) FS&G.

***Mouse of My Heart: A Treasury of Sense & Nonsense.** Margaret Wise Brown. LC 99-87878. 192p. (J). 2000. 19.99 (*0-7868-0628-1*, Pub. by Hyprn Child) Time Warner.

***Mouse of My Heart: A Treasury of Sense & Nonsense.** Margeret Wise Brown. LC 99-87878. 192p. (J). 2000. lib. bdg. 20.49 (*0-7868-2546-4*) Hyprn Child.

***Mouse on a Mission: 54 Bible Review Games to Reinforce Your Lessons.** Ed Dunlop. (Illus.). 220p. (gr. 4-7). 1999. pap. 0.00 (*0-87398-570-2*) Sword of Lord.

Mouse on Mars. Christopher Sergel & Leonard Wibberley. 92p. 1967. pap. 5.50 (*0-87129-104-5*, M35) Dramatic Pub.

Mouse on the Moon. Date not set. 5.95 (*0-89868-347-5*); pap. 4.95 (*0-89868-406-4*); lib. bdg. 10.95 (*0-89868-346-7*) ARO Pub.

***Mouse Pad-Keyboarding,Office Technology.** 1998. 3.00 (*0-538-42597-0*) Thomson Learn.

Mouse Paint. Walsh. 1995. pap. 5.00 (*0-15-201051-3*) Harcourt.

Mouse Paint. Ellen S. Walsh. LC 88-15694. (Illus.). 32p. (J). (ps-1). 1989. 13.00 (*0-15-256025-4*, Voyager Bks) Harcourt.

Mouse Paint. Ellen S. Walsh. LC 88-15694. (Illus.). 32p. (J). (ps-1). 1991. pap. 23.95 (*0-15-256026-2*, Harcourt Child Bks) Harcourt.

Mouse Paint. Ellen S. Walsh. LC 88-15694. (Illus.). 32p. (J). (ps-1). 1995. pap. 5.00 (*0-15-200118-2*, Voyager Bks) Harcourt.

Mouse Paint. Ellen S. Walsh. LC 88-15694. (Illus.). 32p. (J). (ps-1). 1995. pap. 5.95 (*0-15-200265-0*, Red Wagon Bks) Harcourt.

Mouse Paint. Ellen Stoll Walsh. (J). 1989. 10.45 (*0-606-07892-4*) Turtleback.

Mouse Party. Alan Durant. LC 94-38904. (J). 1996. 11.19 (*0-606-09637-X*, Pub. by Turtleback) Demco.

Mouse Party: An Open-the-Door Book. Brigitte Beguinot. LC 91-77598. (Illus.). 12p. (J). (ps-3). 1992. bds. 10.95 (*1-878093-50-9*) Boyds Mills Pr.

Mouse Pours Out. Lee Gurga. 20p. 1988. pap. 2.00 (*0-913719-89-7*, High Coo Pr) Brooks Books.

***Mouse Practice.** Emily Arnold McCully. (YA). (ps up). 1999. write for info. (*0-439-07055-4*) Scholastic Inc.

Mouse Practice. Emily Arnold McCully. LC 98-18522. (J). 1999. pap. 16.95 (*0-590-68267-9*) Scholastic Inc.

Mouse Practice. Emily Arnold McCully. LC 98-18522. 32p. (J). (ps-4). 1999. 15.95 (*0-590-68220-2*) Scholastic Inc.

Mouse Rap. Walter Dean Myers. LC 89-36419. 192p. (J). (gr. 5-9). 1990. lib. bdg. 14.89 (*0-06-024344-9*) HarpC Child Bks.

Mouse Rap. Walter Dean Myers. Ed. & Contrib. by Andy Bacha. LC 89-36419. (Trophy Bk.). 192p. (YA). (gr. 5-9). 1992. pap. 4.95 (*0-06-440356-4*, HarpTrophy) HarpC Child Bks.

Mouse Rap. Walter Dean Myers. 1992. 9.60 (*0-606-01077-7*, Pub. by Turtleback) Demco.

Mouse Soup. Houghton Mifflin Company Staff. (Literature Experience 1991 Ser.). (J). (gr. 2). 1990. pap. 9.48 (*0-395-55148-X*) HM.

Mouse Soup. Houghton Mifflin Company Staff. (Literature Experience 1993 Ser.). (J). (gr. 2). 1992. pap. 9.48 (*0-395-61781-2*) HM.

Mouse Soup. Arnold Lobel. LC 76-41517. (I Can Read Bks.). (Illus.). 64p. (J). (ps-3). 1977. 15.95 (*0-06-023967-0*); lib. bdg. 15.89 (*0-06-023968-9*) HarpC Child Bks.

Mouse Soup. Arnold Lobel. (I Can Read Bks.). (Illus.). 64p. (J). (gr. 1-3). 1983. pap. 3.95 (*0-06-444041-9*, HarpTrophy) HarpC Child Bks.

Mouse Soup. Arnold Lobel. (I Can Read Bks.). (J). (gr. 1-3). 1977. pap. 3.95 (*0-590-20804-7*) Scholastic Inc.

Mouse Soup. Arnold Lobel. (I Can Read Bks.). (J). (gr. 1-3). 1977. 8.95 (*0-606-03215-0*, Pub. by Turtleback) Demco.

Mouse Soup. abr. ed. Arnold Lobel. (I Can Read Bks.). (J). (gr. 1-3). 1990. 8.95 incl. audio (*1-55994-237-1*, TBC 2371) HarperAudio.

Mouse Sticker Paper Doll, Vol. 108. Carolyn Bracken. (Illus.). (J). (gr. k-3). 1993. pap. 1.00 (*0-486-27436-5*) Dover.

Mouse Stroller Songs. Laura Joffe Numeroff. (J). 9.95 (*0-694-01420-6*) HarpC.

Mouse Surprise. Alexandra Whitney. Ed. by Nancy R. Thatch. LC 97-18803. (Books for Students by Students). (Illus.). 32p. (J). (gr. k-3). 1997. lib. bdg. 15.95 (*0-933849-64-8*) Landmark Edns.

***Mouse Tail Moon.** Joanne Ryder. 2001. text 16.95 (*0-8050-6404-4*) St Martin.

Mouse Tale: A Christmas Mouse. unabridged ed. Edythe B. McLeod. LC 98-227232. (Illus.). 24p. (J). (gr. 1-6). 1998. pap. 9.95 (*0-9666869-0-X*) Brooks Bks.

Mouse Tales. Arnold Lobel. LC 66-18654. (I Can Read Bks.). (Illus.). 64p. (J). (ps-3). 1972. 15.95 (*0-06-023941-7*); lib. bdg. 15.89 (*0-06-023942-5*) HarpC Child Bks.

Mouse Tales. Arnold Lobel. LC 72-76511. (I Can Read Bks.). (Illus.). 64p. (J). (gr. 1-3). 1978. pap. 3.95 (*0-06-444013-3*, HarpTrophy) HarpC Child Bks.

Mouse Tales. Arnold Lobel. (I Can Read Bks.). (J). (gr. 1-3). 1972. 8.95 (*0-606-02189-2*, Pub. by Turtleback) Demco.

Mouse Tales. abr. ed. Arnold Lobel. (I Can Read Bks.). (J). (gr. 1-3). 1990. 8.95 incl. audio (*1-55994-239-8*, TBC 2398) HarperAudio.

Mouse Tales: A Behind-the-Ears Look at Disneyland. David Koenig. 240p. 1994. 25.95 (*0-9640605-5-8*) Bonaventure.

Mouse Tales: A Behind-the-Ears Look at Disneyland. David Koenig. 240p. 1995. pap. 13.95 (*0-9640605-6-6*) Bonaventure.

Mouse Tales: A Study Guide. Laurie Diamond. Ed. by J. Friedland & R. Kessler. (Novel-Ties Ser.). (J). (gr. k-2). 1998. pap. text, student ed. 15.95 (*0-7675-0311-2*) Lrn Links.

Mouse That Jack Built. Cyndy Szekeres. LC 96-48182. (Illus.). 32p. (J). (ps-1). 1997. 5.95 (*0-590-69197-X*) Scholastic Inc.

Mouse That Roared. Leonard Wibberley. 20.95 (*0-8488-0190-3*) Amereon Ltd.

Mouse That Roared. Leonard Wibberley. 1963. 5.50 (*0-87129-455-9*, M36) Dramatic Pub.

Mouse That Roared. large type ed. Leonard Wibberley. LC 97-10817. (Perennial Ser.). 242p. 1997. 22.95 (*0-7838-8189-4*, G K Hall Lrg Type) Mac Lib Ref.

Mouse That Roared. Leonard Wibberley. 288p. 1992. reprint ed. lib. bdg. 27.95 (*0-89966-887-9*) Buccaneer Bks.

Mouse That Roared: What Disney Teaches. Henry A. Giroux et al. LC 99-11241. (Culture & Education Ser.). 208p. 1999. 22.95 (*0-8476-9109-8*) Rowman.

***Mouse, the Computer, & the Mouse.** Michael Fiore. (Illus.). 32p. (J). (gr. k-3). 1999. pap. 6.75 (*0-8059-4604-7*) Dorrance.

Mouse, the Rooster & the Cat: Story Pak. Jean de La Fontaine. (Graphic Learning Literature Program Series: Folk Tales). (ENG & SPA., Illus.). (J). 1992. 45.00 (*0-87746-245-3*) Graphic Learning.

Mouse, Timer, & Keyboard Inputs. 5th ed. Richard P. Braden. (Hands-on-Programming Ser.: Bk. 5). 176p. 1995. pap. 15.95 incl. disk (*1-55622-452-4*) Wordware Pub.

Mouse Told His Mother. Bethany Roberts. (Illus.). 32p. (J). (gr. k-3). 1997. 14.95 (*0-316-74982-6*) Little.

***Mouse Told His Mother.** Bethany Roberts. (Illus.). 32p. (J). (ps-2). 1999. pap. 5.95 (*0-316-74958-3*) Little.

Mouse Trap Cars: The Secrets to Success. 4th rev. ed. Alden J. Balmer. Ed. by Chris Cotter. (Illus.). 90p. 1998. pap. 14.00 (*0-9656674-1-3*) Doc Fizzix.

Mouse TV. Matt Novak. LC 93-49399. (Illus.). 32p. (J). (ps-1). 1994. 16.95 (*0-531-06856-0*); lib. bdg. 17.99 (*0-531-08706-9*) Orchard Bks Watts.

Mouse TV. Matt Novak. LC 93-49399. (Illus.). 32p. (J). (ps-1). 1998. pap. 6.95 (*0-531-07099-9*) Orchard Bks Watts.

Mouse under Glass: Secrets of Disney Animation & Theme Parks. David Koenig. LC 96-78506. 270p. 1997. pap. write for info. (*0-9640605-1-5*) Bonaventure.

Mouse under Glass: Secrets of Disney Animation & Theme Parks. David Koenig. LC 96-78506. (Illus.). 270p. 1997. 23.95 (*0-9640605-0-7*) Bonaventure.

Mouse Views: What the Class Pet Saw. Bruce McMillan. LC 92-25921. (Illus.). 32p. (J). (gr. k-3). 1993. lib. bdg. 16.95 (*0-8234-1008-0*) Holiday.

Mouse Views: What the Class Pet Saw. Bruce McMillan. LC 92-25921. (Illus.). 32p. (J). (ps-3). 1993. pap. 6.95 (*0-8234-1132-X*) Holiday.

***Mouse Wedding.** Michelle Cartlidge. (J). 1999. 4.99 (*0-525-46110-8*, Dutton Child) Peng Put Young Read.

Mouse Wedding Dance: A Read-with-Me Story for Grown-Ups & Others, Vol. 2. David P. Williams & Helen C. Williams. (Read-with-Me Mouse Stories Ser.). (Illus.). 12p. (J). 1993. pap. 3.00 (*1-886058-02-4*) D P Williams.

Mouse Who Owned the Sun. Sally Derby. LC 91-40965. (Illus.). 32p. (J). (ps-3). 1993. lib. bdg. 14.95 (*0-02-766965-3*, Four Winds Pr) S&S Childrens.

***Mouse Who Wanted to Stay in the Trap.** Robert E. Wood. (Illus.). 28p. (J). (gr. k-7). 1999. boxed set 16.95 (*1-892458-04-7*) Lifes Footprints.

Mouse Whole: An Epic. Richard Moore. LC 95-69220. 223p. 1996. pap. 15.95 (*0-942544-50-1*) Negative Capability Pr.

Mousedeer & the Tiger Cubs. F. I. Rejab. (Illus.). 24p. (J). 1994. 9.95 (*983-9808-15-X*, Pub. by Delta Edits) Weatherhill.

Mousehole Cat. Antonia Barber. (Illus.). 40p. 1996. mass mkt. 5.99 (*0-689-80837-2*) S&S Childrens.

Mousehole Cat. Antonia Barber. 1996. 11.19 (*0-606-10882-3*, Pub. by Turtleback) Demco.

Mousekin de Viaje. Edna Miller. Tr. by Louis M. Ugalde. (gr. k-3). 1976. pap. 9.95 (*0-13-604355-0*) P-H.

Mousekin's Close Call. Edna Miller. LC 77-27571. (Illus.). (J). (gr. k-3). 1980. 9.95 (*0-13-604207-4*) Simon & Schuster.

Mousekin's Fables. Edna Miller. (Illus.). 28p. (J). (ps-3). 1982. 11.95 (*0-13-604165-5*) P-H.

Mousekin's Family. Edna Miller. (Illus.). (J). (gr. k-3). 1972. lib. bdg. 9.95 (*0-13-604462-X*) Simon & Schuster.

***Mousemazia: Am Amazing Dream House Maze.** Anna Nilsen. LC 99-52865. (Illus.). 24p. (YA). (gr. 2 up). 2000. 11.99 (*0-7636-1251-0*, Pub. by Candlewick Pr) Penguin Putnam.

***Mousery.** Charlotte Pomerantz. LC 99-6116. (Illus.). 40p. (J). (ps-3). 2000. 16.00 (*0-15-202304-6*, Harcourt Child Bks) Harcourt.

Mouse's Baby Blanket. Beverly S. Brown. (Illus.). 8p. (J). (gr. k-1). 1996. pap. 3.75 (*1-880612-51-8*) Seedling Pubns.

Mouse's Birthday. Jane Yolen. (Illus.). 32p. (J). 1995. 5.95 (*0-399-22845-4*, Sandcastle Bks) Putnam Pub Group.

Mouse's Birthday. Jane Yolen. (J). 1993. 11.15 (*0-606-07893-2*, Pub. by Turtleback) Demco.

Mouse's Christmas. Alan Baker. LC 96-2332. (Illus.). 24p. (J). (ps-1). 1996. 12.95 (*0-7613-0503-3*, Copper Beech Bks) Millbrook Pr.

Mouse's Christmas. Marcia Leonard. (Illus.). 16p. 1997. pap. 2.95 (*0-8167-1494-0*) Troll Communs.

Mouse's Christmas Eve. Harry Bornstein & Lillian B. Hamilton. (Signed English Ser.). (Illus.). 44p. (J). (ps-3). 1974. pap. 5.95 (*0-913580-28-7*, Pub. by K Green Pubns) Gallaudet Univ Pr.

Mouse's Christmas House: A Press-Out Model House. Michelle Cartlidge. (Illus.). 16p. (Orig.). (J). 1992. pap. 9.95 (*0-8362-4500-8*) Andrews & McMeel.

Mouse's Family Album. Laura Joffe Numeroff. 32p. (J). 10.95 (*0-06-028561-3*, L Geringer) HarpC Child Bks.

***Mouse's First Christmas!** Lauren Thompson. LC 98-24073. (Illus.). 32p. (J). 1999. 12.00 (*0-689-82325-8*) S&S Bks Yung.

Mouses First Halloween. Lauren Thompson. (J). 2000. per. 12.95 (*0-689-83176-5*) S&S Trade.

Mouse's Halloween. Alan Baker. LC 97-5072. (Illus.). 32p. (J). (ps-2). 1997. 12.95 (*0-7613-0628-5*); lib. bdg. 21.40 (*0-7613-0704-4*, Copper Beech Bks) Millbrook Pr.

Mouse's House. Illus. by Roy Trower. (My Little Fat Bks.). 20p. (J). (ps). 1997. bds. 3.49 (*1-85854-700-8*) Brimax Bks.

Mouse's Story: Jesus & the Storm. Nick Butterworth & Mick Inkpen. (Animal Tales Ser.). (J). (gr. 3-7). 1988. 4.99 (*0-310-55810-7*) Zondervan.

Mouse's Tale. Elaine Anderson. 32p. (J). (gr. k-4). 1991. 8.99 (*0-904748-63-4*) Review & Herald.

Mouse's Tale. Pamela Johnson. Ed. by Diane D'Andrade. LC 90-36805. (Illus.). 32p. (J). (ps-3). 1991. 11.95 (*0-15-256032-7*) Harcourt.

Mouse's Wedding. large type ed. Tr. by Donna Tamaki.Tr. of Nezumi No Yomeiri. (ENG & JPN., Illus.). 12p. (J). (ps-12). 1996. 35.00 (*1-893533-07-7*, 6) Kamish for Kids.

***Mouses's Life.** John Himmelman. LC 00-27012. (Nature Upclose Ser.). (Illus.). (J). 2000. write for info. (*0-516-21167-6*) Childrens.

***Mousetale.com: A Collection of Humorous Stories from the Internet.** Ed. by Dennis Mog. (Illus.). 1999. pap. 6.99 (*0-88270-792-2*) Bridge-Logos.

***Mousetale.com: A Collection of Humorous Stories from the Internet - Includes Mouse Pad.** Ed. by Dennis D. Mog. LC 99-64054. 120p. 1999. pap. 10.99 (*0-88270-774-4*, Bridge) Bridge-Logos.

Mousetracks: A Kid's Computer Idea Book. Peggy L. Steinhauser. LC 96-29330. (Illus.). 104p. (J). (gr. k-5). 1997. pap. 12.95 (*1-883672-48-1*) Tricycle Pr.

Mousetrap: Structure & Meaning in Hamlet. P. J. Aldus. LC 76-42263. 250p. reprint ed. pap. 77.50 (*0-608-15376-1*, 202932300060) Bks Demand.

Mousetrap & Other Plays. Agatha Christie. 752p. 1993. mass mkt. 7.50 (*0-06-100374-3*, Harp PBks) HarpC.

***Mousetrap & Other Plays.** Agatha Christie. (Miss Marple Mysteries Ser.). 752p. 2000. mass mkt. 6.99 (*0-451-20114-0*, Sig) NAL.

MouseTrap Cars: A Teachers Guide. 3rd rev. ed. Alden J. Balmer. Ed. by Chris Cotter. (Illus.). 145p. (gr. 6 up). 1999. pap. 18.00 (*0-9656674-0-5*) Doc Fizzix.

Mousetrap Science Is Fun. 4th rev. ed. Melvyn C. McDaniel. Ed. by Doreen L. McDaniel. (Illus.). 212p. (YA). (gr. 4 up). 1997. pap. 29.95 (*0-9653457-1-8*) Adexell Pub.

***Mousetraps & the Moon: The Strange Ride of Sigmund Freud & the Early Years of Psychoanalysis.** Robert Wilcocks. 320p. 2000. 70.00 (*0-7391-0158-7*) Lxngtn Bks.

M

Moushe' Book: The Soft Diet. Ruth Vorse. 38p. 1995. pap. text 8.00 (*0-614-07329-4*) Strawbry Press.

Mousie Garner: Autobiography of a Vaudeville Stooge. Paul Garner & Sharon Kissane. (Illus.). 224p. 1998. lib. bdg. 29.95 (*0-7864-0581-3*) McFarland & Co.

Mousie up & Down. Norman Gorbaty. (Pet Parade Bks.). (J). 1995. 4.50 (*0-671-89835-3*) Litle Simon.

Mousing Owl. Dick Beyer. LC 96-90439. 278p. 1996. pap. 3.95 (*0-9635404-3-2*) TwoForYou Bks.

Mousses, Bonkei, Bonsai: Un Secret Seculaire du Jardinier Japonais. Ed. by J. Rammeloo. (FRE., Illus.). 137p. 1989. pap. 40.00 (*1-878762-82-6*, Pub. by Natl Botanic Grdn Belgium) Balogh.

Moussorgsky. Montagu Montagu-Nathan. LC 74-24157. 100 p. 1976. reprint ed. 29.50 (*0-404-13050-X*) AMS Pr.

Moussorgsky. Oskar Von Riesemann. Tr. by Paul England. LC 74-121278. reprint ed. 29.50 (*0-404-05334-3*) AMS Pr.

Moussorgsky. Oskar Von Riesemann. Tr. by Paul England from GER. LC 71-100833. 412p. 1971. reprint ed. lib. bdg. 75.00 (*0-8371-4007-2*, RIMO, Greenwood Pr) Greenwood.

Moussorgsky. Oskar Von Riesemann. Tr. by Paul England. 412p. 1990. reprint ed. lib. bdg. 89.00 (*0-7812-9077-5*) Rprt Serv.

Moussorgsky: Music Book Index. Michel D. Calvocoressi. 216p. 1993. reprint ed. lib. bdg. 79.00 (*0-7812-9612-9*) Rprt Serv.

Moustache. Emmanuel Carrere. (FRE.). 192p. 1987. pap. 10.95 (*0-7859-2073-0*, 2070378837) Fr & Eur.

Moustache: Memories of Greg Curnoe. George Bowering. 1993. pap. (*0-88910-457-3*) Talonbks.

Moustache Pete Is Dead. Evviva Moustache Pete! The FraNoi Columns 1985-1988. Fred L. Gardaphe. LC 97-43451. (VIA Folios Ser.: Vol. 13). 96p. 1997. pap. 10.00 (*1-884419-13-5*) Bordighera.

Moustapha's Eclipse. Reginald McKnight. 144p. 1989. reprint ed. pap. 8.95 (*0-88001-179-3*) HarpC.

Mousterian Lithic Technology: Ecological Perspective. Steven L. Kuhn. LC 94-32822. 208p. 1995. text 60.00 (*0-691-03615-2*, Pub. by Princeton U Pr) Cal Prin Full Svc.

Moustique. Henry De Montherlant. (FRE.). 1987. pap. 8.95 (*0-7859-3419-7*) Fr & Eur.

Moutain Lion Maters Math & Science: Fictional Leader Shares Valuable Tips & Encouragement. Lisa Johnson. (Illus.). 5p. (Orig.). (YA). (gr. 5 up). 1997. pap. 6.00 (*0-9634399-4-4*) Funmakers.

***Mouth.** Katherine Goode. LC 00-8315. 32p. 2000. 16.95 (*1-56711-494-6*) Blackbirch.

Mouth. Timothy Gower. 1998. spiral bd. write for info. (*0-201-15832-9*) Addison-Wesley.

Mouth. Robert James. (Human Body Ser.). 1995. lib. bdg. 14.60 (*1-57103-103-0*) Rourke Pr.

***Mouth Madness.** Orr. (C). 1999. pap. text 42.00 (*0-12-785028-7*) Acad Pr.

Mouth Madness. Orr. 1998. 42.00 (*0-7616-4850-X*, W B Saunders Co) Harcrt Hlth Sci Grp.

Mouth of God. Lorenzo Caravella. 1999. pap. text 21.95 (*1-887472-07-X*) Sunstar Pubng.

Mouth of Home: Poems. Janell Moon. LC 98-74910. 63p. 1999. pap. 12.00 (*0-9657015-2-2*) Arctos Pr.

Mouth of Shadows: Hamlet's Ghosts Perform Hamlet & Sunspots. Charles Borkhuis. LC 99-40608. (Illus.). 120p. 2000. pap. 12.00 (*1-881471-32-2*) S Duyvil.

Mouth of the Whale. Elizabeth Sutherland. 50p. 1979. pap. 3.50 (*0-930012-07-0*) J Mudfoot.

Mouth-Piece. Kenneth Gaburo. 1976. 7.00 (*0-939044-08-0*) Lingua Pr.

Mouth That Begs: Hunger, Cannibalism & the Politics of Eating in Modern China. Gang Yue. LC 98-45873. 1999. 64.95 (*0-8223-2308-7*) Duke.

Mouth That Begs: Hunger, Cannibalism & the Politics of Eating in Modern China. Gang Yue. LC 98-45873. 447p. 1999. pap. 20.95 (*0-8223-2341-9*) Duke.

Mouth, the Face & the Mind. Charlotte Feinmann. LC 99-24159. (Illus.). 190p. 1999. text 98.50 (*0-19-263062-8*) OUP.

***Mouth to Mouth.** Michael Kimball. LC 99-39876. 400p. 2000. 24.00 (*0-380-97820-2*, Avon Bks) Morrow Avon.

Mouth to Mouth. Debbie Westbury. 64p. (C). 1989. 40.00 (*0-9587972-5-0*, Pub. by Five Isl Pr) St Mut.

Mouth to Mouth: Poems by Twelve Contemporary Mexican Women. Ed. & Tr. by Forrest Gander from SPA. Tr. by Zoe Anglesey et al from SPA. LC 92-18246. 250p. (Orig.). 1993. pap. 14.95 (0-915943-71-9) Milkweed Ed.

Mouthful of Breath Mints & No One to Kiss: A Cathy Collection. Cathy Guisewite. (Illus.). 128p. 1983. pap. 8.95 (0-8362-1120-0) Andrews & McMeel.

Mouthing Off. Jeffrey A. Kottler. LC 80-82407. 1980. 12.95 (0-87212-141-0) Libra.

Mouthpiece. Kathryn MacLeod. 104p. 1996. pap. 8.95 (0-921331-23-1, Pub. by Tsunami Edits) Barnholden.

Mouthpiece. E. Wallace. 1980. lib. bdg. 14.95 (0-89968-251-0, Lghtyr Pr) Buccaneer Bks.

***Mouthpiece of Thumbs.** limited ed. Derek Sheffield. 48p. 2000. 15.00 (0-911287-38-8) Blue Begonia.

***Mouthpiece of Thumbs.** limited ed. Derek Sheffield. (Working Signs Ser.). (Illus.). 48p. 2000. 25.00 (0-911287-43-4) Blue Begonia.

Mouths. Stephen Savage. (Adaptation for Survival Ser.). (Illus.). 40p. (J). (gr. 2-6). 1995. lib. bdg. 5.00 (1-56847-351-6) Raintree Steck-V.

Mouths & Bits. Toni Webber. (Threshold Picture Guides Ser.). (Illus.). 24p. 1990. pap. 12.00 (1-872082-09-2) Half Halt Pr.

Mouths & Noses. Sally Markham-David. LC 93-29008. (Illus.). (J). 1994. 4.25 (0-383-03764-6) SRA McGraw.

Mouths of People, the Voice of God: Buddhists & Muslims in a Frontier Community of Ladakh. Smriti Srinivas. LC 98-902984. (Illus.). 230p. 1998. text 23.95 (0-19-564229-5) OUP.

Mouths of Stone: Stories of the Ancient Maya from Newly Deciphered Inscriptions & Recent Archaeological Discoveries. Jeffrey Chouinard. LC 93-73799. (Centers of Civilization Ser.). (Illus.). 260p. (C). 1995. lib. bdg. 75.00 (0-89089-565-1) Carolina Acad Pr.

Mouthsounds. Frederick R. Newman. LC 80-51513. (Illus.). 128p. 1980. pap. 6.95 (0-89480-128-7, 427) Workman Pub.

Mouton Rothschild: Paintings for the Labels. Phillipine Rothschild. 1991. write for info. (0-8212-1856-5) Little.

Mouton's Impossible Dream. Arlene A. McGrory. LC 98-47275. (Illus.). 32p. (J). (ps-3). 2000. 16.00 (0-15-202195-7, Gulliver Bks) Harcourt.

Mouvar's Magic. Piers Anthony & Robert E. Margroff. 320p. 1993. mass mkt. 4.99 (0-8125-1982-5, Pub. by Tor Bks) St Martin.

Mouvement d'un Satellite Artificiel de la Terre. Bruno Morando. 256p. 1974. pap. text 77.00 (0-677-50755-0) Gordon & Breach.

Mouvement Perpetuel - Feu de Joie: Ecritures Automatique. Louis Aragon. (FRE.). 1970. pap. 10.95 (0-8288-3811-9, 2070300129) Fr & Eur.

Mouvement Perpetuel & Feu de Joie et Ecritures Automatiques. Louis Aragon. (Poesie Ser.). (FRE.). pap. 7.95 (2-07-030012-9) Schoenhof.

Mouvement Philosophique de 1748 a 1789. Jean-Paul Belin. 381p. 1973. reprint ed. 80.00 (3-487-04822-1) G Olms Pubs.

Mouvements Nationaux Chez les Musulmans de Russie, 2 tomes. Alexandre Bennigsen & Chantal Lemercier-Quelquejay. Incl. No. 3. "Sultangalievisme" au Tatarstan. 1960. pap. 38.25 Tome II. Presse et le Mouvement National Chez les Musulmans De Russie Avant 1920. (Illus.). 1964. pap. 31.60 (90-279-6244-8); (Move with Me Ser.). Set pap. 38.25 (0-685-03444-5) Mouton.

Movable & Wall- or Ceiling-Hung Electric Room Heaters, UL 1278. 2nd ed. (C). 1994. pap. text 290.00 (1-55989-684-1) Underwrtrs Labs.

Movable Bed Physical Models. Ed. by Hsieh W. Shen. (C). 1990. text 139.00 (0-7923-0828-X) Kluwer Academic.

Movable Genetic Elements, 2 pts., Pt. 1. Cold Spring Harbor Symposia on Quantitative Biolog. LC 34-8174. (Cold Spring Harbor Symposia on Quantitative Biology Ser.: No. 45). 467p. reprint ed. pap. 144.80 (0-7837-2016-5, 204229200001) Bks Demand.

Movable Genetic Elements, 2 pts., Pt. 2. Cold Spring Harbor Symposia on Quantitative Biolog. LC 34-8174. (Cold Spring Harbor Symposia on Quantitative Biology Ser.: No. 45). 594p. reprint ed. pap. 184.20 (0-7837-2017-3, 204229200002) Bks Demand.

Movable Harvests: The Simplicity & Bounty of Container Gardens. Chuck Crandall & Barbara Crandall. (Illus.). 128p. 1995. pap. 19.95 (1-881527-70-0, Chapters Bks) HM.

***Movable Mother Goose.** limited ed. Robert Sabuda. (Illus.). (J). 1999. 100.00 (0-689-83149-8) Litle Simon.

***Movable Mother Goose: A Classic Collectible Pop-Up, No. 2.** Robert Sabuda. (Illus.). (J). (ps-3). 1999. per. 19.95 (0-689-81192-6) Litle Simon.

Movable Property in the Nuzi Documents. Dorothy Cross. (American Oriental Ser.: No. 10). 1937. pap. 25.00 (0-527-02684-0) Periodicals Srv.

Movable Roots. David Cornberg. (ENG.). 80p. 1988. pap. text 8.00 (1-57833-021-1) Todd Commns.

Movable School Goes to the Negro Farmer. Thomas M. Campbell. Ed. by Lawrence A. Cremin & Frederick A. Barnard. LC 78-101403. (American Education). 1974. reprint ed. 17.95 (0-405-01398-1) Ayer.

Movable Storage Projects: Ingenious Space-Saving Solutions. Charles R. Self. LC 92-35847. (Illus.). 192p. 1993. pap. 14.95 (0-8069-8631-X) Sterling.

Movable Type: Biography of Legh R. Freeman. Thomas H. Heuterman. LC 79-15511. (Illus.). 182p. 1979. reprint ed. pap. 56.50 (0-608-00160-0, 206094100006) Bks Demand.

Movado History. Fritz Von Osterhausen. LC 96-68730. (Illus.). 234p. (YA). 1996. 89.95 (0-7643-0126-8) Schiffer.

Move Ahead with Possibility Thinking. Robert H. Schuller. 224p. 1986. mass mkt. 5.50 (0-515-08984-2, Jove) Berkley Pub.

Move-Along Math: Grades K-1. Avaril Wedemeyer & Joyce Cejka. 1988. 5.95 (0-89108-187-9, 8814) Love Pub Co.

Move Alpha: Conditions on Its Application & Output. Howard Lasnik & Mamoru Saito. (Current Studies in Linguistics: No. 22). (Illus.). 234p. 1992. 36.00 (0-262-12161-1) MIT Pr.

Move Alpha: Conditions on Its Application & Output. Howard Lasnik & Mamoru Saito. (Current Studies in Linguistics: No. 22). (Illus.). 240p. 1994. pap. text 18.00 (0-262-62091-X) MIT Pr.

Move & Match Colors with Busy Bear. Sondra Rieck & Carol Rutledge. 22p. (J). (ps). 1990. 9.95 (0-9634376-0-7) Woodville Pr.

***Move Closer: An Intimate Philosophy of Art.** John Armstrong. (Illus.). 224p. 2000. 25.00 (0-374-10596-0) FS&G.

MOVE Crisis in Philadelphia: Extremist Groups & Conflict Resolution. Hizkias Assefa & Paul Wahrhaftig. LC 89-39454. (Illus.). 174p. 1990. reprint ed. pap. 12.95 (0-8229-5430-3) U of Pittsburgh Pr.

Move Further South. Ruth Garnett. 1988. pap. 7.95 (0-88378-113-1) Third World.

Move Heaven & Earth. Christina Dodd. 400p. 1995. mass mkt. 5.50 (0-06-108152-3) HarpC.

Move Heaven & Earth. Christina Dodd. 400p. 1999. mass mkt. 3.99 (0-06-103000-7) HarpC.

Move in Our Midst: Looking at Worship in the Life of the Church. Kenneth Morse. LC 77-6411. 159p. 1977. reprint ed. pap. 49.30 (0-608-02166-0, 206283500004) Bks Demand.

Move into Work. Michael Ryan & Michael Weatherley. 138p. (C). 1987. 80.00 (0-946139-56-3, Pub. by Elm Pubns) St Mut.

Move It!!! Sherry Raynor & Richard Drouillard. Ed. by Lou Alonso. (Illus.). 96p. 1978. pap. 6.00 (0-88314-132-9) AAHPERD.

Move It! A Book about Motion. Jill C. Wheeler. LC 95-49660. (Kid Physics Ser.). (J). 1998. lib. bdg. 13.98 (1-56239-631-5) ABDO Pub Co.

Move IT (Information Technology) Moving a Corporate Data Center & Offices. Paul Friday. (Illus.). 251p. 1998. pap. 99.00 (1-883422-08-6) Adams-Blake.

Move Like the Animals. unabridged ed. Stephen Rosenholtz. LC 91-66970. (Illus.). 32p. (J). (ps-3). 1992. 19.95 incl. audio (0-9630979-1-1); pap. 19.95 incl. audio (0-9630979-0-3) Rosewd Pubns.

***Move, Love & Learn: A Compilation of Sermons.** Albert Gani. (Illus.). 388p. 1998. pap. 20.00 (1-882853-12-1) A Gani.

Move of God: Azusa Street to Now. Clara Davis. 80p. (Orig.). 1983. pap. 2.95 (0-88144-016-7, CPS-016) Christian Pub.

Move of God in Man. Witness Lee. 126p. 1994. per. 6.25 (0-87083-807-5, 04-020-001) Living Stream Ministry.

Move of the Holy Spirit in the 10/40 Window. Luis Bush. 1999. pap. 8.99 (1-57658-151-9) YWAM Pub.

Move On! Carol L. Pearson. 50p. (Orig.). 1995. pap. 4.50 (1-57514-171-X, 1140) Encore Perform Pub.

Move on Up. Alan K. Garinger. (Learn to Read TV Ser.). 63p. 1990. student ed. 1.50 (0-910475-43-1) KET.

Move Over! Harriet Ziefert. (Stickerbook Reader). (Illus.). 24p. (J). (ps-3). 1991. mass mkt. 3.95 (0-06-107421-7) HarpC Child Bks.

Move over, Don Porfiro: Tales from the Sierra Madre. Eugene H. Boudreau. LC 75-35308. (Illus.). 96p. 1975. pap. 10.00 (0-686-10963-5) Redbud Press.

***Move over Einstein.** Margaret Springer. (Illus.). 128p. (J). 1998. pap. 7.95 (0-14-037799-9, Pub. by Pnguin Bks Ltd) Trafalgar.

Move over, Elijah: Sermons in Poetry & Prose. Arthur O. Roberts. LC 67-24903. 161p. 1967. 7.95 (0-913342-11-4) Barclay Pr.

Move over, Girl. Brian Peterson. LC 98-96364. 316p. 1998. pap. 12.00 (0-9664587-0-2) C-Twenty Two.

***Move over, Girl.** Brian Peterson. LC 99-53711. 288p. 2000. 19.95 (0-375-50402-8) Villard Books.

Move over Men: God Calls Women into the Pulpit for Boundless Preaching, Theological, Sociological & Logical Support for Women in Ministry. Jacquelyn Donald-Mims. 1998. pap. 12.00 (1-891809-00-8) Pub by Devon.

***Move over Mr. Holland: Insights, Humor & Philosophy on Music & Life.** Trey Reely. LC 99-93450. (Illus.). 198p. 2000. pap. 9.95 (0-9673756-0-6) T Reely.

Move over Monet Birthday Book. Michele Breckenridge et al. (Illus.). (J). 1995. write for info. (0-939979-02-0) Discovery Toys.

Move over, Mother Goose! Finger Plays, Action Verses & Funny Rhymes. Ruth I. Dowell. Ed. by Kathleen Charner. (Illus.). 126p. (Orig.). (J). (ps-1). 1987. pap. 12.95 (0-87659-113-6) Gryphon Hse.

Move over, Mother Goose Young Readers Edition. Ruth I. Dowell. (Illus.). (J). (ps-6). 1991. reprint ed. pap. 8.00 (0-945842-17-1) Pollyanna Prodns.

Move over Mountain: Learning the Lessons of Faith. Eloise C. Henderson. LC 94-14621. 152p. 1994. pap. 12.00 (1-880837-45-5) Smyth & Helwys.

Move over, Picasso! A Young Painter's Primer. Ruth Aukerman. (Illus.). 44p. (Orig.). (J). (gr. 1-6). 1994. pap. 12.95 (1-884555-01-2) P Depke Bks.

Move over Rover. Karen Beaumont. (J). 2005. write for info. (0-15-201979-0) Harcourt.

***Move over Victoria, I Know the Real Secret: Breaking Free from the Lies That Bind You.** Nancy Kennedy. 240p. 2000. 11.95 (1-57856-200-7) Waterbrook Pr.

Move That Horizon. Tessie Marcin. 237p. 1999. pap. 15.95 (0-7414-0059-6) Buy Books.

Move The Crowd: Voices & Faces of the Hip-Hop Nation. Gregor Ehrlich & Dimitri Ehrlich. (Illus.). 192p. 1999. per. 16.95 (0-671-02799-9, MTV Bks) PB.

Move to Learn: Physical Activities for Young Children. Sue Carlyle. (Illus.). 1986. reprint ed. pap. text 8.95 (0-941376-02-8) Bleecker St Pub.

***Move to Strike.** Perri O'Shaughnessy. LC 00-37578. 416p. 2000. 23.95 (0-385-33277-7) Delacorte.

Move to the Market: Trade & Industry Policy Reform in Transitional Economies. Ed. by Frederick I. Nixson & Paul Cook. 250p. 1995. text 79.95 (0-312-12404-X) St Martin.

***Move to the Music: A Musical & Multisensory Resource.** David Howland & Karen Sekiguchi. (Illus.). 70p. (J). (gr. k-5). 1999. pap. text 23.95 (1-882483-59-6) Alta Bk Ctr.

Move up to Ada. Charles G. Petersen & Nancy E. Miller. 115p. (C). 1991. pap. text 25.00 (0-9631838-8-5) P & M Pub Co.

Move up with Manners, Vol. 1. Do Yanney. 57p. 1993. pap. text 10.00 (0-9648815-0-0) Wnng Imprssns.

Move with a Song. Edith Wax & Sydell Roth. 1980. 4.95 (0-934848-01-7) Mostly Movement.

Move with Me 1, 2, 3. unabridged ed. Charlene Schade. Ed. by Pat Ziebarth. LC 88-83287. (Move with Me Ser.). (Illus.). 58p. (J). (ps-1). 1988. 16.90 incl. audio (0-924860-00-6) Exer Fun.

Move with Science: Energy, Force & Motion. Roy Q. Beven. LC 98-84914. (Illus.). 160p. 1998. pap. text 21.95 (0-87355-172-9, PB144X) Natl Sci Tchrs.

Move with the Music. Frances W. Aronoff. LC 81-24070. 133p. 1982. ring bd. 15.95 (0-9602590-1-5) Turning Wheel Pr.

Move Your Church to Action. Kent R. Hunter. LC 99-15046. 2000. pap. text 13.00 (0-687-03134-6) Abingdon.

***Move Your Stuff, Change Your Life: How to Use Feng Shui to Get Love, Money, Respect, & Happiness.** Karen Rauch Carter. LC 99-35705. 240p. 2000. per. 13.00 (0-684-86604-8) S&S Trade.

Moveable Bridge Inspection, Evaluation & Maintenance. (Bridges & Structures Ser.: Vol. MBI-1). (Illus.). 608p. (C). 1998. pap. 96.00 (1-56051-091-9) AASHTO.

Moveable Chords. Ed. by Aaron Stang. 44p. (Orig.). (C). 1991. pap. text 9.95 (0-7692-0960-2, F3095GTX) Wrner Bros.

Moveable Feast. Ernest Hemingway. (Hudson River Editions Ver.). 211p. 1981. 35.00 (0-684-17340-9, Scribners Ref) Mac Lib Ref.

Moveable Feast. Ernest Hemingway. LC 96-30237. 208p. 1996. 21.50 (0-684-83363-8) S&S Trade.

Moveable Feast. Ernest Hemingway. LC 64-15441. (Illus.). 240p. 1996. per. 10.00 (0-684-82499-X, Touchstone) S&S Trade Pap.

Moveable Feast: Pressure Group Conflict & the European Community Shipping Policy. Mark Aspinwall. 208p. 1995. 66.95 (1-85972-069-2, Pub. by Avebry) Ashgate Pub Co.

Moveable Feasts Cookbook. (Illus.). 1994. pap. 14.95 (0-939510-14-6) Mystic Sea Mus.

Moveable Margins: The Narrative Art of Carme Riera. Kathleen M. Glenn et al. LC 98-42630. 336p. 1999. 48.50 (0-8387-5399-X) Bucknell U Pr.

Moveable Shore: The Fate of the Connecticut Coast. Peter C. Patton & James M. Kent. LC 91-9822. (Living with the Shore Ser.). (Illus.). 240p. 1991. text 54.95 (0-8223-1128-3) Duke.

Moveable Shore: The Fate of the Connecticut Coast. Peter C. Patton & James M. Kent. LC 91-9822. (Living with the Shore Ser.). (Illus.). 240p. 1992. pap. text 22.95 (0-8223-1147-X) Duke.

Moved by Love: The Memoirs of Vinoba Bhave. Vinoba Bhave. Ed. by Kalindi. Tr. by Marjorie Sykes from HIN. (Illus.). 271p. 1994. pap. 15.95 (1-870098-54-4, Pub. by Resurgence) Chelsea Green Pub.

Moved Out on the Inside. Julia Vose. 1976. pap. 10.00 (0-935724-78-8) Figures.

Moved Out on the Inside. deluxe ed. Julia Vose. 1976. pap. 15.00 (0-935724-53-2) Figures.

Moved-Outers. Florence C. Means. LC 92-13706. 156p. (J). 1993. pap. 6.95 (0-8027-7386-9) Walker & Co.

Movement. (Jump Ser.). (Illus.). 32p. (J). (gr. 2-7). pap. write for info. (1-882210-24-7) Action Pub.

Movement. Sally Morgan & Adrian Morgan. LC 93-20162. (Illus.). 48p. (J). (gr. 4-9). 1993. 16.95 (0-8160-2979-2) Facts on File.

Movement. Isobel Smales. (Illus.). (J). 1997. write for info. (0-237-51772-8) EVN1 UK.

Movement. Etienne J. Marey. LC 70-169333. (Literature of Cinema, Ser. 2). (Illus.). 344p. 1979. reprint ed. 23.95 (0-405-03900-X) Ayer.

Movement: Anti-Persecution Gazette & Register of Progress, 2 vols. (Nos. 1 - 68) Ed. by George J. Holyoake & M. Q. Ryall. LC 79-120546. 1970. reprint ed. 75.00 (0-678-00679-2) Kelley.

Movement: British Poets of the 1950's. Jerry A. Bradley. LC 93-7653. (English Authors Ser.: Vol. 302). 170p. 1993. 28.95 (0-8057-7040-2, Twyne) Mac Lib Ref.

Movement: From Person to Actor to Character. Theresa Mitchell. LC 97-14861. 1998. 29.95 (0-8108-3328-X) Scarecrow.

Movement: The Muscular & Skeletal System. Jenny Bryan. LC 92-35092. (Body Talk Ser.). (Illus.). 48p. (YA). (gr. 5 up). 1993. lib. bdg. 13.95 (0-87518-565-7, Dillon Silver Burdett) Silver Burdett Pr.

Movement Activities for Children with Learning Difficulties. Bren Pointer. 140p. 1993. pap. 24.95 (1-85302-167-9) Taylor & Francis.

Movement Activities for Early Childhood. Carol T. Hammett. LC 91-42387. (Illus.). 152p. (Orig.). 1992. pap. text 16.00 (0-87322-352-7, BHAM0352) Human Kinetics.

Movement Against Teaching English in Schools of Puerto Rico. Edith A. De Gutierrez. LC 86-30763. 176p. (Orig.). 1987. pap. text 22.00 (0-8191-6088-1); lib. bdg. 40.50 (0-8191-6087-3) U Pr of Amer.

Movement & Allied Disorders in Childhood. Ed. by Mary M. Robertson & Valsamma Eapen. LC 95-9400. 342p. 1996. 215.00 (0-471-95324-5) Wiley.

Movement & Drama in Therapy. 2nd ed. Audrey G. Wethered. 128p. 1993. pap. 27.00 (1-85302-199-7) Taylor & Francis.

Movement & Institution. Francesco Alberoni. LC 84-3181. (European Perspectives Ser.). 448p. 1984. text 81.00 (0-231-04884-X) Col U Pr.

Movement & Meaning: Creativity & Interpretation in Ballet & Mime. Claire G. Moses & Leslie W. Rabine. LC 92-42841. (Illus.). 384p. (C). 1993. pap. 19.95 (0-253-20818-1, MB-818) Ind U Pr.

Movement & Meaning: Creativity & Interpretation in Ballet & Mime. Anya Royce. LC 83-48526. (Illus.). 254p. 1984. pap. 78.80 (0-608-05042-3, 205970300004) Bks Demand.

Movement & Mental Imagery: Outlines of a Motor Theory of the Complexer Mental Processes. Margaret F. Washburn. LC 73-2996. (Classics in Psychology Ser.). 1978. reprint ed. 20.95 (0-405-05168-9) Ayer.

Movement & Modernism: Yeats, Eliot, Williams & Early Twentieth-Century Dance. Terri A. Mester. LC 96-29802. 1997. 30.00 (1-55728-455-5) U of Ark Pr.

Movement & Rhythmic Activities for the Mentally Retarded. Cynthia D. Crain. (Illus.). 136p. 1981. 26.95 (0-398-04174-1) C C Thomas.

Movement & Rhythms of the Stars: A Guide to Naked-Eye Observation of Sun, Moon & Planets. Joachim Schultz.Tr. of Rhythmen der Sterne. (Illus.). 230p. 1986. 25.00 (0-88010-171-7) Anthroposophic.

Movement & the Sixties. Terry H. Anderson. (Illus.). 544p. (C). 1996. pap. text 17.95 (0-19-510457-9) OUP.

Movement As a Way to Agelessness: A Guide to Trager Mentastics. Milton Trager. 1994. pap. 15.95 (0-88268-167-2) Station Hill Pr.

Movement Behavior & Motor Learning. 3rd ed. Bryant J. Cratty. LC 73-1938. (Health Education, Physical Education, & Recreation Ser.). 530p. reprint ed. pap. 164.30 (0-608-17778-4, 205656800074) Bks Demand.

Movement Control. Ed. by Paul Cordo & Stevan R. Harnad. (Illus.). 288p. (C). 1994. pap. text 32.95 (0-521-45607-X) Cambridge U Pr.

Movement Control. Ed. by Paul Cordo & Stevan R. Harnad. (Illus.). 288p. (C). 1994. text 85.00 (0-521-45241-4) Cambridge U Pr.

Movement Control: An Interdisciplinary Forum. Ed. by R. Jacobs & W. E. Rikkert. 108p. (Orig.). 1992. pap. text 18.00 (90-5383-035-9, Pub. by VU Univ Pr) Paul & Co Pubs.

Movement Differences & Diversity in Autism-Mental Retardation: Appreciations & Accommodations People with Communications & Behavior Challenges. Anne M. Donnellan & Martha R. Leary. (Movin' On Ser.). 106p. 1994. pap. text 16.00 (1-886928-00-2) DRI Pr.

***Movement Disorder Surgery: Progress & Challenges.** Ed. by A. M. Lozano. (Progress in Neurological Surgery Ser.: Vol. 15). (Illus.). x, 404p. 2000. 243.50 (3-8055-6990-4) S Karger.

Movement Disorders. Ed. by Nandkumar S. Shah & Alexander G. Donald. LC 86-4884. (Illus.). 424p. (C). 1986. text 120.00 (0-306-42135-6, Kluwer Plenum) Kluwer Academic.

Movement Disorders, No. 3. 3rd ed. Ed. by C. David Marsden & Stanley Fahn. (BIMR Ser.: Vol. 12). (Illus.). 529p. 1994. text 105.00 (0-7506-1412-9) Buttrwrth-Heinemann.

Movement Disorders: A Contemporary Model for Stroke Rehabilitation. Susan Ryerson & Kathryn Levit. LC 96-48529. 1996. text 90.00 (0-443-08913-2) Church.

Movement Disorders: A Neuropsychiatric Approach. James B. Lohr & Alexander A. Wisniewski. LC 86-27163. (Guilford Foundations of Modern Psychiatry Ser.). 387p. 1987. lib. bdg. 63.00 (0-89862-176-3) Guilford Pubns.

Movement Disorders: Neurologic Principles & Practice. Ed. by Raymond L. Watts & William C. Koller. LC 96-35518. (Illus.). 1008p. 1997. text 125.00 (0-07-035203-8) McGraw-Hill HPD.

***Movement Disorders in Childhood.** Harvey S. Singer & Joseph Jankovic. (Illus.). 300p. 2000. 150.00 (0-7506-9852-7) Buttrwrth-Heinemann.

Movement Disorders in Children. Ed. by H. Forssberg & H. Hirschfeld. (Medicine & Sport Science Ser.: Vol. 36). (Illus.). viii, 302p. 1992. 61.00 (3-8055-5556-3) S Karger.

Movement Disorders in Neurology & Neuropsychiatry. 2nd ed. Anthony B. Joseph & Robert R. Young. LC 98-8767. (Illus.). 1998. 165.00 (0-86542-523-X) Blackwell Sci.

Movement Education: A Program for Young Children Ages 2-7. 2nd ed. June G. Munro. (Illus.). 150p. (C). 1995. pap. text 13.95 (0-685-63072-2) M D E A.

Movement Education Leading to Gymnastics: A Session by Session Approach to Key Stage 1. M. E. Carroll & Hazel K. Manners. 168p. (gr. 4-7). 1991. pap. 29.95 (0-7507-0007-6, Falmer Pr) Taylor & Francis.

Movement for Budgetary Reform in the States. William F. Willoughby. (Brookings Institution Reprint Ser.). reprint ed. lib. bdg. 37.50 (0-697-00174-1) Irvington.

Movement for Community Control of New York City's Schools, 1966-1970: Class Wars. Derek Edgell. LC 98-38839. 532p. 1998. text 119.95 (0-7734-8262-8) E Mellen.

An Asterisk (*) at the beginning of an entry indicates that the title is appearing for the first time.

Movement for Indian Assimilation, 1860 to 1890. Henry E. Fritz. LC 81-6650. (Illus.). 244p. 1981. reprint ed. lib. bdg. 65.00 (*0-313-22012-3*, FRMI, Greenwood Pr) Greenwood.

Movement for International Copyright in Nineteenth Century America. Aubert J. Clark. LC 73-9209. ix, 215p. 1973. reprint ed. lib. bdg. 22.50 (*0-8371-6980-1*, CLIC, Greenwood Pr) Greenwood.

Movement for Period Plays. Bari Rolfe. LC 85-73125. (Illus.). 160p. 1985. pap. 12.00 (*0-932456-04-9*) Personabks.

Movement for the Acquisition of All Mexico, 1846-1848. John D. Fuller. LC 78-64161. (Johns Hopkins University. Studies in the Social Sciences. Thirtieth Ser. 1912: 1). reprint ed. 27.50 (*0-404-61271-7*) AMS Pr.

Movement Genesis: Social Movement Theory & the West German Peace Movement. Steven Breyman. LC 98-113391. 256p. (C). 1997. pap. 69.00 (*0-8133-8811-2*, Pub. by Westview) HarpC.

Movement, Gesture & Sign: With Movement, Gesture & Sign Supplement - One Hundred Adapted Signs. Paula Greenhill et al. (Illus.). 54p. (YA). 1995. pap. 24.00 (*1-85878-068-3*, Pub. by Royal Natl Inst) Am Foun Blind.

Movement Improvisation: In the Words of a Teacher & Her Students. Georgette Schneer. LC 93-44419. (Illus.). 216p. 1994. pap. text 22.00 (*0-87322-530-9*, BSCH0530) Human Kinetics.

Movement in Black. Pat Parker. LC 98-55775. 1999. 26.95 (*1-56341-109-1*); pap. 16.95 (*1-56341-108-3*) Firebrand Bks.

Movement in Prayer in a Hasidic Mode. Clifford Trolin. 1979. pap. 3.00 (*0-941500-13-6*) Sharing Co.

Movement in Steady Beat: Activities for Children Age 3 to 7. Phyllis S. Weikart. 96p. (J). (ps-2). 1990. pap. 14.95 (*0-929816-08-0*, M1007) High-Scope.

Movement in Worship: Communicating the Gospel Through Dance. Janet Skidmore. Ed. by Doug Adams. 1987. pap. 3.00 (*0-941500-47-0*) Sharing Co.

Movement Is Fun: A Preschool Movement Program. Susan Young & Liz Keplinger. LC 88-60761. 150p. (Orig.). 1988. pap. 14.00 (*1-882068-01-7*) Sensory Integration.

Movement Is the Rhythm of the World: Lyrical Essays, Poetry & Prophecy from Three Black Men. Sekou Andrews et al. 56p. 1999. 18.95 (*0-9624889-7-6*) Seymour-Smith.

Movement, 1964-1970. Ed. by Clayborne Carson. LC 92-25745. 848p. 1993. lib. bdg. 215.00 (*0-313-28329-X*, CMO, Greenwood Pr) Greenwood.

Movement of a Tickle: Poetry by Children from the Inner-City Neighborhood Art House. Ed. by Mary L. Kownacki. (Illus.). 34p. (J). 1997. pap. 3.00 (*1-890890-04-9*) Benetvision.

Movement of Eros: 25 Years of Lesbian Erotic. Ed. by Heather Findlay. (Orig.). 1996. pap. 12.95 (*1-56333-421-6*, R Kasak Bks) Masquerade.

Movement of Materials Through. Abramoff. Date not set. 1.50 (*0-7167-9086-6*) W H Freeman.

Movement of Poets: Thoughts on Poetry & Feminism. Jan Clausen. 1982. pap. 3.25 (*0-9602284-1-1*) Long Haul.

Movement of the Free Spirit. Raoul Vaneigem. Tr. by Randall Cherry & Ian Patterson from FRE. LC 92-42232. 302p. 1994. 24.95 (*0-942299-70-1*) Zone Bks.

Movement of the Free Spirit. Raoul Vaneigem. 1998. pap. text 12.50 (*0-942299-71-X*) Zone Bks.

Movement of the People. Selwyn R. Cudjoe. 224p. (Orig.). 1983. text 18.95 (*0-686-39680-4*); pap. text 8.95 (*0-911565-22-1*) Calaloux Pubns.

Movement of Theology since the Council. Ed. by Edward Schillebeeckx. (Concilium Ser.: Vol. 170). 128p. (Orig.). 1983. 6.95 (*0-8164-2450-0*) Harper SF.

Movement of Thought: An Essay on Intellect in Seventeenth-Century France. Herbert De Ley. LC 84-16128. 184p. 1985. text 24.95 (*0-252-01165-1*) U of Ill Pr.

Movement of Underground Water in Contact with Natural Gas. Donald L. Katz et al. LC 63-13923. (Illus.). 333p. reprint ed. pap. 103.30 (*0-8357-8237-9*, 203396000087) Bks Demand.

Movement Patterns in a River Population of the Softshell Turtle, Trionyx Muticus. Michael V. Plummer & Hampton W. Shirer. (Occasional Papers: No. 43). 26p. 1975. pap. 1.00 (*0-686-80377-9*) U KS Nat Hist Mus.

Movement Plus Music: Activities for Children Ages 3 to 7. 2nd ed. Phyllis S. Weikart. LC 88-35798. (Illus.). 40p. (Orig.). (J). 1989. pap. text 10.95 (*0-931114-96-9*, M1005) High-Scope.

Movement Plus Rhymes, Songs & Singing Games: Activities for Children. 2nd rev. ed. Phyllis S. Weikart. (Movement Plus Ser.). (Illus.). 100p. (Orig.). (C). 1997. pap. 14.95 (*1-57379-053-2*, M1013) High-Scope.

Movement Science. Antoinette M. Gentile & Jean M. Held. 400p. 1998. text. write for info. (*0-397-55155-X*) Lppncott W & W.

Movement Science. Ed. by Winstein & Knecht. 256p. 1991. pap. 21.00 (*0-912452-78-1*, P-81) Am Phys Therapy Assn.

***Movement Science.** 2nd ed. Janet H. Carr & Shepherd. 2000. 55.00 (*0-8342-1747-3*) Aspen Pub.

Movement Skill Assessment. Allen W. Burton & Daryl E. Miller. LC 97-21938. (Illus.). 416p. 1997. text 35.00 (*0-87322-975-4*, BBUR0975) Human Kinetics.

Movement, Stability & Low Back Pain: The Essential Role of the Pelvis. Andry Vleeming. LC 97-20042. 1997. pap. text 115.00 (*0-443-05574-2*) Church.

Movement Stories for Children. Pamela Gerke. Ed. by Helen Gerke. LC 96-26754. (Young Actors Ser.). 96p. (J). (ps-1). 1996. pap. 19.95 (*1-57525-048-9*) Smith & Kraus.

Movement, Structure & the Work of Santiago Calatrava. Alexander Tzonis & Liane Lefaivre. (Illus.). 184p. 1995. 65.00 (*3-7643-5050-4*, Pub. by Birkhauser) Princeton Arch.

Movement That Fits. Joy Yelin. 142p. 1990. pap. text 19.95 (*0-87487-407-6*) Summy-Birchard.

Movement Therapy Across the Lifespan. Ed. by Andri Vermeer et al. 390p. 1998. pap. 47.50 (*90-5383-551-2*, Pub. by VU Univ Pr) Paul & Co Pubs.

Movement Through Depth. Brendan Tripp. 56p. 1990. pap. 5.00 (*1-57353-019-0*) Eschaton Prods.

Movement to Americanize the Immigrant. Edward G. Hartmann. LC 48-4245. (Columbia University. Studies in the Social Sciences: No. 545). reprint ed. 20.00 (*0-404-51545-2*) AMS Pr.

Movement to Music: Musicians in the Dance Studio, 20. Katherine Teck. LC 90-3141. (Contributions to the Study of Music & Dance Ser.: No. 20). 264p. 1990. 59.95 (*0-313-27288-3*, TMM, Greenwood Pr) Greenwood.

Movement to the Musica Poetica: Movement & Dance Instructions to Accompany the 10 Musica Poetica Recordings. Phyllis S. Weikart. 28p. 1981. pap. 2.50 (*0-918812-18-6*, SE 0754) MMB Music.

Movement Towards Subversion: The English History Play from Skelton to Shakespeare. Eric Sterling. LC 96-24716. 250p. 1996. pap. text 29.50 (*0-7618-0449-8*); lib. bdg. 49.00 (*0-7618-0448-X*) U Pr of Amer.

Movement Training for the Stage & Screen: The Organic Connection Between Mind, Spirit. Jean Sabatine. LC 95-13387. (Illus.). 256p. 1995. pap. text 18.95 (*0-8230-7712-8*, Back Stage Bks) Watsn-Guptill.

Movement with a Purpose: Perceptual Motor-Lesson Plans for Young Children. Madeleine Brehm & Nancy Tindell. LC 83-8023. 208p. (C). 1983. text 24.95 (*0-13-604629-0*) P-H.

Movements. Richard Rodriguez. 1999. pap. write for info. (*0-14-025352-1*, Viking) Viking Penguin.

Movements & Issues in World Religions: A Sourcebook & Analysis of Developments since 1945; Religion, Ideology, & Politics. Ed. by Charles W. Fu & Gerhard E. Spiegler. LC 86-4634. 576p. 1987. lib. bdg. 125.00 (*0-313-23238-5*, FUR/, Greenwood Pr) Greenwood.

Movements & Mimesis: The Idea of Dance in the Sanskritic Tradition. Mandakranta Bose. (Studies of Classical India). 352p. (C). 1991. lib. bdg. 180.50 (*0-7923-1325-9*, Pub. by Kluwer Academic) Kluwer Academic.

Movements, Currents, Trends: Aspects of European Thought in the 19th & 20th Centuries. Ed. by Eugen Weber. (Sources in Modern History Ser.). 619p. (C). 1992. pap. text 32.76 (*0-669-27881-5*) HM Trade Div.

Movements High Plains: Poetry by R. D. Becker. R. D. Becker. (Illus.). 122p. 1998. pap. 20.00 (*1-57502-737-2*, PO2052) Morris Pubng.

Movements in Art since 1945: Issues & Concepts. 3rd rev. ed. Edward Lucie-Smith. LC 94-61061. (World of Art Ser.). (Illus.). 304p. 1995. pap. 14.95 (*0-500-20282-6*, Pub. by Thames Hudson) Norton.

Movements in Chicano Poetry: Against Myths, Against Margins. Rafael Perez-Torres. (Studies in American Literature & Culture: No. 88). 348p. (C). 1995. pap. text 21.95 (*0-521-47803-0*) Cambridge U Pr.

Movements in European History. D. H. Lawrence. Ed. by Philip Crumpton. (Cambridge Edition of the Works of D. H. Lawrence). (Illus.). 400p. (C). 1990. text 95.00 (*0-521-26201-1*) Cambridge U Pr.

Movements of Magic: The Spirit of Tai Chi Chivan. Bob Klein. 163p. 1984. pap. 12.95 (*0-87877-072-0*) Newcastle Pub.

Movements of Political Protest in Canada, 1640-1840. Samuel D. Clark. LC 60-29. (Social Credit in Alberta Ser.: 9). 528p. reprint ed. pap. 163.70 (*0-608-13755-3*, 202651900050) Bks Demand.

Movements of Power Ancient Sector. Bob Klein. 1990. pap. 12.95 (*0-87877-152-2*) Newcastle Pub.

Movements of Sediments in Open Channels. Yu A. Ibad-Zade. 1987. 27.50 (*81-204-0168-9*, Pub. by Oxford IBH) S Asia.

Movements of the British Iron & Steel Industry, 1720 to 1951, Volume 36. Howard G. Roepke. LC 80-23128. (Illinois Studies in the Social Sciences: Vol. 36). (Illus.). 198p. 1981. reprint ed. lib. bdg. 59.50 (*0-8371-9096-7*, ROMB, Greenwood Pr) Greenwood.

Movemt of Substances in & out. Evert. 1998. 1.50 (*0-7167-9353-9*) W H Freeman.

Mover of Men & Mountains. R. G. LeTourneau. mass mkt. 6.99 (*0-8024-3818-0*, 222) Moody.

Movers see Motores

Movers. Dale McCreedy. (National Science Partnership for Girl Scouts & Science Museums Ser.). (Illus.). 38p. (Orig.). 1995. pap. 8.00 (*0-9625622-1-1*) Franklin PA.

Movers: A Saga of the Scotch-Irish. Nancy N. Baxter. LC 86-22859. (Heartland Chronicles Ser.). (Illus.). 515p. 1986. pap. 14.95 (*0-9617367-1-2*) Guild Pr IN.

Movers & Shakers: Deaf People Who Changed the World. Cathryn Carroll & Susan M. Mather. 144p. 1998. pap. text, teacher ed. 14.95 (*0-915035-65-0*) Dawn Sign.

Movers & Shakers: Deaf People Who Changed the World Storybook. Cathryn Carroll & Susan Mozzer-Mather. LC 97-1408. 160p. 1997. 19.95 (*0-915035-64-2*, 9462B) Dawn Sign.

Movers & Shakers: Men Who Have Shaped Saint Louis. Justin L. Faherty et al. Ed. by Verna G. Smith & Guin T. Stemmler. (Illus.). 224p. (Orig.). 1992. pap. 9.95 (*0-935284-96-6*) Patrice Pr.

Movers & Shapers Sarah Angliss. LC 99-10283. (Human Machine Ser.). (Illus.). (J). 1999. lib. bdg. write for info. (*0-382-42177-9*, New Dscvry Bks) Silver Burdett Pr.

***Movers & Shapers: Muscle & Bones.** Sarah Angliss. (Human Machine Ser.). (Illus.). 32p. (J). 1999. lib. bdg. 15.95 (*1-929298-18-8*, Pub. by Thameside Pr) Smart Apple.

Movers & the Shirkers: Representatives & Ideologues in the Senate. Eric M. Uslaner. LC 98-40236. 248p. 1999. text 44.50 (*0-472-10943-X*, 10943) U of Mich Pr.

Movers of Mountains. Elaine M. Ward. 88p. (Orig.). (YA). (gr. 7-12). 1984. pap. 12.95 (*0-940754-24-X*, 8196) Ed Ministries.

Movers, Shakers, & Changemakers. John Dolan. 336p. 1994. per., boxed set 32.95 (*0-8403-9422-5*) Kendall-Hunt.

Moves. Douglas C. Horn. (Orig.). (J). (gr. 3-6). 1995. pap. 9.99 (*0-88092-150-1*) Royal Fireworks.

Moves: A Sourcebook of Ideas for Body Awareness & Creative Movement. Katya Bloom & Rosa Shreeves. (Performing Arts Studies). (Illus.). 136p. 1998. text 25.00 (*90-5702-132-3*, Harwood Acad Pubs); pap. text 23.00 (*90-5702-133-1*, Harwood Acad Pubs) Gordon & Breach.

Moves & Grooves. Elliot Fine. 1996. 14.95 (*0-8497-5503-4*, WD200) Kjos.

Moves from Arm to Arm. E. Waverly Land. Ed. by Ronald H. Bayes. 76p. (Orig.). 1993. pap. 8.95 (*1-879934-07-8*) St Andrews NC.

Moves Make the Man. Bruce Brooks. LC 83-49476. 208p. (YA). (gr. 7-12). 1984. lib. bdg. 15.89 (*0-06-020698-5*) HarpC Child Bks.

Moves Make the Man. Bruce Brooks. LC 83-49476. 320p. (YA). (gr. 7 up). 1984. 15.00 (*0-06-020679-9*) HarpC Child Bks.

Moves Make the Man. Bruce Brooks. LC 83-49476. 256p. (J). (gr. 7-12). 1987. mass mkt. 5.95 (*0-06-447022-9*, HarpTrophy) HarpC Child Bks.

Moves Make the Man. Bruce Brooks. LC 83-49476. (Trophy Bk.). 288p. (YA). (gr. 12 up). 1996. pap. 5.95 (*0-06-440564-8*, HarpTrophy) HarpC Child Bks.

Moves Make the Man. Bruce Brooks. 1987. 10.05 (*0-606-09638-8*, Pub. by Turtleback) Demco.

Moves Make the Man. Bruce Brooks. 1987. 10.30 (*0-606-07894-0*) Turtleback.

***Moves Writers Make.** 1999. teacher ed. write for info. (*0-13-999343-6*) P-H.

Moves Writers Make. 2nd ed. Raymond. 320p. (C). 1998. pap. text 21.70 (*0-536-01270-9*) Pearson Custom.

Movie. Parnell Hall. 288p. 1996. mass mkt. 5.99 (*0-446-40395-4*, Pub. by Warner Bks) Little.

Movie. Don Olson. 1990. pap. 8.95 (*0-8216-2008-8*, Univ Books) Carol Pub Group.

Movie. rev. ed. Ed. by Carol Cuellar. (Showstoppers Ser.). 280p. (Orig.). 1995. pap. text 18.95 (*0-89724-551-2*, F2866SMD) Wrner Bros.

Movie - Made America: A Cultural History of American Movies. rev. ed. Robert Sklar. (Illus.). 416p. 1994. pap. 20.00 (*0-679-75549-7*) Vin Bks.

Movie-A-Day. Nal-Dutton Staff. 736p. 1999. 10.95 (*0-525-94503-2*) NAL.

***Movie & Television Locations: 113 Famous Filming Sites in Los Angeles & San Diego.** Leon Smith. LC 99-54727. (Illus.). 295p. 2000. lib. bdg. 38.50 (*0-7864-0605-4*) McFarland & Co.

***Movie & TV Themes: Play-Aong Solos.** 20p. 1999. pap. 10.95 incl. audio compact disk (*0-634-00458-1*) H Leonard.

Movie Anecdotes. Peter Hay. 336p. 1991. reprint ed. pap. 8.95 (*0-19-504595-5*) OUP.

Movie at the End of the World: Collected Poems. Thomas McGrath. LC 72-91918. 188p. 1972. reprint ed. pap. text 14.95 (*0-8040-0606-7*) Swallow.

Movie Ballads. 160p. 1997. otabind 14.95 (*0-7935-7925-2*) H Leonard.

Movie "Barfly" An Orginal Screenplay. Charles Bukowski. LC 87-18237. (Illus.). 180p. (C). 1998. reprint ed. 25.00 (*0-87685-708-X*); reprint ed. pap. 14.00 (*0-87685-707-1*) Black Sparrow.

***Movie Blockbusters.** 32p. 1998. pap. 7.95 (*0-7935-9300-X*) H Leonard.

Movie Book. Phaidon Press Staff. (Illus.). 512p. 1999. 39.95 (*0-7148-3847-0*) Phaidon Pr.

Movie Buff Checklist: Male Nudity in the Movies. 4th rev. ed. Marvin Jones. (Illus.). 252p. 1993. pap. 19.95 (*0-9623725-2-8*) Campfire Video.

Movie Buff Checklist: Male Nudity in the Movies. 5th ed. Marvin Jones. 1997. pap. 19.95 (*1-888211-04-0*) Campfire Video.

Movie Business. Laurence Snelling. 260p. 1996. 19.95 (*1-885642-04-0*) Kingston NY.

Movie Business Book. Jason E. Squire. LC 82-16126. (Illus.). 414p. 1983. pap. 14.95 (*0-13-604595-2*) P-H.

Movie Business Book. 2nd ed. Ed. by Jason E. Squire. LC 92-20211. 432p. 1992. per. 14.00 (*0-671-75095-X*) S&S Trade Pap.

Movie Cat. Garrison Allen. LC 98-67618. 304p. 1999. text 20.00 (*1-57566-413-5*) Kensgtn Pub Corp.

Movie Censorship & American Culture. Ed. by Francis G. Couvares. (Studies in the History of Film & Television). (Illus.). 256p. 1996. text 45.00 (*1-56098-668-9*); pap. text 17.95 (*1-56098-669-7*) Smithsonian.

Movie Classics. (E-Z Play Today Ser.: Bk. 293). 96p. 1991. otabind 8.95 (*0-7935-8490-6*) H Leonard.

Movie Classics. Ed. by Carol Cuellar. (World's Greatest Music Ser.). 240p. (YA). 1996. pap. text 16.95 (*1-57623-680-3*, MF9645) Wrner Bros.

Movie Classics: Anatomy of a Murder. Robert Traver. 2000. 9.99 (*0-517-20445-2*) Random Hse Value.

***Movie Classics for Piano.** 104p. 1998. otabind 12.95 (*0-7935-9510-X*) H Leonard.

Movie Connection: Piano. 79p. 1996. pap. 10.95 (*1-57623-583-1*, AF9671) Wrner Bros.

Movie Cookbook. Rex Havick. 1998. pap. text 16.95 (*0-9648684-2-3*) InfoPlus.

Movie Critic's Journal. Christy Lamson. (Orig.). 1993. pap. 8.95 (*0-9638778-0-1*) Lamson Ent.

Movie Duets: Intermediate Piano Duets 1 Piano, 4 Hands. 64p. 1995. pap. 8.95 (*0-7935-3993-5*, 00292078) H Leonard.

Movie Extras Guidebook: How to Make Good Money As a Background Actor. rev. ed. Cullen G. Chambers. (Illus.). 320p. 1996. pap. 19.95 (*0-9624577-2-8*) C G Chambers.

Movie Extras Guidebook: How to Make Good Money As a Hollywood Extra. 8th ed. Cullen Chambers. 1997. pap. text 19.95 (*0-9624577-5-2*) C G Chambers.

Movie Fake Book. 2nd ed. Leonard, Hal, Corporation Staff. 352p. 1995. spiral bd. 29.95 (*0-7935-8244-X*, HL00240033) H Leonard.

Movie Favorites: Big Note for Piano. 80p. 1994. pap. 9.95 (*0-7935-3823-8*, 00221826) H Leonard.

Movie Favorites: Trumpet. 1987. pap. 10.95 incl. audio (*0-7935-2781-3*, 00845504) H Leonard.

Movie Favorites for Easy Piano. (Easy Play Ser.). 96p. 1992. otabind 8.95 (*0-7935-1510-6*, 00222551) H Leonard.

Movie Favorites for Piano Solo. 80p. 1992. pap. 9.95 (*0-7935-1511-4*, 00221011) H Leonard.

Movie Game: The Film Business in Britain, Europe & America. Martin Dale. (Film Studies). (Illus.). 416p. 1997. 70.00 (*0-304-33386-7*); pap. 19.95 (*0-304-33387-5*) Continuum.

Movie Greats. 64p. 1995. pap. 10.95 (*0-7935-3899-8*, 00294004) H Leonard.

Movie Greats Barry Norman. LC 81-148525. 319 P. :p. 1981. write for info. (*0-340-25972-8*, Pub. by Hodder & Stought Ltd) Trafalgar.

Movie Guide. James Monaco & Baseline Editors. 1152p. (Orig.). 1995. pap. 25.00 (*0-399-51914-9*, Perigee Bks) Berkley Pub.

Movie Guide: The Most Comprehensive Film Reference of Its Kind. Cinebooks Editors. LC 97-38975. 832p. 1998. pap. 24.95 (*0-399-52393-6*, Perigee Bks) Berkley Pub.

Movie Hits. 96p. 1993. otabind 9.95 (*0-7935-2310-9*, 00221804) H Leonard.

Movie Hits. 64p. 1997. pap. 9.95 (*0-7935-7911-2*) H Leonard.

Movie Hits for 5 Finger Piano. 32p. 1996. pap. 6.95 (*0-7935-6684-3*) H Leonard.

Movie Hits (Import England) 40p. 1987. pap. 8.95 (*0-7692-1176-3*, PF0531) Wrner Bros.

Movie Hooky. Dan Foster. LC 91-72539. 130p. (Orig.). 1992. pap. 9.95 (*1-879603-04-7*) Los Hombres.

Movie Industry Book: Protect Yourself Before You Lose Your Rights & Royalties, Part II. Walter E. Hurst. Ed. by Donato Rico & Annette Kargodorian. (Entertainment Industry Ser.: Vol. 23). (Illus.). 112p. (Orig.). 1982. 20.00 (*0-911370-56-0*) Seven Arts.

Movie Industry Book: Protect Yourself Before You Lose Your Rights & Royalties, Pt. II. Walter E. Hurst. Ed. by Donato Rico & Annette Kargodorian. (Entertainment Industry Ser.: Vol. 23). (Illus.). 112p. (Orig.). 1982. pap. 10.00 (*0-911370-55-2*) Seven Arts.

Movie List. 1997. pap. 24.95 (*0-933997-26-4*) CineBks.

Movie List Book: A Reference Guide to Film Themes, Settings & Series. Richard B. Armstrong & Mary W. Armstrong. LC 89-43692. 400p. 1990. lib. bdg. 36.50 (*0-89950-240-7*) McFarland & Co.

Movie Lot to Beachhead: The Motion Picture Goes to War & Prepares for the Future. Ed. by Look Magazine Staff. LC 79-6696. 1980. reprint ed. lib. bdg. 22.95 (*0-405-12935-1*) Ayer.

***Movie Love Songs Piano Solo.** 64p. 1998. pap. 9.95 (*0-7935-9271-2*) H Leonard.

Movie Lover's Diary. Ed. by Shelagh Wallace. (Illus.). 144p. 1997. 14.95 (*1-55209-148-1*) Firefly Bks Ltd.

Movie-Made America: A Cultural History of American Movies. Robert Sklar. 1976. pap. 18.00 (*0-394-72120-9*) Vin Bks.

Movie Magic. 1997. disk 34.95 (*0-7935-7097-2*) H Leonard.

***Movie Magic.** Anne Cottringer. LC 98-53325. (Eyewitness Readers). 48p. (J). (gr. 2-3). 1999. 12.95 (*0-7894-4009-1*); pap. 3.95 (*0-7894-4008-3*) DK Pub Inc.

Movie Magic: A Behind-the-Scenes Look at Filmmaking. Robin Cross. (Illus.). 64p. (J). 1996. pap. 10.95 (*0-8069-1365-7*) Sterling.

Movie Magic: Behind the Scenes with Special Effects. Elaine Scott. LC 95-2166. (Illus.). 96p. (YA). (gr. 4-7). 1995. 16.00 (*0-688-12477-1*, Wm Morrow) Morrow Avon.

Movie Magic of the 90's. 96p. (Orig.). (YA). 1995. pap. 14.95 (*0-89724-582-2*, MF9512) Wrner Bros.

Movie Making in the New Hollywood. Thomas G. Schatz. Date not set. write for info. (*0-8050-4447-7*); pap. write for info. (*0-8050-4448-5*) H Holt & Co.

Movie Marketing: Opening the Picture & Giving It Legs. Tiiu Lukk. LC 97-31744. xxiv, 274p. (Orig.). 1998. pap. 19.95 (*1-879505-38-X*) Silman James Pr.

Movie Mom's Guide to Family Movies. Nell Morrow. 1997. pap. 12.00 (*0-614-28117-2*, Avon Bks) Morrow Avon.

Movie Mom's [tm] Guide to Family Movies. Nell Minow. LC 99-14406. 720p. 1999. pap. 15.00 (*0-380-78839-X*, Avon Bks) Morrow Avon.

Movie Money: Understanding Hollywood's (Creative) Accounting Practices. Bill Daniels. LC 98-18122. 300p. 1998. pap. 29.95 (*1-879505-33-9*) Silman James Pr.

Movie Monsters. Thomas G. Aylesworth. LC 75-12997. (Illus.). 80p. (J). (gr. 4-7). 1975. 12.95 (*0-397-31639-9*) HarpC Child Bks.

M

Movie Monsters. Thomas G. Aylesworth. LC 75-12997. (Eerie Ser.). (Illus.). 80p. (J). (gr. 4-8). 1990. lib. bdg. 12.89 (0-397-32467-7) HarpC Child Bks.

***Movie Munchies Leader Manual: Grades 1-6.** (Holyword Studios VBS Ser.). 2000. pap., teacher ed. 9.99 (0-7644-2180-8) Group Pub.

Movie Music. 72p. 1997. pap. 9.95 (0-7935-7910-4) H Leonard.

Movie Music. Leonard, Hal, Corporation Staff. 256p. 1998. per. 6.95 (0-7935-8870-7) H Leonard.

Movie Music: Simplified for Piano. Ed. by Tony Esposito. 96p. (Orig.). 1997. pap. text 12.95 (0-7692-0055-9) Wrner Bros.

Movie Music for BN Bradley. 79p. 1997. pap. 10.95 (1-57623-903-9, BP3369A) Wrner Bros.

Movie Musical Magic: Big Note for Piano. 72p. 1994. pap. 9.95 (0-7935-3822-X, 00221825) H Leonard.

Movie Musical Memories, Vol. 143. 80p. 1995. pap. 10.95 (0-7935-4025-9, 00100003) H Leonard.

Movie Musicals on Record: A Directory of Recordings of Motion Picture Musicals, 1927-1987, 32. Compiled by Richard C. Lynch. LC 89-2137. (Discographies Ser.: No. 32). 455p. 1989. lib. bdg. 59.95 (0-313-26540-2, LMV/, Greenwood Pr) Greenwood.

Movie of the Week: Private Stories - Public Events. Elayne Rapping. (American Culture Ser.: Vol. 5). 208p. (C). 1992. pap. 16.95 (0-8166-2018-0); text 42.95 (0-8166-2017-2) U of Minn Pr.

M

Movie Palace Masterpiece: Saving Syracuse's Loew's State/Landmark Theater. Alfred Balk. 80p. 1999. 24.95 (0-8156-8123-2) Syracuse U Pr.

***Movie Palaces.** Lucinda I. Smith. (Architecture & Film Ser.: Vol. 1). (Illus.). 128p. 2000. reprint ed. 29.95 (0-940512-25-4) Hennessey.

Movie Piano Solos. 80p. 1994. pap. 9.95 (0-7935-3335-X, 00311675) H Leonard.

Movie Piano Solos for Kids: Popular Five Finger Arrangements by Pamela & Robert Schultz. Ed. by Robert Schultz. 64p. (Orig.). (YA). 1995. pap. text 8.95 (0-89724-509-1, AF9505) Wrner Bros.

***Movie Poster Design: Film Graphics.** Mike Salisbury. 1999. 39.95 (2-88046-357-2) Watsn-Guptill.

***Movie Poster Price Almanac Vol. 14: Editon 2000.** rev. unabridged ed. Ed. by John Kisch. 1000p. 2000. 49.95 (0-9661482-2-3) Separate Cinema.

Movie Poster Price Almanac 1999. annuals 13th ed. John Kisch. (Illus.). 700p. 1999. lib. bdg. 39.95 (0-9661482-1-5) Separate Cinema.

Movie Posters of the Silent Film Era. Rex Schneider & Christopher Buchman. (International Design Library). (Illus.). 48p. (Orig.). 1981. pap. 5.95 (0-916144-61-5) Stemmer Hse.

Movie Production & Budget Forms . . . Instantly! Ralph S. Singleton. (Ralph S. Singleton Filmmaker's Library: No. 4). 136p. (Orig.). (C). 1985. pap. 19.95 (0-943728-14-2) Lone Eagle Pub.

Movie Psychos & Madmen: Ninety Years of Mad Movies, Maniacs, & Murderous Deeds. John McCarty. LC 92-37552. (Illus.). Date not set. pap. 16.95 (0-8065-1392-6, Citadel Pr) Carol Pub Group.

Movie Queen. Farnham Blair. Ed. by Constance Hunting. 60p. 1996. pap. 8.95 (0-913006-62-9) Puckerbrush.

Movie Quote Each Day. 1998. pap. 10.95 (1-57897-086-5) Language Calendars.

Movie Record Breakers. David Barraclough. 1992. 12.98 (1-55521-771-0) Bk Sales Inc.

Movie Scrapbook. Tommi Lewis. (Prince of Egypt Ser.). (J). 1998. pap. 8.99 (0-8499-5900-4) Tommy Nelson.

Movie Songs of the 80's. CPP Belwin Staff. 1993. pap. 12.95 (0-89898-686-9, F3317SMX) Wrner Bros.

Movie Songs of the 90's. Ed. by Carol Cuellar. 148p. (YA). 1993. pap. 12.95 (0-89898-687-7, F3165SMX) Wrner Bros.

Movie Songs of the 70's. Warner Bros. Staff. 1993. pap. 12.95 (0-89898-685-0, F3322SMX) Wrner Bros.

Movie Songs of the 90's. 128p. (YA). 1991. pap. 12.95 (0-7692-1464-9, F3165SMX) Wrner Bros.

Movie Songs of the 90's, Vol. 2. 148p. (YA). 1993. pap. 12.95 (0-7692-1465-7, F3318SMX) Wrner Bros.

Movie Star Angel. Suzanne Weyn. (Forever Angels Ser.). 160p. (J). (gr. 3-7). 1998. pap. 3.50 (0-8167-4448-3) Troll Communs.

Movie Star Confidential - The Super Adventures of Harry Chess Comics. A. Jay & Mike. (Illus.). 96p. (Orig.). 1989. pap. 10.95 (0-943595-16-9) Leyland Pubns.

***Movie Star Mystery.** Created by Gertrude Chandler Warner. LC 98-54785. (Boxcar Children Ser.: No. 69). (Illus.). 128p. (J). (gr. 2-5). 1999. pap. 3.95 (0-8075-5304-2); lib. bdg. 13.95 (0-8075-5303-4) A Whitman.

***Movie Star Mystery.** Gertrude Chandler Warner. (Boxcar Children Ser.: Vol. 69). (J). 1999. 9.30 (0-606-18762-6) Turtleback.

***Movie Star Pony.** Jeanne Betancourt. (Pony Pals Ser.: No. 26). (Illus.). 96p. (J). (gr. 2-5). 2000. pap. 3.99 (0-439-06492-9) Scholastic Inc.

Movie-Star Portraits of the Forties: 163 Glamour Photos. Ed. by John Kobal. LC 77-80118. (Illus.). 176p. 1977. pap. 12.95 (0-486-23546-7) Dover.

Movie Starring the Late Cary Grant & an As-Yet Unsigned Actress. deluxe ed. Tom Ahern. (Treacle Story Ser.: No. 1). (Illus.). 32p. 1976. 12.50 (0-914232-07-X) McPherson & Co.

***Movie Stars Do the Dumbest Things.** Margaret Moser et al. LC 99-36450. 304p. 1999. pap. 14.95 (1-58063-107-X) Renaissance.

Movie Talk from the Front Lines: Filmmakers Discuss Their Works with the Los Angeles Film Critics Association. Ed. by Jerry Roberts & Steven Gaydos. LC 94-29998. (Illus.). 311p. 1995. lib. bdg. 39.95 (0-7864-0005-6) McFarland & Co.

Movie Themes: Piano/4H. 48p. (Orig.). 1989. pap. 8.95 (0-7692-1118-6, PF0665) Wrner Bros.

Movie Themes for Easy Guitar. 64p. 1997. pap. 10.95 (0-7935-7357-2) H Leonard.

Movie Tie-In Book: A Collector's Guide to Paperback Movie Editions. Moe Wadle. (Illus.). 140p. (Orig.). 1995. pap. 12.50 (0-9637978-0-8) Nostalgia Bks.

Movie Time: A Chronology of Hollywood & the Movie Industry from Its Beginnings to the Present. Gene Brown. LC 95-9091. (Illus.). 448p. 1995. 19.95 (0-02-860429-6, Pub. by Macmillan) S&S Trade.

***Movie Traveller: A Film Fan's Travel Guide to the UK & Ireland.** Allan Foster. 336p. 2000. pap. text 22.95 (0-7486-6249-9) Col U Pr.

***Movie Treasures of the '40s And '50s.** Gynnath Ford. (Illus.). 128p. 2000. 14.95 (0-9676496-4-1) Highlands Pub.

***Movie Wars: How Hollywood & the Media Conspire to Limit What Films We Can See.** Jonathan Rosenbaum. 256p. 2000. 24.00 (1-55652-406-4, Pub. by A Cappella Bks) IPG Chicago.

Movie World Almanac, 2001-2002. Ed. by D. Richard Baer. (Illus.). 360p. 2000. lib. bdg. 75.00 (0-913616-06-0) Hollywd Film Arch.

Movie World Underworld. Norton. 1995. write for info. (0-393-08793-X) Norton.

***Movie Worlds: Production Design in Film.** Heidi Ludi & Tony Ludi. (ENG & GER., Illus.). 128p. 2000. 62.00 (3-932565-13-4) Edition A Menges.

Moviegoer. Walker Percy. LC 96-96687. 1996. pap. 12.00 (0-449-91170-5) Fawcett.

Moviegoer. Walker Percy. 1961. 26.00 (0-394-43703-9) Knopf.

Moviegoer. Walker Percy. 242p. 1998. pap. 12.00 (0-375-70196-6) Vin Bks.

Movieland: Hollywood & the Great American Dream Culture. Jerome Charyn. LC 96-22128. (Illus.). 304p. (C). 1996. pap. text 18.50 (0-8147-1550-8) NYU Pr.

Moviemakers. Mark Dunster. (Rin Ser.: Pt. 16). 49p. (Orig.). 1982. pap. 4.00 (0-89642-089-2) Linden Pubs.

***Movies.** Gilbert Adair. 2000. pap. 14.95 (0-14-118084-6) Viking Penguin.

Movies. Bill Balcziak. (Communication Today & Tomorrow Ser.). (Illus.). 48p. (J). (gr. 4-8). 1989. lib. bdg. 25.27 (0-86592-058-3) Rourke Enter.

Movies. George Coulter & Shirley Coulter. LC 96-11643. (You Make It Work Ser.). (Illus.). 32p. (J). (gr. 3-6). 1996. lib. bdg. 17.27 (0-86625-586-9) Rourke Pubns.

Movies. Diana Gleasner. (Inventions That Changed Our Lives Ser.). (Illus.). (J). (gr. 4-6). 1983. lib. bdg. 8.85 (0-8027-6483-5) Walker & Co.

Movies. Tim Merrison. Ed. by Rebecca Stefoff. LC 90-3964. (Media Story Ser.). (Illus.). 32p. (J). (gr. 4-8). 1991. lib. bdg. 17.26 (0-944483-94-1) Garrett Ed Corp.

Movies. MQ Publications Staff. (Infatuations Ser.). 1998. 12.95 (1-897954-63-8, Pub. by Mus Quilts Pub) Sterling.

Movies. Chris Oxlade & Julian Rowe. LC 96-27563. (Science Encounters Ser.). (J). 1998. 19.92 (1-57572-088-4) Heinemann Lib.

Movies: A Crash Course. John Naughton. (Illus.). 144p. 1998. 14.95 (0-8230-0977-7) Watsn-Guptill.

Movies: A Short History. Gerald Mast. 688p. 1996. pap. text 28.00 (0-205-19670-5) P-H.

Movies: Texts, Receptions, Exposures. Ed. by Laurence Goldstein & Ira Konigsberg. LC 96-31169. 368p. (Orig.). 1996. pap. 16.95 (0-472-06640-4, 06640); text 42.50 (0-472-09640-0, 09640) U of Mich Pr.

Movies: The World on Film. Deborah Hitzeroth & Sharon Heerboth. LC 91-16712. (Encyclopedia of Discovery & Invention Ser.). (Illus.). 96p. (J). (gr. 5-8). 1991. lib. bdg. 23.70 (1-56006-210-X) Lucent Bks.

Movies about the Movies: Hollywood Reflected. Christopher Ames. LC 96-52946. (Illus.). 256p. 1997. 32.50 (0-8131-2018-7) U Pr of Ky.

Movies about the Movies: Hollywood Reflected. Christopher Ames. (Illus.). 264p. (C). 1998. pap. 17.00 (0-8131-0938-8) U Pr of Ky.

Movies & Conduct. Herbert Blumer. LC 76-124023. (Literature of Cinema Ser.: Payne Fund Studies of Motion Pictures & Social Values). 1970. reprint ed. 19.95 (0-405-01640-9) Ayer.

Movies & Mass Culture. John Belton. LC 95-12438. (Depth of Field Ser.). (Illus.). 300p. (C). 1995. text 48.00 (0-8135-2227-7); pap. text 18.00 (0-8135-2228-5) Rutgers U Pr.

***Movies & Meaning.** 2nd ed. (C). 2000. text. write for info. (0-205-32652-8) Allyn.

Movies & Meaning: An Introduction to Film. Stephen R. Prince. LC 95-43380. 397p. 1996. pap. text 51.00 (0-02-396806-0, Macmillan Coll) P-H.

Movies & Meaning: An Introduction to Film. 2nd ed. Rice. 432p. (C). 2000. pap. 36.75 (0-205-31415-5) Allyn.

Movies & Mental Illness. Wedding. LC 98-38002. 272p. 1998. pap. 21.88 (0-07-068990-3) McGraw.

Movies & Methods, Vol. I. Ed. by Bill Nichols. LC 74-22968. 1977. pap. 22.50 (0-520-03151-2, Pub. by U CA Pr) Cal Prin Full Svc.

Movies & Methods, Vol. II. Ed. by Bill Nichols. LC 74-22969. 1985. pap. 22.50 (0-520-05409-1, Pub. by U CA Pr) Cal Prin Full Svc.

Movies & Money: Financing the American Film Industry. Janet Wasko. LC 81-17610. (Communication & Information Science Ser.). 320p. 1982. pap. 39.50 (0-89391-131-3); text 78.50 (0-89391-108-9) Ablx Pub.

Movies & Money: Undeclared War Between Europe & America. David Puttnam. LC 97-31244. 1998. 27.50 (0-679-44664-8) McKay.

Movies & Politics: The Dynamic Relationship. Ed. by James Combs. LC 92-23456. (Illus.). 320p. 1993. text 25.00 (0-8153-0043-3) Garland.

Movies As Artifacts. Michael T. Marsden et al. LC 82-6300. 288p. (C). 1982. text 36.95 (0-88229-453-9) Burnham Inc.

***Movies as History.** Ed. by David Ellwood. (Illus.). 224p. 2000. pap. 24.95 (0-7509-2331-8) Sutton Publng.

Movies As Mass Communication. Garth Jowett & James M. Linton. LC 80-13508. (Sage Commtext Ser.: No. 4). (Illus.). 149p. 1980. reprint ed. pap. 46.20 (0-8357-4811-1, 203774800009) Bks Demand.

Movies As Mass Communication. 2nd ed. Garth Jowett & James M. Linton. (CommText Ser.: Vol. 4). 169p. (C). 1989. text 42.00 (0-8039-3328-2); pap. text 18.95 (0-8039-3329-0) Sage.

Movies As Mass Communication. 2nd ed. Garth Jowett & James M. Linton. LC 89-35235. (Sage Commtext Ser.: No. 4). (Illus.). 160p. 1989. reprint ed. pap. 49.60 (0-7837-9904-7, 206063000006) Bks Demand.

Movies as Politics. Jonathan Rosenbaum. LC 96-9916. 350p. 1997. pap. 18.95 (0-520-20615-0, Pub. by U CA Pr) Cal Prin Full Svc.

Movies As Social Criticism: Aspects of Their Social Psychology. I. C. Jarvie. LC 77-26778. 1978. 32.00 (0-8108-1106-5) Scarecrow.

Movies at Home: How Hollywood Came to Television. Kerry Segrave. LC 99-24239. (Illus.). 263p. 1999. lib. bdg. 38.50 (0-7864-0654-2) McFarland & Co.

Movies Begin: Making Movies in New Jersey, 1887-1920. Paul C. Spehr. Ed. by Marjorie W. Fredricks. LC 77-73649. 1977. 13.95 (0-932828-07-8) Newark Mus.

Movies Blaster. Leo Ewing. (Nutshell Ser.). 80p. 1995. pap. 5.49 (1-885962-64-9) Lincoln Lrning.

Movies Come from America. Gilbert V. Seldes. Ed. by Garth S. Jowett. LC 77-11384. (Aspects of Film Ser.). 1978. reprint ed. lib. bdg. 29.95 (0-405-11144-4) Ayer.

Movies, Delinquency & Crime. Herbert Blumer & Philip M. Hauser. LC 70-124024. (Literature of Cinema Ser.: Payne Fund Studies of Motion Pictures & Social Values). 1977. reprint ed. 18.95 (0-405-01641-7) Ayer.

Movies Go to College: Hollywood & the World of the College-Life Film. Wiley L. Umphlett. LC 81-72048. (Illus.). 240p. 1984. 32.50 (0-8386-3133-9) Fairleigh Dickinson.

Movies Grow up, 1940-1980. rev. ed. Charles Champlin. LC 80-29388. (Illus.). 296p. 1981. reprint ed. pap. 16.95 (0-8040-0364-5) Swallow.

Movies in a Small Town: Poems. W. E. Butts. LC 96-45641. 68p. 1997. pap. 14.95 (0-7734-2705-8, Mellen Poetry Pr) E Mellen.

Movies in Our Midst: Documents in the Cultural History of Films in America. Ed. by Gerald Mast. LC 81-16223. (Illus.). (C). 1983. pap. text 17.95 (0-226-50981-8) U Ch Pr.

Movies in Rockland County: Adolf Zukor & the Silent Era. Ralph Sessions. 1982. pap. 4.00 (0-911183-08-6) Rockland County Hist.

Movies in Society. Mark Koenigil. 1962. 8.95 (0-8315-0000-X) Speller.

Movies in the Age of Innocence. Edward Wagenknecht. LC 97-17182. (Illus.). 348p. 1997. reprint ed. pap. 16.95 (0-87910-098-2) Limelight Edns.

Movies in the Mind: How to Build a Short Story. Colleen M. Rae. 142p. (Orig.). 1996. pap. 14.95 (0-9644196-5-3) Sherman Asher Pub.

Movies, Me, & Us. Edward Perry. LC 99-19624. 1996. 22.95 (0-8050-4917-7) H Holt & Co.

Movies on Trial: The Views & Opinions of Outstanding Personalities Anent Screen Entertainment Past & Present. Ed. by William J. Perlman. LC 78-160245. (Moving Pictures Ser.). xi, 254p. 1971. reprint ed. lib. bdg. 31.95 (0-89198-046-6) Ozer.

Movies Songs & Themes. Ed. by Carol Cuellar. (Warner Brothers Presents Ser.). 328p. 1995. pap. text 18.95 (0-89724-593-8, MF9508A) Wrner Bros.

Movies That Inspire: A Discussion Guide for Families & Groups. Al Quinn. 112p. 1994. 9.95 (0-89944-318-4) Salesiana Pubs.

Movies to Manage By. John K. Clemens & Melora Wolff. LC 99-26801. 240p. 1999. 22.95 (0-8092-2798-3, 279830, Contemporary Bks) NTC Contemp Pub Co.

***Movies to Manage By: Lessons in Leadership from Great Films.** 2000. pap. 14.95 (0-8092-2796-7, Contemporary Bks) NTC Contemp Pub Co.

Movies Unlimited Video Catalog, 1999 Edition. 21st rev. ed. Joseph McLaughlin et al. (Illus.). 750p. 1998. pap. 8.95 (0-9666332-0-2) Movies.

***Movies:Format & Content.** Richard Barsam. 1999. pap. 19.95 (0-393-97436-7) Norton.

Movilizacion del Ahorro: (Spanish - Savings Mobilization) WCCU (World Council of Credit Unions, Inc.) Staff. 160p. (C). 1990. pap. text, per. 10.00 (0-8403-5835-0) Kendall-Hunt.

Movilizacion del Ahorro Technical Systems Package. WCCU (World Council of Credit Unions, Inc.) Staff. (C). 1990. pap. text 60.00 (0-8403-6128-9) Kendall-Hunt.

Moville. Frank Ward. (Illus.). 32p. (J). (ps). 1999. 11.95 (0-9667475-0-X) Renaissance-Atlantic.

Movimiento Anexionista en Puerto Rico. Edgardo Melendez. 1993. pap. 16.95 (0-8477-0186-7) U of PR Pr.

Movimiento de la Fe. John Ankerberg & John Weldon. (Hechos Acerca de...Ser.).Tr. of Faith Movement. (SPA.). 69p. 1995. 3.29 (1-56063-516-9, 497696) Editorial Unilit.

Movimiento en Zigzag. Eliezer Braun. (Ciencia para Todos Ser.). (SPA.). pap. 6.99 (968-16-2457-2, Pub. by Fondo) Continental Bk.

Movimientos de la Tierra. Lynn M. Stone. (Mientras la Tierra Gira Ser.).Tr. of Changing Earth. 24p. (J). (gr. k-4). 1994. lib. bdg. 17.27 (1-55916-059-4) Rourke Bk Co.

***Movin' Teen Poets Take Voice.** Ed. by Dave Johnson. LC 99-49455. 64p. (YA). (gr. 5-9). 2000. pap. 6.95 (0-531-07171-5) Orchard Bks Watts.

***Movin' Teen Poets Take Voice.** Ed. by Dave Johnson. LC 99-49455. 64p. (YA). (gr. 7 up). 2000. 15.95 (0-531-30258-X) Orchard Bks Watts.

Movin & Groovin. Peggy Buchanan & Linda Schwartz. LC 98-156084. (Illus.). 136p. (J). (gr. 1-6). 1997. pap. 12.95 (0-88160-279-5, LW349) Learning Wks.

Movin' On: Bret Clark Story. Bob Schaller. 160p. 1998. pap. 10.95 (1-887002-87-1) Cross Trng.

Movin' On: Living & Traveling Full Time in a Recreational Vehicle. Ron Hofmeister & Barb Hofmeister. LC 94-185084. 392p. 1999. pap. 16.95 (0-9637319-1-2) R & B Pubns.

Movin' On: The Great Migration North. Ed. by Mitch Yamasaki. LC 97-67430. (Perspectives on History Ser.: Pt. II). (Illus.). 68p. 1997. pap. 6.95 (1-57960-004-2) Disc Enter Ltd.

Movin on to Blues B Flat Patterns for Improvisation. F. Mantooth. 32p. 1997. audio compact disk 9.95 (0-7935-6859-5) H Leonard.

Movin on to Blues Bass Clef Patterns for Improvisation. F. Mantooth. 32p. 1997. pap. 9.95 (0-7935-6861-7) H Leonard.

Movin on to Blues C Book Patterns for Improvisation. F. Mantooth. 32p. 1997. pap. 9.95 (0-7935-6858-7) H Leonard.

Movin on to Blues E Flat Patterns for Improvisation. F. Mantooth. 32p. 1997. pap. 9.95 incl. audio compact disk (0-7935-6860-9) H Leonard.

Movin' on Up: A Woman's Guide Beyond Religion to Spirit Living. Rebecca F. Osaigbovo. 1997. 17.95 (1-880560-55-0) DaBaR Srvs.

Movin' Out: Equipment & Technique for Hikers. rev. ed. Harry Roberts. LC 78-26618. (Illus.). 160p. 1979. pap. 9.95 (0-913276-29-4) Stone Wall Pr.

Movin' Right along with Me. Michael Gallina & Jill Gallina. (J). (gr. k-6). 1989. 14.95 (0-931205-51-4) Jenson Pubns.

Moving. Karen Bryant-Mole. LC 97-41944. (Science All Around Me Ser.). (Illus.). 24p. (J). (gr. k-2). 1998. 18.50 (1-57572-630-0) Heinemann Lib.

Moving. Anita Ganeri. 32p. (J). (gr. 1-4). 1996. pap. text 4.95 (0-8114-7990-0) Raintree Steck-V.

Moving. Jackie Hardie & Angela Royston. LC 96-30164. (Body Systems Ser.). (J). 1998. (1-57572-094-9) Heinemann Lib.

Moving. Barbara Howes. LC 82-84115. 70p. (Orig.). 1983. pap. 3.95 (0-941692-00-0) Elysian Pr.

Moving. Mary Rogers. (Foundations Ser.). 32p. (J). (ps). 1992. pap. text 23.00 (1-56843-001-9); pap. text 4.50 (1-56843-051-5) EMG Networks.

Moving. deluxe limited ed. Barbara Howes. LC 82-84115. 70p. (Orig.). 1983. 10.00 (0-941692-01-9) Elysian Pr.

Moving: A Complete Checklist & Guide for Relocation 2nd ed. Karen G. Adams. LC 99-17890. 1999. write for info. (1-893067-00-9) Silvercat Pubns.

Moving: A Parent-Child Manual. Jeffrey Artenstein. 1990. pap. 9.95 (0-8125-0579-4, Pub. by Tor Bks) St Martin.

Moving: The Untold Story: Inside Tips on Making Your Next Move Successful. Patricia E. Zehr. LC 95-69138. (Illus.). 227p. (Orig.). 1995. pap. 15.95 (0-9646550-0-4) Abba Dabba.

Moving: The What, When, Where, & How of It. Patricia O. Neuman. (Illus.). 132p. 1981. pap. 5.95 (0-89651-450-1) M & O Pub.

Moving a Battleship with Your Bare Hands: Governing a University System. Laurence A. Weinstein. LC 93-22814. 294p. 1993. 27.00 (0-912150-27-0) Atwood Pub LLC.

Moving a Public Policy Agenda: The Strategic Philanthropy of Conservative Foundations. Sally Covington. 54p. 1997. pap. 25.00 (1-891465-07-4) Natl Comm Philan.

Moving Abroad, Living Abroad, Returning Home. Elizabeth Fernandez & Diane Ferrabee. 1990. pap. 29.95 (0-614-05757-4) Abbott Langer Assocs.

Moving Across Syllables: Training Articulatory Sound Sequences. Jill Kirkpatrick et al. (Illus.). 208p. 1990. pap. text 47.50 (0-7616-7635-X) Commun Skill.

Moving Ahead: A Training Manual for Children with Motor Disorders. Ed. by Joan O'Connor & E. Yu. LC 98-14892. (Illus.). 530p. 1998. pap. 30.00 (981-3083-27-1, Pub. by Spr-Verlag) Spr-Verlag.

Moving Ahead: Basic Skills for Career Advancement. Jerome M. Rosow & Robert Zager. Ed. by Jill Casner-Lotto. (Job-Linked Literacy: Innovative Strategies at Work Ser.: Pt. III). 97p. 1993. 95.00 (0-89361-047-X) Work in Amer.

Moving Ahead: With Some Luck & Some Chutzpah. Stephen S. Kalmar. LC 98-18719. (Illus.). 272p. (Orig.). 1999. pap. 14.95 (0-89407-116-5) Strawberry Hill.

Moving Ahead in Your Career. Ed. by Howard Cohn & Bill Miller. 256p. (Orig.). 1987. pap. text 6.95 (0-07-606981-8) McGraw.

Moving Ahead with ISO 14000: Improving Environmental Management & Advancing Sustainable Development. Ed. by Phillip A. Marcus & John T. Willig. LC 96-41848. (Wiley Series in Environmental Quality Management). 302p. 1997. 75.00 (0-471-16877-7) Wiley.

Moving Ahead with Your Career. Willet Weeks. 224p. 1994. pap. 44.50 (0-273-60703-0, Pub. by Pitman Pub) Trans-Atl Phila.

Moving Air Through Fans & Ducts. John Gladstone. (Illus.). 96p. 1992. pap. 15.00 (0-930644-17-4) Engineers Pr.

***Moving & Learning.** 4th ed. Nichols. 1999. 50.46 (0-07-092148-2) McGraw.

Moving & Learning: Test & Lessons Plan Manual, No. 2. Nichols. 1990. 46.95 (0-8016-3687-6) Mosby Inc.

An Asterisk (*) at the beginning of an entry indicates that the title is appearing for the first time.

Moving & Learning Across the Curriculum: 315 Activities & Games to Make Learning Fun. abr. rev. ed. Rae Pica. LC 98-4893. 288p. (C). 1998. text 34.95 (*0-8273-8537-4*) Delmar.

Moving & Learning for the Young Child. Ed. by William Stinson. (Illus.). 272p. (Orig.). 1990. pap. text 10.00 (*0-88314-449-2*, A4492) AAHPERD.

Moving & Learning Lesson Plan Manual. 2nd ed. Nichols. 392p. 1990. pap. 18.95 (*0-8016-5802-0*) Mosby Inc.

Moving & Learning Series: Early Elementary. Rae Pica Gardzina. LC 99-47664. 2000. pap. text 52.95 (*0-7668-1604-4*) Delmar.

Moving & Relocation Sourcebook & Directory: Reference Guide to the 100 Largest Metropolitan Areas in the United States. 2nd ed. Kay Gill. LC 98-163827. (Illus.). 1000p. 1998. lib. bdg. 185.00 (*0-7808-0025-7*, B206) Omnigraphics Inc.

***Moving & Relocation Sourcebook & Directory 2001: A Reference Guide to 121 Major Cities in the United States.** 3rd ed. Ed. by Nancy Kniskern. 1100p. 2000. lib. bdg. 210.00 (*0-7808-0431-7*) Omnigraphics Inc.

Moving & Reorganizing a Library. Marianna Wells & Rosemary Young. LC 96-30371. 123p. 1997. 74.95 (*0-566-07701-9*, Pub. by Gower) Ashgate Pub Co.

Moving & Shaking American Medicine: The Structure of a Socioeconomic Transformation, 57. Betty Leyerle. LC 83-22646. (Contributions in Economics & Economic History Ser.: No. 57). 218p. 1984. 55.00 (*0-313-24020-5*, LIP/, Greenwood Pr) Greenwood.

Moving & St. Rage. Kathy Fagan. LC 98-45421. (Vassar Miller Poetry Prize Ser.). 66 p. 1999. pap. 10.95 (*1-57441-066-0*) UNTX Pr.

Moving & the Military Family. Robin Wuebker-Battershell. (Family Forum Library). 16p. 1993. 1.95 (*1-56688-075-0*) Bur For At-Risk.

Moving as One. Elizabeth M. Rees. LC 98-17136. (Heart Beats Ser.: Bk. 1). 233p. (J). (gr. 4-8). 1998. mass mkt. 3.99 (*0-689-81948-X*) S&S Childrens.

***Moving at the Speed of Life: A Youth Survival Handbook.** Ron Sieh. (Illus.). 140p. (YA). (gr. 7 up). 2000. pap. 12.95 (*1-58394-013-8*, Pub. by Frog Ltd CA) Publishers Group.

Moving at the Speed of Light: Sermons for Advent/Christmas/Epiphany. Frank Luchsinger. (Second Lessons Ser.). 1998. pap. 9.50 (*0-7880-1268-1*) CSS OH.

Moving at the Speed of Light: Sermons for Advent/Christmas/Epiphany. Frank Luchsinger. LC 98-5617. (Second Lessons Ser.). 102p. 1998. pap. 9.50 (*0-7880-1265-7*) CSS OH.

Moving Away Vol. 2: More Vignettes of My Childhood. Florence J. Goodman. 53p. 1992. pap. 13.00 (*0-917232-31-3*) Gee Tee Bee.

Moving Away from Diets. Karin Kratina et al. (Illus.). 174p. (Orig.). 1996. pap. 34.95 (*0-9631033-5-0*) Helm Seminars.

Moving Away from Silence: Music of the Peruvian Altiplano & the Experiment of Urban Migration. Thomas Turino. LC 92-26935. (Chicago Studies in Ethnomusicology). (Illus.). 336p. (C). 1993. pap. text 30.00 (*0-226-81700-8*); lib. bdg. 49.95 (*0-226-81699-0*) U Ch Pr.

Moving Balance System: A New Technique for Stock & Option Trading. Humphrey Lloyd. (Illus.). 221p. 1988. pap. 50.00 (*0-930233-28-X*, Pub. by Windsor) Natl Bk Netwk.

Moving Beauty: A Century in Automobile Design. Ed. by Pierre Theberge. LC 96-135287. (Illus.). 240p. 1995. 50.00 (*2-89192-192-5*) Mont Mus Fine Arts.

Moving Between Languages: Immersion, Transition, & Maintenance. Yvonne S. Freeman. pap. text. write for info. (*0-325-00273-8*) Heinemann.

Moving Beyond A. D. D./A. D. H. D. Avery Hart & Rita Kirsch Debroitner. LC 97-14808. 320p. 1997. pap. 16.95 (*0-8092-3076-3*, 307630, Contemporary Bks) NTC Contemp Pub Co.

Moving Beyond Abuse: Questions & Stories for Women Who Have Lived with Abuse. Kay-Laurel Fischer & Michael F. McGrane. Ed. by Jeanne Engelmann & Vincent Hyman. 88p. 1997. per. 10.00 (*0-940069-15-6*) A H Wilder.

Moving Beyond Adultry & Divorce. Corinne Burdett. 75p. 1999. pap. 7.95 (*1-880710-37-4*) Monterey Pacific.

Moving Beyond All Boundaries. Ed. by Carole Boyce-Davies. (C). 1996. pap. text 38.95 (*0-7453-0883-X*) Westview.

Moving Beyond Belief see Mas Alla de la Fe

Moving Beyond Boundaries, Vol. 1. Carole Boyce-Davies. (C). 1996. 66.50 (*0-7453-0758-2*); pap. 19.95 (*0-7453-0759-0*) Westview.

Moving Beyond Boundaries, Vol. 2. Carole Boyce-Davies. (C). 1996. pap. 19.95 (*0-7453-0881-3*) Westview.

Moving Beyond Boundaries Vol. 1: International Dimensions of Black Women's Writing. Ed. by Carole B. Davies & Molara Ogundipe-Leslie. LC 94-31075. 252p. (C). 1995. text 55.00 (*0-8147-1237-1*); pap. text 19.50 (*0-8147-1238-X*) NYU Pr.

Moving Beyond Boundaries Vol. 2: International Dimensions of Black Women's Writing. Ed. by Carole B. Davies & Molara Ogundipe-Leslie. 320p. (C). 1995. text 55.00 (*0-8147-1239-8*); pap. text 19.50 (*0-8147-1240-1*) NYU Pr.

Moving Beyond Confined Circles. LC 90-80048. 1990. 9.00 (*0-914422-20-0*) Glenmary Res Ctr.

Moving Beyond Environmental Compliance: A Handbook for Integrating Pollution Prevention with ISO 14000. Thomas E. Welch. LC 97-27474. 256p. 1997. lib. bdg. 55.00 (*1-56670-295-X*) Lewis Pubs.

Moving Beyond Gridlock: Traffic & Development. Robert T. Dunphy. LC 96-61394. (Illus.). 180p. (Orig.). 1996. pap. 45.95 (*0-87420-803-3*, T03) Urban Land.

Moving Beyond Grief: Lessons from Those Who Have Lived Through Sorrow. Ruth Sissom. LC 94-15196. 160p. 1994. pap. 9.99 (*0-929239-09-1*) Discovery Hse Pubs.

Moving Beyond Myths: Revitalizing Undergraduate Mathematics. National Research Council Staff. 80p. 1991. pap. text 7.95 (*0-309-04489-8*) Natl Acad Pr.

Moving Beyond Secession: The Mennonite Brethren Conference in Russia, 1872-1922. Abe J. Dueck. (Perspectives on Mennonite Life & Thought Ser.: No. 13). (Illus.). 179p. 1998. pap. 16.95 (*0-921788-47-9*) Kindred Prods.

Moving Beyond Traditon: A Turned-Wood Invitational. Steve Loar & Alan DuBois. LC 97-77091. (Illus.). 80p. 1997. pap. 12.95 (*1-884240-15-1*) Arkansas Art Ctr.

Moving Beyond Words. Gloria Steinem. 320p. 1995. per. 12.00 (*0-671-51052-5*) S&S Trade Pap.

Moving Beyond Your Past. Tim Sledge. 224p. 1994. pap. text 12.95 (*0-8054-9927-X*, LifeWay Press) LifeWay Christian.

Moving Bodies. Dana Weimer. (Illus.). 44p. (Orig.). 1992. pap. 6.95 (*0-933313-14-4*) SUN Gemini Pr.

***Moving Book.** Jill Kimball. LC 00-100077. (Illus.). 24p. (J). (ps-7). 2000. pap. 10.00 (*0-9678578-2-1*) E Bks.

Moving Book: A Kid's Survival Guide. Gabriel Davis. LC 95-40604. (Illus.). 128p. (J). 1996. pap. 16.95 (*0-316-17684-2*) Little.

Moving Book: Encouragement for Your Journey. Betsy R. Elliot. LC 98-25015. 86p. 1998. pap. 6.99 (*0-87788-579-6*, H Shaw Pubs) Waterbrook Pr.

Moving Borders: Three Decades of Innovative Writing by Women. Mary M. Sloan. LC 97-52935. 775p. 1998. pap. 27.95 (*1-883689-47-3*) Talisman Hse.

Moving Borders: Three Decades of Innovative Writing by Women. Ed. by Mary M. Sloan. LC 97-52935. 775p. 1998. 52.95 (*1-883689-48-1*) Talisman Hse.

Moving Boundaries V: Computational Modelling of Free & Moving Boundary Problems. Ed. by B. Sarler et al. (Computational & Experimental Methods Ser.: Vol. 1). 206p. 1999. 143.00 (*1-85312-691-8*, 6918, Pub. by WIT Pr) Computational Mech MA.

Moving Boundaries IV: Computational Modelling of Free & Moving Boundary Problems VI. Ed. by R. VanKeer & C. A. Breebia. LC 97-67017. 376p. 1997. 198.00 (*1-85312-465-6*, 4656) Computational Mech MA.

Moving Company: An Easy-to-Understand Guide to Estate Planning, Wills & Trusts. Walter S. Bristow, III. LC 92-71620. (Illus.). 176p. (Orig.). 1992. pap. 20.00 (*0-685-61658-4*); student ed. 50.00 (*0-685-61659-2*); 20.00 (*0-685-61660-6*); audio 10.00 (*0-685-61661-4*); audio 10.00 (*0-685-61662-2*) Hayden Bridge.

Moving Company: An Easy Way to Explain Estate Planning. 2nd rev. ed. Walter S. Bristow, III. LC 89-92022. (Illus.). 150p. 1989. pap. 20.00 (*1-877763-00-4*) Hayden Bridge.

Moving Company: How to Explain Estate Planning Concepts. Walter S. Bristow, III. (Illus.). 56p. (Orig.). 1988. pap. 10.00 (*0-317-93894-0*) Hayden Bridge.

Moving Cultural Frontier of World Order: From Monotheism to North-South Relations. Ali A. Mazrui. 20p. 1982. pap. 14.95 (*0-911646-11-6*) Transaction Pubs.

***Moving DARPA Technologies into the Marketplace.** Frwd. by Bud Durand & Connie Jacobs. (Illus.). 51p. (C). 2000. reprint ed. pap. text 20.00 (*0-7567-0064-7*) DIANE Pub.

Moving Day. (Happy Endings Padded Storybooks Ser.). (Illus.). 32p. (J). (ps-1). 1998. write for info. (*0-7666-0158-7*, Honey Bear Bks) Modern Pub NYC.

Moving Day. Raymond Ehrich. 54p. (J). (gr. 1-3). 1993. pap. 1.00 (*1-886182-02-7*) Heritage Edits.

Moving Day. Robert Kalan. LC 95-2257. (Illus.). 32p. (J). (ps-3). 1996. 14.93 (*0-688-13949-3*, Grenwillow Bks) HarpC Child Bks.

Moving Day: Funeral Mediations. Wayne Brouwer. 1997. pap. text 8.50 (*0-936497-15-7*) Seven Worlds.

Moving Don't Be Taken. Costantino. 1990. pap. 12.95 (*0-945155-04-2*) Trans Pub.

Moving 'Em: A Guide to Low Stress Animal Handling. Burt Smith. Ed. by Dale O. Evans. LC 97-94556. (Illus.). x, 368p. 1998. 29.95 (*0-9662704-3-6*) Graziers Hui.

Moving Envelopes of Stars. Viktor V. Sobolev. Tr. by Sergei Gaposchkin. LC 59-9284. (Harvard Books on Astronomy). 120p. reprint ed. pap. 37.20 (*0-7837-2336-9*, 205742400004) Bks Demand.

Moving Europeans: Migration in Western Europe since 1650. Leslie P. Moch. LC 92-6678. (Interdisciplinary Studies in History). 320p. 1992. 19.95 (*0-253-33859-X*) Ind U Pr.

Moving Europeans: Migration in Western Europe Since 1650. Leslie P. Moch. LC 92-6678. (Interdisciplinary Studies in History). 269p. Date not set. reprint ed. pap. 83.40 (*0-608-20563-X*, 205447700002) Bks Demand.

Moving Experience. Jeanine Jacobson. 56p. 1995. pap. text 8.95 (*0-87487-948-5*); pap. text 8.95 (*0-87487-949-3*) Summy-Birchard.

Moving Experience. Lutton Staff. LC 96-133565. 1997. pap. 29.95 (*0-86196-515-9*, Pub. by J Libbey Med) Bks Intl VA.

Moving Experience: Coping with the Challenge of Moving. Margery Pabst & Rita Goldhammer. (Illus.). (Orig.). 1996. pap. 12.95 (*0-9650260-0-0*) Goldhammer.

Moving Experience: Dance for Lovers of Children & the Child Within. Teresa Benzwie. (Illus.). 224p. 1988. pap. 29.00 (*0-913705-25-X*) Zephyr Pr AZ.

***Moving Experiences.** William Shuttleworth. (Illus.). 96p. 2000. pap. 14.95 (*1-892668-15-7*) Prospect Pr.

Moving Faith into Action: A Facilitator's Guide for Creating Parish Social Ministry Organizations. James R. Lund & Mary Heidkamp. 192p. 1990. pap. 9.95 (*0-8091-3157-9*) Paulist Pr.

***Moving Families: Expatriation, Stress & Coping.** Mary Haour-Knipe. LC 00-30253. 2000. pap. write for info. (*1-85728-815-7*, Pub. by UCL Pr Ltd) Taylor & Francis.

Moving-Field Isodose Charts see Atlas of Radiation Dose Distributions

Moving Finger. Agatha Christie. 208p. 1987. mass mkt. 5.99 (*0-425-10569-5*) Berkley Pub.

Moving Finger. Agatha Christie. 1991. 10.60 (*0-606-12432-2*, Pub. by Turtleback) Demco.

Moving Finger. large type ed. Agatha Christie. (General Ser.). 264p. 1989. lib. bdg. 19.95 (*0-8161-4561-X*, G K Hall Lrg Type) Mac Lib Ref.

Moving Finite Elements. Micael J. Baines. (Monographs on Numerical Analysis). (Illus.). 240p. 1995. text 80.00 (*0-19-853467-1*) OUP.

Moving for Injunctive Relief. Merriann Panarella. LC 94-73530. 1995. pap. text 59.00 (*0-944490-80-8*) Mass CLE.

Moving for Relief from an Automatic Stay in Bankruptcy - Action Guide - Fall 1997. Jeffrey J. Goodrich & Janet R. Walworth. Ed. by Elizabeth M. Johnson. 120p. 1997. ring bd. 58.00 (*0-7626-0167-1*, CP-11215) Cont Ed Bar-CA.

Moving for Relief from the Automatic Stay in Bankruptcy. Mary K. DeNevi. LC 92-60919. 114p. 1992. pap. text 45.00 (*0-944490-87-5*) Mass CLE.

Moving for Seniors. Barbara H. Morris. (Illus.). 42p. 1998. wbk. ed. 10.95 (*0-9671239-0-9*) Smooth Transitns.

Moving for Work: The Sociology of Relocating in the 1990s. Anne B. Hendershott. 210p. (Orig.). (C). 1995. pap. 26.50 (*0-8191-9811-0*); lib. bdg. 48.00 (*0-8191-9810-2*) U Pr of Amer.

Moving Force. Henry I. Meyer. LC 81-66231. 333p. reprint ed. pap. 103.30 (*0-608-11908-3*, 202357200033) Bks Demand.

Moving Fortress. Richardo Barreiro. (Illus.). 64p. (Orig.). 1988. pap. 8.98 (*0-922173-00-1*) Four Winds Pub Group.

Moving Forward: A Book for Ileostomy Patients. Kay Marshall. (Illus.). 32p. 1990. pap. text 3.95 (*0-916999-07-6*) HERC Inc.

***Moving Forward: A Devotional Guide for Finding Hope & Peace in the Midst of Divorce.** Jim Smoke. LC 00-28139. 252p. 2000. 15.95 (*1-56563-544-2*) Hendrickson MA.

***Moving Forward: Procrastination, Self-Worth, Gut Feelings.** Helen Gordon. 14p. 1998. pap. 3.00 (*1-930520-06-9*) H Gordon.

Moving Forward: Tools for Sustainability & Expansion. Elaine Edgcomb et al. 132p. 1996. spiral bd. 15.00 (*1-888753-02-1*) PACT Pubns.

Moving Forward from the Past: Early Writings & Current Reflections of Middle School Founders. Robert J. David et al. LC 98-19634. 1998. pap. write for info. (*1-56090-154-3*) Natl Middle Schl.

Moving Forward, Keeping Still: The Gateway to Eastern Wisdom. Ariel Books Staff. LC 96-85947. 374p. (Orig.). 1997. pap. 5.95 (*0-8362-2593-7*, Arie Bks) Andrews & McMeel.

Moving Forward with Fifty Years of Leadership in Advanced Materials: 39th International SAMPE Symposium & Exhibition, Anaheim, Convention Center, Anaheim, CA, April 11-14, 1994, Bk. 1. International SAMPE Symposium & Exhibition Staff. Ed. by Ken Drake et al. LC TA0418.9.C6A. (Science of Advanced Materials & Process Enginnering Ser.: No. 39). (Illus.). 1800p. 1994. reprint ed. pap. 200.00 (*0-7837-9625-0*, 206038000001) Bks Demand.

Moving Forward with Fifty Years of Leadership in Advanced Materials: 39th International SAMPE Symposium & Exhibition, Anaheim, Convention Center, Anaheim, CA, April 11-14, 1994, Bk. 2. International SAMPE Symposium & Exhibition Staff. Ed. by Ken Drake et al. LC TA0418.9.C6A. (Science of Advanced Materials & Process Enginnering Ser.: No. 39). (Illus.). 1659p. 1994. reprint ed. pap. 200.00 (*0-7837-9626-9*, 206038000002) Bks Demand.

Moving Forward with Literature: Basals, Books, & Beyond. Shelley B. Wepner & Joan T. Feeley. 432p. (C). 1992. pap. text 20.20 (*0-675-21414-9*, Merrill Coll) P-H.

Moving Foward: Expanding Collaborations Between Traffic Safety & Public Health. 30p. 1996. reprint ed. pap. text 15.00 (*0-7881-3328-4*) DIANE Pub.

Moving Free: A Total Program of Post-Mastectomy Exercises. Carol Walter & Lenore H. Miller. LC 80-2735. (Illus.). 1981. pap. write for info. (*0-672-52686-7*) Macmillan.

Moving from Cobol to C. 2nd ed. Morrison J. Budlong. (Illus.). 516p. 1993. pap. 64.95 incl. disk (*1-892856-10-7*, 11) King Computer.

Moving from Cobol to C. 2nd ed. Morrison J. Budlong. (Illus.). 516p. 1998. pap. 49.95 (*1-892856-04-2*, 5) King Computer.

Moving from Parameters to Pathways: A Guide for Developing & Implementing Critical Pathways. Deborah K. Wall & Mitchell M. Proyect. LC 97-24163. 154p. 1997. pap. 40.00 (*0-944496-55-5*) Precept Pr.

Moving from Renewal to Revival. Che Ahn. 168p. 1998. pap. 10.99 (*0-8307-2149-5*) Gospel Lght.

***Moving From Research to Practice: Professional Development to Promote Effective Teaching of Early Reading. A Special Issue of Learning Disabilitites Research & Practice.** Ed. by David Chard & Candace Bos. 88p. 1999. pap. 20.00 (*0-8058-9778-X*) L Erlbaum Assocs.

Moving from Shame to Self-Worth: Preaching & Pastoral Care. Edward P. Wimberly. LC 98-36535. 128p. 1999. pap. 15.00 (*0-687-08226-9*) Abingdon.

Moving from Training to Performance: A Practical Guidebook. Ed. by James C. Robinson et al. LC 98-21647. 300p. 1998. pap. 29.95 (*1-57675-039-6*) Berrett-Koehler.

Moving from Turbo Pascal to Turbo C Plus. Namir C. Shammas. 1992. 29.95 (*0-672-30199-7*) Sams.

Moving from WordPerfect for DOS to WordPerfect for Windows. John Kamper & Donna Kamper. LC 93-12286. (Popular Applications Ser.). 128p. (Orig.). 1993. pap. 15.95 incl. disk (*1-55622-332-3*) Wordware Pub.

Moving Frontier: Social & Economic Change in a Southern Brazilian Community. Maxine L. Margolis. LC 73-7730. (Latin American Monographs: Ser. 2, No. 11). (Illus.). 292p. reprint ed. pap. 90.60 (*0-7837-5074-9*, 204477200004) Bks Demand.

Moving Frontiers. Ed. by Carl S. Meyer. 524p. 1986. pap. 26.00 (*0-570-04461-8*, 12-3069) Concordia.

Moving Frontiers: Economic Restructuring, Regional Development & Emerging Networks. Ed. by Juan R. Cuadrado-Roura et al. 368p. 1994. 96.95 (*1-85628-905-2*, Pub. by Avebry) Ashgate Pub Co.

Moving Frontiers, an American Theme & Its Application to Australian History. Frederick Alexander. (History - United States Ser.). 48p. 1993. reprint ed. lib. bdg. 59.00 (*0-7812-4855-8*) Rprt Serv.

Moving Frontiers in Invertebrate Virology. T. W. Tinsley & K. A. Harrap. Ed. by Joseph L. Melnick. (Monographs in Virology: Vol. 6). (Illus.). 1972. 34.00 (*3-8055-1464-6*) S Karger.

Moving Frontiers in Veterinary Immunology. Ed. by R. Pandey. (Progress in Veterinary Microbiology & Immunology Ser.: Vol. 4). (Illus.). xii, 252p. 1987. 182.75 (*3-8055-4632-7*) S Karger.

Moving Gives Me a Stomach Ache. H. McKend. (Illus.). 32p. (J). (ps-8). 1988. pap. write for info. (*0-88753-178-4*) Black Moss.

Moving Handbook: A Time Saving Workbook to Help Organize Your Move. Sheila Schultz. 1989. ring bd. 22.95 (*0-9621426-0-3*) Abbreviations Pr.

Moving Heaven & Earth: Sexuality, Spirituality, & Social Change. Lucy Goodison. 55.00 (*0-7043-5038-6*, Pub. by Womens Press) Trafalgar.

Moving Heaven & Earth: Sexuality, Spirituality & Social Change. Lucy Goodison. 384p. 1992. pap. text 16.00 (*0-04-440861-7*) NYU Pr.

***Moving Home.** Roberto Rizzon. 1999. pap. text 3.99 (*0-85953-712-9*) Childs Play.

***Moving Home Plate: The Miracle on I-5.** unabridged ed. William D. Tucker & Jerry Walker. LC 99-97554. (Illus.). 340p. 1999. 19.95 (*0-9663169-1-6*) Volcano Press.

Moving House. Anne Civardi. (Illus.). 16p. (J). (ps-3). 1993. pap. 4.50 (*0-7460-1281-0*, Usborne) EDC.

Moving House: Stories. Pawel Huelle. Tr. by Michael Kandel. 256p. 1996. reprint ed. pap. 13.00 (*0-15-600251-5*, Harvest Bks) Harcourt.

Moving House & Other Stories. Pawel Huelle. Tr. by Antonia Lloyd-Jones. LC 93-48587. 248p. 1995. 18.95 (*0-15-162731-2*) Harcourt.

***Moving House with Feng Shui: Use Effective Feng Shui Principles - Create a Feel-Good Factor Inside & Out - Harmonise Your Home.** Jane Purr. (Essentials Ser.). (Illus.). 64p. 2000. pap. 9.95 (*1-85703-569-0*, Pub. by How To Bks) Midpt Trade.

Moving Image. Goldie L. Morales. 24p. 1978. pap. 2.50 (*0-910083-02-9*) Heritage Trails.

Moving Image. large type ed. Annie Ross. 416p. 1996. 27.99 (*0-7089-3523-0*) Ulverscroft.

Moving Image: Immutability, Metaphors, & the Time Clocks Tell. David Suda. LC 88-27984. 164p. (C). 1989. lib. bdg. 41.00 (*0-8191-7251-0*) U Pr of Amer.

Moving In. Alfred Slote. LC 87-45569. 128p. (J). (gr. 3-6). 1988. 15.00 (*0-397-32261-5*); lib. bdg. 14.89 (*0-397-32262-3*) HarpC Child Bks.

Moving in International Circles. 2nd ed. Ya'akov Eden. 364p. 1995. spiral bd. 45.95 (*0-7872-1229-6*) Kendall-Hunt.

Moving in Measure: Essays in Honour of Brian Moloney. Judith Bryce & Doug Thompson. 242p. 1989. 45.00 (*0-85958-475-5*) Denali Press.

Moving in Memory. Poems. Julia Randall. LC 86-27623. 51p. 1987. pap. 6.95 (*0-8071-1388-3*) La State U Pr.

***Moving in on Occupational Injury.** David Worth. (Illus.). 384p. 2000. pap. 0.00 (*0-7506-4198-3*) Buttrwrth-Heinemann.

Moving in on Pain: Conference Proceedings. Ed. by Michael D. Shacklock. LC 96-122656. 224p. 1995. pap. text 44.50 (*0-7506-8926-9*) Buttrwrth-Heinemann.

***Moving in the Apostolic.** John Eckhardt. 1999. write for info. (*0-08-302372-0*) Elsevier.

Moving in the Apostolic: God's Plan for Leading His Church to the Final Victory. John Eckhardt. LC 98-45962. 168p. 1999. pap. 9.99 (*0-8307-2373-0*, Renew) Gospel Lght.

Moving in the Right Direction. Walker Ryan Walker. 51.95 (*1-85628-862-5*) Ashgate Pub Co.

Moving in the Spirit: Becoming a Contemplative in Action. Richard J. Hauser. 144p. 1986. pap. 8.95 (*0-8091-2790-3*) Paulist Pr.

Moving in with Adam. Jeanne Allan. (Romance Ser.). 1996. per. 3.25 (*0-373-03408-3*, 1-03408-1) Silhouette.

Moving into a New Now: Faith for the Later Years. Mildred Tengbom. LC 96-52804. 176p. 1997. pap. 13.99 (*0-8066-3341-7*, 9-3341, Augsburg) Augsburg Fortress.

Moving into Adolescence. Roberta G. Simmons & Dale A. Blyth. 457p. 1987. lib. bdg. 59.95 (*0-202-30328-4*) Aldine de Gruyter.

Moving into Balance: Creating Your Personal Pathway. unabridged ed. Barbara Larrivee. LC 96-92140. (Illus.). x, 202p. (Orig.). 1996. pap. 14.95 (*0-9651780-9-9*) Shoreline Publns.

M

Moving into Economic Development: CDC's & Job Creation. 21p. 1998. pap. 12.00 (*1-889482-05-6*) Nat Congress CED.

Moving into Management. 200p. 1991. 25.00 (*0-317-05767-7*, PB05) Natl Attys General.

***Moving into Management: Prepare Yourself to Be an Effective & Efficient Manager.** 2nd ed. Julie-Ann Amos. (Business & Management Ser.). (Illus.). 160p. 2000. pap. 19.95 (*1-85703-552-6*, Pub. by How To Bks) Trans-Atl Phila.

Moving into the Future: National Standards for Physical Education: A Guide to Content & Assessment. 3rd ed. NASPE Staff. 125p. (Orig.). (C). (gr. 13). 1995. text 22.00 (*0-8151-7338-5*, 304-10083) AAHPERD.

Moving Is Relating: Developing Interpersonal Skills Through Movement. Helen Landalf. LC 98-9253. 96p. (J). (gr. 3-6). 1998. pap. 19.95 (*1-57525-123-X*) Smith & Kraus.

Moving Landscape. Pasquale Verdicchio. (Essential Poets Ser.: No. 23). 48p. 1985. pap. 6.00 (*0-919349-58-7*) Guernica Editions.

***Moving Lessons: Margaret H'Doubler & the Beginning of Dance in American Education.** Janice Ross. 2000. 60.00 (*0-299-16930-8*); pap. 24.95 (*0-299-16934-0*) U of Wis Pr.

Moving Library Collections: A Management Handbook. Elizabeth C. Habich. LC 97-53221. (Greenwood Library Management Collection). 360p. 1998. lib. bdg. 79.50 (*0-313-29330-9*, Greenwood Pr) Greenwood.

***Moving Lila: Novel.** Julie Elaine Fleming. LC 99-55815. 224p. 2000. text 22.95 (*0-312-24409-6*) St Martin.

Moving Loads on Ice Plates. Vernon A. Squire et al. LC 96-1344. (Solid Mechanics & Its Applications Ser.: Vol. 45). 1996. text 144.00 (*0-7923-3953-3*) Kluwer Academic.

Moving Mama to Town. Ronder Thomas Young. LC 96-38993. 224p. (J). (gr. 3-8). 1997. 17.95 (*0-531-30025-0*); lib. bdg. 18.99 (*0-531-33025-7*) Orchard Bks Watts.

Moving Mama to Town. Ronder T. Young. 224p. (J). (gr. 5-9). 1998. reprint ed. pap. 4.50 (*0-440-41455-5*) BDD Bks Young Read.

***Moving Mama to Town, Class Set.** unabridged ed. Ronder T. Young. (J). 1998. pap., boxed set 106.70 incl. audio (*0-7887-2560-2*, 46730) Recorded Bks.

***Moving Mama to Town, Homework Set.** unabridged ed. Ronder T. Young. (J). 1998. 58.24 incl. audio (*0-7887-1936-X*, 40643) Recorded Bks.

Moving Mars. Greg Bear. 512p. 1994. mass mkt. 5.99 (*0-8125-2480-2*, Pub. by Tor Bks) St Martin.

***Moving Medicine.** Jack Liskin. 2000. pap. 17.95 (*1-58177-065-0*) Barrytown Ltd.

Moving Medicine: The Life Work of Milton Trager, M. D. Jack Liskin. LC 96-31343. 1996. 24.95 (*0-88268-196-6*) Station Hill Pr.

Moving Meditation: Enlightenment of the Mind & Total Fitness. Van H. Ho. LC 79-88748. (Illus.). 214p. (C). 1979. pap. 15.00 (*0-9602904-1-9*) V H Ho.

Moving Meetings. Jana M. Kemp. LC 94-14157. (Business Skills Express Ser.). 128p. 1994. text 10.95 (*0-7863-0333-6*, Irwn Prfssnl) McGraw-Hill Prof.

Moving Mom & Dad: Why, Where,How & When to Help Your Parents Relocate. rev. ed. Sarah Morse & Donna Quinn Roberts. (Lanier Guides). 256p. 1998. pap. 14.95 (*0-89087-868-4*) Celestial Arts.

Moving Mosaic. 2nd ed. Kay Ortmans. 46p. 1998. reprint ed. pap. 14.95 (*1-893247-00-7*) Well-Springs.

***Moving Mountains.** Kanai. 2000. mass mkt. 16.95 (*0-8133-1893-9*, Pub. by Westview) HarpC.

Moving Mountains: Japanese Education Reform. Marie H. Roesgaard. LC 98-189528. (Acta Jutlandica 73:1 Ser.: Vol. 71). (Illus.). 265p. 1998. pap. 24.95 (*87-7288-477-0*, Pub. by Aarhus Univ Pr) David Brown.

Moving Mountains: Lessons in Leadership & Logistics from the Gulf War. Harvard Business Review Staff. 272p. 1994. pap. 16.95 (*0-07-103587-7*) McGraw.

Moving Mountains: Lessons in Leadership & Logistics from the Gulf War. William G. Pagonis. 300p. 1992. 29.95 (*0-07-103388-2*) McGraw.

Moving Mountains: Lessons in Leadership & Logistics from the Gulf War. William G. Pagonis & Jeffrey L. Cruikshank. LC 92-15641. 272p. 1992. 29.95 (*0-87584-360-3*) Harvard Busn.

Moving Mountains: Lessons in Leadership & Logistics from the Gulf War. William G. Pagonis & Jeffrey L. Cruikshank. 1994. pap. 16.95 (*0-87584-508-8*) Harvard Busn.

Moving Mountains: Magical Choices for Empowering Your Life's Journey. Steve Frisch. LC 96-84736. 192p. (Orig.). 1997. pap. 12.95 (*0-9651511-1-5*) Alive & Well.

***Moving Mountains: The Principles & Purposes of Leon Sullivan.** Leon H. Sullivan. (Illus.). 304p. 1999. pap. 18.00 (*0-8170-1360-1*) Judson.

Moving Mountains: The Principles & Purposes of Leon Sullivan. Leon H. Sullivan. LC 98-23790. (Illus.). xviii, 300 p. 1998. 22.00 (*0-8170-1289-3*) Judson.

***Moving Nearer to Heaven: The Illusions & Disillusions of Migrants to Scenic Rural Places.** Patrick C. Jobes. LC 99-55875. 256p. 2000. 65.00 (*0-275-96689-5*, Praeger Pubs) Greenwood.

Moving North. Ed. by Catherine Sunshine & Keith Warner. LC 98-28600. (Caribbean Connections Ser.). (Illus.). 1998. pap. 18.00 (*1-878554-12-3*) Netwrk of Educ.

Moving Notation: A Handbook of Musical Rhythm & Elementary Labanotation for the Dancer. Jill Beck & Joseph C. Reiser. (Performing Arts Studies). 367p. 1998. pap. 42.00 incl. cd-rom (*90-5702-179-X*, Harwood Acad Pubs) Gordon & Breach.

***Moving Notation: A Handbook of Musical Rhythm & Elementary Labanotation for the Dancer.** Jill Beck & Joseph C. Reiser. 367p. 1998. text 108.00 (*90-5702-178-1*, Harwood Acad Pubs) Gordon & Breach.

Moving of Income Support: Barriers & Bridges. A. Shaw et al. LC 97-152040. (DSS Research Report Ser.). 1996. write for info. (*0-11-762394-6*, Pub. by Statnry Office) Bernan Associates.

Moving off the Map: A Field Guide to Changing the Congregation. Thomas Bandy. LC 98-40758. 240p. 1998. pap. 17.00 (*0-687-06800-2*) Abingdon.

Moving On. Mary J. Auch. 190p. 1996. 14.95 (*0-8050-4921-5*) H Holt & Co.

Moving On. T. Forest & J. Huizenga. (Illus.). 1989. pap. text 16.31 (*0-8013-0119-X*, 75783) Longman.

Moving On. Larry McMurtry. Ed. by Bill Grose. 1991. per. 7.99 (*0-671-74408-9*) PB.

Moving On. Ralph Thompson. 104p. 1998. pap. 14.95 (*1-900715-17-1*, Pub. by Peepal Tree Pr) Paul & Co Pubs.

***Moving on.** Ralph Thompson. LC 98-203753. 1998. write for info. (*0-19-007517-1*) OUP.

Moving On. Alan J. Whitfield. (C). 1989. text 75.00 (*1-85821-039-9*, Pub. by Pentland Pr) St Mut.

Moving On. Gil Williams. 1969. pap. 4.00 (*0-686-21119-7*) Bellevue Pr.

***Moving On.** large type ed. Peta Taylor. 432p. 1999. 31.99 (*0-7505-1389-6*, Pub. by Mgna Lrg Print) Ulverscroft.

Moving On! A Journey Through Sexual Assault. Louise Phillips. 1996. pap. text 14.95 (*1-86351-156-3*, Pub. by Sally Milner) Seven Hills Bk.

Moving On: A Novel. Larry McMurtry. 800p. 1987. pap. 11.00 (*0-671-63320-1*) S&S Trade.

Moving On: A Novel. Larry McMurtry. 800p. 1999. per. 15.00 (*0-684-85388-4*) S&S Trade Pap.

Moving on: Audio Cassette. T. Forest & J. Huizenga. (Illus.). 1989. audio 41.91 (*0-8013-0120-3*, 75784) Longman.

Moving On: Beginning Listening. J. Huizenga. (Illus.). 1989. pap. text 12.50 (*0-582-90756-X*, 75260); audio 37.95 (*0-582-90755-1*, 75259) Longman.

Moving On: Black Loyalists in the Afro-Atlantic World. Ed. by John W. Pulis. LC 98-41807. (Crosscurrents in African American History Ser.). 222p. 1999. 49.00 (*0-8153-2748-X*, H2049) Garland.

Moving On: New Perspectives on the Women's Movement. Ed. by Tayo Andreasen et al. (Acta Jutlandica Ser.: Vol. 67:1). (Illus.). 224p. (Orig.). (C). 1991. pap. 32.00 (*87-7288-368-5*, Pub. by Aarhus Univ Pr) David Brown.

***Moving On: Quiet Moments for the Divorced.** Dolly Dickinson. 2000. pap. 10.99 (*1-56955-232-0*) Servant.

Moving On: Stories of the West, 1. Jane Candia Coleman. (Love Spell Ser.). 320p. 1999. mass mkt. 4.99 (*0-8439-4545-1*) Dorchester Pub Co.

Moving On: Stories of the West. large type ed. Jane Candia Coleman. LC 96-43960. (Five Star Ser.). 310p. 1997. 17.95 (*0-7862-0732-9*) Five Star.

Moving On: Stories of the West. large type ed. Jane Candia Coleman. LC 97-45642. (G. K. Hall Western Ser.). 1998. 23.95 (*0-7838-8383-8*, G K Hall Lrg Type) Mac Lib Ref.

Moving On: Stories of the West. large type ed. Jane Candia Coleman. 1999. 20.00 (*0-7862-0755-8*) Thorndike Pr.

Moving On: The American People since 1945. George D. Moss. LC 93-27288. 432p. 1994. pap. text 37.60 (*0-13-606138-9*) P-H.

***Moving On: The American People since 1945.** 2nd ed. George Moss. LC 00-20144. 480p. 2000. pap. 36.00 (*0-13-017191-3*) P-H.

Moving On: The Gay Man's Guide for Coping When a Relationship Ends. Dann Hazel. 288p. 1998. pap. 12.00 (*1-57566-378-3*) Kensgtn Pub Corp.

***Moving On: The Gypsies & Travellers of Britain.** Donald Kenrick & Colin Clark. (Illus.). 205p. 1999. pap. 19.95 (*0-900458-99-2*, Pub. by Univ of Herfordshire) Bold Strummer Ltd.

Moving On: The Heroines of Shirley Ann Grau, Anne Tyler, & Gail Godwin. Susan S. Kissel. LC 96-23213. 232p. 1996. pap. 19.95 (*0-87972-712-8*) Bowling Green Univ Popular Press.

Moving On: Women & Society. Ed. by Man Singh Das & Vijay Kumar Gupta. 176p. 1996. pap. 150.00 (*81-7533-023-6*, Pub. by Print Hse) St Mut.

Moving On: Women's Experiences of Childhood Sexual Abuse & Beyond. Yvonne Darlington. LC 96-233040. 140p. 1996. pap. 29.00 (*1-86287-219-8*, Pub. by Federation Pr) Gaunt.

Moving on - Young People & Leaving Care Schemes. N. Biehak et al. LC 96-183828. 320p. 1995. pap. 45.00 (*0-11-321891-5*, HM18915, Pub. by Statnry Office) Bernan Associates.

Moving on after He Moves Out. Jim Conway & Sally Conway. LC 94-23856. 220p. (Orig.). 1995. pap. 10.99 (*0-8308-1643-7*, 1643) InterVarsity.

Moving on & Getting Utilities & Saving Energy. Northwest Regional Educational Laboratory Staff. (Illus.). 1980. text 13.96 (*0-07-047303-X*) McGraw.

***Moving on from Computer Basics: Improve Your Skills & Get More from Your Computer.** Carol Dolman & Marcus Saunders. (Computer Basics Ser.). (Illus.). 160p. 1999. pap. 19.95 (*1-85703-507-0*, Pub. by How To Bks) Trans-Atl Phila.

Moving on in Spelling. Cheryl Lacey. 112p. (J). (gr. k-4). 1994. pap. 14.95 (*0-590-49636-0*) Scholastic Inc.

***Moving on in Your Career: A Guide for Academics & Postgraduates.** Lynda Ali & Barbara Graham. LC 99-44350. 168p. 2000. pap. write for info. (*0-415-17870-3*) Routledge.

Moving on to Greater Things. James C. Lewis. LC 88-50843. 294p. (Orig.). 1990. pap. 10.95 (*0-942482-11-5*) Unity Church Denver.

Moving on Up: A Woman's Guide to Spirit Living. Rebecca F. Osaigbovo. 1996. pap. text 9.95 (*1-880560-54-2*) DaBaR Srvs.

Moving on with Big B. Ed. by Scholastic, Inc. Staff. (J). 1993. pap. 7.95 (*0-590-77253-8*) Scholastic Inc.

***Moving on Without Parents: Planning, Transitions & Sources of Support for Middle-Aged & Older Adults with Intellectual Disability.** Christine Bigby. LC 00-33668. 2000. write for info. (*1-55766-478-1*) P H Brookes.

Moving Onward & Upward: Step-by-Step Guide to Taking the Headache Out of Moving. Jamie Taylor. LC 94-65048. 320p. (Orig.). 1997. 29.95 (*1-884573-06-1*); pap. 19.95 (*1-884573-13-4*) S-By-S Pubns.

Moving Out. David Walker. LC 75-31971. (Virginia Commonwealth University Series for Contemporary Poetry). 94p. reprint ed. pap. 30.00 (*0-608-13931-9*, 202374700033) Bks Demand.

Moving Out of the Target Zone: What to Do When Activitists Attack. James E. Lukaszewski. 5p. 1999. pap. 20.00 (*1-883291-28-3*) Lukaszewski.

Moving out on Your Own: Reflections on Leaving Home for the First Time. Steve Swanson. LC 95-8357. 112p. 1995. pap. 10.99 (*0-8066-2731-X*, 9-2731, Augsburg) Augsburg Fortress.

Moving Pageant: A Literary Sourcebook on London Street-Life, 1700-1914. Richard Allen. LC 97-38277. (Illus.). 264p. (C). 1998. 75.00 (*0-415-15307-7*) Routledge.

Moving Pageant: A Literary Sourcebook on London Street-Life, 1700-1914. Richard Allen. LC 97-38277. 249p. (C). 1998. pap. 24.99 (*0-415-15308-5*) Routledge.

Moving Parts. Steve Katz. LC 76-47782. 1977. 15.95 (*0-914590-32-4*) Fiction Coll.

Moving Parts: Monologues from Contemporary Plays. Ed. by Nina Shengold & Eric Lane. 352p. (Orig.). 1992. pap. 11.95 (*0-14-013992-3*, Penguin Bks) Viking Penguin.

***Moving People: From Street to Platform, 100 Years Underground.** Ray Orton. Tr. by John Gale & Grey Lipley. (Illus.). 77p. 1999. 49.95 (*1-886536-25-2*) Elevator Wrld.

Moving People in Tomorrow's World: Proceedings of the Institution of Civil Engineers. 176p. 1987. 6.00 (*0-7277-0391-9*) Am Soc Civil Eng.

Moving Picture Feast: A Filmgoer's Hemingway. Ed. by Charles M. Oliver. LC 88-32292. 202p. 1989. 55.00 (*0-275-93146-3*, C3146, Praeger Pubs) Greenwood.

Moving Picture Writes. large type ed. Peter Chambers. (Linford Mystery Library). 304p. 1996. pap. 16.99 (*0-7089-7976-9*) Ulverscroft.

Moving Pictures. Anne Hollander. LC 90-43032. (Illus.). 528p. 1991. pap. text 18.95 (*0-674-58828-2*, HOLMOX) HUP.

Moving Pictures. Robert S. Smilie, Jr. 1997. pap. write for info. (*1-57553-514-9*) Watermrk Pr.

Moving Pictures. R. B. Weber. 32p. (Orig.). (C). 1992. pap. text 5.00 (*1-878173-28-6*) Birnham Wood.

Moving Pictures: A New Theory of Film Genres, Feelings & Cognition. Torben Grodal. (Illus.). 320p. 1999. pap. text 24.95 (*0-19-815983-8*) OUP.

Moving Pictures: How They Are Made & Worked. Frederick A. Talbot. LC 71-124038. (Literature of Cinema, Ser. 1). 1970. reprint ed. 23.95 (*0-405-01638-7*) Ayer.

Moving Pictures: Memories of a Hollywood Prince. Budd Schulberg. LC 80-9055. 448p. 1981. pap. 11.95 (*0-8128-6157-4*, Scrbrough Hse) Madison Bks UPA.

Moving Pictures: Trigger Pictures to Help Children Talk about Moves in There Life. H. Alton. 1987. 50.00 (*0-903534-73-8*, Pub. by Brit Ag for Adopt & Fost) St Mut.

Moving Places: A Life at the Movies. Jonathan Rosenbaum. LC 94-28364. (Orig.). 1995. reprint ed. pap. text 18.95 (*0-520-08907-3*, Pub. by U CA Pr) Cal Prin Full Svc.

Moving Points in Nephrology: Festschrift in Honor of Professor Geoffrey M. Berlyne. Ed. by E. Bourke et al. (Contributions to Nephrology Ser.: Vol. 102). (Illus.). xvi, 254p. 1992. 49.75 (*3-8055-5642-X*) S Karger.

Moving Pony. Jeanne Betancourt. (Pony Pals Ser.). 112p. (J). (gr. 2-5). 1999. pap. 3.99 (*0-590-63397-X*) Scholastic Inc.

Moving Pose 1223. (Pose Ser.). (Illus.). 164p. 1995. pap. 34.95 (*4-568-30048-7*, Pub. by Bijutsu Shuppan-Sha) Bks Nippan.

Moving Power & Money: The Politics of Census Taking. Barbara E. Bryant & William Dunn. 234p. 1995. 24.95 (*0-9628092-7-6*) New Strategist.

Moving Psychotherapy: Theory & Application of Pesso System- Psychomotor Therapy. John S. Crandell. Ed. by Albert Pesso. LC 90-1623. 306p. 1990. text 39.95 (*0-914797-72-7*) Brookline Bks.

Moving Questions: A History of Membrane Transport & Bioenergetics. Joseph D. Robinson. LC 96-48139. (People & Ideas Ser.). (Illus.). 392p. 1997. text 85.00 (*0-19-510564-8*) OUP.

Moving Reflections: Gender, Faith & Aesthetics in the Work of Angela Figuera Aymerich. Jo Evans. (Monografias A Ser.: No. 163). 172p. (C). 1996. 63.00 (*1-85566-046-6*, Pub. by Tamesis Bks Ltd) Boydell & Brewer.

Moving Right Along. Kenward Elmslie. 1980. 10.00 (*0-915990-21-0*); pap. 5.00 (*0-915990-20-2*) Z Pr.

Moving Right Along: The Complete Handbook to Survive Packing & Moving. Stephanie Barrett. (Illus.). 128p. 1986. pap. 9.95 (*0-9615962-0-1*) Signals Pub.

Moving Right along after Heart Surgery. large type rev. ed. Susan G. Burrows & Carole A. Gassert. Ed. by Karen Hubbard. (Illus.). 56p. 1999. pap. 6.50 (*0-939838-49-4*) Pritchett & Hull.

Moving River of Tears: Russia's Experience in Finland. Temira Pachmuss. LC 92-25217. (American University Studies: Slavic Languages & Literature: Ser. XII, Vol. 15). (Illus.). XIII, 289p. (C). 1993. text 49.95 (*0-8204-1956-7*) P Lang Pubng.

Moving Sources in Thermoelasticity. Ed. by T. Rosnowski. 1989. text 49.95 (*0-470-21409-0*) P-H.

Moving Stair. Gabriel Fitzmaurice et al. 80p. (J). (gr. 1-4). 1994. pap. 6.95 (*1-85371-267-1*, Pub. by Poolbeg Pr) Dufour.

Moving Stairway: From Home-Making to Business-Making in Eight Dynamic Steps. Lee Mitchell. 156p. 1991. 10.00 (*0-9630693-0-6*) Select Mktg.

Moving Straight Ahead: Linear Relationships. James T. Fey et al. Ed. by Catherine Anderson et al. (Connected Mathematics Ser.). (Illus.). 160p. (Orig.). 1996. teacher ed. 16.50 (*1-57232-171-7*) Seymour Pubns.

Moving Straight Ahead: Linear Relationships. James T. Fey et al. Ed. by Catherine Anderson et al. (Connected Mathematics Ser.). (Illus.). 91p. (Orig.). (J). (gr. 7). 1996. student ed., wbk. ed. 5.95 (*1-57232-170-9*) Seymour Pubns.

Moving Straight Ahead: Linear Relationships. rev. ed. Glenda Lappan et al. Ed. by Catherine Anderson et al. (Connected Mathematics Ser.). (Illus.). 182p. (YA). (gr. 7 up). 1997. pap. text, teacher ed. 16.50 (*1-57232-642-5*, 45837); pap. text, student ed. 5.95 (*1-57232-641-7*, 45836) Seymour Pubns.

Moving Successfully: Money-Saving, Hassle-Free Moving & Storage. Tom Philbin. (Illus.). 106p. 1998. reprint ed. pap. text 15.00 (*0-7881-5203-3*) DIANE Pub.

Moving Target. Carolyn Keene. Ed. by Anne Greenberg. LC 94-125383. (Nancy Drew Files: No. 87). 149p. (J). (gr. 6 up). 1993. mass mkt. 3.99 (*0-671-79479-5*, Archway) PB.

Moving Target. Carolyn Keene. (Nancy Drew Files: No. 87). (YA). (gr. 6 up). 1993. 9.09 (*0-606-05501-0*, Pub. by Turtleback) Demco.

Moving Target. Ross MacDonald, pseud. LC 97-47422. 245p. 1998. pap. 11.00 (*0-375-70146-X*) Vin Bks.

Moving Target. Don Pendelton. (Superbolan Ser.: No. 14). 352p. (Orig.). 1989. mass mkt. 3.95 (*0-373-61414-4*) Harlequin Bks.

Moving Targets. Sean Flannery. 480p. 1992. mass mkt. 5.99 (*0-8125-1013-5*, Pub. by Tor Bks) St Martin.

Moving Targets: An Inside Guide to British Art Now. Louisa Buck. LC 98-157311. (Illus.). 192p. 1997. pap. 25.00 (*1-85437-223-8*, Pub. by Tate Gallery) U of Wash Pr.

Moving Targets: Women, Murder, & Representation. Ed. by Helen Birch. LC 93-25139. 1994. 48.00 (*0-520-08573-6*, Pub. by U CA Pr); pap. 18.95 (*0-520-08574-4*, Pub. by U CA Pr) Cal Prin Full Svc.

***Moving Targets 2: A User's Guide to British Art Now.** Louisa Buck. (Illus.). 256p. 2000. pap. 25.95 (*1-85437-316-1*, Pub. by Tate Gallery) U of Wash Pr.

Moving the Centre: The Struggle for Cultural Freedom. Ngugi wa Thiong'o. LC 92-30303. (Studies in African Literature). 184p. (C). 1993. pap. 17.95 (*0-435-08079-2*, 08079) Heinemann.

Moving the Church into Action: Leader's Guide. Kent R. Hunter & D. Chris Thompson. 1990. pap. 14.95 (*0-911866-19-1*) LifeSprings Res.

Moving the Earth: Cooperative Federalism & Implementation of the Surface Mining Act, 308. Ed. by Uday Desai. LC 92-25744. (Contributions in Political Science Ser.: No. 308). 272p. 1992. 55.00 (*0-313-28698-1*, DMV, Greenwood Pr) Greenwood.

Moving the Earth: Teaching Earth Science Through Movement. Helen Landalf. LC 97-11379. (Illus.). 144p. (Orig.). (J). (gr. 3-6). 1997. pap. 19.95 (*1-57525-108-6*) Smith & Kraus.

Moving the Earth: The Workbook of Excavation. 3rd ed. Herbert L. Nichols, Jr. 1760p. 1988. 99.95 (*0-07-046483-9*) McGraw.

Moving the Earth: The Workbook of Excavation. 4th ed. Herbert L. Nichols, Jr. & David H. Day. LC 98-15161. (Illus.). 1400p. 1998. 105.00 (*0-07-046484-7*) McGraw.

Moving the Force: Desert Storm & Beyond. 88p. 1994. pap. text 30.00 (*1-57979-168-9*) DIANE Pub.

Moving the Force: Desert Storm & Beyond. 1997. lib. bdg. 250.99 (*0-8490-6162-8*) Gordon Pr.

Moving the Force: Desert Storm & Beyond. Scott W. Conrad. 88p. 1995. per. 3.50 (*0-16-061172-5*) USGPO.

Moving the Force: Desert Storm & Beyond. Scott W. Conrad. 81p. (C). 1996. reprint ed. pap. text 20.00 (*0-7881-3679-8*) DIANE Pub.

Moving the Furniture: Liturgical Theory, Practice & Environment William Seth Adams. LC 99-22884. 1999. write for info. (*0-89869-316-0*) Church Pub Inc.

Moving the Glacier: The 2 Koreans. 1989. 15.25 (*0-08-037698-3*) Macmillan.

Moving the Goalposts: Football's Exploitation. Ed Horton. 192p. 1997. 35.00 (*1-85158-863-9*, Pub. by Mainstream Pubng) Trafalgar.

Moving the Housing Market. Ray Forrest & Alan Murie. (Illus.). 110p. 1990. text 72.95 (*1-85628-046-2*, Pub. by Avebry) Ashgate Pub Co.

Moving the Image: Independent Asian Pacific American Media Arts 1970-1990. Intro. by Russell Leong. LC 90-71789. (Illus.). 312p. 1992. pap. 25.00 (*0-934052-13-1*) UCLA Asian Am Studies Ctr.

Moving the Masses: Urban Public Transit in New York, Boston, & Philadelphia, 1880 to 1912. Charles W. Cheape. LC 79-15875. (Studies in Business History: No. 31). (Illus.). 291p. 1980. 18.50 (*0-674-58827-4*) HUP.

M

An Asterisk (*) at the beginning of an entry indicates that the title is appearing for the first time.

Moving the Mountain: My Life in China. Li Lu. 1990. 21.95 (*0-399-13545-6*) Putnam Pub Group.

Moving the Mountain: The Women's Movement in America since 1960. Flora Davis. LC 99-11521. 632p. 1999. pap. 21.95 (*0-252-06782-7*) U of Ill Pr.

Moving the Mountain: Women Working for Social Change. Ellen Cantarow et al. LC 79-11840. (Women's Lives - Women's Work Ser.). (Illus.). 208p. (YA). (gr. 11 up). 1998. pap. 12.95 (*0-912670-61-4*) Feminist Pr.

Moving the Mountain with the Never-Give-Up Diaries, 4 vols., Level 1. rev. ed. Kitty M. Jones. (Illus.). 222p. reprint ed. 15.00 (*1-878502-01-8*) Never-Give-Up Weight.

Moving the Mountain with the Never-Give-Up Diaries, 4 vols., Level 2. rev. ed. Kitty M. Jones. (Illus.). 222p. reprint ed. 15.00 (*1-878502-02-6*) Never-Give-Up Weight.

Moving the Mountain with the Never-Give-Up Diaries, 4 vols., Level 3. rev. ed. Kitty M. Jones. (Illus.). 222p. reprint ed. 15.00 (*1-878502-03-4*) Never-Give-Up Weight.

Moving the Mountain with the Never-Give-Up Diaries, 4 vols., Level 4. rev. ed. Kitty M. Jones. (Illus.). 222p. reprint ed. 15.00 (*1-878502-04-2*) Never-Give-Up Weight.

Moving the Mountain with the Never-Give-Up Diaries, 4 vols., Set. 2nd rev. ed. Kitty M. Jones. (Illus.). 222p. reprint ed. write for info. (*1-878502-00-X*) Never-Give-Up Weight.

Moving the Seasons: Selected Poems of Charles Guenther. Charles Guenther. LC 94-16670. 80p. 1994. pap. 12.00 (*0-933532-98-9*) BkMk.

Moving the Still-Life. Edward Boccia. 26p. 1995. pap. 7.95 (*0-944754-18-X*) Pudding Hse Pubns.

Moving Through Here. Don McNeil. 1990. pap. 9.95 (*0-8065-1165-6*, Citadel Pr) Carol Pub Group.

Moving Through Life Transitions with Power & Purpose. 2nd ed. DiMarco. LC 99-12702. (Illus.). 165p. 1999. pap. text 25.20 (*0-13-919465-7*) P-H.

Moving Through Pregnancy. Elisabeth D. Bing. LC 74-17673. 144p. 1975. pap. write for info. (*0-672-52095-8*) Macmillan.

Moving Through the Ratings: Passing from Private to Professional Pilot. Bill Givens. (Illus.). 304p. 1987. 21.95 (*0-8306-0400-6*, 2400) McGraw-Hill Prof.

Moving to a New Place. Ron Schreiber. LC 74-26380. 72p. 1974. pap. 3.95 (*0-914086-07-3*) Alice James Bks.

Moving to a Windows Word Processor from WordPerfect DOS: How to Leverage Your DOS & WordPerfect Skills into AMI PRO, Word for Windows & WordPerfect for Windows. Nicholas P. Terry. LC 94-36480. (Law Office Ser.). 1995. mass mkt. 35.25 (*0-314-05127-9*) West Pub.

Moving to Antarctica: A Women's Anthology. Ed. by Margaret Kaminski. (American Dust Ser.: No. 2). 150p. 1975. 7.95 (*0-913218-35-9*); pap. 3.95 (*0-913218-36-7*) Dustbooks.

Moving to Arizona: The Complete Arizona Answer Book. 4th ed. Dorothy Tegeler. (Illus.). 162p. (Orig.). 1999. pap. 11.95 (*1-889786-02-0*) Gem Guides Bk.

Moving to Boston: Relocating from Around the World. Karen Rudnick et al. 126p. 1999. pap. write for info. (*0-9672934-0-5*) Interchange Inst.

Moving to Chicago. Alpha Books Staff. LC 96-680495. 208p. 1996. 14.95 (*0-02-861281-7*) IDG Bks.

Moving to Discover the U. S. A. Mike Lee & Rhonda L. Clements. LC 98-11700. (Illus.). 208p. 1998. pap. text 19.00 (*0-88011-799-0*, BLEE0799) Human Kinetics.

Moving to Ireland: A Guide to Living & Investing. Brendan Connolly. 1998. 24.95 (*1-85915-150-7*, Pub. by W & G) Motorbooks Intl.

Moving to Las Vegas. Thersa Mataga & John L. Smith. LC 96-47868. 1997. pap. 12.00 (*1-56980-104-5*) Barricade Bks.

Moving to Las Vegas-1999 Update. Theresa A. Mataga & John L. Smith. 130p. pap. 12.00 (*1-56980-152-5*) Barricade Bks.

Moving to Los Angeles. Alpha Books Staff. 208p. 1996. 14.95 (*0-02-861280-9*) IDG Bks.

***Moving to Maine: The Essential Guide to Get You There.** Victoria Doudera. 144p. 2000. pap. 14.95 (*0-89272-479-X*) Down East.

Moving to Malibu. Mary K. Stillwell. LC 85-50681. (Plains Poetry Ser.: Vol. 6). 72p. (Orig.). pap. 6.95 (*0-911015-13-2*) Sandhills Pr.

Moving to Management: The Role of School Governors in the Late 1990s. Angela Thody. 160p. 1992. pap. 29.95 (*1-85346-177-6*, Pub. by David Fulton) Taylor & Francis.

Moving to Market: Restructuring Transport in the Former Soviet Union. John R. Meyer et al. Ed. by John S. Strong. (Studies in International Development; Institute for International Development Ser.). 232p. 1996. 30.00 (*0-674-58814-2*) HUP.

Moving to Mars. Mike Thaler. (Funny Firsts Ser.). (Illus.). 32p. (Orig.). (J). (ps-3). 1996. pap. 2.95 (*0-8167-3970-6*) Troll Communs.

Moving to Mars. Mike Thaler. (Funny Firsts Ser.). (Orig.). (J). 1996. 8.15 (*0-606-09639-6*, Pub. by Turtleback) Demco.

Moving to New York. Alpha Books Staff. 208p. 1996. pap. text 14.95 (*0-02-861279-5*) IDG Bks.

Moving to Nowhere: Children's Stories of Homelessness. Mary E. Walsh. LC 91-34709. 208p. 1992. 49.95 (*0-86569-017-0*, T017, Auburn Hse); pap. 18.95 (*0-86569-202-5*, R202, Auburn Hse) Greenwood.

Moving to Success: The Astrology of Location. Rose Murray. LC 98-43553. (Illus.). 352p. 1999. 12.95 (*1-56718-478-2*, K478) Llewellyn Pubns.

Moving to Sustainability: How to Keep Small Business Development Centres Alive. Ed. by Daniel Fogel. 128p. 1996. 72.95 (*1-85972-297-0*, Pub. by Avebry) Ashgate Pub Co.

Moving to the Block: Getting Ready to Teach in Extended Periods of Time. Dale V. Eineder et al. LC 97-39906. (Checklist Ser.). (Illus.). 56p. (Orig.). 1997. pap. 5.95 (*0-8106-2159-2*, 2159-2) NEA.

Moving to the Country. Robert McGill. LC 86-50758. (Illus.). 187p. (Orig.). (C). 1987. pap. 8.95 (*0-935069-17-8*) White Oak Pr.

Moving to the Country: How to Buy or Build the Place You've Always Wanted. Don Skillman. (Illus.). 160p. 1996. pap. 12.95 (*0-8117-2445-X*) Stackpole.

Moving to the Market: The World Bank in Transition. Richard W. Richardson & Jonas H. Haralz. LC 94-47640. (Policy Essay Ser.: Vol. 17). 1995. pap. 13.95 (*1-56517-023-7*) Overseas Dev Council.

Moving to Washington D. C. Alpha Books Staff. 208p. 1996. 14.95 (*0-02-861282-5*) IDG Bks.

Moving Toward an Integrated Curriculum in Early Childhood Education. Dianne Lawler-Prince et al. LC 95-42453. (Early Childhood Education Ser.). 1995. 14.95 (*0-8106-0367-5*) NEA.

***Moving Toward Emancipatory Language: A Study of Recent Hymns.** Robin K. Wallace. LC 99-11657. (Drew University Studies in Liturgy: No. 8). 288p. 1999. 57.50 (*0-8108-3640-8*) Scarecrow.

***Moving Toward Harmony.** Eric Oberg. Ed. by Lesley Thomas. (Illus.). 80p. 2000. pap. 14.95 (*0-9678842-0-9*) Far East Pr.

Moving Toward Life: Five Decades of Transformational Dance. Anna Halprin. Ed. by Rachel Kaplan. LC 95-1696. (Illus.). 298p. 1995. pap. 24.95 (*0-8195-6286-6*, Wesleyan Univ Pr); text 45.00 (*0-8195-5284-4*, Wesleyan Univ Pr) U Pr of New Eng.

Moving Toward Maturity: Leader's Guide. Barry St. Clair. (Moving Toward Maturity Series). 264p. 1991. pap. 9.99 (*0-89693-298-2*, 6-1298) Chariot Victor.

***Moving Toward More Effective Public Internet Access: The 1998 National Survey of Public Library Outlet Internet Connectivity.** Government Printing Office Staff. LC 99-205874. 116p. 1999. pap. text 16.00 (*0-16-049974-7*) USGPO.

***Moving Toward Stillness: Lessons in Daily Life from the Martial Ways of Japan.** Dave Lowry. LC 99-29183. (Illus.). 176p. 2000. pap. 16.95 (*0-8048-3160-2*) Tuttle Pubng.

Moving Toward the Mainstream: Twentieth-Century Change among the Brethren of Eastern Pennsylvania. Donald R. Fitzkee. LC 95-17793. (Illus.). 348p. 1995. pap. 9.95 (*1-56148-170-X*) Good Bks PA.

Moving Toward Your Potential: The Athlete's Guide to Peak Performance. M. Jane Miner et al. 157p. (Orig.). 1995. pap., student ed. 18.00 (*1-887476-01-6*) Perf Publns.

Moving Towards Expert Systems Globally in the 21st Century. Ed. by Jay Liebowitz. LC 94-4689. (Illus.). 1573p. (C). 1994. 175.00 (*1-882345-00-2*) Cognizant Comm.

***Moving Towards Home.** Matthew R. K. Haynes. 163p. 1999. 17.95 (*0-7541-0679-9*, Pub. by Minerva Pr) Unity Dist.

Moving Towards Joint Development: The Economic Development-Transit Partnership. Lori Gillen. Ed. by Jenny Murphy. 107p. (Orig.). 1989. pap. 35.00 (*0-317-05499-6*) Natl Coun Econ Dev.

***Moving Towards Precision with Soil & Plant Analysis.** 1998. pap. 60.00 (*0-643-06271-8*, Pub. by CSIRO) Accents Pubns.

Moving Towards the Standards: A National Action Plan for Mathematics Education Reform for the Deaf: A Report on the Recommendations of the NAPMERD Committee. Charles H. Dietz. (Report on the Recommendations of the NAPMERD Committee Ser.). (Illus.). 76p. 1995. pap. text, teacher ed. 8.95 (*0-88095-202-4*) Gallaudet U Pre Coll.

Moving Toy Shop. Edmund Crispin. 20.95 (*0-8488-0104-0*) Amereon Ltd.

Moving Toy Shop. Edmund Crispin. LC 99-996984. 208p. 1989. pap. 6.99 (*0-14-008817-2*, Penguin Bks) Viking Penguin.

Moving U. S. Forces: Options for Strategic Mobility. Rachel Schmidt. (Illus.). 95p. 1999. reprint ed. pap. text. write for info. (*0-7881-8013-4*) DIANE Pub.

Moving United States Forces: Options for Strategic Mobility. Rachel Schmidt. LC 97-152407. 117p. 1997. per. 10.00 (*0-16-048995-4*, Congress) USGPO.

Moving Up. Judy Delton. LC 94-43308. (Lottery Luck Ser.: Bk. 4). (Illus.). 96p. (J). (gr. 2-5). 1995. pap. 3.95 (*0-7868-1021-1*, Pub. by Hyprn Ppbks) Little.

Moving Up. Lauraine Snelling. (High Hurdles Ser.: No. 7). 160p. (YA). (gr. 6-9). 1998. pap. 5.99 (*0-7642-2035-7*) Bethany Hse.

***Moving Up: A Blueprint for Planning Your Entry into the Executive Suite.** Managers Edge Editors. 8p. 1999. pap. 5.00 (*1-878604-31-7*) Briefings Pub Grp.

Moving Up! A Guidebook for Women in Educational Administration. Ed. by Judith T. Witmer. LC 94-62044. 410p. 1995. pap. 24.95 (*1-56676-235-9*) Scarecrow.

Moving Up: Ethnic Succession in America, with a Case History from the Philadelphia School System. Daniel J. Elazar & Murray Friedman. (Illus.). 64p. 1976. pap. 1.95 (*0-87495-005-8*) Am Jewish Comm.

***Moving up in the Music Business.** Jodi Summers. 224p. 2000. pap. 18.95 (*1-58115-061-X*, Pub. by Allworth Pr) Watsn-Guptill.

Moving up the Organization in Facilities Management: Proven Strategies for Improving the Productivity of Your Workforce. A. S. Migs Damiani. (Illus.). 134p. 1998. pap. 24.95 (*1-891121-03-0*) SciTech Pub.

Moving up the Yield Curve: Advances & Obstacles. Ed. by L. S. Murphy et al. (ASA Special Publications: No. 39). (Illus.). 103p. 1980. pap. 3.85 (*0-89118-064-8*) Am Soc Agron.

Moving up to Gloryland. Compiled by Ken Bible. 171p. 1987. 7.99 (*0-8341-9334-5*, MB-579) Lillenas.

Moving up to Supervision. 2nd ed. Martin M. Broadwell. LC 85-29411. (Training & Development Ser.). 256p. 1986. pap. 70.95 (*0-471-83677-X*) Wiley.

Moving Violations: War Zones, Wheelchairs & Declarations of Independence. John Hockenberry. 416p. (J). 1995. 24.45 (*0-7868-6078-2*, Pub. by Hyperion) Time Warner.

Moving Violations: War Zones, Wheelchairs & Declarations of Independence. John Hockenberry. LC 94-37190. 416p. (J). 1996. reprint ed. pap. 14.45 (*0-7868-8162-3*, Pub. by Hyperion) Time Warner.

Moving Water Through Pumps & Pipes for HPAC. John Gladstone. (Illus.). 96p. 1992. pap. 15.00 (*0-930644-18-2*) Engineers Pr.

Moving Western Water: At Whose Cost? Larry Morandi. 37p. 1991. pap. 10.00 (*1-55516-500-1*, 4333) Natl Conf State Legis.

Moving Windows: Evaluating the Poetry Children Write. Jack Collom. LC 85-9803. 225p. (Orig.). 1985. pap. 14.95 (*0-915924-55-2*) Tchrs & Writers Coll.

***Moving with a Purpose: Developing Programs for Preschoolers of All Abilities.** Renee M. McCall & Diane H. Craft. LC 99-88414. (Illus.). 248p. 2000. 22.00 (*0-88011-976-4*) Human Kinetics.

Moving with Children: A Parent's Guide to Moving with Children. Thomas T. Olkowski & Lynn Parker. LC 93-19123. (Illus.). 196p. (Orig.). 1993. pap. 12.95 (*1-880197-08-1*) Gylantic Pub.

Moving with Confidence - Step 1. 7th ed. Gary B. Spindt. 128p. 1992. boxed set 24.90 (*0-8403-5333-2*) Kendall-Hunt.

Moving with Math: AI Numeration. rev. ed. Caryl K. Pierson. (Illus.). 80p. (J). (gr. k-2). 1993. pap. 5.95 (*0-933383-58-4*) Math Teachers Pr.

Moving with Math: AI Numeration Teacher Guide. rev. ed. Caryl K. Pierson. 28p. 1993. pap., teacher ed. 5.95 (*0-933383-57-6*) Math Teachers Pr.

Moving with Math: AII Addition & Subtraction. rev. ed. Caryl K. Pierson. (Illus.). 80p. (J). (gr. k-2). 1993. pap. 5.95 (*0-933383-60-6*) Math Teachers Pr.

Moving with Math: AII Addition & Subtraction Teacher Guide. rev. ed. Caryl K. Pierson. 37p. 1993. pap., teacher ed. 7.95 (*0-933383-59-2*) Math Teachers Pr.

Moving with Math: AIII Fractions, Geometry & Measurement. rev. ed. Caryl K. Pierson. (Illus.). 80p. (J). (gr. k-2). 1993. pap. 5.95 (*0-933383-62-2*) Math Teachers Pr.

Moving with Math: AIII Fractions, Geometry & Measurement Teacher Guide. rev. ed. Caryl K. Pierson. 32p. 1993. pap., teacher ed. 7.95 (*0-933383-61-4*) Math Teachers Pr.

Moving with Math: BI Numeration, Addition & Subtraction Teacher Guide. rev. ed. Caryl K. Pierson. 39p. 1993. pap., teacher ed. 8.95 (*0-933383-54-1*) Math Teachers Pr.

Moving with Math: BI Numeration, Addition, Subtraction. rev. ed. Caryl K. Pierson. (Illus.). 80p. (J). (gr. 3-4). 1993. pap. 5.95 (*0-933383-07-X*) Math Teachers Pr.

Moving with Math: BII Multiplication & Division. rev. ed. Caryl K. Pierson. (Illus.). 80p. (J). (gr. 3-4). 1993. pap. 5.95 (*0-933383-49-5*) Math Teachers Pr.

Moving with Math: BII Multiplication & Division Teacher Guide. rev. ed. Caryl K. Pierson. 39p. 1993. pap., teacher ed. 7.95 (*0-933383-55-X*) Math Teachers Pr.

Moving with Math: BIII Fractions, Geometry & Measurement. rev. ed. Caryl K. Pierson. (Illus.). 80p. (J). (gr. 3-4). 1996. pap. 5.95 (*0-933383-48-7*) Math Teachers Pr.

Moving with Math: BIII Fractions, Geometry & Measurement Teacher Guide. rev. ed. Caryl K. Pierson. (Illus.). 35p. 1993. pap., teacher ed. 8.95 (*0-933383-56-8*) Math Teachers Pr.

Moving with Math: CI Numeration & Problem Solving with Whole Numbers. rev. ed. Caryl K. Pierson. (Illus.). 80p. (J). (gr. 5-6). 1995. pap. 5.95 (*0-933383-89-4*) Math Teachers Pr.

Moving with Math: CI Numeration & Problem Solving with Whole Numbers Teacher Guide. rev. ed. Caryl K. Pierson & Vicki DeVoss. (Illus.). 80p. 1995. pap., teacher ed. 9.95 (*0-933383-90-8*) Math Teachers Pr.

Moving with Math: CII Fractions, Decimals & Percent. rev. ed. Caryl K. Pierson & Vicki DeVoss. (Illus.). 100p. (J). (gr. 5-6). 1995. pap. 6.95 (*0-933383-51-7*) Math Teachers Pr.

Moving with Math: CII Fractions, Decimals & Percent Teacher Guide. rev. ed. Caryl K. Pierson & Vicki DeVoss. (Illus.). 100p. 1995. pap., teacher ed. 9.95 (*0-933383-53-3*) Math Teachers Pr.

Moving with Math: CIII Geometry & Measurement. Caryl K. Pierson. 72p. (J). (gr. 5-6). 1993. pap. 5.95 (*0-933383-15-0*) Math Teachers Pr.

Moving with Math: CIII Geometry, Measurement & Problem Solving Teacher Guide. rev. ed. Caryl K. Pierson. 40p. 1993. pap., teacher ed. 8.95 (*0-933383-70-3*) Math Teachers Pr.

Moving with Math: DI Numeration & Problem Solving with Whole Numbers. rev. ed. Caryl K. Pierson & Vicki DeVoss. (Illus.). 72p. (YA). (gr. 7-8). 1994. pap. 5.95 (*0-933383-18-5*) Math Teachers Pr.

Moving with Math: DI Numeration & Problem Solving with Whole Numbers Teacher Guide. rev. ed. Caryl K. Pierson. 35p. 1990. pap., teacher ed. 8.95 (*0-933383-37-1*) Math Teachers Pr.

Moving with Math: DII Fractions & Decimals. rev. ed. Caryl K. Pierson & Vicki DeVoss. 104p. (YA). (gr. 7-8). 1994. pap. 6.95 (*0-933383-19-3*) Math Teachers Pr.

Moving with Math: DII Problem Solving with Fractions & Decimals Teacher Guide. rev. ed. Caryl K. Pierson. 48p. 1990. pap., teacher ed. 9.95 (*0-933383-38-X*) Math Teachers Pr.

Moving with Math: DIII Problem Solving with Percent. rev. ed. Caryl K. Pierson & Vicki DeVoss. (Illus.). 72p. (YA). (gr. 7-8). 1993. pap. 5.95 (*0-933383-65-7*) Math Teachers Pr.

Moving with Math: DIII Problem Solving with Percent Teacher Guide. rev. ed. Caryl K. Pierson. 37p. 1995. pap., teacher ed. 8.95 (*0-933383-39-8*) Math Teachers Pr.

Moving with Math: DIV Geometry & Measurement. rev. ed. Caryl K. Pierson & Vicki DeVoss. (Illus.). 100p. (YA). (gr. 7-8). 1994. pap. 6.95 (*0-933383-46-0*) Math Teachers Pr.

Moving with Math: DIV Geometry & Measurement Teacher Guide. rev. ed. Caryl K. Pierson. 51p. 1995. pap., teacher ed. 9.95 (*0-933383-40-1*) Math Teachers Pr.

Moving with Math: DV Algebra & Computer. rev. ed. Caryl K. Pierson & Vicki DeVoss. (Illus.). 80p. (YA). (gr. 7-8). 1990. pap. 5.95 (*0-933383-22-3*) Math Teachers Pr.

Moving with Math: DV Algebra & Computer Teacher Guide. rev. ed. Caryl K. Pierson. 47p. 1990. pap., teacher ed. 7.95 (*0-933383-41-X*) Math Teachers Pr.

Moving with Math: Grade 1 Activity Book. rev. ed. Caryl K. Pierson & Susie Whisnant. Ed. by David W. Solberg. (Illus.). 256p. (J). (gr. 1). 1997. pap. 15.95 (*0-933383-93-2*) Math Teachers Pr.

Moving with Math: Grade 1 Teachers Resource Manual. rev. ed. Caryl K. Pierson & Susie Whisnant. Ed. by David W. Solberg. (Illus.). 410p. 1997. pap., teacher ed. 120.00 (*0-933383-94-0*) Math Teachers Pr.

***Moving with Math: Grade 2 Activity Book.** rev. ed. Caryl K. Pierson & Susie Whisnant. Ed. by David W. Solberg. (Illus.). 240p. (J). (gr. 2). 1998. pap. 15.95 (*0-933383-97-5*) Math Teachers Pr.

***Moving with Math: Grade 2 Teachers Resource Manual.** rev. ed. Caryl K. Pierson. (Illus.). 1998. pap., teacher ed. 120.00 (*0-933383-98-3*) Math Teachers Pr.

Moving with Math: Grades 1 & 2 Skill Builders. rev. ed. Caryl K. Pierson et al. (Illus.). 176p. (J). (gr. 1-2). 1994. pap. 29.95 (*0-933383-23-1*) Math Teachers Pr.

Moving with Math: Grades 3 & 4 Skill Builders Using Action Math. rev. ed. Caryl K. Pierson & Judy Heimkes. (Illus.). 192p. (J). (gr. 3-4). 1993. pap. 29.95 (*0-933383-52-5*) Math Teachers Pr.

Moving with Math: Grades 5 & 6 Skill Builders Using Action Math. rev. ed. Caryl K. Pierson. (Illus.). 208p. (J). (gr. 5-6). 1995. pap. 29.95 (*0-933383-86-X*) Math Teachers Pr.

Moving with Math: Grades 7 & 8 Skill Builders. rev. ed. Caryl K. Pierson & Vicki DeVoss. (Illus.). 208p. (YA). (gr. 7-8). 1994. pap. 29.95 (*0-933383-29-0*) Math Teachers Pr.

***Moving with Math: Kindergarten Student Activity Book.** rev. ed. Caryl K. Pierson et al. (Illus.). 176p. (J). (gr. k). 2000. pap. 11.95 (*1-891192-12-4*) Math Teachers Pr.

***Moving with Math: Kindergarten Teachers Resource Manual.** rev. ed. Caryl K. Pierson & Susie Whisnant. 2000. pap., teacher ed. 79.95 (*1-891192-58-2*) Math Teachers Pr.

***Moving with Math: Level A Secondary Workbook.** rev. ed. Caryl K. Pierson. (Illus.). 126p. (YA). (gr. 7-12). 1999. pap., wbk. ed. 7.95 (*1-891192-62-0*) Math Teachers Pr.

Moving with Math: Level A Workbook Teacher Guide. rev. ed. Caryl K. Pierson. 44p. 1995. pap., teacher ed., wbk. ed. 14.95 (*0-933383-91-6*) Math Teachers Pr.

Moving with Math: Level B Math Capsules Diagnostic Tests & Daily Reviews. rev. ed. Caryl K. Pierson. (J). (gr. 3-4). 1994. pap. 19.95 (*0-933383-06-1*) Math Teachers Pr.

Moving with Math: Level C Math Capsules Diagnostic Tests & Daily Reviews. rev. ed. Caryl K. Pierson. (J). (gr. 5-6). 1994. pap. 19.95 (*0-933383-50-9*) Math Teachers Pr.

Moving with Math: Level D Math Capsules Diagnostic Tests & Daily Reviews. Caryl K. Pierson. (YA). (gr. 7-8). 1994. pap. 19.95 (*0-933383-17-7*) Math Teachers Pr.

Moving with Math: Math Capsules Diagnostic Tests & Daily Reviews - Level A. rev. ed. Caryl K. Pierson. (J). (gr. 1-2). 1994. pap. 19.95 (*0-933383-01-0*) Math Teachers Pr.

***Moving with Math: Moviendose Con Matematicas Grade 1.** Caryl K. Pierson & Susie Whisnant. Ed. by David W. Solberg. (SPA., Illus.). (J). (gr. 1). 2000. pap. 180.00 (*0-933383-95-9*) Math Teachers Pr.

***Moving with Math: Moviendose Con Matematicas Grade 2.** rev. ed. Caryl K. Pierson & Susie Whisnant. Ed. by David W. Solberg. (SPA., Illus.). (J). (gr. 2). 1998. pap. 180.00 (*0-933383-99-1*) Math Teachers Pr.

***Moving with Math: Moviendose Con Matematicas Kindergarten.** rev. ed. Caryl K. Pierson & Susie Whisnant. (SPA., Illus.). (J). (gr. k). 2000. pap. 120.00 (*1-891192-59-0*) Math Teachers Pr.

Moving with Math Extensions: Grade 1 Student Book. Caryl Pierson. (Illus.). 80p. (J). (gr. 1). 1998. pap. text 5.95 (*1-891192-14-0*) Math Teachers Pr.

***Moving with Math Extensions: Grade 1 Student Book.** Caryl K. Pierson. Ed. by David W. Solberg. Tr. by Carmen Garcia & Annelise McGuinnes. (SPA.). 80p. (J). (gr. 1). 2000. pap. 6.95 (*1-891192-69-8*) Math Teachers Pr.

M

M

Moving with Math Extensions: Grade 1 Teachers Manual. Caryl Pierson. (Illus.). 228p. 1998. pap. text, teacher ed. 59.95 (*1-891192-23-X*) Math Teachers Pr.

Moving with Math Extensions: Grade 2 Student Book. Caryl Pierson. (Illus.). 80p. (J). (gr. 2). 1998. pap. text 5.95 (*1-891192-15-9*) Math Teachers Pr.

***Moving with Math Extensions: Grade 2 Student Book.** Caryl K. Pierson. Ed. by David W. Solberg. Tr. by Carmen Garcia & Annelise McGuinnes. (SPA.). 80p. (J). (gr. 2). 2000. pap. 6.95 (*1-891192-70-1*) Math Teachers Pr.

Moving with Math Extensions: Grade 2 Teachers Manual. Caryl Pierson. (Illus.). 230p. 1998. pap. text, teacher ed. 59.95 (*1-891192-24-8*) Math Teachers Pr.

***Moving with Math Extensions: Grade 3 Student Book.** Caryl K. Pierson. Ed. by David W. Solberg. Tr. by Carmen Garcia & Annelise McGuinnes. (SPA.). 80p. (J). (gr. 3). 2000. pap. 6.95 (*1-891192-71-X*) Math Teachers Pr.

Moving with Math Extensions: Grade 3 Student Book. Caryle Pierson. (Illus.). 80p. (J). (gr. 3). 1998. pap. text 5.95 (*1-891192-16-7*) Math Teachers Pr.

Moving with Math Extensions: Grade 3 Teachers Manual. Caryle Pierson. (Illus.). 230p. 1998. pap. text, teacher ed. 59.95 (*1-891192-25-6*) Math Teachers Pr.

Moving with Math Extensions: Grade 4 Student Book. Caryl Pierson. (Illus.). 80p. (J). (gr. 4). 1998. pap. text 5.95 (*1-891192-17-5*) Math Teachers Pr.

***Moving with Math Extensions: Grade 4 Student Book.** Caryl K. Pierson. Ed. by David W. Solberg. Tr. by Carmen Garcia & Annelise McGuinnes. (SPA.). 80p. (J). (gr. 4). 2000. pap. 6.95 (*1-891192-72-8*) Math Teachers Pr.

Moving with Math Extensions: Grade 4 Teachers Manual. Caryl Pierson. (Illus.). 230p. 1998. pap. text, teacher ed. 59.95 (*1-891192-26-4*) Math Teachers Pr.

Moving with Math Extensions: Grade 5 Student Book. Caryl Pierson. (Illus.). 80p. (J). (gr. 5). 1998. pap. text 5.95 (*1-891192-18-3*) Math Teachers Pr.

Moving with Math Extensions: Grade 5 Teachers Manual. Caryl Pierson. (Illus.). 230p. 1998. pap. text, teacher ed. 59.95 (*1-891192-27-2*) Math Teachers Pr.

Moving with Math Extensions: Grade 6 Student Book. Caryl Pierson. (Illus.). 80p. (J). (gr. 6). 1998. pap. text 5.95 (*1-891192-19-1*) Math Teachers Pr.

Moving with Math Extensions: Grade 6 Teachers Manual. Caryl Pierson. (Illus.). 230p. 1998. pap., teacher ed. 59.95 (*1-891192-28-0*) Math Teachers Pr.

Moving with Math Extensions: Grade 7 Student Book. Caryl Pierson. (Illus.). 96p. (J). (gr. 7). 1998. pap. text 6.95 (*1-891192-20-5*) Math Teachers Pr.

Moving with Math Extensions: Grade 7 Teachers Manual. Caryl Pierson. (Illus.). 280p. 1998. pap. text, teacher ed. 69.95 (*1-891192-29-9*) Math Teachers Pr.

Moving with Math Extensions: Grade 8 Student Book. Caryl Pierson. (Illus.). 96p. (J). (gr. 8). 1998. pap. text 6.95 (*1-891192-21-3*) Math Teachers Pr.

Moving with Math Extensions: Grade 8 Teachers Manual. Caryl Pierson. (Illus.). 280p. 1998. pap. text, teacher ed. 69.95 (*1-891192-30-2*) Math Teachers Pr.

Moving with Math Extensions: Kindergarten Student Book. Caryl Pierson. (Illus.). 64p. (J). (gr. k). 1998. pap. text 4.95 (*1-891192-13-2*) Math Teachers Pr.

***Moving with Math Extensions: Kindergarten Student Book.** Caryl K. Pierson. Ed. by David W. Solberg. Tr. by Carmen Garcia & Annelise McGuinnes. (SPA.). 64p. (J). (gr. k). 2000. pap. 5.95 (*1-891192-68-X*) Math Teachers Pr.

Moving with Math Extensions: Kindergarten Teacher Manual. Caryl Pierson. (Illus.). 200p. 1998. pap. text, teacher ed. 49.95 (*1-891192-22-1*) Math Teachers Pr.

***Moving with Math Extensions: Moviendose Con Matematicas Grade 1 Resource Pack.** Caryl K. Pierson. Ed. by David W. Solberg. Tr. by Carmen Garcia & Annelise McGuinnes. (SPA.). (J). (gr. 1). 2000. pap. 19.95 (*1-891192-74-4*) Math Teachers Pr.

***Moving with Math Extensions: Moviendose Con Matematicas Grade 2 Resource Pack.** Caryl K. Pierson. Ed. by David W. Solberg. Tr. by Carmen Garcia & Annelise McGuinnes. (SPA.). (J). (gr. 2). 2000. pap. 19.95 (*1-891192-75-2*) Math Teachers Pr.

***Moving with Math Extensions: Moviendose Con Matematicas Grade 3 Resource Pack.** Caryl K. Pierson. Ed. by David W. Solberg. Tr. by Carmen Garcia & Annelise McGuinnes. (SPA.). (J). (gr. 3). 2000. pap. 19.95 (*1-891192-76-0*) Math Teachers Pr.

***Moving with Math Extensions: Moviendose Con Matematicas Grade 4 Resource Pack.** Caryl K. Pierson. Ed. by David W. Solberg. Tr. by Carmen Garcia & Annelise McGuinnes. (SPA.). (J). (gr. 4). 2000. pap. 19.95 (*1-891192-77-9*) Math Teachers Pr.

***Moving with Math Extensions: Moviendose Con Matematicas Kindergarten Resource Pack.** Caryl K. Pierson. Ed. by David W. Solberg. Tr. by Carmen Garcia & Annelise McGuinnes. (SPA.). (J). (gr. k). 2000. pap. 19.95 (*1-891192-73-6*) Math Teachers Pr.

"Moving" with Mattie Lou O'Kelley. Barbara R. Luck. LC 95-11614. (Illus.). 51p. 1995. 9.99 (*0-87935-156-X*) Colonial Williamsburg.

Moving with Skill - Step 2. 7th ed. Gary B. Spindt. 160p. 1992. boxed set 24.90 (*0-8403-5911-X*) Kendall-Hunt.

***Moving with the Ball: The Migration of Professional Footballers.** Pierre Lanfranchi & Matthew Taylor. (Illus.). 256p. 2000. 65.00 (*1-85973-302-6*, Pub. by Berg Pubs); pap. 19.50 (*1-85973-307-7*, Pub. by Berg Pubs) NYU Pr.

Moving with the Elements: Modern Guide to Weather. Steven H. Semken. LC 97-93453. 172p. 1998. pap. 14.95 (*1-888160-35-7*) Ice Cube.

Moving with the Face of the Devil: Art & Politics in Urban West Africa. John W. Nunley. LC 85-16455. (Illus.). 312p. 1987. text 29.95 (*0-252-01015-9*) U of Ill Pr.

Moving Within the Circle: Contemporary Songs & Dances of Native America. J. Bryan Burton. (Illus.). 144p. (Orig.). 1994. pap. 29.95 incl. audio compact disk (*0-937203-65-3*); pap. 63.00 incl. sl., audio compact disk (*0-937203-66-1*) World Music Pr.

Moving Within the Circle: Contemporary Songs & Dances of Native America. annot. ed. J. Bryan Burton. (Illus.). 144p. (Orig.). 1992. pap. 29.95 incl. audio (*0-937203-43-2*); pap. 60.00 incl. audio, sl. (*0-937203-50-5*) World Music Pr.

Moving Without Madness: A Guide to Handling the Stress & Emotions of Moving. Arlene Alpert. (Illus.). ix, 150p. 1997. pap. 14.95 (*1-891076-00-0*) Gemini Press.

Moving Women Up: A Manual for Breaking down Barriers. Judith Pierson. LC 83-60668. 201p. reprint ed. pap. 62.40 (*0-7837-6539-8*, 204567600007) Bks Demand.

Moving Words: Re-Writing Dance. Ed. by Gay Morris. (Illus.). 360p. (C). 1996. 90.00 (*0-415-12542-1*); pap. 27.99 (*0-415-12543-X*) Routledge.

Moving Your Church Through Conflict. Speed B. Leas. 84p. (Orig.). 1985. pap. 13.25 (*1-56699-012-2*, AL82) Alban Inst.

Moving Your Family Overseas. Rosalind Kalb & Penelope Welch. LC 92-21000. (Illus.). 135p. (Orig.). 1992. pap. 15.95 (*1-877864-14-5*) Intercult Pr.

Movings: Poems from Hollywood. Mark Dunster. 11p. 1998. pap. 5.00 (*0-89642-533-9*) Linden Pubs.

Movo Lekrioh. large type ed. Ed. by Y. Y. Lipschitz.Tr. of Introduction to Reading. (HEB.). 32p. (J). (gr. k-2). 1997. pap. 3.00 (*0-8266-0176-6*, Merkos LInyonei Chinuch) Kehot Pubn Soc.

Mowat Adventure Stories. Farley Mowat. 1987. mass mkt. 20.99 (*0-7710-6682-1*) McCland & Stewart.

Mowee: A History of the Hawaiian Island. Cummins E. Speakman. Ed. by Kimo Campbell. (Illus.). 234p. 1981. pap. 9.95 (*0-917850-03-3*) Pueo Pr.

Mower. Ancestors & Descendants of Hannah (Haile) Mower (1780-1855), Including the Bowen, Breck, Bullock, Butterworth, Clapp, Cole, Damon, Davenport, Foxwell, Luther, Mason, Parker, Polly, Sherman, Smith, Tolman & Related Families. 2nd rev. ed. Lyman Mower & Karen H. Mower. (Illus.). 343p. 1997. pap. 52.00 (*0-8328-9477-X*); lib. bdg. 62.00 (*0-8328-9476-1*) Higginson Bk Co.

Mower Maintenance Mechanic. Jack Rudman. (Career Examination Ser.: C-1373). 1994. pap. 23.95 (*0-8373-1373-2*) Nat Learn.

Mowers & Sprayers. 5th rev. ed. Ed. by Deere & Company Staff. (Fundamentals of Service Ser.). (Illus.). 88p. 1993. pap. text 15.95 (*0-86691-179-0*, FOS5605NC) Deere & Co.

Mowgli Has a Party. Heidemarie Lind. (Illus.). 36p. (J). (ps-8). 1997. 15.95 (*1-891126-06-7*); pap. 7.95 (*1-891126-00-8*) Rocky Mtn W.

Mowgli in Arches. Heidemarie Lind. (Illus.). 40p. (J). (ps-8). 1997. 15.95 (*1-891126-09-1*); pap. 7.95 (*1-891126-03-2*) Rocky Mtn W.

Mowgli in Bryce Canyon. Heidemarie Lind. (Illus.). 44p. (J). (ps-8). 1997. 15.95 (*1-891126-07-5*); pap. 7.95 (*1-891126-01-6*) Rocky Mtn W.

Mowgli in Grand Canyon. Heidemarie Lind. (Illus.). 38p. (J). (ps-8). 1997. 15.95 (*1-891126-11-3*); pap. 7.95 (*1-891126-05-9*) Rocky Mtn W.

Mowgli in the Winter Sports. Heidemarie Lind. (Illus.). 64p. (J). (ps-8). 1997. 15.95 (*1-891126-08-3*); pap. 7.95 (*1-891126-02-4*) Rocky Mtn W.

Mowgli in Yellowstone. Heidemarie Lind. (Illus.). 40p. (J). (ps-8). 1997. 15.95 (*1-891126-10-5*); pap. 7.95 (*1-891126-04-0*) Rocky Mtn W.

Mowgli Stories from "The Jungle Book" Rudyard Kipling. LC 94-467. (Illus.). 128p. (Orig.). (J). 1994. pap. 1.00 (*0-486-28030-6*) Dover.

Mowgli's Brothers. Rudyard Kipling. (Illus.). 64p. (YA). (gr. 5 up). 1992. lib. bdg. 26.60 (*1-56846-004-X*, Creat Educ) Creative Co.

Mowgli's Brothers, Set. unabridged ed. Rudyard Kipling. 1994. 16.95 incl. audio (*1-883049-09-1*, 391214, Pub. by Sound Room) Lndmrk Audiobks.

Mowgli's Brothers: Library Edition. unabridged ed. Rudyard Kipling. 1994. lib. bdg. 18.95 incl. audio (*1-883049-28-8*) Sound Room.

Mowing. Jessie Haas. LC 93-12240. (Illus.). 32p. (J). (ps-3). 1994. 14.00 (*0-688-11680-9*, Grenwillow Bks) HarpC Child Bks.

Mowing the Rabbits. Jean Carr. (Illus.). 48p. (Orig.). 1976. pap. 5.00 (*0-942908-03-1*) Pancake Pr.

Mowry: Supplement to the Descendants of Nathaniel Mowry of Rhode Island. William A. Mowry. (Illus.). 95p. 1995. reprint ed. pap. 19.00 (*0-8328-4808-5*); reprint ed. lib. bdg. 29.00 (*0-8328-4807-7*) Higginson Bk Co.

***Moxie.** Kevles. 2000. 27.00 (*0-7382-0209-6*, Pub. by Perseus Pubng) HarpC.

Moxie. Phyllis Rossiter. LC 90-30027. 192p. (J). (gr. 5 up). 1990. text 14.95 (*0-02-777831-2*, Four Winds Pr) S&S Childrens.

Moxie Encyclopedia, Vol. 1. Q. David Bowers. LC 85-5325. (Illus.). 760p. 1999. pap. 19.95 (*0-911572-43-0*, Vestal Pr) Madison Bks UPA.

Moy Qui Me Voy: The Writer & the Self from Montaigne to Leiris. Ed. by George Craig & Margaret McGowan. 240p. 1989. 70.00 (*0-19-815153-5*) OUP.

***Moya Doroga.** Galina Vergules.Tr. of My Road. (RUS.). 1999. text. write for info. (*0-9673753-0-4*) Gelany.

Moyayama: Russian Haiku: A Diary. Alexey V. Andreyev. Ed. by Marek Lugowski & Kim Hodges. LC 96-203571.Tr. of My Ditch. (Illus.). 44p. 1996. pap. 3.00 (*1-888431-08-3*) ASGP.

Moyen Age see Textes & Litterature

Moyen Age see Collection Litteraire

Moyen-Age-Ostie see Grande Encyclopedie

Moyen Age Russe. Alexandre Eck. LC 74-149685. reprint ed. 41.50 (*0-404-02243-X*) AMS Pr.

Moyen Francais. Pierre Guiraud. 123p. 1963. 9.95 (*0-8288-7458-1*) Fr & Eur.

Moyens D'Expression du Pouvoir. E. Peters. 1998. 37.95 (*90-6831-871-3*, Pub. by Peeters Pub) Bks Intl VA.

Moyens du Bord. Michel Mohrt. (FRE.). 1982. pap. 11.95 (*0-7859-4164-9*) Fr & Eur.

Moynihan-Kissinger Doctrine & the "Third World" Henry Winston. 1975. pap. 0.50 (*0-87898-116-0*) New Outlook.

Moys Classification & Thesaurus for Legal Materials. 3rd ed. Ed. by Elizabeth M. Moys. 400p. 1991. 110.00 (*0-86291-903-7*) Bowker-Saur.

Moza de Cantaro. Lope de Vega. Ed. by Jose M. Diez Borque. (Nueva Austral Ser.: No. 105). (SPA.). 1991. pap. text 24.95 (*84-239-1905-6*) Elliots Bks.

Mozambique see Enchantment of the World Series

Mozambique. Colin Darch & Calisto Pacheleke. LC 88-144644. (World Bibliographical Ser.: No. 78). 388p. 1988. lib. bdg. 70.00 (*1-85109-025-8*) ABC-CLIO.

Mozambique. Adam Lechmere. (Travellers Survival Kit Ser.). 1999. pap. 18.95 (*1-85458-223-2*) Seven Hills Bk.

Mozambique. Joseph Sevigny. LC 95-22476. (Oles Country Guide Ser.). 1998. 20.00 (*0-929851-55-2*) Am Assn Coll Registrars.

Mozambique. Jens E. Torp. 250p. 1990. text 49.00 (*0-86187-432-3*, Pub. by P P Pubs); text 17.50 (*0-86187-433-1*, Pub. by P P Pubs) Cassell & Continuum.

Mozambique: A Country Study. Ed. by Harold D. Nelson. LC 85-6027. (DA Pam Area Handbook Ser.: No. 550-61). (Illus.). 375p. 1985. text 16.00 (*0-16-001622-3*, S/N 008-020-01033-2) USGPO.

***Mozambique: A Country Study Guide.** Global Investment & Business Center, Inc. Staff. (World Country Study Guides Library: Vol. 118). (Illus.). 350p. 2000. pap. 59.00 (*0-7397-2416-9*) Intl Business Pubns.

***Mozambique: A Visual Souvenir.** (Illus.). 80p. 2000. 19.95 (*1-86872-207-4*, Pub. by New Holland) BHB Intl.

Mozambique: A War Against the People. Hilary Andersson. LC 92-8426. 1992. text 49.95 (*0-312-08406-4*) St Martin.

Mozambique: Land Mines in Mozambique. Human Rights Watch Africa Staff & Human Rights Watch Arms Project Staff. LC 93-81027. ix, 119p. 1994. pap. 10.00 (*1-56432-121-5*) Hum Rts Watch.

Mozambique: Major Worlds Nations. R. S. James. (Major World Nations Ser.). (Illus.). 144p. (YA). (gr. 5 up). 1999. lib. bdg. 19.95 (*0-7910-4744-X*) Chelsea Hse.

Mozambique: Rising from the Ashes. Rachel Waterhouse. (Oxfam Country Profiles Ser.). (Illus.). 64p. 1996. pap. 9.95 (*0-85598-341-8*, Pub. by Oxfam Pub) Stylus Pub VA.

Mozambique: The Cross & the Crown. Rodney Hein & Ellie Hein. 1989. per. 4.95 (*0-89985-275-0*) Christ for the Nations.

Mozambique: The Revolution & Its Origins. Barry Munslow. LC 82-16204. 207p. reprint ed. pap. 64.20 (*0-8357-6226-2*, 203446800090) Bks Demand.

***Mozambique: The Tortuous Road to Democracy.** Jodao M. Cabrita. LC 00-40457. 2000. write for info. (*0-333-92001-5*) Macmillan.

Mozambique: The Troubled Transition. Hans Abrahamsson & Anders Nilsson. LC 95-21717. (Illus.). 256p. (C). 1995. text 65.00 (*1-85649-323-7*, Pub. by Zed Books) St Martin.

Mozambique: U. N. Peacekeeping in Action, 1992-94. Richard Synge. LC 97-17773. (Illus.). 1997. 32.50 (*1-878379-70-4*); pap. 14.95 (*1-878379-69-0*) US Inst Peace.

Mozambique: Who Calls the Shots? Joseph Hanlon. LC 91-17006. (Illus.). 316p. 1991. 39.95 (*0-253-32696-6*) Ind U Pr.

Mozambique - A Country Study Guide: Basic Information for Research & Pleasure. Global Investment Center, USA Staff. (World Country Study Guide Library: Vol. 118). (Illus.). 350p. 1999. pap. 59.00 (*0-7397-1515-1*) Intl Business Pubns.

Mozambique - A Dream Undone: The Political Economy of Democracy, 1975-1984. Bertil Egero. (Illus.). 230p. (Orig.). 1990. pap. 35.00 (*91-7106-302-1*) Coronet Bks.

Mozambique & Angola: Reconstruction in the Social Sciences. Bertil Egero. (Research Report Ser.: No. 42). 78p. 1977. write for info. (*91-7106-118-5*, Pub. by Nordic Africa) Transaction Pubs.

***Mozambique & the Construction of the New African State: From Negotiations to Nation Building.** Chris Alden. LC 00-33317. 2000. write for info. (*0-312-23594-1*) St Martin.

***Mozambique Business Intelligence Report, 190 vols.** Global Investment & Business Center, Inc. Staff. (World Business Intelligence Library: Vol. 118). (Illus.). 350p. 2000. pap. 99.95 (*0-7397-2616-1*) Intl Business Pubns.

***Mozambique Business Law Handbook, 190 vols.** Global Investment & Business Center, Inc. Staff. (Global Business Law Handbooks Library: Vol. 118). (Illus.). 350p. 2000. pap. 99.95 (*0-7397-2016-3*) Intl Business Pubns.

***Mozambique Business Opportunity Yearbook.** Global Investment & Business Center, Inc. Staff. (Global Business Opportunity Yearbooks Library: Vol. 118). (Illus.). 2000. pap. 99.95 (*0-7397-2216-6*) Intl Business Pubns.

***Mozambique Country Review 2000.** Robert C. Kelly et al. (Illus.). 60p. 1999. pap. 39.95 (*1-58310-542-5*) CountryWatch.

***Mozambique Foreign Policy & Goverment Guide.** Contrib. by Global Investment & Business Center, Inc. Staff. (World Foreign Policy & Government Library: Vol. 114). (Illus.). 350p. 1999. pap. 99.00 (*0-7397-3612-4*) Intl Business Pubns.

***Mozambique Foreign Policy & Goverment Guide.** Global Investment & Business Center, Inc. Staff. (World Foreign Policy & Government Library: Vol. 114). (Illus.). 350p. 2000. pap. 99.95 (*0-7397-3816-X*) Intl Business Pubns.

***Mozambique Investment & Business Guide.** Global Investment & Business Center, Inc. Staff. (Global Investment & Business Guide Library: Vol. 118). (Illus.). 2000. pap. 99.95 (*0-7397-1816-9*) Intl Business Pubns.

***Mozambique Investment & Business Guide: Export-Import, Investment & Business Opportunities.** International Business Publications, USA Staff & Global Investment Center, USA Staff. (World Investment & Business Guide Library-99: Vol. 118). (Illus.). 350p. 1999. pap. 99.95 (*0-7397-0313-7*) Intl Business Pubns.

Mozan No. 2: The Epigraphic Finds of the Sixth Season. L. Milano. (Mesopotamian Studies: No. 5-1). (Illus.). 34p. (C). 1991. pap. text 9.00 (*0-89003-276-9*) Undena Pubns.

Mozan One: The Soundings of the First Two Seasons. Giorgio Buccellati & Marilyn Kelly-Buccellati. LC 87-50698. (Bibliotheca Mesopotamica Ser.: Vol. 20). (Illus.), 164p. 1988. text 31.00 (*0-89003-195-9*); pap. text 22.00 (*0-89003-194-0*) Undena Pubns.

Mozart. (Masterpieces of Piano Music Ser.). (Illus.). 192p. 1986. pap. 15.95 (*0-8256-2423-1*, AM37227) Music Sales.

Mozart. Marcia Davenport. 1976. 30.95 (*0-8488-0976-9*) Amereon Ltd.

Mozart. Marcia Davenport. 440p. 1979. mass mkt. 5.95 (*0-380-45534-X*, Avon Bks) Morrow Avon.

Mozart. Friedman-Fairfax & Sony Music Staff. (Life, Times, & Music Ser.). (Illus.). 72p. 1995. pap. 15.98 incl. audio compact disk (*1-56799-005-3*, Friedman-Fairfax) M Friedman Pub Grp Inc.

Mozart. Peter Gay. LC 98-51912. (Penguin Lives Ser.). 166p. (YA). 1999. 19.95 (*0-670-88238-0*) Viking Penguin.

***Mozart.** Robert Gutman. (Illus.). 864p. 2000. pap. 20.00 (*0-15-601171-9*) Harcourt.

***Mozart.** Ed. by Hal Leonard Publishing Company Staff. (World's Greatest Classical Music Ser.). 224p. 2000. pap. 14.95 (*0-634-01636-9*) H Leonard.

Mozart. Wolfgang Hildesheimer. Tr. by Marion Faber from GER. (Illus.). 408p. 1991. pap. 12.95 (*0-374-52298-7*) FS&G.

Mozart. Martin Hoyle. 160p. 1997. 60.00 (*1-873376-60-X*, Pub. by Spellmnt Pubs) St Mut.

Mozart. Julie Koerner. LC 97-27024. (Illus.). 64p. 1997. 13.50 incl. audio compact disk (*1-56799-543-8*, Friedman-Fairfax) M Friedman Pub Grp Inc.

Mozart. Annette Kolb. (Lost Treasure Ser.). (Illus.). 340p. (Orig.). 1998. pap. 17.95 (*1-85375-285-1*) Prion.

Mozart, 1. Jeroen Koolbergen. 1998. pap. text 7.98 (*1-85501-786-5*) Tiger Bks Intl.

***Mozart.** Jeroen Koolbergen. 1999. 7.95 (*1-57717-073-3*) Todtri Prods.

Mozart. Nancy Loewen. (Profiles in Music Ser.). (Illus.). 112p. (J). (gr. 5 up). 1989. lib. bdg. 25.27 (*0-86592-605-0*) Rourke Enter.

***Mozart.** Wendy Lynch. LC 99-37280. (Lives & Times Ser.). 2000. lib. bdg. write for info. (*1-57572-219-4*) Heinemann Lib.

Mozart. Composed by Wolfgang Amadeus Mozart. 64p. 1996. pap. 9.95 (*0-7935-6737-8*) H Leonard.

Mozart. Ann Rachlin. LC 92-10302. (Famous Children Ser.). (Illus.). 24p. (J). (gr. k-3). 1992. 5.95 (*0-8120-4989-6*) Barron.

Mozart. Ann Rachlin. (Famous Children Ser.). (Illus.). 24p. (J). 1993. 10.95 (*0-8120-6362-7*) Barron.

Mozart. Sacheverell Sitwell. LC 71-114896. (Select Bibliographies Reprint Ser.). 1977. 19.95 (*0-8369-5300-2*) Ayer.

Mozart. Andrew Steptoe. LC 97-217212. 1997. 47.50 (*0-375-40001-X*) Everymns Lib.

***Mozart.** Angelika Taschen. 1999. pap. (*3-8228-6391-2*) Taschen Amer.

Mozart. Eric Tomb. (J). (gr. 1-9). 1992. pap. 3.50 (*0-88388-125-X*) Bellerophon Bks.

***Mozart.** Roland Vernon. (Introducing Composers Ser.). (Illus.). (J). 2000. 16.95 (*0-7910-6041-1*) Chelsea Hse.

Mozart. Neil Wenborn. LC 93-39718. (Compact Companions Ser.). (Illus.). 192p. 1994. 17.50 (*0-671-88791-2*) S&S Trade.

Mozart. Franz E. Gehring. LC 78-37881. (Select Bibliographies Reprint Ser.). 1977. reprint ed. 18.95 (*0-8369-6718-6*) Ayer.

Mozart. Hugh Ottaway. LC 79-91954. (Illus.). 208p. reprint ed. pap. 64.50 (*0-7837-3642-8*, 204351000009) Bks Demand.

Mozart: A Cultural Biography. Robert Gutman. LC 99-31953. 992p. 1999. 40.00 (*0-15-100482-X*, Harvest Bks) Harcourt.

Mozart: A Documentary Biography. Otto E. Deutsch. xii, 680p. 1966. 59.50 (*0-8047-0233-0*) Stanford U Pr.

Mozart: A Life. Maynard Solomon. (Illus.). 656p. 1996. pap. 20.00 (*0-06-092692-9*) HarpC.

Mozart: A Life. Maynard Solomon. 1996. pap. 18.00 (*0-614-14722-0*, Perennial) HarperTrade.

Mozart: A Musical Biography. Konrad Kuster. Tr. by Mary Whittall. LC 95-35042. (Illus.). 428p. 1996. 35.00 (*0-19-816339-8*) OUP.

An Asterisk (*) at the beginning of an entry indicates that the title is appearing for the first time.

Mozart: A Research Guide. 2nd ed. Guy A. Marco & David W. Fenton. (Composer Resource Manuals Ser.). 500p. 1998. text 75.00 (*0-8153-2386-7*) Garland.

***Mozart: Alla Turca.** Ed. by Peter Pickow. (Concert Performer Ser.). 4p. 1999. pap. text 6.95 incl. cd-rom (*0-8256-1749-9*, AM949828) Music Sales.

Mozart: An Illustrated Biography. Richard Baker. (Illus.). 149p. 1997. (*0-316-64133-2*) Little.

Mozart: Clarinet Concerto. Colin J. Lawson. (Cambridge Music Handbks.). (Illus.). 222p. (C). 1996. text 39.95 (*0-521-47384-5*); pap. text 13.95 (*0-521-47929-0*) Cambridge U Pr.

Mozart: From Child Prodigy to Tragic Hero. Michel Parouty. Tr. by Celia Skrine. (Discoveries Ser.). (Illus.). 192p. 1993. pap. 12.95 (*0-8109-2846-9*, Pub. by Abrams) Time Warner.

Mozart: His Character, His Work. Alfred Einstein. Tr. by Arthur Mendel & Nathan Broder. 504p. (Orig.). 1965. reprint ed. pap. 17.95 (*0-19-500732-8*) OUP.

Mozart: Music Book Index. Eric Blom. 387p. 1993. reprint ed. lib. bdg. 89.00 (*0-7812-9610-2*) Rprt Serv.

Mozart: Music Book Index. Sacheverell Sitwell. 191p. 1993. reprint ed. lib. bdg. 69.00 (*0-7812-9718-4*) Rprt Serv.

Mozart: Piano Concertos No. 20 in D Minor, K. 466, & No. 21 in C Major, K. 467. David Grayson, pseud. LC 97-50598. (Cambridge Music Handbks.). (Illus.). 128p. (C). 1998. 39.95 (*0-521-48156-2*); pap. text 13.00 (*0-521-48475-8*) Cambridge U Pr.

Mozart: Piano Solo Complete Edition, 4. Ed. by Tamas Zaszkaliczky. (Urtext Editions for Piano). 1997. boxed set 59.95 (*963-8303-33-6*, 803001) Konemann.

Mozart: Portraits of a Genius. Norbert Elias. Tr. by Edmund Jephcott. (C). 1993. 24.95 (*0-520-08475-6*, Pub. by U CA Pr) Cal Prin Full Svc.

Mozart: Portraits of Greatness. Gino Pugnetti. Tr. by Helen Lawrence from ITA. (Illus.). 75p. 1989. reprint ed. 17.50 (*0-918367-35-2*); reprint ed. pap. 12.50 (*0-918367-29-8*) Elite.

***Mozart: Sonata K. 545.** Ed. by Peter Pickow. (Concert Performer Ser.). 4p. 1999. pap. text 6.95 incl. cd-rom (*0-8256-1750-2*, AM949837) Music Sales.

Mozart: Studies of the Autograph Scores. Alan Tyson. LC 86-33487. (Illus.). 320p. 1987. 46.50 (*0-674-58830-4*) HUP.

Mozart: Studies of the Autograph Scores. Alan Tyson. 320p. 1990. pap. 22.00 (*0-674-58831-2*) HUP.

Mozart: Taschenpartitur, 2 vols. Composed by Wolfgang Amadeus Mozart. (Cloth Bound Pocket Ser.). 1999. boxed set 14.95 (*963-9155-50-0*) Konemann.

Mozart: The Golden Years. H. C. Landon. 256p. 1989. write for info. (*0-318-66745-2*) Macmillan.

Mozart: The 'Haydn' Quartets. John Irving. LC 97-7268. (Music Handbks.). 112p. (C). 1998. text 39.95 (*0-521-58475-2*); pap. text 13.95 (*0-521-58561-9*) Cambridge U Pr.

Mozart: The Illustrated Lives of the Great Composers. 200th anniversary ed. Peggy Woodford. (Illustrated Lives of the Great Composers Ser.). (Illus.). 144p. 1992. pap. text 17.95 (*0-7119-0248-8*, OP 42340) Music Sales.

Mozart: The "Jupiter" Symphony. Ed. by Elaine R. Sisman. LC 92-39074. (Cambridge Music Handbooks Ser.). (Illus.). 122p. (C). 1993. text 39.95 (*0-521-40069-4*); pap. text 13.95 (*0-521-40924-1*) Cambridge U Pr.

Mozart: The Man & His Works. Walter J. Turner. LC 78-60148. 458p. 1979. reprint ed. lib. bdg. 35.00 (*0-313-20550-7*, TUMO, Greenwood Pr) Greenwood.

Mozart: The Man & the Artist As Revealed in His Own Words. Friedrich Kerst. Tr. by Henry E. Krehbiel. 99p. 1965. pap. 4.95 (*0-486-21316-1*) Dover.

Mozart: The Piano Concerti. David Foil. (Black Dog Music Library). 46p. 1995. 9.98 incl. audio compact disk (*1-884822-38-X*) Blck Dog & Leventhal.

Mozart - An Introduction to His Keyboard Works. Ed. by Willard A. Palmer. (Alfred Masterwork Editions Ser.). 64p. 1974. pap. text 7.95 (*0-88284-254-4*, 664) Alfred Pub.

Mozart - Rondo Alla Turca. Ed. by Willard A. Palmer. (Simply Classics Ser.). 4p. 1995. pap. 2.50 (*0-7390-0823-4*, 14315) Alfred Pub.

Mozart - Solo Piano Literature: A Comprehensive Guide: Annotated & Evaluated with Thematics. Ed. by Carolyn Maxwell. (Maxwell Music Evaluation Bks.). (Illus.). 347p. (Orig.). 1987. pap. 13.95 (*0-912531-04-5*) Maxwell Mus Eval.

Mozart - Sonata in C Major, K.545. Ed. by Willard A. Palmer. 16p. 1985. pap. 4.95 (*0-7390-0854-4*, 2543) Alfred Pub.

Mozart - The Easy Way: Easy Piano. Arranged by Charles Bateman. 11.95 (*1-56922-111-1*, 07-2043) Creat Cncpts.

Mozart - 21 of His Most Popular Piano Pieces. Willard A. Palmer. (Alfred Masterwork Edition Ser.). 64p. 1976. pap. 8.50 (*0-7390-0442-5*, 391) Alfred Pub.

Mozart & Beethoven: The Concept of Love in Their Operas. Irving Singer. LC 77-4551. 168p. reprint ed. pap. 52.10 (*0-7837-0048-2*, 20402950016) Bks Demand.

Mozart & Classical Music. Francesco Salvi. LC 98-72291. (Masters of Music Ser.). 64p. (YA). (gr. 6 up). 1998. 14.95 (*0-7641-5131-2*) Barron.

Mozart & Constanze. Francis Carr. 186p. 1985. mass mkt. 4.95 (*0-380-69884-6*, Avon Bks) Morrow Avon.

Mozart & Haydn in London, 2 vols. in 1. C. F. Pohl. LC 70-125059. (Music Ser.). 1970. reprint ed. lib. bdg. 55.00 (*0-306-70024-7*) Da Capo.

Mozart & His Operas. Sadie. Ed. by Stanley Sadie. (Illus.). 256p. 2000. text 24.95 (*0-312-24410-X*) St Martin.

Mozart & His Piano Concertos. Cuthbert M. Girdlestone. LC 52-3317. 511p. reprint ed. pap. 158.50 (*0-608-10968-1*, 200479300046) Bks Demand.

Mozart & Masonry. Paul Nettl. LC 78-114564. (Music Ser.). 1970. reprint ed. lib. bdg. 25.00 (*0-306-71922-3*) Da Capo.

***Mozart & Me.** Joyce T. Stafford. LC 00-37941. 272p. (C). 2001. 24.95 (*1-929490-05-4*) Beil.

Mozart & Posterity. Gernot Gruber. Tr. by R. S. Furness. 1994. text 29.95 (*1-55553-194-6*) NE U Pr.

Mozart & Salieri: The Little Tragedies. Aleksandr Pushkin. Tr. by Antony Wood from RUS. 96p. 1982. reprint ed. 23.00 (*0-946162-02-6*, Pub. by Angel Bks) Dufour.

Mozart & Salieri: The Little Tragedies. Aleksandr Pushkin. Tr. by Antony Wood from RUS. LC 87-13480. 96p. 1987. reprint ed. pap. 15.95 (*0-8023-1282-9*) Dufour.

Mozart & the Enlightenment: Truth, Virtue & Beauty in Mozart's Operas. Nicholas Till. (Illus.). 400p. 1996. pap. 18.95 (*0-393-31395-6*, Norton Paperbks) Norton.

Mozart & the Sonata Form. Joseph R. Tobin. 156p. 1990. reprint ed. lib. bdg. 59.00 (*0-7812-9172-0*) Rprt Serv.

Mozart & the Sonata Form: A Companion Book to Any Edition of Mozart's Piano Sonatas-Including an Analysis of the Form of Each Movement. Joseph R. Tobin. LC 76-109867. 156p. 1971. reprint ed. lib. bdg. 35.00 (*0-8371-4358-6*, TOMS, Greenwood Pr) Greenwood.

Mozart Arias. 64p. 1996. pap. 16.95 incl. audio compact disk (*0-7935-6239-2*) H Leonard.

Mozart Arias. Composed by Wolfgang Amadeus Mozart. 88p. 1996. pap. 16.95 incl. audio compact disk (*0-7935-6241-4*); pap. 16.95 incl. audio compact disk (*0-7935-6242-2*) H Leonard.

Mozart Arias: Mezzo. 88p. 1996. pap. 16.95 incl. audio compact disk (*0-7935-6240-6*) H Leonard.

Mozart Assassine. Rene Fallet. (FRE.). 192p. 1980. pap. 10.95 (*0-7859-2428-0*, 2070371786) Fr & Eur.

Mozart Auf der Reise Nach Prag. unabridged ed. Eduard Morike. (World Classic Literature Ser.). (GER.). pap. 5.95 (*3-89507-018-1*, Pub. by Bookking Intl) Distribks Inc.

***Mozart-Da Ponte Operas: An Annotated Bibliography, 81.** Mary Du Mont. LC 00-21226. (Music Reference Collection: Vol. 81). 224p. 2000. lib. bdg. 79.50 (*0-313-30413-0*, GM0413, Greenwood Pr) Greenwood.

Mozart-Da Ponte Operas: The Cultural & Musical Background to Le Nozze de Figaro, Don Giovanni, & Cosi Fan Tutte. Andrew Steptoe. (Illus.). 284p. 1990. reprint ed. pap. text 29.95 (*0-19-816221-9*) OUP.

Mozart Diary: A Chronological Reconstruction of the Composer's Life, 1761-1791, 58. Peter Dimond. LC 96-29814. (Music Reference Collection: Vol. 58). 248p. 1997. lib. bdg. 65.00 (*0-313-30131-X*, Greenwood Pr) Greenwood.

***Mozart Effect.** Don Campbell. 2000. pap. 14.00 (*0-380-79013-0*, Quil) HarperTrade.

Mozart Effect: Tapping the Power of Music to Heal the Body, Strengthen the Mind & Unlock the Creative Spirit. Don Campbell. LC 97-27570. 352p. 1998. 24.00 (*0-380-97418-5*, Avon Bks) Morrow Avon.

***Mozart Effect (R) for Children: Awakening Your Child's Mind, Health & Creativity With Music.** Don Campbell. 288p. 2000. 25.00 (*0-380-97782-6*, Wm Morrow) Morrow Avon.

Mozart Family: Four Lives in a Social Context. Ruth Halliwell. (Illus.). 772p. (C). 1998. text 49.95 (*0-19-816371-1*) OUP.

***Mozart for a Mother's Soul: With Mozart for a Mother's Soul CD.** Teresa B. Kindred. (BookNotes Ser.). (Illus.). 64p. 2000. 13.99 incl. cd-rom (*0-88088-413-4*) Peter Pauper.

Mozart for Acoustic Guitar. Ben Bolt. 128p. 1997. pap. 22.95 incl. audio compact disk (*0-7866-0597-9*, 95526BCD) Mel Bay.

Mozart for Clarinet. Arranged by Norman Heim. 100p. 1997. pap. 12.95 (*0-7866-0838-2*, 95543) Mel Bay.

***Mozart for Flute.** Mary McCaskill & Dona Gilliam. 112p. 1998. pap. 12.95 (*0-7866-3309-3*, 97063) Mel Bay.

Mozart for Guitar. Composed by Wolfgang Amadeus Mozart. 16p. 1984. pap. 4.95 (*0-7935-2705-8*) H Leonard.

Mozart Handbook: A Guide to the Man & His Music. Louis L. Biancolli. LC 75-32504. (Illus.). 629p. 1975. reprint ed. lib. bdg. 45.00 (*0-8371-8496-7*, BIMH, Greenwood Pr) Greenwood.

Mozart, His Music in His Life. Ivor Keys. LC 79-19028. (Illus.). 248p. 1980. 39.95 (*0-8419-0576-2*) Holmes & Meier.

Mozart in Italy. Iwo Zaluski & Pamela Zaluski. 224p. 2000. 38.95 (*0-7206-1039-7*, Pub. by P Owen Ltd) Dufour.

Mozart in Person: His Character & Health, 14. Peter J. Davies. LC 88-25091. (Contributions to the Study of Music & Dance Ser.: No. 14). 299p. 1989. 57.95 (*0-313-26340-X*, DVM/, Greenwood Pr) Greenwood.

Mozart in Prague: Thirteen Rondels. Jaroslav Seifert. Tr. by Paul Jagasich & Tom O'Grady. LC 85-11907. (Ethnic Diversity Ser.: Vol. 2).Tr. of Mozart V Praze: Trinact Rondels. (CZE & ENG.). 32p. (Orig.). 1985. pap. 6.00 (*0-930370-27-9*) Spirit That Moves.

Mozart in Retrospect. Alexander H. King. LC 76-1016. 278p. 1976. reprint ed. lib. bdg. 65.00 (*0-8371-8760-5*, KIMR, Greenwood Pr) Greenwood.

Mozart in Revolt: Strategies of Resistance, Mischief & Deception. David P. Schroeder. LC 98-45830. (Illus.). 224p. 1999. 25.00 (*0-300-07542-1*) Yale U Pr.

Mozart Masterpieces for Solo Piano: 19 Works. Wolfgang Amadeus Mozart. 128p. 1998. pap. 7.95 (*0-486-40408-0*) Dover.

Mozart Myths: A Critical Reassessment. William Stafford. LC 91-65301. (Illus.). 300p. 1991. 47.50 (*0-8047-1937-3*) Stanford U Pr.

Mozart Myths: A Critical Reassessment. William Stafford. (Illus.). 300p. (C). 1993. pap. 14.95 (*0-8047-2222-6*) Stanford U Pr.

Mozart on the Stage. Frederick C. Benn. LC 74-24041. reprint ed. 22.50 (*0-404-12864-5*) AMS Pr.

Mozart on the Stage: Music Book Index. Frederick C. Benn. 178p. 1993. reprint ed. lib. bdg. 69.00 (*0-7812-9609-9*) Rprt Serv.

Mozart Piano Concerto in C Major. Wolfgang Amadeus Mozart. Ed. by Joseph Kerman. (Critical Scores Ser.). (Illus.). (C). 1970. pap. text 16.75 (*0-393-09890-7*) Norton.

Mozart Season. Virginia E. Wolff. LC 90-23635. 88p. (J). (gr. 6 up). 1995. 15.95 (*0-8050-1571-X*, Bks Young Read) H Holt & Co.

***Mozart Season.** Virginia E. Wolff. (Illus.). 256p. (J). (gr. 5-9). 2000. mass mkt. 4.99 (*0-439-16309-9*, Pub. by Scholastic Inc) Penguin Putnam.

Mozart Speaks: Views on Music, Musicians, & the World. Wolfgang Amadeus Mozart. 446p. 1995. 20.00 (*0-02-871356-7*, Schirmer Books) Mac Lib Ref.

***Mozart Speaks: Views on Music, Musicians & the World.** Robert L. Marshall. (Illus.). 446p. 2000. reprint ed. pap. 20.00 (*0-7881-9321-X*) DIANE Pub.

Mozart Studies. Ed. by Cliff Eisen. (Illus.). 328p. 1992. text 85.00 (*0-19-816191-3*) OUP.

Mozart Studies 2. 2nd ed. Ed. by Cliff Eisen. LC 98-132844. (Illus.). 218p. (C). 1998. text 77.00 (*0-19-816343-6*) OUP.

Mozart the Dramatist. Brigid Brophy. (Quality Paperbacks Ser.). 336p. 1990. pap. 12.95 (*0-306-80389-5*) Da Capo.

Mozart, the Magic Flute & the Salzburg Marionettes. Ellen Switzer. Ed. by Jean Karl. LC 93-47890. (Illus.). 96p. (J). (gr. 3 up). 1995. text 19.95 (*0-689-31851-0*) Atheneum Yung Read.

Mozart Tonight. Julie Downing. LC 93-27445. (Illus.). 40p. (J). (ps-9). 1994. pap. 5.95 (*0-689-71808-X*) Aladdin.

Mozart Tonight. Julie Downing. LC 90-34479. (Illus.). 40p. (J). 1991. lib. bdg. 15.95 (*0-02-732881-3*, Bradbury S&S) S&S Childrens.

Mozart Tonight. large type ed. Julie Downing. 1993. 11.50 (*0-614-09846-7*, L-34083-00) Am Printing Hse.

Mozart Un Genio Musical. Montserrat Albet. 1998. pap. 19.95 (*84-08-01042-5*) Planeta.

Mozart V Praze: Trinact Rondels see Mozart in Prague: Thirteen Rondels

Mozart Very Best for Piano. Ed. by John L. Haag. (Illus.). 144p. (Orig.). 1994. pap. 14.95 (*1-56922-048-4*, 07-2025) Creat Cncpts.

Mozart, Weber & Wagner. Hector Berlioz. 1988. reprint ed. lib. bdg. 49.00 (*0-7812-0566-2*) Rprt Serv.

Mozart, Weber & Wagner. Hector Berlioz. 1976. reprint ed. lib. bdg. 59.00 (*0-403-08963-8*) Scholarly.

Mozart, Young Music Genius. Francene Sabin. LC 89-33980. (Illus.). 48p. (J). (gr. 4-7). 1990. pap. 3.95 (*0-8167-1774-5*) Troll Communs.

Mozart, Young Music Genius. Francene Sabin. LC 89-33980. (Illus.). 48p. (J). (gr. 4-6). 1997. lib. bdg. 17.25 (*0-8167-1773-7*) Troll Communs.

Mozartiana: Two Centuries of Notes, Quotes & Anecdotes about Wolfgang Amadeus Mozart. Illus. & Compiled by Joseph Solman. 1990. 18.00 (*0-394-58445-7*) Vin Bks.

Mozart's Don Giovanni: A Commentary. Charles F. Gounod. LC 78-125050. (Music Ser.). 1970. reprint ed. lib. bdg. 32.50 (*0-306-70015-8*) Da Capo.

Mozart's Don Giovanni: Complete Italian Libretto. Wolfgang Amadeus Mozart. Tr. by Ellen H. Bleiler. (ITA.). 121p. 1985. pap. 2.95 (*0-486-24944-1*) Dover.

Mozart's Early Operas. Carolyn Gianturco. (Music Ser.). 1992. 27.50 (*0-306-79465-9*) Da Capo.

Mozart's Journey to Prague & Selected Poems. Eduard Morike. Tr. by David Luke from GER. 240p. 1997. 55.00 (*1-870352-82-3*, Pub. by Libris) Paul & Co Pubs.

Mozart's Le Nozze Di Figaro. Siegmund Levarie. LC 77-5150. (Music Reprint Ser.). 1977. reprint ed. lib. bdg. 32.50 (*0-306-70897-3*) Da Capo.

***Mozart's Letters, Mozart's Life.** Spaethling. 2000. 35.00 (*0-393-04719-9*) Norton.

Mozart's Nature, Mozart's World: A Program Guide. Stanley Sadie et al. 34p. 1991. pap. write for info. (*0-9616755-4-3*) Westfield Ctr.

Mozart's Operas. Daniel Heartz. 1992. pap. 22.50 (*0-520-07872-1*, Pub. by U CA Pr) Cal Prin Full Svc.

Mozart's Operas: A Critical Study. Edward J. Dent. 276p. reprint ed. lib. bdg. 59.00 (*0-685-14896-3*) Rprt Serv.

Mozart's Operas: A Critical Study. 2nd ed. Edward J. Dent. LC 83-45429. reprint ed. 32.50 (*0-404-20077-X*) AMS Pr.

Mozart's Piano Concertos: Text, Context, Interpretation, 0. Ed. by Neal Zaslaw. LC 96-4416. (Illus.). 496p. (C). 1997. text 105.00 (*0-472-10314-8*, 10314) U of Mich Pr.

Mozart's Piano Sonatas: Contexts, Sources, Style. John Irving. LC 96-14259. (Illus.). 237p. 1997. text 59.95 (*0-521-49631-4*) Cambridge U Pr.

Mozart's Requiem: Historical & Analytical Studies, Documents, & Score. rev. ed. Christoph Wolff. Tr. by Mary Whittall. LC 92-39076. 1993. 48.00 (*0-520-07709-1*, Pub. by U CA Pr) Cal Prin Full Svc.

Mozart's Requiem: Historical & Analytical Studies, Documents, Score. Christoph Wolff. 1998. pap. text 19.95 (*0-520-21389-0*, Pub. by U CA Pr) Cal Prin Full Svc.

***Mozarts Requiem KV 626: Ein Fragment wird erganzt.** Matthias Korten. 2000. 35.95 (*3-631-35825-3*) P Lang Pubng.

Mozart's Starling. Ralph Burns. (Ohio Review Bks.). 72p. 1990. 15.95 (*0-942148-13-4*); pap. 8.95 (*0-942148-12-6*) Ohio Review.

Mozart's String Quartets. Thomas F. Dunhill. LC 77-104260. 1970. reprint ed. lib. bdg. 38.50 (*0-8371-3919-8*, DUMQ, Greenwood Pr) Greenwood.

Mozart's String Quartets, 2 vols. Thomas F. Dunhill. 1990. reprint ed. lib. bdg. 140.00 (*0-7812-9017-1*) Rprt Serv.

Mozart's Symphonies: Context, Performance Practice, Reception. Neal Zaslaw. (Illus.). 642p. 1991. pap. text 35.00 (*0-19-816286-3*) OUP.

Mozart's Symphony in G Minor, K.550. Ed. by Nathan Broder. (Critical Scores Ser.). (C). 1967. pap. text 15.50 (*0-393-09775-7*) Norton.

Mozart/Sonata in G Major, K.283 (189h) Maurice Hinson. (Masterwork Edition Ser.). 16p. 1994. pap. 3.95 (*0-7390-0758-0*, 8006) Alfred Pub.

Mozart/Twelve Songs, High Voice. Wolfgang Amadeus Mozart. Ed. by John G. Paton. 72p. (C). 1992. pap. 8.95 (*0-88284-497-0*, 3389) Alfred Pub.

Mozart/Twelve Songs, Medium Voice. Wolfgang Amadeus Mozart. Ed. by John G. Paton. 72p. (C). 1992. pap. text 9.95 (*0-88284-498-9*, 3390) Alfred Pub.

Mozilla Source Code. J. Eric Townsend. Ed. by Mark Stone. (Illus.). 400p. 2000. pap. 34.95 incl. cd-rom (*1-56592-575-0*) OReilly & Assocs.

Mozote Massacre: Anthropology & Human Rights. Binford. LC 96-10097. (Hegemony & Experience Ser.). (Illus.). 263p. 1996. pap. 19.95 (*0-8165-1662-6*) U of Ariz Pr.

Mozzarella: Inventive Recipes from Leading Chefs with Buffalo Mozzarella. Photos by Sian Irvine. LC 98-41791. (Illus.). 162p. 1999. 21.95 (*962-593-439-1*, Periplus Eds) Tuttle Pubng.

MP & Track: State Initiatives for Young Children & Families. Jane Knitzer & Stephen Page. (Illus.). 144p. (Orig.). 1996. pap. 19.95 (*0-926582-18-6*) NCCP.

M

***MP3 & the Digital Music Revolution: Turn Your PC into a CD-Quality Digital Jukebox!** John Hedtke. LC 98-96890. (Illus.). 247p. 1999. pap. 27.95 incl. cd-rom (*0-9661032-4-6*) Top Floor Pub.

Mpabga o Npabax Zeaobeka (Pravda o Pravah Cheloveka) M. V. Malinin. (RUS.). 8p. 1995. write for info. (*1-887869-50-6*) ASOFSPP.

M.P.B. Aladino. Anonimo. (SPA., Illus.). (ps-3). 1997. pap. text 2.49 (*968-890-138-5*) Edit Diana.

M.P.B. Lechera. Fabian A. Samaniego. (SPA.). (J). (ps-k). 1997. pap. text 2.49 (*968-13-2459-5*) Edit Diana.

MPCB. 1996. pap. text 17.00 (*0-8053-6293-2*) Addison-Wesley.

***MPEG 2.** 2nd ed. John Watkinson. LC 99-203277. 244p. 1998. pap. text 47.95 (*0-240-51510-2*, Focal) Buttrwrth-Heinemann.

***Mpe/Ix System Administrator's Handbook.** Jon Diercks. 2000. pap. 50.00 (*0-13-030540-5*) P-H.

MPG Consumer Annual 1988 (Films of 1987) J. R. Nash & Stanley R. Ross. (Illus.). 320p. (Orig.). 1997. pap. 19.95 (*0-933997-17-5*) CineBks.

MPG Consumer Annual 1989 (Films of 1988) CineBooks Staff. (Illus.). 320p. 1997. pap. 19.95 (*0-933997-21-3*) CineBks.

MPG Consumer Annual 1990 (Films of 1989) CineBooks Staff. (Illus.). 340p. 1997. pap. 19.95 (*0-933997-28-0*) CineBks.

MPI, Bk. 5. (J). (gr. 3 up). 1991. pap. 1.68 (*1-56297-082-8*) Lee Pubns KY.

MPI, Bk. 6. (J). (gr. 3 up). 1991. pap. 1.68 (*1-56297-083-6*) Lee Pubns KY.

MPI - The Complete Reference Vol. 2: The MPI-2 Extensions, 2 vols. William Gropp et al. (Scientific & Engineering Computation Ser.). (Illus.). 800p. 1998. pap. text 55.00 (*0-262-69216-3*) MIT Pr.

MPI--The Complete Reference Vol. 2: The MPI-2 Extensions. William Gropp et al. (Scientific & Engineering Computation Ser.). 350p. 1998. pap. text 30.00 (*0-262-57123-4*) MIT Pr.

MPI Developers Conference, 2nd. LC 96-76653. 224p. 1996. pap. 50.00 (*0-8186-7533-0*, PRO7533) IEEE Comp Soc.

MPI - The Complete Reference Vol. 1: The MPI-1 Core, Vol. 1. 2nd ed. Marc Sner et al. LC 98-25604. (Scientific & Engineering Computation Ser.). (Illus.). 446p. 1998. pap. text 35.00 (*0-262-69215-5*) MIT Pr.

***MPLS: Technology & Applications.** Bruce S. Davie & Yakov Rekhter. (Networking Ser.). 300p. 2000. pap. 44.95 (*1-55860-656-4*) Morgan Kaufmann.

MPs & Defence: A Survey of Parliamentary Knowledge & Opinion Commentary. Philip Towle. (C). 1990. 35.00 (*0-907967-94-9*, Pub. by Inst Euro Def & Strat) St Mut.

MPT Acharya: Reminiscences of an Indian Revolutionary. B. D. Yadav. (C). 1991. 14.00 (*81-7041-470-9*, Pub. by Anmol) S Asia.

***MP3!** 2nd ed. Sybex, Inc. Staff. (I Didn't Know You Could Do That Ser.). (Illus.). 2000. pap. 19.99 (*0-7821-2791-6*) Sybex.

***MP3! I Didn't Know You Could Do That...** 3rd ed. Guy Hart-Davis. 288p. 1999. pap. text 19.99 incl. audio compact disk (*0-7821-2653-7*) Sybex.

***MP3: The Definitive Guide.** Scot Hacker. Ed. by Simon Hayes. (Illus.). 400p. 2000. 27.95 (*1-56592-661-7*) OReilly & Assocs.

***MP3 & Internet Audio.** David E. Weekly. 2000. pap. text 29.99 (*0-7615-2484-3*) Prima Pub.

***MP3 & Internet Audio Handbook: Your Guide to the Digital Music Revolution!** Bruce Fries et al. Ed. by Karen Porterfield. (Illus.). 320p. 2000. pap. 24.95 (*1-928791-10-7*, 1102) TeamCom.

***MP3 & the Infinite Digital Jukebox: A Step-by-Step Guide to Accessing & Downloading CD Quality Music from the Internet.** Chris Gilbey. 256p. 2000. pap. 16.95 (*1-58322-034-8*) Seven Stories.

***MP3 for Musicians: Promote Your Music Career Online.** John Hedtke & Sandy Bradley. (Illus.). 307p. 2000. pap. write for info. (*0-9661032-2-X*) Top Floor Pub.

***MP3 FYI: Digital Music Online.** Jay Lickfett. 240p. 2000. pap. 14.95 (*1-929685-05-X*, Pub. by Muska Lipman) IPG Chicago.

***MP3 for Dummies.** Andy Rathbone. (For Dummies Ser.). 360p. 1999. pap. 19.99 incl. cd-rom (*0-7645-0585-8*) IDG Bks.

MP3 Power! With Winamp. Ben Sawyer et al. 336p. 1999. pap. 29.99 (*0-9662889-3-9*, Pub. by Muska Lipman) IPG Chicago.

***MQSeries Messaging.** Nayan Ruparelia. (Illus.). 400p. 2000. pap. 59.95 (*1-884777-98-8*, Pub. by Manning Pubns) IPG Chicago.

Mr. Ambrose's Letters on the Rebellion. John P. Kennedy. (Notable American Authors Ser.). 1999. reprint ed. lib. bdg. 125.00 (*0-7812-3673-8*) Rprt Serv.

MR Angiography: A Teaching File. Michael Brant-Zawadzki. LC 93-12956. 256p. 1993. text 79.00 (*0-7817-0093-0*) Lppncott W & W.

MR Angiography Applications in Pediatric Intracranial Vascular Lesions. R. Nuri Sener. 1997. pap. 32.50 (*0-87527-526-5*) Green.

MR-Atlas des Muskuloskelettalen Systems see MRI Atlas of the Musculoskeletal System

***Mr. Beans.** Dayton O. Hyde. LC 99-69852. (Illus.). 160p. (YA). (gr. 5 up). 2000. 14.95 (*1-56397-866-0*) Boyds Mills Pr.

Mr. Bear's New Baby. Debi Gliori. LC 98-30530. (Illus.). 32p. (J). (ps-1). 1999. 15.95 (*0-531-30152-4*) Orchard Bks Watts.

***Mr. Bear's Vacation.** Debi Gliori. LC 99-35490. (Illus.). 32p. (J). (ps-1). 2000. 15.95 (*0-531-30255-5*) Orchard Bks Watts.

***Mr. Brightly's Evening Off.** Kathleen Rowntree. (J). 2000. pap. 10.95 (*0-552-99733-1*, Pub. by Transworld Publishers Ltd) Trafalgar.

Mr. Brightly's Evening Off. large type ed. Kathleen Rowntree. 1998. 26.95 (*0-7531-5856-6*) T T Beeler.

Mr. Brown Can Moo! Can You? Dr. Seuss, pseud. (Bright & Early Bks.). (Illus.). (J). (ps-1). 1970. lib. bdg. 11.99 (*0-394-90622-5*, Pub. by Random Bks Yng Read) Random.

Mr. Brown Can Moo! Can You? Dr. Seuss, pseud. LC 73-117538. (Bright & Early Bks.). (Illus.). 27p. (J). (ps-3). 1970. 7.99 (*0-394-80622-0*, Pub. by Random Bks Yng Read) Random.

Mr. Brown Can Moo! Can You? Dr. Seuss, pseud. (Bright & Early Bks.). (J). 1970. 7.99 (*0-606-04052-8*, Pub. by Turtleback) Demco.

Mr. Brown's War: Day by Day Through the Second World War. Helen D. Millgate. LC 99-202590. 288p. 1999. 35.95 (*0-7509-1783-0*) Bks Intl VA.

***Mr. Brown's War: Day by Day Through the Second World War.** Helen D. Millgate. (Illus.). 288p. 1999. pap. 18.95 (*0-7509-2325-3*, Pub. by Sutton Pub Ltd) Bks Intl VA.

***Mr. Buchanan's Administration: On the Eve of the Rebellion.** James Buchanan. x, 296p. 2000. write for info. (*1-58218-180-2*); pap. write for info. (*1-58218-179-9*) Digital Scanning.

Mr. Bumble Buzzes Through the Year. Kim Kennedy. LC 97-81069. (Illus.). 12p. (J). 1998. 5.95 (*0-7868-0425-4*, Pub. by Disney Pr) Time Warner.

Mr. Bunny's Guide to ActiveX. Gary Swanberg. Ed. by Sean Welch. (Illus.). 105p. 1997. pap. 13.95 (*0-9661296-0-1*) Symphonica.

***Mr. Bunny's Internet Startup Game.** Patrick Chan & Carlton Egremont. 12p. 1999. pap. 12.95 (*0-201-65781-3*) Pearson Custom.

***Mr. Cat Plush.** Laura Schlessinger. (ps-2). 2000. pap. 8.95 (*0-694-01503-2*) HarpC.

Mr. Chairman: Power in Dan Rostenkowski's America. James L. Merriner. LC 98-54247. 320p. 1999. 29.95 (*0-8093-2280-3*) S Ill U Pr.

MR Cholangiopancreatography: Techniques, Results & Clinical Indications. P. Pavone & R. Passariello. LC 96-30464. (Illus.). 173p. 1996. 115.00 (*3-540-61349-8*) Spr-Verlag.

Mr Cogito. Zbigniew Herbert. 88p. 1995. pap. 12.00 (*0-88001-381-8*) HarpC.

Mr. Cosmo the Conjuror. Allan Ahlberg. 24p. (J). 1980. pap. 6.95 (*0-14-031237-4*, Pub. by Pnguin Bks Ltd) Trafalgar.

Mr. CPU Complete Educational Package: 3 Fully Illustrated Computer Concept Books & 3 Step by Step Computer Activity Workbooks. Barbara Holliday. (Mr. CPU Complete Educational Package Ser.). (Illus.). (J). (gr. k-5). 1997. pap. text 59.70 (*1-891727-08-7*) Fun Books.

Mr. CPU Fun Package: Meet Mr. CPU, Mr. CPU Gets Organized & Mr. CPU Surfs the Internet. Barbara Holliday. (Mr. CPU Fun Package Ser.: No. 1). (Illus.). (J). (gr. k-5). 1997. pap. text 29.95 (*1-891727-06-0*) Fun Books.

Mr. CPU Gets Organized: An Introduction to File Management on the Personal Computer. Barbara Holliday. (Mr. CPU Ser.: No. 2). (Illus.). 24p. (J). (gr. k-5). 1997. pap. text 9.95 (*1-891727-01-X*) Fun Books.

Mr. CPU Lesson Plan Package: Learning the Hardware, Getting Organized & Learn to Surf. Barbara Holliday. (Mr. CPU Lesson Plan Package Ser.: No. 3). (Illus.). (J). (gr. k-5). 1997. pap. text 29.95 (*1-891727-07-9*) Fun Books.

Mr. CPU Surfs the Net: Introduction to Internet Concepts. Barbara Holliday. (Mr. CPU Ser.: No. 3). (Illus.). 22p. (J). (gr. k-5). 1997. pap. text 9.95 (*1-891727-02-8*) Fun Books.

Mr. Darwin Misread Miss Peacock's Mind: A New Look at Mate Selection in Light of Lessons from Nature. Merle E. Jacobs. LC 98-72865. (Illus.). 248p. 1998. lib. bdg. 21.95 (*0-9665916-1-5*) NatureBooks.

Mr. Eliot's Summer Honeymoon: A Sonnet Sequence. John Gurney. 115p. pap. write for info. (*3-7052-0434-3*, Pub. by Poetry Salzburg) Intl Spec Bk.

***Mr. Elliott Finds a Family: A Little Secret.** Susan Floyd. (Superromance Ser.: Bk. 919). 2000. per. 4.50 (*0-373-70919-6*, 1-70919-5) Harlequin Bks.

***Mr. Emerson's Cook.** Judith B. Schachner. LC 98-10032. (Illus.). 32p. (J). (gr. 4-6). 1998. 15.99 (*0-525-45884-0*, Dutton Child) Peng Put Young Read.

Mr. Executive's Heroic Adventures. Nick Gakis. LC 97-90445. (J). (gr. 3-5). 1998. pap. 7.95 (*0-533-12403-4*) Vantage.

Mr. Fixit Mix Ups Proprietary: Richard Scarry on go Book. Scarry. 1998. 11.99 (*0-689-82486-6*) S&S Childrens.

Mr. Fixit's Opposites. Richard Scarry. (Read-It-Yourself Books Ser.: No. 4). (Illus.). 12p. (J). (ps-3). 1999. bds. 4.99 (*0-689-81627-8*, 076714004993) S&S Childrens.

Mr. Flips Visits The Animals. Quadrillion Media Staff. 1999. 5.95 (*1-58185-217-7*) Quadrillion Media.

Mr. Food a Little Lighter. Art Ginsburg. LC 96-17753. 352p. 1996. 14.95 (*0-688-13139-5*, Wm Morrow) Morrow Avon.

Mr. Food a Taste of Qvc: Food & Fun Behind the Scenes. Art Ginsburg. LC 98-10169. 256p. 1998. 25.00 (*0-688-15897-8*, Wm Morrow) Morrow Avon.

***Mr. Food Christmas: Homemade & Hassle-Free.** Art Ginsburg. LC 98-37986. (Illus.). 224p. 1999. 19.95 (*0-688-15679-7*, Wm Morrow) Morrow Avon.

Mr. Food Cks Like Mama. Art Ginsburg. LC 92-11724. 308p. 1992. 14.95 (*0-688-11127-0*, Wm Morrow) Morrow Avon.

Mr. Food Cookbook. Art Ginsburg. LC 90-37528. 1990. 14.95 (*0-688-09258-6*, Wm Morrow) Morrow Avon.

Mr. Food-Cookies Favorite. Art Ginsburg. LC 94-21802. 257p. 1994. 11.95 (*0-688-13478-5*, Wm Morrow) Morrow Avon.

Mr. Food Cooking By the Calendar: Fifty-Two Weeks of Year-round Favorites. Art Ginsburg. LC 97-39184. (Illus.). 400p. 1999. 14.95 (*0-688-15678-9*, Wm Morrow) Morrow Avon.

Mr Food Cool Cravings: Easy Chilled & Frozen Desserts. Art Ginsburg. LC 97-9547. (Mr. Food Ser.). (Illus.). 256p. 1997. 11.95 (*0-688-14579-5*, Wm Morrow) Morrow Avon.

Mr Food Easy Tex-Mex. Art Ginsburg. LC 96-47462. (Illus.). 224p. 1997. 11.95 (*0-688-14578-7*, Wm Morrow) Morrow Avon.

Mr. Food Grills It All I. Art Ginsburg. LC 95-7357. 166p. 1995. 11.95 (*0-688-13711-3*, Wm Morrow) Morrow Avon.

Mr. Food Meat around the Table. Art Ginsburg. LC 95-46434. 1996. 12.00 (*0-688-14418-7*, Wm Morrow) Morrow Avon.

Mr. Food One Pot, One Meal. Art Ginsburg. LC 97-590. 256p. 1997. 14.95 (*0-688-14577-9*, Wm Morrow) Morrow Avon.

Mr. Food Pasta. Art Ginsburg. LC 93-8501. (Illus.). 158p. 1993. 11.95 (*0-688-11601-9*, Wm Morrow) Morrow Avon.

Mr Food-Real American Ck. Art Ginsburg. LC 94-20870. (Illus.). 1994. 14.95 (*0-688-12637-5*, Wm Morrow) Morrow Avon.

***Mr. Food's Good Times, Good Food Cookbook.** Art Ginsburg. LC 99-13368. (Illus.). 208p. 1999. 14.95 (*0-688-16777-2*, Wm Morrow) Morrow Avon.

Mr. Food's Meals in Minutes. Art Ginsburg. LC 99-17144. 208p. 1999. 14.95 (*0-688-15088-8*, Wm Morrow) Morrow Avon.

Mr Food's Old World Cook. Art Ginsburg. LC 95-37043. 1995. 14.95 (*0-688-13138-7*, Wm Morrow) Morrow Avon.

***Mr. Food's Restaurant Favorites.** Art Ginsburg. LC 99-36710. (Illus.). 224p. 1999. 14.95 (*0-688-15680-0*, Wm Morrow) Morrow Avon.

***Mr. Frumble's Pickle Car.** (Richard Scarry's on the Go Bks.). (J). 1998. 11.99 (*0-689-82487-4*, Simon Spot) Litle Simon.

Mr. Griggs' Work. Cynthia Rylant. LC 88-1484. (Illus.). 32p. (J). (ps-2). 1993. pap. 6.95 (*0-531-07037-9*) Orchard Bks Watts.

Mr. Griggs' Work. Cynthia Rylant. (J). 1989. 11.15 (*0-606-05482-0*, Pub. by Turtleback) Demco.

Mr. Gumpy's Outing. John Burningham. LC 77-159507. (Illus.). 32p. (J). (ps-2). 1995. 14.95 (*0-8050-0708-3*, Bks Young Read); pap. 5.95 (*0-8050-1315-6*, Bks Young Read) H Holt & Co.

Mr. Gumpy's Outing. John Burningham. (J). 1970. 11.15 (*0-606-04482-5*, Pub. by Turtleback) Demco.

***Mr. Hyde's Assets.** Sheridon Smythe. 400p. (Orig.). 2000. pap. 5.99 (*0-505-52356-6*, Love Spell) Dorchester Pub Co.

Mr. Iba: Basketball's Aggie Iron Duke. John Paul Bischoff. (Oklahoma Trackmaker Ser.). (Illus.). 276p. 1980. 12.95 (*0-86546-001-9*) OK Heritage.

MR Imaging & CT of the Spine: A Case Study Approach. 2nd ed. Robert Kricun & Morrie E. Kricun. LC 93-16680. 416p. 1993. text 146.00 (*0-7817-0026-4*) Lppncott W & W.

MR Imaging of Laryngeal Cancer. Gordon B. Snow et al. (Series in Radiology). (C). 1991. text 175.00 (*0-7923-1101-9*) Kluwer Academic.

MR Imaging of the Skull & Brain: A Correlative Text-Atlas. K. Sartor. Ed. by W. Loeffler et al. (Illus.). 820p. 1995. 298.00 (*0-387-52293-X*) Spr-Verlag.

MR in Pediatric Neuroradiology. Samuel M. Wolpert et al. Ed. by H. Verdain Barnes. (Illus.). 491p. (C). (gr. 13). 1991. text 125.00 (*0-8016-5370-3*, 05370) Mosby Inc.

***Mr. Jefferson's Academy: The Real Story Behind West Point.** Norman T. Remick. LC 98-91578. (Illus.). 440p. 1999. 25.00 (*0-9674879-0-0*) N T Remick.

Mr. Jefferson's Private Life. Dumas Malone. 8p. 1974. pap. 3.00 (*0-944026-85-0*) Am Antiquarian.

Mr. Lincoln's Drummer. G. Clifton Wisler. 144p. (YA). (gr. 7 up). 1995. 15.99 (*0-525-67463-2*, Dutton Child) Peng Put Young Read.

Mr. Lincoln's Drummer. G. Clifton Wisler. 144p. (YA). (gr. 6-9). 1997. pap. 4.99 (*0-14-038542-8*) Penguin Putnam.

Mr. Lincoln's Drummer. G. Clifton Wisler. (YA). 1997. 9.09 (*0-606-10986-2*, Pub. by Turtleback) Demco.

***Mr. Littlejohn's Secrets to a Lifetime of Success.** Pat Williams & James D. Denney. LC 99-59460. 272p. 2000. 19.99 (*0-8007-1772-4*) Revell.

Mr. Magoo. Nancy Krulik. LC 97-80025. (Illus.). 96p. (J). (gr. 3-7). 1997. pap. 4.95 (*0-7868-4174-5*, Pub. by Disney Pr) Time Warner.

Mr. Majeika & the Haunted Hot. Humphrey Carpenter. (Illus.). 1989. pap. 7.95 (*0-14-032360-0*, Pub. by Pnguin Bks Ltd) Trafalgar.

Mr. Majeika & the Music Teacher. Humphrey Carpenter. (J). 1988. pap. 7.95 (*0-14-032141-1*, Pub. by Pnguin Bks Ltd) Trafalgar.

MR Mammography (MRM) Werner A. Kaiser. LC 92-49786. 350p. 1993. write for info. (*3-540-55083-6*); 225.00 (*0-387-55083-6*) Spr-Verlag.

Mr. McGratt & the Ornery. Marilyn Helmer & Martine Gourbault. 32p. (J). (gr. k-2). 1999. 14.95 (*1-55074-564-6*) Kids Can Pr.

Mr. Mick Visits Our School. large type ed. Mickey Campaniello. (Illus.). (J). (ps-2). 1999. 12.95 (*0-9673179-0-8*) Someone Special.

Mr. Miracle: By the Year 2000: Celebrate! Carolyn McSparren. 1999. per. 4.25 (*0-373-70852-1*, 1-70852-8) Harlequin Bks.

***Mr. Modem's Internet Guide for Seniors.** 2nd ed. 464p. 2000. pap. 19.99 (*0-7821-2836-X*) Sybex.

Mr. Mombo's Balloon Flight. Fiona Conboy. (Illus.). (J). 1998. 15.99 (*1-884628-62-1*, Flyng Frog) Allied Pub MD.

***Mr. Nice Guy.** Amanda Christie. (7th Heaven Ser.). 132p. (J). (gr. 3-7). 2000. pap. 3.99 (*0-375-80338-6*, Pub. by Random Bks Yng Read) Random.

Mr. Noisy at the Dude Ranch, Vol. 2916. Margaret Allen. Ed. by Joel Kupperstein. (Dr. Maggie's Phonics Readers Ser.). (Illus.). 16p. (J). (ps). 1999. pap. 2.99 (*1-57471-591-7*) Creat Teach Pr.

Mr. Noisy Paints His House, Vol. 4360. Joel Kupperstein. Ed. by Kimberlee Graves. (Fun & Fantasy Ser.). (Illus.). 16p. (J). (ps-1). 1997. pap. 2.49 (*1-57471-257-8*, 4360) Creat Teach Pr.

***Mr. Paint Pig's ABC.** Richard Scarry. (Nifty Lift-&-Look Bks.). (Illus.). 12p. (J). (ps-k). 2000. 5.99 (*0-375-80290-8*, Pub. by Random Bks Yng Read) Random.

Mr. Peters' Connections. Arthur Miller. 1998. pap. 5.25 (*0-8222-1687-6*) Dramatists Play.

Mr. Peters' Connections. Arthur Miller. LC 99-18999. (Plays Ser.). 1999. pap. 7.95 (*0-14-028595-4*) Viking Penguin.

***Mr. Peters' Connections.** Arthur Miller. LC 99-18999. 64p. 1999. pap. 9.95 (*0-14-048245-8*, Penguin Bks) Viking Penguin.

***Mr. Pine's Purple House.** Leonard Kessler. LC 00-104411. (Illus.). 61p. (J). 2000. write for info. (*1-930900-02-3*) Purple Hse Pr.

Mr. Piper & His Cubs. Devon E. Francis. LC 96-84052. xi, 278 p. 1996. 18.95 (*0-911139-26-5*) Flying Bks.

***Mr. Plod's New Whistle.** Gill Davies. (Squeaky Fun Ser.). (Illus.). 14p. (J). (ps-k). 2000. bds. 7.99 (*1-57584-682-9*, Pub. by Rdrs Digest) S&S Trade.

Mr. Popper's Penguins. Rebecca Paigen. (Literature Units Ser.). 48p. (J). (gr. 3-5). 1997. pap. 7.95 (*1-55734-549-X*) Tchr Create Mat.

***Mr. Potato Head's Big Night Out, Vol. 1.** Lucia Monfried. (Mr. Potato Head's Ser.). 1999. pap. 3.49 (*0-525-46277-5*, Dutton Child) Peng Put Young Read.

Mr Potter. Jamaica Kincaid. text. write for info. (*0-374-21494-8*) FS&G.

Mr. Potter's Pets. Dick King-Smith. 1997. 10.05 (*0-606-13624-X*, Pub. by Turtleback) Demco.

Mr. President: The Human Side of America's Chief Executives. David Rubel. LC 97-41135. (Illus.). 256p. (YA). (gr. 11). 1998. 24.95 (*0-7835-5253-X*) Time-Life.

Mr. President, a Book of U.S. Presidents. George A. Sullivan. (Scholastic Biography Ser.). (J). 1997. 9.09 (*0-606-11646-X*, Pub. by Turtleback) Demco.

***Mr. Putter & Tabby Feed the Fish.** Cynthia Rylant. 2001. write for info. (*0-15-202408-5*) Harcourt.

Mr. Putter & Tabby Pour the Tea. Cynthia Rylant. LC 93-21470. (Illus.). 44p. (C). (gr. 1-5). 1994. 13.00 (*0-15-256255-9*) Harcourt.

Mr. Putter & Tabby Pour the Tea. Cynthia Rylant. LC 93-21470. (Illus.). 44p. (J). (gr. 1-5). 1994. pap. 5.95 (*0-15-200901-9*, Harcourt Child Bks) Harcourt.

Mr. Putter & Tabby Pour the Tea. Cynthia Rylant. LC 93-21470. (J). 1994. 10.15 (*0-606-06584-9*, Pub. by Turtleback) Demco.

Mr. Rabbit & the Lovely Present see Senor Conejo y el Hermosa Regalo

Mr Right Next Door: He's My Hero. Arlene James. 1999. per. 3.50 (*0-373-19352-1*, Harlequin) Harlequin Bks.

Mr. Rodeo: The Big Bronco Years of Leo Cremer. Patrick Dawson. 170p. 1986. pap. 25.00 (*0-937959-05-7*) Cayuse Pr MT.

***Mr. Rover Takes Over.** Grace Maccarone & Meredith Johnson. LC 99-462281. (Hello Reader! Ser.). (Illus.). (J). 2000. pap. write for info. (*0-439-20057-1*) Scholastic Inc.

Mr. Santizo's Tasty Treats. Alice K. Flanagan. Ed. by Dana Rau. (Our Neighborhood Ser.). (Illus.). 32p. (J). 1998. pap. 6.95 (*0-516-26296-3*) Childrens.

Mr. Scotts Magical Farm. Sharon Shi. (Illus.). 24p. (J). (gr. k-2). 1998. write for info. (*1-892800-01-2*) Temp Tattoo.

***Mr. Scotts Magical Farm.** rev. ed. Sharon Shi. (Illus.). 24p. (J). 2000. mass mkt. 4.99 (*0-9678636-7-8*, B008, Tattootles Bks) Tattoo Manuf.

Mr. Slaptail's Curious Contraption. rev. ed. Barbara Tharp et al. (My Health My World Ser.: Vol. 3). (Illus.). iv, 36p. (J). (gr. k-5). 1997. pap. write for info. (*1-888997-34-6*) Baylor Coll Med.

Mr. Slaptail's Secret. rev. ed. Judith Dresden et al. (My Health My World Ser.). (Illus.). iv, 36p. (J). (gr. k-5). 1997. pap. write for info. (*1-888997-29-X*) Baylor Coll Med.

Mr. Sugar Came to Town: La Visita del Sr. Azucar. Cruz Gomez. Ed. by Harriet Rohmer. LC 88-38781. (ENG & SPA.). (J). (ps-7). 1990. 22.95 incl. audio (*0-89239-062-X*) Childrens Book Pr.

Mr. Sun & Mr. Sea see Senor Sol y el Senor Mar

Mr. Tick the Teacher. Allan Ahlberg. 24p. (J). (gr. 3-6). 1981. pap. 6.95 (*0-14-031245-5*, Pub. by Pnguin Bks Ltd) Trafalgar.

Mr. Universe: And Other Plays. Jim Grimsley. LC 98-10196. 1998. 24.95 (*1-56512-202-X*); pap. 17.95 (*1-56512-211-9*) Algonquin Bks.

Mr. Vegetable's Garden Tips for Intermountain & High Desert Gardening. Gene Klump. Ed. & Photos by Tova Roseman. LC 99-176291. (Tova's Garden Ser.: No. 2). (Illus.). 104p. 1998. pap. 14.95 (*0-943674-02-6*) Roseman Publng.

Mr. William Shakespeare's Comedies, Histories & Tragedies: A Facsimile of the First Folio, 1623. William Shakespeare. LC 98-12047. 896p. 1998. pap. 50.00 (*0-87830-088-0*) Routledge.

Mr. Willowby's Christmas Tree. Robert E. Barry. (J). 1991. 11.19 (*0-606-05483-9*, Pub. by Turtleback) Demco.

Mr. Wizard's Experiments for Young Scientists. Don Herbert. LC 59-7907. 192p. (J). 1990. pap. 10.95 (*0-385-26585-9*) Doubleday.

Mr. Wizard's Experiments for Young Scientists. Don Herbert. 1990. 16.05 (*0-606-02042-X*, Pub. by Turtleback) Demco.

Mr. Work & Mr. Play Vol. 3: The Adventures of Captain Love & Dr. Smart. large type ed. Patricia Hautland. Ed. by Rollen Foster. (Illus.). 32p. (J). (ps up). 1997. pap. 8.95 (*1-891806-03-3*) LittleKid Pr.

Mr. Worm & His Down-to-Earth Adventures. Anna M. Fabert. (J). 1998. pap. 6.95 (*0-533-12075-6*) Vantage.

Mrcchakatika the Little Clay Cart: A Drama in Ten Acts. Revilo P. Oliver. LC 74-14116. 1975. lib. bdg. 59.50 (*0-8371-7789-8*, SULC, Greenwood Pr) Greenwood.

MRCGP Workbook. Maskrey. LC 94-234055. (C). 1994. pap. text, wbk. ed. 34.00 (*0-443-04985-8*) Harcourt.

MRCOG: MCQS Clinical Obstetrics & Gynecology. K. W. Sharif & J. Jordan. 1997. pap. text 45.00 (*0-7020-2120-2*, Pub. by W B Saunders) Saunders.

MRCOG Pt. 1: MCP's: Basic Science for Obstetrics & Gynaecology. Khaldoun W. Sharif et al. 226p. 1995. pap. text 43.00 (*0-7020-1970-4*, Pub. by W B Saunders) Saunders.

***MRCOG Survival Guide.** 2nd ed. Khaldoun W. Sharif & Judith B. Weaver. LC 99-28975. 2000. write for info. (*0-7020-2545-3*) W B Saunders.

MRCOG Survival Guide: Postgraduate Self-Assessment. Khaldoun W. Sharif & Judith B. Weaver. (Illus.). 258p. 1994. pap. text 34.00 (*0-7020-1828-7*, Pub. by W B Saunders) Saunders.

Mrcogo, Pt. 1. Tim Chard & Richard J. Lilford. 1987. pap. 29.50 (*0-387-19501-7*) Spr-Verlag.

Mrcogo, Pt. 1. 2nd ed. Tim Chard & Richard J. Lilford. LC 92-13661. (Brainscan MCQs Ser.). 136p. 1992. 26.95 (*0-387-19767-2*) Spr-Verlag.

MRCP: 500 MCQ's for MRCP, Pt. 1. Baliga. 1997. pap. text 28.00 (*0-7020-2243-8*) Harcourt.

MRCP (Paediatrics) Pt. 1: MCQ's. Simon Hannam et al. 255p. 1997. pap. text 39.95 (*0-7020-1875-9*, Pub. by W B Saunders) Saunders.

MRCP Pediatrics. Maconochie. (C). 1998. pap. text 39.00 (*0-7020-2381-7*) Harcourt.

MRCPsych Tutor Pt. 1: MCQs. Kam Bhui et al. 72p. 1992. pap. text 19.95 (*0-7020-1642-X*, Pub. by W B Saunders) Saunders.

***MRCS Examination: MCQS & EMQS.** Paul Chatrath & Omar Rahim. LC 99-35373. 1999. write for info. (*0-632-05402-6*, Pub. by Blckwell Science) Iowa St U Pr.

Medieval Russia, 980-1584. Janet L. Martin. (Medieval Textbooks Ser.). (Illus.). 477p. (C). 1996. text 69.95 (*0-521-36276-8*); pap. text 22.95 (*0-521-36832-4*) Cambridge U Pr.

Mr.food-Fun Kitchen Tips. Art Ginsburg. LC 94-45566. (Illus.). 208p. 1995. 14.95 (*0-688-13710-5*, Wm Morrow) Morrow Avon.

Mr.food-Quick & Easy Sid. Art Ginsburg. LC 94-39385. (Illus.). 160p. 1995. 11.95 (*0-688-13712-1*, Wm Morrow) Morrow Avon.

MRI: A Conceptual Overview. Sunder S. Rajan. LC 96-37408. 144p. 1997. pap. 34.95 (*0-387-94911-9*) Spr-Verlag.

***MRI: Principles & Applications.** 2nd ed. Mark Brown & Richard C. Semelka. LC 99-12462. 210p. (C). 1999. pap. 49.95 (*0-471-33062-0*) Wiley.

MRI: Principles & Artifacts. R. Edward Hendrick et al. LC 93-16482. (Raven MRI Teaching File Ser.). 320p. 1993. text 76.00 (*0-88167-709-4*) Lppncott W & W.

MRI: The Basics. Ray H. Hashemi & William G. Bradley, Jr. LC 96-9064. 307p. 1997. pap. 45.00 (*0-683-18240-4*) Lppncott W & W.

MRI & CT Atlas of Correlative Imaging in Otolaryngology. Vijay M. Rao et al. 383p. (C). 1993. pap. text 165.00 (*0-8385-6526-3*, A6526-6, Apple Lange Med) McGraw.

***MRI & CT of the Brain.** Ed. by James E. Gillespie & Alan Jackson. (Illus.). 320p. 2001. text 95.00 (*0-340-76121-0*, Pub. by E A) OUP.

MRI & CT of the Dog. J. Assheuer & M. Sager. (Illus.). 482p. 1996. 199.95 (*0-86542-825-5*) Blackwell Sci.

MRI & CT of the Musculoskeletal System. John L. Bloem & David J. Satoris. (Illus.). 672p. 1991. 150.00 (*0-683-00875-7*) Lppncott W & W.

MRI & CT of the Spine. Krishna C. Rao et al. (Illus.). 608p. 1993. 135.00 (*0-683-07133-5*) Lppncott W & W.

An Asterisk (*) at the beginning of an entry indicates that the title is appearing for the first time.

MRI, Arthroscopy & Surgical Anatomy of the Joints. David W. Stoller. 600p. 1998. 399.00 (*0-7817-1836-8*); text 225.00 (*0-7817-1666-7*) Lppncott W & W.

MRI-Arthroscopy Correlative Atlas. Mark D. Miller et al. Ed. by Richard Lampert. LC 96-44085. (Illus.). 264p. 1997. text 152.00 (*0-7216-6054-1*, W B Saunders Co) Harcrt Hlth Sci Grp.

MRI Atlas for Technologists. Carolyn Kaut. (Radiographic Technology Ser.). (C). 1999. 595.00 (*0-8273-7262-0*) Delmar.

MRI Atlas for Technologists: Clinical Application. Carolyn Kaut. (Radiographic Technology Ser.). 1996. text 79.95 (*0-8273-7264-7*) Delmar.

MRI Atlas for Technologists: Clinical Application. Carolyn Kaut. (Radiographic Technology Ser.). 1999. text, teacher ed. 14.00 (*0-8273-7265-5*) Delmar.

MRI Atlas for Technologists: Clinical Application CTB. Carolyn Kaut. (Radiographic Technology Ser.). 1996. 64.95 (*0-8273-7266-3*) Delmar.

MRI Atlas for Technologists: Clinical Applications. Carolyn Kaut. (Radiographic Technology Ser.). (C). 1999. 595.00 (*0-8273-7267-1*) Delmar.

MRI Atlas for Technologists: Physical Principles. Carolyn Kaut. (Radiographic Technology Ser.). 1999. text, teacher ed. 14.00 (*0-8273-7261-2*) Delmar.

MRI Atlas of Central Nervous System Tumors. L. Cecconi et al. Ed. & Contrib. by E. Tettamanti. (Illus.). 280p. 1992. 274.00 (*0-387-82304-2*) Spr-Verlag.

MRI Atlas of Sectional Anatomy of the Head & Neck. William C. Yuh et al. (Illus.). 384p. 1993. text 205.00 (*0-443-08892-6*) Church.

MRI Atlas of the Abdomen. Ed. by John A. Markisz & Elias Kazam. (Illus.). 256p. 1997. 125.00 (*0-86542-398-9*) Blackwell Sci.

MRI Atlas of the Abdomen. H. Weissleder. Ed. by David D. Stark. 1988. 66.00 (*0-8493-2750-4*) CRC Pr.

MRI Atlas of the Brain. William G. Bradley & Graeme Bydder. LC 89-43377. (Illus.). 353p. 1990. reprint ed. pap. 109.50 (*0-608-05838-6*, 205980400007) Bks Demand.

MRI Atlas of the Chest & Neck: Normal Anatomy & Pathology. John A. Markisz et al. LC 97-4962. (Illus.). 306p. 1997. 125.00 (*0-86542-391-1*) Blackwell Sci.

MRI Atlas of the Corpus Callosum. R. Nuri Sener. Date not set. pap. write for info. (*0-87527-529-X*) Green.

MRI Atlas of the Head & Neck. Anton N. Hasso. LC 93-16858. (Illus.). 216p. 1993. text 133.95 (*0-412-04381-5*) OUP.

***MRI Atlas of the Human Cerebellum.** Schmahmann et al. (Illus.). 220p. (C). 2000. 149.95 (*0-12-625665-9*) Acad Pr.

MRI Atlas of the Musculoskeletal System. Lawrence Bassett et al. 1988. 153.00 (*0-8493-2751-2*) CRC Pr.

MRI Atlas of the Musculoskeletal System. Torsten B. Moller & Emil Reif. LC 93-2493.Tr. of MR-Atlas des Muskuloskelettalen Systems. 308p. 1993. 250.00 (*0-86542-291-5*) Blackwell Sci.

MRI Atlas of the Pelvis: Normal Anatomy & Pathology. John A. Markisz et al. LC 92-14015. (Illus.). 248p. 1993. 135.00 (*0-683-05557-7*) Lppncott W & W.

MRI Bankers' Guide to Foreign Currency: Spring 1993 Issue. Arnoldo Efron. (ENG, GER, POR & SPA., Illus.). 242p. 1993. pap. text 50.00 (*0-9629339-8-8*) Monetary Rsch Intl.

MRI Banker's Guide to Foreign Currency: Summer 1992. Arnoldo Efron. (Illus.). 192p. 1992. pap. 50.00 (*0-9629339-3-7*) Monetary Rsch Intl.

MRI Bankers' Guide to Foreign Currency: Winter 1992-93 Issue. Arnoldo Efron. (ENG, GER, POR & SPA., Illus.). 232p. 1992. pap. text 50.00 (*0-9629339-7-X*) Monetary Rsch Intl.

MRI Contrast Enhancement in the Central Nervous System: A Case Study Approach. Ed. by Robert C. Brasch et al. LC 93-25655. (Illus.). 348p. 1993. reprint ed. pap. 107.90 (*0-608-05841-6*, 205980700007) Bks Demand.

MRI-CT & Pathology in Head & Neck Tumors: A Correlative Study. Roland Chisin et al. (Series in Radiology). (C). 1989. text 213.50 (*0-7923-0227-3*) Kluwer Academic.

MRI for Radiographers. P. T. English & C. Moore. (Illus.). 187p. 1995. 98.00 (*3-540-19750-8*) Spr-Verlag.

MRI for Radiographers. Philip T. English & Christine Moore. LC 94-41660. (Illus.). 195p. 1995. 98.00 (*0-387-19750-8*) Spr-Verlag.

***MRI for Technologists.** Peggy Woodward. 2000. pap. 55.00 (*0-07-135318-6*) McGraw.

MRI in Medicine: The Nottingham Conference. Ed. by Peter Mansfield. LC 95-31244. 333p. 1995. pap. 109.95 (*0-412-07391-9*, Chap & Hall NY) Chapman & Hall.

MRI in Practice. Catherine Westbrook & Carolyn Kaut. LC 93-9653. 296p. 1993. pap. 39.95 (*0-632-03587-0*) Blackwell Sci.

***MRI in Practice.** 2nd ed. Catherine Westbrook & Carolyn Kaut. LC 97-45782. (Illus.). 1999. pap. text 48.95 (*0-632-04205-2*) Blackwell Sci.

MRI Manual. 2nd ed. Robert B. Lufkin. LC 97-20148. (Illus.). 480p. (C). (gr. 13). 1997. pap. text 64.95 (*0-8151-5665-0*, 27077) Mosby Inc.

MRI of Musculoskeletal Masses. Alan Laorr & Clyde A. Helms. LC 96-24302. (Illus.). 384p. 1996. text 139.50 (*0-89640-320-3*) Igaku-Shoin.

MRI of Musculoskeletal System. William E. Palmer. 1994. vdisk 700.00 (*1-56815-021-0*) Mosby Inc.

MRI of Musculoskeletal Tumors. Marc Fenstermacher. (Body MRI Series on CD-ROM). (Illus.). 1999. cd-rom 125.00 (*0-412-14381-X*, Pub. by E A) OUP.

MRI of the Abdomen & Pelvis: A Text-Atlas. Richard C. Semelka et al. LC 96-46195. 744p. 1997. 235.00 (*0-471-16164-0*) Wiley.

MRI of the Abdomen with CT Correlation. Ed. by Richard C. Semelka. LC 92-48523. 192p. 1993. text 108.00 (*0-7817-0019-1*) Lppncott W & W.

MRI of the Body. Peggy Fritsche & David D. Stark. (MRI Teaching File Ser.). 224p. 1993. text 70.00 (*0-88167-706-X*) Lppncott W & W.

MRI of the Brain: Normal Anatomy & Normal Variants. Vimal H. Patel & Lawrence Friedman. Ed. by Sandra Valkoff. LC 96-41701. 325p. 1996. text 89.00 (*0-7216-6945-X*, W B Saunders Co) Harcrt Hlth Sci Grp.

MRI of the Brain I. 2nd ed. William G. Bradley & Michael Brant-Zawadzki. 256p. text 89.95 (*0-7817-2568-2*) Lppncott W & W.

MRI of the Brain II. 2nd ed. Michael Brant-Zawadzki & William G. Bradley. 224p. text 89.95 (*0-7817-2569-0*) Lppncott W & W.

MRI of the Brain One: Non-Neoplastic Disease. William G. Bradley, Jr. & Michael Brant-Zawadzki. (MRI Teaching File Ser.). 256p. 1990. text 76.00 (*0-88167-745-0*) Lppncott W & W.

MRI of the Brain Three: Neoplastic Disease. Anton N. Hasso et al. (MRI Teaching File Ser.). 224p. 1991. text 76.00 (*0-88167-702-7*) Lppncott W & W.

MRI of the Brain Two: Non-Neoplastic Disease. Ed. by Michael Brant-Zawadzki & William G. Bradley, Jr. (MRI Teaching File Ser.). 224p. 1990. text 76.00 (*0-88167-696-9*) Lppncott W & W.

MRI of the Cardiovascular System. Ed. by Andre J. Duerinckx. (MRI Teaching File Ser.). 304p. 1993. text 76.00 (*0-88167-707-8*) Lppncott W & W.

MRI of the Central Nervous System: A Pathology Atlas. Ed. by K. Mori. (Illus.). ix, 241p. 1991. 176.00 (*0-387-70069-2*) Spr-Verlag.

MRI of the Extremities. Kang. 1999. text. write for info. (*0-7216-5264-6*, W B Saunders Co) Harcrt Hlth Sci Grp.

MRI of the Eye & Orbit. Ed. by Patrick De Potter et al. LC 94-41374. 320p. 1995. pap. 99.20 (*0-608-05600-6*, 206605800006) Bks Demand.

MRI of the Female Pelvis. Kaori Togashi. LC 93-38533. (Illus.). 336p. 1993. 125.00 (*0-89640-253-3*) Igaku-Shoin.

MRI of the Foot & Ankle. Ed. by Andrew L. Deutsch et al. 400p. 1992. text 153.00 (*0-88167-899-6*) Lppncott W & W.

MRI of the Foot & Ankle. Marc Fenstermacher & S. Wallace. (Body MRI Series on CD-ROM). 1999. cd-rom 150.00 (*0-412-14371-2*, Pub. by E A) OUP.

MRI of the Head & Neck. Robert B. Lufkin & William N. Hanafee. (MRI Teaching File Ser.). 253p. 1991. text 76.00 (*0-88167-704-3*) Lppncott W & W.

MRI of the Head & Neck. 2nd ed. Robert B. Lufkin. 256p. text 89.95 (*0-7817-2572-0*) Lppncott W & W.

MRI of the Head & Neck: Functional Anatomy - Clinical Findings - Pathology - Imaging. enl. rev. ed. T. J. Vogl. (Illus.). 304p. 1992. 198.00 (*0-387-54306-6*) Spr-Verlag.

MRI of the Knee Marc Fenstermacher. (Body MRI Series on CD-ROM). 1997. cd-rom 149.95 (*0-412-14351-8*, Pub. by E A) OUP.

MRI of the Knee. 2nd ed. Jerrold H. Mink et al. LC 92-17023. 502p. 1992. text 147.00 (*0-88167-936-4*, 2417) Lppncott W & W.

MRI of the Knee. 2nd ed. Ed. by Peter L. Munk & Clyde A. Helms. LC 96-12935. 400p. 1996. text 142.00 (*0-397-51642-8*) Lppncott W & W.

MRI of the Lumbar Spine: A Practical Approach to Image Interpretation. Neil Steinmetz. (Illus.). 218p. 1986. text 49.50 (*0-318-37138-3*, Little Brwn Med Div) Lppncott W & W.

MRI of the Musculoskeletal System. Ed. by John V. Crues, III. (MRI Teaching File Ser.). 242p. 1991. text 76.00 (*0-88167-705-1*) Lppncott W & W.

MRI of the Musculoskeletal System. Harry K. Genant et al. (Illus.). 688p. 1993. text 225.00 (*0-7216-4295-0*, W B Saunders Co) Harcrt Hlth Sci Grp.

MRI of the Musculoskeletal System. Phoebe Kaplan et al. (Illus.). 605p. write for info. (*0-7216-9027-0*, W B Saunders Co) Harcrt Hlth Sci Grp.

***MRI of the Musculoskeletal System.** Vahlensieck. LC 99-52542. (Illus.). 400p. 1999. 139.00 incl. trans. (*0-86577-875-2*) Thieme Med Pubs.

MRI of the Musculoskeletal System. 2nd ed. Mini Nutan Pathria & Karence K. Chan. 256p. text 89.00 (*0-7817-2571-2*) Lppncott W & W.

MRI of the Musculoskeletal System. 3rd ed. Ed. by Thomas H. Berquist. LC 95-31754. (Illus.). 864p. 1995. text 170.00 (*0-7817-0310-7*) Lppncott W & W.

MRI of the Musculoskeletal System. 4th ed. Thomas H. Berquist. 670p. text 170.00 (*0-7817-2574-7*) Lppncott W & W.

MRI of the Musculoskeletal System: A Teaching File. 2nd ed. Andrew Deutsch. 864p. 1996. text 156.00 (*0-397-51672-X*) Lppncott W & W.

MRI of the Pelvis. Hedvig Hricak. (Illus.). 562p. (C). 1992. pap. text 195.00 (*0-8385-6527-1*, A6527-4, Apple Lange Med) McGraw.

MRI of the Shoulder. Lynn Steinbach. LC 97-49684. 250p. 1998. text 155.00 (*0-397-51468-9*) Lppncott W & W.

MRI of the Shoulder. Michael B. Zlatkin. 188p. 1991. text 108.00 (*0-88167-800-7*) Lppncott W & W.

MRI of the Shoulder. 2nd ed. Michael B. Zlatkin. 352p. text 125.00 (*0-7817-1590-3*) Lppncott W & W.

MRI of the Shoulder: Clinical Situations & Management. M. Shannon & P. Tonino. (Illus.). 91p. 1991. text 59.00 (*0-86577-419-6*) Thieme Med Pubs.

MRI of the Spine. Kaiser & Ramos. (Illus.). 168p. 1990. text 112.00 (*0-86577-340-8*) Thieme Med Pubs.

MRI of the Spine. Robert M. Quencer. (MRI Teaching File Ser.). 242p. 1991. text 76.00 (*0-88167-703-5*) Lppncott W & W.

MRI of the Spine. Thomas E. St. Amour et al. LC 93-7902. 864p. 1993. text 211.00 (*0-7817-0027-2*) Lppncott W & W.

MRI of the Spine. 2nd ed. Jeffrey S. Ross. 240p. text 89.00 (*0-7817-2528-3*) Lppncott W & W.

MRI of the Wrist & Hand. Murray A. Reicher & Leland E. Kellerhouse. LC 90-8561. 219p. 1990. reprint ed. pap. 67.90 (*0-608-03440-1*, 206414100008) Bks Demand.

MRI Optimization: A Hands on Approach. Peggy Woodward & Gary Schwartz. LC 96-30379. (Illus.). 256p. 1996. text 39.00 (*0-07-071801-6*) McGraw-Hill HPD.

MRI Physics for Physicians. A. L. Horowitz. (Illus.). xi, 113p. 1990. pap. 25.00 (*0-387-96904-7*) Spr-Verlag.

MRI Physics for Radiologists: A Visual Approach. 2nd ed. A. L. Horowitz. (Illus.). xii, 187p. 1993. pap. 29.00 (*0-387-97717-1*) Spr-Verlag.

MRI Physics for Radiologists: A Visual Approach. 3rd ed. Alfred L. Horowitz. LC 94-33017. (Illus.). 176p. 1997. 38.00 (*0-387-94372-2*) Spr-Verlag.

MRI Primer. William H. Oldendorf, Jr. 240p. 1991. text 53.50 (*0-88167-769-8*) Lppncott W & W.

MRI Principles: A Guide for the Mathematically Illiterate. Donald G. Mitchell. Ed. by Lisette Brawlow. LC 98-12902. (Illus.). 288p. (C). 1998. text 59.00 (*0-7216-6759-7*, W B Saunders Co) Harcrt Hlth Sci Grp.

MRI Study Guide & Exam Review. Stewart C. Bushong. (Illus.). 256p. (C). (gr. 13). 1995. pap. text, student ed. 27.95 (*0-8151-1340-4*, 26666) Mosby Inc.

MRI Study Guide & Exam Review. Rundle. (C). 1997. pap. text, student ed. write for info. (*0-7216-6880-1*, W B Saunders Co) Harcrt Hlth Sci Grp.

MRI Study Guide for Technologists. Kenneth S. Meacham. LC 95-10164. (Illus.). 224p. 1995. 32.95 (*0-387-94489-3*) Spr-Verlag.

MRI Survival Guide. Jim D. Cardoza & Robert J. Herfkens. LC 93-41765. 240p. 1994. text 63.00 (*0-7817-0180-5*) Lppncott W & W.

MRI Workbook for Technologists. Carolyn Kaut-Watson. 288p. 1992. pap. text 44.00 (*0-88167-876-7*) Lppncott W & W.

Mrichchhakatika of Sudraka. Ed. & Tr. by M. R. Kale. (C). 1989. 26.00 (*81-208-0081-8*, Pub. by Motilal Bnarsidass) S Asia.

Mridula Sarabhai: Rebel with a Cause. Aparna Basu. (Illus.). 290p. (C). 1996. text 24.95 (*0-19-563110-2*) OUP.

MRL Detail Print File, No. 1. Elmer G. Osterhoudt. (Illus.). 17p. 1999. reprint ed. pap. write for info. (*1-891501-15-1*) Modern Radio.

MRL Detail Print File, No. 2. Elmer G. Osterhoudt. (Illus.). 17p. 1999. reprint ed. pap. write for info. (*1-891501-16-X*) Modern Radio.

Mrna Formation & Function. Ed. by Joel D. Richter. LC 97-33343. (Illus.). 395p. 1997. text 85.00 (*0-12-587545-2*) Morgan Kaufmann.

MRNA Metabolism & Post-Transcriptional Gene Regulation. David R. Morris & Joe B. Harford. LC 96-39030. (Modern Cell Biology Ser.). 354p. 1997. 135.00 (*0-471-14206-9*) Wiley.

MRO Purchasing. Peter L. Grieco, Jr. LC 96-30412. (Orig.). 1997. pap. text 14.95 (*0-945456-44-1*) PT Pubns.

Mroe Angels Shall I Paint. Robin Tanner. 72p. 1993. 150.00 (*0-907664-23-7*, Pub. by Old Stiles) St Mut.

MROM: Micro Routines for Operations Management. John G. Carlson & Andrew C. Yao. 1991. pap. 40.00 (*0-685-51816-7*) Pearson Custom.

MROM: Micro Routines for Operations Management. 2nd ed. John G. Carlson & Andrew C. Yao. 266p. (C). 1994. text 68.00 (*0-536-58621-7*) Pearson Custom.

MRP: The Adaptation, Enhancement, & Application of MRP II. David A. Turbide. LC 92-30393. (Illus.). 200p. 1993. 39.95 (*0-8311-3046-6*) Indus Pr.

MRP & Beyond: A Toolbox for Integrating People & Systems. Carol A. Ptak. LC 96-3311. 264p. 1996. text 40.00 (*0-7863-0554-1*, Irwn Prfssnl) McGraw-Hill Prof.

***MRP Strategies Made Easy.** 170p. 1999. 36.00 (*1-893570-81-9*) SAP Labs.

MRP II: Making It Happen - The Implementer's Guide to Success with Manufacturing Resource Planning. 2nd ed. Thomas F. Wallace. LC 90-71246. 300p. 1993. 116.00 (*0-939246-20-1*) Wiley.

MRP II: The Implementers' Guide to Success with Manufacturing Resource Planning. 2nd ed. Thomas F. Wallace. 336p. 1995. 50.00 (*0-471-13225-X*) Wiley.

MRP II Standard System - A Handbook for Manufacturing Software Survival. Darryl V. Landvater. LC 88-50484. 250p. 1993. pap., student ed. 67.50 (*0-939246-13-9*) Wiley.

MRP II Standard System - A Handbook for Manufacturing Software. Darryl V. Landvater & Christopher D. Gray. 352p. 1995. 95.00 (*0-471-13275-6*) Wiley.

MRP II Standard System - A Handbook for Manufacturing Software Survival. Darryl V. Landvater & Christopher D. Gray. LC 88-50485. 350p. 1993. 201.00 (*0-939246-12-0*) Wiley.

Mrrarr & Me. Romilda Dilley. (Illus.). 48p. 1982. 24.00 (*0-88014-062-3*) Mosaic Pr OH.

Mrs. Aesop's Fables. Lisa Cofield & Debbie Dongerson. Ed. by Patrick Caton. 168p. (Orig.). 1996. pap. 5.95 (*1-56245-227-4*) Great Quotations.

Mrs. Albert Grundy see Collected Works of Harold Frederic

Mrs. Albert Grundy. Harold Frederic. (Collected Works of Harold Frederic). 1988. reprint ed. lib. bdg. 59.00 (*0-7812-1191-3*) Rprt Serv.

Mrs. Alexander: A Life of the Hymn-Writer: Cecil Frances Alexander 1818-1895. Valerie Wallace. 198p. 1995. pap. 21.00 (*1-874675-46-5*) Dufour.

***Mrs. Appleyard's Kitchen.** Louise Andrew Kent & Elizabeth K. Gay. (Illus.). 319p. 1999. 7.99 (*0-7858-1075-7*) Bk Sales Inc.

Mrs. Arris Goes to Paris. Paul Gallico. LC 89-85722. (Illus.). 158p. 1989. reprint ed. pap. 7.95 (*1-55882-021-3*) Intl Polygonics.

Mrs. Bateman's Low Fat Baking Butter Cookbook. Kristine Bateman. (Illus.). 198p. 1995. pap. text 21.95 (*0-9649109-0-X*) Mrs Batemans.

Mrs. Beauchamp Brown. Jane G. Austin. (Works of Jane (Goodin) Austin). 1989. reprint ed. lib. bdg. 79.00 (*0-7812-1827-6*) Rprt Serv.

Mrs. Beautiful. Lester Goran. 1985. 14.95 (*0-88282-010-9*) New Horizon NJ.

Mrs. Beck's Cookie Cookbook. Dorothy S. Beck. Ed. & Pref. by Doris B. Demou. 138p. (YA). (gr. 6-12). 1988. 10.00 (*0-9604794-2-2*) Doris Demou.

Mrs. Beeton's Best British Home Cooking. Ed. by Bridget Jones. 1998. 35.00 (*0-7063-7620-X*, Pub. by WrLock) Sterling.

***Mrs. Beeton's Book of Household Management.** Isabella Beeton. Ed. by Nicola Humble. LC 99-54236. (Oxford World's Classic Ser.). (Illus.). 672p. 2000. pap. 13.95 (*0-19-283345-6*) OUP.

Mrs. Biddlebox. Smith. (Illus.). 32p. (J). (ps-3). 15.95 (*0-06-028690-3*); 5.95 (*0-06-443620-9*) HarpC.

Mrs. Blackford's Cat. Vogt. (J). Date not set. mass mkt. 16.00 (*0-689-80247-1*) Aladdin.

Mrs. Blackwell's Heart-of-Texas Cookbook. Louise B. Dillow & Dennie B. Carver. (Illus.). 130p. 1980. pap. 9.95 (*0-931722-06-3*) Corona Pub.

Mrs. Blood. 2nd ed. Thomas. 220p. 1992. pap. 14.95 (*0-88922-319-X*, Pub. by Talonbks) Genl Dist Srvs.

Mrs. Boone's Favorite Early-American Recipes. Compiled by Franklin Fox. LC 98-5667. 216p. 1998. pap. 15.95 (*1-879094-56-8*) Momentum Bks.

Mrs. Boone's Wild Game Cookbook. Compiled by Judith McGlinn. (Illus.). 176p. (Orig.). 1991. pap. 12.95 (*1-879094-08-8*) Momentum Bks.

Mrs. Brice's Mice. Syd Hoff. (I Can Read Bks.). (Illus.). 32p. (J). (ps-1). 1988. 14.00 (*0-06-022451-7*) HarpC Child Bks.

Mrs. Brice's Mice. Syd Hoff. LC 87-45680. (I Can Read Bks.). (Illus.). 32p. (J). (ps-3). 1988. lib. bdg. 15.89 (*0-06-022452-5*) HarpC Child Bks.

Mrs. Brice's Mice. Syd Hoff. (I Can Read Bks.). (Illus.). 32p. (J). (ps-1). 1991. pap. 3.95 (*0-06-444145-8*, HarpTrophy) HarpC Child Bks.

Mrs. Brice's Mice. Syd Hoff. (I Can Read Bks.). (J). (ps-1). 1988. 8.95 (*0-606-04755-7*, Pub. by Turtleback) Demco.

Mrs. Bridge. Evan S. Connell. LC 81-81514. 246p. 1990. reprint ed. pap. 9.95 (*0-86547-056-1*) N Point Pr.

Mrs. Bridge: A Novel. large type ed. Evan S. Connell. 1991. pap. 15.95 (*0-8161-5206-3*, G K Hall Lrg Type) Mac Lib Ref.

***Mrs. Broom.** Charles Reasoner. (Halloween Glow Bks.). (Illus.). 14p. (J). (ps-k). 2000. bds. 4.99 (*0-8431-7606-7*, Price Stern) Peng Put Young Read.

Mrs. Brown Went to Town. Wong Herbert Yee. LC 95-23389. (Illus.). 32p. (J). (ps-3). 1996. 14.95 (*0-395-75282-5*) HM.

Mrs. Byrne's Dictionary of Unusual, Obscure, & Preposterous Words. Josefa H. Byrne. Ed. & Intro. by Robert Byrne. LC 93-45370. 1974. 18.95 (*1-55972-233-9*, Birch Ln Pr) Carol Pub Group.

Mrs. Byrne's Dictionary of Unusual, Obscure, & Preposterous Words. Josefa H. Byrne. Ed. & Intro. by Robert Byrne. 1976. pap. 10.95 (*0-8065-0498-6*, Citadel Pr) Carol Pub Group.

Mrs. C. H. Spurgeon. Charles Ray. 1979. pap. 7.00 (*1-56186-305-X*) Pilgrim Pubns.

Mrs. Cage. Nancy Barr. 1993. pap. 5.25 (*0-8222-1313-3*) Dramatists Play.

Mrs. Caldicot's Cabbage War. Chilton Designs Publishers Staff. (C). 1992. 50.00 (*0-9503527-8-0*, Pub. by Chilton Designs) St Mut.

Mrs. Caldwell Speaks to Her Son. Camilo Jose Cela. Tr. by J. S. Bernstein from SPA. LC 68-16379. 232p. 1990. reprint ed. 35.00 (*0-8014-0073-2*); reprint ed. pap. 12.95 (*0-8014-9783-3*) Cornell U Pr.

Mrs. California. Doris Baizley. 1987. pap. 5.25 (*0-8222-0784-2*) Dramatists Play.

Mrs. Carmichael. Ruth Silcock. 84p. 1987. pap. 14.95 (*0-85646-179-2*, Pub. by Anvil Press) Dufour.

Mrs. Chippy's Last Expedition: The Newly Discovered Journal of Shackleton's Polar-Bound Cat. Caroline Alexander. LC 97-15732. (Illus.). 176p. 1997. 16.00 (*0-06-017546-X*) HarpC.

Mrs. Chippy's Last Expedition: The Remarkable Journal of Shackleton's Polar-Bound Cat. Caroline Alexander. LC 97-15732. (Illus.). 176p. 1999. pap. 11.00 (*0-06-093261-9*) HarpC.

***Mrs. Chippy's Last Expedition: The Remarkable Journal of Shackleton's Polar-Bound Cat.** large type ed. Caroline Alexander. LC 99-86698. (Illus.). (J). 2000. pap. 22.95 (*1-56895-847-1*) Wheeler Pub.

Mrs. Claus. Jerry Smath. (J). 1995. pap. 3.95 (*0-8167-3681-2*) Troll Communs.

Mrs. Claus: A Story by Tom Lang. Tom Lang. LC 96-94888. (Illus.). 64p. (J). (gr. 2-12). 1997. pap. 5.00 (*0-9649742-0-7*) Boudelang Pr.

Mrs. Claus Believes. Carol Stone. (J). (gr. 3-5). 1998. pap. 6.95 (*0-533-12780-7*) Vantage.

***Mrs. Claus Invites You.** Carol A. Stone. LC 99-93806. (J). (gr. k-3). 1999. pap. 7.95 (*0-533-13162-6*) Vantage.

Mrs. Cliff's Yacht. Frank Stockton. (Notable American Authors Ser.). 1999. reprint ed. lib. bdg. 125.00 (*0-7812-8935-1*) Rprt Serv.

Mrs. Cole on an Onion Roll: And Other School Poems. Kalli Dakos. LC 94-8018. (Illus.). 40p. (gr. k-3). 1999. pap. 5.99 (*0-689-82687-7*, 076714005990) Aladdin.

M

An Asterisk (*) at the beginning of an entry indicates that the title is appearing for the first time.

Mrs. Cole on an Onion Roll: And Other School Poems. Kalli Dakos. LC 94-8018. (Illus.). 40p. (J). 1995. mass mkt. 14.00 (*0-02-725583-2*) S&S Bks Yung.

Mrs. Cook's Hats see Set 11

***Mrs. Cook's Kitchen: Basics & Beyond.** Gay Cook. 256p. 2000. pap. 16.95 (*1-55285-014-5*) Carlton Bks Ltd.

Mrs. Cottrell's Stretching-the-Food-Dollar Cookbook. Edyth Y. Cottrell. LC 80-36894. (Illus.). 128p. (Orig.). 1982. pap. 4.95 (*0-912800-80-1*) Woodbridge Pr.

Mrs. Craddock. W. Somerset Maugham. 256p. 1992. pap. 11.95 (*0-14-018594-1*, Penguin Classics) Viking Penguin.

Mrs. Craddock. W. Somerset Maugham. LC 75-25358. (Works of W. Somerset Maugham). 1977. reprint ed. 26.95 (*0-405-07817-X*) Ayer.

Mrs. Crump's Cat. Smith. 32p. (J). (ps-3). Date not set. pap. 4.95 (*0-06-443551-2*) HarpC Child Bks.

Mrs. Crump's Cat. Smith. 32p. (J). (ps-3). 2002. 12.95 (*0-06-028302-5*) HarpC Child Bks.

Mrs. Daffodil. Gladys Taber. 23.95 (*0-89190-592-8*) Amereon Ltd.

Mrs. Dahl in the Season of Cub Scouts. Chris Dahl. Ed. by Shirley Warren. 40p. 1991. pap. 5.00 (*1-877801-15-1*) Still Waters.

Mrs. Dalloway. Virginia Woolf. LC 92-54300. 1993. 15.00 (*0-679-42042-8*) Everymns Lib.

Mrs. Dalloway. Virginia Woolf. LC 25-9749. 212p. 1990. 15.95 (*0-15-162862-9*) Harcourt.

Mrs. Dalloway. Virginia Woolf. 194p. 1990. pap. 12.00 (*0-15-662870-8*, Harvest Bks) Harcourt.

Mrs. Dalloway. Virginia Woolf. Ed. by Claire Tomalin. (World's Classics Ser.). (Illus.). 302p. 1992. pap. write for info. (*0-19-281815-5*) OUP.

Mrs. Dalloway. Virginia Woolf. Ed. by Sue Reid. LC 93-9839. (New Casebooks Ser.). 192p. 1993. text 39.95 (*0-312-09688-7*) St Martin.

Mrs. Dalloway. Virginia Woolf. (Classics Library). 160p. 1998. pap. 3.95 (*1-85326-191-2*, 1912WW, Pub. by Wrdsworth Edits) NTC Contemp Pub Co.

Mrs. Dalloway. large type ed. Virginia Woolf. 1996. lib. bdg. 22.95 (*0-7838-1824-6*, G K Hall Lrg Type) Mac Lib Ref.

***Mrs. Dalloway.** Virginia Woolf. 141p. 2000. reprint ed. pap. text 15.00 (*0-7881-9157-8*) DIANE Pub.

***Mrs. Dalloway, Set.** unabridged ed. Virginia Woolf. 1999. 35.95 incl. audio (*1-55685-517-6*) Audio Bk Con.

Mrs. Dalloway: Mapping Streams of Consciousness. David Dowling. (Masterwork Studies: No. 67). 152p. 1991. 29.00 (*0-8057-9414-X*, Twyne) Mac Lib Ref.

Mrs. Dalloway Notes. Gary Carey. (Cliffs Notes Ser.). 64p. 1970. pap. 4.95 (*0-8220-0855-6*, Cliff) IDG Bks.

Mrs. Dalloway's Party: A Short Story Sequence. Virginia Woolf. LC 73-11234. 80p. 1975. reprint ed. pap. 7.00 (*0-15-662900-3*, Harvest Bks) Harcourt.

Mrs. de Winter. large type ed. Susan Hill. LC 93-21205. 483p. 1993. lib. bdg. 24.95 (*0-7862-0051-0*) Thorndike Pr.

Mrs. de Winter. large type ed. Susan Hill. LC 93-21205. 483p. 1995. lib. bdg. 15.95 (*0-7862-0052-9*) Thorndike Pr.

Mrs. Delaney: Her Life & Her Flowers. 2nd ed. Ruth Hayden. (Illus.). 192p. 1993. reprint ed. 35.00 (*1-56131-061-1*, NAB) I R Dee.

Mrs. Dewinter. Susan Hill. 416p. 1994. mass mkt. 6.50 (*0-380-72145-7*, Avon Bks) Morrow Avon.

***Mrs. Digger's Roots.** Eleanor Friedlander. (Illus.). 44p. (J). (ps-3). 1999. 17.95 (*0-9672124-0-5*) Jadeda Pr.

Mrs. Doubtfire (Senora Doubtfire) Anne Fine. Tr. by Flora Pena. (SPA.). 165p. (J). (gr. 5-8). 1992. pap. write for info. (*84-204-4680-7*) Santillana.

Mrs. Duck & the Woman. Kara L. Jones. Ed. by Harry Jones. (Illus.). 16p. 1999. pap. 10.00 (*1-929359-00-4*) Kota Pr.

Mrs. Duff. Joseph N. Ireland. (Notable American Authors Ser.). 1992. reprint ed. lib. bdg. 75.00 (*0-7812-3340-2*) Rprt Serv.

Mrs. Dumpty. Chana Bloch. 80p. (J). 1998. 18.95 (*0-299-16000-9*); pap. 11.95 (*0-299-16004-1*) U of Wis Pr.

Mrs. Dymond (1885) Anne T. Ritchie. (Pocket Classics Ser.). 272p. 1997. pap. 12.95 (*0-7509-1411-4*, Pub. by Sutton Pub Ltd) Intl Pubs Mktg.

Mrs. Eddy. Hugh A. Kennedy. 507p. 1987. 10.95 (*1-878641-01-8*) Aequus Inst Pubns.

Mrs. Egg & Other Americans: Collected Stories. Ed. by Wilson Follett. LC 78-23682. 531p. 1979. reprint ed. lib. bdg. 45.50 (*0-313-20648-1*, BEMO, Greenwood Pr) Greenwood.

Mrs. Einstein: A Novel. Anna McGrail. LC 98-14264. 320p. 1998. 24.95 (*0-393-04611-7*) Norton.

Mrs. Farrell. William Dean Howells. (Notable American Authors Ser.). 1992. reprint ed. lib. bdg. 75.00 (*0-7812-3265-1*) Rprt Serv.

Mrs. Fields Best Cookie Book Ever! 150 Delicious Cookie & Dessert Recipes from the Kitchen of Mrs. Fields. Debbi Fields & Time-Life Books Editors. LC 96-19360. (Illus.). 144p. (J). (gr. 5). 1999. pap. 9.95 (*0-7835-4830-3*) Time-Life.

***Mrs. Fields Best Ever Cookie Book!** Debbi Fields & Time-Life Books Editors. LC 98-156079. (Illus.). 237p. 1999. pap. write for info. (*0-7835-5266-1*) Time-Life.

Mrs. Fields' Cookie Book: One Hundred Recipes from the Kitchen of Mrs. Debbi Fields. Debbi Fields & Time-Life Books Editors. LC 92-9842. (Illus.). 120p. (gr. 7). 1999. 18.95 (*0-8094-6712-7*) Time-Life.

Mrs. Fields' Cookie Book: One Hundred Recipes from the Kitchen of Mrs. Fields. Debbie Fields. (Illus.). 120p. (gr. 5). 1999. pap. 12.95 (*0-8094-6715-1*) Time-Life.

***Mrs. Fields Cookie Chocolate Set.** Time-Life Books Editors. (gr. 7). 1999. pap. 17.95 (*0-7835-4813-3*) Time-Life Educ.

Mrs. Fields' Cookie Secrets. Time-Life Books Editors. (Time-Life Favorite Recipes Ser.). 96p. (YA). (gr. 11). 1999. pap. 6.95 (*0-7370-1117-3*) T-L Custom Pub.

Mrs. Fields I Love Chocolate Cookbook. Debbi Fields. (Illus.). 120p. (gr. 7). 1999. 12.95 (*0-8094-7811-0*) Time-Life.

Mrs. Fields "I Love Chocolate" Cookbook. Debbi Fields. Ed. by Robert A. Doyle. LC 94-2221. (Illus.). 120p. (gr. 7). 1999. 17.95 (*0-8094-7808-0*) Time-Life.

Mrs. Fish, Ape, & Me, the Dump Queen. Norma F. Mazer. 144p. (J). (gr. 4 up). 1981. pap. 3.50 (*0-380-69153-1*, Avon Bks) Morrow Avon.

Mrs. Fisher: or The Future of Humor. Robert Graves. LC 73-21511. (English Literature Ser.: No. 33). 1974. lib. bdg. 75.00 (*0-8383-1755-3*) M S G Haskell Hse.

Mrs. Fiske: Her View on the Stage. Alexander Woollcott. LC 68-56482. (Illus.). 1972. reprint ed. 23.95 (*0-405-09103-6*) Ayer.

Mrs. Fitz's Flamingos. Kevin McCloskey. LC 90-2278. (Illus.). (J). (ps-3). 1992. lib. bdg. 13.93 (*0-688-10475-4*) Lothrop.

***Mrs. Flanagan's Trumpet.** Cookson. 2000. 17.95 (*0-385-40134-5*, Pub. by Transworld Publishers Ltd) Trafalgar.

Mrs. Fox & Mrs. Stork see Dona Zorra y Dona Ciguena

Mrs. Fox & Mrs. Stork see Dame Renard et Dame Cigogne

Mrs. Fox & Mrs. Stork see Ba Cao Va Ba Co

Mrs. Fox & Mrs. Stork. (KOR., Illus.). 24p. (Orig.). (J). (gr. 1-2). 1993. pap. 2.95 (*0-922852-24-3*) Another Lang Pr.

Mrs. Fox & Mrs. Stork. Hanna Hutchinson. Tr. by Naomi Suwa from ENG. (Interlingo Ser.). (JPN., Illus.). 24p. (Orig.). (J). (gr. 1-2). 1993. pap. 2.95 (*0-922852-23-5*) Another Lang Pr.

Mrs. Fox & Mrs. Stork. Hanna Hutchinson. Tr. by May S. Wang from ENG. (Interlingo Ser.). (CHI., Illus.). 24p. (Orig.). (J). (gr. 1-2). 1993. pap. 2.95 (*0-922852-22-7*) Another Lang Pr.

Mrs. Fox & Mrs. Stork. Illus. by Edward Nofziger. 19p. (Orig.). (J). (gr. k-12). 1993. pap. 2.95 (*0-922852-21-9*) Another Lang Pr.

Mrs. Frisby & the Rats of NIMH see Senora Frisby y las Ratas de NIMH

Mrs. Frisby & the Rats of NIMH. Robert C. O'Brien. (Rats of NIMH Ser.). (J). (gr. 4-7). 1999. pap. 2.99 (*0-689-82966-3*) Aladdin.

Mrs. Frisby & the Rats of NIMH. Robert C. O'Brien. LC 74-134818. (Rats of NIMH Ser.). (Illus.). 240p. (J). (gr. 4-7). 1971. 17.00 (*0-689-20651-8*) Atheneum Yung Read.

***Mrs. Frisby & the Rats of NIMH.** Robert C. O'Brien. (Rats of NIMH Ser.). (YA). 1999. 11.95 (*1-56137-532-2*) Novel Units.

***Mrs. Frisby & the Rats of NIMH.** Robert C. O'Brien. (Rats of NIMH Ser.). (J). (gr. 4-7). 1999. 9.95 (*1-56137-273-0*) Novel Units.

Mrs. Frisby & the Rats of NIMH. Robert C. O'Brien. (Rats of NIMH Ser.). (J). (gr. 4-7). 1998. per. 2.65 (*0-689-82171-9*) S&S Childrens.

Mrs. Frisby & the Rats of NIMH. Jane Pryne. (Literature Unit Ser.). (Illus.). 48p. 1998. pap., teacher ed. 7.95 (*1-55734-523-6*) Tchr Create Mat.

Mrs. Frisby & the Rats of NIMH. large type ed. Robert C. O'Brien. (Rats of NIMH Ser.). (Illus.). (J). (gr. 4-7). 1993. 64.50 (*0-614-09848-3*, L-34129-00) Am Printing Hse.

Mrs. Frisby & the Rats of NIMH. large type ed. Robert C. O'Brien. (Rats of NIMH Ser.). (Illus.). (J). (gr. 4-7). 1995. 61.50 (*0-614-09602-2*, L-34828-00) Am Printing Hse.

***Mrs. Frisby & the Rats of NIMH.** large type ed. Robert C. O'Brien. (Rats of NIMH Ser.). (Illus.). 300p. (J). (gr. 4-7). 2000. lib. bdg. 29.95 (*1-58118-056-X*, 23470) LRS.

Mrs. Frisby & the Rats of NIMH. Robert C. O'Brien. (Rats of NIMH Ser.). 248p. (J). (gr. 4-7). 1986. reprint ed. mass mkt. 4.50 (*0-689-71068-2*) Aladdin.

Mrs. Frisby & the Rats of NIMH. 2nd ed. Robert C. O'Brien. (Rats of NIMH Ser.). (J). (gr. 4-7). 1986. 9.60 (*0-606-04055-2*, Pub. by Turtleback) Demco.

Mrs. Frisby & the Rats of Nimh: A Study Guide. Joyce Friedland & Rikki Kessler. (Novel-Ties Ser.). (J). (gr. 5-7). 1984. pap. text, teacher ed., student ed. 15.95 (*0-88122-098-1*) Lrn Links.

Mrs. Frisby & the Rats of Nimh: L-I-T Guide. 1998. pap. 8.95 (*1-56644-962-6*) Educ Impress.

Mrs. Funnywinkle. Susan Morelli. Ed. by Jane Weinberger. LC 93-61196. (Illus.). 54p. (J). (ps-4). 1994. pap. 5.95 (*0-932433-62-6*) Windswept Hse.

Mrs. Gandhi's Second Reign. Arun Shourie. 532p. 1984. 29.95 (*0-7069-2595-5*) Asia Bk Corp.

Mrs. Gaskell & Her Friends. Elizabeth Haldane. LC 73-140356. (Select Bibliographies Reprint Ser.). 1977. 23.95 (*0-8369-5599-4*) Ayer.

Mrs. Gaskell's Tales of Mystery & Horror. Elizabeth Gaskell. Ed. & Intro. by Michael Ashley. LC 79-300393. (Illus.). 231 p. (J). 1978. write for info. (*0-575-02472-0*) V Gollancz.

Mrs. God. Peter Straub. 1999. pap. 9.98 (*0-671-04462-1*) PB.

Mrs. Golightly & Other Stories. Ethel Wilson. 217p. 1996. pap. text 6.95 (*0-7710-8956-2*) McCland & Stewart.

Mrs. Goose's Baby. Charlotte Voake. (Illus.). (J). (ps-1). 1997. 4.99 (*0-614-28641-7*); pap. 4.99 (*0-7636-0092-X*) Candlewick Pr.

Mrs. Greenthumbs. Cassandra Danz. LC 92-17969. 1993. pap. 12.00 (*0-517-58668-1*, Crown) Crown Pub Group.

Mrs. Greenthumbs: How I Turned a Boring Yard into a Glorious Garden & How You Can Too. Cassandra Danz. (Illus.). 256p. 1993. pap. 12.00 (*0-517-88010-5*) C Potter.

Mrs. Greenthumbs Plows Ahead: Five Steps to Drop Dead Gorgeous Gardens of Your Dreams. Cassandra Danz. 224p. (J). 1999. pap. 12.95 (*0-609-80265-8*) Crown Pub Group.

Mrs. Greenthumbs Plows Ahead: Five Steps to Drop Dead Gorgeous Gardens of Your Dreams, 2. Cassandra Danz. (J). 1999. pap. text 12.70 (*0-676-58495-0*) Random.

Mrs. Greenthumbs Plows Ahead: The Five Secrets of a Gorgeous Home Garden. Cassandra Dang. LC 97-30270. 1998. 25.00 (*0-517-70554-0*) Random.

Mrs. Grossman's Basic Sticker Ideabook: How to . . . Andrea Grossman & Mary L. Curtin. Ed. by Mary Clausen. LC 97-93546. (Illus.). 48p. (Orig.). 1997. pap. 12.00 (*0-910299-01-3*) Mrs Grossmans Paper Co.

Mrs. Grossman's Holiday Sticker Idea Book: Celebrate All Year Long with Spectacular Sticker Crafts! Andrea Grossman & Mary L. Curtin. Ed. by Mary Clausen. (Illus.). 48p. 1997. pap. 12.00 (*0-910299-02-1*) Mrs Grossmans Paper Co.

Mrs. Grundy: A History of Four Centuries of Morals Intended to Illuminate Present Problems in Great Britain & the United States. Leo Markun. 1930. 69.00 (*0-403-00130-7*) Scholarly.

Mrs. Hallam's Companion. Mary J. Holmes. (Notable American Authors Ser.). 1992. reprint ed. lib. bdg. 75.00 (*0-7812-3149-3*) Rprt Serv.

Mrs. Harper's Bazaar. Babette Hughes. 1937. pap. 3.25 (*0-8222-0785-0*) Dramatists Play.

Mrs. Harris: The Death of the Scarsdale Diet Doctor. Diana Trilling. LC 80-81991. 272p. 1981. 14.95 (*0-15-176902-8*) Harcourt.

***Mrs. Hen's Big Surprise.** Christel Desmoinaux. (Illus.). 32p. (ps-2). 2000. per. 12.95 (*0-689-83403-9*) S&S Childrens.

Mrs. Hill's Southern Practical Cookery & Recipe Book: A Facsimile of Mrs. Hill's New Cook Book, 1872 Edition. Annabella P. Hill. LC 95-5388. (Illus.). 503p. 1995. 24.95 (*1-57003-048-0*) U of SC Pr.

Mrs. Hobson's Album. Ed. by Elsie Violet Locke & Janet Paul. (Illus.). 168p. 1990. 39.95 (*1-86940-035-6*) OUP.

***Mrs. Hollingsworth's Men: A Novel.** Padgett Powell. 144p. 2000. 20.00 (*0-618-07168-7*) HM.

Mrs. Honey Doll Including Plain Hat. (J). 1999. 16.99 (*0-85953-824-9*) Childs Play.

Mrs. Honey's Dream. Pam Adams. LC 92-40124. (Illus.). 32p. (J). 1993. pap. 3.99 (*0-85953-332-8*) Childs Play.

Mrs. Honey's Glasses. Pam Adams. LC 93-12368. (Illus.). 32p. (J). (ps-3). 1993. 7.99 (*0-85953-757-9*); pap. 3.99 (*0-85953-758-7*) Childs Play.

Mrs. Honey's Hat. Pam Adams. LC 90-46604. (Illus.). 24p. (J). (ps-2). 1980. 7.99 (*0-85953-099-X*, Pub. by Childs Play); pap. 3.99 (*0-85953-325-5*, Pub. by Childs Play) Random House.

Mrs. Honey's Hat. Pam Adams. (GRE.). (J). 1993. pap. 3.99 (*0-85953-821-4*) Childs Play.

Mrs. Honey's Hat - Giant Lap Book. Pam Adams. 32p. (J). (gr. k-3). 26.99 (*0-85953-829-X*) Childs Play.

***Mrs. Honey's Hat Lap Book.** Pam Adams. LC 99-57507. 32p. (J). (ps-3). 1999. 26.99 (*0-85953-814-1*) Childs Play.

Mrs. Honey's Holiday. Pam Adams. LC 92-41886. (Illus.). 32p. (J). 1993. 7.99 (*0-85953-755-2*); pap. 3.99 (*0-85953-756-0*) Childs Play.

Mrs. Honey's List. Sally F. Odgers. LC 93-6572. (Illus.). (J). 1994. write for info. (*0-383-03703-4*) SRA McGraw.

Mrs. Hornstein. large type ed. Fredrica Wagman. LC 97-29616. 1997. 25.95 (*1-56895-481-6*, Compass) Wheeler Pub.

Mrs. Hornstien. Fredrica Wagman. LC 96-52528. 128p. 1997. 17.95 (*0-8050-4956-8*) H Holt & Co.

Mrs. Houblon's Side-Saddle. rev. ed. Rev. by Sylvia Stanier. 79p. (C). 1990. 70.00 (*0-85131-409-0*, Pub. by J A Allen) St Mut.

Mrs. Houdini. Rebecca M. Devet. LC 88-13884. (University of Central Florida Contemporary Poetry Ser.). 72p. 1989. 17.95 (*0-8130-0914-6*) U Press Fla.

***Mrs. Hudson? Mrs. Hudson!! A Conceptual Narrative Treatment of an Original Musical.** James Moss Cardwell. (Illus.). 2000. 30.00 (*1-55246-207-2*) Battered Silicon.

Mrs. Humphrey Ward: A Study in Late-Victorian Feminine Consciousness & Creative Expression. Anne M. Bindslev. 172p. (Orig.). 1985. pap. text 35.00 (*91-22-00731-8*) Coronet Bks.

Mrs. Humphry Ward: Eminent Victorian Pre-Eminent Edwardian. John Sutherland. 432p. 29.95 (*0-685-39465-4*) OUP.

Mrs. Ike. large type ed. Susan Eisenhower. (Niagara Large Print Ser.). 529p. 1997. 29.50 (*0-7089-5868-0*) Ulverscroft.

Mrs. Ike: Memories & Reflections on the Life of Mamie Eisenhower. Susan Eisenhower. LC 96-25019. (Illus.). 320p. 1996. 26.00 (*0-374-21514-6*) FS&G.

***Mrs. Isha's Sugarless Cookbook: Great Desserts Minus the Sugar!** deluxe ed. Isha Eefa. 25p. 1999. 12.95 (*1-929300-09-3*) Just Friends Prod.

Mrs. Jeepers' Batty Vacation. Debbie Dadey & Marcia Thornton Jones. (Adventures of the Bailey School Kids Super Special Ser.: No. 2). (Illus.). (J). (gr. 2-4). 1997. 4.99 (*0-590-21243-5*) Scholastic Inc.

Mrs. Jeepers in Outer Space. Debbie Dadey & Marcia Thornton Jones. (Adventures of the Bailey School Kids Super Special Ser.: No. 4). (Illus.). 124p. (J). (gr. 2-5). 1999. pap. 3.99 (*0-439-04396-4*) Scholastic Inc.

Mrs. Jeepers Is Missing. Debbie Dadey & Marcia Thornton Jones. (Adventures of the Bailey School Kids Super Special Ser.: No. 1). (Illus.). (J). (gr. 2-4). 1996. pap. 4.99 (*0-590-88134-5*) Scholastic Inc.

Mrs. Jeepers' Secret Cave. Debbie Dadey & Marcia Thornton Jones. (Adventures of the Bailey School Kids Super Special Ser.: No. 3). (Illus.). 128p. (J). (gr. 2-4). 1998. pap. 4.99 (*0-590-11712-2*, Little Apple) Scholastic Inc.

Mrs. Jeepers' Secret Cave. Debbie Dadey & Marcia Thornton Jones. (Adventures of the Bailey School Kids Ser.: No. 3). (J). (gr. 2-4). 1998. 10.09 (*0-606-13626-6*, Pub. by Turtleback) Demco.

***Mrs. Jeffries Dusts for Clues.** Emily Brightwell. LC 99-35727. (Orig.). 1999. pap. 23.95 (*0-7838-8721-3*, G K Hall Lrg Type) Mac Lib Ref.

Mrs. Jeffries on the Ball. large type ed. Emily Brightwell. LC 95-2472. (Nightingale Ser.). 282p. 1995. reprint ed. pap. 18.95 (*0-7838-1284-1*, G K Hall Lrg Type) Mac Lib Ref.

Mrs. Jeffries on the Ball: A Victorian Mystery. Emily Brightwell. 208p. (Orig.). 1994. mass mkt. 5.99 (*0-425-14491-7*, Prime Crime) Berkley Pub.

Mrs. Jeffries on the Trail. Emily Brightwell. 240p. (Orig.). 1995. mass mkt. 5.50 (*0-425-14691-X*, Prime Crime) Berkley Pub.

Mrs. Jeffries Plays the Cook. Emily Brightwell. 1995. mass mkt. 5.50 (*0-425-15053-4*) Berkley Pub.

Mrs. Jeffries Questions the Answer. Emily Brightwell. 240p. 1997. mass mkt. 5.99 (*0-425-16093-9*, Prime Crime) Berkley Pub.

Mrs. Jeffries Reveals Her Art. Emily Brightwell. 1998. mass mkt. 5.99 (*0-425-16243-5*, Prime Crime) Berkley Pub.

***Mrs. Jeffries Reveals Her Art.** large type ed. Emily Brightwell. LC 00-39598. 264p. 2000. 23.95 (*0-7838-9104-0*, G K Hall & Co) Mac Lib Ref.

Mrs. Jeffries Rocks the Boat, 1 vol., Emily Brightwell. Vol. 12. 198p. 1999. mass mkt. 5.99 (*0-425-16934-0*) Berkley Pub.

Mrs. Jeffries Stands Corrected. Emily Brightwell. 224p. (Orig.). 1996. mass mkt. 5.99 (*0-425-15580-3*, Prime Crime) Berkley Pub.

Mrs. Jeffries Take the Stage. Emily Brightwell. 1997. mass mkt. 5.99 (*0-425-15724-5*, Prime Crime) Berkley Pub.

Mrs. Jeffries Takes Stock. Emily Brightwell. 208p. (Orig.). 1994. pap. 4.99 (*0-425-14282-5*, Prime Crime) Berkley Pub.

Mrs. Jeffries Takes the Cake. Emily Brightwell. 240p. 1998. pap. 5.99 (*0-425-16569-8*, Prime Crime) Berkley Pub.

***Mrs. Jeffries Takes the Cake.** large type ed. Emily Brightwell. LC 99-45562. (G. K. Hall Paperback Ser.). 1999. pap. 23.95 (*0-7838-8798-1*, G K Hall Lrg Type) Mac Lib Ref.

***Mrs. Jeffries Takes the Stage.** large type ed. Emily Brightwell. LC 00-27602. (Paperback Ser.). 290p. 2000. pap. 23.95 (*0-7838-9035-4*, G K Hall & Co) Mac Lib Ref.

Mrs. Jolly's Joke Shop. Allan Ahlberg. (Illus.). 24p. (J). (gr. 3-6). 1988. pap. 6.95 (*0-14-032347-3*, Pub. by Pnguin Bks Ltd) Trafalgar.

Mrs. Jordan's Profession: The Actress & the Prince. Claire Tomalin. LC 94-28056. (Illus.). 414p. 1995. 27.50 (*0-679-41071-6*) Knopf.

Mrs. Joyce of Zurich & Mr. Forster of King's. limited ed. Ed. by Sandy Campbell. (Illus.). 80p. 1989. 35.00 (*0-917366-09-3*) S Campbell.

Mrs. Katz & Tush. Patricia Polacco. (Illus.). (J). 1992. 15.00 (*0-553-08122-5*, Litl Rooster) BDD Bks Young Read.

Mrs. Katz & Tush. Patricia Polacco. (Illus.). 32p. (J). (ps-3). 1994. pap. 6.99 (*0-440-40936-5*) Dell.

Mrs. Katz & Tush. Patricia Polacco. 1994. 11.19 (*0-606-05930-X*, Pub. by Turtleback) Demco.

***Mrs. Keith's Crime, Set.** unabridged ed. Lucy Clifford. (YA). (gr. 8 up). 1999. 41.95 incl. audio (*1-55685-603-2*) Audio Bk Con.

Mrs. Kennedy. Leo Vroman. (Cross-Cultural Review Chapbook Ser.). 1991. boxed set 100.00 (*0-89304-190-4*) Cross-Cultrl NY.

Mrs. Kennedy. limited ed. Leo Vroman. (Cross-Cultural Review Chapbook Ser.). 1991. 25.00 (*0-89304-189-0*) Cross-Cultrl NY.

Mrs. Kennedy Goes Abroad. Jacqueline Duheme. LC 98-18686. (Illus.). 64p. 1998. 18.95 (*1-57965-123-2*, 85123) Artisan.

Mrs. Keppel & Her Daughter. Diana Souhami. LC 97-7199. 1997. text 25.95 (*0-312-15594-8*) St Martin.

Mrs. Keppel & Her Daughter. Diana Souhami. 368p. 1998. pap. 14.95 (*0-312-19517-6*, St Martin Griffin) St Martin.

Mrs. Kitching's Smith Island Cookbook. Frances Kitching & Susan S. Dowell. LC 81-40043. (Illus.). 128p. 1981. 12.95 (*0-87033-264-3*, Tidewtr Pubs) Cornell Maritime.

Mrs. Klein. Nicholas Wright. 58p. 1989. pap. 14.95 (*1-85459-232-7*, Pub. by N Hern Bks) Theatre Comm.

Mrs. Leicester's School, 1809. Mary Lamb. LC 94-44530. (Revolution & Romanticism, 1789-1834 Ser.). 1995. 48.00 (*1-85477-182-5*) Continuum.

Mrs. Limber's Raffle: or A Church Fair & Its Victims. William A. Butler. LC 71-137724. (American Fiction Reprint Ser.). 1977. 17.95 (*0-8369-7023-3*) Ayer.

Mrs. Lincoln. Thomas Cullinan. 1969. pap. 5.25 (*0-8222-0786-9*) Dramatists Play.

Mrs. Lincoln's Boston Cook Book see Boston Cooking School Cook Book: A Reprint of the 1883 Classic

Mrs. Mack. Patricia Polacco. LC 97-52946. (Illus.). 40p. (J). (ps-3). 1998. 16.99 (*0-399-23167-6*, Philomel) Peng Put Young Read.

Mrs. Magruder & the Purple Hat: A Story about Friendship & Grief. Judy B. Williams. (Illus.). 28p. (Orig.). (J). (gr. 3-6). 1993. pap. 6.95 (*1-884063-53-5*) Mar Co Prods.

An Asterisk (*) at the beginning of an entry indicates that the title is appearing for the first time.

Mrs. Mahoney of the Tenement. Louise Montgomery. LC 74-128741. (Short Story Index Reprint Ser.). (Illus.). 1977. 17.95 (*0-8369-3632-9*) Ayer.

Mrs. Malory: Death of a Dean. Hazel Holt. 176p. 1997. mass mkt. 5.99 (*0-451-19109-9*) NAL.

Mrs. Malory: Death of a Dean. large type ed. Hazel Holt. LC 96-45013. 1996. pap. 22.95 (*1-56895-392-5*) Wheeler Pub.

***Mrs. Malory & the Legacy.** Hazel Holt. 256p. 2000. mass mkt. 5.99 (*0-451-20002-0*, Sig) NAL.

Mrs. Malory & the Only Good Lawyer. Hazel Holt. 1998. mass mkt. 5.99 (*0-451-19264-8*, Sig) NAL.

Mrs. Malory Wonders Why. Hazel Holt. 256p. 1996. mass mkt. 5.50 (*0-451-18286-3*) NAL.

Mrs. Malory Wonders Why. large type ed. Hazel Holt. 1996. pap. 20.95 (*0-7862-0631-4*) Thorndike Pr.

Mrs. Man. Una Stannard. LC 76-58834. (Illus.). 1977. 29.00 (*0-914142-02-X*) Germainbooks.

Mrs. Mauldin's Make-Over Magic: A Diet of Choice (The Absolutely Last Diet You'll Ever Need!) Carol Mauldin. 1997. pap. text 19.95 (*0-9661090-0-7*) C Mauldin.

Mrs. Mayo's Book of Creative Foods: A Complete Guide to Fancy Food Decorating Anyone Can Do. rev. ed. Esther Murphy. Ed. by Del Carnes. (Illus.). 176p. (Orig.). 1987. pap. text 6.95 (*0-937016-01-2*) Deco-Pr Pub.

***Mrs. McGinty's Dead.** Agatha Christie. (Hercule Poirot Mysteries Ser.). 2000. mass mkt. 5.99 (*0-425-17545-6*) Berkley Pub.

Mrs. McGinty's Dead. Agatha Christie. 256p. 1992. mass mkt. 5.99 (*0-06-100375-1*, Harp PBks) HarpC.

Mrs. McGinty's Dead. Agatha Christie. (Hercule Poirot Mystery Ser.). 1992. 10.09 (*0-606-12434-9*, Pub. by Turtleback) Demco.

Mrs. McGinty's Dead. large type ed. Agatha Christie. 320p. 1988. 17.95 (*0-7089-1771-2*) Ulverscroft.

Mrs. McLintock's Recipes for Cookery & Pastry-Work. Intro. by Iseabail MacLeod. 96p. 1986. pap. 3.90 (*0-08-034519-0*, Pub. by Aberdeen U Pr) Macmillan.

***Mrs. McNosh & the Great Big Squash.** Sara T. Weeks. LC 99-64442. (Growing Tree Ser.). (Illus.). 24p. (J). (ps-3). 2000. 9.95 (*0-694-01202-5*, HarpFestival) HarpC Child Bks.

Mrs. McNosh Hangs Up Her Wash. Sarah Weeks. LC 96-38002. (Illus.). 24p. (J). (ps-3). 1998. 9.95 (*0-694-01076-6*, HarpFestival) HarpC Child Bks.

Mrs. McThing. Mary Chase. 1954. pap. 5.25 (*0-8222-0787-7*) Dramatists Play.

Mrs. Medwin see Works of Henry James Jr.: Collected Works

Mrs. Meeker's Money. Doris M. Disney. 1987. mass mkt. 2.95 (*0-8217-2212-3*, Zebra Kensgtn) Kensgtn Pub Corp.

Mrs. Merriwether's Musical Cat. Carol Purdy. LC 92-43934. (J). 1997. 11.15 (*0-606-11647-8*, Pub. by Turtleback) Demco.

Mrs. Meyer the Bird. Wolf Erlbruch. LC 96-41758. (Illus.). 32p. (J). (ps-3). 1997. 14.95 (*0-531-30017-X*); lib. bdg. 15.99 (*0-531-33017-6*) Orchard Bks Watts.

Mrs. Meynell & Her Literary Generation. Anne K. Tuell. (BCL1-PR English Literature Ser.). 286p. 1992. reprint ed. lib. bdg. 79.00 (*0-7812-7600-4*) Rprt Serv.

Mrs. Meynell & Her Literary Generation. Anne K. Tuell. LC 75-145331. 1971. reprint ed. 19.00 (*0-403-01242-2*) Scholarly.

Mrs. Mike. Benedict Freedman. (Illus.). (J). 1968. 12.25 (*0-8085-1442-3*) Econo-Clad Bks.

Mrs. Mike. Benedict Freedman & Nancy Freedman. (YA). (gr. 7 up). 1987. mass mkt. 4.99 (*0-425-10328-5*) Berkley Pub.

Mrs. Mike. Benedict Freeman & Nancy Freedman. 288p. Date not set. 23.95 (*0-8488-2269-2*) Amereon Ltd.

Mrs. Mike. Benedict Freedman. 1981. reprint ed. lib. bdg. 35.95 (*0-89966-396-6*) Buccaneer Bks.

Mrs. Mike: The Story of Katherine Mary Flannigan. Benedict Freedman. 1984. 10.09 (*0-606-01099-8*, Pub. by Turtleback) Demco.

Mrs. Mike & I Heard the Owl Call My Name: Curriculum Unit. Center for Learning Network Staff et al. (Novel Ser.). 76p. (YA). (gr. 7-12). 1994. spiral bd. 18.95 (*1-56077-300-6*) Ctr Learning.

Mrs. Million. Pete Hautman. LC 99-25958. 1999. 30.00 (*0-7862-1986-6*) Mac Lib Ref.

***Mrs. Million.** Pete Hautman. LC 99-52911. 288p. 2000. per. 12.95 (*0-671-03865-6*) PB.

Mrs. Million. Pete Hautman. LC 98-43486. 288p. 1999. 21.50 (*0-684-83243-7*) S&S Trade.

Mrs. Miniver. Jan Struther. 23.95 (*0-88411-677-8*) Amereon Ltd.

Mrs. Miniver. Jan Struther. 162p. 1990. pap. 8.95 (*0-15-663140-7*) Harcourt.

Mrs. Miniver. Jan Struther. 1990. reprint ed. lib. bdg. 19.95 (*0-89968-554-4*) Buccaneer Bks.

Mrs. Miracle. Deborah Funk. LC 97-71098. (Illus.). 144p. (Orig.). 1997. pap. 7.95 (*1-883928-22-2*) Longwood.

Mrs Miracle. large type ed. 353p. 1998. 30.00 (*0-7862-1557-7*, G K Hall Lrg Type) Mac Lib Ref.

Mrs. Miracle. large type ed. Debbie Macomber. LC 98-26228. (G. K. Hall Romance (Large Print) Ser.). 1998. 26.95 (*0-7838-0318-4*, G K Hall Lrg Type) Mac Lib Ref.

***Mrs. Monty & the Birds.** 3rd ed. Marian M. Schoolland. (Illus.). 128p. (J). (gr. 4-6). 1999. reprint ed. pap. write for info. (*0-9673806-0-X*) Kings Bkshelf.

Mrs. Morellis Revenge. Criscuolo. 1999. text 17.95 (*0-312-08853-1*) St Martin.

Mrs. M's Gratitude Journal: Helped Me Survive 18 Major Disasters Because I Still Believe in God, Prayers, Angels & Miracles. M. Callahan. spiral bd. 12.00 (*0-915453-06-1*) Dollars Info Bks.

Mrs. M.'s Quick & Easy Refund & Rebate System: Information in a Nutshell. M. Callahan. 15p. 1982. reprint ed. spiral bd. 12.00 (*0-915453-00-2*) Dollars Info Bks.

Mrs. M's Winning Sweepstakes System. M. Callahan. 9p. (Orig.). 1982. pap. 12.00 (*0-915453-02-9*) Dollars Info Bks.

Mrs. Muggle's Sparkle. Ruth G. Bragg. LC 89-31371. (Illus.). 28p. (J). (ps up). 1991. pap. 15.95 (*0-88708-106-1*, Picture Book Studio) S&S Childrens.

Mrs. Murphy's Crows see Cuervos de la Senora Murphy

Mrs. Murphy's Crows. Janice Boland. (Books for Young Learners). (Illus.). 12p. (J). (gr. k-2). 1999. pap. text 5.00 (*1-57274-141-4*) R Owen Pubs.

Mrs. Murphy's Laws: If Anything Can Go Wrong It Will . . . And It's Usually a Man's Fault. Lisa Cofield et al. 168p. (Orig.). 1995. pap. 5.95 (*1-56245-222-3*) Great Quotations.

Mrs. Murphy's Swedish Cook Book. Linnea S. Murphy. (Illus.). 156p. 1987. 12.98 (*0-9618520-0-3*) J & L Pub.

Mrs. Murray's Farm. Roy London. 1977. pap. 5.25 (*0-8222-0788-5*) Dramatists Play.

Mrs. Mustard's Baby Faces. Jane Wattenberg. (Illus.). 7p. (J). (ps). 1989. bds. 5.95 (*0-87701-659-3*) Chronicle Bks.

Mrs. Mustard's Beastly Babies. Jane Wattenberg. (Illus.). 7p. (J). (ps). 1990. bds. 5.95 (*0-87701-683-6*) Chronicle Bks.

Mrs. Noah's Patchwork Quilt. Janet Bolton. (Illus.). 22p. (J). 1995. 17.95 (*0-8362-4250-5*) Andrews & McMeel.

Mrs. October Was Here. Coleman Dowell. LC 73-89479. 224p. 1974. 9.25 (*0-8112-0518-5*, Pub. by New Directions); pap. 3.75 (*0-8112-0519-3*, NDP368, Pub. by New Directions) Norton.

Mrs. O'Dell's Third-Grade Class is Shrinking. George Edward Stanley. (Scaredy Cats Ser.). 1996. 9.19 (*0-606-10923-4*, Pub. by Turtleback) Demco.

Mrs. O'Leary's Comet: Cosmic Causes of the Great Chicago Fire. Mel Waskin. (Illus.). 170p. 1985. pap. 10.00 (*0-89733-181-8*) Academy Chi Pubs.

Mrs. Oliphant: A Fiction to Herself: A Literary Life. Elisabeth Jay. (Illus.). 366p. 1995. text 45.00 (*0-19-812875-4*) OUP.

Mrs. Oliphant: The Autobiography & Letters of Mrs. M. O. W. Oliphant. Harry Coghill. 510p. (C). 1989. 95.00 (*0-907839-44-4*, Pub. by Brynmill Pr Ltd) St Mut.

Mrs. Palfrey at the Claremont. Elizabeth Taylor. LC 83-2052. (Modern Classic Ser.). 1983. pap. 6.95 (*0-385-27921-3*) BDD Bks Young Read.

Mrs. Pam Polar Bear. Illus. by Lorraine T. Sullo. 32p. (J). (gr. k-2). 1989. 7.95 (*0-9614989-9-4*) Banmar Inc.

Mrs. Pargeter's Package. Simon Brett. 224p. 1992. mass mkt. 4.99 (*0-446-36204-2*, Pub. by Warner Bks) Little.

Mrs. Pargeter's Plot. Simon Brett. (WWL Mystery Ser.: No. 322). 1999. per. 4.99 (*0-373-26322-8*, 1-26322-7, Wrldwide Lib) Harlequin Bks.

Mrs. Pargeter's Plot. Simon Brett. LC 97-24625. (A Mrs Pargeter Mystery Ser.). 208p. 1998. 21.50 (*0-684-83714-5*) Simon & Schuster.

Mrs. Pargeter's Plot. large type ed. Simon Brett. LC 98-3644. 230p. 1998. 28.95 (*0-7838-0172-6*, G K Hall & Co) Mac Lib Ref.

***Mrs. Pargeter's Point of Honour.** Simon Brett. (WWL Mystery Ser.). 256p. 2000. mass mkt. 5.99 (*0-373-26361-9*, 1-26361-5, Wrldwide Lib) Harlequin Bks.

***Mrs. Pargeter's Point of Honour.** Simon Brett. LC 99-32485. 272p. 1999. 22.00 (*0-684-86295-6*) Scribner.

Mrs. Pargeter's Pound of Flesh: A Mrs. Pargeter Mystery. large type ed. Simon Brett. LC 93-17745. 316p. 1993. lib. bdg. 20.95 (*1-56054-771-5*) Thorndike Pr.

Mrs. Parkington. large type ed. Louis Bromfield. 592p. 1992. lib. bdg. 21.95 (*1-56054-354-X*) Thorndike Pr.

Mrs. Parkington. Louis Bromfield. 1976. reprint ed. lib. bdg. 25.95 (*0-88411-502-X*) Amereon Ltd.

Mrs. Parkington. Louis Bromfield. 1994. reprint ed. lib. bdg. 39.95 (*1-56849-546-3*) Buccaneer Bks.

Mrs. Peachtree & the Eighth Avenue Cat. Erica Silverman. (Illus.). 32p. (J). (ps-3). 1996. mass mkt. 5.99 (*0-689-80767-8*) Aladdin.

Mrs. Peachtree & the Eighth Avenue Cat. Erica Silverman. LC 92-16973. (J). 1996. 11.19 (*0-606-09642-6*, Pub. by Turtleback) Demco.

Mrs. Peachtree's Bicycle. Erica Silverman. LC 95-14552. (Illus.). 32p. (J). (ps-3). 1996. 15.00 (*0-689-80477-6*) S&S Bks Yung.

Mrs. Peck's Christmas Puddin' Sylvia Ashby. 1998. 3.00 (*1-57514-297-X*, 3098) Encore Perform Pub.

Mrs. Penn-Lewis: A Memoir. Mayry N. Garrard. Tr. by Lorna Y. Garrard. 1986. pap. write for info. (*0-941598-32-2*) Living Spring Pubns.

Mrs. Pepperpot Again. Alf Proysen. (Illus.). (J). (gr. 1-4). 1961. 12.95 (*0-8392-3023-0*) Astor-Honor.

Mrs. Pepperpot to the Rescue. Alf Proysen. (Illus.). (J). (gr. 1-4). 1988. pap. 3.50 (*0-317-69648-3*, PuffinBks) Peng Put Young Read.

Mrs. Peter Rabbit. Thornton W. Burgess. (J). 18.95 (*0-8488-0390-6*) Amereon Ltd.

Mrs. Peter Rabbit. unabridged ed. Thornton W. Burgess. LC 96-21745. (Children's Thrift Classics Ser.). (Illus.). 96p. (J). 1998. reprint ed. pap. text 1.00 (*0-486-29376-9*) Dover.

Mrs. Piccolo's Easy Chair. Jean Jackson. LC 98-22782. (Illus.). 32p. (J). 1999. text 15.95 (*0-7894-2580-7*) DK Pub Inc.

Mrs. Piggle-Wiggle. Betty B. MacDonald. (J). 1957. 10.05 (*0-606-00728-8*, Pub. by Turtleback) Demco.

Mrs. Piggle-Wiggle. rev. ed. Betty B. MacDonald. LC 47-1876. (Illus.). (J). (gr. k-3). 1957. 15.95 (*0-397-31712-3*) HarpC Child Bks.

Mrs. Piggle-Wiggle. rev. ed. Betty B. MacDonald. LC 47-1876. (Trophy Bk.). (Illus.). 128p. (J). (gr. 1-5). 1985. pap. 4.95 (*0-06-440148-0*, HarpTrophy) HarpC Child Bks.

Mrs. Piggle Wiggle: A Study Guide. Duncan Searl. Ed. by J. Friedland & R. Kessler. (Novel-Ties Ser.). (J). (gr. 2-4). 1994. pap. text, student ed. 15.95 (*1-56982-058-9*) Lrn Links.

Mrs. Piggle-Wiggle's Bad Table-Manners Cure. Ed. by Betty B. MacDonald. LC 97-18055. (Mrs. Piggle-Wiggle Adventure Ser.). (Illus.). (J). 2000. 12.95 (*0-06-027632-0*) HarpC.

***Mrs. Piggle-Wiggle's Bad Table-Manners Cure.** Betty C. MacDonald. LC 97-18055. (Mrs. Piggle-Wiggle Adventure Ser.). (Illus.). (J). 2000. lib. bdg. 12.89 (*0-06-027633-9*) HarpC.

Mrs. Piggle-Wiggle's Farm. Betty B. MacDonald. (Illus.). (J). (gr. 2-6). 14.95 (*0-397-30273-8*, 592801) HarpC Child Bks.

Mrs. Piggle-Wiggle's Farm. Betty B. MacDonald. LC 54-7299. (Illus.). 132p. (J). (gr. k-3). 1954. 15.95 (*0-397-31713-1*) HarpC Child Bks.

Mrs. Piggle-Wiggle's Farm. Betty B. MacDonald. LC 54-7299. (Trophy Bk.). (Illus.). 128p. (J). (gr. 1-5). 1985. pap. 4.95 (*0-06-440150-2*, HarpTrophy) HarpC Child Bks.

Mrs. Piggle-Wiggle's Farm. Betty B. MacDonald. (J). 1985. 10.05 (*0-606-00729-6*, Pub. by Turtleback) Demco.

Mrs. Piggle-Wiggle's Magic. Betty B. MacDonald. 136p. (J). 1976. 17.95 (*0-8488-1087-2*) Amereon Ltd.

Mrs. Piggle-Wiggle's Magic. Betty B. MacDonald. LC 49-11124. (Illus.). 144p. (J). (gr. k-3). 1957. 15.95 (*0-397-31714-X*) HarpC Child Bks.

Mrs. Piggle-Wiggle's Magic. Betty B. MacDonald. LC 49-11124. (Trophy Bk.). (Illus.). 144p. (J). (gr. 1-5). 1985. pap. 4.95 (*0-06-440151-0*, HarpTrophy) HarpC Child Bks.

Mrs. Piggle-Wiggle's Magic. Betty B. MacDonald. (J). 1957. 10.05 (*0-606-00731-8*, Pub. by Turtleback) Demco.

Mrs. Pig's Bulk Buy. Mary Rayner. LC 80-19875. (Illus.). 32p. (J). (gr. k-3). 1981. 14.95 (*0-689-30831-0*) Atheneum Yung Read.

Mrs. Piozzi's Tall Young Beau: William Augustus Conway. John Tearle. LC 89-46415. (Illus.). 256p. 1992. 39.50 (*0-8386-3402-8*) Fairleigh Dickinson.

Mrs. Pirate. Nick Sharratt. LC 93-878. (Illus.). 24p. (J). (ps). 1994. text 8.95 (*1-56402-249-8*) Candlewick Pr.

Mrs. Pollifax. Dorothy Gilman. LC 95-90668. 1996. mass mkt. 5.99 (*0-449-14956-0*) Fawcett.

Mrs. Pollifax & the China Station. Dorothy Gilman. LC 82-45972. 1985. mass mkt. 5.99 (*0-449-20840-0*, Crest) Fawcett.

Mrs. Pollifax & the Golden Triangle. Dorothy Gilman. 1989. mass mkt. 5.99 (*0-449-21515-6*, Crest) Fawcett.

Mrs. Pollifax & the Hong Kong Buddha. Dorothy Gilman. 1986. mass mkt. 5.99 (*0-449-20983-0*, Crest) Fawcett.

Mrs. Pollifax & the Innocent Tourist. Dorothy Gilman. 1997. mass mkt. 5.99 (*0-449-18336-X*, GM) Fawcett.

Mrs. Pollifax & the Lion Killer. Dorothy Gilman. LC 96-96967. 218p. 1997. mass mkt. 5.99 (*0-449-15004-6*, GM) Fawcett.

Mrs. Pollifax & the Second Thief. Dorothy Gilman. 1995. mass mkt. 5.99 (*0-449-14905-6*, GM) Fawcett.

Mrs. Pollifax & the Second Thief. large type ed. Dorothy Gilman. LC 93-40854. 228p. 1994. lib. bdg. 21.95 (*0-8161-5917-3*, G K Hall Lrg Type) Mac Lib Ref.

Mrs. Pollifax & the Whirling Dervish. Dorothy Gilman. 1991. mass mkt. 5.99 (*0-449-14760-6*) Fawcett.

Mrs. Pollifax on Safari. Dorothy Gilman. 1987. mass mkt. 5.99 (*0-449-21524-5*) Fawcett.

Mrs. Pollifax Pursued. large type ed. Dorothy Gilman. LC 94-45327. (Large Print Bks.). 1995. pap. 22.95 (*1-56895-088-8*) Wheeler Pub.

***Mrs. Pollifax Unveiled.** Dorothy Gilman. LC 99-91742. 224p. 2000. 23.00 (*0-345-43652-0*) Ballantine Pub Grp.

***Mrs. Pollifax Unveiled.** large type ed. Dorothy Gilman. LC 99-59960. 2000. 25.95 (*1-56895-826-9*) Wheeler Pub.

Mrs. Porter's New Southern Cookery Book, & Companion for Frugal & Economical Housekeepers. M. E. Porter. LC 72-9802. (Cookery Americana Ser.). 1973. reprint ed. 17.95 (*0-405-05053-4*) Ayer.

Mrs. Potato Head Chooses Her Shoes, 1 vol. Playskool Books Staff. (ps). 1999. pap. 5.99 (*0-525-46191-4*, Dutton Child) Peng Put Young Read.

***Mrs. Potato Head Goes Shopping.** Told to Steffanie Levine. 1999. 6.99 (*0-525-46234-1*, Playskool) Peng Put Young Read.

Mrs. Potter's Pig. Phyllis Root. LC 95-38194. (Illus.). 32p. (J). (ps-2). 1997. reprint ed. pap. 5.99 (*0-7636-0160-8*) Candlewick Pr.

Mrs. Raccoon's Wondrous Tearoom. large type ed. Linda R. Wexler. Ed. by Howard B. Raff. (Illus.). 32p. (Orig.). (J). (gr. k-3). 1997. pap. 9.95 (*1-888230-08-8*) Chelsea St Prods.

Mrs. Rasmussen's Book of One-Arm Cookery. Mary Lasswell. 17.95 (*0-8488-1406-1*) Amereon Ltd.

Mrs. Rasmussen's Book of One-Arm Cookery. Mary Lasswell. 1981. reprint ed. lib. bdg. 18.95 (*0-89966-437-7*) Buccaneer Bks.

Mrs. Red Pepper. Grace S. Richmond. 25.95 (*0-89190-493-X*) Amereon Ltd.

Mrs. Reppert's Twelve Month Herbal: A Day-by-Day Journal in the Herb Garden. Bertha Reppert. (Illus.). 375p. (Orig.). 1996. pap. 17.50 (*0-9617210-8-1*) Remembrance.

Mrs. Reynolds. Gertrude Stein. (Sun & Moon Classics Ser.: No. 1). 336p. 1987. pap. 13.95 (*1-55713-016-7*) Sun & Moon CA.

Mrs. Reynolds & Five Earlier Novelettes, Vol. Two Of Unpublis. Gertrude Stein. LC 70-103663. (Select Bibliographies Reprint Ser.). 1980. 30.95 (*0-8369-5163-8*) Ayer.

Mrs. Richter's Cook-Less Book with Scientific Food Chart. 15th ed. Vera M. Richter. 1996. reprint ed. spiral bd. 11.00 (*0-7873-0720-3*) Hlth Research.

Mrs. Right. Carole Halston. 1997. per. 3.99 (*0-373-24125-9*, 1-24125-6) Silhouette.

Mrs. Rose's Garden. Elaine Greenstein. (Illus.). 32p. (J). (ps-3). 1996. per. 15.00 (*0-689-80215-3*) S&S Bks Yung.

Mrs. Rose's Garden. Elaine Greenstein. (Illus.). 28p. (J). (gr. k up). 1993. 14.95 (*0-88708-264-5*, Picture Book Studio) S&S Childrens.

Mrs. Rosey-Posey, No. 4. (J). Date not set. write for info. (*0-7814-0345-6*, Chariot Bks) Chariot Victor.

Mrs. Rosey-Posey & the Chocolate Cherry Treat. Robin J. Gunn. LC 89-25417. (On My Own Bks.). (Illus.). 32p. (J). (ps-2). 1991. pap. 4.99 (*1-55513-370-3*, 33704, Chariot Bks) Chariot Victor.

Mrs. Rosey-Posey & the Empty Nest. Robin J. Gunn. LC 92-12955. (On My Own Book). (J). (gr. k-3). 1993. pap. 4.99 (*0-7814-0329-4*, Chariot Bks) Chariot Victor.

Mrs. Rosey-Posey & the Treasure Hunt. Robin J. Gunn. LC 89-25244. (On My Own Bks.). (Illus.). 32p. (J). (ps-2). 1991. pap. 4.99 (*1-55513-372-X*, 33720, Chariot Bks) Chariot Victor.

Mrs. Royall's America, 1828 to 1831, 7 vols. in 6. Anne Royall. Incl. Pt. 2. Mrs. Royall's Pennsylvania: or Travels Continued in the United States., **2 vols.** LC 72-37720. 16.00 Pt. 3. Mrs. Royall's Southern Tour: or Second Series of the Black Book., **2 vols.** LC 72-37720. 16.00 LC 72-37720. reprint ed. 95.00 (*0-404-56830-0*) AMS Pr.

Mrs. Royall's Pennsylvania: or Travels Continued in the United States see Mrs. Royall's America, 1828 to 1831

Mrs. Royall's Southern Tour: or Second Series of the Black Book see Mrs. Royall's America, 1828 to 1831

Mrs. S. C. Hall: A Literary Biography. Maureen Keane. (A Colin Smythe Publication). 260p. (C). 1998. 65.00 (*0-86140-394-0*) OUP.

Mrs. Santa Claus. J. Herman. 72p. 1996. otabind 16.95 (*0-7935-7094-8*) H Leonard.

Mrs. Sato's Hens see Gallinas de la Senora Sato

Mrs. Sato's Hens. 2nd ed. Laura Min. (Let Me Read Ser.). (Illus.). 8p. (J). (ps). 1994. text 2.95 (*0-673-36193-4*, GoodYrBooks) Addson-Wesley Educ.

Mrs. Scott's Beautiful Art. Alice K. Flanagan. LC 98-21498. (Our Neighborhood Ser.). 1999. lib. bdg. 6.95 (*0-516-26469-9*) Childrens.

Mrs. Scott's Beautiful Art. Alice K. Flanagan. LC 98-21498. (Our Neighborhood Ser.). 32p. (J). (gr. 1-2). 1999. 19.50 (*0-516-21135-8*) Childrens.

Mrs. Sedgewick's Head. Tom Griffin. LC 97-162140. 1997. pap. 5.25 (*0-8222-1542-X*) Dramatists Play.

Mrs. Seton. Joseph I. Dirvin. 532p. 1993. pap. 10.00 (*0-9639851-0-8*) Nat Shrine St Eliz.

***Mrs. Shakespeare: The Complete Works.** Robert Nye. 2000. 23.95 (*1-55970-552-3*, Pub. by Arcade Pub Inc) Time Warner.

Mrs. Shakespeare's Second Marriage. Ed. by James A. Morgan. LC 75-170138. (Shakespeare Society of New York. Publications: No. 14). reprint ed. 27.50 (*0-404-54214-X*) AMS Pr.

Mrs. Silver's Phonics Workbook I. Claudine Silver. (J). 1986. pap., wbk. ed. 5.99 (*0-88062-131-1*) Mott Media.

Mrs. Silver's Phonics Workbook 1: Teacher's Edition. Claudine Silver. 1994. pap., teacher ed. 5.99 (*0-88062-133-8*) Mott Media.

Mrs. Skagg's Husbands & Other Sketches. Bret Harte. 1972. reprint ed. lib. bdg. 19.50 (*0-8422-8072-3*) Irvington.

***Mrs. Skaggs's Husbands.** Bret Harte. (Works of Bret Harte: Vol. 17). 356p. 1999. reprint ed. lib. bdg. 90.00 (*0-7812-7849-X*) Rprt Serv.

Mrs. Spider Does Lunch. Tedi T. Wixom. (Illus.). 32p. (Orig.). (J). (ps-8). 1995. pap. 5.95 (*1-885227-41-8*) TNT Bks.

Mrs. Spring Fragrance. Sui S. Far & Edith Eaton. Ed. by Kate Falvey. (Masterworks of Literature Ser.). 1994. pap. 16.95 (*0-8084-0447-4*) NCUP.

Mrs. Starkey's Nanny Manager: The Key to a Successful Relationship for the Nanny & the Family. Mary L. Starkey. LC 98-96272. (Illus.). 144p. 1998. 79.95 (*0-9664807-0-8*) Starkey Intl.

Mrs. Stevens Hears the Mermaids Singing. May Sarton. 240p. 1993. pap. 11.00 (*0-393-30929-0*) Norton.

Mrs. Ted Bliss. Stanley Elkin. LC 95-5413. 304p. 1995. 22.45 (*0-7868-6104-5*, Pub. by Hyperion) Time Warner.

Mrs. Ted Bliss. Stanley Elkin. 288p. 1996. pap. 12.00 (*0-380-72896-6*, Avon Bks) Morrow Avon.

Mrs. Ted Bliss. large type ed. Stanley Elkin. LC 96-2291. 1996. pap. 22.95 (*1-56895-314-3*) Wheeler Pub.

Mrs. Temperly see London Life

Mrs. Thatcher's Cultural Policy: A Comparative Study of Globalised Cultural Systems. Christopher Bradley. LC 98-60733. 200p. 1998. 28.00 (*0-88033-400-2*, Pub. by East Eur Monographs) Col U Pr.

Mrs. Thatcher's Minister: The Private Diaries of Alan Clark. Alan Clark. LC 94-6701. 1994. 30.00 (*0-374-13917-2*) FS&G.

Mrs. Thatcher's Revolution: The Ending of the Socialist Era. Peter Jenkins. LC 88-7231. (Illus.). 464p. 1988. reprint ed. 32.00 (*0-674-58832-0*) HUP.

Mrs. Tibbles & the Special Someone. Jeanine Wine. LC 87-14966. (Illus.). 32p. (J). (ps-3). 1987. 12.95 (*0-934672-54-7*) Good Bks PA.

Mrs. Tiggy-Winkle. (Classic Tales Ser.). (Illus.). 24p. (J). 1993. 4.98 (*1-56173-477-2*) Pubns Intl Ltd.

Mrs. Tiggy-Winkle. Illus. by Sam Thiewes et al. (Classic Tales Ser.). 24p. (J). (gr. 2-4). 1992. lib. bdg. 11.95 (*1-56674-007-X*, HTS Bks) Forest Hse.

*__Mrs. Tiggy-Winkle's Colorful Day.__ Beatrix Potter. (Illus.). (J). 2000. pap. 3.99 (*0-7232-4595-9*, F Warne) Peng Put Young Read.

Mrs. Tim Gets a Job. D. E. Stevenson. 282p. 1976. lib. bdg. 27.95 (*0-89966-160-2*) Buccaneer Bks.

Mrs. Tim of the Regiment. D. E. Stevenson. 382p. Date not set. 26.95 (*0-8488-2399-0*) Amereon Ltd.

Mrs. Tim of the Regiment. D. E. Stevenson. 378p. 1976. lib. bdg. 41.95 (*0-89966-157-2*) Buccaneer Bks.

Mrs. Toggle & the Dinosaur. Robin Pulver. (J). 1995. 9.15 (*0-606-07896-7*) Turtleback.

Mrs. Toggle's Beautiful Blue Shoe. Robin Pulver. LC 92-40824. (Illus.). 32p. (J). (ps-2). 1994. mass mkt. 13.95 (*0-02-775456-1*, Four Winds Pr) S&S Childrens.

*__Mrs. Toggle's Class Picture Day.__ Illus. by Robin Pulver & R. W. Alley. LC 99-58609. (J). 2000. pap. write for info. (*0-590-11741-6*) Scholastic Inc.

Mrs. Toggle's Zipper. Robin Pulver. LC 88-37251. (Illus.). 32p. (J). (ps-2). 1990. lib. bdg. 13.95 (*0-02-775451-0*, Four Winds Pr) S&S Childrens.

Mrs. Toggle's Zipper. Robin Pulver. (J). 1993. 10.15 (*0-606-05484-7*, Pub. by Turtleback) Demco.

Mrs. Toggle's Zipper. Robin Pulver. LC 92-39355. (Illus.). 32p. (J). (ps-2). 1993. reprint ed. mass mkt. 4.95 (*0-689-71689-3*) Aladdin.

Mrs. Tooey & the Terrible Toxic Tar. Barbara Dillon. LC 87-45985. 96p. (J). (gr. 3-7). 1988. 10.95 (*0-397-32276-3*); lib. bdg. 11.89 (*0-397-32277-1*) HarpC Child Bks.

Mrs. US: Is Her Time Running Out? Arthur D. Watt. (Illus.). 108p. (Orig.). 1994. pap. 6.95 (*0-9644645-0-0*) Almnd Tree Pr.

Mrs. Vargas & the Dead Naturalist. Kathleen Alcala. LC 92-4469. 192p. 1992. 19.95 (*0-934971-26-9*); pap. 9.95 (*0-934971-25-0*) Calyx Bks.

Mrs. Vole the Vet. Allan Ahlberg. (Illus.). 24p. (J). pap. 6.95 (*0-14-037880-4*, Pub. by Pnguin Bks Ltd) Trafalgar.

Mrs. Waco: The Early Days of the WACO Aircraft Company. Hattie M. Junkin. Ed. by Joe Balmer et al. (Illus.). 36p. (Orig.). 1996. mass mkt. 5.00 (*1-888282-04-5*) Little Otter.

Mrs. Wages New Home Canning Guide. Dacus Food Group, Inc. Staff. 1986. pap. text 5.95 (*0-9649067-1-6*) Precision Foods.

Mrs. Warren's Profession see Six Great Modern Plays

Mrs. Warren's Profession. George Bernard Shaw. Ed. & Pref. by William-Alan Landes. LC 90-53570. 1991. pap. 7.00 (*0-88734-228-0*) Players Pr.

Mrs. Warren's Profession & Others. George Bernard Shaw. 22.95 (*0-8488-0770-7*) Amereon Ltd.

Mrs. Webster's Daily Dictionary. Lisa Cofield et al. 366p. (Orig.). 1994. pap., spiral bd. 8.95 (*1-56245-166-9*) Great Quotations.

Mrs. Webster's Dictionary. Lisa Cofield et al. 168p. (Orig.). 1994. pap. 5.95 (*1-56245-090-5*) Great Quotations.

Mrs. Whaley & Her Charleston Garden. Emily Whaley. 248p. 1998. per. 11.00 (*0-684-84387-0*) S&S Trade Pap.

Mrs. Whaley & Her Charleston Garden. Emily Whaley & William P. Baldwin. LC 96-48731. (Illus.). 224p. 1997. 16.95 (*1-56512-115-5*, 72115) Algonquin Bks.

Mrs. Whaley & Her Charleston Garden. large type ed. Emily Whaley & William P. Baldwin. LC 97-45844. 1998. 23.95 (*0-7862-1318-3*) Mac Lib Ref.

Mrs. Whaley Entertains: Advice, Opinions & 100 Recipes from a Charleston Kitchen. Emily Whaley & William P. Baldwin. LC 98-24665. 266p. 1998. 17.95 (*1-56512-200-3*) Algonquin Bks.

Mrs. Whaley Entertains: Advice, Opinions, & 100 Recipes from A Charleston Kitchen. Emily Whaley & William P. Baldwin. LC 99-14141. 1999. 25.95 (*0-7862-1913-0*) Mac Lib Ref.

Mrs. Whaley's Charleston Kitchen: Advice, Opinion, & 100 Recipes from a Southern Legend. Emily Whaley. 288p. 1999. per. 12.00 (*0-684-86324-3*) S&S Trade.

Mrs. Wide-Mouth Frog: Becomes a Mother. Joan M. Ferrin. (Illus.). ii, 32p. (J). (ps-3). 1997. 16.95 (*0-9662053-0-8*) Golden Ridge Pr.

Mrs. Wiggs. Mark Dunster. 16p. (Orig.). 1992. pap. 4.00 (*0-89642-210-0*) Linden Pubs.

Mrs. Wiggs of the Cabbage Patch. Alice H. Rice. 19.95 (*0-89190-859-5*) Amereon Ltd.

Mrs. Wiggs of the Cabbage Patch. Alice H. Rice. (J). 1992. reprint ed. lib. bdg. 19.95 (*0-89968-273-1*, Lghtyr Pr) Buccaneer Bks.

Mrs. Wiggs of the Cabbage Patch: A Comic Melodrama in 3 Acts. Alice Hogan-Rice. 56p. 1982. pap. 3.50 (*0-88680-132-X*) I E Clark.

Mrs. Wishy-Washy. Joy Cowley. LC 98-67176. (Illus.). 16p. (ps-k). 1999. 5.99 (*0-399-23391-1*) Putnam Pub Group.

*__Mrs. Wishy-Washy.__ Joy Cowley. 1998. write for info. (*0-7802-7466-0*) Wright Group.

Mrs. Witherspoon's Eagles. Jane Weinberger. Ed. by Kate Whitaker. LC 93-61632. (Illus.). 56p. (J). (ps-3). 1994. pap. 8.95 (*1-883650-09-7*) Windswept Hse.

Mrs. Witty's Home-Style Menu Cookbook. Helen Witty. LC 89-40729. (Illus.). 320p. (Orig.). 1990. pap. 12.95 (*0-89480-690-4*, 1690) Workman Pub.

Mrs. Witty's Monster Cookies. Helen Witty. LC 83-40035. (Illus.). 128p. 1983. pap. 6.95 (*0-89480-609-2*, 609) Workman Pub.

Mrs. Wizard's Simplified Reference for Gems & Stones. Wanda M. Vonderhaar. 1988. pap. text 1.50 (*0-9620055-1-7*) Wizards Pr.

MRST '96: Current Ideas in Theoretical Physics. 250p. 1996. lib. bdg. 45.00 (*981-02-2904-6*) World Scientific Pub.

Mrtyu: Concept of Death in Indian Traditions: Transformation of the Body Funeral Rites. Gian Giuseppe Filippi. Tr. by Antonio Rigopoulos. xiii, 258p. 1996. 23.00 (*81-246-0072-4*, Pub. by D K Printwrld) Nataraj Bks.

*__Mr.wrong: A User's Guide: (or, How To Use A Guy)__ Cindy Walker & Don Hehalko. (Illus.). 112p. 2000. 15.95 (*0-688-17025-0*, Wm Morrow) Morrow Avon.

MS: Immunological, Diagnostic & Therapeutic Aspects. F. Clifford Rose & Jones Staff. (Current Problems in Neurology Ser.: Vol. 3). 272p. 1987. 74.95 (*0-86196-109-9*, Pub. by J Libbey Med) Bks Intl VA.

MS - DOS 6.2 Upgrade for Dummies. 400p. 1993. pap. 40.69 (*1-56884-068-3*) IDG Bks.

MS Excel 2000 Advnaced Techniques see MS Excel 2000 Tecnicas Avanzadas

*__MS Access en Espanol: Domine el Programa Mas Temido y Poderoso de Office.__ Mario Tomas Umana. (Manuales para PyMEs (Pequenas y Medianas Empresas) Ser.). (SPA., Illus.). 271p. 1999. pap. 16.90 (*987-9131-93-2*, Pub. by MP Ediciones) Am Wholesale.

MS Access 97 for Window 95. Murphy. (DF - Computer Applications Ser.). 1997. mass mkt. 22.95 (*0-538-67973-5*) S-W Pub.

MS Access 97 for Windows. Sullivan. (IN - Computer Training Ser.). 1998. pap. 20.95 (*0-538-68032-6*) S-W Pub.

MS Access 2000 at a Glance. Perspecti. LC 98-48183. 1998. pap. 19.99 (*1-57231-946-1*) Microsoft.

MS Access '97. Laudon. 1998. text 23.25 incl. cd-rom (*0-07-013732-3*) McGraw.

*__MS Access 97: Complications, Concept & Technology with visible Analyst Software.__ Shelly et al. (C). 1999. pap. 75.50 (*0-7895-5747-9*) Course Tech.

MS Active Directory Networks. Beth Sheresh. (Infraworld Networking Ser.). 1998. pap. 39.99 (*0-7645-3156-5*) IDG Bks.

MS Autobiography Book: An Anthology of Autobiographical Prose & Verse Written by Persons Who Have Multiple Sclerosis. Eric Smirnow. (Illus.). 456p. (Orig.). 1993. pap. 9.95 (*0-9638334-0-5*) Special Computer.

Ms. B's F. Quotations. Jane Bartlett. LC 91-66093. 112p. (Orig.). 1991. pap. 6.95 (*0-9610330-4-5*) J Tabler-Bks.

Ms. Cheap's Guide to Nashville. 2nd rev. ed. Mary Hance. LC 97-3379. (Illus.). 192p. 1998. pap. 8.93 (*1-55853-709-0*) Rutledge Hill Pr.

Ms. Cliff the Climber. Allan Ahlberg. (Illus.). 24p. (J). 1997. pap. 6.95 (*0-14-037879-0*, Pub. by Pnguin Bks Ltd) Trafalgar.

Ms. Davison, Our Librarian. Alice K. Flanagan. (Our Neighborhood Ser.). (Illus.). 32p. (J). 1996. lib. bdg. 19.50 (*0-516-20009-7*) Childrens.

Ms. Davison, Our Librarian. Alice K. Flanagan. (Our Neighborhood Ser.). 32p. (J). 1997. pap. 6.95 (*0-516-26060-X*) Childrens.

*__MS-Directing Shakespeare: Women Direct Shakespeare.__ Elizabeth Schafer. (Illus.). 277p. 2000. text 24.95 (*0-312-22746-9*) St Martin.

MS-DOS. Altenhofen. (C). 1990. text. write for info. (*0-201-52277-2*) Addison-Wesley.

MS-DOS. John D. Hubbard. (Illus.). 376p. 1984. 99.95 (*0-87119-088-5*, EC-1121) Heathkit-Zenith Ed.

MS-DOS. Jonathan Kamin. (Expert Advisor Ser.). 656p. 1988. pap. 21.95 (*0-201-13236-2*) Addison-Wesley.

MS-DOS: Up to & Including Version 6.2. (Prisma Computer Courses Ser.). (Illus.). 200p. (Orig.). 1995. pap. 12.95 (*1-85365-326-8*, Pub. by Spectrum) Seven Hills Bk.

MS-DOS & PC-DOS: A Practical Guide. 2nd ed. Pim Oets. (Computer Science Ser.). (Illus.). 216p. (C). 1988. pap. text 35.00 (*0-333-45440-5*) Scholium Intl.

MS DOS & PC DOS: The Useable Portable Guide. Jon Haber & Herbert R. Haber. (Illus.). (C). 1990. spiral bd. write for info. (*0-945765-20-7*, 14-3440-01) Useable Portable Pubns.

MS-DOS & Windows Essentials. Gerald Lemay. 80p. 1995. pap. text 21.33 (*0-8053-6373-4*) Benjamin-Cummings.

MS-DOS & Windows Essentials. Gerald Lemay. 1995. teacher ed. 11.67 (*0-8053-6548-6*) Benjamin-Cummings.

MS-DOS Batch File Programming. Ronny Richardson. 1988. pap. 19.95 (*0-8306-9328-9*) McGraw-Hill Prof.

MS-DOS Batch File Programming. Ronny Richardson. 1991. 24.95 (*0-8306-6663-X*) McGraw-Hill Prof.

MS-DOS Batch File Programming. 2nd ed. (Illus.). 304p. 1990. pap. 24.95 (*0-8306-3537-8*) McGraw-Hill Prof.

MS-DOS Beyond 640K. 2nd ed. James S. Forney. (Illus.). 352p. 1991. pap. 22.95 (*0-8306-3744-3*) McGraw-Hill Prof.

MS-DOS by Chris: First Common-Sense Manual for MS-DOS. Christopher Fara. LC 91-90358. 144p. 1991. pap., student ed. 19.95 (*1-880099-10-1*) Microdex Bkshelf.

MS-DOS 5.0. M-USA Video Staff. (LogicNotes Ser.). 1991. 24.95 (*0-929978-60-9*) M-USA Busn Systs.

MS-DOS Smart Start. L. Sandler. LC 93-83864. (SmartStart Ser.). (Illus.). 256p. 1993. 25.99 (*1-56529-249-9*) Que.

MS-DOS, Lotus 1-2-3, & DBASE. Joseph G. Massey. 158p. (Orig.). 1987. pap. text 26.00 (*0-685-21222-X*) Forest Res Syst.

MS-DOS Pocket Reference for the IBM-PC & Compatible: Concise Explanations of DOS Commands, Illustrated with Examples. Winfried Hofacker. (Illus.). 85p. (Orig.). (C). 1994. pap. 5.00 (*0-911827-02-1*, 69) Elcomp.

MS-DOS pour les Nuls Jusqu'a 6.22. Dan Gookin. (FRE.). 414p. 1995. 49.95 (*0-7859-9857-8*) Fr & Eur.

MS-DOS Quick Reference. Sally Neuman. 1993. pap. 9.95 (*1-56539-137-3*) Color Cnty.

MS DOS Release 2.3 Quick Reference Guide. 19.95 (*1-56351-018-9*, G163) Microref Educ Systs.

MS-DOS 6.2. Marangraphics Development Group Staff. 1993. pap. 12.95 (*0-685-70706-7*) P-H.

MS DOS 6.2 by Example. Chris Nye. 1994. pap. text 19.95 (*1-86398-035-0*) Prima Pub.

MS-DOS 6.2 pour les Nuls: Special Edition with 2 Diskettes. Dan Gookin. (FRE.). 402p. 1995. 195.00 (*0-7859-9856-X*) Fr & Eur.

MS DOS 6.2 Quick Reference. Sally Neuman. 200p. 1993. 9.99 (*1-56529-645-1*) Que.

MS-DOS 6 QuickStart. Suzanne Weixel. (Illus.). 480p. 1993. 21.95 (*1-56529-096-8*) Que.

MS-DOS Smartstart. 1993. teacher ed. 39.99 (*1-56529-250-2*) Que.

MS-DOS System Programming. 3rd ed. David Burki & Robert Ward. 830p. 1994. pap. 39.95 incl. disk (*0-87930-445-6*) C M P Books.

MS-DOS Technic Control One Technology Pack. Tom Barrowman et al. Ed. by Cathy Helgoe & Tom Lough. (Illus.). 416p. (YA). (gr. 6-12). 1991. 595.00 (*0-914831-78-X*, 968) Lego Dacta.

MS-DOS Techniques. 4th ed. Joseph C. Johnson. (Illus.). 66p. (C). 1993. pap. text 14.95 incl. 3.5 hd (*0-9639214-0-1*); pap. text 14.95 incl. 5.25 hd (*0-9639214-1-X*) CyberTech Communs.

MS-DOS-the Advanced Course. David A. Lien. 1989. pap. 27.95 (*0-932760-49-X*) CompuSoft.

MS-DOS-the Basic Course. David A. Lien. 1989. pap. 14.95 (*0-932760-48-1*) CompuSoft.

MS-DOS Utility Programs. Ronny Richardson. 1991. 14.95 (*0-8306-5384-8*) McGraw-Hill Prof.

MS-DOS Utility Programs (Five & One Quarter) Ronny Richardson. 1991. 14.95 (*0-8306-5414-3*); 14.95 (*0-8306-5415-1*); 14.95 (*0-8306-5416-X*); 14.95 (*0-8306-5417-8*); 14.95 (*0-8306-5418-6*); 14.95 (*0-8306-5419-4*); 14.95 (*0-8306-5420-8*); 14.95 (*0-8306-5421-6*); 14.95 (*0-8306-5422-4*); 14.95 (*0-8306-5423-2*); 14.95 (*0-8306-5424-0*); 14.95 (*0-8306-5426-7*); 14.95 (*0-8306-5427-5*); write for info. (*0-8306-5444-5*) McGraw-Hill Prof.

MS-DOS Utility Programs (Three & One Half) Ronny Richardson. 1991. 14.95 (*0-8306-5428-3*); 14.95 (*0-8306-5430-5*); 14.95 (*0-8306-5431-3*); 14.95 (*0-8306-5432-1*); 14.95 (*0-8306-5433-X*); 14.95 (*0-8306-5434-8*); 14.95 (*0-8306-5435-6*); 14.95 (*0-8306-5436-4*); 14.95 (*0-8306-5437-2*); 14.95 (*0-8306-5438-0*); 14.95 (*0-8306-5439-9*); 14.95 (*0-8306-5440-2*); 14.95 (*0-8306-5441-0*); 14.95 (*0-8306-5442-9*); 14.95 (*0-8306-5443-7*); write for info. (*0-8306-5445-3*) McGraw-Hill Prof.

MS Eighteen Forty Census Vol. 2: Surnames in Census Order. Ed. by Thomas E. Coyle. 652p. 1992. pap. text 60.00 (*1-56088-053-8*) Coyle Data Co.

*__MS Excel 2000 en Espanol/Spanish para Pequenas y Medianas Empresas: Como Extraer Mas Informacion de Sus Datos.__ Claudio Sanchez. (Manuales CM para PyMEs Ser.).Tr. of MS Excel 2000 for Small & Medium Enterprises. (SPA., Illus.). 269p. 1999. pap. 16.90 (*987-526-009-6*, Pub. by MP Ediciones) Am Wholesale.

*__MS Excel 2000: Illustrated 2nd Course.__ O'Keefe. (C). 1999. pap. 21.95 (*0-7600-6063-0*) Thomson Learn.

MS Excel 2000 at a Glance. Perspecti. LC 98-31458. 256p. 1998. pap. 19.99 (*1-57231-942-9*) Microsoft.

*__MS Excel 2000 Tecnicas Avanzadas.__ Claudio Sanchez.Tr. of MS Excel 2000 Advnaced Techniques. (SPA.). 286p. 1999. pap. 17.90 (*987-526-020-7*, Pub. by MP Ediciones) Am Wholesale.

MS Excel 2000 for Small & Medium Enterprises see MS Excel 2000 en Espanol/Spanish para Pequenas y Medianas Empresas: Como Extraer Mas Informacion de Sus Datos

MS Excel 3.0. R. Albrecht. (C). 1991. text. write for info. (*0-201-55931-5*) Addison-Wesley.

MS Excel 5.0 for Windows, Microcomputer & Information Technology. Baumann & Flynn. (Data Processing & Information System Ser.). 1996. pap. 26.50 (*0-314-07122-9*) West Pub.

MS Excel '97. Laudon. 1998. text 22.00 incl. cd-rom (*0-07-013727-7*) McGraw.

MS Exchange 5 Exam Guide. 1998. 99.99 (*0-7897-1506-6*) Que.

MS Faux Pas: A Non Guide to Glitterati Manners. Joan Kron. (Illus.). 86p. 1988. 19.88 (*0-9620612-0-4*) Parvenu Pr.

*__MS Frizzle's Adventures in Egypt.__ Joanna Cole & Bruce Degen. LC 99-18374. 2000. write for info. (*0-590-44680-0*) Scholastic Inc.

*__MS Frontpage 98.__ Pinnacle Software Solutions, Inc. Staff. (Web Development Manuals Ser.). 120p. 1999. 50.00 (*1-930245-13-0*) Pinnacle Soft Solut.

*__MS Frontpage 2000 Complete Concepts & Techniques.__ Shelly & Cashman. (Shelly Cashman Ser.). (C). 2000. pap. 42.95 (*0-7895-5613-8*) Course Tech.

MS Frontpage 2000 Essential Conc & Tech. Shelly & Cashman. (Shelly Cashman Ser.). (C). 1999. pap. text 9.95 (*0-7895-5773-8*) Course Tech.

*__MS Frontpage 98 Introductory Concepts & Techniques.__ Shelly & Cashman. (Shelly Cashman Ser.). (C). 1998. pap. 25.95 (*0-7895-4624-8*) Course Tech.

MS Holmes of Baker Street: The Truth about Sherlock. C. Alan Bradley & William S. Sarjeant. (Illus.). 260p. 1989. 19.95 (*0-938501-09-7*) Wessex.

MS Internet Explorer 4 One Step at a Time. Craig Witherspoon. LC 97-76681. (New Tutorial Ser.). 384p. 1998. pap. 29.99 (*0-7645-3104-2*) IDG Bks.

MS Internet Explorer 4. (Shelly-Cashman Ser.). (C). 1998. pap. 22.95 (*0-7895-4289-7*) Course Tech.

MS Internet Studio Expert Techniques. New Riders Publishing Staff. 1996. 50.00 (*1-56205-615-8*) New Riders Pub.

Ms. Lampedusa Has Vanished. Atanas Slavov. LC 82-62316. 1982. 10.00 (*0-911050-53-1*) Occidental.

MS, Lupus & Me (And That's Not All!) 2nd ed. Bess K. Harvey. 70p. 1992. pap. 7.95 (*0-9640635-0-6*) Golden Lght.

Ms. MacDonald Has a Class. Jan Ormerod. LC 95-38192. (Illus.). 32p. (J). (ps-3). 1996. 15.95 (*0-395-77611-2*, Clarion Bks) HM.

Ms. Mentor's Impeccable Advice for Women in Academia. Emily Toth. LC 97-6259. 240p. (C). (gr. 13). 1997. pap. text 15.95 (*0-8122-1566-4*) U of Pa Pr.

Ms. Moja Makes Beautiful Clothes. Jill D. Duvall. LC 96-34907. (Our Neighborhood Ser.). (Illus.). 1997. lib. bdg. 19.50 (*0-516-20314-2*) Childrens.

Ms. Moja Makes Beautiful Clothes. Jill D. Duvall. (Our Neighborhood Ser.). (J). (gr. k-2). 1997. pap. 6.95 (*0-516-26151-7*) Childrens.

Ms. Murder. Ed. by Marie Smith. 252p. 1989. 14.95 (*0-8065-1139-7*, Citadel Pr) Carol Pub Group.

Ms. Murphy Fights Fires. Alice Flanagan. LC 97-2181. (Our Neighborhood Ser.). (Illus.). (J). (gr. k-2). 1997. lib. bdg. 19.50 (*0-516-20494-7*) Childrens.

Ms. Murphy Fights Fires. Alice K. Flanagan. (Our Neighborhood Ser.). (J). 1998. pap. text 6.95 (*0-516-26249-1*) Childrens.

Ms. Murphy's Law. Faith Hines. 1998. 9.00 (*1-86187-106-6*) Exley Giftbooks.

MS My Story, Merciful Saviour. large type ed. James Haverlock. 160p. 1998. 12.95 (*0-9666429-0-2*) Jims MS Bk.

MS Office for Windows 95 & 3.1 & Mac. Anthony A. Olinzock & Lazarony. (Computer Applications Ser.). 1996. pap. 32.95 (*0-538-71484-0*) Sth-Wstrn College.

*__MS Office 98.__ Murphy. 2000. pap., wbk. ed. 12.95 (*0-538-72434-X*) Thomson Learn.

MS Office '97. Laudon. 1997. text 43.00 incl. cd-rom (*0-07-013735-8*) McGraw.

MS Office 97. Laudon. 1997. text 35.50 (*0-07-561614-9*) McGraw.

MS Office 97 for Windows: Tutorial & Applications. William R. Pasewark. (Df - Computer Applications Ser.). 1997. mass mkt. 41.95 (*0-538-71919-2*) S-W Pub.

MS Office Pro '97. Laudon. 1997. text 56.50 incl. cd-rom (*0-07-013729-3*) McGraw.

MS Office 97 Professional Essentials: Essentials Level 1. Que Education & Training Staff. LC 97-68154. 1997. 49.99 (*1-57576-787-2*) Que Educ & Trng.

MS Office Project Wiindows 95 & Spir. 2nd ed. Philip A. Koneman. LC 96-188844. 832p. (C). 1996. pap. text 64.00 (*0-8053-2749-5*) Addison-Wesley.

*__MS Office 2000.__ Morrison. 2000. pap., wbk. ed. 12.95 (*0-538-72415-3*) Thomson Learn.

*__MS Office 2000 en Espanol Con CD-ROM, 4 vols. in 1.__ Dario Angel Gonzalez. (Manuales PC Users Ser.). (SPA., Illus.). 298p. 1999. pap. 19.90 incl. cd-rom (*987-526-015-0*, Pub. by MP Ediciones) Am Wholesale.

MS Office 2000 Professional at a Glance. Perspecti. LC 98-48182. 352p. 1998. pap. 19.99 (*1-57231-937-2*) Microsoft.

*__MS Office 2000 Tecnicas Avanzadas.__ Dario Angel Gonzales & Adrian Costa.Tr. of MS Office 2000 Advanced Techniques. (SPA.). 316p. 1999. pap. 19.90 incl. cd-rom (*987-526-019-3*, Pub. by MP Ediciones) Am Wholesale.

MS Office Windows 3.1. Pauline Johnson. (C). 1995. pap. text 64.00 (*0-8053-1193-9*) Addison-Wesley.

MS Office 2000. Halvorson. (Illus.). (C). 1999. pap. text 34.95 (*0-7600-6155-6*) Course Tech.

*__MS Office 2000 Advanced Concepts & Techniques__ Shelly Cashman. (C). 1999. ring bd. (*0-7895-5947-1*) Course Tech.

*__MS Office 2000 Advanced Concepts & Techniques.__ Shelly & Cashman. (Shelly Cashman Ser.). 1999. pap. 50.95 (*0-7895-5629-4*) Course Tech.

MS Office 2000 Advanced Techniques see MS Office 2000 Tecnicas Avanzadas

MS Office 2000 Ill Projects. Bob Cram. (C). 1999. pap. text 19.95 (*0-7600-6159-9*) Course Tech.

MS Office 95 Essential. 1997. 36.00 (*0-7686-0079-0*) Quest Custom.

MS Office 97. 1997. write for info. (*0-7686-0134-7*) Quest Custom.

MS Office 97. Halvorson. (Illustrated Ser.). (Illus.). (C). 1997. pap. 34.95 (*0-7600-5841-5*) Course Tech.

MS Office 97: Introduction to Concepts & Techniques. Shelly & Cashman. (Shelly Cashman Ser.). (C). 1997. pap., wbk. ed. 14.95 (*0-7895-4480-6*) Course Tech.

MS Office 97 Illustrated. Marie L. Swanson et al. (C). 1999. pap. text 50.95 (*0-7600-6399-0*) Thomson Learn.

MS Office 97 Introduction to Concepts & Technique & Essentials. 3rd ed. Shelly & Cashman. (Shelly Cashman Ser.). (C). 1997. per. 50.95 (*0-7895-4385-0*) Course Tech.

MS Office 97 Suite Essentials. Que Educational & Training Staff. 1997. 39.99 (*1-57576-972-7*) Que Educ & Trng.

MS Outlook 97 Step by Step. Catapult, Inc., Staff. 368p. 1996. pap. text 29.99 (*1-57231-382-X*) Microsoft.

Ms. Paige Turner's Complete Guide to America's Gentlemen's Clubs. Paige Turner & Nick Spriggs. 212p. 1998. pap. 24.95 (*0-9665530-0-4*, 3004) Paige Turner Pubg.

MS-PC DOS Lab Manual. 2nd ed. Mary S. Auvil et al. 304p. (C). 1991. mass mkt. 17.95 (*0-534-92559-6*) Course Tech.

Ms. Pea's Pet Store & Other Children's Tales. Rachel L. Perez. (J). 1994. 7.95 (*0-533-10836-5*) Vantage.

Ms. Pollywog's Problem-Solving Service. Ellen Javernick. LC 95-1188. (Ready, Set, Read! Ser.: First Chapter Bks.). (Illus.). 64p. (J). (gr. 2-5). 1995. pap. 4.99 (*0-8066-2813-8*, 9-2813) Augsburg Fortress.

MS Powerpoint 97 for Window 95: Quicktorial. Murphy. LC 98-115321. (DF - Computer Applications Ser.). 1997. mass mkt. 22.95 (*0-538-67977-8*) S-W Pub.

An Asterisk (*) at the beginning of an entry indicates that the title is appearing for the first time.

MS PowerPoint 97 for Windows 95. Patricia Murphy. (Quicktorial Ser.). 1997. pap. text 19.95 (*0-538-68427-5*) S-W Pub.

MS Powerpoint 97 for Windows. Sullivan. (IN - Computer Training Ser.). 1998. pap. 20.95 (*0-538-68026-1*) S-W Pub.

***MS Powerpoint 2000.** Pasewark & Skintik. (C). 2000. pap. text 12.95 (*0-538-72443-9*); spiral bd. 36.95 (*0-538-72441-2*) Sth-Wstrn College.

MS PowerPoint 2000 at a Glance. Perspection, Inc. Staff. LC 98-48186. 1998. pap. 19.99 (*1-57231-944-5*) Microsoft.

MS Powerpoint '97. Laudon. 1998. text 17.50 incl. cd-rom (*0-07-013736-6*) McGraw.

Microsoft Project 98 Bible. Nancy Stevenson. LC 97-76683. 560p. 1997. pap. 34.99 incl. cd-rom (*0-7645-3155-7*) IDG Bks.

MS Project X for Dummies. Martin Doucette. 384p. 2000. pap. 24.99 incl. cd-rom (*0-7645-0517-3*) IDG Bks.

MS Publisher for Windows 95 for Dummies. Christopher J. Benz. 352p. 1996. pap. 19.99 (*0-7645-0016-3*) IDG Bks.

Ms Publisher 2000 Essential Conc & Tech. Shelly et al. (Shelly Cashman Ser.). (C). 1999. pap. text 9.95 (*0-7895-5774-6*) Course Tech.

MS Publisher 97. Reding. (Illustrated Ser.). (Illus.). (C). 1997. pap. 21.95 (*0-7600-5591-2*) Course Tech.

Ms. Scrooge. Charles Dickens. 1985. 3.50 (*0-87129-444-3*, M63) Dramatic Pub.

MS SQL Data Warehousing Unleashed. 1997. 49.99 (*0-672-31178-X*) Mac USA.

MS SQL Server 7.0 Professional Reference. McGehee & Kraft. 1997. 59.99 (*1-56205-779-0*) New Riders Pub.

MS SQL Server 7 Programming How-To. Peter Debetta & Joe Lynds. Date not set. 49.99 (*1-57169-126-X*) Sams.

MS SQL Server 7 System Administrator's Guide. Sosinski. 1997. 59.99 (*1-56276-557-4*) Que.

MS SQL Server 6.5 Unleashed. David W. Solomon. 1996. 69.99 incl. cd-rom (*0-614-20290-6*, Sams Sftwre) MCP SW Interactive.

MS SQL Server 6.5 Unleashed MC. Solomon Rankins. 1997. 69.99 (*0-672-31191-7*) Sams.

Microsoft SWL Server 7 Unleashed. 1100p. 1998. 59.99 (*0-672-31227-1*) Sams.

Ms. Thang, Real Knights Don't Show up at 3 in the Morning. Max Elliott. LC 96-48421. 352p. 1997. per. 14.00 (*0-671-00235-X*) PB.

MS 200, Papers of the International Military Tribunal & the Nuremberg Military Tribunals, 1945-49. K. Robson & University of Southampton Hartley Library Staff. LC 93-182980. (Library Archive Lists, Catalogues & Guides Ser.). vi, 61 p. 1993. write for info. (*0-85432-464-X*) Univ of Southampton.

***MS Visual Basic 6.0 - Manual de Referencia en Espanol - Spanish con CD-ROM: Manual de Referencia del Lenguaje mas Utilizado al Alcance.** Baltazar Birnios & Mariano Birnios. (SPA., Illus.). 617p. 1999. pap. 29.90 incl. cd-rom (*987-526-018-5*, Pub. by MP Ediciones) Am Wholesale.

Ms Visual C++ Ver 6. (C). 2000. pap. 10.60 (*0-13-016100-4*) P-H.

***MS Visual FoxPro 6.0 Manual en Espanol: Genere Aplicaciones de Alta Calidad en Tiempo Record.** Adrian Turek. (Manuales CM Ser.). (SPA., Illus.). 344p. 1999. pap. 19.90 (*987-97441-1-X*, Pub. by MP Ediciones) Am Wholesale.

MS Win NT 4.0 WorkStation. Barron & Lyskawa. (Illustrated Ser.). (Illus.). (C). 1997. pap. 10.95 (*0-7600-5180-1*) Course Tech.

***Ms Windows Dna 2000 Programming Unleashed.** 900p. 2000. 49.99 (*0-672-31888-1*) Sams.

***MS Windows 2000 Comprehensive Crs.** Bergerud & Busche. (C). 2000. pap. 54.95 (*0-538-72400-5*) Sth-Wstrn College.

MS Windows 3.1: Hotline. Rainer G. Haselier. (C). 1992. pap. text. write for info. (*0-201-56566-8*) Addison-Wesley.

MS Windows '95. Laudon. 1997. text 23.25 incl. cd-rom (*0-07-013738-2*) McGraw.

MS Windows 98. O'Leary. LC 98-33571. 144p. 1998. pap. 27.50 (*0-07-092041-9*) McGraw.

***MS Windows 98: Essential Concepts & Techniques.** Shelly. (Shelly Cashman Ser.). (C). 1998. pap. 16.95 (*0-7895-4297-8*) Course Tech.

***MS Windows 98 Introduction to Concepts & Techniques Classic Style.** Shelly & Cashman. (Shelly Cashman Ser.). (C). 1998. pap. 27.95 (*0-7895-4299-4*) Course Tech.

MS Windows 98 Simplified: Tutorial. Knowlton. (Computer Applications Ser.). 1998. pap. 41.95 (*0-538-72045-X*) S-W Pub.

***MS Winows98: Concepts & Techniques.** Shelly. (Shelly Cashman Ser.). (C). 1998. pap. 38.95 (*0-7895-4295-1*) Course Tech.

MS Word for Windows 2.0: Hotline. Rainer G. Haselier. (C). 1992. pap. text. write for info. (*0-201-56567-6*) Addison-Wesley.

MS Word 97 for Windows: Tutorial & Application. Morrison. (DF - Computer Applications Ser.). (C). 1997. mass mkt. 41.95 (*0-538-71923-0*) S-W Pub.

MS Word '97. Laudon. 1998. text 23.25 incl. cd-rom (*0-07-013739-0*) McGraw.

MS Word 97. Marie L. Swanson. (Illustrated Ser.). (C). 1997. 12.95 (*0-7600-5995-0*) Course Tech.

MS Works for Windows 3.1 Made Simple. McBride. 160p. Date not set. pap. text 19.95 (*0-7506-2065-X*) Buttrwrth-Heinemann.

MS Works 4.5 for Windows for Dummies. David C. Kay. LC 97-81224. 432p. 1998. pap. 19.99 (*0-7645-0231-X*) IDG Bks.

MS Works 3 for Windows for Dummies. David C. Kay. LC 94-79837. 400p. 1994. pap. 19.99 (*1-56884-214-7*) IDG Bks.

MS Works 2.0 Musterlosungen. Wolfgang Becher. (GER.). (C). 1990. text. write for info. (*0-201-55915-3*) Addison-Wesley.

MS Works 4.5. (Quick Study Computer Ser.). 4p. pap. 4.95 (*1-57222-269-7*) Barcharts.

Ms. Worm. 3rd ed. Lynn Brown. Ed. by Granville Walker, Jr. (Fun & Safety Ser.). (Illus.). (Orig.). (J). (ps-6). 1982. pap. 2.95 (*0-9608466-0-3*) Fun Reading.

MSA - Mechanical Signature Analysis. Ed. by S. Braun. 88p. 1983. pap. text 10.00 (*0-317-02630-5*, G00236) ASME.

MSA Data Banque Report, 1990. Museum Store Association, Inc. Staff. 215p. (Orig.). 1990. pap. text 50.00 (*0-9616104-1-7*) Museum Store.

MSA Minnesota Rules Governing Worker's Compensation Practice & Procedure. 184p. 1986. pap. 8.00 (*0-317-52115-2*) West Pub.

MSAT - Multiple Subject Assessment for Teachers. Research & Education Association Staff. 400p. 1998. pap. text 25.95 (*0-87891-749-7*) Res & Educ.

MSAT Preparation Guide: Multiple Subjects Assessment for Teachers. Jerry Bobrow & Stephen Fisher. (Cliffs Test Preparation Ser.). (Illus.). 580p. (Orig.). (C). 1995. pap. text 24.95 (*0-8220-2048-3*, Cliff) IDG Bks.

MSB Fun Sound. Cole. (J). 1994. 7.98 (*1-57042-137-4*) Warner Bks.

MSB Habitat. Cole. 1995. pap. 7.98 (*1-57042-228-1*) Warner Bks.

MSB Inside Earth. Joanna Cole. (Illus.). (J). (ps-3). 1993. 19.95 (*0-590-72782-6*) Scholastic Inc.

MSB Teacher's Guide. Ed. by Scholastic, Inc. Staff. 1998. pap. 3.95 (*0-590-48771-X*) Scholastic Inc.

MSC - Nastran Advanced Dynamic Analysis User's Guide. rev. ed. David N. Herting. (Illus.). 300p. 1997. pap. text 55.00 (*1-58524-004-4*) MacNeal-Schwendler.

MSC - Nastran Aerolastic Analysis User's Guide. William Rodden & Erwin Johnson. 1994. pap. text 75.00 (*1-58524-006-0*) MacNeal-Schwendler.

MSC - Nastran Basic Dynamic Analysis User's Guide. rev. ed. Ed. by Grant Sitton. (Illus.). 533p. 1997. pap. text 55.00 (*1-58524-003-6*) MacNeal-Schwendler.

MSC - Nastran Common Questions & Answers. 3rd rev. ed. Ed. by John M. Lee. (Illus.). 194p. 1993. pap. text 35.00 (*1-58524-002-8*) MacNeal-Schwendler.

MSC - Nastran Design Sensitivity & Optimization. rev. ed. Gregory J. Moore. (Illus.). 350p. 1994. pap. text 65.00 (*1-58524-005-2*) MacNeal-Schwendler.

MSC - Nastran Linear Static Analysis User's Guide. rev. ed. John M. Lee. (Illus.). 650p. 1997. pap. text 55.00 (*1-58524-001-X*) MacNeal-Schwendler.

MSC - Nastran Numerical Methods User's Guide. rev. ed. Louis Komzsik. (Illus.). 297p. 1998. pap. text 35.00 (*1-58524-007-9*) MacNeal-Schwendler.

MSC - Nastran Primer & Normal Modes Analysis: A Study of Computerized Technology. 2nd rev. ed. Harry G. Shaeffer. (Illus.). 432p. 1999. pap. text 50.00 (*1-58524-008-7*) MacNeal-Schwendler.

MSC - Nastran Quick Reference Guide. rev. ed. Ed. by Kevin Kilroy. (Illus.). 1326p. 1998. reprint ed. pap. text 55.00 (*1-58524-000-1*) MacNeal-Schwendler.

MSC - Patran MSC - Nastran Preference Guide Vol. 1: Structured Analysis. rev. ed. MSC Staff. (Illus.). 289p. 1997. pap. text 25.00 (*1-58524-009-5*) MacNeal-Schwendler.

MSC - Patran MSC - Nastran Preference Guide Vol. 2: Thermal Analysis. rev. ed. MSC Staff. (Illus.). 265p. 1997. pap. text 25.00 (*1-58524-010-9*) MacNeal-Schwendler.

MSCE: Guide to MS Windows 98. 10th ed. Tesch. (C). 1998. mass mkt. 60.95 (*0-7600-1075-7*) Course Tech.

***MSCE: Implementing & Supporting Internet Explorer 5.** Thomas R. Dell. (Microsoft Technology Ser.). 2002. 49.99 (*0-13-014268-9*) P-H.

MSCE Microsoft TCP/IP on Windows NT 4.0: Study Guide Exam 70-59. Syngress Media, Inc. Staff. LC 98-198498. 515p. 1998. student ed. 49.99 incl. cd-rom (*0-07-882489-3*) Osborne-McGraw.

MSCI Handbook of World Stock, Derivative & Commodity Exchanges, 1999. Financial Publications Staff. (Illus.). 1999. 550.00 (*0-9535823-0-2*, Pub. by Financial Pubns) Am Educ Systs.

***MSDE Developer's Guide.** Dan Rahmel. (Illus.). 600p. 2000. pap. text 39.95 (*0-7645-4698-8*) IDG Bks.

MSDS Pocket Dictionary see Diccionario de Bolsillo de las MSDS

MSDS Reference for Crop Protection Chemicals, 1994. 6th ed. C & P Press, Inc. Staff. LC 88-17211. 1500p. 1993. 170.00 (*1-57009-002-5*) Chem & Pharmac.

MSDS Reference for Crop Protection Chemicals, 1994: Update 1. 6th ed. C & P Press, Inc. Staff. LC 88-17211. 306p. 1994. pap. write for info. (*1-57009-004-1*) Chem & Pharmac.

MSDS Reference for Crop Protection Chemicals, 1994: Update 2. 6th ed. C & P Press, Inc. Staff. LC 88-17211. 306p. 1994. pap. write for info. (*1-57009-005-X*) Chem & Pharmac.

MSDS Reference for Crop Protection Chemicals, 1994: Update 3. 5th ed. C & P Press, Inc. Staff. LC 88-17211. 300p. 1993. pap. write for info. (*1-57009-000-9*) Chem & Pharmac.

MSDS Reference for Crop Protection Chemicals, 1994: Update 3. 6th ed. C & P Press, Inc. Staff. LC 88-17211. 306p. 1994. pap. write for info. (*1-57009-006-8*) Chem & Pharmac.

MSDS Reference for Crop Protection Products, 1998. 10th ed. Ed. by Mary Conway. 1998. pap. 170.00 (*1-57009-064-5*, 2108) Chem & Pharmac.

MSDS Software Report. 3rd rev. unabridged ed. Ed. by Elizabeth M. Donley & John W. Donley. (Illus.). vi, 382p. 1997. 239.00 (*1-891682-02-4*) Donley Tech.

***MSDS Software Report.** 4th rev. unabridged ed. Ed. by Elizabeth M. Donley et al. (Illus.). 424p. 1999. lib. bdg. 299.00 (*1-891682-07-5*) Donley Tech.

MSG Is Everywhere. Daniel A. Twogood. 28p. (Orig.). 1996. pap. 7.95 (*0-9631125-2-X*) Wilhelmina.

MSG Missouri State Guard. Carolyn M. Bartels. 1994. pap. 32.95 (*0-9636780-5-1*); text 42.95 (*0-9636780-4-3*) Two Trails Pubg.

MSHA Compliance Manual for Surface Operations. Keller, J. J., & Associates, Inc. Staff. LC 96-79535. 554p. 2000. ring bd. 125.00 (*1-877798-73-8*, 77-M) J J Keller.

MSI-2000 - Multivariate Statistical Analysis in Honor of Professor Minoru Siotani on His 70th Birthday Vol. I: Proceedings of the Multivariate Statistical Inference 2000 Conference (East-West Center, University of Hawaii, Honolulu, Hawaii, U. S. A., August 1995) Ed. by Takesi Hayakawa et al. (Mathematical & Management Sciences Ser.: Vol. 34). (Illus.). ii, 238p. 1996. 195.00 (*0-935950-38-9*) Am Sciences Pr.

MSI-2000 - Multivariate Statistical Analysis in Honor of Professor Minoru Siotani on His 70th Birthday Vol. II: Proceedings of the Multivariate Statistical Inference 2000 Conference (East-West Center, University of Hawaii, Honolulu, Hawaii, U. S. A., August 1995) Ed. by Takesi Hayakawa et al. (Mathematical & Management Sciences Ser.: Vol. 35). (Illus.). 250p. 1996. 195.00 (*0-935950-39-7*) Am Sciences Pr.

MSI-2000 - Multivariate Statistical Analysis in Honor of Professor Minoru Siotani on His 70th Birthday Vol. III: Proceedings of the Multivariate Statistical Inference 2000 Conference (East-West Center, University of Hawaii, Honolulu, Hawaii, U. S. A., August 1995) Ed. by Takesi Hayakawa et al. LC 96-84204. (Mathematical & Management Sciences Ser.: Vol. 36). (Illus.). 206p. 1997. pap. 195.00 (*0-935950-40-0*) Am Sciences Pr.

MSI-2000 - Multivariate Statistical Analysis in Honor of Professor Minoru Siotani on His 70th Birthday Vol. IV: Proceedings of the Multivariate Statistical Inference 2000 Conference (East-West Center, Univ. of Hawaii, Honolulu, Hawaii, U. S. A., August 1995) Ed. by Vidya S. Taneja. (Mathematical & Management Sciences Ser.). 1998. 195.00 (*0-935950-41-9*) Am Sciences Pr.

MSIS Proceedings of the Eighth Annual National Users Group Conference, October 18-19, 1984. Ed. by Jacqueline Franks & Michael S. Levine. (Orig.). 1984. pap. 10.00 (*0-936934-04-2*) N S Kline Inst.

***M16: Inside the Convert World of Her Majesty's Secret Intelligence Service.** Stephen Dorril. LC 00-29385. 880p. 2000. 39.50 (*0-7432-0379-8*) Free Pr.

Msm. Woodland Publishing Staff. 1999. pap. text 3.95 (*1-58054-026-0*) Woodland UT.

MSM: On Our Way Back to Health with Sulfur. Beth M. Ley. 40p. 1998. pap. 3.95 (*1-890766-00-3*) B L Pubns.

***MSM: The Natural Pain Relief Remedy.** Deborah Mitchell & Steven J. Bock. 224p. 1999. mass mkt. 5.99 (*0-380-80899-4*, Avon Bks) Morrow Avon.

MSM - The Super-Supplement of the Decade. Martha M. Christy. 31p. 1997. mass mkt. 3.95 (*0-9632091-4-0*) Wishland Inc.

MSM Miracle. Earl L. Mindell. (Good Health Guides Ser.). pap. 3.95 (*0-87983-841-8*, 38418K, Keats Publng) NTC Contemp Pub Co.

***MSMQ from Scratch.** 400p. 1999. 19.99 (*0-7897-2127-9*) Que.

***MSN Every Day!** Scott Knaster & Barbara Knaster. 208p. 2000. pap. 12.99 (*0-7356-1140-8*) Microsoft.

***MSN.com for Dummies.** Lowe. (For Dummies Ser.). 384p. 2000. pap. 19.99 (*0-7645-0649-8*) IDG Bks.

MSPB Charges & Penalties. Renn C. Fowler & Samuel A. Vitaro. 402p. 1999. pap. 125.00 (*1-878810-53-7*) Dewey Pubns.

MSS R & F in the B-Tradition of Piers Plowman. E. Talbot Donaldson. (Connecticut Academy of Arts & Sciences Ser., Trans.: Vol. 39). 1955. pap. 39.50 (*0-685-22799-5*) Elliots Bks.

MSS Revisited. Robert V. Keeley et al. LC 98-71803. 72p. 1998. pap. 7.00 (*1-892379-07-4*) Five & Ten.

Mstislav Dobuzhinsky Painting, Graphic Art, Stage Design. Alla P. Gusarova. (ENG & RUS.). 204p. 1982. 90.00 (*0-7855-1658-1*) St Mut.

Mstislav Rostropovich & Galina Vishnevskaya: Russia, Music, & Liberty - Conversations with Claude Samuel. Claude Samuel. Tr. by E. Thomas Glasow from FRE. LC 94-11669. (Illus.). 248p. 1995. 24.95 (*0-931340-76-4*, Amadeus Pr) Timber.

Mstrng Skills Elem Alg. Antonios Gonis. 1982. pap. text 32.76 (*0-201-10140-8*) Addison-Wesley.

Mt. Bachelor, Bill Healy's Dream: History & Development of Mt. Bachelor Ski Resort. Peggy C. Lucas. LC 99-70179. (Illus.). 208p. 1999. pap. 19.95 (*0-89288-277-8*) Maverick.

MT CB. Toolkit Staff. 1995. pap. text 15.95 (*0-8053-6184-7*) Addison-Wesley.

MT-80Z Microcomputer Explained: The First Steps. James Desposito. (Series 871). (Orig.). 1983. pap., student ed. 7.00 (*0-8064-0357-8*) Bergwall.

MT-EMAP Data Interchange Standard. D. E. Wight. 91p. 1988. 11.00 (*0-931830-61-3*, 344A) Soc Expl Geophys.

Mt. Holyoke: An Enduring Prospect. David Graci. (Illus.). 105p. (Orig.). 1986. pap. write for info. (*0-9616444-0-0*) Calem Pub Co.

Mt. Hope: America's First Municipal Victorian Cemetery. Richard O. Reisem. (Illus.). 128p. 1995. 39.95 (*0-9641706-3-9*) Landmark Soc.

Mt. Kembla Disaster. Stuart Piggin & Henry Lee. (Illus.). 372p. 1993. text 49.95 (*0-19-553419-0*) OUP.

Mt. Kisco, NY. Historical Briefs, Inc. Staff. Ed. by Thomas Antonucci & Michael Antonucci. 176p. 1991. pap. 19.95 (*0-89677-021-4*) Hist Briefs.

MT Lookout "Where You Can See for Two Days" Ruth M. Colville. LC 97-70484. (Illus.). 226p. (Orig.). 1997. pap. 14.95 (*0-614-30312-5*) Benson Enterp.

Mt. McKinley: The Pioneer Climbs. Terris Moore. LC 81-1002. (Illus.). 224p. 1981. reprint ed. pap. 12.95 (*0-89886-021-0*) Mountaineers.

Mt. Olympus Zoo. Sallie Lowenstein. LC 97-93862. (Illus.). 252p. (Orig.). (J). (gr. 3-8). 1997. pap. 14.99 (*0-9658486-0-4*) Lion Stone.

Mt. Pelee, Martinique: A Study of an Active Island Arc Volcano. Alan L. Smith & M. John Roobol. LC 90-3974. (Geological Society of America Ser.: Vol. 175). (Illus.). 126p. 1990. reprint ed. pap. 39.10 (*0-608-07718-6*, 206780600010) Bks Demand.

Mt. Pulaski & She Held Forth Her Hand: History & Genealogy of Mount Pulaski & Surrounding Vicinity. Compiled by Emagene V. Green. (Illus.). 287p. 1997. reprint ed. lib. bdg. 37.50 (*0-8328-5776-9*) Higginson Bk Co.

Mt. Rainier & South Cascades Fishing Guide: Mt. Rainier National Park & South Cascade Mountain Lakes & Streams. Dave Shorret. LC 98-91474. 144p. 1998. write for info. (*0-9652116-1-4*) Lakestream Pub.

Mt. Shasta Ascended Master Teaching. Nola Van Valer. (Illus.). 224p. 1996. pap. text 11.95 (*0-9641571-1-X*) Seekers & Servers.

Mt. Shasta Book. Andy Selters & Michael Zanger. LC 89-40028. 128p. (Orig.). 1989. pap. 13.95 (*0-89997-101-6*) Wilderness Pr.

Mt. Shasta California's Mystic Mountain. Emilie A. Frank. LC 97-68400. 1998. pap. text 15.95 (*1-888740-08-6*) PhotograFix.

MT Tam: A Hiking, Running & Nature Guide. 2nd ed. Don Martin & Kay Martin. (Illus.). 102p. 1994. pap. 9.95 (*0-9617044-4-6*) Martin Press.

Mt. Whitney: Mountain Lore Whitney Store. Thompson. LC 97-60934. (Illus.). 1997. 9.95 (*0-9653596-0-3*) Wstwind Pub.

MTA - A Word Game Mystery about the 3C's: Conspiracy, Corruption & Control. James McRae. 333p. Date not set. pap. text 15.00 (*0-9651347-2-5*) J McRae.

MTC: Set Apart. Benson Y. Parkinson. LC 95-25066. 302p. 1995. pap. 9.95 (*1-56236-310-7*) Aspen Bks.

***MTH Electric Trains Illustrated Price & Rarity Guide: 1999 Edition.** Tom McComas & Chuck Krone. (Illus.). 192p. 1999. pap. 19.95 (*0-937522-93-7*, Pub. by TM Bks Video) Motorbooks Intl.

***M3 & M5 Stuart Light Tank 1940-45.** Steven J. Zaloga. (New Vanguard Ser.: Vol. 33). (Illus.). 2000. pap. 12.95 (*1-85532-911-5*) Ospry.

M3D III: Mechanics & Mechanisms of Material Damping. Ed. by Alan Wolfenden & Vikram K. Kinra. LC 97-36338. (STP Ser.: Vol. 130). 411p. 1997. text 152.00 (*0-8031-2417-1*, STP1304) ASTM.

Mthunzi's Reed Mats. Janie House. Ed. by Cindy McClain. (Illus.). 24p. (J). (gr. 1-4). 1995. pap. text 3.99 (*1-56309-132-1*, N958101, New Hope) Womans Mission Union.

MTI & Pulsed Doppler Radar. D. Curtis Schleher. (Artech House Radar Library). 730p. 1991. text. write for info. (*0-89006-320-6*) Artech Hse.

MTI & Pulsed Doppler Radar. D. Curtis Schleher. LC 90-26020. (Illus.). 651p. 1991. reprint ed. pap. 200.00 (*0-7837-9697-8*, 206042700005) Bks Demand.

MTI Radar. Ed. by D. Curtis Schleher. LC 78-10858. (Illus.). 507p. reprint ed. pap. 157.20 (*0-608-16027-X*, 203312600083) Bks Demand.

M'Tishrei V'ad Elul. Avivia Langsam. (Illus.). 86p. 1997. pap., teacher ed. 28.00 (*0-915152-04-5*, A042) Langsam Publishing Co.

MTS- DB Management With Paradox 5.0 Windows. 95th ed. Edward G. Martin. 278p. (C). 1995. pap., lab manual ed. 22.50 (*0-03-011072-6*) Dryden Pr.

MTS Lotus1-2-3 Release 5.0 for Windows. Martin. LC 96-104040. (C). 1996. pap. text, lab manual ed. 22.50 (*0-03-016307-2*, Pub. by Harcourt Coll Pubs) Harcourt.

MTS Ninety-Four Challenges & Opportunities in the Marine Environment: Marine Technology Society Annual Conference. 1994. pap. 130.00 (*0-933957-13-0*) Marine Tech Soc.

MTS '91: "An Ocean Cooperative - Industry, Government & Academia", 3 vols., Set. (MTS Annual Proceedings Ser.). (Illus.). 900p. 1991. 130.00 (*0-933957-08-4*) Marine Tech Soc.

MTS '92: A Global Ocean Partnership, 3 vols. (MTS Annual Proceedings Ser.). 1000p. (Orig.). 1992. 140.00 (*0-933957-11-4*) Marine Tech Soc.

MTS Proceedings, 1990: Science & Technology for a New Oceans Decade, 3 vols., Set. 900p. 1990. 75.00 (*0-933957-06-8*) Marine Tech Soc.

***MTS Programming with Visual Basic.** Dan Mezick & Scot Hillier. LC 98-86702. (Illus.). 488p. 1999. pap. 29.99 incl. cd-rom (*0-672-31425-8*) Sams.

MTS: Wordperfect 6.0 for Windows. Martin. LC 95-215612. (C). 1996. pap. text 22.50 (*0-03-016304-8*, Pub. by Harcourt Coll Pubs) Harcourt.

MTS:Lotus 1-2-3 97. Edward G. Martin et al. 256p. (C). 1998. pap. text 26.00 (*0-03-019688-4*) Dryden Pr.

MTS:MS Word 7.0 for Windows. Edward Martin et al. LC 96-164250. 288p. (C). 1995. pap. text, lab manual ed. 24.00 (*0-03-017337-X*) Dryden Pr.

***MTV: The Making of a Revolution.** Tom McGrath. (Illus.). 208p. 1999. reprint ed. text 23.00 (*0-7881-6664-6*) DIANE Pub.

***MTV Celebrity Deathmatch.** Eric Fogel. (Illus.). 2000. pap. 22.50 (*0-7893-0503-8*) Universe.

M

An Asterisk (*) at the beginning of an entry indicates that the title is appearing for the first time.

M

MTV's Beavis & Butt-Head Chicken Soup for the Butt: A Guide to Finding your Inner Butt. Andy Rheingold & Scott Sonneborn. (Bea). 96p. 1998. pap. 14.00 (*0-671-02598-8*, MTV Bks) PB.

MTV's Beavis & Butt-Head Do America: The Official Script Book. Mike Judge. LC 97-120340. 1984. 2.25 (*0-671-00658-4*, MTV Bks) PB.

MTV's Beavis & Butthead: Huh Huh for Hollywood. Larry Doyle. LC 97-109795. 1984. pap. 1.95 (*0-671-00655-X*) PB.

MTV's Beavis & Butthead: This Book Sucks. Mike Judge et al. Ed. by Glenn Eichler. (Illus.). 96p. (Orig.). 1993. pap. 12.00 (*0-671-89034-4*) Callaway Edns.

MTV's Beavis & Butthead the Butt Files: Beavis & Butt Heads Guide to Sci Fi & The Unknown. Greg Grabianski & Aimee Keillor. LC 98-195305. (J). 1997. per. 12.00 (*0-671-01426-9*) PB.

MTV's Daria: Daria's Database. Peggy Nicoll. LC 99-199267. 80p. 1998. per. 14.00 (*0-671-02596-1*, MTV Bks) PB.

MTV's Get a Life: A Guide to Jobs, Money & the Real World. Music Television Video Staff & Joe Heiman. LC 96-163557. 224p. 1996. pap. 12.00 (*0-671-00202-3*) PB.

***MTV's Pieces.** Ed. & Intro. by Stephen Chbosky. 176p. 2000. pap. 11.95 (*0-671-00195-7*, MTV Bks) PB.

***MTV's Real World: New Orleans.** Alison Pollet. 160p. 2000. 16.00 (*0-7434-1127-7*) PB.

MTV's Road Rules: Journals. Alison Pollet. LC 99-199268. 160p. 1998. pap. 18.00 (*0-671-02595-3*) PB.

MTV's Road Rules: Road Trips. MTV Editorial Staff. LC 96-220302. 1996. per. 18.00 (*0-671-00374-7*, MTV Bks) PB.

MTV's Singled Out's Guide to Dating. MTV Editorial Staff. LC 96-225044. 128p. 1996. per. 15.00 (*0-671-00372-0*, MTV Bks) PB.

***MTV's the Real World: True Confessions.** Alison Pollet. 160p. 1999. per. 16.00 (*0-671-03701-3*) PB.

MTV's Travel Log. MTV Staff. LC 98-195301. 1997. per. 12.00 (*0-671-01533-8*, PB Trade Paper) PB.

Mu Lan Chuan Exercise Book: Eight Techniques for Better Health. Sheng Keng Yun. LC 98-7468. (Illus.). 160p. 1998. pap. 14.95 (*1-57863-049-5*) Weiser.

Mu-Lan Shih see Song of Mu Lan

Mu Tau Pankration Vol. 1: Concepts & Skills of "All-Powers" Combat. Jim Arvanitis. (Illus.). 200p. (Orig.). 1997. pap. 40.00 (*0-614-30247-1*) Spartan Pubns.

Mu Tau Pankraton: Concepts & Skills of "All-Powers" Combat. Jim Arvanitis. 198p. 1997. pap. 29.95 (*0-9657442-0-5*) Spartan Pubns.

Mua Thu Cuoi Loi. (VIE.). 368p. (Orig.). 1994. pap. 12.00 (*1-889880-02-7*) Nguoi Dan.

Muae: A Journal of Transcultural Production, Vol. 1. Ed. by Walter K. Lew. (Illus.). 272p. (Orig.). 1995. pap. 19.95 (*1-885030-15-0*) Kaya Prod.

Muae: Contagion. 3rd ed. Lawrence Chua. (Illus.). 200p. 1997. pap. 18.95 (*1-885030-23-1*) Dist Art Pubs.

MUAE 2: Collapsing New Buildings. Ed. by Lawrence Chua. (Illus.). 212p. 1997. pap. 16.95 (*1-885030-22-3*, 620552) Kaya Prod.

***Muay Thai.** Panya Kraitus. (Illus.). 244p. 1999. write for info. (*974-86841-9-9*) TwoP Co Ltd.

***Muay Thai.** Panya Kraitus. (CHI., Illus.). 244p. 2000. write for info. (*974-86680-5-3*) TwoP Co Ltd.

Mubadele: An Ottoman-Russian Exchange of Ambassadors. Ed. by Norman Itzkowitz & Max Mote. LC 77-108933. 1992. lib. bdg. 18.00 (*0-226-38804-2*) U Ch Pr.

Mucas Vidas, Muchas Sabio: Many Lives, Many Masters. Brian L. Weiss. (SPA.). 176p. 1995. per. 11.00 (*0-684-81552-4*, Fireside) S&S Trade Pap.

Mucedorus. LC 70-133711. (Tudor Facsimile Texts. Old English Plays Ser.: No. 83). reprint ed. 49.50 (*0-404-53383-3*) AMS Pr.

Much-Abused Letter. George Tyrrell. LC 72-912. 1906. 5.00 (*0-404-07860-5*) AMS Pr.

Much Ado: The Pogofenokee Trivia Book. Mark Burstein. LC 88-16095. (Illus.). 50p. (Orig.). 1988. pap. 15.00 (*0-945185-02-2*) Spring Hollow Bks.

Much Ado about a Lot: How to Mind Your Manners in Print & in Person. Mary Bruder. LC 99-35897. 288p. 2000. 22.95 (*0-7868-6517-2*, Pub. by Hyperion) Time Warner.

Much Ado about Aldo. Johanna Hurwitz. (Illus.). 96p. (J). (gr. 3-7). 1989. pap. 3.99 (*0-14-034082-3*, PuffinBks) Peng Put Young Read.

Much Ado about Aldo. Johanna Hurwitz. 1989. 9.09 (*0-606-02050-0*, Pub. by Turtleback) Demco.

Much Ado about Aldo. Johanna Hurwitz. LC 78-5434. (Illus.). 1500p. (J). (gr. 4-6). 1978. 15.89 (*0-688-32160-7*, Wm Morrow) Morrow Avon.

***Much Ado about Ballroom Dancing: Pointers on Learning to Dance, Choosing Shoes, Finding Dance Music, & More!** Ronnen Levinson. (Illus.). iv, 68p. 2000. pap. 14.95 (*0-9679909-0-4*) R Levinson.

Much Ado about Calculus: A Modern Treatment with Applications Prepared for Use with the Computer. R. L. Wilson. LC 79-987. (Undergraduate Texts in Mathematics Ser.). (Illus.). 1979. 39.00 (*0-387-90347-X*) Spr-Verlag.

Much Ado about Culture: North American Trade Disputes. Keith Acheson & Christopher Maule. LC 99-48659. (Studies in International Economics). (Illus.). 388p. 1999. text 54.50 (*0-472-11048-9*, 11048) U of Mich Pr.

***Much Ado about Love.** Malia Martin. 384p. 2000. mass mkt. 5.99 (*0-380-81517-6*) Morrow Avon.

Much Ado about Marriage. Shawna Delacorte. 1998. per. 3.50 (*0-373-52069-7*, 1-52069-1) Silhouette.

Much Ado about Me. Fred Allen. 402p. reprint ed. lib. bdg. 27.95 (*0-88411-291-8*) Amereon Ltd.

Much Ado about Murder: Audience Plays Detective. Pat Cook. (Illus.). 64p. 1988. pap. 4.50 (*0-88680-282-2*) I E Clark.

***Much Ado about Nothing.** (YA). 1999. 11.95 (*1-56137-926-3*) Novel Units.

***Much Ado about Nothing.** (YA). 2000. 9.95 (*1-56137-925-5*) Novel Units.

***Much Ado about Nothing.** Cliffs Notes Staff. (Cliffs Notes Ser.). 80p. 1999. pap. 4.95 (*0-7645-8505-3*) IDG Bks.

***Much Ado about Nothing.** Cass Foster. Ed. by Paul M. Howey. (Sixty-Minute Shakespeare Ser.). 75p. 2000. pap. 8.99 (*1-877749-42-7*) Five Star AZ.

Much Ado about Nothing. M.H. Publications Staff. 196p. 1990. 175.00 (*1-872680-04-6*, Pub. by M H Pubns) St Mut.

Much Ado about Nothing. William Shakespeare. 40p. 1997. pap. 3.25 (*0-87440-047-3*) Bakers Plays.

Much Ado about Nothing. William Shakespeare. Ed. by David Bevington et al. (Classics Ser.). 120p. 1988. mass mkt. 3.95 (*0-553-21301-6*, Bantam Classics) Bantam.

Much Ado about Nothing. William Shakespeare. Ed. by F. H. Mares. (New Cambridge Shakespeare Ser.). (Illus.). 176p. 1988. text 44.95 (*0-521-22152-8*); pap. text 11.95 (*0-521-29367-7*) Cambridge U Pr.

Much Ado about Nothing. William Shakespeare. Ed. by Mary Berry & Michael Clamp. (Cambridge School Shakespeare Ser.). (Illus.). 192p. (C). 1992. pap. 11.95 (*0-521-42610-3*) Cambridge U Pr.

Much Ado about Nothing. William Shakespeare. Ed. by John F. Cox. (Shakespeare in Production Ser.). (Illus.). 284p. (C). 1998. text 59.95 (*0-521-47163-X*); pap. text 19.95 (*0-521-59822-2*) Cambridge U Pr.

Much Ado about Nothing. William Shakespeare. 1994. mass mkt. write for info. (*0-451-52615-5*, Sig Classics) NAL.

Much Ado about Nothing. William Shakespeare. (Shakespeare Ser.). 192p. 1998. mass mkt. 4.95 (*0-451-52681-3*, Sig) NAL.

***Much Ado about Nothing.** William Shakespeare. (School Shakespeare Ser.). 160p. 2000. pap. 7.95 (*0-19-832007-8*) OUP.

Much Ado about Nothing. William Shakespeare. (Big Works Collection). (Illus.). 1p. 1999. 29.95 (*1-929142-06-4*) One Page Bk.

Much Ado about Nothing. William Shakespeare. Ed. by Paul Werstine & Barbara A. Mowat. LC 97-184240. (New Folger Library Ser.). (Illus.). 304p. 1995. per. 3.99 (*0-671-72280-8*, Folger Shake Ser) PB.

Much Ado about Nothing. William Shakespeare. Ed. by A. R. Humphreys. 1985. pap. 8.95 (*0-416-19430-3*) Routledge.

Much Ado about Nothing. William Shakespeare. (New Folger Library Shakespeare Ser.). 1995. 9.09 (*0-606-12141-2*, Pub. by Turtleback) Demco.

Much Ado about Nothing. William Shakespeare. Ed. by Josephine W. Bennett. (Pelican Shakespeare Ser.). 1958. pap. 4.95 (*0-14-071412-X*, Pelican Bks) Viking Penguin.

Much Ado about Nothing. William Shakespeare. Ed. by R. A. Foakes. (New Penguin Shakespeare Ser.). 176p. 1981. pap. 5.95 (*0-14-070709-3*, Penguin Classics) Viking Penguin.

Much Ado about Nothing. William Shakespeare. LC 99-462498. (Pelican Shakespeare Ser.). 128p. 1999. pap. 3.95 (*0-14-071480-4*) Viking Penguin.

Much Ado about Nothing. William Shakespeare. (English Ser.). (C). 2001. mass mkt. 9.95 (*0-17-443530-4*) Wadsworth Pub.

Much Ado about Nothing. William Shakespeare. (Classics Library). Date not set. pap. 3.95 (*1-85326-254-4*, 2544WW, Pub. by Wrdsworth Edits) NTC Contemp Pub Co.

Much Ado about Nothing. large type ed. William Shakespeare. (Charnwood Large Print Ser.). 1991. pap. 24.95 (*0-7089-4527-9*, Charnwood) Ulverscroft.

Much Ado about Nothing see New Variorum Edition of Shakespeare

Much Ado about Nothing. William Shakespeare. Ed. by Sheldon P. Zitner. (Oxford World's Classics Ser.). (Illus.). 224p. 1998. reprint ed. pap. 7.95 (*0-19-283418-5*) OUP.

Much Ado about Nothing. unabridged ed. William Shakespeare. (Dover Thrift Editions Ser.). (Illus.). 80p. 1994. pap. 1.00 (*0-486-28272-4*) Dover.

Much Ado about Nothing. 2nd ed. William Shakespeare. (English). 1997. 11.95 (*0-17-443482-0*) Thomson Learn.

Much Ado about Nothing. 3rd ed. William Shakespeare. (English Ser.). (C). 2001. mass mkt. 45.00 (*0-17-443563-0*) Wadsworth Pub.

Much Ado about Nothing, 1. William Shakespeare. 1996. 123.75 (*0-7838-1555-7*, G K Hall & Co) Mac Lib Ref.

Much Ado about Nothing: Arden Playgoers' Edition. 3rd ed. William Shakespeare. Ed. by A. R. Humphreys. 256p. 1997. 19.95 (*0-17-443603-3*) Thomson Learn.

Much Ado about Nothing: Harrison,& Rex, Set. William Shakespeare. LC 67-606. 1991. audio 18.00 (*1-55994-098-0*, CPN 206, Caedmon) HarperAudio.

Much Ado about Nothing: Ready-to-Use Activities for Teaching. John W. Swope. LC 96-38320. (Illus.). 236p. (C). 1996. pap. text 27.95 (*0-87628-914-6*) P-H.

Much Ado about Nothing: Reproducible Teaching Unit. rev. ed. James Scott. 43p. (YA). (gr. 7-12). 1988. teacher ed., ring bd. 29.50 (*1-58049-069-7*, TU31/U) Prestwick Hse.

Much Ado about Nothing: The Making of the Movie. Kenneth Branagh. LC 93-3330. 1993. pap. 15.00 (*0-393-31111-2*) Norton.

Much Ado about Nothing - A Dual Edition. James Scott. 95p. (YA). (gr. 7-12). 1997. pap., wbk. ed. 6.75 (*1-58049-502-8*, SBS14) Prestwick Hse.

Much Ado about Nothing by William Shakespeare: Curriculum Unit. Center for Learning Network Staff. (Novel - Drama Ser.). 95p. 1997. teacher ed., spiral bd. 18.95 (*1-56077-505-X*) Ctr Learning.

MUCH ADO ABOUT NOTHING CD: Harrison,&Rex, Set. William Shakespeare. 1996. audio 25.00 (*0-694-51664-3*) HarperAudio.

Much Ado about Nothing for Young People. William Shakespeare. Ed. & Illus. by Diane Davidson. LC 94-11629. (Shakespeare for Young People Ser.: Vol. 8). 64p. (J). (gr. 5-8). 1994. pap. 5.95 (*0-934048-25-8*) Lrn Links.

Much Ado about Nothing Notes. Salibelle Royster. (Cliffs Notes Ser.). 56p. 1963. pap. 4.95 (*0-8220-0060-1*, Cliff) IDG Bks.

Much Ado about Prom Night. William D. McCants. LC 94-43349. 192p. (YA). (gr. 7 up). 1995. 11.00 (*0-15-200083-6*, Harcourt Child Bks); pap. 5.00 (*0-15-200081-X*, Harcourt Child Bks) Harcourt.

Much Afraid Folio. Jars of Clay. 1997. pap. 14.95 (*0-7601-1856-6*) Brentwood Music.

Much Beloved Daughter: The Story of Florence Li. Ted Harrison. LC 86-725. 112p. 1985. pap. 6.95 (*0-8192-1378-0*) Morehouse Pub.

Much Better Story Book: Stories, Poems & Illustrations from Children & Bestselling Authors & Artists. Michael Coleman. (Illus.). 192p. (J). (gr. 3-5). 1994. pap. 7.95 (*0-09-911531-X*, Pub. by Hutchinson) Trafalgar.

Much Bigger Than Martin. Steven Kellogg. 1992. pap. 5.99 (*0-14-054666-9*) NAL.

Much Bigger Than Martin. Steven Kellogg. LC 75-2799. (Pied Piper Bks.). (Illus.). 32p. (J). (ps-3). 1976. 16.99 (*0-8037-5809-X*, Dial Yng Read) Peng Put Young Read.

Much Bigger Than Martin. Steven Kellogg. (Picture Puffin Ser.). (Illus.). (J). 1976. 11.19 (*0-606-01665-1*, Pub. by Turtleback) Demco.

Much Cry Little Wool: Seventy-One Selected Poems. Ray Freed. 88p. (Orig.). 1990. pap. 6.95 (*0-935252-46-0*) Street Pr.

Much Depends on Dinner: The Extraordinary History & Mythology, Allure & Obsessions, Perils & Taboos, of an Ordinary Meal. Margaret Visser. 352p. 1999. pap. 14.00 (*0-8021-3651-6*, Grove) Grove-Atltic.

Much in Evidence see Henry Cecil Reprint Series

Much Labouring: The Texts & Authors of Yeats's First Modernist Books. David Holdeman. LC 97-4889. (Editorial Theory & Literary Criticism Ser.). 272p. (C). 1997. text 47.50 (*0-472-10851-4*, 10851) U of Mich Pr.

Much Love, Cynny-san. Cynny Robinson. 200p. 1994. 19.95 (*1-878208-49-7*) Guild Pr IN.

Much-Loved Nurse. large type ed. Pauline Ash. 1990. 27.99 (*0-7089-2148-5*) Ulverscroft.

Much Maligned Lord. Barbara Reeves. 192p. (Orig.). 1993. mass mkt. 3.99 (*0-380-77332-5*, Avon Bks) Morrow Avon.

Much Maligned Monsters: A History of European Reactions to Indian Art. Partha Mitter. (Illus.). 376p. 1992. pap. text 21.00 (*0-226-53239-9*) U Ch Pr.

***Much More Early American Pattern Glass: An Important American Heritage.** Alice Metz. (Illus.). 240p. 2000. pap. 17.95 (*1-57432-163-3*) Collector Bks.

***Much More Than a Game: Players, Owners & American Baseball since 1921.** Robert Fredrick Burk. LC 00-41774. (Illus.). 2001. pap. write for info. (*0-8078-4908-1*) U of NC Pr.

***Much More Than Counting: More Math Activities for Preschool & Kindergarten.** Sally Moomaw & Brenda Hieronymus. LC 99-31622. (More Than... Ser.). (Illus.). 320p. 1999. pap. 24.95 (*1-884834-66-3*, 406501, Pub. by Redleaf Pr) Gryphon Hse.

Much More Than Sexuality: Listening to 70 Gay People Talk about Their Lives. Ed. by Liz Sherblom & John Sherblom. LC 96-83147. 328p. (Orig.). (C). 1996. pap. 13.00 (*1-879418-90-8*) Audenreed Pr.

***Much More than the Abcs: The Early Stages of Reading & Writing.** Judith A. Schickedanz & National Association for the Education of Young Children. LC 98-88656. xii, 164p. 1999. 7.00 (*0-935989-90-0*) Natl Assn Child Ed.

Much More than We Imagine. 1997. pap. 1.30 (*0-8341-9660-3*) Lillenas.

Much More to Do About Something: The Guardian Ad Litem in Child Abuse & Neglect Judicial Proceedings. Clara L. Johnson. 174p. 1979. 5.00 (*0-318-16355-1*, B27) Regional Inst Social Welfare.

***Much Prayer - Much Power: Change Your World Through the Power of Prayer.** 2nd ed. Peter Deyneka. 96p. 1999. pap. write for info. (*1-56773-003-5*) Slavic Gospel.

Much Too Loved Quilt. Rachel Waterstone. LC 99-25115. (Illus.). 24p. (J). (gr. k-4). 1999. 13.95 (*1-890326-15-1*, Pub. by First Story Pr) BookWorld.

Much Younger Man. Dianne Highbridge. LC 97-43708. 224p. 1998. 20.00 (*1-56947-114-2*) Soho Press.

Much Younger Man. Dianne Highbridge. 214p. 1999. pap. 11.00 (*1-56947-147-9*) Soho Press.

Mucha. 1995. pap. 8.99 (*3-8228-9430-3*); pap. 5.99 (*3-8228-9438-9*) Taschen Amer.

Mucha: The Triumph of AA Noveau. Arthur Ellridge. (Illus.). 224p. 1997. pap. text 27.50 (*2-87939-006-0*) Stewart Tabori & Chang.

Mucha Art Nouveau Masterpieces, 2 vols. Alphonse M. Mucha. (Illus.). 1986. pap. 10.00 (*0-486-25293-0*) Dover.

Mucha Lana. Jan Henderikse. (Illus.). 30p. 1986. 25.00 (*0-932455-01-8*) Henderikse.

Mucha Notebook. Dover Staff. 1988. text 1.00 (*0-486-25599-9*) Dover.

Muchacha de Las Bragas de Oro. Juan Marse. 1999. pap. text 9.95 (*84-08-02372-1*) Planeta Edit.

Muchachas No More: Household Workers in Latin America & the Caribbean. Ed. by Elsa M. Chaney & Mary G. Castro. (Women in the Political Economy Ser.). 498p. 1988. 39.95 (*0-87722-571-0*) Temple U Pr.

Muchachas No More: Household Workers in Latin America & the Caribbean. Ed. by Elsa M. Chaney & Mary G. Castro. (Women in the Political Economy Ser.). 498p. 1991. pap. 24.95 (*0-87722-835-3*) Temple U Pr.

Muchacho en la Gaveta. Robert Munsch.Tr. of Boy in the Drawer. (SPA., Illus.). 32p. (YA). (ps-2). 1989. pap. 5.95 (*1-55037-097-9*, Pub. by Annick) Firefly Bks Ltd.

Muchacho Que Grito el Lobo! Dorothy S. Bishop et al. (Spanish/English Bilingual Ser.).Tr. of Boy Who Cried Wolf. (ENG & SPA., Illus.). 64p. (J). 1994. pap. 6.95 (*0-8442-7295-7*, 72957, Natl Textbk Co) NTC Contemp Pub Co.

Muchacho Que Grito el Lobo! The Boy Who Cried Wolf. Eugenia De Hoogh. (Bilingual Ser.). 1987. 10.15 (*0-606-01265-6*, Pub. by Turtleback) Demco.

Muchachos No Escriben Historias de Amor (Boys Don't Write Love Stories) Brian Keaney. Tr. by Joaquin Diez-Canedo. (SPA., Illus.). 194p. (YA). 1997. pap. 6.99 (*968-16-5377-7*, Pub. by Fondo) Continental Bk.

Mucha's Figures Decoratives. Alphonse M. Mucha. Orig. Title: Figure Decoratives. (Illus.). 48p. 1981. reprint ed. pap. 8.95 (*0-486-24234-X*) Dover.

Mucha's Floral Borders: Thirty Full-Color Art Nouveau Designs. Alphonse M. Mucha. (Illus.). 32p. (Orig.). 1985. pap. 6.95 (*0-486-24916-6*) Dover.

Muchas Gracias . . . Marielitos . . . Siete Anos Despues: Una Historia Verdadera y Siete Cuentos Imaginados. Angel Perez-Vidal. LC 87-83680. (Coleccion Caniqui). (SPA.). 151p. (Orig.). 1988. pap. 12.00 (*0-89729-473-4*) Ediciones.

Muchas Palabras Sobre Animales. Illus. by Richard Brown. LC 88-21364.Tr. of Hundred Words about Animals. (SPA.). 32p. (J). (ps-1). 1989. pap. 6.00 (*0-15-200531-5*) Harcourt.

Muchas Palabras Sobre Mi Casa. Illus. by Richard Brown. LC 88-21363.Tr. of Hundred Words about My House. (SPA.). 32p. (J). (ps-1). 1989. pap. 6.00 (*0-15-200532-3*, Gulliver Bks) Harcourt.

Mucheke: Race, Status & Politics in a Rhodesian Community. A. K. Weinrich. LC 76-62524. 278p. 1977. 39.50 (*0-8419-0299-2*, Africana) Holmes & Meier.

Mucho Boleto Pero No Train: Many Ticket but No Train. 3rd rev. ed. Randall C. Jimnez. Ed. by Rich Graeber. (Boleto Ser.). (Illus.). 56p. 1999. pap. 9.95 (*0-9661163-0-5*) Hist Science.

Mucho gusto! Que gusto! Mucho gusto! Level 1: Textbook. Robert J. Brett. 39.95 (*0-8219-0246-6*) EMC-Paradigm.

Mucho gusto! Que gusto! Mucho gusto! Level 1: Workbook. Robert J. Brett. 9.50 (*0-8219-0249-0*) EMC-Paradigm.

Mucho gusto! Que gusto! Que gusto! Level 2: Workbook. Robert J. Brett. 9.95 (*0-8219-0270-9*) EMC-Paradigm.

Mucho gusto! Que gusto! Que justo!, Level 2: Textbook. Robert J. Brett. 41.95 (*0-8219-0267-9*) EMC-Paradigm.

Mucho Macho: Tough Talk for Tough Guys. Ed. by Ariel Books Staff. LC 96-83358. 374p. (Orig.). 1996. pap. 5.95 (*0-8362-1514-1*, Arie Bks) Andrews & McMeel.

Mucho Mas Que Numeros. David Y. Cho. Ed. by Luis L. Bernal. Tr. by M. Francisco Lievano.Tr. of More Than Numbers. (SPA.). 208p. 1985. pap. 6.99 (*0-8297-0531-7*) Vida Pubs.

Mucho Mojo. Joe R. Lansdale. 304p. 1995. mass mkt. 5.99 (*0-446-40187-0*, Pub. by Warner Bks) Little.

Muchos Rostros de Cuilapan: El Compendio Historico de un Monasterio Dominico de su Conjunto Eclesiastico, Asi Como del Pueblo Mismo del Siglo Diez y Seis en el Estado de Oaxaca, Mexico. Eleanor F. Sleight. Tr. by Guadalupe C. Harp & Veronica Santos from ENG. LC 93-85007. (SPA., Illus.). 200p. (Orig.). 1993. pap. 20.00 (*0-9619949-1-6*) E F Sleight.

Muchos Rostros de Maria: Una Storia di Amor. Bob Lord & Penny Lord. Tr. by Aminta Valls & Luz E. Sandoval.Tr. of Many Faces of Mary: A Love Story. (SPA., Illus.). 272p. 1994. pap. 9.95 (*0-926143-19-0*, BLOS) Journeys Faith.

Mucial Deprecation. Gracie King. 1984. 30.00 (*0-946270-13-9*, Pub. by Pentland Pr) St Mut.

Muck & Magic: Start Your Own Natural Garden with Colorful, Simple Projects. Jo Readman. (Illus.). 48p. (J). (gr. 4-7). 1994. pap. 12.95 (*0-85532-757-X*, 757-X, Pub. by Srch Pr) A Schwartz & Co.

Muck Arbour. Bruce Marcus. Ed. by John Ashbery. LC 74-5984. 64p. 1975. 7.95 (*0-87955-500-9*) O'Hara.

Muck Luck & Determination. Jeanne E. Sexson. LC 84-91279. (Illus.). 100p. 1984. pap. 7.95 (*0-9613817-0-1*) J E Sexson.

Mucking About: An Autobiography. Paul Hasluck. pap. 24.95 (*1-875560-35-1*, Pub. by Univ of West Aust Pr) Intl Spec Bk.

Muckle Annie. large type ed. Jan Webster. 512p. 1987. 11.50 (*0-7089-1620-1*) Ulverscroft.

Muckle's Naval Architecture. 2nd ed. W. C. Muckle. (Marine Engineering Ser.). (Illus.). 400p. 1987. 110.00 (*0-408-00334-0*) Buttrwrth-Heinemann.

Muckrake Years. David M. Chalmers. LC 79-22780. (Anvil Ser.). 176p. 1980. reprint ed. pap. 10.50 (*0-89874-066-5*) Krieger.

Muckraker. Billy Callahan. LC 99-29501. 224p. 1999. pap. 12.75 (*1-892657-06-6*) Town Bk Pr.

Muckrakers. Louis Filler. (Illus.). 472p. (C). 1993. pap. 17.95 (*0-8047-2236-6*) Stanford U Pr.

***Muckrakers: Evangelical Crusaders.** Ed. by Robert Miraldi. LC 00-25129. 208p. 2000. 63.00 (*0-275-96915-0*, C6915, Praeger Pubs) Greenwood.

Muckraker's Manual: How to Do Your Own Investigative Reporting. 2nd ed. M. Harry. LC 84-80233. 148p. 1984. pap. 14.95 (*0-915179-03-2*) Loompanics.

Muckraking: Three Landmark Articles. Ellen F. Fitzpatrick. 160p. 1994. pap. 11.95 (*0-312-08944-9*); text 39.95 (*0-312-10280-1*) St Martin.

An Asterisk (*) at the beginning of an entry indicates that the title is appearing for the first time.

Muckraking & Objectivity: Journalism's Colliding Traditions, 18. Robert Miraldi. LC 89-26010. (Contributions to the Study of Mass Media & Communications Ser.: No. 18). 184p. 1990. 52.95 (*0-313-27298-0*, MMQ/, Greenwood Pr) Greenwood.

Muckraking & Progressivism in the American Tradition. Louis Filler. 476p. 1996. pap. text 29.95 (*1-56000-875-X*) Transaction Pubs.

Muckraking Sociology: Research As Social Criticism. Ed. by Gary T. Marx. LC 71-186711. 240p. 1972. 32.95 (*0-87855-036-4*); pap. text 18.95 (*0-87855-532-3*) Transaction Pubs.

Mucky Martians. Stephen Cole & Lousie Gardner. (Alien Pop-Ups Ser.). (Illus.). 12p. (J). 1998. 4.95 (*1-899607-62-5*) Sterling.

Mucky Moose. Jonathan Allen. (Illus.). 32p. (J). (ps-3). 1996. per. 5.95 (*0-689-80651-5*) Aladdin.

Mucky Moose. Jonathan Allen. LC 90-6363. (J). 1996. 11.15 (*0-606-09643-4*, Pub. by Turtleback) Demco.

Mucky Pup. Ken Brown. LC 97-220330. (Illus.). 32p. (J). (ps-4). 1997. 14.99 (*0-525-45886-7*) NAL.

Mucky Pup's Christmas Ken Brown. LC 98-47019. 1999. 16.99 (*0-525-46141-8*, Dutton Child) Peng Put Young Read.

Mucopolysaccharides-Glycosaminoglycans of Body Fluids in Health & Disease. R. S. Varma. LC 83-2021. (Illus.). xv, 647p. 1983. 261.55 (*3-11-008471-6*) De Gruyter.

Mucorales. H. Zycha & R. Siepmann. (Illus.). 1970. 65.00 (*3-7682-0145-7*) Lubrecht & Cramer.

Mucosal Biopsy of the Gastrointestinal Tract. 5th ed. Richard Whitehead. Ed. by Lesley Day. LC 96-20545. 416p. 1996. text 95.00 (*0-7216-6192-0*, W B Saunders Co) Harcrt Hlth Sci Grp.

Mucosal Immunity. fac. ed. Ed. by John I. Gallin & Anthony S. Fauci. LC 83-48671. (Advances in Host Defense Mechanisms Ser.: No. 4). (Illus.). 208p. pap. 64.50 (*0-7837-7395-1*, 204699700006) Bks Demand.

Mucosal Immunity in HIV Infection: Proceedings of the International Symposium, Berlin, June 6-7, 1997. Ernst-Otto Riecken. Ed. by Reiner Ullrich et al. (Pathobiology Ser.: Vol. 66, Nos. 3 & 4, 1998). (Illus.). 82p. 1998. pap. 55.75 (*3-8055-6739-1*) S Karger.

Mucosal Immunization: Genetic Approaches & Adjuvants. Ed. by Nancy Mulford. (Biomedical Library). 436p. 1996. pap. 695.00 (*1-57936-008-4*) IBC USA.

Mucosal Immunobiology. Ed. by L. A. Hanson. (Monographs in Allergy: Vol. 24). (Illus.). x, 330p. 1988. 221.75 (*3-8055-4680-7*) S Karger.

Mucosal Immunology. 2nd ed. Ed. by Pearay Ogra et al. LC 98-36839. (Illus.). 1628p. (C). 1998. boxed set 199.95 (*0-12-524725-7*) Acad Pr.

Mucosal Immunology: Intraeithelial Lymphocytes. Ed. by Hiroshi Kiyono & Jerry R. McGhee. LC 93-34356. (Advances in Host Defense Mechanisms Ser.: Vol. 9). (Illus.). 224p. reprint ed. pap. 69.50 (*0-608-09765-9*, 206993800007) Bks Demand.

Mucosal Immunology: Intraepithelial Lymphocytes (IEL) Ed. by Hiroshi Kiyono & Jery R. McGhee. LC 93-34356. (Advances in Host Defense Mechanisms Ser.: No. 9). 224p. 1993. text 98.00 (*0-7817-0117-1*) Lppncott W & W.

***Mucosal Immunology & Ocular Disease.** Ed. by Manfred Zierhut & John V. Forrester. LC 99-48103. (Illus.). 264p. 2000. text 106.00 (*90-70430-37-1*, Pub. by Aeolus Press) Swets & Zeitlinger.

Mucosal T Cells. Ed. by Thomas T. MacDonald. (Chemical Immunology Ser.: Vol. 71 (1998)). (Illus.). xii, 242p. 1998. 208.75 (*3-8055-6722-7*) S Karger.

Mucosal Vaccines. Ed. by Hiroshi Kiyono et al. (Illus.). 479p. (C). 1996. text 89.95 (*0-12-410580-7*) Acad Pr.

Mucus Secretions & Cystic Fibrosis. Ed. by G. G. Forstner. (Modern Problems in Pediatrics Ser.: Vol. 19). (Illus.). 1977. 96.75 (*3-8055-2678-4*) S Karger.

Mucusless Diet Healing System. Arnold Ehret. 1976. pap. 3.95 (*0-87904-004-1*) Lust.

***Mud.** Wendy Cheyette Lewison & Bill Basso. LC 00-35815. (Hello Reader! Ser.). (Illus.). (J). 2001. write for info. (*0-439-17932-7*) Scholastic Inc.

Mud. Mary L. Ray. LC 94-28711. (Illus.). 32p. (J). (ps-3). 1996. 16.00 (*0-15-256263-X*) Harcourt.

Mud! Charnan Simon. LC 98-34284. (Real Kids Readers Ser.). (Illus.). 32p. (J). (ps-1). 1999. pap. 3.99 (*0-7613-2076-8*, Copper Beech Bks); lib. bdg. 16.90 (*0-7613-2051-2*, Copper Beech Bks) Millbrook Pr.

***Mud Actor.** Cyrus Cassells. (Classic Contemporaries Ser.). 2000. pap. text 12.95 (*0-88748-325-9*) Carnegie-Mellon.

Mud & Dust. Charles N. Aronson. LC 76-5966. (Eagle Ser.: No. 2). (Illus.). 1976. 16.00 (*0-915736-09-8*); pap. 10.00 (*0-915736-10-1*) C N Aronson.

Mud & Green Fields. George Kitching. 300p. (C). 1987. 120.00 (*0-920849-02-4*, Pub. by Picton) St Mut.

Mud & Guts: A Look at the Common Soldier of the American Revolution. 1997. lib. bdg. 250.99 (*0-8490-8167-X*) Gordon Pr.

Mud & Guts: A Look at the Common Soldier of the American Revolution. Bill Mauldin. (Illus.). 58p. 1996. reprint ed. pap. text 20.00 (*0-7881-3267-9*) DIANE Pub.

Mud & Guts: The Common Soldier of the American Revolution. Bill Mauldin. 64p. 1995. pap. 8.50 (*0-16-061670-0*) USGPO.

Mud & Magic Shows: Robertson Davies' Fifth Business. Patricia Monk. (Canadian Fiction Studies: No. 13). 88p. (C). 1992. pap. text 14.95 (*1-55022-128-0*, Pub. by ECW) Genl Dist Srvs.

Mud & Manure . . . The Joys of Life with Horses. Debby Thomas. (Illus.). 112p. 1995. pap. 10.95 (*0-9646210-0-2*) TB Enter.

Mud Belly Woman. Jane Farrell. 32p. (Orig.). 1996. pap. 5.95 (*1-889216-02-X*) Meadowcroft.

Mud Between My Toes: Poems for the Womanist. Valerie Davis. 100p. 1992. pap. 9.95 (*1-880299-02-X*) Woman to Woman.

Mud, Blood & Money: English Rugby Union Goes Professional. Ian Malin. (Illus.). 192p. 1998. 35.00 (*1-85158-938-4*, Pub. by Mainstream Pubng) Trafalgar.

Mud Book: How to Make Pies & Cakes. John M. Cage & Lois Long. (Illus.). 46p. 1988. 16.95 (*0-8109-1533-2*, Pub. by Abrams) Time Warner.

Mud Bud & Poxie: Their Very First Adventure. Mary E. Cohon & Helen S. Cohon. LC 98-91218. (Illus.). 30p. (J). (ps-k). 1998. pap. 5.99 (*0-9663116-0-4*) Little Idea.

Mud Cake, Bk. 3A. Groves. (J). Date not set. pap. text. write for info. (*0-582-18794-X*, Pub. by Addison-Wesley) Longman.

Mud Equipment Manual Handbook Vol. 1: IADC Manufacturer--User Conference Series on Mud Equipment Operations. LC 83-161604. 85p. 1981. reprint ed. pap. 25.00 (*0-608-01343-9*, 2062086) Bks Demand.

Mud Equipment Manual Handbook Vol. 8: IADC Manufacturer--User Conference Series on Mud Equipment Operations. LC 83-161604. 80p. 1981. reprint ed. pap. 30.00 (*0-608-01344-7*, 206208600008) Bks Demand.

Mud Equipment Manual Handbook Vol. 10: IADC Manufacturer--User Conference Series on Mud Equipment Operations. LC 83-161604. 55p. 1981. reprint ed. pap. 30.00 (*0-608-01345-5*, 206208600010) Bks Demand.

Mud Equipment Manual Handbook Vol. 11: IADC Manufacturer--User Conference Series on Mud Equipment Operations. LC 83-161604. 66p. 1981. reprint ed. pap. 30.00 (*0-608-01346-3*, 206208600011) Bks Demand.

Mud Family. Betsy James. (Illus.). 32p. (J). 1998. pap. 10.95 (*0-19-512479-0*) OUP.

Mud Flat April Fool. James Stevenson. LC 97-10014. (Illus.). 48p. (J). (gr. k-3). 1998. 15.00 (*0-688-15163-9*, Grenwillow Bks); 15.89 (*0-688-15164-7*, Grenwillow Bks) HarpC Child Bks.

Mud Flat Mystery. James Stevenson. LC 96-46269. (Illus.). 56p. (J). (gr. k-3). 1997. 14.93 (*0-688-14966-9*, Grenwillow Bks) HarpC Child Bks.

Mud Flat Mystery. James Stevenson. LC 96-46269. (Mud Flat Ser.). (Illus.). 56p. (J). (gr. k up). 1997. 15.00 (*0-688-14965-0*, Grenwillow Bks) HarpC Child Bks.

Mud Flat Olympics. James Stevenson. LC 93-28118. 56p. (J). 1994. lib. bdg. 14.93 (*0-688-12924-2*, Grenwillow Bks) HarpC Child Bks.

Mud Flat Olympics. James Stevenson. LC 93-28118. 56p. (J). (gr. k up). 1994. 15.00 (*0-688-12923-4*, Grenwillow Bks) HarpC Child Bks.

***Mud Flat Spring.** James Stevenson. LC 98-2975. (Illus.). 40p. (gr. k-3). 1999. 14.93 (*0-688-15773-4*, Grenwillow Bks) HarpC Child Bks.

Mud Flat Spring. James Stevenson. LC 98-2975. (Illus.). 40p. (YA). (gr. k-3). 1999. 15.00 (*0-688-15772-6*, Grenwillow Bks) HarpC Child Bks.

Mud Grape Pie. Catherine S. Cardinal. 29p. (J). (gr. k-6). 1991. pap. 6.00 (*0-9630655-0-5*) Garden Gate.

Mud-Hut Dwellers. Mihail Sadoveanu. 1964. lib. bdg. 25.00 (*0-8057-5195-5*) Irvington.

Mud Huts & Missionaries. E. V. Thompson. 192p. 1998. 22.00 (*0-7278-5289-2*) Severn Hse.

***Mud Huts & Missionaries.** large type ed. E. V. Thompson. 200p. 1999. 31.99 (*0-7089-9111-4*) Ulverscroft.

Mud in His Eye. large type ed. Gerald Hammond. (Linford Mystery Library). 234p. 1988. pap. 16.99 (*0-7089-6569-5*, Linford) Ulverscroft.

Mud Is Cake. Pamela Munoz Ryan. 32p. Date not set. text 14.99 (*0-7868-0501-3*, Pub. by Hyprn Child) Little.

Mud Is Cake. Pamela Munoz Ryan. 32p. 2005. lib. bdg. 15.49 (*0-7868-2434-4*, Pub. by Hyprn Child) Little.

Mud Makes Me Dance in the Spring. Charlotte Agell. LC 93-33610. (Illus.). 32p. (J). (ps-4). 1994. 7.95 (*0-88448-112-3*) Tilbury Hse.

Mud Man. Diana Stoneberg. (Illus.). 19p. (J). (gr. k-3). 1994. pap. write for info. (*0-9642796-0-6*) Snapping Turtle.

Mud Matters. Jennifer O. Dewey. LC 97-32929. (Illus.). 64p. (J). (gr. 2-5). 1998. lib. bdg. 15.95 (*0-7614-5014-9*) Marshall Cavendish.

Mud, Muscle, & Miracles: Marine Salvage in the United States Navy. Ed. by Charles A. Bartholomew. (Illus.). 505p. (C). 1990. 32.00 (*0-945274-03-3*) Naval Hist Ctr.

Mud on My Feet. Judith Cox. 140p. 1992. pap. 9.95 (*0-9634536-0-2*, TXU 367-733) Healing Design.

Mud on the Stars. William B. Huie. LC 96-23433. (Library of Alabama Classics). 376p. 1996. reprint ed. pap. 19.95 (*0-8173-0872-5*) U of Ala Pr.

Mud on Their Wheels: The Life-Story of Vern & Lois Ellis. Betty M. Hockett. LC 88-81703. (Life-Story Mission Ser.). (Illus.). 80p. (Orig.). (J). (gr. 3-8). 1988. pap. 5.00 (*0-943701-14-7*) George Fox Pr.

Mud Pies. Judith Grey. LC 81-4042. (Illus.). 32p. (J). (gr. k-2). 1981. lib. bdg. 17.25 (*0-89375-541-9*) Troll Communs.

Mud Pies. Judith Grey. LC 81-4042. (Illus.). 32p. (J). (gr. k-2). 1996. pap. 3.95 (*0-89375-542-7*) Troll Communs.

Mud Pies. James Magorian. LC 91-70218. (Illus.). 24p. (Orig.). (J). (gr. 4-6). 1991. pap. 3.00 (*0-930674-35-9*) Black Oak.

Mud Pies. Joan Maynard. 8p. (J). (gr. 1). 1988. pap. text 2.50 (*1-882225-09-0*) Tott Pubns.

Mud Pies & Dirt Cakes: A Collection of Chocolate Delights. 30p. 1995. pap. 3.95 (*0-9629408-9-5*) Cookbook Cup.

Mud Pies & Other Recipes: A Cookbook for Dolls. Marjorie Winslow. LC 96-19049. (Illus.). 48p. (J). (gr. k-3). 1996. pap. 5.95 (*0-8027-7487-3*) Walker & Co.

Mud Pony. Caron L. Cohen. LC 87-23451. 32p. (J). (ps-3). 1989. pap. 4.99 (*0-590-41526-3*) Scholastic Inc.

Mud Pony. Caron L. Cohen. 32p. (J). (ps-3). 1993. 19.95 (*0-590-72838-5*) Scholastic Inc.

Mud Pony: A Traditional Skidi Pawnee Tale. Illus. by Shonto Begay. LC 87-23451. 32p. (J). (gr. k-4). 1988. 15.95 (*0-590-41525-5*) Scholastic Inc.

Mud Pony, a Traditional Skidi Pawnee Tale. Caron Lee Cohen. (J). 1988. 10.15 (*0-606-07897-5*, Pub. by Turtleback) Demco.

Mud Puddle. Robert Munsch. (Annikins Ser.: Vol. 1). (Illus.). 24p. (J). (ps-1). pap. 0.99 (*0-920236-23-5*, Pub. by Annick) Firefly Bks Ltd.

Mud Puddle. Robert Munsch. (Illus.). 32p. (J). (ps-2). 1995. lib. bdg. 16.95 (*1-55037-469-9*, Pub. by Annick) Firefly Bks Ltd.

Mud Puddle. rev. ed. Robert Munsch. (Illus.). 32p. (J). (ps-2). 1982. pap. 5.95 (*1-55037-468-0*, Pub. by Annick) Firefly Bks Ltd.

Mud Puddles. Joan Maynard. 7p. (J). (gr. 1). 1989. pap. text 2.50 (*1-882225-06-6*) Tott Pubns.

Mud Pump Handbook. Samuel L. Collier. LC 82-20743. (Illus.). 256p. 1983. pap. 79.40 (*0-608-04973-5*, 206555300004) Bks Demand.

Mud Pumps & Conditioning Equipment; Circulating Systems see Drilling Fluids, Mud Pumps, & Conditioning Equipment

Mud Racing see MotorSports

Mud Racing. Jeff Savage. (Motorsports Ser.). (Illus.). 48p. (J). (gr. 3-6). 1995. 19.00 (*0-516-35257-1*) Childrens.

***Mud Racing.** Jeff Savage. LC 00-30908. (Action Events Ser.). (Illus.). 2000. write for info. (*0-7660-1713-3*) Enslow Pubs.

Mud Racing. Jeff Savage. LC 95-32757. (Action Events Ser.). (J). 1996. lib. bdg. 14.95 (*0-89686-888-5*, Crstwood Hse) Silver Burdett Pr.

Mud Racing. Jeff Savage. LC 95-32757. (Action Events Ser.). (Illus.). 48p. (J). 1996. pap. 4.95 (*0-382-39297-3*, Crstwood Hse) Silver Burdett Pr.

Mud River. Judy L. Ayyildiz. (Illus.). 80p. (Orig.). 1988. 10.00 (*0-931642-20-5*) Lintel.

Mud River: Poems by Judy Light Ayyildiz. Judy L. Ayyildiz. (Illus.). 80p. (Orig.). 1988. pap. 8.95 (*0-931642-19-1*) Lintel.

Mud, River, Stone. Lynn Nottage. 1998. pap. 5.25 (*0-8222-1660-4*) Dramatists Play.

Mud, Sand, & Water. Dorothy M. Hill. LC 77-72759. (Illus.). 40p. 1977. pap. 3.00 (*0-912674-52-0*, NAEYC 308) Natl Assn Child Ed.

Mud Settling: or Not to Do to Do. George L. Eisberg et al. (To Be Your Own Ser.). (Illus.). 48p. (J). (gr. 3-5). 1994. pap. 6.95 (*1-56721-039-2*) Twnty-Fifth Cent Pr.

Mud Shrimps, Upogebiidae, from the Western Atlantic: Crustacea: Decapoda: Thalassinidea. Austin B. Williams. LC 93-21239. (Smithsonian Contributions to Zoology Ser.: No. 544). (Illus.). 81p. reprint ed. pap. 30.00 (*0-7837-6725-0*, 204635200011) Bks Demand.

Mud Sled. Hans Bender. Tr. by Jeanne Willson from GER. (Modern German Literature in Translation Ser.). 160p. 1993. 24.95 (*0-911173-04-8*) Dimension Pr.

Mud Stoves & Strawberry Jam. Sally Morrissey. 240p. pap. 14.95 (*0-9643963-0-0*) R Paul Pr.

Mud Woman: Poems from the Clay. Naranjo. LC 91-16611. (Sun Tracks Ser.: Vol. 20). (Illus.). 127p. (Orig.). 1992. pap. 17.95 (*0-8165-1281-7*) U of Ariz Pr.

Mud Woman: Poems from the Clay. Nora Naranjo-Morse. LC 91-16611. (Sun Tracks Ser.: Vol. 20). (Illus.). 127p. (Orig.). 1992. 38.50 (*0-8165-1248-5*) U of Ariz Pr.

Mudbaths & Bloodbaths: The Inside Story of the Bears-Packers Rivalry. Gary D'Amato & Cliff Christl. LC 97-27098. (Illus.). 288p. 1997. 25.00 (*1-879483-41-6*); pap. 16.95 (*1-879483-44-0*) Prairie Oak Pr.

***Mudcloth: Poems from the Fabric of Life.** Candy Pettiford. LC 99-90650. 48p. 1999. pap. 10.00 (*1-57921-237-9*) WinePress Pub.

Mudcrack Y. 2nd ed. Craig Schensted & Charles Titus. 160p. 1974. pap. 12.00 (*0-911014-23-3*) Neo Pr.

Mudd in Your Eye. Jerry Oltion. (Star Trek Ser.). 1997. per. 5.99 (*0-671-00260-0*, Star Trek) PB.

Muddle Cuddle see Revoltijo Carinoso

Muddle Cuddle. Laurel D. Gugler & Vlasta van Kampen. LC 96-932214. (Illus.). 24p. (J). (ps-1). 1997. 16.95 (*1-55037-435-4*, Pub. by Annick); pap. 6.95 (*1-55037-434-6*, Pub. by Annick) Firefly Bks Ltd.

Muddle-Headed Republic. Alan Atkinson. 160p. 1994. pap. 24.95 (*0-19-553638-X*) OUP.

Muddling Through. Peter Hennessy. LC 97-122856. 320p. 1998. 40.00 (*0-575-06366-1*, Pub. by V Gollancz); pap. 17.95 (*0-575-40102-8*, Pub. by V Gollancz) Trafalgar.

Muddling Through: Pursuing Science & Truths in the Twenty-First Century. Mike Fortun & Herbert J. Bernstein. LC 98-38517. 272p. 1998. 27.50 (*1-887178-48-1*, Pub. by Counterpt DC) HarpC.

Muddling Through in Madagascar. Dervla Murphy. LC 88-22512. (Illus.). 276p. 1989. 22.95 (*0-87951-342-X*, Pub. by Overlook Pr) Penguin Putnam.

Muddling Through in Madagascar. Dervla Murphy. 276p. 1990. pap. 13.95 (*0-87951-360-8*, Pub. by Overlook Pr) Penguin Putnam.

***Muddling Toward Democracy: Political Change in Grassroots China.** Anne F. Thurston. 56p. 2000. pap. text 20.00 (*0-7567-0047-7*) DIANE Pub.

Muddy Banks. Ruby C. Tolliver. LC 85-20851. (Chaparral Bks.). (Illus.). 154p. (J). (gr. 4). 1987. pap. 6.95 (*0-87565-049-X*) Tex Christian.

Muddy Boots: Ethical in the Construction Field. Merrill. 33.00 (*0-534-55169-6*) Thomson Learn.

Muddy Boots & Ragged Aprons: Images of Working-Class Detroit, 1900-1930. Kevin Boyle & Victoria Getis. LC 96-28256. (Illus.). 208p. 1997. pap. 29.95 (*0-8143-2482-7*) Wayne St U Pr.

Muddy Boots & Sunday Suits. large type ed. Fred Archer. (Reminiscence Ser.). 23.95 (*1-85695-104-9*, Pub. by ISIS Lrg Prnt) Transaction Pubs.

Muddy Cup: A Dominican Family Comes of Age in a New America. Barbara Fischkin. LC 97-3196. 1997. 23.50 (*0-684-80704-1*) S&S Trade.

Muddy Fork & Other Things: Short Fiction & Nonfiction. James Crumley. LC 91-61900. 224p. (Orig.). 1991. pap. 12.95 (*0-944439-39-X*) Clark City Pr.

Muddy Four Paws. Jean Ure. LC 98-48463. (We Love Animals Bks.). (Illus.). 128p. (J). (gr. 4-7). 1999. pap. 3.95 (*0-7641-0968-5*) Barron.

Muddy Glory: America's Indian Wars in the Philippines, 1899 to 1935. Russell Roth. LC 80-70230. 1981. reprint ed. pap. 15.00 (*0-8158-0402-4*) Chris Mass.

***Muddy Shoes.** Majid Naficy. (Illus.). 86p. 1999. pap. 8.00 (*1-892184-01-X*, Pub. by Beyond Baroque) SPD-Small Pr Dist.

Muddy Water. Sally Gunning. (Peter Bartholomew Mystery Ser.). 1997. per. 6.50 (*0-671-56314-9*) PB.

***Muddy Water: A Book about Fishing, Friendships & Wildflowers. 164p. 2000. pap. 16.00 (*1-891609-01-7*) Home Brew Pr.**

Art, photographs, poetry & prose celebrating SPRING! This is the season of kite flying, fishing, discovering wildflowers & exploring friendships. New works blend with some reprints, all are Midwest voices, but most are Wisconsinites.This anthology is the sequel to HBP's award-winning title "the poetry of cold-a collection of writings about winter,wolves & love." Justin Isherwood, Ellen Kort return along with Martin & numerous others, including Kent Meyer, to unearth new thoughts on the "muddy" topics. " Eventually there will be a four season set of books," publisher/contributor/designer, Martin added. She selected "Guidance" by artist Scott Hill for the cover because "it is an arresting portrait, a strong face that honors our Native American heritage; the colors are vivid; & the eagle-feathered, headdress reminded me of the opening of a water lily. Retail: Softcover, $16.00 (From the publisher add $3.50 for shipping & handling.) Published november 1, 2000 by Home brew Press 2540 Abby Lane, P.O. Box 185, Wisconsin Rapids, WI 54495-0185 VOICE: 888-492-4531 EMAIL: or homebrewpress@netscope.net,PH/FAX: 715-421-2429. Publicity contact Mary "Casey: Martin, MARTIN COMMUNICATIONS & MARKETING, P.O. BOX 185, Wisconsin Rapids WI 54495-10852. VOICE: 888-492-4531 or orders PH/FAX: 800-250-2986 or AUTHORS or EMAIL: mcm@wctc.net. *Publisher Paid Annotation.*

Muddy Waters. Astley. 288p. 1997. mass mkt. 12.95 (*0-552-99630-0*) Bantam.

Muddy Waters. Robert Gordon. 2000. write for info. (*0-316-32849-9*) Little.

Muddy Waters. large type ed. Judy Astley. 1998. 26.95 (*0-7531-5593-1*, Pub. by ISIS Lrg Prnt) T T Beeler.

Muddy Waters: Deep Blues. 184p. 1995. per. 24.95 (*0-7935-0955-6*, 00694789) H Leonard.

Muddy Waters: The Army Engineers & the Nation's Rivers. Arthur Maass. LC 73-20238. (FDR & the Era of the New Deal Ser.). 306p. 1974. reprint ed. lib. bdg. 39.50 (*0-306-70607-5*) Da Capo.

Muddy Waters: The Mojo Man. Sandra Tooze. (Illus.). 1997. pap. 22.95 (*1-55022-296-1*, Pub. by ECW) Genl Dist Srvs.

Mudejar Ornament in Manuscripts. Frances Spalding. 1953. 7.00 (*0-87535-078-X*) Hispanic Soc.

Mudeye: An Australian Boyhood & Beyond. Bary Dowling. LC 95-214460. 1999. pap. text 14.95 (*1-86254-345-3*) Wakefield Pr.

Mudfish: A Forum for Contemporary Art & Poetry, No. 2. Ed. by Jill Hoffman & Vladimir Urban. (Illus.). 175p. (Orig.). (C). 1987. pap. 7.00 (*0-9618526-0-7*) Box Turtle Pr.

Mudfish: A Forum for Contemporary Art & Poetry, No. 3. Ed. by Jill Hoffman & Vladimir Urban. (Illus.). 96p. (Orig.). (C). 1988. write for info. (*0-9618526-1-5*) Box Turtle Pr.

Mudflap & Logjam to the Rescue. Stephen Reece. (Illus.). 12p. (J). (ps-3). 1998. pap. 3.65 (*1-892388-05-7*) Lttle Trucker.

Mudflow Rheology & Dynamics. Philippe Coussot. (IAHR Monograph Ser.). (Illus.). 272p. (C). 1997. text 95.00 (*90-5410-693-X*, Pub. by A A Balkema) Ashgate Pub Co.

Mudflows: Experience & Lessons Learned from the Management of Major Disasters. United Nations Department of Humanitarian Affairs. 139p. 1997. pap. 60.00 (*92-1-132020-8*, 85762) UN.

Mudgrump. Jack Greene. LC 80-68130. (Illus.). 56p. (Orig.). (J). (gr. k-6). 1980. pap. text, per. 3.95 (*0-9601258-3-3*) Golden Owl Pub.

Mudhakkarat al-'Amm Sabur, 12 vols., Set. Abd-al-Wahid Ulwani. (J). 1993. pap. 16.95 (*1-57547-184-1*) Dar Al-Fikr.

Mudhakkarat al-'Amm Sabur, Vol. 1. Abd-al-Wahid Ulwani. (J). 1993. pap. write for info. (*1-57547-185-X*) Dar Al-Fikr.

Mudhakkarat al-'Amm Sabur, Vol. 2. Abd-al-Wahid Ulwani. (J). 1993. pap. write for info. (*1-57547-186-8*) Dar Al-Fikr.

Mudhakkarat al-'Amm Sabur, Vol. 3. Abd-al-Wahid Ulwani. (J). 1993. pap. write for info. (*1-57547-187-6*) Dar Al-Fikr.

Mudhakkarat al-'Amm Sabur, Vol. 4. Abd-al-Wahid Ulwani. (J). 1993. pap. write for info. (*1-57547-188-4*) Dar Al-Fikr.

Mudhakkarat al-'Amm Sabur, Vol. 5. Abd-al-Wahid Ulwani. (J). 1993. pap. write for info. (*1-57547-189-2*) Dar Al-Fikr.

Mudhakkarat al-'Amm Sabur, Vol. 6. Abd-al-Wahid Ulwani. (J). 1993. pap. write for info. (*1-57547-190-6*) Dar Al-Fikr.

Mudhakkarat al-'Amm Sabur, Vol. 7. Abd-al-Wahid Ulwani. (J). 1993. pap. write for info. (*1-57547-191-4*) Dar Al-Fikr.

Mudhakkarat al-'Amm Sabur, Vol. 8. Abd-al-Wahid Ulwani. (J). 1993. pap. write for info. (*1-57547-192-2*) Dar Al-Fikr.

Mudhakkarat al-'Amm Sabur, Vol. 9. Abd-al-Wahid Ulwani. (J). 1993. pap. write for info. (*1-57547-193-0*) Dar Al-Fikr.

Mudhakkarat al-'Amm Sabur, Vol. 10. Abd-al-Wahid Ulwani. (J). 1993. pap. write for info. (*1-57547-194-9*) Dar Al-Fikr.

Mudhakkarat al-'Amm Sabur, Vol. 11. Abd-al-Wahid Ulwani. (J). 1993. pap. write for info. (*1-57547-195-7*) Dar Al-Fikr.

Mudhakkarat al-'Amm Sabur, Vol. 12. Abd-al-Wahid Ulwani. (J). 1993. pap. write for info. (*1-57547-196-5*) Dar Al-Fikr.

Mudhakkarat Shahid lil-Qarn. Malik Bin-Nabi. (Mushkilat al-Hadarah Ser.). 456p. 1984. pap. 9.95 (*1-57547-034-9*) Dar Al-Fikr.

Mudhakkirat Dinar. 2nd ed. Dahesh. (ARA & ENG., Illus.). 462p. 1986. 30.00 (*0-935359-01-X*) Daheshist.

Mudhakkirat Yasu' Al-Nasiry Al-Juz' Al-Awwal see Memoirs of Jesus of Nazareth

Mudhakkirati Fi Sijn al-Nisa see Memoirs from the Women's Prison

Mudhole Mystery. Beverly Lewis. LC 96-45853. (Cul-de-Sac Kids Ser.). (Illus.). 80p. (J). (gr. 2-5). 1997. pap. 3.99 (*1-55661-910-3*) Bethany Hse.

Mudlark. Theodore Bonnet. 24.95 (*0-88411-063-X*) Amereon Ltd.

Mudlark. Sheila Simonson. 240p. 1993. 18.95 (*0-685-65328-5*) St Martin.

Mudluscious: Stories & Activities Featuring Food for Preschool Children. Jan Irving & Robin Currie. LC 85-23954. xix, 259p. 1986. pap. text 24.00 (*0-87287-517-2*) Libs Unl.

Mudnoz Marbin Vs. the Bishops: An Approach to Church & State. Marbia M. Alfonso. LC 98-196013. xii, 210p. 1998. write for info. (*1-881713-41-5*) Pubns Intl Ltd.

Mudpack & Me. Joan Thompson. Ed. by Patricia MacDonald. 160p. (Orig.). (J). (gr. 3-6). 1993. per. 3.50 (*0-671-72862-8*, Minstrel Bks) PB.

Mudpie Olympics & Ninety-Nine Other Nonedible Games. Compiled by Debra Ball-Kilbourne. LC 93-37816. 112p. (Orig.). 1994. pap. 13.95 (*0-687-78095-0*) Abingdon.

Mudpies Activity Book: Recipes for Invention. Nancy Blakey. LC 93-26779. (Illus.). 144p. (J). (ps-7). 1994. pap. 8.95 (*1-883672-19-8*) Tricycle Pr.

Mudpies & Building Blocks: Homeschooling Young Children. Ann Lahrson-Fisher. 250p. 1999. pap. write for info. (*0-9640813-4-2*) Nettlepatch Pr.

Mudpies Book of Boredom Busters. Nancy Blakey. LC 99-17791. (Illus.). 120p. (J). (ps-7). 1999. pap. 8.95 (*1-883672-86-4*) Tricycle Pr.

Mudpies to Magnets: A Preschool Science Curriculum. Robert E. Rockwell et al. (Illus.). 156p. (J). (ps-1). 1987. pap. 14.95 (*0-87659-112-8*) Gryphon Hse.

Mudra: A Study of Symbolic Gestures in Japanese Buddhist Sculpture. E. Dale Saunders. LC 84-42937. (Bollingen Ser.: Vol. 58). (Illus.). 320p. 1960. pap. text 21.95 (*0-691-01866-9*, Pub. by Princeton U Pr) Cal Prin Full Svc.

Mudraraksasa. Visakhadatta. Ed. by Alfred Hillebrandt. vi, 226p. 1984. reprint ed. 37.70 (*3-487-07430-3*) G Olms Pubs.

***Mudras: Yoga in Your Hands.** Gertrud Hirschi. LC 99-87141. (Illus.). 240p. 2000. pap. 14.95 (*1-57863-139-4*) Weiser.

Mudrooroo-Muller Project: A Theatrical Casebook. Ed. by Gerhard Fischer. (Illus.). 200p. 1993. pap. 26.95 (*0-86840-237-0*, Pub. by New South Wales Univ Pr) Intl Spec Bk.

Mudros to Lausanne: Britain's Frontier in West Asia, 1918-1923, Vol. 3. Briton C. Busch. LC 76-21641. 430p. (C). 1976. text 24.50 (*0-87395-265-0*) State U NY Pr.

***Muds & Mudstones: Physical & Fluid-Flow Properties.** Ed. by A. C. Aplin et al. (Special Publication Ser.: No. 158). 200p. 1999. 108.00 (*1-86239-044-4*, Pub. by Geol Soc Pub Hse) AAPG.

Mudslides. Zachary Inseth. LC 97-43374. (J). 1998. lib. bdg. 22.79 (*1-56766-488-1*) Childs World.

Mudsock Scrapbook: A Pictorial Perspective of Fishers, Indiana the Early Years. Larry A. Reynolds. LC 93-80648. 200p. 1993. 49.95 (*0-9639445-0-9*) Hoosier Cider.

Mudworks: Creative Clay, Dough, & Modeling Experiences. MaryAnn F. Kohl. LC 88-92897. (Bright Ideas for Learning Ser.: Vol. 2). (Illus.). 152p. (Orig.). (J). (ps-6). 1989. pap. 14.95 (*0-935607-02-1*) Bright Ring.

Mueller State Park Elevenmile Canyon. Bob D'Antonio. (Classic Rock Climbs Ser.: No. 3). (Illus.). 60p. (Orig.). 1996. pap. 9.95 (*1-57540-031-6*) Falcon Pub Inc.

Mueller's Official Puppy Owner Manual. Scott Mueller. (Orig.). pap. text 4.95 (*0-9637183-0-4*) Bridgept Pub.

Muelos: A Stone Age Superstition about Sexuality. Weston La Barre. LC 84-14232. 168p. 1984. text 52.50 (*0-231-05960-4*) Col U Pr.

***Muenscher's Keys to Woody Plants: An Expanded Guide to Native & Cultivated Species.** rev. ed. Edward A. Cope. (Illus.). 2001. 50.00 (*0-8014-3852-7*, Comstock Pub); pap. 22.95 (*0-8014-8702-1*, Comstock Pub) Cornell U Pr.

Muenzpraegung der Lakedaimonier. Susanne Grunauer-Von Hoerschelmann. (Antike Muenzen und Geschnittene Steine Ser.: Vol. 7). (Illus.). (C). 1978. 138.50 (*3-11-007222-X*) De Gruyter.

Muerta En El Barrio. Kadir. Ed. by Alfonso Sastre et al. (SPA.). 235p. (C). 1972. pap. text 25.50 (*0-15-564750-4*) Harcourt Coll Pubs.

***Muerte! Death in Mexican Popular Culture.** Harvey Stafford. Ed. by Adam Parfrey. (Illus.). 208p. 2000. pap. 24.95 (*0-922915-59-8*, Pub. by Feral Hse) Publishers Group.

Muerte a Filo de Obsidiana (Death by the Edge of Obsidian Stone) Eduardo M. Moctezuma. (SPA.). 158p. 1996. pap. 9.99 (*968-16-4991-5*, Pub. by Fondo) Continental Bk.

Muerte Anduvo Por el Guasio. rev. ed. Luis Hernandez Aquino. (UPREX, Ficcion Ser.: No. 1). 172p. (C). 1976. pap. 1.50 (*0-8477-0001-1*) U of PR Pr.

Muerte Arrebatada see Death on the Run

Muerte de Artemio Cruz. Carlos Fuentes.Tr. of Death of Artemio Cruz. (SPA.). pap. 14.95 (*968-16-0973-5*, Pub. by Fondo) Continental Bk.

Muerte de Artemio Cruz. Carlos Fuentes.Tr. of Death of Artemio Cruz. (SPA.). 1989. 9.95 (*0-8288-2565-3*) Fr & Eur.

Muerte de Artemio Cruz. Carlos Fuentes.Tr. of Death of Artemio Cruz. (SPA.). 272p. 1996. pap. 13.95 (*0-14-025582-6*, Viking) Viking Penguin.

Muerte de Artemio Cruz: Secreto Generativo. Santiago Tejerina-Canal. LC 86-63039. (SPA.). 166p. 1987. pap. 30.00 (*0-89295-042-0*) Society Sp & Sp-Am.

Muerte de Artemio Cruz (The Death of Artemio Cruz) Carlos Fuentes. (SPA.). 317p. 1962. pap. 9.99 (*968-16-0972-7*, Pub. by Fondo) Continental Bk.

Muerte de un Escribiente. (SPA.). 214p. 1999. pap. 4.95 (*0-9667602-0-4*, Graphicart) E Morales.

Muerte del Estratega (Death of a Strategist) 2nd ed. Alvao Mutis. (SPA.). 210p. 1995. reprint ed. 18.99 (*968-16-2827-6*, Pub. by Fondo) Continental Bk.

Muerte en el Barrio. Sastre. (SPA.). 117p. (C). 1972. pap. text. write for info. (*0-318-69173-6*) Harcourt Coll Pubs.

Muerte en el Occidente del Mexico Prehispanico. Maria T. Cabrero. 190p. 1995. pap. 23.00 (*968-36-4286-1*, UN41) UPLAAP.

Muerte sin fin see Death Without End

Muerte Sin Fin. Jose Gorostiza. (Fondo 2000 Ser.). (SPA.). pap. 2.99 (*968-16-5050-6*, Pub. by Fondo) Continental Bk.

Muerte Tiene Permiso (Death Has Permission) Edmundo Valades. (SPA.). 136p. 1992. reprint ed. pap. 6.99 (*968-16-0329-X*, Pub. by Fondo) Continental Bk.

Muerte y Ostras Sorpresas, Level 4. Adapted by Mario Benedetti. (Leer en Espanol Ser.). (SPA.). (C). 1998. pap. 6.95 (*84-294-3484-4*) Santillana.

***Muerte y Otras Sorpresas.** Mario Benedetti. (SPA.). 2000. pap. 9.95 (*968-19-0313-7*) Aguilar.

Muertes de Perro. Francisco Ayala. 1995. pap. 14.95 (*0-679-76656-1*) Random.

Muertes de Perro: El Jondo De Vaso. Francisco Ayala. (Nueva Austral Ser.: No. 212). (SPA.). 1991. pap. text 24.95 (*84-239-7212-7*) Elliots Bks.

Museo de la Novela Eterna. Macedonio Fernandez. (Coleccion Archivos de Ediciones Criticas). (SPA.). 30.99 (*84-88344-02-3*, Pub. by Fondo) Continental Bk.

Mufaro's Beautiful Daughters see Bellas Hijas de Mufaro: An African Tale

Mufaro's Beautiful Daughters: An African Tale. John L. Steptoe. LC 84-7158. (Illus.). 32p. (J). (gr. k-3). 1987. lib. bdg. 15.93 (*0-688-04046-2*) Lothrop.

Mufaro's Beautiful Daughters: An African Tale. John L. Steptoe. Tr. by Clarita Kohen. LC 84-7158. (Illus.). 32p. (J). (gr. k-3). 1987. 16.00 (*0-688-04045-4*) Lothrop.

Mufaro's Beautiful Daughters Big Book. John L. Steptoe. 32p. (J). (ps up). 1993. pap. 18.95 (*0-688-12935-8*, Wm Morrow) Morrow Avon.

Muffin, a Palm Beach Pooch. Emilie Peters. (Muffin Ser.: No. 1). 30p. (J). (gr. 3-8). 1992. pap. write for info. (*0-9635568-0-0*) Muffin Pubns.

Muffin & the Lesson of Kokua. Carmen Geshell. 1995. 10.95 (*0-89610-289-0*) Island Heritage.

Muffin Baker's Guide. rev. ed. Bruce Koffler. (Illus.). 138p. 1993. pap. 8.95 (*1-895565-23-5*) Firefly Bks Ltd.

Muffin Child. Stephen Menick. LC 97-51817. 208p. (J). (gr. 5-9). 1998. 17.99 (*0-399-23303-2*, Philomel) Peng Put Young Read.

Muffin Huff 'n Puff Funbook. Susan T. Porcaro. 1997. pap. text 1.50 (*1-890570-04-4*) Huckleberry CT.

Muffin Huff 'n Puff Story: A Mommy & Daddy Book. Noreen Wise. LC 96-94623. (Food & Fun for the Mind, Body, & Soul Ser.: Vol. 1). (Illus.). 32p. (Orig.). (J). (gr. k-3). 1996. pap. 8.95 (*0-9653035-5-1*) Huckleberry CT.

Muffin Lady: Muffins, Cupcakes, & Quickbreads for the Happy Soul. Linda Fisher. LC 97-28736. 224p. 1997. 20.00 (*0-06-039246-0*, ReganBks) HarperTrade.

Muffin Madness: Quick & Healthy Recipes for Today's Busy Family. Marilyn Taylor. LC 96-72268. (Illus.). 176p. (Orig.). 1997. pap. 12.95 (*0-9649401-0-8*) Rhodes & Easton.

Muffin Magic . . . And More: Baking Secrets Your Mother Never Told You. Kathleen Mayes. LC 93-25105. (Illus.). 208p. (Orig.). 1993. 12.95 (*0-88007-201-6*) Woodbridge Pr.

Muffin Mania. Kathy Prange. 1984. spiral bd. 7.95 (*0-89709-187-6*) Liberty Pub.

Muffin Muncher. Stephen Cosgrove. (Serendipity Ser.). 1986. 9.15 (*0-606-02419-0*, Pub. by Turtleback) Demco.

Muffin Pigdoom & the Keeper. Paul Warren. (Adventures of Muffin Pigdoom Ser.). (J). (ps-2). 1996. pap. text 7.99 (*0-7497-2961-9*) London Brdge.

Muffin Pigdoom & the Urgs. Paul Warren. (Adventures of Muffin Pigdoom Ser.). (J). (ps-2). 1996. pap. 7.99 (*0-7497-2962-7*) London Brdge.

Muffin Sampler. Jan Siegrist. (Illus.). 48p. (Orig.). 1989. pap. 3.95 (*0-933050-67-4*) New Eng Pr VT.

***Muffinilogy et. Cetera.** Esther M. Allen. (Illus.). 72p. 1999. pap. text 6.95 (*0-932855-31-8*) Winner Enter.

Muffins. Leon Rooke. 24p. 1995. pap. write for info. (*0-88984-167-5*) Porcup Quill.

Muffins: Applesauce & the Squirrel. Uthman Hutchinson. 56p. (J). 1996. pap. 6.95 (*0-614-21028-3*, 1518) Kazi Pubns.

Muffins: Applesauce & the Squirrel. Uthman Hutchinson. LC 95-80037. (Children Stories Project Ser.). (Illus.). 56p. (J). (gr. 3 up). 1995. pap. 6.95 (*0-915957-41-8*) amana pubns.

***Muffins: Over 300 Recipes & Variations to Accompany Any Meal.** Francesca DiPaolo. 224p. 2000. pap. 12.95 (*1-58062-252-6*) Adams Media.

***Muffins: Poems from Hollywood.** Mark Dunster. 11p. 2000. pap. 5.00 (*0-89642-989-X*) Linden Pubs.

Muffins: Sixty Sweet & Savory Recipes from Old Favorites to New. Elizabeth Alston. 96p. 1984. 11.00 (*0-517-55587-5*) C Potter.

Muffins A to Z. Marie Simmons. Ed. by Rux Martin. (A to Z Cookbook Ser.). (Illus.). 96p. 1995. 14.95 (*1-881527-91-3*, Chapters Bks) HM.

Muffins & Cupcakes. Lawrence M. Rosenberg. Ed. by Marian Levine. (Collector's Ser.: Vol. 18). 64p. (Orig.). 1986. pap., per. 3.95 (*0-942320-13-1*) Am Cooking.

***Muffins & More.** Patricia F. Thonney. (Illus.). 68p. 1999. pap. 7.99 (*1-57753-264-3*) Corn Coop Ext.

Muffins & Other Quick Breads. Cole Group Editors Staff. (Cole's Cooking Companion Ser.). (Illus.). 96p. (Orig.). 1995. pap. 7.95 (*1-56426-811-X*) Cole Group.

Muffins & Quick Breads. (Popular Brands Cookbooks Ser.). (Illus.). 24p. 1995. pap. write for info. (*1-56144-671-8*) Modern Pub NYC.

Muffins & Quick Breads. John P. Carroll. Ed. by Laurie Wertz. LC 92-27837. (Williams-Sonoma Kitchen Library). (Illus.). 108p. 1993. lib. bdg. write for info. (*0-7835-0234-6*) Time-Life.

Muffins & Quick Breads. John P. Carroll. Ed. by Laurie Wertz. LC 92-27837. (Williams-Sonoma Kitchen Library). (Illus.). 108p. (J). (gr. 11). 1999. 18.95 (*0-7835-0233-8*) Time-Life.

Muffin's Book, Bk. I. Patricia Homes. (Illus.). 80p. 1990. pap. 7.95 (*0-9618379-2-6*) Parkside Pubns.

Muffin's Book, Bk. II. Patricia Homes. (Illus.). 40p. (J). 1992. pap. 8.95 (*0-9618379-6-9*) Parkside Pubns.

Muffin's Makapu'u Adventure. Carmen Geshell. LC 98-96366. (Illus.). 40p. (J). (gr. k-6). 1998. 10.95 (*0-9665686-0-5*) Muffin Co.

Muffins, Nut Breads & More. rev. ed. Barbara Kyte & Katherine Greenberg. LC 97-107172. (Illus.). 176p. 1996. pap. 8.95 (*1-55867-147-1*, Nitty Gritty Ckbks) Bristol Pub Ent CA.

Muffins, Scones & Coffeecakes. (Mini Cook Bks.). 148p. pap. 1.95 (*3-8290-0377-3*, 770239) Konemann.

Muffins, Tea Breads & Gems. Sherri Eldridge. (Illus.). 32p. 1998. pap. 2.95 (*1-886862-27-3*, MN MUF, Coastal New England Pubns) Harv Hill ME.

Muffled Cries: The Writer & Literature in Authoritarian Brazil, 1964-1985. Nancy T. Baden. LC 99-15142. 272p. 1999. 55.00 (*0-7618-1420-5*); pap. 34.50 (*0-7618-1421-3*) U Pr of Amer.

Muffled Drums & Mustard Spoons: Cecil County, Maryland, 1860-1865. Jerre Garrett. LC 96-42018. 295p. 1997. 40.00 (*1-57249-043-8*) White Mane Pub.

Muffled Echoes: Oliver North & the Politics of Public Opinion. Amy Fried. LC 96-52988. (Power, Conflict & Democracy Ser.). 336p. 1997. pap. 20.50 (*0-231-10821-4*); lib. bdg. 52.00 (*0-231-10820-6*) Col U Pr.

***Muffler Men.** Timothy Corrigan Correll & Patrick Arthur Polk. LC 00-27338. (Folk Art & Artists Ser.). (Illus.). 128p. 2000. pap. 18.00 (*1-57806-299-3*); lib. bdg. 38.00 (*1-57806-298-5*) U Pr of Miss.

Muffler Shop Manual: How to Start, Manage & Operate a Successful Muffler Service. Ray Teagarden. LC 86-81814. (Illus.). 352p. (Orig.). 1986. pap. 24.95 (*0-938517-25-2*) Auto Pub.

***Muffles in New York.** Anne M. Ronan. (Illus.). 32p. (J). (ps-4). 1999. pap. 8.00 (*1-930248-00-8*) Polka Dot Pr.

Muffs Peer Identification Instrument for Grades 2-5. James Delisle et al. 1984. pap., student ed. 15.00 (*0-89824-124-3*) Trillium Pr.

Muffy & Fluffy: The Kittens Who Didn't Agree. Janet Craig. 1999. pap. text 2.50 (*0-8167-3109-8*); pap. text 16.95 (*0-8167-6282-1*) Troll Communs.

Muffy Vanderbear ID & Price Guide. Ann Gelbach. LC 97-185023. (Illus.). 112p. (Orig.). 1997. pap. 19.95 (*0-87588-477-6*, 5298) Hobby Hse.

***Muffy's Scrapbook.** Muffy Vanderbear & North American Bear Company Inc. Staff. LC 99-57279. (Illus.). 48p. (J). 2000. 16.95 (*0-8118-2763-1*) Chronicle Bks.

Muffy's Secret Admirer. Marc Tolon Brown. LC 99-35312. (Arthur Chapter Book Ser.: No. 17). (Illus.). 64p. (J). (gr. 2-4). 1999. pap. 3.95 (*0-316-12230-0*) Little.

Muffy's Secret Admirer. Marc Tolon Brown. LC 99-35312. (Arthur Chapter Book Ser.: No. 17). (Illus.). 64p. (J). (gr. 3-6). 1999. 12.95 (*0-316-12017-0*) Little.

Mufti of Jerusalem. rev. ed. Philip Mattar. 176p. 1991. pap. text 18.50 (*0-231-06463-2*) Col U Pr.

Mufti of Jerusalem: Al-Hajj Amin Al-Husayni & the Palestinian National Movement. rev. ed. Philip Mattar. (Illus.). 191p. (C). 1998. pap. text 20.00 (*0-7881-5502-4*) DIANE Pub.

Mug Shots: A Police Artist's Guide to Remembering Faces. Douglas P. Hinkle. (Illus.). 128p. 1990. pap. 18.00 (*0-87364-572-3*) Paladin Pr.

Mug Shots: Arresting Photos & Felonious Facts for Hundreds of Stars Behind Bars. Cader Books Staff. LC 96-83356. 144p. (Orig.). 1996. pap. 7.95 (*0-8362-1503-6*, Cader Bks) Andrews & McMeel.

Mugged by Mr. Badwrench. Sal Fariello & Vera Fariello. LC 88-90930. (Illus.). 221p. (Orig.). 1988. pap. 9.95 (*0-929574-00-1*) SFT Pub.

Mugger. Ed McBain, pseud. 192p. 1996. mass mkt. 5.99 (*0-446-60143-8*, Pub. by Warner Bks) Little.

Mugger. Ed McBain, pseud. (Eighty-Seventh Precinct Novel Ser.). 160p. 1986. mass mkt. 3.50 (*0-380-70081-6*, Avon Bks) Morrow Avon.

Muggie Maggie. Beverly Cleary. (SPA., Illus.). (gr. 5 up). 1996. pap. text 7.50 (*84-279-3463-7*) Lectorum Pubns.

Muggie Maggie. Beverly Cleary. LC 89-38959. (Illus.). 80p. (J). (gr. 4-7). 1990. 16.00 (*0-688-08553-9*, Wm Morrow) Morrow Avon.

Muggie Maggie. Beverly Cleary. (J). 1990. 9.70 (*0-606-04980-0*, Pub. by Turtleback) Demco.

Muggie Maggie. Beverly Cleary. (Illus.). 96p. (J). (gr. 2-7). 1990. reprint ed. mass mkt. 4.95 (*0-380-71087-0*, Wm Morrow) Morrow Avon.

Muggie Maggie: A Study Guide. Elizabeth Spencer & J. Friedland. Ed. by R. Kessler. (Novel-Ties Ser.). (J). (gr. 2-4). 1995. pap. text, student ed. 15.95 (*1-56982-276-X*) Lrn Links.

Mugging of Black America. rev. ed. Earl O. Hutchinson. (Illus.). 120p. 1990. pap. 8.95 (*0-913543-21-7*) African Am Imag.

Muggsbottom & Me: A Study in Anglo-Arkansas Relations. Patrick Adcock. LC 93-70993. 268p. 1993. 18.00 (*1-880909-10-3*) Baskerville.

Muggsy & Mopsy. Charles R. Hayes. 46p. (Orig.). 1982. pap. text. write for info. (*0-9621710-2-6*) C R Hayes.

Muggsy Bogues: Tall on Talent. Howard Reiser. LC 95-33637. (Sports Stars Ser.). (Illus.). 48p. (J). (gr. 2-8). 1996. lib. bdg. 19.00 (*0-516-04396-X*) Childrens.

***Muggsy Makes an Assist.** Tess E. Kindig. LC 99-46932. (Slam Dunk Ser.: Vol. 3). (Illus.). 96p. (J). (gr. 1-4). 2000. 4.99 (*0-570-07018-X*) Concordia.

***Muggsy Makes an Assist, 1, 4.** Tess Eileen Kindig. LC 99-46932. Vol. 4. 96p. (J). (gr. 1-4). 1999. pap. text 4.99 (*0-570-07019-8*) Concordia.

Mughal Administration. M. P. Srivastava. (C). 1995. 34.00 (*81-85613-97-4*, Pub. by Chugh Pubns) S Asia.

Mughal Administration in Golconda. J. F. Richards. (Illus.). 1975. 55.00 (*0-19-821561-4*) OUP.

Mughal & Rajput Painting. Milo C. Beach. (New Cambridge History of India Ser.: I: 3). (Illus.). 285p. (C). 1992. text 100.00 (*0-521-40027-9*) Cambridge U Pr.

Mughal Architecture. Ebba Koch et al. (Illus.). 160p. (Orig.). 1991. pap. 25.95 (*3-7913-1070-4*, Pub. by Prestel) te Neues.

***Mughal Art & Imperial Ideology.** Ebba Koch. (Illus.). 384p. 2000. text 45.00 (*0-19-564821-8*) OUP.

Mughal Documents, 1628-1659, Vol. 2. Sai A. Tirmizi. 1995. 28.00 (*81-7304-122-9*, Pub. by Manohar) S Asia.

Mughal Economy. Jagdish N. Sarhar. (C). 1987. 35.00 (*81-85109-47-8*, Pub. by Naya Prokash) S Asia.

Mughal Empire. John F. Richards. (New Cambridge History of India Ser.: I: 5). (Illus.). 338p. (C). 1993. text 59.95 (*0-521-25119-2*) Cambridge U Pr.

Mughal Empire. John F. Richards. (New Cambridge History of India Ser.: Vol. I:5). (Illus.). 337p. 1996. pap. text 22.95 (*0-521-56603-7*) Cambridge U Pr.

Mughal Empire & Its Decline: An Interpretation of the Sources of Social Power. Andrea Hintze. LC 96-52801. 336p. 1997. 83.95 (*0-86078-611-0*, DS461.H5, Pub. by Variorum) Ashgate Pub Co.

Mughal Gardens: Sources, Places, Representations, & Prospects. Ed. by James L. Wescoat, Jr. & Joachim Wolschke-Bulmahn. LC 94-42690. (Colloquium on the History of Landscape Architecture Ser.: No. 16). 1996. 60.00 (*0-88402-235-8*, Dumbarton Rsch Lib) Dumbarton Oaks.

Mughal Glory: Stories of Love, Loyalty, Honour, Courage... Muni Lal. 127p. 1989. text 15.95 (*81-220-0076-2*, Pub. by Konark Pubs Pvt Ltd) Advent Bks Div.

Mughal Harem. K. S. Lal. (C). 1988. 72.00 (*81-85179-03-4*, Pub. by Aditya Prakashan) S Asia.

Mughal India: Encyclopaedic Survey of Islamic Culture. Mohamed Taher. 1998. 88.00 (*81-7488-555-2*) Anmol.

Mughal India: Studies in Polity, Ideas, Society & Culture. M. Athar Ali. (Illus.). 392p. 1999. text 35.00 (*0-19-564860-9*) OUP.

Mughal India & Central Asia. Richard C. Foltz. LC 99-196358. 220p. 1999. text 19.95 (*0-19-577782-4*) OUP.

Mughal Masters: Further Studies. Ed. by Asok Kumar et al. LC 98-902736. (Illus.). 148p. 1998. 94.00 (*81-85026-40-8*, Pub. by Marg Publns) S Asia.

Mughal Painters & Their Work: A Biographical Survey & Comprehensive Catalogue. Som P. Verman. (Illus.). 454p. 1995. text 59.00 (*0-19-562316-9*) OUP.

Mughal Paintings: The School of Jahangir. Stanley C. Clarke. Orig. Title: Indian Drawings. (Illus.). 1983. 45.00 (*0-318-36344-5*) Asia Bk Corp.

Mughal Paintings, Being Thirty Paintings of the School of Jahangir & Four Panels of Calligraphy. Stanley C. Clarke. (Illus.). 60p. 1983. text 32.00 (*0-89563-641-7*) Coronet Bks.

Mughal Religious Policies: Rajputs & the Deccan. Satish Chandra. (C). 1994. 22.00 (*0-7069-8392-0*, Pub. by Vikas) S Asia.

An Asterisk (*) at the beginning of an entry indicates that the title is appearing for the first time.

Mughal Rule in India. Stephen M. Edwardes & Herbert L. Garrett. LC 75-41084. reprint ed. 41.50 (*0-404-14537-X*) AMS Pr.

Mughal Sculpture: Study of Stone Sculptures of Birds, Beasts, Mythical Animals, Human Beings & Deities in Mughal Architecture. R. Nath. LC 97-914268. (Illus.). xx, 218p. 1997. 67.00 (*81-7024-870-1*, Pub. by APH Pubng) Nataraj Bks.

Mughal State, 1526-1750. Ed. by Muzaffar Alam & Sanjay Subrahmanyam. LC 98-909289. (Oxford in India Readings Ser.). 548p. 1998. text 35.00 (*0-19-563905-7*) OUP.

Mughal Weapons in the Babur Nama. G. N. Pant. (C). 1989. 125.00 (*0-8364-2473-5*, Pub. by Agam) S Asia.

Mughals, Maharajas & the Mahatma. K. R. N. Swamy. LC 97-914260. 265 p. 1997. 15.99 (*81-7223-280-2*) HarpC.

Mug's Game: A History of Gaming & Betting in Australia. John O'Hara. 288p. 27.95 (*0-86840-298-2*, Pub. by New South Wales Univ Pr); pap. 27.95 (*0-614-13107-3*, Pub. by New South Wales Univ Pr) Intl Spec Bk.

Mugshots One: The Case of the Pacific Clipper. Dave Arneson. Ed. by Rick Loomis. (Illus.). 80p. 1991. pap. 8.95 (*0-940244-41-1*) Flying Buffalo.

Mugshots Two: Taking Care of Business. Debora Wykle & Michael A. Stackpole. Ed. by Rick Loomis & James Walker. (Illus.). 80p. (Orig.). 1992. pap. 9.95 (*0-940244-42-X*) Flying Buffalo.

Mugwe, a Failing Prophet: A Study of a Religious & Public Dignitary of the Meru of Kenya. Bernardo Bernardi. LC 59-3468. 227p. reprint ed. pap. 70.40 (*0-608-13443-0*, 202278500029) Bks Demand.

Mugworts in May: A Folklore of Herbs. Linda O. Rago. (Illus.). 121p. (Orig.). 1995. pap. 14.95 (*0-9646197-0-9*) Quarrier Pr.

Mugwumps: Public Moralists of the Gilded Age. David M. Tucker. LC 98-20718. 152p. 1998. 27.50 (*0-8262-1187-9*) U of Mo Pr.

Mugwumps, Morals, & Politics, 1884-1920. Ed. by Gerald W. McFarland. LC 74-21242. 292p. 1975. 32.50 (*0-87023-175-8*) U of Mass Pr.

Muhammad. Driss Chraibi. Tr. by Nadia Benabid. LC 98-5353. (Three Continents Ser.). 90p. 1998. lib. bdg. 22.00 (*0-89410-858-1*) L Rienner.

Muhammad. Michael Cook. (Past Masters Ser.). (Illus.). 96p. 1983. pap. text 9.95 (*0-19-287605-8*) OUP.

Muhammad. Maxine Rodinson. 1996. pap. 17.95 (*0-14-024964-8*, Pub. by Pnguin Bks Ltd) Trafalgar.

Muhammad: A Biography of the Prophet. Karen Armstrong. 290p. 1996. 14.95 (*0-614-21088-7*, 806) Kazi Pubns.

Muhammad: A Biography of the Prophet. rev. ed. Karen Armstrong. LC 91-55407. 288p. 1993. pap. 14.00 (*0-06-250886-5*, Pub. by Harper SF) HarpC.

***Muhammad: A Life & a Guide.** F. E. Peters. 252p. (C). 2000. pap. text 19.95 (*1-889119-01-6*) Seven Bridges.

Muhammad: A Prophecy Fulfilled. H. Abdul Al-Dahir. 111p. 1996. pap. 8.00 (*0-614-21674-5*, 807) Kazi Pubns.

Muhammad: A Short Biography. Martin Forward. 184p. 1997. pap. 13.95 (*1-85168-131-0*, Pub. by Onewrld Pubns) Penguin Putnam.

Muhammad: An Islamic Perspective. Ghulam Malik. LC 96-33730. 194p. 1996. lib. bdg. 36.50 (*0-7618-0307-6*) U Pr of Amer.

Muhammad: Encyclopedia of Seerah, Vols. 1-7. Afzalur Rahman. 1000p. 1996. 55.00 (*0-614-21091-7*, 815) Kazi Pubns.

Muhammad: His Life Based on the Earliest Sources. Martin Lings. 368p. 1987. pap. 16.95 (*0-89281-170-6*) Inner Tradit.

Muhammad: His Life Based on the Earliest Sources. Martin Lings. 361p. 1995. reprint ed. write for info. (*0-946621-25-X*, Pub. by Islamic Texts) Intl Spec Bk.

Muhammad: Man & Prophet. M. A. Salahi. LC 95-13547. 768p. 1995. pap. 39.99 (*1-85230-703-X*, Pub. by Element MA) Penguin Putnam.

Muhammad: Man of God. Seyyed Hossein Nasr. 96p. 1994. pap. 8.50 (*1-56744-501-2*) Kazi Pubns.

Muhammad: Prophet & Statesman. William M. Watt. 250p. 1974. pap. text 13.95 (*0-19-881078-4*) OUP.

Muhammad: The Seal. Amina I. Ali. Ed. by J. C. Cinquino. (Prophets' Stories for Children from the Holy Qur'an Ser.: No. 21). (Illus.). 28p. (Orig.). (J). (gr. 4-6). 1996. write for info. (*1-881963-44-6*); pap. 2.50 (*1-881963-45-4*) Al-Saadawi Pubns.

Muhammad - Man & Prophet: A Complete Study of the Life of the Prophet of Islam. Adil Salahi. 1998. pap. 24.95 (*1-86204-290-X*, Pub. by Element MA) Penguin Putnam.

Muhammad Ali. (Little Bks.). (Illus.). 80p. 1998. 4.95 (*0-8362-7159-9*) Andrews & McMeel.

***Muhammad Ali.** Alan Goldstein. (Illus.). 176p. 2000. 29.95 (*1-85868-951-1*, Pub. by Carlton Bks Ltd) Natl Bk Netwk.

***Muhammad Ali.** Clay Latimer. LC 99-47617. (J). 2000. lib. bdg. write for info. (*1-56766-723-6*) Childs World.

Muhammad Ali. Jon E. Lewis. LC 97-26031. (Life & Times of...Ser.). (Illus.). 48p. (YA). (gr. 5 up). 1999. lib. bdg. 15.95 (*0-7910-4641-9*) Chelsea Hse.

Muhammad Ali. Randy Roberts. 1999. pap. write for info. (*0-14-010063-6*, Viking) Viking Penguin.

Muhammad Ali. Kenneth Rudeen. LC 76-12093. (Crowell Biography Ser.). (Illus.). 40p. (J). (gr. 1-4). 1976. lib. bdg. 12.89 (*0-690-01128-8*) HarpC Child Bks.

Muhammad Ali: A View from the Corner. Ferdie Pacheco. (Illus.). 256p. 1992. 21.95 (*1-55972-100-6*, Birch Ln Pr) Carol Pub Group.

Muhammad Ali: Champion. Arlene Schulman. LC 94-47396. (Newsmakers Ser.). (Illus.). 128p. (YA). (gr. 5 up). 1996. lib. bdg. 23.93 (*0-8225-4925-5*) Lerner Pub.

***Muhammad Ali: Champion.** Arlene Schulman. (A&E Biography Ser.). (Illus.). 128p. (YA). (gr. 4-7). 2000. pap. 7.95 (*0-8225-9693-8*, Lerner Publctns) Lerner Pub.

Muhammad Ali: Heavyweight Champion. Jack Rummel. Ed. by Nathan I. Huggins. (Black Americans of Achievement Ser.). (Illus.). 124p. (Orig.). (YA). (gr. 5 up). 1988. lib. bdg. 19.95 (*1-55546-569-2*) Chelsea Hse.

Muhammad Ali: Heavyweight Champion. Jack Rummel. Ed. by Nathan I. Huggins. (Black Americans of Achievement Ser.). (Illus.). 124p. (Orig.). (YA). (gr. 5 up). 1989. pap. 8.95 (*0-7910-0210-1*) Chelsea Hse.

Muhammad Ali: His Life & Times. Thomas Hauser. (Illus.). 544p. 1992. pap. 15.00 (*0-671-77971-0*, Touchstone) S&S Trade Pap.

***Muhammad Ali: In Fighter's Heaven.** Victor Bockris. (Illus.). 2000. pap. write for info. (*0-8154-1062-X*, Pub. by Cooper Sq) Natl Bk Netwk.

Muhammad Ali: In Perspective. Thomas Hauser. 1996. 50.00 (*0-614-25357-8*); pap. 25.00 (*0-614-20474-7*) HarpC.

Muhammad Ali: Ringside. Alex Haley et al. Ed. by John Miller. 128p. 1999. 29.95 (*0-8212-2626-6*, Pub. by Bulfinch Pr) Little.

***Muhammad Ali: The Bird of a Legend, Miami, 1961-1964.** Debra Schulke. LC 99-31473. 1999. text 27.95 (*0-312-20340-3*) St Martin.

Muhammad Ali: The Fight for Respect. Thomas Conklin. (YA). 1992. pap. 5.70 (*0-395-63556-X*) HM.

Muhammad Ali: The Fight for Respect. Thomas Conklin. (New Directions Ser.). 1991. 11.15 (*0-606-07898-3*) Turtleback.

Muhammad Ali: The Fight for Respect. Tom Conklin. LC 91-25950. (New Directions Ser.). (Illus.). 104p. (YA). (gr. 7 up). 1992. pap. 5.95 (*1-56294-832-6*); lib. bdg. 21.90 (*1-56294-112-7*) Millbrook Pr.

Muhammad Ali: The Greatest. Jim Spence. LC 95-5360. (Great Comeback Champions Ser.). (Illus.). (J). (gr. 2-6). 1995. lib. bdg. 18.60 (*1-57103-005-0*) Rourke Pr.

Muhammad Ali: The Greatest of All Time. Timothy J. Dailey. 224p. 1999. mass mkt. 5.99 (*0-451-19784-4*) NAL.

Muhammad Ali: The People's Champ. Ed. by Elliot J. Gorn. (Sport & Society Ser.). 224p. 1995. 24.95 (*0-252-02188-6*) U of Ill Pr.

Muhammad Ali: The People's Champion. William Epes. (Junior Black Americans of Achievement Ser.). (Illus.). 76p. (J). (gr. 3-6). 1993. lib. bdg. 15.95 (*0-7910-1760-5*) Chelsea Hse.

Muhammad Ali: World Heavyweight Boxing Champion. Christopher J. Riccella. (Black American Ser.). (Illus.). 192p. (YA). 1991. mass mkt. 3.95 (*0-87067-574-5*, Melrose Sq) Holloway.

Muhammad Ali Biography. Walter Dean Myers. 40p. 15.95 (*0-06-029131-1*); pap. 5.95 (*0-06-443718-3*); lib. bdg. 15.89 (*0-06-029132-X*) HarpC.

Muhammad Ali Reader. Ed. by Gerald Early. LC 98-37059. 320p. 1999. pap. 15.95 (*0-688-16620-2*, Wm Morrow) Morrow Avon.

Muhammad Ali Reader. Ed. by Gerald Early. LC 97-36846. (Illus.). 320p. 1998. 26.00 (*0-88001-602-7*) HarpC.

Muhammad Ali, the People's Champ. Elliot J. Gorn. (Sport & Society Ser.). 224p. 1998. 14.95 (*0-252-06721-5*) U of Ill Pr.

Muhammad Ali's Greatest Fight: Cassius Clay vs. the United States of America. Howard Bingham & Max Wallace. LC 99-50269. (Illus.). 272p. 2000. 21.95 (*0-87131-900-4*) M Evans.

Muhammad & Jesus: A Comparison of the Prophets & Their Teachings. William E. Phipps. LC 75-29600. 256p. 1996. 27.50 (*0-8264-0914-8*) Continuum.

***Muhammad & Jesus: A Comparison of the Prophets & Their Teachings.** William E. Phipps. 320p. 1999. pap. 19.95 (*0-8264-1207-6*) Continuum.

Muhammad & the Christian: A Question of Response. Kenneth Cragg. 180p. 1996. pap. 18.00 (*0-614-21675-3*, 808) Kazi Pubns.

Muhammad & the Christian: A Question of Response. Kenneth Cragg. 192p. 1999. pap. 17.95 (*1-85168-179-5*, Pub. by Onewrld Pubns) Penguin Putnam.

Muhammad & the Golden Bough: Reconstructing Arabian Myth. Jaroslav Stetkevych. LC 96-12390. 208p. 1996. 39.95 (*0-253-33208-7*) Ind U Pr.

Muhammad & the Islamic Tradition. Emile Dermenghem. Tr. by Jean M. Watt from FRE. LC 81-47412. (Spiritual Masters Ser.). (Illus.). 192p. 1982. 18.95 (*0-87951-130-3*, Pub. by Overlook Pr) Penguin Putnam.

Muhammad & the Islamic Tradition. Emile Dermenghem. Tr. by Jean M. Watt from FRE. LC 81-47412. (Spiritual Masters Ser.). (Illus.). 192p. 1983. pap. 9.95 (*0-87951-170-2*, Pub. by Overlook Pr) Penguin Putnam.

Muhammad & the Origins of Islam. F. E. Peters. 355p. 1996. pap. 19.95 (*0-614-21161-1*, 809) Kazi Pubns.

Muhammad & the Origins of Islam. F. E. Peters. LC 93-10568. (SUNY Series in Near Eastern Studies). 334p. (C). 1994. pap. text 24.95 (*0-7914-1876-6*) State U NY Pr.

Muhammad & the Quran. Rafiq Zakaria. 444p. 1996. pap. 11.95 (*0-614-21063-1*, 810) Kazi Pubns.

Muhammad & the Rise of Islam: The Creation of Group Identity. Subhash C. Inamdar. 260p. 2000. 40.00 (*1-887841-28-8*) Intl Univs Pr.

Muhammad As a Military Leader. Afzalur Rahman. 1993. pap. 16.50 (*1-56744-146-7*) Kazi Pubns.

Muhammad at Mecca. William M. Watt. 192p. 1996. pap. 19.95 (*0-614-21089-5*, 812) Kazi Pubns.

Muhammad at Medina. William M. Watt. 418p. 1996. pap. 15.95 (*0-614-21090-9*, 813) Kazi Pubns.

Muhammad bin Qasim. Fazl Ahmad. (Heroes of Islam Ser.: Bk. 7). 95p. (Orig.). (YA). (gr. 7-12). 1984. pap. 3.50 (*1-56744-245-5*) Kazi Pubns.

Muhammad, His Life Story Introduced. Ed. by Richard L. Burrill. (gr. 9-12). Date not set. 17.95 (*1-878464-59-0*) Anthro Co.

Muhammad in Europe: A Thousand Years of Western Myth-Making. Minou Reeves & P. J. Stewart. LC 99-22794. 1999. text 34.50 (*0-8147-7533-0*) NYU Pr.

Muhammad in the Bible. Abdul A. Dawud. 263p. (C). 1993. pap. 16.50 (*1-56744-487-3*) Kazi Pubns.

Muhammad in the Mirror of Islam. Muhammad Tabatabai. Tr. by William C. Chittick from PER. 21p. 1979. pap. 2.00 (*0-941722-18-X*) Book Dist Ctr.

Muhammad in the Modern Egyptian Popular Ballad. Kamal Abdel-Malek. LC 95-18832. (Studies in Arabic Literature: Vol. 19). 1995. 93.00 (*90-04-10217-5*) Brill Academic Pubs.

Muhammad, the Last Messenger, Pt. 1. Alia N. Athar. 1990. 7.50 (*0-934905-05-3*) Kazi Pubns.

Muhammad, the Last Messenger: Madinah Period, Pt. 2. Alia N. Athar. 110p. 1991. 5.95 (*0-934905-06-1*) Kazi Pubns.

Muhammad, the Last Prophet, Pt. 1. Alia N. Athar. 1990. pap. 5.50 (*0-934905-03-7*) Kazi Pubns.

Muhammad, the Last Prophet, Pt. 2. Alia N. Athar. 1992. pap. 5.50 (*0-934905-04-5*) Kazi Pubns.

Muhammad, the Last Prophet I Workbook. Alia N. Athar. 32p. (J). (gr. 2-4). 1992. pap., student ed. 3.50 (*1-56744-209-9*) Kazi Pubns.

Muhammad, the Last Prophet II Workbook. Alia N. Athar. 32p. (J). (gr. 3-5). 1992. pap. 3.50 (*1-56744-210-2*) Kazi Pubns.

Muhammad the Prophet. 7th ed. Maulana M. Ali. 208p. (Orig.). 1993. pap. 7.95 (*0-913321-07-9*) Ahmadiyya Anjuman.

Muhammad, the Prophet & Statesman. William M. Watt. 250p. 1996. pap. 10.50 (*0-614-21093-3*, 829) Kazi Pubns.

Muhammad the Prophet of Islam. Fazl Ahmad. (Heroes of Islam Ser.: Bk. I). 125p. (Orig.). (YA). (gr. 7-12). 1984. pap. 3.50 (*1-56744-236-6*) Kazi Pubns.

Muhammad, the Prophet of Islam. Chattapadhyaya. 1981. 1.50 (*1-56744-152-1*) Kazi Pubns.

Muhammad, the Qur'an & Islam. N. A. Newman. LC 96-78495. 442p. 1996. 39.95 (*0-944788-85-8*); pap. 19.95 (*0-944788-86-6*) IBRI.

Muhammadan Architecture in Egypt & Palestine. Martin S. Briggs. LC 74-1280. (Architecture & Decorative Art Ser.). (Illus.). 255p. 1974. reprint ed. lib. bdg. 39.50 (*0-306-70590-7*) Da Capo.

Muhammadan Festivals. G. E. Von Grunebaum. 110p. 1996. 39.95 (*0-614-21517-X*, 833) Kazi Pubns.

Muhammadan Law - An Abridgement According to Its Various Schools. Seymour Vesey-Fitzgerald. xv, 252p. 1999. reprint ed. 80.00 (*1-56169-479-7*) Gaunt.

Muhammadan Mysticism in Sumatra. Raymond L. Archer. LC 77-87487. (Royal Asiatic Society, Malayan Branch. Journal Ser.: Vol. 15). reprint ed. 27.50 (*0-404-16695-4*) AMS Pr.

Muhammadan Revelation. Muhammad R. Rida. Tr. by Yusuf T. DeLorenzo from ARA. 160p. 1996. pap. text 9.95 (*1-881963-55-1*) Al-Saadawi Pubns.

Muhammadanea Edessensis: The Rise of Islam in Eastern Christian Historiography under the Early 'Abbasids. Lawrence I. Conrad. (Studies in Late Antiquity & Early Islam: Vol. 12). 150p. 2000. text 24.95 (*0-87850-116-9*) Darwin Pr.

Muhammad's Birthday Festival: Early History in the Central Muslim Lands & Development in the Muslim West until the 10th-16th Century. N. J. Kaptein. LC 92-33004. x, 184p. 1993. 64.50 (*90-04-09452-0*) Brill Academic Pubs.

Muhammad's Companions: Essays on Those Who Bore Witness, Pt. I. Laleh Bakhtiar. 210p. (YA). (gr. 10-12). 1993. pap. 15.95 (*1-56744-426-1*) Kazi Pubns.

Muhammad's Companions: Essays on Those Who Bore Witness, Pt. II. Laleh Bakhtiar. 205p. (YA). (gr. 10-12). 1993. pap. 12.95 (*1-56744-318-4*) Kazi Pubns.

Muhammad's Mecca: History in the Qur'an. William M. Watt. 160p. 1988. 45.00 (*0-85224-565-3*, Pub. by Edinburgh U Pr) Col U Pr.

Muhammad's Prophethood: An Analytical View. Jamal A. Badawi. 26p. 1990. pap. write for info. (*1-882837-19-3*) W A M Y Intl.

Muhammed: The Prophet. rev. unabridged ed. Sirdar Ikbal Ali Shah. LC 98-118945. 285p. 1997. pap. 25.00 (*2-909347-04-4*, Pub. by Tractus Bks) Tractus.

Muhammed Ali. Random House Value Publishing Staff. LC 96-36218. 1997. 20.00 (*0-517-20080-5*) Random Hse Value.

Muhammed Ali: Athlete, Activist, Ambassador. James Duplacey. (Champion Sports Biography Ser.). (Illus.). 96p. (YA). (gr. 7-12). 1999. pap. 8.95 (*1-894020-50-2*) Warwick Publ.

Muhammed Ali: The World's Champion. John Tessitore. LC 97-31204. (Impact Biography Ser.). 144p. (J). 1998. 24.00 (*0-531-11437-6*) Watts.

Muhammed Ali: The World's Champion. John Tessitore. (Impact Biographies Ser.). (Illus.). 144p. (YA). (gr. 7-12). 1999. pap. text 9.95 (*0-531-15927-2*) Watts.

Muhammedan Law of Marriage & Divorce. Ahmed Shukri. (Columbia University. Contributions to Oriental History & Philology Ser.: No. 7). reprint ed. 31.50 (*0-404-50537-6*) AMS Pr.

Muhammedanische Eschatologie. M. Wolff. xiv, 224p. reprint ed. write for info. (*0-318-71572-4*) G Olms Pubs.

Muhammeds Lehre von der Offenbarung Quellenmassig Untersucht. Otto Pautz. 304p. reprint ed. write for info. (*0-318-71550-3*) G Olms Pubs.

Muhlenbergs of Pennsylvania. Paul A. Wallace. LC 75-124264. (Select Bibliographies Reprint Ser.). 1977. 23.95 (*0-8369-5452-1*) Ayer.

Muhurtha (Electional Astrology) Bangalore V. Raman. (C). 1993. 6.50 (*81-85674-68-X*, Pub. by UBS Pubs Dist) S Asia.

Muhy-ud Din Alamgir Aurangzeb. Fazl Ahmad. (Heroes of Islam Ser.: Bk. 9). 103p. (Orig.). (YA). (gr. 7-12). 1984. pap. 3.50 (*1-56744-247-1*) Kazi Pubns.

Muhyiddin Ibn Arabi: A Commemorative Volume. Ed. by S. Hirtenstein Tiernan. 378p. 1996. pap. 30.00 (*0-614-21316-9*, 1347) Kazi Pubns.

Muhyiddin Ibn'Arabi (1165-1240 A.D.) A Volume of Translations & Studies Commemorating the 750th Anniversary of His Life & Work. Ed. by S. Hertenstein & M. Tiernan. 400p. 1993. pap. 65.00 (*1-85230-349-2*, Pub. by Element MA) Penguin Putnam.

Muhyiddin Ibn'Arabi (1165-1240 A.D.) A Volume of Translations & Studies Commemorating the 750th Anniversary of His Life & Work. Ed. by S. Hertenstein & M. Tiernan. 400p. 1993. pap. 30.00 (*1-85230-395-6*, Pub. by Element MA) Penguin Putnam.

Muir-Epes Murder of 1846. Richard L. Jones. 1993. pap. 12.00 (*0-87517-070-6*) Dietz.

Muir Woods: Redwood Refuge. John Hart. (Illus.). 48p. (Orig.). 1991. pap. 7.95 (*0-9625206-4-0*) Gldn Gate Natl Parks Assoc.

Muir Woods: The Ancient Redwood Forest near San Francisco. 2nd ed. James M. Morley. 1992. pap. 10.95 (*0-938765-53-1*) Smith Novelty.

Muir Woods Handbook: An Insider's Guide. Susan Frank & Phil Frank. LC 99-15328. (Illus.). 144p. 1999. pap. 12.95 (*0-7649-1027-2*) Pomegranate Calif.

Muirfield: Home of the Honourable Company (1744-1994) Norman Main. (Illus.). 160p. 1995. 45.00 (*1-85158-617-2*, Pub. by Mainstream Pubng) Trafalgar.

***Muir's Original Log Home Guide for Builders & Buyers.** Ed. by Doris Muir & Allan Muir. (Illus.). 260p. 1999. pap. 25.00 (*0-9677869-0-8*) G J Schroeder.

Muir's Path. 13th ed. Macsween. 1994. 150.00 (*0-340-55145-3*, Pub. by E A) Routldge.

Muir's Textbook of Pathology. 13th ed. write for info. (*0-340-66233-6*, Pub. by E A) Routldge.

Mu'jam al Mustalahat al Iqtisadiyah fi Lughat al Fuqaha: (A Glossary of the Economic Terminology in the Language of the Jurists) Nazih Hammad. LC 93-2200. (Silsilat al Ma'ajim wa al Adillah wa al Kashshafat Ser.: No. 5). (ARA.). 308p. (Orig.). 1993. pap. 10.00 (*1-56564-133-7*) IIIT VA.

Mujer: Su Mision, Posicion y Ministerio. Perry B. Fitzwater. Orig. Title: Woman: Mission, Position, Ministry. (SPA.). 80p. 1972. mass mkt. 3.99 (*0-8254-1233-1*, Edit Portavoz) Kregel.

Mujer: Una Persona de Valor y Dignidad. Charles R. Swindoll. (Serie Realidades - Realities Ser.).Tr. of Woman: A Person of Worth. (SPA.). 36p. 1993. pap. 1.99 (*0-945792-44-1*, 498101) Editorial Unilit.

Mujer Cabalga la Bestia. Dave Hunt. 570p. 1997. pap. 14.99 (*1-928660-00-2*) Berean Call.

***Mujer, Cambia Tu Mundo: Como Dios USA A las Mujeres Para Hacer una Difference.** Jill Briscoe. (SPA.). 96p. 2000. pap. 6.00 (*0-311-04660-6*) Baptist Spanish.

Mujer de Ayer y Hoy. Jose M. Marti. (SPA., Illus.). 28p. (Orig.). 1988. pap. 3.00 (*0-685-24433-4*) Editorial El Coqui.

Mujer de Ciudad (A City Woman) Rita Rainville. (Deseo Ser.: No. 222). (SPA.). 1998. per. 3.50 (*0-373-35222-0*) Harlequin Bks.

Mujer De Excelencia. Gloria Ricardo. 36p. 1992. pap. 1.15 (*1-885630-10-7*) HLM Producciones.

Mujer de Potencia: Cada Gvia Para la Mujer y Viver Affortunado. Louise L. Hay. (SPA.). 173p. 1998. 12.95 (*1-56170-472-5*) Hay House.

Mujer de un Solo Hombre - One-Man Woman. Carole Mortimer. (SPA.). 1997. per. 3.50 (*0-373-33415-X*, 1-33415-0) Harlequin Bks.

Mujer Decidida. M. Duckworth.Tr. of Decisive Woman. 6.99 (*1-56063-636-X*, 495103) Editorial Unilit.

Mujer Desnuda see Naked Woman

Mujer, el SIDA y el Activismo: The Spanish Language Edition of Women, AIDS, & Activism - The ACT UP-NY Women & AIDS Book Group. Ed. by Cynthia Chris & Monica Pearl. 340p. 1992. 25.00 (*0-89608-455-8*); pap. 10.00 (*0-89608-454-X*) South End Pr.

Mujer en el Contexto Epistolar Poetico del Siglo de Oro. Olga M. Muniz. (Iberica Ser.: Vol. 19). (SPA.). 212p. (C). 1996. text 45.95 (*0-8204-3044-7*) P Lang Pubng.

Mujer en la Novela de Mario Vargas Llosa. Nelida Florez. (SPA.). 105p. 1993. write for info. (*0-9635672-0-9*) N Florez.

Mujer en la Obra de Enrique Laguerre. Ruth Ortega-Velez. LC 89-5382. 114p. (Orig.). 1990. pap. text 8.95 (*0-8477-3636-9*) U of PR Pr.

Mujer en las Americas: Como Cerrar la Brecha Entre los Generos. Inter-American Development Bank Staff.Tr. of Women in the Americas: Bridging the Gender Gap. (SPA.). 250p. 1996. pap. text 18.50 (*1-886938-10-5*) IADB.

Mujer en Marti: En Su Pensamiento, Obra y Vida. Onilda A. Jimenez. LC 98-89570. (Coleccion Formacion Martiana Ser.). (SPA., Illus.). 165p. 1999. pap. 16.00 (*0-89729-889-6*) Ediciones.

Mujer en Puerto Rico: Ensayos de Investigacion. Ed. by Yamila Azize-Vargas. LC 87-82377. (Huracan Academia Ser.). (SPA.). 238p. 1987. pap. 9.25 (*0-940238-91-8*) Ediciones Huracan.

Mujer en Soledad (A Woman in Solitude) Dario Puccini. (SPA.). 238p. 1997. pap. 16.99 (*968-16-5036-0*, Pub. by Fondo) Continental Bk.

Mujer en su etapa de Media Vida: Women in Mid-Life Crisis. Jim Conway & Sally Conway. Tr. by Alicia S. De Zorzoli from SPA. 352p. 1986. pap. 9.99 (*0-311-46105-0*) Casa Bautista.

M

An Asterisk (*) at the beginning of an entry indicates that the title is appearing for the first time.

M

Mujer Encantadora: Fascinating Womanhood. Helen Andelin. (SPA.). 234p. 1979. pap. 10.00 (0-911094-08-3) Pacific Santa Barbara.

***Mujer, Eres Libre! Devocional.** T. D. Jakes.Tr. of Woman, Thou Art Loosed! Devotional. 2001. 8.99 (0-7899-0375-X, 498339) Editorial Unilit.

Mujer Ideal. Genova Hilgeman.Tr. of Ideal Woman. (SPA.). 410p. 1975. pap. 8.99 (1-56063-304-2, 498424) Editorial Unilit.

Mujer Integral. Otila Carcamo & Wilfredo Calderon. (SPA.). 88p. 1984. pap. 1.95 (0-938127-03-9) Publ Senda de Vida.

Mujer Involidable (An Unforgettable Woman) Miranda Lee. (Bianca Ser.: No. 442). (SPA.). 1998. per. 3.50 (0-373-33442-7) Harlequin Bks.

Mujer, Jeres Libre! T. D. Jakes.Tr. of Woman, Thou Art Loosed!. (SPA.). 230p. pap. 8.99 (0-7899-0297-4, 498340) Editorial Unilit.

***Mujer, Jesus Se Interesa Por Ti.** Helene Ashker.Tr. of Jesus Cares for Women. (SPA.). 1999. pap. text 5.99 (0-311-12110-1, Edit Mundo) Casa Bautista.

***Mujer Nueva: Cinderella Twin.** Barbara McMahon. (Deseo Ser.: No. 150).Tr. of New Woman. (SPA.). 1999. per. 3.50 (0-373-35280-8, 1-35280-6) Harlequin Bks.

Mujer Que Sabe Latin (Woman Who Speaks Latin) Rosario Castellanos. (SPA.). 216p. 1992. reprint ed. pap. 14.99 (968-16-1673-1, Pub. by Fondo) Continental Bk.

Mujer Sin Eden see Woman Without Eden (Mujer Sin Eden)

Mujer Sujeta al Espiritu. Beverly LaHaye.Tr. of Spirit-Controlled Woman. 208p. 1978. 9.99 (0-88113-210-1) Caribe Betania.

Mujer Two Men Vol. 30: Complete Plays 30: La Divina Cubana; Two Men: The Shit Pit; Pictures Imperfect. Manuel P. Garcia. 82p. 1998. 4.95 (1-885901-80-1, Liberts) Presbyters Peartree.

***Mujer Unica.** Leanne Banks. (Harlequin Deseo Ser.: Vol. 159).Tr. of Unique Woman. (SPA.). 156p. 1999. per. 3.50 (0-373-35289-1, 1-35289-7) Harlequin Bks.

Mujer Virtuosa. Cynthia Heald. (Serie Realidades - Realities Ser.).Tr. of Woman of Virtue. (SPA.). 199p. 1995. 1.99 (1-56063-722-6, 498142) Editorial Unilit.

Mujer y Sus Emociones. Gloria Ricardo. (Estudio Biblico Para Mujeres Ser.). 76p. 1992. pap. 4.00 (1-885630-23-9) HLM Producciones.

***Mujercismas.** Terenci Moix. 1998. pap. text 9.95 (84-08-02013-7) Planeta Edit.

***Mujercitas.** Louisa May Alcott. (SPA., Illus.). (J). 1998. pap. 6.95 (84-01-46257-6) Plaza.

Mujeres: Conversations from a Hispanic Community. Ed. by Nan Elsasser et al. LC 80-20200. (Women's Lives - Women's Work Ser.). (Illus.). 192p. 1980. pap. 12.95 (0-912670-70-3) Feminist Pr.

Mujeres Bautistas en Misiones Guia. 44p. 1995. pap. 3.95 (1-56309-139-9) Womans Mission Union.

Mujeres De Clarin: Espermentos y Camafeos. Sally Ortiz-Aponte & Juan A. Cabezas. 200p. (C). 1971. pap. 3.00 (0-8477-3141-3) U of PR Pr.

Mujeres de Hollywood. Jackie Collins. (SPA.). 16.95 (950-04-0395-1) Emece.

Mujeres de la Biblia. Frances VanderVelde. Orig. Title: Women of the Bible. (SPA.). 272p. 1990. pap. 8.99 (0-8254-1801-1, Edit Portavoz) Kregel.

Mujeres de Ojos Grandes. Angeles Mastretta.Tr. of Women with Big Eyes. (SPA.). 1997. pap. 12.95 (84-322-4660-3, Pub. by E Seix Barral) Continental Bk.

Mujeres de Palabra. Compiled by Angelica Gorodischer. (SPA.). 192p. 1994. pap. 9.95 (0-8477-0218-9) U of PR Pr.

Mujeres de Proposito (Women of Destiny) Cindy Jacobs. (What You Need to Know about ... in 12 Lessons Ser.). (SPA & ENG.). 345p. 10.99 (0-88113-533-X) Caribe Betania.

Mujeres del Mundo: Leyes y Politicas Que Afectan Sus Vidas Reproductivas: Latin America. unabridged ed. Ed. by Gaby O. Aguilar. (Women of the World Ser.: Vol. 2). (SPA.). 225p. Date not set. pap. text 25.00 (1-890671-02-9) Center Reprod.

Mujeres e Iglesia: Sexualidad y Aborto en America Latina. Ed. by Ana M. Portugal. (SPA., Illus.). 146p. (Orig.). 1989. pap. 10.00 (0-915365-15-4) Cath Free Choice.

Mujeres en los Cuentos de Rene Marquez. Neyssa A. Palmer-Bermudez. LC 85-26384. 103p. 1988. pap. 7.50 (0-8477-3803-5) U of PR Pr.

Mujeres en Mexico: Una Historia Olvidada see Women in Mexico: A Past Unveiled

Mujeres Espanolas. Salvador De Madariaga. (Nueva Austral Ser.: Vol. 198). (SPA.). 1991. pap. text 24.95 (84-239-7198-8) Elliots Bks.

Mujeres Grandes Anthology, No. 2. Ed. by Angela De Hoyos. 64p. (Orig.). 1995. pap. 6.00 (0-913983-15-2) M & A Edns.

Mujeres Grandes Anthology: Premier Issue. Ed. by Angela De Hoyos. 63p. 1993. pap. 6.00 (0-913983-11-X) M & A Edns.

***Mujeres Llenas de Gracia.** Betty Jane Grams. (SPA.). 2000. mass mkt. 4.50 (0-7899-0756-9) Spanish Hse Distributors.

Mujeres Mas Famosas de la Historia. Editorial America, S. A. Staff. Ed. by Maria E. Del Real. (SPA., Illus.). (Orig.). 1990. pap. write for info. (0-944499-94-5) Editorial Amer.

***Mujeres Millonarias.** Bettina Flores. (SPA.). 240p. 1999. pap. 16.95 (0-7931-3485-4) Dearborn.

Mujeres, Mitos y Diosas (Women, Myths & Goddesses) Martha Robles. (SPA.). 337p. 1996. pap. 29.99 (968-16-4915-X, Pub. by Fondo) Continental Bk.

Mujeres que Corren Con Los Lobos: Women Who Run with Wolves. Clarissa P. Estes. (SPA.). 1997. pap. write for info. (0-679-77909-4) Vin Bks.

Mujeres que Corren Con Los Lobos: Women Who Run with Wolves. Clarissa P. Estes. 2000. pap. 16.00 (0-375-70753-0) Vin Bks.

***Mujeres Siempre Tienen la Razon & los Hombres Nunca Se Equivocan.** Joey O'Connor. (SPA.). 1999. pap. 9.99 (0-88113-551-8) Caribe Betania.

Mujeres Trabajan Unidas Para el Desarrollo Personal, Economico y de la Comunidad. Suzanne Kindervatter. Tr. by Amparo Giraldo. LC 86-60092. (SPA., Illus.). 100p. (Orig.). 1983. reprint ed. pap. 13.50 (0-912917-03-2) UNIFEM.

Mujeres y el Estres. J. Lusher.Tr. of Women & Stress. (SPA.). pap. 9.99 (1-56063-671-8, 498435) Editorial Unilit.

Mujeres y Sus Emociones. M. Christine Neff.Tr. of Women & Their Emotions. (SPA.). pap. 8.99 (1-56063-579-7, 495012) Editorial Unilit.

Mujerista Theology: A Theology for the Twenty-First Century. Ada M. Isasi-Diaz. LC 96-2913. 224p. (Orig.). 1996. pap. 16.00 (1-57075-081-5) Orbis Bks.

Mu'jizat Wa-Khawariq Al-Duktur Dahesh Yarwyha Al-Sahafi Lutfi Radwan. 2nd rev. ed. Lutfi Radwan. (ARA & ENG., Illus.). 279p. 1997. 15.00 (0-935359-44-3) Daheshist.

Mukara. Muriel Bruce. Ed. by R. Reginald & Douglas Melville. LC 77-84204. (Lost Race & Adult Fantasy Ser.). 1978. reprint ed. lib. bdg. 26.95 (0-405-10960-1) Ayer.

Mukate & Will Underwood. Stanhope Lacy, Jr. 300p. 1984. 14.95 (0-9612362-1-3) L Stanhope.

Mukat's People: The Cahuilla Indians of Southern California. Lowell J. Bean. LC 78-145782. (Illus.). 300p. 1972. pap. 15.95 (0-520-02627-6, Pub. by U CA Pr) Cal Prin Full Svc.

Mukherjee, Mrinalini. Sculpture. Intro. by David Elliott. (Illus.). 1994. pap. 24.00 (0-905836-84-7, Pub. by Museum Modern Art) St Mut.

Mukhtasar Tarikh Dimashq li-Ibn-Asakir, 29 vols., Set. Ibn-Manzur. 11252p. 1990. write for info. (1-57547-072-1) Dar Al-Fikr.

Mukhtasar Tarikh Dimashq li-Ibn-Asakir, Vol. 1. Ibn-Manzur. 1990. 11.95 (1-57547-073-X) Dar Al-Fikr.

Mukhtasar Tarikh Dimashq li-Ibn-Asakir, Vol. 2. Ibn-Manzur. 1990. 11.95 (1-57547-074-8) Dar Al-Fikr.

Mukhtasar Tarikh Dimashq li-Ibn-Asakir, Vol. 3. Ibn-Manzur. 1990. 11.95 (1-57547-075-6) Dar Al-Fikr.

Mukhtasar Tarikh Dimashq li-Ibn-Asakir, Vol. 4. Ibn-Manzur. 1990. 11.95 (1-57547-076-4) Dar Al-Fikr.

Mukhtasar Tarikh Dimashq li-Ibn-Asakir, Vol. 5. Ibn-Manzur. 1990. 11.95 (1-57547-077-2) Dar Al-Fikr.

Mukhtasar Tarikh Dimashq li-Ibn-Asakir, Vol. 6. Ibn-Manzur. 1990. 11.95 (1-57547-078-0) Dar Al-Fikr.

Mukhtasar Tarikh Dimashq li-Ibn-Asakir, Vol. 7. Ibn-Manzur. 1990. 11.95 (1-57547-079-9) Dar Al-Fikr.

Mukhtasar Tarikh Dimashq li-Ibn-Asakir, Vol. 8. Ibn-Manzur. 1990. 11.95 (1-57547-080-2) Dar Al-Fikr.

Mukhtasar Tarikh Dimashq li-Ibn-Asakir, Vol. 9. Ibn-Manzur. 1990. 11.95 (1-57547-081-0) Dar Al-Fikr.

Mukhtasar Tarikh Dimashq li-Ibn-Asakir, Vol. 10. Ibn-Manzur. 1990. 11.95 (1-57547-082-9) Dar Al-Fikr.

Mukhtasar Tarikh Dimashq li-Ibn-Asakir, Vol. 11. Ibn-Manzur. 1990. 11.95 (1-57547-083-7) Dar Al-Fikr.

Mukhtasar Tarikh Dimashq li-Ibn-Asakir, Vol. 12. Ibn-Manzur. 1990. 11.95 (1-57547-084-5) Dar Al-Fikr.

Mukhtasar Tarikh Dimashq li-Ibn-Asakir, Vol. 13. Ibn-Manzur. 1990. 11.95 (1-57547-085-3) Dar Al-Fikr.

Mukhtasar Tarikh Dimashq li-Ibn-Asakir, Vol. 14. Ibn-Manzur. 1990. 11.95 (1-57547-086-1) Dar Al-Fikr.

Mukhtasar Tarikh Dimashq li-Ibn-Asakir, Vol. 15. Ibn-Manzur. 1990. 11.95 (1-57547-087-X) Dar Al-Fikr.

Mukhtasar Tarikh Dimashq li-Ibn-Asakir, Vol. 16. Ibn-Manzur. 1990. 11.95 (1-57547-088-8) Dar Al-Fikr.

Mukhtasar Tarikh Dimashq li-Ibn-Asakir, Vol. 17. Ibn-Manzur. 1990. 11.95 (1-57547-089-6) Dar Al-Fikr.

Mukhtasar Tarikh Dimashq li-Ibn-Asakir, Vol. 18. Ibn-Manzur. 1990. 11.95 (1-57547-090-X) Dar Al-Fikr.

Mukhtasar Tarikh Dimashq li-Ibn-Asakir, Vol. 19. Ibn-Manzur. 1990. 11.95 (1-57547-091-8) Dar Al-Fikr.

Mukhtasar Tarikh Dimashq li-Ibn-Asakir, Vol. 20. Ibn-Manzur. 1990. 11.95 (1-57547-092-6) Dar Al-Fikr.

Mukhtasar Tarikh Dimashq li-Ibn-Asakir, Vol. 21. Ibn-Manzur. 1990. 11.95 (1-57547-093-4) Dar Al-Fikr.

Mukhtasar Tarikh Dimashq li-Ibn-Asakir, Vol. 22. Ibn-Manzur. 1990. 11.95 (1-57547-094-2) Dar Al-Fikr.

Mukhtasar Tarikh Dimashq li-Ibn-Asakir, Vol. 23. Ibn-Manzur. 1990. 11.95 (1-57547-095-0) Dar Al-Fikr.

Mukhtasar Tarikh Dimashq li-Ibn-Asakir, Vol. 24. Ibn-Manzur. 1990. 11.95 (1-57547-096-9) Dar Al-Fikr.

Mukhtasar Tarikh Dimashq li-Ibn-Asakir, Vol. 25. Ibn-Manzur. 1990. 11.95 (1-57547-097-7) Dar Al-Fikr.

Mukhtasar Tarikh Dimashq li-Ibn-Asakir, Vol. 26. Ibn-Manzur. 1990. 11.95 (1-57547-098-5) Dar Al-Fikr.

Mukhtasar Tarikh Dimashq li-Ibn-Asakir, Vol. 27. Ibn-Manzur. 1990. 11.95 (1-57547-099-3) Dar Al-Fikr.

Mukhtasar Tarikh Dimashq li-Ibn-Asakir, Vol. 28. Ibn-Manzur. 1990. 11.95 (1-57547-100-0) Dar Al-Fikr.

Mukhtasar Tarikh Dimashq li-Ibn-Asakir, Vol. 29. Ibn-Manzur. 1990. 11.95 (1-57547-101-9) Dar Al-Fikr.

Mukiwa: A White Boy in Africa. Peter Godwin. LC 96-39341. 432p. 1997. pap. 14.00 (0-06-097723-X, Perennial) HarperTrade.

Mukluk Bk. 2: Collection. Robin Heller. (Illus.). i, 43p. 1998. pap. 5.95 (1-891738-06-2) Creative Prodns.

Mukluk & Honisukle Bk. 3: Collection. Robin Heller. (Illus.). i, 43p. 1998. pap. 5.95 (1-891738-00-3) Creative Prodns.

Mukluk the Eskimo Bk. 1: Collection. Robin Heller. (Illus.). i, 43p. 1998. pap. 5.95 (1-891738-01-1) Creative Prodns.

Mukteshwari. 2nd ed. Swami Muktananda. LC 95-15966. 392p. 1995. pap. 12.95 (0-911307-35-4) SYDA Found.

Muktesvara Temple in Bhubanaswar. Walter Smith. LC 95-900270. (C). 1994. 44.00 (81-208-0793-6, Pub. by Motilal Bnarsidass) S Asia.

Mukun-da-Mala-Stotra: The Prayers of King Kulasekhara. A. C. Bhaktivedanta Swami Prabhupada & Satsvarupa D. Goswami. LC 92-31102. 157p. 1998. pap. 9.95 (0-89213-275-2) Bhaktivedanta.

Mulan. Cathy E. Dubowski. LC 97-80190. (Junior Novelization Ser.). (Illus.). 96p. (J). (gr. 3-7). 1998. pap. 3.95 (0-7868-4222-9, Pub. by Disney Pr) Time Warner.

Mulan. Gina Ingoglia. (Little Golden Bks.). (Illus.). 24p. (J). 1998. 2.29 (0-307-98861-9, 98861, Goldn Books); pap. 3.29 (0-307-13184-X, 13184, Goldn Books) Gldn Bks Pub Co.

Mulan. Mouse Works Staff. 24p. (J). 1998. 3.98 (1-57082-925-X, Pub. by Mouse Works) Time Warner.

Mulan. Schroeder. LC 97-80163. (Illus.). (J). 1998. lib. bdg. 17.49 (0-7868-5065-5, Pub. by Hyperion) Little.

Mulan. Walt Disney Staff. (Disney Read-Alongs Ser.). (J). 7.99 incl. audio (0-7634-0406-3) W Disney Records.

Mulan: Mushu's Story. Justine Korman. (Disney Chapters Ser.). (Illus.). 64p. (J). (gr. 2-4). 1998. pap. 3.95 (0-7868-4225-3, Pub. by Disney Pr) Time Warner.

Mulan: Special Collector's Edition. deluxe ed. Russell Schroder. LC 97-80163. (Illus.). 72p. (J). 1998. 16.95 (0-7868-3173-1, Pub. by Disney Pr) Time Warner.

Mulan - Lady & the Tramp, 2. 75th anniversary ed. Mouse Works Staff. 1998. 9.99 (0-7364-0089-3) Mouse Works.

Mulan Classic Storybook. Mouse Works Staff. LC 99-162498. (Mulan Ser.). 96p. (J). 1998. 7.98 (1-57082-864-4, Pub. by Mouse Works) Time Warner.

Mulan Postcard Book. (Illus.). 64p. (J). 1998. pap. 9.95 (0-7868-8309-X, Pub. by Hyperion) Time Warner.

Mulan Puzzlers. Karen C. Richards. LC 99-158961. (Illus.). 176p. (J). (gr. 3-7). 1998. pap. 9.95 (0-7868-4224-5) Little.

Mulan Saves the Day No. 18. Kathryn McKeon. LC 97-80399. (Disney's First Readers Ser.). (Illus.). 22p. (J). (gr. 2-4). 1998. pap. 2.95 (0-7868-4246-6, Pub. by Disney Pr) Time Warner.

Mulan Spanish Classic Storybook. Mouse Works Staff. (Mulan Ser.). (SPA.). 96p. (J). 1998. 7.98 (1-57082-865-2, Pub. by Mouse Works) Time Warner.

Mulatresse Solitude. Andre Schwarz-Bart. (FRE.). 1983. pap. 11.95 (0-7859-2691-7) Fr & Eur.

Mulatto. Aluisio Azevedo. Ed. & Tr. by Murray G. MacNicoll from POR. LC 89-45755. 304p. 1990. 39.50 (0-8386-3380-3) Fairleigh Dickinson.

Mulatto in the United States. Edward B. Reuter. LC 70-100495. (Studies in Black History & Culture: No. 54). 1970. lib. bdg. 75.00 (0-8383-1216-0) M S G Haskell Hse.

Mulatto in the United States. Edward B. Reuter. LC 69-16569. 417p. 1969. reprint ed. lib. bdg. 52.50 (0-8371-0938-8, REM&) Greenwood.

Mulayam Singh: A Political Biography. Ram Singh & Anshuman Yadav. LC 98-908912. 1998. 24.00 (81-220-0530-6, Pub. by Konark Pubs Pvt Ltd) S Asia.

Mulberries & Prickly Pear. Anne Carter. (Illus.). 161p. (Orig.). 1991. pap. 9.50 (0-9632510-0-7) A Carter.

Mulberry & Peach: Two Women of China. Hualing Nieh. Tr. by Jane P. Young & Linda Lappin. LC 98-12259. 224p. 1998. reprint ed. pap. 12.95 (1-55861-182-7) Feminist Pr.

***Mulberry at Home: A New Approach to Luxurious Country Style.** Roger Saul. (Illus.). 2000. 45.00 (0-09-186812-2, Pub. by Ebury Pr) Trafalgar.

Mulberry Bird: An Adoption Story. rev. ed. Anne B. Brodzinsky. LC 95-2460. (Illus.). 48p. (J). (gr. k-5). 1996. 16.00 (0-944934-15-3) Perspect Indiana.

Mulberry Bush. Cathy Beylon. (Window Bks.). (J). (ps). 1992. 4.95 (1-56288-282-1) Checkerboard.

Mulberry Bush. Sylvia Lynd. LC 78-142886. (Short Story Index Reprint Ser.). 1977. 19.95 (0-8369-3751-1) Ayer.

Mulberry Juice Dress: And Other Stories of Lebanon. Margaret F. Kraushaar. (Illus.). 144p. (Orig.). 1996. pap. 9.95 (1-56474-176-1) Fithian Pr.

Mulberry Tree: Writings of Elizabeth Bowen. Elizabeth Bowen. Ed. by Hermione Lee. LC 86-29446. (Illus.). 1987. 19.95 (0-15-163240-5) Harcourt.

Mulch. Ann Ripley. 304p. 1998. reprint ed. mass mkt. 5.99 (0-553-57734-4) Bantam.

***Mulch Ado About Nothing: A Jane Jeffry Mystery.** Jill Churchill. 224p. 2000. 23.00 (0-380-97735-4, Wm Morrow) Morrow Avon.

Mulch Book: A Complete Guide for Gardeners. rev. ed. Stu Campbell. Ed. by Donna Moore. LC 90-50603. (Illus.). 160p. 1991. reprint ed. pap. 10.95 (0-88266-659-2) Storey Bks.

***Mulch It: A Homeowner's Guide to a Carefree Garden & a More Beautiful Landscape.** rev. ed. Stu Campbell. 128p. 2001. pap. 11.95 (1-58017-316-0) Storey Bks.

Mulch One Through Eight-Nine, Set. 1976. pap. 20.00 (0-685-63382-9) Mulch Pr.

Mulching of America. Harry Crews. 272p. 1996. per. 11.00 (0-684-82541-4) S&S Trade.

Mulching of America: A Novel. Harry Crews. LC 95-11358. 256p. 1995. 22.00 (0-684-80934-6) Simon & Schuster.

Mulder, It's Me: An X-Haustive X-Pose of the Woman Who Is Special Agent Dana Scully. Gil Adamson & Dawn Connolly. (Illus.). 300p. 1997. pap. 16.95 (1-55022-316-X, Pub. by ECW) LPC InBook.

Muldoon. Pamela Duncan Edwards. 32p. (J). Date not set. 14.99 (0-7868-0360-6, Pub. by Hyprn Child); lib. bdg. 15.49 (0-7868-2305-4, Pub. by Hyprn Child) Little.

Mule. Lorraine Travis. 140p. 1990. 65.00 (0-85131-503-8, Pub. by J A Allen) Trafalgar.

Mule Alternative: The Saddle Mule in the American West. Mike Stamm. LC 92-61936. (Illus.). 162p. (Orig.). 1993. pap. 14.95 (0-9640668-8-2) Med Wolf Pr.

Mule & Black-Tailed Deer of North America. Ed. by Olof C. Wallmo et al. LC 80-20128. (Illus.). 623p. 1981. reprint ed. pap. 193.20 (0-608-03368-5, 206407900008) Bks Demand.

***Mule Bone.** Zora Neale Hurston. 2000. pap. 13.00 (0-06-095648-8) HarpC.

Mule Bone: A Comedy of Negro Life in Three Acts. Langston Hughes & Zora Neale Hurston. Ed. by George Houston Bass & Henry Louis Gates, Jr. LC 90-55835. 304p. 2000. pap. 13.00 (0-06-096885-0, Perennial) HarperTrade.

Mule Car & Trolley: The Story of the Santa Barbara Street Railway. William B. Everett & Gary B. Coombs. LC 84-61366. (Illus.). viii, 128p. 1984. 18.50 (0-911773-04-5) Inst Am Res.

Mule Companion: A Guide to Understanding the Mule. 3rd rev. ed. Cynthia Attar. LC 93-92659. Orig. Title: Mule Companion: Essential Mule Wisdom. (Illus.). 188p. 1998. pap. 19.95 (0-9651776-1-0) Prtnr Communs.

Mule Companion: Essential Mule Wisdom see Mule Companion: A Guide to Understanding the Mule

Mule de Corbillard. Marie Cardinal. (FRE.). 1979. pap. 10.95 (0-7859-3210-0, 2266006614) Fr & Eur.

Mule Deer: Behavior, Ecology, Conservation. Erwin A. Bauer. LC 94-39531. (Illus.). 160p. 1995. 35.00 (0-89658-263-9) Voyageur Pr.

***Mule Deer: Behavior, Ecology, Conservation.** Photos by Erwin A. Bauer & Peggy Bauer. (Illus.). 160p. 2000. reprint ed. pap. 19.95 (0-89658-376-7) Voyageur Pr.

Mule Deer: Hunting Today's Trophies. Tom J. Carpenter & Jim Van Norman. LC 98-84096. (Illus.). 256p. 1998. pap. 19.95 (0-87341-563-9, HTMD) Krause Pubns.

Mule Deer Country. Photos by Michael Francis. LC 90-43851. (Illus.). 176p. 1990. 39.00 (1-55971-076-4, 1480, NorthWord Pr) Creat Pub Intl.

Mule Deer Country. Valerius Geist. 1999. pap. text 25.00 (1-55971-680-0, NorthWord Pr) Creat Pub Intl.

Mule Eggs & Topknots. rev. ed. Ed. by King Duncan. LC 86-63997. 220p. (Orig.). 1991. 14.95 (0-936497-05-X) Seven Worlds.

Mule in Southern Agriculture. Robert B. Lamb. LC 63-63464. (University of California Publications in Social Welfare: vol. 15). 106p. reprint ed. pap. 32.90 (0-608-18652-X, 202127200022) Bks Demand.

Mule Musings. Basil Overton. 1983. 8.75 (0-89137-106-0); pap. 6.15 (0-89137-105-2) Quality Pubns.

Mule Thieves. James E. Powell. LC 86-1622. 192p. 1986. 14.95 (0-8027-4058-8) Walker & Co.

Mule Trader: Ray Lum's Tales of Horses, Mules & Men. William R. Ferris. LC 98-28245. (Banner Book Ser.). Orig. Title: You Live & You Learn, Then You Die & Forget It All. (Illus.). 256p. 1998. reprint ed. pap. 16.00 (1-57806-086-9) U Pr of Miss.

Mule Train Journal: A Journey of Hope Remembered. Roland L. Freeman. LC 98-23252. 1998. pap. 14.95 (1-55853-660-4) Rutledge Hill Pr.

Muledred. Kathryn Brown. LC 89-11027. (Illus.). 32p. (J). (ps-3). 1990. 12.95 (0-15-256265-6) Harcourt.

***Mulege Fishing Chart & Guide.** (Illus.). 1999. 14.95 (1-929394-06-3, B006) Baja Directions.

Mules Across the Great Wide Open: A True Western Adventure. Jody Foss. LC 94-96517. (Illus.). 288p. 1995. 19.95 (0-9643413-1-X); pap. 14.95 (0-9643413-0-1) Mules Across Am.

Mules & Dragons: Popular Culture Images in the Selected Writings of African-American & Chinese-American Women Writers. Mary E. Young. LC 92-45119. 176p. 1993. 49.95 (0-313-28735-X, GM8735, Greenwood Pr) Greenwood.

Mules & Early Poems. Paul Muldoon. 72p. 1986. pap. 6.95 (0-916390-22-5) Wake Forest.

Mules & Men. Zora Neale Hurston. LC 89-45672. 352p. 1994. pap. 13.50 (0-06-091648-6, Perennial) HarperTrade.

Mules & Men: Dee, & Ruby. abr. ed. Zora Neale Hurston. 1992. audio 18.00 (1-55994-548-6, CPN 2280) HarperAudio.

Mules & Mountains. Margie E. Hahn. 1993. pap. text 12.95 (0-912299-56-8) Stoneydale Pr Pub.

Mules & Mountains: Walt Hahn, Forest Service Packer. Margie E. Hahn. (Illus.). 142p. 1993. 17.95 (0-912299-55-X) Stoneydale Pr Pub.

Mules Last Bray: WWII & USFS Reminiscences. H. L. Hames. 80p. 1996. pap. 9.95 (1-57510-025-8) Pictorial Hist.

Mules, Mines & Me in Mexico, 1895-1932. Morris B. Parker. Ed. by James M Day. LC 79-15206. (Illus.). 248p. 1979. reprint ed. pap. 76.90 (0-7837-9235-2, 204998600004) Bks Demand.

Mules That Angels Ride. Page Edward, Jr. LC 70-188737. 1972. 9.95 (0-87955-900-4) O'Hara.

Muleshoe & More. William H. Bradfield. LC 98-27975. 300p. 1998. pap. 15.95 (0-88415-865-9, 5865) Gulf Pub.

Mulford Method: A Preschool Teaching Program. Beverley M. Mulford. (Illus.). 96p. (C). teacher ed. write for info. (0-9639125-0-X) Mulford School.

Mulhouse City Plan. (Grafocarte Maps Ser.). 1992. 8.95 (2-7416-0042-2, 80042) Michelin.

***Mulid! Carnivals of Faith.** Sherif Sonbol. 1999. pap. text 19.95 (977-424-519-9, Pub. by Am Univ Cairo Pr) Col U Pr.

Muliebrity: Qualities of a Woman. Joni Arredia. LC 96-92493. (Illus.). 192p. 1997. 17.95 (0-9653203-1-6, PUB-1-6) Perc Pub.

Mulk Raj Anand: The Short Story Writer. Vijay M. Sethi. (C). 1990. 17.50 (81-7024-375-0, Pub. by Ashish Pub Hse) S Asia.

An Asterisk (*) at the beginning of an entry indicates that the title is appearing for the first time.

***Mull & Iona: Highways & Byways, the Fairest of the Inner Hebridean Isles & Scotland's Great Centre of "Celtic Christianity"** Peter Macnab. (Guides to Scotland Ser.). (Illus.). 128p. 1999. pap. 9.95 (*0-946487-58-8*, Pub. by Luath Pr Ltd) Midpt Trade.

Mulla Husayn: Disciple at Dawn. Ruhu'llah Mehrabkhani. 320p. 1987. 19.95 (*0-933770-37-5*) Kalimat.

***Mullah on Mainframe.** Jonah Blank. 2000. 32.50 (*0-226-05676-7*) U Ch Pr.

Mullendore Murder Case. Jonathan Kwitny. 1976. 25.95 (*0-8488-1402-9*) Amereon Ltd.

Mullendore Murder Case. Jonathan Kwitny. 332p. 1991. reprint ed. lib. bdg. 29.95 (*0-89966-820-8*) Buccaneer Bks.

Muller & Kirk's Small Animal Dermatology. 5th ed. Danny W. Scott et al. LC 94-4949. (Illus.). 1232p. 1995. text 135.00 (*0-7216-4850-9*, W B Saunders Co) Harcrt Hlth Sci Grp.

Muller & Kirk's Small Animal Dermatology. 6th ed. Danny W. Scott et al. (Illus.). 1100p. Date not set. text. write for info. (*0-7216-7618-9*, W B Saunders Co) Harcrt Hlth Sci Grp.

Muller in New York. (Easy Reader Ser.: Level 3). 48p. 1995. 6.95 (*3-468-49692-3*) Langenscheidt.

***Muller Journals Vol. 1, 1948-1950: The Washington Years.** Heinrich Muller. Ed. by Gregory Douglas. (Illus.). 272p. 1999. 35.95 (*0-912138-79-3*) Bender Pub CA.

Muller-Kessler, Christa: Grammatik des Christlich - Palastinisch - Aramaischen. (Texte und Studien Zur Orientalistik Ser.: Band 6). (GER.). xxxiv, 342p. 1991. 68.00 (*3-487-09479-7*) G Olms Pubs.

Muller-Lux Drawings, 1958-1963. William Muller-Lux & Ingrid Roltgen. (Illus.). 184p. 1988. 65.00 (*0-9621943-0-1*) Sunrise AZ.

Muller vs. Oregon. Nancy Woloch. LC 95-83525. 206p. 1996. pap. text 12.95 (*0-312-08586-9*) St Martin.

Muller vs. Oregon: A Brief History with Documents. Nancy Woloch. LC 95-83525. (Bedford Series in History & Culture). (Illus.). 192p. 1996. text 39.95 (*0-312-12816-9*) St Martin.

***Mullet: Hairstyle of the Gods.** Mark Larson. 2000. 14.95 (*1-58234-064-1*) Bloomsbury Pubg.

Mullet on the Beach: The Minorcans of Florida, 1768-1788. Patricia C. Griffin. (Florida Sand Dollar Bk.). (Illus.). 224p. 1991. 29.95 (*0-8130-1074-8*); pap. 16.95 (*0-8130-1093-4*) U Press Fla.

***Mullet Run.** G. W. Reynolds, III. LC 99-69399. 510p. 1999. pap. 22.95 (*1-58244-078-6*) Rutledge Bks.

Mulletheads: The Legends, Lore, Magic, & Mania Surrounding the Humble but Celebrated Mullet. Michael Swindle. LC 98-9438. (Illus.). 128p. 1998. pap. 12.95 (*1-57587-084-3*) Crane Hill AL.

Mulligan Affair: Top Cop on the Take. Ian Macdonald & Betty O'Keefe. LC 98-174195. 160p. 1997. pap. 16.95 (*1-895811-45-7*) Heritage Hse.

Mulligan Guide to Sports Journalism Careers. Joseph F. Mulligan & Kevin T. Mulligan. LC 98-8171. 352p. 1999. pap. 15.95 (*0-8442-4540-2*, 45402) NTC Contemp Pub Co.

Mulligan Stew. Gilbert Sorrentino. LC 95-10936. 446p. 1996. pap. 13.95 (*1-56478-087-2*) Dalkey Arch.

Mulligan's Bar Guide: To Mixing, Serving & Otherwise Cinsuming Cocktails, Liqueurs & Shooters. Shawn M. Mulligan. 1998. pap. 3.95 (*0-00-215443-9*) Harper SF.

***Mulligan's Bar Guide: To Mixing, Serving & Otherwise Consuming Cocktails, Liqueurs & Shooters.** rev. ed. Shawn M. Mulligan. 88p. 2000. pap. 5.25 (*0-00-638579-6*) HarpC.

Mulligan's Complete Golf Etiquette Handbook. Larry Maher. Ed. by Robert Bicknell. LC 95-194865. (Illus.). 64p. 1995. pap. 8.95 (*0-9646234-0-4*) Happy Ft Creat.

Mulligans 4 All: 101 Excuses, Alibis & Observations on the Game of Golf. Chuck Carlson. LC 98-24658. (Illus.). 144p. 1998. 9.95 (*1-886110-58-1*) Addax Pubng.

Mulligan's Law: The Wit & Wisdom of William Hughes Mulligan. William H. Mulligan. LC 97-38943. 246p. 1996. 25.00 (*0-8232-1718-3*) Fordham.

Mulligan's Laws. Henry Beard. (Illus.). 128p. 1998. pap. 9.95 (*0-385-49277-4*) Doubleday.

Mulligan's Name Was Ambrose. Tod McGinley. Ed. by Chere Simmons & Eileen Schipper. (Illus.). 128p. 1998. pap. 9.95 (*0-9664987-0-4*) T C McGinley.

Mulliner Nights. P. G. Wodehouse. 21.95 (*0-89190-298-8*) Amereon Ltd.

Mullins Red Cap Utility Trailer: History & Handbook. Robert L. Parmelee. Ed. & Illus. by Get-A-Long Graphics Staff. LC 98-91614. 184p. 1998. 34.95 (*0-9665217-1-4*, 98-300) Milcap Pubg.

Mullion Rock. large type ed. David M. Farrell. 1990. 27.99 (*0-7089-2133-7*) Ulverscroft.

Mullite & Mullite Ceramics. K. Okada et al. LC 93-36459. 266p. 1994. 265.00 (*0-471-94249-9*) Wiley.

Mullyon: Its History, Scenery & Antiquities. Ed. by E. G. Harvey. (C). 1989. 70.00 (*0-907566-70-7*, Pub. by Dyllansow Truran) St Mut.

Mulomedicina Chironis: Concordantia in Mulomedicinam Chironis, 2 vols., Set. Ed. by Gavin G. Betts & D. R. Blackman. write for info. (*0-318-71985-1*) G Olms Pubs.

Mulomedicina Chironis - Concordantia in Mulomedicinam Chironis. Ed. by D. R. Blackman & Gavin G. Betts. 1000p. write for info. (*0-318-70669-5*) G Olms Pubs.

Mulready Advertisements. Malcolm G. Lowe. (Illus.). lib. bdg. 45.00 (*0-911451-00-5*) Mulready Res.

Mulroney: The Politics of Ambition. John Sawatsky. 580p. 1996. mass mkt. 8.99 (*0-7710-7943-5*) McCland & Stewart.

Mulroney & Others. Baron Wormser. LC 99-23169. 104p. 2000. 20.95 (*1-889330-38-8*, Pub. by Sarabande Bks); pap. 12.95 (*1-889330-39-6*, Pub. by Sarabande Bks) Consort Bk Sales.

Multables, Inc. Ed. by Amy Osborne. (Illus.). 3p. (J). (gr. 2-5). 13.99 (*0-9645004-0-X*) Multables.

Multi-Age & More. Colleen Politano & Anne Davies. (Building Connections Ser.). 168p. 1994. pap., teacher ed. 19.00 (*1-895411-65-3*) Peguis Pubs Ltd.

Multi-Age Classroom: A Family of Learners. Wendy C. Kasten & Barbara K. Clarke. LC 93-20195. 84p. 1993. pap. text 13.95 (*1-878450-35-2*, 504) R Owen Pubs.

Multi-Age Classroom: Professional Guide. Jodi McClay. (Professional's Guide Ser.). 80p. 1997. pap. 9.95 (*1-55734-881-2*) Tchr Create Mat.

Multi-Age Classrooms. Ed. by Karen Gutloff. (Teacher-to-Teacher Ser.). (Illus.). 96p. (Orig.). 1995. pap. 12.95 (*0-8106-2907-0*, 2907-0) NEA.

Multi-Age Reading Game. 1999. pap. text 16.95 (*1-56822-754-X*) Instruct Fair.

***Multi-Agency Radiation Survey & Site Investigation Manual (MARSSIM), Final, 1997, December.** 660p. 1998. per. 56.00 (*0-16-062720-6*) USGPO.

Multi-Agent Rationality: 8th European Workshop on Modelling Autonomous Agents in a Multi-Agent World, MAAMAW'97, Ronneby, Sweden, May 13-16, 1997, Proceedings. Ed. by M. Boman et al. LC 97-14896. (Lecture Notes in Artificial Intelligence Ser.: No. 1237). xii, 254p. 1997. pap. 49.00 (*3-540-63077-5*) Spr-Verlag.

***Multi-Agent System Engineering: Proceedings, 9th European Workshop on Modelling Autonomous Agents in a Multi-Agent World, MAAMAW'99, Valencia, Spain, June 30-July 2, 1999.** Ed. by Francisco J. Garijo & Magnus Boman. LC 99-37106. (Lecture Notes in Artificial Intelligence Ser.: Vol. 1647). x, 233p. 1999. pap. 45.00 (*3-540-66281-2*) Spr-Verlag.

Multi-Agent Systems - Theories, Languages & Applications: 4th Australian Workshop on Distributed Artificial Intelligence, Brisbane, QLD, Australia, July 13, 1998: Proceedings. Ed. by Dickson Lukose et al. LC 98-53825. (Lecture Notes in Computer Science Ser.: Vol. 1544). vii, 200p. 1999. pap. 43.00 (*3-540-65477-1*) Spr-Verlag.

Multi-Agent Systems & Agent-Based Simulation: 1st International Workshop, MABS '98, Paris, France, July 4-6, 1998, Proceedings. Ed. by J. S. Sichmann et al. LC 99-10003. (Lecture Notes in Computer Science Ser.: Vol. 1534). viii, 237p. 1998. pap. 43.00 (*3-540-65476-3*) Spr-Verlag.

***Multi-Agent Systems for Concurrent Intelligent Design & Manufacturing.** Weiming Shen et al. LC 00-33764. (Illus.). 2000. write for info. (*0-7484-0882-7*, Pub. by Tay Francis Ltd) Taylor & Francis.

***Multi-Agent Systems in Production (MAS '99) A Proceeding Volume from the IFAC Workshop, Vienna, Austria, 2-4 December, 1999.** IFAC Workshop on Multi-Agent-Systems in Production--MAS '99 Staff et al. LC 00-40089. 2000. pap. write for info. (*0-08-043657-9*, Pergamon Pr) Elsevier.

Multi-Agent Systems Methodologies & Applications: Second Australian Workshop on Distributed Artificial Intelligence, Cairns, QLD, Australia, August 27, 1996, Selected Papers, Vol. 128. Ed. by Chengqi Zhang et al. LC 97-30398. (Lecture Notes in Artificial Intelligence: Vol. 1286). viii, 195p. 1997. pap. 43.00 (*3-540-63412-6*) Spr-Verlag.

Multi-America: Essays on Cultural Wars & Cultural Peace. Ed. by Ishmael Reed. LC 96-9130. xxviii, 468p. 1998. pap. 14.95 (*0-14-025912-0*, Penguin Bks) Viking Penguin.

Multi-Axial Classification of Child Psychiatric Disorders. D. Shaffer et al. 1975. pap. text 16.20 (*92-4-154050-8*, 1150115) World Health.

Multi-Bank Credits Handbook. 1989. pap. 59.95 (*1-55840-376-0*) Exec Ent Pubns.

Multi-Body Dynamics: Vehicles, Machines & Mechanisms. Homer Rahnejat. LC 98-85951. 368p. 1998. 69.00 (*0-7680-0269-9*, R-238) Soc Auto Engineers.

***Multi-Boot Configuration Handbook.** 496p. 2000. 39.99 (*0-7897-2283-6*) Que.

Multi-Camera Camerawork. Peter Ward. LC 97-31110. 350p. 1997. pap. text 26.95 (*0-240-51462-9*) Buttrwrth-Heinemann.

Multi-Camera Director. 2nd ed. Mark Herlinger. (Illus.). 235p. (C). 1998. pap. text 34.00 (*0-9647401-2-5*) Western Media.

Multi-Carrier Spread-Spectrum. Khaled Fazel & Gerhard P. Fettweis. LC 97-26096. 1997. text 125.00 (*0-7923-9973-0*) Kluwer Academic.

Multi-Center Woodturning. Ray Hopper. (Illus.). 168p. 1993. pap. 14.95 (*0-946819-35-1*, Pub. by Guild Master) Sterling.

Multi Channel Marketing: Maximizing Market Share with an Integrated Marketing Strategy. Kevin B. Tynan. LC 94-117728. 225p. 1993. 29.95 (*1-55738-503-3*, Irwn Prfssnl) McGraw-Hill Prof.

Multi-Channel Optical Communication Systems. Willner. 550p. write for info. (*0-471-11835-4*) Wiley.

Multi-Channel Video Competition: Hearing Before the Committee on Commerce, Science & Transportation, United States Senate, 105th Congress, 1st Session, April 10, 1997. USGPO Staff. LC 98-160948. iii, 78 p. 1997. pap. write for info. (*0-16-056166-3*) USGPO.

Multi-Characteristic Correlation of Upper Cretaceous Volcanic Ash Beds from Southwestern Utah to Central Colorado. Bart J. Kowallis et al. (Illus.). 22p. 1989. pap. 3.75 (*1-55791-305-6*) Utah Geological Survey.

Multi-Charity Benefit Greeting Card Concept. rev. ed. Alpha Pyramis Research Division Staff. (Illus.). 68p. 1992. student ed., ring bd. 19.95 (*0-913597-58-9*) Prosperity & Profits.

Multi-Chip Module Conference, 1996 IEEE (MCMC-96) LC 95-35893. 224p. 1996. pap. 50.00 (*0-8186-7286-2*, PR07225) IEEE Comp Soc.

Multi-Chip Module Conference, 1997 IEEE (MCMC-97) LC 96-79698. 250p. 1997. pap. 50.00 (*0-8186-7789-9*, PR07789) IEEE Comp Soc.

Multi-Chip Module Substrate Technology. R. Jones. (Electrical Engineering & Electronics Ser.). Date not set. write for info. (*0-8247-9947-X*) Dekker.

Multi-Chip Module Test Strategies. Ed. by Yervant Zorian. LC 97-8206. 1997. text 101.00 (*0-7923-9920-X*) Kluwer Academic.

Multi-City Study: Drug Misuse Trends in Thirteen European Cities. 1994. 18.00 (*92-871-2392-6*, Pub. by Council of Europe) Manhattan Pub Co.

Multi-Company - Multi-Country Clinical Trials: Implementation, Monitoring, & Regulations. Ed. by Rhona Simmons. (Illus.). 303p. 1993. 159.00 (*0-935184-49-X*) Interpharm.

Multi-Component Archaic & Late Prehistoric Residential Camps Along the Sweetwater River, Rancho San Diego, California. Brian F. Byrd & Carol Serr. (Brian F. Mooney Associates Anthropological Technical Ser.: No. 1). (Illus.). 431p. 1993. pap. write for info. (*0-9639458-0-7*) B Mooney Assocs.

Multi-Coordinate Data Presentation. V. Priel. 1977. 35.00 (*0-8464-0657-8*) Beekman Pubs.

Multi-Copper Oxidases. 500p. 1997. lib. bdg. 69.00 (*981-02-2711-6*) World Scientific Pub.

Multi-Criteria. Massam. (Progress in Planning Ser.). 1988. pap. 32.00 (*0-08-036878-6*, Pergamon Pr) Elsevier.

Multi-Criteria Analyses. 1991. 32.95 (*0-387-54483-6*) Spr-Verlag.

Multi-Criteria Analysis & Regional Decision-Making. A. Van Delft & Peter Nijkamp. (Studies in Applied Regional Science: No. 8). 1977. pap. 15.00 (*90-207-0689-6*) Kluwer Academic.

Multi-criteria Decision Analysis Via Ratio & Difference Judgement. Freerk A. Lootsma. LC 99-14204. (Applied Optimization Ser.). 1999. write for info. (*0-7923-5669-1*) Kluwer Academic.

Multi-Criteria Methods in Alternative Dispute Resolution: With Microcomputer Software Applications. Stuart S. Nagel & Miriam K. Mills. LC 90-8416. 288p. 1990. 77.50 (*0-89930-520-2*, NMC, Quorum Bks) Greenwood.

Multi-Cultural Art Projects: Grades 2-6. Vera J. Griswold & Judith Starke. 1987. pap. 9.95 (*0-89108-170-4*, 8702) Love Pub Co.

***Multi-Cultural Atlas of Skin Conditions.** Darya Samolis. (Illus.). 2000. pap. text 39.95 (*1-873413-42-4*) Merit Pub Intl.

Multi-Cultural Awareness: Consciousness Toward a Process of Personal Transformation. Joseph McNair. 386p. (C). 1996. pap. text, per. 54.95 (*0-7872-2669-6*, 41266901) Kendall-Hunt.

Multi-Cultural Books: Grades 6-8. (J). 1995. lib. bdg. 66.30 (*0-8050-3076-X*) H Holt & Co.

Multi-Cultural Books: K-2. (J). (ps-2). 1995. lib. bdg. 93.71 (*0-8050-3075-1*) H Holt & Co.

***Multi-Cultural Education: Insight on Policies & Pratices in Selected Schools.** Joseph Nwoye. 92p. (C). 1999. per. 41.95 (*0-7872-6499-7*, 41649901) Kendall-Hunt.

Multi Cultural Education in Pennsylvania: Where Are We? Where Are We Going? Barry Kanpol et al. Ed. by Diane Shoop. 17p. 1998. pap. 20.00 (*1-58036-058-0*) Penn State Data Ctr.

Multi-Cultural Literature: Books & Activities. Nancy Polette. (Illus.). 48p. (Orig.). 1993. pap. 7.95 (*1-879287-22-6*, BL032) Pieces of Lrning.

Multi-Cultural Masterpieces. (Illus.). 18p. pap. text 79.00 (*1-56762-045-0*) Modern Learn Pr.

Multi-Cultural Masterpieces Text & Prints. (Illus.). 18p. 1992. pap. text 199.00 (*0-935493-67-0*) Modern Learn Pr.

Multi-Cultural Planet: The Report of a UNESCO International Expert Group. Ervin Laszlo. 212p. 1994. pap. 17.95 (*1-85168-042-X*, Pub. by Onewrld Pubns) Penguin Putnam.

Multi-Cylinder Test Sequences for Evaluating Automotive Engine Oils, Pt. 3: Sequence V-D - STP 315H. Petroleum Products & Lubricants committee D-2. LC 83-68369. 146p. 1991. 20.00 (*0-8031-0238-0*, STP315H) ASTM.

Multi-Dimensional Diffusion Processes. S. S. Varadhan & Daniel W. Stroock. (Grundlehren der Mathematischen Wissenschaften Ser.: Vol. 233). 1997. text 99.00 (*0-387-90353-4*) Spr-Verlag.

***Multi-Dimensional Engine Modeling.** (Special Publications). 208p. 2000. 99.00 (*0-7680-0562-0*, SP-1512) Soc Auto Engineers.

Multi-Dimensional Global Change. LC 96-47601. (Wiley-Praxis Series in Remote Sensing). 776p. 1998. 165.00 (*0-471-97179-0*) Wiley.

Multi-Dimensional Modal Logic. Maarten Marx. LC 96-49525. (Applied Logic Ser.: Vol. 4). 256p. (C). 1996. text 104.00 (*0-7923-4345-X*) Kluwer Academic.

***Multi-Dimensional Simulation of Engine Internal Flows.** Ed. by T. Baritaud. (Oil & Gas Science & Technology Ser.: Vol. 54, No. 2). 310p. 1999. 57.00 (*2-7108-0771-8*) Edits Technip.

Multi-Disciplinary Teamwork: Community Mental Handicap Teams. Morag McGrath. (Care in the Community Studies). 217p. 1991. text 57.95 (*1-85628-152-3*, Pub. by Avebry) Ashgate Pub Co.

Multi-Domain Communication Management Systems. Alex Galis. LC 99-57031. 1999. 99.95 (*0-8493-0587-X*) CRC Pr.

Multi-Engine Flying. Paul A. Craig. LC 93-46034. (Illus.). 212p. 1994. pap. 19.95 (*0-07-013423-5*) McGraw-Hill Prof.

***Multi-Engine Oral Exam Guide: The Comprehensive Guide to Prepare You for the FAA Oral Exam.** 3rd ed. Michael D. Hayes. (Oral Exam Guide Ser.). 94p. 1998. pap. 9.95 (*1-56027-325-9*) ASA Inc.

Multi-Engine Pilot Manual. (Pilot Training Ser.). (Illus.). 128p. 1995. pap. text 28.35 (*0-88487-190-8*, JS314101) Jeppesen Sanderson.

Multi-Ethinic Metropolis: Patterns & Policies. Sako Musterd et al. LC 97-45500. (Geojournal Library: No. 43). 224p. 1997. 110.00 (*0-7923-4854-0*) Kluwer Academic.

Multi-Ethnic Canada: Identities & Inequalities. Leo Driedger. LC 97-120361. 352p. 1996. pap. text 42.00 (*0-19-541161-7*) OUP.

Multi-Ethnic Coalition Building in Los Angeles: A Two-Day Symposium, November 19-20, 1993. Ed. by Eui-Young Yu & Edward T. Chang. LC 95-16251. 1995. 34.95 (*0-941690-66-0*); pap. 16.95 (*0-941690-67-9*) Regina Bks.

Multi-Ethnicity. Isaac Canales. Ed. by Stephen Hayner & Gordon Aeschliman. (Global Issues Bible Study Ser.). 48p. 1990. wbk. ed. 4.99 (*0-8308-4905-X*, 4905) InterVarsity.

Multi-Facility Systems: The VA Experience. Ed. by R. M. Kolodner. LC 96-25988. (Computers in Health Care Ser.). 515p. 1997. pap. text 59.00 (*0-387-94837-6*) Spr-Verlag.

M

Multi-Family: Home Plans. 2nd rev. ed. 50p. 1999. reprint ed. pap. 3.95 (*0-934039-53-4*) Hme Dsgn Altntves.

Multi-Family Housing: Federal Programs for the Private Sector. James W. Jones. 836p. 1986. ring bd. 70.00 (*0-318-22525-5*, 00599) Law Journal.

***Multi-Family Wooden Houses in Japan: A Strategic Entry Report, 1998.** Compiled by Icon Group International Staff. (Illus.). 173p. 1999. ring bd. 1730.00 incl. audio compact disk (*0-7418-1523-0*) Icon Grp.

Multi-Family Wooden Housing in Japan: A Strategic Entry Report, 1996. Compiled by Icon Group International Staff. (Illus.). 126p. 1999. ring bd. 1260.00 incl. audio compact disk (*0-7418-0716-5*) Icon Grp.

Multi-Feed Systems for Radio Telescopes: Proceedings of the Workshop (1994: Tucson, AZ) Ed. by Darrel T. Emerson & John M. Payne. LC 95-75015. (Conference Ser.: Vol. 75). 366p. 1995. 34.00 (*0-937707-94-5*) Astron Soc Pacific.

***Multi-Financial Management.** 6th ed. Shapiro. 848p. 1999. text 95.95 (*0-471-36610-2*) Wiley.

Multi Flying Solo with Hypercard 2.3. Hofmeister. (DA - Computer Education Ser.). (J). (gr. k-8). 1996. pap., teacher ed. 22.95 (*0-538-65106-7*) S-W Pub.

***Multi-Frequency Nonlinear Profile Inversion Methods.** K. F. I. Haak. (Illus.). 206p. 1999. pap. 53.50 (*90-407-1816-4*, Pub. by Delft U Pr) Coronet Bks.

Multi-Gev High Performance Accelerators & Related Technology. Ed. by K. Hatanaka et al. LC 97-41559. 300p. 1997. text 54.00 (*981-02-3210-1*) World Scientific Pub.

Multi-Grid Methods & Applications. M. T. Schlick. (Computational Mathematics Ser.: Vol. 4). (Illus.). 380p. 1985. 143.95 (*0-387-12761-5*) Spr-Verlag.

Multi-Hamiltonian Theory of Dynamical Systems. Maaiej Blaszak & A. Mickiewicz. Ed. by R. Balian et al. LC 98-22162. (Texts & Monographs in Physics). (Illus.). x, 353p. 1998. 59.95 (*3-540-64251-X*) Spr-Verlag.

***Multi Hazard Identification & Risk Assessment: A Cornerstone of the National Mitigation Strategy.** Ed. by Maxine L. Hill. (Illus.). 380p. 1999. pap. text 45.00 (*0-7881-8074-6*) DIANE Pub.

Multi-Image Design & Production. Phiz Mezey. 176p. 1988. pap. text 52.95 (*0-240-51740-7*, Focal) Buttrwrth-Heinemann.

Multi-Image Media. Robert V. Bullough, Sr. Ed. by James E. Duane. LC 80-21341. (Instructional Media Library: Vol. 9). (Illus.). 128p. 1981. 27.95 (*0-87778-169-9*) Educ Tech Pubns.

Multi-Industry R&D Volume-1988: Annual. 1024p. 1988. pap. 25.00 (*0-317-01263-0*) Gov Data Pubns.

Multi-Institutional Management: The Green Bay Experience Presented to the Social & Economic Considerations Committee of the Great Lakes Science Advisory Board. fac. ed. C. Jarrell Yarbrough. LC 91-11179. 95p. 1985. pap. 30.00 (*0-7837-8619-0*, 207522600007) Bks Demand.

Multi-Institutional Systems Management: Concepts & Cases. Ed. by B. Jon Jaeger et al. 1987. teacher ed. 6.95 (*0-910591-03-2*); text 45.00 (*0-910591-02-4*) AUPHA Pr.

Multi-Keyboard Operator. Jack Rudman. (Career Examination Ser.: C-455). 1994. pap. 23.95 (*0-8373-0455-5*) Nat Learn.

Multi-Keyboard Operator II. Jack Rudman. (Career Examination Ser.: C-3073). 1994. pap. 27.95 (*0-8373-3073-4*) Nat Learn.

Multi-Language Glossary on Natural Disasters. Ed. by Kenzo Toki. 251p. (Orig.). (C). 1994. pap. text 85.00 (*0-7881-0184-6*) DIANE Pub.

Multi-Level . . . Hillside Home Plans. Ed. by National Plan Service, Inc. Staff. (Illus.). 32p. reprint ed. pap. 3.95 (*0-934039-16-X*, A41) Hme Dsgn Altntves.

Multi-Level Lot Sizing & Scheduling: Methods for Capacitated, Dynamic, & Deterministic Models. A. Kimms. Ed. by H. Tempelmeier et al. (Production & Logistics Ser.). (Illus.). xxiv, 355p. 1996. pap. 78.00 (*3-7908-0967-5*) Spr-Verlag.

Multi-Level Marketing: The Definitive Guide to America's Top MLM Companies. Upline Financial Press Staff. LC 94-2220. 208p. (Orig.). 1993. pap. 24.95 (*1-56530-059-9*) Summit TX.

Multi-Level Marketing: The Definitive Guide to America's Top MLM Companies. 2nd rev. ed. Will Marks. LC 96-51294. 211p. 1997. pap. 24.99 (*1-56530-215-X*, Pub. by Summit TX) BookWorld.

***Multi-Level Marketing Made E-Z.** Adams. 224p. 2000. pap. 17.95 (*1-56382-457-4*) E-Z Legal.

Multi-Level Money: The Complete Guide to Generating, Closing & Working with All the Prospects You Need to Make Real Money Every Month in Network Marketing. 2nd ed. Jeffrey Lant. LC 95-187301. 250p. (Orig.). 1995. pap. 19.95 (*0-940374-28-5*) JLA Pubns.

Multi-Level Planning & Integrated Rural Development in India. R. P. Misra. 1980. 15.00 (*0-8364-0576-5*, Pub. by Heritage IA) S Asia.

Multi-Level Simulation for VLSI Design. Dwight D. Hill & David R. Coelho. 1986. text 92.00 (*0-89838-184-3*) Kluwer Academic.

Multi-Media & Imaging Databases. Setrag Khoshafian & A. Brad Baker. 586p. (C). 1996. pap. text 51.95 (*1-55860-312-3*) Morgan Kaufmann.

Multi-Media Communications. Ed. by May Katzen. LC 82-3023. 156p. 1982. 45.00 (*0-313-23565-1*, KAC/, Greenwood Pr) Greenwood.

Multi-Media Document Translation: ODA & the EXPRES Project. J. Rosenberg et al. (Illus.). 824p. 1990. 96.95 (*0-387-97397-4*) Spr-Verlag.

Multi-Media Fate Model: A Vital Tool for Predicting the Fate of Chemicals. Society of Environmental Toxicology & Chemistry (S. Ed. by Christina E. Cowan et al. LC 96-113847. 78p. 1995. text 45.00 (*1-880611-02-3*, SETAC Pr) SETAC.

Multi-Media Indexes, Lists, & Review Sources: A Bibliographic Guide. Thomas L. Hart et al. LC 75-15016. (Books in Library & Information Science: No. 13). 283p. reprint ed. pap. 87.80 (*0-7837-0802-5*, 204111700019) Bks Demand.

Multi-Media Investigation Manual. U. S. Environmental Protection Agency Staff. 192p. 1992. pap. 79.00 (*0-86587-300-3*) Gov Insts.

Multi-Media Reviews Index, Vol. 1. Ed. by C. Edward Wall & Penny B. Northern. LC 73-173772. 1972. 40.00 (*0-87650-023-8*) Pierian.

Multi-Media Reviews Index, Vol. 2. Ed. by C. Edward Wall & Penny B. Northern. LC 73-173772. 1973. 45.00 (*0-87650-042-4*) Pierian.

Multi-Media Reviews Index, Vol. 3. Ed. by C. Edward Wall & Penny B. Northern. LC 73-173772. 1973. 45.00 (*0-87650-051-3*) Pierian.

Multi-Media Revolution. Great Britain, Parliament, House of Commons Staff. LC 98-168298. 1998. pap. 25.00 (*0-10-248798-7*, Pub. by Statnry Office) Bernan Associates.

Multi-Member Districting & Minorities. Alan L. Clem & William Farber. 1978. 1.00 (*1-55614-066-5*) U of SD Gov Res Bur.

Multi-Microprocessor Systems for Real-Time Applications. Ed. by Gianni Conte & Dante Del Corso. 1985. text 144.00 (*90-277-2054-1*) Kluwer Academic.

Multi-Modal Approach to Creative Art Therapy. Arthur Robbins. LC 94-236986. 250p. 1994. pap. 23.00 (*1-85302-262-4*) Taylor & Francis.

Multi-National Corporations & Third World Development, 11. Ed. by Pradip K. Ghosh. LC 83-26680. (International Development Resource Bks.: No. 11). (Illus.). 473p. 1984. lib. bdg. 99.50 (*0-313-24147-3*, GMN/, Greenwood Pr) Greenwood.

***Multi-Objective Optimization of Nonstandard Gears Including Robustness.** D. R. Houser et al. (Technical Papers: Vol. 99FTM16). 14p. 1999. pap. 30.00 (*1-55589-754-1*) AGMA.

Multi-Objective Programming & Goal Programming: Theories & Applications. Ed. by M. Tamiz et al. (Lecture Notes in Economics & Mathematical Systems Ser.: Vol. 432). (Illus.). vi, 359p. 1996. pap. 78.00 (*3-540-60662-9*) Spr-Verlag.

Multi-Objective Regional Energy Planning. Peter D. Blair. (Studies in Applied Regional Science: Vol. 14). 1979. lib. bdg. 61.00 (*0-89838-008-1*) Kluwer Academic.

***Multi-Operating System Networking.** Raj Rajagopal. LC 99-40224. (Best Practices Ser.). 1338p. 1999. boxed set 79.95 (*0-8493-9831-2*) CRC Pr.

Multi-Organ Donor: Selection & Management. Robert S. Higgins. LC 97-10438. 1997. 99.95 (*0-86542-395-4*) Blackwell Sci.

Multi-Orgasmic Couple. Chia. 2001. pap. 16.00 (*0-06-251614-0*) HarpC.

Multi-Orgasmic Couple: Sexual Secrets Every Couple Should Know. Mantak Chia et al. 176p. 2000. 24.00 (*0-06-251613-2*) HarpC.

Multi-Orgasmic Man: Sexual Secrets Every Man Should Know. Mantak Chia & Douglas A. Arava. 1997. pap. 13.00 (*0-614-27644-6*) Harper SF.

Multi-Orgasmic Man: Sexual Secrets Every Man Should Know. Mantak Chia & Douglas Abrams Arava. LC 95-51976. (Illus.). 256p. 1997. pap. 15.00 (*0-06-251336-2*, Pub. by Harper SF) HarpC.

Multi-Output Production & Duality: Theory & Applications. Rolf Fare. 184p. (C). 1994. lib. bdg. 106.00 (*0-7923-9518-2*) Kluwer Academic.

***Multi-Party Actions.** Christopher Hodges. 500p. 2000. text 160.00 (*0-19-829896-X*) OUP.

Multi-Party Britain. Ed. by H. M. Drucker. LC 79-52940. (Praeger Special Studies). 256p. 1979. 65.00 (*0-275-90348-6*, C0348, Praeger Pubs) Greenwood.

Multi-Party Politics in America. Ed. by Paul S. Herrnson & John C. Green. LC 97-18719. (People, Passions, & Power Ser.). (Illus.). 216p. (Orig.). 1997. pap. 20.95 (*0-8476-8497-0*); text 68.50 (*0-8476-8496-2*) Rowman.

Multi-Party Politics in Kenya. David Throup & Charles Hornsby. LC 97-49221. 660p. 1997. text 59.95 (*0-8214-1206-X*); pap. text 29.95 (*0-8214-1207-8*) Ohio U Pr.

Multi-Phase Flow Symposium: Proceedings of the Multi-Phase Flow Symposium of ASME, Winter Annual Meeting, Philadelphia, 1963. ASME Staff. Ed. by Norman J. Lipstein. LC TJ0265.M8. 103p. reprint ed. pap. 32.00 (*0-608-11706-4*, 201331600085) Bks Demand.

Multi-Platform Code Management. Kevin Jameson. Ed. by Andy Oram. (Illus.). 354p. (Orig.). 1994. pap. 39.95 (*1-56592-059-7*) Thomson Learn.

Multi Platform Network Security. Andrew Yeomans. (C). 2000. text. write for info. (*0-201-61917-2*) Addison-Wesley.

Multi-Platform Systems Management. Lirov. (C). 1999. text 45.00 (*0-13-915786-7*, Macmillan Coll) P-H.

Multi-Problem Family: A Review & Annotated Bibliography. Benjamin Schlesinger. Ed. by Florence Strakovsky. LC 63-24680. 197p. reprint ed. pap. 61.10 (*0-608-13608-5*, 205121800093) Bks Demand.

Multi-Process Wet Cleaning: Cost & Performance Comparison of Conventional Dry Cleaning & an Alternative Process. 1995. lib. bdg. 249.75 (*0-8490-7433-9*) Gordon Pr.

Multi-Purpose High-Rise Towers & Tall Buildings. Ed. by H. R. Viswanath & J. Tolloczko. LC 98-113372. (Illus.). 424p. (C). (gr. 13). Date not set. 115.00 (*0-419-23300-8*, D5745, E & FN Spon) Routledge.

Multi-script, Multi-lingual, Multi-character. Issues for the On-line Environment: Proceedings of a Workshop Sponsored by the IFLA Section on Cataloguing, Istanbul, Turkey - August 24, 1995. Ed. by John D. Byrum, Jr. & Olivia M. Madison. (IFLA Publications: 85). iv, 123p. 1998. write for info. (*3-598-21814-1*) K G Saur Verlag.

Multi-Sensor & Data Fusion. Richard K. Miller & Terri C. Walker. LC 88-81634. (Survey on Technology & Markets Ser.: No. 43). 50p. 1989. pap. text 200.00 (*1-55865-042-3*) Future Tech Surveys.

Multi-Sensor Fusion. Richard R. Brooks & Sundararaja Iyengar. LC 97-29569. 416p. (C). 1997. text 89.00 incl. disk (*0-13-901653-8*) P-H.

Multi-Sensory Phonics: Mix Workbook (All Vowels) Donna M. Hoiland. (Illus.). 91p. 1987. 9.95 (*1-878880-05-5*, MSPON) Hoiland Pubns.

Multi-Site Pig Production. Hank Harris. LC 99-49092. (Illus.). 280p. 1999. 69.95 (*0-8138-2699-3*) Iowa St U Pr.

Multi-Speed European Integration Process. Featherstone. (C). 1998. pap. text 17.95 (*0-582-30919-0*) Longman.

Multi-Stage Production: Planning & Inventory Control. Ed. by S. Axsater et al. (Lecture Notes in Economics & Mathematical Systems Ser.: Vol. 266). v, 264p. 1986. 37.70 (*0-387-16436-7*) Spr-Verlag.

Multi-State Information System: Proceedings of the Fifth Annual National Users Group Conference. Ed. by Jeffrey Johnsen. 133p. 1981. pap. 10.00 (*0-936934-01-8*) N S Kline Inst.

Multi-State Information System: Proceedings of the Sixth Annual National Users Group Conference, May 4-6, 1981, Orangeburg, N.Y. Ed. by Linda J. Kline & Jane M. Carhart. 225p. (Orig.). 1982. pap. 10.00 (*0-936934-02-6*) N S Kline Inst.

Multi-State Information System - Theoretical & Practical Issues: Proceedings of the Fourth Annual National Users Group Conference. National Users Group Staff. Ed. by James A. King. 206p. 1980. pap. 10.00 (*0-936934-00-X*) N S Kline Inst.

Multi-Storey PreCast Concrete Framed Structures: A Practical Guide. Kim S. Elliott. LC 95-30820. (Illus.). 640p. 1996. text 175.00 (*0-632-03415-7*) Blackwell Sci.

Multi-System Nations & International Law, International Status of Germany, Korea & China. Ed. by Hungdah Chiu & Robert Downen. LC 81-85785. (Occasional Papers-Reprints Series in Contemporary Asian Studies: No. 8-1981). 203p. (Orig.). (C). 1981. pap. text 8.00 (*0-942182-44-8*) Occasional Papers.

Multi-Systemic Auto-Immune Diseases: An Integrated Approach: Dermatological & Internal Aspects. Ed. by Louis Kater & Harold B. De La Faille. LC 95-6498. 372p. 1995. 332.25 (*0-444-81896-0*) Elsevier.

Multi-Systemic Structural-Strategic Interventions for Child & Adolescent Behavior Problems. Ed. by Patrick H. Tolan. LC 89-26684. (Journal of Psychotherapy & the Family: Vol. 6, Nos. 3-4). (Illus.). 168p. 1990. text 4.95 (*0-86656-974-X*) Haworth Pr.

Multi-Threaded Object Oriented MPI-Based Message Passing Interface: The Arch Library. Jean-Marc Adamo. LC 98-18613. (Engineering & Computer Science Ser.). 200p. 1998. 120.00 (*0-7923-8165-3*) Kluwer Academic.

Multi Title Old Woman/Daisies/Grow Old (Papier-Petite), 12 vols. Ed. by Sandra H. Martz. (Illus.). 64p. 1998. 83.40 (*1-57601-035-X*) Papier-Mache Press.

Multi-Track Diplomacy: A Systems Approach to Peace. 3rd ed. Louise Diamond & John McDonald. LC 95-42452. (Books for a World That Works). (Illus.). 192p. 1996. pap. 19.95 (*1-56549-057-6*) Kumarian Pr.

Multi Track Recording for Musicians. Brent Hurtig. (Illus.). 144p. 1988. pap. 19.95 (*0-88284-355-9*, 2608) Alfred Pub.

Multi-Unit Housing. (Architectural Design Ser.). (Illus.). 230p. 1997. 85.00 (*84-921606-4-0*, Pub. by Links Inter) Bks Nippan.

Multi-Unit Wooden Housing in Japan: A Strategic Entry Report, 1998. Compiled by Icon Group International Staff. (Country Industry Report). (Illus.). 116p. 1999. ring bd. 1160.00 incl. audio compact disk (*0-7418-0437-9*) Icon Grp.

Multi-Universe Cosmos: The First Complete Story of the Origin of the Universe. A. K. Velan. (Illus.). 376p. (C). 1992. text 45.00 (*0-306-44267-1*, Kluwer Plenum) Kluwer Academic.

Multi-Use Collapsible Basket Patterns: Over 100 Designs for the Scrollsaw. Rick Longabaugh & Karen Longabaugh. (Illus.). 118p. 1997. pap. 12.95 (*1-56523-088-4*) Fox Chapel Pub.

Multi User America. 4th ed. (C). 1999. pap. text 21.00 (*0-205-31401-5*) Allyn.

Multi-User Communication Systems. Ed. by G. Longe. (CISM International Centre for Mechanical Sciences Ser.: Vol. 265). (Illus.). 259p. 1981. 43.95 (*0-387-81612-7*) Spr-Verlag.

Multi-User Smalltalk. Jay Almarode. (Management Briefings Ser.). 51p. 1996. 85.00 (*1-884842-68-2*, QA76) SIGS Bks & Multimedia.

***Multi-Valued & Universal Binary Neurons: Theory, Learning & Applications.** Igor N. Aizenberg et al. 280p. 2000. 140.00 (*0-7923-7824-5*) Kluwer Academic.

Multi-Vari Chart & Analysis. Mario Perez-Wilson. (Variation Reduction Program Ser.). 86p. 1993. 35.00 (*1-883237-01-7*) Adv Systs Cnslts.

Multi-Variable Calculus. Jerrold E. Marsden. LC 92-38049. 533p. (C). 1993. pap. text 72.95 (*0-7167-2443-X*) W H Freeman.

***Multi View Modeling & Analysis of Visual Scenes: Proceedings of the IEEE Workshop on Multi-View Modeling & Analysis of Visual Scenes, MVIEW '99 Held Fort Collins, Colorado, 1999.** Contrib. by IEEE Computer Society Staff. LC 99-62868. 89p. 1999. pap. 100.00 (*0-7695-0110-9*) IEEE Comp Soc.

Multi-Wavelength Continuum Emission of AGN: Proceedings of the 159th Symposium of the International Astronomical Union Held in Geneva, Switzerland, August 30-September 3, 1993. Ed. by T. J. Courvoisier & A. Blecha. LC 94-4220. (International Astronomical Union Symposia Ser.). 564p. (C). 1994. lib. bdg. 183.00 (*0-7923-2744-6*) Kluwer Academic.

Multi-Year Revenue & Expenditure Forecasting: Report of National Workshops. 126p. 1980. 15.00 (*0-318-17356-5*, DG 80-204) Pub Tech Inc.

***Multi-Year Statewide Strategy for Drugs & Violent Crime Control: State of Texas.** Robert J. Bodisch, Sr. (Illus.). 51p. (C). 1999. pap. text 25.00 (*0-7881-7212-3*) DIANE Pub.

Multiaccess, Mobility & TeleTraffic Advances in Wireless Networks. Ed. by David Everitt & Michael Rumsewicz. LC 97-39046. xi, 357p. 1998. text 137.50 (*0-7923-8091-6*) Kluwer Academic.

Multiaccess, Mobility & Teletraffic for Personal Communications. Ed. by Bi J. Jabbari. (International Series in Engineering & Computer Science, Natural Language Processing & Machine Translation). viii, 364p. (C). 1996. text 133.00 (*0-7923-9742-8*) Kluwer Academic.

***Multiaccess, Mobility & Teletraffic for Wireless Communications.** Kim K. Leung & Branimir Vojcic. LC 99-189927. 1999. write for info. (*0-7923-8353-2*) Kluwer Academic.

Multiage Classroom: A Collection. Ed. by Robin Fogarty. LC 93-80675. (Illus.). 230p. (Orig.). 1993. pap. 24.95 (*0-932935-71-0*) SkyLght.

Multiage Classroom: Choice & Possibility. Maureen Miletta. LC 96-5491. 121p. (Orig.). 1996. pap. text 18.00 (*0-435-08889-0*, 08889) Heinemann.

Multiage Classroom: What Research Tells Us. Sandra J. Stone. LC 98-11534. (What Research Tells Us Ser.). (Illus.). 20p. 1997. pap. 2.00 (*0-912099-33-X*, 404) Kappa Delta Pi.

Multiage Classrooms by Design: Beyond the One-Room School. Tabitha C. Daniel & Kay W. Terry. Ed. by Jerry J. Herman & Janice L. Herman. LC 95-8842. (Practicing Administrator's Leadership Ser.). 88p. 1995. pap. 14.95 (*0-8039-6261-4*) Corwin Pr.

***Multiage Evaluation Book.** Char Forsten et al. LC 99-72753. 86p. 1999. pap. 19.95 (*1-884548-26-1*, 5738, Crystal Spgs) Soc Dev Educ.

Multiage Handbook: A Comprehensive Resource for Multiage Practices. Ed. by Aldene Fredenburg. LC 996. 288p. 1996. pap. 24.95 (*1-884548-05-9*, 4675) Soc Dev Educ.

Multiage Portraits: Teaching & Learning in Mixed-Age Classrooms. Charles Rathbone et al. 185p. 1993. pap. 19.95 (*0-9627389-7-2*, Crystal Spgs) Soc Dev Educ.

Multiage Q & A: 101 Practical Answers to Your Most Pressing Questions. 2nd ed. Jim Grant et al. Ed. by Aldene Fredenburg. 148p. 1996. pap. text, teacher ed. 12.95 (*1-884548-08-3*, Crystal Spgs) Soc Dev Educ.

Multiagent Learning. Ed. by Sandip Sen. (Technical Reports: No. WS-97-03). 76p. 1997. spiral bd. 25.00 (*1-57735-030-8*) AAAI Pr.

Multiagent Platforms: Selected Papers on the 1st Pacific Rim International Workshop on Multi-Agents, PRIMA '98, Singapore, November 23, 1998. Ed. by Toru Ishida et al. LC 99-15830. (Lecture Notes in Computer Science Ser.: Vol. 1599). viii, 187p. 1999. pap. 45.00 (*3-540-65967-6*) Spr-Verlag.

Multiagent Systems: A Modern Approach to Distributed Artificial Intelligence. Ed. by Gerhard Weiss. LC 98-49797. (Illus.). 643p. 1999. 60.00 (*0-262-23203-0*) MIT Pr.

Multiagent Systems: A Theoretical Framework for Intentions, Know-How, & Communications. Munidar P. Singh. LC 94-13877. (Lecture Notes in Artificial Intelligence Ser.: Vol. 799). 1994. 34.95 (*0-387-58026-3*) Spr-Verlag.

Multiattribute Evaluation. Ward Edwards & J. Robert Newman. (Quantitative Applications in the Social Sciences Ser.: Vol. 26). (Illus.). 96p. 1982. pap. 10.95 (*0-8039-0095-3*) Sage.

Multiaxial Classification of Child & Adolescent Psychiatric Disorder: The ICD-10 Classification of Mental & Behavioural Disorders in Children & Adolescents. World Health Organization Staff. 310p. (C). 1997. text 74.95 (*0-521-58133-8*) Cambridge U Pr.

***Multiaxial Fatigue.** Darrell Socie & Gary Marquis. LC 99-32460. 502p. 2000. 69.00 (*0-7680-0453-5*, R-234) Soc Auto Engineers.

Multiaxial Fatigue: Analysis & Experiments. 172p. 1989. 29.00 (*0-89883-780-4*, AE14) Soc Auto Engineers.

Multiaxial Fatigue - STP 853. Ed. by K. J. Miller & M. W. Brown. LC 85-7376. 750p. 1985. text 88.00 (*0-8031-0444-8*, STP853) ASTM.

Multiaxial Fatigue & Deformation Techniques, Vol. STP 1280. Ed. by Sreeramesh Kalluri & Peter J. Bonacuse. LC 96-37368. (STP Ser.). (Illus.). 316p. 1997. text 108.00 (*0-8031-2045-1*, STP1280) ASTM.

***Multiaxial Fatigue & Fracture.** International Conference on Biaxial/Multiaxial Fatigue Staff et al. LC 99-31215. 1999. 175.00 (*0-08-043336-7*, Pub. by Elsevier) Elsevier.

***Multiaxial Fatigue of an Induction Hardened Shaft.** 196th ed. (Advances in Engineering Ser.). 1999. 89.00 (*0-7680-0528-0*, AE-28) Soc Auto Engineers.

Multiaxial Presentation of the ICD-10 for Use in Adult Psychiatry. World Health Organization Staff. LC 96-51767. (Illus.). 158p. (C). 1997. text 59.95 (*0-521-58502-3*) Cambridge U Pr.

Multibank Holding Company Performance. Ronald L. Schillereff. Ed. by Gunter Dufey. LC 82-8583. (Research for Business Decisions Ser.: No. 52). 122p. 1982. reprint ed. pap. 37.90 (*0-8357-1348-2*, 207016000064) Bks Demand.

Multiblock Quilt Designs. Pepper Cory. LC 97-50338. 1998. pap. 8.95 (*0-486-40047-6*) Dover.

Multibody Computer Codes in Vehicle System Dynamics: Supplement to Vehicle System Dynamics, Vol. 22. Ed. by W. Kortum & R. S. Sharp. LC 93-11638. 276p. 1993. 92.00 (*90-265-1365-8*) Swets.

Multibody Dynamics. Ronald L. Huston. LC 89-48799. (Illus.). 432p. reprint ed. pap. 134.00 (*0-608-08851-X*, 206949000004) Bks Demand.

Multibody Dynamics with Unilateral Contacts. Friedrich Pfeiffer & Christoph Glocker. LC 96-12451. (Wiley Series in Nonlinear Science). 336p. 1996. 89.95 (*0-471-15565-9*) Wiley.

Multibody System Dynamics. Ronald L. Huston. 416p. 1990. 130.00 (*0-409-90041-9*) Buttrwrth-Heinemann.

MultiBody System SIMulation No. 7: Numerical Methods, Algorithms & Software. R. M. Phillips. Ed. by M. Griebel et al. LC 99-30072. xv, 251p. 1999. pap. 82.00 (*3-540-65662-6*) Spr-Verlag.

Multibody Systems Handbook. Ed. by W. O. Schiehlen. (Illus.). 435p. 1990. 146.95 (*0-387-51946-7*) Spr-Verlag.

Multicampus System: Perspectives on Practice & Prospects Gerald H. Gaither. LC 98-40753. 1998. write for info. (*1-57922-016-9*) Stylus Pub VA.

***Multicast Communication: Protocols, Programming & Applications.** Ralph Wittmann. (Networking Ser.). 350p. 2000. 44.95 (*1-55860-645-9*) Morgan Kaufmann.

Multicast Networking & Applications. C. Kenneth Miller. LC 98-29715. 304p. (C). 1998. 39.95 (*0-201-30979-3*) Addison-Wesley.

Multicasting on the Internet & Its Applications. Sanjoy Paul. LC 98-20100. 421p. 1998. write for info. (*0-7923-8200-5*) Kluwer Academic.

Multicellular Animals: A New Approach to the Phylogenetic Order in Nature, Vol. 1. Peter Ax. LC 96-15839. 224p. 1996. 89.50 (*3-540-60803-6*) Spr-Verlag.

Multicentre Study on Low Birth Weight & Infant Mortality in India, Nepal, & Sri Lanka. (SEARO Regional Health Papers: No. 25). x, 78p. 1994. pap. text 10.00 (*92-9022-194-1*, 1580025) World Health.

Multicentre Trials. Ed. by H. Helmchen & Norman Sartorius. (Modern Problems of Pharmacopsychiatry Ser.: Vol. 16). (Illus.). xii, 116p. 1981. 68.75 (*3-8055-2806-X*) S Karger.

Multichannel Image Detectors. Ed. by Yair Talmi. LC 79-12441. (ACS Symposium Ser.: No. 102). 1979. 43.95 (*0-8412-0504-3*) Am Chemical.

Multichannel Image Detectors, Vol. 1. Yair Talmi. LC 79-12441. (ACS Symposium Ser.: Vol. 102). 362p. 1979. reprint ed. pap. 112.30 (*0-608-03097-X*, 206355000001) Bks Demand.

Multichannel Image Detectors, Vol. 2. Ed. by Yair Talmi. LC 79-12441. (ACS Symposium Ser.: No. 236). 342p. 1983. lib. bdg. 54.95 (*0-8412-0814-X*) Am Chemical.

Multichannel Image Detectors, Vol. 2. Ed. by Yair Talmi. LC 79-12441. (ACS Symposium Ser.: Vol. 236). 344p. 1983. reprint ed. pap. 106.70 (*0-608-03067-8*, 206352000002) Bks Demand.

Multichannel Integrations of Non Verbal Behavior. Ed. by Aron W. Siegman & Stanley Feldstein. 312p. (C). 1985. text 69.95 (*0-89859-566-5*) L Erlbaum Assocs.

***Multichannel Optical Networks.** Peng J. Wan. LC 99-23435. (Network Theory & Applications Ser.). 1999. write for info. (*0-7923-5776-0*) Kluwer Academic.

Multichannel Optical Networks: Theory & Practice: DIMACS Workshop, March 16-19, 1998. Peng-Jun Wan et al. LC 98-44528. (Discrete Mathematics & Theoretical Computer Science Ser.). 249p. 1998. write for info. (*0-8218-1004-9*) Am Math.

Multichip Module Technologies & Alternatives: The Basics. Ed. by Daryl A. Doane & Paul D. Franzon. LC 92-29779. 1993. text 89.95 (*0-442-01236-5*, VNR) Wiley.

Multichip Module Technology Handbook. Philip E. Garrou et al. LC 97-227212. (Illus.). 688p. 1997. 99.50 (*0-07-022894-9*) McGraw.

Multichip Modules. Business Communications Co., Inc. Staff. 139p. 1990. 2650.00 (*0-89336-750-8*, GB138) BCC.

Multichip Modules. E. S. Kuh. 300p. 1992. text 74.00 (*981-02-0925-8*) World Scientific Pub.

An Asterisk (*) at the beginning of an entry indicates that the title is appearing for the first time.

Multichip Modules: Systems Advantages, Major Constructions & Materials Technologies. R. W. Johnson et al. LC 90-20827. 616p. 1991. 89.95 (*0-87942-267-X*, PC02600) Inst Electrical.

Multichip Modules with Integrated Sensors: Proceedings of the NATO Advanced Research Workshop, Budapest, Hungary, May 18-20, 1995. G. Arbor Hars Anyi. Ed. by W. Kinzy Jones. LC 96-32636. (NATO ASI Series, Partnership SubSeries 3: High Technology). 336p. (C). 1996. text 209.50 (*0-7923-4194-5*) Kluwer Academic.

Multichip Packaging & Bare Chip Systems, No. YGB-138R. Brent J. Knipfer. (Illus.). 263p. 1994. 2650.00 (*1-56965-204-X*, GB-138R) BCC.

***Multiclass Continuum Modelling of Multilane Traffic Flow.** Serge Hoogendoorn. (TRAIL Thesis Series). (Illus.). 385p. 1999. pap. 58.50 (*90-407-1931-4*, Pub. by Delft U Pr) Coronet Bks.

Multicolor Stellar Photometry. V. Straizys. (Astronomy & Astrophysics Ser.: Vol. 15). 584p. 1995. pap. 96.00 (*0-88126-029-0*) Pachart Pub Hse.

Multicolored Mirror: Cultural Substance in Literature for Children & Young Adults. Cooperative Children's Book Center Staff. Ed. by Merri V. Lindgren & Ginny M. Kruse. LC 91-76433. (Illus.). 195p. 1991. pap. 19.00 (*0-917846-05-2*, 95506) Highsmith Pr.

Multicommunity Collaboration: An Evolving Rural Revitalization Strategy. Ed. by Peter F. Korsching et al. 1992. pap. text 13.00 (*0-936913-04-5*, RRD 161) NCRCRD.

Multicomponent & Multilayered Thin Films for Advanced Microtechnologies: Techniques, Fundamentals, & Devices. Ed. by Orlando Auciello & Jurgen Engemann. LC 93-20488. (NATO Advanced Study Institutes Series E, Applied Sciences: Vol. 234). 1993. text 339.00 (*0-7923-2265-7*) Kluwer Academic.

Multicomponent Chromatography: Theory of Interference. Friedrich Helfferich & Geerhard Klein. LC 79-106898. (Chromatographic Science Ser.: Vol. 4). (Illus.). 429p. reprint ed. pap. 133.00 (*0-608-30558-8*, 205038200072) Bks Demand.

Multicomponent Flow Modeling: Modeling & Simulation in Science, Engineering & Technology. V. Giovangigli. LC 99-27050. 332p. 1999. 69.00 (*0-8176-4048-7*) Birkhauser.

Multicomponent Mass Transfer. Ross Taylor & Radha Krishna. LC 92-40667. (Chemical Engineering Ser.). 616p. 1993. 98.95 incl. disk (*0-471-57417-1*) Wiley.

Multicomponent Oxide Films for Electronics Vol. 574: Materials Research Society Symposium Proceedings. Ed. by M. E. Hawley et al. LC 99-42449. 382p. 1999. text 75.00 (*1-55899-481-5*) Materials Res.

Multicomponent Polymer Materials. Ed. by Leslie H. Sperling & D. R. Paul. LC 85-20475. (Advances in Chemistry Ser.: No. 211). (Illus.). xii, 352p. 1986. 87.95 (*0-8412-0899-9*) Am Chemical.

Multicomponent Polymer Materials. Ed. by Leslie H. Sperling & D. R. Paul. LC 85-20475. (Advances in Chemistry Ser.: Vol. 211). 368p. 1986. reprint ed. pap. 114.10 (*0-608-03892-X*, 206433900008) Bks Demand.

Multicomponent Polymer Systems: A Symposium Co-Sponsored by the Division of Industrial & Engineering Chemistry, the Division of Polymer Chemistry, & the Division of Cellulose, Wood, & Fiber Chemistry at the 159th Meeting of the American Chemical Society, Houston, TX, February 23-26, 1970 - Norbert A. J. Platzer, Symposium Chairman. American Chemical Society Staff. LC 70-159768. (Advances in Chemistry Ser.: No. 99). (Illus.). 616p. 1971. reprint ed. pap. 191.00 (*0-608-06759-8*, 206695600009) Bks Demand.

Multicomponent Random Systems. Ed. by R. L. Dobrushin & Ya G. Sinai. LC 80-17688. (Advances in Probability & Related Topics Ser.: No. 6). 622p. reprint ed. pap. 192.90 (*0-7837-7016-2*, 204683200004) Bks Demand.

Multicomponent Seismology in Petroleum Exploration. Robert H. Tatham & M. D. McCormack. (Investigations in Geophysics Ser.: No. 6). (Illus.). 256p. (C). 1991. text 97.00 (*1-56080-051-8*, 106A) Soc Expl Geophys.

Multicomponent Transport Algorithms. Alexandre Ern & Vincent Geovangigli. LC 94-29201. (Lecture Notes in Physics, New Series, Monographs: Vol. 24). 1994. 76.95 (*0-387-58309-2*) Spr-Verlag.

Multicomponent Transport in Polymer Systems for Controlled Release. Alexandre Y. Polishchuk & Gennadi E. Zaikov. (Polymer Science & Engineering Monographs). 1996. text 85.00 (*2-88449-160-0*); pap. text 44.00 (*2-88449-236-4*) Gordon & Breach.

Multicomponent Transport in Polymer Systems for Controlled Release. Alexandreya Polishchuk & Gennadi E. Zaikov. (Polymer Science & Engineering Monograp Ser.). 240p. 1997. text 51.00 (*90-5699-593-6*); pap. text 27.00 (*90-5699-594-4*) Gordon & Breach.

Multicomponent Ultrafine Microstructures Vol. 132: Materials Research Society Symposium Proceedings. Ed. by L. E. McCandlish et al. 243p. 1989. text 17.50 (*1-55899-005-4*) Materials Res.

Multicomputer Networks: Message-Based Parallel Processing. Daniel A. Reed & Richard M. Fujimoto. (Scientific Computation Ser.). 400p. 1987. 52.50 (*0-262-18129-0*) MIT Pr.

Multiconductor Transmission Line Analysis. Sidney Frankel. LC 77-28230. 430p. reprint ed. pap. 133.30 (*0-608-16252-3*, 202715800054) Bks Demand.

Multiconductor Transmission-Line Structures: Modal Analysis Techniques. J. A. Faria. LC 93-10063. (Microwave & Optical Engineering Ser.). 203p. 1993. 122.50 (*0-471-57443-0*) Wiley.

Multicriteria Analysis, Vol. X. Ed. by J. Climaco. LC 97-552. (Illus.). 617p. 1997. 169.00 (*3-540-62074-5*) Spr-Verlag.

Multicriteria Analysis for Land-Use Management. Euro Beinat & Peter Nijkamp. LC 98-35417. (Environment & Management Ser.). vii, 372 p. 1998. 159.00 (*0-7923-5198-3*) Kluwer Academic.

Multicriteria Decision-Aid. P. Vincke. LC 91-30739. 174p. 1992. 159.95 (*0-471-93184-5*) Wiley.

Multicriteria Decision Aid Methods for the Prediction of Business Failure. Constantin Zopounidis & Augustinos I. Dimitras. LC 97-49081. 171p. 1998. lib. bdg. 180.00 (*0-7923-4900-8*) Kluwer Academic.

Multicriteria Decision Making: Advances in MCDM Models, Algorithms, Theory & Applications Tombais Gbal et al. LC 99-30336. (International Operations Research & Management Science Ser.). 15p. 1999. write for info. (*0-7923-8534-9*) Kluwer Academic.

Multicriteria Decision Making - The Analytic Hierarchy Process: Planning, Priority Setting, Resource Allocation. 2nd rev. ed. Thomas L. Saaty. (Illus.). 437p. (C). 1990. reprint ed. pap. 25.00 (*0-9620317-2-0*) RWS Pubns.

Multicriteria Design: Optimization & Identification. R. B. Stanikov. LC 98-52904. (Applied Optimization Ser.). 20p. 1999. write for info. (*0-7923-5560-1*) Kluwer Academic.

Multicriteria Design Optimization: Procedures & Applications. H. A. Eschenauer et al. (Illus.). xxvii, 482p. 1990. 163.95 (*0-387-50604-7*) Spr-Verlag.

Multicriteria Evaluation in a Fuzzy Environment: Theory & Applications in Ecological Economics. G. Munda. (Contributions to Economics Ser.). (Illus.). xiv, 255p. 1995. pap. 71.00 (*3-7908-0892-X*) Spr-Verlag.

Multicriteria Evaluation in Physical Planning. Peter Nijkamp et al. (Contributions to Economic Analysis Ser.: No. 185). 616p. 1990. 125.50 (*0-444-88851-9*, North Holland) Elsevier.

Multicriteria Evaluation in Physical Planning. Peter Nijkamp et al. (Contributions to Economic Analysis Ser.: Vol. 185). 220p. 1990. 131.50 (*0-444-88124-7*) Elsevier.

Multicriteria Methodology for Decision Aiding. Bernard Roy. (Nonconvex Optimization & Its Applications Ser.). 320p. (C). 1996. lib. bdg. 156.00 (*0-7923-4166-X*) Kluwer Academic.

Multicriteria Optimization in Engineering & in the Sciences. W. Stadler. LC 87-32749. (Mathematical Concepts & Methods in Science & Engineering Ser.: Vol. 37). (Illus.). 420p. (C). 1988. text 95.00 (*0-306-42743-5*, Kluwer Plenum) Kluwer Academic.

***Multicultiboho Sideshow, Vol. 1.** Alexs D. Pate. LC 99-29476. 256p. 1999. 23.00 (*0-380-97678-1*, Avon Bks) Morrow Avon.

***Multicultiboho Sideshow: A Novel.** Alexs D. Pate. 2001. write for info. (*0-380-80041-1*, Perennial) HarperTrade.

Multicultural. Sue Boulais. 1993. 6.95 (*1-55708-388-6*, MCC919) McDonald Pub Co.

Multicultural. Susan Brecht Hibbard. 1994. 6.95 (*1-55708-420-3*, MCC910) McDonald Pub Co.

Multicultural Acquisitions. Ed. by Bill Katz & Karen Parrish. LC 93-7657. (Acquisitions Librarian Ser.: No. 5 (9/10)). (Illus.). 322p. 1993. lib. bdg. 49.95 (*1-56024-451-8*) Haworth Pr.

Multicultural Activities. Engleberg. (C). 1997. pap. text 8.76 (*0-395-84192-5*) HM.

Multicultural Activity Workbook: Africa, Asia & the Americas. Jay Monteith. (Illus.). 72p. (Orig.). (J). (gr. 1 up). 1991. pap. text 7.95 (*0-9627366-1-9*) Arts & Comns NY.

Multicultural AIDS Prevention Programs. Ed. by Robert T. Trotter, II. LC 96-33327. (Drugs & Society Ser.: Vol. 9, Nos. 1/2). 235p. (C). 1996. pap. 17.95 (*1-56023-087-8*, Harrington Park) Haworth Pr.

Multicultural AIDS Prevention Programs. Ed. by Robert T. Trotter, II. LC 96-33327. (Drugs & Society Ser.: Vol. 9, Nos. 1/2). 235p. (C). 1996. 49.95 (*1-56024-849-1*, Haworth Pastrl) Haworth Pr.

Multicultural America. 41.95 (*0-382-40673-7*) Cobblestone Pub Co.

Multicultural America: A Resource Book for Teachers of Humanities & American Studies. Ed. by Betty E. Chmaj. LC 92-33140. (C). 1993. pap. text 37.50 (*0-8191-8917-0*); lib. bdg. 64.00 (*0-8191-8916-2*) U Pr of Amer.

Multicultural & Gender Equity in the Mathematics Classroom: The Gift of Diversity (1997 Yearbook) Ed. by Janet Trentacosta & Margaret J. Kenney. LC 97-658. (Illus.). 248p. 1997. 27.00 (*0-87353-432-8*) NCTM.

Multicultural & Interdisciplinary Approaches to Parent-Infant Relations. Ed. by Kevin Nugent et al. (Cultural Context of Infancy Ser.: Vol. 2). 384p. (C). 1991. text 78.50 (*0-89391-627-7*) Ablx Pub.

Multicultural & Racial Conflicts: Role Play Peacegames. David W. Felder. LC 95-90518. 130p. 1996. 24.95 (*0-910959-22-6*, B&G 22H); teacher ed. 44.95 (*0-910959-42-0*, B&G 22T) Wellington Pr.

Multicultural Approaches to the Visual Arts. Patricia Jessup-Woodlin. 138p. (C). 1996. pap. text 37.95 (*0-7872-2766-8*, 41276601) Kendall-Hunt.

Multicultural Art Activities. Partners. 1997. pap. text 10.95 (*1-55734-617-8*) Tchr Create Mat.

Multicultural Art Activities Kit. Dwila Bloom. (Illus.). 384p. 1994. pap. text 59.95 (*0-87628-587-6*) Ctr Appl Res.

***Multicultural Aspects of Disabilities: A Guide to Understanding & Assisting Minorities in the Rehabilitation Process.** Willie V. Bryan. LC 98-52829. 300p. 1999. text 57.95 (*0-398-06941-7*); pap. text 45.95 (*0-398-06942-5*) C C Thomas.

Multicultural Aspects of Library Media Programs. Kathy H. Latrobe & Mildred K. Laughlin. 217p. 1992. 27.50 (*0-87287-879-1*) Libs Unl.

Multicultural Aspects of Sociolinguistics in Deaf Communities. Ed. by Ceil Lucas. (Sociolinguistics in Deaf Communities Ser.: Vol. 2). 246p. 1996. text 39.95 (*1-56368-046-7*) Gallaudet Univ Pr.

Multicultural Assessment. Deleon. 1997. pap. text 24.95 (*0-205-26154-X*) Allyn.

Multicultural Assessment in Counseling & Clinical Psychology. Ed. by Gargi R. Sodowsky & James C. Impara. (Buros-Nebraska Series on Measurement & Testing). 375p. (C). 1996. 49.95 (*0-910674-41-8*) Buros Inst Mental.

Multicultural Assessment Perspectives for Professional Psychology. Richard Dana. LC 92-17630. 320p. (C). 1992. 74.00 (*0-205-14092-0*, Longwood Div) Allyn.

Multicultural Autobiography: American Lives. James R. Payne. LC 91-27130. 376p. (C). 1992. pap. text 18.95 (*0-87049-740-5*); lib. bdg. 41.00 (*0-87049-739-1*) U of Tenn Pr.

Multicultural Books to Make & Share. Susan K. Gaylord. LC 94-234511. (J). 1994. pap. text 15.95 (*0-590-48921-6*) Scholastic Inc.

Multicultural Bulletin. (C). 1992. 0.00 (*0-201-92115-4*) HEPC Inc.

***Multicultural Campus: Strategies for Transforming Higher Education.** Ed. by Leonard A. Valverde & Louis A. Castenell, Jr. 216p. 1998. 62.00 (*0-7619-9165-4*) AltaMira Pr.

***Multicultural Campus: Strategies for Transforming Higher Education.** Ed. by Leonard A. Valverde & Louis A. Castenell, Jr. LC 97-45384. 216p. 1998. pap. 22.95 (*0-7619-9166-2*) AltaMira Pr.

***Multicultural Case Studies: Tools for Training.** Rohini Anand & Laura K. Shipler. ix, 131p. 1998. 24.95 (*1-885077-70-X*) NMCI Pubns.

Multicultural Casebook to Accompany Abnormal Psychology & Modern Life e. 1998 Update. 10th ed. Carson. (C). 1998. pap. text. write for info. (*0-321-01729-3*) Addson-Wesley Educ.

Multicultural Celebrations: Today's Rules of Etiquette for Life's Special Occasions. Norine Dresser. LC 98-29809. 320p. 1999. pap. 14.00 (*0-609-80259-3*) Crown Pub Group.

Multicultural Challenge in Health Education. Ana C. Matiella. LC 93-44540. 1994. 34.95 (*1-56071-355-0*) ETR Assocs.

Multicultural Child Care. Paul Vedder et al. LC 95-24251. 144p. 1995. 59.00 (*1-85359-308-7*, BE9, Pub. by Multilingual Matters); pap. 19.95 (*1-85359-307-9*, BE9, Pub. by Multilingual Matters) Taylor & Francis.

Multicultural Children in the Early Years: Creative Teaching, Meaningful Learning. Peter Woods. LC 98-33348. 1999. 85.00 (*1-85359-435-0*) Multilingual Matters.

***Multicultural Children in the Early Years: Creative Teaching, Meaningful Learning.** Peter Woods. LC 98-33348. 1999. pap. text 24.95 (*1-85359-434-2*) Multilingual Matters.

Multicultural Children's Literature. Norton. 2000. pap. text 19.98 (*0-13-243122-X*) P-H.

Multicultural Children's Literature: An Annotated Bibliography, Grades K-8. Beth B. Lind. LC 96-23847. 279p. (J). (gr. k-8). 1996. lib. bdg. 38.50 (*0-7864-0038-2*) McFarland & Co.

Multicultural Church: A New Landscape in U. S. Theologies. Ed. by William Cenkner. LC 95-31265. 208p. (Orig.). 1996. pap. 14.95 (*0-8091-3607-4*) Paulist Pr.

Multicultural Citizenship: A Liberal Theory of Minority Rights. Will Kymlicka. (Oxford Political Theory Ser.). 290p. 1996. reprint ed. pap. text 19.95 (*0-19-829091-8*) OUP.

Multicultural Clients: Professional Handbook for Health Care Providers & Social Workers. Sybil M. Lassiter. LC 94-30927. 224p. 1995. lib. bdg. 69.50 (*0-313-29140-3*, Greenwood Pr) Greenwood.

Multicultural Clip Art from Around the World. Susan Shneck. 1995. pap. text 15.95 (*0-590-48177-0*) Scholastic Inc.

Multicultural Communication. 2nd ed. Byrd. 1998. 66.00 (*0-07-011663-6*) McGraw.

Multicultural Communication & Pop Culture. Byrd. 1996. text 30.00 (*0-07-011924-4*) McGraw.

Multicultural Communication Strategies: How to Be More Successful with: Customers, Colleagues, Community. Judith A. Starkey. LC 95-80413. 160p. (Orig.). 1995. pap. 19.95 (*0-9648686-0-1*) JAMS Pubng.

Multicultural Connections. 2nd ed. Gerver. (International Math Ser.). 2000. pap. 15.95 (*0-538-69439-4*) Thomson Learn.

Multicultural Cookbook for Students. Carole L. Albyn & Lois S. Webb. LC 92-41634. (Illus.). 312p. 1993. pap. 29.50 (*0-89774-735-6*) Oryx Pr.

***Multicultural Cookbook of Life-Cycle Celebrations.** Lois Sinaiko Webb. 544p. 2000. pap. 35.00 (*1-57356-290-4*) Oryx Pr.

Multicultural Cookbooks, 4 bks. Ann L. Burckhardt. Incl. People of Africa & Their Food. LC 96-25943. (Illus.). 48p. (J). (gr. 3-4). 1996. lib. bdg. 19.00 (*1-56065-434-1*, Cpstone High Low); People of China & Their Food. LC 96-24789. (Illus.). 48p. (J). (gr. 3-4). 1996. lib. bdg. 19.00 (*1-56065-433-3*, Cpstone High Low); People of Mexico & Their Food. LC 96-24787. (Illus.). 48p. (J). (gr. 3-4). 1996. lib. bdg. 19.00 (*1-56065-432-5*, Cpstone High Low); People of Russia & Their Food. (Illus.). 48p. (J). (gr. 3-4). 1996. lib. bdg. 19.00 (*1-56065-435-X*, Cpstone High Low); 76.00 (*1-56065-639-5*, Cpstone High Low) Capstone Pr.

Multicultural Cooking: Light & Easy. Kay Spicer. (Illus.). 222p. 1995. pap. 19.95 (*0-9695688-2-7*) Mghton Hse.

***Multicultural Counseling: Empowerment Strat F/diverse Soc.** Michael J. D'Andrea & Judy A. Daniels. 2001. pap. 35.00 (*0-534-57340-1*) Thomson Learn.

Multicultural Counseling & Psychotherapy: A Lifespan Perspective. 2nd ed. Leroy G. Baruth & Lee M. Manning. LC 98-7606. 426p. 1998. pap. text 67.00 (*0-13-271925-8*, Merrill Coll) P-H.

Multicultural Counseling Competence: Assessment, Education & Training, & Supervision. Ed. by Don Pope-Davis & Hardin L. Coleman. LC 96-25239. (Multicultural Aspects Of Counseling Ser.: Vol. 7). 416p. 1996. 55.00 (*0-8039-7221-0*); pap. 25.95 (*0-8039-7222-9*) Sage.

Multicultural Counseling Competencies: Individual & Organizational Development. Derald W. Sue. LC 97-45323. (Multicultural Aspects of Counseling Ser.). 1998. write for info. (*0-8039-7130-3*); pap. write for info. (*0-8039-7131-1*) Sage.

Multicultural Counseling in a Divided & Traumatized Society: The Meaning of Childhood & Adolescence in South Africa, 32. Joyce Hickson & Susan Kriegler. LC 95-41697. (Contributions in Psychology Ser.: Vol. 32). 200p. 1996. 57.95 (*0-313-28554-3*, Greenwood Pr) Greenwood.

Multicultural Counseling in Schools: A Synergetic Approach. Roger Herring. LC 96-7806. 320p. (Orig.). (C). 1997. pap. text 33.95 (*1-55620-160-5*, 72631) Am Coun Assn.

Multicultural Counseling with Teenage Fathers: A Practical Guide. Mark S. Kiselica. LC 95-12232. (Multicultural Aspects of Counseling Ser.: Vol. 6). 368p. (C). 1995. 56.00 (*0-8039-5336-4*); pap. 28.00 (*0-8039-5337-2*) Sage.

Multicultural Course Transformation in Higher Education: A Broader Truth. Ed. by Ann I. Morey & Margie K. Kitano. 312p. 1996. 38.00 (*0-205-16068-9*) Allyn.

Multicultural Crafts from Recycled Materials. Deborah Whitacre & Becky J. Radtke. Ed. by Judy Mitchell. (Illus.). 80p. (Orig.). (J). (ps-3). 1995. pap. 8.95 (*1-57310-025-0*) Teachng & Lrning Co.

***Multicultural Curriculum: New Directions for Social Theory, Practice & Policy.** Ram Mahalingam & Cameron McCarthy. LC 99-42140. 320p. (C). 2000. text 65.99 (*0-415-92013-2*) Routledge.

***Multicultural Curriculum: New Directions for Social Theory, Practice & Policy.** Ram Mahalingam & Cameron McCarthy. LC 99-42140. 320p. 2000. pap. 21.99 (*0-415-92014-0*) Routledge.

Multicultural Curriculum: Role Play Peacegame. David W. Felder. 57p. 1997. pap. text 8.95 (*1-57501-109-3*, 22D) Wellington Pr.

Multicultural Customer Service. Leslie Aguilar & Linda Stokes. (Business Skills Express Ser.). 160p. 1995. pap. 10.95 (*0-7863-0332-8*, Irwn Prfssnl) McGraw-Hill Prof.

Multicultural Dance. F. Russel Ross & Virginia King. (Illus.). 174p. (Orig.). 1985. pap. 17.95 (*0-9615280-0-1*); pap. text 14.95 (*0-317-31639-7*) Russel & King.

Multicultural Detective Fiction: Murder from the "Other" Side. Ed. by Adrienne J. Gosselin. LC 98-40001. (Reference Library of the Humanities). 384p. 1998. text 60.00 (*0-8153-3153-3*) Garland.

Multicultural Dictionary of Literary Terms. Gary Carey & Mary E. Snodgrass. LC 98-35221. (Illus.). 192p. 1998. pap. 29.50 (*0-7864-0552-X*) McFarland & Co.

Multicultural Dictionary of Proverbs: Over 20,000 Adages from More Than 120 Languages, Nationalities & Ethnic Groups. Harold V. Cordry. LC 96-33264. 416p. 1997. lib. bdg. 47.50 (*0-7864-0251-2*) McFarland & Co.

Multicultural Dimension of the National Curriculum. Ed. by Anna S. King & Michael J. Reiss. LC 92-38078. 306p. 1993. 99.95 (*0-7507-0068-8*, Falmer Pr); pap. 34.95 (*0-7507-0069-6*, Falmer Pr) Taylor & Francis.

Multicultural Discovery Activities for the Elementary Grades. Elizabeth C. Stull. LC 94-13222. 438p. 1994. pap. text 28.95 (*0-87628-586-8*) Ctr Appl Res.

Multicultural Education. Hilda Hernandez. 240p. (C). 1990. pap. text 58.00 (*0-675-21006-2*, Merrill Coll) P-H.

Multicultural Education. 3rd ed. James A. Banks. 446p. 1996. pap. text 52.00 (*0-205-18896-6*) Allyn.

Multicultural Education. 3rd annot. ed. Schultz. 1996. teacher ed. (*0-697-31577-0*, WCB McGr Hill) McGrw-H Hghr Educ.

***Multicultural Education: A Caring-Centered, Reflective Approach.** Valerie Ooka Pang. LC 00-36433. 2001. pap. write for info. (*0-07-236953-1*) McGraw.

Multicultural Education: A Cross-Cultural Training Approach. Ed. by Margaret D. Pusch. LC 79-92379. 276p. (Orig.). 1979. pap. text 14.95 (*0-933662-06-8*) Intercult Pr.

Multicultural Education: A Global Approach. Ed. by Don Bragaw & Scott D. Thomson. 300p. (C). 1992. ring bd. 45.00 (*0-944675-51-4*) Amer Forum.

Multicultural Education: A Global Approach. James Lynch. 220p. 1989. 29.95 (*1-85000-557-5*, Falmer Pr) Taylor & Francis.

Multicultural Education: A Source Book. Patricia C. Ramsay et al. LC 88-31061. (Source Books on Education: Vol. 18). 190p. 1989. text 35.00 (*0-8240-8558-2*) Garland.

Multicultural Education: A Source Book. 2nd ed. Patricia G. Ramsey et al. (Source Books on Education). 300p. 1998. text 45.00 (*0-8153-1744-1*) Garland.

Multicultural Education: A Synopsis. H. Prentice Baptiste, Jr. LC 79-89924. 1979. pap. text 16.00 (*0-8191-0851-0*) U Pr of Amer.

Multicultural Education: A Teacher's Guide to Context, Process & Content. 2nd ed. Hilda Hernandez. 320p. (C). 2000. pap., teacher ed. 47.00 (*0-13-633538-1*, Macmillan Coll) P-H.

Multicultural Education: An International Guide to Research, Policies & Programs. Bruce M. Mitchell & Robert E. Salsbury. LC 95-37337. 400p. 1996. lib. bdg. 85.00 (*0-313-28985-9*, Greenwood Pr) Greenwood.

M

Multicultural Education: Generation of Advocacy. 576p. (C). 1994. text 43.00 (*0-536-58760-4*) Pearson Custom.
Multicultural Education: Inclusion of All. Ed. by Kelly Radzik-Marsh & Marilyn Strutchens. (Illus.). 298p. (Orig.). pap. write for info. (*0-9624818-2-3*) U GA Coll Ed.
Multicultural Education: Instructor's Manual. pap. write for info. (*0-8273-8161-1*) Delmar.
Multicultural Education: Issues & Perspectives. Ed. by James A. Banks & Cherry A. Banks. 400p. 1989. pap. text 33.00 (*0-205-11791-0*, H17916) Allyn.
Multicultural Education: Issues & Perspectives. 3rd ed. James A. Banks. 464p. 1997. pap. 56.95 (*0-471-36457-6*) Wiley.
***Multicultural Education: Issues & Perspectives.** 4th ed. Ed. by James A. Banks & Cheryl A. McGee Banks. 464p. (C). 2000. pap. 108.95 (*0-471-38379-1*) Wiley.
Multicultural Education: Principles & Practice. James Lynch. (Education Bks.). 256p. (C). 1986. text 37.50 (*0-7102-0411-6*, Routledge Thoemms); pap. text 19.95 (*0-7102-0768-9*, Routledge Thoemms) Routledge.
Multicultural Education: Raising Consciousness. Gloria Boutte. LC 97-36020. 352p. (C). 1998. text 51.95 (*0-8273-8159-X*) Delmar.
Multicultural Education: Strategies for Implementation in College & Universities, Vol. 4. Ed. by Janice R. Welsch & J. Q. Adams. (C). 1994. pap. text 10.00 (*1-885890-05-2*) IL Staff & Curriculum.
Multicultural Education: Strategies for Implementation in Colleges & Universities. Ed. by J. C. Adams et al. 152p. (C). Date not set. pap. text. write for info. (*1-885890-00-1*, 346811) IL Staff & Curriculum.
Multicultural Education: Strategies for Implementation in Colleges & Universities, Vol. 2. Ed. by J. Q. Adams & Janice R. Welsch. 139p. (C). 1992. pap. text. write for info. (*1-885890-01-X*, 351921) IL Staff & Curriculum.
Multicultural Education: Strategies for Implementation in Colleges & Universities, Vol. 3. Ed. by J. Q. Adams & Janide R. Welsch. 195p. (C). 1993. pap. text. write for info. (*1-885890-02-8*, 363211) IL Staff & Curriculum.
Multicultural Education 1999-2000 Edition. 6th ed. Schultz. 1999. pap., student ed. 16.56 (*0-07-039824-0*) McGraw.
Multicultural Education As Social Activism. Christine E. Sleeter. LC 95-38596. (SUNY Series, the Social Context of Education). 284p. (C). 1996. pap. text 17.95 (*0-7914-2998-9*) State U NY Pr.
Multicultural Education, Critical Pedagogy, & the Politics of Difference. Ed. by Christine E. Sleeter & Peter L. McLaren. LC 94-32892. (SUNY Series, the Social Context of Education). 465p. (C). 1995. pap. text 24.95 (*0-7914-2542-8*) State U NY Pr.
Multicultural Education Debate in the University: A Bibliography. Ed. by Joan Nordquist. (Contemporary Social Issues: A Bibliographic Ser.: No. 25). 68p. (Orig.). 1992. pap. 20.00 (*0-937855-48-0*) Ref Rsch Serv.
Multicultural Education for the Twenty-First Century. Ed. by Carlos Diaz. 208p. 1992. pap. 18.95 (*0-8106-1849-4*) NEA.
Multicultural Education in a Pluralistic Society. 5th ed. Donna M. Gollnick & Philip C. Chinn. LC 97-7773. 363p. 1997. pap. text 58.00 (*0-13-269572-3*) P-H.
Multicultural Education in All-White Areas. Kishor Patel. 352p. 1994. 77.95 (*1-85628-969-9*, Pub. by Avebry) Ashgate Pub Co.
Multicultural Education in Colleges & Universities: A Transdisciplinary Approach. Ed. by Howard Ball et al. LC 97-31207. 200p. 1988. write for info. (*0-8058-1693-3*); pap. write for info. (*0-8058-1694-1*) L Erlbaum Assocs.
Multicultural Education in Early Childhood Classrooms. Edwina B. Vold. 90p. 1992. pap. 8.95 (*0-8106-0353-5*) NEA.
Multicultural Education in the Everyday: A Renaissance for the Recommitted. Rudolfo C. Chavez. 1995. 18.00 (*0-89333-138-4*) AACTE.
Multicultural Education In the U.S. A Guide to Policies & Programs In the 50 States. Bruce M. Mitchell & Robert E. Salsbury. LC 99-31579. 296p. 2000. lib. bdg. 75.00 (*0-313-30859-4*) Greenwood.
Multicultural Education, 1996-1997. annuals 3rd ed. Fred Schultz. 256p. (C). 1996. text. write for info. (*0-697-31576-2*) Brown & Benchmark.
Multicultural Education, 98-99. 5th ed. Fred Schultz. (Annual Ser.). (Illus.). 240p. 1998. pap. text 12.25 (*0-697-39177-9*, Dshkn McG-Hill) McGrw-H Hghr Educ.
***Multicultural Education of Children & Adolescents.** 3rd ed. Manning & Leroy G. Baruth. LC 99-29162. 382p. 1999. pap. text 54.00 (*0-205-29760-9*) Allyn.
Multicultural Education Resource Guide. Cheryl Gorder. (Illus.). 160p. 1995. pap. 12.95 (*0-933025-37-8*) Blue Bird Pub.
Multicultural Education Teaching Problems. Silverman. 1993. 14.50 (*0-07-057660-2*) McGraw.
Multicultural Education, Transformative Knowledge & Action: Historical & Contemporary Perspectives. James A. Banks. LC 96-1069. (Multicultural Education Ser.). 384p. (C). 1996. text 57.00 (*0-8077-3532-9*); pap. text 26.95 (*0-8077-3531-0*) Tchrs Coll.
Multicultural Experiences, Multicultural Theorizing. Mary F. Rogers. Ed. by George Ritzer. LC 95-25248. 438p. (C). 1995. pap. 38.75 (*0-07-053560-4*) McGraw.
Multicultural Explorations: Joyous Journeys with Books. Mary A. Heltshe & Audrey B. Kirchner. xii, 276p. 1991. pap. text 23.50 (*0-87287-848-1*) Teacher Ideas Pr.
Multicultural Fables & Fairy Tales: Stories & Activities & Promote Literacy. Tara McCarthy. LC 94-226010. 112p. (gr. 1-8). 1993. pap. 14.95 (*0-590-49231-4*) Scholastic Inc.
Multicultural Fables & Fairy Tales Stories & Activities & Promote Literacy. Tara McCarthy. 1993. 20.15 (*0-606-06586-5*, Pub. by Turtleback) Demco.
Multicultural Folk Tales: A Thematic Unit. David Jeffries. (Thematic Units Ser.). (Illus.). 80p. (J). (gr. 3-5). 1992. student ed. 9.95 (*1-55734-230-X*) Tchr Create Mat.
***Multicultural Folktales: Readers Theatre for Elementary Students.** Suzanne I. Barchers. 225p. 2000. pap. 24.50 (*1-56308-760-X*, TIP) Libs Unl.
Multicultural Folktales: Stories to Tell Young Children. Judy Sierra & Robert Kaminski. Tr. by Adela Allen from SPA. LC 91-29533. (Illus.). 136p. 1991. pap. 26.50 (*0-89774-688-0*) Oryx Pr.
Multicultural Folktales & Activities: Grades 1-6. Troll Books Staff. 96p. (J). (gr. 1-6). 1999. pap. text 12.95 (*0-8167-3270-1*) Troll Communs.
Multicultural Folktales for the Feltboard & Readers' Theater. Judy Sierra. LC 96-35370. (Illus.). 197p. 1996. pap. 29.50 (*1-57356-003-0*) Oryx Pr.
Multicultural Friendship Stories & Activities for Children Ages 5-15. Patricia Roberts. LC 97-15975. (School Library Media Ser.). 243p. (gr. k-9). 1998. pap. 22.50 (*0-8108-3359-X*) Scarecrow.
Multicultural Game Book: More Than 70 Traditional Games from 30 Countries. Louise Prlando. LC 94-196979. 110p. 1993. pap., teacher ed. 14.95 (*0-590-49409-0*) Scholastic Inc.
Multicultural Games. Lorraine Barbarash. LC 96-33062. (Illus.). 152p. (Orig.). 1996. pap. text 14.95 (*0-88011-565-3*, BBAR0565) Human Kinetics.
Multicultural Gifted Education. Donna Y. Ford & J. John Harris. LC 98-56046. (Education & Psychology of the Gifted Ser.). 264p. 1999. pap. text 23.95 (*0-8077-3850-6*) Tchrs Coll.
Multicultural Guide to Literature-Based Whole Language Activities for Young Children. Dennis J. Kear & Jeri A. Carroll. 160p. teacher ed. 12.99 (*0-86653-714-7*, GA1431) Good Apple.
Multicultural Guide to Thematic Units for Young Children. Good Apple Staff. (J). 1993. pap. text 10.99 (*0-86653-715-5*) Good Apple.
Multicultural Hawai'i: The Fabric of a Multiethnic Society. Ed. by Michael Haas. LC 97-30365. (Illus.). 362p. 1998. text 60.00 (*0-8153-2377-8*, SS1108) Garland.
Multicultural Healthcare & Rehabilitation of Older People. Ed. by Amanda J. Squires. 192p. (C). 1991. 75.00 (*0-340-54362-0*, Pub. by Age Concern Eng) St Mut.
Multicultural Holidays. Julia Jasmine. (Illus.). 304p. 1994. student ed. 24.95 (*1-55734-615-1*) Tchr Create Mat.
Multicultural Human Services for AIDS Treatment & Prevention: Policy, Perspectives, & Planning. Ed. by Marcia Bok. LC 92-48833. (Journal of Multicultural Social Work: Vol. 2, No. 3). (Illus.). 134p. 1993. 39.95 (*1-56024-414-3*); pap. 12.95 (*1-56023-038-X*, Harrington Park) Haworth Pr.
***Multicultural Iberia: Language, Literature & Music.** Ed. by Dru Dougherty & Milton M. Azevedo. LC 99-22188. (Research Ser.: Vol. 103). 259p. 1999. pap. text 26.50 (*0-87725-003-0*) U of Cal IAS.
Multicultural Imagination: Race, Color, & the Unconscious. Michael V. Adams. LC 96-7561. 296p. (C). 1996. pap. 27.99 (*0-415-13838-8*) Routledge.
Multicultural Imagination: Race, Color, & the Unconscious. Michael V. Adams. LC 96-7561. (Illus.). 296p. (C). 1996. 85.00 (*0-415-13837-X*) Routledge.
***Multicultural Information Quests: Instant Research Lessons, Grades 5-8.** Marle E. Rodgers. LC 99-39119. 250p. 2000. pap. 29.50 (*1-56308-686-7*) Libs Unl.
Multicultural Intervention Perspectives for Professional Psychology. Richard Dana. (C). 2000. 45.95 (*0-205-15897-8*, Macmillan Coll) P-H.
***Multicultural Introduction to Psychology.** 416p. (C). 1999. text 24.00 (*0-321-40153-0*) Addison-Wesley.
***Multicultural Introduction To Psychology.** (C). 1998. 22.00 (*0-321-03490-2*) Addison-Wesley Educ.
***Multicultural Introduction To Psychology.** (C). 1999. write for info. (*0-321-05225-0*) Addison-Wesley Educ.
Multicultural Issues in Child Care. 2nd rev. ed. Janet Gonzalez-Mena. LC 96-20108. x, 117p. (C). 1996. pap. text 16.95 (*1-55934-629-9*, 1629) Mayfield Pub.
Multicultural Issues in Childcare: Early Childhood Education. Janet Gonzalez-Mena. 2000. pap. text. write for info. (*0-7674-0208-1*) Mayfield Pub.
Multicultural Issues in Counseling: New Approaches to Diversity. 2nd rev. ed. Ed. by Courtland C. Lee. LC 96-48042. 368p. (Orig.). 1997. pap. text 40.95 (*1-55620-156-7*, 72627) Am Coun Assn.
Multicultural Issues in Occupational Therapy. Ed. by Zeenat Meghani-Wise. 240p. 1998. pap. 26.95 (*1-85302-474-0*, Pub. by Jessica Kingsley) Taylor & Francis.
Multicultural Issues in Social Work. Ed. by Patricia L. Ewalt et al. 578p. (Orig.). (C). 1996. lib. bdg. 37.95 (*0-87101-266-9*, 2669) Natl Assn Soc Wkrs.
***Multicultural Issues in Social Work: Practice & Research.** Ed. by Patricia L. Ewalt. LC 99-181511. xvii, 709p. 1999. 41.95 (*0-87101-302-9*) Natl Assn Soc Wkrs.
***Multicultural Issues in the Criminal Justice System.** (C). 2000. 20.00 (*0-205-31879-7*) Allyn.
Multicultural Issues Series, 6 vols. (YA). (gr. 6 up). 1995. lib. bdg. 114.70 (*0-89490-564-3*) Enslow Pubs.
Multicultural Japan: Paleolithic to Postmodern. Ed. by Donald Denoon et al. 304p. 1996. text 59.95 (*0-521-55067-X*) Cambridge U Pr.
Multicultural Junior Biographies Series, 4 vols. (Illus.). (J). (gr. 4-10). 1995. lib. bdg. 76.80 (*0-89490-661-5*) Enslow Pubs.
Multicultural Law Enforcement: Strategies for Peace Keeping in a Diverse Society. Robert M. Shusta et al. LC 94-20986. 420p. 1994. 74.00 (*0-13-554080-1*, Pub. by P-H) S&S Trade.
Multicultural Legends & Tales. Vowery D. Carlile. (J). (gr. 1-4). Date not set. teacher ed. 12.95 (*1-56644-974-X*) Educ Impress.
Multicultural Librarianship: An International Handbook. Ed. by Marie F. Zielinska & Francis T. Kirkwood. (IFLA Publications: Vol. 59). 384p. 1992. lib. bdg. 65.00 (*3-598-21787-0*) K G Saur Verlag.
Multicultural Literacies: Dialect, Discourse & Diversity. Patrick L. Courts. LC 96-42973. (Counterpoints Ser.: No. 45). VIII, 196p. (C). 1997. pap. 29.95 (*0-8204-3675-5*) P Lang Pubng.
Multicultural Literacy. 2nd ed. Barbara J. Diamond. (C). 1998. pap. text. write for info. (*0-8013-1862-9*) Addison-Wesley.
Multicultural Literacy: Mirroring the New Reality of the Classroom. Barbara J. Diamond & Margaret A. Moore. 380p. (C). 1994. pap. 60.00 (*0-8013-1141-1*) Longman.
Multicultural Literacy: Mirroring the Reality of the Classroom. 2nd ed. Barbara J. Diamond & Margaret A. Moore. LC 94-27767. (C). 1995. write for info. (*0-8013-1411-9*) Longman.
Multicultural Literature: Essays, Fiction, & Poetry. Center for Learning Network Staff. (English - Language Arts Ser.). 100p. 1996. teacher ed., spiral bd. 19.95 (*1-56077-474-6*) Ctr Learning.
Multicultural Literature & Literacies: Making Space for Difference. Ed. by Suzanne M. Miller & Barbara McCaskill. LC 92-39543. (SUNY Series, Literacy, Culture, & Learning: Theory & Practice). 300p. (C). 1993. text 64.50 (*0-7914-1645-3*); pap. text 21.95 (*0-7914-1646-1*) State U NY Pr.
Multicultural Literature Anthology. Ed. by Reed. (C). 1999. text. write for info. (*0-321-01055-8*) Addson-Wesley Educ.
***Multicultural Literature Circles.** 40p. 1999. pap. text 24.95 (*1-58303-076-X*) Pthways Pubng.
***Multicultural Literature for Children & Young Adults, Vol. 2.** Ginny Moore Kruse et al. 120p. (C). 1999. pap. text 35.00 (*0-7881-8347-8*) DIANE Pub.
Multicultural Literature for Children & Young Adults: A Selected Listed of Books by & about. Ginny Moore Kruse. 1997. pap. 35.00 (*0-931641-07-1*) Friends CCBC.
Multicultural Literature for Children & Young Adults: A Selected Listing of Books, 1980-1990 by & about People of Color. 3rd ed. Ginny M. Kruse & Kathleen T. Horning. Ed. & Frwd. by Herbert J. Grover. 78p. (C). 1993. pap. text 35.00 (*1-56806-323-7*) DIANE Pub.
Multicultural Literatures Through Feminist-Postculturalist Lenses. Barbara F. Waxman. LC 93-8463. 272p. 1994. 36.95 (*0-87049-814-2*) U of Tenn Pr.
Multicultural Management 2000. 2nd ed. Farid Elashmawi & Philip R. Harris. LC 97-53251. (Managing Cultural Differences Ser.). 320p. 1998. 34.95 (*0-88415-494-7*, 5494) Gulf Pub.
Multicultural Manners: New Rules of Etiquette for a Changing Society. Norine Dresser. 304p. 1996. pap. 15.95 (*0-471-11819-2*) Wiley.
Multicultural Marketing: Selling to a Diverse America. Marlene L. Rossman. LC 93-41996. 192p. 1994. 22.95 (*0-8144-5071-7*) AMACOM.
Multicultural Marketing: Selling to a Diverse America. Marlene L. Rossman. LC 93-41996. 176p. 1996. pap. 16.95 (*0-8144-7921-9*) AMACOM.
Multicultural Marketing: Selling to a Diverse America. Marlene L. Rossman. 178p. 1997. reprint ed. text 23.00 (*0-7881-5008-1*) DIANE Pub.
***Multicultural Marketing: Selling to the New America.** Alfred L. Schreiber & Barry Lenson. LC 00-40114. 2000. 34.95 (*0-8442-2601-7*, NTC Business Bks) NTC Contemp Pub Co.
Multicultural Marketing Conference, 1998: Proceedings, Montreal, Quebec, Canada, September 17-20, 1998. Academy of Marketing Science Staff. Ed. by Jean-Charles Chebat & A. Ben Oumlil. LC 99-1285. (Illus.). 567p. reprint ed. pap. 175.80 (*0-608-20286-X*, 207154400001) Bks Demand.
Multicultural Materials. 1993. write for info. (*0-201-96669-7*) Addison-Wesley.
Multicultural Math: Hands-On Math Activities from Around the World. Claudia Zaslavsky. (Illus.). (J). 1994. pap. text 14.95 (*0-590-49646-8*) Scholastic Inc.
Multicultural Math Classroom: Bringing in the World. Claudia Zaslavsky. LC 95-35677. 288p. 1995. pap. text 25.00 (*0-435-08373-2*, 08373) Heinemann.
Multicultural Mathematics. David Nelson et al. LC 92-17031. (Illus.). 238p. 1993. pap. text 14.95 (*0-19-282241-1*) OUP.
Multicultural Mentoring of the Gifted & Talented. E. Paul Torrance et al. 127p. 1997. pap. 19.95 (*1-882664-39-6*) Prufrock Pr.
Multicultural Monologues for Young Actors. Ed. by Craig Slaight et al. LC 94-44188. (Young Actors Ser.). 112p. (YA). (gr. 9 up). 1995. pap. 11.95 (*1-880399-47-4*) Smith & Kraus.
Multicultural Multimodal Multisystems Approach to Working with Culturally Different Families. Sharon-Ann Gopaul-McNicol. LC 96-33195. 160p. 1997. 55.00 (*0-275-95560-5*, Praeger Pubs) Greenwood.
Multicultural Multinational. James Poynter. 176p. (C). 1995. pap. text 52.95 (*0-7872-1069-2*) Kendall-Hunt.
Multicultural Multinational Adjustment & Readjustment. 2nd ed. James Poynter. 196p. (C). 1997. per. 55.95 (*0-7872-4538-0*) Kendall-Hunt.
***Multicultural Multinational Adjustment & Readjustment.** 3rd ed. James Poynter. 206p. (C). 2000. per. 55.95 (*0-7872-7237-X*) Kendall-Hunt.
Multicultural Myths & Legends: Stories & Activities to Promote Cultural Awareness. Tara McCarthy. LC 95-113153. (Illus.). 127p. (J). 1994. pap. text 15.95 (*0-590-49645-X*) Scholastic Inc.
Multicultural Needs Assessment for College & University Student Populations. Ed. by Sally D. Stabb et al. LC 94-33052. (Illus.). 284p. (C). 1995. text 58.95 (*0-398-05933-0*); pap. text 42.95 (*0-398-05948-9*) C C Thomas.
Multicultural Nests: Finding a Writing Voice about Literature by Women of Color. Toni A. McNaron & Pamela J. Olano. Ed. by Lillian Bridwell-Bowles & Susan Batchelder. (Technical Reports: No. 4). 28p. (Orig.). 1993. pap. 3.00 (*1-881221-08-3*) U Minn Ctr Interdis.
Multicultural Neurogenics. Wallace. 1997. 75.00 (*0-7616-3072-4*) Commun Skill.
Multicultural 1 Teacher's Guide. (Thematic Library). 56p. 1996. pap. text, teacher ed. 29.95 (*1-58303-008-5*) Pthways Pubng.
***Multicultural or Immigrant Faculty in American Society.** Cecilia G. Manrique & Gabriel G. Manrique. LC 99-21899. (Studies in Education: Vol. 43). 198p. 1999. text 79.95 (*0-7734-8027-7*) E Mellen.
Multicultural Perspectives. Houghton Mifflin Company Staff. (C). 1992. pap., teacher ed. 364.04 (*0-395-54815-2*) HM.
Multicultural Perspectives: New Approaches. Anne Paolucci et al. (CNL/World Report Ser.: Vol. VI). 128p. 1993. pap. 4.95 (*0-918680-52-2*) Griffon House.
Multicultural Perspectives in Communication Disorders. Robert M. Screen & Noma B. Anderson. LC 93-49681. 142p. 1994. pap. 29.95 (*1-56593-265-X*, 0587) Thomson Learn.
Multicultural Perspectives in Criminal Justice & Criminology. Ed. by James E. Hendricks & Bryan Byers. LC 94-21027. (Illus.). 438p. 1994. pap. 52.95 (*0-398-05975-6*) C C Thomas.
***Multicultural Perspectives in Criminal Justice & Criminology.** 2nd ed. James E. Hendricks & Bryan Byers. LC 00-39213. 2000. write for info. (*0-398-07088-1*) C C Thomas.
Multicultural Perspectives in Music Education. 2nd ed. William M. Anderson & Patricia S. Campbell. (Illus.). 436p. 1996. pap. 48.00 (*1-56545-097-3*, 1509) MENC.
Multicultural Perspectives in Working with Families. Ed. by Elaine P. Congress. LC 96-40363. (Social Work Ser.). (Illus.). 376p. 1997. 47.95 (*0-8261-9560-1*) Springer Pub.
Multicultural Pharmaceutical Education. Ed. by Barry Bleidt. LC 92-49896. (Journal of Pharmacy Teaching: Vol. 3, No. 2). (Illus.). 151p. 1992. 39.95 (*1-56024-356-2*) Haworth Pr.
Multicultural Pharmaceutical Education. Ed. by Barry Bleidt. LC 92-49896. (Journal of Pharmacy Teaching: Vol. 3, No. 2). 151p. 1996. pap. 14.95 (*0-7890-0071-7*, Pharmctl Prods) Haworth Pr.
Multicultural Picture Books: Art for Understanding Others. Kenneth A. Marantz & Sylvia S. Marantz. LC 93-50811. (Professional Growth Ser.). 150p. 1994. pap. text 34.95 (*0-938865-22-6*) Linworth Pub.
Multicultural Picture Books: Art for Understanding Others, Vol. 2. Sylvia Marantz & Kenneth Marantz. (Professional Growth Ser.). (Orig.). 1997. pap. 36.95 (*0-938865-63-3*) Linworth Pub.
Multicultural Plays: A Many-Splendored Tapestry Honoring Our Global Community. July Truesdell Mecca. (Illus.). 128p. (J). (gr. 1-7). 1999. pap. 12.95 (*0-86530-411-4*, IP 411-4) Incentive Pubns.
Multicultural Plays for Children Grades K-3. Ed. by Pamela Gerke. LC 96-164. (Young Actors Ser.). 224p. (J). (gr. k-3). 1996. pap. 19.95 (*1-57525-005-5*) Smith & Kraus.
Multicultural Plays for Children Grades 4-6. Pamela Gerke. (Young Actors Ser.). 224p. (J). (gr. 4-6). 1996. pap. 19.95 (*1-57525-006-3*) Smith & Kraus.
***Multicultural Policies & the State: A Comparison of Two European Societies.** Ed. by Marco Martiniello. (Research in Migration & Ethnic Relations Ser.). 232p. 1999. pap. 20.95 (*90-75719-07-8*, Pub. by Europ Res Centre) Ashgate Pub Co.
Multicultural Practice: A Special Issue of Families in Society. FIS Staff. 64p. 1992. pap. 8.95 (*0-87304-263-8*) Manticore Pubns.
Multicultural Prism: Voices from the Field. Ed. by J. Q. Adams & Janice R. Welsch. (C). 1994. pap. text 10.00 (*1-885890-04-4*) IL Staff & Curriculum.
Multicultural Prism: Voices from the Field, Vol. 2. Ed. by J. Q. Adams & Janice R. Welsch. 232p. (Orig.). 1996. pap. 10.00 (*1-885890-06-0*) IL Staff & Curriculum.
Multicultural Projects Index: Things to Make & Do to Celebrate Festivals, Cultures, & Holidays Around the World. 2nd ed. Mary A. Pilger. LC 98-4445. 300p. 1998. 49.00 (*1-56308-524-0*) Libs Unl.
Multicultural Psychotherapy: An Approach to Individual & Cultural Differences. 2nd ed. Manuel Ramirez, III. 236p. (C). 1998. 42.00 (*0-205-28904-5*) Allyn.
Multicultural Public Health Capacity Building Pilot Projects: Final Report. 78p. pap. text 40.00 (*0-7881-1595-2*) DIANE Pub.
Multicultural Public Relations: A Social-Interpretive Approach. Stephen P. Banks. (Communicating Effectively in Multicultural Contexts Ser.: Vol. 4). 145p. 1995. text 36.00 (*0-8039-4840-9*); pap. text 17.95 (*0-8039-4841-7*) Sage.
***Multicultural Public Relations: A Social-Interpretive Approach.** 2nd ed. Stephen Banks. (Illus.). 184p. 2000. 39.95 (*0-8138-2940-2*) Iowa St U Pr.
Multicultural Queer: Australian Narratives. Ed. by Peter A. Jackson & Gerard Sullivan. LC 98-51298. 233p. 1999. 69.95 (*0-7890-0651-0*); pap. 19.95 (*1-56023-123-8*, Harrington Park) Haworth Pr.

Multicultural Questions. Ed. by Christian Joppke & Steven Lukes. LC 99-24526. 280p. 1999. 52.00 (*0-19-829610-X*) OUP.

Multicultural Readers Theatre Booktalks. Nancy Polette. 128p. 1994. pap. 12.95 (*1-879287-31-5*, BL041) Pieces of Lrning.

Multicultural Readings in Business & Industry. Martin J. Lecker. 272p. (C). 1995. text 38.20 (*0-536-59000-1*) Pearson Custom.

***Multicultural Readings in Business & Industry.** 2nd ed. 294p. (C). 1998. text 30.00 (*0-536-00904-X*) Pearson Custom.

Multicultural Religious Education. Barbara Wilkerson. LC 97-6735. 432p. (Orig.). 1997. pap. 25.95 (*0-89135-101-9*) Religious Educ.

Multicultural Research: A Reflective Engagement with Race, Class, Gender & Sexual Orientation. Ed. by Carl A. Grant. LC 99-158334. 282p. 1999. 75.00 (*0-7507-0881-6*, Falmer Pr) Taylor & Francis.

Multicultural Resource Guide. National Education Association Staff. (Illus.). 1997. pap. 23.75 (*0-8106-2005-7*) NEA.

Multicultural Resources on the Internet: The United States & Canada. Vicki L. Gregory et al. LC 98-38291. 265p. 1999. pap. 28.00 (*1-56308-676-X*) Libs Unl.

Multicultural Riddle: Rethinking National, Ethnic & Religious Identities Gerd Baumann. LC 98-49911. (Zones of Religion Ser.). 1999. pap. 19.99 (*0-415-92213-5*) Routledge.

***Multicultural Riddle: Rethinking National, Ethnic & Religious Identities.** Gerd Baumann. LC 98-49911. 1999. write for info. (*0-415-92212-7*) Routledge.

Multicultural Roots of Success. Emilio S. Rita. 180p. (C). 1995. text 31.80 (*0-536-58719-1*) Pearson Custom.

Multicultural Scenes for Young Actors. Ed. by Craig Slaight & Jack Sharrar. (Young Actors Ser.). 256p. (YA). (gr. 9 up). 1995. pap. 11.95 (*1-880399-48-2*) Smith & Kraus.

Multicultural Sing-Along Big Books Complete Program. Kathleen Beal. 1994. pap. 212.59 (*0-201-52214-4*) Addison-Wesley.

Multicultural Sing & Learn: Folk Songs & Monthly Activities. Carolyn Meyer & Kel Pickens. (Illus.). 144p. (J). (gr. k-5). 1994. 13.99 (*0-86653-830-5*, GA1522) Good Apple.

Multicultural Snacks. Susan Hodges. Ed. by Gayle Bittinger & Jean Warren. LC 94-61057. (Super Snack Ser.). (Illus.). 48p. (Orig.). (J). (ps). 1994. 6.95 (*1-57029-025-3*, WPH 1604) Totline Pubns.

Multicultural Social Studies ESL Library. 1995. 75.19 (*0-201-59149-9*) Addison-Wesley.

Multicultural Social Studies Unit: Who Am I? Joy A. Clarke. (Illus.). 150p. (J). (gr. 3-8). 1991. ring bd. 45.00 (*0-9626984-1-5*) Clarke Enterprise.

Multicultural Societies in Conflict & Coexistence. Ed. & Intro. by R. H. Dekmejian. 100p. (C). 1999. pap. 6.95 (*0-9643432-1-5*) Millenia Pubs.

***Multicultural Spanish Dictionary.** Ed. by Agustin Martinez. LC 99-22373. 234p. 1999. pap. 24.95 (*1-887563-45-8*, Pub. by Schreiber Pub) Natl Bk Netwk.

Multicultural States: Rethinking Difference & Identity. David Bennett. LC 98-17304. 320p. (C). 1998. 75.00 (*0-415-12158-2*); pap. 24.99 (*0-415-12159-0*) Routledge.

Multicultural States of East Africa. Audrey I. Richards. LC 74-101260. (Centre for Developing-Area Studies, McGill University, Keith Callard Lectures: No. 3). 135p. reprint ed. pap. 41.90 (*0-7837-1160-3*, 204168900022) Bks Demand.

Multicultural Stories. James H. Branch, III. Ed. by Dick Ward. LC 92-93449. (Illus.). 29p. (J). 1992. 12.50 (*0-9635840-0-6*) Guttenburg Pub.

***Multicultural Stories Series.** Raintree Steck-Vaughn Publishers Staff. (Illus.). 2000. write for info. (*0-7398-1338-2*) Raintree Steck-V.

Multicultural Strategies for Community Colleges: From Diversity to Synergy. Ed. by Arnold M. Kee & James R. Mahoney. LC 95-163117. 96p. 1995. pap. 15.00 (*0-87117-288-7*, 1385) Comm Coll Pr Am Assn Comm Coll.

Multicultural Student's Guide to Colleges: What Every African American, Hispanic, & Native... Robert Mitchell. 650p. (YA). 1996. pap. text 25.00 (*0-374-52476-9*, Noonday) FS&G.

Multicultural Studio Art Projects for Secondary Students: Ready to Use Lesson Plans, Color . . . Susan Hogan. LC 97-12788. (Illus.). 272p. (C). 1997. spiral bd. 59.95 (*0-13-287442-3*) P-H.

Multicultural Tales from Around the World, Vol. I. Davidson & Associates Inc. Staff. (Story Club Ser.: Vol. 1). (J). (gr. 4-7). 1994. pap. text 14.56 (*0-201-57578-7*) Addison-Wesley.

Multicultural Tales from Around the World, Vol. II. Davidson & Associates Inc Staff. (Story Club Ser.: Vol. 2). (J). (gr. 4-7). 1994. pap. text 14.56 (*0-201-57579-5*) Addison-Wesley.

Multicultural Teacher Education, Vol. 1. American Association of Colleges for Teacher Educa. LC 80-80105. 224p. reprint ed. pap. 69.50 (*0-7837-2596-5*, 204275900001) Bks Demand.

Multicultural Teaching: A Handbook of Activities, Information & Resources. 5th ed. Pamela L. Tiedt & Iris M. Tiedt. LC 98-22408. 432p. 1998. pap. text 56.00 (*0-205-27528-1*) Allyn.

Multicultural Teaching in the University. Ed. by David Schoem et al. LC 92-16141. 376p. 1993. 65.00 (*0-275-93852-2*, C3852, Praeger Pubs) Greenwood.

Multicultural Teaching in the University. Ed. by David Schoem et al. LC 92-16141. 376p. 1995. pap. 22.95 (*0-275-95275-4*) Greenwood.

Multicultural Theatre: Scenes & Monologs from New Hispanic, Asian, & African-American Plays. Ed. by Roger Ellis. LC 96-22150. 232p. (YA). (gr. 9 up). 1996. pap. text 15.95 (*1-56608-026-6*, B205) Meriwether Pub.

Multicultural Theatre II: Contemporary Hispanic, Asian, & African-American Plays. Ed. by Roger Ellis & Ted Zapel. LC 98-28515. 392p. 1998. pap. 15.95 (*1-56608-042-8*, B223) Meriwether Pub.

Multicultural 2 Teacher's Guide. (Thematic Library). 56p. 1996. pap. text, teacher ed. 29.95 (*1-58303-009-3*) Pthways Pubng.

Multicultural Understanding: A Comprehensive Model. Don Locke. (Multicultural Aspects of Counseling Ser.: Vol. 1). 220p. (C). 1992. text 42.00 (*0-8039-4593-0*); pap. text 18.95 (*0-8039-4594-9*) Sage.

Multicultural Voices in Contemporary Literature: A Resource for Teachers. Frances A. Day. LC 94-26262. (Illus.). 244p. 1994. pap. text 26.00 (*0-435-08826-2*, 08826) Heinemann.

Multicultural Workshop: A Reading & Writing Program, Bk. 1. Linda L. Blanton & Linda Lee. LC 93-39447. 192p. (J). 1994. mass mkt. 21.95 (*0-8384-4834-8*) Heinle & Heinle.

Multicultural Workshop: A Reading & Writing Program, Bk. 2. Linda L. Blanton. (College ESL Ser.). 192p. (J). 1994. mass mkt. 26.95 (*0-8384-4835-6*) Heinle & Heinle.

Multicultural Workshop: A Reading & Writing Program, Bk. 3. Linda L. Blanton. (College ESL Ser.). 266p. (J). 1995. mass mkt. 26.95 (*0-8384-5020-2*) Heinle & Heinle.

Multicultural Workshop Box. Lee. (College ESL Ser.). 1995. mass mkt., teacher ed. 6.95 (*0-8384-5027-X*) Heinle & Heinle.

Multicultural Workshop Box-answer Key. Lee. (College ESL). 1995. mass mkt., suppl. ed. 6.95 (*0-8384-5026-1*) Heinle & Heinle.

Multiculturalism. Robert Emmet Long. LC 97-29037. (Reference Shelf Ser.: Vol. 69, No. 5). 1997. pap. 25.00 (*0-8242-0918-4*) Wilson.

***Multiculturalism.** C. W. Watson. LC 00-34014. (Concepts in the Social Sciences Ser.). 2000. pap. write for info. (*0-335-20520-8*, Pub. by OpUniv Pr) Taylor & Francis.

Multiculturalism: A Critical Reader. Ed. by David T. Goldberg. (C). 1994. pap. text 29.95 (*0-631-18912-2*) Blackwell Pubs.

***Multiculturalism: Humanist Perspectives.** Ed. by Robert B. Tapp. 250p. 2000. 25.95 (*1-57392-805-4*) Prometheus Bks.

Multiculturalism: The Changing Australian Paradigm. Lois Foster & David Stockley. 150p. 1984. 69.00 (*0-905028-37-6*, Pub. by Multilingual Matters); pap. 24.00 (*0-905028-38-4*, Pub. by Multilingual Matters) Taylor & Francis.

Multiculturalism & American Democracy. Symposium on Science, Reason, & Modern Democracy S. Ed. by Arthur M. Melzer et al. LC 97-45707. 246p. 1998. 40.00 (*0-7006-0881-8*); pap. 17.95 (*0-7006-0882-6*) U Pr of KS.

Multiculturalism & Economic Growth. Gerald W. Scully. 19p. 1995. pap. 10.00 (*1-56808-061-1*, 196) Natl Ctr Pol.

Multiculturalism & Education: A Select Bibliography. John R. Mallea & Edward C. Shea. LC 80-481969. (Ontario Institute for Studies in Education, Symposium Ser.: No. 9). 300p. reprint ed. pap. 93.00 (*0-608-17710-5*, 203010300067) Bks Demand.

Multiculturalism & Education: Diversity & Its Impact on Schools & Society. Thomas J. La Belle & Christopher R. Ward. LC 93-5712. (SUNY Series, Frontiers in Education). 211p. (C). 1994. pap. text 19.95 (*0-7914-1940-1*) State U NY Pr.

***Multiculturalism & Hybridity in African Literatures.** Hal Wylie. LC 00-29311. 480p. 2000. pap. write for info. (*0-86543-840-4*) Africa World.

***Multiculturalism & Hybridity in African Literatures.** Ed. by Hal Wylie & Bernth Lindfors. LC 00-29311. (Annual Selected Papers of the ALA Ser.: Vol. 7). 480p. 2000. 84.95 (*0-86543-839-0*) Africa World.

Multiculturalism & Intergroup Relations, 75. Ed. by James S. Frideres. LC 88-17786. 194p. 1989. 49.95 (*0-313-26484-8*, FMD/, Greenwood Pr) Greenwood.

Multiculturalism & Learning Style: Teaching & Counseling Adolescents. Rita A. Dunn & Shirley Griggs. LC 94-36775. 200p. 1998. pap. 24.95 (*0-275-96480-9*, Praeger Pubs) Greenwood.

Multiculturalism & Learning Style: Teaching & Counseling Adolescents. Rita Dunn & Shirley A. Griggs. LC 94-36775. 296p. 1995. 59.95 (*0-275-94762-9*, Praeger Pubs) Greenwood.

Multiculturalism & Public Arts Policy. David B. Pankratz. LC 93-25008. 248p. 1993. 57.95 (*0-89789-361-1*, H361, Bergin & Garvey) Greenwood.

Multiculturalism & Representation: Selected Essays. Ed. by John Rieder & Larry R. Smith. (Literary Studies East & West: Vol. 10). (Illus.). 248p. 1996. pap. text 20.00 (*0-8248-1860-1*) Coll Lang Ling & Lit.

Multiculturalism & the Canon of American Culture. Ed. by Hans Bak. 374p. (C). 1993. pap. 49.50 (*90-5383-018-9*, Pub. by VU Univ Pr) Paul & Co Pubs.

Multiculturalism & the School Curriculum: Historical Case Studies. Murray R. Nelson. Ed. by Joe Kincheloe & Shirley R. Steinberg. (Critical Education Practice Ser.). 350p. Date not set. text 52.00 (*0-8153-2106-6*); pap. text 18.95 (*0-8153-2326-3*) Garland.

Multiculturalism & TQE: Addressing Cultural Diversity in Schools. Paula A. Cordeiro et al. LC 93-42325. (Total Quality Education for the World's Best Schools Ser.: Vol. 7). 128p. 1994. pap. 19.95 (*0-8039-6107-3*) Corwin Pr.

Multiculturalism & Ukrainian Canadians: Identity, Homeland Ties, & the Community's Future. Stella Hryniuk. (Illus.). 96p. 1995. pap. text 16.00 (*0-919045-63-4*) U of Toronto Pr.

Multiculturalism As a Fourth Force. Paul Pedersen. LC 98-42486. 300p. 1998. pap. 29.95 (*0-87630-930-9*); boxed set 59.95 (*0-87630-929-5*) Brunner-Mazel.

Multiculturalism As an Educational Policy. Fazal Rizvi. 120p. (C). 1985. 65.00 (*0-7300-0118-0*, Pub. by Deakin Univ) St Mut.

Multiculturalism, Examining the Politics of Recognition. expanded ed. Charles Taylor et al. LC 94-19602. 192p. 1994. pap. text 13.95 (*0-691-03779-5*, Pub. by Princeton U Pr) Cal Prin Full Svc.

Multiculturalism from the Margins: Non-Dominant Voices on Difference & Diversity. Ed. by Dean A. Harris. LC 95-13442. 216p. 1995. 55.00 (*0-89789-449-9*, Bergin & Garvey); pap. 17.95 (*0-89789-455-3*, Bergin & Garvey) Greenwood.

Multiculturalism in a Cross-National Perspective. Michael A. Burayidi. 416p. 1996. 67.50 (*0-7618-0592-3*); pap. 39.50 (*0-7618-0593-1*) U Pr of Amer.

***Multiculturalism in a World of Leaking Boundaries.** Ed. by Dieter Haselbach. 328p. 1999. 32.95 (*3-8258-3664-9*, Pub. by CE24) Transaction Pubs.

Multiculturalism in Academe: A Source Book. Libby V. Morris & Sammy Parker. LC 95-26398. (Source Books on Education: Vol. 47). 200p. 1996. text 39.00 (*0-8153-1798-0*, SS980) Garland.

Multiculturalism in Counseling. Daniel T. Sciarra. LC 98-68252. 203p. 1999. pap. text 27.50 (*0-87581-420-4*) F E Peacock Pubs.

Multiculturalism in Health Education & Health Promotion. Carl A. Grant & Veronica Acosta-Deprez. (C). 1999. pap. text 34.00 (*0-205-26209-0*, Macmillan Coll) P-H.

Multiculturalism in Libraries, 83. Rosemary R. Du Mont et al. LC 93-49543. (Contributions in Librarianship & Information Science Ser.: No. 83). 256p. 1994. 59.95 (*0-313-28418-0*, Quorum Bks) Greenwood.

Multiculturalism in Library Programming for Children. Janice N. Harrington. LC 94-12413. (ALSC Program Support Publications). 15p. 1994. pap. 8.00 (*0-8389-5765-X*) ALA.

Multiculturalism in Mathematics, Science, & Technology: Reading & Activities. Thom Alcoze. pap. 32.00 (*0-201-29595-4*) Addison-Wesley.

Multiculturalism in the College Curriculum: A Handbook of Strategies & Resources for Faculty. Marilyn Lutzker. LC 94-37880. (Greenwood Educators' Reference Collection). 160p. 1995. lib. bdg. 55.00 (*0-313-28918-2*, Greenwood Pr) Greenwood.

Multiculturalism in the United States: A Comparative Guide to Acculturation & Ethnicity. Ed. by John D. Buenker & Lorman A. Ratner. LC 91-35116. 280p. 1992. lib. bdg. 57.95 (*0-313-25374-9*, BUC/, Greenwood Pr) Greenwood.

Multiculturalism in Transit: A German-American Exchange. Ed. by Klaus J. Milich & Jeffrey M. Peck. LC 98-26838. (International Political Currents Ser.: No. 3). 304p. 1998. 59.95 (*1-57181-163-X*) Berghahn Bks.

***Multiculturalism, Liberalism & Democracy.** Ed. by Rajeev Bhargava et al. 444p. 2000. text 29.95 (*0-19-564824-2*) OUP.

***Multiculturalism of Fear.** Jacob T. Levy. 220p. 2000. 29.95 (*0-19-829712-2*) OUP.

Multicurricular Springboards & Starters. Linda Milliken. (Illus.). 144p. 1993. pap. 12.95 (*1-56472-010-1*) Edupress Inc.

Multicylinder Test Sequences for Evaluating Automotive Engine Oils. 10th ed. ASTM Committee B.01 on Automotive Lubricants & D-2. LC 93-14689. (Special Technical Publication Ser.: No. 3151I). 1993. 30.00 (*0-8031-1880-5*, STP315I) ASTM.

Multicylinder Test Sequences for Evaluating Automotive Engine Oils, Pt. II: Sequence IIID - STP 315H. 115p. 1980. pap. 13.00 (*0-8031-0522-3*, STP315H); 16.00 (*0-8031-0523-1*, STP315H) ASTM.

Multicylinder Test Sequences for Evaluating Automotive Engine Oils, Part 1: Sequence IID - STP 315H. 111p. 1980. pap. 13.00 (*0-8031-0520-7*, 04-315080-12); ring bd. 16.00 (*0-8031-0521-5*, STP315H) ASTM.

Multidemensional Hypergeometric Functions the Representation Theory of Lie Algebras & Quantum Groups. Alexander Verchenko. (Advanced Series in Mathematical Physics). 384p. 1995. text 86.00 (*981-02-1880-X*) World Scientific Pub.

Multidiccionario. Nauta Staff. (SPA.). 544p. 1979. 38.95 (*0-8288-4825-4*, S50514) Fr & Eur.

Multidimensional Analysis: Algebras & Systems for Science & Engineering. George W. Hart. LC 94-39139. (Illus.). 236p. 1995. 49.95 (*0-387-94417-6*) Spr-Verlag.

Multidimensional Analysis & Discrete Models. Aleksei A. Dezin. Tr. by Irene Aleksanova from RUS. LC 95-16807. 256p. 1995. boxed set 134.95 (*0-8493-9425-2*, 9425) CRC Pr.

Multidimensional Approaches to Reservoir Fisheries Management. Ed. by L. E. Miranda. LC 96-78695. (Symposium Ser.: Vol. 16). 463p. 1996. 92.00 (*0-913235-92-X*, 540.16) Am Fisheries Soc.

Multidimensional Chromatography: Techniques & Applications. Ed. by Hernan J. Cortes. (Chromatographic Science Ser.: Vol. 50). (Illus.). 424p. 1989. text 170.00 (*0-8247-8136-8*) Dekker.

Multidimensional Chromatography: Techniques & Applications. Mondello. text. write for info. (*0-471-98869-3*) Wiley.

Multidimensional Complex Analysis & Partial Differential Equations: A Collection of Papers in Honor of Fran Cois Treves: Proceedings of the Brazil-U. S. A. Conference on Multidimensional Complex Analysis & Partial Differential Equations, June 12-16, 1995, Sao Carlos, Brazil. Francois Treves et al. LC 96-51034. (Contemporary Mathematics Ser.: Vol. 205). 276p. 1997. pap. 55.00 (*0-8218-0509-6*, CONM/205) Am Math.

Multidimensional Description of Child Personality: A Manual for the Personality Inventory for Children, 1990 Edition. Robert D. Wirt et al. LC 79-57301. 192p. 1990. pap. 58.50 (*0-87424-152-9*, W-152B) Western Psych.

Multidimensional Diffusion Processes, Vol. 233. Daniel W. Stroock & S. R. Varadhan. LC 96-27093. (Grundlehren der Mathematischen Wissenschaften Ser.). 1996. write for info. (*3-540-90353-4*) Spr-Verlag.

Multidimensional Digital Signal. Dan E. Dudgeon & Russell M. Merser. 1995. pap. text 93.33 (*0-13-227638-0*) P-H.

Multidimensional Engine Modeling: 1996 International Congress & Exposition. LC 96-207880. (Special Publications). 184p. 1996. pap. 38.00 (*1-56091-799-7*, SP-1169) Soc Auto Engineers.

Multidimensional Filter Banks & Wavelets: Basic Theory & Cosine Modulated Filter Banks. Bernard Levy. Ed. by Sankar Basu. LC 96-23407. 160p. (C). 1996. text 111.00 (*0-7923-9757-6*) Kluwer Academic.

Multidimensional Filter Banks & Wavelets: Research Developments & Applications. Bernard Levy et al. Ed. by Sankar Basu. LC 96-45465. 244p. (C). 1997. text 125.00 (*0-7923-9848-3*) Kluwer Academic.

M

Multidimensional Fourier Related Transforms & Their Applications. Okan K. Ersoy. 336p. (C). 2001. 28.50 (*0-13-042151-0*) P-H.

Multidimensional Functional Assessment of Older Adults: The Duke Older Americans Resources & Services Procedures. Gerda G. Fillenbaum. 192p. 1988. 39.95 (*0-8058-0241-X*) L Erlbaum Assocs.

Multidimensional Hyperbolic Problems & Computations. Ed. by A. Friedman et al. (IMA Volumes in Mathematics & Its Applications Ser.: Vol. 29). (Illus.). xiv, 386p. 1990. 63.95 (*0-387-97485-7*) Spr-Verlag.

Multidimensional Integral Transformations. Ed. by Yu A. Brychkov et al. LC 91-41471. xiii, 379p. 1992. text 191.00 (*2-88124-839-X*, QA432) Gordon & Breach.

Multidimensional Inverse & Ill-Posed Problems for Differential Equations. Yu. E. Anikonov. (Inverse & Ill-Posed Problems Ser.). 240p. 1994. 120.00 (*90-6764-185-5*, Pub. by VSP) Coronet Bks.

Multidimensional Inverse Scattering Problems. A. G. Ramm. 392p. 1992. 155.00 (*0-582-05665-9*, LM5665, Chap & Hall CRC) CRC Pr.

Multidimensional Microscopy. Ed. by P. C. Cheng et al. LC 93-5146. (Illus.). 408p. 1993. 71.95 (*0-387-94118-5*) Spr-Verlag.

Multidimensional Models of Perception & Cognition. Ed. by F. Gregory Ashby. (Scientific Psychology Ser.). 538p. 1992. text 125.00 (*0-8058-0577-X*) L Erlbaum Assocs.

Multidimensional Palaeobiology. Richard A. Reyment. 426p. 1991. 173.00 (*0-08-037231-7*, Pergamon Pr); pap. 60.00 (*0-08-041001-4*, Pergamon Pr) Elsevier.

Multidimensional Preference Scaling. Gordon C. Bechtel. (Methods & Models in the Social Sciences Ser.: No. 6). 1976. pap. 32.35 (*90-279-7592-2*) Mouton.

Multidimensional Processing of Video Signals. Ed. by Giovanni L. Sicuranza. (International Series in Engineering & Computer Science, VLSI, Computer Architecture, & Digital Screen Processing). 200p. (C). 1992. text 148.50 (*0-7923-9228-0*) Kluwer Academic.

Multidimensional Programming. Edward A. Ashcroft et al. (Illus.). 176p. 1995. text 60.00 (*0-19-507597-8*) OUP.

Multidimensional Residues & Their Applications. A. K. Tsikh. LC 92-8368. (Translations of Mathematical Monographs: Vol. 103). 188p. 1992. text 119.00 (*0-8218-4560-8*, MMONO/103C) Am Math.

Multidimensional Scaling. D. R. Cox. 216p. 1994. ring bd. 68.95 (*0-412-49120-6*, Chap & Hall CRC) CRC Pr.

Multidimensional Scaling. Joseph B. Kruskal & Myron Wish. (Quantitative Applications in the Social Sciences Ser.: Vol. 11). 93p. 1978. pap. 10.95 (*0-8039-0940-3*) Sage.

Multidimensional Scaling. Mark L. Davison. LC 91-30195. 256p. (C). 1992. reprint ed. lib. bdg. 44.95 (*0-89464-662-1*) Krieger.

Multidimensional Scaling: History, Theory & Applications. Ed. by Forrest W. Young & Robert M. Hamer. 336p. 1987. text 69.95 (*0-89859-663-7*) L Erlbaum Assocs.

Multidimensional School Leadership. Larry Lashway. LC 97-69150. (Fastback Ser.: No. 424). 53p. 1997. pap. 3.00 (*0-87367-624-6*, FB#424) Phi Delta Kappa.

Multidimensional Second Order Stochastic Processes. Kakihara. LC 96-37165. (Series on Multivariate Analysis). 1997. write for info. (*981-02-3000-1*) World Scientific Pub.

Multidimensional Signal Processing. Dudgeon. (C). 2001. pap. 78.00 (*0-13-209206-9*, Macmillan Coll) P-H.

Multidimensional Similarity Structure Analysis. I. Borg & J. Lingoes. (Illus.). xiv, 390p. 1987. 54.00 (*0-387-96525-4*) Spr-Verlag.

Multidimensional Singular Integrals & Integral Equations. W. Whyte & Solomon G. Mikhlin. LC 64-21900. (International Series of Monographs on Pure & Applied Mathematics: Vol. 83). 1965. 122.00 (*0-08-010852-0*, Pub. by Pergamon Repr) Franklin.

Multidimensional Solid-State NMR & Polymers. K. Schmidt-Rohr & H. W. Spiess. (Illus.). 512p. 1994. text 111.00 (*0-12-626630-1*) Acad Pr.

Multidimensional Spatial Data & Decision Analysis. Peter Nijkamp et al. LC 79-40518. (Illus.). 334p. reprint ed. pap. 103.60 (*0-608-17610-9*, 203046000069) Bks Demand.

Multidimensional Spectroscopy of Polymers: Vibrational, NMR, & Fluorescence Techniques. Ed. by Theodore Provder & Marek W. Urban. LC 95-17880. (ACS Symposium Ser.: No. 598). (Illus.). 586p. 1995. text 155.00 (0-8412-3262-8, Pub. by Am Chemical) OUP.

Multidimensional Statistical Analysis & Theory of Random Matrices: Proceedings of the Sixth Eugene Lukacs Symposium. Ed. by A. K. Gupta & Vyacheslav L. Girko. (Illus.). 398p. 1996. 200.00 (90-6764-208-8, Pub. by VSP) Coronet Bks.

Multidimensional Strange Attractors & Turbulence, Vol. 8. I. S. Aranson et al. (Mathematical Physics Reviews Ser.: SSR Sec. C, Vol. 8, Pt. 5). ii, 88p. 1989. pap. text 107.00 (3-7186-4868-7) Gordon & Breach.

Multidimensional Systems. Bose Staff. (Mathematics & Its Applications Ser.). 1985. text 184.00 (90-277-1764-8) Kluwer Academic.

Multidimensional Systems: Techniques & Applications. Spyros G. Tzafestas. (Electrical Engineering & Electronics Ser.: Vol. 29). (Illus.). 656p. 1986. text 195.00 (0-8247-7301-2) Dekker.

Multidimensional Wealky Singular Integral Equations. Gennadi Vainikko. LC 93-14009. (Lecture Notes in Mathematics Ser.). xii, 159p. 1993. 37.95 (0-387-56878-6) Spr-Verlag.

Multidisciplinary Analysis of Controversies in the Management of Prostate Cancer. Ed. by D. S. Coffey et al. LC 88-18004. (Illus.). 350p. 1988. 89.50 (0-306-42927-6, Plenum Trade) Perseus Pubng.

***Multidisciplinary Approach to Health Care Ethics.** Drew E. Hinderer & Sara R. Hinderer. LC 00-24568. 2000. write for info. (0-7674-1302-4) Mayfield Pub.

Multidisciplinary Approach to Myelin Diseases. Ed. by G. Serlupi Crescenzi. LC 87-29227. (NATO ASI Series A, Life Sciences: Vol. 142). (Illus.). 416p. 1987. 110.00 (0-306-42776-1, Plenum Trade) Perseus Pubng.

Multidisciplinary Approach to Myelin Diseases 2. S. Salvati. (NATO ASI Ser.: Vol. 258). (Illus.). 274p. (C). 1994. text 95.00 (0-306-44634-0, Kluwer Plenum) Kluwer Academic.

***Multidisciplinary Approach to Rehabilitation.** Shrawan Kumar. 400p. 2000. 45.00 (0-7506-7067-3) Buttrwrth-Heinemann.

Multidisciplinary Approaches to Cholinesterase Functions. A. Shafferman & B. Valen. (Illus.). 310p. (C). 1993. text 95.00 (0-306-44315-5, Kluwer Plenum) Kluwer Academic.

Multidisciplinary Atlas of Breast Surgery. David W. Kinne. LC 97-4343. 275p. 1997. text 150.00 (0-397-51467-0) Lppncott W & W.

Multidisciplinary Care of Cancer Patients. Council of Europe Staff. 1992. 21.00 (92-871-2043-9, Pub. by Council of Europe) Manhattan Pub Co.

Multidisciplinary Child Abuse & Neglect Team Manual. William Chamberlain. 77p. 3.50 (0-318-16356-X, B10) Regional Inst Social Welfare.

Multidisciplinary Competency Assessment: Ensuring Staff Performance. Janice Crabill et al. Ed. by Joseph Jaeger. LC 95-60800. (Illus.). 320p. 1995. pap. 85.00 (1-880254-30-1) Vista.

Multidisciplinary Design & Optimization: State of the Art. Ed. by Natalia Alexandrov & M. Y. Hussaini. LC 96-72047. (Proceedings in Applied Mathematics Ser.: No. 80). xvi, 455p. 1997. pap. 65.50 (0-89871-359-5, PR80) Soc Indus-Appl Math.

***Multidisciplinary Evaluation: Of Suzanne Haik-Vantoura's Musical Interpretation of Tiberian Maso.** Luis A. Schokel. LC 99-6704. 1999. 15.95 (0-941037-54-1) D & F Scott.

Multidisciplinary Gerontology: A Structure for Research in Gerontology in a Developed Country. Ed. by I. R. Mackay. (Interdisciplinary Topics in Gerontology Ser.: Vol. 11). (Illus.). 1977. 53.25 (3-8055-2679-2) S Karger.

Multidisciplinary Pain Center: Organization & Personnel Functions for Pain Management. Ed. by Jawahar N. Ghia. (Current Management of Pain Ser.). (C). 1988. text 134.00 (0-89838-359-5) Kluwer Academic.

Multidisciplinary Perspectives on Family Violence. Klein & Renate. LC 97-30855. (Illus.). 256p. (C). 1998. pap. 27.99 (0-415-15845-1) Routledge.

Multidisciplinary Perspectives on Family Violence. Renate Klein. LC 97-30855. (Illus.). 256p. (C). 1998. 85.00 (0-415-15844-3) Routledge.

Multidisciplinary Perspectives on Population & Conflict. Ed. by Nazli Choucri. LC 84-2641. 240p. 1984. text 45.00 (0-8156-2314-3); pap. text 16.95 (0-8156-2315-1) Syracuse U Pr.

Multidisciplinary Research at Grasshopper Pueblo, Arizona. Ed. by William A. Longacre et al. LC 82-13715. (Anthropological Papers: No. 40). 138p. 1982. pap. 17.95 (0-8165-0425-3) U of Ariz Pr.

Multidisciplinary Teams: How & Why They Make Money. Robert M. Sneider. (Continuing Education Course Notes Ser.: No. 37). (Illus.). 140p. (Orig.). 1996. pap. 27.00 (0-89181-186-9, 907) AAPG.

Multidisciplinary Treatment of Soft Tissue Sarcomas. Ed. by Jaap Verweij et al. LC 93-9299. (Cancer Treatment & Research Ser.: Vol. 67). 208p. (C). 1993. text 198.50 (0-7923-2183-9) Kluwer Academic.

Multidistrict Litigation. D. Herr. 1986. 125.00 (0-316-35871-1, Aspen Law & Bus) Aspen Pub.

Multidistrict Litigation: Handling Cases Before the Judicial Panel on Multidistrict Litigation. David F. Herr. 384p. 1986. 125.00 (0-316-35881-9, Aspen Law & Bus) Aspen Pub.

Multidomain Proteins: Proceedings of the UNESCO Workshop on Structure & Function of Proteins, Budapest, Sept. 13-15, 1984. L. Patthy & P. Friedrich. 221p. (C). 1986. 100.00 (963-05-4306-0, Pub. by Akade Kiado) St Mut.

Multidrug Resistance: Cancer Cells & Multiple Chemotherapeutic Drugs. 1995. lib. bdg. 255.95 (0-8490-7564-5) Gordon Pr.

Multidrug Resistance in Cancer Cells: Molecular, Biochemical, Physiological, & Biological Aspects. Ed. by Sudhir Gupta & Takashi Tsuruo. LC 96-13797. 522p. 1996. 230.00 (0-471-96712-2) Wiley.

Multieffects for Musicians. Craig Anderton. LC 95-140669. (Illus.). 144p. (Orig.). (C). 1995. pap. 19.95 (0-8256-1447-3, AM 91245, Amsco Music) Music Sales.

Multielement Detection Systems for Spectrochemical Analysis. Kenneth W. Busch & Marianna A. Busch. LC 89-30004. 688p. 1990. 210.00 (0-471-81974-3) Wiley.

***Multiemployer & Public Health Care Coalitions Directory, 2000.** 20p. 2000. pap. 250.00 (0-89154-540-9) Intl Found Employ.

***Multiemployer 401(K)/DC Plan Guide.** Eugene B. Burroughs. LC 99-65787. 211p. 1999. pap. 33.00 (0-89154-536-0) Intl Found Employ.

Multiemployer Fund Salaried Administrators Compensation Survey. IF Research Department Staff. 16p. 1996. pap. 50.00 (0-89154-497-6) Intl Found Employ.

Multiemployer Pension Plan Answer Book. Katherine A. Hesse & David W. Healey. 448p. Date not set. boxed set 118.00 (1-56706-303-9, 63039) Panel Pubs.

Multiemployer Plans: A Guide for New Trustees. Joseph A. Brislin. Ed. by Mary Jo Brzezinski. LC 95-78933. 159p. (Orig.). 1995. pap. 29.00 (0-89154-491-7) Intl Found Employ.

Multiengine Flying. 2nd ed. Paul A. Craig. LC 96-44272. 1996. write for info. (0-07-870624-6) McGraw.

Multiengine Flying. 2nd ed. Paul A. Craig. LC 96-44272. (Illus.). 362p. 1997. 44.95 (0-07-013452-9) McGraw.

Multiengine Flying. 2nd ed. Paul A. Craig. LC 96-44272. (Illus.). 362p. 1997. pap. 34.95 (0-07-013453-7) McGraw.

Multiethnic Children's Literature. Gonzalo Ramierez, Jr. & Jan L. Ramierez. LC 93-39662. 158p. (C). 1994. pap. 28.25 (0-8273-5433-9) Delmar.

Multiethnic Education 1987: Theory & Practice. 3rd ed. James A. Banks. LC 93-15713. 350p. 1993. pap. 57.00 (0-205-14745-3) Allyn.

***Multiethnic Feminist Visions of Fatherhood.** 1999. pap. 10.00 (1-877966-64-9) Ctr Women Policy.

***Multiethnic Japan.** John Lie. 288p. 2001. 35.00 (0-674-00299-7) HUP.

Multifacety Ethics 3 Mille. Andrew Marlatt. 1997. pap. text 25.50 (0-07-303668-4) McGraw.

***Multifamily Assisted Housing Reform & Affordability Act of 1997 - S.513: Congressional Hearing.** Ed. by Connie Mack. (Illus.). 155p. (C). 2000. reprint ed. pap. text 30.00 (0-7881-8691-4) DIANE Pub.

Multifamily Development Handbook. Karen Danielson et al. LC 99-61429. 350p. Date not set. 89.95 (0-87420-869-6, M27) Urban Land.

Multifamily Housing: Effects of HUD's Portfolio Reengineering Proposal. (Illus.). 116p. (Orig.). 1997. pap. text 40.00 (0-7881-4052-3) DIANE Pub.

Multifamily Housing: Federal Programs for the Private Sector. James W. Jones. 1986. 33.00 (0-318-37798-5); ring bd. 70.00 (0-318-37797-7) Law Journal.

Multifamily Housing: Federal Programs for the Private Sector. James W. Jones. 836p. 1986. 85.00 (0-317-01812-4) NY Law Pub.

***Multifamily Housing: HUD Missed Opportunities to Reduce Costs on Its Uninsured Section 8 Portfolio.** Ed. by Stanley J. Czerwinski & Christine M. B. Fishkin. (Illus.). 86p. (C). 1999. pap. text 20.00 (0-7881-8459-8) DIANE Pub.

Multifamily Housing: Information on Projects Eligible for Preservation Assistance. (Illus.). 136p. (Orig.). (C). 1994. pap. text 40.00 (0-7881-0896-4) DIANE Pub.

Multifamily Selective Rehabilitation No. 2: Housing Production Manual. Gene Ruckle. Ed. by Jude Cashman & Peter Werwath. (Housing Production Manuals Ser.). 1990. student ed. 35.00 (0-942901-03-7) Enterprise Fnd.

Multifibre Arrangement in Theory & Practice. Choi. 153 p. (C). 1992. text 39.00 (0-86187-552-4) St Martin.

***Multifield Problems in Continuum Mechanics.** Anna-Margarete Shandig et al. LC 00-30797. 2000. write for info. (3-540-67511-6) Spr-Verlag.

***Multifocal IOLS: The New Era of Refractive Cataract Surgery.** R. Bruce Wallace, III. 200p. (C). 2000. text 125.00 (1-55642-460-4) SLACK Inc.

***Multiform Heritage: Studies on Early Judaism & Christianity in Honor of Robert A. Kraft.** Robert A. Kraft. Ed. by Benjamin G. Wright. LC 99-41855. (Homage Ser.). 353p. 1999. 49.95 (0-7885-0583-1, 001624) Duke.

Multiformity of Man. Eugen Rosenstock-Huessy. 1973. pap. 7.00 (0-912148-06-3) Argo Bks.

Multifractals & 1/f Noise. B. Mandelbrot. (Illus.). 400p. 1998. 42.95 (0-387-98539-5) Spr-Verlag.

Multifractals & Turbulence: Fundamentals & Applications in Geophysics. D. Schertzer & S. Lovejoy. 300p. 1999. text 55.00 (981-02-0886-3) World Scientific Pub.

Multifunction Array Radar: System Design & Analysis. Sergio Sabatini & Marco Tarantino. LC 94-21068. 1994. 42.00 (0-89006-576-4) Artech Hse.

***Multifunction Peripherals for PCs: Technology, Troubleshooting & Repair.** Marvin Hobbs. LC 99-50180. 232p. 1999. pap. 32.95 (0-7506-7125-4, Newnes) Buttrwrth-Heinemann.

Multifunctional Materials Vol. 175: Material Research Society Symposium Proceedings. Ed. by D. R. Ulrich et al. 382p. 1990. text 17.50 (1-55899-063-1) Materials Res.

Multifunctional Mesoporous Inorganic Soilds. Ed. by Cesar A. Sequeira & Michael J. Hudson. LC 93-19299. (NATO Advanced Study Institutes Series C, Mathematical & Physical Sciences: Vol. 400). 1993. text 285.50 (0-7923-2289-4) Kluwer Academic.

Multifunctional Proteins: Catalytic Structural & Regulatory. J. Kane. LC 82-12902. 1983. 82.00 (0-8493-6400-0, CRC Reprint) Franklin.

Multifunctions & Integrands. Ed. by G. Salinetti. (Lecture Notes in Mathematics Ser.: Vol. 1091). v, 234p. 1984. 37.95 (0-387-13882-X) Spr-Verlag.

Multigenerational Family Therapy. David S. Freeman. LC 91-7953. (Illus.). 420p. 1991. pap. 24.95 (1-56024-126-8) Haworth Pr.

Multigenerational Family Therapy. David S. Freeman. LC 91-7953. (Illus.). 420p. 1992. lib. bdg. 59.95 (1-56024-125-X) Haworth Pr.

Multiglossia in Judeo-Arabic: With an Edition, Translation & Grammatical Study of the Cairene Purim Scroll. Benjamin H. Hary. LC 92-27530. (Etudes sur le Judaisme Medieval Ser.: Vol. 14). (Illus.). xvii, 359p. 1992. 75.50 (90-04-09694-9) Brill Academic Pubs.

Multigrid Methods. James H. Bramble. 1993. pap. 43.00 (0-582-23435-2, Pub. by Addison-Wesley) Longman.

Multigrid Methods. Stephen F. McCormick. (Lecture Notes in Pure & Applied Mathematics Ser.: Vol. 110). (Illus.). 672p. 1988. pap. text 199.00 (0-8247-7979-7) Dekker.

Multigrid Methods. Ed. by Stephen F. McCormick. LC 87-60444. (Frontiers in Applied Mathematics Ser.: No. 3). xvii, 282p. 1987. text 51.00 (0-89871-214-9) Soc Indus-Appl Math.

***Multigrid Methods.** Ulrich Trottenberg et al. 352p. 1999. 69.95 (0-12-701070-X) Acad Pr.

Multigrid Methods: Proceedings of the Fifth European Multigrid Conference Held in Stuttgart, Germany, October 1-4, 1996. Ed. by W. Hackbusch et al. (Lecture Notes in Computational Science & Engineering Ser.: Vol. 3). vii, 340p. 1998. pap. 79.95 (3-540-63133-X) Spr-Verlag.

Multigrid Methods for Finite Elements. V. V. Shaidurgy. LC 94-43933. (Mathematics & Its Applications Ser.: Vol. 318).Tr. of Mnogosetochnye Metody Konechnykh Elementov. (ENG & RUS.). 331p. 1995. text 166.00 (0-7923-3290-3) Kluwer Academic.

Multigrid Methods for Process Simulation. W. Joppich & S. Mijalkovic. (Computational Microelectronics Ser.). (Illus.). 336p. 1994. 158.95 (0-387-82404-9) Spr-Verlag.

Multigrid Methods IV: Proceedings of the Fourth European Multigrid Conference, Amsterdam, July 6-9, 1993. Ed. by P. W. Hemker & Peter Wesseling. LC 94-10166. (International Series of Numerical Mathematics: Vol. 116). 1994. 99.50 (0-8176-5030-X) Birkhauser.

***Multigrid Methods VI: Proceedings of the Sixth Multigrid Conference Held in Gent, Belgium, September 27-30, 1999.** Ed. by E. Dick et al. (Lecture Notes in Computational Science & Engineering Ser.: Vol. 14). ix, 293p. 2000. pap. 82.00 (3-540-67157-9) Spr-Verlag.

Multigrid Methods III. Ed. by W. Hackbusch et al. (Internationl Series of Numerical Mathematics: Vol. 89). 394p. 1991. 45.00 (3-7643-2632-8) Birkhauser.

Multigrid Methods III. Ed. by M. T. Schlick & Ulrich Trottenberg. (International Series of Numerical Mathematics: Vol. 98). xi, 394p. 1991. 128.50 (0-8176-2632-8) Birkhauser.

Multigrid Methods II. Ed. by M. T. Schlick & Ulrich Trottenberg. (Lecture Notes in Mathematics Ser.: Vol. 1228). vi, 336p. 1986. 53.95 (0-387-17198-3) Spr-Verlag.

Multigrid Tutorial. William L. Briggs. LC 87-62333. (Miscellaneous Bks.: No. 17). (Illus.). ix, 90p. (C). 1987. pap. text 21.50 (0-89871-221-1) Soc Indus-Appl Math.

***Multigrid Tutorial.** 2nd ed. William L. Briggs et al. (Miscellaneous Bks.: Vol. 72). 2000. pap. 39.00 (0-89871-462-1) Soc Indus-Appl Math.

Multihandicapped: Serving the Severely Disabled. Jack M. Gootzeit. 300p. 1981. text 32.50 (0-8290-0556-0); pap. text 16.95 (0-8290-0269-3) Irvington.

Multihousing Management: Advanced Principles & Practices. Frank Basile et al. LC 85-63079. 286p. 1986. pap. 34.00 (0-86718-252-0) Home Builder.

Multihousing Management One. Frank Basile & George C. Caruso. Ed. by Dorris Tennyson. LC 94-15085. 385p. 1994. 45.00 (0-86718-396-9) Home Builder.

Multihull Cruising Fundamentals: The Official American Sailing Association Guide to Cruising & Bareboat Chartering. Rick White & American Sailing Association Staff. (Illus.). 119p. 1997. pap. 17.95 (0-07-001633-X) McGraw.

Multihull Seamanship: An A-Z of Skills for Catamarans & Trim. Gavin LeSueur. (Illus.). 143p. 1998. pap. 21.95 (1-898660-31-X) Motorbooks Intl.

Multihull Voyaging. Thomas F. Jones. (Illus.). 250p. 1994. 27.50 (0-924486-56-2) Sheridan.

Multijurisdictional Drug Law Enforcement Strategies: Reducing Supply & Demand. 127p. (Orig.). (C). 1993. pap. text 30.00 (1-56806-810-7) DIANE Pub.

Multijurisdictional Drug Task Forces in Idaho. (Illus.). 60p. (Orig.). (C). 1993. pap. text 25.00 (1-56806-806-9) DIANE Pub.

***Multikulturalitat und Multiethnizitat in Mittel-, Ost- und Sudosteuropa.** Peter Brezovszky et al. 342p. 1999. 48.95 (3-631-35162-3) P Lang Pubng.

Multilane Design Alternatives for Improving Suburban Highways. (National Cooperative Highway Research Program Report Ser.: No. 282). 71p. 1986. 8.80 (0-309-04015-9) Transport Res Bd.

Multilateral Activities in South East Asia: The 1995 Pacific Symposium. Michael W. Everett. 285p. 1995. per. 13.00 (0-16-047999-1) USGPO.

Multilateral Activities in Southeast Asia: Defense. 1996. lib. bdg. 259.99 (0-8490-6363-9) Gordon Pr.

Multilateral & Bilateral Sources of Financing for Tourism Development. 172p. 1997. pap. 25.00 (92-844-0134-8, WTO4013, Pub. by Wrld Tourism Org) Bernan Associates.

Multilateral Debt Negotiations in the 41st General Assembly of the United States. Thomas G. Weiss. (Pew Case Studies in International Affairs). 59p. (C). 1988. pap. text 3.50 (1-56927-203-4) Geo U Inst Dplmcy.

Multilateral Development: Status of World Bank Reforms. (Illus.). 33p. (Orig.). (C). 1995. pap. text 20.00 (0-7881-1803-X) DIANE Pub.

***Multilateral Development Banking: Environmental Principles & Concepts Reflecting General International Law & Public Policy.** Gunther Handl. LC 00-33091. (International Environmental Law & Policy Ser.). 2000. write for info. (90-411-9807-5) Kluwer Law Intl.

***Multilateral Development Banks: Improving U.S. Leadership.** Barbara Upton. LC 99-57875. (Washington Papers). 168p. 2000. pap. 19.95 (0-275-96967-3, Praeger Pubs) Greenwood.

***Multilateral Development Banks: Improving U.S. Leadership, 178.** Barbara Upton. LC 99-57875. (The Washington Papers). 168p. 2000. 49.95 (0-275-96966-5, Praeger Pubs) Greenwood.

Multilateral Development Banks: Increasing U. S. Exports & Creating U. S. Jobs. 131p. (Orig.). (C). 1994. pap. text 30.00 (0-7881-1427-1) DIANE Pub.

Multilateral Development Banks: Increasing U. S. Exports & Creating U. S. Jobs. 195p. (Orig.). (C). 1997. pap. text 30.00 (0-7881-4715-3) DIANE Pub.

Multilateral Development Banks: Increasing U. S. Exports & Creating U. S. Jobs. (Orig.). 1995. lib. bdg. 255.95 (0-8490-7435-5) Gordon Pr.

Multilateral Development Banks: Increasing U. S. Exports & Creating U. S. Jobs. (Orig.). 1997. lib. bdg. 250.99 (0-8490-7672-2) Gordon Pr.

Multilateral Development Banks: Increasing United States Exports & Creating United States Jobs. Government Printing Office Staff. 135p. 1994. per. 12.00 (0-16-045015-2) USGPO.

Multilateral Development Banks: Public Consulation on Evironmental Assessments. Harold J. Johnson. 78p. (C). 1999. pap. text 20.00 (0-7881-8051-7) DIANE Pub.

Multilateral Development Banks Vol. 1: The African Development Bank. E. Philip English & Harris M. Mule. LC 94-45003. (Multilateral Development Banks Ser.: Vol. 1). 213p. 1996. 38.00 (1-55587-467-3, 87-467-3); pap. text 19.95 (1-55587-493-2, 87-493-2) L Rienner.

Multilateral Development Banks Vol. 2: The Asian Development Bank. Nihal Kappagoda. LC 94-45003. 200p. 1995. 38.00 (1-55587-468-1); pap. text 19.95 (1-55587-494-0) L Rienner.

Multilateral Development Banks Vol. 3: The Caribbean Development Bank. Chandra Hardy. LC 94-45003. 135p. 1995. 38.00 (1-55587-469-X); pap. text 19.95 (1-55587-495-9) L Rienner.

Multilateral Development Banks Vol. 4: The Inter-American Development Bank. Diana Tussie. 165p. 1995. 38.00 (1-55587-466-5); pap. text 19.95 (1-55587-492-4) L Rienner.

Multilateral Development Banks Vol. 5: Titans or Behemoths? Roy Culpeper. 196p. 1997. 38.00 (1-55587-470-3); pap. 19.95 (1-55587-496-7) L Rienner.

Multilateral Diplomacy: The United Nations System at Geneva: A Working Guide - La Diplomatie Multilaterale: Le Systeme des Nations UNIES a Geneve: Guide de Travail. Ed. by M. A. Boisard et al. LC 97-32488. 524p. 1998. 171.00 (90-411-0524-7) Kluwer Law Intl.

Multilateral Diplomacy & the United Nations Today. Ed. by James P. Muldoon, Jr. et al. LC 98-20749. 272p. 1998. 65.00 (0-8133-9959-9, Pub. by Westview) HarpC.

***Multilateral Diplomacy & the United Nations Today.** Ed. by James P. Muldoon, Jr. et al. LC 98-20749. 272p. 1998. pap. text 26.00 (0-8133-9958-0, Pub. by Westview) HarpC.

Multilateral Diplomacy Within the Commonwealth. Athanase Papadopoulos. 1982. lib. bdg. 96.00 (90-247-2568-2) Kluwer Academic.

Multilateral Investment & Private Investment in the Third World. Dietrich Kebschull et al. Ed. by Karl-Wolfgang Menchk. 146p. (C). 1985. pap. 24.95 (0-88738-615-6) Transaction Pubs.

***Multilateral Investment System & Multinational Enterprises.** Thomas L. Brewer & Stephen Young. (Illus.). 320p. 2000. pap. 24.95 (0-19-924110-4) OUP.

Multilateral Investment System Rules & Multinational Enterprises. Thomas L. Brewer & Stephen Young. (Illus.). 320p. 1998. text 75.00 (0-19-829315-1) OUP.

Multilateral Mediation, Practical Experiences & Lessons. 429p. 1989. 60.00 (0-685-50213-9) UN.

Multilateral Negotiations: Lessons from Arms Control, Trade, & the Environment. Fen O. Hampson. 472p. 1995. text 49.95 (0-8018-4999-3) Johns Hopkins.

***Multilateral Negotiations: Lessons from Arms Control, Trade, & the Environment.** Comment by Fen Osler Hansen. 1999. pap. text 17.95 (0-8018-6197-7) Johns Hopkins.

Multilateral Official Debt Rescheduling: Recent Experience. K. Burke Dillon & Gumersindo Oliveros. (World Economic & Financial Surveys Ser.). 22p. 1987. pap. 10.00 (0-939934-83-3) Intl Monetary.

Multilateral Official Debt Rescheduling: Recent Experience. Peter M. Keller & Nissanke Weerasinghe. (World Economic & Financial Surveys Ser.). 23p. 1988. pap. 10.00 (1-55775-018-1) Intl Monetary.

Multilateral Organizations: U. S. Contributions to International Organizations for Fiscal Years 1993-95. Harold J. Johnson. (Illus.). 87p. 1998. pap. text 25.00 (*0-7881-4792-7*) DIANE Pub.

Multilateral System of Payments: Keynes, Convertibility & the International Monetary Fund's Articles of Agreement. Joseph Gold. (Occasional Papers: No. 6). 31p. 1981. pap. 5.00 (*1-55775-077-7*) Intl Monetary.

Multilateral Tax Treaties. Lang. LC 98-177772. 1997. lib. bdg. 103.00 (*90-411-0704-5*) Kluwer Law Intl.

Multilateral Treaties & Conventions on Industrial Property in the Americas. (Treaty Ser.: No. 39). (ENG, POR & SPA.). 1973. pap. 1.00 (*0-685-03622-7*) OAS.

Multilateral Treaties Deposited with the Secretary-General. 1044p. 80.00 (*92-1-133513-2*) UN.

Multilateral Treaties Deposited with the Secretary-General. 931p. 1992. 75.00 (*92-1-133450-0*, E.93.V.11) UN.

Multilateral Treaties Deposited with the Secretary-General. 960p. 1993. 75.00 (*92-1-133471-3*, E.94.V.11) UN.

Multilateral Treaties Deposited with the Secretary-General. 1049p. 1994. 75.00 (*92-1-133484-5*, E.95.V.5) UN.

***Multilateral Treaties Deposited with the Secretary-General: State As of April 30, 1999.** 990p. 1999. 80.00 (*92-1-133610-4*) UN.

Multilateral Treaties Deposited with the Secretary-General Status as at 31 December 1997. Ed. by United Nations Staff. 1014p. 80.00 (*92-1-133527-2*) UN.

Multilateral Treaties Deposited with the Secretary-General: Status As of December 31, 1995. 1010p. 75.00 (*92-1-133508-6*, 70400) UN.

Multilateral Treaties Deposited with the Secretary-General: Status As of 1 December, 1990. 948p. 1991. 75.00 (*92-1-133412-8*, 91.V.8) UN.

Multilateral Treaties Deposited with the Secretary-General: Status As of 31 December, 1986. 871p. 1987. 60.00 (*92-1-133293-1*, E.87.V.6) UN.

Multilateral Treaties Deposited with the Secretary-General: Status As of 31 December, 1987. 883p. 1988. pap. 70.00 (*92-1-133306-7*, E.88.V.3) UN.

Multilateral Treaties Deposited with The Secretary-General: Status As of 31 December, 1988. 947p. 1989. 70.00 (*92-1-133319-9*, E.89.V.6) UN.

Multilateral Treaties Deposited with the Secretary-General: Status As of 31 December, 1989. 70.00 (*92-1-133400-4*, E.90.V.6) UN.

Multilateral Treaties in the Field of the Environment, Vol. 1. Grotius Publications Ltd. Staff. 535p. (C). 1983. 170.00 (*92-807-1025-7*, Pub. by Grotius Pubns Ltd) St Mut.

Multilateral Treaties in the Field of the Environment, Vol. 2. Grotius Publications Ltd. Staff. 537p. (C). 1991. 260.00 (*92-807-1212-8*, Pub. by Grotius Pubns Ltd) St Mut.

Multilateral Treaties Relevant to the United Nations Convention on the Law of the Sea: Multilateral Treaties Relevant to the United Nations Convention. (The Law of the Sea Ser.). 116p. pap. 14.50 (*92-1-133273-7*, E.85.V.II) UN.

Multilateral Treaty Calendar: Repertoire des Trait Es Multilat Eraux, 1648-1995. Christian L. Wiktor. LC 98-6227. (ENG & FRE.). 1998. 278.00 (*90-411-0584-0*) Kluwer Law Intl.

Multilateralism & the United Nations. 325p. 1987. pap. 27.50 (*92-1-104217-8*, E.87.II.A.22) UN.

Multilateralism & Western Strategy. Ed. by Michael Brenner. LC 94-25722. 1994. text 55.00 (*0-312-12361-2*) St Martin.

***Multilateralism in Multinational Perspective.** James P. Sewell. LC 99-38754. (International Political Economy Ser.). 2000. text 68.00 (*0-312-22915-1*) St Martin.

Multilateralism in NATO: Shaping the Postwar Balance of Power, 1945-1961. Steve Weber. LC 91-8260. (Research Ser.: No. 79). ix, 94p. (Orig.). 1995. pap. text 9.50 (*0-87725-179-7*) U of Cal IAS.

Multilateralism Matters: The Theory & Praxis of an Institutional Forum. Ed. by John G. Ruggie. LC 92-31586. (New Directions in World Politics Ser.). 400p. (C). 1993. text 73.50 (*0-231-07980-X*); pap. text 23.00 (*0-231-07981-8*) Col U Pr.

Multilateralism vs. Regionalism: Trade Issues after the Uruguay Round. Elizabeth Ourusoff de Fernandez-Gemenez & E. James Mundy. LC 89-12920. (Illus.). 315p. 1990. text 119.95 (*0-521-39095-8*) Cambridge U Pr.

Multilateralism vs. Regionalism: Trade Issues after the Uruguay Round. Ed. by Meine P. Van Dijk & Sandro Sideri. LC 96-10978. (Eadi Book Ser.: No. 19). 242p. (C). 1996. pap. 24.50 (*0-7146-4270-3*, Pub. by F Cass Pubs) Intl Spec Bk.

Multilayer & Grazing Incidence X-Ray/EUV Optics III. Ed. by Richard B. Hoover & Arthur B. Walker. 358p. 1996. 66.00 (*0-8194-2193-6*) SPIE.

Multilayer & Grazing Incidence X-Ray/EUV Optics III, Vol. 2805. Ed. by Richard B. Hoover & Arthur B. Walker. 306p. 1996. 76.00 (*0-8194-2075-1*) SPIE.

Multilayer & Other Ferroelectric Ceramic Composites: A Special Issue of the Journal Ferroelectrics. Ed. by L. E. Cross et al. ii, 318p. 1986. pap. text 404.00 (*2-88124-150-6*) Gordon & Breach.

Multilayer Bonding Guide. M. Huschka. 130p. 1997. pap. 156.00 (*1-872422-00-4*) St Mut.

Multilayer Ceramic Devices. Ed. by John B. Blum & W. Roger Cannon. LC 86-32080. (Advances in Ceramics Ser.: No. 19). 240p. reprint ed. pap. 74.40 (*0-7837-1382-7*, 204155800021) Bks Demand.

***Multilayer Electronic Ceramic Devices.** Ed. by Jau-Ho Jean et al. (Ceramic Transactions Ser.: Vol. 97). 24p. 1999. text 95.00 (*1-57498-064-5*, CT097) Am Ceramic.

Multilayer Polarized Light: TM-4-97. IESNA Staff. (Illus.). 22p. 1997. pap. 32.00 (*0-87995-144-3*, TM-4-97) Illum Eng.

Multilayer Printed Circuit Board Handbook. J. A. Scarlett. 590p. 1997. pap. 352.00 (*0-901150-15-0*) St Mut.

***Multilayered Aquifer Systems: Fundamentals & Applications.** A. H. D. Cheng. LC 00-31596. (Civil & Environmental Engineering Ser.). (Illus.). 2000. write for info. (*0-8247-9875-9*) Dekker.

Multilayers: Synthesis, Properties, & Nonelectronic Applications. Ed. by T. W. Barbee, Jr. et al. (Materials Research Society Symposium Proceedings Ser.: Vol. 103). 1988. text 17.50 (*0-931837-71-5*) Materials Res.

Multilayers No. IMAM-10: Materials Research Society International Symposium Proceedings. Ed. by T. Ohno & R. Yamamoto. 619p. 1989. text 17.50 (*1-55899-039-9*, IMAM-10) Materials Res.

Multilengua Diccionario de Cartas Comerciales en Cuatro Idiomas, 3 vols., Set. Cantabrica. (ENG, FRE, GER & SPA.). 972p. 1975. 175.00 (*0-8288-5939-6*, S50102) Fr & Eur.

Multilevel Adaptive Methods for Partial Differential Equations. Stephen F. McCormick. LC 89-22034. (Frontiers in Applied Mathematics Ser.: No. 6). ix, 162p. 1989. pap. 33.00 (*0-89871-247-5*) Soc Indus-Appl Math.

Multilevel Analysis of Educational Data. Ed. by R. Darrell Bock. 354p. 1989. text 94.95 (*0-12-108840-5*) Acad Pr.

Multilevel Approach to the Study of Motor Control & Learning. Debra J. Rose. LC 96-24476. 331p. 1996. text 59.00 (*0-02-403621-8*) Allyn.

Multilevel Approach to the Study of Motor Control & Learning. Debra J. Rose. (C). 1997. teacher ed., boxed set. write for info. (*0-02-403623-4*, U5916-4, Macmillan Coll) P-H.

Multilevel Design: A Guide with an Annotated Bibliography, 1980-1993, 23. Harry J. Huttner & Pieter Van den Eeden. LC 94-36760. (Bibliographies & Indexes in Sociology Ser.: 23). 288p. 1995. lib. bdg. 77.95 (*0-313-27310-3*, Greenwood Pr) Greenwood.

Multilevel Health Effects Research: From Molecules to Man. Ed. by J. F. Park & R. A. Pelroy. LC 89-18083. (Proceedings of the 27th Hanford Symposium on Health & the Environment (Oct. 1988) Ser.). 492p. 1990. pap. text 57.50 (*0-935470-55-7*) Battelle.

Multilevel Interconnect Technology II. Ed. by Mart Graef & Divyesh N. Patel. LC 99-196349. (Proceedings of SPIE Ser.: Vol. 3508). 232p. 1998. 69.00 (*0-8194-2967-8*) SPIE.

***Multilevel Interconnect Technology III.** Ed. by Mart Graef & Divyesh N. Patel. 194p. 1999. pap. text 62.00 (*0-8194-3480-9*) SPIE.

Multilevel Marketing: A Legal Primer: A Handbook for Executives, Entrepreneurs, Managers & Distributors. Mario Brossi & Joseph N. Mariano. 78p. (Orig.). 1991. text. write for info. (*0-9630469-0-X*) Direct Selling.

***Multilevel Methods in Lubrication.** C. H. Venner & A. A. Lubrecht. LC 00-41747. 2000. write for info. (*0-444-50503-2*) Elsevier.

Multilevel Models in Education & Social Research. write for info. (*0-85264-288-1*) Lubrecht & Cramer.

Multilevel Optimization: Algorithms & Applications. Ed. by Athanasios Migdalas et al. LC 97-42021. (Nonconvex Optimization & Its Applications Ser.). 406p. 1998. text 214.00 (*0-7923-4693-9*, D Reidel) Kluwer Academic.

Multilevel Projection Methods for Partial Differential Equations. Stephen F. McCormick. LC 91-39536. (CBMS-NSF Regional Conference Series in Applied Mathematics: No. 62). vi, 114p. (C). 1992. pap. text 26.00 (*0-89871-292-0*) Soc Indus-Appl Math.

Multilevel Statistical Models. 2nd ed. Harvey Goldstein. LC 95-207858. (Kendall's Library of Statistics: No. 3). 192p. 1998. 60.00 (*0-340-59529-9*, Pub. by E A) OUP.

***Multilevel Theory, Research & Methods in Organizations: Foundations, Extensions & New Directions.** Katherine J. Klein & Steve W. J. Kozlowski. LC 00-25343. (Frontiers of Industrial & Organizational Psychology Ser.). 2000. 47.95 (*0-7879-5228-1*) Jossey-Bass.

Multilinear Algebra, Vol. 8. Russell Merris. (Algebra, Logic & Applications Ser.). 340p. 1997. text 59.00 (*90-5699-078-0*) Gordon & Breach.

Multilingual Aeronautical Dictionary. Advisory Group Aerospace Research Staff. (DUT, ENG, FRE, GER & ITA.). 876p. 1980. 195.00 (*0-8288-0022-7*, M7770) Fr & Eur.

***Multilingual Anthology of American Literature: A Reader of Original Texts with English Translations.** Marc Shell. 2000. 65.00 (*0-8147-9752-0*); pap. text 26.00 (*0-8147-9753-9*) NYU Pr.

Multilingual Anthology of American Literature: A Reader of Original Texts with English Translations. Ed. by Werner Sollors & Marc Shell. LC 98-6851. 688p. 2000. text 65.00 (*0-8147-8092-X*); pap. text 25.00 (*0-8147-8093-8*) NYU Pr.

Multilingual Apple: Languages in New York City. Ed. by Ofelia Garcia & Joshua A. Fishman. 373p. 1997. 29.95 (*3-11-015707-1*) Mouton.

Multilingual Aspects of Information Technology. J. C. Sager et al. 200p. 1986. text 46.95 (*0-566-03513-8*, Pub. by Gower) Ashgate Pub Co.

***Multilingual Books from Spanish to Portuguese.** Jack L. Ulsh. 1999. pap. 45.00 (*1-58214-055-3*) Mltilingl Bks.

***Multilingual Books FSI Kituba Course, 8 bks., Set.** L. B. Swifa & E. W. Zola. (Multilingual Books Intensive Language Courses Ser.). 470p. 1999. pap. text 185.00 incl. audio (*1-58214-154-1*) Mltilingl Bks.

***Multilingual Books FSI Levantine Arabic Pronunciation, Set.** James Snow. (Multilingual Books Interactive Language Courses Ser.). 100p. 1999. pap. text, wbk. ed. 160.00 incl. audio (*1-58214-051-0*) Mltilingl Bks.

***Multilingual Books FSI Spanish Basic Course 3.** W. A. Swift. (Multilingual Books Interactive Language Courses Ser.). 542p. 1999. pap. text 179.00 (*1-58214-053-7*) Mltilingl Bks.

Multilingual Collection of Terms for Welding & Allied Processes Vol. 2: Gas Welding (15 Languages) 1993. 89.95 (*1-85573-230-0*, Pub. by Woodhead Pubng) Am Educ Systs.

Multilingual Collection of Terms for Welding & Allied Processes Vol. 3: Arc Welding (12 Languages) 1993. 89.95 (*1-85573-231-9*, Pub. by Woodhead Pubng) Am Educ Systs.

Multilingual Collection of Terms for Welding & Allied Processes Vol. 4: Resistance Welding (18 Languages) 1993. 89.95 (*1-85573-232-7*, Pub. by Woodhead Pubng) Am Educ Systs.

Multilingual Collection of Terms for Welding & Allied Processes Vol. 5: Thermal Cutting (18 Languages) 1993. 89.95 (*1-85573-233-5*, Pub. by Woodhead Pubng) Am Educ Systs.

Multilingual Collection of Terms for Welding & Allied Processes Vol. 6: Hot Spraying (18 Languages) 1993. 89.95 (*1-85573-234-3*, Pub. by Woodhead Pubng) Am Educ Systs.

Multilingual Collection of Terms for Welding & Allied Processes Vol. 7: Brazing (17 Languages) 1993. 89.95 (*1-85573-235-1*, Pub. by Woodhead Pubng) Am Educ Systs.

Multilingual Collection of Terms for Welding & Allied Processes Vol. 8: Welding of Plastics (3 Languages) 1993. 89.95 (*1-85573-236-X*, Pub. by Woodhead Pubng) Am Educ Systs.

Multilingual Collection of Terms for Welding & Allied Processes Vol. 9: Special Welding Processes. 1993. 89.95 (*1-85573-237-8*, Pub. by Woodhead Pubng) Am Educ Systs.

Multilingual Commercial Dictionary. Ed. by Alan Isaacs. LC 79-6364. 492p. reprint ed. pap. 152.60 (*0-608-16451-8*, 202722200054) Bks Demand.

Multilingual Compendium of Plant Diseases, Vol. 2. Ed. by P. R. Miller & H. L. Pollard. LC 75-46932. 434p. 1977. 48.00 (*0-89054-020-9*) Am Phytopathol Soc.

Multilingual Computer Advisor. Ed. by Nelson A. Ossorio & Loren Bolinger. (ENG, GER & SPA.). (Orig.). 1995. pap. 29.95 (*1-56721-089-9*) Twnty-Fifth Cent Pr.

Multilingual Dictionary for Mechanics, Salesmen & Engineers in Metal-Working. H. Rieger. (ENG, FRE, GER, ITA & POR.). 519p. 1981. 75.00 (*0-8288-0607-1*, M 15547) Fr & Eur.

Multilingual Dictionary of Agronomic Plants. Ed. by S. Rehm. LC 94-19353. 1994. text 169.50 (*0-7923-2970-8*) Kluwer Academic.

Multilingual Dictionary of Agronomic Plants, English, French, German, Portugese & Spanish. S. Rehm. (ENG, FRE, GER, POR & SPA.). 283p. 1994. 250.00 (*0-7859-9638-9*) Fr & Eur.

Multilingual Dictionary of Analytical Terms. Robert A. Chalmers. LC 94-11359. 288p. 1994. 75.00 (*0-86542-859-X*) Blackwell Sci.

Multilingual Dictionary of Analytical Terms: English, French, German, Spanish, Russian, Chinese & Japanese. Ed. by Robert A. Chalmers. LC 94-11359. 1994. write for info. (*0-08-654285-0*, Pergamon Pr) Elsevier.

Multilingual Dictionary of Animal Production Terminology. 5th ed. Michel Ginguay & A. Lauret. (FRE.). 384p. 1993. pap. 89.95 (*0-8288-1354-X*, M6273) Fr & Eur.

Multilingual Dictionary of Architecture & Building Terms. Grech. LC 98-230262. (GER & FRE., Illus.). 482p. (C). 1998. 90.00 (*0-419-19920-9*, E & FN Spon) Routledge.

Multilingual Dictionary of Artificial Intelligence. Otto Volinhals. LC 91-36370. 432p. (C). 1992. text 160.00 (*0-415-07465-7*, Pub. by Tavistock) Routldge.

Multilingual Dictionary of Automatic Control Technology. H. A. Prime. (IFAC Ser.). 342p. 1994. 96.50 (*0-08-041913-5*, Pergamon Pr) Elsevier.

Multilingual Dictionary of Automatic Control Technology: English, French, German, Spanish, Italian, Japanese, Chinese & Russian. Ed. by H. A. Prime & Ants Work. (IFAC Workshop Ser.). (CHI, ENG, FRE, GER & ITA.). 390p. 1995. 132.25 (*0-08-037192-2*, Pergamon Pr) Elsevier.

Multilingual Dictionary of Banking-Commercial & Financial Terms: Greek, English, German, French, Italian. Delicostopoulos. (ENG, FRE, GER, GRE & ITA.). 300p. 1991. vinyl bd. 95.00 (*0-7859-9048-8*) Fr & Eur.

Multilingual Dictionary of Commercial International Trade & Shipping Terms. Allan E. Branch et al. (ENG, FRE, GER & SPA.). 254p. (C). 1990. 220.00 (*0-948691-90-5*, Pub. by Witherby & Co) St Mut.

Multilingual Dictionary of Copyright, Rights & Contracts. Ed. by Richard Balkwill. 256p. 1994. 49.95 (*0-948905-88-3*) Chapman & Hall.

Multilingual Dictionary of Corrosion Protection Terms: English, French, German, Russian. Anatolij Bakalow. (ENG, FRE, GER & RUS.). 1994. 495.00 (*0-7859-9981-7*) Fr & Eur.

Multilingual Dictionary of Disaster Medicine & International Relief: English, Francais, Espanole, (Arabic) S. W. Gunn. (C). 1989. lib. bdg. 158.50 (*0-89838-409-5*) Kluwer Academic.

Multilingual Dictionary of Electrical Engineering. (DUT, ENG, FRE, GER & RUS.). 479p. 1987. 175.00 (*0-8288-0307-2*, F120890) Fr & Eur.

Multilingual Dictionary of Electronic Publishing: English-German-French-Spanish-Italian. Otto Vollnhals. 420p. 1996. 200.00 (*3-598-11295-5*) K G Saur Verlag.

Multilingual Dictionary of Electronic Publishing, English/French/German/Spanish/Italian. Otto Vollnhals. (ENG, FRE, GER, ITA & SPA.). 384p. 1996. 350.00 (*0-7859-9532-3*) Fr & Eur.

Multilingual Dictionary of Fish & Fish Products. OECD Staff. 1990. pap. 69.95 (*0-8288-7920-6*) Fr & Eur.

Multilingual Dictionary of Fish & Fish Products. OECD Staff. 1990. 180.00 (*0-7855-6946-4*) St Mut.

Multilingual Dictionary of Fish & Fish Products. 4th ed. OECD Staff. 480p. 1995. 59.95 (*0-85238-216-2*) Blackwell Sci.

Multilingual Dictionary of Fishing Gear. 2nd ed. Commission for the European Communities Staff. (Illus.). 360p. 1992. 85.00 (*0-85238-192-1*) Blackwell Sci.

Multilingual Dictionary of Fishing Gear. 2nd ed. Commission of the European Communities Staff. (DAN, DUT, ENG, FRE & GER.). 1360p. 1992. 150.00 (*0-7859-0549-9*, 0-852381921) Fr & Eur.

Multilingual Dictionary of Fishing Vessels & Safety on Board. 2nd ed. Commission for the European Communities Staff. (Illus.). 1038p. 1992. 125.00 (*0-85238-191-3*) Blackwell Sci.

Multilingual Dictionary of Fishing Vessels & Safety on Board. 2nd ed. Commission of the European Communities Staff. (DAN, DUT, ENG, FRE & GER.). 1038p. 1992. 175.00 (*0-7859-0548-0*, 0-852381913) Fr & Eur.

M

Multilingual Dictionary of Foundry. V. Arpad. (ENG, FRE, GER, HUN & RUS.). 435p. 1978. 95.00 (*0-8288-6153-6*) Fr & Eur.

Multilingual Dictionary of Foundry Terms: English, French, German, Italian. 4th ed. Ernst Brunhuber. (ENG, FRE, GER & ITA.). 1158p. 1988. 295.00 (*0-8288-0604-7*, M7424) Fr & Eur.

Multilingual Dictionary of Heat Measurement, 3 vols., Set. Ed. by E. Tyrkiel. 1055p. (C). 1986. text 245.00 (*0-941743-46-2*) Nova Sci Pubs.

Multilingual Dictionary of Local Government & Business. 2nd ed. Clive L. McNeir. 704p. 1997. 130.00 (*0-304-32949-5*) Continuum.

Multilingual Dictionary of Music: Musiikisanakirja. G. Brodin. (ENG, FIN, FRE, GER & ITA.). 375p. 1987. 85.00 (*0-8288-2187-9*, F15060) Fr & Eur.

Multilingual Dictionary of Musical Terms in Seven Languages. Horst Leuchtmann. (ENG, FRE, GER, HUN & ITA.). 798p. Date not set. 95.00 (*0-7859-9628-1*) Fr & Eur.

Multilingual Dictionary of Narcotic Drugs & Psychotropic Substances under International Control. 508p. 42.00 (*92-1-048056-2*, M.93.XI.2) UN.

Multilingual Dictionary of Narcotics Drug & Psychotropic Substances under International Control. 37.00 (*92-1-048005-8*, E/F/R/S.83.XI.5) UN.

Multilingual Dictionary of Politics & Economics: English, French, German. 2nd ed. Harry Back. (ENG, FRE & GER.). 1037p. 1967. 175.00 (*0-7859-9990-6*) Fr & Eur.

Multilingual Dictionary of Print & Publishing Terms. Ed. by John Peacock. (DUT, ENG, FRE, GER & ITA.). 192p. (gr. 13). 1991. mass mkt. 73.95 (*0-948905-35-2*) Chapman & Hall.

Multilingual Dictionary of Printing & Publishing Terms. John Peacock. (DUT, ENG, FRE, GER & ITA.). 242p. 1992. 225.00 (*0-8288-7928-1*, 221200808905352) Fr & Eur.

Multilingual Dictionary of Real Estate: A Guide for the Property Professional in the Single European Market. Ed. by L. Van Breugel et al. LC 93-21713. (Illus.). 408p. (C). 1993. 115.00 (*0-419-18020-6*, E & FN Spon) Routledge.

Multilingual Dictionary of Steam Engineering Terms. Deutsche Babcock-Werke Staff. (GER, ENG, SPA & FRE). (ENG, GER & SPA.). 1994. 225.00 (*0-7859-7040-1*) Fr & Eur.

Multilingual Dictionary of Technical Terms in Cartography. 500p. 1992. 285.00 (*3-598-10764-1*) K G Saur Verlag.

Multilingual Dictionary of Technical Terms in Cartography. J. Neumann. (ENG, FRE & SPA.). 500p. 1992. 450.00 (*0-8288-7914-1*, 3598107641) Fr & Eur.

Multilingual Dictionary of the International Federation of Surveyors in French, German & English. Federation Internationale des Geometres Staff. (ENG, FRE & GER.). 501p. 1963. 275.00 (*0-8288-9248-2*, M15562) Fr & Eur.

Multilingual E. S. L. Teacher Edition, Pt. 1. Candido Sesma. 120p. 1981. pap. text 6.50 (*0-933146-01-9*) Biling Dict.

Multilingual E. S. L. Textbook in 17 Languages. Candido Sesma. 150p. 7.95 (*0-933146-00-0*) Biling Dict.

Multilingual Electronics Dictionary. R. G. Mirimanov. (DUT, ENG, FRE, GER & RUS.). 544p. 1986. 150.00 (*0-8288-0313-7*, F1927) Fr & Eur.

Multilingual Energy Dictionary. Ed. by Alan Isaacs. LC 80-26793. 288p. reprint ed. pap. 89.30 (*0-608-12294-7*, 202515500042) Bks Demand.

***Multilingual Gestutztes Vokabellernen Im Gymnasialen Englischunterricht.** Luise Kemmeter. (Europaische Hochschulschriften Ser.). 340p. 1999. 51.95 (*3-631-32752-8*) P Lang Pubng.

Multilingual Glossary Dendrochronology: English/French/German/Italian/Portuguese/Russian/Spanish. Kaennel & Schweingruber. (ENG, FRE, GER, ITA & POR.). 467p. 1995. 95.00 (*0-320-00559-3*) Fr & Eur.

Multilingual Glossary for Art Libraries. 2nd ed. LC 97-219707. (IFLA Publications: Vol. 75). 183p. 1996. 70.00 (*3-598-21802-8*) K G Saur Verlag.

Multilingual Glossary of Automatic Control. Broadbent. (ENG, FRE, GER, ITA & JPN.). 212p. 1981. 150.00 (*0-8288-7629-0*, M15653) Fr & Eur.

Multilingual Glossary of Biotechnological Terms. Ed. by Hans G. Leuenberger et al. (Verlag Helvetica Chimica Acta Publication Ser.). (ENG, FRE, GER, JPN & POR.). 252p. 1995. 69.95 (*3-906390-13-6*, Wiley-VCH) Wiley.

Multilingual Glossary of Common Plant Names. 2nd ed. H. Koster & F. Schneider. 235p. 1982. pap. 49.95 (*0-8288-0069-3*, M 7990) Fr & Eur.

Multilingual Glossary of Heat Treatment Terms Vol. 1: Theory & Processes. 1986. text 60.00 (*0-904357-70-8*, Pub. by Inst Materials) Ashgate Pub Co.

Multilingual Glossary of Welding & Related Techniques: Recueil Terminologique Multilingue du Soudage et des Techniques Connexes, Vol. 2. Soudure Autogene Staff. 294p. 1983. pap. 95.00 (*0-8288-0603-9*, M6475) Fr & Eur.

Multilingual Health Education Resource Guide. 2nd ed. Pref. by Margot Pfleger & Mizzette Fuenzalida. 151p. 1996. pap. text 25.00 (*0-7881-8939-5*) DIANE Pub.

Multilingual Illustrated Guide to the World's Commercial Coldwater Fish. Claus Frimodt et al. (Illus.). 240p. 1995. 85.00 (*0-85238-213-8*) Blackwell Sci.

Multilingual Illustrated Guide to the World's Commercial Warmwater Fish. Claus Frimodt et al. (Illus.). 240p. 1995. 85.00 (*0-85238-214-6*) Blackwell Sci.

Multilingual International Trade Term Lexicon: Over 7,000 International Trade Terms Entries in 6 Languages. Michelle M. Nicolai. LC 97-80767. 792p. 1998. 95.00 (*1-891628-00-3*) Interlingua Pubns.

Multilingual Japan. Ed. by John C. Maher & Kyoko Yashiro. 180p. 1995. 59.00 (*1-85359-287-0*, Pub. by Multilingual Matters) Taylor & Francis.

Multilingual Lexicon of Higher Education. 1995. write for info. (*3-598-11059-6*) K G Saur Verlag.

Multilingual Lexicon of Higher Education, 2 Vols. Ed. by UNESCO Staff. LC 96-119939. 746p. 1995. lib. bdg. 200.00 (*3-598-10883-4*) K G Saur Verlag.

Multilingual Lexicon of Linguistics & Philology: English, Russian, German, French. Rose Nash. (Miami Linguistic Ser.). 52.50 (*0-685-36678-2*) Fr & Eur.

***Multilingual Literacies: Reading & Writing Different Worlds.** Marilyn Martin-Jones & Kathryn Jones. LC 00-40369. (Studies in Written Language & Literacy). 2000. write for info. (*1-55619-748-9*) J Benjamins Pubng Co.

Multilingual Managers Lexikon Lexique Multilingue du Manager. (ENG & FRE.). 563p. 1996. pap. 61.00 (*2-85608-077-4*) IBD Ltd.

Multilingual Manual for Medical History-Taking. Louis Del Guercio. (FRE.). 178p. 1972. pap. 39.95 (*0-7859-9618-4*) Fr & Eur.

Multilingual Marketing Dictionary: English, French, German, Spanish. Camara Ibanez. (ENG, FRE, GER & SPA.). 693p. 1995. 85.00 (*0-7859-9555-2*) Fr & Eur.

Multilingual Multimedia: Bridging the Language Barrier. Masoud Yazdani. 210p. (Orig.). 1993. pap. text 22.95 (*1-871516-30-7*, Pub. by Intellect) Cromland.

Multilingual PC Directory. Ian Tresman. 1993. 150.00 (*1-873091-02-8*, Pub. by Knowledge Comput) St Mut.

Multilingual Phrase Book. 3.95 (*0-685-36685-5*) Fr & Eur.

Multilingual Phrase Book. FEP Staff. 2.50 (*0-8288-8196-0*, FC2388) Fr & Eur.

Multilingual Phrase Book: French, Spanish, Italian, & German, 4 bks. pap. 3.95 (*0-685-73308-4*) Fr & Eur.

Multilingual Phrase Book: Spanish, French, Dutch, Portugese, German, Italian, Serbo-Croat, Greek. (MUL., Illus.). 144p. 1995. pap. 7.95 (*0-8442-9509-4*, 95094, Natl Textbk Co) NTC Contemp Pub Co.

Multilingual Self: An Inquiry into Language Learning. Natasha Lvovich. LC 97-6164. 1997. pap. 16.50 (*0-8058-2320-4*) L Erlbaum Assocs.

Multilingual Space Sciences Dictionary Vol. 1: Radiation & Matter. Josip Kleczek & H. Kleczkova. (ENG, FRE, GER, POR & RUS.). 664p. 1990. 395.00 (*0-8288-9250-4*) Fr & Eur.

Multilingual Space Sciences Dictionary Vol. 4: Earth Sciences - Solar System - Deep Space. Josip Kleczek & H. Kleczkova. (ENG, FRE, GER, POR & RUS.). 894p. 1992. 395.00 (*0-8288-9253-9*) Fr & Eur.

Multilingual Space Sciences Dictionary, English, French, German, Portuguese, Spanish, Russian Vol. 2: Motion - Space Flight - Data. Josip Kleczek & H. Kleczkova. (ENG, FRE, GER, POR & RUS.). 808p. 1993. 495.00 (*0-8288-9251-2*) Fr & Eur.

Multilingual Spain. Miguel Siguan. (European Studies on Multilingualism: Vol. 2). 308p. 1993. pap. 52.00 (*90-265-1348-8*) Swets.

Multilingual Technical Dictionary on Irrigation & Drainage, Suppl. 1. (ENG & FRE.). 111p. 1980. 8.00 (*81-85068-00-3*) US Comm Irrigation.

Multilingual Terminology of Welding - Soldering & Related Subjects: Receuil Terminologique Multilingue du Soudage et des Techniques Connexes, Vol. 9. 286p. 1981. pap. 49.95 (*0-8288-0602-0*, M6750) Fr & Eur.

Multilingual Text-to-Speech Synthesis: The Bell Labs Approach. Richard W. Sproat & Lucent Technologies Staff. LC 97-31463. 328p. 1997. text 121.00 (*0-7923-8027-4*) Kluwer Academic.

Multilingual Thesaurus for Information Processing in the Field of Education. Jean Viet & George Van Slype. (DAN, DUT, ENG, FRE & GER.). 307p. 1984. 125.00 (*0-8288-0939-9*, M7884) Fr & Eur.

Multilingual Thesaurus of Geosciences. G. N. Rassam. (ENG, FRE, GER, ITA & RUS.). 516p. 1988. 195.00 (*0-8288-7952-4*) Fr & Eur.

Multilingual Thesaurus of Geosciences. 2nd ed. Ed. by J. Gravesteijn et al. LC 96-183176. 645p. 1995. pap. 99.00 (*1-57387-009-9*) Info Today Inc.

Multilingual Vocabulary of Telecommunications. Groupe de Linguistique Appliquee des Telecommunica. 193p. 1992. pap. 38.50 (*0-7859-8908-0*) Fr & Eur.

Multilingual Vocabulary of Telecommunications. Groupe de Linguistique Appliquee des Telecommunica. (ARA, ENG, FRE, GER & POR.). 193p. 1992. pap. 48.00 (*2-85608-044-8*, Pub. by La Maison Du Dict) IBD Ltd.

Multilingualism & Nation Building. Gerda Mansour. LC 92-31458. (Multilingual Matters Ser.: No. 91). 1993. 74.95 (*1-85359-175-0*, Pub. by Multilingual Matters); pap. 29.95 (*1-85359-174-2*, Pub. by Multilingual Matters) Taylor & Francis.

Multilingualism for All. Ed. by Tove Skutnabb-Kangas. (European Studies on Multilingualism: Vol. 4). 294p. 1995. pap. 52.00 (*90-265-1423-9*) Swets.

Multilingualism in Europe & the U. S.: A Communications Challenge for Transatlantic Relations & Global Business: Conclusions from an International Round Table Seminar. Frwd. by Jacques Delors. 38p. (Orig.). 1993. pap. 7.00 (*0-9628287-4-2*) European Inst.

Multilingualism in India. Ed. by Debi P. Pattanayak. (Multilingual Matters Ser.: No. 61). 116p. 1990. 69.00 (*1-85359-073-8*); pap. 24.95 (*1-85359-072-X*) Taylor & Francis.

Multilingualism in International Law & Institutions. Mala Tabory. LC 80-51742. 304p. 1981. lib. bdg. 66.50 (*90-286-0210-0*) Kluwer Academic.

***Multilingualism in Later Medieval Britain.** Ed. by D. A. Trotter. LC 99-42630. (Illus.). 256p. 2000. 60.00 (*0-85991-563-8*, DS Brewer) Boydell & Brewer.

Multilingualism in the British Isles, Vol. 1. Ed. by Safder Alladina & Viv Edwards. LC 89-13672. (Longman Linguistics Library). 299p. 1991. reprint ed. pap. 92.70 (*0-608-03616-1*, 206444300001) Bks Demand.

Multilingualism in the British Isles, Vol. 2. Ed. by Safder Alladina & Viv Edwards. LC 89-13672. (Longman Linguistics Library). 290p. 1991. reprint ed. pap. 89.90 (*0-608-03617-X*, 206444300002) Bks Demand.

Multilingualism in the Soviet Union: Aspects of Language Policy & Its Implementation. E. Glyn Lewis. (Contributions to the Sociology of Language Ser.: No. 3). (Illus.). 332p. (Orig.). 1972. pap. text 70.80 (*90-279-2352-3*) Mouton.

Multilingue Sopena. Sopena Staff. (ENG, FRE & ITA.). 574p. 1981. 95.00 (*0-8288-1456-2*, S16196) Fr & Eur.

Multilink: Activities for the Intermediate Classroom. Stone et al. 48p. (J). (gr. 3-6). 1993. reprint ed. 7.99 (*1-884461-04-2*) NES Arnold.

Multilink: Activities for the Primary Classroom. Stone et al. 48p. (J). (gr. k-3). 1993. reprint ed. 7.99 (*1-884461-03-4*) NES Arnold.

Multilink: Do & Talk. (J). 1994. student ed. 6.99 (*1-884461-11-5*) NES Arnold.

Multilink: Patterns & Relationships. Stone et al. 40p. (J). (gr. k-5). 1993. reprint ed. 7.99 (*1-884461-00-X*) NES Arnold.

Multilink: Problem Solving: Games, Puzzles & Investigations. Stone et al. 48p. (J). (gr. 1-5). 1993. reprint ed. 7.99 (*1-884461-02-6*) NES Arnold.

Multilink: Rediscovering Fractions. Peter Patilla & Bob Stone. Ed. by Cathleen Brady. (Middle School Math Ser.). (Illus.). 37p. (J). (gr. 5-9). 1995. student ed. 8.99 (*1-884461-12-3*) NES Arnold.

Multilink: Shape & Space. Peter Patilla & Bob Stone. Ed. by Cathleen Brady. (Middle School Math Ser.). (Illus.). 36p. (J). (gr. 5-9). 1995. student ed. 8.99 (*1-884461-13-1*) NES Arnold.

Multilink: Spatial Awareness & Geometry. Stone et al. 48p. (J). (gr. 1-5). 1993. reprint ed. 7.99 (*1-884461-01-8*) NES Arnold.

Multilink Beginning Fraction Activities. Bob Stone et al. Ed. by Jane A. Feiler et al. (Middle School Math Ser.). (Illus.). 30p. (J). (gr. 1-4). 1990. reprint ed. pap., wbk. ed. 6.99 (*1-884461-15-8*) NES Arnold.

Multilink Explorations. Peggy McLean et al. (Illus.). 48p. (J). (gr. k-4). 1986. pap. 7.95 (*0-918932-88-2*, A-5560) Activity Resources.

Multilink Problem Solving Fraction Activities. Bob Stone et al. Ed. by Jane A. Feiler & Nancy T. Hootan. (Illus.). 32p. 1990. reprint ed. pap., wbk. ed. 6.99 (*1-884461-16-6*) NES Arnold.

***Multiliteracies: Literacy Learning & Design of Social Futures.** Ed. by Bill Cope & Mary Kalantzis. LC 99-32355. 368p. (C). 1999. text. write for info. (*0-415-21420-3*) Routledge.

Multiliteracies: Literacy Learning & the Design of Social Futures. Bill Cope & Mary Kalantzis. LC 99-32355. (Literacies Ser.). 288p. 1999. pap. 29.99 (*0-415-21421-1*) Routledge.

Multilog User's Guide: Multiple, Categorical Item Analysis & Test Scoring Using Item Response Theory, Version 6. David Thissen. 1991. ring bd. 30.00 (*0-89498-030-0*) Sci Ware.

MultiMate Advantage: The Useable Portable Guide. Jon Haber & Herbert R. Haber. 32p. (Orig.). 1988. pap. 4.95 (*0-317-91107-4*) Useable Portable Pubns.

Multimate Advantage a Practical Applications Approach. Graham. (DF - Computer Applications Ser.). 1987. mass mkt. 20.95 (*0-538-23180-7*) S-W Pub.

Multimate Step by Step. William Grout. 1985. pap. 19.95 (*0-201-11580-8*) Addison-Wesley.

Multimath. Bjorn Felsager. 250p. 1994. pap. 49.00 (*0-387-94312-9*) Spr-Verlag.

Multimedia. David Bowen. 1994. pap. 12.95 (*0-906097-14-2*) LPC InBook.

Multimedia. Randall Packer. 26.95 (*0-393-04979-5*) Norton.

Multimedia. Tannenbaum. (C). Date not set. teacher ed. write for info. (*0-7167-8323-1*) W H Freeman.

Multimedia. Robert S. Tannenbaum. LC 97-44556. 500p. (C). 1998. pap. text 72.95 (*0-7167-8321-5*) W H Freeman.

***Multimedia: A Critical Introduction.** Richard Wise. 2000. 75.00 (*0-415-12150-7*); pap. 22.99 (*0-415-12151-5*) Routledge.

Multimedia: A Hands-On Introduction. David D. Peck. LC 97-22709. (Graphic Communications Ser.). 352p. (C). 1997. pap. 55.95 incl. cd-rom (*0-8273-7190-X*) Delmar.

Multimedia: A Management Perspective. Antone F. Alber. (C). 1995. pap. 72.95 (*0-534-21312-X*) Wadsworth Pub.

Multimedia: Advanced Teleservices & High-Speed Communication Architectures: Proceedings of the Second International Workshop, IWACA '94, Heidelberg, Germany, September 26-28, 1994. Ed. by R. Steinmetz. LC 94-32622. (Lecture Notes in Computer Science Ser.: Vol. 868). x, 451p. 1994. 65.95 (*3-540-58494-3*) Spr-Verlag.

Multimedia: Computing, Communications & Applications. Ralf Steinmetz & Klara Nahrstedt. LC 95-10987. (Innovative Technology Ser.). 880p. 1995. 80.00 (*0-13-324435-0*) P-H.

Multimedia: Concepts & Practice. 600p. 1999. 93.00 (*1-58076-125-9*) Que Educ & Trng.

***Multimedia: Concepts & Practice.** Stephen McGloughlin. 608p. 2000. 73.33 (*0-13-018830-1*) Prntice Hall Bks.

***Multimedia: Digital Photography.** Alex May. LC 99-54350. (Essential Computers Ser.). 72p. 2000. pap. text 6.95 (*0-7894-5531-5*, D K Ink) DK Pub Inc.

Multimedia: Graphics. Pat Johnson et al. 112p. 1997. 49.99 (*1-57576-676-0*) Sams.

Multimedia: ISS in Interactive Communication. Forrest. (C). 1996. pap. text 39.00 (*0-03-015582-7*) Harcourt Coll Pubs.

Multimedia: Law & Practice. Michael D. Scott. LC 93-24357. 1993. 125.00 (*0-13-082984-6*) Aspen Law.

Multimedia: Making It Work. 2nd ed. Tay Vaughan. 608p. 1994. pap. 36.95 (*0-07-882035-9*) Osborne-McGraw.

Multimedia: Making It Work. 3rd ed. Tay Vaughan. LC 97-122059. 608p. 1996. pap. text 39.95 (*0-07-882225-4*) Osborne-McGraw.

Multimedia: Making It Work. 4th ed. Tay Vaughan. 1998. pap. 44.99 incl. cd-rom (*0-07-882552-0*) Osborne-McGraw.

Multimedia: Ophthalmic Surgery, ENT. Jose L. Encarnacao. LC 94-14719. 258p. 1994. 99.95 (*0-387-57413-1*) Spr-Verlag.

Multimedia: Production, Planning & Delivery. Villamil. 148p. 1997. 49.99 (*1-57576-625-6*) Que Educ & Trng.

Multimedia: The Complete Guide. Deni Bown. 192p. 1996. 24.95 (*0-7894-0422-2*) DK Pub Inc.

Multimedia: The Creators. Coupland. 1995. 24.95 (*1-56276-296-6*, Ziff-Davis Pr) Que.

Multimedia - Eine Neue Herausforderung Fuer Den Fremdsprachenunterricht No. 2: Durchgesehene Auflage. 2nd ed. Ed. by Institut Fur Inetrkulturelle Kommunikation e. V. Staff et al. (Deutsch Als Fremdsprache in der Diskussion Ser.: Vol. 3). (GER., Illus.). VII, 278p. 1998. pap. 55.95 (*3-631-33092-8*) P Lang Pubng.

Multimedia Activities for Students: A Teacher's & Librarian's Handbook. Barbara H. Sorrow. LC 96-43907. 199p. 1997. pap. 26.50 (*0-7864-0211-3*) McFarland & Co.

Multimedia Administrator: Planning, Preparing, & Presenting School Budgets Using Computer Multimedia Software. Jonathan T. Hughes. LC 97-35246. 1997. 42.95 (*1-57981-003-9*) Cummngs & Hath.

Multimedia Adventure. Nicholas V. Iuppa & Marc Wade. (Illus.). 179p. 1993. pap. text 34.95 (*0-86729-306-3*, Focal) Buttrwrth-Heinemann.

Multimedia & CD-ROMs. 2nd ed. Andy Rathbone. LC 95-77667. 400p. 1995. pap. 29.99 (*1-56884-909-5*) IDG Bks.

Multimedia & CD-ROMs for Dummies. Andy Rathbone. LC 94-75906. 350p. 1994. pap. 19.95 (*1-56884-089-6*) IDG Bks.

Multimedia & CD-ROMs for Dummies. 2nd ed. Andy Rathbone. 384p. 1995. pap. 19.99 (*1-56884-907-9*) IDG Bks.

Multimedia & CD-ROMs for Dummies: Interactive Multimedia Value Pack. Andy Rathbone. LC 94-76885. 384p. 1994. pap. 29.95 (*1-56884-225-2*) IDG Bks.

Multimedia & CD-ROMs for Dummies: Interactive Multimedia Value Pack. 2nd ed. Andy Rathbone. LC 95-77667. 372p. 1995. pap. 29.99 (*1-56884-908-7*) IDG Bks.

Multimedia & Communications Technology. Steve Heath. LC 98-52393. (Illus.). 352p. 1996. pap. text 49.95 (*0-240-51460-2*, Focal) Buttrwrth-Heinemann.

Multimedia & Communications Technology. 2nd ed. Steve Heath. LC 98-52393. (Illus.). 334p. 1998. pap. 56.95 incl. cd-rom (*0-240-51529-3*, Focal) Buttrwrth-Heinemann.

Multimedia & Computer-Based Training: New Paradigms for Success. Tom S. Calhoon. 150p. 1993. ring bd. 185.00 (*1-56909-008-4*) Info Systs Mgmt.

Multimedia & Groupware for Editing. Adelino Santos. LC 95-34389. (Computer Graphics - Systems & Applications Ser.). 153p. 1995. 69.95 (*3-540-60001-9*) Spr-Verlag.

Multimedia & Hypertext: The Internet & Beyond. Jakob Nielsen. LC 94-44429. (Illus.). xiii, 480p. 1995. pap. text 34.00 (*0-12-518408-5*) Morgan Kaufmann.

Multimedia & Learning: A School Leader's Guide. Ed. by Anne Ward. 116p. (Orig.). 1994. pap. text, teacher ed. 35.00 (*0-88364-181-X*, 03-129) Natl Sch Boards.

Multimedia & Megachange: New Roles for Educational Computing. Ed. by W. Michael Rees et al. (Computers in the Schools Ser.). (Illus.). 438p. 1995. lib. bdg. 59.95 (*1-56024-693-6*) Haworth Pr.

Multimedia & Networking: Proceedings of the Library of Congress Network Advisory Committee Meeting, December 7-9, 1992. LC 93-7826. (Network Planning Papers: No. 24). 1993. write for info. (*0-8444-0788-7*) Lib Congress.

Multimedia & Presentations Graphics Project Guide. Drum. (DF - Computer Applications Ser.). 1997. mass mkt. 13.95 (*0-538-71785-8*) S-W Pub.

***Multimedia & Regional Economic Restructing.** Hans Joachim Braczyk et al. LC 98-51215. 448p. 1999. 115.00 (*0-415-19857-7*) Routledge.

Multimedia & Technology Licensing Agreements: Forms with Commentary. Gregory J. Battersby & Charles W. Grimes. 752p. 1995. 160.00 incl. disk (*0-7913-2377-3*) Warren Gorham & Lamont.

Multimedia & the Law, 1996: Protecting Your Clients' Interests. (Patents, Copyrights, Trademarks, & Literary Property Course Handbook, 1994-95 Ser.). Date not set. pap. 99.00 (*0-614-17242-X*, G4-3955) PLI.

Multimedia & the Virtual Reality Engineering. Richard Brice. LC 97-219489. 320p. 1997. text 48.95 (*0-7506-2987-8*) Buttrwrth-Heinemann.

Multimedia & the Web from A to Z. 2nd enl. rev. ed. David C. Leonard & Patrick M. Dillon. LC 98-34083. 384p. 1998. pap. 39.95 (*1-57356-132-0*) Oryx Pr.

Multimedia Animation. Clarence Lamb. LC 97-65589. (Illus.). 100p. 1997. 49.99 (*1-57576-706-6*) Sams.

Multimedia Applications Development: Using Indeo Video & DVI Technology. 2nd ed. Mark J. Bunzel & Sandra K. Morris. LC 93-23188. (Intel Ser.). 309p. 1993. 45.00 (*0-07-043300-3*) McGraw.

Multimedia Applications for Enterprise Intranets: A Guide to Planning & Implementation. Bohdan O. Szuprowicz. LC 96-30869. (Illus.). 265p. (Orig.). 1996. pap. 270.00 (*1-56607-979-9*) Comput Tech Res.

Multimedia Applications, Services & Techniques - ECMAST '98: Third European Conference, Berlin, Germany, May 26-28, 1998. Proceedings. Ed. by D. Hutchinson et al. LC 98-209984. (Lecture Notes in Computer Science Ser.: Vol. 1425). xvi, 531p. 1998. pap. 75.00 (*3-540-64594-2*) Spr-Verlag.

Multimedia Applications, Services & Techniques - ECMAST'97: Second European Conference, Milan, Italy, May 21-23, 1997 Proceedings. Ed. by Serge Fdida et al. LC 97-20575. (Lecture Notes in Computer Science Ser.: No. 1242). xiv, 772p. 1997. pap. 108.00 (*3-540-63078-3*) Spr-Verlag.

***Multimedia Applications, Services & Techniques - ECMAST'99: Proceedings of the 4th European Conference, Madrid, Spain, May 26-28, 1999.** Ed. by H. Leopold et al. LC 99-34565. (Lecture Notes in Computer Science Ser.: Vol. 1629). xv, 574p. 1999. pap. 85.00 (*3-540-66082-8*) Spr-Verlag.

***Multimedia Authoring on the Cheap: Interactive Laboratory Exercises.** Daniel Everett. 108p. (C). 1999. pap. text 27.95 (*0-7872-6301-X*, 41630101) Kendall-Hunt.

***Multimedia-Based Instructional Design: Computer-Based Training, Web-Based Training, & Distance Learning.** William Lee & Diana Owens. LC 99-51003. 350p. 2000. pap. 59.95 (*0-7879-5159-5*, Pfffr & Co) Jossey-Bass.

***Multimedia Cartography.** Ed. by W. Cartwright et al. LC GA139.5.M85 1999. (Illus.). xviii, 343p. 1999. 59.00 incl. cd-rom (*3-540-65818-1*) Spr-Verlag.

Multimedia Circuitry: Classroom. Murphy. 1997. cd-rom 666.67 (*0-13-237595-8*) P-H.

Multimedia Circuits. Murphy. 1997. cd-rom 37.00 (*0-13-861360-5*, Prentice Hall) P-H.

Multimedia Communication. Andy Sloane. LC 96-36141. 1996. pap. write for info. (*0-07-709222-8*) McGraw.

Multimedia Communication Networks: Technologies & Services. Ed. by Mallikarjun Tatipamula & Bhumip Khasnabish. LC 98-19039. 475p. 1998. 109.00 (*0-89006-936-0*) Artech Hse.

***Multimedia Communications.** Ed. by F. DeNatale & S. Pupolin. LC 98-53818. (Illus.). 592p. 1999. pap. 119.00 (*1-85233-135-6*, Pub. by Spr-Verlag) Spr-Verlag.

***Multimedia Communications.** Fred Halsall. (C). 2000. pap. text. write for info. (*0-201-39818-4*) Addison-Wesley.

Multimedia Communications. Frank Kuo et al. LC 97-36112. 256p. 1997. 68.00 (*0-13-856923-1*) P-H.

Multimedia Communications: Proceedings of Multimedia Communications Conference, 13-16 April 1993, Banff, Canada. Ed. by D. Phillips & P. Desrochers. LC 93-78137. 658p. (gr. 12). 1993. 98.00 (*90-5199-132-0*, Pub. by IOS Pr) IOS Press.

Multimedia Communications & Video Coding: Proceedings of a Symposium Held at Polytechnic University, Brooklyn, New York, October 11-13, 1995. Y. Wang et al. LC 96-21634. (Illus.). 520p. (C). 1996. 162.00 (*0-306-45367-3*, Kluwer Plenum) Kluwer Academic.

***Multimedia Communications Handbook.** Gibson. (Communications, Networking, & Multimedia Ser.). 600p. 2000. 89.95 (*0-12-282160-2*) Acad Pr.

***Multimedia Compendium for Education & Training Vol. 12: 2000 Edition.** rev. ed. Ed. by Richard A. Pollak. 184p. 2000. 69.95 (*0-922649-32-4*) ETC MN.

Multimedia Computer Peripheral in Singapore: A Strategic Entry Report, 1998. Compiled by Icon Group International Staff. (Country Industry Report). (Illus.). 112p. 1999. ring bd. 1120.00 incl. audio compact disk (*0-7418-0153-1*) Icon Grp.

Multimedia Computing. (C). 1995. text. write for info. (*0-201-42061-9*) Addison-Wesley.

Multimedia Computing: Case Studies from MIT Project Athena. Ed. by Mathew E. Hodges & Russell M. Sasnett. (Illus.). 320p. (C). 1993. 40.95 (*0-201-52029-X*) Addison-Wesley.

Multimedia Computing: Preparing for the Twenty-First Century. Ed. by Sorel Reisman. 600p. (C). 1996. text 59.95 (*1-878289-22-5*) Idea Group Pub.

An Asterisk (*) at the beginning of an entry indicates that the title is appearing for the first time.

Multimedia Computing: Proceedings of the Sixth NEC Research Symposium. Ed. by T. Ishiguro. LC 97-66803. (Proceedings in Applied Mathematics Ser.: Vol. 83). ix, 169p. 1997. 36.00 (*0-89871-372-2*, PR83) Soc Indus-Appl Math.

Multimedia Computing & Networking 1999. Ed. by Dilip D. Kandlur et al. V. 334p. pap. text 72.00 (*0-8194-3125-7*) SPIE.

Multimedia Computing & Museums Vol. 1: ICHIM '95 Conference Proceedings. Ed. by David Beaman. LC 96-113982. (Illus.). 388p. 1995. pap. 20.00 (*1-885626-11-8*) Archives & Mus.

Multimedia Computing & Networking,1997, Vol. 3020. Ed. by Martin Freeman & Paul Jardetzky. LC 98-104331. 358p. 1997. 69.00 (*0-8194-2431-5*) SPIE.

Multimedia Computing & Networking, 1998, Vol. 3310. Ed. by Kevin Jeffay et al. LC 98-160784. 272p. 1997. 59.00 (*0-8194-2750-0*) SPIE.

***Multimedia Computing & Systems: Proceedings: IEEE International Conference on Multimedia Computing & Systems (1999: Florence, Italy), 2 vols.** 2036p. 1999. pap. 225.00 (*0-7695-0253-9*) IEEE Comp Soc.

Multimedia Computing & Systems: Proceedings of the International Conference on Multimedia Computing & Systems, Ottawa, Ontario, Canada, 1997. LC 97-71759. 500p. 1997. pap. 145.00 (*0-8186-7819-4*) IEEE Comp Soc.

Multimedia Conference Proceedings 1998. Ed. by ACM Staff & Multimedia Staff. 448p. (C). 1998. pap. text 39.95 (*0-201-30990-4*) Addison-Wesley.

Multimedia Content Development Services in Australia: A Strategic Entry Report, 1997. Compiled by Icon Group International Staff. (Country Industry Report). (Illus.). 141p. 1999. ring bd. 1410.00 incl. audio compact disk (*0-7418-0233-3*) Icon Grp.

Multimedia Contracts, 1996. J. Dianne Brinson & Mark F. Radcliffe. 680p. (Orig.). 1996. pap. 89.95 (*0-9639173-1-5*); disk 99.95 (*0-9639173-5-8*) Ladera Pr.

Multimedia Database Management Systems. Ed. by Jean-Michel Berge et al. (Kluwer International Series in Engineering & Computer Science). 216p. (C). 1997. lib. bdg. 270.00 (*0-7923-9874-2*) Kluwer Academic.

Multimedia Database Management Systems. Guojun Lu. LC 99-41773. 373p. 1999. 79.00 (*0-89006-342-7*) Artech Hse.

Multimedia Database Management Systems. B. Prabhakaran. LC 96-38503. (Kluwer International Series in Engineering & Computer Science: Multimedia Systems & Applications). 1996. text 106.50 (*0-7923-9784-3*) Kluwer Academic.

Multimedia Database Management Systems: Oil Research Issues & Future Directions. Ed. by Bhavani Thuraisingham et al. LC 97-2401. 160p. (C). 1997. text 99.00 (*0-7923-9886-6*) Kluwer Academic.

Multimedia Database Systems: Design & Implementation Strategies. Ed. by Kingsley C. Nwosu et al. LC 96-1595. (Illus.). 400p. (C). 1996. text 131.00 (*0-7923-9712-6*) Kluwer Academic.

Multimedia Database Systems: Issues & Research Directions. Ed. by Sushil G. Jajodia & V. S. Subrahmanian. (Artificial Intelligence Ser.). 327p. 1995. 59.00 (*3-540-58710-1*) Spr-Verlag.

Multimedia Databases in Perspective. P. M. Apers et al. LC 96-52104. 400p. 1997. pap. 49.95 (*3-540-76109-8*) Spr-Verlag.

Multimedia Deals in the Music Industry. Ed. by Willem Roos & Jacqueline Seignette. (Reports Presented at the Meeting of the International Association of Entertainment Lawyers MIDEM 1994, Cannes). 169p. 1996. pap. 100.00 (*90-6715-014-2*, Pub. by Maklu Uitgev) Gaunt.

Multimedia Devices. Murphy. 208p. 1998. pap. text, student ed. 35.20 (*0-13-601907-2*) P-H.

Multimedia Document Systems in Perspectives. Peyia Liu & Arif Ghafoor. LC 98-49293. 1999. write for info. (*0-7923-8416-4*) Kluwer Academic.

Multimedia Education Management Information. 5th ed. Laudon. 1998. text 43.50 (*0-13-888926-0*) P-H.

Multimedia Engineering. John Watkinson. (Illus.). 320p. 2000. pap. text 56.95 (*0-240-51509-9*, Focal) Buttrwrth-Heinemann.

Multimedia Engineering Statics: CD-ROM Hybrid for Windows & Macintosh. Kurt Gramoll. 1996. 42.00 (*0-201-85189-X*) Addison-Wesley.

Multimedia Environmental Management. J. Andy Soesilo & William D. Wiley. LC 99-20384. 328p. 1999. 79.00 (*0-86587-659-2*) Gov Insts.

Multimedia Environmental Models: The Fugacity Approach. Donald Mackay. 272p. 1991. boxed set 85.00 (*0-87371-242-0*, L242) Lewis Pubs.

Multimedia Essentials. John Villamil. LC 96-69865. 196p. 1997. 68.00 (*1-57576-557-8*) Sams.

***Multimedia Fluid Mechanics.** G. M. Homsy et al. (C). 2000. audio compact disk. write for info. (*0-521-78748-3*) Cambridge U Pr.

Multimedia Flying Solo: Featuring HyperCard 2.3! Hofmeister & Rudowski. (Illus.). 224p. 1996. spiral bd. 26.95 incl. cd-rom (*0-538-65108-3*) S-W Pub.

Multimedia Flying Solo with Hypercard 2.3. Rudowski Hofmeister. (Computer Education Ser.). (J). (gr. k-8). 1996. text 24.95 (*0-538-65105-9*) S-W Pub.

Multimedia for Learning: Development, Application, Evaluation. Ed. by Diane M. Gayeski. LC 92-24208. (Illus.). 180p. 1993. 34.95 (*0-87778-250-4*) Educ Tech Pubns.

Multimedia for Windows 95 Made Simple. Collins1. 160p. Date not set. pap. text. write for info. (*0-7506-3397-2*) Buttrwrth-Heinemann.

Multimedia Graphics: The Best of Global Hyperdesign. Ed. by Willem Velthoven & Jorinde Seijdel. 192p. 1996. 60.00 (*0-8118-1404-1*) Chronicle Bks.

Multimedia Guide for America at Odds. Edward Sidlow. (Political Science Ser.). 1998. pap. 12.50 (*0-534-53629-8*) Wadsworth Pub.

Multimedia Guide to Non-Human Primates. F. Burton. 1995. cd-rom 87.00 (*0-13-207168-1*) P-H.

Multimedia Guide to Non-Human Primates: The Print Version. Frances D. Burton. LC 96-134652. 2953p. 1995. pap. text 53.00 (*0-13-209727-3*) P-H.

Multimedia Handbook. Tony Cawkell. LC 96-6079. (Illus.). 480p. (C). 1996. 165.00 (*0-415-13666-0*) Routledge.

Multimedia Hardware Architectures,1997, Vol. 3021. Ed. by Sethuraman Panchanathan & Frans Sijstermans. LC 97-200941. 320p. 1997. 69.00 (*0-8194-2432-3*) SPIE.

Multimedia Hardware Architectures, 1998, Vol. 3311. Ed. by Sethuraman Panchanathan et al. LC 98-191001. 150p. 1998. 59.00 (*0-8194-2751-9*) SPIE.

Multimedia Home Companion. Ed. by Rebecca B. Taylor. 352p. (Orig.). 1994. mass mkt. 21.99 (*0-446-67039-1*, Pub. by Warner Bks) Little.

Multimedia, Hypermedia, & Virtual Reality: Models, Systems, & Applications, Vol. 107. Peter Brusilovsky et al. LC 96-283. (Lecture Notes in Computer Science Ser.). 1996. pap. 56.00 (*3-540-61282-3*) Spr-Verlag.

Multimedia I Ching. Ed. by R. Wilhelm. Tr. by C. F. Baynes. (Bollinger Ser.). 1996. 49.95 (*0-691-01212-1*, Pub. by Princeton U Pr) Cal Prin Full Svc.

***Multimedia Image & Video Processing.** Ling Guan et al. LC 00-30341. 2000. write for info. (*0-8493-3492-6*) CRC Pr.

Multimedia in Action. James E. Shuman. LC 97-9298. (Multimedia Ser.). (C). 1997. 74.95 (*0-534-51370-0*) Wadsworth Pub.

Multimedia in Germany: A Strategic Entry Report, 1996. Compiled by Icon Group International Staff. (Illus.). 117p. 1999. ring bd. 1170.00 incl. audio compact disk (*0-7418-1126-X*) Icon Grp.

Multimedia in Higher Education: A Practical Guide to New Tools for Interactive Teaching & Learning. Helen Carlson & Dennis R. Falk. 176p. 1995. 42.50 (*1-57387-002-1*) Info Today Inc.

Multimedia in Israel: A Strategic Entry Report, 1996. Compiled by Icon Group International Staff. (Illus.). 120p. 1999. ring bd. 1200.00 incl. audio compact disk (*0-7418-1127-8*) Icon Grp.

Multimedia in Mexico: A Strategic Entry Report, 1996. Compiled by Icon Group International Staff. (Illus.). 153p. 1999. ring bd. 1530.00 incl. audio compact disk (*0-7418-1128-6*) Icon Grp.

Multimedia in Practice: Technology & Applications. Judith Jeffcoate. 200p. 1995. pap. 58.00 (*0-13-123324-6*) P-H.

Multimedia in Review Vol. 2: Technologies for the 21st Century. Ed. by Martin Greenberger. 277p. (Orig.). 1992. pap. 24.95 (*1-55940-308-X*) Coun For Tech.

Multimedia in the Classroom. Palmer W. Agnew et al. LC 95-18583. 308p. 1996. pap. text 50.00 (*0-205-16408-0*) Allyn.

Multimedia Information Analysis & Retrieval: Proceedings of the IAPR International Workshop, MINAR '98, Hong Kong, China, August 13-14, 1998. Ed. by Horace H. Ip & Arnoldus W. Smeulders. LC 98-29368. (Lecture Notes in Computer Science Ser.: Vol. 1464). viii, 264p. 1998. pap. 49.00 (*3-540-64826-7*) Spr-Verlag.

Multimedia Information Networking. Sharda. LC 98-18799. 480p. 1998. 99.00 (*0-13-258773-4*) P-H.

Multimedia Information Resources. Paul McNally. 216p. 1998. 69.95 (*0-7329-4092-3*, Pub. by Macmill Educ); pap. 34.95 (*0-7329-4080-X*, Pub. by Macmill Educ) Paul & Co Pubs.

Multimedia Information Retrieval Vol. 397: Content-Based Information Retrieval from Large Text & Audio Databases. Peter SchAuble. LC 97-8939. (International Series in Engineering & Computer Science). 1997. text 96.50 (*0-7923-9899-8*) Kluwer Academic.

Multimedia Information Storage & Management. Ed. by Soon M. Chung. 483p. (C). 1996. lib. bdg. 155.00 (*0-614-19147-5*) Kluwer Academic.

Multimedia Information Systems. Marios C. Angelides & Schahram Dustdar. LC 97-9412. (Multimedia Systems & Application Engineering & Computer Science Ser.). 1997. lib. bdg. 84.00 (*0-7923-9915-3*) Kluwer Academic.

Multimedia Information Systems. V.S. Subrahmanian & S.K. Tripathi. LC 98-7489. 146p. 1998. write for info. (*0-7923-8181-5*) Kluwer Academic.

Multimedia Information Systems in Practice. Ed. by W. S. Chow. 620p. 1999. pap. 59.95 (*981-4021-53-9*) Spr-Verlag.

Multimedia Instruction: Practice. Peter Fenrich. LC 96-86855. 352p. (C). 1997. pap. text 59.00 (*0-03-009264-7*) Dryden Pr.

Multimedia Interface Design in Education. Ed. by Alistair D. Edwards & Simon Holland. LC 92-16387. (NATO ASI Series F: Computer & Systems Science: Vol. 76). xii, 218p. 1996. 64.00 (*0-387-55046-1*) Spr-Verlag.

Multimedia Interface Design Studio. Aaron R. Marcus. 1995. pap. 40.00 (*0-679-75999-9*) Random.

Multimedia, Knowledge-Based & Object-Oriented Databases. Ed. by Joseph Fong et al. LC 96-17841. (Illus.). 400p. 1997. pap. 59.95 (*981-3083-00-X*) Spr-Verlag.

Multimedia Law: Forms & Analysis. Richard Raysman et al. (Commercial Law Intellectual Property Ser.). 1994. write for info. (*0-614-32425-4*) Law Journal.

Multimedia Law & Business. James N. Talbott. (Entertainment Ser.). 1997. ring bd. write for info. (*0-614-06271-3*) West Group.

Multimedia Law & Business Handbook: A Practical Guide for Developers & Publishers. J. Dianne Brinson & Mark F. Radcliffe. LC 96-75898. 468p. (Orig.). 1996. pap. 44.95 (*0-9639173-2-3*) Ladera Pr.

Multimedia Library: Materials Selection & Use. 3rd ed. James Cabeceiras. (Library & Information Science Ser.). (Illus.). 316p. 1991. text 69.95 (*0-12-153953-9*) Acad Pr.

Multimedia Literacy. 2nd ed. Hofstetter. 1997. 68.00 (*0-07-029389-9*) McGraw.

Multimedia Literacy. 2nd ed. Fred T. Hofstetter & Patricia Fox. LC 96-43261. (Illus.). 400p. (C). 1997. pap. 86.56 incl. cd-rom (*0-07-913107-7*) McGraw.

***Multimedia Literacy.** 3rd ed. Fred T. Hofstetter. LC 00-27779. 2001. pap. write for info. (*0-07-365998-3*) McGraw-H Intl.

Multimedia Magic. Arnie H. Abrams. LC 96-126498. 304p. (C). 1995. pap. text 43.00 (*0-205-17867-7*) Allyn.

***Multimedia Magic.** Robert Perry. (Computer Science Library). (Illus.). (J). 2000. pap. 8.95 (*0-531-16472-1*) Watts.

***Multimedia Magic.** Robert L. Perry. LC 99-88787. (Computer Science Library). 2000. 24.00 (*0-531-11755-3*) Watts.

Multimedia Manual Marketing. 7th ed. E. Evans. 1996. pap. text, teacher ed. write for info. (*0-13-283359-X*) Allyn.

Multimedia Marketing for Design Firms. Curtis B. Charles & Karen M. Brown. LC 96-13838. 222p. 1996. pap. 59.95 (*0-471-14609-9*) Wiley.

Multimedia MBA: Small Business Edition 96-97. 2nd ed. Irwin. 1997. 33.75 (*0-256-22838-8*, Irwn Prfssnl) McGraw-Hill Prof.

Multimedia Metadata Management Handbook: Integrating & Applying Digital Data. Ed. by Amit Sheth & Wolfgang Klas. (Illus.). 384p. 1998. 60.00 (*0-07-057735-8*) McGraw.

Multimedia Modeling: MMM '96. LC 97-111734. 500p. 1996. lib. bdg. 82.00 (*981-02-2892-9*) World Scientific Pub.

Multimedia Modeling & Risk Assessment. James L. Regens et al. (Illus.). 1998. pap. write for info. (*0-9657650-1-6*) Medical Univ.

Multimedia Modeling (MMM, '97) Modeling Multimedia Information & Systems Singapore 17-20 November, 1997. Ed. by Pung H. Keng & Chua T. Seng. LC 98-176300. 452p. 1997. pap. 86.00 (*981-02-3351-5*) World Scientific Pub.

Multimedia Modeling (MMM '93) T. S. Chua & Toshiyasu L. Kunii. 300p. 1993. text 109.00 (*981-02-1518-5*) World Scientific Pub.

Multimedia Modeling, Towards Information Superhighway. LC 96-124997. 440p. 1995. 59.00 (*981-02-2502-4*) World Scientific Pub.

Multimedia Network Integration & Management. Larry L. Ball. (McGraw-Hill Computer Communications Series). (Illus.). 416p. 1996. 50.00 (*0-07-005227-1*) McGraw.

Multimedia Networking Handbook. Ed. by James P. Cavanagh. 560p. 1995. 154.00 (*0-7913-2480-X*) Warren Gorham & Lamont.

Multimedia Networking Handbook: 1999 Edition. Jim Cavanaugh. LC 98-37258. 19p. 1998. lib. bdg. 175.00 (*0-8493-9949-1*) Lewis Pubs.

Multimedia Networking, 1997 International Workshop. LC 97-70320. 300p. 1997. pap. 115.00 (*0-8186-7916-6*) IEEE Comp Soc.

Multimedia Networks Vol. 3228: Security, Displays, Terminals & Gateways. Ed. by V. Michael Bove et al. LC 98-145678. 440p. 1998. 89.00 (*0-8194-2661-X*) SPIE.

Multimedia '95: 3rd ACM International Conference on Multimedia. 556p. 1995. pap. text 40.00 (*0-89791-752-9*, 433951) Assn Compu Machinery.

Multimedia '95: 3rd AMC International Conference on Multimedia. Date not set. text 45.00 (*0-89791-751-0*, 433952) Assn Compu Machinery.

Multimedia '94. 1996. 53.00 (*0-387-57963-X*) Spr-Verlag.

Multimedia '94: 2nd Annual Conference on Multimedia. 526p. 1994. pap. text 50.00 (*0-89791-686-7*, 433940) Assn Compu Machinery.

Multimedia, '97: International Conference on Multimedia Held November 9-13, 1997. Date not set. 62.00 (*0-89791-991-2*, 433971) Assn Compu Machinery.

Multimedia '96: Proceedings of the Eurographics Workshop in Rostock, Federal Republic of Germany, May 28-30, 1996. Ed. by B. Urban. (Eurographics Ser.). (Illus.). 178p. 1996. pap. 67.00 (*3-211-82876-1*) Spr-Verlag.

Multimedia '93: 1st International ACM Conference on Multimedia. 480p. 1993. pap. text 50.00 (*0-89791-596-8*, 429932) Assn Compu Machinery.

Multimedia 93 Proceedings. 1993. 69.95 incl. cd-rom (*0-89791-620-4*, 429934) Assn Compu Machinery.

Multimedia Oculosurgical Modules. University of Michigan Staff. 1p. 1999. pap. text 149.95 (*0-8151-2658-1*, 31656) Mosby Inc.

Multimedia Oculosurgical Modules. Ed. by University of Michigan Staff. 1p. 2000. pap. text 495.00 (*0-8151-2654-9*, 31652) Mosby Inc.

Multimedia Oculosurgical Modules: Module 5. University of Michigan Staff. 1p. 1999. pap. text 149.95 (*0-8151-2659-X*, 31657) Mosby Inc.

Multimedia Oculosurgical Modules: Module 6. University of Michigan Staff. 1p. 2000. pap. text 149.95 (*0-8151-2660-3*, 31658) Mosby Inc.

Multimedia on the PC. Ian R. Sinclair. (Illus.). 160p. 1994. pap. 15.95 (*1-870775-35-X*, Pub. by PC Pubg) Cimino Pub Grp.

Multimedia on the Web. Stephen McGrloughlin. LC 96-70682. 193p. 1997. 58.00 (*1-57576-648-5*) Sams.

Multimedia over the Broadband Network: Business Opportunities & Technology. IEC Staff. (Illus.). 380p. 1996. pap. 490.00 (*0-933217-21-8*) Prof Educ Intl.

Multimedia Parallels. Cubic Media, Staff. (C). 1995. 73.33 (*0-13-186347-9*) P-H.

Multimedia Powertool. Billups Jerram. 640p. 1993. pap. 50.00 (*0-553-37105-3*) Bantam.

Multimedia Presentation Technology: With a Sample Presentation on Total Quality Management. Fred T. Hofstetter. 237p. 1993. pap. 42.75 (*0-534-20676-X*) Wadsworth Pub.

Multimedia Presentations on the Go: An Introduction & Buyer's Guide. Martha C. Sammons. LC 95-34464. 200p. 1995. pap. text 30.00 (*1-56308-264-0*) Libs Unl.

Multimedia Processing. (C). Date not set. text. write for info. (*0-13-011393-X*) P-H.

Multimedia Production Guide. Amr Eissa et al. (Illus.). 800p. (Orig.). 1995. pap. 55.00 (*1-56830-225-8*) Hayden.

Multimedia Products in Computer Industry in Hong Kong: A Strategic Entry Report, 1996. Compiled by Icon Group International Staff. (Illus.). 122p. 1999. ring bd. 1220.00 incl. audio compact disk (*0-7418-1146-4*) Icon Grp.

Multimedia Projects. Donna Axelson. 80p. (J). (gr. 3-5). 1997. pap. 9.95 (*1-55734-513-9*) Tchr Create Mat.

Multimedia Projects. Deborah Hayes. 1997. pap. text 9.95 (*1-55734-519-8*) Tchr Create Mat.

Multimedia Projects. Tracee Sudyka & Paul Gardner. (Illus.). 80p. (J). pap., teacher ed. 9.95 (*1-57690-196-3*, TCM2196) Tchr Create Mat.

***Multimedia Projects for Kid Pix.** Marsha Lifter et al. (Illus.). 120p. 1998. ring bd. 29.95 (*1-885830-49-1*, MPI) Pixel Genius.

M

Multimedia Projects in Education: Designing, Producing & Assessing. Karen S. Ivers & Ann E. Barron. LC 97-28332. 200p. 1997. pap. 25.00 (*1-56308-572-0*) Libs Unl.

Multimedia Servers: Applications, Environments, & Design. Dinkar Sitaram & Asit Dan. Ed. by Ed Fox. LC 99-45782. (Multimedia Information & Systems Ser.). 600p. 1999. text 69.95 (*1-55860-430-8*) Morgan Kaufmann.

Multimedia Software Development, 1996 International Workshop on (MMSD '96) LC 96-75129. 192p. 1996. pap. text 50.00 (*0-8186-7511-X*) IEEE Comp Soc.

Multimedia Software for Pc's & Networks in Japan: A Strategic Entry Report, 1998. Compiled by Icon Group International Staff. (Country Industry Report). (Illus.). 156p. 1999. ring bd. 1560.00 incl. audio compact disk (*0-7418-0158-2*) Icon Grp.

***Multimedia Software in Canada: A Strategic Entry Report, 1997.** Compiled by Icon Group International Staff. (Country Industry Report). (Illus.). 128p. 1999. ring bd. 1280.00 incl. audio compact disk (*0-7418-0159-0*) Icon Grp.

Multimedia Sound & Video. Louis Molina et al. LC 96-70684. (Illus.). 192p. 1997. 58.00 (*1-57576-647-7*) Sams.

Multimedia Sourcebook, 1992. Christine Hughes. 350p. 1992. teacher ed. 175.00 (*1-879637-01-4*) Myriad Tech FL.

Multimedia Storage & Archiving Systems. Ed. by C. C. J. Kuo. 406p. 1996. 76.00 (*0-8194-2318-1*) SPIE.

***Multimedia Storage & Archiving Systems IV.** Ed. by Sethuraman Panchanathan et al. 492p. 1999. pap. text 92.00 (*0-8194-3439-6*) SPIE.

Multimedia Storage & Archiving Systems II, Vol. 3229. Ed. by C. C. Kuo et al. LC 98-122108. 426p. 1997. 80.00 (*0-8194-2662-8*) SPIE.

***Multimedia Storage & Archiving Systems III, Vol. 352.** Ed. by C. C. J. Kuo et al. LC 99-170353. 1998. 99.00 (*0-8194-2988-0*) SPIE.

***Multimedia Storytimes.** Robin Works Davis. LC 99-53292. (Illus.). 100p. 2000. pap. text, teacher ed. 15.95 (*1-57950-028-5*, Alleyside) Highsmith Pr.

Multimedia Strategies in Business. Roger L. Fetterman. 1996. 45.00 incl. cd-rom (*0-614-20322-8*) Random.

Multimedia Strategies in the Corporation. Roger Fettereman. 1996. 45.00 (*0-614-95743-5*) Random Ref & Info.

Multimedia Study Guide. 8th ed. Jo Hamblin. 1999. text, student ed. 18.50 (*0-13-889429-9*) P-H.

Multimedia Systems. Ed. by John F. Koegel. LC 93-19184. 464p. (C). 1994. 51.95 (*0-201-53258-1*) Addison-Wesley.

***Multimedia Systems: Delivering, Generating & Interacting with Multimedia.** Tim Morris. LC 00-37377. (Applied Computing Ser.). 2000. write for info. (*1-85233-248-4*) Spr-Verlag.

Multimedia Systems & Applications, Vol. #352. Ed. by Andrew G. Tescher et al. LC 99-200340. 1999. 107.00 (*0-8194-2989-9*) SPIE.

***Multimedia Systems & Applications II.** Ed. by Andrew G. Tescher et al. 1999. pap. text 103.00 (*0-8194-3438-8*) SPIE.

Multimedia Systems & Techniques. Ed. by Borko Furht. LC 95-47658. (International Series in Engineering & Computer Science, Natural Language Processing & Machine Translation). 344p. (C). 1996. text 119.00 (*0-7923-9683-9*) Kluwer Academic.

***Multimedia Systems, Standards & Networks.** Ed. by Atul Puri & Tsuhan Chen. LC 00-24108. (Signal Processing Ser.). 636p. 2000. pap. 195.00 (*0-8247-9303-X*) Dekker.

Multimedia Technologies & Applications for the 21st Century: Visions of World Experts. Ed. by Borko Furht. LC 97-32126. (The Kluwer International Series in Engineering & Computer Science: No. 431). 336p. 1997. text 126.50 (*0-7923-8074-6*, D Reidel) Kluwer Academic.

Multimedia Technologies for Training: An Introduction. Ann E. Barron & Gary W. Orwig. LC 94-36876. (Illus.). xv, 211p. 1994. pap. text 29.00 (*1-56308-262-4*) Libs Unl.

Multimedia Technology & Applications. David Hillman. LC 97-33011. 272p. (C). 1997. mass mkt. 52.95 (*0-8273-8498-X*) Delmar.

Multimedia Technology & Applications: Proceedings of the International Conference. Ed. by V. W. Chow. 600p. (C). 1998. pap. 49.00 (*981-3083-16-6*, Pub. by Spr-Verlag) Spr-Verlag.

*__Multimedia Technology for Applications.__ Mohammed Ismail. Ed. by Bing J. Sheu. LC 97-44804. 688p. 1998. 74.95 (*0-7803-1174-4*, PC5645) Inst Electrical.

Multimedia, Telecommunications, & Applications Vol. XII: Proceedings, Third International COST 237 Workshop, Barcelona, Spain, November 25-27, 1996. Ed. by G. Ventre et al. LC 96-51116. (Lecture Notes in Computer Science Ser.: Vol. 1185). 267p. 1996. pap. 49.00 (*3-540-62096-6*) Spr-Verlag.

Multimedia Tools & Applications. Ed. by Borko Furht. LC 96-10920. (International Engineering & Computer Science Robotic Ser.: No. 359). 416p. (C). 1996. text 125.00 (*0-7923-9721-5*) Kluwer Academic.

Multimedia Tools for Managers. Bohdan O. Szuprowicz. LC 96-9492. 288p. 1996. 29.95 (*0-8144-0254-2*) AMACOM.

Multimedia Training: Developing Technology-Based Systems. Angus Reynolds. LC 95-32922. 1996. pap. text 50.00 incl. disk (*0-07-912012-1*) McGraw.

Multimedia Transport & Fate of Pollutants. Cohan. 372p. (C). 2001. boxed set 64.00 (*0-13-605734-9*) P-H.

Multimedia Transport & Teleservices: Proceedings of the International COST 237 Workshop, Vienna, Austria, November 13-15, 1994. Ed. by D. Hutchison et al. LC 94-40000. (Lecture Notes in Computer Science Ser.: Vol. 882). 1994. write for info. (*0-387-58759-4*) Spr-Verlag.

Multimedia Transport Teleservice. LC 94-40000. 1994. 55.95 (*3-540-58759-4*) Spr-Verlag.

Multimedia Upgrade Kits in Saudi Arabia: A Strategic Entry Report, 1996. Compiled by Icon Group International Staff. (Illus.). 133p. 1999. ring bd. 1330.00 incl. audio compact disk (*0-7418-1147-2*) Icon Grp.

Multimedia Workshop: Action! 3.0 for Windows. Matthew Holtz. (C). 1996. pap. 37.95 (*0-534-31061-3*) Wadsworth Pub.

Multimedia Workshop: Authorware Professional 2.0. Matthew Holtz. (Multimedia Ser.). 162p. 1994. 37.95 (*0-534-31060-5*) Wadsworth Pub.

Multimedia Workshop: Macromedia Director. Matthew Holtz. LC 95-20204. 1995. 37.95 (*0-534-31073-7*) Wadsworth Pub.

Multimedia Workshop: Multimedia ToolBook 3.0. Matthew Holtz. 168p. 1995. pap. 37.95 (*0-534-31059-1*) Wadsworth Pub.

*__Multimedia '99: Proceedings of the Eurographics Workshop in Milan, Italy, September 7-8, 1999.__ Ed. by N. Correia et al. (Eurographics Ser.). ix, 222p. 2000. pap. (*3-211-83437-0*) Spr-Verlag.

Multimensional NMR in Liquids - Basic Principles & Experimental Methods. F. J. Van De Ven. 424p. 1995. 79.95 (*0-471-18594-9*) Wiley.

*__Multimetallic & Macromolecular Inorganic Photochemistry.__ Ed. by V. Ramamurthy & Kirk S. Schanze. (Molecular & Supramolecular Photochemistry Ser.: Vol. 4). (Illus.). 360p. 1999. text 175.00 (*0-8247-7392-6*) Dekker.

Multimeters Explained. William J. Koch. 26p. 1987. pap., wbk. ed. 7.00 (*0-8064-1502-9*, E10) Bergwall.

Multimethod Assessment of Chronic. Paul Karoly & Mark P. Jensen. (C). 1987. 54.95 (*0-205-14386-5*, H4386) Allyn.

Multimethod Research: A Synthesis of Styles. John Brewer & Albert Hunter. (Library of Social Research: Vol. 175). 224p. (C). 1989. text 59.95 (*0-8039-3077-1*) Sage.

Multimethodology: The Theory & Practice of Integrating Management Science Methodologies. John Mingers & Anthony Gill. LC 97-9288. 458p. 1997. 82.95 (*0-471-97490-0*) Wiley.

Multimod Mark III: The Core Dynamic & Steady-State Models, Vol. 164. Douglas Laxton. LC 98-20633. (Occasional Paper Ser.). 1998. write for info. (*1-55775-722-4*) Intl Monetary.

MULTIMOD Mark II: Revised & Extended Model. Paul R. Masson et al. LC 90-37502. (Occasional Papers: No. 71). v, 50p. 1990. pap. 10.00 (*1-55775-141-2*) Intl Monetary.

Multimodal Human-Computer Communication: Systems, Techniques, & Experiments. Ed. by Harry C. Bunt et al. LC 98-3460. (Lecture Notes in Computer Science: Vol. 1374). viii, 345p. 1998. pap. 59.00 (*3-540-64380-X*) Spr-Verlag.

Multimodal Interfaces: A Special Issue of Human Computer Interaction. Ed. by Thomas Moran. 230p. 1997. pap. write for info. (*0-8058-9867-0*) L Erlbaum Assocs.

Multimodal Priority Setting & Application of Geographic Information Systems (TRR 1429) Ed. by Susan Taylor Brown. (Transportation Research Record Ser.). (Illus.). 96p. 1994. pap. text 25.00 (*0-309-05507-5*, R1429) Transport Res Bd.

Multimodal Psychiatric Music Therapy for Adults, Adolescents, & Children: A Clinical Manual. Michael D. Cassity & Julia E. Cassity. 250p. 1993. pap. text 30.00 (*0-9643602-0-9*) MMB Music.

Multimodal Psychiatric Music Therapy for Adults, Adolescents, & Children: A Clinical Manual. 2nd ed. Michael D. Cassity & Julia E. Cassity. LC 95-45524. 1996. 24.95 (*0-918812-85-2*) MMB Music.

Multimodal Reasoning: Papers from the 1998 Spring Symposium. Ed. by Eugene Freuder. (Technical Reports). (Illus.). 174p. 1998. spiral bd. 25.00 (*1-57735-049-9*, SS-98-04) AAAI Pr.

Multimodal Therapy in Oncology Nursing. Ed. by Marcia C. Liebman & Dawn Camp-Sorrell. LC 96-10353. (Illus.). 528p. (C). (gr. 13). 1996. pap. text 37.95 (*0-8151-5422-4*, 25466) Mosby Inc.

Multimodal Transport: Carrier Liability & Documentation. Ralph De Witt. (Lloyd's Shipping Law Library). 500p. 1995. 140.00 (*1-85044-894-9*) LLP.

Multimodal Transport Rules. Mary R. Brooks & Hugh M. Kindred. LC 96-54219. 1997. 102.00 (*90-411-0360-0*) Kluwer Law Intl.

Multimodal/Intermodal Transportation in the United States, Western Europe & Latin America: Governmental Policies, Plans & Programs. Leigh B. Boske. LC TA1215.M84 1998. (Policy Research Project Report Ser.). 540 p. 1998. pap. 30.00 (*0-89940-743-9*) LBJ Sch Pub Aff.

Multimodality Therapy for Gastric Cancer. Ed. by T. Nakajima & T. Yamaguchi. LC 99-27919. (Illus.). xii, 288p. 1999. 169.00 (*4-431-70255-5*) Spr-Verlag.

Multimodality Therapy for Head & Neck Cancer. Ed. by Gordon B. Snow & J. R. Clark. LC 92-3210. (Illus.). 216p. 1992. text 75.00 (*0-86577-433-1*, RC280) Thieme Med Pubs.

Multimodality Therapy in Gynecologic Oncology. Ed. by B. U. Sevin et al. LC 96-14486. 1996. 89.00 (*0-86577-588-5*) Thieme Med Pubs.

*__Multimodality Treatment of Lung Cancer.__ Ed. by Arthur T. Skarin. (Lung Biology in Health & Disease Ser.: Vol. 140). 472p. 2000. 195.00 (*0-8247-0236-0*) Dekker.

Multimode Interference Couplers: Design & Applications. L. B. Soldano. 116p. 1994. pap. 57.50 (*90-407-1044-9*, Pub. by Delft U Pr) Coronet Bks.

Multimode Stellar Pulsations. G. Kovacs et al. 300p. (C). 1988. 180.00 (*0-569-09193-4*, Pub. by Collets) St Mut.

Multinational Accounting: A Research Framework for the Eighties. Frederick D. Choi. LC 81-16448. (Research for Business Decisions Ser.: No. 46). 240p. 1981. reprint ed. pap. 74.40 (*0-8357-1267-2*, 207005500063) Bks Demand.

Multinational Accounting: Segment Disclosure & Risk. Bimal Prodhan. (International Accounting Ser.). 320p. 1986. 55.00 (*0-7099-4010-6*, Pub. by C Helm) Routldge.

Multinational & International Banking. Ed. by Geoffrey Jones. (International Library of Macroeconomic & Financial History: Vol. 2). 640p. 1991. text 250.00 (*1-85278-522-5*) E Elgar.

Multinational Banks: Their Identities & Determinants. Kang R. Cho. LC 85-1123. (Research in Business Economics & Public Policy Ser.: No. 8). (Illus.). 190p. reprint ed. pap. 58.90 (*0-8357-1668-6*, 207036900088) Bks Demand.

Multinational Banks & Their Social & Labour Practices. v, 160p. (Orig.). 1991. pap. 24.75 (*92-2-107285-1*) Intl Labour Office.

Multinational Business Finance. 4th ed. Arthur I. Stonehill. Ed. by David K. Eiteman. LC 85-22915. (C). 1986. text. write for info. (*0-201-11436-4*) Addison-Wesley.

Multinational Business Finance. 5th ed. David K. Eiteman. (Illus.). 700p. (C). 1989. text 39.96 (*0-201-19327-2*) Addison-Wesley.

Multinational Business Finance. 7th ed. David K. Eiteman. (SPA.). (C). 1995. pap. text. write for info. (*0-201-84553-9*) Addison-Wesley.

Multinational Business Finance. 8th ed. 1p. (C). 1997. text. write for info. (*0-201-30934-3*) Addison-Wesley.

Multinational Business Finance. 8th ed. (C). 1997. text 67.00 (*0-201-36016-0*) Addison-Wesley.

*__Multinational Business Finance.__ 8th ed. (C). 1998. text 67.00 (*0-201-39789-7*) Addison-Wesley.

Multinational Business Finance. 8th ed. David K. Eiteman. LC 97-36609. 854p. (C). 1997. 96.00 (*0-201-52485-6*) Addison-Wesley.

*__Multinational Business Finance.__ 9th ed. 672p. (C). 2000. 90.00 (*0-201-63538-0*) Addison-Wesley.

Multinational Business Finance: Includes Instructor's Manual, Lotus Templates, Test Bank & Transparency Masters. 7th ed. David K. Eiteman et al. (C). 1995. text, teacher ed., suppl. ed. 74.33 incl. trans. (*0-201-59558-3*) Addison-Wesley.

Multinational Business in South Africa, 1996: Executive Summary. Peter DeSimone. Ed. by Rosemary Lally & Meg Voorhes. 20p. (Orig.). 1996. pap. text 25.00 (*1-879775-38-7*) IRRC Inc DC.

Multinational Business in South Africa, 1996 Vol. I: U. S. Companies. Peter DeSimone. Ed. by Rosemary Lally & Meg Voorhes. 240p. (Orig.). 1996. pap. text 125.00 (*1-879775-39-5*) IRRC Inc DC.

Multinational Business in South Africa, 1996 Vol. II: Non-U. S. Companies. Peter DeSimone. Ed. by Rosemary Lally & Meg Voorhes. 220p. 1996. pap. text 125.00 (*1-879775-40-9*) IRRC Inc DC.

Multinational Business Service Firms: The Development of Multinational Organization Structures in the U. K. Business Service Sector. Joanne Roberts. LC 97-76945. (Illus.). 320p. 1998. text 67.95 (*1-84014-154-9*, Pub. by Ashgate Pub) Ashgate Pub Co.

Multinational Challenge to Corporation Law: The Search for a New Corporate Personality. Phillip I. Blumberg. LC 92-25046. 336p. 1993. text 70.00 (*0-19-507061-5*) OUP.

Multinational Collective Bargaining Attempts: The Record, the Cases, & the Prospects. Herbert R. Northrup & Richard L. Rowan. (Multinational Industrial Relations Ser.: No. 6). 580p. 1979. 27.50 (*0-89546-016-5*) U PA Ctr Hum Res.

Multinational Companies in China: Winners & Losers. (Research Reports: No. Q189). 1997. 595.00 (*0-85058-916-9*) Economist Intell.

Multinational Companies in U. S. International Trade: A Statistical & Analytical Source Book. F. Steb Hipple. LC 94-46200. 336p. 1995. 72.95 (*0-89930-820-1*, Quorum Bks) Greenwood.

Multinational Company: Instrument for World Growth. Orville Freeman. LC 81-717. 127p. 1981. 49.95 (*0-275-90627-2*, C0627, Praeger Pubs) Greenwood.

Multinational Construction Industry. Howard Seymour. 320p. 1988. lib. bdg. 67.50 (*0-7099-5438-7*, Pub. by C Helm) Routldge.

Multinational Coordinated Arabidopsis Thaliana Genome Research Project: Progress Report: Year Four. Ed. by Anne Moffat. (Illus.). 44p. (C). 1998. pap. text 20.00 (*0-7881-7044-9*) DIANE Pub.

Multinational Corporate Finance. Mark Largan & Virginia Alexandra Featherstone-Witty. 371p. 1999. pap. 120.00 (*0-85297-427-2*, Pub. by Chartered Bank) St Mut.

Multinational Corporate Strategy. James Leontiades. 228p. 1987. pap. 25.95 (*0-669-16038-5*) Lxngtn Bks.

Multinational Corporation. Ed. by David H. Blake & Richard D. Lambert. LC 72-85688. (Annals of the American Academy of Political & Social Science Ser.: No. 403). 300p. (C). 1972. 28.00 (*0-685-00182-2*); pap. 18.00 (*0-87761-153-X*) Am Acad Pol Soc Sci.

Multinational Corporation: Environments & Operations. Parviz Asheghian. LC 98-27526. 432p. 1998. 65.00 (*1-56072-555-9*) Nova Sci Pubs.

Multinational Corporation in the 1980s. Ed. by Charles P. Kindleberger & David B. Audretsch. 300p. (C). 1986. pap. text 18.50 (*0-262-61044-2*) MIT Pr.

Multinational Corporation Plan. Steiner. 1966. 29.95 (*0-02-931130-6*) S&S Trade.

Multinational Corporations. Ed. by M. C. Casson. (International Library of Critical Writings in Economics: Vol. 1). 640p. 1990. text 270.00 (*1-85278-192-0*) E Elgar.

Multinational Corporations. Ed. by Erik R. Peterson. (CSIS Significant Issues Ser.). (C). 1996. pap. text 11.95 (*0-89206-246-0*) Westview.

Multinational Corporations. 2nd rev. ed. Nasrollah S. Fatemi et al. 12.00 (*0-8453-1879-9*, Cornwall Bks) Assoc Univ Prs.

*__Multinational Corporations: Emergence & Evolution.__ Paz Estrella E. Tolentino. LC 00-30429. (Studies in International Business & the World Economy Ser.). 2000. write for info. (*0-415-14575-9*) Routledge.

Multinational Corporations: Investments, Technology, Tax, Labor & Securities: European, North & Latin American Perspectives with Summaries in French & Spanish. Ed. by Alain A. Levasseur & Enrique Dahl. LC 86-13192. 404p. (C). 1986. lib. bdg. 58.00 (*0-8191-5496-2*) U Pr of Amer.

Multinational Corporations: The ECISM Guide to Information Sources. Joseph O. Mekeirle. LC 78-62333. 480p. 1978. 125.00 (*0-275-90307-9*, C0307, Praeger Pubs) Greenwood.

Multinational Corporations & Black Power. Harry G. Matthews. 136p. 1976. text 32.95 (*0-87073-776-7*) Transaction Pubs.

Multinational Corporations & the Environment: A Bibliography. Ed. by Joan Nordquist. LC 95-230996. (Contemporary Social Issues: A Bibliographic Ser.: No. 36). 72p. (C). 1994. pap. 20.00 (*0-937855-70-7*) Ref Rsch Serv.

Multinational Corporations & the Impact of Public Advocacy on Corporate Strategy: Nestle & the Infant Formula Controversy. S. Prakash Sethi. LC 93-32157. (Issues in Business Ethics Ser.: Vol. 6). 432p. (C). 1994. text 148.50 (*0-7923-9378-3*) Kluwer Academic.

Multinational Corporations & the Politics of Dependence: Copper in Chile. Theodore H. Moran. LC 74-2973. 303p. reprint ed. pap. 94.00 (*0-8357-4289-X*, 203708800007) Bks Demand.

Multinational Corporations & the Regionalization of the Latin American Automotive Industry. Russell M. Moore. Ed. by Stuart Bruchey. LC 80-584. (Multinational Corporations Ser.). 1981. lib. bdg. 36.95 (*0-405-13376-6*) Ayer.

Multinational Corporations & the Third World. Som Deo. 1986. 27.50 (*81-7024-051-4*, Pub. by Ashish Pub Hse) S Asia.

Multinational Corporations & Underdevelopment. Volker Bornschier & Christopher K. Chase-Dunn. 192p. 1985. 49.95 (*0-275-90063-0*, 0063, Praeger Pubs) Greenwood.

Multinational Corporations, Environment, & the Third World: Business Matters. Ed. by Charles Pearson. LC 86-19810. (Duke Press Policy Studies). xvi, 295p. 1987. text 54.95 (*0-8223-0707-3*); pap. text 21.95 (*0-8223-0761-8*) Duke.

*__Multinational Corporations in China: Benefiting from Structural Transformation.__ Yadong Luo. 300p. 2000. 54.00 (*87-16-13490-7*, Pub. by Copenhagen Busn Schl) Bks Intl VA.

Multinational Corporations in Democratic Host Countries: U. S. Multinationals & the Vredeling Proposal. Ton DeVos. 288p. 1989. text 82.95 (*1-85521-048-7*, Pub. by Dartmth Pub) Ashgate Pub Co.

Multinational Corporations in Developed Countries: A Review of Recent Research & Policy Thinking. Sperry Lea & Simon Webley. LC 73-77813. (British-North American Committee Ser.). 88p. 1973. 2.00 (*0-902594-07-9*) Natl Planning.

Multinational Corporations in the North American Free Trade Association. Michael J. Twomey. LC 93-6767. 216p. 1993. 62.95 (*0-275-94617-7*, C4617, Praeger Pubs) Greenwood.

Multinational Corporations Series, 35 bks., Set. Ed. by Stuart Bruchey. 1980. lib. bdg. 1048.00 (*0-405-13350-2*) Ayer.

Multinational Corporations 3rd. write for info. (*0-8453-4775-6*) Assoc Univ Prs.

Multinational Crime: The Challenge of Terrorism, Espionage, Drug, & Arms Trafficking. John M. Martin & Anne T. Romano. (Studies in Crime, Law, & Justice: Vol. 9). (Illus.). 220p. 1992. 52.00 (*0-8039-4597-3*); pap. 21.95 (*0-8039-4598-1*) Sage.

Multinational Cross-Cultural Management: An Integrative Context-Specific Process. Robert J. Mockler & D. G. Dologite. LC 96-26270. 336p. 1997. 69.50 (*1-56720-010-9*, Quorum Bks) Greenwood.

Multinational Culture: Social Impacts of a Global Economy, 122. Ed. by Cheryl R. Lehman & Russell M. Moore. LC 91-27. (Contributions in Economics & Economic History Ser.: No. 122). 360p. 1992. 65.00 (*0-313-27822-9*, LMB, Greenwood Pr) Greenwood.

Multinational Direct Marketing: The Methods & the Markets. Richard N. Miller. LC 95-18495. 354p. 1995. 44.95 (*0-07-042356-3*) McGraw.

Multinational Distribution: Channel, Tax & Legal Strategies. R. D. Hall & Ralph J. Gilbert. 160p. 1985. 52.95 (*0-275-90115-7*, C0115, Praeger Pubs) Greenwood.

Multinational Enterprise. Ed. by John H. Dunning. 1971. text 65.00 (*0-04-330189-4*) Routledge.

Multinational Enterprise: International Investment & Host-Country Impacts. Thomas G. Parry. Ed. by Edward I. Altman & Ingo I. Walter. LC 77-24394. (Contemporary Studies in Economic & Financial Analysis: Vol. 20). 225p. 1980. 78.50 (*0-89232-092-3*) Jai Pr.

Multinational Enterprise & Economic Analysis. 2nd ed. Richard E. Caves. (Surveys of Economic Literature Ser.). (Illus.). 336p. (C). 1996. pap. text 20.95 (*0-521-47858-8*) Cambridge U Pr.

Multinational Enterprise & Public Policy: A Study of the Industrial Countries. A. E. Safarian. LC 92-15820. (New Horizons in International Business Ser.). 608p. 1993. 120.00 (*1-85278-714-7*) E Elgar.

Multinational Enterprise in Historical Perspective. 416p. 1989. pap. text 27.95 (*0-521-38914-3*) Cambridge U Pr.

Multinational Enterprise in Transition: Strategies for Global Competitiveness. enl. rev. ed. Ed. by Phillip D. Grub & Dara M. Khambata. LC 93-27751. xvi, 720p. (C). 1993. pap. text 24.95 (*0-87850-105-3*) Darwin Pr.

Multinational Enterprise in Transition: Strategies for Global Competitiveness. 4th enl. rev. ed. Ed. by Phillip D. Grub & Dara M. Khambata. LC 93-27751. xvi, 720p. (C). 1993. 29.95 (*0-87850-104-5*) Darwin Pr.

Multinational Enterprises: Information & Consultation Concerning Their Manpower Plans. xii, 195p. (Orig.). 1985. pap. 22.50 (*92-2-105094-7*) Intl Labour Office.

Multinational Enterprises & Employment in the Caribbean with Special Reference to Trinidad & Tobago. Terisa E. Turner. (Multinational Enterprises Programme Working Papers: No. 20). v, 56p. (Orig.). 1982. pap. 13.50 (*92-2-103030-X*) Intl Labour Office.

Multinational Enterprises & Employment in the Global Economy of the 1990s. P. Bailey et al. xvi, 325p. (Orig.). 1993. pap. 40.50 (*92-2-107105-7*) Intl Labour Office.

Multinational Enterprises & Industrial Organization: The Case of India. Nagesh Kumar. LC 94-21364. 196p. 1995. 28.50 (*0-8039-9183-5*) Sage.

Multinational Enterprises & Technological Spillovers. Tommaso Perez. LC 98-172285. (Studies in Global Competition: Vol. 6). 202p. 1998. text 56.00 (*90-5702-295-8*, ECU40, Harwood Acad Pubs) Gordon & Breach.

*__Multinational Enterprises & the Law.__ Peter Muchlinski. 768p. 1999. pap. 74.95 (*0-631-21676-6*) Blackwell Pubs.

Multinational Enterprises & the Law. Peter Muchlinski. 768p. (C). 1999. 110.95 (*0-631-17311-0*) Blackwell Pubs.

Multinational Enterprises & the OECD Industrial Relations Guidelines. Duncan C. Campbell & Richard L. Rowan. LC 83-81083. (Multinational Industrial Relations Ser.: No. 11). (Illus.). 308p. 1983. reprint ed. pap. 95.50 (*0-608-04371-0*, 206515200001) Bks Demand.

*__Multinational Enterprises & the Social Challenges of the XXIst Century: The ILO Declaration on Fundamental Principles at Work Public & Private Corporate Codes of Conduct.__ Ed. by Roger Blanpain. (Bulletin of Comparative Labour Relations Ser.: Vol. 37). 416p. 1999. pap. text 138.00 (*90-411-1280-4*) Kluwer Law Intl.

Multinational Enterprises & Trade Policy: The Selected Scientific Papers of Alan M. Rugman, Vol. 2. Alan M. Rugman. (Illus.). 432p. (C). 1996. 100.00 (*1-85898-408-4*) E Elgar.

Multinational Enterprises & U. N. Politics: The Quest for Codes of Conduct. Werner J. Feld. (Policy Studies). (Illus.). 1980. 74.00 (*0-08-022488-1*, Pergamon Pr) Elsevier.

Multinational Enterprises from the Netherlands. Ed. by Roger Van Hoesel & Rajneesh Narula. LC 99-193810. (Studies in International Business & the World Economy Ser.: No. 8). (Illus.). xvii, 307 p. (C). 1999. 100.00 (*0-415-17850-9*, D6231) Routledge.

Multinational Enterprises in Development: The Mining Industry of Sierra Leone. Emmanuel Cleeve. LC 96-79950. 160p. 1997. 55.95 (*1-85972-559-7*, Pub. by Avebry) Ashgate Pub Co.

Multinational Enterprises in the West & East. Leon Zurawicki. 218p. 1979. lib. bdg. 88.00 (*90-286-0419-7*) Kluwer Academic.

Multinational Enterprises in the World Economy: Essays in Honour of John Dunning. Ed. by Peter J. Buckley & Mark Casson. (New Horizons in International Business Ser.). 304p. 1992. 95.00 (*1-85278-393-1*) E Elgar.

Multinational Enterprises, Technology & Competitiveness. John H. Dunning. 350p. 1988. text 60.00 (*0-04-445175-X*) Routledge.

Multinational Excursions. Charles P. Kindleberger. 384p. 1984. 33.00 (*0-262-11092-X*) MIT Pr.

Multinational Executive Travel Companion. 24th rev. ed. Dave Strand. Ed. by Janet Tracy. (Illus.). 700p. 1997. 100.00 (*0-614-30214-5*); pap. 60.00 (*0-614-30213-7*) Suburban Pub CT.

Multinational Finance. Kirk Charles Butler. LC 96-34787. (FV - International Finance Ser.). 1996. mass mkt. 70.95 (*0-538-85385-9*) S-W Pub.

***Multinational Finance.** 2nd ed. Butler. LC 99-29724. 682p. 1999. pap. 97.95 (*0-324-00450-8*) Sth-Wstrn College.

Multinational Finance. 3rd ed. 612p. 1996. pap. 68.00 (*0-13-240920-8*) P-H.

***Multinational Finance.** 4th ed. Adrian Buckley. LC 99-41172. 1999. write for info. (*0-13-013166-0*) P-H.

Multinational Financial Accounting. Ahmed R. Belkaoui. LC 91-8400. 240p. 1991. 72.95 (*0-89930-614-4*, BKM, Quorum Bks) Greenwood.

***Multinational Financial Management.** 400p. (C). 1999. 42.00 (*0-536-02447-2*) Pearson Custom.

Multinational Financial Management. 3rd ed. Alan C. Shapiro. 450p. 1989. boxed set 56.00 (*0-205-11777-5*, H17775) Allyn.

Multinational Financial Management. 3rd ed. Alan C. Shapiro. 450p. 1989. teacher ed. write for info. (*0-318-63859-2*, H1778-3); student ed. 19.00 (*0-685-22008-7*, H1779-1) P-H.

Multinational Financial Management. 6th ed. Alan C. Shapiro. LC 98-50571. (C). 1999. text 74.67 (*0-13-010142-7*) P-H.

Multinational Firms & Asian Exports. Benjamin I. Cohen. LC 74-17551. (Publication of the Economic Growth Center, Yale University Ser.). 189p. reprint ed. pap. 58.60 (*0-8357-8741-9*, 203369400087) Bks Demand.

Multinational Firms & International Relocation. Ed. by Peter J. Buckley & Jean-Louis Mucchielli. LC 95-25263. (New Horizons in International Business Ser.). (Illus.). 272p. 1997. 90.00 (*1-85898-302-9*) E Elgar.

***Multinational Firms, Cooperation & Competition in the World Economy.** Peter J. Buckley. LC 99-54659. 240p. 1999. text 69.95 (*0-312-22900-3*) St Martin.

Multinational Force in Beirut, 1982-1984. Ed. by Anthony McDermott et al. (Illus.). 293p. 1991. 49.95 (*0-8130-1051-9*) U Press Fla.

Multinational Institutions & the Third World. Robert H. Girling. LC 84-18131. 212p. 1985. 39.95 (*0-275-90106-8*, C0106, Praeger Pubs) Greenwood.

Multinational Investment in Modern Europe: Strategic Interaction in the Integrated Community. Ed. by John Cantwell. (New Horizons in International Business Ser.). 416p. 1992. 100.00 (*1-85278-421-0*) E Elgar.

Multinational Joint Ventures in Developing Countries. Paul W. Beamish. 160p. 1988. lib. bdg. 52.50 (*0-318-35457-8*, Pub. by C Helm) Routldge.

Multinational Literature of Yugoslavia, 21 vols. Albert B. Lord et al. LC 77-126039. (Review of National Literatures Ser.: Vol. 5, No. 1). 128p. 1974. pap. 4.95 (*0-918680-64-6*) Griffon House.

Multinational Management: A Strategic Approach. John B. Cullen. LC 98-13178. 1998. 87.95 (*0-538-89034-7*) Thomson Learn.

Multinational Management Accounting. Ahmed R. Belkaoui. LC 90-8896. 304p. 1991. 77.50 (*0-89930-529-6*, BMJ/, Quorum Bks) Greenwood.

Multinational Managers & Host Government Interactions. Ed. by Lee A. Tavis. LC 86-40590. 320p. 1988. text 34.50 (*0-268-01364-0*) U of Notre Dame Pr.

Multinational Military Forces: Problems & Prospects: A European Perspective. Roger H. Palin. LC 95-221020. (Adelphi Papers). 88p. 1995. pap. text 23.00 (*0-19-828025-4*) OUP.

Multinational Mission: Balancing Local Demands & Global Vision. C. K. Prahalad & Yves L. Doz. 256p. 1987. 35.00 (*0-02-925050-1*) Free Pr.

Multinational Naval Cooperation & Foreign Policy into the 21st Century. Ed. by Fred W. Crickard et al. LC 97-50012. (Illus.). 305p. 1998. text 72.95 (*1-85521-997-2*, VA40.M85, Pub. by Ashgate Pub) Ashgate Pub Co.

Multinational Pharmaceutical Companies: Principles & Practice. 2nd ed. Bert Spilker. 848p. 1993. text 131.00 (*0-7817-0100-7*) Lppncott W & W.

Multinational Restructuring, Internationalization & Small Economies: The Case of Sweden. Thomas Andersson et al. LC 95-12518. 208p. (C). (gr. 13). 1995. 85.00 (*0-415-12286-4*) Routledge.

Multinational Risk Assessment & Management: Strategies for Investment & Marketing Decisions. Wenlee Ting. LC 87-5970. (Illus.). 262p. 1988. 55.00 (*0-89930-175-4*, TMC/, Quorum Bks) Greenwood.

Multinational Service Firms. Ed. by Peter Enderwick. 272p. 1989. 72.50 (*0-415-00395-4*) Routledge.

***Multinational Strategic Alliance.** Mockler. LC 98-37306. 266p. (C). 1999. 49.95 (*0-471-98775-1*) Wiley.

Multinational Strategic Alliances. Ed. by Refik Culpan. LC 92-20709. (Illus.). 374p. 1993. pap. 24.95 (*1-56024-323-6*) Haworth Pr.

Multinational Strategic Alliances. Ed. by Refik Culpan. LC 92-20709. (Illus.). 374p. 1993. lib. bdg. 79.95 (*1-56024-322-8*) Haworth Pr.

Multinational Union Organizations in the Manufacturing Industries. Richard L. Rowan & Rae A. O'Brien. LC 80-53989. (Multinational Industrial Relations Ser.: No. 7). (Illus.). 232p. (Orig.). 1980. reprint ed. pap. 72.00 (*0-608-04368-0*, 206514900001) Bks Demand.

Multinational Union Organizations in the White-Collar, Service, & Communications Industries. Richard L. Rowan et al. LC 83-48900. (Multinational Industrial Relations Ser.: No. 7). (Illus.). 506p. 1983. reprint ed. pap. 156.90 (*0-608-04369-9*, 206515000001) Bks Demand.

Multinationale Unternehmen & Exportkontrollen: Volkerrechtliche Zulassigkeit & Grenzen Extraterritorialer Ausfuhrbeschrankungen, with an English Summary. Nicolas Baron Von Behr. (ENG & GER.). 347p. 1996. 57.95 (*3-631-30367-X*) P Lang Pubng.

Multinationalism, Japanese Style: The Political Economy of Outward Dependency. Terutomo Ozawa. LC 79-84007. 314p. reprint ed. pap. 97.40 (*0-7837-0561-1*, 204090500019) Bks Demand.

Multinationality & Firm Performance. Ahmed Riahi-Belkaoui. LC 96-15510. 152p. 1996. 59.95 (*1-56720-077-X*, Quorum Bks) Greenwood.

Multinationals: Bank & Corporation Relationships. Olivier Pastre. Ed. by Edward I. Altman & Ingo I. Walter. LC 81-80869. (Contemporary Studies in Economic & Financial Analysis: Vol. 28). 316p. 1981. 78.50 (*0-89232-219-5*) Jai Pr.

Multinationals & Canada - U. S. Free Trade. Alan M. Rugman. LC 89-24814. 192p. 1990. text 34.95 (*0-87249-625-2*) U of SC Pr.

Multinationals & European Integration: Trade, Investment & Regional Development. Nicholas A. Phelps. LC 97-145347. (Regional Policy & Development Ser.: No. 14). 200p. 1996. pap. 36.95 (*1-85302-353-1*, Pub. by Jessica Kingsley) Taylor & Francis.

Multinationals & Indian Exports. K. K. Subrahmanian & P. Mohanan Pillai. 1979. 7.50 (*0-8364-0523-4*) S Asia.

Multinationals & Technology Transfer: The Canadian Experience. Ed. by Alan M. Rugman. LC 82-24650. 204p. 1983. 49.95 (*0-275-91072-5*, C1072, Praeger Pubs) Greenwood.

Multinationals & the National Interest: Playing by Different Rules. 1994. lib. bdg. 250.00 (*0-8490-8555-1*) Gordon Pr.

Multinationals & the Restructuring of the World Economy. Ed. by Michael J. Taylor & Nigel J. Thrift. (Geography & Environment Ser.). 400p. 1986. 65.00 (*0-7099-2457-7*, Pub. by C Helm) Routldge.

Multinationals & the U. S. Technology Base: Final Report of the Multinationals Project. (Illus.). 211p. (Orig.). (C). 1995. pap. text 20.00 (*0-7881-2498-6*) DIANE Pub.

Multinationals & World Trade. Mark Casson. 1986. text 60.00 (*0-04-338125-1*) Routledge.

***Multinationals As Flagship Firms: Regional Business Networks.** Alan Rugman & Joseph R. D'Cruz. LC 99-86516. (Illus.). 300p. 2000. text 72.00 (*0-19-829562-6*) OUP.

Multinationals from the Third World: Indian Firms Investing Abroad. Rajiv B. Lall. 112p. 1987. 14.95 (*0-19-561895-5*) OUP.

Multinationals in a Changing Environment: A Study of Business & Government Relations in the Third World. Adeoye Akinsanya. LC 83-24592. 208p. 1984. 69.50 (*0-275-91115-2*, C1115, Praeger Pubs) Greenwood.

Multinationals in Canada: Theory, Performance, Economic Impact. Alan M. Rugman. 1980. lib. bdg. 60.50 (*0-89838-036-7*) Kluwer Academic.

Multinationals in China: 40 Case Studies. 1996. 595.00 (*0-614-25471-X*) Econ Intel.

***Multinationals in Eastern Europe.** Patrick Artisien-Maksimenko. LC 99-54921. 304p. 2000. 75.00 (*0-312-23131-8*) St Martin.

Multinationals in India: Strategic Product Choices. Sushil Vachani. (C). 1991. 27.50 (*81-204-0550-1*, Pub. by Oxford IBH) S Asia.

Multinationals in Latin America. Robert Grosse. (International Business Ser.). 256p. 1989. 55.00 (*0-685-25041-5*) Routledge.

Multinationals in Latin America: The Politics of Nationalization. Paul E. Sigmund. 448p. 1980. 32.50 (*0-299-08260-1*) U of Wis Pr.

Multinationals in Latin America: The Politics of Nationalization. Paul E. Sigmund. LC 80-5115. 439p. reprint ed. pap. 136.10 (*0-608-09931-7*, 206926900003) Bks Demand.

Multinationals in the New Europe & Global Trade. Ed. by M. W. Klein & Paul J. Welfens. (Illus.). xv, 281p. 1991. 106.95 (*0-387-54634-0*) Spr-Verlag.

Multinationals of the South: New Actors in the International Economy. Ed. by Khushi M. Khan. 200p. 1987. text 45.00 (*0-312-55246-7*) St Martin.

Multinationals, Technology & National Competitiveness. Robert D. Pearce & Marina Papanastassiou. LC 99-31590. (New Horizons in International Business Ser.). 288p. 1999. 95.00 (*1-85898-822-5*) E Elgar.

Multinationals, the State, & Control of the Nigerian Economy. Thomas J. Biersteker. LC 86-25214. (Illus.). 365p. reprint ed. pap. 113.20 (*0-608-06385-1*, 206674600008) Bks Demand.

Multinationals, the State, & the Management of Economic Nationalism: The Case of Trinidad. Chaitram Singh. LC 88-28775. 156p. 1989. 57.95 (*0-275-93075-0*, C3075, Praeger Pubs) Greenwood.

Multinationals' Training Practices & Development. viii, 138p. (Orig.). 1981. pap. 13.50 (*92-2-102569-1*) Intl Labour Office.

Multinomial Probit: The Theory & Its Application to Demand Forecasting. Carlos Daganzo. LC 79-51674. (Economic Theory, Econometrics & Mathematical Economics Ser.). 1979. text 84.95 (*0-12-201150-3*) Acad Pr.

Multinuclear Approach to NMR Spectroscopy. Ed. by Joseph B. Lambert & Frank G. Riddell. 1983. text 247.50 (*90-277-1582-3*) Kluwer Academic.

Multinuclear Magnetic Resonance in Liquids & Solids - Chemical Applications. Ed. by Pierre Granger & Robin K. Harris. (NATO Advanced Science Institutes Series C: Mathematical & Physical Sciences). 488p. (C). 1990. lib. bdg. 200.50 (*0-7923-0986-3*) Kluwer Academic.

Multinuclear NMR. J. Mason. LC 87-12284. (Illus.). 660p. 1987. 155.00 (*0-306-42153-4*, Kluwer Plenum) Kluwer Academic.

Multiobjective Analysis in Water Resources. Ed. by Yacov Y. Haimes. (Conference Proceedings Ser.). 248p. 1984. 5.00 (*0-87262-406-4*) Am Soc Civil Eng.

Multiobjective & Stochastic Optimization Based on Parametric Optimization. Ed. by Collet's Holdings, Ltd. Staff. 1986. 49.00 (*0-7855-1181-4*, Pub. by Collets) St Mut.

Multiobjective & Stochastic Optimization Based on Parametric Optimization. Jurgen Guddat. 176p. (C). 1985. 70.00 (*0-7855-4979-X*, Pub. by Collets) St Mut.

Multiobjective Decision Support for Environmental Management. Ron Janssen. LC 92-24398. (Environment & Management Ser.: Vol. 2). 248p. (C). 1992. text 185.00 (*0-7923-1908-7*) Kluwer Academic.

Multiobjective Optimization: Behavioral & Computational Considerations. Jeffery L. Ringuest. 192p. (C). 1992. lib. bdg. 101.00 (*0-7923-9236-1*) Kluwer Academic.

Multiobjective Problems of Mathematical Programming: Proceedings of the International Conference on Multiobjective Problems of Mathematical Programming Held in Yalta, U. S. S. R., October 26-November 2, 1988. Ed. by A. Lewandowski & V. Volkovich. (Lecture Notes in Economics & Mathematical Systems Ser.: Vol. 351). (Illus.). vii, 314p. 1990. 46.00 (*0-387-53432-6*) Spr-Verlag.

***Multiobjective Scheduling by Genetic Algorithms.** Tapan P. Bagchi. LC 99-37211. 1999. write for info. (*0-7923-8561-6*) Kluwer Academic.

Multiobjective Water Resource Planning. David C. Major. (Water Resources Monograph Ser.: Vol. 4). (Illus.). 81p. 1977. 10.00 (*0-87590-305-3*) Am Geophysical.

Multiparadigm Design for C++ James O. Coplien. LC 98-36336. 304p. (C). 1998. pap. text 34.95 (*0-201-82467-1*) Addison-Wesley.

Multiparadigm Programming in LEDA. Timothy A. Budd. (Illus.). 480p. (C). 1994. 47.81 (*0-201-82080-3*) Addison-Wesley.

Multiparadigmatic Trend in Sociology. Ed. by Ulf Himmelstand. (Studia Sociologica Upsaliencia: No. 25). 197p. (Orig.). 1987. pap. text 41.00 (*91-554-2013-3*) Coronet Bks.

Multiparameter Bifurcation Theory. Ed. by Martin Golubitsky & J. Guckenheimer. LC 86-8106. (Contemporary Mathematics Ser.: Vol. 56). 387p. 1986. pap. 44.00 (*0-8218-5060-1*, CONM/56) Am Math.

Multiparameter Eigenvalue Problems & Expansion Theorems. H. Volkmer. (Lecture Notes in Mathematics Ser.: Vol. 1356). vi, 185p. 1988. 32.95 (*0-387-50479-6*) Spr-Verlag.

***Multiparameter Equations of State: An Accurate Source of Thermodynamic Property Data.** R. Span. LC 00-37341. 2000. write for info. (*3-540-67311-3*) Spr-Verlag.

Multiparameter Spectral Theory for Sturm-Liouville Operators. F. V. Atkinson. LC 92-26872. (Pitman Monographs & Surveys in Pure & Applied Mathematics). 1996. write for info. (*0-582-08175-0*) Longman.

Multiparticle Correlations & Nuclear Reactions, Corinne II. J. Aichelin & D. Ardouin. 500p. 1995. text 124.00 (*981-02-2118-5*) World Scientific Pub.

Multiparticle Dynamics. 500p. 1997. text 60.00 (*981-02-3146-6*) World Scientific Pub.

Multiparticle Dynamics. Ed. by D. Wegener & R. Baier. 716p. (C). 1991. text 164.00 (*981-02-0534-1*) World Scientific Pub.

Multiparticle Dynamics: Festschrift for Leon Van Hove & Proc. Alberto Giovannini & E. W. Kittel. 852p. 1990. text 161.00 (*981-02-0039-0*) World Scientific Pub.

Multiparticle Dynamics: Proceedings of the XXIIIth International Symposium. M. M. Block & A. R. White. 500p. 1994. text 109.00 (*981-02-1780-3*) World Scientific Pub.

Multiparticle Dynamics: Proceedings of the XXIV International Symposium. Alberto Giovannini et al. 628p. 1995. text 124.00 (*981-02-2128-2*) World Scientific Pub.

Multiparticle Dynamics: Proceedings of the XXV International Symposium, Stara Lesna, Slovakia 12 - 16 September 1995. Ed. by D. Bruncko et al. 600p. 1996. text 128.00 (*981-02-2478-8*, Ph-P2949) World Scientific Pub.

Multiparticle Dynamics, 1985. J. Grunhaus. 881p. (C). 1986. text 202.00 (*9971-5-0311-5*) World Scientific Pub.

Multiparticle Dynamics, 1983: Proceedings of the XIV International Symposium on Multiparticle Dynamics Lake Tahoe, U. S. A., June 22-27, 1983. Ed. by J. F. Gunion. 1193p. 1984. 128.00 (*9971-966-41-7*) World Scientific Pub.

Multiparticle Dynamics, 1984: Proceedings of the XV International Symposium on Multiparticle Dynamics, June 11-16, 1984, Lund, Sweden. Ed. by G. Gustafson et al. 904p. 1984. 130.00 (*9971-978-07-5*) World Scientific Pub.

Multiparticle Dynamics, 1986: Proceedings of the 17th International Symposium on Multiparticle Dynamics Seewinke Austria 16-20 June 1986. Ed. by M. Markytan et al. 904p. 1987. text 164.00 (*9971-5-0177-5*) World Scientific Pub.

Multiparticle Dynamics, 1987: Proceedings of the 18th International Symposium on Multiparticle Dynamics. Ed. by I. Dremin & K. Gulamov. 832p. (C). 1988. text 147.00 (*9971-5-0507-X*) World Scientific Pub.

Multiparticle Dynamics, 1982: Proceedings of XIII International Symposium on Multiparticle Dynamics Volendam, Netherlands, June 1982. Ed. by E. W. Kittel et al. 1028p. 1983. 130.00 (*9971-950-53-7*) World Scientific Pub.

Multiparticle Dynamics, 1988: 19th International Symposium. Daniel B. Schiff & J. T. Thanh Van. 732p. 1989. text 121.00 (*2-86332-060-2*) World Scientific Pub.

Multiparticle Dynamics 1981: Proceedings of XII International Symposium on Multiparticle Dynamics Notre Dame, Indiana, U. S. A., June 21-26, 1981. Ed. by W. D. Shephard & X. P. Kenney. xiv, 964p. 1982. 108.00 (*9971-950-30-8*) World Scientific Pub.

Multiparticle Dynamics, 1992: Twenty-Second International Symposium. C. Pajares. 700p. 1993. text 178.00 (*981-02-1239-9*) World Scientific Pub.

Multiparticle Production: Proceedings of the Perugia Workshop. Ed. by G. Pancheri et al. 496p. (C). 1989. text 138.00 (*9971-5-0884-2*) World Scientific Pub.

Multiparticle Production: Proceedings of the Shandong Workshop. Ed. by R. C. Hwa & Q. B. Xie. 568p. (C). 1988. text 139.00 (*9971-5-0490-1*) World Scientific Pub.

Multiparticle Quantum Scattering Applications to Nuclear, Atomic & Molecular Physics. Barry Simon. Ed. by D. G. Truhlar & Donald G. Truhlar. LC 97-2459. (IMA Volumes in Mathematics & Its Applications Ser.: Vol. 89). (Illus.). 416p. 1997. 59.95 (*0-387-94999-2*) Spr-Verlag.

Multiparticulate Oral Drug Delivery. Ghebre-Sellassie. (Drugs & the Pharmaceutical Sciences Ser.: Vol. 65). (Illus.). 496p. 1994. text 199.00 (*0-8247-9191-6*) Dekker.

Multiparty Democracy & Political Change: Constraints to Democratization in Africa. Ed. by John M. Mbaku & Julius O. Ihonvbere. LC 97-77172. (Illus.). 354p. 1998. text 72.95 (*1-84014-379-7*, Pub. by Ashgate Pub) Ashgate Pub Co.

Multiparty Government: The Politics of Coalition in Europe. Michael Laver & Norman Schofield. LC 98-33545. (Ann Arbor Paperbacks Ser.). 328p. 1998. pap. text 19.95 (*0-472-08562-X*, 08562) U of Mich Pr.

Multiparty Politics in Mississippi, 1877-1902. Stephen Cresswell. LC 94-44902. (Illus.). 240p. 1995. text 40.00 (*0-87805-770-6*) U Pr of Miss.

Multipath & Multi-Transmitter Interference in Spread-Spectrum Communication & Navigation Systems. Richard D. Van Nee. vii, 208p. (Orig.). 1995. pap. 67.50 (*90-407-1120-8*, Pub. by Delft U Pr) Coronet Bks.

Multiperson Decision Making Models Using Fuzzy Sets & Possibility Theory. Ed. by Janusz Kacprzyk & Mario Fedrizzi. LC 90-42123. (Theory & Decision Library: Pt. B). 360p. 1990. lib. bdg. 211.50 (*0-7923-0884-0*) Kluwer Academic.

Multiperspective Case Formulation: A Step Towards Treatment Integration. Priyanthy Weerasekera. 348p. (Orig.). (C). 1995. 38.50 (*0-89464-814-4*) Krieger.

Multiperspective Case Formulation: A Step Towards Treatment Integration. Priyanthy Weerasekera. 348p. (Orig.). 1996. pap. 29.50 (*0-89464-976-0*) Krieger.

Multiphase Biomedical Materials. Ed. by T. Tsuruta & A. Nakajima. 202p. 1989. 148.00 (*90-6764-109-X*, Pub. by VSP) Coronet Bks.

Multiphase Catalytic Reactors in the Oil Industry: Design, Modeling Scale-Up, IFP-CEDI, Solaize October, 1990. Ed. by Pierre Trambouze. 112p. 1991. pap. 300.00 (*2-7108-2221-0*, Pub. by Edits Technip) Enfield Pubs NH.

Multiphase Chemical Reactors: Design Methods, Vol. II. A. E. Rodrigues et al. 1981. text 184.00 (*90-286-2821-5*) Kluwer Academic.

Multiphase Flow & Fluidization: Continuum & Kinetic Theory. Dimitri Gidaspow. LC 93-9115. (Illus.). 467p. 1994. text 77.00 (*0-12-282470-9*) Acad Pr.

Multiphase Flow & Heat Transfer in Materials Processing: 1994 International Mechanical Engineering Congress & Exposition, Chicago, Illinois - November 6-11, 1994. (FED - HTD Ser.: Vol. 201, Vol. 297). 68p. 1994. 40.00 (*0-7918-1419-X*, G00914) ASME.

Multiphase Flow & Heat Transfer Second International Symposium, 2 vols., Set. Ed. by Xue-Jun Chen et al. 1500p. 1990. 405.00 (*1-56032-050-8*) Hemisp Pub.

Multiphase Flow & Transport Processes in the Subsurface: A Contribution to the Modeling of Hydrosystems. Rainer Helmig. Tr. by P. Schulz from GER. LC 97-30095. (Environmental Engineering Ser.). 380p. 1997. 84.95 (*3-540-62703-0*) Spr-Verlag.

Multiphase Flow in Porous Media. Ed. by P. M. Adler. 212p. (C). 1995. text 161.50 (*0-7923-3817-0*) Kluwer Academic.

Multiphase Flow in Porous Media. M. B. Allen, III et al. (Lecture Notes in Engineering Ser.: Vol. 34). 310p. 1988. 101.95 (*0-387-96731-1*) Spr-Verlag.

Multiphase Flow in Porous Media. Charles M. Marle. (Illus.). 272p. (C). 1981. 465.00 (*2-7108-0404-2*, Pub. by Edits Technip) Enfield Pubs NH.

Multiphase Flow in Wells & Pipelines. Ed. by U. S. Rohatgi & Madhav P. Sharma. (FED Ser.: Vol. 144). 180p. 1992. 50.00 (*0-7918-1129-8*, G00773) ASME.

Multiphase Flow, 1995: Proceedings of the Second International Conference on Multiphase Flow, April 3-7, 1995, Kyoto, Japan. International Conference on Multiphase Flow Staff. Ed. by Akimi Serizawa et al. LC 95-37508. 820p. 1996. 340.25 (*0-444-81811-1*) Elsevier.

Multiphase Flows with Droplets & Particles. C. T. Crowe et al. LC 97-24341. 496p. 1997. boxed set 79.95 (*0-8493-9469-4*) CRC Pr.

Multiphase Fluid Dynamics. Ed. by Shao L. Soo. 500p. 1990. text 119.95 (*0-566-09033-3*, Pub. by Avebry) Ashgate Pub Co.

Multiphase Migration of Organic Compounds in a Porous Medium: A Mathematical Model. L. M. Abriola. (Lecture Notes in Engineering Ser.: Vol. 8). (Illus.). viii, 232p. 1984. 33.95 (*0-387-13694-0*) Spr-Verlag.

***Multiphase '99: Frontier Technology Comes of Age: Proceedings of the 9th International Conference on Multiphase; Frontier Technology Comes of Age Held in Cannes, France, 1999.** Ed. by A. P. Burns. (BHR Group Conference Ser.: No. 35). 606p. 1999. 530.00 (*1-86058-212-5*) Prof Eng Pubng.

Multiphase Polymers. Ed. by Stuart L. Cooper & Gerald M. Estes. LC 79-10972. (Advances in Chemistry Ser.: No. 176). 1979. 71.95 (*0-8412-0457-8*) Am Chemical.

Multiphase Polymers. Ed. by Stuart L. Cooper & Gerald M. Estes. LC 79-10972. (Advances in Chemistry Ser.: Vol. 176). 656p. 1979. reprint ed. pap. 200.00 (*0-608-03869-5*, 206431600008) Bks Demand.

Multiphase Polymers: Blends & Ionomers. Ed. by R. A. Weiss & Leszek A. Utracki. LC 89-6987. (ACS Symposium Ser.: No. 395). (Illus.). xi, 512p. 1989. 99.95 (*0-8412-1629-0*) Am Chemical.

Multiphase Polymers: Blends & Ionomers. Ed. by R. A. Weiss & Leszek A. Utracki. LC 89-6987. (ACS Symposium Ser.: No. 395). (Illus.). 528p. 1989. reprint ed. pap. 163.70 (*0-608-03205-0*, 206372400007) Bks Demand.

Multiphase Processes in LMFBR Safety Analysis. A. V. Jones. (Ispra Courses on Nuclear Engineering & Technology Ser.: Vol. 5). x, 498p. 1984. text 489.00 (*3-7186-0089-7*) Gordon & Breach.

M

Multiphase Reactor & Polymerization System Hydrodynamics. Ed. by Nicholas P. Cheremisinoff & M. Abid. LC 95-51777. (Advances in Engineering Fluid Mechanics Ser.: Vol. 12). (Illus.). 656p. 1996. 145.00 (*0-88415-497-1*, 5497) Gulf Pub.

Multiphase Science & Technology, Vol. 2. Ed. by Jean-Marc Delhaye et al. (International Centre for Heat & Mass Transfer Ser.). (Illus.). 479p. 1986. 115.00 (*0-89116-282-8*) Hemisp Pub.

Multiphase Science & Technology, Vol. 3. Geoffrey F. Hewitt et al. 501p. 1987. 165.00 (*0-89116-561-4*) Hemisp Pub.

Multiphase Science & Technology, Vol. 5. Geoffrey F. Hewitt et al. (Multiphase Science & Technology Ser.). 750p. 1989. 140.00 (*0-89116-650-5*) Hemisp Pub.

Multiphase Science & Technology, Vol. 6. Geoffrey F. Hewitt et al. 1991. 240.00 (*0-89116-990-3*) Hemisp Pub.

Multiphase Science & Technology, Vol. 7. Hewitt et al. 1991. write for info. (*0-89116-982-2*) CRC Pr.

Multiphase Science & Technology, Vol. 8. Ed. by R. T. Lahey, Jr. et al. 808p. 1995. 99.50 (*1-56700-023-1*) Begell Hse.

Multiphase Transport: Fundamentals, Reactor Safety, Applications: Proceedings of the Multi-Phase Flow & Heat Transfer Symposium, 2nd, Miami Beach, April 16-18, 1979, 5 vols., Set. Multi-Phase Flow & Heat Transfer Symposium Staff. Ed. by T. Nejat Veziroglu. LC 80-11157. (Illus.). 3932p. 1980. text 875.00 (*0-89116-159-7*) Hemisp Pub.

Multiphase Transport in Porous Media, 1993. Ed. by R. R. Eaton et al. LC 91-58411. 155p. 1993. pap. 50.00 (*0-7918-1018-6*) ASME.

Multiphase Transport Particle Phenomena, 1. T. Nejat Veziroglu. 1989. 185.00 (*1-56032-030-3*) Hemisp Pub.

Multiphase Transport Particle Phenomena, Set, Vols. 1[00ad]3. T. Nejat Veziroglu. 1989. 515.00 (*1-56032-026-5*) Hemisp Pub.

Multiphonton Processes: Proceedings of the International Conference. S. L. Chin & D. K. Evans. 496p. 1994. text 109.00 (*981-02-1586-X*) World Scientific Pub.

***Multiphoton & Light Driven Multielectron Processes In.** Francois Kajzar & M. Vladimir Agranovich. 560p. 2000. pap. 90.00 (*0-7923-6272-1*) Kluwer Academic.

***Multiphoton & Light Driven Multielectron Processes in Organics: New Phenomena, Materials & Applications.** F. Kajzar & V. M. Agranovich. LC 00-29637. 2000. write for info. (*0-7923-6271-3*) Kluwer Academic.

***Multiphoton Processes: ICOMP VIII - 8th International Conference.** Ed. by Louis F. DiMauro et al. LC 00-104278. (AIP Conference Proceedings Ser.: Vol. 525). (Illus.). xv, 686p. 2000. 195.00 (*1-56396-946-7*) Am Inst Physics.

Multiphoton Processes: Proceedings of an International Conference at the University of Rochester, Rochester, NY, June 6-9, 1977. Joseph H. Eberly et al. LC 77-13021. (Wiley Series in Pure & Applied Optics). 439p. reprint ed. pap. 136.10 (*0-608-10212-1*, 201739900007) Bks Demand.

Multiphoton Processes in Atoms. N. B. Delone & Vladimir P. Krainov. LC 93-25345. (Atoms & Plasmas Ser.: Vol. 13). 1993. 136.95 (*0-387-56845-X*) Spr-Verlag.

***Multiphoton Processes in Atoms.** 2nd enl. ed. N. B. Delone & V. P. Krainov. LC 99-39037. (Series in Atoms, Molecular, Optical & Plasma Physics: Vol. 13). (Illus.). xii, 350p. 2000. 118.00 (*3-540-64615-9*) Spr-Verlag.

Multiphoton Processes, 1996: Proceedings of the 7th International Conference on Multiphoton Processes Held in Garmisch-Partenkirchen, Germany, 30 September-4 October 1996. Peter Lambropoulos & H. Walther. LC 97-3611. (Conference Ser.). 1997. 168.00 (*0-7503-0443-X*) IOP Pub.

Multiplan for Your Commodore 64. David W. Carroll. LC 84-22352. 200p. 1985. pap. 14.95 (*0-13-605130-8*) P-H.

Multiplan Managerial Accountng. Dascher. (C). 1993. text 45.00 (*0-03-003708-5*) Harcourt Coll Pubs.

Multiplan TM User's Guide. Erwin Schneider. LC 84-13037. 245p. reprint ed. pap. 76.00 (*0-7837-4516-8*, 204429500001) Bks Demand.

Multiplane Transesophageal Echocardiography. Ed. by Jos R. Roelandt & Natesa G. Pandian. 257p. 1995. text 115.00 (*0-443-07950-1*) Church.

Multiplatform Network Management. D. Edgar Taylor. (Computer Engineering Ser.). 1996. text 55.00 (*0-07-063295-2*) McGraw.

Multiple Access Protocols: Performance & Analysis. R. Rom & M. Sidi. Ed. by M. Gerla et al. (Telecommunications Networks & Computer Systems Ser.). (Illus.). viii, 177p. 1990. 60.95 (*0-387-97253-6*) Spr-Verlag.

Multiple AIDS-Related Loss: A Handbook for Understanding & Surviving a Perpetual Fall. David Nord. LC 96-53419. (Series in Death, Dying & Bereavement Ser.). 1997. pap. 29.95 (*1-56032-582-8*); boxed set 64.95 (*1-56032-581-X*) Taylor & Francis.

***Multiple & Generalized Nonparametric Regression.** John Fox. LC 00-24740. (University Papers). 2000. pap. write for info. (*0-7619-2189-3*) Sage.

***Multiple Approaches to Intelligent Systems: Proceedings of the 12th International Conference on Industrial & Engineering Applications of Artificial Intelligence & Expert Systems, IEA/AIE-99, Cairo, Egypt, May 31-June 3, 1999.** Ed. by I. F. Imam et al. LC 99-33306. (Lecture Notes in Computer Science Ser.: Vol. 1611). xix, 899p. 1999. pap. 99.00 (*3-540-66076-3*) Spr-Verlag.

Multiple Assessments for Multiple Intelligences. James Bellanca et al. LC 94-75761. 256p. 1994. pap. 35.95 (*0-932935-72-9*, NB1223) SkyLght.

Multiple Assessments for Multiple Intelligences. 3rd ed. James A. Bellanca et al. LC 97-75330. xii, 264 p. 1997. write for info. (*1-57517-076-0*) SkyLght.

Multiple Attribute Decision Making: An Introduction, No. 104. K. Paul Yoon & Ching-Lai Hwang. (Quantitative Applications in the Social Science Ser.). 96p. 1995. pap. text 10.95 (*0-8039-5486-7*) Sage.

Multiple Attribute Decision Making-Methods & Applications. C. L. Hwang & K. Yoon. (Lecture Notes in Economics & Mathematical Systems Ser.: Vol. 186). (Illus.). 259p. 1981. 38.00 (*0-387-10558-1*) Spr-Verlag.

Multiple Auditory Skills Super Pack. Jean G. DeGaetano. 118p. 1993. pap. text 26.00 (*1-886143-21-8*) Grt Ideas Tching.

Multiple Award Schedules: A Guide for Business & Government. Alison L. Doyle & Robert J. Sherry. 419p. 1995. ring bd. 99.00 (*1-56726-037-3*, B560) Mgmt Concepts.

Multiple Births. Elaine Landau. LC 96-40224. (First Bk.). 64p. (J). 1997. 22.00 (*0-531-20309-3*) Watts.

Multiple Blessings: From Pregnancy Through Childhood, a Guide for Parents of Twins, Triplets, or More. Betty Rothbart. LC 93-36250. 381p. 1994. pap. 12.00 (*0-688-11642-6*, Hearst) Hearst Commns.

***Multiple Bonding Silicon.** Michl. 250p. (C). 2000. text. write for info. (*0-471-32991-6*) Wiley.

Multiple Bonds & Low Coordination in Phosphorous Chemistry. Regitz. 125.00 (*0-86577-380-7*) Thieme Med Pubs.

Multiple Bonds Between Metal Atoms. F. Albert Cotton & Richard A. Walton. LC 88-91. 480p. (C). 1988. reprint ed. lib. bdg. 62.50 (*0-89464-291-X*) Krieger.

Multiple Bonds Between Metal Atoms. 2nd ed. F. Albert Cotton & Richard A. Walton. LC 92-15945. (Illus.). 816p. 1993. 125.00 (*0-19-855649-7*, Clarendon Pr) OUP.

Multiple Cantilevers in Fixed Prosthesis. Edgar O. Schweikert. 70p. 1988. 30.00 (*0-912791-54-3*, Ishiyaku EuroAmerica) Med Dent Media.

***Multiple Cat.** 1999. mass mkt. write for info. (*0-312-97041-2*) St Martin.

Multiple Chemical Interactions. Edward J. Calabrese. (Illus.). 736p. 1990. lib. bdg. 139.00 (*0-87371-146-7*, L146) Lewis Pubs.

Multiple Chemical Sensitivity: A Scientific Overview. Ed. by Frank L. Mitchell. LC 94-74818. (Illus.). 669p. 1995. text 135.00 (*0-911131-53-1*) Specialist Journals.

***Multiple Chemical Sensitivity: A Survival Guide.** Pamela Reed Gibson. 240p. 1999. pap. 16.95 (*1-57224-173-X*) New Harbinger.

Multiple Child. Andree Chedid. Tr. by Judith Radke from FRE. 144p. (Orig.). 1995. pap. 12.95 (*1-56279-079-X*) Mercury Hse Inc.

Multiple Choice. Janet Tashjian. LC 98-43349. (J). (gr. 5-10). 1999. 16.95 (*0-8050-6086-3*) H Holt & Co.

Multiple Choice & Free-Response Questions in Preparation for AP Calculus (AB) Examination. 7th ed. David Lederman. 1998. pap. 21.95 (*1-878621-49-1*) D & S Mktg Syst.

Multiple-Choice & Free Response Questions in Preparation for the AP Calculus (BC) Examination. 6th ed. David Lederman. 1998. pap. 21.95 (*1-878621-51-3*) D & S Mktg Syst.

Multiple Choice Practice Questions for Health Insurance Primer. rev. ed. Denise M. Gavaletz & C. Henry Young. 128p. 1998. pap. text 14.95 (*1-884803-11-3*) Werbel Pub.

Multiple Choice Practice Questions for Law New York Addendum - Life & Health Insurance. rev. ed. Denise M. Gavaletz. 112p. 1999. pap. text 12.95 (*1-884803-07-5*) Werbel Pub.

Multiple Choice Questions. H. L. Beynon et al. (Complete MRCP Ser.). (Illus.). 265p. (Orig.). 1991. pap. text 26.00 (*0-443-04308-6*) Church.

Multiple Choice Questions, Vol. 4. Bailey. 1984. text 8.00 (*0-7216-0951-1*) Harcourt.

***Multiple Choice Questions: For Macroeconomics.** Philip Mayer & Kenneth P. Gilliam. 102p. (C). 1999. spiral bd. 10.00 (*1-929659-01-6*) P Mayer.

***Multiple Choice Questions: For Microeconomics & Macroeconomics.** Philip Mayer & Kenneth P. Gillian. 164p. (C). 1999. spiral bd. 15.00 (*1-929659-00-8*) P Mayer.

Multiple Choice Questions Pt. 1: MRCP. 2nd ed. Ed. by H. L. Beynon et al. 328p. 1998. pap. write for info. (*0-443-05691-9*) Church.

Multiple Choice Questions Clinical Examination. Nicholas J. Talley & Simon O'Connor. (Illus.). 144p. (Orig.). 1996. pap. text 22.95 (*0-632-04153-6*) Blackwell Sci.

Multiple Choice Questions in Anatomy. write for info. (*0-340-50785-3*, Pub. by E A) Routldge.

Multiple Choice Questions in Clinical Pharmacology. James M. Ritter et al. 168p. 1995. pap. text 15.95 (*0-340-55932-2*, Pub. by E A) OUP.

Multiple Choice Questions in Dermatology. S. K. Goolamali. 1992. text 16.00 (*0-7234-1769-5*) Harcrt Hlth Sci Grp.

Multiple Choice Questions in Dermatology. S. K. Goolamali. 144p. (C). (gr. 13). 1992. pap. text 16.00 (*0-8151-3539-4*, 21909) Mosby Inc.

Multiple Choice Questions in Electrical Principles & Technology: Advanced GNVQ. J. O. Bird. LC 95-45356. 64p. 1995. spiral bd. write for info. (*0-7506-2667-4*) Buttrwrth-Heinemann.

Multiple Choice Questions in Human Physiology. 5th ed. Ian C. Roddie & William F. Wallce. 200p. 1997. pap. text 26.50 (*0-340-66234-4*, Pub. by E A) OUP.

Multiple Choice Questions in Mathematics for Engineering Advanced GNVQ. J. O. Bird. LC 95-45357. 64p. 1995. spiral bd. write for info. (*0-7506-2666-6*) Buttrwrth-Heinemann.

Multiple Choice Questions in Orthopaedics. M. Farooque & L. C. Gupta. 182p. (C). 1991. 100.00 (*81-85017-58-1*, Pub. by Interprint) St Mut.

Multiple Choice Questions in Paraclinical Subjects. L. C. Gupta. 292p. (C). 1991. 75.00 (*81-85017-59-X*, Pub. by Interprint) St Mut.

Multiple Choice Questions in Pathology. 3rd ed. Brown. pap. text. write for info. (*0-340-55164-X*, Pub. by E A) Routldge.

Multiple Choice Questions in Pharmacology: With Answers & Explanatory Comments. 2nd ed. D'Mello. pap. text. write for info. (*0-340-54321-3*, Pub. by E A) Routldge.

Multiple Choice Questions in Physiology: With Answers & Explanatory Comments. 3rd ed. Lynn Bindman et al. LC 96-46366. (An Arnold Publication). (Illus.). 144p. 1997. pap. text 17.50 (*0-340-67677-9*, Pub. by E A) OUP.

Multiple Choice Questions in Preparation for the AP Biology Examination. 2nd ed. Ralph V. Ricci. 115p. 1991. student ed. 15.95 (*1-878621-12-2*) D & S Mktg Syst.

Multiple Choice Questions in Preparation for the AP Biology Examination. 2nd ed. Ralph V. Ricci. 71p. (YA). (gr. 11-12). 1991. teacher ed. write for info. (*1-878621-13-0*) D & S Mktg Syst.

Multiple Choice Questions in Preparation for the AP Biology Examination. 3rd ed. Barbara Berthelsen. 1996. pap. 16.95 (*1-878621-41-6*) D & S Mktg Syst.

Multiple Choice Questions in Preparation for the AP Calculus (AB) Examination. David Lederman. 90p. 1991. student ed. 15.95 (*1-878621-01-7*) D & S Mktg Syst.

Multiple Choice Questions in Preparation for the AP Calculus (AB) Examination. 5th ed. David Lederman. 127p. 1991. student ed. 15.95 (*1-878621-00-9*) D & S Mktg Syst.

Multiple Choice Questions in Preparation for the AP Calculus (AB) Examination. 6th ed. David Lederman. 1994. pap. 16.95 (*1-878621-23-8*) D & S Mktg Syst.

Multiple Choice Questions in Preparation for the AP Calculus (BC) Examination. David Lederman. 90p. 1991. student ed. 15.95 (*1-878621-03-3*) D & S Mktg Syst.

Multiple Choice Questions in Preparation for the AP Calculus (BC) Examination. 4th ed. David Lederman. 121p. 1991. student ed. 15.95 (*1-878621-02-5*) D & S Mktg Syst.

Multiple Choice Questions in Preparation for the AP Calculus (BC) Examination. 5th ed. David Lederman. 1994. pap. 16.95 (*1-878621-33-5*) D & S Mktg Syst.

Multiple Choice Questions in Preparation for the AP Chemistry Examination. Kenneth Nealy. 129p. 1992. student ed. 12.95 (*1-878621-20-3*) D & S Mktg Syst.

Multiple Choice Questions in Preparation for the AP Chemistry Examination. 2nd ed. Kenneth Nealy. 116p. 1992. student ed. 15.95 (*1-878621-19-X*) D & S Mktg Syst.

Multiple Choice Questions in Preparation for the AP Chemistry Examination. 3rd ed. Peter E. Demmin. 1996. pap. 16.95 (*1-878621-39-4*) D & S Mktg Syst.

Multiple Choice Questions in Preparation for the AP Computer Science ("A" & "AB") Examination. 2nd ed. James Lyness. 69p. 1989. student ed. 15.95 (*1-878621-18-1*) D & S Mktg Syst.

Multiple Choice Questions in Preparation for the AP Computer Science Examination. 3rd ed. Leon Schram. (YA). (gr. 9-12). 1996. pap. 16.95 (*1-878621-37-8*) D & S Mktg Syst.

Multiple Choice Questions in Preparation for the AP Computer Science Examination. 4th ed. Leon Schram. 1998. pap. 16.95 (*1-878621-53-X*) D & S Mktg Syst.

Multiple Choice Questions in Preparation for the AP Economics ("Macro" & "Micro") Examination. George Davis. 76p. 1992. teacher ed. write for info. (*1-878621-22-X*); student ed. 15.95 (*1-878621-21-1*) D & S Mktg Syst.

Multiple Choice Questions in Preparation for the AP English Language & Composition Examination. Charles F. Winans & Richard Vogel. 71p. 1990. teacher ed. write for info. (*1-878621-17-3*) D & S Mktg Syst.

Multiple Choice Questions in Preparation for the AP English Language & Composition Examination. 2nd ed. Charles F. Winans & Richard Vogel. 85p. 1990. student ed. 15.95 (*1-878621-16-5*) D & S Mktg Syst.

Multiple Choice Questions in Preparation for the AP English Language Examination. 3rd ed. Richard Vogel & Charles F. Winans. 1993. pap. 16.95 (*1-878621-27-0*) D & S Mktg Syst.

Multiple Choice Questions in Preparation for the AP English Language Examination. 4th ed. Richard Vogel & Charles F. Winans. 1997. pap. 16.95 (*1-878621-47-5*) D & S Mktg Syst.

Multiple Choice Questions in Preparation for the AP English Literature & Composition Examination. Charles F. Winans & Richard Vogel. 73p. 1990. teacher ed. write for info. (*1-878621-15-7*) D & S Mktg Syst.

Multiple Choice Questions in Preparation for the AP English Literature & Composition Examination. 3rd ed. Charles F. Winans & Richard Vogel. 115p. 1990. student ed. 15.95 (*1-878621-14-9*) D & S Mktg Syst.

Multiple Choice Questions in Preparation for the AP English Literature Examination. 4th ed. Richard Vogel & Charles F. Winans. 1993. pap. 16.95 (*1-878621-25-4*) D & S Mktg Syst.

Multiple Choice Questions in Preparation for the AP English Literature Examination. 5th ed. Richard Vogel & Charles F. Winans. 1997. pap. 16.95 (*1-878621-45-9*) D & S Mktg Syst.

Multiple Choice Questions in Preparation for the AP European History Examination. Kenneth C. Gutwein. 67p. 1991. teacher ed. write for info. (*1-878621-09-2*) D & S Mktg Syst.

Multiple Choice Questions in Preparation for the AP European History Examination. 2nd ed. Kenneth C. Gutwein. 121p. 1991. student ed. 15.95 (*1-878621-08-4*) D & S Mktg Syst.

Multiple Choice Questions in Preparation for the AP European History Examination. 3rd ed. Ellis Wasson. 1996. pap. 16.95 (*1-878621-35-1*) D & S Mktg Syst.

Multiple Choice Questions in Preparation for the AP Physics ("B" & "C") Examination. Kenneth Cecire. 80p. (YA). (gr. 11-12). 1991. teacher ed. write for info. (*1-878621-11-4*); student ed. 15.95 (*1-878621-10-6*) D & S Mktg Syst.

Multiple Choice Questions in Preparation for the AP Physics (B&C) Examination. 2nd ed. Manu Patel. 1995. pap. 16.95 (*1-878621-31-9*) D & S Mktg Syst.

Multiple Choice Questions in Preparation for the AP United States Government & Politics Examination. Ethel Wood. 38p. 1991. teacher ed. write for info. (*1-878621-05-X*); student ed. 15.95 (*1-878621-04-1*) D & S Mktg Syst.

Multiple Choice Questions in Preparation for the AP United States Government & Politics Examination. 2nd ed. Ethel Wood. 1994. pap. 16.95 (*1-878621-29-7*) D & S Mktg Syst.

***Multiple Choice Questions in Preparation for the AP United States Government & Politics Examination.** 3rd ed. Ethel Wood. (Multiple Choice Questions in Preparation for the AP Examinations Ser.: Vol. 249). (Illus.). 249p. (YA). 2000. pap. 16.95 (*1-878621-55-6*) D & S Mktg Syst.

Multiple Choice Questions in Preparation for the AP United States History Examination. George B. Kirsch. 68p. 1991. teacher ed. write for info. (*1-878621-07-6*) D & S Mktg Syst.

Multiple Choice Questions in Preparation for the AP United States History Examination. 2nd ed. George B. Kirsch. 122p. 1991. student ed. 15.95 (*1-878621-06-8*) D & S Mktg Syst.

Multiple Choice Questions in Preparation for the AP United States History Examination. 3rd ed. Allan Proctor. 1996. pap. 16.95 (*1-878621-43-2*) D & S Mktg Syst.

Multiple Choice Questions in Psychiatry. Chris Ball & Maurice Lipsedge. LC 97-30184. (An Arnold Publication). 144p. 1998. pap. text 16.95 (*0-340-69227-8*) OUP.

Multiple Choice Questions in Veterinary Nursing, Vol. 1. Barbara Cooper. LC 97-185352. 132p. 1997. pap. text 25.00 (*0-7506-3611-4*) Buttrwrth-Heinemann.

Multiple Choice Questions in Veterinary Nursing, Vol. 2. Barbara Cooper. LC 97-185352. 132p. 1997. pap. text 25.00 (*0-7506-3612-2*) Buttrwrth-Heinemann.

***Multiple Choice Questions on Surgical Diagnosis.** R. Visvanathan & J. S. P. Lumley. (Illus.). 127p. 2000. pap. 28.50 (*0-7506-4730-2*) Buttrwrth-Heinemann.

Multiple Choice Questions Vet. Brightling. (C). 1996. pap. text 35.00 (*0-7020-2084-2*) Harcourt.

Multiple Cholecystokinin Receptors in the CNS. Ed. by Colin T. Dourish et al. (Illus.). 580p. 1992. text 130.00 (*0-19-857756-7*) OUP.

Multiple Church Staff Handbook see Church Staff Handbook: How to Build an Effective Ministry Team

Multiple-Class Teaching (UNESCO) John M. Braithwaite & Edward J. King. (Education Studies & Documents: No. 12). 1974. reprint ed. pap. 25.00 (*0-8115-1336-X*) Periodicals Srv.

Multiple Comparison Procedures. Larry E. Toothaker. (Quantitative Applications in the Social Sciences Ser.: Vol. 89). (Illus.). 96p. (C). 1992. pap. 10.95 (*0-8039-4177-3*) Sage.

Multiple Comparisons. Yosef Hochberg et al. LC 87-6226. (Probability & Mathematical Statistics Ser.). 480p. 1987. 164.95 (*0-471-82222-1*) Wiley.

Multiple Comparisons. Alan Klockars & Gilbert Sax. (Quantitative Applications in the Social Sciences Ser.: Vol. 61). 96p. (Orig.). 1986. pap. 10.95 (*0-8039-2051-2*) Sage.

Multiple Comparisons: Theory & Methods. Jason Hsu. 256p. (gr. 13). 1996. lib. bdg. 59.95 (*0-412-98281-1*, Chap & Hall CRC) CRC Pr.

***Multiple Comparisons & Multiple Tests Using the SAS System.** Peter H. Westfall et al. 416p. (C). 1999. pap. 47.95 (*1-58025-397-0*) SAS Publ.

Multiple Comparisons for Researchers. Larry E. Toothaker. 176p. (C). 1991. text 48.00 (*0-8039-4176-5*); pap. text 22.95 (*0-8039-4646-5*) Sage.

An Asterisk (*) at the beginning of an entry indicates that the title is appearing for the first time.

Multiple Comparisons for Researchers. Larry E. Toothaker. LC 91-22011. (Illus.). 176p. reprint ed. pap. 54.60 (*0-608-08562-6*, 206908500002) Bks Demand.

Multiple Comparisons, Selection, & Applications in Biometry: A Festschrift in Honor of Charles W. Dunnett. Fred M. Hoppe. LC 92-31061. (Statistics: Textbooks & Monographs: Vol. 134). (Illus.). 576p. 1992. text 190.00 (*0-8247-8895-8*) Dekker.

Multiple Conflicts over Multiple Uses. Ed. by Terry L. Anderson. 130p. (Orig.). (C). 1994. pap. text 14.95 (*0-8191-9748-3*, Pub. by Pol Eco Res) U Pr of Amer.

Multiple Congenital Anomalies: A Catalogue of Recognizable Syndromes. Robin M. Winter & Michael Baraitser. 1300p. 1991. 279.95 (*0-442-31316-0*) Chapman & Hall.

Multiple Criteria Analysis for Agricultural Designs. Carlos Romero & T. Rehman. (Developments in Agricultural Economics Ser.: No. 5). 258p. 1989. 148.25 (*0-444-87408-9*) Elsevier.

Multiple Criteria & Multiple Constraint Levels Linear Programming: Concept,Techniques & Applications. Shi Yongnan. 1999. 68.00 (*981-02-3738-3*) World Scientific Pub.

Multiple Criteria Decision Analysis in Regional Planning: Concepts, Methods, Applications. Fumiko Seo & Masatoshi Sakawa. (C). 1987. lib. bdg. 282.00 (*90-277-2641-8*) Kluwer Academic.

Multiple Criteria Decision Making. Ed. by A. Goicoechea et al. (Illus.). 485p. 1992. 76.95 (*0-387-97805-4*) Spr-Verlag.

Multiple-Criteria Decision Making: Concepts, Techniques, & Extensions. P. L. Yu. LC 85-16723. (Mathematical Concepts & Methods in Science & Engineering Ser.: Vol. 30). (Illus.). 402p. (C). 1985. 110.00 (*0-306-41965-3*, Plenum Trade) Perseus Pubng.

Multiple Criteria Decision Making: Proceedings of the Tenth International Conference. Ed. by G. H. Tzeng. LC 94-9326. 1994. write for info. (*0-387-94297-1*) Spr-Verlag.

Multiple Criteria Decision Making Vol. XII: Proceedings of the Twelfth International Conference. Ed. by Gunter U. Fandel & Thomas Gal. LC 96-51590. (Lecture Notes in Economics & Mathematical Systems Ser.: Vol. 448). (Illus.). 678p. 1997. pap. 109.00 (*3-540-62097-4*) Spr-Verlag.

Multiple Criteria Decision Making & Its Applications to Economic Problems. Enrique Ballestero & Carlos Romero. LC 98-36003. 1998. write for info. (*0-7923-8238-2*) Kluwer Academic.

Multiple Criteria Decision Making & Risk Analysis Using Microcomputers. Ed. by B. Karpak & S. Zoints. (NATO Asi Series F: Vol. 56). vi, 399p. 1989. 104.95 (*0-387-51396-5*) Spr-Verlag.

Multiple Criteria Decision Methods & Applications. Ed. by Gunter U. Fandel & Jaap Spronk. (Illus.). xiv, 404p. 1985. 104.95 (*0-387-15596-1*) Spr-Verlag.

Multiple Criteria Decision Support: Proceedings of the International Workshop Held in Helsinki, Finland, August 7-11, 1989. Ed. by A. Lewandowski et al. (Illus.). xii, 392p. 1991. 65.00 (*0-387-53895-X*) Spr-Verlag.

Multiple Criteria Decision Support in Engineering Design. Pratyush Sen. LC 98-26520. 1998. 64.95 (*3-540-19932-2*) Spr-Verlag.

Multiple Criteria Problem Solving: Proceedings of a Conference, Buffalo, N.Y., Aug. 22-26, 1977. Ed. by S. Zionts. (Lecture Notes in Economics & Mathematical Systems Ser.: Vol. 155). 1978. 36.00 (*0-387-08661-7*) Spr-Verlag.

Multiple Deformation in Ductile & Brittle Rocks: A Selection of Papers Presented at the International Conference on Multiple Deformation & Foliation Development, Bemagui, NSW, Australia, 4-10 Feb. 1984. Ed. by Paul L. Hancock. 242p. 1985. pap. 54.00 (*0-08-031419-8*, Pub. by PPL) Elsevier.

Multiple Diffraction of X-Rays in Crystals. S. L. Chang. (Solid-State Sciences Ser.: Vol. 50). (Illus.). 320p. 1984. 108.95 (*0-387-12955-3*) Spr-Verlag.

Multiple Discovery. Lamb. 1985. pap. 39.95 (*0-86127-025-8*) Ashgate Pub Co.

Multiple Disjunction Lemma for Smooth Concordance Embeddings. T. Goodwillie. LC 90-31826. (Memoirs Ser.: Vol. 86/431). 317p. 1990. pap. 37.00 (*0-8218-2493-7*, MEMO/86/431) Am Math.

Multiple Dopamine Receptors: Receptor Binding Studies in Dopamine Pharmacology. Milton Titeler. LC 83-1824. (Receptors & Ligands in Intercellular Communications Ser.: No. 1). (Illus.). 189p. reprint ed. pap. 58.60 (*0-7837-4299-1*, 204399100012) Bks Demand.

Multiple Drug Resistance in Cancer: Cellular, Molecular, & Clinical Approaches. Ed. by M. Clynes. LC 93-44250. 400p. (C). 1994. text 204.50 (*0-7923-2669-5*) Kluwer Academic.

Multiple Drug Resistance in Cancer 2: Molecular, Cellular & Clinical Aspects. Ed. by Martin CLynes. LC 98-50221. 344p. 1998. 162.00 (*0-7923-5272-6*) Kluwer Academic.

Multiple Employment Training Programs: Information Crosswalk on 163 Employment Training Programs. 51p. (Orig.). (C). 1995. pap. text 25.00 (*0-7881-1784-X*) DIANE Pub.

Multiple Employment Training Programs: Most Federal Agencies Do Not Know If Their Programs Are Working Effectively. (Illus.). 154p. (Orig.). (C). 1994. pap. text 35.00 (*0-7881-0777-1*) DIANE Pub.

Multiple Employment Training Programs: Overlap among Programs Raises Questions about Efficiency. (Illus.). 68p. (Orig.). (C). 1995. pap. text 20.00 (*0-7881-2221-5*) DIANE Pub.

Multiple Exposure: The Group Portrait in Photography. Leslie Tonkonow & Alan Trachtenberg. 80p. 1995. pap. 25.00 (*0-916365-44-1*) Ind Curators.

Multiple Exposures: Chronicles of the Radiation Age. Catherine Caufield. (Illus.). 312p. 1990. pap. 16.95 (*0-226-09785-4*) U Ch Pr.

Multiple Exposures, Promised Lands: Essays on Canadian Poetry & Fiction. Tom Marshall. 240p. 1992. pap. 18.95 (*1-55082-047-8*, Pub. by Quarry Pr) LPC InBook.

Multiple Facets of Therapeutic Transactions. Chaya Roth & Steven D. Kulb. LC 96-43562. 1997. 45.00 (*0-8236-3487-6*, BN03487) Intl Univs Pr.

Multiple-Factor Analysis: A Development & Expansion of the Vectors of Mind. Louis L. Thurstone. LC 47-2981. 555p. reprint ed. pap. 172.10 (*0-608-11189-9*, 200728500063) Bks Demand.

Multiple Family Housing. David Mackey. (Illus.). 1977. 32.50 (*0-8038-0164-5*) Archit CT.

Multiple-Field Isodose Charts see Atlas of Radiation Dose Distributions

Multiple Forms of Enzymes. Ed. by R. J. Haschen et al. (Advances in Clinical Enzymology Ser.: Vol. 2). 250p. 1982. 121.00 (*3-8055-2921-X*) S Karger.

Multiple Forms of Literacy: Teaching Literacy & the Arts. Piazza. LC 98-33602. 244p. (C). 1998. pap. text 30.00 (*0-13-095503-5*) P-H.

Multiple Frame Agricultural Surveys, 10. FAO Staff. (Fao Statistical Development Ser.). 1998. pap. text 16.00 (*92-5-104074-5*) Bernan Associates.

Multiple Goals in Discourse. Karen Tracy & Nicholas Coupland. 176p. 1990. 59.00 (*1-85359-099-1*, Pub. by Multilingual Matters) Taylor & Francis.

Multiple Gravity Assist Interplanetary Trajectories. A. V. Labunsky et al. (Earth Space Institute Book Series on Public & Private Sector Interest in Space: Vol. 2). (Illus.). 292p. 1998. text 84.00 (*90-5699-090-X*, ECU120, Harwood Acad Pubs) Gordon & Breach.

Multiple Identities & False Memories: A Sociocognitive Perspective. Nicholas P. Spanos. LC 96-9772. 371p. 1996. 29.95 (*1-55798-340-2*) Am Psychol.

Multiple Identities in a Single State. Ed. by Arora & Verney. (C). 1995. 40.00 (*81-220-0414-8*, Pub. by Konark Pubs) S Asia.

Multiple Identities of the Middle East. Bernard Lewis. LC 99-20735. 176p. 1999. pap. text 21.00 (*0-8052-4172-8*) Schocken.

Multiple Impulation for Nonresponse in Surveys. 9th ed. Donald B. Rubin. LC 89-28935. (Probability & Mathematical Statistics Ser.). 288p. 1987. 135.00 (*0-471-08705-X*) Wiley.

Multiple Indicators: An Introduction. John L. Sullivan & Stanley Feldman. (Quantitative Applications in the Social Sciences Ser.: Vol. 15). (Illus.). 87p. 1979. pap. 13.95 (*0-8039-1369-9*) Sage.

Multiple Integrals in the Calculus of Variations. Charles B. Morrey, Jr. (Grundlehren der Mathematischen Wissenschaften Ser.: Vol. 130). 1966. 126.95 (*0-387-03524-9*) Spr-Verlag.

Multiple Intelligence Approaches to Assessment: Solving the Assessment Conundrum. rev. ed. David G. Lazear. LC 94-216. (Illus.). 108p. 1998. pap. 39.00 (*0-913705-95-0*, 1029-F3) Zephyr Pr AZ.

Multiple Intelligences. Ed. by Karen Gutloff. (Teacher-to-Teacher Bks.). 96p. (Orig.). 1996. pap. 12.95 (*0-8106-2910-0*, 2910-0) NEA.

Multiple Intelligences: A Collection. 304p. (C). 1998. pap. text 31.00 (*0-205-29266-6*, Longwood Div) Allyn.

Multiple Intelligences: A Collection. Ed. by Robin Fogarty & James Bellanca. LC 95-75389. 304p. 1995. pap. 26.95 (*0-932935-91-5*) SkyLght.

Multiple Intelligences: Evaluating the Theory. Validating the Vision. Spencer Kagan. (Illus.). 200p. 1997. pap. text 25.00 (*1-879097-45-1*) Kagan Cooperative.

Multiple Intelligences: Helping Kids Discover the Many Ways to Be Smart. Pat Huggins. LC 98-171687. (ASSIST Program Ser.). (Illus.). 340p. 1997. pap. text 30.00 (*1-57035-116-3*, 18MI) Sopris.

Multiple Intelligences: The Theory in Practice. Howard Gardner. LC 92-53241. 272p. 1993. 23.00 (*0-456-01821-2*) Basic.

Multiple Intelligences: The Theory in Practice. Howard Gardner et al. LC 92-53241. 272p. 1999. pap. 18.00 (*0-465-01822-X*, Pub. by Basic) HarpC.

Multiple Intelligences Activities. Ed. by Karen J. Goldfluss. (Illus.). 400p. 1997. pap., teacher ed. 24.95 (*1-57690-464-4*, TCM2464) Tchr Create Mat.

Multiple Intelligences Activities Grades K-4. Deidre Wilkens. 304p. (J). (gr. k-4). 1997. pap. 24.95 (*1-55734-398-5*) Tchr Create Mat.

Multiple Intelligences Activities Grades 5-8. Julia Jasmine. 304p. (J). (gr. 5-8). 1997. pap. 24.95 (*1-55734-399-3*) Tchr Create Mat.

Multiple Intelligences & Assessment: A Collection of Articles. Ed. by Bruce Torff. LC 96-77781. (Illus.). 144p. (Orig.). 1997. pap. 23.95 (*1-57517-065-5*, 1451) SkyLght.

***Multiple Intelligences & Student Achievement: Success Stories from 6 Schools.** Linda Campbell & Bruce Campbell. LC 99-6910. 109p. 1999. pap. 15.95 (*0-87120-360-X*, 199274) ASCD.

Multiple Intelligences Centers & Projects. Carolyn Chapman & Lynn Freeman. LC 96-75264. (Illus.). 192p. (Orig.). 1996. pap. 30.95 (*1-57517-015-9*, 1449) SkyLght.

***Multiple Intelligences in the Classroom.** 2nd ed. Thomas Armstrong. (Illus.). 140p. 2000. pap. 22.95 (*0-87120-376-6*) ASCD.

Multiple Intelligences in the Mathematics Classroom. Hope Martin. LC 95-81187. (Illus.). 208p. (Orig.). 1996. pap. 25.95 (*1-57517-010-8*, 1421) SkyLght.

***Multiple Intelligences in the World: Quotations & Bibliographies for the Study, Understanding & Application of Verbal, Logical Mathematical, Musical, Bodily Kinesthetic, Visual Spatial, Intrapersonal, Interpersonal & Naturalist Intelligence.** 2nd ed. Maurice D. Fisher. 135p. 2000. spiral bd. 22.00 (*0-910609-39-X*) Gifted Educ Pr.

Multiple Intelligences Lesson Plan Book. Anne Bruetsch. 192p. 1995. ring bd. 37.00 (*1-56976-019-5*) Zephyr Pr AZ.

Multiple Intelligences Made Easy: Integrating MI into Your Curriculum. Bonita DeAmicis. LC 96-30400. 1997. pap. 30.00 (*1-56976-060-8*) Zephyr Pr AZ.

***Multiple Intelligences Pathways to Literacy: Making Smilies.** Shirley A. Freed. LC 98-61753. 164p. 1999. 26.95 (*1-57517-141-4*) SkyLght.

Multiple Intelligences Road to a Quality Classroom. Sally Berman. LC 95-79276. (Illus.). 104p. (Orig.). 1995. pap. 24.95 (*1-57517-005-1*, 1346) SkyLght.

Multiple Intelligences Road to an ELT Classroom. Michael Berman. 200p. 1998. pap. 35.00 (*1-899836-23-3*, Pub. by Crown Hse) LPC Group.

Multiple Iteration - Respectable Trial-&-Error. Meriwether L. Baxter. (Nineteen Ninety Fall Technical Meeting Ser.: Vol. 90FTM11). (Illus.). 12p. 1990. pap. text 30.00 (*1-55589-563-8*) AGMA.

Multiple Job-Holding among Farm Families. Ed. by Milton C. Hallberg et al. LC 90-43479. (Illus.). 362p. 1991. reprint ed. pap. 112.30 (*0-608-06859-4*, 206706500009) Bks Demand.

Multiple Journeys to One: Spiritual Stories of Integrating from Dissociative Identity Disorder. Ed. by Judy Dragon & Terry Popp. (Illus.). 240p. 1999. pap. 17.95 (*0-9672458-0-X*) Dancing Serpents.

Multiple Light Scattering Vol. 2: Tables, Formulas & Applications. H. C. Van de Hulst. 436p. 1980. text 140.00 (*0-12-710702-9*) Acad Pr.

Multiple Linear Regression: A Workbook, Syllabus, Readings; Problems & Exams. Isadore Newman & Carolyn Benz. 1979. pap. text 7.25 (*0-917180-07-0*) I Newman.

Multiple-Lines Insurance Production Segment C: Specialized Insurance & Bonds. Jerome Trupin & Daniel P. Hussey, Jr. LC 96-79432. 249p. (C). 1999. pap. text 41.00 (*0-89462-105-X*, 8203) IIA.

Multiple-Lines Insurance Production Segment A: Commercial Liability Insurance. Christopher J. Amrhein & Daniel P. Hussey, Jr. LC 96-79434. 262p. (C). 1999. pap. text 41.00 (*0-89462-103-3*, 8201) IIA.

Multiple-Lines Insurance Production Segment B: Other Commercial Insurance. Jerome Trupin & Daniel P. Hussey, Jr. LC 96-79433. 326p. (C). 1999. pap. text 41.00 (*0-89462-104-1*, 8202) IIA.

Multiple Listing. Anne U. Grant. (Sydney Teague Mystery Ser.: Vol. 1). 272p. 1998. mass mkt. 5.99 (*0-440-22551-5*) Dell.

Multiple Loving Without Jealousy. rev. ed. James L. Park. LC BF575.J4P37 1996. (Love among Authentic Persons Ser.: Vol. 3). 1995. pap. 3.75 (*0-89231-503-2*) Existential Bks.

Multiple Marriage: A Study of Polygamy in Light of the Bible. Robert J. Hitchens & Ernest Gambrell. LC 86-72269. 160p. (Orig.). (C). 1987. pap. 6.95 (*0-9617379-1-3*) Doulos Pubs.

Multiple Mazrui: Scholar, Ideologue, Philosopher & Artist. Chaly Sawere. 28p. 1992. 3.00 (*0-9633277-2-0*, Studies Global) Global Pubns.

Multiple Meanings for the Young Adult. Dorothy McCarr. (C). 1995. pap. text 9.00 (*0-89079-670-X*, 6972) PRO-ED.

***Multiple Measures: Accurate Ways to Assess Student Achievement.** Joan Ardovino et al. LC 00-21527. (Illus.). (J). 2000. write for info. (*0-7619-7680-9*) Corwin Pr.

Multiple Medical Impairment Study. MIB, Inc. Staff & SOA/ AAIM/ HOLUA-IHOU Mortality & Morbidity Liaison Committee. LC 98-39856. 1998. 95.00 (*0-9665356-0-X*) CMAS Bks.

Multiple Methods in Program Evaluation. Ed. by Melvin M. Mark & R. Lance Shotland. LC 85-644749. (New Directions for Evaluation Ser.: No. PE 35). 1987. pap. 22.00 (*1-55542-943-2*) Jossey-Bass.

Multiple Model Approaches to Nonlinear Modelling & Control. Ed. by Roderick Murray-Smith & Tor Johanson. LC 97-153224. (Series in Systems & Control). 416p. 1997. 79.95 (*0-7484-0595-X*, Pub. by Tay Francis Ltd) Taylor & Francis.

Multiple Modern Gods & Other Stories. Stanley Berne. LC 64-21952. (Illus.). 1964. pap. 22.50 (*0-913844-05-5*) Am Canadian.

Multiple Monitores Electro-Convulsive Therapy. Barry M. Maletzky. LC 80-23111. 256p. 1981. 143.00 (*0-8493-5940-6*, RC485, CRC Reprint) Franklin.

Multiple Muses of Virginia Woolf. Ed. by Dianne F. Gillespie. LC 92-36858. (Illus.). 288p. (C). 1993. text 37.50 (*0-8262-0882-7*) U of Mo Pr.

Multiple Myeloma. Gosta Gahrton & Brian G. Durie. (An Arnold Publication). (Illus.). 232p. (C). 1996. text 89.50 (*0-340-57603-0*) OUP.

Multiple Myeloma & Other Paraproteinaemias. I. W. Delamore. LC 86-9666. (Illus.). 377p. 1987. text 92.00 (*0-443-03134-7*) Church.

Multiple Myeloma & Related Disorders, Vol. 1. Henry A. Azar & Michael Potter. LC 72-13525. (Illus.). 440p. reprint ed. 136.40 (*0-8357-9426-1*, 201334900086) Bks Demand.

***Multiple Objective Control Synthesis.** Murti V. Salapaka & Mohammed A. Dahleh. LC 99-57253. (Lecture Notes in Control & Information Sciences Ser.: Vol. 252). xvi, 176p. 1999. pap. 62.80 (*1-85233-256-5*, Pub. by Spr-Verlag) Spr-Verlag.

Multiple Objective Decision Making. Mansooreh Mollaghasemi & J. Pet-Edwards. LC 96-45233. 100p. 1996. pap. 15.00 (*0-8186-7407-5*) IEEE Comp Soc.

Multiple Objective Decision Making for Land, Water & Environmental Management. Ed. by Samir A. El-Swaify. LC 97-48330. (Illus.). 600p. 1998. lib. bdg. 79.95 (*1-57444-091-8*) St Lucie Pr.

Multiple-Objective Decision Making Methods for Transportation. Ernest R. Alexander et al. (Publications in Architecture & Urban Planning: No. R85-3). (Illus.). iv, 85p. 1985. 11.00 (*0-938744-42-9*) U of Wis Ctr Arch-Urban.

Multiple Offense. Gene Cox. (Illus.). vi, 172p. 1997. pap. 18.95 (*0-9669672-0-8*) G Cox.

Multiple-Option Marching Band Techniques. 3rd ed. Robert E. Foster. 48p. (C). 1979. student ed., wbk. ed. 3.95 (*0-88284-087-8*, 5069) Alfred Pub.

Multiple-Option Marching Band Techniques. 3rd ed. Robert E. Foster. 300p. (C). 1978. reprint ed. pap. text 19.95 (*0-88284-066-5*, 5012) Alfred Pub.

Multiple Organ Dysfunction & Failure: Pathophysiology & Clinical Implications. 2nd ed. Ed. by Virginia H. Secor. (Illus.). 480p. (C). (gr. 13). 1996. text 59.95 (*0-8151-4325-7*, 29188) Mosby Inc.

Multiple Organ Dysfunction Syndrome: Examining the Role of Eicosanoids & Procoagulants. John G. Williams. (Medical Intelligence Unit Ser.). 158p. 1996. 99.00 (*1-57059-325-6*) Landes Bioscience.

***Multiple Organ Failure: Pathophysiology, Prevention & Therapy.** Ed. by Arthur Baue et al. LC 99-39600. (Illus.). 600p. 2000. 135.00 (*0-387-98733-9*) Spr-Verlag.

Multiple Organizational Management Software (MOM) Advantage International, Inc. Staff. 1992. 1995.00 (*1-56756-008-3*, OD300I); 995.00 (*1-56756-009-1*, OD301I); student ed. 35.00 (*1-56756-019-9*) Advant Intl.

Multiple Orgasms. limited ed. Wallace Markfield. 1977. 35.00 (*0-89723-006-X*) Bruccoli.

***Multiple Origins: Edward Westermarck in Search of Mankind.** Juhani Ihanus. LC 99-26338. (European Studies in the History of Science & Ideas: Vol. 6). 358p. (C). 1999. pap. text 51.95 (*0-8204-4306-9*) P Lang Pubng.

Multiple Ownership in Television Broadcasting. Herbert H. Howard. Ed. by Christopher H. Sterling. LC 78-21720. (Dissertations in Broadcasting Ser.). 1980. lib. bdg. 35.95 (*0-405-11759-0*) Ayer.

Multiple Paths of Midlife Development. Margie E. Lachman & Jacquelyn B. James. LC 96-29289. (Studies on Successful Midlife Development). 1997. 52.00 (*0-226-46758-9*) U Ch Pr.

Multiple Paths to Literacy. 4th ed. Joan P. Gipe. LC 97-39968. 451p. (C). 1998. pap. text 64.00 (*0-13-785080-8*, Prentice Hall) P-H.

Multiple Periodic Variable Stars: Proceedings of the I.A.U. Symposium, No. 29, Budapest, 1975. rev. ed. International Astronomical Union Staff. Ed. by Walter S. Fitch. (Astrophysics & Space Science Library: No. 60). 1977. lib. bdg. 129.50 (*90-277-0766-9*) Kluwer Academic.

Multiple Persoenlichkeiten: Ueberlebende extremer Gewalt. Michaela Huber. (GER.). 416p. 1995. pap. 18.00 (*3-596-12160-4*, Pub. by Fischer Tasch) Intl Bk Import.

Multiple Personalites, Multiple Disorders: Psychiatric Classification & Media Influence. Carol S. North et al. LC 92-49904. (Oxford Psychiatry Ser.: No. 1). (Illus.). 296p. (C). 1993. text 45.00 (*0-19-508095-5*) OUP.

Multiple Personality, Allied Disorders & Hypnosis. Eugene L. Bliss. 282p. 1986. text 45.00 (*0-19-503658-1*) OUP.

Multiple Personality & Dissociation, 1791-1992: A Complete Bibliography. 2nd ed. Ed. by Carole Goettman et al. LC 94-7179. xii, 156p. 1994. pap. 9.95 (*0-9629164-5-5*) Sidran Pr.

Multiple Personality Disorder: Diagnosis, Clinical Features & Treatment. Colin A. Ross. LC 89-14608. 400p. 1989. 90.00 (*0-471-61515-3*) Wiley.

Multiple Personality Disorder from the Inside Out. Ed. by Barry M. Cohen et al. LC 91-60530. (Illus.). xxii, 245p. (Orig.). 1991. pap. 16.95 (*0-9629164-0-4*) Sidran Pr.

Multiple Personality Disorders in the Netherlands: A Study on Reliability & Validity of the Diagnosis. Suzette Boon & Nel Draijer. 262p. 1993. pap. 46.00 (*90-265-1361-5*) Swets.

Multiple Perspective: Wilhelm Raabe's Third-Person Narratives of the Braunschweig Period. Irene Stocksieker Di Maio. (German Language & Literature Monographs: 11). iv, 149p. 1981. 43.00 (*90-272-4004-3*) J Benjamins Pubng Co.

Multiple Perspective Analyses of Classroom Discourse. Ed. by Judith Green et al. LC 87-33368. (Advances in Discourse Processes Ser.: Vol. 28). 356p. 1988. pap. 42.50 (*0-89391-469-X*); text 78.50 (*0-89391-204-2*) Ablx Pub.

Multiple Perspectives: A Guide to Qualitative Music Therapy Research. Henk Smeijsters. LC 99-164237. 266p. (C). 1997. pap. text 30.00 (*0-9624080-7-7*) Barcelona Pubs.

Multiple Perspectives for Decision Making: Bridging the Gap Between Analysis & Action. Harold A. Linstone. 400p. 1984. 41.00 (*0-444-00803-9*) P-H.

***Multiple Perspectives on Mathematics Teaching & Learning.** Jo Boaler. LC 00-35567. (International Perspectives on Mathematics Education Ser.). 2000. write for info. (*1-56750-535-X*) Ablx Pub.

***Multiple Perspectives on Mathematics Teaching & Learning: International Perspectives on Mathematics Education Ser.** Ed. by Jo Boaler. Vol. V.1. 2000. lib. bdg. write for info. (*1-56750-534-1*) Greenwood.

M

An Asterisk (*) at the beginning of an entry indicates that the title is appearing for the first time.

M

Multiple Perspectives on Play in Early Childhood Education. Ed. by Olivia N. Saracho & Bernard Spodek. LC 97-12087. (SUNY Series, Early Childhood Education). 323p. (C). 1998. text 74.50 (*0-7914-3615-2*); pap. text 24.95 (*0-7914-3616-0*) State U NY Pr.

Multiple Perspectives on Risk & Regulation: The Case of Deliberate Release of Genetically Engineered Organisms into the Environment. Smita K. Siddhanti. LC 91-439. (Environment: Problems & Solutions Ser.). 410p. 1991. text 25.00 (*0-8240-0438-8*) Garland.

Multiple Photon Infrared Laser Photophysics & Photochemistry. V. N. Bagratashvili et al. xii, 512p. 1985. text 237.00 (*3-7186-0269-5*) Gordon & Breach.

Multiple Plot in English Renaissance Drama. Richard Levin. LC 75-130306. 1994. lib. bdg. 22.00 (*0-226-47526-3*) U Ch Pr.

Multiple Points of Immersed Manifolds. Ralph J. Herbert. LC 81-12772. (Memoirs of the American Mathematical Society Ser.: No. 34/250). 60p. 1981. pap. 16.00 (*0-8218-2250-0*, MEMO/34/250) Am Math.

Multiple Points of Immersed Manifolds. Ralph J. Herbert. LC 52-42839. (American Mathematical Society Ser.: No. 250). (Illus.). 75p. reprint ed. pap. 30.00 (*0-608-09181-2*, 205268500002) Bks Demand.

Multiple Poses. Colin Smith. 80p. 1993. pap. 8.95 (*0-921331-24-X*, Pub. by Tsunami Edits) Barnholden.

Multiple Pregnancy: Epidemiology, Gestation & Perinatal Outcome. Louis G. Keith et al. (Illus.). 722p. 1995. 98.00 (*1-85070-666-2*) Prthnon Pub.

Multiple Pregnancy & Delivery. Ed. by Stanley A. Gall. LC 96-3728. (Illus.). 368p. (C). (gr. 13). 1996. text 69.00 (*0-8151-3406-1*, 24729) Mosby Inc.

Multiple Primary Cancers in Connecticut & Denmark. Alfred I. Neugut et al. LC 98-52750. 484p. 1999. write for info. (*0-683-30124-1*) Lppncott W & W.

Multiple Problem Youth. David Huizinga et al. (Research in Criminology Ser.). (Illus.). 240p. 1989. 51.95 (*0-387-96925-X*) Spr-Verlag.

Multiple Psychotherapy. Rudolf Dreikurs et al. LC 84-71164. 146p. (Orig.). 1984. pap. 10.00 (*0-918560-31-4*) Adler Sch Prof Psy.

Multiple Purpose River Development: Studies in Applied Economic Analysis. John V. Krutilla & Otto Eckstein. (Resources for the Future Ser.). 316p. 1970. reprint ed. pap. 10.00 (*0-8018-1091-4*) Johns Hopkins.

Multiple Realities: A Study of Thirteen American High Schools. Barbara B. Tye. 412p. (Orig.). 1985. pap. text 29.00 (*0-8191-4463-0*); lib. bdg. 61.50 (*0-8191-4462-2*) U Pr of Amer.

Multiple Realities in Clinical Practice. John S. Kafka. LC 88-38238. 208p. (C). 1989. 35.00 (*0-300-04350-3*) Yale U Pr.

Multiple Realities of International Mediation. Marieke Kleiboer. LC 97-33555. 252p. 1998. 55.00 (*1-55587-769-9*) L Rienner.

Multiple Reciprocity Boundary Element Method. Ed. by A. J. Nowak & A. C. Neves. 256p. 1994. 110.00 (*1-85312-277-7*) Computational Mech MA.

Multiple Reciprocity Boundary Element Method. Ed. by A. J. Nowak & A. C. Neves. LC 93-74381. (Computational Engineering Ser.). 256p. 1994. 110.00 (*1-56252-201-9*, 2777) Computational Mech MA.

Multiple Reflections: Talks on the Yoga Vasistha. Swami Venkatesananda. 180p. 1988. pap. 8.00 (*0-9612762-1-5*) Chiltern Yoga.

Multiple Regression. Leona S. Aiken & Stephen G. West. (Illus.). 150p. 1991. 48.00 (*0-8039-3605-2*) Sage.

Multiple Regression: A Primer. Paul D. Allison. LC 98-40066. (Pine Forge Press Series in Research Methods & Statistics). 1999. pap. 19.95 (*0-7619-8533-6*) Sage.

Multiple Regression Causal Analysis. McKee J. McClendon. LC 93-86171. 358p. (C). 1994. boxed set 55.00 (*0-87581-384-4*, MR) F E Peacock Pubs.

Multiple-Regression in Behavioral Research: Explanation & Prediction. 3rd ed. Elazar J. Pedhazur. LC 96-78486. 1074p. (C). 1997. text 91.50 (*0-03-072831-2*, Pub. by Harcourt Coll Pubs) Harcourt.

Multiple Regression in Practice. William Berry & Stanley Feldman. (Quantitative Applications in the Social Sciences Ser.: Vol. 50). 1985. 13.95 (*0-8039-2054-7*) Sage.

Multiple Residence Inspector. Jack Rudman. (Career Examination Ser.: C-2842). 1994. pap. 29.95 (*0-8373-2842-X*) Nat Learn.

Multiple Residence Inspector II. Jack Rudman. (Career Examination Ser.: C-3078). 1994. pap. 34.95 (*0-8373-3078-5*) Nat Learn.

Multiple Risk Factors in Cardiovascular Disease: Strategies of Prevention of Coronary Heart Disease, Cardiac Failure, & Stroke. Ed. by Antonio M. Gotto, Jr. et al. LC 98-15831. (Medical Science Symposia Ser.). 388p. 1998. 119.00 (*0-7923-5023-5*) Kluwer Academic.

Multiple Risk Factors in Cardiovascular Diseases. Ed. by Antonio M. Gotto, Jr. et al. LC 92-49870. (Medical Science Symposia Ser.: Vol. 1). 284p. 1992. text 166.50 (*0-7923-1938-9*) Kluwer Academic.

Multiple Risk Factors in Cardiovascular Diseases: Vascular & Organ Protection. Ed. by A. M. Gotto, Jr. et al. LC 95-22833. (Medical Science Symposia Ser.: Vol. 8). 456p. 1995. text 170.00 (*0-7923-3503-1*) Kluwer Academic.

Multiple Roles of Clinical Faculty. Robert L. Gilstrap & Kathleen Beattie. LC 96-67183. (Fastback Ser.: No. 397). 40p. (Orig.). 1996. pap. 3.00 (*0-87367-597-5*) Phi Delta Kappa.

Multiple Scale & Singular Perturbation Methods. J. Kevorkian & J. D. Cole. (Applied Mathematical Sciences Ser.: Vol. 114). (Illus.). 632p. 1996. 59.00 (*0-387-94202-5*) Spr-Verlag.

Multiple Scattering in Solids. A. Gonis & W. H. Butler. LC 99-14736. (Graduate Texts in Contemporary Physics Ser.). (Illus.). 352p. 1999. 59.95 (*0-387-98853-X*) Spr-Verlag.

Multiple Scattering Processes: Inverse & Direct. H. H. Natsuyama et al. LC 75-22363. 1975. write for info. (*0-201-04104-9*) Addison-Wesley.

*__Multiple Sclerosis__ Nathan Aaseng. LC 99-34864. 2000. 25.00 (*0-531-11531-3*) Watts.

Multiple Sclerosis. Jan De Vries. (By Appointment Only Ser.). 125p. 1985. pap. 13.95 (*0-906391-98-9*, Pub. by Mainstream Pubng) Trafalgar.

Multiple Sclerosis. Fitzger. 1998. pap. 11.00 (*0-7225-3142-7*) Thorsons PA.

Multiple Sclerosis. Susan D. Gold. LC 95-33344. (Health Watch Ser.). (J). 1996. lib. bdg. 15.95 (*0-89686-863-X*, Crstwood Hse) Silver Burdett Pr.

Multiple Sclerosis. Susan D. Gold. LC 95-33344. (Health Watch Ser.). (J). (gr. 5). 1998. 5.95 (*0-382-39972-2*, Crstwood Hse) Silver Burdett Pr.

Multiple Sclerosis. Louis J. Rosner & Shelley Ross. 256p. 1992. per. 11.00 (*0-671-77809-9*, Fireside) S&S Trade Pap.

Multiple Sclerosis. Edward Susman. LC 99-17210. (Diseases & People Ser.). (Illus.). 128p. (YA). (gr. 6 up). 1999. lib. bdg. 20.95 (*0-7660-1185-2*) Enslow Pubs.

Multiple Sclerosis. 2nd ed. Ed. by Jorg Kesselring. (Illus.). 226p. (C). 1996. text 69.95 (*0-521-48018-3*) Cambridge U Pr.

Multiple Sclerosis, No. 51. Donald W. Paty & George C. Ebers. LC 97-3052. (Contemporary Neurology Ser.: No. 50). (Illus.). 612p. (C). 1997. text 150.00 (*0-8036-6784-1*) OUP.

Multiple Sclerosis: A Dragon with a Hundred Heads. Peter P. Michael. LC 79-10954. 1981. 22.95 (*0-87949-170-1*) Ashley Bks.

Multiple Sclerosis: A Guide for Families. Rosalind C. Kalb. LC 97-49252. 207p. 1998. pap. 24.95 (*1-888799-14-5*) Demos Medical.

Multiple Sclerosis: A Guide for Patients & Their Families. 2nd ed. Ed. by Labe C. Scheinberg & Nancy J. Holland. 288p. 1987. text 27.50 (*0-88167-254-8*) Lppncott W & W.

Multiple Sclerosis: A Guide for Patients & Their Families. 2nd ed. Ed. by Labe C. Scheinberg & Nancy J. Holland. 288p. 1987. pap. text 20.00 (*0-88167-255-6*) Lppncott W & W.

Multiple Sclerosis: A Guide for the Newly Diagnosed. Nancy J. Holland et al. LC 96-35928. 128p. 1996. pap. 21.95 (*1-888799-06-4*) Demos Medical.

Multiple Sclerosis: A Neuropsychiatric Disorder. Ed. by Uriel Halbreich. LC 92-22041. (Progress in Psychiatry Ser.: No. 37). 192p. 1993. text 32.00 (*0-88048-463-2*, 8463) Am Psychiatric.

Multiple Sclerosis: A Personal Exploration. Alexander Burnfield. (Illus.). 192p. (Orig.). 1997. pap. 14.95 (*0-285-65018-1*, Pub. by Souvenir Pr Ltd) IPG Chicago.

Multiple Sclerosis: A Self-Care Guide to Wellness. Nancy J. Holland et al. LC 98-7854. (Illus.). 164p. 1998. pap., spiral bd. 9.00 (*0-929819-09-8*) Paralyzed Vets.

Multiple Sclerosis: A Self-Help Guide to Its Management. Judy Graham. 160p. (Orig.). 1990. pap. 12.95 (*0-89281-242-7*) Inner Tradit.

*__Multiple Sclerosis: Advances in Clinical Trial Design, Treatment & Future Perspectives.__ Ed. by D. E. Goodkin & R. A. Rudick. (Illus.). xviii, 364p. 1998. pap. 89.00 (*1-85233-033-3*) Spr-Verlag.

Multiple Sclerosis: Advances in Trial Design, Treatment, & Future Perspectives. Ed. by D. E. Goodkin & R. A. Rudick. LC 96-12736. 364p. 1997. 129.50 (*3-540-76018-0*) Spr-Verlag.

Multiple Sclerosis: Approaches to Management. Ed. by Lorraine De Souza & Jo Campling. (Therapy in Practice Ser.). 140p. 1990. pap. 23.00 (*0-412-32230-7*, A4411) Chapman & Hall.

Multiple Sclerosis: Clinical & Pathogenetic Basis. Cedric S. Raine. (Illus.). 448p. 1996. text 125.00 (*0-412-30890-8*, Pub. by E A) OUP.

Multiple Sclerosis: Control of the Disease. W. R. Russell. 84p. 1976. pap. text 18.25 (*0-08-021002-3*, Pergamon Pr) Elsevier.

*__Multiple Sclerosis: Diagnosis, Medical Management & Rehabilitation.__ Jack S. Burks & Kenneth P. Johnson. LC 00-35858. (Illus.). 2000. write for info. (*1-888799-35-8*) Demos Medical.

Multiple Sclerosis: How I Won the Battle. Yvonne A. Fischer. 70p. 1999. pap. write for info. (*0-7392-0134-4*, PO3055) Morris Pubng.

Multiple Sclerosis: Subject, Reference & Research Guide. Oliver A. Fraser. LC 88-47590. 150p. 1988. 47.50 (*0-88164-558-3*); pap. 44.50 (*0-88164-559-1*) ABBE Pubs Assn.

Multiple Sclerosis: The Facts You Need. Paul O'Connor. (Your Personal Health Ser.). 156p. 1999. pap. 14.95 (*1-55209-367-0*) Firefly Bks Ltd.

Multiple Sclerosis: The Questions You Have - The Answers You Need. Rosalind C. Kalb. LC 96-25890. 468p. 1996. pap. 39.95 (*1-888799-04-8*) Demos Medical.

*__Multiple Sclerosis: The Questions You Have - The Answers You Need.__ 2nd rev. ed. Rosalind C. Kalb. 484p. 2000. pap. 39.95 (*1-888799-43-9*, Pub. by Demos Medical) SCB Distributors.

Multiple Sclerosis: Your Legal Rights. 2nd ed. Lanny Perkins & Sara Perkins. LC 99-22996. 224p. 1999. pap. 21.95 (*1-888799-31-5*) Demos Medical.

Multiple Sclerosis - Questions & Answers. David Barne. (Illus.). 120p. 2000. pap. 17.95 (*1-873413-86-6*) Merit Pub Intl.

Multiple Sclerosis & Having a Baby: Everything You Need to Know about Conception, Pregnancy & Parenthood. Judy Graham. LC 99-18416. 160p. 1999. pap. 12.95 (*0-89281-788-7*, Heal Arts VT) Inner Tradit.

Multiple Sclerosis & Other Demyelinating Diseases see Handbook of Clinical Neurology

Multiple Sclerosis Diet Book: A Low-Fat Diet for the Treatment of M.S., Heart Disease & Stroke. Roy L. Swank & Barbara Dugan. LC 86-16819. (Illus.). 416p. 1987. 29.95 (*0-385-23279-9*) Doubleday.

Multiple Sclerosis East & West. Ed. by Y. Kuroiwa & L. T. Kurland. (Illus.). vi, 398p. 1983. 172.25 (*3-8055-3674-7*) S Karger.

Multiple Sclerosis Fact Book. 2nd ed. Richard Lechtenberg. LC 94-25306. (Illus.). 235p. (C). 1995. pap. text 23.95 (*0-8036-0074-7*) Davis Co.

*__Multiple Sclerosis in Clinical Practice.__ Ed. by Stanley Van den Noort & Nancy J. Holland. (Illus.). 256p. 1999. pap. text 34.95 (*1-888799-25-0*) Demos Medical.

Multiple Sclerosis Patient Education Manual. William H. Stuart et al. 304p. 1997. ring bd. 99.00 (*0-8342-0757-5*, 20757) Aspen Pub.

Multiple Sclerosis Research in Europe. Ed. by O. R. Hommes. 1986. text 248.00 (*0-85200-917-8*) Kluwer Academic.

Multiple Sclerosis Through History & Human Life. Richard M. Swiderski. LC 98-37977. 216p. 1998. pap. 29.50 (*0-7864-0562-7*) McFarland & Co.

Multiple Self. Ed. by Jon Elster. (Studies in Rationality & Social Change). 286p. 1987. pap. text 25.95 (*0-521-34683-5*) Cambridge U Pr.

Multiple Selves, Multiple Voices: Working with Trauma, Violation, & Dissociation. Phil Mollon. LC 96-1476. (Series in Clinical Psychology). 228p. 1999. pap. 45.00 (*0-471-96330-5*) Wiley.

Multiple-Service-Level Highway Bridge Railing Selection Procedures. (National Cooperative Highway Research Program Report Ser.: No. 239). 161p. 1981. 10.40 (*0-309-03274-1*, NR239) Transport Res Bd.

Multiple Sigma & PCP Receptor Ligands: Mechanisms for Neuromodulation & Protection? Ed. by J. M. Kamenka & E. F. Domino. LC 91-68518. (Illus.). 971p. 1992. text 95.00 (*0-916182-09-6*) NPP Bks.

Multiple Spaces: The Poetry of Rafael Alberti. Salvador Jimenez-Fajardo. (Monografias A Ser.: No. 106). 166p. (C). 1985. 51.00 (*0-7293-0199-0*, Pub. by Tamesis Bks Ltd) Boydell & Brewer.

Multiple Staff & the Larger Church. Lyle E. Schaller. LC 79-20796. 1980. pap. 9.95 (*0-687-27297-1*) Abingdon.

Multiple Stage in Spain During the Fifteenth & Sixteenth Centuries. William H. Shoemaker. LC 78-137076. 150p. 1973. reprint ed. lib. bdg. 55.00 (*0-8371-5539-8*, SHMS, Greenwood Pr) Greenwood.

Multiple Statistical Decision Theory: Recent Developments. S. S. Gupta & D. Y. Huang. (Lecture Notes in Statistics Ser.: Vol. 6). 112p. 1981. 42.95 (*0-387-90572-3*) Spr-Verlag.

Multiple Stochastic Integral. David D. Engel. LC 82-8740. (Memoirs of the American Mathematical Society Ser.: Vol. 38/265). 83p. 1982. pap. 16.00 (*0-8218-2265-9*, MEMO/38/265) Am Math.

*__Multiple Streams of Income.__ Robert G. Allen. LC 99-58145. (Illus.). 300p. 2000. text 24.95 (*0-471-38180-2*, Wiley Heyden) Wiley.

Multiple Stresses in Ecosystems. Joseph J. Cech et al. LC 97-49109. 224p. 1998. lib. bdg. 59.95 (*1-56670-309-3*) CRC Pr.

Multiple Stressors in Ecological Risk & Impact Assessment. Jeffery Foran & Susan Ferenc. LC 99-17281. (Illus.). 1999. pap. 30.00 (*1-880611-32-5*, SETAC Pr) SETAC.

*__Multiple Stressors in Ecological Risk & Impact Assessment: Approaches to Risk Estimation.__ Ed. by Susan A. Ferenc & Jeffery A. Foran. (Illus.). 2000. write for info. (*1-880611-40-6*, SETAC Pr) SETAC.

Multiple Subject Assessment for Teachers (MSAT) Jack Rudman. (National Teacher Examination Ser.: Vol. NT-9). 1994. pap. 23.95 (*0-8373-8469-9*) Nat Learn.

Multiple System Atrophy. N. Quinn & Gregor Wenning. 256p. 1999. text 85.00 (*0-7506-2359-4*) Buttrwrth-Heinemann.

Multiple Systems Organ Failure: Hepatic Regulation of Systemic Host Defense. George M. Matuschak. (Illus.). 408p. 1993. text 199.00 (*0-8247-9059-6*) Dekker.

Multiple Tabby Weaves, Based on Dr. William G. Bateman's Manuscript. Ed. by Virginia I. Harvey. LC 81-80587. (Guild Monographs: No. 35). (Illus.). 90p. 1981. pap. 14.95 (*0-916658-37-6*) Shuttle Craft.

Multiple-Target Tracking with Radar Applications. Samuel S. Blackman. LC 85-73389. (Artech House Radar Library). (Illus.). 464p. 1986. reprint ed. pap. 143.90 (*0-608-00563-0*, 206144600009) Bks Demand.

Multiple Task Performance. Ed. by Diane Damos. 350p. 1991. 110.00 (*0-85066-757-7*, Pub. by Tay Francis Ltd) Taylor & Francis.

Multiple Teacher Training Programs: Information on Budgets, Services & Target Groups. (Illus.). 35p. (Orig.). (C). 1995. pap. text 25.00 (*0-7881-1785-8*) DIANE Pub.

Multiple Tracking: Math 2: A Self-Instruction Workbook for Visual Accuracy, Reusable Edition. Kitty Wehrli. 88p. 1971. 9.00 (*0-87879-758-0*, Ann Arbor Div) Acad Therapy.

Multiple Trauma. R. Wilder. (Progress in Critical Care Medicine Ser.: Vol. 1). (Illus.). xii, 288p. 1984. 82.75 (*3-8055-3823-5*) S Karger.

Multiple Trigonometric Sums. Ed. by A. A. Karacuba et al. LC 82-18403. (Proceedings of the Steklov Institute of Mathematics Ser.: Vol. 151). 126p. 1982. pap. 67.00 (*0-8218-3067-8*, STEKLO/151) Am Math.

Multiple Unit - Agency Response for Fire. (Training in a Box Ser.). 36p. 1998. ring bd. 49.00 (*1-57927-037-9*) APCO Inst.

Multiple Use Job Descriptions: A Guide to Analysis, Preparation, & Applications for Human Resources Managers. Philip C. Grant. LC 88-23664. 164p. 1989. 55.00 (*0-89930-416-8*, GJI/, Quorum Bks) Greenwood.

Multiple-Use Management: The Economics of Public Forestlands. Michael D. Bowes & John V. Krutilla. LC 89-4018. 357p. 1989. 48.95 (*0-915707-41-1*) Resources Future.

Multiple Uses: Positive Substitution, Problem Solutions, Relaxation, & Goal Achievements, Set-MS. Russell E. Mason. 1975. pap. 60.00 incl. audio (*0-89533-008-3*) F I Comm.

*__Multiple-Valued Logic: ISMVL '98.__ Ed. by IEEE Staff. (Illus.). 1998. 120.00 (*0-8186-8371-6*, IEEE Inst Elec) IEEE Comp Soc.

Multiple-Valued Logic: Proceedings of the 27th International Symposium on Multiple-Valued Logic, Antigonish, Nova Scotia, Canada, 1997. LC 01-95623. 300p. 1997. pap. 115.00 (*0-8186-7910-7*) IEEE Comp Soc.

*__Multiple-Valued Logic: Proceedings of the 29th IEEE International Symposium on Multiple-Value Logic, 1999, Freiburg im Breisgau.__ 302p. 1999. pap. 120.00 (*0-7695-0161-3*) IEEE Comp Soc.

Multiple-Valued Logic Design: An Introduction. G. Epstein. (Illus.). 384p. 1993. 263.00 (*0-7503-0210-0*) IOP Pub.

Multiple-Valued Logic, 26th International Symposium on (ISMVL '96) LC 01-95623. 300p. 1996. pap. 60.00 (*0-8186-7392-3*, PRO7392) IEEE Comp Soc.

Multiple Victimization of Children: Conceptual, Developmental, Research & Treatment Issues. Ed. by B. B. Rossman & Mindy S. Rosenberg. LC 98-10643. 341p. 1998. 49.95 (*0-7890-0361-9*, Maltreatment & Trauma Pr); pap. 24.95 (*0-7890-0382-1*, Maltreatment & Trauma Pr) Haworth Pr.

Multiple Victims, Multiple Causes: How to Recognize & Stop the Disease of Violence. Philip D. Burns. LC 95-69176. 217p. (Orig.). 1995. 12.95 (*1-887431-50-0*) Sytech Res.

Multiple View Geometry. Richard Hartley & Andrew Zisserman. (Illus.). 650p. (C). 1999. text 74.95 (*0-521-62304-9*) Cambridge U Pr.

Multiple Voices: Narrative in Systemic Family Psychotherapy. Renos K. Papadopoulos & John Byng-Hall. LC 97-44057. 304p. (C). 1998. pap. 24.99 (*0-415-92085-X*) Routledge.

Multiple Voices: Narrative in Systemic Family Psychotherapy. Renos K. Papadopoulos & John Byng-Hall. LC 97-44057. 304p. (C). 1998. 75.00 (*0-415-92084-1*) Routledge.

Multiple Voices for Ethnically Diverse Exceptional Learners, 1999. Ed. by Bridgie Alexis Ford. 60p. 1999. pap. 16.00 (*0-86586-295-8*, D5217) Coun Exc Child.

Multiple Voices in Feminist Film Criticism. Ed. by Diane Carson et al. LC 93-13743. 560p. 1994. pap. 19.95 (*0-8166-2273-6*) U of Minn Pr.

Multiple Voices, Multiple Texts: Reading in the Secondary Content Areas. Rosen & Dornan. LC 97-27064. (Orig.). (C). 1997. pap. text 35.00 (*0-86709-417-6*, 0417, Pub. by Boynton Cook Pubs) Heinemann.

Multiple Worlds of Child Writers: Friends Learning to Write. Anne H. Dyson. (Early Childhood Education Ser.). 336p. 1989. text 42.00 (*0-8077-2972-8*); pap. text 22.95 (*0-8077-2971-X*) Tchrs Coll.

Multiple's Guide to Harmonized Family Living: A Healthy Alternative, or Prelude, to Integration. Tammy C. Whitman & Susan C. Shore. LC 94-70635. (Illus.). 128p. (Orig.). 1994. pap. 16.95 (*1-884390-03-X*) Art Endeavors.

Multiplex Man. James Patrick Hogan. 2000. mass mkt. 6.99 (*0-671-57819-7*) PB.

Multiplex Man: And the One Penny Orange Mystery. Morris Ackerman. LC 97-91725. 324p. (Orig.). 1997. pap. 9.95 (*0-9657743-0-9*) Chevy Chase.

Multiplexer Reference Manual. Gilbert Held. LC 92-19944. 200p. 1992. 145.00 (*0-471-93484-4*) Wiley.

Multiplexing. 1997. 44.00 (*1-56091-936-1*, SP-1224) Soc Auto Engineers.

Multiplexing & Fiberoptics: SAE International Congress & Exposition 1994, 28 papers. (Special Publications). 276p. 1994. pap. 86.00 (*1-56091-464-5*, SP-1012) Soc Auto Engineers.

*__Multiplexing & Networking.__ Ed. by Ron Jurgen. (Progress in Technology Ser.). 700p. 1999. 89.00 (*0-7680-0472-1*, PT-78) Soc Auto Engineers.

Multiplicacion Rap in Spanish. unabridged ed. Brad Caudle & Richard Caudle. (Rock 'N Learn Ser.). (SPA., Illus.). 20p. (J). (gr. 3 up). 1994. pap. 9.95 incl. audio (*1-878489-27-5*, RL927) Rock N Learn.

Multiplication see Math Mini-Tests

Multiplication see Discovering Math

Multiplication. (Flashboards Ser.). 60p. (J). (gr. 2-5). bds. 2.99 (*1-56293-596-8*, McClanahan Book) Learn Horizon.

Multiplication. Balloon Books Staff. 1999. pap. text 3.95 (*0-8069-7823-6*) Sterling.

Multiplication. Sheila Cato. LC 98-6377. (Question of Math Book Ser.). (Illus.). 32p. (J). (gr. 1-4). 1999. 25.26 (*1-57505-321-7*, Carolrhoda) Lerner Pub.

Multiplication. S. Harold Collins. (Straight Forward Math Ser.). (Illus.). 34p. (J). (gr. 4-6). 1986. pap. 3.95 (*0-931993-07-5*, GP-007) Garlic Pr OR.

*__Multiplication.__ Dalmatian Press Staff. (J). (gr. 3-4). 1999. pap. text 2.99 (*1-57759-137-2*) Dalmatian Pr.

Multiplication. Fearon Globe Staff. 1991. pap. 8.95 (*0-8224-4487-9*) Fearon Teacher Aids.

Multiplication. Schaffer, Frank, Publications Staff. (Help Your Child Learn Ser.). (Illus.). 24p. (J). (gr. 3-5). 1978. student ed. 3.98 (*0-86734-010-X*, FS-3011) Schaffer Pubns.

Multiplication. Kim Thompson & Karen Hilderbrand. (Rap with the Facts Ser.). (J). (gr. k-6). 1988. 8.99 incl. audio (*0-9632249-7-2*, TWIN 101) Twin Sisters.

Multiplication. Kim Thompson et al. (Rap with the Facts Ser.). (Illus.). 24p. (J). (gr. 2-6). 1993. student ed. 9.98 incl. audio (*1-882331-19-2*, TWIN 401) Twin Sisters.

Multiplication. Contrib. by Twin Sisters Productions Staff. 1997. 19.95 incl. audio compact disk (*1-57583-027-2*) Twin Sisters.

Multiplication. Susan Yelvington. (Basic Skills Ser.). (Illus.). 32p. (J). (gr. 3-4). 1998. pap. text 4.95 (*0-88724-463-7*, CD-2131) Carson-Dellos.

Multiplication see Learn Math Quickly: Addition, Subtraction, the Multiplication Tables, Multiplication, & Division: Video Plus Workbook A

Multiplication: Basic Math for the Job & Personal Use. Wood. (YA - Adult Education Ser.). 1993. pap., wbk. ed. 5.95 (*0-538-70763-1*) S-W Pub.

Multiplication: Factors 1-12. H. S. Lawrence. (Puzzles & Practice Ser.). (ENG & SPA., Illus.). 30p. (Orig.). (J). (gr. 3-6). 1992. pap., student ed. 3.95 (*0-931993-52-0*, GP-052) Garlic Pr OR.

Multiplication: Math Sticker Workbook. DK Publishing Staff. 1997. pap. 4.95 (*0-7894-2189-5*) DK Pub Inc.

Multiplication: Unlock the Biblical Factors to Multiply Your Effectiveness in Ministry. Tommy Barnett. 1997. 14.99 (*0-88419-450-7*) Creation House.

Multiplication - Long Division: Sing & Learn. John Carratello. 1994. pap. 9.95 incl. audio (*0-7604-0020-2*, JPC002) Wrner Bros.

Multiplication & Division. (Home Workbooks Ser.). (Illus.). 64p. (J). (gr. 3-6). 1995. pap., wbk. ed. 2.49 (*0-88724-348-7*, CD-6845) Carson-Dellos.

Multiplication & Division. Kate Cole. (Step Ahead Plus Ser.). (Illus.). 64p. (J). (gr. 3-4). 1986. pap., wbk. ed. 3.49 (*0-307-03656-1*, 03656, Goldn Books) Gldn Bks Pub Co.

***Multiplication & Division.** Dalmatian Press Staff. (J). (gr. 3-4). 1999. pap. text 2.29 (*1-57759-150-X*) Dalmatian Pr.

***Multiplication & Division.** Carol Greenes et al. (Illus.). 60p. (J). (gr. 4-7). 1999. pap. 12.95 (*0-7690-0003-7*) Seymour Pubns.

Multiplication & Division. NCPTA Staff. (Illus.). (J). 1996. mass mkt. 6.95 (*0-340-62984-3*, Pub. by Hodder & Stought Ltd) Trafalgar.

Multiplication & Division. Virginia Slachman. 1997. 4.95 (*1-55708-247-2*, MCR437) McDonald Pub Co.

Multiplication & Division, Vol. 2657. Ed. by Janet Bruno. (Child-Centered Math Ser.: Vol. 7). (Illus.). 80p. 1997. pap. 4.98 (*1-57471-240-3*, 2657) Creat Teach Pr.

Multiplication & Division: Combo. Lorie De Young & Louanne Winkler. (Math Combo Bks.: No. 02203). (Illus.). 64p. (Orig.). (gr. 3). 1997. pap., wbk. ed. 3.25 (*0-88743-139-9*, 02203) Sch Zone Pub Co.

Multiplication & Division in Mammalian Cells. Renato Baserga. LC 75-25166. (Biochemistry of Disease Ser.: No. 6). (Illus.). 255p. reprint ed. pap. 79.10 (*0-7837-0864-5*, 204117200019) Bks Demand.

Multiplication & Division Made Easy. Catherine F. De Bie. Ed. by Betty Weigand. (Illus.). 72p. (Orig.). (J). 1990. pap. 10.95 (*0-9627585-0-7*) M & D Made Easy.

Multiplication & Division Tables. Patricia S. Davidson & Robert E. Willcutt. 1995. pap. 9.50 (*0-201-48021-2*) Addison-Wesley.

Multiplication & Division with Rod Patterns & Graph Paper. Patricia Davidson & Robert E. Willcutt. (Illus.). 64p. (J). (gr. 3-8). 1980. pap. text 9.50 (*0-914040-82-0*) Cuisenaire.

Multiplication & Energy & Construction: Division & Medicine. Learning Achievement Corporation Staff. Ed. by Therese A. Zak. (MATCH Ser.: Bk. 2). (Illus.). 144p. 1981. text 13.96 (*0-07-037112-1*) McGraw.

Multiplication Basic Facts. Bob DeWeese. (Mathematics Ser.). (Illus.). 32p. (J). (gr. 3-5). 1996. pap., teacher ed. 2.95 (*1-55799-464-1*, 4066) Evan-Moor Edu Pubs.

Multiplication Basic Facts. Susan Yelvington. (Basic Skills Ser.). (Illus.). 32p. (J). (gr. 2-3). 1998. pap. text 4.95 (*0-88724-462-9*, CD-2130) Carson-Dellos.

Multiplication Basic Facts: Basic Multiplication Skills. Bob DeWeese. Ed. by Jo Ellen Moore. (Illus.). 30p. (J). (gr. 3-5). 1995. pap., wbk. ed. 2.50 (*1-58610-085-8*, Learn on the Go) Learn Horizon.

Multiplication Book. Becky Daniel & Charlie Daniel. 64p. (J). (gr. 2-6). 1980. 8.99 (*0-916456-76-5*, GA 191) Good Apple.

Multiplication Country. unabridged ed. Jim Ponder et al. (Rock 'N Learn Ser.). (Illus.). 22p. (YA). (gr. 3 up). 1993. pap. 12.99 incl. audio (*1-878489-25-9*, RL925) Rock N Learn.

Multiplication Facts. (Home Workbooks Ser.). (Illus.). 64p. (Orig.). (J). (gr. 3-4). 1995. pap., wbk. ed. 2.49 (*0-88724-346-0*, CD-6843) Carson-Dellos.

Multiplication Facts in Five Minutes a Day. Susan C. Anthony. (Math Facts in Five Minutes a Day Ser.). 120p. 1999. reprint ed. teacher ed., per. 13.95 (*1-879478-22-6*, 072) Instr Res Co.

Multiplication, Grade 3. Marilyn Burns. (Math by All Means Ser.). 144p. 1995. pap. text. write for info. (*0-941355-04-7*) Math Solns Pubns.

***Multiplication I: Facts 0-81.** Dave Hudson. Ed. by Kathy Rogers. (Best Value Drillbooks Ser.). 32p. 1999. 3.99 (*1-56472-137-X*) Edupress Inc.

***Multiplication II: Multi-Digit.** Dave Hudson. Ed. by Kathy Rogers. (Best Value Drillbooks Ser.). 32p. 1999. 3.99 (*1-56472-138-8*) Edupress Inc.

Multiplication in Minutes. pap. text, teacher ed. 24.95 (*0-9651769-0-8*) Krimsten Publng.

Multiplication Memorization Made Fun & Easy. Daniel Quinn & Larry Davis. 128p. (J). (gr. 1-3). 1993. teacher ed. 9.95 (*0-9629746-1-7*) Texas Trends.

***Multiplication Objects in Monoidal Categories.** Jose Escoriza Lopez. 181p. 2000. lib. bdg. 79.00 (*1-56072-823-X*) Nova Sci Pubs.

Multiplication of Distributions: A Tool in Mathematics, Numerical Engineering, & Theoretical Physics. Jean F. Colombeau. LC 92-39265. 1993. write for info. (*3-540-56288-5*); 36.95 (*0-387-56288-5*) Spr-Verlag.

Multiplication of Distributions & Applications to Partial Differential Equations. Michael Oberguggenberger. LC 92-4751. (Pitman Research Notes in Mathematics Ser.: No. 259). 330p. 1992. pap. 102.30 (*0-608-05230-2*, 206576700001) Bks Demand.

Multiplication of Viruses. S. E. Luria. (Protoplasmatologia Ser.: Vol. 4, Pts. 3, 4a, 4b, 5). (ENG & GER., Illus.). iv, 118p. 1958. 32.50 (*0-387-80488-9*) Spr-Verlag.

Multiplication of Whole Numbers see Basic Mathematics

***Multiplication 1 Digit X 1 Digit 0-5.** Robert W. Skarlinski. 25p. 1998. 6.95 (*1-58532-067-6*) Basic Ed Materials.

***Multiplication 1 Digit X 1 Digit 0-9.** Robert W. Skarlinski. 25p. 1998. 6.95 (*1-58532-068-4*) Basic Ed Materials.

Multiplication Practice Puzzles. Marsha Sanger. (Illus.). 128p. (Orig.). (J). (gr. 3-6). 1996. pap. 12.95 (*1-56500-040-4*) Gldn Educ.

Multiplication Rap. unabridged ed. Brad Caudle & Richard Caudle. (Rock 'N Learn Ser.). (Illus.). 24p. (J). (gr. 3 up). 1991. pap. 12.99 incl. audio (*1-878489-07-0*, RL907) Rock N Learn.

Multiplication Rap. unabridged ed. Brad Caudle & Richard Caudle. (Rock n' Learn Ser.). (Illus.). 24p. (J). (gr. 3 up). 1994. pap. 12.95 incl. audio compact disk (*1-878489-37-2*, RL937) Rock N Learn.

Multiplication Rock. unabridged ed. Brad Caudle & Richard Caudle. (Rock 'n Learn Ser.). (Illus.). 24p. (J). (gr. 3 up). 1992. pap. 12.99 incl. audio (*1-878489-05-4*, RL905) Rock N Learn.

Multiplication Songs. Kathy Troxel. (Illus.). 24p. (J). (gr. 3-6). 1998. pap. text 3.00 incl. audio (*1-883028-01-9*) Audio Memory.

Multiplication Table by the "Method of Tricks" - A Pictorially Rapid & Permanent Mastery. Benjamin B. Hughes. (Illus.). 24p. (J). (gr. k up). 1994. pap. text 10.00 (*1-885028-00-8*) Times Table.

Multiplication Tables see Learn Math Quickly: Addition, Subtraction, the Multiplication Tables, Multiplication, & Division: Video Plus Workbook A

***Multiplication Tables: With Re-Usable Stickers.** (Fun to Learn Ser.). (Illus.). 10p. (J). (ps-5). 1999. pap. 1.99 (*1-58279-012-4*) Trident Pr Intl.

Multiplication Tables & Coloring Book. Hillary McElderry. 1993. pap. 8.50 (*0-906212-85-5*, Pub. by Tarquin Pubns) Parkwest Pubns.

***Multiplication Tables Plus.** Nelson A. John. 64p. (YA). (gr. 3 up). 1999. 9.95 (*1-877633-48-8*) Luthers.

***Multiplication 3 Digit X 1 Digit Non-Carrying 0-999.** Robert W. Skarlinski. 25p. 1998. 6.95 (*1-58532-071-4*) Basic Ed Materials.

***Multiplication 3 Digit X 1 Digit Carrying 0-999.** Robert W. Skarlinski. 25p. 1998. 6.95 (*1-58532-072-2*) Basic Ed Materials.

***Multiplication 3 Digit X 3 Digit Non-Carrying 0-999.** Robert W. Skarlinski. 25p. (J). 1998. 6.95 (*1-58532-042-0*) Basic Ed Materials.

***Multiplication 3 Digit X 3 Digit Carrying 0-999.** Robert W. Skarlinski. 25p. (J). 1998. 6.95 (*1-58532-043-9*) Basic Ed Materials.

***Multiplication 2 Digit X 1 Digit Carrying 0-99.** Robert W. Skarlinski. 25p. 1998. 6.95 (*1-58532-070-6*) Basic Ed Materials.

***Multiplication 2 Digit X 1 Digit Non-Carrying 0-99.** Robert W. Skarlinski. 25p. 1998. 6.95 (*1-58532-069-2*) Basic Ed Materials.

***Multiplication 2 Digit X 2 Digit Non-Carrying 0-99.** Robert W. Skarlinski. 25p. 1998. 6.95 (*1-58532-073-0*) Basic Ed Materials.

***Multiplication 2 Digit X 2 Digit Carrying 0-99.** Robert W. Skarlinski. 25p. 1998. 6.95 (*1-58532-074-9*) Basic Ed Materials.

Multiplication Wipe-Off Book. Nancy Salloway. 24p. (Orig.). (J). (gr. 4-7). 1988. pap. 1.95 (*0-590-42009-7*) Scholastic Inc.

Multiplication Wrap-Ups: Individual Sets. Marion W. Stuart. text, teacher ed. write for info. (*0-943343-03-8*) Lrn Wrap-Ups.

Multiplicative Complexity, Convolution, & the DFT. M. T. Heideman. 160p. 1988. 49.00 (*0-387-96810-5*) Spr-Verlag.

Multiplicative Galois Module Structure. A. Weiss. LC 96-10777. (Fields Institute Monographs: No. 5). 95p. 1996. text 39.00 (*0-8218-0265-8*, FIM/5) Am Math.

Multiplicative Homology Operations & Transfer. N. Minami. LC 91-28757. (Memoirs Ser.: No. 457). 74p. 1991. pap. 18.00 (*0-8218-2518-6*, MEMO/94/457) Am Math.

Multiplicative Ideal Theory. Robert W. Gilmer. LC 72-76061. (Pure & Applied Mathematics Ser.: No. 12). 623p. reprint ed. pap. 193.20 (*0-7837-0959-5*, 204126400019) Bks Demand.

Multiplicative Number Theory. H. Davenport. (Graduate Texts in Mathematics Ser.: Vol. 74). 177p. 1980. 39.00 (*0-387-90533-2*) Spr-Verlag.

Multiplicities & Chern Classes in Local Algebra. Paul C. Roberts. LC 97-46135. (Tracts in Mathematics Ser.: No. 133). 316p. (C). 1998. text 59.95 (*0-521-47316-0*) Cambridge U Pr.

Multiplicity: A Collection of Monologues for Student Performance. R. James Scott & Bianca Cowan. (Encore Scene Book Ser.). 1997. pap. 8.95 (*1-57514-021-7*, 5020) Encore Perform Pub.

Multiplicity & Becoming: The Pluralist Empiricism of Gilles Deleuze. Patrick Hayden. LC 97-12506. (Studies in European Thought: Vol. 15). XII, 160p. (C). 1998. text 39.95 (*0-8204-3856-1*) P Lang Pubng.

Multiplicity-Independent, Global Iteration for Meromorphic Functions. Alvis E. McDonald. LC 73-130610. 116p. 1969. 19.00 (*0-403-04516-9*) Scholarly.

Multiplicity of Dreams: Memory, Imagination & Consciousness. Harry T. Hunt. LC 88-27908. (Illus.). 288p. (C). 1989. 42.50 (*0-300-04330-9*) Yale U Pr.

Multiplicity of Dreams: Memory, Imagination, & Consciousness. Harry T. Hunt. 288p. (C). 1991. reprint ed. pap. 18.00 (*0-300-04985-4*) Yale U Pr.

Multiplicity of Mrs. Browns. large type ed. Alan Sewart. (Linford Mystery Library). 336p. 1994. pap. 16.99 (*0-7089-7488-0*, Linford) Ulverscroft.

Multiplier: A Head Start in Multiplication. 2nd rev. ed. Morry Frank. (Illus.). 98p. (J). (gr. 3-4). 1990. pap. text. write for info. (*0-9640912-9-1*) Silverback Bks.

Multiplier Theory. Hugo Hegeland. LC 66-23018. (Reprints of Economic Classics Ser.). (Illus.). x, 261p. 1966. reprint ed. 39.50 (*0-678-00162-6*) Kelley.

Multipliers of Pedersen's Ideal. A. L. Lazar & D. C. Taylor. LC 75-44302. (Memoirs Ser.: No. 5/169). 111p. 1976. pap. 22.00 (*0-8218-1869-4*, MEMO/5/169) Am Math.

Multipliers of Radical Banach Algebras of Power Series. W. G. Bade et al. LC 84-3070. (Memoirs Ser.: No. 49/303). 84p. 1984. pap. 17.00 (*0-8218-2304-3*, MEMO/49/303) Am Math.

Multipliers, Positive Functionals, Positive-Definite Functions & Fourier-Stieltjes Transforms. Kelly McKennon. LC 52-42839. (Memoirs Ser.: No. 1/111). 67p. 1971. pap. 16.00 (*0-8218-1811-2*, MEMO/1/111) Am Math.

***Multiplique el Poder de su Mente.** Jean Stine. (SPA.). 1999. pap. text 24.95 (*0-13-012726-4*) P-H.

***Multiplique el Poder de Su Mente.** Jean Marie Stine. (SPA.). 1999. pap. 13.95 (*0-13-013242-X*) P-H.

***Multiplique el Poder de su Mente.** Jean Marie Stine. (SPA.). 2000. pap. 14.00 (*0-7352-0209-5*) PH Pr.

Multiplique su Capacidad de Lectura. rev. unabridged ed. Jose Escarpanter. Orig. Title: Lea Muy Rapidamente. (SPA., Illus.). 160p. 1994. pap. 5.95 (*0-9648426-6-1*) Brickell Commun.

Multiply see Arithmetic Series

Multiply & Divide. Terry Kane. 1997. pap., wbk. ed. 2.25 (*1-56293-914-9*, McClanahan Book) Learn Horizon.

Multiply Injured Patient with Complex Fractures. Ed. by Marvin H. Meyers. LC 83-9333. (Illus.). 435p. reprint ed. pap. 134.90 (*0-7837-1490-4*, 205718600023) Bks Demand.

Multiply Your Money Trading Soybeans: A Beginner's Guide to Speculating in Soybean Futures. Merrill J. Oster et al. 198p. 1981. 14.95 (*0-914230-10-7*) Investor Pubns.

Multiply Your Profits: A Common-Sense Approach for Small to Midsize Businesses. Richard Peelo. LC 97-46410. xii, 155p. 1999. 24.00 (*0-9661609-0-8*) Inverness Pubs.

Multiply Your Success with Real Estate Assistants: How to Hire, Train & Manage Your Assistant: Featuring 93 Ready-to-Use Forms. Monica Reynolds. LC 93-32671. 247p. (Orig.). 1994. pap. 24.95 (*0-7931-0776-8*, 56088801, Real Estate Ed) Dearborn.

Multiplying & Dividing see Key to Fractions Series

Multiplying & Dividing Puzzles. Karen Bryant-Mole & Robyn Gee. (Math Skills Ser.). (Illus.). 32p. (J). (gr. 2-6). 1993. pap. 6.95 (*0-7460-1073-7*, Usborne) EDC.

Multiplying & Dividing Rational Expressions see Key to Algebra Series

***Multiplying Churches: An Introduction to Church Planting.** Stephen Timmis. 2000. pap. 9.99 (*1-85792-573-4*) Christian Focus.

***Multiplying Identities.** Elizabeth Ann Armstrong. 1999. pap. text 18.00 (*0-226-02694-9*); lib. bdg. 40.00 (*0-226-02693-0*) U Ch Pr.

Multipoint Aerial Refueling: A Review & Assessment. Paul S. Killingsworth. 80p. 1996. pap. text 6.00 (*0-8330-2378-0*, DB-152-CRMAF) Rand Corp.

Multipoint Feedback: A 360 Catalyst for Change. Deborah Jude-York & Susan L. Wise. LC 96-72562. (Fifty-Minute Ser.). (Illus.). 120p. (Orig.). 1997. pap. 10.95 (*1-56052-427-8*) Crisp Pubns.

Multipoint Magnetospheric Measurements: Proceedings of Symposium 8 of the COSPAR 27th Plenary Meeting Held in Espoo, Finland, 18-29 July, 1988. Ed. by C. T. Russell. (Advances in Space Research Ser.: Vol. 8). (Illus.). 472p. 1989. pap. 170.00 (*0-08-037373-9*, Pergamon Pr) Elsevier.

Multipolar Peace? Great-Power Politics in the 21st Century. Charles W. Kegley & Gregory A. Raymond. 278p. 1993. pap. text 29.95 (*0-312-09957-6*) St Martin.

Multipolar Peace? Great-Power Politics in the 21st Century. Charles W. Kegley, Jr. & Gregory A. Raymond. 320p. 1994. text 45.00 (*0-312-10270-4*) St Martin.

Multipreneur: How a Self-Published Writer Parlayed a Single Children's Mystery into 176 Companies. Carole Marsh. (MYOB Ser.). (Illus.). 1994. pap. 19.95 (*0-7933-4389-5*); lib. bdg. 29.95 (*0-7933-4388-7*) Gallopade Intl.

Multipreneur: How a Self-Published Writer Parlayed a Single Children's Mystery into 176 Companies. Carole Marsh. (MYOB Ser.). (Illus.). 1997. disk 29.95 (*0-7933-4390-9*) Gallopade Intl.

Multipreneuring. Thomas Gorman. 256p. 1996. pap. 11.00 (*0-684-81180-4*, Fireside) S&S Trade Pap.

Multiprocess Station. Lab-Volt Ltd. Staff. LC 98-13084. Date not set. write for info. (*2-89289-398-4*) Lab-Volt.

Multiprocessing: Trade-Offs in Computation & Communication. Vijay K. Naik. LC 93-17930. (International Series in Engineering & Computer Science, VLSI, Computer Architecture, & Digital Screen Processing: Vol. 236). 224p. (C). 1993. text 131.50 (*0-7923-9370-8*) Kluwer Academic.

Multiprocessing in Meteorological Models. Ed. by G. R. Hoffmann & D. F. Snelling. (Topics in Atmospheric & Oceanographic Sciences Ser.). xvii, 464p. 1988. 103.95 (*0-387-18457-0*) Spr-Verlag.

Multiprocessor & Array Processor (MAPCON IV) Special Processing, 1988. Ed. by Howard L. Johnson. (Illus.). 132p. (Orig.). (C). 1988. pap. 30.00 (*0-911801-31-6*, MC88-2) Soc Computer Sim.

Multiprocessor & Array Processor (MAPCON V), 1988. Ed. by Walter J. Karplus. (Simulation Ser.: Vol. 21, No. 1). 181p. 1989. 48.00 (*0-911801-48-0*, SS21-1) Soc Computer Sim.

Multiprocessor Execution of Logic Programs. Gopal Gupta. 264p. (C). 1994. text 138.00 (*0-7923-9489-5*) Kluwer Academic.

Multiprocessor Methods for Computer Graphics Rendering. Scott Whitman. (Illus.). 232p. (C). 1992. text 65.00 (*0-86720-229-7*) AK Peters.

Multiprocessor Performance. Erol Gelenbe. (Parallel Computing Ser.). 168p. 1990. 130.00 (*0-471-92392-3*) Wiley.

Multiprocessor Performance Measurement & Evaluation. Ed. by Laxmi N. Bhuyan & Xiaodong Zhang. LC 94-21718. 488p. 1994. 50.00 (*0-8186-6522-X*, BP06522) IEEE Comp Soc.

Multiprocessor Systems - Design & Integration. C. L. Wu. 500p. 1998. text 113.00 (*981-02-2218-1*) World Scientific Pub.

Multiprocessors & Array Processors (Multi '87) (Simulation Ser.: Vol. 18, No. 2). 322p. 1987. 40.00 (*0-911801-19-7*, SS18-2) Soc Computer Sim.

Multiprofessional Education of Health Personnel. 1995. 12.00 (*92-871-2653-4*, Pub. by Council of Europe) Manhattan Pub Co.

Multiprofessional Handbook of Child Sexual Abuse: Integrated Management, Therapy, & Legal Intervention. Tilman Furniss. 384p. (C). 1991. pap. 45.00 (*0-415-05563-6*, A5265) Routledge.

Multiprotocol Network Design & Troubleshooting. Chris Brenton. LC 97-67760. 848p. 1997. 49.99 (*0-7821-2082-2*) Sybex.

Multiprotocol Network Management: A Practical Guide to NetView for AIX. Larry Bennett. 288p. 1996. pap. 45.00 (*0-07-709122-1*) McGraw.

Multiprotocol over ATM: Building State of the Art ATM Intranets, Utilizing RSVP, NHRP, Lane, Flow Switching, & WWW Technology. Andrew Schmidt & Daniel Minoli. LC 97-46424. 1998. 49.00 (*1-884777-42-2*) Manning Pubns.

Multiprotocol Routing over ATM: Bringing Internet Protocols to ATM. Ross W. Callon. (C). 1998. 46.95 (*0-201-57165-X*) Addison-Wesley.

Multiprotocols over ATM: Building State of the Art ATM Intranets. Daniel Minoli & Andrew Schmidt. 325p. (C). 1998. 50.00 (*0-13-889270-9*) P-H.

Multipurpose Australian Trees & Shrubs. Ed. by J. W. Turnbull. 316p. (Orig.). 1986. pap. 165.00 (*0-949511-23-4*) St Mut.

Multipurpose Cadastre: Terms & Definitions. Kenneth J. Ducker & Daniel Kjerne. 12p. 1989. pap. 5.00 (*0-614-06098-2*, G428) Am Congrs Survey.

Multipurpose River Basin Development in China. Ed. by Peter Sun. LC 93-6023. (EDI Seminar Ser.). 118p. 1994. pap. 22.00 (*0-8213-2621-X*, 12621) World Bank.

Multipurpose Serological Serveys & WHO Serum Reference Banks: Proceedings of the WHO Scientific Group, Geneva, 1969. WHO Staff. (Technical Reports: No. 454). 95p. 1970. pap. text 7.00 (*92-4-120454-0*, 1160454) World Health.

Multipurpose Tools for Bible Study. Frederick W. Danker. LC 93-14303. 352p. 1994. pap. 24.00 (*0-8006-2598-6*, 1-2598) Augsburg Fortress.

Multipurpose Transit Payment Media. Daniel Fleishman et al. LC 98-60315. (Report/Transit Cooperative Research Program Ser.). 132 p. 1998. 36.00 (*0-309-06264-0*) Natl Acad Pr.

Multipurpose Trees for Agroforestry & Wasteland Utilisation. R. K. Gupta. (Winrock Ser.). 580p. (C). 1993. text 75.00 (*1-881570-09-6*) Science Pubs.

Multiracial Couples. Richard Powell et al. LC 95-16778. (Understanding Families Ser.: No. 1). 305p. (C). 1995. 48.00 (*0-8039-7258-X*) Sage.

Multiracial Experience: Racial Borders As the New Frontier. Ed. by Maria P. Root. (Illus.). 498p. 1995. 62.00 (*0-8039-7058-7*); pap. 28.00 (*0-8039-7059-5*) Sage.

***Multiracial Identity: an International Perspective.** Mark A. Christian. 2000. text 59.95 (*0-312-23219-5*) St Martin.

Multiracialism As a Social Movement. Simon & Schuster Staff. 1996. 26.95 (*0-8057-3875-4*, Twyne) Mac Lib Ref.

Multiracialism As a Social Movement. Simon & Schuster Staff. 1996. 14.95 (*0-8057-3876-2*, Twyne) Mac Lib Ref.

Multirate & Wavelet Signal Processing. Bruce W. Suter. LC 97-30328. (Wavelet Analysis & Its Applications Ser.: Vol. 8). (Illus.). 199p. 1997. text 59.95 (*0-12-677560-5*) Acad Pr.

Multirate Digital Signal Processing. Ronald E. Crochiere & Lawrence R. Rabiner. (Illus.). 336p. (C). 1983. text 67.51 (*0-13-605162-6*) P-H.

***Multirate Digital Signal Processing: Multirate Systems - Filter Banks - Wavelets.** N. J. Fliege. 352p. 1999. pap. 94.95 (*0-471-49204-3*) Wiley.

M

M

Multirate Switched-Capacitor Circuits for 2-D Signal Processing, Vol. 427. Wang Ping & Jose E. Franca. LC 97-40162. (Kluwer International Series in Engineering & Computer Science). 124p. 1998. text 104.50 (*0-7923-8051-7*) Kluwer Academic.

Multirate Systems & Filter Banks. P. P. Vaidyanathan. 944p. 1992. 96.00 (*0-13-605718-7*) P-H.

Multiregional Demography: Principles, Methods & Extensions. Andrei Rogers. 248p. 1995. 110.00 (*0-471-95892-1*) Wiley.

Multiresidential-Archways. Atrium Press Staff. 1999. pap. 35.00 (*0-688-16223-1*, Wm Morrow) Morrow Avon.

Multiresolution Image Processing & Analysis. Ed. by Azriel Rosenfeld. (Information Sciences Ser.: Vol. 12). (Illus.). 400p. 1984. 74.95 (*0-387-13006-3*) Spr-Verlag.

Multiresolution Image Shape Description. J. M. Gauch. Ed. by R. C. Jain. (Perception Engineering Ser.). (Illus.). 135p. 1992. 102.95 (*0-387-97682-5*) Spr-Verlag.

Multiresolution Signal Decomposition. 2nd ed. Akansu. 450p. 1998. write for info. (*0-12-047141-8*) Acad Pr.

Multiresolution Signal Decomposition: Transforms, Subbands, & Wavelets. Ali N. Akansu & Richard A. Haddad. LC 92-18629. (Telecommunications Ser.). (Illus.). 376p. 1992. text 59.00 (*0-12-047140-X*) Acad Pr.

Multiresource Forest Inventory for Oahu, Hawaii. Michael G. Buck et al. (Illus.). 44p. 1997. reprint ed. 10.40 (*0-89904-929-X*, Ecosytems Resrch); reprint ed. pap. 5.40 (*0-89904-930-3*, Ecosytems Resrch) Crumb Elbow Pub.

Multiresource Management of Ponderosa Pine Forests: November 14-16, 1989, Flagstaff, Arizona. Aregai Tecle et al. (Illus.). 292p. 1998. reprint ed. 37.00 (*0-89904-512-X*, Ecosytems Resrch) Crumb Elbow Pub.

Multiscale Modelling of Materials Vol. 538: Materials Research Society Symposium Proceedings. Ed. by Thomas Diaz de la Rubia et al. LC 99-13247. (Symposium Proceedings Ser.). 591p. 1999. 89.00 (*1-55899-444-0*) Materials Res.

***Multiscale Phenomena in Materials--Experiments & Modeling Vol. 578: Materials Research Society Symposium Proceedings.** Ed. by D. H. Lassila et al. 2000. text 93.00 (*1-55899-486-6*) Materials Res.

***Multiscale Phenomena in Plasticity: From Experiments to Phenomenology, Modelling 7 Materials Engineering.** Johel Lepinoux. LC 00-26055. (NATO Science Ser.). 2000. write for info. (*0-7923-6251-9*) Kluwer Academic.

Multiscale Phenomenon & Their Simulation. LC 97-12537. 400p. 1997. text 60.00 (*981-02-3090-7*) World Scientific Pub.

Multiscale Wavelet Methods for Partial Differential Equations. Ed. by Wolfgang Dahmen et al. LC 97-12672. (Wavelet Analysis & Its Applications Ser.: Vol. 6). (Illus.). 570p. 1997. text 59.95 (*0-12-200675-5*) Morgan Kaufmann.

Multisensor for Computer Vision. Ed. by Jagdishkumar K. Aggarwal. LC 92-42968. 1993. write for info. (*3-540-55044-5*); 126.95 (*0-387-55044-5*) Spr-Verlag.

***Multisensor Fusion A Minimal Representation Framwork.** Rajive Joshi. (Series In Intelligent Control & Intellect). 1999. 55.00 (*981-02-3880-0*) World Scientific Pub.

Multisensory Control of Movement. Ed. by Alain Berthoz. (Illus.). 522p. 1993. 95.00 (*0-19-854785-4*) OUP.

Multisensory Control of Posture: Proceedings of an International Symposium on Sensory Interaction in Posture & Movement Control Held in Smolenice, Slovakia, September 9-11, 1994, As a Satellite Symposium to the European Neuroscience Association Meeting of 1994. Ed. by T. Mergner & F. Hlavacka. LC 95-30547. (Illus.). 370p. 1995. 95.00 (*0-306-45101-8*, Kluwer Plenum) Kluwer Academic.

Multisensory Environments. Paul Pagliano. 1999. pap. text 28.95 (*1-85346-553-4*) Taylor & Francis.

***Multisensory Structured Metacognitive Instruction: An Approach to Teaching a Foreign Language to At-Risk Students.** Elke Schneider. xvii, 305p. 1999. pap. 51.95 (*3-631-33370-6*) P Lang Pubng.

Multisensory Structured Metacognitive Instruction: An Approach to Teaching a Foreign Language to At-Risk Students. Elke Schneider. LC 99-30991. (Theorie und Vermittlung der Sprache Ser.: Vol. 30). (Illus.). XVII, 305p. 1999. pap. 51.95 (*0-8204-3595-3*) P Lang Pubng.

Multisensory Teaching of Basic Language Skills: Theory & Practice. Ed. by Judith R. Birsh. LC 99-21233. 624p. 1999. 59.00 (*1-55766-349-1*, 3491) P H Brookes.

Multisensory Theme-a-Saurus. Ed. by Gayle Bittinger. LC 96-60384. (Illus.). 160p. (Orig.). (J). (ps). 1997. pap. 14.95 (*1-57029-131-4*, 1008) Totline Pubns.

Multiservice Loss Models for Broadband. K. W. Ross. LC 94-47039. (Workshops in Computing Ser.). 343p. 1997. 69.00 (*3-540-19918-7*) Spr-Verlag.

Multishop Handbook. Hugh Foster. Date not set. write for info. (*0-8069-0647-2*) Sterling.

Multisite Evaluations. Ed. by Robin S. Turpin & James M. Sinacore. LC 85-644749. (New Directions for Evalutation Ser.: No. PE 50). 1991. 22.00 (*1-55542-796-0*) Jossey-Bass.

Multiskilled Health Care Workers: Issues & Approaches to Cross-Training. Sherry Makely. Ed. by Lana Christian. 288p. 1997. pap. 34.95 (*0-9652954-3-5*) Pine Ridge Publns.

***Multiskilled Respiratory Therapist: A Competency-Based Program.** 3rd ed. David W. Chang et al. (Illus.). 224p. (C). 2000. pap. text 29.95 (*0-8036-0380-0*) Davis Co.

Multiskilling: Advanced Patient Care Skills for the Health Care Provider. Denise York. LC 97-34658. 152p. (C). 1997. pap., teacher ed. 20.95 (*0-8273-8523-4*) Delmar.

Multiskilling: Dietary Assisting for the Health Care Provider. 2nd rev. abr. ed. Airaghi. LC 98-51789. (Allied Health Ser.). 64p. (C). 1999. pap. 21.95 (*0-7668-0514-X*) Delmar.

Multiskilling: Electrocardiography for the Health Care Provider. Kovanda & Karen Brisindine. LC 97-37683. 80p. (C). 1997. pap. 20.95 (*0-8273-8522-6*) Delmar.

Multiskilling: Electrocardiography for the Health Care Provider - IML. Kovanda & Brisendine. 24p. 1998. teacher ed. 16.00 (*0-7668-0487-9*) Delmar.

Multiskilling: Health Unit Coordination for the Health Care Provider. Emerick & Graham. (Home Care Aide Ser.). 64p. (C). 1998. text 17.95 (*0-7668-0213-2*) Delmar.

Multiskilling: Phlebotomy for the Health Care Provider. Beverly M. Kovanda. LC 97-28487. 144p. (C). 1997. mass mkt. 20.95 (*0-8273-8452-1*) Delmar.

Multiskilling: Phlebotomy for the Health Care Provider - IML. Kovanda. 80p. 1998. teacher ed. write for info. (*0-7668-0737-1*) Delmar.

Multiskilling: Point of Care Testing for the Health Care Provider. Beverly M. Kovanda. LC 97-26293. 96p. (C). 1997. mass mkt. 20.95 (*0-8273-8453-X*) Delmar.

Multiskilling: Point of Care Testing for the Health Care Provider - IML. Kovanda. 56p. 1998. teacher ed. write for info. (*0-7668-0738-X*) Delmar.

Multiskilling: Radiology for Healthcare Providers. Claudia Manning-Weber & Beverlly Kovanda. LC 99-17639. 150p. 1999. pap. 19.95 (*0-7668-0906-4*) Delmar.

***Multiskilling: Rehabilitation Services for the Health Care Provider.** Wyatt. (Physical Therapy Ser.). (C). 2000. pap. 17.95 (*0-7668-0211-6*) Delmar.

Multiskilling: Respiratory Care for the Health Care Provider. Sills. LC 97-42387. 136p. (C). 1997. pap. 20.95 (*0-7668-0075-X*) Delmar.

Multiskilling: Team Building for the Health Care Provider. Makeley Kovanda. (Home Care Aide Ser.). 48p. (C). 1998. text 17.95 (*0-8273-8524-2*) Delmar.

Multiskilling: Waived Laboratory Testing for the Health Care Provider. Kovanda. LC 98-33828. 192p. 1998. text 21.95 (*0-7668-0212-4*) Delmar.

***Multiskilling & Aural Rehabilitation.** Carole E. Johnson & Jeffrey L. Danhauer. LC 99-10767. 365p. 1999. 57.50 (*1-56593-905-0*) Thomson Learn.

***Multiskilling for Television Production.** Alan Bermingham et al. 368p. 2000. pap. 56.95 (*0-240-51557-9*, Focal) Buttrwrth-Heinemann.

Multispectral Imagery Reference Guide. Michael D. Kesiter et al. LC 97-70124. (Illus.). xviii, 205p. 1997. pap. 59.95 (*0-9659086-0-7*) Logicon Geodynamics.

Multispectral Imaging for Terrestrial Applications, Vol. 2818. Ed. by Brian Huberty et al. 234p. 1996. 76.00 (*0-8194-2206-1*) SPIE.

Multispectral Imaging for Terrestrial Applications II, Vol. 3119. Ed. by Jaon B. Lurie & Thomas Delaney. LC 98-122075. 220p. 1997. 59.00 (*0-8194-2541-9*) SPIE.

Multispeed & Standard Squirrel Cage Motors Vol. 1: Standard (Single Speed Only) Motors Only: Testing, Rewinding, Reconnecting, & Redesigning. Samuel Heller. LC 75-36709. (Illus.). 704p. 1976. 85.00 (*0-911740-07-4*) Datarule.

Multistage Fuzzy Control: A Model-Based Approach to Fuzzy Control & Decision Making. Janusz Kacprzyk. LC 96-42340. 338p. 1997. 125.00 (*0-471-96347-X*) Wiley.

Multistage Selection & Ranking Procedures: Second-Order Asymptotics. Nitis Mukhopadhyay & Tumulesh K. Solanky. LC 93-47524. (Statistics: Textbooks & Monographs: Vol. 142). (Illus.). 432p. 1994. text 150.00 (*0-8247-9078-2*) Dekker.

Multistate & Multinational Estate Planning, 2 vols. Jeffrey Schoenblum. 1400p. 1982. suppl. ed. 160.00 (*0-316-77422-7*, Aspen Law & Bus) Aspen Pub.

***Multistate & Multinational Estate Planning.** 2nd ed. Jeffrey A. Schoenblum. LC 99-51884. 1999. boxed set 295.00 (*0-7355-1179-9*) Panel Pubs.

Multistate & Multinational Estate Planning, 2 vols., Vol. 1. Jeffrey Schoenblum. 1400p. 1982. 165.00 (*0-316-77419-7*, Aspen Law & Bus) Aspen Pub.

Multistate & Multinational Estate Planning, 2 vols., Vol. 2. Jeffrey Schoenblum. 1400p. 1982. 165.00 (*0-316-77418-9*) Little.

Multistate Bar Examination (MBE) Jack Rudman. (Admission Test Ser.: ATS-8). 300p. 1994. pap. 39.95 (*0-8373-5008-5*) Nat Learn.

Multistate Bar Review Set. rev. ed. Kimm Walton & Lazar Emanuel. (Law in a Flash Cards Ser.). 1999. pap. text 165.00 (*1-56542-590-1*) E Pub Corp.

Multistate Corporate Tax Almanac, 2 Vol. Set, 1. Panel Publishers, Inc. Staff. write for info. (*1-878375-05-9*) Panel Pubs.

Multistate Corporate Tax Almanac, 2 Vol. Set, 2. Panel Publishers, Inc. Staff. write for info. (*1-878375-06-7*) Panel Pubs.

Multistate Corporate Tax Almanac, 2 Vol. Set, Set. Panel Publishers, Inc. Staff. pap. 185.00 (*1-878375-23-7*) Panel Pubs.

Multistate Corporate Tax Guide Vols. I & II: 1992 Edition, 1. William A. Raabe et al. Ed. by Laura B. Kaiser. 950p. 1991. write for info. (*1-878375-57-1*) Panel Pubs.

Multistate Corporate Tax Guide Vols. I & II: 1992 Edition, 2. William A. Raabe et al. Ed. by Laura B. Kaiser. 950p. 1991. write for info. (*1-878375-58-X*) Panel Pubs.

Multistate Corporate Tax Guide Vols. I & II: 1992 Edition, Set. William A. Raabe et al. Ed. by Laura B. Kaiser. 950p. 1991. pap. text 185.00 (*1-878375-59-8*) Panel Pubs.

Multistate Corporate Tax Guide Supplement, 1991. Steve C. Wells. Ed. by Laura B. Kaiser. 174p. 1991. pap. write for info. (*1-878375-36-9*) Panel Pubs.

Multistate Guide to Benefits Law John F. Buckley, IV. LC 98-106671. 1998. write for info. (*1-56706-378-0*) Panel Pubs.

***Multistate Guide to Benefits Law, 1.** John F. Buckley, IV. 800p. 1999. pap. text 145.00 (*0-7355-0664-7*) Panel Pubs.

***Multistate Payroll Guide.** John F. Buckley IV. 944p. 1999. pap. text 145.00 (*0-7355-0662-0*) Panel Pubs.

Multistate Payroll Guide. John F. Buckley, IV. 600p. 1996. 145.00 (*1-56706-309-8*) Aspen Pub.

Multistate S Corporation Tax Guide. William A. Raabe et al. 641p. 1990. pap. text 96.00 (*1-878375-08-3*) Panel Pubs.

Multistate S Corporation Tax Guide. Rick Taylor et al. 780p. 1994. ring bd. 195.00 (*1-886035-04-0*) Pro Tax & Business.

Multistate S Corporation Tax Guide: Annual. Karen J. Boucher et al. Ed. by Laura B. Kaiser. 600p. 1991. pap. text 96.00 (*1-878375-60-1*) Panel Pubs.

Multistate Sales & Use Tax Compliance Forms Manual, 2 vols. Doris C. Locks. 1993. ring bd. 295.00 (*0-685-69588-3*, CSTC) Warren Gorham & Lamont.

***Multistate Tax Guide to Pass-through Entities, 1.** Robert M. Kozub. 544p. 1999. pap. 168.00 (*0-7355-0343-5*) Panel Pubs.

Multistep Direct Reactions. R. H. Lemmer. 236p. 1992. text 81.00 (*981-02-1171-6*) World Scientific Pub.

Multistrategy Learning. Ed. by Ryszard S. Michalski. LC 93-22647. (International Series in Engineering & Computer Science, VLSI, Computer Architecture, & Digital Screen Processing). 166p. (C). 1993. text 157.50 (*0-7923-9374-0*) Kluwer Academic.

Multisystem Diseases. Ed. by Graeme R. Catto. (New Clinical Applications Nephrology Ser.). (C). 1989. text 91.00 (*0-7462-0060-9*) Kluwer Academic.

Multisystem Skills & Interventions in School Social Work Practice. Edith M. Freeman & National Association of Social Workers Staff. LC 98-25903. 492p. 1998. pap. 29.95 (*0-87101-295-2*) Natl Assn Soc Wkrs.

Multisystemic Treatment of Antisocial Behavior in Children & Adolescents. Scott W. Henggeler et al. LC 98-10618. (Treatment Manuals for Practitioners Ser.). 287p. 1998. lib. bdg. 33.50 (*1-57230-106-6*, C0106) Guilford Pubns.

Multitarget-Multisensor Tracking: Principles & Techniques. Yaakov Bar-Shalom & Xiao-Rong Li. 630p. (C). 1995. pap. text 120.00 (*0-9648312-0-1*) YBS Pubng.

Multitarget-Multisensor Tracking Vol. I: Applications & Advances. Yaakov Bar-Shalom. (Illus.). 365p. (C). 1998. reprint ed. ring bd. 60.00 (*0-9648312-2-8*, MTAA1) YBS Pubng.

Multitarget-Multisensor Tracking Vol. II: Applications & Advances. Yaakov Bar-Shalom. (Illus.). 488p. (C). 1998. reprint ed. ring bd. 60.00 (*0-9648312-3-6*, MTAA2) YBS Pubng.

***Multitarget/Multisensor Tracking Vol. III: Applications & Advances.** Yaakov Bar-Shalom. (Radar Library). 2000. 109.00 (*1-58053-091-5*) Artech Hse.

Multitesting Database Acquisition: Current Approaches; Proceedings of the Washington-Alaska Regional Medical Program Conference, Everett, Wash., 1973. Washington-Alaska Regional Medical Program Confere. LC 73-16454. 197p. 1973. 6.00 (*0-917054-06-7*) Med Communications.

Multithread Program with Win32, 32. Pham & Garg. 320p. 1998. pap. text 49.99 (*0-13-010912-6*) P-H.

Multithreaded Computer Architecture: A Summary of the State of the Art. Ed. by Robert A. Iannucci. LC 94-21605. (International Series in Engineering & Computer Science, VLSI, Computer Architecture, & Digital Screen Processing: 281). 416p. (C). 1994. text 139.00 (*0-7923-9477-1*) Kluwer Academic.

***Multithreaded JAVA Programming.** Bil Lewis & Daniel Berg. LC 99-51538. (Java Ser.). (Illus.). 461p. 1999. pap. text 39.99 (*0-13-017007-0*) P-H.

Multithreaded Processor Design. Simon Moore. (Kluwer International Series in Engineering & Computer Science: Vol. 358). 160p. (C). 1996. text 109.00 (*0-7923-9718-5*) Kluwer Academic.

Multithreaded Programming in C: Posix.1C. Nancy Gilman. (C). 1998. text. write for info. (*0-201-69446-8*) Addson-Wesley Educ.

Multithreaded Programming with Pthreads. Bil Lewis & Daniel J. Berg. LC 97-31758. 432p. (C). 1997. pap. text 34.95 (*0-13-680729-1*) P-H.

Multithreading Applications in Win 32: The Complete Guide to Threads in Windows 95 & Windows NT. Jim Beveridge & Robert Wiener. LC 96-48106. 400p. (C). 1996. pap. 42.95 (*0-201-44234-5*) Addison-Wesley.

Multithreading Programming Techniques for C Programmers. Shashi Prashad. LC 96-34490. (Illus.). 408p. 1997. pap., pap. text 49.95 incl. disk (*0-07-912250-7*) McGraw.

Multitrophic Interactions in Terrestrial Systems: British Ecological Society Symposium Volume. A. C. Gange et al. LC 96-36940. (Illus.). 448p. (Orig.). 1997. pap. text 95.00 (*0-86542-767-4*) Blackwell Sci.

Multitude: Cross-Cultural Readings for Writers. 2nd ed. Chitra Banerjee Divakaruni. LC 96-2699. 624p. (C). 1996. pap. 34.06 (*0-07-017086-X*) McGraw.

Multitude of Blessings. Chris Thornton. (Illus.). 1997. pap. 10.50 (*1-56770-379-8*) S Scheewe Pubns.

***Multitude of Questions.** Juliette Terrell. (Illus.). ii, 34p. 1999. pap. 10.00 (*0-9674900-3-0*) Wordrunner.

Multitude of Sins. large type ed. Pauline Bell. (Magna Large Print Ser.). 314p. 1997. 27.99 (*0-7505-1174-5*, Pub. by Mgna Lrg Print) Ulverscroft.

Multitude of Tigers. John Hepworth. 210p. (C). 1990. 45.00 (*0-947087-21-4*, Pub. by Pascoe Pub) St Mut.

***Multitudes: Poems Selected & New.** Afaa Michael Weaver. LC 99-46428. 160p. 2000. 24.00 (*1-889330-40-X*, Pub. by Sarabande Bks); pap. 14.95 (*1-889330-41-8*, Pub. by Sarabande Bks) Consort Bk Sales.

Multitudes of Love Climaxes: 40's Plus Super Sex. Gustav G. Glenn. 128p. 1993. pap. 14.95 (*1-883500-20-6*) RAMSI Bks.

Multiuser Detection. Sergio Verdu. LC 98-16453. (Illus.). 370p. (C). 1998. text 59.95 (*0-521-59373-5*) Cambridge U Pr.

Multivalence: The Moral Quality of Form in the Modern Novel. Alan W. Friedman. LC 78-17485. 235p. reprint ed. pap. 72.90 (*0-608-09828-0*, 206999600007) Bks Demand.

Multivalent Functions. 2nd ed. W. K. Hayman. LC 93-48417. (Tracts in Mathematics Ser.: No. 110). (Illus.). 275p. (C). 1995. text 59.95 (*0-521-46026-3*) Cambridge U Pr.

Multivalued Analysis: Theory & Applications. Shouchuan Hu & Nikolaos S. Papageorgiou. LC 97-26087. (Mathematics & Its Applications Ser.). 964p. 1997. text 465.00 (*0-7923-4682-3*) Kluwer Academic.

Multivalued Differential Equations. Klaus Deimling. LC 92-16953. (Series in Nonlinear Analysis & Applications: Vol. 1). xii, 260p. (C). 1992. 99.95 (*3-11-013212-5*) De Gruyter.

Multivalued Linear Operators, Vol. 213. Ronald Cross. LC 98-24468. (Monographs & Textbooks in Pure & Applied Mathematics). (Illus.). 352p. 1998. text 150.00 (*0-8247-0219-0*) Dekker.

***Multivari Calculas Stanford.** Ed. by Barr & Edwards. 564p. 1998. pap. text 53.00 (*0-536-01809-X*) P-H.

***Multivariable.** 2nd ed. Finney. 1999. pap., student ed. 25.00 (*0-201-66979-X*) Addison-Wesley.

Multivariable Analysis. G. B. Price. (Illus.). 995p. 1984. 79.95 (*0-387-90934-6*) Spr-Verlag.

Multivariable Analysis: A Guide for Nonstatisticians. Alvan R. Feinstein. LC 95-19489. 1996. 90.00 (*0-300-06299-0*) Yale U Pr.

Multivariable Analysis: A Practical Guide for Clinicians. Mitchell H. Katz. LC 98-39350. (Illus.). 208p. (C). 1999. text 64.95 (*0-521-59301-8*); pap. text 24.95 (*0-521-59693-9*) Cambridge U Pr.

Multivariable Calculus. Lawrence J. Corwin & Szczarba. (Pure & Applied Mathematics Ser.: Vol. 64). (Illus.). 544p. 1982. text 165.00 (*0-8247-6962-7*) Dekker.

Multivariable Calculus. Decker. (C). 2000. pap. text, student ed. 22.67 (*0-13-269440-9*) P-H.

Multivariable Calculus. Hurley. (C). 1995. pap. text 54.50 (*0-15-504301-3*) Harcourt Coll Pubs.

Multivariable Calculus. Jerrold E. Marsden. 1993. pap., student ed. 22.95 (*0-7167-2444-8*) W H Freeman.

Multivariable Calculus. William G. McCallum et al. LC 97-133524. 528p. 1997. pap. 75.95 (*0-471-31151-0*) Wiley.

Multivariable Calculus. Ostebee. (C). 1998. text 39.00 (*0-03-018903-9*); pap. text, teacher ed. 28.00 (*0-03-018904-7*) Harcourt Coll Pubs.

Multivariable Calculus. James Stewart. (Math). 408p. (C). 1989. mass mkt. 47.25 (*0-534-12306-6*) Brooks-Cole.

***Multivariable Calculus.** 2nd ed. 486p. (C). 2000. text 65.00 (*0-536-60096-1*) Pearson Custom.

Multivariable Calculus. 2nd ed. Bradley. 471p. 1998. pap. text 76.00 (*0-13-863945-0*) P-H.

Multivariable Calculus. 2nd ed. Stanley I. Grossman. 876p. (C). 1986. text 93.50 (*0-15-564751-2*) SCP.

Multivariable Calculus. 2nd ed. Leonard I. Holder et al. LC 94-10328. 1994. text 71.95 (*0-534-24912-4*) Brooks-Cole.

Multivariable Calculus. 2nd ed. James Stewart. 440p. (C). 1991. text 48.00 (*0-534-16344-0*) Brooks-Cole.

Multivariable Calculus. 3rd ed. James Stewart. LC 94-41899. 1995. mass mkt. 52.75 (*0-534-25213-3*) Brooks-Cole.

Multivariable Calculus. 4th ed. James Stewart. LC 98-49807. (Mathematics Ser.). (C). 1999. pap. 79.95 (*0-534-35948-5*) Brooks-Cole.

Multivariable Calculus. 4th ed. James Stewart. (Mathematics Ser.). 1999. text, student ed. 20.00 (*0-534-35957-4*) Brooks-Cole.

Multivariable Calculus. 4th ed. James Stewart. (Math). 1999. student ed. 20.00 (*0-534-36445-4*) Brooks-Cole.

Multivariable Calculus. 5th ed. Howard Anton. LC 95-32954. 409p. 1995. pap. 80.95 (*0-471-13909-2*) Wiley.

Multivariable Calculus. 5th ed. Roland E. Larson et al. 413p. (C). 1994. text 67.16 (*0-669-39345-2*) HM Trade Div.

Multivariable Calculus: Complete Solutions Guide, Vol. I, Chpts. 0-6. 5th ed. Roland E. Larson et al. (C). 1994. text. write for info. (*0-614-25395-0*) HM Trade Div.

Multivariable Calculus: Complete Solutions Guide, Vol. II, Chpts. 7-13. Roland E. Larson et al. (C). 1994. text. write for info. (*0-614-25396-9*) HM Trade Div.

Multivariable Calculus: Complete Solutions Guide, Vol. III, Chpts. 14-16. Roland E. Larson et al. (C). 1994. text. write for info. (*0-614-25397-7*) HM Trade Div.

Multivariable Calculus: Concepts & Contexts. James Stewart. (Mathematics Ser.). 1998. mass mkt., student ed. 20.00 (*0-534-34436-4*) Brooks-Cole.

***Multivariable Calculus: Concepts & Contexts.** James Stewart. (C). 1998. text 16.75 (*0-534-35739-3*) Brooks-Cole.

***Multivariable Calculus: Concepts & Contexts.** 2nd ed. James Stewart. (C). 2000. text 15.00 (*0-534-37913-3*); text 15.00 (*0-534-37914-1*) Brooks-Cole.

***Multivariable Calculus: Concepts & Contexts.** 2nd ed. James Stewart. (Mathematics Ser.). (C). 2000. text 20.00 (*0-534-37912-5*) Brooks-Cole.

***Multivariable Calculus: Concepts & Contexts.** 2nd ed. James Stewart. 2000. pap. 55.00 (*0-534-37863-3*) Thomson Learn.

Multivariable Calculus: Solutions Manual. Ostebee. (C). 1998. pap. text, student ed. 12.50 (*0-03-018908-X*) Harcourt Coll Pubs.

Multivariable Calculus: Student Answer Book. Ostebee. 1998. pap. text, student ed. 3.50 (*0-03-018907-1*) Harcourt.

Multivariable Calculus: Study & Solutions Guide. 5th ed. Roland E. Larson et al. (C). 1994. pap. text 27.56 (*0-669-32711-5*) HM Trade Div.

Multivariable Calculus & Mathematica. William G. McCallum et al. 528p. 1997. pap. text, student ed. 139.95 (*0-471-19757-2*) Wiley.

Multivariable Calculus & Mathematica Student Version. William G. McCallum et al. 528p. 1997. pap. text 139.95 (*0-471-19756-4*) Wiley.

Multivariable Calculus & Mathematica(r) With Applications to Geometry & Physics. Kevin R. Coombes et al. LC 97-44764. (Illus.). 272p. 1998. pap. text 34.95 incl. disk (*0-387-98360-0*) Spr-Verlag.

Multivariable Calculus Engineer Preliminary. alternate ed. Philip M. Anselone & John W. Lee. LC 95-33009. 577p. (C). 1995. pap. text 50.67 (*0-13-045279-3*) P-H.

Multivariable Calculus from Graphical, Numerical, & Symbolic Points of View. Arnold Ostebee. 80p. (C). 1997. pap. text, student ed. 14.00 (*0-03-023787-4*) SCP.

Multivariable Calculus from Graphical, Numerical, & Symbolic Points of View. 2nd ed. Arnold Ostebee & Paul Zorn. (C). 1997. pap. text 20.00 (*0-03-023786-6*) SCP.

Multivariable Calculus, Linear Algebra & Differential Equations. 2nd ed. Leon Gerber & Stanley I. Grossman. 876p. (C). 1986. pap. text, teacher ed. 20.75 (*0-15-564752-0*) SCP.

Multivariable Calculus, Linear Algebra & Differential Equations. 3rd ed. Stanley I. Grossman. LC 94-21766. (C). 1994. text 94.50 (*0-03-003038-2*) SCP.

Multivariable Calculus, Student Solutions Manual. William G. McCallum et al. 168p. 1997. pap. 25.95 (*0-471-17356-8*) Wiley.

Multivariable Calculus with Analytic Geometry. 5th ed. Penn & Edwards. 560p. (C). 1997. pap. text 65.00 (*0-13-793084-4*, Prentice Hall) P-H.

Multivariable Calculus with Maple V. Chi-Keung Cheung. 392p. 1993. pap. 34.95 (*0-471-59835-6*) Wiley.

Multivariable Calculus with Vectors. Hartley Rogers. LC 98-3635. 789p. 1998. 89.33 (*0-13-605643-1*) P-H.

Multivariable Control. Ed. by Spyros G. Tzafestas. 1984. text 166.50 (*90-277-1829-6*) Kluwer Academic.

Multivariable Control: An Introduction. Pradip K. Sinha. LC 84-3232. (Electrical Engineering & Electronics Ser.: Vol. 19). (Illus.). 716p. reprint ed. pap. 200.00 (*0-608-08989-3*, 206962400005) Bks Demand.

Multivariable Control - A Graph-Theoretic Approach. K. J. Reinschke. (Lecture Notes in Control & Information Sciences: Vol. 108). 275p. 1988. 51.95 (*0-387-18899-1*) Spr-Verlag.

Multivariable Control for Industrial Applications. J. O'Reilly. (Control Engineering Ser.: No. 32). 466p. 1987. 99.00 (*0-86341-117-7*, CE032) INSPEC Inc.

Multivariable Control Theory. John M. Layton. LC 77-360712. (IEE Control Engineering Ser.: Vol. 1). (Illus.). 246p. reprint ed. pap. 76.30 (*0-608-17788-1*, 203225200079) Bks Demand.

Multivariable Feedback: A Quasi-Classical Approach. Y. S. Hung & A. G. MacFarlane. (Lecture Notes in Control & Information Sciences: Vol. 40). 182p. 1982. 22.95 (*0-387-11902-7*) Spr-Verlag.

Multivariable Feedback Control: Analysis & Design Using Frequency-Domain Methods. Sigurd Skogestad & Ian Postlethwaite. 572p. 1996. pap. 80.00 (*0-471-94330-4*, Wiley-Interscience) Wiley.

***Multivariable Feedback Design.** 2nd ed. Jan Maciejowski. (C). 2000. text. write for info. (*0-201-40364-1*) Addison-Wesley.

Multivariable Feedback Systems. F. M. Callier & C. A. Desoer. (Texts in Electrical Engineering Ser.). (Illus.). 275p. 1982. 116.95 (*0-387-90768-8*) Spr-Verlag.

Multivariable Mathematics. 3rd ed. Richard E. Williamson & Hale F. Trotter. LC 95-36238. 680p. 1995. 89.33 (*0-13-181645-4*) P-H.

Multivariable Operator Theory: Proceedings: A Joint Summer Research Conference on Multivariable Operator Theory (1993: University of Washington, Seattle) Ed. by Raul E. Curto et al. LC 95-2345. (Contemporary Mathematics Ser.: Vol. 185). 380p. 1995. pap. 63.00 (*0-8218-0298-4*, CONM/185) Am Math.

Multivariance PC: An All-Options Computer Program for Univariate & Multivariate Analysis of Variance, Version 7.3. Jeremy D. Finn & R. Darrell Bock. 1988. ring bd. 30.00 (*0-89498-025-4*) Sci Ware.

Multivariate Analysemethoden. 1996. 40.00 (*3-540-60917-2*) Spr-Verlag.

Multivariate Analysis. K. V. Mardia et al. LC 79-40922. (Probability & Mathematical Statistics Ser.). 1980. pap. text 73.00 (*0-12-471252-5*) Acad Pr.

Multivariate Analysis. Anant M. Kshirsagar. LC 78-182214. (Statistics, Textbooks & Monographs: No. 2). 551p. reprint ed. pap. 170.90 (*0-608-15923-9*, 203087800071) Bks Demand.

Multivariate Analysis. 2nd expanded rev. ed. A. M. Kshirsagar. (Statistics Ser.). (Illus.). Date not set. write for info. (*0-8247-9340-4*, 9340-4) Dekker.

Multivariate Analysis: A Selected & Abstracted Bibliography. Kocherlakota Subrahmaniam & Kathleen Subrahmaniam. LC 73-90690. (Statistics Textbooks & Monographs: Vol. 4). 276p. reprint ed. pap. 85.60 (*0-608-30339-9*, 205505200008) Bks Demand.

Multivariate Analysis: Future Directions. Ed. by C. R. Rao. LC 93-16230. (Series in Statistics & Probability: Vol. 5). 488p. 1993. 184.00 (*0-444-89687-2*, North Holland) Elsevier.

Multivariate Analysis: Future Directions 2. Ed. by C. M. Cuadras & C. R. Rao. (North-Holland Series in Statistics & Probability: 7). 504p. 1993. 200.00 (*0-444-81531-7*, North Holland) Elsevier.

Multivariate Analysis: Methods & Application. William R. Dillon & Matthew Goldstein. LC 84-3584. (Probability & Mathematical Statistics Ser.: No. 1-346). 608p. (C). 1984. 109.95 (*0-471-08317-8*) Wiley.

Multivariate Analysis Pt. 1: Distributions, Ordination & Inference. W. J. Krzanowski & F. H. Marriott. (Kendall's Library of Statistics: No. 1). 288p. 1994. 65.00 (*0-340-59326-1*, Pub. by E A) OUP.

Multivariate Analysis Pt. 2: Classification, Covariance Structures & Repeated Measurements. W. J. Krzanowski & F. H. Marriott. (Kendall's Library of Statistics: No. 2). 288p. 1998. 65.00 (*0-340-59325-3*, Pub. by E A) OUP.

Multivariate Analysis & Its Applications. Ed. by T. W. Anderson et al. LC 94-79714. (Lecture Notes-Monographs: Vol. 24). (Illus.). 472p. 1994. pap. 45.00 (*0-940600-35-8*) Inst Math.

Multivariate Analysis in Behavioral Research: For Medical & Social Science Students. 2nd ed. A. E. Maxwell. 164p. (gr. 13). 1977. pap. 54.95 (*0-412-14300-3*, NO. 6193) CRC Pr.

Multivariate Analysis in Ecology & Systematics. J. Podani. (Ecological Computations Ser.: Vol. 6). (Illus.). 316p. 1994. 68.00 (*90-5103-094-0*, Pub. by SPB Acad Pub) Balogh.

Multivariate Analysis in the Human Services. Ed. by John R. Schuerman. (International Series in Social Welfare). 1983. lib. bdg. 85.50 (*0-89838-105-3*) Kluwer Academic.

Multivariate Analysis in Vegetation Research. Laszlo Orloci. 1978. text 155.50 (*90-6193-567-9*) Kluwer Academic.

Multivariate Analysis of Categorical Data: Applications. John P. Van de Geer. (Advanced Quantitative Techniques in the Social Sciences Ser.: Vol. 3). (Illus.). 144p. 1993. 42.00 (*0-8039-4564-7*) Sage.

Multivariate Analysis of Categorical Data: Theory. John P. Van de Geer. (Advanced Quantitative Techniques in the Social Sciences Ser.: Vol. 2). (Illus.). 144p. 1993. 42.00 (*0-8039-4565-5*) Sage.

Multivariate Analysis of Data in Sensory Science. Ed. by Tomrod Naes & Einar Risvik. (Data Handling in Science & Technology Ser.: Vol. 16). 364p. 1996. text 225.50 (*0-444-89956-1*) Elsevier.

Multivariate Analysis of Variance. James H. Bray & Scott E. Maxwell. (Quantitative Applications in the Social Sciences Ser.: Vol. 54). 96p. 1985. pap. text 10.95 (*0-8039-2310-4*) Sage.

Multivariate Analysis of Variance & Repeated Measures. D. J. Hand & C. C. Taylor. (Texts in Statistical Science Ser.). 304p. (gr. 13). 1987. ring bd. 68.95 (*0-412-25800-5*, Chap & Hall CRC) CRC Pr.

Multivariate Analysis of Variance (MANOVA) A Practical Guide to Its Use in Scientific Decision-Making. fac. ed. Harry R. Barker & Barbara M. Barker. LC 82-16122. 131p. 1984. pap. 40.70 (*0-7837-8363-9*, 205917200009) Bks Demand.

Multivariate Analysis Techniques in Social Science Research: From Problem to Analysis. Jacques Tacq. 400p. 1996. 79.95 (*0-7619-5272-1*); pap. 29.95 (*0-7619-5273-X*) Sage.

Multivariate Applications in Substance Use Research. Ed. by Jennifer S. Rose et al. LC 99-28611. (Multivariate Applications Ser.). 450p. 1999. write for info. (*0-8058-2942-3*); pap. write for info. (*0-8058-2943-1*) L Erlbaum Assocs.

Multivariate Applications in the Social Sciences. Nancy Hirschberg & Lloyd G. Humphreys. 304p. (C). 1982. text 59.95 (*0-89859-152-X*) L Erlbaum Assocs.

Multivariate Approaches for the Behavioral Sciences: A Brief Text. G. Frank Lawlis & Douglas Chatfield. (Illus.). 153p. (Orig.). 1974. pap. text 5.00 (*0-89672-051-9*) Tex Tech Univ Pr.

Multivariate Approximation: From Cage to Wavelets - Proceedings of the International Workshop. D. Jetter. (On Approximations & Decomposition Ser.). 348p. 1993. text 109.00 (*981-02-1442-1*) World Scientific Pub.

Multivariate Approximation: Recent Trends & Results. Ed. by Werner Haumann et al. (Mathematical Research Ser.). 320p. 1997. 95.00 (*3-05-501770-6*, Pub. by Akademie Verlag) Wiley.

Multivariate Approximation: Recent Trends & Results. Ed. by Werner Haumann et al. 320p. 1997. 135.00 (*3-527-40117-2*) Wiley.

Multivariate Approximation & Interpolation: Proceedings of an International Workshop Held at the University of Duisburg, August 14-18, 1989. W. Haussmann & K. Jetter. (International Series of Numerical Mathematics: Vol. 94). 334p. 1990. 117.50 (*0-8176-2450-3*) Birkhauser.

Multivariate Approximation & Splines. G. Nurnberger et al. LC 97-37814. (International Series of Numerical Mathematics). 1997. write for info. (*0-8176-5654-5*) Birkhauser.

Multivariate Approximation & Splines. Guido Walz. Ed. by G. Nymberger & Jochen W. Schmidt. LC 97-37814. (International Series of Numerical Mathematics: Vol. 125). 336p. 1997. 98.00 (*3-7643-5654-5*) Spr-Verlag.

Multivariate Approximation Theory: Proceedings of the Conference at the Mathematical Research Institute at Oberwolfach, Black Forest, Feb. 1989, No. IV. Ed. by Charles K. Chui et al. (International Series of Numerical Mathematics: No. 90). 336p. 1989. 122.00 (*0-8176-2384-1*) Birkhauser.

Multivariate Approximation Theory: Selected Topics. E. W. Cheney. LC 86-61533. (CBMS-NSF Regional Conference Series in Applied Mathematics: No. 51). (Illus.). vi, 68p. 1986. pap. text 22.50 (*0-89871-207-6*) Soc Indus-Appl Math.

Multivariate Approximation Theory III. Walter Schempp & Karl Zeller. (International Series of Numerical Mathematics: No. 75). 400p. 1985. 87.50 (*0-8176-1738-8*) Birkhauser.

Multivariate Approximation Theory II. Ed. by Walter Schempp & Karl Zeller. (International Series of Numerical Mathematics: Vol. 61). 1982. 67.50 (*0-8176-1373-0*) Birkhauser.

Multivariate Archaeology: Numerical Approaches in Scandinavian Archaeology. Ed. by Torsten Madsen. (Jutland Archaeological Society Publications: No. 21). (Illus.). 150p. (C). 1988. pap. 16.95 (*87-7288-047-3*, Pub. by Aarhus Univ Pr) David Brown.

Multivariate Birkhoff Interpolation. Rudolph A. Lorentz. LC 92-27388. ix, 192p. 1992. 48.95 (*0-387-55870-5*); pap. 35.00 (*3-540-55870-5*) Spr-Verlag.

Multivariate Calculation. R. H. Farrell. (Series in Statistics). 430p. 1984. 87.95 (*0-387-96049-X*) Spr-Verlag.

Multivariate Calculus & Geometry. S. Dineen. LC 97-31752. (Undergraduate Mathematics Ser.). (Illus.). xii, 262p. 1998. pap. 29.95 (*3-540-76176-4*) Spr-Verlag.

Multivariate Calibration. Harold Martens & Tormod Naes. LC 89-14693. 438p. 1992. pap. 145.00 (*0-471-93047-4*) Wiley.

Multivariate Control System Design Techniques: Dominance & Direct Methods. G. F. Bryant & L. F. Yeung. LC 95-52281. 238p. 1996. 135.00 (*0-471-95866-2*) Wiley.

Multivariate Data Analysis. Fionn Murtagh & Andre Heck. (C). 1986. lib. bdg. 110.00 (*90-277-2425-3*) Kluwer Academic.

Multivariate Data Analysis. Fionn Murtagh & Andre Heck. (C). 1987. pap. text 59.50 (*90-277-2426-1*) Kluwer Academic.

Multivariate Data Analysis. Fionn Murtagh & Andre Heck. (C). 1988. pap. text 88.00 (*90-277-9154-6*) Kluwer Academic.

Multivariate Data Analysis. 5th ed. Joseph F. Hair. LC 97-47031. 730p. (C). 1998. 98.00 (*0-13-894858-5*) P-H.

Multivariate Data Analysis in Industrial Practice. Paul J. Lewi. LC 82-6906. (Chemometrics Research Studies: No. 3). (Illus.). 258p. reprint ed. pap. 80.00 (*0-8357-6228-9*, 203422900089) Bks Demand.

Multivariate Data Analysis in Sensory & Consumer Science. Ed. by Garmt B. Dijksterhuis. LC 97-61692. 309p. 1997. 100.00 (*0-917678-41-9*, 3312) Food & Nut Pr.

***Multivariate Data Reduction & Discrimination with SAS Software.** R. Khattree & D. N. Naik. 416p. 2000. pap. text 59.95 (*0-471-32300-4*) Wiley.

Multivariate Density Estimation: Theory, Practice, & Visualization. David W. Scott. LC 91-43950. (Probability & Mathematical Statistics: Applied Probability & Statistics Section Ser.: No. 1346). 336p. 1992. 125.00 (*0-471-54770-0*) Wiley.

Multivariate Dependencies, 1 vol. D. R. Cox. LC 98-48949. 272p. 1996. boxed set 64.95 (*0-412-75410-X*) CRC Pr.

Multivariate, Design & Sampling. Subir Ghosh. LC 99-14703. (Statistics Ser.). (Illus.). 696p. 1999. text 195.00 (*0-8247-0052-X*) Dekker.

Multivariate Design & Statistics. Steve Miller. (New Essential Psychology Ser.). 224p. 1986. pap. 7.95 (*0-416-34930-7*, 1019) Routledge.

Multivariate Environmental Statistics. Ed. by G. P. Patil & C. R. Rao. LC 93-27385. (North-Holland Series in Statistics & Probability: Vol. 6). 608p. 1994. 201.25 (*0-444-89804-2*, North Holland) Elsevier.

Multivariate Exploratory Data Analysis: A Perspective on Exploratory Factor Analysis. Allen Yates. LC 86-30207. 354p. (C). 1988. pap. text 29.95 (*0-88706-539-2*) State U NY Pr.

Multivariate GARCH in Mean Estimation of the Capital Asset Pricing Model. M. P. Taylor et al. LC HG1581.D57. (Bank of England - Discussion Papers: No. 19). 35p. 1988. reprint ed. pap. 30.00 (*0-608-03152-6*, 206360500007) Bks Demand.

Multivariate Geostatistics: An Introduction with Applications. 2nd rev. ed. H. Wackernagel. LC 98-36206. (Illus.). 312p. 1999. 59.95 (*3-540-64721-X*) Spr-Verlag.

Multivariate Geostatistics: An Introduction with Applications, Vol. XIV. H. Wackernagel. (Illus.). 256p. 1995. 64.95 (*3-540-60127-9*) Spr-Verlag.

Multivariate Interpretation of Clinical Laboratory Data. Adelin Albert & Eugene K. Harris. (Statistics: Textbooks & Monographs: Vol. 75). (Illus.). 328p. 1987. text 137.50 (*0-8247-7735-2*) Dekker.

Multivariate Methods in Aquaculture Research: Case Studies of Tilapias in Experimental & Commercial Systems. Ed. by G. I. Hulata et al. 200p. 1993. pap. 15.00 (*971-10-2285-0*, Pub. by ICLARM) Intl Spec Bk.

Multivariate Methods in Ecological Work. Ed. by Laszlo Orloci et al. (Statistical Ecology Ser.: Vol. 7). 580p. 1980. 50.00 (*0-89974-004-9*) Intl Co-Op.

***Multivariate Methods in High Energy Physics: The Neural Network Revolution.** Pushpalatha C. Bhat & Harrison B. Prosper. 300p. 2000. 58.00 (*981-02-4347-2*) World Scientific Pub.

Multivariate Models & Dependence Concepts. Harry Joe. LC 97-66010. (Monographs on Statistics & Applied Probability: Vol. 73). 399p. 1997. ring bd. 64.95 (*0-412-07331-5*, QA279) Chapman & Hall.

Multivariate Normal Distribution. Y. L. Tong. (Series in Statistics). 265p. 1989. 76.95 (*0-387-97062-2*) Spr-Verlag.

Multivariate Observations. G. A. Seber. LC 83-21741. (Probability & Mathematical Statistics Ser.: No. 1-345). 712p. 1984. 195.00 (*0-471-88104-X*) Wiley.

Multivariate Pattern Recognition in Chemometrics: Illustrated by Case Studies. Ed. by Richard G. Brereton. LC 92-28342. (Data Handling in Science & Technology Ser.: Vol. 2). 326p. (Orig.). 1992. pap. 108.00 (*0-444-89784-4*) Elsevier.

Multivariate Personality Research. Ed. by Ralph Dreger. 1972. 17.50 (*0-87511-029-0*) Claitors.

***Multivariate Probability & Stochastic Processes.** John Hope McColl. (Arnold Texts in Statistics). (Illus.). 288p. 2000. pap. text 34.95 (*0-340-71996-6*) OUP.

Multivariate Quality Control: Theory & Applications. Camil Fuchs & Ron Kenett. LC 98-2764. (Quality & Reliability Ser.). (Illus.). 224p. 1998. text 150.00 (*0-8247-9939-9*) Dekker.

Multivariate Reduced-Rank Regression. G. C. Reinsel & R. P. Velu. Ed. by P. Bickel et al. LC 98-29393. (Lecture Notes in Statistics Ser.: Vol. 136). 272p. 1998. pap. 39.95 (*0-387-98601-4*) Spr-Verlag.

Multivariate Splines. Charles K. Chui. LC 88-61569. (CBMS-NSF Regional Conference Ser.: No. 54). v, 189p. (C). 1988. pap. 29.00 (*0-89871-226-2*) Soc Indus-Appl Math.

Multivariate Statistical Analysis. Narayan C. Giri. LC 95-50252. (Statistics: Textbooks & Monographs: No. 149). (Illus.). 400p. 1996. text 150.00 (*0-8247-9338-2*) Dekker.

Multivariate Statistical Analysis: A Conceptual Introduction. 2nd ed. Sam K. Kachigan. LC 91-52869. (Illus.). 303p. (C). 1991. pap. text 19.95 (*0-942154-91-6*) Radius Pr.

Multivariate Statistical Analysis for Geographers. Daniel A. Griffith & Carl G. Amrhein. LC 96-53264. 345p. (C). 1997. 91.00 (*0-13-605692-X*) P-H.

Multivariate Statistical Inference & Application, Vol. 2. Alvin C. Rencher. LC 97-5255. (Series in Probability & Statistics). 592p. 1997. 89.95 incl. disk (*0-471-57151-2*) Wiley.

Multivariate Statistical Methods. 3rd ed. Donald F. Morrison. 560p. (C). 1989. text 69.74 (*0-07-043187-6*) McGraw.

Multivariate Statistical Methods: A First Course. George A. Marcoulides & Scott L. Hershberger. LC 96-46287. 344p. (C). 1997. text 89.95 (*0-8058-2571-1*); pap. text 39.95 (*0-8058-2572-X*) L Erlbaum Assocs.

Multivariate Statistical Methods: A Primer. 2nd ed. Bryan F. Manly, Jr. 232p. 1994. per. 41.95 (*0-412-60300-4*, Chap & Hall CRC) CRC Pr.

Multivariate Statistical Methods: An Introduction. Marvin J. Karson. LC 82-13057. (Illus.). 317p. 1982. reprint ed. pap. 98.30 (*0-608-06876-4*, 206708400009) Bks Demand.

Multivariate Statistical Methods in Behavioral Research. 2nd ed. R. Darrell Bock. 1985. pap. 40.00 (*0-89498-014-9*) Sci Ware.

Multivariate Statistical Methods in Physical Anthropology. Ed. by G. Van Vark & W. W. Howells. 1984. text 206.50 (*90-277-1734-6*) Kluwer Academic.

Multivariate Statistical Modeling. R. Christensen. LC 81-202346. (Entropy Minimax Sourcebook Ser.: Vol. 5). (Illus.). x, 724p. 1983. lib. bdg. 49.95 (*0-938876-14-7*) Entropy Ltd.

Multivariate Statistical Modeling & Data Analysis. Ed. by H. Bozdogan & A. K. Gupta. (C). 1987. text 122.00 (*90-277-2592-6*) Kluwer Academic.

Multivariate Statistical Modeling Based on Generalized Linear Models. Ludwig Fahrmeir & Gerhard Tutz. LC 93-50900. (Series in Statistics). (Illus.). 440p. 1997. text 60.95 (*0-387-94233-5*) Spr-Verlag.

Multivariate Statistical Simulation. Mark E. Johnson. LC 86-22469. (Probability & Mathematical Statistics Ser.). 240p. 1987. 140.00 (*0-471-82290-6*) Wiley.

***Multivariate Statistics for Wildlife & Ecology Research.** Ed. by K. McGarigal et al. LC 99-16036. (Illus.). 312p. 2000. 79.95 (*0-387-98891-2*) Spr-Verlag.

***Multivariate Statistics for Wildlife & Ecology Research.** Kevin McGarigal et al. LC 99-16036. (Illus.). 312p. 2000. pap. 39.95 (*0-387-98642-1*) Spr-Verlag.

Multivariate Taxometric Procedures: Distinguishing Types from Continua. Niels G. Waller & Paul E. Meehl. LC 97-33826. (Advanced Quantitative Techniques in the Social Sciences Ser.: Vol. 9). 149p. 1997. 32.95 (*0-7619-0257-0*) Sage.

Multivariate Tests for Time Series Models, No. 100. Ed. by Jeff B. Cromwell et al. (Quantitative Applications in the Social Sciences Ser.: Vol. 100). 96p. 1994. pap. 10.95 (*0-8039-5440-9*) Sage.

***Multivarious Data Analysis: Instructors Manual.** 5th ed. Hair. 1998. pap. text. write for info. (*0-13-906025-1*, Prentice Hall) P-H.

Multivectors & Clifford Algebra in Electrodynamics. B. Jancewicz. 332p. (C). 1989. text 79.00 (*9971-5-0290-9*) World Scientific Pub.

Multivendor Networking: Linking PCs, Minis & Mainframes over LANs & WANs. Andres Fortino & Jerry Golick. LC 95-32898. 1995. 65.00 (*0-07-912190-X*) McGraw.

Multiversa Strategy. Penelope O. Colville. LC 99-13. 430p. 1999. 64.35 (*1-55212-244-1*) Trafford Pub.

Multiverse of Democracy: Essays in Honour of Rajni Kothari. Ed. by D. L. Sheth & Ashis Nandy. 280p. (C). 1996. 38.00 (*0-8039-9288-2*) Sage.

Multivoice Magic. Monahan. 1991. pap. text. write for info. (*0-582-86849-1*, Pub. by Addison-Wesley) Longman.

Multiwavelength Optical Networks: A Layered Approach. Thomas E. Stern. LC 99-18432. 512p. (C). 1999. 73.00 (*0-201-30967-X*, Prentice Hall) P-H.

Multiway Contigency Tables Analysis for the Social Sciences. Thomas D. Wickens. 440p. 1989. pap. text 55.00 (*0-8058-0378-5*) L Erlbaum Assocs.

M

An Asterisk (*) at the beginning of an entry indicates that the title is appearing for the first time.

Multiway Contigency Tables Analysis for the Social Sciences. Thomas D. Wickens. 440p. 1989. 99.95 (0-8058-0377-7) L Erlbaum Assocs.

Multiyear Interactive Computer Almanac, 1990-2005: Version 1.5. Astronomical Applications Department, U. S. Naval Observatory Staff. LC 97-46556. 1997. write for info. (0-943396-56-5) Willmann-Bell.

Multiyear Lesson Plan Book. Char Forsten. (Illus.). 192p. 1996. pap. 14.95 (1-884548-10-5, 4861, Crystal Spgs) Soc Dev Educ.

Multnomah County (Oregon) Maintenance & Operations Facility. (PCI Journal Reprints Ser.). 17p. 1981. pap. 12.00 (0-686-40152-2, JR249) P-PCI.

Mulvaney Stories. Rudyard Kipling. LC 70-178444. (Short Story Index Reprint Ser.). 1977. reprint ed. 18.95 (0-8369-4045-8) Ayer.

Mum & Mr. Armitage: Selected Stories of Beryl Bainbridge. Beryl Bainbridge. LC 86-136242. 144 p. 1985. 7.95 (0-7156-2080-0) G Duckworth.

Mum & the Sothsegger. (EETS, OS Ser.: No. 199). 1974. reprint ed. 45.00 (0-527-00199-6) Periodicals Srv.

Mum for Hire. Victoria Pade. (Silhouette Ser.). 1999. 21.95 (0-373-59596-4) Silhouette.

Mum Is... E. Forbes. (J). pap. text 13.95 (0-340-68946-3, Pub. by Hodder & Stought Ltd) Trafalgar.

***Mum-Minder.** Wilson. (J). 2000. pap. 6.95 (0-440-86302-3, Pub. by Transworld Publishers Ltd) Trafalgar.

***Mum-Minder.** Jacqueline Wilson. 1999. 16.95 (0-7540-6073-X) Chivers N Amer.

MuMath: A Microcomputer Algebra System. Chris Wooff & David Hodgkinson. 159p. 1987. pap. text 44.00 (0-12-763070-8) Acad Pr.

***Mumbai (Bombay)** David Collins. (Illus.). 224p. 1999. pap. 14.95 (0-86442-702-6) Lonely Planet.

Mumbet: The Life & Times of Elizabeth Freeman: The True Story of a Slave Who Won Her Freedom. Mary Wilds. LC 99-20017. (Young Adult Ser.). (Illus.). 112p. (YA). (gr. 6-12). 1999. lib. bdg. 19.95 (1-888105-40-2) Avisson Pr.

Mumble Mystery. Jane Norman & Frank Beazley. 24p. (J). (ps-3). 1993. pap. write for info. (1-883585-12-0) Pixanne Ent.

Mumbling in the Dark. Michael W. Gommel. 1997. pap. write for info. (1-57553-677-3) Watermrk Pr.

Mumblings: The Inspirational Poetry of Joseph Hoey. Joseph Hoey. 150p. 1999. pap. 13.95 (0-7414-0101-0) Buy Books.

Mumbo Jumbo. Ishmael Reed. 224p. 1996. per. 11.00 (0-684-82477-9) S&S Trade.

Mumbo Jumbo. Kathryn L. Knight. Ed. by Jane Chelius. 224p. 1992. reprint ed. mass mkt. 4.99 (0-671-68447-7) PB.

Mumford Families in America, 1600-1992: A Biographical, Historical & Genealogical Sketch of the Colonial New England Mumford Family - up Through Present Day. Sherrie A. Styx. LC 92-80817. (Illus.). 400p. (C). 1992. text 53.00 (1-882121-16-3) Styx Enter.

Mumford, Tate, Eiseley: Watchers in the Night. Gale H. Carrithers. LC 91-11860. 257p. 1991. text 37.50 (0-8071-1650-5) La State U Pr.

***Mumia: His Story.** Terry Bisson. 2001. write for info. (0-87486-901-3) Plough.

Mummelmann. unabridged ed. Lons. (World Classic Literature Ser.). (GER.). pap. 5.95 (3-89507-031-9, Pub. by Bookking Intl) Distribks Inc.

***Mummies.** Sylvia Funston. (Strange Science Book Ser.). (Illus.). 40p. (J). (gr. 3-7). 2000. pap. 9.95 (1-894379-04-7, Pub. by GDPB); pap. 19.95 (1-894379-03-9, Pub. by GDPB) Firefly Bks Ltd.

Mummies. Nathaniel Harris. LC 94-39934. (Very Peculiar History Ser.). (Illus.). 48p. (J). (gr. 5-8). 1995. lib. bdg. 23.00 (0-531-14354-6) Watts.

Mummies. Nathaniel Harris. (Very Peculiar History Ser.). (Illus.). 48p. (J). (gr. 4-7). 1995. pap. 5.95 (0-531-15271-5) Watts.

Mummies. Iqbal Hussain. LC 98-84147. (Totally Amazing Ser.). 32p. (J). (gr. 2-6). 1998. pap. text 5.99 (0-307-20162-7, Goldn Books) Gldn Bks Pub Co.

Mummies. Ron Knapp. LC 94-42691. (Weird & Wacky Science Ser.). 48p. (J). (gr. 4-10). 1996. lib. bdg. 18.95 (0-89490-618-6) Enslow Pubs.

***Mummies.** Edith Kunhardt. LC 99-35936. (Road to Reading Ser.). 48p. 2000. 10.99 (0-307-46402-4) Gldn Bks Pub Co.

***Mummies.** Edith Kunhardt. LC 99-35936. (Illus.). 48p. (ps-3). 2000. pap. 3.99 (0-307-26402-5, Goldn Books) Gldn Bks Pub Co.

Mummies. Joyce Milton. LC 96-19295. (All Aboard Reading Ser.: Level 2). (Illus.). 48p. (J). (gr. 1-3). 1996. pap. 3.99 (0-448-41325-6, G & D); lib. bdg. 13.89 (0-448-41326-4, G & D) Peng Put Young Read.

Mummies. Joyce Milton. (All Aboard Reading Ser.). (J). 1996. 9.15 (0-606-11648-6, Pub. by Turtleback) Demco.

Mummies. John Vornholt. 96p. (J). 1991. pap. 3.50 (0-380-76317-6, Avon Bks) Morrow Avon.

Mummies: A Voyage Through Eternity. Francoise Dunand. (Discoveries Ser.). (Illus.). 128p. 1994. pap. 12.95 (0-8109-2886-8, Pub. by Abrams) Time Warner.

Mummies: Life after Death in Ancient Egypt. Renate Germer. LC 97-187482. (Illus.). 144p. 1997. 39.95 (3-7913-1804-7, Pub. by Prestel) te Neues.

Mummies & Mortuary Monuments: A Postprocessual Prehistory of Central Andean Social Organization. William H. Isbell. LC 96-51237. (Illus.). 384p. 1997. 40.00 (0-292-73870-6) U of Tex Pr.

Mummies & Moslems. Charles D. Warner. (Notable American Authors Ser.). 1999. reprint ed. lib. bdg. 125.00 (0-7812-9898-9) Rprt Serv.

***Mummies & Pyramids.** Will Osborne. (J). 2001. lib. bdg. 11.99 (0-375-90298-8) Random Bks Yng Read.

***Mummies & Pyramids.** Will Osborne. (Illus.). (J). 2001. pap. 4.99 (0-375-80298-3) Random Bks Yng Read.

Mummies & Their Mysteries. Charlotte Wilcox. (Carolrhoda Photo Bks.). (Illus.). 48p. (J). (ps-5). 1994. pap. 7.95 (0-87614-643-4, First Ave Edns); lib. bdg. 23.93 (0-87614-767-8, First Ave Edns) Lerner Pub.

Mummies & Their Mysteries. Charlotte Wilcox. 1997. 13.15 (0-606-12435-7, Pub. by Turtleback) Demco.

Mummies & Tombs. Houghton Mifflin Company Staff. (Literature Experience 1993 Ser.). (J). (gr. 6). 1992. pap. 11.04 (0-395-61835-5) HM.

***Mummies & Tombs.** Barbara Taylor. (Illus.). 64p. (gr. 3-7). 2000. 12.95 (0-7548-0505-0, Lorenz Bks) Anness Pub.

***Mummies, Bones & Body Parts.** Charlotte Wilcox. (gr. 4-7). 2000. pap. text 7.95 (1-57505-486-8, Carolrhoda) Lerner Pub.

***Mummies, Bones & Body Parts.** Charlotte Wilcox. LC 99-50516. (Photo Bks.). (Illus.). 64p. (J). (gr. 4-7). 2000. 25.26 (1-57505-428-0, Carolrhoda) Lerner Pub.

Mummies, Dinosaurs, Moon Rocks: How We Know How Old Things Are. James Jesperson & Jane Fitz-Randolph. (Illus.). 96p. (YA). (gr. 7). 1996. 16.00 (0-689-31848-0) Atheneum Yung Read.

Mummies, Disease & Ancient Cultures. 2nd ed. Ed. by Aidan Cockburn et al. LC 97-26894. (Illus.). 424p. (C). 1998. text 74.95 (0-521-58060-9); pap. text 29.95 (0-521-58954-1) Cambridge U Pr.

Mummies Don't Coach Softball. Debbie Dadey & Marcia Thornton Jones. (Adventures of the Bailey School Kids Ser.: No. 21). (J). (gr. 4-7). 1996. pap. 3.99 (0-590-22639-8) Scholastic Inc.

Mummies Don't Coach Softball. Debbie Dadey & Marcia Thornton Jones. (Adventures of the Bailey School Kids Ser.: No. 21). (J). (gr. 2-4). 1996. 8.70 (0-606-09644-2, Pub. by Turtleback) Demco.

Mummies in the Morning. Mary Pope Osborne. (Magic Tree House Ser.: No. 3). (Illus.). 80p. (J). (gr. k-3). 1993. pap. 3.99 (0-679-82424-3, Pub. by Random Bks Yng Read) Random.

Mummies in the Morning. Mary Pope Osborne. (First Stepping Stone Bks.: Vol. 3). (Illus.). 80p. (J). (gr. k-3). 1993. lib. bdg. 11.99 (0-679-92424-8, Pub. by Random Bks Yng Read) Random.

Mummies in the Morning. Mary Pope Osborne. (Magic Tree House Ser.: No. 3). (Illus.). (J). (gr. k-3). 1993. 9.19 (0-606-05932-6, Pub. by Turtleback) Demco.

Mummies Made in Egypt. Aliki. LC 77-26603. (Illus.). 32p. (J). (gr. 2-6). 1979. lib. bdg. 15.89 (0-690-03859-3) HarpC Child Bks.

Mummies Made in Egypt. Aliki. LC 85-42746. (Trophy Nonfiction Bk.). (Illus.). 32p. (J). (gr. 2-6). 1985. pap. 6.95 (0-06-446011-8, HarpTrophy) HarpC Child Bks.

Mummies Made in Egypt. Aliki. 1985. 11.15 (0-606-00342-8, Pub. by Turtleback) Demco.

Mummies, Myth & Magic: In Ancient Egypt. Christine El Mahdy. LC 89-50542. (Illus.). 192p. 1991. reprint ed. pap. 16.95 (0-500-27579-3, Pub. by Thames Hudson) Norton.

Mummies of Egypt. John J. Davis. 1986. pap. 10.99 (0-88469-179-9) BMH Bks.

Mummies of Urumchi. Elizabeth W. Barber. LC 98-18958. (Illus.). 240p. 1999. 35.00 (0-393-04521-8) Norton.

***Mummies of Urumchi.** Elizabeth Wayland Barber. (Illus.). 256p. 2000. pap. text 17.95 (0-393-32019-7) Norton.

Mummies Old & New - Their Health, Disease & Research Investigations: Index of New Information. Andris G. Chien. 150p. 1998. 47.50 (0-7883-2038-6); pap. 44.50 (0-7883-2039-4) ABBE Pubs Assn.

Mummies, Tombs, & Treasure. Houghton Mifflin Company Staff. (Literature Experience 1991 Ser.). (J). (gr. 7). 1990. pap. 11.04 (0-395-55171-4) HM.

Mummies, Tombs, & Treasure: Secrets of Ancient Egypt. Lila Perl. LC 86-17646. (Illus.). 128p. (J). (gr. 4 up). 1987. 16.00 (0-89919-407-9, Clarion Bks) HM.

Mummies, Tombs, & Treasure: Secrets of Ancient Egypt. Lila Perl. LC 86-17646. (Illus.). 128p. (J). (gr. 2-5). 1990. pap. 8.95 (0-395-54796-2, Clarion Bks) HM.

Mummies, Tombs, & Treasure: Secrets of Ancient Egypt. Lila Perl. (J). 1987. 12.15 (0-606-04483-3, Pub. by Turtleback) Demco.

***Mummies Unwrapped.** Kimberly Weinberger. LC 00-29699. (Hello Reader! Ser.). (Illus.). (J). 2001. lib. bdg. write for info. (0-439-20058-X) Scholastic Inc.

Mummies, Pyramids, & Pharaohs: A Book About Ancient Egypt. Gail Gibbons. (J). 2001. write for info. (0-316-30928-1) Little.

***Mummy.** Caroline B. Cooney. (Illus.). 176p. (J). (gr. 7-12). 2000. mass mkt. 4.50 (0-590-67450-1) Scholastic Inc.

Mummy. DK Editors. (Eyewitness Activity Files Ser.). (Illus.). (J). (gr. 3-10). 1998. pap. 9.95 (0-7894-2791-5) DK Pub Inc.

***Mummy.** Jim Putnam. (Eyewitness Books). (Illus.). (J). (gr. 4-8). 2000. 19.99 (0-7894-6593-0) DK Pub Inc.

***Mummy.** Jim Putnam. (Eyewitness Books). (J). (gr. 4-7). 2000. 15.95 (0-7894-5856-X) DK Pub Inc.

Mummy. Jim Putnam. LC 92-1591. (Eyewitness Books). (Illus.). 64p. (J). (gr. 5 up). 1993. 19.00 (0-679-83881-3, Pub. by Knopf Bks Yng Read) Random.

Mummy. Katie Roden. (In the Footsteps of...Ser.). (Illus.). 40p. (J). (gr. 4-6). 1996. lib. bdg. 21.90 (0-7613-0451-7, Copper Beech Bks) Millbrook Pr.

Mummy. Katie Roden. LC 95-39829. (In the Footsteps Of--Ser.). 1996. 12.15 (0-606-09462-8, Pub. by Turtleback) Demco.

Mummy. Barbara Steiner. 176p. (J). (gr. 7-9). 1995. pap. 3.50 (0-590-20353-3) Scholastic Inc.

Mummy. Barbara Steiner. (J). 1995. 8.60 (0-606-07899-1, Pub. by Turtleback) Demco.

Mummy. 2nd ed. E. A. Wallis Budge. LC 64-13391. (Illus.). 1994. pap. 25.00 (0-8196-0139-X) Biblo.

Mummy: A Handbook of Egyptian Funerary Archaeology. E. A. Wallis Budge. 576p. 1989. pap. 10.95 (0-486-25928-5) Dover.

Mummy: A Novel. Max A. Collins. 256p. 1999. mass mkt. 5.99 (0-425-16948-0) Blvd Books.

Mummy! A Tale of the Twenty-Second Century. Jane W. Loudon. LC 87-60458. 500p. 1988. reprint ed. 30.00 (0-915431-03-3); reprint ed. pap. 19.95 (0-915431-04-1) N American Archives.

Mummy: Chapters on Egyptian Funeral Archaeology. E. A. Wallis Budge. (Illus.). 404p. 1998. reprint ed. pap. 42.00 (1-58073-005-1) BCP Bks.

Mummy: Chapters on Egyptian Funeral Archaeology. E. A. Wallis Budge. (Illus.). 404p. 1998. reprint ed. pap. 42.00 (0-933121-69-5) Black Classic.

***Mummy: Unwrap The Ancient Secrets of The Mummies' Tombs.** Joyce A. Tyldesley. 128p. 1999. pap. text 17.95 (1-85868-771-3, Pub. by Carlton Bks Ltd) Natl Bk Netwk.

Mummy & Miss Nitocris: A Phantasy of the Fourth Dimension. George Griffith. Ed. by R. Reginald & Douglas A. Menville. LC 75-46273. (Supernatural & Occult Fiction Ser.). 1976. reprint ed. lib. bdg. 26.95 (0-405-08131-6) Ayer.

Mummy Case. Franklin W. Dixon. (Hardy Boys Mystery Stories Ser.: No. 63). 192p. (J). (gr. 3-6). 1987. mass mkt. 3.99 (0-671-64289-8, Minstrel Bks) PB.

Mummy Case. Elizabeth Peters, pseud. (Amelia Peabody Mystery Ser.). 336p. 1995. mass mkt. 6.99 (0-446-60193-4, Pub. by Warner Bks) Little.

Mummy Case. Dawn Stewardson. (Intrigue Ser.). 1994. per. 2.99 (0-373-22257-2, 1-22257-9) Harlequin Bks.

Mummy Cases & Inscribed Funerary Cones in the Petrie Collection. H. M. Stewart. (Petrie Collection). (Orig.). 1985. pap. 39.95 (0-85668-312-4, Pub. by Aris & Phillips) David Brown.

***Mummy Dearest.** 2000. per. write for info. (0-671-77324-0) S&S Trade.

***Mummy Dearest.** Mel Odom. (Sabrina, the Teenage Witch Ser.: No. 31). 176p. (YA). (gr. 5 up). 2000. per. 4.50 (0-671-04068-5, Archway) PB.

Mummy in Ancient Egypt. Salima Ikram & Aidan Dodson. LC 97-91993. (Illus.). 352p. 1998. 45.00 (0-500-05088-0, Pub. by Thames Hudson) Norton.

Mummy Long Arms. (Young Dragon Readers 1 Ser.). (J). 1995. pap. text. write for info. (962-359-530-1) Addison-Wesley.

Mummy Mess, Vol. 1. Pat Ross. (Puffin Chapters Ser.). 1999. pap. 3.99 (0-14-130654-8, PuffinBks) Peng Put Young Read.

Mummy Musical. Michael Tester. 1996. 5.95 (0-87129-595-4, M93) Dramatic Pub.

Mummy Mysteries: Tales from North America & the Arctic. Guiberson. LC 97-50428. (J). (gr. 2-5). 1998. 15.95 (0-8050-5369-7) H Holt & Co.

***Mummy Mystery: Language Arts.** McGraw-Hill Staff. (J). (gr. 5). 1999. 19.95 (1-57768-335-8) MG-Hill OH.

Mummy of Ramose. Shirley Glubok & Alfred Tamarin. LC 76-21392. (Illus.). (J). 1978. 12.95 (0-06-022039-2) HarpC Child Bks.

Mummy!: or A Tale of the Twenty-Second Century. abr. ed. Jane W. Loudon & Jame W. Loudon. LC 94-12992. 344p. 1994. text 44.50 (0-472-09574-9, 09574, Ann Arbor Bks); pap. text 18.95 (0-472-06574-2, 06574) U of Mich Pr.

Mummy, or Ramses the Damned. Anne Rice. 1989. pap. 14.00 (0-345-36000-1) Ballantine Pub Grp.

Mummy, or Ramses the Damned. Anne Rice. 416p. 1991. mass mkt. 6.99 (0-345-36994-7) Ballantine Pub Grp.

***Mummy Riddles.** Katy Hall. (Easy-to-Read Ser.). 48p. (J). 1999. pap. 3.99 (0-14-130364-6, PuffinBks) Peng Put Young Read.

Mummy Riddles. Katy Hall & Lisa Eisenberg. LC 94-37525. (Illus.). 48p. (J). (ps-3). 1997. 13.99 (0-8037-1846-2, Dial Yng Read) Peng Put Young Read.

Mummy, the Will & the Crypt. John Bellairs. 176p. 1985. pap. 3.99 (0-553-15701-9) Bantam.

Mummy, the Will & the Crypt. John Bellairs. LC 83-7223. (Illus.). 176p. (J). (gr. 3-7). 1996. pap. 4.99 (0-14-038007-8, PuffinBks) Peng Put Young Read.

Mummy, the Will & the Crypt. John Bellairs. (J). 1996. 9.09 (0-606-10883-1, Pub. by Turtleback) Demco.

Mummy Walks. R. L. Stine, pseud. (Goosebumps Series 2000: No. 16). 1999. pap. text 3.99 (0-590-68520-1) Scholastic Inc.

Mummy Who Wouldn't Die. E. A. M. Jakab. (Choose Your Own Nightmare Ser.: No. 9). (J). (gr. 4-8). 1996. 8.60 (0-606-09143-2, Pub. by Turtleback) Demco.

Mummy Who Wouldn't Die see Choose Your Own Nightmare Series

Mummy's Curse. Meredith Costain. LC 99-173652. (Brains & Parker McGoohan Ser.). 64 p. 1999. write for info. (0-7608-1938-6) Sundance Pub.

Mummy's Curse: One Hundred One of the World's Strangest Mysteries. Daniel Cohen. LC 94-4378. 224p. (Orig.). (J). 1994. pap. 3.99 (0-380-77093-8, Avon Bks) Morrow Avon.

Mummys Curse: Universal Filmscripts Classic Horror Films, Vol. 11. Gregory W. Mank. 2000. pap. 19.95 (1-882127-35-8) Magicimage Filmbooks.

Mummy's Footsteps. Cheryl Zach. (Mind Over Matter Ser.). (Orig.). 1997. 9.09 (0-606-11623-0, Pub. by Turtleback) Demco.

Mummy's Gold. Kate McMullan. LC 95-46794. (Eek! Stories to Make You Shriek Ser.). (Illus.). 48p. (J). (gr. 1-3). 1996. pap. 3.95 (0-448-41310-8, G & D); lib. bdg. 13.99 (0-448-41345-0, G & D) Peng Put Young Read.

Mummy's Gold. Kate Mcmullan. (Eek! Stories to Make You Shriek Ser.). 1996. 9.15 (0-606-10884-X, Pub. by Turtleback) Demco.

***Mummy's Home Town: The Curse of the Amulet.** Heather M. Langlais. (Illus.). 144p. (J). (gr. 4-8). 1999. pap. 7.95 (1-930506-00-7) March Forth.

***Mummy's Legs.** Kate Bingham. LC 99-36028. 224p. 2000. 20.00 (0-684-86470-3) S&S Trade.

Mummy's Mirror. Dawn A. Poore. 256p. 1995. mass mkt. 3.99 (0-8217-5050-X, Zebra Kensgtn) Kensgtn Pub Corp.

Mummy's Revenge. Roy Pond. 160p. (J). (gr. 4-6). 1994. pap. 3.50 (0-590-48374-9) Scholastic Inc.

Mummy's Tomb. Roy Pond. (J). 1996. pap. 3.50 (0-590-60370-1) Scholastic Inc.

Mummy's Tomb. Roy Pond. (J). 1996. 8.60 (0-606-09645-0, Pub. by Turtleback) Demco.

***Mummy's Tomb Maze Book.** Golden Books Staff. (Illus.). (J). 2000. 9.99 (0-307-11127-X, Goldn Books) Gldn Bks Pub Co.

Mumps. Nathaniel A. Dickens. (Orig.). 1990. pap. write for info. (0-916191-05-2) Dickens Pubns.

Mum's the Word. Dorothy Cannell. 272p. 1991. mass mkt. 5.99 (0-553-28686-2) Bantam.

***Mum's the Word.** large type ed. Alison Roberts. 288p. 1999. 25.99 (0-263-16025-4, Pub. by Mills & Boon) Ulverscroft.

Mum's the World: The Mamma's Boy Syndrome Revealed. Arlene Gorodensky. 128p. 1997. pap. 29.95 (0-304-33884-2); text 89.50 (0-304-33883-4) Continuum.

Mumwalds. Lee Crawford. (Illus.). 200p. (Orig.). 1994. pap. 12.99 (0-8272-2322-6) Chalice Pr.

Muna-English Dictionary. Rene Van Den Berg. LC 97-121319. (Illus.). 737p. 1996. 84.50 (90-6718-101-3, Pub. by KITLV Pr) Cellar.

Muna Madan: A Play in the Jhyaure Folk Tradition. L. P. Devkota. 1995. pap. write for info. (0-7855-0414-1, Pub. by Ratna Pustak Bhandar) St Mut.

Munajat: The Intimate Prayers. Khwajih A. Ansari. Tr. by Rustam Sarfeh from PER. LC 75-30173. (ENG.). 84p. 1975. 7.50 (0-917220-00-5) Khaneghah & Maktab.

Munch. Jane Avril. 1995. pap. 8.99 (3-8228-9758-2) Taschen Amer.

Munch. Ulrich Bischoff. (SPA.). 1996. pap. 12.99 (3-8228-0224-7) Benedikt Taschen.

Munch. Ulrich Bischoff. 1996. pap. 9.99 (3-8228-0569-6) Taschen Amer.

Munch. Ed. by Jose M. Faerna. LC 96-84011. (Great Modern Masters Ser.). (Illus.). 64p. 1996. pap. 11.98 (0-8109-4694-7, Pub. by Abrams) Time Warner.

Munch. David Loshak. (Illus.). 112p. 1999. pap. 19.95 (1-57715-070-8) Knckerbocker.

Munch. Thomas M. Messer. (Masters of Art Ser.). (Illus.). 128p. 1986. 24.95 (0-8109-1415-8, Pub. by Abrams) Time Warner.

***Munch.** Edvard Munch. (Illus.). 2000. pap. 1.00 (0-486-41066-8) Dover.

Munch. Gabriel Potter. 1994. 5.98 (0-7858-0206-1) Bk Sales Inc.

Munch. John B. Smith. (Color Library). (Illus.). 128p. (C). 1994. pap. 14.95 (0-7148-2732-0, Pub. by Phaidon Press) Phaidon Pr.

Munch. Taschen Staff. (SPA.). Date not set. pap. 4.99 (3-8228-8786-2, Pub. by Benedikt Taschen) Bks Nippan.

Munch: At the Munch Museum, Oslo. Arne Eggum et al. LC 99-183515. 128 p. 1998. write for info. (1-85759-196-8) Scala Books.

Munch: His Life & Work. Reinhold Heller. LC 83-24098. (Illus.). 240p. 1994. pap. 22.50 (0-226-32644-6) U Ch Pr.

Munch: His Life & Work. Reinhold Heller. LC 83-24098. (Illus.). 240p. 1994. lib. bdg. 39.95 (0-226-32643-8) U Ch Pr.

***Munch: The Scream.** Federico Zeri. (One Hundred Paintings Ser.). 48p. 2000. 14.95 (1-55321-015-8, Pub. by NDE Pub) IPG Chicago.

Munch & Photography. Arne Eggum. (C). 1989. 57.00 (0-300-04548-4) Yale U Pr.

Munch & Women: Image & Myth. Patricia G. Berman et al. LC 96-29322. 1997. 24.95 (0-88397-121-6) Art Srvc Intl.

Munch at the Munich-Museet, Oslo. Arne Eggum. 1998. 35.00 (1-85759-185-2) Scala Books.

Munch! What Are You Eating? Rebecca Elgar. 1999. 6.95 (1-899607-57-9) Levinson Bks.

***Muncha! Muncha! Muncha!** Candace Fleming. LC 99-24882. (Illus.). (J). 2001. 20.01 (0-689-83152-8) Atheneum Yung Read.

Munchausen by Proxy Syndrome: Misunderstood Child Abuse. Ed. by Teresa F. Parnell & Deborah O. Day. LC 97-4838. 240p. 1997. text 52.00 (0-8039-5811-0); pap. text 24.95 (0-8039-5812-9) Sage.

Munchausen Exploits. Mark Dunster. 11p. (Orig.). 1992. pap. 4.00 (0-89642-205-4) Linden Pubs.

Munchausen Syndrome by Proxy: Issues in Diagnosis & Treatment. Alex V. Levin & Mary S. Sheridan. LC 95-3324. 479p. 1996. 49.95 (0-02-918606-4) Jossey-Bass.

***Munchausen Syndrome by Proxy Abuse: A Practical Approach.** Ed. by D. Mary Eminson & R. J. Postlethwaite. LC 99-46238. 321p. 2000. pap. text 50.00 (0-7506-4072-3) Buttrwrth-Heinemann.

Munchausen's Syndrome by Proxy: Current Issues in Assessment, Treatment & Research. Ed. by Gwen Adshead & Deborah Brooke. 200p. 1999. 34.00 (1-86094-134-6) World Scientific Pub.

Munchener Phanomenologie. Ed. by H. Kuhn et al. (Phaenomenologica Ser.: No. 65). 194p. 1976. lib. bdg. 106.00 (90-247-1740-X, Pub. by M Nijhoff) Kluwer Academic.

Munchhausen. unabridged ed. Burger. (World Classic Literature Ser.). (GER.). pap. 5.95 (3-89507-001-7, Pub. by Bookking Intl) Distribks Inc.

An Asterisk (*) at the beginning of an entry indicates that the title is appearing for the first time.

Munchhausen Ohnegleichen: Intermediate. (GER.). (C). 1995. 9.95 (*0-8442-2045-0*, X2045-0) NTC Contemp Pub Co.

Munchhausens Abenteuer: Level A. text 7.95 (*0-88436-903-X*) EMC-Paradigm.

Munchies, Dips, Spreads, & Breads. Sue Thraves. 1995. 17.98 (*0-7858-0444-7*) Bk Sales Inc.

Munchies, Meals & Mayhem! Simple Recipes & Fun Projects for Kids. Kris Roeglin & Linda Fullerton. (Illus.). 110p. (J). (ps-6). 1996. pap. 12.95 (*0-9655480-2-3*) Wooden Spoon Pub.

***Munching, Crunching, Sniffing & Snooping.** Brian Moses. LC 99-20404. (Eyewitness Readers). 32p. (J). (gr. 1-3). 1999. 3.95 (*0-7894-4752-5*); 12.95 (*0-7894-4753-3*) DK Pub Inc.

***Munching Maggots, Noah's Flood & TV Heart Attacks: And Other Cataclysmic Science Moments.** Karl Kruszelnicki. LC 99-55614. 189p. 1999. pap. 14.95 (*0-471-37850-X*) Wiley.

Munchkin Tennis: A Parent's Guide to Teaching Tennis Fundamentals. rev. ed. U. S. Professional Registry Staff. (Illus.). 552p. 1998. pap. 14.95 (*1-57243-282-9*) Triumph Bks.

***Munchkin's Guide to Power Gaming.** James Desborough & Steve Mortimer. Ed. by Phil Masters. 128p. 1999. pap. 19.95 (*1-55634-347-7*, Pub. by S Jackson Games) BookWorld.

Munchkins of Oz. rev. ed. Stephen Cox. Orig. Title: The Munchkins Remember. (Illus.). 256p. 1996. pap. 18.95 (*1-888952-04-0*) Cumberland Hse.

Munchkins Remember see Munchkins of Oz

Munchmeyer & Prospero on the Island. Audrey C. Thomas. LC 75-161252. 1972. 5.95 (*0-672-51432-X*, Bobbs) Macmillan.

Munchy Crunchy Book. lib. bdg. 18.90 (*0-8027-6234-4*) Walker & Co.

Munchy Crunchy Bug Book. Ray Nelson, Jr. et al. Ed. by Joseph Siegel. (Illus.). 48p. (J). (gr. 3-6). 1997. 16.95 (*1-883772-08-7*) Flying Rhino.

***Muncie.** Milton Masing & Jeffrey Koenker. (Images of America Ser.). 1999. pap. 18.99 (*0-7385-0111-5*) Arcadia Publng.

Muncy: Descendants of Francis Munch I, with Genealogy of Allied Families. rev. ed. M. E. Shaw. (Illus.). 357p. 1993. reprint ed. pap. 49.50 (*0-8328-3722-9*); reprint ed. lib. bdg. 59.50 (*0-8328-3721-0*) Higginson Bk Co.

Munda Trail. Eric Hammel. 320p. 1991. reprint ed. mass mkt. 4.50 (*0-380-71458-2*, Avon Bks) Morrow Avon.

***Mundaka Upanisad: With the Original Text in Sanskrit & Roman Transliteration, Translation with an Exhaustive Commentary.** Muni Narayana Prasad. LC 98-903086. vii, 142p. 1998. pap. 12.00 (*81-246-0105-4*, Pub. by D K Printwrld) Nataraj Bks.

Mundaka Upanishad with Commentary of Shankara. Tr. by Swami Gambhirananda from SAN. 100p. 1978. pap. 2.00 (*0-87481-203-8*, Pub. by Advaita Ashrama) Vedanta Pr.

Mundakopanisad. Tr. by Swami Sarvananda. (C). pap. 1.25 (*0-87481-460-X*) Vedanta Pr.

Mundane Astrology. H. S. Green & Raphael. LC 77-86746. 205p. 1977. reprint ed. pap. 6.50 (*0-912504-39-0*) Sym & Sign.

Mundane Astrology: An Introduction to the Astrology of Nations & Groups. Michael Baigent et al. 496p. 1988. pap. 12.95 (*0-85030-302-8*, Pub. by Aqrn Pr) Harper SF.

Mundane Astrology: An Introduction to the Astrology of Nations & Groups. rev. ed. Michael Baigent et al. 544p. pap. 19.95 (*1-85538-140-0*, Pub. by Aqrn Pr) HarpC.

Mundane Astrology: Interpreting Astrological Phenomena for Cities, Nations & Groups. C. C. Zain. (Brotherhood of Light Home Study Ser.: Course 13). 1996. pap. 16.95 (*0-87887-350-3*) Church of Light.

Mundane Matter of the Mental Language. J. Christopher Maloney. (Cambridge Studies in Philosophy). (Illus.). 304p. (C). 1989. text 80.00 (*0-521-37031-0*) Cambridge U Pr.

Mundane Perspectives in Astrology: The Expanded Dynamic Horoscopy. Marc E. Jones. (Illus.). 455p. 1975. 19.50 (*0-87878-014-9*) Sabian Pub.

Mundari-English Dictionary. Bhaduri. (ENG.). 228p. 1983. 24.95 (*0-7859-7463-6*) Fr & Eur.

Mundart & Schriftsprache in Bayern, 1450-1800: Untersuchungen zur Sprachnorm & Sprachnormierung im Fruehneuhochdeutschen. Walter Tauber. (Studia Linguistica Germanica: Bd 32). (GER.). xiii, 371p. (C). 1993. lib. bdg. 135.40 (*3-11-013556-6*) De Gruyter.

***Mundartlichen Verhaltnisse in der Region Munchen.** Bernhard Stor. (GER., Illus.). 1999. 96.95 (*3-631-30588-5*) P Lang Pubng.

Mundic Problem: A Guidance Note Recommended Sampling, Examination & Classification Procedure for Suspect Concrete Building Materials in Devon & Cornwall. RICS Books Staff. 1993. pap. 100.00 (*0-85406-586-5*, Pub. by R-I-C-S Bks) St Mut.

Mundjamba: The Life Story of an African Hunter. limited ed. Hugo Seia. LC 95-61364. (Illus.). 383p. 1995. 125.00 (*1-882458-09-5*) Trophy Rm Bks.

Mundo al Que Predicamos. S. Dellutri.Tr. of World We Preach To. (SPA.). 9.99 (*0-7899-0619-8*, 491070) Editorial Unilit.

***Mundo Antiguo (Ancient World)** (ENG & SPA., Illus.). 96p. (YA). (gr. 3 up). 2000. 19.95 (*0-7460-3890-9*, Usborne) EDC.

Mundo Como Voluntad y Representacion: Borges y Schopenhauer. Ana Sierra. 156p. 1998. pap. 49.95 (*1-57309-231-2*) Intl Scholars.

Mundo de Dios: Figuras Que Aparecen. P. Mills. (Figuras Que Aparecen (Chunky Pop-up Bk.)).Tr. of God's World: Chunky Pop-Up Book. (SPA.). 72p. (J). 1993. 3.50 (*1-56063-632-7*, 494606) Editorial Unilit.

Mundo de Dios (God's World) Scandinavia Staff. (SPA.). 4.50 (*0-685-74962-2*, 491396) Editorial Unilit.

***Mundo de Figuras Imposibles.** Bruno Ernst. 1999. 16.99 (*3-8228-8536-3*) Benedikt Taschen.

Mundo de la Cultura: Enciclopedia Formativa Marin, 12 vols., Set. Marin Staff. (SPA.). 2400p. 1978. 395.00 (*0-8288-5255-3*, S50488) Fr & Eur.

Mundo de las Plantas. Francesca Baines. Tr. by Maria T. Sanz. (Biblioteca de Descubrimientos Ser.). (SPA., Illus.). 32p. (J). (gr. k-4). 1998. 11.95 (*1-58087-010-4*) C D Stampley Ent.

Mundo de los Animales: The World of Animals. Planeta Staff. 1990. write for info. (*0-7859-5228-4*) Fr & Eur.

Mundo de los Incas. Felipe Cossio del Pomar. (SPA.). pap. 6.99 (*968-16-0563-2*, Pub. by Fondo) Continental Bk.

Mundo de los Microbios. Georges D. Cortes. (Ciencia para Todos Ser.). (SPA.). pap. 6.99 (*968-16-2703-2*, Pub. by Fondo) Continental Bk.

***Mundo de los Ninos.** World Book Staff. (Illus.). 2538p. (J). (gr. k-8). 1999. write for info. (*0-7166-6426-7*) World Bk.

Mundo de los Ninos, 15 vols. 3rd deluxe ed. Salvat Staff. (SPA.). 4802p. 1987. 895.00 (*0-7859-5111-3*) Fr & Eur.

Mundo de los Ninos, Vol. 1. 3rd ed. Salvat Staff. 320p. 1987. 60.00 (*0-7859-5931-9*, 8434533057) Fr & Eur.

Mundo de los Ninos, Vol. 2. 3rd ed. Salvat Staff. 312p. 1987. 60.00 (*0-7859-5932-7*, 8434533065) Fr & Eur.

Mundo de los Ninos, Vol. 3. 3rd ed. Salvat Staff. 296p. 1987. 60.00 (*0-7859-5933-5*, 8434533073) Fr & Eur.

Mundo de los Ninos, Vol. 4. 3rd ed. Salvat Staff. 350p. 1987. 60.00 (*0-7859-5934-3*, 8434533081) Fr & Eur.

Mundo de los Ninos, Vol. 5. 3rd ed. Salvat Staff. 344p. 1987. 60.00 (*0-7859-6464-9*) Fr & Eur.

Mundo de los Ninos, Vol. 6. 3rd ed. Salvat Staff. 304p. 1987. 60.00 (*0-7859-5935-1*, 8434533103) Fr & Eur.

Mundo de los Ninos, Vol. 8. 3rd ed. Salvat Staff. 320p. 1987. 60.00 (*0-7859-6465-7*) Fr & Eur.

Mundo de los Ninos, Vol. 9. 3rd ed. Salvat Staff. 320p. 1987. 60.00 (*0-7859-5937-8*, 8434533138) Fr & Eur.

Mundo de los Ninos, Vol. 10. 3rd ed. Salvat Staff. 324p. 1987. 60.00 (*0-7859-5938-6*, 8434533146) Fr & Eur.

Mundo de los Ninos, Vol. 11. 3rd ed. Salvat Staff. 320p. 1987. 60.00 (*0-7859-5939-4*, 8434533154) Fr & Eur.

Mundo de los Ninos, Vol. 12. 3rd ed. Salvat Staff. 304p. 1987. 60.00 (*0-7859-5940-8*, 8434533162) Fr & Eur.

Mundo de los Ninos, Vol. 13. 3rd ed. Salvat Staff. 296p. 1987. 60.00 (*0-7859-5941-6*, 8434533170) Fr & Eur.

Mundo de los Ninos, Vol. 14. 3rd ed. Salvat Staff. 304p. 1987. 60.00 (*0-7859-5942-4*, 8434533189) Fr & Eur.

Mundo de los Ninos, Vol. 15. 3rd ed. Salvat Staff. 368p. 1987. 60.00 (*0-7859-5943-2*, 8434533197) Fr & Eur.

Mundo de los Ninos: The Kingfisher Young World Encyclopedia. (SPA., Illus.). 496p. (J). (ps-3). 1996. 29.95 (*1-85697-562-2*, Kingfisher) LKC.

Mundo de los Suenos. Ruben Dario. (Coleccion Mente y Palabra). 233p. (C). 1973. 5.00 (*0-8477-0502-1*); pap. 4.00 (*0-8477-0503-X*) U of PR Pr.

Mundo Del Antiguo Testamento. J. I. Packer.Tr. of World of the Old Testament. (SPA.). 192p. 1985. pap. 8.99 (*0-8297-1416-2*) Vida Pubs.

Mundo del Empleo. Tomas Sarramia. 328p. 1991. pap. write for info. (*0-929441-19-2*) Pubns Puertorriquenas.

Mundo Del Nuevo Testamento. J. I. Packer.Tr. of World of the New Testament. (SPA.). 192p. 1985. pap. 8.99 (*0-8297-1418-9*) Vida Pubs.

Mundo Delicioso de la Papa. deluxe ed. Ed. by Victor D. Marrero. (SPA., Illus.). 112p. 1998. pap. 2.95 (*0-939193-46-9*) Edit Concepts.

Mundo en Llamas: The Whole World Aflame. Billy Graham. (SPA.). 272p. 1981. reprint ed. pap. 7.99 (*0-311-46091-7*) Casa Bautista.

Mundo Es Asi. Y Nessi, Pio Baroja. Ed. by Jose A. Perez Bowie. (Nueva Austral Ser.: No. 142). (SPA.). 1991. pap. text 24.95 (*84-239-1942-0*) Elliots Bks.

Mundo Es Como uno lo Suena-The World Is As You Dream It. John Perkins. (SPA., Illus.). 238p. 1995. pap. 12.95 (*0-89281-465-9*) Inner Tradit.

Mundo Feliz. Aldous Huxley. 1998. pap. 6.50 (*84-01-42321-X*) Lectorum Pubns.

Mundo Hispanp: An Introduction. 4th ed. Terrell. (SPA.). 40p. 1999. pap. 7.19 (*0-07-064728-3*) McGraw.

Mundo Iberoamer Hombre: Hombres en Su Historia. Edilberto Marban. 390p. (YA). (gr. 10-12). 1974. pap. text 6.95 (*0-88345-066-6*, 18084) Prentice ESL.

Mundo Magico del Vidrio. Tessy Lopez. (Ciencia Para Todos Ser.). (SPA.). pap. 6.99 (*968-16-4695-9*, Pub. by Fondo) Continental Bk.

Mundo Maravilloso de las Aves. (SPA.). 10.00 (*84-241-5403-7*) E Torres & Sons.

Mundo Marino. Francesca Baines. (Biblioteca de Descubrimientos Ser.).Tr. of Ocean World. (SPA., Illus.). (J). (gr. 3-6). 1997. 11.95 (*0-915741-88-1*, SY7079) C D Stampley Ent.

Mundo Misterioso de los Peces. (SPA.). 10.00 (*84-241-5404-5*) E Torres & Sons.

***Mundo Nuevo.** Danilo Figueredo. (SPA.). 2000. 15.95 (*1-58430-006-X*); pap. 6.95 (*1-58430-007-8*) Lee & Low Bks.

Mundo Perdido, 1. Michael Crichton. 1998. pap. text 6.95 (*84-01-49240-8*) Lectorum Pubns.

Mundo Psiquico. Aurora Ecchevarria. 1998. pap. 4.50 (*84-01-54043-7*) Lectorum Pubns.

Mundo Que Creo el Azucar. Pedro San Miguel. LC 89-80369. 224p. 1989. pap. 8.50 (*0-940238-98-5*) Ediciones Huracan.

Mundo Que Perecio. John C. Whitcomb. Orig. Title: The World That Perished. (SPA.). 176p. 1991. pap. 7.99 (*0-8254-1867-4*, Edit Portavoz) Kregel.

Mundo Sin Clara. Felix Rizo. (SPA.). 1997. pap. 9.95 (*0-89729-824-1*) Ediciones.

Mundo Submarino (Underwater World) see Enciclopedia Ilustrada de Ciencia Naturaleza (Understanding Science & Nature)

Mundo Tragico de los Griegos y de Shakespeare. Ludiwg Schajowicz. LC 90-30319. 374p. (Orig.). 1990. pap. 12.75 (*0-8477-2831-5*) U of PR Pr.

Mundo 21. Fabian A. Samaniego et al. LC 94-76351. (SPA.). 598p. (C). 1995. pap. text 47.96 (*0-669-21788-3*) HM Trade Div.

Mundo 21. annot. ed. Fabian A. Samaniego et al. (SPA.). (C). 1995. text, teacher ed. 40.36 (*0-669-21791-3*) HM Trade Div.

Mundo Unido: Lectura y Escritura, Vol. 1. Robert Nicholas. (SPA.). 1995. 21.95 (*0-471-10289-X*) Wiley.

Mundo Unido: Repaso y Conversacion, Vol. 2. Maria Dominicis. 432p. 1995. pap. 46.95 (*0-471-58485-1*) Wiley.

Mundo Unido Vol. 1: Lectura y Escritura. Robert Nicholas. 420p. 1995. pap. 36.95 (*0-471-58484-3*) Wiley.

Mundo Unido Grammar Reader Workbook Cassettes Sets. Maria Dominicis & Robert L. Nicholas. 1080p. 1995. pap. 132.80 (*0-471-12856-2*) Wiley.

Mundo Unido Grammar Text & Workbook Set. Dominicis. 660p. 1995. pap. text 76.90 (*0-471-12855-4*) Wiley.

Mundo Unido Grammar Text Workbook & Cassettes Set. Dominicis. 660p. 1995. pap. text 97.85 incl. audio (*0-471-12851-1*) Wiley.

Mundo Visto a los Ochenta Anos: Impresiones de un Arteriosclerotico. Santiago R. Cajal. Ed. by Robert J. Kastenbaum. LC 78-22214. (Aging & Old Age Ser.). (SPA.). 1979. reprint ed. lib. bdg. 21.95 (*0-405-11827-9*) Ayer.

Mundos de Fantasia. 4th ed. Terrell. (SPA.). 40p. 1998. pap. 7.19 (*0-07-064729-1*) McGraw.

Mundos de Ilusion. Susanne McCarthy. (Bianca Ser.). 1996. per. 3.50 (*0-373-33374-9*, 1-33374-9) Harlequin Bks.

Mundos Plausibles, Munos Alternativos - Plausible Worlds: Posibilidad y Comprension en la Historia y En las Ciencias Sociales - Possibility & Understanding in History & the Social Sciences. Geoffrey Hawthorn. Tr. by Gloria Carnevali de Hawthorn. (SPA.). 284p. (C). 1995. pap. 16.95 (*0-521-47646-1*) Cambridge U Pr.

Mundugumor: From the Field Notes of Margaret Mead & Reo Fortune. Nancy McDowell. LC 90-24915. (Series in Ethnographic Inquiry). (Illus.). 352p. (C). 1991. text 50.00 (*1-56098-062-1*) Smithsonian.

Mundus Foppensis & the Levellers. Intro. by Michael S. Kimmel. LC 92-24472. (Augustan Reprints Ser.: No. 248). 1988. reprint ed. 14.50 (*0-404-70248-1*, PR1111) AMS Pr.

Mundus Symbolicus, 2 vols. in 1. Filippo Picinelli. (GER.). 1276p. 1979. reprint ed. write for info. (*3-487-05790-5*); reprint ed. write for info. (*3-487-05970-3*) G Olms Pubs.

Mundy: Nicholas Mundy & Descendants Who Settled in NJ in 1665. E. F. Mundy. (Illus.). 160p. 1991. reprint ed. pap. 25.00 (*0-8328-1698-1*); reprint ed. lib. bdg. 35.00 (*0-8328-1697-3*) Higginson Bk Co.

Muneca de Chocolate. Felix J. Rivera. (SPA., Illus.). 192p. 1995. pap. 8.95 (*1-56328-106-6*) Edit Plaza Mayor.

***Muneca de Elizabeti.** Stephanie Stuve-Bodeen.Tr. of Elizabeti's Doll. (SPA., Illus.). 32p. (YA). (ps up). 2000. 15.95 (*1-58430-000-0*, Pub. by Lee & Low Bks); pap. 6.95 (*1-58430-001-9*, Pub. by Lee & Low Bks) Publishers Group.

Muneca de Trapo: Poesias Infantiles. Carmelina G. De Gutierrez. LC 92-81948. (Coleccion Espejo de Paciencia). (SPA., Illus.). 59p. (Orig.). (J). 1992. pap. 6.00 (*0-89729-642-7*) Ediciones.

Munera Pulveris: Six Essays on the Elements of Political Economy. John Ruskin. LC 69-14065. 218p. 1969. reprint ed. lib. bdg. 35.00 (*0-8371-0642-7*, RUMP, Greenwood Pr) Greenwood.

Mungbean. John M. Poehlman. (C). 1991. text 27.50 (*81-204-0590-0*, Pub. by Oxford IBH) S Asia.

Munger Map Book. 330p. 1989. 100.00 (*0-318-40072-3*) Munger Oil.

Mungo Goes East: A Window Board Book. Rae Lambert. 12p. (J). (ps). 1996. bds. 4.99 (*1-900207-15-X*, Pub. by Little Wizard) Assoc Pubs Grp.

Mungo Goes North: A Window Board Book. Rae Lambert. 12p. (J). (ps). 1996. bds. 4.99 (*1-900207-05-2*, Pub. by Little Wizard) Assoc Pubs Grp.

Mungo Goes South: A Window Board Book. Rae Lambert. 12p. (J). (ps). 1996. bds. 4.99 (*1-900207-10-9*, Pub. by Little Wizard) Assoc Pubs Grp.

Mungo Goes West: A Window Board Book. Rae Lambert. 12p. (J). (ps). 1996. bds. 4.99 (*1-900207-20-6*, Pub. by Little Wizard) Assoc Pubs Grp.

***Mungo Park: Writer, Surgeon & West African Explorer.** Mark Duffill. (Illus.). 112p. 1999. pap. write for info. (*1-901663-15-9*, Pub. by Natl Mus Scotland) A Schwartz & Co.

***Mungo's City: A Glasgow Anthology.** Ronald Armstrong. 400p. 2000. pap. 25.95 (*1-84158-025-2*, Pub. by Birlinn Ltd) Dufour.

Mungo's Hedgerow Tale: A Stopframe Book. Rae Lambert. 12p. (J). (ps). 1996. 7.99 (*1-900207-35-4*, Pub. by Little Wizard) Assoc Pubs Grp.

Mungo's Rainforest Tale: A Stopframe Book. Rae Lambert. 12p. (J). (ps). 1996. 7.99 (*1-900207-40-0*, Pub. by Little Wizard) Assoc Pubs Grp.

Mungo's Riverbank Tale: A Stopframe Book. Rae Lambert. 12p. (J). (ps). 1996. 7.99 (*1-900207-25-7*, Pub. by Little Wizard) Assoc Pubs Grp.

Mungo's Tongues: Glasgow Poems, 1630-1990. Ed. by Hamish Whyte. (Illus.). 192p. 1994. pap. 22.95 (*1-85158-580-X*, Pub. by Mainstream Pubng) Trafalgar.

Mungo's Woodland Tale: A Stopframe Book. Rae Lambert. 12p. (J). (ps). 1996. 7.99 (*1-900207-30-3*, Pub. by Little Wizard) Assoc Pubs Grp.

Mungo's World Tour. Rae Lambert. (Comes to Life Bks.). 16p. (J). (ps-2). 1995. write for info. (*1-57234-058-4*) YES Ent.

Mungo's World Tour: The Exciting Adventures of Munog, Lemmy & Albert Ross. Rae Lambert. 32p. (J). (ps-3). 1996. 5.99 (*1-900207-00-1*, Pub. by Little Wizard) Assoc Pubs Grp.

Muni Photographs. Jeffrey Moreau. LC 91-72515. 64p. 1991. pap. 22.00 (*0-934406-04-9*) Carbarn Press.

Munias & Mannikins. Robin Restall. LC 96-61495. (Illus.). 340p. 1997. 60.00 (*0-300-07109-4*) Yale U Pr.

Munich. 64p. pap. text 9.95 (*88-7009-526-6*, Pub. by Bonechi) Eiron.

Munich. (Panorama Bks.). (FRE., Illus.). 3.95 (*0-685-11409-0*) Fr & Eur.

Munich. Insight Guides Staff. (Insight Guides). 1998. pap. text 7.95 (*0-88729-548-7*) Langenscheidt.

***Munich.** Ed. by Lonely Planet Publications Staff. (Travel Guides Ser.). (Illus.). 232p. 2000. pap. 14.95 (*1-86450-055-7*) Lonely Planet.

Munich. Rand McNally Staff. pap. 6.95 (*0-528-95971-9*) Rand McNally.

Munich. 2nd rev. ed. Lillian Schacherl. (Prestel Guides Ser.). (Illus.). 192p. (Orig.). 1997. pap. 19.95 (*3-7913-1718-0*, Pub. by Prestel) te Neues.

***Munich.** 3rd ed. Ed. by Fodors Travel Publications, Inc. Staff. 2000. pap. write for info. (*0-679-00590-0*) Fodors Travel.

Munich. 3rd ed. Insight Guides Staff. (Insight Guides). 1998. pap. text 21.95 (*0-88729-717-X*); pap. text 12.95 (*0-88729-918-0*) Langenscheidt.

Munich: City of the Arts. Hans F. Noehbauer. (Illus.). 348p. 1994. boxed set 150.00 (*1-55859-865-0*) Abbeville Pr.

Munich: Including Excursions to Castles, Lakes & Mountains. 3rd rev. ed. Nelles Verlag Staff. (Nelles Guides Ser.). (Illus.). 256p. 1999. pap. 15.95 (*3-88618-120-0*) Hunter NJ.

Munich & Bavaria. James Bentley. (Illustrated Travel Guides from Thomas Cook Ser.). (Illus.). 192p. 1994. pap. 12.95 (*0-8442-9062-9*, Passprt Bks) NTC Contemp Pub Co.

Munich & Bavaria. 2nd ed. James Bentley. (Illus.). 192p. 1997. pap. 14.95 (*0-8442-4839-8*) NTC Contemp Pub Co.

***Munich & Memory: Architecture, Monuments & the Legacy of the Third Reich.** Gavriel David Rosenfeld. LC 99-43091. (Weimar & Now Ser.: Vol. 22). (Illus.). 450p. 2000. 45.00 (*0-520-21910-4*, Pub. by U CA Pr) Cal Prin Full Svc.

Munich & Surroundings. Nelles Verlag Staff. (Nelles Guides Ser.). (Illus.). 256p. (Orig.). 1995. pap. 14.95 (*3-88618-039-5*, Pub. by Nelles Verlag) Seven Hills Bk.

Munich & the Bavarian Alps. 2nd ed. Ed. by Macmillan Travel Staff. (Frommer's Travel Guides Ser.). 1999. pap. 14.95 (*0-02-862369-X*, Frommer) Macmillan Gen Ref.

***Munich & the Royal Castles of Bavaria.** Michelin Travel Publication Staff. (In Your Pocket Guides Ser.). 2000. 9.95 (*2-06-653201-0*) Michelin.

Munich & Theatrical Modernism: Politics, Playwriting, & Performance, 1890-1914. Peter Jelavich. (Illus.). 424p. 1985. 46.50 (*0-674-58835-5*) HUP.

Munich & Theatrical Modernism: Politics, Playwriting, & Performance, 1890-1914. Peter Jelavich. (Illus.). 434p. 1996. pap. 19.50 (*0-674-58836-3*) HUP.

Munich, Bayerische Staatsbibliothek, Mus. MS. 10. Ed. by Howard Brown et al. LC 86-751772. (Renaissance Music in Facsimile Ser.: Vol. 14). 460p. 1986. text 35.00 (*0-8240-1463-4*) Garland.

Munich Crisis, 1938: Prelude to World War II. Ed. by Igor Lukes & Erik Goldstein. LC 99-21340. (Diplomacy & Statecraft Ser.: Vol. 10). 374p. 1999. pap. 26.50 (*0-7146-8056-7*, Pub. by F Cass Pubs) Intl Spec Bk.

***Munich Crisis, 1938: Prelude to World War II.** Ed. by Igor Lukes & Erik Goldstein. LC 99-21340. (Diplomacy & Statecraft Ser.: Vol. 10). 402p. 1999. 57.50 (*0-7146-4995-3*, Pub. by F Cass Pubs) Intl Spec Bk.

***Munich et les Chateaux Royaux de Baviere.** Michelin Travel Publication Staff. (In Your Pocket Guides Ser.). 2000. 9.95 (*2-06-658201-8*) Michelin.

***Munich for Less Compact Guide.** Metropolis International Editors. (For Less Compact Guides Ser.). 2000. pap. text 9.95 (*1-901811-43-3*) Metropolis International.

Munich in the Cobwebs of Berlin, Washington, & Moscow: Foreign Political Tendencies in Bavaria, 1917-1919. Siegfried H. Sutterlin. (Studies in Modern European History: Vol. 12). XI, 232p. (C). 1995. text 49.95 (*0-8204-2518-4*) P Lang Pubng.

Munich, 1909 Proceedings see International Congress on the History of Art

Munich Pocket Guide. rev. ed. Berlitz Editors. (Pocket Guides Ser.). (Illus.). 144p. 1999. pap. 8.95 (*2-8315-6988-5*) Berlitz.

Munich Project CIP. F. L. Bauer et al. (Lecture Notes in Computer Science Ser.: Vol. 292). 522p. 1988. 53.00 (*0-387-18779-0*) Spr-Verlag.

Munich Project CIP. Ed. by CIP Group Staff. (Lecture Notes in Computer Science Ser.: Vol. 183). (Illus.). xi, 275p. 1985. pap. 33.00 (*0-387-15187-7*) Spr-Verlag.

Munich Sabbatical. Pat-Ann Morgan. 256p. 1995. 24.95 (*0-947993-67-3*) Mlvrn Pubg Co.

Munich Signature. Bodie Thoene. (Zion Covenant Ser.: Vol. 3). 4p. (Orig.). 1990. pap. 11.99 (*1-55661-079-3*) Bethany Hse.

***Munich Signature.** Bodie Thoene. Vol. 3. 416p. (Orig.). 2000. mass mkt. 7.99 (*0-7642-2429-8*) Bethany Hse.

Munich Ten. Lewis Orde. 1983. mass mkt. 3.95 (*0-8217-1300-0*, Zebra Kensgtn) Kensgtn Pub Corp.

M

Munich to Vietnam: Australia's Relations with Britain & the United States since the 1930s. Ed. by Carl Bridge. 220p. 1991. pap. 19.95 (*0-522-84436-7*, Pub. by Melbourne Univ Pr) Paul & Co Pubs.

Munich up Close. Christopher Middleton. (Illus.). 144p. 1994. pap. 12.95 (*0-8442-9454-3*, Passprt Bks) NTC Contemp Pub Co.

***Munich 1900 Site de la Modernite Munchen 1900 Als Ort der Moderne.** Ed. by Hans-Gert Roloff. (Jahrbuch fur International Germanistik Ser.: Bd. 47). (Illus.). 289p. 1998. 61.95 (*3-906760-79-0*, Pub. by P Lang) P Lang Pubng.

Municipal Administration - A Handbook. 4th ed. D. L. Craythorne. LC 98-218203. 530p. 1998. pap. 85.00 (*0-7021-4206-9*, Pub. by Juta & Co) Intl Spec Bk.

Municipal & Agency Securities after WPPSS. Law & Business Inc. Staff et al. vi, 509p. write for info. (*0-318-58371-2*) Harcourt.

Municipal & Industrial Composting. Richard K. Miller & Marcia E. Rupnow. LC 90-83868. (Survey on Technology & Markets Ser.: No. 163). 50p. 1991. pap. text 200.00 (*1-55865-188-8*) Future Tech Surveys.

Municipal & Industrial Systems see Design Handbook of Wastewater Systems

M

Municipal Bankruptcies: How to Handle a Chapter 9 from Start to Finish. (Commercial Law & Practice Course Handbook Ser.). 200p. 1994. pap. 99.00 (*0-614-17151-2*, A4-4482) PLI.

Municipal Benchmarks: Assessing Local Performance & Establishing Community Standards. David N. Ammons. LC 96-4478. (Illus.). 256p. 1996. 39.95 (*0-8039-7253-9*) Sage.

Municipal Bond: Market Basics. Wilson White. (Illus.). 256p. 1985. 49.95 (*0-9615066-0-1*) Finan Press.

Municipal Bond Finance & Administration: A Practical Guide to the Analysis of Tax-Exempt Securities. Alan Rabinowitz. LC 71-81325. (Illus.). 272p. reprint ed. pap. 84.40 (*0-608-30030-6*, 205157400089) Bks Demand.

Municipal Bond Investment Advisor: Tax-Exempt Investing for High-Bracket Individuals. Wilson White. 275p. 1991. text 27.50 (*1-55738-190-9*, Irwn Prfssnl) McGraw-Hill Prof.

***Municipal Bond Market - Fundamentals.** Wilson White. LC 98-90398. 1999. 24.95 (*0-533-12792-0*) Vantage.

Municipal Bond Portfolio Management. Frank J. Fabozzi et al. LC 94-15558. 384p. 1994. text 80.00 (*1-55623-672-7*, Irwn Prfssnl) McGraw-Hill Prof.

Municipal Bondage: One Man's Anxiety-Producing Adventures in the Big City. Henry Alford. LC 95-1678. 256p. 1995. pap. 10.00 (*1-57322-510-X*, Riverhd Trade) Berkley Pub.

Municipal Bonds see Standard & Poor's Rating Guide

Municipal Bonds: A Century of Experience. Albert M. Hillhouse. LC 75-2640. (Wall Street & the Security Market Ser.). 1975. reprint ed. 51.95 (*0-405-06965-0*) Ayer.

Municipal Bonds: Planning, Sale, & Administration. Lennox L. Moak. (Debt Administration Ser.). (Illus.). 400p. 37.00 (*0-686-84287-1*) Municipal.

Municipal Bonds: The Basics & Beyond. David L. Scott. (Investor's Quick Reference Ser.). 170p. 1992. per. 14.95 (*1-55738-285-9*, Irwn Prfssnl) McGraw-Hill Prof.

Municipal Bonds: The Comprehensive Review of Municipal Securities & Public Finance. 2nd ed. Robert Lamb & Stephen P. Rappaport. LC 86-27539. 288p. 1987. 34.95 (*0-07-036084-7*) McGraw.

Municipal Bonds Coordinator. Jack Rudman. (Career Examination Ser.: C-1342). 1994. pap. 34.95 (*0-8373-1342-2*) Nat Learn.

Municipal Bootstraps: What More Could Cities Be Doing to Help Themselves. 1992. lib. bdg. 75.00 (*0-8490-8764-3*) Gordon Pr.

Municipal Charters: A Discussion of the Essentials of a City Charter with Forms or Models for Adoption. Nathan Matthews. 18.95 (*0-405-19037-9*) Ayer.

Municipal Codes of Minnesota: A Working Bibliography. Ted Kruse. LC 85-26917. (CPL Bibliographies Ser.: No. 163). write for info. (*0-86602-163-9*, Sage Prdcls Pr) Sage.

Municipal Control of Public Utilities: A Study of the Attitudes of Our Courts Toward an Increase of the Sphere of Municipal Activity. Oscar L. Pond. LC 79-76676. (Columbia University. Studies in the Social Sciences: No. 65). reprint ed. 27.50 (*0-404-51065-5*) AMS Pr.

Municipal Court. David Keyko. (Illus.). 402p. 1989. pap. 35.00 (*0-685-14648-0*) NJ Inst CLE.

Municipal Debt. Clayton P. Gillette. 1995. suppl. ed. 75.00 (*0-316-35213-6*, Aspen Law & Bus) Aspen Pub.

Municipal Debt Finance: Law & Theory. Clayton P. Gillette. 1989. write for info. (*0-318-63268-3*, Aspen Law & Bus) Aspen Pub.

Municipal Debt Finance Law: Theory & Practice. Robert S. Amdursky & Clayton P. Gillette. 544p. 1992. boxed set 155.00 (*0-316-31430-7*, Aspen Law & Bus) Aspen Pub.

Municipal Decentralization & Neighborhood Resources: Case Studies of Twelve Cities. George J. Washnis. LC 72-80467. (Special Studies in U. S. Economic, Social & Political Issues). 1972. 42.50 (*0-685-70540-4*) Irvington.

Municipal Decrees of the Roman West. Robert K. Sherk. (Arethusa Monographs: No. 2). vii, 111p. (C). 1970. pap. 6.00 (*0-930881-00-1*) Dept Classics.

Municipal Disclosure Standards Sourcebook see Securities Regulation Series

Municipal Energy Management: A Unit Report from the Energy Task Force of the Urban Consortium. 60p. 1981. 10.00 (*0-318-17344-1*, DG 81-303) Pub Tech Inc.

Municipal Entrepreneurship: A Five Nation Study of Energy Politics, Innovation & Social Change, Vol. 3. Ed. by Alison E. Woodward et al. (International Studies in Global Change). 404p. 1994. text 59.00 (*2-88124-591-9*); pap. text 25.00 (*2-88124-598-6*) Gordon & Breach.

Municipal Environmental Accident & Emergency Response Planning. Pollution Engineering Staff. 164p. 1994. 29.95 (*0-934165-47-5*, 65479) Gulf Pub.

Municipal Environmental Compliance Manual. Ed. by Lisa G. Dowden & John M. McNurney. LC 94-31122. 256p. 1994. lib. bdg. 65.00 (*1-56670-098-1*, L1098) Lewis Pubs.

Municipal Expenditures. Mabel L. Walker. LC 78-64283. (Johns Hopkins University. Studies in the Social Sciences. Thirtieth Ser. 1912: 13). 208p. 1983. reprint ed. 37.50 (*0-404-61383-7*) AMS Pr.

Municipal Expenditures, Revenues, & Services: Economic Models & Their Use by Planners. Ed. by W. Patrick Beaton. LC 82-17786. 266p. 1983. pap. 1.00 (*0-88285-087-3*) Ctr Urban Pol Res.

Municipal Finance: Financing State & Local Governments in the 1990's: Tenth Annual Institute. (Real Estate Law & Practice Course Handbook Ser.). 545p. 1991. pap. 17.50 (*0-685-69467-4*) PLI.

Municipal Finance & Taxation. Peter J. Loughlin. (New Hampshire Municipal Practice Ser.: Vol. 2). 880p. 1991. ring bd. 70.00 (*0-88063-704-8*, MICHIE) LEXIS Pub.

Municipal Finance & Taxation. Peter J. Loughlin. LC 93-33897. (New Hampshire Practice Ser.: Vol. 16). 860p. 1993. 70.00 (*1-56257-362-4*, MICHIE) LEXIS Pub.

Municipal Finance Practices & Preferences for New Development: Survey of Texas Cities. Joel B. Goldsteen & Russell Fricano. 53p. 1988. pap. 5.00 (*0-936440-77-5*) U TX SUPA.

Municipal Financial Disclosure: An Empirical Investigation. Julia H. Magann. Ed. by Richard N. Farmer. LC 83-1106. (Research for Business Decisions Ser.: No. 58). 110p. reprint ed. 34.10 (*0-8357-1394-6*, 207040200088) Bks Demand.

Municipal Financial Reporting & Disclosure Quality. Ronald M. Copeland & Robert W. Ingram. LC 82-11580. (Illus.). 156p. 1983. pap. text. write for info. (*0-201-10197-1*) Addison-Wesley.

Municipal Golf Facilities: A Growth Industry. (InfoPac Ser.). (Illus.). 185p. 1999. pap. 45.00 (*1-57701-065-5*, 99LB056) Natl Golf.

Municipal Government in Michigan & Ohio: A Study in the Relations of City & Commonwealth. Delos F. Wilcox. LC 68-56697. (Columbia University. Studies in the Social Sciences: No. 15). reprint ed. 32.50 (*0-404-51015-9*) AMS Pr.

Municipal Government in North Carolina. Ed. by Warren J. Wicker. 770p. (C). 1996. pap. text 27.00 (*1-56011-248-4*) Institute Government.

Municipal Government in North Carolina. 2nd ed. Ed. by Warren J. Wicker & David M. Lawrence. 770p. (C). 1996. text 32.00 (*1-56011-280-8*, 95.20-HB) Institute Government.

Municipal Grievance Process. Steven Briggs. (Monograph & Research Ser.: No. 36). 185p. 1984. 9.00 (*0-89215-118-8*) U Cal LA Indus Rel.

Municipal Health Department Practice for the Year 1923: In America's 100 Largest Cities. LC 73-11911. (Metropolitan America Ser.). 810p. 1974. reprint ed. 56.95 (*0-405-05429-7*) Ayer.

Municipal Home Rule. Frank J. Goodnow. LC 97-70700. xxiv, 283p. 1997. reprint ed. 55.00 (*1-57588-207-8*, 311180) W S Hein.

Municipal Incinerators: 50 Questions Every Local Government Should Ask. 54p. 1988. 10.00 (*0-933729-42-1*, No. 4006) Natl League Cities.

Municipal Indebtedness: A Study of the Debt-Property Ratio. Leroy A. Shattuck. LC 78-64179. (Johns Hopkins University. Studies in the Social Sciences. Thirtieth Ser. 1912: 2). 152p. 1982. reprint ed. 37.50 (*0-404-61287-3*) AMS Pr.

Municipal Industrial Water Treatment Equipment in Russia: A Strategic Entry Report, 1996. Compiled by Icon Group International Staff. (Illus.). 154p. 1999. ring bd. 1540.00 incl. audio compact disk (*0-7418-1399-8*) Icon Grp.

Municipal Land Use. Ivy Minely. (Illus.). 311p. 1982. pap. 35.00 (*0-685-14650-2*) NJ Inst CLE.

Municipal Lawyer's Formbook. Herbert A. Kline & Nancy Kline. LC 92-53529. 500p. 1992. ring bd. 90.00 (*0-942954-49-1*) NYS Bar.

Municipal Legal Forms, 1964-1992, 10 vols. Samuel Lawton. LC 76-49998. 900.00 (*0-685-09237-2*) West Group.

Municipal Liability: What Should Be Done about Section 1983? 50p. 1987. 15.00 (*0-933729-22-7*) Natl League Cities.

Municipal Liability & Risk Management: Issues & Answers. 56p. 1986. 15.00 (*0-933729-26-X*) Natl League Cities.

***Municipal Management in Poland.** Heather Mckinney & Clark Bradley. (Policy Papers: Vol. 4). 40p. 1999. pap. 6.50 (*0-89940-575-4*) LBJ Sch Pub Aff.

Municipal Monument: A Centennial History of the Municipal Building Serving Minneapolis & Hennepin County, Minnesota. Paul C. Larson. 128p. 1991. 18.95 (*0-9630086-0-9*) Muni Bldg Comm.

Municipal Mother: Portland's Lola Greene Baldwin, America's First Policewoman. Gloria E. Myers. LC 95-16780. 240p. 1995. text 26.95 (*0-87071-386-8*) Oreg St U Pr.

Municipal Ownership in the Electric Utility Industry: A Centennial View. David Schap. LC 85-19418. 144p. 1985. 49.95 (*0-275-92034-8*, C2034, Praeger Pubs) Greenwood.

Municipal Policy Leader Handbook: A Guide for Iowa Mayors & Council Members. Institute of Public Affairs Staff. 1994. pap. 14.00 (*0-317-02836-7*) U Iowa IPA.

***Municipal Population in Pennsylvania 1960 to 1998.** PASDC Staff. 188p. 1999. pap. 40.00 (*1-58036-136-6*) Penn State Data Ctr.

Municipal Pretreatment Programs: Guides to Pollution Prevention. Lynn Knight & David Loughran. (Illus.). 81p. (Orig.). (C). 1995. pap. text 20.00 (*0-7881-2382-3*) DIANE Pub.

Municipal Problems in Medieval Switzerland. John M. Vincent. LC 78-63911. (Johns Hopkins University. Studies in the Social Sciences. Thirtieth Ser. 1912: 11-12). reprint ed. 34.50 (*0-404-61163-X*) AMS Pr.

Municipal Productivity: A Comparison of Fourteen High-Quality Service Cities. David N. Ammons. LC 83-17821. 294p. 1984. 55.00 (*0-275-91118-7*, C1118, Praeger Pubs) Greenwood.

***Municipal Reference Guid: New York - Western, 3.** H. Leslie Shaw. 712p. 1999. lib. bdg. 74.90 (*1-880747-59-6*) Natnl Resce.

***Municipal Reference Guide: California.** H. Leslie Shaw. 546p. 1999. lib. bdg. 74.90 (*1-880747-56-1*) Natnl Resce.

***Municipal Reference Guide: Florida.** H. Leslie Shaw. 600p. 1999. lib. bdg. 74.90 (*1-880747-63-4*) Natnl Resce.

Municipal Reference Guide: Georgia-Northern Edition. Ed. by H. Leslie Shaw. 414p. 1998. lib. bdg. 69.90 (*1-880747-31-6*) Natnl Resce.

Municipal Reference Guide: Georgia-Southern Edition. Ed. by H. Leslie Shaw. 399p. 1998. lib. bdg. 69.90 (*1-880747-32-4*) Natnl Resce.

Municipal Reference Guide: Illinois-East-Central Edition. Ed. by H. Leslie Shaw. 674p. 1997. lib. bdg. 69.90 (*1-880747-29-4*) Natnl Resce.

Municipal Reference Guide: Illinois North-Western Edition. Ed. by H. Leslie Shaw. 714p. 1997. lib. bdg. 69.90 (*1-880747-26-X*) Natnl Resce.

Municipal Reference Guide: Illinois Southern Edition. Ed. by H. Leslie Shaw. 650p. 1997. lib. bdg. 69.90 (*1-880747-28-6*) Natnl Resce.

***Municipal Reference Guide: Massachusetts.** H. Leslie Shaw. 466p. 1998. lib. bdg. 69.90 (*1-880747-35-9*) Natnl Resce.

***Municipal Reference Guide: New Jersey - Northern, 2.** H. Leslie Shaw. 548p. 1999. lib. bdg. 74.90 (*1-880747-61-8*) Natnl Resce.

***Municipal Reference Guide: New Jersey - Southern, 2.** H. Leslie Shaw. 394p. 1999. lib. bdg. 74.90 (*1-880747-62-6*) Natnl Resce.

***Municipal Reference Guide: New York - Northern, 3.** H. Leslie Shaw. 678p. 1999. pap. 74.90 (*1-880747-57-X*) Natnl Resce.

***Municipal Reference Guide: New York - Southern, 3.** H. Leslie Shaw. 528p. 1999. lib. bdg. 74.90 (*1-880747-58-8*) Natnl Resce.

***Municipal Reference Guide: North Carolina.** H. Leslie Shaw. 708p. 1998. lib. bdg. 69.90 (*1-880747-36-7*) Natnl Resce.

***Municipal Reference Guide: Pennsylvania - East Central, 4.** H. Leslie Shaw. 711p. 1999. lib. bdg. 74.90 (*1-880747-68-5*) Natnl Resce.

***Municipal Reference Guide: Pennsylvania - Eastern, 4.** H. Leslie Shaw. 700p. 1999. lib. bdg. 74.90 (*1-880747-69-3*) Natnl Resce.

***Municipal Reference Guide: Pennsylvania - West Central, 4.** H. Leslie Shaw. 760p. 1999. lib. bdg. 74.90 (*1-880747-67-7*) Natnl Resce.

***Municipal Reference Guide: Pennsylvania - Western, 4.** H. Leslie Shaw. 710p. 1999. lib. bdg. 74.90 (*1-880747-66-9*) Natnl Resce.

Municipal Reference Guide: Virginia. Ed. by H. Leslie Shaw. 462p. 1997. lib. bdg. 69.90 (*1-880747-25-1*) Natnl Resce.

Municipal Revenue Sources: Analysis of Omaha's Options. Murray Frost. 170p. (Orig.). 1983. pap. 12.00 (*1-55719-044-5*) U NE CPAR.

Municipal Revolution in America: Origins of Modern Urban Government, 1650-1825. Jon C. Teaford. LC 74-33512. 160p. 1993. lib. bdg. 14.00 (*0-226-79165-3*) U Ch Pr.

Municipal Sales Handbook. unabridged ed. Woody Tatcove & Gloria Leacox. 300p. (Orig.). 1996. pap. 295.00 (*1-890299-03-0*) Gov Technology.

Municipal Securities Principal: License Exam Manual - Questions & Answers. 8th ed. Dearborn Financial Institute, Inc. Editorial Staff. LC 98-131105. (Passtrak Ser.: Series 53). 1997. pap. 165.00 (*0-7931-2535-9*) Dearborn.

Municipal Service Delivery: Thinking Through the Privatization Option. 60p. 1997. 15.00 (*1-886152-44-6*, No. 3540) Natl League Cities.

Municipal Sewage Sludge Management: A Reference Text on Processing, Utilization & Disposal. 2nd ed. Ed. by Cecil Lue-Hing et al. (Water Quality Management Library: Vol. 4). 816p. 1998. 104.95 (*1-56676-621-4*) Technomic.

Municipal Sewage Sludge Management Vol. 4: Processing, Utilization & Disposal. Ed. by Cecil Lue-Hing et al. LC 92-53520. (Water Quality Management Library). 830p. 1992. text 99.95 (*0-87762-930-7*) Technomic.

Municipal Sludge Management. Richard K. Miller & Christy H. Gunter. (Market Research Survey Ser.: No. 323). 50p. 1996. 200.00 (*1-55865-345-7*) Future Tech Surveys.

Municipal Sludge Use in Land Reclamation. William E. Sopper. 176p. 1993. lib. bdg. 85.00 (*0-87371-941-7*, L941) Lewis Pubs.

Municipal Socialism. John Sheldrake. 89p. 1989. text 72.95 (*0-566-05729-8*, Pub. by Dartmth Pub) Ashgate Pub Co.

Municipal Solid Waste: A STS Case Study. John Ramsey et al. 140p. (C). 1996. spiral bd. 10.80 (*0-87563-647-0*) Stipes.

Municipal Solid Waste Incinerator Residues. Hans Van Der Sloot et al. LC 97-9539. (Studies in Environmental Science: 67). 1000p. 1997. 287.50 (*0-444-82563-0*) Elsevier.

Municipal Solid Waste Management. Richard K. Miller & Christy H. Gunter. (Market Research Survey Ser.: No. 308). 50p. 1996. 200.00 (*1-55865-332-5*) Future Tech Surveys.

Municipal Solid Waste Management: Recycling Resource Recovery, & Landfills: A Source Guide. 1991. lib. bdg. 75.00 (*0-8490-4818-4*) Gordon Pr.

Municipal Solid Waste Recycling in Western Europe to 1996. R. Reidy. 246p. 1992. pap. 1110.00 (*1-85617-138-8*, Pub. by Elsvr Adv Tech) Elsevier.

Municipal Solid Wastes: Problems & Solutions. Robert E. Landreth & Paul A. Rebers. LC 96-31106. (Illus.). 288p. 1996. lib. bdg. 99.95 (*1-56670-215-1*) Lewis Pubs.

Municipal Staff Directory. Ed. by Tracey Ryan. 1998. pap. 99.00 (*0-87289-139-9*) C Q Staff.

Municipal State of the Environment Reporting in Canada: Current Status & Future Needs. 81p. pap. text 20.00 (*0-7881-4312-3*) DIANE Pub.

Municipal Storm Water Management. Thomas N. Debo & Andrew J. Reese. 768p. (C). 1995. boxed set 104.95 (*0-87371-981-6*, L981) Lewis Pubs.

Municipal Stormwater Management. Richard K. Miller & Christy H. Gunter. (Market Research Survey Ser.: No. 291). 50p. 1996. 200.00 (*1-55865-315-5*) Future Tech Surveys.

Municipal Strategic Planning: The Reshaping of Israeli Local Government. D. Janner-Klausner. (Progress in Planning Ser.: Vol. 41). 112p. 1994. 69.25 (*0-08-042531-3*, Pergamon Pr) Elsevier.

Municipal Structural Reform in Sioux City: The Perennial Question. Mitchel J. Beville. 1980. 1.00 (*1-55614-067-3*) U of SD Gov Res Bur.

Municipal System in India: Citizens' Involvement. Bijoyini Mohanty. (Illus.). vi, 245p. 1993. 20.00 (*81-7024-530-3*, Pub. by Ashish Pub Hse) Nataraj Bks.

Municipal Technologies: An Assessment of Energy Technologies for the City of Chicago. 114p. 1983. 20.00 (*0-318-17345-X*, DG/83-310) Pub Tech Inc.

Municipal Waste. Ed. by Peter Allen. 1989. pap. 1795.00 (*0-317-01803-5*) FIND-SVP.

Municipal Waste Combustion Study: Assessment of Health Risks Associated with Municipal Waste Combustion Emissions. Radian Corp. Staff. 248p. 1989. 78.95 (*0-89116-071-X*) Hemisp Pub.

Municipal Waste Incineration Risk Assessment: Deposition, Food Chain Impacts, Uncertainty, & Research Needs. C. C. Travis. (Contemporary Issues in Risk Analysis Ser.). (Illus.). 328p. (C). 1991. 110.00 (*0-306-44016-4*, Plenum Trade) Perseus Pubng.

***Municipal Waste Management in Europe: A Comparative Study in Building Regimes** Nicolas Buclet & Olivier Godard. LC 99-36539. (Environment & Management Ser.). 1999. write for info. (*0-7923-5885-6*) Kluwer Academic.

Municipal Wastewater Treatment. Marcia E. Rupnow & Richard K. Miller. (Survey on Technology & Markets Ser.: No. 230). 50p. 1994. 200.00 (*1-55865-261-2*) Future Tech Surveys.

Municipal Wastewater Treatment in Central & Eastern Europe: Present Situation & Cost-Effective Development. Laszlo Somlyody & Peter Shanahan. LC 97-42033. (Report for the Environmental Action Programme for Central & Eastern Europe Ser.). 162p. 1998. pap. 22.00 (*0-8213-4085-9*, 14085) World Bank.

Municipal Wastewater Treatment Technology: Recent Developments. U. S. Environmental Protection Agency Staff. LC 92-25244. (Illus.). 250p. 1993. 69.00 (*0-8155-1309-7*) Noyes.

Municipal Water & Wastewater. Richard K. Miller et al. (Market Research Survey Ser.: No. 272). 50p. 1996. 200.00 (*1-55865-296-5*) Future Tech Surveys.

Municipal Water Environmental Markets. Richard K. Miller. (Illus.). 299p. 1997. spiral bd. 185.00 (*1-881503-68-2*) R K Miller Assocs.

***Municipal Water Supply, Treatment Equip. in Colombia: A Strategic Entry Report, 1996.** Compiled by Icon Group International Staff. (Illus.). 185p. 1999. ring bd. 1850.00 incl. audio compact disk (*0-7418-1398-X*) Icon Grp.

Municipal Water Systems: The Challenge for Urban Resource Management. Ed. by David Holtz & Scott Sebastian. LC 77-74425. 316p. reprint ed. pap. 98.00 (*0-608-17084-4*, 205622900056) Bks Demand.

Municipal Year Book, 1995. Ed. by Evelina Moulder. (Illus.). 416p. 1995. text 79.95 (*0-87326-970-5*, 41001) Intl City-Cnty Mgt.

Municipal Year Book, 1994. Ed. by Evelina Moulder. (Illus.). 416p. 1994. 79.95 (*0-87326-969-1*) Intl City-Cnty Mgt.

Municipal Year Book, 1996. Ed. by Evelina Moulder. (Illus.). 338p. 1996. 79.95 (*0-87326-971-3*, 42023) Intl City-Cnty Mgt.

Municipal Year Book, 1993. Ed. by Evelina Moulder. (Illus.). 416p. 1993. 79.95 (*0-87326-968-3*) Intl City-Cnty Mgt.

Municipal Year Book, 1992. Ed. by Evelina Moulder. (Illus.). 416p. 1992. 77.50 (*0-87326-967-5*) Intl City-Cnty Mgt.

Municipal Yearbook, 1998-1999, 64. International City County Management Staff. 1997. 116.75 (*0-87326-972-1*) Intl City-Cnty Mgt.

Municipalities of Essex County, N. J., 1666-1925, 2 vols. in 1, Vols. 1 & 2. Ed. by Joseph F. Folsom. (Illus.). 888p. 1993. reprint ed. lib. bdg. 89.50 (*0-8328-3218-9*) Higginson Bk Co.

An Asterisk (*) at the beginning of an entry indicates that the title is appearing for the first time.

Municipalities of Essex County, N. J., 1666-1925, 2 vols. in 1, Vols. 3 & 4. Ed. by Joseph F. Folsom. (Illus.). 409p. 1993. reprint ed. lib. bdg. 45.00 (*0-8328-3219-7*) Higginson Bk Co.

Municipalities of the Roman Empire. J. S. Reid. Date not set. 35.00 (*0-89005-551-3*) Ares.

***Municipalities Planning Code.** 1998. 99.00 incl. audio PA Bar Inst.

Municipality of Buffalo: A History, 1720-1923, 4 vols. Ed. by Henry W. Hill. (Illus.). 3440p. 1997. reprint ed. lib. bdg. 145.00 (*0-8328-6108-1*) Higginson Bk Co.

Municipalization of Play. Joseph R. Fulk. LC 71-143056. 1982. 16.95 (*0-8434-0449-3*, Pub. by McGrath NH) Ayer.

Munimenta Academica: or Documents Illustrative of Academical Life & Studies at Oxford, 2 vols. Ed. by Henry Anstey. (Rolls Ser.: No. 50). 1974. reprint ed. 140.00 (*0-8115-1109-X*) Periodicals Srv.

Munimenta Alme Universitatis Glasquensis, 4 vols., Set. Ed. by Cosmos Innes & Joseph Robertson. LC 79-168167. (Maitland Club, Glasgow. Publications: No. 72). reprint ed. 170.00 (*0-404-53100-8*) AMS Pr.

Munimenta Gildhallae Londoniensis: Liber Albus, Liber Custumarum, et Liber Horn, 3 vols., Set. Ed. by Henry T. Riley. Incl. Vol. 1. Liber Albus. 1974. (*0-8115-1015-8*); Vol. 2, Pts. 1 & 2. Liber Custumarum, with Extracts from the Cottonian Ms Claudius D II. 1974. (*0-8115-1016-6*); Vol. 3. Transcript of the Anglo-Norman Passages in Liber Albus, Glossaries, Appendices, & Index. 1974. (*0-8115-1017-4*); (Rolls Ser.: No. 12). 1974. reprint ed. 210.00 (*0-685-09995-4*) Periodicals Srv.

Muniments of the Ancient Saxon Family of Wingfield. Mervyn Edward. (Illus.). 160p. 1987. reprint ed. 155.00 (*0-9619322-0-1*) Wingfield Family Soc.

Munirih Khanum: Memoirs & Letters. Munirih Khanum. Tr. by Sammireh A. Smith. (PER., Illus.). 87p. 1987. 14.95 (*0-933770-51-0*) Kalimat.

Munitions of the Mind: A History of Propaganda from the Ancient World to the Present Era. Philip M. Taylor. LC 95-16756. 272p. 1995. text 79.95 (*0-7190-4829-X*); text 27.95 (*0-7190-4830-3*, Pub. by Manchester Univ Pr) St Martin.

Munjid Fi Al Lugha Wal A'lam: Munjio. Dar El Mashreq. (Illus.). 900p. 69.95 (*0-86685-750-8*) Intl Bk Ctr.

Munkacsy. A. Szekely. (Illus.). 104p. (C). 1979. text 195.00 (*0-7855-5827-6*, Pub. by Collets) St Mut.

Munkman: Damages for Personal Injuries & Death. 10th ed. John Munkman. 279p. 1996. write for info. (*0-406-05360-X*, MDPI10, MICHIE) LEXIS Pub.

Munkman: The Technique of Advocacy. John Munkman. 175p. 1991. boxed set 33.00 (*0-406-00264-9*, UK, MICHIE) LEXIS Pub.

Munro: A Sketch of the Munro Clan, Also of William Munro Who, Deported from Scotland, Settled in Lexington, Mass., & Some of His Posterity. J. P. Munroe. 80p. 1992. reprint ed. pap. 16.00 (*0-8328-2693-6*); reprint ed. lib. bdg. 26.00 (*0-8328-2692-8*) Higginson Bk Co.

Munro Almanac. rev. ed. Cameron McNeish. (Illus.). 144p. 1996. 14.95 (*1-897784-39-2*, Pub. by N Wilson Pubng) Interlink Pub.

Munro Letters: Lieutenant Innes Munro 71st Regiment. Ed. by Arthur H. Haley. 120p. 1990. 70.00 (*0-9511427-8-X*, Pub. by Bullfinch Pubns) St Mut.

Munro Phenomenon. Andrew Dempster. (Illus.). 192p. 1996. 35.00 (*1-85158-698-9*, Pub. by Mainstream Pubng) Trafalgar.

Munroe: History of the Munros of Fowlis, with Genealogies of the Principal Families of the Names, to Which Are Added Those of Lexington & New England. A. MacKenzie. 632p. 1992. reprint ed. pap. 95.00 (*0-8328-2695-2*); reprint ed. lib. bdg. 105.00 (*0-8328-2694-4*) Higginson Bk Co.

Munros: Scotland's Highest Mountains. Cameron McNeish. (Illus.). 228p. 1997. 45.00 (*1-900455-13-7*, Pub. by Colin Baxter Ltd) Voyageur Pr.

Munros & Tops: A Record Setting Walk in the Scottish Highlands. Chris Townsend. (Illus.). 224p. 1997. 35.00 (*1-85158-986-4*, Pub. by Mainstream Pubng) Trafalgar.

Munschworks: The First Munsch Collection. Robert Munsch. (Munsch for Kids Ser.). (Illus.). 128p. (J). (ps-2). 1998. text 19.95 (*1-55037-523-7*, Pub. by Annick Pr) Firefly Bks Ltd.

***Munschworks 3: The Third Munsch Treasury.** Robert N. Munsch. (Illus.). 144p. (J). (ps-2). 2000. 19.95 (*1-55037-633-0*, Pub. by Annick Pr) Firefly Bks Ltd.

Munschworks 2: The Second Munsch Treasury. Robert Munsch. (Illus.). 136p. (J). (ps-2). 1999. text 19.95 (*1-55037-553-9*, Pub. by Annick Pr) Firefly Bks Ltd.

Munshi Premchand of Lamhi Village. Robert O. Swan. LC 77-80813. (Duke University Commonwealth Studies Center: No. 3). 159p. reprint ed. 49.30 (*0-8357-9112-2*, 201793400010) Bks Demand.

Munson Record, III, IV & V. 1984p. 1993. 125.00 (*0-9637119-0-3*) T Munson Fnd.

Munson Record, 1637-1887: A Genealogical & Biographical Account of Captain Thomas Munson (Pioneer of Hartford & New Haven) & His Descendants, 2 vols. in 1. M. A. Munson. (Illus.). 1263p. 1989. reprint ed. pap. 189.00 (*0-8328-0893-8*); reprint ed. lib. bdg. 197.00 (*0-8328-0892-X*) Higginson Bk Co.

Munster City Library: Muster, 1987-1993, Architekturburo Bolles-Wilson. Francisco Sanin. (Architecture in Detail Ser.). (Illus.). 60p. (Orig.). (C). 1994. pap. 29.95 (*0-7148-2996-X*, Pub. by Phaidon Press) Phaidon Pr.

***Munster Raid: Before & after.** Ian Hawkins. LC 99-72570. (Illus.). 1999. write for info. (*0-917678-49-4*) Food & Nut Pr.

Munsters & the Addams Family Reunion. Ed. by Munsters & the Addams Family Fan Club Staff. (Munsters & The Addams Family Television Shows Ser.). (Illus.). 100p. (Orig.). 1997. pap. 30.00 (*0-317-05621-2*) L Wendruck.

Muntadas: Between the Frames, the Forum. Debra B. Balken et al. LC 94-31860. 1994. pap. 15.00 (*0-938437-49-6*) MIT List Visual Arts.

Muntadas: The Games. Christopher Scoates. (SPA.). 1996. pap. text 18.95 (*1-881616-74-6*) Dist Art Pubs.

Muntakhab Siwan Al-Hikmah of Abu Sulaiman As-Sijistani. Ed. by D. M. Dunlop. (Near & Middle East Monographs: No. 4). (ARA.). 1979. text 73.10 (*90-279-3377-4*) Mouton.

Muntu: African Culture & the Western World. Janheinz Jahn. Tr. by Marjorie Grene from GER. LC 90-47010. (Illus.). 352p. 1990. pap. 12.95 (*0-8021-3208-1*, Grove) Grove-Atltic.

Muntzerische Bawren-Krieg. Martin Rinckart. (GER.). 359p. 1991. reprint ed. write for info. (*3-487-09312-X*) G Olms Pubs.

Muntzings & Their Related Families: Five Centuries of Ancestors. William H. Muntzing, II & L. Manning Muntzing. (Illus.). 224p. 1991. 40.00 (*0-9629967-0-X*) McClain.
The history of the Muntzing family & their related families (Franz, Hamstead, Cosner, Nine & their connections) covers five centuries. The book contains pictures, copies of translated letters & other items of interest. ***Publisher Paid Annotation.***

***Munuscula Mesopotamica: Frestschrift fur Johannes Renger.** Barbara Bock. Ed. by Eva C. Cancik-Kirschbaum & Thomas Richter. (Alter Orient und Altes Testament Ser.: No. 267). (GER.). xxix, 704p. 1999. text 135.00 (*3-927120-81-2*, Pub. by Ugarit-Verlag) Eisenbrauns.

Munuscula Romana: Papers Read at a Conference in Lund (October 1-2, 1988) in Celebration of the Re-Opening of the Swedish Institute in Rome. Ed. by Anne-Marie L. Touati et al. (Acta Instituti Romani Regni Sueciae, Series in 4 Degrees: Vol. XVII). (Illus.). 138p. 1991. pap. 49.50 (*91-7042-139-0*, Pub. by P Astroms) Coronet Bks.

Munzen und Medaillen von Koln. Alfred Noss & Walter Havernick. (GER.). 1652p. 1975. reprint ed. write for info. (*3-487-05331-4*) G Olms Pubs.

Munzpragung von Magnesia Am Maander in der Romischen Kaiserzeit. Sabine Schultz. 136p. 1975. write for info. (*3-487-05750-6*) G Olms Pubs.

Muon-Catalyzed Fusion. Ed. by S. E. Jones et al. LC 88-83636. (AIP Conference Proceedings Ser.: No. 181). 482p. 1989. lib. bdg. 70.00 (*0-88318-381-1*) Am Inst Physics.

Muon-Catalyzed Fusion & Fusion with Polarized Nuclei. Ed. by B. Brunelli & G. G. Leotta. LC 87-29171. (Ettore Majorana International Science Series, Life Sciences: Vol. 33). (Illus.). 302p. 1988. 79.50 (*0-306-42784-2*, Plenum Trade) Perseus Pubng.

Muon Method in Science: Proceedings of the Lebedev Physics Institute. Ed. by V. P. Smilga & Yu M. Belousov. LC 93-43319. (Proceedings of the Lebedev Physics Institute Ser.: Vol. 219). (Illus.). 424p. (C). 1994. lib. bdg. 175.00 (*1-56072-161-8*) Nova Sci Pubs.

Muon Physics. Ed. by Vernon Hughes & C. S. Wu. Incl. Vol. 2. Weak Interactions. 1975. 111.00 (*0-12-360602-0*); Vol. 3. Chemistry & Solids. 1975. 80.00 (*0-12-360603-9*); Vol. 1. 1975. 67.50 (*0-12-360601-2*); 1975. 320.00 (*0-685-00060-5*) Acad Pr.

***Muon Science: Proceedings of the 51st Scottish Universities Summer School in Physics, 17-28 August.** S. L. Lee. LC 99-39147. (Physics Ser.: Vol. 51). (Illus.). 482p. 1999. 240.00 (*0-7503-0630-0*) IOP Pub.

Muon Spin Rotation Spectroscopy: Principles & Applications in Solid State Physics. A. Schenk. 335p. 1985. write for info. (*0-318-66774-6*) Taylor & Francis.

Muon Spin Rotation Spectroscopy: Principles & Applications in Solid State Physics. fac. ed. Alexander G. Schenck. LC 85-199870. (Illus.). 335p. 1985. reprint ed. pap. 103.90 (*0-7837-7992-5*, 204774800008) Bks Demand.

Muonic Atoms & Molecules. Ed. by Lukas A. Schaller & Claude Petitjean. LC 92-44349. (Monte Verita Ser.). ix, 370p. 1993. 50.00 (*0-8176-2851-7*) Birkhauser.

MuPAD-Multi Processing Algebra Data Tool: Tutorial. Ed. by B. Fuchssteiner et al. LC 98-107776. 197p. 1994. 23.50 (*0-8176-5017-2*) Birkhauser.

***Mupad Tutorial: A Version & Platform Independent Introduction.** W. Oevel. LC 00-41962. 2000. pap. write for info. (*3-540-67546-9*) Spr-Verlag.

MuPAD User's Manual: Multi-Processing Algebra Data Tool, MuPAD Version 1.2.2. B. Fuchssteiner et al. LC 96-210055. 586p. 1996. pap., pap. text 158.00 incl. cd-rom (*0-471-96716-5*) Wiley.

Muppet Babies' ABC. Illus. by Sue Venning. LC 83-62170. (Chunky Bks. Ser.). 28p. (J). (ps). 1984. 3.99 (*0-394-86363-1*, Pub. by Random Bks Yng Read) Random.

Muppet Babies Invisible. (J). (gr. 3 up). 1991. pap. 1.97 (*1-56297-126-3*, MB-450); pap. 1.97 (*1-56297-128-X*, MUP-401) Lee Pubns KY.

Muppet Babies Magic Pen. (J). (gr. 3 up). 1991. pap. 1.97 (*1-56297-127-1*, MB-450); pap. 1.97 (*1-56297-129-8*, MUP-401) Lee Pubns KY.

Muppet Babies Noisy Book. Francesca Olivieri. (Little Nugget Bks.). (Illus.). 18p. (J). 1998. bds. 3.49 (*0-307-13052-5*, 13052, Goldn Books) Gldn Bks Pub Co.

Muppet Babies Two in One. (J). (gr. 3 up). 1991. pap. 1.97 (*1-56297-157-3*) Lee Pubns KY.

Muppet Christmas Carol. 64p. 1992. per. 14.95 (*0-7935-2007-X*, 00312483) H Leonard.

Muppet Manners. Ellen Weiss. (Muppet Lift-the-Flap Book Ser.). 16p. (J). 1999. pap. 6.99 (*0-14-056518-3*, PuffinBks) Peng Put Young Read.

Muppet Multiplication Flash Cards. American Education Publishing Staff. (Brighter Child Ser.). (Illus.). (J). 1993. pap. text 3.49 (*1-56189-289-0*) Amer Educ Pub.

Muppet Treasure Island. 40p. 1996. pap. 12.95 (*0-7935-6713-0*) H Leonard.

Muppet Treasure Island: The Movie Storybook. Cathy E. Dubowski. (Illus.). 32p. (J). (ps-3). 1996. 10.95 (*0-448-41280-2*, G & D) Peng Put Young Read.

Muppet Two in One Books. (J). (gr. 3 up). 1991. pap. 1.97 (*1-56297-156-5*) Lee Pubns KY.

Muppet Workbook, Beginning Sounds, Phonics. American Education Publishing Staff. (Brighter Child Ser.). 1993. pap. text 2.25 (*1-56189-282-3*) Amer Educ Pub.

Muppet Workbook, Letters, Capital & Small. American Education Publishing Staff. (Brighter Child Ser.). 1993. pap. text 2.25 (*1-56189-281-5*) Amer Educ Pub.

Muppet Workbook, Same & Different. American Education Publishing Staff. (Brighter Child Ser.). 1993. pap. text 2.25 (*1-56189-283-1*) Amer Educ Pub.

Muppet Workbook, Sorting & Ordering. American Education Publishing Staff. (Brighter Child Ser.). 1993. pap. text 2.25 (*1-56189-286-6*) Amer Educ Pub.

Muppet Workbook, Thinking Skills. American Education Publishing Staff. (Brighter Child Ser.). 1993. pap. text 2.25 (*1-56189-285-8*) Amer Educ Pub.

Muppets. Bob Italia. Ed. by Rosemary Wallner. LC 91-73049. (Behind the Creation of Ser.). 202p. (J). 1991. lib. bdg. 12.94 (*1-56239-052-X*) ABDO Pub Co.

Muppets. Colette Morgan & Trudy Nickels. (Look & Find Ser.). (Illus.). 24p. (J). (gr. k-6). 1996. lib. bdg. 14.95 (*1-56674-178-5*, HTS Bks) Forest Hse.

Muppets No. 3: Froggy Mountain Breakdown. Ellen Gilchrist. (Orig.). (J). 1988. pap. 2.50 (*0-8125-7380-3*, Pub. by Tor Bks) St Martin.

Muppets No. 5: On the Town. Ellen Gilchrist. 128p. (Orig.). (J). 1986. pap. 1.95 (*0-8125-7371-4*, Pub. by Tor Bks) St Martin.

***Muppets Big Book of Crafts.** Stephanie St. Pierre. LC 99-38606. (Illus.). 352p. (YA). (gr. 1 up). 1999. pap. 18.95 (*0-7611-0526-3*) Workman Pub.

***Muppets from Space: Gonzo's Book of Out of This World Puzzles.** Laura Driscoll. 24p. (J). 1999. 3.99 (*0-448-42058-9*, G & D) Peng Put Young Read.

***Muppets from Space: Great Gonzos of the Galaxy.** Kiki Thorpe. 24p. 1999. 3.99 (*0-448-42057-0*, G & D) Peng Put Young Read.

***Muppets from Space: The Junior Novelization, 1.** Ellen Weiss. (Illus.). 80p. (J). 1999. pap. text 4.99 (*0-448-42056-2*) Gd Canyon Railway.

***Muppets in Space: The Making of Muppet Movie Magic, 1.** Ben Eastman. (Illus.). 48p. (J). (ps-3). 1999. pap. 8.99 (*0-448-42055-4*) G & D Pubg Co.

Muppets Make Puppets. Cheryl Henson & Muppet Workshop Staff. LC 94-29094. (Illus.). 112p. (Orig.). (J). 1999. pap. 16.95 (*1-56305-708-5*, 3708) Workman Pub.

Muppets, Muppets, Muppets. (J). (ps-2). 1986. 6.98 (*0-685-16866-2*, 618109) Random Hse Value.

***Muppets on the Road.** Grosset & Dunlap Staff. (Sticker Stories Ser.). (Illus.). 16p. (J). (ps-3). 2000. pap. 5.99 (*0-448-42410-X*, Planet Dexter) Peng Put Young Read.

Muppets the Gift of the Magi, Story Book Set & Advent Calendar. O. Henry. LC 97-108928. (Illus.). 4p. 1996. bds. 17.95 (*0-7611-0532-8*, 10532) Workman Pub.

Muppets Tonight Scrapbook. (Golden Paint Box Books). (J). (ps-3). 3.99 (*0-307-09209-7*, Goldn Books) Gldn Bks Pub Co.

Muppie Manual. Emerson L. Lesher. LC 85-80988. (Illus.). 96p. 1985. pap. 4.95 (*0-934672-31-8*) Good Bks PA.

Muqaddimah. abr. ed. Ibn Khaldun. Ed. by N. J. Dowood. Tr. by Franz Rosenthal from ARA. (Bollingen Ser.: No. 43). (Illus.). 480p. 1967. pap. text 18.95 (*0-691-01754-9*, Pub. by Princeton U Pr) Cal Prin Full Svc.

Muqaddimah, 3 vols. 2nd ed. Ibn Khaldun. Tr. by Franz Rosenthal from ARA. (Bollingen Ser.: No. 43). (Illus.). 1700p. 1967. text 225.00 (*0-691-09797-6*, Pub. by Princeton U Pr) Cal Prin Full Svc.

Muqaddimah: An Introduction to History. Ibn Khaldun. Tr. by Franz Rosenthal. 465p. 1996. pap. 16.95 (*0-614-21162-X*, 834) Kazi Pubns.

***Muqarnas.** Ed. by Gulru Necipoglu. (Illus.). 200p. 1999. 54.50 (*90-04-11482-3*) Brill Academic Pubs.

Muqarnas: An Annual on Islamic Art & Architecture, Vol. 3. Ed. by Oleg Grabar. (Historical Studies). (Illus.). 161p. 1985. 53.00 (*90-04-07611-5*) Brill Academic Pubs.

Muqarnas: An Annual on Islamic Art & Architecture, Vol. 3. Ed. by Oleg Grabar. (Historical Studies). (Illus.). vi, 197p. 1987. 54.50 (*90-04-08155-0*) Brill Academic Pubs.

Muqarnas: An Annual on Islamic Art & Architecture, Vol. 3. Ed. by Oleg Grabar. (Historical Studies). (Illus.). 160p. 1988. 53.50 (*90-04-08647-1*) Brill Academic Pubs.

Muqarnas: An Annual on Islamic Art & Architecture, Vol. 3. Ed. by Oleg Grabar. (Illus.). iv, 138p. 1991. 54.50 (*90-04-09372-9*) Brill Academic Pubs.

Muqarnas: An Annual on Islamic Art & Architecture, Vol. 3. Ed. by Oleg Grabar. (Illus.). iv, 188p. 1992. 54.50 (*90-04-09625-6*) Brill Academic Pubs.

Muqarnas: An Annual on the Visual Culture of the Islamic World. Ed. by Gulru Necipoglu. (Muqarnas. An Annual on Islamic Art & Architecture Ser.: Vol. 13). viii, 211p. 1996. 54.50 (*90-04-10633-2*) Brill Academic Pubs.

Muqarnas Vol. 6: An Annual on Islamic Art & Architecture. Ed. by Oleg Grabar. (Illus.). 174p. 1990. 67.50 (*90-04-09050-9*) Brill Academic Pubs.

Muqarnas Vol. 7: An Annual on Islamic Art & Architecture. Ed. by Oleg Grabar. (Illus.). v, 197p. 1991. 54.50 (*90-04-09347-8*) Brill Academic Pubs.

Muqarnas Vol. 14: An Annual on the Visual Culture of the Islamic World. Ed. by Gulru Necipo Lu. (Illus.). iv, 188p. 1997. 54.50 (*90-04-10872-6*) Brill Academic Pubs.

Muqarnas - An Annual on Islamic Art & Architecture: Essays in Honor of Oleg Grabar. Ed. by Oleg Grabar. (Muqarnas Supplements Ser.: Vol. 10). (Illus.). xiv, 390p. 1993. 82.00 (*90-04-09748-1*) Brill Academic Pubs.

Mur. Jean-Paul Sartre. (FRE.). 1977. pap. 10.95 (*0-8288-3775-9*, F125441) Fr & Eur.

Mur. Jean-Paul Sartre. (Folio Ser.: No. 878). (FRE.). 1972. pap. 8.95 (*2-07-036878-5*) Schoenhof.

Mur: C Level. Jean-Paul Sartre. text 8.95 (*0-8219-0856-1*) EMC-Paradigm.

***Mura Migi Kazika: Torres Strait Islander Nursery Rhymes.** Alick Topti. (Illus.). 24p. (J). 2000. pap. 4.95 (*1-875641-55-6*, Pub. by Magabala Bks) Intl Spec Bk.

Murach's Visual Basic 6. Ed Koop et al. LC 99-13011. 617p. 1999. pap. 45.00 (*1-890774-04-9*) M Murach & Assoc.

Muraille, Tome I. John Hersey. (FRE.). 1979. pap. 11.95 (*0-7859-2421-3*, 2070371301) Fr & Eur.

Muraille, Tome II. John Hersey. (FRE.). 1979. pap. 11.95 (*0-7859-2640-2*, 207037131X) Fr & Eur.

Muraille de Chine et Autres Recits. Franz Kafka. (FRE.). 288p. 1975. pap. 10.95 (*0-7859-2357-8*, 2070366545) Fr & Eur.

Muraja'at fi al Fikr wa al Da'wah wa al Harakah: Re-Examinations on Islamic Thought, Da'wah, & Movement. Umar U. Hasanah. LC 91-42630. (Silsilat Qadaya al Fikr al Islami Ser.: No. 7). (ARA.). 127p. (Orig.). 1991. pap. 6.00 (*1-56564-004-7*) IIIT VA.

Mural. Yanitzia Canetti. LC 96-27312. (Illus.). (J). 1996. write for info. (*1-56492-277-8*) Laredo.

Mural: A Formal Development Support System. P. A. Lindsay et al. Ed. by B. Ritchie & A. C. Wills. (Illus.). xiii, 421p. 1991. 98.95 (*0-387-19651-X*) Spr-Verlag.

***Mural by Thomas Dewing: Commerce & Agriculture Bringing Wealth to Detroit.** Bailey Van Hook. (Illus.). 25p. 1998. pap. 12.00 (*0-945936-19-2*) Spanierman Gallery.

Mural of Leaves: Haiku, Senryu, Renku. Ane McKay et al. (Illus.). 48p. (Orig.). (C). 1991. pap. text 5.00 (*0-9618009-7-6*) Vandina Pr.

Mural Painting & Social Revolution in Mexico, 1920-1940: Art of the New Order. Leonard Folgarait. LC 97-32154. (Illus.). 272p. (C). 1998. text 75.00 (*0-521-58147-8*) Cambridge U Pr.

Mural Painting in Ancient Peru. Duccio Bonavia. Tr. by Patricia J. Lyon from SPA. LC 84-47883. (Illus.). 240p. 1985. 26.95 (*0-253-33940-5*) Ind U Pr.

Mural Painting of Teotihuacan. Arthur G. Miller. LC 72-97208. (Illus.). 193p. 1973. 35.00 (*0-88402-049-5*) Dumbarton Oaks.

Mural Project. Peter Wright & John C. Armor. (Illus.). 128p. 1989. 39.95 (*1-55824-162-0*) At-A-Glance Consumer.

Muralla - El Inocente. J. Calvo Sotelo. (SPA.). 192p. 1977. 5.95 (*0-8288-7172-8*) Fr & Eur.

Murals: Cave, Cathedral, to Street. Michael Capek. LC 95-346. (J). 1996. lib. bdg. 23.93 (*0-8225-2065-6*, Lerner Publctns) Lerner Pub.

Murals of Charles Newcomb: A Story of Hagerstown, Indiana. Carolyn Lafeuer. 105p. 1994. 30.00 (*0-932970-96-6*) Prinit Pr.

Murals of Eugene Delacroix at Saint-Sulpice. Jack J. Spector. LC 67-30384. (College Art Association Monographs: Vol. 16). (Illus.). 180p. 1985. reprint ed. 35.00 (*0-271-00408-8*) Pa St U Pr.

Murals of Protest. Alan W. Barnett. LC 79-21552. (Illus.). 520p. 1984. 60.00 (*0-87982-030-6*) Art Alliance.

Murals of Revolutionary Nicaragua, 1979-1992. David Kunzle. LC 94-49437. (Illus.). 288p. 1995. 65.00 (*0-520-08190-0*, Pub. by U CA Pr); pap. 34.95 (*0-520-08192-7*, Pub. by U CA Pr) Cal Prin Full Svc.

Murals of the Mind: Images of a Psychiatric Community. Jay Harris & Cliff Joseph. LC 72-8793. (Illus.). 274p. 1973. 40.00 (*0-8236-3490-6*) Intl Univs Pr.

Murals Without Walls: Arshile Gorky's Aviation Murals Rediscovered. Ruth Bowman. LC 78-13898. 1978. pap. 7.95 (*0-932828-01-9*) Newark Mus.

Muramasa Blades: A Monograph. Yasu Kizu. 10p. 1993. pap. 4.95 (*0-910704-36-8*) Hawley.

***Murano: Poem.** Mark Doty & J. Paul Getty Museum Staff. LC 00-22399. (Illus.). 56p. 2000. 14.95 (*0-89236-598-6*, J P Getty Museum) J P Getty Trust.

***Murano: The Island of Glass.** Ed. by Konemann Inc. Staff. (Illus.). 2000. 19.95 (*3-8290-2124-0*) Konemann.

***Murano Glass.** Gianfranco Toso. (Illus.). 2000. pap. text 9.95 (*88-7743-215-2*) Arsenale Editrice.

Murano, 1910-1970: From Decorative Art to Design. Marc Heiremans. LC 97-117372. (Illus.). 184p. 1997. 95.00 (*3-925369-63-5*, Pub. by Arnoldsche Art Pubs) Antique Collect.

Murasaki's Genji & Proust's Recherche: A Comparative Study. Shirley M. Loui. LC 90-33212. (Studies in Comparative Literature: Vol. 8). 248p. 1991. lib. bdg. 89.95 (*0-88946-424-3*) E Mellen.

Murat Halstead & the Cincinnati Commercial. Donald W. Curl. LC 80-12046. (Illus.). 196p. reprint ed. pap. 60.80 (*0-7837-4943-0*, 204460900004) Bks Demand.

Muratorian Fragment & the Development of the Canon. Geoffrey M. Hahneman. (Oxford Theological Monographs). 248p. 1992. text 58.00 (*0-19-826341-4*) OUP.

Murawina: An Authentic Aboriginal Message. Roberta B. Sykes. (Illus.). 185p. (Orig.). (C). 1996. reprint ed. pap. 18.95 (*0-9652539-0-2*) Smith & Taylor.

M

***Murcheston: The Wolf's Tale.** David Holland. LC 99-55052. 352p. 2000. 23.95 (*0-312-87213-5*, Pub. by Forge NYC) St Martin.

Murchison in Moray: A Geologist on Home Ground with the Correspondence of Roderick Impey Murchison & the Reverend Dr. George Gordon of Birnie. Michael Collie & John Diemer. LC 94-78514. (Transactions Ser.: Vol. 85, Pt. 3). (Illus.). 263p. (C). 1995. pap. 20.00 (*0-87169-853-6*, T853-com) Am Philos.

***Murchison Technologies: Auditing Cases.** 1999. 4.00 (*0-13-016931-5*) P-H.

***Murchison Technologies: Auditing Cases.** 2000. teacher ed. write for info. (*0-13-016933-1*) P-H.

Murcielagos. (Fascinate Mundo de...Ser.).Tr. of Fascinating World of Bats. (SPA.). (J). 1996. lib. bdg. 15.95 (*1-56674-180-7*) Forest Hse.

Murcielagos Serviciales. Arthur Morton. Tr. by Angelita Aguilar. (SPA.). (J). (gr. k-3). 1994. 12.50 (*1-57842-046-6*) Delmas Creat.

***Murder!** Arnold Bennett. 2000. pap. 3.95 (*1-86092-012-8*, Pub. by Travelman Pub) IPG Chicago.

Murder. Jackie Collins. 1998. mass mkt. 3.99 (*0-671-02460-4*) S&S Trade.

Murder. Mark Dunster. (James Ser.: Pt. 3). 38p. (Orig.). 1990. pap. 5.00 (*0-89642-189-9*) Linden Pubs.

Murder. Ed. & Compiled by John Yau. (Illus.). 44p. 1995. pap. 15.00 (*0-614-17704-9*) Smart Art Pr.

Murder: A Tale of Modern American Life. Sara L. Knox. LC 97-23086. 1998. write for info. (*0-8223-2053-3*); pap. 16.95 (*0-8223-2066-5*) Duke.

Murder: An Analysis of Its Forms, Conditions, & Causes. Gerhard Falk. LC 89-13571. 294p. 1990. lib. bdg. 39.95 (*0-89950-478-7*) McFarland & Co.

Murder: From the Chalk Outline to the Execution Chamber. Greg Fallis. LC 99-46772. 256p. 1999. 19.95 (*0-87131-888-1*, Pub. by M Evans) Natl Bk Netwk.

Murder: The Musical. Annette Meyers. 370p. 1998. reprint ed. lib. bdg. 29.95 (*0-7351-0034-9*) Replica Bks.

Murder . . . by Category: A Subject Guide to Mystery Fiction. Tasha Mackler. LC 91-37638. 484p. 1991. 55.50 (*0-8108-2463-9*) Scarecrow.

Murder . . . Now & Then. Jill McGown. 407p. 1993. pap. 13.95 (*0-330-33243-0*, Pub. by Pan) Trans-Atl Phila.

Murder a la Mode. Patricia Moyes. LC 63-12604. 224p. 1995. pap. 5.95 (*0-8050-0706-7*, Owl) H Holt & Co.

Murder Aboard Yorktown. Roy Latall. 200p. 1998. pap. 23.95 (*1-57502-830-1*, P02230) Morris Pubng.

***Murder Ad Nauseam: A Solomon Hunter Mystery.** Arthur Asa Berger. 128p. 2000. pap. 18.00 (*0-7388-2067-9*) Xlibris Corp.

Murder after the Holiday. large type ed. Nicholas Rhea. (Dales Large Print Ser.). 272p. 1998. pap. 19.99 (*1-85389-784-1*, Dales) Ulverscroft.

***Murder American Style.** Bachman Alvarez. (Criminal Justice Ser.). 2001. 25.00 (*0-534-53470-8*) Wadsworth Pub.

***Murder among Friends.** Adams Round Table Group Staff. LC 99-51318. 2000. 21.95 (*0-425-16700-3*, Prime Crime) Berkley Pub.

Murder among Friends. Jonnie Jacobs. 352p. 1996. mass mkt. 4.99 (*1-57566-089-X*, Knsington) Kensgtn Pub Corp.

Murder among Friends: Violations of Philia in Greek Tragedy. Elizabeth S. Beltione. LC 99-13051. 304p. 2000. text 49.95 (*0-19-513149-5*) OUP.

***Murder among Gentlemen: A History of Dueling in Canada.** Hugh A. Halliday. (Illus.). 431p. 2000. pap. 15.95 (*1-896941-09-5*, Pub. by RBST) Midpt Trade.

Murder among Neighbors. Jonnie Jacobs. (Kate Austen Mystery Ser.). 304p. 1994. 16.95 (*0-8217-4680-4*, Zebra Kensgtn) Kensgtn Pub Corp.

Murder among Neighbors. Jonnie Jacobs. 304p. 1995. mass mkt. 4.99 (*0-8217-5039-9*, Zebra Kensgtn); mass mkt. 5.99 (*1-57566-275-2*) Kensgtn Pub Corp.

***Murder Among Strangers.** Jonnie Jacobs. LC 99-66831. (Kate Austen Mystery Ser.). 384p. 2000. 20.00 (*1-57566-540-9*, Knsington) Kensgtn Pub Corp.

Murder among the Angels. Stefanie Matteson. 256p. 1996. pap. 19.95 (*0-425-15149-2*, Prime Crime) Berkley Pub.

Murder among the Angels. Stefanie Matteson. 256p. 1996. mass mkt. 5.99 (*0-425-15548-X*, Prime Crime) Berkley Pub.

Murder among Thieves. large type ed. Peter Alding. 320p. 1992. 27.99 (*0-7089-2564-2*) Ulverscroft.

Murder Among Us. Ann Granger. (Meredith & Markby Mystery Ser.: No. 4). 304p. 1995. mass mkt. 5.99 (*0-380-72476-6*, Avon Bks) Morrow Avon.

Murder among Us: A Kate Austen Mystery. Jonnie Jacobs. LC 97-73786. 336p. 1998. 20.00 (*1-57566-276-0*, Knsington) Kensgtn Pub Corp.

Murder among Us: A Kate Austen Mystery. Jonnie Jacobs. 304p. 1999. mass mkt. 5.99 (*1-57566-398-8*) Kensgtn Pub Corp.

Murder & a Muse. Gillian B. Farrell. 1995. mass mkt. 5.99 (*0-671-75711-3*, Pocket Books) PB.

Murder & Assassination. Albert Ellis & John M. Gullo. 1971. 10.00 (*0-8184-0057-9*) Carol Pub Group.

Murder & Chips. large type ed. Laurie Mantell. 368p. 1989. 27.99 (*0-7089-2028-4*) Ulverscroft.

Murder & Difference: Gender, Genre & Scholarship on Sisera's Death. Mieke Bal. LC 86-42995. (Indiana Studies in Biblical Literature). (Illus.). 160p. 1988. 35.00 (*0-253-33905-7*) Ind U Pr.

Murder & Difference: Gender, Genre & Scholarship on Sisera's Death. Mieke Bal. LC 86-42995. (Indiana Studies in Biblical Literature). (Illus.). 160p. 1992. pap. 11.95 (*0-253-20741-X*, MB 741) Ind U Pr.

Murder & Justice Frontier New Mexico. Jill Mocho. LC 96-10007. (Illus.). 259p. (C). 1997. pap. 19.95 (*0-8263-1800-2*) U of NM Pr.

Murder & Justice Frontier New Mexico. Jill Mocho et al. LC 96-10007. (Illus.). 259p. (C). 1997. 50.00 (*0-8263-1765-0*) U of NM Pr.

Murder & Madness: The Secret Life of Jack the Ripper. David Abrahamsen. 240p. 1993. mass mkt. 4.99 (*0-380-71993-2*, Avon Bks) Morrow Avon.

***Murder & Masculinity: Violent Fictions of Twentieth-Century Latin America.** Rebecca E. Biron. LC 99-6496. 192p. 1999. 45.00 (*0-8265-1342-5*) Vanderbilt U Pr.

Murder & Masculinity: Violent Fictions of Twentieth Century Latin America. Rebecca E. Biron. LC 99-6497. 192p. 1999. pap. 21.95 (*0-8265-1347-6*) Vanderbilt U Pr.

Murder & Misdeeds. Joan Smith. 1997. mass mkt. 4.50 (*0-449-28791-2*, Crest) Fawcett.

Murder & Obsession: New Original Stories. Ed. by Otto Penzler. LC 98-41039. 416p. 1999. 22.95 (*0-385-31800-6*) Delacorte.

***Murder & Obsession: 15 New Original Stories.** Ed. by Otto Penzler. 455p. 2000. mass mkt. 5.99 (*0-440-22318-0*, Dell Trade Pbks) Dell.

Murder & Politics in Colonial Ghana. Richard Rathbone. LC 92-44865. (Illus.). 256p. (C). 1993. 40.00 (*0-300-05504-8*) Yale U Pr.

Murder & Spies, Lovers & Lies: Settling the Great Controversies of American History. Marc Mappen. LC 95-41401. 304p. (Orig.). 1996. pap. 12.50 (*0-380-77514-X*, Avon Bks) Morrow Avon.

Murder & Sullivan: A Joan Spencer Mystery. Sara H. Frommer. (WWL Mystery Ser.). 1998. per. 4.99 (*0-373-26285-X*, 1-26285-6, Wrldwide Lib) Harlequin Bks.

Murder & the First Lady. Elliott Roosevelt. (Eleanor Roosevelt Mystery Ser.). 240p. 1985. mass mkt. 4.99 (*0-380-69937-0*, Avon Bks) Morrow Avon.

Murder & the Monarchy: The Sudden Deaths of 12 English Monarchs. Sessions, William Ltd., Staff. (C). 1988. 35.00 (*1-85072-027-4*, Pub. by W Sessions) St Mut.

Murder As a Business Decision: An Economic Analysis of Criminal Phenomena. Gary E. Marche. LC 98-17072. 356p. 1998. 75.00 (*1-57292-120-X*) Austin & Winfield.

Murder As Usual. large type ed. Hugh Pentecost. (Linford Mystery Library). 368p. 1997. pap. 16.99 (*0-7089-5103-1*, Linford) Ulverscroft.

Murder at Bean & Beluga. Diane Mayo. (Illus.). 64p. 1983. pap. 5.95 (*0-932966-33-0*) Permanent Pr.

Murder at Belgrove Country Club. Manning Spencer, pseud. 230p. (Orig.). 1989. pap. text 9.95 (*0-9621710-4-2*) C R Hayes.

Murder at Bent Elbow. Kate Gamble. 224p. 1998. mass mkt. 5.99 (*0-425-16194-3*, Prime Crime) Berkley Pub.

Murder at Cherry Hill: The Strang-Whipple Case, 1827. Louis C. Jones. LC 82-81376. (Illus.). 124p. (Orig.). 1982. pap. 6.00 (*0-943366-04-6*) Hist Cherry Hill.

Murder at Confederate Headquarters. large type ed. Susan Crites. 200p. (Orig.). 1994. pap. 9.95 (*1-881562-07-7*) Butternut Pubns.

Murder at Crome House. Margaret Cole. 1976. lib. bdg. 13.95 (*0-89968-167-0*, Lghtyr Pr) Buccaneer Bks.

Murder at Ebbets Field. Troy Soos. 1996. mass mkt. 4.99 (*1-57566-027-X*) Kensgtn Pub Corp.

Murder at Fenway Park. Troy Soos. 256p. 1995. mass mkt. 4.99 (*0-8217-4909-9*, Zebra Kensgtn) Kensgtn Pub Corp.

Murder at Fenway Park. large type ed. Troy Soos. (Niagara Large Print Ser.). 277p. 1995. 29.50 (*0-7089-5813-3*) Ulverscroft.

Murder at Fort Christmas. R. Mathews-Danzer & Rinaldo Mathews. 2000. 14.95 (*1-888417-50-1*) Dimefast.

Murder at Gettysburg. Jim Walker. LC 99-17584. (Mysteries in Time Ser.: Vol. 3). 480p. 1999. pap. 13.99 (*0-8054-1970-5*) Broadman.

***Murder at Goose Rapids.** large type ed. Frank Fields. 240p. 2000. 20.99 (*1-84137-023-1*, Pub. by Mgna Lrg Print) Ulverscroft.

Murder at Government House. large type ed. Elspeth Huxley. 304p. 1990. 21.95 (*1-85089-368-3*, Pub. by ISIS Lrg Prnt) Transaction Pubs.

Murder at Hazelmoor. large type ed. Agatha Christie. 1987. 16.95 (*0-85456-203-6*) Ulverscroft.

Murder at Heartbreak Hospital. Henry Slesar. LC 98-19484. 247p. 1998. reprint ed. 21.00 (*0-89733-463-9*) Academy Chi Pubs.

***Murder at Heartbreak Hospital.** Henry Slesar. 247p. 2000. reprint ed. pap. 14.00 (*0-89733-486-8*) Academy Chi Pubs.

Murder at Hobcaw Barony. Elliott Roosevelt. (Eleanor Roosevelt Mystery Ser.). 224p. 1987. mass mkt. 4.50 (*0-380-70021-2*, Avon Bks) Morrow Avon.

Murder at Hockey Camp see Screech Owls Series Boxed Set: Murder at Hockey Camp; Kidnapped in Sweden; Terror in Florida

Murder at Hogans Corner, Washington: An American Destiny. Wallace L. Exum. 227p. 1992. pap. 6.95 (*0-9634866-0-8*) Chart Hse.

Murder at Larinum. Marcus Tullius Cicero. Ed. by Humfrey Grose-Hodge. 1932. text 5.95 (*0-521-04648-3*) Cambridge U Pr.

***Murder at Les Halles.** Elizabeth Cowley-Taylor. 157p. 2000. 21.95 (*0-7541-0980-1*, Pub. by Minerva Pr) Unity Dist.

Murder at Madingley Grange. Caroline Graham. 304p. 1992. mass mkt. 4.99 (*0-380-71295-4*, Avon Bks) Morrow Avon.

Murder at Madingley Grange. large type ed. Caroline Graham. LC 91-550. 465p. 1991. reprint ed. lib. bdg. 18.95 (*1-56054-173-3*) Thorndike Pr.

***Murder @ Maggody.com.** Joan Hess. 2001. mass mkt. 6.99 (*0-671-01685-7*, PB Trade Paper) PB.

***Murder@Maggody.Com: An Arly Hanks Mystery.** Joan Hess. LC 99-46821. 256p. 2000. 22.00 (*0-684-84563-6*) S&S Trade.

***Murder at Manassas.** Michael Kilian. LC 99-33286. 320p. 2000. 21.95 (*0-425-17233-3*, Prime Crime) Berkley Pub.

Murder at Markham. Patricia H. Sprinkle. (Sheila Travis Mystery Ser.). 1992. reprint ed. per. 3.99 (*0-373-26108-X*) Harlequin Bks.

Murder at Medicine Lodge. Mardi Oakley Medawar. LC 98-37611. 272p. 1999. text 23.95 (*0-312-19925-2*) St Martin.

Murder at Midnight: An Eleanor Roosevelt Mystery. Elliott Roosevelt. LC 96-53530. 224p. 1997. 20.95 (*0-312-15596-4*) St Martin.

Murder at Midnight: An Eleanor Roosevelt Mystery. Elliott Roosevelt. (Eleanor Roosevelt Mystery Ser.). 240p. 1998. mass mkt. 5.99 (*0-312-96554-0*) St Martin.

Murder at Mill Hollow, Vol. 1. Peggy Barton & John Quinn. (Illus.). 70p. (J). (gr. 3-8). 1997. pap. 2.95 (*0-9660703-0-5*) Barton Bks.

Murder at Monticello, or, Old Sins. Rita Mae Brown. 320p. 1995. mass mkt. 6.99 (*0-553-57235-0*, Crimeline) Bantam.

Murder at Oklahoma. Jack M. Bickham. 1998. mass mkt. 5.99 (*0-425-16381-4*, Prime Crime) Berkley Pub.

***Murder at Pearl Harbor.** Jim Walker. (Mysteries in Time Ser.). 480p. 2000. pap. 14.99 (*0-8054-2160-2*) Broadman.

Murder at Plum's. Amy Myers. 224p. (Orig.). 1993. mass mkt. 4.50 (*0-380-76586-1*, Avon Bks) Morrow Avon.

Murder at Plum's. large type ed. Amy Myers. (General Ser.). 432p. (Orig.). 1993. pap. 11.50 (*0-7089-2847-1*) Ulverscroft.

***Murder at Rainbow Falls.** Tommy Lovelace & Betty Streett. (Illus.). 144p. (J). (gr. 5-7). 1999. pap. 7.95 (*0-88028-208-8*, 1505) Forward Movement.

Murder at Red Rook Ranch. Dorothy Tell. LC 90-6130. 224p. 1990. pap. 8.95 (*0-941483-80-0*) Naiad Pr.

Murder at Roissy. John Warren. 140p. 1999. pap. 11.95 (*1-890159-09-3*) Greenery Pr.

Murder at San Simeon: A Novel of the Roaring Twenties. Particia Hearst & Cordelia F. Biddle. 186p. 1998. per. 6.99 (*0-671-53402-5*) PB.

Murder at School. Glen Trevor, pseud. reprint ed. lib. bdg. 22.95 (*0-88411-829-0*) Amereon Ltd.

Murder at Stonehenge: An Oxford Mystery. Aaron H. Barken. LC 97-12299. 1997. 25.00 (*0-912526-78-5*) Lib Res.

Murder at Swann's Lake. Sally Spencer. 224p. 1999. 25.00 (*0-7278-2285-3*, Pub. by Severn Hse) Chivers N Amer.

***Murder at Swann's Lake.** large type ed. Sally Spencer. 400p. 2000. pap. 20.99 (*1-84137-001-0*, Pub. by Mgna Lrg Print) Ulverscroft.

Murder at the Ballet: My Gun Is Pink-Chapter II (A Murder Mystery in One Act) Jeffrey Goffin. (Illus.). 32p. (Orig.). 1990. pap. 3.50 (*0-88680-335-7*) I E Clark.

Murder at the Bridge Table. Matthew Granovetter. (Illus.). 310p. (Orig.). 1988. pap. 12.95 (*0-940257-01-7*) Granovetter Bks.

Murder at the Class Reunion. Triss Stein. LC 95-21508. 253p. 1995. per. 3.99 (*0-373-26181-0*, 1-26181-7) Harlequin Bks.

Murder at the Class Reunion. Triss Stein. 205p. 1993. 19.95 (*0-8027-3232-1*) Walker & Co.

Murder at the Fair. Susan Crites. 158p. 1993. pap. 10.00 (*1-881562-02-6*) Butternut Pubns.

Murder at the FBI. Margaret Truman. 320p. 1986. mass mkt. 5.99 (*0-449-20618-1*, Crest) Fawcett.

Murder at the Feast of Rejoicing: A Lord Meren Mystery. Lynda S. Robinson. 240p. (YA). 1996. 20.95 (*0-8027-3274-7*) Walker & Co.

Murder at the Feast of Rejoicing: A Lord Meren Mystery, Vol. 3. 3rd ed. Lynda S. Robinson. LC 96-97154. 248p. 1997. mass mkt. 5.99 (*0-345-39532-8*) Ballantine Pub Grp.

Murder at the Fringe. Gordon DeMarco. LC 87-63291. 190p. 1988. pap. 9.95 (*0-948275-41-3*) Dufour.

Murder at the Gardner. Jane Langton. 352p. 1989. pap. 6.99 (*0-14-011382-7*, Penguin Bks) Viking Penguin.

Murder at the Gardner. large type ed. Jane Langton. LC 88-14728. 468p. 1988. reprint ed. lib. bdg. 7.95 (*0-89621-170-3*) Thorndike Pr.

Murder at the God's Gate. Lynda S. Robinson. 1996. mass mkt. 5.99 (*0-345-39531-X*) Ballantine Pub Grp.

Murder at the God's Gate. Lynda S. Robinson. LC 94-28806. 248p. 1995. 19.95 (*0-8027-3198-8*) Walker & Co.

Murder at the Howard Johnson's. Clark. 1980. pap. 4.00 (*0-573-61202-1*) French.

Murder at the Kabuki. Jack Royce. 1994. 6.95 (*1-884953-01-8*) Eaton St Pr.

Murder at the Kennedy Center. Margaret Truman. 352p. 1990. mass mkt. 5.99 (*0-449-21208-4*, Crest) Fawcett.

***Murder at the Kennedy Center.** Margaret Truman. 1999. 6.99 (*0-449-45926-8*) Fawcett.

Murder at the Kennedy Center. large type ed. Margaret Truman. 559p. 1990. reprint ed. lib. bdg. 20.95 (*0-89621-985-2*) Thorndike Pr.

***Murder at the Library of Congress.** Margaret Truman. 2001. mass mkt. 6.99 (*0-449-00195-4*) Ballantine Pub Grp.

Murder at the Library of Congress. Margaret Truman. LC 99-14953. 336p. 1999. 25.00 (*0-375-50068-5*) Random.

***Murder at the Library of Congress.** Margaret Truman. LC 99-36460. 1999. 25.00 (*0-375-40865-7*) Wheeler Pub.

Murder at the Margin: A Henry Spearman Mystery. Marshall Jevons. LC 93-19771. 192p. 1993. text 39.50 (*0-691-03391-9*, Pub. by Princeton U Pr); pap. text 12.95 (*0-691-00098-0*, Pub. by Princeton U Pr) Cal Prin Full Svc.

Murder at the Masque. Amy Myers. 256p. 1993. mass mkt. 4.99 (*0-380-76584-5*, Avon Bks) Morrow Avon.

***Murder at the Mendel.** Gail Bowen. 216p. 2000. mass mkt. 7.99 (*0-7710-1492-9*) McCland & Stewart.

Murder at the Mendel: A Joanne Kilbourn Mystery. Gail Bowen. 1992. pap. 7.99 (*0-7710-1480-5*) McCland & Stewart.

Murder at the Microphone. large type ed. Freda Bream. (Linford Mystery Library). 1995. pap. 16.99 (*0-7089-7800-2*) Ulverscroft.

Murder at the MLA. D. J. Jones. LC 92-22681. 224p. 1993. text 12.95 (*0-8203-1502-8*) U of Ga Pr.

***Murder at the MLA: A Novel.** D. J. H. Jones. 224p. 2000. pap. 13.95 (*0-8263-2150-X*) U of NM Pr.

Murder at the Monte Carlo. E. Phillips Oppenheim. reprint ed. lib. bdg. 24.95 (*0-89190-413-1*, Rivercity Pr) Amereon Ltd.

Murder at the Mouse Factory. R. Mathews-Danzer. 1999. 14.95 (*1-888417-51-X*) Dimefast.

Murder at the Movies. A. E. Eddenden. LC 95-50689. 159p. 1996. 20.00 (*0-89733-428-0*) Academy Chi Pubs.

Murder at the Movies. Weir et al. 1999. per. 6.99 (*0-373-26305-8*, 1-26305-2, Wrldwide Lib) Harlequin Bks.

Murder at the Murder at the Mimosa Inn. Joan Hess. 192p. 1999. pap. 5.99 (*0-312-97178-8*, St Martins Paperbacks) St Martin.

***Murder at the Museum of Natural History.** Michael Jahn. (Mystery Ser.: No. 337). 2000. per. 4.99 (*0-373-26337-6*, 1-26337-5, Wrldwide Lib) Harlequin Bks.

***Murder at the Music Hall.** Amy Myers. 1999. pap. 11.00 (*0-7472-4843-5*, Pub. by Headline Bk Pub) Trafalgar.

Murder at the National Cathedral. Margaret Truman. 336p. 1999. mass mkt. 5.99 (*0-449-21939-5*, Crest) Fawcett.

***Murder at the National Cathedral.** Margaret Truman. 1999. 6.99 (*0-449-45928-4*) Fawcett.

Murder at the National Gallery. Margaret Truman. 1997. mass mkt. 6.99 (*0-449-21938-0*, Crest) Fawcett.

Murder at the Nightwood Bar. Katherine V. Forrest. LC 86-28458. (Kate Delafield Mystery Ser.: Vol. 2). 240p. 1987. pap. 11.95 (*0-930044-92-4*) Naiad Pr.

Murder at the Old Vicarage. Jill McGown. (Mysteries Around the World Promotion Ser.). 1991. mass mkt. 5.99 (*0-449-21819-8*) Ivy Books.

Murder at the Opera. Ed. by Thomas Godfrey. 1989. 17.45 (*0-89296-379-4*, Pub. by Mysterious Pr) Little.

Murder at the Pageant. Victor L. Whitechurch. (Mystery Classics Ser.). 160p. 1987. reprint ed. pap. 6.95 (*0-486-25528-X*) Dover.

Murder at the Palace. Elliott Roosevelt. 272p. 1989. mass mkt. 4.99 (*0-380-70405-6*, Avon Bks) Morrow Avon.

Murder at the Pentagon. Margaret Truman. 336p. 1993. mass mkt. 5.99 (*0-449-21940-2*, Crest) Fawcett.

***Murder at the Pentagon.** Margaret Truman. 1999. 6.99 (*0-449-45927-6*) Fawcett.

Murder at the Powderhorn Ranch, 1 vol., Vol. 11. Jessica Fletcher & Donald Bain. (Murder She Wrote Ser.: Vol. 11). 266p. 1999. mass mkt. 5.99 (*0-451-19476-4*) NAL.

***Murder at the Powderhorn Ranch: A Murder, She Wrote Mystery.** large type ed. Donald Bain & Jessica Fletcher. LC 99-56673. (Nightingale Ser.). 256p. 2000. pap. 21.95 (*0-7838-8926-7*) Mac Lib Ref.

Murder at the Priory. large type ed. B. Taylor & K. Clarke. (Illus.). 1991. 11.50 (*0-7089-2355-0*) Ulverscroft.

Murder at the PTA Luncheon. Valerie Wolzien. 240p. 1990. mass mkt. 5.99 (*0-449-14639-1*, GM) Fawcett.

Murder at the Races. Ed. by Peter Haining. 487p. 1997. 10.98 (*0-7858-0527-3*) Bk Sales Inc.

Murder at the Red October. Anthony Olcott. (Academy First Mystery Ser.). 320p. 1990. reprint ed. pap. 5.95 (*0-89733-327-6*) Academy Chi Pubs.

Murder at the Reunion. Barbara Steiner. LC 99-189222. (Thumbprint Mysteries Ser.). 128p. (J). (gr. 4). 1999. pap. 5.95 (*0-8092-0692-7*, 069270) NTC Contemp Pub Co.

Murder at the Spirit Cave. Frederic Bean. 336p. 1999. mass mkt. 5.99 (*0-553-58017-5*, Crimeline) Bantam.

Murder at the Strawberry Festival. Warren Carrier. LC 93-77786. 295p. 1993. 19.95 (*1-878044-14-1*) Mayhaven Pub.

Murder at the Tokyo Lawn Tennis Club. Robert J. Collins. 200p. (Orig.). 1994. pap. 9.95 (*0-8048-1934-3*) Tuttle Pubng.

***Murder at the University of Guanajuato: A Culinary Murder Mystery.** Ruthie Wornall. (Illus.). 1999. pap. 8.95 (*1-892931-02-8*) Wornall Pub.

Murder at the Vicarage. Agatha Christie. 240p. 1986. mass mkt. 5.99 (*0-425-09453-7*) Berkley Pub.

***Murder at the Vicarage.** Agatha Christie. (Miss Marple Mysteries Ser.). 224p. 2000. mass mkt. 5.99 (*0-451-20115-9*, Sig) NAL.

***Murder at the Vicarage.** 70th anniversary ed. Agatha Christie. (Miss Marple Mysteries Ser.). 2000. mass mkt. 12.00 (*0-451-19978-2*, Sig) NAL.

Murder at the Vicarage, Set. abr. ed. Agatha Christie. 1997. audio 16.99 (*0-553-47767-6*) BDD Aud Pub.

***Murder at the Wailing Wall.** Gerald Szyszkowitz. Tr. by Todd C. Hanlin from GER. LC 99-52533. (Studies in Austrian Literature, Culture & Thought). 2000. pap. write for info. (*1-57241-087-6*) Ariadne CA.

Murder at the Watergate. Margaret Truman. 1999. mass mkt. 6.99 (*0-449-00194-6*, Crest) Fawcett.

Murder at the Watergate. Margaret Truman. LC 98-3725. 336p. 1998. 25.00 (*0-679-43535-2*) Random Ref & Info.

Murder at the Watergate. large type ed. Margaret Truman. LC 97-51826. 336p. 1998. pap. 25.00 (*0-375-70294-6*) Random.

Murder at Thrippleton Hall. Lagoon Bks Staff. (Illus.). 96p. 1997. 6.95 (*1-899712-49-6*, Pub. by Lagoon Bks) Midpt Trade.

An Asterisk (*) at the beginning of an entry indicates that the title is appearing for the first time.

Murder at Tokyo American Club. Robert J. Collins. 1991. pap. 9.95 (0-8048-1673-5) Tuttle Pubng.

Murder at Wayside Antiques: A True Story of Double Murder in a World Class Antique Shop. Anna Flowers. LC 99-179392. (Illus.). 196p. 1999. pap. 12.95 (0-9666362-0-1) Raven Pr.

***Murder at Witches' Bluff.** Silver RavenWolf. 2000. pap. 14.95 (1-56718-727-7) Llewellyn Pubns.

Murder at Wrigley Field. Troy Soos. 304p. 1997. mass mkt. 5.50 (1-57566-155-1, Knsington) Kensgtn Pub Corp.

***Murder at Yosemite, Vol. 1.** Carlton Smith. 256p. 1999. pap. text 6.50 (0-312-97457-4) St Martin.

Murder Being Once Done. Ruth Rendell. 1998. 21.95 (0-89190-372-0) Amereon Ltd.

Murder Being Once Done. Ruth Rendell. LC 98-52890. (Vintage Crime/Black Lizard Series). 201p. 1999. pap. text 11.00 (0-375-70488-4) Vin Bks.

***Murder Being Once Done: An Inspector Wexford Mystery.** Ruth Rendell. 224p. 1999. pap. 11.00 (0-679-70488-4) Vin Bks.

Murder Beneath the Trees. large type ed. Nicholas Rhea. (Dales Large Print Ser.). 297p. 1996. pap. 18.99 (1-85389-624-1, Dales) Ulverscroft.

Murder Benign. large type ed. Richard Hunt. (Dales Large Print Ser.). 305p. 1997. pap. 18.99 (1-85389-721-3) Ulverscroft.

Murder Bone by Bone. Lora Roberts. 1997. mass mkt. 5.50 (0-449-14946-3) Fawcett.

Murder Book. Richard Rayner. 432p. 1999. mass mkt. 5.99 (0-06-109737-3) HarpC.

Murder by an Aristocrat. Mignon G. Eberhart. 1976. reprint ed. lib. bdg. 24.95 (0-88411-763-4) Amereon Ltd.

Murder by Chemistry. Joseph C. Taylor. 176p. mass mkt. 5.99 (1-55197-595-5) Picasso Publ.

Murder by Contract. 10.95 (0-02-570520-2) Macmillan.

Murder by Contrived Design: Babylon's System Genocidal Plan & Strategies. Ricardo A. Scott. (Ras Cardo Book of Light Ser.). (Illus.). 70p. 1995. pap. text 25.95 (1-883427-49-5) Crnerstone GA.

***Murder by Degrees: A Winnie & Thatch I-95 Mystery.** James A. Noble. 308p. 2000. pap. 18.00 (0-7388-2071-7) Xlibris Corp.

Murder by Design. large type ed. Ray Harrison. (Linford Mystery Library). 416p. 1997. pap. 16.99 (0-7089-5071-X, Linford) Ulverscroft.

Murder by Fax. Henk Elsink, pseud. 241p. 1992. pap. 7.95 (1-881164-52-7) Intercont VA.

Murder by Magic. Franklin W. Dixon. (Hardy Boys Casefiles Ser.: No. 98). (YA). (gr. 6 up). 1995. 9.09 (0-606-07620-4, Pub. by Turtleback) Demco.

Murder by Mail. M. D. Lake. 256p. (Orig.). 1993. mass mkt. 5.99 (0-380-76856-9, Avon Bks) Morrow Avon.

Murder by Membership Only: A Mystery-Comedy in Two Acts for All Women. Thomas Hischak. 52p. 1980. pap. 4.00 (0-88680-133-8) I E Clark.

Murder by Mistake: In 2 Acts. John Kaasik. (Illus.). 61p. (C). 1995. pap. 4.00 (0-88680-417-5, 417-5) I E Clark.

Murder by Natural Causes. Richard Levinson et al. 64p. (YA). (gr. 10 up). 1985. pap. 5.50 (0-87129-850-3, M61) Dramatic Pub.

Murder by Prophecy. Maggie O. Anderson. 280p. 1998. pap. 13.00 (0-9639147-4-X) ReGeJe Press.

Murder by QRM. Walker A. Tompkins. 1989. pap. 5.00 (0-87259-506-4) Am Radio.

Murder by Radio. Judith A. Green. (Adult Basic Learner Ser.). (Illus.). 191p. (Orig.). 1979. pap. text 8.98 (0-89061-152-1, 200, Jamestwn Pub) NTC Contemp Pub Co.

Murder by Reference. D. R. Meredith. 272p. 1991. mass mkt. 4.99 (0-345-36861-4) Ballantine Pub Grp.

Murder by Sacrilege. D. R. Meredith. 1993. mass mkt. 4.99 (0-345-37693-5) Ballantine Pub Grp.

Murder by Tarot. Al Guthrie. 1992. mass mkt. 3.99 (0-8217-3637-X, Zebra Kensgtn) Kensgtn Pub Corp.

Murder by the Book. Cynthia Manson. 1996. mass mkt. 5.99 (0-425-15516-1) Berkley Pub.

Murder by the Book. Margaret St. George. (Intrigue Ser.). 1992. per. 2.89 (0-373-22198-3, 1-22198-5) Harlequin Bks.

Murder by the Book. Pat Welch. 256p. 1990. pap. 9.95 (0-941483-59-2) Naiad Pr.

Murder by the Book? Crime Fiction & Feminism. Sally R. Munt. LC 93-49588. (Narrative Forms & Social Formations Ser.). 200p. (C). 1994. pap. 25.99 (0-415-10919-1, B4244) Routledge.

Murder by the Book: Literary Mysteries from Alfred Hitchcock Mystery Magazine & Ellery Queen's Mystery Magazine. Ed. by Cynthia Manson. LC 96-156448. 304p. 1995. 21.95 (0-7867-0250-8) Carroll & Graf.

Murder by the Glass. large type ed. Peter Haining. 832p. 1996. 27.99 (0-7089-3542-7) Ulverscroft.

Murder by the Lake. large type ed. Nicholas Rhea. (Dales Large Print Ser.). 304p. 1996. pap. 18.99 (1-85389-622-5, Dales) Ulverscroft.

Murder by the Numbers, Set. Max Allan Collins. 1994. 19.95 incl. audio (1-882071-47-6) B&B Audio.

Murder by the Sea. Susan Evans McCloud. LC 97-71249. 192p. 1997. pap. 9.95 (1-57008-314-2) Bookcraft Inc.

Murder by Thirteen. Sisters in Crime, Los Angeles Chapter. Ed. by Priscilla English et al. LC 97-65292. 176p. 1997. pap. 10.95 (0-9647945-3-5) Intrigue Press.

Murder by 13. Sisters in Crime Los Angeles Staff. Ed. by Priscilla English et al. 1997. pap. 10.95 (1-890768-15-4) Intrigue Press.

Murder by Tradition. Katherine V. Forrest. (Kate Delafield Mystery Ser.: Vol. 4). 288p. 1993. reprint ed. pap. 11.95 (1-56280-002-7) Naiad Pr.

Murder Can Be Fun. Fredric Brown. 219p. 1989. pap. 3.95 (0-88184-504-3) Carroll & Graf.

Murder Can Singe Your Old Flame. Selma Eichler. 256p. 1999. mass mkt. 5.99 (0-451-19218-4, Sig) NAL.

***Murder Can Spoil Your Appetite.** Selma Eichler. 261p. 2000. mass mkt. 5.99 (0-451-19958-8, Sig) NAL.

Murder Can Stunt Your Growth. Selma Eichler. 272p. 1996. mass mkt. 5.99 (0-451-18514-5, Sig) NAL.

Murder Can Wreck a Reunion. Selma Eichler. 272p. 1997. mass mkt. 5.99 (0-451-18521-8, Sig) NAL.

***Murder Carries a Torch: A Southern Sisters Mystery.** Anne Carroll George. LC 00-35148. (Southern Sisters Mysteries Ser.). 272p. 2000. 23.00 (0-380-97810-5) Morrow Avon.

Murder Cases of the Twentieth Century: Biographies & Bibliographies of 280 Convicted & Accused Killers. David K. Frasier. LC 96-14984. 570p. 1996. lib. bdg. 65.00 (0-7864-0184-2) McFarland & Co.

Murder Chez Proust. Estelle Monbrun. Tr. by David Martyn. LC 94-39260. (ENG & FRE.). 240p. 1995. 19.45 (1-55970-283-4, Pub. by Arcade Pub Inc) Time Warner.

Murder Chez Proust. Estelle Monbrun. 240p. 1996. pap. 10.45 (1-55970-341-5, Pub. by Arcade Pub Inc) Time Warner.

Murder, Chop Chop. James Norman. 1997. reprint ed. pap. 13.00 (0-915230-16-X) Rue Morgue.

***Murder City.** large type ed. Anthony Lenton. 248p. 1999. pap. 18.99 (0-7089-5595-9, Linford) Ulverscroft.

Murder Club Regional Guides, 2 vols., No. 5: Eastern & Home Countries. Ed. by Brian Lane. (C). 1989. pap. 39.00 (0-245-54679-0) St Mut.

Murder Club Regional Guides, 2 vols., No. 6: South-West England & Wales. Ed. by Brian Lane. (C). 1989. pap. 39.00 (0-245-54686-3) St Mut.

Murder Comes Calling. large type ed. Emma Page. (Magna Large Print Ser.). 363p. 1997. 27.99 (0-7505-1081-1) Ulverscroft.

Murder Comes First. Frances Lockridge & Richard Lockridge. 192p. 1975. reprint ed. lib. bdg. 22.95 (0-89190-902-8, Rivercity Pr) Amereon Ltd.

Murder Comes to Mind. Joan Smith. 1998. mass mkt. 4.99 (0-449-00287-X, Crest) Fawcett.

Murder Confounded. large type ed. Roderic Jeffries. LC 93-37422. 279p. 1994. lib. bdg. 16.95 (0-8161-5902-5, G K Hall Lrg Type) Mac Lib Ref.

Murder, Courts, & the Press: Issues in Free Press - Fair Trial. rev. ed. Peter E. Kane. LC 91-40248. 144p. (C). 1992. 21.95 (0-8093-1780-X); pap. 14.95 (0-8093-1781-8) S Ill U Pr.

Murder Crops Up. Lora Roberts. 240p. 1998. mass mkt. 5.99 (0-449-15048-8, GM) Fawcett.

Murder Crossed: A Clara Gamadge Mystery. Eleanor Boylan. LC 95-34659. 88p. 1995. 20.00 (0-8050-3922-8) H Holt & Co.

Murder Crosses the Equator: A Father Jack Carthier Mystery. David Bergsen. 1999. pap. text 10.95 (1-891874-03-9) Recover Comns.

Murder Did Pay: Nineteenth Century New Jersey Murders. John T. Cunningham & Donald A. Sinclair. (Classics Ser.). (Illus.). 193p. 1981. text 10.95 (0-911020-04-7) NJ Hist Soc.

***Murder Dirty Boogies with Elvis.** Anne George. 2000. 23.00 (0-06-019870-2); mass mkt. 5.99 (0-06-103102-X) HarpC.

Murder Done to Death: Parody & Pastiche in Detective Fiction. John K. Melling. LC 95-15442. 296p. 1996. 46.00 (0-8108-3034-5) Scarecrow.

***Murder.com: The Dark Side of the Net.** Sarah St. Peter. Ed. by Linda J. Dageforde. LC 99-35309. 248p. 1999. pap. 7.99 (1-886225-41-9, 5000) Dageforde Pub.

Murder down Under. Arthur W. Upfield. 304p. 1983. pap. 6.00 (0-684-17887-7, Scribners Ref) Mac Lib Ref.

***Murder down Under.** Arthur W. Upfield. LC 98-21188. 304p. 1998. pap. 11.00 (0-684-85059-1, Scribner Pap Fic) S&S Trade Pap.

Murder Duet: A Musical Case. Batya Gur. LC 98-50456. 448p. 1999. 25.00 (0-06-017268-1) HarpC.

***Murder Duet: A Musical Case.** Batya Gur. 448p. 2000. pap. 14.00 (0-06-093298-8, Perennial) HarperTrade.

Murder Fantastical. Patricia Moyes. LC 84-6752. 256p. 1995. pap. 5.95 (0-8050-0504-8, Owl) H Holt & Co.

Murder First Glass. large type ed. Ron Ellis. (Linford Mystery Library). 287p. 1988. pap. 16.99 (0-7089-6558-X, Linford) Ulverscroft.

Murder Flies Left Seat. Jackie Lewin. LC 97-97218. 192p. 1998. 18.95 (0-8034-9288-X, Avalon Bks) Bouregy.

***Murder Flies Left Seat.** Jackie Lewin. 2000. mass mkt. 5.99 (0-373-26357-0, Wrldwide Lib) Harlequin Bks.

***Murder Follows Money.** Lora Roberts. (Liz Sullivan Mysteries Ser.). 240p. 2000. mass mkt. 6.50 (0-449-00539-9) Fawcett.

Murder for Beltene. Sandra Brewer. 309p. 1999. pap. 18.99 (1-885173-67-9) Write Way.

Murder for Christmas. Ed. & Intro. by Thomas Godfrey. LC 82-60904. (Illus.). 480p. 1987. 35.00 (0-89296-058-2, Pub. by Mysterious Pr) Little.

Murder for Christmas. Ed. & Intro. by Thomas Godfrey. LC 82-60904. (Illus.). 480p. 1999. 19.45 (0-89296-057-4, Pub. by Mysterious Pr) Little.

Murder for Christmas. Ed. by Thomas Godfrey. 304p. 1988. mass mkt. 5.50 (0-445-40774-3, Pub. by Warner Bks) Little.

Murder for Christmas. Ed. by Thomas Godfrey. (Illus.). 480p. 1994. 9.99 (0-517-69040-3) Random Hse Value.

Murder for Christmas. large type ed. Agatha Christie. 416p. 1987. 16.95 (0-7089-1724-0) Ulverscroft.

Murder for Christmas, Vol. II. Ed. by Thomas Godfrey. 336p. 1988. mass mkt. 5.50 (0-445-40752-2, Pub. by Warner Bks) Little.

Murder for Her Birthday. large type ed. Guy Cobden. (Linford Mystery Library). 400p. 1993. pap. 16.99 (0-7089-7381-7, Linford) Ulverscroft.

Murder for Her Majesty. Beth Hilgartner. 252p. (J). (gr. 4-7). 1992. pap. 5.95 (0-395-61619-0) HM.

Murder for Her Majesty. Beth Hilgartner. (J). 1986. 11.05 (0-606-00618-4, Pub. by Turtleback) Demco.

Murder for His Money. large type ed. Guy Cobden. (Linford Mystery Library). 1994. pap. 16.99 (0-7089-7625-5, Linford) Ulverscroft.

Murder for Love. Ed. by Otto Penzler. 1997. mass mkt. 5.50 (0-440-22315-6) Dell.

Murder for Love. Otto Penzler. 368p. 1999. mass mkt. 5.99 (0-440-22105-6) Dell.

Murder for Lunch. large type ed. Haughton Murphy. 1990. 27.99 (0-7089-2225-2) Ulverscroft.

Murder for Pleasure. Howard Haycraft. 445p. Date not set. 29.95 (0-8488-2292-7) Amereon Ltd.

Murder for Pleasure: The Life & Times of the Detective Story. Howard Haycraft. 464p. 1984. pap. 10.95 (0-88184-071-8) Carroll & Graf.

Murder for Reasons Unknown. Cat Lyons. LC 96-95287. 192p. 1997. 18.95 (0-8034-9193-X, Avalon Bks) Bouregy.

Murder for Revenge. Otto Penzler. 400p. 1999. mass mkt. 5.99 (0-440-22321-0) Dell.

***Murder for Sale.** large type ed. Michael Bardsley. 264p. 1999. pap. 18.99 (0-7089-5598-3, Linford) Ulverscroft.

***Murder for the Green.** Andre Murray. LC 00-90507. 2000. 10.95 (0-533-13526-5) Vantage.

***Murder for Treasure.** David Williams. 216p. 2000. 21.95 (0-7540-8559-7, Black Dagger) Chivers N Amer.

Murder Forestalled. large type ed. Peter Chester. (Linford Mystery Library). 352p. 1992. pap. 16.99 (0-7089-7265-9, Linford) Ulverscroft.

Murder from an Academic Angle: An Introduction to the Study of the Detective Narrative. Heta Pyrhonen. (COMLIT Ser.). x, 134p. 1994. 60.00 (1-879751-81-X) Camden Hse.

***Murder from Memory.** large type ed. Sarah J. Mason. 424p. 1999. pap. 18.99 (0-7089-5607-6, Linford) Ulverscroft.

Murder Game. Janice Harrell. Ed. by Ruth Ashby. 160p. (Orig.). (J). 1993. mass mkt. 2.99 (0-671-78541-9, Archway) PB.

Murder Game. Steve Lyons. (Doctor Who Ser.). 1998. pap. 5.95 (0-563-40565-1) BBC.

***Murder Game.** large type ed. Reg Batchelor. 296p. 1999. pap. 18.99 (0-7089-5557-6, Linford) Ulverscroft.

***Murder Gets a Life.** Anne George. LC 99-58850. (Anne George Mystery Ser.). 2000. 25.95 (1-57490-290-3) T T Beeler.

***Murder Gets a Life: A Southern Sisters Mystery.** Anne Carroll George. LC 97-49669. 256p. 1998. 20.00 (0-380-97558-0, Avon Bks) Morrow Avon.

Murder Gets a Life: A Southern Sisters Mystery. Anne Carroll George. LC 97-49669. 259p. 1999. mass mkt. 6.50 (0-380-79366-0, Avon Bks) Morrow Avon.

Murder Goes Mumming. Alisa Craig, pseud. 192p. 1989. mass mkt. 3.99 (0-380-70335-1, Avon Bks) Morrow Avon.

Murder Goes Round & Round. large type ed. Hugh Pentecost. (Linford Mystery Library). 304p. 1998. pap. 17.99 (0-7089-5218-6, Linford) Ulverscroft.

Murder Goes to College: Murder in the Archives. Robert Foster. (Illus.). 246p. 1998. pap. 11.95 (1-57502-761-5, PO2072) Morris Pubng.

Murder Guide to London. Martin Fido. (Illus.). 272p. 1993. reprint ed. pap. 8.95 (0-89733-400-0) Academy Chi Pubs.

Murder Guide to London: An A-Z of Metropolitan Atrocities. Martin Fido. (Illus.). 272p. 1990. 14.95 (0-89733-341-1) Academy Chi Pubs.

Murder Has a Pretty Face. large type ed. Jennie Melville. (Magna Large Print Ser.). 407p. 1996. 27.99 (0-7505-1047-1, Pub. by Mgna Lrg Print) Ulverscroft.

Murder Has a Pretty Face. Jennie Melville. 1991. reprint ed. per. 3.99 (0-373-26079-2) Harlequin Bks.

Murder Has No Calories. Corinne H. Sawyer. 1995. mass mkt. 5.99 (0-449-22338-8) Fawcett.

Murder Hill: A True Story of 19th Century Crime & Punishment on Cape Cod. Thereas Barbo. 1999. pap. text 16.95 (0-940160-81-1) Parnassus Imprints.

***Murder, Honey.** Vinnie Hansen. LC 99-90696. 192p. 1999. 25.00 (0-7388-0466-5); pap. 18.00 (0-7388-0467-3) Xlibris Corp.

Murder, I Presume. large type ed. Gillian Linscott. (Keating's Choice Ser.). 312p. 1992. 21.95 (1-85089-428-0, Pub. by ISIS Lrg Prnt) Transaction Pubs.

Murder in a Cathedral. Ruth Dudley Edwards. LC 97-24203. 317 p. 1997. write for info. (0-7540-3117-9) Chivers N Amer.

Murder in a Cathedral. Ruth Dudley Edwards. LC 97-5498. 1997. 20.95 (0-312-15597-2, Thomas Dunne) St Martin.

Murder in a Cathedral. Ruth Dudley Edwards. 1997. 20.95 (0-614-27895-3) St Martin.

Murder in a Cathedral. large type ed. Ruth Dudley Edwards. LC 97-24203. (Myst-Hall Ser.). 326p. 1997. lib. bdg. 23.95 (0-7838-8284-X, G K Hall Lrg Type) Mac Lib Ref.

Murder in a Hot Flash: A Charlie Greene Mystery. Marlys Millhiser. LC 94-27050. 1995. 20.50 (1-883402-29-8) S&S Trade.

Murder in a Manner of Speaking. large type ed. Hazel W. Jones. (Mystery Ser.). 336p. 1993. 27.99 (0-7089-2827-7) Ulverscroft.

Murder in a Nice Neighborhood. Lora Roberts. LC 94-94033. (Northern California Mysteries Ser.). (Orig.). 1994. mass mkt. 4.99 (0-449-14891-2, GM) Fawcett.

Murder in a Peking Studio. Shunshin Chin. Tr. by Joshua A. Fogel. LC 85-47732. (Occasional Paper Arizona State Univ., Center for Asian Studies: No. 19). 183p. (Orig.). 1986. pap. 10.00 (0-939252-15-5) ASU Ctr Asian.

Murder in America. Ronald M. Holmes & Stephen T. Holmes. (Illus.). 185p. (C). 1993. text 48.00 (0-8039-5054-3); pap. text 21.00 (0-8039-5055-1) Sage.

Murder in America: A History. Roger Lane. LC 96-39626. (History of Crime & Criminal Justice Ser.). (Illus.). 416p. 1998. text 42.50 (0-8142-0732-4, LANMUR); pap. text 16.95 (0-8142-0733-2, LANMUX) Ohio St U Pr.

Murder in Amsterdam: Two "Dekok" Adventures: "Dekok & the Sunday Strangler" & "Dekok & the Corpse on Christmas Eve" Albert C. Baantjer. Tr. by H. G. Smittenaar from DUT. LC 96-36722. 215p. (Orig.). 1996. reprint ed. pap. 9.95 (1-881164-00-4, Pub. by Intercont VA) ACCESS Pubs Network.

***Murder in Belleville.** Cara Black. 368p. 2000. 23.00 (1-56947-211-4) Soho Press.

Murder in Brentwood. Mark Fuhrman. 448p. 1997. mass mkt. 6.99 (0-8217-5855-1, Zebra Kensgtn) Kensgtn Pub Corp.

Murder in Brentwood. Mark Fuhrman. LC 97-363. 275p. 1997. 24.95 (0-89526-421-8) Regnery Pub.

Murder in Brief. Carroll Lachnit. 272p. (Orig.). 1995. mass mkt. 4.99 (0-425-14790-8) Berkley Pub.

Murder in C Major. Sara H. Frommer. 224p. 1988. reprint ed. spiral bd. 3.50 (0-373-26017-2) Harlequin Bks.

Murder in Canton: A Judge Dee Mystery. Robert H. Van Gulik. LC 93-2456. (Illus.). viii, 207p. 1993. pap. 7.95 (0-226-84874-4) U Ch Pr.

Murder in Central Park. Michael Jahn. 352p. 2000. text 24.95 (0-312-24222-0) St Martin.

***Murder in Congo Square.** unabridged ed. Remi Cuvier. Ed. by Lana Wegeng & Julie Price. (New Orleans Murders Ser.: Vol. 2). (Illus.). 1999. pap. 7.95 (1-892651-20-3) Columbia Pubns.

Murder in Cormyr. Chet Williamson. 1998. pap. 5.99 (0-7869-1173-5, Pub. by TSR Inc) Random.

***Murder in Dealey Plaza: What We Know Now That We Didn't Know Then about the Death of JFK.** Ed. by James H. Fetzer. (Illus.). 448p. 2000. pap. 19.95 (0-8126-9422-8) Open Court.

***Murder in Detroit.** Al Parker. LC 99-65321. 192p. 2000. pap. 11.95 (1-56315-260-6, Pub. by SterlingHse) Natl Bk Netwk.

Murder in Drivespace. Richard Dakan. (Alternity Ser.). 1999. 13.95 (0-7869-1407-6, Pub. by TSR Inc) Random.

Murder in East Texas. J. W. Kerr. 320p. 1998. 21.95 (1-891668-01-3) Lions Hd Pub.

Murder in Estoril. Edith Templeton. 1993. 23.95 (1-85702-056-1) Fourth Estate.

***Murder in Foggy Bottom.** Margaret Truman. LC 99-86612. 336p. 2000. 24.95 (0-375-50069-3) Random.

***Murder in Georgetown.** Elliott Roosevelt. LC 99-26719. 230p. 1999. 23.95 (0-312-24221-2, Thomas Dunne) St Martin.

***Murder in Georgetown.** Elliott Roosevelt. 240p. 2000. pap. 5.99 (0-312-97321-7, Minotaur) St Martin.

Murder in Georgetown. Margaret Truman. 336p. 1987. mass mkt. 5.99 (0-449-21332-3, Crest) Fawcett.

***Murder in Georgetown.** large type ed. Elliott Roosevelt. LC 99-56313. (Illus.). 1999. pap. 22.95 (1-56895-807-2) Wheeler Pub.

Murder in Gray & White. large type ed. Corinne H. Sawyer. 427p. 1991. reprint ed. lib. bdg. 18.95 (1-56054-159-8) Thorndike Pr.

Murder in Green Meadows. rev. ed. Douglas Post. 1996. pap. 5.25 (0-8222-1518-7) Dramatists Play.

Murder in Greenwich: Who Killed Martha Moxley? Mark Fuhrman. (Illus.). 432p. 1999. mass mkt. 6.99 (0-06-109692-X, Harp PBks) HarpC.

***Murder in Greenwich: Who Killed Martha Moxley?** large type ed. Mark Fuhrman. LC 00-37698. 445p. 2000. 29.95 (0-7862-2633-1) Thorndike Pr.

***Murder in Greenwich: Who Killed Martha Moxley?, Set.** abr. ed. Mark Fuhrman. 1998. audio 18.00 (0-694-51994-4, 393411, Pub. by HarperAudio) Lndmrk Audiobks.

Murder in Grub Street: A Sir John Fielding Mystery. large type ed. Bruce Alexander. (Ulverscroft Large Print Ser.). 608p. 1997. 27.50 (0-7089-3749-7) Ulverscroft.

Murder in Grub Street: A Sir John Fielding Mystery. Bruce Alexander. 320p. 1996. reprint ed. mass mkt. 5.99 (0-425-15550-1, Prime Crime) Berkley Pub.

***Murder in Guanajuato: A Culinary Murder Mystery.** Ruthie Wornall. (Illus.). 206p. 1998. pap. 8.95 (1-892931-00-1, Pub. by Wornall Pub) Booksource.

Murder in Gutenthal. Armin Wiebe. 1997. pap. 10.95 (0-88801-158-X, Pub. by Turnstone Pr) Genl Dist Srvs.

Murder in Halruaa. Richard S. Meyers. LC 95-62254. (Forgotten Realms Ser.). 280p. 1996. 18.99 (0-7869-0521-2, 8657, Pub. by TSR Inc) Random.

Murder in Hawaii. Steve Allen. LC 98-66231. 320p. 1999. 22.00 (1-57566-375-9) Kensgtn Pub Corp.

***Murder in Hawaii.** Steve Allen. 2000. mass mkt. 5.99 (1-57566-529-8, Knsington) Kensgtn Pub Corp.

Murder in Hawthorn. large type ed. John Armour. 256p. pap. 18.99 (0-7089-5418-9) Ulverscroft.

Murder in High Places. Hugh Pentecost. (Worldwide Library Mysteries: No. 94). 1992. mass mkt. 3.99 (0-373-26094-6, 1-26094-2) Harlequin Bks.

Murder in Hollywood. Steve Allen. write for info. (0-318-62729-9, Zebra Kensgtn) Kensgtn Pub Corp.

Murder in Irvington. Robert Fangmeier. 210p. 1993. 16.95 (1-878208-31-4) Guild Pr IN.

Murder in Jackson Hole. 2nd ed. J. Royal Horton. 290p. (Orig.). 1996. pap. 12.95 (0-9643978-0-3) Sunlght CO.

Murder in Jamaica: The Adventures of Christiana & the Dreadlocks Cop, Mystery. Stan Martin. 359p. 1997. pap. text 18.00 (0-9682646-1-1) CPRE.

Murder-in-Law. Paul Engleman. LC 87-42704. 256p. 1988. mass mkt. 3.95 (0-445-40746-8, Pub. by Mysterious Pr) Little.

An Asterisk (*) at the beginning of an entry indicates that the title is appearing for the first time.

M

Murder in Lincoln County. Stuart Pritchard. LC 98-91569. 177p. 1998. write for info. (*1-892508-03-6*) Jingle Bob Pr.

Murder in Luxury. Hugh Pentecost. 224p. 1991. mass mkt. 3.50 (*0-373-26069-5*) Harlequin Bks.

Murder in Macedon. Anna Apostolou. LC 97-14781. 256p. 1997. text 21.95 (*0-312-16939-6*) St Martin.

Murder in Macedon. Anna Apostolou. 272p. 1998. mass mkt. 5.99 (*0-312-96792-6*) St Martin.

Murder in Mackinac. Ronald J. Lewis. LC 94-72293. 238p. 1994. pap. 12.95 (*0-9642436-0-1*) Agawa Pr.

Murder in Manhattan. Steve Allen. 352p. 1991. mass mkt. 4.95 (*0-8217-3440-7*, Zebra Kensgtn) Kensgtn Pub Corp.

Murder in Manhattan. Lagoon Bks Staff. (Illus.). 96p. 1997. 6.95 (*1-899712-48-8*, Pub. by Lagoon Bks) Midpt Trade.

Murder in Manhattan. large type ed. Eight Mystery Writers. (General Ser.). 360p. 1988. 17.95 (*0-8161-4345-5*, G K Hall Lrg Type) Mac Lib Ref.

Murder in Marrakech. large type ed. Charles Leader. (Linford Mystery Large Print Ser.). 368p. 1998. pap. 17.99 (*0-7089-5289-5*, Linford) Ulverscroft.

Murder in Martinsburg, West Virginia. Susan Crites. 160p. 1992. pap. 10.00 (*1-881562-00-X*) Butternut Pubns.

***Murder in Mayfair.** Robert Barnard. LC 99-46962. (Illus.). 288p. 2000. 23.00 (*0-684-86445-2*) Scribner.

***Murder in Mayfair.** large type ed. Robert Barnard. LC 00-37797. 379p. 2000. pap. 27.95 (*0-7862-2656-0*) Thorndike Pr.

Murder in Mellingham. Susan P. Oleksiw. 288p. 1993. 20.00 (*0-684-19528-3*, Scribners Ref) Mac Lib Ref.

Murder in Memoriam. Didier Daeninckx. Tr. by Liz Heron from FRE. (Masks Ser.). 176p. (Orig.). 1992. pap. 13.95 (*1-85242-206-8*) Serpents Tail.

Murder in Memphis: The FBI & the Assassination of Martin Luther King. Mark Lane & Dick Gregory. LC 92-44534. 336p. 1993. pap. 13.95 (*1-56025-056-9*, Thunders Mouth) Avalon NY.

Murder in Memphis: The True Story of a Family's Quest for Justice. Dorris D. Porch & Rebecca Easley. LC 97-66562. 320p. 1997. 24.95 (*0-88282-157-1*) New Horizon NJ.

Murder in Menomonie. Norm Rockwell. 120p. (Orig.). 1984. pap. 3.95 (*0-9612002-3-5*) Moonlight Press.

Murder in Mesopotamia. Agatha Christie. 240p. 1987. mass mkt. 5.99 (*0-425-10363-3*) Berkley Pub.

Murder in Mesopotamia. Agatha Christie. 1984. 11.09 (*0-606-00965-5*, Pub. by Turtleback) Demco.

Murder in Mesopotamia. large type ed. Agatha Christie. 348p. 1992. 14.95 (*0-8161-4568-7*, G K Hall Lrg Type) Mac Lib Ref.

Murder in Miami: An Analysis of Homicide Patterns & Trends in Dade County (Miami) Florida, 1917-1983. William Wilbanks. LC 84-11969. 396p. 1984. lib. bdg. 57.00 (*0-8191-4024-4*) U Pr of Amer.

Murder in Miniature: The Uncollected Stories of Leo Bruce. Leo Bruce. 208p. 1993. 20.00 (*0-89733-367-5*) Academy Chi Pubs.

Murder in Minnesota: A Collection of True Cases. Walter N. Trenerry. LC 84-20652. (Illus.). xi, 252p. 1962. reprint ed. pap. 12.95 (*0-87351-180-8*) Minn Hist.

Murder in Mixteca. J. Royal Horton. 312p. 1995. pap. 12.95 (*0-9643978-1-1*) Sunlight CO.

Murder in Montparnasse. Howard Engel. LC 99-10504. 304p. 1999. 23.95 (*0-87951-701-8*, Pub. by Overlook Pr) Penguin Putnam.

***Murder in Montparnasse.** Howard Engel. 2000. pap. 14.95 (*1-58567-094-4*, Pub. by Overlook Pr) Penguin Putnam.

Murder in Moscow. Jessica Fletcher & Donald Bain. (Murder She Wrote Ser.: Vol. 9). 302p. 1998. mass mkt. 5.99 (*0-451-19474-8*, Sig) NAL.

Murder in Moscow. large type ed. Andrew Garve. 1974. 27.99 (*0-85456-240-0*) Ulverscroft.

Murder in My Suite: Bienvenidos al Hotel California. Stephen Callis et al. LC 97-74316. (ENG & SPA., Illus.). 70p. 1998. pap. 6.00 (*0-9639050-0-7*, Pub. by Blue Heron OR) Consort Bk Sales.

***Murder in New York City.** Eric H. Monkkonen. (Illus.). 225p. 2000. 29.95 (*0-520-22188-5*, Pub. by U CA Pr) Cal Prin Full Svc.

***Murder in Palm Beach.** Cat Lyons. LC 00-190021. 192p. 2000. 18.95 (*0-8034-9418-1*, Avalon Bks) Bouregy.

***Murder in Palm Springs.** Mike Romano. 190p. 2000. pap. Price not set. (*0-88100-116-3*) Natl Writ Pr.

Murder in Paradise. Created by Francine Pascal. (Sweet Valley High Super Thriller Ser.). 240p. (YA). (gr. 7 up). 1995. mass mkt. 3.99 (*0-553-56710-1*) Bantam.

Murder in Paradise. Kate William. (Sweet Valley High Super Thriller Ser.). (YA). (gr. 7 up). 1995. 9.09 (*0-606-08225-5*, Pub. by Turtleback) Demco.

Murder in Paradise. large type ed. Ann Cleeves. 1990. 27.99 (*0-7089-2200-7*) Ulverscroft.

***Murder In Paradise.** large type ed. Lauran Paine, Jr. LC 99-52855. 2000. 30.00 (*0-7838-8799-X*, G K Hall Lrg Type) Mac Lib Ref.

Murder in Perspective: An Architectural Mystery. Keith Miles. LC 96-35898. 246p. 1997. 21.95 (*0-8027-3298-4*) Walker & Co.

Murder in Pug's Parlour. Amy Myers. 256p. (Orig.). 1992. mass mkt. 4.50 (*0-380-76587-X*, Avon Bks) Morrow Avon.

Murder in Pug's Parlour. large type ed. Amy Myers. 432p. (Orig.). 1993. pap. 27.99 (*0-7089-2732-7*) Ulverscroft.

Murder in Retirement. John Miles. (Worldwide Library Mysteries: No. 243). 1997. per. 4.99 (*0-373-26243-4*, 1-26243-5, Wrldwide Lib) Harlequin Bks.

Murder in Retirement: A Laura Michaels Mystery. John Miles. LC 93-25234. 1994. 19.95 (*0-8027-3246-1*) Walker & Co.

Murder in San Miguel: Culinary Murder Mystery. Ruthie Wornall. (Illus.). Date not set. pap. 8.95 (*1-892931-01-X*) Wornall Pub.

Murder in Scorpio. Martha C. Lawrence. 1996. mass mkt. 5.50 (*0-312-95984-2*) St Martin.

***Murder in Spokane.** Mark Fuhrman. 2000. 25.00 (*0-06-019437-5*) HarpC.

Murder in Store. large type ed. D. C. Brod. 1991. 27.99 (*0-7089-2548-0*) Ulverscroft.

Murder in Store. large type ed. Pamela Hill. 252p. 1997. 25.95 (*0-7531-5569-9*, Pub. by ISIS Lrg Prnt) Transaction Pubs.

***Murder in Store.** large type unabridged ed. Pamela Hill. 243p. 1999. pap. 19.95 (*0-7531-5570-2*, 155702, Pub. by ISIS Lrg Prnt) ISIS Pub.

Murder in Tarsis. John M. Roberts. LC 95-62207. (DragonLance Ser.). 1996. 18.99 (*0-7869-0500-X*, Pub. by TSR Inc) Random.

Murder in Tarsis. John Maddox Roberts. 1999. pap. 5.99 (*0-7869-1587-0*) TSR Inc.

***Murder in Texas.** Smith. 2000. mass mkt. write for info. (*0-312-97033-1*) St Martin.

Murder in the Adirondacks: An American Tradegy Revisited. 2nd rev. ed. Craig Brandon. LC 86-5328. (Illus.). xii, 380p. 1986. pap. 20.00 (*0-932052-58-4*) North Country.

Murder in the Air. Ellen Hart. LC 97-93707. (Sophie Greenway Mystery Ser.). 338p. 1997. mass mkt. 5.99 (*0-345-40203-0*) Ballantine Pub Grp.

Murder in the Blue Room. Elliott Roosevelt. 240p. 1992. mass mkt. 4.99 (*0-380-71237-7*, Avon Bks) Morrow Avon.

Murder in the Blue Room. large type ed. Elliott Roosevelt. (General Ser.). 377p. 1991. lib. bdg. 21.95 (*0-8161-5100-8*, G K Hall Lrg Type) Mac Lib Ref.

Murder in the Carolinas. Nancy Rhyne. 176p. (Orig.). 1998. reprint ed. pap. 12.95 (*1-888105-32-1*) Avisson Pr.

Murder in the Castro. Elaine Beale. LC 97-14674. 192p. 1997. pap. 10.95 (*0-934678-87-1*) New Victoria Pubs.

Murder in the Cathedral. T. S. Eliot. LC 35-1776. 96p. (C). 1964. pap. 7.00 (*0-15-663277-2*, Harvest Bks) Harcourt.

Murder in the Cathedral/Galileo: Curriculum Unit. Center for Learning Network Staff & T. S. Eliot. (Drama Ser.). 102p. (YA). (gr. 9-12). 1995. spiral bd. 18.95 (*1-56077-345-6*) Ctr Learning.

Murder in the Catskills. 2nd ed. Norman J. Van Valkenburgh. LC 92-41885. 109p. 1992. pap. 12.50 (*0-935796-37-1*) Purple Mnt Pr.

Murder in the Central Committee. Manuel V. Montalban. 224p. 1997. pap. text 12.99 (*1-85242-131-2*) Serpents Tail.

Murder in the Charleston Manner. Patricia H. Sprinkle. (Mystery Ser.). 1993. per. 3.99 (*0-373-26119-5*, 1-26119-7) Harlequin Bks.

Murder in the Chateau. Elliott Roosevelt. 1996. 19.95 (*0-614-96760-0*) St Martin.

Murder in the Chateau. Elliott Roosevelt. 1996. mass mkt. 5.99 (*0-312-96050-6*) St Martin.

***Murder in the Chateau.** large type ed. Elliott Roosevelt. LC 99-38385. 1999. 22.95 (*1-56895-769-6*, Wheeler) Wheeler Pub.

Murder in the Church of England of Nine Archbishops, Five of Canterbury Four of York. Ed. by Sessions, William Ltd., Staff. (C). 1988. 30.00 (*1-85072-013-4*, Pub. by W Sessions) St Mut.

***Murder in the CIA.** Margaret Truman. 1999. 6.99 (*0-449-45925-X*) Fawcett.

Murder in the CIA. Margaret Truman. 320p. 1999. reprint ed. mass mkt. 5.99 (*0-449-21275-0*, Crest) Fawcett.

Murder in the Collective. Barbara Wilson. LC 84-10330. 183p. (Orig.). 1984. pap. 9.95 (*1-878067-23-0*) Seal Pr WA.

Murder in the East Room. Elliott Roosevelt. (Eleanor Roosevelt Mystery Ser.). 1995. mass mkt. 4.99 (*0-312-95410-7*) St Martin.

Murder in the Executive Mansion. Elliott Roosevelt. LC 98-23159. 256 p. 1998. write for info. (*0-7540-3423-2*) Chivers N Amer.

Murder in the Executive Mansion. Elliott Roosevelt. 1996. mass mkt. 5.50 (*0-312-95578-2*, Pub. by Tor Bks) St Martin.

Murder in the Executive Mansion. large type ed. Elliott Roosevelt. LC 98-23159. 1998. 19.95 (*0-7838-0284-6*, G K Hall Lrg Type) Mac Lib Ref.

***Murder In The Family.** Burl Barer. 2000. mass mkt. 6.50 (*0-7860-1135-1*) Kensgtn Pub Corp.

Murder in the Family: Poems. Richard Messer. 80p. (Orig.). 1995. pap. 8.95 (*0-933087-37-3*) Bottom Dog Pr.

Murder in the Family: The Inside Story of the Jersey Murders. Jeremy Josephs. (Illus.). 256p. 1995. pap. 11.95 (*0-7472-4455-3*, Pub. by Headline Bk Pub) Trafalgar.

Murder in the First. Dan Gordon. 1995. mass mkt. 4.99 (*0-312-95532-4*) St Martin.

Murder in the Fourth Dimension. Thomas E. Krupowicz. 176p. 1998. pap. 14.95 (*1-881690-05-9*) Terk Bks & Pubs.

Murder in the Gunroom. H. Beam Piper. 272p. 1993. reprint ed. pap. 20.00 (*1-882968-02-6*) Old Earth Bks.

Murder in the Hamptons: A Mystery. Jeanne Toomey. LC 94-15036. 160p. (Orig.). 1994. pap. 12.95 (*0-86534-223-7*) Sunstone Pr.

Murder in the House. Margaret Truman. 1998. pap. 6.99 (*0-449-00172-5*, Crest) Fawcett.

Murder in the House. large type ed. Margaret Truman. LC 96-48623. (Large Print Ser.). 1997. pap. 24.00 (*0-679-77435-1*) Random.

Murder in the Latin Quarter. Tony Hays. 225p. (Orig.). 1993. pap. write for info. (*0-916078-32-9*) Iris Pr.

Murder in the Limelight. Amy Myers. 224p. 1992. mass mkt. 4.50 (*0-380-76585-3*, Avon Bks) Morrow Avon.

Murder in the Limelight. large type ed. Amy Myers. (General Ser.). 1993. 27.99 (*0-7089-2435-2*) Ulverscroft.

***Murder in the Lincoln Bedroom.** Elliott Roosevelt. (Eleanor Roosevelt Mysteries Ser.). 224p. 2000. 22.95 (*0-312-26150-0*, Thomas Dunne) St Martin.

Murder in the Madhouse. Jonathan Latimer. LC 89-85727. 300p. 1989. reprint ed. pap. 7.95 (*1-55882-023-X*, Lib Crime Classics) Intl Polygonics.

Murder in the Mansion & Other Computer Adventures. 2nd ed. Jim Cole. (Illus.). 96p. 1981. pap. 6.95 (*0-86668-501-4*) ARCsoft.

Murder in the Map Room. large type ed. Freda Bream. 1990. pap. 16.99 (*0-7089-6900-3*, Linford) Ulverscroft.

Murder in the Map Room: An Eleanor Roosevelt Mystery. Elliott Roosevelt. (Eleanor Roosevelt Mystery Ser.). 256p. 1998. text 21.95 (*0-312-18168-X*) St Martin.

Murder in the Map Room: An Eleanor Roosevelt Mystery. Elliott Roosevelt. LC 97-37243. (Eleanor Roosevelt Mystery Ser.). 256p. 1999. mass mkt. 5.99 (*0-312-96764-0*) St Martin.

Murder in the Map Room: An Eleanor Roosevelt Mystery. large type ed. Elliott Roosevelt. LC 98-24431. (Large Print Book Ser.). 1998. 22.95 (*1-56895-619-3*) Wheeler Pub.

Murder in the Marais. Cara Black. LC 98-52070. 368p. 1999. 22.00 (*1-56947-159-2*) Soho Press.

***Murder in the Marais.** Cara Black. 360p. 2000. pap. 13.00 (*1-56947-212-2*) Soho Press.

Murder in the Marketplace. Lora Roberts. 1995. mass mkt. 5.50 (*0-449-14890-4*) Fawcett.

***Murder in the Maze.** large type ed. Sarah J. Mason. 448p. 1999. pap. 18.99 (*0-7089-5561-4*, Linford) Ulverscroft.

Murder in the Mews. Agatha Christie. 1984. 11.09 (*0-606-00967-1*, Pub. by Turtleback) Demco.

Murder in the Mews & Other Stories. Agatha Christie. 240p. 1987. mass mkt. 5.99 (*0-425-10435-4*) Berkley Pub.

Murder in the Middle Pasture see **Asesinato en los Pastizales**

***Murder in the Middle Pasture.** John R. Erickson. (Hank the Cowdog Ser.: No. 4). (Illus.). (J). (gr. 2-5). 1999. pap. 14.50 (*0-8335-6817-5*) Econo-Clad Bks.

Murder in the Middle Pasture. John R. Erickson. (Hank the Cowdog Ser.: No. 4). (Illus.). 91p. (J). (gr. 2-5). 1985. 9.95 (*0-916941-08-6*); pap. 6.95 (*0-916941-07-8*) Maverick Bks.

***Murder in the Middle Pasture.** John R. Erickson. (Illus.). 144p. (J). 1998. pap. 14.99 (*0-670-88411-1*, Viking Child) Peng Put Young Read.

Murder in the Middle Pasture. John R. Erickson. LC 98-41854. (Hank the Cowdog Ser.: No. 4). (Illus.). 144p. (J). (gr. 2-5). 1998. pap. 4.99 (*0-14-130380-8*, PuffinBks) Peng Put Young Read.

Murder in the Middle Pasture. John R. Erickson. (Hank the Cowdog Ser.: No. 4). (Illus.). (J). (gr. 2-5). 1988. 12.05 (*0-606-01395-4*, Pub. by Turtleback) Demco.

Murder in the Middle Pasture. unabridged ed. John R. Erickson. (Hank the Cowdog Audio Ser.: No. 4). (Illus.). 91p. (J). (gr. 2-5). 1985. 13.95 incl. audio (*0-916941-09-4*) Maverick Bks.

Murder in the Mirror. Bethany Strong. LC 83-11225. 1984. pap. 5.95 (*0-917250-07-9*) Parable Pr.

***Murder in the Mist.** Willard Scott. 368p. 1999. mass mkt. 6.99 (*0-451-19298-2*) NAL.

Murder in the Mist. Willard Scott & Bill Crider. LC 98-26995. (Stanley Waters Mystery Ser.: 2). 256p. 1999. 23.95 (*0-525-94325-0*) NAL.

***Murder in the Mist.** Eleanor Clarke Yukic. LC 00-190186. 2000. 25.00 (*0-7388-1506-3*); pap. 18.00 (*0-7388-1507-1*) Xlibris Corp.

Murder in the Mist: A Stanley Waters Mystery. Willard Scott. LC 99-12935. (Senior Lifestyles Ser.). 1999. 26.95 (*0-7862-1915-7*, G K Hall & Co) Mac Lib Ref.

***Murder in the Motor Stable.** Amy Myers. 1999. pap. 11.00 (*0-7472-4844-3*, Pub. by Headline Bk Pub) Trafalgar.

Murder in the Museum of Man. Alfred Alcorn. 273p. 1998. pap. 13.00 (*0-944072-78-X*) Zoland Bks.

Murder in the Name of God: The Plot to Kill Yitzhak Rabin. Michael Karpin & Ina Friedman. LC 98-20763. (Illus.). 352p. 1998. 24.95 (*0-8050-5749-8*) H Holt & Co.

Murder in the Napa Valley. David Osborn. 224p. 1995. mass mkt. 4.99 (*0-8217-4844-0*, Zebra Kensgtn) Kensgtn Pub Corp.

Murder in the Napa Valley: A Margaret Barlow Mystery. David Osborn. 224p. 1993. 19.00 (*0-671-70487-7*) S&S Trade.

***Murder in the New Age.** D. J. H. Jones. 192p. 2000. pap. 13.95 (*0-8263-2236-0*) U of NM Pr.

Murder in the New Age. D. J. H. Jones et al. LC 97-4843. 192p. 1997. 19.95 (*0-8263-1813-4*) U of NM Pr.

Murder in the Newsroom: or Andrew Gates, Reporter. Robert Kanehl. Ed. by Jane Weinberger. LC 98-60556. 164p. (J). (gr. 3-10). 1998. pap. 8.00 (*1-883650-52-6*) Windswept Hse.

Murder in the Oval Office. Elliott Roosevelt. 1990. mass mkt. 4.99 (*0-380-70528-1*, Avon Bks) Morrow Avon.

Murder in the Place of Anubis. Lynda S. Robinson. 192p. 1995. mass mkt. 4.99 (*0-345-38922-0*) Ballantine Pub Grp.

Murder in the Place of Anubis. Lynda S. Robinson. 203p. 1994. 18.95 (*0-8027-3249-6*) Walker & Co.

Murder in the Queen's Arms. Aaron J. Elkins. 224p. 1990. mass mkt. 5.99 (*0-445-40913-4*, Mysterious Paperbk) Warner Bks.

***Murder in the Queen's Boudoir.** unabridged ed. Amy Myers. 2000. 26.00 (*0-7278-5561-1*) Severn Hse.

Murder in the Red Room. Elliott Roosevelt. (Eleanor Roosevelt Mystery Ser.). 256p. 1994. mass mkt. 4.99 (*0-380-72143-0*, Avon Bks) Morrow Avon.

***Murder in the Red Room.** large type ed. Elliott Roosevelt. LC 00-39869. 2000. write for info. (*1-56895-901-X*) Wheeler Pub.

Murder in the Rose Garden. Elliott Roosevelt. (Eleanor Roosevelt Mystery Ser.). 256p. 1991. reprint ed. mass mkt. 4.95 (*0-380-70529-X*, Avon Bks) Morrow Avon.

Murder in the Senate. large type ed. William S. Cohen & Thomas B. Allen. LC 93-13140. 533p. 1993. lib. bdg. 18.95 (*1-56054-752-9*) Thorndike Pr.

***Murder in the Shadows.** Ellen Godfrey. (Thumbprint Mysteries Ser.). 128p. 1999. pap. 5.95 (*0-8092-0686-2*, 068620) NTC Contemp Pub Co.

***Murder in the Shawangunks & the Class of '68: A Ward Eastman Mystery.** Norman J. Van Valkenburgh & Airilee Ellyn Blessing. LC 99-76006. 166p. 1999. pap. 12.50 (*1-930098-01-4*) Purple Mnt Pr.

Murder in the Smithsonian. Margaret Truman. 240p. 1985. mass mkt. 5.99 (*0-449-20959-8*, Crest) Fawcett.

Murder in the Smokehouse: An Auguste Didier Whodunit. Amy Myers. LC 97-12327. 1997. 23.95 (*0-312-15598-0*) St Martin.

Murder in the Solid State. Wil McCarthy. 256p. 1996. 22.95 (*0-312-85938-4*) Tor Bks.

Murder in the Stacks. Marion B. Havighurst. 249p. 1989. reprint ed. pap. text 5.00 (*0-918761-03-4*) Miami U Pubns.

Murder in the Supreme Court. Margaret Truman. 288p. 1985. mass mkt. 5.99 (*0-449-20969-5*, Crest) Fawcett.

Murder in the Tiergarten: The Political Life of Vladimer Orlov, Intelligence Agent & Disinformer. unabridged ed. Natalie Grant. Ed. by Jack Dziak et al. LC 97-185323. 61p. (Orig.). 1997. pap. 9.00 (*0-935067-16-7*) Nathan Hale Inst.

Murder in the Tower of High Sorcery. Teri White. (DragonLance Chronicles Ser.). 1997. 16.99 (*0-7869-0780-0*, Pub. by TSR Inc) Random.

Murder in the Tropic Night. large type ed. Frank Arthur. 1990. pap. 16.99 (*0-7089-6997-6*, Linford) Ulverscroft.

Murder in the Tropics. Stuart B. McIver. LC 95-30649. (Florida Chronicles Ser.: Vol. 2). (Illus.). 220p. 1995. 17.95 (*1-56164-079-4*) Pineapple Pr.

Murder in the Tudor Style. rev. ed. Isabel Isaacs. Ed. by Claire Huff. (Orig.). 1998. pap. write for info. (*0-9646184-1-9*) Lucid Pr.

Murder in the West Wing: An Eleanor Roosevelt Mystery. Elliott Roosevelt. (Eleanor Roosevelt Mystery Ser.). 1993. mass mkt. 5.99 (*0-312-95144-2*) St Martin.

Murder in Thebes. Anna Apostolou. LC 98-28727. 240p. 1998. text 21.95 (*0-312-19585-0*) St Martin.

Murder in Thebes: A Mystery of Alexander the Great. Anna Apostolou. 240p. 1999. mass mkt. 5.99 (*0-312-97278-4*) St Martin.

Murder in Their Midst. Sharon Abel Halvorsen. LC 98-89649. 112p. 1999. pap. 13.50 (*0-88739-223-7*) Creat Arts Bk.

Murder in Three Acts. large type ed. Agatha Christie. (General Ser.). 360p. 1989. lib. bdg. 19.95 (*0-8161-4569-5*, G K Hall Lrg Type) Mac Lib Ref.

***Murder in Tinseltown.** Earl Hamner & Don Sipes. 2000. 21.95 (*1-930709-15-3*) HAWK Pubng Grp.

Murder in Vain. large type ed. Laurie Mantell. 357p. 1989. 27.99 (*0-7089-1978-2*) Ulverscroft.

Murder in Victorian Scotland: The Trial of Madeleine Smith. Douglas MacGowan. LC 99-13792. 192p. 1999. 35.00 (*0-275-96431-0*, C6431, Praeger Pubs) Greenwood.

***Murder in Volume.** D. R. Meredith. 2000. mass mkt. 5.99 (*0-425-17309-7*, Prime Crime) Berkley Pub.

Murder in Waiting. Mignon G. Eberhart. 192p. 1983. mass mkt. 4.99 (*0-446-31242-8*, Pub. by Warner Bks) Little.

Murder in Waiting. Mignon G. Eberhart. 215p. reprint ed. lib. bdg. 21.95 (*0-88411-767-7*) Amereon Ltd.

Murder in Washington. Dorothy Woolfolk. (Donna Rockford Mystery Ser.). 208p. (Orig.). (J). (gr. 7 up). 1982. pap. 1.95 (*0-590-32000-9*) Scholastic Inc.

Murder in West Covina: Chronicles of the Finch-Tregoff Case. James L. Jones. LC 93-72153. 395p. 1992. 22.00 (*0-9637102-0-6*) Chaparral Cnslts.

***Murder in Winnetka.** S. C. Pemberton. LC 99-65316. 192p. 2000. pap. 11.95 (*1-56315-251-7*, Pub. by SterlingHse) Natl Bk Netwk.

An Asterisk (*) at the beginning of an entry indicates that the title is appearing for the first time.

Murder in Winter Garden: The Frame-Up of an Innocent Man. Phillip Finch. LC 92-5365. 1992. 20.00 (*0-685-60088-2*) Villard Books.

Murder, Inc. The Story of the Syndicate. Burton B. Turkus & Sid Feder. 512p. 1992. reprint ed. pap. 17.50 (*0-306-80475-1*) Da Capo.

***Murder Included.** large type ed. Joanna Cannan. 344p. 2000. pap. 18.99 (*0-7089-5670-X*, Linford) Ulverscroft.

Murder Inherited. large type ed. Guy Cobden. (Linford Mystery Library). 400p. 1993. pap. 16.99 (*0-7089-7417-1*, Linford) Ulverscroft.

Murder Intercontinental, 1 vol. Cynthia Manson. 1999. mass mkt. 6.99 (*0-425-17123-X*) Berkley Pub.

Murder Is a Collector's Item. Elizabeth Dean. Ed. by Tom Schantz & Enid Schantz. 192p. 1998. reprint ed. pap. 14.00 (*0-915230-19-4*) Rue Morgue.

***Murder Is a Serious Business.** Elizabeth Dean. 256p. 1999. pap. 14.95 (*0-915230-28-3*) Rue Morgue.

Murder Is an Art. Bill Crider. LC 98-41786. 256p. 1999. text 21.95 (*0-312-19927-9*) St Martin.

Murder Is Announced. Agatha Christie. 240p. 1991. mass mkt. 5.99 (*0-425-12962-4*) Berkley Pub.

Murder Is Announced. Agatha Christie. (Miss Marple Mysteries Ser.). 1991. 10.60 (*0-606-12436-5*, Pub. by Turtleback) Demco.

Murder Is Easy. Agatha Christie. 224p. 1992. mass mkt. 5.99 (*0-06-100370-0*, Harp PBks) HarpC.

Murder Is Easy. Agatha Christie. 1992. 11.09 (*0-606-12437-3*, Pub. by Turtleback) Demco.

Murder Is Germane. Karen Saum. LC 91-22262. (Brigid Donovan Mystery Ser.). 224p. (Orig.). 1991. pap. 8.95 (*0-934678-56-1*) New Victoria Pubs.

Murder Is Its Own Reward. large type ed. Peter Chambers. (Linford Mystery Library). 240p. 1995. pap. 16.99 (*0-7089-7797-9*, Linford) Ulverscroft.

Murder Is Material. Karen Saum. LC 94-15389. (Brigid Donovan Mystery Ser.). 192p. (Orig.). 1994. pap. 9.95 (*0-934678-57-X*) New Victoria Pubs.

Murder Is Relative. Karen Saum. LC 90-6134. (Brigid Donovan Mystery Ser.). 256p. 1990. pap. 8.95 (*0-934678-55-3*) New Victoria Pubs.

***Murder Is Ruby Red.** large type ed. E. Radford & M. A. Radford. 288p. 1999. pap. 18.99 (*0-7089-5465-0*, Linford) Ulverscroft.

Murder Is the Deal of the Day. Christine Matthews & Robert J. Randisi. 240p. 1998. text 22.95 (*0-312-19928-7*) St Martin.

***Murder is too Expensive.** Valerie Kershaw. 384p. 2000. 31.99 (*0-7089-4289-X*) Ulverscroft.

Murder League. Robert L. Fish. 168p. 1995. 19.50 (*0-7451-8669-6*, Black Dagger) Chivers N Amer.

Murder Lover. Ellen Rawlings. 1997. mass mkt. 5.99 (*0-449-14988-9*) Fawcett.

Murder Machine: A True Story of Murder, Madness, & the Mafia. Jerry Capeci & Gene Mustain. (Illus.). 496p. 1993. mass mkt. 6.99 (*0-451-40387-8*, Onyx) NAL.

Murder, Magic, & Medicine. John Mann. (Illus.). 240p. 1994. reprint ed. pap. text 24.50 (*0-19-855854-6*) OUP.

Murder Magnified. large type ed. E. Radford & M. A. Radford. (Mystery Library). 368p. 1995. pap. 16.99 (*0-7089-7655-7*, Linford) Ulverscroft.

***Murder Makers.** large type ed. John N. Chance. 240p. 1999. pap. 18.99 (*0-7089-5502-9*, Linford) Ulverscroft.

Murder Makes a Call: A Mystery Jigsaw Puzzle Thriller. Henry Slesar. (BePuzzled Ser.). (Orig.). 1994. 20.00 (*0-922242-63-1*) Bepuzzled.

***Murder Makes Waves.** Anne George. LC 99-58852. (Anne George Mystery Ser.). 2000. 25.95 (*1-57490-274-1*) T T Beeler.

Murder Makes Waves. Anne Carroll George. 272p. 1998. mass mkt. 6.50 (*0-380-78450-5*, Avon Bks) Morrow Avon.

Murder Manual. Steven Womack. 324p. 1998. mass mkt. 5.99 (*0-345-41447-0*) Ballantine Pub Grp.

Murder Map Mystery. Clive Gifford. (Puzzle Adventure Ser.). (J). (gr. 4-7). 1998. pap. 8.95 (*0-7460-2830-X*, Usborne) EDC.

***Murder Matters.** Raymond Joseph Prost. LC 00-190109. 2000. 25.00 (*0-7388-1554-3*); pap. 18.00 (*0-7388-1555-1*) Xlibris Corp.

Murder, Mayhem, Pillage, & Plunder: The History of the Lebanon in the 18th & 19th Centuries by Mikhayil Mishaqa (1800-1873) Tr. by Wheeler M. Thackston, Jr. LC 87-18034. 309p. 1988. text 24.50 (*0-88706-712-3*) State U NY Pr.

***Murder Maze.** large type ed. Hunter Liggett. 304p. 1999. pap. 18.99 (*0-7089-5589-4*, Linford) Ulverscroft.

***Murder Me Now.** Annette Meyers. 288p. 2001. 23.95 (*0-89296-695-5*) Mysterious Pr.

Murder Mile High. Lora Roberts. 1996. mass mkt. 5.50 (*0-449-14947-1*) Fawcett.

Murder, Mischief & Mayhem: A Process for Creative Research Papers. W.Keith Kraus. 149p. 1978. 11.95 (*0-8141-3220-0*) NCTE.

Murder Mistaken. Janet Green. 1954. pap. 5.25 (*0-8222-0790-7*) Dramatists Play.

Murder Most British. Janet Hutchings. (Dead Letter Mysteries Ser.). 1997. mass mkt. 5.99 (*0-312-96182-0*) St Martin.

Murder Most British: Stories from Ellery Queen's Mystery Magazine. Ed. by Janet Hutchings. 272p. 1996. text 22.95 (*0-312-14017-7*) St Martin.

***Murder Most Delectable: Savory Tales of Culinary Crimes.** Martin Harry Greenberg. LC 00-31800. 2000. write for info. (*1-58182-119-0*) Cumberland Hse.

***Murder Most Fair: The Appeal of Murder Mystery.** Michael Cohen. LC 00-37120. 2000. write for info. (*0-8386-3851-1*) Fairleigh Dickinson.

Murder Most Foul: The Killer & the American Gothic Imagination. Karen Halttunen. LC 98-22624. xiv, 322p. 1998. 29.95 (*0-674-58855-X*) HUP.

***Murder Most Foul: The Killer & the American Gothic Imagination.** Karen Halttunen. 368p. 2000. pap. 16.95 (*0-674-00384-5*) HUP.

Murder Most Fouled-Up. Nikki Harmon. 1991. pap. 5.60 (*0-87129-146-0*, M79) Dramatic Pub.

Murder Most Grizzly. Elizabeth Quinn. Ed. by Linda Marrow. 224p. (Orig.). 1993. mass mkt. 4.99 (*0-671-74990-0*) PB.

Murder Most Medical: Stories from Alfred Hitchcock Mystery Magazine & Ellery Queen's Mystery Magazine. Ed. by Cathleen Jordan & Cynthia Manson. 320p. 1995. 21.00 (*0-7867-0198-6*) Carroll & Graf.

***Murder Most Medieval: Noble Tales of Ignoble Demises.** Ed. by Martin H. Greenburg & John Helfers. LC 00-21470. 464p. 2000. 24.95 (*1-58182-087-9*, Cumberland Hearthside) Cumberland Hse.

Murder Most Mellow. Jaqueline Girdner. 1992. mass mkt. 5.50 (*0-425-14707-X*, Prime Crime) Berkley Pub.

Murder Most Merry. Ed. by John Scognamiglio. 352p. 1994. mass mkt. 4.99 (*0-8217-4763-0*, Zebra Kensgtn) Kensgtn Pub Corp.

Murder Most Poetic: The Mystery Novels of Ngaio Marsh. Mary S. Weinkauf. Ed. by Mary A. Burgess. (Brownstone Mystery Guides Ser.: No. 14). 144p. 1996. pap. 19.00 (*0-89370-297-8*) Millefleurs.

Murder Most Puzzling: A Literary Mystery. Lillian S. Robinson. LC 98-4888. 320p. 1998. write for info. (*0-941968-09-X*) Wildcat Pubs.

Murder Most Rare: The Female Serial Killer. Michael D. Kelleher & C. L. Kelleher. LC 97-18718. 224p. 1998. 26.95 (*0-275-96003-X*, Praeger Pubs) Greenwood.

Murder Most Rare: The Female Serial Killer. Michael Kelleher & C. L. Kelleher. 1999. mass mkt. 5.99 (*0-440-23473-5*) Dell.

Murder Moves In. E. X. Ferrars. 200p. 1998. 19.50 (*0-7540-8513-9*, Black Dagger) Chivers N Amer.

Murder, Mrs. Hudson. Sydney Hosier. 1997. mass mkt. 5.50 (*0-380-78176-X*, Avon Bks) Morrow Avon.

Murder! Murder! Burning Bright. large type ed. Jonathan Ross. 304p. 1998. pap. 19.99 (*1-85389-904-6*) Ulverscroft.

Murder, Murder, Polis! Maureen Sinclair. 1989. 45.00 (*0-902859-91-9*, Pub. by Ramsay Head Pr) St Mut.

Murder Must Advertise. Dorothy L. Sayers. 368p. 1995. mass mkt. 5.99 (*0-06-104355-9*, Harp PBks) HarpC.

Murder Must Advertise. Dorothy L. Sayers. 746p. 1992. Not sold separately (*0-614-32008-9*) Random Hse Value.

Murder Must Appetize. H. R. F. Keating. LC 81-83116. 1987. reprint ed. 20.00 (*0-89296-053-1*, Pub. by Mysterious Pr) Little.

Murder Must Wait. Arthur W. Upfield. (Napoleon Bonaparte Mysteries Ser.). reprint ed. lib. bdg. 21.95 (*0-89190-559-6*, Rivercity Pr) Amereon Ltd.

***Murder, My Deer.** Jaqueline Girdner. LC 99-45137. (Kate Jasper Mysteries Ser.). (Illus.). 288p. 2000. 21.95 (*0-425-17328-3*) Berkley Pub.

***Murder, My Suite.** Mary R. Daheim. 272p. (Orig.). 2000. mass mkt. 5.99 (*0-380-77877-7*, Avon Bks) Morrow Avon.

Murder, My Sweet Matilda. Janet Green. 1961. pap. 5.25 (*0-8222-0791-5*) Dramatists Play.

Murder '97. large type ed. Frank Gruber. 1995. 27.99 (*0-7089-3392-0*) Ulverscroft.

Murder, No Doubt: A Widow's Nightmare. Ruth Langlos & Dennis Niemiec. 1993. 22.95 (*0-88282-078-8*) New Horizon NJ.

***Murder No One Committed.** Garrison Flint. 200p. 1999. pap. 12.50 (*1-885631-42-1*, 42-1, Family Of Man Pr) G F Hutchison.

Murder Now & Again. large type ed. J. A. Knipe. (General Ser.). 432p. (Orig.). 1993. 27.99 (*0-7089-2807-2*) Ulverscroft.

Murder of a Dead Man. Katherine John. LC 96-43319. 1996. text 23.95 (*0-312-15369-4*) St Martin.

Murder of a Little Girl. Samuel Roen. LC 73-82981. 343p. 1974. 8.95 (*0-88435-000-2*) Chateau Pub.

Murder of a Moderate Man. John Howlett. 352p. 1988. reprint ed. pap. 4.50 (*0-373-97083-8*) Harlequin Bks.

Murder of a Princess? An Investigational Analysis of the Death of Princess Diana. Isaac I. Omoike. LC 98-91270. (Illus.). 109p. 1998. pap. 13.99 (*0-9632236-4-X*) I Omoike Bks.

***Murder of a Prophet: The Dark Side of Utah Polygamy.** John R. Llewellyn. LC 99-68880. 192p. 2000. pap. 13.95 (*1-888106-93-X*) Agreka Bks.

***Murder of a Small-Town Honey.** Denise Swanson. 2000. mass mkt. 5.99 (*0-451-20055-1*, Sig) NAL.

Murder of a Suicide. large type ed. E. X. Ferrars. (Magna Large Print Ser.). 363p. 1997. 27.99 (*0-7505-1202-4*, Pub. by Mgna Lrg Print) Ulverscroft.

Murder of Adolph Hitler, Vol. 1. Thomas. 1998. 6.99 (*0-312-96734-9*, Pub. by Tor Bks) St Martin.

Murder of Aziz Khan. Zulfikar Ghose. LC 99-176200. 316p. 1998. pap. 11.00 (*0-19-577988-6*) OUP.

Murder of Becket. David Birt. (Resource Units: Middle Ages, 1066-1485 Ser.). (Illus.). 24p. 1974. pap. text, teacher ed. 12.95 (*0-582-39376-0*) Longman.

***Murder of Biggie Smalls.** Cathy Scott. 2000. pap. 6.99 (*0-929712-34-X*) Huntington Pr.

***Murder of Biggie Smalls.** Cathy Scott. LC 00-40250. 2000. write for info. (*0-312-26620-0*) St Martin.

Murder of Brian Jones. Anna Wohlin & Christine Lindsjoo. 1999. 26.00 (*1-85782-316-8*) Seven Hills Bk.

Murder of Charles the Good, Count of Flanders. Galbert. Ed. by James B. Ross. (Medieval Academy Reprints for Teaching Ser.: No. 12). 364p. 1982. reprint ed. pap. text 13.95 (*0-8020-6479-5*) U of Toronto Pr.

Murder of Chief McIntosh. Benjamin Griffith et al. Ed. by J. Caleb Boyd & Pauline D. Gagnon. 72p. 1994. pap. text. write for info. (*1-883199-06-9*) St U W Georgia.

Murder of Convenience. Hannah Blank. 1999. 24.95 (*0-9652778-1-X*, Hightrees Bks) Prism Corp.

Murder of Course. Dennis Harrington. (YA). (gr. 7 up). 1994. 20.00 (*0-922242-72-0*) Bepuzzled.

***Murder of Crows.** Barbara A. Blond. LC 99-72791. 2000. 18.95 (*1-881636-82-8*, Pub. by Windsor Hse Pub Grp) Baker & Taylor.

Murder of Delicia. Marie Corelli. 274p. 1971. reprint ed. spiral bd. 16.50 (*0-7873-0217-1*) Hlth Research.

Murder of Delicia, 1896. Marie Corelli. 274p. 1996. reprint ed. pap. 15.95 (*1-56459-949-3*) Kessinger Pub.

***Murder of Eleaner Lindquist.** Norman Rudnick. (New Voices in American Fiction Ser.). 200p. 2000. pap. 14.95 (*1-883938-80-5*) Dry Bones Pr.

Murder of Helen Jewett: Life & Death of a Prostitute in 19th Century New York. Patricia Cline Cohen. LC 98-14561. (Illus.). 433p. 1998. 27.50 (*0-679-41291-3*) Random.

Murder of Helen Jewett: Life & Death of a Prostitute in 19th Century New York. Patricia Cline Cohen. (Vintage Ser.). (Illus.). 512p. 1999. pap. 14.00 (*0-679-74075-9*) Vin Bks.

Murder of Herodes: And Other Trials from the Athenian Law Courts. Ed. & Tr. by Kathleen Freeman from GRE. 240p. (C). 1994. reprint ed. pap. text 7.95 (*0-87220-306-9*); reprint ed. lib. bdg. 29.95 (*0-87220-307-7*) Hackett Pub.

***Murder of Honor.** Robert Andrews. LC 00-39015. (YA). 2001. write for info. (*0-399-14684-9*, G P Putnam) Peng Put Young Read.

Murder of Hound Dog Bates: A Novel. Robbie Branscum. 1995. 9.09 (*0-606-07900-9*, Pub. by Turtleback) Demco.

Murder of Innocence: The Tragic Life & Final Rampage of Laurie Dann, "The Schoolhouse Killer" Joel Kaplan et al. 1991. mass mkt. 4.99 (*0-446-36002-3*) Warner Bks.

Murder of Jacob. Mary E. Johnson. (Illus.). 300p. (Orig.). 1997. pap. 15.95 (*0-9655668-0-3*) Voices Publishing.

***Murder of Jesus, 1.** John MacArthur. 320p. 2000. 19.99 (*0-8499-1554-6*) J Countryman.

***Murder of Jesus: A Study of How Jesus Died.** John MacArthur. LC 00-20515. 2000. write for info. (*0-8499-6303-6*) Word Pub.

***Murder of Jesus: EZ Lesson Plan.** John MacArthur. (Illus.). 2000. 39.99 (*0-8499-8796-2*) Word Pub.

***Murder of Jesus: Student's Guide.** John MacArthur. (Illus.). (J). 2000. pap. 7.99 (*0-8499-8797-0*) Word Pub.

Murder of Julia Bulette: Virginia City, Nevada, 1867 - With the Life & Confession of John Millian, Convicted Murderer. Charles E. DeLong. Ed. by William R. Jones. 16p. 1978. pap. 2.00 (*0-89646-044-4*) Vistabooks.

Murder of Little Mary Phagan. Mary Phagan. (Illus.). 300p. 1988. 21.95 (*0-88282-039-7*) New Horizon NJ.

Murder of Mercy: Euthanasia on Trial. Stanley M. Rosenblatt. LC 92-25910. (Illus.). 352p. (C). 1992. 28.95 (*0-87975-772-8*) Prometheus Bks.

Murder of Miranda. Margaret Millar. 22.95 (*0-89190-156-6*) Amereon Ltd.

***Murder of Rachel Nickell.** Mike Fielder. 2000. mass mkt. 6.99 (*1-85782-338-9*) Blake Publng.

Murder of Roger Ackroyd. Agatha Christie. 277p. Date not set. 23.95 (*0-8488-2236-6*) Amereon Ltd.

***Murder of Roger Ackroyd.** Agatha Christie. (Hercule Poirot Mysteries Ser.). 2000. mass mkt. 5.99 (*0-425-17389-5*) Berkley Pub.

Murder of Roger Ackroyd. Agatha Christie. LC 84-72782. 288p. 1991. mass mkt. 5.99 (*0-06-100286-0*, Harp PBks) HarpC.

Murder of Roger Ackroyd. Agatha Christie. (Hercule Poirot Mystery Ser.). 1991. 11.09 (*0-606-12438-1*, Pub. by Turtleback) Demco.

***Murder of Roger Ackroyd.** Agatha Christie. (Hercule Poirot Mysteries Ser.). 2000. pap. 12.00 (*0-425-17651-7*) Berkley Pub.

Murder of Sir Edmund Godfrey. John Dickson Carr. 348p. 1989. reprint ed. pap. 12.95 (*1-55882-014-0*, Lib Crime Classics) Intl Polygonics.

***Murder of the Jews in Latvia, 1941-1945.** Bernhard Press. Tr. by Laimdota Mazzarins. 192p. 1999. 54.95 (*0-8101-1728-2*) Northwestern U Pr.

***Murder of the Jews in Latvia, 1941-1945.** Bernhard Press. Tr. by Laimdota Mazzarins. 192p. 2000. pap. 15.95 (*0-8101-1729-0*) Northwestern U Pr.

Murder of the Mind: The Practice of Subtle Discrimination. Claudia Gasparrini. LC TX-3-678-61. 350p. (Orig.). 1993. 25.95 (*0-9627647-2-8*) Space Eagle.

Murder of the Mind: The Practice of Subtle Discrimination. 2nd rev. ed. Claudia Gasparrini. 352p. (Orig.). 1996. pap. 29.95 (*0-9627647-6-0*) Space Eagle.

Murder of the Rosenbergs. Stanley Yalkowsky. 462p. 1990. pap. 25.00 (*0-9620984-2-6*) Crucible Pubns.

Murder of Tutankhamen: A True Story. Bob Brier. LC 97-49193. 288p. 1998. pap. 24.95 (*0-399-14383-1*, Perigee Bks) Berkley Pub.

Murder of Tutankhamen: A True Story. Bob Brier. 288p. 1999. reprint ed. pap. 14.00 (*0-425-16689-9*) Berkley Pub.

***Murder of Woodworm.** Deborah Cox-Stubblefield. 1998. pap. 8.00 (*1-930183-05-4*, DR-0002B-99) Anyanwu.

Murder off the Glass. Michael J. Katz. 1988. pap. 3.50 (*0-317-65526-4*) PB.

Murder off the Rack: Critical Studies of Ten Paperback Masters. Ed. by Jon L. Breen & Martin H. Greenberg. LC 89-33085. 188p. 1989. 24.00 (*0-8108-2232-6*) Scarecrow.

Murder off the Record. Marnie Schulenburg. 304p. 1998. 23.95 (*1-885173-50-4*) Write Way.

Murder Offscreen. Denise Osborne. 1995. write for info. (*0-8050-3113-8*) H Holt & Co.

Murder Ole! Corinne H. Sawyer. LC 96-29906. 256p. 1997. 22.95 (*1-55611-514-8*, Pub. by D I Fine) Penguin Putnam.

Murder on a Bad Hair Day. Anne Carroll George. (Southern Sisters Mysteries Ser.). 246p. 1996. mass mkt. 6.50 (*0-380-78087-9*, Avon Bks) Morrow Avon.

***Murder on a Bad Hair Day.** large type ed. Anne Carroll George. LC 99-39887. (Mystery Ser.). 1999. 25.95 (*1-57490-238-5*, Beeler LP Bks) T T Beeler.

Murder on a Black College Campus. Nathaniel A. Dickens. (Orig.). 1990. pap. write for info. (*0-916191-06-0*) Dickens Pubns.

Murder on a Girl's Night Out. Anne Carroll George. 244p. 1996. mass mkt. 5.99 (*0-380-78086-0*, Avon Bks) Morrow Avon.

***Murder on a Girl's Night Out.** large type ed. Anne Carroll George. LC 99-35650. (Mystery Ser.). 1999. 25.95 (*1-57490-212-1*, Beeler LP Bks) T T Beeler.

Murder on a Kibbutz: A Communal Case. Batya Goor. LC 94-26642. 368p. 1995. pap. 13.00 (*0-06-092654-6*, Perennial) HarperTrade.

Murder on Astor Place. Victoria Thompson. 1999. mass mkt. 5.99 (*0-425-16896-4*, Prime Crime) Berkley Pub.

Murder on Beacon Hill. Ernest Cassara. LC 95-80566. 201p. (Orig.). 1995. pap. 10.00 (*0-9625794-6-7*) A Miniver Pr.

Murder on Boston Common: A Father Ballou & His Dog Spot Mystery. Ernest Cassara. LC 98-72219. 174p. 1998. pap. 9.95 (*0-9662870-0-2*) Cambridge Crnrstone.

Murder on Broadway. Edward Irving Koch. 320p. 1997. mass mkt. 5.99 (*1-57566-186-1*, Knsington) Kensgtn Pub Corp.

Murder on Broadway. Edward Irving Koch & Wendy C. Staub. 192p. 1996. 19.95 (*1-57566-049-0*, Knsington) Kensgtn Pub Corp.

Murder on Center Stage. Jerry L. Twedt. 1976. 5.50 (*0-87129-415-X*, M39) Dramatic Pub.

Murder on Clam Pond. Douglas Kiker. 1986. write for info. (*0-318-61631-9*) Random.

Murder on Cue. Jane Dentinger. 224p. 1992. reprint ed. pap. 5.95 (*0-14-015841-3*, Penguin Bks) Viking Penguin.

Murder on Deck! Shipboard & Shoreline Mystery Stories. Ed. by Rosemary Herbert. LC 97-98078. 352p. 1998. 25.00 (*0-19-508603-1*) OUP.

Murder on Embassy Row. Margaret Truman. 352p. 1985. mass mkt. 5.99 (*0-449-20621-1*, Crest) Fawcett.

Murder on Fifth Avenue, Vol. 1. Michael Jahn. LC 98-4795. Vol. 1. 320p. 1998. text 23.95 (*0-312-18632-0*) St Martin.

***Murder on Fire.** large type ed. Michael Bardsley. 264p. 1999. pap. 18.99 (*0-7089-5586-X*, Linford) Ulverscroft.

***Murder on High.** large type ed. Stefanie Matteson. LC 99-59387. (Mystery Ser.). 2000. 24.95 (*1-57490-261-X*, Beeler LP Bks) T T Beeler.

Murder on Hill Grove: An Adventure in Virtual Reality, Drugs & Police Complicity. Sean Kole. (Adventures in Virtual Reality Ser.: Vol. 1). 180p. 1996. mass mkt. 6.00 (*0-939074-23-0*) Harvest Pubns.

Murder on Hill Grove Vol. 1. Sean Kole. 1998. pap. 14.95 (*0-939074-19-2*) Harvest Pubns.

Murder on Hill Grove Vol. 2: The Feds Close In. Sean Kole. 1998. pap. 14.95 (*0-939074-20-6*) Harvest Pubns.

Murder on Hill Grove Vol. 3: Call of the C. I. A. Sean Kole. Date not set. pap. 14.95 (*0-939074-21-4*) Harvest Pubns.

Murder on Hill Grove Vol. 4: Interpole Out-of-Control. Sean Kole. Date not set. pap. 14.95 (*0-939074-22-2*) Harvest Pubns.

Murder on Ice. Carolyn Keene. (Nancy Drew Files: No. 3). (YA). (gr. 6 up). 1989. mass mkt. 3.75 (*0-671-68729-8*, Archway) PB.

Murder on Ice. Carolyn Keene. (Nancy Drew Files: No. 3). (YA). (gr. 6 up). 1986. 8.85 (*0-606-03067-0*, Pub. by Turtleback) Demco.

***Murder on Ice.** large type ed. Michael Bardsley. 240p. 1999. pap. 18.99 (*0-7089-5556-8*, Linford) Ulverscroft.

Murder on Misty Isle. Patricia A. Stewart & Edna H. Maples. Ed. by Bob Moog. (Murder Mystery Parties Ser.). (Illus.). 52p. 1986. 8.00 (*0-935145-04-4*) Univ Games.

Murder on Mount Desert. David Rawson. LC 95-34706. 304p. 1996. pap. 15.95 (*0-89272-363-7*) Down East.

***Murder on Pawley's.** Margaret Haswell. LC 99-74219. 128p. 1999. pap. 11.95 (*1-57197-189-0*) Pentland Pr.

Murder on Route 66. Ed. by Carolyn Wheat. 294p. 1999. mass mkt. 5.99 (*0-425-17064-0*, Prime Crime) Berkley Pub.

Murder on Safari. Hillary Waugh. (Worldwide Ser.: No. 29). 1989. per. 3.50 (*0-373-26029-6*) Harlequin Bks.

***Murder on St. Mark's Place.** Victoria Thompson. (Gaslight Mysteries Ser.). 2000. mass mkt. 5.99 (*0-425-17361-5*, Prime Crime) Berkley Pub.

Murder on Tape. Ted Sennett. LC 97-15711. (Illus.). 272p. 1997. 16.95 (*0-8230-8335-7*, Billboard Bks) Watsn-Guptill.

Murder on the Air: Television's Great Mystery Series. Ric Meyers. (Illus.). 240p. 1989. pap. 12.95 (*0-89296-977-6*) Mysterious Pr.

Murder on the Appian Way. Steven Saylor. (Dead Letter Mysteries Ser.). 1997. mass mkt. 5.99 (*0-312-96173-1*) St Martin.

Murder on the Astral Plane. Jaqueline Girdner. LC 98-41520. (Kate Jasper Ser.). 320p. 1999. 21.95 (*0-425-16701-1*, Prime Crime) Berkley Pub.

***Murder on the Astral Plane.** Jaqueline Girdner. (Kate Jasper Mysteries Ser.: Vol. 10). 309p. 2000. mass mkt. 5.99 (*0-425-17359-3*, Prime Crime) Berkley Pub.

Murder on the Atlantic. Steve Allen. 288p. 1995. 19.95 (*0-8217-5062-3*, Zebra Kensgtn) Kensgtn Pub Corp.

Murder on the Atlantic. Steve Allen. 304p. 1996. mass mkt. 5.99 (*1-57566-097-0*, Knsington) Kensgtn Pub Corp.

M

*__Murder on the Barbary Coast, 1 vol.__ Kate Bryan. (Maggie Maguire Mysteries Ser.). 1999. mass mkt. 5.99 (*0-425-16933-2*) Berkley Pub.

Murder on the Blackboard. Stuart Palmer. LC 92-70420. 186p. 1992. reprint ed. pap. 5.95 (*1-55882-124-4*, Lib Crime Classics) Intl Polygonics.

Murder on the Boulevard. Anne Sloan. 10.00 (*0-942031-00-8*) Serendipity Comns.

Murder on the Boundary. Medawar. 1999. text. write for info. (*0-312-20938-X*) St Martin.

Murder on the Chesapeake: A Margaret Barlow Mystery. David Osborn. 304p. 1993. mass mkt. 3.99 (*0-8217-4165-9*, Zebra Kensgtn) Kensgtn Pub Corp.

Murder on the Flying Scotsman. Carola Dunn. LC 96-31780. 240p. 1996. text 21.95 (*0-312-15175-6*) St Martin.

Murder on the Fourth of July. Carolyn Keene. (Nancy Drew & Hardy Boys Super Mystery Ser.: No. 28). (YA). (gr. 6 up). 1996. 9.09 (*0-606-10266-3*, Pub. by Turtleback) Demco.

Murder on the Glitter Box. Steve Allen. 352p. 1998. mass mkt. 5.99 (*1-57566-245-0*, Knsington) Kensgtn Pub Corp.

Murder on the Grand. Christopher H. Meehan. 1997. pap. 14.95 (*1-882376-49-8*) Thunder Bay Pr.

Murder on the Gravy Train. Phyllis C. Richman. LC 99-10192. 256p. 1999. 23.00 (*0-06-018390-X*) HarpC.

*__Murder on the Gravy Train.__ Phyllis C. Richman. 336p. 2000. mass mkt. 6.50 (*0-06-109783-7*, Avon Bks) Morrow Avon.

*__Murder on the Gravy Train.__ large type ed. Phyllis C. Richman. LC 99-41960. (Thorndike Mystery Ser.). 398p. 1999. 28.95 (*0-7862-2208-5*) Thorndike Pr.

Murder on the Iditarod Trail. Sue Henry. (Alaska Mystery Ser.). 320p. 2000. reprint ed. mass mkt. 6.50 (*0-380-71758-1*, Avon Bks) Morrow Avon.

Murder on the Line. Created by Francine Pascal. (Sweet Valley High Super Thriller Ser.). 224p. (YA). (gr. 7 up). 1992. mass mkt. 3.50 (*0-553-29308-7*) Bantam.

Murder on the Line. Kate William. (Sweet Valley High Super Thriller Ser.). (YA). (gr. 7 up). 1992. 8.60 (*0-606-02931-1*, Pub. by Turtleback) Demco.

Murder on the Links. Agatha Christie. 240p. 1984. pap. text 5.99 (*0-425-06794-7*) Berkley Pub.

Murder on the Links. Agatha Christie. 1984. 11.09 (*0-606-00970-1*, Pub. by Turtleback) Demco.

Murder on the Links. large type ed. Agatha Christie. (Agatha Christie Ser.). 323p. 1990. lib. bdg. 19.95 (*0-8161-4573-3*, G K Hall Lrg Type) Mac Lib Ref.

Murder on the Loose. Ellen Godfrey. LC 99-189217. (Thumbprint Mysteries Ser.). 128p. 1999. pap. 5.95 (*0-8092-0684-6*, 068460) NTC Contemp Pub Co.

Murder on the Lovers' Bridge. Ellen Godfrey. (Thumbprint Mysteries Ser.). 128p. (J). 1999. pap. 5.95 (*0-8092-0685-4*, 068540) NTC Contemp Pub Co.

*__Murder on the Lusitania.__ Conrad Allen. 2000. mass mkt. 5.99 (*0-312-97571-6*) St Martin.

*__Murder on the Mauretania.__ Conrad Allen. 2000. 23.75 (*0-312-24116-X*) St Martin,

*__Murder on the Menu.__ Mary Blount Christian. (Thumbprint Mysteries Ser.). 128p. 1999. pap. 5.95 (*0-8092-0675-7*, 067570) NTC Contemp Pub Co.

Murder on the Midnight Plane. Gaby Waters & Graham Round. (Puzzle Adventures Ser.). (Illus.). 48p. (J). (gr. 4-9). 1987. pap. 5.50 (*0-86020-952-0*) EDC.

Murder on the Mountain. Ezra Coppin. LC 88-61490. 148p. 1988. pap. 6.95 (*0-89221-158-X*) New Leaf.

*__Murder on the Orient Express.__ Agatha Christie. 2000. mass mkt. 5.99 (*0-425-17375-5*) Berkley Pub.

*__Murder on the Orient Express.__ Agatha Christie. 2000. pap. text 12.00 (*0-425-17393-3*) Berkley Pub.

Murder on the Orient Express. Agatha Christie. 256p. 1991. mass mkt. 5.99 (*0-06-100274-7*, Harp PBks) HarpC.

*__Murder on the Orient Express.__ Agatha Christie. LC 99-35293. 1999. write for info. (*0-7621-0255-1*) RD Assn.

Murder on the Orient Express. Agatha Christie. (Hercule Poirot Mystery Ser.). 1991. 11.09 (*0-606-12439-X*, Pub. by Turtleback) Demco.

Murder on the Orient Express: A Study Guide. Barbara Reeves. Ed. by J. Friedland & R. Kessler. (Novel-Ties Ser.). (YA). (gr. 9-12). 1992. pap. text, student ed. 15.95 (*0-88122-717-X*) Lrn Links.

Murder on the Orient Express: Murder on the Orient Express. Agatha Christie. 1997. mass mkt. 5.99 (*0-06-105881-5*) HarpC.

Murder on the Potomac. Margaret Truman. 1995. reprint ed. mass mkt. 6.99 (*0-449-21937-2*, Crest) Fawcett.

Murder on the Prowl. large type ed. Rita Mae Brown. LC 98-14023. 536p. 1998. 28.95 (*0-7862-1458-9*) Mac Lib Ref.

Murder on the Prowl. Rita Mae Brown. 400p. 1999. reprint ed. mass mkt. 6.99 (*0-553-57540-6*) Bantam.

Murder on the QE2. Jessica Fletcher. Vol. 8. 304p. 1997. mass mkt. 5.99 (*0-451-19291-5*, Sig) NAL.

Murder on the Riviera Express. Lagoon Bks Staff. (Illus.). 96p. 1997. 6.95 (*1-899712-47-X*, Pub. by Lagoon Bks) Midpt Trade.

Murder on the Rocks. L. V. Slyke. 256p. (Orig.). 1995. mass mkt. 4.99 (*0-380-76798-8*, Avon Bks) Morrow Avon.

Murder on the Rocks: A Mystery Jigsaw Puzzle Thriller. Alan Robbins. (BePuzzled Ser.). (Orig.). 1994. 20.00 (*0-922242-62-3*) Bepuzzled.

Murder on the Run. Adams Round Table Staff & Lawrence Block. LC 97-23375. 336p. 1998. pap. 21.95 (*0-425-16146-3*, Prime Crime) Berkley Pub.

Murder on the Santa Fe Trail. Marc Simmons. 120p. 1987. 15.00 (*0-87404-202-X*) Tex Western.

Murder on the Side. large type ed. Day Keene. (Linford Mystery Library). 1991. pap. 16.99 (*0-7089-7075-3*) Ulverscroft.

Murder on the Silk Road. Stefanie Matteson. 1992. mass mkt. 5.50 (*0-425-14820-3*, Prime Crime) Berkley Pub.

Murder on the Thirteenth. A. E. Eddenden. 168p. 1992. 20.00 (*0-89733-380-2*) Academy Chi Pubs.

Murder on the Titanic. Jim Walker. LC 97-42332. 320p. 1998. pap. 13.99 (*0-8054-0198-9*) Broadman.

*__Murder on the Yellow Brick Road.__ Stuart M. Kaminsky. (Toby Peters Mysteries Ser.). 192p. 2000. per. 12.00 (*0-7434-0000-3*, Pub. by ibooks) S&S Trade.

Murder on the Yukon Quest: An Alaska Mystery. Sue Henry. LC 99-21641. 304p. 1999. 22.00 (*0-380-97764-8*, Avon Bks) Morrow Avon.

*__Murder on the Yukon Quest: An Alaska Mystery.__ Sue Henry. Ed. by T. L. Grader. LC 99-21641. 320p. 2000. mass mkt. 6.50 (*0-380-78864-0*, Avon Bks) Morrow Avon.

*__Murder on Theatre Row.__ Michael Jahn. 2000. per. 5.99 (*0-373-26346-5*) Harlequin Bks.

*__Murder on their Hands.__ Hale Bailey. (Criminal Justice Ser.). 2001. 25.00 (*0-534-53480-5*) Wadsworth Pub.

Murder on 34th Street. Edward Irving Koch. LC 97-71433. 192p. 1997. pap. 19.95 (*1-57566-232-9*) Kensgtn Pub Corp.

*__Murder on 34th Street.__ Edward Irving Koch. 288p. 1998. mass mkt. 5.99 (*1-57566-355-4*) Kensgtn Pub Corp.

Murder on Tour: A Rock 'n Roll Mystery. Dick Clark & Paul Francis. 224p. 1989. 16.95 (*0-89296-286-0*) Mysterious Pr.

Murder on Tour: A Rock 'n Roll Mystery. Dick Clark & Paul Francis. 1990. mass mkt. 4.50 (*0-445-40856-1*, Pub. by Warner Bks) Little.

Murder on Wheels. Valerie Frankel. Ed. by Dana Isaacson. 224p. (Orig.). 1992. mass mkt. 4.50 (*0-671-73195-5*) PB.

Murder on Wheels. Stuart Palmer. 307p. 1992. pap. 6.95 (*1-55882-113-9*) Intl Polygonics.

*__Murder on Wheels.__ Mary Scott. 256p. 2000. 26.95 (*0-7490-0460-6*, Pub. by Allison & Busby) Intl Pubs Mktg.

Murder Once Removed. Kathleen Kunz. LC 95-270. (WWL Mystery Ser.). 252p. 1995. per. 3.99 (*0-373-26175-6*, 1-26175-9) Harlequin Bks.

Murder Once Removed. Irving G. Neiman. 1972. pap. 5.25 (*0-8222-0793-1*) Dramatists Play.

Murder One. Dorothy Kilgallen. Date not set. lib. bdg. 22.95 (*0-8488-2148-3*) Amereon Ltd.

Murder One. large type ed. Frank Gruber. 1990. pap. 16.99 (*0-7089-6893-7*, Linford) Ulverscroft.

Murder One: A Writer's Guide to Homicide. Mauro Corvasce & Joseph Paglino. LC 97-26703. (Howdunit Ser.). (Illus.). 216p. 1997. pap. 16.99 (*0-89879-773-X*, Wrtrs Digest Bks) F & W Pubns Inc.

Murder One: Version 3.0. Hugh Gibbons & Thomas Starbranch. 32p. (C). 1997. pap., wbk. ed. 26.20 incl. cd-rom (*0-13-864026-2*) P-H.

Murder Out of Class. large type ed. Howard C. Davis. (Linford Mystery Library). 1991. pap. 16.99 (*0-7089-7070-2*) Ulverscroft.

Murder out of Turn. Frances Lockridge & Richard Lockridge. 18.95 (*0-89190-914-1*) Amereon Ltd.

*__Murder over Dinner: And Other Stories.__ J. P. Taylor. LC 99-65230. 192p. 2000. pap. 12.95 (*1-58501-052-9*, Pub. by CeShore Pubg) Natl Bk Netwk.

Murder Racquet. Ed. by Alfred Hitchcock. 1976. 19.95 (*0-8488-0531-3*) Amereon Ltd.

Murder Reference: Everything You Never Wanted to Know about Murder in America. Ed. by Maureen Harrison & Steve Gilbert. LC 96-83104. 352p. (Orig.). 1996. pap. 16.95 (*1-880780-12-7*) Excellent Bks.

Murder Revisited. Steve Brady & Frank Roderus. 296p. (Orig.). 1996. mass mkt. 5.99 (*0-380-77489-5*, Avon Bks) Morrow Avon.

Murder Runs in the Family. Anne Carroll George. 280p. 1997. mass mkt. 5.99 (*0-380-78449-1*, Avon Bks); mass mkt. 5.99 (*0-614-27699-3*, Avon Bks) Morrow Avon.

*__Murder Runs in the Family.__ large type ed. Anne George. LC 99-58853. (Anne George Mystery Ser.). 2000. 25.95 (*1-57490-258-X*) T T Beeler.

*__Murder Sails at Midnight.__ Marian Babson. 168p. 2000. 21.95 (*0-7540-8555-4*, Black Dagger) Chivers N Amer.

Murder Sees the Light: A Benny Cooperman Mystery. large type ed. Howard Engel. 432p. 1988. 25.99 (*0-7089-1911-1*) Ulverscroft.

*__Murder Sets Seed.__ Janis Harrison. 2000. text 22.95 (*0-312-20382-9*) St Martin.

Murder, She Meowed. Rita Mae Brown. (Mrs. Murphy Mystery Ser.). (Illus.). 300p. 1997. mass mkt. 6.99 (*0-553-57237-7*) Bantam.

Murder She Wrote: A Study of Agatha Christie's Detective Fiction. Patricia D. Maida & Nicholas B. Spornick. 199p. 1982. 16.95 (*0-87972-215-0*) Bowling Green Univ Popular Press.

Murder, She Wrote: Martinis & Mayhem. Jessica Fletcher & Donald Bain. Vol. 4. 304p. 1995. mass mkt. 5.99 (*0-451-18512-9*, Sig) NAL.

*__Murder, She Wrote: Martinis & Mayhem.__ large type ed. Donald Bain. LC 99-15669. 1999. pap. 20.95 (*0-7838-8665-9*, G K Hall Lrg Type) Mac Lib Ref.

Murder, She Wrote Cookbook: Recipes from the Cast & Crew. Ed. by Tom Culver & Nancy G. Iland. LC 97-5961. 288p. 1997. pap. 16.95 (*1-55652-316-5*) Chicago Review.

*__Murder Shoots the Bull.__ Anne George. (Southern Sisters Mysteries Ser.). 272p. 2000. mass mkt. 6.50 (*0-380-80149-3*, Avon Bks) Morrow Avon.

Murder Shoots the Bull: A Southern Sisters Mystery. Anne Carroll George. LC 99-21638. 256p. 1999. 22.00 (*0-380-97688-9*, Avon Bks) Morrow Avon.

*__Murder Shoots the Bull: A Southern Sisters Mystery.__ large type ed. Anne Carroll George. LC 99-45076. 1999. write for info. (*0-07-862222-0*) McGraw.

*__Murder Shoots the Bull: A Southern Sisters Mystery.__ large type ed. Anne Carroll George. LC 99-45076. (Thorndike Americana Ser.). 1999. 25.95 (*0-7862-2222-0*) Thorndike Pr.

Murder Starts from Fishguard. large type ed. Howard C. Davis. (Linford Mystery Library). 1991. pap. 16.99 (*0-7089-7086-9*) Ulverscroft.

Murder Story. large type ed. John Wainwright. LC 94-33674. 248p. 1995. pap. 17.95 (*0-7838-1143-8*, G K Hall Lrg Type) Mac Lib Ref.

Murder Strikes Pink. large type ed. J. Pullein-Thompson. (Linford Mystery Library). 1990. pap. 16.99 (*0-7089-6839-2*, Linford) Ulverscroft.

Murder Take Two. Charlene Weir. LC 97-40421. 336p. 1998. text 23.95 (*0-312-18136-1*) St Martin.

Murder Takes a Break: A Truman Smith Mystery. Bill Crider. LC 97-19939. 246p. 1997. 21.95 (*0-8027-3308-5*) Walker & Co.

*__Murder Takes a Fast Track.__ Barbara Steiner. (Thumbprint Mysteries Ser.). 128p. 1999. pap. 5.95 (*0-8092-0694-3*, 069430) NTC Contemp Pub Co.

Murder Takes a Holiday. large type ed. Tim Kelly. 1991. 27.99 (*0-7089-2434-4*) Ulverscroft.

Murder Takes a Holiday: A Thriller in 2-Acts. Tim Kelly. (Illus.). 52p. 1984. pap. 4.00 (*0-88680-223-7*) I E Clark.

Murder Takes a Partner. large type ed. Haughton Murphy. 1990. 27.99 (*0-7089-2158-2*) Ulverscroft.

Murder Takes the Veil. Margaret A. Hubbard. 103p. 1957. pap. 5.50 (*0-87129-105-3*, M40) Dramatic Pub.

Murder Takes Two. Bernie Lee. 1993. per. 3.99 (*0-373-26127-6*, 1-26127-0) Harlequin Bks.

Murder, They Wrote. Ed. by Elizabeth Foxwell & Martin H. Greenberg. (Murder She Wrote Anthology Ser.: No. 2). 1998. mass mkt. 6.99 (*1-57297-339-0*) Blvd Books.

Murder, They Wrote. Ed. by Martin H. Greenberg. (Jessica Fletcher Presents Ser.). 368p. 1997. mass mkt. 6.99 (*1-57297-194-0*) Blvd Books.

Murder They Wrote. Ed. by Martin H. Greenberg. 1997. mass mkt. 6.99 (*0-425-16702-X*) Blvd Bks FL.

Murder to Burn. large type ed. Laurie Mantell. (Linford Romance Library). 368p. 1987. pap. 16.99 (*0-7089-6391-9*, Linford) Ulverscroft.

Murder to Music. Cynthia Manson. 1998. mass mkt. 5.99 (*0-425-16383-0*, Prime Crime) Berkley Pub.

*__Murder to Music.__ large type ed. John Kilgore. 320p. 2000. 20.99 (*1-84137-003-7*, Pub. by Mgna Lrg Print) Ulverscroft.

Murder to Music: Musical Mysteries from Ellery Queen's Mystery Magazine & Alfred Hitchcock's Mystery Magazine. Ed. by Cynthia Manson & Kathleen Manson. LC 97-517. 272p. 1997. 22.00 (*0-7867-0406-3*) Carroll & Graf.

Murder to Order. Karl Anders. (Illus.). 1967. 6.95 (*0-8159-6207-X*) Devin.

Murder Tonight! Rehearsed Improvisations on a Theme. Ian Wilkes. (Orig.). 1995. pap. 10.00 (*0-88734-904-8*) Players Pr.

Murder Trail. large type ed. Jay H. Potter. (Linford Western Library). 256p. 1996. pap. 16.99 (*0-7089-7882-7*, Linford) Ulverscroft.

Murder Trial of O. J. Simpson. Schmalleger. 1996. pap. text, teacher ed. write for info. (*0-13-256892-6*) Allyn.

Murder Trial Of Wilbur Jackson 2e. 2nd ed. Philip B. Heymann & William H. Kenety. LC 84-13138. (Paralegal). (C). 1984. mass mkt. 36.50 (*0-314-85315-4*) West Pub.

Murder Trials. Marcus Tullius Cicero. Tr. by Michael Grant. (Classics Ser.). 368p. 1975. pap. 13.95 (*0-14-044288-X*, Penguin Classics) Viking Penguin.

Murder, U. S. A. Tom Philbin. (Illus.). 304p. (Orig.). 1992. mass mkt. 4.99 (*0-446-36091-0*, Pub. by Warner Bks) Little.

Murder Under Blue Skies. Willard Scott & Bill Crider. 368p. 1999. mass mkt. 6.99 (*0-451-19297-4*) NAL.

Murder under the Mistletoe: A Dee & Barry Vaughan Mystery. Jennifer Jordan. (WWL Mystery Ser.: No. 295). 1998. per. 4.99 (*0-373-26295-7*, 1-26295-5, Wrldwide Lib) Harlequin Bks.

Murder under the Palms. Stefanie Matteson. LC 96-31429. Vol. 3. 256p. 1997. pap. 21.95 (*0-425-15628-1*, Prime Crime) Berkley Pub.

Murder under the Palms. large type ed. Stefanie Matteson. LC 98-5876. 1998. 24.95 (*1-57490-137-0*) T T Beeler.

Murder under the Palms. Stefanie Matteson. 256p. 1997. reprint ed. mass mkt. 5.99 (*0-425-16035-1*, Prime Crime) Berkley Pub.

*__Murder Undercover: A Denise Cleever Thriller.__ Claire McNab. LC 99-18394. 240p. 1999. pap. 11.95 (*1-56280-259-3*) Naiad Pr.

Murder Unlimited. Emma Fischel. (Whodunnits Ser.). (Illus.). 48p. (J). (gr. 4 up). 1993. pap. 4.95 (*0-7460-0610-1*, Usborne); lib. bdg. 12.95 (*0-88110-522-8*, Usborne) EDC.

*__Murder Unmourned.__ large type ed. George Douglas. 328p. 1999. pap. 18.99 (*0-7089-5588-6*, Linford) Ulverscroft.

*__Murder Unrenovated.__ Pat M. Carlson. LC 99-35100. (Mystery Ser.). 248p. 1999. pap. 19.95 (*0-7862-2077-5*, Five Star MI) Mac Lib Ref.

Murder Update: Modern Murders That Made the Headlines. Brian Lane. 224p. 1991. pap. 9.95 (*0-88184-740-2*) Carroll & Graf.

Murder Ward. Warren Murphy. (Destroyer Ser.: No. 15). 1989. mass mkt. 3.50 (*1-55817-197-5*, Pinncle Kensgtn) Kensgtn Pub Corp.

Murder Was My Neighbour. large type ed. Guy Cobden. (Linford Mystery Library). 496p. 1993. pap. 16.99 (*0-7089-7353-1*, Linford) Ulverscroft.

Murder Was Their Medicine. large type ed. Guy Cobden. (Linford Mystery Library). 432p. 1993. pap. 16.99 (*0-7089-7390-6*, Linford) Ulverscroft.

Murder Wears a Cowl: A Medieval Mystery Featuring Hugh Corbett. large type ed. P. C. Doherty. 400p. 1996. 27.99 (*0-7089-3495-1*) Ulverscroft.

Murder Well-Done. Claudia Bishop. 1996. mass mkt. 5.99 (*0-425-15336-3*) Berkley Pub.

Murder Will Speak. Joan Smith. 208p. 1996. 21.95 (*0-312-14378-8*) St Martin.

Murder with a Twist. L. V. Slyke. 256p. (Orig.). 1994. mass mkt. 4.99 (*0-380-76797-X*, Avon Bks) Morrow Avon.

Murder with Majesty. Amy Myers. 288p. 1999. 25.00 (*0-7278-5415-1*, Pub. by Severn Hse) Chivers N Amer.

Murder with Malice. large type ed. Nicholas Blake. (Linford Mystery Library). 528p. 1997. pap. 16.99 (*0-7089-5094-9*, Linford) Ulverscroft.

Murder with Minarets. large type ed. Charles Forsyte. 1990. 27.99 (*0-7089-2206-6*) Ulverscroft.

*__Murder with Peacocks.__ Donna Andrews. LC 98-46254. 320p. 1999. mass mkt. 5.99 (*0-312-97063-3*, St Martins Paperbacks) St Martin.

*__Murder with Puffins.__ Donna Andrews. LC 00-25476. 288p. 2000. text 24.95 (*0-312-26221-3*, Minotaur) St Martin.

Murder Without Motive. Paine. LC 98-48527. Date not set. 30.00 (*0-7838-0443-1*, G K Hall Lrg Type) Mac Lib Ref.

*__Murder Without Motive.__ Lauran Paine. LC 98-48527. 212p. 1999. write for info. (*0-7540-3646-4*) Chivers N Amer.

Murder Without Reservation. Bernie Lee. (Worldwide Library Mysteries: No. 96). 1992. mass mkt. 3.99 (*0-373-26096-2*, 1-26096-7) Harlequin Bks.

Murder Yet to Come. Isabel B. Myers. LC 93-49476. 256p. 1994. reprint ed. 16.00 (*0-935652-22-1*) Ctr Applications Psych.

Murdered by His Wife. Deborah Navas. LC 99-15160. (Illus.). 193p. 1999. 25.00 (*1-55849-227-5*) U of Mass Pr.

Murdered by Isaac Newton. George Reed. 216p. 1984. 14.95 (*0-89697-146-5*) Intl Univ Pr.

Murdered Heiress: Living Witness. Petti Wagner. 224p. 1992. reprint ed. pap. 10.99 (*0-914903-90-X*) Destiny Image.

*__Murdered House.__ Pierre Magnan. 2000. 26.00 (*1-86046-649-4*) Harvill Press.

Murdered in Central America: The Stories of Eleven U. S. Missionaries. Donna W. Brett & Edward T. Brett. LC 87-37216. (Illus.). 380p. 1988. reprint ed. pap. 117.80 (*0-7837-9858-X*, 206058700005) Bks Demand.

Murdered in Jersey. Gerald Tomlinson. LC 93-35007. (Illus.). 260p. (C). 1994. pap. 17.00 (*0-8135-2078-9*); text 38.00 (*0-8135-2077-0*) Rutgers U Pr.

Murdered My Sweet. Joan Lowery Nixon. 208p. (YA). 1998. mass mkt. 4.50 (*0-440-22005-X*) BDD Bks Young Read.

Murdered My Sweet. Joan Lowery Nixon. LC 96-43431. 176p. (J). (gr. 7). 1997. 15.95 (*0-385-32245-3*) Delacorte.

*__Murdered My Sweet.__ Joan Lowery Nixon. 1998. pap. 11.70 (*0-613-10217-7*) Econo-Clad Bks.

Murdered on Duty: The Killing of Police Officers in America. 2nd ed. Samuel G. Chapman. LC 97-30462. (Illus.). 218p. 1997. text 47.95 (*0-398-06820-8*) C C Thomas.

Murdered on Duty: The Killing of Police Officers in America. 2nd ed. Samuel G. Chapman. LC 97-30462. (Illus.). 218p. 1998. pap. text 32.95 (*0-398-06821-6*) C C Thomas.

Murdered Sun. Christie Golden. (Star Trek: 06). 1996. mass mkt. 5.99 (*0-671-53783-0*) PB.

Murderer. Roy A. Heath. LC 91-44023. 190p. 1992. 19.95 (*0-89255-168-2*) Persea Bks.

Murderer. Anthony Shaffer. LC 97-27381. 96p. 1997. pap. 11.95 (*0-7145-2545-6*) M Boyars Pubs.

Murderer. Georges Simenon. Tr. by Geoffrey Sainsbury. 144p. 1986. 15.95 (*0-15-163270-7*) Harcourt.

Murderer. Roy A. Heath. 190p. 1993. reprint ed. pap. 9.95 (*0-89255-169-0*) Persea Bks.

Murderer & His Murder: A Review of Research. David Lester. LC 85-48007. (Studies in Modern Society: Political & Social Issues: No. 19). 1986. 32.50 (*0-404-61626-7*) AMS Pr.

Murderer & His Victim. 2nd ed. John M. Macdonald. 342p. 1986. pap. 42.95 (*0-398-06254-4*) C C Thomas.

Murderer & His Victim. 2nd ed. John M. Macdonald. 342p. (C). 1986. text 57.95 (*0-398-05205-0*) C C Thomas.

Murderers. large type ed. W. E. B. Griffin. LC 95-5419. 1995. 24.95 (*1-56895-209-0*) Wheeler Pub.

Murderers & Other Friends: Another Part of Life. John Mortimer. 272p. 1996. pap. 11.95 (*0-14-024800-5*, Viking) Viking Penguin.

*__Murderers are Silent.__ large type ed. Robert Clarke. 296p. 1999. pap. 18.99 (*0-7089-5593-2*, Linford) Ulverscroft.

Murderer's Day. E. M. Schorb. LC 97-44480. 1998. pap. 12.95 (*1-55753-120-X*) Purdue U Pr.

Murderers Die, Vol. 1. Brian. 1990. mass mkt. 5.95 (*0-312-92472-0*) St Martin.

*__Murderers Don't Smile.__ large type ed. John Morgan. 304p. 1999. pap. 18.99 (*0-7089-5597-5*, Linford) Ulverscroft.

*__Murderer's Moon.__ large type ed. Richard Dana. 296p. 1999. pap. 18.99 (*0-7089-5600-9*, Linford) Ulverscroft.

Murderers of Katyn. Vladimir Abarinov. 250p. 1992. 19.95 (*0-7818-0032-3*) Hippocrene Bks.

Murderer's Tale. Margaret Frazer. 240p. 1996. mass mkt. 5.99 (*0-425-15406-8*, Prime Crime) Berkley Pub.

Murderess. Alexandros Papadiamantis. Tr. by Peter Levi from GRE. 127p. 1983. 13.95 (*0-904613-94-1*); pap. 5.95 (*0-906495-72-5*) Writers & Readers.

An Asterisk (*) at the beginning of an entry indicates that the title is appearing for the first time.

***Murderess! The Chilling True Story of the Most Infamous Woman Ever Electrocuted.** Leslie Margolin. 1999. mass mkt. 6.50 (*0-7860-1052-5*) Pinal County Schl Office.

Murdering America, Inc. Craig Fraley & Laura Fraley. LC 98-94890. 214p. 1999. pap. 14.95 (*1-57579-139-0*) Pine Hill Pr.

***Murdering Masculinities: Fantasies of Gender & Violence in the American Crime.** Greg Forter. LC 00-9770. 2000. pap. write for info. (*0-8147-2691-7*) NYU Pr.

Murdering Ministers. Beechey. LC 99-36337. 1999. text 24.95 (*0-312-20902-9*) St Martin.

Murdering Mr. Monti. Judith Viorst. 254p. 1994. 21.00 (*0-671-76074-2*) S&S Trade.

***Murdering Mum.** unabridged ed. Mike Tibbets. Ed. by William-Alan Landes. 28p. 2000. pap. 5.00 (*0-88734-843-2*) Players Pr.

Murdering to Dissect: Graverobbing, Frankenstein & the Anatomy Literature. Timothy Marshall. LC 95-1715. 256p. 1996. text 27.95 (*0-7190-4543-6*, Pub. by Manchester Univ Pr) St Martin.

***Murder@maggody.com: An Arly Hanks Mystery.** large type ed. Joan Hess. LC 00-32489. 2000. write for info. (*1-56895-886-2*) Wheeler Pub.

Murderous Memories: One Woman's Hellish Real-Life Struggle to Save Herself. Jean S. Brinson. LC 94-66755. 288p. 1994. 22.95 (*0-88282-126-1*) New Horizon NJ.

Murderous Music. Anneliese Wagner. LC 95-2285. (Crimson Edge Chapbook Ser.). 33p. (Orig.). 1995. pap. 7.95 (*0-9619111-8-2*) Chicory Blue.

Murderous Schemes: An Anthology of Classic Detective Stories. Ed. by Donald E. Westlake. 528p. 1998. pap. 15.95 (*0-19-510487-0*) OUP.

Murderous Schemes: An Anthology of Classic Detective Stories. Ed. by Donald E. Westlake & J. Madison Davis. 528p. 1996. 30.00 (*0-19-510321-1*) OUP.

Murderous Science: Elimination by Scientific Selection of Jews, Gypsies, & Others in Germany, 1933-1945. Benno Mueller-Hill. Tr. by George R. Fraser from GER. LC 97-40085. (Illus.). 200p. (C). 1997. pap. 29.00 (*0-87969-531-5*) Cold Spring Harbor.

Murderously Incorrect. Henry F. Mazel. LC 98-93489. 208p. 1999. pap. 12.95 (*0-9665899-0-4*) Crime & Again.

Murders & Madness: Medicine, Law, & Society in the Fin de Siecle. Ruth Harris. (Oxford Historical Monographs). (Illus.). 384p. 1991. reprint ed. pap. 29.95 (*0-19-820259-8*) OUP.

Murders Anonymous. large type ed. E. X. Ferrars. 1979. 12.00 (*0-7089-0302-9*) Ulverscroft.

Murders at Convict Lake. George J. Williams, III. (Nevada California History Ser.). (Illus.). 1984. 12.95 (*0-935174-14-1*); pap. 5.95 (*0-935174-11-7*) Tree by River.

***Murders at Hollings General.** Jerry Labriola. Ed. by Brian Jud. LC 99-70735. 357p. 1999. 19.95 (*1-928782-00-0*, Pub. by Pubg Directions) ACCESS Pubs Network.

Murders at Moondance. A. B. Guthrie, Jr. LC 92-38605. xiv, 279p. 1993. text 50.00 (*0-8032-2150-9*) U of Nebr Pr.

Murders at Moondance. A. B. Guthrie, Jr. LC 92-38065. xiv, 279p. 1993. pap. 13.95 (*0-8032-7039-9*, Bison Books) U of Nebr Pr.

Murder's Bad But Monday Can Kill You! Pat Cook. 79p. (YA). (gr. 10 up). 1998. pap. 5.60 (*0-87129-866-X*, MA8) Dramatic Pub.

Murders in Musicland. Diana Kirk. 3.50 (*1-891020-12-9*) New Concepts.

Murders in North America. Lionel Martinez. 1991. 15.98 (*1-55521-703-6*) Bk Sales Inc.

Murders in the Bank Vault: The Father's Day Massacre & the Trial of Jim King. Walter Gerash & Phil Goodstein. LC 97-9128. (Illus.). 304p. 1997. pap. 16.95 (*0-9622169-6-8*) New Social.

Murders in the Rue Morgue. Edgar Allan Poe. 240p. 1998. 7.95 (*3-89508-090-X*) Konemann.

Murders in the Rue Morgue & Other Stories. Edgar Allan Poe. 1998. pap. text 7.95 (*1-902058-02-X*, Pub. by Pulp Fictions) Seven Hills Bk.

Murders in the Rue Morgue & Other Tales, Vol. 2. large type ed. Edgar Allan Poe. LC 97-30821. Vol. 2. 240p. 1997. text 22.95 (*1-56000-535-1*) Transaction Pubs.

Murders in the Ruins. large type ed. Richard Hunt. (Dales Mystery Ser.). 296p. 1993. pap. 18.99 (*1-85389-411-7*, Dales) Ulverscroft.

Murders in Volume Two: A Henry Gamadge Mystery. Elizabeth Daly. LC 93-38797. 320p. 1994. reprint ed. pap. 6.95 (*1-883402-52-2*) S&S Trade.

Murder's Long Memory. large type ed. Roderic Jeffries. LC 92-19476. 290p. 1992. reprint ed. lib. bdg. 16.95 (*1-56054-498-8*) Thorndike Pr.

***Murders Most Pleasant.** Norman C. Reddick. 175p. 2000. pap. 10.95 (*0-9701192-0-8*) Carlisle TX.

Murders of Mrs. Austin & Mrs. Beale. Jill McGown. 1994. reprint ed. mass mkt. 5.99 (*0-449-22162-8*, Crest) Fawcett.

Murders of Richard III. Elizabeth Peters, pseud. 230p. 1986. mass mkt. 5.99 (*0-445-40229-6*, Pub. by Warner Bks) Little.

Murder's Out of Tune. Sara Woods. 192p. 1988. pap. 3.50 (*0-380-70586-9*, Avon Bks) Morrow Avon.

Murdoch. William Shawcross. (Illus.). 512p. 1993. 27.50 (*0-671-67327-0*) S&S Trade.

Murdoch. William Shawcross. 496p. 1994. pap. 15.00 (*0-671-87536-1*, Touchstone) S&S Trade Pap.

Murdoch. William Shawcross. 496p. 1997. per. 16.00 (*0-684-83015-9*, Touchstone) S&S Trade Pap.

Murdoch vs. Freud: A Freudian Look at an Anti-Freudian. Jack Turner. LC 92-2925. (American University Studies: English Language & Literature: Ser. IV, Vol. 146). 148p. (C). 1993. text 35.95 (*0-8204-1857-9*) P Lang Pubng.

Murdock Genealogy: Robert Murdock of Roxbury, MA & Some of His Descendants, with Notes on the Descendants of John Munro of Plymouth; George Murdock of Plainfield, CT; Peter Murdock of Saybrook, CT; William Murdock of Philadelphia & Others. Jos. B. Murdock. (Illus.). 274p. 1994. reprint ed. pap. 44.00 (*0-8328-4348-2*); reprint ed. lib. bdg. 54.00 (*0-8328-4347-4*) Higginson Bk Co.

Murdock's Family. Paula D. Riggs. (Desire Ser.). 1994. per. 2.99 (*0-373-05898-5*, 1-05898-1) Silhouette.

***Murdock's Last Stand: (The Protectors)** Beverly Barton. (Intimate Moments Ser.: No. 979). 2000. per. 4.50 (*0-373-07979-6*, 1-07979-7) Harlequin Bks.

Murdos Hispanos Guide, Level 1. Dominguez. (College Spanish Ser.). 1996. pap. 36.95 (*0-8384-6857-8*) Heinle & Heinle.

Muret-Sanders Encyclopedic German Dictionary see Langenscheidt New Muret-Sanders Encyclopedic Dictionary

Muret-Sanders Encyclopedic German Dictionary: A - K see Langenscheidt New Muret-Sanders Encyclopedic Dictionary

Muret-Sanders Encyclopedic German Dictionary: A - M see Langenscheidt New Muret-Sanders Encyclopedic Dictionary

Muret-Sanders Encyclopedic German Dictionary: N - Z see Langenscheidt New Muret-Sanders Encyclopedic Dictionary

Murex Shells of the World: An Illustrated Guide to the Muricidae. George E. Radwin & Anthony D'Attilio. LC 75-7485. (Illus.). 328p. 1976. reprint ed. pap. 30.00 (*0-7837-2164-1*, 204247000004) Bks Demand.

Muria Murder & Suicide. 2nd ed. Verrier Elwin. (Illus.). 322p. 1991. 12.95 (*0-19-562854-3*) OUP.

Muriel & Ruth: A Book about Friendship. Jeffie R. Gordon. LC 91-728718. (Illus.). 24p. (J). (ps-3). 1992. 8.95 (*1-878093-18-5*) Boyds Mills Pr.

Muriel Anderson: Hometown Live! Muriel Anderson. 72p. 1995. 22.95 incl. audio compact disk (*0-7866-1447-1*, MB95664BCD) Mel Bay.

Muriel at Metropolitan: A Novel. Miriam Tlali. LC 79-313912. (Drumbeat Ser.). 190 p. (J). 1979. write for info. (*0-582-64232-9*) Longman.

Muriel Ostriche: Princess of Silent Films. Q. David Bowers. LC 87-1981. (Illus.). 240p. 1987. 24.95 (*0-911572-63-5*, Vestal Pr); pap. 19.95 (*0-911572-64-3*, Vestal Pr) Madison Bks UPA.

Muriel Rukeyser Reader. Jan H. Levi. Ed. by Muriel Rukeyser. 320p. 1995. pap. 15.00 (*0-393-31323-9*) Norton.

Muriel Spark. Alan N. Bold. (Contemporary Writers Ser.). 96p. 1986. pap. 7.50 (*0-416-40360-3*, 9733) Routledge.

Muriel Spark. Karl Malkoff. LC 68-54456. (Columbia Essays on Modern Writers Ser.: No. 36). 48p. (Orig.). 1968. pap. text 12.00 (*0-231-03063-0*) Col U Pr.

Muriel Spark. Derek Stanford. 1989. 30.00 (*0-87556-326-0*) Saifer.

Muriel Spark. Dorothea Walker. (English Authors Ser.: No. 460). 136p. 1988. 22.95 (*0-8057-6960-9*, Twyne) Mac Lib Ref.

***Murielle: The Story of a Model, a Painting & the Artistry of John William Waterhouse.** James Kaye. LC 00-190492. 2000. 25.00 (*0-7388-1790-2*); pap. 18.00 (*0-7388-1791-0*) Xlibris Corp.

Murillo Diego Angulo Iniguez, 3 vols. (SPA.). 1652p. 1982. write for info. (*0-318-65345-1*); write for info. (*0-318-65346-X*); write for info. (*0-318-65347-8*) Elliots Bks.

Murillo's Allegories of Salvation & Triumph: The Parable of the Prodigal Son & the Life of Jacob. Mindy N. Taggard. (Illus.). 168p. 1992. text 32.50 (*0-8262-0872-X*) U of Mo Pr.

***Murine Local Lymph Node Assay: A Test Method for Assessing the Allergic Contact Dermatitis Potential of Chemicals/Compounds.** Ed. by William S. Stokes & Richard N. Hill. (Illus.). 198p. (C). 2000. pap. text 35.00 (*0-7881-8564-0*) DIANE Pub.

Murkin Conspiracy: An Investigation into the Assassination of Dr. Martin Luther King, Jr. Philip H. Melanson. LC 88-15262. 219p. 1989. 39.95 (*0-275-93029-7*, C3029, Praeger Pubs) Greenwood.

***Murky Monster's Birthday Bash.** Ellen Schecter. LC 98-42167. (Bank Street Ready-to-Read Ser.). (Illus.). (J). 1999. trans. 20.01 (*0-553-37588-1*) Bantam.

Murlo & the Etruscans: Art & Society in Ancient Etruria. Ed. by Richard D. De Puma & Jocelyn P. Small. LC 93-14995. (Studies in Classics). (Illus.). 256p. (C). 1994. text 45.00 (*0-299-13910-7*) U of Wis Pr.

Murmansk: Economy, Industry, Government, Business. 2nd rev. ed. Russian Information & Business Center, Inc. Staff. (Russian Regional Business Directories Ser.). (Illus.). 200p. 1997. pap. 99.00 (*1-57751-399-1*) Intl Business Pubns.

***Murmansk Assignment.** large type ed. James A. Pattinson. 336p. 1999. pap. 18.99 (*0-7089-5591-6*, Linford) Ulverscroft.

***Murmansk Oblast Regional Investment & Business Guide.** Global Investment & Business Center, Inc. Staff. (Russian Regional Investment & Business Guides Ser.: Vol. 49). (Illus.). 350p. 1999. pap. 99.00 (*0-7397-0850-3*) Intl Business Pubns.

***Murmansk Oblast Regional Investment & Business Guide.** Contrib. by Global Investment & Business Center, Inc. Staff. (Russian Regional Investment & Business Guides Ser.: Vol. 9). (Illus.). 350p. 2000. pap. 99.95 (*0-7397-2997-7*) Intl Business Pubns.

Murmansk Venture. Charles Maynard. LC 79-115564. (Russia Observed Ser.). (Illus.). 1971. reprint ed. 23.95 (*0-405-03085-1*) Ayer.

Murmel, Murmel, Murmel see Agu, Agu, Agu

Murmel, Murmel, Murmel. Annikin & Robert Munsch. (Annikins Ser.: Vol. 7). (Illus.). 32p. (J). (ps-2). 1989. pap. 0.99 (*1-55037-012-X*, Pub. by Annick) Firefly Bks Ltd.

Murmel, Murmel, Murmel. Robert Munsch. (Illus.). 32p. (J). (gr. k-2). 1982. lib. bdg. 15.95 (*0-920236-29-4*, Pub. by Annick) Firefly Bks Ltd.

Murmel, Murmel, Murmel. Robert Munsch. (Illus.). 32p. (J). (gr. k-3). 1982. pap. 5.95 (*0-920236-31-6*, Pub. by Annick) Firefly Bks Ltd.

Murmel, Murmel, Murmel. Robert Munsch. (Munsch for Kids Ser.). (J). 1982. 11.15 (*0-606-02913-3*, Pub. by Turtleback) Demco.

Murmur see Paperplay Mini-Books

Murmur in the Trees. Emily Dickinson & Ferris Cook. LC 97-40413. (Illus.). 128p. (gr. 8). 1998. 19.95 (*0-8212-2500-6*) Little.

Murmur of Rain. Patricia Vaughn. 1996. pap., mass mkt. 5.99 (*0-671-52004-0*) PB.

Murmuracion: Entretenimiento Social? Gerardo DeAvila. (Serie Guia de Bolsillo - Pocket Guides Ser.).Tr. of Whining: Social Entertainment?. (SPA.). 88p. 1995. 2.79 (*0-7899-0011-4*, 498078) Editorial Unilit.

Murmuring Coast. Lidia Jorge. Tr. by Natalia Costa & Ronald W. Sousa. LC 94-11473. 288p. 1995. 24.95 (*0-8166-2112-8*) U of Minn Pr.

Murmuring Judges. rev. ed. David Hare. 109p. (Orig.). 1995. pap. 11.95 (*0-571-17219-9*) Faber & Faber.

***Murmuring the Judges.** Quintin Jardine. 560p. 2000. 31.99 (*0-7089-4216-4*) Ulverscroft.

Murmurs. Carol Battaglia. Ed. by Carolyn Zagury. LC 96-60060. (Illus.). 96p. 1996. pap. 12.95 (*1-880254-36-0*) Vista.

Murmurs: The Story of a Stethoscope. Tony Miksanek. 131p. 1995. 12.95 (*0-9646089-0-1*) Illusions Pr.

Muro de las Memorias. Pedro Granados. (SPA.). 68p. (Orig.). 1989. pap. 6.50 (*0-9622876-0-1*) Latin Amer Bks.

MUROC: When the Hot Rods Ran, May 15, 1938. William Carroll. LC 90-85257. (Illus.). 80p. (Orig.). 1991. pap. 20.00 (*0-910390-30-4*) Coda Publications.

***Muroki Family Pictures.** Eva Wangui. (Illus.). 2000. pap. 13.95 (*1-878647-69-5*) APU Pub Grp.

Murphy. Samuel Beckett. 208p. 1947. pap. write for info. (*0-7859-4710-8*) Fr & Eur.

Murphy. Samuel Beckett. LC 57-6939. 288p. 1969. pap. 12.00 (*0-8021-5037-3*, Grove) Grove-Atltic.

Murphy: Plays One. Tom Murphy. (Methuen World Dramatists Ser.). 231p. (C). 1992. pap. 14.95 (*0-413-66570-4*, A0660, Methuen Drama) Methn.

Murphy: Plays Three. Tom Murphy. 256p. 1994. pap. 15.95 (*0-413-68350-8*, A0692, Methuen Drama) Methn.

Murphy: Plays Two. Tom Murphy. LC 93-222005. 241p. (C). 1993. pap. 14.95 (*0-413-67560-2*, A0670, Methuen Drama) Methn.

Murphy - Jahn. Editorial Staff. (Master Architect Ser.: Vol. 8). (Illus.). 250p. 1995. 69.95 (*1-875498-19-2*, Pub. by Images Aust AT) Bks Nippan.

Murphy & Kate. Ellen Howard. LC 93-26002. (Illus.). 32p. (J). (ps-2). 1995. per. 15.00 (*0-671-79775-1*) S&S Bks Yung.

Murphy Book. Michael C. O'Laughlin. (Irish Family Histories Ser.). (Illus.). 1981. 15.00 (*0-940134-20-9*) Irish Genealog.

Murphy Family: Genealogy, History, Biography, with Official Statistics of the Part Played by Members of This Numerous Family in the Making & Maintenance of This Great American Republic. M. W. Downes. (Illus.). 363p. 1989. reprint ed. pap. 54.50 (*0-8328-0895-4*); reprint ed. lib. bdg. 62.50 (*0-8328-0894-6*) Higginson Bk Co.

Murphy Federal Taxation, '96. Date not set. pap. text, teacher ed. write for info. (*0-314-05438-3*); pap. text, student ed. write for info. (*0-314-05440-5*) West Pub.

Murphy Gap. Robert W. Taylor. LC 95-69918. 90p. (Orig.). 1997. pap. 11.95 (*1-57197-043-6*) Pentland Pr.

Murphy Goes to Church. Steve Dennie & Rob Suggs. LC 93-18096. (Illus.). 108p. (Orig.). 1993. pap. 6.99 (*0-8308-1837-5*, 1837) InterVarsity.

Murphy Is My Co-Pilot. Harry C. Pellow. (Illus.). 407p. 1983. 29.95 (*0-941210-07-3*) HCP Res.

Murphy on Evidence. 5th ed. Peter Murphy. LC 95-177523. 624p. 1995. pap. 44.00 (*1-85431-373-8*, Pub. by Blackstone Pr) Gaunt.

Murphy on Evidence. 6th ed. Peter Murphy. 565p. 1997. pap. 46.00 (*1-85431-682-6*, Pub. by Blackstone Pr) Gaunt.

***Murphy Portrait Of Amer Politi.** 3rd ed. Murphy. 1999. pap. text 21.57 (*0-395-88547-7*) HM.

Murphy Stories. Mark Costello. LC 72-86409. (Illinois Short Fiction Ser.). 120p. 1973. 9.95 (*0-252-00309-8*) U of Ill Pr.

Murphy Strikes Again! More Murphy's Laws in Cross-Stitch. Jean D. Crowther. Ed. by Duane S. Crowther. 12p. 1987. 5.98 (*0-88290-292-X*, 2799) Horizon Utah.

Murphy Wants to Be Famous. Kathy N. Hasty. (Illus.). 27p. (Orig.). (J). (ps-2). 1991. pap. 3.99 (*0-9631480-0-1*) Story Time Pubns.

Murphy's Ambush. large type ed. Gary Paulsen & Brian Burks. LC 95-20828. (Western Ser.). 175p. 1995. 17.95 (*0-7862-0518-0*) Thorndike Pr.

Murphy's Bed. Sighle Kennedy. LC 75-123433. (Illus.). 325p. 1975. 39.50 (*0-8387-7739-2*) Bucknell U Pr.

Murphy's Boy. Torey L. Hayden. 1983. mass mkt. 5.99 (*0-380-65227-7*, Avon Bks) Morrow Avon.

Murphy's Child: Families Are Forever. Judith Duncan. (Intimate Moments Ser.: No. 946). 1999. per. 4.25 (*0-373-07946-X*, 1-07946-6) Silhouette.

***Murphy's Law.** Arthur Bloch. (J). 1999. pap. 10.99 (*0-8431-7485-4*, Price Stern) Peng Put Young Read.

***Murphy's Law, 1.** Daily. 1998. text 9.99 (*0-8431-7432-3*) Pssblts Denver.

***Murphy's Law: Doctors.** Arthur Bloch. LC 00-28281. (Illus.). 240p. (YA). 2000. pap. 7.99 (*0-8431-7581-8*, Price Stern) Peng Put Young Read.

***Murphy's Law: Lawyers.** Arthur Bloch. LC 00-28288. (Illus.). 240p. (YA). 2000. pap. 7.99 (*0-8431-7580-X*, Price Stern) Peng Put Young Read.

Murphy's Law: Men in Blue. Marilyn Pappano. (Silhouette Intimate Moments Ser.: Vol. 901). 1998. per. 4.25 (*0-373-07901-X*, 1-07901-1, Mira Bks) Harlequin Bks.

Murphy's Law Midi Book. Jeff Burger. Orig. Title: Advanced Midi User's Guide. 94p. (C). 1987. pap. 19.95 (*0-939067-56-0*) Alexander Pub.

Murphy's Law 2000: What Else Can Go Wrong in the 21st Century! Arthur Bloch. LC 98-48575. 96p. 1999. pap. 6.99 (*0-8431-7482-X*, Price Stern) Peng Put Young Read.

***Murphy's Law 2001 Desk Calendar.** Arthur Bloch. 640p. 2000. pap. 10.99 (*0-8431-7570-2*) Peng Put Young Read.

Murphy's Laws: Philosophical Quips in Cross Stitch. Annette Bradshaw & Gwyn Franson. 1984. 5.98 (*0-88290-255-5*) Horizon Utah.

Murphy's Laws of DOS. 2nd ed. Charlie Russel. LC 93-85947. 356p. 1993. pap. 16.99 (*0-7821-1424-5*) Sybex.

Murphy's Laws of Marriage. Steve Dennie & Rob Suggs. LC 96-4165. (Illus.). 104p. (Orig.). 1996. pap. 6.99 (*0-8308-1674-7*, 1674) InterVarsity.

Murphy's Laws of Parenting. Steve Dennie & Rob Suggs. LC 93-41358. (Illus.). 104p. (Orig.). 1994. pap. 6.99 (*0-8308-1839-1*, 1839) InterVarsity.

Murphy's Lore: Tales from Bulfinche's Pub. Patrick Thomas. 288p. (Orig.). 1997. pap. 6.99 (*1-890096-02-4*) Padwolf Pub.

Murphy's Mansion. Elaine K. McEwan. Ed. by LoraBeth Norton. LC 94-7136. (Josh McIntire Ser.). 96p. (J). (gr. 3-6). 1994. pap. 4.99 (*0-7814-0160-7*, Chariot Bks) Chariot Victor.

Murphy's Plays, No. 4. Tom Murphy. 1997. pap. 14.95 (*0-413-71450-0*) Methn.

Murphy's Rules. Ed. by S. John Ross & Steve Jackson. (Illus.). 80p. 1998. pap. 14.95 (*1-55634-363-9*, 9006, Pub. by S Jackson Games) BookWorld.

Murphy's Stand. large type ed. Gary Paulsen & Brian Burks. LC 93-48427. (Western Ser.). 177p. 1994. lib. bdg. 19.95 (*0-7862-0169-X*) Thorndike Pr.

Murphy's Story: The History of Lady's Well Brewery, Cork. Diarmuid O. Drisceoil & Donal O. Drisceoil. (Illus.). 164p. 1997. 29.95 (*0-9531431-0-4*, Pub. by Mercier Pr) Irish Amer Bk.

Murphy's Trail. Gary Paulsen & Brian Burks. 1996. 18.95 (*0-8027-4154-1*) Walker & Co.

Murphy's Trail. large type ed. Gary Paulsen & Brian Burks. LC 96-38779. 208p. 1997. 18.95 (*0-7862-0899-6*) Thorndike Pr.

Murphy's Will Clauses: Annotations & Forms with Tax Effects, 4 vols. Joseph H. Murphy. 1960. ring bd. 980.00 (*0-8205-1441-1*) Bender.

Murray - Conwell: Genealogy & Allied Families. M. L. Lawrence & G. L. Lombard. (Illus.). 115p. 1992. reprint ed. pap. 19.50 (*0-8328-2697-9*); reprint ed. lib. bdg. 29.50 (*0-8328-2696-0*) Higginson Bk Co.

Murray Bookchin Reader. Janet Biehl. 288p. 1999. 53.99 (*1-55164-119-4*); pap. 24.99 (*1-55164-118-6*) Black Rose CA.

Murray Bookchin Reader. Murray Bookchin & Janet Biehl. LC 97-7413. 1997. 70.00 (*0-304-33873-7*); pap. 24.95 (*0-304-33874-5*) Continuum.

Murray Collection: Art of the Twentieth Century - Selections from the Permanent Collection. (Illus.). 48p. 1993. 12.00 (*0-685-72183-3*) Hyde Collect.

***Murray County: Oklahoma.** Roland Earsom. (Images of America Ser.). (Illus.). 128p. 1999. pap. 18.99 (*0-7385-0312-6*) Arcadia Publng.

***Murray Family History: 200 Years in Fayette County, PA.** Donna Allen. (Illus.). 65p. 1999. pap. 15.00 (*0-9658079-1-6*) Donna Allen.

Murray Krieger & Contemporary Critical Theory. Bruce Henricksen. LC 85-19064. (Irvine Studies in the Humanities). 320p. 1986. text 57.50 (*0-231-06118-8*) Col U Pr.

Murray N. Rothbard: In Memoriam. Ed. by Llewellyn H. Rockwell, Jr. 132p. (Orig.). 1995. pap. 14.95 (*0-945466-19-6*) Ludwig von Mises.

Murray on Contracts. 3rd ed. John E. Murray, Jr. 1202p. 1990. 50.00 (*0-87473-613-7*, MICHIE) LEXIS Pub.

Murray on Contracts, 1990. 3rd ed. John E. Murray. 1990. text 50.00 (*0-87473-656-0*, 12191-10, MICHIE) LEXIS Pub.

Murray Resource Directory & Career Guide to Historically Black Colleges & Universities Black College & Career Guide Third Edition. 3rd ed. Vernelle T. Dennis. (Illus.). 342p. (YA). (gr. 9-12). 59.00 (*1-885674-01-5*) LED Pubng.

Murray (S. Carolina) Echoes in Time: The Murray, Connor & Moorer Families of South Carolina. G. Monroe Black. 399p. 1997. pap. 59.00 (*0-8328-7004-8*); lib. bdg. 69.00 (*0-8328-7003-X*) Higginson Bk Co.

Murray Walker, 1996 Grand Prix Year. Murray Walker. (Illus.). 144p. 1996. 12.98 (*1-874557-17-9*, Pub. by Hazelton) Motorbooks Intl.

Murray's Hand-Book for Northern Europe: Finland & Russia. LC 70-115567. (Russia Observed, Series I). 1970. reprint ed. 21.95 (*0-405-03052-5*) Ayer.

Murrays of Murray Hill. Charles Monaghan. (Illus.). x, 166p. 1998. 25.00 (*0-9662430-0-5*) Urban History.

M

An Asterisk (*) at the beginning of an entry indicates that the title is appearing for the first time.

M

Murrieta - Old Town, New Town: A Community History. Mary A. Boyce. (Illus.). 208p. (Orig.). 1995. pap. 14.95 (*0-9648634-0-5*) Rosemar Pubng.

Murrieta Hot Springs Vegetarian Cookbook. Murrieta Foundation Staff. LC 87-21881. (Illus.). 232p. 1987. pap. 9.95 (*0-913990-54-X*) Book Pub Co.

Murrow: His Life & Times. A. M. Sperber. LC 85-27534. 795p. 1986. 25.00 (*0-88191-008-2*) Freundlich.

Murrow Boys: Pioneers on the Frontlines of Broadcast Journalism. Stanley Cloud & Lynne Olson. (Illus.). 464p. 1997. pap. 15.00 (*0-395-87753-9*, Mariner Bks) HM.

***Murrows: His Life & Times.** A. M. Sperber. LC 98-52507. (Communications & Media Studies : No. 1). 816p. 1998. pap. 18.00 (*0-8232-1882-1*) Fordham.

Murrows: His Life & Times. Anne M. Sperber. LC 98-52507. (Communications & Media Studies : No. 1). 816p. 1998. 35.00 (*0-8232-1881-3*) Fordham.

Murry Burnham's Hunting Secrets. Murry Burnham & Russell Tinsley. LC 83-13315. (Illus.). 244p. 1983. 17.95 (*0-8329-0343-4*, Winchester Pr) New Win Pub.

Murs Canadiens de Joseph Lliu. Eugene Ionesco. (Illus.). 48p. 7.50 (*0-686-54196-0*) Fr & Eur.

Murs De Soutenement Tome Ii see Study of Passive Resistance in Foundation Structures, Vol. 2, (Retaining Walls)

Murtagh & the Vikings. Roger C. Newman. (Hawthorn Series in Irish History). (Illus.). 96p. (Orig.). (J). (gr. 5-8). 1986. pap. 9.95 (*0-947962-06-9*, Pub. by Childrens Pr) Irish Bks Media.

Murtagh the Warrior. Roger C. Newman. LC 97-207217. 144p. 1997. pap. 8.95 (*0-947962-98-0*) Dufour.

Murther & Walking Spirits. Robertson Davies. 368p. 1992. reprint ed. pap. 13.95 (*0-14-016884-2*, Penguin Bks) Viking Penguin.

Murvale Eastman: Christian Socialist. Albion W. Tourgee. LC 68-57554. 553p. reprint ed. lib. bdg. 27.00 (*0-8398-1968-4*) Irvington.

Murv's Motoring Memories. Murvin H. Perry. (Illus.). 160p. 1993. pap. 9.95 (*0-932807-72-0*) Overmountain Pr.

Musa: Profile & Background of a Man's Life. Paco Daurella. Tr. by Robert Bacalski from SPA. LC 90-42185. 177p. (C). 1991. text 41.95 (*0-8204-1363-1*) P Lang Pubng.

Musa: The Spoken To. Amina I. Ali. Ed. by J. C. Cinquino. (Prophets' Stories for Children from the Holy Qur'an Ser.: No. 13). (Illus.). 28p. (Orig.). (J). (gr. 4-6). 1996. write for info. (*1-881963-28-4*); pap. 2.50 (*1-881963-29-2*) Al-Saadawi Pubns.

Musa & the All-Seeing-Eye: A History of Moses. Prince A. Cuba. (Illus.). 74p. (Orig.). 1991. pap. 6.95 (*1-56411-009-5*) Untd Bros & Sis.

Musa Lapidaria: A Selection of Latin Verse Inscriptions. E. Courtney. LC 95-30859. (American Philological Association American Classical Studies: No. 36). 457p. (C). 1995. pap. 27.95 (*0-7885-0142-9*, 400436) OUP.

Musa (Moses) Siddiqia Juma. (Illus.). 16p. (J). (ps-1). 1997. 10.00 (*1-879402-46-7*) Tahrike Tarsile Quran.

Musa Pedestris: Three Centuries of Canting Songs & Slang Rhymes, 1536-1896. John S. Farmer. LC 66-2866. 1964. reprint ed. 53.50 (*0-8154-0065-9*) Cooper Sq.

Musa Proterva: Love Poems of the Restoration see Collections of Lyrics & Poems: Sixteenth & Seventeenth Centuries

***Musa the Mouse.** large type ed. John Owhonda. (Illus.). 27p. (J). (gr. 1-4). 1999. 19.95 (*0-9650505-3-X*) CGS Communs.

Musa y el Garabato (The Muse & the Scrawl) Felipe Garrido. (SPA.). 280p. 1992. pap. 8.99 (*968-16-3943-X*, Pub. by Fondo) Continental Bk.

Musaei Lexicon. J. K. Musaeus. Ed. by Domenico Bo. 96p. 1966. write for info. (*0-318-70979-1*) G Olms Pubs.

Musaeus: Musaei Lexicon. Ed. by Domenico Bo. 96p. 1966. 25.00 (*0-318-71967-3*) G Olms Pubs.

Musaics. Burt Kimmelman. LC 92-72540. 52p. 1992. pap. 8.95 (*1-881471-03-9*) S Duyvil.

Musandam: Architecture & Material Culture of a Little Known Region of Oman. Paolo M. Costa. LC 93-166933. (Illus.). 250p. (C). 1995. 84.00 (*0-907151-37-X*, Pub. by IMMEL Pubng) St Mut.

Musarion & Other Rococo Tales. Christoph M. Wieland. Tr. & Intro. by Thomas C. Starnes. (GERM Ser.: Vol. 59). viii, 176p. 1992. pap. 35.00 (*0-938100-91-2*) Camden Hse.

Musarum Deliciae & Wit Restor'd. John Mennes. LC 85-1977. 344p. 1985. 50.00 (*0-8201-1404-9*) Schol Facsimiles.

Musas de Darwin. Jose Sarukhan. (Ciencia para Todos Ser.). (SPA.). pap. 6.99 (*968-16-3035-1*, Pub. by Fondo) Continental Bk.

Musashi: An Epic Novel of the Samurai Era. Eiji Yoshikawa. Tr. by Charles S. Terry from JPN. 992p. 1995. 35.00 (*4-7700-1957-2*) Kodansha.

Musashi No. 5: Way of Life & Death, Bk. 5. Eiji Yoshikawa. 352p. 1989. mass mkt. 4.95 (*0-671-67723-3*) PB.

***Musca Domestica.** Christine Hume. LC 99-87864. 96p. 2000. pap. 15.00 (*0-8070-6859-4*) Beacon Pr.

Muscarinic Agonists & the Treatment of Alzheimer's Disease. Abraham Fisher. LC 95-48062. (Neuroscience Intelligence Unit Ser.). 197 p. 1996. 99.00 (*1-57059-326-4*) Landes Bioscience.

Muscarinic & Nicotinic Stimulant Actions Autonomic Ganglia, Vol. 1. D. Bovet & A. Vurgen. LC 66-22361. (International Encyclopedia of Pharmacology & Therapeutics Ser.: Sec. 12). 1966. 60.00 (*0-08-012062-8*, Pub. by Pergamon Repr) Franklin.

Muscarinic Receptor Subtypes in Smooth Muscle. Eglan. LC 96-26614. (Pharmacology & Toxicology Ser.). 208p. 1997. lib. bdg. 139.95 (*0-8493-8549-0*) CRC Pr.

Muscarinic Receptors. Ed. by Joan Heller Brown. LC 89-15539. (Receptors Ser.). 496p. 1989. 125.00 (*0-89603-156-X*) Humana.

Muscat Command: The Muscat Regiment in Oman in 1967. Peter Thwaites & Simon Sloane. (Illus.). 224p. 1994. 28.95 (*0-85052-411-3*, Pub. by Leo Cooper) Trans-Atl Phila.

***Muscat Explorer.** Explorer Publishing Staff. 1999. pap. text 21.95 (*0-9531647-2-1*) Explorer Pr.

Muscle: Confessions of an Unlikely Bodybuilder. Samuel W. Fussell. 264p. 1992. pap. 12.50 (*0-380-71763-8*, Avon Bks) Morrow Avon.

Muscle - Tendon Changing & Marrow - Brain Washing Chi Kung: The Secret of Youth. 2nd ed. Jwing-Ming Yang. (Illus.). 304p. 1989. pap. 24.95 (*0-940871-06-8*, B012/068) YMAA Pubn.

Muscle Adaptation in the Craniofacial Region. Ed. by D. S. Carlson & J. A. McNamara. (Craniofacial Growth Ser.: Vol. 8). (Illus.). 252p. 1978. 45.00 (*0-929921-05-4*) UM CHGD.

Muscle Afferents & Spinal Control of Movement. IBRO Symposium Staff. Ed. by L. Jami et al. LC 92-48946. 484p. 1992. 185.25 (*0-08-041979-8*, Pergamon Pr) Elsevier.

Muscle & Bone. Paul-Victor Winters. 32p. (Orig.). 1995. pap. 8.00 (*0-9624178-5-8*) Slapering Hol.

Muscle & Fitness & Flex Present Arnold Schwarzenegger: The Icon. Ed. by Jerry Kindela. (Illus.). 188p. (Orig.). 1994. pap. 3.95 (*0-945797-20-6*) Weider Health.

Muscle & Might Training Tracker: The Week-by-Week Journal for Charting Training Success. Stuart McRobert. 136p. 1998. spiral bd. 19.95 (*9963-616-05-4*) CS Pubng Ltd.

Muscle & Nerve, Vol. 6. Ed. by Walter G. Bradley. 1983. text 72.00 (*0-471-88977-6*) Wiley.

Muscle & Sensory Testing. Reese. LC 98-7961. (C). 1999. pap. 45.00 (*0-7216-5958-6*) Harcourt.

Muscle Art. Ray Lawrence. 1995. per. 35.00 (*0-85449-198-8*, Pub. by Gay Mens Pr) LPC InBook.

Muscle As Food. Ed. by Peter J. Bechtel. (Food Science & Technology Ser.). 1986. text 153.00 (*0-12-084190-8*) Acad Pr.

***Muscle Bikes: Ape Hangers, Banana Seats & Cheater Slicks.** Liz Fried. (Illus.). 128p. 2000. pap. 24.95 (*0-933201-96-6*, 129994AP, Pub. by MBI Pubg) Motorbooks Intl.

Muscle Biology, Vol. 1. Ed. by R. G. Cassena. LC 72-81501. 311p. reprint ed. pap. 96.50 (*0-608-16730-4*, 202782200001) Bks Demand.

Muscle Biopsy: Techniques. Mike A. Loughlin. (Illus.). 242p. 1993. text 97.50 (*0-7506-1406-4*) Buttrwrth-Heinemann.

***Muscle Book.** Paul Blakey. 56p. 2000. pap. 12.95 (*0-89389-182-7*) Himalayan Inst.

Muscle Bound. Mel Cebulash. (Author's Signature Collection). (Illus.). 40p. (J). (gr. 3-8). 1993. lib. bdg. 12.79 (*0-89565-883-6*) Childs World.

Muscle Bound. Christopher Morgan. (Orig.). 1992. mass mkt. 4.95 (*1-56333-028-8*, Badboy) Masquerade.

Muscle Building 101: The Fundamentals of Shaping Your Physique. Robert Kennedy & Dwayne Hines, II. LC 97-901205. (Illus.). 112p. 1997. pap. 14.95 (*1-55210-008-1*, Pub. by MuscleMag Intl) BookWorld.

Muscle Car Chronicle. (Illus.). 320p. 1993. 29.95 (*0-7853-0174-7*, 1013000) Pubns Intl Ltd.

Muscle Cars. J. G. Newbery. LC 94-19959. (Illus.). 224p. 1994. 12.99 (*1-57145-007-6*, Thunder Bay) Advantage Pubs.

Muscle Cars. Richard Nichol. 1987. 8.98 (*0-671-07525-X*) S&S Trade.

Muscle Cars: American Thunder. LC 97-65093. (Illus.). 144p. 1997. write for info. (*0-7853-2315-5*) Pubns Intl Ltd.

Muscle Cars: Thunder & Greased Lightening. Michael Benson. 1998. pap. text 10.98 (*1-57717-008-3*) Todtri Prods.

Muscle Cars of the '50s. Consumer Guide Editors. (Illus.). 96p. 1993. 12.98 (*1-56173-301-6*, 1011700) Pubns Intl Ltd.

Muscle Cars of the '60s. Consumer Guide Editors. (Illus.). 96p. 1993. 19.95 (*1-56173-308-3*, 1011800) Pubns Intl Ltd.

Muscle Contraction: Its Regulatory Mechanism. Ed. by Setsuro Ebashi et al. 549p. 1980. 93.95 (*0-387-10411-9*) Spr-Verlag.

Muscle Contraction: Subject, Reference & Research Guidebook. Granger H. Delaney. LC 87-47640. 160p. 1987. 47.50 (*0-88164-584-2*); pap. 44.50 (*0-88164-585-0*) ABBE Pubs Assn.

Muscle Creek. Rosita Boland. 1996. pap. 10.95 (*1-85186-087-8*) Dufour.

Muscle Damage. Ed. by Stanley Salmons. (Illus.). 264p. 1997. text 65.00 (*0-19-262753-8*) OUP.

Muscle Development: Molecular & Cellular Control. Ed. by Mark L. Pearson & Henry F. Epstein. LC 82-72381. 601p. reprint ed. pap. 186.40 (*0-7837-1993-0*, 204226700002) Bks Demand.

***Muscle Diseases.** Anthony H. V. Schapira & Robert C. Griggs. LC 99-20297. 432p. 1999. text 95.00 (*0-7506-7085-1*) Buttrwrth-Heinemann.

Muscle Disorders in Childhood. 2nd ed. Dubowitz. 1995. text 102.00 (*0-7020-1437-0*, W B Saunders Co) Harcrt Hlth Sci Grp.

Muscle Energy Manual Vol. 1: Concepts & Mechanisms the Musculoskeletal Screen Cervical Region Evaluation & Treatment. Fred L. Mitchell, Jr. & P. Kai-Galen Mitchell. LC 95-77816. (Illus.). 228p. 1995. pap. text 59.00 (*0-9647250-1-0*) MET Pr.

Muscle Energy Manual Vol. 2: Evaluation & Treatment of the Thoracic Spine, Lumbar Spine & Rib Cage, 2 vols. Fred L. Mitchell, Jr. & P. Kai-Galen Mitchell. LC 95-77816. (Illus.). 240p. (Orig.). 1998. pap. text 68.00 (*0-9647250-2-9*) MET Pr.

***Muscle Energy Manual Vol. 3: Evaluation & Treatment of the Pelvis & Sacrum, 3 vols.** Fred L. Mitchell, Jr. & Calen P. Mitchell. (Illus.). 200p. 2000. pap. text 63.00 (*0-9647250-3-7*) MET Pr.

Muscle Energy Techniques. Chaitow. 1996. text 44.00 (*0-443-05297-2*, W B Saunders Co) Harcrt Hlth Sci Grp.

Muscle Fatigue Mechanisms in Exercise & Training. Ed. by P. Marconnet et al. (Medicine & Sport Science Ser.: Vol. 34). (Illus.). viii, 244p. 1992. 215.75 (*3-8055-5483-4*) S Karger.

***Muscle Fitness Book: A Practical Guide to Every Day Fitness for Everyone - Beginner & Professional.** St. George. 1998. pap. 17.95 (*0-7318-0064-8*) Simon & Schuster.

Muscle Foods. D. Kinsman. 1992. text. write for info. (*0-442-00610-1*) Chapman & Hall.

Muscle for the Wing: A Rene Shade Mystery. Daniel Woodrell. 224p. 1998. pap. 14.00 (*0-671-00137-X*) S&S Trade.

Muscle Imaging. Ed. by James Fleckenstein et al. LC 95-36652. (Illus.). 461p. 1996. 145.00 (*0-387-94231-9*) Spr-Verlag.

Muscle Mass, Strength & Endurance: The Ultimate Sports Nutrition Protocol with the Power-Sync System. Alex Duarte. 84p. 1994. pap. text 15.00 (*1-891036-05-X*) Nutri Tapes.

Muscle, Matrix & Bladder Function: Proceedings of a Symposium Held in Philadelphia, Pennsylvania, March 18-19, 1994, Vol. 385. Ed. by Stephen A. Zderic. LC 95-45640. (Advances in Experimental Medicine & Biology Ser.: Vol. 385). (Illus.). 282p. 1995. 95.00 (*0-306-45193-X*, RC919, Kluwer Plenum) Kluwer Academic.

Muscle Meals: A Cookbook to Build Muscle & Lose Fat. John Romano. Ed. by Jessica Richmond. LC 97-71088. (Illus.). 224p. 1997. 19.95 (*1-889462-01-2*) Advanced Research Pr.

Muscle Mechanics. Everett Aaberg. LC 98-13154. (Illus.). 224p. 1998. pap. 19.95 (*0-88011-796-6*, PAAB0796) Human Kinetics.

Muscle Membranes in Diseases of Muscle. Ed. by Robert E. Mrak. 168p. 1985. 99.00 (*0-8493-5622-9*, RC925, CRC Reprint) Franklin.

Muscle Memory. Tapply. LC 99-22042. 288p. 1999. text 23.95 (*0-312-20563-5*) St Martin.

Muscle Memory Method: Easy All-Day Fitness for a Stronger, Firmer, Younger Body. Marjorie Jaffe & Jo Sgammato. LC 96-53168. (Illus.). 160p. 1997. 21.95 (*0-87131-819-9*) M Evans.

Muscle Pain: Understanding Its Nature, Diagnosis & Treatment. Siegfried Mense & David Simons. 304p. 65.00 (*0-683-05928-9*) Lppncott W & W.

***Muscle Pain, Myofascial Pain & Fibromyalgia: Recent Advances.** Ed. by Leonardo Vecchiet & Maria Adele Giamberardino. LC 99-39599. (Journal of Musculoskeletal Pain Ser.: Vol. 7, Nos. 1/2). 360p. 1999. 89.95 (*0-7890-0795-9*); pap. text 49.95 (*0-7890-0828-9*) Haworth Pr.

Muscle Pain Relief in Ninety Seconds: The Fold & Hold Method. Dale Anderson. (Illus.). 192p. 1995. 10.95 (*1-56561-058-X*) Wiley.

Muscle Pain Relief in 90 Seconds: The Fold & Hold Method. Dale L. Anderson. 160p. 1994. pap. 11.95 (*0-471-34689-6*) Wiley.

Muscle Pain Syndromes & Fibromyalgia: Pressure Algometry for Quantification of Diagnosis & Treatment Outcome. Ed. by Andrew A. Fischer. LC 98-12625. 158p. 1998. 39.95 (*0-7890-0510-7*, Hawrth Medical) Haworth Pr.

Muscle Physiology & Biochemistry. Shoichi Imai et al. LC 98-36698. (Developments in Molecular & Cellular Biochemistry Ser.). 1998. write for info. (*0-7923-8264-1*) Kluwer Academic.

Muscle Physiology & Cardiac Function. Lincoln E. Ford. (Illus.). 400p. 2000. text 60.00 (*1-884125-72-7*) Cooper Pubng.

Muscle Planes. Michael O'Leary. (Illus.). 128p. 1998. pap. text 20.00 (*0-7881-5493-1*) DIANE Pub.

Muscle Powered Blimps: Ulta Light Gas Blimps. Robert J. Recks. (Illus.). 225p. 1998. pap. text 30.00 (*0-937568-30-9*) Recks Pubns.

Muscle Regeneration. fac. ed. Ed. by Alexander Mauro. LC 77-90593. (Illus.). 576p. pap. 178.60 (*0-7837-7263-7*, 204704200005) Bks Demand.

Muscle Relaxants. 1995. 158.00 (*0-387-70168-0*) Spr-Verlag.

Muscle Relaxants: Physiologic & Pharmacologic Aspects. Ed. by K. Fukushima & R. Ochiai. 415p. 1995. 173.00 (*4-431-70168-0*) Spr-Verlag.

Muscle Relaxants in Anaesthesia. Ed. by Nigel J. N. Harper & M. J. Pollard. (Illus.). 280p. 1995. text 49.95 (*0-340-55155-0*, Pub. by E A) OUP.

Muscle Scanning: Interpreting EMG Scans, 1 of 3. Barbara J. Headley. (Illus.). 95p. (Orig.). 1990. pap. 14.00 (*0-929538-05-6*) Innovat Systems.

Muscle Spasm, Pain & Marijuana Therapy: Testimony from Federal & State Court Proceedings on Marijuana's Medical Use. Ed. by Robert C. Randall. LC 91-71175. (Marijuana, Medicine & the Law Ser.). 237p. 1991. pap. 14.95 (*0-936485-06-X*, Galen Pr DC) Lkng Glass Pubns.

Muscle Strength. Ed. by Karin Harms-Ringdahl. LC 92-48964. (International Perspectives in Physical Therapy Ser.: No. 8). (Illus.). 288p. 1995. pap. text 44.95 (*0-443-04336-1*) Church.

Muscle Testing Handbook. Virginia Pact et al. 194p. 1984. 36.95 (*0-316-68768-5*, Little Brwn Med Div) Lppncott W & W.

Muscle Transplantation. Ed. by G. Freilinger et al. (Illus.). 320p. 1981. 123.00 (*0-387-81636-4*) Spr-Verlag.

Muscle Wires Project Book: A Hands-on Guide to Amazing Robotic Muscles That Shorten When Electrically Powered. rev. ed. Roger G. Gilbertson. Ed. by Celene De Miranda. LC 93-77383. (Illus.). 128p. 1993. pap. 59.95 (*1-879896-16-8*, 3-168); pap. 34.95 (*1-879896-14-1*, 3-141) Mondo-tronics.

Muscle Wires Project Book: A Hands-on Guide to Amazing Robotic Muscles That Shorten When Electrically Powered. 3rd rev. ed. Roger G. Gilbertson. Ed. by Celene De Miranda. LC 93-77383. (Illus.). 128p. 1993. pap. 17.95 (*1-879896-13-3*, 3-133) Mondo-tronics.

***MuscleMag International's Anabolic Edge: Secrets for That Extra Lean Muscle Mass.** Gerard Thorne & Phil Embleton. Ed. & Photos by Robert Kennedy. Photos by Irvin Gelb. (Illus.). 144p. 2000. pap. 24.95 (*1-55210-016-2*, Pub. by MuscleMag Intl) BookWorld.

Musclemag International's Anabolic Primer: An Information-Packed Reference Guide to Ergogenic Aids for Hardcore Body Builders. Phil Embleton & Gerard Thorne. (Illus.). 576p. 1998. pap. 29.95 (*1-55210-010-3*, Pub. by MuscleMag Intl) BookWorld.

***MuscleMag International's North American Bodybuilding & Fitness Directory: Find What You're Looking For.** Mark Shaw. Ed. & Photos by Robert Kennedy. Photos by Irvin Gelb et al. (Illus.). 2000. pap. 19.95 (*1-55210-018-9*, Pub. by MuscleMag Intl) BookWorld.

Muscles. Steve Parker. LC 97-8023. (Look at Your Body! Ser.). (Illus.). 32p. (J). (gr. 4-6). 1997. lib. bdg. 20.90 (*0-7613-0612-9*, Copper Beech Bks) Millbrook Pr.

Muscles: A Study Aid for Students of the Allied Health Professions. Delia Barreto. (Illus.). 48p. (C). 1974. pap. 3.00 (*0-87936-005-4*) Scholium Intl.

Muscles: An Illustrated Guide. Nathan Young. (Illustrated Guide to Anatomy Ser.: Vol. 1). (Illus.). 32p. (C). Date not set. student ed., wbk. ed. 20.00 (*1-893435-08-3*) Lakeshore Comm.

***Muscles: Our Muscular System.** Seymour Simon. LC 97-44758. (Illus.). 32p. (J). (gr. k-3). 1998. 16.00 (*0-688-14642-2*, Wm Morrow); 15.93 (*0-688-14643-0*, Wm Morrow) Morrow Avon.

***Muscles: Our Muscular System.** Seymour Simon. LC 97-44758. (Illus.). 32p. (J). (ps-3). 2000. mass mkt. 6.95 (*0-688-17720-4*, Wm Morrow) Morrow Avon.

Muscles: Testing & Function. 4th rev. ed. Florence P. Kendall et al. LC 92-49150. (Illus.). 448p. 1993. 52.00 (*0-683-04576-8*) Lppncott W & W.

Muscles: Testing & Function with Posture & Pain. 4th ed. Florence Peterson Kendall et al. 451p. text 68.00 (*0-7817-2137-7*) Lppncott W & W.

Muscles Alive: Their Functions Revealed by Electromyography. 5th ed. John V. Basmajian & Carlo J. DeLuca. (Illus.). 562p. 1985. 65.00 (*0-683-00414-X*) Lppncott W & W.

Muscles & Bones see Human Body

Muscles & Bones. Jane Saunderson. LC 90-42882. (Illus.). 32p. (J). (gr. 4-6). 1992. lib. bdg. 18.60 (*0-8167-2088-6*) Troll Communs.

Muscles & Bones. Jane Saunderson. LC 90-42882. (Illus.). 32p. (J). (gr. 4-6). 1997. pap. 4.95 (*0-8167-2089-4*) Troll Communs.

Muscles & Drug Effects: Medical Subject Analysis with Research Bibliography. John C. Bartone, II. LC 84-45657. 150p. 1987. 47.50 (*0-88164-216-9*); pap. 44.50 (*0-88164-217-7*) ABBE Pubs Assn.

Muscles & Molecules: Uncovering the Principles of Biological Motion. Gerald H. Pollack. 300p. (C). 1990. 55.00 (*0-9626895-0-5*) Ebner & Sons.

Muscles & Movements: A Basis for Human Kinesiology. rev. ed. John V. Basmajian & M. A. MacConaill. LC 76-6883. 412p. 1977. 42.50 (*0-88275-398-3*) Krieger.

Muscles & Physiology: Medical Analysis Index with Research Bibliography. Peter B. Zeiderhof. LC 85-47576. 150p. 1987. 47.50 (*0-88164-326-2*); pap. 44.50 (*0-88164-327-0*) ABBE Pubs Assn.

Muscles as Molecular & Metabolic Machines. Peter W. Hochachka. LC 94-6564. 176p. 1994. boxed set 104.95 (*0-8493-2468-8*, 2468) CRC Pr.

Muscles, Bull Moose from Alaska. Douglas DeVries. LC 95-76041. (Illus.). 88p. (Orig.). (J). (gr. k-5). 1995. pap. text 12.00 (*1-877721-02-6*) Jade Ram Pub.

Muscles in Action: An Approach to Manual Muscle Testing. Joan H. Cole et al. (Illus.). 184p. 1988. pap. 29.00 (*0-443-03613-6*) Church.

Muscles in Motion: S-EMG Analysis of the Range of Motion of the Elbow & Wrist. Gabriel E. Sella. 1993. student ed. 30.00 (*1-884325-04-1*) G E Sella.

Muscles in Motion: S-EMG Analysis of the Range of Motion of the Human Body. Gabriel E. Sella. 1993. student ed. 180.00 (*1-884325-00-9*); student ed. 30.00 (*1-884325-01-7*); student ed. 35.00 (*1-884325-05-X*); student ed. 30.00 (*1-884325-06-8*) G E Sella.

Muscles in Motion: S-EMG Analysis of the Range of Motion of the Knee, the Ankle & the Foot. Gabriel E. Sella. 1993. student ed. 30.00 (*1-884325-07-6*) G E Sella.

Muscles in Motion: S-EMG Analysis of the Range of Motion of the Shoulder. Gabriel E. Sella. 1993. student ed. 30.00 (*1-884325-03-3*) G E Sella.

Muscles in Motion: S-EMG Analysis of the Range of Motion of the Trunk. Gabriel E. Sella. 1993. student ed. 30.00 (*1-884325-02-5*) G E Sella.

Muscles, Masses & Motion: The Physiology of Normality, Hypotonicity, Spasticity & Rigidity. E. Geoffrey Walsh. (Clinics in Developmental Medicine Ser.: No. 125). (Illus.). 220p. (C). 1993. text 59.95 (*0-521-43229-4*) Cambridge U Pr.

An Asterisk (*) at the beginning of an entry indicates that the title is appearing for the first time.

Muscles, Myths & Movies: An Acquired Taste on Video Guide to the Cinematic Adventures of Hercules. Stephen Flacassier. (Acquired Taste on Video Ser.). 72p. (Orig.). 1994. pap. 6.95 (*0-9641643-0-2*) Rabbits Garage.

Muscles, Nerves, & Movement: Kinesiology in Daily Living. 2nd ed. Barbara Tyldesley & June I. Grieve. LC 96-13775. (Illus.). 360p. 1996. pap. text 39.95 (*0-632-04096-3*) Blackwell Sci.

Muscles of the Mind Program. Marco Meirovitz & Paul Jacobs. 1992. pap. 14.99 (*0-89824-186-3*) Trillium Pr.

Muscles of the Mind Program: Brain Muscle Builders. Marco Meirovitz & Paul Jacobs. 1992. pap. 14.99 (*0-89824-185-5*) Trillium Pr.

Muscles of the Mind Program: Verbal Thinking. Marco Meirovitz & Stuart Dods. 1992. pap. 14.99 (*0-89824-193-6*) Trillium Pr.

Muscles of the Mind Program: Visual Thinking. Marco Meirovitz & Paul Jacobs. 1992. pap. 14.99 (*0-89824-184-7*) Trillium Pr.

Muscles, the Moose Calf. Douglas DeVries. LC 89-84651. (Illus.). 32p. (Orig.). (J). (ps-3). 1989. pap. text 10.00 (*1-877721-00-X*) Jade Ram Pub.

Muscles Visits Anchorage. Douglas DeVries. LC 90-61154. (Illus.). 32p. (Orig.). (J). (ps-3). 1990. pap. text 10.00 (*1-877721-01-8*) Jade Ram Pub.

Musclesex: A Collection of Erotic Short Stories. Greg Nero. 160p. (Orig.). 1995. pap. 14.95 (*0-943595-59-2*) Leyland Pubns.

Muscle/Tendon & Marrow/Brain Washing Chi Kung see Qigong, the Secret of Youth: Da Mo's Muscle/Tendon & Marrow/Brain Washing Classics

Muscletown USA: Bob Hoffman & the Manly Culture of York Barbell. John Fair. LC 98-39333. (Illus.). 65.00p. 1999. 60.00 (*0-271-01854-2*) Pa St U Pr.

Muscletown USA: Bob Hoffman & the Manly Culture of York Barbell. John D. Fair. LC 98-39333. (Illus.). 420p. 1999. pap. 23.50 (*0-271-01855-0*) Pa St U Pr.

Muscologia Gallica, 1884-94, 2 parts in 1. P. T. Husnot. (Illus.). 1968. 90.00 (*90-6123-082-9*) Lubrecht & Cramer.

Muscovite Law Code (Ulozhenie) of 1649 Pt. 1: Text & Translation. Ed. & Tr. by Richard Hellie. LC 87-32063. (Laws of Russia Ser.: Series I, Vol. 3). 720p. (C). 1988. 195.00 (*1-884445-05-5*) C Schlacks Pub.

Muscovites in California: Or, Rather Demonstration of the Passage from North America. F. Guiseppe Torrubia. 1996. pap. 14.95 (*0-87770-590-9*) Ye Galleon.

Muscovites in California: Or, Rather Demonstration of the Passage from North America. F. Guiseppe Torrubia. LC 96-19882. 1996. 19.95 (*0-87770-563-1*) Ye Galleon.

Muscovy & Sweden in the Thirty Years' War, 1630-1655. B. F. Porshnev. Ed. by Paul Dukes. Tr. by Brian Pearce. 278p. (C). 1996. text 64.95 (*0-521-45139-6*) Cambridge U Pr.

Muscovy & the Mongols: Cross-Cultural Influences on the Steppe Frontier, 1304-1589. Donald Ostrowski. LC 97-21385. 300p. (C). 1998. 59.95 (*0-521-59085-X*) Cambridge U Pr.

Muscovy Duck: Cairina Moschata Domestica: Origins Dispersal Associated Aspects of the Geography of Domestication. R. A. Donkin. 194p. (C). 1989. text 99.00 (*90-6191-544-9*, Pub. by A A Balkema) Ashgate Pub Co.

Muscovy Merchants of 1555. Thomas S. Willan. LC 72-85754. (Reprints of Economic Classics Ser.). 160p. 1973. reprint ed. 35.00 (*0-678-00929-5*) Kelley.

***Muscular Analysis of Everyday Activities.** Elaine Bukowski. 300p. (C). 2000. pap. text 32.00 (*1-55642-462-0*) SLACK Inc.

Muscular Christianity: Embodying the Victorian Age. Ed. by Donald E. Hall. (Cambridge Studies in Nineteenth-Century Literature & Culture: No. 2). 258p. (C). 1994. text 59.95 (*0-521-45318-6*) Cambridge U Pr.

Muscular Christianity: Evangelical Protestants & the Development of American Sport. Tony Ladd & James A. Mathisen. LC 99-10255. (Illus.). 288p. 1999. pap. 20.99 (*0-8010-5847-3*, Bridgept Bks) Baker Bks.

Muscular Contraction. Ed. by Robert M. Simmons. (Illus.). 313p. (C). 1992. text 74.95 (*0-521-41774-0*) Cambridge U Pr.

Muscular Degeneration. Lylas G. Mogk. mass mkt. write for info. (*0-345-42599-5*, Ballantine) Ballantine Pub Grp.

***Muscular Dynamics: Electromyographic Assessment of Energy & Motion.** Gabriel E. Sella. (Illus.). 350p. 2000. text 120.00 (*1-884325-14-9*) G E Sella.

***Muscular Dystrophy.** rev. ed. Gail Lemley Burnett. LC 00-8401. (Health Watch Ser.). (Illus.). 48p. (YA). (gr. 5 up). 2000. lib. bdg. 18.95 (*0-7660-1651-X*) Enslow Pubs.

Muscular Dystrophy: Biomedical Aspects. Ed. by Setsuro Ebashi & E. Ozawa. (Illus.). 302p. 1983. 73.95 (*0-387-12342-3*) Spr-Verlag.

Muscular Dystrophy: Methods & Protocols. Ed. by Katherine M. D. Bushby & Louise V. B. Anderson. (Methods in Molecular Medicine Ser.: Vol. 43). (Illus.). 300p. 2000. 99.50 (*0-89603-695-2*) Humana.

Muscular Dystrophy: Proceedings of the International Symposium on Muscular Dystrophy, Held November 25-27, 1980 in Tokyo. International Symposium on Muscular Dystrophy Staf. Ed. by Setsuro Ebashi. LC 83-160940. (Japan Medical Research Foundation Publication: No. 16). 531p. 1982. reprint ed. pap. 164.70 (*0-608-01197-5*, 206188600001) Bks Demand.

Muscular Dystrophy: The Facts. Alan E. Emery. (Facts Ser.). (Illus.). 152p. 1994. pap. text 19.95 (*0-19-262449-0*) OUP.

***Muscular Dystrophy: The Facts.** 2nd ed. Alan Emery. (Illus.). 176p. 2000. pap. text 19.95 (*0-19-263217-5*) OUP.

Muscular Dystrophy & Allied Diseases: Impact on Patients, Family & Staff. Ed. by Leon I. Charash et al. LC 86-82709. (Current Thanatology Ser.). 90p. 1988. pap. 15.95 (*0-930194-38-1*) Ctr Thanatology.

Muscular Dystrophy & Other Neuromuscular Diseases: Psychosocial Issues. Leon I. Charash et al. (Loss, Grief & Care Ser.: Vol. 4 Nos. 3 & 4). (Illus.). 270p. 1991. text 49.95 (*1-56024-077-6*) Haworth Pr.

Muscular Dystrophy in Children: A Guide for Families. Irwin M. Siegel. LC 99-23878. 136p. 1999. pap. 19.95 (*1-888799-33-1*) Demos Medical.

Muscular Dystrophy, 1976: Proceedings of the Symposium, Jerusalem, 1976. Muscular Dystrophy Symposium Staff. Ed. by Gordon C. Robin & George Falewski de Leon. (Illus.). 1977. 42.75 (*3-8055-2680-6*) S Karger.

Muscular Exercise & the Lung: Proceedings of a Symposium Held at the University of Wisconsin-Madison, 1976, with Support from Syntex Laboratories, Inc., & Boehringer Ingleheim Ltd. Ed. by Jerome A. Dempsey & Charles E. Reed. LC 76-16666. 415p. 1977. reprint ed. pap. 128.70 (*0-608-01954-2*, 206260900003) Bks Demand.

Muscular Fitness Through Resistance Training. 2nd ed. Tom Thomas. 140p. 1991. pap. 16.95 (*0-945483-09-0*) E Bowers Pub.

Muscular Music. Terrance Hayes. 70p. 1999. pap. 10.95 (*1-882688-21-X*) Tia Chucha Pr.

***Muscular System.** Helen Frost. (Human Body Systems Ser.). 24p. (J). (ps-2). 2000. lib. bdg. 13.25 (*0-7368-0650-4*, Pebble Bks) Capstone Pr.

Muscular System. Alvin Silverstein et al. (Human Body Systems Ser.). (Illus.). 96p. (J). (gr. 5-8). 1995. lib. bdg. 21.90 (*0-8050-2836-6*) TFC Bks NY.

Muscle Hypertrophy of Genetic Origin & Its Use to Improve Beef Production. J. W. King & F. Menissier. 1982. text 249.00 (*90-247-2637-9*) Kluwer Academic.

Musculine Cross & Ancient Sex Worship. Sha Rocco. 65p. 1994. reprint ed. spiral bd. 10.00 (*0-7873-1117-0*) Hlth Research.

Musculo Skeletal Diseases & Homeopathy. Luc De Schepper. 200p. (Orig.). (C). 1994. pap. 39.95 (*0-942501-02-0*) Full of Life.

Musculo Skeletal MRI & Ultrasound: A Correlative Atlas & Teaching File. (Illus.). 576p. 2000. text 145.00 (*0-8151-1200-9*, 31718) Mosby Inc.

Musculo-Skeletal Problems in Emergency Medicine. Jim Wardrope. (Illus.). 348p. 1998. text (*0-19-262863-1*) OUP.

Musculo-Skeletal Problems in Emergency Medicine. Jim Wardrope & Bryan English. (Oxford Handbooks in Emergency Medicine Ser.). (Illus.). 348p. 1998. pap. text 47.50 (*0-19-262862-3*) OUP.

Musculocutaneous Flap Reconstruction of the Head & Neck. William R. Panje et al. LC 89-3746. 256p. 1989. reprint ed. pap. 79.40 (*0-608-04678-7*, 206539900004) Bks Demand.

Musculoskeletal Anatomy: A Text & Guide to Dissection for Students in the Allied Health Sciences. Gene L. Colborn & David B. Lause. LC 93-13736. (Illus.). 247p. (C). 1993. pap. 19.95 (*1-85070-523-2*) Prthnon Pub.

Musculoskeletal & Lameness Disorders, Vol. 1. 1996. 79.95 (*0-614-25070-6*) Equistar Pub.

Musculoskeletal Assessment: An Integrated Approach. Barbara M. Edwardson. LC 92-13349. (Illus.). 224p. (Orig.). (C). 1992. pap. text 34.95 (*1-879105-69-1*, 0332) Thomson Learn.

Musculoskeletal Assessment: Joint Range of Motion & Manual Muscle Strength. Hazel Clarkson. (Illus.). 384p. (C). 1989. pap. text 42.00 (*0-683-01711-X*) Lppncott W & W.

Musculoskeletal Assessment: Joint Range of Motion & Manual Muscle Strength. 2nd ed. Hazel M. Clarkson. LC 99-33414. 432p. 2000. pap. 48.00 (*0-683-30384-8*) Lppncott W & W.

Musculoskeletal Clinical Metrology. Nicholas Bellamy. 384p. (C). 1993. text 254.00 (*0-7923-8828-3*) Kluwer Academic.

Musculoskeletal Conditions (aafp) The Academy Collection--Quick Reference Guides for Family Physicians. Walter L. Calmbach. pap. text 29.95 (*0-683-30422-4*) Lppncott W & W.

Musculoskeletal Conditions in the United States. 200p. 1992. 25.00 (*0-89203-063-1*) Amer Acad Ortho Surg.

Musculoskeletal Disease Test & Syllabus. William A. Murphy, Jr. et al. (Professional Self-Evaluation & Continuing Education Program Ser.: Vol. 37). (Illus.). 900p. 1994. 220.00 (*1-55903-036-4*) Am Coll Radiology.

Musculoskeletal Disorders. Barbara M. Edwardson. (Illus.). 318p. (Orig.). (C). 1995. pap. text 42.95 (*1-56593-170-X*, 0469) Thomson Learn.

Musculoskeletal Disorders: A Practical Guide for Diagnosis & Rehabilitation. Ralph Buschbacher. LC 93-36959. (Illus.). 416p. 1993. text 89.00 (*1-56372-077-9*) Buttrwrth-Heinemann.

***Musculoskeletal Disorders: Healing Methods from Chinese Medicine & Orthopaedic Medicine.** Alon Marcus. LC 98-34889. 650p. 1999. 85.00 (*1-55643-282-8*) North Atlantic.

Musculoskeletal Disorders & Congenital Deformities. Arnold J. Rudolph. (Atlas of the Newborn Ser.: Vol. 2). (Illus.). 1997. boxed set 89.95 incl. cd-rom (*1-55009-032-1*) DEKR.

Musculoskeletal Disorders of the Lower Extremities. Ed. by Lawrence M. Oloff. LC 93-7250. 1994. text 142.00 (*0-7216-3716-7*, W B Saunders Co) Harcrt Hlth Sci Grp.

Musculoskeletal Examination. Jeffery Gross et al. LC 95-25651. (Illus.). 300p. 1995. pap. 49.95 (*0-86542-410-1*) Blackwell Sci.

Musculoskeletal Function: An Anatomy & Kinesiology Laboratory Manual. Dortha Esch & Marvin Lepley. LC 73-93577. (Illus.). 134p. 1974. pap. 9.95 (*0-8166-0716-8*) U of Minn Pr.

Musculoskeletal Functional Human Anatomy. Joseph Myrer. 176p. (C). 1996. pap. text, spiral bd. 36.95 (*0-7872-1912-6*, 41191201) Kendall-Hunt.

Musculoskeletal Imaging. John A. Markisz. 1991. 159.95 (*0-316-54613-5*, Little Brwn Med Div) Lppncott W & W.

Musculoskeletal Imaging. Theodore Miller. (Illus.). 546p. 1999. write for info. (*0-07-043257-0*) McGraw-Hill HPD.

Musculoskeletal Imaging: A Teaching File. Felix S. Chew. LC 99-15483. (Illus.). 644p. 1998. write for info. (*0-683-30175-6*) Lppncott W & W.

Musculoskeletal Imaging: Diagnostic & Therapeutic Procedures. Ed. by Jacqueline C. Hodge. LC 96-45275. (Vademecum Series Book). (Illus.). xii, 250p. 1997. 98.00 (*3-8055-6496-1*) S Karger.

Musculoskeletal Imaging: The Requisites. David J. Sartoris. LC 95-25625. (Requisites Ser.). (Illus.). 432p. (C). (gr. 13). 1995. text 85.00 (*0-8151-8002-0*, 26257) Mosby Inc.

Musculoskeletal Infection. Ed. by John L. Esterhai, Jr. et al. 459p. 1991. 95.00 (*0-89203-053-4*) Amer Acad Ortho Surg.

Musculoskeletal Infections. Ed. by Sean P. Hughes & Robert H. Fitzgerald, Jr. LC 85-5295. (Illus.). 254p. reprint ed. pap. 78.80 (*0-8357-7622-0*, 205694500096) Bks Demand.

***Musculoskeletal Injection Skills: Principles & Practice.** Monica Kesson & Elaine Atkins. (Illus.). 208p. 2000. pap. text 50.00 (*0-7506-4372-2*) Buttrwrth-Heinemann.

Musculoskeletal Injuries. William D. Arnold & John P. Lyden. (Illus.). 800p. 1987. text. write for info. (*0-07-044994-5*) McGraw.

Musculoskeletal Magnetic Resonance. Edward J. Easton, Jr. & John A. Powers. 178p. 1985. 41.50 (*0-316-20402-1*, Little Brwn Med Div) Lppncott W & W.

Musculoskeletal Manifestations of AIDS. Jamshid Tehranzadeh. 181p. (Orig.). (C). 1994. pap. text 37.50 (*0-87527-509-5*) Green.

Musculoskeletal Manual. 2nd ed. Jacob S. Birnbaum. LC 79-594. 384p. 1985. text 55.00 (*0-8089-1796-X*, 790594, Grune & Strat) Harcrt Hlth Sci Grp.

Musculoskeletal Medicine: The Spine. Loic Burn. (C). 1990. text 173.50 (*0-7923-8913-1*) Kluwer Academic.

Musculoskeletal Pain: Principles of Physical Diagnosis & Physical Treatment. 2nd ed. David A. Zohn & John M. Mennell. 261p. 1987. 65.00 (*0-316-98897-9*, Little Brwn Med Div) Lppncott W & W.

Musculoskeletal Pain Emanating from the Head & Neck: Current Concepts in Diagnosis, Management, & Cost Containment. Ed. by Murray E. Allen. LC 96-31753. (Journal of Musculoskeletal Pain: Vol. 4, No. 4). 202p. (C). 1996. 34.95 (*0-7890-0005-9*) Haworth Pr.

Musculoskeletal Pain, Myofascial Pain Syndrome, & the Fibromyalgia Syndrome: Proceedings from the Second World Congress on Myofascial Pain & Fibromyalgia. Ed. by Bente Danneskiold-Samsoe & Birger Lund. LC 93-30041. (Journal of Musculoskeletal Pain: Vol. 1, Nos. 3-4). (Illus.). 334p. 1993. pap. text 49.95 (*1-56024-508-5*); lib. bdg. 89.95 (*1-56024-485-2*) Haworth Pr.

Musculoskeletal Primary Care. Sharon J. Gates & Pekka A. Mooar. LC 98-38544. 376p. 1998. pap. text 42.00 (*0-7817-1430-3*) Lppncott W & W.

Musculoskeletal Radiology. Sergio Fern[00a0]ndez Tapia. 400p. 1999. text. write for info. (*0-7817-1662-4*) Lppncott W & W.

Musculoskeletal Soft-Tissue Aging: Impact on Mobility. Ed. by Joseph A. Buckwalter et al. LC 93-41652. 423p. 1994. 105.00 (*0-89203-086-0*) Amer Acad Ortho Surg.

Musculoskeletal Surgery for Cancer. Paul Sugarbaker & Martin Malawar. (Illus.). 413p. 1992. text 115.00 (*0-86577-368-8*) Thieme Med Pubs.

Musculoskeletal System. (Assessment Review Ser.). 1993. pap. text 36.95 incl. VHS (*0-87434-560-X*) Springhouse Corp.

Musculoskeletal System. Brian Feinberg. Ed. by Dale C. Garell & Solomon H. Snyder. (Encyclopedia of Health Ser.). (Illus.). 116p. (YA). (gr. 7 up). 1994. lib. bdg. 19.95 (*0-7910-0028-1*) Chelsea Hse.

Musculoskeletal System: An Integrated Textbook of Diagnosis & Medical Surgical Management of Musculoskeletal Disorders. D. I. Rowley & John A. Dent. LC 96-85637. (Illus.). 352p. 1997. pap. text 19.99 (*0-412-62700-0*, Pub. by E A) OUP.

Musculoskeletal System: Differential Diagnosis from Symptoms & Physical Signs. John M. Mennell. LC 91-4866. 208p. 1992. 79.00 (*0-8342-0255-7*) Aspen Pub.

Musculoskeletal System: Physiological Basics. James G. Gamble. LC 87-16657. 204p. 1988. reprint ed. pap. 63.30 (*0-608-04718-X*, 206543900004) Bks Demand.

Musculoskeletal System Course. Competence Assurance Systems Staff. (Illus.). 1981. pap. text 45.00 (*0-89147-066-2*) CAS.

Musculoskeletal Tissue Banking. William W. Tomford. LC 92-49616. (Illus.). 256p. 1993. reprint ed. pap. 79.40 (*0-608-07203-6*, 206742800009) Bks Demand.

Musculoskeletal Tumor Surgery, Vol. 1. William F. Enneking. LC 83-2045. (Illus.). 789p. reprint ed. pap. 200.00 (*0-8357-6573-3*, 203595900001) Bks Demand.

Musculoskeletal Tumor Surgery, Vol. 2. William F. Enneking. LC 83-2045. (Illus.). 867p. reprint ed. pap. 200.00 (*0-8357-6574-1*, 203595900002) Bks Demand.

Musculoskeletal Ultrasound. Ed. by Bruno D. Fornage. LC 94-44679. (Clinics in Diagnostic Ultrasound Ser.: Vol. 30). 1995. text 95.00 (*0-443-08909-4*) Church.

Musculoskeletal Ultrasound. Marnix Van Holsbeek. (Illus.). 344p. (C). (gr. 13). 1990. text 110.00 (*0-8151-8975-3*, 22127) Mosby Inc.

***Musculoskeletal Ultrasound.** 2nd ed. Marnix Van Holsbeeck. (Illus.). 448p. (C). 1999. text. write for info. incl. cd-rom (*0-323-00018-5*) Mosby Inc.

***Musculoskeletl Imaging: The Requisite.** 2nd ed. Manaster. 2001. text. write for info. (*0-323-01189-6*) Mosby Inc.

Muse. Michael Cecilione. 320p. 1999. text 23.95 (*1-57566-313-9*) Kensgtn Pub Corp.

***Muse.** Michael Cecilione. 2000. mass mkt. 6.99 (*0-7860-1134-3*) Kensgtn Pub Corp.

Muse. Ahmad Nawaz. LC 98-70772. xiv, 120p. 1998. pap. 10.00 (*1-58225-027-8*) Ananta Prakashani.

***Muse.** Ahmad Nawaz. LC 00-131825. 120p. 2000. pap. 10.00 (*1-58225-227-0*) Ananta Prakashani.

Muse: Poems from Hollywood. Mark Dunster. 11p. 1998. pap. write for info. (*0-89642-498-7*) Linden Pubs.

Muse & Drudge. Harryette Mullen. 88p. (Orig.). 1995. pap. 12.50 (*0-935162-15-1*) Singing Horse.

Muse & the Librarian, 10. Roy P. Basler. LC 72-780. (Contributions in American Studies: No. 10). 207p. 1974. 49.95 (*0-8371-6134-7*, BML/, Greenwood Pr) Greenwood.

Muse du Departement & un Prince de la Boheme. Honore de Balzac. (FRE.). (Orig.). 1984. pap. 16.95 (*0-7859-1992-9*, 2070375420) Fr & Eur.

Muse du Departement & un Prince de la Boheme. Honore de Balzac. (Folio Ser.: No. 1542). (FRE.). (Orig.). pap. 13.95 (*2-07-037542-0*) Schoenhof.

Muse Eclectic. Rosemary Schmidt. Ed. by Carry Neumann & Ginny Ballor. 40p. (Orig.). (C). 1997. pap. 3.00 (*1-882294-26-2*) Green Gate.

Muse for Heroes: Nine Centuries of the Epic in France. William Calin. (Romance Ser.). 527p. 1983. text 50.00 (*0-8020-5599-0*) U of Toronto Pr.

Muse from the Bridge. John B. Leach. LC 97-91125. 1998. pap. 8.95 (*0-533-12565-0*) Vantage.

Muse in Council: Being Essays on Poets & Poetry. John Drinkwater. 303p. 1977. 23.95 (*0-8369-1649-2*) Ayer.

Muse in the Machine: Computerizing the Poetry of Human Thought. David Gelernter. LC 93-49721. 209p. 1994. 22.95 (*0-02-911602-3*) Free Pr.

Muse Is Always Half-Dressed in New Orleans & Other Essays. Andrei Codrescu. 208p. 1995. pap. 10.00 (*0-312-13570-X*, Picador USA) St Martin.

Muse Learns to Write: Reflections on Orality & Literacy from Antiquity to the Present. Eric A. Havelock. LC 86-9084. 144p. (C). 1988. reprint ed. pap. 12.00 (*0-300-04382-1*) Yale U Pr.

MUSE Method for Usability Engineering. Kee Y. Lim & John Long. (Series in Human-Computer Interaction: No. 8). (Illus.). 350p. (C). 1995. text 54.95 (*0-521-47494-9*) Cambridge U Pr.

***Muse 'n Washington: Beltway Ballads & Beyond.** James W. Symington. LC 98-67435. (Illus.). 349p. 1999. pap. 22.95 (*1-57197-142-4*) Pentland Pr.

Muse of Abandonment: Origin, Identity, Mastery, in Five American Poets. Lee Upton. LC 98-12153. 1998. 32.50 (*0-8387-5396-5*) Bucknell U Pr.

Muse of Art Vol. 4: Geodyssey. Piers Anthony. LC 99-12905. 448p. 1999. 26.95 (*0-312-86896-0*, Pub. by Tor Bks) St Martin.

Muse of Fire: Literature, Art, & War. A. D. Harvey. LC 97-44896. 1998. 45.00 (*1-85285-168-6*) Hambledon Press.

***Muse of History & the Science of Culture.** Robert L. Carneiro. LC 00-25106. (Illus.). 300p. 2000. pap. 37.50 (*0-306-46273-7*) Kluwer Academic.

Muse of Menus: Stories from Life & Cooking. Constance Crawford. LC 88-7100. (Illus.). 160p. (Orig.). 1988. pap. 9.95 (*0-936784-64-4*) J Daniel.

Muse of Modernity: Essays on Culture as Development in Africa. Philip G. Altbach. LC 97-167780. 1997. pap. text 19.95 (*0-86543-561-8*) Africa World.

Muse of Modernity: Essays on Culture As Development in Africa. Ed. by Philip G. Altbach & Salah M. Hassan. LC 97-167780. 248p. 69.95 (*0-86543-560-X*) Africa World.

***Muse of the Day.** Frank Greenberg. 1999. pap. write for info. (*1-58235-225-9*) Watermrk Pr.

***Muse of Weird.** Lonnie Bailey. 1999. pap. write for info. (*1-58235-220-8*) Watermrk Pr.

Muse Reborn: The Poetry of Antonio Ferreira. T. F. Earle. 224p. 1988. 59.00 (*0-19-815856-4*) OUP.

Muse Spoke French: Selected Poems. Tr. by Kendall Lappin from FRE. LC 94-70671. 128p. (Orig.). 1994. pap. 9.95 (*1-878580-59-0*) Asylum Arts.

Muse Strikes Back: A Poetic Response by Women to Men. Katherine McAlpine. LC 97-25390. 360p. 1997. pap. text 15.95 (*1-885266-49-9*) Story Line.

Muse That Sings: Composers Speak about the Creative Process. Ann McCutchan. LC 98-47028. (Illus.). 288p. 1999. 35.00 (*0-19-512707-2*) OUP.

Mused: Poems from Hollywood. Mark Dunster. 11p. 1998. pap. 5.00 (*0-89642-510-X*) Linden Pubs.

Musee Botanique de M. Benjamin Delessert. A. Lasegue. 1970. reprint ed. 65.00 (*3-7682-0686-6*) Lubrecht & Cramer.

Musee de Caire. Etienne Drioton. (ENG & FRE., Illus.). 1949. lib. bdg. 24.95 (*0-8288-3990-5*) Fr & Eur.

***Musee d'Orsay.** Alexandra Bonfante-Warren. (Illus.). 320p. 2000. 75.00 (*0-88363-502-X*, Pub. by H L Levin) Publishers Group.

***Musee D'orsay.** Vanina Costa. 1998. pap. text 12.95 (*2-86656-123-6*) Scala Edit.

***Musee d'Orsay.** Konemann Inc. Staff. 2000. 14.95 (*3-8290-2671-4*) Konemann.

Musee D'Orsay: Sculpture. Anne Pingeot. (Illus.). 128p. 1999. 30.00 (*1-85759-200-X*) Scala Books.

***Musee d'Orsay: 100 Impressionist Masterpieces.** Laurence Madeline. (Illus.). 144p. 2000. pap. 19.95 (*2-86656-209-7*, Pub. by Scala Edit) Antique Collect.

Musei Lugduno-Batavi Inscriptiones Graecae et Latinae, 2 vols. Leonhard J. Janssen. reprint ed. write for info. (*0-318-72096-5*) G Olms Pubs.

Muselmann: Holocaust Memoirs. Matzner. LC 92-47104. 1993. 20.00 (*0-88125-457-6*) Ktav.

Musenalmanach, 1830-1839. Amadeus Wendt et al. (GER.). lxxi, 3577p. 1988. 698.00 (*3-615-00006-4*, Pub. by Weidmann) Lubrecht & Cramer.

Museo del Prado Inventario General de Pinturas Vol. 1: La Coleccion Real. Ed. by Museo del Prado Staff. (SPA., Illus.). 840p. 1993. 500.00 (*84-239-4311-9*) Elliots Bks.

Museo del Prado Inventario General de Pinturas Vol. 2: El Museo de la Trinidad. Ed. by Museo del Prado Staff. (SPA., Illus.). 514p. 400.00 (*84-239-4312-7*) Elliots Bks.

Museo del Templo Mayor: Diez Anos. Contrib. by Eduardo M. Moctezuma. (SPA., Illus.). 157p. 1997. pap. 40.00 (*970-18-0671-9*, IN92, Pub. by Dir Gen Pubicaiones) UPLAAP.

Museo Immaginario Della Pasta: The "musee Imaginaire" of Pasta. Nigella Lawson. LC 96-160542. (ITA., Illus.). 170p. 1998. 75.00 (*88-422-0544-3*) Allemandi.

Museo J. Paul Getty Guia de la Colecciones. LC 94-42436.Tr. of J. Paul Getty Museum Handbook of Collections. (SPA., Illus.). 226p. (Orig.). 1995. pap. 10.95 (*0-89236-328-2*, Pub. by J P Getty Trust) OUP.

Museology. Richard Ross. (Illus.). 80p. 1989. 65.00 (*0-89381-376-1*) Aperture.

Museos. Jason Cooper. (Lugares Divertidos Para Visitar Ser.).Tr. of Museums. 24p. (J). (gr. k-4). 1994. lib. bdg. 10.95 (*0-86593-239-5*) Rourke Corp.

Muses. Robert S. Dupree et al. LC 94-34955. (Entities Trilogy Ser.). 131p. (Orig.). 1994. pap. 20.00 (*0-911005-26-9*) Dallas Inst Pubns.

Muses. Jean-Luc Nancy. Tr. by Peggy Kamuf. LC 96-10880. (Meridian: Crossing Aesthetics Ser.). 1996. 39.50 (*0-8047-2780-5*) Stanford U Pr.

Muses: Poems from Hollywood. Mark Dunster. 11p. 1998. pap. 5.00 (*0-89642-505-3*) Linden Pubs.

Muses & Masks: Some Classical Genres of Spanish Poetry. Elias L. Rivers. (U. California, Irvine, Hispanic Studies: No. 1). 120p. 1992. 15.50 (*0-936388-53-6*) Juan de la Cuesta.

Muses Common-Weale: Poetry & Politics in the Seventeenth Century. Ed. by Claude J. Summers & Ted-Larry Pebworth. LC 88-4847. 240p. 1989. text 34.95 (*0-8262-0691-3*) U of Mo Pr.

Muses' Concord: Literature, Music & the Visual Arts in the Baroque Age. H. James Jensen. LC 76-11940. (Illus.). 274p. reprint ed. 85.00 (*0-8357-9227-7*, 205521900011) Bks Demand.

Muses Females Are: Martha Moulsworth & Other Women Writers of the English Renaissance. Ed. by Robert C. Evans & Anne C. Little. LC 95-22413. (Locust Hill Literary Studies: No. 20). 315p. (C). 1995. 32.00 (*0-933951-63-9*) Locust Hill Pr.

Muses for the Ammi Shaddai. Astara L. Leopold. 144p. Date not set. pap. 13.95 (*1-885226-26-8*) StarLineage.

***Muses in Arcadia: Cultural Life in the Berkshires.** Timothy Cahill et al. LC 99-58282. (Illus.). 320p. 2000. pap. 19.95 (*1-58157-016-3*, Pub. by Berkshire Hse) Natl Bk Netwk.

Muse's Method: An Introduction to "Paradise Lost" Joseph H. Summers. 230p. 1981. reprint ed. 17.95 (*0-86698-004-0*, P4) Pegasus Pr.

Muses of Gwinn: Art & Nature in a Garden Designed by Warren H. Manning, Charles A. Platt & Ellen Shipman. Robin S. Karson et al. LC 95-8157. (Library of American Landscape History). (Illus.). 216p. 1995. 39.95 (*0-89831-034-2*) Sagapr.

Muses of John Barth: Tradition & Metafiction from Lost in the Funhouse to the Tidewater Tales. Max F. Schulz. LC 89-43483. 240p. reprint ed. pap. 74.40 (*0-608-06140-9*, 206647300008) Bks Demand.

Muses of Resistance: Laboring-Class Women's Poetry in Britain 1739-1796. Donna Landry. (Illus.). 335p. (C). 1990. text 74.95 (*0-521-37412-X*) Cambridge U Pr.

Muses, the Masses, & the Massey Commission. Paul Litt. (Illus.). 336p. (Orig.). 1992. text 50.00 (*0-8020-5003-4*); pap. text 19.95 (*0-8020-6932-0*) U of Toronto Pr.

Muse(sic) John Judson. (Special Ser.: No. 3). 1992. pap. 10.00 (*1-55780-122-3*) Juniper Pr ME.

***Museum.** Susan Canizares & Mark McVeigh. LC 00-23933. (Illus.). (J). 2000. write for info. (*0-439-15375-1*) Scholastic Inc.

Museum. Rita Dove. LC 82-71663. 1983. pap. 12.95 (*0-88748-147-7*) Carnegie-Mellon.

Museum. B. H. Friedman. LC 74-77778. 1974. 15.95 (*0-914590-02-2*); pap. 5.95 (*0-914590-03-0*) Fiction Coll.

Museum. Stuart A. Kallen & Julie Berg. LC 96-22580. (Field Trips Ser.). (Illus.). 24p. (J). (ps-3). 1997. lib. bdg. 13.95 (*1-56239-709-5*) ABDO Pub Co.

Museum: A Reference Guide. Ed. by Michael S. Shapiro & Louis W. Kemp. LC 89-26022. 400p. 1990. lib. bdg. 79.95 (*0-313-23686-0*, SHM/, Greenwood Pr) Greenwood.

Museum: Mixed Metaphors: Fred Wilson. Patterson Sims. 48p. (Orig.). 1993. pap. 6.95 (*0-932216-44-7*) Seattle Art.

Museum Alphabet. Gisela Voss. 1995. 14.00 (*0-87846-384-4*) Mus Fine Arts Boston.

Museum & Gallery Education. Eilean Hooper-Greenhill. (Illus.). 224p. 1992. text 69.00 (*0-7185-1306-1*) St Martin.

Museum & Gallery Education, Vol. 1. Eilean Hooper-Greenhill. 1994. pap. 20.00 (*0-7185-1761-X*) St Martin.

***Museum & Metamorphosis.** Bartolucci. 2000. 25.00 (*1-58243-090-X*, Pub. by Counterpt DC) HarpC.

***Museum & Popular Culture.** Kevin Moore. (Contemporary Issues in Museum Cultures Ser.). 2000. pap. text 24.95 (*0-7185-0227-2*) Leicester U Pr.

Museum & the Photograph: Collecting Photography at the Victoria & Albert Museum, 1853-1990. Mark Haworth-Booth & Anne McCauley. LC 97-46323. (Illus.). 80p. 1998. pap. 17.95 (*0-931102-40-5*) S & F Clark Art.

***Museum & the Web, 2000: Selected Papers from an International Conference.** Ed. by David Bearman & Jennifer Traut. (Illus.). 250p. 2000. pap. 50.00 incl. cd-rom (*1-885626-20-7*) Archives & Mus.

Museum Archaeology in Europe. Ed. by David Gaimster. (Museum Archaeologist; Oxbow Monographs in Archaeology: Vol. 19; No. 39). (Illus.). 192p. 1994. pap. 50.00 (*0-946897-73-5*, Pub. by Oxbow Bks) David Brown.

Museum Architecture. Justin Henderson. (Illus.). 192p. 1998. 50.00 (*1-56496-422-1*) Rockport Pubs.

Museum Architecture in Frankfurt, 1980-1990. Ed. by Vittorio M. Lampugnani. (Illus.). 200p. 1990. 75.00 (*3-7913-1096-8*, Pub. by Prestel) te Neues.

Museum as Muse: Artists Reflect. Kynaston McShine. LC 98-68644. (Illus.). 296p. 1999. 49.50 (*0-8109-6197-0*, Pub. by Abrams) Time Warner.

***Museum as Muse: Artists Reflect.** Kynaston McShine. LC 98-68644. 296p. 1999. 50.00 (*0-87070-091-X*, Pub. by Mus of Modern Art) Abrams.

***Museum as Muse: Artists Reflect.** Kynaston McShine. LC 98-68644. 296p. 1999. pap. 29.95 (*0-87070-092-8*) Mus of Modern Art.

Museum at Midcentury: At Home & Abroad. Ed. by John Elderfield. (Studies in Modern Art: No. 4). (Illus.). 184p. 1994. pap. 19.95 (*0-87070-154-1*, 0-8109-6133-4, Pub. by Mus of Modern Art) Abrams.

Museum at Purgatory. Nick Bantock. LC 98-53766. (Illus.). 128p. 1999. 25.00 (*0-06-757546-3*) HarpC.

Museum Attendant. Jack Rudman. (Career Examination Ser.: C-1374). 1994. pap. 23.95 (*0-8373-1374-0*) Nat Learn.

Museum Basics. Tim Ambrose & Crispin Paine. (Heritage: Care-Preservation-Management Program Ser.). (Illus.). 336p. (C). 1993. pap. 32.99 (*0-415-05770-1*, A7853) Routledge.

Museum Basics. Tim Ambrose & Crispin Paine. (Heritage: Care-Preservation-Management Program Ser.). (Illus.). 196p. (C). (gr. 13). 1993. text 79.95 (*0-415-05769-8*, A7849) Routledge.

Museum Beelden aan Zee. Wim Quist. (Illus.). 128p. 1999. 21.50 (*90-5662-097-5*, 910712, Pub. by NAi Uitgevers) Dist Art Pubs.

Museum Book of Digital Art. Pat Johnson. 1996. 55.00 (*1-56830-268-1*) Hayden.

Museum Builders in the West: The Stanfords As Collectors & Patrons of Art, 1870-1906. Carol M. Osborne et al. LC 85-63383. (Illus.). 1986. pap. 9.95 (*0-937031-10-0*) Stanford Art.

Museum Careers & Training: A Professional Guide. Victor J. Danilov. LC 93-33518. 560p. 1994. lib. bdg. 89.50 (*0-313-28105-X*, Greenwood Pr) Greenwood.

Museum Catalogues: A Foundation for Computer Processing. Brian Abell-Seddon. LC 88-114584. 238p. 1987. reprint ed. pap. 73.80 (*0-7837-9270-0*, 206000700004) Bks Demand.

Museum Collections & Today's Computers. Robert G. Chenhall & David Vance. LC 88-3091. 177p. 1988. lib. bdg. 49.95 (*0-313-25339-0*, CCM/, Greenwood Pr) Greenwood.

Museum Collections of the Essex Institute. Huldah S. Payson. Ed. by Anne Farnam & Bryant F. Tolles. LC 78-67991. (E.I. Museum Booklet Ser.). (Illus.). 1978. pap. 5.95 (*0-88389-070-4*, PEMP192, Essx Institute) Peabody Essex Mus.

Museum Colors. Gisela Voss. (Illus.). 22p. (J). (ps). 1994. bds. 14.00 (*0-87846-369-0*) Mus Fine Arts Boston.

Museum Companion to Los Angeles: A Guidebook to Museums, Historic Houses, Libraries, Botanical Gardens & Zoos. 2nd rev. ed. Borislav Stanic. LC 98-66518. (Illus.). 268p. (Orig.). 1998. pap. 19.95 (*1-889224-02-2*) Museum Pub.

Museum Companion to Los Angeles: A Guidebook to Museums, Historic Houses, Libraries, Botanical Gardens & Zoos in Los Angeles County. Borislav Stanic. LC 96-77668. (Illus.). 270p. (Orig.). 1996. pap. 19.95 (*1-889224-01-4*) Museon Pub.

Museum Culture: Histories, Discourses, Spectacles. Ed. by Daniel J. Sherman & Irit Rogoff. LC 93-27013. (Media & Society Ser.: Vol. 6). 1994. pap. 19.95 (*0-8166-1953-0*) U of Minn Pr.

Museum Curator. Jack Rudman. (Career Examination Ser.: C-1375). 1994. pap. 27.95 (*0-8373-1375-9*) Nat Learn.

Museum Director. Jack Rudman. (Career Examination Ser.: C-2372). 1994. pap. 34.95 (*0-8373-2372-X*) Nat Learn.

Museum Education: History, Theory, & Practice. Ed. by Nancy Berry & Susan Mayers. 257p. 1989. 22.00 (*0-937652-49-0*, 240) Natl Art Ed.

***Museum Educator's Handbook.** Graeme K. Talboys. LC 99-46000. 224p. 2000. 78.95 (*0-566-08173-3*, Pub. by Gower) Ashgate Pub Co.

Museum Environment. 2nd rev. ed. Garry Thomson. 308p. 1986. pap. 54.95 (*0-7506-2041-2*) Buttrwrth-Heinemann.

Museum Ethics. Gary Edson. LC 96-41629. 305p. (C). 1997. 90.00 (*0-415-13811-6*) Routledge.

Museum Ethics. Gary Edson. LC 96-41629. (Illus.). 305p. (C). 1997. pap. 32.99 (*0-415-15290-9*) Routledge.

Museum Exhibition. David Dean. (Illus.). 192p. (C). 1996. pap. 32.99 (*0-415-08017-7*) Routledge.

Museum Experience. John H. Falk & Lynn D. Dierking. Ed. by Mellen Cardage. 210p. 1992. 36.00 (*0-929590-06-6*) Whalesback Bks.

Museum for Everyone! The Honolulu Academy of Arts. Susan Soong. (Illus.). 32p. (Orig.). (J). (gr. 1-6). 1995. pap. 8.95 (*0-937426-32-6*) Honolu Arts.

Museum for the Global Village. George F. MacDonald & Stephen Alsford. (Illus.). 244p. 1989. pap. 19.95 (*0-660-10787-2*, Pub. by CN Mus Civilization) U of Wash Pr.

Museum for the People. Ed. by Emily D. Harvey & Bernard Friedberg. LC 78-155728. 1971. 12.95 (*0-405-02568-8*) Ayer.

Museum Forms Book. 3rd ed. Ed. by Kenneth D. Perry. 463p. 1999. pap. 50.00 (*0-935260-05-6*) Tex Assn Mus.

Museum fur Kunsthandwerk. Michael Brawne. (Architecture in Detail Ser.). (Illus.). 60p. 1993. pap. 29.95 (*0-7148-2765-7*, Pub. by Phaidon Press) Phaidon Pr.

***Museum Gallery Education: A Manual of Good Practice.** Ed. by Hazal Moffatt & Vicky Woollard. 246p. 2000. pap. 42.95 (*0-7425-0408-5*) AltaMira Pr.

Museum Governance: Mission, Ethics, Policy. Marie C. Malaro. LC 93-49384. 208p. (Orig.). 1994. pap. text 16.95 (*1-56098-363-9*) Smithsonian.

Museum Guard. Howard Norman. LC 98-8413. 310p. 1998. 23.00 (*0-374-21649-5*) FS&G.

Museum Guard. Howard Norman. LC 99-34701. 320p. 1999. pap. 14.00 (*0-312-20427-2*) St Martin.

***Museum Guide To Copyright & Trademark.** Michael Steven Shapiro et al. LC 99-43466. 225p. 1999. pap. 25.00 (*0-931201-63-2*) Am Assn Mus.

Museum Guides for Kids: American Art, 3 vols. Ruthie Knapp & Janice Lehmberg. LC 98-60873. (Off the Wall Museum Guides for Kids Ser.). (Illus.). 72p. (YA). (gr. 4-7). 1998. pap. 8.95 (*0-87192-386-6*, Pub. by Davis Mass) Sterling.

Museum Guides for Kids: Egyptian Art, 3 vols. Ruthie Knapp & Janice Lehmberg. LC 98-60874. (Off the Wall Museum Guides for Kids Ser.). (Illus.). 72p. (YA). (gr. 7-12). 1998. pap. 8.95 (*0-87192-384-X*, Pub. by Davis Mass) Sterling.

Museum Guides for Kids: Impressionist Art, 3 vols. Ruthie Knapp & Janice Lehmberg. LC 98-60875. (Off the Wall Museum Guides for Kids Ser.). (Illus.). 72p. (YA). (gr. 4-7). 1998. pap. 8.95 (*0-87192-385-8*, Pub. by Davis Mass) Sterling.

Museum Handbook: Museum Collections, 2 vols. 1997. lib. bdg. 600.95 (*0-8490-8166-1*) Gordon Pr.

Museum Handbook Pt. I: National Parks Service. (Illus.). 850p. (Orig.). (C). 1994. pap. text 65.00 (*0-7881-1032-2*) DIANE Pub.

Museum Impact & Evaluation Study: Roles of Affect in the Museum, Visit & Ways of Assessing Them, 3 vols., Set. Peter Anderson & Bonnie C. Roe. 500p. 1993. 97.50 (*0-9638657-0-6*) Mus of Sci.

Museum Impact & Evaluation Study: Roles of Affect in the Museum, Visit & Ways of Assessing Them, 3 vols., Vol. 1. Peter Anderson & Bonnie C. Roe. 500p. 1993. 12.50 (*0-9638657-1-4*) Mus of Sci.

Museum Impact & Evaluation Study: Roles of Affect in the Museum, Visit & Ways of Assessing Them, 3 vols., Vol. 2. Peter Anderson & Bonnie C. Roe. 500p. 1993. 35.00 (*0-9638657-2-2*) Mus of Sci.

Museum Impact & Evaluation Study: Roles of Affect in the Museum, Visit & Ways of Assessing Them, 3 vols., Vol. 3. Peter Anderson & Bonnie C. Roe. 500p. 1993. 50.00 (*0-9638657-3-0*) Mus of Sci.

Museum in America: Innovators & Pioneers. Edward P. Alexander. LC 97-21127. (American Association for State & Local History Book Ser.). 224p. 1997. 62.00 (*0-7619-8946-3*); pap. 22.95 (*0-7619-8947-1*) AltaMira Pr.

Museum in the Open: The Architectural Treasures of Uzbekistan. G. A. Pugachenkova. 236p. 1981. 275.00 (*0-569-08712-0*) St Mut.

***Museum in Transition: A Philosophical Perspective.** Hilde S. Hein. LC 00-23058. (Illus.). 2000. write for info. (*1-56098-396-5*) Smithsonian.

***Museum in Transition: A Philosophical Perspective.** Hilde S. Hein. 2000. pap. 40.00 (*1-56098-371-X*) Smithsonian.

Museum Instructor. Jack Rudman. (Career Examination Ser.: C-1705). 1994. pap. 27.95 (*0-8373-1705-3*) Nat Learn.

Museum Interactive Multimedia, 1997. Ed. by David Bearman & Jennifer Trant. LC 98-160290. (Illus.). 234p. 1997. pap. 30.00 (*1-885626-14-2*) Archives & Mus.

Museum Intern. Jack Rudman. (Career Examination Ser.: C-1376). 1994. pap. 23.95 (*0-8373-1376-7*) Nat Learn.

Museum Is Born. B. John Zavrel. Ed. by Marco Bodenstein. (Illus.). 48p. (Orig.). 1994. pap. 10.00 (*0-914301-16-0*) West-Art.

Museum Is Born. deluxe ed. B. John Zavrel. Ed. by Marco Bodenstein. (Illus.). 48p. (Orig.). 1994. pap. 85.00 (*0-914301-17-9*) West-Art.

Museum Job Descriptions & Organizational Charts. Mary Lister. Ed. by Roxana J. Adams. (Professional Practice Ser.). (Illus.). 400p. 1999. spiral bd. 30.50 (*0-931201-61-6*, 806) Am Assn Mus.

Museum Jobs from A-Z. Ed. by G. W. Bates. LC 94-153083. 1994. pap. text 9.95 (*0-9629759-4-X*) Batax Mus.

Museum Laboratory Technician. Jack Rudman. (Career Examination Ser.: C-1377). 1994. pap. 27.95 (*0-8373-1377-5*) Nat Learn.

Museum Languages: Objects & Texts. Ed. by Gaynor Kavanagh. 190p. 1992. text 49.00 (*0-7185-1359-2*, Pub. by Leicester U Pr) Cassell & Continuum.

Museum Law: Officers & Counsel. Marilyn E. Phelan. 392p. 1994. pap. 89.00 (*0-9643080-0-2*) Kalos Kapp.

Museum Librarianship: A Guide to the Provision & Management of Information Services. Esther G. Bierbaum. LC 91-23209. (Illus.). 190p. 1994. lib. bdg. 45.00 (*0-89950-971-1*) McFarland & Co.

Museum Lighting: RP-30-96. (Recommended Practices Ser.). (Illus.). 110p. 1996. pap. 60.00 (*0-87995-132-X*, RP-30-96) Illum Eng.

Museum Management. Ed. by Kevin Moore. LC 94-9057. (Leicester Readers in Museums Studies Ser.). (Illus.). 256p. (C). 1994. pap. 32.99 (*0-415-11279-6*, B4634) Routledge.

Museum Management. Ed. by Kevin Moore. LC 94-9057. (Leicester Readers in Museums Studies Ser.). (Illus.). 256p. (C). (gr. 13). 1994. 110.00 (*0-415-11278-8*, B4630) Routledge.

Museum Masters: Their Museums & Their Influence. Edward P. Alexander. LC 95-43139. (American Association for State & Local History Book Ser.). (Illus.). 440p. 1996. reprint ed. pap. 23.95 (*0-7619-9131-X*) AltaMira Pr.

Museum Maze. Wendy Madgwick. 48p. (J). (gr. 4-6). 1999. write for info. (*0-7613-0961-6*, Copper Beech Bks); pap. write for info. (*0-7613-0385-5*, Copper Beech Bks) Millbrook Pr.

Museum, Media, Message. Eilean Hooper-Greenhill. LC 94-10473. (Heritage Ser.). (Illus.). 320p. (C). (gr. 13). 1994. 75.00 (*0-415-11672-4*, B4638) Routledge.

Museum Memories: History, Technology, Art. Didier Maleuvre. LC 98-35055. (Cultural Memory in the Present Ser.). 1999. 49.50 (*0-8047-3202-7*); pap. 19.95 (*0-8047-3604-9*) Stanford U Pr.

Museum Mesdag: Catalogue of Paintings & Drawings. Fred Leeman. LC 97-191988. (Illus.). 460p. 1998. 100.00 (*90-400-9868-9*, Pub. by Waandrs) Consort Bk Sales.

Museum Mission Statements: Building a Distinct Identity. Ed. by Gail Anderson. (Professional Practice Ser.). 137p. 1998. pap. 25.00 (*0-931201-41-1*) Am Assn Mus.

Museum Motifs. (Illus.). 248p. 1997. 42.50 (*89-7059-036-6*, Pub. by Ahn Graphics) Weatherhill.

Museum New York. Tanya Agathocleus. pap. 15.00 (*1-84166-034-5*, Pub. by Ellipsis) Norton.

Museum Numbers. Gisela Voss. (Illus.). 22p. (J). (ps). 1994. bds. 14.00 (*0-87846-370-4*) Mus Fine Arts Boston.

Museum of American Folk Art Encyclopedia of Twentieth-Century American Folk Art & Artists. Chuck Rosenak & Jan Rosenak. (Illus.). 416p. 1991. 75.00 (*1-55859-041-2*) Abbeville Pr.

Museum of Architecture. Atrium Staff. 1999. pap. 35.00 (*0-688-16224-X*, Wm Morrow) Morrow Avon.

Museum of Bad Art: Art Too Bad to Be Ignored. Museum of Bad Art Staff et al. LC 96-19444. (Illus.). 112p. (Orig.). 1996. pap. 14.95 (*0-8362-2185-0*) Andrews & McMeel.

Museum of Clear Ideas: New Poems. Donald Hall. 128p. 1994. pap. 14.00 (*0-395-68085-9*) HM.

Museum of Dreams. Roger Granet. Ed. by Linda Raskin. (Illus.). 96p. 1997. 18.50 (*0-9659661-3-5*, 001-97) Ross-Hunt.

Museum of Early American Tools. Eric Sloane. 105p. 1985. pap. 9.00 (*0-345-32611-3*) Ballantine Pub Grp.

Museum of Faiths: Histories & Legacies of the 1893 World's Parliament of Religions. Ed. by Eric J. Ziolkowski. LC 93-33152. (American Academy of Religion, Classics in Religious Studies: No. 9). 367p. 1993. 44.95 (*1-55540-904-0*, 010509); pap. 29.95 (*1-55540-905-9*, 010509) OUP.

Museum of Fine Arts. Szilvia Bodnar. 144p. 1989. pap. 85.00 (*963-13-3897-5*, Pub. by Corvina Bks) St Mut.

Museum of Fine Arts, Houston: A Permanent Legacy. Peter C. Marzio et al. LC 89-83701. (Illus.). 352p. 1989. 65.00 (*1-55595-022-1*) Hudson Hills.

***Museum of Fine Arts, Houston: Visitor Guide.** Janet Landay. (Illus.). 544p. 2000. 35.00 (*1-85759-231-X*, Pub. by Scala Books) Antique Collect.

Museum of Flight: Seattle Washington. David Gordon. (Illus.). 48p. 1989. pap. 5.95 (*0-917859-31-6*) Sunrise SBCA.

Museum of History & Art in Zagorsk. Galina Makaroskaia. (Illus.). 200p. (C). 1986. text 100.00 (*0-7855-5852-7*, Pub. by Collets) St Mut.

Museum of London: A Souvenir Guide to the Collection. Valerie Cumming et al. (Illus.). 128p. 1997. 35.00 (*1-85759-126-7*, Pub. by P Wilson) Scala Books.

Museum of Love. Steven Weiner. 214p. 1994. 21.95 (*0-87951-531-7*, Pub. by Overlook Pr) Penguin Putnam.

Museum of Love. Steven Weiner. 214p. 1995. 11.95 (*0-87951-583-X*, Pub. by Overlook Pr) Penguin Putnam.

Museum of Modern Art: Collected Poems, 1971-1993. J. H. Kennedy. LC 93-35429. 64p. 1996. pap. 14.95 (*0-7734-2795-3*, Mellen Poetry Pr) E Mellen.

***Museum of Modern Art: Highlights of the Collection.** Museum of Modern Art Staff. (Museum of Modern Art Bks.). 352p. 1999. pap. 18.95 (*0-8109-6201-2*, Pub. by Abrams) Time Warner.

Museum of Modern Art at Mid-Century: Continuity & Change. Ed. by John Elderfield. (Studies in Modern Art: No. 5). (Illus.). 256p. (Orig.). 1996. pap. 19.95 (*0-87070-128-2*, 0-8109-6153-9, Pub. by Mus of Modern Art) Abrams.

Museum of Modern Art at Mid-Century: Studies in Modern Art: Continuity & Change. Ed. by John Elderfield. (Studies in Modern Art.: No. 5). (Illus.). 208p. 1995. pap. 19.95 (*0-8109-6153-9*, Pub. by Abrams) Time Warner.

Museum of Modern Art at Mid-Century: Studies in Modern Art: Studies in ModAtAt Home & Abroad. John Elderfield. (Studies in Modern Art: No. 4). (Illus.). 208p. 1994. pap. 19.95 (*0-8109-6133-4*, Pub. by Abrams) Time Warner.

Museum of Modern Art, Department of Eagles, Section Publicite. Ed. by Benjamin H. Buchloh. (Illus.). (Orig.). 1995. pap. write for info. (*0-944219-12-8*) M Goodman Gallery.

An Asterisk (*) at the beginning of an entry indicates that the title is appearing for the first time.

Museum of Modern Art, Gunma: Takasaki, Gunma Prefecture, Japan, 1971-74. Phillip Drew. (Architecture in Detail Ser.). (Illus.). 60p. (Orig.). 1996. pap. 29.95 (*0-7148-3549-8*, Pub. by Phaidon Press) Phaidon Pr.

Museum of Modern Art, New York: The History & the Collection. Intro. by Sam Hunter. (Illus.). 608p. 1997. reprint ed. 39.98 (*0-8109-8187-4*, Pub. by Abrams) Time Warner.

***Museum of Monster Art.** Random House U. K. Ltd. 16p. (J). 2001. mass mkt. 2.99 (*0-375-81140-0*, Pub. by Random Bks Yng Read) Random.

Museum of My Mother. Ada J. Schneider. (Illus.). 72p. 1996. pap. 10.00 (*0-9636068-1-6*) Gratlau Pr.

Museum of Oriental Art: Moscow. N. Sychova. (Illus.). 231p. (C). 1988. text 300.00 (*0-7855-5851-9*, Pub. by Collets) St Mut.

Museum of Oriental Art, Moscow. N. Sychova. 231p. (C). 1988. 90.00 (*0-569-09124-1*, Pub. by Collets) St Mut.

Museum of Science & Industry Basic List of Children's Science Books, 1973-1984. Bernice Richter & Duane Wenzel. LC 85-18719. 167p. reprint ed. pap. 51.80 (*0-7837-5917-7*, 204571600007) Bks Demand.

Museum of Science & Industry Basic List of Children's Science Books, 1986. Bernice Richter & Duane Wenzel. LC 86-22320. 83p. reprint ed. pap. 30.00 (*0-7837-5953-3*, 204575300007) Bks Demand.

Museum of Science & Industry Basic List of Children's Science Books, 1987. Bernice Richter & Duane Wenzel. LC 87-641170. 85p. reprint ed. pap. 30.00 (*0-7837-5954-1*, 204575400007) Bks Demand.

Museum of the Adirondacks. rev. ed. Craig Gilborn & Alice W. Gilborn. (Illus.). 68p. 1991. reprint ed. 5.95 (*0-910020-36-1*) Adirondack Mus.

Museum of the American Quilters. 1995. pap. 6.95 (*0-89145-837-9*, 3871, Am Quilters Soc) Collector Bks.

Museum of the American Watchmakers Institute, 1993. Henry B. Fried. (Illus.). 125.00 (*0-918845-15-7*) Am Watchmakers.

Museum of the Bargello: Guide to the Collections. Bruna Tomasello. (Illus.). 128p. 1992. 21.95 (*0-8161-0608-8*, G K Hall & Co) Mac Lib Ref.

Museum of the Confederacy: Treasures from the Archives. Ed. by John Coski. (Civil War Regiments Ser.: Vol. 5). (Illus.). 190p. 1996. pap. 12.00 (*1-882810-51-1*) Savas Pub.

Museum of the Hungarian Village at Szentendre. Peter Kecskes. (Illus.). 136p. (C). 1990. pap. 75.00 (*0-7855-5221-9*, Pub. by Collets) St Mut.

Museum of the Hungarian Village at Szentendre: Guided Tour Around the Open Air Ethnographic Museum of Szentendre. Peter Kecskes. (Illus.). 136p. 1999. pap. 21.00 (*963-13-2895-3*, Pub. by Corvina Bks) St Mut.

Museum of the Revolution. Angela Ball. LC 97-76752. (Poetry Ser.). 72p. 1999. pap. 12.95 (*0-88748-275-9*) Carnegie-Mellon.

Museum of the Streets: Minnesota's Contemporary Outdoor Murals. Moira F. Harris. (Illus.). 132p. (Orig.). 1986. pap. 15.00 (*0-9617767-0-6*) Pogo Pr.

Museum of Unconditional Surrender. Dubravka Ugresic. Tr. by Celia Hawkesworth from CRO. LC 99-33134. 256p. 1999. 24.95 (*0-8112-1421-4*, Pub. by New Directions) Norton.

***Museum of Useless Efforts.** Cristina Peri Rossi. Tr. by Tobias Hecht. (European Women Writers Ser.). 2001. pap. 15.00 (*0-8032-8764-X*, Bison Books); text 40.00 (*0-8032-3726-X*) U of Nebr Pr.

Museum of Western & Oriental Art: Kiev. H. Roslavets. (Illus.). 192p. (C). 1985. text 70.00 (*0-7855-5849-7*, Pub. by Collets) St Mut.

Museum of Western & Oriental Art: Odessa. Nelly Lutskevich. (Illus.). 180p. (C). 1985. text 85.00 (*0-7855-5850-0*, Pub. by Collets) St Mut.

Museum of Westward Expansion: A Photographic Collection. Nancy Bikle. 126p. 1997. pap. 5.95 (*0-931056-11-X*) Jefferson Natl.

Museum of Words: The Poetics of Ekphrasis from Homer to Ashbery. Photos by James A. Hefferman. LC 93-4509. (Illus.). 262p. 1993. 29.95 (*0-226-32313-7*) U Ch Pr.

Museum Premieres Exhibitions & Special Events, 1998-1999 Vol. 5: Authorized Nationwide Guidebook of Museum Exhibitions & Special Events for Travelers & Research Professionals. Ed. by Paul D. Groenier et al. (Illus.). 850p. 1998. text 189.00 (*1-888187-00-X*) Info Srvs & Co.

Museum Premieres Exhibitions & Special Events, 1998-1999 Vol. 5: Authorized Nationwide Guidebook of Museum Exhibitions & Special Events for Travelers & Research Professionals. deluxe ed. Ed. by Paul D. Groenier et al. (Illus.). 850p. 1998. 189.00 (*1-888187-02-6*); pap. 99.00 (*1-888187-01-8*) Info Srvs & Co.

Museum Premieres Exhibitions & Special Events, 1998-99 Vol. 5: Authorized Nationwide Guidebook of Museum Exhibitions & Special Events for Travelers & Research Professionals. 4th rev. ed. Ed. by Paul D. Groenier et al. (Illus.). 850p. 1997. pap. text 99.00 (*1-888187-99-9*) Info Srvs & Co.

Museum Premieres Exhibitions & Special Events, 1998/99 Vol. 5: The Only Nationwide Guidebook of Museum Exhibitions & Special Events for Travelers & Research Professionals. 4th large type rev. ed. Ed. by Paul D. Groenier et al. (Illus.). 840p. 1998. per. 159.00 incl. cd-rom (*1-888187-08-5*) Info Srvs & Co.

Museum Premieres Exhibitions & Special Events, 1998/99 Vol. 5: The Only Nationwide Guidebook of Museum Exhibitions & Special Events for Travelers & Research Professionals. 5th ed. Ed. by Paul D. Groenier et al. (Illus.). 850p. 1999. per. 159.00 incl. cd-rom (*1-888187-07-7*) Info Srvs & Co.

***Museum Premieres Exhibitions & Special Events, 1999-2000: Authorized Nationnwide Guidebook of Museum Exhibitions & Special Events for Travelers & Research Professionals.** rev. ed. Ed. by Paul D. Groenier et al. (Illus.). 850p. 1999. pap. 258.95 incl. cd-rom (*1-888187-10-7*) Info Srvs & Co.

Museum Premieres Exhibitions & Special Events, 1999-2000 Vol. 6: Authorized Natuionwide Guidebook of Museum Exhibitions & Special Events for Travelers & Research Professionals. deluxe rev. ed. Ed. by Paul D. Groenier et al. (Illus.). 850p. 1999. 199.95 (*1-888187-05-0*); pap. 109.95 (*1-888187-06-9*) Info Srvs & Co.

Museum Premieres Exhibitions & Special Events, 1999-2000 Vol. 6: Authorized Natuionwide Guidebook of Museum Exhibitions & Special Events for Travelers & Research Professionals. rev. ed. Ed. by Paul D. Groenier et al. (Illus.). 850p. 1999. pap. text 109.95 (*1-888187-04-2*) Info Srvs & Co.

Museum Premieres Exhibitions & Special Events, 1999-2000 Vol. 6: Authorized Natuionwide Guidebook of Museum Exhibitions & Special Events for Travelers & Research Professionals. 6th rev. ed. Ed. by Paul D. Groenier et al. (Illus.). 850p. 1999. text 199.95 (*1-888187-03-4*) Info Srvs & Co.

Museum Premieres Exhibitions & Special Events, 2000-2001: Authorized Nationwide Guidebook of Museum Exhibitions & Special Events for Travelers & Research Professionals. Ed. by Paul D. Groenier et al. (Museum Premieres Exhibitions & Special Events Ser.: Vol. 7). (Illus.). 1000p. 2000. 199.50 (*1-888187-11-5*, 1-888187); pap. 109.50 (*1-888187-12-3*, 1-888187); pap. 258.95 incl. cd-rom (*1-888187-14-X*, 1-888187) Info Srvs & Co.

Museum Profession: Internal & External Relations. Ed. by Gaynor Kavanagh. 190p. 1992. text 49.00 (*0-7185-1387-8*, Pub. by Leicester U Pr) Cassell & Continuum.

Museum Provision & Professionalism. Ed. by Gaynor Kavanagh. LC 94-9484. (Leicester Readers in Museums Studies Ser.). 308p. (C). 1994. pap. 37.99 (*0-415-11281-8*, B4635) Routledge.

Museum Public Relations. G. Donald Adams. LC 83-3708. (American Association for State & Local History Book Ser.). (Illus.). 248p. 1983. reprint ed. 34.95 (*0-910050-65-1*) AltaMira Pr.

Museum Quality Orgasm. 2nd ed. Carl M. Daniels. 48p. 1997. pap. 5.00 (*0-9653194-4-X*) Future Tense.

Museum Robbery. Schultz. (C). 1991. pap. text. write for info. (*0-201-55630-8*) Addison-Wesley.

Museum Security: A Handbook. International Committee on Museum Security Staff. Ed. by Robert W. Burke & David Liston. LC 92-12230. (Heritage: Care-Preservation-Management Program Ser.). (Illus.). 256p. (C). 1993. pap. 37.99 (*0-415-07509-2*, A7600) Routledge.

Museum Shapes. Gisela Voss. (Illus.). 22p. (J). (ps). 1994. bds. 14.00 (*0-87846-368-2*) Mus Fine Arts Boston.

Museum Shop Report: A Guide to Museum Shop Catalogs. Elysa Lazar. 1992. pap. 14.95 (*1-881642-02-X*) Lazar Comms.

Museum Store Management. Mary Miley Theobald. LC 91-16191. (American Association for State & Local History Book Ser.). (Illus.). 240p. (C). 1991. reprint ed. pap. 65.00 (*0-942063-14-7*) AltaMira Pr.

Museum Strategy & Marketing: Designing Missions, Building Audiences & Generating Revenue. Phillip Kotler. LC 98-8964. 608p. 1998. 39.95 (*0-7879-0912-2*) Jossey-Bass.

Museum Studies in Material Culture. Ed. by Susan M. Pearce. 280p. 1990. text 42.50 (*0-7185-1288-X*, Pub. by Leicester U Pr) Cassell & Continuum.

Museum Studies Programs: A Guide to Evaluation. Ed. by Barbara Butler. (Professional Practice Ser.). 37p. (Orig.). 1987. reprint ed. pap. text 14.50 (*0-931201-38-1*) Am Assn Mus.

Museum Supervisor. Jack Rudman. (Career Examination Ser.: C-2941). 1994. pap. 29.95 (*0-8373-2941-8*) Nat Learn.

Museum Technician. Jack Rudman. (Career Examination Ser.: C-522). 1994. pap. 27.95 (*0-8373-0522-5*) Nat Learn.

Museum Theatre: Communicating with Visitors Through Drama. Catherine Hughes. LC 98-23690. 152p. 1998. pap. text 17.95 (*0-325-00056-5*) Heinemann.

Museum Transformed: Design & Culture in the Post-Pompidou Age. Douglas Davis. (Illus.). 240p. 1990. 29.98 (*1-55859-064-1*) Abbeville Pr.

Museum Trusteeship. Alan D. Ullberg & Patricia Ullberg. 136p. 1981. pap. 11.00 (*0-931201-06-3*) Am Assn Mus.

Museum Visits & Activities for Family Life Enrichment. Ed. by Barbara H. Butler & Marvin B. Sussman. LC 89-37694. (Marriage & Family Review Ser.: Vol. 13, Nos. 3-4). (Illus.). 191p. 1989. text 49.95 (*0-86656-758-5*) Haworth Pr.

Museum Volunteers: Good Practice in the Management of Volunteers. Sinclair Goodlad & Stephanie McIvor. LC 97-33485. (Heritage Ser.). 144p. (C). 1998. 60.00 (*0-415-18209-3*) Routledge.

***Museum Watching.** Elliott Erwitt. 160p. 1999. 29.95 (*0-7148-3894-2*) Phaidon Pr.

Museum World of Henry James. Adeline B. Tintner. LC 85-28836. (Studies in Modern Literature: No. 56). (Illus.). 418p. reprint ed. pap. 129.60 (*0-8357-1725-9*, 207061300005) Bks Demand.

***Museumplein: Work in Progress.** Siebe Swart. 2000. pap. 17.95 (*90-5662-130-0*) NAi Uitgevers.

Museums see Museos

Museums. Jason Cooper. LC 92-12556. (J). 1992. 9.50 (*0-685-59389-4*) Rourke Corp.

Museums. Jason Cooper. LC 92-12556. (Great Places to Visit Ser.). 24p. (J). (gr. k-4). 1992. lib. bdg. 10.95 (*0-86593-209-3*) Rourke Corp.

***Museums.** Susan A. Sternau. 1999. 10.95 (*1-57717-147-0*) Todtri Prods.

Museums, Vol. 1. James Russell. (Twentieth-Century Ser.). 1999. 19.95 (*0-7148-3878-0*) Phaidon Pr.

Museums , Vol. 2. James Russell. (Twentieth-Century Ser.). 1999. 19.95 (*0-7148-3879-9*) Phaidon Pr.

Museums: A Place to Work. Jane Glaser & Artemis Zenetou. (Heritage Ser.). 320p. (C). 1996. pap. 32.99 (*0-415-12724-6*, C0599) Routledge.

Museums: A Place to Work. Jane Glaser & Artemis Zenetou. LC 95-16930. (Heritage Ser.). 320p. (C). (gr. 13). 1996. 100.00 (*0-415-12256-2*, C0478) Routledge.

Museums: Places of Learning. George E. Hein & Mary Alexander. Ed. by Ann H. Grogg. (Professional Practice Ser.). (Illus.). 57p. 1998. pap. 9.50 (*0-931201-56-X*, 804) Am Assn Mus.

Museums Vol. 1: Their History & Their Use with a Bibliography, 3 vols. in 2. David Murray. 1999. reprint ed. 150.00 (*1-891396-04-8*) Pober Pub.

Museums along the Arroyo: A History & Guide. Jane Apostol. LC 95-82227. (Illus.). 139p. (Orig.). (C). 1996. pap. 13.95 (*0-914421-17-4*) Hist Soc So CA.

Museums & Adult Education. Hans L. Zetterberg. LC 70-95622. (Illus.). xi, 89p. 1969. lib. bdg. 25.00 (*0-678-07753-3*) Kelley.

Museums & American Intellectual Life, 1876-1925. Conn. 1997. pap. text 13.95 (*0-226-11493-7*) U Ch Pr.

Museums & American Intellectual Life, 1876-1925. Steven Conn. LC 98-16850. (Illus.). 301p. 1998. 32.50 (*0-226-11492-9*) U Ch Pr.

Museums & Anthropology: Acquisitions, Curation, Research. Ed. by Constance Cameron. LC 86-60694. (Occasional Papers of the Archaeological Research Facility: No. 3). (Illus.). 90p. 1986. pap. 10.00 (*0-938217-00-3*) CSU Mus Anthrop.

Museums & Archaeology in West Africa. Ed. by Claude D. Ardonin. LC 98-209036. (Illus.). 163p. (Orig.). 1997. pap. text 26.95 (*1-56098-785-5*) Smithsonian.

Museums & Art Galleries. 1990. 36.00 (*0-86022-254-3*, Pub. by Build Servs Info Assn) St Mut.

Museums & Children: A Design Guide. Uriel Cohen & Ruth McMurtry. (Publications in Architecture & Urban Planning: No. R89-2). (Illus.). vi, 138p. (C). 1989. per. 15.00 (*0-938744-62-3*) U of Wis Ctr Arch-Urban.

Museums & Communities: The Politics of Public Culture. Ed. by Ivan Karp et al. LC 91-31648. (Illus.). 624p. (C). 1992. pap. text 19.95 (*1-56098-189-X*) Smithsonian.

Museums & Consultants: Maximizing the Collaboration. Intro. by Pat Williams. 129p. (Orig.). 1996. pap. text 27.50 (*0-931201-26-8*) Am Assn Mus.

***Museums & Cultural Facilities: Building Type Basics.** Rosenblatt. 304p. 2000. write for info. (*0-471-34915-1*) Wiley.

Museums & Europe, 1992. Ed. by Susan M. Pearce. LC 92-28225. (New Research in Museum Studies: An International Ser.: Vol. 3). 240p. (C). 1992. text 85.00 (*0-485-90003-3*, Pub. by Athlone Pr) Humanities.

Museums & Galleries - Great Britain & Ireland. Johansens Staff. (Johansens Annuals Ser.). 192p. 1999. pap. text 14.95 (*1-86017-726-3*) Nelles Verlag.

***Museums & Galleries of Great Britain & Ireland, 2001.** (Johansens Guides Ser.). (Illus.). 192p. 2001. pap. 17.95 (*1-86017-812-X*) Hunter NJ.

Museums & Galleries of London. 3rd rev. ed. Malcolm Rogers. (Blue Guide Ser.). (Illus.). 408p. 1991. pap. 22.95 (*0-393-30774-3*) Norton.

Museums & Galleries of New York. Carol Von Pressentin Wright. LC 95-1020. (Blue Guide Ser.). 1996. pap. 22.50 (*0-393-31341-7*) Norton.

***Museums & History in West Africa.** Claude Daniel Ardouin et al. LC 99-38643. (Illus.). 192p. 2000. pap. 29.95 (*1-56098-805-3*) Smithsonian.

Museums & Interactive Multimedia: Selected Papers from ICHIM 93. Ed. by Diane Lees. 1993. pap. text 20.00 (*0-905963-89-X*) Archives & Mus.

***Museums & Memory.** Susan A. Crane. LC 99-89384. (Cultural Sitings Ser.). (Illus.). 2000. 55.00 (*0-8047-3564-6*) Stanford U Pr.

***Museums & Memory.** Susan A. Crane. LC 99-89384. (Cultural Sitings Ser.). (Illus.). 2000. pap. 19.95 (*0-8047-3565-4*) Stanford U Pr.

Museums & Money: The Impact of Funding on Exhbitions, Scholarship, & Management. Victoria D. Alexander. LC 95-49863. (IU Center on Philanthropy Series on Governance). 1996. 24.95 (*0-253-33205-2*) Ind U Pr.

Museums & Money: The Impact of Funding on Exhibitions Scholarship & Management. Victoria D Alexander. (IU Center on Philanthropy Series in Governance). (Illus.). 204p. 1996. 27.95 (*0-253-33084-X*) Ind U Pr.

Museums & Other Attractions of Arizona's Smaller Communities, Bk. 1. Korene C. Cohen & Dale C. Cohen. (Illus.). 50p. (Orig.). 1992. 4.95 (*0-9637255-0-5*) Dancing Unicorn.

Museums & Other Attractions of Arizona's Smaller Communities, Bk. 2. Dale C. Cohen & Korene C. Cohen. (Illus.). 61p. (Orig.). 1993. 4.95 (*0-9637255-1-3*) Dancing Unicorn.

Museums & Popular Culture: New Research in Museum Studies #7. Susan M. Pearce. LC 98-30552. (New Research in Museum Studies: 7). (C). 1997. text 90.00 (*0-485-90007-6*) Humanities.

Museums & Sustainable Communities: Summit of the Museums of the Americas. Ed. by Donald Garfield & Oscar Navarro Rojas. LC 98-41080. (ENG & SPA.). 72p. 1998. pap. 14.00 (*0-931201-57-8*) Am Assn Mus.

Museums & the Appropriation of Culture. Ed. by Susan M. Pearce. LC 93-39430. (New Research in Museum Studies: An International Ser.: Vol. 4). 256p. (C). 1994. text 85.00 (*0-485-90004-1*, Pub. by Athlone Pr) Humanities.

Museums & the Community in West Africa. Ed. by Claude D. Ardouin & Emmanuel Arinze. LC 95-68002. (Illus.). 144p. 1995. pap. text 26.95 (*1-56098-611-5*) Smithsonian.

Museums & the First World War: A Social History. Gaynor Kavanagh. LC 94-673. 1994. 39.00 (*0-7185-1713-X*) St Martin.

Museums & the Future of Collecting. Ed. by Simon Knell. LC 98-46336. 1p. 1999. text 69.95 (*0-7546-0000-9*, Pub. by Ashgate Pub) Ashgate Pub Co.

***Museums & the Interpretation of Visual Culture.** Eilean Hooper-Greenhill. LC 00-32182. (Museum Meanings Ser.). (Illus.). 2000. pap. write for info. (*0-415-08633-7*) Routledge.

Museums & the Making of "Ourselves" The Role of Objects in National Identity. Flora E. Kaplan. 448p. 1996. pap. 27.95 (*0-7185-0039-3*) Bks Intl VA.

Museums & the Natural Environment: The Role of Natural History Museums in Biological Conservation. Peter Davis. 208p. 1996. 90.00 (*0-7185-1548-X*) Bks Intl VA.

Museums & the Representation of Native Canadians: Negotiating the Borders of Culture. Moira McCloughlin. LC 99-12896. 1999. 69.00 (*0-8153-2988-1*) Garland.

Museums & the Shaping of Knowledge. Eilean Hooper-Greenhill. LC 91-17628. (Heritage: Care-Preservation-Management Program Ser.). (Illus.). 244p. (C). 1992. pap. 32.99 (*0-415-07031-7*, A7035) Routledge.

Museums & the Web, 1997: Selected Papers. Ed. by David Bearman & Jennifer Trant. LC 97-216909. 380p. 1997. pap. 30.00 (*1-885626-13-4*) Archives & Mus.

Museums & the Web 99: Selected Papers from an International Conference. Ed. by David Bearman & Jennifer Trant. 1999. pap. text 50.00 incl. cd-rom (*1-885626-17-7*) Archives & Mus.

Museums & Their Development: The European Tradition, 1700-1900, 8 vols. fac. ed. Ed. & Intro. by Susan Pearce. 3200p. (C). 1999. 980.00 (*0-415-19307-9*, D6391) Routledge.

Museums & Their Visitors. Eilean Hooper-Greenhill. LC 93-29831. (Hertiage: Care, Preservation, Management Ser.). 224p. (C). (gr. 13). 1994. 60.00 (*0-415-06857-6*, B3900) Routledge.

Museums at Stony Brook: Highlights of the Collection. Museums at Stony Brook Staff. LC 82-81912. (Illus.). 72p. (Orig.). 1982. pap. 3.00 (*0-943924-04-9*) Mus Stony Brook.

Museums, Catalysts for Community Development: Proceeding of the Annual Meeting, 1996. Ed. by Gary Edson & David Dean. (Illus.). 150p. 1999. pap. write for info. (*0-9640188-8-8*) Mus TX Tech.

Museums Count. American Association of Museums Staff. Ed. by Ann Grogg. LC 93-51504. 112p. 1993. pap. 30.00 (*0-931201-17-9*) Am Assn Mus.

Museums Economics & the Community. Ed. by Susan M. Pearce. LC 91-25711. (New Research in Museum Studies: An International Ser.: Vol. 2). 224p. (C). 1991. text 85.00 (*0-485-90002-5*, Pub. by Athlone Pr) Humanities.

Museums Environment Energy. Ed. by May Cassar. 100p. 1994. pap. 30.00 (*0-11-290519-6*, HM05196, Pub. by Statnry Office) Bernan Associates.

Museums for a New Century: A Report of the Commission on Museums for a New Century. Museums for a New Century Commission. LC 84-72051. (Illus.). 144p. 1984. pap. 19.00 (*0-931201-08-X*) Am Assn Mus.

***Museums for a New Millennium: Concepts, Projects & Buildings.** Vittorio M. Lampugnani. (Illus.). 224p. 1999. 65.00 (*3-7913-2219-2*, Pub. by Prestel) te Neues.

Museums for the New Millennium: A Symposium for the Museum Community. Smithsonian Institution, Millennium Symposium Staff. LC 97-11410. 175p. 1997. pap. 25.00 (*0-931201-40-3*) Am Assn Mus.

Museums, Gardens & More in San Diego County: Explore San Diego. William Carroll. (Illus.). 120p. (Orig.). 1994. pap. 10.00 (*0-910390-38-X*) Coda Publications.

Museums, Humanities & Educated Eyes. Marilyn Stokstad et al. 213p. 1982. 5.00 (*0-89338-017-2*) U KS Nat Hist Mus.

Museums in Budapest. Ed. by F. Fulep. (Illus.). 224p. (C). 1989. text 285.00 (*0-7855-5848-9*, Pub. by Collets) St Mut.

Museums in Motion: An Introduction to the History & Functions of Museums. Edward P. Alexander. LC 95-48343. (American Association for State & Local History Book Ser.). (Illus.). 320p. 1979. pap. 24.95 (*0-7619-9155-7*) AltaMira Pr.

Museums in the Life of a City: Strategies for Community Partnerships. Ed. by Ellen C. Hirzy. 48p. 1995. pap. 10.00 (*0-931201-21-7*) Am Assn Mus.

Museums in the Social & Economic Life of a City. Ed. by Reynolds Childress. 80p. 1996. pap. 10.00 (*0-931201-30-6*) Am Assn Mus.

Museums, Magic & Children: Youth Education in Museums. Bonnie Pitman. Ed. by Aubyn Kendall & Carol Bannerman. (Illus.). 262p. (Orig.). 1982. pap. 21.00 (*0-944040-13-6*) AST Ctrs.

Museums, Muses & Me: A Museum Sketchbook. Huntington Art Gallery Staff. 1985. pap. 6.50 (*0-89824-160-X*) Trillium Pr.

Museums, Muses & Me: A Sketchbook for Young Artists. Donna Vliet. (Illus.). 31p. (J). 1991. pap. 9.95 (*0-614-02730-6*) J S Blanton Mus.

M

An Asterisk (*) at the beginning of an entry indicates that the title is appearing for the first time.

Museums Objects & Collections. Pearce. 2000. text. write for info. (*0-7185-1442-4*) St Martin.

Museums, Objects, & Collections: A Cultural Study. Susan M. Pearce. (Illus.). 318p. 1993. pap. text 16.95 (*1-56098-330-2*) Smithsonian.

Museums of Leningrad. V. Mushtukov & L. Tikhonov. (Illus.). 170p. (C). 1982. 40.00 (*0-7855-5192-1*, Pub. by Collets) St Mut.

*__Museums of Modern Science: Nobel Symposium 112.__ Nobel Symposium Staff et al. LC 00-29680. 2000. write for info. (*0-88135-299-3*) Watson Pub Intl.

Museums of New York. 3rd ed. Eloise Danto. (Illus.). 150p. (Orig.). 1998. pap. 12.95 (*0-9615128-9-X*) Eldan Pr.

Museums of the Last Generation. Academy Editions Staff. (Illus.). 144p. 1987. pap. 29.95 (*0-312-00451-6*) St Martin.

Museums of the Mind: Magritte's Labyrinth & Other Essays in the Arts. Ellen H. Spitz. LC 94-12347. (Illus.). 244p. 1995. 37.00 (*0-300-06029-7*) Yale U Pr.

Museums of the Northwest: The Best Collections in Washington, Oregon & Lower British Columbia. Harriet Baskas. LC 98-51573. (Illus.). 320p. 1999. pap. 18.95 (*1-57061-152-1*) Sasquatch Bks.

Museums of the San Francisco Bay Area. 2nd ed. Eloise Danto. (Illus.). 125p. (Orig.). 1998. pap. 12.95 (*0-9615128-8-1*) Eldan Pr.

Museums of the World. 6th ed. Ed. by Saur, K. G., Staff. 750p. 1997. 425.00 (*3-598-20605-4*) K G Saur Verlag.

*__Museums of the World.__ 7th ed. 750p. 1999. 450.00 (*3-598-20606-2*, Pub. by K G Saur Verlag) Bowker.

Museums of Yugoslavia. Vugoslav Srejovic. (Illus.). 172p. (C). 1974. 165.00 (*0-7855-4024-5*, Pub. by Collets) St Mut.

Museums, Sites, & Collections of Germanic Culture in North America: An Annotated Directory of German Immigrant Culture in the United States & Canada. Compiled by Margaret Hobbie. LC 79-6822. 155p. 1980. lib. bdg. 47.95 (*0-313-22060-3*, HGC/) Greenwood.

Museums, Trustees & Communities: Building Reciprocal Relationships. Ed. by Daryl K. Fischer. (Professional Practice Ser.). 100p. 1997. pap. 30.00 (*0-931201-42-X*) Am Assn Mus.

Museums Two-Thousand: Politics, People, Professionals & Profit. Ed. by International Committee of Museums Staff & Patrick Boylan. (Heritage: Care-Preservation-Management Program Ser.). 128p. (C). 1992. pap. 32.99 (*0-415-07129-1*, A7439) Routledge.

Museums Without Barriers: A New Deal for Disabled People. Ed. by Fondation de France Staff & International Committee of Museums Staff. (Heritage: Care-Preservation-Management Program Ser.). (Illus.). 240p. (C). (gr. 13). 1992. text 99.95 (*0-415-05454-0*, A7441) Routledge.

*__Museums You Never Knew Existed.__ David Blevins. 72p. 1999. pap. 15.00 (*0-9672731-2-9*) David Blevins.

Museumsinszenieurungen. Richard-Schone Gesellschaft. (Illus.). 272p. 1995. pap. text 15.00 (*3-364-00325-4*) Gordon & Breach.

Museveni's Long March: From Frelimo to the National Resistance Movement. 320p. 1996. pap. text 21.95 (*0-7453-1133-4*, Pub. by Pluto GBR) Stylus Pub VA.

Museveni's Long March: From Frelimo to the National Resistance Movement. Ondoga O. Amaza. LC 96-16068. 320p. 1996. 65.00 (*0-7453-1134-2*) Pluto GBR.

Musgrave: Notes on the Ancient Family of Musgrave of Musgrave, Westmorland, England, & Its Various Branches in Cumberland, Yorkshire, Northumberland. Percy Musgrave. (Illus.). 351p. 1993. reprint ed. pap. 49.50 (*0-8328-3724-5*); reprint ed. lib. bdg. 59.50 (*0-8328-3723-7*) Higginson Bk Co.

Musgrave Ritual. Arthur Conan Doyle. (Jamestown Classics Ser.). 1995. pap., teacher ed. 7.32 (*0-89061-057-6*, Jamestwn Pub) NTC Contemp Pub Co.

Musgrave Ritual. Arthur Conan Doyle. (Jamestown Classics Ser.). (J). 1995. pap., student ed. 5.99 (*0-89061-056-8*, Jamestwn Pub) NTC Contemp Pub Co.

Musgrave Ritual. Jeremy Paul. 48p. (Orig.). 1992. pap. 11.00 (*0-86025-443-7*, Pub. by I Henry Pubns) Empire Pub Srvs.

*__Musgrave Ritual in Latin.__ Churchill & Fewell. (Sherlockian Scholarship Ser.). 1998. 8.00 (*1-55246-136-X*) Battered Silicon.

Mush: A Beginners Manual of Sled Dog Training. Sierra Nevada Dog Drivers, Inc. Staff. Ed. by Bella Levorsen. LC 75-23913. (Illus.). 250p. 1984. pap. 19.95 (*0-914124-06-4*) Arner Pubns.

Mush! Across Alaska in the Longest Sled-Dog Race. Patricia Seibert. (J). 1994. 10.90 (*0-606-02772-6*, Pub. by Turtleback) Demco.

Mush! Across Alaska in the World's Longest Day Sled Race. Patricia Seibert. (Illus.). 1992. 15.65 (*0-7857-4377-4*) Econo-Clad Bks.

Mush! Across Alaska in the World's Longest Sled-Dog Race. Patricia Seibert. LC 91-38883. (Illus.). 32p. (J). (gr. 2-4). 1992. pap. 7.95 (*1-56294-705-2*) Millbrook Pr.

Mush! Across Alaska in the World's Longest Sled-dog Race! Patricia Seibert. (J). (gr. 4-7). 1992. pap. 5.70 (*0-395-64537-9*) HM.

Mush, a Dog from Space. Daniel M. Pinkwater. LC 94-29212. (Illus.). 40p. (J). (gr. k-3). 1995. 15.00 (*0-689-80317-6*) Atheneum Yung Read.

Mush, a Dog from Space. Daniel M. Pinkwater. LC 94-29212. (Illus.). (J). 1995. 14.95 (*0-02-774634-8*) Macmillan.

Mush-Hole: Memories of a Residential School. Maddie Harper. (Illus.). 24p. (J). 1994. pap. 6.95 (*0-920813-98-4*) LPC InBook.

Musher. Jose Giovanni. (FRE.). 224p. 1987. pap. 10.95 (*0-7859-2532-5*, 2070378101) Fr & Eur.

*__Musher's Journal.__ Brian Leslie Lewis. 16p. 1999. pap. 6.95 (*1-928693-04-0*) Novice Nomad.

*__Mushi & the King of Kings: A Christmas Play for Children.__ Beverly Amstutz. (Illus.). 20p. 1999. pap. 5.50 (*0-937836-11-7*) Precious Res.

Mushkilat al-Afkar fi al-'lam al-Islami. Malik Bin-Nabi. (Mushkilat al-Hadarah Ser.). 184p. 1988. pap. 4.95 (*1-57547-036-5*) Dar Al-Fikr.

Mushkilat al-Thaqafah. Malik Bin-Nabi. (Mushkilat al-Hadarah Ser.). 152p. 1984. pap. 3.95 (*1-57547-037-3*) Dar Al-Fikr.

Mushkilatan wa Qira'ah Fihima: Two Issues & a Critical Study on Them. 2nd ed. Tariq A. Bishri & Taha J. Alwani. (Silsilat Qadaya al Fikr al Islami Ser.: No. 8). (ARA.). 86p. 1992. pap. 4.00 (*1-56564-113-2*) IIIT VA.

Musho! Zulu Popular Praises. Ed. by Mafika Gwala & Elizabeth Gunner. LC 91-39014. (African Historical Sources Ser.). 237p. (C). 1991. 26.95 (*0-87013-306-3*) Mich St U Pr.

Mushroom. Barrie Watts. LC 86-6659. (Stopwatch Ser.). (Illus.). 25p. (J). (gr. k-4). 1986. pap. 3.95 (*0-382-24017-0*); lib. bdg. 9.95 (*0-382-09287-2*, Silver Pr NJ) Silver Burdett Pr.

Mushroom & Toadstools. Jiri Baier. 184p. 1995. write for info. (*1-57215-133-1*) World Pubns.

Mushroom Basket: A Gourmet Introduction to the Best Common Mushrooms of the Southern Rocky Mountains, with Applications Throughout the Northern Hemisphere, & Tidbits of Mushroom Lore from Europe Russia & China. Andrew L. March & Kathryn G. March. LC 82-90153. (Illus.). 162p. (Orig.). 1982. pap. 11.95 (*0-940206-02-1*) Meridian Hill.

Mushroom Biology: Concise Basics & Current Development. 200p. 1997. lib. bdg. 32.00 (*981-02-2877-5*) World Scientific Pub.

Mushroom Book. Storey Publishing Staff. 1997. 29.95 (*0-676-57031-3*) Random.

Mushroom Book: How to Identify, Gather & Cook Wild Mushrooms & Other Fungi. Thomas Laessoe. LC 96-10835. 256p. 1996. 29.95 (*0-7894-1073-7*) DK Pub Inc.

Mushroom Cultivation - with Special Emphasis on Appropriate Techniques for Developing Countries. P. Oei. (Illus.). 284p. 1996. pap. 39.00 (*90-70857-36-7*, Pub. by Tool Bks) Balogh.

Mushroom Feast. Jane Grigson. (Cook's Classic Library). (Illus.). 352p. 1998. reprint ed. pap. 14.95 (*1-55821-194-2*) Lyons Pr.

Mushroom Forest. Phil Baron. Ed. by Ken Forsse & Mary Becker. (Teddy Ruxpin Adventure Ser.). (Illus.). 26p. (J). (ps). 1986. 9.95 (*0-934323-36-4*); audio. write for info. (*0-318-60968-1*) Alchemy Comms.

Mushroom Hunt. Simon Frazer. LC 94-4877. (Read & Wonder Bks.). (Illus.). (J). (ps-3). 1995. 15.99 (*1-56402-500-4*) Candlewick Pr.

Mushroom Hunter's Field Guide. 2nd rev. ed. Alexander Smith & Nancy S. Weber. 316p. 1996. 24.95 (*1-882376-24-2*) Thunder Bay Pr.

Mushroom Hunter's Field Guide: All Color & Enlarged. Alexander H. Smith & Nancy S. Weber. (Illus.). 324p. (Orig.). 1980. 24.95 (*0-472-85610-3*, 85610) U of Mich Pr.

Mushroom Hunters Guide & Common Poisonous Plants. W. G. Farlow. LC 82-72605. (Illus.). 60p. (Orig.). 1982. pap. 4.95 (*0-89708-084-X*) And Bks.

Mushroom Identifier: Practical Handbook. Peter Jordan. 1999. pap. 9.95 (*0-7548-0008-3*, Lorenz Bks) Anness Pub.

Mushroom in the Rain. Mirra Ginsburg. (J). 1997. pap. text 5.99 (*0-689-81475-5*) Aladdin.

Mushroom in the Rain. Mirra Ginsburg. (J). 1990. 12.00 (*0-606-04484-1*, Pub. by Turtleback) Demco.

Mushroom in the Rain. Mirra Ginsburg. LC 90-31814. (Illus.). 32p. (J). (ps-1). 1997. reprint ed. mass mkt. 5.99 (*0-689-71441-6*) Aladdin.

Mushroom Jungle: A History of Postwar Paperback Publishing. Steve Holland. xii, 196p. (Orig.). 1994. lib. bdg. 37.00 (*0-8095-6013-5*) Millefleurs.

Mushroom Jungle: A History of Postwar Paperback Publishing. Steve Holland. (Illus.). 204p. (Orig.). 1993. pap. 29.95 (*1-874113-01-7*, Pub. by Zardoz Bks) Firebird Dist.

*__Mushroom Lover's Mushroom Cookbook & Primer.__ Amy Farges & Christopher Styler. 416p. 2000. 25.95 (*0-7611-2202-8*) Workman Pub.

*__Mushroom Lover's Mushroom Cookbook & Primer.__ Amy Farges & Christopher Styler. (Illus.). 416p. 2000. pap. 16.95 (*0-7611-0660-X*) Workman Pub.

*__Mushroom Magic: 100 Fabulous Fungi Feasts & Marvellous Mushroom Meals.__ Peter Jordan. (Illus.). 2000. pap. 14.95 (*0-7548-0448-8*, Lorenz Bks) Anness Pub.

Mushroom Man. Stuart Pawson. 320p. 1997. mass mkt. 11.95 (*0-7472-4897-4*, Pub. by Headline Bk Pub) Trafalgar.

Mushroom Manual - Tops! Complete for College Class: Simple for You & Me. Lorentz C. Pearson. LC 86-21847. (Illus.). 224p. 1987. pap. 9.95 (*0-87961-161-8*) Naturegraph.

Mushroom Matings: The Best in Mushroom Cookery. Jean Granger. LC 78-5407. 1978. pap. 2.95 (*0-89666-000-1*) Cragmont Pubns.

Mushroom on Mars Hill! The Lowell Observatory & the Discovery of Pluto. Carole Marsh. (Interactive Multimedia Titles Ser.). (J). (gr. 2-9). 1995. 29.95 (*0-7933-7592-4*, C Marsh); pap. 19.95 (*0-7933-7593-2*, C Marsh) Gallopade Intl.

Mushroom on Mars Hill! The Lowell Observatory & the Discovery of Pluto. Carole Marsh. (Interactive Multimedia Titles Ser.). (J). (gr. 2-9). 1996. pap., teacher ed. 19.95 (*0-7933-7837-0*, C Marsh) Gallopade Intl.

Mushroom Science (Systematics) T. N. Kaul. (Illus.). 215p. (C). 1997. 49.00 (*1-886106-95-9*) Science Pubs.

Mushroom Stones of Meso-America. Karl H. Mayer. (Illus.). 1977. pap. 7.95 (*0-916552-09-8*) Acoma Bks.

Mushroom Years: A Story of Survival. Pamela Masters. LC 94-93017. (Illus.). xii, 311p. 1998. pap. 19.95 (*0-9664489-2-8*) Hndrson Hse Pubng.

Mushrooms. LC 97-44418. (Eyewitness Handbooks Ser.). 1998. pap. 18.95 (*0-7894-3335-4*) DK Pub Inc.

Mushrooms. (Magnet Gourmet Ser.). 1997. 5.95 (*0-614-27959-3*) Sterling.

Mushrooms. Audubon Society Staff & Gary H. Lincoff. LC 81-80827. (Illus.). 864p. 1981. 19.00 (*0-394-51992-2*) Knopf.

Mushrooms. Jason Cooper. (Earth's Garden Discovery Library). 24p. (J). (gr. k-4). 1991. lib. bdg. 14.60 (*0-86592-623-9*) Rourke Enter.

Mushrooms. Thomas E. Laess & Gary Lincoff. LC 97-44418. (Eyewitness Handbooks Ser.). 304p. 1998. 29.95 (*0-7894-3286-2*) DK Pub Inc.

Mushrooms. Peter Murray. LC 95-907. (Nature Books Ser.). (Illus.). 32p. (J). (gr. 2-6). 1995. lib. bdg. 22.79 (*1-56766-193-9*) Childs World.

Mushrooms. Ed. by Smallwood & Stewart Staff. LC 96-86646. (Little Books for Cooks). (Illus.). 80p. 1997. 4.95 (*0-8362-2779-4*) Andrews & McMeel.

Mushrooms: A Story Samphlet & Activity Pages. Story Time Stories That Rhyme Staff. (Story Samphlet Edition Ser.). (Illus.). 20p. (J). (gr. 4-7). 1992. 9.95 (*1-56820-010-2*) Story Time.

Mushrooms: Flashguides. Kent Mcnight. (Illus.). 12p. 1996. pap. 7.95 (*0-395-82999-2*) HM.

Mushrooms: Global Recipes from Leading Chefs with Mushrooms. Photos by Sian Irvine. LC 98-47556. (Illus.). 162p. 1999. 21.95 (*962-593-494-4*) Periplus.

Mushrooms: Over 100 Tantalizing International Recipes. Rita Rosenberg. LC 94-37128. (Illus.). 192p. 1995. reprint ed. pap. 12.95 (*1-55561-071-4*) Fisher Bks.

Mushrooms: Poisons & Panaceas: Health Effects of Mushrooms. Denis R. Benjamin. LC 94-44126. (Illus.). 416p. 1995. pap. text 59.95 (*0-7167-2600-9*); pap. text 34.95 (*0-7167-2649-1*) W H Freeman.

Mushrooms: Psychedelic Fungi. Peter E. Furst. (Encyclopedia of Psychoactive Drugs Ser.: No. 1). (Illus.). 124p. (YA). (gr. 7 up). 1986. lib. bdg. 19.95 (*0-87754-767-X*) Chelsea Hse.

Mushrooms: The Photographic Guide to Identify Common & Important Mushrooms. Roger Phillips. 159p. 1986. pap. text 18.00 (*0-241-11756-9*) Lubrecht & Cramer.

Mushrooms & Other Fungi of Great Britain & Europe. Roger Phillips. (Illus.). 288p. (Orig.). 1981. pap. 47.50 (*0-330-26441-9*, Pub. by Pan) Trans-Atl Phila.

Mushrooms & Toadstools. Jens Stordal. (Blanford Mini-Guide Ser.).Tr. of Swedish. (Illus.). 128p. 1981. pap. text 5.00 (*0-7137-1211-2*) Lubrecht & Cramer.

Mushrooms & Toadstools. Marie Taylor. (Mobil New Zealand Nature Ser.). (Illus.). 79p. 1981. pap., spiral bd. 10.95 (*0-589-01354-8*) Lubrecht & Cramer.

Mushrooms & Toadstools. J. Wilkinson & Stefan T. Buczacki. (Collins Gem Guides Ser.). (Illus.). 1982. pap. 7.50 (*0-00-458812-6*) Lubrecht & Cramer.

Mushrooms & Truffles of the Southwest. Jack S. States. LC 89-20693. (Illus.). 232p. 1990. pap. 15.95 (*0-8165-1192-6*) U of Ariz Pr.

Mushrooms Demystified. 2nd rev. ed. David Arora. (Illus.). 959p. 1986. pap. 39.95 (*0-89815-169-4*) Ten Speed Pr.

Mushrooms in the Garden. Hellmut Steineck.Tr. of Pilze im Garten. (Illus.). 151p. (Orig.). 1985. pap. 23.95 (*0-916422-50-X*) Mad River.

Mushrooms Love Herbs. Ruth Bass. LC 96-14312. (Illus.). 64p. 1996. 9.95 (*0-88266-933-8*, Storey Pub) Storey Bks.

*__Mushrooms of Britain & Europe.__ Regis Courtecuisse. (Collins Wild Guide Ser.). (Illus.). 904p. 2000. pap. 29.95 (*0-00-220012-0*, Pub. by HarpC) Trafalgar.

Mushrooms of Colorado: And the Southern Rocky Mountains. Vera S. Evenson. LC 97-181487. (Illus.). 224p. 1997. pap. 25.00 (*1-56579-192-4*) Westcliffe Pubs.

Mushrooms of Idaho & the Pacific Northwest Vol. 1: Discomycetes. Edmund E. Tylutki. (Northwest Naturalist Bks.). 136p. 1994. pap. 13.95 (*0-89301-062-6*) U of Idaho Pr.

Mushrooms of Idaho & the Pacific Northwest Vol. 2: Non-gilled Hymenomycetes. Edmund E. Tylutki. LC 79-64127. (Northwest Naturalist Bks.). (Illus.). 256p. 1987. pap. 14.95 (*0-89301-097-9*) U of Idaho Pr.

Mushrooms of North America: The Most Comprehensive Mushroom Guide Ever. Roger Phillips. 1991. pap. 29.95 (*0-316-70613-2*) Little.

Mushrooms of North America in Color: A Field Guide Companion to Seldom-Illustrated Fungi. Alan E. Bessette et al. LC 95-11781. (Illus.). 188p. 1995. 39.95 (*0-8156-2666-5*); pap. 19.95 (*0-8156-0323-1*) Syracuse U Pr.

Mushrooms of Northeast North America: Midwest to New England. George Barron. (Illus.). 336p. 1999. pap. 19.95 (*1-55105-201-6*) Lone Pine.

Mushrooms of Northeastern North America. Alan E. Bessette et al. (Illus.). xiv, 582p. 1997. 95.00 (*0-8156-2707-6*, BEMU); pap. 45.00 (*0-8156-0388-6*, BEMUP) Syracuse U Pr.

Mushrooms of Northwest North America. Helene M. Schalkwijk-Barendsen. LC 94-910493. (Illus.). 416p. 1994. pap. 19.95 (*1-55105-046-3*) Lone Pine.

Mushrooms of Ontario & Eastern Canada. 3rd ed. George Barron. (Illus.). 336p. (Orig.). 1999. pap. 19.95 (*1-55105-199-0*) Lone Pine.

Mushrooms of the Adirondacks: A Field Guide. Alan E. Bessette. 148p. 1988. pap. 12.95 (*0-932052-64-9*) North Country.

Mushrooms of the World. Guiseppe Pace. (Illus.). 310p. 1998. text 35.00 (*1-55209-212-7*) Firefly Bks Ltd.

Mushrooms of Western Canada. Helene M. Schalkwyk-Barendsen. Ed. by Elaine Butler. 416p. 1991. pap. 19.95 (*0-919433-47-2*) Lone Pine.

Mushrooms of Western North America. Robert T. Orr & Dorothy B. Orr. LC 77-93468. (California Natural History Guides Ser.: No.42). (Illus.). 1979. 45.00 (*0-520-03656-5*, Pub. by U CA Pr); pap. 13.95 (*0-520-03660-3*, Pub. by U CA Pr) Cal Prin Full Svc.

Mushrooms, Sausage & Wine Vol. 1: Life with an Immigrant Father. Edward A. Maruggi. (Illus.). 153p. (Orig.). 1997. pap. 9.95 (*0-9658870-0-6*) Winston NY.

Mushrooms, Turnip Greens & Pickled Eggs. 2nd ed. Fran Parker. 288p. 1975. 5.25 (*0-686-11664-X*) TarPar.

Music see Ideas for Teaching Gifted Students

Music. 25.95 (*0-382-40692-3*) Cobblestone Pub Co.

*__Music.__ Neil Ardley. (Eyewitness Books). (Illus.). 2000. 19.99 (*0-7894-6561-2*) DK Pub Inc.

*__Music.__ Neil Ardley. (Eyewitness Books). (Illus.). (J). (gr. 4-7). 2000. 15.95 (*0-7894-5828-4*) DK Pub Inc.

Music. Bill Balcziak. (Communication Today & Tomorrow Ser.). (Illus.). 48p. (J). (gr. 4-8). 1989. lib. bdg. 25.27 (*0-86592-056-7*) Rourke Enter.

Music. Boardman. (J). (gr. 1-2). 1988. 40.00 (*0-03-005268-8*) Harcourt Schl Pubs.

Music. Jaq Greenspon. (VGM Career Portraits Ser.). (Illus.). 96p. 1994. 13.95 (*0-8442-4360-4*, 43604, VGM Career) NTC Contemp Pub Co.

Music. Ted Greenwald. (Careers Without College Ser.). 1992. 13.15 (*0-606-05189-9*, Pub. by Turtleback) Demco.

Music. William H. Hadow. 256p. 1990. lib. bdg. 69.00 (*0-7812-9021-X*) Rprt Serv.

*__Music.__ Morgan Hughes. LC 00-23698. (Halls of Fame Ser.). 2000. pap. write for info. (*1-55916-269-4*) Rourke Bk Co.

Music! Genevieve Laurencin. Tr. by Vicki Bogard from FRE. LC 89-8892. (Young Discovery Library). (Illus.). (J). (gr. k-5). 1989. 5.95 (*0-944589-25-1*, 025) Young Discovery Lib.

Music. Ken Norris. LC 96-118788. 104p. 1995. pap. 12.00 (*1-55022-260-0*, Pub. by ECW) Genl Dist Srvs.

*__Music.__ Penny Nye. (Bookmates Ser.). (Illus.). 15p. (J). (ps-3). 2000. pap. 12.00 (*1-890703-19-2*, Bkmates) Penny Laine.

Music. Johannes Rademacher. LC 96-83723. (Crash Course Ser.). (Illus.). 192p. 1996. 12.95 (*0-8120-9773-4*) Barron.

Music. Kirk Robertson. (Illus.). 56p. 1995. pap. 10.00 (*0-912449-51-9*) Floating Island.

Music. Julian Rowe. LC 96-17979. (Science Encounters Ser.). (J). 1998. 19.92 (*1-57572-091-4*) Heinemann Lib.

Music. Jack Rudman. (Undergraduate Program Field Tests (UPFT) Ser.: Vol. 16). 43.95 (*0-8373-6066-8*) Nat Learn.

Music. Jack Rudman. (Graduate Record Examination Ser.: GRE-13). 1994. pap. 23.95 (*0-8373-5213-4*) Nat Learn.

Music. Jack Rudman. (Undergraduate Program Field Tests (UPFT) Ser.: Vol. UPFT-16). 1994. pap. 23.95 (*0-8373-6016-1*) Nat Learn.

*__Music.__ Carol Diggory Shields & Svjetlan Junakovic. (Illus.). 32p. (J). 2000. 9.95 (*1-929766-05-X*) Handprint.

Music. Ed. by Jenny Vaughan & Scholastic, Inc. Staff. 1987. pap. 14.95 (*0-590-70700-0*, Scholastic Hardcover) Scholastic Inc.

Music. William H. Hadow. LC 72-137238. reprint ed. 32.50 (*0-404-03021-1*) AMS Pr.

Music. 2nd ed. Christine J. Dillon. (My First Report Ser.). (Illus.). 56p. (J). (gr. 1-3). 1997. reprint ed. ring bd. 5.95 (*1-57896-000-2*, 1763) Hewitt Res Fnd.

Music. 4th ed. Daniel T. Politoske. (Illus.). 576p. (C). 1988. audio. write for info. (*0-318-62496-6*) P-H.

Music. 5th ed. Sufi I. Khan. LC 87-92056. 104p. 1988. pap. 6.95 (*0-89793-059-2*) Hunter Hse.

Music: A Comprehensive Introduction. Steven Porter. LC 85-16847. 336p. 1986. pap. 18.00 (*0-935016-81-3*, Pub. by Zinn Pub Grp) Empire Pub Srvs.

Music: A Comprehensive Introduction, Workbook Number 1: Music Theory, Vol. 2. Steven Porter. 45p. 1986. pap., wbk. ed. 7.00 (*0-935016-84-8*) Zinn Pub Grp.

Music: A Crash Course. Marcus Weeks. (Crash Course Ser.). (Illus.). 144p. 1999. 14.95 (*0-8230-0978-5*) Watsn-Guptill.

Music: A. D. 450 to A. D. 1995. Mark Ammons. (Illus.). 80p. (YA). (gr. 5). 1995. pap. text 9.95 (*1-58037-053-5*, Pub. by M Twain Media) Carson-Dellos.

Music: A Listener's Introduction. Kenneth Levy. 526p. (C). 1997. pap. 68.00 (*0-06-043933-5*) Addson-Wesley Educ.

Music: A Living Language. Tom Manoff. (Illus.). 350p. (C). 1982. write for info. (*0-393-95228-2*); pap. text 36.25 (*0-393-95194-4*) Norton.

Music: A Living Language. Tom Manoff. (Illus.). 350p. (C). 1982. pap. text, teacher ed. write for info. (*0-393-95220-7*) Norton.

Music: A Multicultural Experience. 2nd ed. Davis & Signell. 384p. (C). 1998. per. 39.95 (*0-7872-5270-0*, 41527001) Kendall-Hunt.

Music: A Pictorial Archive of Woodcuts & Engravings. Jim Harter. (Pictorial Archive Ser.). (Illus.). 160p. (Orig.). 1981. pap. 9.95 (*0-486-24002-9*) Dover.

*__Music: A Very Short Introduction.__ 160p. 2000. 8.95 (*0-19-285382-1*) OUP.

Music: A Very Short Introduction. Nicholas Cook. LC 98-12197. (Very Short Introductions Ser.). (Illus.). 156p. 1998. pap. 8.95 (*0-19-285340-6*) OUP.

Music: A Way of Life for the Young Child. 4th ed. Kathleen Bayless. 288p. (C). 1990. pap. text 45.00 (*0-675-21372-X*, Merrill Coll) P-H.

Music: An Appreciation. Roger Kamien. 656p. (C). 1992. 63.00 incl. audio (*0-07-911478-4*) McGraw.

M

An Asterisk (*) at the beginning of an entry indicates that the title is appearing for the first time.

Music: An Appreciation. 2nd ed. Roger Kamien. LC 93-15089. 656p. (C). 1993. pap. text 37.50 (*0-07-034819-7*) McGraw.

Music: An Appreciation. 2nd ed. Roger Kamien. LC 93-15089. 656p. (C). 1993. pap. text, student ed. 15.62 (*0-07-034821-9*) McGraw.

Music: An Appreciation. 3rd ed. Roger Kamien. LC 97-73723. 480p. (C). 1997. 43.13 (*0-07-036521-0*) McGraw.

Music: An Appreciation. 5th ed. Roger Kamien. (C). 1992. pap. text 91.00 (*0-07-911463-6*) McGraw.

Music: An Appreciation. 5th ed. Roger Kamien. 656p. (C). 1992. text 81.50 incl. audio (*0-07-911516-0*) McGraw.

Music: An Appreciation. 5th ed. Roger Kamien. (C). 1992. audio. write for info. (*0-07-911476-8*) McGraw.

Music: An Appreciation. 6th ed. Albert Camus. (C). 1995. pap., student ed., wbk. ed. 28.75 (*0-07-034071-4*) McGraw.

Music: An Appreciation. 6th ed. Roger Kamien. LC 95-21760. (C). 1995. text 45.00 (*0-07-034070-6*) McGraw.

Music: An Appreciation. 7th ed. Roger Kamien. LC 99-12903. 776p. 1999. 56.25 (*0-07-290200-0*) McGraw.

***Music: An Appreciation.** 7th ed. Roger Kamien. 208p. (C). 1999. pap. 27.50 (*0-07-290205-1*) McGrw-H Hghr Educ.

Music: An Appreciation Supplemental. 6th ed. Kamien. 1995. 12.00 (*0-07-912959-5*); 20.00 (*0-07-912961-7*) McGraw.

Music: An Art & a Language. Walter R. Spalding. 342p. 1990. reprint ed. lib. bdg. 79.00 (*0-7812-9132-1*) Rprt Serv.

Music: An Introduction for the New Listener. Greckel. (Music). 2001. student ed. 12.00 (*0-534-52426-5*); mass mkt. 30.00 (*0-534-52425-7*) Wadsworth Pub.

Music: Careers in Music. Mary A. Marshall. LC 93-14832. (Now Hiring Ser.). (Illus.). 48p. (J). (gr. 5-6). 1994. lib. bdg. 15.95 (*0-89686-793-5*, Crstwood Hse) Silver Burdett Pr.

Music: Classical, Romantic & Modern. Arthur E. Hull. (Select Bibliographies Reprint Ser.). 1977. reprint ed. 30.95 (*0-8369-5803-9*) Ayer.

Music: Discipline Analysis, Vol. 7K. J. Michele Edwards. (Women in the Curriculum Ser.). 35p. (Orig.). 1997. pap. 7.00 (*1-885303-24-6*) Towson St Univ.

Music: Its Ideals & Methods, a Collection of Essays for Young Teachers, Amateurs, & Students. William S. Mathews. LC 70-173057. reprint ed. 41.00 (*0-404-07211-9*) AMS Pr.

Music: Its Secret Influence Throughout the Ages. Cyril Scott. 221p. 1996. pap. 20.00 (*0-89540-323-4*, SB-323) Sun Pub.

Music: Physician for Times to Come. Don Campbell. Orig. Title: Music as Physician. 318p. 1995. pap. 15.00 (*0-8356-0668-6*, Quest) Theos Pub Hse.

***Music: Physician for Times to Come.** 2nd rev. ed. Don Campbell. Orig. Title: Music as Physician. 365p. 2000. pap. 15.95 (*0-8356-0788-7*, Pub. by Theos Pub Hse) Natl Bk Netwk.

Music: Role & Importance '94. Charles Fowler. 1993. 50.08 (*0-02-642121-6*) Glencoe.

Music: The Art of Listening. 4th ed. Ferris. 1995. teacher ed. 13.12 (*0-697-26697-4*, WCB McGr Hill) McGrw-H Hghr Educ.

Music: The Art of Listening. 4th ed. Jean Ferris. 400p. (C). 1994. text. write for info. (*0-697-24544-6*) Brown & Benchmark.

Music: The Art of Listening. 4th ed. Jean Ferris. 400p. (C). 1995. text. write for info. (*0-697-24545-4*); text. write for info. (*0-697-24546-2*); text. write for info. (*0-697-26699-0*); audio. write for info. (*0-697-26698-2*) Brown & Benchmark.

Music: The Art of Listening. 5th ed. Ferris. 1999. cd-rom 25.00 (*0-07-229447-7*) McGraw.

Music: The Facts on File Encyclopedia of Black Women in America, Vol. 5-6. Ed. by Darlene Clark Hine. 1997. 29.95 (*0-8160-3431-1*) Facts on File.

Music: The Key of Human Evolution. Corinne Heline. (Illus.). 144p. 1986. pap. text 16.00 (*0-933963-10-6*) New Age Bible.

Music: The New Age Elixir. Lisa Summer & Joseph Summer. LC 96-2765. (Illus.). 303p. 1996. 25.95 (*1-57392-104-1*) Prometheus Bks.

Music: The New Curriculum. Prince L. Dorough & Christopher P. Gordon. 309p. (Orig.). (C). 1995. pap. text 20.80 (*0-87563-577-6*) Stipes.

Music - Cultures in Contact: Convergences & Collisions. Margaret J. Kartomi. (Musicology: A Book Ser.). 248p. 1994. pap. text 18.00 (*2-88449-137-6*) Gordon & Breach.

Music - Cultures in Contact: Convergences & Collisions. Ed. by Margaret J. Kartomi & Stephen Blum. pap. 24.95 (*0-86819-365-8*, Pub. by Currency Pr) Accents Pubns.

Music - Motion & Emotion: The Developmental-Integrative Model in Music Therapy. Chava Sekeles. (Illus.). 181p. (Orig.). 1996. pap. 29.95 (*0-918812-88-7*) MMB Music.

Music - Verse & Verses: A Calendar Book - 2000. Beth Garbo. (Illus.). 116p. 1998. spiral bd. 16.95 (*1-892373-26-2*, 26-2) Especially Bks.

Music - Verse & Verses: A Calendar Book, 1999. Beth Garbo. (Illus.). 116p. 1998. spiral bd. 16.95 (*1-892373-07-6*, 99-13) Especially Bks.

Music, a Short History: Music Book Index. Walter J. Turner. 105p. 1993. reprint ed. lib. bdg. 69.00 (*0-7812-9560-2*) Rprt Serv.

Music: A View from Delft: Selected Essays. Edward T. Cone. Ed. by Robert P. Morgan. LC 88-20659. (Illus.). 352p. 1989. pap. text 22.00 (*0-226-11470-8*) U Ch Pr.

Music: A View from Delft: Selected Essays. Edward T. Cone. Ed. by Robert P. Morgan. LC 88-20659. (Illus.). 344p. 1998. lib. bdg. 78.00 (*0-226-11469-4*) U Ch Pr.

Music Accompaniment for the Funeral Mass. 192p. 1989. pap. 12.95 (*0-8146-1506-6*) Liturgical Pr.

Music Across Curriculum. Holt. 1989. pap. 12.00 (*0-03-025323-3*); pap. 12.00 (*0-03-025324-1*); pap. 12.00 (*0-03-025327-6*); pap. 12.00 (*0-03-025328-4*); pap. 12.00 (*0-03-025329-2*); pap. 12.00 (*0-03-025332-2*) Harcourt Schl Pubs.

Music Activity Book. Ellen J. McHenry. 1996. pap. 2.95 (*0-486-29079-4*) Dover.

Music Address Book. 2nd ed. Michael Levine. LC 93-21463. 240p. 1994. pap. 16.00 (*0-06-273257-9*, Harper Ref) HarpC.

Music Administration: An Annotated Bibliography. Richard Evans. 20p. (Orig.). (C). 1981. pap. text 10.00 (*0-911009-01-9*) Prestige Pubns.

Music Alone: Philosophical Reflections on the Purely Musical Experience. Peter Kivy. LC 89-35570. (Illus.). 240p. 1991. reprint ed. pap. text 14.95 (*0-8014-9960-7*) Cornell U Pr.

Music Analyses: An Annotated Guide to the Literature. Harold J. Diamond. 716p. 1991. 43.00 (*0-02-870110-0*, Schirmer Books) Mac Lib Ref.

Music Analysis in the Nineteenth Century, Vol. 1. Ed. by Ian D. Bent. LC 93-12313. (Cambridge Readings in the Literature of Music Ser.: No. 1). 391p. (C). 1994. text 80.00 (*0-521-25969-X*) Cambridge U Pr.

Music Analysis in the Nineteenth Century Vol. 2: Hermeneutic Approaches. Ed. by Ian D. Bent. (Cambridge Readings in the Literature of Music Ser.). 319p. (C). 1994. text 69.95 (*0-521-46183-9*) Cambridge U Pr.

Music & Art of the Theatre. Adolphe Appia. Ed. by Barnard Hewitt. LC 62-20172. (Books of the Theatre: No. 3). 1962. pap. 19.95 (*0-87024-018-8*) U of Miami Pr.

Music & Ballet. Michel D. Calvocoressi. LC 74-24053. reprint ed. 37.50 (*0-404-12877-7*) AMS Pr.

Music & Bharathanatyam. Z. S. Bhagyalekshmy. (C). 1991. 54.00 (*81-85067-63-5*, Pub. by Sundeep Prak) S Asia.

Music & Black Ethnicity: The Caribbean & South America. Ed. by Gerard H. Behague. LC 94-503. 352p. (C). 1998. pap. 25.95 (*1-56000-708-7*, Pub. by U Miami N-S Ctr) L Rienner.

***Music & British Culture, 1785-1914: Essays in Honour of Cyril Ehrlich.** Ed. by Christina Bashford & Leanne Langley. (Illus.). 448p. 2001. text 105.00 (*0-19-816730-X*) OUP.

Music & Bugling. Boy Scouts of America. (Illus.). 80p. (YA). (gr. 6-12). 1990. pap. 2.90 (*0-8395-3341-1*) BSA.

Music & Child Development. Ed. by J. C. Peery et al. (Illus.). 315p. 1987. 59.00 (*0-387-96422-3*) Spr-Verlag.

Music & Child Development. Ed. by Franz L. Roehmann. (Illus.). 442p. (Orig.). 1990. pap. 25.00 (*0-918812-58-5*, ST011) MMB Music.

***Music & Cinema.** Ed. by James Buhler et al. LC 00-23696. (Music Culture Ser.). (Illus.). 384p. 2000. pap. 24.95 (*0-8195-6411-7*, Wesleyan Univ Pr) U Pr of New Eng.

***Music & Cinema.** Ed. by James Buhler et al. LC 00-23696. (Music Culture Ser.). (Illus.). 384p. 2000. text 70.00 (*0-8195-6410-9*, Wesleyan Univ Pr) U Pr of New Eng.

Music & Conceptualization. Mark DeBellis. (Illus.). 175p. (C). 1995. text 59.95 (*0-521-40331-6*) Cambridge U Pr.

Music & Concert Hall Acoustics: Conference Proceedings from MCHA, 1995. Ed. by Yoichi Ando & Dennis Noson. (Illus.). 448p. 1996. text 95.00 (*0-12-059555-9*) Acad Pr.

Music & Connectionism. Ed. by Peter Todd & D. Gareth Loy. 250p. 1991. 50.00 (*0-262-20081-3*) MIT Pr.

***Music & Consciousness: My Life's Work.** Helen L. Bonny. (C). 2000. pap. text. write for info. (*1-891278-10-X*) Barcelona Pubs.

Music & Context: Essays in Honor of John Milton Ward. Ed. by Anne D. Shapiro. 400p. 1985. 35.00 (*0-674-58888-6*) HUP.

Music & Copyright. Ed. by Simon Frith. (Law & Society Ser.). 208p. 1994. 60.00 (*0-7486-0481-2*, Pub. by Edinburgh U Pr) Col U Pr.

Music & Cultural Theory. John Shepherd & Peter Wicke. LC 97-2730. 232p. (C). 1997. 62.95 (*0-7456-0863-9*); pap. 28.95 (*0-7456-0864-7*) Blackwell Pubs.

Music & Culture in America, 1861-1918. Ed. by Michael Saffle & James R. Heintze. LC 97-49479. (Essays in American Music Ser.: Vol. 2). (Illus.). 387p. 1998. text 75.00 (*0-8153-2125-2*) Garland.

Music & Culture in Eighteenth-Century Europe: A Source Book. Enrico Fubini. Ed. by Bonnie J. Blackburn. Tr. by Wolfgang Freis et al. LC 93-36066. 432p. (C). 1994. pap. text 21.00 (*0-226-26732-6*) U Ch Pr.

Music & Culture in Eighteenth-Century Europe: A Source Book. Enrico Fubini. Ed. by Bonnie J. Blackburn. Tr. by Wolfgang Freis et al. LC 93-36066. 432p. (C). 1994. lib. bdg. 55.00 (*0-226-26731-8*) U Ch Pr.

Music & Culture in Italy from the Middle Ages to the Baroque: A Collection of Essays. Nino Pirrotta. LC 83-12827. (Studies in the History of Music: No. 1). 501p. reprint ed. pap. 155.40 (*0-7837-2313-X*, 205740100004) Bks Demand.

***Music & Culture in South-East New Britain: Unesco Territorial Survey of Oceanic Music Report on Field Research Conducted in August-October 1988.** Wolfgang Laade. 262p. 2000. pap. text 35.95 (*3-906760-41-3*) P Lang Pubng.

***Music & Culture in the Age of Mechanical Reproduction.** Bhesham R. Sharma. LC 99-28063. (New Studies in Aesthetics: No. 31). 232p. (C). 2000. text 49.95 (*0-8204-4516-9*) P Lang Pubng.

Music & Dance see Musica y Baile

Music & Dance. Silvia P. Baeza. LC 95-3718. (Latino Life Ser.). 48p. (J). (gr. 4-8). 1996. lib. bdg. 23.93 (*0-86625-545-1*) Rourke Pubns.

Music & Dance: In the Worship Program of the Church. Constance L. Fisher. (Orig.). 1981. pap. 3.00 (*0-941500-20-9*) Sharing Co.

Music & Dance in Puerto Rico from the Age of Columbus to Modern Times: An Annotated Bibliography. Donald Thompson & Annie F. Thompson. (Studies in Latin American Music). 339p. 1991. 45.00 (*0-8108-2515-5*) Scarecrow.

Music & Dance of the World's Religions: A Comprehensive, Annotated Bibliography of Materials in the English Language, 54. E. Gardner Rust. LC 96-18212. (Music Reference Collection: Vol. 54). 504p. 1996. lib. bdg. 89.50 (*0-313-29561-1*, Greenwood Pr) Greenwood.

Music & Dance Periodicals: An International Directory & Guidebook. Ed. by Doris Robinson. (Orig.). 1989. pap. 65.00 (*0-9617844-4-X*) Peri Press.

Music & Drama. (Studies in the History of Music: Vol. 2). (Illus.). 1988. lib. bdg. 65.00 (*0-8450-7402-4*) Broude.

Music & Drama in the Tragedie en Musique, 1673-1715: Jean-Baptiste Lully & His Successors. rev. ed. Caroline Wood. LC 95-51831. (Outstanding Dissertations in Music from British Universities Ser.). (Illus.). 391p. 1996. text 105.00 (*0-8153-2450-2*) Garland.

Music & Dramatics at Circle Time. Carol Gnojewski & Jean Warren. LC 98-61458. (Circle Time Book Ser.). (Illus.). 96p. (J). (ps-k). 1999. pap. 9.95 (*1-57029-240-X*, 04902) Totline Pubns.

Music & Drum: Voices of War & Peace, Hope & Dreams. Illus. by Debra Lill. LC 92-39312. 32p. (J). (ps up). 1997. 16.95 (*0-399-22024-0*, Philomel) Peng Put Young Read.

Music & Education. D. Kabalevsky. 1988. 19.95 (*1-85302-009-5*, Pub. by Jessica Kingsley) Taylor & Francis.

Music & Education in Vermont, 1700-1900. James A. Keene. LC 87-166730. (Illus.). 214p. 1987. 19.95 (*0-944435-00-9*) Glenbridge Pub.

Music & Feminism. Cusich. 1995. 26.95 (*0-8057-9758-0*, Twyne) Mac Lib Ref.

Music & Feminism. Fontign. 1999. 29.95 (*0-8057-1665-3*, Twyne) Mac Lib Ref.

***Music & Gender** Pirkko Moisala & Beverley Diamond. LC 99-6791. 2000. write for info. (*0-252-06865-3*) U of Ill Pr.

Music & German Literature: Studies on Their Relationship since the Middle Ages. Ed. by James M. McGlathery. (GERM Ser.: Vol. 66). (Illus.). 400p. 1992. 75.00 (*1-879751-03-8*) Camden Hse.

Music & History of the Baroque Trumpet Before 1721. rev. ed. Don L. Smithers. LC 88-23804. (Illus.). 356p. (C). 1989. reprint ed. text 49.95 (*0-8093-1497-5*) S Ill U Pr.

***Music & Humanism: An Essay in the Aesthetics of Music.** R. A. Sharpe. LC 99-50261. 240p. 2000. 35.00 (*0-19-823885-1*) OUP.

Music & Image: Domesticity, Ideology & Socio-Cultural Formation in 18th Century England. Richard D. Leppert. (Illus.). 264p. (C). 1993. pap. text 25.95 (*0-521-44854-9*) Cambridge U Pr.

Music & Imagination. Aaron Copland. LC 52-9385. (Charles Eliot Norton Lectures: 1951-1952). 116p. 1952. pap. text 10.95 (*0-674-58915-7*) HUP.

***Music & Inspiration.** Jonathan Harvey. Ed. by Michael Downes. 176p. 2000. pap. 20.00 (*0-571-20025-7*) Faber & Faber.

Music & Instruments of the Middle Ages: Studies on Text & Performance. Christopher Page. LC 97-2605. (Variorum Collected Studies Ser.: Vol. 562). 352p. 1997. text 98.95 (*0-86078-623-4*, Pub. by Variorum) Ashgate Pub Co.

Music & Irish Cultural History. Ed. by Gerard Gillen & Harry White. (Irish Musical Studies: Vol. 3). (Illus.). 256p. 1995. 45.00 (*0-7165-2536-4*, Pub. by Irish Acad Pr) Intl Spec Bk.

Music & Its Masters. Otis B. Boise. LC 73-39464. (Illus.). reprint ed. 32.50 (*0-404-08367-6*) AMS Pr.

Music & Its Public. Botstein. (C). 1990. lib. bdg. 34.95 (*0-226-06724-6*) U Ch Pr.

Music & Its Social Meanings. Christopher Ballantine. (Monographs on Musicology: Vol. 2). xx, 202p. (C). 1984. pap. text 25.00 (*0-677-22000-6*) Gordon & Breach.

Music & Kabbalah. Matityahu Glazerson. LC 96-49286. 128p. 1997. pap. 30.00 (*1-56821-933-4*) Aronson.

Music & Language. (Studies in the History of Music: Vol. 1). (Illus.). 1983. lib. bdg. 65.00 (*0-8450-7401-6*) Broude.

Music & Literature: A Comparison of the Arts. fac. ed. Calvin S. Brown. LC 86-28914. (Illus.). 303p. 1987. reprint ed. pap. 94.00 (*0-7837-8195-4*, 204790000008) Bks Demand.

Music & Liturgy: The Universa Laus Document & Commentary. Claude Duchesneau & Michel Veuthey. Tr. by Paul Inwood. (Orig.). 1992. pap. text 9.95 (*0-912405-98-8*, Pastoral Press) OR Catholic.

Music & Maestros: The Story of Minneapolis Symphony Orchestra. LC 52-11107. 403p. reprint ed. pap. 125.00 (*0-608-12437-0*, 205591400039) Bks Demand.

Music & Mandrakes: Anthology of Contemporary American Poets. Ed. by Elle Larkin & Leah Maines. 40p. 2000. pap. 8.95 (*0-9664324-5-2*) Finishng Line.

Music & Manners: From Pergolesi to Beethoven. Henry E. Krehbiel. LC 72-154156. (Select Bibliographies Reprint Ser.). 1977. reprint ed. 21.95 (*0-8369-5772-5*) Ayer.

Music & Materials for Analysis: An Anthology. Joseph K. Distefano & James A. Searl. 412p. (C). 1995. pap. text 34.95 (*1-880157-19-5*) Ardsley.

Music & Meaning. Ed. by Jenefer Robinson. LC 96-50450. (Illus.). 296p. 1996. pap. text 16.95 (*0-8014-8367-0*) Cornell U Pr.

Music & Meaning. Ed. by Jennifer Robinson. LC 96-50450. (Illus.). 296p. 1997. text 49.95 (*0-8014-3299-5*) Cornell U Pr.

Music & Media in Local Life: Music Practice in a Newar Neighborhood in Nepal. Ingemar Grandin. (Linkoping Studies in Arts & Sciences: No. 41). (Illus.). 254p. (Orig.). 1989. pap. 72.00 (*91-7870-480-4*) Coronet Bks.

Music & Medicine, 3 vols. Anton Neumayr. Incl. Vol. 1. Haydn, Mozart, Beethoven, Schubert, Notes on Their Lives, Works & Medical Histories. Tr. by Bruce C. Clarke from GER. LC 94-21413.Tr. of Musik und Medizin. (Illus.). 448p. 1994. 32.95 (*0-936741-05-8*); Vol. 2. Hummel, Weber, Mendelssohn, Schumann, Brahms, Bruckner, Notes on Their Lives, Works, & Medical Histories. Tr. by Bruce C. Clarke from GER. LC 94-21413.Tr. of Musk & Medizin, Am Beispielder Deutschen. (Illus.). 600p. 1995. 34.95 (*0-936741-07-4*); Vol. 3. Chopin, Smetana, Tschaikovsky, Notes on Their Lives, Works, & Medical Histories. Tr. by David J. Parent from GER. LC 94-21413. Orig. Title: Musik & Medizin. 1997. 34.95 (*0-936741-08-2*); 102.85 (*0-936741-33-3*) Medi-Ed Pr.

Music & Medicine. Dorothy M. Schullian & Max Schoen. LC 78-142693. (Essay Index Reprint Ser.). 1977. 27.95 (*0-8369-2132-1*) Ayer.

***Music & Memory: An Introduction.** Bob Snyder. LC 99-86731. (Illus.). 370p. (C). 2000. 75.00 (*0-262-19441-4*); pap. 30.00 (*0-262-69237-6*) MIT Pr.

Music & Menus for Christmas. Willi Elsener. 1996. 25.00 (*0-614-19374-5*) Macmillan.

***Music & Menus for Romance: Inspiring Romantic Music, Sensuous Tempting Recipes.** Anton Edelmann. (Illus.). 96p. 2000. 29.95 incl. audio compact disk (*1-85793-997-2*, Pub. by Pavilion Bks Ltd) Trafalgar.

Music & Menus from Italy: A Cookbook with Compact Disc. Antonio Carluccio. (Illus.). 96p. 1996. 24.95 incl. audio compact disk (*1-85793-529-2*, Pub. by Pavilion Bks Ltd) Trafalgar.

Music & Merchants: The Laudesi Companies of Republican Florence. Blake Wilson. (Illus.). 314p. 1992. text 90.00 (*0-19-816176-X*) OUP.

Music & Mind: Philosophical Essays on the Cognition & Meaning of Music. Harold E. Fiske. LC 89-13957. (Studies in the History & Interpretation of Music: Vol. 25). 176p. 1990. lib. bdg. 79.95 (*0-88946-473-1*) E Mellen.

Music & Mind: Philosophical Essays on the Cognition & Meaning of Music. Harold E. Fiske. (Studies in History & Interpretation of Music: Vol. 25). 180p. 1990. write for info. (*0-88946-474-X*) E Mellen.

Music & Ministry: A Biblical Counterpoint. 2nd rev. ed. Calvin Johansson. LC 98-19453. (Illus.). 192p. 1998. pap. 12.95 (*1-56563-361-X*) Hendrickson MA.

Music & Miracles: A Companion to Music: Physician for Times to Come. Ed. by Don Campbell. LC 92-50145. 280p. 1992. pap. 14.00 (*0-8356-0683-X*, Quest) Theos Pub Hse.

Music & Modern Media of Transmission. L. Gordon. 1975. lib. bdg. 250.00 (*0-87968-328-7*) Gordon Pr.

Music & Morals. Hugh R. Haweis. 1977. 20.95 (*0-8369-7223-6*, 8022) Ayer.

Music & Morals: A Theological Appraisal of the Moral & Psychological Effects of Music. Basil Cole. LC 92-36135. 172p. 1993. pap. 8.95 (*0-8189-0660-X*) Alba.

Music & More: Essays, 1968-1991. Samuel Lipman. 318p. (Orig.). 1994. 35.00 (*0-8101-1051-2*); pap. 14.95 (*0-8101-1076-8*) Northwestern U Pr.

Music & Music Education History: A Chronology. George H. Heller. 49p. 1996. pap. 7.50 (*1-879818-08-6*) U KS Art & Music.

Music & Music-Makers. Constance Morse. LC 68-54363. (Essay Index Reprint Ser.). 1977. 22.95 (*0-8369-0724-8*) Ayer.

Music & Musical Instruments of Southern India & the Deccan. C. R. Day. 1990. reprint ed. 12.50 (*81-85395-24-1*, Pub. by Low Price) S Asia.

Music & Musical Instruments of Southern India & the Deccan. C. R. Day. 1996. reprint ed. 11.00 (*81-86142-91-6*, Pub. by Low Price) S Asia.

Music & Musical Life in Soviet Russia, 1917-1981. enl. ed. Boris Schwarz. LC 82-48267. 735p. 1983. reprint ed. pap. 200.00 (*0-8357-3950-3*, 205704500004) Bks Demand.

Music & Musical Thought in Early India. Lewis Rowell. 1998. 68.00 (*81-215-0867-3*, Pub. by M Manoharial) Coronet Bks.

Music & Musical Thought in Early India. Lewis Rowell. (Chicago Studies in Ethnomusicology). 384p. 1992. lib. bdg. 68.00 (*0-226-73032-8*) U Ch Pr.

Music & Musical Thought in Early India. Lewis Rowell. (Chicago Studies in Ethnomusicology). 428p. 1998. pap. text 27.50 (*0-226-73033-6*) U Ch Pr.

Music & Musicians: An Introduction. Donald D. Megill. 1993. pap. text 67.00 incl. audio compact disk (*0-13-103698-X*) P-H.

Music & Musicians: An Introduction. Donald D. Megill. 362p. (C). 1993. pap. text 25.20 (*0-13-605668-7*) P-H.

Music & Musicians: An Introduction (with 2 cassettes) Donald D. Megill. LC 92-38407. 416p. (C). 1993. pap. text 62.67 (*0-13-034919-4*) P-H.

Music & Musicians: Essays & Criticisms. Robert Schumann. Ed. by Fanny R. Ritter. LC 72-8379. (Select Bibliographies Reprint Ser.). 1977. reprint ed. 34.95 (*0-8369-6998-7*) Ayer.

Music & Musicians in Ancient Greece. Warren D. Anderson. (Illus.). 264p. 1995. text 45.00 (*0-8014-3083-6*) Cornell U Pr.

Music & Musicians in Ancient Greece. Warren D. Anderson. (Illus.). 264p. 1996. pap. text 15.95 (*0-8014-8432-4*) Cornell U Pr.

M

An Asterisk (*) at the beginning of an entry indicates that the title is appearing for the first time.

Music & Musicians in Chicago. Florence F. Ffrench. LC 79-9802. (Music Reprint Ser.). 1979. reprint ed. lib. bdg. 32.50 (*0-306-79542-6*) Da Capo.

Music & Musicians in Early 19th Century Cornwall. Richard McGrady. 176p. 1991. pap. text 21.95 (*0-85989-359-6*, Pub. by Univ Exeter Pr) Northwestern U Pr.

Music & Musicians in Israel. Peter Gradenwitz. LC 75-166232. 226p. 1959. reprint ed. 59.00 (*0-403-01568-5*) Scholarly.

Music & Musicians in Nineteenth Century Italy. John Rosselli. (Illus.). 176p. 1991. 29.95 (*0-931340-40-3*, Amadeus Pr) Timber.

Music & Musicians in Renaissance Rome & Other Courts. Richard Sherr. LC 99-11126. (Variorum Collected Studies). 1999. 101.95 (*0-86078-768-0*, Pub. by Variorum) Ashgate Pub Co.

Music & Musicians in the Escorial Liturgy under the Habsburgs, 1563-1700, Vol. 9. Michael Noone. LC 97-41721. (Eastman Studies in Music). (Illus.). 416p. 1998. 100.00 (*1-878822-71-3*) Univ Rochester Pr.

Music & Musicians of Maine. George T. Edwards. LC 74-135736. 1974. reprint ed. 40.00 (*0-404-07231-3*) AMS Pr.

Music & Musicians of Puerto Rico. Fernando Callejo. (Puerto Rico Ser.). 1979. lib. bdg. 59.95 (*0-8490-2974-0*) Gordon Pr.

Music & Musket: Bands & Bandsmen of the American Civil War, 1. Kenneth E. Olson. LC 79-6195. (Contributions to the Study of Music & Dance Ser.: No. 1). (Illus.). 299p. 1981. 65.00 (*0-313-22112-X*, OMM/, Greenwood Pr) Greenwood.

Music & Mysticism, Pt. 1. Ed. by Maxwell Steer. (Contemporary Music Review Ser.). 134p. 1997. pap. text 30.00 (*3-7186-5930-1*, Harwood Acad Pubs) Gordon & Breach.

Music & Mysticism, Pt. 2. Ed. by Maxwell Steer. (Contemporary Music Review Ser.). 134p. 1997. pap. text 22.00 (*3-7186-5931-X*, Harwood Acad Pubs) Gordon & Breach.

Music & Nationalism: A Study of English Opera. Cecil Forsyth. LC 80-2276. Date not set. reprint ed. 37.00 (*0-404-18844-3*) AMS Pr.

Music & New Markets. Ed. by Cees Van Rij. 183p. 1991. pap. 75.00 (*90-6215-302-X*, Pub. by Maklu Uitgev) Gaunt.

Music & Opera: Around the World 1998-99. 3rd ed. Ed. by Editions Le Fil d' Ariane Staff. 1998. pap. 45.00 (*2-911894-04-9*) Stewart Tabori & Chang.

Music & Performance During the Weimar Republic. Ed. by Bryan Gilliam. LC 93-31382. (Studies in Performance Practice: Vol. 3). 234p. (C). 1994. text 64.95 (*0-521-42012-1*) Cambridge U Pr.

Music & Phonorecords - Authors List see National Union Catalog: A Cumulative Author List, 1958-62

Music & Phonorecords - Subject Index see National Union Catalog: A Cumulative Author List, 1958-62

Music & Poetry. Sidney Lanier. 1973. lib. bdg. 250.00 (*0-87968-028-8*) Gordon Pr.

Music & Poetry. Sidney Lanier. LC 68-25292. (Studies in Poetry: No. 38). (C). 1969. reprint ed. lib. bdg. 75.00 (*0-8383-0306-4*) M S G Haskell Hse.

Music & Poetry. Sidney Lanier. (Notable American Authors Ser.). 1999. reprint ed. lib. bdg. 125.00 (*0-7812-3724-6*) Rprt Serv.

Music & Poetry: Essays upon Some Aspects & Interrelations of the Two Arts. Ed. by Sidney Lanier. 248p. 1990. reprint ed. lib. bdg. 69.00 (*0-7812-9013-9*) Rprt Serv.

Music & Poetry in the Middle Ages: A Guide to Research on French & Occitan Song, 1100-1400. Margaret L. Switten. LC 94-33935. (Medieval Bibliographies Ser.: Vol. 1102). 452p. 1995. text 96.00 (*0-8240-4797-4*, H1102) Garland.

Music & Poetry of the English Renaissance. Bruce Pattison. LC 70-127278. (Music Ser.). (Illus.). 1971. reprint ed. lib. bdg. 29.50 (*0-306-71298-9*) Da Capo.

Music & Psychology: A Mutual Regard, Vol 2, No. 1. Stephen McAdams. (Contemporary Music Review Ser.). viii, 320p. 1987. pap. text 74.00 (*3-7186-0382-9*) Gordon & Breach.

Music & Public Entertainment. Ed. by Horatio W. Parker. LC 74-24180. (Illus.). reprint ed. 49.50 (*0-404-13082-8*) AMS Pr.

***Music & Racial Imagination.** Ronald M. Radano. 1999. lib. bdg. 70.00 (*0-226-70199-9*) U Ch Pr.

Music & Religion. Ed. by Stanley A. Hunter. LC 72-1615. reprint ed. 32.50 (*0-404-08316-1*) AMS Pr.

Music & Ritual at Papal Avignon, 1309-1403. Andrew Tomasello. LC 83-18296. (Studies in Musicology: No. 75). 314p. reprint ed. pap. 97.40 (*0-8357-1493-4*, 207034200085) Bks Demand.

Music & Schema Theory: Cognitive Foundations of Systematic Musicology, Vol. 31. Marc Leman. LC 95-4478. (Springer Series in Information Sciences). 1995. 84.95 (*3-540-60021-3*) Spr-Verlag.

Music & Science in the Age of Galileo. Ed. by Victor Coelho. LC 92-33288. (University of Western Ontario Ser. in Philosophy of Science: Vol. 51). 268p. (C). 1992. lib. bdg. 141.50 (*0-7923-2028-X*, Pub. by Kluwer Academic) Kluwer Academic.

Music & Scripts of "In Dahomey" Will M. Cook et al. Ed. by Thomas L. Riis. (Music of the United States of America Ser.: Vol. MUSA5). (Illus.). lxxii, 245p. 1996. pap. 130.00 (*0-89579-342-3*) A-R Eds.

Music & Sea Tattoos. rev. ed. Intro. by Donald E. Hardy. (Tattootime Ser.). (Illus.). 96p. (Orig.). 1988. pap. text 15.00 (*0-945367-04-X*) Hardy Marks Pubns.

Music & Self: Living Your Inner Sound. Pamela Harris. LC 89-84418. (Illus.). 192p. (Orig.). 1989. pap. 10.95 (*0-9623249-5-7*) Intermountain.

Music & Self-Management Methods: A Physicological Model. Joseph P. Scartelli. (Horizon Ser.: Vol. 7). 48p. (Orig.). 1989. pap. text 11.50 (*0-918812-53-4*, ST 150) MMB Music.

***Music & Silence.** Rose Tremain. LC 99-42880. 480p. 2000. 25.00 (*0-374-19989-2*) FS&G.

Music & Social Movements: Mobilizing Traditions in the Twentieth Century. Ron Eyerman & Andrew Jamison. LC 97-25752. (Cultural Social Studies). 204p. (C). 1998. text 59.95 (*0-521-62045-7*); pap. text 18.95 (*0-521-62966-7*) Cambridge U Pr.

Music & Society. Elie Siegmeister. LC 74-2318. (Studies in Music: No. 42). 1974. lib. bdg. 75.00 (*0-8383-2050-3*) M S G Haskell Hse.

Music & Society: The Politics of Composition, Performance, & Reception. Ed. by Richard D. Leppert & Susan McClary. LC 86-31672. (Illus.). 224p. 1989. pap. text 21.95 (*0-521-37977-6*) Cambridge U Pr.

Music & Song. Shawn Woodyard. LC 95-9939. (African American Life Ser.). 48p. (J). (gr. 4-6). 1995. lib. bdg. 23.93 (*1-57103-029-8*) Rourke Pr.

Music & Song in Persia: The Art of Avaz. Lloyd Miller. (Illus.). 400p. 1997. 79.95 (*0-7007-0664-X*, Pub. by Curzon Pr Ltd) Paul & Co Pubs.

***Music & Song in Persia: The Art of Avaz.** Lloyd Miller. LC 99-19892. (Illus.). 360p. 1999. 60.00 (*0-87480-614-3*) U of Utah Pr.

***Music & Sound.** Barron's Educational Editors. (Modern Media Ser.). (Illus.). 32p. 2000. pap. 5.95 (*0-7641-1067-5*) Barron.

Music & Sound. Llewelyn S. Lloyd. LC 70-107815. (Select Bibliographies Reprint Ser.). 1977. 20.95 (*0-8369-5188-3*) Ayer.

Music & Sound. Llewelyn S. Lloyd. (Music Book Index Ser.). 181p. 1992. reprint ed. lib. bdg. 69.00 (*0-7812-9477-0*) Rprt Serv.

Music & Sound for the Macintosh. Bill L. Behrendt. write for info. (*0-318-58192-2*) P-H.

Music & Sound in the Healing Arts: An Energy Approach. John Beaulieu. Ed. by George Quasha. LC 87-10076. 150p. (C). 1987. 19.95 (*0-88268-057-9*); pap. 12.95 (*0-88268-056-0*) Station Hill Pr.

Music & Spectacle in Baroque Rome: Barberini Patronage under Urban VIII. Frederick Hammond. LC 94-10417. (Illus.). 424p. 1995. 45.00 (*0-300-05528-5*) Yale U Pr.

Music & Speech Programs for IBM. Robert J. Traister, Sr. 1991. 35.50 (*0-8306-6607-9*) McGraw-Hill Prof.

Music & Text. P. Driver & R. Christiansen. (Contemporary Music Review Ser.: Vol. 5). vi, 304p. 1989. pap. text 25.00 (*3-7186-4980-2*) Gordon & Breach.

Music & the Apple II: Applications for Music Education, Composition, & Performance. Thomas E. Rudolph. (Illus.). 175p. (Orig.). 1984. pap. text 17.95 (*0-9615386-0-0*) Unsinn Pubns.

Music & the Arts in the Community: The Community Music School in America. Robert F. Egan. LC 89-30492. (Illus.). 489p. 1989. 52.00 (*0-8108-2117-6*) Scarecrow.

***Music & the Celtic Otherworld: From Ireland to Iona.** Karen Ralls-MacLeod. LC 99-58858. 244p. 2000. 49.95 (*0-312-23241-1*) St Martin.

Music & the Child. Erna Czovek. 84p. 1989. pap. 25.00 (*963-13-0700-X*, Pub. by Corvina Bks) St Mut.

Music & the Church: Music & the Church. Ed. by Gerard Gillen & Harry White. (Irish Musical Studies: Vol. 2). (Illus.). 352p. (C). 1992. 45.00 (*0-7165-2486-4*, Pub. by Irish Acad Pr) Intl Spec Bk.

Music & the Cognitive Sciences: Proceedings from the "Symposium on Music & the Cognitive Sciences," 14-18 March 1988 Paris, France. Ed. by Stephen McAdams & I. Deilege. (Contemporary Music Review Ser.: Vol. 4). x, 468p. 1989. pap. text 96.00 (*3-7186-4953-5*) Gordon & Breach.

Music & the Cognitive Sciences, 1990. Ian Cross. (Contemporary Music Review Ser.). 320p. 1994. pap. text 44.00 (*3-7186-5420-2*, Harwood Acad Pubs) Gordon & Breach.

Music & the Cosmic Dance. Cynthia Serjak. 1987. 7.95 (*0-912405-31-7*, Pastoral Press) OR Catholic.

***Music & the Cultures of Print.** Kate Van Orden. LC 99-52664. (Reference Library of the Humanities). 2000. write for info. (*0-8153-2574-6*) Garland.

Music & the Earth Spirit. Bob Dickinson. (Orig.). 1999. pap. write for info. (*1-898307-89-X*, Pub. by Capall Bann Pubng) Holmes Pub.

Music & the Emotions: The Philosophical Theories. Malcolm Budd. (International Library of Philosophy). 224p. 1985. 29.95 (*0-7102-0520-1*, Routledge Thoemms) Routledge.

Music & the Emotions: The Philosophical Theories. Malcolm Budd. (International Library of Philosophy). 224p. (C). 1992. pap. 25.99 (*0-415-08779-1*, A9610) Routledge.

Music & the French Enlightenment: Reconstruction of a Dialogue, 1750-1764. Cynthia Verba. LC 92-17495. 173p. 1993. text 45.00 (*0-19-816281-2*, Clarendon Pr) OUP.

Music & the Historical Imagination. Leo Treitler. LC 88-18066. (Illus.). 352p. 1989. 49.50 (*0-674-59128-3*) HUP.

Music & the Historical Imagination. Leo Treitler. (Illus.). 352p. 1989. pap. 20.50 (*0-674-59129-1*) HUP.

Music & the Macintosh. Geary Yelton. LC 89-91706. (Illus.). 199p. (Orig.). 1990. pap. 16.95 (*0-9623397-6-8*) Midi Amer.

Music & the Mass. David Haas. LC 98-87476. 129p. (Orig.). 1998. pap. 16.00 (*1-56854-198-8*, MUSMAS) Liturgy Tr Pubns.

Music & the Mind. Anthony Storr. 224p. 1993. pap. 11.00 (*0-345-38318-4*) Ballantine Pub Grp.

Music & the Mind. Anthony Storr. LC 92-21743. 212p. 1992. 27.95 (*0-02-931621-9*) Free Pr.

Music & the Mind Machine. Ed. by R. Steinberg. 288p. 1995. 99.95 (*3-540-58528-1*) Spr-Verlag.

Music & the Moderns: The Life & Works of Carol Robinson. Glenda D. Goss. LC 92-37179. (Illus.). 314p. 1993. 41.50 (*0-8108-2626-7*) Scarecrow.

Music & the Occult: French Musical Philosophies, 1750-1950. Joscelyn Godwin. (Eastman Studies in Music: Vol. 3).Tr. of Esoterisme Musical en France, 1750-1950. (ENG & FRE., Illus.). 276p. (C). 1996. 50.00 (*1-878822-53-5*) Univ Rochester Pr.

Music & the Origins of Language: Theories from the French Enlightenment. Downing A. Thomas. (New Perspectives in Music History & Criticism Ser.: No. 3). 207p. (C). 1995. text 69.95 (*0-521-47307-1*) Cambridge U Pr.

Music & the Personal Computer: An Annotated Bibliography, 22A. Compiled by William J. Waters. LC 89-23287. (Music Reference Collection: No. 22). 187p. 1989. lib. bdg. 52.95 (*0-313-26790-1*, WMC/, Greenwood Pr) Greenwood.

***Music & the Racial Imagination.** Ronald M. Radano & Philip V. Bohlman. LC 00-23672. 1999. pap. text 32.00 (*0-226-70200-6*) U Ch Pr.

Music & the Reformation in England, 1549-1660. Peter Le Huray. LC 77-87383. (Cambridge Studies in Music). 484p. reprint ed. pap. 138.00 (*0-608-16450-X*, 2026344) Bks Demand.

Music & the Romantic Movement in France. Arthur W. Locke. 184p. 1977. 15.95 (*0-8369-6859-X*) Ayer.

Music & the Romantic Movement in France. Arthur W. Locke. LC 72-83508. 184p. 1977. reprint ed. 24.95 (*0-405-08751-9*, Pub. by Blom Pubns) Ayer.

Music & the Self-Esteem of Young Children. Jolanta Kalandyk. 224p. (C). 1996. lib. bdg. 39.50 (*0-7618-0154-5*) U Pr of Amer.

Music & the Silent Film: Contexts & Case Studies, 1895-1924. Martin M. Marks. (Illus.). 320p. 1997. text 45.00 (*0-19-506891-2*) OUP.

Music & Theater in Minnesota History. John K. Sherman. LC 58-63622. (History of the Arts in Minnesota Ser.). 67p. reprint ed. pap. 30.00 (*0-608-14150-X*, 205591500039) Bks Demand.

Music & Theatre in France in the 17th & 18th Centuries - Le Grand Siecle: Basic Collection for Musical, Theatrical, Literary & Cultural Historians, 37 titles in 48 vols., Set. reprint ed. 1500.00 (*0-404-60100-6*) AMS Pr.

Music & Theatre in France, 1600-1800. John S. Powell. LC 98-7971. (Illus.). 704p. 2000. text 150.00 (*0-19-816599-4*) OUP.

Music & Trance: A Theory of the Relations Between Music & Possession. Gilbert Rouget. Tr. by Brunhilde Biebuyck. LC 85-1107. (Illus.). xx, 416p. 1985. pap. text 24.00 (*0-226-73006-9*) U Ch Pr.

Music & Trance: A Theory of the Relations Between Music & Possession. Gilbert Rouget. Tr. by Brunhilde Biebuyck. LC 85-1107. (Illus.). xx, 236p. 1996. lib. bdg. 72.00 (*0-226-73005-0*) U Ch Pr.

Music & War: A Research & Information Guide. Ben Arnold. LC 93-24938. (Music Research & Information Guides Ser.: Vol. 17). (Illus.). 464p. 1993. text 20.00 (*0-8153-0826-4*, H1581) Garland.

Music & Women: The Story of Women in Their Relation to Music. Sophie Drinker. LC 95-14816. (Diane Peacock Jezic Series on Women & Music). (Illus.). 394p. 1995. reprint ed. pap. 16.95 (*1-55861-116-9*); reprint ed. lib. bdg. 45.00 (*1-55861-120-7*) Feminist Pr.

Music & Women: The Story of Women in Their Relation to Music. Sophie L. Drinker. LC 75-35730. 1976. reprint ed. 27.95 (*0-89201-011-8*) Zenger Pub.

Music & Worship. Edward W. Nelson. 176p. 1985. spiral bd. 11.99 (*0-311-72642-9*) Casa Bautista.

Music & Worship. Henry W. Davies & Harvey Grace. LC 74-24067. reprint ed. 29.50 (*0-404-12894-7*) AMS Pr.

Music & Worship in Pagan & Christian Antiquity. J. Quasten. 1983. 14.95 (*0-9602378-7-9*, Pastoral Press) OR Catholic.

Music & Worship in the Church: The Complete Resource for Musician, Minister, & Layperson. enl. rev. ed. Austin C. Lovelace & William C. Rice. 1983. pap. 16.95 (*0-687-27357-9*) Abingdon.

Music & Worship Planner see Prepare!: A Weekly Worship Planbook for Pastors & Musicians, 1998-1999

Music & Worship Planner, 1995-1996. 1995. pap. text 15.95 (*0-687-00192-7*) Abingdon.

Music & Worship Planner, 1996-97. David L. Bone & Mary J. Scifres. 144p. 1996. pap. text, spiral bd. 15.95 (*0-687-10961-2*) Abingdon.

Music & Young Children: Expanded Edition. Frances W. Aronoff. LC 72-75917. 224p. 1979. reprint ed. pap. text 13.95 (*0-9602590-0-7*) Turning Wheel Pr.

Music & Your Mind: Listening with a New Consciousness. Helen L. Bonny. 1990. pap. 10.95 (*0-88268-094-3*) Station Hill Pr.

***Music Appreciation.** Larsen. 2000. student ed. 15.00 (*0-534-51635-1*) Wadsworth Pub.

***Music Appreciation.** Larson. (Music Ser.). 2000. 33.00 incl. audio compact disk (*0-534-51634-3*) Wadsworth Pub.

Music Appreciation. Mayall. (Music Ser.). 2002. 30.00 (*0-534-54522-X*) Brooks-Cole.

Music Appreciation. Vicki T. Purslow. (Listener's Notebook Ser.). 98p. 1998. pap. text, wbk. ed. 8.25 (*1-893438-01-5*) Lighthse Pubg.

Music Appreciation. Floyd Skloot. LC 94-26085. 112p. 1994. 19.95 (*0-8130-1313-5*); pap. 10.95 (*0-8130-1314-3*) U Press Fla.

Music, Archetype, & the Writer: A Jungian View. Bettina L. Knapp. LC 87-43122. 234p. 1988. lib. bdg. 35.00 (*0-271-00624-2*) Pa St U Pr.

Music, Art, & Metaphysics: Essays in Philosophical Aesthetics. Jerrold Levinson. LC 90-55138. (Illus.). 432p. 1991. text 57.50 (*0-8014-2342-2*); pap. text 19.95 (*0-8014-9591-1*) Cornell U Pr.

Music As a Way of Knowing. Nick Page. (Strategies for Teaching & Learning Ser.). 80p. (C). 1996. reprint ed. pap. text 15.00 (*1-57110-052-0*) Stenhse Pubs.

Music As Cognition: The Development of Thought & Sound. Mary L. Serafine. (Illus.). 288p. 1988. text 57.50 (*0-231-05742-3*) Col U Pr.

Music As Cultural Practice, 1800-1900. Lawrence Kramer. LC 89-20445. (California Studies in 19th Century Music: No. 8). (Illus.). 241p. 1990. 45.00 (*0-520-06857-2*, Pub. by U CA Pr) Cal Prin Full Svc.

Music As Cultural Practice, 1800-1900. Lawrence Kramer. (C). 1993. pap. 15.95 (*0-520-08443-8*, Pub. by U CA Pr) Cal Prin Full Svc.

Music As Culture. Ed. by Kaye Shelemay. LC 90-3540. (Ethnomusicology Ser.: Vol. 3). 344p. 1990. reprint ed. text 82.00 (*0-8240-6471-2*) Garland.

Music as Medicine. Hordon. 68.95 (*1-84014-299-5*) Ashgate Pub Co.

Music As Metaphor: The Elements of Expression. Donald N. Ferguson. LC 73-9210. (Illus.). 198p. 1973. reprint ed. lib. bdg. 35.00 (*0-8371-6981-X*, FEMM, Greenwood Pr) Greenwood.

***Music as Organized Sound: An Introduction to Basic Music Theory.** Sylvia White. LC 99-46731. 292p. 1999. text 89.95 (*0-7734-7910-4*) E Mellen.

Music as Physician see Music: Physician for Times to Come

Music As Propaganda: Art to Persuade, Art to Control, 8. Arnold Perris. LC 84-27969. (Contributions to the Study of Music & Dance Ser.: No. 8). 247p. 1985. 49.95 (*0-313-24505-3*, PMP/, Greenwood Pr) Greenwood.

Music at Belmont: And Other Essays & Addresses. John T. Sheppard. LC 72-152214. (Essay Index Reprint Ser.). 1977. reprint ed. 18.95 (*0-8369-2860-1*) Ayer.

Music at Christ Church Before 1800: Documents & Selected Anthems. Ed. by Barra Boydell. LC 99-191127. (Christ Church Ser.). 220p. 1998. boxed set 45.00 (*1-85182-413-8*, Pub. by Four Cts Pr) Intl Spec Bk.

Music at Harvard: A Historical Review of Men & Events. Walter R. Spalding. LC 76-58924. (Music Reprint Ser.). 1977. reprint ed. lib. bdg. 37.50 (*0-306-70871-X*) Da Capo.

Music at KU: A History of the University of Kansas Music Department. J. Bunker Clark. 196p. (Orig.). 1985. write for info. (*0-318-60139-7*) U KS Dept Mus Dance.

Music at Midnight. Muriel G. Draper. 327p. 1990. reprint ed. lib. bdg. 79.00 (*0-7812-9028-7*) Rprt Serv.

Music at Nevers Cathedral: Principal Sources of Mediaeval Chant, Vol. 30, Pt.1. Nancy Van Deusen. (Wissenschaftliche Abhandlungen-Musicological Studies). 430p. 1980. lib. bdg. 67.00 (*0-912024-33-X*) Inst Mediaeval Mus.

Music at Nevers Cathedral: Principal Sources of Mediaeval Chant, Vol. 30, Pt.2. Nancy Van Deusen. (Wissenschaftliche Abhandlungen-Musicological Studies). 430p. 1980. lib. bdg. 67.00 (*0-912024-34-8*) Inst Mediaeval Mus.

Music at Night & Other Essays. Aldous Huxley. LC 77-134098. (Essay Index Reprint Ser.). 1977. 20.95 (*0-8369-1960-2*) Ayer.

Music at the Borders: "Not Drowning, Waving" & Their Engagement with Papua New Guinean Culture. Philip Hayward. (Illus.). 248p. 1998. pap. 19.95 (*1-86462-012-9*) Ind U Pr.

Music at the Close: Stravinsky's Last Years. Lillian Libman. (Illus.). 1972. 34.95 (*0-8464-0659-4*) Beekman Pubs.

Music at the Court of Burgundy, 1364-1419. Craig Wright. (Wissenschaftliche Abhandlungen-Musicological Studies: Vol. 28). 300p. 1979. lib. bdg. 107.00 (*0-912024-25-9*) Inst Mediaeval Mus.

Music at the Court of Frederick the Great. Ernest E. Helm. LC ML0279.H4. (Illus.). 292p. reprint ed. pap. 90.60 (*0-608-10884-7*, 201035800068) Bks Demand.

Music at the Edge: Music Therapy with an AIDS Patient. Colin Lee. LC 95-25782. 192p. (C). 1996. pap. 32.99 incl. audio compact disk (*0-415-12464-6*) Routledge.

Music at the Edge: Music Therapy with an AIDS Patient. Colin Lee. LC 95-25782. (Illus.). 192p. (C). 1996. text 85.00 incl. audio compact disk (*0-415-12463-8*) Routledge.

Music at the Margins: Popular Music & Cultural Diversity. Deanna Robinson et al. (Communication & Human Values Ser.: Vol. 8). (Illus.). 320p. 1991. 52.00 (*0-8039-3192-1*); pap. 24.95 (*0-8039-3193-X*) Sage.

Music at the Middle Level: Building Strong Programs. Ed. by June M. Hinckley. LC 94-213091. 160p. 1994. pap. 22.00 (*1-56545-043-4*, 1623) MENC.

Music at the Royal Court & Chapel in Poland, c. 1543-1600. Tomas M. Czepiel. LC 95-51816. (Outstanding Dissertations in Music from British Universities Ser.). 1996. write for info. (*0-614-10485-8*) Garland.

Music at the Royal Court & Chapel in Poland, c. 1543-1600. rev. ed. Tomasz M. Czepiel. LC 95-51816. (Outstanding Dissertations in Music from British Universities Ser.). (Illus.). 432p. 1996. text 105.00 (*0-8153-2237-2*) Garland.

Music at the Turn of the Century: A "Nineteenth-Century Music" Reader. Ed. by Joseph Kerman. (Illus.). 218p. 1990. pap. 16.95 (*0-520-06855-6*, Pub. by U CA Pr) Cal Prin Full Svc.

M

An Asterisk (*) at the beginning of an entry indicates that the title is appearing for the first time.

Music at West Virginia University, 1897-1987: The West Virginia School of Music, 1897. Clifford W. Brown & Clifford W. Brown. Ed. by John Luchok & C. B. Wilson. (Illus.). 100p. (Orig.). 1989. pap. write for info. (*0-925500-00-3*) WV Univ Pubns Servs.

Music at Your Fingertips: Advice for the Artist & Amateur on Playing the Piano. Ruth Slenczynska. LC 74-1018. (Music Ser.). 160p. 1974. reprint ed. lib. bdg. 25.00 (*0-306-70653-9*) Da Capo.

Music at Your Fingertips: Advice for the Artist & Amateur on Playing the Piano. Ruth Slenczynska. LC 74-1018. (Music Ser.). (Illus.). 160p. 1974. reprint ed. pap. 9.95 (*0-306-80034-9*) Da Capo.

Music Basics: An Easy to Understand Guide to Music Fundamentals. Peter L. Alexander. (Illus.). 114p. (C). 1988. pap. text 17.95 (*0-939067-72-2*) Alexander Pub.

Music Behind the Wall Vol. 1: Selected Stories. Anna M. Ortese. Tr. & Intro. by Henry Martin. 160p. 1994. 20.00 (*0-929701-39-9*) McPherson & Co.

***Music Behind the Wall Vol. 2: Selected Stories.** Anna M. Ortese. Tr. by Henry Martin. 224p. 1998. 22.00 (*0-929701-56-9*) McPherson & Co.

Music Beyond Sound: Maria Curcio, a Teacher of Great Pianists. Douglas Ashley. LC 92-44414. (American University Studies: Fine Arts: Ser. XX, Vol. 19). (Illus.). II, 112p. (C). 1993. text 35.95 (*0-8204-2101-4*) P Lang Pubng.

Music Blaster! Leo Ewing. (Nutshell Ser.). 60p. 1994. pap. 5.49 (*1-885962-58-4*) Lincoln Lrning.

Music Booster Manual. 56p. (Orig.). (C). 1989. pap. 13.50 (*0-940796-68-6*, 1504) MENC.

Music Box. Andrea Kane. 1998. per. 6.50 (*0-671-53484-X*) PB.

Music Box. Malpas & Abbs. Date not set. pap. text. write for info. (*0-582-25597-X*, Pub. by Addison-Wesley) Longman.

Music Box: Her Mother's Exquisite Little Gift, Long Hidden Away, Held Such Bittersweet Memories. T. Davis Bunn. LC 96-25299. 192p. 1996. text 11.99 (*1-55661-900-6*) Bethany Hse.

Music Box: Her Mother's Exquisite Little Gift, Long Hidden Away, Held Such Bittersweet Memories. large type ed. T. Davis Bunn. LC 96-40163. 218p. 1997. 21.95 (*0-7862-1011-7*) Thorndike Pr.

Music Box: The Story of Christofori. Suzanne Guy & Donna Lacy. LC 98-23309. (Illus.). 32p. (J). (gr. k-4). 1998. 15.95 (*1-55618-172-8*); pap. 6.95 (*1-55618-173-6*) Brunswick Pub.

***Music Box Murders.** Larry Karp. 344p. 1999. 23.95 (*1-885173-58-X*) Write Way.

Music Box Test. Marcia Hoehne. 150p. (J). 1995. pap. 4.99 (*0-7459-2628-2*) Lion USA.

Music Box Treaty. Richard Duggin. (Illus.). 1982. 20.00 (*0-317-40787-2*) Abattoir.

Music-Brief. 3rd ed. Albert Camus. 176p. 1997. pap., student ed. 12.81 (*0-07-036527-X*) McGraw.

Music Bulletin Boards Activities Kit: Year-Round Displays for the Music Classroom. Nancy Forquer & Marjorie Partin. LC 89-16321. 272p. (C). 1989. pap. text 24.95 (*0-13-606898-7*) P-H.

Music Business. 2nd rev. ed. Dick Weissman. LC 97-12275. 1997. pap. 15.00 (*0-517-88784-3*, Crown) Crown Pub Group.

Music Business: A Legal Perspective. Peter Muller. LC 93-18523. (Music & Live Performances Ser.). 376p. 1993. 69.50 (*0-89930-702-7*, MRQ, Quorum Bks) Greenwood.

Music Business Agreements. Richard Bagehot. (Waterlow Practitioner's Library). 416p. 1989. 90.00 (*0-08-036905-7*, Pergamon Pr) Elsevier.

Music Business (Explained in Plain English) What Every Artist & Songwriter Should Know to Avoid Getting Ripped Off! David Naggar & Jeffrey D. Brandstetter. 122p. 1995. pap. 12.95 (*0-9648709-0-8*) DaJe Pubng.

***Music Business (Explained in Plain English) What Every Artist & Songwriter Should Know to Avoid Getting Ripped Off!** 2nd ed. David Naggar. 136p. 2000. pap. 12.95 (*1-57746-570-9*, Pub. by DaJe Pubng) SCB Distributors.

Music Business Handbook & Career Guide. 6th ed. David Baskerville. LC 95-764. (Illus.). 588p. 1995. 32.00 (*0-8039-7153-2*) Sage.

Music Business Inside Out. Robert A. Livingston. 1997. 97.15 (*0-932303-30-7*) GLGLC Music.

Music Business the Answer to How to Get Started. Geniva F. Jones. 64p. 1997. pap. 25.00 (*0-9663958-1-6*) Lulabell Recs.

Music by Black Women Composers: A Bibliography of Available Scores. Helen Walker-Hill. LC 95-5613. (CBMR Monographs: No. 5). 118p. (Orig.). (C). 1995. 10.00 (*0-929911-04-0*) CCCBMR.

Music by Heart. Lilias MacKinnon. (Music Book Index Ser.). 141p. 1992. reprint ed. lib. bdg. 69.00 (*0-7812-9459-2*) Rprt Serv.

Music by Heart. Lillias Mackinnon. LC 80-26551. 141p. 1981. reprint ed. lib. bdg. 49.50 (*0-313-22810-8*, MAMB, Greenwood Pr) Greenwood.

***Music by Pedro de Cristo (c. 1550-1618)** Ed. by Owen Rees. (Illus.). 231p. 1998. text 60.00 (*90-5755-010-5*, Harwood Acad Pubs) Gordon & Breach.

Music Calligrapher's Handbook: Tools, Materials, & Techniques. Cindy McTee. 44p. (Orig.). 1987. pap. 3.95 (*0-918812-55-0*, SB 0006) MMB Music.

Music Came First: The Memoirs of Theodore Paschedag. Intro. by Thomas J. Hatton. LC 87-28671. (Shawnee Bks.). 110p. 1988. pap. 9.95 (*0-8093-1472-X*) S Ill U Pr.

Music Cataloging Bulletin: Index/Supplement to Volumes 1620, 1985-1989. Compiled by Betsy Gamble. 112p. 1993. pap. 22.50 (*0-914954-40-7*) Scarecrow.

Music Cataloging Decisions: As Issued by the Music Section, Special Materials Cataloging Division, Library of Congress in the Music Cataloging Bulletin, Through December 1991. Ed. by Betsy Gamble. 1992. pap. 25.00 (*0-914954-39-3*) Scarecrow.

Music Cataloging Policy in the General Libraries. (Contributions to Librarianship Ser.: No. 8). 112p. 1984. pap. 15.00 (*0-930214-13-7*).U TX Austin Gen Libs.

***Music CDs in Japan: A Strategic Entry Report, 1995.** Compiled by Icon Group International Staff. (Illus.). 158p. 1999. ring bd. 1580.00 incl. audio compact disk (*0-7418-1573-7*) Icon Grp.

Music City Babylon: Inside the World of Country Music. Scott Faragher. (Illus.). 288p. 1992. 18.95 (*1-55972-134-0*, Birch Ln Pr) Carol Pub Group.

Music City Blues. unabridged ed. Steven S. Fielden. (Illus.). 170p. 1997. mass mkt. 11.95 (*0-9663643-1-7*) Hindsight Pr.

Music Cognition. W. Jay Dowling & Dane L. Harwood. (Cognition & Perception Ser.). 1985. text 59.95 (*0-12-221430-7*) Acad Pr.

Music Cognition & Aesthetic Attitudes. Harold E. Fiske. LC 93-2117. (Studies in the History & Interpretation of Music: Vol. 41). 184p. 1993. text 79.95 (*0-7734-9334-4*) E Mellen.

Music, Cognition & Computerized Sound: An Introduction to Psychoacoustics. Ed. by Perry R. Cook. LC 98-16783. (Illus.). 734p. 1999. 60.00 (*0-262-03256-2*) MIT Pr.

Music Collections in American Libraries: A Chronology. Carol J. Bradley. LC 81-2907. (Detroit Studies in Music Bibliography: No. 46). xi, 249p. 1981. 25.00 (*0-89990-002-X*) Harmonie Park Pr.

Music Columns from the Nation, 1962-68. Benjamin Boretz. LC 91-90386. 168p. 1991. write for info. (*0-9629865-0-X*) Open Space NY.

Music, Communication, Ideology. Michael Jenne. Tr. by Michael Fleming from GER.Tr. of Musik, Kommunikation, Ideologie. 202p. 1984. reprint ed. pap. text 13.95 (*0-87487-405-X*) Summy-Birchard.

Music Composed for Shakespeare's A Midsummer Night's Dream. Felix Mendelssohn. 1976. lib. bdg. 59.95 (*0-8490-2307-6*) Gordon Pr.

Music Concepts & Vocabulary for Violin. rev. ed. Margie Chan. (C.A.V.E. Concepts & Vocabulary Exploration Ser.: Bk. 2). 48p. 1988. reprint ed. student ed., spiral bd. 8.95 (*0-9615006-8-9*); reprint ed. student ed., ring bd. 7.95 (*0-9615006-2-X*) Gim-Ho.

Music Concepts & Vocabulary for Violin. rev. ed. Margie Chan. (C.A.V.E. Concepts & Vocabulary Exploration Ser.: Bk. 1). 61p. 1988. student ed., spiral bd. 8.95 (*0-9615006-5-4*); student ed., ring bd. 8.95 (*0-9615006-9-7*) Gim-Ho.

Music Concepts & Vocabulary for Violin, Bk. 1. Margie Chan. (C.A.V.E. Concepts & Vocabulary Exploration Ser.). 41p. (J). (gr. 2 up). 1984. student ed. 4.95 (*0-9615006-0-3*) Gim-Ho.

Music Concepts & Vocabulary for Violin, Bk. 2. Margie Chan. (C.A.V.E. Concepts & Vocabulary Exploration Ser.). 48p. (J). (gr. 2 up). 1985. student ed. 4.95 (*0-9615006-1-1*) Gim-Ho.

***Music Connection.** (gr. 3). 1999. write for info. (*0-382-34502-9*, Silver Pr NJ) Silver Burdett Pr.

***Music Connection.** (gr. 5). 1999. write for info. (*0-382-34504-5*, Silver Pr NJ) Silver Burdett Pr.

***Music Connection.** (gr. 6). 1999. write for info. (*0-382-34505-3*, Silver Pr NJ) Silver Burdett Pr.

***Music Connection.** (gr. 8). 1999. write for info. (*0-382-34507-X*, Silver Pr NJ) Silver Burdett Pr.

***Music Connection.** (gr. 4). 1999. write for info. (*0-382-34503-7*, Silver Pr NJ) Silver Burdett Pr.

***Music Connection: C 2000, Big Book Shipper, Grade K.** 1999. write for info. (*0-382-34519-3*) Silver Burdett Pr.

***Music Connection: C 2000, Big Book Shipper, Grade 1.** (gr. 1). 1999. write for info. (*0-382-34520-7*) Silver Burdett Pr.

***Music Connection: National Edition, 2000C,** (gr. 1). 1999. write for info. (*0-382-34564-9*, Silver Pr NJ) Silver Burdett Pr.

***Music Connection: National Edition, 2000C,** (gr. 2). 1999. write for info. (*0-382-34565-7*, Silver Pr NJ) Silver Burdett Pr.

***Music Connection: National Edition, 2000C,** (gr. 3). 1999. write for info. (*0-382-34566-5*, Silver Pr NJ) Silver Burdett Pr.

***Music Connection: National Edition, 2000C,** (gr. 6). 1999. write for info. (*0-382-34569-X*, Silver Pr NJ) Silver Burdett Pr.

***Music Connection: National Edition, 2000C,** (gr. 8). 1999. teacher ed. write for info. (*0-382-34571-1*, Silver Pr NJ) Silver Burdett Pr.

***Music Connection: National Edition, 2000C, Grade 5.** 1999. teacher ed. write for info. (*0-382-34568-1*) Silver Burdett Pr.

***Music Connection: 2000C, Sample Package, Grade K.** 1999. write for info. (*0-382-34623-8*) Silver Burdett Pr.

***Music Connection 2000c Keyboard Accompaniments Grade K.** 1999. write for info. (*0-382-34521-5*, Silver Pr NJ) Silver Burdett Pr.

***Music Connection 2000c Keyboard Accompaniments Grade K.** (gr. 1). 1999. write for info. (*0-382-34522-3*, Silver Pr NJ) Silver Burdett Pr.

***Music Connection 2000c Keyboard Accompaniments Grade K.** (gr. 3). 1999. write for info. (*0-382-34524-X*, Silver Pr NJ) Silver Burdett Pr.

***Music Connection 2000c Keyboard Accompaniments Grade K.** (gr. 4). 1999. write for info. (*0-382-34525-8*, Silver Pr NJ) Silver Burdett Pr.

***Music Connection 2000 Keyboard Accompaniments.** (gr. 5). 1999. write for info. (*0-382-34526-6*, Silver Pr NJ) Silver Burdett Pr.

***Music Connection 2000c: Teacher Resource.** (gr. 2). 1999. write for info. (*0-382-34532-0*, Silver Pr NJ) Silver Burdett Pr.

***Music Connection 2000c: Teacher Resource Book.** (gr. 4). 1999. write for info. (*0-382-34534-7*, Silver Pr NJ) Silver Burdett Pr.

***Music Connection 2000c: Teacher Resource Book.** (gr. 5). 1999. write for info. (*0-382-34535-5*, Silver Pr NJ) Silver Burdett Pr.

***Music Connection 2000c: Teacher Resource Book.** (gr. 6). 1999. write for info. (*0-382-34536-3*, Silver Pr NJ) Silver Burdett Pr.

***Music Connection, 2000c: Teacher Resource Book Grade K.** 1999. write for info. (*0-382-34530-4*, Silver Pr NJ) Silver Burdett Pr.

***Music Connection, 2000c: Teachers Resource Book.** (gr. 8). 1999. write for info. (*0-382-34538-X*, Silver Pr NJ) Silver Burdett Pr.

***Music Connection, 2000c Grade 1: Teacher Resource Book.** 1999. write for info. (*0-382-34531-2*, Silver Pr NJ) Silver Burdett Pr.

***Music Connection 2000c Keyboard Accompaniments.** (gr. 7). 1999. write for info. (*0-382-34528-2*, Silver Pr NJ) Silver Burdett Pr.

***Music Connection 2000c Keyboard Accompaniments.** (gr. 8). 1999. write for info. (*0-382-34529-0*, Silver Pr NJ) Silver Burdett Pr.

***Music Connection 2000c, Teacher Resource Book Grade 3: Teacher Resource Book.** (gr. 3). 1999. write for info. (*0-382-34533-9*, Silver Pr NJ) Silver Burdett Pr.

***Music Contracts.** Nigel Lipton. 350p. 2000. pap. 62.75 (*1-85811-215-X*, Pub. by CLT Prof) Gaunt.

Music Crafts for Kids: The How-To Book of Music Discovery. Noel Fiarotta & Phyllis Fiarotta. LC 93-24114. (Illus.). 160p. (Orig.). (J). (gr. 3 up). 1993. 19.95 (*0-8069-0406-2*) Sterling.

Music Crafts for Kids: The How-To Book of Music Discovery. Noel Fiarotta & Phyllis Fiarotta. (Illus.). 160p. (Orig.). (J). (gr. 3-7). 1995. pap. 9.95 (*0-8069-0407-0*) Sterling.

Music Creativity: Conductor Score & Manual, Alto/Baritone Sax. Thomas Dodson. 84p. 1992. 4.95 (*0-8497-0491-X*, L205E) Kjos.

Music Creativity: Conductor Score & Manual, Clarinet/Trumpet. Thomas Dodson. 84p. 1992. 4.95 (*0-8497-0490-1*, L205TP) Kjos.

Music Creativity: Conductor Score & Manual, Flute/Oboe. Thomas Dodson. 84p. 1992. 4.95 (*0-8497-0489-8*, L205C) Kjos.

Music Creativity: Conductor Score & Manual, French Horn. Thomas Dodson. 84p. 1992. 4.95 (*0-8497-0492-8*, L205HF) Kjos.

Music Creativity: Conductor Score & Manual, Mallet Percussion. Thomas Dodson. 84p. 1992. 4.95 (*0-8497-0496-0*, L205M) Kjos.

Music Creativity: Conductor Score & Manual, Percussion. Thomas Dodson. 84p. 1992. 4.95 (*0-8497-0495-2*, L205PR) Kjos.

Music Creativity: Conductor Score & Manual, Score & Manual. Thomas Dodson. 84p. 1994. 19.95 (*0-8497-0487-1*, L205F) Kjos.

Music Creativity: Conductor Score & Manual, Tenor Sax/Baritone TC. Thomas Dodson. 84p. 1992. 4.95 (*0-8497-0497-9*, L205XB) Kjos.

Music Creativity: Conductor Score & Manual, Trombone/Baritone BC/Bassoon. Thomas Dodson. 84p. 1992. 4.95 (*0-8497-0493-6*, L205BC) Kjos.

Music Creativity: Conductor Score & Manual, Tuba. Thomas Dodson. 84p. 1992. 4.95 (*0-8497-0494-4*, L205BS) Kjos.

Music Criticism, 1846-1899. Eduard Hanslick. 312p. 1990. reprint ed. lib. bdg. 79.00 (*0-7812-9212-3*) Rprt Serv.

Music Criticism in Nineteenth-Century France: La Revue et Gazette Musicale de Paris. Katharine Ellis. 315p. (C). 1995. text 69.95 (*0-521-45443-3*) Cambridge U Pr.

Music Criticism in Vienna, 1896-1897: Critically Moving Forms. Sandra McColl. (Oxford Monographs on Music). (Illus.). 260p. 1996. text 69.00 (*0-19-816564-1*) OUP.

Music Criticism of Hugo Wolf. Ed. by Henry Pleasants. LC 77-11092. 291p. 1979. 39.50 (*0-8419-0331-X*) Holmes & Meier.

Music, Culture, & Experience: Selected Papers of John Blacking. John Blacking. Ed. by Reginald Byron. 282p. 1995. pap. text 17.95 (*0-226-08830-8*) U Ch Pr.

Music, Culture, & Experience: Selected Papers of John Blacking. John Blacking & Bruno Nettl. LC 94-25598. 282p. 1995. lib. bdg. 45.95 (*0-226-08829-4*) U Ch Pr.

***Music, Culture & Society: A Reader.** Ed. by Derek B. Scott. (Illus.). 304p. 2000. pap. 24.95 (*0-19-879012-0*); text 60.00 (*0-19-879011-2*) OUP.

Music Cultures of the Pacific, the Near East & Asia. 3rd ed. William P. Malm. LC 94-48578. (History of Music Ser.). 278p. (C). 1995. pap. text 48.00 (*0-13-182387-6*) P-H.

Music Curriculum Activities Library. Audrey Adair. LC 87-8829. 112p. (C). 1987. pap. text 18.95 (*0-13-065707-7*) P-H.

Music Curriculum Guidelines for Moderately Retarded Adolescents. Mary R. Beal & Janet P. Gilbert. 122p. (C). 1982. pap., spiral bd. 27.95 (*0-398-04757-X*) C C Thomas.

Music, Dance & Religion: The Performing Arts in Worship. Norman Mealy & Judith Rock. (Illus.). 192p. 1985. 15.95 (*0-13-607219-4*); pap. 8.95 (*0-13-607201-1*) P-H.

Music, Dance & Theater Scholarships: A Complete Guide. Intro. by David Cerone et al. 450p. (Orig.). 1995. pap. 20.95 (*1-884669-07-7*) Conway Greene.

Music, Dance & Theater Scholarships: A Guide to Undergraduate Awards. Conway Greene Editorial Staff. 1998. pap. 24.95 (*1-884669-18-2*) Conway Greene.

Music Dictionary. Roy Bennett. 414p. (C). 1996. pap. 23.95 (*0-521-56930-3*) Cambridge U Pr.

Music Dictionary: Musikordboken. G. Brodin. (SWE.). 306p. 1985. 95.00 (*0-8288-2185-2*, F17030) Fr & Eur.

Music Dictionary Pocketbook. L. Dean Bye. 32p. 1994. pap. 0.95 (*0-7866-0060-8*, 95221) Mel Bay.

***Music Directors: Emmaus Library.** Sandy Stickney. Ed. by Rita Collett. LC 99-16329. 56p. 2000. pap. 3.00 (*0-8358-0911-0*) Upper Room Bks.

Music Director's Guide to the Drum Set. F. May. 32p. 1992. pap. 7.95 (*0-7935-1791-5*, 06621760) H Leonard.

***Music Director's Necessary Book.** 2nd rev. ed. George M. D. Frink. (Illus.). 124p. 2000. pap. 19.95 (*0-9679882-4-1*, CB9005) Carol Pr.

Music Discourse from Classical to Early Modern Times: Editing & Translating Texts. Maria R. Maniates. (Illus.). 158p. 1998. text 40.00 (*0-8020-0972-7*) U of Toronto Pr.

Music Documents: Music in Catholic Worship & Liturgical Music Today. U. S. Bishops. 54p. 1995. pap. 4.25 (*0-915531-41-0*) OR Catholic.

Music Dramas of Richard Wagner. Albert Lavignac. Tr. by Esther Singleton. LC 77-121292. 1977. reprint ed. 22.75 (*0-404-03890-5*) AMS Pr.

Music Dramas of Richard Wagner & His Festival Theatre in Bayreuth. Albert Lavignac. 515p. 1990. reprint ed. lib. bdg. 99.00 (*0-7812-9157-7*) Rprt Serv.

Music Dramas of Richard Wagner & His Musical Theatre in Bayreuth. A. Lavignac. LC 68-25293. (Studies in Music: No. 42). 1969. reprint ed. lib. bdg. 75.00 (*0-8383-0284-X*) M S G Haskell Hse.

Music Ed see Songs of Praise

Music Education. Joseph A. Labuta & Deborah Smith. 158p. (C). 1996. 51.00 (*0-13-489444-8*) P-H.

Music Education. Jack Rudman. (National Teacher Examination Ser.: NT-11). 1994. pap. 23.95 (*0-8373-8421-4*) Nat Learn.

Music Education: Concepts & Innovations. Sherman D. Vanderark. 258p. (Orig.). 1996. pap. text 29.95 (*0-9652371-8-4*) Gldn Clef.

Music Education: Tradition & Innovation. Robert Walker, Jr. 180p. 1983. pap. 23.95 (*0-398-06655-8*) C C Thomas.

Music Education: Tradition & Innovation. Robert Walker, Jr. (Illus.). 180p. (C). 1983. 33.95 (*0-398-04861-4*) C C Thomas.

Music Education, an Artificial Intelligence Approach: Proceedings of a Workshop Held As Part of the World Conference, Edinburgh, Scotland, 25 August 1993. Ed. by Matt Smith et al. LC 93-48464. 1994. 55.95 (*0-387-19873-3*) Spr-Verlag.

Music, Education & Multiculturalism: Foundations & Principles. Terese M. Volk. LC 96-53476. (Illus.). 288p. (C). 1997. text 39.95 (*0-19-510609-1*) OUP.

Music Education & the Art of Performance in the German Baroque. John Butt. (Cambridge Musical Texts & Monographs). (Illus.). 257p. (C). 1994. text 64.95 (*0-521-43327-4*) Cambridge U Pr.

Music Education as Praxis: Reflecting on Music-Making as Human Action. Kathryn A. Martin et al. Ed. by Marie McCarthy. LC 99-22115. (State-of-the-Arts Ser.: Vol. 3). 142p. (C). 1992. pap. write for info. (*0-9655233-2-2*) Univ MD Coll Pk.

Music Education for the Deaf. Eleanor M. Edwards. LC 74-76260. 248p. (Orig.). (C). 1974. pap. 6.00 (*0-914562-00-2*) Merriam-Eddy.

Music Education in Canada: A Historical Account. J. Paul Green & Nancy F. Vogan. 544p. 1991. text 125.00 (*0-8020-5891-4*) U of Toronto Pr.

Music Education in the Christian Home. Mary A. Froehlich. 1996. pap. text 10.95 (*1-56857-031-7*) Noble Pub Assocs.

Music Education in the United States: Contemporary Issues. J. Terry Gates. LC 87-5836. (Illus.). 344p. 1988. pap. 98.10 (*0-608-05138-1*, 2065699) Bks Demand.

Music Education in Theory & Practice. Charles Plummeridge. (Falmer Press Library on Aesthetic Education). 184p. 1991. 65.00 (*1-85000-765-9*, Falmer Pr) Taylor & Francis.

Music Education Research: An Anthology from the Journal of Research in Music Education. Harry Edward Price & Music Educators National Conference (U. S.) Staff. LC 98-211644. xviii, 840p. 1998. 40.00 (*1-56545-109-0*) MENC.

Music Educator & Community Music: The Best of M. E. J. Ed. by Michael Mark. (Best of MEJ Ser.). (Illus.). 104p. 1992. teacher ed. 20.00 (*1-56545-006-X*, 1612) MENC.

***Music Engineering.** Richard Brice. 416p. 2001. pap. 37.95 (*0-7506-5040-0*, Newnes) Buttrwrth-Heinemann.

Music Engraving & Printing: Historical & Technical Treatise. William Gamble. LC 72-173166. (Illus.). 1979. reprint ed. 23.95 (*0-405-08549-4*, Pub. by Blom Pubns) Ayer.

Music Every Day. Richardson. 2000. 34.00 (*0-07-052396-7*) McGraw.

Music Experience. 2nd ed. (C). 1996. write for info. (*0-8087-7794-7*) Pearson Custom.

Music Explained to the World. Francis J. Fetis & Peter Bloom. (Music Reprint Ser.).Tr. of Musique mise a la Portee de Tout le Monde. xvi, 320p. 1987. reprint ed. lib. bdg. 32.50 (*0-306-76276-5*) Da Capo.

Music Explosion Book & Tape: Teacher's Manual. rev. ed. Stephanie K. Burton. Date not set. teacher ed. 34.95 incl. audio (*1-889163-05-8*) Panda Bear Pub.

M

Music Facilities: Building, Equipping, & Renovating. rev. ed. Harold P. Geerdes. Orig. Title: Planning & Equipping Music Facilities. 136p. 1987. reprint ed. 36.25 (*0-940796-55-4*, 1034) MENC.

*__Music Festival Mystery.__ Carolyn Keene. 160p. 2000. 3.99 (*0-671-04265-3*, Minstrel Bks) PB.

Music Festivals - From Bach to the Blues: A Traveler's Guide. Tom Clyness. (Illus.). 632p. 1996. 18.95 (*0-7876-0823-8*) Gale.

Music, Film & Art, Vol. 3. Haig Khatchadourian. (Monographs on Musicology). xii, 222p. 1985. text 42.00 (*2-88124-008-9*); pap. text 10.00 (*2-88124-024-0*) Gordon & Breach.

Music First. 3rd ed. White. 1995. teacher ed. 21.25 (*0-697-29382-3*, WCB McGr Hill) McGrw-H Hghr Educ.

Music First. 4th ed. White. 2001. 27.00 (*0-07-228768-3*) McGraw.

Music First! An Introduction to the Fundamentals of Music & Music Reading & Songbook. 3rd ed. Gary C. White. 288p. (C). 1995. spiral bd. write for info. (*0-697-25836-X*) Brown & Benchmark.

*__Music Flash Cards: Set A.__ 120p. 1998. pap. text 3.95 (*0-7935-7775-6*) H Leonard.

Music for a Broken Piano. James B. Hall. LC 82-84670. 163p. 1983. pap. 6.95 (*0-914590-79-0*) Fiction Coll.

Music for a King: George Herbert's Style & the Metrical Psalms. Coburn Freer. LC 76-179136. 270p. reprint ed. pap. 83.70 (*0-608-15151-3*, 202581500046) Bks Demand.

Music for a Lifetime. Setzer. 1997. text 50.00 (*0-697-34061-9*) McGraw.

Music for a Pannykhida: The Orthodox Service for the Departed. Ed. by Timothy Clader. Tr. by Laurence Campbell from SLA. 60p. 1994. spiral bd. 10.00 (*0-912927-84-4*, D021) St John Kronstadt.

Music for a Summer's Evening. (In Classical Mood Ser.: Vol. 1). (Illus.). 1997. write for info. incl. cd-rom (*1-886614-23-7*) Intl Masters Pub.

Music for All: Developing Music in the Curriculum with Pupils with Special Educational Needs. Peter Wills & Melanie Peter. 112p. 1995. pap. 21.95 (*1-85346-280-2*, Pub. by David Fulton) Taylor & Francis.

Music for All Occasions: Nostalgic Love Songs. Ed. by Tony Esposito. 112p. 1997. pap. 12.95 (*0-7692-0065-6*) Warner Bros.

Music for All Occasions: Wedding & Special Events. Ed. by Tony Esposito. 112p. (Orig.). 1997. pap. 12.95 (*0-7692-0064-8*, FB9701) Wrner Bros.

Music for All Occasions - Broadway Showstoppers. Ed. by Tony Esposito. 112p. 1997. pap. 12.95 (*0-7692-0988-2*, FB9710) Wrner Bros.

Music for All Occassions: Jazz, Swing & Big Band. Ed. by Tony Esposito. 112p. (Orig.). 1997. pap. 12.95 (*0-7692-0066-4*, FB9704) Wrner Bros.

Music for All Occasions: Movie & T. V. Hits. Ed. by Tony Esposito. 96p. (Orig.). 1997. pap. 12.95 (*0-7692-0068-0*, FB9706) Wrner Bros.

Music for Analysis: Examples from the Common Practice Period & the Twentieth Century. 2nd ed. Thomas Benjamin et al. 418p. (C). 1989. pap. write for info. (*0-534-13428-9*) Wadsworth Pub.

Music for Analysis: Examples from the Common Practice Period & the Twentieth Century. 3rd ed. Thomas Benjamin et al. 418p. (C). 1991. mass mkt. 41.95 (*0-534-16674-1*) Wadsworth Pub.

Music for Analysis: Examples from the Common Practice Period & the Twentieth Century. 4th ed. Thomas Benjamin et al. 480p. (C). 1995. spiral bd. 67.95 (*0-534-25506-X*) Wadsworth Pub.

Music for Cello & Orchestra. J. Tower. 44p. 1991. pap. 30.00 (*0-7935-0914-9*) H Leonard.

Music for Chameleons. Truman Capote. LC 93-42198. 1994. pap. 12.00 (*0-679-74566-1*) Vin Bks.

Music for Chamelons. Truman Capote. 283p. Date not set. 23.95 (*0-8488-2227-7*) Amereon Ltd.

Music for Children, 3 vols., 1. Ed. by Hermann Regner. (Orff-Schulwerk Ser.). 1977. pap. 24.95 (*0-930448-12-X*, STAP012) Eur-Am Music.

Music for Children, 3 vols., 2. Ed. by Hermann Regner. (Orff-Schulwerk Ser.). 1977. pap. 39.95 (*0-930448-00-6*, STAP006) Eur-Am Music.

Music for Children, 3 vols., 3. Ed. by Hermann Regner. (Orff-Schulwerk Ser.). 1977. pap. 39.95 (*0-930448-08-1*, STAP008) Eur-Am Music.

Music for Cittern see Complete Works

Music for Conducting Class. 2nd ed. James McKelvy. LC 88-82200. (Illus.). xi, 143p. 1988. pap. text 23.95 (*0-916656-26-8*, MFBK 10) Mark Foster Mus.

Music for Daily Vespers & Matins. Ed. by Timothy Clader. Tr. by Holy Transfiguration Monastery Staff et al from SLA. 98p. 1996. pap., spiral bd. 20.00 (*0-912927-73-9*, D038) St John Kronstadt.

Music for Developing Speech & Language Skills in Children: A Guide for Parents & Therapists. Donald E. Michel & Janet L. Jones. (MMB Horizon Ser.: No. 9). 56p. (Orig.). 1991. pap. 9.95 (*0-918812-69-0*, ST 233) MMB Music.

Music for Divine Services: Traditional Chants & Chant Settings. Theodore Heckman. 165p. (Orig.). 1984. spiral bd. 10.00 (*1-878997-11-4*) St Tikhons Pr.

Music for Elizabethan Lutes: The Osborn Commonplace-Book Tablatures & Related Sources, 2 vols., Set. Ed. by John M. Ward. (Illus.). 380p. 1992. text 185.00 (*0-19-315264-9*) OUP.

Music for Films. Peter Gizzi. 36p. 1992. 20.00 (*0-945926-36-7*) Paradigm RI.

Music for Films. Peter Gizzi. 36p. 1996. pap. 5.00 (*0-945926-35-9*) Paradigm RI.

Music for Flute & Guitar. Frederic Hand. 47p. (YA). 1995. pap. 17.95 (*0-89524-854-9*); pap. 14.95 (*0-89524-853-0*) Cherry Lane.

Music for Fun & Profit. large type ed. Arthur Mitchell. (For Fun & Profit Ser.). (Illus.). 300p. Date not set. pap. 24.95 (*1-56559-905-5*) HGI-Over Fifty.

Music for Hire: A Study of Professional Musicians in Washington, 1877-1900. Katherine K. Preston. LC 85-28399. (Sociology of Music Ser.: No. 6). (Illus.). 280p. 1992. lib. bdg. 47.00 (*0-918728-66-5*) Pendragon NY.

Music for Keyboard, Bk. 1A. Robert Pace. 32p. 1994. pap. 5.95 (*0-7935-3992-7*, 00372365) H Leonard.

Music for Keyboard, Bk. 1B. Robert Pace. 1995. pap. 5.95 (*0-7935-4939-6*, 00372367) H Leonard.

Music for Life: Aspects of Creative Music Therapy with Adult Clients. Gary Ansdell. LC 95-14419. 237p. 1995. pap. 29.95 (*1-85302-299-3*, Pub. by Jessica Kingsley) Taylor & Francis.

Music for Little Mozarts. E. L. Lancaster et al. (Music Flashcards Ser.: Bk. 3). (J). (ps-1). Date not set. write for info. (*0-7390-0646-0*, 17183); pap. write for info. (*0-7390-0645-2*, 17182); pap. write for info. (*0-7390-0644-4*, 17180) Alfred Pub.

Music for Little Mozarts. E. L. Lancaster et al. (Music Flashcards Ser.: Bk. 4). (J). (ps-1). Date not set. write for info. (*0-7390-0653-3*, 17189); pap. write for info. (*0-7390-0650-9*, 17186); pap. write for info. (*0-7390-0652-5*, 17188) Alfred Pub.

Music for Little Mozarts. E. L. Lancaster et al. (Music Workbks.: No. 4). (J). (ps-1). Date not set. pap., wbk. ed. write for info. (*0-7390-0651-7*, 17187) Alfred Pub.

Music for Little Mozarts, Workbk. 3. E. L. Lancaster et al. wbk. ed. write for info. (*0-7390-0643-6*, 17181) Alfred Pub.

*__Music for Little Mozarts: Deluxe Package.__ deluxe ed. E. L. Lancaster et al. 1999. 69.95 (*0-7390-0796-3*, 17194) Alfred Pub.

Music for Little Mozarts, Teacher's Handbook, Nos. 3 & 4. E. L. Lancaster et al. Date not set. pap. write for info. (*0-7390-0656-8*, 17192) Alfred Pub.

Music for Lute & Bandora see Complete Works

Music for Minors. Ed. by Christine J. Dillon. (Illus.). 130p. 1995. pap. 8.95 (*0-913717-81-9*, 2087) Hewitt Res Fnd.

Music for Monet. Robert H. Schuller. 80p. 1983. pap. 3.95 (*0-933180-57-8*) Spoon Riv Poetry.

Music for More Than One Piano: An Annotated Guide. Maurice Hinson. LC 82-49245. 248p. 1983. 39.95 (*0-253-33952-9*) Ind U Pr.

Music for New Musicians: A Beginner's Guide. 3rd ed. Douglas Smith. LC 97-171378. 284p. (C). 1997. pap. text 38.95 (*0-7872-2931-8*, 41293101) Kendall-Hunt.

Music for Oboe, Oboe d'Amore, & English Horn: A Bibliography of Materials at the Library of Congress, 1. Compiled by Virginia S. Gifford. LC 83-8517. (Music Reference Collection: No. 1). 431p. 1983. lib. bdg. 55.00 (*0-313-23762-X*, GMO/) Greenwood.

Music for Oboe, 1650-1800: A Bibliography. 2nd expanded rev. ed. Bruce Haynes. LC 91-34794. (Reference Books in Music: No. 16). xxv, 432p. 1992. 49.50 (*0-914913-15-8*, Fallen Lef Pr) Scarecrow.

Music for Orchestra Score. L. Kirchner. 48p. 1991. pap. 15.00 (*0-7935-0971-8*) H Leonard.

Music for Our Time. Winter. (Music Ser.). 1991. 19.50 (*0-534-13105-0*) Wadsworth Pub.

Music for Our Time. Robert Winter. 728p. (C). 1991. 51.75 (*0-534-13104-2*) Wadsworth Pub.

Music For Piano. Robert Pace. (Pace Piano Education Ser.: Bk. 4). 1988. pap. 6.95 (*0-7935-8378-0*) H Leonard.

Music for Piano, Bk 1. Robert Pace. 48p. 1988. pap. 5.95 (*0-7935-2787-2*, 00372121) H Leonard.

Music for Piano: A Short History. F. E. Kirby. LC 94-42642. (Illus.). 464p. 1995. 39.95 (*0-931340-86-1*, Amadeus Pr) Timber.

Music for Piano & Orchestra: An Annotated Guide. enl. ed. Maurice Hinson. LC 93-20035. 384p. 1993. 49.95 (*0-253-33953-7*); pap. 29.95 (*0-253-20835-1*) Ind U Pr.

Music for Piano 2. 48p. 1988. pap. 5.95 (*0-7935-9826-5*) H Leonard.

Music for Pleasure: Essays in the Sociology of Pop. Simon Frith. 208p. 1988. 37.50 (*0-415-90051-4*) Routledge.

Music for Sharing, Bk. 2. Margaret Goldston. 32p. 1994. pap. 6.95 (*0-7390-0342-9*, 11717) Alfred Pub.

Music for Sharing Bk. 1: 10 Early Elementary Piano Duets with Student Appeal. Margaret Goldston. 32p. 1994. pap. 6.50 (*0-7390-0359-3*, 11716) Alfred Pub.

Music for Shelley's Poetry. Burton R. Pollin. LC 74-4446. (Music Reprint Ser.). 174p. 1974. lib. bdg. 29.50 (*0-306-70640-7*) Da Capo.

Music for Sight Singing. Thomas E. Benjamin et al. 318p. (C). 1989. pap. 32.95 (*0-534-13416-5*) Wadsworth Pub.

Music for Sight Singing. 2nd ed. Thomas E. Benjamin et al. 336p. 1993. 37.50 (*0-534-20823-1*) Wadsworth Pub.

*__Music for Sight Singing.__ 2nd ed. Thomas E. Benjamin et al. (Music Ser.). 1999. 40.50 (*0-534-76773-7*) Wadsworth Pub.

Music for Sight Singing. 4th ed. Robert W. Ottman. 360p. 1996. spiral bd. 48.00 (*0-13-234360-6*) P-H.

Music for Silent Films: A Guide. 1991. lib. bdg. 79.95 (*0-8490-4229-1*) Gordon Pr.

Music for Study. 3rd ed. Robert A. Melcher et al. 256p. 1988. pap. write for info. (*0-318-62256-4*) P-H.

Music for Study. 3rd ed. Willard F. Melcher & Warch. 256p. 1988. 70.00 (*0-13-607474-X*) P-H.

Music for Summer Nights see Musica Para Noches de Verano

Music for the Ballet: Piano. 96p. (Orig.). 1993. pap. 10.95 (*0-7692-1119-4*, PF0859) Wrner Bros.

Music for the Cathedral of Treviso in the Late Sixteenth Century: A Reconstruction of the Lost Manuscripts 29 & 30. Bonnie J. Blackburn. (Royal Musical Association Monographs: No. 3). 168p. 1993. 29.95 (*0-947854-02-9*) U Ch Pr.

Music for the Christian Wedding. 52p. 1968. pap. 10.99 (*0-8341-9449-X*, MB-139) Lillenas.

Music for the Dance: Reflections on a Collaborative Art, 15. Katherine Teck. LC 88-38551. 264p. 1989. 59.95 (*0-313-26376-0*, TMU/, Greenwood Pr) Greenwood.

Music for the Divine Liturgy: Multiple Settings for the Unvarying Portions of the Divine Liturgy. Ed. by Timothy Clader. Tr. by Holy Transfiguration Monastery Staff et al from SLA. 332p. 1996. pap., spiral bd. 55.00 (*0-912927-75-5*, D040) St John Kronstadt.

Music for the Divine Liturgy of the Presanctified Gifts. Ed. by Timothy Clader. Tr. by Isaac E. Lambertsen & Laurence Campbell from GRE. 73p. 1994. pap. 12.00 (*0-912927-59-3*, D019) St John Kronstadt.

Music for the Eleven Evangelical Stichera. Ed. by Timothy Clader. Tr. by Isaac Lambertsen from SLA. 58p. 1997. spiral bd. 12.00 (*0-912927-83-6*, D020) St John Kronstadt.

Music for the Exceptional Child. Richard M. Graham. LC 75-850. 259p. 1975. reprint ed. pap. 80.30 (*0-608-04218-8*, 206496000011) Bks Demand.

*__Music for the Feet.__ Frank Ferrel. 90p. 1998. spiral bd. 17.95 (*0-7866-2959-2*, 96726) Mel Bay.

Music for the Films. Leonid L. Sabaneev. Ed. by Garth S. Jowett. Tr. by S. W. Pring. LC 77-11382. (Aspects of Film Ser.). 1979. reprint ed. lib. bdg. 11.95 (*0-405-11142-8*) Ayer.

Music for the Flute of Bali. Julia Hansen. 12p. 1997. pap. 15.00 (*0-9619498-4-8*) Linaria Pr.

Music for the Hearing Impaired & Other Special Groups: A Resource Manual & Curriculum Guide. Carol Robbins & Clive Robbins. (Illus.). 480p. 1980. pap., spiral bd. 24.95 (*0-918812-11-9*, ST 027) MMB Music.

*__Music for the Heather Folk.__ Sue Richards. 48p. 1998. pap. 8.95 (*0-7866-2543-0*, 96324) Mel Bay.

Music for the Listener. Daniel Binder. 304p. (C). 1995. ring bd. 66.95 (*0-7872-1087-0*) Kendall-Hunt.

Music for the Mass I. Ed. by Ernest Warburton. (Johann Christian Bach Ser.: Vol. 19). 350p. 1987. text 105.00 (*0-8240-6068-7*) Garland.

Music for the Mass II: Settings of the Gloria & Credo for Soloists, Choir, & Orchestra from Eighteenth-Century Manuscript Sources. Ed. by Ernest Warburton. LC 83-48727. (Johann Christian Bach Ser.: Vol. 20). 376p. 1986. text 105.00 (*0-8240-6069-5*) Garland.

*__Music for the Millennium: Modern Landscapes for the Piano.__ 1998. pap. 12.95 (*1-57560-120-6*, Pub. by Cherry Lane) H Leonard.

Music for the Millions: Antebellum Democratic Attitudes & the Birth of American Popular Music. Nicholas E. Tawa. LC 83-26222. (Sociology of Music Ser.: No. 3). (Illus.). 160p. 1984. lib. bdg. 59.00 (*0-918728-38-X*) Pendragon NY.

Music for the Movies. 2nd expanded ed. Tony Thomas. (Illus.). 280p. 1997. pap. 19.95 (*1-879505-37-1*) Silman James Pr.

Music for the Office of the Dead. Ed. by Ernest Warburton. (Johann Christian Bach Ser.: Vol. 21). 225p. 1987. text 127.00 (*0-8240-6070-9*) Garland.

Music for the Paschal Canon: According to the Liturgy of the Orthodox Church, As Chanted During Paschaltide. Ed. by Timothy Clader. Tr. by Laurence Campbell from SLA. 98p. 1994. spiral bd. 15.00 (*0-912927-85-2*) St John Kronstadt.

Music for the Piano: A Handbook of Concert & Teaching Material from 1580 to 1952. rev. ed. James Friskin & Irwin Freundlich. LC 72-93608. 448p. 1973. pap. 9.95 (*0-486-22918-1*) Dover.

*__Music for the Recorder - Folk Songs of the U. S. Beginning-Intermediate Level.__ Mark Lepiane. 64p. 1999. pap. 9.95 (*0-7866-3080-9*, 96738) Mel Bay.

Music for the Soul. Alexander Maclaren. LC 96-79878. (Walk in the Word Ser.). 400p. 1996. 24.99 (*0-89957-218-9*) AMG Pubs.

Music for the Sunday Vigil in the Eight Tones, 8 vols., Set. Ed. by Timothy Clader. Tr. by Isaac E. Lambertsen & Laurence Campbell from GRE. (Orig.). 1992. spiral bd. 100.00 (*0-912927-47-X*, D010) St John Kronstadt.

Music for the Tsar of the Sea. Celia Barker Lottridge. (Illus.). (J). (gr. 1-4). 1998. 16.95 (*0-88899-328-5*, Pub. by Gro1undwood-Douglas) Publishers Group.

Music for the Vigil Service: Multiple Settings for the Unvarying Portions of the Vigil Service. Ed. by Timothy Clader. Tr. by Holy Transfiguration Monastery Staff et al from SLA. 196p. 1996. pap., spiral bd. 40.00 (*0-912927-74-7*, D039) St John Kronstadt.

Music for the Voice: A Descriptive List of Concert & Teaching Material. rev. ed. Sergius Kagen. LC 68-27348. 800p. reprint ed. pap. 200.00 (*0-7837-1756-3*, 205729200024) Bks Demand.

Music for the Voice: A Descriptive List of Concert & Teaching Material. rev. ed. Sergius Kagen. LC 68-27348. 800p. 1969. 59.95 (*0-253-33955-3*) Ind U Pr.

Music for the Voice: A Descriptive List of Concert & Teaching Material. rev. ed. Sergius Kagen. LC 68-27348. 800p. 1997. pap. 39.95 (*0-253-21142-5*) Ind U Pr.

Music for the Wedding Service. pap. 10.95 (*0-7935-3976-5*, 00199001) H Leonard.

Music for Three or More Pianists: A Historical Survey & Catalogue. Grant T. Maxwell. LC 92-37842. 387p. 1993. 47.50 (*0-8108-2631-3*) Scarecrow.

*__Music for Three Viols: (Or String Trio)__ Will Ayton. (Contemporary Consort Ser.: Vol. 35). 23p. 1999. pap. 8.00 (*1-56571-176-9*, CC035) PRB Prods.

Music for Tired Lovers see Muzyka dlia Ustalykh Liubovnikov

Music for Today's Preschoolers. Jane Burdeshaw & Cindy McClain. (Illus.). 39p. (Orig.). (J). (ps-k). 1995. pap. text 10.95 (*1-56309-158-5*, N958103, New Hope) Womans Mission Union.

Music for Torching. A. M. Homes. LC 98-55252. 368p. 1999. 26.00 (*0-688-16711-X*, Wm Morrow) Morrow Avon.

*__Music for Torching.__ A. M. Homes. 368p. 2000. pap. 14.00 (*0-688-17762-X*) Morrow Avon.

Music for Twelve: For Chamber Ensemble Full Score. L. Kirchner. 96p. 1993. pap. 20.00 (*0-7935-2522-5*) H Leonard.

Music for Two Instruments. Ed. by Ernest Warburton. (Johann Christian Bach Ser.: Vol. 38). 280p. 1991. text 165.00 (*0-8240-6087-3*) Garland.

Music for Two or More Players at Clavichord, Harpsichord, Organ: An Annotated Bibliography, 29. Compiled by Sally J. Sloane. LC 91-11404. (Music Reference Collection: No. 29). 128p. 1991. lib. bdg. 49.95 (*0-313-27910-1*, SXM/, Greenwood Pr) Greenwood.

Music for Two Theatre Pieces: Pizarro (1799) & Love Laughs at Locksmiths (1803) Michael Kelly. LC 79-18565. (Music Reprint Ser.: 1979). 1979. reprint ed. lib. bdg. 29.50 (*0-306-79562-0*) Da Capo.

Music for Vespers & Compline: Vesper & Compline Music for Two Principal Voices. Jeffrey Kurtzman & Anne Schnoebelen. LC 56-5. (Seventeenth-Century Italian Sacred Music Ser.: Vol. 12). 280p. 1996. text 105.00 (*0-8153-2359-X*) Garland.

Music for Vespers I. Ed. by Ernest Warburton. (Johann Christian Bach Ser.: Vol. 22). 350p. 1985. text 105.00 (*0-8240-6071-7*) Garland.

Music for Vespers II. Ed. by Ernest Warburton. (Johann Christian Bach: The Collected Works: Vol. 23). 400p. 1985. text 110.00 (*0-8240-6072-5*) Garland.

Music for Viola Bastarda. fac. ed. Jason Paras. LC 84-43068. (Music Scholarship & Performance Ser.). (Illus.). 252p. 1986. pap. text 15.95 (*0-253-38824-4*) Ind U Pr.

Music for Violin & Viola. Hans Letz. 107p. 1993. reprint ed. lib. bdg. 69.00 (*0-7812-9690-0*) Rprt Serv.

Music for Voice & Classical Guitar, 1945-1996: An Annotated Catalog. James Maroney. LC 97-19848. 152p. 1997. lib. bdg. 42.50 (*0-7864-0384-5*) McFarland & Co.

Music for Wedding Services: An Ecumenical Collection, Congregational bklt. 48p. (Orig.). 1993. pap. 2.95 (*0-8146-2302-6*) Liturgical Pr.

Music for Wedding Services: An Ecumenical Collection, Musician's copy. 250p. (Orig.). 1993. pap., spiral bd. 42.50 (*0-8146-2301-8*) Liturgical Pr.

Music for Wedding Services: An Ecumenical Collection Couples Planner. 48p. (Orig.). 1993. pap. 3.50 (*0-8146-2300-X*) Liturgical Pr.

Music for Weddings. Margaret Daly. 96p. 1989. pap. 55.00 (*1-85390-131-8*, Pub. by Veritas Pubns); pap. 22.00 (*1-85390-631-X*, Pub. by Veritas Pubns); audio 22.00 (*0-7855-6982-0*, Pub. by Veritas Pubns) St Mut.

Music for Wind Band. J. C. Bach. LC 83-48727. (Collected Works of Johann Christian Bach). 225p. 1990. reprint ed. text 94.00 (*0-8240-6086-5*) Garland.

Music for Young Children. Barbara Andress. LC 96-79966. 208p. (C). 1997. pap. text 42.00 (*0-15-503071-X*, Pub. by Harcourt Coll Pubs) Harcourt.

Music Forum, Vol. 4. Music Forum Staff. 1977. text 65.00 (*0-231-03934-4*) Col U Pr.

Music Forum, Vol. 6, Pt. I. Ed. by William J. Mitchell & Felix Salzer. 256p. 1988. text 64.50 (*0-231-05832-2*) Col U Pr.

*__Music Four Fun Pack, Set.__ 1998. 24.95 incl. audio (*1-887120-09-2*, Pub. by Prodn Assocs) Penton Overseas.

Music from a Blue Well. Torborg Nedreaas. Tr. by Bibbi Lee. LC 87-19026. (European Women Writers Ser.). 244p. 1988. reprint ed. pap. 75.70 (*0-608-02669-7*, 206332200004) Bks Demand.

Music from a Place Called Half Moon. Jerrie Oughton. LC 94-25368. 176p. (YA). (gr. 5-9). 1997. mass mkt. 3.99 (*0-440-21999-X*, YB BDD) BDD Bks Young Read.

Music from a Place Called Half Moon. Jerrie Oughton. LC 94-25368. 176p. (J). (gr. 5-8). 1995. 15.00 (*0-395-70737-4*) HM.

Music from a Place Called Half Moon. Jerrie Oughton. 1997. 9.09 (*0-606-11003-8*, Pub. by Turtleback) Demco.

Music from Batman - 15 Great Themes. Ed. by Tony Esposito. 56p. (Orig.). (YA). 1997. pap. 10.95 (*0-7692-0186-5*, 0081B) Wrner Bros.

Music from Batman - 15 Great Themes: Alto Sax. Ed. by Tony Esposito. 24p. (Orig.). 1997, pap. 10.95 (*0-7692-0184-9*, 0078B) Wrner Bros.

Music from Batman - 15 Great Themes: Clarinet. Ed. by Tony Esposito. 24p. (Orig.). (YA). 1997. pap. 10.95 (*0-7692-0181-4*, 0076B) Wrner Bros.

Music from Batman - 15 Great Themes: Flute. Ed. by Tony Esposito. 24p. (Orig.). (YA). 1997. pap. 10.95 (*0-7692-0180-6*, 0075B) Wrner Bros.

Music from Batman - 15 Great Themes: Tenor Sax. Ed. by Tony Esposito. 24p. (Orig.). (YA). 1997. pap. 10.95 (*0-7692-0183-0*, 0079B) Wrner Bros.

Music from Batman - 15 Great Themes: Trombone. Ed. by Tony Esposito. 24p. (Orig.). 1997. pap. 10.95 (*0-7692-0185-7*, 0080B) Wrner Bros.

Music from Batman - 15 Great Themes: Trumpet. Ed. by Tony Esposito. 24p. (Orig.). 1997. pap. 10.95 (*0-7692-0182-2*, 0077B) Wrner Bros.

Music from Ireland. Ed. by John Loesburg. 56p. pap. 7.95 (*0-946005-55-9*, Pub. by Ossian) Music Sales.

Music from Missouri: Dance Tunes for the Autoharp. Tom Schroeder. Ed. by Becky Blackley. (Illus.). 30p. 1988. pap. 6.95 (*0-912827-11-4*) I A D Pubns.

Music from Star Wars Trilogy: Arranged by Dan Coates. Ed. by Carol Cuellar. (Illus.). 36p. (Orig.). (J). 1997. pap. text 12.95 (*1-57623-938-1*, 0020B) Wrner Bros.

An Asterisk (*) at the beginning of an entry indicates that the title is appearing for the first time.

Music from Strings. Josephine Paker. LC 92-5162. (Millbrook Arts Library). (Illus.). 48p. (J). (gr. 2-6). 1992. lib. bdg. 22.90 (*1-56294-283-1*) Millbrook Pr.

Music from the Days of George Washington. Ed. by Carl Engel & John T. Howard. LC 82-2331. (Music Reprint Ser.). 103p. 1983. reprint ed. lib. bdg. 29.50 (*0-306-76086-X*) Da Capo.

Music from the Days of George Washington. Ed. by Carl Engel & W. Oliver Strunk. LC 73-36418. reprint ed. 38.50 (*0-404-07230-5*) AMS Pr.

Music from the Evening of the World. Michael Brownstein. (New American Fiction Ser.: No. 17). 104p. 1987. pap. 10.95 (*1-55713-038-8*) Sun & Moon CA.

Music from the Evening of the World. Michael Brownstein. (New American Fiction Ser.: No. 17). 104p. 1989. 15.95 (*1-55713-036-1*) Sun & Moon CA.

Music from the Heart. Rod Kennedy. LC 98-205040. (Illus.). 408p. 1998. 39.95 (*1-57168-173-6*); pap. 29.95 (*1-57168-230-9*) Sunbelt Media.

Music from the Heart: Compositions of a Folk Fiddler. Colin Quigley. LC 93-39721. (Illus.). 288p. 1995. 35.00 (*0-8203-1637-7*) U of Ga Pr.

Music from the House of Hammer: Music in the Hammer Horror Films, 1950-1980. Randall D. Larson. 234p. 1996. 32.50 (*0-8108-2975-4*) Scarecrow.

Music from the Middle Ages Through the Twentieth Century: A Seventieth Birthday Tribute to Gwynn S. McPeek. C. P. Comberiati & M. C. Steel. xiv, 394p. 1988. text 86.00 (*2-88124-216-2*) Gordon & Breach.

Music from the Middle Passage. George Buggs. pap. 1.50 (*0-918476-02-X*) Cornerstone Pr.

Music from the Motion Picture "For the Boys" Ed. by Sy Feldman. 72p. (Orig.). (C). 1991. pap. text 18.95 (*0-7692-0455-4*) Wrner Bros.

Music from the Mountains Vol. 1: New York State Music Camp, 1947-1996. Robert F. Swift. LC 97-180963. (Illus.). xiv, 124p. 1996. 20.00 (*0-9653933-1-3*); spiral bd. 12.00 (*0-9653933-0-5*) NYSMC Pr.

***Music from the Silence.** Gilbert Levine. 2001. 24.00 (*0-609-60457-0*, Pub. by Crown Pub Group) Random House.

Music from the Star Wars Trilogy. Ed. by Sy Feldman. (Illus.). 60p. (Orig.). 1997. pap. text 16.95 (*1-57623-953-5*, 5204A) Wrner Bros.

Music from the Tang Court 6. Laurence Picken & Noel Nickson. 308p. (C). 1997. text 85.00 (*0-521-62100-3*) Cambridge U Pr.

***Music from the Tang Court 7: Some Ancient Connections Explored.** Ed. by Laurence E. R. Picken & Noel J. Nickson. (Illus.). 320p. (C). 2000. 89.95 (*0-521-78084-5*) Cambridge U Pr.

***Music from the Wayang Kulit of Bali: For Bamboo Ensemble or Gender.** Julia Hansen. 58p. 1999. pap. 20.00 (*0-9619498-5-6*) Linaria Pr.

***Music from Titanic.** 16p. 1998. pap. 5.95 (*0-7935-9469-3*); pap. 5.95 (*0-7935-9470-7*); pap. 5.95 (*0-7935-9471-5*); pap. 5.95 (*0-7935-9472-3*); pap. 5.95 (*0-7935-9473-1*); pap. 5.95 (*0-7935-9474-X*); pap. 9.95 (*0-7935-9475-8*) H Leonard.

***Music from Titanic.** 12p. 1998. pap. 4.95 (*0-7935-9874-5*) H Leonard.

Music Fundamentals. L. Dean Bye. 32p. 1981. pap. 0.95 (*0-87166-549-2*, 93753) Mel Bay.

Music Fundamentals. Vito Puopolo. LC 75-4316. (Illus.). 219p. (C). 1976. 19.00 (*0-02-871890-9*, Schirmer Books) Mac Lib Ref.

Music Fundamentals: A Performance Approach. Phyllis Irwin. (C). 1982. pap. text, student ed. 48.00 (*0-03-054021-6*, Pub. by Harcourt Coll Pubs) Harcourt.

Music Fundamentals: Pitch Structures & Rhythmic Design. Elvo S. D'Amante. (C). 1994. pap. text 35.95 (*1-880157-12-8*) Ardsley.

Music Fundamentals: Through Pitch Structures & Rhythmic Design. Elvo S. D'Amante. 1994. pap. text, teacher ed. 10.95 (*1-880157-22-5*) Ardsley.

Music Fundamentals for the Recreational Musician. 2nd rev. ed. Vicki T. Purslow. (Illus.). 49p. 1998. pap. text 9.95 (*1-893438-00-7*) Lighthse Pubg.

Music Fundamentals, Methods & Materials for the Elementary Classroom Teacher. 2nd ed. Michon Rozmajzl & Rene Boyer-White. LC 95-9934. (Orig.). (C). 1996. pap. text 62.81 (*0-8013-1580-8*) Longman.

***Music Fundamentals, Methods & Materials for the Elementary Classroom Teacher.** 3rd ed. Michon Rozmajzl. 416p. (Orig.). (C). 1999. pap. text. write for info. (*0-8013-3082-3*) Longman.

***Music Fundamentals, Methods & Materials for the Elementary Classroom Teacher.** 3rd ed. Rozmanjzl & Boyer-Alexander. 1999. spiral bd. 70.00 (*0-13-088109-0*) P-H.

Music, Gender, Education. Lucy Green. 294p. 1997. text 59.95 (*0-521-55517-5*); pap. text 21.95 (*0-521-55522-1*) Cambridge U Pr.

***Music Genres & Corporate Cultures.** Keith Negus. LC 98-51909. 1999. pap. 22.99 (*0-415-17400-7*); text. write for info. (*0-415-17399-X*) Routledge.

Music, Gestalt, & Computing: Studies in Cognitive & Systematic Musicology, Vol. 131. Ed. by Marc Leman. LC 97-39887. (Lecture Notes in Artificial Intelligence: Vol. 1317). ix, 524p. 1997. pap. 69.00 (*3-540-63526-2*) Spr-Verlag.

***Music God Likes.** Joseph Nicholson. (Spiritual Discovery Ser.). 112p. 1998. pap., teacher ed. 9.95 (*0-88243-228-1*, 02-0228); pap., student ed. 4.95 (*0-88243-128-5*, 02-0128) Gospel Pub.

Music Goes Round. Frederick W. Gaisberg. Ed. by Andrew Farkas. LC 76-29936. (Opera Biographies Ser.). (Illus.). 1977. reprint ed. lib. bdg. 29.95 (*0-405-09678-X*) Ayer.

Music Graphics. Compiled by Rockport Publishers Editorial Staff. (Design Library). (Illus.). 80p. 1996. pap. 14.99 (*1-56496-291-1*) Rockport Pubs.

Music Grooves: Essays & Dialogues. Charles Keil & Steven Feld. 410p. (C). 1994. pap. text 21.00 (*0-226-42957-1*) U Ch Pr.

Music Grooves: Essays & Dialogues. Charles Keil & Steven Feld. 410p. (C). 1994. lib. bdg. 47.95 (*0-226-42956-3*) U Ch Pr.

Music Hall: Performance & Style. Ed. by J. S. Bratton. LC 86-12608. (Popular Music in Britain Ser.). 224p. 1987. pap. 33.95 (*0-335-15131-0*) OpUniv Pr.

Music Hall: The Business of Pleasure. Ed. by Peter Bailey. LC 86-12837. (Popular Music in Britain Ser.). 208p. 1987. 123.95 (*0-335-15278-3*); pap. 33.95 (*0-335-15129-9*) OpUniv Pr.

Music Hall in Britain. D. F. Cheshire. LC 74-2581. (Illus.). 112p. 1974. 26.50 (*0-8386-1563-5*) Fairleigh Dickinson.

Music Halls to Movie Places. John L. Scherer. (Illus.). 28p. 1985. 10.00 (*0-934483-07-8*) Gal Assn NY.

Music Handbook. (C). 1996. write for info. (*0-8087-2468-1*) Pearson Custom.

Music Handbook. John B. Whitlock. LC 72-6832. 183p. (C). 1972. text 32.50 (*0-8422-5023-9*) Irvington.

Music, History, & Ideas. Hugo Leichtentritt. LC 38-17551. 320p. reprint ed. pap. 99.20 (*0-608-17492-0*, 202999200067) Bks Demand.

Music History During the Renaissance Period, 1425-1580: A Documented Chronology, 28. Blanche M. Gangwere. LC 91-2163. (Music Reference Collection: No. 28). 512p. 1991. lib. bdg. 65.00 (*0-313-25309-9*, GMY, Greenwood Pr) Greenwood.

Music History from the Late Roman Through the Gothic Periods, 313-1425: A Documented Chronology, 6. Blanche M. Gangwere. LC 85-21934. (Music Reference Collection: No. 6). (Illus.). 260p. 1986. lib. bdg. 55.00 (*0-313-24764-1*, GMH/, Greenwood Pr) Greenwood.

Music Ho. Constant Lambert. 1967. 8.95 (*0-8079-0086-9*) October.

Music Ho! A Study of Music in Decline. Constant Lambert. (Music Book Index Ser.). 342p. 1992. reprint ed. lib. bdg. 89.00 (*0-7812-9507-6*) Rprt Serv.

Music Hound Rock: The Essential Album Guide. 2nd ed. Gary Graff & Daniel Durchholz. LC 98-40006. (Illus.). 1550p. 1999. 24.95 (*1-57859-061-2*) Visible Ink Pr.

Music I No Longer Heard. Leslie Simon & Jan J. Drantell. LC 97-35471. 1998. 23.50 (*0-684-81319-X*) S&S Trade.

Music-Ideology: Resisting the Aesthetic. Adam Krims & Henry Klumoenhouwer. 160p. 1997. pap. 18.95 (*90-5701-321-5*) Dist Art Pubs.

Music-Ideology: Resisting the Aesthetic. Adam Krims & Henry Klumpenhouwer. 160p. 1997. 35.00 (*90-5701-241-3*) Dist Art Pubs.

Music, Imagination & Culture. Nicholas Cook. (Illus.). 272p. 1992. pap. text 21.00 (*0-19-816303-7*) OUP.

Music Improvisation As a Classroom Method. Bert Konowitz. LC 72-96015. 102p. 1973. pap. text 6.95 (*0-88284-003-7*, 696) Alfred Pub.

Music, in a Foreign Language. Andrew Crumey. Date not set. 22.00 (*0-614-25847-2*, Picador USA) St Martin.

Music in African American Fiction: Representing Music in African American Fiction. rev. ed. Robert H. Cataliotti. LC 95-35215. (Studies in African American History & Culture). 272p. 1995. text 70.00 (*0-8153-2330-1*) Garland.

Music in American Life. Crawford. Date not set. write for info. (*0-393-04736-9*) Norton.

Music in American Life. Richard Crawford. (C). pap. text. write for info. (*0-393-97410-3*) Norton.

Music in American Life. Richard Crawford. (C). 2000. pap. text. write for info. (*0-393-97409-X*) Norton.

Music in American Life. Augustus D. Zanzig. LC 71-143075. Date not set. 39.95 (*0-8434-0442-6*, Pub. by McGrath NH) Ayer.

Music in American Society, 1776-1976. Ed. by George McCue. LC 76-24527. (Illus.). 201p. 1976. text 39.95 (*0-87855-209-X*); pap. text 24.95 (*0-87855-634-6*) Transaction Pubs.

Music in Ancient Arabia & Spain: Being la Musica de las Cantigas. Julian Ribera. LC 70-87614. (Music Ser.). 1970. reprint ed. lib. bdg. 45.00 (*0-306-71622-4*) Da Capo.

Music in Ancient Greece & Rome. John G. Landels. LC 98-3051. (Illus.). 306p. (C). 1998. 85.00 (*0-415-16776-0*) Routledge.

Music in Art: Through the Ages. Tom Phillips. LC 98-186539. (Illus.). 128p. 1997. 39.95 (*3-7913-1864-0*, Pub. by Prestel) te Neues.

Music in Biblical Perspective. John Coblentz. 1986. pap. 1.75 (*0-87813-524-3*) Christian Light.

Music in Boston: Readings from the First Three Centuries. John C. Swan. 1977. 4.00 (*0-89073-052-0*, 194) Boston Public Lib.

Music in British Libraries: A Directory of Resources. Compiled by Barbara Penney. LC 92-16596. 109p. Date not set. reprint ed. pap. 33.80 (*0-608-20732-2*, 207183000002) Bks Demand.

Music in Canada. Ernest Macmillan. 1988. reprint ed. lib. bdg. 49.00 (*0-7812-0198-5*) Rprt Serv.

Music in Canada. Ed. by Ernest Macmillan. LC 77-18206. 232p. 1955. reprint ed. 49.00 (*0-403-01616-9*) Scholarly.

Music in Canada: A Research & Information Guide. Carl Morey. LC 96-29156. (Garland Reference Library of the Humanities). 304p. 1997. text 50.00 (*0-8153-1603-8*) Garland.

Music in Childhood: From Preschool Through the Elementary Grades. Patricia S. Campbell & Carol Scott-Kassner. LC 94-30663. (Illus.). 384p. 1995. 38.00 (*0-02-870552-1*, Schirmer Books) Mac Lib Ref.

Music in Churches: Nourishing Your Congregation's Musical Life. Linda J. Clark. LC 94-78334. 140p. 1994. pap. 13.25 (*1-56699-134-X*, AL155) Alban Inst.

Music in Classic Period. 4th ed. Reinhard G. Pauly. LC 99-30849. 272p. 1999. pap. 39.20 (*0-13-011502-9*) P-H.

Music in Colonial Massachusetts, 1630-1820: A Conference Held by the Colonial Society of Massachusetts, May 17 & 18, 1973, Vol. 1: Music in Public Places. Colonial Society of Massachusetts Staff. LC 80-66188. (Publications of the Colonial Society of Massachusetts: Nos. 53-54). 451p. reprint ed. pap. 139.90 (*0-7837-3739-4*, 204342200001) Bks Demand.

Music in Colonial Massachusetts, 1630-1820: A Conference Held by the Colonial Society of Massachusetts, May 17 & 18, 1973, Vol. 2: Music in Homes & in Churches. Colonial Society of Massachusetts Staff. LC 80-66188. (Publications of the Colonial Society of Massachusetts: Nos. 53-54). 840p. reprint ed. pap. 200.00 (*0-7837-3740-8*, 204342200002) Bks Demand.

Music in Cultural Context: Eight Views on World Music Education. Patricia S. Campbell. (Illus.). 88p. (Orig.). 1996. pap. 16.50 (*1-56545-100-7*, 1634) MENC.

Music in Culture. Vicki Curry. 96p. (C). 1995. student ed., spiral bd., suppl. ed. 8.95 (*0-7872-1896-0*) Kendall-Hunt.

Music in Derrick's Heart. Gwendolyn Battle-Lavert. LC 97-34115. (Illus.). 32p. (J). (ps-3). 2000. 16.95 (*0-8234-1353-5*) Holiday.

Music in Eighteenth-Century Austria. Ed. by David W. Jones. (Illus.). 303p. (C). 1996. text 69.95 (*0-521-45349-6*) Cambridge U Pr.

***Music in Eighteenth-Century Britain.** (Illus.). 300p. 2000. 79.95 (*1-84014-688-5*, Pub. by Ashgate Pub) Ashgate Pub Co.

Music in Eighteenth-Century Georgia. Ron Byrnside. LC 96-3280. 1997. 45.00 (*0-8203-1853-1*) U of Ga Pr.

Music in Elizabethan England. Dorothy E. Mason. LC 59-1448. (Folger Guides to the Age of Shakespeare Ser.). 1958. pap. 4.95 (*0-918016-21-5*) Folger Bks.

Music in England. Eric Blom. 1988. reprint ed. lib. bdg. 49.00 (*0-317-90766-2*) Rprt Serv.

Music in England. Eric Blom. LC 71-181112. 220p. 1942. reprint ed. 49.00 (*0-403-01511-1*) Scholarly.

Music in English Children's Drama, 1597-1613. Linda P. Austern. LC 92-14000. 374p. 1992. text 30.00 (*2-88124-558-7*) Gordon & Breach.

Music in English Children's Drama of the Later Renaissance. Linda P. Austern. (Musicology: A Book Ser.). 374p. 1992. pap. text 14.00 (*2-88124-564-1*) Gordon & Breach.

Music in English Drama. John S. Manifold. 1988. reprint ed. lib. bdg. 75.00 (*0-7812-0242-6*) Rprt Serv.

Music in English Drama from Shakespeare to Purcell. John S. Manifold. LC 70-181207. 208p. 1956. reprint ed. 49.00 (*0-403-01617-7*) Scholarly.

Music in English Renaissance Drama. John H. Long. LC 68-12969. 200p. reprint ed. pap. 62.00 (*0-608-10978-9*, 200160900080) Bks Demand.

Music in Europe & the United States: A History. 2nd ed. Edith Borroff. 60p. 1990. pap. text, teacher ed. write for info. (*0-912675-46-2*) Ardsley.

Music in Europe & the United States: A History. 2nd ed. Edith Borroff. (Illus.). 794p. 1990. text 44.95 (*0-912675-44-6*) Ardsley.

Music in Every Classroom: A Resource Guide for Integrating Music Across the Curriculum, Grades K-8. James D. Sporborg. LC 98-19823. 128p. 1998. 28.00 (*1-56308-610-7*) Libs Unl.

Music in Every Room: Around the World in a Bad Mood. John Krich. LC 88-3445. (Travel Ser.). 320p. 1988. pap. 12.00 (*0-87113-194-3*, Atlntc Mnthly) Grove-Atltic.

Music in General Education. Music Educators National Conference, Music in Gene. Ed. by Karl D. Ernst & Charles L. Gary. LC 65-19741. 231p. 1965. reprint ed. pap. 71.70 (*0-608-04210-2*, 206494800011) Bks Demand.

Music in Georgia. Ed. by Frank W. Hoogerwerf. (Music Ser.). (Illus.). 328p. 1981. lib. bdg. 39.50 (*0-306-76096-7*) Da Capo.

Music in Greek & Roman Culture. Giovanni Comotti. Tr. by Rosaria V. Munson from ITA. LC 88-45413. (Ancient Society & History Ser.). 192p. 1991. reprint ed. pap. text 14.95 (*0-8018-4231-X*) Johns Hopkins.

Music in Human Life: Anthropological Perspectives on Music. John E. Kaemmer. LC 92-14937. (Sourcebooks in Anthropology: No. 17). (Illus.). 259p. (C). 1993. pap. 24.95 (*0-292-74314-9*); text 45.00 (*0-292-74313-0*) U of Tex Pr.

Music in Human Life: Anthropological Perspectives on Music. John E. Kaemmer. LC 92-14937. (Texas Press Sourcebooks in Anthropology Ser.: Vol. 17). (Illus.). 259p. reprint ed. pap. 80.30 (*0-608-20866-3*, 207196500003) Bks Demand.

Music in India: The Classical Traditions. Bonnie C. Wade. (C). 1994. 24.00 (*81-85054-25-8*, Pub. by Manohar) S Asia.

Music in Indian Art. M. Hariharan & Gowri Kuppuswamy. (C). 1985. text 38.50 (*0-8364-2619-3*, Pub. by Sundeep Prak) S Asia.

Music in Institutions. William Van de Wall & Clara M. Liepmann. LC 79-143074. 1982. 48.95 (*0-8434-0443-4*, Pub. by McGrath NH) Ayer.

Music in Late Medieval Bruges. 2nd rev. ed. Reinhard Strohm. (Oxford Monographs on Music). (Illus.). 296p. 1991. reprint ed. pap. text 37.50 (*0-19-316418-3*) OUP.

Music in Latin American Culture. Schechter. LC 99-13859. 9p. 1999. 40.00 (*0-02-864750-5*, Schirmer Books) Mac Lib Ref.

Music in Lexington Before 1840. Joy C. Carden. LC 80-83683. 148p. 1980. pap. 9.95 (*0-912839-05-8*) Lexington-Fayette.

***Music in London, 3 vols.** George Bernard Shaw. 2000. reprint ed. lib. bdg. 225.00 (*0-7812-0960-9*) Rprt Serv.

Music in London, 1890-1894, 3 vols., Set. George Bernard Shaw. LC 77-181257. 1956. reprint ed. 125.00 (*0-403-01680-0*) Scholarly.

***Music in Lubavitcher Life.** Ellen Koskoff. LC 99-51007. (Music in American Life Ser.). 320p. 2000. text 39.95 (*0-252-02591-1*) U of Ill Pr.

Music in Lutheran Worship. Carl F. Schalk. 16p. (Orig.). 1983. reprint ed. pap. 2.00 (*0-570-01323-2*, 99-1253) Concordia.

Music in Medieval Europe. Jeremy Yudkin. 640p. 1989. pap. text 52.00 incl. audio (*0-13-608192-4*, Pub. by P-H) S&S Trade.

Music in Motion: Twenty-Two Songs in Signing Exact English, for Children. Michael D. Wojcio et al. (Illus.). 112p. (Orig.). (J). 1982. pap. 13.95 (*0-916708-07-1*) Modern Signs.

Music in Mourning: A Novel of the Gulf Coast. rev. ed. Regina C. Rapier. (Illus.). 196p. 1995. reprint ed. 20.00 (*0-685-48990-6*) R C Rapier.

Music in My Time: And Other Reminiscences. Daniel G. Mason. (American Biography Ser.). 409p. 1991. reprint ed. lib. bdg. 89.00 (*0-7812-8274-8*) Rprt Serv.

Music in My Time & Other Reminiscences. Daniel G. Mason. LC 71-107818. (Select Bibliographies Reprint Ser.). 1977. 36.95 (*0-8369-5189-1*) Ayer.

Music in My Time & Other Reminiscences. Daniel G. Mason. LC 71-109784. 409p. 1970. reprint ed. lib. bdg. 49.50 (*0-8371-4274-1*, MAMT, Greenwood Pr) Greenwood.

Music in New Jersey, 1655-1860. Charles H. Kaufman. LC 78-75180. 304p. 1982. 85.00 (*0-8386-2270-4*) Fairleigh Dickinson.

Music in New Orleans: The Formative Years, 1791-1841. Henry A. Kmen. LC 66-25723. (Illus.). 332p. reprint ed. pap. 103.00 (*0-608-10821-9*, 205530200013) Bks Demand.

Music in New York During the American Revolution: An Inventory of Musical References in Rivington's New York Gazette. Gillian B. Anderson. (Music Library Association Index & Bibliography Ser.: No. 24). 135p. 1987. pap. 15.00 (*0-914954-33-4*) Scarecrow.

Music in Our Culture. Ellen Kravitz. 180p. (C). 1996. per. 77.95 (*0-7872-2808-7*, 41280801) Kendall-Hunt.

Music in Our Lives: The Early Years. Dorothy T. McDonald. LC 79-51509. 68p. 1979. pap. text 4.00 (*0-912674-65-2*, NAEYC #107) Natl Assn Child Ed.

Music in Our Time: Trends in Music since the Romantic Era. Adolfo Salazar. Tr. by Isabel Pope. LC 75-97391. 367p. 1970. reprint ed. lib. bdg. 38.50 (*0-8371-3014-X*, SAMT, Greenwood Pr) Greenwood.

***Music in Our World: An Active-Listening Approach.** Gary White et al. LC 00-33923. 2001. pap. write for info. (*0-07-027212-3*) McGraw.

Music in Painting. Idiko Ember. 132p. (C). 1989. 90.00 (*0-7855-4517-4*, Pub. by Collets) St Mut.

Music in Paintings of the Low Countries in the 16th & 17th Centuries. Pieter Fischer. 122p. 1975. pap. text 31.50 (*90-265-0185-4*) Swets.

Music in Performance & Society: Essays in Honor of Roland Jackson. Roland J. Jackson. LC 97-29311. (Detroit Monographs in Musicology: Studies in Music: Vol. 20). 1997. 75.00 (*0-89990-106-9*) Harmonie Park Pr.

Music in Philadelphia. Robert A. Gerson. (Music Book Index Ser.). 422p. 1992. reprint ed. lib. bdg. 99.00 (*0-7812-9501-7*) Rprt Serv.

Music in Prekindergarten: Planning & Teaching. Ed. by Mary Palmer & Wendy L. Sims. (Illus.). 80p. (C). 1993. pap. text 20.00 (*1-56545-017-5*, 1031) MENC.

Music in Primitive Culture. Bruno Nettl. LC 56-8551. 220p. reprint ed. 68.20 (*0-8357-9167-X*, 201673000005) Bks Demand.

Music in Print Master Composer Index, 1988. LC 89-3361. (Music in Print Ser.: Vol. XC). 824p. lib. bdg. 120.00 (*0-88478-023-6*) Musicdata.

***Music in Print Master Composer Index 1999, 2 vols.** LC 89-3361. (Music in Print Ser.). 1151p. 1999. lib. bdg. 150.00 (*0-88478-049-X*) Musicdata.

Music in Print Master Title Index, 1988. LC 89-13822. (Music in Print Ser.: Vol. XT). 581p. lib. bdg. 120.00 (*0-88478-024-4*) Musicdata.

***Music in Print Master Title Index 1999.** LC 89-13822. (Music in Print Ser.). 803p. 1999. lib. bdg. 130.00 (*0-88478-050-3*) Musicdata.

Music in Renaissance Cities & Courts: Studies in Honor of Lewis Lockwood. Jessie A. Owens. Ed. by Anthony Cummings. LC 96-41999. (Detroit Monographs in Musicology: No. 18). 533p. 1996. 65.00 (*0-89990-102-6*) Harmonie Park Pr.

Music in Renaissance Magic: Toward a Historiography of Others. Gary Tomlinson. (Illus.). xvi, 308p. 1994. pap. text 17.95 (*0-226-80792-4*) U Ch Pr.

Music in Renaissance Magic: Toward a Historiography of Others. Gary Tomlinson. LC 92-17755. (Illus.). 308p. 1997. lib. bdg. 38.50 (*0-226-80791-6*) U Ch Pr.

Music in Russian Poetry. Paul Friedrich. LC 96-16460. (Middlebury Studies in Russian Languages & Literature: Vol. 10). XVII, 344p. (C). 1998. pap. text 32.95 (*0-8204-3347-0*) P Lang Pubng.

Music in Sequence. William Lloyd. 1997. pap. write for info. (*0-8081-5416-8*) Bonus Books.

Music in Silence. Charles Bivins. Ed. by C. Natale Peditto. LC 94-12722. (Open Mouth Poetry Ser.). 129p. (Orig.). 1994. pap. 9.95 (*1-884773-00-1*) Heat Press.

Music in Society. Ivo Supicic. LC 85-28414. (Sociology of Music Ser.: No. 4). 361p. 1988. lib. bdg. 62.00 (*0-918728-35-5*) Pendragon NY.

Music in Spain During the Eighteenth Century. Ed. by Malcolm Boyd & Juan J. Carreras. LC 97-41924. (Illus.). 275p. (C). 1998. 69.95 (*0-521-48139-2*) Cambridge U Pr.

Music in State Clothing: The Story of the Kettledrummers, Trumpeters & Band of the Life Guards. G. R. Lawn. (Illus.). 194p. 1995. 31.95 (*0-85052-454-7*, Pub. by Leo Cooper) Trans-Atl Phila.

M

An Asterisk (*) at the beginning of an entry indicates that the title is appearing for the first time.

Music in Terezin, 1941-1945. Joza Karas. LC 84-24411. (Illus.). 212p. 1985. pap. 16.95 (*0-918728-34-7*) Pendragon NY.
Music in the Aegean Bronze Age. John G. Younger. (Illus.). 119p. 1998. pap. 49.50 (*91-7081-124-5*, Pub. by P Astroms) Coronet Bks.
*__Music in the Age of Chaucer.__ rev. ed. Nigel Wilkins. (Chaucer Studies: No. 0261-9822). (Illus.). 224p. 1999. pap. 45.00 (*0-85991-565-4*, DS Brewer) Boydell & Brewer.
Music in the Age of Chaucer: With "Chaucer Songs" 2nd rev. ed. Nigel Wilkins. (Chaucer Studies: Vol. I). (Illus.). 224p. (C). 1995. 75.00 (*0-85991-461-5*) Boydell & Brewer.
Music in the Age of the Renaissance. Leeman L. Perkins. LC 98-28961. (Illus.). 750p. 1999. 49.95 (*0-393-04608-7*) Norton.
Music in the Baroque. 3rd ed. Harold Gleason & Warren Becker. LC 79-66417. (Music Literature Outlines Ser.: No. II). 188p. 1988. pap. 19.95 (*0-88284-378-8*, 2892) Alfred Pub.
Music in the Baroque Era. Manfred F. Bukofzer. (Illus.). (C). 1947. text 35.50 (*0-393-09745-5*) Norton.
Music in the Blood. large type ed. Margaret Duffy. (Dales Large Print Ser.). 356p. 1998. pap. 19.99 (*1-85389-813-9*, Dales) Ulverscroft.
Music in the Castle: Troubadours, Books & Orators in Italian Courts of the Thirteenth, Fourteenth & Fifteenth Centuries. F. Alberto Gallo. Tr. by Anna Herklotz & Kathryn Krug from ITA. (Illus.). 156p. 1996. pap. text 19.95 (*0-226-27969-3*); lib. bdg. 45.00 (*0-226-27968-5*) U Ch Pr.
Music in the Christian Community. Dale Topp. LC 76-20471. 205p. reprint ed. 63.60 (*0-8357-9130-0*, 201934000011) Bks Demand.
Music in the Church. Peter C. Lutkin. LC 72-135722. reprint ed. 42.50 (*0-404-04069-1*) AMS Pr.
Music in the Classic Period: An Anthology with Commentary. F. E. Kirby. LC 77-84939. 928p. 1979. 35.00 (*0-02-870710-9*, Schirmer Books) Mac Lib Ref.
Music in the Classic Period: Essays in Honor of Barry S. Brook. Ed. by Allan A. Atlas. LC 84-27391. (Festschrift Ser.: No. 5). 400p. 1985. lib. bdg. 48.00 (*0-918728-37-1*) Pendragon NY.
Music in the Culture of Northern Afghanistan. Mark Slobin. LC 74-31998. (Viking Fund Publications in Anthropology: No. 54). 297p. 1976. pap. 12.95 (*0-8165-0498-9*) U of Ariz Pr.
Music in the Culture of the Renaissance & Other Essays, 2 vols. Edward E. Lowinsky. (Illus.). 1023p. 1989. lib. bdg. 300.00 (*0-226-49478-0*) U Ch Pr.
Music in the Distance. Nicholas Gage. 1988. write for info. (*0-318-63912-2*) HM.
Music in the Early Years. Aelwyn Pugh & Lesley Pugh. LC 97-45590. (Teaching & Learning in the First Three Years of School Ser.). 224p. (C). 1998. pap. 20.99 (*0-415-14181-8*) Routledge.
Music in the Early Years. Susan Young & Jo Glover. 70p. 1997. pap. 22.95 (*0-7507-0659-7*, Falmer Pr) Taylor & Francis.
Music in the Education of Children. 3rd ed. Swanson. (Music Ser.). 1969. mass mkt. 15.25 (*0-534-00673-6*) Wadsworth Pub.
Music in the English Courtly Masque, 1604-1640. Peter Walls. LC 95-16156. (Oxford Monographs on Music). (Illus.). 391p. 1996. text 75.00 (*0-19-816141-7*) OUP.
Music in the French Royal Academy of Sciences: A Study in the Evolution of Musical Thought. Albert Cohen. LC 81-47118. 169p. 1981. reprint ed. pap. 52.40 (*0-7837-9321-9*, 206006100004) Bks Demand.
Music in the German Renaissance: Sources, Styles & Contexts. Ed. by John Kmetz. (Illus.). 307p. (C). 1995. text 69.95 (*0-521-44045-9*) Cambridge U Pr.
Music in the Harvard Libraries: A Catalogue of Early Printed Music & Books on Music in the Houghton Library & the Eda Kuhn Loeb Music Library. David A. Wood. (Illus.). 318p. 1980. 50.00 (*0-674-59125-9*) HUP.
Music in the Hills. D. E. Stevenson. 256p. 1976. lib. bdg. 38.95 (*0-89966-165-3*) Buccaneer Bks.
Music in the History of the Western Church. Edward Dickinson. LC 77-127454. reprint ed. 37.50 (*0-404-02127-1*) AMS Pr.
Music in the History of the Western Church. Edward Dickinson. LC 68-25286. (Studies in Music: No. 42). 1969. reprint ed. lib. bdg. 75.00 (*0-8383-0301-3*) M S G Haskell Hse.
Music in the History of the Western Church: With an Introduction in Religious Music among the Primitive & Ancient Peoples. Edward Dickinson. 426p. 1990. reprint ed. lib. bdg. 89.00 (*0-7812-9120-8*) Rprt Serv.
Music in the History of the Western Church, with an Introduction in Religious Music among the Primitive & Ancient Peoples. Edward Dickinson. 1977. reprint ed. 49.00 (*0-403-08194-7*) Scholarly.
Music in the Jewish Community of Palestine 1880-1948: A Social History. Jehoash Hirshberg. (Illus.). 312p. 1996. reprint ed. pap. text 29.95 (*0-19-816651-6*) OUP.
Music in the Junior College. Music Educators National Conference, Music in Gene. LC 71-122451. 62p. 1970. reprint ed. pap. 30.00 (*0-608-04211-0*, 206494900011) Bks Demand.
Music in the Key of C. Theodore Enslin. (Bloody Twin Press Ser.). 32p. (Orig.). 1995. pap. 30.00 (*1-886350-30-2*) Bloody Twin Pr.
Music in the Life of Albert Schweitzer. Albert Schweitzer. Ed. by Charles R. Joy. LC 76-117840. (Essay Index Reprint Ser.). 1977. 20.95 (*0-8369-2200-X*) Ayer.
Music in the Life of Man. Julius Portnoy. LC 73-9265. (Illus.). 300p. 1973. reprint ed. lib. bdg. 35.00 (*0-8371-7000-1*, POMU, Greenwood Pr) Greenwood.
Music in the Making. Grace C. Nash & Janice Rapley. 160p. 1990. pap. 27.95 (*0-88284-448-2*, 3557) Alfred Pub.
Music in the Market. Don Cusic. LC 95-47158. 189p. 1996. pap. 22.95 (*0-87972-694-6*) Bowling Green Univ Popular Press.
Music in the Marquesas Islands. E. S. Handy & J. L. Winne. (BMB Ser.: No. 17). 1974. reprint ed. pap. 25.00 (*0-527-02120-2*) Periodicals Srv.
Music in the Medieval & Renaissance Universities. Nan Cooke Carpenter. LC 70-171380. (Music Ser.). (Illus.). 394p. 1972. reprint ed. lib. bdg. 45.00 (*0-685-01357-X*) Da Capo.
Music in the Medieval English Liturgy: Plainsong & Mediaeval Music Society Centennial Essays. Ed. by Susan K. Rankin & David Hiley. (Illus.). 422p. 1993. text 105.00 (*0-19-316125-7*) OUP.
Music in the Medieval World. 2nd ed. Albert Seay. (Illus.). 182p. (C). 1991. reprint ed. pap. text 18.95 (*0-88133-635-1*) Waveland Pr.
Music in the Middle Ages. Gustave Reese. (Illus.). (C). 1940. text 52.25 (*0-393-09750-1*) Norton.
Music in the Middle Ages & Renaissance. 3rd ed. Harold Gleason & Warren Becker. (Music Literature Outlines Ser.: No. I). 224p. 1988. pap. text 19.95 (*0-88284-379-6*, 2891) Alfred Pub.
*__Music in the Midst of Chaos: One Family's Saga on the Human Rights Battlefield.__ Jean Conklin. LC 99-90747. (Illus.). 268p. 1999. pap. 16.95 (*0-9673440-0-X*, Pub. by Carico Pr) Good Shepherd Pubns.
Music in the Mind: The Concepts of Music & Musician in Afghanistan. Hiromi L. Sakata. LC 82-23296. 261p. 1983. reprint ed. pap. 81.00 (*0-608-07361-X*, 206758900009) Bks Demand.
Music in the Mist. Laura Pender. (Intrigue Ser.). 1993. per. 2.99 (*0-373-22249-1*, 1-22249-6) Harlequin Bks.
Music in the Modern World: Music Book Index. Rollo H. Myers. 211p. 1993. reprint ed. lib. bdg. 79.00 (*0-7812-9576-9*) Rprt Serv.
Music in the Moment. Jerrold Levinson. LC 97-19847. 176p. 1997. 25.00 (*0-8014-3129-8*) Cornell U Pr.
Music in the Nachtwachen. Paul Davies. LC 90-27765. (American University Studies: Germanic Languages & Literature: Ser. I, Vol. 94). 191p. (C). 1991. text 35.95 (*0-8204-1559-6*) P Lang Pubng.
Music in the Nation. Bernard H. Haggin. LC 71-167350. (Essay Index Reprint Ser.). 1977. reprint ed. 25.95 (*0-8369-2503-3*) Ayer.
Music in the New World. Charles Hamm. (Illus.). (C). 1983. text 51.15 (*0-393-95193-6*) Norton.
Music in the Night. V. C. Andrews. LC 98-169961. 1998. 24.00 (*0-671-53467-X*); per. 7.99 (*0-671-53474-2*) PB.
Music in the Night. V. C. Andrews. 1998. 12.60 (*0-606-13627-4*, Pub. by Turtleback) Demco.
Music in the Night. large type ed. V. C. Andrews. LC 98-56121. 1999. 28.95 (*0-7838-8533-4*, G K Hall Lrg Type) Mac Lib Ref.
*__Music in the Old Bones: Jezebel Through the Ages.__ Janet Howe Gaines. LC 99-24189. (Illus.). 224p. 2000. 34.95 (*0-8093-2274-9*) S Ill U Pr.
Music in the Paris Academy of Sciences: 1666-1793. Albert Cohn & Leta E. Miller. LC 78-70025. (Detroit Studies in Music Bibliography: No. 43). 69p. 1979. 16.00 (*0-911772-96-0*) Harmonie Park Pr.
Music in the Pentecostal Church. Delton L. Alford. 113p. 1969. pap. 4.25 (*0-87148-562-1*) Pathway Pr.
Music in the Renaissance. rev. ed. Gustave Reese. (Illus.). (C). 1959. text 50.75 (*0-393-09530-4*) Norton.
Music in the Renaissance. 2nd ed. Brown & Stein. LC 98-12248. 396p. 1998. pap. 41.00 (*0-13-400045-5*) P-H.
Music in the Romantic Era. Alfred Einstein. (Illus.). (C). 1947. text 33.50 (*0-393-09733-1*) Norton.
Music in the Romantic Period: An Anthology with Commentary. F. E. Kirby. 986p. 1986. 35.00 (*0-02-871330-3*, Schirmer Books) Mac Lib Ref.
Music in the Ruben Cobos Collection of Spanish New Mexican Folklore: A Descriptive Catalogue. Victoria L. Levine. Ed. by Amanda Chace. (ENG & SPA.). 200p. 1998. pap. 25.00 (*0-935052-30-5*) Colorado College.
Music in the Service of the Church: The Funeral Sermon for Heinrich Schuetz. Robin A. Leaver. 68p. (Orig.). 1985. pap. 6.75 (*0-570-01331-3*, 99-1261) Concordia.
Music in the Southwest, 1825-1950. Howard Swan & Howard Swan. LC 77-5421. (Music Reprint Ser.). 1977. reprint ed. lib. bdg. 39.50 (*0-306-77418-6*) Da Capo.
Music in the Street: Photographs of New Orleans by Ralston Crawford. Ralston Crawford. Ed. & Intro. by John H. Lawrence. LC 83-80537. (Illus.). xii, 36p. (Orig.). 1983. pap. 10.00 (*0-917860-14-4*) Historic New Orleans.
Music in the Theater: Essays on Verdi & Other Composers. Pierluigi Petrobelli. Tr. by Roger Parker. LC 93-3440. (Opera Studies). 208p. (C). 1994. text 45.00 (*0-691-09134-X*, Pub. by Princeton U Pr) Cal Prin Full Svc.
*__Music in the Theater, Church & Villa: Essays in Honor of Robert Lamar Weaver & Norma Wright Weaver.__ Robert Lamar Weaver et al. LC 00-31977. (Detroit Monographs in Musicology). 2000. write for info. (*0-89990-092-5*) Harmonie Park Pr.
Music in the Theatre. Ronald Settle. 1988. reprint ed. lib. bdg. 49.00 (*0-685-55958-0*) Rprt Serv.
Music in the Theatre of Ben Jonson. Mary Chan. (Illus.). 400p. 1980. text 89.00 (*0-19-812632-8*) OUP.
Music in the Twentieth Century, 3 vols., Set. LC 98-8564. 800p. (C). 1998. text 299.00 (*0-7656-8012-2*, Sharpe Prof) M E Sharpe.
Music in the 20th Century. Mary Booker. 1981. 30.00 (*0-7223-1397-7*, Pub. by A H S Ltd) St Mut.
Music in the West. Ed. by Paul Shull. (Illus.). 104p. (Orig.). 1983. pap. text 15.00 (*0-89745-047-7*) Sunflower U Pr.
Music in the Western Tradition. Claire Detels. LC 99-178818. 76p. 1997. pap. text 7.95 (*0-7674-0015-1*); pap. text 7.95 (*0-7674-0073-9*) Mayfield Pub.
Music in the Western World. Piero Weiss. LC 83-16171. 1984. 26.95 (*0-02-872910-2*, Schirmer Books) Mac Lib Ref.
Music in the Western World: A History in Documents. Piero Weiss & Richard F. Taruskin. (Illus.). 550p. 1984. 28.00 (*0-02-872900-5*, Schirmer Books) Mac Lib Ref.
Music in the 21st Century: The New Language. William Lee. Ed. by Jack Bullock. 84p. (Orig.). 1995. 14.95 incl. disk (*0-7604-0067-9*, EL03947IBM); 14.95 (*0-7604-0068-7*, EL03947MAC) Wrner Bros.
Music in the 21st Century: The New Language. William Lee. Ed. by Jack Bullock. (Orig.). (C). 1995. pap. text 4.95 (*0-7604-0065-2*, EL03948) Wrner Bros.
Music in the 21st Century: The New Language. William Lee. Ed. by Jack Bullock. 84p. (Orig.). 1995. pap. text 9.95 (*1-57623-841-5*, EL03947) Wrner Bros.
Music in Theory & Practice. 6th ed. Bruce Benward & Gary C. White. 288p. (C). 1996. text, wbk. ed. 21.87 (*0-697-28789-0*) Brown & Benchmark.
Music in Theory & Practice, 2. 6th ed. Bruce Benward & Gary C. White. LC 96-83191. 416p. (C). 1997. text. write for info. (*0-697-32874-0*, WCB McGr Hill) McGrw-H Hghr Educ.
Music in Theory & Practice, 2. 6th ed. Bruce Benward & Gary C. White. 288p. (C). 1997. text, student ed. 21.87 (*0-697-32876-7*, WCB McGr Hill) McGrw-H Hghr Educ.
Music in Theory & Practice, I. 5th ed. Bruce Benward & Gary C. White. 288p. (C). 1992. text 26.87 (*0-697-12532-7*) Brown & Benchmark.
Music in Theory & Practice, Vol. 1. 5th ed. Bruce Benward. 432p. (C). 1993. spiral bd. write for info. (*0-318-69096-9*) Brown & Benchmark.
Music in Theory & Practice, Vol. I. 6th ed. Bruce Benward & Gary White. 1997. teacher ed. 12.81 (*0-697-28787-4*, WCB McGr Hill) McGrw-H Hghr Educ.
Music in Theory & Practice, Vol. II. 6th ed. Bruce Benward & Gary White. 1998. teacher ed. write for info. (*0-697-32875-9*, WCB McGr Hill) McGrw-H Hghr Educ.
Music in Theory & Practice, Vols. I-II. 5th ed. Bruce Benward & Gary C. White. 256p. (C). 1992. text 26.87 (*0-697-12528-9*) Brown & Benchmark.
Music in Transition: A Study of Tonal Expansion & Atonality, 1900-1920. Jim Samson. (Illus.). 256p. 1995. pap. text 26.00 (*0-460-86150-6*) OUP.
Music in Video Production. Rosanne Soifer. 160p. 1997. pap. text 21.95 (*0-240-80292-6*, Focal) Buttrwrth-Heinemann.
Music in Western Civilization. Paul H. Lang. LC 97-5883. 1100p. (C). 1997. 45.00 (*0-393-04074-7*) Norton.
Music in Willa Cather's Fiction. Richard Giannone. LC 67-10664. 266p. reprint ed. pap. 82.50 (*0-608-10818-9*, 202255600028) Bks Demand.
Music in Winter. large type ed. Suzanne Ebel. 299p. 1981. 27.99 (*0-7089-0634-6*) Ulverscroft.
Music in World Cultures: Understanding Multiculturalism Through the Arts. James O'Brien. LC 94-214490. 400p. (C). 1996. pap. text, per. 40.95 (*0-8403-9122-6*) Kendall-Hunt.
Music in Worship: A Mennonite Perspective. Bernie Neufeld. LC 99-188757. 260p. 1999. pap. text 14.99 (*0-8361-9459-4*) Herald Pr.
Music in Your Life: Concise Music Companion. 84p. (C). 1997. 9.00 (*0-536-00456-0*) Pearson Custom.
*__Music in Your Life: Concise Music Companion.__ 2nd ed. 112p. (C). 1999. 43.00 (*0-536-02719-6*) Pearson Custom.
Music Index Vol. 41: A Subject Author Guide to Music Periodical Literature, 1989. Harmonie Park Press Staff. 1991. 450.00 (*0-89990-055-0*) Harmonie Park Pr.
Music Index Vol. 42: A Subject-Author Guide to Music Periodical Literature, 1990. Harmonie Park Press Staff. 1992. 475.00 (*0-89990-056-9*) Harmonie Park Pr.
Music Index Vol. 43: A Subject-Author Guide to Music Periodical Literature, 1991. Harmonie Park Press Staff. 1993. 500.00 (*0-89990-066-6*) Harmonie Park Pr.
Music Index Vol. 44: A Subject-Author Guide to Music Periodical Literature, 1992. Harmonie Park Press Staff. 1994. 530.00 (*0-89990-068-2*) Harmonie Park Pr.
Music Index Vol. 45: A Subject-Author Guide to Music Periodical Literature 1993. Harmonie Park Press Staff. 1995. 565.00 (*0-89990-100-X*) Harmonie Park Pr.
Music Index Vols. 33 & 34: A Subject-Author Guide to Music Periodical Literature, 1981-1982. Harmonie Park Press Staff. 1982. 475.00 (*0-89990-041-0*) Harmonie Park Pr.
Music Index Vols. 35-36: A Subject-Author Guide to Music Periodical Literature, 1979-1980. Harmonie Park Press Staff. 1986. 450.00 (*0-89990-029-1*) Harmonie Park Pr.
Music Index Vols. 35-36: A Subject-Author Guide to Music Periodical Literature, 1983-1984. Harmonie Park Press Staff. 1984. 495.00 (*0-89990-044-5*) Harmonie Park Pr.
Music Index Vols. 37 & 38: A Subject-Author Guide to Music Periodical Literature, 1985-1986. Harmonie Park Press Staff. 1989. 550.00 (*0-89990-048-8*) Harmonie Park Pr.
Music Index Vols. 39-40: A Subject-Author Guide to Music Periodical Literature, 1987-1988. Harmonie Park Press Staff. 1990. 590.00 (*0-89990-049-6*) Harmonie Park Pr.
*__Music India.__ Manorama Sharma. LC 99-938880. 1999. 68.00 (*81-7648-031-2*, Pub. by Ashish Pub Hse) S Asia.
Music Industry. 69p. 1996. pap. 7.00 (*0-16-061985-8*) USGPO.
Music Industry Book. Walter E. Hurst. 1971. 15.00 (*0-911370-51-X*); pap. 10.00 (*0-87505-367-X*) Borden.
Music Industry Book: Protect Yourself Before You Lose Your Rights & Royal Ties. Walter E. Hurst. (Entertainment Industry Service Ser.: Vol. 2). 1981. pap. 10.00 (*0-911370-52-8*) Seven Arts.
*__Music Industry Economics: A Global Demand Model for Pre-Recorded Music.__ K. Brad Stamm. LC 00-41831. (Studies in Economics). 2000. write for info. (*0-7734-7646-6*) E Mellen.
Music Is for Children Level 4: Kit B Advanced, Level 4. (J). pap., student ed. 5.95 (*0-7814-4971-5*, 83709) Cook.
Music Is Magic for Your Child & You: Black & White Nellie Edge I Can Read & Sing Big Book. Nellie Edge. (Illus.). 1988. pap. 22.00 (*0-922053-00-6*) N Edge Res.
Music Is My Life. Adella Hughes. (American Autobiography Ser.). 319p. 1995. reprint ed. lib. bdg. 89.00 (*0-7812-8561-5*) Rprt Serv.
Music Is My Mistress. Edward K. Ellington. LC 75-31665. (Illus.). 544p. 1976. pap. 17.50 (*0-306-80033-0*) Da Capo.
Music Is the Master Key. Karen J. Reed. LC 97-40440. (Illus.). 160p. 1999. 18.95 (*0-944957-70-6*) Rivercross Pub.
Music Is You. Rosita Perez. (Illus.). 1994. audio 29.95 (*0-9611354-2-5*) T Knox Pub.
Music Is You: A Guide to Thinking Less & Feeling More. 4th ed. Rosita Perez. (Illus.). 124p. (Orig.). 1994. pap. 12.50 (*0-9611354-7-6*) T Knox Pub.
Music is Your Forte: In Appreciation of Your Musical Gifts. Mary Horner Collins. LC 98-46732. (Shaw Greetings Ser.). 96p. 1999. pap. text 6.99 (*0-87788-568-0*, H Shaw Pubs) Waterbrook Pr.
Music, Its Secret Influence Throughout the Ages. Cyril Scott. 1974. 250.00 (*0-8490-0676-7*) Gordon Pr.
Music, Jr. H. S. Jack Rudman. (Teachers License Examination Ser.: T-42). 1994. pap. 27.95 (*0-8373-8042-1*) Nat Learn.
Music Keeps on Playing. Audre Pitts. 96p. (Orig.). 1988. pap. 7.99 (*0-8341-1250-7*) Beacon Hill.
Music Kit. 2nd ed. Tom Manoff. (C). Date not set. pap. write for info. (*0-393-95988-0*) Norton.
Music Kit. 3rd ed. Tom Manoff. (C). Date not set. pap. write for info. (*0-393-99945-9*) Norton.
Music Kit. 3rd ed. Tom Manoff. (C). 1994. pap. text, teacher ed. write for info. (*0-393-96326-8*) Norton.
Music Kit: Computer - Assisted Instruction. 3rd ed. Tom Manoff & John Miller. (C). 1994. pap. 44.00 (*0-393-96330-6*); pap. text. write for info. (*0-393-96327-6*) Norton.
Music Kit: Rhythm Reader. 3rd ed. Tom Manoff. (C). Date not set. pap. write for info. (*0-393-99203-9*) Norton.
Music Kit: Wkbk., Rhythm Reader, Scorebook. 3rd ed. Tom Manoff. 391p. (C). 1994. pap. text 37.50 incl. digital audio (*0-393-96325-X*) Norton.
Music Kit: Workbook. 3rd ed. Tom Manoff. (C). Date not set. pap. write for info. (*0-393-99199-7*) Norton.
Music Lab. Joseph W. Landon. (Mini-Modular Series in Music Education). (Illus.). 182p. (Orig.). (J). (gr. 3-8). 1982. pap. 14.95 (*0-943988-00-4*) Music Educ Pubns.
Music Language & Fundamentals. 2nd ed. Ronald Gretz. 272p. (C). 1993. text. write for info. (*0-697-12497-5*) Brown & Benchmark.
Music Law: How to Run Your Band's Business. Richard Stim. Ed. by Patti Gima. LC 98-11389. (Orig.). 1998. pap. 29.95 (*0-87337-438-X*) Nolo com.
Music Leadership in the Church. Erik Routley & Carlton R. Young. 136p. 1985. reprint ed. pap. text 11.95 (*0-916642-24-0*) Agape IL.
Music, Learning & Your Child. Julie Wylie. (Illus.). 120p. (Orig.). (C). 1996. pap. 24.95 (*0-908812-46-9*, Pub. by Canterbury Univ) Accents Pubns.
*__Music Lesson: Novel.__ Katharine Weber. LC 99-54978. 192p. 2000. pap. 12.00 (*0-312-25285-4*, Picador USA) St Martin.
Music Lesson: Stories. Martha L. Hall. LC 83-24151. (Illinois Short Fiction Ser.). 136p. 1984. 14.95 (*0-252-01129-5*) U of Ill Pr.
Music Lessons for Children with Special Needs. T. M. Perry. 140p. 1995. pap. 19.95 (*1-85302-295-0*) Taylor & Francis.
Music Librarianship: A Bibliography of Principles. Wagstaff. 110.95 (*1-85928-134-6*) Ashgate Pub Co.
Music Librarianship: A Practical Guide. Eric T. Bryant. 503p. 1990. reprint ed. lib. bdg. 99.00 (*0-7812-9269-7*) Rprt Serv.
Music Librarianship: A Practical Guide. 2nd ed. Eric T. Bryant & Guy A. Marco. LC 84-27731. (Illus.). 473p. 1985. 47.50 (*0-8108-1785-3*) Scarecrow.
*__Music Librarianship at the Turn of the Century.__ Richard Griscom & Amanda Maple. LC 00-32949. (Technical Reports). 2000. write for info. (*0-8108-3866-4*) Scarecrow.
Music Librarianship in America. Ed. by Michael Ochs. 144p. 1991. pap. 22.00 (*0-8108-3521-5*) Scarecrow.
Music Library. George M. D. Frink. (Illus.). 20p. 1992. pap. 5.95 (*0-9679882-3-3*, CB9004) Carol Pr.
*__Music Listening: A Syllabus.__ Hanley Jackson. 112p. (C). 1999. per. 17.95 (*0-7872-5963-2*, 41596301) Kendall-Hunt.
Music Listening Bingo. C. Lavender. 1992. pap. text 29.95 incl. audio (*0-7935-2912-3*) H Leonard.
Music Listening Today. Hoffer. (Music Ser.). 1998. mass mkt. 54.95 (*0-534-51360-3*) Wadsworth Pub.
*__Music Listening Today.__ 2d ed. Hoffer. 2001. 39.00 incl. audio compact disk (*0-534-51571-1*) Wadsworth Pub.
Music Literature. Fink. LC 98-33452. xiii, 301 p. 1999. 50.00 (*0-02-864844-7*, Schirmer Books) Mac Lib Ref.
Music Literature. Fink. 1998. teacher ed. 35.00 (*0-02-864847-1*) S&S Trade.

M

An Asterisk (*) at the beginning of an entry indicates that the title is appearing for the first time.

Music Living Language. 2nd ed. Manoff. pap. text 0.00 (*0-393-96072-2*); pap. text, teacher ed. 0.00 (*0-393-96073-0*) Norton.

Music, Love, Death & Mann's "Doctor Faustus" John F. Fetzer. (GERM Ser.: Vol. 45). (Illus.). xii, 156p. 1991. 50.00 (*0-938100-71-8*) Camden Hse.

Music Lover's Book of Lists. (C). 1997. 24.95 (*0-13-896572-2*, Macmillan Coll) P-H.

Music Lovers' Cookbook, Vol. 1. unabridged ed. Frances E. Gibson & Edwin W. Gibson, Sr. (Illus.). 152p. 1992. lib. bdg. 25.95 (*0-9644871-0-1*, TX3-449-150) MusiBook.

Music Lovers' Cyclopedia. Rupert Hughes. 948p. 1991. reprint ed. lib. bdg. 119.00 (*0-7812-9354-5*) Rprt Serv.

Music Lover's Diary. Ed. by Shelagh Wallace. (Illus.). 144p. 1996. 14.95 (*1-55209-024-8*) Firefly Bks Ltd.

Music Lover's Guide to Europe: A Compendium of Festivals, Concerts, & Opera. Ed. by Roberta Gottesman. LC 91-14409. 448p. 1992. pap. 14.95 (*0-471-53310-6*) Wiley.

Music Lover's Guide to Great Britain. Anne Bianchi. Ed. by Dan Spinella. (Illus.). 350p. (Orig.). 1995. pap. 14.95 (*0-8442-9006-8*, Passprt Bks) NTC Contemp Pub Co.

Music Lover's Literary Companion. Dannie Abse & Joan Abse. 330p. 1995. pap. 14.95 (*0-86051-654-7*, Robson-Parkwest) Parkwest Pubns.

Music Lovers Postcards. Starhill Press Staff. 1990. pap. text 6.95 (*0-913515-57-4*, Starrhill Press) Black Belt Communs.

Music Lovers' Quotations. Ed. by Helen Exley. (Quotable Quotations Ser.). (Illus.). 60p. 1992. 9.00 (*1-85015-267-5*) Exley Giftbooks.

Music-Lovers's Birthday Book. Metropolitan Museum of Art Staff. (Illus.). 128p. 1987. boxed set 14.95 (*0-317-61333-2*) Abrams.

Music Machine: Selected Readings from Computer Music Journal. Ed. by Curtis Roads. (Illus.). 740p. 1992. reprint ed. pap. text 35.00 (*0-262-68078-5*) MIT Pr.

Music Made Easy, Pt. 1. B. Lee. (Made Easy Ser.). 1990. 7.95 (*0-685-32064-2*, 8413) Hansen Ed Mus.

Music Madness. (J). pap. 1.85 (*0-8066-0871-4*, 15-0954) Augsburg Fortress.

Music Madness. (J). 1984. pap. 1.20 (*0-8066-0872-2*, 15-0953) Augsburg Fortress.

Music Maker. Gail Gibbons. 1996. 15.00 (*0-689-80466-0*) S&S Childrens.

Music Maker, Pt. A. Frances Clark & Louise Goss. (Music Maker Ser.). (Illus.). 56p. (J). (gr. 2 up). 1986. pap. text, student ed. 6.95 (*0-913277-20-7*) Summy-Birchard.

Music Maker, Pt. B. Frances Clark & Louise Goss. (Music Maker Ser.). 56p. 1987. pap. text 6.95 (*0-913277-21-5*) Summy-Birchard.

Music Makers. Bernard Rosenberg & Deena Rosenberg. LC 78-15564. 1979. text 64.50 (*0-231-03953-0*) Col U Pr.

Music Makers see Homeplay: Joyful Learning for Children & Adults, Series I

Music Makers: Some Outstanding Musical Performers of Our Day. Roland Gelatt. LC 72-2334. (Music Ser.). 1972. reprint ed. lib. bdg. 37.50 (*0-306-70519-2*) Da Capo.

Music Makes a Difference Series, Bks. I. Elizabeth L. Mayer & John M. Langstaff. 48p. 1994. pap. 5.95 (*1-886380-04-X*) Langstaff Vid.

***Music Makes the Difference: Music, Brain Development, & Learning.** (Music Makes the Difference). 152p. (Orig.). 2000. pap. 12.50 (*1-56545-129-5*, 1668) MENC.

***Music Makes the Difference: Programs & Partnerships.** (Music Makes the Difference). 176p. (Orig.). 1999. pap. 12.50 (*1-56545-117-1*, 1669) MENC.

Music-Making in the British Isles from 1890 to 1990. Mary Booker. (C). 1993. 65.00 (*0-7223-2745-5*) St Mut.

Music Man. (Vocal Score Ser.). 176p. 1983. per. 45.00 (*0-88188-210-0*, 00448253) H Leonard.

Music Man, Vol. 172. M. Wilson. 24p. 1983. pap. 5.95 (*0-7935-2650-7*, 00101796) H Leonard.

Music Man: The Story of Frank Simon. Michael Freedland. LC 93-48238. (Illus.). 300p. (C). 1994. 22.50 (*0-85303-280-7*, Pub. by F Cass Pubs); pap. 16.95 (*0-85303-284-X*, Pub. by F Cass Pubs) Intl Spec Bk.

Music Management Made Easy: Practical Ways to Market & Sell Your Music. Barbara L. Hughes. (Illus.). 144p. (Orig.). 1991. pap. 12.95 (*1-878036-03-3*) Hughes Taylor.

Music Mania. Stephanie K. Burton. 153p. (Orig.). 1994. pap., teacher ed. 29.95 incl. audio (*1-889163-00-7*); pap., teacher ed. 19.95 (*1-889163-02-3*) Panda Bear Pub.

Music Mania Book & CD: Teacher's Manual. Stephanie K. Burton. 153p. 1994. teacher ed. 33.95 incl. audio compact disk (*1-889163-03-1*) Panda Bear Pub.

Music Manuscript Preparation: A Concise Guide. Mona Mender. LC 90-8373. (Illus.). 222p. 1991. 34.50 (*0-8108-2294-6*) Scarecrow.

Music Manuscripts at Harvard. Barbara M. Wolff. (C). 1992. write for info. (*1-882477-00-6*) Harv U Lib.

Music Master: The CD-Five Singles Directory, 1994, Vol. One. 2nd ed. Ed. by Paul C. Mawhinney. 194p. 1994. reprint ed. pap. 30.00 (*0-910925-07-0*) Record-Rama.

Music Master: The Forty-Five RPM Christmas Singles Directory, 1994, Vol. One. 2nd ed. Ed. by Paul C. Mawhinney. 142p. 1994. reprint ed. pap. 30.00 (*0-910925-08-9*) Record-Rama.

Music Master of the Middle West: The Story of F. Melius Christiansen & the St. Olaf Choir. 2nd ed. Leola N. Bergmann. LC 68-16222. (Music Ser.). 1968. reprint ed. 32.50 (*0-306-71057-9*) Da Capo.

Music Masters: Music Book Index, 4 vols., Set. Alfred L. Bacharach. 1993. reprint ed. lib. bdg. 300.00 (*0-7812-9579-3*) Rprt Serv.

Music Masters Old & New. J. F. Cooke. 1972. 59.95 (*0-8490-0682-1*) Gordon Pr.

Music Matters: A New Philosophy of Music Education. David J. Elliott. (Illus.). 400p. (C). 1995. text 39.95 (*0-19-509171-X*) OUP.

Music Melting Round: A History of Music in the United States. Edith Borroff. (Illus.). 387p. (C). 1995. text 39.95 (*1-880157-17-9*) Ardsley.

Music Melting Round: A History of Music in the United States. Edith Borroff. (Illus.). 387p. (C). 1995. pap. text. write for info. (*1-880157-18-7*) Ardsley.

Music Men: The Guys Who Sang with the Bands & Beyond. Richard Grudens. 240p. 1998. pap. 17.95 (*1-57579-097-1*) Pine Hill Pr.

Music Men: The Story of Professional Gospel Quartet Singing in America. Bob Terrell. 1990. 19.95 (*1-878894-00-5*) B Terrell.

Music, Menus & Magnolias. Charleston Symphony Orchestra. 320p. 1996. 17.95 (*0-9648219-1-5*, Pub. by CSOL) Wimmer Bks.

Music Menus & Magnolias: Charleston Shares Its Culture & Cuisine. Charleston Symphony Orchestra League Staff. LC 95-70790. (Illus.), 350p. 1996. reprint ed. 17.95 (*0-9648219-0-7*) CSOL.

Music, Mind & Brain: The Neuropsychology of Music. Ed. by Manfred Clynes. LC 82-546. (Illus.). 444p. (C). 1982. text 107.00 incl. lp (*0-306-40908-9*, Kluwer Plenum) Kluwer Academic.

Music, Mind & Structure, Vol. 3, No. 1. Eric Clarke & Simon Emmerson. Ed. by Nigel Osborne. (Contemporary Music Review Ser.: Vol. 3, Pt. 1). iv, 236p. 1989. text 23.00 (*3-7186-4879-2*) Gordon & Breach.

Music Mind Games, Level 1. Michiko Yurko. Ed. by Debbie Cavalier. (Illus.). (J). 1993. pap. text 159.95 (*1-57623-707-9*, MY1946) Wrner Bros.

Music Mind Games - Level One: Blue Jello Cards. Michiko Yurko. Ed. by Debbie Cavalier. 28p. (J). (gr. k-3). 1992. pap. text 13.95 (*0-7692-1782-6*, MY1927) Wrner Bros.

***Music Minder, 1999-2000.** 1999. 12.00 (*0-687-07303-0*) Abingdon.

Music Minus One. Jane Shore. 1996. pap. 20.00 (*0-614-20816-5*, Picador USA) St Martin.

Music Minus One. Jane Shore. 128p. 1997. pap. 10.00 (*0-312-16944-2*, Picador USA) St Martin.

Music Mode & Words in Lasso's Last Works. Robert C. Luoma. LC 87-28228. (Studies in the History & Interpretation of Music: Vol. 11). 200p. 1988. lib. bdg. 79.95 (*0-88946-435-9*) E Mellen.

Music, Modernity, & the Global Imagination: South Africa & the West. Veit Erlmann. LC 98-7806. (Illus.). 320p. 1999. text 65.00 (*0-19-512367-0*) OUP.

Music Moods & Memories: Lounge Favorites. Ed. by Tony Esposito. 160p. (Orig.). (C). 1997. pap. text 14.95 (*0-7692-0079-6*) Wrner Bros.

Music, Movement, Mind & Body. Bridget Watson. 1995. 27.95 (*0-943873-36-3*) Elder Bks.

Music, Music for Everyone. Vera B. Williams. LC 83-14196.Tr. of iMusica para todo el mundo!. (Illus.). 32p. (J). (gr. k-3). 1984. 16.00 (*0-688-02603-6*, Grenwillow Bks) HarpC Child Bks.

Music, Music for Everyone. Vera B. Williams. LC 83-14196.Tr. of iMusica para todo el mundo!. (SPA., Illus.). 32p. (J). (gr. k up). 1995. 15.00 (*0-688-14035-1*, Grenwillow Bks) HarpC Child Bks.

Music, Music for Everyone. Vera B. Williams. LC 83-14196.Tr. of iMusica para todo el mundo!. (Illus.). 32p. (J). (ps up). 1988. mass mkt. 4.95 (*0-688-07811-7*, Wm Morrow) Morrow Avon.

Music, Musicians & Health Influences: Index of Modern Authors & Subjects with Guide for Rapid Research. Melvin M. Galloway. 160p. 1996. 47.50 (*0-7883-0942-0*); pap. 44.50 (*0-7883-0943-9*) ABBE Pubs Assn.

Music, Musicians, & the Saint-Simonians. Ralph P. Locke. LC 85-20915. (Illus.). xviii, 418p. (C). 1986. pap. text 24.95 (*0-226-48902-7*); lib. bdg. 55.00 (*0-226-48901-9*) U Ch Pr.

Music My Love: An Autobiography. Jean-Pierre Rampal & Deborah Wise. 1989. 18.95 (*0-318-42516-5*) Random.

Music, Myth & Consciousness. George Champion. 112p. (C). 1994. pap. text, per. 21.95 (*0-8403-9893-X*) Kendall-Hunt.

Music, Myth, & Nature, or, the Dolphins of Arion. rev. ed. Francois-Bernard Mache. Tr. by Susan Delaney from FRE. LC 92-39112. (Contemporary Music Studies: Vol. 6). 200p. 1993. text 46.00 (*3-7186-5321-4*); pap. text 20.00 (*3-7186-5322-2*) Gordon & Breach.

Music 1988. Boardman. 1988. 75.00 (*0-03-005269-6*) Harcourt Schl Pubs.

Music 1988. Boardman. (J). (gr. k-2). 1988. student ed. 43.25 (*0-03-005302-1*) Harcourt Schl Pubs.

Music 1988. Boardman. (J). (gr. k-6). 1988. student ed. 43.25 (*0-03-005309-9*) Harcourt Schl Pubs.

Music 1988. Boardman. (J). (gr. k-8). 1989. student ed. 52.50 (*0-03-005327-7*) Harcourt Schl Pubs.

Music, 1988: Holiday Songbook. Boardman. (J). 1988. pap., teacher ed. 21.75 (*0-03-005253-X*) Harcourt Schl Pubs.

Music, 1900-1930. Alfred J. Swan. 86p. 1990. reprint ed. lib. bdg. 59.00 (*0-7812-9030-9*) Rprt Serv.

Music, No Staves. Katy Lederer. 22p. 1998. 6.00 (*0-937013-80-3*) Potes Poets.

Music Notation. Mark McGrain. 207p. 1990. pap. 16.95 (*0-7935-0847-9*, 50449399, Berklee Pr) H Leonard.

Music Notation. Gardner Read. LC 68-54213. (Illus.). (C). 1979. reprint ed. pap. 23.95 (*0-8008-5453-5*, Crescendo) Taplinger.

Music Notation Evaluation Procedure, 1994: With Summary. Douglas F. Keislar. LC 94-69390. 110p. 1994. pap. 25.00 (*0-9638849-1-3*) Music Notation.

Music Notation in the Twentieth Century: A Practical Guidebook. Kurt Stone. (Illus.). (C). 1980. text. write for info. (*0-393-95053-0*) Norton.

Music Now. Dorothy Taylor. 160p. 1979. pap. 24.00 (*0-335-00253-6*) OpUniv Pr.

Music Observed: The Selection Made by Steuart Wilson. Arthur H. Fox-Strangways. LC 68-16931. (Essay Index Reprint Ser.). 1977. 19.95 (*0-8369-0452-4*) Ayer.

Music of a Poet's Heart. Teresa A. Pitts. (Illus.). 147p. (Orig.). (YA). (gr. 7 up). 1987. pap. 10.00 (*0-9618600-0-6*) T A Pitts.

Music of a Thousand Autumns: The Togaku Style of Japanese Court Music. Robert Garfias. LC 75-13865. (Illus.). 371p. reprint ed. pap. 115.10 (*0-608-18007-6*, 202904300058) Bks Demand.

Music of Acoma, Isleta, Cochiti, & Zuni Pueblos. Frances Densmore. (Bureau of American Ethnology Bulletins Ser.). 117p. 1995. lib. bdg. 79.00 (*0-7812-4165-0*) Rprt Serv.

Music of Acoma, Isleta, Cochiti, & Zuni Pueblos. Frances Densmore. LC 72-1877. (Music Ser.). (Illus.). 142p. 1972. reprint ed. lib. bdg. 22.50 (*0-306-70505-2*) Da Capo.

Music of Africa. Joseph H. Nketia. (Illus.). 278p. (C). 1974. pap. text 18.75 (*0-393-09249-6*) Norton.

Music of Alban Berg. Dave Headlam. LC 95-46936. (Composers of the Twentieth Century Ser.). (Illus.). 456p. (C). 1996. 47.50 (*0-300-06400-4*) Yale U Pr.

Music of Albeniz: Carlos Barbosa-Lima Guitar Editions. Ed. by Aaron Stang. (Orig.). (YA). 1994. pap. text 19.95 incl. audio compact disk (*0-89898-772-5*, EL03954CD) Wrner Bros.

Music of Angels: A Beginner's Guide to Sacred Music from Chant to Christian Rock. Patrick Kavanaugh. LC 98-45505. (Illus.). 312p. 1999. pap. 16.95 (*0-8294-1019-8*) Loyola Pr.

***Music of Another World.** Szymon Laks. LC 99-88812. (Jewish Lives Ser.). 2000. pap. 15.95 (*0-8101-1802-5*) Northwestern U Pr.

Music of Anthony Braxton, 43. Mike Heffley. LC 95-43113. (Contributions to the Study of Music & Dance Ser.: No. 43). 504p. 1996. 69.50 (*0-313-29956-0*, Greenwood Pr) Greenwood.

Music of Arthur Honegger. Geoffrey K. Spratt. 651p. 1987. 75.00 (*0-902561-34-0*, Pub. by Cork Univ) Intl Spec Bk.

Music of Arthur Sullivan. Gervase Hughes. LC 73-9128. (Illus.). 180p. 1973. reprint ed. lib. bdg. 55.00 (*0-8371-6985-2*, HUMA, Greenwood Pr) Greenwood.

Music of Bela Bartok. Paul Wilson. LC 91-36107. (Composers of the Twentieth Century Ser.). (Illus.). 224p. (C). 1992. 40.00 (*0-300-05111-5*) Yale U Pr.

Music of Bela Bartok: A Study of Tonality & Progression in Twentieth Century Music. Elliott Antokoletz. LC 82-17352. (Illus.). 472p. (C). 1984. pap. 22.50 (*0-520-06747-9*, Pub. by U CA Pr) Cal Prin Full Svc.

Music of Ben Johnston. Heidi Von Gunden. LC 86-13954. (Illus.). 212p. 1986. 39.50 (*0-8108-1907-4*) Scarecrow.

Music of Benjamin Britten. 2nd rev. ed. Peter Evans. (Illus.). 602p. 1996. pap. text 21.00 (*0-19-816590-0*) OUP.

Music of Black America: A History. 3rd ed. Eileen Southern. LC 96-28811. (Illus.). 640p. 1997. 37.95 (*0-393-03843-2*) Norton.

Music of Black Americans: A History. 3rd ed. Eileen Southern. LC 96-28811. (C). 1997. pap. text 37.50 (*0-393-97141-4*) Norton.

Music of Brahms. Michael Musgrave. (Illus.). 340p. 1994. pap. text 28.00 (*0-19-816401-7*) OUP.

Music of Brahms. Michael Musgrave. (Companions to the Great Composers Ser.). (Illus.). 320p. 1985. 39.95 (*0-7100-9776-X*, Routledge Thoemms) Routledge.

Music of Brazil. David P. Appleby. LC 82-13613. (Illus.). 223p. reprint ed. pap. 69.20 (*0-608-08650-9*, 206917300003) Bks Demand.

Music of Brendan Tonra. Helen Kisiel. 28p. 1988. pap. 8.00 (*0-934665-10-9*) Quinlin C Pubs.

Music of Bruce Hornsby. Ed. by Milton Okun. (Easy Piano Ser.). pap. 9.95 (*0-89524-339-3*) Cherry Lane.

Music of Canada. Timothy J. McGee. LC 84-27318. 257p. (C). 1985. pap. text 22.25 (*0-393-95376-9*) Norton.

Music of Chance. Paul Auster. (Contemporay American Fiction Ser.). 224p. 1991. reprint ed. pap. 12.95 (*0-14-015407-8*, Penguin Bks) Viking Penguin.

Music of Charles Ives. Philip Lambert. LC 96-38979. (Composers of the Twentieth Century Ser.). 256p. 1997. 35.00 (*0-300-06522-1*) Yale U Pr.

Music of Chopin. Jim Samson. LC 93-30977. (Illus.). 252p. 1994. pap. text 19.95 (*0-19-816402-5*, Clarendon Pr) OUP.

Music of Chopin. Jim Samson. (Companions to the Great Composers Ser.). 304p. 1985. 39.95 (*0-7100-9688-7*, Routledge Thoemms) Routledge.

***Music of Christmas: Piano, Vocal, Chords.** Ed. by Warner Brothers Publications Staff. (Illus.). 1999. pap. 12.95 (*0-7692-8936-3*) Wrner Bros.

Music of Claude Debussy. Richard S. Parks. 360p. (C). 1990. 50.00 (*0-300-04439-9*) Yale U Pr.

Music of Cole Porter. (Easy Piano Ser.). 64p. 1986. pap. 6.95 (*0-88188-733-1*, 00365875) H Leonard.

Music of Conlon Nancarrow. Kyle Gann. (Music in the Twentieth Century Ser.: No. 7). 315p. (C). 1996. text 64.95 (*0-521-46534-6*) Cambridge U Pr.

***Music of Creation: Foundations of a Christian Life.** John Michael Talbot. 256p. 2000. pap. 13.95 (*1-58542-037-9*, Tarcher Putnam) Putnam Pub Group.

Music of Creation: Fundamentals of the Christian Faith. John M. Talbot. LC 99-15574. (Illus.). 256p. 1999. 22.95 (*0-87477-983-9*, Tarcher Putnam) Putnam Pub Group.

Music of Czechoslovakia. Rosa H. Newmarch. LC 77-26269. (Music Reprint Ser.: 1978). 1978. reprint ed. lib. bdg. 32.50 (*0-306-77563-8*) Da Capo.

Music of Czechoslovakia. Rosa H. Newmarch. (Music Book Index Ser.). 244p. 1992. reprint ed. lib. bdg. 79.00 (*0-7812-9510-6*) Rprt Serv.

Music of David Bowie. David Buckley. (Illus.). 160p. (Orig.). 1996. pap. 8.95 (*0-7119-5301-5*, OP4799) Omnibus NY.

Music of David Friesen: Years Through Time. 80p. 1995. otabind 14.95 (*0-7935-3670-7*, 00673253) H Leonard.

Music of Death & New Creation: Experiences in the World of Balinese Gamelan Beleganjur. Michael B. Bakan. LC 98-42727. (Chicago Studies in Ethnomusicology). 370p. 1999. pap. text 30.00 (*0-226-03488-7*) U Ch Pr.

Music of Death & New Creation: Experiences in the World of Balinese Gamelan Beleganjur. Michael B. Bakan. LC 98-42727. 1999. lib. bdg. 60.00 (*0-226-03487-9*) U Ch Pr.

Music of Dmitri Shostakovich. Roy Blokker & Robert Dearling. LC 78-68623. 192p. 1979. 32.50 (*0-8386-1948-7*) Fairleigh Dickinson.

Music of Dolphins. Karen Hesse. (J). Date not set. 14.95 (*0-8050-3558-3*) H Holt & Co.

Music of Dolphins. Karen Hesse. 244p. (J). pap. 4.50 (*0-8072-1542-2*) Listening Lib.

Music of Dolphins. Karen Hesse. LC 96-3494. (Illus.). 196p. (YA). (gr. 4-7). 1996. 14.95 (*0-590-89797-7*) Scholastic Inc.

Music of Dolphins. Karen Hesse. 192p. (J). (gr. 4-7). 1998. pap. 4.50 (*0-590-89798-5*) Scholastic Inc.

***Music of Dolphins.** Karen Hesse. (Apple Signature Edition Ser.). (J). 1998. 9.60 (*0-606-13628-2*, Pub. by Turtleback) Demco.

***Music of Dolphins.** unabridged ed. Karen Hesse. (J). (gr. 5-7). 1999. 21.98 incl. audio (*0-8072-8135-2*, YA113SP) Listening Lib.

Music of Duke Ellington. Duke Ellington. (Easy Piano Ser.). 64p. 1995. pap. 12.95 (*0-7935-4912-4*, 00110035) H Leonard.

Music of Earlier Times: Reprint from "Kleine Musikgeschichte," 2nd edn., Leipzig, 1931. Ed. by Johannes Wolf. 158p. (C). 1952. reprint ed. pap. 5.00 (*0-8450-2576-7*) Broude.

Music of Eastern Europe. Rough Guides Staff. (Orig.). 1998. audio compact disk 14.95 (*1-85828-368-X*) Penguin Putnam.

Music of Eastern India. Sukumar Ray. 1986. 20.00 (*0-8364-1581-7*) S Asia.

Music of Edgard Varese. Jonathan W. Bernard. LC 86-22431. (Composers of the Twentieth Century Ser.). 296p. reprint ed. pap. 91.80 (*0-7837-3281-3*, 205768300006) Bks Demand.

Music of Edmund Rubbra. Ralph S. Grover. 643p. 1992. 113.95 (*0-85967-910-1*, Pub. by Scolar Pr) Ashgate Pub Co.

Music of Elliott Carter. 2nd ed. David Schiff. LC 98-33956. (Illus.). 356p. 1998. 35.00 (*0-8014-3612-5*) Cornell U Pr.

Music of Exile: Poems by Matthew Brennan. Matthew Brennan. 76p. pap. text 12.00 (*1-55605-250-2*) Wyndham Hall.

Music of Failure. Bill Holm. (Illus.). 128p. (Orig.). 1986. pap. 6.95 (*0-918461-04-9*) Plains Press.

Music of France: International Guitar Editions. Ed. by Aaron Stang. (International Guitar Editions Ser.). 32p. (Orig.). 1995. pap. text 19.95 (*0-89724-542-3*, GF9507) Wrner Bros.

Music of Francis Poulenc 1899-1963: A Catalogue. Carl B. Schmidt. (Illus.). 632p. 1995. text 105.00 (*0-19-816336-3*) OUP.

Music of Franz Schmidt: The Orchestral Music, Vol. 1. Harold Truscott. (Eulenburg Music Ser.). (Illus.). 190p. 1985. lib. bdg. 25.00 (*0-907689-11-6*) Da Capo.

***Music of Frederick Sommer.** Frederick Sommer. (Illus.). 15p. 2000. 75.00 (*3-923922-81-7*) Nazraeli Press.

Music of George Washington's Time. U. S. George Washington Bicentennial Commission. Ed. by John T. Howard. LC 74-24120. reprint ed. 27.50 (*0-404-12976-5*) AMS Pr.

Music of Germany: International Guitar Editions. Ed. by Aaron Stang. (International Guitar Editions Ser.). 32p. (Orig.). 1995. pap. text 19.95 (*0-89724-541-5*, GF9506) Wrner Bros.

Music of Gershwin. Steven E. Gilbert. LC 95-12086. (Composers of the Twentieth Century Ser.). 257p. 1995. 37.00 (*0-300-06233-8*) Yale U Pr.

Music of Grace: The Sacred in Contemporary American Poetry. Jeanne Foster. LC 93-34673. (American University Studies, Series XXIV: Vol. 55). 135p. (C). 1995. text 37.95 (*0-8204-2349-1*) P Lang Pubng.

Music of Gustav Mahler. James Burnett. LC 84-29790. 232p. 1985. 36.50 (*0-8386-3167-3*) Fairleigh Dickinson.

Music of Hans Pfitzner. John Williamson. (Oxford Monographs on Music). (Illus.). 396p. 1992. text 95.00 (*0-19-816160-3*) OUP.

***Music of Harrison Birtwistle.** Robert Adlington. (Music in the Twentieth Century Ser.: No. 12). (Illus.). 244p. (C). 2000. 59.95 (*0-521-63082-7*) Cambridge U Pr.

Music of Harry Partch: A Descriptive Catalog. Thomas McGeary. LC 91-70674. (I.S.A.M. Monographs: No. 31). (Illus.). xiv, 186p. (Orig.). 1991. pap. 20.00 (*0-914678-34-5*) Inst Am Music.

Music of Henry Ainsworth's Psalter (Amsterdam, 1612) Lorraine Inserra & H. Wiley Hitchcock. LC 81-81547. (I.S.A.M. Monographs: No. 15). 126p. (Orig.). 1981. pap. 10.00 (*0-914678-15-9*) Inst Am Music.

Music of Henry Fillmore & Will Huff. Paul E. Bierley. LC 82-81491. (Music Catalog Ser.). 71p. 1982. pap. 5.95 (*0-918048-02-8*) Integrity.

Music of Hindostan. A. H. Strangways. (C). 1994. reprint ed. 26.00 (*81-215-0643-3*, Pub. by M Manoharial) Coronet Bks.

Music of Hindu Trinidad: Songs from the India Diaspora. Helen Myers. LC 97-25692. (Illus.). 480p. 1998. pap. text 39.00 (*0-226-55453-8*); lib. bdg. 85.00 (*0-226-55451-1*) U Ch Pr.

*__Music of His Promises: Listening to God with Love, Trust & Obedience.__ Elisabeth Elliot. 2000. pap. 10.99 (*1-56955-216-9*) Servant.

*__Music of Home.__ Edward L. Johnson. (Illus.). 134p. (YA). 1999. pap. 9.75 (*0-7392-0197-2*, PO3189) Morris Pubng.

Music of Ideas. James Laughlin. 44p. 1995. 75.00 (*0-918116-88-0*) Brooding Heron Pr.

Music of Ideas. deluxe limited ed. James Laughlin. 44p. 1995. 125.00 (*0-918116-87-2*) Brooding Heron Pr.

Music of India. S. Bandopadhyaya. 80p. 1978. 7.95 (*0-318-36332-1*) Asia Bk Corp.

Music of India. Atiya B. Fyzee-Rahamin. (Illus.). 1979. text 22.50 (*0-89563-395-7*) Coronet Bks.

Music of India. Jamila Massey & Reginald Massey. (C). 1993. 22.00 (*81-7017-332-9*, Pub. by Abhinav) S Asia.

Music of India. Atiya B. Fyzee-Rahamin. 1990. reprint ed. 8.00 (*81-85418-05-5*, Pub. by Low Price) S Asia.

Music of India. H. A. Popley. 1990. reprint ed. 8.00 (*81-85418-06-3*, Pub. by Low Price) S Asia.

Music of Ireland. Compiled by Stefan Grossman. 32p. 1992. pap. 5.95 (*1-56222-047-0*, 94510) Mel Bay.

Music of Israel: From the Biblical Era to Modern Times. 2nd rev. ed. Peter E. Gradenwitz. (Illus.). 420p. 1996. 39.95 (*1-57467-012-3*, Amadeus Pr) Timber.

*__Music of J. S. Bach: Analysis & Interpretation, 4.__ David Schulenberg. (Bach Perspectives Ser.). 1999. text 65.00 (*0-8032-1051-5*) U of Nebr Pr.

Music of Jean Sibelius. Burnett D. James. LC 82-24214. 174p. 1983. 32.50 (*0-8386-3070-7*) Fairleigh Dickinson.

*__Music of Jelly Roll Morton for Fingerstyle Guitar.__ Stefan Grossman. 60p. 1998. pap. 17.95 (*0-7866-3475-8*, 95267BCD) Mel Bay.

Music of Johann Sebastian Bach: The Choral Works. Stephen Daw. LC 78-68624. (Illus.). 240p. 1981. 36.50 (*0-8386-1682-8*) Fairleigh Dickinson.

Music of Johann Sebastian Bach: The Sources, the Style, the Significance. Robert L. Marshall. 375p. 1989. reprint ed. 36.00 (*0-02-871781-3*, Schirmer Books) Mac Lib Ref.

Music of John Coltrane: Over One Hundred Compositions by Jazz Saxophone Great John Coltrane. John Coltrane. (Jazz Giants Ser.). 128p. (Orig.). 1991. spiral bd. 22.95 (*0-7935-0409-0*, 00660165) H Leonard.

Music of John Denver Made Easy for Guitar. Ed. by Milton Okun. (Easy Guitar Ser.). pap. 9.95 (*0-89524-018-1*) Cherry Lane.

Music of Joseph Haydn. Antony Hodgson. LC 75-21259. (New Ser. of Music Bks). (Illus.). 208p. 1977. 32.50 (*0-8386-1684-4*) Fairleigh Dickinson.

Music of Latin America. (Music Ser.). 58p. 1979. 3.00 (*0-8270-3975-1*) OAS.

Music of Leo Kottke: Transcriptions & Instruction. rev. ed. Mark Hanson. 48p. (C). 1991. pap. text 19.95 (*0-936799-18-8*, AC72672, Pub. by Accent Music) Music Sales.

Music of Life. 2nd ed. Anahat I. Khan. 353p. 1998. reprint ed. pap. 18.00 (*0-930872-38-X*) Omega Pubns NY.

Music of Light. Lindsley Cameron. LC 97-49506. 240p. 1998. 24.00 (*0-684-82409-4*) Free Pr.

Music of Light. large type ed. Lindsley Cameron. LC 98-28957. 1998. 23.95 (*0-7838-0286-2*, G K Hall Lrg Type) Mac Lib Ref.

Music of Lou Harrison. Heidi Von Gunden. LC 94-8059. (Illus.). 380p. 1995. 47.50 (*0-8108-2887-1*) Scarecrow.

Music of Love. large type ed. Karen West. (Linford Romance Large Print Ser.). 240p. 1998. pap. 17.99 (*0-7089-5261-5*, Linford) Ulverscroft.

Music of Love: Piano Solos. 64p. 1984. pap. 10.95 (*0-7935-5095-5*, 00202133) H Leonard.

*__Music of Luigi Dallapiccola.__ Raymond Fearn. (Eastman Studies in Music). (Illus.). 320p. 2000. 75.00 (*1-58046-078-X*, Pub. by Univ Rochester Pr) Boydell & Brewer.

Music of Lutoslawski. 3rd ed. Charles B. Rae. (Illus.). 318p. 1999. pap. 22.95 (*0-7119-6910-8*, OP48072) Omnibus NY.

Music of Many Cultures. Carol Fisher Mathieson. (Illus.). 80p. (J). (gr. 10-13). 1996. pap. text 9.95 (*1-58037-102-7*, Pub. by M Twain Media) Carson-Dellos.

Music of Many Means: Sketches & Essays on the Music of Robert Erickson. Robert Erickson & John Mackay. LC 95-2191. (Composers of North America Ser.: Vol. 17). 491p. 1995. 62.50 (*0-8108-3014-0*) Scarecrow.

*__Music of Memory.__ Muriel Cooper. 64p. 2000. pap. 7.50 (*0-920635-13-X*) Genl Dist Srvs.

Music of Mexico Acoustic Guitar, Vol. 1. Ruben Delgado. 56p. 1996. 19.95 incl. audio compact disk (*0-7866-2718-2*, 94863BCD) Mel Bay.

*__Music of Mexico for Acoustic Guitar, Vol. 2.__ Ruben Delgado. 48p. 1998. pap. 19.95 incl. audio compact disk (*0-7866-4504-0*, 95347BCD) Mel Bay.

Music of Mexico for Acoustic Guitar, Vol. 3. Ruben Delgado. 40p. 1997. pap. 17.95 incl. audio compact disk (*0-7866-2666-6*, 96517BCD) Mel Bay.

Music of Michael Jackson & Family. Geoff Brown. (Illus.). 152p. 1996. pap. 8.95 (*0-7119-5303-1*, OP47801) Omnibus NY.

*__Music of Miracles.__ Byron Janis. 2000. write for info. (*0-688-16828-0*, Wm Morrow) Morrow Avon.

Music of Morton Feldman, 36. Thomas DeLio. LC 95-24022. (Contributions to the Study of Music & Dance Ser.: Vol. 36). 260p. 1996. 65.00 (*0-313-29803-3*, Greenwood Pr) Greenwood.

Music of Mozart. Cavett. (C). Date not set. write for info. (*0-415-03352-7*) Routledge.

Music of Mozart: The Symphonies. Robert Dearling. LC 78-68625. (Illus.). 232p. 1982. 36.50 (*0-8386-2335-2*) Fairleigh Dickinson.

Music of My Soul. Ellen G. Massey. LC 97-97116. 192p. 1998. 18.95 (*0-8034-9277-4*, Avalon Bks) Bouregy.

Music of My Time. Joan Peyser. (Illus.). 496p. 1995. 35.00 (*0-912483-99-7*) Pro-Am Music.

Music of Neil Young Made Easy for Guitar. Ed. by Aaron Stang. 48p. (Orig.). 1994. pap. 9.95 (*0-89724-171-1*, GF0122) Wrner Bros.

Music of Nightnoise. 64p. 1997. otabind 14.95 (*0-7935-7611-3*) H Leonard.

Music of Noel Bauldeweyn. Edgar H. Sparks. (Studies & Documents: Vol. 6). (Illus.). 158p. 1972. pap. 10.00 (*1-878528-08-4*) Am Musicological.

Music of O'Carolan. Compiled by Stefan Grossman. audio 10.98 (*1-56222-850-1*, 94989C) Mel Bay.

Music of O'Carolan. Compiled by Stefan Grossman. 1987. 15.95 incl. audio (*1-56222-851-X*, 94989P) Mel Bay.

Music of O'Carolan. Compiled by Stefan Grossman. 24p. 1993. pap. 5.95 (*1-56222-832-3*, 94989) Mel Bay.

Music of Our Day. Lazare Saminsky. LC 78-117838. (Essay Index Reprint Ser.). 1977. 23.95 (*0-8369-1682-4*) Ayer.

Music of Our Lives. Kathleen M. Higgins. 288p. 1990. 37.95 (*0-87722-756-X*) Temple U Pr.

Music of Paul Ben-Haim: A Performace Guide. Hadassah Guttmann. LC 92-5279. (Illus.). 265p. 1992. 37.50 (*0-8108-2551-1*) Scarecrow.

Music of Per Norgard: Fourteen Interpretative Essays. Anders Byer. (Illus.). 300p. 1996. 56.95 (*1-85928-313-6*, Pub. by Scolar Pr) Ashgate Pub Co.

Music of Ralph Vaughan Williams. Frank S. Howes. LC 75-3737. (Illus.). 372p. 1975. reprint ed. lib. bdg. 35.00 (*0-8371-8064-3*, HOMR, Greenwood Pr) Greenwood.

Music of Reason: Experience the Beauty of Mathematics Through Quotations. Theoni Pappas. LC 95-38362. (Illus.). 128p. (Orig.). 1995. pap. 9.95 (*1-884550-04-5*) Wide World-Tetra.

Music of Richard Marx: Easy Guitar. Ed. by Mark Phillips. (Illus.). 52p. (Orig.). 1990. pap. text 10.95 (*0-89524-500-0*) Cherry Lane.

Music of Richard Marx (Easy Piano) Ed. by Milton Okun. (Illus.). 56p. (Orig.). 1990. pap. text 10.95 (*0-89524-478-0*) Cherry Lane.

Music of Richard Rodgers. 32p. 1987. pap. 7.95 (*0-7935-3686-3*, 00365950) H Leonard.

*__Music of Robert Burns for Dulcimer.__ Edward Schelb. 56p. 1998. pap. 11.95 (*0-7866-2749-2*, 96555) Mel Bay.

*__Music of Robert Cray.__ 72p. 1998. otabind 19.95 (*0-7935-8373-X*) H Leonard.

Music of Russia: International Guitar Editions. Ed. by Aaron Stang. (International Guitar Editions Ser.). 48p. (Orig.). 1995. pap. text 19.95 (*0-89724-540-7*, GF9505) Wrner Bros.

Music of Ruth Crawford Seeger. Joseph N. Straus. (Music in the Twentieth Century Ser.: No. 6). 272p. (C). 1995. text 69.95 (*0-521-41646-9*) Cambridge U Pr.

Music of Santeria: Traditional Rhythms of the Bata Drums. 2nd rev. ed. John Amira & Steven Cornelius. LC 99-29426. (Performance in World Music Ser.: No. 5). (Illus.). 128p. (YA). (gr. 9-12). 1999. pap. 24.95 (*0-941677-70-2*, Pub. by White Cliffs Media) Words Distrib.

Music of Santo Domingo Pueblo, New Mexico. Frances Densmore. 186p. 1938. pap. 5.00 (*0-916561-53-4*) Southwest Mus.

Music of Sergei Prokofiev. Neil Minturn. LC 96-27064. (Composers of the Twentieth Century Ser.). 352p. 1997. 35.00 (*0-300-06366-0*) Yale U Pr.

Music of Sibelius. Ed. by Gerald Abraham. LC 74-23413. (Music Reprint Ser.). 218p. 1975. reprint ed. lib. bdg. 29.50 (*0-306-70716-0*) Da Capo.

Music of Sibelius: Music Book Index. Gerald E. Abraham. 218p. 1993. reprint ed. lib. bdg. 79.00 (*0-7812-9621-8*) Rprt Serv.

Music of Sigmund Romberg. Ed. by Carol Cuellar. 104p. 1977. pap. text 12.95 (*0-7692-1504-1*, SF0018) Wrner Bros.

*__Music of Silence: A Composer's Testament.__ John Tavener. Ed. by Brian Keeble. (Illus.). 208p. 2000. pap. 15.00 (*0-571-20088-5*) Faber & Faber.

Music of Silence: A Sacred Journey Through the Hours of the Day. David Steindl-Rast & Sharon Lebell. LC 97-51683. (Illus.). 144p. 1998. pap. 12.00 (*1-56975-137-4*) Ulysses Pr.

Music of Sir Peter Maxwell Davies: An Annotated Catalogue. Ed. by Colin Bayliss. 304p. (C). 1991. text 80.00 (*0-948929-46-4*) St Mut.

Music of Solid Objects. John Dickson. LC 97-61511. (Illus.). 112p. 1997. pap. 7.95 (*0-939395-22-3*) Thorntree Pr.

Music of Southslavic Epics from the Bihac Region of Bosnia. rev. ed. Stephen Erdely. LC 94-39321. (Milman Parry Studies in Oral Tradition). 656p. 1995. text 10.00 (*0-8153-1237-7*) Garland.

Music of Spain: Piano Solo. 12.95 (*0-7935-4988-4*, 50482476) H Leonard.

Music of Star Trek. Jeff Bond. LC 98-31903. (Illus.). 250p. 1999. pap. 21.95 incl. audio compact disk (*1-58065-012-0*, Pub. by Lone Eagle Pub) Natl Bk Netwk.

Music of Stravinsky. Stephen Walsh. (Illus.). 326p. 1993. pap. text 24.00 (*0-19-816375-4*) OUP.

Music of Stuart Saunders Smith, 38. John P. Welsh. LC 95-4475. (Contributions to the Study of Music & Dance Ser.: Vol. 38). 400p. 1996. 67.95 (*0-313-29805-X*, Greenwood Pr) Greenwood.

Music of Summer. Rosa Guy. 1992. 12.95 (*0-385-30704-7*) Doubleday.

Music of Szymanowski. Jim Samson. 1990. reprint ed. pap. 15.95 (*0-912483-34-2*) Pro-Am Music.

Music of the Alaska-Klondike Gold Rush: A Songbook & History. Jean A. Murray. (LanternLight Library: Vol. 3). (Illus.). 440p. 1999. 54.95 (*1-889963-13-5*); spiral bd. 35.95 (*1-889963-14-3*) U of Alaska Pr.

Music of the Ancient Near East. Claire C. Polin. LC 73-20879. (Illus.). 138p. 1974. reprint ed. lib. bdg. 49.50 (*0-8371-5796-X*, PONE, Greenwood Pr) Greenwood.

Music of the Angels. Michael Tippett. (Eulenburg Music Ser.). 1982. reprint ed. pap. 19.50 (*0-903873-60-5*) Da Capo.

Music of the Arabs. Habib H. Touma. Tr. by Laurie Schwartz from GER. LC 94-43650. (Illus.). 260p. 1996. 29.95 (*0-931340-88-8*, Amadeus Pr) Timber.

Music of the Bach Family: An Anthology. Karl Geiringer. (Music Reprint Ser.). (Illus.). viii, 248p. 1980. reprint ed. lib. bdg. 45.00 (*0-306-79597-3*) Da Capo.

Music of the Ballads see **Frank C. Brown Collection of North Carolina Folklore**

Music of the Bauls of Bengal. Charles Capwell. LC 84-27824. (Illus.). 254p. 1986. reprint ed. pap. 78.80 (*0-608-07347-4*, 206757500009) Bks Demand.

Music of the Bible in Christian Perspective. Garen L. Wolf. 419p. 1996. pap. 19.99 (*0-88019-353-0*) Schmul Pub Co.

Music of the Bible Revealed. Suzanne Hack-Vantoura. Ed. by John Wheeler, Jr. Tr. by Dennis Weber. LC 90-25315. 1991. pap. 29.95 (*0-941037-10-X*, BIBAL Press) D & F Scott.

*__Music of the Birds: A Celebration of Bird Song.__ Lang Elliott. (Illus.). 136p. 1999. 35.00 (*0-618-00698-2*); pap. 25.00 (*0-618-00697-4*) HM.

Music of the Close: The Final Scenes of Shakespeare's Tragedies. Walter C. Foreman, Jr. LC 77-75484. 240p. 1978. 28.00 (*0-8131-1366-0*) U Pr of Ky.

Music of the Common Tongue: Survival & Celebration in African American Music. Christopher Small. LC 98-23578. 509p. 1998. reprint ed. pap. 19.95 (*0-8195-6357-9*, Wesleyan Univ Pr) U Pr of New Eng.

Music of the Common Tongue: Survival & Celebration in Afro-American Music. Christopher Small. LC 86-31381. 448p. 1994. pap. 19.95 (*0-7145-4096-X*) Riverrun NY.

Music of the Comte de St. Germain. Frwd. by Manly P. Hall. pap. 12.95 (*0-89314-416-9*) Philos Res.

Music of the Dance: Stravinsky. Prod. by Zobeida Perez. 16p. (Orig.). (YA). 1994. pap. 17.00 (*0-89898-799-7*, BMR05084) Wrner Bros.

Music of the Drama. 16p. (Orig.). (YA). 1994. pap. 17.00 (*0-89898-806-3*, BMR05094) Wrner Bros.

Music of the Eagles Made Easy for Guitar. Ed. by Aaron Stan. 48p. (Orig.). 1994. pap. 9.95 (*0-89724-169-X*, GF0232) Wrner Bros.

Music of the Earth: Volcanoes, Earthquakes, & Other Geological Wonders. Ron L. Morton. (Illus.). 326p. (C). 1996. 28.95 (*0-306-45263-4*, Plenum Trade) Perseus Pubng.

Music of the English Church. Kenneth R. Long. (Illus.). 480p. 1991. lib. bdg. 87.50 (*0-340-14962-0*, Pub. by Hodder & Stought Ltd) Lubrecht & Cramer.

Music of the Ephrata Cloister. Julius F. Sachse. LC 77-134386. (Communal Societies in America Ser.). reprint ed. 32.50 (*0-404-05500-1*) AMS Pr.

Music of the Folk Songs see **Frank C. Brown Collection of North Carolina Folklore**

Music of the Ghetto & the Bible. Lazare Saminsky. LC 74-24220. reprint ed. 20.00 (*0-404-12833-5*) AMS Pr.

Music of the Gods: Hera, Aphrodite see **Greek Mythology**

*__Music of the Golden Age, 1900-1950 & Beyond: A Guide to Popular Composers & Lyricists.__ Arthur L. Iger. LC 98-12203. 288p. 1998. lib. bdg. 69.50 (*0-313-30691-5*, Greenwood Pr) Greenwood.

Music of the Heart: John & Charles Wesley on Music & Musicians - An Anthology. Carlton R. Young. LC 94-73036. 200p. 1995. pap. 18.95 (*0-916642-58-5*, 1592) Hope Pub.

Music of the Heart: The Roberta Guaspari Story. Roberta Tzavaras & Larkin Warren. LC 99-40757. (Illus.). 208p. 1999. pap. 12.95 (*0-7868-8487-8*, Pub. by Hyperion) Time Warner.

Music of the Heavens: Kepler's Harmonic Astronomy. Bruce Stephenson. LC 93-44916. 272p. (C). 1994. text 42.50 (*0-691-03439-7*, Pub. by Princeton U Pr) Cal Prin Full Svc.

Music of the Highest Class: Elitism & Populism in Antebellum Boston. Michael Broyles. LC 92-12422. (Illus.). 384p. (C). 1992. 45.00 (*0-300-05495-5*) Yale U Pr.

Music of the Hutchinson Family Singers. Hutchinson Family. (Earlier American Music Ser.). 1991. 29.50 (*0-306-77328-7*) Da Capo.

Music of the Indians of British Columbia. Frances Densmore. LC 72-1879. (Music Ser.). (Illus.). 118p. 1972. reprint ed. lib. bdg. 21.50 (*0-306-70507-9*) Da Capo.

Music of the Inferno. Frank Lentricchia. LC 99-14974. (SUNY Series in Italian/American Culture). 220p. (C). 1999. 24.50 (*0-7914-4347-7*) State U NY Pr.

Music of the Inferno. Frank Lentricchia. LC 99-14974. 220p. (C). 2000. pap. 19.95 (*0-7914-4348-5*) State U NY Pr.

*__Music of the Inner Lakes.__ Roger Sheffer. LC 98-89720. 1999. pap. text 14.95 (*0-89823-193-0*, Pub. by New Rivers Pr) Consort Bk Sales.

Music of the Louvin Brothers: Heaven's Own Harmony. Thomas L. Wilmeth. LC 98-44403. (Studies in the History & Interpretation of Music: Vol. 61). vi, 153p. 1999. text 79.95 (*0-7734-8255-5*) E Mellen.

Music of the Manger. Jeff Lahr. 40p. (Orig.). 1994. pap. 3.49 (*0-87227-183-8*, RBP5220) Reg Baptist.

Music of the Mind: An Adventure into Consciousness. Darryl Reanney. (Illus.). 192p. 1997. pap. 14.95 (*0-285-63288-4*, Pub. by Souvenir Pr Ltd) IPG Chicago.

Music of the Minnesinger & Early Meistersinger. Robert W. Linker. LC 73-181946. (North Carolina. University. Studies in the Germanic Languages & Literatures: No. 32). reprint ed. 35.00 (*0-404-50932-0*) AMS Pr.

Music of the Moppets: Pace Piano Education, Bk. I. 48p. (J). 1988. pap. 7.95 (*0-7935-5853-0*) H Leonard.

Music of the Most Ancient Nations, Particularly of the Assyrians, Egyptians & Hebrews. Carl Engel. 380p. 1990. reprint ed. lib. bdg. 79.00 (*0-7812-9027-9*) Rprt Serv.

Music of the Most Ancient Nations, Particularly of the Assyrians, Egyptians, & Hebrews, with Special Reference to Recent Discoveries in Western Asia & in Egypt. Carl Engel. LC 73-114875. (Select Bibliographies Reprint Ser.). 1980. 29.95 (*0-8369-5279-0*) Ayer.

Music of the Nations (a Comparative Study) Swami Prajnananda. 223p. 1973. 12.00 (*0-614-16457-5*) Theodore Front.

*__Music of the North American Indians for Acoustic Guitar.__ Steven Eckels. 48p. 2000. pap. 17.95 incl. audio compact disk (*0-7866-2146-X*, 96015BCD) Mel Bay.

Music of the Old South: Colony to Confederacy. Albert Stoutamire. LC 74-149827. (Illus.). 349p. 1975. 39.50 (*0-8386-7910-2*) Fairleigh Dickinson.

Music of the Past. Wanda Landowska. 185p. 1990. reprint ed. lib. bdg. 59.00 (*0-7812-9012-0*) Rprt Serv.

Music of the Past. Wanda Landowska. LC 75-181199. 184p. 1924. reprint ed. 39.00 (*0-403-01609-6*) Scholarly.

Music of the Pilgrims: A Description of the Psalm-Book Brought to Plymouth in Sixteen Twenty. Waldo S. Pratt. 1980. lib. bdg. 59.00 (*0-8490-3180-X*) Gordon Pr.

Music of the Planet: A Musical Journey about the World & Wonders of Our Solar System. Tobin J. Mueller. (J). (ps-8). 1990. pap. 14.95 (*1-56213-017-X*) Ctr Stage Prodns.

*__Music of the Raj: A Social & Economic History of Music in Late Eighteenth Century Anglo-Indian Society.__ Ian Woodfield. (Illus.). 288p. 2000. text 74.00 (*0-19-816433-5*) OUP.

Music of the Repressed Russian Avant-Garde, 1900-1929, 31. Larry Sitsky. LC 93-35836. (Contributions to the Study of Music & Dance Ser.: No. 31). 368p. 1994. 69.50 (*0-313-26709-X*, Greenwood Pr) Greenwood.

Music of the Sea & Sky. 16p. (Orig.). (J). 1994. pap. 17.00 (*0-89898-796-2*, BMR05085) Wrner Bros.

Music of the Shakers for Mountain Dulcimer: Intermediate Level. Neal Hellman. 80p. 1997. spiral bd. 11.95 (*0-7866-2597-X*, 96468) Mel Bay.

Music of the Soul: Sufi Teachings. 2nd ed. Shaykh Muhammad al-Jamal. 524p. 1996. pap. 29.95 (*1-892595-00-1*) Sidi Muha Pr.

*__Music of the Spheres.__ Maso. 2000. 25.00 (*1-58243-088-8*, Pub. by Counterpt DC) HarpC.

Music of the Spheres: Music, Science, & the Natural Order of the Universe. Jamie James. 263p. 1995. 14.00 (*0-387-94474-5*) Spr-Verlag.

Music of the Spheres & the Dance of Death. Kathi Meyer-Baer. LC 83-18905. (Music Reprint Ser.). (Illus.). 376p. 1984. reprint ed. lib. bdg. 47.50 (*0-306-76224-2*) Da Capo.

Music of the Sumerians & Their Immediate Successors, the Babylonians & Assyrians. Francis W. Galpin. LC 73-109625. (Select Bibliographies Reprint Ser.). 1977. 20.95 (*0-8369-5234-0*) Ayer.

Music of the Sumerians & Their Immediate Successors, the Babylonians & Assyrians. Francis W. Galpin. LC 75-104273. 110p. 1970. reprint ed. lib. bdg. 55.00 (*0-8371-3928-7*, GAMS, Greenwood Pr) Greenwood.

Music of the Sumerians & Their Immediate Successors, the Babylonians & Assyrians. Francis W. Galpin. (Music Book Index Ser.). 110p. 1992. reprint ed. lib. bdg. 69.00 (*0-7812-9476-2*) Rprt Serv.

Music of the Swamp. Lewis Nordan. 210p. 1991. 15.95 (*0-945575-76-9*) Algonquin Bks.

Music of the Swamp. Lewis Nordan. (Front Porch PB Ser.). 210p. 1992. pap. 7.95 (*1-56512-016-7*) Algonquin Bks.

Music of the Troubadours. Elizabeth Aubrey. LC 96-10358. (Music: Scholarship & Performance Ser.). (Illus.). 352p. 1996. lib. bdg. 49.95 (*0-253-33207-9*) Ind U Pr.

*__Music of the Troubadours.__ Elizabeth Aubrey. (Illus.). 352p. 2000. pap. 24.95 (*0-253-21389-4*) Ind U Pr.

Music of the Twentieth Century: Style & Structure. Bryan R. Simms. 1996. audio 60.00 (*0-02-864603-7*, Schirmer Books) Mac Lib Ref.

Music of the Twentieth Century: Style & Structure. 2nd ed. Bryan R. Simms. 1996. 40.00 (*0-02-864602-9*, Schirmer Books) Mac Lib Ref.

Music of the Venetian Ospedali: A Thematic Catalogue, Vol. 21. Joan Whittemore. LC 95-24548. (Thematic Catalogues Ser.: No. 21). (Illus.). 192p. 1995. lib. bdg. 56.00 (*0-945193-72-6*) Pendragon NY.

*__Music of the Vietnam War.__ Lee Andresen. (Illus.). 192p. 2000. pap. 14.95 (*1-886028-05-2*, Pub. by Savage Pr) Bookmen Inc.

Music of the Warao of Venezuela: Song People of the Rain Forest. Dale A. Olsen. LC 95-46549. (Illus.). 432p. (C). 1996. lib. bdg. 49.95 incl. cd-rom (*0-8130-1390-9*) U Press Fla.

Music of the Whole Earth. unabridged ed. David B. Reck & Carol Reck. LC 96-50895. (Illus.). 559p. 1997. pap. 27.50 (*0-306-80749-1*) Da Capo.

Music of the Work & Glory Vol. 2: Songbook. Lynn S. Lund & Gerald N. Lund. 1997. pap. 10.95 (*1-57008-349-5*) Bookcraft Inc.

Music of the Work & the Glory, Vol. 1. Lynn S. Lund & Gerald N. Lund. 1995. pap. 10.95 (*1-57008-188-3*) Bookcraft Inc.

*__Music of the World.__ Andrea Bergamini. 64p. 1999. 14.95 (*0-7641-5135-5*) Barron.

Music of the Zeros. D. S. Black. 52p. (Orig.). 1996. pap. 4.95 (*0-9626708-9-8*) Talisman IN.

Music of Time: Words & Music & Spiritual Friendship. John S. Dunne. LC 95-47364. 232p. (C). 1996. text 25.00 (*0-268-01423-X*) U of Notre Dame Pr.

An Asterisk (*) at the beginning of an entry indicates that the title is appearing for the first time.

Music of To-Morrow & Other Studies. Lawrence Gilman. LC 71-128246. (Essay Index Reprint Ser.). 1977. 17.95 (*0-8369-1830-4*) Ayer.

Music of Tree Limbs. Marsh Cassady. (Amelia Chapbooks Ser.). 20p. (Orig.). 1993. pap. 5.00 (*0-936545-18-6*) Amelia.

Music of Victor Herbert. Ed. by Carol Cuellar. 116p. 1976. pap. text 14.95 (*0-7692-1506-8*, SF0011) Wrner Bros.

Music of Viguen & Ravanbakhsh. (PER.). 24p. 1992. pap. 4.95 (*0-936347-27-9*) IBEX.

***Music of Vivian Fine.** Heidi Von Gunden. LC 98-49550. (Illus.). 208p. 1999. 56.00 (*0-8108-3617-3*) Scarecrow.

Music of What Happens. Ghita Orth. LC 82-10280. (Eileen W. Barnes Award Ser.). (Illus.). 70p. (Orig.). 1982. pap. 5.50 (*0-938158-01-5*) Saturday Pr.

Music of What Happens. John Straley. 272p. 1997. mass mkt. 5.99 (*0-553-57205-9*, Crimeline) Bantam.

Music of What Happens: Celtic Spirituality: A View from the Inside. John J. O'Riordain. 120p. 1996. pap. 9.95 (*0-88489-514-9*) St Marys.

Music of What Happens: Poems, Poets, Critics. Helen H. Vendler. LC 87-21240. 487p. 1988. 42.50 (*0-674-59152-6*) HUP.

Music of What Happens: Poems, Poets, Critics. Helen H. Vendler. 487p. 1988. pap. text 20.50 (*0-674-59153-4*) HUP.

Music of Wild, Pt. 1. Gene S. Porter. 19.95 (*0-8488-0611-5*) Amereon Ltd.

Music of Wild, Pt. 2. Gene S. Porter. 17.95 (*0-8488-0612-3*) Amereon Ltd.

Music of Wild, Pt. 3. Gene S. Porter. 17.95 (*0-8488-0613-1*) Amereon Ltd.

Music of William Walton: Music Book Index, 2 vols., Set. Frank S. Howes. 1993. reprint ed. lib. bdg. 150.00 (*0-7812-9668-4*) Rprt Serv.

Music of Yes: Structure & Vision in Progressive Rock. Bill Martin, Jr. 298p. (Orig.). 1996. pap. 19.95 (*0-8126-9333-7*) Open Court.

Music on Demand: Composers & Careers in the Hollywood Film Industry. Robert R. Faulkner. LC 82-2676. (Illus.). 281p. 1982. 34.95 (*0-87855-403-3*) Transaction Pubs.

Music on My Beat: An Intimate Volume of Shop Talk. H. Howard Taubman. LC 76-57173. 267p. 1977. reprint ed. lib. bdg. 65.00 (*0-8371-9433-4*, TAMU, Greenwood Pr) Greenwood.

Music on Record: A Critical Guide, 4 vols., Set. Peter Gammond & James Burnett. Incl. Vol. 1. Orchestral Music., **2 vols.** LC 78-8183. 1978. lib. bdg. 50.00 (*0-313-20515-9*, GAMR01, Greenwood Pr); Vol. 2. Orchestral Music., **2 vols.** LC 78-8183. 1978. lib. bdg. 50.00 (*0-313-20516-7*, GAMR02, Greenwood Pr); Vol. 3. Chamber & Instrumental Music. LC 78-8183. 1978. lib. bdg. 50.00 (*0-313-20517-5*, GAMR03, Greenwood Pr); Vol. 4. Opera & Vocal Music. LC 78-8183. 1978. lib. bdg. 50.00 (*0-313-20518-3*, GAMR04, Greenwood Pr); LC 78-8183. 1978. reprint ed. Set lib. bdg. 145.00 (*0-313-20514-0*, GAMR, Greenwood Pr) Greenwood.

Music on the Internet: And Where to Find It. Ian Waugh. (Music How-To Ser.). 1998. pap. text 17.95 (*1-878427-69-5*) Cimino Pub Grp.

Music on the Internet 1997-1998. Stull. 96p. (C). 1997. write for info. (*0-13-646209-X*, Macmillan Coll) P-H.

Music on the Shakespearian Stage. George H. Cowling. LC 74-24063. reprint ed. 27.50 (*0-404-12889-0*) AMS Pr.

***Music Online for Dummies.** David Kushner. (For Dummies Ser.). (Illus.). 360p. 2000. pap. 24.99 (*0-7645-0705-2*) IDG Bks.

Music over Manhattan. Mark Karlins. (Illus.). 32p. 1999. pap. 6.99 (*0-440-41187-4*) BDD Bks Young Read.

Music over Manhattan. Mark Karlins. LC 96-47668. (Illus.). 32p. (J). (ps-3). 1998. 15.95 (*0-385-32225-9*) Doubleday.

Music, Past & Present, at Kamehameha Schools: Lei Mele No Pauahi. Jonathan K. Osorio & Kanalu G. Young. LC 98-165854. Orig. Title: Lei Mele No Pauahi. (Illus.). 96p. 1997. pap. 16.95 (*0-87336-050-8*) Kamehameha Schools.

Music Pedagogy: The Proceedings of the Workshop on Music Pedagogy, Conducted at the Catholic University of America, June 15-16, 1962. Catholic University of America, Music Education Wo. Ed. by Richard H. Werder. LC 64-66051. 96p. reprint ed. pap. 30.00 (*0-608-10887-1*, 200535900053) Bks Demand.

Music Performance Practice in the Early Abbasid Era, 132-320 AH/750-932 AD. George D. Sawa. xviii, 251p. pap. text 30.29 (*0-88844-092-8*) Brill Academic Pubs.

Music Periodical Literature: An Annotated Bibliography of Indexes & Bibliographies. Joan M. Meggett. LC 77-19120. 126p. 1978. 26.50 (*0-8108-1109-X*) Scarecrow.

Music, Physics, & Engineering. enl. rev. ed. Harry F. Olson. (Illus.). 460p. 1966. pap. 10.95 (*0-486-21769-8*) Dover.

Music Play: The Early Childhood Music Curriculum Guide for Parents, Teachers, & Caregivers. Wendy H. Valerio et al. 144p. 1998. pap. 44.95 incl. audio compact disk (*1-57999-027-4*) GIA Pubns.

Music, Politics, & the Academy. Pieter C. Van den Toorn. LC 94-42446. (Illus.). 1996. pap. 16.95 (*0-520-20116-7*, Pub. by U CA Pr) Cal Prin Full Svc.

Music Power & Harmony: A Workbook of Music & Inner Forces. R. J. Stewart. (Illus.). 192p. (Orig.). 1990. pap. 16.95 (*0-7137-2121-9*, Pub. by Blandford Pr) Sterling.

Music Preparation: A Guide to Music Copying. Ken J. Williams. LC 79-56140. (Illus.). 149p. 1980. 16.95 (*0-9603742-0-5*) K J Williams Pubns.

Music Principles for the Skeptical Guitarist Vol. 1: The Big Picture. Bruce Emery. Ed. by Mary Pickering. (Illus.). iv, 136p. 1997. pap. 24.95 (*0-9665029-0-6*) Skeptical Guitarist.

Music Principles for the Skeptical Guitarist Vol. 2: The Fretboard. Bruce Emery. Ed. by Mary Pickering. LC 99-165868. (Illus.). 140p. 1998. pap. 24.95 (*0-9665029-1-4*) Skeptical Guitarist.

Music Principles for the Skeptical Guitarist Vol. 3: Blues-N-Jazz. Bruce Emery. Ed. by Mary Pickering. (Illus.). 140p. 1999. pap. 24.95 (*0-9665029-2-2*) Skeptical Guitarist.

Music, Print & Culture in Early Sixteenth Century Italy. Iain Fenlon. (Illus.). 125p. 1996. pap. 30.00 (*0-7123-0412-6*, Pub. by B23tish Library) U of Toronto Pr.

Music Printing in Renaissance Venice: The Scotto Press (1539-1572) Jane A. Bernstein. (Illus.). 1200p. 1998. 175.00 (*0-19-510231-2*) OUP.

Music Processing. Ed. by Geoffredo Haus. (Computer Music & Digital Audio Ser.: Vol. 9). (Illus.). 360p. (C). 1993. pap. 39.95 (*0-89579-268-0*) A-R Eds.

Music Producers: Conversations with Today's Top Hit Makers! Leonard Hall. LC 99-62536. 140p. 1999. pap. text 24.95 (*0-87288-730-8*) Intertec Pub.

Music Profession in Britain since the Eighteenth Century: A Social History. Cyril Ehrlich. (Illus.). 280p. 1986. reprint ed. 65.00 (*0-19-822665-9*) OUP.

Music Profession in Britain since the Eighteenth Century: A Social History. Cyril Ehrlich. (Illus.). 276p. 1989. reprint ed. pap. text 23.00 (*0-19-822743-4*) OUP.

Music Programme. Paul Micou. 1990. 16.95 (*1-55972-023-9*, Birch Ln Pr) Carol Pub Group.

Music Publisher Directory. Robert A. Livingston. (Livingston's Complete Music Business Directory Ser.). 94p. 1995. pap. 29.95 (*0-932303-21-8*) GLGLC Music.

Music Publisher's International ISMN Directory, 1998/99. 2nd ed. Bowker Staff. 1999. 210.00 (*3-598-22248-3*) K G Saur Verlag.

Music Publishing: A Songwriter's Guide. rev. ed. Randy Poe. LC 97-25566. (Illus.). 144p. 1997. pap. 18.99 (*0-89879-754-3*, Wrtrs Digest Bks) F & W Pubns Inc.

Music Publishing: The Real Road to Music Business Success. 4th expanded rev. ed. Tim Whitsett. LC 97-71973. 208p. 1997. pap. 49.95 (*0-918371-16-3*, HL00330316, MixBooks) Intertec Pub.

***Music Publishing: The Real Road to Music Business Success.** 5th ed. Tim Whitsett. 200p. 2000. pap. 49.95 (*0-87288-758-8*) Intertec Pub.

Music Publishing & Collecting: Essays in Honor of Donald W. Krummel. Ed. by David Hunter. (Illus.). 252p. 1994. 45.00 (*0-87845-095-5*) U of Ill Grad Sch.

Music Publishing, Copyright & Piracy in Victorian England, 1881-1906: A Twenty-Five Year Chronicle from the Pages of the Musical Times & Other English Music Journals of the Period. J. Coover. 184p. 1985. text 120.00 (*0-7201-1749-6*) Continuum.

***Music Publishing 101: Crash Course.** Regina Smith. 103p. 2000. pap. 16.95 (*0-9677020-0-3*) No Walls Prod.

***Music, Race & Nation: Musica Tropical in Colombia.** Peter Wade. LC 99-88600. (Studies in Ethnomusicology). 1999. pap. text 20.00 (*0-226-86845-1*) U Ch Pr.

***Music, Race & Nation: Musica Tropical in Colombia.** Peter Wade. LC 99-88600. (Chicago Studies in Ethnomusicology). (Illus.). 1999. lib. bdg. 40.00 (*0-226-86844-3*) U Ch Pr.

Music Reading & Theory Skills Level 1 & 2: A Sequential Method for Practice & Mastery. Carolyn Francis. 228p. (J). (gr. 4-12). 1986. 249.95 (*0-931303-04-4*); ring bd. 249.95 (*0-931303-02-8*) Innovative Learn.

Music Reading & Theory Skills Level 3: A Sequential Method for Practice & Mastery. Carolyn Francis. 90p. 1984. 49.95 (*0-685-09764-1*); teacher ed. 29.95 (*0-931303-00-1*); student ed. 59.95 (*0-685-09765-X*); 298.55 (*0-685-09763-3*) Innovative Learn.

Music Reading & Theory Skills Level 3: A Sequential Method for Practice & Mastery. Carolyn Francis. 90p. (YA). (gr. 7-12). 1984. student ed. 329.50 (*0-931303-01-X*) Innovative Learn.

Music Reading by Intervals: A Modern Sight-Reading & Ear-Training Method. Brock McElheran. LC 98-73279. (Illus.). 140p. (C). 1998. spiral bd. 14.95 (*0-9658910-0-3*, BRM-1) Brichtmark Music.

Music Reading for Bass: By Wendi Hrehovcsik. 64p. 1997. pap. 9.95 (*0-7935-8197-4*) H Leonard.

Music Reading for Beginners. Julia Hansen. (Illus.). 95p. (Orig.). 1986. pap. 15.00 (*0-9619498-0-5*) Linaria Pr.

Music Reading for Guitar. David Oates. 160p. 1998. otabind 16.95 (*0-7935-8188-5*) H Leonard.

Music Reading for Keyboard. Larry Steelman. 104p. 1998. otabind 12.95 (*0-7935-8200-8*) H Leonard.

Music-Record Business & Law: Your Introduction to Music-Record Copyright, Contracts & Other Business & Law. Walter E. Hurst & William S. Hale. (Entertainment Industry Ser.). (Illus.). 234p. (YA). (gr. 12). 1974. text 15.00 (*0-911370-21-8*) Seven Arts.

Music Reference & Research Materials: An Annotated Bibliography. 4th rev. ed. Vincent H. Duckles & Michael A. Keller. 740p. 1998. text 40.00 (*0-7881-5554-7*) DIANE Pub.

Music Reference & Research Materials: An Annotated Bibliography. 4th rev. ed. Vincent H. Duckles & Michael A. Keller. LC 92-12386. 740p. 1994. 45.00 (*0-02-870822-9*, Schirmer Books) Mac Lib Ref.

Music Research in Italian Libraries. Walter H. Rubsamen. 1993. reprint ed. lib. bdg. 89.00 (*0-7812-9699-4*) Rprt Serv.

***Music Research Reference Techniques.** 2000. pap. 23.00 (*0-02-865325-4*, Schirmer Books) Mac Lib Ref.

Music, Right & Left. Virgil Thomson. LC 69-14115. (Illus.). 214p. 1969. reprint ed. lib. bdg. 59.50 (*0-8371-0685-0*, THMU, Greenwood Pr) Greenwood.

Music, Ritual, & Falasha History. rev. ed. Kay K. Shelemay. LC 86-71246. (Ethiopian Ser.: Monograph No. 17). (Illus.). 420p. (C). 1989. reprint ed. text 29.95 (*0-87013-274-1*) Mich St U Pr.

Music Road, Bk. 1. Constance Starr. 72p. 1981. pap. text 8.50 (*0-87487-610-9*) Summy-Birchard.

Music Road, Bk. 2. Constance Starr. 72p. (YA). 1996. pap. 8.50 (*0-87487-611-7*, 0611) Summy-Birchard.

Music Road, Bk. 3. Constance Starr. 96p. 1985. pap. text 11.95 (*0-87487-612-5*) Summy-Birchard.

Music Room. Dennis McFarland. 288p. 1991. reprint ed. pap. 12.00 (*0-380-71456-6*, Avon Bks) Morrow Avon.

***Music, Saddles & Flapjacks: Dudes at the OTO Ranch.** Roberta Cheney & Clyde Erskine. (Illus.). 302p. 2000. reprint ed. pap. 16.00 (*0-87842-422-9*) Mountain Pr.

Music School. John Updike. 1966. 25.00 (*0-394-43727-6*) Knopf.

Music, Science, & Natural Magic in Seventeenth-Century England. Penelope Gouk. (Illus.). 352p. 1999. 35.00 (*0-300-07383-6*) Yale U Pr.

***Music Seen, Music Heard: A Picture Book of Musical Design.** Robert Cogan. (Illus.). 127p. 1998. pap. 35.00 (*0-9634500-3-4*) Pubn Contact Intl.

Music since 1945: Issues, Materials, & Literature. Elliott Schwartz & Daniel Godfrey. 544p. 1993. 38.00 (*0-02-873040-2*, Schirmer Books) Mac Lib Ref.

Music since 1900. 6th ed. Slonimsky. 1750p. 2002. 150.00 (*0-02-864787-4*) S&S Trade.

Music since the First World War. Arnold Whittall. (Illus.). 288p. 1995. pap. text 16.95 (*0-19-816533-1*) OUP.

Music Skills for Classroom Teachers. 8th ed. Robert W. Winslow & Leon Dallin. 344p. (C). 1991. text. write for info. (*0-697-10439-7*) Brown & Benchmark.

***Music Skills for Classroom Teachers.** 9th ed. Robert W. Winslow et al. LC 00-42714. 2000. pap. write for info. (*0-07-232465-1*) McGraw.

Music Smart: Ready-to-Use Listening Tapes & Activities for Teaching Music Appreciation. Gwen Hotchkiss. LC 89-25487. 368p. (C). 1990. pap. text 69.95 (*0-13-607714-5*) P-H.

Music, Society & Imagination in Contemporary France. Francois-Bernard Mache. (Contemporary Music Review Ser.). 212p. 1994. pap. text 25.00 (*3-7186-5421-0*, Harwood Acad Pubs) Gordon & Breach.

Music, Society, Education. Christopher Small. LC 96-20010. (Music - Culture Ser.). 248p. 1996. reprint ed. pap. 17.95 (*0-8195-6307-2*, Wesleyan Univ Pr) U Pr of New Eng.

Music, Songs, & Poems. Marilyn LaPenta. Ed. by Susan Evento. (Macmillan Early Skills Program - Conversion Ser.). 64p. (J). (ps-2). 1995. pap. 9.95 (*1-56784-506-1*) Newbridge Educ.

Music, Sound & Sensation: A Modern Exposition. Fritz Winckel. Tr. by Thomas Binkley. (Illus.). 189p. 1967. pap. text 7.95 (*0-486-21764-7*) Dover.

Music, Sound, & Technology. 2nd ed. John M. Eargle. (Electrical Engineering Ser.). 1995. text 54.95 (*0-442-02034-1*, VNR) Wiley.

Music Sound & Technology. 3rd ed. John Eargle. (Electrical Engineering Ser.). 1996. pap. 59.95 (*0-442-02036-8*, VNR) Wiley.

Music Sources: A Collection of Excerpts & Complete Movements. 2nd ed. Mary I. Arlin et al. 592p. (C). 1989. pap. text 50.00 (*0-13-608282-3*) P-H.

Music Speech Audio. William J. Strong & George R. Plitnik. (Illus.). 520p. (Orig.). (C). 1992. pap. text 35.00 (*0-9611938-2-4*) Soundprint.

Music Speed Reading. 2nd ed. David Hickman. 43p. 1981. pap. 9.95 (*0-938170-02-3*) Wimbledon Music.

Music Speed Reading for Beginners. David Hickman. 48p. 1986. pap. 8.95 (*0-938170-07-4*) Wimbledon Music.

Music, Sr. H. S. Jack Rudman. (Teachers License Examination Ser.: T-43). 1994. pap. 27.95 (*0-8373-8043-X*) Nat Learn.

Music Study in Germany. Amy Fay. 1991. pap. 9.95 (*0-486-26562-5*) Dover.

Music Subject Headings Used in Printed Catalog Cards of the Library of Congress. Ed. by Library of Congress Staff. (Library Science Ser.). 1980. lib. bdg. 59.95 (*0-8490-3178-8*) Gordon Pr.

Music Subject Heaings, Compiled from Library of Congress Subject Headings. 2nd ed. Compiled by Harriette Hemmasi & Fred Rowley. LC 98-39597. (Soldier Creek Music Ser.). 1998. pap. 90.00 (*0-936996-76-5*) Soldier Creek.

Music Tablature Analysis. Robben Ford. 16p. 1992. pap., student ed. 15.95 incl. audio (*0-7935-1489-4*) H Leonard.

Music Teacher. Robert Starer. LC 96-29263. 200p. 1997. 23.95 (*0-87951-756-5*, Pub. by Overlook Pr) Penguin Putnam.

***Music Teacher from the Black Lagoon.** Mike Thaler. LC 99-89828. (Illus.). 32p. (J). (gr. 1-4). 2000. pap. 3.25 (*0-439-18873-3*) Scholastic Inc.

Music Teacher's Almanac: Read-to-Use Music Activities for Every Month of the Year. Loretta Mitchell. 256p. (C). 1992. pap. text 27.95 (*0-13-605601-6*) P-H.

Music Teacher's Book of Lists. Cynthia M. Ross & Karen M. Strangl. LC 94-2407. 256p. (C). 1994. spiral bd. 29.95 (*0-13-093832-7*, Parker Publishing Co) P-H.

Music Teacher's Survival Guide: Practical Techniques & Materials for the Elementary Music Teacher. Rosalie A. Haritun. LC 93-43240. 448p. (C). 1994. pap. text 27.95 (*0-13-121302-4*, Parker Publishing Co) P-H.

Music Techniques in Therapy, Counseling & Special Education. Jayne Standley. LC 91-30003. 240p. (Orig.). 1991. pap. 18.95 (*0-918812-64-X*, ST230) MMB Music.

Music Technology Reference Book. Peter Buick & Vic Lennard. (Illus.). 160p. 1995. pap. 15.95 (*1-870775-34-1*, Pub. by PC Pubg) Cimino Pub Grp.

Music That Changed Our Lives: An In-Depth Look. Wolf Marshall. (Guitar Presents Ser.). 1999. pap. 14.95 (*1-57560-222-9*) Cherry Lane.

Music, the Arts, & Ideas. Leonard B. Meyer. LC 67-25515. 1993. pap. text 12.95 (*0-226-52141-9*, P336) U Ch Pr.

Music, the Arts, & Ideas: Patterns & Predictions in Twentieth-Century Culture. Leonard B. Meyer. LC 93-45855. xii, 354p. 1994. pap. text 20.00 (*0-226-52143-5*) U Ch Pr.

Music, The Brain, And Ecstasy: How Music Captures Our Imagination. Robert Jourdain. 400p. 1998. pap. 13.50 (*0-380-78209-X*, Avon Bks) Morrow Avon.

Music, the Hidden Talent. Richard L. Carper. (Illus.). 126p. (Orig.). (C). 1988. pap. 8.95 (*0-9620443-0-X*) Minimax Pub.

Music Theory. (Four Bass Superchops Ser.). 1992. pap. 14.95 incl. audio compact disk (*0-7935-1030-9*, 00660305) H Leonard.

Music Theory. (Four Bass Superchops Ser.). 1992. pap. 12.95 incl. audio (*0-7935-1029-5*, 00660304) H Leonard.

Music Theory. George T. Jones. (HarperCollins College Outline Ser.). (Illus.). 288p. (Orig.). 1994. pap. 16.00 (*0-06-467168-2*, Harper Ref) HarpC.

Music Theory. Jack Rudman. (Advanced Placement Test (AP) Ser.: Vol. AP-15). 1997. pap. 23.95 (*0-8373-6215-6*) Nat Learn.

Music Theory: Problems & Practices in the Middle Ages & Renaissance. Lloyd Ultan. LC 77-75597. 283p. 1977. reprint ed. pap. 87.80 (*0-608-00842-7*, 206163300010) Bks Demand.

Music Theory & Arranging Techniques for Folk Harps. Sylvia Woods. 112p. 1987. 16.95 (*0-936661-02-X*) Woods Mus Bks.

Music Theory & Composition Step by Step. Joseph A. Tomei. 129p. (Orig.). 1991. pap. text 14.95 (*0-9629973-0-7*) J A Tomei.

Music Theory & Its Sources: Antiquity & the Middle Ages. Ed. by Andre Barbera. LC 89-40390. (Conferences in Medieval Studies: Vol. 1). (C). 1990. text 57.50 (*0-268-01379-9*) U of Notre Dame Pr.

Music Theory & the Exploration of the Past. Ed. by Christopher Hatch & David W. Bernstein. LC 92-46985. (Illus.). 576p. 1993. pap. text 27.00 (*0-226-31902-4*) U Ch Pr.

Music Theory & the Exploration of the Past. Ed. by Christopher Hatch & David W. Bernstein. LC 92-46985. (Illus.). 576p. 1997. lib. bdg. 65.00 (*0-226-31901-6*) U Ch Pr.

Music Theory for Beginners. Emma Danes. (Music Bks.). (Illus.). 48p. (J). (gr. 1 up). 1997. text 7.95 (*0-7460-2416-9*, Usborne); lib. bdg. 15.95 (*0-88110-902-9*, Usborne) EDC.

Music Theory for Guitar: With Tablature. M. Wolfsohn. 32p. 1992. pap. 7.95 (*0-7935-0989-0*, 00699329) H Leonard.

Music Theory for Non-Music Majors. Peter A. Spencer. LC 95-24023. 280p. (C). 1995. pap. text 52.00 (*0-13-192501-6*) P-H.

***Music Theory for Non-Music Majors.** 2nd ed. Peter Spencer. LC 00-25558. 304p. 2000. pap. 42.67 (*0-13-026264-1*) P-H.

Music Theory for the Contemporary Guitarist Vol. 1: Note Reading Made Exciting. Mike DiGiacomo. (C). 1989. pap. text 4.95 (*1-880462-11-7*); pap. text 10.95 incl. audio (*0-685-50700-9*) Mad Music.

Music Theory for the Music Professional. Richard Sorce. 114p. 1995. pap. text, teacher ed. write for info. (*1-880157-24-1*) Ardsley.

Music Theory for the Music Professional: A Comparison of Common-Practice & Popular Genres. Richard Sorce. (C). 1995. text 47.95 (*1-880157-20-9*) Ardsley.

Music Theory for the Rock Guitarist. pap. 7.95 (*0-7935-3382-1*, 00696545); pap. 7.95 (*0-7935-3383-X*, 00696546) H Leonard.

Music Theory for the Rock Guitarist. Ben Bolt. 40p. 1996. 9.95 incl. audio compact disk (*0-7866-2720-4*, 94525BCD) Mel Bay.

Music Theory from Zarlino to Schenker: A Bibliography & Guide. David Damschroder & David R. Williams. LC 90-6952. (Harmonologia Ser.: No. 4). 550p. 1991. lib. bdg. 84.00 (*0-918728-99-1*) Pendragon NY.

Music Theory Grade One. Andrew Scott. (Progressive Ser.). (Illus.). 1997. pap. text 16.95 (*0-947183-11-6*) Koala Pubns.

Music Theory Grade Two. Andrew Scott. 1997. pap. 16.95 (*0-947183-30-2*) Koala Pubns.

Music Theory Handbook. Marjorie Merryman. LC 96-76368. 272p. (C). 1996. pap. text 18.00 (*0-15-502662-3*, Pub. by Harcourt Coll Pubs) Harcourt.

Music Theory in Concept & Practice. Ed. by James M. Baker et al. LC 96-53956. (Eastman Studies in Music: Vol. 8). 544p. 1997. 130.00 (*1-878822-79-9*) Univ Rochester Pr.

Music Theory in Practice, Bk. 1. Carmela Mercuri. 32p. 1984. pap. 5.95 (*0-935474-01-3*) Carousel Pubns Ltd.

Music Theory in the Age of Romanticism. Ed. by Ian D. Bent. 255p. (C). 1996. text 64.95 (*0-521-55102-1*) Cambridge U Pr.

***Music Theory in the Real World - A Practical Guide - Todays Music.** Michael Perlowin. 48p. 2000. pap. 9.95 (*0-7866-4526-1*, 98207) Mel Bay.

Music Theory Made Easy. Kelly Dean. (Illus.). 96p. 1998. per. 12.95 (*0-7935-4254-5*, 00841002) H Leonard.

Music Theory Made Easy. 2nd ed. David Harp. (Illus.). 80p. 1995. pap. 12.95 incl. audio (*0-918321-52-2*, DH10070) Musical I Pr.

Music Theory Made Easy. 2nd rev. ed. David Harp. (Illus.). 80p. 1994. pap. 5.95 (*0-918321-99-9*) Musical I Pr.

Music Theory of Godfrey Winham. Leslie D. Blasius. LC 97-5562. 208p. 1997. text 35.00 (*0-691-01227-X*, Pub. by Princeton U Pr) Cal Prin Full Svc.

M

An Asterisk (*) at the beginning of an entry indicates that the title is appearing for the first time.

*Music Theory Resource Book. Harold Owen. LC 99-21158. (Illus.). 272p. (C). 2000. spiral bd. 35.00 (0-19-511539-2) OUP.

Music Theory, Scales & Chords for the Percussion Drum Student: Recommended for All Students & All Instruments. Phil Zampino. (Illus.). 130p. (YA). (gr. 4 up). 1998. spiral bd. 19.95 (0-942253-10-8) PAZ Pub.

Music Theory Workbook. Bruce Pearson. (Standard of Excellence Ser.: Bk. 3). 1996. wbk. ed. 6.45 (0-8497-0517-7, L23) Kjos.

Music Theory Workbook for Guitar: Intervals & Chords, Vol. 1: Intervals & Chords. Bruce Arnold. (Illus.). 194p. 1997. pap. 31.50 (0-9648632-4-3) Muse Eek.

Music Theory Workbook for Guitar Vol. 2: Scale Construction & Application. Bruce Arnold. (Illus.). 215p. 1999. pap., wbk. ed. 31.50 (0-9648632-5-1) Muse Eek.

Music Therapy: An Introduction. Jacqueline S. Peters. 186p. 1987. pap. 25.95 (0-398-06321-4) C C Thomas.

Music Therapy: An Introduction. Jacqueline S. Peters. 186p. (C). 1987. text 37.95 (0-398-05284-0) C C Thomas.

*Music Therapy: An Introduction. 2nd ed. Jacqueline Schmidt Peters. LC 99-88599. 2000. pap. write for info. (0-398-07043-1) C C Thomas.

Music Therapy: An Introduction, Including Music in Special Education. 2nd ed. Donald E. Michel. (Illus.). 152p. (C). 1985. 29.95 (0-398-05063-5) C C Thomas.

M

Music Therapy: Art Beyond Words. Leslie Bundt. 224p. (C). 1994. pap. 27.99 (0-415-08703-1) Routledge.

Music Therapy: Group Vignettes. Ronald Borczon. LC 99-163039. 200p. (C). 1997. pap. text 24.00 (0-9624080-9-3) Barcelona Pubs.

Music Therapy: Improvisation, Communication & Culture. Even Ruud. LC 99-163042. 204p. (C). 1998. pap. text 26.00 (1-891278-04-5) Barcelona Pubs.

*Music Therapy & Medicine: Theoretical & Clinical Approaches. Ed. by Cheryl Dileo. 1999. write for info. (1-884914-00-4) Amer Music Therapy.

Music Therapy & Music Education of the Handicapped - Developments & Limitations in Practice & Research: Proceedings of the Fifth International Congress, Leeuwenhorst Congress Center, Noordwijkerhout, The Netherlands, August 23-27, 1989. Ed. by Rosalie R. Pratt. LC 92-12557. 190p. 1993. 14.95 (0-918812-73-9) MMB Music.

Music Therapy & Music in Special Education Vol. 1: The International State of the Art. Ed. by Barbara Hesser. (ISME Edition Ser.: No. 3). 192p. (Orig.). 1989. pap. 11.95 (0-918812-61-5, ST 189) MMB Music.

Music Therapy & Music in Special Education Vol. 2: The International State of the Art. Pref. by Rosalie R. Pratt. (ISME Edition Ser.: No. 4). 176p. 1989. pap. 11.95 (0-918812-62-3, ST 191) MMB Music.

Music Therapy & the Dementias: Improving the Quality of Life. Ruth Bright. (Horizon Ser.: No. 4). 80p. (Orig.). (C). 1988. pap. 9.75 (0-918812-56-9, ST 178) MMB Music.

Music Therapy Clinical Training Manual. Robert M. Krout. 84p. (Orig.). (C). 1988. pap. 12.00 (0-918812-52-6, ST 003) MMB Music.

Music Therapy for Living: The Principle of Normalization Embodied in Music Therapy. Edith H. Boxill. (Horizon Ser.: Vol. 6). 100p. (Orig.). 1989. pap. 10.50 (0-918812-54-2, ST 179) MMB Music.

Music Therapy for Non-Musicians. Ted Andrews. Ed. by Pagan Alexander-Harding. (Beginnings, a Dragonhawk Ser.). (Illus.). 324p. 1996. pap. 9.95 (1-888767-31-6) Dragonhawk Pubg.

Music Therapy for the Autistic Child. 2nd ed. Juliette Alvin & Auriel Warwick. (Illus.). 164p. 1992. pap. text 22.00 (0-19-816276-6) OUP.

Music Therapy for the Developmentally Disabled. Edith H. Boxill. LC 84-15752. (Illus.). 270p. 1985. text 36.00 (0-89079-190-2, 2054) PRO-ED.

Music Therapy in Context: Music, Meaning & Relationship. Mercedes Pavlicevic. LC 97-202351. 224p. 1997. pap. 26.95 (1-85302-434-1, Pub. by Jessica Kingsley) Taylor & Francis.

Music Therapy in Health & Education. Ed. by Margaret Heal & Tony Wigram. 304p. 1993. pap. write for info. (1-85302-175-X, Pub. by Jessica Kingsley) Taylor & Francis.

Music Therapy in Palliative Care: New Voices. David Aldridge. LC 98-45893. 1999. pap. text 26.95 (1-85302-739-1) Taylor & Francis.

Music Therapy in Palliative Hospice Care. Susan Munro. 112p. (Orig.). (C). 1984. pap. 12.95 (0-918812-37-2) MMB Music.

Music Therapy in Special Education. 2nd rev. ed. Paul Nordoff & Clive Robbins. (Illus.). 272p. 1983. pap. 17.50 (0-918812-22-4, ST 035) MMB Music.

Music Therapy in Special Education: Developing & Maintaining Social Skills Necessary for Mainstreaming. Robert M. Krout. (MMB Horizon Ser.: No. 3). 27p. 1986. pap. 7.75 (0-918812-48-8, ST 029) MMB Music.

Music Therapy in the Treatment of Adults with Mental Disorders. Ed. by Robert F. Unkefer. 225p. 1990. 45.00 (0-02-873032-1, Schirmer Books) Mac Lib Ref.

Music Therapy Intimate Notes. Mercedes Pavlicevic. LC 98-45894. 1999. 24.95 (1-85302-692-1) Taylor & Francis.

Music Therapy, Remedial Music Making & Musical Activities for People with a Developmental Disability. F. W. Schalkwijk. LC 93-44007. 160p. 1993. pap. 24.95 (1-85302-226-8) Taylor & Francis.

Music Therapy Research: Quantitative & Qualitative Perspectives. Ed. by Barbara L. Wheeler. 616p. (C). 1995. pap. text 45.00 (0-9624080-3-4) Barcelona Pubs.

Music Therapy Research & Practice in Medicine: From Out of the Silence. David Aldridge. 352p. 1996. pap. text 32.95 (1-85302-296-9, Pub. by Jessica Kingsley) Taylor & Francis.

Music Therapy Sourcebook: A Collection of Activities Categorized & Analyzed. Cecilia Schulberg. LC 80-12945. 296p. 1981. pap. 22.95 (0-89885-281-1, Kluwer Acad Hman Sci) Kluwer Academic.

*Music Therapy Supervision. Ed. by Michele Forinash. 2001. pap. text. write for info. (1-891278-11-8) Barcelona Pubs.

Music Therapy, Theory & Manual: Contributions to the Knowledge of Nonverbal Contexts. 2nd ed. Rolando O. Benenzon. LC 96-6334. (Illus.). 296p. 1996. text 59.95 (0-398-06611-6); pap. text 44.95 (0-398-06612-4) C C Thomas.

Music Therapy with Children, Vol. 1. David Aldridge. 1999. pap. 27.95 (1-85302-757-X) Jessica Kingsley.

Music Through Children's Literature: Theme & Variations. Donna B. Levene. (Illus.). viii, 117p. (Orig.). 1993. pap. text 22.50 (1-56308-021-4) Teacher Ideas Pr.

*Music Through the Dark: A Tale of Survival in Cambodia. Bree Lafreniere. LC 99-53430. (Intersections Ser.). 176p. 2000. pap. 17.95 (0-8248-2266-8); text 36.00 (0-8248-2227-7) UH Pr.

Music Through the Eyes of Faith. Harold Best. LC 92-53911. 240p. 1993. pap. 15.00 (0-06-060862-5, Pub. by Harper SF) HarpC.

Music, Time, Any Time! Andrew Clements. (Allegra's Window 8 by 8s Ser.). (Illus.). (J). (ps-1). 1997. pap. 3.25 (0-614-29073-2) Aladdin.

Music to Me: Songs by Bill Staines. 104p. 1994. otabind 16.95 (0-7935-2343-5, 00699387) H Leonard.

Music to My Ears: The Billboard Essays. Timothy White. 384p. 1997. pap. text 14.95 (0-8050-5596-7) H Holt & Co.

Music Translation Dictionary: An English, Czech, Danish, Dutch, French, German, Hungarian, Italian, Polish, Portuguese, Russian, Spanish, Swedish Vocabulary of Music. Compiled by Carolyn D. Grigg. LC 78-60526. (CZE, DAN, DUT, ENG & FRE.). 336p. 1978. lib. bdg. 75.00 (0-313-20559-0, GMT/) Greenwood.

Music Tree, 3 pts. Frances Clark & Louise Goss. 1993. write for info. (0-318-55882-3) Summy-Birchard.

Music Tree, Pt. C. Frances Clark & Louise Goss. 1973. 9.95 (0-87487-123-9) Summy-Birchard.

Music Tree, Pt. C. Frances Clark & Louise Goss. 56p. 1995. pap. text, wbk. ed. 7.95 (0-87487-952-3) Summy-Birchard.

Music Tree, Pt. C. rev. ed. Frances Clark & Louise Goss. 72p. 1994. pap. text 7.95 (0-87487-688-5) Summy-Birchard.

Music Tree, Pt. A. Frances Clark & Louise Goss. 1973. 9.95 (0-87487-121-2) Summy-Birchard.

Music Tree, Pt. A. rev. ed. Frances Clark & Louise Goss. 64p. 1993. pap. text 7.95 (0-87487-686-9) Summy-Birchard.

Music Tree, Pt. B. Frances Clark & Louise Goss. 1973. 9.95 (0-87487-122-0) Summy-Birchard.

Music Tree, Pt. B. rev. ed. Frances Clark & Louise Goss. 64p. 1993. pap. text 7.95 (0-87487-687-7) Summy-Birchard.

Music Tree: A Handbook for Teachers, A, B, C. Contrib. by Frances Clark & Louise Goss. 72p. 1996. pap. text 4.95 (0-87487-955-8) Summy-Birchard.

Music Tree: Workbook, Pt. A. Frances Clark & Louise Goss. 64p. 1993. pap. text 7.95 (0-87487-950-7) Summy-Birchard.

Music Tree B Workbook. Frances Clark & Louise Goss. 64p. 1994. pap. text 7.95 (0-87487-951-5) Summy-Birchard.

Music Tree Time to Begin. rev. ed. Frances Clark & Louise Goss. 72p. 1993. reprint ed. pap. text 7.95 (0-87487-685-0) Summy-Birchard.

Music U. S. A. Prod. by Zobeida Perez. 16p. (Orig.). (YA). 1994. pap. 17.00 (0-89898-790-3, BMR05078) Wrner Bros.

Music U. S. A. America's Country & Western Tradition. Charles T. Brown. 1986. 14.95 (0-13-608167-3) P-H.

Music U. S. A., 1988, rev. ed. Ed. by Paul Bjorneberg. 28p. 1988. pap. 40.00 (0-918196-13-2) American Music.

Music U. S. A., 1985. Ed. by Paul Bjorneberg & Betty Stearns. (Illus.). 1985. pap. text 35.00 (0-918196-10-8) American Music.

Music U. S. A., 1989. rev. ed. Paul Bjorneberg. 28p. 1989. pap. 40.00 (0-918196-15-9) American Music.

Music U. S. A., 1987. rev. ed. Paul Bjorneberg & Betty Stearns. (Illus.). 24p. 1987. pap. text 35.00 (0-918196-12-4) American Music.

Music U. S. A., 1986. rev. ed. Paul Bjorneberg & Betty Stearns. (Illus.). 20p. 1986. pap. text 35.00 (0-918196-11-6) American Music.

Music U. S. A., 1998: Statistical Review of the Music Products Industry. Ed. by John Maher. (Illus.). 72p. 1998. pap. text 45.00 (0-9641677-4-3) Natl Music Merchants.

Music U. S. A., 1995: Statistical Review of the Music Products Industry. Ed. by Jerry Derloshon. (Illus.). 68p. (Orig.). 1995. pap. text 20.00 (0-9641677-1-9) Natl Music Merchants.

Music U. S. A., 1994: Statistical Review of the Music Products Industry. 48p. 1994. pap. text 20.00 (0-9641677-0-0) Natl Music Merchants.

*Music U. S. A., 1999: Statistical Review of the Music Products Industry. Ed. by John Maher. (Illus.). 48p. 1999. pap. text 45.00 (0-9641677-5-1) Natl Music Merchants.

Music U. S. A., 1991. rev. ed. Paul Bjorneberg. 32p. 1991. pap. write for info. (0-918196-18-3) American Music.

Music U. S. A., 1996: Statistical Review of the Music Products Industry. Ed. by Jerry Derloshon. 68p. 1996. pap. 20.00 (0-9641677-2-7) Natl Music Merchants.

Music under the Soviets: The Agony of an Art, No. 11--11. Andrey Olkhovsky. LC 74-20341. (Studies of the Research Program of the U. S. S. R.: No. 11). 427p. 1975. reprint ed. lib. bdg. 72.50 (0-8371-7856-8, OLMS, Greenwood Pr) Greenwood.

Music Universe, Music Mind: Revisiting the Creative Music Studio, Woodstock, New York. Robert E. Sweet. LC 96-83108. (Illus.). 280p. (Orig.). 1996. pap. 14.95 (0-9650438-4-3) Arborvlle Pubng.

Music Unlimited! The Performer's Guide to New Audiences. Isabel Farrell & Kenton Mann. LC 94-2405. (Performing Arts Studies: Vol. 1). 61p. 1994. text 30.00 (3-7186-5525-X); pap. text 15.00 (3-7186-5526-8) Gordon & Breach.

*Music USA 2000: Statistical Review of the Music Products Industry. Ed. by John Maher. (Illus.). 48p. 2000. pap. text 45.00 (0-9641677-6-X) Natl Music Merchants.

Music, Value, & the Passions. Aaron Ridley. LC 98-29695. (Illus.). 216p. 1995. text 29.95 (0-8014-3035-6) Cornell U Pr.

Music Videodiscs: An Annotated Guide. Richard M. Jacobs & Edward Schwartz. 160p. (C). 1991. text. write for info. (0-697-13996-4) Brown & Benchmark.

*Music Violence. LC 98-159881. (S. Hrg. Ser.). iii, 86 p. 1998. write for info. (0-16-056324-0) USGPO.

Music Was Our Passport. Greta Milius. Ed. & Pref. by Lydia Thayer. LC 96-85964. (Illus.). (Orig.). 1996. pap. 12.95 (0-9603832-8-X) Anthony Pub Co.

Music We Dance To: Poems. Rebecca Seiferle. LC 99-41100. 112p. 1999. pap. 13.95 (1-878818-76-7, Pub. by Sheep Meadow) U Pr of New Eng.

Music Western World. 2nd ed. Weiss. 400p. 1999. 27.00 (0-02-864746-7) Macmillan.

Music Window (Musica Cercana) Antonio Buero-Vallejo. Ed. by Martha T. Halsey. Tr. by Marion P. Holt from SPA. LC 93-74274. (Contemporary Spanish Plays Ser.: Vol. 5). xiv, 66p. 1994. pap. 6.00 (0-9631212-4-3) Estreno.

Music with Words: A Composer's View. Virgil Thomson. LC 89-30709. 112p. (C). 1989. 27.00 (0-300-04505-0) Yale U Pr.

Music Within You. 2nd ed. Shelley Katsh & Carol Merle-Fishman. LC 99-174718. 268p. (C). 1985. pap. text 28.00 (1-891278-02-9) Barcelona Pubs.

Music Word Search Puzzles. Vicki T. Purslow. 56p. 1999. pap. 7.95 (1-893438-02-3) Lighthse Pubg.

Music! Words! Opera!, 4 vols., Level 1. Sandra Purrington et al. LC 90-19274. (Illus.). 264p. (J). (gr. k-2). 1990. teacher ed. 65.00 (0-918812-65-8, SE0694) MMB Music.

Music! Words! Opera!, 4 vols., Level 2. Clifford Brooks et al. LC 91-45210. (Illus.). 460p. (J). (gr. 3-5). 1991. teacher ed. 82.50 (0-918812-66-6, SE 0706) MMB Music.

Music! Words! Opera!, 3 vols., Set, Level 1. Sandra Purrington et al. LC 90-19274. (Illus.). 264p. (J). (gr. k-2). 1990. student ed. 3.50 (0-918812-67-4, SE0695-SE0697) MMB Music.

Music! Words! Opera!, 3 vols., Set, Level 2. Clifford Brooks et al. LC 91-45210. (Illus.). (J). (gr. 3-5). 1991. student ed. 4.95 (0-918812-68-2, SE 0707, SE 0708, SE 0709) MMB Music.

Music Workbook, Bk. 1A. (Frances Clark Library for Piano Students). 63p. 1957. pap. text 7.95 (0-87487-180-8) Summy-Birchard.

Music Workbook, Bk. 1B. (Frances Clark Library for Piano Students). 63p. 1957. pap. text 7.95 (0-87487-181-6) Summy-Birchard.

Music Workbook, Bk. 2. (Frances Clark Library for Piano Students). 64p. 1957. pap. text 7.95 (0-87487-182-4) Summy-Birchard.

Music Workbook, Bk. 3. (Frances Clark Library for Piano Students). 63p. 1958. pap. text 7.95 (0-87487-183-2) Summy-Birchard.

*Music Works: A Professional Notebook for Music Therapists. 3rd ed. Dellinda J. Henry et al. 165p. 1999. ring bd. 35.00 (0-9617272-5-X) Music Works.

Music Works: Funstation, 5 vols. (J). (gr. 3-7). 1998. 17.95 (1-57145-347-4, Silver Dolph) Advantage Pubs.

Music World of Stamps. Marshall J. Whitehead. (Illus.). 115p. (Orig.). 1975. pap. 6.00 (0-614-25045-5) Am Topical Assn.

Music Writing Book. (Illus.). 48p. 1963. pap. 6.95 (0-8256-2118-6, AM40494) Music Sales.

Music Yearbook, 1994. Joel Whitburn. 240p. 1995. pap. 19.95 (0-7935-5039-4, 00330157) H Leonard.

Music, Youth & Opportunity: A Survey of Settlement & Community Schools. Janet Schenck. 113p. 1986. 26.00 (0-318-21720-1) NGCSA.

Music (Zoran) The Graphic Work, 1947-81. Rolf Schmucking. (GER., Illus.). 242p. 1986. 300.00 (1-55660-228-6) A Wofsy Fine Arts.

*Musica! Salsa, Rhumba, Merengue & More. Sue Steward. LC 99-10083. (Illus.). 176p. 1999. pap. 22.95 (0-8118-2566-3) Chronicle Bks.

Musica: The First Guide to Classical Music on U. S. & Canadian Radio Stations. Ed. by Ben Jacobs. LC 76-18472. 1978. pap. 5.45 (0-9600964-3-4) Musica.

Musica Andaluza Medieval en las Canciones de Trovadores, Troveros, 3 vols. in 1. Julian Ribera Y Tarrago. LC 71-178588. reprint ed. 57.50 (0-404-56665-0) AMS Pr.

Musica Asiatica, No. 4. Ed. by Laurence Picken. 280p. 1984. pap. text 80.00 (0-521-27837-6) Cambridge U Pr.

Musica Asiatica, No. 6. Ed. by Allan Marett. (Illus.). 144p. (C). 1991. text 69.95 (0-521-39050-8) Cambridge U Pr.

Musica, Ballo e Drammatica Alla Corte Medicea dal 1600 al 1637. Angelo Solerti. LC 67-12470. (ITA.). 1972. reprint ed. 42.95 (0-405-08987-2) Ayer.

Musica Baltica: Interregionale Musikkulturelle Beziehungen im Ostseeraum. Ed. by Ekkehard Ochs et al. (Greifswalder Beitrage zur Musikwissenschaft Ser.: Bd. 4). (GER., Illus.). 322p. 1996. 57.95 (3-631-30480-3) P Lang Pubng.

Musica Brasileira: Bilingual Edition. Claus Schreiner. Tr. by Mark Weinstein from GER. LC 92-19894. 368p. 1993. 35.00 (0-7145-2946-X) M Boyars Pubs.

Musica Celestis: String Orchestra Score. A. Kernis. 16p. 1994. pap. 10.95 (0-7935-3868-8, 50482276) H Leonard.

Musica Cercana. Antonio B. Vallejo. (Nueva Austral Ser.: No. 132). (SPA.). 1991. pap. text 24.95 (84-239-1932-3) Elliots Bks.

*Musica Clasica Para Toda Ocasion Series, Binder I. Orig. Title: In Classical Mood. (SPA., Illus.). 2000. ring bd. write for info. (1-892207-54-0) Intl Masters Pub.

*Musica Clasica Para Toda Ocasion Series, Binder II. Orig. Title: In Classical Mood. (SPA., Illus.). 2000. ring bd. write for info. (1-892207-55-9) Intl Masters Pub.

Musica Cubana del Areyto a la Neuva Trova. 3rd ed. Cristobal D. Ayala. LC 81-23127. (Coleccion Arte). (Illus.). 416p. 1993. pap. 29.00 (0-89729-703-2) Ediciones.

Musica Cubana para Piano: Cuarenta Danzas y Una Contradanza. Rene Touzet. LC 90-80578. (Coleccion Arte). (ENG & SPA.). 172p. (Orig.). 1990. pap. 19.95 (0-89729-564-1) Ediciones.

Musica de Guatemala en el Siglo XVIII: Music from Eighteenth Century Guatemala. Alfred E. Lemmon. LC 85-63627. (ENG & SPA., Illus.). 174p. (Orig.). 1986. pap. 14.00 (0-910443-03-3) Plumsock Meso Studies.

Musica de la Raza: Mexican & Chicano Music in Minnesota. Maya Lopez-Santamaria. LC 98-43709. (Minnesota Musical Traditions Ser.). (Illus.). 76p. 1999. pap. 16.95 incl. audio compact disk (0-87351-366-5, 366-5, Borealis Book) Minn Hist.

Musica de los Viejitos. Jack Loeffler et al. (SPA., Illus.). 192p. 1999. 49.95 (0-8263-2168-2) U of NM Pr.

*Musica de los Viejitos: Hispano Folk Music of the Rio Grande del Norte. Jack Loeffler et al. 192p. 1999. pap. 19.95 (0-8263-1884-3) U of NM Pr.

Musica Duorum, Vol. 6. Romano Eustachio. (Monuments of Renaissance Music Ser.). 200p. 1975. lib. bdg. 120.00 (0-226-22646-8) U Ch Pr.

Musica, 1855, 1857-1859. Ed. by H. Robert Cohen. (Repertoire International de la Presse Musicale Ser.). (ITA.). 282p. 1989. 120.00 (0-8357-0873-X); 120.00 (0-8357-0872-1) Univ Microfilms.

Musica en el Caribe, Vol. 1. Carlos Cabrer et al. (SPA.). 145p. 1990. pap. 5.00 (0-8477-2505-7) U of PR Pr.

*Musica en la Noche. V. C. Andrews. 1999. 24.95 (84-08-02872-3) Planeta Edit.

Musica en Puerto Rico. Munoz. 1966. 12.95 (0-87751-012-1) E Torres & Sons.

Musica Enchiriadis: And Scolica Enchiriadis. Ed. by Claude V. Palisca. Tr. & Intro. by Raymond Erickson. LC 94-34601. (Music Theory Translation Ser.). 106p. 1995. 35.00 (0-300-05818-7) Yale U Pr.

Musica Ficta: Figures of Wagner. Phillippe L. Labarthe. Tr. by Felicia McCarren. LC 94-15594. xxvi, 161p. 1995. pap. 13.95 (0-8047-2385-0) Stanford U Pr.

Musica Ficta: Figures of Wagner. Philippe Lacoue-Labarthe. LC 94-15594. xxvi, 161p. 1995. 35.00 (0-8047-2376-1) Stanford U Pr.

Musica Folklorica de Puerto Rico. Lopez Cruz. 1967. 19.95 (0-87751-008-3) E Torres & Sons.

Musica Franca: Essays in Honor of Frank A. D'Accone. Frank A. D'Accone et al. LC 96-21129. (Festschrift Ser.). 1996. 54.00 (0-945193-92-0) Pendragon NY.

Musica Getutscht, 1511. Sebastian Virdung. Ed. by Robert Eitner. (Publikation Alterer Praktischer und Theoretischer Musikwerke, XV. & XVI. Jhs. Ser.: Vol. 11). (GER.). 1966. reprint ed. lib. bdg. 75.00 (0-8450-1711-X) Broude.

Musica Ilustrada Hispano-Americana 1898-1902. Ed. by H. Robert Cohen. (Repertoire International de la Presse Musicale Ser.). (SPA.). 286p. 1997. lib. bdg. 145.00 (0-608-06502-1) UMI.

Musica Instrumentalis Deutsch 1528 und 1545, Erste und Vierte. Martin Agricola. Ed. by Robert Eitner. (Publikation alterer praktischer und theoretischer Musikwerke Ser.: Vol. 20). (GER., Illus.). 1966. reprint ed. lib. bdg. 55.00 (0-8450-1720-9) Broude.

Musica Nova: Accommodata per Cantar et Sonar Sopra Organi et Altri Strumenti, Composta per Diversi Eccellentissimi Musici. Harry C. Slim. LC 64-12258. (Monuments of Renaissance Music Ser.: No. 1). 169p. reprint ed. pap. 52.40 (0-608-09532-X, 205433400005) Bks Demand.

*Musica Para Noches de Verano. (Musica Clasica Para Toda Ocasion Ser.: Vol. 1).Tr. of Music for Summer Nights. (SPA., Illus.). 30p. 2000. write for info. (1-892207-56-7) Intl Masters Pub.

Musica para Ocasiones Especiales: Music for Special Occasions. Ed. by Salom Mussiett. (SPA.). 48p. (Orig.). 1993. pap. 4.50 (0-311-32219-0) Casa Bautista.

Musica para Todo el Mundo! Vera B. Williams. (J). 1995. 11.15 (0-606-07901-7, Pub. by Turtleback) Demco.

Musica para Todo el Mundo! Music, Music for Everyone. Vera B. Williams. Tr. by Aida E. Marcuse from ENG. LC 83-14196. (SPA., Illus.). 32p. (J). (gr. k-3). 1995. pap. 5.95 (0-688-14021-1, Wm Morrow) Morrow Avon.

Musica Poetica: Musical-Rhetorical Figures in German Baroque Music. Dietrich Bartel. LC 97-2450. (Illus.). xv, 471p. 1997. text 60.00 (0-8032-1276-3) U of Nebr Pr.

An Asterisk (*) at the beginning of an entry indicates that the title is appearing for the first time.

Musica Popular Brasileira. Oneyda Alvarenga. 1976. lib. bdg. 59.95 (*0-8490-2308-4*) Gordon Pr.

Musica "Rock" John Ankerberg & John Weldon. (Hechos Acerca de...Ser.).Tr. of Rock Music. (SPA.). pap. 3.29 (*1-56063-694-7*, 497700) Editorial Unilit.

Musica Scientia: Musical Scholarship in the Italian Renaissance. Ann E. Moyer. LC 91-55057. (Illus.). 336p. 1992. text 49.95 (*0-8014-2426-7*) Cornell U Pr.

Musica Significans Pt. 1, Vol. 2. 4th ed. Ed. by Raymond Monelle. 88p. 1998. pap. text 14.00 (*90-5755-013-X*, Harwood Acad Pubs) Gordon & Breach.

Musica Significans Pt. 3, Vol. 3. Ed. by Raymond Monelle. 71p. 1998. pap. text 22.00 (*90-5755-015-6*, Harwood Acad Pubs) Gordon & Breach.

Musica Significans Pt. 4, Vol. 4. Ed. by Raymond Monelle. 101p. 1998. pap. text 22.00 (*90-5755-017-2*, Harwood Acad Pubs) Gordon & Breach.

Musica Significans Pt. 5, Vol. 5. Ed. by Raymond Monelle. 94p. 1998. pap. text 22.00 (*90-5755-019-9*, Harwood Acad Pubs) Gordon & Breach.

Musica Significans Pt.1, Vol. 1. Ed. by Raymond Monelle. 78p. 1998. pap. text 22.00 (*90-5755-012-1*, Harwood Acad Pubs) Gordon & Breach.

Musica Speculative of Johannes de Muris. Ed. by Susan Fast. (Wissenschaftliche Abhandlungen-Musicological Studies Ser.: No. 61). (ENG & LAT.). lxxx, 352p. 1994. lib. bdg. 124.00 (*0-931902-85-1*) Inst Mediaeval Mus.

Musica Tejana: The Cultural Economy of Artistic Transformation. Manuel Pena. LC 98-47951. (University of Houston Series in Mexican American Studies: Vol. 1). (Illus.). 224p. 1999. 27.95 (*0-89096-877-2*); pap. 15.95 (*0-89096-888-8*) Tex A&M Univ Pr.

Musica Theorica. fac. ed. Lodovico Fogliani. (Monuments of Music & Music Literature in Facsimile Ser., Series II: Vol. 93). 1969. lib. bdg. 50.00 (*0-8450-2293-8*) Broude.

Musica Transalpina. Madrigales Translated 4, 5 & 6 Parts. Nicholas Yonge. LC 77-38232. (English Experience Ser.: No. 496). 346p. 1972. reprint ed. 75.00 (*90-221-0496-6*) Walter J Johnson.

Musica y Arte (Art & Music) (Primera Biblioteca Infantil de Aprendizaje - A Child's First Library of Learning). (SPA., Illus.). 88p. (J). (gr. 1-4). 1996. 16.95 (*0-7835-4009-4*) Time-Life.

Musica y Baile. Silvia P. Baeza. (Vida Latina Ser.).Tr. of Music & Dance. (SPA.). 48p. (J). (gr. 4-8). 1995. lib. bdg. 23.93 (*0-86625-565-6*) Rourke Pubns.

MusiCache: An Index to the Microfiche Collection. Ed. by Mary E. Morrison. iv, 216p. reprint ed. 40.00 (*0-8357-0927-2*) Univ Microfilms.

Musicae Compendium. fac. ed. Rene Descartes. (Monuments of Music & Music Literature in Facsimile Ser., Series II: Vol. 87). 1968. lib. bdg. 32.50 (*0-8450-2287-3*) Broude.

Musicage: Cage Muses on Words * Art * Music. John Cage. LC 95-9497. (Illus.). 408p. 1996. pap. 22.95 (*0-8195-6311-0*, Wesleyan Univ Pr); text 40.00 (*0-8195-5285-2*, Wesleyan Univ Pr) U Pr of New Eng.

Musical: A Concise History. Kurt Ganzl. LC 97-3008. 1997. 50.00 (*1-55553-311-6*) NE U Pr.

Musical! A Grand Tour. Denny M. Flinn. (Orig.). 1997. pap. 40.00 (*0-614-27463-X*, Schirmer Books) Mac Lib Ref.

Musical: A Grand Tour, the Rise, Glory, & Fall of an American Institution. Denny M. Flinn. LC 96-46030. 556p. 1997. 40.00 (*0-02-864610-X*) Macmillan.

Musical: A Look at the American Musical Theatre. expanded rev. ed. Richard Kislan. (Illus.). 324p. 1995. pap. 18.95 (*1-55783-217-X*) Applause Theatre Bk Pubs.

Musical! Where to Find It. Ed. by Clyde Primm. 219p. 1984. pap. 24.95 (*0-918933-00-5*) Magnetic Inds.

Musical! Where to Find It. Ed. by Clyde Primm. 371p. 1985. pap. 29.95 (*0-918933-01-3*) Magnetic Inds.

Musical ABC Book. Illus. by Judith Stuchley. 6p. (J). (ps-k). 1996. vinyl bd. 5.00 (*1-883043-00-X*) Straight Edge.

Musical Ability in Children & Its Measurement. Arnold Bently. 1966. 9.95 (*0-8079-0187-3*) October.

Musical Accompaniment of Moving Pictures. Edith M. Lang & George West. LC 72-124014. (Literature of Cinema, Ser. 1). 1975. reprint ed. 11.95 (*0-405-01620-4*) Ayer.

Musical Acoustics. 2nd ed. Donald E. Hall. LC 90-2374. 475p. (C). 1990. mass mkt. 60.75 (*0-534-13248-0*) Brooks-Cole.

***Musical Acoustics.** 3rd ed. Hall. (Physics Ser.). 2001. 52.00 (*0-534-37728-9*) Brooks-Cole.

Musical Acoustics: An Introduction. Donald E. Hall. 1980. pap. 29.50 (*0-534-00758-9*) Wadsworth Pub.

Musical Acoustics: Selected Reprints. Ed. by Thomas D. Rossing. (Reprint Bks.). (Illus.). 227p. (C). 1988. per. 15.00 (*0-917853-30-X*, RB-51) Am Assn Physics.

Musical Acoustics or the Phenomena of Sound As Connected with Music. John Broadhouse. 425p. 1990. reprint ed. lib. bdg. 89.00 (*0-7812-9126-7*) Rprt Serv.

Musical Acoustics: or The Phenomena of Sound As Connected with Music. John Broadhouse. LC 72-181115. 425p. 1926. reprint ed. 35.00 (*0-403-01630-4*) Scholarly.

Musical Aesthetics: A Historical Reader - The Eighteenth Century, 1 of 3 vols., Vol. I. Ed. by Edward A. Lippmann. LC 85-28415. (Aesthetics in Music Ser.: Vol. 1, No. 4). 430p. 1986. text 73.00 (*0-918728-41-X*) Pendragon NY.

Musical Aesthetics: A Historical Reader - The Nineteenth Century. Ed. by Edward A. Lippmann. LC 85-28415. (Aesthetics in Music Ser.: No. 4, Vol.II). 450p. 1988. lib. bdg. 73.00 (*0-918728-90-8*) Pendragon NY.

Musical Aesthetics: A Historical Reader - The Twentieth Century. Ed. by Edward A. Lippman. LC 85-28415. (Aesthetics in Music Ser.: No. 4, Vol. 3). 350p. 1990. lib. bdg. 73.00 (*0-945193-10-6*) Pendragon NY.

Musical Allusions in the Works of James Joyce: Early Poetry Through "Ulysses" Zack R. Bowen. LC 74-13314. 372p. (C). 1974. text 24.50 (*0-87395-248-0*) State U NY Pr.

Musical Alphabet. Bellerophon Books Staff. (J). (gr. 1-9). 1992. pap. 3.95 (*0-88388-137-3*) Bellerophon Bks.

Musical Amateur: A Book on the Human Side of Music. Robert H. Schauffler. LC 74-167411. (Essay Index Reprint Ser.). 1977. reprint ed. 20.95 (*0-8369-2858-X*) Ayer.

Musical Amateur: A Book on the Human Side of Music. Robert H. Schauffler. 261p. 1990. reprint ed. lib. bdg. 69.00 (*0-7812-9005-8*) Rprt Serv.

Musical America, 1998: International Directory of the Performing Arts. Ed. by Therese Schneider. (Illus.). 912p. 1997. pap. 95.00 (*1-891131-00-1*) Primedia Directories.

Musical America 1999: International Directory of the Performing Arts. Sedgwick Clark. 832p. 1998. pap. 105.00 (*1-891131-01-X*) Primedia Directories.

Musical America, 1997: International Directory of the Performing Arts. Ed. by Therese Schneider. (Illus.). 862p. 1996. pap. text 95.00 (*0-9649630-4-3*) Primedia Directories.

Musical America, 1996: International Directory of the Performing Arts. Ed. by Therese Schneider. (Illus.). 832p. 1995. pap. text 85.00 (*0-9649630-1-9*) Primedia Directories.

***Musical America 2000: International Directory of the Performing Arts.** Ed. by Sedgwick Clark. (Illus.). 840p. 1999. pap. 105.00 (*1-891131-05-2*) Primedia Directories.

Musical Americans: A Biographical Dictionary, 1918-1926. Mary DuPree. LC 97-18294. (Reference Books in Music: Vol. 23). 317p. 1997. 37.95 (*0-914913-13-1*, Fallen Lef Pr) Scarecrow.

Musical Analysis. Henry C. Banister. 81p. 1991. reprint ed. lib. bdg. 59.00 (*0-7812-9362-6*) Rprt Serv.

Musical Anthologies for Analytical Study: A Annotated Bibliography, 48. Compiled by James E. Perone. LC 95-21762. (Music Reference Collection: Vol. 48). 200p. 1995. lib. bdg. 59.95 (*0-313-29595-6*, Greenwood Pr) Greenwood.

Musical Articles from the Encyclopedia Britannica. Donald F. Tovey. 1988. reprint ed. lib. bdg. 49.00 (*0-7812-0186-1*) Rprt Serv.

Musical Articles from the Encyclopedia Britannica. Donald F. Tovey. LC 79-181279. 251p. 1944. reprint ed. 39.00 (*0-403-01702-5*) Scholarly.

Musical Artifacts of Pre-Hispanic West Mexico: Towards an Interdisciplinary Approach. Peter Crossley-Holland. LC 80-50811. (Monograph Series in Ethnomusicology: No. 1). vii, 45p. (Orig.). 1980. pap. text 6.00 (*0-88287-013-0*) UCLA Dept Ethnom.

Musical Arts & Styles. William Fleming & Frank Macomber. 528p. 1990. 59.95 (*0-8130-0961-8*); pap. 29.95 (*0-8130-0990-1*) U Press Fla.

Musical As Social Text. John Shepherd. 1991. pap. 27.95 (*0-7456-0826-4*, Pub. by Polity Pr) Blackwell Pubs.

Musical Ascent of Herman Being: A How-To Novel. 3rd rev. ed. Robert Danziger. LC 95-75889. (Illus.). 112p. (C). 1995. pap. 11.95 (*0-9613427-8-1*) Jordan Pr.

Musical Autobiography. Theodore Thomas. (American Biography Ser.). 378p. 1991. reprint ed. lib. bdg. 79.00 (*0-7812-8383-3*) Rprt Serv.

Musical Autographs: A Comparative Guide, Suppl. 1. J. B. Muns. (Illus.). 1992. pap. 15.00 (*1-881858-01-4*) J B Muns.

Musical Autographs: A Comparative Guide, Suppl. 2. J. B. Muns. (Illus.). 36p. 1994. pap. 15.00 (*1-881858-02-2*) J B Muns.

Musical Autographs: A Comparative Guide see Musical Autographs: A Comparative Guide

Musical Autographs: A Comparative Guide, Suppls. 1-4. Incl. Suppl. 3. Musical Autographs: A Comparative Guide. (Illus.). 40p. 1996. pap. 15.00 (*1-881858-05-7*); (Illus.). 1996. Set pap. 60.00 (*1-881858-03-0*) J B Muns.

Musical Backgrounds for English Literature, 1580-1650. Gretchen L. Finney. LC 75-35024. 292p. 1976. reprint ed. lib. bdg. 65.00 (*0-8371-8572-6*, FIMB, Greenwood Pr) Greenwood.

Musical Basis of Verse. Julia P. Dabney. LC 79-119650. (BCL Ser. I). reprint ed. 22.50 (*0-404-01916-1*) AMS Pr.

Musical Beginnings: Origins & Development of Musical Competence. Ed. by Irene Deliege & John A. Sloboda. (Illus.). 238p. 1996. pap. text 29.95 (*0-19-852332-7*) OUP.

Musical Beliefs: Psychoacoustic, Mythical & Educational Perspectives. Robert Walker, Jr. 272p. (C). 1990. pap. text 22.95 (*0-8077-3007-6*) Tchrs Coll.

Musical Berks & Beyond. Cedric Elmer & Wesley Fisher. 382p. 1995. pap. text 34.95 (*1-887762-00-0*) His Soc Brks Cnty.

Musical Blunders: And Other Musical Curiosities. Fritz Spiegl. LC 97-66448. (Illus.). 1997. 28.95 (*1-86105-075-5*, Robson-Parkwest) Parkwest Pubns.

Musical Blunders: And Other Off-Beat Curiosities. Fritz Spiegl. (Illus.). 236p. 1998. pap. 12.95 (*1-86105-141-7*, Pub. by Robson Bks) Parkwest Pubns.

Musical Blunders & Other Off-beat Curiosities. pap. text. write for info. (*0-7881-9001-6*) DIANE Pub.

Musical Book for Children & Adult. Rebecca Wooley. 1978. write for info. (*0-9601654-1-X*) R S Wooley.

Musical Box. Arthur W. Ord-Hume. LC 94-37334. (Illus.). 336p. 1995. 79.95 (*0-88740-764-1*) Schiffer.

Musical Boxes & Other Musical Marvels. Ed. by Angelo Rulli. (Illus.). 500p. 1991. pap. 15.00 (*0-915000-02-4*) Musical Box Soc.

Musical Careers in the Third Reich: Musicians & Their Music in the Third Reich. Michael H. Kater. LC 96-6339. 344p. 1997. 45.00 (*0-19-509620-7*) OUP.

Musical Century. fac. ed. Henry Carey. (Monuments of Music & Music Literature in Facsimile, I Ser.: Vol. 22). 9p. 1976. lib. bdg. 65.00 (*0-8450-2022-6*) Broude.

Musical Chairs: Childhood Haiku. Alexis K. Rotella. (Illus.). 50p. 1994. pap. text, per. 11.00 (*0-917951-26-3*) Jade Mtn.

Musical Chairs: or Between Two Stools: Music Book Index. Cecil Gray. 324p. 1993. reprint ed. lib. bdg. 89.00 (*0-7812-9638-2*) Rprt Serv.

Musical Charlatan. Johann Kuhnau. Tr. by John Russell from GER. LC 97-10212. (Studies in German Literature, Linguistics & Culture). xviii, 163 p. 1997. 50.00 (*1-57113-142-6*) Camden Hse.

Musical Christmas for Easy Piano. 20p. 1984. pap. 5.95 (*0-7935-6020-9*) H Leonard.

Musical Chronicle, 1917-1923. Paul Rosenfeld. LC 77-175877. 17.00 (*0-685-26463-7*) Ayer.

Musical Classroom: Backgrounds, Models & Skills for Elementary Teaching. 4th ed. Patrica Hackett & Carolynn A. Lindeman. LC 96-39597. 440p. 1997. spiral bd. 62.00 (*0-13-262833-3*) P-H.

***Musical Classroom: Backgrounds, Models & Skills for Elementary Teaching.** 5th ed. Patricia Hackett & Carolynn A. Lindeman. LC 00-41678. 2001. write for info. (*0-13-026262-5*) P-H.

Musical Comedy in America: From the Black Crook Through Sweeney Todd. Cecil Smith & Glenn Litton. LC 80-51638. (Illus.). 367p. (C). 1987. pap. 19.99 (*0-87830-564-5*, Thtre Arts Bks) Routledge.

Musical Comedy Murders of 1940. John Bishop. 1987. pap. 5.25 (*0-8222-0792-3*) Dramatists Play.

Musical Companion. Ed. by A. L. Bachrach & J. R. Pearce. 800p. 1984. pap. 13.95 (*0-15-662321-8*, Harvest Bks) Harcourt.

Musical Composition. Reginald Smith-Brindle. (Illus.). 196p. (C). 1986. pap. text 24.95 (*0-19-317107-4*) OUP.

Musical Composition: A Short Treatise for Students: Music Book Index. Charles V. Stanford. 193p. 1993. reprint ed. lib. bdg. 69.00 (*0-7812-9661-7*) Rprt Serv.

Musical Composition: Projects in Ways & Means. Ellis B. Kohs. LC 79-26990. 248p. 1980. 45.00 (*0-8108-1285-1*) Scarecrow.

Musical Composition in the Twentieth Century. Arnold Whittall. LC 99-49858. (Illus.). 432p. 2000. text 60.00 (*0-19-816684-2*) OUP.

***Musical Composition in the Twentieth Century.** Arnold Whittall. LC 99-49858. (Illus.). 432p. 2000. pap. text 19.95 (*0-19-816683-4*) OUP.

Musical Concepts Level 2. June Montgomery & Martha Mier. (Alfred's Basic Piano Library Ser.). 1996. pap. 7.50 (*0-7390-0003-9*, 14521) Alfred Pub.

Musical Concordance of the Bible. Compiled by Doug Jeffries. 1986. 1.99 (*0-685-68745-7*, MB-570) Lillenas.

***Musical Constructions of Nationalism: Essays on the History & Ideology of European Musical Culture, 1800-1945.** Ed. by Harry White & Michael Murphy. 320p. 2000. 65.00 (*1-85918-153-8*, Pub. by Cork Univ) Stylus Pub VA.

Musical Creativity in Twentieth Century China: Abing, His Music & Its Changing Meaning. LC 96-28056. (Eastman Studies in Music: Vol. 6). (Illus.). 224p. 1997. 90.00 (*1-878822-76-4*) Univ Rochester Pr.

Musical Critic's Holiday. Ernest Newman. 330p. 1990. reprint ed. lib. bdg. 79.00 (*0-7812-9129-1*) Rprt Serv.

Musical Day. Illus. by Paula Martyr. (My First Piano Ser.). (J). 7.98 (*1-57717-112-8*) Todtri Prods.

Musical Design in Aeschylean Theater. William C. Scott. LC 83-40560. 252p. 1984. text 35.00 (*0-87451-291-3*) U Pr of New Eng.

Musical Design in Sophoclean Theater. William C. Scott. LC 95-21611. 352p. 1996. text 45.00 (*0-87451-739-7*) U Pr of New Eng.

Musical Development for the Classroom Teacher. Edward J. Bostley. 368p. (C). 1994. pap. text, spiral bd. 37.95 (*0-8403-9522-1*) Kendall-Hunt.

Musical Development for the Classroom Teacher. 3rd ed. Edward J. Bostley. 240p. (C). 1997. spiral bd. 38.95 (*0-7872-4386-8*) Kendall-Hunt.

Musical Development for the Classroom Teacher. 4th ed. Edward Bostley. 246p. (C). spiral bd. 47.95 (*0-7872-6683-3*) Kendall-Hunt.

Musical Dialogue: Thoughts on Monteverdi, Bach & Mozart. Nikolaus Harnoncourt. Tr. by Mary O'Neill. 220p. 1997. pap. 14.95 (*1-57467-023-9*, Amadeus Pr) Timber.

Musical Dictionary. fac. ed. James Grassineau. (Monuments of Music & Music Literature in Facsimile Ser., Series II: Vol. 40). 1966. lib. bdg. 45.00 (*0-8450-2240-7*) Broude.

Musical Dilettante: A Treatise on Composition by J. F. Daube. Ed. by Susan P. Snook-Luther. (Studies in Music Theory & Analysis: No. 3). 300p. (C). 1992. text 95.00 (*0-521-36564-3*) Cambridge U Pr.

Musical Director: In the Amateur Theatre. William Hoare. (Illus.). 112p. 1994. pap. 15.00 (*0-85343-593-6*, Pub. by J G Miller Ltd) Empire Pub Srvs.

Musical Director in the Amateur Theatre. William Hoare. (Illus.). (Orig.). 1994. pap. 17.00 (*0-85353-593-0*, Pub. by J G Miller Ltd) Empire Pub Srvs.

Musical Discourse, from the New York Times. Richard Aldrich. LC 67-28740. (Essay Index Reprint Ser.). 1977. 20.95 (*0-8369-0144-4*) Ayer.

Musical Discoveries: A Story about Music, History & Friendship, Bk. 1. Julia Fraser. LC 95-6266. (Grammy Musical Discoveries Ser.: Bk. 1). (Illus.). (J). (gr. 6-8). 1995. 6.95 (*0-88284-656-6*, 4707) Alfred Pub.

Musical Ear. L. S. Lloyd. LC 88-31967. 104p. 1990. reprint ed. lib. bdg. 49.50 (*0-313-26666-2*, LLME, Greenwood Pr) Greenwood.

***Musical Edge of Therapeutic Dialogue.** Steven H. Knoblauch. 184p. 2000. 33.50 (*0-88163-297-X*) Analytic Pr.

Musical Elaborations. Edward W. Said. 1991. 32.50 (*0-231-07318-6*) Col U Pr.

Musical Elaborations. Edward W. Said. 1993. pap. 18.00 (*0-231-07319-4*) Col U Pr.

Musical Entertainer, Bickham's Musical Entertainer. fac. ed. George Bickham. (Monuments of Music & Music Literature in Facsimile Ser., Series I: Vol. 6). (Illus.). 1965. lib. bdg. 125.00 (*0-8450-2006-4*) Broude.

Musical Events. Andrew Porter. 1990. 16.95 (*0-671-69656-4*) S&S Trade.

Musical Experience of Composer, Performer, Listener. Roger Sessions. LC 72-160545. 135p. 1971. reprint ed. pap. 41.90 (*0-7837-9289-1*, 206002800004) Bks Demand.

Musical Feast: Recipes from over 100 of the World's Most Famous Musical Artists. Ed. by Wendy Diamond. (Illus.). 113p. 1999. text 22.00 (*0-7881-6014-1*) DIANE Pub.

Musical Feast: Recipes from over 100 of the World's Top Musical Artist: Proceeds Help the Homeless. Wendy Diamond. Ed. by Lori Narlock et al. LC 95-78322. (Illus.). 117p. 1995. 19.95 (*0-9647316-0-6*) Global Liaisons.

Musical Fingers, Bk. 1. Frances Clark et al. (Illus.). 32p. 1983. pap. 4.95 (*0-913277-09-6*) Summy-Birchard.

Musical Fingers, Bk. 2. Frances Clark et al. (Illus.). 40p. 1984. pap. 4.95 (*0-913277-10-X*) Summy-Birchard.

Musical Fingers, Bk. 3. Frances Clark et al. (Illus.). 40p. 1985. pap. 4.95 (*0-913277-11-8*) Summy-Birchard.

Musical Fingers, Bk. 4. Frances Clark et al. (Illus.). 48p. 1986. pap. 5.95 (*0-913277-12-6*) Summy-Birchard.

Musical Form. Hugo Leichtentritt. LC 51-11139. 479p. reprint ed. pap. 148.50 (*0-7837-2292-3*, 205738000004) Bks Demand.

Musical Form. Ebenezer Prout. 257p. 1990. reprint ed. lib. bdg. 69.00 (*0-7812-9147-X*) Rprt Serv.

Musical Form. Ebenezer Prout. LC 78-108526. 1970. reprint ed. 6.50 (*0-403-00327-X*) Scholarly.

Musical Form see Score Reading

Musical Form & Analysis. Glenn Spring & Jere T. Hutcheson. 416p. (C). 1994. text. write for info. (*0-697-15367-3*) Brown & Benchmark.

Musical Form & Musical Performance. Edward T. Cone. LC 68-11157. (Illus.). (C). 1968. pap. text 12.50 (*0-393-09767-6*) Norton.

Musical Form in the Age of Beethoven: Selected Writings on Theory & Method. A. B. Marx. Ed. by Scott Burnham. LC 96-49875. (Studies in Music Theory & Analysis: Vol. 12). 214p. (C). 1998. text 64.95 (*0-521-45274-0*) Cambridge U Pr.

Musical from the Inside Out. Stephen Citron. 336p. 1992. text 27.50 (*0-929587-79-0*) I R Dee.

Musical from the Inside Out. Stephen Citron. LC 97-19905. 312p. 1997. pap. 14.95 (*1-56663-176-9*, Elephant Paperbacks) I R Dee.

Musical Games & Activities to Learn By. Judith N. Henneberger. Ed. by Marjorie R. Hershey. (Illus.). 33p. 1976. reprint ed. pap. text 5.95 (*1-929187-00-9*, CGBK17, Pub. by Choristers) Lorenz Corp.

Musical Games, Fingerplays & Rhythmic Activities for Early Childhood. Marian J. Wirth et al. LC 82-22371. (Illus.). 224p. (C). 1983. pap. text 24.95 (*0-13-607085-X*) P-H.

Musical Gems: Concert Arias by W. A. Mozart & F. Schubert. Ed. & Tr. by Dietrich Erbelding from GER. Tr. by Lisa Kaborycha from GER. (ENG, GER & ITA.). 79p. 1990. spiral bd. 10.95 (*1-58126-967-6*, MG-Bk) Pocket Coach.

Musical Gift: Organ Preludes on Fourteen Familiar Hymn Tunes by Austin C. Lovelace. Composed by Austin C. Lovelace. 32p. 1994. pap., student ed. 8.00 (*1-889079-07-3*) Darcey Pr.

Musical Gift Bk. 2: 20 Organ Preludes on Familiar Hymn Tunes. Composed by Robert J. Powell. 42p. (Orig.). 1996. pap., student ed. 10.00 (*1-889079-08-1*) Darcey Pr.

Musical Gift Bk. 3: 25 Improvisations on Familiar Hymn Tunes for Organ or Piano by Peter J. Hodgson. Composed by Peter J. Hodgson. 62p. 1996. pap., student ed. 12.50 (*1-889079-16-2*) Darcey Pr.

Musical Growth & Development: Birth Through Six. Dorothy C. McDonald & Gene M. Simons. 304p. 1989. 12.00 (*0-02-871347-8*, Schirmer Books) Mac Lib Ref.

Musical Growth in the Elementary School. 6th ed. Bjornar Bergethon et al. LC 96-75034. 448p. (C). 1996. pap. text 51.50 (*0-15-501648-2*, Pub. by Harcourt Coll Pubs) Harcourt.

Musical Guide, Pts. I-III: 1700-1721. Friederich E. Niedt. Ed. & Tr. by Irmgard C. Taylor. Tr. by Pamela L. Poulin. (Early Music Ser.). (Illus.). 312p. 1989. text 98.00 (*0-19-315251-7*) OUP.

Musical Guide to Hungary. Istvan Balazs. 160p. 1999. pap. 21.00 (*963-13-3399-X*, Pub. by Corvina Bks) St Mut.

Musical Guide to Richard Wagner's Ring of the Nibelung. Ernest Hutcheson. LC 76-169462. reprint ed. 32.50 (*0-404-03462-4*) AMS Pr.

***Musical Healing in Cultural Contexts.** Ed. by Penelope Gouk. LC 99-40654. (Illus.). 256p. (C). 2000. text 78.95 (*1-84014-279-0*) Ashgate Pub Co.

Musical Highlights from the White House. Elise K. Kirk. 272p. 1992. 39.50 (*0-89464-664-8*); pap. 32.50 (*0-89464-699-0*) Krieger.

Musical Humanism & Its Legacy: Essays in Honor of Claude V. Palisca. Ed. by Nancy K. Baker & Barbara R. Hanning. LC 91-45586. (Festschrift Ser.: No. 11). (Illus.). 525p. 1992. lib. bdg. 54.00 (*0-945193-29-7*) Pendragon NY.

Musical Iconography: A Manual for Cataloguing Musical Subjects in Western Art Before 1800. Howard Mayer Brown & Joan Lascelle. LC 76-180151. (Illus.). 236p. 1972. 34.95 (*0-674-59220-4*) HUP.

M

An Asterisk (*) at the beginning of an entry indicates that the title is appearing for the first time.

Musical Idea & the Design Aesthetic in Contemporary Music: A Text for Discerning Appraisal of Musical Thought in Western Culture. Clifford Taylor. LC 88-9466. (Studies in the History & Interpretation of Music: Vol. 7). 386p. 1990. lib. bdg. 99.95 (*0-88946-432-4*) E Mellen.

Musical Idea & the Logic, Technique, & Art of Its Presentation. Arnold Schoenberg. Ed. & Tr. by Patricia Carpenter & Severine Neff from GER. LC 93-20009.Tr. of Musikalische Gedanke und die Logik, Technik und Kunst seiner Darstellung. (Illus.). 462p. 1994. 94.00 (*0-231-06428-4*) Col U Pr.

***Musical Ideas Manuscript Book.** William Bay. 112p. 1998. pap. 7.95 (*0-7866-4113-4*, 98170) Mel Bay.

Musical Image: A Theory of Content, 30. Laurence D. Berman. LC 92-32210. (Contributions to the Study of Music & Dance Ser.: No. 30). 408p. 1993. 65.00 (*0-313-28434-2*, BLI, Greenwood Pr) Greenwood.

Musical Impressions: Resphighi. 16p. (Orig.). (YA). 1994. pap. 17.00 (*0-89898-798-9*, BMR05100) Wrner Bros.

Musical Improvisation for Children. Alice Kanack. 44p. 1998. pap. text 14.95 (*0-87487-772-5*) Summy-Birchard.

Musical Impulse. 2nd ed. Christopher N. Bonds. LC 95-120081. 368p. 1994. pap., per. 60.95 (*0-8403-9802-6*, 40980201) Kendall-Hunt.

Musical Information in Musicology & Desktop Publishing. Eleanor Selfridge-Field & Edmund Correia, Jr. (Illus.). 75p. (Orig.). 1994. pap. text 15.00 (*0-936943-09-2*) CCARH.

***Musical Instrument Auction 2000.** String Letter Publishing Staff. 408p. 2000. pap. 44.95 (*1-890490-23-7*) String Letter.

Musical Instrument Collector. J. Robert Willcutt & Kenneth R. Ball. Ed. by Steven F. Brines. LC 78-68088. (Illus.). 1978. reprint ed. pap. 6.95 (*0-933224-00-1*, T035) Bold Strummer Ltd.

Musical Instrument Design: Practical Information for Instrument Making. Bart Hopkin. (Illus.). 181p. (Orig.). 1996. pap. 18.95 (*1-884365-08-6*) See Sharp Pr.

Musical Instrument Makers of New York: A Directory of 18th & 19th Century Urban Craftsmen. Nancy J. Groce. LC 89-37076. (Annotated Reference Tools in Music Ser.: No. 4). (Illus.). 450p. 1991. lib. bdg. 64.00 (*0-918728-97-5*) Pendragon NY.

Musical Instruments. Denys Darlow. (Junior Reference Ser.). (Illus.). (J). (gr. 6 up). 1983. 14.95 (*0-7136-2043-9*) Dufour.

Musical Instruments. Claude Delafosse. LC 96-181854. (First Discovery Book). (Illus.). 24p. (J). (ps-2). 1994. 11.95 (*0-590-47729-3*, Cartwheel) Scholastic Inc.

Musical Instruments. B. Chaitanya Deva. 108p. 1977. 8.95 (*0-318-36330-5*) Asia Bk Corp.

Musical Instruments. Meryl Doney. LC 95-18099. (World Crafts Ser.). (Illus.). 32p. (J). (gr. 4-7). 1996. lib. bdg. 21.00 (*0-531-14398-8*) Watts.

Musical Instruments. Meryl Doney. (World Crafts Ser.). (J). (gr. 4). 1997. pap. text 5.95 (*0-531-15871-3*) Watts.

Musical Instruments. Ed. by Amrita Kumar. (C). 1993. 7.50 (*81-7167-161-6*, Pub. by Rupa) S Asia.

Musical Instruments. Johannes Rademacher. Tr. by Ann Jeffers-Brown & Sally Schreiber. LC 96-78858. (Crash Course Ser.). (Illus.). 192p. 1997. pap. text 12.95 (*0-7641-0052-1*) Barron.

Musical Instruments. Sturman. Date not set. pap. text. write for info. (*0-582-33163-3*, Pub. by Addison-Wesley) Longman.

Musical Instruments, 8 vols. Barrie Carson Turner. (Illus.). 32p. (J). lib. bdg. 170.40 (*1-887068-50-3*) Smart Apple.

Musical Instruments. Louise Tythacott. (Traditions Around the World Ser.). (Illus.). 48p. (J). (gr. 4-6). 1995. lib. bdg. 24.26 (*1-56847-228-5*) Raintree Steck-V.

Musical Instruments: From Flutes Carved of Bone, to Lutes, to Modern Electric Guitars. Ed. by Scholastic, Inc. Staff. LC 94-9150. (Scholasitc Voyages of Discovery Ser.). 48p. (J). (gr. 4-6). 1994. 19.95 (*0-590-47638-6*) Scholastic Inc.

***Musical Instruments: Traditions & Craftsmanship from Pre-History to the Present.** Lucie Rault. (Illus.). 240p. 2000. 60.00 (*0-8109-4384-0*, Pub. by Abrams) Time Warner.

Musical Instruments & Accessories, UL 469. 3rd ed. (C). 1997. pap. text 195.00 (*1-55989-386-9*) Underwrtrs Labs.

Musical Instruments & the Voices Grades 3-9: Fifty Ready-to-Use Activities. Audrey J. Adair. LC 87-8834. Vol. 4. 112p. (C). 1987. pap. text 18.95 (*0-13-606963-0*) P-H.

Musical Instruments & Their Music, 1500-1750, 2 vols. in 1. Gerald R. Hayes. LC 74-26053. reprint ed. 47.50 (*0-404-12958-7*) AMS Pr.

Musical Instruments & Their Symbolism in Western Art: Studies in Musical Iconology. Emanuel Winternitz. LC 78-65482. 349p. reprint ed. pap. 108.20 (*0-7837-3314-3*, 20577160006) Bks Demand.

Musical Instruments (Collection of the Cincinnati Art Museum) 1993. reprint ed. lib. bdg. 89.00 (*0-7812-9531-9*) Rprt Serv.

Musical Instruments from A to Z see Alphabasics Series

Musical Instruments from Around the World. Judy L. Hasday. LC 98-36094. (Costume, Tradition, & Culture Ser.). (Illus.). 64p. 1998. 16.95 (*0-7910-5168-4*) Chelsea Hse.

Musical Instruments from the Tomb of Tutankhamun. Lise Manniche. (Tutankhamuns Tomb Ser.: Vol. 6). 48p. 1976. 30.00 (*0-900416-05-X*, Pub. by Aris & Phillips) David Brown.

***Musical Instruments in Germany: A Strategic Entry Report, 1996.** Compiled by Icon Group International Staff. (Illus.). 97p. 1999. ring bd. 970.00 incl. audio compact disk (*0-7418-1340-8*) Icon Grp.

***Musical Instruments in Germany: A Strategic Entry Report, 2000.** Compiled by Icon Group International. (Illus.). 95p. 1999. ring bd. 950.00 incl. audio compact disk (*0-7418-2181-8*) Icon Grp.

***Musical Instruments in Japan: A Strategic Entry Report, 1996.** Compiled by Icon Group International Staff. (Illus.). 161p. 1999. ring bd. 1610.00 incl. audio compact disk (*0-7418-1341-6*) Icon Grp.

Musical Instruments in Sculpture in Karnataka. Chaitanya Deva. 1989. 38.50 (*81-208-0641-7*, Pub. by Motilal Bnarsidass) S Asia.

Musical Instruments in the Viennese Tradition, 1750-1850: An Exhibition of Instruments by Austrian Makers with Supplementary Exhibits of Contemporary Graphics, Printed Music & Books. Nicholas Renouf. (Illus.). 32p. (Orig.). 1981. pap. 4.00 (*0-929530-02-0*) Yale U Coll Musical Instruments.

Musical Instruments in Tibetan Legend & Folklore. Peter Crossley-Holland. LC 82-50350. (Monograph Series in Ethnomusicology: No. 3). 42p. (Orig.). 1982. pap. text 5.00 (*0-88287-015-7*) UCLA Dept Ethnom.

Musical Instruments of India: Their History & Development. B. Chaitanya Deva. 1987. 32.00 (*81-215-0048-6*, Pub. by M Manoharial) Coronet Bks.

Musical Instruments of North India: Eighteenth Century Portraits. Balt Solvyns et al. LC 97-914054. 1997. write for info. (*81-7304-165-2*) Manohar.

Musical Instruments of the Punjab, 1. Alka Pande. 1999. 27.50 (*1-890206-15-6*) Grantha.

Musical Instruments of the Southern Appalachian Mountains. John R. Irwin. (Illus.). 108p. 1983. pap. 9.95 (*0-916838-80-3*) Schiffer.

Musical Instruments of the Violin Family & the Geometry of Positioning & Cutting Out Their F-Shaped Sound Holes. Andrew Dipper. LC 98-108242. (Technical Studies in the Arts of Musical Instrument Making: Vol. 1). (Illus.). 80p. (Orig.). 1997. pap., spiral bd. 25.00 (*0-9657095-0-7*) Dipper Pr.

Musical Instruments of the Violin Family & the Geometry of Positioning & Cutting Out Their F-Shaped Sound Holes. 4th ed. Andrew Dipper. LC 98-108242. (Technical Studies in the Arts of Musical Instrument Making: No. 1). (Illus.). 80p. (Orig.). 1997. reprint ed. pap., spiral bd. 25.00 (*0-9657095-1-5*) Dipper Pr.

***Musical Instruments of Tribal India.** Dillip Bhattacharya. LC 98-915699. 1998. 142.00 (*81-7049-092-8*, Pub. by Manas Pubns) S Asia.

Musical Interludes in Boston, 1795-1830. H. Earle Johnson. LC 43-11010. reprint ed. 29.50 (*0-404-03588-4*) AMS Pr.

Musical Interpretation: Its Laws & Principles, No. 3713. Tobias A. Matthay. 1913. pap. text 8.95 (*0-686-30014-9*) Boston Music.

Musical Interpretation, Its Laws & Principles, & Their Application in Teaching & Performing. Tobias A. Matthay. LC 70-107820. (Select Bibliographies Reprint Ser.). 1977. 17.95 (*0-8369-5191-3*) Ayer.

Musical Interpretation, Its Laws & Principles, & Their Application in Teaching & Performing. Tobias A. Matthay. LC 72-109787. 163p. 1970. reprint ed. lib. bdg. 35.00 (*0-8371-4277-6*, MAMU, Greenwood Pr) Greenwood.

Musical Interpretation, Its Laws & Principles, & Their Application in Teaching & Performing. Tobias A. Matthay. 163p. 1990. reprint ed. lib. bdg. 59.00 (*0-7812-9152-6*) Rprt Serv.

Musical Journey Through India, 1963-1964. Nazir A. Jairazbhoy. Ed. by Eran Fraenkel. (Illus.). x, 64p. (C). 1988. 40.00 incl. audio (*0-88287-023-8*) UCLA Dept Ethnom.

Musical Journeys of Louis Spohr. Louis Spohr. Ed. by Henry Pleasants. LC 61-9003. (Illus.). 283p. reprint ed. pap. 87.80 (*0-608-10833-2*, 201626900002) Bks Demand.

Musical Journeys of Louis Spohr. Louis Spohr. Tr. by Henry Pleasants from GER. LC 86-29436. (Illus.). 273p. 1987. reprint ed. lib. bdg. 77.50 (*0-313-25834-1*, SPMJ, Greenwood Pr) Greenwood.

Musical Kaleidoscope. Prod. by Zobeida Perez. 20p. (Orig.). (J). 1994. pap. 17.00 (*0-89898-786-5*, BMR05093) Wrner Bros.

Musical Knowledge: Intuition, Analysis, & Music Education. Keith Swanwick. LC 93-24935. 208p. (C). 1994. pap. 22.99 (*0-415-10097-6*) Routledge.

***Musical Landscapes in Color: Conversations with Black American Composers.** William C. Banfield. 480p. 1999. 59.50 (*0-8108-3706-4*) Scarecrow.

Musical Language of Hugo Wolf. Jean I. Haywood. 48p. 1986. 35.00 (*0-7223-2013-2*, Pub. by A H S Ltd) St Mut.

Musical Languages. Joseph P. Swain. LC 96-38351. (Illus.). 384p. (C). 1997. 32.50 (*0-393-04079-8*) Norton.

Musical Legacy of 100 Years: The Story of the NFMC National Federation of Music Clubs. Lucile P. Ward. (Illus.). 350p. (C). 1995. 32.95 (*1-884416-11-X*) A Press.

Musical Licensing in Restaurants & Retail & Other Establishments: Hearing Before the Subcommittee on Courts & Intellectual Property of the Committee on the Judiciary, House of Representatives, One Hundred Fifth Congress, First Session . . . July 17, 1997. United States Government. LC 98-156787. iv, 154 p. 1997. write for info. (*0-16-056279-1*) USGPO.

Musical Life: Reflections on What It Is & How to Live It. W. A. Mathieu. LC 93-39776. 1994. pap. 17.00 (*0-87773-670-7*, Pub. by Shambhala Pubns) Random.

Musical Life in a Changing Society: Aspects of Musical Sociology. Kurt Blaukopf. Tr. by David Marinelli from GER. LC 92-17805. (Illus.). 328p. 1992. pap. 22.95 (*0-931340-55-1*, Amadeus Pr) Timber.

Musical Life in Poland. Lidia Rappoport-Gelfand. (Musicology: A Book Ser.). xviii, 248p. 1991. text 39.00 (*2-88124-319-3*) Gordon & Breach.

Musical Life of Gustav Mole. Kathryn Meyrick. (GRE.). (J). 1990. pap. 6.99 (*0-85953-802-8*); pap. 6.99 (*0-85953-550-9*) Childs Play.

Musical Life of Gustav Mole. Kathryn Meyrick. LC 90-49100. 32p. (J). (ps-3). 1990. 13.99 (*0-85953-303-4*); pap. 6.99 (*0-85953-347-6*) Childs Play.

***Musical Life of Gustav Mole.** Kathryn Meyrick. (Child's Play Library). (J). 1999. pap. 13.99 incl. audio (*0-85953-333-6*) Childs Play.

Musical Life of Gustav Mole. Michael Twinn. 1996. 15.95 (*0-85953-893-1*) Childs Play.

Musical Life of Gustav Mole. unabridged ed. Kathryn Meyrick. (Theatre Ser.). (J). (gr. k-5). 1990. audio 6.99 (*0-85953-376-X*) Childs Play.

Musical Life of the Crystal Palace. Michael Musgrave. (Illus.). 286p. (C). 1995. text 59.95 (*0-521-37562-2*) Cambridge U Pr.

Musical London. Edward Lee. 192p. pap. 19.95 (*0-7119-3083-X*, OP 47094) Omnibus NY.

Musical London. Spellmount Ltd. Publishers Staff. (C). 1986. 140.00 (*0-946771-15-4*, Pub. by Spellmnt Pubs) St Mut.

Musical Lynn Essays Vol. 1: A Baker's Dozen. Musical Lynn. 13p. (Orig.). (YA). (gr. 12). 1991. pap. 8.95 (*1-880718-02-2*); pap. text 8.95 (*1-880718-03-0*) Genius New.

Musical Manuscript Montecassino 871: A Neapolitan Repertory of Sacred & Secular Music. Ed. by Isabel Pope & Masakata Kanazawa. (Illus.). 1979. 95.00 (*0-19-816132-8*) OUP.

Musical Massage Sound Therapy Vol. 1: A Chronic Pain Syndrome Case Study. Dorothy Gundling. Ed. by Beth Bywater. LC 96-94240. (Illus.). iv, 85p. (Orig.). 1996. pap. 10.00 (*0-9618621-1-4*) Casa De Maria.

Musical Meaning & Expression. Stephen Davies. LC 93-39890. (Illus.). 400p. (C). 1994. text 57.50 (*0-8014-2930-7*); pap. text 22.50 (*0-8014-8151-1*) Cornell U Pr.

Musical Meaning in Beethoven: Markedness, Correlation, & Interpretation. Robert S. Hatten. LC 93-26001. (Advances in Semiotics Ser.). 1994. 29.95 (*0-253-32742-3*) Ind U Pr.

Musical Memories. Camille Saint-Saens. 1990. reprint ed. lib. bdg. 79.00 (*0-7812-9003-1*) Rprt Serv.

Musical Memories. William Spark. 366p. 1991. reprint ed. lib. bdg. 89.00 (*0-7812-9332-4*) Rprt Serv.

Musical Memories of Laura Ingalls Wilder. Diana Waring. 1997. pap. 19.99 (*1-888306-26-2*) Holly Hall.

Musical Migration & Ernst Toch. Diane P. Jezic. LC 89-11224. (Illus.). 232p. 1989. reprint ed. pap. 72.00 (*0-608-00092-2*, 206085700006) Bks Demand.

Musical Mind: An Introduction to the Cognitive Psychology of Music. John A. Sloboda. (Oxford Psychology Ser.). (Illus.). 304p. 1986. pap. text 45.00 (*0-19-852128-6*) OUP.

Musical Mind Benders. Arthur Cohn. (Musical Quizzical II Ser.). 192p. (Orig.). 1992. pap. 13.95 (*0-911318-16-X*) E C Schirmer.

Musical Ministries in the Church. Waldo S. Pratt. LC 74-24193. reprint ed. 36.00 (*0-404-13095-X*) AMS Pr.

Musical Moment: And Other Stories. Yehoshua Kenaz. Tr. by Dalya Bilu & Betsy Rosenberg from HEB. LC 95-4306. 200p. 1995. 19.50 (*1-883642-18-3*); pap. 12.00 (*1-883642-47-7*) Steerforth Pr.

Musical Morphology: A Discourse & a Dictionary. Siegmund Levarie & Ernest Levy. LC 82-21274. 355p. reprint ed. pap. 110.10 (*0-7837-5124-9*, 204485200004) Bks Demand.

Musical Motifs in Swedish Church Art: The Pictorial Representations of Music & Music-Making in Sweden's Medieval Churches up to 1630. I. B. Magnus & B. Kjellstorn. Tr. by Michael Stevens from SWE. (ENG & SWE., Illus.). 408p. 1993. 82.50 (*91-972117-0-2*) Coronet Bks.

Musical Motley. Ernest Newman. LC 76-10332. (Music Reprint Ser.). 1976. lib. bdg. 35.00 (*0-306-70784-5*) Da Capo.

Musical Motley. Ernest Newman. 291p. 1990. reprint ed. lib. bdg. 69.00 (*0-7812-9001-5*) Rprt Serv.

Musical Movie Posters. Ed. by Bruce Hershenson & Richard Allen. (The/Illustrated History of Movies Through Posters Ser.: Vol. 9). (Illus.). 80p. 1999. 50.00 (*1-887893-32-6*) B Hershenson.

***Musical Movie Posters.** Ed. by Bruce Hershenson & Richard Allen. (The/Illustrated History of Movies Through Posters Ser.: Vol. 9). (Illus.). 80p. 1999. pap. 20.00 (*1-887893-31-8*) B Hershenson.

Musical Musings. Petr Beckmann. LC 89-84833. (Illus.). 197p. (Orig.). 1989. pap. 15.00 (*0-911762-40-X*) Golem.

Musical Mysteries. Kathleen M. Ferguson. (Illus.). 144p. (J). (gr. 4-8). 1985. student ed. 13.99 (*0-86653-282-X*, GA 684) Good Apple.

Musical Mystery. Dandi Daley Mackall. LC 98-169815. (Puzzle Club Mystery Ser.). 80p. (J). (ps-3). 1998. pap. 4.99 (*0-570-05059-6*) Concordia.

Musical Nationalism: American Composers' Search for Identity, 66. Alan H. Levy. LC 82-12168. (Contributions in American Studies: No. 66). 168p. 1983. 47.95 (*0-313-23709-3*, LMN/, Greenwood Pr) Greenwood.

Musical Networks: Parallel Distributed Perception & Performance. Ed. by Niall Griffith & Peter M. Todd. LC 98-25671. (Illus.). 350p. 1999. 37.50 (*0-262-07181-9*, Bradford Bks) MIT Pr.

Musical New York: An Informal Guide to Its History & Legends & a Walking Tour of Its Sites & Landmarks. Carol J. Binkowski. LC 98-11733. (Illus.). 304p. 1999. pap. 12.95 (*0-940159-47-3*) Camino Bks.

Musical Notation of Latin Liturgical Chants see Notation Musicale des Manuscrits Liturgiques Latins

Musical Notations of the Orient: Notational Systems of Continental, East, South & Central Asia. Walter Kaufmann. LC 66-64235. (Indiana University Humanities Ser.: No. 60). 512p. reprint ed. pap. 158.80 (*0-7837-2027-0*, 205730200002) Bks Demand.

Musical Notes: A Practical Guide to Staffing & Staging Standards of the American Musical Theatre. Carol Lucha-Burns. LC 85-10017. 598p. 1986. lib. bdg. 85.00 (*0-313-24648-3*, BMN/, Greenwood Pr) Greenwood.

Musical Notes by Honore Daumier: Prints from the Collection of Egon & Belle Gartenberg. Joyce H. Robinson. (Illus.). 24p. 1998. pap. 6.00 (*0-911209-47-6*) Palmer Mus Art.

Musical Notes of a Physician. rev. ed. F. William Sunderman. 320p. 1992. 24.95 (*0-9632927-0-6*) Inst Clin Sci.

Musical Notes on Math: A Math Music Program. Madeline Frank. (How Music Can Make Your Child Brighter Ser.). (Illus.). 60p. (Orig.). 1997. pap., teacher ed. 20.00 (*0-9658583-1-6*) M Frank.

Musical Offering: Essays in Honor of Martin Bernstein. Ed. by Edward Clinkscale & Claire Brook. LC 76-53128. (Festschrift Ser.: No. 1). 1977. lib. bdg. 42.00 (*0-918728-03-7*) Pendragon NY.

***Musical Offering: Hymnfest for the Church Year.** Ruth Buenting et al. 40p. 1999. pap. 5.75 (*0-7880-1527-3*) CSS OH.

Musical Openings: Using Music in the Language Classroom. D. Cranmer & C. Laroy. 111p. 1995. audio 28.00 (*0-582-07503-3*, 79846) Longman.

Musical Patronage in 17th-Century England: Christopher, First Baron Hatton, 1605-1670. Jonathan P. Wainwright. LC 97-2418. (Illus.). 512p. 1997. text 91.95 (*1-85928-278-4*, Pub. by Scolar Pr) Ashgate Pub Co.

Musical PC. Marc Apfestadt. 1991. pap. 19.95 (*0-9623397-8-4*) Midi Amer.

Musical Perceptions. Ed. by Rit Aiello & John A. Sloboda. (Illus.). 304p. (C). 1994. pap. text 28.95 (*0-19-506476-3*) OUP.

Musical Performance: A Philosophical Study. Stan Godlovitch. 184p. (C). 1998. pap. 24.99 (*0-415-19129-7*, D6237) Routledge.

Musical Performance: A Philosophical Study. Stan Godlovitch. 184p. (C). (gr. 13). 1998. 75.00 (*0-415-19128-9*, D6233) Routledge.

Musical Performance: Learning Theory & Pedagogy. Daniel L. Kohut. 230p. (C). 1992. reprint ed. pap. 18.80 (*0-87563-415-X*) Stipes.

Musical Pictures: Mussorgsky. 20p. (Orig.). (YA). 1994. pap. 17.00 (*0-89898-793-8*, BMR05097) Wrner Bros.

Musical Poetics. Joachim Burmeister. Ed. by Claude V. Palisca. Tr. & Intro. by Benito V. Rivera. LC 92-33207. (Music Theory Translation Ser.). (ENG & LAT.). 336p. (C). 1993. 62.00 (*0-300-05110-7*) Yale U Pr.

Musical Portraits: Interpretations of Twenty Modern Composers. Paul Rosenfeld. LC 68-29243. (Essay Index Reprint Ser.). 1977. 20.95 (*0-8369-0837-6*) Ayer.

Musical Processes, Resources, & Technologies. Ed. by Kaye Shelemay. LC 90-3537. (Ethnomusicology Ser.: Vol. 6). 364p. 1990. reprint ed. text 95.00 (*0-8240-6474-7*) Garland.

Musical Prodigies: Perilous Journeys, Remarkable Lives. Claude Kenneson. LC 98-28636. (Illus.). 386p. 1999. 29.95 (*1-57467-046-8*, Amadeus Pr) Timber.

Musical Pronouncing Dictionary. Dudley Buck. 1976. reprint ed. lib. bdg. 39.00 (*0-403-03787-5*) Scholarly.

Musical Punstruments. Zach M. Arnold. (Illus.). 287p. 1994. pap. 14.95 (*0-940168-28-6*) Boxwood.

Musical Puzzles of Note, Vol. I. rev. ed. Victor Sazer. (Illus.). (Orig.). 1991. pap. 8.95 (*0-944810-00-4*) Ofnote.

Musical Puzzles of Note, Vol. II. Victor Sazer. (Illus.). 80p. (Orig.). 1989. pap. 8.95 (*0-944810-01-2*) Ofnote.

Musical Quizzical. Arthur Cohn. 96p. 1985. pap. 5.95 (*0-7935-0015-X*, HL00123471) H Leonard.

Musical References & Song Texts in the Bible. Geary Larrick. LC 90-13480. (Studies in the History & Interpretation of Music: Vol. 9). (Illus.). 172p. 1990. lib. bdg. 79.95 (*0-88946-492-8*) E Mellen.

Musical References in the Gazzetta di Napoli, 1681-1725. Thomas Griffin. LC 92-354474. (Reference Books in Music: No. 17). xxxv, 140p. 1993. 35.00 incl. disk (*0-914913-18-2*, Fallen Lef Pr) Scarecrow.

Musical Reflections of Scotland. John Loesberg. 1994. 10.95 (*0-946005-82-6*, OS00097) Omnibus NY.

Musical Reflections or Ireland. John Loesburg. 1997. pap. text 10.95 (*0-946005-36-2*) Dufour.

Musical Repercussions of 1492: Encounters in Text & Performance. Ed. by Carol E. Robertson. LC 92-6895. (Illus.). 496p. (C). 1992. text 65.00 (*1-56098-183-0*) Smithsonian.

Musical Resources for the Revised Common Lectionary. Compiled by Arthur Wenk. LC 94-11481. 613p. 1994. write for info. (*0-8108-2909-6*) Scarecrow.

***Musical Rexicon.** Bruce Adolphe. (Illus.). 24p. (J). (ps-6). 2000. 3.95 (*0-9701249-0-2*) PollyRhythm.

Musical Ride of the Royal Canadian Mounted Police. William Kelly & Nora Kelly. LC 98-30204. 1998. write for info. (*0-9625898-5-3*); pap. write for info. (*0-9625898-4-5*) EquiMedia.

Musical Savants: Exceptional Skill in Mentally Retarded. Leon K. Miller. 272p. (C). 1989. text 49.95 (*0-8058-0034-4*) L Erlbaum Assocs.

Musical Scales of the Hindus. Sourindo M. Tagore. LC 74-24225. reprint ed. 39.50 (*0-404-12837-8*) AMS Pr.

Musical Scotland Past & Present. David Baptie. 253p. 1972. reprint ed. lib. bdg. 60.00 (*3-487-04292-4*) G Olms Pubs.

Musical Setting for the Liturgy of St. John Chrysostom. (Illus.). 42p. 1998. pap. 2.00 (*0-911726-05-5*, MJC) Alleluia Pr.

An Asterisk (*) at the beginning of an entry indicates that the title is appearing for the first time.

Musical Settings of American Poetry: A Bibliography, 8. Compiled by Michael Hovland. LC 86-402. (Music Reference Collection: No. 8). 572p. 1986. lib. bdg. 65.00 (*0-313-22938-4*, HWT/, Greenwood Pr) Greenwood.

Musical Signal Processing. Ed. by Curtis Roads et al. LC 97-2598. (Studies on New Music Research). 480p. 1997. pap. 39.00 (*90-265-1483-2*) Swets.

Musical Signal Processing. Ed. by Curtis Roads et al. LC 97-2598. (Studies on New Music Research). 480p. 1997. 99.00 (*90-265-1482-4*) Swets.

Musical Signification: Essays in the Semiotic Theory & Analysis of Music. Ed. by Eero Tarasti. LC 95-9941. (Approaches to Semiotics Ser.: No. 121). (C). 1995. lib. bdg. 229.25 (*3-11-014040-3*) Mouton.

Musical Skills: A Computer-Based Assessment. G. David Peters. 1992. 8.00 (*0-317-05525-9*) U IL Sch Music.

***Musical Snapshots.** Martha Mier. 24p. 1999. pap. 5.95 (*0-7390-0336-4*, 18199) Alfred Pub.

Musical Sources for Domenico Corri's: A Select Collection of the Most Admired Songs, Duets, & C., 3 Vols., Vols. 1 - 3. Ed. by Richard Maunder. LC 93-8550. (Domenico Corri's Treatises on Singing Ser.: No. 2). 608p. 1994. text 40.00 (*0-8153-0680-6*) Garland.

Musical Sources for Domenico Corri's: A Select Collection of the Most Admired Songs, Duetts, & C., the Singer's Preceptor. Ed. by Richard Maunder. LC 93-8550. (Domenico Corri's Treatises on Singing Ser.: Vol. 4). 272p. 1995. text 40.00 (*0-8153-0845-0*) Garland.

Musical Stages: An Autobiography. Richard Rodgers. (Illus.). 379p. 1995. reprint ed. pap. 14.95 (*0-306-80634-7*) Da Capo.

Musical Standard, 1862-1871 (First Series), 3 vols., Set. Ed. by H. Robert Cohen. (Repertoire International de la Presse Musicale Ser.). 1991. lib. bdg. 360.00 (*0-8357-2123-X*) Univ Microfilms.

***Musical Structure: Harmony, Form & Counterpoint.** Benjamin. 2003. pap. 37.50 (*0-534-55766-X*) Thomson Learn.

Musical Structure & Cognition. Ed. by Peter Howell et al. 1985. text 145.00 (*0-12-357170-7*) Acad Pr.

Musical Structure & Design. Cedric T. Davie. (Illus.). 181p. 1966. pap. 6.95 (*0-486-21629-2*) Dover.

***Musical Structures in Wagnerian Opera.** Marshall Tuttle. LC 00-41821. (Studies in History & Interpretation of Music). 372p. 2000. 99.95 (*0-7734-7642-3*) E Mellen.

Musical Studies. Ernest Newman. LC 68-25297. (Studies in Music: No. 42). 1969. reprint ed. lib. bdg. 75.00 (*0-8383-0309-9*) M S G Haskell Hse.

Musical Studies: Music Book Index. Ernest Newman. 319p. 1993. reprint ed. lib. bdg. 89.00 (*0-7812-9706-0*) Rprt Serv.

***Musical Style & Genre: History & Modernity.** Marina Lobanova. Tr. by Kate Cook. (Illus.). 220p. 2000. text 50.00 (*90-5755-067-9*, Harwood Acad Pubs) Gordon & Breach.

Musical Supervisor. Jack Rudman. (Career Examination Ser.: C-525). 1994. pap. 29.95 (*0-8373-0525-X*) Nat Learn.

Musical Symbol. Gordon Epperson. (Music Reprint Ser.). xvi, 323p. 1987. reprint ed. lib. bdg. 32.50 (*0-306-76291-9*) Da Capo.

Musical Taste & Socio-Economic Background. Karl F. Schuessler. Ed. by Harriet Zuckerman & Robert K. Merton. LC 79-9024. (Dissertations on Sociology Ser.). 1980. lib. bdg. 16.95 (*0-405-12992-0*) Ayer.

Musical Taste As a Religious Question in Nineteenth Century America: The Development of Episcopal Church Hymnody. Jane Rasmussen. LC 86-12774. (Studies in American Religion: Vol. 20). 632p. 1986. lib. bdg. 129.95 (*0-88946-664-5*) E Mellen.

Musical Temperament: Psychology & Personality of Musicians. Anthony E. Kemp. (Illus.). 296p. 1996. pap. text 26.00 (*0-19-852362-9*) OUP.

Musical Temperaments. Erich Neuwirth. Tr. by R. Steblin. LC 97-40405. 80p. 1997. pap. 49.95 incl. cd-rom (*3-211-83040-5*) Spr-Verlag.

Musical Terminology: A Practical Compendium in Four Languages. Composed by David Boccagna. LC 99-31743. (Illus.). 243p. 1999. pap. 9.99 (*1-57647-015-6*) Pendragon NY.

***Musical Terms.** Sales Corporation Music Staff. Ed. by Peter Pickow. (Pocket Manual Ser.). 151p. 1999. pap. text 7.95 (*0-8256-1716-2*, SSM00764) Music Sales.

Musical Terms, Symbols & Theory. 1990. 41.00 (*1-55862-054-0*, 00000282) St James Pr.

Musical Terms, Symbols & Theory: An Illustrated Dictionary. Michael C. Thomsett. LC 89-42758. 287p. 1989. lib. bdg. 43.50 (*0-89950-392-6*) McFarland & Co.

Musical Theater Synopses: An Index. Jeanette M. Drone. LC 98-12198. 352p. 1998. 75.00 (*0-8108-3489-8*) Scarecrow.

Musical Theatre: A Celebration. Alan J. Lerner. (Quality Paperbacks Ser.). (Illus.). 256p. 1989. pap. 16.95 (*0-306-80364-X*) Da Capo.

Musical Theatre at the Court of Louis XIV: Le Mariage de la Grosse Cathos. Rebecca Harris-Warrick & Carol G. Marsh. LC 93-31380. (Musical Texts & Monographs). (Illus.). 358p. (C). 1995. text 120.00 (*0-521-38012-X*) Cambridge U Pr.

Musical Theatre Classics. 64p. 1996. pap. 19.95 incl. audio compact disk (*0-7935-6237-6*); pap. 19.95 incl. audio compact disk (*0-7935-6238-4*) H Leonard.

Musical Theatre Classics, Vol. 1. 64p. 1996. pap. 19.95 incl. audio compact disk (*0-7935-6233-3*); pap. 19.95 incl. audio compact disk (*0-7935-6235-X*) H Leonard.

Musical Theatre Classics, Vol. 2. 64p. 1996. pap. 19.95 incl. audio compact disk (*0-7935-6234-1*); pap. 19.95 incl. audio compact disk (*0-7935-6236-8*) H Leonard.

Musical Theatre Classics: Baritone Bass. (Vocal Collections). 64p. 1990. pap. 14.95 (*0-7935-0096-6*, 00660153) H Leonard.

Musical Theatre Classics: Mezzo Soprano Alto, Vol. 1. (Vocal Collections). 1990. pap. 14.95 incl. audio (*0-7935-0093-1*, 00660150) H Leonard.

Musical Theatre Classics: Mezzo Soprano Alto, Vol. 2. (Vocal Collections). 1990. pap. 14.95 incl. audio (*0-7935-0094-X*, 00660151) H Leonard.

Musical Theatre Classics: Soprano, Vol. 1. 1990. pap. 14.95 incl. audio (*0-7935-0091-5*, 00660148) H Leonard.

Musical Theatre Classics: Soprano, Vol. 2. 1990. pap. 14.95 incl. audio (*0-7935-0092-3*, 00660149) H Leonard.

Musical Theatre Cookbook: Recipes from Best Loved Musicals. Mollie A. Meserve. 208p. 1993. pap. 9.95 (*0-937657-16-6*) Feedbk Theabks & Prospero.

Musical Theatre in America: Papers & Proceedings of the Conference on the Musical Theatre in America, 8. Ed. by Glenn M. Loney. LC 83-8913. (Contributions in Drama & Theatre Studies: No. 8). (Illus.). 441p. 1984. 59.95 (*0-313-23524-4*, LMT/) Greenwood.

Musical Thought. Carlos Chavez. LC 60-15236. (Charles Norton Lectures: 1958-1959). (Illus.). 134p. reprint ed. pap. 41.60 (*0-608-11019-1*, 200641600059) Bks Demand.

Musical Thought at Ircam, Vol. 1, No. 1. Tod Machover. (Contemporary Music Review Ser.). ii, 230p. 1984. pap. text 48.00 (*3-7186-0272-5*) Gordon & Breach.

Musical Thought in Ancient Greece. Edward A. Lippman. LC 74-23415. (Music Reprint Ser.). 1975. reprint ed. lib. bdg. 32.50 (*0-306-70669-5*) Da Capo.

Musical Thoughts & Afterthoughts. Alfred Brendel. 168p. 1991. pap. 12.95 (*0-374-52278-2*) FS&G.

Musical Time: The Sense of Order. Barbara R. Barry. LC 89-71132. (Harmonologia Ser.: No. 5). (Illus.). 325p. 1990. lib. bdg. 56.00 (*0-945193-01-7*) Pendragon NY.

Musical Times 1844-1900, 9 vols. Ed. by H. Robert Cohen. (Repertoire International de la Presse Musicale Ser.). 1995. lib. bdg. 1285.00 (*0-8357-2330-5*) UMI.

Musical Tour Through the Land of the Past. Romain Rolland. Tr. by Bernard Miall. LC 67-30229. (Essay Index Reprint Ser.). 1977. 19.95 (*0-8369-0830-9*) Ayer.

Musical Transcription. Ed. by Kaye Shelemay. LC 90-3537. (Ethnomusicology Ser.: Vol. 4). 296p. 1990. reprint ed. text 83.00 (*0-8240-6472-0*) Garland.

Musical Transformation & Musical Intuition: Eleven Essays in Honor of David Lewin. Ed. by Rafael Atlas & Michael Cherlin. (Illus.). 241p. (Orig.). (C). 1994. pap. 40.00 (*1-886464-00-6*) Ovenbird Pr.

Musical Travels. (In Classical Mood Ser.: Vol. 26). (Illus.). 1998. write for info. incl. cd-rom (*1-886614-52-0*) Intl Masters Pub.

Musical Tree. large type ed. S. Bernadine Riske. LC 94-96424. (Illus.). 20p. (Orig.). (J). (ps-12). 1994. pap. 9.95 (*1-885981-02-3*) Brisk Pubng.

Musical Trends in the Twentieth Century. Norman Demuth. LC 73-6258. (Illus.). 359p. 1975. reprint ed. lib. bdg. 59.75 (*0-8371-6896-1*, DEMT, Greenwood Pr) Greenwood.

Musical Trivia see Juguemos con Musica

***Musical Twinkle, Twinkle, Little Star.** Janice Castiglione. (Rub-a-Dub-Tub Musical Bks.). (Illus.). (J). 2000. pap. 5.99 (*1-883043-18-2*) Straight Edge.

Musical Uproar in Moscow. Alexander Werth. LC 73-5211. 103p. 1973. reprint ed. lib. bdg. 49.50 (*0-8371-6864-3*, WEMU, Greenwood Pr) Greenwood.

Musical Uproar in Moscow: Music Book Index. Alexander Werth. 103p. 1993. reprint ed. lib. bdg. 69.00 (*0-7812-9568-8*) Rprt Serv.

Musical Wesleys. Erik Routley. LC 75-36511. (Illus.). 272p. 1976. reprint ed. lib. bdg. 77.50 (*0-8371-8644-7*, ROMW, Greenwood Pr) Greenwood.

Musical Wind Instruments. Adam V. Carse. (Music Book Index Ser.). 381p. 1992. reprint ed. lib. bdg. 89.00 (*0-7812-9496-7*) Rprt Serv.

Musical Wind Instruments: A History of the Wind Instruments Used in European Orchestras & Wind Bands, from the Later Middle Ages up to the Present Time. 2nd ed. Adam Carse. LC 65-18502. (Music Ser.). 1975. reprint ed. 45.00 (*0-306-70906-6*); reprint ed. pap. 9.95 (*0-306-80005-5*) Da Capo.

Musical Wisdom: Songs & Drawings for the Child in Us All. Tom Robson. (Illus.). 88p. (Orig.). (J). (gr. k-6). 1992. pap. 16.95 (*0-9633332-0-8*) Laughing Cat.

Musical Woman: An International Perspective, 1983, Vol. 1. Ed. by Judith L. Zaimont et al. LC 83-1637. (Illus.). 406p. 1984. lib. bdg. 79.50 (*0-313-23587-2*, ZMW/01, Greenwood Pr) Greenwood.

Musical Woman: An International Perspective, 1984-1985, Vol. 2. Ed. by Judith L. Zaimont et al. LC 84-64917. (Illus.). 583p. 1987. lib. bdg. 85.00 (*0-313-23588-0*, ZMW/02, Greenwood Pr) Greenwood.

Musical Woman: An International Perspective, 1986-1990, Vol. 3. Ed. by Judith L. Zaimont et al. LC 84-64917. (Musical Women Ser.). 848p. 1991. lib. bdg. 95.00 (*0-313-23589-9*, ZMW03, Greenwood Pr) Greenwood.

Musical Women in England. Gilett. LC 99-42809. 1999. text 49.95 (*0-312-12156-3*) St Martin.

***Musical Work: Reality or Invention?** Ed. by Michael Talbot. 288p. 2000. 52.95 (*0-85323-825-1*, Pub. by Liverpool Univ Pr); pap. 21.95 (*0-85323-835-9*, Pub. by Liverpool Univ Pr) Intl Spec Bk.

Musical Works. William Dunlap. LC 79-24504. 1979. 50.00 (*0-8201-1348-4*) Schol Facsimiles.

Musical Works of Frederick the Great, 4 vols. in 3. Frederick The Great. Ed. by Philip Spitta. LC 67-27453. (Music Ser.). 1967. reprint ed. lib. bdg. 135.00 (*0-306-70980-5*) Da Capo.

Musical Works of Maharaja Swati Tirunal. Ed. by G. Kuppaswamy & M. Hariharan. 1990. 115.00 (*81-85067-24-4*, Pub. by Sundeep Prak) S Asia.

Musical Workshop. Frederick Dorian. LC 77-138109. (Illus.). 368p. 1971. reprint ed. lib. bdg. 69.50 (*0-8371-5685-8*, DOMW, Greenwood Pr) Greenwood.

Musical World of Frances James & Murray Adaskin. Gordana Lazarevich. 331p. 1988. text 40.00 (*0-8020-5738-1*) U of Toronto Pr.

Musical World of J. J. Johnson. Joshua Berrett & Louis G. Bourgois. LC 99-10077. (Studies in Jazz: No. 35). (Illus.). 464p. 1999. text 65.00 (*0-8108-3648-3*) Scarecrow.

Musical World of Robert Schumann, Schumann on Music: A Selection from the Writings. Robert Schumann. reprint ed. lib. bdg. 79.00 (*0-7812-0303-1*) Rprt Serv.

Musical World of Walt Disney. David Tietyen. (Illus.). 160p. 1990. 19.95 (*0-88188-476-6*, HL 00183514) H Leonard.

Musical World 1836-1865, 11 vols. Ed. by H. Robert Cohen. Incl. Vol. 1. Musical World 1836-1865. 1996. lib. bdg. 145.00 (*0-8357-2431-X*); Vol. 2. Musical World 1836-1865. 1996. lib. bdg. 145.00 (*0-8357-2432-8*); Vol. 3. Musical World 1836-1865. 1996. lib. bdg. 145.00 (*0-8357-2433-6*); Vol. 4. Musical World 1836-1865. 1996. lib. bdg. 145.00 (*0-8357-2434-4*); Vol. 5. Musical World 1836-1865. 1996. lib. bdg. 145.00 (*0-8357-2435-2*); Vol. 6. Musical World 1836-1865. 1997. lib. bdg. 145.00 (*0-8357-2436-0*); Vol. 7. Musical World 1836-1865. 1997. lib. bdg. 145.00 (*0-8357-2437-9*); Vol. 8. Musical World 1836-1865. 1997. lib. bdg. 145.00 (*0-8357-2438-7*); Vol. 9. Musical World 1836-1865. 1997. lib. bdg. 145.00 (*0-8357-2439-5*); Vol. 10. Musical World 1836-1865. 1997. lib. bdg. 145.00 (*0-8357-2440-9*); Vol. 11. Musical World 1836-1865. 1997. lib. bdg. 145.00 (*0-8357-2441-7*); (Repertoire International de la Presse Musicale Ser.). Set lib. bdg. 1570.00 (*0-8357-2430-1*) UMI.

Musical World 1836-1865 see Musical World 1836-1865

Musical Worlds: New Directions in the Philosophy of Music. Philip Alperson. LC 97-33027. 1998. pap. 14.95 (*0-271-01769-4*) Pa St U Pr.

Musicality. Barbara Guest & June Felter. LC 88-8089. (Illus.). 40p. (Orig.). 1988. pap. 9.00 (*0-932716-23-7*) Kelsey St Pr.

Musically Incorrect: Conversations about Music at the End of the 20th Century. Hayes Biggs & Susan Orzel. LC 98-28553. 1998. pap. 12.95 (*0-938856-07-3*) C F Peters Corp.

Musically Mixed. Beatrice Miller. 32p. 1995. pap. text 5.95 (*0-87487-746-6*) Summy-Birchard.

Musicals. Rudiger Bering. (Crash Course Ser.). (Illus.). 192p. 1998. pap. 13.95 (*0-7641-0436-5*) Barron.

Musicals. Michael P. Kennedy & John Muir. 412p. 1998. 24.95 (*0-00-472067-9*, Pub. by HarpC) Trafalgar.

Musicals! Directing School & Community Theatre. Robert Boland & Paul Argentini. LC 97-11996. (Illus.). 208p. 1997. pap. 29.50 (*0-8108-3323-9*) Scarecrow.

Musicals: The Guide to Amateur Production. Peter A. Spencer. (Illus.). 240p. 1994. pap. 22.00 (*0-85343-592-8*, Pub. by J G Miller Ltd) Empire Pub Srvs.

***Musicals - Hollywood & Beyond.** Ed. by Bill Marshall & Robynn Stilwell. 192p. 2000. pap. 24.95 (*1-84150-003-8*, Pub. by Intellect) Intl Spec Bk.

Musicbook: O Songs, Games, Movement Activities for Teaching Music to Young Children. Erling Bisgaard & Gulle Stehouwer. Ed. by Tossi Aaron. 80p. 1976. pap. 8.95 (*0-918812-04-6*, SE 0016) MMB Music.

***Music.Dot.Com.** (Illus.). 184p. 2000. pap. 39.95 (*0-8230-8347-0*) Watsn-Guptill.

Musichound Blues. 2nd ed. Date not set. 24.95 (*1-57859-082-5*) Visible Ink Pr.

Musichound Classical: The Essential Album Guide. David Wagner. (Illus.). 800p. 2000. pap. 24.95 (*1-57859-034-5*, 00157595) Visible Ink Pr.

Musichound Country. 2nd ed. Date not set. 24.95 (*1-57859-081-7*) Visible Ink Pr.

MusicHound Country: The Essential Album Guide. Ed. by Gary Graff. 1997. pap. 24.95 (*0-614-27469-9*) Visible Ink Pr.

Musichound Electronica: The Essential Album Guide. 1998. 24.95 (*1-57859-035-3*, 00157596) Visible Ink Pr.

MusicHound Folk: The Essential Album Guide. Neal Walters et al. LC 99-162267. 960p. 1998. pap. 24.95 incl. cd-rom (*1-57859-037-X*, 00157598) Music Sales.

Musichound Lounge: The Essential Album Guide to Martini Music & Easy Listening. Steve Knopper. LC 98-19584. (MusicHound Ser.). 600p. 1998. text 24.95 (*1-57859-048-5*) Visible Ink Pr.

MusicHound Soundtracks: The Essential Album Guide to Film, Television & Stage Music. 2nd ed. Didier C Deutsch. LC 99-42807. (Illus.). 872p. 1999. pap. text 26.95 (*1-57859-101-5*) Visible Ink Pr.

***Musichound World: The Essential Album Guide.** Ed. by Adam Mcgovern. (Illus.). 1096p. 1999. pap. text 26.95 incl. cd-rom (*1-57859-039-6*) Visible Ink Pr.

MusicHound's Swing! The Essential Album Guide. Steve Knopper. LC 99-27950. (MusicHound Ser.). 461p. 1999. pap. 19.95 (*1-57859-091-4*) Visible Ink Pr.

Musici Scriptores Graeci. Ed. by Jan. (GRE.). 1995. reprint ed. 115.00 (*3-519-01776-8*; T1776, Pub. by B G Teubner) U of Mich Pr.

Musici Scriptores Graeci: Supplementum. Ed. by Jan. (GRE.). 1995. reprint ed. 19.95 (*3-519-01777-6*, T1777, Pub. by B G Teubner) U of Mich Pr.

Musician. Lyn Murray. 384p. 1987. 17.95 (*0-8184-0432-9*) Carol Pub Group.

Musician. I. S. Roverso. 1975. pap. 3.50 (*0-913054-08-9*) Poet Gal Pr.

Musician. Eve Shelnutt. LC 87-11764. 180p. 1987. pap. 9.00 (*0-87685-698-9*) Black Sparrow.

Musician, signed ed. deluxe ed. Eve Shelnutt. LC 87-11764. 180p. 1987. 30.00 (*0-87685-700-4*) Black Sparrow.

Musician as Athlete: Alternative Approaches to Healthy Performance. Dorothy Bishop. Ed. by Jude Carlson. (Illus.). 395p. (Orig.). (C). 1992. pap. 18.95 (*0-9695590-0-3*, Pub. by Kava Pubns) Rosenthals.

Musician at Court: An Autobiography of Franz Benda. Franz Benda & Douglas A. Lee. LC 98-23705. (Detroit Monographs in Musicology/Studiesin Music: Vol. 23). 1998. 27.50 (*0-89990-083-6*) Harmonie Park Pr.

Musician at Large. Harvey Grace. LC 78-107703. (Essay Index Reprint Ser.). 1977. 20.95 (*0-8369-1506-2*) Ayer.

Musician Looks at the Psalms: A Journal of Daily Meditations. Don Wyrtzen. 416p. 1988. 19.95 (*0-310-36360-8*, 18331) Zondervan.

Musician Talks. Donald F. Tovey. 1988. reprint ed. lib. bdg. 49.00 (*0-7812-5970-3*) Rprt Serv.

Musician Talks, 2 vols. in 1. Donald F. Tovey. LC 73-181280. 1946. reprint ed. 39.00 (*0-403-01703-3*) Scholarly.

Musicians see Women in Profile Series

Musicians. Laura Conlon. LC 94-17029. (Performers Discovery Library). (J). 1994. 14.60 (*1-57103-062-X*) Rourke Pr.

Musicians. Peggy Roalf. (Looking at Paintings Ser.). (J). 1993. 11.90 (*0-606-05911-3*, Pub. by Turtleback) Demco.

Musicians. Jean-Jacques Sempe. LC 80-51894. (Illus.). 96p. 1980. 14.95 (*0-89480-099-X*, 330); pap. 9.95 (*0-89480-508-8*, 1508) Workman Pub.

***Musicians & Composers.** Nathan Levy. Ed. by Renee Kristensen & Jeffrey A. Sculthorp. LC 99-69276. (Whose Clues? Ser.). 32p. (YA). (gr. 3-12). 2000. pap., teacher ed. 5.99 (*1-889319-41-4*, MindMotion) Trend Enterprises.

Musicians & Mummers. Hermann Klein. LC 80-2284. (Illus.). reprint ed. 38.50 (*0-404-18850-8*) AMS Pr.

Musicians & Music-Lovers. William F. Apthorp. 1972. 59.95 (*0-8490-0684-8*) Gordon Pr.

Musicians & Music-Lovers: And Other Essays. William F. Apthorp. LC 74-39633. (Essay Index Reprint Ser.). 1977. reprint ed. 23.95 (*0-8369-2736-2*) Ayer.

Musicians & the Prevention of Hearing Loss. Marshall Chasin. (Illus.). 204p. (Orig.). 1996. pap. 45.00 (*1-56593-626-4*, 1298) Thomson Learn.

Musicians & Watchmakers. Alicia Steimberg. Tr. by Andrea G. Labinger from SPA. LC 98-21585. (Discoveries Ser.). 128p. 1998. pap. 13.95 (*0-935480-96-X*) Lat Am Lit Rev Pr.

Musician's Atlas. Ed. by Martin Folkman. 352p. 1999. pap. 19.95 (*0-9669368-0-9*) Mus Res.

***Musician's Atlas 1999: The Ultimate Resource for Working Musicians.** Music Resource Group Staff. (Illus.). 1999. pap. 19.95 (*0-634-00145-0*) H Leonard.

Musician's Atlas 2000, 1. Leonard Hall. 1999. pap. text 19.95 (*0-634-00597-9*) H Leonard.

***Musician's Book of the Mass.** John Hajda & Diana Kaulback. LC 99-59953. (Illus.). 1999. pap. 7.95 (*0-89390-481-3*) Resource Pubns.

Musician's Business & Legal Guide. 2nd rev. ed. Ed. & Compiled by Mark E. Halloran. LC 95-26842. 462p. (C). 1996. pap. text 35.95 (*0-13-237322-X*) P-H.

***Musician's Business & Legal Guide.** 3rd ed. Mark E. Halloran. 456p. 2001. pap. text 36.00 (*0-13-031681-4*, Prentice Hall) P-H.

Musician's Dictionary. 2nd rev. ed. David W. Barber. (Illus.). 96p. (Orig.). 1997. pap. 11.95 (*0-920151-21-3*, Pub. by Sound & Vision) Firefly Bks Ltd.

Musician's Gig Library - Christmas Songs. Ed. by Tony Esposito. 112p. 1997. pap. 12.95 (*0-7692-0938-6*, FB9707) Wrner Bros.

Musician's Gig Library: Praise Songs, Spirituals & Hymns: Music for All Occasions. Ed. by Tony Esposito. 104p. 1997. pap. 17.95 (*0-7692-0984-X*, FB9708) Wrner Bros.

***Musician's Guide Through the Legal Jungle: Answers to Frequently Asked Questions about Music Law.** unabridged ed. Joy R. Butler. (Guide Through the Legal Jungle Audiobook Ser.). (Orig.). 2000. pap. 29.95 incl. audio (*0-9672940-0-2*) Sashay Commns.

Musician's Guide to Copyright & Publishing: New Copyright Law. Willis Wagner. 1978. pap. 10.95 (*0-912483-60-1*, T096) Bold Strummer Ltd.

Musician's Guide to Desktop Computing with Macintosh Computers. Benjamin Suchoff. LC 93-20276. 252p. (C). 1993. pap. 22.40 (*0-13-605726-8*) Prntice Hall Bks.

Musician's Guide to Home Recording: How to Make Great Recordings at Home. rev. ed. Peter Mclan & Larry Wichman. 320p. 1994. pap. 24.95 (*0-8256-1378-7*, AM91470) Omnibus NY.

Musician's Guide to Making & Selling Your Own CDs & Cassettes. Jana Stanfield. LC 97-25566. 160p. 1997. pap. 18.99 (*0-89879-808-6*, Wrtrs Digest Bks) F & W Pubns Inc.

Musician's Guide to Perception & Cognition. David E. Butler. 265p. 1992. 63.00 incl. cd-rom (*0-02-870341-3*, Schirmer Books) Mac Lib Ref.

Musician's Guide to Reading & Writing Music. Dave Stewart. LC 99-24983. (Illus.). 110p. 1999. pap. 9.95 (*0-87930-570-3*) Miller Freeman.

***Musician's Guide to the Internet.** 2nd ed. Gary Hustwit. 2000. pap. 14.95 (*0-634-01012-3*) H Leonard.

Musician's Handbook. M. Carlyle Hume. LC 97-41853. 225p. (C). 1998. pap. text 55.00 incl. audio compact disk (*0-13-856709-3*) P-H.

***Musician's Handbook.** M. Carlyle Hume. (Illus.). 1998. pap. 53.33 (*0-13-996034-1*) P-H.

Musician's Home Recording Handbook: Practical Techniques for Recording Great Music at Home. Ted Greenwald. (Illus.). 173p. 1992. pap. 19.95 (*0-87930-237-2*) Miller Freeman.

Musicians in Action: Fifty Ready-to-Use Activities for Grades 3-9, Unit 7. Audrey J. Adair. LC 87-8833. (Classroom Music Activities Library: Vol. 7). 112p. (C). 1987. pap. text 18.95 (*0-13-607144-9*) P-H.

Musicians in English Society from Elizabeth to Charles First. Walter L. Woodfill. LC 69-12694. (Music Ser.). (Illus.). 1969. reprint ed. lib. bdg. 42.50 (*0-306-71225-3*) Da Capo.

Musician's Little Book of Wisdom. Scott Power. LC 96-22582. 160p. 1996. pap. 5.95 (*1-57034-048-X*) Globe Pequot.

Musician's Manual for Chord Substitution. Dom Minasi. Ed. by Thomas Gambino. 30p. (Orig.). 1973. pap., student ed. 6.00 (*0-936519-03-7*) Sunrise Artistries.

Musician's Notebook: Manuscript Paper for Inspiration & Composition. Illus. by Martin Mayo. 96p. 1998. 5.95 (*0-7624-0369-1*) Running Pr.

Musicians of Bremen: A Tale from Germany. Jane Yolen. LC 94-30732. (Illus.). 32p. (J). (ps-2). 1996. mass mkt. 14.00 (*0-689-80501-2*) S&S Bks Yung.

Musicians of Bremen, Rapunzel & Sleeping Beauty. (Once upon a Time Children's Classics Retold in ASL Ser.: Vol. 4). 44p. (J). (ps-5). VHS 24.95 (*0-915035-42-1*, 4504) Dawn Sign.

Musicians of India: Past & Present, Gharanas of Hindustani Music & Genealogies. Amal Das Sharma. (C). 1993. 22.00 (*81-85421-18-8*, Pub. by Naya Prokash) S Asia.

Musicians of the Sun. Gerald McDermott. (J). 1997. write for info. (*0-614-29297-2*) S&S Childrens.

Musicians of the Sun. Gerald McDermott. LC 93-44050. (J). 1994. 14.95 (*0-590-47337-9*, Blue Sky Press) Scholastic Inc.

Musicians of the Sun, No. 1. Retold by Gerald McDermott. LC 96-19891. (Illus.). 40p. (J). (gr. k-4). 1997. per. 17.00 (*0-689-80706-6*) S&S Childrens.

Musicians of To-Day. Romain Rolland. Tr. by M. Blaiklock. LC 72-86777. (Essay Index Reprint Ser.). 1977. 21.95 (*0-8369-1188-1*) Ayer.

Musician's Practice Log. Burton Kaplan. 84p. (Orig.). (gr. 7-12). 1985. pap. 8.95 (*0-918316-04-9*) Percept Dev Tech.

***Musician's Practice Planner.** 86p. 1999. spiral bd. 6.95 (*0-9674012-0-8*) Molto Music.

Musician's Quest. George MacDonald. Ed. by Michael Phillips. LC 84-18508. Orig. Title: Robert Falconer. 272p. 1984. reprint ed. pap. 8.99 (*0-87123-444-0*) Bethany Hse.

Musician's Resource: The Watson-Guptill Guide to Workshops, Conferences, Artists' Colonies & Academic Programs. Gwendolyn Freed. LC 97-11997. (Getting Your Act Together Ser.). (Illus.). 176p. 1997. pap. 19.95 (*0-8230-7652-0*) Watsn-Guptill.

Musicians since 1900: Performers in Concert & Opera. Ed. & Compiled by David Ewen. LC 78-12727. 970p. 1978. 82.00 (*0-8242-0565-0*) Wilson.

***Musician's Soul.** James Jordan. 181p. 1999. 19.95 (*1-57999-058-4*, G-5095) GIA Pubns.

Musician's Studio Theory Workbook. 2nd rev. ed. Robert Grieco. 75p. 1995. wbk. ed. write for info. (*0-9650382-1-1*) Musicians Studio.

Musician's Survival Guide. Roger R. Clark. 60p. 1993. pap. text 12.95 (*0-9639190-0-8*) Time Traveler.

Musician's Survival Guide: To Life on the Road. Stella Hemmings. (Music How-To Ser.). 1998. pap. text 17.95 (*1-878427-68-7*) Cimino Pub Grp.

Musician's Survival Manual: A Guide to Preventing & Treating Injuries in Instrumentalists. Richard Norris. 1993. pap. text 19.95 (*0-918812-74-7*) MMB Music.

Musicians Talk. Leonora W. Armsby. LC 76-99679. (Essay Index Reprint Ser.). 1977. 21.95 (*0-8369-1338-8*) Ayer.

Musician's Theory Book: Reference to Fundamentals, Harmony, Counterpoint, Fugue & Form. Date not set. pap. 12.95 (*0-912483-61-X*) Pro-Am Music.

Musician's Theory Book: Reference to Fundamentals, Harmony, Counterpoint, Fugue & Form. Asger Hamerik. LC 83-71221. 1983. pap. text 15.95 (*0-935474-14-5*) Carousel Pubns Ltd.

Musicians Wrestle Everywhere: Emily Dickinson & Music. Carlton Lowenberg. LC 92-9923. (Reference Books in Music: No. 19). xxviii, 210p. 1992. 39.50 (*0-914913-20-4*, Fallen Lef Pr) Scarecrow.

Musicianship: For Singers, Jazz & Pop Vocalists. 84p. 1995. pap. 28.00 (*0-7935-5597-3*, 00740030) H Leonard.

Musicianship in Action: Piano Book. 68p. (YA). 1985. pap. 7.50 (*0-7692-0991-2*, EL02755) Warner Bros.

Musicien Francais Oublie, Marc-Antoine Charpentier, 1634-1704. Claude Crussard. LC 76-43912. (Music & Theatre in France in the 17th & 18th Centuries Ser.). reprint ed. 32.50 (*0-404-60155-3*) AMS Pr.

Musiciens de la Cour de Bourgogne au XVe Siecle, 1420-1467. Ed. by Janne Marix. LC 76-4478. (Illus.). reprint ed. 55.00 (*0-404-56627-8*) AMS Pr.

Musiciens Romains de l'Antiquite. Alain Baudot. LC 74-183208. (FRE., Illus.). 167p. reprint ed. pap. 51.80 (*0-7837-6950-4*, 204677900003) Bks Demand.

Musick Fyne. D. James Ross. 176p. 1996. 68.00 (*1-873644-17-5*, Pub. by Mercat Pr Bks) St Mut.

Musick of the Mocking Birds, the Roar of the Cannon: The Civil War Diary & Letters of William Winters. William Winters. Ed. by Steven E. Woodworth. (Illus.). 154p. 1998. text 35.00 (*0-8032-4773-7*, WINMUS) U of Nebr Pr.

Musicking: The Meanings of Performing & Listening. Christopher Small. LC 97-49996. (Music/Culture Ser.). 238p. 1998. pap. 16.95 (*0-8195-2257-0*, Wesleyan Univ Pr); text 40.00 (*0-8195-2256-2*, Wesleyan Univ Pr) U Pr of New Eng.

Musick's Monument. fac. ed. Thomas Mace. (Monuments of Music & Music Literature in Facsimile, II Ser.: Vol. 17). (Illus.). 1966. lib. bdg. 75.00 (*0-8450-2217-2*) Broude.

Musicmakers of West Africa. John Collins. LC 81-51651. (Illus.). 177p. 1985. 25.00 (*0-89410-075-0*, Three Contnts) L Rienner.

MusicMaster: The 45 RPM Record Directory by Artist (1997 Edition) rev. ed. Ed. by Paul C. Mawhinney. 1500p. 1997. pap. 100.00 (*0-910925-09-7*) Record-Rama.

MusicMaster: The 45 RPM Record Directory by Label (1997 Edition) rev. ed. Ed. by Paul C. Mawhinney. 1500p. 1997. pap. 100.00 (*0-910925-11-9*) Record-Rama.

MusicMaster: The 45 RPM Record Directory by Title (1997 Edition) rev. ed. Ed. by Paul C. Mawhinney. 1500p. 1997. pap. 100.00 (*0-910925-10-0*) Record-Rama.

MusicMasters & Gramophone Annuals, 1996, 3 vols., Set. Retail Entertainment Data Publishing Staff. (C). 1996. 175.00 (*0-02-864521-9*, Schirmer Books) Mac Lib Ref.

MusicMasters & Gramophone Annuals, 1996, 3 vols., Set. Retail Entertainment Data Publishing Staff. (C). 1996. text 350.00 incl. cd-rom (*0-02-864523-5*, Schirmer Books) Mac Lib Ref.

MusicMasters Annual Guide to Popular Recordings, 1996, 2 vols., Set. Retail Entertainment Data Publishing Staff. 1996. 115.00 (*0-02-864576-6*, Hall Reference) Macmillan.

Musicmasters Annual Guide to Popular Recordings, 1996, Vol. 1. Music Master Staff. 1996. 60.00 (*0-02-864515-4*, Schirmer Books) Mac Lib Ref.

***Musicmatch Jukebox Deluxe French.** 1999. 48.70 (*1-57595-381-1*) Macmillan Digit.

***Musicmatch Jukebox Deluxe German.** 1999. 69.95 (*1-57595-379-X*) Macmillan Digit.

MusicMedicine: International Society for Music in Medicine, Fourth International MusicMedicine Symposium. Ed. by Ralph Spintge & Roland Droh. 424p. (Orig.). 1992. pap. 29.95 (*0-918812-72-0*, ST 249) MMB Music.

Musico Prattico. Giovanni M. Bononcini. (Illus.). 164p. 1969. reprint ed. 65.00 (*0-318-71581-3*) G Olms Pubs.

Musicologie Medievale, Histoire et Methodes see Melanges de Musicologie Critique

Musicology: The Princeton Studies: Humanistic Scholarship in America. Frank L. Harrison. LC 73-21288. (Illus.). 337p. 1974. lib. bdg. 35.00 (*0-8371-6144-4*, HAMU, Greenwood Pr) Greenwood.

Musicology & Difference: Gender & Sexuality in Music Scholarship. Ed. by Ruth A. Solie. 353p. 1995. pap. 17.95 (*0-520-20146-9*, Pub. by U CA Pr) Cal Prin Full Svc.

Musicology & Other Delights see Paperplay Mini-Books

Musicology & Performance. Paul H. Lang et al. LC 96-39636. 272p. 1997. 35.00 (*0-300-06805-0*) Yale U Pr.

***Musicology & Sister Disciplines: Past, Present, Future: Proceedings of the 16th International Congress of the International Musicological Society, London 1997.** Ed. by David Greer. (Illus.). 712p. 2000. text 120.00 (*0-19-816734-2*) OUP.

Musicology in Ireland, No. 1. Ed. by Gerard Gillen & Harry White. LC 91-116055. (Irish Musical Studies: Vol. 1). (Illus.). 320p. (C). 1990. 45.00 (*0-7165-2456-2*, Pub. by Irish Acad Pr) Intl Spec Bk.

Musicology in the Nineteen Eighties: Methods, Goals, Opportunities. Ed. by D. Kern Holoman & Claude V. Palisca. LC 82-14966. (Music Reprint Ser.). 170p. 1982. lib. bdg. 23.50 (*0-306-76188-2*) Da Capo.

Musicplay: Learning Activities for Young Children. Leon Burton. 1979. pap. text 23.95 (*0-201-00883-1*) Addison-Wesley.

Musicplay: Recordings & Learning Activities for Young Children. Leon Burton. 1979. text 44.00 (*0-201-20940-3*) Addison-Wesley.

Music's All That Matters: A History of Progressive Rock. Paul Stump. 400p. 1998. pap. 16.95 (*0-7043-8036-6*, Pub. by Quartet) Interlink Pub.

***Music's Bride.** Marius Kociejowski. 60p. 2000. pap. 18.95 (*0-85646-318-3*, Pub. by Anvil Press) Dufour.

Musics Many Cultures. Dale A. Olsen. 280p. (C). 1996. pap. text 23.95 (*0-7872-1245-8*) Kendall-Hunt.

Musics of Hawaii: "It all Comes from the Heart": An Anthology of Musical Traditions in Hawaii (Compact Disc/ Book Package) Ed. & Tr. by Lynn J. Martin. (Illus.). 152p. 1998. pap. text 95.00 (*0-8248-2139-4*) UH Pr.

Musics of Hawaii: "Talking Story": A Series of Educational Programs Featuring Interviews with Traditional Musicans in Hawaii (Book/Cassette Package) Ed. & Tr. by Lynn J. Martin. Tr. & Photos by Clarence Lee Design & Associates Staff. (Illus.). 64p. 1998. pap. text 85.00 incl. audio (*0-8248-2140-8*) UH Pr.

Musics of Many Cultures: An Introduction. Ed. by Elizabeth May. LC 76-50251. (Illus.). 454p. 1980. pap. 27.50 (*0-520-04778-8*, Pub. by U CA Pr) Cal Prin Full Svc.

***Music's Social Powers: Soundtrack, Self & Embodiment in Everyday Life.** Tia DeNora. LC 99-52606. 2000. write for info. (*0-521-62206-9*); write for info. (*0-521-62732-X*) Cambridge U Pr.

Music's the Very Best Thing Vol. 1: Bill Black Irish Tune Collection. Bill Black. 1996. spiral bd. 28.00 (*0-9652458-0-2*) Sunphone.

Musicville Parade. Carol A. Hanshaw. (Interactive Books - Zoundies Ser.). 12p. (J). (ps-2). 1994. write for info. (*1-57234-024-X*) YES Ent.

Musik - Und die Geschichte der Philosophie und Naturwissenschaften im Mittelalter: Fragen zur Wechselwirkung von Musica und Philosophie im Mittelalter. Frank Hentschel. (Studien und Texte zur Geistesgeschichte des Mittelalters Ser.: No. 62). (Illus.). 380p. 1998. 135.00 (*90-04-11093-3*) Brill Academic Pubs.

***Musik als Lebensprogramm: Festschrift fur Constantin Floros zum 70. Geburtstag.** Gottfried Krieger & Matthias Spindler. 2000. 49.95 (*3-631-35406-1*) P Lang Pubng.

Musik & Dramaturgie: 15 Studien Fritz Hennenberg Zum 65. Geburtstag. Beate Hiltner-Hennenberg. (GER.). 207p. 1997. 42.95 (*3-631-31799-9*) P Lang Pubng.

Musik der Zwanziger Jahre. Ed. by Werner Keil. (Hildesheimer Musikwissenschaftliche Arbeiten Ser.: Vol. 3). (GER.). 1996. write for info. (*3-487-10263-3*) G Olms Pubs.

Musik des Altertums. Curt Sachs. 96p. 1980. reprint ed. write for info. (*3-487-06912-1*) G Olms Pubs.

Musik fur den Stummfilm: Analysierende Beschreibung originaler Filmkompositionen. Rainer Fabich. 1993. 54.80 (*3-631-45391-4*) P Lang Pubng.

***Musik Im Fernsehwerbespot.** Hildegund Leo. (GER., Illus.). 164p. 1999. 32.00 (*3-631-34527-5*) P Lang Pubng.

Musik in Deutschen Texten des Mittelalters. Kerstin Bartels. (Europaische Hochschulschriften Ser.: Reihe 1, Bd. 1601). (GER.). 518p. 1996. 82.95 (*3-631-31106-0*) P Lang Pubng.

Musik in Geschichte und Gegenwart: Allegemeine Enzyklopaedie der Musik, 17 vols., Set. Ed. by F. Blume. write for info. (*3-7618-0641-8*); write for info. (*3-7618-5913-9*) Adlers Foreign Bks.

Musik, Kommunikation, Ideologie see Music, Communication, Ideology

Musik und Geschichte. Hellmut Federhofer. (Musikwissenschaftliche Publikationen: Bd. 5). (Illus.). viii, 570p. 1996. write for info. (*3-487-10199-8*) G Olms Pubs.

Musik und Literatur: Komparatistische Studien zur Strukturverwandtschaft 2., Veranderte Auflage. 2nd ed. Albert Gier & Gerold W. Gruber. (Europaische Hochschulschriften, Reihe 36: No. 127). (GER.). 335p. 1997. 57.95 (*3-631-31939-8*) P Lang Pubng.

Musik-Welt, 1880-1882. Ed. by H. Robert Cohen. (Repertoire International de la Presse Musicale Ser.). (GER.). 229p. 1992. lib. bdg. 120.00 (*0-8357-2210-4*) Univ Microfilms.

Musikalisch-Kritische Bibliothek, 3 vols. in 1. Johann N. Forkel. xl, 1066p. 1964. reprint ed. write for info. (*0-318-71780-8*) G Olms Pubs.

Musikalisch-Literarischer Monatsbericht Neuer Musikalien, Musikalischer Schriften und Abbildungen. Carl F. Whistling. x, 718p. reprint ed. write for info. (*0-318-71878-2*) G Olms Pubs.

Musikalische Dialogen. Johann J. Heinse. (GER.). 238p. 1977. reprint ed. write for info. (*3-487-06257-7*) G Olms Pubs.

Musikalische Erscheinungsform der Trouverepoesie. Hans-Herbert S. Raekel. 391p. 1977. pap. 35.00 (*3-258-01149-4*) Theodore Front.

Musikalische Gedanke und die Logik, Technik und Kunst seiner Darstellung see Musical Idea & the Logic, Technique, & Art of Its Presentation

***Musikalische Interpretation: Reflexionen Im Spannungsfeld Von Notentext, Werkcharakter Und Auffuhrung Symposion Zum 80. Geburtstag Von Kurt Von Fischer, Zurich 1993 in Zusammenarbeit Mit Dorothea Baumann.** Joseph Willimann. 148p. 1999. 25.95 (*3-906762-32-7*) P Lang Pubng.

Musikalische Phrasierung Aus Historischer und Kognitionspsychologischer Sicht. Gunter Kreutz. Ed. by Helga De La Motte-Haber. (Schriften Zur Musikpsychologie und Musikasthetik Ser.: Vol. 10). (Illus.). 231p. 1998. pap. 39.95 (*3-631-32427-8*) P Lang Pubng.

Musikalische Spicilegien Ueber das Liturgische Drama, Orgelbau und Orgelspiel, das Ausserliturgische Lied und die Instrumentalmusik Desmittelalters. P. Anselm Schubiger. Ed. by Robert Eitner. (Publikation Alterer Praktischer und Theoretischer Musikwerke, XV. & XVI. Jhs. Ser.: Vol. 5). (GER & LAT.). 1966. reprint ed. lib. bdg. 55.00 (*0-8450-1705-5*) Broude.

Musikalische Werke: Erste Kritische Gesamtausgabe, 3 vols., Set. Carl M. Weber. (Musikalische Werke Ser.). (Illus.). 1977. reprint ed. lib. bdg. 300.00 (*0-89371-020-2*) Broude Intl Edns.

Musikalischer Almanach fur Deutschland Auf das Jahr 1782, Desgleichen 1783, 1784 und 1789, 4 vols., Set. Ed. by Johann N. Forkel. 1974. reprint ed. write for info. (*3-487-05215-6*) G Olms Pubs.

Musikalisches Lexikon. 4th ed. Johann G. Walther. (GER.). 732p. 1986. pap. 125.00 (*0-8288-2180-1*, M7565) Fr & Eur.

Musikanschauung, Musikpraxis, Kantatenkompositionen in der Herrnhuter Brudergemeine. Anja Wehrend. 1995. 79.95 (*3-631-48224-8*) P Lang Pubng.

***Musikermigrationen Im Deutschen Ostseeraum in der Ersten Halfte des 19, Jahrhunderts: Die Kleinstadt Greifswald - Ein Schnittpunkt Zahlreicher Reiserouten.** Kathleen Raatz. (Europaische Hochschulschriften, Reihe 36). Viii, 387p. 1999. 56.95 (*3-631-34756-1*) P Lang Pubng.

Musikerziehung in der Schweiz. Paul Kaelin. 269p. 1976. pap. 12.25 (*3-425-03764-1*) Theodore Front.

Musikkritischen Schriften Robert Schumanns: Versuch eines Literaturwissenschaftlichen Zugangs. Hans-Peter Fricker. (European University Studies: German Language & Literature: Ser. 1, Vol. 677). (GER.). 286p. 1983. 46.00 (*3-261-03275-8*) P Lang Pubng.

***Musikkultur Altisraels/Palastinas: Studien zu Archaologischen, Schriftlichen und Verleichenden Quellen.** Joachim Braun. (Orbis Biblicus et Orientalis Ser.: Vol. 164). (Illus.). xii, 388p. 1999. text 80.50 (*3-7278-1246-X*, Pub. by Ed Univ Fri) Eisenbrauns.

Musikpsychologie. Ernst Kurth. (GER.). xii, 324p. 1995. reprint ed. write for info. (*3-487-02696-1*) G Olms Pubs.

***Musiktherapie und Sauglingsforschung: Zusammenspiel. Einschatzung der Beziehungsqualitat am Beispiel des instrumentalen Ausdrucks eines autistischen Kindes 2., durchgesehene Auflage.** Karin Schumacher. 2000. 42.95 (*3-631-36052-5*) P Lang Pubng.

Musikwirtschaft und Neue Musik: Das Unternehmerische Entscheidungsverhalten Zwischen Asthetik und Okonomie. Axel Sikorski. (Europaische Hochschulschriften: Reihe 5: Bd. 2163). (GER., Illus.). 242p. 1997. 51.95 (*3-631-32291-7*) P Lang Pubng.

***Musil-Paraphrasen II/Musil-Paraphrases II: Eine Kunstlerische Auseinandersetzung Mit Musils Mann Ohne Eigenschaften/An Artist's Approach to Musils Man Without Qualities.** Brigitta Westphal. (Illus.). 75p. 1999. 55.95 (*3-906761-90-8*, Pub. by P Lang) P Lang Pubng.

Musil's Socratic Discourse in "Der Mann Ohne Eigenschaften" A Comparative Study of Ulrich & Socrates. Daniel J. Brooks. (American University Studies: Germanic Languages & Literature: Ser. I, Vol. 81). IX, 169p. (C). 1989. text 32.95 (*0-8204-0923-5*) P Lang Pubng.

Musing: Poems from Hollywood. Mark Dunster. 11p. 1998. pap. 5.00 (*0-89642-509-6*) Linden Pubs.

Musing in Rhyme. George F. Brown, Sr. (Illus.). 46p. (Orig.). 1998. pap. 10.00 (*0-9663188-1-1*) Oceanfront Pub.

Musing on the Vernacular. Alastair Johnston. 36p. 1988. 12.00 (*0-918395-09-7*) Poltroon Pr.

***Musing Through Towns in Mississippi.** Wynelle Scott Deese. (Postcard History Ser.). (Illus.). 128p. 1999. pap. 18.99 (*0-7385-0038-0*) Arcadia Publng.

Musings. 425p. (Orig.). 1995. 45.00 (*1-885206-22-4*, Iliad Pr) Cader Pubng.

Musings . . . A Collection of Poems for & about Children. Emory H. Jennings. (Collection of Poems for & about Children). 64p. (J). (gr. k-6). 1991. pap. 7.95 (*1-885754-00-0*) E H Jennings.

Musings: One Man's Thoughts. James M. Kemp. LC 98-91346. 60p. 1998. pap. 7.50 (*0-9630899-2-7*) J M Kemp.

***Musings: Poems & Essays.** James M. Kemp. 70p. 2000. pap. text 7.50 (*0-9630899-3-5*) J M Kemp.

***Musings: Poems from Hollywood.** Mark Dunster. 11p. 1999. pap. 5.00 (*0-89642-809-5*) Linden Pubs.

***Musings: Tales of Truth & Wisdom.** Linda M. Ford. (Illus.). 272p. 2000. pap. 22.95 (*1-55591-980-4*) Fulcrum Pub.

Musings: The Musical Worlds of Gunther Schuller. Gunther A. Schuller. 336p. 1989. reprint ed. pap. 11.95 (*0-19-505921-2*) OUP.

Musings: The Musical Worlds of Gunther Schuller--A Collection of His Writings. Gunther Schuller. LC 98-48220. (Illus.). 320p. 1999. reprint ed. mass mkt. 15.95 (*0-306-80902-8*, Pub. by Da Capo) HarpC.

Musings & Forebodings. Grant E. Perry. LC 93-71088. (Illus.). 60p. (Orig.). 1993. pap. 7.95 (*1-878149-22-9*) Counterpoint Pub.

Musings & Memories of a Musician. George Henschel. (Music Reprint Ser.). 1979. reprint ed. lib. bdg. 45.00 (*0-306-79540-X*) Da Capo.

Musings by Luci . . . Lucille G. Williams. 1998. pap. write for info. (*1-57553-653-6*) Watermrk Pr.

Musings for a Mellow Mood. Jacquie Hoffman. (Illus.). 65p. (Orig.). 1979. reprint ed. pap. 4.95 (*0-9604082-0-7*) I J Hoffman.

Musings for Meditation. Arleen Lorrance. LC 76-14783. (Illus.). 180p. (Orig.). 1976. pap. 7.95 (*0-916192-03-2*) L P Pubns.

Musings from a Sufi. Kismet D. Stam. 62p. 1980. 8.95 (*0-85692-025-8*, Pub. by East-West) Omega Pubns NY.

Musings from the Menopause. Jeanne LaVasque. LC 90-91722. (Illus.). 61p. (Orig.). 1990. pap. 9.95 (*0-9628454-0-X*) Polliwog Pr.

***Musings of a Barrio Sack Boy.** L. Luis Lopez. LC 00-132264. x, 81p. 2000. pap. 10.00 (*0-9679844-0-8*) Farolito Pr.

Musings of a Biophilious Metaphysician, Vol. 1. Mona Feirson. ii, 55p. 1997. spiral bd. 10.00 (*0-9661982-0-4*) Ensoulment Educ.

***Musings of a Lagniappe Lover: On Reaching the Last Third of the Last Third Of Life.** Hymie Samuelson. LC 99-35287. 1999. 14.00 (*1-57168-335-6*, Eakin Pr) Sunbelt Media.

Musings of a Modern Mystic. Peter O. Childs. LC 95-92015. 160p. (Orig.). 1995. pap. text 12.50 (*0-9644830-0-9*) Dos Plumas Pub.

Musings of an Average African-American Man. Tom Wyche. 84p. 1999. pap. 10.00 (*0-9671687-0-8*) Sincere Thoughts.

Musings on a Misspent Youth. John R. Judge. 130p. (Orig.). 1994. pap. write for info. (*0-9638059-0-8*) Buono Pubng.

Musings with God. Dottie Denton. (Illus.). 90p. (Orig.). 1987. reprint ed. 7.00 (*0-9625420-0-8*); reprint ed. pap. 5.00 (*0-9625420-1-6*) Dottie May Pub.

Musiphysicality for Piano. S. Bernstein. 72p. 1991. pap. 9.95 (*0-7935-0609-3*) H Leonard.

Musique. R. De Cande. (FRE.). 550p. 75.00 (*0-686-56978-4*, M-6105) Fr & Eur.

Musique Anodine-Album Italiano: The Critical Edition of the Works of Gioachino Rossini. Gioachino Rossini. 1996. lib. bdg. 80.00 (*0-226-72853-6*) U Ch Pr.

Musique au Theatre. Antoine L. Maillot. LC 80-2288. 1981. reprint ed. 44.00 (*0-404-18856-7*) AMS Pr.

An Asterisk (*) at the beginning of an entry indicates that the title is appearing for the first time.

Musique Cajun et Musique Noires: Cajun Music & Black Music. Robert Sacre. (FRE., Illus.). (Orig.). 1990. spiral bd. 15.95 (*0-913714-74-7*, Pub. by Editions Creatal) Random House.
Musique Chinoise: A Study of Chinese Music. Louis Laloy. (Illus.). 96p. 1993. pap. 18.50 (*0-910704-75-9*) Hawley.
Musique des Troubadours. Johann B. Beck. (Illus.). reprint ed. 34.50 (*0-404-56526-3*) AMS Pr.
Musique, Deuxieme Fascicule see Maitres Musiciens de la Renaissance Francaise
Musique d'Orgue au XVe Siecle et au Debut du XVIe. Yvonne Rokseth. (GER.). xviii, 418p. 1996. reprint ed. 150.00 (*3-487-10036-3*) G Olms Pubs.
Musique et Liturgie: Le Graduel et l'Antiphonaire Romains; Histoire et Description. Amedee Gastoue. LC 70-178577. (FRE.). reprint ed. 45.00 (*0-404-56608-1*) AMS Pr.
Musique Fantastique: A Survey of Film Music in the Fantastic Cinema. Randall D. Larson. LC 84-13954. 602p. 1984. 52.00 (*0-8108-1728-4*) Scarecrow.
Musique Francaise de Piano Avant 1830. Georges Favre. LC 76-43917. (Music & Theatre in France in the 17th & 18th Centuries Ser.). reprint ed. 40.00 (*0-404-60158-8*) AMS Pr.
Musique Instrumentale: Pieces de Clavecin en Concerts, Six Concerts en Sextour see Oeuvres Completes de Jean-Philippe Rameau
Musique mise a la Portee de Tout le Monde see Music Explained to the World
Musique Piano 1: Dictionnaire des Compositeurs Ouevres, A-I. G. Sacre. (FRE.). 1998. 89.95 (*0-320-00295-0*) Fr & Eur.
Musique Piano 2: Dictionnaire des Compositeurs Ouevres, J-Z. G. Sacre. (FRE.). 1998. 89.95 (*0-320-00296-9*) Fr & Eur.
Musique pour Cameleon. Truman Capote. (FRE.). 308p. 1991. pap. 11.95 (*0-7859-2144-3*, 2070382672) Fr & Eur.
Musique, Premier Fascicule see Maitres Musiciens de la Renaissance Francaise
Musique, Troiseme Fascicule see Maitres Musiciens de la Renaissance Francaise
Musiques de Scenes: Level C. Sagan. text 8.95 (*0-88436-745-2*) EMC-Paradigm.
*__Musk Ox: And Other Poems.__ Anne H. Greet. LC 98-33509. (Illus.). 107 p. 1999. pap. 10.00 (*1-56474-287-3*) Fithian Pr.
Musk Ox Babies of the Far North. Helen Von Ammon. LC 96-96232. (Illus.). 52p. (Orig.). (J). 1997. pap. text 12.95 (*0-9647756-5-4*) Doodlebug Bks.
Musk Oxen: Bearded Ones of the Arctic. Margaret Rau. LC 75-26538. (Illus.). 40p. (J). (gr. 3-7). 1976. lib. bdg. 10.89 (*0-690-01040-0*) HarpC Child Bks.
Muskeg & the Northern Environment in Canada. Muskeg Research Conference Staff. Ed. by N. W. Radforth & C. O. Brawner. LC 76-54734. (Illus.). 417p. reprint ed. pap. 129.30 (*0-8357-8238-7*, 203398000088) Bks Demand.
Muskeg Engineering Handbook. National Research Council of Canada, Associate Com. Ed. by Ivan C. MacFarlane. LC 78-447167. (Canadian Building Ser.: No. 3). 320p. reprint ed. pap. 99.20 (*0-608-16673-1*, 205611400050) Bks Demand.
Muskegon - At the Peak of the Lumber Area: A Pictorial Companion to the Novel "Sawdust Fires" Thomas Carlson. (Illus.). 30p. 1998. pap. 8.50 (*0-9665487-1-X*) T Carlson.
Muskegon's Jewish Community: A Centennial History, 1888-1988. Dennis S. Devlin. (Illus.). 84p. (Orig.). 1988. pap. text 9.95 (*0-9620751-0-8*) Congr Bnai Israel.
Muskerry. Robert Welch. (C). 1991. 24.00 (*0-948268-94-8*, Pub. by Dedalus); pap. 15.00 (*0-948268-93-X*, Pub. by Dedalus) St Mut.
Musket, Anchor, & Plow: The Story of River Edge, 1677-1976. Naomi Howitt & George Howitt. 1976. 15.95 (*0-405-09859-6*, 19430) Ayer.
Muskets & Altars: Jeremy Taylor & the Last of the Anglicans. Reginald Askew. 1998. pap. write for info. (*0-264-67462-6*, Pub. by A R Mowbray) Cassell & Continuum.
*__Muskets of Gascony.__ John Salmon. (Illus.). 307p. 2000. 27.95 (*0-7541-1211-X*) Minerva Pr.
Muskie, Muskie, on the Wall. George W. Sandell. LC 86-90547. (True Facts of Life along the Muskie Trail Ser.). (Illus.). 160p. (Orig.). 1986. pap. 9.95 (*0-940107-03-1*) Muskie Mem Pr.
Muskingum County Footprints, Vol. 7, 1987. 70p. 1987. pap. 9.00 (*0-917033-06-X*) Muskingum.
Muskingum County Footprints, Vol. 8, 1987. 132p. 1987. pap. 13.25 (*0-917033-07-8*) Muskingum.
Muskingum County Footprints, Vol. 9, 1988. 102p. 1988. pap. 11.25 (*0-917033-08-6*) Muskingum.
Muskingum County Footprints Vol. 2: Miscellaneous Records, Muskingum County, Ohio. Sylvia S. Hargrove & Hilda E. Yinger. 60p. (Orig.). 1984. pap. text 9.00 (*0-917033-01-9*) Muskingum.
Muskingum County Footprints Vol. 3: 1860 Mortality Schedule, Death Records 1900-1901, Land Records, Various Church Records. Sylvia S. Hargrove & Hilda E. Yinger. 58p. 1986. pap. 8.00 (*0-917033-02-7*) Muskingum.
Muskingum County Footprints Vol. 4: Will Book Index, 1804-1831. Sylvia S. Hargrove & Hilda E. Yinger. 1986. pap. 8.00 (*0-917033-03-5*) Muskingum.
Muskingum County Footprints Vol. 5: Naturalizations, 1860-1875. Sylvia S. Hargrove & Hilda E. Yinger. 1986. pap. 8.00 (*0-917033-04-3*) Muskingum.
Muskingum County Footprints Vol. 6: Will Book Index, 1832. Sylvia S. Hargrove & Hilda E. Yinger. 1986. pap. 8.00 (*0-917033-05-1*) Muskingum.
Muskingum County, Ohio: J. F. Everhart History Index & Muskingum County Duplicate Tax Lists of 1807. Fay Maxwell. 53p. 1976. 12.00 (*1-885463-19-7*) Ohio Genealogy.
Muskingum County, Ohio: Marriages, 1804-1818 & Some of 1818-1835. Fay Maxwell. 86p. 1977. 19.00 (*1-885463-18-9*) Ohio Genealogy.
Muskoka. John De Visser. (Illus.). 120p. 1995. pap. text 24.00 (*1-55046-049-8*, Pub. by Boston Mills) Genl Dist Srvs.
Muskoka Souvenir. John De Visser & Judy Ross. (Illus.). 80p. 1995. 15.95 (*1-55046-125-7*, Pub. by Boston Mills) Genl Dist Srvs.
Muskoka II. Judy Ross. (Illus.). 120p. 1998. 39.95 (*1-55046-237-7*, Pub. by Boston Mills) Genl Dist Srvs.
Muskoka's Grand Hotels. Barbaranne Boyer. (Illus.). 192p. 1992. pap. 24.95 (*1-55046-051-X*, Pub. by Boston Mills) Genl Dist Srvs.
*__Muskoxen & Their Hunters: A History.__ Peter C. Lent. LC 99-15298. (Animal Natural History Ser.). 352p. 1999. 57.50 (*0-8061-3170-5*) U of Okla Pr.
Muskrat: A Surprise Bid for the America's Cup. 3rd ed. Douglas Hanks, Jr. 239p. (Orig.). 1989. reprint ed. pap. 12.00 (*0-9624156-0-X*, TXU-270-198) Creekside Pubs.
*__Muskrat Courage.__ Philip Lawson. LC 00-24756. 288p. 2000. text 23.95 (*0-312-26207-8*, Minotaur) St Martin.
Muskrat Farm. Dan Cushman. LC 59-6988. 1977. 12.95 (*0-911436-05-7*) Stay Away.
Muskrat Trapper's Guide. Mitchell S. Ricketts. LC 88-81827. (Illus.). 182p. (Orig.). 1988. pap. 13.95 (*0-9617720-1-8*) Elk River Pr.
Muskrat Will Be Swimming. Cheryl Savageau. LC 95-40293. (Illus.). 32p. (J). (gr. 1-3). 1996. lib. bdg. 14.95 (*0-87358-604-2*, Rising Moon Bks) Northland AZ.
Muskulistaya Smert: Raskazi. Mikhail Armalinskii, pseud. (RUS.). 150p. (Orig.). 1984. pap. 6.00 (*0-916201-00-7*, 83-63508) M I P Co.
Musky Mastery: The Techniques of Top Guides. Steve Heiting. LC 91-77559. (Illus.). 160p. 1992. pap. 9.95 (*0-87341-198-6*) Krause Pubns.
Muslim Almanac I. Azim Nanji. LC 95-17324. 581p. 1995. 105.00 (*0-8103-8924-X*) Gale.
Muslim & a Christian in Dialogue. 2nd ed. Badru D. Kateregga & David W. Shenk. LC 96-49805. Orig. Title: Islam & Christianity: A Muslim & a Christian Response. 224p. 1997. pap. 14.99 (*0-8361-9052-1*) Herald Pr.
Muslim & Parsi Castes & Tribes of Gujarat. James M. Campbell. 1990. reprint ed. 41.00 (*81-85326-29-0*, Pub. by Vintage) S Asia.
Muslim Architecture of Egypt, 2 vols. K. A. Creswell. LC 75-11056. (Illus.). 1978. reprint ed. lib. bdg. 500.00 (*0-87817-175-4*) Hacker.
Muslim Bonaparte: Diplomacy & Orientalism in Ali Pasha's Greece. K. E. Fleming. LC 98-36435. 1999. 45.00 (*0-691-00194-4*, Pub. by Princeton U Pr) Cal Prin Full Svc.
*__Muslim Bonaparte: Diplomacy & Orientalism in Ali Pasha's Greece.__ K. E. Fleming. LC 98-36435. 1999. pap. 19.95 (*0-691-00195-2*, Pub. by Princeton U Pr) Cal Prin Full Svc.
Muslim Brotherhood. S. Hawwa. 1988. 9.95 (*1-56744-153-X*) Kazi Pubns.
Muslim Brotherhoods & Politics in Senegal. Lucy Behrman. LC 70-95918. 240p. 1970. 30.50 (*0-674-59490-8*) HUP.
Muslim Brothers & the Palestine Question, 1928-1947. Al-Fattah. (Modern Middle East Studies). 256p. 1998. text 59.50 (*1-86064-214-4*, Pub. by I B T) St Martin.
Muslim Cemetery in Fields V & VI-IX (Stratum II) J. Kenneth Eakins. LC 80-21724. (Joint Archaeological Expedition to Tell el-Hesi Ser.: No. 5). (Illus.). xvii, 214p. 1993. text 35.00 (*0-931464-78-1*) Eisenbrauns.
Muslim Character. Al-Ghazali. 220p. 1988. pap. 6.50 (*1-56744-154-8*) Kazi Pubns.
*__Muslim Child.__ Inayat I. Kahn. 72p. 1999. pap. text 11.95 (*0-929141-61-X*) Napoleon Publ.
Muslim Chinese: Ethnic Nationalism in the People's Republic. Dru C. Gladney. (East Asian Monographs: Vol. No. 149). (Illus.). 473p. (C). 1991. 38.00 (*0-674-59495-9*) HUP.
Muslim Chinese: Ethnic Nationalism in the People's Republic. 2nd ed. Dru C. Gladney. (East Asian Monographs: No. 149). (Illus.). 493p. 1996. pap. 24.00 (*0-674-59497-5*) HUP.
Muslim-Christian Dialogue: Promise & Problems. Ed. by M. Darrol Bryant & Syed A. Ali. LC 98-26383. 275p. 1998. pap. 14.95 (*1-55778-764-6*) Paragon Hse.
Muslim-Christian Marriages in the Philippines: Studies Made in North Cotabato. Luis Q. Lacar. (Humanities Publications Ser., Silliman University: No. 2). (Illus.). 100p. (C). 1981. pap. 7.50 (*0-686-31074-8*, Pub. by New Day Pub) Cellar.
Muslim-Christian Relations: Dialogue in Lebanon. John J. Donohue. (Occasional Papers Ser.). iii, 24p. 1996. pap. 3.95 (*1-929218-10-9*) Georgetwn U Ctr Muslim.
Muslim-Christian Relations: Past, Present, Future. Ovey N. Mohammed. LC 98-47530. 196p. 1999. pap. 16.00 (*1-57075-257-5*) Orbis Bks.
Muslim-Christian Relations & Inter-Christian Rivalries in the Middle East. John Joseph. 240p. 1996. pap. 19.95 (*0-614-21677-X*, 859) Kazi Pubns.
Muslim-Christian Relations & Inter-Christian Rivalries in the Middle East: The Case of the Jacobites in an Age of Transition. John Joseph. LC 82-870. 240p. (C). 1984. text 24.50 (*0-87395-600-1*) State U NY Pr.
Muslim Cities, No. 3. IIIT Staff. 440p. 1995. ring bd. 24.95 (*0-7872-1623-2*) Kendall-Hunt.
Muslim Civilization & the Crisis in Iran. Ravi Batra. 218p. (Orig.). 1980. pap. 3.95 (*0-686-95468-8*) Ananda Marga.
Muslim Communities in North America. Ed. by Yvonne Y. Haddad & Jane I. Smith. LC 93-36564. (SUNY Series in Middle Eastern Studies). 545p. (C). 1994. text 89.50 (*0-7914-2019-1*); pap. text 29.95 (*0-7914-2020-5*) State U NY Pr.
Muslim Communities in the New Europe. Gerd Nonneman. 1998. pap. text 19.95 (*0-86372-223-7*, Pub. by Garnet-Ithaca) LPC InBook.
Muslim Communities of South Asia: Culture, Society, & Power. Ed. by Triloki N. Madan. LC 95-906177. (C). 1995. reprint ed. 28.50 (*81-7304-090-7*, Pub. by Manohar) S Asia.
Muslim Communities Reemerge. F. Kappeler. 132p. 1996. pap. 24.95 (*0-614-21163-8*, 1354) Kazi Pubns.
Muslim Communities Reemerge: Historical Perspectives on Nationality, Politics, & Opposition in the Former Soviet Union & Yugoslavia. Andreas Kappeler et al. Ed. by Gerhard Simon et al. Tr. by Caroline Sawyer from GER. LC 93-43021. (Central Asia Book Ser.).Tr. of Die Muslime in der Sowjetunion und in Jugoslawien. 384p. 1994. text 64.95 (*0-8223-1447-9*); pap. text 24.95 (*0-8223-1490-8*) Duke.
Muslim Contribution to Civilization. Haidar Bammate. 1985. 2.75 (*0-89259-029-7*) Am Trust Pubns.
Muslim Contribution to Geography. N. Ahmad. 1993. pap. 15.50 (*1-56744-155-6*) Kazi Pubns.
Muslim Contribution to Science & Culture. M. A. Khan. 1991. pap. 3.50 (*1-56744-156-4*) Kazi Pubns.
Muslim Cooking of Pakistan. K. G. Saiyidain. 160p. (Orig.). 1991. pap. 7.50 (*1-56744-341-9*) Kazi Pubns.
Muslim Creed: Its Genesis & Historical Development. Arent J. Wensinck. 311p. 1932. reprint ed. text 24.00 (*0-685-13805-4*) Coronet Bks.
Muslim Cross Word Puzzles. Muhammad Gamiet. 32p. (J). 1996. pap. 3.50 (*0-614-21029-1*, 841) Kazi Pubns.
Muslim Devotions: A Study of Prayer-Manuals in Common Use. Constance E. Padwick. 313p. 1996. pap. 19.95 (*1-85168-115-9*, 574, Pub. by Onewrld Pubns) Penguin Putnam.
*__Muslim Diaspora: A Comprehensive Reference to the Spread of Islam in Asia, Africa, Europe & the Americas.__ Everett Jenkins, Jr. LC 98-49332. (Illus.). 437p. 1999. lib. bdg. 75.00 (*0-7864-0431-0*) McFarland & Co.
*__Muslim Diaspora Vol. 2, 1500-1799: A Comprehensive Reference to the Spread of Islam in Asia, Africa, Europe & the Americas.__ Everett Jenkins, Jr. (Illus.). 423p. 2000. lib. bdg. 75.00 (*0-7864-0744-1*) McFarland & Co.
Muslim Discovery of Europe. Bernard Lewis. (Illus.). 352p. 1985. pap. 13.95 (*0-393-30233-4*) Norton.
Muslim Diversity: Local Islam in Global Contexts. Leif Manger. 288p. 1998. 75.00 (*0-7007-1104-X*, Pub. by Curzon Pr Ltd) Paul & Co Pubs.
Muslim Doctorine of God. S. W. Zwimmer. 130p. 1987. 195.00 (*1-85077-903-1*, Pub. by Darf Pubs Ltd) St Mut.
Muslim Economic Thinking: A Survey of Contemporary Literature. Muhammad N. Siddiqi. 130p. (Orig.). 1981. 10.50 (*0-86037-082-8*, Pub. by Islamic Fnd); pap. 5.25 (*0-86037-081-X*, Pub. by Islamic Fnd) New Era Publns MI.
Muslim Education in Medieval Times. Bayard Dodge. LC 63-144. 1962. 3.75 (*0-916808-02-5*) Mid East Inst.
Muslim Educational Institutions. Hisham Nashabe. 183p. 1989. 16.95 (*0-86685-470-3*, LDL4703, Pub. by Librairie du Liban) Intl Bk Ctr.
Muslim Etiquettes. Abdur-Rahman Shad. 1981. 16.50 (*1-56744-157-2*) Kazi Pubns.
Muslim Eurasia: Conflicting Legacies. Ed. by Yaacov Ro'i. 1995. pap. 24.50 (*0-7146-4142-1*, Pub. by F Cass Pubs) Intl Spec Bk.
Muslim Eurasia: Conflicting Legacies. Ed. by Yaacov Ro'i. LC 94-40028. (Cummings Center Ser.). 330p. 1995. 52.50 (*0-7146-4615-6*, Pub. by F Cass Pubs) Intl Spec Bk.
Muslim European Youth: Reproducing Ethnicity, Religion, Culture. Ed. by Steven Vertovec & Alisdair Rogers. LC 98-70995. (Research in Ethnic Relations Ser.). 224p. 1998. text 59.95 (*1-84014-341-X*, Pub. by Ashgate Pub) Ashgate Pub Co.
Muslim Extremism in Egypt: The Prophet & Pharaoh. Gilles Kepel. 250p. 1986. pap. 15.95 (*0-520-08543-4*, Pub. by U CA Pr) Cal Prin Full Svc.
Muslim Family: A Study of Women's Rights in Islam. Tove S. Dahl. 211p. (C). 1997. text 31.00 (*82-00-22420-1*) Scandnvan Univ Pr.
Muslim Family Reader. Saidi J. El Liwaru & Maisha Z. El Liwaru. Ed. by Hamid Quinlan. pap. 6.50 (*0-89259-108-0*) Am Trust Pubns.
Muslim Family Reader, 2. Saidi J. El Liwaru & Maisha Z. El Liwaru. Ed. by Hamid Quinlan. LC 82-74126. 1991. 6.50 (*0-89259-080-7*) Am Trust Pubns.
Muslim Festival in India & Other Essays. Garcin de Tassy. Ed. by M. Waseem. (Illus.). 208p. (C). 1996. 18.95 (*0-19-563677-5*) OUP.
Muslim Filipinos: Heritage & Horizon. Peter G. Gowing. (Illus.). 1979. pap. 17.50 (*971-10-0239-6*, Pub. by New Day Pub) Cellar.
Muslim Friends: Their Faith & Feeling. Roland E. Miller. 1996. 19.00 (*0-570-04624-6*, 12-3205) Concordia.
Muslim Fundamentalism in Israel. Raphael Israeli. 200p. 1993. text 58.00 (*0-08-041793-0*, Pub. by Brasseys) Brasseys.
Muslim Hausa Women in Nigeria: Tradition & Change. Barbara J. Callaway. LC 87-6464. (Illus.). 264p. 1987. text 39.95 (*0-8156-2406-9*) Syracuse U Pr.
Muslim Heroes of the Twentieth Century. S. M. Mashoor. 112p. (Orig.). 1985. pap. 6.95 (*1-56744-342-7*) Kazi Pubns.
Muslim Holidays see Ethnic Holidays Series
Muslim Holidays. Nunir A. Shaikh & Kamran S. Aghaie. 36p. 1997. pap. 7.00 (*1-930109-01-6*) Council on Islamic.
Muslim Identity & Community Consciousness. Asim P. Chakrabarti. (C). 1993. 22.00 (*81-85195-58-7*, Pub. by Minerva) S Asia.
Muslim Identity & Social Change in Sub-Saharan Africa. Ed. by Louis Brenner. LC 93-10131. (Illus.). 260p. (C). 1994. 36.95 (*0-253-31269-8*); pap. 15.95 (*0-253-31271-X*) Ind U Pr.
Muslim Identity & the Balkan State. Suha Taji-Farouki. LC 97-28044. 1997. text 40.00 (*0-8147-8228-0*) NYU Pr.
Muslim Inmates & Prison Officials: Answers to Most Frequently Asked Questions. 1998. pap. 6.95 (*1-56744-573-X*) Kazi Pubns.
Muslim Intellectual & Social History: A Collection of Essays. Franz Rosenthal. (Collected Studies: No. CS309). 336p. 1990. text 115.95 (*0-86078-257-3*, Pub. by Variorum) Ashgate Pub Co.
Muslim Intellectuals & National Developments in Indonesia. Howard M. Federspiel. 215p. (C). 1992. pap. text 95.00 (*1-56072-033-6*) Nova Sci Pubs.
Muslim-Jewish Encounters: Intellectual Expressions & Modern Politics, Vol. 4. Ed. by Ronald L. Nettler & Suha Taji-Farouki. (Studies in Mulsim-Jewish Relations). 219p. 1998. text 30.00 (*90-5702-195-1*, Harwood Acad Pubs); pap. text 14.00 (*90-5702-196-X*, Harwood Acad Pubs) Gordon & Breach.
Muslim, Jews & Pagans: Studies on Early Islamic Medina. Michael Lecker. 160p. 1996. 51.50 (*0-614-21164-6*, 1364) Kazi Pubns.
Muslim Jurisprudence & Qur'anic Laws of Crimes. Mir Waliullah. 175p. 1996. 18.50 (*0-614-21203-0*, 846) Kazi Pubns.
Muslim Jurisprudence & the Qur'anic Laws of Crimes. Mir Waliullah. 1992. 21.50 (*1-56744-158-0*) Kazi Pubns.
*__Muslim Kingship in India.__ Ed. by Nagendra K. Singh. 1999. 34.00 (*81-261-0436-8*, Pub. by Anmol) S Asia.
Muslim Law. 2nd ed. Rashid Khalid. (C). 1990. 60.00 (*0-7855-5143-3*) St Mut.
Muslim Law: Syed Khalid Rashid's. Syed K. Rashid & V. P. Bharatiya. 1999. pap. 30.00 (*81-7012-562-6*, Pub. by Eastern Book) St Mut.
Muslim Law Courts & the French Colonial State in Algeria. Allan Christelow. LC 84-42878. 334p. reprint ed. pap. 103.60 (*0-608-06368-1*, 206672900008) Bks Demand.
Muslim Law of Inheritance. Muhammed U. Al-Haj. 225p. 1986. 19.95 (*0-318-37194-4*) Asia Bk Corp.
Muslim Law of Marriage, Divorce & Maintenance. 2nd ed. Vijay Malik. (C). 1988. 60.00 (*0-7855-5474-2*) St Mut.
Muslim Military History: A Preliminary Bibliography. Muhammad Naeem. (Orig.). 1992. pap. 12.00 (*1-56744-460-1*) Kazi Pubns.
Muslim Mind. Charis Waddy. (Illus.). 218p. (C). 1990. pap. 19.95 (*1-56131-014-X*, NAB) I R Dee.
Muslim Minorities in the World: Research Papers & Proceedings of the 6th International Conference of Wamy. Ed. & Frwd. by Aal Al-Sheikh. (ARA.). 507p. (Orig.). pap. write for info. (*1-882837-08-8*) W A M Y Intl.
Muslim Minorities in the World Vol. 2: Research Papers & Proceedings of the 6th International Conference of Wamy. Intro. by Tawfik Al-Kausar. (ARA.). 479p. (Orig.). pap. write for info. (*1-882837-07-X*) W A M Y Intl.
Muslim Minorities in the World Vol. 3: Research Papers & Proceedings of the 6th International Conference of Wamy. 438p. (Orig.). pap. write for info. (*1-882837-06-1*) W A M Y Intl.
Muslim Mosque see Places of Worship
Muslim Mosque. Umar Heredus. (Keystones Ser.). (Illus.). 32p. (J). (gr. 2-6). 1998. 16.95 (*0-7136-4335-8*, Pub. by A & C Blk) Midpt Trade.
*__Muslim Mosque.__ Umar Heredus. (Keystones Ser.). (Illus.). 32p. (J). (gr. 2-6). 2000. pap. write for info. (*0-7136-5344-2*, Pub. by A & C Blk) Midpt Trade.
Muslim Mothers' Child-Rearing Method: Islamic Child-Rearing in 5 Steps. Yuhaayaa L. Kaahena. Ed. by Latifa Ismail. 56p. (Orig.). 1993. pap. 5.00 (*1-883781-00-0*) Yuhaaya.
Muslim Mystic Movement in Bengal, 1301-1550. S. Abdul Latif. (C). 1993. 14.00 (*81-7074-136-X*, Pub. by KP Bagchi) S Asia.
Muslim Names. 1985. pap. 3.25 (*0-89259-030-0*) Am Trust Pubns.
Muslim Names & Their Meanings. Muhammad A. Nu'Man & Muhammad A. Nu'man. 20p. (Orig.). reprint ed. pap. 2.50 (*0-933821-02-6*) New Mind Prod.
Muslim National Communism in the Soviet Union: A Revolutionary Strategy for the Colonial World. Alexandre A. Benningsen & Enders S. Wimbush. LC 78-8608. xxii, 304p. 1980. pap. text 7.95 (*0-226-04236-7*, P915) U Ch Pr.
Muslim Neoplatonism. Ian R. Netton. 1991. pap. text 27.00 (*0-7486-0251-8*, Pub. by Edinburgh U Pr) Col U Pr.
Muslim Nursery Rhymes. Mustafa Y. McDermott. 40p. (J). 1996. pap. 3.50 (*0-614-21030-5*, 1588) Kazi Pubns.
Muslim Peoples: A World Ethnographic Survey, 2 vols., Set. 2nd ed. Ed. by Richard V. Weekes. LC 83-18494. (Illus.). 953p. 1984. lib. bdg. 150.00 (*0-313-23392-6*, WMP/) Greenwood.
Muslim Peoples: A World Ethnographic Survey, 2 vols., Vol. 1. 2nd ed. Ed. by Richard V. Weekes. LC 83-18494. (Illus.). 953p. 1984. lib. bdg. 100.00 (*0-313-24639-4*, WMP/01) Greenwood.
Muslim Peoples: A World Ethnographic Survey, 2 vols., Vol. 2. 2nd ed. Ed. by Richard V. Weekes. LC 83-18494. (Illus.). 953p. 1984. lib. bdg. 100.00 (*0-313-24640-8*, WMP/02) Greenwood.

M

M

Muslim Perceptions of Other Religions Throughout History. Ed. by Jacques Waardenburg. LC 97-29982. 368p. 1999. text 85.00 (*0-19-510472-2*) OUP.
Muslim Philosopher on the Soul & Its Fate: Al-Amiri's Kitab al-Amad ala L-Abad. Everett Rowson. 375p. 1996. 42.50 (*0-614-21210-3*, 2) Kazi Pubns.
Muslim Philosopher on the Soul & Its Fate: Al-Amiri's Kitab al-Amad 'ala l'abad. Everett K. Rowson. (Amer. Oriental Ser.: Vol. 70). vi, 375p. 1988. 42.50 (*0-940490-70-6*) Am Orient Soc.
Muslim Philosophy & Philosophers. Mohammad S. Khan & Mohammad A. Saleem. viii, 130p. 1994. 16.00 (*81-7024-623-7*, Pub. by Ashish Pub Hse) Nataraj Bks.
Muslim Poems for Children. Mymona Hendricks. 48p. (J). 1996. pap. 3.50 (*0-614-21031-3*, 848) Kazi Pubns.
Muslim Political Thought in India. Ed. by Mohamed Taher. 1998. 44.00 (*81-7488-943-4*) Anmol.
Muslim Politics. Dale F. Eickelman & James P. Piscatori. LC 95-41203. (Princeton Studies in Muslim Politics). 240p. 1996. text 39.50 (*0-691-03184-3*, Pub. by Princeton U Pr); pap. text 14.95 (*0-691-00870-1*, Pub. by Princeton U Pr) Cal Prin Full Svc.
Muslim Politics in India. S. K. Ghosh. 1986. 18.50 (*81-7024-070-0*, Pub. by Ashish Pub Hse) S Asia.
Muslim Politics in the Punjab. J. S. Rakkar. 1986. 36.00 (*0-8364-1904-9*, Pub. by Deep & Deep Pubns) S Asia.
Muslim Preacher in the Modern World: A Jordanian Case Study in Comparative Perspective. Richard T. Antoun. LC 88-21482. 305p. 1989. reprint ed. pap. 94.60 (*0-608-02938-6*, 206400400008) Bks Demand.
***Muslim Primer: Beginner's Guide to Islam.** 2nd ed. Ira G. Zepp, Jr. 356p. 2000. pap. 22.50 (*1-55728-595-0*) U of Ark Pr.
Muslim Recipe Book for MGT/GCC: How to Cook What You Eat to Live. Elijah Muhammad. Ed. by Reda F. Khalifah. 1995. reprint ed. pap. 5.95 (*1-56411-082-6*, 4BBG0087) Untd Bros & Sis.
***Muslim Reformist Political Thought Revivalists, Modernist & Free Will.** Sarfraz Kahn. 288p. 2000. 80.00 (*0-7007-1237-2*, Pub. by Curzon Pr Ltd) Paul & Co Pubs.
Muslim Resistance to the Tsar: Shamil & the Conquest of Chechnia & Daghestan. Moshe Gammer. (Illus.). 452p. 1994. text 62.50 (*0-7146-3431-X*, Pub. by F Cass Pubs) Intl Spec Bk.
Muslim Response to Western Education. Masroor Hashmi. (C). 1989. 31.00 (*81-7169-005-X*, Pub. by Gian Publng Hse) S Asia.
Muslim Revivalist Movements in Northern India in the 16th & 17th Century: In the Sixteenth & Seventeenth Centuries. Saiyid A. Rizvi. 376p. (C). 1995. reprint ed. 42.00 (*81-215-0590-9*, Pub. by M Manoharial) Coronet Bks.
Muslim Rule in Deccan: Encyclopaedic Survey of Islamic Culture. 1998. 42.00 (*81-7488-540-4*) Anmol.
Muslim Rule in Kashmir: 1554 A. D. to 1586 A. D. Nizam-Ud-Din-Wani. (C). 1993. 30.00 (*81-7041-831-3*, Pub. by Anmol) S Asia.
Muslim Rulers & Rebels: Everyday Politics & Armed Separatism in the Southern Philippines. Thomas M. McKenna. LC 97-49422. (Comparative Studies on Muslim Societies). 343p. 1998. 50.00 (*0-520-21015-8*, Pub. by U CA Pr); pap. 20.00 (*0-520-21016-6*, Pub. by U CA Pr) Cal Prin Full Svc.
Muslim Sects & Divisions: The Section on Muslim Sects in Kitab Al-Milal Wa L-Nihal. Muhammad B. Shahrastani. Tr. by A. K. Kazi & J. G. Flynn. 180p. 1984. 45.00 (*0-7103-0063-8*) Routledge.
Muslim Sister to Sister: Understanding Muslim Women. Yuhaayaa L. Kaahena. Ed. by Latifa Ismail. 68p. (Orig.). 1992. pap. 8.00 (*1-883781-02-7*) Yuhaaya.
Muslim Slave System in Medieval India. K. S. Lal. LC 94-905167. (C). 1995. 17.50 (*81-85689-67-9*, Pub. by Aditya Prakashan) S Asia.
Muslim Society. Ernest Geller. LC 80-41103. (Cambridge Studies in Social & Cultural Anthropology: No. 32). 267p. 1983. pap. text 24.95 (*0-521-27407-9*) Cambridge U Pr.
Muslim Society. Ernest Gellner. 267p. 1996. pap. 16.95 (*0-614-21518-8*, 849) Kazi Pubns.
Muslim Society in a Transition. Arifa K. Javed. (C). 1990. 34.00 (*81-7169-096-3*, Pub. by Commonwealth) S Asia.
Muslim Society in Northern India: 15th & Early Half of the 16th Century. M. Zaki. (C). 1996. 20.00 (*81-7074-175-0*, Pub. by KP Bagchi) S Asia.
Muslim Society in Transition: Titu Meer's Revolt. Dutta Abhijit. 241p. (C). 1987. 21.00 (*0-8364-2175-2*, Pub. by Minerva) S Asia.
Muslim Spain & Portugal: A Political History of Al-Andalus. Hugh Kennedy. LC 96-22764. 360p. (C). 1997. pap. 28.00 (*0-582-49515-6*) Longman.
Muslim Spain, Its History & Culture. Anwar G. Chejne. LC 73-87254. (Illus.). 587p. reprint ed. pap. 182.00 (*0-608-15949-2*, 203321200084) Bks Demand.
Muslim Theologian's Response to Christianity: A Translation of Ibn Taymiyya's Jawab al-Sahih li-man Baddala din al-Masih. Ibn Taymiya. Tr. by Thomas F. Michel. LC 83-15430. (Studies in Islamic Philosophy & Science). 480p. 1985. 75.00 (*0-88206-058-9*) Caravan Bks.
Muslim Theologian's Response to Christianity: Ibn Taymiya's al-Jawab al-Sahih li-Man Baddal Din Al-Masih. Ibn Taymiya. Tr. by Thomas F. Michel. 480p. 1996. 75.00 (*0-614-21676-1*, 1365) Kazi Pubns.
Muslim Thought, Its Origin & Achievements. A. A. Shariff. 1994. pap. 8.50 (*1-56744-159-9*) Kazi Pubns.
Muslim Tradition in Psychotherapy & Modern Trends. Syed A. Rizvi. 1995. 25.50 (*1-56744-160-2*) Kazi Pubns.
Muslim Travellers: Pilgrimage, Migration & the Religious Imagination. Ed. by Dale F. Eickelman & James P. Piscatori. LC 90-33657. 310p. 1990. pap. 18.95 (*0-520-07252-9*, Pub. by U CA Pr) Cal Prin Full Svc.
Muslim Travellers: Pilgrimage, Migration & the Religious Imagination. Dale F. Eickelman & James P. Piscatori. 1990. 55.00 (*0-520-07019-4*, Pub. by U CA Pr) Cal Prin Full Svc.
Muslim Tribes of Lakshadweep Islands: An Anthropological Appraisal of Island Ecology & Cultural Perceptions. Makhan Jha. LC 98-901916. 82p. 1997. pap. 150.00 (*81-7533-032-5*, Pub. by Print Hse) St Mut.
***Muslim Turkistan: Razak Religion & Collective Memory.** Bruce G. Privratsky. (Illus.). 336p. 2000. 85.00 (*0-7007-1297-6*, Pub. by Curzon Pr Ltd) Paul & Co Pubs.
Muslim Vidhi: Muslim Law in Hindi. 2nd ed. S. L. Agarwal. (HIN.). (C). 1980. 35.00 (*0-7855-5477-7*) St Mut.
Muslim Wives Have Comfort, Ease & Happiness: She's Not a Housewife, She Is a Man's Wife. Yuhaayaa L. Kaahena. Ed. & Tr. by Latifa Ismail. 48p. (Orig.). 1995. pap. 5.00 (*1-883781-09-4*) Yuhaaya.
Muslim Woman Believer: The Journey of Becoming. Laleh Bakhtiar. 80p. 1989. pap. text 5.60 (*1-871031-08-7*) Abjad Bk.
Muslim Women: In Purdah & Out of It. J. Brijbhushan. 133p. 1980. 14.95 (*0-318-37060-3*) Asia Bk Corp.
Muslim Women: In the Family & the Society. Fathi Osman. 60p. 1991. pap. text 3.00 (*1-881504-02-6*) Minaret Pubns.
Muslim Women: Problems & Prospects. Ed. by Zakia A. Siddiqi & Arwar Jahan Zuberi. 158p. 1993. pap. 140.00 (*81-85880-04-2*, Pub. by Print Hse) St Mut.
Muslim Women & Higher Education. Anis Ahmad. 107p. 1992. pap. 4.95 (*1-56744-447-4*) Kazi Pubns.
Muslim Women & the Politics of Participation: Implementing the Beijing Platform. Ed. by Mahnaz Afkhami & Erika Friedl. LC 97-25582. (Gender, Culture & Politics in the Middle East Ser.). 192p. 1997. 39.95 (*0-8156-2759-9*); pap. 19.95 (*0-8156-2760-2*) Syracuse U Pr.
Muslim Women in Changing Perspective. Talat A. Ashrafi. (C). 1992. 28.50 (*81-7169-172-2*, Pub. by Commonwealth) S Asia.
Muslim Women in India. Ed. by Mohini Anjum. 225p. 1992. text 22.50 (*81-7027-153-3*, Pub. by Radiant Pubs) S Asia.
Muslim Women in India: Political & Private Realities, 1890s-1980s. Shahida Lateef. LC 90-39964. 240p. (C). 1990. text 62.50 (*0-86232-954-X*, Pub. by St Martin); text 19.95 (*0-86232-955-8*, Pub. by St Martin) St Martin.
Muslim Women in Medieval India. Zinat Kausar. ix, 340p. 1992. 31.00 (*81-85078-74-2*, Pub. by Janaki) Nataraj Bks.
Muslim Women in Mombasa, 1890-1975. Margaret Strobel. LC 79-10721. 271p. reprint ed. pap. 84.10 (*0-7837-3280-5*, 205767800006) Bks Demand.
Muslim Women in the Midst of Change. Zakaria Bashier. 32p. 1996. pap. 3.75 (*0-614-21391-6*, 855) Kazi Pubns.
Muslim Women in West Bengal. K. N. Jehangir. (C). 1992. 17.50 (*81-85195-42-0*, Pub. by Minerva) S Asia.
***Muslim Women Mystics: The Life & Work of Rabi'a & Other Women Mystics in Islam.** Margaret Smith. 2001. pap. 19.95 (*1-85168-250-3*, Pub. by Onewrld Pubns) Element MA.
Muslim Women of the British Punjab: From Seclusion to Politics. Dushka H. Saiyid. LC 98-11477. 192p. 1998. text 59.95 (*0-312-21459-6*) St Martin.
Muslim Women (Protection of Rights on Divorce) Act. V. R. Iyer. (C). 1989. 50.00 (*0-89771-753-8*, Pub. by Eastern Book) St Mut.
***Muslim Women Through the Centuries.** Kamran S. Aghaie. Ed. by Munir A Shaikh. 51p. 1998. spiral bd. 15.00 (*1-930109-02-4*) Council on Islamic.
Muslim Women Throughout the World: A Bibliography with Selected Annotations. Michelle Kimball & Barbara R. Von Schlegell. LC 96-25718. 285p. 1997. lib. bdg. 75.00 (*1-55587-680-3*, 876803) L Rienner.
Muslim Women's Choices: Religious Belief & Social Reality. Ed. by Camillia F. El-Solh & Judy Mabro. LC 93-36551. (Cross-Cultural Perspectives on Women Ser.). 224p. 1996. 39.50 (*0-85496-835-0*, Pub. by Berg Pubs); pap. 17.50 (*0-85496-836-9*, Pub. by Berg Pubs) NYU Pr.
Muslim World: Geography & Development. Ed. by Mushtaqur Rahman. LC 87-14087. (Illus.). 202p. (Orig.). (C). 1987. pap. text 21.50 (*0-8191-6559-X*); lib. bdg. 38.00 (*0-8191-6558-1*) U Pr of Amer.
Muslim World Cook Book. Women's Committee. 134p. 1996. pap. 5.50 (*0-614-21519-6*, 1382) Kazi Pubns.
Muslim World (Islam Breaks Fresh Ground) T. C. Rastogi. 1986. 29.00 (*81-7024-039-5*, Pub. by Ashish Pub Hse) S Asia.
Muslim World Issues & Challenges. Fathi Osman. 510p. 1989. pap. text 10.00 (*1-881504-06-9*) Minaret Pubns.
Muslim Youth Speak: Voices of Muslim Youth. Ed. by Yahiya Emerick. 110p. (J). (gr. 6-9). 1998. pap. write for info. (*1-889720-21-6*, Pub. by Amirah Pubng) Intl Bks & Tapes.
Muslims. Ernest Hahn. LC 95-8309. (Response Ser.). 64p. 1995. 3.99 (*0-570-04677-7*, 12-6010) Concordia.
Muslims: Their Religious Beliefs & Practices, Vol. 1, The Formative Period, Vol. 1. Andrew Rippin. LC 89-10442. 192p. (C). (gr. 13). 1990. pap. 25.99 (*0-415-04519-3*, A4179) Routledge.
Muslims Vol. 2: Their Religious Beliefs & Practices, Vol. 2. Andrew Rippin. (Library of Religious Beliefs & Practices). 192p. (C). 1993. pap. 25.99 (*0-415-04528-2*) Routledge.
Muslims Vols. 1 & 2: Their Religious Beliefs & Practices: The Formative Years & the Contemporary Period. Andrew Rippin. 400p. 1996. pap. 36.00 (*0-614-21471-8*, 1434) Kazi Pubns.
Muslims & Christians: Enemies or Brothers? Jean-Rene Milot. Tr. by Mary T. Noble from FRE. LC 96-36972.Tr. of Musulmans & Chretiens: Des Freres Ennemis?. 88p. (Orig.). 1997. mass mkt. 4.95 (*0-8189-0779-7*) Alba.
***Muslims & Christians at the Table: Promoting Biblical Understanding among North American Muslims.** Bruce A. McDowell & Anees Zaka. LC 99-45496. 342p. 1999. pap. 14.99 (*0-87552-473-7*) P & R Pubng.
Muslims & Christians Face to Face. Kate Zebiri. LC 98-185624. 288p. 1997. pap. 22.95 (*1-85168-133-7*, Pub. by Onewrld Pubns) Penguin Putnam.
Muslims & Christians on the Emmaus Road. Ed. by J. Dudley Woodberry. 392p. reprint ed. pap. 15.95 (*0-912552-65-4*) MARC.
Muslims & Indian National Congress. Moin Shakir. 1987. 16.50 (*81-202-0186-8*, Pub. by Ajanta) S Asia.
Muslims & Islamization in North America: Problems & Prospects. Amber Haque. LC 99-30397. 492p. 1999. 19.95 (*0-915957-91-4*) amana pubns.
Muslims & Missionaries in Pre-Mutiny India. Avril A. Powell. (SOAS London Studies on South Asia: No. 7). 368p. (C). 1996. text 50.00 (*0-7007-0210-5*, Pub. by Curzon Pr Ltd) UH Pr.
Muslims & Modernization. Sushila Jain. 1986. 27.50 (*81-7033-009-2*, Pub. by Rawat Pubns) S Asia.
Muslims & the Congress: Correspondence of Dr. M. A. Ansari. M. A. Ansari. Ed. by Masud U. Hasan. 1979. 18.50 (*0-8364-0381-9*) S Asia.
Muslims & the Third World Politics. Attar Chand. (C). 1993. 24.00 (*81-7041-625-6*, Pub. by Anmol) S Asia.
***Muslims & the West: Quest for "Change" & Conflict Resolution.** Mahboob A. Khawaja. 240p. 2000. 42.50 (*0-7618-1652-6*) U Pr of Amer.
Muslim's Character. M. Al-Ghazali. 240p. pap. write for info. (*1-882837-23-1*) W A M Y Intl.
***Muslims in America.** F. Denny. (Illus.). 2000. pap. 0.00 (*0-19-510919-8*) OUP.
Muslims in America: Seven Centuries of History, 1312-1998: Collections & Stories of American Muslims. Amir N. Muhammad. LC 97-52570. 1998. 8.95 (*0-915957-78-7*) amana pubns.
Muslims in Assan Politics. M. Kar. LC 97-903297. (C). 1997. 44.00 (*81-259-0169-8*, Pub. by Vikas) S Asia.
Muslims in Central Asia. F. Gross. 132p. 1996. pap. 21.95 (*0-614-21165-4*, 1353) Kazi Pubns.
Muslims in Central Asia: Expressions of Identity & Change. Ed. by Jo-Ann Gross. LC 91-13772. (Central Asia Book Ser.). 240p. 1991. pap. text 23.95 (*0-8223-1190-9*) Duke.
Muslims in Central Asia: Expressions of Identity & Change. Ed. by Jo-Ann Gross. LC 91-13772. (Central Asia Book Ser.). 240p. 1992. text 49.95 (*0-8223-1187-9*) Duke.
Muslims in Dialogue: The Evolution of a Dialogue. Ed. by Leonard Swidler. LC 92-9459. 564p. 1992. lib. bdg. 119.95 (*0-88946-499-5*) E Mellen.
Muslims in Europe. Ed. by Bernard Lewis & Dominique Schnapper. LC 94-13756. (Social Change in Western Europe Ser.). 1994. 39.00 (*1-85567-250-2*); pap. 15.00 (*1-85567-214-6*) St Martin.
Muslims in India: A Bibliography of Their Religious, Socio-Economic & Political Literature. Satyaprakash. 1986. 34.00 (*0-8364-1558-2*, Pub. by Indian Doc Serv) S Asia.
Muslims in India: A Biographical Dictionary, Vol. II. Ed. by Naresh K. Jain. 1984. 40.00 (*0-8364-1150-1*, Pub. by Manohar) S Asia.
Muslims in India: Recent Contributions to Literature on Religion, Philosophy, History, & Social Aspects. Mohamed Taher. 1993. 29.50 (*81-7041-620-5*, Pub. by Anmol) S Asia.
Muslims in India Vol. 1: Their Educational, Demographic & Socio-Economic Status with Comparative Indicators for Hindus, Sikhs, Christians & Other Communities, Based on a Singular & Systematic Field Survey 1990-1993, No. 1. Bihar A. Ahmad. (C). 1993. 42.00 (*81-210-0317-2*, Pub. by Inter-India Pubns) S Asia.
Muslims in India & Abroad: Caste & Ethnicity. Abdul Matin. (C). 1996. 26.00 (*81-7024-755-1*, Pub. by Ashish Pub Hse) S Asia.
Muslims in Our Community & Around the World, Grade 2. IIIT (Douglass) Staff. 80p. 1995. ring bd. 14.95 (*0-8403-9940-5*) Kendall-Hunt.
Muslims in Singapore: A Shared Vision. Zuraidah Ibrahim. (Illus.). 126p. 1996. pap. 29.00 (*0-614-21470-X*, 1502) Kazi Pubns.
***Muslims in the Philippines.** Cesar Adib Majul. (Illus.). 488p. 1999. pap. text 40.00 (*971-542-188-1*, Pub. by U of Philippines Pr) UH Pr.
Muslims in the West: The Message & the Mission. A. Nadwi. Ed. by Khurram Murad. 191p. (Orig.). 1983. pap. 6.95 (*0-86037-130-1*) New Era Publns MI.
Muslims in Western Europe. Jorgen S. Nielsen. (Islamic Surveys Ser.). (Illus.). 192p. 1992. 42.50 (*0-7486-0309-3*, Pub. by Edinburgh U Pr) Col U Pr.
Muslims in Western Europe. Jorgen S. Nielsen. (Islamic Surveys Ser.). 192p. 1992. pap. 17.50 (*0-7486-0364-6*, Pub. by Edinburgh U Pr) Col U Pr.
Muslims in Western Europe. 2nd ed. Jorgen S. Nielsen. 192p. 1995. pap. 17.50 (*0-7486-0617-3*, Pub. by Edinburgh U Pr) Col U Pr.
Muslims, Jews, & Pagans: Studies on Early Islamic Medina. Michael Lecker. LC 95-9833. (Islamic History & Civilization, Studies & Text Ser.: Vol. 13). xviii, 180p. 1995. 68.50 (*90-04-10247-7*) Brill Academic Pubs.
***Muslims, Magic & the Kingdom of God.** Rick Lovell. LC 00-31222. 2000. pap. write for info. (*0-87808-443-6*) William Carey Lib.
Muslims of America. Ed. by Yvonne Y. Haddad. 250p. 1996. 39.95 (*0-614-21442-4*, 860); pap. 19.95 (*0-614-21441-6*, 860) Kazi Pubns.
Muslims of America. Ed. by Yvonne Y. Haddad. (Religion in America Ser.). (Illus.). 272p. (C). 1993. reprint ed. pap. text 19.95 (*0-19-508559-0*) OUP.
Muslims of Bosnia - Herzegovina: Their Historic Development from the Middle Ages to the Dissolution of Yugoslavia. rev. ed. Ed. by Mark Pinson. (C). 1996. reprint ed. pap. 14.95 (*0-932885-12-8*) Harvard CMES.
Muslims of British India. Peter Hardy. LC 77-184772. (Cambridge South Asian Studies: No. 13). 317p. reprint ed. pap. 90.40 (*0-608-13311-6*, 2025585) Bks Demand.
Muslims of India. Mohammed Haroon. (C). 1989. 52.00 (*81-85004-16-1*, Pub. by Manohar) S Asia.
Muslims of Jammu & Kashmir. R. Hari Om. 160p. 1986. 150.00 (*0-7855-1822-3*, Pub. by Archives Pubs) St Mut.
Muslims of Jammu & Kashmir: A Study in the Spread of Education & Consciousness, 1857-1925. R. Hari Om. 156p. 1986. 12.00 (*0-685-58187-X*, Pub. by Archives Pubs) Nataraj Bks.
Muslims of Sri Lanka under the British Rule. M. N. Asad. (C). 1993. 22.00 (*81-7013-099-9*, Pub. by Navarang) S Asia.
Muslims of Valencia in the Age of Fernando & Isabel. Mark D. Meyerson. 370p. 1996. 49.95 (*0-614-21628-1*, 861) Kazi Pubns.
Muslims of Valencia in the Age of Fernando & Isabel: Between Coexistence & Crusade. Mark D. Meyerson. LC 90-35502. (Illus.). 382p. 1991. 58.00 (*0-520-06888-2*, Pub. by U CA Pr) Cal Prin Full Svc.
***Muslims on the Americanization Path?** Ed. by Yvonne Yazbeck Haddad & John L. Esposito. (Illus.). 376p. 2000. pap. 18.95 (*0-19-513526-1*) OUP.
Muslims Through Discourse: Religion & Ritual in Gayo Society. John R. Bowen. LC 92-34217. (Illus.). 370p. (C). 1993. text 57.50 (*0-691-09475-6*, Pub. by Princeton U Pr); pap. text 21.95 (*0-691-02870-2*, Pub. by Princeton U Pr) Cal Prin Full Svc.
Muslims under Latin Rule, 1100-1300. James M. Powell. LC 90-34238. 229p. reprint ed. pap. 71.00 (*0-608-20142-1*, 207141400011) Bks Demand.
Musocal Immunity & the Gut Epithelium: Interactions in Health & Disease. Ed. by S. Auricchio et al. (Dynamic Nutrition Research Ser.: Vol. 4). (Illus.). viii, 188p. 1995. 186.25 (*3-8055-6063-X*) S Karger.
Musonii Rufi. Ed. by Hense. (GRE.). 1990. reprint ed. pap. 24.95 (*3-322-00747-2*, T1542, Pub. by B G Teubner) U of Mich Pr.
Musonius Rufus. Amand Jagu. (Studien und Materialien Zur Geschichte der Philosophie Ser.: No. 5). 116p. 1979. write for info. (*3-487-06628-9*) G Olms Pubs.
Musorgsky: Eight Essays & an Epilogue. Richard F. Taruskin. 449p. 1992. pap. text 19.95 (*0-691-01623-2*, Pub. by Princeton U Pr) Cal Prin Full Svc.
Musorgsky: Eight Essays & an Epilogue. Richard F. Taruskin. (Illus.). 460p. 1992. text 55.00 (*0-691-09147-1*, Pub. by Princeton U Pr) Cal Prin Full Svc.
Musorgsky: "Pictures at an Exhibition" Michael Russ. (Cambridge Music Handbooks Ser.). (Illus.). 111p. (C). 1992. pap. text 13.95 (*0-521-38607-1*) Cambridge U Pr.
Musorgsky Reader: A Life of Modeste Petrovich Musorgsky in Letters & Documents. Ed. by Jay Leyda & Sergei Bertensson. LC 70-87393. (Music Ser.). (Illus.). 1970. reprint ed. lib. bdg. 49.50 (*0-306-71534-1*) Da Capo.
Musorgsky's Days & Works: A Biography in Documents. Aleksandra A. Orlova. Ed. & Tr. by Roy J. Guenther. LC 82-4826. (Russian Music Studies: No. 4). 719p. reprint ed. pap. 200.00 (*0-8357-1324-5*, 207043600089) Bks Demand.
Mussadiq & the Struggle for Power in Iran. Katouzian. 305p. 2000. text 22.50 (*1-86064-290-X*, Pub. by I B T) St Martin.
Mussaurus see New Dinosaur Collection
Musse ou l'Ecole de l'Hypocrisie. Jules Romains, pseud. (FRE.). 144p. 1959. pap. 10.95 (*0-7859-1312-2*, 2070255255) Fr & Eur.
Musse und Kult - Was Heisst Philosophieren? see Leisure: The Basis of Culture
Mussel Cookbook. Sarah Hurlburt. (Illus.). 168p. 1977. pap. text 8.95 (*0-674-59542-4*) HUP.
Mussel Mytilus: Ecology, Physiology, Genetics, & Culture. Ed. by Elizabeth Gosling. LC 92-24364. (Developments in Aquaculture & Fisheries Science Ser.: Vol. 25). 590p. 1992. 171.75 (*0-444-88752-0*) Elsevier.
Mussel Slough Tragedy. James L. Brown. (Illus.). 153p. 1980. reprint ed. pap. 6.00 (*0-686-31567-7*) J L Brown.
Musselman's Guide to Minor League Basketball, Vol. I, No. 1. rev. ed. Christian S. Anderson & Eric P. Musselman. 250p. (Orig.). 1995. pap. text 45.00 (*0-9636968-0-7*) Goose Prods.
Mussels: Hard-Shelled Mollusks see Secrets of the Animal World New Releases
Mussels at Midnight. S. Anderson. Date not set. pap. 6.99 (*0-906731-93-3*, Pub. by Christian Focus) Spring Arbor Dist.
Musset: Five Plays, No. 5. Alfred De Musset. (Methuen Anthologies Ser.). 1995. pap. 15.95 (*0-413-69240-X*, A0747) Heinemann.
***Musset: Lorenzaccio.** Alfred De Musset. Ed. by Derek Connon. (Modern Language Ser.). (FRE.). 192p. 1998. pap. text 20.95 (*1-85399-516-9*, Pub. by Brist Class Pr) Focus Pub-R Pullins.
Musset et Shakespeare: Etude Analytique de l'Influence de Shakespeare sur le Theatre d'Alfred de Musset. Cecil Malthus. Ed. by Rex A. Barrell. (American University Studies: Romance Languages & Literature: Ser. II, Vol. 62). XIV, 449p. (C). 1988. text 56.50 (*0-8204-0490-X*) P Lang Pubng.

An Asterisk (*) at the beginning of an entry indicates that the title is appearing for the first time.

Mussolini. Laura Fermi. LC 63-9728. (Phoenix Bks.). (Illus.). 485p. reprint ed. pap. 150.40 (*0-608-09296-7*, 205417000004) Bks Demand.

***Mussolini: A Biography.** Jasper Ridley. (Illus.). 2000. pap. 19.95 (*0-8154-1081-6*, Pub. by Cooper Sq) Natl Bk Netwk.

Mussolini: A Biography. Jasper Ridley. LC 98-37813. 448p. 1998. 27.50 (*0-312-19303-3*, Thomas Dunne) St Martin.

Mussolini: A Biography. Denis M. Smith. LC 83-5759. 464p. 1983. pap. 18.00 (*0-394-71658-2*) Vin Bks.

Mussolini: His Part in My Downfall. large type ed. Spike Milligan. 21.95 (*1-85695-182-0*, Pub. by ISIS Lrg Prnt) Transaction Pubs.

Mussolini: Red & Black. Armando Borghi. LC 73-20389. (Studies in Political Science: No. 94). 1974. lib. bdg. 75.00 (*0-8383-1765-0*) M S G Haskell Hse.

Mussolini: The Birth of the New Democracy. Gertrude M. Godden. 1977. lib. bdg. 59.95 (*0-8490-2309-2*) Gordon Pr.

Mussolini & Fascism. Marco Palla. LC 99-44263. (Illustrated Histories Ser.). (Illus.). 160p. 2000. pap. 15.00 (*1-56656-340-2*) Interlink Pub.

Mussolini & Fascist Italy. Martin Blinkhorn. (Lancaster Pamphlets Ser.). 64p. 1984. pap. text 6.95 (*0-415-04022-1*, NO. 4164) Routledge.

Mussolini & Fascist Italy. 2nd ed. Martin Blinkhorn. LC 93-45640. (Lancaster Pamphlets Ser.). 80p. (C). 1994. pap. 11.99 (*0-415-10231-6*, B2466) Routledge.

Mussolini & Italian Fascism. Hamish Macdonald. (Pathfinder History Ser.). (Illus.). 64p. (YA). (gr. 11 up). 1999. pap. 15.95 (*0-7487-3386-8*, Pub. by S Thornes Pubs) Trans-Atl Phila.

Mussolini & the British. Richard Lamb. LC 98-180709. (Illus.). 336p. 1998. 45.00 (*0-7195-5592-2*, Pub. by John Murray) Trafalgar.

Mussolini & the Cult of Italian Youth. P. Roy. 1972. 250.00 (*0-8490-0685-6*) Gordon Pr.

Mussolini As Diplomat: Il Duce's Italy on the World Stage. Richard Lamb. LC 99-38378. (Illus.). 368p. 1999. 30.00 (*0-88064-244-0*, Pub. by Fromm Intl Pub) FS&G.

Mussolini, the Man of Destiny: Studies in Fascism: Ideology & Practice. Vittorio E. De Fiori. Tr. by Mario A. Pei from ITA. LC 78-63673. (Illus.). 288p. 1982. reprint ed. 34.50 (*0-404-16933-3*) AMS Pr.

Mussolini's Afrika Korps: The Italian Army in North Africa, 1940-1943. Rex Trye. (Illus.). 200p. 1999. 36.00 (*1-891227-14-9*, Axis Europa Bks) Axis Europa.

Mussolini's Empire: The Rise & Fall of the Fascist Vision. Edwin P. Hoyt. 298p. 1994. 24.95 (*0-471-59151-3*) Wiley.

Mussolini's Enemies: The Italian Anti-Fascist Resistance. Charles F. Delzell. LC 61-7406. 641p. reprint ed. pap. 198.80 (*0-608-09164-2*, 200056200030) Bks Demand.

***Mussolini's Shadow: The Double Life of Count Galeazzo Ciano.** Ray Moseley. LC 99-34242. (Illus.). 302p. 2000. 29.95 (*0-300-07917-6*) Yale U Pr.

Mussolini's Soldiers. Rex Trye. (Illus.). 167p. 1995. 29.95 (*0-7603-0022-4*) MBI Pubg.

Must a Jew Believe Anything? Menachem Kellner. LC 98-39900. (Library of Jewish Civilization). 192p. 1999. pap. 19.95 (*1-874774-49-8*) Intl Spec Bk.

Must Be the Music Vol. I: Memoirs of a Musical Dynasty. Sederick C. Rice. (Illus.). 220p. 1999. pap. 15.95 (*0-7392-0245-6*, PO3250) Morris Pubng.

Must Canada Fail? Ed. by Richard Simeon. 1977. pap. 24.95 (*0-7735-0313-7*, Pub. by McG-Queens Univ Pr) CUP Services.

Must Canada Fail? Ed. by Richard Simeon. LC 78-307029. 317p. reprint ed. pap. 98.30 (*0-7837-1151-4*, 204168000022) Bks Demand.

Must Carry Rules. 36p. 1983. 3.00 (*0-318-18630-6*) Station Reps Assn.

Must Christians Suffer? Kenneth E. Hagin. 1982. pap. 3.95 (*0-89276-404-X*) Faith Lib Pubns.

Must Corporate Income Be Taxed Twice? Charles E. McLure, Jr. LC 78-27905. (Studies of Government Finance). 262p. 1979. 34.95 (*0-8157-5620-8*); pap. 14.95 (*0-8157-5619-4*) Brookings.

***Must Global Politics Constrain Democracy? Great-Power Realism, Democratic Peace & Democratic Internationalism.** Alan Gilbert. LC 99-12203. 256p. 1999. 55.00 (*0-691-00181-2*, Pub. by Princeton U Pr) Cal Prin Full Svc.

***Must Global Politics Constrain Democracy? Great-Power Realism, Democratic Peace & Democratic Internationalism.** Alan Gilbert. LC 99-12203. 256p. 1999. 17.95 (*0-691-00182-0*, Pub. by Princeton U Pr) Cal Prin Full Svc.

Must I Turn the Other Cheek: Premature Forgiveness Obstructs Recovery from Sexual Abuse. Elaine Ducharme. 128p. pap. write for info. (*0-9701695-0-7*) denlan prodns.

Must Jesus Be Lord to Be Savior? rev. ed. William Webster. 131p. pap. 8.95 (*1-879737-24-8*, Christ Res) Calvary Press.

Must Philosophers Disagree? And Other Essays in Popular Philosophy. Ferdinand C. Schiller. LC 75-3347. 1976. reprint ed. 37.50 (*0-404-59346-1*) AMS Pr.

***Must-See Amsterdam.** (Illus.). 2000. pap. 14.95 (*1-84157-033-8*, Pub. by Thomas Cook Pub) Globe Pequot.

***Must-See Brussels, Bruges, Ghent & Lille.** (Illus.). 2000. pap. 14.95 (*1-84157-034-6*, Pub. by Thomas Cook Pub) Globe Pequot.

***Must-See Dublin.** (Illus.). 2000. pap. 14.95 (*1-84157-036-2*, Pub. by Thomas Cook Pub) Globe Pequot.

Must See in Kyoto. Ed. by Japan Travel Bureau Staff. (JTB's Illustrated Japan in Your Pocket Ser.: No. 5). (Illus.). 192p. 1985. pap. 17.95 (*4-533-00528-4*, Pub. by Japan Trvl Bur) Bks Nippan.

Must See in Nikko. Ed. by Japan Travel Bureau Staff. (JTB's Illustrated Japan in Your Pocket Ser.: No. 6). (Illus.). 192p. 1985. pap. 17.95 (*4-533-00529-2*, Pub. by Japan Trvl Bur) Bks Nippan.

***Must-See New York.** (Illus.). 2000. pap. 14.95 (*1-84157-038-9*, Pub. by Thomas Cook Pub) Globe Pequot.

***Must-See Paris.** (Illus.). 2000. pap. 14.95 (*1-84157-039-7*, Pub. by Thomas Cook Pub) Globe Pequot.

***Must-See Rome.** (Illus.). 2000. pap. 14.95 (*1-84157-040-0*, Pub. by Thomas Cook Pub) Globe Pequot.

Must the Maiden Die? Miriam G. Monfredo. LC 99-29295. (Seneca Falls Historical Mystery Ser.: No. 6). 1999. 21.95 (*0-425-16699-6*, Prime Crime) Berkley Pub.

***Must the Maiden Die?** Miriam G. Monfredo. (Seneca Falls Historical Mysteries Ser.). 2000. mass mkt. 6.99 (*0-425-17610-X*) Berkley Pub.

***Must there be Scapegoats? Violence & Redemption in the Bible.** Raymund Schwager. 264p. 2000. pap. 29.95 (*0-8245-1867-5*, Pub. by Crossroad NY) Natl Bk Netwk.

***Must We Burn Sade?** Simone de Beauvoir. LC 99-40738. 375p. 2000. text 59.95 (*1-57392-726-0*, Humanity Bks) Prometheus Bks.

Must We Burn Sade? Deepak Narang Sawhney. LC 99-40738. 375p. 1999. pap. 19.95 (*1-57392-739-2*) Prometheus Bks.

***Must We Defend Nazis? Hate Speech, Pornography & the New First Amendment.** Richard Delgado. 1999. pap. text 20.00 (*0-8147-1923-6*) NYU Pr.

Must We Defend Nazis? Hate Speech, Pornography, & the New First Amendment. Richard Delgado & Jean Stefancic. 280p. (C). 1997. text 45.00 (*0-8147-1858-2*) NYU Pr.

Must We Grow Old: From Pauling to Prigogine to Toynbee. Daniel Hershey. LC 83-71510. (Illus.). 249p. (Orig.). 1984. pap. 10.00 (*0-916961-00-1*) Basal Books.

Must We Hide? Ralph E. Lapp. LC 81-6440. (Illus.). 182p. 1981. reprint ed. lib. bdg. 55.00 (*0-313-23102-8*, LAMW, Greenwood Pr) Greenwood.

Must We Mean What We Say? Stanley Cavell. LC 75-32911. 394p. 1976. pap. text 35.95 (*0-521-29048-1*) Cambridge U Pr.

Must We Suffer Our Way to Death? Cultural & Theological Perspectives on Death by Choice. Ed. by Ronald P. Hamel & Edwin R. DuBose. LC 96-13818. 408p. (Orig.). 1996. 35.00 (*0-87074-392-9*); pap. 18.95 (*0-87074-393-7*) SMU Press.

Must Words: The Six Thousand Most Important Words for a Successful & Profitable Vocabulary. Peter Norback & Craig T. Norback. 312p. 1983. pap. 12.95 (*0-07-047141-X*) McGraw.

Mustache Cups: Timeless Victorian Treasures. Pauline C. Peck & Glenn Erardi. (Illus.). 176p. 1999. 49.95 (*0-7643-0924-2*) Schiffer.

Mustaches & Other Stories. G. W. Clift. LC 95-43280. 92p. 1995. pap. 14.00 (*1-886157-02-2*) BkMk.

Mustafas Geheimnis: Ein Moslemischer Junge auf der Suche nach Gott. Sandra Klaus.Tr. of Mustapha's Secret - A Muslim Boy's Search to Know God. (GER., Illus.). (J). (gr. 2-7). Date not set. pap. write for info. (*0-9617490-6-7*) Gospel Missionary.

Mustang. Jim Campisano. 1997. 16.98 (*1-56799-438-5*, MetroBooks) M Friedman Pub Grp Inc.

Mustang. Consumer Guide Editors. (Illus.). 96p. 1993. 12.98 (*1-56173-276-1*, 1011900) Pubns Intl Ltd.

Mustang. Sharon Curtin. LC 96-83438. (Illus.). 192p. 1996. 40.00 (*0-9649915-1-9*) Rufus Pubns Inc.

Mustang. Randy Leffingwell. (Illus.). 192p. 1995. 29.95 (*0-7603-0048-8*) MBI Pubg.

Mustang. A. T. McKenna. LC 98-29328. (Ultimate Cars Ser.). 2000. lib. bdg. 21.35 (*1-57765-126-X*) ABDO Pub Co.

Mustang. Ian Penberthy. 72p. 1995. 10.98 (*0-7858-0226-6*) Bk Sales Inc.

Mustang. Ed. by Penguin Books Staff. 1999. pap. 6.99 (*0-7214-5688-X*, Ladybrd) Penguin Putnam.

Mustang. Jay Schleifer. LC 91-27908. (Cool Classics Ser.). (Illus.). 48p. (J). (gr. 5). 1992. lib. bdg. 13.95 (*0-89686-699-8*, Crstwood Hse) Silver Burdett Pr.

Mustang. Alvin Silverstein et al. LC 96-42682. (Endangered in America Ser.). (Illus.). 64p. (J). (gr. 4-6). 1997. lib. bdg. 22.40 (*0-7613-0048-1*) Millbrook Pr.

***Mustang: A Gathering of Legends.** Paul Coggan. (Illus.). 160p. 2000. 34.95 (*1-57427-094-X*) Howell Pr VA.

Mustang: An American Classic. Nicky Wright. 1998. pap. text 10.98 (*1-57717-082-2*) Todtri Prods.

Mustang: Anniversary Edition, 1964-1994. Nicky Wright. (Illus.). 224p. 1997. 45.00 (*1-85375-167-7*) Trafalgar.

Mustang: Ford's Wild Pony. Linda Craven. LC 93-20243. (Car Classics Ser.). 32p. (YA). (gr. 5-12). 1993. lib. bdg. 15.95 (*0-86593-255-7*) Rourke Corp.

Mustang: North American P-51. Photos by Dan Patterson. (Living History Ser.: No. 3). (Illus.). 64p. 1995. pap. 15.95 (*0-943231-75-2*) Howell Pr VA.

Mustang: Selling the Legend. Andy Willsheer. LC 97-116835. (Illus.). 112p. 1997. pap. 12.98 (*0-7603-0317-7*) MBI Pubg.

Mustang! The Complete History of America's Ponycar. Gary L. Witzenburg. LC 79-89754. (Illus.). 204p. 1979. 29.95 (*0-915038-13-7*, 3-AQ-0018) Auto Quarterly.

Mustang: The Racing Thoroughbred. Dustin W. Carter & Birch J. Matthews. LC 91-60015. (Illus.). 208p. 1992. text 39.95 (*0-88740-391-3*) Schiffer.

Mustang, a Lost Tibetan Kingdom. M. Peissel. (C). 1993. 120.00 (*0-7855-0193-2*, Pub. by Ratna Pustak Bhandar) St Mut.

Mustang Ace: Memoirs of a P-51 Fighter Pilot. Robert J. Goebel. LC 91-13477. (Illus.). 242p. 1991. 24.95 (*0-935553-03-7*) Pacifica Military.

Mustang Aces of Ninth & Fifteenth Air Force & the R. A. F., Vol. 7. Jerry Scutts. (Aircraft of the Aces Ser.: Vol. 8). (Illus.). 96p. 1995. pap. 17.95 (*1-85532-583-7*, Pub. by Ospry) Motorbooks Intl.

Mustang Aces of the Eighth Air Force, Vol. 1. Jerry Scutts. (Aircraft of the Aces Ser.). (Illus.). 96p. 1994. pap. 17.95 (*1-85532-447-4*, Pub. by Ospry) Motorbooks Intl.

***Mustang, America's Favorite Pony Car.** 2nd rev. ed. John Gunnell. LC 94-77379. (Illus.). 328p. 2000. pap. 21.95 (*0-87341-946-4*, MS02) Krause Pubns.

Mustang & Ford Small Block V8, 1962-1969. Bob Mannel. LC 98-91185. (Illus.). 736p. 1998. pap. 49.95 (*0-9662741-0-5*) RPM Press.

***Mustang & Mercury Cougar Parts Locating Guide.** David R. Gimbel & Adam Gimbel. 152p. 1999. reprint ed. pap. 18.95 (*1-891752-28-6*) Jalopy Joe.

***Mustang Annie.** Rachelle Morgan. 336p. 2000. mass mkt. 5.99 (*0-380-80921-4*) Morrow Avon.

Mustang Bhot in Fragments. M. Thapa. (C). 1992. 43.00 (*0-7855-0191-6*, Pub. by Ratna Pustak Bhandar) St Mut.

***Mustang Chronicle** Jerry Heasley. LC 99-212249. 264p. 1998. write for info. (*0-7853-3262-6*) Pubns Intl Ltd.

Mustang Desert. Dodge Tyler. (Dan'l Boone Ser.: No. 11). 176p. 1999. mass mkt. 3.99 (*0-8439-4509-5*) Dorchester Pub Co.

***Mustang Designer: Edgar Schmued & the P-51.** Ray Wagner. LC 99-42023. (Illus.). 240p. 2000. pap. 19.95 (*1-56098-994-7*) Smithsonian.

Mustang Does It. Ray Miller. LC 77-78278. (Ford Road Ser.: Vol. 6). (Illus.). 320p. 1978. lib. bdg. 44.95 (*0-913056-09-X*) Evergreen Pr.

Mustang 5.0 Projects: Performance & Upgrade How-To's for 1979-1995 5.0 Mustangs. Mark Houlahan. LC 97-25718. 176p. 1997. pap. 17.95 (*1-55788-275-4*, HP Books) Berkley Pub.

Mustang 5.0 & 4.6, 1979-1998. Matthew L. Stone. LC 97-46055. (Muscle Car Color History Ser.). 128p. 1998. pap. 21.95 (*0-7603-0334-7*) MBI Pubg.

Mustang Flats. G. Clifton Wisler. LC 96-29899. 128p. (YA). (gr. 5-9). 1997. 14.99 (*0-525-67544-2*, Dutton Child) Peng Put Young Read.

Mustang Flats. G. Clifton Wisler. (YA). (gr. 5-9). 1999. pap. 5.99 (*0-14-130410-3*, PuffinBks) Peng Put Young Read.

Mustang: Fury Over Europe see Mustang: Fury Over Europe: 8th Air Force Fighter Command, World War II

Mustang, Fury over Europe: Fury over Europe. F. Franklin Craig. LC 95-13108. (Illus.). 104p. (Orig.). 1995. pap. 9.95 (*1-878815-07-5*) Reflected Images.

***Mustang: Fury Over Europe: 8th Air Force Fighter Command, World War II.** large type ed. F. Franklin Craig. Ed. by Bert Webber. LC 95-13108. Orig. Title: Mustang: Fury Over Europe. (Illus.). 104p. 2000. pap. Price not set. (*1-878815-14-8*) Reflected Images.

Mustang Heart. Margot Dalton. (Crystal Creek Ser.). 1994. per. 3.99 (*0-373-82525-0*, 1-82525-6) Harlequin Bks.

Mustang How-To, Vol. 1. Ed. by Donald N. Farr. (Illus.). 98p. 1991. reprint ed. pap. 6.95 (*0-9624908-3-0*) CA Mustang Sales.

Mustang How-To, Vol. 2. Ed. by Jim Smart. (Illus.). 87p. 1990. reprint ed. pap. 7.95 (*0-9624908-1-4*) CA Mustang Sales.

Mustang Interior Restoration. A. Trantafello. (Illus.). 80p. 1986. pap. 12.95 (*0-87938-211-2*) MBI Pubg.

Mustang Man. Louis L'Amour. 176p. 1966. mass mkt. 4.50 (*0-553-27681-6*) Bantam.

Mustang Man. Louis L'Amour. LC 96-41329. (Thorndike Large Print Western Ser.). 248 p. 1999. write for info. (*0-7540-3670-7*) Chivers N Amer.

Mustang Man. large type ed. Louis L'Amour. LC 96-41329. 1999. 20.00 (*0-7862-0873-2*, G K Hall Lrg Type) Mac Lib Ref.

Mustang, 1965-1973. Ed. by ADP Hollander Interchange Staff. (Illus.). 252p. 1998. pap. 19.95 (*1-58132-004-3*) ADP-Hollander.

Mustang 1964 1/2-73 Restoration Guide. 2nd ed. Tom Corcoran. LC 98-19123. (Illus.). 448p. 1998. pap. 29.95 (*0-7603-0552-8*) MBI Pubg.

***Mustang, 1964-1/2-1973.** Mike Mueller. (Illus.). 156p. 2000. 29.95 (*0-7603-0734-2*, 130124AP, Pub. by MBI Pubg) Motorbooks Intl.

Mustang Performance Handbook. William R. Mathis. LC 94-18029. 224p. (Orig.). 1994. pap. 17.95 (*1-55788-193-6*, HP Books) Berkley Pub.

Mustang Performance Handbook 2: Chassis & Suspension Modifications for Street, Strip, & Road Racing Use for All Models of the Ford Mustand, 1979 to Present, No. 2. William R. Mathis. LC 94-24719. (Illus.). 188p. (Orig.). 1995. pap. 17.95 (*1-55788-202-9*, HP Books) Berkley Pub.

Mustang Performance, 1988-1996, Vol. 4. Hot Rod Magazine Staff. (Best Of "Hot Rod Magazine" Ser.). 1999. pap. 18.95 (*1-884089-36-4*) CarTech.

Mustang Professor: The Story of J. Frank Dobie. Mark Mitchell. (Illus.). 96p. (J). (gr. 6-7). 1993. 12.95 (*0-89015-823-1*) Sunbelt Media.

Mustang Professor: The Story of J. Frank Dobie. Mark Mitchell. (Illus.). 96p. (J). 1997. pap. 7.95 (*1-57168-134-5*, Eakin Pr) Sunbelt Media.

Mustang Recognition Guide, 1965-1973. rev. ed. Larry Dobbs et al. (Illus.). 226p. 1989. pap. 16.95 (*0-685-59726-1*) CA Mustang Sales.

***Mustang Red Book 1964 1/2 to 2000.** 3rd ed. Peter Sessler. LC 99-86575. (Red Bks.). (Illus.). 160p. 2000. pap. 11.95 (*0-7603-0800-4*, 130001AP, Pub. by MBI Pubg) Motorbooks Intl.

Mustang Restoration Tips & Techniques. R. M. Clarke. 163p. 1986. pap. 18.95 (*0-948207-97-3*, Pub. by Brooklands Bks) Motorbooks Intl.

Mustang Sally. Edward Allen. 1994. pap. 9.95 (*0-393-31156-2*) Norton.

Mustang Sixty-Four & One Half - Sixty-Eight. Tom Corcoran. (Muscle Car Color History Ser.). (Illus.). 128p. 1993. pap. 21.95 (*0-87938-630-4*) MBI Pubg.

***Mustang Story.** Ken Delve. (Illus.). 2000. 34.95 (*1-85409-259-6*) Arms & Armour.

Mustang The Affordable Sports Car: A 30 Year Pony Ride. John Gunnell. LC 94-77379. (Illus.). 304p. 1994. pap. 16.95 (*0-87341-310-5*, MS01) Krause Pubns.

Mustang, the Next Generation. Bob McClurg. LC 94-70071. (Illus.). 208p. 1994. 39.95 (*0-9640895-0-5*) Bolder Ventures.

Mustang War. large type ed. Frank Roderus. (Sagebrush Large Print Westerns Ser.). 292p. 1995. lib. bdg. 17.95 (*1-57490-011-0*) T T Beeler.

Mustang Weekend Projects 2. rev. ed. Jerry Hensley. 176p. (Orig.). 1996. pap. 17.95 (*1-55788-253-3*, HP Books) Berkley Pub.

Mustang, Wild Spirit of the West. Marguerite Henry. LC 91-25187. (Illus.). 224p. (J). (gr. 3-7). 1992. mass mkt. 4.50 (*0-689-71601-X*) Aladdin.

Mustang, Wild Spirit of the West. Marguerite Henry. (J). (gr. 3-7). 1996. 19.25 (*0-8446-6888-5*) Peter Smith.

Mustang, Wild Spirit of the West. Marguerite Henry. 1966. 9.60 (*0-606-01832-8*, Pub. by Turtleback) Demco.

Mustang Wranglers: A True Adventure Story from the Canadian West. Russell V. Gunter. LC 98-109227. 224p. 1999. pap. 10.95 (*1-895618-91-6*) Fifth Hse Publ.

***Mustang 5.0: Technical Reference & Performance Handbook, 1979-1993.** Al Kirschenbaum. LC 99-32419. (Illus.). 440p. 1999. pap. 34.95 (*0-8376-0210-6*, GFM5) Bentley Pubs.

***Mustangers.** Gary McCarthy. 192p. 1999. mass mkt. 3.99 (*0-8439-4518-4*, Leisure Bks) Dorchester Pub Co.

Mustangers. Lauran Paine. LC 99-35274. (Westerns Ser.). 250p. 1999. 19.95 (*0-7862-1577-1*) Five Star.

Mustangers. large type ed. Lauran Paine. 275p. 2000. 30.00 (*0-7862-1586-0*) Thorndike Pr.

Mustangs see High Performance

Mustangs see Great American Muscle Cars

***Mustangs.** J Frank Dobie. 1999. 9.99 (*0-7858-1131-1*) Book Sales.

Mustangs. Lorrine Gillespie. (High Performance Ser.). (Illus.). 48p. (J). (gr. 3-7). 1996. 19.00 (*0-516-20244-8*) Childrens.

Mustangs. J. Frank Dobie. (Illus.). 392p. 1984. reprint ed. pap. 14.95 (*0-292-75081-1*) U of Tex Pr.

Mustangs: America's Wild Horse see Great American Horses

Mustangs & Unicorn: A History of the 359th F. G. Jack H. Smith. LC 97-68918. (Illus.). 473p. 1997. pap. 19.95 (*1-57510-029-0*) Pictorial Hist.

Mustangs & Wild Horses see Learning about Horses Series

Mustangs & Wild Horses. Gail B. Stewart. (Illus.). 48p. (J). (gr. 3-7). 1995. lib. bdg. 19.00 (*0-516-35301-2*) Childrens.

Mustangs in Korea. Warren Thompson. (Frontline Color 1 Ser.). 128p. 1999. pap. 19.95 (*1-85532-917-4*) Ospry.

Corvettes, 1953-1988: A Collector's Guide. Richard Langworth. (Collector's Guide Ser.). (Illus.). 128p. 1996. pap. 19.95 (*1-899870-11-3*, Pub. by Motor Racing) Motorbooks Intl.

Mustangs, 1965-1973: A Collector's Guide. Richard Langworth. (Collector's Guide Ser.). (Illus.). 128p. 1996. pap. 19.95 (*1-899870-12-1*, Pub. by Motor Racing) Motorbooks Intl.

Mustangs over Korea: The North American F-51 at War, 1950-1953. David R. McLaren. LC 98-87295. (Illus.). 184p. 1999. 45.00 (*0-7643-0721-5*) Schiffer.

Mustapha & His Wise Dog. Esther M. Friesner. (Twelve Kingdoms Ser.: No. 1). 160p. 1985. pap. 2.95 (*0-380-89676-1*, Avon Bks) Morrow Avon.

Mustapha et Zeangir. Chamfort. Ed. by Davies. (Exeter French Texts Ser.: Vol. 83). (FRE.). 99p. Date not set. pap. text 19.95 (*0-85989-377-4*, Pub. by Univ Exeter Pr) Northwestern U Pr.

Mustapha's Secret: A Muslim Boy's Search to Know God. 2nd ed. Sandra Klaus. (Illus.). 42p. (J). (gr. 2-7). 1997. spiral bd. 11.95 (*1-890940-00-3*) Gospel Missionary.

Mustapha's Secret - A Muslim Boy's Search to Know God see Mustafas Geheimnis: Ein Moslemischer Junge auf der Suche nach Gott

Mustard: A Story about Soft Love & Strong Values. Jessel Miller. Ed. by Carolynne Gamble. (Soft Love Strong Values Ser.). (Illus.). 48p. (J). (ps-6). 1998. 24.00 (*0-9660381-7-7*) Jessel Gallery.

Mustard Bk. II: A Journey to Love. Jessel Miller. Ed. by Carolynne Gamble. (Illus.). 48p. (J). (ps-6). 1998. 24.95 (*0-9660381-1-8*) Jessel Gallery.

***Mustard Bk. III: Lessons from Old Souls.** Jessel Miller. Ed. by Carolynne Gamble. (Illus.). 48p. (ps-6). 1999. 24.95 (*0-9660381-5-0*) Jessel Gallery.

Mustard Book: How to Make Your Own - From Dijon to Creole - At Home. Jan Roberts-Dominguez. 176p. 1997. pap. text 12.95 (*0-02-861856-4*) Macmillan.

***Mustard Book: The Quintessential Guide to History, Lore, Varieties & Curiosities of Mustard.** Nikki Antol. 224p. 1999. pap. 11.95 (*0-89529-920-8*, Avery) Penguin Putnam.

Mustard Magic. R. Marilyn Schmidt. 58p. 1992. spiral bd. 6.95 (*0-937996-19-X*) Pine Barrens Pr.

Mustard Seed. (Adventures of Hacker Ser.: Vol. 2). (Illus.). 160p. (Orig.). (J). (gr. 4-8). 1995. pap. 3.50 (*1-57414-012-4*) Value Network.

Mustard Seed. Monica Brett-Serle. (Illus.). 30p. (Orig.). 1996. pap. 5.00 (*1-890702-00-5*) Latitude Ent.

Mustard Seed: Commentaries on the Fifth Gospel of St. Thomas. 6th ed. Osho. (Illus.). 498p. 1975. reprint ed. 26.95 (*3-89338-137-6*, Pub. by Rebel Hse) Oshos.

Mustard Seed: Discourses on the Sayings of Jesus from the Gospel According to Thomas. 6th ed. Osho. 1994. pap. 14.95 (*1-85230-498-7*, Pub. by Element MA) Penguin Putnam.

Mustard Seed Garden Manual of Painting: A Facsimile of the 1887-1888 Shanghai Edition. Ed. by M. Sze. LC 77-312. 648p. 1977. pap. 27.50 (*0-691-01819-7*, Pub. by Princeton U Pr) Cal Prin Full Svc.

Mustard Seed of Magic. Norma Johnston. LC 99-60484. (Keeping Days Ser.). 184p. (YA). 1999. reprint ed. pap. 16.00 (*1-892323-31-1*, Pierce Harris Pr) Vivisphere.

Mustard Seed vs. McWorld: Reinventing Life & Faith for the Future. Tom Sine. LC 99-25951. 256p. (C). 1999. pap. 14.99 (*0-8010-9088-1*) Baker Bks.

Mustard Seeds, Vol. 1. G & R Publishing Company Staff. 368p. (Orig.). 1995. pap. 7.50 (*1-56383-046-9*, 5010) G & R Pub.

Mustard Seeds: Daily Thoughts to Grow With. Matthew Kelly. 128p. 1998. pap. 7.95 (*1-878718-48-7*, Resurrection Pr) Catholic Bk Pub.

Mustards. Ann Creber. LC 94-66. (Williams-Sonoma Essentials Ser.). (Illus.). 1994. 9.95 (*1-875137-19-X*) Weldon Owen.

M

Mustards, Ketchups & Vinegars: Making the Most of Seasonal Abundance. Carol W. Costenbader. LC 95-42378. (Well Stocked Pantry Ser.). (Illus.). 96p. 1996. 16.95 (*0-88266-813-7*, 813-7, Storey Pub) Storey Bks.

Muster & Pay Rolls of the War of the Revolution, 1775-1783. 707p. 1996. reprint ed. text 45.00 (*0-8063-1512-1*) Genealog Pub.

***Muster Days at Muster Field Farm: New Hampshire's Muster Day Tradition, 1787-1850.** Jack Noon. (Illus.). xii, 121p. 2000. 20.00 (*0-9677202-0-6*) Muster Fld Frm Mus.

Muster Roll: Men from Oswego County Who Served in Other Regiments. David K. Parsons. (Bugles Echo Across the Valley Ser.: Vol. 3). (Illus.). 165p. (Orig.). (J). (gr. 6). 1996. pap. 18.00 (*1-886303-11-8*) Write to Print.

Muster Roll of Prince Charles Edward Stuart's Army, 1745-1746. Ed. by Alasdair Livingstone et al. 228p. 1984. 29.50 (*0-08-030385-4*, Pergamon Pr) Elsevier.

Muster Rolls & Prisoner-of-War Lists in American Archival Collections Pertaining to the German Mercenary Troops Who Served with the British Forces During the American Revolution, 3 pts., Set. Clifford N. Smith. (German-American Genealogical Research Monographs: No. 3). 200p. (Orig.). 1975. pap. 60.00 (*0-915162-02-4*) Westland Pubns.

Muster Rolls of the Pennsylvania Volunteers in the War of 1812-1814: (From the Pennsylvania Archives, Second Series, Vol. XII, 1890) John B. Linn & William H. Egle. LC 67-30758. 560p. 1994. reprint ed. pap. 39.95 (*0-8063-0211-9*) Clearfield Co.

Muster Rolls of the Soldiers of the War of 1812 Detached from the Militia of North Carolina in 1812 & 1814: Detached from the Militia of North Carolina in 1812 & 1814. With an Added Index. North Carolina Adjutant, General's Office Staff & Maurice S. Toler. LC 76-20239. 193p. 1998. reprint ed. pap. 22.50 (*0-8063-0728-5*) Clearfield Co.

Mustering of Support for World War I by the Ladies' Home Journal. Joanne L. Karetzky. LC 97-31898. (Illus.). 160p. 1997. 69.95 (*0-7734-2250-1*) E Mellen.

Mustique. Roger Vaughan. 304p. 1994. 100.00 (*0-9640272-9-1*) Hasselqvist & Schweitzman.

Musubi Man: Hawaii's Gingerbread Man. Sandi Takayama. (Illus.). 24p. (J). (ps-3). 1996. 9.95 (*1-57306-053-4*) Bess Pr.

Musubime Riron to Sono Oyo see Knot Theory & Its Applications

Musuem of Fine Arts, Houston: Visitor Guide Houston Museum of Fine Arts Staff & Janet Landay. LC 99-31022. 2000. write for info. (*0-89090-091-4*) Mus Fine TX.

Musui's Story: The Autobiography of a Tokugawa Samurai. Katsu. LC 87-36545. (Illus.). 178p. 1991. reprint ed. pap. 17.95 (*0-8165-1256-6*) U of Ariz Pr.

Musulman Painting, 12th-17th Century. Edgar Blochet. Tr. by C. M. Binyon from FRE. (Illus.). 1975. reprint ed. lib. bdg. 50.00 (*0-87817-155-X*) Hacker.

Musulmanes Que Encontraron a Cristo. R. F. Wootan.Tr. of Jesus More Than a Prophet. (SPA.). 82p. 1987. pap. 3.99 (*1-56063-316-6*, 498528) Editorial Unilit.

Musulmans & Chretiens: Des Freres Ennemis? see Muslims & Christians: Enemies or Brothers?

Musurgia Universalis, 2 vols. Athanasius Kircher. (Documenta Technica Ser.). (GER.). lvii, 1152p. 1999. reprint ed. 475.00 (*3-487-10911-5*) G Olms Verlag.

Mut-Ants! David Jacobs. (Bug Files Ser.). (YA). (gr. 7 up). 1996. mass mkt. 4.50 (*0-425-15417-3*) Berkley Pub.

Mut zum Sein. Paul Johannes Tillich. (GER.). ii, 129p. (Orig.). (C). 1991. pap. text 22.70 (*3-11-013382-2*, 223-91) De Gruyter.

Mutable Self: A Self Concept for Social Change. Louis A. Zurcher. LC 77-21026. (Sage Library of Social Research: No. 59). 279p. reprint ed. pap. 86.50 (*0-8357-8410-X*, 203468100091) Bks Demand.

Mutagen-Induced Chromosome Damage in Man. Harold J. Evans & D. Lloyd. LC 78-60354. 355p. 1979. 55.00 (*0-300-02315-4*) Yale U Pr.

Mutagenesis. Helen Collins. 320p. 1994. mass mkt. 4.99 (*0-8125-2163-3*) Tor Bks.

Mutagenicity, Carcinogenicity, & Teratogenicity of Industrial Pollutants. Ed. by Micheline Kirsch-Volders. LC 83-11126. 350p. 1984. 85.00 (*0-306-41148-2*, Plenum Trade) Perseus Pubng.

Mutagens & Mutagenicity Tests: Directory of Authors of New Medical & Scientific Reviews with Subject Index. Science & Life Consultants Association Staff. 160p. 1995. 47.50 (*0-7883-0600-6*); pap. 44.50 (*0-7883-0601-4*) ABBE Pubs Assn.

Mutagens in Food: Detection & Prevention. Hikoya Hayatsu. 296p. 1990. lib. bdg. 219.00 (*0-8493-5877-9*, RA1258) CRC Pr.

***Mutant Aliens.** Bill Plympton. (Illus.). 192p. 2000. pap. 10.95 (*1-56163-236-8*) NBM.

Mutant Beach. Victor Appleton. Ed. by Anne Greenberg. (Tom Swift Ser.: No. 11). 160p. (Orig.). (YA). (gr. 7 up). 1992. pap. 2.99 (*0-671-75657-5*, Archway) PB.

Mutant Empire: Sanctuary. Christopher Golden. (X-Men Ser.: No. 2). 352p. (Orig.). 1996. mass mkt. 6.50 (*1-57297-268-8*) Blvd Books.

Mutant Hell. Mark Grant. (Mutants Amok Ser.: No. 2). 240p. 1991. pap. 2.95 (*0-380-76048-7*, Avon Bks) Morrow Avon.

Mutant Mandarin: A Guide to New Chinese Slang. James J. Wang & Zhou Yimin. (CHI & ENG.). 175p. 1995. pap. 12.95 (*0-8351-2543-2*) China Bks.

Mutant Message Down Under. Marlo Morgan. 208p. 1995. pap. 13.00 (*0-06-092631-7*, Perennial) HarperTrade.

Mutant Message down Under. large type ed. Marlo Morgan. LC 94-33225. 289p. 1994. lib. bdg. 21.95 (*0-7862-0330-7*) Thorndike Pr.

Mutant Message Down Under: Morgan,&Marlo. abr. ed. Marlo Morgan. 1994. audio 18.00 (*0-694-51515-9*, CPN 2461) HarperAudio.

Mutant Message from Forever: A Novel of Aboriginal Wisdom. Marlo Morgan. 336p. 1999. pap. 13.00 (*0-06-093026-8*) HarpC.

***Mutant Monsters: Make Hundreds of Funny Faces with Re-Usable Stickers!** (Funny Faces Ser.). (Illus.). 10p. (J). (ps-7). 1999. pap. 1.99 (*1-86091-125-0*) Trident Pr Intl.

Mutant Mule Review: Anthology of Contemporary American Poets. Ed. by Elle Larkin & Leah Maines. 40p. 1999. pap. 7.95 (*0-9664324-4-4*) Finishng Line.

Mutant Oncogenes: Targets for Therapy. Ed. by Nicholas R. Lemoine & Agamemnon A. Epenetos. LC 92-48907. 224p. (gr. 13). 1993. text 132.95 (*0-412-48110-3*) Chapman & Hall.

Mutants Amok, No. 1. Mark Grant. 240p. 1991. pap. 2.95 (*0-380-76047-9*, Avon Bks) Morrow Avon.

Mutants Amok No. 3: Rebel Attack. Mark Grant. 192p. (Orig.). 1991. pap. 2.95 (*0-380-76191-2*, Avon Bks) Morrow Avon.

Mutants Amok No. 4: Holocaust Horror. Mark Grant. 224p. (Orig.). 1991. pap. 2.99 (*0-380-76192-0*, Avon Bks) Morrow Avon.

Mutants Amok No. 5: Christmas Slaughter. Mark Grant. 192p. (Orig.). 1991. pap. 3.50 (*0-380-76457-1*, Avon Bks) Morrow Avon.

Mutants down Under. Erick Wujcik. Ed. by Alex Marciniszyn. (After the Bomb Ser.: Bk. 3). (Illus.). 48p. (Orig.). (YA). (gr. 8 up). 1988. pap. 7.95 (*0-916211-34-7*, 507) Palladium Bks.

Mutants in Avalon. James Wallis & Kevin Siembieda. Ed. by Alex Marciniszyn & Thomas Bartold. (After the Bomb Ser.: Bk. 5). (Illus.). 80p. (Orig.). (YA). (gr. 8 up). 1991. pap. 9.95 (*0-916211-47-9*, 513) Palladium Bks.

Mutants in Orbit. James Wallis & Kevin Sienbieda. Ed. by Alex Marciniszyn et al. (After the Bomb Ser.: Bk. 6). (Illus.). 112p. (Orig.). (YA). (gr. 8 up). 1992. pap. 11.95 (*0-916211-48-7*, 514) Palladium Bks.

Mutants of Maize. M. G. Neuffer et al. LC 96-44280. (Illus.). 468p. (C). 1997. 150.00 (*0-87969-443-2*); pap. 60.00 (*0-87969-444-0*) Cold Spring Harbor.

Mutants of the Yucatan. Erick Wujcik. Ed. by Alex Marciniszyn. (After the Bomb Ser.: Bk. 4). (Illus.). 48p. (Orig.). (YA). (gr. 8 up). 1990. pap. 7.95 (*0-916211-44-4*, 511) Palladium Bks.

Mutatio Valentia: The Late Roman Baths at Valesio, Salento. Johannes Boersma. (Scrinium IX). (Illus.). 424p. 1995. 157.00 (*90-5170-337-6*, Pub. by Thesis Pubs) D Brown Bk Co.

***Mutation.** K. A. Applegate. (Animorphs Ser.: No. 36). (Illus.). 142p. (J). (gr. 4-7). 1999. mass mkt. 4.99 (*0-439-10675-3*) Scholastic Inc.

***Mutation.** K. A. Applegate. (Animorphs Ser.: Vol. 36). (Illus.). (J). 1999. 10.34 (*0-606-18507-0*) Turtleback.

Mutation. Robin Cook. 1990. mass mkt. 7.50 (*0-425-11965-9*) Berkley Pub.

Mutation. Robin Cook. 1990. 12.09 (*0-606-00933-7*, Pub. by Turtleback) Demco.

Mutation & Evolution. Ed. by R. C. Woodruff & James N. Thompson. (Contemporary Issues in Genetics & Evolution Ser.: Vol. 7). 592p. 1998. write for info. (*0-7923-4971-7*) Kluwer Academic.

Mutation & Evolution. R. C. Woodruff & John N. Thompson. LC 98-9254. (Contemporary Issues in Genetics & Evolution Ser.). 580p. 1998. write for info. (*0-7923-4973-3*) Kluwer Academic.

Mutation Breeding: Theory & Practical Applications. A. M. Van Harten. LC 97-28369. (Illus.). 360p. (C). 1998. text 120.00 (*0-521-47074-9*) Cambridge U Pr.

Mutation Detection. Richard G. Cotton. (Illus.). 216p. 1997. text 85.00 (*0-19-854888-5*); pap. text 45.00 (*0-19-854889-3*) OUP.

Mutation Detection: A Practical Approach. Ed. by E. Edkins et al. LC 97-51537. (The Practical Approach Ser.: No. 188). (Illus.). 262p. 1998. text 105.00 (*0-19-963657-5*); pap. text 49.95 (*0-19-963656-7*) OUP.

Mutation Detection Protocols. Lisa Baumbach. (Methods in Molecular Biology Ser.). (Illus.). 1998. 69.50 (*0-89603-496-8*) Humana.

Mutation, Developmental Selection, & Plant Evolution. Edward J. Klekowski, Jr. (Illus.). 448p. 1988. text 96.50 (*0-231-06528-0*) Col U Pr.

Mutation Factor in Evolution (with Particular References to Oenothera) R. R. Gates. 354p. 1985. pap. 180.00 (*0-7855-0383-8*, Pub. by Intl Bks & Periodicals) St Mut.

Mutation in Welsh. Martin J. Ball & Nicole Muller. LC 91-30393. 288p. (C). (gr. 13). 1992. text 89.95 (*0-415-03165-6*, A6067) Routledge.

Mutational & Morphological Analysis. Jean-Pierre Aubin. LC 98-2857. (Systems & Control Ser.). xxxvii, 425 p. 1998. write for info. (*3-7643-3935-7*) Birkhauser.

Mutational & Morphological Analysis: Tools for Shape Evolution & Morphogenesis. Ed. by Jean P. Aubin. LC 98-2857. 400p. 1998. 74.50 (*0-8176-3935-7*) Birkhauser.

Mutations in Plant Breeding 2. (Panel Proceedings Ser.). (Illus.). 315p. 1968. pap. 35.00 (*92-0-111368-4*, ISP182, Pub. by IAEA) Bernan Associates.

Mutations of Alternative Algebras. Alberto Elduque & Hyo C. Myung. LC 94-2765. (Mathematics & Its Applications Ser.). 240p. (C). 1994. text 148.50 (*0-7923-2735-7*) Kluwer Academic.

Mutatis Mutandis: 27 Invoices. William Harmon. LC 84-25633. (Wesleyan Poetry Ser.). 55p. 1985. pap. 12.95 (*0-8195-6115-0*, Wesleyan Univ Pr) U Pr of New Eng.

Mutative Metaphors in Psychotherapy. Murray Cox & Alice Theilgaard. 280p. (C). 1987. pap. 18.95 (*0-422-61810-1*, Pub. by Tavistock); lib. bdg. 49.50 (*0-422-61800-4*, Pub. by Tavistock) Routldge.

Mutative Metaphors in Psychotherapy: The Aeolian Mode. Murray Cox & Alice Theilgaard. 308p. 1997. reprint ed. pap. write for info. (*1-85302-459-7*, Pub. by Jessica Kingsley) Taylor & Francis.

Mutch Touch. Mutch. 1991. 14.95 (*0-13-608696-9*) P-H.

Mute. Piers Anthony. 448p. (Orig.). 1981. mass mkt. 4.50 (*0-380-77578-6*, Avon Bks) Morrow Avon.

Mute. Greg Wilkovich. (Orig.). 1996. pap. write for info. (*1-57553-236-0*) Watermrk Pr.

Mute Horseman of Dragon's Bay. Selwyn J. Lloyd. (J). (gr. 4). 1992. pap. 7.95 (*0-8464-4877-7*, Gomer Pr) Beekman Pubs.

Mute Music. Roberto Schmitz. (Illus.). 128p. 1997. 17.00 (*0-8059-4020-0*) Dorrance.

Mute Phone Calls & Other Stories. Ruth Zernova. Tr. by Helen Reeve et al. 280p. (C). 1991. pap. 13.95 (*0-8135-1736-2*); text 35.00 (*0-8135-1735-4*) Rutgers U Pr.

Mute Stones Speak: The Story of Archaeology in Italy. 2nd ed. Paul MacKendrick. (Illus.). 1983. pap. 14.95 (*0-393-30119-2*) Norton.

Mute Swan. Janet Kear. (Natural History Ser.: No. 27). (Illus.). 24p. 1989. pap. 5.25 (*0-85263-948-1*, Pub. by Shire Pubns) Parkwest Pubns.

Mute Swans. Wendy Pfeffer. LC 95-52709. (Creatures in White Ser.). (Illus.). 32p. (J). 1996. pap. 5.95 (*0-382-39324-4*, Silver Pr NJ); lib. bdg. 18.95 (*0-382-39325-2*) Silver Burdett Pr.

Mute Swans of the Atlantic Coast. James E. Twining. LC 87-51129. (Illus.). 104p. (Orig.). 1987. 10.95 (*0-934881-05-7*); pap. 6.95 (*0-934881-04-9*) Dutch Island.

Muted Conscience: Moral Silence & the Practice of Ethics in Business. Frederick B. Bird. LC 96-591. 280p. 1996. 59.95 (*0-89930-652-7*, Quorum Bks) Greenwood.

Muted Consent: A Casebook in Modern Medical Ethics. Jan Wojcik. LC 77-89472. (Science & Society: Series in Science, Technology, & Human Values: Vol. 1). 169p. 1978. pap. 7.95 (*0-931682-02-9*) Purdue U Pubns.

Muted Differences: The Negotiations to Normalize U. S. - Chinese Relations. Thomas P. Bernstein. (Pew Case Studies in International Affairs). 69p. (C). 1995. pap. text 3.50 (*1-56927-426-6*) Geo U Inst Dplmcy.

Muted Fury: Populists, Progressives, & Labor Unions Confront the Courts, 1890-1937. William G. Ross. LC 93-13698. 368p. 1993. text 49.50 (*0-691-03264-5*, Pub. by Princeton U Pr) Cal Prin Full Svc.

Muted Grooves Bass Builders. J. Des Pres. 64p. 1995. pap. 16.95 (*0-7935-3455-0*, 00696555) H Leonard.

Muted Voices. Eugene Relgis. 1972. reprint ed. lib. bdg. 250.00 (*0-87968-001-6*) Gordon Pr.

***Muted Voices: The Recovery of Democracy in the Shaping of Technology.** Jesse S. Tatum. LC 99-32780. 184p. 2000. 35.00 (*0-934223-58-0*) Lehigh Univ Pr.

Mutes & Earthquakes: Bill Manhire's Creative Writing Course at Victoria. Bill Manhire. LC 98-103421. 333p. 1997. write for info. (*0-86473-318-6*) Victoria Univ Pr.

***Mute's Soliloquy.** Pramoedya A. Toer. Tr. by Willem Samuels. 400p. 1999. 27.50 (*0-7868-6416-8*, Pub. by Hyperion) Time Warner.

Mute's Soliloquy: A Memoir. Pramoedya A. Toer. 704p. 1999. text. write for info. (*0-7868-6500-8*, Pub. by Disney Pr) Little.

***Mute's Soliloquy: A Memoir.** Pramoedya A. Toer. 400p. 2000. pap. 14.95 (*0-14-028904-6*, Penguin Bks) Viking Penguin.

***Multi-Threaded Programming in C++** Mark Walmsley. LC 99-40885. x, 239p. 1999. 49.95 (*1-85233-146-1*, Pub. by Spr-Verlag) Spr-Verlag.

***Mutiagent Systems: A Modern Approach to Distributed Artificial Intelligence.** Gerhard Weiss. (Illus.). 648p. (C). 2000. reprint ed. pap. 35.00 (*0-262-73131-2*) MIT Pr.

Mutige Narr im Dramatischen Werk Friedrich Duerrenmatts. Sigrun R. Gottwald. Ed. by Joseph Strelka. LC 83-48647. (New Yorker Studien zur Neueren Deutschen Literaturgeschichte Ser.: Vol. 3). (GER.). 331p. (Orig.). (C). 1983. pap. text 32.65 (*0-8204-0027-0*) P Lang Pubng.

Mutilated. Tennessee Williams. 1967. pap. 3.25 (*0-8222-0794-X*) Dramatists Play.

Mutilated Monkey Meat. Todd Strasser. (Camp Run-a-Muck Ser.: No. 2). (J). (gr. 4-7). 1997. mass mkt. 3.99 (*0-590-74262-0*, Apple Paperbacks) Scholastic Inc.

Mutilating God: Authorship & Authority in the Narrative of Conversion. Gerald P. Peters. LC 93-22151. 192p. 1993. lib. bdg. 29.95 (*0-87023-891-4*) U of Mass Pr.

Mutilating the Body: Identity in Blood & Ink. Kim Hewitt. LC 96-35524. (Illus.). 155p. 1997. pap. 18.95 (*0-87972-710-1*) Bowling Green Univ Popular Press.

Mutilingual Space Sciences Dictionary Vol. 3: Space Technology & Space Research. Josip Kleczek & H. Kleczkova. (ENG, FRE, GER, POR & RUS.). 742p. 1994. 247.00 (*0-444-98817-3*) Elsevier.

Mutilingual Space Sciences Dictionary Vol. 3: Space Technology & Space Research. Josip Kleczek & H. Kleczkova. (ENG, FRE, GER, POR & RUS.). 742p. 1994. 450.00 (*0-8288-9252-0*) Fr & Eur.

Mutineers' Moon. David Weber. 320p. 1992. per. 5.99 (*0-671-72085-6*) Baen Bks.

Mutineers of the Bounty & Their Descendants in Pitcairn. Belcher. 1972. 250.00 (*0-87968-342-2*) Gordon Pr.

Mutineers of the Bounty & Their Descendants in Pitcairn & Norfolk Islands. Diana Belcher. LC 75-3439. reprint ed. 49.50 (*0-404-14443-8*) AMS Pr.

Mutiny: A History of Naval Insurrection. Leonard F. Guttridge. LC 92-6616. (Illus.). 318p. 1992. 31.95 (*0-87021-281-8*) Naval Inst Pr.

Mutiny Amid Repression: Russian Soldiers in the Revolution of 1905-1906. John Bushnell. LC 84-48849. (Indiana-Michigan Series in Russian & East European Studies). 346p. reprint ed. pap. 107.30 (*0-7837-3693-2*, 205787100009) Bks Demand.

Mutiny & the Mainstream: Talk That Changed Art, 1975-1990. Ed. by Judy Seigel. LC 90-64244. (Orig.). 1992. pap. text 22.00 (*1-877675-05-9*) Midmarch Arts.

Mutiny at Almack's. Judith A. Lansdowne. 1999. mass mkt. 4.99 (*0-8217-6388-1*, Zebra Kensgtn) Kensgtn Pub Corp.

Mutiny at Brandy Station: The Last Battle of the Hooker Brigade: A Controversial Army Reorganization, Courts Martial, & the Bloody Days That Followed. Frederick B. Arner. LC 93-73405. (Illus.). 210p. 1993. 29.95 (*0-9638523-4-5*) Bates & Blood.

Mutiny at Crossbones Bay. Felicity Everett. (Puzzle Adventures Ser.). (Illus.). 24p. (J). (gr. 3-8). 1995. pap. 5.95 (*0-7460-1642-5*, Usborne) EDC.

Mutiny at Crossbones Bay. Felicity Everett. (Puzzle Adventures Ser.). (Illus.). 24p. (J). (gr. 3-8). 1999. lib. bdg. 13.95 (*0-88110-734-4*, Usborne) EDC.

Mutiny at Salerno: An Injustice Exposed. Saul David. (Illus.). 241p. (C). 1995. 29.95 (*1-85753-146-9*, Pub. by Brasseys) Brasseys.

Mutiny in Meerut. large type ed. Vivian Stuart. 432p. 1994. 27.99 (*0-7089-3085-9*) Ulverscroft.

Mutiny in Space. Cherith Baldry. (Illus.). 128p. (J). pap. 7.95 (*0-14-038489-8*, Pub. by Pnguin Bks Ltd) Trafalgar.

***Mutiny in the Civil War.** Webb Garrison, Sr. (Illus.). 328p. 2000. 29.95 (*1-57249-215-5*, WM Books) White Mane Pub.

Mutiny in the Indies. John Black. 26p. 1993. pap. 2.50 (*0-89567-114-X*) World View Forum.

***Mutiny of the Elsinore.** Jack London. (Collected Works of Jack London). 365p. 1998. reprint ed. lib. bdg. 98.00 (*1-58201-729-8*) Classic Bks.

Mutiny on Board H. M. S. Bounty. William Bligh. (Illustrated Classics Collection 5). 64p. 1994. pap. 4.95 (*0-7854-0781-2*, 40562) Am Guidance.

Mutiny on Board H. M. S. Bounty. William Bligh. 486p. 1984. lib. bdg. 23.95 (*0-89968-256-1*, Lghtyr Pr) Buccaneer Bks.

Mutiny on Board H. M. S. Bounty. William Bligh. (Now Age Illustrated V Ser.). (Illus.). 64p. (J). (gr. 4-12). 1979. pap. text 2.95 (*0-88301-392-4*); student ed. 1.25 (*0-88301-416-5*) Pendulum Pr.

Mutiny on Board H. M. S. Bounty Readalong. William Bligh. (Illustrated Classics Collection 5). 64p. 1994. pap. 14.95 incl. audio (*0-7854-0797-9*, 40564) Am Guidance.

Mutiny on the Amistad: The Saga of a Slave Revolt & Its Impact on American Abolition, Law & Diplomacy. Howard Jones. (Illus.). 281p. (C). 1987. reprint ed. 25.00 (*0-19-503828-2*) OUP.

Mutiny on the Amistad: The Saga of a Slave Revolt & Its Impact on American Abolition, Law & Diplomacy. Howard Jones. (Illus.). 304p. 1997. reprint ed. pap. 12.95 (*0-19-503829-0*) OUP.

Mutiny on the Bounty. William Bligh. Ed. by Malvina Vogel. (Great Illustrated Classics Ser.: Vol. 19). (Illus.). 240p. (J). (gr. 3-6). 1992. 9.95 (*0-86611-970-1*) Playmore Inc.

Mutiny on the Bounty. Ed. by Tricia Hedge. (Illus.). 44p. 1995. pap. text 5.95 (*0-19-421672-1*) OUP.

***Mutiny on the Bounty.** Nordhoff C & Hall J. N. 1998. pap. 14.95 (*0-316-19012-8*, Back Bay) Little.

Mutiny on the Bounty. Charles Nordhoff. (J). 1989. 20.05 (*0-606-12854-9*, Pub. by Turtleback) Demco.

Mutiny on the Bounty. Charles Nordhoff & James N. Hall. (Illus.). 379p. 1989. pap. 14.95 (*0-316-61168-9*) Little.

Mutiny on the Bounty Charles Nordhoff & James N. Hall. LC 84-672646. viii, 416p. 1982. write for info. (*0-86220-511-5*, Pub. by Chivers Pr) Chivers N Amer.

Mutiny on the Bounty. Charles Nordhuff. 1976. 26.95 (*0-8488-0597-6*) Amereon Ltd.

Mutiny on the Bounty & the Story of Pitcairn's Island, 1790-1894. Rosalind Young. 1978. lib. bdg. 300.00 (*0-87968-369-4*) Gordon Pr.

Mutiny on the Elsinore: A Novel of Seagoing Gangsters. Jack London. 378p. 1987. mass mkt. 5.95 (*0-935180-40-0*) Mutual Pub HI.

Mutiny on the Enterprise. Robert E. Vardeman. (Star Trek Ser.: No. 12). 1990. per. 5.50 (*0-671-70800-7*, Pocket Star Bks) PB.

Mutiny on the H. M. S. Bounty. William Bligh. 24.95 (*0-8488-1278-6*) Amereon Ltd.

An Asterisk (*) at the beginning of an entry indicates that the title is appearing for the first time.

Mutiny on the Harvard Bounty: The Harvard Business School & the Decline of the Nation. Kenton W. Elderkin. LC 96-96420. (Illus.). 300p. 1996. text 29.95 (*0-923965-03-3*) Elderkin Assocs.

Mutiny on the High Seas. Edgar A. Haine. LC 84-45017. (Illus.). 136p. 1992. 29.50 (*0-8453-4785-3*, Cornwall Bks) Assoc Univ Prs.

***Mutiple Choice Questions: For Microeconomics.** Philip Mayer & Kenneth P. Gilliam. 90p. (C). 1999. spiral bd. 10.00 (*1-929659-02-4*) P Mayer.

Mutism. Lebrun. 1990. 65.00 (*1-56593-539-X*, 0042) Singular Publishing.

Mutley Goes Diving! Gene Alba. (Mutley's True Life Adventures Ser.). 1998. 14.95 (*0-89346-878-9*) Heian Intl.

Mutley Goes to Snow Mountain. Gene Alba. (Mutley's True Life Adventures Ser.). 32p. (J). (ps-6). 1999. 14.95 (*0-89346-877-0*) Heian Intl.

Mutlimedia MBA: Corporate Edition 96-97. 2nd ed. 1997. 33.75 (*0-256-22837-X*, Irwn Prfssnl) McGraw-Hill Prof.

Mutliply & Divide. Terry Kane. 1997. pap., wbk. ed. 2.25 (*1-56293-917-3*, McClanahan Book) Learn Horizon.

Mutsun Dialect of Costanoan Based on the Vocabulary of de la Cuesta. fac. ed. J. Alden Mason. (University of California Publications in American Archaeology & Ethnology: Vol. 11: 7). 73p. (C). 1916. reprint ed. pap. text 8.44 (*1-55567-199-3*) Coyote Press.

Mutt in the Iron Muzzle. Michael J. Friedman. LC 97-73287. (Adventures of Wishbone Ser.: No. 7). (Illus.). 141p. (J). (gr. 3-7). 1997. mass mkt. 3.99 (*1-57064-274-5*, Big Red) Lyrick Pub.

Mutt in the Iron Muzzle see Adventures of Wishbone

Mutter und Kose Lieder: 1844 Edition. Friedrich Froebel. Ed. & Intro. by Jeffrey Stern. (Classics in Education Ser.). (GER.). 110p. 1996. reprint ed. 65.00 (*1-85506-283-6*) Bks Intl VA.

Muttketeer! Bill Crider. LC 97-73288. (Adventures of Wishbone Ser.: No. 8). (Illus.). (J). (gr. 3-6). 1997. mass mkt. 3.99 (*1-57064-272-9*, Big Red) Lyrick Pub.

Muttketeer! see Adventures of Wishbone

Mutts. Ariel Books Staff. LC 96-83369. 1996. 4.95 (*0-8362-2111-7*, Arie Bks) Andrews & McMeel.

Mutts. Stuart A. Kallen. LC 95-928. (Dogs Ser.). (Illus.). 24p. (J). (ps-4). 1995. lib. bdg. 13.98 (*1-56239-450-9*) ABDO Pub Co.

Mutts. Patrick McDonnell. (Illus.). 127p. (Orig.). 1996. pap. 9.95 (*0-8362-1025-5*) Andrews & McMeel.

Mutts: A Complete Pet Owner's Manual. Fredric L. Frye. 1989. pap. 6.95 (*0-8120-4126-7*) Barron.

Mutts: America's Dogs. Brian Kilcommons & Matthew J. Costello. 224p. 1996. 21.95 (*0-446-51949-9*, Pub. by Warner Bks) Little.

Mutts: Little Big Book. Andrews & McMeel Staff. (Little Bks.). (Illus.). 80p. 1998. 4.95 (*0-8362-6980-2*) Andrews & McMeel.

Mutts in Love: A Romantic Tail. Mindy Felinton. (Illus.). 35p. 1997. pap. 12.95 (*0-9658706-0-X*) Paw Prints.

***Mutts of the Masters.** Michael Patrick. 64p. 1999. 5.98 (*1-56731-336-1*, MJF Bks) Fine Comms.

***Mutt's Sundays.** Patrick McDonnell. 144p. 1999. pap. 12.95 (*0-7407-0010-3*) Andrews & McMeel.

Muttsey, an Unforgettable Mutt. DiAnna Mahry. 1991. 7.95 (*0-924663-16-2*) Alaskan Viewpoint.

Muttsy's Mystery. Helen Lester & Robin Lester. LC 94-24224. (Gund Children's Library). (Illus.). (J). 1995. write for info. (*1-56402-499-7*) Candlewick Pr.

Muttwutter's Adventure in Wappleland. Marjorie Ilich. (Muttwutter Tales Ser.: No. 3). (Illus.). 60p. (J). (gr. 1-4). 1998. 13.95 (*0-935650-52-0*) Bengal Pr.

Muttwutter's Tale. Marjorie Ilich. (Mutterwutter Book Ser.). (Illus.). 56p. (Orig.). (J). (ps-7). 1995. pap. 11.95 (*0-935650-50-4*) Bengal Pr.

Mutu Finds the Way to Heaven. Sue Delaney. (Literature Crusade Ser.). pap. 0.95 (*0-89985-378-1*) Christ for the Nations.

Mutu Finds the Way to Heaven. Sue Delaney. 1974. pap. 1.95 (*0-89985-996-8*) Christ for the Nations.

Mutu Finds the Way to Heaven (Pablo Encuentra el Camino al Cielo) Gordon Lindsay. (Literature Crusade Ser.). (SPA.). pap. 0.95 (*0-89985-376-5*) Christ for the Nations.

Mutual Accommodation: Ethnic Conflict & Cooperation. Robin M. Williams. LC 77-90060. 476p. reprint ed. pap. 147.60 (*0-7837-2904-9*, 205755000006) Bks Demand.

Mutual Accusation: Seventeenth-Century Body & Soul Dialogues in Their Literary & Theological Context. Rosalie Osmond. 272p. 1970. text 50.00 (*0-8020-5843-4*) U of Toronto Pr.

Mutual Agreement - Procedure & Practice. (Cahiers de Droit Fiscal International Ser.: Vol. LXVIa). 550p. 1981. pap. 105.50 (*90-6544-006-2*) Kluwer Law Intl.

Mutual Aid: A Factor in Evolution. Peter Kropotkin. (Freedom Press Anarchist Classics Ser.). 278p. 1987. reprint ed. pap. 12.00 (*0-900384-36-0*) Left Bank.

Mutual Aid: A Factor of Evolution. Peter Kropotkin. 362p. 1988. 48.99 (*0-921689-27-6*, Pub. by Black Rose); pap. 19.99 (*0-921689-26-8*, Pub. by Black Rose) Consort Bk Sales.

Mutual Aid: A Factor of Evolution & Including: "The Struggle for Existence" by Thomas H. Huxley. Peter Kropotkin. (Extending Horizons Ser.). 400p. (C). 1976. reprint ed. pap. 6.95 (*0-87558-024-6*) Porter Sargent.

Mutual Aid for Survival: The Case of the Mexican-American. Jose A. Hernandez. LC 82-21246. 170p. (C). 1983. lib. bdg. 19.50 (*0-89874-546-2*) Krieger.

Mutual Aid Groups, Vulnerable Populations, & the Life Cycle. 2nd ed. Ed. by Alex Gitterman & Lawrence Shulman. LC 93-31667. 448p. 1994. 47.50 (*0-231-08288-6*) Col U Pr.

Mutual Assistance in Criminal & Business Regulatory Matters. Ed. by William C. Gilmore. (Cambridge International Documents Ser.: No. 8). 451p. (C). 1995. text 95.00 (*0-521-47297-0*) Cambridge U Pr.

***Mutual Attraction.** Diana Waldhuber. 140p. 2000. pap. 10.00 (*1-58345-382-2*) Domhan Bks.

***Mutual Attraction.** large type ed. Margaret Mayo. 352p. 1999. 31.99 (*0-7505-1464-7*, Pub. by Mgna Lrg Print) Ulverscroft.

Mutual Banking. William B. Greene. 1972. 250.00 (*0-87968-048-2*) Gordon Pr.

Mutual Benefit Life. Robert Patrick. 1979. pap. 5.25 (*0-8222-0795-8*) Dramatists Play.

Mutual Causality in Buddhism & General Systems Theory: The Dharma of Natural Systems. Joanna Macy. LC 90-39937. (SUNY Series in Buddhist Studies). 254p. (C). 1991. pap. text 21.95 (*0-7914-0637-7*) State U NY Pr.

Mutual Concern: The Story of the American University of Beirut. John M. Munro. LC 77-22003. 212p. 1977. 25.00 (*0-88206-014-7*) Caravan Bks.

Mutual Contempt: Lyndon Johnson, Robert Kennedy & the Feud That Defined a Decade. Jeff Shesol. LC 97-710. (Illus.). 576p. 1997. 32.50 (*0-393-04078-X*) Norton.

Mutual Contempt: Lyndon Johnson, Robert Kennedy & the Feud That Defined a Decade. Jeff Shesol. (Illus.). 624p. 1998. pap. 17.95 (*0-393-31855-9*, Norton Paperbks) Norton.

Mutual Criticism see Hand-book of the Oneida Community, with a Sketch of Its Founder, & an Outline of Its Constitution & Doctrines

Mutual Criticism. John H. Noyes. 128p. 1975. reprint ed. pap. 17.95 (*0-8156-2170-1*) Syracuse U Pr.

Mutual Dreaming. Linda L. Magallon. LC 97-3114. 384p. 1997. per. 12.00 (*0-671-52684-7*) PB.

Mutual Effects of the Islamic & Judeo-Christian Worlds: The East European Pattern. Ed. by A. Ascher et al. LC 77-90629. (Studies on Society in Change: No. 3). 1979. write for info. (*0-930888-00-6*) Brooklyn Coll Pr.

Mutual Effects of the Islamic & Judeo-Christian Worlds: The East European Pattern. Ed. by Abraham Ascher et al. 244p. (C). 1986. reprint ed. lib. bdg. 45.00 (*0-8191-5564-0*) U Pr of Amer.

Mutual Exchanges: Sheffield-Munster Colloquium I. Ed. by R. J. Kavanagh. 334p. 1998. pap. text 51.95 (*0-8204-3646-1*) P Lang Pubng.

***Mutual Exchanges: Sheffield-Munster Colloquium II.** Dirk Jurgens. 418p. 1999. 52.95 (*3-631-35723-0*) P Lang Pubng.

Mutual Exclusivity Bias in Children's Word Learning. William E. Merriman & Laura L. Bowman. (Monographs of the Society for Research in Child Development: No. 220). 138p. 1990. pap. text 15.00 (*0-226-52066-8*) U Ch Pr.

Mutual Friend. Frederick Busch. LC 93-31458. 240p. 1994. reprint ed. pap. 9.95 (*0-8112-1258-0*, NDP774, Pub. by New Directions) Norton.

Mutual Fund Activities of Banks. Melanie L. Fein. LC 93-35858. 1056p. 1998. ring bd. 165.00 (*0-13-109190-5*) Aspen Law.

Mutual Fund Bible: The Complete Guide to Mutual Funds. William A. Kelly. (Illus.). 237p. Date not set. pap. 29.95 (*0-9665630-0-X*) W A Kelly Pub.

Mutual Fund Business. Robert C. Pozen. LC 98-4894. 743p. 1998. 65.00 (*0-262-16177-X*); pap. text 37.50 (*0-262-66141-1*) MIT Pr.

Mutual Fund Buyer's Guide. Norman G. Fosback. (Illus.). 475p. (Orig.). 1996. pap. 17.95 (*0-917604-45-8*) Inst Econometric.

Mutual Fund Buyer's Guide: Performing Ratings, Five Year Projections, Safety Ratings, Sales. Norman G. Fosback. 500p. 1994. pap. 17.95 (*1-55738-586-6*, Irwn Prfssnl) McGraw-Hill Prof.

Mutual Fund Fact Book, 1997. 37th ed. Investment Company Institute Staff. (Illus.). 132p. 1997. pap. 25.00 (*1-878731-19-X*) Invest Co Inst.

***Mutual Fund Faqs: Answering You Customers' Most Frequently Asked Questions.** LC 99-204271. 88p. 1999. write for info. (*0-7931-3124-3*) Dearborn.

Mutual Fund Fee Index. Richard L. Spellman, Jr. (Illus.). 1025p. (Orig.). 1989. pap. text, ring bd. 250.00 (*0-685-26837-3*) Connaught Muse.

Mutual Fund Industry: The WetFeet.com Insider Guide. 4th ed. WetFeet.com Staff. (Insider Guides Ser.). 78p. 1999. per. 25.00 (*1-58207-002-4*) WetFeet.

Mutual Fund Investment Strategies. J. W. Dicks. 1997. 17.95 (*0-02-861441-0*) Macmillan.

***Mutual Fund Investments by Fuzzy Logic** Kurt E. Peray. LC 99-12298. 1999. 39.95 (*1-57444-264-3*) St Lucie Pr.

Mutual Fund Kit. Bay Gruber. LC 97-19758. 208p. (Orig.). 1997. pap. 16.95 (*0-7931-2492-1*, 5680-4501) Dearborn.

Mutual Fund Masters: A Revealing Look into the Minds & Strategies of Wall Street's Best & Brightest. Bill Griffeth. 240p. 1994. text 22.95 (*1-55738-582-3*, Irwn Prfssnl) McGraw-Hill Prof.

Mutual Fund Rules: 50 Esential Axioms to Explain & Examine Mututal Funds Investing. Michael D. Sheimo. LC 99-32835. 247p. 1999. 18.95 (*0-07-135025-X*) McGraw.

Mutual Fund Strategies. J. W. Dicks. 1997. 17.95 (*0-614-19918-2*) Macmillan Gen Ref.

Mutual Fund Superstars: Invest in the Best, Forget about the Rest. William E. Donoghue. 1994. 24.95 (*0-9637899-0-2*) Elliott & James Pubs.

Mutual Fund Superstars: Invest in the Best, Forget about the Rest, 1996 Edition. 2nd ed. William E. Donoghue. (Illus.). 300p. 1995. 24.95 (*0-9637899-1-0*); pap. 14.95 (*0-9637899-2-9*) Elliott & James Pubs.

Mutual Fund Switch Strategies & Timing Tactics. Warren Boroson. (Investor's Self-Teaching Seminar Ser.). 225p. 1991. per. 24.95 (*1-55738-184-4*, Irwn Prfssnl) McGraw-Hill Prof.

Mutual Fund Tax Guide, 1990. 4th ed. Donna S. Carpenter. (Illus.). 129p. 1990. pap. 7.95 (*0-317-92282-3*) Fidelity MA.

***Mutual Fund Wealth Builder: A Profit-Building Guide for the Savvy Mutual Fund Investor.** Dick Fabian. (Illus.). 288p. 2000. 24.95 (*0-07-136247-9*) McGraw.

Mutual Funds: Analysis, Allocation, & Performance Evaluation. Joan Lamm-Tennant. LC 94-73423. 200p. (C). 1995. text 43.00 (*0-943590-66-3*) Amer College.

Mutual Funds: Your Key to Sound Financial Planning. Lyle Allen. 144p. (Orig.). 1994. pap. 10.00 (*0-380-77690-1*, Avon Bks) Morrow Avon.

Mutual Funds & Federal Regulation. Larry D. Barnett. 458p. 1999. ring bd. 65.00 (*1-879581-64-7*) Lupus Pubns.

Mutual Funds & Your Investment Portfolio. 2nd ed. Gerald W. Perritt. 129p. 1987. pap. 8.95 (*0-930369-18-1*) Invest Info.

Mutual Funds Buyers Guide: 1996 Edition. Norman G. Fosback. 464p. 1996. text 17.95 (*0-7863-1073-1*, Irwn Prfssnl) McGraw-Hill Prof.

Mutual Funds Explained: The Basics & Beyond. Robert C. Upton, Jr. (Investor's Quick Reference Ser.). 150p. 1991. per. 14.95 (*1-55738-211-5*, Irwn Prfssnl) McGraw-Hill Prof.

Mutual Funds for Dummies. 2nd ed. Eric Tyson. LC 98-85433. 432p. 1998. pap. 19.99 (*0-7645-5112-4*) IDG Bks.

Mutual Funds in India: Marketing Strategies & Investment Practices. H. Sadhak. LC 97-14442. 1997. pap. write for info. (*0-8039-9369-2*) Sage.

Mutual Funds in India: Marketing Strategies & Investment Practices. H. Sadhak. LC 97-14442. 272p. 1997. 39.95 (*0-8039-9368-4*) Sage.

Mutual Funds on the Net: Making Money Online. Paul B. Farrell. LC 96-48416. (Wiley Investing Ser.). (Illus.). 416p. 1997. pap. 24.95 (*0-471-17486-6*) Wiley.

Mutual Gains: A Guide to Union-Management Cooperation. Edward Cohen-Rosenthal & Cynthia E. Burton. LC 86-25249. 302p. 1986. 57.95 (*0-275-92204-9*, C2204, Praeger Pubs) Greenwood.

Mutual Gains: A Guide to Union-Management Cooperation. 2nd rev. ed. Edward Cohen-Rosenthal & Cynthia E. Burton. LC 93-11918. 360p. 1993. pap. text 26.95 (*0-87546-312-6*, ILR Press) Cornell U Pr.

Mutual Gains Enterprise: Forging a Winning Partnership Among Labor, Management & Government. Thomas A. Kochan & Paul Osterman. LC 94-5930. 272p. 1994. 27.95 (*0-87584-394-8*) Harvard Busn.

Mutual Goal Setting in Patient Care. Jo Anne Horsley. (Using Research to Improve Nursing Practice Ser.). 1982. pap. text 44.00 (*0-8089-1510-X*, 792061, Grune & Strat) Harcrt Hlth Sci Grp.

Mutual Hostages: Canadian & Japanese During the Second World War. Patricia E. Roy et al. 320p. 1990. 24.95 (*0-8020-5774-8*) U of Toronto Pr.

Mutual Hostages: Canadian & Japanese During the Second World War. Patricia E. Roy et al. 298p. 1992. pap. text 18.95 (*0-8020-7366-2*) U of Toronto Pr.

Mutual Impact of Computing Power & Control Theory. M. Karny & K. Warwick. (Illus.). 398p. (C). 1993. 110.00 (*0-306-44590-5*, Plenum Trade) Perseus Pubng.

***Mutual Impressions: Writers from the Americas Reading One Another.** Ed. by Ilan Stavans. LC 99-34818. 314p. 1999. 49.95 (*0-8223-2400-8*); pap. text 17.95 (*0-8223-2423-7*) Duke.

Mutual Interaction of People & Their Built Environment: A Cross-Cultural Perspective. Ed. by Amos Rapoport. (World Anthropology Ser.). (Illus.). xvi, 506p. 1976. 58.50 (*3-10-800169-8*) Mouton.

Mutual Interference in Fast-Frequency-Hopped, Multiple Frequency-Shift-Keyed, Spread-Spectrum Communication Satellite Systems. Edward Bedrosian. LC 96-19534. (Illus.). 83p. (Orig.). 1996. pap. 15.00 (*0-8330-2393-4*, MR-672-AF/A) Rand Corp.

Mutual Irradiation: A Quaker View of Ecumenism. Douglas V. Steere. LC 73-146680. (Orig.). 1971. pap. 4.00 (*0-87574-175-4*) Pendle Hill.

Mutual Legal Assistance Treaties. 2nd rev. ed. Mark Nestmann. 15p. 1998. spiral bd. 25.00 (*1-891266-10-1*, Pub. by Asset Protection Intl) Pathway Bk Serv.

Mutual Ministry: New Vitality for the Local Church. James C. Fenhagen. 1982. 10.45 (*0-8164-0332-5*) Harper SF.

Mutual Misunderstanding: Scepticism & the Theorizing of Language & Interpretation. Talbot J. Taylor. LC 92-6934. (Post-Contemporary Interventions Ser.). 279p. 1992. text 49.95 (*0-8223-1238-7*); pap. text 17.95 (*0-8223-1249-2*) Duke.

Mutual Reflections: Jews & Blacks in American Art. Milly Heyd. LC 98-34696. (Illus.). 272p. (C). 1999. text 50.00 (*0-8135-2617-5*); pap. text 24.00 (*0-8135-2618-3*) Rutgers U Pr.

Mutual Relations of the Four Castes. E. W. Hopkins. 114p. 1986. 14.00 (*0-8364-1759-3*, Pub. by Usha) S Asia.

Mutual Savings Banks & Savings & Loan Associations: Aspects of Growth. Alan Teck. LC 68-18999. (Illus.). 208p. reprint ed. pap. 64.50 (*0-608-30019-5*, 201969990014) Bks Demand.

***Mutual Shores.** Phillip Sterling. 2000. pap. 12.00 (*0-932826-95-4*) WMU Poetry & Prose.

Mutual Upholding: Fashioning Jewish Philosophy Through Letters. Michael Oppenheim. LC 91-36045. (Revisioning Philosophy Ser.: Vol. 9). 186p. (C). 1992. text 36.95 (*0-8204-1685-1*) P Lang Pubng.

Mutualism & Community Organization: Behavioural, Theoretical, & Food-Web Approaches. Ed. by Hiroya Kawanabe et al. LC 92-39578. (Illus.). 438p. 1993. text 115.00 (*0-19-854027-2*) OUP.

Mutualities in Dialogue. Ed. by Ivana Markova et al. (Illus.). 300p. (C). 1996. text 59.95 (*0-521-49595-4*); pap. text 19.95 (*0-521-49941-0*) Cambridge U Pr.

Mutuality: A Formal Norm for Christian Social Ethics. Dawn M. Nothwehr. LC 97-2614. 224p. 1997. 74.95 (*1-57309-158-8*, Cath Scholar Pr); pap. 54.95 (*1-57309-157-X*, Cath Scholar Pr) Intl Scholars.

***Mutuality in the Rhetoric & Composition Classroom.** David L. Wallace & Helen R. Ewald. LC 99-51750. 2000. pap. 14.95 (*0-8093-2324-9*) S Ill U Pr.

Mutuality of Care. Roy H. Steinhoffsmith. LC 99-12978. 224p. 1999. pap. 21.99 (*0-8272-2324-2*, 985880, Pub. by Chalice Pr) Abingdon.

Mutuk & Mukluks. Bob Aiken & Lew Freedman. 14.95 (*0-9671504-0-X*) Todd Commns.

Mutumin Kirkii: The Concept of the Good Man in Hausa. Anthony H. Kirk-Greene. (Hans Wolff Memorial Lectures). (Orig.). 1974. pap. text 3.00 (*0-941934-08-X*) Indiana Africa.

Mutwutter in a Storm at the Zoo. Majorie Illich. LC 98-165308. (Muttwutter Tales Ser.: No. 2). (Illus.). 60p. (J). (gr. 1-4). 1998. 13.95 (*0-935650-51-2*) Bengal Pr.

Muu Muu. (Libros de Carton Con Sonido Ser.). (SPA.). 1995. bds. 4.98 (*1-85854-294-4*) Brimax Bks.

Muwata. Imam Malik & M. R. Din. 1991. 25.50 (*1-56744-162-9*) Kazi Pubns.

Muwatalli's Prayer to the Storm-God of Lightning Through the Assembly of Gods. Itamar Singer. LC 96-9169. (ASOR Bks.: Vol. 2). (Illus.). 204p. (C). 1996. pap. text 30.00 (*0-7885-0281-6*, 850302, Pub. by Am Sch Orient Res) David Brown.

***Muy Alto Muy Bajito.** Concordia Publishing House Staff. (Hear Me Read Ser.). (SPA., Illus.). 24p. (J). (ps-k). 2000. 2.95 (*0-570-09917-X*) Concordia.

***Muy Caliente! Afro-Cuban Play-Along CD & Book.** Chuck Sher. (SPA.). 50p. 2000. pap. 18.00 incl. cd-rom (*1-883217-08-3*) Sher Music.

Muy Macho: Latino Men Confront Their Manhood. Ed. & Intro. by Ray Gonzalez. (Illus.). 256p. 1996. pap. 14.00 (*0-385-47861-5*, Anchor NY) Doubleday.

Muybridge's Complete Human & Animal Locomotion: All 781 Plates from the 1887 Animal Locomotion, 3 vols., Set. Eadweard Muybridge. Incl. Vol. 1. LC 77-1665. 1979. 75.00 (*0-486-23792-3*); Vol. 2. LC 77-1665. 1979. 75.00 (*0-486-23793-1*); Vol. 3. LC 77-1665. 1979. 75.00 (*0-486-23794-X*); (Illus.). 1979. reprint ed. 225.00 (*0-685-01500-9*) Dover.

Muzeeka. John Guare. 1968. pap. 3.25 (*0-8222-0796-6*) Dramatists Play.

Muzio Clementis Leben. Max Unger. LC 72-158959. (Music Ser.). 1971. reprint ed. lib. bdg. 37.50 (*0-306-70192-8*) Da Capo.

Muzyka dlia Ustalykh Liubovnikov. Roman Jarov. LC 84-73268.Tr. of Music for Tired Lovers. (RUS.). 216p. (Orig.). 1985. 11.00 (*0-911971-05-X*) Effect Pub.

Muzzle Blasts: Early Years Plus Vol. I & II, 1939-41. Nation Muzzle Loading Rifle Association Staff. LC 74-11637. 352p. 1974. pap. 20.00 (*0-87387-069-7*) Shumway.

Muzzle-Loading Caplock Rifle. Ned Roberts. 1991. 30.00 (*0-935632-96-4*) Wolfe Pub Co.

Muzzle-Loading Rifle Then & Now. Walter M. Cline. 1993. 32.00 (*1-879356-34-1*) Wolfe Pub Co.

Muzzle Thyself. Lauren Fairbanks. LC 90-14058. 64p. 1991. pap. 9.95 (*0-916583-74-0*) Dalkey Arch.

Muzzle Velocity: The Weaponry Guide for Thundering Steel. Edwin M. Dyer, III. (Illus.). 24p. (Orig.). (C). 1993. pap. text 5.00 (*0-9631504-1-3*) Minds In One Prods.

Muzzled Muse: Literature & Censorship in South Africa. Margreet De Lange. LC 97-6145. (Utrecht Publications in General & Comparative Literature Ser.: Vol. 32). xiii, 181p. 1997. pap. 24.95 (*1-55619-432-3*); lib. bdg. 59.00 (*1-55619-431-5*) J Benjamins Pubng Co.

Muzzleloader's Little Library. R. O. Ackerman. 1994. 6.00 (*1-877704-13-X*) Pioneer Pr.

Muzzleloading. Toby Bridges. LC 97-3876. (Hunting & Fishing Library). (Illus.). 128p. 1997. 19.95 (*0-86573-066-0*) Creat Pub Intl.

Muzzleloading for Whitetails. Toby Bridges. Ed. by Glenn Helgeland. LC 94-49359. (On Target Ser.: No. 12). (Illus.). 156p. 1995. pap. 12.95 (*0-913305-12-X*) Target Comm.

Muzzlers, Guzzlers,& Good Yeggs. Joe Coleman. 1998. pap. 12.95 (*0-87816-636-X*) Kitchen Sink.

Muzzy Readers, 6 bks., Set, Series I. BBC Staff. (J). 1990. 59.95 incl. audio (*1-85497-327-4*) Audio-Forum.

Muzzy Readers, 6 bks., Set, Series II. BBC Staff. (Illus.). (J). 1990. 59.95 incl. audio (*1-85497-262-6*) Audio-Forum.

***MV Agusta Fours.** Mick Walker. (Illus.). 200p. 2000. 35.95 (*1-86126-329-5*, 130659AE, Pub. by Cro1wood) Motorbooks Intl.

MV Herald of Free Enterprise: Report of Court No. 8074. Formal Investigation. 75p. (Orig.). 1987. pap. 30.00 (*0-11-550828-7*, HM916, Pub. by Statnry Office) Balogh.

MVA in the Treatment of Incomplete Abortion see Ameu en el Tratamiento del Aborto Incompleto: Experiencia Clinica y Programatica

MVA in the Treatment of Incomplete Abortion. Traci L. Baird et al. LC 95-4492. 1995. pap. write for info. (*1-882220-08-0*) IPAS.

MVIP Book: The Definitive Reference Manual for the Multi-Vendor Integration Protocol - The Worldwide Computer Telephony Standard. GO-MVIP Staff. 400p. 1995. pap. 34.95 (*0-936648-76-7*) Telecom Bks.

M

MVP-FORTH Expert System Toolkit. Jack Park. Ed. by Glen B. Haydon. (MVP-Forth Bks.: Vol. 4). 80p. (Orig.). 1984. pap. 22.00 (0-317-56526-1) Mntn View Pr.

MVP-FORTH Expert System Tutorial. M. Derick & L. Derick. Ed. by Glen B. Haydon. (MVP-Forth Bks.: Vol. 6). 80p. (Orig.). 1984. pap. 22.00 (0-317-56527-X) Mntn View Pr.

MVP-FORTH File Management System. Pierre Moreton. Ed. by Glen B. Haydon. (MVP-Forth Bks.: Vol. 5). 278p. (Orig.). 1984. pap. 30.00 (0-317-56529-X) Mntn View Pr.

MVP-FORTH Math & Floating Point. Philip Koopman, Jr. (MVP-Forth Bks.: Vol. 3). 320p. 35.00 (0-914699-28-8) Mntn View Pr.

MVP-FORTH Source Listing. Glen B. Haydon & R. Kuntze. (MVP-Forth Bks.: Vol. 2). 320p. 1984. 25.00 (0-914699-01-6) Mntn View Pr.

MVP-FORTH User's Manual: AMIGA. Glen Tenney. Ed. by Glen B. Haydon. (MVP-Forth Bks.). 50p. (Orig.). 1985. pap. 20.00 (0-914699-54-7) Mntn View Pr.

MVP-FORTH User's Manual: APPLE. R. Kuntze. Ed. by Glen B. Haydon. (MVP-Forth Bks.). 50p. (Orig.). 1983. pap. 20.00 (0-914699-51-2) Mntn View Pr.

MVP-FORTH User's Manual: CP-M. Glen B. Haydon. (MVP-Forth Bks.). 50p. (Orig.). pap. 20.00 (0-914699-53-9) Mntn View Pr.

MVP-FORTH User's Manual: MACINTOSH. Edward Wischmeyer. Ed. by Glen B. Haydon. (MVP-Forth Bks.). 50p. pap. 20.00 (0-914699-55-5) Mntn View Pr.

MVP-FORTH User's Manual: PC-MS DOS. Glen B. Haydon. (MVP-Forth Bks.). 50p. (Orig.). 1984. pap. 20.00 (0-914699-52-0) Mntn View Pr.

MVP Sports Puzzles. Brad Herzog. (J). 1994. pap. 4.50 (0-553-54185-4) BDD Bks Young Read.

MVP Sports Puzzles. Brad Herzog. (J). 1995. pap. 4.50 (0-553-54214-1) BDD Bks Young Read.

MVP Sports Puzzles. rev. ed. Brad Herzog & Sports Illustrated for Kids Editors. (Sports Illustrated for Kids Bks Ser.). (Illus.). 64p. (J). (gr. 4-6). 1999. pap. text 3.99 (1-886749-60-4) SI For Kids.

MVP Sports Puzzles. rev. ed. Brad Herzog & Sports Illustrated for Kids Editors. Ed. by Scott Gramling. (Sports Illustrated for Kids Bks.). (Illus.). 48p. (J). (gr. 4-6). 1999. pap. write for info. (1-886749-70-1) SI For Kids.

MVPs. Renardo Barden. (Baseball Heroes Ser.). (J). 1991. 12.50 (0-685-66095-8) Rourke Corp.

MVPs. Renardo Barden. (Baseball Heroes Ser.). 48p. (J). (gr. 3-8). 1991. lib. bdg. 15.95 (0-86593-127-5) Rourke Corp.

MVPs. John Marino. 80p. 1996. 11.98 (1-56799-243-9, MetroBooks) M Friedman Pub Grp Inc.

MVRDV at VPRO. Ed. by Jaime Salazar. (Illus.). 250p. 1998. pap. 27.00 (84-89698-60-0, 820871, Pub. by Actar) Dist Art Pubs.

MVS - JCL: Mastering Job Control Language. Gabriel F. Gargiulo. 436p. 1993. 54.95 (0-471-56164-9) Wiley.

MVS - TSO: Mastering CLISTs. Barry K. Nirmal. 272p. 1993. pap. 49.95 (0-471-58441-X, GC3195) Wiley.

MVS - VSAM for the Application Programmer. 10th ed. Gary D. Brown & S. A. Smith. 484p. 1993. pap. 49.95 (0-471-56045-6, GD423X) Wiley.

MVS & UNIX: A Survival Handbook for Multi-Platform Users, Developers & Managers. Richard J. Bambara. LC 98-6457. (Illus.). 608p. 1998. pap. 65.00 (0-07-006663-9) McGraw.

MVS Answer Book. David Sacks. 296p. 1994. pap. 42.95 (0-471-60821-1) Wiley.

MVS Assembler Language. rev. ed. Kevin McQuillen & Anne Prince. LC 86-63830. 528p. 1987. pap. 45.00 (0-911625-34-8) M Murach & Assoc.

MVS Capacity Planning for a Balanced System. Brian A. Macfarlane. LC 94-21735. (IBM Ser.). 1994. write for info. (0-07-709053-5) McGraw.

MVS Cobol Application Developers Toolbox. Alex Varsegi. (IBM Ser.). 450p. 1993. 65.00 (0-07-067175-3) McGraw.

MVS JCL. 2nd ed. Doug Lowe. LC 94-37779. 496p. 1994. pap. 49.50 (0-911625-85-2) M Murach & Assoc.

MVS-JCL & Utilities: A Comprehensive Treatment. 2nd ed. Michael Trombetta & Sue C. Finkelstein. (Illus.). 608p. (C). 1989. text 60.00 (0-201-08318-3) Addison-Wesley.

MVS-JCL (OS-390) Quick Reference Guide. 2nd rev. ed. Olivia R. Carmandi. (Mainframe Ser.). 80p. 1998. pap. text 22.00 (1-892559-00-5) M V S Train.

MVS JCL Primer. Saba Zamir. 384p. 1992. pap. 42.95 (0-07-072702-3) McGraw.

MVS Performance Management. 5th ed. Stephen L. Samson. LC 96-53004. (Illus.). 467p. 1997. 65.00 (0-07-057700-5) McGraw.

MVS Primer. David S. Kirk. 141p. 1993. pap. 29.95 (0-471-57715-4, GD3993) Wiley.

MVS TSO Pt. 1: Concepts & ISPF. 2nd ed. Doug Lowe. LC 90-19907. 467p. 1990. pap. 42.50 (0-911625-56-9) M Murach & Assoc.

MVS TSO Pt. 2: Commands & Procedures. 2nd ed. Doug Lowe. LC 90-19907. 450p. 1991. pap. 42.50 (0-911625-57-7) M Murach & Assoc.

MVS-TSO (OS-390) Quick Reference Guide. 2nd rev. ed. Olivia R. Carmandi. (Mainframe Ser.). 113p. 1998. pap. text 22.00 (1-892559-01-3) M V S Train.

MVS TSO/ISPF: A Guide for Users & Developers. Kurt Bosler. 1993. 55.00 (0-07-006565-9) McGraw.

MW ClarisWorks 3.0 Companion. 3rd ed. Steven A. Schwartz. 600p. 1995. pap. 24.99 (1-56884-481-6) IDG Bks.

MW Freehand 5 Bible. 2nd ed. Deke McClelland. 784p. 1995. pap. 29.99 (1-56884-492-1) IDG Bks.

MW Office 98 Bible. Bob LeVitus. 880p. 1998. pap. 39.99 (0-7645-4041-6) IDG Bks.

MW Quarkxpress 4 Bible. Galen Gruman. LC 97-77230. 950p. 1998. pap. 39.99 (0-7645-4029-7) IDG Bks.

Mwalimu: The Influence of Nyerere. Ed. by Colin Legum & Geoffrey Mmari. LC 95-3926. 1995. 49.95 (0-86543-478-6); pap. 16.95 (0-86543-479-4) Africa World.

Mwalimu Wa Kiswahili: A Language Teaching Manual. Lioba Moshi et al. 123p. 1998. pap. text, teacher ed. 22.00 (1-883058-61-9) Global Pubns.

Mwindo Epic from the Banyanga (Congo Republic) Ed. by Daniel P. Biebuyck & Kahombo C. Mateene. 1969. pap. 12.95 (0-520-02049-9, Pub. by U CA Pr) Cal Prin Full Svc.

MWSS: Object - Oriented Design in Java. Tom Cabanski. LC 97-46425. (Mitchell Waite Signature Ser.). 768p. 1999. 49.99 (1-57169-134-0) Sams.

MX ICBM & National Security. Colin S. Gray. LC 81-2557. 173p. 1981. 57.95 (0-275-90637-X, C0637, Praeger Pubs) Greenwood.

MXM: Man Out of Mutant, a Personal Quest for a Creed to Live By. Maya De Montaudouin. LC 95-77658. (Illus.). 104p. 1996. pap. 7.95 (0-9624648-4-8) Good Earth Pubns.

My Feelings see Ayuqucinka

My A, B, C, D, E Thinking, Feeling & Doing Book. Margaret F. Goldman. LC 83-90397. (Illus.). 48p. (J). (ps up). 11.95 (0-914237-00-4) L & M Bks.

My A, B, C's. (Jr. Academic Ser.). (Illus.). 32p. (J). (ps). 1998. wbk. ed. 2.25 (1-57768-228-9) MG-Hill OH.

My A-B-Cs Say Be Kind to You & Me see Tena, Joshua, & Friends

My "a" Sound Box. Jane Belk Moncure. LC 84-17024. (Sound Box Library). (Illus.). 32p. (J). (ps-2). 1984. lib. bdg. 21.36 (0-89565-296-X) Childs World.

My ABC. Lorna Read. (My Big Little Fat Bks.). (Illus.). 20p. (J). (ps). 1996. bds. 3.49 (1-85854-173-5) Brimax Bks.

My ABC Bible Verses: Hiding God's Word in Little Hearts. Susan Hunt. LC 98-17102. (Illus.). 64p. (J). (ps-2). 1998. 12.99 (1-58134-005-2) Crossway Bks.

My ABC Book. Nancy Bennett & Pearl Bennett. (Illus.). 54p. (J). (ps-1). 1988. student ed. 12.00 (0-9622242-0-0) Red Baron Pub Co.

My ABC Book of Cancer. Shannin Chamberlain. (Illus.). 40p. (J). 1991. pap. 6.95 (0-912184-07-8) Synergistic Pr.

My ABC of Health Coloring Book. David Hakim. pap. 1.50 (0-686-11513-9) Hakims Pubs.

My ABC Signs of Animal Friends. Ben Bahan & Joe Dannis. (Illus.). 32p. (J). 1994. pap. 8.95 (0-915035-31-6, 4201) Dawn Sign.

My ABC's. (Fisher-Price Bubble - Bath Bks.). (Illus.). 6p. (J). (ps). 1998. vinyl bd. write for info. (0-7666-0145-5, Honey Bear Bks) Modern Pub NYC.

***My ABC's.** Don L. Curry. LC 99-50152. (Illus.). 1999. pap. write for info. (0-7368-7048-2) Capstone Pr.

My ABC's Lowercase. Beth A. Wise. 32p. (J). 1997. pap. text, wbk. ed. 2.25 (1-56293-949-1, McClanahan Book) Learn Horizon.

My ABC's Uppercase. Beth A. Wise. 32p. (J). 1997. pap. text, wbk. ed. 2.25 (1-56293-950-5, McClanahan Book) Learn Horizon.

My Acres of Diamonds Prosperity Workbook. Clark & Hixson. 192p. 1985. pap. 14.50 (0-8187-0064-5) Harlo Press.

My Adam & Eve Book of Opposites. Glenda Palmer. (Early Learner's Picture Books Ser.). (Illus.). 32p. (J). 1995. 6.99 (0-570-04780-3, 56-1800) Concordia.

My Address Is Earth. Dorothy Jacobson. (Illus.). (Orig.). 1978. pap. 4.00 (0-932460-00-3) Summer Stream.

***My Advent Fun Book: Daily Activities for Children.** Francine M. O'Connor. 32p. 1998. pap. text 1.95 (0-7648-0217-8) Liguori Pubns.

My Advent Journal. William F. Maestri. 110p. 1990. pap. 5.95 (0-8189-0599-9) Alba.

***My Adventure to the Enchanted Forest.** Jennifer Anna. (My Adventure Ser.). (Illus.). 30p. 1999. pap. 10.00 (1-886383-72-3, Little Blue) Pride & Imprints.

***My Adventure to the Moon.** Jennifer Anna. (Illus.). 20p. (J). 1999. pap. 10.00 (1-886383-73-1, Little Blue) Pride & Imprints.

My Adventure with Lupus: Living with a Chronic Illness. Robert L. Yocum. 180p. (Orig.). 1995. pap. text 12.95 (1-888824-02-6) Bridgeport Bks.

My Adventurers in Zuni: Including Father of the Pueblos & an Aboriginal Pilgrimage. Frank H. Cushing & Sylvester Baxter. (American Historical Reprints Ser.). (Illus.). 79p. 1999. pap. 8.95 (0-86541-045-3) Filter.

My Adventures As a Spy. Robert Baden-Powell. (Illus.). 132p. (Orig.). (YA). 1993. pap. 16.95 (0-9632054-8-X) Stevens Pub.

My Adventures in the Golden Age of Music. Henry T. Finck. LC 70-87496. (Music Ser.). 462p. 1971. reprint ed. lib. bdg. 55.00 (0-306-71448-5) Da Capo.

My Adventures in the Golden Age of Music. Henry T. Finck. (American Biography Ser.). 462p. 1991. reprint ed. lib. bdg. 89.00 (0-7812-8130-X) Rprt Serv.

My Adventures in Zuni: American Autobiography. Frank H. Cushing. 125p. 1995. lib. bdg. 69.00 (0-7812-8494-5) Rprt Serv.

My Adventures with Mankind: A Layman's Profile of the Bible. James P. Whitlock. 136p. 1991. pap. 4.95 (0-914733-15-X) Desert Min.

My Adventures with Your Money. George Rice. (Illus.). 332p. 1986. 25.00 (0-913814-75-X) Nevada Pubns.

My Adventures with Your Money. George G. Rice. 1975. 10.00 (0-685-54481-8) Bookfinger.

My Aeroplane. (C). 1977. write for info. (0-201-13832-8) Addison-Wesley.

My Affair with Christianity. L. Blue. text 35.00 (0-340-66906-3, Pub. by Hodder & Stought Ltd) Trafalgar.

***My African Heritage.** Shegita Kiflom. (Illus.). 26p. (J). (ps-k). 2000. pap. 9.98 (0-9675581-0-7) Papyrus Pubng Inc.

My African Roots: A Child's Create Your Own Keepsake Book of Family History & African-Awareness. Jacqueline Galloway-Blake. 32p. (J). (ps-7). 1992. student ed. 5.95 (0-9637243-6-3) Brwn Sug & Spice.

My African Safari. Kim Capehart. LC 99-70088. (Illus.). 96p. 1999. pap. 11.95 (1-57197-165-3) Pentland Pr.

My Afterlife Guaranteed: And Other Narratives. Nanos Valaoritis. 140p. (Orig.). 1990. pap. 6.95 (0-87286-248-8) City Lights.

My Alef-Bet Coloring Book. David Sokoloff. (Illus.). 24p. (Orig.). (J). (ps-5). 1998. pap. 1.00 (1-889655-04-X) Jewish Educ Toys.

My Alexandria: Poems. Mark Doty. LC 92-21564. (National Poetry Ser.). 102p. (C). 1993. 11.95 (0-252-06317-1) U of Ill Pr.

My Alexandria: Poems. Mark Doty. 102p. (C). 1995. 18.95 (0-252-02210-6) U of Ill Pr.

My All for Him. M. Basilea Schlink. 16p. 1972. mass mkt. 4.99 (0-87123-370-3) Bethany Hse.

My All His All. J. Edwin Orr. Ed. by Richard O. Roberts. xiv, 170p. 1989. 14.95 (0-940033-40-2) R O Roberts.

My All, His All. rev. ed. James E. Orr. 215p. 1989. reprint ed. lib. bdg. 14.95 (0-926474-02-2) Intl Awakening Pr.

My All Sufficient One. Sharon Price. 159p. (Orig.). 1985. pap. 5.95 (0-917595-08-4) Kingdom Pubs.

My All-Time Favorites - Songs for Kids: Piano. 48p. (Orig.). 1993. pap. 8.95 (0-7692-1121-6, PF0822) Wrner Bros.

My All-Time Favorites/Melodies: Piano. 128p. (Orig.). 1993. pap. 14.95 (0-7692-1120-8, PF0824) Wrner Bros.

My All-Time Favorites/T. V. & Movie Songs: Piano. 80p. (Orig.). 1993. pap. 9.95 (0-7692-1122-4, PF0823) Wrner Bros.

My Almost Perfect Plan. David Gooding & Sarah J. Verney. (Full House Michelle Ser.: Vol. 18). (J). (gr. 4-7). 1984. per. 1.75 (0-671-00837-4) PB.

My Alphabet: Seek 'n Sound. (Illus.). (J). 1996. write for info. (0-307-74159-1, Goldn Books) Gldn Bks Pub Co.

My Alphabet & Bible Verse Coloring Book. Illus. by Elaine Cole. 28p. (J). (ps). 1994. pap. 2.50 (1-883426-02-2) Chldrns Outrch.

My Alphabet Book. (Wipe-Off Activity Bks.). (Illus.). 16p. (J). (ps-k). 1997. wbk. ed. 3.79 (1-889319-15-5) Trend Enterprises.

My Alphabet Book. Ed. by Penguin Books Staff. (Early Readers Ser.: No. S8711-5). (Illus.). (J). (ps-2). 3.95 (0-7214-5145-4, Ladybrd) Penguin Putnam.

***My Alphabet Letter Books, AA to ZZ.** Robert S. Brown. (Illus.). (J). 2000. pap. 3.95 (0-13-014808-3) P-H.

My Amazing Body see Mi Asombroso Cuerpo

My Amazing Body. Kathryn Breighner & Deborah Rohe. 1990. teacher ed. 24.95 (0-88671-371-4, 4352) Am Guidance.

My Amazing Body. Rachel Wright. (Illus.). 32p. (J). (gr. k-4). 1997. 11.95 (0-915741-78-4) C D Stampley Ent.

***My Amazing Human Body Explorer.** Paul Robert Dawson. LC 00-29469. (Illus.). (J). 2000. pap. write for info. (0-7894-6707-0) DK Pub Inc.

***My Amazon River Day.** Kris Nesbitt. (Illus.). 48p. (J). (gr. 3-8). 2000. 23.95 (0-9701035-0-6) Shedd Aquarium.

My America: 1928-1938. Louis Adamic. LC 76-2050. (FDR & the Era of the New Deal Ser.). 1976. reprint ed. lib. bdg. 59.50 (0-306-70801-9) Da Capo.

My America: 1928-1938. Louis Adamic. (American Biography Ser.). 669p. 1991. reprint ed. lib. bdg. 109.00 (0-7812-8002-8) Rprt Serv.

My American Century. Studs Terkel. LC 96-52779. 1997. 25.00 (1-56584-365-7, Pub. by New Press NY) Norton.

My American Century. Studs Terkel. 544p. 1998. pap. 14.95 (1-56584-469-6, Pub. by New Press NY) Norton.

My American Dream. Dinesh Shah. (Save the Democracy Ser.). (Illus.). 200p. Date not set. pap. write for info. (0-9634764-1-6) Fnding Fathers.

My American Dream. Dinesh Shah. (Save the Democracy Ser.). (Illus.). 200p. 1996. write for info. (0-9634764-6-7) Fnding Fathers.

My American History: Lesbian & Gay Life During the Reagan-Bush Years. Sarah Schulman. LC 94-9261. 320p. (C). (gr. 13). 1994. pap. 20.99 (0-415-90853-1) Routledge.

My American Journey: An Autobiography. Colin L. Powell & Joseph E. Persico. 1996. mass mkt. 6.99 (0-345-40728-8) Ballantine Pub Grp.

My American Journey: An Autobiography. Colin L. Powell & Joseph E. Persico. (Illus.). 643p. 1995. 25.95 (0-679-43296-5) Random.

My American Visit. Frederick Smith. LC 73-13150. (Foreign Travelers in America, 1810-1935 Ser.). (Illus.). 340p. 1974. reprint ed. 28.95 (0-405-05473-4) Ayer.

My Amiable Uncle: Recollections about Booth Tarkington. Susanah Mayberry. LC 82-81021. (Illus.). 160p. 1983. 24.95 (0-911198-66-0) Purdue U Pr.

My Analysis with Freud. Joseph Wortis. LC 94-34614. 234p. 1994. pap. text 45.00 (1-56821-394-8) Aronson.

My Ancestor Was a Merchant Seaman. (C). 1987. 45.00 (0-7855-2077-5, Pub. by Birmingham Midland Soc) St Mut.

My Ancestors Came with the Conqueror: Those Who Did & Some of Those Who Probably Did Not. Anthony J. Camp. 89p. 1998. reprint ed. pap. 9.50 (0-8063-1390-0, 878) Genealog Pub.

My Ancestors Were Baptists. (C). 1987. 60.00 (0-7855-2076-7, Pub. by Birmingham Midland Soc) St Mut.

My Ancestors Were Jewish. (C). 1987. 50.00 (0-7855-2079-1, Pub. by Birmingham Midland Soc) St Mut.

My Ancestors Were Quakers. (C). 1987. 60.00 (0-7855-2078-3, Pub. by Birmingham Midland Soc) St Mut.

***My Angel.** Yuko Green. (Little Activity Bks.). (Illus.). (J). 1998. pap. text 1.00 (0-486-40127-8) Dover.

***My Angel.** Christine Young. 2000. mass mkt. 5.99 (0-8217-6643-0, Zebra Kensgtn) Kensgtn Pub Corp.

My Angel & Other Poems. Jane Hathaway. Ed. & Pref. by Michael Hathaway. 48p. (Orig.). 1994. pap. 12.00 (0-943795-26-5) Chiron Rev.

My Angel, Daniel: Early Dawn of True Life in God. Vassula Ryden. (True Life in God Ser.: Vol.). 314p. 1995. pap. 9.95 (1-883225-17-5) Trinitas.

My Angel Named Herman. Elmer Townes. LC 98-4896. (Illus.). 128p. (J). (gr. 3-7). 1998. 7.99 (0-8499-5839-3) Tommy Nelson.

My Angel Will Go Before You. Georges Huber.Tr. of Mon Ange Marchera Devant Toi. 128p. 1995. pap. 9.95 (0-905127-72-2) Scepter Pubs.

***My Angelica.** Carol Lynch Williams. 2001. pap. 4.99 (0-440-22778-X) BDD Bks Young Read.

My Angelica. Carol Lynch Williams. LC 98-23139. 160p. (YA). (gr. 6-9). 1999. 15.95 (0-385-32622-X) Delacorte.

My Animal Book. Harry Bornstein et al. (Signed English Ser.). (Illus.). 16p. (J). (ps). 1973. pap. 3.50 (0-930323-38-6, Pub. by K Green Pubns) Gallaudet Univ Pr.

My Animal-Free Kitchen! deluxe ed. Sharon L. Davies-Tight. 184p. 1996. reprint ed. pap. 22.95 (1-885099-00-2) Rainbow Sunshine.

My Animal-Free Kitchen! Small Edition. 2nd ed. Sharon L. Davies-Tight. 184p. 1996. pap. 15.95 (1-885099-01-0) Rainbow Sunshine.

***My Animal Friends.** rev. ed. David La Jars. (Talk Together Ser.). (Illus.). (J). 2000. 9.95 (1-58728-013-2); pap. 4.95 (1-58728-017-5) Two Can Pub.

***My Answer Journal: What Kids Wonder about God & the Bible.** Mary J. Davis. 136p. (J). (gr. 4). 1999. pap. 9.99 (1-885358-72-5, Lgacy Pr) Rainbow CA.

***My Antiques Organizer.** Hobby House Press Staff. 24p. (YA). 2000. 19.95 (0-87588-579-9) Hobby Hse.

***My Antiques Organizer Fact Sheets Album.** Hobby House Press Staff. 128p. 2000. pap. 11.95 (0-87588-574-8) Hobby Hse.

***My Antonia.** (YA). 1999. 11.95 (1-56137-759-7) Novel Units.

My Antonia. Willa Cather. 24.95 (0-88411-287-X) Amereon Ltd.

My Antonia. Willa Cather. 320p. 1994. mass mkt. 4.95 (0-553-21418-7, Bantam Classics) Bantam.

My Antonia. Willa Cather. (Barron's Book Notes Ser.). 1985. pap. 2.50 (0-8120-3528-3) Barron.

My Antonia. Willa Cather. LC 95-30223. (Illus.). 244p. 1995. pap. 5.95 (0-395-75514-X) HM.

My Antonia. Willa Cather. 288p. 1994. mass mkt. 4.95 (0-451-52579-5, Sig Classics) NAL.

My Antonia. Willa Cather. (Critical Editions Ser.). (C). 1997. pap. text. write for info. (0-393-96790-5, Norton Paperbks) Norton.

My Antonia. Willa Cather. 1996. 15.95 (0-679-60205-4) Random.

My Antonia. Willa Cather. LC 96-223945. 1996. 16.00 (0-679-44727-X) Random.

My Antonia. Willa Cather. (Signet Classics). 1994. 10.05 (0-606-05933-4, Pub. by Turtleback) Demco.

My Antonia. Willa Cather. LC 94-20031. (Enriched Classics Ser.). 1994. 10.60 (0-606-06588-1, Pub. by Turtleback) Demco.

My Antonia. Willa Cather. 240p. 1997. pap. 5.95 (0-460-87723-2, Everyman's Classic Lib) Tuttle Pubng.

My Antonia. Willa Cather. Ed. by Charles W. Mignon & Kari Ronning. LC 93-50941. (Willa Cather Scholarly Edition Ser.). (Illus.). xx, 415p. 1997. pap. 14.95 (0-8032-6372-4, Bison Books) U of Nebr Pr.

My Antonia. Willa Cather. LC 93-2491. (Illus.). 304p. 1994. pap. 9.95 (0-14-018764-2, Penguin Classics) Viking Penguin.

My Antonia. Willa Cather. 1997. pap. write for info. (0-14-771198-3) Viking Penguin.

My Antonia. Willa Cather. (C). 1999. pap. 10.95 (0-14-028327-7) Viking Penguin.

My Antonia. Willa Cather. 1999. audio 16.95 (0-14-086313-3) Viking Penguin.

My Antonia. Willa Cather. 256p. 1994. pap. 9.00 (0-679-74187-9) Vin Bks.

My Antonia. Willa Cather. LC 95-206306. 125 p. 1994. write for info. (0-573-69499-0) S French Trade.

***My Antonia.** large type ed. Willa Cather. 352p. 2000. pap. 22.00 (0-06-095694-1, HarpCollins) HarperTrade.

My Antonia. large type ed. Willa Cather. 400p. 1996. reprint ed. lib. bdg. 24.00 (0-939495-05-8) North Bks.

My Antonia. Willa Cather. 1992. reprint ed. lib. bdg. 25.95 (0-89966-977-8) Buccaneer Bks.

My Antonia. Willa Cather. (Collected Works of Willa Cather). 418p. 1998. reprint ed. lib. bdg. 108.00 (1-58201-570-8) Classic Bks.

My Antonia. Willa Cather. 240p. 1998. reprint ed. lib. bdg. 24.00 (1-58287-051-9) North Bks.

My Antonia. Willa Cather. Ed. & Intro. by Sharon O'Brien. 344p. 1994. reprint ed. mass mkt. 5.50 (0-671-89086-7, WSP) PB.

My Antonia. Willa Cather. Ed. by Charles W. Mignon & Kari A. Ronning. LC 93-50941. (Willa Cather Scholarly Edition Ser.: Vol. 2). (Illus.). xxv, 543p. 1995. reprint ed. text 65.00 (0-8032-1468-5) U of Nebr Pr.

My Antonia. unabridged ed. Willa Cather. 176p. 1994. pap. text 2.00 (0-486-28240-6) Dover.

My Antonia: A Study Guide. Melissa Klapper. Ed. by J. Friedland & R. Kessler. (Novel-Ties Ser.). (YA). (gr. 9-12). 1996. pap. text 15.95 (1-56982-670-6) Lrn Links.

An Asterisk (*) at the beginning of an entry indicates that the title is appearing for the first time.

My Antonia: A Unit Plan. Mary B. Collins. 180p. 1994. teacher ed., ring bd. 26.95 (*1-58337-124-9*) Teachers Pet Pubns.

My Antonia: Curriculum Unit. Center for Learning Network Staff & Willaim K. Carter. (Novel Ser.). 71p. (YA). (gr. 9-12). 1990. spiral bd. 18.95 (*1-56077-357-X*) Ctr Learning.

My Antonia: Notes. David Kubicek. (Cliffs Notes Ser.). (Illus.). 88p. (Orig.). (C). 1962. pap., student ed. 4.95 (*0-8220-0861-0*, Cliff) IDG Bks.

My Antonia: Reproducible Teaching Unit. James Scott. 54p. (YA). (gr. 7-12). 1999. ring bd. 29.50 (*1-58049-144-8*, TU65) Prestwick Hse.

My Antonia: The Road Home. John J. Murphy. (Masterwork Studies: No. 31). 136p. (C). 1989. 25.95 (*0-8057-7986-8*, MWS-31, Twyne); mass mkt. 14.95 (*0-8057-8035-1*, Twyne) Mac Lib Ref.

My Anxieties Have Anxieties. Charles M. Schulz. 128p. 1995. pap. 5.95 (*0-8050-1691-0*, Owl) H Holt & Co.

My Apartment. Patricia T. Cousin et al. (Visions: African-American Experiences: No. 16). (Illus.). 8p. (Orig.). (J). (gr. k-1). 1995. pap. text 3.00 (*1-57518-015-4*) Arborlake.

My Appalachian Heritage: Yes, I'm a Hillbilly. Dorlous Barth. LC 96-69807. 1996. pap. 12.95 (*1-881908-16-X*) PanPress.

My Apple see First Step Science

My Apple Tree. Harriet Ziefert. (Stickerbook Reader Ser.). (Illus.). 24p. (J). (ps-3). 1991. mass mkt. 3.95 (*0-06-107420-9*) HarpC Child Bks.

My Apple Tree & Me. Katherine Miller. (Food & Fun for the Mind, Body, & Soul Ser.: No. 3). (Illus.). 32p. (Orig.). (J). (gr. k-3). 1996. pap. 8.95 (*0-9653035-1-9*) Huckleberry CT.

My Appointed Round: 929 Days As Postmaster General. J. Edward Day. 160p. 1965. reprint ed. 8.00 (0-87012-149-9) McClain.

The funniest-&-wisest book ever written about the post office. By the father of the zip code, President Kennedy's postmaster general, this book is rollicking humor with political revelations. A wonderful gift for friends who work, or have worked, for the post office. Third Printing, 1973. ***Publisher Paid Annotation.***

My April Fool Book. Arlene Popkin. (Illus.). (J). (ps-1). 1974. lib. bdg. 11.86 (*0-914844-04-0*) J Alden.

My April Journal. Alana Trisler & Patrice Cardiel. (Illus.). 48p. (J). (gr. 1-2). 1999. pap., wbk. ed. 1.75 (*1-56762-102-3*) Modern Learn Pr.

My Apron. Eric Carle. (Illus.). 32p. (J). (gr. k). 1994. 22.95 (*0-399-22824-1*, Philomel) Peng Put Young Read.

My Apron. Eric Carle. LC 93-36342. (Illus.). 40p. (J). (gr. 1 up). 1995. 13.95 (*0-399-22685-0*, Philomel) Peng Put Young Read.

My Arabic Alphabet Book. Siddiqa Juma. (ARA., Illus.). (J). (gr. k-6). Date not set. 10.00 (*1-879402-33-5*) Tahrike Tarsile Quran.

My Arctic Journal: A Year among Ice-Fields & Eskimos. Josephine D. Peary. LC 74-5863. reprint ed. 54.50 (*0-404-11669-8*) AMS Pr.

My Arctic Journal, a Year among Ice-Fields & Eskimos: With an Account of the Great White Journey Across Greenland by Robert E. Peary. Josephine D. Peary. (American Biography Ser.). 240p. 1991. reprint ed. lib. bdg. 69.00 (*0-7812-8309-4*) Rprt Serv.

My Arctic 1, 2, 3. Michael A. Kusugak. (Illus.). 24p. (J). (gr. k-2). 1996. 16.95 (*1-55037-505-9*, Pub. by Annick); pap. 6.95 (*1-55037-504-0*, Pub. by Annick) Firefly Bks Ltd.

My Argument with the Gestapo: A Macaronic Journal. Thomas Merton. LC 69-20082. 256p. 1975. pap. 10.95 (*0-8112-0586-X*, NDP403, Pub. by New Directions) Norton.

My Army Life. Frances C. Carrington. LC 72-150173. (Select Bibliographies Reprint Ser.). 1977. 27.95 (*0-8369-5686-9*) Ayer.

My Art, My Life: An Autobiography (with Gladys March) Diego Rivera. (Illus.). 224p. 1992. reprint ed. pap. 7.95 (*0-486-26938-8*) Dover.

***My Asakusa: Coming of Age in Pre-War Tokyo.** Sadako Sawamura. Tr. by Norman E. Stafford & Yasuhiro Kawamura. 2000. pap. 16.95 (*0-8048-2135-6*) Tuttle Pubng.

My Attitude. Maurine Fergueson. pap. 16.95 (*0-614-16305-6*) Noble Hse.

My Attitude. Maurine Ferguson. LC 96-68092. (Illus.). Date not set. 16.95 (*1-56167-305-6*) Noble Hse MD.

***My August Journal.** Alana Trisler & Patrice Cardiel. 48p. (J). (gr. 1-2). 1999. wbk. ed. 1.75 (*1-56762-114-7*) Modern Learn Pr.

My Aunt Came Back. Pat Cummings. LC 96-49374. (Illus.). 14p. (J). (ps up). 1998. write for info. (*0-694-01059-6*) HarpC.

My Aunt Came Back Big Book: Black & White Nellie Edge I Can Read & Sing Big Book. Illus. by Melissa Saylor. (J). (ps-2). 1988. pap. text 21.00 (*0-922053-12-X*) N Edge Res.

My Aunt Is a Pilot Whale. Anne Provoost. Tr. by Ria Bleumer. 150p. (YA). pap. 8.95 (*0-88961-202-1*, Pub. by Womens Pr) LPC InBook.

My Aunt Otilia's Spirits (Los Espiritus de Mi Tia Otilia) Richard Garcia. Tr. by Jesus Guerrero Rea. LC 86-17129. (ENG & SPA., Illus.). 24p. (YA). (gr. 1 up). 1987. 15.95 (*0-89239-029-8*) Childrens Book Pr.

My Aunt Ruth. Iris Rosofsky. LC 90-4940. (Charlotte Zolotow Bk.). 224p. (YA). (gr. 7 up). 1991. 13.95 (*0-06-025087-9*) HarpC Child Bks.

My Aunt, the Monster. Mary Stanton. (Magical Mystery Ser.: Vol. 1). 144p. (J). (gr. 3-7). 1997. mass mkt. 3.99 (*0-425-15227-8*) Berkley Pub.

***My Auntie Bean, She Is a Scream.** Arlene McFarlane. Ed. by Noreen Wise. (Lemonade Collection). (Illus.). 64p. (J). (ps-2). 2000. pap. 5.95 (*1-58584-258-3*) Huckleberry CT.

My Austin: Remembering the Teens & Twenties. Emmett Shelton, Sr. (Texas History Ser.). (Illus.). 83p. 1994. pap. 9.95 (*0-89641-268-7*) American Pr.

My Autobiography. Benito Mussolini. xix, 318p. 1928. 15.25 (*0-8371-4294-6*) Greenwood.

My Autobiography. Samuel S. McClure. (American Biography Ser.). 266p. 1991. reprint ed. lib. bdg. 69.00 (*0-7812-8281-0*) Rprt Serv.

***My Autobiography: Chapters from the North American Review.** Mark Twain, pseud. LC 99-50284. 288p. 2000. pap. 8.95 (*0-486-40898-1*) Dover.

My Autobiography & the Fall of Mussolini see My Rise & Fall

***My Autobiography, Bill Carling.** W. Carling. 1998. text 35.00 (*0-340-69658-3*, Pub. by Hodder & Stought Ltd) Trafalgar.

My Awakening: A Path to Racial Understanding. David Duke. LC 98-86509. (Illus.). 736p. 1998. 29.95 (*1-892796-00-7*) Free Speech Pr.

***My B-I-B-L-E.** Cathy Drinkwater Better. (Illus.). 10p. (J). (ps-k). 2000. 8.99 (*0-570-07041-4*) Concordia.

My "b" Sound Box. Jane Belk Moncure. LC 77-23588. (Sound Box Library). (Illus.). 32p. (J). (ps-2). 1977. lib. bdg. 21.36 (*0-913778-92-3*) Childs World.

My Baba & I. John S. Hislop. LC 85-61733. 1985. pap. 9.00 (*0-9600958-8-8*) Birth Day.

My Babies & Me: By the Year 2000: Baby. Tara T. Quinn. (Superromance Ser.: No. 864). 1999. per. 4.25 (*0-373-70864-5*, 1-70864-3) Harlequin Bks.

My Baby. Roger Generazzo. LC 97-74282. (Shaped Little Nugget Bks.). (Illus.). 18p. (J). 1998. bds. 3.99 (*0-307-12721-4*, 12721, Goldn Books) Gldn Bks Pub Co.

***My Baby.** Jeanette Winter. 2001. text (*0-374-35103-1*) FS&G.

My Baby & Me: A Journal for the Single Parent. Judith Levy. (Illus.). 64p. 1999. text 17.95 (*1-55670-890-4*) Stewart Tabori & Chang.

My Baby Book. 1410p. Date not set. 14.95 (*0-88271-135-0*, 1415); 14.95 (*0-88271-557-7*, 10344) Regina Pr.

***My Baby Bro is Little Monster.** Sarah Albee. 24p. (J). 2001. mass mkt. 1.99 (*0-375-81148-6*) Random Bks Yng Read.

My Baby Brother. (C). 1977. write for info. (*0-201-13838-7*) Addison-Wesley.

***My Baby Brother: A Fill-In & Keep Book.** Richard Dawson. (Illus.). 32p. (J). 2000. pap. 3.99 (*0-330-36970-9*) Mcm Child Bks.

***My Baby Brother & Me: Memory Scrapebook for Kids.** Jane Drake & Ann Love. (Memory Scrapbook for Kids Ser.). (Illus.). 32p. (YA). (gr. k-3). 2000. pap. 5.95 (*1-55074-639-1*, Pub. by Kids Can Press) Genl Dist Srvs.

My Baby Brother Has Ten Tiny Toes. Laura Leuck. LC 96-32815. (Illus.). 24p. (J). (ps). 1997. lib. bdg. 14.95 (*0-8075-5310-7*) A Whitman.

My Baby Brother Has Ten Tiny Toes. Laura Leuck. (Prairie Paperback Bks.). (Illus.). 24p. (J). 1999. pap. 5.95 (*0-8075-5311-5*) A Whitman.

My Baby Daddy: Another Baby - No Husband. Joyce Ameen. (Illus.). 100p. 1998. pap. text 7.95 (*0-9664325-0-9*) Four Malse.

***My Baby Face.** Caryn Jenner. (Changing Faces Ser.). (Illus.). 16p. (J). (ps). 2000. 3.95 (*0-7641-5220-3*) Barron.

My Baby Jesus Book of Numbers. Glenda Palmer. (Early Learner's Picture Books Ser.). (Illus.). 32p. (J). 1995. 6.99 (*0-570-04782-X*, 56-1802) Concordia.

***My Baby Journal.** Sylvia Long. (Illus.). 64p. 1998. 16.95 (*0-8118-1890-X*) Chronicle Bks.

My Baby Manual: An Easy Reference Guide to Your Baby's First Year. Linda Levin & Eileen Bropson. LC 98-60125. (ENG & SPA., Illus.). 192p. 1998. spiral bd. 19.95 (*0-9655703-2-0*) Square Peg Pr.

***My Baby, My Love.** Dani Sinclair. (Intrigue Ser.: No. 551). 2000. per. 4.25 (*0-373-22551-2*, 1-22551-5, Harlequin) Harlequin Bks.

My Baby Photograph Album: Victorian Photograph Album. Ed. by Nancy C. Akmon. (Illus.). 14p. 1997. 10.95 (*1-884807-11-9*) Blushing Rose.

***My Baby Sister: Fill-In & Keep Book.** Richard Dawson. (Illus.). 32p. (J). 2000. pap. 3.99 (*0-330-36971-7*) Mcm Child Bks.

***My Baby Sister & Me: Memory Scrapbooks for Kids.** Jane Drake & Ann Love. (Memory Scrapbook for Kids Ser.). (Illus.). 32p. (YA). (gr. k-3). 2000. pap. 5.95 (*1-55074-641-3*, Pub. by Kids Can Press) Genl Dist Srvs.

My Baby, Your Child. Nikki Benjamin. (Special Edition Ser.). 1994. per. 3.50 (*0-373-09880-4*, 5-09880-1) Silhouette.

My Baby, Your Son. Anne Peters. (Fabulous Fathers Ser.). 1997. per. 3.25 (*0-373-19222-3*, 1-19222-8) Silhouette.

My Baby's Father: A Politics of Black Love Novel. G. Dan Buford. LC 95-83300. 1996. pap. 12.00 (*0-9647635-1-6*) La Caille-Nous.

My Babysitter Bites Again. Ann Hodgman. Ed. by Ruth Ashby. (Illus.). 144p. (Orig.). (J). (gr. 3-6). 1993. pap. 3.50 (*0-671-79378-0*, Minstrel Bks) PB.

My Babysitter Flies at Night. Ann Hodgman. Ed. by Ruth Ashby. (Illus.). 144p. (Orig.). (YA). 1994. pap. 3.50 (*0-671-88450-6*, Minstrel Bks) PB.

My Babysitter Flies by Night. Ann Hodgman. 1994. 8.60 (*0-606-06589-X*, Pub. by Turtleback) Demco.

My Babysitter Goes Bats. Ann Hodgman. Ed. by Ruth Ashby. (My Babysitter Ser.: No. 5). 144p. (Orig.). (J). 1994. pap. 3.50 (*0-671-88451-4*, Minstrel Bks) PB.

My Babysitter Has Fangs. Ann Hodgman. Ed. by Ruth Ashby. (Illus.). 128p. (Orig.). (J). 1992. pap. 3.50 (*0-671-75868-3*, Minstrel Bks) PB.

My Babysitter Is a Movie Monster. Ann Hodgman. (Illus.). 144p. (J). (gr. 3-6). 1995. pap. 3.50 (*0-671-88452-2*, Minstrel Bks) PB.

My Babysitter Is a Movie Monster. Ann Hodgman. (J). 1995. 8.60 (*0-606-07902-5*, Pub. by Turtleback) Demco.

My Babysitter Is a Vampire. Ann Hodgman. Ed. by Ruth Ashby. LC 91-196766. (Illus.). 121p. (J). (gr. 4-7). 1991. per. 3.50 (*0-671-64751-2*, Minstrel Bks) PB.

My Babysitter is a Vampire. Ann Hodgman. (J). 1991. 8.60 (*0-606-04981-9*, Pub. by Turtleback) Demco.

My Back Is Normal. large type ed. Sitare Ltd. Staff. Ed. by Alistair MacLean. (Self Help Ser.). (Illus.). 75p. (YA). 1998. spiral bd. 10.00 (*0-940178-95-8*) Sitare.

My Back is Normal: Back Problems. large type ed. Ed. by Alistair MacLean. (Illus.). 100p. 1999. spiral bd. 10.00 (*0-940178-01-X*) Sitare.

My Back Yardstick. Tom Plante. 56p. 1998. pap. 4.95 (*0-9647373-2-9*) Marimbo Commun.

My Backpack. Eve Bunting. LC 96-83934. (Illus.). 32p. (J). (ps). 1997. 14.95 (*1-56397-433-9*) Boyds Mills Pr.

My Backyard Garden. Carol Lerner. LC 97-6460. (Illus.). 48p. (J). (gr. 4-6). 1998. lib. bdg. 15.93 (*0-688-14756-9*, Wm Morrow) Morrow Avon.

My Backyard Garden. Carol Lerner. LC 97-6460. (Illus.). 48p. (J). (ps-3). 1998. 16.00 (*0-688-14755-0*, Wm Morrow) Morrow Avon.

My Backyard Garden. Carol Lerner. 1998. 16.00 (*0-676-57322-3*) Random.

My Backyard History Book. David Weitzman. (Brown Paper School Bks.). (Illus.). 128p. (J). (gr. 4 up). 1975. pap. 13.95 (*0-316-92902-6*) Little.

My Backyard History Book. David L. Weitzman. (Brown Paper School Bks.). (J). 1975. 18.05 (*0-606-04026-9*, Pub. by Turtleback) Demco.

My Bad: Forgiveness. Kent Kramer et al. (Inter Acta Ser.). (Illus.). 6p. (C). 1994. teacher ed., ring bd. 1.25 (*1-885702-01-9*, 741-010t, Inter Acta); student ed., ring bd. 3.25 (*1-885702-00-0*, 741-010s, Inter Acta) WSN Pr.

My Bad Boy. large type ed. Margot Neville. (Linford Mystery Library). 400p. 1992. pap. 16.99 (*0-7089-7234-9*, Linford) Ulverscroft.

My Badge Is My Integrity: The Life of a Harness Bull. Edward A. Stein, Sr. LC 97-77347. (Illus.). vii, 389p. 1997. 24.50 (*0-9661937-1-7*); pap. 18.50 (*0-9661937-0-9*) Ashco Pubns.

***My Ballet Activity Book.** Winky Adam. 1999. pap. text 1.00 (*0-486-40493-5*) Dover.

My Ballet Book. Tom Ettinger & William Jaspersohn. (Illus.). 48p. (J). (gr. 3-7). 1993. 10.95 (*0-694-00477-4*, HarpFestival) HarpC Child Bks.

My Ballet Book: An Introduction to the Magical World of Ballet. Kate Castle. LC 98-22803. (Illus.). 61p. (J). (gr. 1-6). 1998. pap. 15.95 (*0-7894-3432-6*) DK Pub Inc.

My Ballet Collection: Sleeping Beauty. Oyster Books Staff. (Illus.). 32p. (J). 1995. 4.95 (*0-8362-0769-6*) Andrews & McMeel.

My Ballet Collection: Swan Lake. Oyster Books Staff. (Illus.). 32p. (J). 1995. 4.95 (*0-8362-0771-8*) Andrews & McMeel.

My Ballet Collection: The Nutcracker. Tim Wood & Jenny Wood. LC 96-119846. (Illus.). 32p. (J). 1995. 4.95 (*0-8362-0772-6*) Andrews & McMeel.

***My Balloon at the Zoo.** 2nd large type ed. Linda Garber. (Illus.). 21p. (J). (gr. 1-4). 1999. spiral bd. 9.95 (*1-892218-05-4*) Murlin Pubns.

My Banking Workbook. Stephen J. Pigott. (Illus.). 80p. 1999. pap. text, wbk. ed. 14.95 (*0-9672932-2-7*) S J Pubg Inc.

My Baptism. Bev Milton. (Illus.). 24p. 1998. pap. 23.95 (*1-55145-296-0*, Pub. by Wood Lake Bks) Logos Prods.

My Baptism Activity & Memory Book. Allan K. Burgess & Max H. Molgard. (Illus.). 21p. 1997. pap., student ed. 4.95 (*1-57345-250-5*) Deseret Bk.

My Baptism Book. Ilona Obrien. 1998. pap. 5.95 (*0-687-08716-3*) Abingdon.

My Baptism Memory Book. Beth B. McNamara. (Illus.). 40p. (Orig.). 1996. pap. 9.95 (*0-87973-367-5*) Our Sunday Visitor.

My Bar Mitzvah. Illus. & Des. by Marlene Lobell Ruthen. 36p. 1995. 13.00 (*0-8074-0542-6*, 510010) UAHC.

My Bar/Bat Mitzvah. Illus. by Marlene L. Ruthern. 36p. (YA). 1994. 10.00 (*0-8074-0200-1*, 510000) UAHC.

My Barbie Slumber Party Book. Golden Books Staff. (Barbie Ser.). 20p. (J). 1998. 4.99 (*0-307-30451-5*, 30451, Goldn Books) Gldn Bks Pub Co.

My Baseball Book. Gail Gibbons. LC 99-32945. (Illus.). 24p. (J). (ps-2). 2000. 5.95 (*0-688-17137-0*, Wm Morrow) Morrow Avon.

My Baseball Book: A Write-in-Me Book for Young Players. Tom Ettinger & William Jaspersohn. (Illus.). 48p. (J). (gr. 3-7). 1993. 10.95 (*0-694-00466-9*, HarpFestival) HarpC Child Bks.

My Baseball Diary. James T. Farrell. LC 97-43794. (Writing Baseball Ser.). 304p. 1998. pap. 14.95 (*0-8093-2189-0*) S Ill U Pr.

My Basic Missal. large type ed. Paul Trinchard. LC 96-76329. (Illus.). 96p. (Orig.). 1996. pap. 8.00 (*1-889168-00-9*) MAETA.

***My Basketball Book.** Gail Gibbons. LC 99-87902. (Illus.). 24p. (J). (ps-2). 2000. 5.95 (*0-688-17140-0*, Wm Morrow) Morrow Avon.

***My Basketball Book.** Gail Giggons. 2000. 5.89 (*0-06-029224-5*) HarpC.

My Bat Mitzvah. Illus. & Des. by Marlene Lobell Ruthen. 36p. 1995. 13.00 (*0-8074-0543-4*, 510020) UAHC.

My Beanie Baby Binder: Expressly for Casual to Compulsive Collectors. Peg Fugal et al. 384p. 1998. 29.95 (*0-9666105-0-4*) Beanie Stuff.

My Beanieography: A Journal of Beanie Baby Experiences. Dawna Foucht. (Illus.). 68p. (J). (gr. 1-12). 1998. 14.95 (*1-885628-17-X*) Buckaroo Bks.

My Bear & Me. Barbara Maitland. LC 97-75775. (Illus.). 32p. (J). (ps-2). 1999. 16.00 (*0-689-82085-2*) McElderry Bks.

My Bears' Schoolhouse, 6 bks. Gina Bencraft. (Illus.). (J). 1995. bds. write for info. (*1-85479-762-X*, Pub. by M OMara) Assoc Pubs Grp.

My Beastiary. Julianne Leigh. Ed. by Edward Mycue. (Took Modern Poetry in English Ser.: No. 11). (Illus.). 28p. (Orig.). 1993. pap. 3.00 (*1-879457-05-9*) Norton Coker Pr.

My Beautiful, Broken Shell (Discovering Beauty in Our Brokenness) see My Beautiful Broken Shell Gift Book: Words of Hope to Refresh the Soul

My Beautiful Broken Shell Gift Book: Words of Hope to Refresh the Soul. Carol Hamblet Adams. Orig. Title: My Beautiful, Broken Shell (Discovering Beauty in Our Brokenness). (Illus.). 64p. 1998. 9.99 (*1-881830-93-4*) Garborgs.

***My Beautiful Broken Shell Journal.** Garborg's Inc. Staff. 168p. 1999. 11.99 (*1-58375-420-2*) Garborgs.

My Beautiful Fat Friend. Josephine Carr. 1988. reprint ed. write for info. (*0-318-62360-9*) S&S Trade.

My Beautiful Lady. 3rd ed. Thomas Woolner. LC 79-148334. reprint ed. 32.50 (*0-404-07031-0*) AMS Pr.

My Beautiful Launderette & Others. Hanif Kureishi. LC 97-209473. 108p. 1997. pap. 16.95 (*0-571-17738-7*) Faber & Faber.

***My Beautiful Life: How Macrobiotics Brought Me from Cancer to Radiant Health.** Mina Dobic. LC 99-67783. (Illus.). 198p. 2000. pap. 15.95 (*1-899171-13-4*, Pub. by Findhorn Pr) Words Distrib.

My Bedtime: A Book about Getting Ready for Bed see PowerKids Readers Set 1: My World

My Bedtime Bible. Carolyn Larsen. LC 95-217315. (Illus.). 384p. (J). (ps). 1994. 19.99 (*0-529-10248-X*, MB1) World Publng.

My Bedtime Book of the Saints. rev. ed. Frank Lee. LC 93-78437. (Illus.). 64p. (J). 1993. pap. 3.95 (*0-89243-585-2*) Liguori Pubns.

My Bedtime Prayer. Tony McCaffrey. LC 97-16411. (Illus.). 32p. (J). 1997. 12.95 (*0-8294-0966-1*) Loyola Pr.

My Bedtime Prayer Bear. Zoe Crutchley & Veronica Parnell. (Illus.). 12p. (J). (ps-k). 1999. bds. 8.99 (*0-8054-1796-6*) Broadman.

My Beginning Mass Book. JoAnn M. Angers. (Illus.). 48p. (Orig.). (J). (gr. 1-4). 1978. pap. 2.95 (*0-89622-082-6*) Twenty-Third.

My Beloved. Charles Penn. 1981. pap. 4.75 (*1-57836-085-4*, BW-105) Sathya Sai Bk Ctr.

***My Beloved.** Karen Ranney. LC 99-94775. 372p. 1999. mass mkt. 5.99 (*0-380-80590-1*, Avon Bks) Morrow Avon.

***My Beloved Angel.** LeRoy F. Oates. 2000. pap. write for info. (*1-58235-329-8*) Watermrk Pr.

My Beloved Community: Selected Sermons & Speeches. Herbert D. Daughtry, Sr. 1998. 59.95 (*0-86543-589-8*); pap. 18.95 (*0-86543-590-1*) Africa World.

My Beloved Is Mine. John W. Bramhall. Ed. by J. Boyd Nicholson. 127p. 1994. pap. 5.95 (*1-882701-10-0*) Uplook Min.

***My Beloved Marconi.** Maria C. Marconi & Elettra Marconi. LC 99-44852. Orig. Title: Mio Marito Guglielmo. (Illus.). 1999. 29.95 (*0-937832-36-7*) Dante U Am.

My Beloved Son. Catherine Cookson. 432p. 1992. mass mkt. 6.99 (*0-552-13302-7*) Bantam.

My Beloved Son. Joan K. Ireland. LC 95-185831. 192p. Date not set. pap. 10.99 (*0-8280-0944-9*) Review & Herald.

My Beloved Son. large type ed. Catherine Cookson. 524p. 1993. reprint ed. lib. bdg. 22.95 (*1-56054-694-8*) Thorndike Pr.

My Beloved Son: A Novel. Catherine Cookson. LC 92-10143. 1993. 22.00 (*0-671-75865-9*) S&S Trade.

***My Beloved Wife.** Lloyd Adams. 256p. 1999. pap. write for info. (*0-9636577-7-1*) Trego-Hill.

My Best Book: A Year-Long Record of "Personal Bests" Claire Martin & Steve Martin. (Illus.). 40p. (Orig.). (J). (gr. 3-5). 1988. pap. 7.95 (*0-929545-00-1*) Black Birch Bks.

My Best Day: Remembrances of Celebrities & Other Prominent Americans. Mark S. Keyes. LC 97-12741. 125p. 1997. text 13.95 (*0-929765-57-5*) Seven Locks Pr.

My Best Defense. Bob Riggs. LC 96-60283. 208p. (Orig.). (J). (gr. 4-9). 1996. pap. 5.95 (*1-886747-01-6*) Ward Hill Pr.

***My Best Fiend.** Sheila Lavelle. (Illus.). 1998. pap. 9.95 (*0-14-037182-6*, Pub. by Pnguin Bks Ltd) Trafalgar.

***My Best Friend.** Pam Huizenga. (Illus.). 12p. (J). (ps-3). 2000. 7.95 (*1-929774-00-1*, Greenleaf Bk Grp) Grnlf Ent.

My Best Friend. Pat Hutchins. LC 91-48354. (Illus.). 32p. (J). (ps-3). 1993. 15.95 (*0-688-11485-7*, Grenwillow Bks) HarpC Child Bks.

My Best Friend, Vol. 2, Bk. 2. Jalon E. Lies. Ed. by David Holland. (Illus.). (J). (ps-2). 1996. 7.50 (*1-889994-03-0*) For His Kingdom.

My Best Friend: A Book about Friendship see PowerKids Readers Set 1: My World

My Best Friend: A Pet Owners Journal. Iris L. Solomon & Ronald Solomon. (Illus.). 50p. (YA). (gr. k up). 1999. spiral bd. 14.95 (*0-9658167-2-9*) Swingset Pr.

My Best Friend Mini Edition. Ariel, pseud. 1999. 4.95 (*0-8362-8172-1*) Andrews & McMeel.

My Best Friend & Me. A. Child. (Foundations Ser.). 19p. (J). (gr. 1). 1992. pap. text 4.50 (*1-56843-072-8*) EMG Networks.

M

My Best Friend & Me: Big Book. A. Child. (Foundations Ser.). 19p. (J). (gr. 1). 1992. pap. text 23.00 (*1-56843-022-1*) EMG Networks.

My Best Friend Is a Movie Star. Cathy East Dubowski. (Full House Michelle Ser.: Vol. 10). 144p. (J). (gr. 4-7). 1996. per. 3.99 (*0-671-56835-3*) PB.

My Best Friend is Invisible. R. L. Stine, pseud. (Goosebumps Ser.: No. 57). 144p. (J). (gr. 3-7). 1997. pap. text 3.99 (*0-590-56894-9*) Scholastic Inc.

My Best Friend is Invisible. R. L. Stine, pseud. (Goosebumps Ser.: No. 57). 1997. 9.09 (*0-606-11649-4*, Pub. by Turtleback) Demco.

My Best Friend Is Me. Beth A. Marcozzi & Lawrence E. Shapiro. (Illus.). 45p. (J). (ps-3). 1995. pap. 10.50 (*1-882732-25-1*) Childswork.

My Best Friend Is Out of This World. Sarah Albee. LC 98-12754. (Road to Reading Ser.). (Illus.). 32p. (J). 1998. pap. 3.99 (*0-307-26202-2*, 26202) Gldn Bks Pub Co.

*__My Best Friend Jesus: 180 Devotions & Worship Activities for Preschoolers.__ Cheryl L. Woolsey. LC 98-226817. (Illus.). (J). (ps). 1998. 12.99 (*0-8280-1308-X*) Review & Herald.

*__My Best Friend, My Blanket.__ Charles M. Schulz. (Peanuts Gang Ser.). (Illus.). 32p. (J). (ps-3). 1998. pap. 3.50 (*0-694-01044-8*) HarpC.

My Best Friends. Photos by Margaret Miller. LC 96-157695. (Super Chubby Board Bks.). (Illus.). 12p. (J). (ps). 1996. 4.99 (*0-689-80049-5*) Litle Simon.

My Best Friends. Sterling Publishing Staff. (J). 1999. 5.95 (*0-8069-1950-7*) Strlng Pub CA.

My Best Friends & Me: Fun Things to Do Together. Emilie Barnes & Anne Christian Buchanan. LC 99-17715. (Illus.). 32p. (J). (ps-3). 1999. 14.99 (*0-7369-0121-3*) Harvest Hse.

My Best Friend's Boyfriend. Kate William. (Sweet Valley High Ser.: No. 87). (YA). (gr. 7 up). 1992. 8.60 (*0-606-00684-2*, Pub. by Turtleback) Demco.

My Best Friend's Girlfriend. Wendy Loggia. (Love Stories Super Edition Ser.). 224p. (YA). (gr. 7-12). 1997. mass mkt. 4.50 (*0-553-49214-4*) BDD Bks Young Read.

My Best Friends Wedding. 64p. 1997. otabind 16.95 (*0-7935-8661-5*) H Leonard.

My Best Game of Chess. L. Szabo. (Chess Ser.). (Illus.). 232p. 1986. 19.95 (*0-08-032034-1*, Pub. by PPL) Elsevier.

*__My Best Games of Chess.__ Vishy Anand. 1998. pap. write for info. (*1-901983-00-5*, Pub. by Gambit) BHB Intl.

My Best Games of Chess, 1908-1937. Alexander Alekhine. 581p. 1985. reprint ed. pap. 13.95 (*0-486-24941-7*) Dover.

My Best Games of Chess, 1905-1954. S. G. Tartakower. (Chess Ser.). 480p. 1985. reprint ed. pap. 11.95 (*0-486-24807-0*) Dover.

*__My Best Man.__ Andy Schell. 2000. 23.00 (*1-57566-549-2*, Knsington) Kensgtn Pub Corp.

My Best Mathematical & Logic Puzzles. Martin Gardner. (Illus.). 96p. 1994. pap. 4.95 (*0-486-28152-3*) Dover.

*__My Best Pet.__ Michelle Knudsen. (Pop-Up Play Ser.). (J). (ps). 2001. 6.99 (*1-57584-744-2*, Pub. by Rdrs Digest) S&S Trade.

My Best Pet. Teacher Created Materials Staff. (Go Bks.). 8p. (J). (gr. k-1). 1997. pap. 2.49 (*1-57690-817-8*) Tchr Create Mat.

My Best Poems. John M. Denney. (Illus.). 40p. 1996. pap. 4.95 (*0-9654698-1-6*) Denney Literary.

My Best Puzzles in Logic & Reasoning. 81st ed. Hubert C. Phillips. (Orig.). 1961. pap. 4.95 (*0-486-20119-8*) Dover.

My Best Puzzles in Mathematics. Hubert C. Phillips. (Orig.). 1961. pap. 4.95 (*0-486-20091-4*) Dover.

My Best Self: Using the Enneagram to Free the Soul. Kathleen V. Hurley & Theodore E. Dobson. LC 92-53922. 304p. 1993. pap. 15.00 (*0-06-250332-4*, Pub. by Harper SF) HarpC.

My Best Shoes. Marilee R. Burton. LC 92-33863. (Illus.). 32p. (J). 1994. 14.89 (*0-688-11757-0*, Wm Morrow) Morrow Avon.

My Best to You: A Collection of Choice Recipes for the New Cook. Bonnie S. Paiva. (Orig.). 1994. pap. 12.50 (*0-9639227-1-8*) B S Paiva.

My Best to You from the Lilley Pad. Mary B. Lilley. LC 91-90243. 152p. 1991. pap. 9.95 (*0-9629488-0-2*) Lilley Pub.

*__My Best Work Is Done at the Office.__ Roland Cheek. Ed. by Robert Elman. Tr. by Laura Donavan. LC 99-76467. 320p. 2000. pap. 19.95 (*0-918981-06-9*) Skyline Pub.

My Bible ABCs. Tracy Harrast. LC 97-61397. (Illus.). 32p. (J). (ps). 1998. 4.99 (*0-310-91778-6*) Zondervan.

My Bible Animals. Tracy Harrast. LC 97-61402. (Illus.). 32p. (J). (ps). 1998. 4.99 (*0-310-91780-8*) Zondervan.

My Bible Colors. Tracy Harrast. LC 97-61401. (One to Grow on Bible Ser.). (Illus.). 32p. (J). (ps). 1998. 4.99 (*0-310-91779-4*) Zondervan.

*__My Bible Dress-Up Book.__ Carla Williams. (Illus.). (J). 2000. pap. 12.99 (*0-7814-3436-X*) Chariot Victor.

My Bible Friend's: Mary & the Baby Jesus. Alice J. Davidson. LC 98-138317. (My Bible Friends Board Books). (Illus.). 12p. (J). 1997. bds. 3.99 (*0-310-97327-9*) Zondervan.

My Bible Friends: Read-&-Do Book. Robin Currie. LC 97-14056. (Illus.). 175p. (J). (ps-3). 1998. 19.95 (*0-8198-4795-X*) Pauline Bks.

*__My Bible Journal: A Journey Through the Word for Kids.__ Mary J. Davis. 152p. (J). 1999. pap. 9.99 (*1-885358-70-9*, Lgacy Pr) Rainbow CA.

*__My Bible Journal (KJV Edition) A Journey Through the Word for Kids.__ 152p. 1999. pap. 9.99 (*1-885358-86-5*, Lgacy Pr) Rainbow CA.

My Bible 1-2-3s. Tracy Harrast. LC 97-61398. (Illus.). 32p. (J). (ps). 1998. 4.99 (*0-310-91781-6*) Zondervan.

My Bible Pals Present the First Thanksgiving. rev. ed. Dana Stewart. (My Bible Pals Present Ser.). (Illus.). 12p. (J). (ps). 1997. bds. 4.99 (*0-7847-0722-7*, 03472) Standard Pub.

My Bible Pals Spinner Games. Diane Stortz. (Illus.). 10p. (J). (ps). 1996. bds. 8.99 (*0-7847-0517-8*, 02657) Standard Pub.

My Bible Pals Storybook: Learning with Friends from the Bible & Today. Illus. by Jodie McCallum. (My Bible Pals Ser.). 128p. (J). (ps-k). 1996. 9.99 (*0-7847-0529-1*, 02749) Standard Pub.

My Bible Stories: The Hop-Aboard Handbook & Sing-along. Carol Greene. (Illus.). 64p. (J). (ps). 1993. pap. 13.99 incl. audio (*0-570-04752-8*, 56-1771) Concordia.

My Bible Story Book. Sarah Fletcher. LC 73-91810. (Illus.). 72p. (J). (ps-3). 1974. 9.99 (*0-570-03423-X*, 56-1171) Concordia.

My Bible Story Book. Dena Korfker. LC 88-7236. (Illus.). 512p. 1988. pap. 12.99 (*0-8254-3045-3*) Kregel.

My Bible Story Book of ABCs. Glenda Palmer. (Early Learner's Picture Books Ser.). (Illus.). 32p. (J). 1995. 6.99 (*0-570-04783-8*, 56-1803) Concordia.

My Bible Story Book of ABCs, Colors, Numbers & Opposites. Glenda Palmer. 128p. (J). 1999. 9.99 (*0-88486-258-5*) Galahad Bks.

My Bible Story Coloring Book. Rick Incrocci. (My Bible Story Coloring Books). (J). (ps-3). 1998. pap. 1.99 (*0-570-05032-4*); pap. 1.99 (*0-570-05034-0*); pap. 1.99 (*0-570-05035-9*) Concordia.

My Bible Story Coloring Book, 2. Ruth Geisler. (My Bible Story Coloring Books Ser.). (ps-3). 1998. pap. 1.99 (*0-570-05033-2*, 56-1857) Concordia.

*__My Bible Story Coloring Book, 8.__ Concordia Publishing Company Staff. 1998. pap. 1.99 (*0-570-05085-5*) Concordia.

My Bible Story Coloring Book No. 6. Concordia Publishing Staff. (Illus.). 32p. (ps-2). 1998. pap. 2.95 (*0-570-05073-1*) Concordia.

My Bible Story Library. Tommy Nelson Publishers Staff. (J). 1999. 14.99 (*0-8499-5981-0*) Tommy Nelson.

My Bible Story Reader, 6 vols., Set. Lillie A. Faris. (J). 1979. pap. 17.99 (*0-88019-089-2*) Schmul Pub Co.

My Bible Study Notebook. Jerold Potter. 108p. (YA). 1992. spiral bd. 3.97 (*1-55748-280-2*) Barbour Pub.

My Bible Study Notebook. Jerold Potter. 1994. pap. text 2.49 (*1-55748-480-5*) Barbour Pub.

*__My Bible Talks to Me: A Bible Verse for Every Day, to Help Me Live a Better Way, 1.__ Nelson Word Publishing Staff. (Jesus in My Pocket Ser.). (Illus.). 64p. (J). (ps-3). 2000. pap. 2.99 (*0-7852-0023-1*) W1CL.

My Bible Teaches Me about God, Vol. 5. (Junior Kids Church Ser.). 160p. (J). (ps). 1998. 129.95 incl. audio, vdisk (*1-57405-436-8*) CharismaLife Pub.

My Bible Teaches Me about God Vol. 5: Extra Leader's Manual. 160p. 1998. teacher ed. 15.00 (*1-57405-437-6*) CharismaLife Pub.

My Bible Teaches Me about God's Good News Vol. 7: Leader's Manual. (Junior Kids Church Ser.). 160p. 1999. teacher ed. 15.00 (*1-57405-464-3*) CharismaLife Pub.

My Bible Teaches Me about Jesus Vol. 6: Extra Leader's Manual. (Junior Kids Church Ser.). 160p. 1998. teacher ed. 15.00 (*1-57405-463-5*) CharismaLife Pub.

My Bible Treasury - The New Testament. Tim Wood & Jenny Wood. (Illus.). 28p. (YA). (ps up). 1999. pap. 9.99 (*0-8054-1883-0*) Broadman.

My Bible Treasury - The Old Testament. Tim Wood & Jenny Wood. (Illus.). 28p. (YA). (ps up). 1999. pap. 9.99 (*0-8054-1882-2*) Broadman.

My Bible Word Book. Ann Adams. LC 97-197416. (Illus.). 48p. (ps-2). 1997. 9.99 (*0-570-04882-6*, 56-1831) Concordia.

My Bicycle Trip. Monna Dingman. 232p. 1995. pap. 9.95 (*0-88961-212-9*) Womans Pr.

*__My Big Alphabet Book.__ Kindersley Publishing Dorling. 8p. (J). (ps-k). 1999. 9.95 (*0-7894-4681-2*) DK Pub Inc.

My New Bed: From Crib to Bed. 2nd ed. Stan Berenstain & Jan Berenstain. (Berenstain Bears Baby Board Books Ser.). (J). (ps). 1999. pap. 3.99 (*0-679-89333-4*, Pub. by Random Bks Yng Read) Random.

My Big Book. D K Publishing Staff. LC 99-191131. (J). 1999. 9.95 (*0-7894-4325-2*) DK Pub Inc.

*__My Big Book of Animal Stories.__ Smithmark Publishing Staff. LC 98-60615. (Illus.). 256p. (J). (ps-3). 1998. 14.98 (*0-7651-0889-5*) Smithmark.

*__My Big Book of Animals.__ Lowell House Juvenile Staff. (My Big Board Books Ser.). (Illus.). 24p. (J). (ps-k). 2000. bds. 8.95 (*0-7373-0410-3*, 04103W, Pub. by Lowell Hse Juvenile) NTC Contemp Pub Co.

*__My Big Book of Bedtime Stories.__ Smithmark Publishing Staff. LC 98-60617. (Illus.). 256p. (J). (ps-3). 1998. 14.98 (*0-7651-0695-7*) Smithmark.

My Big Book of Bible Stories. Kari James. (At Your Fingertips Ser.). (Illus.). 5p. (J). (ps-3). 1999. mass mkt. 6.95 (*0-7681-0103-4*, McClanahan Book) Learn Horizon.

My Big Book of Bible Stories: At Your Fingertips. Kari James & McClanahan Book Co., Inc. Staff. (At Your Fingertips Ser.). (Illus.). 24p. (J). (ps-3). 1996. bds. 6.99 (*1-56293-834-7*, McClanahan Book) Learn Horizon.

My Big Book of Everything. (Illus.). 64p. (J). (ps). 1996. 14.95 (*0-7894-0998-4*) DK Pub Inc.

My Big Book of Fairy Tales: A Treasury of Favorite Stories for Children/08503. (J). 1987. 8.98 (*0-671-08503-4*) S&S Trade.

*__My Big Book of Words.__ Lowell House Juvenile Staff. (My Big Board Books Ser.). (Illus.). 24p. (J). (ps-k). 2000. bds. 8.95 (*0-7373-0407-3*, 04073W, Pub. by Lowell Hse) NTC Contemp Pub Co.

My Big Box. Diane Foley. LC 92-31910. (Voyages Ser.). (Illus.). (J). 1993. 3.75 (*0-383-03584-8*) SRA McGraw.

*__My Big Boy Potty.__ Joanna Cole. LC 99-50286. (Illus.). 32p. (J). (ps up). 2000. 5.95 (*0-688-17042-0*, Wm Morrow) Morrow Avon.

*__My Big Boy Potty Book.__ Cole. 2000. lib. bdg. 5.89 (*0-06-029223-7*) HarpC.

*__My Big, Bright World.__ Sarah Weeks. (Fisher-Price Step-by-Step Ser.). (J). 2001. 5.99 (*1-57584-715-9*, Pub. by Rdrs Digest) S&S Trade.

*__My Big Buddy.__ (Books to Go Ser.). 1998. pap. write for info. (*0-8136-8308-4*) Modern Curr.

My Big Christmas Book. Hayden McAllister. (J). 1988. 5.98 (*0-671-07565-9*) S&S Trade.

My Big Coloring Bible. Illus. by Jonielle Emery. 320p. (J). 1997. pap. 6.99 (*1-57673-122-7*, Gold n Honey) Zondervan.

*__My Big Counting Book.__ Kindersley Publishing Dorling. 8p. (J). (ps-k). 1999. 9.95 (*0-7894-4682-0*) DK Pub Inc.

My Big Day: A Diary of Your Toddler's Day. 2nd ed. Beth Kalish. (Illus.). 69p. (J). (ps). 1996. 11.95 (*1-929501-04-8*) Hanky Kids.

My Big Dictionary. LC 93-33756. 40p. (J). (gr. 4 up). 1994. pap. 22.00 (*0-395-66377-6*) HM.

My Big Dictionary. Ahd. (C). 1994. pap. 18.95 (*0-395-70912-1*) HM.

My Big Dictionary. Read. 1995. pap. 27.28 (*0-395-76202-2*) HM.

My Big Dog. Janet Stevens & Susan Stevens Crummel. LC 98-84183. (Family Storytime Ser.: No. 1). (Illus.). 32p. (J). (ps-2). 1999. pap. 9.95 (*0-307-10220-3*, 10220, Goldn Books) Gldn Bks Pub Co.

My Big Family at Church. Helen Caswell. LC 88-30630. (J). 1989. pap. 5.95 (*0-687-27533-4*) Abingdon.

My Big Father see Mi Gran Padre

My Big Father. Bruce Farnham. 206p. 1992. reprint ed. pap. text 5.99 (*0-9630908-2-8*) O M Lit.

*__My Big Girl Potty.__ Joanna Cole. LC 99-50287. (Illus.). 32p. (J). (ps up). 2000. 5.95 (*0-688-17041-2*, Wm Morrow) Morrow Avon.

*__My Big Girl Potty Book.__ Cole. 2000. lib. bdg. 5.89 (*0-06-029222-9*) HarpC.

My Big Lie. Bill Cosby. LC 98-42049. (Little Bill Books for Beginning Readers Ser.). (Illus.). 40p. (J). (gr. k-3). 1999. 15.95 (*0-590-52160-8*) Scholastic Inc.

*__My Big Lie.__ Bill Cosby. LC 98-42049. (Little Bill Books for Beginning Readers Ser.). (Illus.). 40p. (J). (gr. 1-5). 1999. pap. 3.99 (*0-590-52161-6*) Scholastic Inc.

My Big Machine Book. D K Publishing Staff. LC 99-191139. (J). 1999. 9.95 (*0-7894-4326-0*) DK Pub Inc.

My Big Phonics Word Book. (Illus.). 128p. (Orig.). (J). (ps-3). 1997. pap. 9.95 (*1-56293-466-X*, McClanahan Book) Learn Horizon.

My Big Pocket Book of God's Promises. 320p. (J). 1996. write for info. (*0-7814-0228-X*, Chariot Bks) Chariot Victor.

My Big Reading & Math Book: K-1 Advanced. McClanahan Book Company Staff. (High Q Ser.). (Illus.). 160p. (J). (gr. k-2). 1997. mass mkt. 9.99 (*0-7681-0017-8*, McClanahan Book) Learn Horizon.

My Big Reading & Math Book: K-1 Beginning. McClanahan Book Company Staff. (High Q Ser.). (Illus.). 160p. (J). (gr. k-2). 1997. mass mkt. 9.99 (*0-7681-0016-X*, McClanahan Book) Learn Horizon.

My Big Reading & Math Books: Preschool - Advanced. Mcclanahan Book Company Staff. 1997. pap. text 9.99 (*0-7681-0015-1*, McClanahan Book) Learn Horizon.

My Big Reading & Math Books: Preschool - Beginning. Mcclananhan Book Company Staff. (Illus.). 160p. 1997. pap. text 9.99 (*0-7681-0013-5*, McClanahan Book) Learn Horizon.

My Big Sister. Gina Mayer & Mercer Mayer. (Look-Look Bks.). (Illus.). (J). 1997. pap. text 1.79 (*0-307-11619-0*, 11619, Goldn Books) Gldn Bks Pub Co.

*__My Big Sister & Me.__ Golden Books Staff. 1999. pap. text 2.99 (*0-307-29050-6*) Gldn Bks Pub Co.

My Big Sister Takes Drugs. Judith Vigna. LC 89-70736. (J). (gr. k-3). 1995. pap. 5.95 (*0-8075-5316-6*) A Whitman.

My Big Sister Takes Drugs. Judith Vigna. (J). 1990. 11.15 (*0-606-07903-3*, Pub. by Turtleback) Demco.

My Big Sourcebook: For People Who Work with Words & Pictures. EEI Communications Staff. LC 96-19386. 400p. 1996. pap. 19.95 (*0-935012-19-2*) E E I Pr.

My Big Wheel. Patricia T. Cousin et al. (Visions: African-American Experiences: No. 17). (Illus.). 8p. (Orig.). (J). (gr. k-1). 1995. pap. text 3.00 (*1-57518-016-2*) Arborlake.

My Biggest Bedtime Book Ever. (J). 1988. 8.98 (*0-671-07571-3*) S&S Trade.

My Biggest O: Gay Men Describe "the Best Sex They Ever Had" Ed. by Jack Hart. 159p. 1993. pap. 9.95 (*1-55583-241-5*) Alyson Pubns.

My Biggest Playtime Book Ever/07933. (J). 1987. 8.98 (*0-671-07933-6*) S&S Trade.

My Bird Book. Norma Cole. (Littoral Bks.). 112p. 1991. pap. 9.95 (*1-55713-090-6*) Sun & Moon CA.

My Birthday. (St. Joseph's Coloring Bks.). (Illus.). 32p. (Orig.). (J). (ps-3). 1991. pap. 0.99 (*0-89942-693-X*, 693/00) Catholic Bk Pub.

My Birthday Book: Five Years of Birthday Memories. Catherine Hoesterey. (Illus.). 48p. 1998. 14.95 (*0-8212-2399-2*, Pub. by Bulfinch Pr) Little.

My Birthday! (Boy) Illus. by Michele Eargle. 15p. (J). (ps-4). 1998. pap. 12.00 (*1-890703-10-9*, Bkmates) Penny Laine.

My Birthday (Girl) Illus. by Michele Eargle. 15p. (J). (ps-4). 1998. pap. 12.00 (*1-890703-11-7*, Bkmates) Penny Laine.

My Birthday Memories. Laurel Green & Trudy Beck. (Illus.). (J). (ps-12). 1985. 5.00 (*0-9613079-1-9*) Greenbeck.

My Birthday Party. Patricia T. Cousin et al. (Visions: African-American Experiences: No. 18). (Illus.). 8p. (Orig.). (J). (gr. k-1). 1995. pap. text 3.00 (*1-57518-017-0*) Arborlake.

My Birthday Story Album. Harriet Ziefert. (Illus.). 10p. (J). (ps-2). 1993. 6.95 (*0-694-00445-6*) HarpC Child Bks.

My Birthday/Jesus Birthday. Holly Davis. LC 98-11305. (J). 1998. 12.99 (*0-310-21968-X*) Zondervan.

*__My Black Horse: New & Selected Poems.__ Tess Gallagher. 256p. 2000. pap. 19.95 (*1-85224-306-6*, Pub. by Bloodaxe Bks) Dufour.

My Black Me: A Beginning Book of Black Poetry. Ed. by Arnold Adoff. (Illus.). 96p. (J). (gr. 4-7). 1994. 14.99 (*0-525-45216-8*, Dutton Child) Peng Put Young Read.

My Black Me: A Beginning Book of Black Poetry. Arnold Adoff. 84p. (J). (gr. 3-7). 1995. pap. 4.99 (*0-14-037443-4*, PuffinBks) Peng Put Young Read.

My Black Me: A Beginning Book of Black Poetry. Arnold Adoff. (J). 1995. 10.09 (*0-606-08573-4*, Pub. by Turtleback) Demco.

My Blanket. Hui Chuan Chen. (Illus.). 48p. (J). (gr. k-3). 1997. pap. 9.00 (*0-8059-4123-1*) Dorrance.

My Bleeding Punjab. Khushwant Singh. (C). 1992. 17.50 (*81-85674-64-7*, Pub. by UBS Pubs Dist) S Asia.

My Blessings for Food. Illus. by Michael Horen. (J). 7.99 (*0-89906-702-6*, YBER) Mesorah Pubns.

My Blessings for Food: Birchas Hamozon. Meir Zlotowitz. (ArtScroll Youth Ser.). (Illus.). 32p. (J). (gr. 1-6). 1988. 7.95 (*0-89906-799-9*) Mesorah Pubns.

*__My Bloody Life: The Making of a Latin King.__ Reymundo Sanchez. LC 99-54261. 2000. 24.00 (*1-55652-401-3*, Pub. by Chicago Review) IPG Chicago.

*__My Bloody Valentine.__ Jo Gibson. 2000. mass mkt. 3.99 (*0-7860-1250-1*, Pinncle Kensgtn) Kensgtn Pub Corp.

My Blue Blanket. Joyce Landorf Heatherley. LC 91-27280. 253p. 1991. 16.95 (*0-8407-7599-7*) Balcony Pub Inc.

My Blue Boat. Chris L. Demarest. LC 94-10924. (Illus.). 32p. (J). 1998. pap. 6.00 (*0-15-201701-1*, Harcourt Child Bks) Harcourt.

*__My Blue Boat.__ Chris L. Demarest. 1998. 11.20 (*0-606-13629-0*, Pub. by Turtleback) Demco.

My Blue Book of God's Different Things. Mary Landis. (Illus.). 32p. (J). (ps-2). 1993. pap. 2.55 (*0-7399-0045-5*, 2539) Rod & Staff.

My Blue Book of God's Different Things. Mary Landis. (SPA., Illus.). 32p. (J). (ps-2). 1995. pap. 2.05 (*0-7399-0290-3*, 2539.1) Rod & Staff.

My Blue-Checker Corker & Me. Paul J. Radley. 1986. 15.45 (*0-89919-432-X*, Pub. by Ticknor & Fields) HM.

My Blue Goddess: Poems by R. D. Baker. R. D. Baker. (Poetry Chapbook Ser.). (Illus.). 28p. (Orig.). 1995. pap. 4.00 (*1-887641-10-6*) Argonne Hotel Pr.

My Blue Heaven. Jane Chambers. LC 81-83856. (Gay Play Script Ser.). (Illus.). 91p. 1986. pap. 7.95 (*0-935672-03-6*) T n T Class.

*__My Blue Zoo.__ Lynn Brunelle. (Gymboree Colorblock Ser.). (Illus.). 20p. (J). 1999. reprint ed. 4.95 (*1-892374-13-7*) Weldon Owen.

My Bluebird Family. Arnette Heidcamp. LC 97-186329. 1997. 18.00 (*0-517-70496-X*) Random.

My Boat see First Step Science

*__My Body.__ Brighter Vision Staff. (Learning Adventure Preschool Bks.). 32p. (J). 1998. pap. text 2.25 (*1-55254-005-7*) Brighter Vision.

My Body. Patricia Carratello. (Illus.). 38p. (J). (gr. 1-4). 1980. student ed. 7.95 (*1-55734-211-3*) Tchr Create Mat.

My Body. DK Publishing Staff. (What's Inside? Ser.). 24p. 1999. pap. text 3.95 (*0-7894-4293-0*) DK Pub Inc.

My Body. Adrianne Holden. (Fun to Learn Ser.). (Illus.). 32p. (J). 1999. 7.95 (*1-85967-833-5*, Pub. by Anness Pub) Random.

My Body. Grace Jasmine. (Thematic Unit Ser.). (Illus.). 80p. 1996. pap., teacher ed. 9.95 (*1-55734-584-8*) Tchr Create Mat.

My Body, 4 vols. Angela Wilkes. LC 98-16282. (Ladders Ser.). (Illus.). 32p. (J). (gr. k-3). 1999. write for info. (*0-7166-7709-1*) World Bk.

My Body: Easy Readers Science. Ann Flagg. (Easy Readers Ser.). 16p. (J). (ps-k). 1997. pap. 2.49 (*1-57690-278-1*) Tchr Create Mat.

My Body . . . Handle with Care: Your Personal Life History . . . of Medical & Health Care. unabridged ed. Edward P. Swertz. 144p. 1997. pap. 12.95 (*0-9661764-0-5*) Exten Inc.

My Body - God's Temple: Are You Using Your Body for Jesus? Joseph Christiano. LC 99-166171. 152p. 1997. write for info. (*0-9623058-2-0*) Trinity Pub & Mktg.

My Body Belongs to Me. Marilyn Kile & Kristin Baird. (BodyRights: a DUSO Approach to Preventing Sexual Abuse of Children Ser.). (J). (gr. k-2). 1986. text 18.95 (*0-88671-173-8*, 7202) Am Guidance.

*__My Body Fell Off! A Novel.__ B. J. Rowley. (Light Traveler Adventure Ser.: Vol. 1). 206p. (YA). 2000. pap. 11.95 (*0-9700103-1-1*) Goldn Wings.

My Body Is a Flute. Jim Cody. LC 92-28770. (Illus.). 80p. 1993. 35.00 (*0-916908-50-X*); pap. 9.95 (*0-916908-51-8*) Place Herons.

My Body Is a War Toy. Joie Cook. 24p. (Orig.). 1990. pap. 3.00 (*0-929730-26-7*) Zeitgeist Pr.

My Body Is Mine, My Feelings Are Mine: A Storybook about Body Safety for Young Children. Susan Hoke. (Illus.). 78p. (J). (ps-3). 1995. pap. 18.95 (*1-882732-24-3*) Childswork.

My Body Is My House: A Coloring Book about Alcohol, Drugs & Health. Jeanne Engelmann. (Illus.). 16p. (J). (gr. k-5). 1990. pap. 1.75 (*0-89486-735-0*, 5100B) Hazelden.

My Body Is My Planet: Surfing the Cosmic Wave. Maheshsvari. Ed. by Jeff Cline & C. Cline. LC 97-92812. (Illus.). 200p. 1998. pap. 19.95 (*1-892009-00-5*) Maheshsvari Pub.

An Asterisk (*) at the beginning of an entry indicates that the title is appearing for the first time.

My Body Is Private. Linda W. Girard. Ed. by Kathleen Tucker. LC 84-17220. (Illus.). 32p. (J). (ps-3). 1984. pap. 5.95 (*0-8075-5319-0*); lib. bdg. 13.95 (*0-8075-5320-4*) A Whitman.

My Body Is Something Special. Howard I. Bogot & Daniel B. Syme. (Illus.). (J). (ps). 1982. pap. 4.00 (*0-8074-0152-8*, 101715) UAHC.

My Body Is Where I Live. Dorothy Chapman. (Drug Free Ser.). (J). (gr. k-4). 1989. text 18.95 (*0-88671-297-1*, 5102) Am Guidance.

My Body Lies over the Ocean. J. S. Borthwick. LC 98-41754. 304p. 1998. text 22.95 (*0-312-19991-0*) St Martin.

***My Body Lies over the Ocean.** J. S. Borthwick. 304p. 1999. mass mkt. 5.99 (*0-312-97040-4*, St Martins Paperbacks) St Martin.

My Body Machine. Janeen Brady. (Illus.). (J). (ps-6). 1989. 10.95 (*0-944803-71-7*); student ed. 4.95 (*0-944803-65-2*) Brite Music.

My Body Machine. Janeen Brady. 29p. (J). (ps-6). 1990. 4.95 (*0-944803-73-3*) Brite Music.

My Body, My Choice. Cynthia L. Phiffer. Ed. by Stanley C. Coy. 40p. (Orig.). (YA). (gr. 7-12). 1994. pap. 2.00 (*1-881459-17-9*) Eagle Pr SC.

My Body, My Health: The Concerned Woman's Guide to Gynecology. Felicia H. Stewart et al. LC 78-31499. (Illus.). 590p. 1979. reprint ed. pap. 182.90 (*0-608-08432-8*, 201783200009) Bks Demand.

***My Body, My Self for Boys: A "What's Happening to My Body?" Quizbook.** Lynda Madaras & Area Madaras. (Illus.). 2000. reprint ed. pap. 12.95 (*1-55704-440-6*) Newmarket.

My Body, My Self for Boys: The "What's Happening to My Body?" Workbook for Boys. Lynda Madaras & Area Madaras. LC 95-40401. (Illus.). 112p. (YA). (gr. 6-12). 1995. pap., wbk. ed. 11.95 (*1-55704-230-6*, Pub. by Newmarket) Norton.

***My Body, My Self for Girls: A "What's Happening to My Body?" Quizbook.** Lynda Madaras & Area Madaras. (Illus.). 2000. reprint ed. pap. 12.95 (*1-55704-441-4*) Newmarket.

My Body, My Self for Girls: The "What's Happening to My Body?" Workbook for Girls. Area Madaras & Lynda Madaras. LC 93-19189. (Illus.). 128p. (YA). (gr. 6-12). 1993. pap., wbk. ed. 11.95 (*1-55704-150-4*, Pub. by Newmarket) Norton.

***My Body, the Buddhist.** Deborah Hay. LC 00-8647. 2000. write for info. (*0-8195-6328-5*, Wesleyan Univ Pr) U Pr of New Eng.

My Body to You. Elizabeth Searle. LC 92-34205. (Iowa Short Fiction Award Ser.). 196p. (C). 1993. 11.50 (*0-87745-387-X*) U of Iowa Pr.

My Body Was Eaten by Dogs: Selected Poems. David McFadden. Ed. & Intro. by George Bowering. 120p. 1981. 12.95 (*0-916696-19-7*); pap. 6.95 (*0-916696-18-9*) Cross Country.

My Body, Your Body. Mick Manning & Brita Granstrom Om. LC 97-10727. (Wonderwise Ser.). (J). 1997. pap. write for info. (*0-531-15324-X*) Watts.

My Body, Your Body. Mick Manning & Brita Granstrom Om. LC 97-10727. (Wonderwise Ser.). 32p. (J). (ps-2). 1997. lib. bdg. 20.00 (*0-531-14486-0*) Watts.

***My Bold Decision to Walk with Christ.** Richard K. Meredith. (Illus.). 32p. 1999. pap. write for info. (*0-9674471-0-0*, 555) Harv Evangel Min.

***My Bologna.** Loretta Paganini. LC 00-24272. (Illus.). 256p. 2000. text 23.95 (*0-312-26208-6*) St Martin.

***My Bondage & My Freedom.** Elizabeth Anderson. (Illus.). 244p. 1999. pap. 14.95 (*1-881524-57-4*, Pub. by Milligan Bks) Baker & Taylor.

My Bondage & My Freedom. Frederick Douglass. Ed. & Intro. by William L. Andrews. LC 87-5002. (Blacks in the New World Ser.). 344p. (C). 1988. text 34.95 (*0-252-01409-X*); pap. text 16.95 (*0-252-01410-3*) U of Ill Pr.

My Bondage & My Freedom. Frederick Douglass. LC 68-28994. (American Negro: His History & Literature. Series 1). (Illus.). 480p. 1968. reprint ed. 37.95 (*0-405-01813-4*) Ayer.

My Bondage & My Freedom. Frederick Douglass. (Black Rediscovery Ser.). 1969. reprint ed. pap. 8.95 (*0-486-22457-0*) Dover.

My Bondage & My Freedom. Frederick Douglass. (American Biography Ser.). 464p. 1991. reprint ed. lib. bdg. 89.00 (*0-7812-8111-3*) Rprt Serv.

My Bondage & My Freedom. Frederick Douglass. (Notable American Authors Ser.). 1992. reprint ed. lib. bdg. 75.00 (*0-7812-2675-9*) Rprt Serv.

My Book. 1989. spiral bd. 20.00 (*0-941016-65-X*) Penfield.

My Book. Regina Alston. Ed. by Mary J. Mason. (Illus.). 10p. (J). (ps-6). 1997. pap., spiral bd. 8.00 (*1-890864-02-1*) Breath of Life.

My Book: A Proactive "Life-Book" Technique for Children: Sensory-Based Treatment Approach for Victims of Child Abuse. Vijai P. Sharma & Jan Hindman. (Illus.). 46p. 1998. pap. 13.95 (*0-9628382-5-X*) Mind Pubns.

My Book: Growing up with Family & Friends. Y. Ganz. 1993. 14.99 (*0-89906-994-0*) Mesorah Pubns.

My Book: Memories & Other Stuff. Ed. by Dorothy Coe. (Illus.). 1994. pap. 10.00 (*0-9661569-0-0*) D Coe.

My Book about Abraham Lincoln. Lucille Wallower. Ed. by Patricia L. Gump. (J). (gr. 2-4). 1967. pap. 3.00 (*0-931992-10-9*) Penns Valley.

My Book about Bartimaeus. Good. (Say It Again Ser.). (Illus.). 24p. (J). 1978. pap. 2.35 (*0-7399-0001-3*, 2391) Rod & Staff.

My Book about Confession. Anthony Bullen. (Illus.). (C). 1996. pap. 39.95 (*0-85439-248-3*, Pub. by St Paul Pubns) St Mut.

My Book about Hudson. Sheila Miller. 1975. pap. 2.95 (*9971-972-20-4*) OMF Bks.

My Book about Life in Jesus' Time. Robert Baden. LC 97-27909. (Illus.). 96p. (J). (ps-3). 1998. 9.99 (*0-570-05036-7*, 56-1860) Concordia.

My Book about Me. Val Bagley. (J). pap. 4.95 (*1-57734-341-7*, 01113682) Covenant Comms.

My Book about Me. Sandy Jenkins. (Illus.). 24p. (J). 1997. 9.95 (*0-7894-1511-9*) DK Pub Inc.

My Book about Me: By Me, Myself. Dr. Seuss, pseud et al. LC 75-85289. (I Can Read It All by Myself: Beginner Books). (Illus.). 60p. (J). (ps-3). 1969. 12.00 (*0-394-80093-1*, Pub. by Random Bks Yng Read) Random.

My Book about Me: My Homeschool Yearbook. L. S. McClaine. (Illus.). 26p. (Orig.). (J). (gr. 1-6). 1995. pap. text 2.95 (*1-890537-02-0*) Nutmeg Pubns.

My Book about the Mass. Anthony Bullen. (Illus.). (C). 1996. pap. 39.95 (*0-85439-249-1*, Pub. by St Paul Pubns) St Mut.

My Book for Kids with Cancer. Jason Gaes. (J). 1999. pap. write for info. (*0-14-011869-1*, Viking) Viking Penguin.

My Book for Kids with Cansur: A Child's Autobiography of Hope. Jason Gaes. LC 90-63822. (Illus.). 34p. (J). (gr. 1-8). 1991. reprint ed. pap. 8.95 (*0-937603-09-0*) Melius Pub.

My Book House, 12 vols. rev. ed. United Educators Staff. LC 74-155096. (Illus.). (J). (ps-8). write for info. (*0-87566-012-6*); write for info. (*0-87566-006-1*) United Ed.

My Book Journal. Amy Tucker. 105p. 1997. pap. 8.95 (*0-9661222-3-2*, GWS1001) Graphic Web.

My Book of Baby Forest Animals. Ladybird Books Staff. (Early Readers Ser.: No. S8711-12). (Illus.). (J). (ps-2). 1989. 3.95 (*0-7214-5150-0*, Ladybird) Penguin Putnam.

My Book of Baby Pet Animals. Ladybird Books Staff. (Early Readers Ser.: No. S8711-9). (Illus.). (J). (ps-2). 1989. 3.95 (*0-7214-5151-9*, Ladybird) Penguin Putnam.

My Book of Baby Zoo Animals. Ladybird Books Staff. (Early Readers Ser.: No. S8711-11). (Illus.). (J). (ps-2). 1989. 3.95 (*0-7214-5149-7*, Ladybird) Penguin Putnam.

My Book of Bedtime Prayers. Paul Wilkes. LC 92-70386. (Illus.). 32p. (J). (ps). 1992. lib. bdg. 15.99 (*0-8066-2592-9*, 9-2592, Augsburg) Augsburg Fortress.

My Book of Bible Promises. Compiled by Clarence L. Blasier. 303p. 1998. lthr. 4.97 (*1-55748-154-7*) Barbour Pub.

My Book of Bible Stories see Meu Livro de Historias Biblicas

My Book of Birthdays. Julia Nelson. Date not set. write for info. (*0-9673230-1-0*) Allyn Group Pubns.

My Book of Favorite Fairy Tales. Random House Value Publishing Staff. LC 97-51198. 128p. (J). 1998. 6.99 (*0-517-20302-2*) Random Hse Value.

My Book of Friendship. Nicola Baxter. LC 97-62148. (Illus.). 32p. 1998. 7.98 (*0-7651-9147-4*) Smithmark.

My Book of Funny Valentines. Margo Lundell. LC 93-178587. (Read with Me Paperback Ser.). (Illus.). 32p. (J). (ps-3). 1993. pap. 2.50 (*0-590-44187-6*) Scholastic Inc.

My Book of Gray. Helen E. Simcox. Ed. by Jane Weinberger. LC 89-50682. (Illus.). 44p. (J). (ps-4). 1989. pap. 3.95 (*0-932433-61-8*) Windswept Hse.

My Book of Gymnastics. Amanda Durrant. LC 93-24978. (Illus.). 32p. (J). (gr. k-4). 1993. lib. bdg. 21.40 (*1-56847-125-4*) Raintree Steck-V.

My Book of Little House Christmas Paper Dolls: Christmas on the Prairie. Laura Ingalls Wilder. (Illus.). 24p. (J). (ps-3). 1996. 6.95 (*0-694-00751-X*, HarpFestival) HarpC Child Bks.

My Book of Little House Paper Dolls: A Day on the Prairie. Laura Ingalls Wilder. (Illus.). 24p. (J). (ps-3). 1997. 6.95 (*0-694-00900-8*, HarpFestival) HarpC Child Bks.

My Book of Little House Paper Dolls: The Big Woods Collection. Illus. by Renee Graef. 24p. (J). (ps-3). 1995. 7.95 (*0-694-00638-6*) HarpC Child Bks.

***My Book of Mormon ABC's.** Val Bagley. (J). 1999. 8.95 (*1-57734-517-7*, 01114174) Covenant Comms.

***My Book of Mormon Activity Book.** Laura Lee Rostrom. 32p. (J). (ps-5). 1999. pap. 2.99 (*1-55517-425-6*) CFI Dist.

***My Book of Mormon Storybook.** Laura Lee Rostrom. (Illus.). (J). (ps-6). 1999. 19.95 (*1-55517-352-7*) CFI Dist.

My Book of One Minute Stories & Verses. (J). 1987. 3.98 (*0-671-08500-X*) S&S Trade.

My Book of Opposites. Shereen G. Rutman. (J). 1997. pap. text, wbk. ed. 2.25 (*1-56293-951-3*, McClanahan Book) Learn Horizon.

***My Book of Poems.** 2nd rev. ed. Tommy L. Johnson. (Illus.). 80p. (J). 1999. pap. 8.00 (*1-892196-00-X*) D J Ent.

***My Book of Prayer.** Geof Farrar. 2000. write for info. (*1-58235-277-1*) Watermrk Pr.

My Book of Prayers. Maria L. Benigni. Tr. by Edmund C. Lane. (Illus.). 32p. (Orig.). 1995. pap. 3.50 (*0-8189-0678-2*) Alba.

My Book of Prayers. Illus. by Carla Cortesi. 48p. (Orig.). (J). (gr. 1-4). pap. 3.50 (*0-8198-4776-3*) Pauline Bks.

***My Book of Psalms.** Pino Madero. Tr. by Mary David Wickenhiser. (Illus.). 56p. (J). (gr. 2-5). 2000. pap. 3.95 (*0-8198-4807-7*) Pauline Bks.

My Book of Rainbows: A Delightful Book of Children's Poems. Constance Scoglietti & Siglinda Parker. LC 96-85478. (Illus.). 32p. (J). (ps-5). 1996. 11.95 (*0-9652902-0-4*) Beevinwood.

My Book of Shapes & Colors. Ladybird Books Staff. (Early Readers Ser.: No. S8711-7). (Illus.). (J). (ps-2). 1992. 3.95 (*0-7214-5148-9*, Ladybird) Penguin Putnam.

***My Book of States.** Donna R. Fisher. (Illus.). 54p. (J). (gr. 1). 1999. 5.00 (*1-57896-054-1*, 2820, Hewitt Homeschl Res) Hewitt Res Fnd.

My Book of Thanks: And Thoughts. Shirley A. Uhlhorn. (Illus.). (Orig.). 1995. pap. 20.00 (*0-9645576-0-6*) S Uhlhorn.

My Book of Things & Stuff: An Interest Questionnaire for Young Children. Ann McGreevy. 1982. pap. 14.95 (*0-936386-17-7*) Creative Learning.

My Book of Words, Songs & Sentences. Ursula O. Ronnholm & Paul F. Ronnholm. (Illus.). 91p. (J). (gr. k-3). 1986. pap. text 7.00 (*0-941911-03-9*) Two Way Bilingual.

My Box of Bible Stories, 4 vols. Smithmark Publishers, Inc. Staff. (Illus.). (J). (ps-3). 1997. boxed set 7.98 (*0-7651-9252-7*) Smithmark.

My Box of Color. Lorianne Siomades. LC 97-77912. (Illus.). 32p. (J). (ps-1). 1998. 8.95 (*1-56397-711-7*) Boyds Mills Pr.

My Boy Elvis: The Colonel Tom Parker Story. Sean O'Neal. LC 98-3056. 1998. write for info. (*1-56980-127-4*) Barricade Bks.

My Boy Jack. David Haig. 1999. pap. 5.95 (*0-8222-1694-9*) Dramatists Play.

My Boy Jack. David Haig. LC 99-216609. (Nick Hern Books, Drama Classics). 80p. 1998. pap. 13.95 (*1-85459-314-5*, Pub. by N Hern Bks) Consort Bk Sales.

My Boy Jack: The Search for John Kipling. Toni Holt & Valmai Holt. LC 99-490991. 1998. 39.95 (*0-85052-407-5*, Pub. by Leo Cooper) Combined Pub.

My Boyfriend's Back: The Story of the Girl Groups. Friedman-Fairfax & Sony Music Staff. (CD Ser.). 1995. pap. 16.98 incl. audio compact disk (*1-56799-181-5*, Friedman-Fairfax) M Friedman Pub Grp Inc.

My Boyhood. John Burroughs. (Works of John Burroughs). 1989. reprint ed. lib. bdg. 79.00 (*0-7812-2201-X*) Rprt Serv.

***My Boys Can Swim: The Official Guy's Guide to Pregnancy.** Ian Davis. LC 99-32679. 1999. pap. 9.99 (*0-7615-2167-4*) Prima Pub.

My Brain & Senses. Paul Bennett. LC 97-6028. (Bodyworks Ser.). (J). 1997. lib. bdg. 16.95 (*0-382-39783-5*) Silver Burdett Pr.

My Brain & Senses. Paul Bennett. LC 97-6028. (Bodyworks Ser.). (J). (gr. 2-5). 1997. pap. 5.95 (*0-382-39784-3*) Silver Burdett Pr.

My Brain Escapes Me. Robert S. Rhine. LC 99-19398. 352p. 1999. pap. 16.95 (*0-941543-18-8*) Sun Dog Pr.

My Brain Escapes Me: Signed Paper. Robert S. Rhine. LC 99-19398. 352p. 1999. pap. 21.95 (*0-941543-19-6*) Sun Dog Pr.

My Brain Is Open: The Mathematical Journeys of Paul Erdos. Bruce Schechter. LC 98-22293. 224p. (YA). 1998. 25.00 (*0-684-84635-7*) S&S Trade.

***My Brain Is Open: The Mathematical Journeys of Paul Erdos.** Bruce Schechter. 224p. 2000. pap. 13.00 (*0-684-85980-7*) S&S Trade.

My Breakfast: A Book about a Great Morning Meal see PowerKids Readers Set 1: My World

My Breakin' Heart. 1995. 12.95 (*0-89524-880-8*, 02502147) Cherry Lane.

My Breast. Joyce Wadler. Ed. by Julie Rubenstein. 192p. 1994. reprint ed. mass mkt. 5.50 (*0-671-87970-7*) PB.

My Breast: One Woman's Cancer Story. Joyce Wadler. 176p. 1997. pap. 10.00 (*0-671-01775-6*) PB.

My Breath in Art: Acting from Within. Beatrice Manley. LC 97-19329. 320p. 1998. pap. text 16.95 (*1-55783-281-1*) Applause Theatre Bk Pubs.

***My Bridal Shower Record Keeper & Photo Album.** Evelyn L. Beilenson. (Illus.). 48p. 2000. 11.99 (*0-88088-648-X*) Peter Pauper.

My Bridges of Hope. (J). 2001. pap. 4.99 (*0-689-82577-3*) Aladdin.

***My Bridges of Hope: Searching for Life & Love after Auschwitz.** Livia Bitton-Jackson. LC 98-8046. 272p. (YA). (gr. 7 up). 1999. per. 17.00 (*0-689-82026-7*) S&S Childrens.

My Bro Stealing 2nd. Jim Naughton. LC 88-22035. (Trophy Keypoint Bk.). 288p. (YA). (gr. 7 up). 1991. mass mkt. 3.95 (*0-06-447017-2*, HarpTrophy) HarpC Child Bks.

My Brother. Jamaica Kincaid. LC 97-16190. 197p. 1997. 19.00 (*0-374-21681-9*) FS&G.

My Brother. Jamaica Kincaid. 208p. 1998. pap. 10.00 (*0-374-52562-5*) FS&G.

My Brother & I. Lara Day. (Foundations Ser.). 15p. (J). (ps). 1992. pap. text 4.50 (*1-56843-054-X*) EMG Networks.

My Brother & I: Big Book. Lara Day. (Foundations Ser.). 15p. (J). (ps). 1992. pap. text 23.00 (*1-56843-004-3*) EMG Networks.

My Brother & I Like Cookies. 2nd ed. Anna L. Carlson & Diana Wynne. LC 80-81624. (Illus.). 96p. (Orig.). (J). (gr. 1-7). 1980. pap. 4.95 (*0-939938-00-6*) Karwyn Ent.

My Brother, Ant. Betsy C. Byars. LC 95-23725. (Easy-to-Read Classics Ser.). (Illus.). 31p. (J). (gr. k-3). 1996. 13.99 (*0-670-86664-4*, Viking Child) Peng Put Young Read.

My Brother Ant. Betsy C. Byars. (Puffin Easy-to-Read Ser.). (J). 1998. 9.19 (*0-606-12996-0*, Pub. by Turtleback) Demco.

My Brother Ant. Betsy C. Byars. 32p. (J). (ps-3). 1998. pap. 3.99 (*0-14-038345-X*) Viking Penguin.

***My Brother Ant.** unabridged ed. Betsy C. Byars. (J). (gr. k-3). 1999. 24.95 incl. audio (*0-87499-517-5*) Live Oak Media.

My Brother Bill. John Faulkner. LC 98-73550. (Illus.). 215p. 1998. reprint ed. pap. 16.50 (*1-892514-00-1*) Hill St Pr.

My Brother Blubb. Mel Gilden. 144p. (J). (gr. 3-6). 1994. pap. 3.50 (*0-671-79898-7*, Minstrel Bks) PB.

My Brother Daniel: And Other Stories of Brothers & Sisters. Highlights Staff. LC 94-78466. 96p. (J). (gr. 2-5). 1996. pap. 3.95 (*1-56397-456-8*) Boyds Mills Pr.

My Brother Death. Cyrus Sulzberger. Ed. by Robert J. Kastenbaum. LC 76-19589. (Death & Dying Ser.). 1977. reprint ed. lib. bdg. 24.95 (*0-405-09584-8*) Ayer.

My Brother, Ernest Hemingway. 4th ed. Leicester Hemingway. LC 95-39104. (Illus.). 320p. 1996. 21.95 (*1-56164-098-0*) Pineapple Pr.

My Brother George Seferis. Ioanna Tsatsos. Tr. by Jean Demos from GRE. (Modern Greek History & Culture Ser.). 1982. 20.00 (*0-935476-10-5*) Nostos Bks.

My Brother Gloucester. Michael Schmidt. LC 75-43116. 1976. 13.95 (*0-8023-1255-1*) Dufour.

My Brother, Grant Wood. Nan W. Graham et al. LC 93-28241. 1993. 16.95 (*0-89033-012-3*) State Hist Iowa.

My Brother, Hail & Farewell. Edward Zebrowski. LC 94-60021. 200p. 1994. pap. 15.95 (*0-9640096-0-9*) Woodstock Books.

My Brother Has AIDS. Deborah Davis. 192p. (J). (gr. 4-8). 1994. 15.00 (*0-689-31922-3*) Atheneum Yung Read.

My Brother Is a Superhero. Dyan Sheldon. LC 95-33665. (Illus.). 123p. (J). (gr. 3-6). 1996. 15.99 (*1-56402-624-8*) Candlewick Pr.

My Brother Is a Superhero. Dyan Sheldon. LC 97-20615. 128p. (J). (gr. 3-6). 1998. pap. 4.99 (*0-7636-0383-X*) Candlewick Pr.

My Brother Is a Visitor from Another Planet. Dyan Sheldon. LC 92-53420. (Illus.). (J). (gr. 3-6). 1995. pap. 3.99 (*1-56402-517-9*) Candlewick Pr.

My Brother is a Visitor from Another Planet. Dyan Sheldon. (J). 1995. 9.09 (*0-606-07904-1*) Turtleback.

***My Brother Is an Ape.** Andrew Griffin. (Illus.). 32p. (J). 2001. 15.99 (*0-7868-0684-2*, Pub. by Disney Pr) Time Warner.

My Brother Is from Outer Space: The Book of Proof. Vivian Ostrow. LC 95-38321. (Illus.). 32p. (J). (gr. k-4). 1996. lib. bdg. 14.95 (*0-8075-5325-5*) A Whitman.

My Brother Is from Outer Space: (The Book of Proof) Vivian Ostrow. (Illus.). 32p. (J). (gr. k-4). 1999. pap. 6.95 (*0-8075-5326-3*) A Whitman.

My Brother Joseph: The Spirit of a Cardinal & the Story of a Friendship. Eugene Kennedy. LC 97-13306. (Illus.). 176p. 1997. text 17.95 (*0-312-17118-8*) St Martin.

My Brother Joseph: The Spirit of a Cardinal & the Story of a Friendship. Eugene Kennedy. 192p. 1998. pap. 11.95 (*0-312-19515-X*) St Martin.

My Brother Louis Measures Worms: And Other Louis Stories. Barbara Robinson. LC 87-45302. (Charlotte Zolotow Bk.). 160p. (J). (gr. 3-7). 1988. lib. bdg. 15.89 (*0-06-025083-6*) HarpC Child Bks.

My Brother Louis Measures Worms: And Other Louis Stories. Barbara Robinson. LC 87-45302. (Charlotte Zolotow Bk.). 160p. (J). (gr. 3-7). 1991. pap. 4.95 (*0-06-440362-9*, HarpTrophy) HarpC Child Bks.

***My Brother Made Me Do It.** Peg Kehert. LC 99-89173. 144p. (J). 2000. 16.00 (*0-671-03418-9*, Minstrel Bks) PB.

My Brother, Matthew. Mary Thompson. LC 92-9858. (Illus.). 28p. (J). (gr. k-5). 1992. 14.95 (*0-933149-47-6*) Woodbine House.

My Brother Michael. Janis Owens. LC 96-51172. 304p. 1997. 18.95 (*1-56164-124-3*) Pineapple Pr.

My Brother, My Enemy. Madge Harrah. LC 96-19963. 144p. (YA). (gr. 5-9). 1997. per. 16.00 (*0-689-80968-9*) S&S Bks Yung.

My Brother, My Sister, & I. Yoko Kawashima Watkins. LC 93-23535. 240p. (YA). (gr. 6-12). 1996. per. 4.50 (*0-689-80656-6*) Aladdin.

My Brother, My Sister, & I. Yoko Kawashima Watkins. LC 93-23535. 224p. (YA). (gr. 5 up). 1994. mass mkt. 17.00 (*0-02-792526-9*, Bradbury S&S) S&S Childrens.

My Brother, My Sister, & I. Yoko Kawashima Watkins. LC 93-23535. (YA). (gr. 5 up). 1996. 9.60 (*0-606-09646-9*, Pub. by Turtleback) Demco.

***My Brother, My Sister & Me: A First Look at Sibling Rivalry.** Pat Thomas. (First Look at Bks.). (Illus.). 32p. (J). (gr. k-2). 2000. pap. 5.95 (*0-7641-1460-3*) Barron.

My Brother Needs an Operation. Anna M. Jaworski. LC 98-92847. (Illus.). 57p. (J). (ps-5). 1998. 20.00 (*0-9652508-2-2*) Baby Hearts.

My Brother Peter: Murder or Suicide? Nomi Berger. 288p. 1998. pap. text 16.99 (*1-55207-010-7*, Pub. by R Davies Pub) Genl Dist Srvs.

***My Brother Sam Is Dead.** 1999. 11.95 (*1-56137-823-2*) Novel Units.

***My Brother Sam Is Dead.** (YA). 1999. 9.95 (*1-56137-380-X*) Novel Units.

My Brother Sam Is Dead. (Assessment Packs Ser.). 15p. 1998. pap. text 15.95 (*1-58303-052-2*) Pthways Pubng.

My Brother Sam Is Dead. James L. Collier & Christopher Collier. LC 84-28787. 224p. (YA). (gr. 7 up). 1984. lib. bdg. 17.00 (*0-02-722980-7*, Four Winds Pr) S&S Childrens.

My Brother Sam Is Dead. James L. Collier & Christopher Collier. LC 84-28787. (Illus.). 224p. (YA). (gr. 5-9). 1985. pap. 4.50 (*0-590-42792-X*) Scholastic Inc.

My Brother Sam Is Dead. James L. Collier & Christopher Collier. (Scholastic Literature Guide Ser.). 16p. (J). 1997. pap. text 3.95 (*0-590-37362-5*) Scholastic Inc.

My Brother Sam Is Dead. James L. Collier & Christopher Collier. (J). 1974. 9.60 (*0-606-00962-0*, Pub. by Turtleback) Demco.

My Brother Sam Is Dead: A Unit Plan. Janine Sherman. 160p. 1998. teacher ed., ring bd. 26.95 (*1-58337-212-1*) Teachers Pet Pubns.

My Brother Sam Is Dead: L-I-T Guide. (J). (gr. 6-9). 1993. 8.95 (*1-56644-952-9*) Educ Impress.

***My Brother Sam Is Dead: Literature Unit.** Corinne Coombs. (Illus.). 48p. 1999. pap., teacher ed. 7.95 (*1-57690-507-1*, TCM2507) Tchr Create Mat.

My Brother Sam Is Dead - Study Guide. Michael Murphy. Ed. by Joyce Friedland & Rikki Kessler. (Novel-Ties Ser.). (J). (gr. 6-8). 1993. pap. text 15.95 (*0-88122-119-8*) Lrn Links.

My Brother Sammy. Becky Edwards. LC 98-28179. 32p. (J). (gr. k-3). 1999. 14.95 (*0-7613-0439-8*, Copper Beech Bks); lib. bdg. 21.90 (*0-7613-1417-2*, Copper Beech Bks) Millbrook Pr.

My Brother Says There's a Monster Living in Our Toilet. Rosalind Welcher. (Illus.). 96p. (Orig.). (J). 1987. pap. 6.95 (*0-939775-01-8*) West Hill Pr.

My Brother Sebastian. Annika Idstrom. Tr. by Joan Tate from FIN. 130p. (Orig.). 1991. pap. 21.00 (*1-85610-002-2*, Pub. by Forest Bks) Dufour.

My Brother Stevie: A Study Guide. Joyce Friedland & Rikki Kessler. (Novel-Ties Ser.). (J). (gr. 3-5). 1982. pap. text, teacher ed., student ed. 15.95 (*0-88122-007-8*) Lrn Links.

My Brother, the Brat. Kirsten Hall. LC 94-32420. (My First Hello Reader Ser.). (Illus.). 32p. (J). (ps-1). 1995. 3.95 (*0-590-48504-0*, Cartwheel) Scholastic Inc.

My Brother, the Pest. Margery Bernstein. LC 98-35822. (Real Kids Readers Ser.). (Illus.). 32p. (J). (gr. k-2). 1999. pap. 3.99 (*0-7613-2080-6*, Copper Beech Bks); lib. bdg. 16.90 (*0-7613-2055-5*, Copper Beech Bks) Millbrook Pr.

My Brother, the Werewolf. Nancy Garden. LC 93-46795. (J). 1995. lib. bdg. 7.99 (*0-679-95414-7*, Bullseye Bks) Random Bks Yng Read.

My Brother, the Werewolf. Nancy Garden. LC 93-46795. (J). 1995. 9.60 (*0-606-09647-7*, Pub. by Turtleback) Demco.

My Brother Wants to Be Like Me. large type ed. Jan Mader. (Illus.). 16p. (J). (gr. k-2). 1998. text 4.95 (*1-879835-27-4*, Kaeden) Kaeden Corp.

My Brother's a Pain in the Back Seat. Dale Bulla. LC 95-92283. (Illus.). 28p. (J). (gr. 2-6). 1995. 14.95 (*1-884197-05-1*); pap. 6.95 (*1-884197-06-X*) N Horizon Educ.

My Brother's a World-Class Pain: A Sibling's Guide to ADHD - Hyperactivity. Michael Gordon. (Illus.). 35p. (J). (gr. 4 up). 1992. pap. 11.00 (*0-9627701-2-4*) GSI Pubns.

My Brother's Bar Mitzvah. Janet Gallant. LC 90-4879. (Illus.). 32p. (J). (ps-3). 1990. 8.95 (*0-929371-20-8*) Kar-Ben.

***My Brother's Battle: A Novel.** Meredith Allard. LC 00-103987. 359p. 2000. 25.00 (*0-7388-2120-9*); pap. 18.00 (*0-7388-2121-7*) Xlibris Corp.

My Brother's Face: Portraits of the Civil War. Charles Phillips & Alan Axelrod. LC 92-13958. (Illus.). 1993. 27.50 (*0-8118-0386-4*) Chronicle Bks.

***My Brother's Farm: Reflection on Life, Farming & the Pleasures of Food.** Doug Jones. LC 98-54599. 224p. 1999. 19.95 (*0-399-14502-8*, G P Putnam) Peng Put Young Read.

***My Brother's Farm: Reflections on Life, Farming & the Pleasures of Food.** Doug Jones. 2000. pap. text 12.95 (*0-399-52586-6*, Perigee Bks) Berkley Pub.

My Brother's Gun: A Novel of Disposable Lives, Immediate Fame, & a Big Black Automatic. Ray Loriga. Tr. by Kristina Cordero. LC 97-16233. 128p. 1997. text 18.95 (*0-312-16947-7*) St Martin.

***My Brothers Keeper.** C. Barry Denham. (Orig.). 2000. pap. 14.95 (*1-891929-61-5*) Four Seasons.

***My Brother's Keeper.** Cortez R. Law, III. viii, 194p. 1999. pap. 10.99 (*0-9673478-0-7*) Issues of Blood.

***My Brother's Keeper.** Charles Sheffield. 288p. 2000. per. 5.99 (*0-671-57873-1*) PB.

My Brother's Keeper. Marcia Davenport. LC 78-74646. 1979. reprint ed. 24.00 (*0-8376-0429-X*) Bentley Pubs.

My Brother's Keeper, Bk. 1. Michael J. Friedman. (Star Trek My Brother's Keeper Ser.: Vol. 85). 267p. 1998. per. 6.50 (*0-671-01914-7*, Star Trek) PB.

My Brothers Keeper, Vol. I. Naftoli Gottleib. (Pillar of Chesed Ser.). 170p. (C). 1989. 15.95 (*1-56062-012-9*); pap. 12.95 (*1-56062-013-7*) CIS Comm.

My Brothers Keeper, Vol. II. Naftoli Gottleib. (Pillar of Chesed Ser.). (Illus.). 156p. 1989. 15.95 (*1-56062-014-5*); 12.95 (*1-56062-015-3*) CIS Comm.

My Brothers' Keeper: A Civil War Story. Nancy Johnson. LC 97-27186. 152p. (J). (gr. 4-7). 1997. 14.95 (*0-89272-414-5*) Down East.

My Brother's Keeper: Fostering Projects in the Jewish National Home. Aaron Klieman. LC 90-44347. (American Zionism Ser.: Vol. 5). 389p. 1991. text 40.00 (*0-8240-7353-3*) Garland.

My Brother's Keeper: Reflections on Jews, Social Science & Public Policy. Eli Ginzberg. 308p. 1989. 39.95 (*0-88738-291-6*) Transaction Pubs.

***My Brother's Keeper: Virginia's Diary, Gettysburg, Pennsylvania, 1863.** Mary Pope Osborne. LC 00-20200. (My America Ser.). (Illus.). 112p. (J). (gr. 2-5). 2000. 8.95 (*0-439-15307-7*) Scholastic Inc.

My Brother's Killer. large type ed. Dominic Devine. 388p. 1983. 27.99 (*0-7089-1026-2*) Ulverscroft.

***My Brother's Letters Home.** Lawrence P. Hall. LC 98-91025. 1999. pap. 12.95 (*0-533-13023-9*) Vantage.

My Brother's Motorcycle. Claudette C. Mitchell et al. (Visions: African-American Experiences: Vol. 10). (Illus.). 8p. (J). (gr. k-1). 1996. pap. text 3.00 (*1-57518-052-9*) Arborlake.

My Brother's Poems. Peter T. Ferrero, 3rd. (Illus.). 100p. (Orig.). 1997. pap. 17.50 (*0-9657096-1-2*) P T Ferrero.

My Brother's Train. Heather Kellerhals-Stewart. LC 96-932116. (Illus.). 32p. (J). (ps-2). 1997. 15.95 (*0-88899-282-3*) Publishers Group.

My Brown Bear Barney. Dorothy Butler. LC 88-21199. (Illus.). 32p. (J). (ps up). 1989. 15.95 (*0-688-08567-9*, Grenwillow Bks) HarpC Child Bks.

***My Brown Bear Barney.** Dorothy Butler. 2000. pap. 4.95 (*0-688-17723-9*, Wm Morrow) Morrow Avon.

***My Brown Bear Barney at the Party.** Dorothy Butler. (J). 2000. lib. bdg. 15.89 (*0-688-17549-X*, Grenwillow Bks) HarpC Child Bks.

***My Brown Bear Barney at the Party.** Dorothy Butler. (J). 2001. 15.95 (*0-688-17548-1*, Grenwillow Bks) HarpC Child Bks.

My Bubbe - My Grandmother. Lili Steiner. (Illus.). 24p. (J). 1998. pap. 14.95 (*1-891397-02-8*) L Steiner Pubns.

My Bubbe's Arms: Reudor's the Doodle Family. Reudor Staff. (Rhyme Time Doodles Ser.). (Illus.). 24p. (J). (gr. 1-12). 1998. 7.95 (*1-886611-00-9*) Atara Publ.

My Bucket's Got a Hole in It: New Poems by Mike O'Connell. Mike O'Connell. LC 95-95237. (Illus.). 80p. (Orig.). 1995. pap. write for info. (*0-9640408-1-6*) Hugger Mugger.

My Buddhist Writings: Based on Pali Tipitaka & Adi Grantha. Harcharan S. Sobti. xiv, 230p. (C). 1994. 20.00 (*81-86339-01-9*, Pub. by Eastern Bk Linkers) Nataraj Bks.

My Buddy. Audrey Osofsky. LC 92-3028. (Illus.). 32p. (J). (gr. k-3). 1995. 14.95 (*0-8050-1747-X*, Bks Young Read) H Holt & Co.

My Buddy. Audrey Osofsky. (Illus.). (J). (gr. 3). 1995. pap. 5.95 (*0-8050-3546-X*) H Holt & Co.

My Buddy. Audrey Osofsky. (Illus.). (J). (gr. 3). 1995. 8.60 (*0-395-73228-X*) HM.

My Buddy. Themistocle Sordellini. 96p. (Orig.). 1995. pap. 7.00 (*0-9651262-0-X*) T Sordellini.

My Buddy. large type ed. Audrey Osofsky. (Illus.). 54p. (J). (gr. 3). 13.50 (*0-614-20607-3*, L-38215-00 APHB) Am Printing Hse.

My Buddy, My Friend. Claudette C. Mitchell et al. (Visions: African-American Experiences: Vol. 11). (Illus.). 8p. (Orig.). (J). (gr. k-1). 1996. pap. text 3.00 (*1-57518-053-7*) Arborlake.

My Buddy, the King. Bill Brittain. LC 88-35704. (Trophy Bk.). 144p. (J). (gr. 5-8). 1992. pap. 3.95 (*0-06-440339-4*, HarpTrophy) HarpC Child Bks.

My Budget Workbook. Stephen J. Pigott. (Illus.). 80p. 1999. pap. text, wbk. ed. 14.95 (*0-9672932-1-9*) S J Pubg Inc.

***My Buffalo Soldier.** Bk Reeves. 2000. pap. 8.95 (*1-58571-013-X*, Pub. by Genesis Press) BookWorld.

My Bug. Ed. by Michael J. Rosen. LC 99-32504. (Illus.). 160p. 1999. 19.95 (*1-57965-135-6*, 85135) Artisan.

My Bug Box see Mi Caja de Insectas

My Bug Box. Pat Blanchard & Joanne Suhr. (Books for Young Learners). (Illus.). 12p. (J). (gr. k-2). 1999. pap. text 5.00 (*1-57274-273-9*) R Owen Pubs.

***My Building.** Robin I. Ahrens. LC 97-62300. (Illus.). 32p. (J). (ps-1). 1998. 15.95 (*1-890817-06-6*, Pub. by Winslow Pr) Publishers Group.

My Bundjalung People. Ruby L. Ginibi. LC 94-233284. 1994. pap. 16.95 (*0-7022-2637-8*, Pub. by Univ Queensland Pr) Intl Spec Bk.

My Bunny. James Young. LC 98-6931. (Read with Me Paperback Ser.). (Illus.). 32p. (J). (ps-1). 1999. 3.25 (*0-590-18375-3*) Scholastic Inc.

My Bunny & Me. Lindsay B. George. LC 99-16408. (J). 2001. write for info. (*0-688-16074-3*, Grenwillow Bks); lib. bdg. 15.89 (*0-688-16075-1*, Grenwillow Bks) HarpC Child Bks.

My Bunny Book: A Press 'n Dress Paper Doll. Jennifer Selby. LC 96-70371. (Illus.). 12p. (J). (ps-k). 1997. 9.95 (*0-531-30018-8*) Orchard Bks Watts.

***My Bunny Slippers Didn't Match His Career.** Lois Dickey. 319p. 2000. pap. 9.95 (*0-9678882-5-5*) MBrio Bks.

My Burning Heart. Satprem Staff. Tr. by Luc Venet from FRE. Orig. Title: Sept Jours en Inde. 205p. 1989. pap. text 8.95 (*0-938710-15-X*) Inst Evolutionary.

My Business Was to Fight the Devil: Recollections of Rev. Adam Wallace, Peninsula Circuit Rider, 1847-1865. Adam Wallace & Joseph DiPaolo. LC 98-16576. 1998. 22.50 (*1-56888-266-1*) Tapestry MA.

My Busy, Busy Day. Kelly Kim. 12p. 2000. 5.99 (*0-310-23206-6*, Zonderkidz) Zondervan.

My Busy Day. Joan Walsh Anglund. (Illus.). 14p. (J). (ps-k). 1999. bds. 4.99 (*0-689-82023-2*) S&S Childrens.

My Busy Day. Shereen G. Rutman. (LTFT Toddler Time Ser.). (Illus.). 16p. (J). (ps). 1994. wbk. ed. 2.95 (*1-56293-464-3*, McClanahan Book) Learn Horizon.

My Busy Little Dreidel. Dorothy Fish & Betty Cohen. (Illus.). 20p. (J). (ps-3). 1997. 5.99 (*0-914080-08-3*) Shulsinger Sales.

***My Busy World.** Sarah Weeks. (Fisher-Price Step-by-Step Tab Bks.). (Illus.). 10p. (J). (ps). 2001. 5.99 (*1-57584-728-0*, Pub. by Rdrs Digest) S&S Trade.

My Busy Year. Joan Walsh Anglund. (Illus.). 14p. (J). (ps). 1999. bds. 4.99 (*0-689-82024-0*) S&S Childrens.

My Butterfly Net see Take Along Stories

My Buttons Are Blue & Other Love Poems from the Digital Heart of an Electronic Computer. Ed. by Ron Clark. (Illus.). 96p. 1983. 4.95 (*0-86668-013-6*) ARCsoft.

My "c" Sound Box. Jane Belk Moncure. LC 78-23638. (Sound Box Library). (Illus.). 32p. (J). (ps-2). 1979. lib. bdg. 21.36 (*0-89565-052-5*) Childs World.

My Calling: Poems by Jack Curtis. Jack Curtis. LC 98-84881. (Illus.). 152p. 1998. pap. 8.95 (*0-9640537-8-0*) Monterey Pubng.

My Calvary Road. Roy Hession & Stanley Voke. 1996. 10.99 (*1-85792-154-2*, Pub. by Christian Focus) Spring Arbor Dist.

My Cambridge. Ed. by Ronald Hayman. 214p. (Orig.). 1987. pap. 8.95 (*0-86051-382-3*, Pub. by Robson Bks) Parkwest Pubns.

My Camp Book: Campers! Write up Your Own Adventures & Experiences! Marlor Press Staff. (Illus.). 96p. (J). 1994. pap. 8.95 (*0-943400-77-5*) Marlor Pr.

My Camp Book Diary. Anna Pomaska. (J). (gr. k-3). 1991. pap. 1.00 (*0-486-26641-9*) Dover.

My Camp Memories. Linda Schwartz. LC 93-86210. (Illus.). 32p. (J). (gr. 3-6). 1994. pap. 4.95 (*0-88160-226-4*, LW321) Learning Wks.

My Camp Memory Book: A Camp Sunnyside Friends Special. Marilyn Kaye. 144p. (Orig.). 1990. pap. 5.95 (*0-380-76081-9*, Avon Bks) Morrow Avon.

My Camp-Out. Marcia Leonard. (Real Kids Readers Ser.). (Illus.). 32p. (J). (gr. k-1). 1999. lib. bdg. 16.90 (*0-7613-2052-0*, Copper Beech Bks) Millbrook Pr.

***My Camp-Out.** Marcia Leonard. LC 98-38106. (Real Kids Readers Ser.). (Illus.). 32p. (J). (gr. k-1). 1999. pap. 3.99 (*0-7613-2077-6*, Copper Beech Bks) Millbrook Pr.

My Canyonlands. Kent Frost & Rosalie Goldman. LC 97-66770. (Illus.). 160p. 1997. reprint ed. pap. 10.00 (*0-925685-33-X*) Canyon Country Pubns.

My Cap. Patty Carratello. (Easy Reader Ser.). (Illus.). 1996. teacher ed. 2.49 (*1-57690-016-9*, TCM2016) Tchr Create Mat.

My Captains. Tommy Ralston. 112p. 1990. pap. 21.00 (*1-898218-27-7*) St Mut.

My Captive. Joseph Altsheler. Date not set. lib. bdg. 25.95 (*0-8488-2124-6*) Amereon Ltd.

My Captivity. Connie Roop. 64p. 1999. pap. 4.99 (*0-14-037719-0*, Viking) Viking Penguin.

My Captivity among the Sioux Indians. Fanny Kelly. 1973. pap. 10.95 (*0-8065-0389-0*, Citadel Pr) Carol Pub Group.

My Car. (Illus.). 32p. 1996. pap. 4.95 (*0-913515-30-2*, Elliott Clark) Black Belt Communs.

My Car in Managua. Forrest D. Colburn. (Illus.). 148p. 1991. pap. 10.95 (*0-292-75124-9*); text 17.95 (*0-292-75123-0*) U of Tex Pr.

My Career Adventure. Olga B. Weston. 100p. (Orig.). (J). 1996. pap. 9.95 (*1-57502-181-1*, PO805) Morris Pubng.

My Career with the Leafs & Other Stories. Brian Fawcett. 192p. pap. 13.95 (*0-88922-199-5*, Pub. by Talonbks) Genl Dist Srvs.

My Carousel Horse. Mary L. Ray. LC 93-45876. (Illus.). (J). 1994. text 13.95 (*0-15-200023-2*) Harcourt.

My Cassette Player. Harriet Ziefert. (Illus.). 14p. (J). (ps). 1993. 4.50 (*0-694-00418-9*) HarpC Child Bks.

My Castle. (Illus.). (J). (ps-1). 1991. 26.00 (*1-56021-098-2*) W J Fantasy.

My Cat. David Alderton. (Pet Photo Album Ser.). (Illus.). 24p. (J). (gr. 2-6). 1997. 15.95 (*0-7613-0249-2*) Millbrook Pr.

My Cat. Jonathan Allan. (Illus.). (J). 1999. pap. write for info. (*0-14-055272-3*) NAL.

My Cat. Marilyn Baillie.Tr. of Mon Chat. (Illus.). 32p. (J). 1993. 12.95 (*1-55074-125-X*, Pub. by Kids Can Pr); pap. 5.95 (*1-55074-206-X*, Pub. by Kids Can Pr) Genl Dist Srvs.

My Cat. Penny Nye. (Illus.). (J). (ps-5). 1999. pap. 12.00 (*1-890703-16-8*, Bkmates) Penny Laine.

My Cat: Companion Animals. Sam B. Basilious. (My Companion Ser.). (Illus.). 100p. (Orig.). 1993. pap. write for info. incl. disk (*0-9630843-5-6*) Infoconnect.

My Cat, Herman Bernard Fred Tigger Dusty Geronimo Mike: Animal Stories from Highlights. Highlights for Children Editors. 96p. (J). (gr. 2-5). 1996. pap. 3.95 (*1-56397-585-8*) Boyds Mills Pr.

My Cat Is Going to the Dogs. Mike Thaler. LC 93-18596. (Funny Firsts Ser.). (Illus.). 32p. (J). (ps-3). 1993. lib. bdg. 15.85 (*0-8167-3022-9*) Troll Communs.

My Cat Jack. Patricia Casey. LC 93-39669. (Illus.). (J). (ps-3). 1996. pap. 5.99 (*1-56402-660-4*) Candlewick Pr.

My Cat Jack. Patricia Casey. (Read & Wonder Ser.). 1996. 11.19 (*0-606-08827-X*, Pub. by Turtleback) Demco.

***My Cat Saved My Life.** Phillip Schreibman. 128p. 2000. 18.95 (*1-58542-063-8*, Tarcher Putnam) Putnam Pub Group.

My Cat Saved My Life. unabridged ed. Phillip Schreibman. LC 99-226603. 128p. 1999. pap. write for info. (*0-9683273-0-3*) DogByte Develop.

***My Cat Spit McGee.** Willie Morris. (J). 2000. pap. 11.00 (*0-375-70693-3*, Pub. by Knopf Bks Yng Read) Random.

***My Cat Spit McGee.** Willie Morris. LC 99-31086. 144p. 1999. 18.95 (*0-375-50321-8*) Random.

***My Cat Spit McGee.** large type ed. Willie Morris. LC 99-54228. 1999. 23.95 (*1-57490-247-4*, Beeler LP Bks) T T Beeler.

***My Cat Tuna.** Lynn W. Reiser. LC 98-50518. (J). 2001. 9.95 (*0-688-16874-4*, Grenwillow Bks) HarpC Child Bks.

***My Catholic Faith: A Manual of Religion.** Louis L. Morrow. (Illus.). 415p. (YA). (gr. 6 up). 2000. 39.95 (*0-9639032-6-8*) Sarto Hse.

My Cat's Book: The Who, What, When & Where of My Cat's Life - An Essential Book for All Cat Owners. S. K. Bollin. 32p. 1992. pap. 4.95 (*0-914846-63-9*) Golden West Pub.

My Cats Nick & Nora. Isabelle Harper. LC 94-31981. (Illus.). 32p. (J). (ps-3). 1995. 14.95 (*0-590-47620-3*, Blue Sky Press) Scholastic Inc.

My Cat's Not Fat, He's Just Big-Boned. Nicole Hollander. LC 99-158000. (Illus.). 112p. 1998. pap. 9.95 (*1-887166-43-2*, Hysteria Pubns) Sourcebks.

My Cave Life in Vicksburg. Mary A. Loughborough. 212p. 1989. reprint ed. 25.00 (*0-916107-65-5*) Broadfoot.

My Cave Life in Vicksburg with Letters of Trial & Travel. Jas. M. Loughborough. LC 75-46574. 196p. 1988. reprint ed. 25.00 (*0-87152-217-9*) Reprint.

My Celestial. Luqiu Wang. 102p. 1997. pap. text 6.00 (*1-888065-12-5*) New Wrld Poetry.

***My Century.** Gunter Grass. Tr. by Michael Henry Heim from GER. LC 99-38690.Tr. of Mein Jahrhundert. 280p. (C). 1999. 25.00 (*0-15-100496-X*, Harvest Bks) Harcourt.

***My Century.** Gunter Grass.Tr. of Mein Jahrhundert. 288p. 2000. pap. 13.00 (*0-15-601141-7*) Harcourt.

My Century: An Outspoken Memoir. Evangeline Lindsley & Nancy Diggs. (Illus.). 192p. (Orig.). 1996. pap. 10.00 (*0-913428-79-5*) Landfall Pr.

My Changing Body. Kino Learning Center Staff et al. (Changing Years Ser.). (Illus.). 64p. (J). (gr. 5-9). 1987. pap. 8.99 (*0-86653-420-2*, GA1030) Good Apple.

My Chanukah Activity Book. David Sokoloff. (Illus.). 24p. (Orig.). (J). (ps-5). 1998. pap. 1.00 (*1-889655-06-6*) Jewish Educ Toys.

My Chanukah Coloring & Activity Book. (Illus.). 144p. (Orig.). (J). (gr. k-2). 1994. pap. 5.95 (*1-56144-517-7*, Honey Bear Bks) Modern Pub NYC.

My Chapbook: Toiling in the Groves. H. K. Henisch. (Illus.). 83p. 1998. pap. 8.50 (*0-87601-009-5*) Carnation.

My Character Growth Journal: Intermediate & Middle Grades. Jo Neal. Ed. by Sally E. Warren. (Word of the Week Ser.). 152p. 1997. pap. 10.00 (*1-57074-350-9*) Greyden Pr.

My Character Growth Journal: Primary Grades. Jo Neal. Ed. by Sally E. Warren. (Word of the Week Ser.). 80p. (J). (gr. 1-3). 1997. pap. 8.00 (*1-57074-324-X*) Greyden Pr.

My Cheetah Family. Matto Barfuss. LC 98-33998. 48p. (J). (gr. 4-6). 1999. 23.93 (*1-57505-377-2*, Carolrhoda) Lerner Pub.

My Cherished Enemy. Samantha James. 400p. (Orig.). 1992. mass mkt. 4.50 (*0-380-76692-2*, Avon Bks) Morrow Avon.

My Chess Career. Jose R. Capablanca. (Illus.). 194p. 1966. pap. 7.95 (*0-486-21548-2*) Dover.

My Chicken Soup for the Soul Personal Journal. Jack Canfield & Mark Victor Hansen. 192p. 1997. 12.95 (*1-55874-484-3*) Health Comm.

***My Chickens.** Heather Miller. (Welcome Bks.). (Illus.). (J). 2000. 13.50 (*0-516-23105-7*) Childrens.

***My Chickens.** Heather Miller. LC 00-24385. (My Farm Ser.). (Illus.). 24p. (J). (ps-2). 2000. pap. write for info. (*0-516-23030-1*) Childrens.

My Chief & I. Frances E. Colenso. Ed. by Margaret Daymond. 250p. 1994. pap. 22.00 (*0-86980-886-9*, Pub. by Univ Natal Pr) Intl Spec Bk.

My Child Is a Mother. Mary Stephenson. LC 91-70759. 253p. 1991. 17.95 (*0-931722-87-X*) Corona Pub.

My Child Is a Mother. Mary Stephenson. LC 91-70759. 253p. 1994. pap. 8.95 (*0-931722-88-8*) Corona Pub.

My Child Is Gay: How Parents React When They Hear the News. Bryce McDougall. 189p. 1998. pap. 12.95 (*1-86448-658-9*) IPG Chicago.

My Child, Let Me Take the Wheel! Dealing with Depression. Lila W. Burrows et al. (Illus.). 172p. 1991. 6.95 (*0-936369-29-9*) Son-Rise Pubns.

My Child Loses Control? Polly Greenberg. (What Do I Do When... Ser.). (Illus.). 48p. 1997. pap. text 3.95 (*0-590-36680-7*) Scholastic Inc.

My Child, My Disciple: A Practical, Torah-Based Guide to Effective Discipline in the Home. Noach Orlowek. LC 93-46947. 1994. 17.95 (*0-87306-645-6*) Feldheim.

My Child, My Friend. Dorothy Nielsen & Claudia Evans. 1991. pap. 4.95 (*1-55503-273-7*, 0111813) Covenant Comms.

My Child Our Child (New York Time's Best Selling Author) Patricia Hagan. (Special Edition Ser.: No. 1277). 1999. per. 4.25 (*0-373-24277-8*, 1-24277-5) Silhouette.

My Childhood. Maxim Gorky. 1976. 21.95 (*0-8488-0508-9*) Amereon Ltd.

My Childhood. Maxim Gorky. Tr. by Ronald Wilks. 240p. 1991. pap. 12.95 (*0-14-018285-3*, Penguin Classics) Viking Penguin.

My Childhood: As I Remember It. Joan C. Baez, Sr. (Illus.). 124p. (Orig.). 1996. pap. 12.00 (*0-945131-04-6*) Terrace Pr.

My Childhood at the Gate of Unrest: A Romanian Memoir. Paul Goma. Tr. by Angela Clark from ROM. 250p. (Orig.). 1990. 17.95 (*0-930523-73-3*); pap. 10.95 (*0-930523-74-1*) Readers Intl.

My Children: A Photo Essay of Swami Chinmayananda with Children from Around the World. Text by Swami Chinmayananda. LC 94-94101. (Illus.). 130p. (Orig.). 1994. pap. 15.00 (*1-880687-16-X*) Chinmaya Pubns.

My Children Are Words. Ivan Radoev. Tr. by Don D. Wilson from BUL. 56p. 1994. pap. 7.50 (*1-880286-32-7*) Singular Speech Pr.

***My Children Don't Eat Dogfood: Natural Pet Recipes.** Sandra K. Hughes. Ed. by Laura Karth. (Illus.). v, 55p. 1999. pap. 15.95 (*0-9674110-0-9*) Kaye-Hughes.

My Children, Listen. Catherine H. Toye. LC 98-70377. xviii, 360p. 1998. 24.00 (*0-9663088-0-8*) Caritas Communs.

My Children! My Africa! Athol Fugard. LC 90-11252. 96p. 1990. 16.95 (*1-55936-013-5*); pap. 10.95 (*1-55936-014-3*) Theatre Comm.

My Children, My Gold. Debbie Taylor. (Illus.). 208p. 1994. pap. 6.99 (*1-85381-706-6*, Pub. by Oxfam Pub) Stylus Pub VA.

My Children, My Gold: A Journey to the World of Seven Single Mothers. Debbie Taylor. LC 94-36741. 1995. 45.00 (*0-520-20144-2*, Pub. by U CA Pr); pap. 16.95 (*0-520-20145-0*, Pub. by U CA Pr) Cal Prin Full Svc.

My Children's Struggles. Roosevelt Baums. Ed. by Edwin A. Ellis & Joanne Michels. LC 82-60222. (Illus.). 126p. 1983. pap. 2.25 (*0-934138-02-8*) Rosey-Royce.

My Child's Care. Laura Nieboer. 50p. 1992. 25.00 (*1-881782-00-X*) State Art.

***My Child's Medical Journal.** rev. ed. Deitra D. Pickett. Orig. Title: Innocence...a Child's Medical Portfolio. 2000. spiral bd. write for info. (*0-9655577-1-5*) Princess Pubns.

My Child's PHJ: Personal Health Journal. Latrice Collins. 112p. 1996. spiral bd. 14.95 (*0-9660451-0-6*) Empower Press.

My China: Jewish Life in the Orient, 1900-1950. Yaacov Liberman. LC 97-36231. (Illus.). 248p. 1997. 24.95 (*965-229-171-4*, Pub. by Gefen Pub Hse) Gefen Bks.

An Asterisk (*) at the beginning of an entry indicates that the title is appearing for the first time.

My China: The Metamorphosis of a Country & a Man. Sidney Shapiro. 351p. 1997. 19.95 (*7-80005-338-5*, Pub. by New World Pr) China Bks.

My China Odyssey. Emilie Johnson. LC 81-50672. (Illus.). 192p. (Orig.). 1981. pap. 5.95 (*0-9605910-0-1*) Silver Fox.

My Choices & Decisions. Kino Learning Center Staff & Corinne Sanders. (Changing Years Ser.). (Illus.). 64p. (J). (gr. 5-9). 1987. pap. 8.99 (*0-86653-421-0*, GA1031) Good Apple.

My Chosen Trails: A Wyoming Woman's Recollections Through the Twentieth Century. Vema Burger Davis. LC 98-96028. (Illus.). 200p. 1998. pap. 12.95 (*0-9663347-0-1*) Deep Creek.

*__My Christian Dictionary.__ Charlene Stout. Ed. by Kathy Rogers. 32p. 1998. 1.99 (*1-56472-142-6*) Edupress Inc.

My Christian Passport. 16p. (J). 1989. pap. 2.95 (*0-8146-1576-7*) Liturgical Pr.

*__My Christian Values Bible.__ 1999. pap. text 9.99 (*0-529-11119-5*) World Publng.

My Christina & Other Stories. Merce Rodoreda. Tr. by David H. Rosenthal from CAT. LC 84-81626. (Short Fiction Ser.). 133p. 1984. pap. 11.00 (*0-915308-65-7*) Graywolf.

My Christmas: A Photolog Book. Kathy Faggella. (Illus.). 48p. (J). (ps-3). 1993. 4.50 (*1-55670-330-9*) Stewart Tabori & Chang.

My Christmas ABC Book. Mary Erickson. (Illus.). 32p. (J). (ps-2). 1995. 5.99 (*0-7814-0239-5*, Chariot Bks) Chariot Victor.

My Christmas Activity Book. Carolyn Owens. 32p. 1995. pap. text 3.99 (*0-570-04785-4*, 56-1805) Concordia.

My Christmas Angel: A Hide & Seek Story. Sarah R. Chisholm. (Illus.). 32p. (J). (ps). 1993. pap. 6.99 (*0-8066-2601-1*, 9-2601) Augsburg Fortress.

My Christmas Book. (Illus.). 8p. (J). (ps). 1997. 35.00 (*1-888074-52-3*) Pckts Lrning.

My Christmas Counting Book. Illus. by Stephanie Longfoot. 20p. (J). (ps). 1996. bds. 5.98 (*0-86112-758-7*) Brimax Bks.

My Christmas Diary: A Journal for the Holiday Season Through the Years. Marjorie Merena. 240p. 1998. 16.00 (*0-380-97753-2*, Avon Bks) Morrow Avon.

My Christmas List. (Illus.). (J). (ps-1). 1996. 34.99 (*1-888074-40-X*) Pckts Lrning.

My Christmas Memories. Penny Nye. (Illus.). 15p. (J). 1998. pap. 12.00 (*1-890703-13-3*, Bkmates) Penny Laine.

My Christmas Poem. Mark Wallace. (Poetry New York Pamphlet Ser.: Vol. 1). 18p. 1998. pap. 5.00 (*0-923389-14-8*) Meet Eyes Bind.

My Christmas Prayer Book. Arch Books Staff. LC 98-228009. (Illus.). 16p. (J). (gr. k-5). 1998. pap. 1.99 (*0-570-07546-7*) Concordia.

My Christmas Present. (Christmas Board Bks.: No. S8823-2). (Illus.). (J). (ps). 1990. text 3.95 (*0-7214-9128-6*, Ladybrd) Penguin Putnam.

My Christmas Star: A Hide & Seek Story. Sarah R. Chisholm. (Illus.). 32p. (J). (ps). 1993. pap. 6.99 (*0-8066-2600-3*, 9-2600) Augsburg Fortress.

My Christmas Story Album. Harriet Ziefert. (Illus.). 10p. (J). (ps up). 1992. 6.95 (*0-694-00430-8*) HarpC Child Bks.

My Christmas Treasury. Norman Vincent Peale. 160p. Date not set. 15.00 (*0-88365-928-X*) Galahad Bks.

My Church. J. B. Moody. 325p. 1974. reprint ed. 9.50 (*0-87921-030-3*) Attic Pr.

My Church. rev. ed. Gordon G. Johnson. LC 73-87817. (Foundation Ser.). 186p. 1987. reprint ed. pap. 3.99 (*0-935797-25-4*) Harvest IL.

My Church: Developing Congregational Ownership. Sanford G. Kulkin. 125p. 1992. ring bd. 195.00 incl. audio (*1-58034-008-3*) IML Pubns.

My Church, My Family: How to Have a Healthy Relationship with the Church. James B. Richards. 153p. (Orig.). 1995. pap. 9.00 (*0-924748-09-5*) Impact Ministries.

My Circus Family. Mary D. Lake. LC 95-17745. (Illus.). 8p. (J). (ps-1). 1995. pap. 2.95 (*1-57255-034-1*) Mondo Pubng.

My Class. Josie Stewart & Lynn Salem. (Illus.). 8p. (J). (gr. k-1). 1995. pap. 3.75 (*1-880612-35-6*) Seedling Pubns.

My Cleveland Story. Greg Cielec. LC 98-96292. 288p. 1998. 22.00 (*0-9665724-0-8*) Pink Flamngo Pr.

My Clothes. abr. ed. Sian Tucker. (Sian Tucker Board Bks.). (Illus.). 16p. (J). (ps). 1998. 4.99 (*0-689-81982-X*) Litle Simon.

*__My Clubhouse.__ Cathy Beylon. (Little Activity Bks.). (Illus.). (J). 1999. pap. 1.00 (*0-486-40746-2*) Dover.

*__My Collectibles Organizer.__ Hobby House Press Staff. 2000. 19.95 (*0-87588-578-0*) Hobby Hse.

*__My Collectibles Organizer Fact Sheets Album.__ Hobby House Press Staff. 128p. 2000. pap. 11.95 (*0-87588-575-6*) Hobby Hse.

My Collection of Poems: Expressions. Veronica L. Cook. 70p. (Orig.). 1989. pap. text 10.00 (*0-685-29993-7*) Ronnie Two Pub.

My Collection of Recipes & Memories in Culinary Arts. Wendell R. Dorne. LC 97-90567. (Illus.). 239p. 1997. pap. 15.00 (*0-9658806-0-5*) W R Dorne.

My Collective Mind. Jeff Massengale. 1997. pap. 56.95 (*1-57553-679-X*) Watermrk Pr.

My College Ring Between My Toes. Philip A. Bumb. (Illus.). 106p. (Orig.). 1996. pap. 12.95 (*0-9652388-5-7*) M C Bumb.

My Color. William J. Middleton. LC 96-90743. (Illus.). 52p. (Orig.). 1996. pap. 5.00 (*1-886467-14-5*) WJM Press.

My Color & Play Book A. 48p. (YA). 1985. pap. 5.95 (*0-7692-1431-2*, EL03144) Wrner Bros.

My Color Is Panda. Deborah Winograd. LC 92-17423. (Illus.). 32p. (J). (ps-1). 1993. 13.00 (*0-671-79152-4*, Green Tiger S&S) S&S Childrens.

My Color Is Skin Deep. Disha Dewan. LC 97-74758. (Illus.). 48p. (J). (ps-6). 1997. pap. 5.99 (*1-883477-18-2*) Lone Oak MN.

My Colored Battalion. Warner A. Ross. 17.95 (*0-8488-1142-9*) Amereon Ltd.

My Colorful Counting Zoo. Walt Disney Staff. 5p. (J). 1997. 9.98 (*1-57082-439-8*, Pub. by Mouse Works) Time Warner.

My Coloring Book of Salah. unabridged ed. Abidullah Ghazi et al. (Illus.). 27p. (Orig.). (J). (ps-k). 1994. pap. 4.00 (*1-56316-052-8*) Iqra Intl Ed Fdtn.

*__My Colors.__ Rebecca Emberley. (Illus.). 20p. (J). 2000. 5.95 (*0-316-23347-1*) Little.

My Colors. Keith Faulkner. LC 95-158553. (Illus.). 24p. (J). (ps up). 1995. 7.95 (*0-671-89829-9*) Litle Simon.

My Colors . . . & the Rainbow. unabridged ed. Yvonne R. Whitmore. (Midwest Women Poets Ser.). 28p. 1988. pap. 6.00 (*1-891476-08-4*) Wild Dove.

My Colors Go Round. (Jr. Academic Ser.). (Illus.). 32p. (J). (ps). 1998. wbk. ed. 2.25 (*1-57768-208-4*) MG-Hill OH.

My Command. Olusegun Obasanjo. (African Writers Ser.). (Illus.). 178p. (C). 1981. reprint ed. pap. 9.95 (*0-435-90249-0*, 90249) Heinemann.

My Commitment. John C. Reid. 68p. 1993. pap. 3.95 (*0-914733-14-1*) Desert Min.

My Community. Norris & Davis. (Illus.). 48p. (J). (gr. 1-3). 1996. pap., teacher ed. 9.95 (*1-55799-566-4*, 552) Evan-Moor Edu Pubs.

My Commute. Alison A. Axel. LC 98-68529. 76p. 1998. pap. 14.00 (*1-892379-09-0*) Five & Ten.

My Companion Through Grief: Comfort for Your Darkest Hours. Gary Kinnaman. 200p. (Orig.). 1996. pap. 12.99 (*0-89283-947-3*, Vine Bks) Servant.

My Companions in the Bleak House. Eva Kanturkova & Vaclav Havel. LC 87-5688. (ENG.). 304p. 1987. 19.95 (*0-87951-289-X*, Pub. by Overlook Pr) Penguin Putnam.

My Company. Carroll J. Swan. (American Biography Ser.). 263p. 1991. reprint ed. lib. bdg. 69.00 (*0-7812-8376-0*) Rprt Serv.

My Complete Story of the Flute. rev. ed. Leonardo De Lorenzo. LC 92-8525. (Instrument, the Performer, the Music Ser.). (Illus.). 675p. 1992. reprint ed. pap. 35.00 (*0-89672-285-6*) Tex Tech Univ Pr.

My Computer Signs. Ed. by Robin S. Stevens. 70p. (C). 1988. 35.00 (*0-7300-0581-X*, Pub. by Deakin Univ) St Mut.

My Confederate Girlhood. Kate V. Logan. Ed. by Annette K. Baxter. LC 79-8803. (Signal Lives Ser.). (Illus.). 1980. reprint ed. lib. bdg. 26.95 (*0-405-12849-5*) Ayer.

My Confession: The Recollections of a Rogue. Samuel E. Chamberlain. Ed. by William H. Goezman. LC 96-31788. (Illus.). 400p. 1996. 60.00 (*0-87611-156-8*) Tex St Hist Assn.

My Confession: The Recollections of a Rogue. limited ed. Samuel Chamberlain. LC 96-31788. (Illus.). 400p. 1996. 165.00 (*0-87611-157-6*, Pub. by Tex St Hist Assn) Tex A&M Univ Pr.

My Confession Book: A Child's Preparation for the Sacrament of Penance. M. Andrine Welters. LC 97-60767. Orig. Title: Pax: A Preparation for the Sacrament of Penance for Children. (Illus.). 39p. (J). (gr. 1-4). 1997. reprint ed. pap. 2.00 (*0-89555-600-6*, 1505) TAN Bks Pubs.

My Confessional. Havelock Ellis. LC 79-121464. (Essay Index Reprint Ser.). 1977. 20.95 (*0-8369-1918-1*) Ayer.

My Confessional. Havelock Ellis. (Essay Index Reprint Ser.). 245p. 1982. reprint ed. lib. bdg. 17.00 (*0-8290-0783-0*) Irvington.

My Confirmation: A Guide for Confirmation Instruction. 2nd rev. ed. UCBHM Editorial Staff. LC 94-8457. (Illus.). 232p. 1994. pap. 12.95 (*0-8298-0991-0*) Pilgrim OH.

*__My Confirmation Journal.__ Debbie Repp. (Illus.). 48p. 1998. pap. 1.95 (*0-7648-0257-7*) Liguori Pubns.

My Confirmation Journal. rev. ed. Bill Coleman & Patty Coleman. 112p. (J). (gr. 6-9). 1991. pap. 4.95 (*0-89622-483-X*, B67) Twenty-Third.

My Confirmation Memories. Concordia Staff. 24p. 1994. 14.99 (*0-570-04693-9*, 12-3252) Concordia.

My Connecticut Garden: Personal Experiences of an Amateur Gardener. George Valchar. LC 92-21134. (Illus.). 277p. 1993. 39.95 (*0-88192-227-7*) Timber.

My Connemara: The Carl Sandburg Story. Paula Steichen. LC 69-14844. (Illus.). 178p. 1989. reprint ed. pap. 3.95 (*0-915992-46-9*) Eastern National.

My Continuing Quest: Sociological Perspectives on Mormonism. Ray R. Canning. Ed. by Stan Larson. LC 96-29378. 160p. 1996. text 12.95 (*0-9634732-4-7*) Freethinker.

My Conversation, Bk. 2. Chavez & Hojel. (C). 1997. pap. text, teacher ed. 20.19 (*0-673-19192-3*) Addson-Wesley Educ.

My Conversation, Bk. 3. Chavez & Hojel. (C). 1997. text, teacher ed. 15.14 (*0-673-19193-1*) Addson-Wesley Educ.

My Conversation Book, Bk. 1. Chavez. (My English Book Ser.). 1987. pap. text 8.10 (*0-673-19181-8*) Addison-Wesley.

My Conversation Book, Bk. 2. Chavez. (My English Book Ser.). 1987. pap. text 8.10 (*0-673-19182-6*) Addison-Wesley.

My Conversation Book, Bk. 3. Chavez. (My English Book Ser.). 96p. 1997. pap. text 8.11 (*0-673-19183-4*) Addison-Wesley.

My Conversation Book, Bk. 4. Chavez. (My English Book Ser.). 1987. pap. text 8.10 (*0-673-19184-2*) Addison-Wesley.

My Conversations with Martin Luther: In Which I Learn about God, Faith, Marriage, Sexuality, Family, Education, War, Spirituality, Church Life, the Future, Heaven & Hell & Other Things, Too. Timothy F. Lull. LC 99-28310. 128p. 1999. pap. 6.99 (*0-8066-3898-2*, 9-3898, Augsburg) Augsburg Fortress.

My Conversion. Charles H. Spurgeon. 93p. 1996. mass mkt. 5.99 (*0-88368-405-5*) Whitaker Hse.

My Conversion to Christ. Paul Photiou. Ed. by Orthodox Christian Educational Society Staff. (GRE.). (Orig.). 1970. reprint ed. 2.00 (*0-938366-41-6*) Orthodox Chr.

My Cook Book. R. M. Marshall. 136p. 1985. 49.00 (*0-906054-34-6*) St Mut.

My Cookbook . . . Where All Your Favorite Recipes Live: Do-It-Yourself Cookbook. Cosmo Appleduck. 1982. spiral bd. 19.95 (*0-911505-06-7*) Lifecraft.

My Cool Friends. Jennifer Harris. (I-See-You Ser.). (Illus.). 8p. (J). 1996. 3.50 (*1-56293-829-0*, McClanahan Book) Learn Horizon.

*__My Cosmic Pessimism.__ Luis Alberto Santander. LC 99-80016. 160p. 2000. pap. write for info. (*1-57197-211-0*, Pub. by Pentland Pr) Assoc Pubs Grp.

My Counting Book. Ladybird Books Staff. (Early Readers Ser.: No. S8711-6). (Illus.). (J). (ps-2). 3.95 (*0-7214-5146-2*, Ladybrd) Penguin Putnam.

My Country. Ed. by Burton E. Stevenson. LC 70-133075. (Granger Index Reprint Ser.). 1977. 30.95 (*0-8369-6205-2*) Ayer.

My Country: The African Diaspora's Country Music Heritage. Pamela E. Foster. LC 97-92592. (Illus.). viii, 378p. 1998. 32.00 (*0-9662680-0-8*) MY COUNTRY.

My Country: The African Diaspora's Country Music Heritage. Pamela E. Foster. LC 97-92592. (Illus.). viii, 378p. 1998. pap. 32.00 (*0-9662680-1-6*) MY COUNTRY.

My Country & My Rulers. V. B. Kulkarni. 317p. 1977. 14.95 (*0-318-36635-5*) Asia Bk Corp.

My Country Home. Eula F. Long. 1998. pap. write for info. (*1-57553-761-3*) Watermrk Pr.

My Country Is Called Earth: A Mythology from the Twenty-First Century. Lawrence Brown. LC 94-94555. 144p. (Orig.). 1994. pap. 12.95 (*0-9642458-0-9*) Gorilla Pr CA.

My Country Right or Left, 1940-1943 see Collected Essays, Journalism, & Letters of George Orwell

My Country Tears of Thee. Fred J. Jackson. 24p. 1999. write for info. (*1-891934-02-3*) Black Rose CA.

*__My Country, Too: The Other Black Music.__ Pamela E. Foster. 2000. pap. 13.95 (*0-9662680-2-4*) MY COUNTRY.

My Cousin Has Eight Legs. Jasper Tomkins. (Illus.). 40p. (Orig.). (J). (ps up). 1992. pap. 9.95 (*0-912365-68-4*) Sasquatch Bks.

My Cousin Justin. Margaret Barrington. Orig. Title: Turn Ever Northward. 288p. (Orig.). (YA). (gr. 10-12). 1990. pap. 11.95 (*0-85640-456-X*, Pub. by Blackstaff Pr) Dufour.

My Cousin Mandy. large type ed. Jill Murray. 1989. 27.99 (*0-7089-2107-8*) Ulverscroft.

My Cousin, Mark Twain. Cyril Clemens. LC 74-16297. (American Literature Ser.: No. 49). 1974. lib. bdg. 75.00 (*0-8383-1744-8*) M S G Haskell Hse.

My Cousin, My Gastroenterologist. Mark Leyner. LC 93-15505. 1995. pap. 10.00 (*0-679-74579-3*) Vin Bks.

My Cousin Rachel. adapted ed. Daphne Du Maurier. 1980. pap. 5.25 (*0-8222-0797-4*) Dramatists Play.

My Cousin Rachel. Daphne Du Maurier. LC 74-184731. 352p. 1971. reprint ed. lib. bdg. 20.00 (*0-8376-0413-3*) Bentley Pubs.

My Cousin Rachel. Daphne Du Maurier. 1993. reprint ed. lib. bdg. 28.95 (*1-56849-142-5*) Buccaneer Bks.

*__My Covenant over Your Children & Children's Children.__ Linda Greene. 175p. 1999. write for info. (*0-9676644-5-4*) HIS LOVE.

My Cow Comes to Haunt Me: European Explorers, Travellers & Novelists Constructing Textual Selves & Imagining the Unthinkable in Lands & Islands Beyond the Sea, from Christopher Columbus to Alexander von Humboldt. Norman Simms. LC 94-19523. 380p. (C). 1995. pap. text 36.50 (*0-944473-19-9*); lib. bdg. 77.00 (*0-944473-18-0*) Pace Univ Pr.

My Cowboy's Gift. Andy Wilkinson. 38p. 1998. pap. 25.00 incl. audio compact disk (*1-888609-10-9*) Grey Hrse Pr.

*__My Cows.__ Heather Miller. LC 00-24386. (My Farm Ser.). (Illus.). 24p. (J). (ps-2). 2000. pap. 4.95 (*0-516-23031-X*) Childrens.

*__My Cows.__ Heather Miller. (Welcome Bks.). (Illus.). (J). 2000. 13.50 (*0-516-23106-5*) Childrens.

My Crayons Talk. Patricia Hubbard. LC 95-12786. (Illus.). 32p. (J). (ps-2). 1995. 15.95 (*0-8050-3529-X*) H Holt & Co.

My Crayons Talk. Patricia Hubbard. (ps-3). 1999. pap. text 5.95 (*0-8050-6150-9*) H Holt & Co.

My Crazy Cousin Courtney Comes Back. Judi Miller. Ed. by Pat MacDonald. 160p. (J). 1994. pap. 3.50 (*0-671-88734-3*, Minstrel Bks) PB.

My Crazy Cousin Courtney Comes Back. Judi Miller. 1993. 8.09 (*0-606-11650-8*, Pub. by Turtleback) Demco.

My Crazy Cousin Courtney Comes Back. Judi Miller. 1994. 8.60 (*0-606-11651-6*, Pub. by Turtleback) Demco.

My Crazy Cousin Courtney Gets Crazier. Judi Miller. (Crazy Courtney Ser.). 1997. 8.60 (*0-606-11652-4*, Pub. by Turtleback) Demco.

My Crazy Cousin Courtney Returns Again. Judi Miller. Ed. by Pat MacDonald. 160p. (Orig.). 1995. pap. 3.50 (*0-671-88733-5*, Minstrel Bks) PB.

My Crazy Cousin Courtney Returns Again. Judi Miller. (Orig.). 1995. 8.60 (*0-606-11653-2*, Pub. by Turtleback) Demco.

My Crooked Family. James L. Collier. LC 90-27747. 288p. (YA). (gr. 5-9). 1991. pap. 15.00 (*0-671-74224-8*) S&S Bks Yung.

My Crowd: The Original Addams Family & Other Ghoulish Creatures. Charles Addams. 1991. pap. 10.95 (*0-671-77812-9*) S&S Trade.

My Crystal Glass: A Poetic Journey Through Recovery. Illus. by RAM Staff. iii, 23p. 1992. pap. 5.00 (*1-893035-00-X*) Encircle Pubns.

My Crystal Glass: A Poetic Journey Through Recovery. rev. ed. Illus. by RAM Staff. iii, 23p. 1998. pap. 6.45 (*1-893035-04-2*) Encircle Pubns.

My Cube. Erno Rubek. 1999. pap. write for info. (*0-14-006250-5*, Penguin Bks) Viking Penguin.

My Cuddly Toys. Rachel Elliot. (I-See-You Ser.). (Illus.). 8p. (J). 1996. 3.50 (*1-56293-828-2*, McClanahan Book) Learn Horizon.

My Culinary Journey. Irene T. Pieper. (Illus.). 168p. 1993. 19.93 (*0-9638234-0-X*) I K Pieper.

My Cup Overflows: With the Comfort of His Love. Emilie Barnes. LC 98-4084. 170p. 1998. 12.99 (*1-56507-907-8*) Harvest Hse.

My Cup Ranneth Over. Robert Patrick. 1979. pap. 5.25 (*0-8222-0798-2*) Dramatists Play.

My Cup Runneth Over. Vera E. Johansen. LC 98-90583. 1999. 9.95 (*0-533-12855-2*) Vantage.

My Cup Runneth Over (Most of the Time) 52 Light & Not-So-Light Devotions for Teachers. Delia T. Halverson. LC 98-36979. 1999. pap. 8.00 (*0-687-05692-6*) Dimen for Liv.

My "d" Sound Box. Jane Belk Moncure. LC 78-8450. (Sound Box Library). (Illus.). 32p. (J). (ps-2). 1978. lib. bdg. 21.36 (*0-89565-044-4*) Childs World.

My Dad see Mi Papa

My Dad see Mon Papa

*__My Dad.__ Anthony Browne. LC 99-47083. (J). 2000. write for info. (*0-7894-2681-1*) DK Pub Inc.

*__My Dad.__ Anthony Browne. LC 00-37951. (Illus.). (J). 2001. write for info. (*0-374-35101-5*) FS&G.

My Dad. Niki Daly. LC 94-14455. (Illus.). 32p. (J). (ps-3). 1995. per. 16.00 (*0-689-50620-1*) McElderry Bks.

My Dad. Janet Horowitz & Kathy Faggella. (Photolog Bk.). (Illus.). 48p. (J). (gr. 1-7). 1991. 4.50 (*1-55670-174-8*) Stewart Tabori & Chang.

My Dad. 6th ed. Debbie Bailey. (Talk-about-Books Ser.: Vol. 6). (Illus.). 14p. (J). (ps-k). 1991. bds. 5.95 (*1-55037-164-9*, Pub. by Annick) Firefly Bks Ltd.

My Dad Drives a Big Truck. Stephen Reece. (Illus.). 12p. (J). (ps-3). 1998. pap. 2.95 (*1-892388-02-2*) Lttle Trucker.

My Dad Drives an AFV (Alternative Fuel Vehicle) Jenna Denning. Ed. by Steve McCrea. (Illus.). 28p. (J). 1995. pap. text 7.00 (*1-57074-245-6*) Greyden Pr.

My Dad Has HIV. Earl Alexander et al. (Illus.). 32p. (J). (gr. k-4). 1996. 14.95 (*0-925190-99-3*) Fairview Press.

My Dad Is Awesome. Nick Butterworth. LC 91-71832. (Illus.). 24p. (J). (ps up). 1992. pap. 4.99 (*1-56402-033-9*) Candlewick Pr.

My Dad Is Getting Married Again. Lisa M. Schab. (Illus.). 34p. (J). (gr. k-7). 1995. pap. 15.95 (*1-882732-43-X*) Childswork.

My Dad Lost His Job. Mary Kalifon. (Illus.). 32p. (Orig.). (J). (ps-4). 1995. pap. 5.95 (*0-9641981-0-X*) Cedrs Sinai Hlth Sys.

My Dad Loves Me, My Dad Has a Disease: A Child's View: Living with Addiction. 3rd rev. ed. Claudia Black. (Illus.). 84p. (J). (gr. k-6). 1997. pap. 12.95 (*0-910223-23-8*) MAC Pub.

*__My Dad Moved Yesterday.__ Maryum Muhammad. (J). (gr. k-2). 2000. 10.95 (*0-533-13230-4*) Vantage.

*__My Dad Says.__ John E. Fry. (Illus.). 256p. 1999. pap. 14.95 (*0-9674279-0-8*) Wheatland View.

My Dad Sells Insurance. Richard C. Shaw. (Illus.). 40p. (J). (ps-5). 1988. lib. bdg. write for info. (*0-944900-00-3*) Shaw & Co.

My Dad Takes Care of Me. Patricia M. Quinlan. (Illus.). 24p. (J). (ps-3). 1987. pap. 4.95 (*0-920303-76-5*, Pub. by Annick); lib. bdg. 15.95 (*0-920303-79-X*, Pub. by Annick) Firefly Bks Ltd.

My Dad Was Not Hamlet. Saul Landau. Ed. by Carol Ferry. 85p. (Orig.). 1993. pap. 9.95 (*0-89758-049-4*) Inst Policy Stud.

My Daddy. Susan Paradis. LC 97-45857. (Illus.). 32p. (J). (ps-1). 1998. 15.95 (*1-886910-30-8*) Front Str.

*__My Daddy.__ Susan Paradis. (Illus.). 30p. (J). (ps-1). 1999. bds. 8.95 (*1-886910-50-2*, Pub. by Front Str) Publishers Group.

My Daddy & I... Eloise Greenfield. (Illus.). 12p. (J). 1991. bds. 4.95 (*0-86316-206-1*) Writers & Readers.

My Daddy & Me. Judy B. Mack. (Illus.). 40p. (Orig.). (J). (gr. k-4). 2000. pap. write for info. (*0-9637795-7-5*) MinervaPress.

My Daddy Died. Heather Teakle. 1993. 12.00 (*1-86371-095-7*) Harper SF.

My Daddy Died: When Someone You Love Dies, & You Need to Tell a Child. Roberta C. Andresen. (Illus.). 50p. (J). (ps-5). 1994. lib. bdg. 6.95 (*0-9641718-0-5*) Andresen Ent.

My Daddy Is a Soldier. Kirk Hilbrecht & Sharron Hilbrecht. (Illus.). 30p. (Orig.). (J). (gr. k-2). 1996. pap. 5.75 (*1-889658-01-4*) New Canaan Pub.

My Daddy Is a Stranger. Vicki Cochran. Ed. by Joy Johnson. (Illus.). 24p. (Orig.). (J). (gr. 1-5). 1992. pap. 3.95 (*1-56123-049-9*) Centering Corp.

My Daddy Likes to Be with Me. Michelle Castronovo. LC 95-92266. (Kids Comfort Inc. Ser.: No. 2). (Illus.). 16p. (Orig.). (J). 1995. pap. 9.95 (*1-887453-17-2*) Kids Comfort.

My Daddy the Duke. Judy Christenberry. (American Romance Ser.: Vol. 735). 1998. per. 3.99 (*0-373-16735-0*, 1-16735-2) Harlequin Bks.

My Daddy Used to Say . . . Al Westbrook. 150p. (Orig.). 1996. pap. write for info. (*1-57502-200-1*, PO830) Morris Pubng.

M

M

My Daddy's Cancer. Cindy K. Cohen & John T. Heiney. (Illus.). 32p. (J). (ps-6). 1999. pap. 7.95 (*0-9656498-1-4*) Promise Pubns.

My Daddy's Going Working. Michelle Castronovo. LC 95-92265. (Kids Comfort Inc. Ser.: No. 1). (Illus.). 16p. (Orig.). (J). 1995. pap. 9.95 (*1-887453-09-1*) Kids Comfort.

My Dads a Wizard. H. Roche. LC 99-166908. (Illus.). (J). (ps). 1998. pap. 4.95 (*1-84089-013-4*, 868236Q) Zero to Ten.

My Dad's Definitely Not a Drunk! Elisa L. Carbone. Ed. by Susan B. Weber. LC 92-53883. (Illus.). 116p. (Orig.). (J). (gr. 4-9). 1992. pap. text 7.95 (*0-914525-22-0*) Waterfront Bks.

***My Dad's St. Louis Boyhood: German Immigrants' Life 1900-1915, Including Visits to Louisiana Purchase Exposition.** Marian Wenzel. LC 99-48896. (Illus.). 95p. 2000. pap. 9.95 (*0-930887-33-6*) Wenzel Pr.

My Daily Affirmation. Kathleen Shedaker. 22p. (Orig.). 1997. pap. 10.00 (*0-614-30230-7*) Morning NY.

My Daily Devotion: God's Promises for Joyful Living. Stephen J. Carter. 372p. (Orig.). 1988. pap. 14.99 (*0-570-03077-3*, 06-1192) Concordia.

My Daily Eucharist. Ed. & Compiled by Joan C. McHugh. 384p. (Orig.). 1995. pap. text 10.00 (*0-9640417-3-1*) Witness Min.

My Daily Eucharist, Vol. II. Ed. & Compiled by Joan C. McHugh. 392p. (Orig.). 1997. pap. 12.00 (*0-9640417-5-8*) Witness Min.

My Daily Journey with My Utmost for His Highest: Personal Reflections That Draw Us Closer to God. Carolyn Reeves. LC 95-33978. 192p. 1995. pap., student ed. 12.99 (*1-57293-005-5*) Discovery Hse Pubs.

My Daily Prayer see Daily Prayers: A Classic Collection

My Daily Prayer Journal. 368p. 1989. lthr. 4.97 (*0-916441-61-X*) Barbour Pub.

My Daily Prayers & Inspirations - Lift up Your Hearts. Anthony A. Petrusic. Ed. by Sue H. Parker. (Illus.). 1999. 7.95 (*0-937739-44-8*, 10042) Roman IL.

My Daily Success Journal: A Workbook Designed to Create a Happy, Satisfying Life. Andrea S. Glass. 200p. (Orig.). 1990. pap. 12.95 (*0-9628131-0-9*) Ideal Enter.

My Daily Walk: Living a Life of Praise. Dimensions for Living Staff. 1999. write for info. (*0-687-07479-7*) Abingdon.

***My Daily Walk, 1999: Living a Life of Hope.** Dimensions for Living Staff. (Illus.). 264p. 1998. pap., spiral bd. 14.00 (*0-687-05723-X*) Dimen for Liv.

My Daily Walk, 1999 & 365 Days of Spiritual Growth. Paul E. Miller & Phyllis Cole-Dai. 1998. pap. 21.00 (*0-687-05726-4*) Dimen for Liv.

My Daily Walk, 1997. 1996. 20.75 (*0-687-04792-7*) Abingdon.

***My Daily Walk 2001: Living an Abundant Life.** 264'p. 1999. spiral bd. 15.00 (*0-687-09021-0*) Dimen for Liv.

My Daily Walk, 2000: Living a Life of Praise. 140.00 (*0-687-07786-9*) Abingdon.

My Daisy Girl Scout Activity Scrapbook. Girl Scouts of the U. S. A. Staff. (Illus.). 64p. (J). (gr. k-1). 1993. 5.95 (*0-88441-277-6*, 20-907) Girl Scouts USA.

***My Dangerous Desires: A Queer Girl Dreaming Her Way Home.** Amber L. Hollibaugh. LC 00-30307. (Series Q). (Illus.). 264p. 2000. pap. 17.95 (*0-8223-2619-1*); lib. bdg. 49.95 (*0-8223-2625-6*) Duke.

My Daniel. Pam Conrad. LC 88-19850. 144p. (J). (gr. 4-7). 1989. lib. bdg. 15.89 (*0-06-021314-0*) HarpC Child Bks.

My Daniel. Pam Conrad. LC 88-19850. 144p. (YA). (gr. 5 up). 1989. 13.95 (*0-06-021313-2*) HarpC Child Bks.

My Daniel. Pam Conrad. LC 88-19850. (Trophy Bk.). 144p. (YA). (gr. 4-7). 1991. pap. 4.95 (*0-06-440309-2*, HarpTrophy) HarpC Child Bks.

***My Dark Brother: The Illins, A Russian - Aboriginal Family.** Elena Gover. 320p. 2000. pap. 29.95 (*0-86840-594-9*, Pub. by New South Wales Univ Pr) Intl Spec Bk.

My Dark Companion & Their Strange Stories. Henry Morton Stanley. 1977. 28.95 (*0-8369-9175-3*, 9048) Ayer.

My Dark Places. James Ellroy. 1997. pap. 14.00 (*0-679-76205-1*) Random Hse Value.

My Dark Places: An L. A. Crime Memoir. James Ellroy. LC 96-36673. 355p. 1996. 25.00 (*0-679-44185-9*) Knopf.

***My Dark Prince.** Jean Ross Ewing. 2000. mass mkt. 6.99 (*0-515-12883-X*, Jove) Berkley Pub.

My Darling Bride. Valerie King et al. (Zebra Regency Romance Ser.). 256p. 1998. mass mkt. 4.99 (*0-8217-5904-3*, Zebra Kensgtn) Kensgtn Pub Corp.

My Darling Buffy: The Early Life of the Queen Mother. Grania Forbes. (Illus.). 224p. 1998. 35.00 (*1-86066-091-6*, Pub. by R Cohen Bks) Trafalgar.

My Darling Buffy: The Early Life of the Queen Mother. large type ed. Grania Forbes. (Charnwood Large Print Ser.). (Illus.). 272p. 1998. 29.99 (*0-7089-8986-1*, Charnwood) Ulverscroft.

My Darling Caroline. Adele Ashworth. 352p. 1998. mass mkt. 5.99 (*0-515-12369-2*, Jove) Berkley Pub.

My Darling Danny: Letters from Mary O'Connell to Her Son Daniel, 1830-1832. Ed. by Erin Bishop. LC 99-175819. (Irish Narrative Ser.). 96p. 1998. pap. 12.95 (*1-85918-173-2*, Pub. by Cork Univ) Intl Spec Bk.

My Darling Dominatrix. 3rd ed. Grant Antrews. (Orig.). 1997. reprint ed. mass mkt. 7.95 (*1-56333-566-2*, Rhinoceros) Masquerade.

My Darling Duke. Constance Hall. 352p. 1998. pap. 4.99 (*0-8217-5929-9*) Kensgtn Pub Corp.

My Darling Elia. Eugenie Melnyk. LC 99-13110. 278p. 1999. text 23.95 (*0-312-20565-1*) St Martin.

My Darling Kate. Elizabeth Graham. 320p. 1997. mass mkt. 4.99 (*0-8217-5686-9*, Zebra Kensgtn) Kensgtn Pub Corp.

My Darling Melissa. Linda Lael Miller. Ed. by Linda Marrow. 336p. 1991. mass mkt. 6.99 (*0-671-73771-6*) PB.

My Darling Melissa. Linda Lael Miller. 1995. mass mkt. 5.99 (*0-671-53419-X*) PB.

My Darling, My Hamburger. Paul Zindel. 128p. (YA). (gr. 7-12). 1984. mass mkt. 4.50 (*0-553-27324-8*) Bantam.

My Darling, My Hamburger: A Novel. Paul Zindel. (J). 1969. 9.60 (*0-606-04074-9*, Pub. by Turtleback) Demco.

My Darling My Hamburger: A Student Response Journal. rev. ed. James Scott. 14p. (YA). (gr. 7-12). 1998. ring bd. 19.95 (*1-58049-754-3*, RJ06R) Prestwick Hse.

My Darling Valentine. 256p. 1999. mass mkt. 4.99 (*0-8217-6125-0*) Kensgtn Pub Corp.

My Darling Villain. Lynne Reid Banks. LC 76-58718. 240p. (YA). (gr. 7 up). 1977. 11.25 (*0-06-020392-7*) HarpC Child Bks.

My Date with Satan: Stories. Stacey Richter. LC 99-13146. 224p. 1999. 21.50 (*0-684-85701-4*) S&S Trade.

***My Date with Satan: Stories.** Stacey Richter. 224p. 2000. pap. 11.00 (*0-684-85702-2*) Scribner.

My Datebook: A Keepsake Book of Special Days. Lois G. Leppard. 112p. (J). 1997. text 7.99 (*0-7642-2021-7*) Bethany Hse.

My Daughter Maria Callas. Evangelia Callas & Lawrence G. Blochman. Ed. by Andrew Farkas. LC 76-29928. (Opera Biographies Ser.). (Illus.). 1979. reprint ed. lib. bdg. 21.95 (*0-405-09671-2*) Ayer.

My Daughter, My Daughter. Dee Brestin. LC 99-39736. 1999. pap. text 12.99 (*1-56476-784-1*) SP Pubns.

***My Daughter, My Son, the Eagle, the Dove: An Aztec Chant.** Ana Castillo. (Illus.). 48p. (J). 2000. 12.99 (*0-525-45856-5*, Dutton Child) Peng Put Young Read.

My Daughter, My Special Friend. Roy Honegger. LC 96-78976. 168p. 1997. pap. 5.95 (*1-56245-280-0*) Great Quotations.

***My Daughter Susan Smith.** Linda Russell & Shirley Stephens. (Illus.). 304p. 2000. pap. 16.95 (*0-615-11644-2*) Authors Bk Nook.

***My Daughter Susan Smith.** Linda Russell & Shirley Stephens. (Illus.). 304p. 2000. pap. 16.95 (*0-9701076-1-7*) Authors Bk Nook.

My Daughter, the Teacher: Jewish Teachers in the New York City Schools. Ruth J. Markowitz. LC 92-37565. 288p. (C). 1993. text 40.00 (*0-8135-1974-8*); pap. text 16.00 (*0-8135-1975-6*) Rutgers U Pr.

My Day. (Active Minds Ser.). (Illus.). 24p. (J). 1993. 4.98 (*1-56173-480-2*) Pubns Intl Ltd.

My Day. Mike Barney. (World of Discovery Ser.). 1997. text 4.95 (*1-879835-30-4*) Kaeden Corp.

My Day. Donatella Bazzucchi. (Illus.). 14p. (J). (ps). 1994. pap. 3.99 (*1-881445-35-6*) Sandvik Pub.

My Day. Elizabeth S. Buchanan. 32p. (J). 1997. pap. 9.95 (*0-385-48264-7*, Main St Bks) Doubleday.

My Day. Michael Evans. (Little Surprises Ser.). (Illus.). 24p. (J). (ps). 1992. bds. 2.95 (*0-8249-8526-5*, Ideals Child) Hambleton-Hill.

***My Day.** Debbie Mackinnon. (Illus.). 8p. (J). (ps-3). 1999. 7.95 (*0-316-64898-1*) Little.

My Day. P. Mills. (Chunky Pop up Book). (J). (ps). 1994. bds. 3.99 (*0-7814-1514-4*) Chariot Victor.

My Day. large type ed. Mike Barney. (Illus.). 16p. (J). (gr. k-2). 1998. pap. 4.95 (*1-879835-26-6*, Kaeden) Kaeden Corp.

My Day: Active Minds. Photos by George Siede & Donna Preis. (Active Minds-English Ser.). (Illus.). 24p. (J). (ps-3). 1992. lib. bdg. 11.95 (*1-56674-002-9*, HTS Bks) Forest Hse.

My Day: Chubby Board Book. (Chubby Board Bks.). 16p. (J). (ps). 1980. pap. 2.95 (*0-671-41344-9*) S&S Trade.

My Day at the Baseball Game: A Book about a Special Day see PowerKids Readers Set 1: My World

My Day: Chunky Pop-Up Book see Mi Dia: Figuras Que Aparecen

My Day in the Garden. Miela Ford. LC 97-34450. (Illus.). 24p. (J). (ps-3). 1999. 16.00 (*0-688-15541-3*, Grenwillow Bks) HarpC Child Bks.

***My Day in the Garden.** Miela Ford. LC 97-34450. (Illus.). 24p. (J). (ps-3). 1999. 15.89 (*0-688-15542-1*, Grenwillow Bks) HarpC Child Bks.

***My Day (Mi Dia) A Book in Two Languages (Un Libro en Dos Lenguas)** Rebecca Emberley. (ENG & SPA.). 28p. (J). (ps-3). 2000. pap. 5.95 (*0-316-22983-0*) Little.

My Day with Anka. Nan F. Nelson. LC 95-25425. (Illus.). 24p. (J). (ps up). 1996. 16.00 (*0-688-11058-4*); lib. bdg. 15.93 (*0-688-11059-2*) Lothrop.

My Day with Jesus. Lawrence G. Lovasik. (Saint Joseph Picture Bks.). (Illus.). 1987. pap. text 1.25 (*0-89942-294-2*, 294-00) Catholic Bk Pub.

***My Day, Your Day.** Robin Ballard. (J). 2001. write for info. (*0-688-17796-4*, Grenwillow Bks); lib. bdg. write for info. (*0-06-029187-7*, Grenwillow Bks) HarpC Child Bks.

My Days: A Memoir. R. K. Narayan. LC 98-14082. 192p. 1999. reprint ed. 14.00 (*0-88001-625-6*) HarpC.

My Days As a Youngling, John Jacob Niles: Playscript. Nancy N. Sexton et al. (J). (gr. 4 up). 1982. 7.00 (*0-87602-239-5*) Anchorage.

My Days with Albert Schweitzer. Frederick Franck. (Illus.). 190p. 1996. reprint ed. pap. 14.99 (*0-88092-326-1*, 3261) Royal Fireworks.

My Days with Errol Flynn. Buster Wiles & William Donati. LC 88-61235. (Illus.). 272p. 1989. 21.95 (*0-915677-36-9*) Roundtable Pub.

My Days with Nehru. M. O. Mathai. 270p. 1979. 14.95 (*0-7069-0823-6*) Asia Bk Corp.

My Days...My Pictures Vol. I: A Daily Drawing Journal for 4 to 6 Year Olds. Kathleen Lashier. (Memory Journals for Young Writers Ser.). 375p. (J). (ps-1). 1995. pap. text 9.99 (*1-56383-054-X*, 5055) G & R Pub.

My Days...My Writings: A Daily Journal for 6 to 9 Year Olds, Vol. I. Joanne Farrell. (Memory Journals for Young Writers Ser.). 374p. (J). (gr. 1-4). 1995. pap. text 9.99 (*1-56383-055-8*, 5056) G & R Pub.

My Deadly Valentine. Carolyn Keene. Ed. by Anne Greenberg. (Nancy Drew Files: No. 92). 160p. (YA). (gr. 6 up). 1994. per. 3.99 (*0-671-79484-1*, Archway) PB.

My Deadly Valentine. Carolyn Keene. (Nancy Drew Files: No. 92). (YA). (gr. 6 up). 1994. 9.09 (*0-606-05945-8*, Pub. by Turtleback) Demco.

My Dear Alex: Letters from the KGB. Dinesh D'Souza & Gregory Fossedal. LC 87-9720. 160p. 1987. 14.95 (*0-89526-576-1*) Regnery Pub.

My Dear Alexias. 187p. 1979. 9.95 (*0-85978-038-4*, Pub. by C W Daniel) Natl Bk Netwk.

My Dear Alexias: Extracts from the Letters of W. Tudor Pole to Rosamond Lehmann. (Illus.). 220p. 14.95 (*0-8464-4256-6*) Beekman Pubs.

My Dear America Diary. Scholastic, Inc. Staff. 144p. 1998. 7.95 (*0-590-25989-X*) Scholastic Inc.

My Dear Aunt Flora. large type ed. Elizabeth Cadell. 448p. 1996. 27.99 (*0-7089-3512-5*) Ulverscroft.

My Dear Boy: Gay Love Letters Through the Centuries. Ed. by Rictor Norton. LC 97-28335. (Illus.). 288p. 1998. 50.00 (*0-943595-70-3*); pap. 15.95 (*0-943595-71-1*) Leyland Pubns.

My Dear Brother M... Why Ellen White Wrote the Letters in Testimonies for the Church. Paul A. Gordon. LC 96-33565. 1997. pap. 7.97 (*0-8163-1369-5*) Pacific Pr Pub Assn.

My Dear Carrie: The Civil War Letters of George K. Pardee & Family. Robert H. Jones & Caroline J. Pardee. LC 94-239574. (Illus.). 286p. 1994. text 29.95 (*1-883916-00-3*) Summit Cty Hist Soc.

My Dear Friend: A Basic Writing Program for Adults. Marilyn Gerstner-Horvath. Ed. by Jane H. Combs. (Illus.). 96p. (Orig.). 1992. pap., student ed. 6.95 (*0-9614330-5-1*) Longmuir Jones Pub.

My Dear Fugitive. large type ed. Olga Sinclair. (Lythway Ser.). 208p. 1991. 21.95 (*0-7451-1278-1*, G K Hall Lrg Type) Mac Lib Ref.

My Dear Gogarty: Previously Unpublished Critical Essay Together with Selections from the Correspondence of Oliver St John Gogarty. limited ed. Ed. by Mary C. Stratton. (Illus.). 52p. 1991. pap. 150.00 (*0-916375-12-9*) Press Alley.

My Dear Jenny. Madeleine Robins. 224p. 1980. pap. 1.75 (*0-449-50041-7*, Coventry) Fawcett.

My Dear Lady: The Story of Anna Ella Carroll, the "Great Unrecognized Member of Lincoln's Cabinet" Marjorie B. Greenbie. LC 74-3953. (Women in America Ser.). (Illus.). 330p. 1974. reprint ed. 29.95 (*0-405-06101-3*) Ayer.

***My Dear Miss: The Civil War Letters of David M. Poor & Mary O. Mussey.** David M. Poor & Mary O. Mussey. Ed. by Douglas N. Travers & Mary I. Travers. (Illus.). 609p. 1999. 85.00 (*1-929013-02-7*) Oakhill Pubg.

My Dear Mollie: Love Letters of a Texas Sheep Rancher. Compiled & Intro. by Agnesa L. Reeve. LC 90-41891. (Illus.). 192p. (J). (gr. 7 up). 1990. 8.95 (*0-937460-62-1*) Hendrick-Long.

***My Dear Mom.** Deborah Hansen. (Illus.). (J). 1999. 7.95 (*1-56245-370-X*) Great Quotations.

My Dear Mother: Stormy, Boastful, & Tender Letters by Distinguished Sons - From Dostoevsky to Elvis. Karen E. Gordon & Holly Johnson. LC 97-14494. 224p. 1997. 18.95 (*1-56512-121-X*) Algonquin Bks.

My Dear Mother & Sisters: Civil War Letters of Capt. A. B. Mulligan, Co. B, 5th South Carolina Cavalry - Butler's Division - Hampton's Corps, 1861-1865. Ed. by Olin F. Hutchinson, Jr. LC 92-11129. 1992. 25.00 (*0-87152-456-2*) Reprint.

My Dear Mr. Bell: Letters from Dr. Jonathan Pereira to Mr. Jacob Bell, London, 1844 to 1853. Ed. by Cecil Cloughly et al. 129p. (Orig.). 1987. pap. 12.00 (*0-931292-18-2*) Am Inst Hist Pharm.

My Dear Noel: The Story of a Letter from Beatrix Potter. Jane Johnson. Ed. by Phyllis Fogelman. LC 96-11074. (Illus.). 40p. (J). (ps-3). 1999. 15.99 (*0-8037-2050-5*, Dial Yng Read); 15.89 (*0-8037-2051-3*, Dial Yng Read) Peng Put Young Read.

My Dear Ones . . . Mercy. LC 94-65100. 112p. 1994. pap. 2.75 (*1-882972-22-8*, 3152) Queenship Pub.

My Dear Runemeister: A Voyage Through the Alphabet. Lloyd Reynolds. LC 89-16400. (Illus.). 80p. (Orig.). 1990. reprint ed. pap. 9.95 (*0-87595-219-4*) Oregon Hist.

My Dear Watson: Being the Annals of Sherlock Holmes. David L. Hammer et al. (Illus.). 104p. (Orig.). 1995. pap. 12.95 (*0-938501-22-4*) Wessex.

My Dearest Cal. Sherryl Woods. (Special Ser.: No. 669). 1991. per. 3.25 (*0-373-09669-0*) Silhouette.

My Dearest Enemy. Connie Brockway. 384p. 1998. mass mkt. 6.50 (*0-440-22375-X*) Doubleday.

My Dearest Friend. Nancy Thayer. 1991. mass mkt. 4.95 (*1-55817-485-0*, Pinncle Kensgtn) Kensgtn Pub Corp.

***My Dearest Friend: The Civil War Correspondence of Cornelia McGimsey & Lewis Warlick.** Ed. by Mike Lawing & Carolyn Lawing. LC 99-69190. 224p. 2000. pap. 20.00 (*0-89089-832-4*) Carolina Acad Pr.

My Dearest Julia: The Love Letters of Dr. Benjamin Rush to Julia Stockton, 1775-1776. 1979. 17.50 (*0-88202-187-7*) Watson Pub Intl.

My Dearest Love. Diana Haviland. 352p. 1996. mass mkt. 4.99 (*0-8217-5407-6*, Zebra Kensgtn) Kensgtn Pub Corp.

My Dearest Love. Emilie Loring. 1976. reprint ed. lib. bdg. 21.95 (*0-88411-359-0*) Amereon Ltd.

My Dearest Love: Love Letters from Him to Her. Ronald L. Moss. 142p. (Orig.). 1996. pap. 14.95 (*0-9655693-0-6*) Moss & Moss.

My Dearest Minette: Letters Between Charles II & His Sister. Ed. by Ruth Norrington. LC 96-224077. (Illus.). 240p. 1996. 39.95 (*0-7206-0991-7*, Pub. by P Owen Ltd) Dufour.

My Dearly Beloved. Alaina Hawthorne. (Romance Ser.). 1995. per. 2.99 (*0-373-19069-7*, 1-19069-3) Silhouette.

My Debut As a Literary Person. Samuel L. Clemens. 367p. 1998. reprint ed. lib. bdg. 79.00 (*0-7812-4780-2*) Rprt Serv.

My Debut As a Literary Person: With Other Essays & Stories. Mark Twain, pseud. (Works of Samuel Clemens). 1989. reprint ed. lib. bdg. 79.00 (*0-685-28371-2*) Rprt Serv.

My December Journal. Alana Trisler & Patrice Cardiel. 48p. (J). (gr. 1-2). 1999. pap., wbk. ed. 1.75 (*1-56762-098-1*) Modern Learn Pr.

My Deep Dark Pain Is Love: A Collection of Latin American Gay Fiction. Ed. by Winston Leyland. Tr. by E. A. Lacey from POR. (Illus.). 384p. (Orig.). 1983. pap. 14.95 (*0-917342-03-8*) Gay Sunshine.

***My Deepest Sympathies: Meaningful Sentiments for Times of Loss Plus a Guide to Eulogies.** Florence Isaacs. LC 99-59905. 160p. 2000. 17.00 (*0-609-60565-8*) C Potter.

My Denali: Exploring Alaska's Favorite National Park with Hannah Corral. Kimberly Corral & Hannah Corral. LC 95-21169. (Illus.). 32p. (YA). (gr. 5 up). 1995. 15.95 (*0-88240-467-9*, Alaska NW Bks) Gr Arts Ctr Pub.

My Dentist. Harlow Rockwell. LC 75-6974. (Illus.). 32p. (J). (ps-3). 1975. 16.00 (*0-688-80011-4*, Wm Morrow) Morrow Avon.

My Dentist. Harlow Rockwell. LC 75-6974. (Illus.). 32p. (J). (ps up). 1987. mass mkt. 4.95 (*0-688-07040-X*, Wm Morrow) Morrow Avon.

***My Dentist & the Tooth Fairy: Educational Acitvity & Coloring Book.** Karen Jean Hood. 160p. (J). (ps-11). 2000. pap. 9.95 (*0-9679368-1-0*) Whsprng Pine.

My Dentist Is a Vampire. M. T. Coffin. LC 97-93867. (Spinetinglers Ser.: No. 29). 128p. (J). (gr. 3-7). 1998. pap. 3.99 (*0-380-79163-3*, Avon Bks) Morrow Avon.

My Dentist, My Friend. P. K. Hallinan. LC 95-37592. (Illus.). 24p. (Orig.). (J). (ps-3). 1996. pap. 4.95 (*1-57102-086-1*, Ideals Child) Hambleton-Hill.

***My Descent into Death: And the Message of Love Which Brought Me Back.** Howard Storm. (Illus.). 184p. 2000. pap. 16.95 (*1-902636-16-3*, Pub. by Temple Lodge) Anthroposophic.

My Desert Storm Diary: Write Your Story for Your Children & Grandchildren. Ed. by J. Forbes. (Illus.). 112p. 1991. 7.50 (*0-941402-09-6*) Devon Pub.

My Destiny. large type ed. Rosemary Hammond. 1990. reprint ed. lib. bdg. 18.95 (*0-263-12077-5*) Mac Lib Ref.

My Destiny: Survivor of the Holocaust. Georgia M. Gabor. LC 81-68276. (Illus.). 319p. (Orig.). 1981. pap. 6.95 (*0-941204-00-6*) Amen Pub.

My Detour on Life's Highway: A Survivor's Story of Stem Cell Transplant. Rosemary Champagne. (Illus.). 80p. 1999. pap. 7.95 (*0-9650315-7-8*) Glacier Publng.

My Devotional Diary: The Teen Years. Jan Duda. 96p. 1992. pap. 5.99 (*0-570-03997-5*, 12-3025) Concordia.

My Diary. (Illus.). 208p. (J). (gr. k-1). 1988. 12.95 (*0-685-24081-9*) Childrens Reading Inst.

My Diary. Margaret O'Brien. (American Autobiography Ser.). 117p. 1995. reprint ed. lib. bdg. 69.00 (*0-7812-8602-6*) Rprt Serv.

My Diary North & South. Eugene H. Berwanger & William H. Russell. LC 94-48487. 384p. (C). 1987. pap. 22.19 (*0-07-554025-8*) McGraw.

My Diary Secrets. Freda Lindsay. 1976. per. 9.95 (*0-89985-021-9*) Christ for the Nations.

My Dinner with Andre. Wallace Shawn & Andre Gregory. LC 81-47639. 128p. 1988. pap. 8.95 (*0-8021-3063-1*, Grove) Grove-Atltic.

My Dinner with Andrew: A Novel. Martha Williamson. LC 98-19479. (Touched by an Angel Novel Ser.). 256p. 1998. mass mkt. 5.99 (*0-7852-7130-9*) Nelson.

***My Dinner with Auden.** Larry Woiwode. 2000. 25.00 (*0-465-09232-2*, Pub. by Basic); pap. 14.00 (*0-465-09233-0*, Pub. by Basic) HarpC.

My Dinosaur. Mark Alan Weatherby. LC 95-42020. (Illus.). 32p. (J). (ps-2). 1997. pap. 15.95 (*0-590-97203-0*) Scholastic Inc.

My Dinosaur. Mark Alan Weatherby. 1997. write for info. (*0-614-09434-8*, Scholastic Hardcover) Scholastic Inc.

My Dinosaur Sticker Album. Mel Greifinger. (Illus.). (J). (gr. k-3). 1994. pap. 1.00 (*0-486-28125-6*) Dover.

My Disciple, My Child: A Practical, Torah-Based Guide to Effective Discipline in the Classroom. Noach Orlowek. LC 93-46948. 1994. 18.95 (*0-87306-646-4*) Feldheim.

My Disillusionment in Russia. Emma Goldman. (American Biography Ser.). 263p. 1991. reprint ed. lib. bdg. 69.00 (*0-7812-8148-2*) Rprt Serv.

My Disney Princess Book: A Book for Keepsakes, Memories & Dreams. Illus. by Disney Studio Archives. 96p. (J). (gr. 3 up). 1998. 10.95 (*0-7868-3159-6*, Pub. by Disney Pr) Time Warner.

My Ditch see Moyayama: Russian Haiku: A Diary

My Divided Brain. W. R. Baker. LC 98-41210. 80p. 1999. pap. 11.00 (*1-56474-298-9*) Fithian Pr.

***My Divine Love.** LC 99-65935. (Illus.). 152p. 2000. pap. 15.00 (*0-912322-57-8*) Mark-Age.

My Divorce Workbook: Your Self-Empowerment Guide for Dealing with Professionals, Managing the Ex-Spouse, & Saving Money in Your Divorce. Godwin O. Igein. Ed. by Ruth L. Wilson. (Illus.). 160p. 1995. pap. 19.95 (*0-9646581-1-9*) Destiny Publns.

An Asterisk (*) at the beginning of an entry indicates that the title is appearing for the first time.

My DJ Book: Packed Full with Information for the General Public, the Music Industry, Club Owners - Managers, Beginning DJs, Professional Mobile DJs, Radio & Street DJs. John L. Jones. LC 89-91287. (Illus.). 179p. 1989. 19.98 (*0-9623147-0-6*) All Together.

My D'Nealian Handwriting Word Book. Donald N. Thurber. (Illus.). 64p. (Orig.). 1989. pap. 6.95 (*0-673-38477-2*, GoodYrBooks) Addson-Wesley Educ.

***My Do It!** Ros Asquith. LC 00-25737. (Toddlers Storybook Ser.). (Illus.). 24p. (ps-k). 2000. pap. write for info. (*0-7894-5648-6*, Pub. by DK Pub Inc) Pub Resources Inc.

My Doctor Does Hypnosis. Gary R. Elkins. LC 97-10739. (Illus.). (J). 1997. write for info. (*1-886610-03-7*) Am Soc Clin Hyp Pr.

My Doctor, My Friend. P. K. Hallinan. LC 95-37593. (Illus.). 24p. (Orig.). (J). (ps-3). 1996. pap. 4.95 (*1-57102-071-3*, Ideals Child) Hambleton-Hill.

My Doctor Says I Have a Little Diabetes: A Guide to Understanding & Controlling Type 2 Non-Insulin-Dependent Diabetes. Martha H. McCool & Sandra Woodruff. LC 98-51136. 144p. 1999. pap. 9.95 (*0-89529-860-0*, Avery) Penguin Putnam.

My Dodgers. Chuck McAnulla. (Illus.). 48p. (Orig.). 1995. pap. text 6.95 (*0-9649095-1-0*) C McAnulla.

My Dog. David Alderton. (Pet Photo Album Ser.). (Illus.). 24p. (J). (gr. 2-6). 1997. 15.95 (*0-7613-0239-5*) Millbrook Pr.

My Dog. Penny Nye. (Illus.). (J). (ps-5). 1999. pap. 12.00 (*1-890703-17-6*, Bkmates) Penny Laine.

My Dog. unabridged ed. Marilyn Baillie.Tr. of Mon Chien. (Illus.). 32p. (J). (gr. 2-6). 1993. 12.95 (*1-55074-127-6*, Pub. by Kids Can Pr); pap. 5.95 (*1-55074-208-6*, Pub. by Kids Can Pr) Genl Dist Srvs.

My Dog: A Book about a Special Pet see PowerKids Readers Set 1: My World

My Dog & His Bone, Vol. I. Vivian A. Phillips. (Illus.). 15p. (J). Date not set. pap. text. write for info. (*1-888413-03-4*) Seasoning Quilting.

My Dog & His Bone, Vol. II. Vivian A. Phillips. (Illus.). 14p. (J). Date not set. text. write for info. (*1-888413-07-7*) Seasoning Quilting.

My Dog & His Bone, Vol. III. Vivian A. Phillips. (Illus.). Date not set. pap. text. write for info. (*1-888413-11-5*) Seasoning Quilting.

My Dog Ate It. Saragail K. Benjamin. LC 93-25218. 176p. (J). (gr. 4-6). 1994. 14.95 (*0-8234-1047-1*) Holiday.

My Dog Ben. Cecily Matthews. LC 92-31946. (Voyages Ser.). (Illus.). (J). 1993. 3.75 (*0-383-03585-6*) SRA McGraw.

My Dog Can Fly. Leigh Tresder. 112p. (J). (gr. 4-6). 1995. pap. 2.99 (*0-590-22504-9*) Scholastic Inc.

My Dog Can Fly. Leigh Treseder. (J). 1995. 8.09 (*0-606-07905-X*, Pub. by Turtleback) Demco.

***My Dog, Cat.** Marty Crisp. (Illus.). 64p. (J). (gr. 2-5). 2000. 15.95 (*0-8234-1537-6*) Holiday.

***My Dog Clifford Plush Book.** Norman Bridwell. (Clifford, the Big Red Dog Ser.). (Illus.). 12p. (J). (ps-k). 2000. bds. 7.95 (*0-439-06046-X*, Cartwheel) Scholastic Inc.

My Dog Is an Elephant. Remy Simard. (Illus.). 32p. (J). (ps-3). 1994. pap. 6.95 (*1-55037-976-3*, Pub. by Annick); lib. bdg. 15.95 (*1-55037-977-1*, Pub. by Annick) Firefly Bks Ltd.

My Dog Is Jewish: Reudor's the Doodle Family. Reudor Staff. (Rhyme Time Doodles Ser.). (Illus.). 24p. (J). (gr. 1-12). 1998. 7.95 (*1-886611-03-3*) Atara Publ.

My Dog is Lost. Ezra Jack Keats. 32p. (J). (ps-3). 1999. pap. 5.99 (*0-14-056569-8*, PuffinBks) Peng Put Young Read.

***My Dog is Lost!** Ezra Jack Keats & Pat Cherr. LC 98-37755. (Illus.). 56p. (J). (ps-3). 1999. 15.99 (*0-670-88550-9*, Viking Child) Peng Put Young Read.

My Dog, Miffy. Claudette C. Mitchell et al. (Illus.). 8p. (Orig.). (J). (gr. k-1). 1996. pap. text 3.00 (*1-57518-054-5*) Arborlake.

My Dog Never Says Please. Suzanne Williams. LC 96-11950. (Illus.). 32p. (J). 1997. 15.99 (*0-8037-1679-6*, Dial Yng Read) Peng Put Young Read.

***My Dog Never Says Please.** Suzanne Williams. (Picture Puffin Ser.). (Illus.). 32p. (J). (ps-3). 2000. pap. 5.99 (*0-14-056725-9*, PuffinBks) Peng Put Young Read.

***My Dog Rosie.** Isabelle Harper & Barry Moser. (Illus.). 32p. (J). (ps-2). 1999. pap. 5.99 (*0-590-48634-9*) Scholastic Inc.

My Dog Skip. Willie Morris. 1996. 15.35 (*0-606-14278-9*) Turtleback.

My Dog Skip. Willie Morris. 144p. 1996. pap. 10.00 (*0-679-76722-3*) Vin Bks.

My Dog Skip. large type ed. Willie Morris. LC 98-8369. 122p. 1998. 21.95 (*1-57490-154-0*, Beeler LP Bks) T T Beeler.

My Dog Talks. Gail Herman. LC 94-38908. (Hello Reader! Ser.). (Illus.). 32p. (J). (ps-3). 1995. pap. 3.50 (*0-590-22196-5*, Cartwheel) Scholastic Inc.

My Dog Talks. Gail Herman. (Hello Reader! Level 1 Ser.). (J). 1995. 8.70 (*0-606-07906-8*, Pub. by Turtleback) Demco.

My Dog Toby. David Clemesha & Andrea Zimmerman. LC 98-35246. (Illus.). 32p. (J). 2000. 15.00 (*0-15-202014-4*) Harcourt.

My Dog Truffle. Lynn W. Reiser. LC 98-50913. (J). 2001. 9.95 (*0-688-16875-2*, Grenwillow Bks) HarpC Child Bks.

My Dog Tulip. J. R. Ackerley. LC 99-14568. 200p. 1999. reprint ed. pap. 12.95 (*0-940322-11-0*, Pub. by NY Rev Bks) Midpt Trade.

My Dog Was a Redneck, but We Got Him Fixed. Roger Pond. LC 96-72170. (Illus.). 176p. (Orig.). 1997. pap. 11.95 (*0-9617766-4-1*) Pine Forest Pub.

My Dog's a Democrat. Curt Brummett. (Illus.). 96p. reprint ed. pap. 6.95 (*1-879894-01-7*) Saratoga Pub.

My Dog's Book: The Who, What, When & Where of My Dog's Life - An Essential Book for All Dog Owners. S. K. Bollin. 32p. 1992. pap. 4.95 (*0-914846-62-0*) Golden West Pub.

My Dog's Brain. Stephen Huneck. LC 98-109799. 96p. 1997. 27.50 (*0-670-87736-0*) Viking Penguin.

My Dog's the Best. Stephanie Calmenson. LC 97-9726. (Hello Reader! Ser.). (Illus.). (J). (ps-1). 1997. 3.50 (*0-590-33072-1*) Scholastic Inc.

My Dog's the Best. Stephanie Calmenson. 1997. 9.44 (*0-606-11655-9*) Turtleback.

My Dog's the World's Best Dog. Suzy Becker. LC 95-34378. (Illus.). 96p. 1995. pap. 6.95 (*0-7611-0105-5*, 10105) Workman Pub.

My Doll see Set 5

My Doll House. Yes! Entertainment Corporation Staff. (Pop-Up Sound-Up Bks.). 2p. (J). (ps-2). 1993. write for info. (*1-883366-04-6*) YES Ent.

My Doll Is Missing! Elizabeth Anders. LC 96-76135. (Puzzle Place Ser.). (Illus.). 32p. (Orig.). (J). (ps-1). 1996. pap. 4.95 (*0-448-41313-2*, G & D) Peng Put Young Read.

My Doll, Keshia. Eloise Greenfield. (Illus.). 12p. (J). (ps-1). 1991. bds. 5.95 (*0-86316-203-7*) Writers & Readers.

***My Doll Organizer.** (Illus.). 1999. ring bd. 19.95 (*0-87588-556-X*) Hobby Hse.

***My Doll Organizer Fact Sheets Album.** Hobby House Press Staff. 128p. 2000. pap. 11.95 (*0-87588-572-1*) Hobby Hse.

My Dolly. Alana Willoughby. Ed. by Dan Wasserman. (Ten Word Book Ser.). (Illus.). (J). (gr. k-1). 1979. 9.95 (*0-89868-075-1*); pap. 3.95 (*0-89868-086-7*) ARO Pub.

My Doomsday Sampler. Sue Owen. LC 99-14900. 72p. 1999. pap. 12.95 (*0-8071-2403-6*); text 19.95 (*0-8071-2402-8*) La State U Pr.

My Double Life. Derek Adams. (Orig.). 1995. mass mkt. 5.95 (*1-56333-314-7*, Badboy) Masquerade.

My Double Life: Memoirs of a Naturalist. Frances Hamerstrom. LC 94-17999. (Illus.). 328p. 1994. pap. 18.95 (*0-299-14204-3*) U of Wis Pr.

My Double Life: The Memoirs of Sarah Bernhardt. Sarah Bernhardt. Tr. by Victoria Tietze Larson from FRE. LC 98-30036. (SUNY Series, Women Writers in Translation). 352p. (C). 1999. pap. text 24.95 (*0-7914-4054-0*) State U NY Pr.

My Double Life: The Memoirs of Sarah Bernhardt. Sarah Bernhardt. Tr. by Victoria Tietze Larson from FRE. LC 98-30036. (SUNY Series, Women Writers in Translation). 352p. (C). 1999. text 73.50 (*0-7914-4053-2*) State U NY Pr.

My Dream: American Edition. Brian Wildsmith. LC 97-173750. (Cat on the Mat Book). (Illus.). 16p. (J). (gr. k-6). 1997. pap. 4.25 (*0-19-849008-9*) OUP.

My Dream: Memoirs of a One-of-a-Kind Disciple. George E. Vandeman. LC 95-38961. 1995. pap. 2.97 (*0-8163-1305-9*) Pacific Pr Pub Assn.

***My Dream Has Red Fingers.** Stella V. Radulescu. LC 99-65225. 64p. 2000. pap. 9.95 (*1-58501-050-2*, Pub. by CeShore Pubg) Natl Bk Netwk.

My Dream Is You: A Collection of Poems on Love. Ed. by Susan Polis Schutz. LC 87-72258. (Illus.). 64p. (Orig.). 1987. pap. 7.95 (*0-88396-259-4*) Blue Mtn Art.

My Dream of Heaven. Rebecca R. Springer. 148p. 1993. pap. 10.00 (*0-9636435-1-7*) M A P.

My Dream of Martin Luther King. Faith Ringgold. (Illus.). 32p. (J). (ps-4). 1995. 18.00 (*0-517-59976-7*) Crown Pub Group.

My Dream of Martin Luther King. Faith Ringgold. (J). 1998. pap. 6.99 (*0-517-88577-8*) Crown Pub Group.

My Dream Slipped Away: Inside Football - Clemson University, NCAA, Other Colleges & the Cleveland Browns. Terry Minor. 47p. pap. write for info. (*1-882194-13-6*) TN Valley Pub.

My Dreams & Visions: An Autobiography. Ted Choy & Leona Choy. 255p. 1997. pap. 15.95 (*1-889283-09-6*) Golden Morning.

My Drowning. Jim Grimsley. (Reading Group Guides Ser.). 1997. pap. write for info. (*0-684-00605-7*, Touchstone) S&S Trade Pap.

My Drowning. Jim Grimsley. LC 97-34648. 272p. 1998. per. 11.00 (*0-684-84123-1*, Scribner Pap Fic) S&S Trade Pap.

My Drowning: A Novel. Jim Grimsley. LC 96-24630. 266p. 1997. 18.95 (*1-56512-141-4*) Algonquin Bks.

My Drum see First Step Science

***My Duck.** Tanya Linch. (Illus.). 32p. (J). (ps-2). 2000. 14.95 (*0-439-20670-7*) Scholastic Inc.

***My Ducks Love to Quack.** Catherine Rollin. 4p. 1998. pap. 2.50 (*0-7390-0731-9*, 18176) Alfred Pub.

My Duel with the Vatican: The Autobiography of a Catholic Modernist. Alfred F. Loisy. Tr. by Richard W. Boynton. LC 68-19290. 357p. 1968. reprint ed. lib. bdg. 65.00 (*0-8371-0148-4*, LODV, Greenwood Pr) Greenwood.

My Dysfunctional Life. Jennifer Worick & Kerry Tessaro. (Illus.). 96p. 1999. spiral bd. 10395.00 (*0-8118-2244-3*) Chronicle Bks.

My "e" Sound Box. Jane Belk Moncure. LC 84-17021. (Sound Box Library). (Illus.). 32p. (J). (ps-2). 1984. lib. bdg. 21.36 (*0-89565-297-8*) Childs World.

My Early Life. Charles Dickens. LC 98-215834. (Illus.). 224p. 1997. 24.95 (*1-85410-518-3*, Pub. by Aurum Pr) London Brdge.

My Early Life. William Second Ex-Emperor of Germany. LC 71-137306. (Illus.). reprint ed. 35.00 (*0-404-06947-9*) AMS Pr.

My Early Life: A Roving Commission. Winston L. S. Churchill. (Illus.). 384p. 1987. pap. 15.00 (*0-684-18803-1*, Scribners Ref) Mac Lib Ref.

My Early Life: A Roving Commission. Winston L. S. Churchill. (Illus.). 385p. 1989. reprint ed. 24.95 (*0-85052-257-9*, Pub. by Leo Cooper) Trans-Atl Phila.

My Early Life, 1874-1904. Winston L. S. Churchill. 400p. 1996. per. 14.00 (*0-684-82345-4*) S&S Trade Pap.

My Early Travels & Adventures in America. Henry Morton Stanley. LC 81-15941. (Illus.). 329p. reprint ed. pap. 102.00 (*0-7837-1836-5*, 204203700001) Bks Demand.

My Early Years. Adrienne Von Speyr. LC 94-73063. 427p. (Orig.). 1995. pap. 17.95 (*0-89870-541-X*) Ignatius Pr.

My Earthly Possessions. (Illus.). 32p. 1996. pap. 4.95 (*0-913515-08-6*, Elliott Clark) Black Belt Communs.

My Easter Book. (J). (ps-3). 1989. pap. 1.95 (*0-8167-0004-4*) Troll Communs.

My Easy to Read Fairy Tale. Illus. by Gill Guile. 96p. (J). (ps-3). 1996. 5.98 (*1-85854-515-3*) Brimax Bks.

My Economic Affair. Ashok V. Desai. (C). 1994. text 24.00 (*81-224-0582-7*) S Asia.

My Education: A Book of Dreams. William S. Burroughs. 208p. 1996. pap. 11.95 (*0-14-009454-7*, Penguin Bks) Viking Penguin.

My Ego. Mary K. Bryant. (Illus.). 64p. (Orig.). 1986. 6.95 (*0-934391-06-8*) Quotidian.

My Ego, Higher Self & I. Jerry Hirschfield. 281p. (Orig.). 1986. pap. 11.95 (*0-87418-014-7*, 151) Coleman Pub.

My Ego, My Higher Power, & I: A Transformational Journey from Ego to Higher Self Millennium Edition 1999. Jerry Hirschfield. LC 91-1309. (Illus.). 279p. 1987. reprint ed. pap. 14.95 (*0-9626597-0-3*) HI Prodns.

My Eight Book. Jane Belk Moncure. LC 85-30962. (My Number Bks.). (Illus.). 32p. (J). (ps-2). 1986. lib. bdg. 21.36 (*0-89565-319-2*) Childs World.

My Eighty Years in Texas. William P. Zuber. Ed. by Janis B. Mayfield. LC 73-161971. (Personal Narratives of the West Ser.). 303p. reprint ed. pap. 94.00 (*0-7837-2086-6*, 204236100004) Bks Demand.

My Elders. Charles Hodge. 80p. (Orig.). 1974. pap. 2.95 (*0-933672-24-1*, C-1435) Star Bible.

My Elders Taught Me: Aspects of Western Great Lakes American Indian Philosophy. John Boatman. 73p. (Orig.). (C). 1992. text 32.50 (*0-8191-8691-0*); pap. text 17.50 (*0-8191-8692-9*) U Pr of Amer.

My Eldest Son. Paula FitzGerald & Edward FitzGerald. (Son of Man Trilogy Ser.: Pt. 2). 175p. (Orig.). 1986. pap. 6.50 (*0-935915-01-X*) Corinth Pub.

My Elected Representatives Went to Washington. Tom Toles. (Illus.). 128p. 1993. pap. 8.95 (*0-8362-1716-0*) Andrews & McMeel.

My Elephant Can Do Almost Anything. Anke De Vries. LC 95-40267. (Illus.). 28p. (J). (gr. k-3). 1996. 14.95 (*1-886910-06-5*, Front Street) Front Str.

My Emerald Life & Other Poems. Elsie F. Gerald. 105p. (Orig.). 1983. pap. 10.00 (*0-9610096-0-8*) E F Gerald.

My Emily Dickinson. Susan Howe. 150p. 1988. 25.00 (*0-938190-53-9*); pap. 14.95 (*0-938190-52-0*) North Atlantic.

My Emperor's New Clothes: Musical. Larry Shue. 1985. pap. 7.00 (*0-8222-0799-0*) Dramatists Play.

My Encounters with the Light: Jesus & the Janitor. rev. ed. Myles D. Ferguson. LC 96-36183. 184p. 1999. pap. 12.95 (*1-880090-36-8*) Galde Pr.

My Enemy Is My Guest: Jesus & Violence in Luke. Josephine F. Ford. LC 84-5812. 192p. reprint ed. pap. 59.60 (*0-7837-5511-2*, 204528100005) Bks Demand.

My Enemy, My Ally. Diane Duane E. Ed. by Dave Stern. (Star Trek Ser.: No. 18). 320p. (Orig.). 1989. mass mkt. 5.50 (*0-671-70421-4*) PB.

My Enemy, My Brother: Men & Days of Gettysburg. Joseph E. Persico. LC 95-45864. (Illus.). 288p. 1996. reprint ed. pap. 16.00 (*0-306-80692-4*) Da Capo.

My Enemy, My Love. large type ed. Robert T. Stevens. Orig. Title: Appointment in Sarajevo. 512p. 1983. 27.99 (*0-7089-8136-4*, Charnwood) Ulverscroft.

***My Enemy, My Patient.** E. M. Morris. LC 00-91498. 2000. pap. 12.95 (*0-533-13584-2*) Vantage.

My Enemy's Enemy: Lebanon in the Early Zionist Imagination, 1900-1948. Laura Z. Eisenberg. LC 93-45499. (Illus.). 220p. 1994. text 29.95 (*0-8143-2424-X*) Wayne St U Pr.

My Escape: Shipwrecked. Judy Donnelly & Sydelle A. Kramer. Ed. by Ruth Ashby. LC 94-152967. 112p. (Orig.). (J). (gr. 4-7). 1994. pap. 2.99 (*0-671-67895-7*, Minstrel Bks) PB.

My Escape from the Auto de Fe. Don F. Del La Mina. (Illus.). 112p. 1997. pap. 9.95 (*0-9643914-2-2*) Shiloh Med.

My Escaping Self: Poems by Wilson Reid Ogg. Wilson R. Ogg. (Illus.). 250p. (Orig.). 1988. pap. 8.50 (*0-929707-03-6*) Pinebrook CA.

My Estate Planner: Information for My Family. Marion J. Caffey. 92p. (Orig.). 1990. pap. 9.95 (*0-9622993-9-1*) Sunshine Pubns.

My Estate Planning Record Book. Robert S. Hunter. (Klear-E-Lex Ser.). 210p. (Orig.). 1993. pap., student ed. 14.95 (*1-884177-02-6*) Justice IL.

My Eucharistic Day: Rules & Practices Recommended by St. Peter Julian Eymard. 84p. (Orig.). 1954. pap. 4.00 (*0-913382-20-5*, 107-1) Marytown Pr.

My European Heritage: Life among Great Men of Letters. Brigitte B. Fischer. Tr. by Harry Zhon from GER. (Illus.). 324p. 1986. 25.95 (*0-8283-1897-2*) Branden Bks.

My Ever Dear Daughter, My Own Dear Mother: The Correspondence of Julia Stone Towne & Mary Julia Towne, 1868-1882. Ed. by Katherine R. Morgan. LC 96-24991. (Illus.). 328p. 1996. pap. 16.95 (*0-87745-564-3*); text 32.95 (*0-87745-563-5*) U of Iowa Pr.

My Every Christmas Wish. Barbara J. Damon. (Illus.). (J). (gr. 3-6). 1997. 7.95 (*0-533-11102-1*) Vantage.

My Everyday Book, Vol. 6. Stan Berenstain & Jan Berenstain. 7p. 2000. pap. 4.99 (*0-679-89337-7*) Random.

My Everyday Spanish Word Book. Michele Kahn. (SPA & ENG., Illus.). 46p. (J). (gr. 3-9). 1982. 10.95 (*0-8120-5429-6*) Barron.

My Evil Twin. Thomas Mckean. 160p. 1998. pap. 3.99 (*0-380-79082-3*, Avon Bks) Morrow Avon.

My Ex-Best Friend. Erika Tamar et al. (Party of Five Ser.: No. 8). (J). (gr. 7-12). 1966. pap. 12.50 (*0-671-01895-7*, Minstrel Bks) PB.

My Expanding World: Second Grade Student Book see Philosophy for Young Thinkers Program

My Experience with Clinical Depression. rev. ed. Gerald F. Mundfrom. Orig. Title: Purged. (Illus.). 191p. 1990. reprint ed. pap. 7.50 (*0-9615494-1-6*) Mercy & Truth.

My Experience with Depression: And How I Overcame It. 150p. 16.00 (*0-9624825-3-6*) Achivmnt USA.

My Experience with Gear Tooth Forms. A. A. Ross. (Technical Papers: Vol. P207). (Illus.). 18p. 1940. pap. text 30.00 (*1-55589-451-8*) AGMA.

My Experience with Living Food. Kristine Nolfi. 23p. 1994. reprint ed. spiral bd. 10.00 (*0-7873-1034-4*) Hlth Research.

My Experiences in Astrology. Bangalore V. Raman. (BVR Astrology Ser.). (C). 1992. 6.00 (*81-85273-73-1*, Pub. by UBS Pubs Dist) S Asia.

My Experiences in Service: or A Nine Months Man. James F. Dargan. Ed. by Norman E. Tanis & Jack Matcha. (American Classics Facsimile Ser.: Pt. I). 416p. 1974. pap. 10.00 (*0-937048-00-3*) Santa Susana.

My Experiences in the First World War. John J. Pershing. (Illus.). 868p. 1995. reprint ed. pap. 19.95 (*0-306-80616-9*) Da Capo.

My Experiences in the First World War. John J. Pershing. (Military Classics Ser.: Vol. 2). 472p. 1989. reprint ed. 24.95 (*0-8306-9407-2*) McGraw-Hill Prof.

***My Experiences in War & Business: One Man's Story of Success in America.** Otis E. Hawkins. LC 99-91063. 317p. 1999. 24.95 (*1-878802-21-6*); pap. 12.95 (*1-878802-22-4*) J M Ashbrook Ctr Pub Affairs.

My Exploding World. Louise F. Underhill. (Illus.). 59p. 1983. pap. 5.00 (*0-9616734-4-3*) Underhill Ent.

***My Eyes.** Kathy Furgang. LC 99-45245. (My Body Ser.). (Illus.). (J). 2000. write for info. (*0-8239-5573-7*) Rosen Group.

My Eyes Have a Cold Nose: American Autobiography. Hector Chevigny. 273p. 1995. lib. bdg. 79.00 (*0-7812-8478-3*) Rprt Serv.

My "f" Sound Box. Jane Belk Moncure. LC 77-9377. (Sound Box Library). (Illus.). 32p. (J). (ps-2). 1977. lib. bdg. 21.36 (*0-913778-93-1*) Childs World.

My Fables Book. rev. ed. Donna R. Fisher. (Bee Sees Ser.). 73p. (J). (gr. 1). 1996. reprint ed. pap. text 5.00 (*0-913717-04-5*, 2328) Hewitt Res Fnd.

My Fabulous New Life. Sheila Greenwald. LC 92-44928. (Illus.). 128p. (J). (gr. 3-7). 1993. 10.95 (*0-15-277693-1*, Harcourt Child Bks); pap. 3.95 (*0-15-276716-9*, Harcourt Child Bks) Harcourt.

My Face see Kegginaqa

My Face. Marcia Abbott. Ed. by Barbara Abbott. (Illus.). 44p. (J). (gr. 1-5). 1998. 12.50 (*0-9666097-0-0*) Forward Face.

***My Face.** large type ed. Karen Paul. (Illus.). 8p. (J). (gr. k-3). 2000. pap. text 6.00 (*1-58084-197-X*) Lower Kuskokwim.

My Face among Strangers. Seymour Shubin. 239p. 1999. 23.95 (*1-885173-57-1*) Write Way.

***My Face (Cup'ik)** large type ed. Karen Paul. (Illus.). 8p. (J). (gr. k-3). 2000. pap. text 6.00 (*1-58084-199-6*) Lower Kuskokwim.

My Face for the World to See: The Diaries of Candy Darling. Ed. by Jeremiah Newton & Francesca Passalacqua. 1997. 29.95 (*0-614-28045-1*) DAP Assocs.

My Face for the World to See: The Diaries of Candy Darling. Ed. by Jeremiah Newton & Francesca Passalacque. 1997. 29.95 (*0-945367-21-X*) Hardy Marks Pubns.

My Face to the Rising Sun. Dorothy L. Smith. 110p. Date not set. 16.95 (*1-928762-04-2*) Grio Pr.

My Fading Full Moon: A Husband's Journal. Boen Hallum. LC 84-61706. 200p. 1984. 14.00 (*0-9608854-3-9*) B Hallum.

My Fair Gentleman. Jan Freed. (Superromance Ser.). 1996. per. 3.99 (*0-373-70713-4*, 1-70713-2) Harlequin Bks.

My Fair Lady. Garebia. 1998. 12.95 (*0-88962-653-7*) Mosaic.

My Fair Lady. Louis Hemon. Tr. by William A. Bradley. LC 72-10773. (Short Story Index Reprint Ser.). 1977. reprint ed. 21.95 (*0-8369-4219-1*) Ayer.

My Fair Lady, Vol. 77. Lerner & Loewe. (EZ Play Today Ser.: Series B). 24p. 1981. pap. 5.95 (*0-7935-2651-5*, 00100489) H Leonard.

My Fair Lady: Easy Piano. 16p. 1956. pap. 7.95 (*0-7692-1123-2*, 00301700) Wrner Bros.

My Fair Lady: Vocal Score. Ed. by Michael Lefferts. (Vocal Score Ser.). 256p. (Orig.). (C). 1981. per. 45.00 (*0-88188-036-1*, 00312266) H Leonard.

***My Fair Lady Vet.** Jeanette Sparks. LC 99-91305. 192p. 2000. 18.95 (*0-8034-9392-4*, Avalon Bks) Bouregy.

***My Fair Lord.** Julie Beard. 352p. 2000. mass mkt. 6.99 (*0-425-17481-6*) Berkley Pub.

***My Fairy Tale Princess Activity Kit.** Kay Barnham. LC 98-182863. (Illus.). 24p. (J). (ps-3). 1998. 9.98 (*0-7651-0702-3*) Smithmark.

My Faith. Bernard Leach. (Illus.). 1966. pap. 40.00 (*0-685-45124-0*) R S Barnes.

My Faith Is Taking Me Someplace. Andrew Merritt. LC 97-65689. 1997. pap. 11.99 (*0-88419-458-2*) Creation House.

My Faith Journal. Karen Hill. 1999. 9.99 (*0-8499-5964-0*); 9.99 (*0-8499-5965-9*) Tommy Nelson.

My Faith Journal (Fish) Karen Hill. (Illus.). 96p. (J). (gr. 1-7). 1997. 9.99 (*0-8499-1453-1*) Tommy Nelson.

M

My Faith Journal (Flowers) Karen Hill. (Illus.). 96p. (J). (gr. 1-7). 1997. 9.99 (*0-8499-1506-6*) Tommy Nelson.

***My Faith Journal for Leaders-Fall 2000: FW Friends.** Group Publishing Inc. Staff. 2000. pap. 5.99 (*0-7644-1051-2*) Group Pub.

***My Faith Journal I-Fall 2000: FW Friends-Lower Elementary.** Group Publishing Inc. Staff. 2000. pap. 4.99 (*0-7644-1049-0*) Group Pub.

***My Faith Journal II-Fall 2000: FW Friends-Upper Elementary.** Group Publishing Inc. Staff. 2000. pap. 4.99 (*0-7644-1050-4*) Group Pub.

My Faith Still Holds: A Worship Celebration for Easter Arranged by Mosie Lister. 1993. 5.99 (*0-8341-9003-6*, ME-43) Lillenas.

My Faithful Goodwin. Prevrajikc Urajaprana. 116p. 1994. pap. text 1.95 (*81-85301-25-5*, Pub. by Advaita Ashrama) Vedanta Pr.

My Fake Eye: The Story of My Prosthesis. Nancy Chernus-Mansfield & Marilyn Horn. LC 91-73190. 24p. (J). (ps-9). 1991. pap. write for info. (*0-9630118-0-4*) Inst Fam Blind Child.

My Fall Journal. Alana Trisler & Patrice Cardiel. 72p. (J). (gr. 2-3). 1999. pap., wbk. ed. 2.00 (*1-56762-104-X*) Modern Learn Pr.

***My Fallen Angel.** Pamela Britton. 352p. 2000. mass mkt. 5.99 (*0-06-101431-1*) HarpC.

My False Heart. Liz Carlyle. 1999. per. 6.50 (*0-671-04054-5*) S&S Trade.

My False Impressions. Christina Ekengren-Hawkins. LC 97-32631. 1997. 15.00 (*1-889833-02-9*) Memoirs Unltd.

My False Teeth Fit Fine but I Sure Miss My Mind. (Illus.). 128p. (Orig.). 1996. pap. 8.95 (*1-889116-07-6*) Penbrooke Pub.

My Family. (Little Lessons Ser.). Date not set. 3.95 (*0-88271-555-0*, 10335) Regina Pr.

***My Family.** Sanduik Bokforlag. (Illus.). 11p. 1998. bds. 5.99 (*1-58048-013-6*) Sandvik Pub.

***My Family.** Miriam Dickman. 1999. pap. write for info. (*1-58235-018-3*) Watermrk Pr.

***My Family.** Penny Nye. (Bookmates Ser.). (Illus.). 15p. (J). (ps). 2000. pap. 12.00 (*1-890703-18-4*, Bkmates) Penny Laine.

My Family, No. 11. Debbie Bailey. (Talk-about-Books Ser.: Vol. 11). (Illus.). 14p. (J). (ps). 1998. bds. 5.95 (*1-55037-510-5*, Pub. by Annick) Firefly Bks Ltd.

My Family: Journal. Raquel Benatar. (Illus.). 24p. (YA). (gr. 3 up). 1997. pap., wbk. ed. 6.95 (*1-56492-179-4*) Laredo.

***My Family: Past, Present & Future.** 2nd ed. Scott Williams. 114p. (C). 1999. per. 18.95 (*0-7872-6402-4*, 41640201) Kendall-Hunt.

My Family . . . Remembered. Florence M. Hayes. LC 87-91705. (Illus.). 214p. 1987. 59.95 (*0-9619646-0-X*); pap. 49.95 (*0-9619646-1-8*) F M S Hayes.

***My Family & Friends.** 2000. student ed. write for info. (*0-13-019759-9*) P-H.

My Family & Friends. Gretchen D. Van Kleef. wbk. ed. 4.95 (*0-89486-978-7*, 5557 B) Hazelden.

My Family & Me. Barbara M. Wolff. (Illus.). 16p. (J). (ps-1). 1993. lib. bdg. 13.95 (*0-685-59697-4*, Valeria Bks) Wonder Well.

My Family & Other Animals. Gerald Durrell. 1983. 22.50 (*0-8446-6073-6*) Peter Smith.

My Family & Other Animals. Gerald Durrell. 1959. pap. 12.99 (*0-14-001399-7*, Penguin Bks) Viking Penguin.

***My Family & Other Animals.** Gerald Durrell. LC 99-46458. (Penguin Nature Classics Ser.). 288p. (J). 2000. pap. 12.95 (*0-14-028902-X*, Penguin Bks) Viking Penguin.

My Family & the Constitution. 1956. reprint ed. pap. write for info. (*0-614-28381-7*) B R Landes.

My Family Helps. Melissa Becker. Ed. by Karen Gross. (Illus.). 24p. (J). (ps-1). 1993. pap. text 4.95 (*1-56309-080-5*, N938102, New Hope) Womans Mission Union.

My Family Heritage. Carriage House Staff. 1993. 19.95 (*0-89786-144-2*); 19.95 (*0-89786-145-0*); 19.95 (*0-89786-146-9*); 19.95 (*0-89786-147-7*) CHP Ltd Redding.

My Family Heritage: Adult Personal History Starter Kit. Duane S. Crowther. LC 78-52120. 52p. 1981. pap. 9.98 (*0-88290-087-0*) Horizon Utah.

My Family History. Nancy Burgeson. LC 92-3086. (Family Guide Ser.). (Illus.). 32p. (J). (gr. 4-7). 1997. pap. 1.95 (*0-8167-2794-5*) Troll Communs.

My Family Is Living with Cancer: Helps Children Understand the Changes That Occur in Families When One Member Becomes Seriously Ill. Sandra P. Hazouri & Miriam S. McLaughlin. LC 95-75124. (Illus.). 24p. (Orig.). (J). (ps-6). 1994. pap. 8.95 (*1-884063-51-9*) Mar Co Prods.

My Family Is Living with Cancer Workbook: Ten Activities Give Children the Opportunity for Personal Expression & Interaction with Others. Sandra P. Hazouri & Miriam S. McLaughlin. (Illus.). 24p. (Orig.). (J). (ps-6). 1994. pap. 6.95 (*1-884063-52-7*) Mar Co Prods.

My Family Lariviere-Morin. Susan Salisbury. 401p. 1998. pap. 30.00 (*0-7884-0935-2*, S044) Heritage Bk.

My Family Plays & Prays. Kendra Thomason. Ed. by Karen Gross. (Illus.). 32p. (J). (ps-k). 1992. pap. text 4.95 (*1-56309-050-3*, N928105, New Hope) Womans Mission Union.

My Family Plays Music. Judy Cox. LC 96-35009. (Illus.). (J). 2001. lib. bdg. write for info. (*0-8234-1285-7*) Holiday.

My Family Says Please & Thank You. Kendra Thomason. (Illus.). 24p. (J). (ps-k). 1996. pap. text 4.95 (*1-56309-178-X*, N968102, New Hope) Womans Mission Union.

My Family Secrets. Robert Rosdhal. (Illus.). 272p. 1998. pap. write for info. (*1-57579-108-0*) Pine Hill Pr.

My Family Seder. Norma Simon. (Festival Series of Picture Storybooks). (Illus.). (J). (ps). 1961. spiral bd. 4.50 (*0-8381-0710-9*, 10-710) USCJE.

My Family Story. 4th ed. Herbert Goldenberg. (Counseling Ser.). 148p. 1995. pap., wbk. ed. 19.50 (*0-534-33917-4*) Brooks-Cole.

My Family Story: Told & Examined. 5th ed. Goldenberg. (Counseling Ser.). 1999. pap. 22.50 (*0-534-36651-1*) Brooks-Cole.

My Family Tells This Story. Snow Flower. (Illus.). 156p. 1999. pap. 19.00 (*0-7884-1136-5*, S558) Heritage Bk.

My Family, the Jewish Immigrants: The Jewish Immigrants. Norman Beim. LC 97-19410. (Illus.). 400p. 1997. pap. 18.95 (*0-931231-08-6*) Newconcept Pr.

My Family Tree: A Bird's Eye View. Nina Laden. LC 96-9633. (Illus.). 32p. (J). 1997. pap. 9.95 (*0-8118-1528-5*) Chronicle Bks.

My Family Tree Workbook: Genealogy for Beginners. Rosemary A. Chorzempa. (Illus.). 64p. (J). (gr. 5 up). 1982. pap. 2.95 (*0-486-24229-3*) Dover.

My Family Vacation. Dayal K. Khalsa. (Illus.). 24p. (J). (gr. 1-3). 1988. 16.95 (*0-88776-226-3*) Tundra Bks.

***My Family's Best.** Bob Bowersox. (In the Kitchen with Bob Ser.: Vol. 1). (Illus.). 128p. 1999. 24.00 (*1-928998-00-3*) Q V C Pubg.

My Family's Changing: A First Look at Family Break-Up. Pat Thomas. LC 98-73952. (Illus.). 32p. (J). (ps-3). 1999. pap. 5.95 (*0-7641-0995-2*) Barron.

My Family's Role in the World Revolution & Other Prose. Bora Cosic. Tr. by Ann C. Bigelow. LC 97-15118. 1997. pap. text 16.95 (*0-8101-1368-6*) Northwestern U Pr.

My Family's Role in the World Revolution & Other Prose. Bora Cosic. Tr. by Ann C. Bigelow. LC 97-15118. (Writings from an Unbound Europe Ser.). 1997. 49.95 (*0-8101-1367-8*) Northwestern U Pr.

My Fantastic Feet! Toes Press Piggy Staff. 12p. (J). (gr. k). 1999. pap. text 6.95 (*1-58117-046-7*, Piggy Toes Pr) Intervisual Bks.

***My Fantastic Voyage.** Melvin Branker. 1999. pap. write for info. (*1-58235-102-3*) Watermrk Pr.

My Fantasy Dream Date With... H. B. Gilmour. 128p. (J). (gr. 4-7). 1999. pap. 4.99 (*0-590-40894-1*) Scholastic Inc.

My Fare, Lady. St. Ann's Altar Society Staff. Ed. by Nell Partin. (Illus.). 148p. 1989. reprint ed. pap. text 8.95 (*0-9622871-0-5*) Frog Inc Pub.

My Farm. Alison Lester. LC 93-30894. (Illus.). 32p. (J). 1994. 14.95 (*0-395-68193-6*) HM.

My Farm. Alison Lester. (Illus.). 32p. (J). (ps-3). 1999. pap. 5.95 (*0-395-97721-5*, W Lorraine) HM.

My Farm of Edgewood. Donald G. Mitchell. (Notable American Authors Ser.). 1999. reprint ed. lib. bdg. 125.00 (*0-7812-4564-8*) Rprt Serv.

My Father. Judy Collins. (Illus.). 32p. (J). (gr. k-3). 1997. pap. 4.95 (*0-316-15238-2*) Little.

My Father. Judy Collins. 1997. 10.15 (*0-606-13630-4*, Pub. by Turtleback) Demco.

My Father Always Embarrasses Me. Meir Shalev. Ed. by Zanvel Klein. Tr. by Dagmar Herrmann from HEB. LC 89-27709. (Illus.). 30p. (J). (gr. k-3). 1990. 12.95 (*0-922984-02-6*) Wellington IL.

My Father & I: How the Bible Teaches Fatherhood. Judson Cornwall. 1998. pap. 10.99 (*1-884369-78-2*) McDougal Pubng.

***My Father & Me.** unabridged ed. Jane Drake & Ann Love. (Memory Scrapbook for Kids Ser.). (Illus.). 32p. (J). (gr. k up). 2000. pap. 5.95 (*1-55074-637-5*, Pub. by Kids Can Pr) Genl Dist Srvs.

***My Father & Mother on Earth & in Heaven.** Sister Mary Alphonsine. (Our Holy Faith Ser.: Vol. I). (Illus.). 96p. (J). (gr. 1-2). 1998. 15.00 (*0-911845-77-1*) Neumann Pr.

My Father & Myself. J. R. Ackerley. LC 75-6884. (Illus.). 219p. 1975. reprint ed. pap. 3.95 (*0-15-662325-0*, Harvest Bks) Harcourt.

My Father & Myself. J. R. Ackerley. LC 99-14566. 280p. 1999. reprint ed. pap. 12.95 (*0-940322-12-9*, Pub. by NY Rev Bks) Midpt Trade.

My Father As I Recall Him. M. Dickens. LC 73-21523. (Studies in Dickens: No. 52). 1974. lib. bdg. 75.00 (*0-8383-1814-7*) M S G Haskell Hse.

My Father Becomes the Wind. R. D. Drexler. (CRP Chapbook Ser.: No. 1). (Illus.). 32p. (Orig.). 1995. pap. 4.00 (*0-9636959-1-6*) Coe Review Pr.

My Father, Bertrand Russell. Katharine Tait. 224p. 1996. pap. 14.95 (*1-85506-390-5*) Bks Intl VA.

My Father Bleeds History: A Survivor's Tale, Vol. 1. Art Spiegelman. LC 86-42642. (Maus Ser.). (Illus.). 159p. 1986. pap. 14.00 (*0-394-74723-2*) Pantheon.

***My Father, Dancing.** Bliss Broyard. LC 00-35066. (Harvest Bks.). 208p. 2000. pap. text 13.00 (*0-15-601396-7*) Harcourt.

My Father, Dancing. Bliss Broyard. LC 99-31090. 224p. 1999. 22.00 (*0-375-40060-5*) Knopf.

My Father, Daniel Boone: The Draper Interviews with Nathan Boone. Ed. by Neal O. Hammon. LC 99-19263. (Illus.). 192p. 1999. 22.00 (*0-8131-2103-5*) U Pr of Ky.

My Father, Edward Branstein: His Life & Letters. Frances Rothman. (Illus.). 109p. 1983. pap. 5.00 (*0-943376-18-1*) Magnes Mus.

My Father Forgets. Lynn McAndrews. LC 90-91658. 110p. (Orig.). 1991. pap. 8.95 (*0-9626683-0-3*) Nrthrn Expressions.

My Father, Frank Lloyd Wright. John L. Wright. Orig. Title: My Father Who Is on Earth. (Illus.). 192p. 1992. reprint ed. pap. 6.95 (*0-486-26986-8*) Dover.

***My Father Gave Me Scarsdale: A Memoir, 1933-1950.** Mary Greenlee. LC 99-96889. 2000. 13.95 (*0-533-13361-0*) Vantage.

My Father, His Son. Reidar Jonsson. 256p. 1993. pap. 9.70 (*1-55970-201-X*, Pub. by Arcade Pub Inc) Time Warner.

My Father I Trust You. M. Basilea Schlink. 1976. pap. 1.25 (*3-87209-617-6*) Evang Sisterhood Mary.

My Father Immortal. Michael D. Weaver. 240p. 1991. mass mkt. 3.99 (*0-380-70863-9*, Avon Bks) Morrow Avon.

My Father-in-Law: Memories of Karl Barth. Max Zellweger-Barth. Tr. by Martin Rumscheidt from GER. LC 86-2411. (Princeton Theological Monographs: No. 5).Tr. of Mein Schwiegervater. (Orig.). 1986. pap. 6.00 (*0-915138-84-0*) Pickwick.

My Father in the Night. Terence Clarke. LC 90-49561. 304p. 1991. 19.95 (*0-916515-93-1*) Mercury Hse Inc.

My Father, Marconi. 2nd rev. ed. Degna Marconi. (Prose Ser.: No. 40). 282p. (YA). 1996. reprint ed. pap. 13.00 (*1-55071-044-3*) Guernica Editions.

My Father, Mark Twain. Clara Clemens. LC 74-6024. (BCL Ser.: No. I). (Illus.). reprint ed. 45.00 (*0-404-11544-6*) AMS Pr.

My Father More or Less. Jonathan Baumbach. LC 81-71644. 152p. 1982. 15.95 (*0-914590-66-9*); pap. 6.95 (*0-914590-67-7*) Fiction Coll.

My Father My Hero: Becoming Your Child's Best Friend. Terry Olsen. LC 95-200756. 191p. (Orig.). 1995. pap. 9.95 (*1-883893-13-5*) WinePress Pub.

My Father, My King. Pliskin. 19.99 (*0-89906-315-2*, MYFH); pap. 16.99 (*0-89906-316-0*, MYFP) Mesorah Pubns.

***My Father, My Rebbe: The Life & Times of Rabbi Benzion Rakow, Zt "l.** Chani Zahn. 380p. 1998. 14.95 (*1-56871-120-4*) Feldheim.

My Father My Self: A Son's Memoir of His Father, Rabbi Yehudah D. Goldman, America's Oldest Practicing Rabbi. Alex J. Goldman. LC 97-69562. (Doris Minsky Memorial Fund Publications: No. 4). (Illus.). x, 109p. 1997. pap. 3.00 (*1-884703-02-X*) Chi Jewish Hist.

My Father, My Self: Understanding Dad's Influence on Your Life, a Guide to Reconciliation & Healing for Sons & Daughters. Masa A. Goetz. 224p. 1998. 21.95 (*1-86204-348-5*, Pub. by Element MA) Penguin Putnam.

My Father, My Self: Understanding How Dad Influenced Your Life: A Guide to Reconciliation & Healing for Sons & Daughters. Masa A. Goetz. LC 98-11276. 1998. 21.95 (*1-86204-341-8*) Element MA.

My Father, My Sons & Me in Between. LC 98-101535. 104p. 1997. pap. 9.95 (*0-9660779-0-3*) Radnor Pr.

My Father, My Teacher: A Spiritual Journey. Nichiko Niwano. Tr. by Richard L. Gage from JPN. 144p. (Orig.). 1982. pap. 5.95 (*4-333-01095-0*, Pub. by Kosei Pub Co) Tuttle Pubng.

My Father Owns This Place. Gary Swanson. (Orig.). (YA). (gr. 8-11). 1997. pap. 8.99 (*0-8280-1252-0*) Review & Herald.

My Father Owns This Place: Devotional Stories for Teens about Getting along in God's World. Gary B. Swanson. LC 97-28974. (J). 1997. write for info. (*0-08-201252-0*, Pergamon Pr) Elsevier.

My Father Paul Gauguin. Pola Gauguin & Pola Gauguin. LC 87-80029. (Illus.). xv, 292p. 1988. reprint ed. lib. bdg. 40.00 (*0-87817-315-3*) Hacker.

My Father, Sholom Aleichem. Marie Waife-Goldberg. LC 78-370959. 333 p. 1968. write for info. (*0-575-00166-6*) V Gollancz.

My Father Spoke French: Nationalism & Legitimacy in Alsace, 1871-1914. Bonnie M. Kahn. LC 90-45126. (Harvard Studies in Sociology: Vol. 8). 208p. 1990. text 20.00 (*0-8240-9828-5*) Garland.

***My father Taught Me How to Cry, but Now I Have Forgotten: Semantics of Religious Concepts with an Emphasis on Meaning, Interpretation & Translatability.** Kjell Magne Yri. (Acta Humaniora). 220p. 1998. pap. 28.00 (*82-00-12853-9*) Scandnvan Univ Pr.

My Father, the Chef. Illus. by Dorothy Louis. 148p. (Orig.). 1978. pap. 15.00 (*0-9609624-0-9*) Bookworm Rochester NY.

My Father the Czar. deluxe ed. Author22 Publishing Staff. LC 98-96138. 510p. 1999. pap. 22.95 (*1-892183-00-5*) DTTN.

My Father the Horse Thief. Jerry Jerman. (Journeys of Jessie Land Ser.). 132p. (Orig.). (J). (gr. 3-8). 1995. pap. 5.99 (*1-56476-347-1*, 6-3347, Victor Bks) Chariot Victor.

My Father the Spirit-Priest: Religion & Social Organization in the Amaa Tribe (Southwestern Sudan) Ayyoub-Awaga Bushara Gafour. LC 87-31491. (African Studies: Vol. 4). 150p. 1988. lib. bdg. 69.95 (*0-88946-178-3*) E Mellen.

My Father Took a Cake to France. Cynthia Flood. LC 92-91271. 184p. (Orig.). 1992. pap. 13.95 (*0-88922-310-6*, Pub. by Talonbks) Genl Dist Srvs.

My Father Took Me to the Circus: Religious Life from Within. Prue Wilson. 144p. 1985. pap. 5.95 (*0-87193-218-0*) Dimension Bks.

My Father, Uncle Miltie. William Berle & Brad Lewis. 1999. 22.00 (*1-56980-149-5*) Barricade Bks.

My Father Was a Toltec & Selected Poems. Ana Castillo. 192p. 1996. pap. 12.00 (*0-393-31354-9*) Norton.

My Father Was Born on Trafalgar Street: An American Finds His Way Home to England. unabridged ed. Harvey L. Gotliffe. (Incredible Odyssey Ser.). (Illus.). 36p. (Orig.). 1997. pap. 4.50 (*1-882302-98-2*) Cogitator Pubns.

My Father Was Shiva: A Family Tragedy in Prose & Poetry. Jim Flosdorf. LC 93-38755. 192p. 1994. pap. 39.50 (*1-56750-062-5*); text 73.25 (*0-89391-972-1*) Ablx Pub.

My Father Who Is on Earth see My Father, Frank Lloyd Wright

My Father Who Is on Earth: Including Comments, Responses, & Documents by Frank Lloyd Wright & John Lloyd Wright. 2nd rev. ed. John L. Wright. Ed. & Intro. by Narcisco G. Menocal. LC 92-1316. (Illus.). 256p. (C). 1994. 26.95 (*0-8093-1749-4*) S Ill U Pr.

My Father with the Sweet Name see My Lord, You Are Magic

My Father's Angels. Gloria Gaither. LC 99-10194. 32p. (J). (ps-3). 1999. 14.99 incl. audio (*0-310-23104-3*) Zondervan.

My Father's Assassins. Ibrahima K. Diallo. 1997. pap. 10.95 (*0-533-12369-0*) Vantage.

My Father's Bitter Gift. Dorothy E. Watts. LC 88-28137. 95p. reprint ed. pap. 30.00 (*0-7837-6400-6*, 204611600010) Bks Demand.

My Father's Boat. Sherry Garland. LC 97-19021. (Illus.). 32p. (J). (gr. k-3). 1998. 15.95 (*0-590-47867-2*) Scholastic Inc.

My Father's Business. English Bradshaw. LC 95-61464. 260p. (Orig.). 1996. pap. 12.95 (*1-887798-03-X*) WriteMore Pubns.

***My Father's Daughter.** 480p. 2000. 25.50 (*0-7432-0433-6*) S&S Trade.

***My Father's Daughter: A Memoir.** Tina Sinatra & Jeff Coplon. (Illus.). 320p. 2000. 25.50 (*0-684-87076-2*) S&S Trade.

My Father's Daughter: Continuing the Dream. Victoria W. Darrah. (Illus.). 209p. (Orig.). 1994. pap. text 11.95 (*0-9644039-0-0*) Servant Warriors.

My Father's Dragon. Ruth S. Gannett. LC 86-27635. (Borzoi Sprinters Ser.). (Illus.). 96p. (J). (gr. 2-5). 1987. pap. 4.99 (*0-394-89048-5*, Pub. by Knopf Bks Yng Read) Random.

My Fathers Dragon. Ruth S. Gannett. 1987. 9.84 (*0-606-02929-X*, Pub. by Turtleback) Demco.

My Father's Dragon. Ruth Stiles Gannett. 87p. (J). (gr. 1-3). pap. 4.99 (*0-8072-1286-5*) Listening Lib.

My Father's Dragon. Ruth S. Gannett. 88p. 1990. reprint ed. lib. bdg. 29.95 (*0-89966-701-5*) Buccaneer Bks.

My Father's Dragon: 50th Anniversary Edition. anniversary ed. Ruth S. Gannett. LC 97-25215. (J). 1997. lib. bdg. 17.99 (*0-679-98911-0*, Pub. by Random Bks Yng Read) Random.

My Father's Face: Entrusting Our Lives to a God Who Loves Us. James Robison. LC 97-6733. 224p. 1997. 18.99 (*1-57673-030-1*, Multnomah Bks) Multnomah Pubs.

My Father's Geisha. James G. Bennett. Ed. by Jane Rosenman. 176p. 1991. reprint ed. pap. 8.00 (*0-671-74000-8*, WSP) PB.

My Father's Glory & My Mother's Castle: Marcel Pagnol's Memories of Childhood. Marcel Pagnol. Tr. by Rita Barisse. LC 86-60989. 342p. 1986. pap. 13.00 (*0-86547-257-2*) N Point Pr.

My Father's God: A Novel. Lynn N. Austin. LC 97-13729. (Chronicles of the Kings Ser.). 284p. 1997. pap. 12.99 (*0-8341-1675-8*) Beacon Hill.

My Father's Greatest Gift: A Father & Son Share an Extraordinary Journey. Stephen J. Balkun. 110p. 1995. pap. 12.95 (*0-9649184-0-4*) Lionbird Pr.

***My Father's Gun: One Family, Three Badges: One Hundred Years in the NYPD.** Brian McDonald. LC 98-51156. 312p. 2000. pap. 12.95 (*0-452-27924-0*, Plume) Dutton Plume.

***My Father's Guru: A Journey Through Spirituality & Disillusion.** Jeffrey Moussaieff Masson. 192p. 1998. pap. 14.00 (*0-671-02573-2*) PB.

My Father's Hands. Terry Marshall. (Northway Ser.). vi, 193p. 1992. 19.95 (*0-89672-274-0*) Tex Tech Univ Pr.

My Father's Hands. Joanne Ryder. LC 93-27116. (Illus.). 32p. (J). (ps up). 1994. 16.95 (*0-688-09189-X*, Wm Morrow) Morrow Avon.

My Father's Hands. Joanne Ryder. LC 93-27116. (Illus.). 32p. (YA). (ps up). 1994. lib. bdg. 15.93 (*0-688-09190-3*, Wm Morrow) Morrow Avon.

My Father's Harmonica. Madeline Tiger. Ed. by Roy Zarucchi & Carolyn Page. (Chapbook Ser.). (Illus.). 48p. (Orig.). 1991. pap. 8.95 (*1-879205-09-2*) Nightshade Pr.

My Father's House. Timothy Cross. 1997. pap. 5.99 (*0-907927-88-2*) Emerald House Group Inc.

***My Father's House.** large type ed. Kathleen Conlon. 400p. 1999. 31.99 (*0-7089-4058-7*) Ulverscroft.

My Father's House. Pierrepont B. Noyes. 312p. 1993. reprint ed. lib. bdg. 89.00 (*0-7812-5312-8*) Rprt Serv.

My Father's House: A Memoir of Incest & of Healing. Sylvia Fraser. 256p. 1988. 17.45 (*0-89919-779-5*, Pub. by Ticknor & Fields) HM.

My Father's House: An Oneida Boyhood. Pierrepont B. Noyes. (American Biography Ser.). 312p. 1991. reprint ed. lib. bdg. 79.00 (*0-7812-8300-0*) Rprt Serv.

My Father's Martial Art: Poems. Stephen S. Liu. LC 99-36762. (Western Literature Ser.). 80p. 2000. pap. 11.00 (*0-87417-342-6*) U of Nev Pr.

My Father's Mountain: Mt. Rushmore National Memorial & How It Was Carved. rev. ed. Lincoln Borglum. 16p. 1997. pap. text. write for info. (*0-913062-02-2*) Fenwyn Pr.

My Father's Prayer. Phyllis Tickle. 1995. pap. 12.25 (*0-687-60766-3*) Abingdon.

My Father's Scar. Michael Cart. 208p. (YA). (gr. 7 up). 1996. mass mkt. 16.00 (*0-689-80749-X*) S&S Childrens.

My Fathers Scar. Michael Cart. LC 97-43657. 1998. pap. 11.95 (*0-312-18137-X*) St Martin.

My Father's Shadow: Intergenerational Conflict in African American Men's Autobiography. David L. Dudley. LC 91-8377. 192p. (C). 1991. text 27.95 (*0-8122-3081-7*) U of Pa Pr.

My Father's Son. Farley Mowat. 384p. 1993. mass mkt. 7.99 (*0-7704-2576-3*) Bantam.

My Father's Son. Frank O'Connor. LC 94-185540. 200 p. 1994. write for info. (*0-85640-522-1*) Blackstaff Pr.

My Father's Son. Frank O'Connor. 1999. pap. 17.95 (*0-8156-0564-1*) Syracuse U Pr.

***My Father's Son: The Story Behind the Greek Mafia in Houston.** Alex Keaton. 240p. 1999. pap. 24.95 (*1-885373-24-4*, Pub. by Emerald Ink) ACCESS Pubs Network.

An Asterisk (*) at the beginning of an entry indicates that the title is appearing for the first time.

My Father's Spats & Other Poems. Mark Goldman. Ed. by Patricia Schultz. LC 91-3058. (Mellen Poetry Ser.: Vol. 15). 72p. 1991. pap. 12.95 (0-7734-9777-3) E Mellen.
My Father's Testament: Memoir of a Jewish Teenager, 1938-1945. Edward Gastfriend. Ed. & Afterword by Bjorn Krondorfer. LC 99-30263. (Illus.). 256p. 2000. 59.50 (1-56639-734-0); pap. 19.95 (1-56639-735-9) Temple U Pr.
My Father's War: A Novel. Adriaan Van Dis. Tr. by Claire N. White from DUT. LC 95-49084. (International Fiction Ser.). 261p. 1996. 23.00 (1-56584-033-X, Pub. by New Press NY) Norton.
***My Father's War: Stories of Midwestern Men.** Barton Sutter. 2000. pap. 14.95 (0-8166-3685-0) U of Minn Pr.
My Father's Watch: Lodz Ghetto Underground. Michael M. Checinski. 248p. (Orig.). 1994. pap. text 14.95 (965-229-112-9, Pub. by Gefen Pub Hse) Gefen Bks.
My Father's World. Michael Phillips & Judith Pella. (Journals of Corrie Belle Hollister: No. 1). 288p. 1990. pap. 9.99 (1-55661-104-8) Bethany Hse.
My Father's World. large type ed. write for info. (0-318-68660-0, 6003) LBW.
My Father's World. large type ed. Michael Phillips & Judith Pella. LC 94-14261. 366p. 1994. lib. bdg. 20.95 (0-8161-5994-7, G K Hall Lrg Type) Mac Lib Ref.
My Father's World: Masterpieces & Memories of the Great Outdoors. Thomas Kinkade. (Illus.). 128p. 2000. 12.99 (0-7852-6963-0) Nelson.
***My Fault.** Billy Childish. 2001. pap. 15.95 (1-899598-18-9) Codex.
My Fault: The Saga of Chatham Jack. Billy Childish. 354p. (Orig.). 1997. pap. 16.95 (1-899598-06-5, Pub. by Codex) AK Pr Dist.
***My Fav Things.** Rodgers. 2000. lib. bdg. 15.89 (0-06-029233-4) HarpC.
My Favorite American Quick Print. Austin. 328p. (C). 1998. pap. text 18.50 (0-536-00649-0) Pearson Custom.
My Favorite American Stories. Austin. 328p. (C). 1998. pap. text 26.50 (0-536-01165-6) Pearson Custom.
My Favorite Animals. Cassandra Eason. LC 98-130612. (Illus.). 16p. (J). 1998. 6.95 (0-8069-0384-8) Sterling.
My Favorite Author's Reading Lesson Plans. Marty Kusmierski. 50p. 1992. teacher ed. 17.50 (1-886210-10-1) Tyketoon Yng Author.
***My Favorite Baby Animals.** Ed. by Sterling Publishing Staff. (Illus.). (J). 2000. 5.95 (0-8069-2671-6) Sterling.
***My Favorite Barbie Stories.** Golden Books Staff. (Illus.). (J). 2000. 9.99 (0-307-34093-7, Goldn Books) Gldn Bks Pub Co.
***My Favorite Bear.** Peter Ackerman. (Books for Young Learners). (Illus.). 12p. (J). (gr. k-2). 1999. pap. text 5.00 (1-57274-336-0, A2759) R Owen Pubs.
My Favorite Bedtime Stories. Helen Bramos & Ann S. Bramos. LC 91-76687. (Illus.). 63p. (J). (gr. k-7). 1992. pap. 7.00 (1-56002-152-7) A S Bramos.
My Favorite Bible Stories. Allan H. Jahsmann. LC 67-15957. 95p. (J). 1967. pap. 6.99 (0-570-03415-9, 56-1064) Concordia.
***My Favorite Bible Stories.** Philippa Moyle. LC 98-60694. (Read Aloud Ser.). (Illus.). 20p. (J). (ps-3). 1998. bds. 9.98 incl. audio (0-7651-0694-9) Smithmark.
My Favorite Chanukah Activity & Coloring Book. Arthur Friedman. (Illus.). 32p. (Orig.). (J). (ps-3). 1996. pap. 2.50 (1-889655-03-1) Jewish Educ Toys.
My Favorite Christmas Carols. Illus. by Kathy Wilburn. LC 90-22390. (Merry Christmas Bk.). 24p. (J). (ps up). 1991. 2.95 (0-694-00366-2) HarpC Child Bks.
My Favorite Christmas Carols: Big Note Piano. 24p. 1984. pap. 4.95 (0-7935-0937-8, 00009291) H Leonard.
My Favorite Classics, Bk. 1. Brimhall. (Children's Classics Ser.). 1990. 13.95 (0-685-32040-5, O114) Hansen Ed Mus.
My Favorite Classics Bach: Piano. 40p. (Orig.). Date not set. pap. 8.95 (0-7692-1124-0, PF0634) Wrner Bros.
My Favorite Classics Beethoven: Piano. 40p. (Orig.). Date not set. pap. 8.95 (0-7692-1125-9, PF0635) Wrner Bros.
My Favorite Classics Best Of: Piano. 128p. (Orig.). Date not set. pap. 12.95 (0-7692-1126-7, PF0674) Wrner Bros.
My Favorite Classics Handel: Piano. 48p. (Orig.). 1987. pap. 8.95 (0-7692-1127-5, PF0469) Wrner Bros.
My Favorite Classics Level One. John Brimhall. 120p. (J). (gr. 3-6). pap. text 13.95 (0-8494-2180-2, 0114) Hansen Ed Mus.
My Favorite Classics Level Two. John Brimhall. 120p. (Orig.). 1985. pap. text 13.95 (0-317-39977-2, 0124); 13.95 (0-8494-2184-5) Hansen Ed Mus.
My Favorite Cookies from the Old Country: Loved Recipes Assembled by . . . Olli Leeb. (Illus.). 189p. 1985. 20.50 (3-921799-97-X, Pub. by Olli Leeb) Lubrecht & Cramer.
My Favorite Dolls, Vol. 1. Kim Bell Gatto. 1999. pap. 4.99 (0-448-42076-7, G & D) Peng Put Young Read.
My Favorite Duet Album. Maxwell Eckstein. 159p. 1948. pap. 9.95 (0-8258-0163-X, 03253) Fischer Inc NY.
My Favorite Fairy Tales: A Sticker Book. Anna Nilsen. (Illus.). 16p. (J). (ps-1). 1999. pap. text 3.99 (0-7636-0501-8) Candlewick Pr.
My Favorite Family Haggadah: A Fun, Interactive Passover Service for Children & Their Families. Shari Faden Donahue. (Illus.). 31p. (J). (ps-3). 1994. pap. 5.95 (0-9634287-1-3) Arimax.
***My Favorite Fantasy Story.** Ed. by Martin H. Greenberg. 384p. 2000. 6.99 (0-88677-905-7, Pub. by DAW Bks) Penguin Putnam.
My Favorite Ghost. Stephen Roos. LC 87-15186. (Illus.). 128p. (J). (gr. 3-7). 1988. lib. bdg. 13.95 (0-689-31301-2) Atheneum Yung Read.
My Favorite Ghost. Stephen Roos. (J). 1996. pap. 2.95 (0-8167-1824-5) Troll Communs.
***My Favorite Hanukkah Book.** Phoebe Phillips. LC 98-60693. (Read Aloud Ser.). (Illus.). 20p. (J). (ps-3). 1998. bds. 9.98 (0-7651-0804-6) Smithmark.
My Favorite Herb: How North America's Great Chefs Savor the Flavor of Herbs. Laurel Keser. (Illus.). 240p. 1999. pap. 19.95 (1-896511-12-0, Pub. by Callawind) Firefly Bks Ltd.
My Favorite Holiday Recipes. Ed. by Nancy Ludwig. (Illus.). 50p. 1998. write for info. (1-893296-06-7) Meadowsweet Kit.
***My Favorite Horror Story.** Mike Baker. 2000. mass mkt. 6.99 (0-88677-914-6, Pub. by DAW Bks) Penguin Putnam.
My Favorite Husband. Sally Carleen. (Romance Ser.). 1996. per. 3.25 (0-373-19183-9, 1-19183-2) Silhouette.
My Favorite Jewish Holiday. Illus. by David Sokoloff. 12p. (Orig.). (J). (ps-1). 1998. bds. 5.00 (1-889655-12-0) Jewish Educ Toys.
My Favorite Martian. Brigandi. 96p. (J). 1999. pap. 4.95 (0-7868-4239-3, Pub. by Hyperion) Time Warner.
My Favorite Maryland Recipes. Helen A. Tawes. LC 96-54735. (Illus.). 192p. 1997. reprint ed. pap. 9.95 (0-87033-500-6, Tidewtr Pubs) Cornell Maritime.
My Favorite Messages: Sermon Outlines by Walter Schell. Elizabeth M. Schell. LC 98-91044. viii, 100p. 1999. pap. 20.00 (0-9670726-0-3) Light House Evang.
My Favorite Nurse. Herb Kavet. (Illus.). 1998. pap. 5.95 (1-889647-41-1) Boston Am.
My Favorite Nursery Rhymes. 8p. (J). 1993. 37.99 (1-888074-11-6) Pckts Lrning.
My Favorite Passover Activity & Coloring Book. David Sokoloff et al. (Illus.). 32p. (Orig.). (J). (ps-3). 1996. pap. 2.50 (1-889655-02-3) Jewish Educ Toys.
My Favorite Patterns: For Dressing Antique Dolls, 1865-1925. Evelyn Ackerman. (Illus.). 133p. 1993. pap. 29.95 (0-912823-34-8, BT-131, Pub. by Gold Horse) Dollmasters.
My Favorite Patterns: For Dressing Antique Dolls 1865-1925. Evelyn Ackerman. (Illus.). 119p. 1994. pap. 9.95 (0-912823-47-X, BT-143, Pub. by Gold Horse) Dollmasters.
***My Favorite Plant: Writers & Gardeners on the Plants They Love.** Ed. by Jamaica Kincaid. LC 98-22779. (Illus.). xix, 329p. 1998. 20.00 (0-374-28193-9) FS&G.
My Favorite Program Album. Ed. by Maxwell Eckstein. 158p. 1943. pap. 11.95 (0-8258-0161-3, 03198) Fischer Inc NY.
My Favorite Quotations. Norman Vincent Peale. LC 89-45895. 144p. 1990. 17.00 (0-06-066483-5, Pub. by Harper SF) HarpC.
My Favorite Quotes, Bk. 1. Larry W. Smith. 68p. 1997. pap. 5.95 (1-57914-008-4) Campbell-Smith.
My Favorite Recipe Register. Barbara Deede. (Illus.). 72p. 1990. pap. 9.95 (0-9627619-0-7) Deede Pr.
My Favorite Recipe Register. Barbara Deede. (Illus.). 144p. reprint ed. spiral bd. 6.95 (0-9622412-5-3) Pickle Point.
My Favorite Recipes. Karen G. Culpepper. 150p. 1998. pap. 12.95 (1-57502-928-6, PO2558) Morris Pubng.
My Favorite Recipes. Donna C. Watson. 129p. 1987. 5.95 (0-939035-02-2) Watson Pub Hse.
My Favorite Saints. Maggie Swanson. 1999. 3.95 (0-88271-708-1) Regina Pr.
My Favorite Science Fiction Story. Ed. by Martin H. Greenberg. 320p. 1999. mass mkt. 6.99 (0-88677-830-1, Pub. by DAW Bks) Penguin Putnam.
My Favorite Solo Album. Ed. by Maxwell Eckstein. 160p. 1944. pap. 11.50 (0-8258-0154-0, 03223) Fischer Inc NY.
My Favorite Teacher. Herb Kavet. (Illus.). 64p. 1998. pap. 5.95 (1-889647-40-3) Boston Am.
My Favorite Teacher. Diane Muldrow. LC 97-76904. (Look-Look Bks.). (Illus.). 24p. (J). (ps-3). 1998. pap. 2.99 (0-307-13180-7, 13180, Goldn Books) Gldn Bks Pub Co.
My Favorite Teacher Coupons. Sourcebooks Staff. 128p. 1997. pap. 5.95 (1-57071-231-X) Sourcebks.
My Favorite Thing. Gyo Fujikawa. (Illus.). 16p. (J). (ps). 1989. reprint ed. bds. 6.95 (1-55987-004-4, Sunny Bks) J B Comns.
***My Favorite Things.** Sanduik Bokforlag. (Illus.). 5p. (J). 1998. pap. 4.99 (1-58048-050-0) Sandvik Pub.
***My Favorite Things.** Vicki Day & Nola Cabral. (Illus.). 44p. 1999. pap. 12.95 (0-936459-45-X) Stained Glass.
***My Favorite Things.** Nancy Parent. (Barbie Scented Flap Bk.). 10p. (J). (ps-k). 2001. 6.99 (1-57584-731-0, Pub. by Rdrs Digest) S&S Trade.
My Favorite Things. Richard Rodgers. 32p. pap. 5.95 (0-06-443627-6) HarpC Child Bks.
***My Favorite Things.** Richard Rodgers. LC 99-63086. 32p. (J). 2000. 15.95 (0-06-028710-1) HarpC Child Bks.
My Favorite Things. large type ed. Agnes Kairaiuak et al. (Illus.). 8p. (J). (gr. k-3). 1999. pap. text 6.00 (1-58084-160-0) Lower Kuskokwim.
My Favorite Things: From the Sound of Music. Richard Rodgers & Oscar Hammerstein, II. (Piano-Vocal-Guitar Ser.). 6p. 1981. 3.95 (0-7935-1149-6, 00304530) H Leonard.
My Favorite Things: 5-Finger Piano Solos with Optional Accompaniment. 16p. 1985. pap. 6.95 (0-7935-2282-X, 00240258) H Leonard.
My Favorite Things: 75 Works of Art from Around the World. Wendy Beckett. LC 98-53881. (Illus.). 160p. 1999. 29.95 (0-8109-4387-5, Pub. by Abrams) Time Warner.
My Favorite Things to Do. Michael S. Tracy. (Foundations Ser.). 31p. (J). (ps). 1992. pap. text 4.50 (1-56843-055-8) EMG Networks.
My Favorite Things to Do: Big Book. Michael S. Tracy. (Foundations Ser.). 31p. (J). (ps). 1992. pap. text 23.00 (1-56843-005-1) EMG Networks.
My Favorite Time of Year. Susan Pearson. LC 87-45296. (Illus.). 32p. (J). (ps-3). 1988. 12.95 (0-06-024681-2) HarpC Child Bks.
My Favorite Toy. Carole B. Weatherford. LC 96-22743. (Illus.). 12p. (J). (ps). 1994. bds. 5.95 (0-86316-215-0) Writers & Readers.
My Favorite Tree: Terrific Trees of North America. Diane Iverson. LC 98-47623. (Sharing Nature with Children Book Ser.). (Illus.). 64p. (J). (ps-7). 1999. 19.95 (1-883220-94-7); pap. 9.95 (1-883220-93-9) Dawn CA.
My Favorite War: A Novel. Christopher John Farley. LC 95-47730. 220p. 1996. 23.00 (0-374-21696-7) FS&G.
My Favorite Wines. Rick Breckenridge. (Illus.). 120p. 1999. 11.95 (0-9669840-0-5) Lexus Pub.
My Favorite Word Book: Words & Pictures for the Very Young. Selina Young. (Illus.). 72p. (J). (ps-1). 1999. 17.95 (0-385-32683-1) Bantam.
My Favorite Works of Poetry. Frederick M. Markham. 1998. pap. write for info. (1-57553-757-5) Watermrk Pr.
My Favorite Year: Vocal Selections. Ed. by Carol Cuellar. 96p. (Orig.). (C). 1993. pap. text 22.95 (0-7692-0771-5, VF1945) Wrner Bros.
My Favourite English Poems. Ed. by John Masefield. LC 75-76947. (Granger Index Reprint Ser.). 1977. 21.95 (0-8369-6028-9) Ayer.
My Favourite Year: A Collection of New Football Writing. Ed. by Nick Hornby. 288p. 1997. pap. 15.95 (0-575-40063-3, Pub. by V Gollancz) Trafalgar.
My February Journal. Alana Trisler & Patrice Cardiel. 48p. (J). (gr. 1-2). 1999. pap., wbk. ed. 1.75 (1-56762-100-7) Modern Learn Pr.
My Feelings see Mihigimanitka
My Feelings see Qanuqitpit
My Feelings. Gretchen D. Van Kleef. wbk. ed. 4.95 (0-89486-980-9, 5559 B) Hazelden.
My Feelings. large type ed. Veronica Michael & Frances Caole. (Illus.). 8p. (J). (gr. k-3). 1999. pap. text 6.00 (1-58084-054-X) Lower Kuskokwim.
My Feelings. 2nd ed. Marcia K. Morgan. (Illus.). (J). (ps-5). 1984. reprint ed. pap. text 4.95 (0-930413-00-8, TX-1-361-947) Migima Designs.
My Feelings & Me: Feelings: Experiencing Feelings. Betty Gouge et al. Ed. by J. Thomas Morse et al. LC 85-81270. (KidSkills Interpersonal Skill Ser.). (Illus.). 44p. (J). (ps). 1986. 8.95 (0-934275-10-6) Fam Skills.
My Feelings Are Like Wild Animals! How Do I Tame Them? A Practical Guide to Help Teens (& Former Teens) Feel & Deal with Painful Emotions. Gary Egeberg. LC 97-53267. 96p. (YA). 1998. pap. 9.95 (0-8091-9575-5) Paulist Pr.
My Feelings, My Self: A Growing-Up Guide for Girls. rev. ed. Lynda Madaras & Area Madaras. LC 93-9877. Orig. Title: Lynda Madaras' Growing-Up Guide for Girls. (Illus.). 160p. (J). (gr. 3-10). 1993. pap. 11.95 (1-55704-157-1, Pub. by Newmarket) Norton.
My Feet. Aliki. LC 89-49357. (Let's-Read-&-Find-Out Science Bks.). (Illus.). 32p. (J). (ps-1). 1990. lib. bdg. 16.89 (0-690-04815-7) HarpC Child Bks.
My Feet. Aliki. LC 89-49357. (Trophy Let's-Read-&-Find-Out Bk.). (Illus.). 32p. (J). (ps-1). 1992. pap. 5.95 (0-06-445106-2, HarpTrophy) HarpC Child Bks.
My Feet Are Big. Donna E. Chotvacs. (J). (gr. 4-7). 1996. pap. text 4.95 (0-9644076-2-0) Calliope Pub.
My Feet Are Killing Me. Edith Courtney. 203p. (C). 1977. 30.00 (0-85088-416-0, Pub. by Gomer Pr) St Mut.
My Fellow Americans: A Family Album. Alice Provensen. LC 95-15527. (Illus.). 64p. (J). (gr. 4 up). 1995. 19.95 (0-15-276642-1, Harcourt Child Bks) Harcourt.
My Fellow Americans: Presidential Addresses That Shaped History. James C. Humes. LC 91-27248. 312p. 1992. 65.00 (0-275-93507-8, C3507, Praeger Pubs) Greenwood.
My Fellow Texans: Governors of Texas in the 20th Century. Dede W. Casad. (Illus.). 128p. (J). 1997. 12.95 (0-89015-996-3, Eakin Pr) Sunbelt Media.
My Female, My Male, My Self, & God: A Modern Woman in Search of Her Soul. Anneliese Widman. LC 99-169955. 192p. 1997. pap. 14.95 (0-9655067-0-3, Ant Hill Press) N Star Pubns.
My Fifth Grade Yearbook. Bearl Brooks. (My Yearbook Ser.). 832p. (gr. 5). 1981. 18.00 (0-8209-0085-0, MFG-5) ESP.
My Fifty Favorite Arches. Virginia Allen. (Illus.). 88p. 1998. pap. 6.95 (1-891858-02-5, 4010) Arch Hunter Bks.
My Fifty Favorite Restaurants from New Brunswick to New Hope, 1995 Edition. Suzanne Goldenson. 125p. (Orig.). 1994. pap. 9.95 (0-9637022-2-X) Gldn Sun Bks.
My 55 Ways to Lower Your Golf Score. Jack Nicklaus. 1998. per. 14.00 (0-684-84754-X, Fireside) S&S Trade Pap.
My Fifty-Five Ways to Lower Your Golf Score. Jack Nicklaus. (Illus.). 128p. 1985. pap. 10.00 (0-671-55395-X) S&S Trade.
My Fifty-Five Years in Medicine. Constance Friess. 1995. 12.95 (0-533-11165-X) Vantage.
My Fifty-One Years in Oil Exploration. W. O. Bazhaw. (Illus.). 135p. 1990. 23.95 (0-929566-05-X) Post Point Pr.
My Fifty Years in America: English Summary. Peter Suski. 50p. 1986. pap. 7.95 (0-910704-25-2) Hawley.
My Fifty Years of Nursing: Give Us to Go Blithely. 2nd ed. Doris Schwartz. LC 94-24237. 216p. 1995. 28.95 (0-8261-8920-2) Springer Pub.
My Fight for Birth Control see Works
***My Fight for Guyana's Freedom: With Reflections on My Father by Nadira Jagan-Brancier.** Cheddi Jagan & Nadira Jagan-Brancier. (Illus.). 1998. 45.00 (0-9684059-0-8) Hrpy.
My Fight for Irish Freedom. Dan Breen. 218p. 1981. reprint ed. pap. 15.95 (0-947962-33-6, Pub. by Anvil Books Ltd) Irish Bks Media.
My Fill of Phil. Evan Skolnick. (Disney's Action Club Ser.). 1997. pap. text 4.50 (1-57840-076-7, Pub. by Acclaim Bks) Penguin Putnam.
My Final Planner Workbook. 330p. 1997. text, wbk. ed. 49.95 (0-9656951-0-7) N Wells & Co.
My Financial Career & Other Follies. Raymond Leacock. 208p. 1996. pap. text 5.95 (0-7710-9892-8) McCland & Stewart.
***My Fire Engine.** Michael Rex. LC 98-6611. (Illus.). (J). (ps-k). 1999. 15.95 (0-8050-5391-3) H Holt & Co.
My First ABC. Purnima Aggarwal. (Illus.). (J). (ps). 1997. pap. 20.00 (81-7289-131-8, Pub. by Pitambar Pub) St Mut.
My First ABC. Jane Bunting. LC 93-15153. (Illus.). 32p. (J). (gr. k-1). 1993. 12.95 (1-56458-403-8) DK Pub Inc.
My First ABC. Jane Bunting. (Illus.). (J). (ps). 15.95 (0-590-24127-3) Scholastic Inc.
My First ABC: English-Arabic. (ARA & ENG.). 1997. 19.95 (0-86685-687-0) Intl Bk Ctr.
My First ABC Board Book. Deni Bown. LC 97-36186. (Illus.). 32p. (J). (ps). 1998. bds. 6.95 (0-7894-2781-8) DK Pub Inc.
My First ABC Book, 4 vols. Silver Dolphin Staff. (My First Books Ser.). (Illus.). 16p. 1998. 16.95 (1-57145-313-X, Silver Dolph) Advantage Pubs.
My First ABCs. (Butterfly Bks.). (ENG & ARA., Illus.). 1997. 14.95 (0-86685-682-X) Intl Bk Ctr.
My First Acquaintance with Poets. William C. Hazlitt. LC 93-17428. 40p. 1993. reprint ed. 35.00 (1-85477-129-9) Continuum.
***My First Action Rhymes.** Lynne W. Cravath. LC 99-69949. (Illus.). 24p. (J). (ps). 2000. pap. 9.95 (0-694-01418-4, HarpFestival) HarpC Child Bks.
My First Action Word Book: A Picture Dictionary of 1,000 First Words. Jane Bunting. LC 95-44260. 40p. (J). (ps-3). 1996. 14.95 (0-7894-0463-X) DK Pub Inc.
My First Action Word Book: A Picture Dictionary of 1,000 First Words. Jane Bunting. (Illus.). 48p. (J). 17.99 (0-590-24897-9) Scholastic Inc.
My First Activity Book. Donatella Bazzucchi. (J). 1995. pap. text 26.95 (1-884832-06-7) JTG Nashville.
My First Alphabet Book. Illus. by Julie Park. 36p. (J). 1995. (0-19-910332-1) OUP.
My First Amazing Diary. (J). (gr. k-4). 1998. 19.95 incl. cd-rom (0-7894-3891-7) DK Pub Inc.
My First Amazing Words & Pictures. DK Multimedia Staff. 1997. 29.95 (0-7894-1663-8) DK Pub Inc.
My First Amazing Words & Pictures. Dorling Kindersley Staff. 1997. 29.95 (0-7894-1693-X) DK Pub Inc.
My First Animal Board Book. Deni Bown. LC 97-32131. (Illus.). 32p. (J). (ps). 1998. bds. 6.95 (0-7894-2783-4) DK Pub Inc.
My First Animal Ride. Julia Allen. (My First Ser.). (Illus.). (J). (gr. k-3). 1987. 9.95 (0-89868-179-0); pap. 3.95 (0-89868-180-4) ARO Pub.
My First Animals. Bettina Paterson. LC 89-17275. (Illus.). 32p. (J). (ps). 1990. 8.95 (0-690-04775-4) HarpC Child Bks.
My First Atlas. Bill Boyle. LC 94-10467. (Illus.). 40p. (J). (gr. k-4). 1994. 14.95 (1-56458-624-3) DK Pub Inc.
My First Atlas. Bill Boyle & Dave Hopkins. (FRE., Illus.). (J). 21.99 (0-590-24520-1); text 18.95 (0-590-24339-X) Scholastic Inc.
My First Atlas. Alan Snow. LC 91-24303. (Illus.). 32p. (J). (gr. k-3). 1992. pap. text 4.95 (0-8167-2518-7) Troll Communs.
My First Atlas, Vol. 1. Kate Petty. LC 90-37926. (Illus.). (J). (ps-8). 1991. 9.95 (1-55782-361-8) Little.
***My 1st Baby Games.** Manning. 14p. (J). 2001. 5.95 (0-694-01435-4) HarpC Child Bks.
My First Backpack. Carol North. (Illus.). 24p. (Orig.). (J). (ps-1). 1996. pap. 2.25 (1-56293-909-2, McClanahan Book) Learn Horizon.
My First Backseat Books: See the U. S. A. Rand McNally Staff. 64p. (J). 1997. pap. text 3.95 (0-528-83849-0) Rand McNally.
My First Backseat Books Travel Time. Rand McNally Staff. (Illus.). 64p. (J). 1997. pap. text 3.95 (0-528-83846-6) Rand McNally.
My First Baking Book. Rena Coyle. LC 87-40646. (Bialosky & Friends Bks.). (Illus.). 144p. (J). (gr. 1-5). 1988. pap. 9.95 (0-89480-579-7, 1579) Workman Pub.
My First Ballet Class. Edwina Riddell. LC 92-24450. (Illus.). 32p. (J). (ps-2). 1993. pap. 5.95 (0-8120-1674-2) Barron.
My First Barbie: A Colorful Beach Day. Diane Muldrow. LC 97-74275. (Naptime Tales Ser.). (Illus.). 16p. (J). (ps). 1998. bds. 3.99 (0-307-12994-2, 12994, Goldn Books) Gldn Bks Pub Co.
My First Barbie: Shapes at the Ballet. Diane Muldrow. LC 97-74276. (Naptime Tales Ser.). (Illus.). 16p. (J). 1998. bds. 3.99 (0-307-12993-4, 12993, Goldn Books) Gldn Bks Pub Co.
My First Batteries & Magnets. Jack Challoner. LC 92-52825. (Illus.). 48p. (J). (gr. k-4). 1992. 12.95 (1-56458-133-0) DK Pub Inc.
My First Bible see Mi Primera Biblia
My First Bible. Linda Hayward. (Illus.). 12p. (J). (ps-1). 1994. 7.99 (0-679-85621-8, Pub. by Random Bks Yng Read) Random.
***My First Bible Board Book.** Dorling Kindersley Publishing Co. Staff. LC 99-44314. (Illus.). 36p. (J). (gr. k-2). 2000. bds. 6.95 (0-7894-5213-8, D K Ink) DK Pub Inc.
My First Bible Brain Quest. Brain Quest Editors. (Brain Quest Ser.). (Illus.). 116p. (J). (ps-k). 1997. pap. 10.95 (0-7611-0928-5) Workman Pub.
My First Bible Stories in Pictures. Ed. by Kenneth N. Taylor. (Illus.). 272p. (J). (gr. 1-3). 1990. 11.95 (0-87973-246-6, 246) Our Sunday Visitor.

M

An Asterisk (*) at the beginning of an entry indicates that the title is appearing for the first time.

My First Bible Words: A Kid's Devotional. William O. Noller & Kenneth N. Taylor. LC 97-27171. (Illus.). (J). 1998. 10.99 *(0-8423-4399-7)* Tyndale Hse.

My First Birds. Cecilia Fitzsimons. LC 84-48347. (Illus.). 12p. (J). (gr. k-4). 1985. 8.95 *(0-06-021892-4)* HarpC Child Bks.

***My First Biscuit Library, 3 bks.** Alyssa Satin Capucilli. (Illus.). (J). (ps up). 2000. pap. 9.95 *(0-694-01457-5)* HarpC Child Bks.

My First Blue Picture. John Dillon. 1997. pap. write for info. *(0-7214-5525-5)* Viking Penguin.

***My First Body Board Book.** DK Publishing Staff. (My First Bks.). (Illus.). 36p. (ps-k). 2000. 6.95 *(0-7894-6516-7)* DK Pub Inc.

My First Body Book. Christopher Rice. (Illus.). (J). 22.99 *(0-590-24611-9)* Scholastic Inc.

My First Body Book. Melanie Rice & Christopher J. Rice. LC 94-40835. (Illus.). 48p. (J). (gr. k-3). 1995. 16.95 *(1-56458-893-9, 5-70553)* DK Pub Inc.

My First Book. Jane Belk Moncure. LC 84-17455. (Sound Box Library). (Illus.). 32p. (J). (ps-2). 1984. lib. bdg. 21.36 *(0-89565-271-4)* Childs World.

My First Book: Picture Puzzles & Word Fun for the Very Young. LC 91-71831. 64p. (J). (ps up). 1994. pap. 9.99 *(1-56402-370-2)* Candlewick Pr.

My First Book about Alabama. Carole Marsh. (Carole Marsh Alabama Bks.). (J). (gr. k-4). 1994. pap. 19.95 *(0-7933-5570-2)*; lib. bdg. 29.95 *(0-7933-5569-9)*; disk 29.95 *(0-7933-5571-0)* Gallopade Intl.

My First Book about Alaska. Carole Marsh. (Carole Marsh Alaska Bks.). (J). (gr. k-4). 1994. pap. 19.95 *(0-7933-5573-7)*; lib. bdg. 29.95 *(0-7933-5572-9)*; disk 29.95 *(0-7933-5574-5)* Gallopade Intl.

My First Book about Arizona. Carole Marsh. (Carole Marsh Arizona Bks.). (J). (gr. k-4). 1994. pap. 19.95 *(0-7933-5576-1)*; lib. bdg. 29.95 *(0-7933-5575-3)*; disk 29.95 *(0-7933-5577-X)* Gallopade Intl.

My First Book about Arkansas. Carole Marsh. (Carole Marsh Arkansas Bks.). (J). (gr. k-4). 1994. pap. 19.95 *(0-7933-5579-6)*; lib. bdg. 29.95 *(0-7933-5578-8)*; disk 29.95 *(0-7933-5580-X)* Gallopade Intl.

My First Book about California. Carole Marsh. (Carole Marsh California Bks.). (J). (gr. k-4). 1994. pap. 19.95 *(0-7933-5582-6)*; lib. bdg. 29.95 *(0-7933-5581-8)*; disk 29.95 *(0-7933-5583-4)* Gallopade Intl.

***My First Book about California.** Carole Marsh. (California Experience! Ser.). (Illus.). (J). (gr. 2-6). 2000. pap. 7.95 *(0-7933-9503-8)* Gallopade Intl.

My First Book about Colorado. Carole Marsh. (Carole Marsh Colorado Bks.). (J). (gr. k-4). 1994. pap. 19.95 *(0-7933-5585-0)*; lib. bdg. 29.95 *(0-7933-5584-2)*; disk 29.95 *(0-7933-5586-9)* Gallopade Intl.

***My First Book about Colorado.** Carole Marsh. (Colorado Experience! Ser.). (Illus.). (J). (gr. 2-6). 2000. pap. 7.95 *(0-7933-9603-4)* Gallopade Intl.

My First Book about Connecticut. Carole Marsh. (Carole Marsh Connecticut Bks.). (J). (gr. k-4). 1994. pap. 19.95 *(0-7933-5588-5)*; lib. bdg. 29.95 *(0-7933-5587-7)*; disk 29.95 *(0-7933-5589-3)* Gallopade Intl.

***My First Book about Connecticut.** Carole Marsh. (Connecticut Experience! Ser.). (Illus.). (J). (gr. 2-6). 2000. pap. 7.95 *(0-7933-9579-8)* Gallopade Intl.

My First Book about Delaware. Carole Marsh. (Carole Marsh Delaware Bks.). (J). (gr. k-4). 1994. pap. 19.95 *(0-7933-5591-5)*; lib. bdg. 29.95 *(0-7933-5590-7)*; disk 29.95 *(0-7933-5592-3)* Gallopade Intl.

My First Book about Florida. Carole Marsh. (Carole Marsh Florida Bks.). (J). (gr. k-4). 1994. pap. 19.95 *(0-7933-5597-4)*; lib. bdg. 29.95 *(0-7933-5596-6)*; disk 29.95 *(0-7933-5598-2)* Gallopade Intl.

***My First Book about Florida.** Carole Marsh. (Florida Experience! Ser.). (Illus.). (J). (gr. 2-6). 2000. pap. 7.95 *(0-7933-9506-2)* Gallopade Intl.

My First Book about Georgia. Carole Marsh. (Carole Marsh Georgia Bks.). (J). (gr. k-4). 1994. pap. 19.95 *(0-7933-5600-8)*; lib. bdg. 29.95 *(0-7933-5599-0)*; disk 29.95 *(0-7933-5601-6)* Gallopade Intl.

***My First Book about Georgia.** Carole Marsh. (Georgia Experience! Ser.). (Illus.). (J). (gr. 2-6). 2000. pap. 7.95 *(0-7933-9509-7)* Gallopade Intl.

My First Book about Hawaii. Carole Marsh. (Carole Marsh Hawaii Bks.). (J). (gr. k-4). 1994. pap. 19.95 *(0-7933-5603-2)*; lib. bdg. 29.95 *(0-7933-5602-4)*; disk 29.95 *(0-7933-5604-0)* Gallopade Intl.

My First Book about Idaho. Carole Marsh. (Carole Marsh Idaho Bks.). (J). (gr. k-4). 1994. pap. 19.95 *(0-7933-5606-7)*; lib. bdg. 29.95 *(0-7933-5605-9)*; disk 29.95 *(0-7933-5607-5)* Gallopade Intl.

My First Book about Illinois. Carole Marsh. (Carole Marsh Illinois Bks.). (J). (gr. k-4). 1994. pap. 19.95 *(0-7933-5609-1)*; lib. bdg. 29.95 *(0-7933-5608-3)*; disk 29.95 *(0-7933-5610-5)* Gallopade Intl.

***My First Book about Illinois.** Carole Marsh. (Illinois Experience! Ser.). (Illus.). (J). (gr. 2-6). 2000. pap. 7.95 *(0-7933-9512-7)* Gallopade Intl.

My First Book about Indiana. Carole Marsh. (Carole Marsh Indiana Bks.). (J). (gr. k-4). 1994. pap. 19.95 *(0-7933-5612-1)*; lib. bdg. 29.95 *(0-7933-5611-3)*; disk 29.95 *(0-7933-5613-X)* Gallopade Intl.

My First Book about Iowa. Carole Marsh. (Carole Marsh Iowa Bks.). (J). (gr. k-4). 1994. pap. 19.95 *(0-7933-5615-6)*; lib. bdg. 29.95 *(0-7933-5614-8)*; disk 29.95 *(0-7933-5616-4)* Gallopade Intl.

My First Book about Jesus, 4 bks. Elspeth C. Murphy & Wayne Hanna. Incl. Bk. 3. Jesus Loves Children. 1981. 2.95 *(0-89191-333-5)*; (Illus.). 1981. write for info. *(0-318-51433-8)* Chariot Victor.

My First Book about Kansas. Carole Marsh. (Carole Marsh Kansas Bks.). (J). (gr. k-4). 1994. pap. 19.95 *(0-7933-5618-0)*; lib. bdg. 29.95 *(0-7933-5617-2)*; disk 29.95 *(0-7933-5619-9)* Gallopade Intl.

My First Book about Kentucky. Carole Marsh. (Carole Marsh Kentucky Bks.). (J). (gr. k-4). 1994. pap. 19.95 *(0-7933-5621-0)*; lib. bdg. 29.95 *(0-7933-5620-2)*; disk 29.95 *(0-7933-5622-9)* Gallopade Intl.

***My First Book about Kentucky.** Carole Marsh. (Kentucky Experience! Ser.). (Illus.). (J). (gr. 2-6). 2000. pap. 7.95 *(0-7933-9515-1)* Gallopade Intl.

My First Book about Louisiana. Carole Marsh. (Carole Marsh Louisiana Bks.). (J). (gr. k-4). 1994. pap. 19.95 *(0-7933-5624-5)*; lib. bdg. 29.95 *(0-7933-5623-7)*; disk 29.95 *(0-7933-5625-3)* Gallopade Intl.

***My First Book about Louisiana.** Carole Marsh. (Louisiana Experience! Ser.). (Illus.). (J). (gr. 2-6). 2000. pap. 7.95 *(0-7933-9547-X)* Gallopade Intl.

My First Book about Maine. Carole Marsh. (Carole Marsh Maine Bks.). (J). (gr. k-4). 1994. pap. 19.95 *(0-7933-5627-X)*; lib. bdg. 29.95 *(0-7933-5626-1)*; disk 29.95 *(0-7933-5628-8)* Gallopade Intl.

My First Book about Mary. Christine V. Orfeo. LC 96-20218. (Illus.). 80p. (Orig.). (J). (ps-2). 1996. pap. 9.95 *(0-8198-4789-5)* Pauline Bks.

My First Book about Maryland. Carole Marsh. (Carole Marsh Maryland Bks.). (J). (gr. k-4). 1994. pap. 19.95 *(0-7933-5630-X)*; lib. bdg. 29.95 *(0-7933-5629-6)*; disk 29.95 *(0-7933-5631-8)* Gallopade Intl.

***My First Book about Maryland.** Carole Marsh. (Maryland Experience! Ser.). (Illus.). (J). (gr. 2-6). 2000. pap. 7.95 *(0-7933-9611-5)* Gallopade Intl.

My First Book about Massachusetts. Carole Marsh. (Massachuseets Bks.). (J). (gr. k-4). 1994. pap. 19.95 *(0-7933-5633-4)*; lib. bdg. 29.95 *(0-7933-5632-6)*; disk 29.95 *(0-7933-5634-2)* Gallopade Intl.

My First Book about Michigan. Carole Marsh. (Carole Marsh Michigan Bks.). (J). (gr. k-4). 1994. pap. 19.95 *(0-7933-5636-9)*; lib. bdg. 29.95 *(0-7933-5635-0)*; disk 29.95 *(0-7933-5637-7)* Gallopade Intl.

***My First Book about Michigan.** Carole Marsh. (Michigan Experience! Ser.). (Illus.). (J). (gr. 2-6). 2000. pap. 7.95 *(0-7933-9563-1)* Gallopade Intl.

My First Book about Minnesota. Carole Marsh. (Carole Marsh Minnesota Bks.). (J). (gr. k-4). 1994. pap. 19.95 *(0-7933-5639-3)*; lib. bdg. 29.95 *(0-7933-5638-5)*; disk 29.95 *(0-7933-5640-7)* Gallopade Intl.

My First Book about Mississippi. Carole Marsh. (Carole Marsh Mississippi Bks.). (J). (gr. k-4). 1994. pap. 19.95 *(0-7933-5642-3)*; lib. bdg. 29.95 *(0-7933-5641-5)*; disk 29.95 *(0-7933-5643-1)* Gallopade Intl.

***My First Book about Mississippi.** Carole Marsh. (Mississippi Experience! Ser.). (Illus.). (J). (gr. 2-6). 2000. pap. 7.95 *(0-7933-9555-0)* Gallopade Intl.

My First Book about Missouri. Carole Marsh. (Carole Marsh Missouri Bks.). (J). (gr. k-4). 1994. pap. 19.95 *(0-7933-5645-8)*; lib. bdg. 29.95 *(0-7933-5644-X)*; disk 29.95 *(0-7933-5646-6)* Gallopade Intl.

***My First Book about Missouri.** Carole Marsh. (Missouri Experience! Ser.). (Illus.). (J). (gr. 2-6). 2000. pap. 7.95 *(0-7933-9571-2)* Gallopade Intl.

My First Book about Montana. Carole Marsh. (Carole Marsh Montana Ser.). (J). (gr. k-4). 1994. pap. 19.95 *(0-7933-5648-2)*; lib. bdg. 29.95 *(0-7933-5647-4)*; disk 29.95 *(0-7933-5649-0)* Gallopade Intl.

My First Book about Nebraska. Carole Marsh. (Carole Marsh Nebraska Bks.). (J). (gr. k-4). 1994. pap. 19.95 *(0-7933-5651-2)*; lib. bdg. 29.95 *(0-7933-5650-4)*; disk 29.95 *(0-7933-5652-0)* Gallopade Intl.

My First Book about Nevada. Carole Marsh. (Carole Marsh Nevada Bks.). (J). (gr. k-4). 1994. pap. 19.95 *(0-7933-5654-7)*; lib. bdg. 29.95 *(0-7933-5653-9)*; disk 29.95 *(0-7933-5655-5)* Gallopade Intl.

My First Book about New Hampshire. Carole Marsh. (Carole Marsh New Hampshire Bks.). (J). (gr. k-4). 1994. pap. 19.95 *(0-7933-5657-1)*; lib. bdg. 24.95 *(0-7933-5656-3)*; disk 29.95 *(0-7933-5658-X)* Gallopade Intl.

My First Book about New Jersey. Carole Marsh. (Carole Marsh New Jersey Bks.). (J). (gr. k-4). 1994. pap. 19.95 *(0-7933-5660-1)*; lib. bdg. 29.95 *(0-7933-5659-8)*; disk 29.95 *(0-7933-5661-X)* Gallopade Intl.

***My First Book about New Jersey.** Carole Marsh. (New Jersey Experience! Ser.). (Illus.). (J). (gr. 2-6). 2000. pap. 7.95 *(0-7933-9521-6)* Gallopade Intl.

My First Book about New Mexico. Carole Marsh. (Carole Marsh New Mexico Bks.). (J). (gr. k-4). 1994. pap. 19.95 *(0-7933-5663-6)*; lib. bdg. 29.95 *(0-7933-5662-8)*; disk 29.95 *(0-7933-5664-4)* Gallopade Intl.

My First Book about New York. Carole Marsh. (Carole Marsh New York Bks.). (J). (gr. k-4). 1994. pap. 19.95 *(0-7933-5666-0)*; lib. bdg. 29.95 *(0-7933-5665-2)*; disk 29.95 *(0-7933-5667-9)* Gallopade Intl.

My First Book about North Carolina. Carole Marsh. (Carole Marsh North Carolina Bks.). (J). (gr. k-4). 1994. pap. 19.95 *(0-7933-5669-5)*; lib. bdg. 29.95 *(0-7933-5668-7)*; disk 29.95 *(0-7933-5670-9)* Gallopade Intl.

***My First Book about North Carolina.** Carole Marsh. (North Carolina Experience! Ser.). (J). (gr. 2-6). 2000. pap. 7.95 *(0-7933-9518-6)* Gallopade Intl.

My First Book about North Dakota. Carole Marsh. (Carole Marsh North Dakota Bks.). (J). (gr. k-4). 1994. pap. 19.95 *(0-7933-5672-5)*; lib. bdg. 29.95 *(0-7933-5671-7)*; disk 29.95 *(0-7933-5673-3)* Gallopade Intl.

My First Book about Ohio. Carole Marsh. (Carole Marsh Ohio Bks.). (J). (gr. k-4). 1994. pap. 19.95 *(0-7933-5675-X)*; lib. bdg. 29.95 *(0-7933-5674-1)*; disk 29.95 *(0-7933-5676-8)* Gallopade Intl.

***My First Book about Ohio.** Carole Marsh. (Ohio Experience! Ser.). (Illus.). (J). (gr. 2-6). 2000. pap. 7.95 *(0-7933-9524-0)* Gallopade Intl.

My First Book about Oklahoma. Carole Marsh. (Oklahoma Bks.). (J). (gr. k-4). 1994. pap. 19.95 *(0-7933-5678-4)*; lib. bdg. 24.95 *(0-7933-5677-6)*; disk 29.95 *(0-7933-5679-2)* Gallopade Intl.

***My First Book about Oklahoma.** Carole Marsh. (Oklahoma Experience! Ser.). (Illus.). (J). (gr. 2-6). 2000. pap. 7.95 *(0-7933-9595-X)* Gallopade Intl.

My First Book about Oregon. Carole Marsh. (Oregon Bks.). (J). (gr. k-4). 1994. pap. 19.95 *(0-7933-5681-4)*; lib. bdg. 29.95 *(0-7933-5680-6)*; disk 29.95 *(0-7933-5682-2)* Gallopade Intl.

My First Book about Pennsylvania. Carole Marsh. (Pennsylvania Bks.). (J). (gr. k-4). 1994. pap. 19.95 *(0-7933-5684-9)*; lib. bdg. 29.95 *(0-7933-5683-0)*; disk 29.95 *(0-7933-5685-7)* Gallopade Intl.

***My First Book about Pennsylvania.** Carole Marsh. (Pennsylvania Experience! Ser.). (Illus.). (J). (gr. 2-6). 2000. pap. 7.95 *(0-7933-9587-9)* Gallopade Intl.

My First Book about Rhode Island. Carole Marsh. (Rhode Island Bks.). (J). (gr. k-4). 1994. pap. 19.95 *(0-7933-5687-3)*; lib. bdg. 29.95 *(0-7933-5686-5)*; disk 29.95 *(0-7933-5688-1)* Gallopade Intl.

My First Book about South Carolina. Carole Marsh. (South Carolina Bks.). (J). (gr. k-4). 1994. pap. 19.95 *(0-7933-5690-3)*; lib. bdg. 29.95 *(0-7933-5689-X)*; disk 29.95 *(0-7933-5691-1)* Gallopade Intl.

My First Book about South Dakota. Carole Marsh. (South Dakota Bks.). (J). (gr. k-4). 1994. pap. 19.95 *(0-7933-5693-8)*; lib. bdg. 29.95 *(0-7933-5692-X)*; disk 29.95 *(0-7933-5694-6)* Gallopade Intl.

My First Book about Tennessee. Carole Marsh. (Tennessee Bks.). (J). (gr. k-4). 1994. pap. 19.95 *(0-7933-5696-2)*; lib. bdg. 29.95 *(0-7933-5695-4)*; disk 29.95 *(0-7933-5697-0)* Gallopade Intl.

My First Book about Texas. Carole Marsh. (Texas Bks.). (J). (gr. k-4). 1994. pap. 19.95 *(0-7933-5699-7)*; lib. bdg. 29.95 *(0-7933-5698-9)*; disk 29.95 *(0-7933-5700-4)* Gallopade Intl.

***My First Book about Texas.** Carole Marsh. (Texas Experience! Ser.). (Illus.). (J). (gr. 2-6). 2000. pap. 7.95 *(0-7933-9527-5)* Gallopade Intl.

My First Book about the Internet. Sharon Cromwell. (Illus.). (J). 1997. pap. 3.50 incl. disk *(0-8167-4320-7)* Troll Communs.

My First Book about Utah. Carole Marsh. (Utah Bks.). (J). (gr. k-4). 1994. pap. 19.95 *(0-7933-5702-0)*; lib. bdg. 29.95 *(0-7933-5701-2)*; disk 29.95 *(0-7933-5703-9)* Gallopade Intl.

My First Book about Vermont. Carole Marsh. (Vermont Bks.). (J). (gr. k-4). 1994. pap. 19.95 *(0-7933-5705-5)*; lib. bdg. 29.95 *(0-7933-5704-7)*; disk 29.95 *(0-7933-5706-3)* Gallopade Intl.

My First Book about Virginia. Carole Marsh. (Virginia Bks.). (J). (gr. k-4). 1994. pap. 19.95 *(0-7933-5708-X)*; lib. bdg. 29.95 *(0-7933-5707-1)*; disk 29.95 *(0-7933-5709-8)* Gallopade Intl.

***My First Book about Virginia.** Carole Marsh. (Virginia Experience! Ser.). (Illus.). (J). (gr. 2-6). 2000. pap. 7.95 *(0-7933-9500-3)* Gallopade Intl.

My First Book about Washington D. C. Carole Marsh. (Washington Bks.). (J). (gr. k-4). 1994. pap. 19.95 *(0-7933-5711-X)*; lib. bdg. 29.95 *(0-7933-5710-1)*; disk 29.95 *(0-7933-5712-8)* Gallopade Intl.

My First Book about Washington DC. Carole Marsh. (Washington, D.C. Bks.). (J). (gr. k-4). 1994. pap. 19.95 *(0-7933-5594-X)*; lib. bdg. 29.95 *(0-7933-5593-1)*; disk 29.95 *(0-7933-5595-8)* Gallopade Intl.

My First Book about West Virginia. Carole Marsh. (West Virginia Bks.). (J). (gr. k-4). 1994. pap. 19.95 *(0-7933-5714-4)*; lib. bdg. 29.95 *(0-7933-5713-6)*; disk 29.95 *(0-7933-5715-2)* Gallopade Intl.

My First Book about Wisconsin. Carole Marsh. (Wisconsin Bks.). (J). (gr. k-4). 1994. pap. 19.95 *(0-7933-5717-9)*; lib. bdg. 29.95 *(0-7933-5716-0)*; disk 29.95 *(0-7933-5718-7)* Gallopade Intl.

***My First Book about Wisconsin.** Carole Marsh. (Wisconsin Experience! Ser.). (Illus.). (J). (gr. 2-6). 2000. pap. 7.95 *(0-7933-9539-9)* Gallopade Intl.

My First Book about Wyoming. Carole Marsh. (Wyoming Bks.). (J). (gr. k-4). 1994. pap. 19.95 *(0-7933-5720-9)*; lib. bdg. 29.95 *(0-7933-5719-5)*; disk 29.95 *(0-7933-5721-7)* Gallopade Intl.

My First Book of ABC's. (Step Ahead Sticker Starters Ser.). (Illus.). 16p. (J). (ps-3). 1995. pap., wbk. ed. 2.79 *(0-307-03503-4, 03503, Goldn Books)* Gldn Bks Pub Co.

My First Book of Animal Sounds. Chuck Murphy. (Lift-the-Flap Concept Bks.). (Illus.). 12p. (J). (ps-k). 1995. 6.95 *(0-590-20301-0, Cartwheel)* Scholastic Inc.

My First Book of Animals. Sanduik Bokforlag. (Illus.). (J). 1998. bds. 12.98 *(1-58048-008-X)* Sandvik Pub.

My First Book of Animals from A to Z: More Than 150 Animals Every Child Should Know. Illus. by Turi MacCombie. LC 92-19284. (Cartwheel Learning Bookshelf Ser.). 64p. (J). (ps-2). 1994. 13.95 *(0-590-46305-5, Cartwheel)* Scholastic Inc.

My First Book of Bible Animals. Mark Water & Karen Donnelly. 24p. (J). 1996. 7.99 *(1-56476-549-0, 6-3549, Victor Bks)* Chariot Victor.

My First Book of Bible Devotions see My Primer Libro Devocional de la Biblia

My First Book of Bible Devotions. LC 90-37714. (Illus.). 80p. (J). (ps). 1991. 7.99 *(1-55513-416-5, 64162, Chariot Bks)* Chariot Victor.

My First Book of Bible People. Mark Water. (Illus.). 24p. (J). 1996. 7.99 *(1-56476-548-2, 6-3548, Victor Bks)* Chariot Victor.

My First Book of Biographies. Jean Marzollo. LC 92-27623. (Illus.). 80p. (J). (gr. k-4). 1994. 14.95 *(0-590-45014-X)* Scholastic Inc.

My First Book of Catholic Bible Stories. Sam Butcher. 1999. 9.95 *(0-88271-752-9)* Regina Pr.

My First Book of Catholic Prayers. Regina Press Staff. 1999. 5.95 *(0-88271-753-7)* Regina Pr.

My First Book of Christmas Carols. Illus. by Susan Harrison. 24p. (J). 1992. pap. 3.95 *(0-8249-8568-0, Ideals Child)* Hambleton-Hill.

My First Book of Christmas Songs. Bergerac. (Illus.). 1997. pap. 3.50 *(0-486-29718-7)* Dover.

***My First Book of Classical Music: 20 Themes by Beethoven, Mozart, Chopin & Other Great Composers.** Bergerac. (J). 2000. pap. 3.95 *(0-486-41092-7)* Dover.

My First Book of Classics: Bach. (Easy Classics Ser.). 1990. 6.95 *(0-685-32057-X, H705)* Hansen Ed Mus.

My First Book of Classics: Beethoven. Ludwig van Beethoven. (Easy Classics Ser.). 1990. 6.95 *(0-685-32054-5, H702)* Hansen Ed Mus.

My First Book of Classics: Haydn. (Easy Classics Ser.). 1990. 6.95 *(0-685-32056-1, H704)* Hansen Ed Mus.

My First Book of Classics: Mozart. Composed by Wolfgang Amadeus Mozart. (Easy Classics Ser.). 1990. 6.95 *(0-685-32053-7, H701)* Hansen Ed Mus.

My First Book of Classics: Schumann. Schumann. (Easy Classics Ser.). 1990. 6.95 *(0-685-32055-3, H703)* Hansen Ed Mus.

***My First Book of College.** Suzette Tyler. 2000. pap. 13.95 *(0-9656086-3-8)* Front Porch.

My First Book of Embroidery: With 44 Iron-on Transfer Patterns. Judith H. Corwin. (Illus.). 80p. (Orig.). 1992. pap. 4.95 *(0-486-27100-5)* Dover.

My First Book of Facts. Carol Watson. (Illus.). (J). 18.95 *(0-590-74341-4)* Scholastic Inc.

My First Book of How Things Are Made: Crayons, Jeans, Guitars, Peanut Butter, & More. George Jones. LC 94-45667. (Cartwheel Learning Bookshelf Ser.). (Illus.). 64p. (J). (gr. 3-5). 1995. 12.95 *(0-590-48004-9, Cartwheel)* Scholastic Inc.

My First Book of Irish Songs & Celtic Dances: 21 Favorite Pieces in Easy Piano Arrangements. Ed. by Bergerac. (Illus.). 48p. 1998. pap. 3.95 *(0-486-40405-6)* Dover.

My First Book of Knowledge. Jenny Vaughn. (J). 1997. 10.98 *(0-7651-9406-6)* Smithmark.

My First Book of Marches. Dolly M. Moon. 48p. 1998. pap. 3.95 *(0-486-26338-X)* Dover.

My First Book of Mitzvos. Isaiah Karlinsky & Ruth Karlinsky. (Illus.). (J). (gr. k-3). 1986. 10.95 *(0-87306-388-0)* Feldheim.

My First Book of 123's. (Step Ahead Sticker Starters Ser.). (Illus.). 16p. (J). (ps-3). 1995. pap., wbk. ed. 2.79 *(0-307-03501-8, 03501, Goldn Books)* Gldn Bks Pub Co.

My First Book of Poems Coloring Book. Victoria Fremont. (Illus.). (J). (gr. k-3). 1993. pap. 1.00 *(0-486-27824-7)* Dover.

My First Book of Prayers: A Collection of Everyday Prayers from a Child's Heart. Maureen Bradley. (Illus.). 96p. (J). 1997. 5.99 *(0-88486-181-3, Inspirational Pr)* Arrowood Pr.

My First Book of Prayers: Boy's Baptismal Remembrance Edition. (Precious Moments Ser.). (J). 12.95 *(0-614-22067-X)* Regina Pr.

My First Book of Prayers: General Edition. (Precious Moments Ser.). (J). 8.95 *(0-614-22076-9)* Regina Pr.

My First Book of Prayers: Girls Catholic Padded Gift Edition. (Precious Moments Ser.). (J). 12.95 *(0-614-22075-0)* Regina Pr.

My First Book of Proverbs (Mi Primer Libro de Dichos) Ralfka Gonzalez & Ana Ruiz. LC 95-7288.Tr. of Mi Primer Libro de Dichos. (ENG & SPA., Illus.). 32p. (YA). (gr. 1 up). 1995. 15.95 *(0-89239-134-0)* Childrens Book Pr.

My First Book of Questions. Jennifer Daniel et al. (Illus.). 128p. (J). (ps-2). 1992. 12.95 *(0-590-44942-7, 032, Cartwheel)* Scholastic Inc.

My First Book of Seasons. (Butterfly Bks.). (ARA., Illus.). 14.95 *(0-86685-711-7)* Intl Bk Ctr.

My First Book of Shapes. Chuck Murphy. LC 93-178664. (Illus.). 12p. (J). (ps-k). 1993. 6.95 *(0-590-46303-9)* Scholastic Inc.

My 1st Book of Shapes & Colors. Ian Winton. LC 99-474389. (Illus.). 18p. (J). (ps-1). 1995. 9.95 *(0-671-51119-X)* Litle Simon.

My First Book of Sign. Pamela J. Baker. (Awareness & Caring Ser.). (Illus.). 76p. (J). (gr. k up). 1992. reprint ed. lib. bdg. 18.95 *(1-878363-92-1)* Forest Hse.

My First Book of Sign Language. Joan Holub. (Illus.). 32p. (J). (ps-2). 1996. pap. 3.50 *(0-8167-4033-X, Whistlstop)* Troll Communs.

My First Book of Sign Language. Joan Holub. LC 96-133227. (J). 1996. 8.15 *(0-606-09648-5, Pub. by Turtleback)* Demco.

My First Book of Space. Rosanna Hansen & Robert Bell. (Illus.). 48p. (J). (gr. 1-5). 1985. 13.00 *(0-671-60262-4)* S&S Bks Yung.

My First Book of Space Coloring & Activity Book. Robert Bell. (Illus.). 160p. (J). (gr. 1 up). 1986. pap. 6.95 *(0-671-62407-5)* Litle Simon.

My First Book of the Alphabet. Chuck Murphy. (Illus.). 12p. (J). 1993. 6.95 *(0-590-46304-7)* Scholastic Inc.

My First Book of Time. Claire Llewellyn. LC 91-58194. (Illus.). 32p. (J). (ps-3). 1992. 14.95 *(1-879431-78-5)* DK Pub Inc.

My First Book of Time. Ed. by Scholastic, Inc. Staff. (Illus.). (J). 1992. 18.95 *(0-590-74283-3)* Scholastic Inc.

My First Book of Words. Illus. by Lena Shiffman. (Cartwheel Learning Bookshelf Ser.). 64p. (J). (ps-k). 1992. 13.95 *(0-590-45142-1, Cartwheel)* Scholastic Inc.

My First Box of Prayers, 4 bks. Hanna Barbera. (Illus.). (J). (gr. 2 up). 1988. 8.95 *(0-687-27539-3)* Abingdon.

***My First Boxed Set.** DK Publishing Staff. (Illus.). 100p. (ps-k). 2000. 19.95 *(0-7894-5561-7)* DK Pub Inc.

***My 1st Brain Quest.** Brain Quest. (Brain Quest Ser.). 75p. (Orig.). 1999. pap. 10.95 *(0-7611-1517-X)* Workman Pub.

An Asterisk (*) at the beginning of an entry indicates that the title is appearing for the first time.

My First Brain Quest: Ages Two-Three. Chris W. Feder. (Illus.). 75p. (J). (ps). 1994. pap. 10.95 (*1-56305-634-8*, 3634) Workman Pub.

My First Bus Ride. Harry W. Faircloth. (Illus.). 26p. (J). (ps-4). Date not set. pap. 9.95 (*0-9668650-1-4*) Maximilian Pr.

My First Butterflies. Cecilia Fitzsimons. LC 84-48348. (Illus.). 12p. (J). (gr. k-4). 1985. 8.95 (*0-06-021893-2*) HarpC Child Bks.

My First Camera Book. Anne Kostick. LC 88-40560. (Bialosky & Friends Bks.). (Illus.). 64p. (J). (ps-3). 1989. pap. 9.95 (*0-89480-381-6*, 1381) Workman Pub.

My First Camping Trip. Julia Allen. (My First Ser.). (Illus.). (J). (gr. k-3). 1987. 9.95 (*0-89868-181-2*); pap. 3.95 (*0-89868-182-0*) ARO Pub.

My First Camping Trip: Big Big Book. Julia Allen. (My First Ser.). (Illus.). (J). (gr. k-3). 1987. 22.00 (*0-614-24513-3*) ARO Pub.

My First Canadian Atlas. Nicola Wright et al. (Illus.). 40p. (J). 1997. reprint ed. text 10.00 (*0-7881-5161-4*) DIANE Pub.

My First Catechism. Lawrence G. Lovasik. (Saint Joseph Picture Bks.). (Illus.). 1985. pap. 1.25 (*0-89942-382-5*, 382-00) Catholic Bk Pub.

My First Catholic Picture Dictionary. Lawrence G. Lovasik. (Saint Joseph Picture Bks.). (Illus.). 1984. pap. 1.25 (*0-89942-306-X*, 306-00) Catholic Bk Pub.

My First Christmas Activity Book. Angela Wilkes. LC 94-638. (Illus.). 48p. (J). 1994. 12.95 (*1-56458-674-X*) DK Pub Inc.

My First Christmas Board Book. LC 99-24057. (My First Bks.). 36p. (J). (gr. k-2). 1999. 6.95 (*0-7894-4735-5*) DK Pub Inc.

My First Christmas Book. Ladybird Books Staff. (Christmas Board Bks.: No. S8823-1). (Illus.). (J). (ps). 1990. pap. 3.95 (*0-7214-9093-X*, Ladybrd) Penguin Putnam.

My First Christmas Carols. Mary E. Erickson. (Illus.). 32p. (J). (ps-3). 1995. 5.99 (*0-7814-0238-7*, Chariot Bks) Chariot Victor.

My First Christmas Carols. Gayle Kowalchyk & E. L. Lancaster. 16p. 1989. pap. 5.50 (*0-7390-0678-9*, 233) Alfred Pub.

My First Christmas Carols. Laura Rader. LC 94-17170. (Illus.). 32p. 1994. lib. bdg. 16.65 (*0-8167-3596-4*) Troll Communs.

My First Christmas Carols. Laura Rader. LC 94-17170. (Illus.). 32p. (J). (gr. k-2). 1996. pap. 2.95 (*0-8167-3513-1*) Troll Communs.

***My First Christmas Fun Book.** Box & Sage. (J). 1998. pap. 6.95 (*0-7459-3691-1*, Pub. by Lion Pubng) Trafalgar.

My First Clock. Playskool Staff. (Illus.). 6p. (J). 1997. 11.99 (*0-525-45772-0*) NAL.

My First Clock Book. (Illus.). 8p. (J). (ps). 1997. 35.00 (*1-888074-57-4*) Pckts Lrning.

My First Cold. Julia Allen. (My First Thirty Word Book Ser.). (Illus.). (J). (gr. k-3). 1994. pap. 3.95 (*0-89868-232-0*, Read Res); lib. bdg. 9.95 (*0-89868-224-X*, Read Res) ARO Pub.

My First Coloring Book. Keith Haring. (Illus.). 32p. (Orig.). (J). (ps-5). 1993. pap. 4.95 (*1-881270-61-0*) FotoFolio.

My First Communion: A Day to Remember. Nadia Bonaldo. Tr. by Janet Alampi & Frank Alampi from ITA. (Illus.). 114p. (J). (gr. 2). 1993. reprint ed. 14.95 (*0-8198-4770-4*) Pauline Bks.

My First Communion: For Boys. Victor Hoagland. (Precious Moments Ser.). 1992. 14.95 (*0-88271-502-X*) Regina Pr.

My First Communion - Boy Image. 2nd rev. ed. Anthony A. Petrusic. Ed. by Sue H. Parker. (Illus.). 128p. (J). (gr. 1-3). 1999. 6.00 (*0-937739-35-9*, 10248) Roman IL.

My First Communion - Boy Image, Padded Cover. 2nd rev. ed. Anthony A. Petrusic. Ed. by Sue H. Parker. (Illus.). 128p. (J). (gr. 1-3). 1999. 10.00 (*0-937739-37-5*, 10288) Roman IL.

My First Communion - Faux Mother of Pearl, Grey. 2nd rev. ed. Anthony A. Petrusic. Ed. by Sue H. Parker. (Illus.). 128p. (J). (gr. 1-3). 1999. 15.00 (*0-937739-41-3*, 10278) Roman IL.

My First Communion - Faux Mother of Pearl, White. 2nd rev. ed. Anthony A. Petrusic. Ed. by Sue H. Parker. (Illus.). 128p. (J). (gr. 1-3). 1999. 15.00 (*0-937739-42-1*, 10279) Roman IL.

My First Communion - Girl Image. 2nd rev. ed. Anthony A. Petrusic. Ed. by Sue H. Parker. (Illus.). 128p. (J). (gr. 1-3). 1999. 6.00 (*0-937739-36-7*, 10249) Roman IL.

My First Communion - Girl Image, Padded Cover. 2nd rev. ed. Anthony A. Petrusic. Ed. by Sue H. Parker. (Illus.). 128p. (J). (gr. 1-3). 1999. 10.00 (*0-937739-38-3*, 10289) Roman IL.

My First Communion - Symbol Design, Black. 2nd rev. ed. Anthony A. Petrusic. Ed. by Sue H. Parker. (Illus.). 128p. (J). (gr. 1-3). 1999. 4.50 (*0-937739-39-1*, 10268) Roman IL.

My First Communion - Symbol Design, White. 2nd rev. ed. Anthony A. Petrusic. Ed. by Sue H. Parker. (Illus.). 128p. (J). (gr. 1-3). 1999. 4.50 (*0-937739-40-5*, 10269) Roman IL.

My First Communion Album. Victor Hoagland. (Illus.). (J). 1996. 17.95 (*0-88271-500-3*) Regina Pr.

My First Communion Book. 56p. (J). 1988. pap. 4.95 (*0-8146-1547-3*) Liturgical Pr.

My First Computer Book. Advantage International, Inc. Staff. (Illus.). 50p. 1992. student ed. 19.95 (*1-56756-002-4*, SAC200) Advant Intl.

My First Cookbook. Rena Coyle. LC 84-40683. (Bialosky & Friends Bks.). (Illus.). 128p. (J). (gr. 1-5). 1985. pap. 10.95 (*0-89480-846-X*, 846) Workman Pub.

My First Cookbook. V. Mae Hoover. (Illus.). 104p. (Orig.). 1988. pap., spiral bd. 6.95 (*0-9621686-0-2*) A & H Pubns.

My First Counting Book see Mi Primer Libro de Contar

My First Counting Book. Lilian Moore. (Little Golden Treasures Ser.). 26p. (J). (ps). 1998. 5.99 (*0-307-20311-5*, 20311, Goldn Books) Gldn Bks Pub Co.

My First Cousin Once Removed: Money, Madness, & the Family of Robert Lowell. Sarah P. Stuart. LC 98-7787. (Illus.). 256p. 1998. 25.00 (*0-06-017689-X*) HarpC.

***My First Cousin Once Removed: Money, Madness & the Family of Robert Lowell.** Sarah Payne Stuart. 256p. 1999. pap. 13.00 (*0-06-093036-5*) HarpC.

My First Crossword Puzzle Book. Anna Pomaska. (J). pap. 1.00 (*0-486-26299-5*) Dover.

My First Day at Camp see Bank Street Ready-to-Read Books: Levels 1, 2 & 3

My First Day at Camp. Ellen Weiss. LC 98-21928. (Bank Street Ready-to-Read Ser.). (Illus.). 32p. (J). 1999. pap. 4.50 (*0-553-37587-3*) Bantam.

My First Day at Preschool. Edwina Riddell. LC 91-18374. (Illus.). 32p. (J). (ps). 1992. 9.95 (*0-8120-6261-2*) Barron.

My First Day at Preschool. Edwina Riddell. (Illus.). 32p. 1995. pap. 5.95 (*0-8120-1878-8*) Barron.

***My First Day at School.** Harry W. Faircloth. (Illus.). 24p. (J). 1999. pap. 12.95 (*0-9668650-3-0*) Maximilian Pr.

***My First Day at School.** Erin Gathrid. (Illus.). (J). 2000. 9.99 (*0-307-33103-2*) Gldn Bks Pub Co.

My First Day at School. Ronnie Sellers. (J). 1985. 12.45 (*0-89845-373-9*, Caedmon) HarperAudio.

My First Day of School. P. K. Hallinan. (Illus.). 24p. (J). (ps-3). 1987. per. 4.95 (*0-8249-8533-8*, Ideals Child) Hambleton-Hill.

My First Day Of School. P. K. Hallinan. 24p. 1999. 6.95 (*1-57102-154-X*) Hambleton-Hill.

My First Day of School. Patrick Hallinan. (Illus.). (J). 1987. pap. write for info. (*0-8249-8166-9*) Ideals.

My First Days in the White House. Huey Long. 1992. lib. bdg. 88.95 (*0-8490-5514-8*) Gordon Pr.

My First Dentist Visit. Julia Allen. (My First Ser.). (Illus.). (J). (gr. k-3). 1987. 9.95 (*0-89868-185-5*); pap. 3.95 (*0-89868-186-3*) ARO Pub.

My First Design Book: Projects to Make with Stencil Shapes. Lone Morton. (Illus.). 24p. (J). (gr. 1-4). 1993. pap. 4.95 (*0-8120-1744-7*) Barron.

My First Diary. Mary M. Simon. (Illus.). 80p. (Orig.). (J). (gr. 2-5). 1992. pap. 4.99 (*0-570-04721-8*, 56-1680) Concordia.

***My First Dictionary.** S. Brimax. (J). 1998. 60.00 (*81-86982-64-7*, Pub. by Business Pubns) St Mut.

My First Dictionary. Illus. by Terry Burton. 48p. (J). (ps-1). 1997. 7.98 (*1-85854-600-1*) Brimax Bks.

My First Dictionary. Diana Fisher. 1999. 9.95 (*1-56010-405-8*) W Foster Pub.

My First Dictionary. Harper Collins Staff. (Illus.). 240p. 1997. 15.50 (*0-673-28509-X*) Harper SF.

My First Dictionary. Betty Root. LC 93-20145. (Illus.). 96p. (J). (gr. k-4). 1993. 17.95 (*1-56458-277-9*) DK Pub Inc.

My First Dictionary. Betty Root & Jonathan Langley. (Illus.). (J). text 23.95 (*0-590-74595-6*) Scholastic Inc.

My First Dictionary. Alan Snow. LC 91-23485. (Illus.). 32p. (J). (gr. k-3). 1992. pap. text 4.95 (*0-8167-2516-0*) Troll Communs.

My First Dictionary: Four Thousand Words & Meanings for Young Readers. (Illus.). 448p. (J). 1991. pap. 15.50 (*0-06-275001-1*, Harper Ref) HarpC.

My First Dictionary of the Zoo in Arabic & English. Librarie Du Liban. 1981. 5.50 (*0-86685-297-2*) Intl Bk Ctr.

My First Disney ABC Word Book. Ellen Weiss. LC 98-87222. (Big Bks.). (Illus.). 48p. (J). 1999. 12.99 (*0-7364-0070-2*, Pub. by Mouse Works) Time Warner.

My First Doctor Visit. Julia Allen. (My First Ser.). (Illus.). (J). (gr. k-3). 1987. 9.95 (*0-89868-187-1*); pap. 3.95 (*0-89868-188-X*) ARO Pub.

My First Doll Book Level 3: Hand Sewing. Winky Cherry. Ed. by Pati Palmer & Linda Wisner. LC 94-66067. (My First Sewing Book Ser.). (Illus.). 40p. (Orig.). (J). (gr. k-5). 1994. pap. 12.95 (*0-935278-36-2*) Palmer-Pletsch.

My First Dot-to-Dots. rev. ed. Illus. by Peter Kingston. (Super Activity Juniors Ser.). 48p. (Orig.). (J). (ps-k). 1992. pap. 3.99 (*0-8431-3456-9*, Price Stern) Peng Put Young Read.

My First Drawing Book. Tedd Arnold. LC 87-134510. (My First Bks.). (Illus.). 16p. (J). (ps-3). 1986. pap. 5.95 (*0-89480-350-6*, 1350) Workman Pub.

My First 81 Years. Dorcas Cavett. Ed. by Linda J. Dageforde. (Illus.). 224p. 1999. pap. 16.95 (*1-886225-33-8*, 2000) Dageforde Pub.

My First 80 Years. Martha Stelter. LC 97-72212. (Illus.). 123p. 1997. pap. 9.95 (*1-890352-01-2*) Jackson Harbor.

My First Embroidery Book Level 2: A Name Sampler. Winky Cherry. Ed. by Pati Palmer. (My First Sewing Book Ser.). (Illus.). 40p. (J). (ps-6). 1995. pap. 12.95 (*0-935278-31-1*) Palmer-Pletsch.

***My First Encounter with an Angel: Revelations of Ancient Wisdom, Vol. 1.** Sidney Schwartz. 300p. 1999. pap. 24.00 (*1-891850-21-0*, Pub. by Med Bear) New Leaf Dist.

My First Encyclopedia. Alan Snow. LC 91-24320. (Illus.). 32p. (J). (gr. k-3). 1992. pap. 4.95 (*0-8167-2520-9*) Troll Communs.

My First Encyclopedia. Carol Watson. LC 92-53477. (Illus.). 80p. (J). (gr. k-3). 1993. 16.95 (*1-56458-214-0*) DK Pub Inc.

***My First "Essential Preschool Learning Tools" Display.** DK Publishing Staff. 2000. 750.00 (*0-7894-6906-5*) DK Pub Inc.

My First European Dictionary. (J). (gr. 2-5). 1995. 7.98 (*1-85854-148-4*) Brimax Bks.

***My First Fairy Tale Treasury.** (Illus.). 288p. (J). 2000. write for info. (*0-307-37501-3*) Gldn Bks Pub Co.

My First Family Tree Book. Catherine Bruzzone. (Illus.). 24p. (J). (gr. k-3). 1992. pap., per. 3.95 (*0-8249-8546-X*, Ideals Child) Hambleton-Hill.

***My First Farm Book.** DK Publishing Staff. LC 99-39924. (Illus.). 64p. (J). (gr. k-2). 2000. 16.95 (*0-7894-5214-6*, D K Ink) DK Pub Inc.

My First Fishes & Other Waterlife: Pop-Up Field Guide. Cecilia Fitzsimons. LC 86-45489. (Illus.). 12p. (J). (gr. k-4). 1987. 8.95 (*0-06-021873-8*) HarpC Child Bks.

My First Five Hundred Words. 64p. (J). 1994. 7.98 (*0-86112-753-6*) Brimax Bks.

***My First Five Years.** Anne Geddes. 88p. 1999. 21.95 (*0-7683-2082-8*) CEDCO Pub.

My First Five Years: A Developmental Photo Album. Shirley Shufer. Ed. by Jane Shufer. (Illus.). 110p. (Orig.). 1997. pap., spiral bd. 14.95 (*0-9655660-0-5*) Serenity Books.

My First Five Years: A Record Book. Freidman & Fairfa. 48p. 1997. text 9.95 (*1-56799-516-0*, Friedman-Fairfax) M Friedman Pub Grp Inc.

My First Five Years: Apricot Bouquet. Anne Geddes. (Illus.). 82p. 1996. 21.95 (*1-55912-022-3*) CEDCO Pub.

My First Five Years: Atop of Towels. Anne Geddes. (Illus.). 82p. 1996. 21.95 (*1-55912-021-5*) CEDCO Pub.

My First Five Years: Daffodils Multicultural Edition. Anne Geddes. (My First Five Years Ser.). 82p. (J). 1997. 21.95 (*1-55912-288-9*) CEDCO Pub.

My First Five Years: Wet Sparrow. Anne Geddes. (Illus.). 82p. 1998. 21.95 (*0-7683-2019-4*) CEDCO Pub.

My First Five Years: Wrapped in Blanket. Anne Geddes. (Anne Geddes Line Ser.). (Illus.). 81p. 1995. 21.95 (*1-55912-002-9*) CEDCO Pub.

My First Flashlight: A Book & Flashlight. Dawn Bentley. LC 97-180869. (Illus.). 14p. (J). (ps). 1997. 12.95 (*0-590-10099-8*, Cartwheel) Scholastic Inc.

My First Flight see Our Flight

My First Folk Songs, Pre-Reading. Gayle Kowalchyk & E. L. Lancaster. 16p. 1990. pap. 5.50 (*0-7390-0781-5*, 227) Alfred Pub.

My First French Vocabulary. Bookmaker & Michele Raquin. (Illus.). 48p. 1991. pap. 12.00 (*0-13-377607-7*, Harraps IN) Macmillan Gen Ref.

My First French Words. Illus. by David Melling. LC 98-46154. (My First ...Words to See Ser.). (FRE.). 48p. 1999. 11.95 (*0-8442-2406-5*, 24065, Passprt Bks) NTC Contemp Pub Co.

My First Gamebook. Katy Dobbs. LC 85-40524. (My First Bks.). (Illus.). 16p. (J). (ps-3). 1985. pap. 5.95 (*0-89480-945-8*, 945) Workman Pub.

My First Garden. Julia Allen. (My First Thirty Word Books Ser.). (Illus.). (J). (gr. k-3). 1994. pap. 3.95 (*0-89868-221-5*, Read Res); lib. bdg. 9.95 (*0-89868-220-7*, Read Res) ARO Pub.

My First Garden. Tomek Bogacki. LC 99-24503. (Illus.). 40p. (YA). (ps-3). 2000. 16.00 (*0-374-32518-9*) FS&G.

My First Garden Book. NK Lawn & Garden Co. Staff. (NK Lawn & Garden Step-by-Step Visual Guides Ser.). (Illus.). 80p. (J). 1992. pap. 6.95 (*0-380-76667-1*, Avon Bks) Morrow Avon.

My First Garden Book. NK Lawn & Garden Co. Staff. (Step-by-Step Visual Guide Ser.). 80p. 1991. pap. 7.95 (*1-880281-05-8*) NK Lawn & Garden.

My First German Vocabulary. Bookmaker & Michele Raquin. (Illus.). 48p. 1991. pap. 11.00 (*0-13-377599-2*, Harraps IN) Macmillan Gen Ref.

***My First Golden Bible.** (Illus.). 192p. (J). 2000. pap. 9.99 (*0-307-16854-9*) Gldn Bks Pub Co.

My First Golden Book of ABC's. Golden Books Staff. 48p. 1999. 9.99 (*0-307-45351-0*) Gldn Bks Pub Co.

My First Golden Book of 123's. Golden Books Staff. 48p. 1999. 9.99 (*0-307-45350-2*) Gldn Bks Pub Co.

My First Golf Book. James D. Smith & Lauren M. Smith. LC 99-72074. (My First Book Ser.). (Illus.). 44p. (J). (ps-1). 2000. 14.95 (*0-9669116-0-1*, Pub. by CTL Pubg) ACCESS Pubs Network.

My First Grade. Julia Allen. (My First Thirty Word Book Ser.). (Illus.). (J). (gr. k-3). 1994. pap. 3.95 (*0-89868-223-1*, Read Res); lib. bdg. 9.95 (*0-89868-222-3*, Read Res) ARO Pub.

My First Grade Music Book. rev. ed. Ann M. Eisen & Lamar Robertson. (My Music Book Ser.: Vol. 1). (Illus.). 64p. (J). (gr. 1-3). 1994. pap. text, wbk. ed. 30.00 (*1-889967-03-3*) Sneaky Snake.

My First Grade Yearbook. Bearl Brooks. (My Yearbook Ser.). 544p. (gr. 1). 1979. 18.00 (*0-8209-0081-8*, MFG-1) ESP.

My First Grieg see Mio Primo Grieg Piano Solo - My First Grieg: Piano Solo

My First Handwriting. Longman Publishing Staff. (J). Date not set. pap. text. write for info. (*0-582-51112-7*, Pub. by Addison-Wesley) Longman.

My First Health & Nutrition Coloring Book: Mr. Carrots Coloring Book. David Greenbaum & Edward Wasser. (Health & Nutrition Coloring Book Ser.). (Illus.). 40p. (Orig.). (J). (gr. 2). 1988. pap. 0.99 (*0-9621833-0-X*) D Greenbaum.

My First Hebrew Alphabet Book. Jennifer Lapine & Susan Lapine. (Illus.). 48p. (J). (ps-1). 1977. pap. 3.95 (*0-8197-0399-0*) Bloch.

My First Hidden Picture Coloring Book. Lynn Adams. (Illus.). (J). (gr. k-3). 1993. pap. 1.00 (*0-486-27478-0*) Dover.

My First Holy Communion. Marita Conlon-McKenna. 1989. pap. 22.00 (*1-85390-116-4*, Pub. by Veritas Pubns) St Mut.

My First Holy Communion: For Girls. Victor Hoagland. (Precious Moments Ser.). 1992. 12.95 (*0-88271-501-1*) Regina Pr.

My First Holy Communion: For Girls. Victor Hoagland. (Precious Moments Ser.). (J). 1992. 12.95 (*0-88271-503-8*) Regina Pr.

My First Horse. Marilyn S. Rose. 53p. (Orig.). (J). (gr. 3-4). 1991. pap. 9.95 (*0-9632117-0-6*) AMI & Arabian Mktg.

My First Horse: No Problem! Tommie Kirksmith. LC 97-20696. 178p. 1997. 19.95 (*0-87605-605-2*) Macmillan.

My First Hymnal: Seventy-Five Favorite Bible Songs & What They Mean. Karyn Henley & Randall Dennis. (Illus.). 160p. (J). (ps-3). 1994. 14.95 (*0-917143-35-3*) Sparrow TN.

My First I Can Read. Judyann Grant. (Illus.). 32p. (ps up). 12.95 (*0-06-028723-3*) HarpC.

My First Incredible, Amazing Dictionary. (ps-3). text 29.95 incl. cd-rom (*1-56458-902-1*) HM.

My First Insects, Spiders & Crawlers: Pop-Up Field Guide. Cecilia Fitzsimons. LC 86-45490. (Illus.). 12p. (J). (gr. k-4). 1987. 8.95 (*0-06-021889-4*) HarpC Child Bks.

My First Jewish Word Book. Rosalyn Schanzer. LC 92-12697. (J). (ps). 1992. 13.95 (*0-929371-36-4*) Kar-Ben.

My First Job. Julia Allen. (My First Ser.). (Illus.). (J). (gr. k-3). 1987. 3.95 (*0-89868-183-9*); pap. 9.95 (*0-89868-184-7*) ARO Pub.

***My First Joke Book.** Anderson. (J). 2000. pap. 5.95 (*0-552-54278-4*, Pub. by Transworld Publishers Ltd) Trafalgar.

My First Joke Book. Shoo Rayner. 32p. 1999. pap. 3.99 (*0-14-054822-X*) NAL.

My First Kwanzaa Book. Deborah M. Newton Chocolate. LC 92-1200. (Illus.). 32p. (J). (ps-2). 1992. 10.95 (*0-590-45762-4*, Cartwheel) Scholastic Inc.

***My First Kwanzaa Book.** Deborah M. Newton Chocolate. (Illus.). 32p. (J). (ps-2). 1999. mass mkt. 5.99 (*0-439-12926-5*) Scholastic Inc.

My First Last Day at School: Daily Devotions for Living in the Real World. Al Cadenhead, Jr. 192p. 1995. pap. 15.00 (*1-57312-011-1*) Smyth & Helwys.

My First Learn & Do Jewish Holiday Book. Rifka Gootel. (Illus.). 64p. (J). (gr. k-2). pap. 4.95 (*0-87441-475-X*) Behrman.

My First Lessons. Phyllis Chvostal. (Illus.). (Orig.). 1993. pap. 6.00 (*0-9631050-6-X*) Safe Harbour.

My First Library Carry Case, 4 vols. Whitecap Bks. (J). 1998. 9.95 (*1-55110-814-3*) Whitecap Bks.

***My First Lift the Flap Animals.** DK Publishing Staff. (My First Bks.). (Illus.). 12p. (ps-k). 2000. 9.95 (*0-7894-6515-9*) DK Pub Inc.

My First Lift the Flap Board Book. LC 99-21186. (My First Bks.). (Illus.). 12p. (J). (ps-k). 1999. 9.95 (*0-7894-4736-3*) DK Pub Inc.

My First Little Bible Story Book. Linda Parry. LC 95-48118. (Illus.). 200p. (J). 1996. 3.00 (*1-57312-035-9*) Smyth & Helwys.

My First Little 12 Story Book Set. Rochelle Larkin. (J). (ps-2). 1994. 29.95 (*1-886520-00-3*) Micro R&D.

My First Look at Numbers. Photos by Stephen Oliver. LC 89-63088. (Illus.). 24p. (J). (ps). 1990. 9.00 (*0-679-80533-8*, Pub. by Random Bks Yng Read) Random.

My First Love. Callie West. (Love Stories Ser.). 192p. (YA). (gr. 7-12). 1995. mass mkt. 4.50 (*0-553-56661-X*) Bantam.

My First Love & Other Disasters. Francine Pascal. 176p. (J). (gr. 7 up). 1986. mass mkt. 2.95 (*0-440-95447-9*, LLL BDD) BDD Bks Young Read.

My First Loves. Ivan Klima. Tr. by Ewald Osers from CZE. LC 88-38798.Tr. of Moje Prvni Lasky. 1989. pap. 9.95 (*0-393-30601-1*) Norton.

My First Lunch Box. Eric Suben. (Story Shapes Ser.). (Illus.). 24p. (Orig.). (J). (gr. k-1). 1997. pap. 2.25 (*1-56293-933-5*, McClanahan Book) Learn Horizon.

My First Machine Sewing Book Level 4: Straight Stitching. Winky Cherry. Ed. by Lynette R. Black et al. (My First Sewing Book Ser.). (Illus.). 40p. (Orig.). (J). (gr. k-6). 1994. pap. 12.95 (*0-935278-40-0*) Palmer-Pletsch.

My First Magic Book. Lawrence Leyton. LC 93-22104. (Illus.). 48p. (J). (gr. k-4). 1993. 12.95 (*1-56458-319-8*) DK Pub Inc.

My First Mass Book. M. Bernard. (J). (ps-3). Date not set. pap. text 1.95 (*0-88271-165-2*) Regina Pr.

My First Mass Book: Little Angel. K. Cavanagh. (J). (ps-3). Date not set. pap. text 1.25 (*0-88271-200-4*) Regina Pr.

My First Math Book. (SPA.). (Orig.). (J). write for info. (*0-7894-0312-9*, 5-70666) DK Pub Inc.

My First Math Book. Beth A. Wise. (J). 1997. pap. text, wbk. ed. 2.25 (*1-56293-952-1*, McClanahan Book) Learn Horizon.

My First Mazes. rev. ed. Peter Kingston. (Super Activity Juniors Ser.). (Illus.). 48p. (J). (ps-k). 1992. pap. 3.99 (*0-8431-3457-7*, Price Stern) Peng Put Young Read.

***My First Meal, Vol. 2.** Phyllis Adams-Crymes. (Children's Diary Ser.). (Illus.). (J). (gr. k-3). 2000. pap. text. write for info. (*1-930659-02-4*) P Adams-Crymes.

***My First Millennium.** Lathika Sadasivan. LC 00-102530. (Illus.). 20p. (J). (ps-3). 2000. pap. 7.99 (*0-9700318-0-7*) Peek A Bks.

My First Missal. 1995. pap. 3.50 (*0-8189-0679-0*) Alba.

My First Missal. Illus. by Carla Cortesi. 56p. (J). (gr. 1-4). pap. 3.50 (*0-8198-4775-5*) Pauline Bks.

My First Monolingual English Words. Neil Morris & David Melling. LC 98-37176. (My First ...Words to See Ser.). 48p. (J). 1999. 11.95 (*0-8442-2405-7*, 24057, Passprt Bks) NTC Contemp Pub Co.

My First Mother Goose. Illus. by Lisa McCue. 20p. (J). (gr. k-3). 1999. bds. 11.99 (*1-57584-254-8*, RD Childrens) Rdrs Digest.

My First Mother Goose , 1 Vol. Kathy Wilburn. LC 98-235407. (J). 1998. write for info. (*0-7853-2669-3*) Pubns Intl Ltd.

M

An Asterisk (*) at the beginning of an entry indicates that the title is appearing for the first time.

My First Music Book. Helen Drew. LC 92-54306. (Illus.). 48p. (J). (gr. k-3). 1993. 12.95 (*1-56458-215-9*) DK Pub Inc.

My First Nature Books, 11 bks. Incl. Air. Kitty Benedict & Andrienne Soutter-Perrot. 32p. (J). (gr. 1-3). 1993. lib. bdg. 14.60 (*0-88682-547-4*, Creat Educ); Ant. Kitty Benedict. LC 92-15122. (Illus.). 32p. (J). (gr. 1-3). 1993. lib. bdg. 14.60 (*0-88682-564-4*, Creat Educ); Cow. Kitty Benedict. LC 92-14456. (Illus.). 32p. (J). (gr. 1-3). 1993. lib. bdg. 14.60 (*0-88682-567-9*, Creat Educ); Earth. Andrienne Soutter-Perrot. (Illus.). 32p. (J). (gr. 1-3). 1993. lib. bdg. 14.60 (*0-88682-548-2*, Creat Educ); Earthworm. Andrienne Soutter-Perrot. LC 92-15024. (Illus.). 32p. (J). (gr. 1-3). 1993. lib. bdg. 14.60 (*0-88682-566-0*, Creat Educ); Fire. Andrienne Soutter-Perrot. (Illus.). 32p. (J). (gr. 1-3). 1993. lib. bdg. 14.60 (*0-88682-553-9*, Creat Educ); Oak. Andrienne Soutter-Perrot. (Illus.). 32p. (J). (gr. 1-3). 1993. lib. bdg. 14.60 (*0-88682-550-4*, Creat Educ); Toad. Illus. by Monique Felix. LC 92-14165. 32p. (J). (gr. 1-3). 1993. lib. bdg. 14.60 (*0-88682-568-7*, Creat Educ); 160.60 (*0-88682-570-9*, Creat Educ) Creative Co.

My First Nature Treasury. Lizann Flatt. (Illus.). 48p. (J). (ps-3). 1995. 12.95 (*0-87156-362-2*) Sierra Club Childrens.

My First Ninety Days. (Gifts of Growth Ser.). 96p. (Orig.). 1987. pap. text 3.00 (*0-934391-09-2*) Quotidian.

My First Ninety Years. Leon S. Medalia, Jr. 300p. 1974. 12.00 (*0-685-41734-4*) Fountainhead.

***My First Number Bath Book.** DK Publishing Staff. (Bath Bks.). (Illus.). 10p. (ps-k). 2000. pap. 4.95 (*0-7894-6517-5*) DK Pub Inc.

My First Number Board Book. DK Publishing Staff. LC 99-209609. (My First Bks.). 1999. bds. 6.95 (*0-7894-3450-4*) DK Pub Inc.

My First Number Book. (Illus.). (J). 16.95 (*0-590-74282-5*) Scholastic Inc.

My First Number Book. Marie Heinst. LC 91-58193. (Illus.). 48p. (J). (ps-3). 1992. 14.95 (*1-879431-73-4*) DK Pub Inc.

My First Number Book. Ed. by Scholastic, Inc. Staff. (FRE., Illus.). (J). 19.99 (*0-590-74416-X*) Scholastic Inc.

My First Numbers. Judy Nayer. (J). 1997. pap. text, wbk. ed. 2.25 (*1-56293-953-X*, McClanahan Book) Learn Horizon.

My First Nursery Rhymes. HarperCollins Publishing Staff & Bruce Whatley. LC 98-70415. (Illus.). 24p. (YA). (ps up). 1999. 9.95 (*0-694-01205-X*, HarpFestival) HarpC Child Bks.

My First 100 Hebrew Words: A Young Person's Dictionary of Judaism. Howard I. Bogot. (Illus.). (J). (gr. k-3). 1993. 11.95 (*0-8074-0509-4*, 101716) UAHC.

My First One Hundred Words in French & English. Keith Faulkner. (Illus.). 14p. (J). (ps-3). 1993. 11.95 (*0-671-86447-5*) S&S Bks Yung.

My First 123 Book, 4 vols. Silver Dolphin Staff. (My First Books Ser.). (Illus.). 16p. (J). 1998. 16.95 (*1-57145-312-1*, Silver Dolph) Advantage Pubs.

My First Origami No. 1: Airplanes, Penguin, Ivy & Pinwheel. (J). (gr. 1-3). 1989. bds. 3.95 (*0-89346-317-5*) Heian Intl.

My First Origami No. 2: Waterbird, Hat, Bat & Turtle. (J). (gr. 1-3). 1989. bds. 3.95 (*0-89346-318-3*) Heian Intl.

My First Origami No. 3: Cap, Piano, Pigeon & Snake. (J). (gr. 1-3). 1989. bds. 3.95 (*0-89346-319-1*) Heian Intl.

My First Origami No. 4: Grasshopper, Cat, Fish & Boat. (J). (gr. 1-3). 1989. bds. 3.95 (*0-89346-320-5*) Heian Intl.

My First Origami No. 5: Crow, Flower, Cicada & Boots. (J). (gr. 1-3). 1989. bds. 3.95 (*0-89346-321-3*) Heian Intl.

My First Origami No. 6: Box, Sailboat, Table & Chair, & Angelfish. (J). (gr. 1-3). 1989. bds. 3.95 (*0-89346-322-1*) Heian Intl.

***My First Oxford Book of Poems.** John Foster. (Illus.). 96p. 2000. 19.95 (*0-19-276201-X*) OUP.

***My First Oxford Book of Stories.** Geraldine McCaughrean. (Illus.). 96p. 2000. 19.95 (*0-19-278115-4*) OUP.

My First Painting Book. Dawn Sirett. LC 93-34261. (Illus.). 48p. (J). (gr. k-5). 1994. 12.95 (*1-56458-466-6*) DK Pub Inc.

My First Party. Julia Allen. (My First Thirty Word Book Ser.). (Illus.). (J). (gr. k-3). 1994. pap. 3.95 (*0-89868-234-7*, Read Res); lib. bdg. 9.95 (*0-89868-233-9*, Read Res) ARO Pub.

My First Patchwork Book: Hand & Machine Sewing. Winky Cherry. (My First Sewing Book Ser.). (Illus.). 40p. (J). (gr. 1-6). 1997. pap. 12.95 (*0-935278-48-6*) Palmer-Pletsch.

My First Peek-a-Boo Game. Mouse Works Staff. (Disney Babies Ser.). (J). 1998. 4.98 (*1-57082-713-3*, Pub. by Mouse Works) Little.

My First Phone. Illus. by Francese Rigol. (J). (ps up). 1996. 12.99 (*0-614-15713-7*) Random.

My First Phone Call. Julia Allen. (My First Ser.). (Illus.). (J). (gr. k-3). 1987. 9.95 (*0-89868-189-8*); pap. 3.95 (*0-89868-190-1*) ARO Pub.

My First Phonebook. Iris L. Solomon & Ronald B. Solomon. (Illus.). 40p. (Orig.). (J). (ps-3). 1997. spiral bd. 9.95 (*0-9658167-0-2*) Swingset Pr.

***My First Phonics Board Book.** DK Publishing Staff. LC 99-39928. (Illus.). 36p. (J). (gr. k-2). 2000. 6.95 (*0-7894-5215-4*, D K Ink) DK Pub Inc.

My First Phonics Book. DK Publishing Staff & Diane McGuinness. LC 99-21465. (My First Bks.). (Illus.). 48p. (J). (ps-k). 1999. 16.95 (*0-7894-4737-1*) DK Pub Inc.

My First Photography Book. Dave King. LC 94-7359. (Illus.). 48p. (J). (gr. k-3). 1994. 12.95 (*1-56458-673-1*) DK Pub Inc.

My First Picnic. Mouse Works Staff. 5p. (J). 1997. 6.98 (*1-57082-569-6*, Pub. by Mouse Works) Time Warner.

My First Picture Bible see Mi Primera Biblia Ilustrada

My First Picture Bible. (J). Date not set. 8.95 (*0-88271-532-1*, 10520) Regina Pr.

My First Picture Bible. Eira Reeves. LC 98-206083. (Illus.). 128p. (J). 1998. 9.99 (*0-8024-6023-2*) Moody.

My First Picture Dictionary see Big Blue Box of Books: Five Picture-Book Favorites

My First Picture Dictionary. Illus. by Huck Scarry. LC 76-24174. (Pictureback Ser.). (J). (ps-2). 1978. pap. 3.25 (*0-394-83486-0*, Pub. by Random Bks Yng Read) Random.

***My First Picture Dictionary.** Schofield & Sims Staff. (Illus.). (J). 1999. pap. 24.00 (*0-7217-0723-8*, Pub. by Schofield) St Mut.

My First Plane Ride. Erin Gathrid. 16p. 1999. 9.99 (*0-307-33304-3*) Gldn Bks Pub Co.

My First Pop-Up Book of Prehistoric Animals. Roma Bishop. (Illus.). (J). (ps-3). 1994. 12.95 (*0-671-89556-7*) S&S Bks Yung.

My First Prayer Book. 1998. 3.95 (*0-88271-575-5*) Regina Pr.

My First Prayer Book. Ed. by Jeanette Gojoy. (Illus.). 80p. (J). (ps-4). 1998. text 5.00 (*1-888765-50-X*) Devon Trading.

My First Prayer Book. Frances C. Heerey. (J). 1986. 3.95 (*0-88271-131-8*) Regina Pr.

My First Prayer Book. Lawrence G. Lovasik. (Saint Joseph Picture Bks.). (Illus.). 1987. pap. text 1.25 (*0-89942-288-8*, 288-00) Catholic Bk Pub.

My First Prayer Book: Little Angel. K. Cavanagh. (J). (ps-3). Date not set. pap. text 1.25 (*0-88271-204-7*) Regina Pr.

My First Prayerbook. Lawrence G. Lovasik. (Saint Joseph Beginner Ser.). (Illus.). (J). 1991. 3.50 (*0-89942-205-5*, 205/22) Catholic Bk Pub.

My First Prayers. (Saint Joseph Picture Bks.). (Illus.). 1978. pap. 1.25 (*0-89942-490-2*, 490-00) Catholic Bk Pub.

***My First Prayers.** Bessie Pease Gutmann et al. 48p. 2000. 12.95 (*1-884807-52-6*, EC 752) Blushing Rose.

My First Prayers: A Book about Talking to Jesus. Debby Anderson & L. B. Norton. (Illus.). 320p. (J). (ps). 1995. 10.99 (*0-7814-0210-7*, Chariot Bks) Chariot Victor.

My First Prayers: Play-a-Sound Book. Illus. by Judith Pfeiffer & Tish Tenud. 12p. (J). (ps-k). 1999. 9.99 (*0-7847-0890-8*, 03750) Standard Pub.

My First Prayers & Psalms. Illus. by Anna Curti. (ps-3). 1999. 7.99 (*0-375-80235-5*, Pub. by Random Bks Yng Read) Random.

My First Quilt Book: Machine Sewing. Winky Cherry. (My First Sewing Book Ser.). (Illus.). 40p. (J). (gr. k-6). 1997. pap. 12.95 (*0-935278-49-4*) Palmer-Pletsch.

My First Raggedy Ann: Raggedy Ann & the Birthday Surprise. Illus. by Stephanie T. Peters & Kathy Mitter. LC 99-24899. 2000. per. 15.00 (*0-689-83136-6*) S&S Bks Yung.

My First Reader & Skills Book: One Hundred Words Plus. Alfred G. Prather & Gloria A. Prather. Ed. by Arden C. Prather. (Illus.). 36p. (Orig.). (J). (gr. 1-3). 1988. pap. write for info. (*0-9619655-2-5*) Academic Parks Co.

***My First Readers: Hooked on Phonics - Learn to Read.** (Illus.). 128p. (J). (ps-1). 2000. pap. 14.95 (*1-887942-85-8*) Gateway Learning.

***My First Readers: Hooked on Phonics Companion Books.** (Illus.). 112p. (J). (ps-1). 1998. pap. 19.95 (*1-887942-66-1*) Gateway Learning.

***My First Real Mother Goose Board Book.** Illus. by Blanche Fisher Wright. LC 00-21425. 30p. (J). (ps-k). 2000. bds. 6.99 (*0-439-14671-2*) Scholastic Inc.

My First Recorder Book. Janet Bunting. (Illus.). 32p. (J). (gr. 2-6). 1989. pap. 14.95 (*0-8120-7618-4*) Barron.

My First Report: Set of Fourteen Unit Studies. Christine J. Dillon. (Illus.). (J). (gr. 1-4). 1998. ring bd. 49.95 (*1-57896-038-X*, 9212) Hewitt Res Fnd.

My First Riddles. Judith H. Corwin. LC 97-73144. (Illus.). 24p. (J). (ps up). 1998. 9.95 (*0-694-01109-6*) HarpC Child Bks.

My First Sewing Book Level 1: Hand Sewing. Winky Cherry. (My First Sewing Book Ser.). Orig. Title: Is That Sew?. (Illus.). 40p. (J). (ps-6). 1994. pap. 12.95 (*0-935278-29-X*) Palmer-Pletsch.

My First Shapes & Colors Book. (Illus.). 16p. (J). (ps-1). 1998. 16.95 (*1-57145-361-X*, Silver Dolph) Advantage Pubs.

My First Siddur: A Selection of Prayers & Blessings for Boys & Girls. LC 89-12717. 32p. (Orig.). (J). (ps up). 1989. pap. 1.00 (*0-8266-0178-2*, Neshei Chabad) Kehot Pubn Soc.

My First Siddur: A Selection of Prayers for Jewish Boys & Girls. Ed. & Tr. by Berl Haskelevich from ENG. LC 90-82127. (RUS., Illus.). 32p. (Orig.). (J). (gr. k-8). 1990. pap. 1.50 (*1-878860-01-1*) Noviysvet.

My First Soccer Book: A Story, Coloring & Parent-Child Activity Book. Tom McLoughlin. (Soccer Kids Ser.). (Illus.). 16p. (J). (ps-k). 1998. pap. 4.95 (*0-9666681-8-9*) United Pubg.

My First Songs. Jane Manning. LC 97-73142. 24p. (J). (ps up). 1998. 9.95 (*0-694-00983-0*) HarpC Child Bks.

My First Spanish ABC Picture Coloring Book. Deb T. Bunnell. (Illus.). 24p. (J). 1998. pap. 2.50 (*0-486-40358-0*) Dover.

My First Spanish & English Dictionary. Passport Books Publishing Staff. (ENG & SPA.). (J). 1992. 12.15 (*0-606-02341-0*, Pub. by Turtleback) Demco.

My First Spanish & English Dictionary. Passport Books Staff. LC 99-86167. (SPA & ENG., Illus.). 64p. (J). (gr. 4-7). 2000. pap. 6.95 (*0-8442-0055-7*, 00557, Natl Textbk Co) NTC Contemp Pub Co.

My First Spanish Vocabulary. Bookmaker & Michele Raquin. (Illus.). 48p. 1991. pap. 11.00 (*0-13-377581-X*, Harraps IN) Macmillan Gen Ref.

My First Spanish Word Book. Angela Wilkes. LC 92-54500. (ENG & SPA., Illus.). 64p. (J). (gr. k-4). 1993. 16.95 (*1-56458-255-8*) DK Pub Inc.

My First Spanish Words. Melling. (My First ...Words to See Ser.). (SPA., Illus.). 48p. 1999. 11.95 (*0-8442-2399-9*, 23999, Passprt Bks) NTC Contemp Pub Co.

My First Stamp Album. 1988. pap. 9.95 (*0-912236-25-6*, Minkus Pubns) Novus Debut.

My First Stamp Album Starter Kit. (Illus.). (Orig.). (J). (gr. 3-9). 1988. pap. 15.95 (*0-912236-26-4*, Minkus Pubns) Novus Debut.

***My First Sticker Book.** Kindersley Publishing Dorling. (My First Bks.). 16p. (J). (gr. k-2). 1999. pap. text 6.95 (*0-7894-4686-3*) DK Pub Inc.

My First Storybook Dictionary see Mi Primer Diccionario

***My First Storybook Treasury.** (Padded Storybook Bind-Ups Ser.). (Illus.). 288p. (J). 2000. 12.99 (*0-307-37502-1*, 37502, Goldn Books) Gldn Bks Pub Co.

My First Study Bible: Exploring God's Word on My Own. Paul Loth. 528p. (J). (gr. 1-5). 1994. 14.99 (*0-7852-8274-2*) Tommy Nelson.

My First Summer in the Sierra. John Muir. 1992. 22.50 (*0-8446-6523-1*) Peter Smith.

My First Summer in the Sierra. John Muir. LC 89-6081. (Illus.). 208p. 1990. pap. 10.00 (*0-87156-748-2*, Pub. by Sierra) Random.

My First Summer in the Sierra. John Muir. 336p. 1987. pap. 9.95 (*0-14-025570-2*) Viking Penguin.

My First Summer in the Sierra. John Muir. LC 90-47834. (Illus.). 361p. 1990. reprint ed. 34.95 (*0-87797-192-7*) Cherokee.

My First Summer in the Sierra. John Muir. (BCL1 - United States Local History Ser.). 353p. 1991. reprint ed. lib. bdg. 89.00 (*0-7812-6342-5*) Rprt Serv.

My First Summer in the Sierras, 001. John Muir. LC 98-16599. 336p. 1998. pap. 10.00 (*0-395-35351-3*) HM.

My First Tea Journal. large type ed. Linda R. Wexler. Ed. by Howard B. Raff. (Illus.). 112p. (Orig.). (J). (gr. 4 up). 1997. pap. 5.95 (*1-888230-04-5*) Chelsea St Prods.

My First Theory Book: Note Names for Coloring. Carmela Mercuri. (Illus.). 32p. (Orig.). (J). (gr. 1-6). 1987. pap. text 5.95 (*0-935474-20-X*) Carousel Pubns Ltd.

My First Thirty Quiet Times. T. Saltzgiver. 1991. pap. text 2.50 (*0-9616562-0-4*) Salt Resources Inc.

My First Thirty-Two Words: Level 1. Robert Lado. (Reading Playhouse Ser.). (Illus.). 34p. (J). (ps). 1985. 9.95 (*1-879580-51-9*) Lado Intl Pr.

My First Three Hundred Babies. rev. ed. Gladys W. Hendrick. LC 78-50853. (Illus.). 173p. (Orig.). 1964. reprint ed. pap. 13.95 (*0-9600400-2-1*) Hurst Pub.

My First Three Hundred Babies. rev. ed. Gladys N. Hendrick. (Illus.). pap. 13.95 (*0-9600400-0-5*) Hurst Pub.

***My First 300 Babies.** rev. ed. Gladys West Hendrick. LC 97-62173. (Illus.). xx, 116p. 1999. spiral bd. 13.95 (*0-9600400-1-3*) Hurst Pub.

My First Time: Gay Men Describe Their First Same-Sex Experience. Ed. by Jack Hart. 180p. (Orig.). 1996. pap. 11.95 (*1-55583-283-0*) Alyson Pubns.

***My First Time: True Stories of Love & Sex from the Internet.** Suzi Landolphi. Ed. by Craig Paddock & Peter Foldy. 201p. 1999. pap. 14.95 (*0-9672635-0-6*) Good 2 Go Entertain.

My First Time at a Swim Meet: Poetry from Summer Camp. Ed. by Lynne M. Cohn. 52p. (YA). 1998. pap. text 20.00 (*1-56439-100-0*, Pub. by Ridgeway) Partners Pubs Grp.

My First Time II: Gay Men Describe Their First Same - Sex Experience. Jack Hart. 240p. 1999. pap. 12.95 (*1-55583-487-6*, Pub. by Alyson Pubns) Consort Bk Sales.

My First Tool Box. Dale Keene. (Story Shapes Ser.). (Illus.). 24p. (Orig.). (J). (ps-1). 1997. pap. 2.25 (*1-56293-934-3*, McClanahan Book) Learn Horizon.

***My First Train Trip.** Emily Neye. LC 99-37709. (All Aboard Bks.). 32p. 1999. pap. 2.99 (*0-448-41998-X*, G & D) Peng Put Young Read.

My First Trip to Africa. Atlantis T. Browder & Anthony T. Browder. Ed. by Anne Browder. LC 91-70328. (Illus.). 38p. (Orig.). (J). 1991. pap. 16.95 (*0-924944-02-1*); pap. 8.95 (*0-924944-01-3*) Inst Karmic.

My First Truck Board Book. DK Publishing Staff. LC 98-44421. (DK's "My First" Ser.). 36p. 1999. bds. 6.95 (*0-7894-3978-6*) DK Pub Inc.

My First Two Thousand Years: The Autobiography of the Wandering Jew. George S. Viereck & Paul Eldridge. 501p. 1984. reprint ed. 25.00 (*0-911378-16-2*) Sheridan.

My First Visit to a Farm. J. M. Parramon. (Illus.). 32p. (J). 1990. pap. 5.95 (*0-8120-4305-7*) Barron.

My First Visit to the Aviary. J. M. Parramon. (My First Visit Ser.). (Illus.). 32p. (J). (ps). 1990. pap. 4.95 (*0-8120-4303-0*) Barron.

My First Visit to the Zoo. J. M. Parramon. (My First Visit Ser.). (Illus.). 32p. (J). (ps). 1990. pap. 6.95 (*0-8120-4302-2*) Barron.

My First White Friend. Patricia Raybon. 256p. 1997. pap. 11.95 (*0-14-024436-0*) Viking Penguin.

My First White Friend: Confessions on Race, Love & Forgiveness. Patricia Raybon. 233p. 1996. 22.95 (*0-670-85956-7*, Viking); 22.95 (*0-614-95763-X*, Viking) Viking Penguin.

My First Wild Animals. Bettina Paterson. LC 89-17305. (Illus.). 32p. (J). (ps). 1991. 8.95 (*0-690-04771-1*) HarpC Child Bks.

My First Winnie the Pooh. 8p. (J). 1999. 10.99 (*0-7868-3241-X*, Pub. by Disney Pr) Time Warner.

My First Word & Picture Book. (Passport's Pull-Tab Language Bks.). (Illus.). 10p. (J). 1995. 10.95 (*0-8442-9184-6*, Passprt Bks) NTC Contemp Pub Co.

My First Word Bath Book. DK Publishing Staff. (DK's "My First" Ser.). 10p. 1999. 4.95 (*0-7894-4297-3*) DK Pub Inc.

My First Word Board Book. Angela Wilkes. (Illus.). 32p. (J). 1997. bds. 6.95 (*0-7894-1514-3*) DK Pub Inc.

***My First Word Book.** S. Brimax. (J). 1998. pap. 40.00 (*81-86982-65-5*, Pub. by Business Pubns) St Mut.

My First Word Book. Illus. by Stewart Lees. 48p. (J). (ps-1). 1997. 7.98 (*1-85854-519-6*) Brimax Bks.

My First Word Book. Carole Osterink. (Illus.). 64p. (Orig.). (J). (ps-3). 1996. pap. 6.95 (*1-56293-845-2*, McClanahan Book) Learn Horizon.

My First Word Book. Pat Thorne. (Illus.). (J). (ps up). 16.95 (*0-590-74011-3*) Scholastic Inc.

My First Word Book. Angela Wilkes. LC 91-60897. (Illus.). 64p. (J). (ps-3). 1991. 16.95 (*1-879431-21-1*) DK Pub Inc.

My First Word Book. rev. ed. DK Publishing Staff. LC 99-206690. (DK's "My First" Ser.). 64p. 1999. 16.95 (*0-7894-3977-8*) DK Pub Inc.

My First Word Book: English-Arabic. Librairie du Liban Staff. (ARA., Illus.). 64p. (J). 1993. 19.95 (*0-86685-598-X*, LDL598X, Pub. by Librairie du Liban) Intl Bk Ctr.

My First Words. (ENG & HEB., Illus.). 12p. (J). (ps-1). 1993. 9.95 (*0-943706-17-3*) Pitspopany.

My First Words. Schaffer, Frank, Publications Staff. (Help Your Child Learn Ser.). (Illus.). 24p. (J). (gr. 1-3). 1978. student ed. 3.98 (*0-86734-005-3*, FS-3006) Schaffer Pubns.

My First Words. Beth A. Wise. (J). 1997. pap. text, wbk. ed. 2.25 (*1-56293-954-8*, McClanahan Book) Learn Horizon.

My First World. unabridged ed. Edward F. Keller. (Illus.). 86p. 1995. spiral bd. 17.50 (*0-9660833-0-X*) E F Keller.

My First Year. 1995. 10.95 (*0-7459-3365-3*, Pub. by Lion Pubng) Trafalgar.

My First Year: A Beatrix Potter Baby Book. Beatrix Potter. 48p. 1998. 10.00 (*0-7232-4380-8*, F Warne) Peng Put Young Read.

My First Year As a Doctor: Real World Stories from America's M. D.s. Ed. by Melissa S. Ramsdell. LC 94-4990. (First Year Career Ser.). 144p. 1994. 19.95 (*0-8027-1290-8*); pap. 9.95 (*0-8027-7418-0*) Walker & Co.

My First Year As a Lawyer: Real World Stories from America's Lawyers. Ed. by Mark Simenhoff. LC 94-13585. (First Year Career Ser.). 120p. 1994. 19.95 (*0-8027-1289-4*); pap. 9.95 (*0-8027-7417-2*) Walker & Co.

My First Year As a Print Journalist: Real World Stories from America's Newspaper & Magazine Journalists. Ed. by Diane Selditch. LC 94-30748. (First Year Career Ser.). 160p. 1995. 21.95 (*0-8027-1295-9*) Walker & Co.

My First Year As a Print Journalist: Real World Stories from America's Newspaper & Magazine Journalists. Ed. by Diane Selditch. LC 94-30748. (First Year Career Ser.). 160p. 1995. pap. 11.95 (*0-8027-7426-1*) Walker & Co.

My First Year As a Teacher. Ed. by Pearl R. Kane. 176p. (C). 1996. mass mkt. 5.99 (*0-451-18891-8*, Sig) NAL.

My First Year in Book Publishing: Real World Stories from America's Book Publishing Professionals. Ed. by Lisa Healy. LC 94-9607. (First Year Career Ser.). 192p. 1994. 21.95 (*0-8027-1294-0*); pap. 11.95 (*0-8027-7425-3*) Walker & Co.

My First Year in Television. Ed. by L. Carol Ritchie. (First Year Career Ser.). 160p. (J). 1995. pap. 9.95 (*0-8027-7424-5*) Walker & Co.

My First Yellow Picture. John Dillon. 1997. pap. write for info. (*0-7214-5526-3*) Viking Penguin.

My First 100 Words. Illus. by Stephanie Ryder. 20p. (J). (ps). 1997. bds. 5.98 (*1-85854-547-1*) Brimax Bks.

My First 500 Words see Mis Primeras 500 Palabras

***My First 79 Years: Isaac Stern written with Chaim Potok.** Isaac W. Stern & Chaim Potok. LC 99-30918. 320p. 1999. 27.50 (*0-679-45130-7*) Knopf.

My Five Book. Jane Belk Moncure. LC 85-9699. (My Number Bks.). (Illus.). 32p. (J). (ps-2). 1985. lib. bdg. 21.36 (*0-89565-316-8*) Childs World.

My Five Cambridge Friends. Yuri Modin. 1995. 23.00 (*0-374-21698-3*) FS&G.

***My Five Cambridge Friends: Burgess, Maclean, Philby, Blunt, & Cairncross.** Yuri Modin. Tr. by Anthony Roberts. (Illus.). 282p. 2000. reprint ed. pap. 17.00 (*0-7881-9413-5*) DIANE Pub.

My 5 Cambridge Friends: Burgess, Maclean, Philby, Blunt, & Cairncross by Their KGB Controller. Yuri Modin. Tr. by Anthony Roberts. (Illus.). 282p. 1998. text 23.00 (*0-7881-5594-6*) DIANE Pub.

My Five Senses see Mis Cinco Sentidos

My Five Senses see Mis Cinco Sentidos: Cuento de un Leon

My 5 Senses. Aliki. (J). 1962. 12.89 (*0-690-56763-4*) HarpC Child Bks.

My 5 Senses. Susan Aliki. 1984. mass mkt. 4.95 (*0-06-445009-0*) HarpC.

My Five Senses. Aliki Brandenberg. (Let's-Read-And-Find-Out Book Ser.). (J). 1985. 10.15 (*0-606-02342-9*, Pub. by Turtleback) Demco.

My Five Senses. Margie Burton et al. Ed. by Susan Evento. (Early Connections Ser.). 16p. (J). (gr. k-2). 1998. pap. 4.25 (*1-892393-64-6*) Benchmark Educ.

My Five Senses. Margaret Miller. (Illus.). 24p. (J). 1998. per. 5.99 (*0-689-82009-7*) Aladdin.

My Five Senses. Margaret Miller. LC 93-1956. (Illus.). 24p. (J). (ps up). 1994. 16.00 (*0-671-79168-0*) S&S Bks Yung.

An Asterisk (*) at the beginning of an entry indicates that the title is appearing for the first time.

My Five Senses. Margaret Miller. 1998. 11.19 (*0-606-13631-2*, Pub. by Turtleback) Demco.

My Five Senses. Moore & Evans. (Illus.). 16p. (J). (gr. 1-3). 1994. pap., teacher ed. 5.95 (*1-55799-094-8*, 804) Evan-Moor Edu Pubs.

My Five Senses. Judy Nayer. (Whole-Language Big Bks.). (Illus.). 16p. (Orig.). (J). (ps-2). 1994. pap. 16.95 (*1-56784-067-1*) Newbridge Educ.

My Five Senses. rev. ed. Aliki. LC 88-35350. (Trophy Let's-Read-&-Find-Out Bk.). (Illus.). 32p. (J). (ps-1). 1989. pap. 4.95 (*0-06-445083-X*, HarpTrophy); lib. bdg. 15.89 (*0-690-04794-0*) HarpC Child Bks.

My Five Senses. rev. ed. Aliki. LC 88-853500. (Let's-Read-&-Find-Out Science Bks.). (Illus.). 32p. (J). (ps-3). 1989. 15.95 (*0-690-04792-4*) HarpC Child Bks.

My Five Senses Big Book. rev. ed. Aliki. LC 88-35350. (Let's-Read-&-Find-Out Science Bks.). (Illus.). 32p. (J). (ps-1). 1991. 21.95 (*0-06-020050-2*) HarpC Child Bks.

My Five Senses (Spanish edition) Mis cinco sentitidos. Aliki. Tr. by Daniel Santacruz. LC 94-24656. (SPA., Illus.). 32p. (J). (ps-3). 1995. pap. 5.95 (*0-06-445138-0*, HarpTrophy) HarpC Child Bks.

My Flag. Babette Katz. (Artists' Books Ser.). (Illus.). 64p. (Orig.). 1995. pap. 12.00 (*0-89822-116-1*) Visual Studies.

My Flesh the Sound of Rain. Heather MacLeod. LC 99-487822. 96p. 1999. pap. 7.95 (*1-55050-141-0*) Genl Dist Srvs.

***My Floral Roots: A Scottish Garden Odyssey.** Martha Smith. (Illus.). 320p. 2000. 22.95 (*1-55921-241-1*) Moyer Bell.

My Florida. Ernest Lyons. LC 69-14559. (Florida Classics Ser.). (Illus.). 136p. 1977. reprint ed. pap. 9.95 (*0-912451-01-7*) Florida Classics.

***My Florida Garden: A Gardener's Journal.** Cool Springs Press Publications Staff. 2000. 19.95 (*1-888608-84-6*) Cool Springs Pr.

***My Florida Garden: A Gardener's Journal.** Tom MacCubbin. (Illus.). 2000. spiral bd. 19.95 (*1-930604-03-3*) Cool Springs Pr.

My Florida Soul: Florida History with Humor. Edward T. Winn. (Illus.). 175p. 1997. pap. 7.00 (*0-9658489-0-6*, 1621) E T Winn.

My Folks Don't Want Me to Talk about Slavery. Ed. by Belinda Hurmence. LC 84-16891. 104p. 1984. pap. 6.95 (*0-89587-039-8*) Blair.

My Folks in Maine, Vol. 1. Charles A. Stephens. LC 72-3380. (Short Story Index Reprint Ser.). 1977. reprint ed. 20.95 (*0-8369-4161-6*) Ayer.

My Foolish Heart. James Pendergrast. LC 97-136642. 96p. 1997. pap. 12.00 (*0-671-53666-4*, PB Trade Paper) PB.

***My Football Book.** Gibbons. 2000. lib. bdg. 5.89 (*0-06-029221-0*) HarpC.

***My Football Book.** Gail Gibbons. LC 99-87202. (Illus.). 24p. (J). (ps-2). 2000. 5.95 (*0-688-17139-7*, Wm Morrow) Morrow Avon.

My Foots in the Stirrup - My Pony Won't Stand. large type ed. Stephen A. Bly. LC 98-18672. (Code of the West Ser.). 316p. 1998. 21.95 (*0-7838-0177-7*, G K Hall Lrg Type) Mac Lib Ref.

My Foot's in the Stirrup--My Pony Won't Stand, No. 5. Stephen A. Bly. LC 96-31445. (Code of the West Ser.: Vol. 5). 192p. 1996. pap. 9.99 (*0-89107-898-3*) Crossway Bks.

***My Footsteps Echo: The Yemen Journal of Rabbi Yaakov Sapir.** Tr. by Yaakov Lavon. 1998. 17.95 (*1-56871-184-0*, Pub. by Targum Pr) Feldheim.

My Foreign Country: Trevor Fishlock's Britain. Trevor Fishlock. 276p. 1998. 35.00 (*0-7195-5228-1*, Pub. by John Murray) Trafalgar.

My Forest Friends. Judy Mullican. (Big Bks.). (Illus.). 8p. (J). (ps-k). 1994. pap. text 10.95 (*1-57332-003-X*) HighReach Lrning.

***My Forest Friends.** large type ed. Judy Mullican. (LB Ser.). (Illus.). 8p. (J). (ps-1). 2000. pap. text 10.95 (*1-57332-172-9*); pap. text 10.95 (*1-57332-180-X*) HighReach Lrning.

My Foster Family: A Story for Children Entering Foster Care. Jennifer Levine. (Illus.). (J). (gr. k-6). 1994. pap. 6.95 (*0-87868-537-5*) Child Welfare.

My Four Book. Jane Belk Moncure. LC 85-9700. (My Number Bks.). (Illus.). 32p. (J). (ps-2). 1985. lib. bdg. 21.36 (*0-89565-315-X*) Childs World.

My Four Decades with Alabama Baptists: An Oral History Memoir. George E. Bagley. LC 89-85560. (Illus.). 272p. 1990. 15.95 (*0-9624149-0-5*) AL Baptist.

My Four Lions. Bernice Gold. (Illus.). 24p. (J). 1999. pap. 6.95 (*1-55037-602-0*, Pub. by Annick Pr) Firefly Bks Ltd.

***My Four Lions.** Bernice Gold. (Illus.). 24p. (J). 1999. lib. bdg. 17.95 (*1-55037-603-9*, Pub. by Annick Pr) Firefly Bks Ltd.

My Four Lives. Beth Armstrong. LC 89-61703. (Illus.). 164p. 1989. pap. 15.95 (*0-88100-064-7*) Natl Writ Pr.

***My Four Lives: Memoirs of a Singing Psychoanalyst.** Manfred Hecht. LC 99-15169. (Biography, Autobiography, Memoirs Ser.). (Illus.). 202p. 1999. pap. write for info. (*1-57241-085-X*) Ariadne CA.

My Fourscore Years: Autobiography by Sculptor Thomas Ball. Thomas Ball. Ed. by Shirley St. Leon. LC 93-1771. (Illus.). 200p. (C). 1993. 34.95 (*0-9620635-2-5*) TreCavalli Pr.

My Fourth-Grade Mess. Cathy East Dubowski. (Full House Michelle Ser.). 96p. (J). (gr. 2-4). 1996. per. 3.99 (*0-671-53576-5*, PB Trade Paper) PB.

My Fourth Grade Music Book. Ann M. Eisen & Lamar Robertson. (My Music Book Ser.: Vol. 4). (Illus.). 102p. (J). (gr. 4-7). 1999. pap. text, wbk. ed. 35.00 (*1-889967-02-5*) Sneaky Snake.

My Fourth Grade Yearbook. Bearl Brooks. (My Yearbook Ser.). 832p. (gr. 4). 1979. 18.00 (*0-8209-0084-2*, MFG-4) ESP.

My France: Politics, Culture, Myth. Eugen Weber. LC 90-35780. (Belknap Ser.). 424p. 1991. text 37.95 (*0-674-59575-0*, WEBMYF) HUP.

My France: Politics, Culture, Myth. Eugen Weber. 424p. 1992. pap. text 14.95 (*0-674-59576-9*) HUP.

My Freedom Trip: A Child's Escape to South Korea. Frances Park & Ginger Park. LC 97-77911. (Illus.). 32p. (J). (gr. k-3). 1998. 15.95 (*1-56397-468-1*) Boyds Mills Pr.

My Freshman Manual: The Official College Handbook. Joe P. Turton. 132p. pap. 6.95 (*0-9644302-0-7*) Joe Turton.

My Friend & I. Lisa Jahn-Clough. LC 98-30519. (Illus.). 32p. (J). (gr. k-3). 1999. 15.00 (*0-395-93545-8*) HM.

My Friend Anne Frank. Jacqueline Van Maarsen. Tr. by Debra F. Onkenhout from DUT. LC 96-90350. 80 p. (Orig.). 1996. pap. 8.95 (*0-533-12013-6*) Vantage.

My Friend at School. Patricia T. Cousin et al. (Visions: African-American Experiences: No. 29). (Illus.). 8p. (Orig.). (J). (gr. k-1). 1996. pap. text 3.00 (*1-57518-028-6*) Arborlake.

My Friend Bear. Jez Alborough. LC 97-32557. (Illus.). 32p. (J). (ps-2). 1998. 16.99 (*0-7636-0583-2*) Candlewick Pr.

My Friend Ben. Wanda G. Kachur. LC 97-65270. (Illus.). 50p. (J). 1997. pap. 6.95 (*0-9644271-4-1*) Peytral Pubns.

My Friend Can't Read: Christian Living - Encouragement. Doris Harris. Ed. by Becky Nelson. 21p. (YA). (gr. 7-12). 1994. pap. text 1.95 (*1-56309-097-X*, C946104, Wrld Changers Res) Womans Mission Union.

My Friend Chicken. Adam McCauley. LC 98-36187. (Illus.). 28p. (J). 1999. 9.95 (*0-8118-2327-X*) Chronicle Bks.

My Friend Consider. Dru A. Kenner. LC 84-51459. 100p. (Orig.). 1985. pap. 4.95 (*0-930551-00-1*) Vistara Pubns.

My Friend Cousin Emmie. large type ed. Jane Duncan. 1978. 27.99 (*0-7089-0136-0*) Ulverscroft.

My Friend Degas. Hilaire G. Degas. Ed. by Mina Curtiss. LC 64-22375. (Illus.). 138p. reprint ed. pap. 42.80 (*0-608-18588-4*, 200523600051) Bks Demand.

My Friend Emily. Susanne M. Swanson. LC 94-238020. (Illus.). 36p. (Orig.). (J). (gr. k-5). 1994. pap. 6.99 (*1-885101-04-X*) Writers Pr ID.

My Friend Fellow: Pets Are Friends Too. Elizabeth Hager. (Illus.). 36p. (J). (gr. k-2). 1998. pap. 4.95 (*1-881524-25-6*) Milligan Bks.

My Friend Flicka. Mary O'Hara. (J). 1988. 10.85 (*0-606-02855-2*, Pub. by Turtleback) Demco.

My Friend Flicka. Mary O'Hara. (Illus.). 320p. (YA). 1999. reprint ed. 37.95 (*1-56849-725-3*) Buccaneer Bks.

My Friend Flicka. Mary O'Hara. LC 87-45654. 304p. (YA). (gr. 4-7). 1988. reprint ed. mass mkt. 6.00 (*0-06-080902-7*, P-902, Perennial) HarperTrade.

My Friend Flicka. rev. ed. Mary O'Hara. LC 73-6611. (Illus.). 272p. (J). (gr. 7-9). 1973. 15.95 (*0-397-00981-X*, Lippncott) Lppncott W & W.

My Friend Frank. Meredith Gardner. (Illus.). 20p. (Orig.). 1985. pap. text 5.95 (*0-935703-00-4*) Too Young.

My Friend Godefroy see Mon Ami Godefroy

My Friend Goes Left. Barbara Gregorich. Ed. by Joan Hoffman. (Start to Read! Ser.). (Illus.). 16p. (J). (gr. k-2). 1984. pap. 2.29 (*0-88743-008-2*, 06008) Sch Zone Pub Co.

My Friend Goes Left. Barbara Gregorich. Ed. by Joan Hoffman. (Start to Read! Ser.). (Illus.). 32p. (J). (ps-3). 1993. pap. 3.99 (*0-88743-406-1*, 06058) Sch Zone Pub Co.

My Friend Gorila see Mi Amigo Gorila (My Friend Gorilla)

My Friend Gorilla. Atsuko Morozumi. LC 97-60546. (Illus.). (J). (ps-k). 1998. text 15.00 (*0-374-35458-8*) FS&G.

My Friend Harry. Kim Lewis. LC 94-38903. (Illus.). 32p. (J). (ps-3). 1995. 15.95 (*1-56402-617-5*) Candlewick Pr.

My Friend Harry. Kim Lewis. LC 94-38903. (Illus.). 32p. (J). (ps-1). 1997. reprint ed. pap. 5.99 (*0-7636-0285-X*) Candlewick Pr.

My Friend Has Asthma. Charlotte L. Casterline. (Illus.). 24p. (Orig.). (J). (ps-6). 1985. pap. 4.95 (*0-9617218-0-4*) Info All Bk.

My Friend in Africa. rev. ed. Frederick Franck. 59p. (J). (gr. 3-6). 1996. pap. 9.99 (*0-88092-325-3*) Royal Fireworks.

My Friend Is Dying: Prayers & Reflections. Mary E. Latela. LC 92-75204. 64p. 1993. pap. 3.95 (*0-89243-517-8*) Liguori Pubns.

***My Friend Is Struggling With-- Death of a Loved One.** Josh McDowell. LC 00-24466. (Friendship 911 Ser.). (Illus.). 64p. (gr. 8-12). 2000. pap. write for info. (*0-8499-3791-4*) Word Pub.

My Friend Jesus. Lawrence G. Lovasik. (Saint Joseph Picture Bks.). (Illus.). 1989. pap. 1.25 (*0-89942-293-4*, 293-00) Catholic Bk Pub.

My Friend Jesus. Etta B. Degering. (J). 1993. reprint ed. pap. 5.99 (*0-8280-0755-1*) Review & Herald.

My Friend Jesus. Margaret Wyatt. LC 86-90051. (Illus.). 20p. (Orig.). (J). (ps-12). 1994. reprint ed. pap. 2.95 (*0-9616117-0-7*) M Wyatt.

My Friend John. Charlotte Zolotow. LC 98-54582. (Illus.). 32p. (J). (gr. k-3). 2000. 14.95 (*0-385-32651-3*) BDD Bks Young Read.

My Friend Josh. John K. Seagrove. 54p. (YA). (gr. 12). 1997. per. 12.00 (*0-9647633-3-8*) Kendall Pubng.

My Friend, Julia Lathrop. Jane Addams. LC 74-1660. (Children & Youth Ser.). 246p. 1974. reprint ed. 24.95 (*0-405-05942-6*) Ayer.

My Friend Julian see Companero Julian: Artifices de Malos Destinos

***My Friend Lenny: A Memoir.** Ouida Blatt Mintz. viii, 357p. 2000. pap. 14.95 (*0-615-11879-8*) Bravura Bks.

My Friend Luke, the Stenciller. Margaret W. Fabian. LC 83-50689. (Illus.). 35p. (J). (gr. 3-4). 1987. pap., bds. 8.95 (*0-931474-25-6*) TBW Bks.

My Friend Martha's Aunt. large type ed. Jane Duncan. 416p. 1983. 27.99 (*0-7089-1041-6*) Ulverscroft.

My Friend Mr. Morris. Illus. by Satoshi Kitamura. LC 87-542. (Share-a-Story Bks.). (J). (gr. k-2). 1988. 8.95 (*0-385-29603-7*) Delacorte.

My Friend Mr. Morris. Pat Thompson. (Share-a-Story Ser.: No. 6). (J). (gr. k-6). 1988. reprint ed. pap. 2.50 (*0-440-40061-9*) Dell.

My Friend Muriel. large type ed. Jane Duncan. 434p. 1982. 27.99 (*0-7089-0846-2*) Ulverscroft.

My Friend Muriel. Jane Duncan. 1993. reprint ed. lib. bdg. 18.95 (*1-56849-235-9*) Buccaneer Bks.

My Friend, My Friend: The Story of Thoreau's Relationship with Emerson. Harmon Smith. LC 98-53492. (Illus.). 248p. 1999. 29.95 (*1-55849-186-4*) U of Mass Pr.

My Friend, My King: John's Vision of Our Hope of Heaven. Calvin Miller. LC 99-29723. 1999. 14.99 (*0-7814-3315-0*) Chariot Victor.

My Friend, My Lover, My Husband. Avis L. Brown. LC 96-95415. 132p. (Orig.). 1997. pap. 12.99 (*0-9656554-0-7*) Lamb Pub TX.

My Friend Noah. Debby Anderson. LC 87-72710. (Cuddle & Sing Bks.). (Illus.). 18p. (J). (ps). 1988. bds. 4.29 (*1-55513-665-6*, Chariot Bks) Chariot Victor.

My Friend, O'Connell. Mary C. Ryan. 112p. (Orig.). (J). (gr. 3-4). 1991. pap. 2.95 (*0-380-76145-9*, Avon Bks) Morrow Avon.

My Friend Penguin. Stephen Bachand. (Booktime Buddies Ser.). (Illus.). (J). (ps-2). 1999. 4.25 (*1-928972-01-2*) Critter Pubns.

My Friend Sandy. large type ed. Jane Duncan. 432p. 1983. 27.99 (*0-7089-0955-8*) Ulverscroft.

My Friend Sashie. Jane Duncan. 1993. reprint ed. lib. bdg. 18.95 (*1-56849-232-4*) Buccaneer Bks.

My Friend Sneezy: Making Choices. LaGretta M. Walker. (Illus.). 42p. (Orig.). (J). (gr. k-6). 1990. pap. 7.95 (*1-884063-98-5*) Mar Co Prods.

My Friend the Dog. Albert Pason Terhune. 25.95 (*0-89190-365-8*) Amereon Ltd.

My Friend the Fox. William Glennon. 72p. 1968. pap. 3.50 (*0-87129-064-2*, M76) Dramatic Pub.

My Friend, the Holy Spirit. 159p. (Orig.). (C). 1995. write for info. (*0-614-09370-8*) I J Hager.

My Friend the Manatee: An Ocean Magic Book. Jeff Schneider. LC 90-61576. (Ocean Magic Ser.). (Illus.). 12p. (J). (ps). 1991. 4.95 (*1-877779-08-3*) Schneider Educational.

My Friend the Monster. Clyde R. Bulla. LC 79-7826. (Trophy Bk.). (Illus.). 96p. (J). (gr. 2-5). 1990. pap. 3.50 (*0-06-440378-5*, HarpTrophy) HarpC Child Bks.

My Friend the Monster. Clyde Robert Bulla. (J). 1980. 12.95 (*0-690-04031-8*) HarpC Child Bks.

My Friend the Murderer: And Other Mysteries & Adventures. Arthur Conan Doyle. LC 76-37267. (Short Story Index Reprint Ser.). 1977. reprint ed. 18.95 (*0-8369-4078-4*) Ayer.

My Friend the Painter. Lygia Bojunga-Nunes. LC 90-46047. (J). 1995. 10.10 (*0-606-09649-3*, Pub. by Turtleback) Demco.

My Friend the Painter. Lygia B. Nunes. Tr. by Giovanni Pontiero from POR. LC 90-46043. 96p. (J). (gr. 3-7). 1991. 13.95 (*0-15-256340-7*) Harcourt.

My Friend the Painter. Lygia B. Nunes. Tr. by Giovanni Pontiero. LC 90-46043. (Illus.). 96p. (J). (gr. 3-7). 1995. pap. 5.00 (*0-15-200872-1*) Harcourt.

My Friend the Partridge: Memories of New England Shooting. Stephen T. Hammond. 148p. 1984. reprint ed. 17.95 (*0-936075-00-7*) Gunnerman Pr.

My Friend the Penguin: An Ocean Magic Book. Jeff Schneider. LC 90-61577. (Ocean Magic Ser.). (Illus.). 12p. (J). (ps). 1991. 4.95 (*1-877779-09-1*) Schneider Educational.

My Friend the Piano. Catherine Cowan. LC 93-37437. (Illus.). 32p. (J). (gr. k-3). 1998. 16.00 (*0-688-13239-1*, Wm Morrow) Morrow Avon.

***My Friend the Piano.** Catherine Cowan. LC 93-37437. (Illus.). 32p. (J). (gr. k-3). 1998. 15.89 (*0-688-13240-5*, Wm Morrow) Morrow Avon.

My Friend the Polar Bear: An Ocean Magic Book. Jeff Schneider. LC 90-61579. (Ocean Magic Ser.). (Illus.). 12p. (J). (ps). 1991. 4.95 (*1-877779-12-1*) Schneider Educational.

My Friend the Porpoise: An Ocean Magic Book. Jeff Schneider. LC 90-61572. (Ocean Magic Ser.). (Illus.). 12p. (J). (ps). 1991. 4.95 (*1-877779-07-5*) Schneider Educational.

My Friend the Sea Otter: An Ocean Magic Book. Jeff Schneider. LC 90-61578. (Ocean Magic Ser.). (Illus.). 12p. (J). (ps). 1991. 4.95 (*1-877779-10-5*) Schneider Educational.

My Friend the Swallow. large type ed. Jane Duncan. 1985. 15.95 (*0-7089-1253-2*) Ulverscroft.

My Friend the Trout. Eugene V. Connett, III. (Illus.). 176p. 1991. reprint ed. 50.00 (*0-9620609-4-1*) Meadow Run Pr.

My Friend the Walrus: An Ocean Magic Book. Jeff Schneider. LC 90-61581. (Ocean Magic Ser.). (Illus.). 12p. (J). (ps). 1991. 4.95 (*1-877779-11-3*) Schneider Educational.

My Friend Will. Charles F. Lummis. 1972. pap. 5.00 (*0-87516-161-8*) DeVorss.

My Friend Ziggy. Peter W. Huebner. 160p. 1995. 6.95 (*0-9649464-0-8*) P W Huebner.

My Friendly Contemporaries see Collected Works of Hamlin Garland

My Friendly Contemporaries. Hamlin Garland. (Collected Works of Hamlin Garland). 1988. reprint ed. lib. bdg. 59.00 (*0-7812-1254-5*) Rprt Serv.

***My Friends.** 96p. 1999. write for info. (*1-56148-296-X*) Good Bks PA.

My Friends. (Little Lessons Ser.). Date not set. 3.95 (*0-88271-556-9*, 10334) Regina Pr.

My Friends. B Small Publishing Staff. 1999. pap. 5.95 (*1-874735-50-6*) B Small Publishing.

My Friends. Emmanuel Bove. Tr. by Janet Louth. 152p. 2000. pap. 15.95 (*0-8101-6058-7*) Northwestern U Pr.

My Friends. Catherine Bruzzone & Lone Morton. (Illus.). 24p. (Orig.). (J). (gr. k-3). 1994. pap., per. 3.95 (*0-8249-8650-4*, Ideals Child) Hambleton-Hill.

My Friends. Taro Gomi. LC 95-17991. (Illus.). 40p. (J). (ps-1). 1995. pap. 5.95 (*0-8118-1237-5*) Chronicle Bks.

My Friends. Taro Gomi. 1990. 11.15 (*0-606-08924-1*, Pub. by Turtleback) Demco.

My Friends. Bob Jones, Sr. 131p. 1983. pap. 6.50 (*0-89084-230-2*, 020669) Bob Jones Univ.

My Friends. Francine Oomen. (Peephole Board Bks). (Illus.). 6p. (J). 1995. 2.25 (*0-689-80260-9*, Mac Bks Young Read) S&S Childrens.

My Friends Vol. 2, Bk. 1: Russian Language Sunday School. Life Publishers Staff. (RUS., Illus.). (J). (gr. 1-3). 1999. pap., student ed. write for info. (*0-7361-0094-6*) Life Pubs Intl.

My Friends Vol. 2, Bk. 2: Russian Language Sunday School. Life Publishers Staff. (RUS., Illus.). (J). (gr. 1-3). 1999. pap., student ed. write for info. (*0-7361-0095-4*) Life Pubs Intl.

M

My Friends Vol. 2, Bks. 1 & 2: Russian Language Sunday School. Life Publishers Staff. (RUS., Illus.). (J). (gr. 1-3). 1999. pap., teacher ed. write for info. (*0-7361-0093-8*) Life Pubs Intl.

My Friends - Russian Language Student Quarterly for Sunday School, Vol. 3, Bk. 1. (RUS.). 48p. (J). (gr. 1-3). 1998. student ed. write for info. (*0-7361-0050-4*) Life Pubs Intl.

My Friends - Russian Language Student Quarterly for Sunday School, Vol. 3, Bk. 2. (RUS.). (J). (gr. 1-3). 1998. student ed. write for info. (*0-7361-0051-2*) Life Pubs Intl.

My Friends - Russian Language Teachers Manual for Sunday School, Vol. 3, Bks. 1 & 2. (RUS., Illus.). 80p. 1998. teacher ed. write for info. (*0-7361-0049-0*) Life Pubs Intl.

***My Friends - Student Book Vol. 3: Russian Lanaguage Sunday School Manual.** Prod. by Life Publishers Staff. (RUS., Illus.). 48p. (J). (gr. 1-3). 2000. pap., student ed. write for info. (*0-7361-0163-2*) Life Pubs Intl.

***My Friends - Student Book Vol. 3: Russian Language Student Sunday School Manual.** Prod. by Life Publishers Staff. (RUS., Illus.). 48p. (J). (gr. 1-3). 2000. pap., student ed. write for info. (*0-7361-0165-9*) Life Pubs Intl.

***My Friends - Teachers Manual Vol. 3: Russian Language Sunday School.** Prod. by Life Publishers Staff. (RUS., Illus.). 80p. (J). (gr. 1-3). 2000. pap., teacher ed. write for info. (*0-7361-0162-4*) Life Pubs Intl.

***My Friends - Visual Aids Vol. 3: Russian Language Visual Aids for Sunday School.** Prod. by Life Publishers Staff. (RUS., Illus.). 24p. 2000. pap. write for info. (*0-7361-0164-0*) Life Pubs Intl.

***My Friend's a Werewolf.** Johnson. (J). 2000. pap. 6.95 (*0-440-86342-2*, Pub. by Transworld Publishers Ltd) Trafalgar.

My Friends ABC Book. Arissa Hammond et al. LC 88-70949. (Illus.). 32p. (J). (gr. 2 up). 1988. 10.00 (*0-9605968-4-4*) Bright Bks.

***My Friends & Me.** Marlene Rimler. (Illus.). 1999. pap. 6.50 (*1-56245-386-6*) Great Quotations.

My Friends & Me Activity Manual. rev. ed. Duane Davis. (My Friends & Me Ser.). (J). (ps). 1988. pap. text 72.95 (*0-88671-325-0*, 4601) Am Guidance.

My Friends & Me Story Book. rev. ed. Duane Davis. (My Friends & Me Ser.). (J). (ps). 1988. pap. text 86.95 (*0-88671-326-9*, 4605) Am Guidance.

My Friends Are Dying! Ray Comfort. 224p. 1991. write for info. (*1-878859-32-3*) Living Wat CA.

My Friends Are Dying! The Seductive Voice of Cocaine Whispers to the Simple, "Give Me Your Hand...& I Will Take Your Life!" 8th ed. Ray Comfort. Ed. by Living Waters Pubns. Staff. (Illus.). 210p. 1991. reprint ed. pap. write for info. (*1-878859-07-2*) Living Wat CA.

My Friends at Brook Farm. John V. Sears. LC 72-8250. reprint ed. 41.50 (*0-404-11004-5*) AMS Pr.

My Friends' Beliefs. Hiley Ward. 1988. pap. 12.95 (*0-8027-7376-1*) Walker & Co.

My Friend's Book 2. 1997. text, student ed. 11.31 (*0-673-43815-5*) Addison-Wesley.

My Friends Call Me C. C. The Story of Courtney Chauncey Julian. William G. Hutson. Ed. by James C. Smith, Jr. LC 90-35789. (Illus.). 228p. (Orig.). 1990. pap. 10.95 (*0-86534-143-5*) Sunstone Pr.

My Friends George & Tom. Jane Duncan. 1993. reprint ed. lib. bdg. 18.95 (*1-56849-234-0*) Buccaneer Bks.

My Friend's Got This Problem, Mr. Chandler. Mel Glenn. (YA). 1992. write for info. (*0-318-69268-6*, Clarion Bks) HM.

My Friends in the Barrios. Juan M. Flavier. 190p. 1974. 2.00 (*0-942717-11-2*) Intl Inst Rural.

My Friends in the Barrios. Juan M. Flavier. 1974. 8.75 (*971-10-0317-1*, Pub. by New Day Pub) Cellar.

My Friends Obey My Voice. Joseph C. Hedgecock. Ed. by Patricia T. Ross. 69p. 1987. pap. 4.95 (*0-945255-09-8*) J C Hedgecock Pubns.

***My Friends' Secrets.** Joan Collins. (Illus.). 144p. 2000. 24.95 (*0-233-99494-7*, Pub. by Andre Deutsch) Trafalgar.

My Friends That Rhyme with Orange. Barry Rudner. LC 95-90526. 29p. (J). (ps). 1995. pap. 6.95 (*0-9642206-2-8*) Windword Pr.

My Friends the Miss Boyds. large type ed. Jane Duncan. 414p. 1982. 27.99 (*0-7089-0818-7*) Ulverscroft.

My Friends the Miss Boyds. Jane Duncan. 1993. reprint ed. lib. bdg. 18.95 (*1-56849-233-2*) Buccaneer Bks.

My Friends the Mrs. Millers. large type ed. Jane Duncan. 1984. 15.95 (*0-7089-1157-9*) Ulverscroft.

My Friends the Saints. Lawrence G. Lovasik. (J). 1992. 5.75 (*0-89942-271-3*, 270/22) Catholic Bk Pub.

My Friends Were Robbed. Uri Zohar. Tr. by M. Weinberg. 1995. 17.95 (*0-87306-701-0*) Feldheim.

My Friendship Cross. William H. Klein. (Illus.). 48p. (J). 1998. pap. text 12.99 (*0-8054-1716-8*) Broadman.

***My Front Porch: An Invitation to the Charm & Tradition.** Alda Ellis. LC 98-31112. 48p. 1999. 15.99 (*0-7369-0010-1*) Harvest Hse.

My Frozen Turbulence in Kashmir. enl. rev. ed. Jagmohan. (C). 1992. 36.00 (*81-7023-352-6*, Pub. by Allied Pubs) S Asia.

***My Fun-tastic Personal Progress Journal Beehive, No. 1.** Ross. 1999. pap. 8.95 (*1-57734-440-5*, 01113879) Covenant Comms.

***My Fun-tastic Personal Progress Journal Beehive, No. 2.** Ross & Guymon-King. 1999. pap. 8.95 (*1-57734-441-3*, 01113887) Covenant Comms.

***My Funny Faces.** Marianne Borgardt. (Illus.). 12p. (J). 1999. 5.95 (*1-892374-17-X*) Weldon Owen.

My Funny Therapist. Kristin Brase. Ed. by Linda J. Dageforde. 32p. 1998. pap. 6.95 (*1-886225-32-X*, 1000) Dageforde Pub.

***My Furry Friends.** Golden Books Staff. 10p. 1999. 5.99 (*0-307-14575-1*) Gldn Bks Pub Co.

My Futurist Years. Roman Jakobson. 210p. 1997. pap. text 19.95 (*1-56886-049-8*) Marsilio Pubs.

***My Fuzzy Friends.** Tad Hills. 14p. (J). 1999. 9.99 (*0-689-82357-6*) Litle Simon.

My Fuzzy Valentine. Golden Books Staff. 32p. (J). (ps-4). 1997. pap. text 1.69 (*0-307-02679-5*, Goldn Books) Gldn Bks Pub Co.

My G-r-r-r-reat Uncle Tiger. James Riordan. LC 95-13109. (Illus.). (J). (ps-3). 1995. 14.95 (*1-56145-110-X*) Peachtree Pubs.

My "g" Sound Box. Jane Belk Moncure. LC 78-22037. (Sound Box Library). (Illus.). 32p. (J). (ps-2). 1979. lib. bdg. 21.36 (*0-89565-053-3*) Childs World.

***My Gal Sunday.** 2000. 23.00 (*0-7432-0628-2*) Simon & Schuster.

My Gal Sunday. Mary Higgins Clark. 1997. per. 6.99 (*0-671-01491-9*) PB.

My Gal Sunday. Mary Higgins Clark. LC 96-230890. 240p. 1996. 23.00 (*0-684-83229-1*) S&S Trade.

My Gal Sunday. Mary Higgins Clark. 1997. 11.60 (*0-606-13632-0*, Pub. by Turtleback) Demco.

My Gal Sunday: Henry & Sunday Stories. Mary Higgins Clark. 1996. pap. text 23.00 (*0-684-83238-0*, Scribner Pap Fic) S&S Trade Pap.

My Galaxy of Memories, Feelings, & Dreams: A Writing Journal for Kids. George Tomek & Marilee Tomek. (Illus.). 80p. (Orig.). (J). (gr. 2-6). 1996. pap. 11.95 (*1-883790-17-4*, 111-1634, EDINFO Pr) Grayson Bernard Pubs.

***My Gallant Knight.** Tara O'Dell. (Zebra Splendor Historical Romances Ser.). 1999. mass mkt. 4.99 (*0-8217-6352-0*, Zebra Kensgtn) Kensgtn Pub Corp.

My Garden & I. Olive Pitkin. 160p. 1992. 19.95 (*1-55821-180-2*) Lyons Pr.

My Garden (Book) Jamaica Kincaid. LC 99-26204. (Illus.). 244p. 1999. 23.00 (*0-374-28186-6*) FS&G.

My Garden in Autumn & Winter. E. A. Bowles. LC 98-17491. (Illus.). 348p. 1998. 24.95 (*0-88192-459-8*) Timber.

My Garden in Spring. E. A. Bowles. LC 96-38286. 308p. 1997. 24.95 (*0-88192-375-3*) Timber.

My Garden in Spring. Edward A. Bowles. LC 78-178004. (Illus.). 1971. reprint ed. 12.50 (*0-685-61145-0*) Theophrastus.

My Garden in Summer. E. A. Bowles. LC 97-41260. (Illus.). 393p. 1998. reprint ed. 24.95 (*0-88192-413-X*) Timber.

My Garden Journal. Illus. by Suzanne Feaman & Christine Felicelli. text. write for info. (*0-937739-23-5*) C F Miller.

My Garden Journal: A Monthly Guide to Healthier Food. Rita Engelken. (Illus.). 120p. 1996. pap. 12.00 (*1-56383-063-9*) G & R Pub.

My Garden Visits. Justin Matott. LC 96-46792. 1997. 18.00 (*0-345-41251-6*) Ballantine Pub Grp.

My Gender Workbook: How to Become a Real Man, a Real Woman, the Real You or Something Else Entirely. Kate Bornstein. LC 98-134184. (Illus.). 272p. 1997. pap. 17.99 (*0-415-91673-9*) Routledge.

My Gender Workbook: How to Become a Real Man, a Real Woman, the Real You or Something Else Entirely. Kate Bornstein. LC 98-134184. (Illus.). 272p. (C). 1998. 75.00 (*0-415-91672-0*) Routledge.

My Generation: Collective Autobiography & Identity Politics. John D. Hazlett. LC 97-47292. (Wisconsin Studies in American Autobiography). 288p. (Orig.). 1998. pap. text 19.95 (*0-299-15784-9*) U of Wis Pr.

My Generation: Collective Autobiography & Identity Politics. John D. Hazlett. LC 97-47292. (Wisconsin Studies in American Autobiography). 263p. (Orig.). 1998. text 45.00 (*0-299-15780-6*) U of Wis Pr.

My Generation: Fifty Years of Sex, Drugs, Rock, Revolution, Glamour, Greed, Valor, Faith & Silcon Chips. Michael Gross. LC 99-55384. (Illus.). 416p. 2000. 25.00 (*0-06-017594-X*, Cliff Street) HarperTrade.

My Generation: Rock 'n Roll Remembered: An Imperfect History. Ed. by Antony Farrell et al. LC 97-116223. 338p. 1996. pap. 25.95 (*1-874675-51-1*, Pub. by Lilliput Pr) Irish Bks Media.

***My Generation, An Autobiography of the Life Experiences of Colonel Frederick Paul Howland, Sr. Pop Pop's Story.** Frederick Paul Howland, Sr. (Illus.). v, 204p. 1999. pap. text. write for info. (*0-9676966-0-7*, 01) Fred Howland.

My Generations: A Course in Jewish Family History. Arthur Kurzweil. (Illus.). 128p. 1984. pap. 9.95 (*0-87441-383-4*) Behrman.

***My Genes Made Me Do It: A Scientific Look at Sexual Orientation.** Neil L. Whitehead & Briar Whitehead. LC 90-75710. 240p. 1999. pap. text 13.99 (*1-56384-165-7*, Pub. by Huntington Hse) BookWorld.

***My Georgia Garden: A Gardener's Journal.** Cool Springs Press Publications Staff. 2000. 19.95 (*1-888608-82-X*) Cool Springs Pr.

***My Georgia Garden: A Gardener's Journal.** Erica Glasener & Walter Reeves. (Illus.). 128p. 2000. spiral bd. 19.95 (*1-930604-01-7*) Cool Springs Pr.

My German Question: Growing up in Nazi Berlin. Peter Gay. LC 98-26686. (Illus.). 256p. 1998. 27.50 (*0-300-07670-3*) Yale U Pr.

***My German Question: Growing up in Nazi Berlin.** Peter Gay. (Illus.). 256p. 1999. pap. 10.95 (*0-300-08070-0*) Yale U Pr.

My Getting-Ready-for-Christmas Book. Harriet Ziefert. LC 90-55148. (Illus.). 12p. (J). (ps-1). 1991. pap. 13.95 (*0-06-107404-4*) HarpC Child Bks.

My Ghost. (C). 1977. write for info. (*0-201-13835-2*) Addison-Wesley.

***My Ghost.** Adam Fuss. 48p. 1999. 75.00 (*0-944092-73-X*) Twin Palms Pub.

***My Ghost: Adam Fuss.** Photos by Adam Fuss. (Illus.). 48p. 1999. boxed set 200.00 (*0-944092-74-8*) Twin Palms Pub.

My Giant Preschool Lift-the-Flap Book: With Sixty Five Fun Flaps to Open! Playskool Books Staff. (Illus.). 10p. (J). (ps up). 1999. 9.99 (*0-525-46196-5*) Penguin Putnam.

My Giant Treasury of Fairy Tales. Jane Carruth. (J). 1988. 9.98 (*0-671-09118-2*) S&S Trade.

My Gift to You. Ronalyn Choco. LC 88-71341. (Illus.). 80p. 1988. 7.95 (*0-939596-02-4*) Country Rd.

My Gingerbread House. Mouse Works Staff. LC 97-222171. 5p. (J). 1997. 5.98 (*1-57082-718-4*, Pub. by Mouse Works) Time Warner.

***My Giraffe.** Lynn Salem & Josie Stewart. (Illus.). 8p. (J). (gr. k-2). 2000. pap. 3.75 (*1-58323-006-8*) Seedling Pubns.

My Girl. Patricia Hermes. (YA). (gr. 6 up). 1991. pap. 3.99 (*0-671-75929-9*) S&S Trade.

My Girl & Frozen Assets. Barrie Keeffe. (Methuen New Theatrescripts Ser.). 144p. (Orig.). (C). 1989. pap. write for info. (*0-413-62200-2*, A0401, Methuen Drama) Methn.

My Girl Two. Patricia Hermes. 192p. (YA). (gr. 6 up). 1994. per. 4.50 (*0-671-88828-5*) PB.

My Girlhood among Outlaws. Lily Klasner. Ed. by Eve Ball. LC 77-165206. 404p. 1972. reprint ed. pap. 125.30 (*0-608-02352-3*, 206299300004) Bks Demand.

***My Girls' Camp Journal.** Kelly Heaps. 120p. 1999. 11.95 (*1-56236-241-0*, Pub. by Aspen Bks) Origin Bk Sales.

***My Glass Is Cracked.** Ed. by Candace Catlin Hall. 36p. 1998. pap. 10.95 (*0-916897-34-6*) Andrew Mtn Pr.

My Glimpse of Eternity. Betty Malz. LC 77-22671. 128p. (gr. 10). 1979. mass mkt. 4.99 (*0-8007-8363-8*, Spire) Revell.

My Global Address, Vol. 2927. Tamara Nunn. Ed. by Rozanne L. Williams. (Social Studies Learn to Read Ser.). (Illus.). 16p. (J). (ps-2). 1996. pap. 2.75 (*1-57471-132-6*, 3927) Creat Teach Pr.

My Global Address, Vol. 3971. Tamara Nunn. Ed. by Rozanne L. Williams. (Social Studies Big Bks.). (Illus.). 16p. (J). (ps-2). 1997. pap. 12.98 (*1-57471-178-4*, 3970) Creat Teach Pr.

My Glorious Brothers. Howard Fast. 23.95 (*0-89190-579-0*) Amereon Ltd.

My Goals. Gretchen D. Van Kleef. wbk. ed. 4.95 (*0-89486-977-9*, 5556 B) Hazelden.

***My Goats.** Heather Miller. (Welcome Bks.). (Illus.). (J). 2000. 13.50 (*0-516-23107-3*) Childrens.

***My Goats.** Heather Miller. LC 00-24384. (My Farm Ser.). (Illus.). 24p. (J). (ps-2). 2000. pap. write for info. (*0-516-23032-8*) Childrens.

My God - They're Real! Robert Matyi. LC 78-32013. 1979. 22.95 (*0-87949-150-7*) Ashley Bks.

My God & My All. Marion A. Habig. 288p. 1997. reprint ed. vinyl bd. 3.75 (*0-8199-0659-X*, Frncscn Herld) Franciscan Pr.

My God & My Dogs. Danford Austin. 100p. 1998. pap. write for info. (*1-57502-878-6*, PO2392) Morris Pubng.

My God, Do You Love Me? A Woman's Conversations with God. Brenda Hunter. 208p. 1998. 14.95 (*1-57856-030-6*) Waterbrook Pr.

My God Is a God of Knowledge. Ralph Sexton, Sr. 82p. (Orig.). 1997. pap. 9.95 (*1-57090-059-0*, Mountain Chrch) Alexander Dist.

My God Is Real. 1992. 1.25 (*0-8341-9015-X*) Nazarene.

My God Is So Great! 62 Games to Help Preschoolers Know & Love God. Group Publishing Staff. LC 99-21480. 96p. 1999. 14.99 (*0-7644-2094-1*) Group Pub.

My God Is Yahweh. M. B. Van't Veer. Tr. by Theodore Plantinga from DUT. 440p. 1980. 12.95 (*0-88815-035-0*) Inhtce Pubns.

My God, My God, Why Hast Thou Forsaken Me. David W. Dolive. (Illus.). 192p. 1998. pap. write for info. (*0-9662785-0-X*) David Publng.

My God, My Life. 71p. pap. 5.95 (*0-9616007-0-5*) M F Turner Pub.

My God, Why? A Mastectomy from a Husbands Point of View. Jim Pollnow. LC 79-55888. 127p. 1980. pap. 2.95 (*0-9603708-0-3*) J L Pollnow.

My Gold Coast: South Florida in Earlier Years. Lora S. Britt. (Illus.). 245p. 1984. 10.95 (*0-9613982-0-5*) Brittany Hse.

My Golden Age of Singing. Frieda Hempel et al. LC 97-35976. (Operabio Ser.: Vol. 10). (Illus.). 452p. 1998. 39.95 (*1-57467-036-0*, Amadeus Pr) Timber.

My Golf Book. Laurance Benefield. Ed. & Illus. by Marilyn E. Davis. 1996. lthr. write for info. (*1-880981-03-3*) A Diff View.

My Good Manners Book. (Illus.). 8p. (J). (ps). 1998. 35.00 (*1-888074-78-7*) Pckts Lrning.

My Good Night Bible. Susan L. Lingo. Ed. by Laura Ring. LC 99-22435. (Illus.). 208p. (J). (ps-1). 1999. 12.99 (*0-7847-0406-6*, Bean Sprouts) Standard Pub.

My Good Shepherd Bible Story Book. A. C. Mueller. LC 70-89876. 175p. (J). (gr. 3-5). 1969. bds. 15.99 (*0-570-03400-0*, 56-1126) Concordia.

***My Goodnight Book.** Bessie Pease Gutmann et al. 48p. (J). 2000. 12.95 (*1-884807-51-8*, EC 751) Blushing Rose.

My Goose Betsy. Trudi Braun. LC 98-3456. (Illus.). 32p. (J). 1999. text 16.99 (*0-7636-0449-6*) Candlewick Pr.

***My Gorilla Journey.** Helen Attwater. (Illus.). 384p. 2000. 31.99 (*0-7089-9155-6*) Ulverscroft.

***My Gr-r-r-reat Uncle Tiger.** James Riordan. (Illus.). 32p. (J). (ps-2). 2000. pap. 6.95 (*1-56145-228-9*) Peachtree Pubs.

My Gradual Demise & Honeysuckle. Douglas A. Martin. 84p. 1995. pap. 7.00 (*0-9641196-2-5*) Champion Bks.

My Grammar Dictionary. Concetta D. Ryan. Ed. by Kathy Rogers. (Illus.). 32p. 1999. pap., teacher ed., wbk. ed. 1.99 (*1-56472-611-8*) Edupress Inc.

My Grammy: A Book about Alzheimer's Disease. Marsha Kibbey. (Illus.). (J). (gr. 1-4). 1991. pap. 4.95 (*0-87614-544-6*, First Ave Edns) Lerner Pub.

My Grampa's Woods: The Adirondacks. Laurence T. Beahan. 2000. pap. write for info. (*0-925168-75-0*) North Country.

My Gran. Illus. by Debbie Boon. LC 97-31892. 32p. (J). (gr. k-2). 1998. lib. bdg. 19.90 (*0-7613-0312-X*) Millbrook Pr.

My Grandchild: Photo Album & Journal. Nancy Cogan. (Illus.). 1998. 13.95 (*1-884807-29-1*, EC724) Blushing Rose.

My Granddaddy Was a Ramblin' Man. William C. Berdine. LC 97-94443. 264p. 1997. 20.00 (*0-9631802-3-1*) Berdine.

My Granddaughter Has Fleas! Cathy Guisewite. (Cathy Collection Ser.). (Illus.). 128p. (Orig.). 1989. pap. 9.95 (*0-8362-1855-8*) Andrews & McMeel.

My Grandfather. Denis Constanduros. (Illus.). 136p. 1989. pap. 8.95 (*0-563-20864-3*, Pub. by BBC) Parkwest Pubns.

My Grandfather. large type ed. Denis Constanduros. (Illus.). 112p. 1991. 19.95 (*1-85089-471-X*, Pub. by ISIS Lrg Prnt) Transaction Pubs.

***My Grandfather & Me: A Memory Scrapbook for Kids.** Jane Drake & Ann Love. (Illus.). 32p. (YA). (gr. k up). 1999. 5.95 (*1-55074-630-8*) Kids Can Pr.

***My Grandfather Jack the Ripper.** Claudio Adone.Tr. of Mio Nonno Jack Lo Squartatore. 192p. (YA). (gr. 7-12). 2000. 19.00 (*1-928746-16-0*) Herodias.

My Grandfather the Spy. Corinne Gerson. (J). 1990. 14.95 (*0-8027-6955-1*) Walker & Co.

My Grandfather, Thornton W. Burgess: An Intimate Portrait. Frances B. Meigs. LC 98-17258. (Illus.). 192p. 1998. 21.95 (*1-889833-05-3*, Commonwealth Eds) Memoirs Unltd.

***My Grandfather's Blessings: Stories of Strength, Refuge & Belonging.** Rachel N. Remen. LC 99-58061. 368p. 2000. 24.95 (*1-57322-150-3*, Riverhead Books) Putnam Pub Group.

My Grandfather's Finger. Edward Swift. LC 98-43406. (Illus.). 272p. 1999. 24.95 (*0-8203-2100-1*) U of Ga Pr.

***My Grandfather's Finger.** large type ed. Edward Swift. LC 00-25194. (Senior Lifestyles Ser.). 350p. 2000. 26.95 (*0-7862-2523-8*) Thorndike Pr.

My Grandfather's House. Bruce Coville. LC 95-3630. (Illus.). 32p. (J). (gr. k-3). 1996. 14.95 (*0-8167-3804-1*) BrdgeWater.

My Grandfather's House. Bruce Coville. (Illus.). (J). (gr. 3 up). 1997. pap. 4.95 (*0-8167-3805-X*) Troll Communs.

My Grandfather's House. 2nd ed. Robert Clark. LC 99-27746. 288p. 1999. text 24.00 (*0-312-20932-0*, Picador USA) St Martin.

***My Grandfather's House: A Genealogy of Doubt & Faith.** Robert Clark. 304p. 2000. pap. 13.00 (*0-312-24314-6*, Picador USA) St Martin.

My Grandfather's House: Tlingit Songs of Death & Sorrow. David Cloutier. LC 80-15499. (Illus.). 40p. (Orig.). 1980. pap. 8.95 (*0-914974-26-2*) Holmgangers.

***My Grandfather's Tale.** Ulfat Idilbi. 1999. pap. 12.95 (*0-7043-8100-1*, Interlink Bks) Interlink Pub.

***My Grandma Always Told Me.** Patricia Phipps. 176p. 1999. pap. 15.25 (*0-9671542-0-0*) Five Dreams Pubns.

My Grandma & I. Zainabu Renner. 16p. 1998. pap. write for info. (*1-57579-107-2*) Pine Hill Pr.

My Grandma Is a Pilot. Cheryl J. Young. 58p. (J). 1995. 14.95 (*0-9648881-0-6*) Chandelle Publns.

My Grandma Is Great. H. Roche. LC 99-166963. (Illus.). (J). (ps). 1998. pap. 4.95 (*1-84089-014-2*, 868237Q) Zero to Ten.

My Grandma Is Wonderful. Nick Butterworth. LC 91-58747. (Illus.). 32p. (J). (ps up). 1992. pap. 4.99 (*1-56402-100-9*) Candlewick Pr.

My Grandma Lived in Gooligulch. Graeme Base. (Illus.). 42p. 1990. 16.95 (*0-8109-1547-2*, Pub. by Abrams) Time Warner.

My Grandma Lived in Gooligulch. Graeme Base. LC 96-102798. (Illus.). 18p. (J). 1995. 19.95 (*0-8109-4288-7*, Pub. by Abrams) Time Warner.

My Grandma Says... Audrey H. Winslow. LC 97-76680. (Illus.). 28p. (J). (ps-3). 1997. pap. 6.95 (*1-880218-28-3*) Mktg Dir Inc.

My Grandma the Monster. Ascher Davis. (Illus.). 32p. (J). reprint ed. pap. 2.95 (*0-88961-099-1*, Pub. by Womens Pr) LPC InBook.

***My Grandma's the Mayor.** Marjorie White Pellegrino. LC 99-16771. (Illus.). 32p. (J). (gr. k-8). 1999. 14.95 (*1-55798-608-8*, 441-6088, Magination Press) Am Psychol.

My Grandmother & Me: A Memory Scrapbook. Jane Drake & Ann Love. (Illus.). 32p. (J). (gr. k up). 1999. 4.95 (*1-55074-628-6*) Kids Can Pr.

My Grandmother Wears Crazy Hats. Katy Perry. Ed. by Mary E. Minor. (Illus.). 16p. (J). (gr. k-5). 1993. pap. 4.95 (*0-9626823-4-9*) Perry ME.

My Grandmother's Cactus: Stories by Egyptian Women. Tr. & Intro. by Marilyn Booth. 208p. 1991. 19.95 (*0-7043-2649-3*, Pub. by Quartet) Interlink Pub.

My Grandmother's Family: The Strocks from Andrew County, Missouri. Judith T. McGarvey. (Illus.). 174p. 1986. 16.00 (*0-932619-00-2*) JD McG Pubns.

My Grandmother's House Plant. Najiyyah Avery. 16p. (J). (gr. k-6). 1999. 7.00 (*0-8059-4539-3*) Dorrance.

My Grandmother's Journey. John Cech. LC 90-35731. (Illus.). 40p. (J). (ps-4). 1991. lib. bdg. 16.00 (*0-02-718135-9*, Bradbury S&S) S&S Childrens.

My Grandmother's Journey. John Cech. (Illus.). 40p. (J). (ps-4). 1998. per. 5.99 (*0-689-81890-4*) S&S Childrens.

My Grandmother's Journey. John Cech. 1998. 11.15 (*0-606-13633-9*, Pub. by Turtleback) Demco.

My Grandmother's Posture. Wanda Olugbala. pap. 6.00 (*0-9657107-1-8*) Olugbalas Way.

My Grandmother's Story Quilt. Faith Ringgold. (J). 1998. lib. bdg. write for info. (*0-517-70948-1*) Crown Bks Yng Read.

My Grandmother's Story Quilt. Faith Ringgold. (J). 1999. write for info. (*0-517-70947-3*) Crown Bks Yng Read.

My Grandmother's Table: Simple, Low-Fat, Family Meals. Amy Simon. (Illus.). 128p. 1999. 11.95 (*0-9671670-0-0*, 7000) Gardner Pbg.

My Grandmother's Treasure. Jackie Torrence. (American Storytelling Ser.). (J). (gr. 3 up). 1993. 12.00 incl. audio (*0-87483-328-0*) August Hse.

My Grandpa & the Sea. Katherine S. Orr. LC 89-23876. (Illus.). 32p. (J). (gr. k-4). 1990. lib. bdg. 19.95 (*0-87614-409-1*, Carolrhoda) Lerner Pub.

My Grandpa & the Sea. Katherine S. Orr. (Illus.). 32p. (J). (gr. k-4). 1991. pap. 5.95 (*0-87614-525-X*, Carolrhoda) Lerner Pub.

My Grandpa Died Today. Joan Fassler. LC 71-147126. (Illus.). 32p. (J). (ps-3). 1983. pap. 9.95 (*0-89885-174-2*, Kluwer Acad Hman Sci) Kluwer Academic.

My Grandpa Has No Garbage. Ann Sutherland. (Illus.). 24p. (Orig.). (J). (gr. 2-6). 1996. pap. 7.95 (*1-56550-027-X*) Vis Bks Intl.

My Grandpa is a Tugboat Captain. Ken Kreisler. Ed. by John P. O'Connor. LC 99-72230. (Illus.). 32p. (J). (ps-k). 1999. spiral bd. 9.95 (*1-892216-13-2*, No. 1892216132) Bristol Fash.

My Grandpa Is Amazing. Nick Butterworth. LC 91-58746. (Illus.). 32p. (J). (ps up). 1992. pap. 4.99 (*1-56402-099-1*) Candlewick Pr.

My Grandpa Says . . . Audrey H. Winslow. (Illus.). 24p. (Orig.). (J). (ps-3). 1996. pap. 6.95 (*1-880218-23-2*) Mktg Dir Inc.

My Grandparents. Penny Nye. (Illus.). 16p. (Orig.). (J). (ps-4). 1997. pap. 12.00 (*1-890703-05-2*) Penny Laine.

***My Grandson Lew.** rev. ed. Charlotte Zolotow. 32p. (J). (ps-1). 1999. 14.95 (*0-06-028299-1*) HarpC Child Bks.

***My Grandson Lew.** rev. ed. Charlotte Zolotow. 32p. (J). (ps-1). 1999. lib. bdg. 14.89 (*0-06-028300-9*) HarpC Child Bks.

***My Grandson Lew.** rev. ed. Charlotte Zolotow. 32p. (J). (ps-1). 1999. pap. 5.95 (*0-06-443549-0*) HarpC Child Bks.

My Granny's Great Escape. Jeremy Strong. (Illus.). 96p. (J). pap. 7.95 (*0-14-038390-5*, Pub. by Pnguin Bks Ltd) Trafalgar.

***My Granny's Great Escape.** large type ed. Jeremy Strong. (Illus.). (J). 1998. pap. 16.95 (*0-7540-6031-4*, Galaxy Child Lrg Print) Chivers N Amer.

My Grapes. Meggan McGrath. LC 93-24057. (Illus.). 48p. (Orig.). (J). 1993. pap. 16.95 (*0-938586-99-8*) Pfeifer-Hamilton.

My Grass Cradle. Joanne Arnott. 72p. 1993. pap. 10.95 (*0-88974-048-8*, Pub. by Press Gang Pubs) LPC InBook.

My Great-Aunt Arizona. Gloria M. Houston. LC 90-44112. (Illus.). 32p. (J). (gr. 1-4). 1992. lib. bdg. 15.89 (*0-06-022607-2*) HarpC Child Bks.

My Great-Aunt Arizona. Gloria M. Houston. LC 90-44112. (Illus.). 32p. (J). (ps-3). 1992. 15.95 (*0-06-022606-4*) HarpC Child Bks.

My Great-Aunt Arizona. Gloria M. Houston. LC 90-44112. (Trophy Picture Bk.). (Illus.). 32p. (J). (gr. 1-4). 1997. pap. 5.95 (*0-06-443374-9*, HarpTrophy) HarpC Child Bks.

My Great-Aunt Arizona. Gloria M. Houston. 1997. 11.15 (*0-606-11656-7*, Pub. by Turtleback) Demco.

My Great-Grandfather Was Stonewall Jackson: The Story of a Negro Boy Growing up in the Segregated South. David J. Sawyer. LC 92-74120. (Illus.). 288p. 1994. pap. 14.00 (*0-9635159-1-8*) Pub Concepts.

My Great-Grandfather Was Stonewall Jackson Vol. 1: The Story of a Negro Boy Growing up in the Segregated South. 2nd rev. ed. David J. Sawyer. Ed. by Paul Evans. (Illus.). 304p. (gr. 10-11). 1994. reprint ed. pap. 16.00 (*0-9634206-1-5*) Jonathan MD.

An Asterisk (*) at the beginning of an entry indicates that the title is appearing for the first time.

My Great-Grandfather Was Stonewall Jackson Vol. 2: Stonewalling in the Shadow of a Legend. rev. ed. David J. Sawyer. Ed. by Paul Evans. 317p. (Orig.). (YA). (gr. 10-11). 1994. reprint ed. pap. 16.00 (*0-9634206-9-0*) Jonathan MD.

My Great-Grandfather's House in Exeter, New Hampshire. James E. Brooks. (Illus.). 64p. 1997. reprint ed. pap. 13.00 (*0-8328-5991-5*) Higginson Bk Co.

***My Great-Grandmother's Gourd.** Cristina Kessler. LC 99-56553. (Illus.). 32p. (J). (gr. k-4). 2000. 16.95 (*0-531-30284-9*); 17.99 (*0-531-33284-5*) Orchard Bks Watts.

My Great Redeemer's Praise: An Introduction to Christian Hymns. Carlton R. Young. Ed. by Timothy J. Crouch. 143p. (Orig.). 1995. pap. 14.95 (*1-878009-22-2*, OSL Pubns) Order St Luke Pubns.

My Great Redeemer's Praise: Duets for Piano & Synthesizer. Des. by Teresa Wilhelmi. 44p. 1994. 10.99 (*0-8341-9035-4*, MB-676) Lillenas.

My Great Wide Beautiful World: African-American Women Writers 1910-1940 by J. Harrison. Gates. LC 96-43473. 1996. 25.00 (*0-7838-1433-X*, Hall Reference) Macmillan.

My Greatest Day in Baseball. John P. Carmichael. LC 95-40142. xii, 245p. 1996. pap. 12.95 (*0-8032-6368-6*, Bison Books) U of Nebr Pr.

My Greatest Day in Baseball, 1946-1997: Baseball's Greatest Share Their Triumphs. Bob McCullough. LC 98-10673. 273p. 1998. pap. text 22.95 (*0-87833-989-2*) Taylor Pub.

***My Greatest Day in NASCAR.** Bob McCullough. LC 99-55496. (Illus.). 320p. 2000. text 24.95 (*0-312-25254-4*, Thomas Dunne) St Martin.

My Greatest Day in Show Business: Screen Legends Share Their Fondest Memories. Raymond Richmond. LC 99-18436. 1999. pap. 15.95 (*0-87833-224-3*) Taylor Pub.

My Greatest Fight. Ken Gorman. (Illus.). 192p. 1997. pap. 22.95 (*1-84018-018-8*, Pub. by Mainstream Pubng) Trafalgar.

My Greatest Game-Cricket. Ed. by Bob Holmes & Vic Marks. (Illus.). 207p. 1995. pap. 22.95 (*1-85158-742-X*, Pub. by Mainstream Pubng) Trafalgar.

My Greatest Game-Rugby. Ed. by Bob Holmes & Chris Thau. (Illus.). 191p. 1995. pap. 19.95 (*1-85158-741-1*, Pub. by Mainstream Pubng) Trafalgar.

My Green Age. Tom MacDonagh. 148p. 1986. pap. 8.95 (*0-905169-76-X*, Pub. by Poolbeg Pr) Dufour.

My Green Book of God's Different Things. Mary Landis. (Jewel Book Ser.: Set 4). (Illus.). 32p. (J). 1993. pap. 2.55 (*0-7399-0044-7*, 2529) Rod & Staff.

My Green Book of God's Different Things. Mary Landis. (Jewel Book Ser.). (SPA., Illus.). 32p. (J). 1995. pap. 2.05 (*0-7399-0289-X*, 2529.1) Rod & Staff.

***My Grieving Journey Book.** Donna Shavatt & Eve Shavatt. 32p. (J). (gr. k-12). 1999. 14.95 (*0-9678630-0-7*) Shavatt Ent.

My Guardian Angel. Date not set. 8.95 (*0-88271-559-3*, 10523) Regina Pr.

My Guardian Angel. S. First. (J). 1996. bds. 4.95 (*0-88271-455-4*) Regina Pr.

My Guardian Angel: Helper & Friend. Thomas J. Donaghy. LC 97-203015. (Illus.). 32p. (J). 1994. 5.95 (*0-89942-125-3*, 125/22) Catholic Bk Pub.

My Guardian Angel: The Invisible Crewman. 2nd ed. William Purser. LC 97-94118. (Illus.). vi, 178p. 1997. pap. 18.95 (*0-9659414-0-X*) Bonnie Pr.

My Guardian Angel - The Invisible Crewman. 2nd rev. ed. William Purser. Ed. by Kathy P. Giddens. LC 97-94118. (Illus.). 210p. 1997. pap. 12.95 (*0-9659414-2-6*) Bonnie Pr.

My Guardian Angel in My Mourning. Regina A. Shay. LC 96-164321. (Illus.). 28p. (Orig.). (J). 1996. pap. 6.95 (*0-7880-0715-7*) CSS OH.

My Guardian Angels. unabridged ed. Rory Morse. (Illus.). 60p. 1997. spiral bd. 15.00 (*1-929326-49-1*) Hal Bar Pubg.

My Guardian Dear (Mi Angel de la Guarda) A Story of the Angels (Un Cuento Acerca de los Angeles) Miriam A. Lademan & Susan A. Brindle. Tr. by Carmen A. Emmanuelli Klosterman. (Stories of the Faith Ser.). (ENG & SPA., Illus.). 64p. (gr. k-10). 1996. pap. 9.95 (*1-889733-03-2*, 01005) Precious Life Bks.

My Guess Was Murder. large type ed. Guy Cobden. (Linford Mystery Library). 448p. 1993. pap. 16.99 (*0-7089-7377-9*, Linford) Ulverscroft.

***My Guide to America's Animals & Plants.** Bob Dewire. (Illus.). 48p. (J). (gr. 1-2). 2000. 2.50 (*1-56762-126-0*) Modern Learn Pr.

***My Guide to America's Habitats.** Bob Dewire. (Illus.). 72p. 2000. 2.95 (*1-56762-128-7*) Modern Learn Pr.

***My Guide to Our Habitat.** Bob Dewire. (Illus.). 64p. (J). (gr. 2-3). 2000. 2.75 (*1-56762-127-9*) Modern Learn Pr.

***My Gum Is Gone.** Richard P. Yurcheshen. LC 99-57728. (Illus.). 32p. (J). (ps-3). 2000. pap. 8.95 (*1-55798-662-2*, 441-6622, Magination Press) Am Psychol.

My Gun Is Pink: A Mystery Comedy. Jeffrey Goffin. (Illus.). 32p. 1987. pap. 3.50 (*0-88680-280-6*) I E Clark.

My Gun Is Quick. Mickey Spillane, pseud. 20.95 (*0-89190-836-6*) Amereon Ltd.

My Gun, My Brother: The World of the Papua New Guinea Colonial Police, 1920-1960. August I. Kituai. LC 97-38820. (Pacific Islands Monographs: Vol. 15). (Illus.). 376p. 1998. text 48.00 (*0-8248-1747-8*) UH Pr.

My Guru & His Disciple. Christopher Isherwood. LC 96-178374. (Michael di Capua Bks.). 4494p. 1988. pap. 13.00 (*0-374-52087-9*) FS&G.

My Guru & His Disciple. Christopher Isherwood. LC 81-102777. 338p. 1980. write for info. (*0-413-46930-1*) Heinemann.

My Guru & Me: A Path to Spiritual Enlightenment. Gerald Kuwada. (Self-Mastery II Ser.). 200p. 1997. 21.95 (*0-9643386-5-3*) Self Mastery.

My Guru, My Midwife: Poems 1981-1994, 1. Padma Jared Thornlyre. 1994. pap. text 13.00 (*1-880046-09-1*) Baculite Pub.

***My Guy.** Sarah Weeks. 128p. (J). (gr. 3-7). 2001. 14.95 (*0-06-028369-6*, L Geringer); lib. bdg. 14.89 (*0-06-028370-X*, L Geringer) HarpC Child Bks.

My "H" Sound Box. Jane Belk Moncure. LC 77-8977. (Sound Box Library). (Illus.). 32p. (J). (ps-2). 1977. lib. bdg. 21.36 (*0-913778-94-X*) Childs World.

***My "H" Sound Box.** Jane Belk Moncure. LC 99-56560. (Illus.). (J). 2000. lib. bdg. write for info. (*1-56766-774-0*) Childs World.

My Haggadah. Ila Cherney. (Illus.). 66p. (J). (gr. 4-7). 1985. pap. text 4.95 (*0-87441-483-0*) Behrman.

My Hair Is Beautiful . . . Because It's Mine. Paula Dejoie. 12p. (J). 1994. 5.95 (*0-86316-219-3*) Writers & Readers.

My Hair Is in the Outbox. Marjory L. McGrath. 116p. (Orig.). 1995. pap. 7.95 (*0-9649200-0-X*) M&C Pubng.

My Hair, My Glory: Is There Really Any Significance? Juli Jasinski. Ed. by Jeanne Austin. (Illus.). 250p. 1995. pap. 11.95 (*0-9650467-0-2*) Pentecstals.

My Hair Turning Gray among Strangers. Leroy V. Quintana. LC 95-31049. 88p. (Orig.). (C). 1996. pap. 9.00 (*0-927534-57-6*) Biling Rev-Pr.

My Hairiest Adventure. R. L. Stine, pseud. (Goosebumps Ser.: No. 26). 160p. (J). (gr. 3-7). 1994. pap. 3.99 (*0-590-48350-1*) Scholastic Inc.

My Hairiest Adventure. R. L. Stine, pseud. (Goosebumps Ser.: No. 26). 1994. 9.09 (*0-606-07046-X*, Pub. by Turtleback) Demco.

My Hairiest Adventure. Adapted by Diane Umansky. (Goosebumps Presents Ser.: No. 6). (Illus.). 64p. (J). 1996. pap. 3.99 (*0-590-82519-4*) Scholastic Inc.

My Hairiest Adventure. Adapted by Diane Umansky. (Goosebumps Presents Ser.: No. 6). 1996. 9.19 (*0-606-10827-0*, Pub. by Turtleback) Demco.

My Half-Century: Selected Prose. Anna Andreevena Akhmatova. Ed. by Ronald Meyer. LC 97-14774. 1997. pap. 18.95 (*0-8101-1485-2*) Northwestern U Pr.

My Hand in His. J. G. Malphurs. 1961. 5.00 (*0-88027-012-8*) Firm Foun Pub.

***My Hand in His: Ancient Truths in Modern Parables.** rev. ed. Herman W. Gockel. LC 99-31571. 240p. 1999. 12.99 (*0-570-05233-5*) Concordia.

My Hand Will Write What My Heart Dictates: The Unsettled Lives of Women in New Zealand 1820-1915 As Revealed in Letters to Sisters, Family & Friends. Ed. by Frances Porter & Charlotte Macdonald. 480p. 1996. pap. 34.95 (*1-86940-129-8*) Paul & Co Pubs.

My Hands. Aliki. LC 62-12810. (Let's-Read-&-Find-Out Science Bks.). (Illus.). 40p. (J). (gr. k-3). 1962. lib. bdg. 12.89 (*0-690-56834-7*) HarpC Child Bks.

My Hands. rev. ed. Aliki. LC 89-49158. (Let's-Read-&-Find-Out Science Bks.). (Illus.). 32p. (J). (ps-1). 1990. lib. bdg. 15.89 (*0-690-04880-7*) HarpC Child Bks.

My Hands. rev. ed. Aliki. LC 89-49158. (Trophy Let's-Read-&-Find-Out Bk.). (Illus.). 32p. (J). (ps-1). 1992. pap. 4.95 (*0-06-445096-1*, HarpTrophy) HarpC Child Bks.

My Hands Held Out to You: The Use of Body & Hands in Prayer. Giancarlo Moroni. 112p. 1994. pap. 35.00 (*0-86012-194-1*, Pub. by Srch Pr) St Mut.

My Hanukkah Book: Questions, Answers, Activities. Kimberly Colen. (Illus.). 24p. (Orig.). (J). (gr. 4-6). 1987. pap. 3.95 (*0-590-40965-4*) Scholastic Inc.

My Happy Birthday Book. Lisa Jahn-Clough. LC 95-37602. (Illus.). 32p. (J). (ps-k). 1996. 5.95 (*0-395-77260-5*) HM.

My Happy Days. Jane D. Shakelford. (Illus.). (J). 1990. 7.95 (*0-87498-004-6*) Assoc Pubs DC.

My Happy Easter Book. Arch Books Staff. LC 96-132987. (Arch Bks.). (Illus.). (J). (gr. k-4). 1996. 1.99 (*0-570-07520-3*, 59-1493) Concordia.

My Happy Hours. Ethel V. Hodge. 1998. pap. write for info. (*1-57553-889-X*) Watermrk Pr.

My Happy Ones. Joan Hutson. (Illus.). 23p. (J). (ps). 1987. 3.95 (*0-8198-4723-2*) Pauline Bks.

My Hard Bargain. Walter Kirn. Ed. by Maryanne Sacco. 160p. 1992. reprint ed. pap. 9.00 (*0-671-79379-9*, WSP) PB.

My Harvard Library Years, 1937-1955: A Sequel to Random Recollections of an Anachronism. Keyes D. Metcalf. Ed. by Edwin E. Williams. 320p. 1988. 25.00 (*0-674-59600-5*) HUP.

My Harvest Home: A Celebration of Polish Songs, Dances, Games & Customs. Andrea Schafer. (Illus.). 76p. (Orig.). 1996. pap. 17.95 incl. audio (*0-937203-68-8*); pap. 20.95 incl. audio compact disk (*0-937203-69-6*) World Music Pr.

My Hat Flies on Again. James Crenner. LC 79-25793. 62p. (Orig.). 1980. pap. 4.25 (*0-934332-23-1*) LEpervier Pr.

My Hatreds. Emile Zola. Tr. by Palomba Paves-Yashinsky & Jack Yashinsky from FRE. LC 91-42114. (Studies in French Literature: Vol. 12).Tr. of Mes Haines. xiv, 182p. 1992. lib. bdg. 79.95 (*0-7734-9736-6*) E Mellen.

My, Haven't the Flowers Been? Harriet Zinnes. LC 95-79163. 128p. (Orig.). 1995. pap. 12.00 (*0-913660-26-4*) Magic Cir Pr CT.

My Hawaiian Smile. C. A. Bridgman. (J). 14.95 (*0-681-32826-6*) Booklines Hawaii.

My Hawaiian Smile. C. A. Bridgman. LC TXU645-473. (Illus.). 32p. (J). (ps-4). 1996. 14.95 (*0-9659382-1-2*) Immanuel Pr.

***My Head & My Heart: Sex, Love, Life & the Unconscious.** Jorge Degregorio. 2000. 24.95 (*0-679-46297-X*) Random.

My Head Is Bloody but Unbowed. Matsu Crawford. 111p. (Orig.). 1983. pap. 5.00 (*0-9612862-0-2*) R E F Typesetting Pub.

My Head Is Full of Colors. Catherine Friend. LC 93-5787. (Illus.). 32p. (J). (ps-3). 1994. 14.95 (*1-56282-360-4*, Pub. by Hyprn Child); lib. bdg. 14.89 (*1-56282-361-2*, Pub. by Hyprn Child) Little.

My Head Is Full of Colors. Catherine Friend. LC 93-5787. (Illus.). 32p. (J). (ps-3). 1995. pap. 4.95 (*0-7868-1071-8*, Pub. by Hyprn Ppbks) Little.

My Head is Full of Colors. Catherine Friend. 1995. 10.15 (*0-606-08828-8*, Pub. by Turtleback) Demco.

My Head Is Opening. E. Conlon. (C). 1991. 34.95 (*0-946211-32-9*) St Mut.

My Head, My Head. Robert Graves. LC 73-20386. (English Literature Ser.: No. 33). 1974. lib. bdg. 75.00 (*0-8383-1757-X*) M S G Haskell Hse.

My Head Was a Sledgehammer: Six Plays. Richard Foreman. 380p. 1995. 24.95 (*0-87951-575-9*, Pub. by Overlook Pr) Penguin Putnam.

My Head Was a Sledgehammer: Six Plays. Richard Foreman. 380p. 1995. pap. 14.95 (*0-87951-622-4*, Pub. by Overlook Pr) Penguin Putnam.

My Healing from Breast Cancer. Barbara Joseph. Ed. by Phyllis Herman. 392p. 1996. pap. 14.95 (*0-87983-711-X*, 3711XK, Keats Publng) NTC Contemp Pub Co.

My Health Is Better in November: Thirty-Five Stories of Hunting & Fishing in the South. Havilah Babcock. LC 85-225748. (Illus.). 298p. 1985. 24.95 (*0-87249-440-3*) U of SC Pr.

My Health Record: Help the Doctor Help You. 2nd rev. ed. Sandra Lewis. 80p. 2000. pap. 8.95 (*0-9662129-1-6*, Pub. by SDL Pubs) ACCESS Pubs Network.

My Healthy Heart. Phillip G. Kelley. (Big Bks.). (Illus.). 8p. (J). (ps-k). 1994. pap. text 10.95 (*1-57332-000-5*) HighReach Lrning.

***My Heart.** Kathy Furgang. LC 99-88032. (My Body Ser.). (Illus.). (J). 2000. lib. bdg. write for info. (*0-8239-5574-5*, PowerKids) Rosen Group.

My Heart - Christ's Home. Robert B. Munger. (Horizon Ser.). 1996. pap. 4.99 (*1-56570-033-3*) Meridian MI.

My Heart - Christ's Home: Retold for Children. Robert B. Munger & Carolyn Nystrom. LC 97-12919. (Illus.). 32p. (J). (gr. 2-6). 1997. 14.99 (*0-8308-1907-X*, 1907) InterVarsity.

My Heart a Hiding Place. Paul Lee. 1986. pap. 7.95 (*0-87508-316-1*) Chr Lit.

My Heart, Christ's Home. Meridian Publishing Staff. 1995. pap. text 14.95 (*1-56570-058-9*) Meridian MI.

My Heart, Christ's Home. Robert B. Munger. (Christian Classics Ser.). 1995. pap. 2.99 (*1-56570-014-7*) Meridian MI.

My Heart-Christ's Home. Robert B. Munger. LC 92-5678. (Stories for Old & Young Ser.). (Illus.). 48p. 1992. reprint ed. 12.99 (*0-8308-1842-1*, 1842) InterVarsity.

My Heart-Christ's Home see IVP Booklets

My Heart, Christ's Home, 5 vols. rev. ed. Robert Boyd Munger. 1986. pap. 5.00 (*0-8308-6575-6*) InterVarsity.

My Heart Cries Out to Thee. John-Charles Duffy. pap. write for info. (*0-88290-690-9*) Horizon Utah.

My Heart Flies. Kathy Adkisson. 128p. 1998. pap. write for info. (*0-9670067-0-8*) K Adkisson.

My Heart Goes Home: A Hudson Valley Memoir. Thomas S. Lossing. Ed. by Peter D. Hannaford. LC 97-14258. (Illus.). 190p. 1997. pap. 17.50 (*0-935796-87-8*) Purple Mnt Pr.

My Heart in a Suitcase. Anne L. Fox. LC 95-38174. (Library of Holocaust Testimonies). (Illus.). 184p. (Orig.). 1996. pap. 17.50 (*0-85303-311-0*, Pub. by M Vallentine & Co) Intl Spec Bk.

My Heart in His Hands. Sharon L. James. 1999. pap. text 12.99 (*0-85234-421-X*) Evangelical Pr.

***My Heart in My Mouth: Prayers for Soul-Searching Worship.** Ted Loder. 160p. 2000. pap. 14.95 (*1-880913-49-6*) Innisfree Pr.

My Heart Is a Glowing Sunset: My Voice Is a Warming Song. Ed. by Roy McBride. (Illus.). 177p. (Orig.). 1990. pap. 8.00 (*0-927663-15-5*) COMPAS.

My Heart Is Full of Wishes. Joshua Grishaw. LC 94-40435. (Publish-a-Book Ser.). (Illus.). (J). (gr. 1-6). 1995. lib. bdg. 22.83 (*0-8114-7269-8*) Raintree Steck-V.

***My Heart Is Not Disabled: People with Disabilities in Kampot Province, 6 vols., Vol. 4.** Rebecca Catalla et al. 63p. 2000. pap. 4.00 (*0-910082-40-5*) Am Fr Serv Comm.

My Heart is on the Ground: The Diary of Nannie Little Rose, a Sioux Girl, Carlisle Indian School, Pennsylvania, 1880. Ann Rinaldi. LC 98-26767. (Dear America Ser.). (Illus.). 197p. (J). (gr. 4-9). 1999. 10.95 (*0-590-14922-9*) Scholastic Inc.

My Heart Is Ready: Feasts & Fasts from Fifth Avenue. John Andrew. LC 94-41666. (Church Year Sermons Ser.). 195p. 1995. pap. 11.95 (*1-56101-107-X*) Cowley Pubns.

My Heart Is So Rebellious: The Caldwell Letters, 1861-1865. John K. Gott et al. (Illus.). 295p. (Orig.). 1991. 24.95 (*0-9630128-1-9*); pap. 14.95 (*0-9630128-0-0*) Fauquier Bank.

My Heart Laid Bare. Joyce Carol Oates. 544p. 1999. pap. 13.95 (*0-452-28006-0*, Plume) Dutton Plume.

My Heart Laid Bare & Other Prose Writings. Charles Baudelaire. Ed. by Peter Quennell. LC 75-34313. (Studies in French Literature: No. 45). 1974. lib. bdg. 75.00 (*0-8383-1870-3*) M S G Haskell Hse.

My Heart Laid Bare & Other Prose Writings. Charles Baudelaire. Ed. by Peter Quennell. Tr. by Norman Cameron from FRE. 225p. 1986. reprint ed. pap. 13.95 (*0-948166-07-X*, Pub. by Soho Bk Co) Dufour.

My Heart Leaps Up, Chapters 7 & 8. R. A. Lafferty. (Booklet Ser.: No. 29). 49p. (Orig.). 1988. pap. text 2.75 (*0-936055-37-5*) C Drumm Bks.

My Heart Leaps Up, Chapters 9 & 10. R. A. Lafferty. (Booklet Ser.: No. 35). 63p. (Orig.). 1990. pap. text 3.50 (*0-936055-41-3*) C Drumm Bks.

My Heart Leaps Up, Chapters 9 & 10. deluxe ed. R. A. Lafferty. (Booklet Ser.: No. 35). 63p. (Orig.). 1990. pap. 6.00 (*0-936055-42-1*) C Drumm Bks.

My Heart Leaps Up, Chs. 5 & 6. R. A. Lafferty. (Booklet Ser.: No. 28). 53p. (Orig.). 1987. pap. 2.95 (*0-936055-33-2*) C Drumm Bks.

My Heart Leaps Up: Chapters 3 & 4, Chpts. 3 & 4. R. A. Lafferty. (Drumm Booklet Ser.: No. 26). 44p. (Orig.). 1987. pap. 2.75 (*0-936055-30-8*) C Drumm Bks.

My Heart, My Country: The Story of Dorothea MacKellar. Adrienne Howley. 1989. pap. 16.95 (*0-7022-2188-0*, Pub. by Univ Queensland Pr) Intl Spec Bk.

My Heart, My Life, My All: Love's Response: A Living Sacrifice. William MacDonald. 1997. pap. 8.95 (*1-882701-44-5*) Uplook Min.

My Heart on the Yukon River. Monique Dykstra. LC 97-26116. (Illus.). 136p. (Orig.). 1997. pap. 24.95 (*0-87422-157-9*) Wash St U Pr.

My Heart Soars. Dan George. (Illus.). 96p. 1989. pap. 7.95 (*0-88839-231-1*) Hancock House.

***My Heart Speaks: Wisdom from Pope John XXIII.** Ed. by Jeanne Kun. LC 00-35914. 144p. 2000. pap. 12.00 (*0-932085-34-2*) Word Among Us.

My Heart Speaks to Thee, Vol. 1. Ed. by Carolyn E. Cardwell. (Illus.). 250p. 1985. pap. 10.95 (*0-916395-02-2*, MH-1) Hieroglyphics.

My Heart Speaks to Thee, Vol. 2. Ed. by Carolyn E. Cardwell. (Illus.). 250p. 1985. pap. 10.95 (*0-916395-05-7*, MH-2) Hieroglyphics.

***My Heart 2 Heart Autograph Album.** Ed. by Ninda Dumont. (Illus.). 80p. (J). 1999. 5.95 (*1-892951-01-0*) Fine Print.

***My Heart 2 Heart Girlfriends' Book.** Ed. by Ninda Dumont. (Illus.). 64p. (J). 1999. 11.95 (*1-892951-02-9*) Fine Print.

My Heart Two Heart Diary: Blue Dog Edition. Ed. by Ninda Dumont. (Illus.). 128p. (J). 1996. 11.95 (*0-9640713-4-7*) Fine Print.

My Heart 2 Heart Diary: Broccoli Edition. Ed. by Ninda Dumont. (Illus.). 128p. (J). 1998. 11.95 (*0-9640713-9-8*) Fine Print.

My Heart 2 Heart Diary: Indigo Puppy Edition. Ed. by Ninda Dumont. (Illus.). 64p. (J). 1998. 11.95 (*0-9640713-8-X*) Fine Print.

My Heart 2 Heart Diary: Keyhole Edition. Ed. by Ninda Dumont. 128p. (J). (gr. 4-8). 1994. 10.95 (*0-9640713-0-4*) Fine Print.

My Heart 2 Heart Diary: Wordy Birdy Edition. Ed. by Ninda Dumont. 1997. 12.95 (*0-9640713-6-3*) Fine Print.

My Heart 2 Heart Scraps & Pockets. Ed. by Ninda Dumont. (J). 1997. 14.95 (*0-9640713-3-9*) Fine Print.

My Heart 2 Heart Travel Diary. Ed. by Ninda Dumont. (Illus.). 64p. (J). 1998. pap. 11.95 (*0-9640713-7-1*) Fine Print.

***My Heart Will Go On: (Celine Dion)** 8p. 1998. pap. 3.95 (*0-7935-9716-1*) H Leonard.

***My Heart Will Go On: (Celine Dion)** 64p. 1999. pap. 9.95 (*0-634-00466-2*) H Leonard.

***My Heart Will Go On (Love Theme From Titanic) & 15 other Top Movie Hits.** 112p. 1998. per. 10.95 (*0-7935-9605-X*) H Leonard.

***My Heart Will Go On (Love Theme From Titanic) & 15 other Top Movie Hits.** 56p. 1998. pap. 7.95 (*0-7935-9652-1*) H Leonard.

My Heart's a Suitcase & Low Level Panic. Clare McIntyre. 128p. 1997. pap. 14.95 (*1-85459-246-7*, Pub. by N Hern Bks) Theatre Comm.

My Heart's at Home. Mary Larmoyeux. LC 98-31336. 224p. 1999. pap. 12.99 (*0-8054-1658-7*) Broadman.

My Heart's Desire. Andrea Kane. Ed. by Carolyn Tolley. 336p. 1991. mass mkt. 5.50 (*0-671-73584-5*) PB.

My Heart's Health: A New Revolutionary View. D. Sodi-Pallares. 198p. 1989. pap. text 15.00 (*1-57235-064-4*) Piccin Nuova.

My Heart's Health: A New Revolutionary View. D. Sodi-Pallares. (Illus.). 198p. 1989. text 17.00 (*88-299-0725-1*, Pub. by Piccin Nuova) Gordon & Breach.

My Heart's Memory. Robert A. Clay. 63p. 1998. 9.95 (*0-9662444-0-0*) R A Clay.

***My Heart's Treasures: Collection of Poetry.** Marie Ford Smith. 40p. 1999. pap. 7.00 (*0-8059-4598-9*) Dorrance.

My Heart's World: Stories by David Mazel. David Mazel. Ed. & Illus. by Niki Adam-Casimiro. LC 84-62148. 144p. 1985. pap. 9.95 (*0-931762-02-2*) Phunn Pubs.

My Heavenly Bank Account. Sherry Poff. (Orig.). 1995. pap. 5.99 (*1-883602-07-6*) Atlantic Digital.

***My Heavenly Happys & My Secretly Sads: A Childs Workbook.** Ruth-Ann Robinson. (Illus.). 56p. (J). (gr. 3-10). 1999. pap. 20.00 (*1-929010-01-X*) Epiphany IL.

My Hen Is Dancing. Karen Wallace. LC 93-930. (Read & Wonder Bks.). (Illus.). 32p. (J). (ps up). 1994. 14.95 (*1-56402-303-6*) Candlewick Pr.

My Hen Is Dancing. Karen Wallace. LC 93-930. (Read & Wonder Bks.). (Illus.). 32p. (J). (ps-3). 1996. reprint ed. pap. 5.99 (*1-56402-961-1*) Candlewick Pr.

My Herbal Water Cure: An Encyclopedia of Herbology. Sebastian Kneipp. 1991. lib. bdg. 79.95 (*0-8490-4255-0*) Gordon Pr.

My Heritage. Mary F. Dever. LC 96-90827. 1997. 12.95 (*0-533-12182-5*) Vantage.

My Heritage Cookbook. Lorna D. Smith. (Illus.). 136p. 1992. pap. 5.00 (*0-9632467-5-5*) ApronStrings.

My Hero. Debbie Macomber. (Romance Ser.: No. 180). 1992. per. 2.79 (*0-373-03180-7*, 1-03180-6) Harlequin Bks.

My Hero, Hercules. Priscilla Galloway. (Tales of Ancient Lands Ser.). 120p. (J). (gr. 4-8). 1999. 16.95 (*1-55037-569-5*, Pub. by Annick Pr); pap. 6.95 (*1-55037-568-7*, Pub. by Annick Pr) Firefly Bks Ltd.

M

An Asterisk (*) at the beginning of an entry indicates that the title is appearing for the first time.

M

My Hero, My Friend: The Life of Henry Arthur Callis. Jerald L. Hoover. 166p. (Orig.). pap. 7.95 (*1-56411-043-5*) Untd Bros & Sis.

My Hero, My Friend Jimmy Bryan. Phil Sampaio & Len Gasper. (Illus.). 346p. 1993. write for info. (*0-942078-44-6*) R Tanner Assocs Inc.

My Hero, My Friend Jimmy Bryan. deluxe ed. Phil Sampaio & Len Gasper. (Illus.). 346p. 1993. write for info. (*0-942078-45-4*) R Tanner Assocs Inc.

My Heroes, My People: African Americans & Native Americans in the West. Morgan Monceaux & Ruth Katcher. LC 98-45400. (Illus.). 64p. (YA). (gr. 5-9). 1999. 18.00 (*0-374-30770-9*, Frances Foster) FS&G.

My Hero's a Mutt: True Stories of Dogs Who Save Lives: True Stories of Dogs Who Saved Lives. Barry Hoffman. (Illus.). 226p. 2002. 17.45 (*0-7868-6358-7*, Pub. by Hyperion) Little.

My Hideous Progeny: Mary Shelly, William Godwin & the Father-Daughter Relationship. Katherine C. Hill-Miller. LC 94-18535. 1995. 38.50 (*0-87413-535-4*) U Delaware Pr.

My Highland Kellas Cats. D. Francis. 1994. 35.00 (*0-224-03608-4*, Pub. by Random) Trafalgar.

My Highland Kellas Cats. large type ed. Di Francis. (Illus.). 416p. 1996. 27.99 (*0-7089-3539-7*) Ulverscroft.

*__My Him Book.__ Linda Ekins. (Illus.). 30p. 1999. pap. text 10.95 (*1-57636-071-7*) SunRise Pbl.

My Hiroshima: A Personal Epic. Richard J. Schoeck. LC 97-30529. 100p. 1997. pap. 14.95 (*0-7734-2846-1*, Mellen Poetry Pr) E Mellen.

*__My History Is America's History: 15 Things You Can Do to Save America's Stories.__ 98p. 1999. pap. 13.00 (*0-16-050212-8*) USGPO.

*__My History is America's History: 15 Things You Can Do to Save America's Stories.__ Robert D. Selim. Ed. by Patti VanTuyl. (Illus.). 97p. 2000. pap. text 25.00 (*0-7881-8904-2*) DIANE Pub.

*__My History Is America's History Guidebook.__ LC 99-76568. (Illus.). 98p. 1999. write for info. (*0-942310-00-4*) National Endowment for Humanities.

My History, Not Yours: The Formation of Mexican American Autobiography. Genaro M. Padilla. LC 93-3457. (Studies in American Autobiography). (Illus.). 224p. (Orig.). (C). 1993. pap. 18.95 (*0-299-13974-3*); lib. bdg. 40.00 (*0-299-13970-0*) U of Wis Pr.

My Hitch in Hell: The Bataan Death March. Lester I. Tenney. (World War II Commemorative, Association of the U. S. Army Book Ser.). (Illus.). 240p. 1995. 24.95 (*0-02-881125-9*) Brasseys.

*__My Hitch in Hell: The Bataan Death March.__ Lester I. Tenney. 2000. reprint ed. pap. 15.95 (*1-57488-298-8*) Brasseys.

My Ho- Ho- Horrible Christmas. Cathy East Dubowski. (Full House Michelle Ser.: Vol. 17). 96p. (J). (gr. 4-7). 1997. per. 3.99 (*0-671-00836-6*) PB.

*__My Holiday Journal.__ Brian Leslie Lewis. 16p. (J). 1999. pap. 6.95 (*1-928693-05-9*) Novice Nomad.

My Holiday Story Book. rev. ed. Morris Epstein. (J). (gr. 4-5). 1958. pap. 4.95 (*0-87068-368-3*) Ktav.

My Hollywood - When Both of Us Were Young: The Memories of Patsy Ruth Miller, 2 bks. in 1. Philip J. Riley. (Illus.). 1991. 39.95 (*0-929127-01-3*) Magicimage Filmbooks.

My Home. (Little Book of Questions & Answers Ser.). (Illus.). 32p. (J). 1993. 4.98 (*1-56173-472-1*) Pubns Intl Ltd.

*__My Home.__ Anness Publications Staff. 1999. pap. 4.95 (*0-7548-0280-9*, Lorenz Bks) Anness Pub.

My Home. Photos by Bill Thomas et al. LC 97-23459. (Baby's Big Board Bks.). (Illus.). 12p. (J). (ps). 1997. bds. 6.95 (*1-887734-32-5*) Star Brght Bks.

My Home. Nicola Tuxworth. (Let's Look Ser.). (Illus.). 24p. (J). (ps). 1997. 3.95 (*1-85967-411-9*, Lorenz Bks) Anness Pub.

My Home - The Home of Many. Barbara M. Alusi. LC 86-80685. (Illus.). 128p. 1986. 17.00 (*0-934188-20-3*) Evans Pubns.

My Home Afloat: Taken from My Journal of a Two Year Voyage Aboard Prime Time. Dorothy I. Hoekwater. LC 92-93407. (Illus.). 224p. 1992. pap. 9.95 (*0-9632888-4-9*) Prime Time FL.

*__My Home & My Neighborhood: Thematic Unit.__ Rachel C. Oetken. Ed. by David Cook. 80p. (J). 1999. pap., teacher ed. 9.95 (*1-57690-469-5*, TCM2469) Tchr Create Mat.

My Home Country, 6 bks. 48p. (J). (gr. 2-8). 1992. lib. bdg. 127.60 (*0-8368-1701-X*) Gareth Stevens Inc.

My Home Is Africa: Who Am I? Valerie Tracqui. Tr. by Boston Language Institute Staff from FRE. LC 96-84445. (Little Nature Bks.). (Illus.). 10p. (J). (ps-k). 1997. bds. 4.95 (*0-88106-942-6*) Charlesbridge Pub.

My Home Is Far Away. Dawn Powell. LC 95-3238. 295p. 1995. pap. 14.00 (*1-883642-43-4*) Steerforth Pr.

My Home Is in the Smoky Mountains. Herbert L. Hyde. LC 98-60860. 194p. 1998. pap. 14.99 (*1-56664-133-0*) WorldComm.

*__My Home Is over Jordan.__ Sandra Forrester. 160p. (J). 2000. pap. 4.99 (*0-14-038802-8*, PuffinBks) Peng Put Young Read.

My Home Is over Jordan: Sequel to "Sound the Jubilee" Sandra Forrester. LC 97-15591. Orig. Title: Fire & Shadow. 176p. (J). (gr. 5-9). 1997. 15.99 (*0-525-67568-X*, Dutton Child) Peng Put Young Read.

My Home Is the Desert: Who Am I? Valerie Tracqui. LC 95-41034. (Little Nature Bks.). (Illus.). 10p. (J). (ps-k). 1996. bds. 4.95 (*0-88106-934-5*) Charlesbridge Pub.

My Home Is the Farm: Who Am I? Valerie Tracqui. LC 95-72222. (Little Nature Bks.). (Illus.). 10p. (J). (ps-k). 1996. bds. 4.95 (*0-88106-939-6*) Charlesbridge Pub.

My Home Is the Mountains: Who Am I? Valerie Tracqui. LC 95-41033. (Little Nature Bks.). (Illus.). 10p. (J). (ps-k). 1996. bds. 4.95 (*0-88106-936-1*) Charlesbridge Pub.

My Home Is the Polar Regions: Who Am I? Valerie Tracqui. LC 95-41031. (Little Nature Bks.). (Illus.). 10p. (J). (ps-k). 1996. bds. 4.95 (*0-88106-937-X*) Charlesbridge Pub.

My Home Is the Sea: Who Am I? Valerie Tracqui. LC 95-41032. (Little Nature Bks.). (Illus.). 10p. (J). (ps-k). 1996. bds. 4.95 (*0-88106-935-3*) Charlesbridge Pub.

My Home Is Washington County, North Carolina. Ed. by Shirleyan B. Phelps et al. LC 98-73085. (Illus.). v, 200p. 1999. 20.00 (*0-9663776-1-3*) Wash Cty NC.

My Home on the Crimean Steppe: Memoirs of David Weigum. David Weigum. LC 87-72581. 1987. pap. 15.00 (*0-914222-15-5*) Am Hist Soc Ger.

My Home, Sweet Home. Giovanni Guareschi. Date not set. 20.95 (*0-8488-2435-0*) Amereon Ltd.

My Homeword Assignment Book! A Record Keeping Forms Book for Organizing Daily Homework Assignments! Karen Sevaly. (Illus.). 88p. (J). (gr. 2-6). 1998. pap. 2.99 (*1-57882-018-9*, TF-1402) Teachers Friend Pubns.

My Homework Ate My Dog: The Best Cartoons from the Phi Delta Kappan, 1991-1996. Illus. by Carol Bucheri. 130p. 1996. pap. 18.00 (*0-87367-803-6*) Phi Delta Kappa.

My Honey Valentine. LC 97-116805. (J). 1997. 5.98 (*1-57082-441-X*, Pub. by Mouse Works) Time Warner.

*__My Hope for the Church: Critical Encouragement for the 21st Century.__ Bernard Haring. LC 98-40685. 1999. pap. text 16.95 (*0-7648-0379-4*) Liguori Pubns.

My Horse & Other Stories. Stacey Levine. (New American Fiction Ser.: No. 28). 150p. (Orig.). 1990. pap. 11.95 (*1-55713-124-4*) Sun & Moon CA.

My Horse Can Outrun Your Horse. J. E. Knott. (Illus.). 400p. reprint ed. 16.00 (*0-9623471-3-2*) Mesa Pub Corp.

My Horse Coloring Book. John Green. (Illus.). (J). (gr. k-3). 1994. pap. 2.95 (*0-486-28064-0*) Dover.

My Horse of the North. Bruce McMillan & Stan Berenstain. LC 96-45241. (Illus.). 32p. (J). (gr. k-3). 1997. 15.95 (*0-590-97205-7*) Scholastic Inc.

*__My Horses.__ Heather Miller. LC 00-20922. (My Farm Ser.). (Illus.). 24p. (J). (ps-2). 2000. pap. 4.95 (*0-516-23033-6*) Childrens.

*__My Horses.__ Heather Miller. (Welcome Bks.). (Illus.). (J). 2000. 13.50 (*0-516-23108-1*) Childrens.

My Horse's Book: The Who, What, When & Where of My Horse's Life - An Essential Book for All Horse Owners. S. K. Bollin. 32p. 1992. pap. 4.95 (*0-914846-64-7*) Golden West Pub.

My Horses, My Teachers. Alois Podhajsky. 1997. pap. 75.00 (*0-85131-692-1*) Trafalgar.

My Horses, My Teachers. Alois Podhajsky. Tr. by Eva Podhajsky. LC 96-50410. (Illus.). 202p. 1997. pap. 17.95 (*1-57076-091-8*, Trafalgar Sq Pub) Trafalgar.

My Host the Enemy, & Other Tales. Franklin W. Calkins. LC 72-81265. (Short Story Index Reprint Ser.). 1977. 21.95 (*0-8369-3017-7*) Ayer.

My House. Lisa Desimini. (J). 1995. write for info. (*0-8050-3144-8*) H Holt & Co.

My House. Lisa Desimini. 1997. 11.15 (*0-606-13634-7*, Pub. by Turtleback) Demco.

My House. David Drew. LC 92-30424. (Voyages Ser.). (Illus.). (J). 1993. 2.50 (*0-383-03586-4*) SRA McGraw.

My House. Leslie Wood. (Illus.). 16p. (J). (gr. k-6). 1988. pap. 4.25 (*0-19-272186-0*) OUP.

My House. large type ed. Helen Morris. (Illus.). 8p. (J). (gr. k-3). 1999. pap. text 17.00 (*1-58084-157-0*) Lower Kuskokwim.

My House. Nikki Giovanni. LC 72-116. 96p. 1974. reprint ed. pap. 9.00 (*0-688-05021-2*, Quil) HarperTrade.

My House, Vol. 1. Lisa Disimini. (Illus.). 32p. (J). 1997. reprint ed. pap. 5.95 (*0-8050-5516-9*) H Holt & Co.

My House Has Stars. Megan McDonald. LC 95-53798. (Illus.). 32p. (J). (gr. k-3). 1996. lib. bdg. 17.99 (*0-531-08879-0*) Orchard Bks Watts.

My House Has Stars. Megan McDonald. LC 95-53798. (Illus.). 32p. (J). (ps-3). 1996. 16.95 (*0-531-09529-0*) Orchard Bks Watts.

My House Has Two Door: China, Autobiography, History Suyin Han. LC 82-184021. 655 p. 1980. write for info. (*0-224-01702-0*) Jonathan Cape.

My House Is Your House Audio (Spanish edition) Mi casa es su casa. abr. ed. Michele Valeri. LC 82-740049. (J). (ps-3). 1986. audio 11.95 (*0-89845-175-2*, CPN 1708, Caedmon) HarperAudio.

My House (Mi Casa) A Book in Two Languages (Un Libro en Dos Lenguas) Rebecca Emberley. (ENG & SPA.). (J). 1993. 11.15 (*0-606-05487-1*, Pub. by Turtleback) Demco.

My House, My Paradise: The Construction of the Ideal Domestic Universe. Gustav Gili. (Illus.). 192p. 1999. 50.00 (*1-58423-015-0*) Gingko Press.

*__My House of Shapes.__ (Point & Peek Books Ser.). (Illus.). 6p. (J). 2000. bds. write for info. (*1-57584-362-5*) Rdrs Digest.

My House or Yours? Lass Small. (Desire Ser.). 1996. per. 3.25 (*0-373-05974-4*, 1-05974-0) Silhouette.

My House to Yours: How to Look Younger, Feel Better, & Live a Happier Life. Doris B. Gill. LC 87-71395. 159p. 1987. 9.95 (*0-9618693-1-3*) Crab Cove Bks.

My House, Your House. Shirley J. Miller. (Illus.). 60p. (Orig.). (J). (gr. 2-6). 1993. pap. 6.95 (*1-878580-91-4*) Asylum Arts.

My Houseful of Hints. Doris B. Gill. LC 89-91761. (Illus.). 176p. 1989. pap. 12.95 (*0-9618693-6-4*) Crab Cove Bks.

My House/Mi Casa: A Book in Two Languages. Rebecca Emberley. 32p. (J). (gr. k-3). 1993. pap. 5.95 (*0-316-23448-6*) Little.

*__My Hugger Is Empty.__ Greg Hancock. (Illus.). 24p. (J). (ps-3). 1999. pap. 7.95 (*1-894303-14-8*) RRP.

*__My Hungarian Family.__ Kruger. 2001. write for info. (*0-15-100591-5*) Harcourt.

My Hurt Is Over: The Miserable Experience of a Combat Infantryman in the Vietnam War. William B. Butler. 128p. 1997. pap. 12.95 (*0-89896-395-8*) Larksdale.

My Husband. Irene Castle. LC 78-12730. (Series in Dance). (Illus.). 1979. reprint ed. lib. bdg. 29.50 (*0-306-79505-1*) Da Capo.

My Husband, Arthur Murray. K. Murray. (Ballroom Dance Ser.). 1985. lib. bdg. 100.00 (*0-87700-693-8*) Revisionist Pr.

My Husband Gabrilowitsch. Clara Clemens. LC 79-11316. (Music Reprint Ser.). 1979. reprint ed. 39.50 (*0-306-79563-9*) Da Capo.

My Husband Is Not a Christian see Mi Esposo No Es Cristiano

My Husband, Jimmie Rodgers. 2nd ed. Carrie Rodgers. LC 95-68521. (Illus.). 222p. 1995. reprint ed. pap. 14.95 (*0-915608-16-2*) Country Music Found.

My Husband, My Love. Marlene Rimler. Ed. by Patrick Caton. LC 96-78980. 68p. 1997. 6.50 (*1-56245-283-5*) Great Quotations.

My Husband Said He Needed More Space, So I Locked Him Outside: Reflections on Life by Women. Cynthia W. McCullough. LC 98-2626. 112p. 1998. per. 10.00 (*0-684-84189-4*, Fireside) S&S Trade Pap.

My Husband Wears My Clothes. 2nd ed. Peggy J. Rudd. LC 98-67950. 174p. 1999. pap. text 14.95 (*0-9626762-5-X*) P M Publng.

My "i" Sound Box. Jane Belk Moncure. LC 84-17022. (Sound Box Library). (Illus.). 32p. (J). (ps-2). 1984. lib. bdg. 21.36 (*0-89565-298-6*) Childs World.

My Idea of Fun: A Cautionary Tale. Will Self. 1995. pap. 14.00 (*0-679-75093-2*) Vin Bks.

My Ideal-Jesus, Son of Mary. Emil Neubert. LC 88-50578. 111p. 1988. reprint ed. pap. 4.00 (*0-89555-338-4*) TAN Bks Pubs.

My Ideal Woman see Mi Mujer Ideal

*__My Illinois Garden: A Gardener's Journal.__ Jennifer Brennan. (Illus.). 128p. 2000. spiral bd. 19.95 (*1-930604-07-6*) Cool Springs Pr.

*__My Illinois Garden: A Gardener's Journal.__ Cool Springs Press Publications Staff. 2000. 19.95 (*1-888608-88-9*) Cool Springs Pr.

My Illustrated Dictionary. Librairie du Liban Staff. (ARA & ENG.). (J). (gr. 5-12). 1983. 11.95 (*0-86685-317-0*); 9.95 (*0-86685-318-9*); 9.95 (*0-86685-319-7*); 9.95 (*0-86685-320-0*); 9.95 (*0-86685-321-9*) Intl Bk Ctr.

My Illustrated Dictionary: Arabic & English. Librairie du Liban Staff. (ARA & ENG., Illus.). 64p. (J). 1983. 9.95 (*0-86685-314-6*, LDL3146, Pub. by Librairie du Liban) Intl Bk Ctr.

My Imac. Andrew Gore et al. LC 99-22753. (Illus.). 384p. 1999. pap. text 19.99 (*0-7645-3317-7*) IDG Bks.

My Image Is My Choice: How to Create the Perfect Haircut for Your Lifestyle. Tisha Lee. (Illus.). 260p. (Orig.). 1988. pap. text 24.95 (*0-9620833-0-5*) Castle Pubn.

My Impossible Dreams. Kristin E. Andalis. LC 97-91319. (Orig.). 1999. pap. 8.95 (*0-533-12640-1*) Vantage.

My Impressions of America. Charles L. Wagner. Tr. by Mary L. Hendee. LC 73-13155. (Foreign Travelers in America, 1810-1935 Ser.). 318p. 1974. reprint ed. 24.95 (*0-405-05477-7*) Ayer.

My Indian Boyhood. Luther Standing Bear. LC 88-12222. (Illus.). viii, 200p. 1988. reprint ed. pap. 9.95 (*0-8032-9186-8*, Bison Books) U of Nebr Pr.

My Indian Friends. F. Max Muller. (Auld Lang Syne Second Ser.). (C). 1993. reprint ed. 18.50 (*81-206-0839-9*, Pub. by Asian Educ Servs) S Asia.

My Indian Reminiscences. Paul Deussen. Tr. by A. King. 1995. 17.00 (*81-206-1054-7*, Pub. by Asian Educ Servs) S Asia.

*__My Indoor Garden.__ Carol Lerner. LC 98-18929. (Illus.). 48p. (J). 1999. 15.89 (*0-688-14754-2*, Wm Morrow) Morrow Avon.

My Indoor Garden. Carol Lerner. LC 98-18929. (Illus.). 48p. (J). (ps-3). 1999. 16.00 (*0-688-14753-4*, Wm Morrow) Morrow Avon.

My Infant: Off to a Good Start see Mi Bebe: Un Buen Comienzo

My Inner Self. Remigio M. Maradona.Tr. of Dentro de Mis Entranas. (Illus.). 76p. (Orig.). 1996. pap. 12.95 (*0-9650878-0-8*) Intl Diplomatic News.

*__My Inner Thoughts.__ John Rodriguez. LC 98-90946. 1999. pap. 9.95 (*0-533-12999-0*) Vantage.

My Inspiration: An Assortment of Poems for Various Occasions. Gloria Stella-Felder. 80p. (Orig.). 1997. pap. 6.95 (*1-57502-451-9*, PO1355) Morris Pubng.

*__My Intended.__ Brandi Scollins-Mantha. LC 99-36973. 240p. 2000. 18.00 (*0-688-17404-3*) Morrow Avon.

My Internet Address Book. (Illus.). 186p. 1996. pap. 8.99 (*0-9654580-0-8*) P L Publns.

My Inventions. Nikola Tesla. (Nikola Tesla Ser.). 1991. lib. bdg. 79.95 (*0-8490-4318-2*) Gordon Pr.

My Inventions: The Autobiography of Nikola Tesla. Nikola Tesla. Ed. by Ben Johnston. LC 82-82495. (Illus.). 111p. 1982. reprint ed. 12.95 (*0-910077-01-0*); reprint ed. pap. 7.95 (*0-910077-00-2*) Hart Bro Pub.

*__My Iowa Journey: The Life Story of the University of Iowa's First African American Professor.__ Philip G. Hubbard. LC 99-14788. (Singular Lives Ser.). (Illus.). 228p. (C). 1999. text 22.95 (*0-87745-672-0*) U of Iowa Pr.

My Irish Enchantress, 1. Julia Hanlon. 384p. 1999. mass mkt. 5.99 (*0-8217-6283-4*) Kensgtn Pub Corp.

My Irish Heritage: The Story of My Family . . . an Exquisite Tribute to All Those of Irish Ancestry. Carriage House Staff. 1993. 19.95 (*0-89786-149-3*) CHP Ltd Redding.

*__My Irish Love.__ Maggie James. 1999. mass mkt. 5.99 (*0-8217-6436-5*, Zebra Kensgtn) Kensgtn Pub Corp.

My Ishmael. Daniel Quinn. 288p. 1998. pap. 13.95 (*0-553-37965-8*) Bantam.

My Island. Ricky A. Lauren. (Illus.). 140p. 1994. 100.00 (*0-679-43711-8*) Random.

My Island: A Picture Storybook. Lorraine F. Joseph. (Illus.). 23p. (Orig.). (J). (gr. k-3). 1985. pap. 2.95 (*0-935357-00-9*) CRIC Prod.

My Ivory Cellar. John N. Ott. (Illus.). 12.95 (*0-8159-6217-7*) Devin.

My "j" Sound Box. Jane Belk Moncure. LC 78-23178. (Sound Box Library). (Illus.). 32p. (J). (ps-2). 1979. lib. bdg. 21.36 (*0-89565-049-5*) Childs World.

My Jack. Iza Trapani. LC 98-13229. (J). (ps-2). 1999. pap. 5.95 (*1-58089-013-X*, Whispering Coyote) Charlesbridge Pub.

My Jack. Iza Trapani. LC 98-13229. (J). (ps-3). 1999. 15.95 (*1-58089-012-1*, Whispering Coyote) Charlesbridge Pub.

My January Journal. Alana Trisler & Patrice Cardiel. 48p. (J). (gr. 1-2). 1999. pap., wbk. ed. 1.75 (*1-56762-099-X*) Modern Learn Pr.

My Jerusalem. Bronwyn Drainie. 304p. 1995. pap. 14.95 (*0-385-25520-9*) Doubleday.

My Jesus, I Love Thee. 1992. 1.30 (*0-8341-9033-8*, AN-2635) Lillenas.

My Jesus Pocketbook Lords. Victor Publishing Chariot. 1983. pap. text 7.90 (*1-55513-014-3*) Cook.

My Jesus Pocketbook of a Very Special Birthday. Chariot Family Staff. 32p. (J). 1986. pap. text 7.90 (*1-55513-131-X*) Chariot Victor.

My Jesus Pocketbook of Prayer. Jeannie Harmon. 1992. pap. text 0.79 (*1-55513-733-4*) Chariot Victor.

My Jesus Storybook. Carrie L. Goddard. LC 93-49650. 32p. (Orig.). (J). 1994. pap. 5.95 (*0-687-19924-7*) Abingdon.

My Jewelry Box. LC 98-141039. (Illus.). 32p. (J). (gr. 3-9). 1996. pap. 14.95 (*0-8118-1459-9*) Chronicle Bks.

My Jewels Are Broken Glass: A True Story of Childhood Sexual Abuse & the Recovery Process. Ella M. Heady. 337p. (Orig.). 1997. pap. 11.95 (*1-880451-24-7*) Rainbows End.

My Jewish A. B. C.'s. Draizy Zelcer. LC 93-81028. (Illus.). 32p. (J). (ps-1). 1994. 9.95 (*0-922613-62-1*) Hachai Pubng.

My Jewish Brother Jesus. Rolf Gompertz. 208p. 1977. pap. 12.95 (*0-918248-02-7*) Word Doctor.

My Jewish Brother Jesus. limited ed. Rolf Gompertz. 208p. 1977. 19.95 (*0-918248-03-5*) Word Doctor.

My Jewish Counting Book. Ann D. Koffsky. (HEB & ENG., Illus.). 10p. (J). (ps-k). 1998. spiral bd. 5.99 (*0-914080-12-1*) Shulsinger Sales.

*__My Jewish Days of the Week.__ Dvora Waysman. Ed. by D. L. Rosenfeld. LC 00-103137. (Illus.). 32p. (J). (ps-k). 2000. 9.95 (*1-929628-03-X*) Hachai Pubng.

My Jewish Discovery. Craig Taubman. (J). (ps up). 1995. 10.00 incl. audio (*1-886926-00-X*) Craig n Co.

My Jewish Face & Other Stories. Melanie Kaye-Kantrowitz. LC 90-9427. 256p. (Orig.). 1990. pap. 9.95 (*0-933216-71-8*); lib. bdg. 19.95 (*0-933216-72-6*) Aunt Lute Bks.

My Jewish Heroes Crossword Puzzle Book. David Sokoloff. (Illus.). 24p. (Orig.). (J). (ps-5). 1998. pap. 1.00 (*1-889655-05-8*) Jewish Educ Toys.

My Jewish Holiday Activity Book. David Sokoloff. (Illus.). 24p. (Orig.). (J). (ps-5). 1998. pap. 1.00 (*1-889655-09-0*) Jewish Educ Toys.

*__My Jewish Holiday Fun Book.__ (Illus.). (J). 2000. 6.95 (*0-8074-0727-5*) UAHC.

My Jewish Holidays. Azriel Eisenberg & Jessie B. Robinson. 208p. (J). (gr. 5-6). 3.95 (*0-8381-0176-3*, 10-176) USCJE.

My Jewish Home. Martin Lemelman. (Illus.). 10p. (J). (ps). 1988. bds. 3.95 (*0-8074-0415-2*, 102002) UAHC.

My Jewish Home: Bath Book. Illus. by Martin Lemelman. 10p. (J). (ps). 1987. vinyl bd. 3.95 (*0-8074-0327-X*, 102001) UAHC.

My Jewish People. Ruth Lascelle. LC 97-77833. (Illus.). 256p. 1998. pap. 13.00 (*0-9654519-1-7*) Bedrock Pub.

My Jewish World. Robert Thum & Susan Dworski. (Illus.). (Orig.). (J). (gr. 3-4). 1989. pap. text 8.95 (*0-87441-478-4*) Behrman.

My Jewish World. Robert Thum et al. (Illus.). (Orig.). 1989. pap., teacher ed. 14.95 (*0-87441-489-X*) Behrman.

My Jewish Year: Celebrating Our Holidays. Adam Fisher. (Illus.). 160p. (J). (gr. 2-3). 1995. pap. 8.95 (*0-87441-540-3*) Behrman.

My Jewish Year: Celebrating Our Holidays. Jessica Weber. (J). 1995. pap., teacher ed. 14.95 (*0-87441-541-1*) Behrman.

My Jingle Bell Baby. Leandra Logan. (Temptation Ser.: No. 663). 1997. per. 3.50 (*0-373-25763-5*, 1-25763-3) Harlequin Bks.

*__My Job, My Self: Work & Creation of Modern Individual.__ Al Gini. LC 99-48225. 272p. 2000. 23.95 (*0-415-92635-1*) Routledge.

My Job-Search Record: Records Project. Alan M. Levin & Wayne E. Page. LC 93-71441. 142p. 1993. student ed., ring bd. write for info. (*1-883552-03-6*) Career Adv MD.

My Jobs in Italy. Rosa B. Champine. Ed. by Barry Lane. (Opening Doors Ser.: No. 1). (Illus.). 32p. (Orig.). 1989. pap. 4.00 (*1-877829-02-1*) Homegrown Bks.

My Journal. 2nd ed. Narcissa P. Whitman. 74p. 1985. 9.95 (*0-87770-482-1*); pap. 5.95 (*0-87770-348-5*) Ye Galleon.

*__My Journal: A Place to Begin.__ Marijo Grogan. Ed. by Doreen Skardarasy. (Illus.). 72p. (YA). (gr. 5-8). 1999. 9.95 (*0-9678801-2-2*) Acorn MI.

My Journal: A Place to Write about God & Me. Janet R. Knight & Lynn W. Gilliam. Ed. by JoAnn E. Miller. (Illus.). 112p. (J). (gr. 2-6). 1997. pap. 15.00 (*0-8358-0791-6*, UR791) Upper Room Bks.

An Asterisk (*) at the beginning of an entry indicates that the title is appearing for the first time.

***My Journal: Primary.** Linda Milliken. Ed. by Kathy Rogers. (Illus.). 32p. 1998. 1.99 (*1-56472-143-4*) Edupress Inc.

***My Journal: Upper Grade.** Linda Milliken. Ed. by Kathy Rogers. (Illus.). 32p. 1998. 1.99 (*1-56472-144-2*) Edupress Inc.

***My Journal (14 Page Version)** Brian Leslie Lewis. 16p. (J). (gr. k). 1999. pap. 6.95 (*1-928693-01-6*) Novice Nomad.

***My Journal of Love.** Algerrie Jones. (Illus.). 65p. 1999. spiral bd. 15.00 (*0-9669179-1-X*) Fifth Wrld.

My Journal of Personal Growth. Kino Learning Center Staff et al. (Changing Years Ser.). (Illus.). 64p. (J). (gr. 5-9). 1987. pap. 8.99 (*0-86653-418-0*, GA 1028) Good Apple.

My Journey. Nicolas Radoui. 544p. 1991. 22.95 (*0-8187-0134-X*) Harlo Press.

My Journey: Poems & Reflections. Illus. by Irene Werley. 96p. 1998. reprint ed. pap. 18.69 (*0-9666434-0-2*) Shin Pubg.

My Journey: Selected Poems of Ali Sardar Jafri : Urdu Poems with English Translation. Ali Sardar Jafri et al. LC 98-917643. viii, 409 p. 1999. write for info. (*81-207-2156-X*) Sterling Pubs.

***My Journey in Karate: The Sabaki Way.** Joko Ninomiya & Ed Zorensky. LC 99-87452. (Illus.). 240p. 2000. pap. 16.95 (*1-58394-017-0*, Pub. by Frog Ltd CA) Publishers Group.

My Journey in the House of Prayer. Ann E. Chester. (Illus.). (Orig.). 1991. pap. 8.95 (*0-9628739-0-X*) Sstrs Srvnts.

My Journey into Alzheimer's Disease. Robert Davis. 140p. 1989. pap. 7.99 (*0-8423-4645-7*) Tyndale Hse.

My Journey into Self Phase One. Diane K. Pike. LC 79-12179. 161p. 1979. pap. 9.95 (*0-916192-13-X*) L P Pubns.

My Journey, My Prayer. Center for Learning Network Staff. 96p. (YA). (gr. 9-12). 1991. reprint ed. pap. text 5.95 (*1-56077-128-3*) Ctr Learning.

My Journey Through Arhab & Hashid. Eduard Glaser. Tr. by David Warburton. (Yemen Translation Ser.). xi, 31p. 1993. 5.00 (*1-882557-02-6*) Am Inst Yemeni.

My Journey Through Art: Create Your Own Masterpieces. Barron's Educational Editors. (Illus.). 48p. (J). (gr. 2 up). 1994. pap. 6.95 (*0-8120-1924-5*) Barron.

***My Journey Through Life.** James R. Brown. LC 99-93732. 1999. 22.95 (*0-533-13134-0*) Vantage.

My Journey Through Life: From the Steppes of Russia to America, an Octogenarian Writes about Her Family, 1880-1997. Esther R. Goldman. 194p. 1998. pap. 12.95 (*1-890622-12-5*) Leathers Pub.

My Journey Through Life, In Verse. Sarah L. Shaw. 1998. pap. write for info. (*1-57553-961-6*) Watermrk Pr.

My Journey to Betterment. George M. Shuffer, Jr. LC 97-91373. 1998. 18.95 (*0-533-12654-1*) Vantage.

My Journey to Lhasa. Alexandra David-Neel. LC 93-16631. (Illus.). 346p. 1993. pap. 17.00 (*0-8070-5903-X*) Beacon Pr.

My Journey with a Mystic. Fritz Peters. Ed. by Richard Weaver & Ron Baron. 312p. 1989. reprint ed. 22.50 (*0-942139-00-3*); reprint ed. pap. 11.95 (*0-942139-10-0*) Tale Weaver.

My Journey with Aristotle to the Anarchist Utopia. Graham Purchase. 128p. (Orig.). 1994. pap. 7.00 (*0-9622937-6-8*) III Pub.

My Journey with the Grandmaster: Reflections of an American Martial Artist on Okinawa. William R. Hayes. LC 95-92115. (Illus.). 224p. (Orig.). 1997. pap. write for info. (*1-57502-554-X*, P01613) Morris Pubng.

My Joy Cometh in the Morning: Though the Road Be Rough, Dark & Dreary. Ricardo Scott & Giancarlo T. Scott. (Ras Crado Spiritual Revelations & Prophesy Ser.). (Illus.). 75p. (Orig.). 1995. pap. 9.95 (*1-883427-78-9*) Crnerstone GA.

***My Juliet.** John Ed Bradley. LC 99-89051. 288p. 2000. 23.95 (*0-385-49803-9*) Doubleday.

***My July Journal.** Alana Trisler & Patrice Cardiel. 48p. (J). (gr. 1-2). 1999. wbk. ed. 1.75 (*1-56762-113-9*) Modern Learn Pr.

***My June Journal.** Alana Trisler & Patrice Cardiel. 48p. (J). (gr. 1-2). 1999. wbk. ed. 1.75 (*1-56762-112-0*) Modern Learn Pr.

My Just War: The Memoir of a Jewish Red Army Soldier in World War II. Gabriel Temkin. LC 97-36778. (Illus.). 272p. 1998. 24.95 (*0-89141-645-5*) Presidio Pr.

My "k" Sound Box. Jane Belk Moncure. LC 78-22034. (Sound Box Library). (Illus.). 32p. (J). (ps-2). 1979. lib. bdg. 21.36 (*0-89565-050-9*) Childs World.

My Kaleidoscope of Poetry & Stories. Ida Olivia Hurst. LC 91-92380. (Illus.). 96p. (Orig.). (J). 1992. pap. 11.95 (*0-9632521-0-0*) Gemstone OR.

My Kantian Ways. Ermanno Bencivenga. LC 94-34350. 148p. 1995. 30.00 (*0-520-08984-7*, Pub. by U CA Pr) Cal Prin Full Svc.

My Karma Just Ran over Your Dogma: 1050-2050 A. D. Uncle Yrret. 72p. (Orig.). 1997. pap. 4.95 (*1-882196-03-1*) Baja Bks.

My Kate. large type ed. Ann Hardy. (Linford Romance Large Print Ser.). 208p. 1996. pap. 16.99 (*0-7089-7970-X*) Ulverscroft.

My Keepsake Recipes: A Personal Journal of Meals, Memories, & Traditions. Sandy L. Clough. 92p. (Orig.). 1996. 12.99 (*1-56507-494-7*) Harvest Hse.

***My Kentucky Garden: A Gardener's Journal.** Cool Springs Press Publications Staff. 2000. 19.95 (*1-888608-93-5*) Cool Springs Pr.

***My Kentucky Garden: A Gardener's Journal.** Denny McKeown. (Illus.). 128p. 2000. spiral bd. 19.95 (*1-930604-09-2*) Cool Springs Pr.

My Khyber Marriage. Morag Murray Abdullah. 272p. 1990. 24.00 (*0-86304-055-1*, Pub. by Octagon Pr) ISHK.

My Kid Can't Spell! Understanding & Assisting Your Child's Literacy Development. J. Richard Gentry. LC 96-25778. 128p. 1996. pap. 13.95 (*0-435-08135-7*) Heinemann.

My Kid Won't Eat Cookbook. Sharon Otis. (Orig.). 1986. pap. 5.00 (*0-9617737-1-5*) Total Lrn.

My Kid's Allergic to Everything Dessert Cookbook: Sweets & Treats the Whole Family Will Enjoy. Mary Harris & Wilma Nachsin. LC 96-42047. 112p. (Orig.). 1996. pap. 13.95 (*1-55652-303-3*) Chicago Review.

My Kids Grow & So Do I: A Parent's Toolbox for Practical Spirituality. Johanna Van Zwet. LC 96-85592. (Illus.). xiii, 220p. pap. 16.95 (*0-9653566-0-4*) Ascad Communs.

***My Kids, My Teachers Vol. I: What the Students Taught the Teacher.** (C). 2000. spiral bd. write for info. (*0-9678791-0-8*) Tahoe Advent Learn.

My Kind of Angel: I. M. William Burroughs. Ed. by Rupert Loydell. LC 99-218805. 1998. 19.95 (*1-900152-42-8*, Pub. by Stride Pubns) SPD-Small Pr Dist.

My Kind of Country: Favorite Writings about New York. Carl Carmer. LC 94-42338. 292p. 1995. pap. 15.95 (*0-8156-0310-X*) Syracuse U Pr.

My Kind of Family: A Book for Kids in Single-Parent Homes. Michele Lash et al. LC 90-31471. (Illus.). 208p. (J). (ps-6). 1990. pap., spiral bd. 16.95 (*0-914525-12-3*); spiral bd. 16.95 (*0-914525-13-1*) Waterfront Bks.

My Kind of Garden. Richard W. Brown. LC 97-22927. (Illus.). 160p. 1997. 40.00 (*0-395-79123-5*) HM.

My Kind of Garden. David Hicks. 1998. 49.50 (*1-870673-30-1*) Garden Art Pr.

My Kind of Garden. Storey Publishing Staff. 1997. 40.00 (*0-676-57063-1*) Random.

My Kind of Kathmandu. B. Bhagat. 1994. pap. 310.50 (*0-7855-0461-3*, Pub. by Ratna Pustak Bhandar) St Mut.

My Kind of People: Achievement, Identity & Aboriginality. Wayne Coolwell. 1993. pap. 14.95 (*0-7022-2543-6*, Pub. by Univ Queensland Pr) Intl Spec Bk.

My Kinder Journal. Beth Garbo. (Illus.). 86p. 1998. spiral bd. 12.95 (*1-892373-13-0*, 99-20) Especially Bks.

My Kindergarten Yearbook. Bearl Brooks. (My Yearbook Ser.). 544p. (gr. k). 1980. 18.00 (*0-8209-0080-X*, MKY_K) ESP.

My King. F. R. Havergal. pap. 3.99 (*0-87377-042-0*) GAM Pubns.

My Kingdom for a Horse. Betty Schwartz. 1950. pap. text 17.95 (*0-8050-6212-2*) St Martin.

***My Kingdom Is a Horse: The Really, Really, Really Difficult Way to Find a Husband.** Emma C. Spurling. Ed. by Adolph Caso. LC 99-33949. (Illus.). 256p. 1999. pap. 16.95 (*0-8283-2050-0*) Branden Bks.

***My Kingdom of Books.** Richard Booth. 318p. 1999. 24.95 (*0-86243-495-5*, Pub. by Y Lolfa) Intl Spec Bk.

My Kitchen in Spain. JANET MENDELL. 25.00 (*0-06-019526-6*) HarpC.

My Kitchen to Your Kitchen. Hiam I. Nidzi. (Illus.). 80p. 1998. pap. 16.95 (*0-9664045-0-5*) H I Nidzi.

***My Kitchen Wars.** Betty H. Fussell. LC 00-33754. 2000. write for info. (*0-7862-2697-8*) Thorndike Pr.

***My Kitchen Wars: A Memoir.** Betty Fussell. LC 99-25954. 240p. 1999. 23.00 (*0-86547-577-6*) N Point Pr.

***My Kitchen Wars: A Memoir.** Betty Fussell. 256p. 2000. pap. 13.00 (*0-86547-603-9*) N Point Pr.

My Kite. large type ed. Deborah Williams. (Illus.). 8p. (Orig.). (J). (gr. k-1). 1997. pap. 4.25 (*1-879835-96-7*) Kaeden Corp.

My Kite Is the Magic Me. Helen Webber. (Illus.). (J). (gr. k-6). 1968. 8.95 (*0-8392-3055-9*) Astor-Honor.

My Knight in Shining Armor. Linda Knight. 300p. (Orig.). 1993. pap. 11.95 (*0-9630796-1-1*) Rock Church NW.

My Kwanzaa Book. 48p. (J). (gr. 1-7). 1991. 5.95 (*1-877610-06-2*) Sea Island.

My Kwanzaa Story. Bobbie Ballard. (Illus.). 48p. (J). (gr. k-6). 1993. 6.95 (*0-9639349-0-2*) Ujamaa Ent.

My "l" Sound Box. Jane Belk Moncure. LC 78-8373. (Sound Box Library). (Illus.). 32p. (J). (ps-2). 1978. lib. bdg. 21.36 (*0-89565-045-2*) Childs World.

My Lace. Ondori Publishing Company Staff. (Illus.). 94p. 1987. pap. 11.95 (*0-87040-736-8*) Japan Pubns USA.

My Lady Belinda. Linda Ladd. 1997. mass mkt. 5.99 (*0-451-40557-9*, Onyx) NAL.

My Lady Captor. Anna Jennet. 1996. mass mkt. 5.99 (*0-515-11858-3*, Jove) Berkley Pub.

My Lady Caroline. Jill Jones. 1996. mass mkt. 5.99 (*0-312-95836-6*, Pub. by Tor Bks) St Martin.

***My Lady Deceiver.** large type ed. June Francis. 336p. 1999. pap. 20.99 (*1-85389-876-7*, Dales) Ulverscroft.

My Lady Ghost. June Calvin. 224p. 1998. mass mkt. 4.99 (*0-451-19541-8*, Sig) NAL.

***My Lady Governess.** Wilma Counts. (Regency Romance Ser.). 2000. mass mkt. 4.99 (*0-8217-6483-7*, Zebra Kensgtn) Kensgtn Pub Corp.

My Lady in Time. Angie Ray. 1998. mass mkt. 5.99 (*0-515-12227-0*, Jove) Berkley Pub.

My Lady King Hatshepsut. Catherine M. Andronik. LC 98-52675. (J). 2000. 17.00 (*0-689-82562-5*) Atheneum Yung Read.

My Lady Ludlow. Elizabeth Gaskell. (Academy Victorian Classics Ser.). 240p. 1995. pap. 11.00 (*0-89733-409-4*) Academy Chi Pubs.

My Lady Madness. Michele Hauf. (Zebra Splendor Historical Romances Ser.). 352p. 1998. mass mkt. 4.99 (*0-8217-5981-7*, Zebra Kensgtn) Kensgtn Pub Corp.

My Lady Midnight. Laurie Grant. 1996. per. 4.99 (*0-373-28940-5*, 1-28940-4) Harlequin Bks.

My Lady Mischief. Valerie King. 224p. 1999. mass mkt. 4.99 (*0-8217-6207-9*) Kensgtn Pub Corp.

My Lady Nicotine, Etc. see Works of J. M. Barrie: Peter Pan Edition

***My Lady Nightingale.** Evelyn Richardson. 224p. 1999. mass mkt. 4.99 (*0-451-19858-1*, Sig) NAL.

My Lady Notorious. Jo Beverley. 384p. 1993. mass mkt. 4.50 (*0-380-76785-6*, Avon Bks) Morrow Avon.

My Lady of Hy-Brasil. Peter Tremayne. (Illus.). 1987. 30.00 (*0-937986-83-6*) D M Grant.

My Lady of the Chimney Corner. deluxe ed. Alexander Irvine. 160p. 1994. pap. 9.95 (*0-86281-464-2*, Pub. by Appletree Pr) Irish Bks Media.

My Lady of the North. Randall Parrish. 1976. lib. bdg. 16.30 (*0-89968-086-0*, Lghtyr Pr) Buccaneer Bks.

My Lady of the South. Randall Parrish. 1976. lib. bdg. 16.30 (*0-89968-087-9*, Lghtyr Pr) Buccaneer Bks.

My Lady Pirate. Danelle Harmon. 400p. (Orig.). 1994. mass mkt. 4.50 (*0-380-77228-0*, Avon Bks) Morrow Avon.

***My Lady Pocahontas.** John Esten Cooke. 252p. 2000. pap. 9.95 (*0-594-00027-0*) Eightn Hundrd.

My Lady Pocahontas. John E. Cooke. LC 68-20009. (Americans in Fiction Ser.). reprint ed. pap. text 5.95 (*0-89197-862-3*) Irvington.

My Lady Pokahontas. John E. Cooke. LC 68-20009. (Americans in Fiction Ser.). reprint ed. lib. bdg. 22.00 (*0-8398-0272-2*) Irvington.

***My Lady Reluctant.** Laurie Grant. (Historical Ser.: No. 497). 2000. per. 4.99 (*0-373-29097-7*, 1-29097-2, Harlequin) Harlequin Bks.

***My Lady Vixen.** Connie Mason. 448p. (Orig.). 1999. pap. 5.99 (*0-8439-4607-5*, Leisure Bks) Dorchester Pub Co.

My Ladye Nevells Booke. William Byrd. Ed. by Hilda Andrews & Richard Terry. (Illus.). 292p. 1948. reprint ed. lib. bdg. 30.00 (*0-8450-0101-9*) Broude.

My Ladye Nevells Booke of Virginal Music. William Byrd. Ed. by Hilda Andrews. LC 68-55532. 245p. 1969. reprint ed. pap. 13.95 (*0-486-22246-2*) Dover.

My Lady's Champion. Claire Delacroix. (Harlequin Historical Ser.: No. 326). 1996. per. 4.99 (*0-373-28926-X*, 1-28926-3) Harlequin Bks.

***My Lady's Choice.** Lyn Stone. (Historical Ser.: Vol. 511). 296p. 2000. mass mkt. 4.99 (*0-373-29111-6*) Harlequin Bks.

***My Lady's Dare.** Gayle Wilson. (Historical Ser.: Bk. 516). 2000. per. 4.99 (*0-373-29116-7*, 1-29116-0) Harlequin Bks.

My Lady's Desire. Claire Delacroix. (Historical Ser.). 1998. per. 4.99 (*0-373-29009-8*, 1-29009-7) Harlequin Bks.

***My Lady's Guardian.** Gayle Callen. 384p. 2000. mass mkt. 5.99 (*0-380-81376-9*, Avon Bks) Morrow Avon.

My Lady's Money. E. F. Bielier. 17.95 (*0-8488-0062-1*) Amereon Ltd.

My Lady's Servant. Cindy Holbrook. 256p. 1998. pap. 4.99 (*0-8217-5911-6*) Kensgtn Pub Corp.

My Lai Massacre. Olson. LC 97-74967. 222p. 1998. pap. text 11.95 (*0-312-14227-7*) St Martin.

My Lamp Still Burns. Robert Morgan. 141p. (C). 1981. text 39.00 (*0-85088-504-3*, Pub. by Gomer Pr) St Mut.

My Land & My People. Dalai Lama XIV. LC BL1489.N44A3. (Illus.). 271p. 1983. reprint ed. 6.95 (*0-9611474-0-7*) Potala.

My Land & My People: The Original Autobiography of His Holiness the Dalai Lama of Tibet. Dalai Lama XIV. LC 97-23849. xiv, 238p. 1997. mass mkt. 12.99 (*0-446-67421-4*, Pub. by Warner Bks) Little.

My Land of Israel. Elizabeth Z. Nover. (Illus.). 32p. (Orig.). (J). (gr. k-2). 1987. pap. 4.95 (*0-87441-447-4*) Behrman.

My Land of Tears & Laughter: The Story of "Zonik" (Col. Ze'ev Shaham), a Man of Many Friends. Amos Ettinger. Tr. by Peretz Kidron from HEB. LC 92-54397. 1994. 24.50 (*0-8453-4848-5*, Cornwall Bks) Assoc Univ Prs.

***My Land Sings.** Rudolfo A. Anaya. (J). 2000. pap. write for info. (*0-380-72902-4*) Morrow Avon.

My Land Sings: Stories from the Rio Grande. Rudolfo A. Anaya. LC 99-19040. (Illus.). 144p. (J). (gr. 5-9). 1999. 17.00 (*0-688-15078-0*, Wm Morrow) Morrow Avon.

***My Laocohon, or Yours, or Theirs.** Richard Brilliant. LC 99-41240. (Discovery Ser.). 160p. 2000. 45.00 (*0-520-21682-2*, Pub. by U CA Pr) Cal Prin Full Svc.

My Last Chance to Be a Boy: Theodore Roosevelt's South American Expedition of 1913-1914. Joseph Ornig. (Illus.). 320p. 1994. 29.95 (*0-8117-1098-X*) Stackpole.

My Last Chance to Be a Boy: Theodore Roosevelt's South American Expedition of 1913-1914. Joseph R. Ornig. LC 97-51138. (Illus.). 320p. 1998. pap. 16.95 (*0-8071-2271-8*) La State U Pr.

My Last Days As Roy Rogers. Pat Cunningham Devoto. LC 98-22788. 358p. 1999. 20.00 (*0-446-52388-7*, Pub. by Warner Bks) Little.

***My Last Days As Roy Rogers.** Pat Cunningham Devoto. 368p. 2000. mass mkt. 12.95 (*0-446-67564-4*, Pub. by Warner Bks) Little.

My Last Duchess, & Other Poems. Robert Browning. LC 93-22085. (Thrift Editions Ser.). 128p. (Orig.). 1993. reprint ed. pap. 1.00 (*0-486-27783-6*) Dover.

My Last Forty Days: A Visionary Journey among the Pueblo Spirits. Felicitas D. Goodman. LC 97-5108. 1997. pap. 9.95 (*0-253-21135-2*) Ind U Pr.

My Last Forty Days: A Visionary Journey among the Pueblo Spirits. Felicitas D. Goodman. LC 97-5108. (Illus.). 112p. 1997. 25.00 (*0-253-33310-5*) Ind U Pr.

My Last Kambaku. limited ed. Leo Kroger. 1997. 60.00 (*1-57157-044-6*) Safari Pr.

***My Last Martini.** Barry Gifford. LC 00-27682. 64p. 2000. pap. 8.95 (*1-57587-136-X*) Crane Hill AL.

My Last Million Readers. Emile Gauvreau. LC 74-15741. (Popular Culture in America Ser.). 492p. 1975. reprint ed. 40.95 (*0-405-06376-8*) Ayer.

My Lawman. Deana James. (Zebra Bks.). 352p. 1998. mass mkt. 5.99 (*0-8217-6040-8*, Zebra Kensgtn) Kensgtn Pub Corp.

My Lead Dog Was a Lesbian: An Iditarod Rookie's Tale. Brian P. O'Donoghue. (Departures Ser.). Date not set. write for info. (*0-614-10310-X*) Vin Bks.

My Lead Dog Was a Lesbian: Mushing Across Alaska in the Iditarod - The World's Most Grueling Race. Brian P. O'Donoghue. 320p. 1996. pap. 13.00 (*0-679-76411-9*) Vin Bks.

My Leafs Sweater. Mike Lionetti. (Illus.). 32p. (J). (ps-3). 1998. 15.95 (*1-55192-194-4*) Raincoast Bk.

My Lee Comes to America. Elmira K. Beyer. LC 97-216187. (Illus.). 74p. (Orig.). (J). (gr. 4-5). 1997. pap. 9.99 (*0-88092-044-0*) Royal Fireworks.

My Left Foot. Christy Brown. 192p. (C). 1995. reprint ed. pap. 9.95 (*0-7493-9177-4*, A0571) Heinemann.

***My Legacy Book: Student Workbook.** F. M. Avey. (Illus.). 50p. (YA). (gr. 5-10). 2000. pap., student ed., wbk. ed. 12.95 (*1-930758-60-X*, Legacy Kids) Yeva Corp.

My Lemonade Days. Richard Trone. 152p. Date not set. pap. 12.00 (*1-887150-09-9*) Millennia Bks.

My Lenten Fun Book: Daily Activities for Children. Francine M. O'Connor. 48p. 1998. pap. text 2.95 (*0-7648-0218-6*) Liguori Pubns.

My Lenten Journal. William F. Maestri. 132p. 1990. pap. 6.95 (*0-8189-0576-X*) Alba.

My Lenten Walk with Jesus. Francine M. O'Connor. (Cycle C Ser.). (Illus.). 32p. (J). (gr. 1-3). 1993. pap., pap. text 2.50 incl. audio (*0-89243-421-X*); pap., pap. text, teacher ed. 9.95 incl. audio (*0-89243-420-1*) Liguori Pubns.

My Lenten Walk with Jesus, Cycle A. Francine M. O'Connor. (Cycle A Ser.). (Illus.). 32p. (J). (gr. 1-3). 1993. pap. text 2.50 (*0-89243-453-8*) Liguori Pubns.

My Lenten Walk with Jesus: Cycle B. Francine M. O'Connor. (J). (gr. 1-3). 1991. pap., pap. text, teacher ed. 9.95 incl. audio (*0-89243-666-2*) Liguori Pubns.

My Lenten Walk with Jesus: Cycle B, Cycle B. Francine M. O'Connor. 32p. (J). (gr. 1-3). 1991. pap., pap. text 2.50 incl. audio (*0-89243-665-4*) Liguori Pubns.

My Lesbian Husband. Barrie Jean Borich. 294p. 1999. 24.95 (*1-55597-292-6*, Pub. by Graywolf) SPD-Small Pr Dist.

***My Lesbian Husband.** Barrie Jean Borich. 294p. 2000. reprint ed. pap. 14.00 (*1-55597-310-8*) Graywolf.

***My Lessons with Kumi: How I Learned to Perform with Confidence in Life & Work.** Michael Colgrass. LC 99-88119. (Illus.). 440p. 2000. pap. 18.50 (*0-911226-40-0*) Real People.

My Letter Book. Thomas Wasylyk. (Illus.). 64p. (J). (gr. k-1). 1997. wbk. ed. 2.75 (*1-56762-071-X*) Modern Learn Pr.

***My Letters to God.** Theresa Just. LC 98-90812. 1999. pap. 7.95 (*0-533-12926-5*) Vantage.

My Letters to the Editor, 1977-1986. Everett Dehmer. write for info. (*0-9619584-1-3*) Caril.

My Life. Marc Chagall. (Illus.). 192p. 1996. pap. 29.95 (*0-7206-0969-0*, Pub. by P Owen Ltd) Dufour.

My Life. Isadora Duncan. 384p. 1996. pap. 14.00 (*0-87140-158-4*, Norton Paperbks) Norton.

My Life. Rebecca Emberley. (J). 2000. write for info. (*0-316-23324-2*) Little.

My Life. Lyn Hejinian. (Sun & Moon Classics Ser.: No. 11). 120p. 1998. pap. 9.95 (*1-55713-024-8*) Sun & Moon CA.

My Life. Corinne Jacker. 1977. pap. 5.25 (*0-8222-0800-8*) Dramatists Play.

My Life. Earvin "Magic" Johnson & William Novak. (Black History Titles Ser.). 384p. 1993. mass mkt. 5.99 (*0-449-22254-3*) Fawcett.

My Life. Edith Piaf. Tr. by Margaret Crosland from FRE. (Illus.). 144p. 1990. 30.00 (*0-7206-0797-3*, Pub. by P Owen Ltd) Dufour.

***My Life.** Erich Raeder. 2000. pap. text 18.00 (*0-306-80962-1*) Da Capo.

My Life. Burt Reynolds. (Illus.). 352p. (J). 1994. 22.45 (*0-7868-6130-4*, Pub. by Hyperion) Time Warner.

My Life, 2 vols. Richard Wagner. LC 78-181292. 911p. 1936. 89.00 (*0-403-01715-7*); pap. 59.00 (*0-685-47617-0*) Scholarly.

My Life. deluxe ed. Lyn Hejinian. (Sun & Moon Classics Ser.: No. 11). 120p. 1987. 30.00 (*1-55713-007-8*) Sun & Moon CA.

My Life. Emma Calve. Ed. by Andrew Farkas. Tr. by Rosamond Gilder. LC 76-29929. (Opera Biographies Ser.). (Illus.). 1977. reprint ed. lib. bdg. 33.95 (*0-405-09672-0*) Ayer.

My Life. Marc Chagall. (Illus.). 227p. 1994. reprint ed. pap. 14.95 (*0-306-80571-5*) Da Capo.

My Life. Marc Chagall. (Illus.). 173p. 1985. reprint ed. boxed set 30.00 (*0-685-18787-X*, Pub. by P Owen Ltd) Dufour.

My Life. Isadora Duncan. (American Biography Ser.). 376p. 1991. reprint ed. lib. bdg. 79.00 (*0-7812-8115-6*) Rprt Serv.

My Life. Erich Raeder. Tr. by Henry W. Drexel. LC 79-6121. (Navies & Men Ser.). (Illus.). 1980. reprint ed. lib. bdg. 44.95 (*0-405-13075-9*) Ayer.

My Life. Richard Wagner. 1988. reprint ed. lib. bdg. 120.00 (*0-7812-0537-9*) Rprt Serv.

My Life, 2 vols. Alfred R. Wallace. LC 72-1668. (Illus.). reprint ed. 84.50 (*0-404-08184-3*) AMS Pr.

My Life: An Attempt at an Autobiography. Leon Trotsky. LC 73-108715. 604p. 1970. reprint ed. lib. bdg. 75.00 (*0-87348-143-7*) Pathfinder NY.

My Life: An Attempt at an Autobiography. Leon Trotsky. LC 73-108715. 604p. 1970. reprint ed. pap. 26.95 (*0-87348-144-5*) Pathfinder NY.

My Life: Autobiography of Havelock Ellis. Havelock Ellis. LC 83-45749. reprint ed. 42.50 (*0-404-20087-7*) AMS Pr.

My Life - In Spite of Myself! Roy Clark & Marc Eliot. 1994. 22.00 (*0-671-86434-3*) S&S Trade.

M

An Asterisk (*) at the beginning of an entry indicates that the title is appearing for the first time.

My Life - Truths, Tales, Memories & Dreams: A Way to Write Your Life Story. 2nd ed. Maureen Lomasney. 224p. 1994. reprint ed. pap. 24.95 (*1-889451-00-2*) Tannery Creek.

My Life, A Journal. Hartley & Marks Publishers Staff. 192p. 1998. 14.95 (*0-88179-170-9*) Hartley & Marks.

My Life According to Me: A Journal for Girls. Klutz Editors. (Illus.). 66p. (YA). (gr. 5 up). 1999. spiral bd. 14.95 (*1-57054-354-2*) Klutz.

My Life among the Aliens. Gail Gauthier. LC 95-5233. (Illus.). 112p. (J). (gr. 3-7). 1996. 14.95 (*0-399-22945-0*, G P Putnam) Peng Put Young Read.

My Life among the Aliens. Gail Gauthier. (Illus.). 112p. (J). (gr. 3-7). 1998. pap. 3.99 (*0-698-11636-4*, PapStar) Peng Put Young Read.

My Life among the Aliens. Gail Gauthier. (J). 1998. 9.09 (*0-606-12997-9*, Pub. by Turtleback) Demco.

***My Life An Open Book.** Bill Zimmerman. 208p. 2000. pap. 16.95 (*1-57071-441-X*) Sourcebks.

My Life & An Era: The Autobiography of Buck Colbert Franklin. Buck Franklin. Ed. by John H. Franklin & John W. Franklin. LC 97-24771. (Illus.). 336p. 1998. 29.95 (*0-8071-2213-0*) La State U Pr.

***My Life & an Era: The Autobiography of Buck Colbert Franklin.** Ed. by John Hope Franklin & John Whittington Franklin. (Illus.). 320p. 2000. pap. 16.95 (*0-8071-2599-7*) La State U Pr.

My Life & Books. S. M. Houghton. 173p. 1988. 14.99 (*0-85151-537-1*) Banner of Truth.

My Life & Experiences among Our Hostile Indians. Oliver O. Howard. LC 76-87436. (American Scene Ser.). 1972. reprint ed. lib. bdg. 55.00 (*0-306-71506-6*) Da Capo.

My Life & Experiences among Our Hostile Indians. Oliver O. Howard. (American Biography Ser.). 570p. 1991. reprint ed. lib. bdg. 99.00 (*0-7812-8197-0*) Rprt Serv.

My Life & Hard Times. James Thurber. 17.95 (*0-8488-0338-8*) Amereon Ltd.

My Life & Hard Times. James Thurber. LC 99-15618. (Illus.). 128p. 1999. pap. 11.00 (*0-06-093308-9*) HarpC.

My Life & Hard Times. James Thurber. LC 89-45725. (Illus.). 112p. 1995. reprint ed. pap. 11.00 (*0-06-091642-7*, Perennial) HarperTrade.

My Life & Hard Times. James Thurber. (American Biography Ser.). 114p. 1991. reprint ed. lib. bdg. 59.00 (*0-7812-8390-6*) Rprt Serv.

My Life & Hard Times. James Thurber. 1993. reprint ed. lib. bdg. 89.00 (*0-7812-5407-8*) Rprt Serv.

My Life & Lives: The Story of a Tibetan Incarnation. 2nd rev. ed. Khyongla Rato. 280p. Date not set. reprint ed. pap. 14.95 (*0-9630293-0-4*) Rato Pubns.

My Life & Loves. Frank Harris. Ed. & Intro. by John F. Gallagher. LC 91-20044. (Illus.). 1024p. 1971. pap. 16.95 (*0-8021-5161-2*, Grove) Grove-Atltic.

***My Life & Loves.** Frank Harris. LC 99-39269. (Literary Classics). 360p. 1999. pap. 9.95 (*1-57392-774-0*) Prometheus Bks.

My Life & Music. Artur Schnabel. (Illus.). 288p. 1988. reprint ed. pap. 9.95 (*0-486-25571-9*) Dover.

My Life & My Art see Ma Vie et Mon Art Souvenirs

My Life & My Country. Alexander Lebed. LC 97-33323. 399p. 1997. 29.95 (*0-89526-422-6*) Regnery Pub.

My Life & My Films. Jean Renoir. Tr. by Norman Denny from FRE. (Quality Paperbacks Ser.). (Illus.). 287p. 1991. reprint ed. pap. 14.95 (*0-306-80457-3*, Pub. by Da Capo) HarpC.

My Life & Other Stories. Anton Chekhov. Tr. by Samuel S. Koteliansky & Gilbert Cannan. LC 77-169544. (Short Story Index Reprint Ser.). 1977. reprint ed. 18.95 (*0-8369-4005-9*) Ayer.

My Life & Some Letters. Patrick Campbell. LC 71-173104. (Illus.). 1972. reprint ed. 30.95 (*0-405-08340-8*, Pub. by Blom Pubns) Ayer.

***My Life & the Paradise Garage: Keep on Dancin'** Mel Cheren. (Illus.). 495p. 2000. 24.95 (*0-9678994-0-0*) TWENTY-FOUR HRS.

My Life & the Story of the Gospel Hymns & of Sacred Songs & Solos. Ira D. Sankey. LC 72-1682. reprint ed. 37.50 (*0-404-08332-3*) AMS Pr.

My Life & the Story of the Gospel Hymns & of Sacred Songs & Solos. Ira D. Sankey. (American Biography Ser.). 410p. 1991. reprint ed. lib. bdg. 89.00 (*0-7812-8339-6*) Rprt Serv.

***My Life & Time in Rhyme.** Georgette Innes-Brown. 1999. pap. write for info. (*1-58235-290-9*) Watermrk Pr.

My Life & Times. Elwood W. Pierce. LC 90-91579. 389p. 1990. 19.50 (*0-9626545-0-7*) Power Pub Co.

My Life & Times. Mir Qasim. (C). 1992. 24.00 (*81-7023-355-0*, Pub. by Allied Pubs) S Asia.

My Life & Travels. Levi B. Branham. LC 88-18944. 64p. 1994. reprint ed. pap. 7.95 (*0-87797-107-2*) Cherokee.

My Life & Work. Henry J. Ford & Samuel Crowther. LC 73-2507. (Big Business; Economic Power in a Free Society Ser.). 1980. reprint ed. 39.95 (*0-405-05088-7*) Ayer.

My Life As a Battered Woman. Rebecca Pollock. Ed. by Steven Mitchell. 96p. 1998. pap. 9.00 (*0-9664975-0-3*) Cocozza Pub.

My Life As a Bigfoot Breath Mint. Bill Myers. LC 96-32349. (Incredible Worlds of Wally McDoogle Ser.: No. 12). 128p. (J). (gr. 3-7). 1997. pap. 5.99 (*0-8499-3876-7*) Tommy Nelson.

My Life As a Blundering Ballerina. Bill Myers. LC 97-34366. (Incredible Worlds of Wally McDoogle Ser.: No. 13). 128p. (Orig.). (J). (gr. 3-7). 1997. pap. 5.99 (*0-8499-4022-2*) Tommy Nelson.

My Life As a Boy: A Woman's Story. Kim Chernin. LC 96-53978. 196p. 1997. 16.95 (*1-56512-163-5*, 72163) Algonquin Bks.

My Life As a Broken Bungee Cord. Bill Myers. (Incredible Worlds of Wally McDoogle Ser.: No. 3). 128p. (J). (gr. 3-7). 1993. pap. 5.99 (*0-8499-3404-4*) Tommy Nelson.

***My Life as a Busted-Up Basketball Backboard.** Bill Myers. LC 00-25058. (Incredible Worlds of Wally McDoogle Ser.: No. 18). 128p. (J). (gr. 3-7). 2000. pap. 5.99 (*0-8499-4027-3*) Tommy Nelson.

My Life As a Cartoon: A Ziggy Collection. Tom Wilson. (Illus.). 104p. 1995. pap. 6.95 (*0-8362-1786-1*) Andrews & McMeel.

My Life As a Crow. Francois Gravel. (Blue Kite Adventure Ser.). (Illus.). 80p. (J). (gr. 2 up). 1995. pap. 8.95 (*1-55028-417-7*); bds. 16.95 (*1-55028-425-8*) Formac Dist Ltd.

***My Life as a Dog.** Brian Hargrove. LC 00-42567. 2000. write for info. (*0-7862-2784-2*) Thorndike Pr.

My Life As a Dog. Reidar Jonsson. Tr. by Eivor Martinus. 224p. 1993. pap. 12.00 (*0-374-52379-7*, Noonday) FS&G.

***My Life as a Dog,** Moose. LC 99-57695. (Illus.). 144p. 2000. 19.95 (*0-06-105172-1*, HarpEntertain) Morrow Avon.

***My Life as a Dog in Vermont: The Many Moods of Lucy, the Dog of a Thousand Faces.** Geof Hanson. LC 99-18475. 96p. 1999. 8.95 (*0-7407-0033-2*) Andrews & McMeel.

My Life As a Dragonfly: Swimmer to Flyer! William S. Cruscial. LC 96-92629. (Illus.). 28p. (Orig.). (J). (ps-3). 1996. pap. 4.50 (*0-9654099-0-2*) Sawtooth Pr.

My Life as a Fifth-Grade Comedian. Elizabeth Levy. LC 97-3842. 192p. (J). (gr. 3-7). 1998. pap. 4.95 (*0-06-440723-3*) HarpC.

My Life As a Fifth-Grade Comedian. Elizabeth Levy. LC 97-3842. 192p. (J). (gr. 3-7). 1997. 15.95 (*0-06-026602-3*) HarpC Child Bks.

My Life as a Girl. Elizabeth Mosier. LC 98-8688. 193p. (YA). (gr. 7-12). 1999. lib. bdg. 18.99 (*0-679-99035-6*) Random.

***My Life as a Girl.** Elizabeth Mosier. 208p. (YA). (gr. 7-12). 2000. pap. 4.99 (*0-375-80194-4*, Pub. by Random Bks Yng Read) Random.

My Life As a Girl. Elizabeth Mosier. LC 98-8688. 212p. (YA). (gr. 7-12). 1999. 17.00 (*0-679-89035-1*, Pub. by Random Bks Yng Read) Random.

My Life As a Half-Baked Christian: More Tales from the Far Side of Christian Life. Tim Wildmon. 240p. 1999. pap. 12.99 (*1-57748-571-8*) Barbour Pub.

My Life As a Hand, Set of 1-4. rev. ed. Karen A. Gardner. (Sense Bks.). (Illus.). 37p. (J). (ps-2). 1984. lib. bdg. 1.70 (*0-931421-03-9*) Psychol Educ Pubns.

My Life As a Human Hairball. Bill Myers. LC 98-7219. (Incredible Worlds of Wally McDoogle Ser.: No. 15). (J). (gr. 3-7). 1998. 5.99 (*0-8499-4024-9*) Tommy Nelson.

My Life As a Human Hockey Puck. Bill Myers. (Incredible Worlds of Wally McDoogle Ser.: No. 7). 128p. (J). (gr. 3-7). 1994. pap. 5.99 (*0-8499-3601-2*) Tommy Nelson.

My Life As a List: 207 Things about My Bronx Childhood. Linda Rosenkranz. LC 98-27681. (Illus.). 89p. 1999. 15.00 (*0-609-60367-1*) Crown Pub Group.

My Life As a Maine-iac. Muriel Young. Ed. by Constance Hunting. (Illus.). 150p. 1984. pap. 6.95 (*0-913006-30-0*) Puckerbrush.

My Life As a Male Anorexic. Michael Krasnow. LC 95-43399. (Illus.). 152p. 1996. pap. 12.95 (*1-56023-883-6*, Harrington Park) Haworth Pr.

My Life As a Male Anorexic. Michael Krasnow. LC 95-43399. (Illus.). 152p. 1996. 29.95 (*0-7890-6029-9*) Haworth Pr.

My Life As a Man. Philip Roth. LC 73-20847. 330p. 1974. write for info. (*0-03-012646-0*) Holt R&W.

My Life As a Man. Philip Roth. LC 75-312299. 6p. (J). 1974. 2.95 (*0-224-00987-7*) Jonathan Cape.

My Life As a Man. Philip Roth. LC 93-15504. 334p. 1994. pap. 12.00 (*0-679-74827-X*) Vin Bks.

***My Life As a Middle School Mom: My Kids May Be Deductible, but They're Still Taxing.** Angela Elwell Hunt. 190p. 2000. pap. 10.99 (*1-56955-203-7*) Servant.

***My Life As a Miracle: The Wizard of New Zealand.** Wizard of New Zealand staff. (Illus.). 168p. (Orig.). 1998. pap. 29.95 (*0-908812-73-6*, Pub. by Canterbury Univ) Accents Pubns.

***My Life as a Mixed-Up Millennium Bug.** Bill Myers. LC 99-35244. (Incredible Worlds of Wally McDoogle Ser.: No. 17). 128p. (J). (gr. 3-7). 1999. 5.99 (*0-8499-4026-5*) Tommy Nelson.

My Life As a Nose, Set of 1-4. rev. ed. Karen A. Gardner. (Sense Bks.). (Illus.). 37p. (J). (ps-2). 1984. lib. bdg. 1.70 (*0-931421-04-7*) Psychol Educ Pubns.

My Life As a Pornographer & Other Indecent Acts. John Preston. (Orig.). 1993. pap. 12.95 (*1-56333-135-7*, R Kasak Bks) Masquerade.

My Life As a Radical Lawyer. William M. Kunstler & Sheila Isenberg. LC 94-11590. (Illus.). 432p. 1994. 22.50 (*1-55972-265-7*, Birch Ln Pr) Carol Pub Group.

My Life As a Radical Lawyer. William M. Kunstler & Sheila Isenberg. LC 96-18494. (Illus.). 448p. 1996. pap. 16.95 (*0-8065-1755-7*, Citadel Pr) Carol Pub Group.

My Life As a Screaming Skydiver. Bill Myers. LC 98-11458. (Incredible Worlds of Wally McDoogle Ser.: No. 14). (Illus.). 128p. (J). (gr. 3-7). 1998. 5.99 (*0-8499-4023-0*) Tommy Nelson.

My Life As a Search for the Meaning of Mediumship. Eileen J. Garrett. LC 75-7380. (Perspectives in Psychical Research Ser.). 1975. reprint ed. 23.95 (*0-405-07030-6*) Ayer.

My Life As a Search for the Meaning of Mediumship. Eileen J. Garrett. (American Biography Ser.). 224p. 1991. reprint ed. lib. bdg. 69.00 (*0-7812-8142-3*) Rprt Serv.

My Life As a Seer: The Lost Memoirs. Edgar Cayce. Ed. & Compiled by A. Robert Smith. LC 99-31180. 400p. 1999. text 25.95 (*0-312-20419-1*) St Martin.

My Life As a Smashed Burrito. Bill Myers. (Incredible Worlds of Wally McDoogle Ser.: No. 1). 128p. (J). (gr. 3-7). 1993. pap. 5.99 (*0-8499-3402-8*) Tommy Nelson.

My Life As a Smashed Burrito. Bill Myers. (Incredible Worlds of Wally McDoogle Ser.: No. 1). (J). (gr. 3-7). 1999. pap. 1.99 (*0-8499-7508-5*) Tommy Nelson.

***My Life as a Ten-Year-Old Boy: Bart, the Simpsons & Me.** Nancy Cartwright. (Illus.). 224p. (J). 2000. pap. 19.95 (*0-7868-6696-9*, Pub. by Hyprn Child) Time Warner.

My Life As a Toasted Time Traveler. Bill Myers. (Incredible Worlds of Wally McDoogle Ser.: No. 10). 128p. (Orig.). (J). (gr. 3-7). 1996. pap. 5.99 (*0-8499-3867-8*) Tommy Nelson.

My Life As a Tongue, Set of 1-4. rev. ed. Karen A. Gardner. (Sense Bks.). (Illus.). 37p. (J). (ps-2). 1984. lib. bdg. 1.70 (*0-931421-05-5*) Psychol Educ Pubns.

My Life As a Torpedo Test Target. Bill Myers. (Incredible Worlds of Wally McDoogle Ser.: No. 6). 128p. (J). (gr. 3-7). 1994. pap. 5.99 (*0-8499-3538-5*) Tommy Nelson.

My Life as a Walrus Whoopee Cushion. Bill Myers. LC 99-13459. (Incredible Worlds of Wally McDoogle Ser.: No. 16). 116p. (J). (gr. 3-7). 1999. pap. text 5.99 (*0-8499-4025-7*) Tommy Nelson.

My Life As Alien Monster Bait. Bill Myers. (Incredible Worlds of Wally McDoogle Ser.: No. 2). 128p. (J). (gr. 3-7). 1993. pap. 5.99 (*0-8499-3403-6*) Tommy Nelson.

My Life As an Afterthought Astronaut. Bill Myers. LC 94-45373. (Incredible Worlds of Wally McDoogle Ser.: No. 8). 128p. (J). (gr. 3-7). 1989. pap. 55.99 (*0-8499-3602-0*) Tommy Nelson.

My Life As an Artist Blacksmith. Francis Whitaker. 1995. 42.50 (*0-9646389-0-8*); lib. bdg. 100.00 (*0-9646389-1-6*) F Whitaker.

My Life As an Ear, Set of 1-4. rev. ed. Karen A. Gardner. (Sense Bks.). (Illus.). 37p. (J). (ps-2). 1984. lib. bdg. 1.70 (*0-931421-01-2*) Psychol Educ Pubns.

My Life As an Explorer: The Great Adventurer's Classic Memoir. Sven A. Hedin. Ed. by Philip Turner. Tr. by Alfild Huebsch. LC 96-23143. (Illus.). 576p. 1996. pap. 16.00 (*1-56836-142-4*, Kodansha Globe) Kodansha.

My Life As an Explorer: The Great Adventurer's Classic Memoir. Sven Anders Hedin. LC 98-905016. xi, 544 p. 1998. write for info. (*81-206-1057-1*) Asian Educ Servs.

My Life As an Eye, Set of 1-4. rev. ed. Karen A. Gardner. (Sense Bks.). (Illus.). 37p. (J). (ps-2). 1984. lib. bdg. 1.70 (*0-931421-02-0*) Psychol Educ Pubns.

My Life As an Indian. James W. Schultz. (American Biography Ser.). 204p. 1991. reprint ed. lib. bdg. 69.00 (*0-7812-8343-4*) Rprt Serv.

My Life As an Indian: The Story of a Red Woman & a White Man in the Lodges of the Blackfeet. James W. Schultz. LC 97-7577. (Illus.). 288p. 1997. reprint ed. pap. text 8.95 (*0-486-29614-8*) Dover.

My Life As an Indian: The Story of a Red Woman & a White Man in the Lodges of the Blackfeet. 3rd unabridged ed. James W. Schultz. (Illus.). 472p. 1996. reprint ed. pap. 18.95 (*0-87928-112-X*) Corner Hse.

My Life As Author & Editor. H. L. Mencken. Ed. & Intro. by Jonathan Yardley. 1993. 30.00 (*0-679-41315-4*) Knopf.

My Life As Crocodile Junk Food. Bill Myers. (Incredible Worlds of Wally McDoogle Ser.: No. 4). 128p. (J). (gr. 3-7). 1993. pap. 5.99 (*0-8499-3405-2*) Tommy Nelson.

My Life as Dinosaur Dental Floss. Bill Myers. (Incredible Worlds of Wally McDoogle Ser.: No. 5). 128p. (J). (gr. 3-7). 1994. pap. 5.99 (*0-8499-3537-7*) Tommy Nelson.

My Life As Polluted Pond Scum. Bill Myers. LC 96-8256. (Incredible Worlds of Wally McDoogle Ser.: No. 11). 128p. (Orig.). (J). (gr. 3-7). 1996. pap. 5.99 (*0-8499-3875-9*) Tommy Nelson.

My Life As Reindeer Road Kill. Bill Myers. (Incredible Worlds of Wally McDoogle Ser.: No. 9). 128p. (J). (gr. 3-7). 1995. pap. 5.99 (*0-8499-3866-X*) Tommy Nelson.

My Life at a Glance. J. Daryl Lippencott. Ed. by Gail B. Fisher. 170p. 1995. write for info. (*1-885001-09-6*) Via Press.

My Life Between the Cross & the Bars. unabridged ed. George R. Castillo & Daniel J. Bayse. LC 96-230393. (Illus.). 295p. 1996. 21.95 (*0-9649916-0-8*) G & M Pubns.

My Life, by August Bebel. August Bebel. LC 83-1556. 343p. (C). 1983. reprint ed. lib. bdg. 69.50 (*0-313-23927-4*, BEMY, Greenwood Pr) Greenwood.

My Life East & West. William S. Hart. LC 68-20228. (Illus.). 363p. 1972. reprint ed. 19.95 (*0-405-08601-6*, Pub. by Blom Pubns) Ayer.

My Life for the Poor: Mother Teresa of Calcutta. Ed. by Jose L. Gonzalez & Jane Playfoot. 128p. 1987. reprint ed. mass mkt. 5.99 (*0-345-33780-8*, Ballantine Epiphany) Ballantine Pub Grp.

My Life from Brigand to King. Amir Habibulah. 276p. 1990. 24.00 (*0-86304-047-0*, Pub. by Octagon Pr) ISHK.

***My Life Full of Cars.** Paul Frere. (Illus.). 256p. 2000. 39.95 (*1-85960-670-9*, 130423AE, Pub. by Haynes Manuals) Motorbooks Intl.

My Life Has Just Started Yesterday Was Not the End: Inspiration & Healing Poems from the Heart. Jim Schutte. Ed. by Kris P. Neal. LC 95-70218. (Illus.). 60p. (Orig.). Date not set. pap. 7.95 (*0-9647807-0-4*) Picnic Pubng.

My Life in Advertising: Scientific Advertising. Claude C. Hopkins. (American Biography Ser.). 318p. 1991. reprint ed. lib. bdg. 79.00 (*0-7812-8191-1*) Rprt Serv.

My Life in Advertising & Scientific Advertising. Claude C. Hopkins. LC 97-30305. 336p. 1995. pap. 11.95 (*0-8442-3101-0*, NTC Business Bks) NTC Contemp Pub Co.

My Life in Art. Constantin Stanislavski. 582p. 1987. pap. 24.99 (*0-87830-550-5*, Thtre Arts Bks) Routledge.

My Life in Art, Vol. 4. Konstantin Stanislavsky. (The Collected Works of Konstantin Stanislavsky). 448p. (C). (gr. 13). 1999. 45.00 (*0-87830-083-X*, Thtre Arts Bks) Routledge.

My Life in Baseball: The True Record. Ty Cobb & Al Stump. LC 92-35297. xiv, 315p. 1993. reprint ed. pap. 12.95 (*0-8032-6359-7*, Bison Books) U of Nebr Pr.

My Life in Baseball - Ty Cobb. Ty Cobb & Al Stump. Date not set. lib. bdg. 27.95 (*0-8488-1562-9*) Amereon Ltd.

My Life in China & America. Ed. by Wing Yung & Roger Daniels. LC 78-54850. (Asian Experience in North America Ser.). 1979. reprint ed. lib. bdg. 23.95 (*0-405-11301-3*) Ayer.

My Life in Christ: A Momento of My Confirmation. S. H. Fenske. LC 76-5729. (J). (gr. 8 up). 1976. pap. 3.50 (*0-8100-0056-3*, 16N0514) Northwest Pub.

My Life in Court. Louis Nizer. 1993. reprint ed. lib. bdg. 35.95 (*1-56849-145-X*) Buccaneer Bks.

My Life in Dog Years. Gary Paulsen. 144p. (J). 1999. pap. 4.99 (*0-440-41471-7*) BDD Bks Young Read.

My Life in Dog Years. Gary Paulsen. LC 97-40254. (Illus.). 144p. (YA). (gr. 5 up). 1998. 15.95 (*0-385-32570-3*) Delacorte.

My Life in E-Flat. Chan Parker. LC 98-19682. (Illus.). 256p. 1999. pap. 16.95 (*1-57003-245-9*) U of SC Pr.

My Life in Flux & Vice Versa. Emmett Williams. LC 91-67359. (Illus.). 512p. 1992. 40.00 (*0-500-97398-9*, Pub. by Thames Hudson) Norton.

My Life in Germany Before & after 1933: A Report. Karl Lowith. Tr. by Elizabeth King. LC 93-43772. (Illus.). 192p. 1994. text 32.95 (*0-252-02121-5*); pap. text 14.95 (*0-252-06409-7*) U of Ill Pr.

My Life in Hiding. Jean Nordhaus. (QRL Poetry Bks.: Vol. XXX). 1991. 20.00 (*0-614-06432-5*) Quarterly Rev.

My Life in High Heels. Loni Anderson. 1997. mass mkt. 6.99 (*0-380-72854-0*, Avon Bks) Morrow Avon.

My Life in High Heels. Loni Anderson & Larkin Warren. 1997. mass mkt. 6.99 (*0-614-27698-5*, Avon Bks) Morrow Avon.

My Life in Living Color: Story of Bernice Kentner, Author of Color Me a Season & Rainbow in Your Eyes. Bernice Kentner. (Illus.). 160p. (Orig.). 1994. spiral bd. 15.95 (*0-941522-11-3*) Ken Kra Pubs.

My Life in Music. John Erskine. LC 73-8158. (Illus.). 283p. 1974. reprint ed. lib. bdg. 65.00 (*0-8371-6950-X*, ERLM, Greenwood Pr) Greenwood.

My Life in My Hands: Living on with Cystic Fibrosis. Doug Lab & Olivia K. Lab. Ed. by Robyn Witkin. 163p. 1990. pap. 7.50 (*0-9629216-0-2*) LabPro Pr.

My Life in Search of Africa. John Henrik Clarke. LC 97-48939. 1997. 30.00 (*0-88378-158-1*) Third World.

My Life in Search of Africa. John Henrik Clarke. LC 97-48939. 104p. 1999. pap. 15.95 (*0-88378-178-6*) Third World.

My Life-In Spite of Myself. Roy Clark. (Illus.). (J). 1995. mass mkt. 6.99 (*0-671-52686-3*) PB.

My Life in the Foreign Legion. H. R. H. Prince Aage of Denmark. (European War Ser.: No. 1). (Illus.). 204p. 1994. reprint ed. 34.95 (*0-89839-196-2*) Battery Pr.

My Life in the Irish Brigade: The Civil War Memoirs of Private William McCarter, 116th Pennsylvania Infantry. Ed. by Kevin E. O'Brien. (Illus.). 288p. 1997. reprint ed. 24.95 (*1-882810-07-4*, 07-4) Savas Pub.

My Life in the Mountains & on the Plains: The Newly Discovered Autobiography. David Meriwether. Ed. by Robert A. Griffen. LC 65-11240. (American Exploration & Travel Ser.: 46). 324p. reprint ed. pap. 100.50 (*0-608-12408-7*, 205213200039) Bks Demand.

My Life in the Negro Leagues. Wilmer Fields. (Illus.). 100p. 1992. lib. bdg. 29.50 (*0-88736-850-6*) Mecklermedia.

My Life in the Old Army: The Reminiscences of Abner Doubleday. Abner Doubleday. Ed. & Anno. by Joseph E. Chance. LC 97-34316. (Illus.). 1998. 27.95 (*0-87565-185-2*) Tex Christian.

My Life in the Russian Theatre. Vladimir Nemirovitch-Dantchenko. LC 67-18053. (Illus.). 365p. 1987. pap. 69.90 (*0-87830-520-3*, Thtre Arts Bks) Routledge.

My Life in Three Acts. large type ed. Helen Hayes. LC 90-44225. 403p. 1990. reprint ed. lib. bdg. 21.95 (*1-56054-051-6*) Thorndike Pr.

***My Life in 'Toons: From Flatbush to Bedrock in Under a Century.** Joe Barbera. 250p. 2000. reprint ed. 20.00 (*0-7881-9308-2*) DIANE Pub.

My Life in Two Worlds, 2 vols., Set. Francis Neilson. 1971. 300.00 (*0-87700-004-2*) Revisionist Pr.

***My Life in Verse & Rhyme.** Joan Robertson. 129p. 2000. 19.95 (*0-7541-1148-2*, Pub. by Minerva Pr) Unity Dist.

My Life in Writing. Knowles. 256p. 1997. 19.95 (*0-684-19353-1*, Scribners Ref) Mac Lib Ref.

My Life Infused with Music. Stella Star. Ed. by Frances B. Goodman. (Illus.). 64p. (Orig.). 1993. pap. 7.95 (*0-89896-185-8*) Larksdale.

My Life Is a Three Ring Circus. Cathy East Dubowski. (Full House Michelle Ser.). (J). (gr. 2-4). 1998. per. 3.99 (*0-671-01730-6*, Minstrel Bks) PB.

My Life Is Great, Why Do I Feel So Awful? Successful Women, Hidden Passions. Steve R. Pieczenik. LC 89-39118. 1990. 18.45 (*0-446-51458-6*) Warner Bks.

My Life Is in Your Hands: Devotions to Help You Fall More in Love with Jesus. Kathy Troccoli. LC 97-26778. 144p. 1997. 15.99 (*0-310-21061-5*) Zondervan.

***My Life Is in Your Hands & Take My Life: The Autobiographies of Eddie Cantor.** Eddie Cantor. (Illus.). 2000. pap. 22.95 (*0-8154-1057-3*) Cooper Sq.

My Life Is on Hold see Angel in Disguise: Bridging This World to the Other Side

My Life Is on Hold: One Family's Struggle with Terminal Illness. large type ed. MarJoe Davidson. LC 94-96007. 160p. (Orig.). 1994. pap. 13.00 (*0-9639866-1-9*) MDees Pubng.

My Life, Melinda's Story. Melinda Lawrence. 15p. 1987. pap. 4.95 (*0-317-61838-5*) Child Hospice VA.

My Life, My Choices: Key Issues for Young Adults. Mary A. Wojno. LC 97-197676. 320p. (Orig.). 1997. pap. 14.95 (*0-8091-3682-1*) Paulist Pr.

My Life My Love My Lasagne. Steven Herrick. LC 98-144955. (Storybridge Ser.). 80p. (J). 1997. pap. 10.95 (*0-7022-2955-5*, Pub. by Univ Queensland Pr) Intl Spec Bk.

My Life, My Trees. 2nd ed. Richard St. Barbe Baker. 192p. 1989. reprint ed. pap. 10.95 (*0-905249-63-1*, Pub. by Findhorn Pr) Words Distrib.

My Life, My Way. Al Olshan. 300p. (Orig.). 1992. pap. write for info. (*0-9632134-0-7*) Al Olshan.

My Life 'N' Doins. LuLu M. O'Neal. Ed. by Reta Spears-Stewart. 1998. pap. 10.00 (*1-892477-06-8*) Barnabs Pub.

My Life of Absurdity: The Autobiography of Chester Himes - The Later Years. 2nd ed. Chester B. Himes. LC 98-161421. (Illus.). 400p. 1995. reprint ed. pap. 13.95 (*1-56025-094-1*, Thunders Mouth) Avalon NY.

My Life of Adventure. Norman D. Vaughan & Cecil B. Murphey. (Illus.). 256p. 1995. 24.95 (*0-8117-0892-6*) Stackpole.

My Life of Music. Henry J. Wood. LC 72-157359. (Select Bibliographies Reprint Ser.). 1977. reprint ed. 24.95 (*0-8369-5820-9*) Ayer.

My Life of Song. Luisa Tetrazzini. Ed. by Andrew Farkas. LC 76-29970. (Opera Biographies Ser.). (Illus.). 1977. reprint ed. lib. bdg. 30.95 (*0-405-09709-3*) Ayer.

My Life on a Napkin: Pillow Mints, Playground Dreams & Coaching the Runnin' Utes. Rick Majerus. LC 99-190566. (Illus.). 256p. 1999. 22.95 (*0-7868-6527-X*, Pub. by Hyperion) Time Warner.

***My Life on a Plate: A Novel.** India Knight. 224p. 2000. 21.00 (*0-618-09397-4*) HM.

My Life on Either Side of the Rockies. Henry C. Brown. Ed. by Carolyn W. Greenlee. LC 98-35630. 167p. 1999. pap. 19.95 (*1-887400-20-6*) Earthen Vessel Prodns.

My Life on Mountain Railroads. William J. Gould & William R. Gould. (Illus.). 264p. 1995. 36.95 (*0-87421-197-2*); pap. 17.95 (*0-87421-193-X*) Utah St U Pr.

My Life on the Plains. George A. Custer. 1995. 9.98 (*0-88394-091-4*) Promntory Pr.

My Life on the Plains. George A. Custer. Ed. & Intro. by Milo M. Quaife. LC 67-2618. (Illus.). xlii, 632p. 1966. pap. 15.00 (*0-8032-5042-8*, Bison Books) U of Nebr Pr.

My Life on the Plains: Or Personal Experiences with Indians. George A. Custer. (Western Frontier Library: No. 52). 1977. pap. 12.95 (*0-8061-1357-X*) U of Okla Pr.

***My Life on the Road: The Autobiography of a Traveller.** Nancy Joyce. Ed. by Anna Farmar. (Illus.). 128p. 2000. pap. 11.95 (*1-899047-58-1*, Pub. by A A Farmar) Irish Bks Media.

My Life on the Street: Memoirs of a Faceless Man. Joe Homeless. 1994. pap. 12.95 (*0-88282-091-5*) New Horizon NJ.

***My Life Planner: 400 Years Calendar/Vurtual Calendar.** Phiet Bui. (Illus.). 68p. 1999. pap. 8.99 (*0-9671141-0-1*) Suhasian.

My Life-Politics & Diplomacy in Turbulent Times. Maurice Czikann-Zichy. LC 86-51433. (Program of the Hungarian Historical Research Society Ser.). 105p. (Orig.). 1986. pap. 9.00 (*0-935484-12-4*) Universe Pub Co.

My Life, So Far: Edith Ann. Jane Wagner. (Illus.). 192p. (J). 1995. pap. 7.70 (*0-7868-8133-X*, Pub. by Hyperion) Time Warner.

My Life, Starring Dara Falcon. Ann Beattie. 320p. 1998. pap. 13.00 (*0-679-78132-3*) Vin Bks.

***My Life Story: A Memoir.** James Kay. Ed. by Doris Lora. (Illus.). 107p. 1999. write for info. (*1-888069-22-8*) Biography For Everyone.

My Life Story: The Autobiography of a Berber Woman. Fadhma Amrouche. Tr. by Dorothy Blair. 197p. (C). 1989. text 35.00 (*0-8135-1425-8*); pap. text 17.00 (*0-8135-1426-6*) Rutgers U Pr.

My Life Story: The LGP Autobiography System. Ed. by Loup Garou Press Staff. 250p. 1988. student ed., ring bd. 35.00 (*0-9621860-1-5*) Loup Garou Pr.

My Life Story Vol. 1: From Birth Through Grandparenthood. unabridged ed. Christine O'Brien. (Illus.). 100p. 1997. 29.95 (*1-889972-84-3*) Newpt Media.

***My Life, Take Two.** Paul Many. LC 99-55396. 204p. (YA). (gr. 7-12). 2000. 16.95 (*0-8027-8708-8*) Walker & Co.

My Life Turned Upside down, but I Turned It Rightside Up. Hennie M. Shore & Mary B. Field. (Self-Esteem Ser.). (Illus.). 71p. (J). (gr. k-7). 1994. pap. 14.95 (*1-882732-06-5*) Childswork.

My Life Was Like the Storm at Sea. M. Emiko R. (Illus.). 72p. 1997. pap. 10.00 (*0-8059-4074-X*) Dorrance.

My Life Was Meaningless & So Was My Death. Blacky Hix. 160p. (Orig.). 1992. pap. 12.00 (*1-885466-06-4*) Smoke The Soul.

My Life with Barbra: A Love Story. Barry Dennen. LC 97-24796. (Illus.). 281p. 1997. 24.95 (*1-57392-160-2*) Prometheus Bks.

***My Life with Benjamin Franklin.** Claude Anne Lopez. LC 99-46231. 288p. 2000. 25.00 (*0-300-08192-8*) Yale U Pr.

My Life with Bing. Kathryn Crosby. LC 82-74361. (Illus.). 358p. 1983. 29.95 (*0-938728-01-6*) Collage Bks Inc.

My Life with Boxers. Friderun Stockmann. LC 68-92392. xii, 236p. 1968. write for info. (*0-09-086010-1*) Arrow Bks.

***My Life with Boxers: The Classic Memoirs of the Most Important Boxer Breeder.** rev. ed. Friederun Stockmann. Tr. by Calvin D. Gruver from GER.Tr. of Mein Leben Mit Boxern. (Illus.). 333p. 1998. 39.95 (*0-9675747-0-6*) Classic Pet Bks.

My Life with Darwin. Molly B. Tinsley. reprint ed. 9.95 (*0-931848-89-X*) Dryad Pr.

***My Life with Dogs.** Gayle Bunney. 144p. 1999. pap. 11.95 (*1-55105-152-4*) Lone Pine.

My Life with God. (Saint Joseph Picture Bks.). (Illus.). 1978. pap. 1.25 (*0-89942-304-3*, 304-00) Catholic Bk Pub.

My Life with Groucho. Arthur Marx. LC 91-41254. (Illus.). 287p. 1992. pap. 12.95 (*0-942637-45-3*) Barricade Bks.

My Life with Janacek: The Memoirs of Zdenka Janackova. Ed. & Tr. by Chia-ning Chang. (Illus.). 304p. 1998. 33.95 (*0-571-17540-6*) Faber & Faber.

My Life with Martin Luther King, Jr. rev. ed. Coretta Scott King. LC 92-23525. (Illus.). xiii, 335p. (YA). (gr. 6 up). 1995. 17.95 (*0-8050-2445-X*, Bks Young Read) H Holt & Co.

***My Life with Nature.** John Muir & Joseph Bharat Cornell. LC 00-8827. 2000. pap. write for info. (*1-58469-009-7*) Dawn Pub Co.

My Life with Noel Coward. Graham Payn. LC 94-42525. (Illus.). 320p. 1996. 24.95 (*1-55783-190-4*) Applause Theatre Bk Pubs.

My Life with Noel Coward. Graham Payn. (Illus.). 320p. 1996. pap. 16.95 (*1-55783-247-1*) Applause Theatre Bk Pubs.

My Life with President Kennedy. Christopher Clausen. LC 94-16527. 143p. 1994. pap. 9.95 (*0-87745-485-X*) U of Iowa Pr.

My Life with Radiation: Hiroshima Plus 50 Years. Ralph L. Lapp. LC 95-36596. (Illus.). 168p. 1995. pap. 17.95 (*0-944838-52-9*, Cogito Bks) Med Physics Pub.

My Life with Sri Shirdi Sai Baba: Thrilling Memories of Shivamma Thayee. Satya Pal Ruhela. (Thrilling Memories of Shivamma Thayee Ser.). 78p. 1996. pap. 50.00 (*81-7533-003-1*, Pub. by Print Hse) St Mut.

My Life with Suzuki. Waltraud Suzuki. 70p. (Orig.). 1987. pap. text 10.95 (*0-87487-585-4*) Summy-Birchard.

***My Life with Sylvia Browne: A Son Reflects on Life with His Psychic Mother.** Chris Dufresne. LC 99-44831. (Illus.). 176p. 2000. pap. 12.95 (*1-56170-667-1*, 5014) Hay House.

My Life with the Chimpanzees. Jane Goodall. 160p. (J). (gr. 3-6). 1996. per. 3.99 (*0-671-56271-1*, Minstrel Bks) PB.

My Life with the Chimpanzees. Jane Goodall. 1996. 9.09 (*0-606-09650-7*, Pub. by Turtleback) Demco.

My Life with the Chimpanzees. Houghton Mifflin Company Staff. (J). (gr. 7). 1992. pap. 11.04 (*0-395-61849-5*) HM.

My Life with the Chimpanzees. rev. ed. Jane Goodall. (J). (gr. 3-7). 14.00 (*0-614-15697-1*, Minstrel Bks) PB.

My Life with the Great Pianists. Franz Mohr. Tr. by Life Publishers International Staff. (RUS., Illus.). 400p. (C). 1999. pap. write for info. (*0-7361-0081-4*) Life Pubs Intl.

My Life with the Great Pianists. 2nd ed. Franz Mohr & Edith Schaeffer. LC 96-216092. 200p. (YA). (gr. 10). 1996. pap. 14.99 (*0-8010-5710-8*, Ravens Ridge) Baker Bks.

My Life with the Indians: The Story of Mary Jemison. Robin Moore. LC 97-13606. (Incredible Journey Ser.). (Illus.). (J). 1997. 16.95 (*0-382-39922-6*); pap. write for info. (*0-382-39923-4*) Silver Burdett Pr.

My Life with the Printed Circuit. Paul Eisler. LC 88-81397. (Illus.). 176p. 1989. 35.00 (*0-934223-04-1*) Lehigh Univ Pr.

My Life with the Samurai: A POW in Indonesia. Anthony Crowling. LC 96-176259. 1996. pap. text 16.95 (*0-86417-812-3*, Pub. by Kangaroo Pr) Seven Hills Bk.

My Life with the Spirits: The Adventures of a Modern Magician. Lon M. DuQuette. LC 99-20559. (Illus.). 208p. 1999. pap. 14.95 (*1-57863-120-3*) Weiser.

***My Life with the Wave: Based on the Story by Octavio Paz.** Catherine Cowan. 2000. pap. write for info. (*0-688-17524-4*, Wm Morrow) Morrow Avon.

My Life with the Wave: Based on the Story by Octavio Paz. Catherine Cowan & Octavio Paz. LC 93-33625. (Illus.). 32p. (J). (gr. k-3). 1997. 16.00 (*0-688-12660-X*) Lothrop.

My Life with the Wave: Based on the Story by Octavio Paz. Catherine Cowan & Octavio Paz. LC 93-33625. (Illus.). 32p. (J). (gr. k-3). 1997. lib. bdg. 15.93 (*0-688-12661-8*) Lothrop.

My Life with Thomas Aquinas. Carol Robinson. (Integrity Magazine Anthology Ser.: Vol. 1). (Illus.). 307p. (Orig.). 1992. pap. text 13.50 (*0-935952-83-7*) Angelus Pr.

My Life with Vanessa: The Plagued Years. Myst Wismer. (Illus.). 68p. 1999. pap. 11.95 (*1-884873-30-8*) My Bros Keeper.

My Life Without God. enl. rev. ed. William Murray. LC 92-10586. 1992. mass mkt. 5.99 (*1-56507-029-1*) Harvest Hse.

***My Life Without God: The Rest of the Story.** William Murray. 375p. 2000. pap. 11.99 (*0-7369-0315-1*) Harvest Hse.

My Life...My Thoughts: A Daily Journal for 9 to 13 Year Olds, Vol. I. Contrib. by Susan Kolling. (Memory Journals for Young Writers Ser.). 374p. (J). (gr. 4-7). 1995. pap. text 9.99 (*1-56383-056-6*, 5057) G & R Pub.

***My Life's Passages.** Jane Hu. LC 99-94418. 96p. 1999. pap. 10.00 (*1-880016-29-X*, Ink Drop Pr) Road Pubs.

My Life's Soul-Journey: Daily Meditations for Ever-Increasing Spiritual Fulfillment. Sri Chinmoy. 430p. 1995. pap. text 13.95 (*0-88497-244-5*) Aum Pubns.

My Lifetime of Sex & How to Handle It. Carole Marsh. (Smart Sex Stuff Ser.). (Orig.). (J). (gr. ps-12). 1994. pap. 19.95 (*1-55609-211-3*) Gallopade Intl.

My Lifetime Tidbits of Preventive Medicine. Frank Smith. (Illus.). 110p. (Orig.). 1997. pap. 12.95 (*1-57502-345-8*, PO1140) Morris Pubng.

***My Light @ Night.** Johnny Mascari. Ed. by Rebecca Taff. LC 99-97810. (Illus.). 32p. (J). (ps up). 2000. 15.95 (*1-930413-00-9*) Mascari & Co.

My Linda. Ernest C. Grigg. 430p. mass mkt. 5.99 (*1-896329-21-7*) Picasso Publ.

My Lips Are Sealed: Unjust Reliance - What Is America? Ricardo Scott. (Rastafars Truths As Observed & Revealed Ser.). (Illus.). 85p. 1999. pap. write for info. (*1-58470-021-1*, RAS1949) Crnerstone GA.

My Listen & Learn Bible. Illus. by David Barnett. LC 94-23391. 96p. (J). 1994. 5.99 (*0-7814-0092-9*, Chariot Bks) Chariot Victor.

My Literary Passions. William Dean Howells. (Notable American Authors Ser.). 1992. reprint ed. lib. bdg. 75.00 (*0-7812-3273-2*) Rprt Serv.

My Literary Passions. William Dean Howells. LC 74-131753. 1970. reprint ed. 11.00 (*0-403-00640-6*) Scholarly.

My Literary Zoo. Kate Sanborn. LC 72-4751. (Essay Index Reprint Ser.). 1977. reprint ed. 19.95 (*0-8369-2973-X*) Ayer.

My Litter Box Was Dirty . . .So I Left You a Present in Your Shoe! Behavior Modification from a Cat's Point of View. Isabel G. Pomphrey. Ed. by Patrick J. Pomphrey, Jr. (Illus.). 114p. 1997. pap. 16.98 (*0-9661487-0-3*) Tunabreath.

My Little Angel. James Pada, Jr. 76p. 1997. pap. write for info. (*1-57502-561-2*, PO1624) Morris Pubng.

My Little Angel Is Watching over Me. Jeanne Ludwig. (Illus.). 24p. (J). (gr. 1-3). 1996. 9.95 (*1-56550-060-1*) Vis Bks Intl.

My Little Aquarius. J. Astrop. (Little Stars Ser.). (Illus.). 64p. 1994. pap. 5.95 (*1-85230-547-9*, Pub. by Element MA) Penguin Putnam.

My Little Aries. J. Astrop. (Little Stars Ser.). (Illus.). 64p. 1994. text 5.95 (*1-85230-537-1*, Pub. by Element MA) Penguin Putnam.

***My Little Artist.** Donna Green. LC 99-20004. (Illus.). 32p. (J). (ps-3). 1999. 11.98 (*0-7651-1742-8*) Smithmark.

My Little Artist. Donna Green. (Illus.). 32p. (J). 1999. 12.95 (*1-883746-20-5*) Vermilion.

My Little Artist. deluxe ed. Donna Green. (Illus.). 32p. (J). 1999. 15.95 (*1-883746-21-3*) Vermilion.

My Little Bible, Pink. Stephanie M. Britt. (My Little Bible Ser.). (Illus.). 98p. (J). (ps-k). 1993. 5.99 (*0-8499-1077-3*) Tommy Nelson.

My Little Bible, White. Stephanie M. Britt. (My Little Bible Ser.). (Illus.). 98p. (J). (ps-k). 1993. 5.99 (*0-8499-0824-8*) Tommy Nelson.

My Little Bible Blue. Stephanie Britt. (Illus.). 98p. (Orig.). (J). (ps-k). 1993. 5.99 (*0-8499-1078-1*) Tommy Nelson.

My Little Bible in Pictures. Kenneth N. Taylor. 1998. 5.99 (*0-8423-5180-9*); 7.99 (*0-8423-5176-0*) Tyndale Hse.

My Little Bible Picture Book. LC 88-4575. (Illus.). 80p. (J). (ps). 1988. 7.99 (*1-55513-513-7*, Chariot Bks) Chariot Victor.

My Little Bible Picture Book. 80p. (J). 1997. write for info. (*0-7814-0283-2*, Chariot Bks) Chariot Victor.

My Little Bible Promises. Stephanie M. Britt. LC 94-17707. (My Little Bible Ser.). (Illus.). 98p. (J). (ps-k). 1994. 5.99 (*0-8499-1145-1*) Tommy Nelson.

***My Little Black Book.** William Barnes. 68p. 1999. pap. write for info. (*0-7392-0428-9*, PO3708) Morris Pubng.

My Little Black Book. Jarrold Publishing Staff. 1999. 3.95 (*0-7117-1040-6*) Seven Hills Bk.

My Little Book about Allah. Mohammad M. Hussaini. 76p. (J). 1996. pap. 4.95 (*0-614-21032-1*, 864) Kazi Pubns.

My Little Book about God. Jane W. Watson. (Little Golden Treasures Ser.). 26p. (J). (ps). 1998. 5.99 (*0-307-20312-3*, 20312, Goldn Books) Gldn Bks Pub Co.

My Little Book about the Quran. Mohammad M. Hussaini. 72p. (J). (gr. 1-6). 1996. pap. 4.95 (*0-614-21033-X*, 865) Kazi Pubns.

My Little Book about the Voyages of Paul Etta Wilson. LC 96-137218. (Leap Frog Bks.). 1993. write for info. (*0-7853-0088-0*) Pubns Intl Ltd.

My Little Book of Big Bible Promises. Linda J. Sattgast. LC 97-146472. 80p. (J). (ps-3). 1996. 9.99 (*1-57673-021-2*, Gold n Honey) Zondervan.

My Little Book of Burrowing Owls. Hope I. Marston. LC 95-36480. (Illus.). 48p. (Orig.). (J). (gr. k-5). 1996. pap. 6.95 (*1-55971-547-2*, NorthWord Pr) Creat Pub Intl.

My Little Book of Caring & Sharing. Mohammad M. Hussaini. 72p. (J). (gr. 1-6). 1996. pap. 4.95 (*0-614-21034-8*, 72) Kazi Pubns.

My Little Book of Du'a. Mohammad M. Hussaini. 72p. (J). 1996. pap. 4.95 (*0-614-21035-6*, 867) Kazi Pubns.

My Little Book of Halal & Haram. unabridged ed. Mohammad M. Hussaini. Ed. by Abidullah Ghazi & Tasneema Ghazi. (Islamic Akhlaq Ser.). (Illus.). 45p. (J). (gr. 1-3). 1987. pap. text 6.00 (*0-911119-12-4*) Iqra Intl Ed Fdtn.

My Little Book of Painted Turtles. Hope I. Marston. LC 96-11583. (Illus.). 36p. (J). (gr. k-5). 1996. pap. 6.95 (*1-55971-569-3*, NorthWord Pr) Creat Pub Intl.

***My Little Book of Poems.** Golden Books Staff. (First Little Golden Book Ser.). (Illus.). (J). 2000. 12.99 (*0-307-10142-8*, Goldn Books) Gldn Bks Pub Co.

***My Little Book of Prayer.** S. M. Henriques. 1999. pap. 6.95 (*1-58334-034-3*) Walnut Gr Pr.

My Little Book of River Otters. Hope Marston. LC 97-5958. (Illus.). 32p. (Orig.). (J). (gr. k-5). 1997. pap. 6.95 (*1-55971-639-8*, NorthWord Pr) Creat Pub Intl.

My Little Book of Timber Wolves. Hope I. Marston. LC 96-48183. (Illus.). 36p. (Orig.). (J). (ps-5). 1997. pap. 4.95 (*1-55971-582-0*, NorthWord Pr) Creat Pub Intl.

My Little Book of Wood Ducks. Hope I. Marston. LC 94-40917. (Illus.). 32p. (Orig.). (J). (gr. 1-5). 1995. pap. 6.95 (*1-55971-467-0*, NorthWord Pr) Creat Pub Intl.

My Little Books about the Bible Series: David & Goliath; Joseph's Coat of Many Colors; Noah's Ark; Jonah & the Whale; Prayers & Poems; Daniel in the Lions' Den; The Birth of Jesus; Jesus & the Children; The Miracle of Easter; The Miracles of Jesus; Stories Jesus Told; The Travels of Paul, 12 bks., Set. (Illus.). (J). 1993. pap. 15.48 (*1-56173-716-X*) Pubns Intl Ltd.

My Little Books, Based on Original Stories by Beatrix Potter: Mrs. Tiggy-Winkle; Benjamin Bunny; Jemima Puddle-Duck; Mr. Jeremy Fisher; Two Bad Mice; Peter Rabbit; Pigling Bland; Miss Moppet; The Flopsy Bunnies; Ginger & Pickles; Squirrel Nutkin; Tom Kitten, 12 bks., Set. (Illus.). (J). 1993. pap. 15.48 (*1-56173-498-5*) Pubns Intl Ltd.

***My Little Box of ABC's: Featuring the Art of MaryJo Koch, 4 vols.** Illus. by MaryJo Koch. 12p. (J). (ps-k). 2000. 7.98 (*0-7651-1746-0*) Smithmark.

***My Little Box of 1 2 3's: Featuring the Art of MaryJo Koch, 4 vols.** MaryJo Koch. (Illus.). 12p. (J). (ps-k). 2000. 7.98 (*0-7651-1747-9*) Smithmark.

My Little Brother. Debi Gliori. LC 91-58748. (Illus.). 32p. (J). (ps up). 1992. 13.95 (*1-56402-079-7*) Candlewick Pr.

My Little Brother. Debi Gliori. LC 91-58748. (Illus.). (J). (ps up). 1995. pap. 4.99 (*1-56402-455-5*) Candlewick Pr.

My Little Brother. Debi Gliori. 1995. 10.19 (*0-606-08829-6*, Pub. by Turtleback) Demco.

My Little Brother Ben see Mi Hermanito Ben

My Little Brother Ben. Karen Cogan. (Books for Young Learners). (Illus.). 12p. (J). (gr. k-2). 1999. pap. text 5.00 (*1-57274-142-2*) R Owen Pubs.

My Little Cancer. J. Astrop. (Little Stars Ser.). (Illus.). 64p. 1994. pap. 5.95 (*1-85230-540-1*, Pub. by Element MA) Penguin Putnam.

My Little Capricorn. J. Astrop. (Little Stars Ser.). (Illus.). 64p. 1984. pap. 5.95 (*1-85230-546-0*, Pub. by Element MA) Penguin Putnam.

My Little Christmas Books: Rudolph's Adventure; Frosty's Snowy Day; Santa Claus Is Coming to Town; Twas the Night Before Christmas; The Nutcracker; The Little Drummer Boy, 6 bks., Set. (Illus.). (J). 1993. pap. 7.74 (*1-56173-717-8*) Pubns Intl Ltd.

My Little Christmas Calendar: A Flap Book & Lantern. Mark Water. (Illus.). 14p. (J). (ps-2). 1995. pap. 8.99 (*0-8499-5100-3*) Word Pub.

My Little Christmas Pop-Up Book. Carol Gildar. (Illus.). 12p. (J). (ps-k). 1994. 6.95 (*0-590-48016-2*, Cartwheel) Scholastic Inc.

My Little Christmas Treasury. Henrietta D. Gambill. 80p. 1999. 7.99 (*0-88486-261-5*) Galahad Bks.

My Little Christmas Treasury, 12 bks., Set. (Illus.). 24p. (J). 1993. boxed set 19.98 (*0-7853-0200-X*) Pubns Intl Ltd.

My Little Christmas Tree: And Other Christmas Bedtime Stories. Chip Davis. LC 98-138707. (J). 1997. 29.95 (*0-9656909-0-3*) American Gramaphone.

My Little Corner of the World. Beth B. Smith. 31p. lib. bdg. write for info. (*1-878096-36-2*, Epigram Pr) Best E TX Pubs.

***My Little Everest: A Story about Dealing with Fear.** Dan Culver. (Illus.). 48p. 2000. 11.95 (*1-55039-105-4*) Sono Nis Pr.

My Little First Bible see Mi Primera Biblia Bolsillo

***My Little Flap Book of Colors, Vol. 1.** Fair Ideal Instructional Staff. LC 99-474916. 1999. 6.95 (*1-56451-223-1*) Ideal School.

***My Little Flap Book of Letters.** INSTRUCTIONAL FAIR Ideal Instructional Fair. 1999. 6.95 (*1-56451-222-3*) Ideal School.

***My Little Flap Book of Shapes.** Fair Ideal Instructional Staff. 1999. 6.95 (*1-56451-220-7*) Ideal School.

***My Little Flip Book of Numbers.** Fair Ideal Instructional Staff. 1999. 6.95 (*1-56451-221-5*) Ideal School.

My Little Fountain of Youth Book. Edita M. Kaye. 1995. pap. text 5.95 (*0-9635150-2-0*) Fntain of Yth.

My Little Friend Goes to a Baseball. Evelyn M. Finnegan. (My Little Friend Ser.). (Illus.). 32p. (J). (gr. k-2). 1997. pap. 8.95 incl. audio (*1-890453-05-6*) Little Frnd.

My Little Friend Goes to a Baseball Game. Evelyn M. Finnegan. LC 94-96099. (Illus.). 32p. (J). (ps-3). 1995. 14.95 (*0-9641285-0-0*) Little Frnd.

My Little Friend Goes to a Baseball Game. Evelyn M. Finnegan. LC 94-96099. (My Little Friend Ser.). (Illus.). 32p. (J). (ps-3). 1997. pap. 6.95 (*0-9641285-9-4*) Little Frnd.

My Little Friend Goes to a Baseball Game. 2nd ed. Evelyn M. Finnegan. LC 94-96099. (Illus.). 32p. (J). (gr. k-2). 1994. reprint ed. pap. 11.95 incl. audio (*1-890453-09-9*) Little Frnd.

My Little Friend Goes to School. Evelyn M. Finnegan. LC 96-75797. (My Little Friend Ser.). (Illus.). 32p. (J). (ps-3). 1996. 14.95 (*0-9641285-3-5*); pap. 6.95 (*0-9641285-6-X*) Little Frnd.

My Little Friend Goes to School. Evelyn M. Finnegan. (My Little Friend Ser.). (Illus.). 32p. (J). (gr. k-2). 1997. pap. 8.95 incl. audio (*1-890453-07-2*) Little Frnd.

My Little Friend Goes to the Dentist. Evelyn M. Finnegan. LC 95-77741. (My Little Friend Ser.). (Illus.). 32p. (J). (ps-3). 1995. 14.95 (*0-9641285-1-9*) Little Frnd.

My Little Friend Goes to the Dentist. Evelyn M. Finnegan. (My Little Friend Ser.). (Illus.). 32p. (J). (ps-3). 1997. pap. 6.95 (*1-890453-00-5*) Little Frnd.

My Little Friend Goes to the Dentist. Evelyn M. Finnegan. (My Little Friend Ser.). (Illus.). 32p. (J). (gr. k-2). 1997. pap. 8.95 incl. audio (*1-890453-06-4*) Little Frnd.

M

An Asterisk (*) at the beginning of an entry indicates that the title is appearing for the first time.

M

My Little Friend Goes to the Dentist. 2nd ed. Evelyn M. Finnegan. LC 95-77741. (Illus.). 32p. (J). (gr. k-2). 1995. reprint ed. pap. 11.95 incl. audio (1-890453-10-2) Little Frnd.

My Little Friend Goes to the Zoo. Evelyn M. Finnegan. (My Little Friend Ser.). (Illus.). 32p. (J). (gr. k-2). 1997. pap. 8.95 incl. audio (1-890453-08-0) Little Frnd.

My Little Friend Goes to the Zoo. Evelyn M. Finnegan. LC 97-71682. (My Little Friend Ser.). (Illus.). 32p. (J). (gr. k-3). 1998. pap. 6.95 (1-890453-03-X) Little Frnd.

My Little Friend Goes to the Zoo. Evelyn M. Finnegan. LC 97-71682. (My Little Friend Ser.). (Illus.). 32p. (J). (ps-2). 1998. 14.95 (1-890453-02-1); pap. 11.95 incl. audio (1-890453-12-9) Little Frnd.

My Little Friends Goes to School. 2nd ed. Evelyn M. Finnegan. LC 96-75797. (Illus.). 32p. (J). (ps-2). 1996. reprint ed. pap. 11.95 incl. audio (1-890453-11-0) Little Frnd.

My Little Gemini. J. Astrop. (Little Stars Ser.). (Illus.). 64p. 1994. pap. 5.95 (1-85230-539-8, Pub. by Element MA) Penguin Putnam.

My Little Golden Storybook about God. Jane W. Watson. (J). 1997. 3.99 (0-307-16141-2, 16141, Goldn Books) Gldn Bks Pub Co.

My Little Guardian Storybook. Edie C. Benchabbat et al. (Illus.). 28p. (J). (ps-5). Date not set. pap. 5.99 (0-9660879-0-9) Little Guardians.

My Little Hanukkah Pop-Up Book. Carol Gildar. (Illus.). 12p. (J). (ps-k). 1994. 6.95 (0-590-48017-0, Cartwheel) Scholastic Inc.

My Little House Birthday Book. Laura Ingalls Wilder. (Illus.). 40p. (J). (gr. 3-7). 1997. 7.95 (0-694-00875-3, HarpFestival) HarpC Child Bks.

My Little House Book & Diary Set. Laura Ingalls Wilder. (Illus.). (J). (gr. 3-7). 1999. 14.95 (0-694-01253-X) HarpC Child Bks.

My Little House Book of Animals. Laura Ingalls Wilder. LC PZ7.W6461Myb 1998. (My First Little House Baby Bks.). (Illus.). (J). (ps). 1998. lib. bdg. write for info. (0-06-025993-0) HarpC Child Bks.

My Little House Book of Family. Laura Ingalls Wilder. LC PZ7.W6461Myf 1998. (My First Little House Baby Bks.). (Illus.). (J). (ps). 1998. lib. bdg. write for info. (0-06-025989-2) HarpC Child Bks.

My Little House Chapter Book Boxed Set: Animal Adventures; School Days; Pioneer Sisters; The Adventures of Laura & Jack, 4 bks. Laura Ingalls Wilder. (Little House Chapter Bks.). (Illus.). (J). (gr. 2-5). 1998. pap. 16.95 (0-06-449438-1) HarpC Child Bks.

My Little House Christmas Crafts Book. Carolyn Strom Collins et al. LC TT900.C4M93 1997. (Illus.). 48p. (J). (gr. 3 up). 1997. 9.95 (0-694-01016-2, HarpFestival) HarpC Child Bks.

My Little House Cookbook. Laura Ingalls Wilder. LC 94-48529. (Illus.). 32p. (J). (ps-3). 1996. 12.95 (0-06-024296-5) HarpC Child Bks.

***My Little House Crafts Book: 18 Projects from Laura Ingalls Wilder's Little House Stories.** Carolyn Strom Collins & Christina Wyss Eriksson. LC TT160.C643 1998. (Illus.). 64p. (J). (gr. 3 up). 1998. pap. 9.95 (0-06-446204-8, HarpTrophy) HarpC Child Bks.

My Little House Crafts Book: 18 Projects from Laura Ingalls Wilder's Little House Stories. Carolyn Strom Collins. 1998. 14.05 (0-606-13635-5, Pub. by Turtleback) Demco.

My Little House Diary. Illus. by Pat Schories. 160p. (J). (gr. 4-7). 1995. 12.95 (0-694-00697-1) HarpC Child Bks.

My Little House Sewing Book: 8 Projects form Laura Ingalls Wilder's Classic Stories. Margaret E. Irwin. LC 97-107314. (Illus.). 64p. (J). (gr. 3-7). 1997. 10.95 (0-694-00903-2, HarpFestival) HarpC Child Bks.

My Little House Sticker Book: A Day in the Big Woods. Laura Ingalls Wilder. (Illus.). 6p. (J). (ps-3). 1996. 7.95 (0-694-00749-8, HarpFestival) HarpC Child Bks.

My Little Huggy Pup. Sanduik Bokforlag. (Illus.). (J). 1997. 5.99 (1-58048-015-2) Sandvik Pub.

My Little International Christmas Book. Larry W. Smith. 94p. 1997. pap. 5.95 (1-57914-010-6) Campbell-Smith.

My Little Island. Frane Lessac. LC 84-48355. (Illus.). 48p. (J). (gr. 1-4). 1985. 14.00 (0-397-32114-7); lib. bdg. 15.89 (0-397-32115-5) HarpC Child Bks.

My Little Island. Frane Lessac. LC 84-48355. (Trophy Picture Bk.). (Illus.). 48p. (J). (gr. 1-4). 1987. reprint ed. pap. 5.95 (0-06-443146-0, HarpTrophy) HarpC Child Bks.

My Little Leo. J. Astrop. (Little Stars Ser.). (Illus.). 64p. 1994. pap. 5.95 (1-85230-541-X, Pub. by Element MA) Penguin Putnam.

My Little Libra. J. Astrop. (Little Stars Ser.). (Illus.). 64p. 1994. pap. 5.95 (1-85230-543-6, Pub. by Element MA) Penguin Putnam.

***My Little Little Golden Book Holiday Pack.** Golden Books Publishing Company Staff. 1999. 24.99 (0-307-10706-X) Gldn Bks Pub Co.

My Little Memory Verses. Stephanie M. Britt. (My Little Bible Ser.). (Illus.). 98p. (J). (ps-k). 1994. 5.99 (0-8499-1140-0) Tommy Nelson.

My Little Ole Pickup Truck: (And Other Thoughts about Women) 81p. 1998. spiral bd. 8.85 (0-9661787-1-8) Hermits Cave.

***My Little One.** Flavia Weedn. (Illus.). 26p. (J). (ps). 1999. bds. 7.95 (0-7683-2066-6) CEDCO Pub.

***My Little One: With Child...** Linda Randall Wisdom. (American Romance Ser.: Bk. 831). 2000. per. 4.25 (0-373-16831-4, 1-16831-9) Harlequin Bks.

My Little People Farm. Doris Tomaselli. (Fisher-Price Lift the Flap Bks.). (Illus.). 10p. (J). (gr. k-3). 1997. bds. 7.99 (1-57584-188-6, Pub. by Rdrs Digest) Random.

***My Little People Safari, 4 bks.** Mutt Singer & Matt Mitter. (Fisher-Price Sidesqueakers Ser.). (Illus.). 14p. (J). (ps-k). 2000. bds. write for info. (1-57584-661-6, Pub. by Rdrs Digest) S&S Trade.

My Little People School Bus: A Lift-the-Flap Playbook. Fisher-Price Staff & Doris Tomaselli. (Fisher-Price Lift the Flap Bks.). (Illus.). 10p. (J). (gr. k-3). 1997. bds. 7.99 (1-57584-184-3, Pub. by Rdrs Digest) Random.

***My Little People Town.** Ellen Weiss. (Lift-the-Flap Playbook Ser.). (Illus.). 10p. (J). (ps-k). 2000. bds. 7.99 (1-57584-424-9) Rdrs Digest.

My Little Pisces. J. Astrop. (Little Stars Ser.). (Illus.). 64p. 1994. pap. 5.95 (1-85230-548-7, Pub. by Element MA) Penguin Putnam.

My Little Prayers. Stephanie M. Britt. LC 93-578. (My Little Bible Ser.). (Illus.). 98p. (J). (ps-k). 1995. 5.99 (0-8499-1064-1) Tommy Nelson.

My Little Promise Bible. Linda J. Sattgast. LC 95-179256. 96p. (J). 1994. 6.99 (0-88070-697-X, Gold n Honey) Zondervan.

My Little Psalms. Stephanie M. Britt. LC 95-1446. (My Little Bible Ser.). (Illus.). 98p. (J). (ps-k). 1995. 5.99 (0-8499-1193-1) Tommy Nelson.

My Little Red Kite Vol. 8: Pasitos English Language Development Books. Darlyne F. Schott. (Pasitos Hacia la Lectura Ser.). 11p. (J). (gr. k-1). 1990. pap. text 11.50 (1-56537-067-8) D F Schott Educ.

***My Little Red Toolbox.** Stephen T. Johnson. (Illus.). 14p. (J). (ps-3). 2000. 16.90 (0-15-202154-X, Harcourt Child Bks) Harcourt.

***My Little Red Wagon: Radio Flyer Memories, 1.** Roberto Pasini & Paul Pasin. LC 99-31516. 1999. pap. 18.95 (0-7407-0044-8) Andrews & McMeel.

My Little Sagittarius. J. Astrop. (Little Stars Ser.). (Illus.). 64p. 1994. pap. 5.95 (1-85230-545-2, Pub. by Element MA) Penguin Putnam.

My Little Scorpio. J. Astrop. (Little Stars Ser.). (Illus.). 64p. 1994. pap. 5.95 (1-85230-544-4, Pub. by Element MA) Penguin Putnam.

My Little Siddur. Azriel Dvir & Mazal Mashat. 68p. (J). 8.95 (0-915361-87-6) Lambda Pubs.

My Little Sister & Selected Poems. Abba Kovner. Tr. & Pref. by Shirley Kaufman. LC 85-73146. (Field Translation Ser.: No. 11). 159p. (C). 1986. 13.50 (0-932440-20-7); pap. 7.95 (0-932440-21-5) Oberlin Coll Pr.

My Little Sister Ate One Hare. Bill Grossman. LC 95-7539. (Illus.). (J). 1996. 17.00 (0-517-59600-8, Crown); lib. bdg. 18.99 (0-517-59601-6, Crown) Crown Pub Group.

My Little Sister Ate One Hare. Bill Grossman. (J). (ps-3). 1998. pap. 6.99 (0-517-88576-X, Crown) Crown Pub Group.

My Little Sister Hugged an Ape. Bill Grossman. 1999. 17.00 (0-517-80017-9); lib. bdg. 18.99 (0-517-80018-7) Random Hse Value.

My Little Sticker Album. Phyllis Marner. (Illus.). (J). 1991. pap. text 1.00 (0-486-26624-9) Dover.

My Little Storybook. Helen Bramos & Ann S. Bramos. (Illus.). 63p. (Orig.). (J). (gr. k-7). 1992. pap. 7.00 (0-9635333-0-4) A S Bramos.

My Little Supermarket. Caroline Repchuk. LC 96-42691. (Illus.). 1996. 12.95 (0-7613-0145-3) Millbrook Pr.

My Little Taurus. J. Astrop. (Little Stars Ser.). (Illus.). 64p. 1994. pap. 5.95 (1-85230-538-X, Pub. by Element MA) Penguin Putnam.

My Little Teddy Bear. Tony Geiss. (Jewelry Board Bks.). (Illus.). 8p. (J). (ps up). 1994. 4.99 (0-679-85860-1, Pub. by Random Bks Yng Read) Random.

***My Little Treasures.** Havoc Publishing Staff. 1999. 8.00 (1-57977-624-8) Havoc Pub.

My Little Treasury of Stories & Rhymes. Friedman-Fairfax Publishing Staff. 1998. pap. text 9.98 (1-56799-671-X, Friedman-Fairfax) M Friedman Pub Grp Inc.

My Little Troll Tales Series: The Enchanted Frog; The Sword & the Troll; Magic Hair; The Princess Troll; Lucky Rainbow; The Littlest Troll, 6 bks., Set. (Illus.). (J). 1993. pap. 7.74 (0-7853-0033-3) Pubns Intl Ltd.

My Little Unicorn. Tony Geiss. (Jewelry Board Bks.). (Illus.). 8p. (J). (ps up). 1994. 4.99 (0-679-85859-8, Pub. by Random Bks Yng Read) Random.

My Little Virgo. J. Astrop. (Little Stars Ser.). (Illus.). 64p. 1994. pap. 5.95 (1-85230-542-8, Pub. by Element MA) Penguin Putnam.

My Little World Book, Vol. 4. Judy Mohr-Stephens. Ed. by Evelyn Riegert. (Please Understand Us Ser.). (Illus.). 500p. 1990. student ed. write for info. (0-935323-04-X) Barrington Hse.

My Little World Book, Vol. 5. Judy Mohr-Stephens. Ed. by Evelyn Riegert. (Please Understand Us Ser.). (Illus.). 500p. 1990. teacher ed. write for info. (0-935323-05-8) Barrington Hse.

My Little World Book, Vol. 6. Judy Mohr-Stephens. Ed. by Evelyn Riegert. (Please Understand Us Ser.). (Illus.). 500p. 1990. write for info. incl. audio (0-935323-06-6) Barrington Hse.

My Little World Book, Vol. 7. Judy Mohr-Stephens. Ed. by Evelyn Riegert. (Please Understand Us Ser.). (Illus.). 500p. 1990. teacher ed. write for info. (0-935323-07-4) Barrington Hse.

My Little World Book, Vol. 8. rev. ed. Judy Mohr-Stephens. Ed. by Evelyn Riegert. (Please Understand Us Ser.). (Illus.). 500p. 1990. teacher ed. write for info. (0-935323-08-2) Barrington Hse.

My Little World Book, Vol. 9. rev. ed. Judy Mohr-Stephens. Ed. by Evelyn Riegert. (Please Understand Us Ser.). (Illus.). 500p. 1990. student ed. write for info. (0-935323-09-0) Barrington Hse.

My Little World Book, Vol. 10, Bk. 1: Text. Judy Mohr-Stephens. Ed. by Evelyn Riegert. (Please Understand Us Ser.). (Illus.). 1990. write for info. (0-935323-10-4) Barrington Hse.

My Little World Book, Vol. 11: Teacher's Tips. Judy Mohr-Stephens. Ed. by Evelyn Riegert. (Please Understand Us Ser.). (Illus.). 1990. write for info. (0-935323-11-2) Barrington Hse.

My Little World Book, Vol. 12: Teacher's Tips. Judy Mohr-Stephens. Ed. by Evelyn Riegert. (Please Understand Us Ser.). (Illus.). 1990. write for info. (0-935323-12-0) Barrington Hse.

My Little World Book, Vol. 13, Bk. 2: Text. Judy Mohr-Stephens. Ed. by Evelyn Riegert. (Please Understand Us Ser.). (Illus.). 1990. write for info. (0-935323-13-9) Barrington Hse.

My Little World Book, Vol. 14, Bk. 2: Teacher's Tips. Judy Mohr-Stephens. Ed. by Evelyn Riegert. (Please Understand Us Ser.). (Illus.). 1990. write for info. (0-935323-14-7) Barrington Hse.

My Little World Book, Vol. 15, Bk. 2: Role Plays. Judy Mohr-Stephens. Ed. by Evelyn Riegert. (Please Understand Us Ser.). (Illus.). 1990. write for info. (0-935323-15-5) Barrington Hse.

My Lives & How I Lost Them. Christopher Cat & Countee Cullen. LC 92-46738. (Illus.). 174p. (J). (gr. 3-5). 1993. pap. 7.95 (0-8136-7209-0) Silver Burdett Pr.

My Lives Between Hitler & Stalin. George Lewens. (Illus.). 160p. (Orig.). 1992. pap. 12.95 (0-9631336-0-8) Lewens Pub.

My Lomzynskie Dzieci. Jan Dobkowski. (POL., Illus.). 360p. (Orig.). 1992. pap. text 14.95 (0-930401-52-2) Artex Pub.

My Lone Star Summer. D. Anne Love. 192p. (J). (gr. 7-12). 1996. 15.95 (0-8234-1235-0) Holiday.

***My Lone Star Summer.** D. Anne Love. 1998. 9.09 (0-606-13636-3, Pub. by Turtleback) Demco.

My Lone Star Summer. D. Anne Love. 192p. (J). (gr. 4-7). 1998. reprint ed. pap. 3.99 (0-440-41375-3, YB BDD) BDD Bks Young Read.

My Long Island: Growing up on Hal B. Fullerton's Blessed Isle, 1902-1942. Eleanor F. Ferguson. LC 93-84734. (Illus.). xii, 209p. (Orig.). 1993. pap. 24.00 (0-9637126-1-6) Scrub Oak Pr.

My Long Life: An Autobiographic Sketch. Mary C. Clarke. LC 12-31352. 1969. reprint ed. 25.00 (0-403-00105-6) Scholarly.

My Long Life, an Autobiographic Sketch. Mary C. Clarke. (BCL1-PR English Literature Ser.). 276p. 1992. reprint ed. lib. bdg. 79.00 (0-7812-7498-5) Rprt Serv.

My Long Walk with Jesus: The Georgia Benton Story. Linda M. Smith. (Illus.). 86p. 1997. pap. 5.00 (0-9618060-6-0) Sheer Joy Pr.

My Longest Night: A Twelve-Year-Old Heroine's Stirring Account of D-Day & After. Genevieve Duboscq. Tr. by Richard S. Woodward from FRE. LC 94-13980. (Illus.). 304p. 1994. reprint ed. pap. 11.45 (1-55970-277-X, Pub. by Arcade Pub Inc) Time Warner.

My Loop Creek Country Friends. John Kincaid. 145p. 1994. 9.95 (0-941092-29-1) Mtn St Pr.

My Loose Tooth. Stephen Krensky. LC 97-11829. (Step into Reading Ser.: A Step 1 Book). (Illus.). 32p. (J). (ps-1). 1999. lib. bdg. 11.99 (0-679-98847-5, Pub. by Random Bks Yng Read) Random.

My Loose Tooth. Stephen Krensky. LC 97-11829. (Step into Reading Ser.: A Step 1 Book: Vol. 1). (Illus.). 32p. (J). (gr. k-3). 1999. pap. 3.99 (0-679-88847-0, Pub. by Random Bks Yng Read) Random.

My Lord & My God. large type ed. Charles L. Allen. (Large Print Inspirational Ser.). 80p. 1987. pap. 5.95 (0-8027-2588-0) Walker & Co.

My Lord & My God: Essays on Modern Religion, the Bible, & Emanuel Swedenborg. Theodore Pitcairn. (Illus.). 312p. 1967. 7.50 (1-883270-03-0); pap. 5.00 (1-883270-04-9) Swedenborg Assn.

My Lord & My God: Thomas' Incredible Account of Jesus' Resurrection. Calvin Miller. LC 97-44952. (Illus.). (J). 1998. 14.99 (0-7814-3032-1) Chariot Victor.

My Lord & My God: Thomas Meets the Risen Christ. Bert Polman. (Scripture Alive Ser.). 17p. 1998. pap. text 14.95 (1-56212-336-X, 2280-0030) CRC Pubns.

***My Lord Bag of Rice: New & Selected Stories.** Carol Bly. LC 99-47930. 326p. 2000. pap. 16.95 (1-57131-031-2) Milkweed Ed.

My Lord Beaumont. Madris Dupree. (Intrigue Ser.). 1994. per. 3.99 (0-373-28813-1, 1-28813-3) Harlequin Bks.

My Lord Conqueror. Samantha James. 416p. (Orig.). 1995. mass mkt. 5.99 (0-380-77548-4, Avon Bks) Morrow Avon.

***My Lord de Burgh.** Deborah Simmons. (Historical Ser.: Bk. 533). 2000. mass mkt. 4.99 (0-373-29133-7, 1-29133-5) Harlequin Bks.

My Lord Destiny. Eve Byron. 384p. 1999. mass mkt. 5.99 (0-380-80365-8, Avon Bks) Morrow Avon.

My Lord Enemy. large type ed. Joanna Makepeace. (Large Print Ser.). 512p. 1997. 27.99 (0-7089-3670-9) Ulverscroft.

My Lord Footman. Marcy Stewart. 224p. 1995. mass mkt. 3.99 (0-8217-4877-7, Zebra Kensgtn) Kensgtn Pub Corp.

My Lord John. Georgette Heyer. 1998. lib. bdg. 21.95 (1-56723-053-9) Yestermorrow.

My Lord Lion. Rebecca Ward. 192p. (Orig.). 1995. mass mkt. 3.99 (0-380-77804-1, Avon Bks) Morrow Avon.

My Lord Loves a Pure Heart: The Yoga of Divine Virtues. Swami Chidvilasananda. LC 94-14948. 192p. (Orig.). 1994. pap. 12.95 (0-911307-29-X) SYDA Found.

My Lord Murderer. Elizabeth Mansfield. 256p. 1986. mass mkt. 4.50 (0-515-08743-2, Jove) Berkley Pub.

My Lord of Belmont: A Biography of Leo Haid. Paschal M. Baumstein. (Illus.). xxii, 396p. 1995. reprint ed. pap. 18.00 (0-9614976-5-3) Archives Belmont.

My Lord of Belmont: A Biography of Leo Haid. Paschal M. Baumstein. (Illus.). xxii, 396p. 1985. reprint ed. 21.00 (0-9614976-0-2) Archives Belmont.

***My Lord Pirate.** Laura Renken. (Seduction Romance Ser.). 2000. mass mkt. 5.99 (0-515-12984-4, Jove) Berkley Pub.

My Lord Protector. Deborah Hale. (Historical Ser.: No. 452). 1999. per. 4.99 (0-373-29052-7, 1-29052-7) Harlequin Bks.

My Lord Stranger. Eve Byron. 384p. 1999. mass mkt. 5.99 (0-380-80364-X, Avon Bks) Morrow Avon.

My Lord, What a Morning: An Autobiography. Marian Anderson. 312p. reprint ed. lib. bdg. 59.00 (0-685-14834-3) Rprt Serv.

My Lord, You Are Magic. George Goulding. Orig. Title: My Father with the Sweet Name. 81p. (Orig.). 1989. pap. 4.95 (0-9624831-0-9) DeVorss.

***My Lost Dream.** Kim L. Dulaney. (Fuzzy-Feeling Bks.). (J). 1999. pap. 8.25 (1-891636-07-3) Unique Exp.

My Lost Mexico. James A. Michener. LC 92-26953. (Illus.). 176p. 1992. 24.95 (0-938349-93-7) State House Pr.

My Lost Mexico. James A. Michener. 224p. 1993. mass mkt. 4.99 (0-8125-3437-9, Pub. by Tor Bks) St Martin.

My Lost Mexico. limited ed. James A. Michener. LC 92-26953. (Illus.). 176p. 1992. 125.00 (0-938349-94-5) State House Pr.

My Lost World: A Survivor's Tale. Sara Rosen. (Library of Holocaust Testimonies). 320p. 1993. pap. text 19.50 (0-85303-254-8, Pub. by M Vallentine & Co) Intl Spec Bk.

My Louisiana Sky. Kimberly Willis Holt. LC 98-12345. 176p. (YA). (gr. 6-9). 1998. 15.95 (0-8050-5251-8) H Holt & Co.

My Louisiana Sky. Kimberly Willis Holt. 208p. (YA). (gr. 5 up). 4.99 (0-8072-8291-X) Listening Lib.

My Love, a Stranger. large type ed. Renee Shahn. 288p. 1989. 23.95 (0-7451-0936-5, G K Hall Lrg Type) Mac Lib Ref.

***My Love Affair with America: The Cautionary Tale of a Cheerful Conservative.** Norman Podhoretz. LC 99-462225. 256p. 2000. 25.00 (0-7432-0051-9) Free Pr.

My Love Affair with Charles. Frances Hunter. 1971. pap. 5.95 (0-8307-0098-6) Hunter Bks.

My Love Affair with England: A Traveler's Memoir. Susan A. Toth. 336p. 1994. pap. 10.00 (0-345-38565-9) Ballantine Pub Grp.

My Love Affair with the State of Maine. 2nd ed. Scotty Mackenzie & Ruth Goode. LC 97-929. (Illus.). 328p. 1997. reprint ed. pap. 14.95 (0-89272-407-2) Down East.

My Love for Lucy: Real Romance in the 1880s. Ed. by Catherine A. Bennett & Robert T. Bennett. (Illus.). 250p. 1998. boxed set 100.00 (0-9601718-4-3) Melrose Plantation.

My Love for You. Donald Pelton. (Illus.). 1984. pap. 5.95 (0-933169-00-0) Heldon Pr.

My Love for You. Susan L. Roth. LC 95-53759. (Illus.). 32p. (J). 1997. 12.99 (0-8037-2031-9, Dial Yng Read) Peng Put Young Read.

My Love for You: Board Book. Susan L. Roth. Ed. by Andra Serlin. LC 99-228243. (Illus.). 24p. (J). (ps). 1999. pap. 5.99 (0-8037-2352-0, Dial Yng Read) Peng Put Young Read.

My Love Has Wings. large type ed. Joan Mandover. (Linford Romance Library). 224p. 1989. pap. 16.99 (0-7089-6688-8, Linford) Ulverscroft.

My Love Is Free: But the Rest of Me Don't Come Cheap. P.S. Wall. 210p. 1999. pap. 11.95 (0-345-42887-0) Ballantine Pub Grp.

***My Love Is Your Love.** Whitney Houston. (Illus.). 2000. pap. 19.95 (0-7692-7734-9) Wrner Bros.

My Love, My Care, My Spouse: A Chronicle of Parkinson's Disease. Eva B. Popper. LC 88-90551. 75p. (Orig.). 1988. pap. text 6.95 (0-945520-09-3) PSGA.

My Love, My Country. Lee Hee-Ho. Tr. by Rhee Tong-Chin from KOR. Orig. Title: Naeui Sarang, Naeui Joguk. 298p. Date not set. 22.95 (1-884445-34-9); pap. 10.95 (1-884445-35-7) C Schlacks Pub.

My Love, My Friend & My Dreams. Gabriela Freitas. LC 93-79491. 1994. 6.95 (0-8158-0495-4) Chris Mass.

My Love, My Friend or the Peasant Girl. Rosa Guy. 128p. 1995. pap. 9.95 (0-8050-1659-7, Owl) H Holt & Co.

My Love Remembers. Betty R. Salls. pap. 1.75 (0-686-12740-4) Grace Pub Co.

My Love You, My Children: One Hundred & One Stories for Children of All Ages. LC 81-9847. (Illus.). 425p. 1981. pap. 17.00 (0-914390-44-9) Fellowship Pr PA.

My Love You, My Children: One Hundred & One Stories for Children of All Ages. M. R. Bawa Muhaiyaddeen. LC 81-9847. (Illus.). 425p. 1981. 23.00 (0-914390-20-1) Fellowship Pr PA.

My Love You My Children: One Hundred & One Stories for Children of All Ages. M. R. Muhaiyaddeen. 475p. (J). 1996. 24.95 (0-614-21036-4, 868) Kazi Pubns.

My Loved One Is Dying. John E. Biegert. (Looking up Ser.). 24p. (Orig.). 1990. pap. 1.95 (0-8298-0846-9) Pilgrim OH.

***My Lovely Executioner.** large type ed. Peter Rabe. (Star Mystery Ser.). 1999. 19.95 (0-7862-2024-4) Five Star.

My Lover & His Half-Leg. Dierdre McKee. 24p. 1993. pap. 5.00 (1-882827-03-1) Insight to Riot.

My Lover Is a Woman: Contemporary Lesbian Love Poems. Lesléa Newman. 240p. 1996. 18.50 (0-345-39483-6) Ballantine Pub Grp.

My Lover is a Woman: Contemporary Lesbian Love Poems. Lesléa Newman. LC 99-90324. 304p. 1999. pap. 12.00 (0-345-42114-0, Ballantine) Ballantine Pub Grp.

***My Lover, Myself: Self-Discovery Through Relationship.** David Kantor. 2000. pap. 12.95 (1-57322-787-0, Riverhd Trade) Berkley Pub.

***My Lover, Myself: Self-Discovery Through Relationship.** David Kantor. LC 98-51090. 336p. 1999. 24.95 (1-57322-140-6, Riverhead Books) Putnam Pub Group.

My Lover's Secret. Jean Barrett. 1999. per. 3.99 (0-373-22528-8, 1-22528-3) Harlequin Bks.

An Asterisk (*) at the beginning of an entry indicates that the title is appearing for the first time.

My Loving Enemy. Lisa A. Verge. Ed. by Linda Marrow. 416p. (Orig.). 1993. mass mkt. 5.50 (*0-671-74073-3*) PB.

***My Loving Familiar.** C. J. Card. (Magical Love Ser.). 2000. mass mkt. 5.99 (*0-515-12728-0*, Jove) Berkley Pub.

My Lucky Face. May-Lee Chai. 272p. 2000. 13.00 (*1-56947-181-9*) Soho Press.

My Lucky Hat. Kevin O'Malley. LC 98-43057. (Illus.). 32p. (J). (gr. 5-9). 1999. 15.95 (*1-57255-710-9*) Mondo Pubng.

My Lucky Lady. Casey Claybourne. 224p. (Orig.). 1994. mass mkt. 4.50 (*0-515-11504-5*, Jove) Berkley Pub.

***My Lucky Penny.** deluxe large type ed. Joseph Scaglione. (Illus.). 64p. (J). (ps-4). 1999. pap. 24.95 incl. cd-rom (*0-9675011-0-5*) New Day Enter.

My Lucky Stars: A Hollywood Memoir. Shirley MacLaine. 400p. 1996. mass mkt. 6.99 (*0-553-57233-4*) Bantam.

My Lucky Stars: A Hollywood Memoir. large type ed. Shirley MacLaine. LC 95-24495. 552p. 1995. 24.95 (*0-7838-1476-3*, G K Hall Lrg Type) Mac Lib Ref.

***My Lungs.** Kathy Furgang. LC 99-88033. (My Body Ser.). (Illus.). (J). 2000. lib. bdg. write for info. (*0-8239-5575-3*) Rosen Group.

My "m" Sound Box. Jane Belk Moncure. LC 78-24458. (Sound Box Library). (Illus.). 32p. (J). (ps-2). 1979. lib. bdg. 21.36 (*0-89565-051-7*) Childs World.

My Magic Alphabet Book. Sally Hewitt. LC 97-72040. (Magic Screen Bks.). 16p. 1998. 12.99 (*0-448-41729-4*, G & D) Peng Put Young Read.

My Magic Numbers Book. Sally Hewitt. LC 97-72042. (Magic Screen Bks.). 16p. (J). (ps-1). 1998. 12.99 (*0-448-41731-6*, G & D) Peng Put Young Read.

My Magic Pours Secret Libations. Monifa A. Love. (Illus.). 80p. (Orig.). 1997. pap. 19.95 (*1-889282-01-4*) FSU Mus Fine Arts.

My Magic Shapes Book. Sally Hewitt. LC 97-72043. (Magic Screen Bks.). 16p. 1998. 12.99 (*0-448-41732-4*, G & D) Peng Put Young Read.

My Magic Time Book. Sally Hewitt. LC 97-72041. (Magic Screen Bks.). 16p. (J). 1998. pap. text 12.99 (*0-448-41730-8*, G & D) Peng Put Young Read.

My Maine Summer. Matthew Rossignol. (Illus.). 120p. (Orig.). 1996. pap. 12.95 (*0-9646054-8-1*) Moosehead Communs.

My Major Is Philosophy, Vol. 2. Canyn L. Whals. (Illus.). 139p. 1985. pap. 9.00 (*0-9610254-1-7*) Walsh Pub Hse.

My Major Is Philosophy: A Student Handbook. Canyn L. Whals. (Illus.). 229p. 1982. pap. 9.00 (*0-9610254-0-9*) Walsh Pub Hse.

My Major Is Philosophy: A Student Handbook, 2 vols., Set. Canyn L. Whals. (Illus.). 229p. 1982. pap. write for info. (*0-9610254-2-5*) Walsh Pub Hse.

My Make Believe Briefcase. Dawn Bentley. (What's Inside? Bks.). (Illus.). (J). (ps-2). 1997. 9.99 (*0-614-28725-1*) NAL.

My Make Believe Purse. Dawn Bentley. (What's Inside? Bks.). (Illus.). (J). (ps-2). 1997. 9.99 (*0-614-28724-3*) NAL.

My Mama. Patricia T. Cousin et al. (Visions: African-American Experiences: No. 19). (Illus.). 8p. (Orig.). (J). (gr. k-1). 1995. pap. text 3.00 (*1-57518-018-9*) Arborlake.

My Mama Always Said . . . Advice - Good & Bad - from Mothers Everywhere. Ed. by Faith Brynie. (Illus.). 112p. 1998. pap. 9.95 (*0-9660944-0-9*) Verity West.

My Mama Had a Dancing Heart. Libba M. Gray. LC 94-48802. (Illus.). 32p. (J). (ps-3). 1996. 15.95 (*0-531-09470-7*); lib. bdg. 16.99 (*0-531-08770-0*) Orchard Bks Watts.

***My Mama Had a Dancing Heart.** Libba Moore Gray. LC 94-48802. (Illus.). 32p. (J). (ps-3). 1999. pap. 5.95 (*0-531-07142-1*) Orchard Bks Watts.

My Mama Says There Aren't Any Zombies, Ghosts, Vampires, Creatures, Demons, Monsters, Fiends, Goblins, or Things. Judith Viorst. LC 73-76331. (Illus.). 48p. (J). (gr. k-4). 1973. 16.00 (*0-689-30102-2*) Atheneum Yung Read.

My Mama Says There Aren't Any Zombies, Ghosts, Vampires, Creatures, Demons, Monsters, Fiends, Goblins, or Things. 2nd ed. Judith Viorst. LC 87-18733. (Illus.). 48p. (J). (gr. k-4). 1987. reprint ed. mass mkt. 5.99 (*0-689-71204-9*) Aladdin.

My Mama's Dead Squirrel: Lesbian Essays on Southern Culture. Mab Segrest. LC 85-20534. 240p. (Orig.). 1985. pap. 9.95 (*0-932379-06-0*); lib. bdg. 20.95 (*0-932379-07-9*) Firebrand Bks.

My Mama's Little Ranch on the Pampas. Maria C. Brusca. LC 93-28113. (J). 1995. 15.95 (*0-8050-2782-3*) H Holt & Co.

My Mama's Waltz: A Book for Daughters of Alcoholic Mothers. Eleanor Agnew & Sharon Robideaux. LC 98-150433. 336p. 1998. 24.00 (*0-671-01385-8*, PB Hardcover) PB.

My Mama's Waltz: A Book for Daughters of Alcoholic Mothers. Eleanor Agnew & Sharon Robideaux. 336p. 1999. pap. 14.00 (*0-671-01386-6*, PB Trade Paper) PB.

***My Man Blue: Poems.** Nikki Grimes. LC 98-28229. (Illus.). (J). 1999. lib. bdg. 15.89 (*0-8037-2328-8*, Dial Yng Read) Peng Put Young Read.

My Man Blue: Poems. Nikki Grimes. Ed. by Toby Sherry. LC 98-28229. (Illus.). 32p. (J). (gr. 1 up). 1999. 15.99 (*0-8037-2326-1*, Dial Yng Read) Peng Put Young Read.

My Man Pendleton. Elizabeth Bevarly. 384p. 1998. mass mkt. 5.99 (*0-380-80019-5*, Avon Bks) Morrow Avon.

My Manhattan. Conger Beasley, Jr. 96p. (Orig.). 1986. pap. 3.95 (*0-9617499-0-3*) Woods Colt Pr.

My Many Colored Days. Dr. Seuss, pseud. LC 95-18893. (Illus.). 40p. (J). (ps-3). 1996. 16.00 (*0-679-87597-2*) Knopf.

My Many Colored Days. Dr. Seuss, pseud. (Illus.). 40p. (J). (ps). 1998. 6.99 (*0-679-89344-X*) Knopf.

My Many Colored Days. Dr. Seuss, pseud. (Illus.). 40p. (J). 1996. lib. bdg. 17.99 (*0-679-97597-7*) Random.

My Many Faces. Kathy Robinson. Date not set. per. 16.00 (*0-9673326-0-5*) K L Robinson.

***My Many Hats.** Nancy I. Sanders. (Soft Tabs Bk.). (Illus.). 10p. (J). 2000. write for info. (*1-57584-705-1*, Pub. by Rdrs Digest) S&S Trade.

My Many Lives. Lotte Lehmann. Tr. by Frances Holden from GER. LC 74-3689. (Illus.). 262p. 1975. reprint ed. lib. bdg. 38.50 (*0-8371-7361-2*, LEML, Greenwood Pr) Greenwood.

My Many Lives. Lotte Lehmann. (American Autobiography Ser.). 262p. 1995. reprint ed. lib. bdg. 79.00 (*0-7812-8576-3*) Rprt Serv.

My Many Lives: Music Book Index. Lotte Lehmann. 262p. 1993. reprint ed. lib. bdg. 79.00 (*0-7812-9633-1*) Rprt Serv.

My March Journal. Alana Trisler & Patrice Cardiel. 48p. (J). (gr. 1-2). 1999. pap., wbk. ed. 1.75 (*1-56762-101-5*) Modern Learn Pr.

My Mariah. Jean Wilson. (Zebra Bks.). 352p. 1998. mass mkt. 4.99 (*0-8217-6044-0*, Zebra Kensgtn) Kensgtn Pub Corp.

My Mark Twain. William Dean Howells. LC 76-53025. (Studies in Mark Twain: No. 76). 1977. lib. bdg. 75.00 (*0-8383-2176-3*) M S G Haskell Hse.

My Mark Twain. William Dean Howells. LC 96-39016. (Illus.). 192p. 1997. reprint ed. pap. text 7.95 (*0-486-29640-7*) Dover.

My Mark Twain. William Dean Howells. (Notable American Authors Ser.). 1992. reprint ed. lib. bdg. 75.00 (*0-7812-3282-1*) Rprt Serv.

My Mark Twain: Reminiscences & Criticisms. William Dean Howells. (BCL1-PS American Literature Ser.). 186p. 1992. reprint ed. lib. bdg. 69.00 (*0-7812-6690-4*) Rprt Serv.

My Mary-Kate & Ashley Diary: For All My Words. Harper Entertainment Staff. (Illus.). 128p. (gr. 2-7). 1999. 12.99 (*0-06-107567-1*, Pub. by Harper SF) HarpC.

***My Mask Is, Prison Poems & Stories by Women.** Ed. by Deborah Kilgore. (Illus.). 30p. 1999. 3.00 (*1-888431-23-7*) ASGP.

My Mass see Learning My Prayers

My Mass & Holy Communion Book, Black Ed., Boys. Ed. by Jeannette Gojny. (Illus.). 128p. (J). (gr. 2-3). 1996. text 3.70 (*1-888765-01-1*) Devon Trading.

My Mass & Holy Communion Book, Boys Ed. deluxe ed. Ed. by Jeannette Gojny. (Illus.). 128p. (J). (gr. 2-3). 1996. 8.95 (*1-888765-05-4*) Devon Trading.

My Mass & Holy Communion Book, Full Color Ed., Boys. Ed. by Jeannette Gojny. (Illus.). 128p. (J). (gr. 2-3). 1996. 5.95 (*1-888765-03-8*) Devon Trading.

My Mass & Holy Communion Book, Full Color Ed., Girls. Ed. by Jeannette Gojny. (Illus.). 128p. (J). (gr. 2-3). 1996. 5.95 (*1-888765-02-X*) Devon Trading.

My Mass & Holy Communion Book, Girls Ed. deluxe ed. Ed. by Jeannette Gojny. (Illus.). 128p. (J). (gr. 2-3). 1996. 8.95 (*1-888765-04-6*) Devon Trading.

My Mass & Holy Communion Book, White Ed., Girls. Ed. by Jeannette Gojny. (Illus.). 128p. (J). (gr. 2-3). 1996. text 3.70 (*1-888765-00-3*) Devon Trading.

My Mass & Holy Communion Book: Boys Edition. alternate ed. Ed. by Jeanette Gojoy. (Illus.). 128p. (J). (gr. 2-3). 1996. text 6.50 (*1-888765-11-9*) Devon Trading.

My Mass & Holy Communion Book: Girls Edition. alternate ed. Ed. by Jeanette Gojoy. (Illus.). 128p. (J). (gr. 2-3). 1996. text 6.50 (*1-888765-10-0*) Devon Trading.

My Mass & Holy Communion Book: Mother of Pearl, Boy. Ed. by Jeannette Gojny. (Illus.). 128p. (J). (gr. 2-3). 1996. im. lthr. 18.50 (*1-888765-07-0*) Devon Trading.

My Mass & Holy Communion Book: Mother of Pearl, Girl. Ed. by Jeannette Gojny. (Illus.). 128p. (J). (gr. 2-3). 1996. im. lthr. 18.50 (*1-888765-06-2*) Devon Trading.

My Mass & Holy Communion Book: With Silver Medallion. Ed. by Jeanette Gojny. (Illus.). 128p. (gr. 2-3). 1996. text 22.95 (*1-888765-08-9*) Devon Trading.

My Mass & Holy Communion Book: With Silver Medallion. Ed. by Jeanette Gojny. (Illus.). 128p. (J). (gr. 2-3). 1996. text 22.95 (*1-888765-09-7*) Devon Trading.

My Mass Book. (J). Date not set. 1.50 (*0-88271-542-9*, 10356) Regina Pr.

My Mass Book. 1998. 3.95 (*0-88271-629-8*) Regina Pr.

My Mass Book. (Illus.). 79p. (J). (gr. 1-3). 1997. reprint ed. 14.00 (*0-911845-65-8*) Neumann Pr.

My Master. Parthasarathi Rajagopalachari. 184p. 1989. reprint ed. 10.00 (*0-945242-12-3*) Shri Ram Chandra.

My Master: The Inside Story of Sam Houston & His Times by His Former Slave Jeff Hamilton. Jeffrey Hamilton. LC 92-4923. (Illus.). 165p. 1992. 24.95 (*0-938349-84-8*) State House Pr.

My Master: The Inside Story of Sam Houston & His Times by His Former Slave Jeff Hamilton. limited ed. Jeffrey Hamilton. LC 92-4923. (Illus.). 165p. 1992. 60.00 (*0-938349-85-6*) State House Pr.

My Master Is My Self: The Birth of a Spiritual Teacher. 2nd ed. Andrew Cohen. LC 95-75484. 103p. 1995. pap. 10.95 (*1-883929-07-5*) Moksha Pr.

***My Master Mariner.** large type ed. Judith Saxton. 336p. 1999. pap. 20.99 (*1-85389-884-8*, Dales) Ulverscroft.

My Master's Touch: A Heartwarming Tale of Love, Loyalty, & Devotion. Lynda Nelson. LC 97-51820. (Illus.). 120p. (J). 1998. 13.00 (*0-399-52443-6*, Perigee Bks) Berkley Pub.

My Math Fact Booklet. Ella D. Davis. 14p. (J). (gr. k-6). 1992. pap. text 12.95 (*1-888185-51-1*) Davis Pubng LA.

My Maui. Gordon Morse. pap. 9.95 (*1-885129-09-2*) My Island.

My May Journal. Alana Trisler & Patrice Cardiel. 48p. (J). (gr. 1-2). 1999. pap., wbk. ed. 1.75 (*1-56762-103-1*) Modern Learn Pr.

My Meadow. Margaret H. Morris. (Illus.). 144p. (Orig.). 1996. pap. 14.95 (*0-9632687-6-7*) PenRose Pub.

My Mechanicsburg in the Thirties. Josephine F. Collitt. 34p. (Orig.). 1995. pap. 6.00 (*0-9648441-1-7*) J F Collitt.

***My Medical Records.** Sandrajeanne Bushell. 208p. 1999. ring bd. 25.00 (*1-58499-003-1*, 150) Full Spectrums.

My Meeting with the Masters on Mount Shasta. 2nd rev. ed. Nola Van Valer. 144p. 1994. pap. 7.95 (*0-9641571-0-1*) Seekers & Servers.

My Melungeon Heritage: A Story of Life on Newman's Ridge. Mattie R. Johnson. LC 97-205604. (Illus.). xii, 156p. 1997. pap. 12.95 (*1-57072-063-0*) Overmountain Pr.

My Memoir. Edith B. Wilson. Ed. by Annette K. Baxter. LC 79-8824. (Signal Lives Ser.). (Illus.). 1980. reprint ed. lib. bdg. 48.95 (*0-405-12868-1*) Ayer.

My Memoir, in Chinese: Sorting Out Chinese Writings of the Ever-Green House. John Kiang. 315p. (Orig.). 1996. pap. 14.95 (*0-916301-08-7*) One World Pub.

My Memoirs. Marguerite Steinheil. 1976. lib. bdg. 49.95 (*0-8490-2310-6*) Gordon Pr.

My Memoirs, 2 vols. Alfred P. Von Tirpitz. LC 77-111779. reprint ed. 65.00 (*0-404-06464-7*) AMS Pr.

My Memoirs of World War Two. Nicholas G. Myers. Ed. by Paul N. Harris. (Illus.). 144p. (Orig.). 1988. pap. 8.95 (*0-915180-31-6*) Harrowood Bks.

My Memorial. Nona Freeman. Ed. by Nell Perry. 335p. 1989. pap. 6.00 (*1-878366-02-5*) Nonas Bk Sales.

My Memories of Eighty Years. Chauncey M. Depew. (American Biography Ser.). 417p. 1991. reprint ed. lib. bdg. 89.00 (*0-7812-8106-7*) Rprt Serv.

My Memory Book: A Journal for Grieving Children. 2nd ed. Gretchen G. Lane. 68p. (J). (ps-13). 1997. pap., wbk. ed. 10.95 (*1-888493-12-7*) Chi Rho Pr.

My Memory Book: A Personal Yearbook. Tom Wilson. (Illus.). 104p. 1999. 9.95 (*0-8362-2059-5*) Andrews & McMeel.

My Memory Box Journal. Lory M. Goetsch. (J). 1998. spiral bd. 19.95 (*0-9663436-0-3*) Grote Publ.

My Merry Christmas Arch Book: Luke 2: 1-20. (Arch Bks.). (J). (ps-4). 1996. 1.99 (*0-570-07515-7*, 59-1488) Concordia.

My Merry Christmas Songbook. rev. ed. (Illus.). 24p. (J). (ps-3). 1995. pap. 2.49 (*1-57102-077-2*, Ideals Child) Hambleton-Hill.

My Merry Mornings: Stories from Prague. Ivan Klima. Tr. by George Theiner from CZE. LC 85-181206. (Illus.). 156p. (C). 1985. pap. 14.95 (*0-930523-05-9*) Readers Intl.

My Messy Bedroom: Love & Sex in the 90s. Josey Vogels. 160p. (Orig.). 1995. pap. 13.95 (*1-55065-064-5*, Pub. by Vehicule Pr) LPC Group.

My Messy Room. Mary Packard. LC 92-36006. (Illus.). 32p. (J). 1993. pap. 3.95 (*0-590-46191-5*) Scholastic Inc.

My Method. Emile Coue. 97p. 1983. pap. 10.00 (*0-89540-147-9*, SB-147) Sun Pub.

My Method: Including American Impressions. Emile Cove. 221p. 1996. reprint ed. pap. 19.95 (*1-56459-622-2*) Kessinger Pub.

My Method: Writings & Interviews. Roberto Rossellini. 256p. 1995. pap. 12.95 (*0-941419-65-7*) Marsilio Pubs.

My Method: Writings & Interviews. Roberto Rossellini. Tr. by Annapaola Cancogni from ITA. LC 92-82645. (Illus.). 256p. 1995. 24.00 (*0-941419-64-9*) Marsilio Pubs.

My Mexico: Half a Lifetime of Culinary Adventures with More Than 300 Recipes. Diana Kennedy. LC 98-9181. (Illus.). 512p. 1998. 35.00 (*0-609-60247-0*) C Potter.

My Mexico - Mexico Mio. Tony Johnston. LC 91-12180. (Illus.). 36p. (J). (ps-3). 1996. 15.95 (*0-399-22275-8*, G P Putnam) Peng Put Young Read.

***My Mexico - Mexico Mio.** Tony Johnston. (Illus.). (J). (gr. k up). 1999. pap. 5.99 (*0-698-11757-3*, PapStar) Peng Put Young Read.

My Michael. Amos Oz. 1999. pap. 7.95 (*0-14-011729-6*, Viking) Viking Penguin.

My Middle-Aged Baby Book: A Record of Milestones, Millstones, & Gallstones. Mary-Lou Weisman. LC 95-19449. (Illus.). 96p. 1995. bds. 12.95 (*1-56305-817-0*, 3817) Workman Pub.

***My Midnight.** Betty Pontes DeOliveira & Eddy Bral. LC 99-91945. 2000. 25.00 (*0-7388-1444-X*); pap. 18.00 (*0-7388-1445-8*) Xlibris Corp.

My Midwest: Rural Writings from the Heartland. Ed. by Philip Martin. LC 99-166309. 160p. 1998. pap. 10.95 (*1-883953-26-X*, Face to Face) Midwest Trad.

***My Miffy.** Dick Bruna. (Illus.). (J). 2000. pap. 10.95 (*1-56836-307-9*) Kodansha.

***My Millennium Memoir: Who I Am, How I Feel, What I Think in the 21st Century.** Christine Tate. 96p. 1999. 14.00 (*0-385-33431-1*) Delacorte.

My Millennium Record Book. D K Publishing Staff. (DK Millennium Ser.). 1999. 9.95 (*0-7894-4713-4*) DK Pub Inc.

My Mind & Its Thoughts, in Sketches, Fragments, & Essays. Sarah W. Morton. LC 74-28388. 336p. 1975. reprint ed. lib. bdg. 50.00 (*0-8201-1150-3*) Schol Facsimiles.

My Mind Is Out to Get Me: Humor & Wisdom in Recovery. Compiled by Ron B. 180p. pap. 6.95 (*1-56838-010-0*) Hazelden.

"My Mind Set on Freedom" A History of the Civil Rights Movement, 1954-1968. John A. Salmond. LC 96-31675. (American Ways Ser.). 192p. 1997. 22.50 (*1-56663-140-8*, Pub. by I R Dee) Natl Bk Netwk.

"My Mind Set on Freedom" A History of the Civil Rights Movement, 1954-1968. John A. Salmond. LC 96-31675. (American Ways Ser.). 192p. 1998. pap. text 12.95 (*1-56663-141-6*, Pub. by I R Dee) Natl Bk Netwk.

***My MindWalks Journal: A Record of Discoveries.** Mary H. Frakes. LC 98-96993. 300p. 1999. pap. 7.95 (*0-9667879-1-9*, MindWalks) Life Lessons.

My Mini ABC's: 24 Bible Alphabet Board Books. Illus. by Jill Dubin. (Read to Me Mommy Ser.). 144p. (J). 1998. bds. 14.99 (*0-8499-5831-8*) Tommy Nelson.

My Miracle Is You. Clinton Weyand. (Illus.). 176p. (Orig.). 1979. 7.95 (*0-938292-08-0*) Being Bks.

My Miracle Manifestation Manual. Jacquelyn Aldana. Ed. by Gillian Sands & Supreme Editing Team Staff. 128p. 1999. pap. 15.95 (*0-9656741-4-2*) Inner Wisdom CA.

My Miscellanies see Works of Wilkie Collins

***My Miserable Mother-in-Law: The Big Nightmare.** D. M. Campbell. 2000. pap. 5.95 (*0-533-13467-6*) Vantage.

My Mission Book: Needful Things. Claudia Kaelin. 95p. 1996. 19.95 (*1-885425-14-7*) Restorat Source.

My Mission to Russia & Other Diplomatic Memories. George Buchanan. LC 78-115510. (Russia Observed, Series I). 1970. reprint ed. 28.95 (*0-405-03008-8*) Ayer.

***My Missionary Book.** Val Bagley. 1999. pap. 3.95 (*1-57734-518-5*, 01114182) Covenant Comms.

My Missions for Revolutionary Bolivia, 1944-1962. Victor Andrade. LC 76-6656. (Pitt Latin American Ser.). 217p. reprint ed. 67.30 (*0-8357-9758-9*, 201786300009) Bks Demand.

***My Mississippi.** Willie Morris. (Illus.). 256p. 2000. 37.00 (*1-57806-193-8*) U Pr of Miss.

***My Mississippi.** limited ed. Willie Morris. (Illus.). 256p. 2000. 100.00 (*1-57806-309-4*) U Pr of Miss.

***My Missouri Garden: A Gardener's Journal.** Cool Springs Press Publications Staff. 2000. 19.95 (*1-888608-90-0*) Cool Springs Pr.

***My Missouri Garden: A Gardener's Journal.** Mike Miller. (Illus.). 128p. 2000. spiral bd. 19.95 (*1-930604-08-4*) Cool Springs Pr.

My Misty Diary. Bill Farnsworth. (Illus.). 160p. (J). (gr. 2-7). 1997. per. 12.95 (*0-689-81769-X*) S&S Trade.

My Moline: An Illegal Immigrant Dreams. John R. Cervantes. LC 86-71156. (Illus.). 192p. 1986. pap. 7.95 (*0-942568-12-5*) Canyon Pub Co.

My Mom see Mi Mama

My Mom see Ma Maman

My Mom. Janet Horowitz & Kathy Faggella. (Photolog Bk.). (Illus.). 48p. (J). (gr. 1-7). 1991. 4.50 (*1-55670-173-X*) Stewart Tabori & Chang.

My Mom Talk About Books, No.5. 5th ed. Debbie Bailey. (Talk-about-Books Ser.: Vol. 5). (Illus.). 14p. (J). (ps-k). 1991. bds. 5.95 (*1-55037-163-0*, Pub. by Annick) Firefly Bks Ltd.

My Mom & Dad Make Me Laugh. Nick Sharratt. 1996. 10.19 (*0-606-08830-X*, Pub. by Turtleback) Demco.

My Mom & Dad Make Me Laugh. Nick Sharrett. LC 93-3558. (Illus.). (J). (ps-3). 1996. pap. 4.99 (*1-56402-580-2*) Candlewick Pr.

My Mom Drives an Electric Car. Abby Yuzenas. Ed. by Steve McCrea. (Illus.). 22p. (J). 1995. pap. text 6.00 (*1-57074-247-2*) Greyden Pr.

***My Mom Has a Bad Temper.** Beverly H. Hopkins. LC 98-47301. (J). 2000. 8.95 (*0-87868-722-X*) Child Welfare.

My Mom Has Cancer. Shari Lichtenstein. (Illus.). 60p. (Orig.). (J). (gr. k-12). 1997. pap. 15.50 (*1-890867-00-4*) Justice Research.

***My Mom Has Hepatitis C.** Hedy Weinberg et al. (Illus.). 30p. (J). (gr. k-7). 2000. 15.95 (*1-57826-075-2*, Pub. by Hatherleigh) Norton.

My Mom Is Different. Deborah Sessions. LC 93-46388. (Illus.). 32p. (Orig.). (J). 1994. pap. 8.95 (*0-9629164-3-9*) Sidran Pr.

My Mom Is Excellent. Nick Butterworth. LC 92-43769. (Illus.). 32p. (J). (ps up). 1994. pap. 4.99 (*1-56402-289-7*) Candlewick Pr.

My Mom Is Magic. H. Roche. LC 99-166958. (Illus.). (J). (ps). 1998. pap. 4.95 (*1-84089-012-6*, 868235Q) Zero to Ten.

My Mom Is My Show-&-Tell. Dolores Johnson. LC 98-8703. (Illus.). 32p. (J). (gr. k-3). 1999. 15.95 (*0-7614-5041-6*, Cav Child Bks) Marshall Cavendish.

My Mom Is Pregnant! Lucinda H. Kennaley. (Illus.). 60p. (Orig.). (J). (ps). 1990. pap. text 9.95 (*0-9628067-0-6*) Thoth MO.

My Mom Loves Me. 16p. (J). 1990. pap. write for info. (*1-55513-441-6*, Chariot Bks) Chariot Victor.

My Mom Made Me Go to Camp. Judy Delton. (J). 1993. pap. 2.99 (*0-440-40838-5*) Dell.

My Mom Married the Principal. Margaret Bechard. LC 97-22653. (J). 1998. 14.99 (*0-670-87394-2*) Viking Penguin.

My Mom, the Professional. Diane Dannhaus. (Illus.). 24p. (Orig.). (J). (gr. k-4). 1994. pap. 7.95 (*0-89896-104-1*) Larksdale.

My Mom the Professional. Dianne Dannhauss. Ed. by Debbie Bowen. LC 98-37897. (Professional Mom Ser.). (Illus.). 23p. (J). (gr. 1-4). 1998. lib. bdg. 12.95 (*1-56763-147-9*) Ozark Pub.

My Mom Travels a Lot. Caroline Feller Bauer. (Illus.). (J). (gr. k-3). 1983. flmstrp 32.95 (*0-941078-24-8*) Live Oak Media.

***My Moment in History: An Autobiography.** Robert L. Edwards, Jr. (Illus.). 300p. 1999. 25.00 (*0-9653670-1-0*) Immanuel Chur.

My Mommy & Daddy Didn't Divorce Me. Richard Esterman. (Illus.). 23p. (Orig.). (J). (ps-6). 1996. pap. 6.95 (*0-9646173-1-5*) R A Esterman.

My Mommy Has AIDS: Angels of Love: Celebrating Diversity & Adoption. Lynda Arnold. (Illus.). 32p. (J). (gr. k-5). 1998. 18.95 (*1-892073-01-3*) Dream Pub.

M

An Asterisk (*) at the beginning of an entry indicates that the title is appearing for the first time.

My Mommy Has Cancer. Carolyn S. Parkinson. (Illus.). 20p. (J). (ps-4). 1991. pap. 8.95 (*0-9630287-0-7*) Solace Pub.

My Mommy Hung the Moon. Jamie Lee Curtis. 32p. (ps-1). pap. 6.95 (*0-06-443696-9*) HarpC.

My Mommy Hung the Moon. Jamie Lee Curtis. 32p. (ps-3). 16.95 (*0-06-029016-1*); lib. bdg. 16.89 (*0-06-029017-X*) HarpC.

My Mommy Likes Me see Mi Mama' Me Ama

My Mommy Likes to Be with Me. Michelle Castronovo. LC 95-92267. (Kids Comfort Inc. Ser.: No. 3). (Illus.). 16p. (Orig.). (J). 1995. pap. 9.95 (*1-887453-08-3*) Kids Comfort.

***My Mommy's Cancer.** Cindy Klein Cohen & John T. Heiney. Ed. by Sharon R. Baseman. (Illus.). 32p. (J). 1999. pap. 7.95 (*0-9656498-2-2*) Promise Pubns.

My Mommy's Going Working. Michelle Castronovo. LC 95-92268. (Kids Comfort Inc. Ser.: No. 4). 16p. (Orig.). (J). 1995. pap. 9.95 (*1-887453-02-4*) Kids Comfort.

My Mommy's Having a Baby. Gloria Shelley. (Illus.). 20p. (J). (ps-3). 1997. pap. 12.95 incl. audio (*0-9659094-0-9*) Growing Up Great.

***My Mommy's Having a Baby.** 2nd rev. ed. Gloria Newman. (Illus.). 20p. (J). (gr. k-3). 2000. pap. 12.95 (*0-9659094-1-7*) Growing Up Great.

My Mom's a Vet. Henry Horenstein. LC 93-24964. (Illus.). 64p. (J). (gr. 4-7). 1994. 17.95 (*1-56402-234-X*) Candlewick Pr.

My Mom's a Vet. Henry Horenstein. LC 93-24964. 1996. 13.19 (*0-606-10263-9*, Pub. by Turtleback) Demco.

My Mom's a Vet. Henry Horenstein. LC 93-24964. (Illus.). 64p. (J). (gr. 4-7). 1996. reprint ed. pap. 7.99 (*1-56402-922-0*) Candlewick Pr.

My Mom's Okay. Guy Gilchrest. LC 91-10722. (Mudpie Bks.). (Illus.). 24p. (J). (ps-3). 1991. 5.95 (*1-56288-088-8*) Checkerboard.

My Mom's Purse. Charlotte Hutchinson. (Illus.). 36p. (J). (ps-3). 1996. pap. write for info. (*0-88753-199-7*) Black Moss.

My Mom's Taxi. Houghton Mifflin Company Staff. (Mathematics Big Book Ser.). (J). 1994. pap. 44.32 (*0-395-70376-X*) HM.

***My Mom's the Best Mom.** Illus. & Compiled by Stuart Hample. 96p. 2000. pap. text 7.95 (*0-7611-1968-X*) Workman Pub.

***My Monarch Journal: Parent-Teacher Edition.** Connie Muther & Anita Bibeau. (Sharing Nature with Children Book Ser.). (Illus.). 32p. 2000. pap. 7.95 (*1-58469-006-2*) Dawn CA.

***My Monarch Journal: Student Edition.** Connie Muther & Anita Bibeau. (Sharing Nature with Children Book Ser.). (Illus.). 32p. (J). 2000. pap., student ed. 7.95 (*1-58469-005-4*) Dawn CA.

My Money, Myself: Leader's Guide. Josephine Swanson et al. (Illus.). 100p. 1991. ring bd. 8.75 (*1-57753-040-3*, 322RENMMDC) Corn Coop Ext.

***My Monster Mama Loves Me So.** Laura Leuck. LC 98-48141. (Illus.). (J). (ps). 1999. lib. bdg. 15.93 (*0-688-16867-1*) Lothrop.

***My Monster Mama Loves Me So.** Laura Leuck. LC 98-48141. (Illus.). 24p. (J). (ps-k). 1999. 16.00 (*0-688-16866-3*) Lothrop.

***My Monthly Organizer.** 1999. pap. 20.00 (*1-57977-277-3*) Havoc Pub.

***My More-Than-Coloring Book About Christmas, Vol. 1.** Cathy Spieler. (My More-Than-Coloring Books Ser.). 1999. pap. 5.00 (*0-570-05555-5*) Concordia.

***My More-Than-Coloring Book about God's Creation, Vol. 1.** Cathy Spieler. (My More-Than-Coloring Books Ser.). 1999. pap. 5.00 (*0-570-05556-3*) Concordia.

My Mortal Enemy. Willa Cather. 1976. 17.95 (*0-8488-0452-X*) Amereon Ltd.

My Mortal Enemy. Willa Cather. LC 90-50169. (Vintage Classics Ser.). 144p. 1990. pap. 8.95 (*0-679-73179-2*) Vin Bks.

My Most Memorable Shots in the Majors: And What You Can Learn from Them. Jack Nicklaus & Ken Bowden. (Illus.). 128p. 1988. 14.95 (*0-8129-1750-2*, Times Bks) Crown Pub Group.

My Mother. 2000. write for info. (*0-671-03624-6*) S&S Trade.

My Mother. 2001. per. write for info. (*0-671-03625-4*) S&S Trade.

My Mother. Augustine, Saint. Ed. by John E. Rotelle. Tr. by Matthew J. O'Connell from ITA. LC 87-70277. 144p. (Orig.). 1987. pap. 4.00 (*0-941491-01-3*) Augustinian Pr.

My Mother: Demonology: A Novel. Kathy Acker. LC 94-21534. 268p. 1994. pap. 11.00 (*0-8021-3403-3*, Grove) Grove-Atltic.

My Mother Always Called Me by My Brother's Name. Daniel Ort. 128p. (Orig.). 1994. pap. 14.95 (*0-914061-45-3*) Orchises Pr.

***My Mother Always Used to Say That Too...** Anna Tochter. 80p. 2000. 9.00 (*0-207-19912-4*) CARP.

My Mother & I Are Growing Strong (Mi Mama y Yo Nos Hacemos Fuertes) Inez Maury. Tr. by Anna Munoz. (Illus.). 28p. (J). (ps-5). 1979. pap. 5.95 (*1-884244-17-3*) Volcano Pr.

***My Mother & Me.** unabridged ed. Jane Drake & Ann Love. (Memory Scrapbook for Kids Ser.). (Illus.). 32p. (J). (gr. k-3). 2000. pap. 5.95 (*1-55074-635-9*, Pub. by Kids Can Pr) Genl Dist Srvs.

My Mother Before Me: When Daughters Discover Mothers. Julie K. Gundlach. LC 91-41297. 1992. pap. 14.95 (*0-942637-52-6*) Barricade Bks.

My Mother Doesn't Like to Cook. Wanda C. Phillips. (Illus.). 28p. (Orig.). (J). (gr. 1-5). 1935. pap. 6.95 (*0-936981-20-2*) ISHA Enterprises.

My Mother Dying. Hilary Johnson. LC 99-19236. 192p. 1999. text 25.00 (*0-312-19930-9*, St Martins Paperbacks) St Martin.

My Mother Gets Married. Moa Martinson. Tr. & Afterword by Margaret S. Lacy. LC 88-21405. 304p. 1988. 35.00 (*0-935312-99-4*); pap. 9.95 (*0-935312-81-1*) Feminist Pr.

***My Mother Goose Library, 2 vols.** Iona Opie. (Illus.). 108p. (J). 2000. boxed set 40.00 (*0-7636-1177-8*) Candlewick Pr.

My Mother Had One Like That: An Easy Handbook to Learn the Worth of Your Heirlooms, Antiques & Treasures. Mary Chumas-Ernst. (Illus.). 32p. (Orig.). 1995. pap. text 9.95 (*1-880971-09-7*) Light&Life Pub Co MN.

***My Mother Is a Fish: A Commonplace Reader of William Faulkner's Fiction.** William Faulkner. LC PS3511.A86A6 1999A. 216p. 2000. 30.00 (*1-57309-379-3*, Pub. by Intl Scholars) Natl Bk Netwk.

My Mother Is the Most Beautiful Woman in the World. Becky Reyher. (Illus.). 40p. (J). (gr. k-3). 1944. lib. bdg. 16.93 (*0-688-51251-8*) Lothrop.

My Mother Is the Smartest Woman in the World. Eleanor Clymer. LC 82-1685. (Illus.). 96p. (J). (gr. 4-6). 1982. 13.95 (*0-689-30916-3*) Atheneum Yung Read.

My Mother Is Weird. Rachna Gilmore. (Illus.). 24p. (J). (ps-3). 1994. pap. 6.95 (*0-920304-83-4*, Pub. by Gynergy-Ragweed) U of Toronto Pr.

My Mother, Madame Edwarda & the Dead Man. Georges Bataille et al. Tr. by Austryn Wainhouse from FRE. 224p. 1994. pap. 14.95 (*0-7145-3004-2*) M Boyars Pubs.

My Mother Made Me Do It see Overcoming the Legacy of Overeating: How Your Mother Influenced Your Eating Patterns & How You Can Change Them

***My Mother, My Friend: The Ten Most Important Things to Talk about with Your Mother.** Marcdante. 208p. 2001. pap. 12.00 (*0-684-86606-4*, Fireside) S&S Trade Pap.

My Mother, My Mother Africa: The Mothers of Civilization. Ricardo A. Scott. (Ras Cardo Speaks Ser.). (Illus.). 75p. (Orig.). 1995. pap. 9.95 (*1-883427-64-9*) Crnerstone GA.

My Mother Played the Piano: More Touching Stories of Home to Inspire & Encourage the Heart. gif. ed. John William Smith. LC 97-4348. (Illus.). 265p. 1997. 15.99 (*1-878990-75-6*) Howard Pub LA.

***My Mother Prayed for Me: Faith Journaling for African American Women.** LaVerne McCain Gill. LC 00-36452. 2000. pap. write for info. (*0-8298-1396-9*) Pilgrim OH.

***My Mother Ruth.** Hillary Johnson. 256p. 2000. pap. 14.95 (*0-312-26763-0*) St Martin.

My Mother Said. Gwendolyn Jansma. LC 90-63145. 1991. pap. 10.95 (*0-87212-244-1*) Libra.

My Mother Said I Never Should. C. Keatley. 1994. pap. 10.95 (*0-413-68470-9*) Methn.

My Mother Said I Never Should. Charlotte Keatley. (Royal Court Writers Ser.). 53p. (C). 1989. pap. write for info. (*0-413-61720-3*, A0385, Methuen Drama) Methn.

My Mother Talks to Trees. Doris Gove. LC 98-36188. (Illus.). 32p. (J). (ps-3). 1999. 15.95 (*1-56145-166-5*, 51665) Peachtree Pubs.

My Mother, the Detective: The Complete "Mom" Short Stories. James Yaffe. 175p. 1996. pap. 15.00 (*1-885941-11-0*) Crippen & Landru.

My Mother the Mail Carrier - Mi Mama la Cartera. Inez Maury. Tr. by Norah Alemany. LC 76-14275. (ENG & SPA., Illus.). 32p. (J). (ps-4). 1976. pap. 7.95 (*0-935312-23-4*) Feminist Pr.

My Mother the Witch Lady. Shannon. (J). 13.00 (*0-671-75440-8*) S&S Bks Yung.

My Mother Told Me. Dorothy G. Fraembs. (Illus.). 32p. 1984. 22.00 (*0-88014-068-2*) Mosaic Pr OH.

My Mother Walked Out. Michael Hannon. 1989. write for info. (*0-318-65387-7*) Pr MacDonald & Reinecke.

My Mother Was a Grapevine. Guri Duncan. LC 93-73403. 1994. 10.00 (*0-9638803-1-4*) Driftwood Pr.

My Mother Was Right: How Today's Women Reconcile with Their Mothers. Barbara McFarland & Virginia Watson-Rouslin. LC 97-24510. 248p. 1997. mass mkt. 24.50 (*0-7879-0875-4*) Jossey-Bass.

My Mother, Your Mother: She Is for All God's Children. James F. Lupton. Ed. by Sandra Bissex & Margaret Tanner. (Illus.). 120p. (Orig.). 1996. pap. write for info. (*0-614-25692-5*) Jabbok Encounter.

My Mother/My Self: The Daughter's Search for Identity. Nancy Friday. LC 98-115632. 448p. 1997. pap. 13.95 (*0-385-32015-9*) Doubleday.

My Mother's Arm Swings the Broom with Mine. Marijane D. Duncan. Ed. by Nancy G. Duncan. LC 93-73402. (Illus.). 900p. 1994. 30.00 (*0-9638803-0-6*) Driftwood Pr.

My Mother's Betrothal. Shih Hu. Ed. by Mary Rouse. 1946. 5.95 (*0-88710-050-3*) Yale Far Eastern Pubns.

My Mother's Betrothal. Shih Hu. Ed. by Mary Rouse. 1946. audio 8.95 (*0-88710-051-1*) Yale Far Eastern Pubns.

My Mother's Body. Marge Piercy. Ed. by Nancy Nicholas. LC 84-48661. 160p. 1985. pap. 14.00 (*0-394-72945-5*) Knopf.

My Mother's Book. Joan Lyons. (Illus.). 48p. (Orig.). 1993. pap. 10.00 (*0-89822-104-8*) Visual Studies.

My Mother's Breast: Daughters Face Their Mothers' Cancer. Laurie Tarkan. LC 99-12047. 212p. 1999. pap. 14.95 (*0-87833-227-8*) Taylor Pub.

***My Mother's Daughter.** Judith Henry Wall. 432p. 2000. 25.00 (*0-684-83766-8*) S&S Trade.

My Mother's Favorite Song: Tender Stories of Home to Deepen Your Faith. John William Smith. LC 96-157342. 300p. 1995. 15.99 (*1-878990-46-2*) Howard Pub LA.

My Mother's Ghost. Fergus M. Bordewich. 2000. 23.95 (*0-385-49129-8*) Bantam.

My Mother's Ghost. Margaret Buffie. 224p. (J). 1992. mass mkt. 4.95 (*1-55074-091-1*) Kids Can Pr.

My Mother's Hands. Paul Cline. (Illus.). 32p. (J). 1991. pap. 7.95 (*0-9625261-2-6*) Medlicott Pr.

***My Mother's Hands: Celebrating Her Special Touch.** John Trent & Erin M. Healy. 112p. 2000. 9.95 (*1-57856-327-5*) Waterbrook Pr.

My Mother's House & Sido. Sidonie-Gabrielle Colette. Tr. by Una V. Troubridge & Enid McLeod from FRE. 219p. 1975. pap. 10.00 (*0-374-51218-3*) FS&G.

My Mother's House & Sido. Colette Rossant. 224p. 1995. 14.50 (*0-679-60157-0*) Random.

My Mother's Kitchen Cabinet: A Story of the Depression & World War II Years. Contrib. by Doris Young & Kimberly J. Wightman. 80p. 1998. pap. 9.00 (*1-888911-07-7*) Benson Smythe.

My Mother's Last Dance: And Other Poems. Honor Ford-Smith. 128p. 1996. pap. text. write for info. (*1-896705-12-X*) Sister Vis Pr.

My Mother's Loves. Stephane Poulin. (Illus.). 32p. (J). (ps-3). 1990. 15.95 (*1-55037-149-5*, Pub. by Annick); pap. 5.95 (*1-55037-148-7*, Pub. by Annick) Firefly Bks Ltd.

My Mother's Music. Paul West. 208p. 1999. pap. 11.95 (*0-14-025531-1*) Viking Penguin.

***My Mother's Pearls.** Catherine Myler Fruisen. (Illus.). 2000. 12.95 (*0-7683-2177-8*) CEDCO Pub.

My Mother's People, to Colorado They Came. Patricia K. Kaufman. LC 94-66708. (Illus.). 109p. 1994. pap. 16.95 (*0-938274-06-6*) Paddlewheel.

My Mother's Sabbath Days: A Memoir. Chaim Grade. Tr. by Channa Kleinerman Goldstein & Inna Hecker Grade from YID. LC 97-12723. 400p. 1997. pap. 30.00 (*1-56821-962-8*) Aronson.

My Mother's Secret Life. Rebecca Emberley. LC 97-19931. (Illus.). 32p. (J). (gr. k-2). 1998. 15.95 (*0-316-23496-6*) Little.

My Mother's Shadow. (Illus.). 1997. write for info. (*1-889582-08-5*) Lavine Publns.

My Mother's Sin & Other Stories by Georgios Vizyenos. Georgios Vizyenos. Tr. by William F. Wyatt, Jr. LC 87-23218. 249p. 1988. pap. 17.95 (*0-87451-443-6*) U Pr of New Eng.

My Mother's Southern Desserts. James Villas & Martha P. Villas. Ed. by Pam Hoenig. LC 97-51399. (Illus.). 320p. 1998. 25.00 (*0-688-15695-9*, Wm Morrow) Morrow Avon.

***My Mother's Southern Entertaining.** James Villas. (Illus.). 336p. 2000. 26.00 (*0-688-17184-2*, Wm Morrow) Morrow Avon.

My Mother's Southern Kitchen. James Villas. LC 94-2627. 1994. pap. 25.00 (*0-02-622015-6*) Macmillan.

***My Mother's Southern Kitchen: Recipes & Reminiscences.** James Villos & Martha P. Villos. LC 99-33178. (Illus.). 352p. 1999. 25.00 (*0-688-17174-5*, Wm Morrow) Morrow Avon.

My Mother's Voice. Sally Callahan. 357p. 2000. pap. 12.95 (*0-943873-49-5*, Pub. by Elder Bks) Midpt Trade.

My Mother's Words of Wisdom: A Collection of Slavic/Russian Proverbs. Mary B. Kuhtik. (Illus.). 64p. (Orig.). 1996. per. 12.95 (*0-9652033-0-1*, 0001) M B Kuhtik.

My Motto Is . . . unabridged ed. Victor C. Klein. LC 98-67340. (Illus.). 1998. pap. 6.95 (*0-9661812-1-2*, 04) Lycanthrope Pr.

***My Movie Business.** John Irving. 2000. pap. 12.95 (*0-345-44130-3*) Ballantine Pub Grp.

***My Movie Business: A Memoir.** John Irving. LC 99-15800. 208p. 1999. 19.95 (*0-375-50368-4*) Random.

My Mud Puddle Ran Away. Valerie Mazza. LC 98-66127. (Illus.). 34p. 1998. pap. 7.95 (*1-882792-63-7*) Proctor Pubns.

My Mum & Other Horror Stories. Meg Harper. (J). 1997. pap. 7.50 (*0-7459-3726-8*, Pub. by Lion Pubng) Trafalgar.

My Mum & Our Dad. Rose Impey. (Illus.). 32p. (J). pap. 9.95 (*0-14-055361-4*, Pub. by Pnguin Bks Ltd) Trafalgar.

My Muse Was Supposed to Meet Me Here. Erik Anderson-Reece. 72p. 1992. pap. 10.00 (*0-917453-25-5*) Bamberger.

***My Museum Journal: A Writing & Sketching Book.** Shelly Kale & Lisa Vihos. (Illus.). 48p. 2000. pap. 14.95 (*0-89236-570-6*) J P Getty Trust.

My Music. Ed. by Daniel Cavicchi & Charles Keil. LC 92-56907. (Music - Culture Ser.). 244p. 1993. pap. 17.95 (*0-8195-6264-5*, Wesleyan Univ Pr) U Pr of New Eng.

My Music Is My Flag: Puerto Rican Musicians & Their New York Communities, 1917-1940. Ruth Glasser. LC 94-9015. 1995. 40.00 (*0-520-08122-6*, Pub. by U CA Pr) Cal Prin Full Svc.

My Music Is My Flag: Puerto Rican Musicians & Their New York Communities, 1917-1940. Ruth Glasser. LC 94-9015. (Illus.). 1997. pap. 17.95 (*0-520-20890-0*, Pub. by U CA Pr) Cal Prin Full Svc.

***My Music Journal International: HI Student Piano Library.** 48p. 1998. spiral bd. 3.95 (*0-634-00109-4*) H Leonard.

My Music Workbook. Kenneth W. Osbeck. 144p. 1982. pap. 8.99 (*0-8254-3415-7*) Kregel.

My Musical Life. Walter J. Damrosch. 376p. 1990. reprint ed. lib. bdg. 79.00 (*0-7812-9105-4*) Rprt Serv.

My Musical Life. Walter J. Damrosch. (American Biography Ser.). 376p. 1991. reprint ed. lib. bdg. 79.00 (*0-7812-8098-2*) Rprt Serv.

My Mysterious World. Margaret Mahy. LC 95-1291. (Meet the Author Ser.). (Illus.). 32p. (J). (gr. 2-5). 1995. 14.95 (*1-878450-58-1*, 710) R Owen Pubs.

My "n" Sound Box. Jane Belk Moncure. LC 78-22053. (Sound Box Library). (Illus.). 32p. (J). (ps-2). 1979. lib. bdg. 21.36 (*0-89565-054-1*) Childs World.

My Naked Soul. Alan Burke. (Illus.). 1968. 3.95 (*0-87212-021-X*) Libra.

My Name Escapes Me: The Diary of a Retiring Actor. Alec Guinness. 224p. 1998. pap. 12.95 (*0-14-027745-5*) Viking Penguin.

My Name Escapes Me: The Diary of a Retiring Actor. large type ed. Alec Guinness. LC 97-24578. 1997. lib. bdg. 21.95 (*0-7862-1203-9*) Thorndike Pr.

My Name Happens Also: Poems. deluxe limited ed. Elizabeth Robinson. (Poetry Chapbooks). 32p. 1987. pap. 15.00 (*0-930901-44-4*) Burning Deck.

My Name in Books: A Guide to Character Names in Children's Literature. Katharyn Tuten-Puckett. xvi, 242p. 1993. pap. text 24.00 (*0-87287-979-8*) Libs Unl.

My Name Is . . . "Ritta" Poetry With A Story. 2nd large type rev. ed. LC 95-96141. (Illus.). 74p. (YA). (gr. 12 up). 1997. reprint ed. pap. write for info. (*0-9650676-1-0*) R T Elliott.

***My Name Is A: Meeting the Letters of the Alphabet.** Trish Nelson. LC 99-93419. (Illus.). 32p. (J). (ps-1). 1999. pap. 6.95 (*0-9673943-0-9*) Nelson Bldg Blk.

My Name Is Amanda. Dorothy Peterson. (Amanda Ser.: Vol. 1). (Illus.). 13p. (Orig.). (J). (ps-1). 1996. pap. 8.95 (*1-890547-00-X*) Hse Amanda Built.

My Name Is Amelia. Donald J. Sobol. LC 94-18540. 128p. (J). (gr. 4-8). 1994. 14.00 (*0-689-31970-3*) Atheneum Yung Read.

My Name Is Ana. Lori M. Poe. LC 91-91466. (Illus.). 208p. 1992. pap. 23.95 (*0-9624804-9-5*) Place Light.

My Name Is Aram. William Saroyan. LC 40-34075. (Modern Classic Ser.). (Illus.). 205p. 1989. 15.95 (*0-15-163827-6*) Harcourt.

My Name Is Asher Lev. Chaim Potok. 352p. 1984. mass mkt. 6.99 (*0-449-20714-5*, Crest) Fawcett.

My Name Is Asher Lev. Chaim Potok. 369p. 1996. pap. 11.00 (*0-449-91168-3*) Fawcett.

***My Name Is Big Bird.** Kate Klimo. 1999. 1.99 (*0-375-80391-2*) Random.

***My Name Is Blue, from Me to You, All about PTSD.** Rain, Blue & the Crew Publishers Staff. 16p. 1999. pap. text 6.00 (*1-929396-00-7*) Rain Blue.

***My Name Is Blue, from Me to You, All about PTSD, Vol. 2.** Blue & the Crew Publishers Staff. Ed. by Rain & the Crew Publishers Staff. 16p. 2000. pap. 6.00 (*1-929396-01-5*) Rain Blue.

My Name Is Brain Brian. Jeanne Betancourt. LC 92-16513. 144p. (J). (gr. 3-7). 1993. 14.95 (*0-590-44921-4*) Scholastic Inc.

My Name Is Brain Brian. Jeanne Betancourt. (J). 1993. 9.09 (*0-606-07907-6*, Pub. by Turtleback) Demco.

My Name Is Brian. Jeanne Betrancourt. (gr. 4-7). 1995. pap. text 3.99 (*0-590-44922-2*) Scholastic Inc.

My Name Is Chellis, & I'm in Recovery from Western Civilization. Chellis Glendinning. LC 93-39136. 1994. pap. 16.95 (*0-87773-996-X*, Pub. by Shambhala Pubns) Random.

My Name Is Christian Woman. Ed. by Mary H. Wallace. (Illus.). 288p. 2000. reprint ed. pap. 6.95 (*0-912315-20-2*) Word Aflame.

My Name Is David: Fun with Colors. Diane Stortz. (My Bible Pals Tall Shaped Board Bks.). (Illus.). 12p. (J). (ps-k). 1996. bds. 5.49 (*0-7847-0537-2*, 03447) Standard Pub.

***My Name Is Elmo.** Kate Klimo. 1999. 1.99 (*0-375-80390-4*) Random.

***My Name Is Gene.** N. L. Eskeland & N. C. Bailey. (Illus.). 92p. (YA). (gr. 5-8). 1999. pap. 19.95 (*0-9673811-1-8*) ScienceTwoDiscover.

My Name Is Georgia: A Portrait. Jeanette Winter. LC 97-7087. (Illus.). 48p. (J). (gr. k-3). 1998. 16.00 (*0-15-201649-X*) Harcourt.

***My Name Is Grover.** Random House Staff. 24p. (J). 2000. 1.99 (*0-375-80446-3*, Pub. by Random Bks Yng Read) Random.

My Name Is Izzy. Isabel J. Covalt. LC 99-24091. (Illus.). 192p. 1999. pap. 14.95 (*0-89407-128-9*) Strawberry Hill.

My Name Is Jack. Anne T. Perkins. (Big Books - Mini Bks.). (Illus.). 8p. (J). (ps). 1993. 12.00 (*1-884204-05-8*) Teach Nxt Door.

My Name Is Jesus: Fun with Counting. Diane Stortz. (My Bible Pals Tall Shaped Board Bks.). (Illus.). 12p. (J). (ps-k). 1996. bds. 5.49 (*0-7847-0538-0*, 03448) Standard Pub.

My Name Is Johari. Anne Sibley-O'Brien. Ed. by Lisa Trumbauer. (Multicultural Big Bks.). (Illus.). 16p. (J). (ps-2). 1994. pap. 16.95 (*1-56784-501-0*) Newbridge Educ.

My Name Is John. Thomas D. Eno. LC 94-45947. 1995. pap. 9.95 (*1-55503-770-4*, 01111868) Covenant Comms.

My Name Is Jorge: On Both Sides of the River. Jane Medina. LC 99-60227. (SPA., Illus.). 48p. (YA). (gr. 2-5). 1999. 14.95 (*1-56397-811-3*) Boyds Mills Pr.

***My Name Is Jorge: On Both Sides of the River.** Jane Medina. (SPA., Illus.). 48p. (YA). (gr. 4-7). 1999. 7.95 (*1-56397-842-3*, Wordsong) Boyds Mills Pr.

My Name is Jose & I Think You'll Like Me! see I'm Jose & I'm Okay: Three Stories from Bolivia

My Name Is Kathryn - Whole in One: From Multiple Personality Disorder to Wholeness. K. C. Findley. Ed. by Carolyn DeLozier & Kathleen Fox. (Illus.). 201p. (Orig.). 1995. pap. text 23.95 (*0-9628178-5-6*) Strong Stock Pr.

My Name Is Legion. Sheila M. Berry. LC 99-31286. 308p. 1999. 25.00 (*0-9662299-1-6*, Pub. by Archer Books) Midpt Trade.

My Name Is Legion. Charles Morgan. (Literature Ser.). 346p. 1972. reprint ed. 39.00 (*0-403-01115-9*) Scholarly.

My Name Is Louis. Janet C. James. 96p. (YA). (gr. 9-12). 1988. 9.95 (*0-921254-06-7*, Pub. by Penumbra Pr) U of Toronto Pr.

My Name Is Love: Darlene Love. Darlene Love et al. LC 98-19242. (Illus.). 320p. 1998. 24.00 (*0-688-15657-6*, Wm Morrow) Morrow Avon.

My Name Is Maria Isabel. Alma F. Ada. Tr. by Ana M. Cerro from SPA. LC 91-44910. (Illus.). 64p. (J). (gr. 2-5). 1993. 13.00 (*0-689-31517-1*) Atheneum Yung Read.

An Asterisk (*) at the beginning of an entry indicates that the title is appearing for the first time.

My Name is Maria Isabel. Alma Flor Ada. (J). 1995. 9.40 (*0-606-07908-4*) Turtleback.

My Name Is Maria Isabel. Alma Flor Ada. Tr. by Ana M. Cerro. LC 91-44910. (Illus.). 64p. (J). (gr. 2-5). 1995. per. 3.95 (*0-689-80217-X*) Aladdin.

My Name Is Maria Isabel: Spanish. Alma F. Ada. (SPA.). 64p. (J). 1996. per. 4.99 (*0-689-81099-7*) S&S Childrens.

My Name Is Maria Isabel: Spanish. Alma Flor Ada. (J). 1996. pap. 4.95 (*0-689-31980-0*) S&S Bks Yung.

My Name Is Mary . . . Anita Katzman. xi, 122p. 1995. reprint ed. pap. 12.00 (*0-9663284-0-X*) Corbino Art.

My Name Is Million: An Illustrated History of the Poles in America. W. S. Kunicizak. LC 99-48176. (Illus.). 170p. 2000. 24.95 (*0-7818-0760-3*) Hippocrene Bks.

My Name Is Mister Ryan. Matt Chaney. LC 94-173383. (Greatness in People Ser.). (Illus.). 450p. (Orig.). 1994. 27.95 (*0-9639316-0-1*); pap. 15.95 (*0-9639316-1-X*) Four Walls.

My Name Is Moses: Fun with Words. Greg Holder. (My Bible Pals Tall Shaped Board Bks.). (Illus.). 12p. (J). (ps-k). 1996. bds. 5.49 (*0-7847-0539-9*, 03449) Standard Pub.

My Name Is Nabil. Wendy Heller. (Illus.). 48p. (J). (gr. 3-6). 1981. 14.95 (*0-933770-17-0*) Kalimat.

***My Name Is Neofytos.** Toulla Palazeti. Ed. by Noreen Wise. (Book-a-Day Collection). (Illus.). 32p. (YA). (ps up). 2000. pap. 5.95 (*1-58584-387-3*) Huckleberry CT.

My Name Is Nina, BK. 1. Bochorisvili. (Play & Say Ser.). 48p. 1995. pap. text 13.23 (*0-201-60973-8*) Addison-Wesley.

My Name Is Nina, Bk. 2. Bochorishvili. (Play & Say Ser.). 48p. 1995. pap. text 13.23 (*0-201-83260-7*) Addison-Wesley.

My Name Is Nina!, Bk. 2. Natalia Bochorishvili & Vitalij Palkus. (C). 1996. text, teacher ed. 18.17 (*0-201-83264-X*) Addison-Wesley.

My Name Is Noah: Fun with Shapes. Greg Holder. (My Bible Pals Tall Shaped Board Bks.). (Illus.). 12p. (J). (ps-k). 1996. bds. 5.49 (*0-7847-0540-2*, 03450) Standard Pub.

My Name is Nobody. Maureen C. Wartski. 1988. 15.95 (*0-8027-6770-2*) Walker & Co.

My Name Is Not Angelica. Scott O'Dell. 144p. (J). (gr. k-6). 1990. pap. 4.99 (*0-440-40379-0*, YB BDD) BDD Bks Young Read.

My Name Is Not Angelica. Scott O'Dell. 144p. (J). (gr. 5-9). 1989. 18.00 (*0-395-51061-9*) HM.

My Name Is Not Angelica. Scott O'Dell. (J). 1989. 9.60 (*0-606-04485-X*, Pub. by Turtleback) Demco.

My Name Is Not Dummy. 2nd rev. ed. Elizabeth Crary. LC 96-20259. (Children's Problem Solving Bk.). (Illus.). 32p. (Orig.). (J). (ps-3). 1996. pap. 6.95 (*1-884734-16-2*); lib. bdg. 16.95 (*1-884734-17-0*) Parenting Pr.

***My Name Is Not Gussie.** Mikki Machlin. LC 99-19160. (Illus.). 32p. (J). (gr. k-3). 1999. 16.00 (*0-395-95646-3*) HM.

***My Name Is Not Magilla Gorilla.** Arlene McFarlane. Ed. by Noreen Wise. (Lemonade Collection). (Illus.). 48p. (J). (ps up). 2000. pap. 5.95 (*1-58584-210-9*) Huckleberry CT.

My Name is Peter. Stephanie Britt. 1999. pap. text 3.95 (*0-687-05328-5*) Abingdon.

My Name Is Polly Winter. large type ed. Veronica Black. (Ulverscroft). 352p. 1994. 27.99 (*0-7089-3036-0*) Ulverscroft.

My Name Is Rachamim. Jonathan P. Kendall. (Illus.). (J). (gr. 2-3). 1987. 7.95 (*0-8074-0321-0*, 123925) UAHC.

My Name Is... "Ritta" Poetry with a Story. 2nd large type rev. ed. LC 95-96141. (Illus.). 74p. (YA). (gr. 12 up). 1997. reprint ed. 15.66 (*0-9650676-0-2*) R T Elliott.

***My Name Is Ron & I'm a Recovering Legislator: Memoirs of a Louisiana State Representative, Vol. 1.** 275p. 2000. 18.75 (*0-9700156-0-7*) Zemog.

My Name Is Sara. Bonnie Doss. 24p. 1999. 5.00 (*0-9653895-9-6*) Bookmark Pubg.

My Name Is Scrambled Eggs. HarBrace Staff. (J). 1995. pap. text 13.10 (*0-15-305618-5*) Harcourt.

My Name Is Seepeetza. Shirley Sterling. LC 93-202302. 128p. (gr. 5-7). 1998. pap. 7.95 (*0-88899-165-7*) Grndwd Bks.

My Name Is Selah. J. Noel. (Illus.). 22p. 1994. pap. 4.95 (*0-930422-19-8*) Dennis-Landman.

***My Name Is York.** Elizabeth Van Steenwyk. 2000. pap. write for info. (*0-87358-758-8*, Rising Moon Bks) Northland AZ.

My Name Is York. Elizabeth Van Steenwyk. LC 97-8816. (Illus.). 32p. (J). (gr. 1-3). 1997. lib. bdg. 14.95 (*0-87358-650-6*, Rising Moon Bks) Northland AZ.

***My Name Is Zoe.** Kate Klimo. 1999. 1.99 (*0-375-80392-0*) Random.

My Name Isn't Martha but I Can Decorate My Home. Robie Hanby. 1998. per. 14.00 (*0-671-01542-7*, PB Trade Paper) PB.

My Name Isn't Martha, But I Can Renovate My Home: The Real Person's Guide to Renovating & Improving Your Home. Sharon Hanby-Robie. 288p. 1999. per. 15.95 (*0-671-01543-5*, PB Trade Paper) PB.

My Name Was Fientje. 2nd ed. Faye A. Warschauer. Ed. by Barbara Robidoux. (Illus.). 96p. (Orig.). 1997. pap. 10.00 (*0-9659274-0-7*) Pulpt Rck.

My Name Was Martha: A Renaissance Woman's Autobiographical Poem. Martha Moulsworth. Ed. by Robert C. Evans & Barbara Wiedemann. LC 93-27167. 117p. (C). 1993. lib. bdg. 22.50 (*0-933951-53-1*) Locust Hill Pr.

My Name with a Sigh Breathin' Fred Wah. LC 81-91382. 88p. 1981. pap. 10.95 (*0-88922-188-X*, Pub. by Talonbks) Genl Dist Srvs.

My Name's Not Susie: A Life Transformed by Literacy. Sharon J. Hamilton. LC 95-18077. 153p. 1995. 19.95 (*0-86709-361-7*, 0361, Pub. by Boynton Cook Pubs) Heinemann.

My Name's Not Susie: A Life Transformed by Literacy. Sharon J. Hamilton. LC 95-18077. 153p. 1997. pap. 13.95 (*0-86709-404-4*, 0404, Pub. by Boynton Cook Pubs) Heinemann.

My Nanny: From a Small Country Town, to the Entertainment Capital of the World. Leslie S. O'Neil. Ed. by Michael Moreau & Colleen O'Neil. LC 97-94475. 368p. 1998. pap. 16.95 (*0-9660519-0-4*) Crown Pt Publ.

My Napoleon. Catherine Brighton. LC 96-7663. (Illus.). 32p. (J). (gr. k-4). 1997. 16.95 (*0-7613-0106-2*) Millbrook Pr.

My Nasty Neighbours. Creina Mansfield. (J). 1997. pap. 6.95 (*0-86278-462-X*, Pub. by OBrien Pr) Irish Amer Bk.

My Natchez Years. Morris Raphael. (Illus.). 160p. (YA). (gr. 5 up). 1998. 19.95 (*0-8187-0312-1*) M Raphael.

My Native American School. large type ed. Carol Gould. (Illus.). 16p. (Orig.). (J). (gr. k-2). 1996. text 4.95 (*1-879835-77-0*) Kaeden Corp.

My Native Cradle. Alfred A. Warren. 149p. 1998. pap. 14.95 (*1-892227-06-1*) Lasana Pubg.

My Native English: Criticisms of an Unnecessary Crisis in English Studies. Ed. by Roger Knight & Ian Robinson. 204p. (C). 1989. 95.00 (*0-907839-37-1*, Pub. by Brynmill Pr Ltd) St Mut.

My Native Land: A Celebration of Britain. Ed. by Sean McMahon. 360p. 1987. pap. 12.95 (*0-905169-97-2*, Pub. by Poolbeg Pr) Dufour.

My Native Land: An Anthology by New Writers. Ed. by Literacy Volunteers of New York City Staff. 64p. (Orig.). 1992. pap. text 3.50 (*0-929631-65-X*, Signal Hill) New Readers.

My Native Land: Chilean Reminiscence, Folklore, Panorama, Writers. Agustin Edwards. 1976. lib. bdg. 59.95 (*0-8490-2311-4*) Gordon Pr.

***My Nature: Works with Paper by Kiki Smith.** Olivia Lahs-Gonzales. Ed. by Mary Ann Steiner. 1999. pap. 19.95 (*0-89178-081-5*) St Louis Art Mus.

My Nature Crafts Book. Cheryl Owen. LC 92-10187. (Illus.). 96p. (J). 1993. 15.95 (*0-316-67715-9*) Little.

My Nature Is Fire: Saint Catherine of Siena. Catherine M. Meade. LC 91-9224. 1991. pap. 12.50 (*0-8189-0615-4*) Alba.

My Nature Journal: A Personal Nature Guide for Young People. unabridged ed. Adrienne Olmstead. Ed. & Des. by Donald Olmstead. (ACE., Illus.). 176p. (gr. 3-8). 2000. 17.95 (*0-9672459-1-5*) Pajaro.

My Navajo Sister. Eleanor Schick. (Illus.). 32p. (J). (gr. k-3). 1996. 16.00 (*0-689-80529-2*) S&S Childrens.

My Navy Too. Beth F. Coye. LC 97-92277. 432p. (Orig.). 1997. pap. 16.95 (*0-9658578-0-8*) Cedar Hollow.

My Neck of the Woods. Louise D. Rich. LC 98-28401. 256p. 1998. reprint ed. pap. 12.95 (*0-89272-453-6*) Down East.

My Neckline & the Collapse of Western Civilization. Sue H. Brown et al. (Orig.). 1987. pap. 7.95 (*0-9617736-0-X*, 1) Smartweed Pr.

My Neighbor: A Study of City Conditions, a Plea for Social Service. James S. Woodsworth. LC 77-163839. (Social History of Canada Ser.). 236p. reprint ed. pap. 73.20 (*0-7837-0298-1*, 204061900019) Bks Demand.

My Neighbor, My Sister, My Friend. Ardeth Greene Kapp. LC 89-71486. xii, 206p. 1995. pap. 7.95 (*0-87579-958-2*) Deseret Bk.

My Neighbor, My Sister, My Friend. Ardeth Greene Kapp. (POR.). 260p. 1999. write for info. (*1-57345-481-8*) Deseret Bk.

My Neighborhood. Norris & McMahon. (Illus.). 48p. (J). (ps-1). 1996. pap., teacher ed. 9.95 (*1-55799-560-5*, 546) Evan-Moor Edu Pubs.

***My Neighborhood.** Merry North. (Giant Flap Bks.). (Illus.). 10p. (J). (ps-k). 1999. bds. write for info. (*1-57584-346-3*, Pub. by Rdrs Digest) Random.

My Neighborhood: The Words & Pictures of Inner-City Children. Linda Waldman. (Illus.). 120p. (Orig.). 1993. pap. 15.95 (*0-9637517-0-0*) Hyde Pk Bank.

My Neighborhood & Me. Margaret Hargreaves & Pat Davis. (J). (gr. 2). 1988. student ed. 259.00 (*0-318-41081-8*) Southwinds Pr.

My Neighbors: Stories of the Welsh People. Caradoc Evans. LC 73-121539. (Short Story Index Reprint Ser.). 1977. 19.95 (*0-8369-3495-4*) Ayer.

My New Baby & Me: A First Year Record Book for Big Brothers & Sisters. Dian G. Smith & Metropolitan Museum of Art Staff. (Illus.). 48p. (Orig.). (J). 1987. mass mkt. 12.95 (*0-684-18712-4*) Scribner.

My New Boy. Joan Phillips. LC 85-30129. (Step into Reading Ser.: A Step 1 Book). (Illus.). 32p. (J). (ps-1). 1986. pap. 3.99 (*0-394-88277-6*, Pub. by Random Bks Yng Read) Random.

My New Boy. Joan Phillips. (Step into Reading Ser.: A Step 1 Book). (J). (ps-1). 1986. 9.19 (*0-606-12443-8*, Pub. by Turtleback) Demco.

My New Boy. 93rd ed. Joan Phillips. (Step into Reading Ser.: A Step 1 Book). (J). (ps-1). 1993. pap. text 10.80 (*0-15-300313-8*, Harcourt Child Bks) Harcourt.

My New Eye Patch: A Book for Parents & Children. Nancy Chernus-Mansfield & Marilyn Horn. LC 93-80042. (Illus.). 24p. (Orig.). (J). (ps-9). 1993. pap. write for info. (*0-9630118-1-2*) Inst Fam Blind Child.

My New Family: Foster Family Activity Book. Jim Boulden & Joan Boulden. Ed. by JoAnn Farness. (Illus.). 16p. (J). (gr. k-2). 1996. pap. 5.95 (*1-878076-75-2*) Boulden Pub.

My New Friend: Advanced Reader. Gary Harbo. (If You Want to Succeed, You Need to Read! Ser.: Bk. 1). (Illus.). 33p. (J). (gr. 1-4). 1988. 9.95 (*1-884149-01-4*) Kutie Kari Bks.

My New Friends. Barbara J. Crane. (Crane Reading System-English Ser.). (gr. k-2). 1977. pap. text 5.15 (*0-89075-102-1*) Bilingual Ed Serv.

My New Friends: A Funny Fingers Book. Karin Blume & Brigitte Pokornik. (Funny Fingers Ser.). (Illus.). 16p. (J). (ps-1). 1996. 6.95 (*0-7892-0180-1*, Abbeville Kids) Abbeville Pr.

My New Friends Were Barefoot. John Gray. LC 94-14536. 73p. 1994. 12.50 (*0-933249-13-6*) Mid-Peninsula Lib.

My New Home in Northern Michigan. Charles W. Jay. 1979. reprint ed. 15.00 (*0-915056-10-0*) Hardscrabble Bks.

My New Kitten. Joanna Cole. LC 94-20295. (Illus.). 40p. (J). (ps up). 1995. 15.00 (*0-688-12901-3*, Wm Morrow) Morrow Avon.

My New Kitten. Joanna Cole. LC 94-20295. (Illus.). 40p. (J). (ps up). 1995. 14.93 (*0-688-12902-1*, Wm Morrow) Morrow Avon.

My New Life. Ron Molen. LC 96-14254. 240p. (Orig.). 1996. pap. 14.95 (*1-56085-073-6*) Signature Bks.

***My New Pet Is the Greatest.** Sarah Albee. LC 98-8772. (Road to Reading Ser.). (Illus.). 32p. (J). 1999. pap. 3.99 (*0-307-26208-1*, Whitman Coin) St Martin.

My New Sandbox. Donna Jakob. LC 95-21784. (Illus.). 32p. (J). (ps-2). 1996. 13.95 (*0-7868-0172-7*, Pub. by Hyprn Child) Little.

***My New Toolbox.** Karen Hooker. 8p. 1999. pap. 3.75i (*1-880612-96-8*) Seedling Pubns.

***My New Yellow Shirt.** Eileen Spinelli. 2000. text 15.95 (*0-8050-6242-4*) St Martin.

My New York. Kathy Jakobsen. 32p. (J). (gr. k-3). 1993. 16.95 (*0-316-45653-5*) Little.

***My New York Diary.** Julie Doucet. 124p. 1999. 24.95 (*1-896597-23-8*, Pub. by Drawn & Quarterly) LPC InBook.

***My New York Garden: A Gardener's Journal.** Liz Ball. (Illus.). 128p. 2000. spiral bd. 19.95 (*1-930604-10-6*) Cool Springs Pr.

***My New York Garden: A Gardener's Journal.** Cool Springs Press Publications Staff. 2000. 19.95 (*1-888608-94-3*) Cool Springs Pr.

My NICU Baby Book: For NICU Infants. Joy Johnson. (Illus.). 48p. (Orig.). (J). (gr. 3 up). 1994. pap. 9.95 (*1-56123-073-1*, MNIC) Centering Corp.

My Night at Maud's. Eric Rohner. LC 92-32891. (Films in Print Ser.: Vol. 19). (Illus.). 220p. (C). 1993. text 40.00 (*0-8135-1939-X*); pap. text 17.00 (*0-8135-1940-3*) Rutgers U Pr.

My Night Forest. Roy Owen. LC 93-45666. (Illus.). 32p. (J). (ps-2). 1994. mass mkt. write for info. (*0-02-769005-9*) S&S Bks Yung.

My Night with Federico Garcia Lorca - Mi Noche Con Federico Garcia Lorca. Jaime Manrique. Tr. by Edith Grossman & Eugene Richie. LC 96-48543. (ENG & SPA.). 127p. 1997. pap. 12.00 (*0-9651558-3-8*) Painted Leaf.

***My Night with Reg.** Kevin Elyot. 80p. (C). 1998. pap. 5.60 (*0-87129-860-0*, MA5) Dramatic Pub.

My Night with Reg. Kevin Elyot. 96p. 1994. pap. 14.95 (*1-85459-358-7*) N Hern Bks.

***My Night with the Language Thieves.** Tad Richards. (Illus.). 150p. 1999. pap. 14.00 (*1-889289-31-0*) Ye Olde Font Shoppe.

My Nighttime Book. Stephanie C. Oda. (Good Little Books for Good Little Children). 12p. (J). (ps). 1986. 3.25 (*0-8378-5091-6*) Gibson.

My Nine Book. Jane Belk Moncure. LC 85-30959. (My Number Bks.). (Illus.). 32p. (J). (ps-2). 1986. lib. bdg. 21.36 (*0-89565-320-6*) Childs World.

My Nine Innings: An Autobiography of 50 Years in Baseball. Lee MacPhail. 1989. 21.95 (*0-88736-387-3*) Mecklermedia.

My Nine Lives by Clio. Marjorie Priceman & Clio. LC 97-47565. (Illus.). 48p. (J). (gr. 2-6). 1998. 16.00 (*0-689-81135-7*) S&S Childrens.

My Nine Month Diary. Linda J. Black. (Illus.). 42p. (Orig.). 1993. pap. 7.50 (*1-881459-05-5*) Eagle Pr SC.

My 911 Book for Help. Julie Melle. LC 92-71606. (Illus.). 16p. (J). (ps-6). 1992. pap. text 9.99 (*1-881402-00-2*) CA Storybook.

My 911 Book & Tape for Help. 2nd rev. ed. Julie Melle. Ed. by Maureen Hagan. Tr. & Illus. by Work for Hire. Illus. by Liz Hutnick. LC 97-69634. (ENG & SPA.). 36p. (J). (gr. k-5). 1997. per. 15.99 (*1-881402-01-0*) CA Storybook.

My 9-1-1 Telephone Book. 2nd rev. ed. Vivian Laube. Orig. Title: Picture Me Telephone Book. (Illus.). 12p. (Orig.). (J). (gr. k-4). 1996. write for info. (*0-9625912-1-1*) Novel Tees.

My Noah's Ark. M. B. Goffstein. LC 77-25666. (Illus.). 32p. (J). (ps-3). 1978. 13.95 (*0-06-022022-8*) HarpC Child Bks.

My Noah's Ark Activity Book. David Sokoloff. (Illus.). 24p. (J). (ps-5). 1998. pap. 1.00 (*1-889655-08-2*) Jewish Educ Toys.

My North Carolina Ancestors Vol. 1: Of Beaufort, Bladen, Columbus, Martin & Washington Cos. NC & Isle of Wight, Co, VA. Jennifer M. Sheppard. LC 90-60847. (Illus.). 138p. (Orig.). 1990. pap. 29.95 (*1-878916-01-7*) Modlins Ancestral.

***My North Carolina Garden: A Gardener's Journal.** Toby Bost. (Illus.). 2000. spiral bd. 19.95 (*1-930604-04-1*) Cool Springs Pr.

***My North Carolina Garden: A Gardener's Journal.** Cool Springs Press Publications Staff. 2000. 19.95 (*1-888608-85-4*) Cool Springs Pr.

***My North Carolina Heritage Vol. 2: Rollins, Ealy, Morgan & Smelser Families.** Marshall Styles. 408p. 1999. 72.00 (*0-8328-9881-3*); pap. 62.00 (*0-8328-9882-1*) Higginson Bk Co.

My North Dakota Prairie Childhood. Rose M. Brauer. LC 94-79031. 138p. 1990. pap. 15.00 (*0-9643204-0-1*) Gregory Pubs.

***My Nose.** Kathy Furgang. LC 99-45240. (My Body Ser.). (Illus.). (J). 2000. write for info. (*0-8239-5576-1*) Rosen Group.

My Nose Is a Gherkin Pickle Gone Wrong. Marilyn Gear Pilling. LC 97-151273. 192p. 1996. pap. text 16.95 (*0-920953-96-4*) Stoddart Publ.

My Nose Is a Hose! Kent Salisbury. 12p. 1997. 6.99 (*1-56293-930-0*, McClanahan Book) Learn Horizon.

My Nose Is Frostbitten: Useful Phrases for Russian-American Exchanges. Melissa C. Chapin. Ed. by Lena Makarova. (Illus.). 58p. 1992. pap. write for info. (*0-9633522-0-2*) Taiga.

***My Nose Is Running.** Louise Bonnet-Rampersaud. LC 99-14242. 1999. 12.95 (*1-886388-14-8*) Flower Valley Pr.

My Nose, My Toes! Playskool Books Staff. (Illus.). 24p. 1995. 5.99 (*0-525-45472-1*, Dutton Child) Peng Put Young Read.

My Notebook: (With Help from Amelia) Marissa Moss. (Amelia (American Girl) Ser.). (Illus.). 48p. (J). (gr. 3-7). 1999. pap. 5.95 (*1-56247-792-7*) Pleasant Co.

My Notebook (with Help from Amelia) Marissa Moss. (Illus.). 48p. (J). (gr. 2-7). 1997. pap. 9.95 (*1-883672-47-3*) Tricycle Pr.

My Notre Dame: Memories & Reflections of Sixty Years. Thomas Stritch. LC 91-50572. (C). 1992. pap. text 17.50 (*0-268-01402-7*) U of Notre Dame Pr.

M

My Novel. Edward Bulwer Lytton. 602p. 1999. reprint ed. pap. 35.00 (*0-7661-0784-1*) Kessinger Pub.

My November Journal. Alana Trisler & Patrice Cardiel. 48p. (J). (gr. 1-2). 1999. pap., wbk. ed. 1.75 (*1-56762-097-3*) Modern Learn Pr.

My Number Book. Leesa Krampe. (Illus.). 126p. (J). (ps-1). 1986. pap. text 3.95 (*0-932957-99-4*) Natl School.

My Number Word Book. Leesa Krampe. Ed. by Doris Ehrlich. (Illus.). 100p. (Orig.). (J). (ps-1). 1987. pap. text 3.95 (*0-932957-94-3*) Natl School.

My Number 1-887379- Mark Sonnenfeld. 32p. 1997. pap. 3.00 (*1-887379-11-8*) M Sonnenfeld.

***My Numbers.** Rebecca Emberley. (Illus.). 20p. (J). 2000. 5.95 (*0-316-23350-1*) Little.

***My Numbers, My Friends.** Paulo Ribenboim. LC 99-42458. 450p. 2000. pap. 39.95 (*0-387-98911-0*) Spr-Verlag.

My Nursery Rhyme Collection. Illus. by Fran Thatcher. 96p. (J). 1997. 15.99 (*1-884628-48-6*, Flyng Frog) Allied Pub MD.

My "o" Sound Box. Jane Belk Moncure. LC 84-17023. (Sound Box Library). (Illus.). 32p. (J). (ps-2). 1984. lib. bdg. 21.36 (*0-89565-299-4*) Childs World.

My Ocean Liner: Across the North Atlantic on the Great Ship Normandie. Peter Mandel. (Illus.). 48p. (J). (gr. 3-6). 2000. 16.95 (*0-88045-149-1*) Stemmer Hse.

My October Journal. Alana Trisler & Patrice Cardiel. 48p. (J). (gr. 1-2). 1999. pap., wbk. ed. 1.75 (*1-56762-096-5*) Modern Learn Pr.

My Odyssey in Mother's Womb. Josef Ben-Porat. 1979. 6.95 (*0-9603256-0-3*) Brighton House.

My Official X-Files Pictorial Price Guide. Duane Dimock. 80p. 1995. pap. 13.00 (*1-888239-00-X*) E Finn Prods.

***My Ohio Garden: A Gardener's Journal.** Cool Springs Press Publications Staff. 2000. 19.95 (*1-888608-81-1*) Cool Springs Pr.

***My Ohio Garden: A Gardener's Journal.** Denny McKeown. (Illus.). 128p. 2000. spiral bd. 19.95 (*1-930604-00-9*) Cool Springs Pr.

My Ol' Man. Patricia Polacco. LC 94-15395. (Illus.). 40p. (J). (gr. k-3). 1995. 15.95 (*0-399-22822-5*, Philomel) Peng Put Young Read.

My Ol' Man. Patricia Polacco. (Illus.). 40p. (YA). (gr. k-3). 1999. pap. 6.99 (*0-698-11770-0*, PapStar) Peng Put Young Read.

My Old Cowboy Boots. Dwight E. Burgess. LC 92-81560. (Illus.). 83p. 1992. pap. 11.95 (*1-879984-00-8*) Premier KS.

My Old Gold Boat. Patty Carratello. (Easy Readers Ser.). 16p. (J). (gr. k-1). 1997. pap. 2.49 (*1-57690-013-4*) Tchr Create Mat.

My Old Kentucky Home, Good-Night: Shamrocks in the Bluegrass. Mary A. Kelly. LC 78-71897. (Illus.). 310p. 1979. 25.00 (*0-682-49143-8*) M A Kelly.

My Old Man & the Sea. large type ed. David Hays & Daniel Hays. 432p. 1997. 31.50 (*0-7089-3687-3*) Ulverscroft.

My Old Man & the Sea: A Father & Son Sail Around Cape Horn. David Hays & Daniel Hays. (Illus.). 256p. 1995. 19.95 (*1-56512-102-3*) Algonquin Bks.

My Old Man & the Sea: A Father & Son Sail Around Cape Horn. David Hays & Daniel Hays. 256p. 1996. pap. 13.00 (*0-06-097696-9*) HarpC.

My Old Man & the Sea: A Father & Son Sail Around Cape Horn. David Hays & Daniel Hays. 1996. pap. text 12.50 (*0-07-027418-5*) McGraw.

My Old Sweetheart. Nikolai Vasilevich Gogol. LC 96-28797. 1997. pap. 12.00 (*0-679-77641-9*) Random.

My Old Teddy. Dom Mansell. LC 91-71830. (Illus.). 32p. (J). (ps). 1992. 12.95 (*1-56402-035-5*) Candlewick Pr.

***My One & Only.** Katherine O'Neal. 352p. 2000. mass mkt. 5.99 (*0-553-58121-X*) Bantam.

***My One & Only Bomb Shelter: Stories.** John Smolens. LC 99-74434. (Series in Short Fiction). 178p. 2000. pap. 15.95 (*0-88748-329-1*, Pub. by Carnegie-Mellon) CUP Services.

My One & Only Love. large type ed. D. H. Thomson. (Linford Romance Large Print Ser.). 320p. 1998. pap. 17.99 (*0-7089-5255-0*, Linford) Ulverscroft.

My One Book. Jane Belk Moncure. LC 85-5897. (My Number Bks.). (Illus.). 32p. (J). (ps-2). 1985. lib. bdg. 21.36 (*0-89565-312-5*) Childs World.

My One Good Nerve. Ruby Dee. LC 98-25196. 178p. 1998. 16.95 (*0-471-31704-7*) Wiley.

My 132 Semesters of Studies of Chemistry. V. Prelog. (Profiles, Pathways & Dreams Ser.). 120p. 1991. text 36.00 (*0-8412-1772-6*) OUP.

My One Life to Give. Stine T. Smith. (Illus.). 46p. 1998. pap. 8.95 (*0-533-12453-0*) Vantage.

My 1-2-3 Book. Pearl Bennett. (Illus.). 12p. (Orig.). (J). (ps-1). 1990. student ed. 4.00 (*0-9622242-1-9*) Red Baron Pub Co.

My 1, 2, 3's. (Jr. Academic Ser.). (Illus.). 32p. (J). (ps). 1998. wbk. ed. 2.25 (*1-57768-218-1*) MG-Hill OH.

My 1-2-3s Say Be Kind to You & Me see Tena, Joshua, & Friends

My Oneness with God. Josephine C. Natividad. Tr. by M. Gabrawy. LC 89-90122. (ARA., Illus.). 160p. (Orig.). 1989. pap. 4.95 (*0-685-25931-5*) J C Natividad.

***My Only Comfort: Death, Deliverance & Discipleship in the Music of Bach.** Calvin R. Stapert. LC 99-462207. 232p. 2000. pap. 16.00 (*0-8028-4472-3*) Eerdmans.

***My Only Great Passion: The Life & Films of Carl the Dreyer.** Jean Drum & Dale D. Drum. LC 99-86373. (Filmmakers Ser.). 320p. 2000. 45.00 (*0-8108-3679-3*) Scarecrow.

***My Only Love.** Cheryl Holt. 2000. mass mkt. 4.99 (*0-8217-6576-0*, Zebra Kensgtn) Kensgtn Pub Corp.

My Only Love. Katherine Sutcliffe. 352p. (Orig.). 1993. mass mkt. 5.99 (*0-515-11074-4*, Jove) Berkley Pub.

***My Only Story: Novel.** Monica Wood. LC 99-55112. 320p. 2000. 22.95 (*0-8118-2714-3*) Chronicle Bks.

My Ontario Beautiful. Mary A. Nangini. LC 94-5676. 64p. 1995. pap. 14.95 (*0-7734-2726-0*, Mellen Poetry Pr) E Mellen.

My Opinions: Incest & Illegitimacy. 3rd expanded rev. ed. Alfred Jordan. LC 97-94183. (Illus.). 160p. (Orig.). 1998. reprint ed. pap. 9.95 (*0-9648652-3-8*) AL-jay Pubng.

***My Opposites.** Rebecca Emberley. (Illus.). 20p. (J). 2000. 5.95 (*0-316-23345-5*) Little.

My Orchestras & Other Adventures: The Memoirs of Boyd Neel. Ed. by J. David Finch. 256p. 1985. text 24.95 (*0-8020-5674-1*) U of Toronto Pr.

My Other Family: An Artist-Wife in Singapore, 1946-48. Patricia Morley. (Illus.). 160p. 1994. text 39.50 (*1-85043-823-4*, Pub. by I B T) St Martin.

My Other Islands. large type ed. Evelyn M. Richardson. 1991. 27.99 (*0-7089-2542-1*) Ulverscroft.

My Other Life. Paul Theroux. 464p. 1997. pap. 13.00 (*0-395-87752-0*, Mariner Bks) HM.

My Other Life. Paul Theroux. 488p. 1996. 33.99 (*0-7710-8575-3*) McCland & Stewart.

My Other Life. Paul Theroux. 1999. text 22.95 (*0-670-86583-4*) Viking Penguin.

My Other Life. unabridged ed. Paul Theroux. 12p. 1998. pap. write for info. incl. audio (*0-7871-1127-9*, 134321, Pub. by NewStar Media) Lndmrk Audiobks.

My Other Loneliness: Letters of Thomas Wolfe & Aline Bernstein. Thomas Wolfe. Ed. by Suzanne Stutman & Richard S. Kennedy. LC 82-20102. (Illus.). xxvi, 390p. 1983. pap. text 19.95 (*0-8078-4117-X*) U of NC Pr.

My Other Self. Clarence J. Enzler. 1958. pap. 11.95 (*0-87193-056-0*) Dimension Bks.

My Other Self: The Letters of Olive Schreiner & Havelock Ellis, 1884- 1920. Ed. by Yaffa C. Draznin. LC 90-5906. XI, 583p. (C). 1993. text 79.95 (*0-8204-1360-7*) P Lang Pubng.

***My Outdoor Buddy. Jack O. Moore. 208p. 2000. pap. 19.95 (*0-87012-608-3*) McClain.**

MY OUTDOOR Buddy is the ultimate book for hikers, backpackers & campers. For unforgettable campfire memories keep records of all your outings in your outdoor diary. It will help you prepare for a more enjoyable & safer outing. Includes basic first aid. Loads of trivia for question games; scary tale starters & even bible time. This book will become your OUTDOOR Buddy. *Publisher Paid Annotation.*

My Outer Banks Coloring Book. Mary Maden. (Illus.). 24p. (Orig.). (J). (gr. k-5). 1996. pap. 2.95 (*0-9646970-4-1*) Dog & Pony Pub.

My Outlaw. Rachel Davis. 384p. 1997. mass mkt. 5.99 (*0-8217-5680-X*, Zebra Kensgtn) Kensgtn Pub Corp.

My Outlaw. Linda Lael Miller. 320p. 1997. per. 6.99 (*0-671-87318-0*) PB.

My Own. Ed. & Illus. by Christian F. Hensler. 112p. (Orig.). 1995. pap. write for info. (*1-883331-11-0*) Anderie Poetry.

My Own Alphabet. Bobbie L. Hawkins. LC 89-7354. 144p. (Orig.). 1989. pap. 9.95 (*0-918273-52-8*) Coffee Hse.

My Own Backyard. Maryl Barker. LC 99-94045. (Gracie's Great Adventures Ser.: Vol. 3). (Illus.). 40p. (J). (ps-4). 1999. pap. 14.95 (*0-9662234-2-X*) GraceMar Prodns.

My Own Big Bed. Anna G. Hines. LC 97-34476. (Illus.). 24p. (J). (ps-3). 1998. 15.00 (*0-688-15599-5*, Grenwillow Bks) HarpC Child Bks.

***My Own Big Bed.** Anna G. Hines. LC 97-34476. (Illus.). 24p. (J). (ps-3). 1998. 14.93 (*0-688-15600-2*, Grenwillow Bks) HarpC Child Bks.

My Own Book! Reading Is Fundamental (RIF) 20th Anniversary. Roger A. Hammer. LC 86-30410. (Illus.). 128p. 1987. pap. 14.95 (*0-932991-50-5*) Place in the Woods.

My Own Book of Feelings. Linda P. Silbert & Alvin J. Silbert. (Little Twirps Creative Thinking Workbook Ser.). (Illus.). (J). (gr. k-8). 1977. 4.98 (*0-89544-017-2*, 017) Silbert Bress.

My Own Book of Prayers. Mary Batchelor. (Illus.). 64p. (J). (gr. k-3). 1996. 11.95 (*0-687-01879-X*) Abingdon.

My Own Book of Special Things. Linda P. Silbert & Alvin J. Silbert. (Little Twirps Creative Thinking Workbook Ser.). (Illus.). (J). (ps-4). 1977. student ed. 4.98 (*0-89544-019-9*, 019) Silbert Bress.

My Own Book of Wishes. Linda P. Silbert & Alvin J. Silbert. (Little Twirps Creative Thinking Workbook Ser.). (Illus.). (J). (gr. k-6). 1976. student ed. 4.98 (*0-89544-016-4*) Silbert Bress.

My Own Cape Cod. Gladys Taber. reprint ed. lib. bdg. 22.95 (*0-89190-595-2*, Rivercity Pr) Amereon Ltd.

My Own Cape Cod. Gladys Taber. (Illus.). 256p. 1981. reprint ed. pap. 8.95 (*0-940160-10-2*) Parnassus Imprints.

My Own Circus. Ed Gillies. (Illus.). (J). (gr. k-4). 1993. pap. 14.95 (*1-882954-07-6*) Aspen Press.

My Own Cookbook. Gladys Taber. 24.95 (*0-8488-1194-1*) Amereon Ltd.

My Own Cookbook: From Stillmeadow & Cape Cod. Gladys Taber. 312p. 1982. reprint ed. pap. 9.95 (*0-940160-15-3*) Parnassus Imprints.

My Own Country. Abraham Vergehese. 1995. pap. 15.00 (*0-679-75292-7*) Random.

My Own Cruising Journal. Pat R. Anderson. LC 92-97098. 80p. 1997. spiral bd. 19.95 (*0-9634391-0-3*) P Russel Anderson.

My Own Fun: Creative Learning Activities for Home & School. Carolyn B. Haas & Anita C. Friedman. LC 90-44181. (Illus.). 208p. (Orig.). (J). (gr. 2-7). 1990. pap. 9.95 (*1-55652-093-X*) Chicago Review.

My Own Ground. Hugh Nissenson. LC 97-21602. (Library of Modern Jewish Literature). 180p. 1997. pap. 17.95 (*0-8156-0485-8*) Syracuse U Pr.

My Own Hanukah Story. Daniel D. Stuhlman. (Illus.). (Orig.). (J). (ps-5). 1980. 2.50 (*0-934402-12-4*); pap. 3.95 (*0-934402-07-8*); 1.00 (*0-934402-08-6*) BYLS Pr.

My Own Harlem. Pellom McDaniels, III. Ed. by Nawah McDaniels. LC 98-129906. (Illus.). 66p. 1997. pap. write for info. (*0-9661814-0-9*) P McDaniels.

***My Own Harlem.** 2nd ed. Pellom McDaniels, III. LC 98-43009. 80p. 1998. pap. 12.95 (*1-886110-67-0*, Pub. by Addax Pubng) Midpt Trade.

My Own Home. Lyn L. Hooper. LC 90-4386. (Charlotte Zolotow Bk.). (Illus.). 32p. (J). (gr. k-3). 1991. 13.95 (*0-06-022570-X*) HarpC Child Bks.

My Own Hundred Doors. Pam Bernard. Ed. by Bertha Rogers. (Poetry Award Ser.). 60p. (Orig.). 1996. pap. 10.95 (*0-9646844-4-6*) Bright Hill.

My Own Life & Times, 1741-1814. Thomas Somerville. (Contemporary Memoirs Ser.: Vol. 1). 397p. 1996. 85.00 (*1-85506-396-4*) Bks Intl VA.

My Own Life & Times, 1741-1814. Thomas Somerville. Ed. by William Lee. LC 78-67543. reprint ed. 44.50 (*0-404-17206-7*) AMS Pr.

My Own Los Angeles, 1894 to 1982. Warren S. Rogers. (Los Angeles Miscellany Ser.: No. 13). (Illus.). 53p. 1982. 15.00 (*0-87093-313-2*) Dawsons.

***My Own Manger: The Read & Play Christmas Story.** Zonderskidz Staff. (Illus.). (J). 2000. 12.99 (*0-310-97870-X*, Zonderkidz) Zondervan.

My Own Nativity. Ed Gillies. (Illus.). 12p. (J). (gr. k-4). 1993. pap. 14.95 (*1-882954-01-7*) Aspen Press.

My Own Noah's Ark. Ed Gillies. (Illus.). 10p. (J). (gr. k-4). 1993. pap. 14.95 (*1-882954-02-5*) Aspen Press.

My Own Opinions upon Libraries & Librarianship. William E. Henry. LC 67-23231. (Essay Index Reprint Ser.). 1977. 20.95 (*0-8369-0536-9*) Ayer.

***My Own Pages: A Journal for 2000.** Ed. by Highlights Editors. (Illus.). 176p. (YA). (gr. 3 up). 2000. pap. 19.95 (*1-56397-857-1*) Boyds Mills Pr.

***My Own Pages: A Journal for 2001.** Ed. by Highlights Editors. (Illus.). 176p. (YA). (gr. 3 up). 2000. pap. 19.95 (*1-56397-914-4*) Boyds Mills Pr.

My Own Personal Experience & Observation As a Soldier in the Confederate Army During the Civil War, 1861-1865, Also During the Period of Reconstruction. J. E. Robuck. (Illus.). 136p. 1977. reprint ed. 14.00 (*0-937130-03-6*) Burkes Bk Store.

My Own Pesah Story. Daniel D. Stuhlman. (My Own Holiday Stories Ser.: No. 2). (Illus.). (Orig.). (J). (gr. 1-6). 1981. pap. 3.95 (*0-934402-09-4*); pap. 3.00 (*0-934402-10-8*); 1.50 (*0-934402-11-6*) BYLS Pr.

My Own Pet. Lynn Offerman. LC 98-68543. (Illus.). 10p. (YA). (ps-k). 1999. pap. 6.95 (*0-7613-1034-7*) Millbrook Pr.

My Own Place. Michael Bosworth. LC 93-27058. (Voyages Ser.). (Illus.). (J). 1994. 4.25 (*0-383-03766-2*) SRA McGraw.

***My Own Private Cuba: Essays on Cuban Literature & Culture.** Gustavo Perez Firmat. LC 99-71350. 260p. 1999. pap. 25.00 (*0-89295-096-X*) Society Sp & Sp-Am.

My Own Private Germany: Daniel Paul Schreber's Secret History of Modernity. Eric L. Santner. LC 95-43738. 240p. 1996. text 35.00 (*0-691-02628-9*, Pub. by Princeton U Pr); pap. text 14.95 (*0-691-02627-0*, Pub. by Princeton U Pr) Cal Prin Full Svc.

My Own Recipes. Ed. by G & R Publishing Staff. (Uni-Bks.). 160p. (Orig.). 1994. pap. text 3.00 (*1-56383-025-6*, 3300) G & R Pub.

My Own Reflections. Peter Vallas. 78p. (Orig.). (C). pap. 6.00 (*0-9606106-0-X*) Beddoe Pub.

My Own Right Time: An Exploration of Clockwork Design. Philip Woodward. (Illus.). 176p. 1995. 55.00 (*0-19-856522-4*) OUP.

My Own Sea Kingdom. Ed Gillies. (Illus.). (J). (gr. k-4). 1993. pap. 14.95 (*1-882954-08-4*) Aspen Press.

My Own Sense of Place: A Southern View with a Northern Exposure. 2nd rev. ed. Anne Wells Branscomb. LC 98-74410. 160p. 1999. 22.95 (*1-57736-126-1*) Providence Hse.

***My Own Small Place: Developing the Writing Life.** Madeleine L'Engle. LC 98-23519. 1998. write for info. (*0-87788-571-0*, H Shaw Pubs) Waterbrook Pr.

My Own Song. Michael Strikland. LC 97-70582. (Illus.). 64p. (J). (gr. 5). 1997. 14.95 (*1-56397-686-2*, Wordsong) Boyds Mills Pr.

My Own Story. Emmeline Pankhurst. LC 85-952. (Illus.). 364p. 1985. reprint ed. lib. bdg. 59.75 (*0-313-24926-1*, PMOS, Greenwood Pr) Greenwood.

My Own Story. John Robinson. (American Autobiography Ser.). 172p. 1995. reprint ed. lib. bdg. 69.00 (*0-7812-8627-1*) Rprt Serv.

My Own Story. John T. Trowbridge. (Notable American Authors). 1999. reprint ed. lib. bdg. 125.00 (*0-7812-9820-2*) Rprt Serv.

My Own Story. rev. ed. Fremont Older. (BCL1 - United States Local History Ser.). 340p. 1991. reprint ed. lib. bdg. 89.00 (*0-7812-6343-3*) Rprt Serv.

My Own Thoughts & Feelings: A Growth & Recovery Workbook for Young Boys. Wendy Deaton. 64p. (J). (gr. 2-6). 1993. 17.95 (*0-89793-134-3*); pap., student ed. 9.95 (*0-89793-131-9*) Hunter Hse.

My Own Thoughts & Feelings: A Growth & Recovery Workbook for Young Girls. Wendy Deaton. 64p. (J). (gr. 2-6). 1993. 17.95 (*0-89793-133-5*); pap., student ed. 9.95 (*0-89793-130-0*) Hunter Hse.

My Own Thoughts on Stopping the Hurt. Wendy Deaton. 64p. (J). (gr. 2-6). 1993. 17.95 (*0-89793-135-1*); pap., student ed. 9.95 (*0-89793-132-7*) Hunter Hse.

My Own Time: The Authorized Biography of John Wetton. Kim Dancha. LC 96-70725. (Illus.). 180p. (Orig.). 1997. pap. 19.95 (*0-9654847-1-8*) Northern Line.

My Own Trail. Howard Luke. 10.00 (*1-877962-32-5*) Todd Commns.

***My Own True Name: New & Selected Poems for Young Adults, 1984-1999.** Pat Mora. LC 00-23969. (Illus.). 81p. (YA). 2000. pap. 11.95 (*1-55885-292-1*, Pub. by Arte Publico) SPD-Small Pr Dist.

My Own True Psychic Adventures. Nora P. Grafton. LC 75-28590. 270p. 1977. vinyl bd. 10.95 (*0-916498-01-8*) Tolff.

My Own Two Feet. Robert G. Lowe. Ed. by Thelma L. Hill. LC 94-77361. 110p. (Orig.). 1994. pap. text 10.00 (*1-878455-10-9*) Markas Pub.

My Own Two Feet: A Memoir. Beverly Cleary. LC 95-1764. (Illus.). 288p. (YA). (gr. 8-12). 1995. 15.00 (*0-688-14267-2*, Wm Morrow) Morrow Avon.

My Own Two Feet: A Memoir. Beverly Cleary. 272p. (J). (gr. 4-7). 1996. pap. 10.00 (*0-380-72746-3*, Avon Bks) Morrow Avon.

My Own Two Feet: A Memoir. Beverly Cleary. LC 95-1764. 1996. 15.35 (*0-606-10264-7*) Turtleback.

My Own Very Special Book about Me. Vijai P. Sharma & Jan Hindman. LC 98-66496. (Illus.). 54p. 1998. pap. 7.95 (*0-9628382-8-4*) Mind Pubns.

My Own Words, Bk. 5. Ed. by Simon & Schuster Children's. (J). 1998. 14.98 (*0-671-74167-5*) S&S Childrens.

My Own Worst Enemy. Carol Sonenklar. LC 98-41952. 144p. (YA). (gr. 5 up). 1999. 15.95 (*0-8234-1456-6*) Holiday.

***My Own Yearbook.** Trish Frederick. 150p. 1999. 17.98 (*1-57532-255-2*) Press-Tige Pub.

My Oxford. Martin Amis. Ed. & Intro. by Ann Thwaite. (Illus.). 214p. (Orig.). 1987. pap. 8.95 (*0-86051-381-5*, Pub. by Robson Bks) Parkwest Pubns.

My "p" Sound Box. Jane Belk Moncure. LC 78-7841. (Sound Box Library). (Illus.). 32p. (J). (ps-2). 1978. lib. bdg. 21.36 (*0-89565-047-9*) Childs World.

My Painted House, My Friendly Chicken & Me. Maya Angelou. LC 93-45735. (Illus.). 48p. (J). (ps-5). 1994. 16.00 (*0-517-59667-9*) C Potter.

My Painted House, My Friendly Chicken & Me. Maya Angelou. 48p. 1996. pap. 6.99 (*0-517-88815-7*) C Potter.

My Painted House, My Friendly Chicken & Me. Maya Angelou. (J). 1994. 12.19 (*0-606-10885-8*, Pub. by Turtleback) Demco.

My Pal Al. Marcia Leonard. LC 97-40289. (Real Kids Readers Ser.). (Illus.). 32p. (J). (ps-1). 1998. pap. 3.99 (*0-7613-2026-1*, Copper Beech Bks); lib. bdg. 16.90 (*0-7613-2001-6*, Copper Beech Bks) Millbrook Pr.

***My Pal Grubby.** Tony Lamke & Sue Lamke. (Illus.). 112p. (Orig.). (J). 2000. pap. 9.95 (*1-882203-68-2*) Orange Frazer.

***My Pals from the Pickle Patch: 101 Playful Verses Written & Illustrated by Paul Agosto.** (Illus.). 108p. 1999. 6.00 (*0-9675280-0-3*) Pickle Gas Pr.

My Pamet: Cape Cod Chronicle. Thomas Kane. 480p. 1989. 14.95 (*0-918825-91-1*) Moyer Bell.

My Pants Are Wet, But I Didn't Do It! enl. ed. George Wilkins. Orig. Title: Dere Prisabel, or My Pants Are Wet, But I Didn't Do It!. (Illus.). 128p. 1997. pap. 7.95 (*0-914875-30-2*) Bright Mtn Bks.

My Paper Route. Alex N. Holland. (Illus.). 16p. (J). (gr. k-5). 1995. pap. 10.95 (*1-56606-033-8*) Bradley Mann.

My Parable, Reminiscences see Mia Parabola, Memorie

My Pardner. Max Evans. LC 75-187421. (Illus.). 104p. (J). (gr. 5-9). 1972. 3.95 (*0-395-13725-X*) HM.

My Parents. Herve Guibert. (Masks Ser.). 160p. 1994. pap. 12.99 (*1-85242-286-6*) Serpents Tail.

My Parents Are Divorced. Mark DiSanto. (J). (gr. 3-6). 1997. 8.95 (*0-533-12371-2*) Vantage.

My Parents Are Divorced, Too: A Book for Kids by Kids. Melanie Ford et al. LC 96-46699. (Illus.). 64p. (J). (gr. 3-8). 1997. pap. 11.95 (*0-945354-69-X*) Am Psychol.

My Parents Are Divorced, Too: A Book for Kids by Kids. Melanie Ford et al. 64p. (J). (gr. 3-8). 1997. pap. 11.95 (*1-55798-450-6*, 441-4506, Magination Press) Am Psychol.

My Parents Are Users: Christian Living - Encouragement. Ron Climer. Ed. by Becky Nelson. 21p. (YA). (gr. 7-12). 1994. pap. text 1.95 (*1-56309-096-1*, C946105, Wrld Changers Res) Womans Mission Union.

My Parents Cried Too. 3rd rev. ed. Dennis A. Van Wingerden & J. Marilyn Van Wingerden. (Illus.). 17p. 1998. pap. 6.00 (*0-9661782-0-3*) Fam Life Today.

My Parents' Divorce. Julia Cole. LC 98-16956. (How Do I Feel About... Ser.). (Illus.). 24p. (J). (gr. k). 1998. lib. bdg. 19.90 (*0-7613-0869-5*, Copper Beech Bks) Millbrook Pr.

My Parent's Keeper: Adult Children of the Emotionally Disturbed. Eva Brown. 152p. (Orig.). 1989. pap. 11.95 (*0-934986-78-9*) New Harbinger.

***My Parents' Last Years: A Daughter's Journey with Death & Alzheimer's Disease.** Janet M. Stone. 2000. pap. 12.95 (*0-533-13551-6*) Vantage.

My Parents Married on a Dare & Other Favorite Essays on Life. Carlfred B. Broderick. LC 96-19270. viii, 150p. 1996. 14.95 (*1-57345-190-8*) Deseret Bk.

***My Parents, My Children: Spiritual Help for Caregivers.** Cecil Murphey. 244p. 2000. pap. 16.95 (*0-664-22246-3*) Westminster John Knox.

My Parents Never Had Sex: Myths & Facts of Sexual Aging. Doris B. Hammond. LC 87-20818. 180p. (Orig.). 1987. 26.95 (*0-87975-409-5*); pap. 17.95 (*0-87975-413-3*) Prometheus Bks.

My Parents Still Love Me, Even Though They're Getting Divorced: An Interactive Tale for Children. Lois V. Nightingale. LC 96-92679. (Illus.). 128p. (J). (gr. k-6). 1996. pap. 14.95 (*1-889755-00-1*) Nightngale Rose.

My Parents Think I'm Sleeping. Jack Prelutsky. LC 84-13640. (Illus.). 48p. (J). (gr. 2-4). 1985. lib. bdg. 15.93 (*0-688-04019-5*, Grenwillow Bks) HarpC Child Bks.

My Parents Think I'm Sleeping. Jack Prelutsky. LC 84-13640. (Illus.). 48p. (J). (ps-3). 1985. 16.00 (*0-688-04018-7*, Grenwillow Bks) HarpC Child Bks.

My Parents Think I'm Sleeping. Jack Prelutsky. LC 84-13640. (Illus.). 48p. (J). (ps-3). 1995. reprint ed. mass mkt. 4.95 (*0-688-14028-9*, Wm Morrow) Morrow Avon.

My Parents Think I'm Sleeping Poems. Jack Prelutsky. (J). 1995. 10.15 (*0-606-07909-2*, Pub. by Turtleback) Demco.

My Parrot, My Friend: An Owner's Guide to Parrot Behavior. Bonnie M. Doane & Thomas Qualkinbush. (Illus.). 256p. 1995. 25.00 (*0-87605-970-1*) Howell Bks.

My Parsha Bereishis Learn & Play Book, Vol. I. Libby Chein. (Illus.). 150p. (Orig.). (J). pap., student ed. 9.95 (*1-884535-93-3*) Empire Press.

My Partner Prayer Notebook. Becky Tirabassi. 276p. 1998. spiral bd. 19.99 (*0-7852-7479-0*) Nelson.

My Parts of Speech Dictionary. Linda Milliken. Ed. by Kathy Rogers. (Illus.). 32p. 1999. pap., teacher ed., wbk. ed. 1.99 (*1-56472-610-X*) Edupress Inc.

My Passage at the New Orleans Tribune: A Memoir of the Civil War Era. Jean-Charles Houzeau. Ed. by David C. Rankin. Tr. by Gerard F. Denault. LC 84-7185. (Library of Southern Civilization). 184p. 1984. reprint ed. pap. 57.10 (*0-608-00867-2*, 206165900010) Bks Demand.

My Passage Through Life. Abraham Weisberg. 188p. 1995. 15.00 (*0-9644801-4-X*) Mgt Servs Corp Invest Tr.

My Passover Activity Book. David Sokoloff. (Illus.). 24p. (Orig.). (J). (ps-5). 1998. pap. 1.00 (*1-889655-10-4*) Jewish Educ Toys.

My Past & Thoughts, 6 vols. Aleksandr Herzen. 1972. 600.00 (*0-8490-0689-9*) Gordon Pr.

My Past & Thoughts: The Memoirs of Alexander Herzen. Aleksandr Herzen. Ed. by Dwight MacDonald & Dwight Macdonald. LC 73-15933. 752p. 1999. pap. 18.95 (*0-520-04210-7*, Pub. by U CA Pr) Cal Prin Full Svc.

My Patchwork Spirit. Kathryn W. Lazenby. (Illus.). 96p. 1998. 22.95 (*1-57736-089-3*) Providence Hse.

My Path Through Life. Lilli Lehman. Ed. by Andrew Farkas. Tr. by Alice B. Seligman. LC 76-29947. (Opera Biographies Ser.). (Illus.). 1977. reprint ed. lib. bdg. 53.95 (*0-405-09689-5*) Ayer.

My Path Through Life. Lilli Lehmann. Tr. by Alice B. Seligman. LC 80-2286. (Illus.). reprint ed. 54.50 (*0-404-18855-9*) AMS Pr.

My Path to Easter: Initiation Journal for Children. Kathy Coffey. (Children & Christian Initiation Ser.). (Illus.). 40p. (J). (gr. 1-4). 1997. 5.95 (*1-889108-35-9*) Liv Good News.

My Path to Easter: Initiation Journal for Youth. Kathy Coffey. (Children & Christian Initiation Ser.). (Illus.). 40p. (J). (gr. 5-9). 1997. 5.95 (*1-889108-36-7*) Liv Good News.

My Path to Heaven: A Young Person's Guide to the Faith. Geoffrey Bliss. LC 97-13452. Orig. Title: A Retreat with St. Ignatius: In Pictures for Children. (Illus.). 96p. (Orig.). (J). (gr. 4-6). 1997. reprint ed. pap. 12.95 (*0-918477-48-4*) Sophia Inst Pr.

My Path to Peace & Justice. Richard T. McSorley. 350p. (Orig.). 1996. pap. 17.00 (*1-879175-19-3*) Fortkamp.

My Patient God's Gift: Mariette, a Saint for Our Time. Mariette Do-Nguyen & Gerald E. Nelson. Ed. by Beverly Trainer. (Revelations Ser.). (Illus.). 200p. (Orig.). 1996. pap. 25.00 (*0-9652169-0-X*, 1) Rebuild My Church.

My Patients with Tales: The Experiences of a Wisconsin Veterinarian. Robert W. Pope. (Illus.). 120p. 1999. pap. 11.25 (*0-9669829-0-8*, 0101) Pause Pub Co.

My Pee Dee River Hills: A Remembered Place. Chris Florance. (Illus.). 234p. 1995. pap. 13.95 (*1-878086-41-3*, Pub. by Down Home NC) Blair.

My Pen & I. John R. Terry. 132p. 1985. pap. 10.95 (*0-933704-52-6*) Dawn Pr.

My Pen Pal, Pat. Lisa Papademetriou. LC 98-16596. (Real Kids Readers Ser.). (Illus.). 48p. (J). (gr. 1-3). 1998. pap. 3.99 (*0-7613-2048-2*, Copper Beech Bks); lib. bdg. 17.90 (*0-7613-2023-7*, Copper Beech Bks) Millbrook Pr.

An Asterisk (*) at the beginning of an entry indicates that the title is appearing for the first time.

My Pen Pal Scrapbook: An Educational Journey Through World Cultures. Shelley Aliotti. Ed. by Diane Tapscott. LC 95-61366. (Illus.). 66p. (Orig.). (J). (gr. 3-8). 1995. pap. 19.95 (*0-9647396-0-7*) Wrld View CA.

My Penitente Land: Reflections on Spanish New Mexico. Fray A. Chavez. 272p. 1993. pap. 14.95 (*0-89013-255-0*) Museum NM Pr.

***My Pennsylvania Garden: A Gardener's Journal.** Liz Ball. (Illus.). 128p. 2000. spiral bd. 19.95 (*1-930604-06-8*) Cool Springs Pr.

***My Pennsylvania Garden: A Gardener's Journal.** Cool Springs Press Publications Staff. 2000. 19.95 (*1-888608-89-7*) Cool Springs Pr.

My People see Mayn Folk ALEF

My People see Mayn Folk, Vol. 2, Beyz

My People: Abba Eban's History of the Jews, Vol. II. David Bamberger. (Illus.). 1979. pap. 10.95 (*0-87441-280-3*) Behrman.

My People: Abba Eban's History of the Jews, Vol. II. Geoffrey Horn & David Bamberger. (Illus.). 1979. pap., teacher ed. 14.95 (*0-87441-341-9*) Behrman.

My People: Abba Eban's History of the Jews Genesis to 1776, Vol. I. David Bamberger. LC 77-10667. (Illus.). 1978. pap. text 10.95 (*0-87441-263-3*) Behrman.

My People: Abba Eban's History of the Jews Genesis to 1776, Vol. I. David Bamberger & Geoffrey Horn. LC 77-10667. (Illus.). 1978. pap., teacher ed. 14.95 (*0-87441-296-X*) Behrman.

My People: Abba Eban's History of the Jews Genesis to 1776, Vol. I. David Bamberger & Miriam P. Kurinsky. LC 77-10667. (Illus.). 1978. pap., wbk. ed. 4.95 (*0-87441-329-X*) Behrman.

My People: The Story of Those Christians Sometimes Called Plymouth Brethren. Robert H. Baylis. LC 95-41247. 336p. 1995. pap. 24.99 (*0-87788-577-X*, H Shaw Pubs) Waterbrook Pr.

My People - Stuff Directory. Iris L. Solomon & Ronald B. Solomon. 114p. (J). (gr. 3 up). 1998. ring bd. 14.95 (*0-9658167-1-0*) Swingset Pr.

My People Are Destroyed for a Lack of Knowledge: A Biblical Account in Chart Form. Jackie Fowler. (Illus.). 80p. (Orig.). 1992. reprint ed. pap. 7.95 (*0-9633722-0-3*) Fowler Ent.

My People, My Poetry. Tonye Joiner. (Illus.). 80p. 1997. pap. 10.99 (*0-9657539-0-5*) Essence of Liv.

My People Says Your God: Jeremiah. Burton Yost. Ed. by Maynard Shelly. LC 88-81700. (Faith & Life Bible Studies). 116p. 1988. pap. 1.95 (*0-87303-122-9*) Faith & Life.

My People the Sioux. Luther Standing Bear. Ed. by E. A. Brininstool. LC 74-77394. (Illus.). xx, 292p. 1975. reprint ed. pap. 11.95 (*0-8032-5793-7*, Bison Books) U of Nebr Pr.

My People's Prayer Book - Traditional Prayers, Modern Commentaries Vol. 1: The Sh'ma & Its Blessings. Ed. by Lawrence A. Hoffman. LC 97-26836. 168p. 1997. 23.95 (*1-879045-79-6*) Jewish Lights.

My People's Prayer Book - Traditional Prayers, Modern Commentaries Vol. 2: The Amidah. Ed. by Lawrence A. Hoffman. 240p. 1998. 23.95 (*1-879045-80-X*) Jewish Lights.

My People's Prayer Book - Traditional Prayers, Modern Commentaries Vol. 3: P'sukei D'zimrah (Morning Psalms) Ed. by Lawrence A. Hoffman. 200p. 1999. 23.95 (*1-879045-81-8*) Jewish Lights.

***My People's Prayer Book - Traditional Prayers, Modern Commentaries Vol. 4: Seder K'riyat Hatorah (Shabbat Torah Service),** Ed. by Lawrence A. Hoffman. 240p. 1999. 23.95 (*1-879045-82-6*) Jewish Lights.

***My People's Waltz: Stories.** Dale R. Phillips. 2000. pap. 13.00 (*0-380-73336-6*) Morrow Avon.

My People's Waltz: Stories. Dale R. Phillips. LC 98-37090. 192p. 1999. 22.95 (*0-393-04715-6*) Norton.

***My Perfect Guy.** Created by Francine Pascal. (Sweet Valley Junior High Ser.: No. 14). (J). (gr. 3-7). 2000. pap. 4.50 (*0-553-48702-7*, Sweet Valley) BDD Bks Young Read.

My Perfect Neighborhood. Leah Komaiko. LC 89-37871. (Illus.). 32p. (J). (ps-3). 1990. 13.95 (*0-06-023287-0*) HarpC Child Bks.

My Perfect Pet. Christopher Carrie. (Crayola So Big Bks.). (Illus.). 40p. (Orig.). (J). (ps up). 1989. pap. 1.99 (*0-86696-218-2*) Binney & Smith.

My Persian Pilgrimage: An Autobiography. rev. ed. William M. Miller. LC 89-995. (Illus.). 408p. 1995. pap. 21.95 (*0-87808-243-3*, WCL243-3) William Carey Lib.

My Personal Bowling Diary. Rachel A. Holmes. iv, 81p. (Orig.). 1996. pap. 15.95 (*0-9652658-0-3*) Eloquent Express.

My Personal Health History. William E. Pitts. 95p. 1999. 19.95 (*0-9671388-0-9*) Bea Pubg.

My Personal Pet Rememberance Journal. Enid S. Traisman. 44p. (Orig.). 1997. pap. write for info. (*0-9651131-0-8*) Dove Lewis Comm Serv.

My Personal Prayer Book. Alvin N. Rogness. LC 88-28625. (Illus.). 64p. 1988. kivar 8.99 (*0-8066-2358-6*, 10-4599, Augsburg) Augsburg Fortress.

***My Personal Prayer Journal.** Doris Lyon. 162p. 1999. pap. 9.99 (*1-57921-173-9*, Pub. by WinePress Pub) BookWorld.

***My Personal Thoughts.** Mercedes Vega. 2000. pap. write for info. (*1-58235-313-1*) Watermrk Pr.

My Personal Touch: A Child's Story about Good & Bad Touch. Kathleen Shelly-Amoriello. (Illus.). 20p. (J). (gr. k-3). 1996. pap. 5.50 (*0-9649372-6-3*) K Shelly-Amoriello.

My Personal Tribute to President Ronald Reagan: The President in Verse. Carol A. Osley. (Orig.). (C). 1983. pap. 4.00 (*0-910119-07-4*) SOCO Pubns.

My Personal Yearbook. Illus. by Patricia Howard. 52p. (J). (gr. 5-8). 1993. pap. 6.95 (*1-877673-20-X*, YB) Cottonwood Pr.

My Personalized Journal & Life Organizer. John D. Hawkes. 1979. 12.95 (*0-89036-074-X*) Liahona Pub Trust.

My Perversion is the Belief in True Love. Ellen Cantor. (Illus.). 112p. 1999. pap. 29.95 (*3-908247-02-0*) Scalo Pubs.

My Pesach Book: Halachos of Pesach & the Seder. Yossi Lieman. LC 98-165911. (Illus.). 69p. (J). (gr. 2-4). 1998. 8.00 (*0-9666133-0-9*) Yamban.

***My Pest.** Kim L. Dulaney. (Fuzzy-Feeling Bks.). (Illus.). (J). (gr. 1-4). 1999. pap. 8.25 (*1-891636-05-7*, 1006) Unique Exp.

My Pet. Lynn Salem & Josie Stewart. (Illus.). 8p. (J). (gr. k-1). 1992. pap. 3.75 (*1-880612-11-9*) Seedling Pubns.

My Pet: A Photolog Book. Janet Horowitz et al. (Illus.). 48p. (J). (gr. 1-7). 1992. bds. 4.50 (*1-55670-268-X*) Stewart Tabori & Chang.

My Pet Cat. Leeanne Engfer. LC 96-47304. (All about Pets Ser.). (Illus.). 64p. (J). (gr. 3-6). 1997. lib. bdg. 22.60 (*0-8225-2258-6*, Lerner Publctns) Lerner Pub.

My Pet Cats. Leeanne Engfer. (All about Pets Ser.). (Illus.). 64p. (J). (gr. 3-7). 1997. pap. text 7.95 (*0-8225-9793-4*) Lerner Pub.

My Pet Crocodile: And Other Slightly Outrageous Verse. John Billings. LC 93-72718. (Illus.). 128p. (J). (gr. k-12). 1994. 16.95 (*1-884035-55-8*) Chokecherry.

My Pet Died: A Let's Make a Book About It Book. Rachel Biale. (Let's Make a Book about It Ser.). (Illus.). 48p. (J). (ps-3). 1997. pap. 7.95 (*1-883672-51-1*) Tricycle Pr.

My Pet Dinosaur. Pam Howard. (HRL Little Bks.). (Illus.). 8p. (Orig.). (J). (ps-k). 1996. pap. text 10.95 (*1-57332-073-0*) HighReach Lrning.

My Pet Dinosaur. large type ed. Pam Howard. (HRL Big Bks.). (Illus.). 8p. (Orig.). (J). (ps-k). 1996. pap. text 10.95 (*1-57332-074-9*) HighReach Lrning.

My Pet Dog. Ruth Berman. LC 98-50709. (All about Pets Ser.). (Illus.). 64p. (J). (gr. 3-6). 2000. 22.60 (*0-8225-2259-4*, Lerner Publctns) Lerner Pub.

***My Pet Ferrets.** Amy Gelman. LC 99-6865. (All about Pets Ser.). (Illus.). 64p. (J). (gr. 3-6). 2000. 22.60 (*0-8225-2264-0*, Lerner Publctns) Lerner Pub.

My Pet Fish. Lori Coleman. LC 97-10861. (All about Pets Ser.). (Illus.). 64p. (J). (gr. 3-6). 1997. lib. bdg. 22.60 (*0-8225-2262-4*) Lerner Pub.

My Pet Hamster. Anne Rockwell. 40p. (ps-1). pap. 4.95 (*0-06-445205-0*) HarpC.

My Pet Hamster & Gerbils. Leeanne Engfer. LC 96-37908. (All about Pets Ser.). (Illus.). 64p. (gr. 3-6). 1997. lib. bdg. 22.60 (*0-8225-2261-6*) Lerner Pub.

My Pet Hamster & Gerbils. Leeanne Engfer. (All about Pets Ser.). (Illus.). 64p. (J). (gr. 3-6). 1997. pap. text 7.95 (*0-8225-9794-2*) Lerner Pub.

My Pet Hamster & Gerbils. Rockwell. 40p. (J). (ps-1). 15.95 (*0-06-028564-8*); lib. bdg. 15.89 (*0-06-028565-6*) HarpC Child Bks.

My Pet Iguana. large type ed. Amy Adams. (Illus.). 32p. (J). (gr. 1-5). 1997. pap. 10.00 (*1-888166-54-1*) Shining Lght.

My Pet Lizards. Leeanne Engfer. LC 98-2871. (All about Pets Ser.). (Illus.). 64p. (J). (gr. 3-6). 1999. 22.60 (*0-8225-2263-2*, Lerner Publctns) Lerner Pub.

My Pet Rabbit. Kristine Spangard. (All about Pets Ser.). (Illus.). 64p. (J). (gr. 3-7). 1997. pap. text 7.95 (*0-8225-9795-0*) Lerner Pub.

My Pet Rabbit. Kristine I. Spangard. LC 96-40245. (All about Pets Ser.). (Illus.). 64p. (J). (gr. 3). 1997. lib. bdg. 22.60 (*0-8225-2257-8*) Lerner Pub.

My Pet Rat. Arlene Erlbach. LC 97-24709. (All about Pets Ser.). (Illus.). 64p. (J). (gr. 3-6). 1998. lib. bdg. 22.60 (*0-8225-2260-8*, Lerner Publctns) Lerner Pub.

My Pet Tyrannosaurus. Jane Murphy. LC 88-81468. (Illus.). 32p. (J). (ps-2). 8.95 incl. audio (*0-937124-17-6*, KIM 11C) Kimbo Educ.

My Pet Zoo. Date not set. 5.95 (*0-89868-321-1*); pap. 4.95 (*0-89868-402-1*); lib. bdg. 10.95 (*0-89868-320-3*) ARO Pub.

My Peter Rabbit Cloth Book. Beatrix Potter. (Illus.). 10p. (J). (ps). 1994. pap. 4.99 (*0-7232-0020-3*, F Warne) Peng Put Young Read.

My Pets. Jane Brettle. (Animal Noises Ser.). 1999. 2.98 (*1-57717-099-7*) Todtri Prods.

My Pets. Ed. by Intervisual Books Staff. (Cuddly Cloth Bks.). (Illus.). 6p. (J). 1997. 14.95 (*0-8362-2828-6*) Andrews & McMeel.

My Pets. Jo E. Moore. (Illus.). 48p. (J). (ps-1). 1988. pap. 9.95 (*1-55799-131-6*, EMC 185) Evan-Moor Edu Pubs.

My Pets: Cuddly Cloth Books. Intervisual Books Staff. (J). 1997. text 14.95 (*1-888443-00-6*) Intervisual Bks.

My Phantom Husband. Marie Darrieussecq. Tr. by Esther Allen from FRE. LC 98-55513. 160p. 1999. 19.95 (*1-56584-538-2*, Pub. by New Press NY) Norton.

***My Phillipe.** Barbara Miller. 448p. 2000. 6.50 (*0-671-77453-0*, Sonnet Bks) PB.

My Philosophical Development. Bertrand Russell. (Unwin Paperbacks Ser.). 1975. pap. 9.95 (*0-04-192030-9*) Routledge.

My Philosophical Development. Bertrand Russell. LC 96-163548. 224p. (C). 1995. pap. 17.99 (*0-415-13601-6*) Routledge.

My Philosophy: Why My Paintings are Signed "A Friend of Civilization" Robert G. Bowen, Jr. LC 81-69045. (Orig.). 1982. 30.00 (*0-9607512-1-1*); 30.00 (*0-9607512-3-8*); pap. 4.00 (*0-9607512-0-3*); pap. 6.00 (*0-9607512-2-X*) R G Bowen.

My Philosophy & My Religion. Ralph W. Trine. 130p. 1997. pap. 11.00 (*0-89540-349-8*, SB-349) Sun Pub.

My Philosophy & Other Essays on the Moral & Political Problems of Our Time. Benedetto Croce. Tr. by E. F. Caritt. LC 75-41068. (BCL Ser. II). reprint ed. 37.50 (*0-404-14526-4*) AMS Pr.

My Philosophy of Law: Credos of Sixteen American Scholars. (Illus.). xii, 321p. 1987. reprint ed. 45.00 (*0-8377-2431-7*, Rothman) W S Hein.

My Phoenix Song. Mary J. Richeimer. 1997. pap. 56.95 (*1-57553-646-3*) Watermrk Pr.

My Phone Book. Suzann M. Olah. 18p. (J). (ps-2). 1991. pap. 3.50 (*0-9630985-0-0*) RJB Enter.

My Phonics Dictionary. Nancy Shaw & Charlene Stout. Ed. by Linda Milliken. (Illus.). 32p. 1998. pap., wbk. ed. 1.99 (*1-56472-112-4*) Edupress Inc.

My Phonics Word Book. Cass Hollander. (Illus.). 64p. (J). (ps-2). 1995. pap. 6.95 (*1-56293-825-8*, McClanahan Book) Learn Horizon.

My Phonics Word Book II. Cass Hollander. 64p. (J). (ps-2). 1995. 6.95 (*1-56293-812-6*, McClanahan Book) Learn Horizon.

My Phony Valentine, Bk. 13. Marie Ferrarella. (Love & Laughter Ser.). 1997. per. 3.50 (*0-373-44013-8*, 1-44013-0) Harlequin Bks.

My Picture Book about Me. Donna Rumney. (Illus.). 20p. (J). (ps). 1988. write for info. (*0-318-64233-6*) My Picture Bks.

My Picture Book of the Planets. Nancy E. Krulik. 32p. (J). (ps-3). 1991. pap. 2.99 (*0-590-43907-3*) Scholastic Inc.

My Picture Book of the Planets. Nancy E. Krulik. (J). 1991. 8.19 (*0-606-04982-7*, Pub. by Turtleback) Demco.

***My Picture Dictionary.** Compiled by Betty Matthews. (Illus.). (J). (ps-2). 1999. pap. 29.00 (*0-7217-0390-9*, Pub. by Schofield) St Mut.

My Picture Dictionary. Ed. by Diane Snowball & Robyn Green. LC 94-30179. (Illus.). 72p. (J). (ps-2). 1994. pap. 8.95 (*1-879531-56-9*); lib. bdg. 15.95 (*1-879531-57-7*) Mondo Pubng.

My Picture Missal. Lawrence G. Lovasik. (Saint Joseph Picture Bks.). (Illus.). (J). (ps-3). 1978. pap. 1.25 (*0-89942-275-6*, 275-00) Catholic Bk Pub.

My Picture of Jenny. James E. Comer. 123p. (Orig.). (J). (gr. 7-12). 1997. pap. 10.00 (*0-9650690-3-6*) Lyndel Publns.

My Picture Prayer Book. Lawrence G. Lovasik. (Illus.). (J). (ps-3). 1987. 5.75 (*0-89942-134-2*, 134/22) Catholic Bk Pub.

My Picture Reading Bible to See & Share. V. Gilbert Beers. (Illus.). 384p. (J). 1994. 15.99 (*1-56476-297-1*, 6-3297, Victor Bks) Chariot Victor.

***My Pigs.** Heather Miller. LC 00-24625. (My Farm Ser.). (Illus.). 24p. (J). (ps-2). 2000. pap. 4.95 (*0-516-23034-4*) Childrens.

***My Pigs.** Heather Miller. (Welcome Bks.). (Illus.). (J). 2000. 13.50 (*0-516-23109-X*) Childrens.

My Pilgrimage for Peace. George Lansbury. LC 70-147723. (Library of War & Peace; Peace Leaders: Biographies & Memoirs). 1972. lib. bdg. 46.00 (*0-8240-0251-2*) Garland.

My Pilgrimage of Faith. Corazon M. Torrevillas. 85p. (Orig.). 1984. pap. 6.50 (*971-10-0150-0*, Pub. by New Day Pub) Cellar.

My Pilgrimage to Haifa, November 1919. Bahiyyih Winkler. LC 96-4389. (Illus.). 120p. (Orig.). 1996. 9.95 (*0-87743-254-6*) Bahai.

***My Pilgrim's Progress: Media Studies, 1950-1997.** George W. Trow. LC 98-5967. 288p. 1998. 24.00 (*0-375-40134-2*) Pantheon.

***My Pilgrim's Progress: Media Studies, 1950-1998.** George W. S. Trow. 288p. 2000. pap. 13.00 (*0-375-70138-9*) Vin Bks.

My Pillow Book. Alice H. Rice. 17.95 (*0-8488-1134-8*) Amereon Ltd.

***My Pinkie Finger.** Betsy Franco. LC 00-29530. (Rookie Reader Ser.). (Illus.). (J). 2001. write for info. (*0-516-22221-X*) Childrens.

My Pirate Coloring Book. Mary Maden. Ed. by Eric Schroeder. (Illus.). (J). (ps-6). 1999. pap. 3.95 (*1-890479-57-8*) Dog & Pony Pub.

My Place. Nadia Wheatley. (Illus.). 40p. (J). (gr. 3-7). 1994. pap. 7.95 (*0-916291-54-5*) Kane-Miller Bk.

My Place: Adventures of a Lifetime in the Outdoors. Montague Rhodes James. LC 92-3961. (Illus.). 192p. 1992. 19.95 (*0-8117-1097-1*) Stackpole.

My Place in God's Purpose: A Commentary for Women: Galatians & Ephesians. Monte M. Clendinning. Ed. by Becky Nelson. (Illus.). 112p. 1994. pap. text 6.95 (*1-56309-100-3*, N944102, New Hope) Womans Mission Union.

My Place in Space. Robin Hirst. (J). 1990. 12.15 (*0-606-02774-2*, Pub. by Turtleback) Demco.

My Place in Space. Robin Hirst & Sally Hirst. LC 89-37893. (Illus.). 40p. (J). (ps-2). 1992. pap. 6.95 (*0-531-07030-1*) Orchard Bks Watts.

My Place in the United States Marine Corps History. Jess Walker. (Illus.). 105p. 1996. pap. 15.00 (*1-882194-27-6*) TN Valley Pub.

My Plans for a Second Term. Bill Clinton. 112p. 1995. 6.95 (*0-8216-1004-X*) Carol Pub Group.

My Plant. (C). 1977. write for info. (*0-201-13839-5*) Addison-Wesley.

***My Platonic Sweetheart.** Mark Twain, pseud. 48p. 1999. write for info. (*1-893766-00-4*) Aeon Pub Co.

My Play a Tune Book: American Songs. Ed. by Toni Ellis. (Sing a Song, Play along Series with Electronic Keyboard). (Illus.). 26p. (J). 1988. lib. bdg. 14.95 (*0-938971-12-3*) JTG Nashville.

My Play a Tune Book: Children's Songs. Ed. by John S. Ellis & Mary B. Leary. (Sing a Song, Play along Series with Electronic Keyboard). (Illus.). 26p. (J). (ps up). 1985. 14.95 (*0-938971-00-X*) JTG Nashville.

My Play a Tune Book: Christmas Songs. Ed. by Etta Wilson. (Sing a Song, Play along Series with Electronic Keyboard). (Illus.). 26p. (J). (gr. k up). 1987. 14.95 (*0-938971-05-0*) JTG Nashville.

My Play a Tune Book: Jewish Songs. Ed. by Hebrew Workshop Educators. (Illus.). 26p. 1988. 14.95 (*0-938971-10-7*) JTG Nashville.

My Play a Tune Book: Mother Goose Songs. J. Ellis. (J). 1990. 15.95 incl. audio (*0-938971-44-1*) JTG Nashville.

My Play a Tune Book: Shake It to the One That You Love the Best. Cheryl W. Mattox. (Sing a Song, Play along Series with Electronic Keyboard). (J). 1991. 14.95 (*0-938971-11-5*) JTG Nashville.

My Play a Tune Book: The Berenstain Bears' Family Favorites. (Sing a Song, Play along Series with Electronic Keyboard). (J). (gr. k-5). 1990. 14.95 (*0-938971-08-5*) JTG Nashville.

My Play & Learn Book. Sandra Jenkins. (Illus.). (J). (ps). 19.99 (*0-590-24537-6*) Scholastic Inc.

My Play Book, One see Learn-To-Read Series

My Play-Doh Book of Words see Mi Gran Libro de Palabras

***My Play Kitchen.** C. Beylon. (Little Activity Bks.). (J). 2000. pap. 1.00 (*0-486-40981-3*) Dover.

My Playful Pets. Kees Moerbeek. (Little Spinners Ser.). 10p. (J). (ps-k). 1998. 7.95 (*0-7613-0392-8*, Copper Beech Bks) Millbrook Pr.

***My Playground Sticker Picture.** Cathy Beylon. (Illus.). (J). 1999. pap. 4.50 (*0-486-40584-2*) Dover.

My Playthings see Mis Juguetes

My Plea for the Old Sword. Ian R. Paisley. 111p. (Orig.). 1997. pap. text 8.99 (*1-84030-015-9*) Ambassador Prodns Ltd.

My Pleasure. Laura Chester. 1980. pap. 10.00 (*0-935724-03-6*) Figures.

***My Pocket Guide to the New Testament.** Rebecca L. Wilke. 2000. pap. 7.95 (*0-9673989-3-2*) Sonkist Min.

My Pocket Writing Assistant. Sandra E. Haven. 44p. (Orig.). 1996. pap. 3.95 (*0-9651358-1-0*) Bristol Servs.

My Poempire: 50 Selected Poems. Ferenc Mozsi. Tr. by Peter Hargitai. 130p. 1997. write for info. (*963-85315-8-4*) Framo Pub.

***My Poems of Faith, Hope, Love.** Ruth George. 1999. write for info. (*1-58235-499-5*) Watermrk Pr.

***My Poetic Journey into the Soul of a Black Woman.** L. E. Jones. (Illus.). 102p. 2000. 15.95 (*0-9702514-0-8*) L M D Pub.

***My Poetry Book.** Sue Petersen. 48p. 1999. pap. 9.95 (*0-9660705-6-9*) Dykema Pub Co.

My Point . . . & I Do Have One. Ellen DeGeneres. 211p. 1996. mass mkt. 6.50 (*0-553-57361-6*) Bantam.

My Poke & Look Busy Book. Nicoletta Costa. (Poke & Look Bks.). (Illus.). 44p. (J). (ps-2). 1990. spiral bd. 14.95 (*0-448-21034-7*, G & D) Peng Put Young Read.

My Polly & Paul Activity Book. Linda Schwartz. 16p. (J). (ps). 1991. student ed. 3.95 (*0-9631987-0-X*) Put-Together Dev Toys.

My Ponies. K. A. Alistir. LC 95-13238. (Hello Reader! Ser.: Level 2). (Illus.). (J). 1996. 3.50 (*0-590-25489-8*) Scholastic Inc.

My Ponies. K. A. Alistir & Lucinda McQueen. (Hello Reader! (Je Peux Lire!) Ser.). (FRE., Illus.). 32p. (J). 1996. pap. 5.99 (*0-590-16030-3*) Scholastic Inc.

My Pop-Up Garden Friends. rod Campbell. (J). 1993. 59.40 (*0-689-71650-8*) Litle Simon.

My Pop-Up Garden Friends. Rod Campbell. LC 92-4382. (Illus.). 14p. (J). (ps). 1993. mass mkt. 4.95 (*0-689-71643-5*) Aladdin.

My Pop-Up Surprise A B C. Robert Crowther. LC 96-72255. (Illus.). 14p. (J). (ps-1). 1997. 16.95 (*0-531-30038-2*) Orchard Bks Watts.

My Pop-Up Surprise 1 2 3. Robert Crowther. LC 96-72254. (Illus.). 12p. (J). (ps-1). 1997. 16.95 (*0-531-30039-0*) Orchard Bks Watts.

My Poppie. Jeannine D. Bray. Ed. by Imani Kenyatta. LC 98-66324. (Illus.). 80p. (J). (gr. k-6). 1998. 14.95 (*1-886580-62-6*) Pinnacle-Syatt.

My Portion (An Autobiography) Rebekah Kohut. LC 74-27995. (Modern Jewish Experience Ser.). 1975. reprint ed. 28.95 (*0-405-06722-4*) Ayer.

My Potty & I: A Friend In Need. 4th ed. Stan Berenstain & Jan Berenstain. (Berenstain Bears Baby Board Books Ser.). (Illus.). 7p. (J). (ps). 1999. pap. 3.99 (*0-679-89335-0*, Pub. by Random Bks Yng Read) Random.

My Power Book. Dan Lena & Marie Lena. (Self Help Motivation Ser.). (Illus.). 60p. (YA). 1991. student ed. 10.00 (*0-9617032-0-2*) D & M Lena.

My Power Diary. Rhonda Paisley. 1998. pap. 11.99 (*1-84030-028-0*) Ambassador Prodns Ltd.

***My Power Words File: Big Bible Words Made Small.** Rhonda Paisley. 192p. (J). (gr. 1-6). 1998. pap. 9.99 (*1-84030-027-2*) Ambassador Prodns Ltd.

My Practice Record Staff Paper Music Dictionary. 32p. 1997. pap. 0.75 (*0-7935-8474-4*) H Leonard.

My Prairie Christmas. Brett Harvey. (Illus.). (J). (ps-3). 1990. pap. 5.95 (*0-8234-1064-1*) Holiday.

My Prairie Christmas. Brett Harvey. LC 90-55104. (Illus.). 32p. (J). (gr. k-3). 1990. lib. bdg. 16.95 (*0-8234-0827-2*) Holiday.

My Prairie Summer. Glasscock. (Folktales Ser.). 24p. (J). (gr. 1-2). 1995. 19.97 (*0-8172-5161-8*) Raintree Steck-V.

***My Praise Journal: A Celebration of Psalms for Kids.** Legacy Press Staff & Mary J. Davis. (Illus.). 144p. (J). (gr. 4-7). 1999. pap. 9.99 (*1-885358-71-7*, Lgacy Pr) Rainbow CA.

My Prayer: Daily Prayers, Vol. 1. Nissan Mindel. (My Prayer Ser.). 332p. 1972. reprint ed. 14.00 (*0-8266-0310-6*, Merkos LInyonei Chinuch) Kehot Pubn Soc.

My Prayer: Shabbat Prayers, Vol. 2. Nissan Mindel. (My Prayer Ser.). 208p. 1989. reprint ed. 14.00 (*0-8266-0311-4*, Merkos LInyonei Chinuch) Kehot Pubn Soc.

M

An Asterisk (*) at the beginning of an entry indicates that the title is appearing for the first time.

My Prayer Book. LC 56-12420. 235p. 1983. 6.99 (*0-570-03059-5*, 06-1184) Concordia.

My Prayer Book, Black. deluxe ed. (J). 1994. boxed set, lthr. 24.95 (*0-88271-260-8*) Regina Pr.

My Prayer Book, Brown. 1981. pap. 9.95 (*0-88271-041-9*) Regina Pr.

My Prayer Book, White. deluxe ed. (J). 1994. boxed set, lthr. 24.95 (*0-88271-261-6*) Regina Pr.

My Prayer Book: Bridal, Pearl. (J). 1994. pap. 19.95 (*0-88271-052-4*) Regina Pr.

My Prayer for You Is a Hungry Heart. Bobbie G. Talley. LC 95-68645. 136p. (Orig.). 1995. pap. 8.95 (*1-884570-32-1*) Research Triangle.

***My Prayer Journal.** Karen Hill. (Illus.). 96p. 2000. 9.99 (*0-8499-5989-6*) Tommy Nelson.

***My Prayer Journal.** Karen Hill. (Illus.). 96p. (J). (gr. 2-6). 2000. 9.99 (*0-8499-5982-9*) Tommy Nelson.

My Prayer Journal: A Keepsake for Kids Who Love the Lord. Mary J. Davis. 144p. (J). (gr. 4-7). pap. 9.99 (*1-885358-37-7*, LP46841, Lgacy Pr) Rainbow CA.

My Prayer Journal Book. Gregory Backman. 150p. 1997. pap. 6.95 (*1-57502-611-2*, PO1755) Morris Pubng.

My Prayer Notebook. Review & Herald Publishing Editors. 1995. ring bd. 17.99 (*0-8280-0776-4*) Review & Herald.

My Prayer Partner Notebook. Becky Tirabassi. 1990. pap. text 9.99 (*0-8407-9110-0*) Nelson.

***My Prayer/Tefilati.** Congregation Bnai Jeshurun, New York, NY Staff. 128p. 2000. pap. 15.00 (*0-87441-715-5*) Behrman.

My Pre Reading Book. Chavez. (My English Book Ser.). 88p. 1997. pap. text 8.10 (*0-673-19400-0*) Addison-Wesley.

My Precious Child: Affirmations for the Child-Within. Mary L. Williams. (Illus.). 48p. (Orig.). 1991. pap. 6.95 (*1-55874-149-6*) Health Comm.

My Precious Moments with God: Quiet Time Devotionals for Girls & Boys, White. (Precious Moments Ser.). (J). 19.95 (*1-55976-449-X*) CEF Press.

My Pregnancy: A Record Book. Linda Spivey. 1997. 20.00 (*1-57977-114-9*) Havoc Pub.

***My Pregnancy Journal.** Whitecap Books Staff. 1999. 6.95 (*1-55285-005-6*) Whitecap CAN.

***My Pregnancy Journal: A Guided Journal.** Lynn Rosen. (Guided Journals). (Illus.). 128p. 2000. 11.99 (*0-88088-219-0*) Peter Pauper.

***My Pregnancy Journal (Mother & Child)** gif. ed. Anne Geddes. (Illus.). 88p. 1999. spiral bd. 21.95 (*0-7683-2078-X*) CEDCO Pub.

My Pregnancy Record Book. DK Publishing Staff. 64p. 1999. 9.95 (*0-7894-4122-5*) DK Pub Inc.

My Preschooler: Ready for New Adventures see Mi Preescolar: Listo para Nuevas Aventuras

My Present Age. Guy Vanderhaeghe. 252p. 1985. 15.95 (*0-685-11126-1*) HM.

My Presidential Years. R. Venkataraman. (C). 1994. text 38.00 (*81-7223-155-5*, Pub. by Indus Pub) S Asia.

My Pretty Princess, Set. Nicola Baxter. LC 95-13701. (Illus.). 19p. (J). 1995. pap. 14.95 (*0-8120-8393-8*) Barron.

My Priceless Prayerbook: A Childhood Keepsake of Building Blocks to Faith, Values & Self Esteem. Steve Viglione. Ed. by Sue Asci. (Illus.). 130p. (Orig.). (J). (ps-5). 1995. pap., per. 12.95 (*0-9645224-0-3*) Lghthse Publ.

My Priceless Prayerbook, New Thought Edition: A Childhood Keepsake of Building Blocks to Faith, Values & Self-Esteem. Steve Viglione. Ed. by Beverly Craig et al. (Illus.). 130p. (J). (ps-5). 1996. pap. 12.95 (*0-9645224-1-1*) Lghthse Publ.

My Primer Libro Devocional de la Biblia. David C. Cook.Tr. of My First Book of Bible Devotions. (SPA.). 80p. (J). 1981. write for info. (*0-614-27082-0*) Editorial Unilit.

My Prince Charming. Molly McGuire. (American Romance Ser.). 1993. per. 3.39 (*0-373-16484-X*, 1-16484-7) Harlequin Bks.

My Printing Book. 4th rev. ed. Jan Z. Olsen. (Illus.). 72p. (J). (gr. 1). 1997. pap. text, teacher ed. 4.75 (*1-891627-01-5*) Handwriting.

My Private Gift. (Illus.). 64p. 1992. 27.50 (*0-9634249-0-4*) Gift Future Two Thous.

My Private Life: Real Experiences of a Dominant Woman. Mistress Nan. Ed. by Joseph Bean. LC 94-69814. 196p. (Orig.). 1995. pap. 14.95 (*1-881943-11-9*) Daedalus Pub.

***My Private Military Odyssey.** Harry J. Wade. LC 98-91006. 1999. pap. 7.95 (*0-533-13017-4*) Vantage.

My Private Spider Webs. Pierrette Pancrazi. 1998. pap. write for info. (*1-57553-932-2*) Watermrk Pr.

My Private War: One Man's Struggle to Survive the Soviets & the Nazis. Jakub Gerstenfeld-Maltiel. LC 92-34654. (Library of Holocaust Testimonies). 336p. 1993. pap. text 19.50 (*0-85303-260-2*, Pub. by M Vallentine & Co) Intl Spec Bk.

***My Professional Life, 1929-98: With a Selected Bibliography.** Ester Boserup. 69p. 1999. (*87-7289-520-9*, Pub. by Mus Tusculanum) Paul & Co Pubs.

***My Promise Book.** Honor Books Publishing Staff. (Beginners Bible Ser.). (Illus.). (J). 2000. 9.99 (*1-56292-933-X*) Honor Bks OK.

My Promise Is the Palace: So What Am I Doing in the Pit? Rod Parsley. 155p. (Orig.). 1993. pap. 8.99 (*1-880244-14-4*) Wrld Harvest Church.

My Prophetic Soul & Other Poems. Faith S. Green. LC 92-31911. 72p. 1992. pap. 14.95 (*0-7734-0043-5*, Mellen Poetry Pr) E Mellen.

My Psalms. Rachel Y. Baldwin. Ed. by Elizabeth Harris-Charity. (Illus.). 35p. 1998. pap. 9.95 (*0-9651866-4-4*) Youth Corp.

My Psychosis, My Bicycle, & I: The Self-Organization of Madness. Fritz B. Simon. 304p. 1996. 45.00 (*1-56821-647-5*) Aronson.

***My Puffer Train.** Mary Murphy. LC 98-47803. (Illus.). 32p. (J). 1999. 9.95 (*0-395-97105-5*) HM.

My Pulse Is Not What It Used to Be: The Leadership Challenges in Health Care. Irwin M. Rubin & C. Raymond Fernandez. LC 91-65593. 104p. (Orig.). 1991. pap. 40.00 (*0-9629561-0-4*) Temenos Found.

My Puppy see Mi Perrito

***My Puppy.** Metrobooks Staff. (Illus.). 8p. (ps-k). 2000. 8.99 (*1-58663-104-7*) M Friedman Pub Grp Inc.

My Puppy. 2nd ed. Inez Greene. (Let Me Read Ser.). (Illus.). 8p. (J). (ps-1). 1994. text 2.95 (*0-673-36192-6*, GoodYrBooks) Addson-Wesley Educ.

My Puppy Book: A Press 'n Dress Paper Doll. Jennifer Selby. LC 96-70370. (Illus.). 12p. (J). (ps-k). 1997. 9.95 (*0-531-30019-6*) Orchard Bks Watts.

My Puppy Is Born. Joanna Cole. (J). 1991. 10.15 (*0-606-04983-5*, Pub. by Turtleback) Demco.

My Puppy Is Born. rev. ed. Joanna Cole. LC 90-42011. (Illus.). 48p. (J). (ps-3). 1991. mass mkt. 5.95 (*0-688-10198-4*, Wm Morrow) Morrow Avon.

My Puppy Pack. (J). 1996. 7.98 (*1-57082-462-2*, Pub. by Mouse Works) Time Warner.

My Puppy's Record Book. Carl Day & Alexandra Day. (Illus.). 32p. (J). (ps-3). 1994. 9.95 (*0-374-36151-7*) FS&G.

My Pushkin. unabridged ed. Marina I. Tsvetaeva. (World Classic Literature Ser.). (RUS.). pap. 6.95 (*2-87714-269-8*, Pub. by Bookking Intl) Distribks Inc.

My Pygmy & Negro Hosts. Paul Schebesta. Tr. by Gerald Griffin from GER. LC 74-15086. reprint ed. 52.00 (*0-404-12136-5*) AMS Pr.

My "q" Sound Box. Jane Belk Moncure. LC 79-13085. (Sound Box Library). (Illus.). 32p. (J). (ps-2). 1979. lib. bdg. 21.36 (*0-89565-100-9*) Childs World.

My Quarter Century of American Politics, 2 vols., Set. Champ Clark. (History - United States Ser.). 1992. reprint ed. lib. bdg. 150.00 (*0-7812-6195-3*) Rprt Serv.

My Queenly Mother. James A. Stewart. 1969. pap. 0.79 (*1-56632-068-2*) Revival Lit.

My Quest: Voices from the Heart. William J. Crockett. 15p. 1985. pap. 3.00 (*0-934383-32-4*) Pride Prods.

My Quest for Beauty. Rollo May. LC 85-61687. 243p. 1985. 9.95 (*0-933071-01-9*) Saybrook Pub Co.

My Quest for Beauty. Rollo May. LC 85-61687. (Illus.). 244p. 1987. reprint ed. pap. 9.95 (*0-933071-13-2*) Saybrook Pub Co.

***My Quest for Bram Stoker.** Harry Ludlam. 110p. 2000. pap. 15.00 (*1-888893-02-8*) Dracula Pr.

My Quest for El Dorado. large type ed. Ross Salmon. 469p. 1981. 27.99 (*0-7089-0657-5*) Ulverscroft.

***My Quest for Freedom.** George Knava. 340p. 2000. 24.95 (*1-58244-051-4*) Rutledge Bks.

***My Quest for the Yeti: Confronting the Himalayas' Deepest Mystery.** Reinhold Messner. Tr. by Peter Constantine from GER. LC 99-55091. (Illus.). 192p. 2000. text 23.95 (*0-312-20394-2*) St Martin.

***My Questions - God's Questions.** Ramon. LC 99-56443. 160p. Date not set. 16.00 (*1-57312-294-7*) Smyth & Helwys.

My Quiet Book. 8p. (J). 1989. 34.99 (*1-888074-16-7*) Pckts Lrning.

My Quilts & Me: The Diary of an American Quilter. Nora Ezell. LC 96-1815. (Illus.). 208p. Date not set. 45.00 (*1-881320-21-9*, Black Belt) Black Belt Communs.

My "r" Sound Box. Jane Belk Moncure. LC 78-7842. (Sound Box Library). (Illus.). 32p. (J). (ps-2). 1978. lib. bdg. 21.36 (*0-89565-048-7*) Childs World.

***My Race Car.** Michael Rex. LC 99-31773. 32p. 2000. 15.95 (*0-8050-6101-0*) H Holt & Co.

***My Rain Forest Sticker Activity Book.** Cathy Beylon. (Illus.). (J). 1999. pap. 1.00 (*0-486-40509-5*) Dover.

My Ranger Years. William G. Wallace. Ed. by Susan McDonald. 160p. (Orig.). 1992. pap. text 9.95 (*1-878441-04-3*) Sequoia Nat Hist Assn.

***My Rattle Book.** Leslie McGuire. (Illus.). 12p. (J). 1999. 5.95 (*1-892374-14-5*) Weldon Owen.

My Reader, My Fellow-Labourer: A Study of English Romantic Prose. John R. Nabholtz. LC 85-20118. 144p. 1986. text 24.95 (*0-8262-0491-0*) U of Mo Pr.

My Reading Book. Chavez. (My English Book Ser.). 88p. 1997. pap. text 8.11 (*0-673-19186-9*) Addison-Wesley.

My Reading List: A Child's Personal Reading Record. Emily Ellison. LC 94-74238. 48p. (J). (ps-3). 1995. pap. 8.95 (*1-56352-205-5*) Longstreet.

My Real Family. Emily Arnold McCully. LC 92-46290. (Illus.). 32p. (J). (ps-3). 1994. 14.00 (*0-15-277698-2*, Harcourt Child Bks) Harcourt.

My Real Family. Emily Arnold McCully. 32p. (C). 1999. pap. 6.00 (*0-15-201957-X*, Voyager Bks) Harcourt.

My Real Name Is Lisa. David Alexander. 288p. 1996. 21.00 (*0-7867-0310-5*) Carroll & Graf.

My Really Cool Baby Book. Todd Parr. (J). 2000. 13.95 (*0-316-69241-7*) Little.

My Rebel Son. Joyce Bell. 288p. 25.00 (*0-7278-5219-1*) Severn Hse.

My Rebellious Bride. Constance Hall. 384p. 1999. mass mkt. 5.99 (*0-8217-6215-X*) Kensgtn Pub Corp.

My Rebellious Heart. Samantha James. 400p. (Orig.). 1993. mass mkt. 4.50 (*0-380-76937-9*, Avon Bks) Morrow Avon.

***My Recipe Box.** Katharine E. Giles. LC 00-190184. 621p. 2000. 25.00 (*0-7388-1502-0*); pap. 18.00 (*0-7388-1503-9*) Xlibris Corp.

My Recipes Are for the Birds: Finch Fries, Dove Delights, Robin Russe, Wren Rolls, & More! Irene Cosgrove. LC 99-24942. (Illus.). 96p. 1999. pap. 7.95 (*0-385-49547-1*, Main St Bks) Doubleday.

My Recitations. Cora V. Potter. LC 75-39380. (Granger Index Reprint Ser.). 1977. reprint ed. 20.95 (*0-8369-6347-4*) Ayer.

My Reckless Heart. Jo Goodman. 448p. 1998. mass mkt. 5.99 (*0-8217-5843-8*, Zebra Kensgtn) Kensgtn Pub Corp.

My Recollection of Cherokee Alabama. Jack Daniel. (Illus.). 232p. 1998. pap. 20.00 (*1-884289-25-8*) Grandmother Erth.

My Recollection of Chicago & the Doctrine of Laissez Faire. Stephen Leacock. LC 99-172372. (Illus.). 160p. 1998. text 35.00 (*0-8020-4286-4*); pap. text 14.95 (*0-8020-8121-5*) U of Toronto Pr.

My Recollections. Jules E. Massenet. Tr. by H. Villiers Barnett. LC 75-107819. (Select Bibliographies Reprint Ser.). 1977. 26.95 (*0-8369-5190-5*) Ayer.

My Recollections. Mary Slechta. LC 87-82456. (Illus.). 88p. 1987. 15.95 (*0-943498-65-1*) Friis-Pioneer Pr.

My Recollections (1848-1912) Jules E. Massenet. 304p. 1990. reprint ed. lib. bdg. 79.00 (*0-7812-9073-2*) Rprt Serv.

My Record Book of Dreams, Quotes & Other Thoughts. Whole Works Staff. Ed. by Ettie Steg. (Illus.). 100p. 1988. student ed. 13.00 (*0-942751-07-8*) Whole Works.

My Record Treasure Chest, No. 1, No. 1000. Marene P. Fassina. 1998. mass mkt. 12.95 (*1-892996-10-3*) M Fassina.

***My Recovery.** Eugene Thomas. 2000. write for info. (*1-58235-480-4*) Watermrk Pr.

My Red Storybook. Helen Bramos & Ann S. Bramos. (Illus.). 77p. (Orig.). (J). (gr. k-7). 1993. pap. 8.00 (*0-9635333-1-2*) A S Bramos.

***My Reel Story.** Ted Perry. 2001. 26.00 (*1-58465-076-1*) U Pr of New Eng.

My Relations with Carlyle: Together with a Letter from the Late Sir James Stephen, Dated Dec. 9, 1886. James A. Froude. LC 70-154150. (Select Bibliographies Reprint Ser.). 1977. reprint ed. 15.95 (*0-8369-5766-0*) Ayer.

My Relationship with God see Bridge: Student to Student Discipleship

My Relationship with My World see Bridge: Student to Student Discipleship

My Relationships with Others. Kino Learning Center Staff et al. (Changing Years Ser.). (Illus.). 64p. (J). (gr. 5-9). 1987. pap. 8.99 (*0-86653-419-9*, GA 1029) Good Apple.

My Religion. Emil G. Hirsch. Ed. by Gerson B. Levi. Incl. Crucifixion Viewed from a Jewish Standpoint, 1908. LC 73-2207. LC 73-2207. (Jewish People; History, Religion, Literature Ser.). 1973. reprint ed. 36.95 (*0-405-05271-5*) Ayer.

My Religion: The Spiritual Texts & Holy Meanings. Don Steele. LC 98-89978. 365p. 1999. 25.00 (*0-7388-0311-1*); pap. 15.00 (*0-7388-0312-X*) Xlibris Corp.

My Remarkable Uncle. Raymond Leacock. 248p. 1996. pap. text 6.95 (*0-7710-9965-7*) McCland & Stewart.

My Remembers: A Black Sharecropper's Recollections of the Depression. Eddie Stimpson, Jr. LC 95-33312. (Illus.). 167p. 1999. reprint ed. pap. 16.95 (*1-57441-067-9*) UNTX Pr.

My Reminiscences. Rabindranath Tagore. 1972. 300.00 (*0-8490-0691-0*) Gordon Pr.

My Reminiscences. Luigi Arditi. LC 77-5500. (Music Reprint Ser.). (Illus.). 1977. reprint ed. lib. bdg. 39.50 (*0-306-77417-8*) Da Capo.

My Reminiscences. Joseph S. Bloch. LC 73-2188. (Jewish People; History, Religion, Literature Ser.). 1973. reprint ed. 48.95 (*0-405-05254-5*) Ayer.

My Reminiscences of East Africa. 6th ed. Paul Von Lettow Vorbeck. (Battery Classics Ser.: No. 6). (Illus.). 346p. 1990. reprint ed. 39.95 (*0-89839-154-7*) Battery Pr.

My Reminiscences of Ezra Cornell. Andrew D. White. (Notable American Authors Ser.). 1999. reprint ed. lib. bdg. 125.00 (*0-7812-9935-7*) Rprt Serv.

My Report of Findings: More Observations of a Chiropractic Advocate. William D. Esteb. 240p. (Orig.). 1993. pap. text 24.95 (*0-9631711-1-9*) Back Talk Systs.

My Residence at the Court of the Amir. J. A. Gray. 544p. 1987. 350.00 (*1-85077-904-X*, Pub. by Darf Pubs Ltd) St Mut.

My Response see Mi Respuesta

My Return. Jack H. Abbott & Naomi Zack. LC 86-43236. 213p. 1987. 29.95 (*0-87975-355-2*) Prometheus Bks.

My Return to Normandy see Return to Normandy: Still Brave at Heart

My Return to Normandy. Robert L. Williams. (Illus.). 52p. (Orig.). 1995. pap. 2.75 (*0-9627534-1-6*) Skyspec Pub.

My Revelation. abr. ed. Loula L. Combs. LC 91-65172. (Illus.). 351p. 1991. reprint ed. 25.95 (*0-9625511-2-0*) Storm Ridge Pr.

My Rhyming Bible: Bible Stories in Rhyme. Rob Suggs. LC 96-60870. (Illus.). 144p. (J). (ps-6). 1996. 12.99 (*0-529-10694-9*, MRB) World Publng.

My Ride with Gus. Charles Carillo. 256p. 1996. 22.00 (*0-671-53568-4*, PB Hardcover) PB.

My Ride with Gus. Charles Carillo. 1997. per. 5.99 (*0-671-53569-2*) PB.

My Riding Book: A Write-in-Me Book for Young Riders. Tom Ettinger & William Jaspersohn. (Illus.). 48p. (J). (gr. 3-7). 1993. 10.95 (*0-694-00465-0*, HarpFestival) HarpC Child Bks.

My Rise & Fall. Benito Mussolini. Ed. & Tr. by Max Ascoli. LC 98-217204. Orig. Title: My Autobiography & the Fall of Mussolini. (Illus.). 590p. 1998. reprint ed. pap. 18.95 (*0-306-80864-1*) Da Capo.

My Rites of Passage. Rita Dodson. 52p. 1986. pap. 5.00 (*0-9615511-0-0*) R Dodson.

My River Speaks: The History & Lore of the Magothy River. Marianne Taylor & Energy Recovery Corp Staff. LC 98-73314. xi, 243 p. 1998. 29.00 (*0-9665239-0-3*) Genl Cnsvtn.

My Road see Moya Doroga

My Road to Emeritus. Elmer Ellis. LC 89-212510. (Illus.). 256p. (Orig.). 1989. 19.95 (*0-9622891-1-6*) SHS MO.

My Road to Rotary. Paul Harris. 304p. 1984. 9.25 (*0-915062-17-8*); pap. 7.00 (*0-685-42715-3*) Rotary Intl.

My Road to Rotary. Paul Harris. (American Autobiography Ser.). 318p. 1995. reprint ed. lib. bdg. 89.00 (*0-7812-8551-8*) Rprt Serv.

My Road to the Sundance. Manny Twofeathers. (Illus.). 204p. (Orig.). 1995. pap. 14.95 (*1-886340-04-8*) Wo-Pila Pub.

My Robot Buddy. Alfred Slote. LC 75-9922. (Illus.). 96p. (J). (gr. 3-5). 1975. 12.95 (*0-397-31641-0*) HarpC Child Bks.

My Robot Buddy. Alfred Slote. LC 85-45393. (Trophy Bk.). (Illus.). 80p. (J). (gr. 2-5). 1986. pap. 4.95 (*0-06-440165-0*, HarpTrophy) HarpC Child Bks.

My Robot Buddy. Alfred Slote. LC 75-9922. (Illus.). 80p. (J). (gr. 2-5). 1991. lib. bdg. 13.89 (*0-397-32505-3*) HarpC Child Bks.

My Robot Buddy. Alfred Slote. (J). 1986. 9.70 (*0-606-03113-8*, Pub. by Turtleback) Demco.

My Rock Garden. Reginald Farrer. LC 72-161605. (Illus.). 1971. reprint ed. 8.50 (*0-913728-04-7*) Theophrastus.

My Roman Britain. Richard Reece. 164p. 1988. pap. 14.00 (*0-905853-21-0*) David Brown.

***My Room of Mirrors & Other Reflective Thoughts.** Victor Schmidt. 1999. pap. write for info. (*1-58235-115-5*) Watermrk Pr.

My Roosevelt Years. Norman M. Littell. Ed. by Jonathan Dembo. LC 87-10523. (Illus.). 436p. 1987. 35.00 (*0-295-96525-8*) U of Wash Pr.

***My Roots Go Back to Loving: And Other Stories from "Year of the Family"** Ed. by Becky C. Powers. 192p. 2000. pap. 9.95 (*0-9672134-1-X*) Canaan Home Commun.

My Rosary Journal: The Great Mysteries. William F. Maestri. (Illus.). 112p. (Orig.). 1993. pap. 7.95 (*0-8189-0673-1*) Alba.

My Rose: An African American Mother's Story of AIDS. Geneva Bell. LC 97-3419. 104p. (Orig.). 1997. pap. 12.95 (*0-8298-1160-5*) Pilgrim OH.

My Rotten, Redheaded Older Brother. Patricia Polacco. (Illus.). 40p. (J). (ps-2). 1994. 16.00 (*0-671-72751-6*) S&S Bks Yung.

My Rotten, Redheaded Older Brother. Patricia Polacco. LC 93-13980. (Illus.). 32p. (J). (ps-3). 1998. per. 5.99 (*0-689-82036-4*) S&S Childrens.

My Rottweiler Babe: A Collection of Poems. unabridged ed. Mary L. Christie. (Illus.). 47p. (Orig.). 1995. pap. 13.95 (*0-9651756-0-X*) M L Christie.

My Rows & Piles of Coins. Tololwa M. Mollel. LC 98-21586. (Illus.). 32p. (J). (gr. k-3). 1999. 15.00 (*0-395-75186-1*, Clarion Bks) HM.

My Royal Service. Zane Clark. (Illus.). 165p. (J). (gr. 4-12). 1989. pap. 12.95 (*0-89114-164-2*) Baptist Pub Hse.

My Rules: The Lauryn Hill Story. Marc Shapiro. 1999. mass mkt. 5.99 (*0-425-17211-2*) Berkley Pub.

My Runaway Heart. Miriam Minger. 400p. (Orig.). 1995. mass mkt. 5.50 (*0-380-78301-0*, Avon Bks) Morrow Avon.

My Russia: The Political Autobiography of Gennady Zyuganov. Gennady A. Zyuganov. Ed. by Vadim Medish. LC 96-39545. (Illus.). 224p. (C). (gr. 13). 1997. 44.95 (*1-56324-995-2*) M E Sharpe.

***My Russian.** Deirdre McNamer. 304p. 2000. pap. 14.00 (*0-345-43951-1*) Ballantine Pub Grp.

My Russian. Deirdre McNamer. LC 99-19140. 278p. 1999. 24.00 (*0-395-95637-4*) HM.

My Russian Love. Dan Franck. 1996. 19.00 (*0-614-20636-7*) Doubleday.

My Russian Memoirs. Bernard Pares. LC 78-96471. reprint ed. write for info. (*0-404-04878-1*) AMS Pr.

My Russian Yesterdays. Catherine D. Doherty. 136p. 1990. pap. 11.95 (*0-921440-18-9*) Madonna Hse.

My Rustic Tree Etchings. Denver Keels. 1999. pap. write for info. (*1-58235-069-8*) Watermrk Pr.

My "s" Sound Box. Jane Belk Moncure. LC 77-8970. (Sound Box Library). (Illus.). 32p. (J). (ps-2). 1977. lib. bdg. 21.36 (*0-913778-95-8*) Childs World.

My Sadie. Efner T. Holmes. (Illus.). 128p. (J). (gr. 3-6). 1993. pap. 3.50 (*1-56288-350-X*) Checkerboard.

My Samoan Chief. Fay G. Calkins. (Pacific Classics Ser.: No. 2). (Illus.). 216p. 1971. reprint ed. pap. 9.95 (*0-87022-932-X*) UH Pr.

My Savage Heart. Christine Dorsey. 448p. 1994. mass mkt. 4.50 (*0-8217-4523-9*, Zebra Kensgtn) Kensgtn Pub Corp.

My Savior, My Friend: A Daily Devotional. Kay Arthur. 1995. 17.99 (*1-56507-351-7*) Harvest Hse.

My Say: A Mentor's Guide to Success. Edwin E. Bobrow. LC 98-89738. 304p. 1999. 15.95 (*1-886284-36-9*, Pub. by Chandler Hse) Natl Bk Netwk.

My Say: One Woman's Slightly Skewed Perception of Life. Donna Allen. (Illus.). 80p. 1997. pap. 9.95 (*0-9658079-0-8*) Donna Allen.

***My School.** Cathy Beylon. (Little Activity Bks.). (Illus.). (J). 1999. pap. text 1.00 (*0-486-40510-9*) Dover.

My School. Janet Horowitz & Kathy Faggella. (Photolog Bk.). (Illus.). 48p. (J). (gr. 1-7). 1991. 4.50 (*1-55670-176-4*) Stewart Tabori & Chang.

My School. Tott Publications Staff. 8p. (J). (gr. 1). 1990. pap. text 2.50 (*1-882225-03-1*) Tott Pubns.

My School Bus: A Book about School Bus Safety see PowerKids Readers Set 1: My World

An Asterisk (*) at the beginning of an entry indicates that the title is appearing for the first time.

My School Days: A Keepsake Album. Norman Rockwell. (Illus.). 42p. 1994. 16.95 (*0-8109-4450-2*, Pub. by Abrams) Time Warner.
My School Days Memories: Grades K-6. Judith M. Hough. (Illus.). 40p. (J). (gr. k-6). 1992. pap. 7.95 (*0-9633769-0-X*) Touch The Sky.
My School is Worse Than Yours. Tom Toles. 80p. 1999. pap. 3.99 (*0-14-130358-1*, PuffinBks) Peng Put Young Read.
***My School Memories: Scrapbook.** (gr. 3-7). 1999. 12.95 (*0-439-09253-1*) Scholastic Inc.
My School Record. Elliott. 13p. 1995. 10.95 (*1-57359-001-0*, Starrhill Press) Black Belt Communs.
My School Years: Kindergarten Through Graduation. Barbara Benavidez. (Illus.). (J). (gr. 5-12). 24.95 (*0-9619463-0-X*) Barmarle Pubns.
My School, Your School. Bette Birnbaum. (Ready-Set-Read Ser.). (Illus.). 32p. (J). (ps-3). 1990. lib. bdg. 21.40 (*0-8172-3583-3*) Raintree Steck-V.
My School, Your School. Bette Birnbaum. 28p. (J). (ps-3). 1990. pap. text 4.95 (*0-8114-6743-0*) Raintree Steck-V.
My School's a Zoo Smith. LC 99-63978. 40p. (J). (gr. k-3). 2000. 5.95 (*0-06-443588-1*) HarpC Child Bks.
My School's a Zoo. Smith. LC 99-63978. (Illus.). 40p. (J). (gr. k-3). Date not set. 15.95 (*0-06-028510-9*) HarpC.
My School's a Zoo. Smith. LC 99-63978. 40p. (J). (gr. k-3). 2000. lib. bdg. 15.89 (*0-06-028511-7*) HarpC Child Bks.
My Scrapbook Memories of Dark Shadows. Kathryn L. Scott. (Illus.). 152p. 1986. pap. 15.95 (*0-938817-04-3*) Pomegranate Pr.
My Scribblings: From the Side of the Rock. large type ed. Vera H. Johnson. Ed. by Joseph Naylor. LC 96-95446. (Illus.). 108p. (Orig.). 1997. pap. 9.95 (*1-888106-21-2*) Agreka Bks.
***My Scriptural Rosary.** Lauren S. Roddy. (Illus.). 48p. (J). (gr. 2-5). 1999. 3.95 (*0-8198-4797-6*) Pauline Bks.
My Sea Log: Missile-Salvage Boat Captain & Ocean Tracker Mate. Alfred M. Huger. (Illus.). 122p. 1982. pap. 10.00 (*0-89745-031-0*) Sunflower U Pr.
My Search for Augusta Pierce Tabor: Leadville's First Lady. Evelyn E. Furman. 213p. 1993. write for info. (*0-9635005-0-3*) E E L Furman.
My Search for B. Traven. Jonah Raskin. LC 80-15834. 249 p. 1980. write for info. (*0-416-00751-1*) Routledge.
***My Search for Bill W.** Mel B. 160p. 2000. pap. 14.00 (*1-56838-374-6*) Hazelden.
My Search for Radionic Truths. R. Murray Denning. LC 88-70943. (Illus.). 118p. (Orig.). 1988. pap. 9.95 (*0-945685-01-7*) Borderland Sciences.
My Search for Ruth. large type ed. Anna Clarke. (General Ser.). 263p. 1989. lib. bdg. 16.95 (*0-8161-4709-4*, G K Hall Lrg Type) Mac Lib Ref.
My Search for the Burial Sites of Great Sioux Indian Chiefs. Veryl Walstrom. Ed. by Linda J. Dageforde. LC 95-90016. (Illus.). 148p. 1995. pap. 15.00 (*1-886225-09-5*) Dageforde Pub.
My Search for the Real Killer: Not by OJ Simpson. large type ed. William A. Crawford. LC 97-164616. (Illus.). 120p. (Orig.). 1997. pap. 10.95 (*0-9657235-0-X*) Windfall Pr.
My Search for Traces of God. Philip S. Callahan. 204p. 1997. pap. 18.00 (*0-911311-54-8*) Acres USA.
My Search "Outside" for the Lord "Within" Imagery & Style Collection. Addie Holt. Ed. by Patricia Williams. 124p. 1996. pap. 10.95 (*1-886493-07-3*) NBC Study Pub.
My Seasons. 2nd ed. Haniel Long. Ed. by James H. Maguire. LC 77-72389. (Ahsahta Press Modern & Contemporary Poets of the West Ser.). 68p. 1977. pap. 6.95 (*0-916272-06-0*) Ahsahta Pr.
My Seaswept Heart. Christine Dorsey. 384p. 1996. pap. 2.99 (*0-8217-5487-4*) Kensgtn Pub Corp.
My Second Grade Music Book. Ann M. Eisen & Lamar Robertson. (My Music Book Ser.: Vol. 2). (Illus.). 82p. (J). (gr. 2-5). 1994. pap. text, wbk. ed. 30.00 (*1-889967-04-1*) Sneaky Snake.
My Second Grade Yearbook. Bearl Brooks. (My Yearbook Ser.). 640p. (gr. 2). 1979. 18.00 (*0-8209-0082-6*, MSG-2) ESP.
My Second Handwriting. Longman Publishing Staff. (J). Date not set. pap. text. write for info. (*0-582-51113-5*, Pub. by Addison-Wesley) Longman.
My Second 25 Years. Emanuel Haldeman-Julius. (American Autobiography Ser.). 117p. 1995. reprint ed. lib. bdg. 69.00 (*0-7812-8542-9*) Rprt Serv.
My Secret: Parental Substance Abuse Activity Book. Jim Boulden. (Illus.). 32p. (J). (gr. 1-7). 1991. pap. 5.95 (*1-878076-13-2*) Boulden Pub.
My Secret Admirer. Albert Ellis. 192p. (J). (gr. 7-9). 1989. pap. 3.25 (*0-590-44768-8*) Scholastic Inc.
My Secret Admirer. Anne Stuart et al. 384p. 1999. per. 5.99 (*0-373-83398-9*, 1-83398-7, Harlequin) Harlequin Bks.
My Secret Boat: A Notebook of Prose & Poems. Michael Burkard. 1991. pap. 8.95 (*0-393-30748-4*) Norton.
My Secret Brother. Fiona Dunbar. (Illus.). 32p. (J). (ps-1). 1994. 17.95 (*0-09-176402-5*, Pub. by Hutchnson) Trafalgar.
***My Secret Camera: Life in the Lodz Ghetto.** Frank Dabba Smith. LC 99-6268. (Illus.). 32p. (YA). (ps-3). 2000. 16.00 (*0-15-202306-2*, Gulliver Bks) Harcourt.
***My Secret Camera: Life in the Lodz Ghetto.** Frank Dabba Smith. (Illus.). 40p. (gr. 4-7). 2000. 24.26 (*0-7398-2198-9*) Raintree Steck-V.
My Secret Camp. limited ed. J. J. Scot. (Illus.). 450p. 1994. pap. 100.00 (*0-317-05751-0*) Harvestman.
***My Secret Closet.** Hyancinth. LC 99-93673. 1999. pap. 8.95 (*0-533-13111-1*) Vantage.
My Secret Diary. Janine Phillips. 160p. 1982. 10.95 (*0-317-54333-4*) Dufour.
My Secret Diary. Anne Simpson. LC 92-20177. (Illus.). 64p. (J). (gr. 4-6). 1992. pap. 2.95 (*0-8167-2941-7*) Troll Communs.
My Secret Fishing Line. Nick Lyons. LC 99-13921. (Illus.). 208p. 1999. 23.00 (*0-87113-750-X*, Atlntc Mnthly) Grove-Atltic.
My Secret Garden. Nancy Friday. 352p. 1991. pap. 6.50 (*0-671-74252-3*, Pocket Star Bks) PB.
My Secret Garden: Women's Sexual Fantasies. Nancy Friday. LC 99-196748. 363p. 1998. per. 6.99 (*0-671-01987-2*, Pocket Books) PB.
My Secret Hiding Place. Rose Greydanus. (Illus.). 32p. (J). (gr. k-2). 1997. pap. 2.50 (*0-89375-283-5*) Troll Communs.
My Secret History. Paul Theroux. LC 96-96618. 1996. pap. 12.95 (*0-449-91200-0*) Fawcett.
My Secret Life. James Jennings. 656p. 1996. pap. 11.95 (*0-929654-37-4*, 27) Blue Moon Bks.
My Secret Life. Ed. & Intro. by James Kincaid. LC 95-74999. 544p. 1996. mass mkt. 7.95 (*0-451-52602-3*, Sig Classics) NAL.
My Secret Life. Walter. 608p. 1996. mass mkt. 7.95 (*0-7867-0346-6*) Carroll & Graf.
My Secret Life, Vol. 2. 418p. 1998. pap. 9.95 (*1-56201-086-7*) Blue Moon Bks.
***My Secret Life: Sexual Revelations from Long-Term Lovers.** Brigid McConville. 192p. 1998. pap. 13.00 (*0-7225-3662-3*, Pub. by Thorsons MD) Natl Bk Netwk.
My Secret Life with an Angel: Earth in the Seventh Circle. Julia M. Busch. LC 96-79343. (Illus.). 208p. (Orig.). 1997. pap. 14.95 (*1-886369-16-X*, SAN297-6986, Kosmic Kurrents) Anti Aging Pr.
My Secret Lover: Lorna Moon. Richard De Mille. LC 97-48280. (Illus.). 311p. 1998. 25.00 (*0-374-21757-2*) FS&G.
***My Secret Pal.** Matthew Lansfield. 2000. 4.99 (*1-56245-400-5*) Great Quotations.
My Secret Power, Vol. 2. Lou Austin. (J). (gr. 1-6). 1960. 4.95 (*0-934538-22-0*) Partnership Foundation.
My Secret Secret Admirer. Diane Umansky. (Full House Stephanie Ser.: Vol. 22). 144p. (J). (gr. 3-6). 1997. per. 3.99 (*0-671-00363-1*) PB.
***My Secret War: The World War II Diary of Madeline Beck.** Mary Pope Osborne. LC 00-21918. (Dear America Ser.). (Illus.). 208p. (YA). (gr. 4-7). 2000. 10.95 (*0-590-68715-8*) Scholastic Inc.
My Secret Wars Scrapbook: Adventures in Combat, Covert Action & Espionage Operations. David A. Phillips. 260p. 1988. pap. 15.00 (*0-317-90861-8*) Stone Trail Pr.
My See & Pray Missal: Based on the Traditional Mass. M. Joan Therese. LC 97-60766. (Illus.). 41p. (J). (gr. k-2). 1997. reprint ed. pap. 2.00 (*0-89555-601-4*, 1506) TAN Bks Pubs.
My Self Esteem. Gretchen D. Van Kleef. wbk. ed. 4.95 (*0-89486-979-5*, 5558 B) Hazelden.
***My Self, My Family, My Friends: 26 Experts Explore Young Children's Self-Esteem.** Ed. by Betty Farber. LC 99-89706. (Illus.). 320p. 2000. pap. 24.95 (*1-881425-07-X*) Preschl Pubns.
My Sensational Sticker Set. (Illus.). (J). (ps-3). 1993. pap. 2.95 (*0-8167-3098-9*) Troll Communs.
My Sense of Self. Donald Pelton. (Illus.). 1984. pap. 7.95 (*0-933169-01-9*) Heldon Pr.
***My Sense of Silence: Memoirs of a Childhood with Deafness.** Lennard J. Davis. LC 99-6618. (Creative Non-Fiction Ser.). (Illus.). 176p. 2000. 23.95 (*0-252-02533-4*) U of Ill Pr.
My Senses Work for Me. Rice & Deborah P. Cerbus. (Easy Theme Reader Ser.). (Illus.). 16p. (J). (ps-1). 1996. pap. 2.49 (*1-55734-929-0*) Tchr Create Mat.
***My Sentiments Exactly.** Keith Baxter. 1999. pap. 35.00 (*1-84002-053-9*, Pub. by Theatre Comm) Consort Bk Sales.
My September Journal. Alana Trisler & Patrice Cardiel. 48p. (J). (gr. 1-2). 1999. pap., wbk. ed. 1.75 (*1-56762-095-7*) Modern Learn Pr.
My Sergei: A Love Story. Ekaterina Gordeeva & E. M. Swift. 352p. 1997. mass mkt. 6.50 (*0-446-60533-6*, Pub. by Warner Bks) Little.
My Sergei: A Love Story. large type ed. Ekaterina Gordeeva & E. M. Swift. LC 96-44818. (Core Ser.). 284p. 1997. lib. bdg. 25.95 (*0-7838-1963-3*, G K Hall Lrg Type) Mac Lib Ref.
My Servant Brigham: Portrait of a Prophet. Richard N. Holzapfel & R. Q. Shupe. 1997. 19.95 (*1-57008-351-7*) Bookcraft Inc.
My Servants the Prophets, Vol. 1. John T. Willis. LC 76-180789. (Way of Life Ser.: No. 116). 1971. pap. 6.95 (*0-89112-116-1*) Abilene Christ U.
My Servants the Prophets, Vol. 2. John T. Willis. LC 76-180789. (Way of Life Ser.: No. 117). 1972. pap. 6.95 (*0-89112-117-X*) Abilene Christ U.
My Servants the Prophets, Vol. 4. John T. Willis. (Way of Life Ser.: No. 119). 1982. pap. 6.95 (*0-89112-119-6*) Abilene Christ U.
My Seven Book. Jane Belk Moncure. LC 86-2594. (My Number Bks.). (Illus.). 32p. (J). (ps-2). 1986. lib. bdg. 21.36 (*0-89565-318-4*) Childs World.
My Seventy-Two Friends: Encounters with Refuseniks in the U. S. S. R. Dov Peretz Elkins. LC 89-80116. 1989. pap. 12.00 (*0-918834-11-2*) Growth Assoc.
My Seventy Years: At Paramount Studios & the Directors Guild of America. Joseph C. Youngerman. Ed. by Ira Skutch. LC 95-68414. (Oral History Ser.). 144p. 1995. 15.00 (*1-882766-02-4*) Dirs Guild Am.
My Seventy Years in California, 1857-1927. Jackson A. Graves. 1992. reprint ed. lib. bdg. 75.00 (*0-7812-5038-2*) Rprt Serv.
My Several Lives: Memoirs of a Social Inventor. James B. Conant. (American Biography Ser.). 701p. 1991. reprint ed. lib. bdg. 119.00 (*0-7812-8088-5*) Rprt Serv.
My Several Worlds. Pearl Synderstricker Buck. 1992. reprint ed. lib. bdg. 27.95 (*0-89966-987-5*) Buccaneer Bks.
My Sex My Soul. (Red Stripe Ser.). 1989. pap. 3.95 (*0-8216-5069-6*) Carol Pub Group.
My Shabbat Activity Book. David Sokoloff. (Illus.). 24p. (Orig.). (J). (ps-5). 1998. pap. 1.00 (*1-889655-07-4*) Jewish Educ Toys.
My Shabbos 123's. Surie Fettman. LC 96-76744. (Illus.). 32p. (J). (ps-1). 1996. 9.95 (*0-922613-61-3*) Hachai Pubng.
My Shadow. Robert Louis Stevenson. LC 98-51834. (Illus.). (J). 1999. text 12.99 (*0-7636-0923-4*) Candlewick Pr.
My Shadow. Robert Louis Stevenson. (Illus.). 32p. (J). 1989. pap. 9.95 (*1-56792-108-6*) Godine.
My Shadow. Robert Louis Stevenson. LC 88-46107. (Illus.). 32p. (J). (gr. 1 up). 1989. 17.95 (*0-87923-788-0*) Godine.
My Shadow. Robert Louis Stevenson. LC 89-24265. 1996. 10.15 (*0-606-09652-3*, Pub. by Turtleback) Demco.
My Shadow & I. Patty Wolcott. LC 84-40770. (Illus.). (J). 1975. 6.95 (*0-201-14251-1*) HarpC Child Bks.
My Shadow Ran Fast: Who Cares about Me? rev. ed. Bill Sands. 240p. 1995. pap. 11.95 (*1-880369-05-2*) N Hill Found.
My Shameless St. Augustine Scrapbook. Ed. by Ruth M. Kempher. (Illus.). 210p. 1998. pap. 18.95 (*1-888832-11-8*) Kings Estate.
***My Shapes.** Rebecca Emberley. (Illus.). 20p. (J). 2000. 5.95 (*0-316-23355-2*) Little.
My Shaping-Up Years: The Early Life of Labor's Great Reporter. Art Shields. LC 82-21176. (Illus.). 292p. (Orig.). 1983. 14.00 (*0-7178-0597-2*); pap. 4.95 (*0-7178-0571-9*) Intl Pubs Co.
***My Sheep.** Heather Miller. (Welcome Bks.). (Illus.). (J). 2000. 13.50 (*0-516-23110-3*) Childrens.
***My Sheep.** Heather Miller. LC 00-24363. (My Farm Ser.). (Illus.). 24p. (J). (ps-2). 2000. pap. write for info. (*0-516-23035-2*) Childrens.
My Sheep Hear My Voice. Joseph C. Hedgecock. Ed. by Patricia T. Ross. (Illus.). 94p. (Orig.). 1988. pap. 4.95 (*0-945255-00-4*); pap. 5.95 (*0-945255-01-2*); pap. 4.95 (*0-945255-02-0*); pap. 1.95 (*0-945255-05-5*) J C Hedgecock Pubns.
My Shimmery Learning Book: Colors, Shapes, Counting, Opposites, Getting Dressed. Salina Yoon. 10p. (J). 1999. 8.95 (*1-58117-060-2*) Intervisual Bks.
***My Shimmery Play Time Book.** Salina Yoon. (Illus.). (J). 2000. 8.95 (*1-58117-082-3*, Piggy Toes Pr) Intervisual Bks.
My Shining Archipelago. Talvikki Ansel. LC 96-45321. (Yale Series of Younger Poets). 64p. 1997. 18.00 (*0-300-07031-4*); pap. 11.00 (*0-300-07032-2*) Yale U Pr.
My Shooting Box. Henry W. Herbert. (Notable American Authors Ser.). 1992. reprint ed. lib. bdg. 75.00 (*0-7812-3094-2*) Rprt Serv.
My Siddur. Deborah U. Miller. (Illus.). 35p. (J). (gr. k-2). 1984. pap. text 4.95 (*0-87441-389-3*) Behrman.
My Side of the Mountain. 44p. (YA). 1998. 11.95 (*1-56137-494-6*, NU4946SP) Novel Units.
My Side of the Mountain. Jean Craighead George. LC 87-27556. (Illus.). 177p. (J). (gr. 3-7). 1991. pap. 4.99 (*0-14-034810-7*, PuffinBks) Peng Put Young Read.
My Side of the Mountain. Jean Craighead George. (Illus.). (J). (gr. 3 up). 1997. pap. 9.99 (*0-14-774425-3*, PuffinBks) Peng Put Young Read.
My Side of the Mountain. Jean Craighead George. (J). 1959. 10.05 (*0-606-00726-1*, Pub. by Turtleback) Demco.
***My Side of the Mountain.** Phyllis A. Green. 32p. 1999. 9.95 (*1-56137-106-8*) Novel Units.
My Side of the Mountain. rev. ed. Jean Craighead George. (Illus.). (J). 1988. 15.99 (*0-525-46346-1*, Dutton Child) Peng Put Young Read.
My Side of the Mountain: A Study Guide. Joyce Friedland & Rikki Kessler. (Novel-Ties Ser.). (J). (gr. 4-6). 1982. pap. text 15.95 (*0-88122-008-6*) Lrn Links.
My Side of the Mountain: A Unit Plan. Janine Sherman. 171p. 1997. teacher ed., ring bd. 26.95 (*1-58337-170-2*) Teachers Pet Pubns.
***My Side of the Mountain Trilogy.** Jean Craighead George. (Illus.). 640p. (J). (gr. 4 up). 2000. 24.95 (*0-525-46269-4*, Dutton Child) Peng Put Young Read.
My Side of the Story: My Life, Love, & Work from Harlem to Hollywood. Erik Estrada. (Illus.). 256p. 1997. 22.00 (*0-614-22047-5*, Wm Morrow) Morrow Avon.
My Side of the War: How Meatballs Saved My Life. Willy A. Schauss. LC 96-110903. 165p. 1994. write for info. (*0-9617626-9-1*) Scott Publishing Co.
My Sign Is...Aquarius: Astrology for Young Adults, 12 vols. (Illus.). 72p. 1999. pap. 4.95 (*965-494-073-6*) Astrolog Pub.
My Sign Is...Aries, 12 vols. (Illus.). 72p. 1999. pap. 4.95 (*965-494-063-9*) Astrolog Pub.
My Sign Is...Cancer: Astrology for Young Adults, 12 vols. (Illus.). 72p. 1999. pap. 4.95 (*965-494-066-3*) Astrolog Pub.
My Sign Is...Capricorn: Astrology for Young Adults, 12 vols. (Illus.). 72p. 1999. pap. 4.95 (*965-494-072-8*) Astrolog Pub.
My Sign Is...Display, 1. 1999. pap. text 118.80 (*965-494-087-6*) Astrolog Pub.
My Sign Is...Gemini: Astrology for Young Adults. (Illus.). 72p. 1999. pap. 4.95 (*965-494-065-5*) Astrolog Pub.
My Sign Is...Leo: Astrology for Young Adults, 12 vols. (Illus.). 72p. 1999. pap. 4.95 (*965-494-067-1*) Astrolog Pub.
My Sign Is...Libra: Astrology for Young Adults, 12 vols. Amanda Starr. (Illus.). 72p. 1999. pap. 4.95 (*965-494-069-8*) Astrolog Pub.
My Sign Is...Pisces: Astrology for Young Adults, 12 vols. (Illus.). 72p. 1999. pap. 4.95 (*965-494-074-4*) Astrolog Pub.
***My Sign Is...Sagittarius: Astrology for Young Adults, 12 vols.** Amanda Starr. (Illus.). 72p. 1999. pap. 4.95 (*965-494-071-X*) Astrolog Pub.
My Sign Is...Scorpio: Astrology for Young Adults, 12 vols. (Illus.). 72p. 1999. pap. 4.95 (*965-494-070-1*) Astrolog Pub.
***My Sign Is...Taurus: Astrology for Young Adults, Vol. 12.** Amanda Starr. (Illus.). 72p. 1999. pap. 4.95 (*965-494-064-7*) Astrolog Pub.
My Sign Is...Virgo: Astrology for Young Adults, 12 vols. (Illus.). 72p. 1999. pap. 4.95 (*965-494-068-X*) Astrolog Pub.
My Signing Book of Numbers. Patricia Bellan Gillen. LC 87-28758. (Illus.). 64p. (J). (ps up). 1988. 14.95 (*0-930323-37-8*, Pub. by K Green Pubns) Gallaudet Univ Pr.
My Signing Book of Numbers. 2nd ed. Patricia B. Gillen. (Awareness & Caring Ser.: Vol. 9). (Illus.). 56p. (J). (gr. k-5). 1997. reprint ed. lib. bdg. 18.95 (*1-56674-208-0*) Forest Hse.
My Silent Partner. Ben A. Savelli. 1997. pap. 9.95 (*0-7880-0906-0*, Fairway Pr) CSS OH.
My Silk Purse & Yours: The Publishing Scene & American Literary Art. George P. Garrett. 328p. 1992. 34.95 (*0-8262-0866-5*) U of Mo Pr.
My Silly Book of ABCs. Amerikaner. (J). 1994. pap. 3.95 (*0-382-24677-2*) Silver Burdett Pr.
My Silly Book of ABCs. Susan Amerikaner. Ed. by Bonnie Brook. (Silly Me Ser.). (Illus.). 32p. (J). (ps-1). 1989. pap. 3.95 (*0-382-24672-1*); lib. bdg. 6.95 (*0-671-68363-2*) Silver Burdett Pr.
My Silly Book of Colors. Susan Amerikaner. Ed. by Bonnie Brook. (Silly Me Ser.). (Illus.). 32p. (J). (ps-1). 1989. pap. 3.95 (*0-382-24674-8*); lib. bdg. 6.95 (*0-671-68364-0*) Silver Burdett Pr.
My Silly Book of Colors. Susan Amerikaner. (Silly Me Ser.). (SPA.). 32p. (J). 1994. pap. 3.95 (*0-382-24679-9*) Silver Burdett Pr.
My Silly Book of Counting. Susan Amerikaner. Ed. by Bonnie Brook. (Silly Me Ser.). (Illus.). 32p. (J). (ps-1). 1989. pap. 3.95 (*0-382-24673-X*); lib. bdg. 6.95 (*0-671-68365-9*) Silver Burdett Pr.
My Silly Book of Counting. Susan Amerikaner. (Silly Me Ser.). (SPA., Illus.). 32p. (J). 1994. pap. 3.95 (*0-382-24678-0*) Silver Burdett Pr.
My Silly Book of Opposites. Susan Amerikaner. Ed. by Bonnie Brook. (Silly Me Ser.). (Illus.). 32p. (J). (ps-1). 1989. pap. 3.95 (*0-382-24675-6*); lib. bdg. 6.95 (*0-671-68366-7*) Silver Burdett Pr.
My Silly Book of Opposites. Susan Amerikaner. (Silly Me Ser.). (SPA., Illus.). 32p. (J). 1994. pap. 3.95 (*0-382-24680-2*) Silver Burdett Pr.
My Simple Life & Revelation Plus. Clarence Rice. 140p. (Orig.). 1996. pap. write for info. (*1-57502-230-3*) Morris Pubng.
My Sin: Poems from Hollywood. Mark Dunster. 11p. 1998. pap. 5.00 (*0-89642-523-1*) Linden Pubs.
My Sin & Nothing More. Rebecca Gilman. 79p. 1997. pap. 5.60 (*0-87129-798-1*, MA2) Dramatic Pub.
My Sins upon You All. Betty Balsam. LC 98-61469. 546p. 1999. pap. 17.95 (*1-881636-62-3*) Windsor Hse Pub Grp.
My Sister: A Giftbook with Envelope. Nancy C. Akmon. (Illus.). 49p. 1998. 6.95 (*1-884807-26-7*, EC709) Blushing Rose.
My Sister: A Special Friend. Compiled by Liesl Vazquez. (Gift Editions Ser.). (Illus.). 64p. 1996. 7.99 (*0-88088-491-6*) Peter Pauper.
My Sister--Life. Boris Pasternak. Ed. & Tr. by Bohdan Boychuk from RUS. Tr. by Mark Rudman from RUS. 106p. 1993. reprint ed. pap. 13.95 (*0-8101-1090-3*) Northwestern U Pr.
***My Sister Alison, Who Moved Away.** Vivian Vande Velde. LC 00-32032. (Illus.). (J). 2001. write for info. (*0-618-04585-6*) HM.
My Sister & I. Friedrich Wilhelm Nietzsche. Tr. by Oscar Levy from GER. (Illus.). 340p. (C). 1990. reprint ed. pap. 9.95 (*1-878923-01-3*) Amok Bks.
My Sister Annie. Bill Dodds. LC 91-77599. (Illus.). 96p. (J). (gr. 3-7). 1997. pap. 7.95 (*1-56397-554-8*) Boyds Mills Pr.
My Sister Disappears: Stories & a Novella. Lee M. Byrd. LC 93-19647. 200p. (Orig.). 1993. 22.50 (*0-87074-351-1*); pap. 10.95 (*0-87074-359-7*) SMU Press.
My Sister Eileen. Jerome Chodorov & Joseph Fields. 1946. pap. 5.25 (*0-8222-0801-6*) Dramatists Play.
My Sister Eileen. Ruth McKenney. 1993. reprint ed. lib. bdg. 89.00 (*0-7812-5388-8*) Rprt Serv.
My Sister, Esther. Martha Baillie. 118p. 1997. pap. 14.95 (*0-88801-200-4*, Pub. by Turnstone Pr) Genl Dist Srvs.
My Sister from the Black Lagoon: A Novel of My Life. Laurie Fox. LC 98-6466. 304p. 1998. 22.50 (*0-684-84745-0*) S&S Trade.
***My Sister from the Black Lagoon: A Novel of My Life.** Laurie Fox. 336p. 1999. pap. 13.00 (*0-684-85538-0*) S&S Trade Pap.
My Sister Gone. Kathryn Marshall. LC 91-58685. 240p. 1992. reprint ed. pap. 9.95 (*0-944439-49-7*) Clark City Pr.
***My Sister Gracie.** Gillian Johnson. (Illus.). 32p. (J). (ps-k). 2000. 16.95 (*0-88776-514-9*) Tundra Bks.
My Sister Has Lived a Nightmare / 0'C8. Martha Ulrich. 80p. 1996. pap. 8.00 (*0-8059-3780-3*) Dorrance.
My Sister Is Missing!! Kimball R. Crum. (Illus.). 24p. (Orig.). (J). (gr. k-2). 1995. pap. 3.00 (*0-9645022-0-8*) Read Me Publ.

M

An Asterisk (*) at the beginning of an entry indicates that the title is appearing for the first time.

M

My Sister Is Special. rev. ed. Larry Jansen. Ed. by Lise Caldwell. LC 97-47524. (Illus.). 24p. (J). (ps-1). 1998. pap. 1.99 (*0-7847-0797-9*, 24-04255) Standard Pub.

My Sister Is Super. H. Roche. LC 99-166916. (Illus.). (J). (ps). 1998. pap. 4.95 (*1-84089-015-0*, 868238Q) Zero to Ten.

My Sister-Life. Katherine O'Connor. 200p. 1989. 32.50 (*0-88233-778-5*) Ardis Pubs.

My Sister Life. Maria Flook. LC 98-30823. 352p. 1999. reprint ed. pap. 13.00 (*0-7679-0315-3*) Broadway BDD.

My Sister Life: The Story of My Sister's Disappearance. Maria Flook. LC 97-6769. 353p. 1998. 25.00 (*0-679-44208-1*) Pantheon.

My Sister Lotta & Me. Helena Dahlback. Tr. by Rika Lesser from SWE. (Illus.). 32p. (J). (gr. k-3). 1995. 15.95 (*0-8050-2558-8*, Bks Young Read) H Holt & Co.

My Sister Marilyn: A Memoir of Marilyn Monroe. Berniece B. Miracle & Mona R. Miracle. LC 94-8652. 232p. 1994. 19.95 (*1-56512-070-1*) Algonquin Bks.

My Sister Marilyn: A Memoir of Marilyn Monroe. Berniece B. Miracle & Mona R. Miracle. (Illus.). 256p. 1995. pap. 12.00 (*1-57297-026-X*) Blvd Books.

My Sister, My Brother: Womanist & Xodus God-Talk. Karen Baker-Fletcher & Garth Baker-Fletcher. LC 97-12080. (Bishop Henry McNeal Turner/Sojourners Truth Series in Black Religion: No. 12). 325p. (Orig.). 1996. pap. 18.00 (*1-57075-099-8*) Orbis Bks.

My Sister, My Friend. (Little Treasures Ser.). (Illus.). 88p. 1993. 4.99 (*1-57051-001-6*) Brownlow Pub Co.

My Sister, My Science Report. Margaret Bechard. (Illus.). 96p. (J). 1992. pap. 4.99 (*0-14-034408-X*, PuffinBks) Peng Put Young Read.

My Sister, My Science Report. Margaret E. Bechard. (J). 1992. 9.09 (*0-606-01724-0*, Pub. by Turtleback) Demco.

My Sister Rose Has Diabetes. Monica D. Beaty. LC 97-35095. (Illus.). 32p. (J). (gr. 3-7). 1997. pap. 8.95 (*0-929173-27-9*) Health Press.

My Sister Roseanne. Geraldine Barr. LC 93-44653. 1994. 19.95 (*1-55972-230-4*, Birch Ln Pr) Carol Pub Group.

***My Sister Roseanne: The True Story of Roseanne Barr Arnold.** Geraldine Barr. (Illus.). 293p. 1999. text 25.00 (*0-7881-6789-8*) DIANE Pub.

My Sister Saint Therese: By Sister Genevieve of the Holy Face. Celine Martin. LC 97-60610. Orig. Title: A Memoir of My Sister St. Therese (Counseils et Souvenirs). 249p. 1997. reprint ed. pap. 8.00 (*0-89555-598-0*, 1522) TAN Bks Pubs.

My Sister Sif. Ruth Park. 1997. 10.50 (*0-606-11657-5*, Pub. by Turtleback) Demco.

My Sister the Moon Co. Sue Harrison. 416p. 1995. mass mkt. 6.99 (*0-380-71836-7*, Avon Bks) Morrow Avon.

My Sister the Sausage Roll, Vol. 1. Barbara W. Holmes. LC 96-32512. Vol. 1. (Illus.). 64p. (J). (gr. 3-4). 1997. lib. bdg. 14.49 (*0-7868-2260-0*, Pub. by Hyprn Child) Little.

***My Sister the Supermodel.** Megan Stine. (Two of a Kind Ser.: No. 6). 112p. (J). (gr. 1-3). 1999. mass mkt. 4.25 (*0-06-106576-5*) HarpC.

My Sister the Unicorn: The Green Lion. Aurora Terrenus. (Orig.). 1988. pap. 8.95 (*0-945717-90-3*) Celestial Comns.

My Sister the Witch. Ellen Conford. (Norman Newman Ser.). (Illus.). 96p. (J). (gr. 3-5). 1997. lib. bdg. 15.35 (*0-8167-3815-7*) Troll Communs.

My Sister the Witch. Ellen Conford. (Norman Newman Ser.). (J). 1995. 7.60 (*0-606-07959-9*, Pub. by Turtleback) Demco.

My Sisters: A Calendar Book - 1999. Beth Garbo. (Illus.). 54p. 1998. spiral bd. 16.95 (*1-892373-04-1*, 99-05) Especially Bks.

My Sisters: A Calendar Book - 2000. Beth Garbo. (Illus.). 54p. 1998. spiral bd. 16.95 (*1-892373-23-8*, 23-8) Especially Bks.

My Sister's Bones. Cathi Hanauer. 272p. 1997. pap. 11.95 (*0-385-31704-2*) Doubleday.

My Sister's Hand in Mine: The Collected Works of Jane Bowles. rev. ed. Jane Bowles. 476p. 1966. pap. 17.00 (*0-374-50652-3*) FS&G.

***My Sister's Keeper.** Kerry Duke. LC 99-52032. 1999. pap. write for info. (*0-929540-23-9*) Pub Designs.

My Sisters Love My Clothes. Brendan Hanrahan. (Illus.). 32p. (J). (gr. 1-4). 1992. 12.95 (*0-9630181-0-8*) Perry Heights.

My Sister's Rusty Bike. Jim Aylesworth. LC 94-20117. (Illus.). 32p. (J). (gr. k-3). 1996. 16.00 (*0-689-31798-0*) Atheneum Yung Read.

***My Sisters Telegraphic: Women in the Telegraph Office, 1846-1950.** Thomas C. Jepsen. (Illus.). 256p. 2000. 49.95 (*0-8214-1343-0*); pap. 21.95 (*0-8214-1344-9*) Ohio U Pr.

My Six Book. Jane Belk Moncure. LC 85-30961. (My Number Bks.). (Illus.). 32p. (J). (ps-2). 1985. lib. bdg. 21.36 (*0-89565-317-6*) Childs World.

My Sixteen: A Self-Help Guide to Finding Your Sixteen Great-Great Grandparents. Robert W. Marlin. LC 96-232653. (Illus.). 229p. (Orig.). 1996. pap. 14.95 (*0-9650513-0-7*) Land Yacht Pr.

My Sixth Grade Yearbook. Bearl Brooks. (My Yearbook Ser.). 832p. 1981. 18.00 (*0-8209-0086-9*, MSG-6) ESP.

My 66 Years in the Big Leagues. Connie Mack. Date not set. lib. bdg. 21.95 (*0-8488-1587-4*) Amereon Ltd.

My 60 Years As a Labor Activist. Harry Kelber. 272p. 1996. pap. text 17.50 (*0-9632071-4-8*) AG Pub.

My Sixty Years in Recreation Working for Life Enrichment: An Autobiography: a Story of the Leisure Movement in the Twentieth Century. Thomas E. Rivers. Ed. by Paul Douglass. LC 83-61662. (Illus.). 108p. reprint ed. pap. 33.50 (*0-7837-1548-X*, 204183600024) Bks Demand.

My Sixty Years on the Plains: Trapping, Trading, & Indian Fighting. William T. Hamilton. (American Biography Ser.). 184p. 1991. reprint ed. lib. bdg. 59.00 (*0-7812-8163-6*) Rprt Serv.

My Sixty Years with Norwegian Elghunds. Olav P. Campbell. (Illus.). 124p. 1988. 27.95 (*0-9621512-0-3*) Show Quality Pet Prod.

My Sixty Years with Rural Youth. Theodore A. Erickson & Anna N. Colt. LC 56-7810. 192p. reprint ed. pap. 59.60 (*0-608-14645-5*, 205586000039) Bks Demand.

My Skeleton & Muscles. Jo E. Moore & Joy Evans. (Illus.). 16p. (J). (gr. 1-3). 1987. pap., teacher ed. 5.95 (*1-55799-101-4*, 811) Evan-Moor Edu Pubs.

My Sketchbook. Arthur Babb. Ed. by Neill Cameron. LC 96-69675. (Illus.). 122p. (Orig.). 1996. pap. 14.95 (*0-917898-19-2*) NSU Pr LA.

My Skin Aches: Fifteen Women Talk about Divorce. Jane Staw. 1996. write for info. (*0-201-58121-3*) Addison-Wesley.

My Skin Is Brown. Paula DeJoie. (Illus.). 12p. (J). (ps-1). 1996. bds. 5.95 (*0-86316-239-8*) Writers & Readers.

My Small Country Living. Jeanine McMullen. (Illus.). 224p. 1985. mass mkt. 8.95 (*0-446-38305-8*, Pub. by Warner Bks) Little.

My Smoky Mountain Coloring Book. Mary Maden. (Illus.). 16p. (Orig.). (J). (gr. k-5). 1997. pap. 2.95 (*1-890479-54-3*) Dog & Pony Pub.

My So-Called Boyfriend. Elizabeth Winfrey. (Love Stories Ser.). 192p. (YA). (gr. 7-12). 1996. mass mkt. 3.99 (*0-553-56668-7*) BDD Bks Young Read.

My So-Called Life. Catherine Clark. (Illus.). 176p. (YA). (gr. 9). 1995. pap. 4.99 (*0-679-87789-4*) McKay.

My So-Called Life Goes On. Catherine Clarke. 212p. (YA). (gr. 9-11). 1999. pap. 4.99 (*0-375-80111-1*, Pub. by Random Bks Yng Read) Random.

My Soccer Book. Tom Ettinger & William Jaspersohn. (Illus.). 48p. (J). (gr. 3-7). 1993. 10.95 (*0-694-00478-2*, HarpFestival) HarpC Child Bks.

My Soccer Book. Gail Gibbons. LC 99-34514. (Illus.). 24p. (J). (ps-2). 2000. 5.95 (*0-688-17138-9*, Wm Morrow) Morrow Avon.

My Sodium Poppa: The Komplete Kat Komics. George Herriman. 1991. pap. 9.95 (*0-913666-50-5*) Turtle Isl Foun.

My Sojourn in Heaven & Stopover in Hell. John Bunyan. Ed. by Mary S. Relfe. 128p. Date not set. pap. 6.00 (*0-9607986-3-3*) League Prayer.

My Soliloquy. Leah J. Reynolds. (Illus.). 43p. (Orig.). 1992. pap. 5.95 (*1-56411-022-2*) Untd Bros & Sis.

My Son, Beloved Stranger. Kate McLaughlin. LC 95-3295. 1995. pap. 1.97 (*0-8163-1257-5*) Pacific Pr Pub Assn.

My Son Eric. Mary V. Borhek. LC 79-16161. 168p. (Orig.). 1984. pap. 11.95 (*0-8298-0729-2*) Pilgrim OH.

My Son, Ikhnaton. Ann R. Colton. LC 91-76904. (Illus.). 172p. 1992. 15.95 (*0-917189-09-4*) A R Colton Fnd.

My Son Jimi. James A. Hendrix. (Illus.). 185p. 1999. 29.95 (*0-9667857-0-3*) AL-JAS Ent.

***My Son Jimi.** James A. Hendrix. (Illus.). 1999. pap. 17.95 (*0-9667857-1-1*) AL-JAS Ent.

My Son John. Jim Aylesworth. 1997. 11.15 (*0-606-13637-1*, Pub. by Turtleback) Demco.

My Son John. Jim Aylesworth. (Illus.). 32p. (J). (ps-2). 1997. reprint ed. pap. 5.95 (*0-8050-5517-7*) H Holt & Co.

My Son, My Brother, My Friend: A Novel in Letters. rev. ed. Dale Willard. LC 94-4053. 102p. 1995. pap. 8.95 (*0-940895-17-X*) Cornerstone IL.

My Son, My King. Linda C. Shute. 1.25 (*0-687-02700-4*) Abingdon.

***My Son, My Son.** C. Anthony. 1998. text 35.00 (*0-7195-5416-0*, Pub. by John Murray) Trafalgar.

My Son... My Son: A Guide to Healing after Death, Loss or Suicide. rev. ed. Iris Bolton. 120p. 1995. pap. 32.50 incl. audio (*0-9616326-4-X*) Bolton Pr.

My Son... My Son: A Guide to Healing after Death, Loss or Suicide. rev. ed. Iris Bolton. 120p. 1995. 39.00 incl. audio (*0-9616326-5-8*) Bolton Pr.

My Son... My Son: A Guide to Healing after Death, Loss or Suicide. rev. ed. Iris Bolton & Curtis Mitchell. 120p. 1983. pap. 12.95 (*0-9616326-0-7*) Bolton Pr.

My Son... My Son: A Guide to Healing after Death, Loss or Suicide. 12th rev. ed. Iris Bolton & Curtis Mitchell. 120p. 1983. 17.95 (*0-9616326-1-5*) Bolton Pr.

My Son, My Sorrow: The Tragic Tale of Dr. Kevorkian's Youngest Patient. Carol Loving. LC 97-66563. (Illus.). 300p. 1998. 22.95 (*0-88282-161-X*) New Horizon NJ.

My Son on the Galley. Jacob Wallenberg et al. Tr. by Peter Graves et al from SWE. LC 94-165680. 196p. 1994. pap. 24.00 (*1-870041-23-2*) Norvik Pr.

My Son the Fanatic. Hanif Kureishi. (Illus.). 112p. 1999. pap. 13.95 (*0-571-19234-3*) Faber & Faber.

My Son, the Time Traveler. Dan Greenburg. LC 97-2243. (Zack Files: No. 8). (Illus.). 64p. (J). (gr. 2-5). 1997. pap. 3.95 (*0-448-41341-8*, G & D); lib. bdg. 12.99 (*0-448-41587-9*, G & D) Peng Put Young Read.

My Son, the Time Traveler. Dan Greenburg. LC 97-2243. (Zack Files: No. 8). (J). (gr. 2-5). 1997. 9.15 (*0-606-12133-1*, Pub. by Turtleback) Demco.

My Son the Wizard. Christopher Stasheff. LC 97-14769. (Wizard in Rhyme Ser.: No. 5). 352p. 1997. 11.95 (*0-345-37602-1*) Ballantine Pub Grp.

My Son the Wizard. Christopher Stasheff. (A Wizard in Rhyme Ser.: No. 5). 1998. mass mkt. 6.99 (*0-345-42480-8*, Del Rey) Ballantine Pub Grp.

My Son, Yo-Yo: A Biography of the Early Years of Yo-Yo Ma. Marina Mas & John A. Rallo. LC 97-195180. (Illus.). 150p. 1997. pap. text 18.95 (*962-201-640-5*, Pub. by Chinese Univ) U of Mich Pr.

My Song for Piano. B. Sheng. 20p. 1994. pap. 7.50 (*0-7935-3836-X*, 50482268) H Leonard.

My Song Is Beautiful: A Celebration of Multicultural Poems & Pictures. Selected by Mary A. Hoberman. LC 93-24976. 32p. (J). (gr. k-3). 1994. 16.95 (*0-316-36738-9*) Little.

My Song Is My Weapon: People's Songs, American Communism, & the Politics of Culture, 1930-1950. Robbie Lieberman. (Music in American Life Ser.). (Illus.). 232p. 1989. text 24.95 (*0-252-01559-2*) U of Ill Pr.

My Song Is My Weapon: People's Songs, American Communism, & the Politics of Culture, 1930-1950. Robbie Lieberman. (Music in American Life Ser.). (Illus.). 232p. (C). 1995. 16.95 (*0-252-06525-5*) U of Ill Pr.

My Song Is of Mercy: Writings of Matthew Kelty, Including Flute Solo. Matthew Kelty. Ed. by Michael Downey. LC 94-30801. 280p. (Orig.). 1994. pap. 15.95 (*1-55612-606-9*) Sheed & Ward WI.

My Son's Story. Nadine Gordimer. 1990. 19.95 (*0-374-21751-3*) FS&G.

My Son's Story. Nadine Gordimer. 292p. 1991. reprint ed. pap. 12.95 (*0-14-015975-4*, Penguin Bks) Viking Penguin.

My Sons Were Faithful & They Fought the Irish Brigade at Antietam: An Anthology. Ed. by Joseph G. Bilby & Stephan D. O'Neill. LC 98-220798. (Illus.). 131p. 1997. pap. 18.00 (*0-944413-42-0*, 132) Longstreet Hse.

***My Soul & I.** Adam Misterka. 1999. pap. write for info. (*1-58235-246-1*) Watermrk Pr.

My Soul in China: A Novella & Stories. Anna Kavan. 192p. 1975. pap. 16.95 (*0-7206-0786-8*) Dufour.

My Soul Is a Witness: A Chronology of the Civil Rights Era in the United States, 1954-1965. Bettye Collier-Thomas. Ed. by V. P. Franklin. LC 99-27987. 256p. 2000. text 30.00 (*0-8050-4769-7*) St Martin.

My Soul Is a Witness: African-American Women's Spirituality. Ed. by Gloria Wade-Gayles. 384p. 1996. pap. 15.00 (*0-8070-0935-0*) Beacon Pr.

My Soul Is a Woman: The Feminine in Islam. Annemarie Schimmel. Tr. by Susan H. Ray. LC 83-14816. 176p. 1997. 22.95 (*0-8264-1014-6*) Continuum.

My Soul Is Free Vivianna Reich. LC 92-236428. iv, 108p. 1992. write for info. (*1-56043-506-2*) Destiny Image.

My Soul Is Rested: Movement Days in the Deep South Remembered. Howell Raines. 472p. 1983. pap. 14.95 (*0-14-006753-1*, Penguin Bks) Viking Penguin.

My Soul Lives in a Daisy see Moja Dusha Zhivet V Romanshke

My Soul Look Back & Wonder... A Collection of Poems by Evelyn Phosia Holmes. Evelyn P. Holmes. LC 96-94072. (Illus.). 70p. 1997. per. 10.00 (*0-9661321-5-7*) E P Holmes.

My Soul Looks Back. James H. Cone. 144p. 1986. pap. 13.50 (*0-88344-355-4*) Orbis Bks.

My Soul Looks Back, 'Less I Forget. Dorothy W. Riley. 332p. (YA). 1991. write for info. (*1-880234-06-8*); pap. write for info. (*1-880234-00-9*) Winbush Pub.

My Soul Looks Back, 'Less I Forget. rev. ed. Ed. by Dorothy W. Riley. 512p. 1995. pap. 20.00 (*0-06-272057-0*, Harper Ref) HarpC.

My Soul Looks Back, 'Less I Forget, Vol. 2. Dorothy W. Riley. 332p. (YA). 1992. pap. write for info. (*1-880234-01-7*) Winbush Pub.

***My Soul Magnifies the Lord: Discovering the Riches of the Magnificant.** Martyn Lloyd-Jones. 112p. 2000. pap. 9.99 (*1-58134-209-8*) Crossway Bks.

My Soul Purpose. Heidi Von Beltz. 1998. mass mkt. 6.99 (*0-312-96431-5*) St Martin.

My Soul Sings Acappella: Poetry & Prose. Shia S. Barnett. LC 96-94860. (Illus.). xiv, 90p. (Orig.). 1996. pap. 11.95 (*0-9655430-7-2*) Blckberry Bks.

My Soul Speaks Truth. Bettye S. Coney. (Illus.). 119p. (Orig.). 1996. pap. 14.95 (*0-9648337-0-0*) SteBreCo.

***My Soul Thirsts: An Invitation to Intimacy with God.** Steve Korch. LC 99-49495. 176p. 2000. pap. 15.00 (*0-8170-1345-8*) Judson.

My Soul to Keep. Tananarive Due. LC 97-4992. 352p. 1998. pap. 15.00 (*0-06-105366-X*, HarperPrism) HarpC.

My Soul to Keep. Jean M. Favors. 160p. (Orig.). (YA). (gr. 5 up). 1994. mass mkt. 3.99 (*0-380-77478-X*, Avon Bks) Morrow Avon.

My Soul to Keep. Judith Hawkes. 416p. 1997. mass mkt. 6.99 (*0-451-18414-9*, Sig) NAL.

My Soul to Take. Dale Freeman. 122p. 1993. pap. 6.95 (*1-880365-64-2*) Prof Pr NC.

My Soul to Take. large type ed. Steven Spruill. LC 94-20146. (Cloak & Dagger Ser.). 550p. 1994. lib. bdg. 24.95 (*0-7862-0274-2*) Thorndike Pr.

My Soul's Been Anchored: A Preacher's Heritage of Faith. H. Beecher Hicks, Jr. LC 98-10395. 208p. 1998. 14.99 (*0-310-22136-6*) Zondervan.

My Soul's Delights: God's Comfort in Sorrow. Merna B. Shank. (Illus.). 1991. pap. 2.75 (*0-87813-540-5*) Christian Light.

***My Soul's on a Journey.** Anne Marie Legon. 50p. 1999. 6.95 (*1-885206-68-2*) Cader Pubng.

My Sound Parade. Jane Belk Moncure. LC 79-15930. (Sound Box Library). (Illus.). 32p. (J). (ps-2). 1979. lib. bdg. 21.36 (*0-89565-103-3*) Childs World.

My Sourdough Dad. Olivia Casberg. LC 89-8644. 168p. (Orig.). 1989. pap. 8.00 (*0-933380-07-0*) Olive Pr Pubns.

My Sourh Block Years: Memoirs of a Foreign Secretary. J. N. Dixit. 1997. pap. 18.50 (*81-7476-183-7*, Pub. by UBS Pubs) S Asia.

My Southern Friends. James R. Gilmore. LC 78-83964. (Black Heritage Library Collection). 1977. 20.95 (*0-8369-8580-X*) Ayer.

My Southern Friends by Edmund Kirke. James Gilmore. LC 72-101143. (Southern Literature & History Ser.: No. 65). 1969. reprint ed. lib. bdg. 75.00 (*0-8383-1218-7*) M S G Haskell Hse.

My Southern Home: The South & Its People. William W. Brown. LC 70-78570. (Muckrakers Ser.). (Illus.). 260p. reprint ed. lib. bdg. 32.95 (*0-8398-0177-7*) Irvington.

My Spanish Speaking Left Foot. Jose A. Cardenas. 135p. (Orig.). 1997. pap. 9.00 (*1-878550-59-4*) Inter Dev Res Assn.

My Special Book of Jewish Celebrations. Grace C. Mack. (Illus.). 36p. (Orig.). (J). (ps-2). 1984. pap. 8.95 (*0-9602338-4-9*) Rockdale Ridge.

My Special Brother. Lena Schiff. 250p. (C). 1991. pap. 14.95 (*1-56062-101-X*) CIS Comm.

My Special Brother. Lena Schiff. 250p. (C). 1991. 17.95 (*1-56062-102-8*) CIS Comm.

My Special Day. 1995. 7.50 (*0-7459-3360-2*, Pub. by Lion Pubng) Trafalgar.

My Special Family: A Children's Book about Open Adoption. Kathleen Silber & Debra M. Parelskin. (Illus.). 28p. (Orig.). (J). (ps-4). 1994. pap. 12.95 (*0-9640009-1-1*) Open Adoption.

My Special Friend. BHB International Staff. 1997. 6.95 (*1-85833-612-0*, Pub. by CLib Bks) Whitecap Bks.

My Special Place. Bill Martin, Jr. 136p. (gr. 4-9). 1980. pap. 8.95 (*0-89114-111-1*) Baptist Pub Hse.

My Spellbound Heart. Ed. by John Scognamiglio. 384p. 1994. mass mkt. 4.99 (*0-8217-4731-2*, Zebra Kensgtn) Kensgtn Pub Corp.

My Spelling Book. Chavez. (My English Book Ser.). 88p. 1997. pap. text 8.11 (*0-673-19187-7*) Addison-Wesley.

My Spelling Dictionary. Nancy Shaw & Charlene Stout. Ed. by Linda Milliken. (Illus.). 32p. 1998. pap., wbk. ed. 1.99 (*1-56472-111-6*) Edupress Inc.

My Spirit Flies: Portraits & Prose of Women in Their Power. M. Cathy Angell. LC 96-95260. (Illus.). 96p. (Orig.). 1997. pap. 19.95 (*0-9655459-3-8*) Bay City Pr.

My Spirit Helpers. Judith Pleasant. LC 98-93410. 136p. 1998. pap. text 12.95 (*0-9666446-0-3*) BootSun Pub.

My Spirit Rejoices: The Diary of a Christian Soul in an Age of Unbelief. Elisabeth Leseur. LC 96-6442. 265p. 1996. pap. 16.50 (*0-918477-40-9*) Sophia Inst Pr.

My Spirit Soars. Dan George. (Illus.). 96p. 1989. pap. 7.95 (*0-88839-233-8*) Hancock House.

My Spiritual Aeroplane. Augusta E. Stetson. LC 91-815605. 57p. 1989. reprint ed. pap., per. 5.00 (*1-879135-04-3*) Emma Pub Soc.

My Spiritual Alphabet Book. Holly Bea. LC 98-32194. (Illus.). 32p. (J). (ps-2). 2000. 14.00 (*0-915811-83-9*) H J Kramer Inc.

My Spiritual Heritage. Faithe H. Musser. LC 98-90153. 1998. pap. 8.95 (*0-533-12729-7*) Vantage.

My Spiritual Journey: New Testament. Stephen Arterburn. LC 96-109302. 857p. 1995. pap. 14.99 (*0-8423-4501-9*) Tyndale Hse.

My Spring Journal. Alana Trisler & Patrice Cardiel. 72p. (J). (gr. 2-3). 1999. pap., wbk. ed. 2.00 (*1-56762-106-6*) Modern Learn Pr.

My Spring Robin. Anne Rockwell. (Illus.). 24p. (J). (ps-1). 1996. per. 4.95 (*0-689-80447-4*) Aladdin.

My Spring Robin. Anne F. Rockwell. LC 88-13333. (J). 1996. 10.85 (*0-606-09656-6*, Pub. by Turtleback) Demco.

My Spurgeon Souvenirs. Eric Hayden. 1997. pap. 7.99 (*1-898787-75-1*) Emerald House Group Inc.

***My Spy: Memoir of a CIA Wife.** Bina Cady Kiyonaga. LC 99-50096. (Illus.). 320p. 2000. 24.00 (*0-380-97587-4*) Morrow Avon.

***My SQL.** Paul DuBois. 756p. 1999. pap. text 49.99 (*0-7357-0921-1*) New Riders Pub.

***My SQL & PHP from Scratch.** 550p. 2000. 34.99 (*0-7897-2440-5*) Que.

My Staggerford Journal. Jon Hassler. LC 99-46993. 112p. 1999. 14.00 (*0-345-43288-6*) Ballantine Pub Grp.

My Stand up Baby Animals. (Illus.). (J). (ps). 1993. 6.00 (*1-56021-199-7*) W J Fantasy.

My Stand up Farm Animals. (Illus.). (J). (ps). 1993. 6.00 (*1-56021-200-4*) W J Fantasy.

My Stars, It's Mrs. Gaddy! Wilson Gage. LC 90-478577. (Illus.). 96p. (J). (ps-3). 1991. 15.95 (*0-688-10514-9*, Grenwillow Bks) HarpC Child Bks.

My State. Kathy L. Balsamo. (Illus.). 144p. 1997. pap. 14.95 (*1-880505-50-9*, CLC0202) Pieces of Lrning.

My State. Schneider & Shipman. (Illus.). 48p. (J). (gr. 3-6). 1996. pap., teacher ed. 5.95 (*1-55799-569-9*, 555) Evan-Moor Edu Pubs.

My Statement to the World. Mary E. Baguio. 1997. 6.95 (*0-533-08440-7*) Vantage.

***My Steadfast Heart.** Jo Goodman. LC 00-24498. 2000. write for info. (*0-7862-2501-7*) Five Star.

My Steadfast Heart. Jo Goodman. 416p. 1997. mass mkt. 5.50 (*0-8217-5595-1*, Zebra Kensgtn) Kensgtn Pub Corp.

My Stepfamily. Julie Johnson. LC 98-16957. (How Do I Feel About... Ser.). (Illus.). 24p. (J). (gr. 1-3). 1998. lib. bdg. 19.90 (*0-7613-0868-7*, Copper Beech Bks) Millbrook Pr.

My Stepfather Shrank! Barbara Dillon. LC 91-23901. (Illus.). 128p. (J). (gr. 3-7). 1992. 13.00 (*0-06-021574-7*) HarpC Child Bks.

***My Stepping Stones to Prayer: Prayer Channel.** Dell McPherson. 236p. 1999. pap. 13.00 (*0-7392-0468-8*, PO3784) Morris Pubng.

My Steps. Sally Derby. LC 96-33847. (Illus.). 32p. (J). (ps-4). 1999. 14.95 (*1-880000-40-7*) Lee & Low Bks.

My Steps. Sally Derby. LC 96-33847. (Illus.). 32p. (J). (gr. 1-4). 1999. pap. 6.95 (*1-880000-84-9*, Pub. by Lee & Low Bks) Publishers Group.

My Steve Sax Connection: How a Hero Led an Abused Boy to Manhood. Alan B. Waldman. 272p. (Orig.). 1990. pap. 12.95 (*0-9626298-1-2*) Astor Street Pub.

My Sticker Atlas of the United States & Canada. Ann D. Hardy. (Illus.). 48p. (J). 1995. 3.99 (*0-517-12082-8*) Random Hse Value.

My Sticker Book Atlas. Deni Bown. (Illus.). 20p. (J). (ps-2). 1994. pap. 6.95 (*1-56458-714-2*) DK Pub Inc.

An Asterisk (*) at the beginning of an entry indicates that the title is appearing for the first time.

My Sticker Book of the Body. Deni Bown. (Illus.). 20p. (J). (ps-2). 1996. pap. 6.95 (*0-7894-1196-2*) DK Pub Inc.

My Sticker Book of Time. Deni Bown. (Illus.). 20p. (J). (ps-2). 1996. pap. 6.95 (*0-7894-1197-0*) DK Pub Inc.

My Sticker Book of Words. Deni Bown. (Illus.). 20p. (J). (ps-2). 1994. pap. 6.95 (*1-56458-715-0*) DK Pub Inc.

My Sticker Dictionary. Cass Hollander. (Illus.). 64p. (J). (ps-2). 1992. pap. 6.95 (*1-56293-250-0*, McClanahan Book) Learn Horizon.

My Sticker Dictionary. Random House Value Publishing Staff. (J). 1998. 3.99 (*0-517-16040-4*) Random Hse Value.

My Stories about Jesus. Sarah Fletcher. (Illus.). 32p. (J). (ps-3). 1974. pap. 2.89 (*0-570-03427-2*, 56-1182) Concordia.

My Story. write for info. (*0-8154-1102-2*) Cooper Sq.

My Story. Kamala Das. (C). 1996. pap. write for info. (*81-207-1324-9*) Sterling Pubs.

My Story. Sarah Ferguson. 1998. pap. 9.98 (*0-671-04464-8*) PB.

My Story. Sarah Ferguson & Jeff Coplan. 1997. per. 6.99 (*0-671-00439-5*) PB.

My Story. Amy Fisher. 1994. mass mkt. 5.50 (*0-671-86559-5*, Pocket Star Bks) PB.

My Story. Emily Moore. 10p. 1998. pap. 2.50 (*1-891972-01-4*) Beastkraft Pubg.

My Story. George Polley. 27p. 1999. pap. 3.00 (*1-893901-03-3*) T & H Pubns.

***My Story.** C. Richard. 1998. text 29.95 (*0-233-99300-2*, Pub. by Andre Deutsch) Trafalgar.

My Story. Gabriela Sabatini. Ed. by Feldman. 112p. (Orig.). (J). (gr. 3 up). 1994. pap. 4.95 (*1-886612-00-5*) Avatar Gen.

My Story. Vicky Van Meter. 1999. pap. 14.99 (*0-670-86417-X*) Viking Penguin.

My Story. large type ed. Sarah M. York & Jeff Coplon. LC 96-53536. 1997. 26.95 (*0-7838-8084-7*, G K Hall Lrg Type) Mac Lib Ref.

My Story. Tom L. Johnson. Ed. by Elizabeth J. Hauser. LC 77-127899. reprint ed. 18.95 (*0-404-03593-0*) AMS Pr.

My Story. Tom L. Johnson. Ed. by Elizabeth J. Hauser. LC 92-37745. (Black Squirrel Bks.: No. 3). (Illus.). 448p. 1993. reprint ed. pap. 17.00 (*0-87338-487-3*) Kent St U Pr.

My Story. Tom L. Johnson. (American Biography Ser.). 326p. 1991. reprint ed. lib. bdg. 79.00 (*0-7812-8223-3*) Rprt Serv.

My Story. Tom L. Johnson. (BCL1 - United States Local History Ser.). 326p. 1991. reprint ed. lib. bdg. 89.00 (*0-7812-6318-2*) Rprt Serv.

My Story. Mary Roberts Rinehart. Ed. by Annette K. Baxter. LC 79-8806. (Signal Lives Ser.). (Illus.). 1980. reprint ed. lib. bdg. 69.95 (*0-405-12852-5*) Ayer.

My Story. Mary Roberts Rinehart. 1993. reprint ed. lib. bdg. 89.00 (*0-7812-5824-3*) Rprt Serv.

My Story. Mary Roberts Rinehart. (American Autobiography Ser.). 570p. 1995. reprint ed. lib. bdg. 109.00 (*0-7812-8625-5*) Rprt Serv.

My Story: A Champion's Memoirs. William Tilden. (American Autobiography Ser.). 335p. 1995. reprint ed. lib. bdg. 89.00 (*0-7812-8652-2*) Rprt Serv.

My Story: A Journal. Susan Paul. 130p. (Orig.). 1997. spiral bd. 10.95 (*0-9650231-2-5*) Inner Edge.

My Story: Divorce & Remarriage Activity Book. Jim Boulden & Joan Boulden. (J). (gr. 1-7). 1991. pap., student ed. 5.95 (*1-878076-06-X*) Boulden Pub.

My Story: Life History Outline - Non-Denominational. 4th ed. Lynda Nelson. 97p. 1992. reprint ed. ring bd. 13.95 (*0-9652557-1-9*, NDE) Hist Happenings.

My Story: Life History Outline for Latterday Saints. 4th ed. Lynda Nelson. 127p. 1992. reprint ed. ring bd. 16.95 (*0-9652557-0-0*, LDSE) Hist Happenings.

My Story - Wrinkles & All. Kathy Staff. mass mkt. 13.95 (*0-340-69470-X*, Pub. by Hodder & Stought Ltd) Trafalgar.

***My Story about Cancer.** Charles B. Wolford & Fay Wolford. LC 99-58273. 56p. 1999. pap. 5.95 (*0-929765-75-3*) Seven Locks Pr.

My Story & I'm Sticking to It. Alex Hawkins. 272p. 1990. pap. 8.95 (*0-945575-54-8*) Algonquin Bks.

***My Story Book.** G. Huggins. (J). (gr. 1-5). 2000. pap. 5.95 (*0-533-13450-1*) Vantage.

***My Story Book: Primary.** Linda Milliken. Ed. by Kathy Rogers. (Illus.). 32p. 1998. 1.99 (*1-56472-145-0*) Edupress Inc.

***My Story Book: Upper Grade.** Linda Milliken. Ed. by Kathy Rogers. (Illus.). 32p. 1998. 1.99 (*1-56472-146-9*) Edupress Inc.

My Story Life History Outline for Latter-Day Saints see Mi Historia Compendio Historico de Vida: Para Miembros de la Iglesia de los Santos de los Ultimos Dias

My Story: Life History Outline Non-Denominational see Mi Historia: Compendio Historico de Vida Tradicional - Non-Denominational

***My Story, My Song: A Novel.** Bret Lott. 2001. 24.00 (*0-375-50377-3*) Random.

My Story of the War: A Woman's Narrative of Four Year's Personal Experience As Nurse in the Union Army. Mary A. Livermore. LC 72-2612. (American Women Ser.: Images & Realities). (Illus.). 704p. 1975. reprint ed. 44.95 (*0-405-04466-6*) Ayer.

My Story of the War: A Women's Narrative of Four Years Personal Experience As Nurse in the Union Army. Mary A. Livermore. 700p. 1978. reprint ed. 39.95 (*0-87928-100-6*) Corner Hse.

My Story of the War: The Civil War Memoirs of the Famous Nurse, Relief Organizer, & Suffragette. Mary A. Livermore. (Illus.). 710p. 1995. reprint ed. pap. 19.95 (*0-306-80658-4*) Da Capo.

My Strange Cyberlife. R. E. Berney. 126p. 1998. pap. 11.95 (*1-892896-33-8*) Buy Books.

My Street. Ed. by Rebecca Treays & Racheal Wells. (Young Geography Ser.). (Illus.). 24p. (J). (ps-3). 1999. pap. text 8.95 (*0-7460-3077-0*, Usborne) EDC.

My Struggle: The Explosive Views of Russias Most Controversial Political Figure. Vladimir Zhirinovsky. LC 95-26654. 144p. 1996. 18.00 (*1-56980-074-X*) Barricade Bks.

My Students' Favorite Chinese Recipes. Norma Chang. (Illus.). 200p. (Orig.). 1987. pap. 9.75 (*0-9618759-0-9*) Travelling Gourmet.

My Study Windows. James Russell Lowell. LC 70-126664. reprint ed. 31.50 (*0-404-04057-8*) AMS Pr.

My Study Windows. James Russell Lowell. (BCL1-PS American Literature Ser.). 433p. 1992. reprint ed. lib. bdg. 99.00 (*0-7812-6788-9*) Rprt Serv.

My Study Windows. James Russell Lowell. (Notable American Authors Ser.). 1999. reprint ed. lib. bdg. 125.00 (*0-7812-3895-1*) Rprt Serv.

My Stupid Illness. Katy Tartakoff. Ed. by Droy Advertising Staff. (Illus.). 54p. (Orig.). 1991. student ed. 14.95 (*0-9629365-0-2*) Childrens Lgcy.

My Stupid Illness. Katy Tartakoff. 54p. (Orig.). 1994. wbk. ed. 14.95 (*0-9629365-4-5*) Childrens Lgcy.

My Substitute Teacher's Gone Batty! Louise Munro Foley. (Vampire Cat Ser.). (J). (gr. 3-7). 1996. pap. 3.99 (*0-614-15787-0*) Tor Bks.

My Substitute Teacher's Gone Batty! Louise Munro Foley. (Vampire Cat Ser.: No. 1). 96p. (J). (gr. 3-6). 1996. mass mkt. 4.50 (*0-8125-5366-7*, Pub. by Tor Bks) St Martin.

My Subtle Shift from Baptist Fundamentalist to... Sermons of a Newly Liberated Ministry. Terry J. Moore. LC 98-85959. 325p. 1998. 25.00 (*0-7388-0002-3*); pap. 15.00 (*0-7388-0041-4*) Xlibris Corp.

My Success Journal. 2nd ed. Lila Swell. 80p. (C). 1993. pap. text, per. 7.95 (*0-8403-8153-0*) Kendall-Hunt.

My Success Journal: Teacher's Guide. 2nd ed. Lila Swell. 144p. 1995. per. 17.80 (*0-8403-8154-9*) Kendall-Hunt.

My Sudan Year. E. S. Stevens. 400p. 1990. 155.00 (*1-85077-079-4*, Pub. by Darf Pubs Ltd) St Mut.

***My Sugar Babies: Proven Techniques on Controlling Type 1 Diabetes from a Mother's Perspective.** Victoria Peurrung. (Illus.). 250p. 1999. pap. 15.95 (*1-884707-91-2*) Lifestyles.

My Summer As a Bride. Cathleen Calbert. 26p. 1995. pap. 5.00 (*1-890044-05-9*) Riverstone PA.

My Summer Camp Diary. Stephanie Calmenson. 96p. (J). (ps-3). 1995. pap. 2.99 (*0-590-48398-6*) Scholastic Inc.

My Summer in a Garden. Charles D. Warner. (BCL1-PS American Literature Ser.). 183p. 1992. reprint ed. lib. bdg. 69.00 (*0-7812-6893-1*) Rprt Serv.

My Summer in a Garden. Charles D. Warner. (Notable American Authors Ser.). 1999. reprint ed. lib. bdg. 125.00 (*0-7812-9887-3*) Rprt Serv.

My Summer Journal. Alana Trisler & Patrice Cardiel. 72p. (J). (gr. 2-3). 1999. pap., wbk. ed. 2.00 (*1-56762-107-4*) Modern Learn Pr.

My Summer on the Choo-Choo Express. Arlene Erlbach. 1988. reprint ed. write for info. (*0-318-62361-7*) S&S Trade.

My Summer with George. large type ed. Marilyn French. 304p. 1996. 29.99 (*0-7089-9022-3*) Ulverscroft.

***My Summer with Julia.** Sarah Woodhouse. 2000. 23.95 (*0-312-26622-7*) St Martin.

My Summer with Molly: The Journal of a Second Generation Father. Larry L. Meyer. LC 89-840. (Illus.). 192p. 1989. 16.95 (*0-942273-04-4*) Calafia Pr.

***My Sunday Missal: "Explained"** rev. ed. Joseph Stedman. Ed. by Paul Trinchard. 352p. 1999. reprint ed. pap. 15.00 (*1-889168-08-4*) MAETA.

My Super Duper Sticker Set. (J). (ps-3). 1993. pap. 2.95 (*0-8167-3099-7*) Troll Communs.

My Super Sleepover Book. Linda Williams Aber. (Full House Michelle Ser.). 112p. (J). (ps-3). 1999. pap. 3.99 (*0-671-02701-8*) PB.

My Survival As an African in America: A Story of My Struggle. R. Fola Adeshina. Ed. by Noni Ford. LC 96-107110. (Illus.). 152p. (Orig.). 1995. pap. text 12.95 (*0-9645896-0-5*) R F Adeshina.

My Sweet Audrina. V. C. Andrews. Ed. by Linda Marrow. 1990. mass mkt. 7.99 (*0-671-72946-2*) PB.

My Sweet Audrina. V. C. Andrews. (J). 1989. 12.65 (*0-606-02956-7*, Pub. by Turtleback) Demco.

My Sweet Baby. Patricia Coughlin. 1993. per. 3.50 (*0-373-09837-5*, 5-09837-1) Silhouette.

My Sweet Folly. Laura Kinsale. 416p. 1997. mass mkt. 6.50 (*0-425-15687-7*) Berkley Pub.

My Sweet Folly. large type ed. Laura Kinsale. LC 97-49395. 590p. 1998. pap. 26.95 (*0-7838-8410-9*, G K Hall Lrg Type) Mac Lib Ref.

My Sweet Untraceable You. Sandra Scoppettone. 320p. 1995. mass mkt. 5.99 (*0-345-39162-4*) Ballantine Pub Grp.

My Sweetheart's House: Memories, Fictions. Robert Drake. LC 93-46129. (C). 1994. 18.95 (*0-86554-437-9*, MUP/P105) Mercer Univ Pr.

My Symphony. Mary Englebreit. (Illus.). 48p. (J). (gr. 1). 1997. 14.95 (*0-8362-3674-2*) Andrews & McMeel.

My Symptoms. John Yau. LC 98-14838. 203p. 1998. 27.50 (*1-57423-062-X*); pap. 15.00 (*1-57423-061-1*) Black Sparrow.

My Symptoms. deluxe ed. John Yau. LC 98-14838. 203p. 1998. 35.00 (*1-57423-063-8*) Black Sparrow.

My Synagogue. M. Weisser. (Illus.). 25p. (J). (gr. k-5). 1984. pap. text 4.95 (*0-87441-386-9*) Behrman.

My System. Aron Nimzowitsch. 1995. pap. 17.95 (*1-85744-089-7*) S&S Trade.

My System. rev. ed. Aron Nimzowitsch. 1979. pap. 18.00 (*0-679-14025-5*) McKay.

My System - 21st Century Edition: The Landmark Positional Chess Training Classic in an Easy-to-Study Algebraic. Aron Nimzowitsch & Lou Nimzowitsch. Ed. by Lou Hays. 260p. 1993. pap. 17.50 (*1-880673-85-1*) Hays Pub.

My "t" Sound Box. Jane Belk Moncure. LC 77-23587. (Sound Box Library). (Illus.). 32p. (J). (ps-2). 1977. lib. bdg. 21.36 (*0-913778-96-6*) Childs World.

My Tacoma Dome. David C. Helstrom. (Color-A-Story Ser.). (Illus.). 24p. (Orig.). (J). (gr. 1-4). 1983. pap. 2.75 (*0-933992-29-7*) Coffee Break.

My Tale of Two Worlds. Lement Harris. Ed. by Betty Smith. LC 86-10671. (Illus.). 300p. 1986. pap. 6.95 (*0-7178-0641-3*) Intl Pubs Co.

My Talks with Arab Leaders. David Ben-Gurion. LC 72-94298. 342p. 1973. 30.00 (*0-89388-076-0*) Okpaku Communications.

My Tangs Tungled. Sara Westbrook Brewton. (J). 1973. 12.95 (*0-690-57223-9*) HarpC Child Bks.

My Taoist Vision or Art. Sal Kupunan. LC 98-37584. (Illus.). 64p. 1999. pap. 14.95 (*1-887905-12-X*) Pkway Pubs.

My Tea Journal. Linda Wexler. LC 95-83099. (Spot of Tea Ser.). (Illus.). 104p. (Orig.). 1995. pap., spiral bd. 8.95 (*1-888230-01-0*) Chelsea St Prods.

My Tea Journal. Linda R. Wexler. Ed. by Howard B. Raff. (Spot of Tea Ser.). (Illus.). 104p. (Orig.). 1997. pap. 8.95 (*1-888230-03-7*) Chelsea St Prods.

My Teacher Doesn't Like Me. Valerie F. Harris & Eula V. Jones. 22p. (J). (gr. k-6). Date not set. pap. write for info. (*1-889654-00-0*) Enricharamics.

My Teacher Flunked the Planet. Bruce Coville. (J). 1992. per. 3.99 (*0-671-79199-0*) PB.

My Teacher Flunked the Planet. Bruce Coville. Ed. by Pat MacDonald. (Illus.). 176p. (J). (gr. 3-8). 1992. pap. 3.99 (*0-671-75081-X*, Minstrel Bks) PB.

My Teacher Flunked the Planet. Bruce Coville. (My Teacher Is an Alien Ser.). (J). 1992. 8.60 (*0-606-02087-X*, Pub. by Turtleback) Demco.

My Teacher Fried My Brains. Coville. (J). 1991. per. 2.99 (*0-671-74610-3*) PB.

My Teacher Fried My Brains. Bruce Coville. Ed. by Patricia MacDonald. 128p. (J). (gr. 3-7). 1991. per. 3.99 (*0-671-72710-9*, Minstrel Bks) PB.

My Teacher Fried My Brains. Bruce Coville. (J). 1991. 9.09 (*0-606-04984-3*, Pub. by Turtleback) Demco.

My Teacher Glows in the Dark. Bruce Coville. Ed. by Patricia MacDonald. (Illus.). 144p. (J). (gr. 4-7). 1991. per. 3.99 (*0-671-72709-5*, Minstrel Bks) PB.

My Teacher Glows in the Dark. Bruce Coville. (J). 1991. 9.09 (*0-606-04985-1*, Pub. by Turtleback) Demco.

My Teacher Helps Me. Claudette C. Mitchell et al. (Visions: African-American Experiences: Vol. 23). (Illus.). 8p. (Orig.). (J). (gr. k-1). 1996. pap. text 3.00 (*1-57518-065-0*) Arborlake.

My Teacher Is a Song: Based on the Album among Friends. Breeze Bryson. Ed. by Aimee Conn et al. (Illus.). 56p. (Orig.). 1988. pap. 6.00 (*0-9621411-0-0*) New Breeze Prodns.

My Teacher Is a Vampire. Mercer Mayer. (Schooltime Tales Ser.). (Illus.). 48p. (J). (gr. 1-3). 1994. 4.69 (*0-307-15957-4*, 15957) Gldn Bks Pub Co.

My Teacher Is an Alien. Bruce Coville. 123p. (J). (gr. 3-6). pap. 4.50 (*0-8072-1528-7*) Listening Lib.

My Teacher Is an Alien. Bruce Coville. (Camp Haunted Hills Ser.). (Illus.). 123p. (J). (gr. 3-7). 1989. pap. 3.99 (*0-671-73729-5*, Minstrel Bks) PB.

My Teacher Is an Alien. Bruce Coville. (J). 1997. per. 3.99 (*0-671-31189-1*) PB.

My Teacher Is an Alien. Bruce Coville. 1997. cd-rom 34.95 (*0-671-57662-3*) S&S Childrens.

***My Teacher Is an Alien.** Bruce Coville. (J). 1999. pap. 16.00 (*0-671-03571-1*) S&S Trade.

My Teacher Is an Alien. Bruce Coville. (J). 1989. 9.09 (*0-606-04280-6*, Pub. by Turtleback) Demco.

My Teacher is the Best. Sharon Gordon. 1999. pap. text 2.95 (*0-8167-4915-9*) Troll Communs.

My Teacher Is the Tooth Fairy. Mary Smith. LC 96-221702. (Illus.). 32p. (Orig.). (J). (ps-3). 1996. pap. 3.50 (*0-8167-4126-3*) Troll Communs.

My Teacher Said Goodbye Today: Planning for the End of the School Year. 2nd ed. Judy Osborne. (Illus.). 39p. (J). (ps-6). 1987. reprint ed. pap. text 9.95 (*0-9618303-8-7*) Emijo Pubns.

***My Teacher Said Goodbye Today: Planning for the End of the School Year.** 2nd rev. ed. Judy Osborne. (Illus.). (J). (ps-2). 1999. spiral bd. 9.95 (*0-9618303-7-9*) Emijo Pubns.

My Teacher Sleeps in School. Leatie Weiss. LC 85-40449. (Illus.). 32p. (J). (ps-3). 1985. pap. 5.99 (*0-14-050559-8*, PuffinBks) Peng Put Young Read.

My Teacher Sleeps in School. Leatie Weiss. (Picture Puffin Ser.). (J). 1985. 10.19 (*0-606-00344-4*, Pub. by Turtleback) Demco.

My Teacher's a Bug. M. T. Coffin. (Spinetinglers Ser.: No. 3). 160p. (Orig.). (J). (gr. 3-6). 1995. pap. 3.50 (*0-380-77785-1*, Avon Bks) Morrow Avon.

My Teacher's a Bug. M. T. Coffin. (Spinetinglers Ser.). (Orig.). (J). 1995. 8.60 (*0-606-07911-4*) Turtleback.

My Teacher's My Friend. P. K. Hallinan. (Illus.). 24p. (J). (ps-3). 1989. pap., per. 4.95 (*0-8249-8542-7*, Ideals Child) Hambleton-Hill.

My Teacher's My Friend. P. K. Hallinan. 24p. 1999. 6.95 (*1-57102-155-8*) Hambleton-Hill.

My Teacher's Secret Life. Stephen Krensky. (Illus.). 32p. (J). (ps-1). 1996. mass mkt. 15.00 (*0-689-80271-4*) Aladdin.

My Teacher's Secret Life. Stephen Krensky. (Illus.). 32p. (J). (gr. k-3). 1999. per. 5.99 (*0-689-82982-5*) Aladdin.

My Tears Spoiled My Aim. John S. Reed. 168p. 1994. pap. 8.95 (*0-15-600006-7*) Harcourt.

My Tears Spoiled My Aim: And Other Reflections on Southern Culture. John S. Reed. LC 92-37623. (Illus.). 168p. (C). 1993. 19.95 (*0-8262-0886-X*) U of Mo Pr.

My Teddy Bear Diary. Elizabeth K. Brownd. (Illus.). (J). (gr. k-3). 1992. pap. 1.00 (*0-486-27206-0*) Dover.

My Teddy Bear Library, 1, Set. Bruce Degen et al. (Illus.). (J). (ps-2). 1999. 19.95 (*0-694-01252-1*) HarpC Child Bks.

My Teddy Bears, Vol. 12. Shirley A. Barone. (Illus.). 44p. (Orig.). (J). (ps-2). 1989. pap. write for info. (*0-318-66622-7*) Toad Hse Bks.

***My Teddy Organizer.** (Illus.). 1999. ring bd. 19.95 (*0-87588-557-8*) Hobby Hse.

***My Teddy Organizer Fact Sheet Book.** 128p. 2000. pap. 11.95 (*0-87588-570-5*) Hobby Hse.

***My Teddy Organizer Fact Sheets Album.** Hobby House Press Staff. 2000. pap. 11.95 (*0-87588-573-X*) Hobby Hse.

My Teeming Brain: Creativity in Creative Writers. Jane Piirto. (Perspectives on Creativity Ser.). 256p. 1999. text 52.50 (*1-57273-275-X*); pap. text 21.95 (*1-57273-276-8*) Hampton Pr NJ.

My Teen Years. April R. Rogers. (YA). (gr. 6-12). 1993. spiral bd. 12.95 (*0-9643763-1-8*) U-Talk Pubns.

My Teen Years Memory Journal see Teen Yearbook: My Life in My Own Words

My Teen Years Memory Journal. April R. Rogers. (YA). (gr. 6-12). 1995. spiral bd. 12.95 (*0-9643763-2-6*) U-Talk Pubns.

My Teenage Heart. deluxe ed. Author22 Publishing Staff. LC 98-96140. 440p. 1999. pap. 19.95 (*1-892183-01-3*) DTTN.

My Telephone. (C). 1977. write for info. (*0-201-13836-0*) Addison-Wesley.

My Telephone. Harriet Ziefert. (Illus.). 14p. (J). (ps). 1993. 4.50 (*0-694-00419-7*) HarpC Child Bks.

My Television. Harriet Ziefert. (Illus.). 14p. (J). (ps) 1993. 4.50 (*0-694-00420-0*, HarpFestival) HarpC Child Bks.

My Ten Book. Jane Belk Moncure. LC 86-2293. (My Number Bks.). (Illus.). 32p. (J). (ps-2). 1986. lib. bdg. 21.36 (*0-89565-321-4*) Childs World.

My Ten Years in a Quandry. Robert Benchley. (Illus.). 1976. reprint ed. lib. bdg. 26.95 (*0-88411-303-5*, 303) Amereon Ltd.

***My Tenant, "Bobo"** Harvey W. Black. LC 99-94958. 1999. 21.95 (*0-533-13234-7*) Vantage.

***My Tender Soul: A Story of Survival.** Peggy McNamara. 160p. 2000. pap. 12.95 (*1-890676-61-6*, Pub. by Beavers Pond) Bookman Bks.

My Territory. Mark Insingel. Tr. by Adrienne Dixon. LC 86-61608. 128p. 1987. 6.95 (*0-87376-049-2*) Red Dust.

***My Testimony Before & after Grace: Before Grace.** Cornelia K. Gail. (Illus.). v, 154p. (YA). (gr. 7-12). 1999. write for info. (*0-9674454-0-X*) Godiva Girl.

***My Testimony Before & after Grace Pt. 1: Before Grace.** Cornelia K. Gail. (Illus.). v, 154p. (YA). (gr. 7-12). 1999. pap. 21.95 (*0-9674454-1-8*) Godiva Girl.

***My Texas Family: An Uncommon Journey to Prosperity.** Rick Hyman & Ronda Hyman. (Image of America Ser.). (Illus.). 128p. 1999. 34.99 (*0-7385-0181-6*) Arcadia Publng.

***My Texas Garden: A Gardener's Journal.** Cool Springs Press Publications Staff. 2000. 19.95 (*1-888608-83-8*) Cool Springs Pr.

***My Texas Garden: A Gardener's Journal.** Dale Groom. (Illus.). 128p. 2000. spiral bd. 19.95 (*1-930604-02-5*) Cool Springs Pr.

My Texas 'Tis of Thee. Owen P. White. LC 76-169568. (Short Story Index Reprint Ser.). 1977. reprint ed. 20.95 (*0-8369-4031-8*) Ayer.

My Thank You Book. Mary Landis. (Jewel Book Ser.: Set 3). (Illus.). 24p. (J). (ps-2). 1990. pap. 2.55 (*0-7399-0040-4*, 2333) Rod & Staff.

***My Thanks to You: Mini Edition.** Andrews & McMeel Staff. 272p. 2000. mass mkt. 5.95 (*0-7407-0545-8*) Andrews & McMeel.

My Theodosia. Anya Seton. 24.95 (*0-8488-0624-7*) Amereon Ltd.

My Theodosia. Anya Seton. 1995. reprint ed. lib. bdg. 36.95 (*1-56849-650-8*) Buccaneer Bks.

My Theory of Life A to Z. Jacqueline C. Marshall & Marie Shepard-Moore. Incl. Straws Blowing in the Air. 1988. 99p. 1988. 8.95 (*0-318-35389-X*) Shepherd-Moore Ed Foun.

My Theory of Relativity. Albert Einstein. 1996. pap. 8.95 (*0-8065-1765-4*, Citadel Pr) Carol Pub Group.

My Thing & I. Carlos Yban. LC 98-90301. 1998. pap. 9.95 (*0-533-12758-0*) Vantage.

My Third Escape. Ludwig Gelb. (Illus.). 120p. 1992. 14.95 (*0-940646-62-5*) Rossel Bks.

My Third Grade Music Book. Ann M. Eisen & Lamar Robertson. (My Music Book Ser.: Vol. 3). (Illus.). 98p. (J). (gr. 3-7). 1995. pap. text, wbk. ed. 35.00 (*1-889967-05-X*) Sneaky Snake.

My Third Grade Yearbook. Bearl Brooks. (My Yearbook Ser.). 768p. (gr. 3). 1979. 18.00 (*0-8209-0083-4*, MTG-3) ESP.

My Thirteen Colors & How I Use Them. Helen Van Wyk. Ed. by Herbert Rogoff. (Illus.). 64p. (Orig.). 1993. pap. 19.95 (*0-929552-07-5*) Art Instr Assocs.

My Thirty Third Year. Gerhard A. Fittkau. 263p. 1993. pap. 9.95 (*0-614-07025-2*) Fidelity Pr.

My Thirty-Three Years' Dream: The Autobiography of Miyazaki Toten. Toten Miyazaki. Tr. by Eto Shinkichi & Marius B. Jansen. LC 81-47925. (Princeton Library of Asian Translations). (Illus.). 327p. 1982. reprint ed. pap. 101.40 (*0-7837-9444-4*, 2060800004) Bks Demand.

My Thirty Year Black-Out. Harley H. Hess. (Illus.). 200p. 1979. 13.00 (*0-931068-00-2*) Purcells.

M

My Thirty Years in Baseball. John J. McGraw. LC 95-14325. (Illus.). xxiii, 311p. (C). 1995. pap. 12.95 (*0-8032-8139-0*, Bison Books) U of Nebr Pr.

My Thirty Years in Baseball. John J. McGraw. LC 74-15746. (Popular Culture in America Ser.). (Illus.). 314p. 1975. reprint ed. 28.95 (*0-405-06381-4*) Ayer.

My Thirty Years Out of the Senate. Seba Smith. LC 75-164786. reprint ed. 52.50 (*0-404-02169-7*) AMS Pr.

My Thirty Years' War, an Autobiography. Margaret Anderson. LC 76-136511. (Illus.). 320p. 1971. reprint ed. lib. bdg. 69.50 (*0-8371-5429-4*, ANTY, Greenwood Pr) Greenwood.

My Thoughts on Music & Musicians. H. Heathcote Statham. LC 72-3354. 1977. 33.95 (*0-8369-2924-1*) Ayer.

My Thoughts on Piano Technique. Haruko Kataoka. 38p. 1988. pap. text 5.95 (*0-87487-284-7*) Summy-Birchard.

***My Thoughts with Love: A Grandparents Keepsake Journal (Cradled in Hands)** gif. ed. Anne Geddes. (Illus.). 96p. 1999. spiral bd. 17.95 (*0-7683-2079-8*) CEDCO Pub.

***My Thoughts with Love: A Grandparents Keepsake Journal (Green Butterfly)** gif. ed. Anne Geddes. (Illus.). 96p. 1999. spiral bd. 17.95 (*0-7683-2084-4*) CEDCO Pub.

***My Thoughts with Love: A Parents Keepsake Journal (Orange Butterfly)** gif. ed. Anne Geddes. (Illus.). 96p. 1999. spiral bd. 17.95 (*0-7683-2085-2*) CEDCO Pub.

***My Thoughts with Love: A Parents Keepsake Journal (Ruler Baby)** gif. ed. Anne Geddes. (Illus.). 96p. 1999. pap. 17.95 (*0-7683-2080-1*) CEDCO Pub.

My Three Angels. Samuel Spewack & Bella Spewack. 1954. pap. 5.25 (*0-8222-0802-4*) Dramatists Play.

My Three Book. Jane Belk Moncure. LC 85-5898. (My Number Bks.). (Illus.). 32p. (J). (ps-2). 1985. lib. bdg. 21.36 (*0-89565-314-1*) Childs World.

My Three Countries. Joan Kunhardt. LC 84-2993. (Orig.). 1984. pap. 10.00 (*0-87233-076-1*) Bauhan.

My 3 Lives in Headlines. Mary Carey. LC 96-29630. (Illus.). 360p. 1997. 27.95 (*1-57168-125-6*, 125-6, Eakin Pr) Sunbelt Media.

My Three Mothers & Other Passions. Sophie Freud. 351p. (C). 1991. pap. text 17.50 (*0-8147-2600-3*) NYU Pr.

My Three Weeks As a Spy. Ellen Steiber. (Full House Stephanie Ser.). (J). (gr. 4-6). 1998. per. 3.99 (*0-671-00832-3*) PB.

My Three Worlds. Isolde M. Patton. 167p. 1985. 9.95 (*0-87770-316-7*) Ye Galleon.

My Three Worlds. Darlene Sizemore & Janet Smith. (Orig.). 1996. pap. 8.00 (*0-9650967-0-X*) V Larson.

My Three Worlds. Darlene Sizemore-Larson. Ed. by Chuck Dean. (Illus.). 230p. (Orig.). 1993. pap. 10.00 (*0-9622413-7-7*) WinePress Pub.

My Tibet. Photos & Intro. by Galen Rowell. LC 90-10868. (Illus.). 168p. 1990. 45.00 (*0-520-07109-3*, Pub. by U CA Pr) Cal Prin Full Svc.

My Tibet. Photos & Intro. by Galen Rowell. (Illus.). 162p. 1995. pap. 29.95 (*0-520-08948-0*, Pub. by U CA Pr) Cal Prin Full Svc.

My Ticket to Tomorrow: Activities for Exploring the Past, Present & Future. Betty Lies. LC 97-225319. 1997. pap. 15.95 (*1-55591-285-0*) Fulcrum Pub.

My Tiger Cat see Set 5

My Time in Hell: Memoir of an American Soldier Imprisoned by the Japanese in World War II. Andrew D. Carson. LC 97-23520. 264p. 1997. pap. 29.95 (*0-7864-0403-5*) McFarland & Co.

My Time in His Hands. C. Wood. 6.99 (*1-85792-091-0*, Pub. by Christian Focus) Spring Arbor Dist.

***My Time with Antonioni.** Wim Wenders. Tr. by Michael Hofmann from GER. (Illus.). 240p. 2000. pap. 16.00 (*0-571-20076-1*, Pub. by Faber & Faber) Penguin Books.

***My Time with God: 150 Ways to Start Your Own Quiet Time.** Jeanette Dall et al. LC 00-21068. (Heritage Builders Ser.). 208p. (J). (gr. 3-7). 2000. 9.99 (*1-56179-802-9*) Tyndale Hse.

My Times: Living. Pierre Berton. (Illus.). 448p. 1995. 34.95 (*0-385-25528-4*) Doubleday.

My Times in the Hudson Valley: The Insider's Guide to Historic Homes, Scenic Drives, Restaurants, Museums, Farm Produce & Points of Interest. Harold Faber. LC 97-33995. (Illus.). 264p. 1997. pap. 16.95 (*1-883789-14-1*) Blk Dome Pr.

***My Times with the Sisters: And Other Events.** unabridged ed. Franklyn E. Dailey, Jr. (Illus.). vi, 134p. 2000. per. 9.50 (*0-9666251-1-0*) Dailey Intl Pub.

My Tiny Life: Crime & Passion in a Virtual World. Julian Dibbell. LC 98-13636. 324p. 1999. 14.95 (*0-8050-3626-1*, Owl) H Holt & Co.

***My Tired Father.** Gellu Naum. Tr. by James Brook. (Green Integer Bks.: No. 19). 80p. 1999. pap. 8.95 (*1-892295-07-5*, Pub. by Green Integer) SPD-Small Pr Dist.

My Toddler: The Beginning of Independence see Mi Parvulo: El Comienzo de la Independencia

My Toes Are Starting to Wiggle. Jackie Silberg. (J). (ps-5). 1991. pap. 14.95 (*0-939514-12-5*) Miss Jackie.

My Tokyo. Frederick Seidel. 64p. 1994. pap. 11.00 (*0-374-52396-7*, Noonday) FS&G.

My Tokyo: Poems. Frederick Seidel. LC 92-41936. 50p. 1993. 18.00 (*0-374-21754-8*) FS&G.

My Tom Kitten. Beatrix Potter. (J). 1994. pap. 4.99 (*0-7232-4159-7*, F Warne) Peng Put Young Read.

My Tom Kitten Cloth Book. Beatrix Potter. (Illus.). 10p. (J). (ps). 1999. 4.99 (*0-7232-0021-1*, F Warne) Peng Put Young Read.

My Tomb Was Empty: Seven Sermons for Lent & Easter. Joe Barone. LC 92-32776. 1992. pap. 6.25 (*1-55673-564-2*, 9311) CSS OH.

My Tongue Is the Pen: How Audiocassettes Can Serve the Nonreading World. Marilyn Malmstrom. LC 91-66074. 224p. (Orig.). 1991. pap. 17.00 (*0-88312-812-8*) S I L Intl.

My Tool Box Book. LC 97-132002. 5p. (J). 1996. 9.98 (*1-57082-438-X*, Pub. by Mouse Works) Time Warner.

My Tooth Is about to Fall Out. Grace Maccarone. LC 94-9772. (Hello Reader! Ser.).Tr. of Ma Dent Va Tomber. (Illus.). 32p. (J). (ps-1). 1995. 3.50 (*0-590-48376-5*, Cartwheel) Scholastic Inc.

My Tooth Is about to Fall Out. Grace Maccarone.Tr. of Ma Dent Va Tomber. (J). 1995. 8.70 (*0-606-07912-2*, Pub. by Turtleback) Demco.

My Tooth Is Loose. Susan Hood. LC 99-19687. (Fisher-Price All-Star Readers Ser.). (Illus.). 32p. (J). (gr. k-3). 1999. pap. 3.99 (*1-57584-310-2*, Pub. by Rdrs Digest) Random.

My Tooth Is Loose! Martin Silverman. (Hello, Reader! Ser.). (J). 1991. 8.70 (*0-606-00627-3*, Pub. by Turtleback) Demco.

My Tooth Is Loose. Harriet Ziefert. LC 94-223599. (Easy-to-Read Bks.). (Illus.). 30p. (J). (ps-3). 1994. pap. 3.99 (*0-14-037001-3*, PuffinBks) Peng Put Young Read.

My Tooth Ith Loothe. George Ulrich. 48p. (J). 1996. pap. 3.50 (*0-440-91307-1*) BDD Bks Young Read.

My Tooth Ith Loothe: Funny Poems to Read Instead of Doing Your Homework. George Ulrich. (J). 1995. 8.70 (*0-606-07913-0*) Turtleback.

My Totally Awesome Holiday Friendship Book. Linda Williams Aber. (Full House Michelle Ser.). (Illus.). 96p. (J). (gr. 2-4). 1997. per. 3.99 (*0-671-00840-4*) PB.

My Tot's Tales. Jeannie Kellogg. (Illus.). 96p. 1995. pap. text 5.95 (*1-56383-041-8*, 9220) G & R Pub.

"My Toughest Mentor" Theodore Roethke & William Carlos Williams (1940-1948) Robert Kusch. LC 98-50628. 96p. 1999. 28.50 (*0-8387-5406-6*) Bucknell U Pr.

My Town. Drew Harrington. LC 93-71841. (Illus.). 320p. (Orig.). 1993. pap. 14.95 (*1-56883-006-8*) Colonial Pr AL.

My Town. Janet Horowitz & Kathy Faggella. (Photolog Bk.). (Illus.). 48p. (J). (gr. 1-7). 1991. 9.95 (*1-55670-175-6*) Stewart Tabori & Chang.

My Town. David Lee. LC 95-17053. 132p. 1995. pap. 12.00 (*1-55659-074-1*) Copper Canyon.

My Town. Mouse Works Staff. LC 97-216088. 9p. (J). 1997. 5.98 (*1-57082-715-X*, Pub. by Mouse Works) Time Warner.

My Town. Rebecca Treays. (Young Geography Ser.). (Illus.). 24p. (J). (ps-k). 1998. text 8.95 (*0-7460-3079-7*, Usborne) EDC.

My Town. Rebecca Treays. (Young Geography Ser.). (Illus.). 24p. (J). (ps up). 1998. lib. bdg. 16.95 (*1-58086-129-6*, Usborne) EDC.

My Town. William Wegman. LC 98-5315. (Illus.). 40p. (J). (ps-3). 1998. 16.95 (*0-7868-0410-6*, Pub. by Disney Pr) Time Warner.

My Town. William Wegman. LC 98-5315. (Illus.). (J). (ps-4). 1998. lib. bdg. 17.49 (*0-7868-2360-7*, Pub. by Disney Pr) Little.

My Town. large type ed. Pam Jarrell. (Big Bks.). (Illus.). 8p. (J). (ps-k). 1998. pap. text 10.95 (*1-57332-125-7*); pap. text 10.95 (*1-57332-127-3*) HighReach Lrning.

My Town: Santa Maria, California, 1941-45. Milton E. Shriner. 1991. pap. 10.95 (*0-9631851-0-1*) M E Shriner.

***My Town Is in Development.** Craig D. Reader. (Illus.). 73p. 2000. 14.99 (*0-9678522-0-X*) Zero to One.

My Toy Book. Harry Bornstein et al. (Signed English Ser.). (Illus.). 16p. (J). (ps). 1973. pap. 3.50 (*0-913580-22-8*, Pub. by K Green Pubns) Gallaudet Univ Pr.

My Toys. (Peek-a-Boo Bks.). (Illus.). 20p. (J). 1998. bds. 3.95 (*0-8069-3762-9*, Balloon Books) Sterling.

My Toys. Sanduik Bokforlag. (Illus.). 12p. (J). (ps). 1992. pap. 7.99 (*1-881445-10-0*) Sandvik Pub.

My Toys. Ed. by Intervisual Books Staff. (Cuddly Cloth Bks.). (Illus.). 6p. (J). 1997. 14.95 (*0-8362-2829-4*) Andrews & McMeel.

My Toys. abr. ed. Sian Tucker. (Sian Tucker Board Bks.). (Illus.). 16p. (J). (ps). 1998. 4.99 (*0-689-81983-8*) Litle Simon.

My Toys: Cuddly Cloth Books. Intervisual Books Staff. (Illus.). (J). 1997. text 14.95 (*1-888443-01-4*) Intervisual Bks.

My Traitor's Heart. Rian Malan. LC 90-50145. (Vintage International Ser.). 432p. 1991. pap. 14.00 (*0-679-73215-2*) Vin Bks.

***My Traitor's Heart: A South African Exile Returns to Face His Country, His Tribe & His Conscience.** Rian Malan. 368p. 2000. reprint ed. pap. 13.00 (*0-8021-3684-2*, Pub. by Grove-Atltic) Publishers Group.

My Treasure Is My Friend. Michael Talbott. (Illus.). 29p. 1982. 14.95 (*0-317-11168-X*) Joyce Media.

My Treasured Pleasures: "Down Home Cooking" Central Louisiana Style. large type ed. Alice P. Mathews. Ed. by Marita Mathews. (Illus.). 416p. 1998. pap. 22.98 (*1-887303-20-0*) Blu Lantern Pub.

My Treasury of Chaplets. 3rd ed. Patricia S. Quintiliani. LC 97-102611. (Illus.). 240p. 1992. pap. 7.95 (*0-911218-25-4*) Ravengate Pr.

My Tree. Evelyn Marie. (Illus.). 24p. (J). (gr. k-2). 1987. pap. 3.50 (*0-9614746-5-3*) Berry Bks.

***My Treehouse.** Lynn Duryee. Ed. by Noreen Wise. (Lemonade Collection). 160p. (YA). (gr. 5 up). 2000. pap. 8.95 (*1-58584-283-4*) Huckleberry CT.

***My Trek: Reflections II, the Sequel.** Oscar L. Guzman. LC 99-91287. 2000. 25.00 (*0-7388-0738-9*); pap. 18.00 (*0-7388-0739-7*) Xlibris Corp.

My Tribute: The Songs of Andrae Crouch. Devries. 1995. pap. 6.95 (*0-7601-0163-9*) Brentwood Music.

***My Triduum Journey: Celebrating the Easter Mysteries.** Kass P. Dotterweich. (Illus.). 32p. 1998. 1.95 (*0-7648-0332-8*) Liguori Pubns.

My Trip. Jackie Nelson & Janice Halpern-Segal. (Illus.). 24p. (Orig.). (J). (ps-3). 1989. pap. 6.95 (*0-685-29177-4*) Take Along Pubns.

My Trip 'n a Ship. Jean T. Fredeking. 16p. (J). 1987. pap. 30.00 (*0-7855-1748-0*, Pub. by A H S Ltd) St Mut.

My Trip to Alpha I. Alfred Slote. LC 78-6463. (Illus.). 96p. (J). (gr. 2-5). 1978. 12.95 (*0-397-31810-3*) HarpC Child Bks.

My Trip to Alpha I. Alfred Slote. LC 85-45394. (Trophy Bk.). (Illus.). 96p. (J). (gr. 4-7). 1986. pap. 4.95 (*0-06-440166-9*, HarpTrophy) HarpC Child Bks.

My Trip to Alpha I. Alfred Slote. LC 78-6463. (Illus.). 96p. (J). (gr. 2-5). 1992. lib. bdg. 14.89 (*0-397-32510-X*) HarpC Child Bks.

My Trip to Alpha I. Alfred Slote. 96p. (J). (gr. 3-5). pap. 96.00 (*0-8072-1402-7*) Listening Lib.

My Trip to Alpha I. Alfred Slote. (J). 1986. 9.70 (*0-606-03114-6*, Pub. by Turtleback) Demco.

My Trip to California in 1849. James Carstarphen. 8p. 1971. reprint ed. pap. 3.95 (*0-87770-038-9*) Ye Galleon.

My Trip to Felicity's Williamsburg: An American Girl's Journal. Pleasant Company Staff. (Illus.). 14p. (J). (gr. 2-5). 1991. 1.00 (*1-56247-029-9*) Pleasant Co.

My Trip to New York City. Bill Luoma. 1994. pap. 5.00 (*0-935724-65-6*) Figures.

My Trip to the Big Chicken. Sherry L. Lewis. LC 93-80806. 32p. (J). 1996. pap. 10.00 (*0-9639319-0-3*) K S Jewels.

My Trips to India. Jason K. Bhattacharya. (Illus.). viii, 24p. (Orig.). (J). 1995. pap. 3.95 (*1-881338-43-6*) Nataraj Bks.

***My Triumph on Everest: A Photobiography of Sir Edmund Hillary.** 64p. (gr. 4-6). 2000. per. 17.95 (*0-7922-7114-9*) Natl Geog.

My Triumphant Life. Harvey A. Childress. 1978. pap. 2.25 (*0-88027-087-X*) Firm Foun Pub.

"My Trouble Is My English" Asian Students & the American Dream. Danling Fu. LC 94-44918. 230p. 1995. pap. text 23.50 (*0-86709-355-2*, 0355, Pub. by Boynton Cook Pubs) Heinemann.

My Troubles Are Going to Have Trouble with Me: Everyday Trials & Triumphs of Women Workers. Karen B. Sacks & Dorothy Remy. LC 83-23079. 1984. 40.00 (*0-8135-1038-4*); pap. 16.95 (*0-8135-1039-2*) Rutgers U Pr.

My Troubles with Women. R. Crumb. 80p. 1991. pap. 16.95 (*0-86719-374-3*) Last Gasp.

My Truck & My Pup: Easy Reader. Patty Carratello. (Easy Readers Ser.). 16p. (J). (gr. k-1). 1997. pap. 2.49 (*1-57690-020-7*) Tchr Create Mat.

My Truck is Stuck. Kevin Lewis. LC 99-31527. 32p. (J). Date not set. lib. bdg. 13.49 (*0-7868-2465-4*, Pub. by Disney Pr) Little.

***My Truck Is Stuck.** Kevin Lewis. LC 99-31527. (Illus.). 32p. (J). 2000. write for info. (*0-7868-0534-X*) Hyprn Child.

My True Feelings. Helen E. Meaney. 1998. pap. write for info. (*1-57553-763-X*) Watermrk Pr.

***My True Love.** Karen Ranney. 384p. 2000. mass mkt. 5.99 (*0-380-80591-X*, Avon Bks) Morrow Avon.

My True Love. large type ed. Theresa Charles. 304p. 1988. 27.99 (*0-7089-1770-4*) Ulverscroft.

My True Story. Manuel Rodriguez. 136p. 1994. pap. 14.95 (*1-56097-141-X*) Fantagraph Bks.

My Trusty Car Seat: Buckle Up For Safety. 3rd ed. Stan Berenstain & Jan Berenstain. (Berenstain Bears Baby Board Books Ser.). (J). (ps). 1999. pap. 3.99 (*0-679-89334-2*, Pub. by Random Bks Yng Read) Random.

My Trusty Indian Guide: And Other Alaskan Tales. Carl W. Mathisen. 256p. (Orig.). 1992. pap. 12.95 (*1-882756-00-2*) Alaska Eagle.

***My Truth, Your Truth, Whose Truth? Discovering Absolutes in a Relative World.** Tyndale House Publishers Staff. (Life on the Edge Ser.). 2000. pap. 10.99 (*1-56179-868-1*) Focus Family.

My Tryst with Secularism: An Autobiography Sohan Singh Josh. Sohan S. Josh. (C). 1991. 28.50 (*81-7050-127-X*, Pub. by Patriot Pubs) S Asia.

***My Tryst with the Projects: Bhakra & Beas.** Jagman Singh. LC 98-909656. 1998. 42.00 (*81-85565-99-6*, Pub. by Uppal Pub Hse) S Asia.

My Turn. Nancy Lee. (Illus.). 150p. 1982. pap. 10.95 (*0-933704-23-2*) Dawn Pr.

My Turn. Nancy Reagan. 4.98 (*0-394-68388-9*) Random.

My Turn. Patricia G. Shapiro. 256p. 1997. pap. text 14.95 (*1-56079-946-3*) Petersons.

My Turn, Vol. 1. large type ed. Nancy Reagan. LC 90-41187. 650p. 1990. reprint ed. lib. bdg. 22.95 (*1-56054-056-7*) Thorndike Pr.

My Turn: Caring for Aging Parents & Other Elderly Loved Ones. Sandra W. Haymon. LC 96-227803. 192p. (Orig.). 1996. pap. 19.95 (*0-9652965-0-4*) Magnolia Prods.

My Turn: The Memoirs of Nancy Reagan. Nancy Reagan & William Novak. (Illus.). 1989. 21.95 (*0-394-56368-9*) Random.

My Turn: Women's Search for the Self after the Children Leave. Patricia G. Shapiro. 256p. 1996. 21.95 (*1-56079-632-4*) Petersons.

My Turn at Bat: The Story of My Life. Ted Williams & John W. Underwood. 320p. 1988. pap. 12.00 (*0-671-63423-2*, Fireside) S&S Trade Pap.

***My Turn Bible Stories about ABCs.** Sarah Fletcher. (My Turn Bible Stories Ser.). (Illus.). 32p. (J). (ps-1). 1999. 7.00 (*0-570-05493-1*, 56-1956GJ) Concordia.

My Turn Bible Stories about Colors. Carol Greene. LC 97-47371. (Illus.). 32p. (J). (ps-1). 1998. 6.99 (*0-570-05061-8*) Viking Penguin.

My Turn Bible Stories about Numbers. Sarah Fletcher. (Illus.). 32p. (ps-1). 1998. 6.99 (*0-570-05060-X*) Concordia.

***My Turn Bible Stories about Opposites.** Sarah Fletcher. (My Turn Bible Stories Ser.). (Illus.). 32p. (J). (ps-1). 1999. 7.00 (*0-570-05492-3*, 56-1955GJ) Concordia.

My Turn to Count. Illus. by Louise Gardner. 12p. (J). (ps-k). 1997. bds. 6.98 (*1-85854-713-X*) Brimax Bks.

My Turn to Speak: Iran, the Revolution & Secret Deals with the U. S. Abol H. Bani-Sadr. 240p. 1991. 24.95 (*0-08-040563-0*, 3883M) Brasseys.

My Turn to Weep: Salvadoran Refugee Women in Costa Rica. Robin O. Quizar. LC 97-40996. 216p. 1998. 55.00 (*0-89789-540-1*, Bergin & Garvey) Greenwood.

My Tussle with the Devil & Other Stories, by O. Henry's Ghost. LC 72-160947. (Short Story Index Reprint Ser.). 1977. reprint ed. 17.95 (*0-8369-3926-3*) Ayer.

My TV's Alive! Real Life Robots, Future Computers & Clones. James Stazzer. 128p. 1999. pap. 4.95 (*1-902618-35-1*, Pub. by Element Childrns) Penguin Putnam.

My 20th Century. David Kirby. LC 98-12928. 128p. 1999. pap. 13.95 (*0-914061-76-3*) Orchises Pr.

My Twenty-Five Years in China. John B. Powell. LC 76-27721. (China in the 20th Century Ser.). 1976. reprint ed. lib. bdg. 45.00 (*0-306-70761-6*) Da Capo.

My 20 Years of RV Adventures: Help! - Full-Time - Part-Time? 2nd ed. Everett L. Gracey. (Illus.). 52p. 1998. per. 9.95 (*0-9665842-1-X*) E L Gracey.

My Twin & I. Bette G. Wahlfeldt. 300p. (Orig.). 1988. student ed. 10.95 (*0-317-92298-X*); pap. text 10.95 (*0-317-92297-1*) BW Enterprises.

My Two Best Friends. Cathy East Dubowski. (Full House Michelle Ser.). (Orig.). (J). (gr. 4-7). 1995. pap. 3.99 (*0-671-52271-X*, Minstrel Bks) PB.

My Two Book. Jane Belk Moncure. LC 85-7885. (My Number Bks.). (Illus.). 32p. (J). (ps-2). 1985. lib. bdg. 21.36 (*0-89565-313-3*) Childs World.

My Two Families. Althea Braithwaite. 1997. 11.95 (*0-7136-4542-3*, Pub. by A & C Blk) Midpt Trade.

***My Two Grandmothers.** Effin Older. LC 99-6092. (Illus.). 32p. (J). (ps-3). 2000. 16.00 (*0-15-200785-7*, Harcourt Child Bks) Harcourt.

***My Two Hands, My Two Feet.** Rick Walton. LC 98-32153. (Illus.). 40p. (J). (ps-1). 2000. 20.01 (*0-399-23338-5*) Putnam Pub Group.

My Two Homes Magic Words Handbook for Kids. Kent Winchester. (Illus.). 28p. (J). (gr. 2-6). 1998. spiral bd. 5.95 (*0-9650296-1-1*) LadyBug Press.

***My Two Lights.** Felix Padilla. Ed. by Rebecca Padilla. (Illus.). 32p. 2000. 16.00 (*0-9675413-0-1*) Libros Latin Treas.

My Two Thousand Year Psychic Memory As Mary of Bethany: 13th Disciple to Jesus of Nazareth. 2nd ed. Ruth E. Norman. (Illus.). 74p. 1988. 6.00 (*0-932642-32-2*) Unarius Acad Sci.

My Two Uncles. Judith Vigna. LC 94-22007. (Albert Whitman Concept Bks.). (Illus.). 32p. (J). (gr. 1-4). 1995. lib. bdg. 14.95 (*0-8075-5507-X*) A Whitman.

My Two Wars. Moritz Thomsen. LC 96-1203. 317p. 1996. 25.00 (*1-883642-06-X*) Steerforth Pr.

My Two Worlds. Jana Coman. 256p. (Orig.). 1997. mass mkt. 9.95 (*0-89914-048-3*) Third Party Pub.

My Two Year Honeymoon in Turkey. Ellen Greene, pseud. 64p. 1996. pap. 7.50 (*1-884680-02-X*) Gabelmann Pr.

My Tyrannosaurus Rex Notebook. Dover Publications Inc. Staff. (Illus.). (J). 1991. pap. text 1.00 (*0-486-25604-9*) Dover.

My "u" Sound Box. Jane Belk Moncure. LC 84-17012. (Sound Box Library). (Illus.). 32p. (J). (ps-2). 1984. lib. bdg. 21.36 (*0-89565-300-1*) Childs World.

My Ukrainian Footprints. Melvin H. Pickrell & Vera T. Siegmund. (Illus.). 232p. 1995. 24.95 (*0-9655652-0-3*) M H Pickrell.

***My Ultimate Pink Book.** Melinda Lilly. 12p. 1999. 10.99 (*0-307-12158-5*, Goldn Books) Gldn Bks Pub Co.

My Uncle Max. Les Casson. (Annikins Ser.: Vol. 10). (Illus.). 32p. (Orig.). (J). (ps-2). 1990. pap. 0.99 (*1-55037-130-4*, Pub. by Annick) Firefly Bks Ltd.

My Uncle Napoleon. Iraj Pezeshkzad. Tr. by Dick Davis from PER. LC PK6561.P54 D313 1996. 512p. 1996. 29.95 (*0-934211-48-5*) Mage Pubs Inc.

***My Uncle Napoleon.** Iraj Pezeshkzad. Tr. by Dick Davis. LC PK6561.P54 D313 1996. 512p. 2000. pap. 19.95 (*0-934211-62-0*) Mage Pubs Inc.

My Uncle Nikos. Julie Delton. LC 81-43317. (Illus.). 32p. (J). (gr. 1-4). 1983. lib. bdg. 11.89 (*0-690-04165-9*) HarpC Child Bks.

My Uncle Oswald. Roald Dahl. 208p. 1990. pap. 11.95 (*0-14-005577-0*, Penguin Bks) Viking Penguin.

My Uncle Sam. Len Jenkin. 1984. pap. 5.25 (*0-8222-0803-2*) Dramatists Play.

My Uncle, Stephen Leacock. Elizabeth Kimball. (Illus.). 174p. 1970. mass mkt. 4.95 (*0-88780-124-2*, Pub. by Formac Publ Co) Formac Dist Ltd.

My Uncle the Netziv: The Life of Rabbi Naftali Zvi Yehudah Berlin. Baruch H. Epstein. Ed. by N. T. Erline. Tr. by Moshe Dombey from HEB. (ArtScroll History Ser.). 230p. 1988. 15.99 (*0-89906-492-2*); pap. 12.99 (*0-89906-493-0*) Mesorah Pubns.

My Uncle's Truck. Patricia T. Cousin et al. (Visions: African-American Experiences: No. 20). (Illus.). 8p. (Orig.). (J). (gr. k-1). 1995. pap. text 3.00 (*1-57518-019-7*) Arborlake.

My Underrated Year. Randy Powell. LC 87-46401. 184p. (YA). (gr. 7 up). 1991. pap. 4.95 (*0-374-45453-1*, Sunburst Bks) FS&G.

My Underwear's Inside Out: The Care & Feeding of Young Poets. Diane Dawber. (Illus.). 64p. (J). 1991. 14.95 (*1-55082-010-9*, Pub. by Quarry Pr); pap. 8.95 (*1-55082-011-7*, Pub. by Quarry Pr) LPC InBook.

An Asterisk (*) at the beginning of an entry indicates that the title is appearing for the first time.

My Unforgettable Season, 1970. Red Holzman & Leonard Levin. 1994. pap. 4.99 (*0-8125-5056-0*, Pub. by Forge NYC) St Martin.
My Unforgettable Season, 1970. Red Holzman & Leonard Levin. 320p. 1993. 21.95 (*0-312-85453-6*, Pub. by Tor Bks) St Martin.
My Unicorn Has Gone Away. Robert J. Publicover. 112p. 1993. 14.00 (*0-9634759-0-8*) Powder Hse Pub.
My Unicorn Thinks He Is Real: And Similar Confusions. Carolyn Muentner. 68p. 1982. reprint ed. 8.95 (*0-9606240-2-3*) Pearl-Win.
My United States & World Map. Illus. by TNI Stone & Associates Staff & Petertil Design Partners Staff. (Powertools for Kids Ser.: No. 18). 4p. (J). (gr. k-8). 1998. pap. 4.95 (*1-58220-017-3*, 32508, PowerTools for Kids) Navigator.
***My Unity with All Women.** Anne Toensmeier. 1999. pap. 0.25 (*1-58429-029-3*) Rational Isl.
My Universe: Selected Reviews Ya. B. Zeldovich. Ed. by Boris Y. Zeldovich. xv, 252p. 1992. text 141.00 (*3-7186-5004-5*, Harwood Acad Pubs); pap. text 53.00 (*3-7186-5238-2*, Harwood Acad Pubs) Gordon & Breach.
My University Life: The First Steps. T. Y. Okosun. 1998. pap. write for info. (*0-9637979-5-6*) T Y Okosun.
***My University Life: The First Steps.** 2nd ed. 186p. (C). 1999. 23.00 (*0-536-02852-4*) Pearson Custom.
My University, My God. Daniel Hershey. 77p. 1998. reprint ed. pap. 10.00 (*0-916961-07-9*) Basal Books.
My Unknown Child. Noreen Riols. LC 99-12862. 208p. 1999. pap. text 10.99 (*1-57673-466-8*) Multnomah Pubs.
My Unknown Chum. Aguecheek. 1912. 25.00 (*0-8159-6208-8*) Devin.
My Unusual Adventures on the Five Continents in Search for the Ageless. Edmond B. Szekely. (Search for the Ageless Ser.: Vol. 1). (Illus.). 212p. 1977. pap. 7.80 (*0-89564-022-8*) IBS Intl.
My Unusual Journey to Success: Based on a True Story. Ruby L. Oliver. LC 96-92997. 160p. 12.95 (*0-9655770-9-0*) Oliver Prods.
My Ups & Downs. (Illus.). 32p. (J). (ps). 1998. wbk. ed. 2.25 (*1-57768-238-6*) MG-Hill OH.
My Upsheren Book. Yaffa L. Gottlieb. (Illus.). 32p. (J). (ps-1). 1991. 8.95 (*0-922613-37-0*); pap. 6.95 (*0-922613-38-9*) Hachai Pubng.
My Urban Wilderness in the Hollywood Hills: A Year of Years on Quito Lane. Richard G. Lillard. (Illus.). 218p. (Orig.). (C). 1983. pap. text 24.00 (*0-8191-3318-3*); lib. bdg. 52.00 (*0-8191-3317-5*) U Pr of Amer.
My Usual Game: Adventures in Golf. David Owen. 288p. 1996. pap. 14.95 (*0-385-48338-4*) Doubleday.
My Utmost for His Highest see En Pos de Lo Supremo
My Utmost for His Highest. Oswald Chambers. (Essential Christian Library Ser.). 384p. 1998. 9.97 (*1-57748-264-6*) Barbour Pub.
***My Utmost for His Highest.** Oswald Chambers. (Deluxe Christian Classics). 384p. 2000. 9.97 (*1-57748-914-4*) Barbour Pub.
My Utmost for His Highest. Oswald Chambers & Bargain Books Staff. 384p. 1997. lthr. 9.97 (*1-57748-142-9*) Barbour Pub.
My Utmost for His Highest. Logos Research Systems Inc. Staff. 1998. pap. 14.95 (*1-57799-128-1*) Logos Res Sys.
My Utmost for His Highest. anniversary ed. Oswald Chambers. (Christian Library Ser.). 282p. 1987. reprint ed. bond lthr. 9.97 (*1-55748-054-0*) Barbour Pub.
My Utmost for His Highest. deluxe ed. Oswald Chambers. 1988. bond lthr. 14.97 (*1-55748-059-1*) Barbour Pub.
My Utmost for His Highest. large type ed. Oswald Chambers. 384p. 1999. pap. 12.97 (*1-57748-589-0*) Barbour Pub.
My Utmost for His Highest. large type ed. Oswald Chambers. (Christian Library Ser.). 282p. 1987. reprint ed. bond lthr. 14.97 (*0-916441-83-0*) Barbour Pub.
My Utmost for His Highest. anniversary ed. Oswald Chambers. (Christian Library Ser.). 384p. 2000. reprint ed. lthr. 4.97 (*0-916441-82-2*) Barbour Pub.
My Utmost for His Highest: An Updated Edition in Today's Language - the Golden Book of Oswald Chambers. Oswald Chambers. Ed. by James Reimann. LC 95-18752. 400p. 1995. 14.99 (*0-929239-99-7*) Discovery Hse Pubs.
My Utmost for His Highest: An Updated Edition in Today's Language:The Golden Book of Oswald Chambers. rev. ed. Oswald Chambers. LC 92-15394. 395p. 1992. 14.99 (*0-929239-57-1*) Discovery Hse Pubs.
My Utmost for His Highest: Prayer Edition. Oswald Chambers. 384p. 1999. 12.97 (*1-57748-590-4*) Barbour Pub.
My Utmost for His Highest: Updated Edition in Today's Language. Ed. by Oswald Chambers & James Reimann. (Believer's Life System Ser.). 1997. ring bd. 14.99 (*0-8024-2786-3*) Moody.
My Utmost for His Highest Journal. Oswald Chambers. 1995. bond lthr. 19.97 (*1-55748-737-5*) Barbour Pub.
My Utmost for His Highest, Updated Language: An Updated Edition in Today's Language. large type ed. Oswald Chambers. LC 98-7253. 384p. 1998. pap. 14.99 (*1-57293-037-3*) Discovery Hse Pubs.
My "v" Sound Box. Jane Belk Moncure. LC 79-13084. (Sound Box Library). (Illus.). 32p. (J). (ps-2). 1979. lib. bdg. 21.36 (*0-89565-101-7*) Childs World.
My Vacation. Penny Nye. (Illus.). 16p. (J). (ps-5). 1997. pap. 12.00 (*1-890703-09-5*) Penny Laine.
My Vacation Book: For Kids, by Kids. Kellan Ilse & Trevor Ilse. 74p. (J). (gr. 1-7). 1994. spiral bd. 9.95 (*1-883525-00-4*) Wntergrn.
My Vacation Diary. Ideals Children's Books Editors. (Illus.). 24p. (Orig.). (J). (gr. 1-6). 1995. pap. 9.95 (*1-57102-029-2*, Ideals Child) Hambleton-Hill.
My Vagabond Life. Kurt Winkler. 236p. (C). 1988. 35.00 (*0-7212-0708-1*, Pub. by Regency Pr GBR) St Mut.
My Vagabond Lover: An Intimate Biography of Rudy Vallee. Eleanor Vallee & Jill Amadio. (Illus.). 272p. 1996. 22.95 (*0-87833-918-3*) Taylor Pub.
My Valentine Counting Book. Duncan Maxfield. (Chubby Board Bk.). (Illus.). 8p. (J). (ps). 1999. bds. 2.99 (*0-689-82237-5*) S&S Childrens.
My Valentine '94. Margot Dalton et al. (Promo Ser.). 1994. mass mkt. 4.99 (*0-373-83294-X*, 1-83294-8) Harlequin Bks.
My Valiant Knight. Hannah Howell. 320p. 1995. pap. 5.50 (*0-8217-5186-7*, Zebra Kensgtn) Kensgtn Pub Corp.
My Van Gogh Art Museum: A Sticker Book of Paintings. Carole Armstrong. (Illus.). 16p. (J). (gr. 1-5). 1996. pap. 11.95 (*0-399-23012-2*, Philomel) Peng Put Young Read.
My Vast Fortune: The Money Adventures of a Quixotic Capitalist. Andrew Tobias. LC 98-21198. 224p. (C). 1998. pap. 13.00 (*0-15-600622-7*, Harvest Bks) Harcourt.
My Vegetable Love: A Journal of a Growing Season. Carl H. Klaus. LC 96-17836. 320p. 1996. 22.95 (*0-395-78587-1*) HM.
***My Vegetable Love: A Journal of a Growing Season.** Carl H. Klaus. (Bur Oak Ser.). 352p. 2000. reprint ed. pap. 19.95 (*0-87745-707-7*) U of Iowa Pr.
My Venice. Harold Brodkey. LC 97-28899. 1998. 20.00 (*0-8050-4833-2*) H Holt & Co.
My Vertical World. Jerzy Kukuczka. 192p. 1992. 29.95 (*0-89886-344-9*) Mountaineers.
My Very Best Friend Vol. 12: A Book about Jesus. Linda Porter Carlyle. Ed. by Kim Justinen & Aileen Sox. (Child's Steps to Jesus Ser.). (Illus.). 24p. (J). (ps-2). 1994. 7.99 (*0-8163-1184-6*) Pacific Pr Pub Assn.
My Very Dear Sean: George Jean Nathan on Sean O'Casey, Letters & Articles. George J. Nathan. Ed. by Patricia Angelin & Robert Lowery. LC 82-48549. 192p. 1985. 32.50 (*0-8386-3166-5*) Fairleigh Dickinson.
My Very First. Beverly P. Faaborg. (Illus.). 184p. (Orig.). 1992. pap. 9.95 (*1-878488-68-6*) Quixote Pr IA.
My Very 1st Book of Colors. Eric Carle. LC 72-83776. (My Very First Library). (Illus.). 10p. (J). (ps-1). 1985. 4.95 (*0-694-00011-6*) HarpC Child Bks.
My Very First Book of Colors. Eric Carle. LC 72-83776. (My Very First Library). (Illus.). 10p. (J). (ps). 1985. 2.95 (*0-690-57365-0*) HarpC Child Bks.
My Very 1st Book of Food. Eric Carle. LC 85-45259. (My Very First Library). (Illus.). 10p. (J). (ps). 1986. 2.95 (*0-694-00130-9*) HarpC Child Bks.
My Very 1st Book of Heads. Eric Carle. LC 85-45260. (My Very First Library). (Illus.). 10p. (J). (ps). 1986. 2.95 (*0-694-00128-7*) HarpC Child Bks.
***My Very First Book of Manners.** Michal Sparks. 10p. (J). 2000. bds. 5.99 (*0-7369-0244-9*) Harvest Hse.
My Very First Book of Numbers. Eric Carle. LC 72-8377. (My Very First Library). (Illus.). 10p. (J). (ps). 1985. 2.95 (*0-690-57366-9*) HarpC Child Bks.
My Very 1st Book of Numbers. Eric Carle. LC 72-83777. (My Very First Library). (Illus.). 10p. (J). (ps-1). 1985. 4.95 (*0-694-00012-4*) HarpC Child Bks.
My Very First Book of Poetry & Other Things. Peggy S. Moore. (Poetry & Essays Ser.: No. I). (Illus.). 16p. (J). (gr. 3-5). 1982. pap. 1.98 (*0-9613078-0-3*) Detroit Black.
My Very First Book of Shapes. Eric Carle. LC 72-83778. (My Very First Library). (Illus.). 10p. (J). (ps). 1985. 2.95 (*0-690-57367-7*) HarpC Child Bks.
My Very 1st Book of Shapes. Eric Carle. LC 72-83778. (My Very First Library). (Illus.). 10p. (J). (ps-1). 1985. 4.95 (*0-694-00013-2*) HarpC Child Bks.
My Very 1st Book of Tools. Eric Carle. LC 85-45258. (My Very First Library). (Illus.). 10p. (J). (ps). 1986. 2.95 (*0-694-00129-5*) HarpC Child Bks.
My Very 1st Book of Touch. Eric Carle. LC 84-47894. (My Very First Library). (Illus.). 10p. (J). (ps). 1986. 2.95 (*0-694-00095-7*) HarpC Child Bks.
My Very First Book of Words. Eric Carle. LC 72-83779. (My Very First Library). (Illus.). 10p. (J). (ps-1). 1985. 2.95 (*0-690-57368-5*) HarpC Child Bks.
My Very 1st Book of Words. Eric Carle. LC 72-83779. (My Very First Library). (Illus.). 10p. (J). (ps-1). 1985. 4.95 (*0-694-00014-0*) HarpC Child Bks.
My Very First Books to Make & Read. Jeri Carroll & Kathy Dunlavy. 144p. (J). (ps-2). 1990. 13.99 (*0-86653-557-8*, GA1163) Good Apple.
***My Very First Christmas Book.** Michal Sparks. 10p. (J). 2000. bds. 5.99 (*0-7369-0318-6*) Harvest Hse.
My Very First Christmas Story. Lois Rock. (J). 1999. 10.99 (*0-7459-4096-X*) Lion USA.
My Very First Colors, Shapes, Sizes & Opposite Book. (Butterfly Bks.). (ARA., Illus.). 22p. 1997. 14.95 (*0-86685-710-9*) Intl Bk Ctr.
My Very First Colors, Shapes, Sizes, & Opposites Book. (J). 1993. write for info. (*1-56458-377-5*) DK Pub Inc.
My Very First Colors, Shapes, Sizes & Opposites Book in Arabic Language. (Butterfly Bks.). (Illus.). (J). 1996. 14.95 (*0-86685-666-8*, Pub. by Librairie du Liban) Intl Bk Ctr.
***My Very First Devotional Bible.** Catherine DeVries. (Illus.). (J). 2000. 14.99 (*0-310-93251-3*) Zondervan.
***My Very First Disney 123 Counting Book: Big Book.** (Illus.). 48p. (J). 2000. 12.99 (*0-7364-0146-6*, Pub. by Mouse Works) Time Warner.
My Very First Mother Goose. Ed. by Iona Opie. LC 96-4904. (Illus.). 108p. (J). (ps-k). 1996. 19.99 (*1-56402-620-5*) Candlewick Pr.
My Very First Number Book. DK 93-7623. (J). 1993. write for info. (*1-56458-376-7*) DK Pub Inc.
My Very First Number Book in Arabic. (Butterfly Bks.). (Illus.). (J). 1996. 14.95 (*0-86685-667-6*, Pub. by Librairie du Liban) Intl Bk Ctr.
My Very First Piano Book of Cowboy Songs: Twenty-Two Favorite Songs Easy in Piano Arrangement. Dolly M. Moon. (Illus.). 46p. (J). (gr. 2 up). 1998. pap. 3.50 (*0-486-24311-7*) Dover.
My Very First Pow Wow. Donna Whitford-Garner. (Illus.). 24p. (J). (gr. k-5). 1997. pap. 7.00 (*0-8059-4133-9*) Dorrance.
***My Very First Tea Party.** Michal Sparks. 10p. 2000. bds. 5.99 (*0-7369-0243-0*) Harvest Hse.
***My Very First Winnie the Pooh.** Tk. 192p. (J). 2000. 14.99 (*0-7868-3271-1*, Pub. by Disney Pr) Time Warner.
My Very First Winnie the Pooh, No. 12. Kathleen Zoehfeld. LC 98-89405. (Illus.). 32p. (J). (ps-k). 1999. 12.99 (*0-7868-3242-8*, Pub. by Disney Pr) Time Warner.
My Very First Word Book. Dorling Kindersley Staff. LC 93-1112. (J). 1993. write for info. (*1-56458-375-9*) DK Pub Inc.
My Very First Word Book in Arabic & English. (Butterfly Bks.). (Illus.). (J). 1996. 14.95 (*0-86685-669-2*, Pub. by Librairie du Liban) Intl Bk Ctr.
***My Very Last Possession: And Other Stories by Pak Wanso.** Pak Wanso. Tr. by Kyung-Ja Chun from KOR. LC 99-10681. 240p. 1999. text 45.00 (*0-7656-0428-0*, East Gate Bk) M E Sharpe.
***My Very Last Possession: And Other Stories by Pak Wanso.** Pak Wanso & Kyung-Ja Chun. LC 99-10681. 240p. 1999. pap. text 22.95 (*0-7656-0429-9*, East Gate Bk) M E Sharpe.
My Very Own Bible. Alda Ellis. (J). 1991. 6.99 (*0-89081-918-1*) Harvest Hse.
***My Very Own Bible for Toddlers.** Juliana Nothnagel. 1999. 14.95 (*0-86997-635-4*) Lux Verbi.
My Very Own Big Dictionary. (Illus.). 40p. (J). 1996. 11.95 (*0-395-76320-7*) HM.
My Very Own Birthday: A Book of Cooking & Crafts. Robin West. (My Very Own Holiday Bks.). (Illus.). 64p. (J). 1996. lib. bdg. 19.95 (*0-87614-980-8*, Carolrhoda) Lerner Pub.
My Very Own Book about Me see Mi Gua de DeFensa Personal
***My Very Own Book about Me! Personal Safety Book.** Jo Stowell & Mary Dietzel. (Illus.). 64p. (J). (gr. 3-7). 1999. wbk. ed. 15.25 (*1-930489-00-5*) Act For Kids.
My Very Own Book of ABCs. Illus. by Guy Smalley. (My Very Own Ser.). 32p. (J). (ps-2). 1989. 9.95 (*0-929793-02-1*) Camex Bks Inc.
My Very Own Book of Mother Goose Animals. Illus. by Guy Smalley. (My Very Own Ser.). 24p. (J). (ps-2). 1989. 9.95 (*0-929793-01-3*) Camex Bks Inc.
My Very Own Book of Numbers. Illus. by Guy Smalley. (My Very Own Ser.). 28p. (J). (ps-2). 1989. 9.95 (*0-929793-00-5*) Camex Bks Inc.
My Very Own Book of Sizes. Illus. by Guy Smalley. (My Very Own Ser.). 24p. (J). (ps-2). 1989. 9.95 (*0-929793-04-8*) Camex Bks Inc.
My Very Own Book of Toys. Illus. by Guy Smalley. (My Very Own Ser.). 24p. (J). (ps-2). 1989. 9.95 (*0-929793-03-X*) Camex Bks Inc.
My Very Own Book of What's for Lunch. Illus. by Guy Smalley. (My Very Own Ser.). 24p. (J). (ps-2). 1989. 9.95 (*0-929793-05-6*) Camex Bks Inc.
My Very Own Bulletin, Vol. 1. 22.25 (*0-87162-673-X*) Warner Pr.
My Very Own Bulletin, Vol. 2. 22.25 (*0-87162-699-3*) Warner Pr.
***My Very Own Bulletin Vol. 6: Creative Activities to Increase Children's Knowledge of the Bible.** Warner Press Staff. (Illus.). (J). 1999. pap. 14.95 (*0-87162-844-9*) Warner Pr.
My Very Own Christmas. Robin West. (My Very Own Holiday Bks.). (Illus.). 64p. (J). (gr. k-4). 1997. pap. text 9.95 (*1-57505-231-8*, Carolrhoda) Lerner Pub.
My Very Own Christmas: A Book of Cooking & Crafts. Robin West. LC 92-8653. (My Very Own Holiday Bks.). (Illus.). (J). (gr. k-4). 1992. lib. bdg. 19.95 (*0-87614-722-8*, Carolrhoda) Lerner Pub.
***My Very Own Fairy Stories.** Johnny Gruelle. (Illus.). 100p. (J). (gr. k-5). 2000. reprint ed. 22.95 (*1-57860-076-6*) Guild Pr IN.
My Very Own Fairy Tales Treasury, 12 bks. (Illus.). 94p. (J). 1993. boxed set 19.98 (*0-7853-0032-5*) Pubns Intl Ltd.
My Very Own Family Divorce. Anna Dunwell Friedler. (Illus.). 16p. (J). (gr. k-12). 2000. spiral bd. 24.95 (*1-891657-35-6*, S3091) Lift Every Voice.
***My Very Own Haggadah.** 3rd rev. ed. Judyth R. Saypol & Madeline Wikler. LC 83-6. (Illus.). 32p. (J). (ps-3). 1999. pap. 3.95 (*1-58013-023-2*) Kar-Ben.
My Very Own Halloween. Robin West. (J). (gr. k-4). 1992. lib. bdg. 19.95 (*0-87614-725-2*, Carolrhoda) Lerner Pub.
My Very Own Halloween. Robin West. (My Very Own Holiday Bks.). (Illus.). 64p. (J). (gr. k-4). 1997. pap. text 9.95 (*1-57505-232-6*, Carolrhoda) Lerner Pub.
***My Very Own Halloween Box, 4 bks.** Phoebe Phillips. LC 98-183739. (Carry Cases Ser.). (Illus.). 10p. (J). (ps-3). 1998. bds. 7.98 (*0-7651-0802-X*) Smithmark.
My Very Own Hanukkah Box, 4 bks. (Carry Cases Ser.). (Illus.). 10p. (J). (ps-3). 1997. bds. 7.98 (*0-7651-9255-1*) Smithmark.
My Very Own Library Treasure Hunt. Candace Jackson. Ed. by Richard Greenwood & Susan Erickson. (Dewee & Libby Literacy Ser.: Vol. II). (Illus.). 44p. (J). (gr. k-7). 1998. pap. 4.45 (*1-892240-01-7*) Museum Mania.
My Very Own Mother's Day: A Book of Cooking & Crafts. Robin West. LC 95-22625. (My Very Own Holiday Bks.). (Illus.). 64p. (J). (gr. 3-5). 1996. lib. bdg. 19.95 (*0-87614-981-6*, Carolrhoda) Lerner Pub.
My Very Own Multicultural Family. Anna Dunwell Friedler. (Illus.). 16p. (J). (gr. k-12). 2000. spiral bd. 24.95 (*1-891657-34-8*, S3090) Lift Every Voice.
My Very Own Octopus. Bernard Most. Ed. by Diane D'Andrade. LC 80-12786. (Illus.). 32p. (J). (ps-3). 1991. pap. 6.00 (*0-15-256345-8*, Voyager Bks) Harcourt.
My Very Own Parent's Training Manual. LaVerne Bell-Tolliver. 36p. 1994. student ed. 9.95 (*0-9642551-0-3*) Empowerment.
My Very Own Parent's Training Manual Trainer's Guide. LaVerne Bell-Tolliver. 42p. 1994. teacher ed. 9.95 (*0-9642551-1-1*) Empowerment.
My Very Own Phone Book. Adventure Publications. (J). (ps-3). 1993. pap. 7.95 (*0-9635490-0-6*) Just Mom & Me.
***My Very Own Room.** Amada Irma Perez. LC 00-20769. (Illus.). 32p. (J). (ps-3). 2000. 15.95 (*0-89239-164-2*) Childrens Book Pr.
***My Very Own Room.** Michal Sparks. 10p. (J). 2000. bds. 5.99 (*0-7369-0331-3*) Harvest Hse.
My Very Own Rosh Hashanah see All about Rosh Hashanah
My Very Own Stories. Alice K. Taylor. (Illus.). 16p. (J). (gr. 2-8). 1993. lib. bdg. 11.95 (*0-9638873-0-0*) J Taylor Ltd.
My Very Own Sukkot see All about Sukkot
My Very Own Thanksgiving. Robin West. (My Very Own Holiday Bks.). (Illus.). 64p. (J). (gr. k-4). 1997. pap. text 9.95 (*1-57505-233-4*, Carolrhoda) Lerner Pub.
My Very Own Thanksgiving: A Book of Cooking & Crafts. Robin West. LC 92-33234. (My Very Own Holiday Bks.). (Illus.). 63p. (J). (gr. k-4). 1993. lib. bdg. 19.95 (*0-87614-723-6*, Carolrhoda) Lerner Pub.
My Very Own Valentine's Day: A Book of Cooking & Crafts. Robin West. LC 92-22254. (My Very Own Holiday Bks.). (Illus.). (J). (gr. k-4). 1993. lib. bdg. 19.95 (*0-87614-724-4*, Carolrhoda) Lerner Pub.
My Very Own Yom Kippur see All about Yom Kippur
My Very Worst Friend: A Survivor's Report on the Twentieth Century. Mike Layton. LC 97-94775. (Illus.). 311p. 1998. pap. 16.00 (*0-9654533-1-6*) DragonRed Pr.
***My Vice Is Verses: Poetry.** Bernard Yaeger. 240p. 2000. pap. 12.95 (*1-55618-187-6*) Brunswick Pub.
***My View.** Ardenelle Mason. 1999. pap. write for info. (*1-58235-087-6*) Watermrk Pr.
My View of the World. Erwin Schrodinger. LC 83-60548. viii, 110p. 1983. reprint ed. 26.00 (*0-918024-29-3*); reprint ed. pap. 14.00 (*0-918024-30-7*) Ox Bow.
My Village. Illus. by Klaus Blieseuer. 16p. (J). (gr. k-3). 1995. 20.00 (*1-56021-247-0*, 0099) W J Fantasy.
My Village by the Sea: Folktales of Greece. Vilma L. Chantiles. (Illus.). 120p. (Orig.). 1993. pap. text 10.00 (*0-918618-58-4*) Pella Pub.
My Village in Israel. Sonia Gidal & Tim Gidal. (Illus.). (J). (gr. 5-6). 1963. lib. bdg. 5.69 (*0-394-91912-2*) Pantheon.
My Virginia Childhood. Louisa V. Kyle. (Illus.). 45p. (J). (gr. 3). 1976. write for info. (*0-318-64827-X*) Four OClock Farms.
My Visit to Me-Maw. Gale Davis. (Illus.). 18p. (J). (ps-6). 1997. pap. 3.59 (*0-9661299-0-3*) Unika Pubns.
My Visit to My Doctor: A Coloring Book for Kids. Betsy Monroe. (Medical Ser.: No. 4). (Illus.). 24p. (Orig.). (J). (gr. k-4). 1989. pap. write for info. (*1-878083-01-5*) Color Me Well.
My Visit to the Aquarium. Aliki. LC 92-18678. (Illus.). 40p. (J). (ps-3). 1993. 15.95 (*0-06-021458-9*); lib. bdg. 15.89 (*0-06-021459-7*) HarpC Child Bks.
My Visit to the Aquarium. Aliki. LC 92-18678. (Trophy Picture Bk.). (Illus.). 40p. (J). (ps-2). 1996. pap. 6.95 (*0-06-446186-6*, HarpTrophy) HarpC Child Bks.
My Visit to the Aquarium. Aliki. LC 92-18678. (J). 1993. 11.15 (*0-606-09657-4*, Pub. by Turtleback) Demco.
My Visit to the Dentist. Pam Howard. (HRL Little Bks.). (Illus.). 8p. (J). (ps-k). 1995. pap. text 10.95 (*1-57332-024-2*); pap. text 10.95 (*1-57332-050-1*) HighReach Lrning.
My Visit to the Dinosaurs. Aliki. LC 85-42748. (Trophy Let's-Read-&-Find-Out Bk.). (Illus.). 32p. (J). (ps-3). 1985. pap. 4.95 (*0-06-445020-1*, HarpTrophy) HarpC Child Bks.
My Visit to the Dinosaurs. Aliki. (Let's-Read-And-Find-Out Book Ser.). (J). 1985. 10.15 (*0-606-00343-6*, Pub. by Turtleback) Demco.
My Visit to the Dinosaurs. rev. ed. Aliki. LC 85-47538. (Let's-Read-&-Find-Out Science Bks.). (Illus.). 32p. (J). (ps-3). 1985. lib. bdg. 15.89 (*0-690-04423-2*) HarpC Child Bks.
My Visit to the Dinosaurs Book & Tape. Aliki. (J). 1990. pap. 7.95 incl. audio (*1-55994-247-9*) HarperAudio.
My Visit to the Emergency Room: A Coloring Book for Kids. Betsy Monroe. (Medical Ser.: No. 1). (SPA., Illus.). 32p. (J). (gr. k-4). 1990. reprint ed. pap. write for info. (*1-878083-03-1*) Color Me Well.
My Visit to the Hospital: A Coloring Book for Kids. Betsy Monroe. (Medical Ser.: No. 2). (Illus.). 32p. (Orig.). (J). (gr. k-4). 1986. pap. write for info. (*1-878083-02-3*) Color Me Well.
"My Visit to the Kentucky Horse Park" Joyce Yaes. (Illus.). 26p. (YA). (gr. 5-6). 1996. 7.00 (*0-9677295-0-5*) Harmony Hse KY.
My Visit to the Nursing Home: A Children's Story of Loving & Sharing Between the Generations. Steven Ross. Tr. & Illus. by Jill Pabich. LC 95-24142. 48p. (J). (ps-2). 1995. pap. 5.95 (*0-942963-59-8*) Distinctive Pub.
My Visit to the Outpatient Department: A Coloring Book for Kids. Betsy Monroe. (Medical Ser.: No. 3). (Illus.). 24p. (J). (gr. k-4). 1986. pap. write for info. (*1-878083-04-X*) Color Me Well.
My Visit to the Sun. 2nd ed. Phoebe M. Holmes. 135p. 1996. reprint ed. spiral bd. 12.00 (*0-7873-1203-7*) Hlth Research.
My Visit to the Sun (1933) Phoebe M. Holmes. 135p. 1996. reprint ed. pap. 11.00 (*1-56459-953-1*) Kessinger Pub.
My Visit to the Zoo. Aliki. LC 96-9897. (Illus.). 40p. (J). (ps-3). 1997. 14.95 (*0-06-024939-0*) HarpC.
My Visit to the Zoo. Aliki. LC 96-9897. (Illus.). 40p. (J). (ps up). 1997. lib. bdg. 15.89 (*0-06-024943-9*) HarpC.
My Visit to the Zoo. Aliki. LC 96-9897. (Illus.). 40p. (YA). (ps-3). 1999. pap. 6.95 (*0-06-446217-X*, HarpTrophy) HarpC Child Bks.

M

An Asterisk (*) at the beginning of an entry indicates that the title is appearing for the first time.

My Visit to Venus. T. Lobsang Rampa. 75p. 1992. 10.00 (0-938294-61-X) Inner Light.

My Vita, If You Will: The Uncollected Ed McClanahan. Ed McClanahan. Ed. by Tom Marksbury. LC 98-34792. 256p. 1998. pap. 13.50 (1-887178-77-5, Pub. by Counterpt DC) HarpC.

My Vocation, by Eminent Americans: or What Eminent Americans Think of Their Callings. Compiled by Earl G. Lockhart. LC 72-5602. (Essay Index Reprint Ser.). 1977. reprint ed. 35.95 (0-8369-2997-7) Ayer.

My Vocation Is Love see St. Therese of Lisieux: Her Life, Times & Teaching, Centenary Edition

My Vocation Is Love. Jean Lafrance. 175p. (C). 1990. 45.00 (0-85439-393-5, Pub. by St Paul Pubns) St Mut.

My Voice to the Lord. John A. Shalhoub. 185p. 1998. pap. 9.95 (1-55630-515-X) Brentwood Comm.

My Voice Will Go with You. Sidney Rosen. 1991. pap. 13.95 (0-393-30135-4) Norton.

My "w" Sound Box. Jane Belk Moncure. LC 78-8614. (Sound Box Library). (Illus.). 32p. (J). (ps-2). 1978. lib. bdg. 21.36 (0-89565-046-0) Childs World.

My Walk-a-Mile, No. 1000. Marene P. Fassina. 54p. 1999. mass mkt. 5.95 (1-892996-00-6) M Fassina.

My Walk Across the Church. 112p. 1986. pap. 6.99 (0-8341-1128-4) Nazarene.

My Walk with Jesus: Miracles in the Snow. Helen R. Bechtel. LC 98-61307. (Illus.). 64p. 1998. pap. 11.99 (1-57921-151-8, Pub. by WinePress Pub) BookWorld.

My Walking Cane see Ayaruqa

My War. Catherine Chrisman. 200p. (Orig.). 1989. pap. 12.00 (1-882021-22-3) Summer.

***My War.** Andy Rooney. (Illus.). 2000. 20.00 (1-58648-010-3) PublicAffairs NY.

***My War: A Love Story in Letters & Drawings from World War II.** Tracy Sugarman. LC 00-32345. (Illus.). 224p. 2000. 30.00 (0-375-50513-X) Random.

My War Against Sleep: Poems. R. D. Baker. (Poetry Chapbook Ser.). (Illus.). 28p. (Orig.). 1995. pap. 4.00 (1-887641-02-5) Argonne Hotel Pr.

My War Diary: Lebanon June 5 - July 1, 1982. Dov Yermiya. Tr. by Hillel Schenker from HEB. LC 83-51286. 160p. 1983. 25.00 (0-89608-201-6); pap. 7.00 (0-89608-200-8) South End Pr.

***My War Gone by, I Miss It So.** Anthony Loyd. LC 99-43963. 336p. 2000. 25.00 (0-87113-769-0, Pub. by Grove-Atltic) Publishers Group.

***My War Gone By, I Miss It So.** Anthony Loyd. 2001. pap. 13.00 (0-14-029854-1) Penguin Putnam.

My War Memoirs. Edvard Benes. LC 70-114467. (Illus.). 512p. 1971. reprint ed. lib. bdg. 38.50 (0-8371-4763-8, BEMW, Greenwood Pr) Greenwood.

My War Memories. Edvard Benes. LC 70-135794. (Eastern Europe Collection). 1971. reprint ed. 30.95 (0-405-02736-2) Ayer.

My War: or How I Surved in the Royal Air Force. Ed. by Andy Padbury. (C). 1989. 45.00 (0-7855-6629-5) St Mut.

My War with Brian. Ted Rall. (Illus.). 80p. (YA). 1998. pap. 8.95 (1-56163-215-5, Comics Lit) NBM.

My Warrior's Heart. Betina M. Krahn. 432p. (Orig.). 1992. mass mkt. 4.99 (0-380-76771-6, Avon Bks) Morrow Avon.

***My Wartime Encounter with Geography.** Harm De Blij. (Illus.). 180p. 2000. 29.50 (1-85776-457-9, Pub. by Book Guild Ltd) Trans-Atl Phila.

My Wartime Summers. Jane Cutler. LC 94-9845. 176p. (J). (gr. 5 up). 1994. 15.00 (0-374-35111-2) FS&G.

My Wartime Summers. Jane Cutler. LC 94-9845. 160p. (YA). (gr. 5-9). 1997. pap. 4.95 (0-374-45463-9, Sunburst Bks) FS&G.

My Wartime Summers. Jane Cutler. LC 94-9845. 1997. 10.05 (0-606-11658-3, Pub. by Turtleback) Demco.

My Washington D. C. Kathy Jakobsen. (Illus.). 32p. (J). 2000. write for info. (0-316-45622-5) Little.

My Water Cure. Sebastian Kneipp. 400p. 1997. reprint ed. pap. 25.00 (0-7873-0507-3) Hlth Research.

My Way: Speeches & Poems. Charles Bernstein. LC 98-30345. 321p. 1999. pap. 18.00 (0-226-04410-6); lib. bdg. 46.00 (0-226-04409-2) U Ch Pr.

***My Way: The Universe & the Truth.** Peter Maurer. 224p. 2000. pap. write for info. (1-57733-068-4) B Dolphin Pub.

My Way of Looking at It: An Autobiography. 2nd ed. Willia Van Til. LC 96-24631. 478p. 1996. 29.95 (1-880192-17-9) Caddo Gap Pr.

My Way of the Cross Journal: A Lenten Journey with Jesus. William F. Maestri. 98p. (Orig.). 1993. pap. 5.95 (0-8189-0663-4) Alba.

My Way Sally. Penelope C. Paine & Mindy Bingham. LC 88-2653. (Illus.). 48p. (J). (ps up). 1988. 14.95 (0-911655-27-1) Advocacy Pr.

My Way, the Way of White Clouds. Osho. 192p. 1995. pap. 14.95 (1-85230-699-8, Pub. by Element MA) Penguin Putnam.

My Way with Trout. Arthur Cove. (Illus.). 186p. 1993. pap. 24.95 (1-85223-680-9, Pub. by Crolwood) Trafalgar.

***My Wedding Organizer.** 1999. pap. 20.00 (1-57977-279-X) Havoc Pub.

My Wedding Planner. Ed. by Helen Exley. (Record Bks.). (Illus.). 80p. 1994. 12.00 (1-85015-515-1) Exley Giftbooks.

***My Weeds: A Gardener's Botany.** Sarah B. Stein. (Illus.). 240p. 2000. reprint ed. pap. 16.95 (0-8130-1739-4) U Press Fla.

My Weekly Chores. Claudette C. Mitchell et al. (Visions: African-American Experiences: Vol. 36). (Illus.). 8p. (Orig.). (J). (gr. k-1). 1996. pap. text 3.00 (1-57518-078-2) Arborlake.

My Weekly Sidra. Melanie Berman & Joel Lurie Grishaver. (Illus.). 192p. (gr. k-3). 1988. pap. 8.50 (0-933873-21-2) Torah Aura.

My Well-Balanced Life on a Wooden Leg. Al Capp. LC 91-6728. (Illus.). 128p. 1991. 15.95 (0-936784-93-8) J Daniel.

My Wetland Coloring Book. Government Printing Office Staff. 28p. 1991. pap. 3.50 (0-16-035860-4) USGPO.

My, What Sharp Teeth: Chewing & Biting Problems, Vol. 3. September B. Morn. (Illus.). 16p. 1996. pap. text 3.75 (0-9633884-4-4) Pawprince Pr.

My Whole Food ABC's. David Richard. LC 98-171176. (Illus.). 32p. (J). (gr. k-2). 1997. pap. 8.95 (1-890612-07-3) Vital Health.

My Wholly Terra: A Father's Diary. Will Kilkeary. (Illus.). (Orig.). 1998. pap. 12.95 (1-889406-09-0) Prell Pub.

My Wicked Enchantress. Meagan McKinney. LC 97-23464. (Five Star Romances Ser.). 408p. (Orig.). 1997. pap. 21.95 (0-7862-1206-3) Five Star.

My Wicked Enchantress. Meagan McKinney. 416p. (Orig.). 1997. pap. 5.99 (0-8217-5661-3, Zebra Kensgtn) Kensgtn Pub Corp.

My Wicked Fantasy. Karen Ranney. LC 97-94075. 384p. 1998. mass mkt. 5.99 (0-380-79581-7, Avon Bks) Morrow Avon.

***My Wicked Marquess.** Constance Hall. 1999. mass mkt. 5.99 (0-8217-6302-4, Zebra Kensgtn) Kensgtn Pub Corp.

My Wicked Stepmother. Norman Leach. LC 92-19674. (Illus.). 32p. (J). (ps-3). 1993. lib. bdg. 13.95 (0-02-754700-0, Mac Bks Young Read) S&S Childrens.

My Wicked, Wicked Ways. Sandra Cisneros. LC 92-14852. (Orig.). 1992. 24.00 (0-679-41821-0) Random.

My Wicked, Wicked Ways. Errol Flynn. 1976. 28.95 (0-8488-1316-2) Amereon Ltd.

My Wicked, Wicked Ways. Errol Flynn. 1976. reprint ed. lib. bdg. 35.95 (0-89966-093-2) Buccaneer Bks.

***My Wife.** Photos & Text by Petter Hegre. (Illus.). 2000. 39.95 (3-908163-28-5, Pub. by Edit Stemmle) Abbeville Pr.

My Wife & I: The Story of Louise & Sidney Homer. Sidney Homer. LC 77-10561. (Music Reprint Ser.). (Illus.). 1978. reprint ed. lib. bdg. 39.50 (0-306-77526-3) Da Capo.

My Wife Bernadette: A Poetic Remembrance. Abraham J. Heller. (Orig.). 1997. pap. write for info. (1-57553-457-6) Watermrk Pr.

My Wife, the Politician: A Play in Three Acts. H. J. Roberts. 137p. 1993. pap. 17.95 (0-9633260-5-8) Sunshine Sentinel.

My Wife's Last Lover. Martin Golan. LC 98-83088. 224p. 2000. pap. 14.95 (0-88739-237-7) Creat Arts Bk.

My Wild Friends: Free Food from Field & Forest. Blanche C. Derby. LC 96-90924. (Illus.). 264p. (Orig.). 1997. pap., ring bd. 22.50 (0-9626131-2-6) White Star MA.

My Wild Rose. Deborah Camp. 416p. (Orig.). 1992. mass mkt. 4.50 (0-380-76738-4, Avon Bks) Morrow Avon.

My Wilderness. William O. Douglas. 256p. 1989. 5.95 (0-89174-054-6) Comstock Edns.

My Will, a Legacy to the Healthy & the Sick. Sebastian Kneipp. 380p. 1996. reprint ed. pap. 22.50 (0-7873-0505-7) Hlth Research.

My Will Be Done. Clayton A. Parker. 201p. 1982. pap. 3.00 (0-686-86578-2, 0-9606438) C A Parker Pubns.

My Window. Mary Martha Brown. 1999. 24.00 (1-891721-55-0) McBrown S&S.

My Winds of Change Wilhelm Verwoerd. LC 98-107032. 176 p. 1997. write for info. (0-86975-513-7) Ohio U Pr.

My Wine. Noah Bertoleio. LC 97-72091. 88p. 1997. pap. 20.00 (0-9658823-0-6) Love St Publ.

My Wings. Terry Page. (Illus.). 24p. (J). (gr. 2-6). 1995. pap. text 4.00 (1-887864-52-0); lib. bdg. 7.00 (1-887864-04-0) Boo Bks.

My Wings Coloring Book. Terry Page. (Illus.). 32p. (J). (ps-5). 1995. pap. 3.00 (1-887864-05-9) Boo Bks.

My Winter Journal. Alana Trisler & Patrice Cardiel. 72p. (J). (gr. 2-3). 1999. pap., wbk. ed. 2.00 (1-56762-105-8) Modern Learn Pr.

***My Wisconsin Garden: A Gardener's Journal.** Cool Springs Press Publications Staff. 2000. 19.95 (1-888608-86-2) Cool Springs Pr.

***My Wisconsin Garden: A Gardener's Journal.** Melinda Myers. (Illus.). 128p. 2000. spiral bd. 19.95 (1-930604-05-X) Cool Springs Pr.

***My Wisdom Journal: A Discovering of Proverbs for Kids.** Mary J. Davis. 160p. (J). 1999. pap. 9.99 (1-885358-73-3, Lgacy Pr) Rainbow CA.

My Wish for Tomorrow: Words & Pictures from Children Around the World: In Celebration of the Fiftieth Anniversary of the United Nations. Contrib. by Henson, Jim, Productions Staff. (Illus.). 48p. (J). (ps up). 1995. 16.00 (0-688-14455-1, Wm Morrow) Morrow Avon.

My Wish for Tomorrow: Words & Pictures from Children Around the World: In Celebration of the Fiftieth Anniversary of the United Nations. Intro. by Nelson Mandela. (Illus.). 48p. (J). (ps up). 1995. lib. bdg. 15.93 (0-688-14456-X, Wm Morrow) Morrow Avon.

***My Wish for You: Blessings from A Mother's Heart.** Cheri Fuller & Sandra P. Aldrich. LC 99-58074. 144p. 2000. 12.99 (1-56955-132-4, Vine Bks) Servant.

***My Wish List & Other Stories.** Lisa-Marie Calderone-Stewart & Ed Kunzman. (Stories for Teens Ser.: Vol. 2). 72p. (YA). 1999. pap. 4.95 (0-88489-590-4) St Marys.

My Witness. William Winter. (Notable American Authors Ser.). 1999. reprint ed. lib. bdg. 125.00 (0-7812-7763-9) Rprt Serv.

***My Wonderful Christmas Tree.** Dahlov Ipcar. LC 99-37003. 1999. pap. 9.95 (0-89272-475-7) Down East.

My Wonderful Salvation. Harvey A. Childress. 1978. pap. 1.75 (0-88027-088-8) Firm Foun Pub.

"My Word!" Celebrities Reveal Their Favorite Words & the Reasons Behind Their Selections. Ed. & Compiled by Vick Knight, Jr. LC 95-83087. (Illus.). 180p. 1996. pap. 9.95 (0-931407-03-6) Aristan Pr.

My Word Bk. 1: We Borrowed Their Names. Masahiro Hori. LC 95-92315. (Illus.). 104p. (Orig.). 1995. pap. 12.95 (0-9644573-6-9) Shamrock Sky Bks.

My Word Bk. 2: We Borrowed Their Place Names. Gerald D. Sullivan & Masahiro Hori. LC 96-92200. (Illus.). 104p. (Orig.). 1996. pap. 12.95 (0-9644573-7-7) Shamrock Sky Bks.

My Word Bk. 3: Our Favorite Word Stories. Gerald D. Sullivan & Masahiro Hori. 1998. pap. 12.95 (0-9644573-9-3) Shamrock Sky Bks.

My Word Book. Alana Trisler & Patrice H. Cardiel. (Illus.). 56p. (Orig.). (J). 1994. pap. text 2.50 (1-56762-055-8) Modern Learn Pr.

My Word Booklet. Ella D. Davis. 6p. (J). (gr. k-6). 1993. pap. text 15.95 (1-888185-53-8) Davis Pubng LA.

***My Word Dictionary.** Nancy Shaw. Ed. by Charlene Stout & Kathy Rogers. 32p. 1998. 1.99 (1-56472-141-8) Edupress Inc.

My Word Works. Alana Trisler & Patrice Cardiel. 64p. (Orig.). (J). (gr. 1-3). 1997. pap., wbk. ed. write for info. (1-56762-067-1) Modern Learn Pr.

My Words...Exactly. L. Charles McLain. 1999. pap. write for info. (1-58235-033-7) Watermrk Pr.

My Work: In Retrospect. Hans U. Von Balthasar. Tr. by Brian McNeil from GER. LC 92-74535. 120p. (Orig.). 1993. pap. 9.95 (0-89870-435-9) Ignatius Pr.

My Work in Films. Eugene Lourie. (Illus.). 384p. 1985. pap. 16.95 (0-15-662342-0, Harvest Bks) Harcourt.

My Work with Borderline Patients. Harold F. Searles. LC 86-20639. 432p. 1986. 60.00 (0-87668-930-6) Aronson.

My Working Mom. Peter Glassman. LC 93-22036. (Illus.). (J). (ps-3). 1994. 16.00 (0-688-12259-0, Wm Morrow) Morrow Avon.

My Working Mom. Peter Glassman. LC 93-22036. (Illus.). (J). (ps-3). 1994. 15.93 (0-688-12260-4, Wm Morrow) Morrow Avon.

***My World, 6 vols.** 192p. (J). (gr. 2-7). 1999. write for info. (0-7166-9418-2) World Bk.

***My World.** Prue Greener. LC 00-24163. (Illus.). 20p. (ps-k). 2000. write for info. (0-7894-6513-2, Pub. by DK Pub Inc) Pub Resources Inc.

My World. Michele Lucien. 44p. (J). (gr. k-3). 1994. spiral bd. 10.95 (0-9639678-0-0) Write For You.

My World. Leona E. Murray. 1997. pap. write for info. (1-57553-512-2) Watermrk Pr.

My World. Jesse Stuart. LC 92-17549. (Kentucky Bicentennial Bookshelf Ser.). 104p. 1992. 18.00 (0-8131-0211-1) U Pr of Ky.

My World, Bk. 1. Regents. 24p. (J). 1996. pap. text, student ed. 7.80 (0-13-349705-4) P-H.

My World: A Thematic Unit. Diane Williams. (Thematic Units Ser.). (Illus.). 80p. (J). (ps-1). 1990. student ed. 9.95 (1-55734-252-0) Tchr Create Mat.

My World: Nature - Peace. Ed. by Richard Exley & Helen Exley. (Illus.). 256p. 1995. boxed set 29.95 (0-8442-9621-X, Natl Textbk Co) NTC Contemp Pub Co.

***My World: Ramblings of an Aging Gutter Punk.** Jeff Ott. 2000. pap. 15.00 (0-9677287-0-3) Sub City.

My World - Nature. Ed. by Richard Exley & Helen Exley. (Illus.). 127p. 1985. 14.95 (0-8442-9622-8, Natl Textbk Co) NTC Contemp Pub Co.

My World - Peace. Ed. by Richard Exley & Helen Exley. (Illus.). 127p. 1985. text 14.95 (0-8442-9620-1, Natl Textbk Co) NTC Contemp Pub Co.

My World & Globe. Ira Wolfman. LC 91-50382. (Illus.). 64p. (Orig.). (J). (ps-2). 1991. pap. 13.95 (0-89480-993-8, 1993) Workman Pub.

My World & Welcome to It. James Thurber. reprint ed. lib. bdg. 20.95 (0-89190-269-4, Rivercity Pr) Amereon Ltd.

My World & Welcome to It. James Thurber. LC 42-36350. (Illus.). 324p. 1969. reprint ed. pap. 13.00 (0-15-662344-7, Harvest Bks) Harcourt.

My World As a Jew, Vol. 1. Israel Goldstein. LC 82-42721. (Illus.). 352p. 1984. 22.50 (0-8453-4765-9, Cornwall Bks) Assoc Univ Prs.

My World As a Jew, Vol. 2. Israel Goldstein. LC 82-42621. (Illus.). 416p. 1984. 22.50 (0-8453-4780-2, Cornwall Bks) Assoc Univ Prs.

My World at War. Richard Lyons. 158p. 1998. pap. text 7.50 (1-881604-33-0) Scopcraeft.

My World Cup. Mark Mascarenhas. LC 97-71687. 1997. 50.00 (0-944142-34-6) Grantha.

My World in French. Tamara Mealer. (My World in...Coloring Book Ser.). (FRE., Illus.). 96p. (J). 1994. pap. 4.95 (0-8442-1393-4, 13934, Natl Textbk Co) NTC Contemp Pub Co.

My World in German Coloring Book. Tamara Mealer. LC 97-43146. (My World in...Coloring Book Ser.). (GER., Illus.). 96p. (J). 1994. pap. 4.95 (0-8442-2169-4, 21694, Natl Textbk Co) NTC Contemp Pub Co.

My World in Italian Coloring Book. Tamara Mealer. (ITA., Illus.). 96p. (J). (ps-3). 1994. pap. 4.95 (0-8442-8067-4, 80674, Natl Textbk Co) NTC Contemp Pub Co.

My World in Spanish Coloring Book. Tamara Mealer. (SPA., Illus.). 96p. (J). 1994. pap. 4.95 (0-8442-7552-2, 75522, Natl Textbk Co) NTC Contemp Pub Co.

My World Indoors: Activities Guide for Teachers. rev. ed. Nancy Moreno et al. (My Health My World Ser.). (Illus.). vi, 48p. 1997. pap. write for info. (1-888997-11-7) Baylor Coll Med.

My World Is an Island. Elisabeth Ogilvie. LC 90-80510. (Illus.). 288p. 1990. reprint ed. pap. 12.95 (0-89272-288-6) Down East.

My World Is an Island. Elizabeth Ogilvie. reprint ed. lib. bdg. 23.95 (0-88411-334-5) Amereon Ltd.

My World Is Burning & Other Poems. George Beecher. 1998. pap. write for info. (1-57553-985-3) Watermrk Pr.

My World Is Not Flat. Nussbaum. 1993. 12.95 (1-55550-895-2, Pub. by Universe) St Martin.

My World, My Fingerhold, My Bygod Apple. Neva V. Hacker. LC 95-52070. (First Ser.). 80p. (Orig.). 1996. pap. 11.00 (0-922811-25-3) Mid-List.

My World, My Responsibility. Michael Exeter. 1987. pap. 2.50 (0-935427-14-7) Foundation Hse.

My World of Astrology. Sydney Omar. 1976. pap. 10.00 (0-87980-103-4) Wilshire.

My World of Colors & Shapes, 1 vol. (Barbie Learn 'n' Tell Sticker Bks.: Vol. 4). (J). 1998. pap. write for info. (0-7666-0201-X, Honey Bear Bks) Modern Pub NYC.

***My World of Knowledge.** Ed. by McGraw-Hill Book Company Staff. (Young Learner's Ser.). (Illus.). (J). 2000. pap. 12.95 (1-57768-770-1) MG-Hill OH.

My World of Reality. Hildrus A. Poindexter. LC 72-85752. (Illus.). 349p. 1973. 9.95 (0-913642-03-7) Balamp Pub.

My World of Spanish Words. Debbie MacKinnon. LC 94-42967.Tr. of Mi Mundo de Palabras. (Illus.). 128p. (J). 1995. 8.95 (0-8120-6505-0) Barron.

My World of Words. Debbie MacKinnon. LC 94-42966.Tr. of Mon Monde de Mots. (ENG & FRE., Illus.). 128p. (J). 1995. 8.95 (0-8120-6506-9) Barron.

My World of Words. Debbie MacKinnon. LC 94-43792.Tr. of Mon Monde de Mots. (Illus.). 128p. (J). (ps). 1995. 7.95 (0-8120-6507-7) Barron.

My World of Yesterdays: A Collection of Stories. Frances J. Kontos. (Illus.). 92p. 1993. 22.50 (0-9639063-0-5) A Cornell Pubng.

My World Set, 6 bks. Incl. Cars. (Illus.). 8p. (J). (ps-2). 1997. pap. 2.49 (0-395-88929-4); Dad. Catherine Peters. 8p. (J). 1997. pap. 2.49 (0-395-88309-1); Foods to Eat. Catherine Peters. (J). 1997. pap. 2.49 (0-395-88289-3); Friends. Catherine Peters. 8p. (J). 1997. pap. 2.49 (0-395-88310-5); Hats. Catherine Peters. 8p. (J). 1997. pap. 2.49 (0-395-88297-4); I Am. Catherine Peters. 8p. (J). 1997. pap. 2.49 (0-395-88303-2); (Little Readers Book Bag Ser.). 1997. 15.00 (0-395-88288-5) HM.

My World War II Experience Revisited. Lyle D. Green. LC 96-67609. (Illus.). 128p. (Orig.). 1996. pap. 9.95 (1-882792-21-1) Proctor Pubns.

My Worship Planner & Organizer. Gloria Meurant. 1992. pap. 8.50 (1-55673-439-5, 9242) CSS OH.

My Worst Date. 3rd ed. David Leddick. 272p. 1998. pap. 12.95 (0-312-18138-8) St Martin.

My Worst Days Diary see Bank Street Ready-to-Read Books: Levels 1, 2 & 3

My Worst Days Diary. Ellen Schecter. (J). 1995. 19.95 (0-553-53120-4) BDD Bks Young Read.

My Worst Friend. P.J. Petersen. LC 98-3219. (J). (gr. 3-4). 1998. 15.99 (0-525-46028-4, Dutton Child) Peng Put Young Read.

My Write & Read Music Workbook: Worksheets for Reading Music Through Writing Music. Vicki Jorgensen. (Recorder & "Flute" "Let's Sing & Play" Ser.). (Illus.). 72p. 1987. wbk. ed. 4.25 (0-913500-24-0, L-7WB) Peg Hoenack MusicWorks.

***My Writing Day.** David A. Adler. LC 99-11049. (Meet the Author Ser.). (Illus.). 32p. (J). (gr. 2-5). 1999. 14.95 (1-57274-326-3, 723) R Owen Pubs.

My Writing Tablet. Dalmatian Press Staff. (J). 1998. pap. 2.29 (1-888567-10-4) Dalmatian Pr.

My WWII Diary & the War Effort. Walbrook D. Swank. LC 96-35261. (Illus.). 142p. 1996. 20.00 (1-57249-023-3, Burd St Pr) White Mane Pub.

My "x, y, z" Sound Box. Jane Belk Moncure. LC 79-13086. (Sound Box Library). (Illus.). 32p. (J). (ps-2). 1979. lib. bdg. 21.36 (0-89565-102-5) Childs World.

My Year. Roald Dahl. (J). 1999. pap. 3.99 (0-14-037680-1, Viking) Viking Penguin.

My Year: Worthy Matron's Year Book. enl. rev. ed. 1994. reprint ed. ring bd. 20.00 (0-88053-333-1, 8003) Macoy Pub.

My Year in a Log Cabin. William Dean Howells. (Illus.). 56p. 1996. reprint ed. pap. 7.50 (0-913428-80-9) Landfall Pr.

My Year in the No-Man's-Bay. Peter Handke. Tr. by Krishna Winston. LC 97-48948. 356p. 1998. 25.00 (0-374-21755-6) FS&G.

My Year in the Word, 1999: Through the Gospels with Bob Russell. Bob Russell. Ed. by Jim Eichenberger. 208p. 1998. pap. 14.99 (0-7847-0800-2, 11-41000) Standard Pub.

***My Year of Fun Book.** Full House Michelle Staff. (Full House Michelle & Friends Ser.). 96p. (J). (gr. 2-4). 2000. 3.99 (0-671-04200-9, Minstrel Bks) PB.

My Year of Meats: A Novel. Ruth L. Ozeki. LC 97-52319. 364p. 1998. 23.95 (0-670-87904-5, Viking) Viking Penguin.

***My Year of Meats: A Novel.** Ruth L. Ozeki. LC 97-52319. 384p. 1999. pap. 12.95 (0-14-028046-4) Viking Penguin.

My Year Off: Recovering Life after a Stroke. Robert McCrum. LC 99-27259. 256p. 1999. pap. 13.00 (0-7679-0400-1) Bantam.

My Year Off: Rediscovering Life after a Stroke. Robert McCrum. LC 98-29629. 224p. 1998. 23.95 (0-393-04656-7) Norton.

My Year Off: Rediscovering Life after a Stroke. large type ed. Robert McCrum. LC 99-18677. 285p. 1999. write for info. (0-7838-8584-9, G K Hall & Co) Mac Lib Ref.

My Years with Louis St. Laurent: A Political Memoir. J. W. Pickersgill. LC 75-24675. (Illus.). 352p. reprint ed. pap. 109.20 (0-8357-8239-5, 203400800088) Bks Demand.

My Yearbook. (Illus.). 1995. 5.95 (1-56472-055-1) Edupress Inc.

My Years in Communist China. Eva Diao. 1993. 13.95 (0-533-10480-7) Vantage.

My Years in Theresienstadt: How One Woman Survived the Holocaust. Gerty Spies. Tr. by Jutta R. Tragnitz. LC 97-271. (Illus.). 214p. 1997. 26.95 (1-57392-141-6) Prometheus Bks.

An Asterisk (*) at the beginning of an entry indicates that the title is appearing for the first time.

My Years of Exile: Reminiscences of a Socialist. Eduard Bernstein. Tr. by Bernard Miall from GER. LC 86-1865.Tr. of Vo-ker zu Hause. 287p. 1986. reprint ed. lib. bdg. 65.00 (*0-313-25114-2*, BMYY, Greenwood Pr) Greenwood.
My Years Through Raj to Swaraj. T. N. Kaul. (C). 1995. 28.00 (*0-7069-9700-X*, Pub. by Vikas) S Asia.
My Years with Ayn Rand: The Truth Behind the Myths. Nathaniel Branden. LC 98-25440. 480p. 1999. pap. 19.00 (*0-7879-4513-7*) Jossey-Bass.
My Years with Bob Wills. 2nd rev. ed. Al Stricklin. (Illus.). 160p. 1996. pap. 16.95 (*1-57168-119-1*, Eakin Pr) Sunbelt Media.
My Years with Capone: Jack Woodford & Al Capone. 2nd ed. Neil Elliott. LC 85-51231. 160p. 1990. pap. 10.95 (*0-9601574-4-1*) Woodford Mem.
My Years with General Motors. Alfred P. Sloan, Jr. LC 64-11306. 496p. 1990. reprint ed. pap. 21.00 (*0-385-04235-3*) Doubleday.
My Years with Gorbachev & Shevardnadze: The Memoir of a Soviet Interpreter. Pavel Palazchenko & Don Oberdorfer. LC 96-25686. 1997. 35.00 (*0-271-01603-5*) Pa St U Pr.
My Years with Indira Gandhi. P. Alexander. (C). 1991. 18.00 (*81-7094-087-7*, Pub. by Vision) S Asia.
My Years with Ludwig Von Mises. rev. ed. Margit Von Mises. (Illus.). 242p. 1984. pap. 7.95 (*0-915513-01-3*) Ctr Futures Ed.
My Years with Ludwig Von Mises. 2nd rev. ed. Margit Von Mises. (Illus.). 230p. 1984. 14.95 (*0-915513-00-5*) Ctr Futures Ed.
My Years with the Arabs. John Glubb. 19p. 1971. pap. 6.00 (*0-9500029-6-8*, Pub. by Octagon Pr) ISHK.
My Yellowstone Years. Donald C. Stewart. LC 88-51698. (Illus.). 369p. 1989. pap. 12.95 (*0-923568-01-8*) Wilderness Adventure Bks.
My Yo-Yo. Date not set. 9.95 (*0-89868-295-9*); pap. 3.95 (*0-89868-294-0*) ARO Pub.
My Yoke Is Easy & My Burden Is Light: A Current Technology Translation of the Bible. William E. Adams. LC 97-91645. 100p. (Orig.). 1997. pap. text 6.95 (*0-9639623-1-0*) Old Drum.
My Young Master. Novel. Opie Read. LC 86-27443. (Library of Southern Civilization). 352p. 1987. pap. text 18.95 (*0-8071-1395-6*) La State U Pr.
My Yup'ik Eskimo Toys see Yugtaat Naanguat
My Yup'ik Eskimo Toys see Cup'igtat Laanguarrutenka
***My Yupik Eskimo Toys.** large type ed. James Berlin, Sr. (Illus.). 12p. (J). (gr. k-3). 1999. pap. text 17.00 (*1-58084-074-4*) Lower Kuskokwim.
My Zaidah - My Grandfather. Lili Steiner. (My Jewish Family Series with a Bissel Yiddish). (Illus.). 24p. (J). 1998. pap. 14.95 (*1-891397-01-X*) L Steiner Pubns.
My Zayde: A Recollection. Richard M. Usatinsky. LC 93-86375. (Illus.). 80p. (Orig.). 1994. 18.00 (*1-884341-01-2*); pap. 10.00 (*1-884341-00-4*) Satin Sky Pr.
My Zeesa Jessica My Sweet Jessica. Lili Steiner. (My Jewish Family Series with a Bissel Yiddish). (Illus.). 24p. 1997. pap. 14.95 (*1-891397-00-1*) L Steiner Pubns.
My Zeppelins. Hugo Eckener. Ed. by James B. Gilbert. Tr. by Douglas H. Robinson. LC 79-7250. (Flight: Its First Seventy-Five Years Ser.). (Illus.). 1980. reprint ed. lib. bdg. 27.95 (*0-405-12162-8*) Ayer.
My Zombie Valentine. Dian Curtis Regan. 112p. (J). (gr. 4-6). 1993. pap. 2.95 (*0-590-46038-2*) Scholastic Inc.
***My 360 Best-loved Bible Verses: A Daily Devotional.** Solly Ozrovech. 1999. 14.95 (*0-86997-765-2*) Lux Verbi.
Myanmar see Countries of the World
***Myanmar: A Country Study Guide.** Global Investment & Business Center, Inc. Staff. (World Country Study Guides Library: Vol. 119). (Illus.). 350p. 2000. pap. 59.00 (*0-7397-2417-7*) Intl Business Pubns.
Myanmar: Trade & Investment Potential in Asia. (Studies in Trade & Investment: No. 19). 166p. 25.00 (*92-1-119729-5*, DS530) UN.
Myanmar - A Country Study Guide: Basic Information for Research & Pleasure. Global Investment Center, USA Staff. (World Country Study Guide Library: Vol. 119). (Illus.). 350p. 1999. pap. 59.00 (*0-7397-1516-X*) Intl Business Pubns.
Myanmar - English Dictionary. Ed. by Myanmar Language Commission. 672p. 1997. reprint ed. 94.00 (*1-881265-47-1*) Dunwoody Pr.
Myanmar (Burma) Nelles Verlag Staff. (Nelles Guides Ser.). (Illus.). 256p. 1999. pap. 15.95 (*3-88618-415-3*) Hunter NJ.
Myanmar (Burma) Karen L. Niesen & Christine Onaga. LC 95-22467. (Oles Country Guide Ser.). 1996. 22.00 (*0-929851-54-4*) Am Assn Coll Registrars.
***Myanmar (Burma)** 7th ed. Joe Cummings & Michael Clark. (Illus.). 432p. 1999. pap. 16.95 (*0-86442-703-4*) Lonely Planet.
Myanmar (Burma) Handbook. Joshua Eliot. (Footprint Handbooks Ser.). (Illus.). 250p. 1997. 16.95 (*0-8442-4919-X*, 4919X, Natl Textbk Co) NTC Contemp Pub Co.
Myanmar (Burma), "In the National Interest" Prisoners of Conscience, Torture, Summary Trials under Martial Law. 52p. 1990. 6.00 (*0-939994-60-7*) Amnesty Intl USA.
Myanmar (Burma), Prisoners of Conscience. 86p. 1989. 3.00 (*0-685-50862-5*, ASA 16-23-89 -) Amnesty Intl USA.
***Myanmar Business Intelligence Report, 190 vols.** Global Investment & Business Center, Inc. Staff. (World Business Intelligence Library: Vol. 119). (Illus.). 350p. 2000. pap. 99.95 (*0-7397-2617-X*) Intl Business Pubns.
***Myanmar Business Law Handbook, 190 vols.** Global Investment & Business Center, Inc. Staff. (Global Business Law Handbooks Library: Vol. 119). (Illus.). 350p. 2000. pap. 99.95 (*0-7397-2017-1*) Intl Business Pubns.
***Myanmar Business Opportunity Yearbook.** Global Investment & Business Center, Inc. Staff. (Global Business Opportunity Yearbooks Library: Vol. 119). (Illus.). 2000. pap. 99.95 (*0-7397-2217-4*) Intl Business Pubns.
***Myanmar Business Opportunity Yearbook: Export-Import, Investment & Business Opportunities.** International Business Publications, U. S. A. Staff & Global Investment Center, U. S. A. Staff. (Global Business Opportunity Yearbooks Library: Vol. 119). (Illus.). 350p. 1999. pap. 99.95 (*0-7397-1317-5*) Intl Business Pubns.
***Myanmar Country Review 2000.** Robert C. Kelly et al. (Illus.). 60p. 1999. pap. 39.95 (*1-58310-543-3*) CountryWatch.
***Myanmar Foreign Policy & Government Guide.** Contrib. by Global Investment & Business Center, Inc. Staff. (World Foreign Policy & Government Library: Vol. 350). (Illus.). 350p. 1999. 99.00 (*0-7397-3613-2*) Intl Business Pubns.
***Myanmar Foreign Policy & Government Guide.** Global Investment & Business Center, Inc. Staff. (World Foreign Policy & Government Library: Vol. 115). (Illus.). 350p. 2000. pap. 99.95 (*0-7397-3817-8*) Intl Business Pubns.
***Myanmar Investment & Business Guide.** Global Investment & Business Center, Inc. Staff. (Global Investment & Business Guide Library: Vol. 119). (Illus.). 2000. pap. 99.95 (*0-7397-1817-7*) Intl Business Pubns.
***Myanmar Investment & Business Guide: Export-Import, Investment & Business Opportunities.** International Business Publications, USA Staff & Global Investment Center, USA Staff. (World Investment & Business Guide Library-99: Vol. 119). (Illus.). 350p. 1999. pap. 99.95 (*0-7397-0314-5*) Intl Business Pubns.
Myanmar Newspaper Reader. Ed. by Luzor. LC 96-86039. 328p. 1997. 54.00 (*1-881265-48-X*) Dunwoody Pr.
Myanmar Style. Elizabeth Moore et al. 220p. 1998. 45.00 (*962-593-397-2*, Periplus Eds) Tuttle Pubng.
Myart. C. Seejoy Belk. 1998. pap. text 11.95 (*0-9620258-8-7*, 26A) Babe Pub.
Myaskovsky: His Life & Work: Music Book Index. Aleksei A. Ikonnikov. 162p. 1993. reprint ed. lib. bdg. 69.00 (*0-7812-9608-0*) Rprt Serv.
Myasthenia Gravis. Ed. by Marc H. De Baets & Hans J. Oosterhuis. LC 92-49515. 288p. 1993. lib. bdg. 198.00 (*0-8493-6343-8*, RC935) CRC Pr.
Myasthenia Gravis. Christian Hermann, Jr. et al. (Illus.). 220p. (C). 1973. text 32.50 (*0-8422-7074-4*) Irvington.
Myasthenia Gravis: European Conference on Myasthenia Gravis, Maastricht, 1st, June 1987. Ed. by M. De Baets et al. (Monographs in Allergy: Vol. 25). (Illus.). viii, 160p. 1988. 109.75 (*3-8055-4736-6*) S Karger.
Myasthenia Gravis: Pathogenesis & Treatment. International Symposium on Myasthenia Gravis, Path. LC 82-113776. (Japan Medical Research Foundation Publication: No. 14). 441p. 1981. reprint ed. pap. 136.80 (*0-608-01548-2*, 206195700001) Bks Demand.
Myasthenia Gravis: The Immunobiology of an Autoimmune Disease. Bianca M. Conti-Fine et al. LC 96-41316. (Neuroscience Intelligence Unit Ser.). 212p. 1996. 99.00 (*1-57059-406-6*) Landes Bioscience.
Myasthenia Gravis & Myasthenic Disorders. Ed. by Andrew Engel. LC 99-10443. (Contemporary Neurology Ser.: No. 56). (Illus.). 336p. 1999. text 98.50 (*0-19-512970-9*) OUP.
Myasthenia Gravis & Related Diseases: Disorders of the Neuromuscular Junction. Ed. by David P. Richman. LC 97-52826. (Annals of the New York Academy of Sciences Ser.: No. 841). 838p. 1998. pap. 160.00 (*1-57331-120-0*) NY Acad Sci.
Myasthenia Gravis & Related Diseases: Disorders of the Neuromuscular Junction. Ed. by David P. Richman. LC 97-52826. (Annals of the New York Academy of Sciences Ser.: No. 841). 838p. 1998. 160.00 (*1-57331-119-7*) NY Acad Sci.
Myasthenia Gravis & Related Disorders: Experimental & Clinical Aspects. Ed. by Audrey S. Penn et al. LC 93-8239. (Annals Ser.: Vol. 681). 1993. write for info. (*0-89766-755-7*); pap. 165.00 (*0-89766-756-5*) NY Acad Sci.
Mybia Cartier. Charlotte Whaley. 397p. 1992. pap. write for info. (*0-9632929-4-3*) Jentry Whaley.
Mycenae. Heinrich Schliemann. LC 66-29424. (Illus.). 1972. reprint ed. 43.95 (*0-405-08931-7*, Pub. by Blom Pubns) Ayer.
Mycenae & the Mycenaean Age. George E. Mylonas. LC 65-17154. (Illus.). 340p. reprint ed. pap. 105.40 (*0-8357-6229-7*, 203428500089) Bks Demand.
Mycenae Paranaenses. Ed. by R. A. Geesteranus & A. A. De Meijer. LC 98-122488. (Verhandelingen der Koninklijke Nederlandse Akademie van Wetenschappen, Afd. Letterkunde, Nieuwe Reeks Ser.: Vol. 97). 172p. 1997. 72.00 (*0-444-85817-2*) Elsevier.
Mycenaean Achaea Pts. 1 & 2: Text & Figures. Athanasios J. Papadopoulos. (Studies in Mediterranean Archaeology: Vol. LV:1-2). (Illus.). 573p. (Orig.). 1979. pap. 165.00 (*91-85058-83-1*) P Astroms.
Mycenaean Athens. P. A. Mountjoy. (Studies in Mediterranean Archaeology & Literature: No. 127). (Illus.). 140p. 1995. pap. 45.00 (*91-7081-073-7*, Pub. by P Astroms) Coronet Bks.
Mycenaean Cult Buildings: A Study of Their Architecture & Function in the Context of the Aegean & the Eastern Mediterrean. Helene Whittaker. (Monographs from the Norwegian Institute at Athens: Vol. 1). (Illus.). 355p. 1997. 87.50 (*82-91626-03-0*) Coronet Bks.
Mycenaean Decorated Pottery: A Guide to Identification. P. A. Mountjoy. (Studies in Mediterranean Archaeology: Vol. LXXIII). (Illus.). 241p. (Orig.). 1986. pap. 125.00 (*91-86098-32-2*, Pub. by P Astroms) Coronet Bks.
Mycenaean Dictionary. Kazansky. (Illus.). (C). text. write for info. (*0-472-10752-6*) U of Mich Pr.
Mycenaean IIIC: LB & Related Pottery in Cyprus. Barbara Kling. (Illus.). 472p. (Orig.). 1989. pap. 157.00 (*91-86098-93-4*) Coronet Bks.
Mycenaean Palace at Knossos. Erik Hallager. (Museum of Mediterranean & Near Eastern Antiquities: Memoir 1). (Illus.). 119p. (Orig.). 1977. pap. 49.50 (*91-7192-367-5*, Pub. by P Astroms) Coronet Bks.
Mycenaean Pictorial Vase Painting. Emily D. Vermeule & Vassos Karageorghis. (Illus.). 424p. 1982. 98.50 (*0-674-59650-1*) HUP.
Mycenaean Pottery: An Introduction. Penelope Mountjoy. (Illus.). 215p. 1993. pap. 32.00 (*0-947816-36-4*, Pub. by Oxford Univ Comm Arch) David Brown.
Mycenaean Pottery III: Plates. Arne Furumark. Ed. by Paul Astrom et al. (Acta Instituti Atheniensis Regni Sueciae Ser.: Series 4, XX: 3). (Illus.). 193p. (Orig.). 1992. pap. 62.50 (*91-7916-026-3*, Pub. by P Astroms) Coronet Bks.
Mycenaean World. John Chadwick. (Illus.). 218p. 1976. text 69.95 (*0-521-21077-1*); pap. text 22.95 (*0-521-29037-6*) Cambridge U Pr.
Mycenaeans. William Taylour. LC 82-50813. (Ancient Peoples & Places Ser.). (Illus.). 180p. 1990. pap. 15.95 (*0-500-27586-6*, Pub. by Thames Hudson) Norton.
Mycenaeans & Europe. Anthony Harding. 1984. text 125.00 (*0-12-324760-8*) Acad Pr.
Mycenaeans & Minoans: Aegean Prehistory in the Light of the Linear B Tablets. 2nd ed. Leonard R. Palmer. LC 79-22315. (Illus.). 368p. 1980. reprint ed. lib. bdg. 37.50 (*0-313-22160-X*, PAMY, Greenwood Pr) Greenwood.
Mycenean World. K. A. Wardle & Diane Wardle. (Classical World Ser.). (Illus.). 140p. (C). 1997. pap. text 18.95 (*1-85399-355-7*, Pub. by Brist Class Pr) Focus Pub-R Pullins.
Mycerinus: The Temples of the Third Pyramid at Giza. George A. Reisner. (Illus.). 400p. 1998. reprint ed. 125.00 (*1-57898-145-X*) Martino Pubng.
Mycobacteria: A Sourcebook, Set, Pt. A. George P. Kubica. Ed. by Lawrence G. Wayne. (Microbiology Ser.: Vol. 15). (Illus.). 704p. 1984. text 550.00 (*0-8247-7009-9*) Dekker.
Mycobacteria: A Sourcebook, Set, Pt. B. George P. Kubica. Ed. by Lawrence G. Wayne. (Microbiology Ser.: Vol. 15). (Illus.). 1024p. 1984. text 550.00 (*0-8247-1917-4*) Dekker.
Mycobacteria: Chemotherapy, Vol. 2. P. A. Jenkins & Pattisapu R. Gangadharam. LC 97-3970. 512p. (C). (gr. 13). 1997. write for info. (*0-412-05441-8*) Kluwer Academic.
***Mycobacteria: Molecular Biology & Virulence.** Colin Ratledge & Jeremy Dale. LC 99-24452. (Illus.). 1999. pap. 185.00 (*0-632-05304-6*) Blackwell Sci.
Mycobacteria Vol. 1: Basic Aspects, Vol. 1. Pattisapu R. Gangadharam & P. A. Jenkins. LC 97-3970. 448p. (C). (gr. 13). 1997. pap. write for info. (*0-412-05451-5*) Kluwer Academic.
Mycobacteria & Human Disease. 2nd ed. John M. Grange. (Arnold Publication). (Illus.). 240p. (C). 1996. text 75.00 (*0-340-64563-6*) OUP.
Mycobacteria Protocols. Tanya Parish & Neil G. Stoker. LC 98-22177. (Methods in Molecular Biology Ser.: Vol. 101). (Illus.). 488p. 1998. 89.50 (*0-89603-471-2*) Humana.
Mycobacterial Infections of Zoo Animals. Ed. by Richard J. Montali. LC 77-60860. (Research Symposia of the National Zoological Park Ser.: No. 1). (Illus.). 276p. 1979. text 30.00 (*0-87474-644-2*, MOMI); pap. text 18.95 (*0-87474-645-0*, MOMIP) Smithsonian.
Mycobacterial Skin Disease. Ed. by Marwali Harahap. (New Clinical Applications Dermatology Ser.). (C). 1989. text 121.50 (*0-7462-0119-2*) Kluwer Academic.
Mycobacterium Avium--Complex Infection: Progress in Research & Treatment. Ed. by Joyce A. Korvick & Constance A. Benson. (Lung Biology in Health & Disease Ser.: Vol. 87). (Illus.), 344p. 1995. text 150.00 (*0-8247-9403-6*) Dekker.
Mycobacterium Tuberculosis: Interactions with the Immune System. M. Bendinelli & H. Friedman. LC 88-4128. (Infectious Agents & Pathogenesis Ser.). (Illus.). 448p. (C). 1988. text 115.00 (*0-306-42724-9*, Kluwer Plenum) Kluwer Academic.
Mycoflora Australis. Rolf Singer. 1969. pap. 160.00 (*3-7682-5429-1*) Lubrecht & Cramer.
Mycogenetics: An Introduction to the General Genetics of Fungi. John H. Burnett. LC 74-13143. 389p. reprint ed. pap. 120.60 (*0-608-18413-6*, 203043500069) Bks Demand.
Mycologia Index, 1967-1988, Vols. 59-80. Ed. by Mary E. Palm et al. LC 57-51730. 496p. 1991. lib. bdg. 82.00 (*0-89327-357-0*) NY Botanical.
Mycological Contributions Celebrating the 70th Birthday of Clark T. Rogerson. Frwd. by Gary J. Samuels. LC 88-29648. (Memoirs Ser.: No. 49). (Illus.). 374p. 1989. pap. text 37.00 (*0-89327-336-8*) NY Botanical.
Mycological Dictionary. 2nd ed. Karl Berger. (CZE, ENG, FRE, GER & LAT.). 432p. 1980. 125.00 (*0-8288-0068-5*, M15339) Fr & Eur.
Mycological Dictionary in Eight Languages: German, English, French, Spanish, Latin, Czech, Polish, Russian. 2nd rev. ed. Karl Berger. (Illus.). 432p. 1980. lib. bdg. 80.00 (*3-437-20220-0*) Lubrecht & Cramer.
Mycological English-Latin Glossary, 1965. Edith K. Cash. (Mycologia Memoirs Ser.: No. 1). 152p. 1965. pap. text 12.50 (*0-945345-37-2*) Lubrecht & Cramer.
Mycological Papers No. 156: A Reappraisal of Asochytula & Ascochytella (Coelomycetes) P. K. Buchanan. 83p. (C). 1987. pap. text 31.50 (*0-85198-579-3*) C A B Intl.
Mycological Papers No. 157: The Tubeufiaceae & Similar Loculoascomycetes. A. Y. Rossman. 71p. (C). 1987. pap. text 31.50 (*0-85198-580-7*) C A B Intl.
Mycological Papers No. 159: Ascochyta II. Species on Monocotyledons (excluding grasses), Cryptograms & Gymnosperms. E. Punithalingam. 235p. (C). 1987. pap. text 41.50 (*0-85198-592-0*) C A B Intl.
Mycological Papers No. 160: Cercospora & Similar Fungi on Yams - Dioscorea Species. N. Pons & B. C. Sutton. (Mycological Paper Ser.: No. 160). 78p. 1989. pap. 36.00 (*0-85198-622-6*) C A B Intl.
Mycological Papers No. 161: Aspergillus Species on Stored Products. Z. Kozakiewicz. 188p. 1989. 63.00 (*0-85198-632-3*) C A B Intl.
Mycological Papers No. 162: Revised Tabular Key to the Species of Phytophthora. D. J. Stamps et al. (Illus.). 1990. pap. 27.00 (*0-85198-683-8*) C A B Intl.
Mycological Papers Vol. 158: Graminicolous Species of Bipolaris, Curvularia, Drechslera, Exserohilum & Their Teleomorphs. A. Sivanesan. 261p. (C). 1987. pap. text 52.00 (*0-85198-587-4*) C A B Intl.
Mycologist's Handbook. D. L. Hawksworth. 231p. 1974. text 21.30 (*0-685-09603-3*) Lubrecht & Cramer.
***Mycology: Proceedings of the 4th China-Japan International Congress of Mycology Zhuhai, China 17 - 19 July 1998 with Poster.** 280p. 1998. 98.00 (*7-80003-419-4*) Intl Academic Pubs.
Mycology in Sustainable Development: Expanding Concepts & Vanishing Borders. Ed. by Mary E. Palm & Ignacio H. Chapela. LC 96-3693. 150p. (C). 1997. 40.00 (*1-887905-01-4*) Pkway Pubs.
Mycoplasma Diseases of Crops. Ed. by Karl Maramorosch & S. P. Raychaudhuri. (Illus.). 450p. 1987. 208.00 (*0-387-96646-3*) Spr-Verlag.
Mycoplasma Protocols. Ed. by Roger J. Miles & Robin A. J. Nicholas. LC 98-4288. (Methods in Molecular Biology Ser.). (Illus.). 336p. 1998. 89.50 (*0-89603-525-5*) Humana.
Mycoplasmas: Molecular Biology & Pathogenesis. Ed. by Jack Maniloff et al. LC 92-49746. (Illus.). 609p. 1992. 109.00 (*1-55581-050-0*) ASM Pr.
Mycoplasmatales & the L-Phase of Bacteria. Ed. by Leonard Hayflick. LC 68-54562. 753p. reprint ed. pap. 200.00 (*0-608-12390-0*, 205568600030) Bks Demand.
Mycoplasmosis in Animals: Laboratory Diagnosis. Ed. by Howard W. Whitford et al. LC 93-24447. (Illus.). 186p. (C). 1994. text 69.95 (*0-8138-2491-5*) Iowa St U Pr.
Mycorhizes, Band XIII. Desire G. Strullu. (Handbuch der Pflanzenanatomie Encyclopedia of Plant Anatomy - Traite d' Anatomie Vegetale Ser.: Teil 2). (GER., Illus.). ix, 198p. 1985. 57.00 (*3-443-14016-5*, DM 96, Pub. by Gebruder Borntraeger) Balogh.
Mycorrhiza. Ed. by A. Varma & B. Hock. 728p. 1995. 249.00 (*3-540-58525-7*) Spr-Verlag.
Mycorrhiza: Structure, Function, Molecular Biology & Biotechnology. Ed. by A. Varma & B. Hock. LC 95-1417. 1995. write for info. (*0-387-58525-7*) Spr-Verlag.
Mycorrhiza: Structure, Function, Molecular Biology & Biotechnology. 2nd ed. Ed. by A. Varma & B. Hock. LC 98-22470. (Illus.). xviii, 702p. 1998. 250.00 (*3-540-63981-0*) Spr-Verlag.
Mycorrhiza Manual. Ed. by A. Varma. LC 97-29903. (Springer Lab Manual Ser.). (Illus.). 350p. 1998. text 99.95 (*3-540-62437-6*) Spr-Verlag.
Mycorrhizae & Plant Health. Ed. by F. L. Pfleger & R. G. Linderman. LC 93-72994. (APS Symposium Ser.). 360p. 1994. pap. 42.00 (*0-89054-158-2*) Am Phytopathol Soc.
Mycorrhizae in Sustainable Agriculture. Ed. by G. J. Bethlenfalvay & R. G. Linderman. LC 92-32096. (Special Publications: No. 54). 124p. 1992. pap. 12.00 (*0-89118-112-1*) Am Soc Agron.
***Mycorrhizal Biology.** K. G. Mukerji et al. LC 99-49587. 340p. 2000. write for info. (*0-306-46294-X*, Kluwer Plenum) Kluwer Academic.
Mycorrhizal Symbiosis. 2nd ed. Ed. by Sally Smith & David J. Read. LC 96-45949. (Illus.). 624p. 1996. text 74.95 (*0-12-652840-3*) Morgan Kaufmann.
Mycoses--Index of New Information & Medical Research Bible. Martha R. Stein. LC 95-16710. 150p. 1995. write for info. (*0-7883-0102-0*); pap. write for info. (*0-7883-0103-9*) ABBE Pubs Assn.
Mycoses in AIDS Patients. Ed. by H. Vanden Bossche et al. (Illus.). 348p. (C). 1990. text 114.00 (*0-306-43704-X*, Kluwer Plenum) Kluwer Academic.
Mycoses International Nomenclature of Diseases Vol. II: Infectious Diseases, 2. (International Nomenclature of Diseases Ser.: No. 2). Date not set. pap. text 15.00 (*92-9036-007-0*) World Health.
Mycosis of the Eye & Its Adnexa. W. Behrens-Baumann. LC 99-35330. (Developments in Ophthalmology Ser.: Vol. 32). (Illus.). xii, 202p. 1999. 195.00 (*3-8055-6915-7*) S Karger.
Mycospaerella Spp. & Their Anamorphs Associated with Leaf Spot Diseases of Eucalyptus. Pedro W. Crous. LC 97-77522. (Mycologia Memoir Ser.: Vol. 21). (Illus.). 170p. 1998. pap. text 49.00 (*0-89054-190-6*) Am Phytopathol Soc.
Mycota: A Comprehensive Treatise on Fungi as Experimental System for Basic & Applied Research. D. T. Wicklow. Ed. by K. Esser et al. (Environmental & Microbial Relationships Ser.: Vol. IV). (Illus.). 385p. 1997. pap. 235.00 (*0-387-58005-0*) Spr-Verlag.
Mycota: A Comprehensive Treatise on Fungi As Experimental Systems for Basic & Applied Research, Vol. 2. A. C. Melton. Ed. by Karl Esser & P. A. Lemke. 648p. 1995. 299.95 (*0-387-58003-4*) Spr-Verlag.

An Asterisk (*) at the beginning of an entry indicates that the title is appearing for the first time.

M

Mycota - a Comprehensive Treatise in Fungi as Experimental Systems for Basic & Applied Research, Vol. 1: Grow, Differentiation & Sexuality, Vol. 1. Ed. by Karl Esser & P. A. Lemke. LC 94-19413. 1994. 219.95 (*0-387-57781-5*) Spr-Verlag.

Mycotaxon Cumulative Index for Volumes XLI-LX (1991-1996) Karen D. Gettelman et al. 296p. 1998. pap. 35.00 (*0-930845-07-2*) Mycotaxon Ltd.

Mycotaxon Cumulative Index for Volumes I-XX, 1974-1984. Richard P. Korf & Susan C. Gruff. LC 75-640802. 232p. (Orig.). 1985. pap. text 17.50 (*0-930845-00-5*) Mycotaxon Ltd.

Mycotaxon Cumulative Index for Volumes XXI-XL, 1984-1991. Richard P. Korf & Susan C. Gruff. 352p. (Orig.). 1991. pap. 30.00 (*0-930845-01-3*) Mycotaxon Ltd.

Mycotic Diseases in Europe. (Euro Reports & Studies Ser.: No. 105). 84p. 1987. pap. text 9.00 (*92-890-1271-4*) World Health.

Mycotoxic Fungi & Chemistry of Mycotoxins. Ed. by Thomas D. Wyllie & Lawrence G. Morehouse. LC 76-43380. (Mycotoxic Fungi, Mycotoxins, Mycotoxicoses Ser.: No. 1). 568p. 1977. reprint ed. pap. 176.10 (*0-7837-8330-2*, 204911700001) Bks Demand.

Mycotoxicoses of Man & Plants: Mycotoxin Control & Regulatory Aspects. Ed. by Thomas D. Wyllie & Lawrence G. Morehouse. LC 78-5168. (Mycotoxic Fungi, Mycotoxins, Mycotoxicoses Ser.: No. 3). (Illus.). 232p. reprint ed. pap. 72.00 (*0-8357-8570-X*, 203493600091) Bks Demand.

Mycotoxin Induced Physiological Responses in Crop Plants. K. K. Sinha. 124p. 1996. pap. 100.00 (*81-7533-016-3*, Pub. by Print Hse) St Mut.

***Mycotoxin Protocols.** Ed. by Mary W. Trucksess & Albert E. Pohland. LC 00-20616. (Methods in Molecular Biology Ser.: Vol. 157). 232p. 2000. 79.50 (*0-89603-623-5*) Humana.

Mycotoxin Teratogenicity & Mutagenicity. A. Wallace Hayes. 144p. 1981. 81.00 (*0-8493-5651-2*, QP632, CRC Reprint) Franklin.

Mycotoxins. (Environmental Health Criteria Ser.: No. 11). 127p. 1979. pap. text 19.00 (*92-4-154071-0*, 1160011) World Health.

Mycotoxins: Formation, Analysis & Significance. John E. Smith & M. O. Moss. LC 84-26953. (Illus.). 154p. 1985. reprint ed. pap. 47.80 (*0-608-02601-8*, 206325900004) Bks Demand.

Mycotoxins & Animal Foods. John E. Smith & Rachel S. Henderson. (Illus.). 864p. 1991. lib. bdg. 395.00 (*0-8493-4904-4*, SF757) CRC Pr.

Mycotoxins & N-Nitroso Compounds: Environmental Risks, 2 vols., Vol. I. Ronald C. Shank. 296p. 1981. 167.00 (*0-8493-5307-6*, RA1242, CRC Reprint) Franklin.

Mycotoxins & N-Nitroso Compounds: Environmental Risks, 2 vols., Vol. II. Ronald C. Shank. 248p. 1981. 141.00 (*0-8493-5308-4*, CRC Reprint) Franklin.

Mycotoxins & Other Fungal Related Food Problems. Ed. by Joseph V. Rodricks. LC 76-4547. (Advances in Chemistry Ser.: No. 149). 1976. 49.95 (*0-8412-0222-2*) Am Chemical.

Mycotoxins & Other Fungal Related Food Problems. Ed. by Joseph V. Rodricks. LC 76-4547. (Advances in Chemistry Ser.: Vol. 149). 422p. 1976. reprint ed. pap. 130.90 (*0-608-03889-X*, 206433600008) Bks Demand.

Mycotoxins & Phycotoxins: Developments in Chemistry, Toxicology & Food Safety. Ed. by M. Miraglia et al. LC 98-70629. 620p. 1998. 175.00 (*1-880293-09-9*) Alaken.

Mycotoxins & Phytoalexins. Raghubir P. Sharma et al. (Telford Press Ser.). 800p. 1991. boxed set 195.00 (*0-8493-8833-3*) CRC Pr.

Mycotoxins & Their Control: Constraints & Opportunities. R. Coker. 73p. 1997. pap. 60.00 (*0-85954-478-8*, Pub. by Nat Res Inst) St Mut.

Mycotoxins, Cancer, & Health. Donna H. Ryan. Ed. by George A. Bray. LC 90-13706. (Pennington Center Nutrition Ser.: Vol. 1). (Illus.). 352p. 1991. text 50.00 (*0-8071-1679-3*) La State U Pr.

Mycotoxins in Agriculture & Food Safety. Ed. by Sinha & Bhatnagar. LC 98-25610. (Illus.). 520p. 1998. text 175.00 (*0-8247-0192-5*) Dekker.

Mycotoxins in Ecological Systems. Ed. by Dilip K. Arora et al. (Handbook of Applied Mycology Ser.: Vol. 5). (Illus.). 464p. 1991. text 235.00 (*0-8247-8551-7*) Dekker.

Mycotoxins in Food. Ed. by Palle Krogh. (Food Science & Technology Ser.). 263p. 1988. text 104.00 (*0-12-426670-3*) Acad Pr.

Mycotoxins in Grain: Compounds Other Than Aflatoxin. Ed. by J. David Miller & Locksley Trenholm. LC 93-73623. (Illus.). 552p. 1994. 159.00 (*0-9624407-5-2*) Eagan Pr.

Mycotoxins, Nephropathy & Urinary Tract Tumors. M. Castegnaro et al. (IARC Scientific Publications: No. 115). (Illus.). 358p. 1992. pap. text 98.00 (*92-832-2115-X*) OUP.

Mycotrophy in Plants: Lectures on the Biology of Mycorrhizae & Related Structures. A. P. Kelley. (Illus.). 223p. 1990. reprint ed. text 37.50 (*0-685-41269-5*, Pub. by Mahendra Pal Singh) Lubrecht & Cramer.

Mycozoenosen Von Wurzel und Stamm Von Jungbaumen Unterschiedlicher Bestandsbegrundungen. Claudia Gorke. (Bibliotheca Mycologica: Vol. 173). (GER.). 1998. 106.00 (*3-443-59075-6*, Pub. by Gebruder Borntraeger) Balogh.

Myel. Oreste Joseph. Ed. by Rita Parisse. (CPR, Illus.). 19p. (J). 1995. pap. 3.00 (*1-885566-04-2*) Oresjozef.

Myelin. 2nd ed. Ed. by Pierre Morell. LC 84-9975. (Illus.). 566p. (C). 1984. text 132.00 (*0-306-41540-2*, Kluwer Plenum) Kluwer Academic.

Myelin: Biology & Chemistry. Russel E. Martenson. 976p. 1992. lib. bdg. 229.00 (*0-8493-8849-X*, QP752) CRC Pr.

Myelination & Demyelination: Implications for Multiple Sclerosis. Ed. by S. U. Kim. (Illus.). 284p. 1989. 75.00 (*0-306-43118-1*, Plenum Trade) Perseus Pubng.

Myelodysplastic Syndromes. Ed. by G. J. Mufti & D. A. Galton. (Illus.). 256p. 1992. text 89.95 (*0-443-04083-4*) Church.

Myelodysplastic Syndromes. Ed. by F. Schmalzi & G. J. Mufti. (Illus.). 340p. 1992. 181.00 (*0-387-52966-7*) Spr-Verlag.

Myelodysplastic Syndromes: Approach to Diagnosis & Treatment. Harold R. Schumacher & Sucha Nand. LC 94-13053. (Illus.). 264p. 1995. 98.50 (*0-89640-266-5*) Igaku-Shoin.

Myelodysplastic Syndromes - Advances in Research & Treatment: Proceedings of the International Symposium on Myelodysplastic Syndrdomes, National Cancer Center, Tokyo, Japan, 13-14 October 1994. International Symposium on Myelodyspastic Syndromes Staff. Ed. by Takeo Nomura. LC 95-4214. (International Congress Ser.: No. 1080). 428p. 1995. 227.25 (*0-444-82050-7*) Elsevier.

Myelography. 4th ed. Robert Shapiro. LC 83-21577. (Illus.). 704p. reprint ed. pap. 200.00 (*0-8357-6313-7*, 203558600096) Bks Demand.

Myeloma: Biology & Management. 2nd ed. Ed. by James Malpas et al. LC 97-18025. (Illus.). 686p. 1998. text 175.00 (*0-19-262882-8*) OUP.

Myeloma Poetry. Muriel R. Kulwin. 60p. 1996. 15.00 (*1-889080-11-X*) Doublem Bks.

Myelopeptides. Rem V. Petrov et al. 200p. 1998. 34.00 (*981-02-3507-0*) World Scientific Pub.

Myers Avenue: Cripple Creek's Red Light District. Leland Feitz. (Illus.). 1990. pap. 2.95 (*0-936564-16-4*) Little London.

Myers-Briggs Type Indicator: A Critical Review & Practical Guide. R. Bayne. 186p. 1996. pap. text 55.00 (*1-56593-353-2*, 0677) Singular Publishing.

Myers-Briggs Type Indicator: Australian Perspectives. Ed. by Mary McGuiness. (C). 1992. 75.00 (*0-86431-128-1*, Pub. by Aust Council Educ Res) St Mut.

Myers' History of West Virginia, 2 vols., Set. S. Myers. 1993. reprint ed. lib. bdg. 105.00 (*0-8328-3087-9*) Higginson Bk Co.

Myers' Literary Guide: The North East. Alan Myers. LC 95-211452. 192p. (Orig.). pap. 17.95 incl. Apple II (*1-85754-199-5*, Pub. by Carcanet Pr) Paul & Co Pubs.

Myersville, Md., Lutheran Baptisms. Margaret E. Myers. Ed. by Donna V. Russell. (Illus.). 70p. 1986. pap. 11.00 (*0-914385-04-6*) Catoctin Pr.

Mykhailo Hrushevsky: The Politics of National Culture. Thomas M. Prymak. 432p. 1987. text 40.00 (*0-8020-5737-3*) U of Toronto Pr.

Mykolas Paskevicius. Mykolas Paskevicius. Ed. & Intro. by Danas Lapkus. LC 94-77355. (LIT., Illus.). 168p. 1995. 35.00 (*0-9617756-9-6*) Galerija.

Myl Life with the Lord. Cassie Vidal. 1999. 12.95 (*0-938645-60-9*) In His Steps.

Myles Keogh: The Life & Legend of an Irish Dragoon with the Seventh Cavalry. Compiled by John P. Langellier. LC 91-65910. (Montana & the West Ser.: Vol. 9). (Illus.). 206p. 1991. 100.00 (*0-912783-21-4*) Upton & Sons.

Myles Munroe on Leadership. Myles Munroe. 1997. pap. 5.99 (*1-56229-115-7*) Pneuma Life Pub.

Myles Textbook for Midwives. 12th ed. Ed. by V. Ruth Bennett & Linda K. Brown. LC 93-3748. 876p. 1993. pap. text 55.95 (*0-443-04581-X*) Church.

Mymaridae (Insecta: Hymenoptera): Introduction & Review of Genera see Fauna of New Zealand Series

Mynarski's Lanc. Bette Page. LC 90-112140. (Illus.). 192p. 1996. 32.00 (*1-55046-006-4*, Pub. by Boston Mills) Genl Dist Srvs.

Myne Owne Ground: Race & Freedom on Virginia's Eastern Shore, 1640-1676. T. H. Breen & Stephen Innes. (Illus.). 152p. 1982. pap. text 19.95 (*0-19-503206-3*) OUP.

***MYOB Accounting Plus Training Guide.** (Illus.). iv, 241p. 2000. pap. text 49.95 (*0-9701403-0-4*) MYOB US Inc.

Myoblast Transfer Therapy. Ed. by R. C. Griggs & G. Karpati. (Advances in Experimental Medicine & Biology Ser.: Vol. 280). (Illus.). 330p. (C). 1990. text 132.00 (*0-306-43714-7*, Kluwer Plenum) Kluwer Academic.

Myocardial & Skeletal Muscle Bioenergetics. Ed. by Nachman Brautbar. LC 86-4883. (Advances in Experimental Medicine & Biology Ser.: Vol. 194). 692p. 1986. 130.00 (*0-306-42237-9*, Plenum Trade) Perseus Pubng.

Myocardial Biopsy: Diagnostic Significance. H. D. Bolte. (Illus.). 180p. 1980. 43.00 (*0-387-10063-6*) Spr-Verlag.

Myocardial Contrast Two Dimensional Echocardiography. Ed. by Samuel Meerbaum & Richard Melzer. (Developments in Cardiovascular Medicine Ser.). (C). 1989. text 182.50 (*0-7923-0205-2*) Kluwer Academic.

Myocardial Damage: Early Detection by Novel Biochemical Markers, Vol. 205. Juan C. Kaski & David W. Holt. LC 98-8191. (Developments in Cardiovascular Medicine Ser.). 212p. 1998. 82.00 (*0-7923-5140-1*) Kluwer Academic.

Myocardial Energy Metabolism. Ed. by J. W. De Jong. (Developments in Cardiovascular Medicine Ser.). (C). 1988. text 195.50 (*0-89838-394-3*) Kluwer Academic.

Myocardial Hypertrophy. Franklin & Harold Sandler. 1990. 60.00 (*0-88258-023-X*) Howard U Pr.

Myocardial Hypertrophy & Failure. fac. ed. Ed. by Norman R. Alpert. LC 83-3407. (Perspectives in Cardiovascular Research Ser.: No. 7). (Illus.). 720p. pap. 200.00 (*0-7837-7414-1*, 204720900006) Bks Demand.

***Myocardial Infarction.** Springhouse Corporation Staff. LC 99-32918. 1999. pap. 18.95 (*1-58255-009-3*) Springhouse Corp.

Myocardial Infarction: From Trials to Practice. Ed. by Stephen G. Ball. 224p. 1995. 75.00 (*1-871816-26-2*, Pub. by Wrightson Biomed) Taylor & Francis.

Myocardial Infarction: Measurement & Intervention, Developments in Cardiovascular Medicine, No. 14. Ed. by Galen S. Wagner. 500p. 1982. text 249.00 (*90-247-2513-5*) Kluwer Academic.

Myocardial Infarction: Proceedings of the Cardiovascular Disease Conference, 3rd, Snowmass at Aspen, CO, Jan. 1972. Cardiovascular Disease Conference Staff. Ed. by J. H. Vogel. (Advances in Cardiology Ser.: Vol. 9). 1973. 85.25 (*3-8055-1373-9*) S Karger.

Myocardial Infarction at Young Age: Proceedings. Ed. by H. Roskamm. (Illus.). 228p. 1982. 39.95 (*0-387-11090-9*) Spr-Verlag.

Myocardial Infarction Community Registers. (Public Health in Europe Ser.: No. 5). 232p. 1976. 22.00 (*92-9020-124-X*, 1320005) World Health.

Myocardial Infarction in the Spectrum of Ischemic Heart Disease: Proceedings of the Symposium, March 1977. Symposium, Palm Springs, Calif. Staff. Ed. by J. R. See et al. (Advances in Cardiology Ser.: Vol. 23). (Illus.). 1978. 76.75 (*3-8055-2753-5*) S Karger.

Myocardial Injury: Laboratory Diagnosis. Johannes Mair & Bernd Puschendorf. LC 96-27642. (Medical Intelligence Unit Ser.). 204p. 1996. 89.95 (*1-57059-303-5*) Landes Bioscience.

Myocardial Ischemia. Ed. by Naranjan S. Dhalla et al. (Developments in Cardiovascular Medicine Ser.). 1987. text 161.50 (*0-89838-866-X*) Kluwer Academic.

Myocardial Ischemia: Mechanisms, Reperfusion, Protection. Ed. by M. Karmazyn. 1996. 189.95 (*0-8176-5269-8*) Birkhauser.

Myocardial Ischemia: Mechanisms, Reperfusion, Protection, Vol. 76. Ed. by M. Karmazyn. 528p. 1996. 189.95 (*3-7643-5269-8*) Birkhauser.

Myocardial Ischemia & Arrhythmia. Ed. by M. Zehender et al. 276p. 1995. 67.00 (*0-387-91455-2*) Spr-Verlag.

Myocardial Ischemia & Reperfusion. Michael V. Cohen. LC 98-7849. (Developments in Molecular & Cellular Biochemistry Ser.). 1998. write for info. (*0-7923-8173-4*) Kluwer Academic.

Myocardial Ischemia Arrhytmia. 1995. 73.95 (*3-7985-0956-5*) Spr-Verlag.

Myocardial Metabolism, 2. V. N. Smirnov & A. Katz. (Cardiology of the Soviet Medical Reviews Supplement, Section A,: Vol 2). xii, 674p. 1987. text 436.00 (*3-7186-0311-X*) Gordon & Breach.

Myocardial Perfusion, Reperfusion, Coronary Venous Retroperfusion. Ed. by Samuel Meerbaum. 160p. 1990. 102.00 (*0-387-91362-9*) Spr-Verlag.

Myocardial Preconditioning. Cherry L. Wainwright & James R. Parratt. (Medical Intelligence Unit Ser.). 266p. 1995. 99.00 (*1-57059-333-7*) Landes Bioscience.

Myocardial Preservation, Preconditioning & Adaptation. Dipak K. Das et al. LC 96-21067. (Annals of the New York Academy of Sciences: Vol. 793). 1996. 150.00 (*1-57331-024-7*) NY Acad Sci.

Myocardial Preservation, Preconditioning, & Adaptation. Dipak K. Das et al. LC 96-21067. (Annals of the New York Academy of Sciences). 1996. pap. 150.00 (*1-57331-025-5*) NY Acad Sci.

Myocardial Protection: The Pathophysiology of Reperfusion & Reperfusion Injury. Ed. by Derek M. Yellon & Robert B. Jennings. LC 91-32899. (Illus.). 224p. reprint ed. pap. 69.50 (*0-608-05794-0*, 205975900007) Bks Demand.

Myocardial Protection & the KATP Channel, No. 179. Ed. by Derek M. Yellon & Garrett J. Gross. LC 95-41178. (DICM - Developments in Cardiovascular Medicine Ser.: Vol. 179). 232p. (C). 1996. text 151.50 (*0-7923-3791-3*) Kluwer Academic.

Myocardial Protection by Calcium Antagonists. Ed. by Lionel H. Opie. 195p. 1994. pap. 79.95 (*0-471-07669-4*) Wiley.

Myocardial Protection in Cardiac Surgery. Ed. by Arthur J. Roberts. (Cardiothoracic Surgery Ser.: Vol. 3). (Illus.). 640p. 1987. text 250.00 (*0-8247-7638-0*) Dekker.

Myocardial Revascularization: A Surgical Atlas. Quentin R. Stiles et al. LC 75-30304. 1976. 49.00 (*0-316-81500-4*, Little Brwn Med Div) Lppncott W & W.

Myocardial Revascularization Bibliography. Ed. by Joe R. Utley. LC 89-81062. (Cardiothoracic Surgery Monographs). 600p. 1989. pap. text 50.00 (*0-9623617-7-1*) Cardiothoracic Rsch.

Myocardial Revascularization in Acute Conditions. Ed. by S. G. Degre. (Bibliotheca Cardiologica Ser.: No. 39). (Illus.). vi, 146p. 1986. 100.00 (*3-8055-4142-2*) S Karger.

***Myocardial Viability.** 2nd ed. Ami E. Iskandrian & E. Van Der Wall. LC 99-89525. (Illus.). 2000. write for info. (*0-7923-6161-X*) Kluwer Academic.

***Myocardial Viability: A Clinical & Scientific Treatise.** Ed. by Vasken Dilsizian. LC 99-39509. (Illus.). 550p. 1999. 125.00 (*0-87993-437-9*) Futura Pub.

Myocardial Viability: Detection & Clinical Relevance. Ed. by Abdulmassih S. Iskandrian & Ernst E. Van Der Wall. LC 94-13373. (Developments in Cardiovascular Medicine Ser.: Vol. 154). 212p. (C). 1994. text 148.50 (*0-7923-2813-2*) Kluwer Academic.

Myocardium. 2nd ed. Ed. by Glenn A. Langer. LC 97-15596. (Illus.). 405p. 1997. text 69.95 (*0-12-436570-1*) Morgan Kaufmann.

Myocardium: Proceedings. Conference on Canberra, 1973. Ed. by Ralph Reader. (Advances in Cardiology Ser.: Vol. 12). 300p. 1974. 117.50 (*3-8055-1690-8*) S Karger.

Myoclonus. fac. ed. Ed. by Stanley Fahn et al. LC 85-25798. (Advances in Neurology Ser.: No. 43). (Illus.). 750p. pap. 200.00 (*0-7837-7192-4*, 204710700005) Bks Demand.

Myodocopid Ostracoda (Halocypridina Cladocopina) from Anchialine Caves in the Bahamas, Canary Islands & Mexico. Louis S. Kornicker & Thomas M. Iliffe. LC 97-35364. (Smithsonian Contributions to Zoology Ser.: Vol. 599). (Illus.). 97p. reprint ed. pap. 30.10 (*0-608-09837-X*, 207080700007) Bks Demand.

Myodocopid Ostracoda of Enewetak & Bikini Atolls. Louis S. Kornicker. LC 90-10359. (Smithsonian Contributions to Zoology Ser.: No. 505). 144p. reprint ed. pap. 44.70 (*0-8357-2795-5*, 203992200014) Bks Demand.

Myodocopid Ostracoda of Hydrothermal Vents in the Eastern Pacific Ocean. Louis S. Kornicker. LC 90-23102. (Smithsonian Contributions to Zoology Ser.: No. 516). (Illus.). 50p. reprint ed. pap. 30.00 (*0-7837-0545-X*, 204087300019) Bks Demand.

Myodocopid Ostracoda of the Benthedi Expedition, 1977, to the NE Mozambique Channel, Indian Ocean. Louis S. Kornicker. LC 92-20590. (Smithsonian Contributions to Zoology Ser.: No. 531). (Illus.). 247p. reprint ed. pap. 76.60 (*0-7837-4412-9*, 204415600012) Bks Demand.

Myoe the Dreamkeeper: Fantasy & Knowledge in Early Kamakura Buddhism. George J. Tanabe, Jr. LC 92-31990. (Illus.). 295p. 1993. text 35.00 (*0-674-59700-1*) HUP.

***Myofascial & Fascial-Ligamentous Approaches in Osteopathic Manipulative Medicine.** Harry Friedman et al. LC 00-131503. (Illus.). 120p. 2000. pap. 39.95 (*0-9701841-1-5*) S F I M M S Pr.

Myofascial Exams & Biofeedback: Can EMG Validate Trigger Points?, 3 of 3. Barbara J. Headley & Barbara A. North. (Illus.). 101p. (Orig.). 1990. pap. 14.00 (*0-929538-08-0*) Innovat Systems.

Myofascial Manipulation. Robert Cantu. 190p. 1992. 75.00 (*0-8342-0310-3*) Aspen Pub.

***Myofascial Manipulation.** 2nd ed. Robert Cantu. 2000. 75.00 (*0-8342-1779-1*) Aspen Pub.

Myofascial Pain & Dysfunction: The Trigger Point Manual, Vol. 1. Janet G. Travell & David G. Simons. (Illus.). 714p. 1983. 95.00 (*0-683-08366-X*) Lppncott W & W.

Myofascial Pain & Dysfunction: The Trigger Point Manual, Vol. 2. Janet G. Travell & David G. Simons. (Illus.). 626p. 1992. 95.00 (*0-683-08367-8*) Lppncott W & W.

Myofascial Release & It's Application to Neuro-Developmental Treatment. Regi Boehme. (Illus.). 87p. (Orig.). (C). 1991. pap. text 20.00 (*1-879801-00-0*) Boehme Wkshps.

Myofascial Release Manual. 2nd ed. Carol J. Manheim. LC 94-13677. (Illus.). 214p. (C). 1994. pap. 39.00 (*1-55642-241-5*) SLACK Inc.

***Myofascial Release Manual.** 3rd ed. Carol J. Manheim. 214p. (C). 2000. pap. text 40.00 (*1-55642-452-3*) SLACK Inc.

Myologik Vol. 3: Atlas of Human Pectoral Musculature in Clay. Jon Zahourek. (Myologic Anatomy Ser.). (Illus.). 122p. 1995. pap. text 19.95 (*1-887087-03-6*) Zahourek Systs.

Myologik Vol. 4: Atlas of Human Pelvic Musculature in Clay. Jon Zahourek. (Myologic Anatomy Ser.). (Illus.). 126p. 1995. pap. text 19.95 (*1-887087-04-4*) Zahourek Systs.

Myologik Vol. 5: Atlas of Human Extrinsic Musculature in Clay. Jon Zahourek. (Myologic Anatomy Ser.). 123p. (C). 1995. pap. text 19.95 (*1-887087-05-2*) Zahourek Systs.

Myologik Atlas Series: Axial, Viceral, Pectoral, Pelvic, Extrinsic. 2nd ed. Jon Zahourek. Ed. by Kenneth Morgareidge. (Atlas of Human Musculature in Clay Ser.: Vols. 1-5). (Illus.). (Orig.). 1997. pap. 19.95 (*1-887087-02-8*, ZSP-MA-0009) Zahourek Systs.

Myology, 1. 2nd ed. Andrew G. Engel. write for info. (*0-07-019558-7*) McGraw.

Myology, 2. 2nd ed. Andrew G. Engel. write for info. (*0-07-019559-5*) McGraw.

Myology, 2 vols., Set. 2nd ed. Ed. by Andrew G. Engel & Clara Franzini-Armstrong. (Illus.). 1932p. 1994. 350.00 (*0-07-911134-3*) McGraw-Hill HPD.

***Myomectomy.** Eric J. Bieber & Victoria M. Maclin. LC 98-21524. (Illus.). 310p. 1998. 105.00 (*0-86542-381-4*) Blackwell Sci.

Myopain '95: Abstracts from the 3rd World Congress of Myofacial Pain & Fibromyalgia, San Antonio, Texas, U. S. A. July 30-August 3, 1995. Ed. by I. Jon Russell. LC 95-23108. 1995. 35.00 (*0-7890-0000-8*, Hawrth Medical) Haworth Pr.

Myopain '98: Abstracts from the 4th World Congress on Myofascial Pain & Fibromyalgia, Silvi Marina, Italy, August 24-27, 1998. Leonardo Vecchiet & Maria A. Giamberardino. LC 98-22001. (Journal of Musculoskeletal Pain Ser.). 1998. 40.00 (*0-7890-0549-2*, Hawrth Medical) Haworth Pr.

Myopathies. Ed. by Pierre J. Vinken et al. LC 92-48375. 686p. 1992. 307.00 (*0-444-81281-4*) Elsevier.

Myopia: Prevalence & Progression. National Research Council, Committee on Vision Sta. 126p. 1989. pap. text 15.00 (*0-309-04081-7*) Natl Acad Pr.

Myopia & Nearwork. Mark Rosenfield & Bernard Gilmartin. LC 98-10422. 232p. 1998. text 65.00 (*0-7506-3784-6*) Buttrwrth-Heinemann.

Myopia & the Control of Eye Growth - Symposium No. 155. CIBA Foundation Staff. LC 90-13012. (CIBA Foundation Symposium Ser.: No. 155). 266p. 1991. 128.00 (*0-471-92692-2*) Wiley.

An Asterisk (*) at the beginning of an entry indicates that the title is appearing for the first time.

*Myopia Control Vol. 39-3: Behavioral Aspects of Vision Care. (Illus.). 162p. 1998. pap. 20.00 (0-943599-25-3) OEPF.

Myopia Myth: The Truth about Nearsightedness & How to Prevent It. Donald S. Rehm. LC 83-80453. (Illus.). 165p. 1983. reprint ed. pap. 15.00 (0-9608476-0-X) Intl Myopia.

Myopia Updates: Proceedings of the 6th International Conference on Myopia. Ed. by Takashi Tokoro. LC 97-30100. (Illus.). xiv, 414p. 1997. text 149.00 (4-431-70199-0) Spr-Verlag.

*Myopia Updates II. International Conference on Myopia Staff. Ed. by L. L. Lin et al. LC 99-51551. (Illus.). xii, 176p. 2000. pap. 90.00 (4-431-70275-X) Spr-Verlag.

Myopic Development & Cultural Lens. Sukant K. Chaudhury. (C). 1992. 19.00 (81-210-0309-1, Pub. by Inter-India Pubns) S Asia.

Myopic Grandeur: The Ambivalence of French Foreign Policy Toward the Far East, 1919-1945. John E. Dreifort. LC 91-11434. 352p. 1992. 35.00 (0-87338-441-5) Kent St U Pr.

Myosin. 2nd ed. James R. Sellers. LC 99-13741. (Protein Profile Ser.). (Illus.). 252p. 1999. pap. text 50.00 (0-19-850509-4) OUP.

MYP-FORTH Professional Applications Development System (PADS) Manual. Thomas E. Wempe. Ed. by Glen B. Haydon. (MVP-Forth Bks.: Vol. 8). 320p. pap. 55.00 (0-317-56528-1) Mntn View Pr.

Myra Bradwell: First Woman Lawyer. Elizabeth Wheaton. LC 96-37082. (Notable Americans Ser.). (Illus.). 96p. (YA). (gr. 5 up). 1997. lib. bdg. 18.95 (1-883846-17-X) M Reynolds.

Myra Breckinridge & Myron. Gore Vidal. LC 87-40002. 416p. 1997. pap. 14.95 (0-14-118028-5) Viking Penguin.

Myra Breckinridge & Myron. Gore Vidal. LC 87-40002. (Vintage Contemporaries Ser.). 432p. 1987. pap. 15.00 (0-394-75444-1) Vin Bks.

*Myra Inman: A Diary of the Civil War in East Tennessee. Ed. by William R. Snell. (Illus.). 304p. 2000. 29.95 (0-86554-590-1) Mercer Univ Pr.

Myra Sims. Janis Owens. LC 98-24079. 480p. 1999. 21.95 (1-56164-177-4) Pineapple Pr.

Myra's Lightning. 1993. pap. 4.50 (0-8216-5098-X, Univ Books) Carol Pub Group.

Myrelaion (Bodrum Camii) in Istanbul: With an Appendix on the Excavated Pottery by John W. Hayes. Cecil L. Striker. LC 81-5863. (Illus.). 99p. 1981. reprint ed. pap. 30.70 (0-7837-9456-8, 206019800004) Bks Demand.

Myriad Chronicles. Michales W. Joy. 349p. 1999. 17.95 (0-7414-0153-3) Buy Books.

Myriad Global Crises of the 1980's & the Nuclear World since World War II. Raya Dunayevskaya. 64p. 1986. pap. 2.00 (0-914441-27-2) News & Letters.

Myriad-Minded Shakespeare: Essays on the Tragedies, Problem Comedies & Shakespeare the Man. 2nd ed. E. A. Honigmann. LC 97-26827. 290p. 1997. pap. 18.95 (0-312-17753-4) St Martin.

Myriad of Autumn Leaves: Japanese Art from the Kurt & Millie Gitter Collection. Stephen Addiss et al. LC 83-43150. (Illus.). 295p. 1983. pap. 29.95 (0-89494-017-1) New Orleans Mus Art.

Myriad of Minstrels. Marinell Harriman & Robert Harriman. (Illus.). 32p. (Orig.). (J). (gr. 5-7). pap. 3.50 (0-940920-00-X) Drollery Pr.

Myriad Worlds: Buddhist Cosmology in Abhidharma, Kalachakra & Dzog-Chen. Jamgon Kongtrul. 304p. 1995. pap. 22.95 (1-55939-033-6) Snow Lion Pubns.

Myriadminded Man: Jottings on Joyce. Ed. by R. M. Bosinelli et al. 296p. 1995. pap. 22.95 (88-8091-438-3) Paul & Co Pubs.

Myriam & the Mystic Brotherhood. Maude L. Howard. 370p. 1981. pap. 32.00 (0-89540-105-3, SB-105) Sun Pub.

Myriam & the Mystic Brotherhood. Maude L. Howard. 370p. 1963. reprint ed. spiral bd. 18.50 (0-7873-1202-9) Hlth Research.

Myriam & the Mystic Brotherhood (1924) Maude L. Howard. 370p. 1996. reprint ed. pap. 24.95 (1-56459-903-5) Kessinger Pub.

Myriam Mendilow: The Mother of Jerusalem. Phyllis Cytron. LC 93-15119. (YA). (gr. 5 up). 1993. lib. bdg. 23.93 (0-8225-4919-0, Lerner Publctns) Lerner Pub.

Myricks Massachusetts: A Frming Settlement, a Railroad Village. Gail E. Terry. LC 99-173659. 200 p. 1998. 21.50 (0-7884-1005-9) Heritage Bk.

Myrna: Rin, Pt. 10. Mark Dunster. 30p. 1982. pap. 4.00 (0-89642-084-1) Linden Pubs.

Myrna Mack Case: An Update. National Academy of Sciences Staff et al. LC 98-231770. 16p. (C). 1998. pap. text 10.00 (0-309-06077-X) Natl Acad Pr.

Myrna Never Sleeps. Beth Peterson. LC 93-8301. (J). (gr. 2-6). 1995. 13.00 (0-689-31893-6) Atheneum Yung Read.

Myron Cohen's Big Joke Book. Myron Cohen. 410p. 1983. reprint ed. pap. 5.95 (0-8065-0853-1, Citadel Pr) Carol Pub Group.

Myron Goldfinger Architect. Myron Goldfinger. 220p. 1993. 50.00 (0-9633144-0-8) Artium Bks.

Myron Hunt, 1868 to 1952: The Search for a Regional Architecture. Ed. by Jay Belloli. LC 84-81891. (California Architecture & Architects Ser.: No. 4). (Illus.). 120p. (Orig.). 1984. pap. 24.50 (0-912158-90-5) Hennessey.

Myron Lechay (1898-1972) Lewis Kachur. (Illus.). 1994. pap. 5.00 (0-945936-13-3) Spanierman Gallery.

Myron Safford Webb: His Log Book, 1840-1841. Myron S. Webb. (Illus.). 122p. (Orig.). 1985. pap. 7.50 (0-9607906-5-9) ACETO Bookmen.

Myron Smith Towne & the Meaning of Success, 1829-1918. Ruth W. Towne. LC 97-26674. (Illus.). 298p. 1998. 25.00 (0-943549-50-7) Truman St Univ.

Myron T. Herrick, Friend of France. Thomas B. Mott. 1993. reprint ed. lib. bdg. 89.00 (0-7812-5392-6) Rprt Serv.

Myrour of Recluses: A Middle English Translation of Speculum Inclusorum. Ed. by Marta P. Harley. 128p. (C). 1995. 26.50 (0-8386-3589-X) Fairleigh Dickinson.

Myroure of Our Lady. Ed. by J. H. Blunt. (EETS, ES Ser.: No. 19). 1974. reprint ed. 54.00 (0-527-00232-1) Periodicals Srv.

Myrrh. Judith Roche. 100p. (Orig.). 1993. pap. 11.00 (0-930773-30-6) Black Heron Pr.

Myrrh, Aloes, Pollen & Other Traces. Silvano Scannerini. 1996. pap. 39.95 (0-85439-538-5, Pub. by St Paul Pubns) St Mut.

Myrrhs: A Book of Poems for the Los Angeles Bicentennial. Mark Dunster. 20p. (Orig.). 1981. pap. 4.00 (0-89642-078-7) Linden Pubs.

Myrrour of Modestie: Incl: Morando: The Tritameron of Love, Pts. 1 & 2: Arbasto: The Anatomie of Fortune, 1584-1587 see Life & Complete Works in Prose & Verse of Robert Greene

Myrsilus of Methymna: Hellenistic Paradoxographer. Steven Jackson. 124p. 1995. pap. 34.00 (90-256-1086-2, Pub. by AM Hakkert) BookLink Distributors.

Myrtilla Miner. Ed. by Ellen M. O'Connor. LC 79-89384. (Black Heritage Library Collection). 1977. 16.95 (0-8369-8640-7) Ayer.

Myrtilla Miner: A Memoir. Ellen M. O'Connor & Myrtilla Miner. LC 73-92235. (American Negro, Ser. 3). 1970. reprint ed. 18.95 (0-405-01933-5) Ayer.

*Myrtle Allen's Cooking at Ballymaloe House. Myrtle Allen. 2000. 27.50 (1-58479-042-3) Stewart Tabori & Chang.

Myrtle & the Rose. Annie Messina. Tr. & Intro. by Jessie Bright. LC 97-41902. 158p. (Orig.). 1997. pap. 12.50 (0-934977-45-3) Italica Pr.

Myrtle Beach Dine-a-Mate Book. 208p. 1996. pap. text 25.00 (1-57393-070-9) Dine-A-Mate.

Myrtle Fillmore: Mother of Unity. Thomas E. Witherspoon. LC 77-78221. (Illus.). 306p. 1977. 12.95 (0-87159-102-2) Unity Bks.

*Myrtle Fillmore: Mother of Unity. 3rd rev. ed. Thomas E. Witherspoon. LC 99-42591. 295p. 2000. pap. 12.95 (0-87159-258-4, 23) Unity Bks.

Myrtle Fillmore's Healing Letters. Myrtle Fillmore. 152p. 1936. 7.95 (0-87159-103-0) Unity Bks.

Myrtle Learns About Asthma see Myrtle Teachable Moments Series

Myrtle Learns About Dangerous Situations see Myrtle Teachable Moments Series

Myrtle Learns About Diabetes see Myrtle Teachable Moments Series

Myrtle Learns About Hygiene see Myrtle Teachable Moments Series

Myrtle Learns About Lice see Myrtle Teachable Moments Series

Myrtle Learns About Medicine see Myrtle Teachable Moments Series

Myrtle Learns About Safety see Myrtle Teachable Moments Series

Myrtle Learns About Seizures see Myrtle Teachable Moments Series

Myrtle Learns How You Catch an Illness see Myrtle Teachable Moments Series

Myrtle Learns to Eat Well see Myrtle Teachable Moments Series

Myrtle Learns to Get Along see Myrtle Teachable Moments Series

Myrtle Learns to Make Friends see Myrtle Teachable Moments Series

Myrtle Learns to Take Care of Boo Boos see Myrtle Teachable Moments Series

Myrtle Learns Why Exercise is Important see Myrtle Teachable Moments Series

Myrtle Makes a Choice see Myrtle Teachable Moments Series

*Myrtle of Willendorf. Rebecca O'Connell. 128p. (YA). (gr. 7 up). 2000. 15.95 (1-886910-52-9, Pub. by Front Str) Publishers Group.

Myrtle Point: The Changing Land & People of a Lower Patuxent River Community. Stuart A. Reeve et al. (Occasional Papers: No. 3). (Illus.). 209p. 1991. spiral bd. 18.00 (1-878399-09-8) Div Hist Cult Progs.

Myrtle Teachable Moments Series, 16 vols. Saitofi Anne Deem. Incl. Myrtle Learns About Asthma. (Illus.). 8p. (J). (ps-3). 1998. pap. text 7.95 (1-930694-00-8); Myrtle Learns About Dangerous Situations. (Illus.). 8p. (J). (ps-3). 1998. pap. text 7.95 (1-930694-03-2); Myrtle Learns About Diabetes. (Illus.). 12p. (J). (ps-3). 1998. pap. text 7.95 (1-930694-04-0); Myrtle Learns About Hygiene. (Illus.). 8p. (J). (ps-3). 1998. pap. text 7.95 (1-930694-09-1); Myrtle Learns About Lice. (Illus.). 12p. (J). (ps-3). 1998. pap. text 7.95 (1-930694-11-3); Myrtle Learns About Medicine. (Illus.). 8p. (J). (ps-3). 1998. pap. text 7.95 (1-930694-12-1); Myrtle Learns About Safety. (Illus.). 8p. (J). (ps-3). 1998. pap. text 7.95 (1-930694-13-X); Myrtle Learns About Seizures. (Illus.). 8p. (J). (ps-3). 1998. pap. text 7.95 (1-930694-14-8); Myrtle Learns How You Catch an Illness. (Illus.). 8p. (J). (ps-3). 1998. pap. text 7.95 (1-930694-10-5); Myrtle Learns to Eat Well. (Illus.). 12p. (J). (ps-3). 1998. pap. text 7.95 (1-930694-05-9); Myrtle Learns to Get Along. (Illus.). 8p. (J). (ps-3). 1998. pap. text 7.95 (1-930694-08-3); Myrtle Learns to Make Friends. (Illus.). 8p. (J). (ps-3). 1998. pap. text 7.95 (1-930694-07-5); Myrtle Learns to Take Care of Boo Boos. (Illus.). 12p. (J). (ps-3). 1998. pap. text 7.95 (1-930694-01-6); Myrtle Learns Why Exercise is Important. (Illus.). 8p. (J). 1998. pap. text 7.95 (1-930694-06-7); Myrtle Makes a Choice. (Illus.). 8p. (J). (ps-3). 1998. pap. text 7.95 (1-930694-02-4); Myrtle's Friend is Very Sick. (Illus.). 8p. (J). (ps-3). 1998. pap. text 7.95 (1-930694-15-6); (Illus.). (J). Set pap. text 114.48 (1-930694-16-4) Myrtle Learns.

Myrtle's Friend is Very Sick see Myrtle Teachable Moments Series

Myrtlewood Grove. La Plante Royal Staff. 1994. pap. text 12.95 (1-881116-94-8) Black Forest Pr.

*Myrtlewood Grove-Revisited. Royal LaPlante. Ed. by Mary Inbody. 226p. 2000. pap. 12.95 (1-58275-015-7) Black Forest Pr.

Myself. rev. ed. Marlene J. McCracken & Robert A. McCracken. (Themes Ser.). (Illus.). 92p. 1984. pap. 12.00 (0-920541-78-X) Peguis Pubs Ltd.

Myself: The Autobiography of John R. Commons. John R. Commons. (Illus.). 222p. 1963. pap. 9.95 (0-299-02924-7) U of Wis Pr.

Myself & I. Janet Lambert. 20.95 (0-8488-0128-8) Amereon Ltd.

Myself & I. Norma Johnston. LC 99-60482. (Keeping Days Ser.). 210p. (YA). 1999. reprint ed. pap. 16.00 (1-892323-33-8, Pierce Harris Pr) Vivisphere.

Myself & Other Strangers. Phyllis Katz. LC 94-96751. (Illus.). 108p. (Orig.). 1995. pap. 9.95 (0-9631335-1-9) LChaim Pub.

Myself & Others. 1979. 5.00 (0-944675-31-X) Amer Forum.

Myself Exactly. Jack Libert. (Illus.). (Orig.). 1971. pap. 10.00 (0-911732-56-X) Irego.

Myself Has Come Home. Pennimo. (Illus.). 75p. 1997. 24.95 (0-9661543-1-2); pap. 11.95 (0-9661543-0-4) D A Meaux.

Myself in Family Context. 3rd ed. Herbert Goldenberg. (Counseling Ser.). 1991. pap. 20.95 (0-534-13747-4) Brooks-Cole.

Myself in the Street: Poems. Tyler Bootman. (Orig.). 1966. 4.50 (0-8079-0087-7); pap. 1.95 (0-8079-0088-5) October.

*Myself When I Am Real: The Life & Music of Charles Mingus. Gene Santoro. LC ML418.M45S26 2000. (Illus.). 448p. 2000. 30.00 (0-19-509733-5) OUP.

Myself When Young. Florence M. Ratcliffe. (C). 1989. text 39.00 (1-872795-42-0, Pub. by Pentland Pr) St Mut.

Myself with Others: Selected Essays. Carlos Fuentes. LC 87-7448. 320p. 1988. 19.95 (0-374-21750-5) FS&G.

*Mysery Shopping. 2nd ed. James Poynter. 134p. 1998. per. 44.00 (0-7872-5540-8, 41554001) Kendall-Hunt.

Myshlenie (Thinking) The Sixth Book of Poems. Michael Jupp. (RUS., Illus.). 224p. (Orig.). 1991. pap. 35.00 (0-911971-75-0) Effect Pub.

Mysids in Fisheries. T. P. Nesler & E. P. Bergersen. LC 91-71560. (Symposium Ser.: No. 9). 199p. 1991. pap. 42.00 (0-913235-71-7, 540.09) Am Fisheries Soc.

Mysore & Coorg from the Inscriptions. B. Lewis Rice. (Illus.). 256p. 1986. reprint ed. write for info. (0-8364-1700-3, Pub. by Manohar) S Asia.

Mysore Royal Dasara. Swami Sivapriyananda. 1995. 150.00 (81-7017-331-0, Pub. by Abhinav) S Asia.

Mysore Tribes & Castes, 5 vols. L. K. Iyer. 1988. reprint ed. 280.00 (0-8364-2535-9, Pub. by Mittal Pubs Dist) S Asia.

*MySQL. (Sams Teach Yourself... in 21 Days Ser.). 650p. 2000. 39.99 (0-672-31914-4) Sams.

MySQL & mSQL. Randy J. Yarger et al. Ed. by Andy Oram. (Nutshell Ser.). (Illus.). 500p. 1999. pap. 34.95 (1-56592-434-7) OReilly & Assocs.

Myst. Straub. pap. 9.98 (0-671-04525-3) S&S Trade.

*Myst: Prima's Official Strategy Guide. Rick Barba & Rusel DeMaria. (Value Ser.). 2000. pap. 9.99 (0-7615-2894-6) Prima Pub.

Myst: The Book of Atrus. David Wingrove & Robyn Miller. (Illus.). 304p. (J). 1995. 22.95 (0-7868-6159-2, Pub. by Hyperion) Time Warner.

Myst: The Book of Atrus. David Wingrove et al. (Illus.). 422p. (J). 1996. mass mkt. 5.99 (0-7868-8188-7, Pub. by Hyperion) Time Warner.

Myst: The Book of D'Ni. Rand Miller & David Wingrove. LC 97-23999. (Illus.). 336p. (J). 1997. 23.45 (0-7868-6161-4, Pub. by Hyperion) Time Warner.

Myst: The Book of D'Ni. Rand Miller & David Wingrove. 528p. (J). 1998. mass mkt. 6.99 (0-7868-8942-X, Pub. by Hyperion) Time Warner.

Myst: The Book of Ti'Ana. Rand Miller & David Wingrove. (Illus.). 336p. (J). 1996. 22.95 (0-7868-6160-6, Pub. by Hyperion) Time Warner.

Myst: The Book of Ti'Ana. Rand Miller & David Wingrove. (Illus.). 528p. (J). 1997. mass mkt. 6.99 (0-7868-8920-9, Pub. by Hyperion) Time Warner.

Myst: The Official Strategy Guide. expanded rev. ed. Rick Barba & Rusel DeMaria. (Illus.). 192p. 1997. pap. 19.95 (0-7615-0102-9, Prima Games) Prima Pub.

Myst Express. Pam Adams. LC 90-45758. 24p. (J). 1989. 6.99 (0-85953-180-5) Childs Play.

Myst M31. (J). (gr. 4 up). 1991. pap. 2.47 (1-56297-015-1, M-33) Lee Pubns KY.

Myst M32. (J). (gr. 4 up). 1991. pap. 2.47 (1-56297-016-X, M-33) Lee Pubns KY.

Myst Strategies & Secrets: For DOS. Anne Ryman. LC 95-67585. 112p. 1995. pap. 12.99 (0-7821-1678-7, Strategies & Secrets) Sybex.

Mystagogical Quintology. A. E. Waite. 1987. pap. text 4.95 (0-916411-70-2, Sure Fire) Holmes Pub.

Mystagogy: A Theology of Liturgy in the Patristic Age. Enrico Mazza. 228p. 1992. pap. 14.50 (0-8146-6093-2, Pueblo Bks) Liturgical Pr.

Mystagogy of the Holy Spirit. Joseph P. Farrell. 116p. 1997. pap. text 6.95 (0-916586-88-X) Holy Cross Orthodox.

Mystara Karameikos. Jeff Grubb. (Advanced Dungeons & Dragons, 2nd Edition: Mystara Campaign World Ser.). 1994. 30.00 (1-56076-853-3) TSR Inc.

Mystari. Nancy Northrop. (Illus.). 16p. (J). 1991. spiral bd. 5.95 (0-9627894-1-0) LNR Pubns.

MYSTAT: Statistical Applications (DOS) Robert L. Hale. (Illus.). 176p. (C). 1992. pap. text 14.95 incl. 5.25 hd (1-878748-63-7) Course Tech.

MYSTAT: Statistical Applications (Macintosh) Robert L. Hale. (Illus.). 208p. (C). 1993. pap. text 18.25 incl. mac hd (1-878748-62-9) Course Tech.

Mystat Mnl Statistics For The Behavioral Sciences. 4th ed. Gravetter & Wallnau. 1996. pap. text 5.00 (0-314-08822-9) Thomson Learn.

*Mystat Mnl Statistics For The Behavioral Sciences. 5th ed. Gravetter & Wallnau. (Psychology Ser.). 1999. pap. text 4.50 (0-534-37079-9) Wadsworth Pub.

Mystere. Marie-Aude Murail. (Folio - Cadet Bleu Ser.: No. 217). (FRE., Illus.). 64p. (J). (gr. 1-5). 1987. pap. 9.95 (2-07-031217-8) Schoenhof.

Mystere a Amboise. (FRE.). (C). 1990. pap. 7.95 (0-8442-1225-3, VF1225-3) NTC Contemp Pub Co.

Mystere a Toronto. (FRE.). (C). 1985. pap. 7.95 (0-8442-1216-4, VF1216-4) NTC Contemp Pub Co.

Mystere D'Adam. Paul Aebischer. 119p. 1964. 9.95 (0-8288-7496-4) Fr & Eur.

Mystere de la Charite de Jeanne D'Arc. Charles Peguy. (Gallimard Ser.). (FRE.). pap. 11.95 (2-07-010656-X) Schoenhof.

Mystere de la Passion. Arnoul Greban. (FRE.). 554p. 1987. pap. 17.95 (0-7859-2547-3, 2070378810) Fr & Eur.

Mystere de la Passion. Arnoul Greban. (Folio Ser.: No. 1881). (FRE.). 543p. 1987. pap. 16.95 (2-07-037881-0) Schoenhof.

Mystere de la Pizza Disparue: Teenage Mutant Ninja Turtles. Stephen Murphy. Tr. by DigiPro Staff from ENG. (Comes to Life Bks.).Tr. of Mystery of the Missing Pizza. (FRE.). 16p. (J). (ps-2). 1994. write for info. (1-883366-66-6) YES Ent.

Mystere de l'Iles aux Epices: The Nutmeg Princess. Richardo Keens-Douglas. (FRE., Illus.). 32p. (J). (gr. k-2). 1992. pap. 6.95 (1-55037-250-5, Pub. by Annick) Firefly Bks Ltd.

Mystere de l'Iles aux Epices: The Nutmeg Princess. Richardo Keens-Douglas. (FRE., Illus.). 32p. (J). (ps-2). 1992. lib. bdg. 15.95 (1-55037-249-1, Pub. by Annick) Firefly Bks Ltd.

Mystere de Sainte Venice. Ed. by Runnalls. (Exeter French Texts Ser.: Vol. 38). (FRE.). 60p. Date not set. pap. text 19.95 (0-85989-186-0, Pub. by Univ Exeter Pr) Northwestern U Pr.

Mystere des Caves Saint Emilion. Cavalie. text 4.25 (0-8219-1032-9) EMC-Paradigm.

Mystere D'Israel. Jacques Maritain. (FRE.). 302p. 1990. pap. 29.95 (0-7859-1601-6, 222003173X) Fr & Eur.

Mystere du Lac Carre. Sylvie Desrosiers. (Novels in the Roman Jeunesse Ser.). (FRE.). 96p. (J). (gr. 4-7). 1988. pap. 8.95 (2-89021-079-0, Pub. by La Courte Ech) Firefly Bks Ltd.

Mystere Frontenac. Francois Mauriac. 9.95 (0-686-55470-1) Fr & Eur.

Mystere Frontenac. Francois Mauriac. (Coll. Diamant). (FRE.). 1957. 7.95 (0-8288-9869-3, F113200) Fr & Eur.

Mysteres de Chine. Chrystine Brouillet. (Novels in the Roman Jeunesse Ser.). (FRE.). 96p. (J). (gr. 4-7). 1993. pap. 8.95 (2-89021-189-4, Pub. by La Courte Ech) Firefly Bks Ltd.

Mysteres de Marseille. Emile Zola. (FRE.). 361p. 1992. pap. 18.95 (0-7859-1547-8, 2740100280) Fr & Eur.

Mysteres de Marseille, 2 vols. Emile Zola. (FRE.). 886p. 1984. pap. 79.95 (0-7859-1656-3, 2728706093) Fr & Eur.

Mysteres D'Eleusis. Paul F. Foucart. LC 75-10636. (Ancient Religion & Mythology Ser.). (FRE.). 1976. reprint ed. 53.95 (0-405-07013-6) Ayer.

Mysteria: History of the Secret Doctrines & Mystic Rites of Ancient Religions & Medieval & Modern Secret Orders. Otto H. Am Rhyn. 245p. 1996. reprint ed. pap. 19.95 (1-56459-606-0) Kessinger Pub.

Mysteria, Jung & the Ancient Mysteries: Extracts from the Collected Works of C. G. Jung. Richard Nool. LC 94-34815. (C). 1994. pap. 14.95 (0-691-03647-0, Pub. by Princeton U Pr) Cal Prin Full Svc.

Mysterie of Rhetorique Unvail'd. John Smith. (Anglistica & Americana Ser.: No. 124). 267p. 1973. reprint ed. 70.20 (3-487-04581-8) G Olms Pubs.

Mysteries. 1988. write for info. (0-318-67249-9, Scribners Ref) Mac Lib Ref.

Mysteries. Knut Hamsun. 340p. 1984. pap. 8.95 (0-88184-031-9) Carroll & Graf.

Mysteries. Knut Hamsun. 352p. 1997. pap. 14.00 (0-374-52527-7, Noonday) FS&G.

*Mysteries. Knut Hamsun & Sverre Lyngstad. LC 00-40651. 2001. write for info. (0-14-118618-6) Penguin Putnam.

Mysteries. Ita Wegman. Tr. & Compiled by Crispian Villeneuve. 144p. 1995. pap. 15.95 (0-904693-75-9, Pub. by Temple Lodge) Anthroposophic.

Mysteries see Papers from Eranos Yearbooks

Mysteries: Creation. Adapted by Bernard Sahlins. (Plays for Performance Ser.). 68p. 1992. pap. 7.95 (1-56663-004-5, Pub. by I R Dee); lib. bdg. 15.95 (1-56663-005-3, Pub. by I R Dee) Natl Bk Netwk.

Mysteries: Rudolf Steiner's Writings on Spiritual Initiation. Andrew Welburn. 1997. 34.95 (0-86315-243-0, Pub. by Floris Bks) Anthroposophic.

Mysteries: The Creation & The Passion, Vol. 1. James Jennings. (Nick Hern Books, Drama Classics). 96p. 1997. pap. 6.95 (1-85459-391-9, Pub. by N Hern Bks) Theatre Comm.

Mysteries: The Creation & The Passion, Vol. 2. James Jennings. (Nick Hern Books, Drama Classics). 96p. 1997. pap. 6.95 (1-85459-396-X, Pub. by N Hern Bks) Theatre Comm.

Mysteries: The Passion. Adapted by Bernard Sahlins. (Plays for Performance Ser.). 72p. 1993. pap. 7.95 (1-56663-024-X, Pub. by I R Dee); lib. bdg. 15.95 (1-56663-023-1, Pub. by I R Dee) Natl Bk Netwk.

M

M

Mysteries & Adventures along the Atlantic Coast. Edward Rowe Snow. (Illus.). 352p. 1977. 23.95 (*0-8369-1066-4*) Ayer.

Mysteries & Histories of the Great Lakes: Shipwrecks of the Great Lakes. Wes Oleszewski. LC 97-70282. (Illus.). 312p. 1997. pap. 13.95 (*0-932212-92-1*) Avery Color.

Mysteries & Intrigues of the Bible. Livingstone Editorial Group et al. LC 97-17546. 250p. 1997. pap. 12.99 (*0-8423-4674-0*) Tyndale Hse.

***Mysteries & Magic.** J. A. Spencer & Anne Spencer. (True Life Encounters Ser.). 304p. 1999. pap. 12.95 (*1-57500-030-X*, Pub. by TV Bks) HarpC.

Mysteries & Marvels of Nature. Barbara Cork & R. Morris. (Mysteries & Marvels Ser.). (Illus.). 192p. (J). (gr. 3-7). 1983. 24.95 (*0-7460-0421-4*) EDC.

Mysteries & Miracles of Arizona. Jack Kutz. (Mysteries & Miracles of the Southwest Ser.). (Illus.). 235p. (Orig.). 1991. pap. text 8.95 (*0-936455-04-7*) Rhombus Pub.

Mysteries & Miracles of California: Guidebook to the Genuinely Bizarre in the Golden Gate State. Jack Kutz. (Mysteries & Miracles Ser.). (Illus.). 207p. (Orig.). 1997. pap. 8.95 (*0-936455-07-1*) Rhombus Pub.

Mysteries & Miracles of Colorado: Guidebook to the Genuinely Bizarre. Jack Kutz. (Illus.). 255p. (Orig.). 1993. pap. 7.95 (*0-936455-05-5*) Rhombus Pub.

Mysteries & Miracles of New Mexico: Guide Book to the Genuinely Bizarre in the Land of Enchantment. Jack Kutz. (Illus.). 226p. 1989. pap. 8.95 (*0-936455-02-0*) Rhombus Pub.

Mysteries & Miracles of Texas: Guidebook to the Genuinely Bizarre in the Lone Star State. Jack Kutz. 211p. Date not set. pap. 8.95 (*0-936455-06-3*) Rhombus Pub.

***Mysteries & Monsters of Sea.** FATE Magazine Editorial Staff. 2001. 8.99 (*0-517-16349-7*) Crown Pub Group.

Mysteries & Revelations: Apocalyptic Studies since the Uppsala Colloquium. Ed. by John J. Collins & James H. Charlesworth. (Journal for the Study of the Pseudepigrapha Supplement Ser.: No. 9). 172p. (C). 1991. 52.50 (*1-85075-299-0*, Pub. by Sheffield Acad) CUP Services.

Mysteries & Secrets of Magic. John Teal. Ed. by Thorguard Templar. (Illus.). 435p. 1994. 25.00 (*1-57179-004-7*) Intern Guild ASRS.

Mysteries & Unknown, Bk. 4. Regents. 24p. 1996. pap. text, student ed. 7.80 (*0-13-349796-8*) P-H.

Mysteries Confucius Couldn't Solve/Genesis & Mystery Confucius Couldn't Solve see God's Promise to the Chinese

***Mysteries for the New Millennium.** Bennett. 216p. 2000. 25.00 (*0-321-02971-2*) Benjamin-Cummings.

Mysteries from the Finger Lakes. Beals. 1989. pap. 12.50 (*0-9624738-0-4*) Six Lakes Arts.

Mysteries from the Finger Lakes, 2 vols., Set. Buchholz. 1991. pap. 8.95 (*0-9624738-4-7*) Six Lakes Arts.

Mysteries from the Finger Lakes: Short Stories from In-Between Magazine. Jack Lavalley et al. (Illus.). 128p. 1989. pap. 8.95 (*0-685-29418-8*) Six Lakes Arts.

Mysteries in God's New Testament Economy. Witness Lee. 83p. 1990. pap. 4.50 (*0-87083-527-0*, 04-011-001) Living Stream Ministry.

Mysteries in Space. Michael Uslan. 1980. 7.95 (*0-686-61048-2*, 24775, Fireside) S&S Trade Pap.

Mysteries in the Public Domain. Walter Bargen. LC 89-15049. (Target Poetry Ser.). 64p. (Orig.). 1990. pap. 6.50 (*0-933532-74-1*) BkMk.

Mysteries in the Scriptures: Enlightenment Through Ancient Beliefs. Vicki Alder. 326p. 1991. 13.95 (*0-9626559-1-0*) V Alder.

Mysteries, Marvels, Miracles: In the Lives of the Saints. Joan C. Cruz. LC 96-60581. (Illus.). 581p. 1997. pap. 24.00 (*0-89555-541-7*, 1383) TAN Bks Pubs.

Mysteries, Nicknames, & Medals. John A. Hurst. LC 87-2293. (And so the Story Goes...Ser.: No. 3). 80p. (Orig.). 1987. pap. 7.95 (*0-89196-134-8*, 31706) Quality Bks IL.

Mysteries of Africa. Ed. by Eugene Schleh. 120p. (C). 1991. 24.95 (*0-87972-511-7*); pap. 12.95 (*0-87972-512-5*) Bowling Green Univ Popular Press.

Mysteries of Algiers. Robert Irwin. 203p. 1997. reprint ed. pap. 9.99 (*1-873982-60-7*, Pub. by Dedalus) Subterranean Co.

Mysteries of All Nations. James Grant. 2000. reprint ed. 70.00 (*1-55888-190-5*) Omnigraphics Inc.

Mysteries of Almsgiving. Muhammad Al-Ghazali. Tr. by N. A. Faris. 1994. pap. 4.95 (*1-56744-163-7*) Kazi Pubns.

Mysteries of Almsgiving. Al-Ghazzali. Tr. by Nabik A. Faris. 1966. 19.95 (*0-8156-6002-2*, Pub. by Am U Beirut) Syracuse U Pr.

***Mysteries of Ancient South America.** Harold T. Wilkins. (Atlantis Reprint Ser.). 236p. 2000. pap. 14.95 (*0-932813-26-7*, Pub. by Adventures Unltd) SCB Distributors.

Mysteries of Ancient South America. Harold T. Wilkins. 1977. lib. bdg. 59.95 (*0-8490-2312-2*) Gordon Pr.

Mysteries of Animal Intelligence. Brad Steiger et al. 128p. (Orig.). (J). (gr. 5 up). 1995. pap. 4.99 (*0-8125-5191-5*, Pub. by Tor Bks) St Martin.

Mysteries of Astrology & the Wonders of Magic. Charles W. Roback. 1996. reprint ed. spiral bd. 15.50 (*0-7873-0728-9*) Hlth Research.

Mysteries of Astrology & the Wonders of Magic, 1854. Charles W. Roback. 239p. 1996. reprint ed. pap. 14.95 (*1-56459-799-7*) Kessinger Pub.

Mysteries of Atlantis Revisited. Edgar E. Cayce et al. LC 97-138785. 212p. 1997. mass mkt. 5.99 (*0-312-96153-7*) St Martin.

Mysteries of Attention. James S. Hans. LC 92-9021. 292p. (C). 1993. text 64.50 (*0-7914-1391-8*); pap. text 21.95 (*0-7914-1392-6*) State U NY Pr.

Mysteries of Bizarre Animals & Freaks of Nature. Phyllis R. Emert. 128p. (Orig.). (YA). (gr. 6 up). 1994. pap. 2.99 (*0-8125-3630-4*, Pub. by Tor Bks) St Martin.

Mysteries of Bizarre Animals & Freaks of Nature. Phyllis Raybin-Emert. (Strange Unsolved Mysteries Ser.). (J). 1994. 8.09 (*0-606-11929-9*, Pub. by Turtleback) Demco.

Mysteries of Borobudur. John Miksic. (Asia's Cultural Attractions Ser.). (Illus.). 32p. 2000. 9.95 (*962-593-198-8*) Tuttle Pubng.

Mysteries of Britain. Lewis Spence. 256p. 1996. reprint ed. spiral bd. 16.00 (*0-7873-0807-2*) Hlth Research.

Mysteries of Britain: The Secret Rites & Traditions of Ancient Britain Restored. Lewis Spence. Ed. by Gina R. Gross. (Illus.). 256p. 1993. reprint ed. pap. 12.95 (*0-87877-185-9*) Newcastle Pub.

Mysteries of Creation: The Genesis Story. Rocco A. Errico. 176p. 1993. pap. 16.95 (*0-9631292-3-6*) Noohra Found.

Mysteries of Deep Space: Black Holes, Pulsars & Quasars see Isaac Asimov's New Library of the Universe

Mysteries of Demeter: Rebirth of the Pagan Way. Jennifer Reif. LC 99-29771. (Illus.). 344p. 1999. 35.00 (*1-57863-133-5*) Weiser.

***Mysteries of Demeter: Rebirth of the Pagan Way.** Jennifer Reif. LC 99-29771. (Illus.). 320p. 2000. pap. 19.95 (*1-57863-141-6*) Weiser.

Mysteries of Development: Studies Using Political Elasticity Theory. Herbert H. Werlin. (Illus.). 418p. (C). 1998. 68.00 (*0-7618-1178-8*); pap. 25.00 (*0-7618-1179-6*) U Pr of Amer.

Mysteries of Draco & Leona. Fra Draco. (Illus.). 40p. 1981. pap. 7.00 (*0-939622-22-X*) Four Zoas Night Ltd.

Mysteries of Egypt: Secret Rites & Traditions of the Nile. Lewis Spence. LC 79-183056. 256p. 1992. pap. 13.95 (*0-89345-241-6*, Steinerbks) Garber Comm.

Mysteries of Egypt or the Secret Rites & Traditions of the Nile. Lewis Spence. 285p. 1996. pap. 22.00 (*0-89540-239-4*, SB-239) Sun Pub.

Mysteries of Egypt or the Secret Rites & Traditions of the Nile. Lewis Spence. 256p. 1994. reprint ed. pap. 17.95 (*1-56459-419-X*) Kessinger Pub.

***Mysteries of Faith.** Mark Allen McIntosh. LC 99-46467. 200p. 1999. pap. 11.95 (*1-56101-175-4*) Cowley Pubns.

Mysteries of Fasting. Nabih A. Faris. 1989. pap. 4.95 (*1-56744-164-5*) Kazi Pubns.

Mysteries of Fire & Water. Omraam M. Aivanhov. (Izvor Collection: No. 232). 173p. 1993. pap. 7.95 (*2-85566-545-0*, Pub. by Prosveta) Prosveta USA.

Mysteries of Freemasonry or an Exposition of the Religious Dogmas & Customs of the Ancient Egyptians. John Fellows. 368p. 1999. reprint ed. pap. 24.95 (*0-7661-0819-8*) Kessinger Pub.

Mysteries of Freemasonry (The Morgan Espose) Ed. by George R. Crafts. 206p. 1993. reprint ed. pap. 17.95 (*1-56459-342-8*) Kessinger Pub.

Mysteries of Genesis. Charles Fillmore. LC 97-44069. (Classic Library). 432p. 2000. reprint ed. 12.95 (*0-87159-219-3*, 92) Unity Bks.

Mysteries of God Revealed. Carol Crook. 300p. 2001. ring bd. 100.00 (*0-939399-34-2*) Bks of Truth.

***Mysteries of God Revealed.** Ronald C. Dubrul. (Illus.). 262p. 1999. pap. 19.95 (*1-929138-24-5*, MYSTER) Christ Fellow Min.

Mysteries of Godliness: A History of Mormon Temple Worship. David J. Buerger. LC 94-37828. (Illus.). 244p. 1994. 24.95 (*1-56085-042-6*, Smith Res) Signature Bks.

Mysteries of Harris Burdick, 001. Harris Burdick & Chris Van Allsburg. 32p. 1984. 17.95 (*0-395-35393-9*) HM.

Mysteries of Harris Burdick: Portfolio Edition. Chris Van Allsburg. LC 84-9006. (Illus.). 32p. (YA). (gr. 5 up). 1996. ring bd. 19.95 (*0-395-82784-1*) HM.

Mysteries of Human Reproduction. Raymond W. Bernard. 126p. 1994. reprint ed. spiral bd. 14.50 (*0-7873-1157-X*) Hlth Research.

Mysteries of Identity: A Theme in Modern Literature. Robert Langbaum. LC 81-21894. (Phoenix Ser.). 400p. (C). 1998. pap. text 14.95 (*0-226-46873-9*) U Ch Pr.

Mysteries of Isis: Her Worship & Magick. De Traci Regula. LC 95-20520. (Llewellyn's World Religion & Magic Ser.). (Illus.). 320p. 1999. pap. 19.95 (*1-56718-560-6*) Llewellyn Pubns.

Mysteries of John. 14th ed. Charles Fillmore. 215p. 2000. reprint ed. 12.95 (*0-87159-204-5*, 38) Unity Bks.

Mysteries of Life & Death. Osho. Tr. by Malini Bisen from HIN. 1978. reprint ed. pap. 3.50 (*0-89684-045-X*, Pub. by Motilal Bnarsidass) S Asia.

Mysteries of Life & the Universe. William H. Shore. 356p. (C). 1994. pap. 15.00 (*0-15-600136-5*) Harcourt.

Mysteries of Life & the Universe: New Essays from America's Finest Writers on Science. Ed. by William H. Shore. LC 92-15677. 1992. 24.95 (*0-15-163972-8*) Harcourt.

Mysteries of Life Explained. 2nd ed. Ed. by Hank Krastman. 136p. 1998. pap. 9.95 (*0-935551-00-X*) Krastman.

Mysteries of Light. David A. Winnett et al. Ed. by Catherine Anderson & Mali Apple. (Discovery Science Ser.). (Illus.). 76p. (Orig.). (J). 1996. pap. text 11.95 (*0-201-49660-7*, 36838) Seymour Pubns.

Mysteries of London. William Reynolds. Ed. by Trefor Thomas. (Illus.). 384p. 1998. 50.00 (*1-85331-111-1*, Pub. by Edinburgh U Pr) Col U Pr.

Mysteries of London, 4 vols., 2 bks., Set. George W. Reynolds. LC 79-8192. reprint ed. 84.50 (*0-404-62106-6*) AMS Pr.

Mysteries of Lost & Hidden Treasure, Vol. 1. Phyllis R. Emert. (Illus.). (J). 1996. mass mkt. 3.99 (*0-8125-4360-2*, Pub. by Tor Bks) St Martin.

Mysteries of Lost & Hidden Treasures, 9. Phyllis Raybin Emert. (Strange Unsolved Mysteries Ser.). 1996. 8.09 (*0-606-13820-X*, Pub. by Turtleback) Demco.

Mysteries of Love: Eros & Spirituality. Arthur Versluis. LC 96-94131. 165p. 1996. 34.00 (*0-9650488-8-8*) Grail Pubng.

Mysteries of Magic. Arthur E. Waite. 349p. 1996. reprint ed. spiral bd. 26.00 (*0-7873-0921-4*) Hlth Research.

Mysteries of Magic: A Digest of the Writings of Eliphas Levi. Arthur E. Waite. 540p. 1993. reprint ed. pap. 24.95 (*1-56459-374-6*) Kessinger Pub.

Mysteries of Magritte. Harold Norse. (Orig.). (C). 1984. pap. 5.00 (*0-912377-07-0*) Atticus Pr.

Mysteries of Magritte. limited ed. Harold Norse. (Orig.). (C). 1984. 15.00 (*0-912377-06-2*) Atticus Pr.

Mysteries of March: Hans Urs Von Balthasar on the Incarnation & Easter. John Saward. LC 90-30902. 186p. 1990. 22.95 (*0-8132-0726-6*); pap. 12.95 (*0-8132-0727-4*) Cath U Pr.

***Mysteries of Mary: The Fullness of Discipleship.** Bernard Haring. LC 98-67383. (Liguori Celebration Ser.). 80p. 1999. pap. text 6.95 (*0-7648-0356-5*) Liguori Pubns.

Mysteries of Mind. Yuvacharya Mahaprajna. 225p. 1982. 11.00 (*0-88065-223-3*, Pub. by Today Tomorrow) Scholarly Pubns.

Mysteries of Mind, Space & Time: The Unexplained, 26 vols., Set. (Illus.). 1992. 285.48 (*0-87475-575-1*) Websters Unified.

Mysteries of Mithra. Franz Cumont. 256p. 1996. reprint ed. pap. 14.95 (*1-56459-690-7*) Kessinger Pub.

Mysteries of Mithra. G. R. Mead. 90p. 1992. reprint ed. pap. 5.95 (*1-56459-249-9*) Kessinger Pub.

Mysteries of Mithra. 2nd ed. Franz Cumont. Tr. by Thomas J. McCormack. (Illus.). 239p. 1956. pap. 8.95 (*0-486-20323-9*) Dover.

Mysteries of Mithra. 2nd ed. Franz Cumont. 239p. 1996. reprint ed. spiral bd. 15.50 (*0-7873-0231-7*) Hlth Research.

Mysteries of Mithras. G. R. Mead. 1993. reprint ed. pap. 6.95 (*1-55818-209-8*) Holmes Pub.

Mysteries of Modern Science. Brian M. Stableford. (Quality Paperback Ser.: No. 360). 270p. 1980. reprint ed. pap. 13.00 (*0-8226-0360-8*) Littlefield.

Mysteries of Osiris: Egyptian Initiation. R. Swinburne Clymer. 287p. 1951. 10.95 (*0-932785-31-X*) Philos Pub.

Mysteries of Osiris: Egyptian Initiation. deluxe ed. R. Swinburne Clymer. 287p. 1951. lthr. 20.00 (*0-932785-93-X*) Philos Pub.

Mysteries of Paris. 2nd ed. Eugene Lue. 423p. 1997. reprint ed. pap. 11.99 (*0-946626-30-8*, Pub. by Dedalus) Subterranean Co.

Mysteries of Paris: The Quest for Morton Fullerton. Marion Mainwaring. (Illus.). 384p. 2000. 30.00 (*1-58465-008-7*) U Pr of New Eng.

Mysteries of Paris & London. Richard Maxwell. (Victorian Literature & Culture Ser.). (Illus.). 416p. 1992. text 39.50 (*0-8139-1341-1*) U Pr of Va.

Mysteries of People & Places, 3. Phyllis Raybin-Emert. (Strange Unsolved Mysteries Ser.). (J). 1992. 7.60 (*0-606-11927-2*, Pub. by Turtleback) Demco.

Mysteries of Pittsburgh. Michael Chabon. LC 88-45708. 304p. 1989. reprint ed. pap. 12.00 (*0-06-097212-2*, PL 7212, Perennial) HarperTrade.

Mysteries of Purity. Nabih A. Faris. 1991. pap. 5.95 (*1-56744-165-3*) Kazi Pubns.

Mysteries of Purity: Ibn al-'Arabi's Asrar al-Taharah. Eric Winkel. LC 95-68663. 275p. (C). 1995. 38.95 (*0-940121-32-8*, H302) Cross Cultural Pubns.

In this translation of a portion of the FIGH section of the Futuhat al-Makkiyyah, at least two startling key issues emerge. Being startled, in itself, is the first key. And the second is the "arabic language" which means that language which the original audience of the Qur'an understood. Also startling are all the twists & turns, all the secrets & mysteries, all the bizarre & strange permutations of the original text. This translation is quite literal, but with careful reading special academic preparation is not necessary. Both spiritual & intellectual in content, this book gives great hope for a more authentic & deep Islamic discourse on a neglected subject: the Sufi meditation upon the meaning of Islamic Law.
Publisher Paid Annotation.

Mysteries of Radiance Unfolded: Relative Connections, Vol. II. Gyeorgos C. Hatonn. (The Phoenix Journals). 241p. 1993. pap. 6.00 (*1-56935-019-1*) Phoenix Source.

Mysteries of Research. 2nd ed. Sharron Cohen. LC 95-43103. 135p. 1996. pap. 16.95 (*0-917846-76-1*, Alleyside) Highsmith Pr.

Mysteries of Righteousness: The Literary Composition & Genre of the Sentences of Pseudo-Phocylides. Walter T. Wilson. (Text und Studien Zum Antiken Judentum Ser.: No. 40). 255p. 1994. text 125.00 (*3-16-146211-4*, Pub. by JCB Mohr) Coronet Bks.

Mysteries of St. Louis. Henry Boernstein. Ed. by Steven Rowan & Elizabeth Sims. Tr. by Freidrich Munch from GER. (Foreign-Language American Left Ser.). (Illus.). 320p. (C). 1990. reprint ed. 35.00 (*0-88286-169-7*); reprint ed. pap. 18.00 (*0-88286-168-9*) C H Kerr.

Mysteries of Science. John Rowland. LC 78-105035. (Essay Index Reprint Ser.). 1977. 21.95 (*0-8369-1624-7*) Ayer.

Mysteries of Science: Research Activities for Investigating Scientific Fact & Fiction. Thomas Christie. (Illus.). 64p. (J). (gr. 4-8). 1994. 8.99 (*0-86653-796-1*, GA1490) Good Apple.

Mysteries of Sedona: The New Age Frontier. 2nd ed. Tom Dongo. (Illus.). 84p. 1988. reprint ed. pap. 6.95 (*0-9622748-0-1*) T Dongo.

Mysteries of Sedona Bk. III: The Quest. Tom Dongo. (Illus.). 146p. (Orig.). 1993. pap. 9.95 (*0-9622748-2-8*) T Dongo.

Mysteries of Sherlock Holmes. Arthur Conan Doyle. LC 96-6275. (Illustrated Junior Library). (Illus.). 240p. (YA). (gr. 4 up). 1996. 14.95 (*0-448-40957-7*, G & D) Peng Put Young Read.

Mysteries of Sherlock Holmes. Arthur Conan Doyle. (Bullseye Step into Classics Ser.). (Illus.). 96p. (J). (gr. 2-6). 1994. pap. 3.50 (*0-679-85086-4*, Bullseye Bks) Random Bks Yng Read.

Mysteries of Sherlock Holmes. Arthur Conan Doyle. Ed. by Judith Conaway. LC 81-15751. (Step into Classics Ser.). (Illus.). 96p. (J). (gr. 4-7). 1994. pap. 3.99 (*0-394-85086-6*, Pub. by Random Bks Yng Read) Random.

Mysteries of Shetaut Pautti: Mystical Teachings of the Ancient Egyptian Creation Myth. Mnata A. Ashbi. (Illus.). 64p. 1997. pap. 5.99 (*1-884564-38-0*) Cruzian Mystic.

Mysteries of Ships & Planes. Phyllis R. Emert. (Strange Unsolved Mysteries Ser.: No. 1). 128p. (YA). 1990. pap. 2.50 (*0-8125-9427-4*, Pub. by Tor Bks) St Martin.

Mysteries of Ships & Planes. Phyllis Raybin-Emert. (Strange Unsolved Mysteries Ser.). (J). 1990. 7.60 (*0-606-11925-6*, Pub. by Turtleback) Demco.

Mysteries of Small Houses. Alice Notley. LC 97-42195. (Penguin Poets Ser.). 160p. 1998. pap. 14.95 (*0-14-058896-5*) Viking Penguin.

Mysteries of Sound & Number. Habeeb Ahmad. 1991. lib. bdg. 79.95 (*0-8490-4992-X*) Gordon Pr.

Mysteries of Sound & Number. abr. ed. Sheikh H. Ahmad. 89p. 1983. reprint ed. pap. 10.00 (*0-7873-0020-9*) Hlth Research.

Mysteries of Space: Opposing Viewpoints. Richard M. Rassmussen. LC 93-13592. (Great Mysteries Ser.). 128p. 1994. lib. bdg. 22.45 (*1-56510-097-2*) Greenhaven.

Mysteries of Space & the Universe. Phyllis Raybin-Emert. (Strange Unsolved Mysteries Ser.). (J). 1994. 8.09 (*0-606-11930-2*, Pub. by Turtleback) Demco.

Mysteries of Strange Appearances from Beyond. Phyllis R. Emert. (Strange Unsolved Mysteries Ser.: No. 7). (Orig.). (YA). (gr. 6-12). 1995. pap. 2.99 (*0-8125-3632-0*, Pub. by Tor Bks) St Martin.

Mysteries of the Alphabet. Marc-Alain Ouaknin. LC 98-44840. (Illus.). 384p. 1999. 39.95 (*0-7892-0523-8*); pap. 24.95 (*0-7892-0521-1*) Abbeville Pr.

Mysteries of the Ancients. Brian Innes. LC 98-15505. (Unsolved Mysteries Ser.). (J). 1999. 24.26 (*0-8172-5481-1*) Raintree Steck-V.

***Mysteries of the Ancients.** Steck-Vaughn Company Staff. (Unsolved Mysteries Ser.). (Illus.). (J). 2000. pap. 6.95 (*0-8172-4278-3*) Raintree Steck-V.

Mysteries of the Backwoods: Sketches of the Southwest. Thomas B. Thorpe. LC 71-104579. (Illus.). reprint ed. pap. text 10.95 (*0-8290-1691-0*); reprint ed. lib. bdg. 25.00 (*0-8398-1958-7*) Irvington.

***Mysteries of the Bible Now Revealed.** Grant Jeffrey et al. Ed. by Jim Combs & David Lewis. LC 99-70075. 240p. 1999. pap. 12.99 (*0-89221-459-7*) New Leaf.

Mysteries of the Body & the Mind. John Taylor. LC 97-44625. 130p. 1998. pap. text 12.95 (*1-885266-53-7*) Story Line.

Mysteries of the Book of Daniel. Jim Combs. (Illus.). 176p. (Orig.). (C). 1994. pap. 9.95 (*1-884764-01-0*) Baptist Bible.

Mysteries of the Children of Og. Rikki. (Story of Og & Man Ser.: Part 2). (Illus.). 216p. (Orig.). 1983. pap. 10.00 (*0-910149-03-8*) Msng Link AZ.

Mysteries of the City: Culture Politics & the Underworld in New York, 1870-1920. Daniel Czitrom. (C). (gr. 13). 1999. 25.00 (*0-415-90470-6*) Routledge.

***Mysteries of the Cold War.** Ed. by Stephen J. Cimbala. LC 98-31001. (Policy Studies Organization Ser.). 200p. 1999. text 78.95 (*1-84014-425-4*, Pub. by Ashgate Pub) Ashgate Pub Co.

Mysteries of the Creation. Dovid Brown. (Illus.). 400p. 1987. 19.99 (*0-939833-23-7*) Mosdos Pubs.

Mysteries of the Creation: A Cosmology Derived from the Tanuch & Chazal. Dovid Brown. 402p. 1997. 21.95 (*1-56871-145-X*) Targum Pr.

Mysteries of the Dark Moon: The Healing Power of the Dark Goddess. Demetra George. LC 91-55318. 304p. 1992. pap. 17.00 (*0-06-250370-7*, Pub. by Harper SF) HarpC.

Mysteries of the Deep. Ed. by Frank Spaeth. LC 98-5869. (Illus.). 256p. 1999. pap. 9.95 (*1-56718-260-7*) Llewellyn Pubns.

Mysteries of the Deep: Exploring Life in the Deep Sea. Christina Joie Slager & Monterey Bay Aquarium Staff. LC 98-47583. 1999. 5.95 (*1-878244-24-8*) Monterey Bay Aquarium.

Mysteries of the Dreamtime: The Spiritual Life of Australian Aborigines. James G. Cowan. (Illus.). 164p. (Orig.). 1989. pap. 11.95 (*1-85327-077-6*, Pub. by Prism Pr) Assoc Pubs Grp.

Mysteries of the Dreamtime: The Spiritual Life of the Australian Aborigine. James Cowan. 192p. (Orig.). 1990. pap. write for info. (*1-85327-038-5*, Pub. by Prism Pr) Assoc Pubs Grp.

Mysteries of the East. (In Classical Mood Ser.: Vol. 41). (Illus.). 1998. write for info. incl. cd-rom (*1-886614-67-9*) Intl Masters Pub.

Mysteries of the East & of Christianity, Vol. 33. rev. ed. Rudolf Steiner. LC 88-92551. 96p. 1989. lib. bdg. 10.00 (*0-89345-059-6*, Spir Sci Lib) Garber Comm.

Mysteries of the Glorious Resurrection. B. R. Hicks. (Illus.). 95p. 1985. pap. 6.95 (*1-58363-061-9*, MD-4010) Christ Gospel.

***Mysteries of the Glory Unveiled: A New Wave of Signs & Wonders.** David Herzog. 250p. 2000. pap. 12.99 (*1-58158-012-6*) McDougal Pubng.

Mysteries of the Goddess: Astrology, Tarot & the Magical Arts. Ffiona Morgan. (Illus.). 194p. (Orig.). 1995. pap. 13.00 (*1-880130-37-8*) Daughters Moon.

Mysteries of the Great Cities: The Politics of Urban Design, 1877-1937. John D. Fairfield. LC 93-18133. (Urban Life & Urban Landscape Ser.). (Illus.). 322p. 1993. text 62.50 (*0-8142-0604-2*) Ohio St U Pr.

Mysteries of the Great Cities: The Politics of Urban Design, 1877-1937. John D. Fairfield. LC 93-18133. (Urban Life & Urban Landscape Ser.). 1997. pap. text 18.95 (*0-8142-0754-5*) Ohio St U Pr.

Mysteries of the Great Operas. Max Heindel. 178p. 1998. reprint ed. pap. 19.95 (*0-7661-0419-2*) Kessinger Pub.

Mysteries of the Holy Grail. Corinne Heline. 128p. (Orig.). 1999. reprint ed. pap. 18.00 (*0-933963-15-7*) New Age Bible.

Mysteries of the Holy Stones. Joseph Schenck. LC 82-62509. (Illus.). 179p. 1982. pap. 10.00 (*0-936978-02-3*) Pheasant Run.

Mysteries of the Human Body. Time-Life Books Editors. (Library of Curious & Unusual Facts). 1990. 17.27 (*0-8094-7679-7*); lib. bdg. 23.27 (*0-8094-7680-0*) Time-Life.

Mysteries of the Human Soul. Muhammad Al-Ghazali. Tr. by Abdul Qayyum Hazarvi. 64p. (Orig.). 1985. pap. 7.50 (*1-56744-343-5*) Kazi Pubns.

***Mysteries of the Kabbalah.** Marc-Alain Ouaknin. 2000. 39.95 (*0-7892-0654-4*) Abbeville Pr.

Mysteries of the Kingdom: An Exposition of the Parables. Herman Hanko. LC 75-13930. 342p. 1991. reprint ed. pap. 14.50 (*0-916206-39-4*) Refrd Free Pub Assn.

Mysteries of the Limpid Butterfly. Mary Olkowski. LC 99-94342. (Illus.). 300p. 1999. pap. 14.99 (*0-9668781-1-6*, 1002) Limpid Butterfly.

Mysteries of the Mind. LC 99-170054. 1997. pap. text. write for info. (*1-57259-540-X*) Worth.

***Mysteries of the Mind.** Richard Restak. 2000. 35.00 (*0-7922-7941-7*) Natl Geog.

***Mysteries of the Mind.** Richard M. Restak. LC 00-27668. 2000. write for info. (*0-7922-7640-X*) Natl Geog.

Mysteries of the Mind. Mariam Weist-Meyer. (Great Unsolved Mysteries Ser.). 1997. pap. 4.95 (*0-8114-6859-3*) Raintree Steck-V.

Mysteries of the Mind & the Senses No. 8. Phyllis Raybin-Emert. (Strange Unsolved Mysteries Ser.). (J). 1995. 8.09 (*0-606-11932-9*, Pub. by Turtleback) Demco.

Mysteries of the Mind & the Senses No. 8: Strange Unsolved Mysteries. Phyllis R. Emert. (Strange Unsolved Mysteries Ser.: No. 8). 128p. (Orig.). (YA). (gr. 6-12). 1995. 2.99 (*0-8125-3633-9*, Pub. by Tor Bks) St Martin.

Mysteries of the Moon & Star: A Collectors Guide to Moon & Star Pattern Glass with Price Guide. George Breeze & Linda Breeze. 128p. pap. 29.95 (*0-9649326-0-1*) G & L Breeze.

Mysteries of the Most Holy Rosary. Michael O'Brien. (Illus.). 40p. 1994. spiral bd. 14.95 (*0-9696391-0-4*) Whi4te Horse.

Mysteries of the New Testament. Arthur Jackson. 167p. (Orig.). 1996. pap. 10.95 (*1-885904-10-X*) Focus Pubng.

Mysteries of the Opposite Sex. David Feldman. 1999. write for info. (*0-316-27272-8*) Little.

***Mysteries of the Planet Earth.** Karl P. Shuker. 1999. pap. text 22.95 (*1-85868-802-7*, Pub. by Carlton Bks Ltd) Natl Bk Netwk.

Mysteries of the Psalms. George E. Drew. 55p. (Orig.). 1989. pap. 7.95 (*0-940754-68-1*) Ed Ministries.

***Mysteries of the Qabalah.** Eliphas Levi. (Illus.). 288p. 2000. (*1-57863-940-9*) Weiser.

Mysteries of the Qabalah. Elias Gewurz. 1922. reprint ed. 11.00 (*0-911662-32-4*) Yoga.

***Mysteries of The Qabalah: or Occult Agreement of the Two Testaments.** Eliphas Levi. (Illus.). 288p. 2000. pap. 18.95 (*0-87728-940-9*) Weiser.

Mysteries of the Qaballah, Vol. II. Elias Gewurz. 99p. 1996. reprint ed. spiral bd. 10.00 (*0-7873-1236-3*) Hlth Research.

Mysteries of the Rain Forest. Reader's Digest Editors. LC 98-21012. (Earth, Its Wonders, Its Secrets Ser.). 1998. 19.98 (*0-7621-0110-5*) RD Assn.

Mysteries of the Rainforest: 20th Century Medicine Man. Elaine Pascoe. LC 96-47736. (New Explorers Ser.). (Illus.). 48p. (YA). (gr. 5 up). 1997. lib. bdg. 17.95 (*1-56711-229-3*) Blackbirch.

Mysteries of the Rosary. Edith Myers. (Illus.). 41p. 1977. reprint ed. 3.00 (*0-912414-13-8*) Stella Maris Bks.

***Mysteries of the Rosary: Mirror of Scripture & Gateway to Prayer.** Roy Barkley. (Illus.). 2000. pap. 16.95 (*0-8189-0848-3*, Saint Pauls) Alba.

Mysteries of the Rosie Cross: The History of That Curious Sect of the Middle Ages Known As the Resicrucians. 134p. 1993. reprint ed. spiral bd. 23.00 (*0-7873-0037-3*) Hlth Research.

Mysteries of the Rosie Cross of the History of That Curious Sect of the Middle Ages Known as the Rosicrucians (1891) 139p. 1996. reprint ed. pap. 16.95 (*1-56459-698-2*) Kessinger Pub.

Mysteries of the Runes. Michael Howard. 1994. pap. 22.95 (*1-898307-07-5*, Pub. by Capall Bann Pubng) Holmes Pub.

Mysteries of the Sahara. Ed. by Arthur Meier Schlesinger, Jr. & Fred L. Israel. (Cultural & Geographical Exploration Ser.). (Illus.). 144p. (YA). (gr. 5 up). 1999. lib. bdg. 19.95 (*0-7910-5097-1*) Chelsea Hse.

Mysteries of the Seed. Rodney Collin. 1987. pap. 7.95 (*1-55818-100-8*, Sure Fire) Holmes Pub.

Mysteries of the Sky: Activities for Collaborative Groups. Adams & Slater. 232p. (C). 1998. per. 38.95 (*0-7872-5126-7*) Kendall-Hunt.

Mysteries of the Unexplained. H. G. Carlson. LC 95-100126. (Illus.). 192p. 1994. pap. 15.95 (*0-8092-3497-1*, 349710, Contemporary Bks) NTC Contemp Pub Co.

Mysteries of the Universe. Colin Wilson. LC 97-15424. (Unexplained Ser.). 40p. (J). (gr. 4-6). 1997. 14.95 (*0-7894-2165-8*) DK Pub Inc.

Mysteries of the Universe: The Latest Secrets Revealed in the Light of Recent Scientific Discoveries. Nigel Hawkes. (Mysteries of...Ser.). (Illus.). 40p. (J). (gr. 4-6). 1995. pap. 6.95 (*1-56294-195-X*, Copper Beech Bks) Millbrook Pr.

Mysteries of the Unknown. Usborne Books Staff. (Illus.). 96p. (YA). (gr. 6 up). lib. bdg. 21.95 (*1-58086-032-X*, Usborne) EDC.

Mysteries of the Unknown: Master Index. Time-Life Books Editors. Ed. by Jim Hicks. LC 92-26586. (Mysteries of the Unknown Ser.). (Illus.). 160p. 1993. lib. bdg. 26.93 (*0-8094-6509-4*) Time-Life.

Mysteries of the World (Geklarte u. Ungeklarte Phanomene) Quadrillion Media Staff. (Start Me Up Ser.: Vol. 4). 48p. (J). (gr. 3-8). 1998. mass mkt. 12.95 (*1-58185-003-4*, Tessloff Publishing) Quadrillion Media.

Mysteries of Time & Space. Brad Steiger. LC 89-50670. (Illus.). 256p. 1989. pap. 12.95 (*0-914918-95-8*, Whitford) Schiffer.

Mysteries of Udolpho. 2nd ed. Ann Radcliffe. Ed. by Bonamy Dobree. (Oxford World's Classics Ser.). 736p. 1998. pap. 11.95 (*0-19-282523-2*) OUP.

Mysteries of UFOs. Brian Innes. LC 98-9354. (Unsolved Mysteries Ser.). (J). 1999. 24.26 (*0-8172-5477-3*) Raintree Steck-V.

Mysteries of UFO's. Brian Innes. 1999. pap. text 6.95 (*0-8172-4274-0*) Raintree Steck-V.

Mysteries of Unknown (B - U) C. Miller et al. (World of the Unknown Ser.). (Illus.). 96p. (YA). (gr. 6 up). 1992. pap. 12.95 (*0-86020-492-8*) EDC.

Mysteries of Venus. Mark Lerner. (Illus.). 208p. (Orig.). 1986. pap. 10.95 (*0-938559-00-1*) Great Bear Pr.

Mysteries of Willpower. Torkom Saraydarian. LC 94-60982. 283 p. 1995. pap. 14.95 (*0-929874-41-2*) TSG Pub Found.

Mysteries of Witchcraft: Pagan Mysteries & Universal Laws. Rhuddlwm Gawr. LC 85-73761. (Illus.). 144p. (Orig.). 15.95 (*0-931760-38-0*, CP 10116); pap. 12.95 (*0-931760-16-X*) Camelot GA.

Mysteries of Witchcraft & the Occult. Bob Jackson. 1991. 12.98 (*1-55521-711-7*) Bk Sales Inc.

Mysteries of Witchcraft & the Occult. Robert Jackson. 128p. 10.99 (*1-57215-228-1*, JG2281) World Pubns.

Mysteries of Women. mass mkt. 6.95 (*0-7472-4401-4*, Pub. by Headline Bk Pub) Trafalgar.

Mysteries of Worship in Islam. E. E. Calverley. 1981. 6.95 (*1-56744-166-1*) Kazi Pubns.

Mysteries of Yesod. 3rd ed. Omraam M. Aivanhov. (Complete Works: Vol. 7). (Illus.). 217p. 1988. pap. 14.95 (*2-85566-109-9*, Pub. by Prosveta) Prosveta USA.

Mysteries of Zigomar: Poems & Stories. Allan Ahlberg. LC 97-2035. (Illus.). 64p. (J). (gr. 1-7). 1997. 17.99 (*0-7636-0352-X*) Candlewick Pr.

Mysteries on Monroe Street. Sandra Belton. LC 97-45013. (Ernestine & Amanda Ser.). 153p. (J). (gr. 4-7). 1998. per. 16.00 (*0-689-81612-X*) S&S Childrens.

Mysteries on Monroe Street. Sandra Belton & Nancy Carpenter. LC 97-45013. (Ernestine & Amanda Ser.: No. 4). 176p. (J). (gr. 4-6). 1999. per. 4.50 (*0-689-81662-6*, 076714004504) Aladdin.

Mysteries, Puzzles & Paradoxes in Quantum Mechanics. Ed. by Rodalfo Bonifacio. LC 99-60523. (AIP Conference Proceedings Ser.). (Illus.). 362p. 1999. 95.00 (*1-56396-852-5*) Am Inst Physics.

Mysteries Revealed: A Handbook of Esoteric Psychology, Philosophy & Spirituality. Andrew Schneider. LC 95-74966. (Illus.). 192p. (Orig.). 1995. pap. 12.95 (*1-56184-124-2*) New Falcon Pubns.

***Mysteries since Creation.** Christopher Sun. (CHI., Illus.). 288p. 2000. 12.00 (*0-9668519-0-0*) Christopher Sun.

Mysteries Through the Ages. Jillian Powell et al. LC 96-13227. (Illus.). 192p. (J). (gr. 4-6). 1996. 16.95 (*0-7613-0518-1*, Copper Beech Bks) Millbrook Pr.

Mysteries Today & Other Essays. Laurence J. Bendit. 1994. 5.95 (*0-7229-5024-1*) Theos Pub Hse.

Mysteries, True & False. Barron's Educational Editors. (Megascope Ser.). (Illus.). 64p. (J). (gr. 5). 1998. 6.95 (*0-7641-5095-2*) Barron.

Mysteries with a Message. Tom Letchworth & Celesta Letchworth. 1995. pap. 8.99 (*0-8341-9351-5*, MP-762) Nazarene.

Mysteries with a Message, No. 2. 1997. pap. 8.99 (*0-8341-9654-9*) Lillenas.

***Mysteries Within: A Surgeon Reflects on Medical Myths.** Sherwin B. Nuland. LC 99-88659. 288p. 2000. 24.00 (*0-684-85486-4*) S&S Trade.

***Mysteries 3 Bk Set-hde.** Time-Life Books Editors. (gr. 7). 1999. (*0-7835-4773-0*) Time-Life Educ.

***Mysteries 3 Bk Set-tpm.** Time-Life Books Editors. (gr. 7). 1999. 44.85 (*0-7835-4772-2*) Time-Life Educ.

Mysterieuse Attirance. Charlotte Walker. (FRE.). 1998. mass mkt. 4.99 (*0-373-38307-X*, 1-38307-4) Harlequin Bks.

Mysterieux Heritage. Liz Fielding. (Azur Ser.: Vol. 700). (FRE.). 1998. mass mkt. 3.50 (*0-373-34700-6*, 1-34700-4) Harlequin Bks.

Mysteriose Konzert: Teacher's guide. EMC Publishing Company Staff & Hans J. Konig. text 5.95 (*0-8219-0041-2*) EMC-Paradigm.

Mysteriose Konzert: Textbook. Hans J. Konig. text 5.95 (*0-8219-0039-0*) EMC-Paradigm.

Mysteriose Konzert: Workbook. EMC Publishing Company Staff & Hans J. Konig. pap., wbk. ed. 5.95 (*0-8219-0040-4*) EMC-Paradigm.

Mysterious. Fabio. 352p. 1998. pap. 6.99 (*0-7860-0491-6*, Pinncle Kensgtn) Kensgtn Pub Corp.

***Mysterious Addie Destima Taylor Hester: Solving Puzzles of Family History.** Albert L. Hester. (Illus.). 76p. 1999. pap. 19.95 (*0-9673027-1-4*) Green Berry Pr.

Mysterious Adventures of Sherlock Holmes. Arthur Conan Doyle. (Classics for Young Readers Ser.). (Illus.). 256p. (YA). (gr. 5 up). 1996. pap. 3.99 (*0-14-037262-8*, PuffinBks) Peng Put Young Read.

Mysterious Affair at Styles. Agatha Christie. 22.95 (*0-88411-385-X*) Amereon Ltd.

Mysterious Affair at Styles. Agatha Christie. 1992. 19.95 incl. audio (*1-882071-21-2*) B&B Audio.

Mysterious Affair at Styles. Agatha Christie. 208p. 1991. mass mkt. 5.99 (*0-425-12961-6*) Berkley Pub.

Mysterious Affair at Styles. Agatha Christie. LC 97-1451. (Dover Mystery Classics Ser.). 160p. 1997. reprint ed. pap. text 2.00 (*0-486-29695-4*) Dover.

Mysterious Affair at Styles & the Secret Adversary: An Agatha Christie Omnibus. Agatha Christie. LC 97-4269. 464p. 1998. pap. 12.95 (*0-7867-0434-9*) Carroll & Graf.

Mysterious Alabaster Bottle. Elizabeth R. Handford & Joy R. Martin. 28p. (Orig.). 1987. pap. 2.50 (*0-912623-04-7*) Joyful Woman.

Mysterious Apocalypse: Interpreting the Book of Revelation. Arthur W. Wainwright. 288p. (Orig.). 1993. pap. 21.95 (*0-687-27641-1*) Abingdon.

Mysterious Barricades. Bengt Soderbergh. Tr. by Elivor Martinus from SWE. LC 86-62822. 267p. (Orig.). 1986. 29.95 (*0-7206-0639-X*, Pub. by P Owen Ltd) Dufour.

Mysterious Bible Codes. Grant Jeffrey. LC 98-38284. 256p. 1998. 19.99 (*0-8499-1325-X*) Word Pub.

Mysterious Bible Codes. Grant R. Jeffrey. 208p. 1999. pap. text 12.99 (*0-8499-3718-3*) Tommy Nelson.

Mysterious Britain. Homer Sykes. (Country Ser.). (Illus.). 160p. 1998. pap. 17.95 (*0-7538-0432-8*, Pub. by Orion Pubng Grp) Trafalgar.

Mysterious Cairo. (Torg Ser.). 352p. 4.95 (*0-87431-346-5*, 20608) West End Games.

Mysterious Cape Cod Manuscript. Marie Lee. LC 97-93460. (Cape Cod Mystery Ser.: Bk. 3). 192p. 1997. 18.95 (*0-8034-9238-3*, Avalon Bks) Bouregy.

Mysterious Caravan. Franklin W. Dixon. (Hardy Boys Mystery Stories Ser.: No. 54). (Illus.). 180p. (J). (gr. 3-6). 1975. 5.95 (*0-448-08954-8*, G & D) Peng Put Young Read.

Mysterious Cargo. Galila Ben-Uri. (Illus.). 285p. (J). (gr. 5-7). 1989. pap. 14.95 (*1-56062-007-2*) CIS Comm.

Mysterious Case. Dave Gustaveson. (Reel Kids Adventures Ser.: Bk. 4). 150p. (J). (gr. 3-8). 1995. pap. 5.99 (*0-927545-78-0*) YWAM Pub.

Mysterious Case of Nancy Drew & the Hardy Boys. Marvin Heiferman & Carole Kismaric. LC 98-29839. (Illus.). 136p. 1998. 20.00 (*0-684-84689-6*, Fireside) S&S Trade Pap.

Mysterious Case of Sir Arthur Conan Doyle. Cynthia Adams. LC 99-11668. (World Writers Ser.). (Illus.). 112p. (YA). (gr. 5 up). 1999. lib. bdg. 18.95 (*1-883846-34-X*) M Reynolds.

Mysterious Cases of Mr. Pin. Mary E. Monsell. Ed. by Patricia MacDonald. (Illus.). 64p. (J). 1992. pap. 3.50 (*0-671-74084-9*, Minstrel Bks) PB.

Mysterious Cat Stories. John R. Stephens. 1994. 11.98 (*0-88365-872-0*) Galahad Bks.

Mysterious Catalytic Foods. Brown Landone. 63p. 1994. reprint ed. spiral bd. 11.00 (*0-7873-1033-6*) Hlth Research.

Mysterious Cave: Includes Audio Cassette, Coloring Pad & Crayons. A. L. Parr. (Illus.). 16p. (J). (gr. k-4). 1998. pap. 12.50 incl. audio (*0-9662994-1-8*) Adven Meadow.

Mysterious Chronicles of Oz: or Tip & the Sawhorse of Oz. Onyx Madden. LC 83-73621. (Illus.). 240p. 1985. 14.95 (*0-930422-34-1*) Dennis-Landman.

Mysterious Creatures. Time-Life Books Editors. (Mysteries of the Unknown Ser.). (Illus.). 144p. 1988. 14.95 (*0-8094-6332-6*); pap. write for info. (*0-8094-6335-0*); text. write for info. (*0-8094-6334-2*); lib. bdg. 23.27 (*0-8094-6333-4*) Time-Life.

Mysterious Death of Mary Rogers: Sex & Culture in 19th-Century New York. Amy G. Srebnick. (Studies in the History of Sexuality). (Illus.). 240p. 1997. reprint ed. pap. text 14.95 (*0-19-511392-6*) OUP.

Mysterious Detectives: Psychics. Tamara Wilcox. (Great Unsolved Mysteries Ser.). 1997. pap. 4.95 (*0-8114-6860-7*) Raintree Steck-V.

Mysterious Disappearance of Leon (I Mean Noel) Ellen Raskin. (Illus.). 160p. (J). (gr. 5-9). 1989. pap. 5.99 (*0-14-032945-5*, PuffinBks) Peng Put Young Read.

Mysterious Disappearance of Leon (I Mean Noel) Ellen Raskin. (J). 1971. 10.09 (*0-606-04096-X*, Pub. by Turtleback) Demco.

Mysterious Document. Loretta B. Staley. iv, 234p. 1997. pap. 12.00 (*1-891142-02-X*) Book Bench.

Mysterious Document. Jules Verne. lib. bdg. 22.95 (*0-8488-2064-9*) Amereon Ltd.

Mysterious Doom: And Other Ghostly Tales of the Pacific Northwest. Jessica A. Salmonson. (Illus.). 216p. (Orig.). 1992. pap. 11.95 (*0-912365-65-X*) Sasquatch Bks.

Mysterious Dr. Q. Created by Francine Pascal. (Sweet Valley Twins Ser.: No. 102). 144p. (J). (gr. 3-7). 1996. pap. 3.50 (*0-553-48433-8*) Bantam.

Mysterious Dr. Q. Jamie Suzanne. (Sweet Valley Twins Ser.: No. 102). (J). (gr. 3-7). 1996. 8.60 (*0-606-10334-1*, Pub. by Turtleback) Demco.

Mysterious Erotic Tales. 256p. 1997. 8.98 (*0-7858-0725-X*) Bk Sales Inc.

Mysterious Fayum Portraits: Faces from Ancient Egypt. Euphrosyne Doxiadis. (Illus.). 256p. 1995. 85.00 (*0-8109-3331-4*, Pub. by Abrams) Time Warner.

Mysterious Flame: Conscious Minds in a Material World. Colin McGinn. 256p. 1999. 24.00 (*0-465-01422-4*, Pub. by Basic) HarpC.

***Mysterious Flame: New SubTitle.** McGinn. 256p. 2000. pap. 14.00 (*0-465-01423-2*) HarpC.

Mysterious Giant of Barletta. Tomie De Paola. LC 83-18445. (Illus.). 32p. (J). (ps-3). 1988. pap. 6.00 (*0-15-256349-0*, Voyager Bks) Harcourt.

Mysterious Giant of Barletta: An Italian Folktale. Tomie De Paola. LC 83-18445. (Illus.). 32p. (J). (ps-3). 1984. 13.95 (*0-15-256347-4*) Harcourt.

Mysterious Gunfighter: The Story of Dave Mather. Jack DeMattos. LC 92-4022. (Illus.). 200p. 1992. 21.95 (*0-932702-95-3*) Creative Texas.

Mysterious Healing. Brian Innes. LC 98-38216. (Unsolved Mysteries Ser.). (J). 1999. 24.26 (*0-8172-5489-7*) Raintree Steck-V.

***Mysterious Healing.** Steck-Vaughn Company Staff. (Unsolved Mysteries Ser.). (Illus.). (J). 2000. pap. 6.95 (*0-8172-5851-5*) Raintree Steck-V.

Mysterious Hideaway. Lois W. Johnson. (Adventures of the Northwoods Ser.: Bk. 6). 16p. (J). (gr. 4-7). 1992. pap. 5.99 (*1-55661-238-9*) Bethany Hse.

Mysterious Island. Tony Abbott. (Secrets of Droon Ser.: No. 3). (Illus.). (J). (gr. 2-5). 1999. pap. 2.99 (*0-590-10840-9*, Pub. by Scholastic Inc) Penguin Putnam.

Mysterious Island. Jules Verne. 1997. mass mkt. 4.99 (*1-57840-033-3*, Pub. by Acclaim Bks) Penguin Putnam.

Mysterious Island. Jules Verne. Ed. by Isaac Asimov. 512p. (YA). 1986. mass mkt. 5.95 (*0-451-52491-8*, Sig Classics) NAL.

Mysterious Island. Jules Verne. LC 88-3167. (Scribners Illustrated Classics Ser.). (Illus.). 493p. (J). 1988. 25.95 (*0-684-18957-7*) Scribner.

Mysterious Island. Jules Verne. 1986. 11.05 (*0-606-02969-9*, Pub. by Turtleback) Demco.

Mysterious Island. Jules Verne. (Airmont Classics Ser.). (J). (gr. 8 up). 1965. mass mkt. 1.95 (*0-8049-0077-9*, CL-77) Airmont.

Mysterious Island. Jules Verne. (Illustrated Classics Collection 2). 64p. 1994. pap. 4.95 (*0-7854-0721-9*, 40409) Am Guidance.

Mysterious Island. Jules Verne. 1997. pap. 2.95 (*0-89375-708-X*) Troll Communs.

Mysterious Island. large type ed. Jules Verne. 400p. 1998. lib. bdg. 24.00 (*0-939495-59-7*) North Bks.

Mysterious Island. Jules Verne. 620p. 1998. reprint ed. lib. bdg. 25.00 (*1-58287-052-7*) North Bks.

Mysterious Island: Student Activity Book. Marcia Sohl & Gerald Dackerman. (Now Age Illustrated Ser.). (Illus.). (J). (gr. 4-10). 1976. student ed. 1.25 (*0-88301-193-X*) Pendulum Pr.

Mysterious Island Readalong. Jules Verne. (Illustrated Classics Collection 2). 64p. 1994. pap. 14.95 incl. audio (*0-7854-0687-5*, 40411) Am Guidance.

Mysterious Islands: Forgotten Tales of the Great Lakes. Andrea Gutsche & Barbara Chisholm. 320p. 1999. pap. 19.95 (*1-894073-11-8*) Lynx Images.

Mysterious Journey: Amelia Earhart's Last Flight. Martha Wickham. (Odyssey Ser.). (J). (gr. 2-5). 1997. audio 7.95 (*1-56899-414-1*, C6006) Soundprints.

Mysterious Journey: Amelia Earhart's Last Flight. Martha Wickham. (Odyssey Ser.). (Illus.). 32p. (J). (gr. 2-5). 1997. 19.95 incl. audio (*1-56899-412-5*, BC6006); 14.95 (*1-56899-407-9*); pap. 5.95 (*1-56899-408-7*) Soundprints.

Mysterious Journey: Amelia Earhart's Last Flight, Incl. toy. Martha Wickham. (Smithsonian Odyssey Ser.). (Illus.). 32p. (J). (gr. 2-5). 1997. 29.95 (*1-56899-409-5*); 35.95 incl. audio (*1-56899-413-3*); pap. 17.95 (*1-56899-410-9*); pap. 25.95 incl. audio (*1-56899-411-7*) Soundprints.

Mysterious Jungles. Illus. by Luis Rizo. LC 95-15155. 32p. (J). (gr. 3-12). 1996. lib. bdg. 15.95 (*0-7910-3465-8*) Chelsea Hse.

Mysterious Kitties. Andrews & McMeel Publishing Staff. 1999. 7.95 (*0-8362-8275-2*) Andrews & McMeel.

***Mysterious Knoxville.** Charles Edwin Price. (Illus.). 112p. 1999. pap. 12.95 (*1-57072-103-3*, Silver Dagger) Overmountain Pr.

Mysterious Kundalini. Vasant G. Rele. 92p. (Orig.). 1985. reprint ed. spiral bd. 13.00 (*0-7873-1032-8*) Hlth Research.

Mysterious Lands: A Naturalist Explores the Four Great Deserts of the Southwest. Ann Zwinger. (Illus.). 388p. 1996. pap. 16.95 (*0-8165-1650-2*) U of Ariz Pr.

Mysterious Lands & Peoples. Time-Life Books Editors. Ed. by Jim Hicks. (Mysteries of the Unknown Ser.). (Illus.). 144p. 1991. 14.95 (*0-8094-6520-5*); lib. bdg. 17.45 (*0-8094-6521-3*) Time-Life.

***Mysterious Life of the Body: A New Look at Psychosomatics.** Jennifer Bullington. (Linkoping Studies in Arts & Science). (Illus.). 336p. 1999. pap. 52.50 (*91-22-01844-1*, Pub. by Almqvist) Coronet Bks.

Mysterious Light. Jane Norman & Frank Beazley. 24p. (J). (ps-3). 1993. pap. write for info. (*1-883585-05-8*) Pixanne Ent.

***Mysterious Lights & Other Cases.** Seymour Simon. LC 96-41766. (Einstein Anderson, Science Detective Ser.). (Illus.). 96p. (J). (gr. 3-6). 1998. 15.00 (*0-688-14445-4*, Wm Morrow) Morrow Avon.

***Mysterious Lights & Other Cases.** Seymour Simon. (Einstein Anderson, Science Detective Ser.). (Illus.). 96p. (J). (gr. 3-6). 1999. mass mkt. 3.99 (*0-380-72660-2*, Avon Bks) Morrow Avon.

Mysterious Love. Shirley Brinkerhoff. (Nikki Sheridan Ser.: Bk. 2). 192p. (YA). (gr. 9-13). 1998. pap. 5.99 (*1-56179-485-6*) Focus Family.

***Mysterious, Magical Cat.** D. J. Conway. LC 00-37143. (Illus.). 224p. (J). 2000. pap. 8.99 (*0-517-16301-2*) Bell T.

M

Mysterious, Magickal Cat. D.J. Conway. LC 98-2501. (Illus.). 256p. 1998. pap. 15.95 (*1-56718-180-5*) Llewellyn Pubns.

Mysterious Mannequin. Carolyn Keene. LC 77-100115. (Nancy Drew Mystery Stories Ser.: No. 47). (Illus.). 178p. (J). (gr. 4-7). 1970. 5.95 (*0-448-09547-5*, G & D) Peng Put Young Read.

Mysterious Mansion. (Get a Clue Mystery Puzzles Ser.). 16p. (J). (gr. 5). 12.99 (*0-7847-0734-0*) Standard Pub.

Mysterious Marching Vegetables. Barbara Tharp et al. (My Health My World Ser.: Vol. 4). (Illus.). vi, 36p. pap. write for info. (*1-888997-37-0*) Baylor Coll Med.

Mysterious Mask. Cragie. Date not set. pap. text. write for info. (*0-17-556001-3*) Addison-Wesley.

Mysterious Message. Stephen B. Castleberry & Susie L. Castleberry. (Farm Mystery Ser.). 160p. 1997. pap. 7.50 (*1-891907-04-2*) Castleberry.

***Mysterious Message in Montana.** Bob Schaller. (Arlington Family Adventures Ser.). 144p. (gr. 3-7). 2000. pap. 5.99 (*0-8010-4454-5*) Baker Bks.

Mysterious Messengers: A Course of Hebrew Prophecy from Amos Onwards. John Eaton. LC 98-24505. x, 214 p. 1998. pap. 18.00 (*0-8028-4495-2*) Eerdmans.

***Mysterious Mew.** Hidenori Kusaka. (Pokemon Adventures Ser.: No. 1). (Illus.). 48p. (J). (gr. 4-7). 1999. pap. 5.95 (*1-56931-387-3*, Pub. by Viz Commns Inc) Publishers Group.

M

Mysterious Minds. Gillian Cross. (Illus.). 48p. (J). pap. 7.95 (*0-14-130140-6*, Pub. by Pnguin Bks Ltd) Trafalgar.

***Mysterious Misadventures of Foy Rin Jin: A Decidedly Dysfunctional Dragon.** Jim Friedman. LC 98-12140. (Illus.). 32p. (J). (ps-3). 1999. lib. bdg. 15.89 (*0-06-028551-6*) HarpC Child Bks.

Mysterious Misadventures of Foy Rin Jin: A Decidedly Dysfunctional Dragon. Jim Friedman. LC 98-12140. (Illus.). 32p. (J). (ps-3). 1999. 15.95 (*0-06-028000-X*, Perennial) HarperTrade.

Mysterious Miss Marie Corelli: Queen of Victorian Bestsellers. Teresa Ransom. 1999. 39.95 (*0-7509-1570-6*, Pub. by Sutton Publng) Intl Pubs Mktg.

***Mysterious Miss Slade.** Dick King-Smith. LC 99-46886. (Illus.). 128p. (J). (gr. 3-5). 2000. 15.95 (*0-517-80045-4*, Pub. by Crown Bks Yng Read); lib. bdg. 17.99 (*0-517-80046-2*, Pub. by Crown Bks Yng Read) Random.

Mysterious Monday. Colleen L. Reece. (Juli Scott, Super Sleuth Ser.). 176p. (J). (gr. 4-10). 1997. pap. text 2.97 (*1-55748-983-1*) Barbour Pub.

Mysterious Mountain Man: Man of the Month. Annette Broadrick. (Desire Ser.). 1995. mass mkt. 3.25 (*0-373-05925-6*, 1-05925-2) Silhouette.

Mysterious Mountain Score. A. Hovhaness. 64p. 1991. pap. 18.95 (*0-7935-1023-6*) H Leonard.

Mysterious Mr. Blot. Elihu Blotnick & Barbara Robinson. Ed. by Ariel Fragment. LC 79-51994. (Illus.). 1979. 5.00 (*0-915090-09-0*) Calif Street.

Mysterious Mr Love: A Play Karoline Leach. LC 98-232331. 51 p. 1997. write for info. (*0-573-01830-8*) French.

Mysterious Mr. Moon. Anne Stephenson. 160p. (Orig.). (J). (gr. 4-7). 1990. pap. 3.95 (*0-7736-7284-2*) Stoddart Publ.

Mysterious Mr. Quin. Agatha Christie. 256p. 1987. mass mkt. 5.99 (*0-425-10353-6*) Berkley Pub.

Mysterious Mr. Ross. Vivien Alcock. LC 87-5455. 160p. (YA). (gr. 5-9). 1987. 14.95 (*0-385-29581-2*) Delacorte.

Mysterious Music: Rhythm & Free Verse. G. Burns Cooper. LC 97-49161. 262p. 1998. 49.50 (*0-8047-2938-7*) Stanford U Pr.

Mysterious Neighbor. Vivian A. Velasco. (Illus.). (J). 1995. 7.95 (*0-533-11357-1*) Vantage.

Mysterious Numbers see Et les Nombres Mysterieux: The Berenstain Bears

Mysterious Numbers see En De Geheimzinnige Getallen: The Berenstain Bears

Mysterious Numbers: The Berenstain Bears. Stan Berenstain & Jan Berenstain. (Comic Tale Easy Reader Ser.). 16p. (J). (ps-2). 1993. write for info. (*1-883366-00-3*) YES Ent.

Mysterious Numbers: The Berenstain Bears. Stan Berenstain & Jan Berenstain. (Comes to Life Bks.). 16p. (J). (ps-2). 1994. write for info. (*1-883366-74-7*) YES Ent.

Mysterious Numbers of the Hebrew Kings. Edwin R. Thiele. LC 94-25569. 256p. 1995. pap. 12.99 (*0-8254-3825-X*) Kregel.

Mysterious Numbers of the Hebrew Kings. rev. ed. Edwin R. Thiele. 256p. 1984. reprint ed. pap. 17.95 (*0-310-36011-0*, 10116P) Zondervan.

Mysterious Numbers of the Sealed Revelation see Science & Religion Series

Mysterious Nurse. large type ed. Valerie Scott. LC 97-35652. 287p. 1998. lib. bdg. 18.95 (*0-7838-8289-0*, G K Hall Lrg Type) Mac Lib Ref.

***Mysterious Ocean Highway: Benjamin Franklin & the Gulf Stream.** Deborah Heiligman. LC 99-11476. (Ocean Pilot Ser.). (Illus.). 48p. (J). 1999. lib. bdg. 25.69 (*0-7398-1226-2*) Raintree Steck-V.

Mysterious Ocean Highway: Benjamin Franklin & the Gulf Stream. Deborah Heiligman. LC 99-11476. (Turnstone Ocean Pilot Book Ser.). 48p. (J). (gr. 3-7). 1999. 7.95 (*0-7398-1227-0*) Raintree Steck-V.

Mysterious Oceans. Jon Erickson. 208p. 1988. 22.95 (*0-07-157342-9*) McGraw.

Mysterious Oceans. Jon S. Erickson. (Discovering Earth Science Ser.). (Illus.). 208p. 1988. 22.95 (*0-8306-9142-1*, 3042); pap. 15.95 (*0-8306-9342-4*) McGraw-Hill Prof.

Mysterious Oklahoma: Eerie True Tales from the Sooner State. David A. Farris. LC 96-190423. (Illus.). (Orig.). 1995. pap. 12.95 (*0-9646922-0-1*) D A Farris.

Mysterious Old Church, Vol. 1. Neil Wilson. (Choice Adventures Ser.). (J). (gr. 4-7). 1991. pap. 4.99 (*0-8423-5025-X*) Tyndale Hse.

Mysterious Parable: A Literary Study. Madeleine Boucher. Ed. by Bruce Vawter. LC 76-51260. (Catholic Biblical Quarterly Monographs: No. 6). ix, 101p. 1977. pap. 2.50 (*0-915170-05-1*) Catholic Bibl Assn.

Mysterious Passover Visitors. Ann B. Herold. LC 89-1946. (Illus.). 112p. (Orig.). (J). (gr. 3-7). 1989. pap. 5.99 (*0-8361-3494-X*) Herald Pr.

Mysterious Pen Pal. Eli Cantillon. (J). (ps-5). 1994. 16.95 (*0-938971-83-2*) JTG Nashville.

Mysterious Persons in History. Fred Neff. LC 96-51182. 1996. lib. bdg. 19.93 (*0-8225-3932-2*, Lerner Publctns) Lerner Pub.

Mysterious Places. Jennifer Westwood. 1996. 22.98 (*0-88365-938-7*) Galahad Bks.

***Mysterious Places of the World, 1.** Ronald Pearsall. 1999. 16.95 (*1-57717-157-8*) Todtri Prods.

***Mysterious Play, Vol. 2.** Yu Watase. (Illus.). 192p. 2000. pap. text 15.95 (*1-56931-439-X*, Pub. by Viz Commns Inc) Publishers Group.

Mysterious Play of Kali: An Interpretive Study of Ramakrishna. Carl Olson. 140p. 1990. 29.95 (*1-55540-339-5*, 01 00 56); pap. 19.95 (*1-55540-340-9*) OUP.

Mysterious Power of Ki: The Force Within. Kouzo Kaku. (Illus.). 224p. 2000. boxed set 24.95 (*1-901903-25-7*, Pub. by Global Oriental) Midpt Trade.

***Mysterious Presence.** Copland Mini Kenneth. 1999. pap. text 6.99 (*1-57794-149-7*) Harrison Hse.

Mysterious Presence. Christopher P. Maselli. LC 97-46152. (Commander Kellie & the Superkids' Early Adventures Ser.). 1998. pap. write for info. (*1-57562-215-7*) K Copeland Pubns.

Mysterious Rays of Dr. Rontgen. Beverly Gherman. LC 92-38966. (Illus.). 32p. (J). (gr. 2-5). 1994. lib. bdg. 14.95 (*0-689-31839-1*) Atheneum Yung Read.

Mysterious Realms: Functions of Imagery in Traditional Spanish Lyric & Balladry. Elizabeth Boretz. viii, 178p. 1998. pap. 14.00 (*0-936388-25-0*) Juan de la Cuesta.

Mysterious Realms: Probing Paranormal, Historical, & Forensic Enigmas. Ed. by Joe Nickell & John F. Fischer. LC 92-36998. (Illus.). 221p. 1992. 26.95 (*0-87975-765-5*) Prometheus Bks.

Mysterious Rider. Zane Grey. 1976. 23.95 (*0-8488-0277-2*) Amereon Ltd.

Mysterious Rider. Zane Grey. 1998. mass mkt. 4.99 (*0-8125-9040-6*, Pub. by Tor Bks) St Martin.

***Mysterious Robbery.** Radhika Kaula. (Illus.). 16p. (J). (gr. k-5). 2000. pap. 12.00 (*0-9653862-3-6*) Transnatl Computing.

Mysterious Ruins. Natalie J. Prior. 1996. pap. 6.95 (*1-86448-247-8*) IPG Chicago.

Mysterious Samadhi. 1984. write for info. (*0-318-59380-7*) Ranney Pubns.

***Mysterious Science.** Lisa McCourt. (Brain Builders Ser.). 48p. (J). 2000. pap. 7.95 (*0-7373-0465-0*, 04650W, Pub. by Lowell Hse Juvenile) NTC Contemp Pub Co.

Mysterious Science of the Law. Daniel J. Boorstin. (Illus.). 288p. 1996. pap. text 14.95 (*0-226-06498-0*) U Ch Pr.

Mysterious Scotland. M. Balfour. LC 97-136345. 1997. text 35.00 (*1-85158-695-4*, Pub. by Mainstream Pubng) Trafalgar.

Mysterious Scott: The Monte Cristo of Death Valley. Orin S. Merrill. LC 72-93067. (Illus.). 216p. 1972. reprint ed. pap. 8.50 (*0-912494-10-7*) Commun Print.

Mysterious Sea. Ferdinand Lane. LC 73-128268. (Essay Index Reprint Ser.). 1977. 24.95 (*0-8369-1971-8*) Ayer.

Mysterious Sea Monsters of California's Central Coast. Randall A. Reinstedt. Ed. by John Bergez. LC 80-114610. (Illus.). 74p. 1993. pap. 6.95 (*0-933818-06-8*) Ghost Town.

Mysterious Secrets of the Dark Kingdom: The Battle for Planet Earth. Jonathan P. Timmons. Ed. by Ralph Rideout. (Illus.). 414p. 1991. 24.95 (*1-56350-000-0*) CCI Pub.

Mysterious Signal. Lois W. Johnson. LC 97-33958. (Riverboat Adventures Ser.). 176p. (J). 1998. pap. 5.99 (*1-55661-355-5*) Bethany Hse.

Mysterious Signs. Mark Weinrich. LC 93-74958. (Light Chaser Mysteries Ser.: Bk. 2). 111p. (J). 1994. pap. 4.99 (*0-88965-107-8*, Pub. by Horizon Books) Chr Pubns.

Mysterious Skin: A Novel. Scott Heim. LC 95-52882. 304p. 1996. pap. 13.00 (*0-06-092686-4*) HarpC.

Mysterious Space Chase. 1997. pap. 1.50 (*0-8167-0891-6*) Troll Communs.

Mysterious Sphinx. Hilton Hotema. 41p. 1996. reprint ed. spiral bd. 9.00 (*0-7873-0456-5*) Hlth Research.

Mysterious Spirit: The Bell Witch of Tennessee. Charles B. Bell & Harriett P. Miller. 1972. reprint ed. pap. 9.95 (*0-918450-13-6*) C Elder.

Mysterious Stories from the Bible. Charles Mills & Ruth Brands. LC 94-186085. (Professor Appleby & the Maggie B. Tapes Ser.: Vol. 1). 128p. (J). (gr. 4-7). 1993. pap. 8.99 (*0-8280-0709-8*) Review & Herald.

Mysterious Stranger. Susan Mallery. 1997. per. 3.99 (*0-373-24130-5*, 1-24130-6) Silhouette.

Mysterious Stranger. Mark Twain, pseud. 22.95 (*0-8488-0652-2*) Amereon Ltd.

Mysterious Stranger. Mark Twain, pseud. (Signet Classics Ser.). 1962. mass mkt. 4.95 (*0-451-52458-6*, Sig Classics) NAL.

Mysterious Stranger. Eric Wiggin. (Hannah's Island Ser.: Bk. 3). 152p. (Orig.). (J). (gr. 3-7). 1995. pap. 5.99 (*1-883002-26-5*) Emerald WA.

***Mysterious Stranger.** large type ed. E. G. Bartlett. 264p. 2000. pap. 18.99 (*0-7089-5646-7*, Linford) Ulverscroft.

Mysterious Stranger. large type ed. Brenda Castle. (Linford Romance Library). 240p. 1997. pap. 16.99 (*0-7089-5008-6*, Linford) Ulverscroft.

Mysterious Stranger. Mark Twain, pseud. LC 95-9644. (Literary Classics Ser.). 121p. 1995. reprint ed. pap. 5.95 (*1-57392-039-8*) Prometheus Bks.

Mysterious Stranger. Mark Twain, pseud. (Works of Samuel Clemens). 1989. reprint ed. lib. bdg. 79.00 (*0-685-28382-8*) Rprt Serv.

Mysterious Stranger: And Other Stories. Mark Twain, pseud. 1916. 10.05 (*0-606-01908-1*, Pub. by Turtleback) Demco.

Mysterious Stranger Aboard: A Couple's Courageous 40-Year Battle with Multiple Sclerosis. John Johnson & Alice Johnson. 288p. 1995. pap. 9.95 (*0-9648271-0-7*) Mal-Jonal Prodns.

Mysterious Stranger & Other Stories. Mark Twain, pseud. (Thrift Editions Ser.). (Illus.). 128p. 1992. pap. 1.00 (*0-486-27069-6*) Dover.

***Mysterious Strangler.** Peter J. Heck. 2000. mass mkt. 6.50 (*0-425-17704-1*) Berkley Pub.

Mysterious Tadpole. Steven Kellogg. (Illus.). 40p. (J). (ps-3). 1992. pap. 5.99 (*0-14-054870-X*) NAL.

Mysterious Tadpole. Steven Kellogg. 1977. 11.19 (*0-606-05057-4*, Pub. by Turtleback) Demco.

Mysterious Tail of a Charleston Cat. Ruth P. Chappell & Bess P. Shipe. LC 96-26065. (Illus.). 80p. (J). (gr. 4-7). 1996. 15.95 (*0-87844-130-1*) Sandlapper Pub Co.

Mysterious Tales of Japan. Rafe Martin. LC 94-43464. (Illus.). 80p. (YA). (gr. 3 up). 1996. 18.95 (*0-399-22677-X*, G P Putnam) Peng Put Young Read.

Mysterious Thelonious. Chris Raschka. LC 97-6994. (Illus.). 32p. (J). (ps up). 1997. 13.95 (*0-531-30057-9*); lib. bdg. 14.99 (*0-531-33057-5*) Orchard Bks Watts.

Mysterious Transformation: or When Does History Become Literature. Lawrence C. Powell. 276p. 1993. 32.50 (*0-9632966-2-0*) Bks West SW.

Mysterious Transformation: or When Does History Become Literature. deluxe ed. Lawrence C. Powell. 276p. 1993. boxed set 100.00 (*0-9632966-3-9*) Bks West SW.

Mysterious Treasure Map. Glenn Robinson. LC 94-46118. (Shoebox Kids Ser.: Vol. 1). (J). 1995. pap. 6.99 (*0-8163-1256-7*) Pacific Pr Pub Assn.

***Mysterious Treasure of the Slimy Sea Cave.** Rod Randall. LC 98-37534. (Heebie Jeebies Ser.: Vol. 3). 144p. (YA). 1999. pap. 5.99 (*0-8054-1000-7*) Broadman.

Mysterious Universe. James H. Jeans. LC 75-41156. reprint ed. 20.00 (*0-404-14742-9*) AMS Pr.

Mysterious Universe: A Handbook of Astronomical Anomalies. William R. Corliss. LC 78-65616. (Illus.). 1979. 19.95 (*0-915554-05-4*) Sourcebook.

Mysterious Valley. Maurice Champagne. Tr. by Bill Bucko from FRE. (Illus.). 256p. (J). 1994. pap. 19.95 (*0-9626854-9-6*) Atlantean Pr.

Mysterious Valley. Maurice Champagne. Tr. by Bill Bucko from FRE. LC 94-78488. (Illus.). 256p. (J). (gr. 3 up). 1994. 29.95 (*0-9626854-6-1*) Atlantean Pr.

Mysterious Valley. Christopher O'Brien. 1996. mass mkt. 6.99 (*0-312-95883-8*) St Martin.

Mysterious Visitor: Stories of the Prophet Elijah. Nina Jaffe. LC 96-7534. (Illus.). 112p. (J). 1997. 19.95 (*0-590-48422-2*) Scholastic Inc.

Mysterious Voices. William DeAndrea. 1997. 27.50 (*0-614-28227-6*) Macmillan USA.

Mysterious West. Ed. by Tony Hillerman. 464p. 1995. mass mkt. 6.50 (*0-06-109262-2*, Harp PBks) HarpC.

Mysterious World. Time-Life Books Editors. Ed. by Jim Hicks. LC 92-20196. (Mysteries of the Unknown Ser.). (Illus.). 160p. 1993. lib. bdg. 25.93 (*0-8094-6550-7*) Time-Life.

***Mysterious World of Janitorial Brokers.** Robert Jack Kravitz. 110p. 2000. 21.95 (*0-9676187-4-6*) Altura Solutn.

Mysterious World of Marcus Leadbeater. Ivan Southall. 192p. 1990. 14.95 (*0-374-35113-9*) FS&G.

Mysterious Wu Fang - the Case of the Suicide Tomb. Robert J. Hogan. Ed. & Intro. by John P. Gunnison. (High Adventure Ser.: 42). (Illus.). 96p. (C). 1998. pap. 6.00 (*1-886937-29-X*) Adventure Hse.

Mysteriously Meant: The Rediscovery of Pagan Symbolism & Allegorical Interpretation in the Renaissance. Don C. Allen. LC 77-105363. 366p. reprint ed. 113.50 (*0-8357-9279-X*, 201516000092) Bks Demand.

Mysteriously Yours, Maggie Marmelstein. Marjorie Weinman Sharmat. LC 81-48656. (Illus.). 160p. (J). (gr. 3-6). 1982. 12.95 (*0-06-025516-1*) HarpC Child Bks.

Mysterium & Mystery: The Clerical Crime Novel. William D. Spencer. LC 91-28207. 360p. (C). 1992. pap. 21.95 (*0-8093-1809-1*) S Ill U Pr.

Mysterium & Mystery: The Clerical Crime Novel. William D. Spencer. LC 91-28207. 360p. (C). 1992. 36.95 (*0-8093-1808-3*) S Ill U Pr.

Mysterium & Mystery: The Clerical Crime Novel. William D. Spencer. LC 88-39773. (Studies in Religion: No. 6). 356p. reprint ed. pap. 110.40 (*0-8357-1936-7*, 207063700011) Bks Demand.

Mysterium Cosmographicum. Johannes Kepler. Tr. by E. J. Aiton & A. M. Duncan. LC 77-86245. (Janus Ser.).Tr. of Secret of the Universe. 267p. lib. bdg. 35.00 (*0-913870-64-1*) Abaris Bks.

Mysterium Lectures: A Journey through C. G. Jung's Mysterium Coniunctionis. Edward F. Edinger. (Studies in Jungian Psychology by Jungian Analysts: No. 66). (Illus.). 352p. 1995. pap. 20.00 (*0-919123-66-X*, Pub. by Inner City Bks) BookWorld.

Mysterium Liberationis: Fundamental Concepts of Liberation Theology - Conceptos Fundamentales de la Teologia de Liberacion, 2 vols. Ignacio Ellacuria & Jon Sobrino. Tr. by Robert R. Barr et al from SPA. 650p. 1993. reprint ed. 45.00 (*0-88344-917-X*) Orbis Bks.

Mysterium Magnum or an Exposition of the First Book of Moses Called Genesis. Jacob Boehme. Ed. by John Sparrow. 1030p. 1992. reprint ed. pap. 50.00 (*1-56459-212-X*) Kessinger Pub.

Mysterium Paschale. Hans Urs Von Balthasar. Tr. by Aidan Nichols. 310p. pap. 31.95 (*0-567-29171-5*) T&T Clark Pubs.

Mysterium Trinitatis? Fallstudien Zur Trinitaetslehre In der Evangelischen Dogmatik des 20. Jahrunderts. Michael Murrmann-Kahl. (Theologische Biblithek Toepelmann Ser.: Vol. 79). (GER.). viii, 376p. (C). 1997. lib. bdg. 134.30 (*3-11-015262-2*) De Gruyter.

Mystery. C. Mills. (Shadow Creek Ranch Ser.). 1994. pap. 5.99 (*1-878951-19-X*) Review & Herald.

***Mystery.** Steck-Vaughn Company Staff. (Illus.). (J). 2000. pap., teacher ed. 6.45 (*0-8114-9330-X*) Raintree Steck-V.

Mystery. Peter Straub. 560p. 1991. mass mkt. 7.99 (*0-451-16869-0*, Sig) NAL.

Mystery. Peter Straub. 1990. write for info. (*0-318-66856-4*, Penguin Bks) Viking Penguin.

Mystery. Stewart E. White & Samuel H. Adams. LC 74-16525. (Science Fiction Ser.). (Illus.). 296p. 1975. reprint ed. 26.95 (*0-405-06317-2*) Ayer.

Mystery, Level D. (Reading Power Modules Software Ser.). 1997. pap. 3.75 (*1-55855-789-X*) Raintree Steck-V.

Mystery, Level G. (Reading Power Modules Software Ser.). 1997. pap. 3.75 (*1-55855-798-9*) Raintree Steck-V.

Mystery, Level H. (Reading Power Modules Software Ser.). 1997. pap. 3.75 (*1-55855-344-4*) Raintree Steck-V.

Mystery Colossians 1:25-27. Richard Mallette. LC 99-175353. 330 p. 1998. write for info. (*1-878146-09-2*) A C Design NY.

Mystery - Drama from Ancient to Modern Times. Albert Steffen. (Illus.). 40p. 1977. pap. 5.50 (*0-932776-10-8*) Adonis Pr.

Mystery! A Celebration: Stalking Public Television's Greatest Sleuths. Ron Miller. LC 96-42130. (Illus.). 320p. 1996. pap. 27.95 (*0-912333-89-8*) BB&T Inc.

Mystery Amulet of Twelve Words of Love. Erik Kryukov. Date not set. pap. 12.95 (*1-889668-12-5*) S & D.

Mystery & Crime: The New York Public Library Book of Answers-Ingriguing & Entertaining Questions & Answers About the Who's Who & What's What of Whodunnits. Jay Pearsall. 192p. 1995. pap. 11.00 (*0-671-87237-0*, Fireside) S&S Trade Pap.

Mystery & Detection: Thinking & Problem Solving with the Sleuths. Jerry D. Flack. (Gifted Treasury Ser.). xx, 246p. 1990. pap. text 24.00 (*0-87287-815-5*) Teacher Ideas Pr.

Mystery & Detective Fiction in the Library of Congress Classification Scheme. Michael Burgess. LC 84-12344. (Borgo Cataloging Guides Ser.: No.2). 184p. 1987. pap. 23.00 (*0-89370-918-2*) Millefleurs.

Mystery & Glory in John's Gospel. Dorotha W. Fry. LC 92-54261. (Covenant Bible Studies). 96p. 1992. pap. 5.95 (*0-87178-597-8*, 8978) Brethren.

***Mystery & History of the Menger Hotel.** Docia Schultz Williams. (Illus.). 250p. 2000. pap. 16.95 (*1-55622-792-2*, Rep of TX Pr) Wordware Pub.

Mystery & Imagination. 2nd ed. (Illus.). 110p. 1993. 5.95 (*0-19-585463-2*) OUP.

Mystery & Its Fictions: From Oedipus to Agatha Christie. David I. Grossvogel. LC 78-20516. 224p. reprint ed. pap. 69.50 (*0-7837-4262-2*, 204395400012) Bks Demand.

Mystery & Lure of Perfume. C. J. Thompson. 1981. 250.00 (*0-8490-0693-7*) Gordon Pr.

Mystery & Magic, 4 vols. Robert R. Ingpen. LC 95-40726. (Mystery & Magic Ser.). 1998. 69.83 (*0-7910-3925-0*) Chelsea Hse.

Mystery & Magic of Trees & Flowers. Lesley Gordon. (Illus.). 112p. 1999. reprint ed. text 15.00 (*0-7881-6065-6*) DIANE Pub.

Mystery & Manners: Occasional Prose. Flannery O'Connor. Ed. by Robert Fitzgerald & Sally Fitzgerald. LC 69-15409. 256p. 1969. pap. 12.00 (*0-374-50804-6*) FS&G.

Mystery & Mayhem: Tales of Lust, Murder, Madness & Disappearance. Michelle Ghaffari. 120p. 1995. 16.98 (*1-56799-176-9*, MetroBooks) M Friedman Pub Grp Inc.

Mystery & Meaning of Love & Marriage. Lazar Puhalo. 45p. Date not set. pap. 4.00 (*1-879038-54-4*, 9024) Synaxis Pr.

Mystery & Meaning of the Dead Sea Scrolls. Hershel Shanks. 272p. 1999. pap. 14.00 (*0-679-78089-0*) Knopf.

Mystery & Meaning of the Dead Sea Scrolls. Hershel Shanks. LC 97-29391. 384p. 1998. 25.00 (*0-679-45757-7*) Random.

***Mystery & Meaning of the Mass.** Joseph Champlin. LC 98-43977. (Illus.). 126p. 1999. pap. 9.95 (*0-8245-1782-2*) Crossroad NY.

Mystery & Method: The Other in Rahner & Levinas. Michael Purcell. LC 98-8986. (Studies in Theology: Vol. 15). 400p. 1998. 40.00 (*0-87462-639-0*) Marquette.

Mystery & Ministry of Angels. Herbert Lockyer. 111p. (YA). 1994. text 9.95 (*0-942516-13-3*) Plymouth Rock Found.

Mystery & Morality. Neil King. (Drama Ser.). 96p. 1984. pap. 12.95 (*0-7175-1231-2*) Dufour.

Mystery & Myth in the Philosophy of Eric Voegelin. Glenn Hughes. LC 92-34192. 144p. (C). 1993. text 27.50 (*0-8262-0875-4*) U of Mo Pr.

Mystery & Promise: A Theology of Revelation. John F. Haught. (New Theology Studies). 224p. (Orig.). 1993. pap. text 14.95 (*0-8146-5792-3*, M Glazier) Liturgical Pr.

Mystery & Prophecy of the Great Pyramid (1928) Charles S. Knight. 214p. 1999. reprint ed. pap. 17.95 (*0-7661-0820-1*) Kessinger Pub.

Mystery & Religion: Newman's Epistemology of Religion. Clyde M. Nabe. 76p. (Orig.). (C). 1988. pap. text 13.00 (*0-8191-6712-6*) U Pr of Amer.

An Asterisk (*) at the beginning of an entry indicates that the title is appearing for the first time.

Mystery & Significance of Numbers. C. M. Kelland. 55p. 1996. spiral bd. 9.00 (*0-7873-1256-8*) Hlth Research.

Mystery & Suspense see Young Adult Reading Activities Library

Mystery & Suspense. J. Steffens & J. Carr. (Language Arts Ser.). (Illus.). (J). (gr. 5-8). 1983. pap. 10.95 (*0-88160-096-2*, LW 1006) Learning Wks.

Mystery & Suspense Writers: The Literature of Crime Detection & Espionage, Vol. 1. Ed. by Robin W. Winks & Maureen Corrigan. LC 98-36812. 1998. 120.00 (*0-684-80519-7*) S&S Trade.

Mystery & Suspense Writers: The Literature of Crime Detection & Espionage, Vol. 2. Ed. by Robin W. Winks & Maureen Corrigan. 1998. 120.00 (*0-684-80520-0*) S&S Trade.

Mystery & Truth. John MacQuarrie & John Macquarrie. (Pere Marquette Lectures). 1970. 15.00 (*0-87462-518-1*) Marquette.

Mystery-Anti-Coloring Book. Susan Striker. (Illus.). 64p. (Orig.). (J). (gr. 1 up). 1995. pap. 6.95 (*0-8050-1600-7*, Owl) H Holt & Co.

Mystery at Bellwood Estate. Hilda Stahl. LC 92-41738. (Best Friends Ser.: Vol. 11). 160p. (J). (gr. 4-7). 1993. pap. 4.99 (*0-89107-713-8*) Crossway Bks.

Mystery at Blarney Castle, Vol. 1. Barbara M. Bersaw. (Illus.). viii, 40p. (J). (gr. 4-6). 1997. pap. 3.50 (*0-9660535-0-8*) Castle Pubns MA.

Mystery at Camp Galena. Joan R. Biggar. LC 97-12849. (Megan Parnell Mysteries Ser.). (J). (gr. 5-9). 1997. pap. text 5.99 (*0-570-05016-2*, 56-1843) Concordia.

Mystery at Captain's Cove. Ruth N. Moore. LC 91-40805. (Sara & Sam Mysteries Ser.: Vol. 7). (Illus.). 160p. (Orig.). (J). (gr. 4-7). 1992. pap. 6.99 (*0-8361-3581-4*) Herald Pr.

Mystery at Claudia's House. Ann M. Martin. (Baby-Sitters Club Mystery Ser.: No. 6). 176p. (J). (gr. 4-6). 1992. 3.50 (*0-590-44961-3*) Scholastic Inc.

Mystery at Claudia's House. Ann M. Martin. (Baby-Sitters Club Mystery Ser.: No. 6). (J). 1992. 8.60 (*0-606-02502-2*, Pub. by Turtleback) Demco.

Mystery at Devil's Paw. Franklin W. Dixon. (Hardy Boys Mystery Stories Ser.: No.38). (Illus.). 192p. (J). (gr. 3-6). 1959. reprint ed. 5.99 (*0-448-08938-6*, G & D) Peng Put Young Read.

Mystery at Dragon Bone Hill: Beijing. Boaz. 1997. 25.00 (*0-02-903711-5*) Free Pr.

Mystery at Echo Cliffs. Kate Abbott. LC 93-33849. (Illus.). 184p. (J). (gr. 5-9). 1994. pap. 11.95 (*1-878610-37-6*) Red Crane Bks.

Mystery at Hanover School. Dian Curtis Regan. (Ghost Twins Ser.: No. 7). 128p. (J). (gr. 4-6). 1995. pap. text 3.25 (*0-590-53884-5*) Scholastic Inc.

Mystery at Hanover School. Dian Curtis Regan. (Ghost Twins Ser.). (J). 1995. 8.35 (*0-606-07914-9*, Pub. by Turtleback) Demco.

Mystery at Kickingbird Lake. Dian Curtis Regan. (Mystery at Kickingbird Lake Ser.: No. 01). 128p. (J). (gr. 4-6). 1994. pap. 3.25 (*0-590-48253-X*) Scholastic Inc.

Mystery at Lake Placid see Screech Owls Series Boxed Set: Mystery at Lake Placid; The Night They Stole the Stanley Cup; The Screech Owls' Northern Adventure

***Mystery at Lighthouse Point: A Smugglers Revenge.** Kim Wolf-Tau & Jeanne Wolf. (Cliffhanger Adventure Mystery Ser.: Vol. Cliff 1). 122p. (J). (gr. 4-7). 1999. 24.95 (*0-9668491-1-6*) Mental Interact.

Mystery at Lilac Inn. Carolyn Keene. (Nancy Drew Mystery Stories Ser.: No. 4). (Illus.). 180p. (J). (gr. 4-7). 1930. 5.99 (*0-448-09504-1*, G & D) Peng Put Young Read.

Mystery at Lilac Inn. fac. ed. Carolyn Keene. LC 94-9297. (Nancy Drew Mystery Stories Ser.: No. 4). (Illus.). iv, 200p. (J). (gr. 4-7). 1994. reprint ed. 14.95 (*1-55709-158-7*, Pub. by Applewood) Consort Bk Sales.

***Mystery at Lilac Inn; The Secret of Shadow Ranch; The Secret of Red Gate Farm, Vol. 1-6.** Carolyn Keene. (Nancy Drew Mystery Stories Ser.: 2). 560p. (J). (gr. 4-7). 2000. boxed set 9.98 (*0-7651-1766-5*) Smithmark.

Mystery at Magnolia Mansion. Carolyn Keene. Ed. by Ann Greenberg. LC 91-130243. (Nancy Drew Mystery Stories Ser.: No. 97). 148p. (Orig.). (J). (gr. 3-6). 1990. pap. 3.99 (*0-671-69282-8*, Minstrel Bks) PB.

Mystery at Manatee Creek. Robert Tylander. 192p. 2000. pap. 11.95 (*1-56315-204-5*) SterlingHse.

Mystery at Maple Street Park. Mary H. Duplex. LC 93-28466. (J). 1994. pap. 1.97 (*0-8163-1187-0*) Pacific Pr Pub Assn.

***Mystery at Melbeck.** large type ed. Gillian Kaye. 192p. 1999. pap. 18.90 (*0-7089-5510-X*, Linford) Ulverscroft.

Mystery at Midnight Museum. Stefan Czernecki. 32p. (J). 14.95 (*0-06-026199-4*) HarpC Child Bks.

Mystery at Midnight Museum. Lattimore. 32p. (J). lib. bdg. 14.89 (*0-06-026202-8*) HarpC Child Bks.

Mystery at Miss Abigail's. Lois G. Leppard. 128p. 1999. pap. 4.50 (*0-553-48661-6*) Bantam.

Mystery at Monster Lake. James Pirone & Paula Sweeney. (Jake Montana Ser.: Bk. 3). (YA). (gr. 6 up). 2000. pap. 9.99 (*0-88092-407-1*, 2958) Royal Fireworks.

Mystery at Moorsea Manor. Carolyn Keene. (Nancy Drew Mystery Stories Ser.: No. 150). 148p. (J). (gr. 3-7). 1999. per. 3.99 (*0-671-02787-5*) PB.

Mystery at Natural Bridge. Bea Carlton. (Orig.). (J). (gr. 4-7). Date not set. pap. 5.95 (*0-9658103-2-1*) SonLife Pub.

Mystery at Peacock Hall. Created by Gertrude Chandler Warner. LC 98-3148. (Boxcar Children Ser.: No. 63). 128p. (J). (gr. 2-5). 1998. pap. 3.95 (*0-8075-5445-6*); lib. bdg. 13.95 (*0-8075-5444-8*) A Whitman.

***Mystery at Peacock Hall.** Created by Gertrude Chandler Warner. (Boxcar Children Ser.: No. 63). (J). (gr. 2-5). 1998. 9.05 (*0-606-13212-0*, Pub. by Turtleback) Demco.

Mystery at Pier Fourteen. Betty Swinford. LC 87-82753. (Illus.). 144p. (YA). (gr. 7-11). 1988. pap. 3.50 (*0-88243-654-6*, 02-0654) Gospel Pub.

***Mystery at Ricena's Pond.** Riki Lipe. Ed. by Reta Spears-Stewart. (Illus.). 36p. (J). (ps-6). 2000. 10.00 (*0-9659381-2-3*, Pub. by Hoot N Cackle) Booksource.

Mystery at Salvage Rock. E. A. Olsen. LC 68-16401. (Oceanography Ser.). (Illus.). 48p. (J). (gr. 3 up). 1970. lib. bdg. 10.95 (*0-87783-027-4*); audio 10.60 (*0-87783-195-5*) Oddo.

Mystery at Salvage Rock. deluxe ed. E. A. Olsen. LC 68-16401. (Oceanography Ser.). (Illus.). 48p. (J). (gr. 3 up). 1970. pap. 3.94 (*0-87783-101-7*) Oddo.

Mystery at Shawme Pond. Elsie S. Santos. Ed. by Albert M. Alvaro. (Stories for Young Grandchildren by Grandma Elsie Ser.). (Illus.). 20p. (Orig.). (J). (ps-2). 1983. pap. 4.25 (*0-914151-01-0*) E S Santos.

Mystery at Smokey Mountain. Dave Gustaveson. (Reel Kids Adventures Ser.: Bk. 2). 144p. (J). (gr. 3-8). 1994. pap. 5.99 (*0-927545-65-9*) YWAM Pub.

Mystery at Snowflake Inn. Created by Gertrude Chandler Warner. (Boxcar Children Special Ser.: No. 3). (Illus.). 192p. (J). (gr. 2-5). 1994. pap. 3.95 (*0-8075-5346-8*); lib. bdg. 13.95 (*0-8075-5345-X*) A Whitman.

Mystery at Snowflake Inn. Created by Gertrude Chandler Warner. (Boxcar Children Special Ser.: No. 3). (J). (gr. 2-5). 1994. 9.05 (*0-606-13221-X*, Pub. by Turtleback) Demco.

Mystery at the Alamo. Created by Gertrude Chandler Warner. LC 98-106164. (Boxcar Children Ser.: No. 58). (J). (gr. 2-5). 1997. pap. 3.95 (*0-8075-5437-5*); lib. bdg. 13.95 (*0-8075-5436-7*) A Whitman.

Mystery at the Alamo. Created by Gertrude Chandler Warner. (Boxcar Children Ser.: No. 58). (J). (gr. 2-5). 1997. 9.05 (*0-606-11161-1*, Pub. by Turtleback) Demco.

Mystery at the Ballpark. Created by Gertrude Chandler Warner. (Boxcar Children Special Ser.: No. 4). (J). (gr. 2-5). 1995. pap. 3.95 (*0-8075-5341-7*); lib. bdg. 13.95 (*0-8075-5340-9*) A Whitman.

Mystery at the Ballpark. Created by Gertrude Chandler Warner. (Boxcar Children Special Ser.: No. 4). (J). (gr. 2-5). 1995. 9.05 (*0-606-13222-8*, Pub. by Turtleback) Demco.

Mystery at the Baseball Hall of Fame: Who Stole Babe's Bat?, 1. Nancy Ann Van Wie. LC 97-92933. (Max's Mystery Travels Ser.). (Illus.). 135p. (J). (gr. 1-7). 1997. pap. 5.95 (*1-888575-07-7*) Maxs Pubns.

Mystery at the Big Blue House. Janelle Cherrington. (Bear in the Big Blue House Ser.: No. 5). (J). (gr. k-3). 2000. pap. 3.50 (*0-689-83339-3*, Simon Spot) Litle Simon.

Mystery at the Broken Bridge see Home School Detectives Series

Mystery at the Crystal Palace. Carolyn Keene. (Nancy Drew Mystery Stories Ser.: No. 133). (J). (gr. 3-6). 1996. per. 3.99 (*0-671-50515-7*) PB.

Mystery at the Crystal Palace. Carolyn Keene. (Nancy Drew Mystery Stories Ser.: No. 133). (J). (gr. 3-6). 1996. 9.09 (*0-606-10886-6*, Pub. by Turtleback) Demco.

Mystery at the Dog Show. Created by Gertrude Chandler Warner. (Boxcar Children Ser.: No. 35). (Illus.). 128p. (J). (gr. 2-5). 1993. pap. 3.95 (*0-8075-5394-8*); lib. bdg. 13.95 (*0-8075-5395-6*) A Whitman.

Mystery at the Dog Show. Created by Gertrude Chandler Warner. LC 93-20458. (Boxcar Children Ser.: No. 35). (J). (gr. 2-5). 1993. 9.05 (*0-606-08937-3*, Pub. by Turtleback) Demco.

Mystery at the Fair. Created by Gertrude Chandler Warner. (Boxcar Children Special Ser.: No. 6). (Illus.). 128p. (J). (gr. 2-5). 1996. pap. 3.95 (*0-8075-5337-9*); lib. bdg. 13.95 (*0-8075-5336-0*) A Whitman.

Mystery at the Fair. Created by Gertrude Chandler Warner. (Boxcar Children Special Ser.: No. 6). (J). (gr. 2-5). 1996. 9.05 (*0-606-08701-X*, Pub. by Turtleback) Demco.

Mystery at the Fairgrounds. Janet H. McHenry. LC 96-50884. (Annie Shepard Mysteries Ser.). (J). 1997. pap. 4.99 (*1-56476-566-0*) Chariot Victor.

Mystery at the Gym: Read-Along. Denholtz. (Illus.). 32p. (J). (gr. 3-6). 1984. pap. 9.95 (*0-87386-308-9*) Jan Prods.

***Mystery at the Haunted House.** David A Adler. (Cam Jansen Ser.). 64p. (J). 1999. pap. 3.99 (*0-14-130649-1*, PuffinBks) Peng Put Young Read.

Mystery at the Lighthouse. Joan Weir. 160p. (Orig.). (J). (gr. 3-6). 1991. pap. write for info. (*0-614-17729-4*) Stoddart Publ.

Mystery at the Masked Ball. Eric Weiner. (Clue Ser.: No. 4). 112p. (J). (gr. 3-6). 1993. pap. 2.95 (*0-590-45633-4*) Scholastic Inc.

Mystery at the Masked Ball. Eric Weiner. (Clue Ser.: No. 4). (J). (gr. 3-6). 1993. 8.05 (*0-606-02775-0*, Pub. by Turtleback) Demco.

Mystery at the Old Stamp Mill, Vol. 3. Janet H. McHenry. LC 96-51183. (Annie Shepard Mysteries Ser.: Vol. 3). 129p. (J). (gr. 3-7). 1997. pap. 4.99 (*0-7814-1547-0*) Chariot Victor.

Mystery at the Ski Jump. rev. ed. Carolyn Keene. (Nancy Drew Mystery Stories Ser.: No. 29). (Illus.). 180p. (J). (gr. 4-7). 1952. 5.95 (*0-448-09529-7*, G & D) Peng Put Young Read.

Mystery at the Spanish Castle. Ruth N. Moore. LC 89-29290. 112p. (Orig.). (J). (gr. 4-8). 1990. pap. 6.99 (*0-8361-3515-6*) Herald Pr.

Mystery at the Statue of Liberty: The Unwanted Ghooost! Nancy Ann Van Wie. LC 97-94174. (Max's Mystery Travels Ser.). (Illus.). 135p. (J). (gr. 1-7). 1997. pap. 5.95 (*1-888575-10-7*) Maxs Pubns.

Mystery at the White House: A President is Missing! Nancy Ann VanWei. LC 97-92932. (Illus.). 133p. (J). (gr. 1-7). 1997. pap. 5.95 (*1-888575-04-2*) Maxs Pubns.

Mystery at Witch Creek. Mary Crawford. (J). (gr. 3-6). 1995. pap. 9.99 (*0-88092-177-3*) Royal Fireworks.

Mystery Athletes: Can You Guess the Mystery Athlete? Ed. by Scott Gramling. 32p. (J). (gr. 3-8). 1998. pap. text 3.95 (*1-886749-49-3*) SI For Kids.

Mystery Baby. Dani Sinclair. (Intrigue Ser.). 1996. per. 3.75 (*0-373-22371-4*, 1-22371-8) Harlequin Bks.

Mystery Behind the Wall. Gertrude Chandler Warner. LC 72-13356. (Boxcar Children Ser.: No. 17). (Illus.). 128p. (J). (gr. 2-5). 1973. pap. 3.95 (*0-8075-5367-0*); lib. bdg. 13.95 (*0-8075-5364-6*) A Whitman.

Mystery Behind the Wall. Gertrude Chandler Warner. (Boxcar Children Ser.: No. 17). (J). (gr. 2-5). 1973. 9.05 (*0-606-04986-X*, Pub. by Turtleback) Demco.

Mystery Believed, Pt. 1. Illus. by Mark Melone. LC 96-77418. (Light for Life Ser.). 112p. (Orig.). 1995. pap. text 10.00 (*1-887158-07-3*) God With Us.

Mystery Beyond. Bede Griffiths. 1997. pap. 7.95 (*0-85305-426-6*, 1941, Pub. by Arthur James) Morehouse Pub.

Mystery Bookstore. Illus. by Charles Tang. LC 95-17794. (Boxcar Children Ser.: No. 48). (J). (gr. 2-5). 1995. pap. 3.95 (*0-8075-5422-7*); lib. bdg. 13.95 (*0-8075-5421-9*) A Whitman.

Mystery Bookstore. Created by Gertrude Chandler Warner. (Boxcar Children Ser.: No. 48). (J). (gr. 2-5). 1995. 9.05 (*0-606-08497-5*, Pub. by Turtleback) Demco.

***Mystery Box.** Ellen McPeek Glisan. 50p. 1998. teacher ed. 39.95 (*1-884074-69-3*, PCI 736) PCI Educ Pubg.

Mystery Box. Frederick Highland. LC 97-73702. (Illus.). 240p. 1998. 24.95 (*0-9659409-5-0*); pap. 16.95 (*0-9659409-6-9*) Ana Libri Pr.

***Mystery Bridge.** Omatseyin Mark Edah. Ed. by Martin M. Eda. (Illus.). (J). (gr. 3 up). 2000. pap. write for info. (*1-928903-04-5*) Edah Bks.

***Mystery Bruise.** Terry Wolverton. 128p. 1999. pap. 9.95 (*1-888996-14-5*, Red Hen Press) Valentine CA.

Mystery Castle see Castillo Misterioso

Mystery Cave see Sugar Creek Gang Series

Mystery Cave of Many Faces: A History of Burrows Cave, Bk. I. Russell E. Burrows & Fred Rydholm. LC 92-80160. 240p. 1992. 22.00 (*0-9639948-3-2*) Superior Hrtland.

Mystery Celebrated. Illus. by Mark Melone. LC 96-77418. (Light for Life Ser.: Pt. 2). 108p. (Orig.). 1996. pap. 10.00 (*1-887158-09-X*) God With Us.

Mystery Child. Carla Cassidy. (Shadows Ser.). 1996. per. 3.50 (*0-373-27061-5*, 1-27061-0) Silhouette.

Mystery Cities: Exploration & Adventure in Labaantun. Thomas W. Gann. LC 76-44721. (Illus.). 320p. 1977. reprint ed. 55.00 (*0-404-15925-7*) AMS Pr.

Mystery Cities of Central America. Thomas Gann. 1977. lib. bdg. 59.95 (*0-8490-2313-0*) Gordon Pr.

Mystery Cities of the Maya: Exploration & Adventure in Lubaantun & Belize; Harmonic. Thomas Gann. (Mystic Traveller Ser.). 252p. 1997. pap. 16.95 (*0-932813-17-8*) Adventures Unltd.

Mystery Code. Harold Silvani. (Illus.). 45p. (J). (gr. 4-8). 1989. student ed. 7.95 (*1-878669-35-4*, CTA-4330) Crea Tea Assocs.

Mystery Creek. Christopher Barry. 1992. pap. 9.99 (*0-88092-187-0*) Royal Fireworks.

Mystery Cruise. Created by Gertrude Chandler Warner. (Boxcar Children Ser.: No. 29). (Illus.). 192p. (J). (gr. 2-5). 1992. pap. 3.95 (*0-8075-5368-9*); lib. bdg. 13.95 (*0-8075-5362-X*) A Whitman.

Mystery Cruise. Created by Gertrude Chandler Warner. (Boxcar Children Ser.: No. 29). (J). (gr. 2-5). 1992. 8.60 (*0-606-02333-X*, Pub. by Turtleback) Demco.

Mystery Dad. Leona Karr. (Intrigue Ser.: Vol. 487). 1998. per. 3.99 (*0-373-22487-7*, 1-22487-2) Harlequin Bks.

Mystery Date. Created by Francine Pascal. (Sweet Valley High Super Edition Ser.). 240p. (YA). (gr. 7 up). 1998. mass mkt. 4.50 (*0-553-57073-0*, Sweet Valley) BDD Bks Young Read.

Mystery, Detective, & Espionage Magazines. Michael L. Cook. LC 82-20977. (Historical Guides to the World's Periodicals & Newspapers Ser.). 793p. 1983. lib. bdg. 105.00 (*0-313-23310-1*, CMD/, Greenwood Pr) Greenwood.

***Mystery Doctor.** Claire Vernon. LC 99-42645. 2000. 30.00 (*0-7838-8759-0*, G K Hall Lrg Type) Mac Lib Ref.

Mystery Driver. Jean Graton.Tr. of Pilot Sans Visage. (Illus.). 64p. 1997. pap. 9.95 (*0-9651380-1-1*) MediaVision.

Mystery Driver, Vol. 1. unabridged ed. Jean Graton. Tr. by Intex Staff from FRE.Tr. of Pilot Sans Visage. (FRE., Illus.). 64p. 1996. 7.95 (*0-9651380-0-3*) MediaVision.

Mystery Era of American Pewter, 1928-1931. Carolyn A. Smith & Peggy R. Hixon. 75p. (Orig.). 1979. pap. 7.95 (*0-9606292-0-3*) C A Smith.

***Mystery Explosion.** Johnnie Tuitel & Sharon E. Lamson. (Gun Lake Adventure Ser.: No. 2). 115p. (J). (gr. 3-7). 1998. pap. 5.99 (*0-9658075-1-7*) Cedar Tree Pub.

Mystery Fancier: An Index to Volumes I-XIII, November 1976-Fall 1992. William F. Deeck. LC 93-341. (Brownstone Mystery Guides Ser.: Vol. 9). (Illus.). ix, 169p. 1993. pap. 21.00 (*0-941028-12-7*, 27642983); lib. bdg. 31.00 (*0-941028-11-9*, 27642983) Millefleurs.

Mystery Fanfare: A Composite Annotated Index to Mystery & Related Fanzines 1963-1981. Michael L. Cook. LC 82-73848. 1983. pap. 13.95 (*0-87972-230-4*) Bowling Green Univ Popular Press.

Mystery Festival. rev. ed. Kevin Beals & Carolyn Willard. Ed. by Lincoln Bergman et al. (Great Explorations in Math & Science (GEMS) Ser.). (Illus.). 268p. (J). (gr. 2-8). 1998. pap. 25.50 (*0-924886-10-2*, GEMS) Lawrence Science.

Mystery Fiction & Modern Life. R. Gordon Kelly. LC 97-21530. (Studies in Popular Culture Ser.). 272p. 1998. 45.00 (*1-57806-005-2*); pap. 18.00 (*1-57806-032-X*) U Pr of Miss.

***Mystery Files.** Ed. by Phil Roxbee Cox. (Puzzle Adventure Kits Ser.). (Illus.). (J). (gr. 4-7). 2000. 15.95 (*0-7460-3677-9*, Pub. by Usbrne Pbng UK) EDC.

Mystery Flag. Glenwood High School Library Club. (WeWrite Kids! Ser.: No. 15). (Illus.). 43p. (J). (ps-3). 1995. pap. 3.95 (*1-884987-49-4*) WeWrite.

Mystery Flowers. Grace Livingston Hill. 21.95 (*0-89190-070-5*) Amereon Ltd.

Mystery Flowers. Grace Livingston Hill. (Grace Livingston Hill Ser.: Vol. 61). 1991. 5.99 (*0-8423-4613-9*) Tyndale Hse.

Mystery Fold: Stories to Tell, Draw & Fold. Valerie Marsh. (Illus.). 80p. (J). (ps-5). 1993. pap. 14.95 (*0-913853-31-3*, 32540, Alleyside) Highsmith Pr.

Mystery Fossil 1: A Physical Anthropology Laboratory Exercise for the Macintosh. John T. Omohundro & Kathleen Goodman. (Mystery Fossil Ser.). (C). 1993. pap. text 24.95 incl. disk (*1-55934-264-1*, 1264) Mayfield Pub.

Mystery Fossil 2: A Physical Anthropology Laboratory Exercise for the Macintosh. John T. Omohundro & Kathleen Goodman. (Mystery Fossil Ser.). (C). 1993. pap. text 24.95 incl. disk (*1-55934-275-7*, 1275) Mayfield Pub.

Mystery Girl. Created by Gertrude Chandler Warner. (Boxcar Children Ser.: No. 28). (Illus.). 192p. (J). (gr. 2-5). 1992. pap. 3.95 (*0-8075-5371-9*); lib. bdg. 13.95 (*0-8075-5370-0*) A Whitman.

Mystery Girl. Created by Gertrude Chandler Warner. (Boxcar Children Ser.: No. 28). (J). (gr. 2-5). 1992. 8.60 (*0-606-02332-1*, Pub. by Turtleback) Demco.

Mystery Heiress. Suzanne Carey. (Fortune's Children Ser.). 256p. 1997. per. 4.50 (*0-373-50185-4*, 1-501857) Harlequin Bks.

Mystery Hid from All Ages & Generations. Charles Chauncy. LC 70-83414. (Religion in America, Ser. 1). 1980. reprint ed. 25.95 (*0-405-00235-1*) Ayer.

Mystery Hidden for Ages in God. Paul M. Quay. LC 93-17286. (American University Studies VII: Vol. 161). XVI, 438p. (C). 1995. text 63.95 (*0-8204-2221-5*) P Lang Pubng.

***Mystery Hidden for Ages in God, 161.** 2nd ed. Paul M. Quay. (American University Studies: Ser.). XVI, 438p. 1998. pap. 35.95 (*0-8204-4039-6*) P Lang Pubng.

Mystery Horse. Created by Gertrude Chandler Warner. (Boxcar Children Ser.: No. 34). (Illus.). 128p. (J). (gr. 2-5). 1993. pap. 3.95 (*0-8075-5339-5*); lib. bdg. 13.95 (*0-8075-5338-7*) A Whitman.

Mystery Horse. Created by Gertrude Chandler Warner. LC 93-700. (Boxcar Children Ser.: No. 34). (J). (gr. 2-5). 1993. 9.05 (*0-606-08936-5*, Pub. by Turtleback) Demco.

Mystery House. Kathleen Norris. reprint ed. lib. bdg. 17.95 (*0-89190-309-7*, Rivercity Pr) Amereon Ltd.

Mystery House. unabridged ed. Jean Booker. 112p. (J). (gr. 3-6). 1996. mass mkt. 4.95 (*0-7736-7448-9*) STDK.

***Mystery in Acambaro: Did Dinosaurs Survive Until Recently?** Charles H. Hapgood. 256p. 2000. pap. 14.95 (*0-932813-76-3*, Pub. by Adventures Unltd) SCB Distributors.

Mystery in Bugtown. William Boniface. LC 96-49312. (Illus.). (J). 1997. 15.95 (*0-939251-90-6*) Accord CO.

Mystery in Lost Canyon. John Bibee. LC 97-15600. (Home School Detectives Ser.: Vol. 7). 128p. (J). (gr. 3-7). 1997. mass mkt. 4.99 (*0-8308-1917-7*, 1917) InterVarsity.

Mystery in New York. Illus. by Charles Tang. LC 99-34254. (Boxcar Children Ser.: No. 13). 144p. (J). (gr. 2-5). 1999. lib. bdg. 13.95 (*0-8075-5459-6*); mass mkt. 3.95 (*0-8075-5460-X*) A Whitman.

***Mystery in New York.** Gertrude Chandler Warner. (Boxcar Children Special Ser.). (Illus.). (J). 1999. 9.30 (*0-606-18771-5*) Turtleback.

Mystery in Old Quebec. Mary C. Jane. 10.00 (*0-89064-074-2*) NAVH.

Mystery in Peru: The Lines of Nazca. David McMullen. (Great Unsolved Mysteries Ser.). 1997. pap. 4.95 (*0-8114-6861-5*) Raintree Steck-V.

Mystery in Room 11. Rena J. Berlin et al. 178p. 1994. wbk. ed. 29.95 (*1-888528-00-1*) Res Develop.

Mystery in San Francisco. Created by Gertrude Chandler Warner. LC 97-6127. (Boxcar Children Ser.: No. 57). (J). (gr. 2-5). 1997. pap. 3.95 (*0-8075-5434-0*) A Whitman.

Mystery in San Francisco. Created by Gertrude Chandler Warner. LC 97-6127. (Boxcar Children Ser.: No. 57). (J). (gr. 2-5). 1997. lib. bdg. 13.95 (*0-8075-5433-2*) A Whitman.

Mystery in San Francisco. Created by Gertrude Chandler Warner. LC 97-6127. (Boxcar Children Ser.: No. 57). (J). (gr. 2-5). 1997. 9.05 (*0-606-11160-3*, Pub. by Turtleback) Demco.

Mystery in Space: Pulp Fiction Library. Gardner Fox. (Illus.). 223p. 1999. pap. text 19.95 (*1-56389-494-7*, Pub. by DC Comics) Diamond Comic Distributors Inc.

Mystery in the Attic. Charles Mills. (Shadow Creek Ser.: Vol. 2). (J). (gr. 4-7). 1994. pap. 5.99 (*0-8280-0831-0*) Review & Herald.

Mystery in the Cave. Illus. by Charles Tang. (Boxcar Children Ser.: No. 50). (J). (gr. 2-5). 1996. pap. 3.95 (*0-8075-5412-X*); lib. bdg. 13.95 (*0-8075-5411-1*) A Whitman.

Mystery in the Cave. Created by Gertrude Chandler Warner. (Boxcar Children Ser.: No. 50). (J). (gr. 2-5). 1995. 8.60 (*0-606-08499-1*, Pub. by Turtleback) Demco.

***Mystery in the Computer Game.** Created by Gertrude Chandler Warner. (Boxcar Children Ser.: No. 78). 128p. (J). (gr. 2-5). 2000. pap. 3.95 (*0-8075-5469-3*); lib. bdg. 13.95 (*0-8075-5468-5*) A Whitman.

Mystery in the Drood Family. Montagu Saunders. LC 74-6448. (Studies in Dickens: No. 52). 1974. lib. bdg. 75.00 (*0-8383-1973-4*) M S G Haskell Hse.

M

Mystery in the Farrowing Barn. Colene Copeland. LC 91-62326. (Priscilla Ser.: No. 4). (Illus.). 150p. (Orig.). (J). (gr. 3-7). 1991. 9.95 (*0-939810-13-1*); pap. 3.95 (*0-939810-14-X*) Jordan Valley.

Mystery in the Mall. Created by Gertrude Chandler Warner. LC 99-35489. (Boxcar Children Ser.: No. 72). (Illus.). 128p. (J). (gr. 2-5). 1999. lib. bdg. 13.95 (*0-8075-5456-1*); mass mkt. 3.95 (*0-8075-5457-X*) A Whitman.

*__Mystery in the Mall.__ Gertrude Chandler Warner. (Boxcar Children Ser.: Vol. 72). (J). 1999. 9.30 (*0-606-18765-0*) Turtleback.

Mystery in the Moonlight. Marie Jacks. (Clue Ser.: No. 9). 112p. (J). (gr. 3-6). 1995. pap. 3.50 (*0-590-48935-6*) Scholastic Inc.

Mystery in the Moonlight. Marie Jacks. (Clue Ser.: No. 9). (J). (gr. 3-6). 1995. 8.60 (*0-606-09662-0*, Pub. by Turtleback) Demco.

Mystery in the Old Attic. Created by Gertrude Chandler Warner. LC 97-25372. (Boxcar Children Ser.: No. 9). (Illus.). 144p. (J). (gr. 2-5). 1997. pap. 3.95 (*0-8075-5439-1*); lib. bdg. 13.95 (*0-8075-5438-3*) A Whitman.

Mystery in the Old Attic. Created by Gertrude Chandler Warner. (Boxcar Children Special Ser.: No. 9). (J). (gr. 2-5). 1997. 9.05 (*0-606-12636-8*, Pub. by Turtleback) Demco.

M

Mystery in the Old Cave. Helen F. Orton. (Illus.). (J). (gr. 4-6). 1950. 11.95 (*0-397-30173-1*) HarpC Child Bks.

*__Mystery in the Old Dark Attic.__ Charles Edwin Price. 2000. 22.50 (*1-57072-118-1*); pap. 12.50 (*1-57072-134-3*) Overmountain Pr.

Mystery in the Plays of T. S. Eliot. S. K. Tikoo. 1990. text 25.00 (*81-214-0301-4*, Pub. by Natl Pub House) Advent Bks Div.

Mystery in the Sand. Gertrude Chandler Warner. LC 70-165823. (Boxcar Children Ser.: No. 16). (Illus.). 128p. (J). (gr. 2-5). 1971. pap. 3.95 (*0-8075-5372-7*); lib. bdg. 13.95 (*0-8075-5373-5*) A Whitman.

Mystery in the Sand. Gertrude Chandler Warner. (Boxcar Children Ser.: No. 16). (J). (gr. 2-5). 1971. 8.60 (*0-606-04987-8*, Pub. by Turtleback) Demco.

Mystery in the Snow. Created by Gertrude Chandler Warner. (Boxcar Children Ser.: No. 32). (Illus.). 192p. (J). (gr. 2-5). 1992. pap. 3.95 (*0-8075-5393-X*); lib. bdg. 13.95 (*0-8075-5392-1*) A Whitman.

Mystery in the Snow. Created by Gertrude Chandler Warner. (Boxcar Children Ser.: No. 32). (J). (gr. 2-5). 1992. 9.05 (*0-606-02337-2*, Pub. by Turtleback) Demco.

Mystery in the Sunshine State. Ed. by Stuart M. Kaminsky. LC 99-33326. 272p. 1999. pap. 14.95 (*1-56164-185-5*) Pineapple Pr.

*__Mystery in Tornado Alley.__ Carolyn Keene. (Nancy Drew Mystery Stories Ser.: No. 155). 160p. (J). (gr. 3-6). 2000. per. 3.99 (*0-671-04264-5*, Minstrel Bks) PB.

Mystery in Washington, D. C. Created by Gertrude Chandler Warner. (Boxcar Children Special Ser.: No. 2). (J). (gr. 2-5). 1994. pap. 3.95 (*0-8075-5410-3*); lib. bdg. 13.95 (*0-8075-5409-X*) A Whitman.

Mystery in Washington, D. C. Created by Gertrude Chandler Warner. (Boxcar Children Special Ser.: No. 2). (J). (gr. 2-5). 1994. 9.05 (*0-606-13220-1*, Pub. by Turtleback) Demco.

Mystery in Western Medicine. David Greaves. (Avebury Series in Philosophy). 176p. 1996. text 63.95 (*1-85972-441-8*, Pub. by Avebury) Ashgate Pub Co.

Mystery in Wisdonsin Dells: The Ghost Town of Newport Mystery. Sandra D. Sweeney. 128p. (J). (gr. 1-6). 1997. pap. 3.25 (*0-9659570-0-4*) Advent for Kids.

Mystery Index: Subjects, Settings, & Sleuths of 10,000 Mystery Novels. Steven Olderr. LC 87-1294. 448p. 1987. text 20.00 (*0-8389-0461-0*) ALA.

Mystery Knowledge & Mystery Centres: Fourteen Lectures by Rudolf Steiner. Rudolf Steiner. Tr. by P. Wehrle from GER. 266p. 1998. pap. 19.95 (*1-85584-061-8*, 98, Pub. by R Steiner Pr) Anthroposophic.

Mystery Lady. Jackie Merritt. (Desire Ser.). 1994. per. 2.99 (*0-373-05849-7*, 5-05849-0) Silhouette.

Mystery Lights of Navajo Mesa, 1. Jake Thoene & Luke Thoene. LC 94-30426. (Last Chance Detectives Ser.: No. 1). (J). (gr. 3-7). 1994. pap. 5.99 (*0-8423-2082-2*) Tyndale Hse.

Mystery Lover. large type ed. Lilian Woodward. (Linford Romance Library). 1991. pap. 16.99 (*0-7089-6990-9*) Ulverscroft.

Mystery Lovers' Book of Quotations. Compiled by Jane E. Horning. LC 87-73209. 288p. 1988. 17.45 (*0-89296-201-1*, Pub. by Mysterious Pr) Little.

Mystery Lovers' Book of Quotations. Compiled by Jane E. Horning. 1989. pap. 12.45 (*0-89296-948-2*, Pub. by Mysterious Pr) Little.

Mystery Machine. Herbie Brennan. LC 94-4185. (Illus.). 96p. (J). (gr. 4-7). 1995. per. 14.00 (*0-689-50615-5*) McElderry Bks.

*__Mystery Magazine, Vol. 10.__ Steck-Vaughn Publishing Staff. 2000. pap. 15.95 (*0-8114-9336-9*) Raintree Steck-V.

Mystery Man. Diana Palmer. (Romance Ser.). 1997. per. 3.25 (*0-373-19210-X*, 1-192103) Silhouette.

*__Mystery Man.__ large type ed. Diana Palmer. (Romance Ser.). 2000. 22.95 (*0-373-59699-5*) Silhouette.

Mystery Man: William Rhodes Davis, Nazi Agent. Dale Harrington. LC 99-29911. (Illus.). 276p. 1999. 27.50 (*1-57488-181-7*) Brasseys.

Mystery Man of Darkness, No. 666. Frank E. Stranges. 14p. 1994. pap. text 4.95 (*0-933470-05-3*) Intl Evang.

Mystery Man of the Bible. Hilton Hotema. 61p. (Orig.). 1997. reprint ed. spiral bd. 11.00 (*0-7873-0450-6*) Hlth Research.

*__Mystery Man S. I. X. One Man's Struggle to Become the (666) Beast of Revelation.__ Harold G. Murray, Sr. LC 99-73462. 214p. 1999. pap. 14.95 (*1-890622-94-X*) Leathers Pub.

*__Mystery Manor.__ D. H. Masi. Ed. by Robert G. Schuyler. 78p. 1999. pap. 8.95 (*1-886623-06-6*) Canal Side Pubs.

Mystery Mansion: House Math see I Love Math Series

Mystery Mark of the New Age: Satan's Design for World Domination. Texe Marrs. LC 87-72056. 1988. pap. 11.99 (*0-89107-479-1*) Crossway Bks.

*__Mystery Mazes & Puzzles.__ Golden Books Staff. (Illus.). (J). 2000. pap. 3.99 (*0-307-10479-6*, Goldn Books) Gldn Bks Pub Co.

*__Mystery Men.__ Lara Rice Bergen. LC 99-24492. 1999. pap. 4.99 (*0-440-41574-8*) Dell.

Mystery Midrash: An Anthology of Jewish Mystery & Detective Fiction. Ed. by Lawrence W. Raphael. LC 99-30222. 304p. 1999. pap. 16.95 (*1-58023-055-5*) Jewish Lights.

Mystery Mile see Margery Allingham Omnibus

Mystery Mile. Margery Allingham. 250p. 1994. 4.50 (*0-7867-0168-4*) Carroll & Graf.

Mystery Mile. Margery Allingham. 264p. 1998. lib. bdg. 25.95 (*1-56723-014-8*) Yestermorrow.

Mystery Mother. Marilyn Kaye. (Replica Ser.: No. 8). 160p. (J). (gr. 4-7). 1999. pap. 4.50 (*0-553-48692-6*) Bantam.

Mystery Museum. Susan Wilcox School 1994-95 Fourth-Grade Classes S. (WeWrite Kids! Ser.: No. 24). (Illus.). (J). (ps-4). 1995. pap. 3.95 (*1-884987-82-6*) WeWrite.

*__Mystery Mutt.__ Beverly Lewis. LC 99-6754. (Cul-de-Sac Kids Ser.: Vol. 21). (Illus.). 80p. (J). (gr. 2-5). 2000. pap. 3.99 (*0-7642-2126-4*) Bethany Hse.

Mystery, Novelty & Fantasy Clocks. Derek Roberts. LC 99-30136. (Illus.). 256p. 1999. 150.00 (*0-7643-0873-4*) Schiffer.

Mystery of a Hansom Cab. Fergus W. Hume. LC 75-32754. (Literature of Mystery & Detection Ser.). 1976. reprint ed. lib. bdg. 26.95 (*0-405-07878-1*) Ayer.

Mystery of Alzheimer's: A Guide for Carers. Elizabeth Forsythe. (Illus.). 202p. 1997. pap. 13.95 (*1-85626-220-0*, Pub. by Cathie Kyle) Trafalgar.

Mystery of Alzheimer's: Sunrise to Sunset & Beyond. abr. ed. Harold E. Wagner. Ed. by Fern Wagner & Laura Aymond. LC 98-93223. (Illus.). 160p. 1998. pap. 19.50 (*0-9665600-0-0*) H E W.

Mystery of Angelina Frood. R. Austin Freeman. 298p. 1987. pap. 3.95 (*0-88184-311-3*) Carroll & Graf.

Mystery of Animal Intelligence. Brad Steiger & Sherry H. Steiger. (Orig.). (YA). 1994. mass mkt. 3.99 (*0-8125-3367-4*, Pub. by Tor Bks) St Martin.

Mystery of Animal Migration. Matthieu Ricard. LC 72-172577. 235p. reprint ed. pap. 72.90 (*0-608-13596-8*, 205128200093) Bks Demand.

Mystery of Arafat. Danny Rubinstein. Tr. by Dan Leon. 140p. (C). 1998. text 18.00 (*0-7881-5430-3*) DIANE Pub.

Mystery of Arafat. Danny Rubinstein. LC 95-9748. 144p. 1995. 18.00 (*1-883642-10-8*) Steerforth Pr.

Mystery of Art. D. K. Chandra. (C). 1995. 16.00 (*81-208-1190-9*, Pub. by Motilal Bnarsidass) S Asia.

Mystery of Arthur at Tintagel. Richard Seddon. pap. 22.95 (*0-85440-436-8*, 432, Pub. by R Steiner Pr) Anthroposophic.

Mystery of Arthur Gordon Pym with Edgar Allen Poe. Jules Verne. lib. bdg. 22.95 (*0-8488-2048-7*) Amereon Ltd.

*__Mystery of Atlantis.__ Anita Ganeri & Holly Wallace. LC 98-54490. (Can Science Solve Ser.). 32p. (J). 1999. 22.79 (*1-57572-803-6*) Heinemann Lib.

Mystery of Baptism in the Anglican Tradition. Kenneth Stevenson. LC 98-33529. 224p. 1998. pap. 15.95 (*0-8192-1774-3*) Morehouse Pub.

Mystery of Bat Cave Set. Carole Marsh. (Carole Marsh Mysteries Ser.). 1994. teacher ed. 125.00 (*0-7933-6956-8*) Gallopade Intl.

Mystery of Beautiful Nell Cropsey: A Nonfiction Novel. Bland Simpson. LC 93-3324. (Illus.). xii, 172p. 1993. 24.95 (*0-8078-2120-9*); pap. 14.95 (*0-8078-4432-2*) U of NC Pr.

Mystery of Being, 2 vols., bk. 1. Gabriel Marcel. Tr. by Rene Hague from FRE. LC 77-27179. (Gifford Lectures: 1949-50). 432p. reprint ed. 61.50 (*0-404-60504-4*) AMS Pr.

Mystery of Being: or Oriental Teachings vs. Occidental Theories. Heeralal Dhole. 69p. 1997. pap. 6.00 (*0-89540-262-9*, SB-262) Sun Pub.

Mystery of Being or Oriental Teachings vs. Occidental Theories (1907) Ed. by Heeralal Dhole. 74p. 1998. reprint ed. pap. 5.50 (*0-7661-0486-9*) Kessinger Pub.

Mystery of Bethlehem: Devotional Reading for the Christmas Season. rev. ed. Herman Hoeksema. LC 86-50844. 197p. 1986. pap. 4.95 (*0-916206-31-9*) Refrd Free Pub Assn.

Mystery of Bhowal. Cole S. Brembeck. LC 98-915246. 384p. 1998. write for info. (*81-241-0492-1*) Har-Anand Pubns.

Mystery of Black Holes. Chris Oxlade. LC 99-17399. (Can Science Solve Ser.). (Illus.). 32p. (J). (gr. 4-6). 1999. lib. bdg. 15.95 (*1-57572-808-7*) Heinemann Lib.

Mystery of Black Mesa. Carol Hamilton. LC 95-14262. (Illus.). 121p. (J). (gr. 4-6). 1995. pap. 6.49 (*0-89084-827-0*, 088401) Bob Jones Univ.

Mystery of Blue Mines. Anderson. 1992. pap. text. write for info. (*0-582-05478-8*, Pub. by Addison-Wesley) Longman.

Mystery of Briar Rose Manor. Doris Davis. LC 89-82583. (Illus.). 122p. (YA). 1990. pap. 3.95 (*0-88243-652-X*, 02-0652) Gospel Pub.

Mystery of Cabin Island. Franklin W. Dixon. LC 98-56443. (Hardy Boys Mystery Stories Ser.: No. 8). 210p. (J). (gr. 2-5). 1999. 14.95 (*1-55709-266-4*, Pub. by Applewood) Consort Bk Sales.

Mystery of Cabin Island. Franklin W. Dixon. (Hardy Boys Mystery Stories Ser.: No. 8). (Illus.). 180p. (J). (gr. 4-7). 1929. 5.99 (*0-448-08908-4*, G & D) Peng Put Young Read.

*__Mystery of Capital: Why Capitalism Succeeds in the West & Fails Everywhere Else.__ Hernando De Soto. 2000. 27.50 (*0-465-01614-6*, Pub. by Basic) HarpC.

Mystery of Case D. Luc. Beverly Lewis. (Cul-de-Sac Kids Ser.). (Illus.). 80p. (J). (gr. 2-5). 1995. pap. 3.99 (*1-55661-646-5*) Bethany Hse.

Mystery of Cavanaugh's Mansion. Diane Woo. (Hidden Picture Hunt Ser.). (Illus.). 64p. (Orig.). (J). (gr. 2-6). 1992. pap. 3.95 (*1-56288-219-8*) Checkerboard.

Mystery of Choice. Robert W. Chambers. LC 73-94710. (Short Story Index Reprint Ser.). 1977. 20.95 (*0-8369-3089-4*) Ayer.

Mystery of Christ see Misterio de Cristo

Mystery of Christ. Watchman. 70p. 1998. per. 6.50 (*1-57593-395-0*, 08-045-002) Living Stream Ministry.

Mystery of Christ: And Why We Don't Get It. Robert F. Capon. LC 93-26653. 202p. (Orig.). 1993. pap. 14.00 (*0-8028-0121-8*) Eerdmans.

Mystery of Christ: Knowing Christ in the Church & As the Church. Watchman Nee. 70p. 1997. per. 6.50 (*1-57593-954-1*, 08-045-001) Living Stream Ministry.

Mystery of Christ: The Liturgy As Christian Experience. Thomas Keating. LC 97-174714. 136p. (C). 1994. reprint ed. pap. 12.95 (*0-8264-0697-1*) Continuum.

Mystery of Christ (Colossians) Guy Appere. (Welwyn Commentary Ser.). 1984. pap. 8.99 (*0-85234-180-6*, Pub. by Evangelical Pr) P & R Pubng.

Mystery of Christ in You: The Mystical Vision of Saint Paul. George A. Maloney. LC 97-27145. 112p. 1998. pap. 8.95 (*0-8189-0802-5*) Alba.

Mystery of Christ Made Present see Mystery of Christ Made Present: Selected Texts for the Christian Year

Mystery of Christ Made Present: Selected Texts for the Christian Year. Odo Casel. Ed. by Arno Schilson. Tr. by Ronald Walls from GER. LC 99-12918. Orig. Title: Gegenwart des Christus-Mysterium: Ausgewahlte Textezum Kirchenjahr. 101p. 1999. pap. 10.95 (*1-879007-38-X*, MYST) St Bedes Pubns.

Mystery of Christian Worship. John Cast & Odo Casel. Ed. by Burkhard Neunheuser. LC 99-11630. 99p. 1999. pap. 12.95 (*0-8245-1808-X*) Crossroad NY.

Mystery of Christmas. Raniero Cantalamessa. 80p. (C). 1989. pap. 6.95 (*0-8146-1813-8*) Liturgical Pr.

Mystery of Christmas: A Commentary on the Magnificat, Gloria & Nunc Dimittis. Raniero Cantalamessa. 127p. (C). 1996. pap. 39.95 (*0-85439-282-3*, Pub. by St Paul Pubns) St Mut.

Mystery of Christmas Reflections on the Magnificat, Gloria & Nunc Dimittis. Ed. by Raniero Cantalamessa. 112p. (C). 1988. 39.00 (*0-7855-2321-9*, Pub. by St Paul Pubns) St Mut.

Mystery of Coniunctio. Edward F. Edinger. Ed. by Joan D. Blackmer. (Illus.). 112p. 1996. pap. 16.00 (*0-919123-67-8*, Pub. by Inner City Bks) BookWorld.

Mystery of Consciousness. John R. Searle. LC 97-26044. 224p. 1997. pap. text 12.95 (*0-940322-06-4*) NY Rev Bks.

Mystery of Continuity: Time & History, Memory & Eternity in the Thought of Saint Augustine. Jaroslav J. Pelikan. LC 86-7788. (Richard Lectures, University of Virginia: No. 1984). 189p. reprint ed. pap. 58.60 (*0-608-20051-4*, 207132300011) Bks Demand.

*__Mystery of Courage.__ William Ian Miller. LC 00-29559. 384p. 2000. 29.95 (*0-674-00307-1*) HUP.

Mystery of Coyote Canyon. Timothy Green. LC 93-44119. (Illus.). 150p. (Orig.). (J). (gr. 5-9). 1994. pap. 12.95 (*0-941270-83-1*) Ancient City Pr.

Mystery of Creation. Paul Haffner. 224p. (Orig.). 1996. pap. 19.95 (*0-85244-316-1*, Pub. by Gra1cewing) Morehouse Pub.

Mystery of Creation. Watchman Nee. Tr. by Stephen Kaung. 149p. 1981. pap. 4.50 (*0-935008-52-7*) Christian Fellow Pubs.

Mystery of Creation According to Rashi. Pinchas Doron. 154p. 1982. 12.00 (*0-940118-58-0*) Moznaim.

Mystery of Crocodile Island. Carolyn Keene. LC 77-76128. (Nancy Drew Mystery Stories Ser.: No. 55). (Illus.). 180p. (J). (gr. 4-7). 1978. 5.99 (*0-448-09555-6*, G & D) Peng Put Young Read.

Mystery of Crop Circles. Chris Oxlade. LC 98-54489. (Can Science Solve Ser.). 32p. (J). 1999. 22.79 (*1-57572-804-4*) Heinemann Lib.

Mystery of Culture Contacts, Historical Reconstruction & Text Analysis: An Emic Approach. Kenneth L. Pike et al. Ed. by Kurt R. Jankowsky. LC 95-14739. 120p. 1995. 29.95 (*0-87840-295-0*) Georgetown U Pr.

Mystery of Darkness. B. R. Hicks. (Illus.). 78p. 1976. pap. 5.00 (*1-58363-062-7*, MD-4011) Christ Gospel.

Mystery of Death. Ed. by Russell Standish & Colin Standish. 123p. (Orig.). 1996. pap. 8.95 (*0-923309-36-5*) Hartland Pubns.

Mystery of Death. Lester Sumrall. LC 95-69896. Vol. 1. 192p. 1995. pap. 9.95 (*0-89221-300-0*) New Leaf.

Mystery of Death. Adrienne Von Speyr. Tr. by Graham Harrison from GER. LC 88-80726. 125p. 1988. pap. 24.95 incl. audio (*0-89870-204-6*, 945) Ignatius Pr.

Mystery of Death: A Study of the Katha Upanishad. Swami Abhedananda. 312p. 1987. 15.00 (*0-87481-617-3*, Pub. by Rama Ved Math) Vedanta Pr.

Mystery of Dr. Fu Manchu. Longman Publishing Staff. Date not set. pap. text. write for info. (*0-17-556692-5*) Addison-Wesley.

Mystery of Drear House. Virginia Hamilton. LC 86-9829. 224p. (J). (gr. 7 up). 1987. 15.95 (*0-688-04026-8*, Greenwillow Bks) HarpC Child Bks.

Mystery of Drear House. Virginia Hamilton. 1997. mass mkt. 4.50 (*0-590-95627-2*) Scholastic Inc.

Mystery of Drear House. Virginia Hamilton. (Apple Signature Edition Ser.). (J). 1997. 9.09 (*0-606-12775-5*, Pub. by Turtleback) Demco.

Mystery of E Troop: Custer's Gray Horse Company at the Little Bighorn. Gregory F. Michno. LC 97-13581. 352p. 1994. pap. 18.00 (*0-87842-304-4*) Mountain Pr.

Mystery of Easter. Dietrich Bonhoeffer. Ed. by Manfred Weber. LC 97-69106. (Illus.). 48p. 1997. 14.95 (*0-8245-1722-9*, Crsrd) Crossroad NY.

Mystery of Easter. Raniero Cantalamessa. Tr. by Alan Neame. 126p. (Orig.). 1994. pap. 9.95 (*0-8146-2129-5*) Liturgical Pr.

Mystery of Easter Island. Katherine Routledge. 1997. pap. 16.95 (*0-932813-48-8*) Adventures Unltd.

Mystery of Easter Island: The Story of an Expedition. Katherine Routledge. LC 77-18690. reprint ed. 84.50 (*0-404-14231-1*) AMS Pr.

Mystery of Edisto Island. Idella F. Bodie. Ed. by Barbara Stone. LC 94-618. (Illus.). 157p. (Orig.). (J). (gr. 5-7). 1994. pap. 9.95 (*0-87844-123-9*) Sandlapper Pub Co.

Mystery of Education. Barrett Wendell. LC 71-134154. (Essay Index Reprint Ser.). 1977. 18.95 (*0-8369-2085-6*) Ayer.

Mystery of Edwin Drood see Oxford Illustrated Dickens

Mystery of Edwin Drood. Charles Dickens. 22.95 (*0-88411-276-4*) Amereon Ltd.

Mystery of Edwin Drood. Charles Dickens. LC 75-42303. (Studies in Dickens: No. 52). 1974. lib. bdg. 75.00 (*0-8383-1962-9*) M S G Haskell Hse.

*__Mystery of Edwin Drood.__ Charles Dickens. (Oxford World's Classics Ser.). (Illus.). 266p. 1999. pap. 6.95 (*0-19-283660-9*) OUP.

Mystery of Edwin Drood. Charles Dickens. Ed. by Steven Connor. 352p. 1996. pap. 6.95 (*0-460-87663-5*, Everyman's Classic Lib) Tuttle Pubng.

Mystery of Edwin Drood. Charles Dickens. Ed. by A. Cox. (English Library). 320p. 1974. pap. 7.95 (*0-14-043092-X*, Penguin Classics) Viking Penguin.

Mystery of Edwin Drood. Charles Dickens. (Classics Library). 1998. pap. 3.95 (*1-85326-729-5*, 7295WW, Pub. by Wrdsworth Edits) NTC Contemp Pub Co.

Mystery of Edwin Drood. large type ed. Charles Dickens. (Isis Clear Type Classic Ser.). 323p. 1991. 24.95 (*1-85089-399-3*, Pub. by ISIS Lrg Prnt) Transaction Pubs.

Mystery of Edwin Drood: An Annotated Bibliography. Don R. Cox. (Dickens Bibliographies Ser.: Vol. 11). 400p. 74.00 (*0-8240-8511-6*, H707) Garland.

Mystery of Edwin Drood: Vocal Selections. Ed. by Carol Cuellar. 88p. (Orig.). (C). 1986. pap. text 16.95 (*0-7692-0772-3*, VF1299) Wrner Bros.

*__Mystery of Errors.__ Simon Hawke. 2000. text 22.95 (*0-312-87372-7*) Forge NYC.

Mystery of Evelin Delorme: A Hypnotic Story. Albert B. Paine. Ed. by R. Reginald & Douglas A. Menville. LC 75-46299. (Supernatural & Occult Fiction Ser.). 1976. reprint ed. lib. bdg. 17.95 (*0-405-08159-6*) Ayer.

*__Mystery of Everest: A Photobiography of George Mallory.__ 64p. (gr. 4-6). 2000. per. 17.95 (*0-7922-7222-6*) Natl Geog.

Mystery of Faith: A Christian Creed for Today. William V. Dych. 104p. 1995. pap. text 7.95 (*0-8146-5514-9*, M Glazier) Liturgical Pr.

Mystery of Feeling Great: Discover the World's Greatest Secret. Dori O'Rourke. 191p. (Orig.). 1996. pap. 14.95 (*0-9628854-1-X*) On Target Life.

Mystery of Fidelity. Joseph Allen. 121p. 1984. pap. 9.95 (*0-916586-59-6*, Pub. by Holy Cross Orthodox) BookWorld.

Mystery of Francis Bacon. William T. Smedley. 1991. lib. bdg. 75.95 (*0-8490-5004-9*) Gordon Pr.

Mystery of Francis Bacon. William T. Smedley. 195p. 1996. reprint ed. spiral bd. 16.00 (*0-7873-0801-3*) Hlth Research.

Mystery of Francis Bacon. William T. Smedley. 200p. 1992. reprint ed. pap. 14.95 (*1-56459-135-2*) Kessinger Pub.

Mystery of Freemasonry Unveiled. unabridged ed. Caro Rodriguez. 254p. 1962. reprint ed. pap. 15.00 (*0-945001-27-4*) GSG & Assocs.

Mystery of Ghostly Vera & Other Haunting Tales of Southwest Virginia. Charles E. Price. 128p. 1993. 12.95 (*0-932807-88-7*) Overmountain Pr.

Mystery of God. Compiled by A. M. Muhajir. 328p. 1984. 19.95 (*0-900125-44-6*) Bahai.

Mystery of God. Scott Allen Taylor. 1999. pap. text 14.99 (*0-933451-43-1*) Prescott Pr.

Mystery of God. Thomas K. Watts. 120p. (Orig.). 1997. pap. 10.00 (*0-9657533-0-1*) T R Watts.

Mystery of God: Karl Barth & the Postmodern Foundations of Theology. William S. Johnson. LC 96-40011. (Columbia Series in Reformed Theology). 216p. 1997. 19.00 (*0-664-22094-0*) Westminster John Knox.

Mystery of God: St. Augustine on the Trinity. Edmund Hill. (Catholic Theology Ser.). 200p. 1986. 14.95 (*0-225-66470-4*) Harper SF.

Mystery of Godliness & Other Sermons. John Clavin. 212p. 1999. reprint ed. 20.95 (*1-57358-094-5*) Soli Deo Gloria.

Mystery of God's Opened Doors. Ora O. Turner. (Illus.). 152p. (Orig.). 1996. pap. text 10.95 (*0-9656504-0-5*) Ora Turner.

Mystery of God's Supreme Sovereignty in the Book of Daniel. B. R. Hicks. (Illus.). 237p. 1985. 15.95 (*1-58363-064-3*, PR-2402) Christ Gospel.

Mystery of God's Will. Charles R. Swindoll. LC 99-43573. 300p. 1999. 21.99 (*0-8499-1133-8*) Word Pub.

An Asterisk (*) at the beginning of an entry indicates that the title is appearing for the first time.

Mystery of God's Word. Raniero Cantalamessa. 96p. (Orig.). 1995. pap. 7.95 (*0-8146-2127-9*) Liturgical Pr.

Mystery of Golf. Arnold Haultain. Date not set. lib. bdg. 18.95 (*0-8488-1662-5*) Amereon Ltd.

Mystery of Golf. Arnold Haultain. 160p. 1998. pap. 9.95 (*0-939218-18-6*) Chapman Billies.

***Mystery of Golf.** Arnold Haultain. 160p. 2000. 19.00 (*0-618-05522-3*) HM.

Mystery of Golf. rev. ed. Arnold Haultain. Ed. & Intro. by John Updike. (Classics of Golf Ser.). 152p. 1988. reprint ed. 28.00 (*0-940889-09-9*) Classics Golf.

Mystery of Goodness & the Positive Moral Consequences of Psychotherapy. Mary Nicholas. 288p. (C). 1994. 30.00 (*0-393-70166-2*) Norton.

Mystery of Great Price. Dandi Daley Mackall. (Puzzle Club Mystery Ser.). 1997. pap. text 4.99 (*0-570-05027-8*, 56-1851) Concordia.

Mystery of Half Moon Cove: A Kimmy O'Keefe Mystery. Dan Montgomery. LC 96-5207. (Kimmy O'Keefe Mystery Ser.: Vol. 2). 204p. (Orig.). (YA). (gr. 8-11). 1996. pap. 6.95 (*0-8198-4785-2*) Pauline Bks.

Mystery of Handshake: The Rest of My Story. Clayton Jennings. (Illus.). 316p. (Orig.). 1995. 25.00 (*0-9638624-2-1*); pap. 20.00 (*0-9638624-3-X*) C Jennings.

Mystery of Haunted Houses. Holly Wallace. LC 99-17405. (Can Science Solve Ser.). 1999. 22.79 (*1-57572-809-5*) Heinemann Lib.

Mystery of He. Michel Gagne. (Illus.). 32p. 1999. 24.95 (*0-9666404-1-1*) Gagne Intl Pr.

Mystery of Healing. Paul Rymniak. 256p. (Orig.). 1996. pap. write for info. (*0-614-14973-8*) P Rymniak.

Mystery of Healing: Journeys Through Alternative Medicine. Stephen A. Appelbaum. LC 98-38700. 288p. 1998. pap. 16.95 (*1-57129-062-1*) Brookline Bks.

Mystery of Holy Night. Dietrich Bonhoeffer. Ed. by Manfred Weber. LC 96-85500. (Illus.). 48p. 1996. 14.95 (*0-8245-1591-9*) Crossroad NY.

Mystery of Hope in the Philosophy of Gabriel Marcel, 1888-1973: Hope & "Homo Viator" Albert B. Randall. LC 92-26572. (Problems in Contemporary Philosophy Ser.: Vol. 33). 420p. 1992. text 109.95 (*0-7734-9160-0*) E Mellen.

***Mystery of Horses.** Kim Marie Wood. (Illus.). 2000. pap. 14.95 (*0-9671978-5-6*) Syncopated Pr.

Mystery of Horseshoe Mountain. Laura Sanborn & Jane Sanborn. (Illus.). 108p. (Orig.). (J). (gr. 4-12). 1983. pap. 4.95 (*0-910715-01-7*) Search Public.

Mystery of Human Relationship: Alchemy & the Transformation of Self. Nathan Schwartz-Salant. LC 97-21851. (Illus.). 264p. 1998. pap. 24.99 (*0-415-15389-1*) Routledge.

Mystery of Human Relationship: Alchemy & the Transformation of Self. Nathan Schwartz-Salant. LC 97-21851. (Illus.). 264p. (C). 1998. 90.00 (*0-415-08971-9*) Routledge.

Mystery of Humanity: Tranquility & Survival. 2nd ed. Molana S. Angha. LC 95-441128. 86p. (Orig.). 1997. reprint ed. pap. 9.95 (*0-8191-9793-9*) U Pr of Amer.

Mystery of Hunting's End. Mignon G. Eberhart. LC 98-9956. (Illus.). v, 341p. 1998. pap. 15.00 (*0-8032-6737-1*, Bison Books) U of Nebr Pr.

Mystery of Huntings End. Mignon G. Eberhart. 1976. reprint ed. lib. bdg. 25.95 (*0-88411-764-2*) Amereon Ltd.

Mystery of Immortality. Lester Sumrall. 120p. (C). 1988. pap. text 1.95 (*0-937580-09-0*) Sumrall Pubng.

Mystery of Iniquity: An Indepth & Electrifying Message of End Time Prophesy. Richard B. Glenn. 171p. (Orig.). 1994. pap. text 11.95 (*0-9641535-0-5*) R Glenn Minist.

Mystery of Iniquity: Melville As Poet, 1857-1891. William H. Shurr. LC 70-190535. 295p. reprint ed. 91.50 (*0-8357-9791-0*, 201107200074) Bks Demand.

Mystery of Irma Vep & Other Plays. Charles Ludlum. LC 99-44196. 300p. 1999. pap. 16.95 (*1-55936-173-5*, Pub. by Theatre Comm) Consort Bk Sales.

Mystery of Jesus Christ. F. Ocariz et al. LC 95-149485. 123p. 1997. pap. 24.95 (*1-85182-127-9*, Pub. by Four Cts Pr) Intl Spec Bk.

Mystery of King Karfu. Doug Cushman. LC 95-31064. (Illus.). 32p. (J). (ps-3). 1996. 14.95 (*0-06-024796-7*) HarpC Child Bks.

Mystery of King Karfu. Doug Cushman. LC 95-31064. (Illus.). 32p. (J). (ps-3). 1998. pap. 5.95 (*0-06-443503-2*) HarpC Child Bks.

Mystery of King Karfu. Doug Cushman. 1998. 11.15 (*0-606-13638-X*, Pub. by Turtleback) Demco.

***Mystery of Knots: Computer Programming for Knot Tabulation, 20.** Charilaos Aneziris. (Series on Knots & Everything: Vol. 20). (Illus.). 1999. 55.00 (*981-02-3878-9*) World Scientific Pub.

Mystery of Leopold Stokowski. William A. Smith. LC 88-46154. (Illus.). 288p. 1990. 48.50 (*0-8386-3362-5*) Fairleigh Dickinson.

Mystery of Light: The Life & Teaching of Omraam Mikhael Aivanhor. rev. ed. Georg Feuerstein. LC 97-35200. (Illus.). 280p. 1998. pap. 14.95 (*0-941255-51-4*) Integral Pub.

Mystery of Lost Shoes. Vern Rutsula. LC 85-160. 37p. 1985. 5.00 (*0-89924-046-1*) Lynx Hse.

***Mystery of Lost Trail Pass: A Quest for Lewis & Clark's Campsite of September 3, 1805.** James R. Fazio et al. (Illus.). 76p. (C). 2000. 12.00 (*0-9678887-1-9*) L & C Trail.

Mystery of Love. Hume. 11.95 (*0-340-67113-0*, Pub. by Hodder & Stought Ltd) Trafalgar.

Mystery of Macbeth. Daniel Amneus. 1983. 10.00 (*0-9610864-0-8*); pap. 7.00 (*0-9610864-1-6*) Primrose Pr.

Mystery of Magnets. Melvin Berger. Ed. by Lisa Trumbauer. (Early Science Big Bks.). (Illus.). 16p. (J). (ps-2). 1995. pap. 16.95 (*1-56784-022-1*) Newbridge Educ.

Mystery of Magnets: Mini Book. Melvin Berger. Ed. by Lisa Trumbauer. (Early Science Big Bks.). 16p. (J). (ps-2). 1995. pap. 3.95 (*1-56784-047-7*) Newbridge Educ.

Mystery of Magnets Theme Pack. Melvin Berger. Ed. by Susan Evento. (Macmillan Early Science Big Bks.). (Illus.). (J). (ps-2). 1995. pap. 49.95 (*1-56784-179-1*) Newbridge Educ.

Mystery of Magritte. Abrams, Harry N., Staff. 1997. 45.00 (*0-8109-5152-5*, Pub. by Abrams) Time Warner.

Mystery of Majesty: An Intimate Look at a Loving God. Dennis Jernigan. LC 97-38189. (Artists Devotional Ser.). 288p. 1997. 14.99 (*1-878990-78-0*) Howard Pub LA.

***Mystery of Mallory & Irvine.** rev. ed. Tom Holzel & Audrey Salkeld. (Illus.). 362p. 2000. pap. 18.95 (*0-89886-726-6*) Mountaineers.

Mystery of Man. Hilton Hotema. 41p. 1998. reprint ed. pap. 10.00 (*0-7873-0457-3*) Hlth Research.

Mystery of Manna: The Psychedelic Sacrament of the Bible. Dan Merkur. LC 99-42800. 208p. 1999. pap. 16.95 (*0-89281-772-0*) Inner Tradit.

Mystery of Marriage. Mike Mason. LC 96-177234. 185p. 1996. 16.99 (*0-88070-895-6*, Multnomah Bks) Multnomah Pubs.

Mystery of Mars. Sally Ride. LC 98-52929. (Illus.). 48p. (gr. 3-5). 1998. lib. bdg. 20.99 (*0-517-70972-4*, Pub. by Crown Bks Yng Read) Random.

***Mystery of Mars.** Sally Ride. LC 98-52929. (Illus.). 48p. (gr. 3-5). 1998. 19.00 (*0-517-70971-6*, Pub. by Crown Bks Yng Read) Random.

Mystery of Mary. Grace Livingston Hill. (Grace Livingston Hill Ser.: Vol. 86). 128p. 1995. pap. 4.99 (*0-8423-4632-5*, 074632-5) Tyndale Hse.

Mystery of Mary. Grace Livingston Hill. reprint ed. lib. bdg. 22.95 (*0-89190-043-8*, Rivercity Pr) Amereon Ltd.

Mystery of Mary Stuart. Andrew Lang. LC 78-111771. reprint ed. 52.50 (*0-404-03858-1*) AMS Pr.

Mystery of Masochism: Art of Sex. Andrey Romanov. Ed. by Irina Romanova. 112p. 1998. pap. write for info. (*1-57502-002-5*, P01945) Morris Pubng.

Mystery of Master Romuald: History of Camaldolese Benedictines. Thomas Matus et al. LC 94-31045. 220p. 1994. pap. 12.95 (*0-940147-33-5*) Source Bks CA.

Mystery of Matter. Trusted. LC 98-54238. (C). 1999. text 65.00 (*0-312-22145-2*) St Martin.

Mystery of Matter: Nonlocality, Morphic Resonance, Synchronicity & the Philosophy of Nature of Thomas Aquinas. James Arraj. 171p. (Orig.). 1996. pap. 12.00 (*0-914073-09-5*) Inner Growth Bks.

Mystery of Melchisedec. Stephen Everett, Jr. 196p. (Orig.). 1991. pap. 10.99 (*1-56043-036-2*) Destiny Image.

***Mystery of Meteors: Poems.** Eleanor Lerman. LC 00-41309. 2001. write for info. (*1-889330-55-8*) Sarabande Bks.

Mystery of Metropolisville see Collected Works of Edward Eggleston

Mystery of Metropolisville. Edward Eggleston. LC 70-104446. (Illus.). 320p. reprint ed. pap. text 9.95 (*0-8290-1692-9*); reprint ed. lib. bdg. 19.00 (*0-8398-0454-7*) Irvington.

Mystery of Metropolisville. Edward Eggleston. (Collected Works of Edward Eggleston). 1988. reprint ed. lib. bdg. 59.00 (*0-7812-1174-3*) Rprt Serv.

Mystery of Mineral Gorge. Julia Van Nutt. LC 98-13567. 32p. (J). 1999. 15.95 (*0-385-32562-2*) BDD Bks Young Read.

Mystery of Mister E. Mike Sadler. (Junior African Writers Ser.). (Illus.). 80p. (J). (gr. 3 up). 1992. pap. write for info. (*0-7910-2924-7*) Chelsea Hse.

***Mystery of Mr. Nice: A Chet Gecko Mystery.** Bruce Hale. LC 99-50914. (Illus.). (J). 2000. 14.00 (*0-15-202271-6*) Harcourt.

Mystery of Misty. Carol Kopec. LC 98-119418. 141p. (J). (gr. 3-6). 1998. pap. 9.99 (*0-88092-406-3*, 4063) Royal Fireworks.

Mystery of Misty Canyon. Carolyn Keene. (Nancy Drew Mystery Stories Ser.: No. 86). (J). (gr. 3-6). 1988. mass mkt. 3.99 (*0-671-63417-8*, Minstrel Bks) PB.

Mystery of Monk Island. Gordon Snell. 154p. 1996. pap. 7.95 (*1-85371-765-7*, Pub. by Poolbeg Pr) Dufour.

Mystery of Morgan Castle. John Rambeau & Nancy Rambeau. (Morgan Bay Mysteries Ser.). 10.00 (*0-614-30535-7*) NAVH.

Mystery of Mortimore Strange. Arthur W. Marchmont. 1976. lib. bdg. 16.70 (*0-89968-068-2*, Lghtyr Pr) Buccaneer Bks.

Mystery of My Story. Paula F. Sullivan. 1991. pap. 5.95 (*0-8091-3211-7*) Paulist Pr.

***Mystery of Mysteries: Cultural Differences & Designs.** Samuel Coale. LC 99-55806. 242p. 2000. 51.95 (*0-87972-813-2*); pap. 25.95 (*0-87972-814-0*) Bowling Green Univ Popular Press.

Mystery of Mysteries: Is Evolution a Social Construction? Michael Ruse. LC 98-41969. 320p. 1999. 27.50 (*0-674-46706-X*) HUP.

Mystery of New Orleans. William H. Holcombe. LC 78-39090. (Black Heritage Library Collection). 1977. reprint ed. 22.95 (*0-8369-9028-5*) Ayer.

Mystery of Numbers. Annemarie Schimmel. 320p. 1996. pap. 13.95 (*0-614-21317-7*, 1390) Kazi Pubns.

Mystery of Numbers. Annemarie Schimmel. (Illus.). 336p. 1993. 30.00 (*0-19-506303-1*) OUP.

Mystery of Numbers. Annemarie Schimmel. (Illus.). 336p. 1994. reprint ed. pap. 15.95 (*0-19-508919-7*) OUP.

Mystery of Old Salem Activity Book. Carole Marsh. (History Mystery Ser.). 12p. (Orig.). (J). (gr. 4-8). 1994. pap. 19.95 (*0-935326-67-7*) Gallopade Intl.

Mystery of Old Salem Gamebook. Carole Marsh. (History Mystery Ser.). (Orig.). (J). (gr. 4-8). 1994. pap. 19.95 (*0-935326-66-9*) Gallopade Intl.

Mystery of Old Salem S. P. A. R. K. Kit. Carole Marsh. (History Mystery Ser.). (Illus.). (Orig.). (J). (gr. 3-9). 1994. pap. 19.95 (*0-935326-74-X*) Gallopade Intl.

Mystery of Old Salem Set. Carole Marsh. (Carole Marsh Mysteries Ser.). 1994. teacher ed. 125.00 (*0-7933-6952-5*) Gallopade Intl.

Mystery of One Wish Pond. Dian Curtis Regan. (Ghost Twins Ser.: No. 02). 128p. (J). (gr. 4-6). 1994. pap. 3.25 (*0-590-48254-8*) Scholastic Inc.

Mystery of Orcival. Emile Gaboriau. 320p. 1977. reprint ed. lib. bdg. 14.25 (*0-89968-183-2*, Lghtyr Pr) Buccaneer Bks.

***Mystery of Our Lord Jesus Christ.** Marcel Lefebvre. LC 00-29324. 2000. pap. write for info. (*1-892331-02-0*) Angelus Pr.

Mystery of Pelican Cove. Milly Howard. LC 93-25966. 134p. (J). 1993. pap. 6.49 (*0-89084-711-8*, 070458) Bob Jones Univ.

Mystery of Physical Life. E. L. Watson. 224p. 1992. reprint ed. pap. 16.95 (*0-940262-53-3*, Lindisfarne) Anthroposophic.

***Mystery of Playland Park.** Richard K. DePaola, Sr. LC 99-91123. (J). 1999. 25.00 (*0-7388-0628-5*); pap. 18.00 (*0-7388-0629-3*) Xlibris Corp.

Mystery of Pony Hollow. Lynn Hall. (J). 1992. 9.19 (*0-606-01507-8*, Pub. by Turtleback) Demco.

Mystery of Providence. John Flavel. (Puritan Paperbacks Ser.). 221p. 1991. reprint ed. pap. 6.99 (*0-85151-104-X*) Banner of Truth.

Mystery of Robert Emmet's Grave: A Fascinating Story of Deception, Intrigue & Misunderstanding Michael Barry. LC 91-151802. 77p. 1991. write for info. (*0-9515387-2-1*, Pub. by Saturn Bks-AerRianta) St Mut.

Mystery of Romans: The Jewish Context of Paul's Letter. Mark D. Nanos. LC 95-47643. 424p. 1996. pap. 29.00 (*0-8006-2937-X*, 1-2937, Fortress Pr) Augsburg Fortress.

Mystery of Ruby's Ghost. Lael J. Littke. LC 92-25015. (Bee There Ser.: No. 2). 166p. (Orig.). (J). (gr. 3-7). 1992. pap. 5.95 (*0-87579-656-7*, Cinnamon Tree) Deseret Bk.

Mystery of Runes. Andrews & McMeel Staff. (Little Bks.). 1998. 4.95 (*0-8362-5224-1*) Andrews & McMeel.

Mystery of Sadler Marsh. Kim D. Pritts. LC 92-26454. (Illus.). 112p. (Orig.). (J). (gr. 3-7). 1993. pap. 5.99 (*0-8361-3618-7*) Herald Pr.

Mystery of Salvation: The Story of God's Gift. Doctrine Commission of the Church of England Staff. 223p. (Orig.). 1996. pap. 17.95 (*0-8192-1671-2*) Morehouse Pub.

Mystery of Samba: Popular Music & National Identity in Brazil. Hermano Vianna. Tr. by John C. Chasteen from POR. LC 98-22170. (Latin America in Translation/en Traduccion/em Traducao Series). 168p. 1999. pap. 15.95 (*0-8078-4766-6*); lib. bdg. 34.95 (*0-8078-2464-X*) U of NC Pr.

Mystery of San Gottardo. H. R. Giger. 1998. 39.99 (*3-8228-7291-1*) Taschen Amer.

Mystery of Sara Beth. (Illus.). (J). (ps-2). 1991. pap. 5.10 (*0-8136-5616-8*); lib. bdg. 7.95 (*0-8136-5116-6*) Modern Curr.

Mystery of Self Image. Torkom Saraydarian. LC 93-79459. 250p. (Orig.). 1993. pap. 10.95 (*0-929874-38-2*) TSG Pub Found.

Mystery of Sex: Race Regeneration. R. Swinburne Clymer. 273p. 1950. 9.95 (*0-932785-32-8*) Philos Pub.

Mystery of Sex: Race Regeneration. deluxe ed. R. Swinburne Clymer. 273p. 1950. lthr. 20.00 (*0-932785-94-8*) Philos Pub.

Mystery of Shakespeare's Sonnets. John C. Walters. LC 78-39283. (Studies in Shakespeare: No. 24). 119p. 1972. reprint ed. lib. bdg. 75.00 (*0-8383-1398-1*) M S G Haskell Hse.

Mystery of Sleep (1905) John Bigelow. 224p. 1998. reprint ed. pap. 17.95 (*0-7661-0579-2*) Kessinger Pub.

Mystery of Statistical Science. rev. ed. V. V. Shvyrkov. (Illus.). 151p. (Orig.). 1997. pap. text 41.25 (*0-942004-66-3*) Throwkoff Pr.

Mystery of Stone Mountain. Carole Marsh. (Real People-Real Places Ser.). (Orig.). (J). (gr. 3-7). 1994. pap. 19.95 (*0-935326-25-1*); lib. bdg. 29.95 (*1-55609-180-X*) Gallopade Intl.

Mystery of Stonehenge. Nancy Lyon. (Great Unsolved Mysteries Ser.). 1997. pap. 4.95 (*0-8114-6862-3*) Raintree Steck-V.

Mystery of Survival & Other Stories. Alicia Gaspar de Alba. LC 93-14834. 128p. 1993. pap. 11.00 (*0-927534-32-0*) Biling Rev-Pr.

Mystery of Swordfish Reef. Arthur W. Upfield. (Napoleon Bonaparte Mysteries Ser.). 20.95 (*0-89190-562-6*) Amereon Ltd.

Mystery of Swordfish Reef. Arthur W. Upfield. LC 98-23512. 256p. 1998. pap. 11.00 (*0-684-85060-5*) S&S Trade.

Mystery of Swordfish Reef. Arthur W. Upfield. 1994. reprint ed. lib. bdg. 32.95 (*1-56849-351-7*) Buccaneer Bks.

Mystery of the Abominable Snowman. Holly Wallace. LC 99-17396. (Can Science Solve Ser.). (Illus.). 32p. (J). (gr. 4-6). 1999. lib. bdg. 15.95 (*1-57572-810-9*) Heinemann Lib.

Mystery of the Acts of John: An Interpretation of the Hymn & the Dance in Light of the Acts' Theology. Paul G. Schneider. LC 90-28187. (Distinguished Dissertations Ser.: Vol. 10). 260p. 1991. lib. bdg. 89.95 (*0-7734-9956-3*) E Mellen.

Mystery of the African Gray. Elizabeth C. Murphy. 64p. 1998. pap. 3.99 (*0-7642-2130-2*) Bethany Hse.

***Mystery of the Aleph: Mathematics, the Kabbalah & the Search for Infinity.** Amir D. Aczel. (Illus.). 304p. 2000. 24.95 (*1-56858-105-X*, Pub. by FWEW) Publishers Group.

Mystery of the Anasazi. Leonard Everett Fisher. LC 96-26642. (Illus.). 32p. (J). (gr. k-4). 1997. 16.00 (*0-689-80737-6*) S&S Childrens.

Mystery of the Anchor. G. G. Thomson. LC 97-66529. (Illus.). 30p. 1997. pap. text 15.95 (*1-887003-28-2*, Dancing Dagger) Dancng Jester.

Mystery of the Ancient Maya. rev. ed. Carolyn Meyer & Charles Gallenkamp. (Illus.). 192p. (J). (gr. 7 up). 1995. mass mkt. 15.00 (*0-689-50619-8*) McElderry Bks.

Mystery of the Aspen Bandits: A Kimmy O'Keefe Mystery. Dan Montgomery. LC 96-5209. (Kimmy O'Keefe Mystery Ser.: Vol. 1). 204p. (YA). (gr. 8-11). 1996. pap. 6.95 (*0-8198-4788-7*) Pauline Bks.

***Mystery of the Attic Lion.** Elspeth Campbell Murphy. (Three Cousins Detective Club Ser.: Vol. 27). (Illus.). 64p. (J). (gr. 2-5). 2000. pap. 3.99 (*0-7642-2135-3*) Bethany Hse.

Mystery of the Avatar: The Divine Descent. Helena Petrovna Blavatsky & Raghavan N. Iyer. (Theosophical Texts Ser.). 80p. 1987. pap. 12.75 (*0-88695-035-X*) Concord Grove.

Mystery of the Aztec Warrior. Franklin W. Dixon. (Hardy Boys Mystery Stories Ser.: No. 43). (Illus.). 180p. (J). (gr. 4-7). 1964. 5.95 (*0-448-08943-2*, G & D) Peng Put Young Read.

***Mystery of the Backdoor Bundle.** Elspeth Campbell Murphy. LC 99-50982. (Three Cousins Detective Club Ser.: Vol. 28). (Illus.). 64p. (J). (gr. 2-5). 2000. pap. 3.99 (*0-7642-2136-1*) Bethany Hse.

Mystery of the Bayeux Tapestry. David J. Bernstein. LC 86-30864. (Illus.). 272p. 1987. 29.95 (*0-226-04400-9*) U Ch Pr.

Mystery of the Beatitudes. Jan Van Rijckenborgh. 138p. (Orig.). 1987. pap. 9.50 (*90-70196-55-7*) Rosycross Pr.

Mystery of the Bermuda Triangle. Chris Oxlade. LC 99-18042. (Can Science Solve Ser.). (Illus.). 32p. (J). (gr. 4-6). 1999. lib. bdg. 15.95 (*1-57572-811-7*) Heinemann Lib.

Mystery of the Biltmore House Set. Carole Marsh. (Carole Marsh Mysteries Ser.). 1994. teacher ed. 125.00 (*0-7933-6948-7*) Gallopade Intl.

Mystery of the Biltmore House Set. Carole Marsh. (History Mystery Ser.). (Illus.). (J). (gr. 3-9). 1994. 29.95 (*0-935326-07-3*) Gallopade Intl.

Mystery of the Birthday Party. Elspeth C. Murphy. LC 97-21121. (Three Cousins Detective Club Ser.: No. 17). 64p. (J). 1997. pap. 3.99 (*1-55661-855-7*) Bethany Hse.

Mystery of the Black Hole Mine. Lee Roddy. (D.J. Dillon Adventure Ser.). 132p. (J). 1996. pap. 5.99 (*1-56476-508-3*, 6-3508, Victor Bks) Chariot Victor.

***Mystery of the Black Raven.** Created by Gertrude Chandler Warner. LC 98-54886. (Boxcar Children Ser.: No. 12). (Illus.). 144p. (J). (gr. 2-5). 1999. pap. 3.95 (*0-8075-2989-3*); lib. bdg. 13.95 (*0-8075-2988-5*) A Whitman.

***Mystery of the Black Raven Jewels.** Gertrude Chandler Warner. (Boxcar Children Special Ser.: Vol. 12). (Illus.). (J). 1999. 9.30 (*0-606-18770-7*) Turtleback.

Mystery of the Blanket: A Fictional Tale of Life . . . (of Truth) Mirian Rubinson. 200p. 1998. pap. 12.00 (*0-9668684-0-4*) Robinson Publ.

Mystery of the Blue-Gowned Ghost. Linda Wirkner. 171p. (J). (gr. 3-7). 1994. pap. 4.50 (*0-87935-128-4*) Colonial Williamsburg.

Mystery of the Blue Heron: New Reader Novel. G. G. Thomson. LC 97-66531. (Illus.). 30p. 1997. pap. text 15.95 (*1-887003-30-4*, Dancing Dagger) Dancng Jester.

Mystery of the Blue Ring. Patricia Reilly Giff. (Polka Dot Private Eye Ser.: No. 1). 80p. (J). (gr. k-6). 1987. pap. 3.99 (*0-440-45998-2*, YB BDD) BDD Bks Young Read.

Mystery of the Blue Ring. Patricia Reilly Giff. (J). (gr. 1-4). 1990. 18.50 (*0-8446-6375-1*) Peter Smith.

Mystery of the Blue Ring. Patricia Reilly Giff. 73p. (J). (gr. 1-2). pap. 3.99 (*0-8072-1272-5*) Listening Lib.

Mystery of the Blue Ring. Patricia Reilly Giff. (Polka Dot Private Eye Ser.). (J). 1987. 9.19 (*0-606-03624-5*, Pub. by Turtleback) Demco.

Mystery of the Blue Train. Agatha Christie. Date not set. lib. bdg. 20.95 (*0-8488-2138-6*) Amereon Ltd.

Mystery of the Blue Train. Agatha Christie. (Hercule Poirot Mystery Ser.). 224p. 1991. reprint ed. mass mkt. 5.99 (*0-425-13026-6*) Berkley Pub.

Mystery of the Book Fair, Vol.24. Elspeth Campbell Murphy. LC 99-6449. (Three Cousins Detective Club Ser.). 64p. (J). (gr. 2-5). 1999. pap. text 3.99 (*0-7642-2132-9*) Bethany Hse.

Mystery of the Boule Cabinet: A Detective Story. Burton E. Stevenson. LC 75-32786. (Literature of Mystery & Detection Ser.). 1976. reprint ed. 31.95 (*0-405-07901-X*) Ayer.

Mystery of the Brass Bound Trunk. Carolyn Keene. LC 76-8371. (Nancy Drew Mystery Stories Ser.: No. 17). (Illus.). 180p. (J). (gr. 3-6). 1940. 5.95 (*0-448-09517-3*, G & D) Peng Put Young Read.

Mystery of the Brass Bound Trunk. Carolyn Keene. LC 76-8371. (Nancy Drew Mystery Stories Ser.: No. 17). (Illus.). 180p. (J). (gr. 3-6). 1974. write for info. (*0-448-19517-8*, G & D) Peng Put Young Read.

Mystery of the Buried Crosses see Collected Works of Hamlin Garland

Mystery of the Buried Crosses. Hamlin Garland. (Collected Works of Hamlin Garland). 1988. reprint ed. lib. bdg. 59.00 (*0-7812-1258-8*) Rprt Serv.

Mystery of the Butterfly Garden, Vol. 23. Elspeth Campbell Murphy. LC 99-6448. (Three Cousins Detective Club Ser.). 64p. 1999. pap. text 3.99 (*0-7642-2131-0*) Bethany Hse.

Mystery of the Campus Crook see Home School Detectives Series

Mystery of the Cape Cod Tavern. Phoebe Atwood Taylor. (Asey Mayo Cape Cod Mystery Ser.). 288p. 1985. pap. 7.95 (*0-88150-047-X*, Foul Play) Norton.

An Asterisk (*) at the beginning of an entry indicates that the title is appearing for the first time.

Mystery of the Chinese Junk. Franklin W. Dixon. (Hardy Boys Mystery Stories Ser.: No. 39). (Illus.). 180p. (J). (gr. 3-6). 1959. 5.95 (*0-448-08939-4*, G & D) Peng Put Young Read.

Mystery of the Church: The Pilgrimage of an Orthodox Convert. William Bush. 158p. 1999. pap. 22.95 (*0-9649141-7-4*) Regina Orthodox.

Mystery of the City upon Seven Hills. John T. Ferrier. 80p. 1962. pap. text 6.00 (*0-900235-60-8*) Order Of The Cross.

***Mystery of the Compass Rose.** Jeffrey P. Jacobson. LC 99-91833. 191p. 2000. pap. 14.95 (*0-9677814-0-X*) Bluewater Pub.

***Mystery of the Coon Cat.** Elspeth Campbell Murphy. LC 99-6561. (Three Cousins Detective Club Ser.). 64p. (J). 1999. pap. text 3.99 (*0-7642-2133-7*) Bethany Hse.

Mystery of the Copycat Clown. Elspeth C. Murphy. LC 96-45765. (Three Cousins Detective Club Ser.: Vol. 11). (Illus.). 64p. (J). (gr. 2-5). 1996. pap. 3.99 (*1-55661-849-2*) Bethany Hse.

Mystery of the Counterfeit Money. Anthony G. Bollback. LC 98-226248. 127p. (J). (gr. 4-9). 1997. pap. 7.95 (*1-885729-15-4*) Toccoa Falls.

***Mystery of the Crooked House.** Created by Gertrude Chandler Warner. (Boxcar Children Ser.: No. 79). 128p. (J). (gr. 2-5). 2000. pap. 3.95 (*0-8075-5472-3*); lib. bdg. 13.95 (*0-8075-5471-5*) A Whitman.

***Mystery of the Cross.** Basil Hume. LC 99-54440. 127p. 2000. pap. 12.95 (*1-55725-245-9*, 930-048, Pub. by Paraclete MA) BookWorld.

Mystery of the Cross. Alister E. McGrath. 160p. 1988. 11.95 (*0-310-29980-2*, 18406) Zondervan.

Mystery of the Cross. Alister E. McGrath. 1990. pap. 8.99 (*0-310-29981-0*) Zondervan.

Mystery of the Crystal Skulls: A Real-Life Detective Story of the Ancient World. Chris Morton & Ceri L. Thomas. LC 98-23740. (Illus.). 400p. 1998. pap. 22.00 (*1-879181-54-1*) Bear & Co.

Mystery of the Cupboard. Lynne Reid Banks. LC 92-39295. (Indian in the Cupboard Ser.: No. 4). (Illus.). 256p. (J). (gr. 4-7). 1993. 16.95 (*0-688-12138-1*, Wm Morrow); 15.93 (*0-688-12635-9*, Wm Morrow) Morrow Avon.

***Mystery of the Cupboard.** Lynne Reid Banks. (Indian in the Cupboard Ser.: No. 4). 256p. (J). (gr. 4-7). 1999. mass mkt. 4.95 (*0-380-72013-2*, Avon Bks) Morrow Avon.

Mystery of the Cupboard. Lynne Reid Banks. (Indian in the Cupboard Ser.: No. 4). (J). (gr. 4-7). 1993. 9.60 (*0-606-05934-2*, Pub. by Turtleback) Demco.

Mystery of the Cupboard. Lynne Reid Banks. (Indian in the Cupboard Ser.: No. 4). 246p. (J). (gr. 4-7). pap. 4.99 (*0-8072-1459-0*) Listening Lib.

Mystery of the Cupboard. Lynne Reid Banks. (Indian in the Cupboard Ser.: No. 4). 224p. (J). (gr. 4-7). 1995. reprint ed. mass mkt. 4.50 (*0-380-72595-9*, Avon Bks) Morrow Avon.

Mystery of the Dancing Angels. Elspeth C. Murphy. (Three Cousins Detective Club Ser.: No. 4). 64p. (J). (gr. 2-5). 1995. pap. 3.99 (*1-55661-408-X*) Bethany Hse.

Mystery of the Desert Giant. Franklin W. Dixon. LC no-na1090. (Hardy Boys Mystery Stories Ser.: No. 40). (Illus.). 180p. (J). (gr. 4-7). 1960. 5.95 (*0-448-08940-8*, G & D) Peng Put Young Read.

Mystery of the Disappearing Dogs. Dian Curtis Regan. (Ghost Twins Ser.: No. 5). 128p. (J). (gr. 4-6). 1995. pap. 3.25 (*0-590-25241-0*) Scholastic Inc.

Mystery of the Disappearing Dogs. Dian Curtis Regan. (Ghost Twins Ser.). (J). 1995. 8.35 (*0-606-07915-7*, Pub. by Turtleback) Demco.

Mystery of the Dolphin Detective. Elspeth C. Murphy. LC 95-45258. (Three Cousins Detective Club Ser.: Vol. 8). (Illus.). 64p. (Orig.). (J). (gr. 2-5). 1995. pap. 3.99 (*1-55661-412-8*) Bethany Hse.

Mystery of the Dragon in the Dungeon Vol. 3: The Red Door Detective Club. Janet Riehecky. (Red Door Detective Club Ser.: Bk. 3). (Illus.). 100p. (J). (gr. 3-6). 1999. lib. bdg. 12.95 (*1-56674-089-4*) Forest Hse.

Mystery of the Eagle Feather. Elspeth C. Murphy. LC 95-45260. (Three Cousins Detective Club Ser.: Vol. 9). (Illus.). 64p. (Orig.). (J). (gr. 4-7). 1995. pap. 3.99 (*1-55661-413-6*) Bethany Hse.

Mystery of the Eagle's Eye. James R. Adams. Ed. by Patricia Adams. (Illus.). 108p. (Orig.). (J). (gr. 3-6). 1995. pap. 7.95 (*0-9618060-7-9*) Sheer Joy Pr.

Mystery of the Earth's Mantle. A. Malakhov. (Illus.). 204p. 1975. 14.95 (*0-8464-0664-0*) Beekman Pubs.

***Mystery of the Electric Lemon: An Introduction to Electrochemistry, Student Science Journal.** Peter R. Bergethon. (Illus.). 47p. (YA). (gr. 6-9). 1999. pap. text. write for info. (*1-58447-059-3*) Symmetry Lrng.

***Mystery of the Electric Lemon: An Introduction to Electrochemistry, Teacher Manual.** Peter R. Bergethon. (Illus.). 47p. 1999. pap. text, teacher ed. write for info. (*1-58447-058-5*) Symmetry Lrng.

***Mystery of the Empty Safe.** Created by Gertrude Chandler Warner. LC 99-56190. (Boxcar Children Ser.: No. 75). 128p. (J). (gr. 2-5). 2000. pap. 3.95 (*0-8075-5463-4*); lib. bdg. 13.95 (*0-8075-5462-6*) A Whitman.

***Mystery of the Empty Safe.** Gertrude Chandler Warner. (Boxcar Children Ser.: Vol. 75). (Illus.). (J). 2000. 9.30 (*0-606-18768-5*) Turtleback.

Mystery of the Eucharist in the Anglican Tradition. Henry R. McAdoo & Kenneth Stevenson. 206p. (Orig.). 1995. pap. 16.95 (*1-85311-113-9*, 851, Pub. by Canterbury Press Norwich) Morehouse Pub.

Mystery of the Eye & the Shadow of Blindness. Rod Michalko. 224p. 1998. pap. text 17.95 (*0-8020-8093-6*) U of Toronto Pr.

Mystery of the Fiery Eye see Alfred Hitchcock & the Three Investigators

Mystery of the Fire Dragon. Carolyn Keene. (Nancy Drew Mystery Stories Ser.: No. 38). (Illus.). 180p. (J). (gr. 4-7). 1961. 5.99 (*0-448-09538-6*, G & D) Peng Put Young Read.

Mystery of the Fire in the Sky. Gloria Skurzynski & Alane Ferguson. (Mystery Solvers Ser.). (Illus.). 64p. (J). (gr. 1-4). 1997. pap. 2.95 (*0-8167-4313-4*) Troll Communs.

Mystery of the Flying Elephants. Jane Norman & Frank Beazley. 24p. (J). (ps-3). 1993. pap. write for info. (*1-883585-02-3*) Pixanne Ent.

Mystery of the Flying Express. Franklin W. Dixon. LC 73-106327. (Hardy Boys Mystery Stories Ser.: No. 20). (Illus.). 180p. (J). (gr. 4-7). 1941. 5.95 (*0-448-08920-3*, G & D) Peng Put Young Read.

Mystery of the Flying Monk. Antonio Tarzia. Tr. by Edmund C. Lane. (ITA., Illus.). 44p. 1990. 9.95 (*0-8189-0583-2*) Alba.

Mystery of the Flying Orange Pumpkin. Steven Kellogg. (Illus.). (J). (ps-3). 1992. pap. 5.99 (*0-14-054670-7*, Dial Yng Read) Peng Put Young Read.

Mystery of the Forest Phantom. Christopher Carrie. (Crayola Color & Activity Ser.). (Illus.). 40p. (J). (gr. k up). 1990. pap. 1.59 (*0-86696-243-3*) Binney & Smith.

Mystery of the Four Crosses Surrounding the Cross of Jesus Christ. B. R. Hicks. (Illus.). 70p. 1997. pap. 6.00 (*1-58363-063-5*, MD-4012) Christ Gospel.

Mystery of the French Mist. Neil F. Fogarty. 184p. (Orig.). 1988. pap. 4.95 (*0-929260-02-3*) Cricklewood Pr.

Mystery of the Gingerbread House. Elspeth C. Murphy. LC 96-45911. (Three Cousins Detective Club Ser.: Vol. 13). (Illus.). 64p. (J). (gr. 2-5). 1997. pap. 3.99 (*1-55661-851-4*) Bethany Hse.

Mystery of the Glowing Eye. Carolyn Keene. LC 73-13372. (Nancy Drew Mystery Stories Ser.: No. 51). (Illus.). 180p. (J). (gr. 4-7). 1974. 5.99 (*0-448-09551-3*, G & D) Peng Put Young Read.

***Mystery of the Golden Reindeer.** Elspeth Campbell Murphy. (Three Cousins Detective Club Ser.: Vol. 30). (Illus.). 64p. (J). (gr. 2-5). 2000. pap. 3.99 (*0-7642-2138-8*) Bethany Hse.

Mystery of the Goldfish Pond, Vol. 15. Elspeth C. Murphy. LC 97-4645. (Three Cousins Detective Club Ser.). (Illus.). 64p. (J). (gr. 2-5). 1997. pap. 3.99 (*1-55661-853-0*) Bethany Hse.

Mystery of the Gospel. A. E. Knoch. 297p. 1976. reprint ed. pap. text 7.00 (*0-910424-55-1*) Concordant.

Mystery of the Grail: Initiation & Magic in the Quest for the Spirit. Julius Evola. LC 96-26858. 240p. 1996. pap. 14.95 (*0-89281-573-6*, Inner Trad) Inner Tradit.

Mystery of the Green Ghost. Robert Arthur. Ed. by Alfred Hitchcock. (Three Investigators Ser.: No. 4). (Illus.). 160p. (J). (gr. 3-7). 1985. pap. 3.99 (*0-394-86404-2*, Pub. by Random Bks Yng Read) Random.

Mystery of the Hairy Tomatoes. George E. Stanley. LC 98-17142. (Third Grade Detectives Ser.: No. 3). (J). 1999. pap. 3.99 (*0-689-82209-X*) Aladdin.

Mystery of the Hansom Cab. Fergus Hume. 239p. 1999. reprint ed. pap. 14.95 (*0-947533-42-7*, Pub. by Breese Bks) Firebird Dist.

Mystery of the Hansom Cab, Set. unabridged ed. Fergus Hume. (C). 1995. 41.95 incl. audio (*1-55685-609-1*) Audio Bk Con.

Mystery of the Haunted Castle. Dian Curtis Regan. (Ghost Twins Ser.: No. 8). (J). 1995. pap. 3.50 (*0-590-53885-3*) Scholastic Inc.

Mystery of the Haunted Castle. Dian Curtis Regan. (Ghost Twins Ser.). 1995. 8.60 (*0-606-08574-2*, Pub. by Turtleback) Demco.

Mystery of the Haunted House. M. Masters. (Can You Solve the Mystery? Ser.). 96p. (J). (gr. 3-8). 1992. 21.37 (*1-56239-182-8*) ABDO Pub Co.

Mystery of the Haunted Lighthouse. Elspeth C. Murphy. (Three Cousins Detective Club Ser.: Vol. 7). (Illus.). 64p. (Orig.). (J). (gr. 2-5). 1995. pap. 3.99 (*1-55661-411-X*) Bethany Hse.

Mystery of the Haunted Lighthouse/The Mystery of the Dolphin Detective. Elspeth C. Murphy. (Three Cousins Detective Club Ser.). (J). 1997. boxed set 23.99 (*0-7642-8159-3*) Bethany Hse.

Mystery of the Haunted Silver Mine. Gloria Skurzynski & Alane Ferguson. (Mystery Solvers Ser.). (Illus.). 64p. (J). (gr. 1-4). 1997. pap. 2.95 (*0-8167-4312-6*) Troll Communs.

Mystery of the Hidden Beach. Created by Gertrude Chandler Warner. (Boxcar Children Ser.: No. 41). (J). (gr. 2-5). 1994. pap. 3.95 (*0-8075-5404-9*); lib. bdg. 13.95 (*0-8075-5403-0*) A Whitman.

Mystery of the Hidden Beach. Created by Gertrude Chandler Warner. LC 94-5674. (Boxcar Children Ser.: No. 41). (J). (gr. 2-5). 1994. 9.05 (*0-606-06247-5*, Pub. by Turtleback) Demco.

Mystery of the Hidden Hand. Phyllis A. Whitney. 234p. Date not set. 21.95 (*0-8488-2415-6*) Amereon Ltd.

Mystery of the Hidden Painting. Created by Gertrude Chandler Warner. (Boxcar Children Ser.: No. 24). (Illus.). (J). (gr. 2-5). 1992. pap. 3.95 (*0-8075-5379-4*); lib. bdg. 13.95 (*0-8075-5383-2*) A Whitman.

Mystery of the Hidden Painting. Created by Gertrude Chandler Warner. (Boxcar Children Ser.: No. 24). (J). (gr. 2-5). 1992. 9.09 (*0-606-00631-1*, Pub. by Turtleback) Demco.

Mystery of the Hidden Painting. large type ed. Illus. by Charles Tang. (Boxcar Children Ser.: No. 24). (J). (gr. 2-5). 1995. 9.00 (*0-395-73243-3*) HM.

***Mystery of the Hieroglyphs.** Carol Donoughue. (Illus.). 48p. (YA). 1999. lib. bdg. 18.95 (*0-19-521553-2*) OUP.

Mystery of the Hieroglyphs: The Story of the Rosetta Stone & the Race to Decipher Egyptian Hieroglyphs. Carol Donoughue. (Illus.). 48p. (YA). 1999. pap. 16.95 (*0-19-521554-0*) OUP.

Mystery of the Hobo's Message. Elspeth C. Murphy. (Three Cousins Detective Club Ser.: No. 5). (Illus.). 64p. (J). (gr. 2-5). 1995. pap. 3.99 (*1-55661-409-8*) Bethany Hse.

Mystery of the Holy Grail - A Modern Path of Initiation. Rene Querido. 1991. pap. 14.95 (*0-945803-12-5*) R Steiner Col.

Mystery of the Holy Spirit. Manly P. Hall. pap. 4.95 (*0-89314-333-2*) Philos Res.

Mystery of the Holy Spirit. R. C. Sproul. (Trinity Ser.: No. 2). 191p. 1994. pap. 10.99 (*0-8423-4378-4*) Tyndale Hse.

Mystery of the Homeless Treasure see Home School Detectives Series

Mystery of the Honeybees' Secret. Elspeth C. Murphy. LC 96-45766. (Three Cousins Detective Club Ser.: Vol. 12). (Illus.). 64p. (J). (gr. 2-5). 1996. pap. 3.99 (*1-55661-850-6*) Bethany Hse.

Mystery of the Hot Air Balloon. Created by Gertrude Chandler Warner. (Boxcar Children Ser.: No. 47). (J). (gr. 2-5). 1995. pap. 3.95 (*0-8075-5420-0*); lib. bdg. 13.95 (*0-8075-5419-7*) A Whitman.

Mystery of the Hot Air Balloon. Created by Gertrude Chandler Warner. (Boxcar Children Ser.: No. 47). (J). (gr. 2-5). 1995. 8.60 (*0-606-07315-9*, Pub. by Turtleback) Demco.

Mystery of the Ice Cream House. Isabel R. Marvin. Ed. by Kate Whitaker. LC 93-61532. 64p. (J). (gr. 5-8). 1994. pap. 6.95 (*0-932433-87-1*) Windswept Hse.

***Mystery of the Incarnation.** Basil Hume. 166p. 2000. pap. 13.95 (*1-55725-250-5*, 930-052, Pub. by Paraclete MA) BookWorld.

Mystery of the Incarnation. Christoph Von Schonborn. Tr. by Graham Harrison from GER. (Illus.). 67p. (Orig.). 1992. pap. 8.95 (*0-89870-393-X*) Ignatius Pr.

Mystery of the Invisible Knight. Bill Myers. LC 97-21043. (Bloodhounds, Inc. Ser.: No. 2). 128p. (J). (gr. 3-8). 1997. pap. 5.99 (*1-55661-891-3*) Bethany Hse.

Mystery of the Island Jungle. Lee Roddy. (Ladd Family Adventure Ser.: Vol. 3). 160p. (Orig.). (J). (gr. 3-7). 1989. pap. 5.99 (*0-929608-19-4*) Focus Family.

Mystery of the Ivory Charm. fac. ed. Carolyn Keene. LC 99-16571. (Nancy Drew Mystery Stories Ser.: No. 13). (Illus.). (J). (gr. 3-6). 1999. 14.95 (*1-55709-259-1*, Pub. by Applewood) Consort Bk Sales.

Mystery of the Ivory Charm. Carolyn Keene. LC 74-3868. (Nancy Drew Mystery Stories Ser.: No. 13). (Illus.). 196p. (J). (gr. 4-7). 1936. reprint ed. 5.95 (*0-448-09513-0*, G & D) Peng Put Young Read.

Mystery of the Jade Tiger. Carolyn Keene. Ed. by Anne Greenberg. LC 06-337589. (Nancy Drew Mystery Stories Ser.: No. 104). 160p. (J). (gr. 4-7). 1991. per. 3.99 (*0-671-73050-9*, Minstrel Bks) PB.

Mystery of the Jade Tiger. Carolyn Keene. (Nancy Drew Mystery Stories Ser.: No. 104). (J). (gr. 3-6). 1991. 9.09 (*0-606-00632-X*, Pub. by Turtleback) Demco.

Mystery of the Jelly Bean Trail: Read-Along. Denholtz. (Illus.). 32p. (J). (gr. 3-6). 1983. pap. 9.95 (*0-87386-288-0*) Jan Prods.

Mystery of the Kaifeng Scroll: A Vivi Hartman Adventure. Harriet K. Feder. LC 94-24651. 160p. (YA). (gr. 5 up). 1995. lib. bdg. 19.93 (*0-8225-0739-0*) Lerner Pub.

Mystery of the Kingdom. Theron Messer & Scott Hadden. (Illus.). 240p. (Orig.). 1997. pap. 9.95 (*1-886965-04-8*) Grace Minist.

***Mystery of the Kingdom: On the Gospel of Matthew.** Edward P. Sri. LC 00-100215. 160p. 2000. pap. 9.95 (*0-9663223-5-5*) Emmaus Road.

Mystery of the Kingdom of God: The Secret of Jesus' Messiahship & Passion. Albert Schweitzer. LC 85-60625. 196p. 1985. pap. 21.95 (*0-87975-294-7*) Prometheus Bks.

Mystery of the Kingdom of Heaven. 8.95 (*0-913343-60-9*) Inst Psych Inc.

Mystery of the Lake Monster. Created by Gertrude Chandler Warner. LC 97-40301. (Boxcar Children Ser.: No. 62). (Illus.). 128p. (J). (gr. 2-5). 1998. pap. 3.95 (*0-8075-5442-1*); lib. bdg. 13.95 (*0-8075-5441-3*) A Whitman.

***Mystery of the Lake Monster.** Created by Gertrude Chandler Warner. (Boxcar Children Ser.: No. 62). (J). (gr. 2-5). 1998. 9.05 (*0-606-13211-2*, Pub. by Turtleback) Demco.

Mystery of the Lascaux Cave. Dorothy H. Patent. LC 97-48276. (Frozen in Time Ser.). (Illus.). 64p. (YA). (gr. 4 up). 1998. 18.95 (*0-7614-0784-7*) Benchmark Books.

Mystery of the Light: The Life & Teaching of Omraam Mikhael Aivanhov. Georg Feuerstein. 1994. pap. 14.95 (*1-878423-20-7*) Morson Pub.

Mystery of the Light Within Us. John T. Ferrier. (Illus.). 242p. 1932. text 26.00 (*0-900235-12-8*) Order Of The Cross.

Mystery of the Loch Ness Monster. Chris Oxlade & Holly Wallace. LC 98-54481. (Can Science Solve Ser.). 32p. (J). 1999. write for info. (*1-57572-805-2*) Heinemann Lib.

Mystery of the Locks see Collected Works of E. W. Howe

Mystery of the Locks. E. W. Howe. (Collected Works of E. W. Howe). 1988. reprint ed. lib. bdg. 59.00 (*0-7812-1287-1*) Rprt Serv.

Mystery of the Lost Chord. William Zinn & George S. Grosser. LC 82-82899. 216p. 1994. pap. 15.00 (*0-935016-76-7*, Pub. by Zinn Pub Grp) Empire Pub Srvs.

Mystery of the Lost Colony. Carole Marsh. (History Mystery Ser.). (Illus.). (J). (gr. 4-9). 1994. pap. 19.95 (*0-935326-05-7*); lib. bdg. 29.95 (*1-55609-182-6*) Gallopade Intl.

Mystery of the Lost Colony Set. Carole Marsh. (Carole Marsh Mysteries Ser.). 1994. teacher ed. 125.00 (*0-7933-6949-5*) Gallopade Intl.

Mystery of the Lost Island. Elspeth C. Murphy. LC 97-21123. (Three Cousins Detective Club Ser.: No. 18). 64p. (J). 1997. pap. 3.99 (*1-55661-856-5*) Bethany Hse.

Mystery of the Lost Letter. Helen F. Orton. LC 46-7568. (Illus.). (J). (gr. 4-6). 1946. 11.95 (*0-397-31598-8*, Lippnctt) Lppncott W & W.

Mystery of the Lost Mine. Created by Gertrude Chandler Warner. (Boxcar Children Ser.: No. 52). (J). (gr. 2-5). 1996. pap. 3.95 (*0-8075-5428-6*); lib. bdg. 13.95 (*0-8075-5427-8*) A Whitman.

Mystery of the Lost Mine. Created by Gertrude Chandler Warner. LC 96-6778. (Boxcar Children Ser.: No. 52). (J). (gr. 2-5). 1996. 9.05 (*0-606-09095-9*, Pub. by Turtleback) Demco.

Mystery of the Lost Village. Created by Gertrude Chandler Warner. (Boxcar Children Ser.: No. 37). (J). (gr. 2-5). 1993. pap. 3.95 (*0-8075-5401-4*); lib. bdg. 13.95 (*0-8075-5400-6*) A Whitman.

Mystery of the Lost Village. Created by Gertrude Chandler Warner. (Boxcar Children Ser.: No. 37). (J). (gr. 2-5). 1993. 8.60 (*0-606-05766-8*, Pub. by Turtleback) Demco.

Mystery of the Lunchbox Criminal. Alison Lohans. (Shooting Star: Vol. 3). (J). 1990. pap. 4.50 (*0-590-73367-2*) Scholastic Inc.

Mystery of the Magi's Treasure. Elspeth C. Murphy. (Three Cousins Detective Club Ser.: No. 6). (Illus.). 64p. (J). (gr. 2-5). 1995. pap. 3.99 (*1-55661-410-1*) Bethany Hse.

Mystery of the Mammoth Bones & How It Was Solved. James C. Giblin. LC 98-6701. 112p. (J). (gr. 3-7). 1999. 15.95 (*0-06-027493-X*) HarpC Child Bks.

Mystery of the Mammoth Bones & How It Was Solved. James C. Giblin. LC 98-6701. 112p. (J). (gr. 3-7). 1999. lib. bdg. 15.89 (*0-06-027494-8*) HarpC Child Bks.

Mystery of the Manchild. Drennon D. Stringer & Willard E. Thomas. 168p. 1993. 12.95 (*0-8059-3358-1*) Dorrance.

Mystery of the Marble Angle. John Rambeau & Nancy Rambeau. (Morgan Bay Mysteries Ser.). 10.00 (*0-614-30532-2*) NAVH.

Mystery of the Masked Man's Music: A Search for the Music Used on "The Lone Ranger" Radio Program, 1933-1954. Reginald M. Jones, Jr. LC 86-33872. (Illus.). 233p. 1987. 26.50 (*0-8108-1982-1*) Scarecrow.

Mystery of the Masked Rider. Carolyn Keene. Ed. by Ellen Winkler. LC 94-135919. (Nancy Drew Mystery Stories Ser.: No. 109). 160p. (Orig.). (J). (gr. 3-6). 1992. pap. 3.99 (*0-671-73055-X*, Minstrel Bks) PB.

Mystery of the Matching Lockets. M. Lowengert & B. Yasgur. Ed. by Ilana Felder. (Bina Gold Mystery Ser.). (Illus.). (YA). Date not set. pap. 9.95 (*0-911643-23-0*) Aura Bklyn.

Mystery of the Maya: The Golden Age of the Classic Maya. Nancy Ruddell. (Illus.). 56p. 1995. pap. 8.95 (*0-660-14036-5*, Pub. by CN Mus Civilization) U of Wash Pr.

Mystery of the Maya: The Golden Age of the Classic Maya. Nancy Ruddell. (Illus.). 56p. 1996. 8.95 (*0-660-14040-3*, Pub. by CN Mus Civilization) U of Wash Pr.

Mystery of the Melted Diamonds. Carol Farley. 1986. pap. 2.50 (*0-380-89865-9*, Avon Bks) Morrow Avon.

Mystery of the Menorah. J. R. Church. pap. 11.95 (*0-941241-13-0*) Prophecy Pubns.

***Mystery of the Messiah.** Hugh Schonfield. LC 99-208832. 149p. 1999. pap. 16.95 (*1-871871-38-7*, Pub. by Open Gate Pr) Paul & Co Pubs.

Mystery of the Mexican Graveyard see Home School Detectives Series

Mystery of the Midnight Menace, Case 2. Nancy Garden. Ed. by Patricia MacDonald. (Monster Hunters Ser.: Case No. 2). 208p. (J). 1991. pap. 2.99 (*0-671-70735-3*, Minstrel Bks) PB.

Mystery of the Midnight Visiter. John Rambeau & Nancy Rambeau. (Morgan Bay Mysteries Ser.). 10.00 (*0-614-30533-0*) NAVH.

Mystery of the Midnight Visitor see Morgan Bay Mysteries: Low Vocabulary, High Interest Level

Mystery of the Mind. 2nd rev. ed. Swami Muktananda. LC 81-50159. 72p. (Orig.). 1992. pap. 8.95 (*0-911307-51-6*) SYDA Found.

Mystery of the Mind: A Critical Study of Consciousness & the Human Brain. Wilder Penfield. LC 74-25626. 154p. reprint ed. pap. 47.80 (*0-7837-0102-0*, 204038000016) Bks Demand.

Mystery of the Missing Bagpipes. Kathy L. Emerson. 128p. (Orig.). (J). (gr. 5). 1991. pap. 2.95 (*0-380-76138-6*, Avon Bks) Morrow Avon.

Mystery of the Missing Cat. Created by Gertrude Chandler Warner. (Boxcar Children Ser.: No. 42). (Illus.). 192p. (J). (gr. 2-5). 1994. pap. 3.95 (*0-8075-5406-5*); lib. bdg. 13.95 (*0-8075-5405-7*) A Whitman.

Mystery of the Missing Cat. Created by Gertrude Chandler Warner. (Boxcar Children Ser.: No. 42). (J). (gr. 2-5). 1994. 9.05 (*0-606-07147-4*, Pub. by Turtleback) Demco.

Mystery of the Missing Crew. Michael J. Friedman. Ed. by Lisa Clancy. (Stargazer Trilogy Ser.: No. 6). (Illus.). 128p. (J). (gr. 3-6). 1995. pap. 3.99 (*0-671-50108-9*, Minstrel Bks) PB.

Mystery of the Missing Crew. Michael Jan Friedman. (Star Trek Next Generation Starfleet Acad Ser.). (Orig.). 1995. 9.09 (*0-606-11905-1*, Pub. by Turtleback) Demco.

Mystery of the Missing Dog. Elizabeth Levy. LC 94-38765. (Invisible Inc. Ser.: Vol. 2). (Illus.). 48p. (J). (ps-3). 1995. pap. 3.50 (*0-590-47484-7*, Cartwheel) Scholastic Inc.

Mystery of the Missing Map. Lois W. Johnson. LC 93-43770. (Adventures of the Northwoods Ser.: No. 9). 16p. (J). (gr. 3-8). 1994. pap. 5.99 (*1-55661-241-9*) Bethany Hse.

Mystery of the Missing Marlin. John Rambeau & Nancy Rambeau. (Morgan Bay Mysteries Ser.). 10.00 (*0-614-30534-9*) NAVH.

An Asterisk (*) at the beginning of an entry indicates that the title is appearing for the first time.

Mystery of the Missing Mascot. Carolyn Keene. Ed. by Anne Greenberg. (Nancy Drew Mystery Stories Ser.: No. 119). 160p. (YA). (gr. 4-7). 1994. pap. 3.99 (*0-671-87202-8*, Minstrel Bks) PB.

Mystery of the Missing Mascot. Carolyn Keene. (Nancy Drew Mystery Stories Ser.: No. 119). (J). (gr. 3-6). 1994. 9.09 (*0-606-06597-0*, Pub. by Turtleback) Demco.

Mystery of the Missing Microchips see Home School Detectives Series

Mystery of the Missing Millionairess. Carolyn Keene. Ed. by Anne Greenberg. (Nancy Drew Mystery Stories Ser.: No. 101). 160p. (J). (gr. 3-6). 1991. pap. 3.99 (*0-671-69287-9*, Minstrel Bks) PB.

Mystery of the Missing Money. Janet Riehecky. (Illus.). 120p. (J). (gr. 3-6). 1996. pap. 6.95 (*1-56674-701-5*) Forest Hse.

Mystery of the Missing Money. Janet Riehecky. LC 94-928. (Red Door Detective Club Ser.: Bk. 1). (Illus.). 120p. (J). (gr. 3-6). 1996. lib. bdg. 12.95 (*1-56674-087-8*) Forest Hse.

Mystery of the Missing Pearls. Haji U. Hutchinson. Ed. by Zeba Siddiqui. (Invincible Abdullah Ser.: Vol. 3). (Illus.). 131p. (YA). (gr. 6-12). 1993. pap. 6.00 (*0-89259-124-2*) Am Trust Pubns.

Mystery of the Missing Pitom. Beverly Geller. LC 99-52667. 24p. (J). (gr. 2-4). 1999. 12.95 (*965-229-202-8*) Gefen Pub Hse.

Mystery of the Missing Pizza see Mistero Delle Pizze Scomparse: Teenage Mutant Ninja Turtles

Mystery of the Missing Pizza see Mystere de la Pizza Disparue: Teenage Mutant Ninja Turtles

Mystery of the Missing Pizza see Het Mysterie Van De Verdwenen Pizza: Teenage Mutant Ninja Turtles

Mystery of the Missing Pizza see Mistero Della Pizza Scomparsa: Teenage Mutant Ninja Turtles

Mystery of the Missing Pizza: Teenage Mutant Hero Turtles. Stephen Murphy. (Comes to Life Bks.). 16p. (J). (ps-2). 1994. write for info. (*1-883366-75-5*) YES Ent.

Mystery of the Missing Pizza: Teenage Mutant Ninja Turtles. Stephen Murphy. (Comes to Life Bks.). 16p. (J). (ps-2). 1993. write for info. (*1-883366-08-9*) YES Ent.

Mystery of the Missing Red Mitten. Steven Kellogg. 1992. pap. 4.99 (*0-14-054671-5*) NAL.

Mystery of the Missing Red Mitten. Steven Kellogg. (J). 1974. 9.19 (*0-606-02763-7*, Pub. by Turtleback) Demco.

Mystery of the Missing Tooth see Bank Street Ready-to-Read Books: Levels 1, 2 & 3

Mystery of the Missing Tooth. William H. Hooks. (Bank Street Ready-to-Read Ser.). (Illus.). (J). (ps-3). 1997. pap. 3.99 (*0-614-28635-2*) BDD Bks Young Read.

Mystery of the Mixed-Up Zoo. Created by Gertrude Chandler Warner. (Boxcar Children Ser.: No. 26). (Illus.). 192p. (J). (gr. 2-5). 1992. pap. 3.95 (*0-8075-5385-9*); lib. bdg. 13.95 (*0-8075-5386-7*) A Whitman.

Mystery of the Mixed-Up Zoo. Created by Gertrude Chandler Warner. (Boxcar Children Ser.: No. 26). (J). (gr. 2-5). 1992. 8.60 (*0-606-02330-5*, Pub. by Turtleback) Demco.

Mystery of the Moaning Cave see Alfred Hitchcock & the Three Investigators

Mystery of the Monkey's Maze. Doug Cushman. LC 98-39424. (Illus.). 32p. (J). (ps-3). 1999. 15.95 (*0-06-027719-X*); lib. bdg. 15.89 (*0-06-027720-3*) HarpC Child Bks.

Mystery of the Monster Movie, 8 vols., Vol. 1 David A. Adler. (Cam Jansen Ser.: No. 8). (Illus.). 64p. (gr. 2-5). 1999. pap. 3.99 (*0-14-130460-X*, PuffinBks) Peng Put Young Read.

Mystery of the Monster Party. Deri Robins. LC 97-14745. (Gamebook Preschool Puzzles Ser.). (Illus.). 32p. (Orig.). (J). 1998. pap. 5.99 (*0-7636-0300-7*) Candlewick Pr.

Mystery of the Morgan Castle see Morgan Bay Mysteries: Low Vocabulary, High Interest Level

Mystery of the Moss-Covered Mansion. Carolyn Keene. LC 77-155244. (Nancy Drew Mystery Stories Ser.: No. 18). (Illus.). 177p. (J). (gr. 4-7). 1941. 5.95 (*0-448-09518-1*, G & D) Peng Put Young Read.

Mystery of the Mountain. Carolyn Swift. (J). 1997. pap. 6.95 (*0-86278-413-1*, Pub. by OBrien Pr) Irish Amer Bk.

Mystery of the Muddled Marsh. Nancy Moreno et al. (My Health My World Ser.: Vol. 2). (Illus.). 36p. (J). (gr. k-5). 1996. write for info. (*1-888997-16-8*) Baylor Coll Med.

Mystery of the Muddled Marsh. rev. ed. Barbara Tharp et al. (My Health My World Ser.: Vol. 2). (Illus.). iv, 36p. (J). (gr. k-5). 1997. pap. write for info. (*1-888997-30-3*) Baylor Coll Med.

Mystery of the Night Raiders. Nancy Garden. LC 87-45829. (Monster Hunters Case Ser.: No. 1). 144p. (J). (gr. 4-7). 1987. 14.00 (*0-374-35221-6*) FS&G.

Mystery of the Night Raiders. Nancy Garden. Ed. by Patricia MacDonald. (Monster Hunters Ser.: No. 1). 176p. (J). 1991. reprint ed. per. 2.99 (*0-671-76064-5*, Minstrel Bks) PB.

Mystery of the Night Raiders, Case 1. Nancy Garden. (Monster Hunters Ser.: No. 1). 176p. (J). 1991. pap. 2.99 (*0-671-70734-5*, Minstrel Bks) PB.

Mystery of the Ninety-Nine Steps. Carolyn Keene. (Nancy Drew Mystery Stories Ser.: No. 43). (Illus.). 180p. (J). (gr. 3-6). 1965. 5.99 (*0-448-09543-2*, G & D) Peng Put Young Read.

***Mystery of the Painted Snake.** Elspeth Campbell Murphy. (Three Cousins Detective Club Ser.: Vol. 29). (Illus.). 64p. (J). (gr. 2-5). 2000. pap. 3.99 (*0-7642-2137-X*) Bethany Hse.

Mystery of the Passion: The Third Day. Arnoul Greban. Ed. by Martin Stevens & Stephen Wright. Tr. by Paula Giuliano. LC 94-41936. (Early European Drama in Translation Ser.). 205p. 1996. pap. 12.95 (*1-889818-01-1*, P30) Pegasus Pr.

Mystery of the Peanut-Butter Spacemen. Phil Gilbreath. (Illus.). 19p. (Orig.). 1995. pap. 3.25 (*0-88680-411-6*, 411-6) I E Clark.

Mystery of the Phantom Billionaire. Marjel Jean DeLauer. Ed. by Billie Young. LC 72-83301. 1972. 22.95 (*0-87949-005-5*) Ashley Bks.

Mystery of the Phantom Gold. Lee Roddy. (American Adventure Ser.: Bk. 7). 176p. (Orig.). (J). (gr. 3-8). 1991. pap. 5.99 (*1-55661-210-9*) Bethany Hse.

Mystery of the Phantom Ranger. Evan Skolnick. (Power Rangers Turbo Ser.). (J). 1997. pap. text 4.50 (*1-57840-164-X*, Pub. by Acclaim Bks) Penguin Putnam.

***Mystery of the Pharoah's Tomb.** Susan Korman. (Magic Attic Club Ser.). (J). (gr. 2-6). 2001. 12.95 (*1-57513-165-X*); pap. 5.95 (*1-57513-164-1*) Magic Attic.

Mystery of the Pier: New Reader Novel. G. G. Thomson. LC 97-66530. (Illus.). 30p. 1997. pap. text 15.95 (*1-887003-29-0*, Dancing Dagger) Dancng Jester.

Mystery of the Pig Killer's Daughter: Four Plays. Lawrence Russell. LC 75-12079. 134p. 1975. pap. 6.95 (*0-914580-03-5*) Angst World.

Mystery of the Pink Waterfall. Dwayne Moulton. LC 80-84116. (Illus.). 192p. (J). (gr. 3-8). 1980. 14.95 (*0-9605236-0-X*) Pandoras Treasures.

Mystery of the Pirate Ghost. Geoffrey Hayes. LC 84-18228. (Step into Reading Ser.: A Step 3 Book). (Illus.). 48p. (J). (gr. 2-3). 1985. pap. 3.99 (*0-394-87220-7*, Pub. by Random Bks Yng Read) Random.

Mystery of the Pirate Ghost. Geoffrey Hayes. (Step into Reading Ser.: A Step 3 Book). (J). (gr. 2-3). 1985. 9.19 (*0-606-03434-X*, Pub. by Turtleback) Demco.

***Mystery of the Pirate's Map.** Created by Gertrude Chandler Warner. LC 99-21474. (Boxcar Children Ser.: No. 70). (Illus.). 128p. (J). (gr. 2-5). 1999. lib. bdg. 13.95 (*0-8075-5453-7*); mass mkt. 3.95 (*0-8075-5454-5*) A Whitman.

***Mystery of the Pirate's Map.** Gertrude Chandler Warner. (Boxcar Children Ser.: Vol. 70). (J). 1999. 9.30 (*0-606-18763-4*) Turtleback.

Mystery of the Pirate's Treasure. Idella F. Bodie. LC 84-5451. (Illus.). 136p. (J). (gr. 5 up). 1984. reprint ed. pap. 6.95 (*0-87844-059-3*) Sandlapper Pub Co.

Mystery of the Plant That Ate Dirty Socks. Nancy McArthur. (Plant That Ate Dirty Socks Ser.: No. 7). (J). (gr. 2-5). 1996. 9.09 (*0-606-09663-9*, Pub. by Turtleback) Demco.

Mystery of the Plant That Ate Dirty Socks, Bk. 7. Nancy McArthur. (Plant That Ate Dirty Socks Ser.: Bk. 7). 160p. (J). (gr. 2-5). 1996. mass mkt. 3.99 (*0-380-78318-5*, Avon Bks) Morrow Avon.

Mystery of the Plumed Serpent. Houghton Mifflin Company Staff. (Literature Experience 1993 Ser.). (J). (gr. 4). 1992. pap. 10.24 (*0-395-61805-3*) HM.

Mystery of the Poison Pen. Gayle Roper. LC 94-6755. 128p. (J). 1994. write for info. (*0-7814-1507-1*, Chariot Bks) Chariot Victor.

Mystery of the Princes: An Investigation into a Supposed Murder. Audrey Williamson. (Illus.). 215p. 1992. reprint ed. pap. 12.00 (*0-89733-208-3*) Academy Chi Pubs.

Mystery of the Princes: An Investigation into a Supposed Murder. Audrey Williamson. (Illus.). 222p. 1993. reprint ed. pap. text 12.95 (*0-904387-58-5*, Pub. by Sutton Pub Ltd) Intl Pubs Mktg.

Mystery of the Puerto Rican Penny. Isabel R. Marvin. Ed. by Jane Weinberger. LC 93-61533. (The Marisa Blake Mystery Ser.). 72p. (Orig.). (J). (gr. 5-8). 1995. pap. 6.95 (*1-883650-01-1*) Windswept Hse.

Mystery of the Purple Pool. Created by Gertrude Chandler Warner. (Boxcar Children Ser.: No. 38). (J). (gr. 2-5). 1993. lib. bdg. 13.95 (*0-8075-5407-3*) A Whitman.

Mystery of the Purple Pool. Created by Gertrude Chandler Warner. (Boxcar Children Ser.: No. 38). (J). (gr. 2-5). 1994. pap. 3.95 (*0-8075-5408-1*) A Whitman.

Mystery of the Purple Pool. Created by Gertrude Chandler Warner. (Boxcar Children Ser.: No. 38). (J). (gr. 2-5). 1994. 9.05 (*0-606-05767-6*, Pub. by Turtleback) Demco.

Mystery of the Quantum World. 2nd ed. Euan J. Squires. (Illus.). 208p. 1994. pap. 28.00 (*0-7503-0178-3*) IOP Pub.

Mystery of the Queen's Jewels. Created by Gertrude Chandler Warner. LC 98-24725. (Boxcar Children Ser.: No. 11). (Illus.). 144p. (J). (gr. 2-5). 1998. pap. 3.95 (*0-8075-5451-0*); lib. bdg. 13.95 (*0-8075-5450-2*) A Whitman.

***Mystery of the Queen's Jewels.** Gertrude Chandler Warner. (Boxcar Children Special Ser.: Vol. 11). (J). 1998. 9.30 (*0-606-18769-3*) Turtleback.

***Mystery of the Rainbow & the Showdown Between Two Angels.** Wanda Codper Amick & Sandra Codper Jharpe. Ed. by Lea Hardy. 104p. (J). 1999. pap. 7.95 (*0-9675187-0-9*) Rainbow Angel.

Mystery of the Roman Ransom. Henry Winterfeld. LC 89-24510. Orig. Title: Caius Geht Ein Licht Auf. 192p. (J). (gr. 3-7). 1990. pap. 6.00 (*0-15-256614-7*, Odyssey) Harcourt.

Mystery of the Rosary. Marc Tremeau. 1985. pap. 3.25 (*0-89942-105-9*, 105/04) Catholic Bk Pub.

Mystery of the Runaway Russian. Neil F. Fogarty. (Illus.). 156p. (Orig.). 1989. pap. 4.95 (*0-929260-03-1*) Cricklewood Pr.

***Mystery of the Runaway Scarecrow.** Elspeth Campbell Murphy. LC 99-6565. (Three Cousins Detective Club Ser.). 64p. (J). (gr. 2-5). 1999. pap. text 3.99 (*0-7642-2134-5*) Bethany Hse.

Mystery of the Russian Circus School. Judith M. Austin. (GlobalFriends Adventures Ser.). (Illus.). 64p. (J). (gr. 2-6). 1996. pap. 5.95 (*1-58056-003-2*, GlobalFr Pr) GlobalFriends.

Mystery of the Sand Castle. Elspeth C. Murphy. LC 97-53761. (Three Cousins Detective Club Ser.). (Illus.). 64p. (J). 1998. pap. 3.99 (*1-55661-858-1*) Bethany Hse.

Mystery of the Screaming Clock. Robert Arthur. (Three Investigators Ser.: No. 9). (J). (gr. 3-7). 1999. pap. 3.99 (*0-679-82173-2*, Pub. by Random Bks Yng Read) Random.

Mystery of the Sea. Bram Stoker. (Pocket Classics Ser.). 288p. 1997. pap. 12.95 (*0-7509-1468-8*, Pub. by Sutton Pub Ltd) Intl Pubs Mktg.

Mystery of the Sea. Bram Stoker. 1994. reprint ed. lib. bdg. 28.95 (*1-56849-516-1*) Buccaneer Bks.

Mystery of the Sea Dog's Treasure. P. J. Stray. LC 95-25764. (Passport Mystery Ser.: No. 2). (Illus.). 144p. (J). 1996. pap. 4.95 (*0-382-39265-5*); lib. bdg. 13.95 (*0-382-39264-7*) Silver Burdett Pr.

Mystery of the Secret Code. Ruth N. Moore. LC 85-5441. (Sara & Sam Mysteries Ser.: Vol. 2). (Illus.). 128p. (Orig.). (J). (gr. 7-9). 1985. pap. 6.99 (*0-8361-3394-3*) Herald Pr.

Mystery of the Secret Marks, Case 3. Nancy Garden. Ed. by Patricia MacDonald. (Monster Hunters Ser.: Case No. 3). 240p. (J). 1992. reprint ed. pap. 2.99 (*0-671-70736-1*, Minstrel Bks) PB.

Mystery of the Secret Message. Created by Gertrude Chandler Warner. LC 96-39833. (Boxcar Children Ser.: No. 55). (Illus.). 128p. (J). (gr. 2-5). 1996. pap. 3.95 (*0-8075-5430-8*); lib. bdg. 13.95 (*0-8075-5429-4*) A Whitman.

Mystery of the Secret Message. Created by Gertrude Chandler Warner. (Boxcar Children Ser.: No. 55). (J). (gr. 2-5). 1996. 9.05 (*0-606-10147-0*, Pub. by Turtleback) Demco.

Mystery of the Serpent Mound. Ross Hamilton. LC 99-29926. (Illus.). 250p. 2000. pap. 16.95 (*1-58394-003-0*) Frog Ltd CA.

Mystery of the Seven Vowels: In Theory & Practice. Joscelyn Godwin. LC 90-47432. (Illus.). 120p. (Orig.). 1991. pap. 10.95 (*0-933999-86-0*) Phanes Pr.

Mystery of the Several Sevens. Bill Brittain. LC 93-47076. (Illus.). 88p. (J). (gr. 2-5). 1994. lib. bdg. 12.89 (*0-06-024462-3*) HarpC Child Bks.

Mystery of the Sexes: Secrets of Past & Future Human Creationism. Francis H. Buzzacott. 183p. 1996. reprint ed. spiral bd. 16.50 (*0-7873-0138-8*) Hlth Research.

Mystery of the Shark & the Poi. Susan Entz & Sheri Galarza. (Hawaiian Values Ser.: Vol. 1). (Illus.). 24p. (J). (ps-2). 1999. pap. 4.95 (*1-57306-087-9*) Bess Pr.

Mystery of the Shroud of Turin: New Scientific Evidence. John C. Iannone. LC 97-31297. (Illus.). 250p. 1998. pap. 14.95 (*0-8189-0804-1*) Alba.

Mystery of the Shrunken Heads. Beverly Van Hook. (Supergranny Ser.: No. 1). (Illus.). 96p. (J). (gr. 3-7). 1985. pap. 2.95 (*0-916761-10-X*); lib. bdg. 7.95 (*0-916761-11-8*); lib. bdg. 9.95 (*0-916761-17-7*) Holderby & Bierce.

Mystery of the Shrunken Heads #1. Beverly Van Hook. (Supergranny Ser.: No. 1). (Illus.). 96p. (J). (gr. 3-7). 1985. pap. 3.25 (*0-916761-16-9*) Holderby & Bierce.

Mystery of the Silent Nightingale. Elspeth C. Murphy. LC 94-16718. (Three Cousins Detective Club Ser.: Vol. 1). 64p. (J). (gr. 2-5). 1994. pap. 3.99 (*1-55661-406-3*) Bethany Hse.

Mystery of the Silent Wolf. Gloria Skurynski & Alane Ferguson. (Illus.). (J). 1997. write for info. (*0-614-29273-5*) Natl Geog.

Mystery of the Silly Goose. Elspeth C. Murphy. LC 96-45764. (Three Cousins Detective Club Ser.: Vol. 10). (Illus.). 64p. (J). (gr. 4-7). 1996. pap. 3.99 (*1-55661-848-4*) Bethany Hse.

Mystery of the Silver Cord. George Snelling. 80p. 1981. pap. 2.95 (*0-934142-00-9*) Vancento Pub.

Mystery of the Silver Spider see Alfred Hitchcock & the Three Investigators

Mystery of the Singing Ghost. Created by Gertrude Chandler Warner. (Boxcar Children Ser.: No. 31). (Illus.). 192p. (J). (gr. 2-5). 1992. pap. 3.95 (*0-8075-5398-0*); lib. bdg. 13.95 (*0-8075-5397-2*) A Whitman.

Mystery of the Singing Ghost. Created by Gertrude Chandler Warner. (Boxcar Children Ser.: No. 31). (J). (gr. 2-5). 1992. 9.05 (*0-606-02336-4*, Pub. by Turtleback) Demco.

Mystery of the Smoking Chimney. 112p. (J). (gr. 3-7). 1999. pap. 6.95 (*1-889062-04-9*) Artel.

***Mystery of the Smuggler's Treasure.** Sarah Masters Buckey. LC 98-47808. 176p. (gr. 5-9). 1999. 7.96 (*1-56247-813-3*) Pleasant Co.

Mystery of the Smuggler's Treasure. Sarah Masters Buckley. LC 98-47808. 1999. pap. text 4.76 (*1-56247-757-9*) Pleasant Co.

Mystery of the Sock Monkeys. Elspeth Campbell Murphy. (Three Cousins Detective Club Ser.: No. 21). (Illus.). 64p. (J). 1998. pap. 3.99 (*1-55661-859-X*) Bethany Hse.

Mystery of the Soul: Katha Upanishad. Swami Jyotirmayananda. (Illus.). 1976. pap. 4.95 (*0-934664-07-2*) Yoga Res Foun.

Mystery of the Spiral Bridge. Franklin W. Dixon. (Hardy Boys Mystery Stories Ser.: No. 45). (Illus.). 180p. (J). (gr. 3-6). 1965. 5.95 (*0-448-08945-9*, G & D) Peng Put Young Read.

Mystery of the Spooky Shadow. Gloria Skurzynski. LC 96-228950. 1997. pap. 2.95 (*0-8167-4214-6*) Troll Communs.

Mystery of the "Star Ship" Movie. M. Masters. (Can You Solve the Mystery? Ser.). 96p. (J). (gr. 3-8). 1992. 21.37 (*1-56239-178-X*) ABDO Pub Co.

Mystery of the Stolen Bike. Marc Tolon Brown. (Arthur Chapter Book Ser.: No. 8). 59p. (J). (gr. 3-6). pap. 3.95 (*0-8072-1304-7*) Listening Lib.

Mystery of the Stolen Bike. Marc Tolon Brown. LC 98-65411. (Arthur Chapter Book Ser.: No. 8). (Illus.). 64p. (J). (gr. 3-6). 1998. 12.95 (*0-316-11570-3*); pap. 3.95 (*0-316-11571-1*) Little.

***Mystery of the Stolen Bike.** unabridged ed. Marc Tolon Brown. (Arthur Chapter Book Ser.). (J). (gr. 3-6). 1999. pap. 15.98 incl. audio (*0-8072-0401-3*, EFTR199SP) Listening Lib.

Mystery of the Stolen Blue Paint. Steven Kellogg. 1993. pap. 4.99 (*0-14-054672-3*, PuffinBks) Peng Put Young Read.

Mystery of the Stolen Blue Paint. Steven Kellogg. 1986. 10.19 (*0-606-03305-X*, Pub. by Turtleback) Demco.

Mystery of the Stolen Boxcar. Illus. by Charles Tang. LC 95-30926. (Boxcar Children Ser.: No. 49). (J). (gr. 2-5). 1995. pap. 3.95 (*0-8075-5424-3*); lib. bdg. 13.95 (*0-8075-5423-5*) A Whitman.

Mystery of the Stolen Boxcar. Created by Gertrude Chandler Warner. (Boxcar Children Ser.: No. 49). (J). (gr. 2-5). 1995. 8.60 (*0-606-08498-3*, Pub. by Turtleback) Demco.

Mystery of the Stolen Football. T. J. Edwards. (Sports Mystery Ser.: No. 3). 1995. pap. text 2.99 (*0-590-48454-0*) Scholastic Inc.

Mystery of the Stolen Football. T. J. Edwards. (Sports Mysteries Ser.). (J). 1995. 8.09 (*0-606-07916-5*, Pub. by Turtleback) Demco.

Mystery of the Stolen Jewels: Royal Adventures from Highlights. Highlights Staff. (Illus.). 96p. (J). (gr. 2-5). 1996. pap. 3.95 (*1-56397-609-9*) Boyds Mills Pr.

Mystery of the Stolen Music. Illus. by Charles Tang. LC 94-36420. (Boxcar Children Ser.: No. 45). (J). (gr. 2-5). 1995. pap. 3.95 (*0-8075-5416-2*); lib. bdg. 13.95 (*0-8075-5415-4*) A Whitman.

Mystery of the Stolen Music. Created by Gertrude Chandler Warner. (Boxcar Children Ser.: No. 45). (J). (gr. 2-5). 1995. 8.60 (*0-606-07313-2*, Pub. by Turtleback) Demco.

Mystery of the Stolen Sword. Illus. by Charles Tang. LC 98-39740. (Boxcar Children Ser.: No. 67). 121p. (J). (gr. 2-5). 1998. pap. 3.95 (*0-8075-7623-9*) A Whitman.

Mystery of the Stolen Sword. Created by Gertrude Chandler Warner. LC 98-39740. (Boxcar Children Ser.: No. 67). (Illus.). 128p. (J). (gr. 2-5). 1998. lib. bdg. 13.95 (*0-8075-7622-0*) A Whitman.

Mystery of the Suffocated Seventh Grader: A Play to Read Aloud in Class. Cheryl M. Thurston. 23p. (Orig.). (J). (gr. 5-9). 1988. pap. text 9.95 (*1-877673-03-X*, MYS) Cottonwood Pr.

Mystery of the Sunken Steamboat. Eric Wiggin. (Hannah's Island Ser.: Bk. 2). 144p. (Orig.). (J). (gr. 3-7). 1995. pap. 5.99 (*1-883002-25-7*) Emerald WA.

Mystery of the Supernatural. Henri De Lubac. Tr. by Rosemary Sheed. LC 97-42442. 300p. 1998. pap. 27.50 incl. audio (*0-8245-1699-0*, Crsrd) Crossroad NY.

***Mystery of the 13th Volume.** P. M. Butler. LC 99-91731. 2000. 25.00 (*0-7388-1210-2*); pap. 18.00 (*0-7388-1211-0*) Xlibris Corp.

Mystery of the Tolling Bell. Carolyn Keene. LC 73-2183. (Nancy Drew Mystery Stories Ser.: No. 23). (Illus.). 192p. (J). (gr. 4-7). 1946. reprint ed. 5.99 (*0-448-09523-8*, G & D) Peng Put Young Read.

Mystery of the Tooth Gremlin. Bonnie Graves. LC 96-26832. (Illus.). 64p. (J). (gr. 2-4). 1997. lib. bdg. 14.49 (*0-7868-2238-4*, Pub. by Hyprn Child) Little.

Mystery of the Traveling Button. Elspeth C. Murphy. LC 97-21122. (Three Cousins Detective Club Ser.: No. 16). 64p. (J). 1997. pap. 3.99 (*1-55661-854-9*) Bethany Hse.

Mystery of the Treasure Map. Andrew Richardson. LC 96-44839. (Publish-a-Book Clippers Ser.). (Illus.). (J). (gr. 1-6). 1997. lib. bdg. 22.83 (*0-8172-4435-2*) Raintree Steck-V.

Mystery of the Trinity: Trinitarian Experience & Vision in the Biblical & Patristic Tradition. Boris Bobrinskoy. Tr. by Anthony P. Gythiel from FRE. LC 98-50071. 1999. write for info. (*0-88141-182-5*) St Vladimirs.

Mystery of the Trinity & the Mission of the Spirit. Rudolf Steiner. (Illus.). 128p. 1991. 24.95 (*0-88010-353-1*); pap. 12.95 (*0-88010-352-3*) Anthroposophic.

***Mystery of the Trinity in the Theological Thought of Pope John Paul II.** Antoine E. Nachef. LC 99-17572. (American University Studies, VII: Vol. 211). 289p. 1999. text 33.00 (*0-8204-4524-X*) P Lang Pubng.

Mystery of the UFO. Date not set. pap. 6.95 (*1-56674-702-3*) Forest Hse.

Mystery of the UFO. Janet Riehecky. LC 94-929. (Red Door Detective Club Ser.: Bk. 2). (Illus.). 128p. (J). (gr. 3-6). 1996. lib. bdg. 12.95 (*1-56674-088-6*) Forest Hse.

Mystery of the Vanishing Cave see Home School Detectives Series

Mystery of the Vanishing Creatures. Gloria Skurzynski & Alane Ferguson. (Illus.). (J). (gr. 1-4). 1997. pap. 2.95 (*0-8167-4215-4*) Troll Communs.

Mystery of the Vanishing Treasure. Robert Arthur. Ed. by Alfred Hitchcock. LC 99-197945. (Three Investigators Ser.: No. 5). (Illus.). (J). (gr. 3-7). 1985. pap. 3.99 (*0-394-86405-0*, Pub. by Random Bks Yng Read) Random.

Mystery of the Voodoo Queen's Treasure. M. L. Tureaud & A. R. Tureaud. 64p. 1996. pap. 8.00 (*0-8059-3858-3*) Dorrance.

Mystery of the Wagner Whacker. Joseph Romain. (Warwick Young Adult Sports Ser.). 208p. (Orig.). (YA). (gr. 5 up). 1997. pap. 8.95 (*1-895629-94-2*) Warwick Publ.

Mystery of the Wax Museum. Ed. & Intro. by Richard Koszarski. LC 78-53296. (Warner Bros. Screenplay Ser.). (Illus.). 164p. 1979. pap. 9.95 (*0-299-07674-1*) U of Wis Pr.

M

Mystery of the Wax Museum. Ed. & Intro. by Richard Koszarski. LC 78-53296. (Wisconsin/Warner Bros. Screenplay Ser.). (Illus.). 167p. reprint ed. pap. 51.80 (*0-608-20414-5*, 207166700002) Bks Demand.

Mystery of the Wedding Cake. Elspeth C. Murphy. LC 97-45440. (Three Cousins Detective Club Ser.). (Illus.). 64p. (J). 1998. pap. 3.99 (*1-55661-857-3*) Bethany Hse.

Mystery of the Whale Tattoo. Franklin W. Dixon. LC 68-12750. (Hardy Boys Mystery Stories Ser.: No. 47). (Illus.). 180p. (J). (gr. 4-7). 1967. 5.95 (*0-448-08947-5*, G & D) Peng Put Young Read.

Mystery of the Whispering Mummy. Robert Arthur. Ed. by Alfred Hitchcock. LC 99-192344. (Three Investigators Ser.: No. 3). (Illus.). 160p. (J). (gr. 3-7). 1985. pap. 3.99 (*0-394-86403-4*, Pub. by Random Bks Yng Read) Random.

Mystery of the White Elephant. Elspeth C. Murphy. LC 94-16719. (Three Cousins Detective Club Ser.). 64p. (J). (ps-3). 1994. pap. 3.99 (*1-55661-405-5*) Bethany Hse.

Mystery of the White Elephant/The Mystery of the Silent Nightingale. Elspeth C. Murphy. (Three Cousins Detective Club Ser.). (J). 1997. boxed set 23.99 (*0-7642-8158-5*) Bethany Hse.

Mystery of the Widow's Watch. John Bibee. LC 98-21210. (Home School Detectives Ser.: Vol. 8). 128p. (J). 1998. mass mkt. 4.99 (*0-8308-1918-5*, 1918) InterVarsity.

*__Mystery of the Widow's Watch Bk. 8.__ John Bibee. (Home School Detectives Ser.). (Illus.). (J). 1999. 18.99 (*0-8308-8661-3*) InterVarsity.

*__Mystery of the Wild Ponies.__ Created by Gertrude Chandler Warner. (Boxcar Children Ser.: No. 77). 128p. (J). (gr. 2-5). 2000. mass mkt. 3.95 (*0-8075-5466-9*) A Whitman.

*__Mystery of the Wild Ponies.__ Created by Gertrude Chandler Warner. LC 00-24334. (Boxcar Children Ser.: No. 77). (Illus.). 128p. (J). (gr. 2-7). 2000. lib. bdg. 13.95 (*0-8075-5465-0*) A Whitman.

*__Mystery of the Wild Ponies.__ Gertrude Chandler Warner. (Boxcar Children Ser.: Vol. 77). (Illus.). (J). 2000. 9.30 (*0-606-18908-4*) Turtleback.

Mystery of the Wild Surfer. Lee Roddy. (Ladd Family Adventure Ser.: Vol. 6). 160p. (Orig.). (J). (gr. 3-7). 1990. pap. 5.99 (*0-929608-64-X*) Focus Family.

Mystery of the Windswept Cruise. Neil F. Fogarty. 257p. (Orig.). 1987. pap. 5.95 (*0-929260-00-7*) Cricklewood Pr.

Mystery of the Winged Lion. Carolyn Keene. (Nancy Drew Mystery Stories Ser.: No. 65). (J). (gr. 3-6). 1989. pap. 3.50 (*0-318-41224-1*, Minstrel Bks) PB.

Mystery of the World's Fair. Carole Marsh. (Real People-Real Places Ser.). (Illus.). (Orig.). (J). (gr. 3-9). 1994. pap. 19.95 (*0-935326-04-9*) Gallopade Intl.

Mystery of the Wrong Dog. Elspeth C. Murphy. LC 94-16717. (Three Cousins Detective Club Ser.: Vol. 3). 64p. (J). (gr. 2-5). 1994. pap. 3.99 (*1-55661-407-1*) Bethany Hse.

Mystery of the Yellow Hands. Jake Thoene & Luke Thoene. (Baker Street Mysteries Ser.: Vol. 1). 168p. (J). (gr. 4-9). 1998. pap. 5.99 (*0-7852-7078-7*) Nelson.

*__Mystery of the Yellow Room, Set.__ unabridged ed. Gaston Leroux. 1999. 35.95 incl. audio (*1-55685-594-X*) Audio Bk Con.

Mystery of the Yellow Room: Extraordinary Adventures of Joseph Rouletabille, Reporter. Gaston Leroux. 1992. lib. bdg. 27.95 (*0-89966-141-6*) Buccaneer Bks.

Mystery of the Yellow Room: Extraordinary Adventures of Joseph Rouletabille, Reporter. Gaston Leroux. Ed. by Terry Hale. (European Classics). 256p. 1997. pap. 11.99 (*1-873982-38-0*, Pub. by Dedalus) Subterranean Co.

Mystery of the Yellow Room: Extraordinary Adventures of Joseph Rouletabille, Reporter. Gaston Leroux. LC 75-32762. (Literature of Mystery & Detection Ser.). 1976. reprint ed. 33.95 (*0-405-07883-8*) Ayer.

Mystery of the Zoo Camp. Elspeth C. Murphy. LC 96-45912. (Three Cousins Detective Club Ser.: Vol. 14). (Illus.). 64p. (J). (gr. 2-5). 1997. pap. 3.99 (*1-55661-852-2*) Bethany Hse.

Mystery of Things. Christopher Bollis. LC 98-53607. 1999. pap. 29.99 (*0-415-21232-4*); text. write for info. (*0-415-21231-6*) Routledge.

Mystery of Things: Stories for Sharing. Elizabeth Wenzel. pap. 7.95 (*0-8488-0868-1*) Amereon Ltd.

*__Mystery of Time: Humanity's Quest for Order & Measure.__ John Langone. (Illus.). 256p. 2000. 35.00 (*0-7922-7910-7*) Natl Geog.

*__Mystery of Time: Humanity's Quest for Order & Measure.__ John Langone. LC 00-41812. 2000. write for info. (*0-7922-7911-5*) Natl Geog.

*__Mystery of True Israel.__ 189p. 2000. pap. 7.50 (*0-944379-17-6*) CPA Bk Pub.

Mystery of Tryon Palace Activity Book. Carole Marsh. (History Mystery Ser.). (Orig.). (J). (gr. 3-6). 1994. pap. 19.95 (*0-935326-69-3*) Gallopade Intl.

Mystery of Tryon Palace Gamebook. Carole Marsh. (History Mystery Ser.). (Orig.). (J). (gr. 2-6). 1994. pap. 19.95 (*0-935326-70-7*) Gallopade Intl.

Mystery of Tryon Palace Set. Carole Marsh. (Carole Marsh Mysteries Ser.). 1994. teacher ed. 125.00 (*0-7933-6950-9*) Gallopade Intl.

Mystery of UFOs. Judith Herbst. LC 95-45845. (Illus.). 40p. (J). (gr. 2-6). 1997. 16.00 (*0-689-31652-6*) Atheneum Yung Read.

Mystery of UFOs. Chris Oxlade. LC 98-54488. 32p. (YA). 1999. 22.79 (*1-57572-806-0*) Heinemann Lib.

Mystery of Unity: Theme & Technique in the Novels of Patrick White. Patricia A. Morley. LC 77-188136. 261p. reprint ed. pap. 81.00 (*0-7837-6932-6*, 204676100003) Bks Demand.

Mystery of Witch-Face Mountain & Other Stories. Mary N. Murfree. 1972. reprint ed. lib. bdg. 29.00 (*0-8422-8099-5*) Irvington.

Mystery of Witch-Face Mountain & Other Stories. Mary N. Murfree. (Notable American Authors Ser.). 1999. reprint ed. lib. bdg. 125.00 (*0-7812-4601-6*) Rprt Serv.

Mystery of Womanhood see Christian Woman's Guide to Sexuality

Mystery of Y'Barbo's Tunnel. Martha T. Jones. LC 91-2980. (Illus.). 112p. (J). (gr. 3-7). 1991. 14.95 (*0-937460-68-0*) Hendrick-Long.

Mystery on City Street. Robert Hinson. (YA). (gr. 6-12). 1998. pap. 5.95 (*1-890424-05-6*) Dyn-Novel.

Mystery on Mackinac Island. 5th rev. ed. Anna W. Hale. (Illus.). 183p. (Orig.). (J). (gr. 4-9). 1997. pap. 10.95 (*1-882376-48-X*) Thunder Bay Pr.

Mystery on Main Street. S. Dixon. (Advanced Puzzle Adventures Ser.). (Illus.). 48p. (YA). (gr. 7 up). 1994. pap. 4.95 (*0-7460-0660-8*, Usborne); lib. bdg. 12.95 (*0-88110-700-X*, Usborne) EDC.

Mystery on Maui. Carolyn Keene. (Nancy Drew Mystery Stories Ser.: No. 143). (J). (gr. 3-6). 1998. 9.09 (*0-606-13645-2*, Pub. by Turtleback) Demco.

Mystery on Maui. Elizabeth Nugent & Carolyn Keene. (Nancy Drew Mystery Stories Ser.: No. 143). 147p. (J). (gr. 3-6). 1998. per. 3.99 (*0-671-00753-X*, Minstrel Bks) PB.

Mystery on Mirror Mountain. W. Fraser. LC 89-9757. 112p. (J). (gr. 3-7). 1989. pap. 4.99 (*1-55513-588-9*, Chariot Bks) Chariot Victor.

Mystery on Oak Street & Other Stories. Mary H. Duplex. (Illus.). 96p. (Orig.). (J). (gr. 6-8). 1995. pap. 5.95 (*0-8198-4778-X*) Pauline Bks.

Mystery on October Road. Alison C. Herzig. (J). 1993. 9.19 (*0-606-05936-9*, Pub. by Turtleback) Demco.

Mystery on October Road. Alison C. Herzig & Jane L. Mali. LC 93-7487. 64p. (J). (gr. 3-7). 1993. pap. 4.99 (*0-14-034614-7*, PuffinBks) Peng Put Young Read.

Mystery on Stage. Created by Gertrude Chandler Warner. (Boxcar Children Ser.: No. 43). (Illus.). 192p. (J). (gr. 2-5). 1994. pap. 3.95 (*0-8075-5418-9*); lib. bdg. 13.95 (*0-8075-5417-0*) A Whitman.

Mystery on Stage. Created by Gertrude Chandler Warner. (Boxcar Children Ser.: No. 43). (J). (gr. 2-5). 1994. 9.05 (*0-606-07148-2*, Pub. by Turtleback) Demco.

Mystery on the Docks. Thacher Hurd. LC 82-48261. (Trophy Picture Bk.). (Illus.). 32p. (J). (ps-3). 1984. pap. 6.95 (*0-06-443058-8*, HarpTrophy) HarpC Child Bks.

Mystery on the Docks. Thacher Hurd. (J). 1983. 11.15 (*0-606-01899-9*, Pub. by Turtleback) Demco.

Mystery on the Ice. Created by Gertrude Chandler Warner. (Boxcar Children Special Ser.: No. 1). (J). (gr. 2-5). 1993. pap. 3.95 (*0-8075-5413-8*); lib. bdg. 13.95 (*0-8075-5414-6*) A Whitman.

Mystery on the Ice. Created by Gertrude Chandler Warner. (Boxcar Children Special Ser.: No. 1). (J). (gr. 2-5). 1993. 9.05 (*0-606-13218-X*, Pub. by Turtleback) Demco.

Mystery on the Island. (Key Words Readers Ser.: A Series, No. 641-11a). (Illus.). (J). (ps-5). pap. 3.50 (*0-7214-0011-6*, Ladybrd) Penguin Putnam.

Mystery on the Menu. Carolyn Keene. Ed. by Anne Greenberg. LC 94-152984. (Nancy Drew Mystery Stories Ser.: No. 117). 152p. (J). (gr. 3-6). 1994. per. 3.99 (*0-671-79303-9*, Minstrel Bks) PB.

Mystery on the Mississippi. Laura Lee Hope. (New Bobbsey Twins Ser.: No. 6). (Illus.). 96p. (J). (gr. 3-6). 1988. pap. 2.95 (*0-671-62657-4*, Minstrel Bks) PB.

Mystery on the Mississippi. Laura Lee Hope. (New Bobbsey Twins Ser.: No. 6). (J). (gr. 3-5). 1988. 8.05 (*0-606-03868-X*, Pub. by Turtleback) Demco.

Mystery on the Queen Mary. Bruce Graeme. (Black Dagger Crime Ser.). 320p. 1992. 19.50 (*0-86220-847-5*, Black Dagger) Chivers N Amer.

Mystery on the Train. Created by Gertrude Chandler Warner. (Boxcar Children Ser.: No. 51). (Illus.). 128p. (J). (gr. 2-5). 1996. pap. 3.95 (*0-8075-5426-X*); lib. bdg. 13.95 (*0-8075-5425-1*) A Whitman.

Mystery on the Train. Created by Gertrude Chandler Warner. (Boxcar Children Ser.: No. 51). (J). (gr. 2-5). 1996. 9.05 (*0-606-08699-4*, Pub. by Turtleback) Demco.

Mystery on Walrus Mountain. Dian Curtis Regan. (Ghost Twins Ser.: No. 03). 128p. (J). (gr. 4-6). 1995. pap. 3.25 (*0-590-48255-6*) Scholastic Inc.

Mystery on Walrus Mountain. Dian Curtis Regan. (Ghost Twins Ser.). (J). 1995. 8.35 (*0-606-07917-3*, Pub. by Turtleback) Demco.

Mystery Parables of the Kingdom. Kevin J. Conner. 341p. 1998. pap. 24.99 (*0-949829-29-3*) City Bible Pub.

Mystery Patient's Guide to Gaining & Retaining Patients. Suzanne Boswell. LC 96-50954. 1997. 49.95 (*0-87814-654-7*) PennWell Bks.

Mystery Pictures to Draw. Anthony Tallarico. (Illus.). 64p. (Orig.). (J). 1990. pap. 1.95 (*0-942025-19-9*) Kidsbks.

Mystery Play. G. Morrison. Ed. by Bob Kahan. (Illus.). 80p. 1995. mass mkt. 9.95 (*1-56389-189-1*, Pub. by DC Comics) Time Warner.

Mystery Play. Jean-Claude Van Itallie. 1973. pap. 5.25 (*0-8222-0804-0*) Dramatists Play.

Mystery Plays: 8 Plays for the Classroom Based on Stories by Famous Writers. Tom Conklin. 96p. (gr. 4-8). 1997. pap. 12.95 (*0-590-20939-6*) Scholastic Inc.

Mystery Quilt. Schultz. (C). 1991. pap. text. write for info. (*0-201-55628-6*) Addison-Wesley.

Mystery Ranch. Gertrude Chandler Warner. (Boxcar Children Ser.: No. 4). 128p. (J). (gr. 2-5). pap. 3.95 (*0-8072-1450-7*) Listening Lib.

Mystery Ranch. Gertrude Chandler Warner. (Boxcar Children Ser.: No. 4). (J). (gr. 2-5). 1986. 9.05 (*0-606-02084-5*, Pub. by Turtleback) Demco.

Mystery Ranch. Gertrude Chandler Warner. LC 58-9953. (Boxcar Children Ser.: No. 4). (Illus.). 128p. (J). (gr. 2-5). 1958. reprint ed. lib. bdg. 13.95 (*0-8075-5390-5*) A Whitman.

Mystery Ranch. Gertrude Chandler Warner. LC 58-9953. (Boxcar Children Ser.: No. 4). (Illus.). 127p. (J). (gr. 2-5). 1989. reprint ed. pap. 3.95 (*0-8075-5391-3*) A Whitman.

Mystery Range. Charles A. Seltzer. 1976. reprint ed. lib. bdg. 24.95 (*0-88411-114-8*) Amereon Ltd.

Mystery Reader's Walking Guide: Chicago. Alzina S. Dale & Barbara S. Hendershott. LC 94-33414. (Illus.). 400p. 1995. 16.95 (*0-8442-9607-4*, Passprt Bks) NTC Contemp Pub Co.

Mystery Reader's Walking Guide: England. Alzina S. Dale & Barbara S. Hendershott. (Illus.). 416p. 1988. 16.95 (*0-8442-9551-5*, Passprt Bks) NTC Contemp Pub Co.

Mystery Reader's Walking Guide: London. Stone Dale & Barbara S. Hendershott. 320p. 1993. 16.95 (*0-8442-9550-7*) NTC Contemp Pub Co.

Mystery Reader's Walking Guide: London. Stone Dale & Barbara S. Hendershott. (Illus.). 320p. 1994. pap. 12.95 (*0-8442-9552-3*) NTC Contemp Pub Co.

Mystery Reader's Walking Guide: London. 2nd ed. Barbara S. Hendershott & Alzina S. Dale. (Illus.). 320p. 1995. pap. 14.95 (*0-8442-9610-4*, Passprt Bks) NTC Contemp Pub Co.

Mystery Reader's Walking Guide: New York. Alzina S. Dale & Barbara S. Hendershott. (Illus.). 360p. 1995. 16.95 (*0-8442-9481-0*, Passprt Bks) NTC Contemp Pub Co.

Mystery Reader's Walking Guide: New York. Alzina Stone Dale. (Illus.). 360p. 1997. pap. text 14.95 (*0-8442-9611-2*) NTC Contemp Pub Co.

Mystery Reader's Walking Guide: Washington, D. C. Alzina S. Dale. LC 97-34072. (Mystery Reader's Walking Guide Ser.). (Illus.). 400p. 1998. pap. 16.95 (*0-8442-9480-2*, Passprt Bks) NTC Contemp Pub Co.

Mystery Reading. Sandy Kelley. Ed. by Joe Burleson & Scholastic, Inc. Staff. 1994. pap., teacher ed. 5.95 (*0-590-48895-3*) Scholastic Inc.

Mystery Religions. Samuel Angus. (Citadel Library of the Mystic Arts). 1989. pap. 9.95 (*0-8065-1142-7*, Citadel Pr) Carol Pub Group.

Mystery Religions. Samuel Angus. LC 74-12637. 359p. 1975. reprint ed. pap. 8.95 (*0-486-23124-0*) Dover.

Mystery Religions & the New Testament. Henry C. Sheldon. 155p. 1994. reprint ed. pap. 16.95 (*1-56459-460-2*) Kessinger Pub.

Mystery Revealed: The Handbook of Weltmerism. Sidney A. Weltmer. 80p. 1993. reprint ed. spiral bd. 16.50 (*0-7873-0948-6*) Hlth Research.

Mystery Ride. Bonnie Bryant. (Saddle Club Ser.: No. 48). 144p. (J). (gr. 4-7). 1995. pap. 3.99 (*0-553-48266-1*, Skylark BDD) BDD Bks Young Read.

Mystery Ride. Bonnie Bryant. (Saddle Club Ser.: No. 48). (J). (gr. 4-6). 1995. 8.60 (*0-606-08595-5*, Pub. by Turtleback) Demco.

Mystery Ride. large type ed. Robert Boswell. LC 93-10508. 665p. 1993. lib. bdg. 23.95 (*1-56054-750-2*) Thorndike Pr.

Mystery Ride. Robert Boswell. LC 93-27188. 352p. 1994. reprint ed. pap. 13.00 (*0-06-097585-7*, Perennial) HarperTrade.

Mystery Ride: A Novel. Robert Boswell. 1993. 22.00 (*0-679-41292-1*) Knopf.

Mystery Roast. Peter Gadol. LC 96-33272. 320p. 1996. pap. 13.00 (*0-312-15176-4*) St Martin.

Mystery Schools. 2nd ed. Grace F. Knoche. LC 99-45623. 108p. 1999. pap. 7.50 (*1-55700-066-2*) Theos U Pr.

*__Mystery Schools.__ 2nd rev. ed. Grace F. Knoche. LC 99-45623. 108p. 2000. 12.95 (*1-55700-067-0*) Theos U Pr.

Mystery Science Theater 3000: Amazing Colossal Episode Guide. Mystery Science Theater 3000 Writers & Performers. 208p. 1996. pap. 17.95 (*0-553-37783-3*) Bantam.

*__Mystery Ship! A History of the Travel Air Type R Monoplanes.__ Edward H. Phillips. LC 99-40372. (Historic Aircraft Ser.). 1999. 29.95 (*0-911139-29-X*) Flying Bks.

Mystery Soundvalue. Straub. 1999. pap. 9.98 (*0-671-04463-X*) PB.

Mystery Stories. Illus. by Adrian Reynolds. LC 96-1435. (Story Library). 260p. (J). (gr. 1 up). 1996. pap. 7.95 (*0-7534-5025-9*) LKC.

*__Mystery Stories: A Journey Through the Rosary.__ unabridged ed. James L. Carney. LC 99-64130. (Illus.). xviii, 404p. 2000. pap. 24.95 (*0-9673328-0-X*) Crown of Mary Pubg Co.

Mystery Streams in Europe & the New Mysteries. B. C. Lievegoed. Tr. by J. M. Van Houten et al from DUT. 87p. (Orig.). 1982. pap. 8.95 (*0-88010-002-8*) Anthroposophic.

Mystery Teacher's Guide. (Thematic Library). 56p. 1996. pap. text, teacher ed. 29.95 (*1-58303-010-7*) Pthways Pubng.

Mystery Teacher's Resource Guide. Irene Welch. Ed. by Liz Parker. (Take Ten Bks.). 35p. (Orig.). 1992. pap. text 16.95 (*1-56254-061-0*) Saddleback Pubns.

Mystery Thief see Sugar Creek Gang Series

Mystery Title to Come. Munoz. 2000. pap. 17.25 (*0-07-232616-6*) McGraw.

Mystery Title to Come, Vol. 1. 1998. 5.99 (*0-312-96616-4*, Pub. by Tor Bks) St Martin.

Mystery to a Solution: Poe, Borges, & the Analytic Detective Story. John T. Irwin. LC 93-15474. 482p. 1994. 49.95 (*0-8018-4650-1*) Johns Hopkins.

Mystery to a Solution: Poe, Borges, & the Analytic Detective Story. John T. Irwin. 520p. 1996. reprint ed. pap. text 19.95 (*0-8018-5466-0*) Johns Hopkins.

Mystery to Come, Vol. 1. 1998. write for info. (*0-312-96652-0*) Tor Bks.

*__Mystery Toothpaste.__ Omatseyin Mark Edah. Ed. by Martin M. Eda. (Illus.). 32p. (J). (gr. 4 up). 2000. pap. write for info. (*1-928903-03-7*) Edah Bks.

Mystery Tour. J. Cunliffe. (Illus.). (J). mass mkt. 8.95 (*0-340-71333-X*, Pub. by Hodder & Stought Ltd) Trafalgar.

Mystery Tracks in the Snow. Hap Gilliland. LC 90-5816. (Illus.). 128p. 1990. pap. 7.95 (*0-87961-199-5*) Naturegraph.

Mystery Train. Carolyn Keene & Franklin W. Dixon. Ed. by Ann Greenberg. (Nancy Drew & Hardy Boys Super Mystery Ser.: No. 8). 224p. (YA). (gr. 6 up). 1990. mass mkt. 3.99 (*0-671-67464-1*, Archway) PB.

Mystery Train. Carolyn Keene & Franklin W. Dixon. (Nancy Drew & Hardy Boys Super Mystery Ser.: No. 8). (YA). (gr. 6 up). 1990. 9.09 (*0-606-04758-1*, Pub. by Turtleback) Demco.

Mystery Train. David Wojahn. LC 89-39343. (Poetry Ser.). 112p. 1990. pap. 10.95 (*0-8229-5429-X*); text 19.95 (*0-8229-3637-2*) U of Pittsburgh Pr.

Mystery Train. 4th ed. Greil Marcus. LC 96-53338. 288p. 1997. reprint ed. pap. 15.95 (*0-452-27836-8*, Plume) Dutton Plume.

Mystery Tribe of Camp Blackeagle. rev. ed. Sigmund Brouwer. (Accidental Detective Ser.: Vol. 2). 132p. (J). (gr. 3-7). 1994. pap. 4.99 (*1-56476-371-4*, 6-3371, Victor Bks) Chariot Victor.

*__Mystery Unfolds in Massachusetts.__ Bob Schaller. (Arlington Family Adventures Ser.). 144p. (gr. 3-7). 2000. pap. 5.99 (*0-8010-4452-9*) Baker Bks.

Mystery Voices: Interviews with British Crime Writers. Dale Salwak. LC 84-3115. (Brownstone Mystery Guides Ser.: Vol. 8). 112p. 1991. pap. 17.00 (*0-89370-278-1*) Millefleurs.

Mystery Walk. Robert R. McCammon. Ed. by Sally Peters. 432p. 1992. reprint ed. per. 10.99 (*0-671-76991-X*) PB.

*__Mystery We Proclaim: Catechesis for the Third Millenium.__ 2nd rev. ed. Francis D. Kelly. 160p. 1999. 14.95 (*0-87973-597-X*) Our Sunday Visitor.

Mystery Wife. Annette Broadrick. (Special Edition Ser.). 1994. per. 3.50 (*0-373-09877-4*, 5-09877-7) Silhouette.

Mystery with a Dangerous Beat. Franklin W. Dixon. LC MLC R CP01285. (Hardy Boys Mystery Stories Ser.: No. 124). 160p. (J). (gr. 3-6). 1994. pap. 3.99 (*0-671-79314-4*, Minstrel Bks) PB.

Mystery with a Dangerous Beat. Franklin W. Dixon. (Hardy Boys Mystery Stories Ser.: No. 124). (J). (gr. 3-6). 1994. 9.09 (*0-606-05859-1*, Pub. by Turtleback) Demco.

*__Mystery Wolf.__ large type ed. Frank Vander Pyle. 104p. 1999. pap. 3.79 (*0-9673203-0-5*) Vanova Bks.

Mystery Woman of Old Tascosa: The Legend of Frenchy McCormick. 2nd ed. Pauline D. Robertson & R. L. Robertson. (Illus.). 1995. pap. 3.95 (*0-942376-16-1*) Paramount TX.

Mystery Women 1980-89: An Encyclopedia of Leading Women Characters in Mystery Fiction, 2. Colleen A. Barnett. write for info. (*0-938313-41-X*) E B Houchin.

Mystery Writer. R. Mathews-Danzer. 1999. pap. 14.95 (*1-888417-41-2*) Dimefast.

Mystery Writer's Sourcebook: Where to Sell Your Manuscripts. 2nd ed. Ed. by David Borcherding. 475p. 1995. 19.99 (*0-89879-724-1*, Wrtrs Digest Bks) F & W Pubns Inc.

*__Mystery Writers Work Book.__ R. Mathews-Danzer. (Illus.). 130p. 1999. pap. 14.99 (*1-888417-69-2*) Dimefast.

Mystery's Most Wanted: Staff of Mystery Scene. Mystery Scene Magazine Staff. 1997. mass mkt. 5.99 (*0-312-96476-5*) St Martin.

Mysterys of Nature & Art: In Foure Tretises. John Bate. LC 77-6850. (English Experience Ser.: No. 845). 1977. reprint ed. lib. bdg. 45.00 (*90-221-0845-7*) Walter J Johnson.

Mysti & the Mystery of Manana. Judith Ellis. (Illus.). 48p. (J). (ps-4). 1996. 14.95 (*1-887527-27-3*) Wonder Whales.

Mystic: From Charismatic to Mystical Prayer see Torkington Trilogy on Prayer

Mystic Americanism: The Spiritual Heritage of America Revealed. Grace K. Morey & R. Swinburne Clymer. 328p. 1975. 9.95 (*0-932785-33-6*) Philos Pub.

Mystic & Love Poetry of Medieval Hindi with Introductions, Texts, Grammar, Notes, Translations & Glossary. Anoop Chandola. 147p. 1982. 12.50 (*0-88065-236-5*, Pub. by Today Tomorrow) Scholarly Pubns.

Mystic & Pilgrim: The "Book" & the World of Margery Kempe. Clarissa W. Atkinson. LC 82-22219. 242p. (C). 1983. pap. text 16.95 (*0-8014-9895-3*) Cornell U Pr.

Mystic & Pilgrim: The Book & the World of Margery Kempe. Clarissa W. Atkinson. LC 82-22219. (Illus.). 245p. reprint ed. pap. 76.00 (*0-608-20087-5*, 207135900011) Bks Demand.

Mystic & the Professor: An Interview of Baba Fagir Chano. Mark Juergensmeyer. Ed. by David C. Lane. 54p. 1992. pap. 2.00 (*1-56543-004-2*) Mt SA Coll Philos.

Mystic Aquarium Cookbook. Ed. & Intro. by Tonia Binder. (Illus.). 160p. (Orig.). 1995. write for info. (*0-915897-06-7*) Mystic Marinelife Aquarium.

*__Mystic Artist: The Artist Is the Channel for a Higher Force.__ Sandra Frazier. (Illus.). 240p. 1998. pap. 19.95 (*1-884039-15-4*) Mystic-Art Media.

Mystic Arts of the Ninja. Stephen K. Hayes. (Illus.). 160p. (Orig.). 1985. pap. 15.95 (*0-8092-5343-7*, 534370, Contemporary Bks) NTC Contemp Pub Co.

Mystic Bayou. Morris Raphael. LC 85-81338. 88p. 1985. 12.95 (*0-9608866-4-8*) M Raphael.

Mystic Beauty: The Holy Art of Imperial Russia 1660-1917. James Jackson, Jr. Ed. by Sara Rathban. (Illus.). 80p. 1996. pap. 5.00 (*0-9656482-2-2*) J&M Hearst.

Mystic Bridge: A Calendar Book - 1999. Beth Garbo. (Illus.). 110p. 1998. spiral bd. 12.95 (*1-892373-00-9*, 99-01) Especially Bks.

An Asterisk (*) at the beginning of an entry indicates that the title is appearing for the first time.

Mystic Bridge: A Calendar Book - 2000. Beth Garbo. (Illus.). 110p. 1998. spiral bd. 12.95 (*1-892373-19-X*, 19-x) Especially Bks.

Mystic Built: Ships & Shipyards of the Mystic River, Connecticut, 1784-1919. William N. Peterson. (Illus.). xvi, 254p. 1989. 36.00 (*0-913372-51-X*) Mystic Seaport.

Mystic China: Ninjas & Superspies Sourcebook. Erick Wujcik. Ed. by Alex Marciniszyn et al. (Ninjas & Superspies Ser.). (Illus.). 208p. (Orig.). 1994. pap. 19.95 (*0-916211-77-0*, 526) Palladium Bks.

Mystic Chords of Memory: Civil War Battlefields & Historic Sites Recaptured. David J. Eicher. LC 98-20247. (Illus.). 232p. 1998. 39.95 (*0-8071-2309-9*) La State U Pr.

Mystic Chords of Memory: The Transformation of Tradition in American Culture. Michael G. Kammen. LC 92-50069. 1993. pap. 25.00 (*0-679-74177-1*) Vin Bks.

Mystic Christianity. Yogi Ramacharaka. reprint ed. 15.00 (*0-911662-08-1*) Yoga.

Mystic Christianity or the Inner Teachings of the Master. Yogi Ramacharaka. 274p. 1998. reprint ed. pap. 19.95 (*0-7661-0168-1*) Kessinger Pub.

***Mystic Coast, Stonington to New London: A Photographic Portrait.** (Illus.). 128p. 2000. 24.95 (*1-885435-09-6*, PilotPress Pubs) Twin Lights.

Mystic Dream Book: 2500 Dreams Explained. Ano. 1998. pap. 7.95 (*0-572-02411-8*, Pub. by W Foulsham) Trans-Atl Phila.

Mystic Dream Book: 2500 Dreams Explained. Foulsham Editors. 186p. 1995. pap. 3.95 (*0-572-00207-6*, Pub. by Foulsham UK) Assoc Pubs Grp.

Mystic Dreamers. Rosanne Bittner. LC 98-50567. 1999. 22.95 (*0-312-86511-2*, Pub. by Forge NYC) St Martin.

***Mystic Dreamers.** Rosanne Bittner. 384p. 2000. mass mkt. 6.99 (*0-8125-6540-1*, Pub. by Tor Bks) St Martin.

Mystic Endowment: Religious Ethnography of the Warao Indians. Johannes Wilbert. LC 93-10164. (Religions of the World Ser.). 1993. 28.95 (*0-945454-04-X*); pap. 25.95 (*0-945454-05-8*) Harvard U Wrld Relig.

***Mystic Experience: Bhagwan Shree Rajneesh.** Ed. by Ma Ananda Prem. Tr. by Dolly Diddee. 1998. 32.00 (*81-208-1377-4*, Pub. by Motilal Bnarsidass); pap. 22.00 (*81-208-1378-2*, Pub. by Motilal Bnarsidass) S Asia.

Mystic Eye-Manifestations of Psychic Phenomenon. Olga Brosten. Ed. by Sylvia Ashton. LC 78-54162. 1981. 22.95 (*0-87949-122-1*) Ashley Bks.

Mystic Fable: The Sixteenth & Seventeenth Centuries. Michel De Certeau. Tr. by Michael B. Smith. 384p. 1995. pap. text 22.00 (*0-226-10037-5*) U Ch Pr.

Mystic Fable: The Sixteenth & Seventeeth Centuries. Michel De Certeau. Tr. by Michael B. Smith. (Religion & Postmodernism Ser.). (Illus.). 384p. 1992. 37.50 (*0-226-10036-7*) U Ch Pr.

***Mystic Fan.** Chronicle Staff. 1999. 9.95 (*0-8118-2399-7*) Chronicle Bks.

Mystic Fire: The Love Poems of James Kavanaugh. 3rd ed. James Kavanaugh. LC 91-90572. 112p. 1991. pap. 12.95 (*1-878995-19-7*) S J Nash Pub.

***Mystic Forest: A Fantasy Quest Screenplay for Children.** James Russell. 118p. 1999. pap. 34.95 (*0-916367-27-4*, MF) James Russell.

Mystic Gateways. Friedrich Hechelmann. 44p. 1996. pap. 9.50 (*1-885394-11-X*) Bluestar Communs.

Mystic, Geometer & Intuitionist: The Life of L. E. J. Brouwer: The Dawning Revolution. Dirk Van Dalen. LC 99-214056. (Illus.). 456p. 1999. text 140.00 (*0-19-850297-4*) OUP.

Mystic Gleams from the Holy Grail. F. Rolt-Wheeler. 1972. 59.95 (*0-8490-0694-5*) Gordon Pr.

Mystic Gnosis. J. M. Fisher. 1977. lib. bdg. 59.95 (*0-8490-2316-5*) Gordon Pr.

Mystic Healers: A History of Magical Medicine. rev. ed. Paris Flammonde. LC 98-52363. xxiv, 272p. 1999. pap. 17.95 (*0-8128-3149-7*, Pub. by Madison Bks UPA) Natl Bk Netwk.

Mystic Healers & Medicine Shows: Blazing Trails to Wellness in the Old West & Beyond. Gene Fowler, Jr. LC 96-34432. (Illus.). 200p. 1997. 29.95 (*0-941270-94-7*); pap. 14.95 (*0-941270-95-5*) Ancient City Pr.

Mystic Heart: Discovering a Universal Spirituality in the World's Religions. Wayne Teasdale. LC 99-41879. (Illus.). 308p. 1999. text 23.95 (*1-57731-102-7*, Pub. by New Wrld Lib) Publishers Group.

Mystic Hours of Spiritual Experiences. G. A. Redman. 388p. 1997. reprint ed. pap. 24.95 (*0-7661-0035-9*) Kessinger Pub.

Mystic in the Marketplace: A Spiritual Journey. William F. Sturner. (Illus.). 175p. 1994. pap. 16.95 (*0-930222-99-7*) Creat Educ Found.

Mystic in the New World: Marie de l'Incarnation, 1599-1672. Anya Mali. LC 96-32576. (Studies in the History of Christian Thought). 1996. 87.00 (*90-04-10606-5*) Brill Academic Pubs.

Mystic in the Theatre: Eleonora Duse. Eva Le Gallienne. LC 72-11975. (Arcturus Books Paperbacks). 189p. 1973. pap. 14.95 (*0-8093-0631-X*) S Ill U Pr.

***Mystic Knight: The Legend of the Ancient Scroll, No. 1.** Michael Teitelbaum. (Mystic Knights of Tir Na Nog Ser.). 96p. (J). (gr. 1-5). 1999. pap. text 3.99 (*0-06-107160-9*) HarpC.

***Mystic Knights: Draganta Revealed!, No. 5.** Michael Teitelbaum. (Mystic Knights Ser.: No. 5). 96p. (gr. 1-5). 1999. mass mkt. 4.25 (*0-06-107164-1*, Pub. by Harper SF) HarpC.

***Mystic Knights: Fire Within, Air Above!, No. 2.** Robert Simpson. (Mystic Knights Ser.: No. 2). 112p. (J). (gr. 1-5). 1999. 3.99 (*0-06-107161-7*) HarpC.

***Mystic Knights: The Taming of Pyre, No. 4.** John Whitman. (Mystic Knights Ser.: Vol. 4). 96p. (gr. 1-5). 1999. mass mkt. 4.25 (*0-06-107163-3*, Pub. by Harper SF) HarpC.

***Mystic Knights: Water Around, Earth Below!, No. 3.** R. Brightfield. (Mystic Knights Ser.: No. 3). 96p. (J). (gr. 1-5). 1999. mass mkt. 3.99 (*0-06-107162-5*) HarpC.

Mystic Lake Sioux: Sociology of the Mdewakantonwan Santee. Ruth Landes. LC 68-9019. 232p. reprint ed. pap. 72.00 (*0-7837-5589-9*, 204538200005) Bks Demand.

Mystic Life of Alfred Deakin. Al Gabay. 216p. (C). 1992. text 59.95 (*0-521-41494-6*) Cambridge U Pr.

Mystic Life of Animals. Ann Walker. 1998. pap. 19.95 (*1-86163-016-6*) Holmes Pub.

Mystic Link with India: Life Story of Two Pilgrims Painters of Hungary. R. K. Raju. (C). 1991. 22.00 (*81-7023-317-8*, Pub. by Allied Pubs) S Asia.

***Mystic Magic Words.** Orlo Marlatt. LC 99-93676. 1999. pap. 8.95 (*0-533-13114-6*) Vantage.

Mystic Magic Words. Orlo Marlatt. 1997. pap. 56.95 (*1-57553-631-5*) Watermrk Pr.

***Mystic Mantra: Om Mani Padme Aum.** Robert Chaney. LC 99-72963. 112p. 1999. pap. 12.95 (*0-918936-34-9*) Astara.

Mystic Masonry or the Symbols of Freemasonry & the Greater Mysteries of Antiquity. J. D. Buck. 290p. 1990. reprint ed. pap. 16.95 (*1-56459-271-5*) Kessinger Pub.

Mystic Masseur. V. S. Naipaul. (Caribbean Writers Ser.). 214p. (C). 1971. pap. 8.95 (*0-435-98646-5*, 98646) Heinemann.

Mystic Masters. Allen Varney. Ed. by Rob Bell. (Champions Ser.). (Illus.). 112p. (Orig.). (C). 1989. pap. 13.00 (*1-55806-075-8*, 405) Hero Games.

Mystic Masters Speak. Vernon Howard. 1974. pap. 8.95 (*0-911203-23-0*) New Life.

Mystic Memories. Susan L. Liepitz. 1998. mass mkt. 5.99 (*0-515-12262-9*, Jove) Berkley Pub.

***Mystic Mind.** Crystal Love. (Illus.). 224p. 2000. pap. 14.95 (*1-58394-023-5*, Pub. by Frog Ltd CA) Publishers Group.

Mystic Minerals: Wisdom of the Ancients. rev. ed. Barbara J. Matteson. LC 86-71607. (Illus.). 64p. 1986. pap. 4.95 (*0-9620524-0-X*) Cosmic Resources.

Mystic Moments in Poet's Corner. 2nd rev. ed. Roderic Vickers. (Illus.). 44p. (YA). 1996. reprint ed. pap. text 9.95 (*1-886956-06-5*) Star Concepts.

Mystic Monkey. Baba Hari Dass. LC 81-51051. (Illus.). 64p. (Orig.). (J). (gr. 4-8). 1984. pap. 9.95 (*0-918100-05-4*) Sri Rama.

Mystic Muse. Ed. by Hannah R. Lurie et al. LC 76-20284. 1976. pap. 3.00 (*0-9600728-2-9*) H R Lurie.

Mystic of Liberation: A Portrait of Pedro Casaldaliga. Teofilo Cabestrero. Tr. by Donald D. Walsh from SPA. LC 80-25402. (Illus.). 222p. reprint ed. pap. 68.90 (*0-8357-4065-X*, 203675500005) Bks Demand.

Mystic of Tunja: The Writings of Madre Castillo, 1671-1742. Kathryn J. McKnight. LC 96-40881. (Illus.). 304p. 1997. text 45.00 (*1-55849-074-4*) U of Mass Pr.

Mystic Path. Raymond Andrea. LC 87-63342. 163p. (Orig.). 1990. pap. 11.95 (*0-912057-56-4*, 502080) GLELJ AMORC.

Mystic Path. Karl Pruter. LC 96-48219. (St. Willbrords Studies in Philosophy & Religion: No. 5). 80p. 1997. 23.00 (*0-912134-32-1*); pap. 13.00 (*0-912134-33-X*) Millefleurs.

***Mystic Path to Cosmic Power.** Vernon Howard. 264p. 1999. reprint ed. pap. 11.95 (*0-911203-40-0*) New Life.

Mystic Places. (Mysteries of the Unknown Ser.). (Illus.). 144p. 1987. 14.95 (*0-8094-6312-1*); lib. bdg. 23.27 (*0-8094-6313-X*) Time-Life.

Mystic Poetry: Hamsadutta & Uddhava Sandesh. Rupa Goswami. Tr. by Jan Brzezenski. 115p. 1999. pap. 15.95 (*1-886069-09-3*, 1052, Pub. by Mandala Pub Grp) Words Distrib.

Mystic Quest: An Introduction to Jewish Mysticism. David S. Ariel. LC 88-10431. 256p. 1988. 30.00 (*0-87668-928-4*) Aronson.

Mystic Quests. Time-Life Books Editors. Ed. by Jim Hicks. (Mysteries of the Unknown Ser.). (Illus.). 144p. 1991. 14.95 (*0-8094-6529-9*); lib. bdg. 17.45 (*0-8094-6530-2*) Time-Life.

Mystic Reality of Christ Consciousness: The Series Introduction. Beverly F. Brandt. Ed. by Mari L. Paquette. LC 99-94499. (Consciousness of Commitment Ser.: Vol. 8). 525p. 2000. pap. 23.45 (*1-929064-00-4*, 2000-1) Brandt Pubns.

Mystic Rebels: The Lives of Appollonius Tyaneus; Jan Van Leyden; Sabbatai Zevij Cagliostro. Harry C. Schnur. 316p. 1995. reprint ed. pap. 19.95 (*1-56459-504-8*) Kessinger Pub.

Mystic Rebels No. 2: Apollonius Tyaneus, Jan Van Leyden, Sabbatai Zevi, Cagliostro. Harry C. Schnur. LC 74-179741. (Biography Index Reprint Ser.). 1977. reprint ed. 22.95 (*0-8369-8109-X*) Ayer.

Mystic River Anthology. Ed. by Judith A. Hicks. (Illus.). 160p. (Orig.). 1988. pap. 6.95 (*0-934881-03-0*) Dutch Island.

Mystic Road of Love. John S. Dunne. LC 99-22330. 200p. 1999. 25.00 (*0-268-01445-0*); pap. 16.00 (*0-268-01446-9*) U of Notre Dame Pr.

Mystic Rose. Alan Robinson. 112p. 1996. pap. 39.95 (*0-85439-525-3*, Pub. by St Paul Pubns) St Mut.

Mystic Russia. Kevin Siembieda. Ed. by Alex Marciniszyn et al. (Rifts Worldbook Ser.: Vol. 18). (Illus.). 176p. (YA). (gr. 8 up). 1998. pap. 16.95 (*1-57457-011-0*, 833) Palladium Bks.

Mystic Seals & Columns. Rudolf Steiner. 155p. 1996. reprint ed. spiral bd. 18.00 (*0-7873-1294-0*) Hlth Research.

Mystic Seaport Museum Watercraft. 2nd rev. ed. Maynard Bray. (Illus.). xx, 300p. 1986. pap. 29.95 (*0-913372-38-2*) Mystic Seaport.

Mystic Sense of Equality. Millard Hansen. LC 83-8875. 170p. (Orig.). 1984. pap. 6.00 (*0-8477-2464-6*) U of PR Pr.

Mystic Shrine Illustrated: The Fully Illustrated Ritual of the Nobles of the Mystic Shrine. John Blanchard. (Illus.). 50p. 1994. reprint ed. pap. 8.95 (*1-56459-444-0*) Kessinger Pub.

Mystic Spiral: Journey of the Soul. Jill Purce. (Art & Imagination Ser.). (Illus.). 128p. 1980. reprint ed. pap. 15.95 (*0-500-81005-2*, Pub. by Thames Hudson) Norton.

Mystic Spirituality of A. W. Tozer, a Twentieth-Century Protestant. E. Lynn Harris. LC 92-10799. 184p. 1992. lib. bdg. 79.95 (*0-7734-9872-9*) E Mellen.

Mystic Stories: The Sacred & the Profane. Mircea Eliade. Tr. by Ana Cartianu from RUM. 280p. 1993. text 43.50 (*0-88033-227-1*, Pub. by East Eur Monographs) Col U Pr.

Mystic Sweet Communion. Jane Kirkpatrick. LC 98-30162. 300p. 1998. pap. 12.99 (*1-57673-293-2*) Multnomah Pubs.

Mystic Tales from the Zohar. Aryeh Wineman. (Illus.). 200p. 1996. 24.95 (*0-8276-0515-3*) JPS Phila.

Mystic Tales from the Zohar. Tr. by Aryeh Wineman from ARC. LC 97-49575. (Mythos Ser.). 184p. 1998. pap. text 12.95 (*0-691-05833-4*, Pub. by Princeton U Pr) Cal Prin Full Svc.

***Mystic Tarot.** 1999. pap. 29.95 (*1-85868-719-5*, Pub. by Carlton Bks Ltd) Natl Bk Netwk.

Mystic Tendencies in Islam. M. Zuhur-Ud-Din. 225p. 1985. 14.95 (*1-56744-344-3*) Kazi Pubns.

Mystic Test Book. Olney H. Richmond. Date not set. pap. text 14.95 (*0-87877-245-6*) Newcastle Pub.

Mystic Test Book: Magic of the Cards. 6th annot. ed. Olney H. Richmond. Ed. by Iain McLaren-Owens. LC 97-77161. (Astro-Cards Reprints Ser.). (Illus.). 387p. 1998. reprint ed. pap. text 40.00 (*1-885500-13-0*, AR:11) Astro-Cards.

Mystic Test Book: The Magic of the Cards. Olney H. Richmond. 1997. reprint ed. pap. 17.50 (*0-7873-0717-3*) Hlth Research.

Mystic Test Book of "The Hindu Occult Chambers" Magic & Occultism of India Hindu & Egyptian Crystal Gazing, the Hindu Magic Mirror. L. W. DeLaurence. 1996. spiral bd. 16.50 (*0-7873-0988-5*) Hlth Research.

Mystic Test Book of "The Hindu Occult Chambers" The Magic & Occultism of India Hindu & Egyptian Crystal Gazing the Hindu Magic Mirror, 1909. L. W. DeLaurence. 180p. 1996. reprint ed. pap. 15.50 (*1-56459-920-5*) Kessinger Pub.

Mystic Thesaurus: Occultism Simplified. abr. ed. Willis F. Whitehead. Ed. & Intro. by Iain McLaren-Owens. (Astro-Cards Reprints Ser.). 90p. 1995. pap. text 9.00 (*1-885500-09-2*, AR7) Astro-Cards.

Mystic Tie. Allen E. Roberts. xvi, 296p. 1994. 16.50 (*0-88053-086-3*, M331) Macoy Pub.

Mystic Triangle: A Modern Magazine of Rosicrucian Philosophy, 1925. Ed. by H. Spencer Lewis. 136p. 1998. reprint ed. pap. 17.95 (*0-7661-0702-7*) Kessinger Pub.

Mystic Triangle: A Modern Magazine of Rosicrucian Philosophy (1926) Ed. by H. Spencer Lewis. 310p. 1998. reprint ed. pap. 24.95 (*0-7661-0703-5*) Kessinger Pub.

Mystic Triangle: A Modern Magazine of Rosicrucian Philosophy (1927) Ed. by H. Spencer Lewis. 402p. 1998. reprint ed. pap. 29.95 (*0-7661-0704-3*) Kessinger Pub.

Mystic Triangle: A Modern Magazine of Rosicrucian Philosophy (1928) Ed. by H. Spencer Lewis. 416p. 1998. reprint ed. pap. 29.95 (*0-7661-0705-1*) Kessinger Pub.

Mystic Triangle: A Modern Magazine of Rosicrucian Philosophy (1929) Ed. by H. Spencer Lewis. 434p. 1998. reprint ed. pap. 29.95 (*0-7661-0706-X*) Kessinger Pub.

Mystic Union: An Essay in the Phenomenology of Mysticism. Nelson Pike. LC 91-55553. (Cornell Studies in the Philosophy of Religion). (Illus.). 240p. 1992. text 39.95 (*0-8014-2684-7*) Cornell U Pr.

Mystic Union: An Essay in the Phenomenology of Mysticism. Nelson Pike. (Cornell Studies in the Philosophy of Religion). (Illus.). 240p. 1994. pap. text 15.95 (*0-8014-9969-0*) Cornell U Pr.

Mystic Vision in the Grail Legend & in the Divine Comedy. Lizette A. Fisher. LC 79-168029. reprint ed. 20.00 (*0-404-02389-4*) AMS Pr.

***Mystic Visions.** Rosanne Bittner. 320p. 2000. 22.95 (*0-312-86512-0*) Forge NYC.

***Mystic Vista.** Robert W. Hutmacher. 1999. pap. 10.95 (*5-550-72036-1*) Nairi.

***Mystic Vista.** Robert W. Hutmacher. (Illus.). 1999. 15.95 (*5-550-72032-9*) Nairi.

***Mystic Warriors.** Rosanne Bittner. 2001. text. write for info. (*0-312-86513-9*) St Martin.

Mystic Warriors of the Plains. Thomas E. Mails. 1976. 22.95 (*0-8488-1091-0*) Amereon Ltd.

Mystic Warriors of the Plains: The Culture, Arts, Crafts, & Religion of the Plains Indians. Thomas E. Mails. (Illus.). 618p. 1995. pap. 29.95 (*1-56924-843-5*) Marlowe & Co.

Mystic Warriors of the Yellowstone. large type ed. Elizabeth Laden. Ed. by Jan Cooper. (Orig.). 1996. pap. 12.95 (*0-9654107-1-4*) My Office Pubng.

Mystic Way. Evelyn Underhill. 304p. 1991. pap. 12.95 (*0-89804-138-4*) Ariel GA.

Mystic Way. Raymund Andrea. 142p. 1998. reprint ed. pap. 16.95 (*0-7661-0467-2*) Kessinger Pub.

Mystic Way: A Psychological Study in Christian Origins (1913) Evelyn Underhill. 400p. 1998. reprint ed. pap. 24.95 (*0-7661-0175-4*) Kessinger Pub.

Mystic Way: A Spiritual Autobiography. Nicholas Hagger. 1994. pap. 30.00 (*1-85230-478-2*, Pub. by Element MA) Penguin Putnam.

Mystic Will. Charles G. Leland. 1976. reprint ed. 11.00 (*0-911662-58-8*) Yoga.

Mystic Will: Based upon a Study of the Philosophy of Jacob Boehme. Howard H. Brinton. 285p. 1994. reprint ed. pap. 19.95 (*1-56459-453-X*) Kessinger Pub.

Mystic Words of Mighty Power. Walter DeVoe. 213p. 1971. reprint ed. spiral bd. 15.00 (*0-7873-0282-1*) Hlth Research.

Mystic Words of Mighty Power: The Power of "I Am" Walter DeVoe. 1991. lib. bdg. 79.95 (*0-8490-4994-6*) Gordon Pr.

Mystic Words of Mighty Power, 1905. Walter DeVoe. 214p. 1996. reprint ed. pap. 13.95 (*1-56459-941-8*) Kessinger Pub.

Mystic Writing Pad. Gene Frumkin. 1977. per. 2.50 (*0-88031-037-5*) Invisible-Red Hill.

Mystic Year of Animals. Ann Walker. (Orig.). 1997. pap. 19.95 (*1-86163-021-2*, Pub. by Capall Bann Pubng) Holmes Pub.

Mystical & Ethical Experience. Gerry C. Heard. LC 84-29569. viii, 82p. 1985. 8.50 (*0-86554-149-3*, MUP/H140) Mercer Univ Pr.

Mystical & Mythological Explanatory Works of Assyrian & Babylonian Scholars. Alasdair Livingstone. 280p. 1986. 85.00 (*0-19-815462-3*) OUP.

Mystical & Visionary Treatises of Shihabuddin Yahya Suhrawardi. Shihabuddin Yahya Suhrawardi. Tr. by W. H. Thackston, Jr. LC 87-672827. 118p. 1982. 25.00 (*0-900860-92-8*, Pub. by Octagon Pr) ISHK.

Mystical Arts: Dream Interpretation. Lauren D. Peden. 60p. 1995. write for info. (*0-446-51905-7*) Warner Bks.

Mystical Arts: I Ching. Lauren D. Peden. 60p. 1995. write for info. (*0-446-51903-0*) Warner Bks.

Mystical Arts: Numerology. Lauren D. Peden. 60p. 1995. write for info. (*0-446-51902-2*) Warner Bks.

Mystical Arts: Numerology. Lauren D. Peden. LC 96-161731. 60p. 1996. 6.95 (*0-446-91012-0*, Pub. by Warner Bks) Little.

Mystical Arts: Palmistry. Lauren D. Peden. 60p. 1995. write for info. (*0-446-51904-9*) Warner Bks.

Mystical Astrology According to Ibn Arabi. 2nd ed. Titus Burckhardt. Tr. by Bulent Rauf from FRE. (Illus.). 52p. (Orig.). 1977. reprint ed. pap. 8.00 (*0-904975-09-6*, Pub. by Beshara) New Leaf Dist.

Mystical Babylon. 31p. (Orig.). pap. 0.95 (*0-937408-21-2*) GMI Pubns Inc.

Mystical Body of Christ & the Reorganization of Society. unabridged ed. Denis Fahey. 589p. 1943. reprint ed. pap. 15.00 (*0-945001-62-2*) GSG & Assocs.

Mystical Child: The Human Spirit from the Heart & Mind of a Child. Janet B. Simmons. LC 95-90216. 220p. 1996. pap. 22.95 (*0-9643469-6-6*) Enlghtmnt Pr.

Mystical Chorus: Jung & the Religious Dimension. Donald Broadribb. LC 95-193988. 276p. (Orig.). 1996. pap. 12.95 (*1-86429-019-6*, Pub. by Millennium Bks) Morehouse Pub.

Mystical Christ. Manly P. Hall. 1994. pap. 14.95 (*0-89314-514-9*) Philos Res.

Mystical Christianity: A Psychological Commentary on the Gospel of John. John A. Sanford. 352p. 1994. reprint ed. pap. 19.95 (*0-8245-1412-2*) Crossroad NY.

Mystical City of God. abr. ed. Mary of Agreda & Mary Of Agreda. 794p. 1993. pap. 12.50 (*0-911988-31-9*, 38263) AMI Pr.

Mystical City of God, 4 vols., 1. Mary Of Agreda. 610p. 1996. 12.50 (*0-911988-27-0*) AMI Pr.

Mystical City of God, 4 vols., 2. Mary Of Agreda. 608p. 1996. 12.50 (*0-911988-28-9*) AMI Pr.

Mystical City of God, 4 vols., 3. Mary Of Agreda. 790p. 1996. 12.50 (*0-911988-29-7*) AMI Pr.

Mystical City of God, 4 vols., 4. Mary Of Agreda. 661p. 1996. 12.50 (*0-911988-30-0*) AMI Pr.

Mystical City of God, 4 vols., Set. Mary Of Agreda. 2676p. 1996. 50.00 (*0-911988-26-2*, 38229) AMI Pr.

Mystical City of God: A Popular Abridgement, Vol. 1. abr. ed. Mary Agreda. Tr. by Fiscar Marison & George J. Blatter from SPA. LC 78-62255. 1993. reprint ed. pap. 18.50 (*0-89555-070-9*) TAN Bks Pubs.

Mystical Concepts in Chassidism: An Introduction to Kabbalistic Concepts & Doctrines. Jacob I. Schochet. 174p. 1979. reprint ed. 14.00 (*0-8266-0412-9*) Kehot Pubn Soc.

Mystical Creations. Sally A. Denno. 48p. 1996. pap. 11.95 (*1-879825-27-9*) Jones Publish.

Mystical Crystal. Geoffrey Keyte. 272p. (Orig.). 1993. pap. 32.95 (*0-8464-4176-4*) Beekman Pubs.

Mystical Crystal. Geoffrey Keyte. 187p. 1994. pap. 21.95 (*0-85207-269-4*, Pub. by C W Daniel) Natl Bk Netwk.

Mystical Delights: The Mystical Experiences of Famous Poets. Hilary Huttner. LC 95-61718. 240p. 1996. 19.95 (*0-9647057-9-6*) Frntline Systs.

Mystical Design of "Paradise Lost" Galbraith M. Crump. 194p. 1975. 29.50 (*0-8387-1519-2*) Bucknell U Pr.

Mystical Diets: Paranormal, Spiritual, & Occult Nutrition & Practices. Jack Raso & Stephen Barrett. LC 92-40828. (Consumer Health Ser.). 299p. 1993. 26.95 (*0-87975-761-2*) Prometheus Bks.

Mystical Dimension: An Essay on Unknowingness. David C. Lane. (Jewels of India Ser.). (Orig.). 1992. pap. 2.00 (*1-56543-010-7*) Mt SA Coll Philos.

Mystical Dimensions of Islam. Annemarie Schimmel. 506p. 1996. pap. 19.95 (*0-614-21318-5*, 875) Kazi Pubns.

Mystical Dimensions of Islam. Annemarie Schimmel. LC 73-16112. (Illus.). xxi, 506p. 1975. pap. 19.95 (*0-8078-1271-4*) U of NC Pr.

M

Mystical Element in Heidegger's Thought. rev. ed. John D. Caputo. LC 77-92257. xxvi, 292p. 1986. pap. 17.50 (*0-8232-1153-3*) Fordham.

Mystical Element in the Metaphysical Poets of the 17th Century. Itrat-Husain. LC 66-23522. 1948. 30.00 (*0-8196-0177-2*) Biblo.

Mystical Element of Religion As Studied in Saint Catherine of Genoa & Her Friends, 2 vols. F. Von Huegel. 1977. lib. bdg. 200.00 (*0-8490-2317-3*) Gordon Pr.

Mystical Element of Religion As Studied in Saint Catherine of Genoa & Her Friends. Friedrich von Hugel. LC 99-33007. 1999. pap. 39.95 (*0-8245-1790-3*) Crossroad NY.

Mystical Elements in Mohammed. John C. Archer. LC 80-26396. (Yale Oriental Series: Researches: No. 11 Pt. 1; All Published). reprint ed. 39.50 (*0-404-60281-9*) AMS Pr.

Mystical Epistemology of Mulla Sadra. Ali Mesbah et al. (Nur Ser.). 349p. (Orig.). 1997. pap. 17.00 (*1-883058-24-4*, Nur) Global Pubns.

Mystical Evolution, 2 vols., I. John G. Arintero. Tr. by Jordan Aumann from SPA. LC 78-62254. Orig. Title: La Evolucion Mistica. 1979. reprint ed. pap. write for info. (*0-89555-072-5*) TAN Bks Pubs.

Mystical Evolution, 2 vols., II. John G. Arintero. Tr. by Jordan Aumann from SPA. LC 78-62254. Orig. Title: La Evolucion Mistica. 1979. reprint ed. pap. write for info. (*0-89555-073-3*) TAN Bks Pubs.

Mystical Evolution, 2 vols., Set. John G. Arintero. Tr. by Jordan Aumann from SPA. LC 78-62254. Orig. Title: La Evolucion Mistica. 1979. reprint ed. pap. 36.00 (*0-89555-071-7*) TAN Bks Pubs.

Mystical Experience & Religious Doctrine: An Investigation of the Study of Mysticism in World Religions. Philip C. Almond. (Religion & Reason Ser.: No. 26). 197p. 1982. text 52.35 (*90-279-3160-7*) Mouton.

Mystical Experience in Abraham Abulafia. Moshe Idel. LC 87-1869. (SUNY Series in Judaica: Hermeneutics, Mysticism, & Religion). 240p. (C). 1987. pap. text 21.95 (*0-88706-553-8*) State U NY Pr.

Mystical Experiences of True Buddha Disciples. rev. ed. Sheng-Yen Lu. Tr. by Siong-Chow Ho et al from CHI. 192p. 1993. pap. 10.00 (*1-881493-01-6*) Purple Lotus Soc.

***Mystical Gesture: Essays on Medieval & Early Modern Spiritual Culture in Honor of Mary E. Giles.** Mary E. Giles & Robert Boenig. LC 99-54068. 240p. 2000. 78.95 (*0-7546-0123-4*, Pub. by Ashgate Pub) Ashgate Pub Co.

Mystical Heart: Fifty-Two Weeks in the Presence of God. Edwina Gateley. (Illus.). 128p. 1998. pap. 9.95 (*0-8245-1764-4*, Crsrd) Crossroad NY.

***Mystical Illusions.** Christie Pekish. 1999. write for info. (*1-58235-449-9*) Watermrk Pr.

Mystical Initiation. Dom S. Louismet. 233p. 1996. reprint ed. pap. 18.95 (*1-56459-544-7*) Kessinger Pub.

Mystical Islam: An Introduction to Sufism. Julian Baldick. 192p. (C). 1989. text 50.00 (*0-8147-1138-3*); pap. text 18.50 (*0-8147-1139-1*) NYU Pr.

Mystical Journey. M. R. Muhaiyaddeen. LC 89-1102. 150p. 1990. 14.00 (*0-914390-28-7*); pap. 11.00 (*0-914390-29-5*) Fellowship Pr PA.

Mystical Key to the English Language. Robert M. Hoffstein. 192p. (Orig.). 1992. pap. 12.95 (*0-89281-309-1*) Inner Tradit.

Mystical Key to the Psalms. Thessalonia DePrince. LC 92-62658. (Illus.). 110p. (Orig.). 1994. pap. 7.95 (*0-935611-11-8*) United Spirit.

Mystical Knowledge of God: An Essay in the Art of Knowing & Loving the Divine Majesty. Dom S. Louismet. 159p. 1996. reprint ed. pap. 17.95 (*1-56459-565-X*) Kessinger Pub.

Mystical Land of Kubble. William Grundy. (Illus.). 72p. (J). (gr. k-6). 1999. pap. 9.00 (*0-8059-4492-3*) Dorrance.

Mystical Languages of Unsaying. Michael A. Sells. 232p. 1996. pap. 18.95 (*0-614-21319-3*, 1425) Kazi Pubns.

Mystical Languages of Unsaying. Michael A. Sells. LC 93-23488. 256p. (C). 1994. pap. text 18.95 (*0-226-74787-5*); lib. bdg. 49.95 (*0-226-74786-7*) U Ch Pr.

Mystical Legends of the Shamans. Brad Steiger & Sherry H. Steiger. 96p. 1991. 12.95 (*0-938294-54-7*) Inner Light.

Mystical Life of Jesus. H. Spencer Lewis. LC 54-20988. (Illus.). 248p. 1929. pap. 14.95 (*0-912057-46-7*, 501980) GLELJ AMORC.

Mystical Lore of Precious Stones Vol. 2: Astrology, Birthstones, Therapeutic & Religious..., Vol. II. George F. Kunz. 199p. 1986. pap. 9.95 (*0-87877-095-X*) Newcastle Pub.

Mystical Machine: Issues & Ideas in Computing. John E. Savage et al. LC 85-6096. 320p. (C). 1986. pap. text 31.25 (*0-201-06462-6*) Addison-Wesley.

Mystical Magical Marvelous World of Dreams. Wilda B. Tanner. (Illus.). 400p. 1996. pap. 17.75 (*0-945027-02-8*) Sparrow Hawk Pr.

Mystical Marriage: Symbol & Meaning of the Human Experience. Gerhard Wehr. 159p. 1990. pap. 14.95 (*1-85274-060-4*, Pub. by Aqrn Pr) Harper SF.

Mystical Marriage of Science & Spirit. Frances Paelian. LC 81-70272. (Illus.). 200p. 1981. pap. 11.95 (*0-918936-11-X*) Astara.

Mystical Meaning of Jesus the Christ: Significant Episodes in the Life of the Master. 2nd ed. Helen Brungardt. (Illus.). 64p. 1983. pap. 5.25 (*0-941992-03-9*) Los Arboles Pub.

Mystical Medicine. Warren Peters. LC 95-61242. 96p. 1995. per. 7.95 (*1-57258-044-5*) Teach Servs.

Mystical Meditations on the Collects. Dion Fortune. LC 91-12148. 193p. 1991. reprint ed. pap. 12.95 (*0-87728-734-1*) Weiser.

Mystical Mind: Probing the Biology of Religious Experience. Eugene D'Aquili & Andrew B. Newberg. LC 99-24098. (Theology & the Sciences Ser.). 240p. 1999. pap. 20.00 (*0-8006-3163-3*, 1-3163, Fortress Pr) Augsburg Fortress.

Mystical Mirrors: Russian Icons in the Maryhill Museum of Art. A. Dean McKenzie. (Illus.). 64p. (Orig.). 1986. pap. 14.95 (*0-9617180-0-5*) Maryhill Art.

Mystical Moments & Unitive Thinking. Dan Merkur. LC 98-20221. 256p. (C). 1999. text 65.50 (*0-7914-4063-X*); pap. text 21.95 (*0-7914-4064-8*) State U NY Pr.

Mystical Now: Art & the Sacred. Wendy Beckett. LC 92-24967. 1993. 25.95 (*0-87663-647-4*, Pub. by Universe) St Martin.

Mystical Opuscula. St. Bonaventure. Tr. by Jose De Vinck. 266p. 1960. 15.00 (*0-8199-0527-5*, Frncscn Herld) Franciscan Pr.

Mystical Paths. Susan Howatch. 1993. mass mkt. 6.99 (*0-449-22122-9*, Crest) Fawcett.

Mystical Paths: Open Market Edition. Susan Howatch. 1992. mass mkt. 5.99 (*0-449-22205-5*, Crest) Fawcett.

Mystical Philosophy of Avicenna. Parviz Morewedge. (Nur Ser.). 250p. (Orig.). (C). 1998. pap. 17.00 (*1-883058-23-6*, Intl Medieval) Global Pubns.

Mystical Philosophy of T. S. Eliot. Fayek M. Ishak. 1970. 16.95 (*0-8084-0224-2*); pap. 13.95 (*0-8084-0225-0*) NCUP.

Mystical Poems of Kabir. Swami Rama & Robert B. Regli. LC 90-20832. 121p. 1990. pap. 8.95 (*0-89389-121-5*) Himalayan Inst.

Mystical Poems of Rumi. Jalal Al-Din Rumi. Tr. by Arthur J. Arberry from PER. LC 68-29935. vi, 208p. 1974. pap. 13.00 (*0-226-73151-0*, P584) U Ch Pr.

Mystical Poems of Rumi, Vol. 1. Jalal Al-Din Rumi. Tr. by Arthur J. Arberry. 202p. 1996. pap. 21.90 (*0-614-21320-7*, 877) Kazi Pubns.

Mystical Poems of Rumi, Vol. 2. Jalal Al-Din Rumi. Tr. by A. J. Arberry. 202p. 1996. pap. 10.95 (*0-614-21321-5*, 877) Kazi Pubns.

Mystical Poems of Rumi: Second Selection, Poems 201-400. Ed. by Ehsan Yarshater. Tr. by A. J. Arberry from PER. LC 79-5101. (Persian Heritage Ser.: Vol. 23). xiv, 187p. 1991. pap. 13.00 (*0-226-73152-9*) U Ch Pr.

Mystical Poems of Rumi: Second Selection, Poems 201-400, Vol. 34. Ed. by Ehsan Yarshater. Tr. by A. J. Arberry from PER. LC 79-5101. (Persian Heritage Ser.: Vol. 23). xiv, 187p. 1979. text 19.50 (*0-89158-477-3*) Bibliotheca Persica.

Mystical Poets of the English Church. P. Osmond. 1972. 59.95 (*0-8490-0696-1*) Gordon Pr.

Mystical Prayer in Ancient Judaism: An Analysis of Ma'aseh Merkavah. Michael D. Swartz. (Texte und Studien zum Antiken Judentum: No. 28). 250p. 1991. 110.00 (*3-16-145679-3*, Pub. by JCB Mohr) Coronet Bks.

***Mystical Presence.** John Williamson Nevin. 244p. 2000. pap. 22.00 (*1-57910-348-0*) Wipf & Stock.

Mystical Qabalah. Dion Fortune. LC 92-46987. 320p. 1979. pap. 12.95 (*0-87728-596-9*) Weiser.

***Mystical Qabalah.** rev. ed. Dion Fortune. (Illus.). 360p. 2000. pap. 14.95 (*1-57863-150-5*) Weiser.

Mystical Quest in Freemasonry. A. E. Waite. 1994. pap. 5.95 (*1-55818-296-9*, Sure Fire) Holmes Pub.

Mystical Quest of Christ. Robert F. Horton. 317p. 1997. pap. 27.00 (*0-89540-321-8*, SB-321) Sun Pub.

***Mystical Rites of our Creator: Version 1.0.** Errol Mueller. (HomeWorship 101 Ser.). 250p. 1999. pap. 15.00 (*0-9675266-0-4*) White Stone Comm.

Mystical Rosary with the Mystical Mass Prayer. Luke Zimmer. (Orig.). 1996. pap. 1.00 (*1-882972-67-8*, 3085) Queenship Pub.

Mystical Rose of Tepeyac. Cora Hussey. LC 97-94846. (Illus.). vii, 57p. 1997. pap. 4.95 (*0-9661830-0-2*) C Hussey.

Mystical Secrets of the Last Days. Shaykh M. An-Naqshbandi et al. LC 96-161285. 144p. 1995. pap. 12.50 (*0-934905-27-4*) Kazi Pubns.

***Mystical Secrets of the Stars.** Mary Gemming. (Illus.). 75p. 2000. mass mkt. 11.00 (*0-86690-497-2*) Am Fed Astrologers.

***Mystical Seductress Handbook.** Tannis Blackman. Ed. by Gina Clark. (Illus.). 96p. 2000. 4.95 (*0-9652540-5-4*) Swing St Pub.

Mystical Sense of the Gospels: A Handbook for Contemplatives. James M. Somerville. LC 97-28873. 180p. 1997. pap. text 17.95 (*0-8245-1710-5*) Crossroad NY.

Mystical Sex: Love, Ecstasy & the Mystical Experience. Louis W. Meldman. LC 96-42203. 208p. 1997. pap. 14.95 (*1-85230-957-1*, Pub. by Element MA) Penguin Putnam.

***Mystical Society: Revitalization in Culture, Theory & Education.** Philip Wexler. (Edge Ser.). 192p. 2000. pap. 27.00 (*0-8133-9143-1*) Westview.

Mystical Sources of German Romantic Philosophy. Ernest Benz. Tr. by Blair Reynolds et al from FRE. LC 83-21154. (Pittsburgh Theological Monographs, New Ser.: No. 6). vi, 133p. 1983. pap. 10.00 (*0-915138-50-6*) Pickwick.

***Mystical Stories from the Bhagavatam: Twenty Timeless Lessons in Self-Discovery.** Amal Bhakta. (Illus.). 224p. 2000. 18.95 (*1-887089-27-6*, Pub. by Torchlght Pub) Natl Bk Netwk.

***Mystical Stories from the Mahabharata: Twenty Timeless Lessons in Wisdom & Virtue.** Amal Bhakta. LC 99-53807. (Illus.). 264p. 2000. 17.95 (*1-887089-19-5*, Pub. by Torchlght Pub) Natl Bk Netwk.

Mystical Studies in the Apocalypse. H. Erskine Hill. 272p. 1997. reprint ed. pap. 19.95 (*0-7661-0081-2*) Kessinger Pub.

Mystical Tarot. Rosemary E. Gurley. 304p. (Orig.). 1990. mass mkt. 5.99 (*0-451-16800-3*, Sig) NAL.

Mystical Teachings of Al-Shadhili. Ibn Al-Sabbagh. Tr. by Elmer Douglas. 274p. 1996. pap. 19.95 (*0-614-21322-3*, 880) Kazi Pubns.

Mystical Teachings of Al-Shadhili: Including His Life, Prayers, Letters, & Followers. A Translation from the Arabic of Ibn Al-Sabbagh's Durrat Al-Asrar Wa Tuhfat Al-Abrar. Tr. by Elmer H. Douglas. LC 92-33632. (SUNY Series in Islam). 274p. (C). 1993. pap. text 19.95 (*0-7914-1614-3*) State U NY Pr.

Mystical Teachings of Al-Shadhili: Including His Life, Prayers, Letters, & Followers. A Translation from the Arabic of Ibn Al-Sabbagh's Durrat Al-Asrar Wa Tuhfat Al-Abrar. Tr. by Elmer H. Douglas. LC 92-33632. (SUNY Series in Islam). 274p. (C). 1993. text 59.50 (*0-7914-1613-5*) State U NY Pr.

Mystical Teachings of Christianity. Jim Lewis. 150p. 1980. pap. 7.95 (*0-942482-01-8*) Unity Church Denver.

Mystical Teachings of the Ausarian Resurrection. unabridged ed. Abhaya A. Muata. (Illus.). 237p. (Orig.). 1997. pap. 15.99 (*1-884564-22-4*) Cruzian Mystic.

***Mystical Themes in Le Corbuster's architecture in the Chapel Notre Dame Du Hout at Ronchamp: The Ronchamp Riddle.** Robert Coombs. LC 00-23741. (Mellen Studies in Architecture: 2). 232p. 2000. 89.95 (*0-7734-7746-2*) E Mellen.

Mystical Theology. Dionysius the Areopagite. Ed. by Evelyn Sire. (Orig.). 1997. pap. 5.95 (*1-55818-381-7*) Holmes Pub.

Mystical Theology: The Integrity of Spirituality & Theology. Mark A. McIntosh. LC 97-44977. (Challenges in Contemporary Theology Ser.). 288p. 1998. 62.95 (*1-55786-906-5*); pap. 26.95 (*1-55786-907-3*) Blackwell Pubs.

Mystical Theology: The Science of Love. William Johnston. LC 97-43303. 374p. 1998. reprint ed. pap. 18.00 (*1-57075-175-7*) Orbis Bks.

Mystical Theology of St. Bernard. Etienne Gilson. Tr. by A. H. Downes from FRE. (Cistercian Studies: No. 120). 266p. 1990. pap. 10.95 (*0-87907-960-6*) Cistercian Pubns.

Mystical Theology of the Eastern Church. Vladimir Lossky. LC 76-25448. Orig. Title: Essai sur la Theologie Mystique de l'Eglise d'Orient. 252p. 1976. reprint ed. pap. 13.95 (*0-913836-31-1*) St Vladimirs.

Mystical Tradition. Jacob I. Schochet. (Mystical Dimension Ser.: Vol. 1). 168p. 1990. reprint ed. 18.00 (*0-8266-0528-1*) Kehot Pubn Soc.

Mystical Traditions (1909) Isabel Cooper-Oakley. 305p. 1998. reprint ed. pap. 24.95 (*0-7661-0346-3*) Kessinger Pub.

Mystical Transformations: The Imagery of Liquids in the Work of Mechthild von Magdeburg. James C. Franklin. LC 75-5248. 192p. (C). 1976. 28.50 (*0-8386-1738-7*) Fairleigh Dickinson.

Mystical Union in Judaism, Christianity & Islam: An Ecumenical Dialogue. Ed. by Bernard McGinn & Moshe Idel. 264p. 1996. pap. 24.95 (*0-8264-0882-6*) Continuum.

Mystical Universal Mother: The Teachings of Mother of Yellow Altar. Hua-Ching Ni. LC 90-60709. 210p. (Orig.). 1992. pap. 14.95 (*0-937064-45-9*) SevenStar Comm.

Mystical Verses of a Mad Dalai Lama. Glenn H. Mullin. LC 94-2560. 288p. 1994. pap. 14.00 (*0-8356-0700-3*, Quest) Theos Pub Hse.

Mystical Vision of Existence in Classical Islam. Gerhard Boewering. (Studien zur Sprache, Geschichte und Kultur des Islamischen Orients). 296p. (C). 1979. text 142.35 (*3-11-007546-6*) De Gruyter.

Mystical Vocabulary of Venerable Mere Marie De L'Incarnation & Its Problems. Mother Aloysius G. L'Heureux. LC 72-94190. (Catholic University of America. Studies in Romance Languages & Literatures: No. 53). (FRE.). reprint ed. 37.50 (*0-404-50353-5*) AMS Pr.

Mystical Way & the Arthurian Quest. Derek Bryce. LC 96-3309. 160p. 1996. pap. 9.95 (*0-87728-863-1*) Weiser.

Mystical Way in the Fourth Gospel: Crossing over into God. L. William Countryman. LC 94-40675. 176p. 1995. pap. 16.00 (*1-56338-103-6*) TPI PA.

***Mystical Women, Mystical Body.** Owen F. Cummings. LC 00-33963. 2000. pap. write for info. (*1-56929-036-9*, Pastoral Press) OR Catholic.

Mystical World of Indonesia: Culture & Economic Development in Conflict. Allen M. Sievers. LC 74-6838. 448p. reprint ed. pap. 138.90 (*0-608-15155-6*, 202587100046) Bks Demand.

Mystical Writings of St. Isaac the Syrian. Isaac The Syrian. Tr. by A. J. Wensinck from SYR. 1977. pap. 5.00 (*0-89981-062-4*) Eastern Orthodox.

Mystical Year. Time-Life Books Editors. Ed. by Jim Hicks. (Mysteries of the Unknown Ser.). (Illus.). 144p. 1991. lib. bdg. 17.45 (*0-8094-6538-8*) Time-Life.

Mysticism. Frank C. Happold. (Orig.). 1991. pap. 14.95 (*0-14-013746-7*) Viking Penguin.

Mysticism. Annie W. Besant. 150p. 1997. reprint ed. pap. 19.95 (*0-7661-0095-2*) Kessinger Pub.

Mysticism: An Evangelical Option? Winfred Corduan. 160p. 1991. pap. 10.99 (*0-310-52901-8*) Zondervan.

Mysticism: Buddhist & Christian: Encounters with Jan van Ruusbroec. Paul Mommaers & Jan Van Bragt. LC 94-31692. (Nanzan Studies in Religion & Culture). 272p. 1995. 29.95 (*0-8245-1455-6*) Crossroad NY.

Mysticism: Experience, Response, & Empowerment. Jess B. Hollenbeck. LC 95-47064. (Hermeneutics, Studies in the History of Religions). 672p. (C). 1996. pap. 25.00 (*0-271-01552-7*) Pa St U Pr.

Mysticism: Experience, Response, & Empowerment. Jess B. Hollenbeck. LC 95-47064. (Hermeneutics, Studies in the History of Religions). (C). 1996. 90.00 (*0-271-01551-9*) Pa St U Pr.

Mysticism: Holiness East & West. Denise L. Carmody & John T. Carmody. 336p. 1996. pap. text 24.95 (*0-19-508819-0*) OUP.

Mysticism: Its History & Challenge. Bruno Borchert. LC 93-17157. (Illus.). 464p. (Orig.). 1994. pap. 19.95 (*0-87728-772-4*) Weiser.

Mysticism: Spiritual Quest or Psychic Disorder? Group for the Advancement of Psychiatry Staff. LC 76-45931. (Group for the Advancement of Psychiatry, Symposium Ser.: Vol. 9, No. 97). 125p. reprint ed. pap. 38.80 (*0-7837-2107-2*, 204238500004) Bks Demand.

Mysticism: The Common Foundation of World Religion. unabridged ed. William L. Brown. 52p. (Orig.). 1997. pap. 13.00 (*0-9657531-0-7*) Strange As Angels.

Mysticism: The Journey Within. Robert G. Chaney. LC 79-52959. 192p. 1979. pap. 13.95 (*0-918936-06-3*) Astara.

Mysticism: The Nature & Development of Spiritual Consciousness. Evelyn Underhill. 520p. 1994. pap. 11.95 (*1-85168-196-5*, Pub. by Onewrld Pubns) Penguin Putnam.

Mysticism: The Search for Ultimate Meaning. John Chrisci. 78p. (C). 1986. text 32.00 (*0-8191-5609-4*); pap. text 14.50 (*0-8191-5610-8*) U Pr of Amer.

Mysticism - The Ultimate Experience. Cecil A. Poole. LC 81-86628. 166p. 1982. 16.95 (*0-912057-33-5*, 501900) GLELJ AMORC.

Mysticism after Modernity. Ed. by Don Cupitt. LC 97-11925. 200p. (C). 1997. text 57.95 (*0-631-20763-5*); pap. text 23.95 (*0-631-20764-3*) Blackwell Pubs.

Mysticism & Catholicism. Hugh E. Stutfield. 1977. lib. bdg. 59.95 (*0-8490-2318-1*) Gordon Pr.

***Mysticism & Cognition: The Cognitive Development of John of the Cross As Revealed in His Works.** Birgitta Mark. (Studies in Religion: Vol. 1). 256p. 2000. pap. 24.95 (*87-7288-804-0*, Pub. by Aarhus Univ Pr) David Brown.

***Mysticism & Dissent: Socioreligious Thought in Qajar Iran.** Mangol Bayat. LC 99-48925. 224p. 1999. pap. text 22.95 (*0-8156-2853-6*) Syracuse U Pr.

Mysticism & Dissent: Socioreligious Thought in Qajar Iran. Mangol Bayat. 228p. (C). 1997. reprint ed. pap. text 25.00 (*0-7881-3967-3*) DIANE Pub.

Mysticism & Experience. Russell H. Hvolbek. LC 98-23954. 144p. 1998. 44.00 (*0-7618-1159-1*); pap. 24.50 (*0-7618-1160-5*) U Pr of Amer.

Mysticism & Guilt-Consciousness in Schelling's Philosophical Development. Paul Johannes Tillich. Ed. by Catherine McKnight. LC 88-23760. 155p. (Orig.). 1975. 26.50 (*0-8387-1493-5*); pap. 8.95 (*0-912761-34-2*) Bucknell U Pr.

Mysticism & Kingship in China: The Heart of Chinese Wisdom. Julia Ching. LC 96-51602. (Studies in Religious Traditions: Vol. 11). 324p. (C). 1997. text 69.95 (*0-521-46293-2*); pap. text 22.95 (*0-521-46828-0*) Cambridge U Pr.

Mysticism & Language. Ed. by Steven T. Katz. 272p. 1992. text 45.00 (*0-19-505455-5*) OUP.

Mysticism & Magic in Turkey: An Account of the Religious Doctrines, Monastic Organisation & Ecstatic Powers of the Dervish Orders. Lucy M. Garnett. LC 77-87628. (Illus.). reprint ed. 47.50 (*0-404-16453-6*) AMS Pr.

Mysticism & Mental Healing. Manly P. Hall. pap. 4.95 (*0-89314-336-7*) Philos Res.

Mysticism & New Paradigm Psychology. John E. Collins. 282p. (C). 1991. lib. bdg. 49.50 (*0-8476-7669-2*) Rowman.

Mysticism & Philosophical Analysis. Steven T. Katz. 272p. 1978. pap. text 21.95 (*0-19-520011-X*) OUP.

Mysticism & Philosphical Rationalism, Vol. III. Israel Zinberg. 25.00 (*0-87068-482-5*) Ktav.

Mysticism & Plurality Meaning. Keshavjee. 1998. text 9.95 (*1-86064-231-4*, Pub. by I B T) St Martin.

Mysticism & Prophecy: The Dominican Tradition. Richard Woods. LC 98-19019. (Traditions of Christian Spirituality Ser.). 128p. 1998. pap. 14.00 (*1-57075-206-0*) Orbis Bks.

Mysticism & Religion. 2nd ed. Robert S. Ellwood. LC 98-26078. 224p. 1999. pap. text 19.95 (*1-889119-02-4*) Seven Bridges.

***Mysticism & Sacred Scripture.** Steven T. Katz. LC 99-28187. 2000. write for info. (*0-19-509704-1*) OUP.

***Mysticism & Sacred Scripture.** Ed. by Steven T. Katz. LC 99-28187. 304p. 2000. text 55.00 (*0-19-509703-3*) OUP.

Mysticism & Social Change: The Social Witness of Howard Thurman. Alton B. Pollard, III. (Martin Luther King, Jr., Memorial Studies in Religion, Culture, & Social Development: Vol. 2). 219p. (Orig.). (C). 1992. text 39.95 (*0-8204-1612-6*) P Lang Pubng.

Mysticism & Social Change: The Social Witness of Howard Thurman. 2nd ed. Alton B. Pollard, III. (Martin Luther King, Jr., Memorial Studies in Religion, Culture, & Social Development: Vol. 2). 219p. (Orig.). (C). 1992. pap. text 29.95 (*0-8204-1981-8*) P Lang Pubng.

Mysticism & Spirituality in Medieval England. Ed. by Robert Boenig & William F. Pollard. LC 97-10759. (Illus.). 272p. 1997. 60.00 (*0-85991-516-6*, DS Brewer) Boydell & Brewer.

Mysticism & Symbolism. B. D. Dhawan. 1988. 24.95 (*81-212-0094-6*) Asia Bk Corp.

Mysticism & the Early South German-Austrian Anabaptist Movement, 1525-1531. Werner O. Packull. LC 76-46557. (Studies in Anabaptist & Mennonite History: No. 19). 254p. reprint ed. pap. 72.40 (*0-608-06024-0*, 2066353) Bks Demand.

An Asterisk (*) at the beginning of an entry indicates that the title is appearing for the first time.

Mysticism & the Eastern Church. Nicholas Arseniev. LC 96-27837. 173p. 1979. pap. 11.95 (*0-913836-55-9*) St Vladimirs.

Mysticism & the Experience of Love. Howard Thurman. LC 61-13708. (Orig.). 1961. pap. 4.00 (*0-87574-115-0*) Pendle Hill.

Mysticism & the Hindu Tradition. Ashok K. Malhotra. 42p. 1993. 3.00 (*1-883058-04-X*, Oneonta Philosophy) Global Pubns.

Mysticism & the Institutional Crisis. Ed. by Christian Duquoc et al. (Concilium Ser.). 130p. (Orig.). 1994. pap. 15.00 (*0-88344-879-3*) Orbis Bks.

Mysticism & the Mystical Experience: East & West. Ed. by Donald H. Bishop. LC 94-35278. 1995. 49.50 (*0-945636-73-3*) Susquehanna U Pr.

Mysticism & the New Physics. Michael Talbot. (Illus.). 208p. 1993. pap. 13.95 (*0-14-019328-6*, Arkana) Viking Penguin.

Mysticism & Vocation. James R. Horne. 110p. 1996. pap. 19.95 (*0-88920-264-8*) W Laurier U Pr.

***Mysticism & Yoga Tentra.** Ed. by Sadhu Santideva. 2000. 62.00 (*81-7020-997-8*, Pub. by Cosmo Pubn) S Asia.

Mysticism at the Dawn of a Modern Age. Rudolf Steiner. 1997. 19.95 (*0-8334-0753-8*, 1495) Garber Comm.

Mysticism at the Dawn of the Modern Age see Mystics after Modernism: Discovering the Seeds of a New Science in the Renaissance

Mysticism at the Dawn of the Modern Age. 2nd ed. Rudolf Steiner. Ed. by Paul M. Allen. Tr. by Karl E. Zimmer from GER. 256p. 1981. reprint ed. pap. 12.95 (*0-8334-1786-X*, Steinerbks) Garber Comm.

Mysticism, Death, & Dying. Christopher Nugent. LC 93-50159. (SUNY Series in Western Esoteric Traditions). 127p. (C). 1994. text 16.50 (*0-7914-2205-4*) State U NY Pr.

Mysticism Debate. Paul Murray. 1978. pap. 1.00 (*0-8199-0722-7*, Frncscn Herld) Franciscan Pr.

Mysticism Examined: Philosophical Inquiries into Mysticism. Richard H. Jones. LC 92-16480. (SUNY Series in Western Esoteric Traditions). 304p. (C). 1993. text 21.50 (*0-7914-1435-3*) State U NY Pr.

***Mysticism for Beginners.** Adam Zagajewski. Tr. by Clare Cavanagh from POL. 80p. 1999. pap. 12.00 (*0-374-52687-7*) FS&G.

Mysticism, Freudianism & Scientific Psychology. Knight Dunlap. (Select Bibliographies Reprint Ser.). 1977. reprint ed. 19.95 (*0-8369-5838-1*) Ayer.

Mysticism in Blake & Wordsworth. Jacomina Korteling. LC 68-2111. (Studies in Poetry: No. 38). 1969. reprint ed. lib. bdg. 75.00 (*0-8383-0577-6*) M S G Haskell Hse.

Mysticism in Christianity. W. K. Fleming. 300p. 1996. reprint ed. pap. 24.95 (*1-56459-577-3*) Kessinger Pub.

Mysticism in English Literature, 1913. Caroline F. Spurgeon. 172p. 1996. reprint ed. pap. 17.95 (*1-56459-564-1*) Kessinger Pub.

Mysticism in India: The Poet-Saints of Maharashtra. R. D. Ranade. LC 82-10458. (Illus.). 494p. (C). 1983. reprint ed. text 23.50 (*0-87395-669-9*) State U NY Pr.

Mysticism in Jewish Art. Ori Z. Soltes. (Illus.). (Orig.). 1996. pap. text. write for info. (*1-881456-28-5*) B B K Natl Jew Mus.

Mysticism in Maharashtra (Indian Mysticism) R. D. Ranade. (C). 1988. 31.00 (*81-208-0575-5*, Pub. by Motilal Bnarsidass) S Asia.

Mysticism in Religion. William R. Inge. LC 76-15407. 168p. 1976. reprint ed. lib. bdg. 35.00 (*0-8371-8953-5*, INMR, Greenwood Pr) Greenwood.

Mysticism in Robert Browning. Rufus M. Jones. LC 70-117596. (Studies in Browning: No. 4). 1970. reprint ed. lib. bdg. 49.00 (*0-8383-1029-X*) M S G Haskell Hse.

Mysticism in Seventeenth Century English Literature. Elbert N. Thompson. LC 78-100788. 1970. reprint ed. pap. 39.95 (*0-8383-0076-6*) M S G Haskell Hse.

***Mysticism in the Gospel of John: An Inquiry into Its Background.** Jey J. Kanagaraj. LC 98-156609. (JSNT Supplement Ser.: No. 158). 356p. 1998. 85.00 (*1-85075-865-4*, Pub. by Sheffield Acad) CUP Services.

Mysticism in the Neo-Romanticists. B. C. Broers. LC 68-767. (Studies in Comparative Literature: No. 35). 1969. reprint ed. lib. bdg. 75.00 (*0-8383-0514-8*) M S G Haskell Hse.

Mysticism in the World's Religions. Geoffrey Parrinder. 220p. 1995. pap. 14.95 (*1-85168-101-9*, Pub. by Onewrld Pubns) Penguin Putnam.

Mysticism in World Religion. Sidney Spencer. 1990. 21.75 (*0-8446-0927-7*) Peter Smith.

Mysticism, Magic, & Kabbalah in Ashkenazi Judaism: International Symposium Held in Frankfurt A.M. 1991. Ed. by Karl E. Groezinger et al. (Studia Judaica: Vol. 13). vi, 331p. (C). 1995. lib. bdg. 121.55 (*3-11-013744-5*) De Gruyter.

Mysticism, Metaphysics & Maritain: On the Road to the Spiritual Unconscious. James Arraj. 182p. 1993. pap. 12.00 (*0-914073-07-9*) Inner Growth Bks.

Mysticism, Mind, Consciousness. Robert K. Forman. LC 98-47983. 224p. (C). 1999. text 49.50 (*0-7914-4169-5*); pap. text 16.95 (*0-7914-4170-9*) State U NY Pr.

Mysticism of Dante. Henry C. Sartorio. 22p. 1997. reprint ed. pap. 9.95 (*0-7661-0061-8*) Kessinger Pub.

Mysticism of Everyday. Edward Carter. LC 90-63487. 88p. (Orig.). (C). 1991. pap. 7.95 (*1-55612-410-4*, LL1410) Sheed & Ward WI.

Mysticism of Hindu Gods & Goddesses. Swami Jyotirmayananda. (Illus.). 1974. pap. 5.95 (*0-934664-08-0*) Yoga Res Foun.

Mysticism of Innerworldly Fulfillment: A Study of Jacob Boehme. David Walsh. LC 83-6554. (University of Florida Humanities Monographs: No. 53). x, 142p. (Orig.). 1983. pap. 17.95 (*0-8130-0751-8*) U Press Fla.

Mysticism of Masonry. R. Swinburne Clymer. 184p. 1993. 15.95 (*0-932785-95-6*) Philos Pub.

Mysticism of Now. Rafael Catala. LC 97-41081. 1998. pap. 13.95 (*1-889051-19-5*, Awakening) Acrpls Bks CO.

Mysticism of Paul the Apostle. Albert Schweitzer. LC 98-27098. 430p. 1998. pap. 18.95 (*0-8018-6098-9*) Johns Hopkins.

Mysticism of Ramanuja. Cyril Veliath. (C). 1993. text 25.00 (*81-215-0561-5*, Pub. by M Manoharial) Coronet Bks.

Mysticism of Sound. Inayat Khan. 94p. 1972. reprint ed. spiral bd. 8.00 (*0-7873-1196-0*) Hlth Research.

Mysticism of Sound & Music. Hazrat I. Khan. LC 96-22762. 336p. 1996. pap. 18.00 (*1-57062-231-0*, Pub. by Shambhala Pubns) Random.

Mysticism of St. Francis of Assisi. D. H. Nicholson. 1977. lib. bdg. 250.00 (*0-8490-2319-X*) Gordon Pr.

***Mysticism of the Cloud of Unknowing.** William Johnston. 2000. pap. 30.00 (*0-8232-2074-5*) Fordham.

***Mysticism of the Cloud of Unknowing.** William Johnston. 2000. pap. 17.00 (*0-8232-2075-3*) Fordham.

Mysticism of the Cloud of Unknowing: A Modern Interpretation. 2nd ed. William Johnston. LC 74-30738. (Religious Experience Ser.: Vol. 8). 297p. reprint ed. pap. 92.10 (*0-608-16246-9*, 205217200049) Bks Demand.

Mysticism of the Devi Mahatmya. Swami Jyotirmayananda. (Illus.). 200p. 1994. pap. 10.00 (*0-934664-58-7*) Yoga Res Foun.

Mysticism of the Mahabharata. Swami Jyotirmayananda. (Illus.). 268p. 1993. pap. 9.95 (*0-934664-56-0*) Yoga Res Foun.

Mysticism of the Ramayana. Swami Jyotirmayananda. (Illus.). 312p. 1994. pap. 11.95 (*0-934664-57-9*) Yoga Res Foun.

Mysticism of the Wesleyan Tradition. Robert G. Tuttle, Jr. 192p. 1989. 14.99 (*0-310-75430-5*) Zondervan.

Mysticism of Ushet Rekhat: Worship of the Goddess. unabridged ed. Abhaya A. Muata. (Illus.). 64p. 1997. 9.99 (*1-884564-18-6*) Cruzian Mystic.

Mysticism of William Blake. Helen C. White. (BCL1-PR English Literature Ser.). 276p. 1992. reprint ed. lib. bdg. 79.00 (*0-7812-7446-X*) Rprt Serv.

Mysticism of William Law. George E. Clarkson. LC 91-18018. (American University Studies: Philosophy: Ser. V, Vol. 124). 194p. (C). 1992. text 38.95 (*0-8204-1634-7*) P Lang Pubng.

Mysticism Through the Ages. E. Gall. 1972. 59.95 (*0-8490-0697-X*) Gordon Pr.

Mysticism Throughout the Ages (1920) Edward Gall. 218p. 1998. reprint ed. pap. 17.95 (*0-7661-0508-3*) Kessinger Pub.

Mysticism True & False. Dom S. Louismet. 178p. 1996. reprint ed. pap. 17.95 (*1-56459-548-X*) Kessinger Pub.

Mystics. Mark Dunster. 13p. (Orig.). 1993. pap. 4.00 (*0-89642-218-6*) Linden Pubs.

***Mystics after Modernism: Discovering the Seeds of a New Science in the Renaissance.** Rudolf Steiner & Paul M. Allen. Tr. by Karl E. Zimmer from GER. (Classics in Anthroposophy). Orig. Title: Mysticism at the Dawn of the Modern Age. 208p. 2000. pap. 18.95 (*0-88010-470-8*) Anthroposophic.

Mystics & Heretics in Italy at the End of the Middle Ages. E. Gebhart. 1977. lib. bdg. 59.95 (*0-8490-2321-1*) Gordon Pr.

Mystics & Heretics in Italy at the End of the Middle Ages (1922) Emile Gebhart. 300p. 1998. reprint ed. pap. 24.95 (*0-7661-0371-4*) Kessinger Pub.

Mystics & Medics: A Comparison of Mystical & Psychotherapeutic Encounters. Ed. by Reuven P. Bulka. LC 79-87593. 120p. 1979. pap. 16.95 (*0-87705-377-4*, Kluwer Acad Hman Sci) Kluwer Academic.

Mystics & Men of Miracles in India. Mayah Balse. (Illus.). 1976. 7.95 (*0-91234-10-4*) Hapi Pr.

***Mystics & Messiahs: Cults & New Religions in Modern America.** Philip Jenkins. LC 99-28732. 304p. 2000. 27.50 (*0-19-512744-7*) OUP.

Mystics & Mysteries of Alexandria. Manly P. Hall. (Adepts Ser.). 1988. pap. 8.50 (*0-89314-544-0*) Philos Res.

Mystics & Zen Masters. Thomas Merton. 320p. 1999. pap. 14.00 (*0-374-52001-1*) FS&G.

Mystics, Ascetics & Saints of India: A Study of Sadhmaism with an Account of the Yogis, Sanyasis, Bairagis, & other Strange Hindu Sectarians. John C. Oman. 308p. 1984. text 38.50 (*0-89563-650-6*) Coronet Bks.

Mystics at Prayer. Ed. by Many Cihlar. LC 36-17108. 83p. 1931. pap. 9.95 (*0-912057-58-0*, 501650) GLELJ AMORC.

Mystics Come to Harley St. Basil Douglas-Smith. 48p. 1984. 15.00 (*0-7212-0608-5*, Pub. by Regency Pr GBR) St Mut.

Mystics for Our Time. Noel D. O'Donoghue. (Orig.). 1997. 39.95 (*0-567-09526-6*, Pub. by T & T Clark) Bks Intl VA.

Mystic's Goal. Julia Seton. 103p. 1968. reprint ed. spiral bd. 10.00 (*0-7873-0773-4*) Hlth Research.

Mystics, Magicians & Medicine People: Tales of a Wanderer. Doug Boyd. 173p. (C). 1995. pap. 11.95 (*1-56924-880-X*) Marlowe & Co.

Mystics of Engelthal: Writings from a Medieval Monastery. Leonard P. Hindsley. LC 98-21081. 240p. 1998. text 45.00 (*0-312-16251-0*) St Martin.

Mystics of Islam. Manly P. Hall. (Adepts Ser.). pap. 8.50 (*0-89314-532-7*) Philos Res.

Mystics of Islam. Reynold A. Nicholson. 178p. 1996. pap. 9.95 (*0-614-21323-1*, 1346) Kazi Pubns.

***Mystics of Islam, Vol. 8.** Reynold Alleyne Nicholson. LC 99-46556. (Orientalism Ser.). 2000. write for info. (*0-415-20905-6*) Routledge.

Mystics of Spain. E. Allison Peers. 1977. lib. bdg. 59.95 (*0-8490-2322-X*) Gordon Pr.

Mystics of the Book: Themes, Topics, & Typologies. Ed. by Robert A. Herrera. LC 92-32887. VIII, 415p. (C). 1993. text 64.95 (*0-8204-2007-7*) P Lang Pubng.

Mystics of the Church. Evelyn Underhill. LC 88-13217. 264p. 1988. reprint ed. pap. 13.95 (*0-8192-1435-3*) Morehouse Pub.

Mystics of the Renaissance. Rudolf Steiner. 278p. 1967. reprint ed. spiral bd. 18.50 (*0-7873-0823-4*) Hlth Research.

Mystics of the Renaissance & Their Relation to Modern Thought Including: Meister Eckhart, Tavler, Paracelsus, Jacob Boehme, Giordano Bruno & Others (1911) Rudolf Steiner. 288p. 1996. reprint ed. pap. 17.50 (*1-56459-722-9*) Kessinger Pub.

Mystic's Passion: The Spirituality of Johannes von Staupitz in His 1520 Lenten Sermons. Rudolf K. Markwald. LC 89-2259. (Renaissance & Baroque Studies & Texts: Vol. 3). XIV, 210p. 1990. text 47.95 (*0-8204-0950-2*) P Lang Pubng.

Mystics, Visionaries & Prophets: A Historical Anthology of Women's Spiritual Writings. Ed. by Shawn Madigan. LC 98-36261. 512p. 1998. 39.00 (*0-8006-3145-5*, 9-3145) Augsburg Fortress.

Mysticus. Randall Silvis. 466p. 1999. 26.00 (*0-9672117-0-0*) Wolfhawk Bks.

Mystification et Creativite dans l'Oeuvre Romanesque de Marguerite Yourcenar: Cinq Lectures Genetiques. Beatrice Ness. LC 93-85869. (North Carolina Studies in the Romance Languages & Literatures). 210p. (C). 1994. pap. text 32.50 (*0-8078-9251-3*) U of NC Pr.

Mystification of George Chapman. Gerald Snare. LC 89-1605. xv, 295p. (Orig.). 1989. text 37.95 (*0-8223-0937-8*) Duke.

Mystified Fortune-Teller & Other Tales from Psychotherapy. Gerald Amada. LC 97-34255. 216p. 1998. 24.95 (*1-56833-099-5*) Madison Bks UPA.

***Mystified Magistrate: And Other Tales.** Marquis de Sade. Tr. by Richard Seaver from FRE. 256p. 2000. 23.45 (*1-55970-432-2*, Pub. by Arcade Pub Inc) Time Warner.

Mystified Magistrate: Four Stories. Marquis De Sade, pseud. Tr. by Margaret Crosland from FRE. Orig. Title: Contes et fabliaux d'un troubadour provencal du XVIII siecle. 158p. 1993. pap. 17.95 (*0-7206-0849-X*, Pub. by P Owen Ltd) Dufour.

Mystified Magistrate: Four Stories. Marquis De Sade, pseud. Orig. Title: Contes et fabliaux d'un troubadour provencal du XVIII siecle. 158p. 1996. pap. 18.95 (*0-7206-1022-2*, Pub. by P Owen Ltd) Dufour.

Mystified Magistrate: Four Stories. Marquis De Sade, pseud. Tr. by Margaret Crosland from FRE. LC 87-60409. Orig. Title: Contes et fabliaux d'un troubadour provencal du XVIII siecle. 158p. 1986. reprint ed. 27.00 (*0-7206-0653-5*, Pub. by P Owen Ltd) Dufour.

Mystifying Card Tricks. Bob Longe. LC 96-35887. (Illus.). 128p. 1997. 5.95 (*0-8069-9454-1*) Sterling.

Mystifying Logic Puzzles. Norman Willis. LC 97-37300. (Illus.). 96p. 1997. 5.95 (*0-8069-9720-6*) Sterling.

Mystifying Logic Puzzles. Norman Willis. LC 98-44561. (Illus.). 96p. (J). 1999. 6.95 (*0-8069-9721-4*) Sterling.

Mystifying Math Puzzles. Steve Ryan. (Illus.). 96p. 1996. pap. 5.95 (*0-8069-1304-5*) Sterling.

Mystifying Mazes. Dave Phillips. 48p. 1984. pap. 3.50 (*0-486-24722-8*) Dover.

Mystifying Mind. (Library of Curious & Unusual Facts). (Illus.). 1991. 14.95 (*0-8094-7707-6*); lib. bdg. write for info. (*0-8094-7708-4*) Time-Life.

Mystik im Aufgange des Neuzeitlichen Geisteshebens und ihr Verahtnis zur Modernen Wertanschruung see Mystics after Modernism: Discovering the Seeds of a New Science in the Renaissance

Mystik im Johannesevangelium: Eine Hermeneutische Untersuchung Aufgrund der Auseinandersetzung mit Zen-Meister Hisamatsu Shin'Ichi. B. Neuenschwander. (Biblical Interpretation Ser.: No. 31). (GER.). xiv, 370p. 1998. 134.00 (*90-04-11035-6*) Brill Academic Pubs.

Mystique. Marion Clarke. 1997. mass mkt. 4.99 (*0-8217-5753-9*) Kensgtn Pub Corp.

Mystique. Amanda Quick, pseud. 352p. 1996. mass mkt. 6.99 (*0-553-57159-1*) Bantam.

Mystique. large type ed. Amanda Quick, pseud. 1995. 25.95 (*0-7838-1630-8*, G K Hall Lrg Type) Mac Lib Ref.

Mystique & Identity: Women's Fashion of the 50's. Barbara Schreier. LC 83-63525. (Illus.). 106p. 1984. pap. 12.00 (*0-940744-45-7*) Chrysler Museum.

Mystique of Arkansas. Irene Keesee. LC 95-79994. (Illus.). 122p. (Orig.). 1996. pap. 14.95 (*0-938041-64-9*) Arc Pr AR.

Mystique of Dreams: A Search for Utopia Through Senoi Dream Theory. G. William Domhoff. 156p. 1985. pap. 14.95 (*0-520-06021-0*, Pub. by U CA Pr) Cal Prin Full Svc.

Mystique of Enlightenment. Alvin Bobroff & U. G. Krishnamurti. 190p. 1985. pap. 9.95 (*0-87418-020-1*, 156) Coleman Pub.

Mystique of Entertaining in Texas. Betsy Nozick & Tricia Henry. LC 97-6987. (Illus.). 232p. 1997. 21.95 (*1-57168-074-8*) Sunbelt Media.

Mystique of God: As Revealed to Virginia Testa. Virginia Testa. LC 95-60656. (Illus.). 96p. 1995. pap. 12.95 (*1-881539-09-1*) Tabby Hse Bks.

Mystique of Hebrew: An Ancient Language in the New World. Alvin I. Schiff. 180p. (C). 1996. 20.00 (*0-88400-190-3*, Shengold Bks) Schreiber Pub.

***Mystique of Ojai.** Phil Harvey. (Mystique of ... Ser.). (Illus.). 12p. 1999. 12.00 (*0-9676346-0-1*) Topa Topa Pr.

Mystique of Printing: A Half Century of Books Designed by Ward Ritchie. Ward Ritchie. 30p. 1984. pap. 2.50 (*0-929722-00-0*) CA State Library Fndtn.

Mystique of the Tall Ships. Cy Libberman. 1989. 14.98 (*0-88365-747-3*) Galahad Bks.

Mystique Poetica: Living Philosophy Through Revealed Wisdom. John Bright-Fey. LC 98-96499. (Illus.). xii, 190p. 1998. 23.00 (*0-9665247-0-5*) Rubrica.

Mystiques, Theosophes et Illumines au Siecle des Lumieres. Antoine Faivre. (Stueien und Materialien Zur Geschichte der Philosophie Ser.: No. XX). xii, 263p. 1976. write for info. (*3-487-06114-7*) G Olms Pubs.

Myth. Laurence Coupe. LC 97-7292. (New Critical Idiom Ser.). 240p. (C). 1997. pap. 12.99 (*0-415-13494-3*) Routledge.

Myth. Laurence Coupe. LC 97-7292. (New Critical Idiom Ser.). 240p. (C). 1998. 50.00 (*0-415-13493-5*) Routledge.

Myth: A Poem. Thomas Sanfilip. LC 89-85583. 115p. 1996. pap. 12.00 (*0-9625306-0-3*) Iliad Press.

Myth: Its Meaning & Functions in Ancient & Other Cultures. Geoffrey S. Kirk. LC 72-628267. (Sather Classical Lectures: No. 40). 1970. pap. 18.95 (*0-520-02389-7*, Pub. by U CA Pr) Cal Prin Full Svc.

Myth: Matter of Mind? Francesco A. Ancona. LC 94-4718. 186p. (Orig.). pap. 27.50 (*0-8191-9494-8*); lib. bdg. 46.00 (*0-8191-9493-X*) U Pr of Amer.

Myth: Myths & Legends of the World Explained & Explored. Kenneth McLeish. 800p. 1996. 50.00 (*0-8160-3237-8*) Facts on File.

Myth: The Extinction Factor. Rick Lawler. 176p. (Orig.). 1994. pap. 8.50 (*0-9624394-2-8*) MinRef Pr.

Myth about Safe Sex see Mito del Acto Sexual Seguro

Myth Abroad. Nye. 1993. 4.50 (*0-446-77755-2*) Warner Bks.

Myth Absolutism. Nicholas Henshall. (C). 1992. text 58.95 (*0-582-05618-7*) Addison-Wesley.

Myth, Allegory & Gospel: An Interpretation of J. R. R. Tolkien - C. S. Lewis - G. K. Chesterton - Charles Williams. Edmund Fuller et al. Ed. by John W. Montgomery. 159p. (C). 1994. pap. text 8.95 (*1-885914-03-2*) Trinity Bible Coll.

Myth, Allegory & Gospel: An Interpretation of J. R. R. Tolkien, C. S. Lewis, G. K. Chesterton [&] Charles Williams. Edmund Fuller. LC 74-1358. 159 p. 1974. write for info. (*0-87123-357-6*) Bethany Fellow.

***Myth, Allegory & Gospel: An Interpretation of J. R. R. Tolkien, C. S. Lewis, G. K. Chesterton, Charles Williams.** 2nd ed. Ed. by John W. Montgomery. 159p. 2000. reprint ed. pap. 12.50 (*1-896363-11-3*) CN Inst for Law.

Myth America Vol. 1: A Historical Anthology. Ed. by Patrick Gerster & Nicholas Cords. (Illus.). 272p. 1997. pap. text 18.50 (*1-881089-37-1*) Brandywine Press.

Myth America Vol. II: A Historical Anthology. Ed. by Patrick Gerster & Nicholas Cords. (Illus.). 272p. 1997. pap. text 18.50 (*1-881089-97-5*) Brandywine Press.

Myth & Archive: A Theory of Latin American Narrative. Echevarria R. Gonzalez. LC 97-32274. 1998. write for info. (*0-8223-2194-7*) Duke.

Myth & Archive: Toward a Theory of Latin American Narrative. Roberto G. Echevarria. (Cambridge Studies in Latin American & Iberian Literature: No. 3). 259p. (C). 1990. text 64.95 (*0-521-30682-5*) Cambridge U Pr.

Myth & Cult: The Iconography of the Eleusinian Mysteries. Kevin Clinton. (Acta Instituti Atheniensis Regni Sueciae Ser.: Series 8, XI). (Illus.). 157p. (Orig.). 1992. pap. 57.50 (*91-7916-025-5*, Pub. by P Astroms) Coronet Bks.

Myth & Cult among Primitive Peoples. Adolf E. Jensen. Tr. by Marianna T. Choldin & Wolfgang Weissleder. LC 63-20909. 359p. reprint ed. pap. 111.30 (*0-8357-8960-8*, 205678500085) Bks Demand.

Myth & Epos in Early Greek Art: Representation & Interpretation. Gudrun Ahlberg-Cornell. (Studies in Mediterranean Archaeology: Vol. C). (Illus.). 410p. (Orig.). 1992. pap. 97.50 (*91-7081-017-6*, Pub. by P Astroms) Coronet Bks.

Myth & Fiction in Early Norse Lands. Ursula Dronke. (Collected Studies: No. CS524). 336p. 1996. text 101.95 (*0-86078-545-9*, Pub. by Variorum) Ashgate Pub Co.

Myth & Guilt - Consciousness in Balzac's la Femme de Trente Ans. J. H. Mazaheri. LC 98-48616. (Studies in French Literature: Vol. 32). 128p. 1999. text 59.95 (*0-7734-8267-9*) E Mellen.

Myth & Hate. Albert Schweitzer. 1999. text. write for info. (*0-312-16561-7*) St Martin.

Myth & History. Ed. by Jean Holm & John Bowker. LC 94-15089. (Themes in Religious Studies). 1994. 45.00 (*1-85567-098-4*); pap. 16.95 (*1-85567-099-2*) St Martin.

Myth & History in the Historiography of Early Burma: Paradigms, Primary Sources, & Prejudices. Michael A. Aung-Thwin. LC 97-49191. (Monographs in International Studies, Southeast Asia Ser.: No. 102). 220p. (C). 1998. pap. text 25.00 (*0-89680-201-9*) Ohio U Pr.

***Myth & Identity in the Epic of Imperial Spain.** Elizabeth B. Davis. 2000. 34.95 (*0-8262-1277-8*) U of Mo Pr.

Myth & Ideology in Contemporary Brazilian Fiction. Daphne Patai. LC 81-71313. 256p. 1983. 37.50 (*0-8386-3132-0*) Fairleigh Dickinson.

Myth & Legend Study Partner. Terry Moss. (Final Exam Ser.). 72p. 1996. pap. 5.49 (*1-885962-66-5*) Lincoln Lrning.

Myth & Literature: Contemporary Theory & Practice. Ed. by John B. Vickery. LC 65-11563. 403p. reprint ed. pap. 125.00 (*0-608-15038-X*, 202622200048) Bks Demand.

Myth & Literature in the American Renaissance. Robert D. Richardson. LC 77-22638. 317p. reprint ed. pap. 98.30 (*0-8357-6684-5*, 205686300094) Bks Demand.

Myth & Madness: The Psychodynamics of Antisemitism. Mortimer Ostow. LC 95-36973. 208p. 1995. 34.95 (*1-56000-224-7*) Transaction Pubs.

Myth & Magic. (In Classical Mood Ser.: Vol. 30). (Illus.). 1998. write for info. incl. cd-rom (*1-886614-56-3*) Intl Masters Pub.

M

An Asterisk (*) at the beginning of an entry indicates that the title is appearing for the first time.

Myth & Magic Calendar, 1994. Illus. by Hrana Janto & William Giese. 24p. 1993. pap. 10.00 (0-87542-909-2) Llewellyn Pubns.

Myth & Magic of Cats. Herbert Axelrod. (Cats & Dogs). (Illus.). 84p. (YA). (gr. 3 up). 1999. 19.95 (0-7910-4808-X) Chelsea Hse.

Myth & Magic of Cats. Arianna Reynolds. (Illus.). 64p. 1998. 12.95 (0-7938-0240-7, WW074) TFH Pubns.

*__Myth & Magic of Embroidery.__ Helen M. Stevens. (Illus.). 144p. 2000. 29.95 (0-7153-0774-6, Pub. by D & C Pub) Sterling.

*__Myth & Mankind: Persian Myth.__ 144p. (J). 2000. 29.95 (0-7054-3633-0) Time-Life Educ.

Myth & Meaning. Claude Levi-Strauss. LC 78-25833. 80p. 1995. pap. 10.00 (0-8052-1038-5) Schocken.

Myth & Meaning: Five Talks for Radio. Claude Levi-Strauss. LC 78-5212. (Massey Lectures: 1977). 64p. reprint ed. pap. 30.00 (0-8357-8240-9, 203403000088) Bks Demand.

Myth & Meaning, Myth & Order. Stephen C. Ausband. LC 83-5478. xiv, 126p. 1983. 10.45 (0-86554-089-6, MUP-H079) Mercer Univ Pr.

Myth & Measurement: The New Economics of the Minimum Wage. David Card. 432p. 1995. pap. text 16.95 (0-691-04823-1, Pub. by Princeton U Pr) Cal Prin Full Svc.

Myth & Measurement: The New Economics of the Minimum Wage. David Card & Alan Krueger. 384p. 1995. text 55.00 (0-691-04390-6, Pub. by Princeton U Pr) Cal Prin Full Svc.

*__Myth & Memory in the Construction of Community: Historical Patterns in Europe & Beyond.__ Ed. by Bo Strath. (Illus.). 432p. 2000. 42.95 (90-5201-910-X, Pub. by College of Europe) P Lang Pubng.

*__Myth & Memory in the Construction of Community: Historical Patterns in Europe & Beyond.__ Ed. by Bo Strath. (Multiple Europes Ser.: Vol. 9). 432p. 2000. pap. 42.95 (0-8204-4654-8) P Lang Pubng.

Myth & Memory in the Mediterranean: Remembering Fascism's Empire. Nicholas Doumanis. 256p. 1997. text 65.00 (0-312-17243-5) St Martin.

*__Myth & Metamorphosis: Picasso's Classical Prints of the 1930's.__ Lisa Florman. (Illus.). 216p. (C). 2000. 39.95 (0-262-06213-5) MIT Pr.

Myth & Metaphysics in Plato's Phaedo. David A. White. LC 88-43053. 320p. 1990. 45.00 (0-945636-01-6) Susquehanna U Pr.

Myth & Method. Ed. by Laurie L. Patton & Wendy Doniger. (Studies in Religion & Culture). 448p. (C). 1996. pap. text 22.50 (0-8139-1657-7) U Pr of Va.

Myth & Method. Ed. by Laurie L. Patton & Wendy Doniger. (Studies in Religion & Culture). 448p. (C). 1996. text 57.50 (0-8139-1656-9) U Pr of Va.

Myth & Method: Modern Theories of Fiction. James E. Miller. LC 60-12941. (Bison Book Ser.: No. BB105). 177p. reprint ed. pap. 54.90 (0-608-18779-8, 202982100065) Bks Demand.

Myth & Metropolis: Walter Benjamin & the City. Graeme Gilloch. Ed. by Sue Leigh. 227p. (C). 1997. text 23.95 (0-7456-1125-7, Pub. by Polity Pr) Blackwell Pubs.

Myth & Metropolis: Walter Benjamin & the City. Graeme Gilloch. 227p. (C). 1997. pap. text 23.95 (0-7456-2010-8, Pub. by Polity Pr) Blackwell Pubs.

Myth & Miracle: An Essay on the Mystic Symbolism of Shakespeare. G. Wilson Knight. 1972. 59.95 (0-8490-0699-6) Gordon Pr.

Myth & Mobilization in Revolutionary Iran: The Use of the Friday Congregational Sermon. Haggay Ram. LC 94-20284. 278p. (C). 1994. lib. bdg. 65.50 (1-879383-21-7) Am Univ Pr.

Myth & Modern American Drama. Thomas E. Porter. LC 68-21543. (Waynebook Ser.: No. 36). 286p. reprint ed. pap. 88.70 (0-608-10601-1, 207122200009) Bks Demand.

Myth & Modern Man in Sherlock Holmes: Sir Arthur Conan Doyle & the Uses of Nostalgia. David S. Payne. LC 91-70565. 325p. 1992. 25.00 (0-934468-29-X, Pub. by Gaslight) Empire Pub Srvs.

Myth & Modern Philosophy. Stephen H. Daniel. 256p. (C). 1990. 37.95 (0-87722-644-X) Temple U Pr.

Myth & Modernity: Postcritical Reflections. Milton Scarborough. LC 93-17790. (SUNY Series, The Margins of Literature). 152p. (C). 1994. text 49.50 (0-7914-1879-0); pap. text 16.95 (0-7914-1880-4) State U NY Pr.

Myth & Music: A Semiotic Approach to the Aesthetics of Myth in Music... Eero Tarasti. (Approaches to Semiotics Ser.: No. 51). 1979. pap. text 63.10 (90-279-7918-9) Mouton.

Myth & Mystery: An Introduction to Pagan Religions of the Biblical World. Jack Finegan. 336p. 1997. pap. 19.99 (0-8010-2160-X) Baker Bks.

Myth & Mythmaking: Continuous Evolution in Indian Tradition. Ed. by Julia Leslie. LC 96-153476. (SOAS Collected Papers on South Asia: No. 12). 260p. (C). 1996. text 45.00 (0-7007-0303-9, Pub. by Curzon Pr Ltd) UH Pr.

Myth & Narrative: Structure & Meaning in Some Ancient Near Eastern Text. John Evers. (Alter Orient und Altes Testament Ser.: Vol. 241). 133p. 1995. text 49.50 (3-7887-1535-9) NeukirchenerV.

*__Myth & Narrative in Jewish & Israeli Culture.__ Nurith Gertz. (Illus.). 224p. 2000. 52.50 (0-85303-386-2); pap. 24.50 (0-85303-383-8) Intl Spec Bk.

*__Myth & National Identity in Nineteenth Century Britain: The Legends of King Arthur & Robin Hood.__ Stephanie L. Barczewski. LC 99-40054. 288p. 2000. write for info. (0-19-820728-X) OUP.

Myth & Philosophy. Ed. by George F. McLean. LC 72-184483. (Proceedings of the American Catholic Philosophical Association Ser.: Vol. 45). 1971. pap. 20.00 (0-918090-05-9) Am Cath Philo.

Myth & Philosophy. Ed. by Frank E. Reynolds & David Tracy. LC 89-48910. (SUNY Series, Toward a Comparative Philosophy of Religions). 382p. (C). 1990. pap. text 21.95 (0-7914-0418-8) State U NY Pr.

Myth & Philosophy. Ed. by Frank E. Reynolds & David Tracy. LC 89-48910. (SUNY Series, Toward a Comparative Philosophy of Religions). 382p. (C). 1990. text 64.50 (0-7914-0417-X) State U NY Pr.

Myth & Philosophy: A Contest of Truths. Lawrence J. Hatab. LC 90-40804. 397p. 1990. 38.95 (0-8126-9115-6) Open Court.

Myth & Philosophy: A Contest of Truths. Lawrence J. Hatab. LC 90-40804. 397p. 1990. pap. 19.95 (0-8126-9116-4) Open Court.

*__Myth & Philosophy from the Pre-Socratics to Plato.__ Kathryn A. Morgan. LC 99-49056. 2000. write for info. (0-521-62180-1) Cambridge U Pr.

Myth & Poetry in Homer: A Handbook. 2nd rev. ed. Lowell Edmunds. 120p. 1993. pap. text. write for info. (0-9634516-1-8) Mill Brook Pr.

Myth & Poetry in Lucretius. Monica R. Gale. (Cambridge Classical Studies). 274p. (C). 1994. text 59.95 (0-521-45135-3) Cambridge U Pr.

Myth & Prayers of the Great Star Chant & the Myth of the Coyote Chant. Des. by Mary C. Wheelwright. LC 85-161304. (Illus.). 191p. 1989. pap. 27.00 (0-912586-61-3) Dine College Pr.

Myth & Reality. Mircea Eliade. 204p. (C). 1998. reprint ed. pap. text 12.95 (1-57766-009-9) Waveland Pr.

Myth & Reality: Studies in the Formation of Indian Culture. Dharmanmanda D. Kosambi. (C). 1992. reprint ed. 17.50 (81-7154-245-X, Pub. by Popular Prakashan) S Asia.

Myth & Reality: The Struggle for Freedom in India, 1945-47. Ed. by Amit K. Gupta. 525p. 1987. 44.00 (81-85054-18-5, Pub. by Manohar) S Asia.

Myth & Reality in the Rain Forest: How Conservation Strategies are Failing in West Africa. John F. Oates. LC 99-20220. 340p. 1999. 50.00 (0-520-21782-9, Pub. by U CA Pr) Cal Prin Full Svc.

Myth & Reality in the Rain Forest: How Conservation Strategies Are Failing in West Africa. John F. Oates. LC 99-20220. 340p. 1999. pap. 19.95 (0-520-22252-0, Pub. by U CA Pr) Cal Prin Full Svc.

Myth & Reality of Aging, 1974. National Council on Aging Staff. LC 79-84576. 1979. write for info. (0-89138-971-7) ICPSR.

Myth & Reality of the Protection of Civil Rights Law: A Case Study of Untouchability in Rural India. Dinesh Khosla. 190p. 1987. 27.50 (81-7075-000-8, Pub. by Hindustan) S Asia.

Myth & Religion: A Thorn in the Flesh. Alan Watts. (Alan Watts Love of Wisdom Library). 128p. 1996. 16.95 (0-8048-3055-X) Tuttle Pubng.

Myth & Religion in European Painting, 1270-1700: The Stories As the Artists Knew Them. Satia Bernen & Robert Bernen. LC 73-162220. 280p. 1973. write for info. (0-09-458650-0) Constable & Co.

Myth & Religion in Mircea Eliade. Douglas Allen & Adriana Berger. LC 98-30209. (Theorists of Myth Ser.: Vol. 11). 386p. 1998. 75.00 (0-8240-3720-0, H1168) Garland.

Myth & Religion of the North. E. Gabriel Turville-Petre. LC 75-5003. (Illus.). 340p. 1975. reprint ed. lib. bdg. 85.00 (0-8371-7420-1, TUMR, Greenwood Pr) Greenwood.

Myth & Ritual in Christianity. Alan W. Watts. (Illus.). 1968. reprint ed. pap. 17.50 (0-8070-1375-7) Beacon Pr.

Myth & Ritual in the Plays of Samuel Beckett. Ed. by Katherine H. Burkman. LC 86-46026. 176p. 1987. 32.50 (0-8386-3299-8) Fairleigh Dickinson.

Myth & Ritual Theory: An Anthology. Ed. by Robert A. Segal. LC 97-20350. 450p. (C). 1997. text 68.95 (0-631-20679-5); pap. text 31.95 (0-631-20680-9) Blackwell Pubs.

Myth & Romance: The Art of J. W. Waterhouse. J. W. Waterhouse. (Miniature Editions Ser.). (Illus.). 160p. (Orig.). (C). 1994. pap. 8.95 (0-7148-3264-2, Pub. by Phaidon Press) Phaidon Pr.

Myth & Rural Culture. Paul J. Cloke et al. 192p. 1992. text 69.95 (0-340-55048-1, A9522, Pub. by E A) Routldge.

Myth & Science: An Essay. Tito Vignoli. Ed. by Kees W. Bolle. LC 77-79156. (Mythology Ser.). 1978. reprint ed. lib. bdg. 23.95 (0-405-10565-7) Ayer.

Myth & Society in Ancient Greece. Jean-Pierre Vernant. Tr. by Janet Lloyd from FRE. LC 87-33786. 279p. 1988. 26.95 (0-942299-16-7); pap. 14.95 (0-942299-17-5) Zone Bks.

Myth & Southern History Vol. 1: The Old South. 2nd ed. Ed. by Patrick Gerster & Nicholas Cords. 224p. 1989. pap. text 13.95 (0-252-06024-5) U of Ill Pr.

Myth & Southern History Vol. 2: The New South. 2nd ed. Ed. by Patrick Gerster & Nicholas Cords. 208p. 1989. pap. text 13.95 (0-252-06025-3) U of Ill Pr.

Myth & Symbol: Critical Approaches & Applications, by Northrop Frye, L. C. Knights & Others. A Selection of Papers Delivered at the Joint Meeting of the Midwest Modern Language Association & the Central Renaissance Conference, 1962. Ed. by Bernice Slote. LC 63-9960. 207p. reprint ed. pap. 64.20 (0-608-15533-0, 202974900064) Bks Demand.

Myth & Symbol in Ancient Egypt. R. T. Clark. 1991. pap. 15.95 (0-500-27112-7, Pub. by Thames Hudson) Norton.

Myth & Symbol in Soviet Fiction: Images of the Savior Hero, Great Mother, "Anima," & Child in Selected Novels & Films. Thomas F. Rogers. LC 91-46783. (Illus.). 348p. 1992. lib. bdg. 99.95 (0-7734-9849-4) E Mellen.

Myth & Territory in the Spartan Mediterranean. Irad Malkin. LC 93-30357. (Illus.). 296p. (C). 1994. text 74.95 (0-521-41183-1) Cambridge U Pr.

Myth & the Body: A Colloquy With Joseph Campbell. Stanley Keleman. 90p. 1999. pap. 14.95 (0-934320-17-9) Center Pr.

Myth & the Cold War. Dante A. Puzzo. 98p. (Orig.). 1995. pap. 12.00 (0-9634503-2-8) Randatamp Pr.

Myth & the Crisis of Historical Consciousness. Ed. by Lee W. Gibbs & W. Taylor Stevenson. LC 75-33049. 117p. reprint ed. pap. 36.30 (0-608-08841-2, 206948000004) Bks Demand.

*__Myth & the Fiction of Michel Tournier & Patrick Grainville.__ Rachel Edwards. LC 99-16646. (Studies in French Literature: Vol. 36). 324p. 1999. text 99.95 (0-7734-7938-4) E Mellen.

Myth & the History of the Hispanic Southwest: Essays. David J. Weber. LC 88-12035. (Calvin P. Horn Lectures in Western History & Culture). (Illus.). 191p. 1988. reprint ed. pap. 59.30 (0-608-07860-3, 205404300011) Bks Demand.

Myth & the Mirage: Six Essays on Revolution. Mario Llerena. Ed. by Adolfo Leyva. LC 95-83543. 217p. 1995. pap. 15.00 (1-884619-07-X) Endowment CAS.

Myth & the Movies: Discovering the Mythic Structure of over 50 Unforgettable Films using "The Writer's Journey" Stuart Voytilla. LC 99-27626. (Illus.). 300p. 1999. pap. 26.95 (0-941188-66-3, 38RLS) M Wiese.

Myth & the Polis. Ed. by Dora C. Pozzi & John M. Wickersham. LC 90-55716. (Myth & Poetics Ser.). 248p. 1991. text 37.50 (0-8014-2473-9); pap. text 14.95 (0-8014-9734-5) Cornell U Pr.

Myth & the Reality of Judaism: 82 Misconceptions Set Straight. Simon Glustrom. (Orig.). (C). 1989. pap. text 8.95 (0-87441-479-2) Behrman.

Myth & Today's Consciousness. Ean Begg. 1991. pap. 10.95 (0-904575-30-6) Sigo Pr.

Myth & Tragedy in Ancient Greece. Jean-Pierre Vernant & Pierre Vidal-Naquet. Tr. by Janet Lloyd from FRE. LC 87-34050. (Illus.). 527p. 1988. 32.95 (0-942299-18-3); pap. 18.95 (0-942299-19-1) Zone Bks.

Myth As Argument: The Brhaddevata As Canonical Commentary. Laurie L. Patton. LC 96-20603. (Religionsgeschichtliche Versuche und Vorarbeiten Ser.: Vol. 41). xxviii, 549p. (C). 1996. lib. bdg. 207.40 (3-11-013805-0) De Gruyter.

Myth as Foundation for Society & Values: A Sociological Analysis. Pierre H. Hegy. LC 91-27320. (Mellen Studies in Sociology: Vol. 10). 236p. 1991. lib. bdg. 89.95 (0-7734-9680-7) E Mellen.

Myth As Genre in British Romantic Poetry. Paul M. Wiebe. LC 98-25161. (American University Studies: Series IV, Vol. 170). 185p. (C). 1998. text 40.95 (0-8204-2153-7) P Lang Pubng.

Myth Become Reality: History & Development of the Miao Written Language, Vol. 1. Joakim Enwall. LC 96-149666. (Stockholm East Asian Monographs: No. 5). 263p. 1995. pap. 97.50 (91-7153-269-2, Pub. by Almqvist Wiksell) Coronet Bks.

Myth Become Reality: History & Development of the Miao Written Language, Vol. 2. Joakim Enwall. (Stockholm East Asian Monographs: No. 6). 239p. 1995. pap. 97.50 (91-7153-423-7, Pub. by Almqvist Wiksell) Coronet Bks.

Myth Becomes History: Pre-Classical Greece. Carol G. Thomas. LC 93-7199. (Publications of the Association of Ancient Historians: No. 4). 96p. 1993. 19.95 (0-941690-52-0); pap. 11.95 (0-941690-51-2) Regina Bks.

Myth Conceptions. Robert L. Asprin. 224p. 1986. mass mkt. 5.99 (0-441-55521-7) Ace Bks.

Myth Directions. Robert L. Asprin. (Myth Ser.). 1986. mass mkt. 5.99 (0-441-55529-2) Ace Bks.

Myth, Emblem, & Music in Shakespeare's "Cymbeline" An Iconographic Reconstruction. Peggy M. Simonds. LC 90-50930. (Illus.). 400p. 1992. 60.00 (0-87413-429-3) U Delaware Pr.

Myth, Ethos, & Actuality: Official Art in Fifth-Century B. C. Athens. David Castriota. LC 92-50247. (Studies in Classics). (Illus.). 354p. (C). 1992. pap. 24.95 (0-299-13354-0) U of Wis Pr.

Myth, Ethos, & Actuality: Official Art in Fifth-Century B.C. Athens. David Castriota. LC 92-50247. (Studies in Classics). (Illus.). 354p. (Orig.). (C). 1992. lib. bdg. 50.00 (0-299-13350-8) U of Wis Pr.

Myth for Moderns: Erwin Ramsdell Goodenough & Religious Studies in America, 1938-1955. Eleanor B. Mattes. LC 97-8875. (ATLA Monograph Ser.: No. 43). 256p. 1997. 42.00 (0-8108-3339-5) Scarecrow.

Myth from the Ice Age to Mickey Mouse. Robert W. Brockway. LC 93-2690. 187p. (C). 1993. pap. text 21.95 (0-7914-1714-X) State U NY Pr.

Myth from the Ice Age to Mickey Mouse. Robert W. Brockway. LC 93-2690. 187p. (C). 1993. text 64.50 (0-7914-1713-1) State U NY Pr.

Myth, History & the Industrial Revolution. D. C. Coleman. 225p. 1992. 55.00 (1-85285-074-4) Hambledon Press.

Myth II: Exclusive Strategy Guide. Talon. 1999. pap. text 19.95 (1-56893-926-4) GT Interactive Software.

Myth in Indo-European Antiquity. Ed. by Gerald J. Larson et al. LC 72-93522. (Publications of the UCSR Institute of Religious Studies). 205p. reprint ed. pap. 63.60 (0-608-18008-4, 202904900058) Bks Demand.

Myth in Literature. Ed. by Andrej Kodjak et al. (New York University Slavic Papers: Vol. V). 207p. (Orig.). 1985. pap. 15.95 (0-89357-137-7) Slavica.

Myth in Old Testament Interpretation. John W. Rogerson. LC 73-78234. (Beiheft zur Zeitschrift fuer die Alttestamentliche Wissenschaft Ser.). (C). 1974. 76.95 (3-11-004220-7) De Gruyter.

Myth in Surrealist Painting, 1929-1939. Whitney Chadwick. LC 79-26713. (Studies in the Fine Arts: The Avant-Garde: No. 1). (Illus.). 261p. 1980. reprint ed. pap. 81.00 (0-8357-1907-3, 207068500017) Bks Demand.

Myth in the Works of Chingiz Aitmatov. Nina Kolesnikoff. LC 99-13400. 144p. 1999. 34.00 (0-7618-1362-4) U Pr of Amer.

Myth Information. Allen J. Varasdi. 1996. pap. 12.00 (0-345-41049-1) Ballantine Pub Grp.

Myth-ing Persons. Robert L. Asprin. 176p. 1986. mass mkt. 5.50 (0-441-55276-5) Ace Bks.

Myth into Art: Poet & Painter in Classical Greece. Harvey A. Shapiro. LC 93-2262. (Illus.). 192p. (C). 1994. pap. 25.99 (0-415-06793-6) Routledge.

Myth, Legend & Custom in the Old Testament: A Comparative Study with Chapters from Sir James G. Frazer's Folklore in the Old Testament, 2 vols., Set. Theodor H. Gaster. 1990. 37.00 (0-8446-5189-3) Peter Smith.

Myth Legend Dust: Critical Responses To Cormac Mccarthy. Rick Wallach. text. write for info. (0-7190-5947-X, Pub. by Manchester Univ Pr) St Martin.

Myth Legends Dust: Critical Responses To Cormac Mccarthy. Rick Wallach. pap. write for info. (0-7190-5948-8, Pub. by Manchester Univ Pr) St Martin.

Myth, Literature & the African World. Wole Soyinka. (Canto Book Ser.). 180p. (C). 1990. pap. 11.95 (0-521-39834-7) Cambridge U Pr.

Myth, Magic, & Morals. Fred C. Conybeare. 184p. 1996. reprint ed. spiral bd. 32.00 (0-7873-0196-5) Hlth Research.

Myth, Magic & Mystery: 100 Years of American Children. Trinkett Clark & H. Nichols Clark. (Illus.). 240p. 1996. pap. 29.95 (1-57098-079-9) Roberts Rinehart.

Myth Maker: J. R. R. Tolkien. Diaz. LC 96-50032. 1998. write for info. (0-15-200835-7) Harcourt.

Myth Maker: J. R. R. Tolkien. Anne E. Neimark. LC 96-4196. (Illus.). 128p. (J). 1996. 17.00 (0-15-298847-5) Harcourt.

Myth Maker: J. R. R. Tolkien. Anne E. Neimark. LC 97-50380. (Illus.). 128p. (YA). (gr. 5-9). 1998. mass mkt. 4.95 (0-688-15741-6, Wm Morrow) Morrow Avon.

Myth Maker: J. R. R. Tolkien. Anne E. Neimark. (J). 1998. 10.05 (0-606-13639-8, Pub. by Turtleback) Demco.

Myth Makers. Joanne Kalnitz & Kathy R. Judd. 192p. (C). 1986. pap. text 18.00 (0-03-001287-2, Pub. by Harcourt Coll Pubs) Harcourt.

*__Myth Makers & Storytellers: How to Unleash the Power of Myths, Stories & Metaphors to Understand the Past, Envisage the Future.__ Michael Kaye. 202p. 1999. pap. 29.95 (1-875680-26-8) Business Prof of Amer.

Myth Man. Elizabeth Swados. 1999. pap. 9.95 (0-14-015981-9, Viking) Viking Penguin.

Myth Man: A Storyteller's Jesus. John R. Aurelio. 240p. 1993. reprint ed. pap. 11.95 (0-8245-1210-3) Crossroad NY.

Myth, Manifesto, Meltdown: Communist Strategy, 1848-1991. Edward M. Collins. LC 97-22806. 256p. 1998. 59.95 (0-275-95938-4, Praeger Pubs) Greenwood.

Myth, Meaning, & Memory on Roman Sarcophagi. Michael Koortbojian. LC 94-36581. (Illus.). 225p. 1995. text 48.00 (0-520-08518-3, Pub. by U CA Pr) Cal Prin Full Svc.

Myth, Media & the Southern Mind. Stephen A. Smith. LC 84-28021. 207p. 1985. pap. 16.00 (0-938626-41-8) U of Ark Pr.

*__Myth, Memory & Imagination: Universal Themes in the Life & Culture of the South.__ Julia J. Norrell et al. (Illus.). 84p. 1999. pap. 20.00 (0-938983-13-X) U of SC Pr.

Myth Men: Hercules the Strong Man: Guardians of the Legend. Laura Geringer. LC 97-191492. (Myth & Men Ser.). (Illus.). 32p. (J). (ps-3). 1996. pap. text 4.99 (0-590-84500-4) Scholastic Inc.

Myth Men: Ulysses: Guardians of the Legend. Laura Geringer. LC 97-193258. (Myth & Men Ser.). (Illus.). 32p. (J). (ps-3). 1996. pap. text 4.99 (0-590-84531-4) Scholastic Inc.

Myth, Mensch & Umwelt. Ed. by Adolf E. Jensen & Kees W. Bolle. LC 77-79134. (Mythology Ser.). (GER., Illus.). 1978. reprint ed. lib. bdg. 40.95 (0-405-10544-4) Ayer.

Myth, Music & Dance of the American Indian. Ruth DeCesare. Ed. by Sandy Feldstein et al. (Illus.). 80p. (J). (gr. 4-12). 1988. teacher ed. 12.95 (0-88284-371-0, 3518); student ed. 4.95 (0-88284-372-9, 3520) Alfred Pub.

Myth, Music & Dance of the American Indian. Ruth DeCesare. Ed. by Sandy Feldstein et al. (Illus.). 80p. (J). (gr. 4-12). 1988. teacher ed. 19.95 incl. audio (0-88284-383-4, 3534) Alfred Pub.

Myth, Music & Dance of the American Indian: Teachers Handbook. Ruth DeCesare. 1997. pap. 21.95 incl. audio compact disk (0-88284-845-3, 16415) Alfred Pub.

Myth, Music & Dance of the American Indian, Songbook. Ruth DeCesare. Ed. by Sandy Feldstein et al. (Illus.). 24p. (J). (gr. 4-12). 1988. student ed. 6.95 (0-88284-373-7, 3519) Alfred Pub.

Myth-Nomers & Im-Pervections, No. 8. Robert L. Asprin. 1988. mass mkt. 5.99 (0-441-55279-X) Ace Bks.

Myth of a Nation: Literature & Politics in Prussia under Napoleon. Otto Johnston. LC 87-70864. (GERM Ser.: Vol. 32). (Illus.). xvi, 240p. 1989. pap. 35.00 (0-938100-53-X) Camden Hse.

Myth of a Progressive Reform: Railroad Regulation in Wisconsin, 1903-1910. Stanley P. Caine. LC 75-630131. (Illus.). 250p. 1970. 7.95 (0-87020-110-7) State Hist Soc Wis.

An Asterisk (*) at the beginning of an entry indicates that the title is appearing for the first time.

Myth of A. S. Pushkin in Russia's Silver Age: M. O. Gershenzon, Pushkinist. Brian Horowitz. (Studies in Russian Literature & Theory). 136p. 1996. text 49.95 (*0-8101-1355-4*) Northwestern U Pr.

Myth of Absolutism: Change & Continuity in Early Modern European Monarchy. Nicholas Henshall. 256p. (C). 1995. pap. 40.06 (*0-582-05617-9*, 79355) Longman.

***Myth of Adam Smith.** Salim Rashid. LC 97-30625. 240p. 1998. 85.00 (*1-85898-532-3*) E Elgar.

Myth of Addiction. 2nd ed. John Booth Davies. 192p. 1997. text 40.00 (*90-5702-246-X*, Harwood Acad Pubs); pap. text 20.00 (*90-5702-237-0*, Harwood Acad Pubs) Gordon & Breach.

Myth of Addiction: An Application of the Psychological Theory of Attribution to Illicit Drug Use. John B. Davies. xii, 180p. 1992. text 71.00 (*3-7186-5197-1*, Harwood Acad Pubs); pap. text 43.00 (*3-7186-5243-9*, Harwood Acad Pubs) Gordon & Breach.

Myth of Adolescence: Raising Responsible Children in an Irresponsible Society. David A. Black. LC 98-89234. 166p. 1999. 17.00 (*1-891833-51-0*) Davidson Pr.

Myth of Adolescent Culture. Frederick Elkin & William A. Westley. (Reprint Series in Social Sciences). (C). 1993. reprint ed. pap. text 5.00 (*0-8290-3846-9*, S-79) Irvington.

Myth of Africa. Dorothy Hammond & Alta Jablow. LC 76-62996. 1977. 20.00 (*0-915042-03-7*) Lib Soc Sci.

Myth of America: Essays in the Structures of Literary Imagination. Viola Sachs. LC 72-93158. 162p. 1973. text 53.80 (*90-279-7263-X*) Mouton.

Myth of American Eclipse: The New Global Age. Alfred Balk. 246p. (C). 1990. 39.95 (*0-88738-369-6*) Transaction Pubs.

Myth of American Individualism: The Protestant Origins of American Political Thought. Barry A. Shain. LC 94-15826. 408p. 1994. text 52.50 (*0-691-03382-X*, Pub. by Princeton U Pr) Cal Prin Full Svc.

Myth of Analysis: Three Essays in Archetypal Psychology. James Hillman. LC 97-32837. 320p. 1998. pap. 17.95 (*0-8101-1651-0*) Northwestern U Pr.

Myth of Apollo & Daphne from Ovid to Quevedo: Love, Agon, & the Grotesque. Mary Barnard. LC 86-29142. (Duke Monographs in Medieval & Renaissance Studies: No. 8). (Illus.). xi, 222p. 1987. text 34.95 (*0-8223-0701-4*) Duke.

Myth of Apollo & Marsyas in the Art of the Italian Renaissance: An Inquiry into the Meaning of Images. Edith Wyss. LC 94-23887. 184p. 1996. 69.50 (*0-87413-540-0*) U Delaware Pr.

Myth of Arab Piracy in the Gulf. Sultan Muhammad Al-Qasimi. LC 85-22411. 450p. 1986. 49.95 (*0-7099-2106-3*, Pub. by C Helm) Routldge.

Myth of Aristotle's Development: The Betrayal of Metaphysics. Walter E. Wehrle. 320p. (C). 2000. pap. text 24.95 (*0-8476-8161-0*); lib. bdg. 67.50 (*0-8476-8160-2*) Rowman.

Myth of Atlas: Families & the Therapeutic Story. Maurizio Andolfi et al. LC 89-32190. 256p. 1989. text 35.95 (*0-87630-549-4*) Brunner-Mazel.

Myth of Aunt Jemima: Representations of Race & Religion. Diane Roberts. LC 93-50574. 208p. (C). 1994. pap. 24.99 (*0-415-04919-9*, B4245) Routledge.

Myth of Black Corporate Mobility. Ulwyn L. Pierre. LC 98-42967. (Studies in African American History & Culture). 1998. 60.00 (*0-8153-3138-X*) Garland.

Myth of Black Ethnicity: Monophylety, Diversity, & the Dilemma of Identity. Richard A. Davis. LC 96-34171. (Illus.). 250p. 1997. pap. 39.50 (*1-56750-293-8*); text 73.25 (*1-56750-292-X*) Ablx Pub.

Myth of Black Progress. Alphonso Pinkney. LC 84-1912. 208p. 1986. pap. text 17.95 (*0-521-31047-4*) Cambridge U Pr.

***Myth of Certainty: The Reflective Christian & the Risk of Commitment.** Daniel Taylor. 1999. pap. 10.99 (*0-8308-2237-2*) InterVarsity.

Myth of Christian America: What You Need to Know about the Separation of Church & State. Mark W. Whitten. LC 99-14806. 128p. 1999. pap. 12.00 (*1-57312-287-4*) Smyth & Helwys.

Myth of Christian Uniqueness: Toward a Pluralistic Theology of Religions. Ed. by John Hick & Paul F. Knitter. LC 87-23992. (Faith Meets Faith Ser.). 264p. (Orig.). 1988. pap. 20.00 (*0-88344-602-2*) Orbis Bks.

Myth of Community: Gender Issues in Participatory Development. Ed. by Irene Guijt & Meera K. Shah. 320p. 1998. pap. 17.50 (*1-85339-421-1*, Pub. by Intermed Tech) Stylus Pub VA.

Myth of Community Care: An Alternative Neighbourhood Model of Care. Steve Baldwin. LC 93-30442. 186p. 1993. pap. 31.75 (*1-56593-225-0*, 0563) Singular Publishing.

Myth of Consensus, 1945-1964. Jones Staff. 208p. 1996. text 65.00 (*0-312-16154-9*) St Martin.

Myth of Constitutionalism in Pakistan. Zulfikar K. Maluka. 374p. 1996. text 42.00 (*0-19-577572-4*) OUP.

Myth of Continents: A Critique of Metageography. Martin W. Lewis & Karen Wigen. LC 96-30294. (Illus.). 383p. 1997. 55.00 (*0-520-20742-4*, Pub. by U CA Pr); pap. 19.95 (*0-520-20743-2*, Pub. by U CA Pr) Cal Prin Full Svc.

Myth of Cosmic Rebellion: A Study of Its Reflexes in Ugaritic & Biblical Literature. Hugh Rowland Page, Jr. (Vetus Testamentum, Supplements Ser.: Vol. 65). (Illus.). Xvi, 232p. 1996. text 100.00 (*90-04-10563-8*) Brill Academic Pubs.

Myth of Creation: A Puppet Show in Three Acts. Sadiq Hidayat. Tr. by M. R. Ghanoonparvar from PER. (Bibliotheca Tranica: Vol. 4).Tr. of Afsaneh-Ye Afarinesh. (Illus.). 78p. 1998. 19.95 (*1-56859-066-0*) Mazda Pubs.

Myth of Deliverance: Reflections of Shakespeare's Problem Comedies. Northrop Frye. 1993. pap. text 15.95 (*0-8020-7781-1*) U of Toronto Pr.

Myth of Deliverance: Reflections on Shakespeare's Problem Comedies. Northrop Frye. LC 83-181165. 98p. reprint ed. pap. 30.40 (*0-7837-2663-5*, 204302700006) Bks Demand.

Myth of Democracy. Ferdinand Lundberg. 1989. 11.95 (*0-8184-0500-7*) Carol Pub Group.

Myth of Democratic Failure: Why Political Institutions Are Efficient. Donald A. Wittman. x, 230p. 1996. pap. text 17.95 (*0-226-90423-7*) U Ch Pr.

Myth of Democratic Failure: Why Political Institutions Are Efficient. Donald A. Wittman. LC 94-46186. (American Politics & Political Economy Ser.). 240p. 1997. 29.95 (*0-226-90422-9*) U Ch Pr.

Myth of Dialectics: Reinterpreting the Marx-Hegel Relation. John Rosenthal. LC 97-8402. 276p. 1998. text 65.00 (*0-312-17600-7*) St Martin.

Myth of Dietrich Bonhoeffer: Is His Theology Evangelical? Richard Weikart. LC 96-52499. 248p. 1997. 74.95 (*1-57309-150-2*); pap. 54.95 (*1-57309-149-9*) Intl Scholars.

Myth of Egypt & Its Hieroglyphs in European Tradition. Erik Iversen. LC 93-19325. (Mythos: The Princeton - Bollingen Series in World Mythology). (Illus.). 178p. 1993. pap. text 17.95 (*0-691-02124-4*, Pub. by Princeton U Pr) Cal Prin Full Svc.

Myth of "Ethnic Conflict" Politics, Economics & "Cultural" Violence. Ed. by Beverly Crawford & Ronnie D. Lipschutz. LC 98-28697. (Research Ser.). vii, 580p. 1998. pap. text 28.50 (*0-87725-198-3*) U of Cal IAS.

Myth of Freedom. Chogyam Trungpa. (Orig.). 1976. pap. 7.95 (*0-394-73180-8*) Random.

Myth of Freedom. Chogyam Trungpa. LC 87-28358. (Dragon Editions Ser.). 176p. (Orig.). 1988. pap. 13.00 (*0-87773-084-9*, Pub. by Shambhala Pubns) Random.

Myth of Generational Conflict: The Family & State in Ageing Societies Sara Arber & Claudine Attias-Donfut. LC 99-28669. (ESA Studies in European Society). 1999. write for info. (*0-415-20770-3*) Routledge.

Myth of Government Information. Alastair J. Allan. LC 91-105582. (Viewpoints in Library & Information Science: Vol. 6). 72p. reprint ed. pap. 30.00 (*0-608-20966-X*, 207183800002) Bks Demand.

Myth of Green Marketing: Tending Our Goats at the Edge of Apocalypse. Toby Smith. LC 99-173158. (Illus.). 208p. 1998. text 50.00 (*0-8020-4175-2*); pap. text 19.95 (*0-8020-8035-9*) U of Toronto Pr.

Myth of Guillaume. David Schenck. LC 88-60711. 150p. 1988. lib. bdg. 19.95 (*0-917786-54-8*) Summa Pubns.

Myth of Hercules, Vol. 1. Lasky. (J). 1997. 15.95 (*0-7868-1278-8*, Pub. by Hyperion) Little.

Myth of Heterosexual AIDS: How a Tragedy Has Been Distorted by the Media & Partisan Politics. Michael Fumento. LC 93-26358. 496p. 1993. pap. 14.95 (*0-89526-729-2*) Regnery Pub.

Myth of Human Races. Alain F. Corcos. LC 97-17769. 1997. pap. 17.95 (*0-87013-439-6*) Mich St U Pr.

Myth of Icarus in Spanish Renaissance Poetry. John H. Turner. (Monografias A Ser.: No. 56). 160p. (C). 1976. 51.00 (*0-7293-0035-8*, Pub. by Tamesis Bks Ltd) Boydell & Brewer.

Myth of Inevitable Progress, 115. Franco Ferrarotti. LC 84-589. (Contributions in Political Science Ser.: No. 115). 208p. 1985. 49.95 (*0-313-24329-8*, FMY/, Greenwood Pr) Greenwood.

Myth of Innocence: Mark & Christian Origins. Burton L. Mack. LC 86-45906. (Foundations & Facets Ser.). 448p. 1991. pap. 25.00 (*0-8006-2549-8*, 1-2549) Augsburg Fortress.

Myth of Invariance: The Origin of the Gods, Mathematics & Music from the Rg Veda to Plato. Ernest G. McClain. LC 76-28411. (Illus.). 216p. 1985. pap. 8.95 (*0-89254-012-5*) Nicolas-Hays.

Myth of Japanese Homogeneity: Social-Ecological Diversity in Education & Socialization. Herman W. Smith. (Illus.). 259p. (C). 1994. lib. bdg. 80.00 (*1-56072-169-3*) Nova Sci Pubs.

Myth of Liberal Individualism. Colin Bird. LC 98-38601. (Social Philosophy & Policy Ser.). (Illus.). 280p. (C). 1999. text 54.95 (*0-521-64128-4*) Cambridge U Pr.

***Myth of Magic.** Adam Cole. LC 99-91485. 1999. 25.00 (*0-7388-0824-5*); pap. 18.00 (*0-7388-0825-3*) Xlibris Corp.

Myth of Male Power. Warren Farrell. 448p. 1994. pap. 13.00 (*0-425-14381-3*) Berkley Pub.

Myth of Male Power. Warren Farrell. 1996. mass mkt. 6.99 (*0-425-15523-4*) Berkley Pub.

Myth of Market Failure: Employment & the Labor Market in Mexico. Peter Gregory. LC 85-45927. 307p. reprint ed. pap. 95.20 (*0-7837-4232-0*, 204392000012) Bks Demand.

Myth of Mary. Cesar Vidal. LC 94-80004. (Illus.). 192p. (Orig.). 1995. pap. 8.50 (*0-937958-47-6*) Chick Pubns.

***Myth of Matriarchal Prehistory: Why An Invented Past Won't Give Women a Future.** Cynthia Eller. LC 99-57360. (Illus.). 304p. 2000. 26.00 (*0-8070-6792-X*) Beacon Pr.

Myth of Meaning: In the Work of C. G. Jung. Aniela Jaffe. 214p. 1995. pap. 14.00 (*3-85630-500-9*) Continuum.

Myth of Medea & the Murder of Children, 89. Lillian Corti. LC 97-26892. (Contributions to the Study of World Literature Ser.: Vol. 89). 264p. 1998. 59.95 (*0-313-30536-6*, Greenwood Pr) Greenwood.

Myth of Mental Illness, Revised Edition. rev. ed. Thomas S. Szasz. LC 84-47742. 320p. 1984. pap. 14.00 (*0-06-091151-4*, CN 1151, Perennial) HarperTrade.

Myth of Mondragon: Cooperatives, Politics, & Working-Class Life in a Basque Town. Sharryn Kasmir. LC 95-40339. (SUNY Series in the Anthropology of Work). 243p. (C). 1996. text 68.50 (*0-7914-3003-0*); pap. text 23.95 (*0-7914-3004-9*) State U NY Pr.

***Myth of Monogamy Clothbound.** Carol Barash. 2001. pap. text. write for info. (*0-7167-4004-4*) W H Freeman.

***Myth of More: And Other Lifetraps That Sabotage the Happiness You Deserve.** Joseph R. Novello. 2001. pap. 16.95 (*0-8091-3941-3*) Paulist Pr.

Myth of Natural Origins: How Science Points to Divine Creation. Ashby L. Camp. LC 94-77024. 136p. (Orig.). 1994. pap. 9.95 (*0-9642076-2-1*) Ktisis Pubng.

Myth of New Orleans in Literature: Dialogues of Race & Gender. Violet H. Bryan. LC 92-42846. 248p. (C). 1993. text 33.00 (*0-87049-789-8*) U of Tenn Pr.

Myth of Objectivity: Data Collection in Social Science. A. C. Higgins. 214p. (Orig.). (C). 1995. pap. text 26.50 (*1-885343-08-6*) Exams Unltd.

Myth of Open Borders. Wayne Lutton. 47p. 1988. pap. 2.00 (*0-936247-09-6*) Amer Immigration.

Myth of Our Own: Adventures in World Religions. Jamake Highwater. LC 95-41251. (J). 1995. 14.95 (*0-8050-3721-7*) H Holt & Co.

***Myth of Pain.** Valerie Gray Hardcastle. LC 99-30099. (Philosophical Psychopathology Ser.). (Illus.). 296p. 1999. 37.50 (*0-262-08283-7*) MIT Pr.

Myth of Papal Infallibility. Ed. by Cenacle Staff. (Illus.). 112p. (Orig.). 1990. pap. 5.00 (*0-912927-41-0*, X041) St John Kronstadt.

Myth of Political Correctness: The Conservative Attack on Higher Education. John K. Wilson. LC 95-22495. 224p. 1995. pap. 16.95 (*0-8223-1713-3*); text 49.95 (*0-8223-1703-6*) Duke.

Myth of Population Control: Family, Caste & Class in an Indian Village. Mahmood Mamdani. LC 72-81761. (Illus.). 176p. 1973. pap. 15.00 (*0-85345-284-9*, Pub. by Monthly Rev) NYU Pr.

Myth of Post-Cold War Chaos: Bosnia & Myths about Ethnic Conflict. Yahya M. Sadowsi. LC 98-8943. 250p. 1998. 28.95 (*0-8157-7664-0*) Brookings.

Myth of Primitivism. Ed. by Susan Hiller. (Illus.). 368p. (C). 1991. pap. 24.99 (*0-415-01481-6*, A3783) Routledge.

Myth of Privilege: Aboriginal Status, Media Visions & Public Ideas. Steve Mickler. 346p. 1998. 19.95 (*1-86368-249-X*, Pub. by Fremantle Arts) Intl Spec Bk.

Myth of Property: Toward an Egalitarian Theory of Ownership. John Christman. LC 93-31713. 240p. 1994. text 45.00 (*0-19-508594-9*) OUP.

Myth of Psychology. Fred Newman. LC 91-76608. 229p. 1991. pap. 12.95 (*0-9628621-2-6*) Castillo Intl.

Myth of Psychotherapy: Mental Healing As Religion, Rhetoric, & Repression. Thomas Szasz. (Illus.). 238p. (C). 1988. reprint ed. pap. 17.95 (*0-8156-0223-5*) Syracuse U Pr.

Myth of Quetzalcoatl. Enrique Florescano & Raul Velazquez. LC 98-8733. (Illus.). 291p. 1999. 45.00 (*0-8018-5999-9*) Johns Hopkins.

Myth of Religious Neutrality: An Essay on the Hidden Role of Religious Belief in Theories. Roy A. Clouser. LC 90-50928. (C). 1992. pap. text 22.00 (*0-268-01399-3*) U of Notre Dame Pr.

Myth of Replacement: Stars, Gods, & Order in the Universe. Thomas D. Worthen. LC 90-20202. (Illus.). 318p. 1991. 45.00 (*0-8165-1200-0*) U of Ariz Pr.

Myth of Repressed Memory: False Memories & Allegations of Sexual Abuse. Elizabeth F. Loftus & Katherine Ketcham. 304p. 1996. pap. 13.95 (*0-312-14123-8*) St Martin.

***Myth of Repressed Memory: False Memories & Allegations of Sexual Abuse.** Elizabeth Loftus & Katherine Ketcham. 290p. 2000. reprint ed. 23.00 (*0-7881-9282-5*) DIANE Pub.

Myth of Rescue: Why the Democracies Could Not Have Saved More Jews from the Nazis. William D. Rubinstein. LC 97-203027. 288p. 1997. 32.99 (*0-415-12455-7*) Routledge.

Myth of Rescue: Why the Democracies Could Not Have Saved More Jews from the Nazis. William D. Rubinstein. LC 99-27372. 1999. pap. 20.99 (*0-415-21249-9*) Routledge.

Myth of Return in Early Greek Epic. Douglas Frame. LC 77-76306. 190p. reprint ed. pap. 58.90 (*0-8357-8241-7*, 203372600087) Bks Demand.

Myth of Ritual: A Native's Ethnography of Zapotec Life-Crisis Rituals. Fadwa El Guindi & Abel Hernandez. LC 86-25018. 147p. 1986. 27.95 (*0-8165-0907-7*) U of Ariz Pr.

Myth of Ritual Murder: Jews & Magic in Reformation Germany. R. Po-Chia Hsia. 248p. (C). 1988. 42.50 (*0-300-04120-9*) Yale U Pr.

Myth of Ritual Murder: Jews & Magic in Reformation Germany. R. Po-Chia Hsia. 256p. (C). 1990. reprint ed. pap. 17.00 (*0-300-04746-0*) Yale U Pr.

Myth of Romance see Mito del Romance

Myth of Rome's Fall. Richard M. Haywood. LC 78-12128. 178p. 1979. reprint ed. lib. bdg. 35.00 (*0-313-21108-6*, HAMY, Greenwood Pr) Greenwood.

Myth of Santa Fe: Creating a Modern Regional Tradition. Chris Wilson. LC 95-50222. 410p. 1996. pap. 29.95 (*0-8263-1746-4*) U of NM Pr.

Myth of Scientific Literacy. Morris H. Shamos. LC 94-41057. 300p. (C). 1995. text 27.95 (*0-8135-2196-3*) Rutgers U Pr.

Myth of Scientific Public Policy. Robert Formaini. 160p. (C). 1990. 39.95 (*0-88738-352-1*); text 24.95 (*0-88738-852-3*) Transaction Pubs.

Myth of Self-Esteem. John P. Hewitt. 285p. 1998. text 29.95 (*0-312-17556-6*) St Martin.

Myth of Self-Esteem: Finding Happiness & Solving Problems in America. John P. Hewitt. LC 97-66312. (Contemporary Social Issues Ser.). 160p. 1997. pap. text 14.95 (*0-312-13715-X*) St Martin.

Myth of Shangri-la: Tibet, Travel Writing & the Western Creation of Sacred Landscape. Peter Bishop. 400p. 1989. 48.00 (*0-520-06686-3*, Pub. by U CA Pr) Cal Prin Full Svc.

Myth of Sisyphus & Other Essays. Albert Camus. Tr. by Justin O'Brien. LC 90-50476. 192p. 1991. pap. 12.00 (*0-679-73373-6*) Vin Bks.

Myth of Social Action. Colin Campbell. 207p. (C). 1996. text 54.95 (*0-521-55079-3*) Cambridge U Pr.

Myth of Social Action. Colin Campbell. 230p. (C). 1998. pap. text 19.95 (*0-521-64636-7*) Cambridge U Pr.

Myth of Social Cost. Steven N. Cheung. LC 80-26083. (Cato Papers: No. 16). 74p. 1980. reprint ed. pap. 1.00 (*0-932790-21-6*) Cato Inst.

Myth of Southern History: Historical Consciousness in Twentieth-Century Southern Literature. Francis Garvin Davenport. LC 76-112600. 224p. reprint ed. pap. 69.50 (*0-8357-3253-3*, 203947400013) Bks Demand.

Myth of Teaching. Nelson A. Ossorio. (Orig.). 1995. pap. 8.95 (*1-56721-122-4*) Twnty-Fifth Cent Pr.

Myth of the A. D. D. Child: 50 Ways to Improve Your Child's Behavior & Attention Span Without Drugs, Labels or Coercion. Thomas Armstrong. 320p. 1997. pap. 13.95 (*0-452-27547-4*, Plume) Dutton Plume.

M

Myth of the Appalachian Brain Drain. Richard D. Raymond. LC 72-187762. 78p. 1972. pap. 7.95 (*0-937058-06-8*) West Va U Pr.

Myth of the Bad Mother: Parenting Without Guilt. Jane Swigart. 272p. 1992. pap. 10.00 (*0-380-71806-5*, Avon Bks) Morrow Avon.

Myth of the Bagre. Jack Goody. LC 73-155639. (Oxford Library of African Literature Ser.). 403p. reprint ed. pap. 125.00 (*0-7837-2355-5*, AU0042000006) Bks Demand.

Myth of the Balanced Budget: Why the Budget Can Never Be Balanced & If Balanced Would Lead to a Major Depression. 1996. lib. bdg. 251.95 (*0-8490-5870-8*) Gordon Pr.

Myth of the Blitz. Angus Calder. (Illus.). 320p. 1996. pap. 24.95 (*0-7126-9820-5*, Pub. by Pimlico) Trafalgar.

Myth of the British Monarchy. Edgar Wilson. 227p. (C). pap. 18.95 (*1-85172-025-1*, Pub. by Pluto GBR) Stylus Pub VA.

Myth of the Coming Labor Shortage: Jobs, Skills, & Incomes of America's Workforce 2000. Lawrence R. Mishel & Ruy A. Teixeira. 1991. 12.00 (*0-944826-33-4*) Economic Policy Inst.

Myth of the Conqueror: Prince Henry Stuart, a Study of 17th Century Personation. Jerry W. Williamson. LC 77-78318. (Studies in the Renaissance: No. 2). 1978. 34.50 (*0-404-16004-2*) AMS Pr.

Myth of the Cross. A. D. Ajijola. 1996. pap. 10.50 (*1-56744-167-X*) Kazi Pubns.

Myth of the Electronic Library: Librarianship & Social Change in America, 82. William F. Birdsall. LC 93-49534. (Contributions in Librarianship & Information Science Ser.: No. 82). 224p. 1994. 59.95 (*0-313-29210-8*, Greenwood Pr) Greenwood.

Myth of the Eternal Return: or Cosmos & History. Mircea Eliade. Tr. by Willard R. Trask. (Bollingen Ser.: Vol. 46). 212p. 1991. text 39.50 (*0-691-09798-4*, Pub. by Princeton U Pr); pap. text 10.95 (*0-691-01777-8*, Pub. by Princeton U Pr) Cal Prin Full Svc.

Myth of the Explorer. Beau Riffenburgh. (Polar Research Ser.). (Illus.). 224p. 1993. text 59.00 (*1-85293-260-0*) St Martin.

Myth of the Fall & Walker Percy's Last Gentleman. Bernadette Prochaska. LC 91-42105. (American University Studies: American Literature: Ser. XXIV, Vol. 32). XI, 148p. 1993. pap. 29.95 (*0-8204-1806-4*) P Lang Pubng.

Myth of the First Three Years: A New Understanding of Early Brain Development & Lifelong Learning. John T. Bruer. LC 99-34934. 256p. 1999. pap. text 24.50 (*0-684-85184-9*) Free Pr.

Myth of the Framework. Karl Raimund Popper. 248p. (C). 1996. pap. 24.99 (*0-415-13555-9*) Routledge.

Myth of the Global Corporation. Paul N. Doremus et al. 1999. pap. 16.95 (*0-691-01007-2*, Pub. by Princeton U Pr) Cal Prin Full Svc.

Myth of the Goddess: The Evolution of an Image. Anne Baring & Jules Cashford. 800p. 1993. pap. 24.95 (*0-14-019292-1*, Arkana) Viking Penguin.

Myth of the Good Corporate Citizen: Democracy under the Rule of Big Business. Murray Dobbin. 320p. 1998. 23.95 (*0-7737-3087-7*) Stoddart Publ.

***Myth of the Great War.** John Mosier. 2001. write for info. (*0-06-019676-9*) HarpC.

Myth of the Greener Grass. rev. ed. J. Allan Petersen. 233p. 1984. pap. 9.99 (*0-8423-4651-1*) Tyndale Hse.

Myth of the Heroine: The Female Bildungsroman in the Twentieth-Century. 2nd ed. Esther K. Labovitz. (American University Studies: General Literature: Ser. XIX, Vol. 4). 272p. 1987. text 49.95 (*0-8204-0360-1*) P Lang Pubng.

Myth of the Independent Voter. Bruce E. Keith et al. (C). 1992. pap. 16.95 (*0-520-07720-2*, Pub. by U CA Pr) Cal Prin Full Svc.

Myth of the Jacobite Clans. Murray G. Pittock. 240p. 1996. pap. 25.00 (*0-7486-0715-3*, Pub. by Edinburgh U Pr) Col U Pr.

Myth of the Jew in France, 1967-1982. Henry Weinberg. 160p. 1993. pap. 14.95 (*0-88962-354-6*) Mosaic.

Myth of the Jewish Race. rev. ed. Raphael Patai & Jennifer Patai. LC 88-27721. (Illus.). 470p. reprint ed. pap. 145.70 (*0-608-10631-3*, 207125300009); reprint ed. pap. 145.70 (*0-608-06269-3*, 206659800008) Bks Demand.

An Asterisk (*) at the beginning of an entry indicates that the title is appearing for the first time.

Myth of the Lazy Native. Syed H. Alatas. 267p. 1977. 49.50 (*0-7146-3050-0*, BHA-03050, Pub. by F Cass Pubs) Intl Spec Bk.

*__Myth of the Liberal Media: An Edward Herman Reader.__ Edward S. Herman. LC 99-35205. (Media & Culture Ser.: Vol. 2). 344p. (C). 1999. pap. text 29.95 (*0-8204-4186-4*) P Lang Pubng.

Myth of the Llama. Jeri Massi. (Illus.). 118p. (Orig.). (J). (gr. 6). 1989. pap. 5.95 (*1-877778-00-1*) Llama Bks.

*__Myth of the Lost Cause & Civil War History.__ Gary W. Gallagher & Alan T. Nolan. LC 00-36978. 2000. 24.95 (*0-253-33822-0*) Ind U Pr.

Myth of the Lost Paradise in the Novels of Jacques Poulin. Paul G. Socken. LC 92-55126. 1993. 26.50 (*0-8386-3513-X*) Fairleigh Dickinson.

Myth of the Machine. Lewis Mumford. (Illus.). 1997. 14.98 (*1-56731-201-2*, MJF Bks) Fine Comms.

Myth of the Machine, 2 vols. Lewis Mumford. Incl. Vol. 1. Technics & Human Development. (Illus.). 384p. 1971. reprint ed. pap. 19.95 (*0-15-662341-2*, Harvest Bks); Vol. 2. Myth of the Machine. (Illus.). 544p. 1974. reprint ed. pap. 19.95 (*0-15-671610-0*, Harvest Bks); (Illus.). pap. write for info. (*0-318-52958-0*, Harvest Bks) Harcourt.

Myth of the Machine see Myth of the Machine

Myth of the Madding Crowd. Clark McPhail. (Social Institutions & Social Change Ser.). 295p. (Orig.). 1991. pap. text 27.95 (*0-202-30375-6*) Aldine de Gruyter.

Myth of the Madding Crowd. Clark McPhail. (Social Institutions & Social Change Ser.). 295p. 1991. lib. bdg. 51.95 (*0-202-30424-8*) Aldine de Gruyter.

Myth of the Magus. E. M. Butler. (Canto Book Ser.). 296p. (C). 1993. pap. 11.95 (*0-521-43777-6*) Cambridge U Pr.

Myth of the Maiden: On Being a Woman. Joan E. Childs. 250p. (Orig.). 1995. pap. 9.95 (*1-55874-315-4*, 3154) Health Comm.

*__Myth of the Male Breadwinner.__ Safa. 2000. pap. 24.00 (*0-8133-3729-1*, Pub. by Westview) HarpC.

Myth of the Male Breadwinner: Women & Industrialization in the Caribbean. Helen I. Safa. (Conflict & Social Change Ser.). 208p. (C). 1995. pap. 25.00 (*0-8133-1212-4*, Pub. by Westview) HarpC.

Myth of the Market: Promises & Illusions. Jeremy Seabrook. 189p. 1991. 47.99 (*1-895431-09-3*, Pub. by Black Rose); pap. 18.95 (*1-895431-08-5*, Pub. by Black Rose) Consort Bk Sales.

Myth of the Modern Homosexual: Queer History & the Search for Cultural Unity. Rictor Norton. LC 97-7785. 1997. 69.95 (*0-304-33891-5*); pap. 19.95 (*0-304-33892-3*) Continuum.

Myth of the Modern Presidency. David K. Nichols. 192p. (C). 1994. 35.00 (*0-271-01316-8*); pap. 15.95 (*0-271-01317-6*) Pa St U Pr.

Myth of the Nation & the Vision of Revolution: The Origins of Ideological Polarisation in the Twentieth Century. Jacob L. Talmon. LC 80-6167. 650p. reprint ed. pap. 200.00 (*0-7837-4680-6*, 204442700003) Bks Demand.

Myth of the Nation & Vision of Revolution: Ideological Polarization in the Twentieth Century. Jacob L. Talmon. 643p. (C). 1990. pap. 24.95 (*0-88738-844-2*) Transaction Pubs.

Myth of the Negro Past. Melville Jean Herskovits. LC 89-43083. 416p. 1990. reprint ed. pap. 17.00 (*0-8070-0905-9*) Beacon Pr.

*__Myth of the Noble Savage.__ Terry J. Ellingson. LC 99-59341. (Illus.). 504p. 2001. pap. 24.95 (*0-520-22610-0*, Pub. by U CA Pr) Cal Prin Full Svc.

*__Myth of the Noble Savage.__ Terry Jay Ellingson. LC 99-59341. (Illus.). 504p. 2001. 60.00 (*0-520-22268-7*, Pub. by U CA Pr) Cal Prin Full Svc.

Myth of the Other: Lacan, Foucault, Deleuze, Bataille. Franco Rella. Tr. & Intro. by Nelson Moe. (Post Modern Positions Ser.: Vol. 7). 120p. (C). 1994. pap. text 11.95 (*0-944624-21-9*); lib. bdg. 29.95 (*0-944624-20-0*) Maisonneuve Pr.

Myth of the Perfect Mother. Jane Swigart. LC 98-24864. 272p. 1998. pap. 14.95 (*0-8092-2938-2*, 293820, Contemporary Bks) NTC Contemp Pub Co.

Myth of the Picaro: Continuity & Transformation of the Picaresque Novel, 1554-1954. Alexander Blackburn. LC 78-23605. 279p. reprint ed. pap. 86.50 (*0-7837-2070-X*, 204234400004) Bks Demand.

Myth of the Powerless State. Linda Weiss. LC 97-48666. (Cornell Studies in Political Economy). 256p. 1998. text 45.00 (*0-8014-3547-1*); pap. text 17.95 (*0-8014-8543-6*) Cornell U Pr.

Myth of the Reine Margot Vol. 15: Toward the Elimination of a Legend. Robert J. Sealy. LC 93-46256. (Studies in the Humanities: Vol. 15). XIII, 226p. (C). 1995. text 45.95 (*0-8204-2480-3*) P Lang Pubng.

Myth of the Renaissance in Nineteenth-Century Writing. J. B. Bullen. LC 93-5373. (Illus.). 348p. 1994. text 75.00 (*0-19-812888-6*, Clarendon Pr) OUP.

Myth of the Resurrection & Other Essays. Joseph McCabe. LC 92-46038. (Freethought Library). 168p. (Orig.). (C). 1993. pap. 14.95 (*0-87975-833-3*) Prometheus Bks.

Myth of the Revolution: Hero Cults & the Institutionalization of the Mexican State, 1920-1940, 1. Ilene V. O'Malley. LC 85-30488. (Contributions to the Study of World History Ser.: No. 1). 211p. 1986. 49.95 (*0-313-25184-3*, OMR/, Greenwood Pr) Greenwood.

Myth of the Robber Barons. 3rd rev. ed. Burton W. Folsom, Jr. 170p. 1996. pap. 9.95 (*0-9630203-1-5*) Young Am Found.

Myth of the Ruling Class: Gaetano Mosca & the "Elite" Pref. by James H. Meisel. LC 80-13080. 432p. 1980. reprint ed. lib. bdg. 65.00 (*0-313-22346-7*, MEMR, Greenwood Pr) Greenwood.

Myth of the Starlite Dance: I Used to Be a Rock & Roll Star. Larry Vernieri. LC 97-67921. 1997. mass mkt., per. 19.95 (*1-889131-16-4*) CasAnanda.

Myth of the State. Ernst Cassirer. (C). 1961. pap. 15.00 (*0-300-00036-7*, y33) Yale U Pr.

Myth of the State. Ernst Cassirer. LC 82-18392. 303p. 1983. reprint ed. lib. bdg. 38.50 (*0-313-23790-5*, CAMO, Greenwood Pr) Greenwood.

Myth of the Titanic. Howelss. LC 98-53552. (Illus.). 272p. 1999. text 29.95 (*0-312-22148-7*) St Martin.

Myth of the Twentieth Century. Alfred Rosenberg. Orig. Title: Der Mythos des 20. Jahrhunderts. 1984. lib. bdg. 250.00 (*0-87700-605-9*) Revisionist Pr.

Myth of the University: Ideal & Reality in Higher Education. Paul Shore. 250p. (C). 1991. pap. text 27.00 (*0-8191-8269-9*); lib. bdg. 52.00 (*0-8191-8268-0*) U Pr of Amer.

Myth of the Virgin of Guadalupe. Rius. Orig. Title: El Mito Guadalupano. 69p. 1988. pap. 9.00 (*0-910309-52-3*, 5439) Am Atheist.

Myth of the Welfare Queen: A Pulitzer Prize-Winning Journalist's Portrait of Women on the Line. David Zucchino. 320p. 1999. pap. 13.00 (*0-684-84006-5*) S&S Trade.

Myth of the Welfare State. Jack D. Douglas. 505p. (C). 1990. pap. 24.95 (*0-88738-874-4*) Transaction Pubs.

Myth of the World Food Shortage. 1991. lib. bdg. 79.95 (*0-8490-4422-7*) Gordon Pr.

Myth of Theory. William Righter. LC 93-30388. 234p. (C). 1994. text 54.95 (*0-521-44544-2*) Cambridge U Pr.

Myth of Victory: What Is Victory in War? Richard Hobbs. LC 79-4703. (Westview Special Studies in Peace, Conflict & Conflict Resolution). 566p. 1979. 40.00 (*0-89158-388-2*) ColDoc Pubng.

Myth of Warmth. Jesse W. Nash. LC 93-72178. 78p. (Orig.). 1994. pap. 12.95 (*0-9625762-4-7*) Art Review Pr.

Myth of Wild Africa: Conservation Without Illusion. Jonathan S. Adams & Thomas O. McShane. (Illus.). 266p. 1997. pap. 16.95 (*0-520-20671-1*, Pub. by U CA Pr) Cal Prin Full Svc.

Myth of Women's Masochism. 2nd ed. Paula J. Caplan. 280p. 1993. pap. 18.95 (*0-8020-7745-5*) U of Toronto Pr.

Myth of Workers Control. Arthur Scargill & Peggy Kahn. (C). 1988. text 35.00 (*0-7855-3169-6*, Pub. by Univ Nottingham) St Mut.

Myth, Oil & Politics: Introduction to the Political Economy of Petroleum. Charles F. Doran. LC 77-4571. (Illus.). 1977. 22.95 (*0-02-907580-7*) Free Pr.

Myth or Reality: Adaptive Strategies of Asian Americans in California. Lilly Cheng et al. LC 92-38080. 212p. 1992. pap. 27.95 (*0-7507-0073-4*, Falmer Pr) Taylor & Francis.

Myth, Origins, Magic: A Study of Form in Eli Mandel's Writing. Andrew Stubbs. 1997. pap. 14.95 (*0-88801-170-9*, Pub. by Turnstone Pr) Genl Dist Srvs.

Myth Persephone: Demeter Artemis see Greek Mythology

Myth, Realism & the African Writer. Richard K. Priebe. Ed. by Stephen H. Arnold & George Lang. LC 88-71174. (Comparative Studies in African-Caribbean Literature Ser.). 200p. (C). 1988. 35.00 (*0-86543-097-7*); pap. 11.95 (*0-86543-098-5*) Africa World.

Myth, Reality & History: Selected Essays. Charles W. Toth. LC 76-26548. 207p. 1980. pap. 7.20 (*0-8477-0847-0*) U of PR Pr.

Myth, Reality & Reform: Higher Education Policy in Latin America. Claudio De Moura Castro & Daniel C. Levy. (Inter-American Development Bank Ser.). 122p. 2000. pap. 19.95 (*1-886938-60-1*) IADB.

Myth, Rhetoric, & Fiction: A Reading of Longus's Daphnis & Chloe. Bruce D. MacQueen. LC 90-12054. 297p. 1990. reprint ed. pap. 92.10 (*0-608-01856-2*, 206250600003) Bks Demand.

Myth, Ritual & Religion, 2 vols. Andrew Lang. 1993. 59.00 (*1-881338-46-0*) Nataraj Bks.

Myth, Ritual & Religion, 2 vols. in 1. Andrew Lang. LC 68-54280. reprint ed. 55.00 (*0-404-03868-9*) AMS Pr.

Myth, Symbol & Language: A Modern Perspective with Reference to India & Her Religions, Including Mythologem & Mythologene. Ananda. LC 98-906958. xi, 404 p. 1998. 58.00 (*81-7305-117-8*, Pub. by Aryan Bks Intl) S Asia.

Myth That Kills. Don Boone. (Illus.). 76p. 1997. pap. 9.95 (*1-56664-117-9*) WorldComm.

Myth the Fallen Lords: Unauthorized Secrets & Solutions. Joe G. Bell. LC 97-69251. 224p. 1997. per. 19.99 (*0-7615-1204-7*) Prima Pub.

Myth II: Soulblighter Official Strategies & Secrets. Bart Farkas. LC 98-88754. 256p. 1998. pap. 19.99 (*0-7821-2442-9*) Sybex.

Mythago Wood. Robert Holdstock. 288p. 1991. pap. 3.95 (*0-380-76276-5*, Avon Bks) Morrow Avon.

Mythago Wood. Robert Holdstock. 252p. 1984. pap. 25.00 (*0-89366-283-6*) Ultramarine Pub.

Mythanalysis. Pierre Solie. LC 98-21897. 160p. (Orig.). 1998. pap. 24.95 (*1-888602-03-1*, 031) Chiron Pubns.

*__Mythatypes: Signatures & Signs of African/Diaspora & Black Goddesses, 198.__ De Vita Brooks. LC 99-56463. (Contributions in Afro-American & African Studies: Vol. 198). 200p. 2000. 59.95 (*0-313-31068-8*, Greenwood Pr) Greenwood.

Mythe de Sisyphe. Albert Camus. (Folio Essais Ser.: No. 11). (FRE.). 1942. pap. 8.50 (*2-07-032288-2*) Schoenhof.

Mythe et Roman en Egypte Ancienne. E. Peters. 1998. 63.95 (*90-6831-890-X*, Pub. by Peeters Pub) Bks Intl VA.

Mythematics. Michael Stephans. 80p. 1993. 7.95 (*1-881168-45-X*) Red Danceflr.

Mythematics & Extropy II: Selected Literary Criticism of Boleslaw Lesmian. Boleslaw Lesmian. Ed. & Tr. by Alexandra Chciuk-Celt from POL. LC 91-20519. (American University Studies: Slavic Languages & Literature: Ser. XII, Vol. 3). 158p. (C). 1992. text 29.95 (*0-8204-1636-3*) P Lang Pubng.

*__Mythenbehandlung und Kompositionstechnik in Christa Wolfs Medea. Stimmen.__ Birgit Roser. 2000. 26.95 (*3-631-35480-0*) P Lang Pubng.

Mythenbildung und Erkenntnis: Eine Abhandlung Uber die Grundlagen der Philosophie. Gottlob F. Lipps. Ed. by Kees W. Bolle. LC 77-79141. (Mythology Ser.). 1978. lib. bdg. 30.95 (*0-405-10550-9*) Ayer.

*__Mythenbildungen Und Nationalismus.__ Wolfgang Reinbold. 319p. 1999. 47.95 (*3-906762-04-1*) P Lang Pubng.

Mythengeschichte der Asiatischen Welt: Mit Einen Anhang: Beitrage aus den Heidelberger Jahrbuchern. Joseph Gorres. Ed. by Kees W. Bolle. (Mythology Ser.). (GER.). 1978. reprint ed. lib. bdg. 59.95 (*0-405-10538-X*) Ayer.

Mythes de Platon: Etude Philosophique & Litteraire. Perceval Frutiger. LC 75-13269. (History of Ideas in Ancient Greece Ser.). (FRE.). 1980. reprint ed. 34.95 (*0-405-07310-0*) Ayer.

Mythic Archetypes in Ralph Waldo Emerson: A Blakean Reading. Richard R. O'Keefe. LC 95-1707. 232p. 1995. text 35.00 (*0-87338-518-7*) Kent St U Pr.

Mythic Artery: The Magic of Music Therapy. Carolyn B. Kenny. xiv, 154p. (Orig.). (C). 1982. pap. text 12.00 (*0-917930-60-6*); lib. bdg. 27.00 (*0-917930-74-6*) Ridgeview.

Mythic Astrology. Liz Greene. LC 94-12162. 224p. 1994. per. 24.95 (*0-671-50094-5*, Fireside) S&S Trade Pap.

Mythic Astrology: Archetypal Powers in the Horoscope. Ariel Guttman & Kenneth Johnson. LC 93-20514. (Illus.). 400p. 1999. pap. 17.95 (*0-87542-248-9*) Llewellyn Pubns.

*__Mythic Beings: Spirit Art of the Northwest Coast.__ Gary R. Wyatt. (Illus.). 144p. 1999. pap. text. write for info. (*90-5703-532-4*, Pub. by Craftsman House) Gordon & Breach.

Mythic Beings: Spirit Art of the Northwest Coast. Gary R. Wyatt. LC 99-22928. (Illus.). 160p. 1999. pap. 19.95 (*0-295-97798-1*) U of Wash Pr.

Mythic Black Fiction: The Transformation of History. Jane Campbell. LC 86-6909. 200p. (C). 1986. text 28.00 (*0-87049-508-9*) U of Tenn Pr.

Mythic Dimension: A Course on Mythology. J. Campbell. LC 96-46156. 272p. 1997. pap. 15.00 (*0-06-096612-2*) HarpC.

Mythic Dog, Friend Dog, Friends since the First Morning, Dog Myths from Around the World see Dogs of Myth

Mythic Family: An Essay. Judith Guest. LC 88-42974. 16p. (Orig.). 1988. pap. 3.50 (*0-915943-30-1*) Milkweed Ed.

Mythic Image. Joseph Campbell & M. J. Abadie. LC 79-166363. (Bollingen Ser.: No. C). (Illus.). 560p. 1981. pap. 39.50 (*0-691-01839-1*, Pub. by Princeton U Pr) Cal Prin Full Svc.

Mythic Image. J. Campbell. (Illus.). 552p. 1996. reprint ed. 10.98 (*1-56731-122-9*, MJF Bks) Fine Comms.

Mythic Imagination. J. Campbell. 2000. pap. 14.95 (*0-06-096610-6*) HarpC.

Mythic Imagination. J. Campbell. 2000. 30.00 (*0-06-055309-X*) HarperTrade.

Mythic Imagination: The Quest for Meaning Through Personal Mythology. Stephen Larsen. LC 95-54017. (Illus.). 432p. 1996. pap. 16.95 (*0-89281-574-4*, Inner Trad) Inner Tradit.

Mythic Ireland. Michael Dames. LC 91-67303. (Illus.). 272p. 1996. pap. 16.95 (*0-500-27872-5*, Pub. by Thames Hudson) Norton.

Mythic Journey: Gunter Grass's Tin Drum. Edward Diller. LC 73-86402. 224p. reprint ed. pap. 69.50 (*0-608-13085-0*, 201951600013) Bks Demand.

Mythic Journey: The Meaning of Myth As A Guide for Life. Liz Greene & Juliet Sharman-Burke. LC 99-41554. 288p. 2000. per. 18.00 (*0-684-86947-0*) S&S Trade.

Mythic Land Apart: Reassessing Southerners & Their History, 173. John D. Smith & Thomas H. Appleton. LC 96-27389. (Contributions in American History Ser.). 216p. 1997. 62.95 (*0-313-29304-X*, Greenwood Pr) Greenwood.

Mythic Life: Learning to Live Our Greater Story. Jean Houston. LC 95-21245. 352p. 1996. pap. 14.00 (*0-06-250282-4*, Pub. by Harper SF) HarpC.

Mythic Masks in Self-Reflexive Poetry: A Study of Pan & Orpheus. Dorothy Z. Baker. LC 85-16468. (Studies in Comparative Literature: No. 62). x, 186p. 1986. 29.95 (*0-8078-7062-5*) U of NC Pr.

Mythic Masks in Self-Reflexive Poetry: A Study of Pan & Orpheus. Dorothy Z. Baker. LC 85-16468. (University of North Carolina Studies in Comparative Literature: Vol. 62). 196p. reprint ed. pap. 60.80 (*0-608-08602-9*, 206912500003) Bks Demand.

Mythic Past: Biblical Archaeology & the Myth of Israel. Thomas L. Thompson. LC 99-186293. 432p. 1999. text 30.00 (*0-465-00622-1*, Pub. by Basic) HarpC.

Mythic Path: Discovering the Guiding Stories of Your Past - Creating a Vision for Your Future. David Feinstein & Stanley Krippner. LC 96-26397. (Inner Work Bks.). (Illus.). 336p. (Orig.). 1997. pap. 17.95 (*0-87477-857-3*, Tarcher Putnam) Putnam Pub Group.

Mythic Patterns in Ibsen's Last Plays. Orley I. Holtan. LC 74-139960. 223p. 1970. reprint ed. pap. 69.20 (*0-7837-2947-2*, 205750700006) Bks Demand.

*__Mythic Places.__ Judith Tate O'Brien. (Chapbook Ser.: Vol. 3). 32p. 2000. 5.00 (*0-9659832-3-4*) ByLine Pr.

Mythic Present. Max F. Schulz. (Illus.). 20p. (Orig.). 1995. pap. 20.00 (*0-945192-17-7*) USC Fisher Gallery.

Mythic Seas. Alan Smithee & Roderick Robertson. (Ars Magica Ser.). (Illus.). 96p. 1998. pap. 16.95 (*1-887801-69-3*, AG0259) Trident MN.

Mythic Symbolism & Cultural Anthropology in Three Early Works of Marguerite Yourcenar: Nouvelles Orientales, Le Coup de Grace, Comme l'Eau qui Coule. Patricia E. Frederick. LC 94-18376. 204p. 1994. text 89.95 (*0-7734-9079-5*) E Mellen.

Mythic Tarot. Juliet Sharman-Burke et al. 224p. 1986. per. 24.95 (*0-671-61863-6*, Fireside) S&S Trade Pap.

Mythic Tarot Workbook. Juliet Sharman-Burke. (Illus.). 160p. 1988. per. 10.95 (*0-671-65842-5*, Fireside) S&S Trade Pap.

*__Mythic Texas.__ Bryan Wooley. LC 99-39123. 1999. pap. 18.95 (*1-55622-696-9*) Wordware Pub.

Mythic Voice of Statius: Power & Politics in Thebaid. William J. Dominik. LC 94-16658. (Mnemosyne, Bibliotheca Classica Batava. Supplementum: Vol. 136). 1994. 81.00 (*90-04-09972-7*) Brill Academic Pubs.

Mythic West in Twentieth-Century America. Robert G. Athearn. LC 86-11106. (Illus.). xii, 324p. 1986. 35.00 (*0-7006-0304-2*); pap. 14.95 (*0-7006-0377-8*) U Pr of KS.

*__Mythic Women/Real Women: Plays & Performance Pieces by Women.__ Selected & Intro. by Lizbeth Goodman. 544p. 2000. pap. 18.00 (*0-571-19140-1*) Faber & Faber.

Mythic World of the Zuni: As Written by Frank Hamilton Cushing. Barton Wright. LC 87-22902. (Illus.). 167p. 1992. pap. 14.95 (*0-8263-1387-6*) U of NM Pr.

Mythical & Fabulous Creatures: A Sourcebook & Research Guide. Ed. by Malcolm South. LC 86-14964. (Illus.). 422p. 1987. lib. bdg. 49.95 (*0-313-24338-7*, SMY/, Greenwood Pr) Greenwood.

Mythical Animals Dot-to-Dot. Monica Russo. 1997. pap. text 59.50 (*0-8069-9883-0*) Sterling.

Mythical Animals Dot-to-Dot. Monica Russo. (Illus.). 64p. (J). 1997. pap. 5.95 (*0-8069-9716-8*) Sterling.

*__Mythical Aryans & Their Invasion.__ 2nd ed. N. R. Waradpande. 2000. 34.00 (*81-85016-57-7*, Pub. by Bks & Bks) S Asia.

*__Mythical Beasts.__ Alexandra Bonfante-Warren. (Illus.). 176p. 2000. 19.98 (*1-56799-985-9*) M Friedman Pub Grp Inc.

Mythical Beasts: Gift Anthologies. 1999. 11.95 (*1-85967-286-8*, Pub. by Lorenz Anness) Random.

Mythical Beasts Coloring Book. Fridolf Johnson. (Illus.). (J). (gr. k-3). 1976. pap. 2.95 (*0-486-23353-7*) Dover.

Mythical Beasts Stained Glass Coloring Book. Copeland. (Illus.). pap. 3.95 (*0-486-28899-4*) Dover.

Mythical Beasts Stickers. John O'Brien. (Illus.). (J). 1994. pap. 1.00 (*0-486-28282-1*) Dover.

Mythical Body of Christ in the Modern World. unabridged ed. Denis Fahey. 364p. 1939. reprint ed. pap. 15.00 (*0-945001-48-7*) GSG & Assocs.

Mythical Creatures of the U. S. A. & Canada. Walker D. Wyman. (Illus.). 105p. 1978. pap. 4.95 (*0-686-27300-1*) U Wisc-River Falls Pr.

Mythical Expressions of Siege in Israeli Films. Nitzan S. Ben-Shaul. LC 97-12630. (Studies in Art & Religious Interpretation: No. 17). 156p. 1997. text 69.95 (*0-7734-8608-9*) E Mellen.

Mythical Image: The Ideal of India in German Romanticism. Leslie A. Willson. LC 64-14083. 275p. reprint ed. pap. 85.30 (*0-608-15045-2*, 202621900048) Bks Demand.

Mythical Intentions in Modern Literature. Eric Gould. LC 81-47132. 290p. reprint ed. pap. 89.90 (*0-7837-1409-2*, 204176300023) Bks Demand.

Mythical Journeys, Legendary Quests: The Spiritual Search - Traditional Stories from World Mythology. Moyra Caldecott. LC 96-229518. (Illus.). 176p. 1996. 27.95 (*0-7137-2546-X*, Pub. by Blandford Pr) Sterling.

*__Mythical Land, Legal Boundaries: Land Rites & Land Rights in Cultural & Historical Context.__ Allen Abramson. 2000. pap. text 22.50 (*0-7453-1570-4*) Pluto GBR.

Mythical Lands: Artography. Larry Elmore. (Illus.). 1999. pap. 20.00 (*1-892519-05-4*) Archangel Ent.

Mythical Lovers, Divine Desires The World's Great Love Legends. Sarah Bartlett. 1999. 24.95 (*0-7137-2718-7*) Blandford Pr.

Mythical Man-Month: Essays on Software Engineering. anniversary ed. Frederick P. Brooks, Jr. (Illus.). 336p. (C). 1995. pap. text 24.95 (*0-201-83595-9*) Addison-Wesley.

Mythical Monsters. Charles Gould. 1976. lib. bdg. 134.95 (*0-8490-2324-6*) Gordon Pr.

Mythical Monsters. Charles Gould. LC 81-50199. (Secret Doctrine Reference Ser.). (Illus.). 412p. 1981. reprint ed. 22.00 (*0-913510-38-6*) Wizards.

Mythical Monsters: Fact or Fiction? Charles Gould. (Illus.). 407p. 1998. reprint ed. pap. text 20.00 (*0-7881-5368-4*) DIANE Pub.

Mythical Mufferaw. Bernie Bedore. (Illus.). 96p. (J). Date not set. pap. 10.95 (*1-55082-087-7*, Pub. by Quarry Pr) LPC InBook.

Mythical Past Elusive Future: History & Society in an Anxious Age. Furedi. 310p. (C). 49.95 (*0-7453-0530-X*, Pub. by Pluto GBR); pap. 18.95 (*0-7453-0531-8*, Pub. by Pluto GBR) Stylus Pub VA.

Mythical Sand Painting of the Navajo Indians, No. 8. James Stevenson. (Smithsonian Institution, Bureau of Ethnology Ser.). (Illus.). 77p. pap. text 9.06 (*1-55567-819-X*) Coyote Press.

Mythical Trickster Figures: Contours, Contexts & Criticisms. Ed. by William J. Hynes & William G. Doty. LC 92-19629. 328p. (C). 1993. text 44.95 (*0-8173-0599-8*) U of Ala Pr.

*__Mythical West: An Encyclopedia of Legend, Lore, & Popular Culture.__ Richard W. Slatta. 2001. lib. bdg. 65.00 (*1-57607-151-0*) ABC-CLIO.

An Asterisk (*) at the beginning of an entry indicates that the title is appearing for the first time.

Mythical World of Nazi War Propaganda, 1939-1945. Jay W. Baird. LC 74-83132. (Illus.). 349p. reprint ed. pap. 108.20 (*0-8357-8961-6*, 203320300085) Bks Demand.

Mything Link: A Study Guide on Gospel, Culture & Media. Dave Pomeroy. 1990. pap. 5.95 (*0-377-00208-9*) Friendship Pr.

Mythistory & Other Essays. William H. McNeill. LC 85-8584. x, 226p. 1995. 23.95 (*0-226-56135-6*) U Ch Pr.

***Mythmaker: The Life & Work of George Lucas.** John Baxter. 464p. 2000. pap. 14.00 (*0-380-81188-X*, HarpEntertain) Morrow Avon.

***Mythmaker: The Life & Work of George Lucas, Vol. 1.** John Baxter. LC 99-37051. (Illus.). 496p. 1999. 27.50 (*0-380-97833-4*, Avon Bks) Morrow Avon.

Mythmakers. Mary Barnard. LC 66-20061. 213p. 1986. reprint ed. 12.95 (*0-932576-36-2*) Breitenbush Bks.

Mythmakers: Gospel, Culture & the Media. William F. Fore. 1990. pap. 7.95 (*0-377-00207-0*) Friendship Pr.

Mythmakers: Intellectuals & the Intelligentsia in Perspective, 63. Ed. by Raj P. Mohan. LC 86-29597. (Contributions in Sociology Ser.: No. 63). 159p. 1987. 49.95 (*0-313-25836-8*, MMY/, Greenwood Pr) Greenwood.

Mythmaker's Magic: Behind the Illusion of "Creation Science" Delos McKown. LC 92-34549. 180p. (C). 1993. 27.95 (*0-87975-770-1*) Prometheus Bks.

Mythmakers of the American Dream. Wiley L. Umphlett. LC 81-67781. (Illus.). 224p. 1983. 40.00 (*0-8453-4739-X*, Cornwall Bks) Assoc Univ Prs.

Mythmakers of the American Dream: The Nostalgic Vision in Popular Culture. Wiley L. Umphlett. LC 78-75342. (Illus.). 192p. 1983. 40.00 (*0-8387-3123-6*) Bucknell U Pr.

Mythmaking: Heal Your Past, Claim Your Future. Patricia Montgomery. LC 95-167758. 224p. 1994. pap. 14.95 (*0-9638327-3-5*) Sibyl Pubns.

Mythmaking & Metaphor in Black Women's Fiction. Jacqueline De Weever. 200p. 1992. pap. 15.95 (*0-312-06533-7*); text 35.00 (*0-312-06532-9*) St Martin.

Mythmaking Frame of Mind: Social Imagination & American Culture. James Gilbert et al. 325p. (C). 1992. 23.50 (*0-534-19038-3*) Wadsworth Pub.

Mytho-Cycle Heroique dans l'Aire. E. Peters. 1998. 60.95 (*90-6831-813-6*, Pub. by Peeters Pub) Bks Intl VA.

***Mytho-Empiricism of Gnosticism: Triumph of the Vanquished.** S. Giora Shoham. 272p. 1999. pap. 24.95 (*1-902210-26-3*, Pub. by Sussex Acad Pr) Intl Spec Bk.

Mythographi Graeci Vol. I: Apollodori, Pediasmi. Ed. by Wagner. (GRE.). 1996. reprint ed. 95.00 (*3-519-11543-3*, T1543, Pub. by B G Teubner) U of Mich Pr.

Mythographic Art: Classical Fable & the Rise of the Vernacular in Early France & England. Ed. by Jane Chance. 350p. 1990. 49.95 (*0-8130-0974-X*); pap. 19.95 (*0-8130-0984-7*) U Press Fla.

Mythographic Chaucer: The Fabulation of Sexual Politics. Jane Chance. LC 94-10265. 1994. pap. 19.95 (*0-8166-2277-9*) U of Minn Pr.

Mythography: The Study of Myths & Rituals. William G. Doty. LC 85-991. 352p. 1987. pap. text 22.95 (*0-8173-0398-7*) U of Ala Pr.

***Mythography: The Study of Myths & Rituals.** William G. Doty. LC 99-6781. 2000. 54.95 (*0-8173-1005-3*) U of Ala Pr.

***Mythography: The Study of Myths & Rituals.** 2nd ed. William G. Doty. LC 99-6781. 2000. pap. 24.95 (*0-8173-1006-1*) U of Ala Pr.

Mytholog: Poems. Robley E. Whitson. 100p. 1995. pap. text 12.00 (*1-55605-254-5*) Wyndham Hall.

Mythological Astronomy of the Ancients Demonstrated, Pt. 1. Samson A. Mackey. LC 73-84043. (Secret Doctrine Reference Ser.). 380p. 1973. reprint ed. 17.00 (*0-913510-06-8*) Wizards.

Mythological Bonds Between East & West. Dorothea Chaplin. 1976. lib. bdg. 59.95 (*0-8490-2325-4*) Gordon Pr.

Mythological Creatures & the Chinese Zodiac in Origami. John Montroll. LC 95-83963. (Illus.). 120p. 1996. pap. 9.95 (*1-877656-11-9*) Antroll Pub.

Mythological Creatures & the Chinese Zodiac in Origami. John Montroll. (Illus.). 128p. 1996. pap. 10.95 (*0-486-28971-0*) Dover.

Mythological Creatures Iron-On Transfer Patterns. Marty Noble. (Illus.). 48p. 1998. pap. 3.95 (*0-486-40093-X*) Dover.

Mythological Expressions of Southwestern Design. Leo J. Korte & Judith Adamson. (Illus.). 136p. 1997. 42.00 (*0-9661655-1-9*); pap. 28.00 (*0-9661655-0-0*); lib. bdg. 28.00 (*0-9661655-2-7*) Kortes Pub.

Mythological Foundations of the Epic Genre: The Solar Voyage as the Hero's Journey. Hugh Fox. LC 88-37960. (Studies in Epic & Romance Literature: Vol. 1). 250p. 1989. lib. bdg. 89.95 (*0-88946-109-0*) E Mellen.

Mythological Monsters: Visuals & Learning Activities. Stern Sloan Price. 32p. (Orig.). 1999. pap. 5.99 (*0-8431-7517-6*, Price Stern) Peng Put Young Read.

Mythological Monsters: Visuals & Learning Activities. Ian Thompson. (Illus.). 23p. 1991. pap. 3.25 (*0-939507-26-9*, B309) Amer Classical.

Mythologie der Chinesischen Antike: Mit Ausblick auf Spatere Entwicklungen. Wolfgang Munke. (GER., Illus.). 457p. 1998. 82.95 (*3-631-32776-5*) P Lang Pubng.

Mythologie des Plantes: Ou les Legendes du Regne Vegetal. Angelo De Gubernatis. Ed. by Kees W. Bolle. LC 77-79128. (Mythology Ser.). 1978. reprint ed. lib. bdg. 57.95 (*0-405-10539-8*) Ayer.

Mythologie Matriarche Chez Claudel, Montherlant, Crommelynck, Ionesco, et Genet. Gisele Feal. LC 92-27580. (American University Studies: Romance Languages & Literature: Ser. II, Vol. 195). XI, 174p. (C). 1993. text 38.95 (*0-8204-1971-0*) P Lang Pubng.

Mythologie Primitive. 2nd ed. Lucien Levy-Bruhl. LC 75-35138. 1976. reprint ed. 57.50 (*0-404-14154-4*) AMS Pr.

Mythologie Universelle (Universal Mythology) Alexandre H. Krappe. Ed. by Kees W. Bolle. LC 77-79135. (Mythology Ser.). 1978. reprint ed. lib. bdg. 40.95 (*0-405-10545-2*) Ayer.

Mythologies. Roland Barthes. Tr. by Annette Lavers. 159p. 1972. pap. 10.00 (*0-374-52150-6*) FS&G.

Mythologies. Roland Barthes. (FRE.). 256p. 1970. 34.95 (*0-686-53938-9*, F80570); pap. 14.95 (*0-7859-0665-7*, F80570) Fr & Eur.

Mythologies. Roland Barthes. 1983. 22.50 (*0-8446-5982-7*) Peter Smith.

Mythologies, 2 vols. Ed. by Yves Bonnefoy. Tr. by Wendy Doniger. LC 90-46982. 1312p. 1991. lib. bdg. 300.00 (*0-226-06453-0*) U Ch Pr.

Mythologies. William Butler Yeats. 384p. 1998. per. 14.00 (*0-684-82621-6*) S&S Trade Pap.

Mythologies: The Sculpture of Helaine Blumenfeld. Nicola Upson & Helaine Blumenfeld. LC 98-17327. (Illus.). 248p. 1998. 65.00 (*0-87951-880-4*, Pub. by Overlook Pr) Penguin Putnam.

Mythologies of Danger. Jacqueline Berger. 86p. 1998. 24.00 (*1-878325-18-3*); pap. 11.00 (*1-878325-19-1*) Bluestem Press.

Mythologies of the East: A Detailed Description & Explanation of the Mythologies of All the Great Nations of Asia, 2 vols. J. Hackin et al. 1996. reprint ed. 175.00 (*81-7305-020-1*, Pub. by Aryan Bks Intl) S Asia.

Mythologies of the East: Indian Subcontinent, Middle East, Nepal & Tibet, Indo-China & Java: A Detailed Description & Explanation of the Mythologies of All the Great Nations of Asia. Ed. by J. Hackin et al. (Illus.). 240p. 1996. 110.00 (*81-7305-018-X*, Pub. by Aryan Bks Intl) Nataraj Bks.

Mythologies of the East Vol. 2: Central Asia, China, Japan: A Detailed Description & Explanation of the Mythologies of All the Great Nations of Asia. Ed. by J. Hackin et al. (Illus.). xxi, 220p. 1996. 110.00 (*81-7305-019-8*, Pub. by Aryan Bks Intl) Nataraj Bks.

Mythologies of the Heart. Gerard Malanga. LC 95-53182. (Illus.). 179p. (Orig.). (C). 1996. 25.00 (*0-87685-994-5*); pap. 13.50 (*0-87685-993-7*) Black Sparrow.

Mythologies of the Heart, signed ed. deluxe ed. Gerard Malanga. LC 95-53182. (Illus.). 179p. (Orig.). (C). 1996. 35.00 (*0-87685-995-3*) Black Sparrow.

Mythologies of Violence in Postmodern Media. Ed. by Christopher Sharrett. LC 99-24232. (Contemporary Film & Television Ser.). 528p. 1999. pap. 24.95 (*0-8143-2742-7*) Wayne St U Pr.

Mythologies of Violence in Postmodern Media. Ed. by Christopher Sharrett. LC 99-24232. (Contemporary Film & Television Ser.). 528p. 1999. 49.95 (*0-8143-2879-2*) Wayne St U Pr.

***Mythologies of Vision: Image, Culture & Visuality.** Eduardo Neiva. LC 98-25975. (Semiotics & the Human Sciences Ser.: Vol. 15). 254p. (C). 1999. text 50.95 (*0-8204-4184-8*, 41848) P Lang Pubng.

Mythologische Forschungen Aus Dem Nachlasse, 2 vols. Wilhelm Mannhardt. Ed. by Kees W. Bolle. LC 77-79142. (Mythology Ser.). (GER.). 1978. reprint ed. lib. bdg. 42.95 (*0-405-10551-7*) Ayer.

Mythologizing Uruguayan Reality in the Works of Jose Pedro Diaz. Marie J. Peck. LC 85-5910. 130p. 1985. pap. 8.00 (*0-87918-058-7*) ASU Lat Am St.

***Mythology.** (Collins Gem Ser.). (Illus.). 256p. 2000. pap. 7.95 (*0-00-472370-8*, Pub. by HarpC) Trafalgar.

Mythology. Thomas Bulfinch. (Laurel Classic Ser.). 1959. 12.09 (*0-606-00434-3*, Pub. by Turtleback) Demco.

Mythology. Center for Learning Network Staff. 269p. (YA). (gr. 9-12). spiral bd. 37.95 (*1-56077-395-2*) Ctr Learning.

***Mythology.** D K Publishing Staff. (Eyewitness Books). (Illus.). (J). (gr. 4-7). 2000. 19.99 (*0-7894-6627-9*) DK Pub Inc.

Mythology. Edith Hamilton. 1976. 31.95 (*0-8488-1037-6*) Amereon Ltd.

Mythology. Edith Hamilton. (Illus.). 497p. (YA). (gr. 7 up). 1942. 27.95 (*0-316-34114-2*) Little.

***Mythology.** Edith Hamilton. 1998. mass mkt. 13.00 (*0-316-19152-3*, Back Bay) Little.

Mythology. Edith Hamilton. 1969. 11.05 (*0-606-00198-0*, Pub. by Turtleback) Demco.

***Mythology.** Gloria Levine. 44p. (YA). 1999. 11.95 (*1-56137-817-8*) Novel Units.

Mythology. Kathryn Petras & Ross Petras. (Fandex Family Field Guide Ser.). (Illus.). 1998. pap. 9.95 (*0-7611-1207-3*) Workman Pub.

***Mythology.** Neil Philip. (Eyewitness Books). (J). (gr. 4-7). 2000. 15.95 (*0-7894-6288-5*) DK Pub Inc.

Mythology. Neil Philip. LC 98-32234. 1999. lib. bdg. 20.99 (*0-375-90135-3*) Knopf.

***Mythology.** Neil Philips. LC 98-32234. 60p. (YA). (gr. 5-9). 1999. 19.00 (*0-375-80135-9*) Knopf.

Mythology. rev. ed. James Weigel, Jr. (Cliffs Notes Ser.). 216p. 1973. pap. 7.95 (*0-8220-0865-3*, Cliff) IDG Bks.

Mythology, No. 4. Rebecca Stark. Date not set. teacher ed. 5.95 (*1-56644-967-7*, 967-7ADB) Educ Impress.

Mythology, No. 4 Rebecca Stark. Date not set. teacher ed. 10.95 (*1-56644-965-0*) Educ Impress.

Mythology: A Cooperative Learning Unit. James Scott. 64p. (YA). (gr. 7-12). 1996. pap., wbk. ed. 4.50 (*1-58049-107-3*, CO07A) Prestwick Hse.

Mythology: A Short Story about Creation, Gods, & Revenge. Nicholas J. Cipriani. 34p. (Orig.). 1996. pap. 5.95 (*0-9653570-2-3*) N J Cipriani.

Mythology: Classical. Arthur Cotterell. 1999. 12.95 (*1-85967-993-5*, Lorenz Bks) Anness Pub.

Mythology: From Ancient to Post-Modern. Ed. by Jurgen Kleist & Bruce A. Butterfield. LC 91-44219. (Plattsburgh Studies in the Humanities: Vol. 1). (Illus.). 219p. (C). 1992. text 39.95 (*0-8204-1742-4*) P Lang Pubng.

Mythology: Greek & Roman. Thomas H. Carpenter & Robert J. Gula. (Illus.). (gr. 10). 1977. pap. text 9.25 (*0-88334-089-5*) Longman.

Mythology: Tales of Ancient Civilizations. Timothy R. Roberts et al. LC 97-53045. (Illus.). 448p. 1998. 29.98 (*1-56799-664-7*, Friedman-Fairfax) M Friedman Pub Grp Inc.

Mythology: The Voyage of the Hero. 3rd ed. David A. Leeming. (Illus.). 288p. 1998. 30.00 (*0-19-512153-8*); pap. 16.95 (*0-19-511957-6*) OUP.

Mythology: Timeless Tales of Gods & Heroes. Edith Hamilton. (Illus.). 512p. 1998. pap. 12.95 (*0-316-34151-7*, Back Bay) Little.

Mythology: Timeless Tales of Gods & Heroes. Edith Hamilton. (Illus.). 352p. 1999. mass mkt. 6.99 (*0-446-60725-8*, Pub. by Warner Bks) Little.

Mythology Vol. 61-65: Chinese Children's Stories. Hwa-I Publishing Co., Staff. Ed. by Emily Ching et al. Tr. by Wonder Kids Publications Staff from CHI. (Mythology Ser.). (Illus.). 28p. (J). (gr. 3-6). 1991. reprint ed. 39.75 (*1-56162-061-0*) Wonder Kids.

Mythology & Folklore of the Hui, a Muslim Chinese People. Shuiang Li. 459p. 1996. pap. 19.95 (*0-614-21520-X*, 1356) Kazi Pubns.

Mythology & Folklore of the Hui, a Muslim Chinese People. Shujiang Li & Karl W. Luckert. Tr. by Fenglan Yu et al. LC 93-21529. (Illus.). 459p. (C). 1994. text 22.50 (*0-7914-1823-5*) State U NY Pr.

Mythology & Folktales: Their Relation & Interpretation. Edwin S. Hartland. LC 75-144519. (Popular Studies in Mythology, Romance & Folklore: No. 7). reprint ed. 27.50 (*0-404-53507-0*) AMS Pr.

Mythology & History: The Great Paintings of the Prada. Rosa Lopez Torrijos. 1998. 35.00 (*1-85759-189-5*) Scala Books.

Mythology & Meatballs: A Greek Island Diary-Cookbook. Daniel Spoerri. Tr. by Emmett Williams from FRE. LC 82-16355. (Illus.). 238p. 1982. 16.95 (*0-943186-01-3*); pap. 10.95 (*0-943186-02-1*, 0-671-55843-9) Aris Bks.

Mythology & Misogyny: The Social Discourse of Nineteenth-Century British Classical-Subject Painting. Joseph A. Kestner. LC 87-40365. (Illus.). 440p. reprint ed. pap. 136.40 (*0-608-20446-3*, 207169900002) Bks Demand.

Mythology & the Bible. Corinne Heline. 75p. 1972. pap. text 12.00 (*0-933963-13-0*) New Age Bible.

Mythology & the Tolerance of the Javanese. 2nd rev. ed. Benedict R. Anderson. LC 97-208972. (Modern Indonesia Project Ser.: Vol. 37). (Illus.). 104p. (C). 1997. pap. 12.00 (*0-87763-041-0*) Cornell SE Asia.

Mythology & You. Donna Rosenberg. 304p. 1992. pap., student ed. 22.53 (*0-8442-5561-0*) NTC Contemp Pub Co.

Mythology & You. Donna Rosenberg & Sorelle Baker. (Illus.). 304p. 1993. pap. 19.95 (*0-8442-5594-7*, 55947, Natl Textbk Co) NTC Contemp Pub Co.

Mythology & You: Classical Mythology & Its Relevance to Today's World. (C). pap., teacher ed. 6.99 (*0-8442-5562-9*, X5562-9) NTC Contemp Pub Co.

Mythology As Metaphor: Romantic Irony, Critical Theory & Wagner's Ring, 46. Mary A. Cicora. LC 98-9606. (Contributions to the Study of Music & Dance Ser.: Vol. 46). 184p. 1998. 59.95 (*0-313-30528-5*, Greenwood Pr) Greenwood.

***Mythology, Edith Hamilton's: Reproducible Teaching Unit.** James Scott. 54p. (YA). (gr. 7-12). 1999. ring bd. 29.50 (*1-58049-189-8*, TU126) Prestwick Hse.

***Mythology for Children of the Twenty-First Century: Book One -- In the Beginning.** Paul Gershowitz. (Illus.). 32p. 2000. pap. 9.00 (*0-8059-4902-X*) Dorrance.

Mythology for the 21st Century: Mythologie pour le Vingt-et-Unieme Siecle. Allen A. Dutton. Ed. by Pat Eason & Mary Hawkins. Tr. by Edwin P. Grobe. (ENG & FRE., Illus.). 70p. (Orig.). 1990. pap. 25.00 (*0-9625682-0-1*) Jeckwoe Pub.

Mythology of Cats: Feline Legend & Lore Through the Ages. Gerald Hausman & Loretta Hausman. LC 98-5921. 224p. 1998. text 21.95 (*0-312-18633-9*) St Martin.

***Mythology of Cats: Feline Legend & Lore Through the Ages.** Gerald Hausman & Loretta Hausman. 224p. 2000. pap. 12.95 (*0-425-17449-2*) Berkley Pub.

***Mythology of Crime & Criminal Justice.** 3rd ed. Victor E. Kappeler et al. 354p. (C). 2000. pap. 19.95 (*1-57766-078-1*) Waveland Pr.

Mythology of Dogs: Canine Legend. Gerald Hausman et al. (Illus.). 288p. 1997. pap. 12.95 (*0-312-18139-6*) St Martin.

Mythology of Mexico & Central America. John Bierhorst. LC 90-5879. (Illus.). 256p. (YA). (gr. 7 up). 1990. 17.00 (*0-688-06721-2*, Wm Morrow) Morrow Avon.

Mythology of Middle-earth. Ruth S. Noel. LC 78-303237. 198p. 1977. write for info. (*0-500-01187-7*) Thames Hudson.

Mythology of Modern Law. Peter Fitzpatrick. LC 92-296. (Sociology of Law & Crime Ser.). 256p. (C). 1992. pap. 27.99 (*0-415-08263-3*, A7806) Routledge.

***Mythology of Native America.** David Leeming. 224p. 2000. pap. text 11.95 (*0-8061-3239-6*) U of Okla Pr.

Mythology of Native North America. David Leeming & Jake Page. LC 97-18451. 224p. 1998. 22.95 (*0-8061-3012-1*) U of Okla Pr.

Mythology of North America: Introduction to Classic Native American Gods, Heroes & Tricksters. John Bierhorst. LC 85-281. (Illus.). 272p. (YA). (gr. 7 up). 1986. pap. 13.00 (*0-688-06666-6*, Wm Morrow) Morrow Avon.

Mythology of Sex. Sarah Dening. (Illus.). 224p. 1996. 27.50 (*0-02-861207-8*) Macmillan.

Mythology of Sex: An Illustrated Exploration of Sexual Customs & Practices from Ancient Times to the Present. Sarah Dening. (Illus.). 224p. 1998. text 28.00 (*0-7881-5536-9*) DIANE Pub.

Mythology of the Bella Coola Indians. Franz Boas. LC 73-3510. (Jesup North Pacific Expedition. Publications: Vol. 1, Pt. 2). reprint ed. 40.00 (*0-404-58113-7*) AMS Pr.

Mythology of the Blackfoot Indians. Tr. by Clark Wissler & D. C. Duvall. LC 94-40882. (Sources of American Indian Oral Literature Ser.). xxxiii, 168p. 1995. pap. 9.95 (*0-8032-9762-9*, Bison Books) U of Nebr Pr.

Mythology of the Blackfoot Indians. Clark Wissler & D. C. Duvall. LC 74-9019. (Anthropological Papers of the American Museum of Natural History: Vol. 2, Pt. 1). (Illus.). reprint ed. 39.50 (*0-404-11916-6*) AMS Pr.

Mythology of the British Isles. Geoffrey Ashe. (Illus.). 304p. 1992. pap. 19.95 (*0-413-66540-2*) Random.

Mythology of the Hindus. Charles Coleman. (C). 1995. reprint ed. 88.00 (*81-206-0971-9*, Pub. by Asian Educ Servs) S Asia.

Mythology of the Lenape: Guide & Texts. John Bierhorst. LC 95-11567. 147p. 1995. 36.00 (*0-8165-1523-9*); pap. 19.95 (*0-8165-1573-5*) U of Ariz Pr.

Mythology of the Thompson Indians. James A. Teit. LC 73-3529. (Jesup North Pacific Expeditions. Publications: No. 8, Pt. 2). reprint ed. 54.00 (*0-404-58125-0*) AMS Pr.

Mythology of the Wichita. George A. Dorsey. LC 95-2857. 368p. 1995. pap. 12.95 (*0-8061-2778-3*, 2778) U of Okla Pr.

Mythology of the Zodiac: Tales of the Constellations. Marianne McDonald. (Illus.). 120p. 2000. 19.98 (*1-56799-581-0*, Friedman-Fairfax) M Friedman Pub Grp Inc.

Mythology of Transgression: Homosexuality As Metaphor. Jamake Highwater. LC 96-20576. 272p. 1997. 25.00 (*0-19-510180-4*) OUP.

***Mythology of Voice** Darsie Bowden. LC 99-34080. (Crosscurrents Ser.). 1999. 21.00 (*0-86709-481-8*, Pub. by Boynton Cook Pubs) Heinemann.

Mythology 101. Nye. 1993. 4.95 (*0-446-77754-4*) Warner Bks.

Mythology Series, 39 vols., Set. Ed. by Kees W. Bolle. (Illus.). 1978. lib. bdg. 1807.50 (*0-405-10529-0*); lib. bdg. 669.00 (*0-405-18984-2*) Ayer.

Mythology Smart Junior. Princeton Review Publishing Staff. LC 97-27239. 1997. pap. 10.00 (*0-679-78375-X*) Random.

Mythology Songbook. Ann Edwards et al. (Illus.). 29p. 1992. pap. 4.90 (*0-939507-20-X*, B208) Amer Classical.

Mythology, Spirituality, & History in an Amazonian Community. Andrew Gray. LC 95-37322. (Arakmbut of Amazonian Peru Ser.: Vol. 1). (Illus.). 272p. 1996. 59.95 (*1-57181-876-6*) Berghahn Bks.

Mythology's Last Gods: Yahweh & Jesus. William N. Harwood. LC 92-15252. 416p. (C). 1992. 49.95 (*0-87975-742-6*) Prometheus Bks.

Mythomania: Fantasies, Fables, & Sheer Lies in Contemporary American Popular Art. Bernard Welt. (Illus.). 128p. (Orig.). 1996. pap. 12.95 (*0-9637264-3-9*, 620481, Art Issues) Fnd Adv Crit.

Mythomanias: The Nature of Deception & Self-Deception. Ed. by Michael S. Myslobodsky. LC 96-13605. 416p. 1996. text 79.95 (*0-8058-1919-3*) L Erlbaum Assocs.

Mythopoeic Reality: The Postwar American Nonfiction Novel. Mas'ud Zavarzadeh. 272p. 1976. pap. text 11.95 (*0-252-00645-3*) U of Ill Pr.

Mythopoesis: Mythic Patterns in the Literary Classics. Harry Slochower. LC 96-11337. (Waynebooks Ser.: No. 35). 364p. 1970. pap. text 19.95 (*0-8143-1511-9*) Wayne St U Pr.

Mythopoesis & the Crisis of Postmodernism: Toward Integrating Image & Story. Lois J. Parker. 220p. 1998. pap. text 25.00 (*0-913412-79-1*) Brandon Hse.

***Mythopoetic Perspectives of Men's Healing Work: An Anthology for Therapists & Others.** Ed. by Edward Read Barton. LC 99-54739. 300p. 2000. 64.00 (*0-89789-646-7*, H646, Bergin & Garvey) Greenwood.

Mythos: The Shaping of Our Mythic Tradition. Joseph Campbell. (Illus.). 256p. 1999. text 39.95 (*1-86204-527-5*, Pub. by Element MA) Penguin Putnam.

Mythos & Logos in the Thought of Carl Jung: The Theory of the Collective Unconscious in Scientific Perspective. Walter A. Shelburne. LC 87-10210. 180p. (C). 1988. text 64.50 (*0-88706-693-3*); pap. text 21.95 (*0-88706-695-X*) State U NY Pr.

Mythos der Weiblichkeit im Werke Max Frischs. Liette Bohler. (Studies on the Themes & Motifs in Literature: Vol. 36). (GER.). VII, 237p. (C). 1998. 46.95 (*0-8204-3886-3*) P Lang Pubng.

Mythos-Kerygma-Wahrheit: Gesammelte Aufsatze Zum Alten Testament in Seiner Umwelt und Zur Biblischen Theologie. Hans-Peter Muller. (Beiheft zur Zeitschrift fuer die Alttestamentliche Wissenschaft Ser.: Band 200). (GER.). xiv, 319p. (C). 1991. lib. bdg. 101.55 (*3-11-012885-3*) De Gruyter.

Mythos of the Ark. J. W. Lake. 1993. reprint ed. pap. 8.95 (*1-55818-199-7*, Sure Fire) Holmes Pub.

Mythos und Komodie. Untersuchungen Zu Den "Vogeln" Des Aristophanes. Heinz Hofmann. (Spudasmata Ser.: Bd. 33). (GER.). x, 229p. 1976. write for info. (*3-487-05888-X*) G Olms Pubs.

***Mythos Von Der Osterreichischen Identitat: Uberlegungen Zu Aspekten Der Wirklichkeitsmythisierung In Romanen Von Albert Paris Gutersloh, Heimito Von Doderer Und Herbert Eisenreich.** Slawomir Piontek. 250p. 1999. 45.95 (*3-631-33437-0*) P Lang Pubng.

Myths: Gods, Heroes & Saviors. Leonard J. Biallas. LC 85-52140. 312p. (Orig.). 1986. pap. 12.95 (*0-89622-290-X*) Twenty-Third.

M

An Asterisk (*) at the beginning of an entry indicates that the title is appearing for the first time.

Myths: Reading Level 2-3, Reading Level 2-3. (Timeless Tales Ser.). 1993. audio 9.95 (*0-88336-268-6*) New Readers.

Myths: Reading Level 2-3, Reading Level 2-3. Tara Reiff. (Timeless Tales Ser.). 1993. 4.95 (*0-88336-272-4*) New Readers.

Myths: Universal Roots. Silo. Ed. by Paul Tooby & Daniel Zuckerbrot. (Illus.). 210p. 1998. lib. bdg. 12.95 (*1-878977-19-9*) Latitude Pr.

***Myths about Condom Safety.** Benjamin Hicks. 86p. 1999. pap. 6.00 (*1-929883-04-8*, 99-5EB) Ingleside Pr MD.

Myths about Gun Control. Morgan O. Reynolds & W. W. Caruth, III. 1992. pap. 10.00 (*0-943802-99-7*, 176) Natl Ctr Pol.

Myths about Modern Bible Versions. David W. Cloud. 248p. 1999. pap. 19.95 (*1-58318-059-1*) Way of Life.

Myths about Our Health Care System: Lessons for Policy Makers. Merrill Matthews, Jr. & John C. Goodman. 18p. 1995. pap. 5.00 (*1-56808-055-7*, BG136) Natl Ctr Pol.

Myths about the King James Bible, 5 vols., Set. 2nd rev. ed. David W. Cloud. 176p. 1993. 7.50 (*1-58318-013-3*, WOL021B) Way of Life.

Myths about the King James Bible Vol. 1: Erasmus Was a Humanist. 2nd rev. ed. David W. Cloud. 25p. 1993. pap. 2.00 (*1-58318-014-1*, WOL021B(1)) Way of Life.

Myths about the King James Bible Vol. 2: Reformation Editors Locked Sufficient Manuscript Evidence. 2nd rev. ed. David W. Cloud. 19p. 1993. pap. 2.00 (*1-58318-015-X*, WOL021B(2)) Way of Life.

Myths about the King James Bible Vol. 3: No Doctrinal Differences Between Text & Versions. 2nd rev. ed. David W. Cloud. 39p. 1993. pap. 2.00 (*1-58318-016-8*, WOL021B(3)) Way of Life.

Myths about the King James Bible Vol. 4: Inspiration Is Perfect But Preservation Is General. 2nd rev. ed. David W. Cloud. 34p. 1993. pap. 2.00 (*1-58318-017-6*, WOL021B(4)) Way of Life.

Myths about the King James Bible Vol. 5: True Scholars Reject the Received Text. 2nd rev. ed. David W. Cloud. 37p. 1993. pap. 2.00 (*1-58318-018-4*, WOL021B(5)) Way of Life.

Myths about the Powerless. Ed. by M. Brinton Lykes et al. LC 95-47188. 336p. (C). 1996. pap. 22.95 (*1-56639-422-8*); lib. bdg. 69.95 (*1-56639-421-X*) Temple U Pr.

Myths about the St. Bartholomew's Day Massacres, 1572-1576. Robert M. Kingdon. LC 87-13540. (Illus.). 28p. 1988. 43.00 (*0-674-59831-8*) HUP.

***Myths & Civilization of the Ancient Chinese.** Sonia Cheng. (Myths & Civilization Ser.). (Illus.). 48p. (J). (gr. 3-7). 2000. 16.95 (*0-87226-592-7*, 65927B, P Bedrick Books) NTC Contemp Pub Co.

Myths & Civilization of the Ancient Greeks. Hazel Martell. (Myths & Civilization Ser.). (Illus.). 48p. (gr. 3-7). 1999. lib. bdg. 16.95 (*0-87226-283-9*, 62839B, P Bedrick Books) NTC Contemp Pub Co.

***Myths & Civilization of the Ancient Mesopotamians.** Elena Gambino. (Myths & Civilization Ser.). 48p. 2000. 16.95 (*0-87226-593-5*, 65935B, P Bedrick Books) NTC Contemp Pub Co.

Myths & Civilization of the Ancient Romans. John Malam. (Myths & Civilization Ser.). 48p. (J). 1999. lib. bdg. 16.95 (*0-87226-590-0*, 65900B, P Bedrick Books) NTC Contemp Pub Co.

Myths & Civilization of the Celts. Hazel Mary Martell. (Myths & Civilization Ser.). 48p. 1999. lib. bdg. 16.95 (*0-87226-591-9*, 65919B, P Bedrick Books) NTC Contemp Pub Co.

Myths & Civilization of the Native Americans. Marion Wood. (Myths & Civilization Ser.). (Illus.). 48p. (J). (gr. 3-7). 1998. lib. bdg. 16.95 (*0-87226-284-7*, 62847B, P Bedrick Books) NTC Contemp Pub Co.

Myths & Civilization of the Vikings. Hazel M. Martell. (Myths & Civilization Ser.). (Illus.). 48p. (gr. 3 up). 1999. lib. bdg. 16.95 (*0-87226-285-5*, 62855B, P Bedrick Books) NTC Contemp Pub Co.

Myths & Civilizations of the Ancient Egyptians. Sarah Quie. (Myths & Civilization Ser.). (Illus.). 48p. (J). (gr. 3-7). 1999. lib. bdg. 16.95 (*0-87226-282-0*, 62820B, P Bedrick Books) NTC Contemp Pub Co.

Myths & Dreams. Edward Clodd. 1993. reprint ed. pap. 23.50 (*1-55818-226-8*, Pub. by Mandrake Pr) Holmes Pub.

Myths & Fables. J. Steffens & J. Carr. (Language Arts Ser.). (Illus.). (J). (gr. 5-8). 1984. pap. 10.95 (*0-88160-113-6*, LW 1008) Learning Wks.

Myths & Facts about AIDS. Anna Forbes. LC 96-2500. (AIDS Awareness Library). (Illus.). 24p. (J). (gr. k-4). 1996. lib. bdg. 15.93 (*0-8239-2366-5*, PowerKids) Rosen Group.

Myths & Facts about Colorectal Cancer: What You Need to Know. Richard Pazdur & Delanie Royce. 48p. 1998. pap. text 9.95 (*0-9641823-9-4*) PRR.

Myths & Facts About Lung Cancer. John Ruckdeschel. (Illus.). 1999. pap. 9.95 (*1-891483-04-8*) PRR.

Myths & Facts about Ovarian Cancer. M. Steven Piver. 1997. pap. text 9.95 (*0-9641823-5-1*) PRR.

***Myths & Facts about Ovarian Cancer: What You Need to Know.** 2nd ed. M. Steven Piver & Gamal Eltabbakh. LC 00-132234. (Illus.). 64p. 2000. pap. 9.95 (*1-891483-07-2*) PRR.

Myths & Fictions. Ed. by Shlomo Biderman & Ben-Ami Scharfstein. LC 93-29158. (Philosophy & Religion Ser.: Vol. 3). 1993. 137.50 (*90-04-09838-0*) Brill Academic Pubs.

Myths & Folk: Tales of the Russians, Western Slavs & Magyars. Jeremiah Curtin. LC 99-45507. 584p. 2000. pap. 16.95 (*0-486-40905-8*) Dover.

Myths & Folk-Tales of Ireland. Jeremiah Curtin. LC 69-18206. 245p. 1975. reprint ed. pap. 6.95 (*0-486-22430-9*) Dover.

Myths & Folk-Tales of the Alabama-Coushatta Indians. Howard N. Martin. (Illus.). 1976. 22.50 (*0-88426-052-6*) Encino Pr.

Myths & Folk-Tales of the Russians, Western Slavs & Magyars. Jeremiah Curtin. LC 74-160611. 1972. reprint ed. 34.95 (*0-405-08414-5*, Pub. by Blom Pubns) Ayer.

Myths & Folk-Tales of the Russians, Western Slavs & Magyars. Jeremiah Curtin. (Works of Jeremiah Curtin). 1990. reprint ed. lib. bdg. 79.00 (*0-685-44766-9*) Rprt Serv.

Myths & Folklore of Ireland. Jeremiah Curtin. 352p. 1995. 9.99 (*0-517-18570-9*) Wings Bks.

Myths & Folklore of Ireland. Jeremiah Curtin. (Works of Jeremiah Curtin). 1990. reprint ed. lib. bdg. 79.00 (*0-685-44780-4*) Rprt Serv.

Myths & Folktales from Many Lands. Betty-Lou Kratoville. (Illus.). 80p. (J). (gr. 1-3). 1998. pap. text 14.00 (*1-57128-098-7*) High Noon Bks.

Myths & Gods of India. Alain Danielou. (Classic Work on Hindu Polytheism from the Princeton Bollingen Ser.). (Illus.). 480p. 1991. pap. 35.00 (*0-89281-354-7*) Inner Tradit.

Myths & Hero Tales: A Cross-Cultural Guide to Literature for Children & Young Adults. Alethea K. Helbig & Agnes R. Perkins. LC 97-8778. 304p. 1997. 49.95 (*0-313-29935-8*, Greenwood Pr) Greenwood.

Myths & Hunting Stories of the Mandan & Hidatsa Sioux. Martha W. Beckwith. LC 76-43665. (Vassar College Folklore Foundation: Publication No. 10). 1977. reprint ed. 39.50 (*0-404-15498-0*) AMS Pr.

Myths & Legend from Around the World. Sandy Shepherd. (Illus.). 96p. (J). (gr. 3-7). 1995. mass mkt. 17.95 (*0-02-762355-6*, Mac Bks Young Read) S&S Childrens.

Myths & Legends see **Artists' Workshop Series**

Myths & Legends. (Time Travel Activity Bks.). 48p. (J). (gr. 3 up). 1992. 1.95 (*0-88679-917-1*) Educ Insights.

Myths & Legends. David Barraclough. 1992. 19.98 (*1-55521-812-1*) Bk Sales Inc.

Myths & Legends. Illus. by Francis Mosley. LC 93-11878. (Story Library). 260p. (Orig.). (J). (gr. 1 up). 1994. pap. 7.95 (*1-85697-975-X*) LKC.

Myths & Legends, 4 vols. Oxford Staff. 1995. 80.00 (*0-19-521154-5*) OUP.

Myths & Legends, Level C. (Reading Power Modules Software Ser.). 1997. pap. 3.75 (*1-55855-788-1*) Raintree Steck-V.

Myths & Legends, Level F. (Reading Power Modules Software Ser.). 1997. pap. 3.75 (*1-55855-796-2*) Raintree Steck-V.

Myths & Legends: Babylonia & Assyria. Lewis Spence. 412p. 1995. reprint ed. pap. 29.95 (*1-56459-500-5*) Kessinger Pub.

***Myths & Legends: Read & Understand: Grade 4-6.** Tekla White & Jill Norris. Ed. by Marilyn Evans. (Read & Understand Ser.). (Illus.). 144p. 2000. pap., teacher ed. 12.95 (*1-55799-752-7*, 759) Evan-Moor Edu Pubs.

Myths & Legends: Viking, Oriental, Greek. David Bellingham et al. (Illus.). 208p. 1997. 17.98 (*0-7858-0627-X*) Bk Sales Inc.

Myths & Legends Ancient Egypt. Lewis Spence. 476p. 1997. reprint ed. pap. 35.00 (*0-7661-0048-0*) Kessinger Pub.

Myths & Legends of All Nations. Herbert S. Robinson. 1976. 17.05 (*0-606-02094-2*, Pub. by Turtleback) Demco.

Myths & Legends of All Nations. Herbert S. Robinson & Knox Wilson. (Quality Paperback Ser.: No. 319). 244p. 1978. reprint ed. pap. 11.95 (*0-8226-0319-5*) Littlefield.

Myths & Legends of Bantu. Alice Werner. 289p. 1968. reprint ed. 37.50 (*0-7146-1735-0*, Pub. by F Cass Pubs) Intl Spec Bk.

Myths & Legends of California & the Old Southwest. Ed. by Katharine B. Judson. LC 93-46686. (Illus.). x, 255p. (C). 1994. pap. 8.95 (*0-8032-7580-3*, Bison Books) U of Nebr Pr.

Myths & Legends of China. E. T. Werner. LC 94-5790. (Illus.). 496p. 1994. pap. 10.95 (*0-486-28092-6*) Dover.

Myths & Legends of China. E. T. Werner. LC 71-172541. (Illus.). 454p. 1980. reprint ed. 36.95 (*0-405-09059-5*, Pub. by Blom Pubns) Ayer.

Myths & Legends of Hawaii. William D. Westervelt. 266p. 1987. reprint ed. mass mkt. 6.95 (*0-935180-43-5*) Mutual Pub HI.

Myths & Legends of India: An Introduction to the Study of Hinduism. J. M. Macfie. (C). 1994. pap. 9.50 (*81-7167-131-4*, Pub. by Rupa) S Asia.

Myths & Legends of Ireland Tales of a Magical & Mysterious Past. Ronald Pearsall. 1998. 16.98 (*1-880908-43-3*) Todtri Prods.

Myths & Legends of Japan. F. Hadland Davis. Date not set. lib. bdg. 28.95 (*0-8488-2096-7*) Amereon Ltd.

Myths & Legends of Japan. F. Hadland Davis. (Illus.). 432p. 1989. reprint ed. pap. 19.50 (*9971-4-9125-7*) Heian Intl.

Myths & Legends of Japan. Hadland F. Davis. (Illus.). 432p. 1992. reprint ed. pap. 10.95 (*0-486-27045-9*) Dover.

Myths & Legends of Mount Olympos. Charles F. Baker, III & Rosalie F. Baker. 96p. 1994. pap. 12.95 (*0-942389-06-9*) Cobblestone Pub Co.

Myths & Legends of Pacific Northwest. Ed. by Katharine B. Judson. LC 96-39239. (Illus.). iv, 193p. 1997. pap. 10.00 (*0-8032-7595-1*, Bison Books) U of Nebr Pr.

Myths & Legends of the Bantu. Alice Werner. LC 78-63237. (Folktale Ser.). (Illus.). reprint ed. 34.00 (*0-404-16176-6*) AMS Pr.

Myths & Legends of the British Isles. Richard Barber. LC 99-21492. (Illus.). 640p. 1999. 55.00 (*0-85115-748-3*, Suffolk Records Soc) Boydell & Brewer.

Myths & Legends of the Mackinacs & the Lake Region. 2nd ed. Grace F. Kane. (Illus.). 164p. 1972. reprint ed. pap. 10.00 (*0-912382-09-0*) Black Letter.

Myths & Legends of the Martial Arts. Peter Lewis. 192p. 1998. pap. 13.95 (*1-85375-271-1*) Prion.

Myths & Legends of the Middle Ages. Helene A. Guerber. (Illus.). 464p. 1994. reprint ed. pap. text 10.95 (*0-486-27862-X*) Dover.

Myths & Legends of the North American Indians. pap. text. write for info. (*0-7881-9190-X*) DIANE Pub.

Myths & Legends of the North American Indians. Lewis Spence. 474p. 1997. reprint ed. pap. 35.00 (*0-7661-0119-3*) Kessinger Pub.

Myths & Legends of the Polynesians. Johannes C. Andersen. (Illus.). 592p. 1995. pap. text 12.95 (*0-486-28582-0*) Dover.

Myths & Legends of the Polynesians. Johannes C. Andersen. LC 75-35170. (Illus.). reprint ed. 52.50 (*0-404-14200-1*) AMS Pr.

Myths & Legends of the Rhine. Helene A. Guerber. 1976. lib. bdg. 59.95 (*0-8490-2329-7*) Gordon Pr.

Myths & Legends of the Sioux. Marie L. McLaughlin. LC 90-33804. (Illus.). 200p. 1990. reprint ed. pap. 9.00 (*0-8032-8171-4*, Bison Books) U of Nebr Pr.

Myths & Legends of the Vikings. John Lindow. (Illus.). 1980. pap. 3.95 (*0-88388-071-7*) Bellerophon Bks.

Myths & Legends of the Vikings. Judith Mileage. 1999. 7.99 (*0-7858-1077-3*) Bk Sales Inc.

***Myths & Legends of the World , 4 vol. set.** 2000. 295.00 (*0-02-865439-0*) Macmillan.

***Myths & Legends of the World.** 2000. 75.00 (*0-02-865435-8*) Macmillan.

***Myths & Legends of the World, Vol. 2.** 2000. 75.00 (*0-02-865436-6*) Macmillan.

***Myths & Legends of the World , vol. 3.** 2000. 75.00 (*0-02-865437-4*) Macmillan.

***Myths & Legends of the World , vol.4.** 2000. 75.00 (*0-02-865438-2*) Macmillan.

Myths & Magic of the Yeats Country. Eily Kilgannon. 96p. 1998. pap. 7.95 (*1-85635-218-8*, Pub. by Mercier Pr) Irish Amer Bk.

Myths & Magical Fantasies. Peter Schjeldahl & Reesey Shaw. LC 96-86108. (Illus.). 41p. (Orig.). 1996. pap. 20.00 (*1-885088-06-X*) CA Ctr Arts.

***Myths & Memories of the Nation.** Anthony D. Smith. LC 99-36963. 296p. 2000. pap. 24.95 (*0-19-829684-3*); text 65.00 (*0-19-829534-0*) OUP.

Myths & Methods of Being a Manager. Kandy Kidd. (Illus.). 100p. 1986. 14.95 (*0-937751-31-6*) Brendon Hill Pub.

Myths & [Mis] Perceptions: Changing U. S. Elite Visions of Mexico. Sergio Aguayo. LC 97-51682. (U. S.-Mexico Contemporary Perspectives Ser.). 1998. pap. write for info. (*1-878367-36-6*) UCSD Ctr US-Mex.

Myths & Motifs in Literature. David J. Burrows et al. LC 72-90546. 448p. (Orig.). (C). 1973. pap. 16.95 (*0-02-905030-8*) Free Pr.

Myths & Mysteries of Same-Sex Love. rev. ed. Christine Downing. LC 82-40283. 348p. (C). 1996. pap. 19.95 (*0-8264-0918-0*) Continuum.

Myths & Myth-Makers. John Fiske. (Notable American Authors Ser.). 1992. reprint ed. lib. bdg. 75.00 (*0-7812-2840-9*) Rprt Serv.

Myths & Myth Makers. John Fiske. 262p. 1997. reprint ed. pap. 19.95 (*0-7661-0093-6*) Kessinger Pub.

Myths & Nationhood. Ed. by George Schopflin & Geoffrey Alan Hosking. LC 97-213820. 256p. (C). 1997. 65.00 (*0-415-91974-6*); pap. 17.99 (*0-415-91973-8*) Routledge.

Myths & New World Explorations. Gordon Speck. 1979. 19.95 (*0-87770-214-4*) Ye Galleon.

Myths & Politics in Western Societies: Evaluating the Crisis of Modernity in the United States, Germany, & Great Britain. John Girling. LC 92-21504. 192p. (C). 1993. text 34.95 (*1-56000-092-9*) Transaction Pubs.

Myths & Realities: A Report of the National Commission on the Insanity Defense. National Commission on the Insanity Defense, (U. S & National Mental Health Association (U. S.) Staff. LC 83-60609. (Illus.). 50p. 1983. 3.95 (*0-317-00680-0*, PE0902SH) Natl Mental Health.

Myths & Realities: Best Practices for Language Minority Students. Katharine D. Samway & Denise Mckeon. LC 98-50063. 1999. pap. text 13.00 (*0-325-00057-3*) Heinemann.

Myths & Realities: Guidelines for Designing an Extraordinary Life! Gary R. Blair. 48p. 1998. pap. 6.95 (*1-889770-02-7*, MRG) GoalsGuy.

Myths & Realities: Hearing Transcript of the National Commission on the Insanity Defense. National Commission on the Insanity Defense, (U. S & National Mental Health Association (U. S.) Staff. LC 83-60608. 214p. 1983. 9.95 (*0-317-00681-9*, PE0903SH) Natl Mental Health.

Myths & Realities: Societies of the Colonial South. Carl Bridenbaugh. LC 80-25280. (Walter Lynwood Fleming Lectures in Southern History). 208p. 1981. reprint ed. lib. bdg. 55.00 (*0-313-22770-5*, BRMR) Greenwood.

Myths & Realities about the Decentralization of Health Systems. Ed. by Riitta-Liisa Kolehmainen-Aitken. LC 99-25251. 192p. 1999. pap. 19.95 (*0-913723-52-5*); lib. bdg. 39.95 (*0-913723-56-8*) Mgmt Sci Health.

Myths & Realities of Academic Administration. Patricia R. Plante & Robert L. Caret. (ACE-Oryx Series on Higher Education). 160p. 1990. 27.95 (*0-02-897335-6*) Oryx Pr.

Myths & Realities of Blended Families. 34p. 1990. 2.50 (*0-936098-62-7*) Intl Marriage.

Myths & Realities of Contemporary French Theater: Comparative Views. Ed. by Patricia M. Hopkins & Wendell M. Aycock. LC 85-50604. (Proceedings of the Comparative Literature Symposium Ser.). 196p. 1985. 24.95 (*0-89672-134-5*); pap. 12.95 (*0-89672-185-X*) Tex Tech Univ Pr.

Myths & Realities of Foreign Investment in Poor Countries: The Modern Leviathan in the Third World. John M. Rothgeb, Jr. LC 88-34026. 162p. 1989. 57.95 (*0-275-93255-9*, C3255, Praeger Pubs) Greenwood.

Myths & Realities of French Imperialism in India, 1763-1783. Sudipta Das. LC 91-30733. (American University Studies: History: Ser. IX, Vols. 117). (Illus.). XVII, 459p. (C). 1993. text 54.95 (*0-8204-1676-2*) P Lang Pubng.

Myths & Realities of Managerial Accounting & Finance. L. Chadwick. (Financial Times Management Briefings Ser.). 1997. pap. 94.50 (*0-273-63262-0*, Pub. by F T P-H) Trans-Atl Phila.

Myths & Realities of Pesticide Reduction: A Reader's Guide to Understanding the Full Economic Impacts. Edward C. Jaenicke. (Policy Studies Report: No. 8). (Illus.). 35p. 1997. pap. 6.00 (*1-893182-10-X*) H A Wallace Inst.

Myths & Reality of External Constraints on Development. James Riedel. (Thames Essays Ser.: No. 47). 100p. 1987. text 19.95 (*0-566-05336-5*, Pub. by Avebry) Ashgate Pub Co.

Myths & Recipes of the Last Frontier, Alaska. Judy Kivi. Ed. by Alisa B. Oliver. LC 97-121309. (Illus.). 304p. 1996. pap. 24.95 (*0-9641606-1-7*) Easy Break.

Myths & Science of Soils of the Tropics. R. Lal & P. A. Sanchez. (SSSA Special Publications: No. 29). 185p. 1992. 15.00 (*0-89118-800-2*) Soil Sci Soc Am.

Myths & Songs from the South Pacific. William W. Gill. Ed. by Richard M. Dorson. LC 77-70596. (International Folklore Ser.). 1980. reprint ed. lib. bdg. 28.95 (*0-405-10095-7*) Ayer.

Myths & Symbols in Hindu Mythology: A Legal Interpretation. D. C. Varshney. 1990. 27.50 (*81-202-0279-1*, Pub. by Ajanta) S Asia.

Myths & Symbols in Indian Art & Civilization. Heinrich Zimmer. Ed. by Joseph Campbell. (Works by Heinrich Zimmer: Vol. 6). 282p. 1946. pap. text 11.95 (*0-691-01778-6*, Pub. by Princeton U Pr) Cal Prin Full Svc.

Myths & Symbols in Pagan Europe: Early Scandinavian & Celtic Religions. H. R. Davidson. (Illus.). 270p. (C). 1988. pap. text 17.95 (*0-8156-2441-7*) Syracuse U Pr.

Myths & Symbols of Vedic Astrology. Bepin Behari. 280p. (Orig.). (C). 1990. pap. 14.95 (*1-878423-06-1*) Morson Pub.

Myths & Tales from the San Carlos Apache. Pliny E. Goddard. LC 76-43715. (AMNH. Anthropological Papers: Vol. 29, Pt. 1). reprint ed. 29.50 (*0-404-15548-0*) AMS Pr.

Myths & Tales of the Chiricahua Apache Indians. Compiled by Morris E. Opler. LC 94-12396. (Sources of American Indian Oral Literature Ser.). xxvi, 115p. 1994. pap. 6.95 (*0-8032-8602-3*, Bison Books) U of Nebr Pr.

Myths & Tales of the Jicarilla Apache Indians. Morris E. Opler. LC 94-27548. (Sources of American Indian Oral Literature Ser.). xxxviii, 407p. 1994. reprint ed. pap. 14.95 (*0-8032-8603-1*, Bison Books) U of Nebr Pr.

Myths & Tales of the Jicarilla Apache Indians. unabridged ed. Morris E. Opler. 406p. 1994. pap. text 9.95 (*0-486-28324-0*) Dover.

Myths & Tales of the Southeastern Indians. John R. Swanton. (Bureau of American Ethnology Bulletins Ser.). 275p. 1995. lib. bdg. 89.00 (*0-7812-4088-3*) Rprt Serv.

Myths & Tales of the Southeastern Indians. John R. Swanton. LC 95-11004. 296p. 1995. pap. 12.95 (*0-8061-2784-8*) U of Okla Pr.

Myths & Tales of the Southeastern Indians. John R. Swanton. LC 74-9011. (Smithsonian Institution. Bureau of American Ethnology. Bulletin Ser.: 88). reprint ed. 41.50 (*0-404-11908-5*) AMS Pr.

Myths & Tales of the White Mountain Apache. Ed. by Grenville Goodwin. LC 39-33959. (AFS Memoirs Ser.). 1974. reprint ed. 30.00 (*0-527-01085-5*) Periodicals Srv.

Myths & Tales of the White Mountain Apache. Grenville Goodwin. 223p. 1994. reprint ed. pap. 17.95 (*0-8165-1451-8*) U of Ariz Pr.

Myths & Texts. rev. ed. Gary Snyder. LC 77-25378. 54p. 1978. pap. 7.95 (*0-8112-0686-6*, NDP457, Pub. by New Directions) Norton.

Myths & Texts: Strategies of Incorporation & Displacement. fac. ed. John B. Vickery. LC 83-9337. 230p. 1983. reprint ed. pap. 71.30 (*0-7837-7925-9*, 204768100008) Bks Demand.

Myths & the American West. Richard W. Etulain. LC 98-209196. 112 p. 1998. pap. 17.95 (*0-89745-224-0*) Sunflower U Pr.

Myths & the Malay Ruling Class. Sharifah M. Omar. 144p. 1993. pap. 12.50 (*981-210-025-3*, Pub. by Times Academic) Intl Spec Bk.

Myths & the Truth about Selecting a Marine Sextant. Joel H. Jacobs. LC 75-4318. 56p. 1975. reprint ed. pap. 30.00 (*0-608-02459-7*, 206310300004) Bks Demand.

***Myths & Tradeoffs: The Role of Tests in Undergraduate Admissions.** National Research Council Staff. Ed. by Alexandra Beatty et al. 58p. 1999. pap. 18.00 (*0-309-06597-6*) Natl Acad Pr.

Myths & Traditions of the Arikara Indians. Compiled by Douglas R. Parks. LC 95-43855. (Sources of American Indian Oral Literature Ser.). (Illus.). xix, 406p. 1996. pap. 17.95 (*0-8032-8742-9*, Bison Books) U of Nebr Pr.

Myths & Traditions of the Crow Indians. Robert H. Lowie. LC 74-7981. reprint ed. 41.50 (*0-404-11872-0*) AMS Pr.

Myths & Voices: New Canadian Short Fiction. Ed. by David Lampe. 420p. 1993. pap. 17.00 (*1-877727-28-8*) White Pine.

Myths Away, or Myths Are a Way. rev. ed. Michael C. Giammatteo. (Illus.). (Orig.). 1999. pap. 8.95 (*0-918428-04-1*) Sylvan Inst.

An Asterisk (*) at the beginning of an entry indicates that the title is appearing for the first time.

Myths, Dreams & Dances: Poems, 1968-1973. David B. Axelrod. (Illus.). 110p. 1974. pap. 12.00 (*0-925062-31-6*); pap. 8.00 (*0-925062-33-2*) Writers Ink Pr.

Myths, Dreams & Religion. Ed. by Campbell. 256p. 1999. 6.98 (*1-56731-340-X*, MJF Bks) Fine Comms.

Myths Every Child Should Know. Hamilton W. Mabie. 1990. pap. 20.00 (*0-8195-1235-4*) Biblo.

Myths from Mesopotamia: Creation, the Flood, Gilgamesh & Others. Stephanie Dalley. (Illus.). 360p. 1998. pap. 9.95 (*0-19-283589-0*) OUP.

Myths from the Mahabharata. Sadashiv Ambadas Dange. LC 97-905056. 1997. write for info. (*81-7305-116-X*) Aryan Bks Intl.

Myths, Gods & Fantasy: A Dictionary. Pamela Allardice. 200p. (Orig.). 1991. lib. bdg. 40.00 (*0-87436-660-7*) ABC-CLIO.

Myths Greece & Rome. (C). 1986. write for info. (*0-8087-6938-3*) Pearson Custom.

Myths, Heroes & Anti-Heroes: The Literature of the Asia-Pacific Region. Ed. by Bruce Bennett & Dennis Haskell. pap. 19.00 (*0-86422-221-1*, Pub. by Univ of West Aust Pr) Intl Spec Bk.

Myths in Adventism: An Interpretive Study of Ellen White, Education & Related Issues. George R. Knight. LC 85-11889. 273p. reprint ed. pap. 84.70 (*0-7837-6430-8*, 204642800012) Bks Demand.

***Myths in Stone: Religious Dimensions of Washington, D. C.** Jeffrey F. Meyer. LC 00-20172. 2001. write for info. (*0-520-21481-1*) U CA Pr.

***Myths, Legends & Folktales of America: An Anthology.** David Leeming & Jake Page. (Illus.). 240p. 2000. pap. 15.95 (*0-19-511784-0*) OUP.

Myths, Legends & Tales. Phillis Jean Perry. LC 98-48773. 102p. 1999. pap. text 16.95 (*1-57950-017-X*) Highsmith Pr.

Myths, Legends & Tales of Europe for Travellers. Charles Leocha. 360p. (Orig.). Date not set. pap. 14.95 (*0-915009-15-3*) World Leis Corp.

Myths, Lies, & Denial: Christian & Secular Counseling in America. John J. Frank. 232p. 1996. pap. text. write for info. (*1-887835-00-8*) Minstrel Missions.

***Myths, Magic & Mysticism: The Rituals, Rites & Superstitions of the World's Unorthodox Religions.** Vivianne Crowley & Chris Crowley. (Illus.). 224p. 2000. 35.00 (*1-85868-987-2*, Pub. by Carlton Bks Ltd) Natl Bk Netwk.

Myths, Misconceptions & Heroics: The Story of the Treatment of Hypertension from the 1930's. Marvin Moser. 68p. 1997. pap. 22.00 (*0-9626020-4-3*) Le Jacq Commns.

Myths, Misdeeds, & Misunderstandings: The Roots of Conflict in U. S. - Mexican Relations. Ed. by Jaime E. Rodriguez & Kathryn Vincent. LC 97-1217. (Latin American Silhouettes Ser.). (Illus.). 274p. 1997. 45.00 (*0-8420-2662-2*) Scholarly Res Inc.

Myths, Models, & Methods in Sport Pedagogy. Adelphi-AIESEP 85 World Sport Conference (1985: Ad. Ed. by Gary T. Barrette et al. LC 86-20094. (Illus.). 284p. 1987. reprint ed. pap. 88.10 (*0-608-06449-1*, 206728700009) Bks Demand.

Myths, Models, & U. S. Foreign Policy: The Cultural Shaping of Three Cold Warriors. Stephen W. Twing. LC 98-3322. 224p. 1998. lib. bdg. 49.95 (*1-55587-766-4*, Three Contnts) L Rienner.

Myths of Ancient Mexico. Michel Graulich. Tr. by Bernard R. Ortiz de Montellano & Thelma Ortiz de Montellano. LC 96-49255. (Civilization of the American Indian Ser.: Vol. 222). (Illus.). 320p. 1997. 32.95 (*0-8061-2910-7*) U of Okla Pr.

Myths of August: A Personal Exploration of Our Tragic Cold War Affair with the Atom. Stewart L. Udall. LC 97-53053. (Illus.). 399p. (C). 1998. pap. text 19.00 (*0-8135-2546-2*) Rutgers U Pr.

***Myths of Childhood.** Joel Paris. LC 00-21546. 272p. 2000. 34.95 (*0-87630-966-X*) Brunner-Mazel.

Myths of Consciousness in the Novels of Charles Maturin. Shirley C. Scott. Ed. by Devendra P. Varma. LC 79-8479. (Gothic Studies & Dissertations). 1980. lib. bdg. 28.95 (*0-405-12661-1*) Ayer.

Myths of Educational Choice. Judy Pearson. LC 92-19594. 168p. 1992. 42.95 (*0-275-94169-8*, C4169, Praeger Pubs) Greenwood.

Myths of Empire: Domestic Politics & International Ambition. Jack Snyder. LC 91-55052. (Cornell Studies in Security Affairs). 344p. 1991. text 42.50 (*0-8014-2532-8*) Cornell U Pr.

Myths of Empire: Domestic Politics & International Ambition. Jack Snyder. LC 91-55052. (Cornell Studies in Security Affairs). 344p. 1993. pap. text 15.95 (*0-8014-9764-7*) Cornell U Pr.

Myths of Ethnicity & Nation: Immigration, Work, & Identity in the Belize Banana Industry. Mark Moberg. LC 96-51261. (Illus.). 256p. 1997. 38.00 (*0-87049-970-X*) U of Tenn Pr.

Myths of Freedom: Equality, Modern Thought & Philosophical Radicalism, 62. Stephen L. Gardner. LC 98-11105. (Contributions in Philosophy Ser.: Vol. 62). 216p. 1998. 59.95 (*0-313-30724-5*, Greenwood Pr) Greenwood.

Myths of Gender: Biological Theories about Women & Men. 2nd rev. ed. Anne Fausto-Sterling. LC 85-47561. 272p. 1992. 16.50 (*0-465-04792-0*, Pub. by Basic) HarpC.

Myths of Greece & Rome. Helene A. Guerber. (Illus.). 1990. pap. 25.00 (*0-8196-2069-6*) Biblo.

Myths of Greece & Rome. Christopher Holme. 288p. 1981. pap. 24.95 (*0-14-005643-2*, Penguin Bks) Viking Penguin.

Myths of Greece & Rome. Helene A. Guerber. LC 92-40392. (Illus.). 480p. 1993. reprint ed. pap. 9.95 (*0-486-27584-1*) Dover.

Myths of Herakles in Ancient Greece: Survey & Profile. Mark W. Padilla. LC 98-2650. 112p. (C). 1998. 40.00 (*0-7618-1050-1*); pap. 21.50 (*0-7618-1051-X*) U Pr of Amer.

Myths of Idaho Indians. rev. ed. Deward E. Walker, Jr. LC 79-57484. (Illus.). 204p. (Orig.). 1980. pap. 11.95 (*0-89301-066-9*) U of Idaho Pr.

Myths of Love: Classical Lovers in Medieval Literature. Katherine Heinrichs. LC 89-43498. 248p. 1990. lib. bdg. 32.50 (*0-271-00689-7*) Pa St U Pr.

Myths of Male Dominance: Collected Articles on Women Cross-Culturally. Eleanor B. Leacock. LC 79-3870. 352p. reprint ed. pap. 109.20 (*0-7837-6993-8*, 204680500004) Bks Demand.

Myths of Mastery & Drama of Decomposition in Moliere. Larry W. Riggs. (Sociocritisim: Literature, Society & History Ser.: Vol. 1). 275p. (C). 1989. text 44.95 (*0-8204-0912-X*) P Lang Pubng.

Myths of Mexico & Peru. Lewis Spence. LC 94-22661. (Illus.). 448p. 1994. pap. text 10.95 (*0-486-28332-1*) Dover.

Myths of Middle India. Verrier Elwin. 552p. 1992. 24.95 (*0-19-562963-9*) OUP.

Myths of Modern Art. Alberto Boixados. 144p. (Orig.). (C). 1990. pap. text 20.00 (*0-8191-7953-1*); lib. bdg. 37.00 (*0-8191-7952-3*) U Pr of Amer.

Myths of Modern Individualism: Faust, Don Quixote, Don Juan, Robinson Crusoe. Ian Watt. (Illus.). 305p. (C). 1996. 29.95 (*0-521-48011-6*) Cambridge U Pr.

Myths of Modern Individualism: Faust, Don Quixote, Don Juan, Robinson Crusoe. Ian Watt. (Illus.). 309p. 1997. pap. 12.95 (*0-521-58564-3*) Cambridge U Pr.

Myths of Narasimha & Vamana: Two Avatars in Cosmological Perspective. Deborah A. Soifer. LC 90-21260. (SUNY Series in Hindu Studies). 335p. (C). 1991. pap. text 19.95 (*0-7914-0800-0*) State U NY Pr.

Myths of Norsemen. Helene A. Guerber. 1972. 69.95 (*0-87968-280-9*) Gordon Pr.

Myths of Northern Lands. Helene A. Guerber. 1995. pap. 24.00 (*0-8196-2070-X*) Biblo.

Myths of Oz: Reading Australian Popular Culture. John Fiske et al. 204p. 1988. text 39.95 (*0-04-330391-9*, Pub. by Allen & Unwin Pty); pap. text 17.95 (*0-04-306005-6*, Pub. by Allen & Unwin Pty) Paul & Co Pubs.

Myths of Power: A Study of Royal Power & Ideology in Ugaritic & Biblical Tradition. Nick Wyatt. 492p. 1996. text 75.00 (*3-927120-43-X*) Ugarit-Verlag.

Myths of Power: Norbert Elias & the Early-Modern European Court. Jeroen Duindam. 200p. (C). 1994. pap. 39.50 (*90-5356-136-6*, Pub. by Amsterdam U Pr); text 62.50 (*90-5356-111-0*, Pub. by Amsterdam U Pr) U of Mich Pr.

Myths of Pre-Columbian America. D. Mackenzie. 1972. 75.00 (*0-8490-0701-1*) Gordon Pr.

Myths of Pre-Columbian America. Donald A. Mackenzie. (LC History-America-E). 351p. 1999. reprint ed. lib. bdg. 99.00 (*0-7812-4299-1*) Rprt Serv.

Myths of Pre-Columbian America. unabridged ed. Donald A. Mackenzie. LC 96-32395. (Illus.). 416p. 1996. reprint ed. pap. text 9.95 (*0-486-29379-3*) Dover.

Myths of Reason: Vagueness, Rationality, & the Lure of Logic. Murray Code. LC 94-41693. 260p. (C). 1995. text 60.00 (*0-391-03901-6*) Humanities.

Myths of Religion. Andrew M. Greeley. 656p. 1989. mass mkt. 16.95 (*0-446-38818-1*, Pub. by Warner Bks) Little.

Myths of Rich & Poor: Why We're Better off Than We Think. W. Michael Cox & Richard Alm. LC 99-177815. (Illus.). 256p. 1998. 25.00 (*0-465-04784-X*, Pub. by Basic) HarpC.

***Myths of Rich & Poor: Why We're Better Off Than We Think.** W. Michael Cox & Richard Alm. 1999. pap. 14.00 (*0-465-04783-1*, Pub. by Basic) HarpC.

Myths of School Self-Renewal. David Gordon. (C). 1984. text 27.95 (*0-8077-2755-5*) Tchrs Coll.

Myths of Sexuality. Thomas Hardy. LC 82-14853. 1983. 12.00 (*0-89444-036-5*) John Jay Pr.

Myths of the Atonement. Ralph A. Letch. 1985. 30.00 (*0-7223-1657-7*, Pub. by A H S Ltd) St Mut.

Myths of the Chemical Industry. ICHEM Engineering Staff. 1985. pap. 16.50 (*0-08-032632-3*, Pergamon Pr) Elsevier.

Myths of the Cherokee. James Mooney. LC 70-108513. (American Indian History Ser.). 1970. reprint ed. 89.00 (*0-403-00221-4*) Scholarly.

Myths of the Cherokee. unabridged ed. James Mooney. LC 95-22350. (Illus.). 608p. 1996. reprint ed. pap. text 14.95 (*0-486-28907-9*) Dover.

Myths of the Cherokee & Sacred Formulas of the Cherokees. James Mooney. LC 72-188151. (Illus.). 1982. reprint ed. 29.95 (*0-918450-22-5*); reprint ed. pap. 16.95 (*0-918450-05-5*) C Elder.

Myths of the Dog-Man. David G. White. LC 90-43597. (Illus.). 368p. 1991. pap. 21.95 (*0-226-89509-2*) U Ch Pr.

Myths of the Dog-Man. David G. White. LC 90-43597. (Illus.). 368p. 1991. lib. bdg. 51.00 (*0-226-89508-4*) U Ch Pr.

Myths of the Dreaming: Interpreting Aboriginal Legends. James G. Cowan. (Illus.). 192p. (Orig.). (C). 1994. pap. 14.95 (*1-85327-085-7*, Pub. by Prism Pr) Assoc Pubs Grp.

Myths of the English. Ed. by Roy Porter. LC 92-28892. 272p. 1993. pap. 31.95 (*0-7456-1306-3*) Blackwell Pubs.

Myths of the Greeks & Romans. Michael Grant. 1989. pap. 5.95 (*0-317-02799-9*) NAL.

Myths of the Greeks & Romans. Michael Grant. LC 95-10012. 448p. 1995. pap. 16.95 (*0-452-01162-0*, Mer) NAL.

Myths of the Hindus & Buddhists. Ananda K. Coomaraswamy & Sr. Nivedita. (Illus.). 400p. (J). (gr. 4-8). 1967. pap. 10.95 (*0-486-21759-0*) Dover.

Myths of the Lechuza. David E. Alexander. (Illus.). 78p. (Orig.). (J). Date not set. pap. 12.95 (*0-9623078-5-8*) Alexander Forney.

Myths of the Middle Ages. Sabine Baring-Gould. Ed. by John Matthews. LC 96-225932. (Illus.). 176p. 1996. 27.95 (*0-7137-2607-5*, Pub. by Blandford Pr) Sterling.

Myths of the Modocs. Jeremiah Curtin. (Works of Jeremiah Curtin). 1990. reprint ed. lib. bdg. 79.00 (*0-685-44783-9*) Rprt Serv.

Myths of the Modocs: Indian Legends from the Northwest. Jeremiah Curtin. LC 74-170711. 1972. reprint ed. 23.95 (*0-405-08415-3*, Pub. by Blom Pubns) Ayer.

Myths of the Moon see **Leyendas de la Luna**

Myths of the Nation: National Identity & Literary Representations. Rumina Sethi. LC 98-51996. 232p. 1999. text 70.00 (*0-19-818339-9*) OUP.

Myths of the New World: A Treatise on the Symbolism & Mythology of the Red Race of America. D. G. Brinton. LC 68-24972. (American History & Americana Ser.: No. 47). 1969. reprint ed. lib. bdg. 75.00 (*0-8383-0918-6*) M S G Haskell Hse.

Myths of the New World: A Treatise on the Symbolism & Mythology of the Red Race of America. 2nd ed. Daniel G. Brinton. LC 69-13839. 331p. 1969. reprint ed. lib. bdg. 49.75 (*0-8371-2040-3*, BRMN, Greenwood Pr) Greenwood.

***Myths of the New World, a Treatise on the Symbolism & Mythology of the Red Race of America.** Daniel G. Brinton. (LC History-America-E). 360p. 1999. reprint ed. lib. bdg. 99.00 (*0-7812-4296-7*) Rprt Serv.

Myths of the Norsemen: From the Eddas & the Sagas. unabridged ed. Helene A. Guerber. LC 92-23003. (Illus.). 480p. 1992. reprint ed. pap. text 10.95 (*0-486-27348-2*) Dover.

Myths of the Norsemen: Retold from the Old Norse Poems & Tales. Roger Lancelyn Green. (Puffin Classics). (J). 1994. 9.09 (*0-606-03626-1*, Pub. by Turtleback) Demco.

Myths of the North American Indians. Lewis Spence. 480p. 1989. pap. 8.95 (*0-486-25967-6*) Dover.

***Myths of the North-East Frontier of India.** Verrier Elwin. 470p. 1999. 47.50 (*81-215-0915-7*, Pub. by M Manoharial) Coronet Bks.

Myths of the Odyssey in Art & Literature. J. Ellen Harrison. (Illus.). xxv, 219p. (C). 1993. reprint ed. lib. bdg. 50.00 (*0-89241-437-5*) Caratzas.

Myths of the Opossum: Pathways of Mesoamerican Mythology. Alfredo Lopez Austin. Tr. by Bernard R. Ortiz de Montellano & Thelma Ortiz de Montellano. LC 92-27258. (Illus.). 434p. 1993. reprint ed. pap. 134.60 (*0-608-04129-7*, 206486200011) Bks Demand.

Myths of the Owens Valley Paiute. fac. ed. Julian H. Steward. (University of California Publications in American Archaeology & Ethnology: Vol. 34: 5). 89p. (C). 1936. reprint ed. pap. text 10.00 (*1-55567-296-5*) Coyote Press.

Myths of the Peoples of the World Encyclopaedia, 2 vols., Bk. 2. Ed. by S. Tokarev. (RUS.). 718p. (C). 1988. 150.00 (*0-7855-6473-X*, Pub. by Collets) St Mut.

Myths of the Peoples of the World Encyclopedia, 2 vols., Bk. 1. Ed. by S. Tokarev. (RUS.). 672p. (C). 1987. 160.00 (*0-569-09034-2*, Pub. by Collets) St Mut.

Myths of the Sacred Tree. Moyra Caldecott. (Illus.). 224p. (Orig.). 1993. pap. 12.95 (*0-89281-414-4*, Destiny Bks) Inner Tradit.

Myths of the Southern Sierra Miwok. fac. ed. Samuel A. Barrett. (University of California Publications in American Archaeology & Ethnology: Vol. 16: 1). 28p. (C). 1919. reprint ed. pap. text 3.13 (*1-55567-221-3*) Coyote Press.

Myths of the Toba & Pilaga Indians of the Gran Chaco. Alfred Metraux. LC 46-4565. (American Folklore Society Memoirs Ser.). 1974. reprint ed. 30.00 (*0-527-01092-8*) Periodicals Srv.

Myths of the Tribe: When Religion, Economics, Government & Ethics Converge. J. David Rich. LC 93-17732. 296p. (C). 1993. 32.95 (*0-87975-824-4*) Prometheus Bks.

Myths of the World: A Thematic Encyclopedia. Michael Jordan. 302p. 1995. pap. 13.95 (*1-85626-156-5*, Pub. by Cathie Kyle) Trafalgar.

Myths of Wyoming Vol. I: Jackson Hole. Joseph R. Brockett. (Myths of Wyoming Ser.). (Illus.). 32p. 1985. pap. 1.50 (*0-942345-19-3*) Dovehaven Pr Ltd.

Myths, Rituals & Beliefs in Himachal Pradesh. Molu Ram Thakur. LC 97-914468. 188p. 1997. write for info. (*81-7387-071-3*) Indus Pub.

Myths, Saints & Legends in Medival India. Charlotte Vaudeville. (Illus.). 342p. (C). 1996. text 35.00 (*0-19-563414-4*) OUP.

Myths That Cause Crime. 3rd rev. ed. Harold E. Pepinsky & Paul Jesilow. LC 92-18307. 186p. 1992. pap. 12.95 (*0-932020-91-7*) Seven Locks Pr.

Myths That Divide Us: How Lies Have Poisoned American Race Relations. John Perazzo. LC 96-60240. 544p. 1998. pap. 19.95 (*0-9651268-0-3*) Wrld Studies.

***Myths That Divide Us: How Lies Have Poisoned American Race Relations.** John Perazzo. LC 99-73860. 629p. 1999. pap. 24.00 (*0-9651268-1-1*) Wrld Studies.

Myths the World Taught Me see **Reasonable Doubts**

Myths to Lie By. Dorothy Bryant. LC 83-51600. 192p. 1984. 20.00 (*0-931688-11-6*); pap. 9.95 (*0-931688-12-4*) Ata Bks.

Myths to Live By. Joseph Campbell. 304p. 1993. pap. 14.95 (*0-14-019461-4*, Arkana) Viking Penguin.

Mythus. Gary Gygax. Ed. by Lester Smith. (Dangerous Journeys Ser.). (Illus.). 416p. (Orig.). 1992. pap. 26.00 (*1-55878-131-5*) Game Designers.

Mythus des 20 Jahrhunderts. Alfred Rosenberg. LC 78-63710. (Studies in Fascism: Ideology & Practice). reprint ed. 64.50 (*0-404-16983-X*) AMS Pr.

Mythus Magick. Gary Gygax & Lester Smith. (Dangerous Journeys Ser.). 384p. (YA). 1992. pap. 24.00 (*1-55878-133-1*) Game Designers.

Mythus und Kultur (Myth & Culture) Arthur Liebert. Ed. by Kees W. Bolle. (Mythology Ser.). (GER.). 1978. reprint ed. lib. bdg. 19.95 (*0-405-10549-5*) Ayer.

Myxobacteria: Development & Cell Interactions. Ed. by Eugene Rosenberg. (Molecular Biology Ser.). (Illus.). 325p. 1984. 159.00 (*0-387-90962-1*) Spr-Verlag.

Myxobacteria 2. Ed. by Martin Dworkin & Dale Kaiser. LC 92-48477. (Illus.). 385p. 1993. 69.00 (*1-55581-060-8*) ASM Pr.

Myxomatosis. Frank Fenner & F. N. Ratcliffe. LC 65-17207. 412p. reprint ed. pap. 117.50 (*0-608-13571-2*, 2022448) Bks Demand.

Myxomycetes. Marie L. Farr. LC 76-19370. (Flora Neotropica Monographs: No. 16). 304p. 1976. pap. 22.50 (*0-89327-003-2*) NY Botanical.

***Myxomycetes: A Handbook of Slime Molds.** Steven L. Stephenson & Henry Stempen. (Illus.). 200p. 2000. pap. 19.95 (*0-88192-439-3*) Timber.

Myxomycetes, I. Ceratiomyxales, Echinosteliales, Liceales, Trichiales. Carlos Lado & Francisco Pando. (Flora Mycologica Iberica Ser.: Vol. 2). (ENG & SPA., Illus.). 323p. 1997. pap. 71.00 (*3-443-65007-4*, Pub. by Gebruder Borntraeger) Balogh.

***Myxomycetes of Ohio: Their Systematics, Biology & Use in Teaching.** Harold W. Keller & Karl L. Braun. LC 99-74757. (Bulletin Ser.: Vol. 13, No. 2). (Illus.). 182p. (C). 1999. pap. text 35.00 (*0-86727-133-7*) Ohio Bio Survey.

Myxophyceae of North America & Adjacent Regions. J. Tilden. (Bibliotheca Phycologica Ser.: Vol. 4). (Illus.). 1968. reprint ed. pap. 64.00 (*3-7682-0546-0*) Lubrecht & Cramer.

Myxosporidia of the U. S. S. R. S. S. Shul'man. Tr. by S. Sharma from RUS. (Russian Translation Ser.: No. 75). 643p. (C). 1990. text 149.00 (*90-6191-986-X*, Pub. by A A Balkema) Ashgate Pub Co.

Mz Goose & Her Wonderful Rhymes: They Make You Happy All of the Time. Elyse F. Aronson. (Illus.). 56p. (J). (ps-3). 2000. pap. 12.95 incl. audio (*0-9669510-1-8*, Pub. by Good Things) Penton Overseas.

Mzala. Mbulelo Mzamane. (Writers Ser.). 185p. 1995. reprint ed. pap. text 12.95 (*0-86975-465-3*, Pub. by Ravan Pr) Ohio U Pr.

***Mzumi.** Greg Knepp. LC 00-190651. 436p. 2000. 25.00 (*0-7388-1904-2*); pap. 18.00 (*0-7388-1905-0*) Xlibris Corp.

Mzungu. Junior African Writers Staff & Carolyn B. Mitchell. (Junior African Writers Ser.). (Illus.). 80p. (J). (gr. 3 up). 1995. pap. 4.95 (*0-7910-3017-2*) Chelsea Hse.

M31 Budgeting & Accounting for Nonaccounting Managers. Cuna. 176p. per. 33.26 (*0-7872-6273-0*) Kendall-Hunt.

***M4 Sherman Walk Around.** Jim Mesko. (On Deck Ser.: Vol. 1). (Illus.). 80p. 2000. pap. 14.95 (*0-89747-410-4*) Squad Sig Pubns.

N

N

N: A Romantic Mystery. Louis Edwards. 240p. 1998. pap. 12.95 (*0-452-27788-4*, Plume) Dutton Plume.

N. A. Automotive Chemical, Filter, Tire & Motor Oil: Creativity Is Essential for Growth. Frost & Sullivan Staff. 476p. 1996. spiral bd. 2495.00 (*0-7889-0461-2*, 5364) Frost & Sullivan.

N. A. Automotive OEM Undercarriage Component Markets: Leveraging Innovation for Growth. Frost & Sullivan Staff. 342p. 1996. spiral bd. 2495.00 (*0-7889-0452-3*, 5362-18) Frost & Sullivan.

N. A. D. A. Retail Consumer Edition. NADA Official Used Car Guide Co. Staff. Ed. by Lynn A. Weaver. 320p. 1992. pap. 9.95 (*1-881406-00-8*) NADA VA.

N. A. P. B. L. Umpire Manual. rev. ed. Umpire Development Program Staff. 112p. 1998. pap. 15.95 (*1-57243-259-4*) Triumph Bks.

N. A. Tink Tinkham: Watchmaker, Music Maker. Intro. by Jocelyn Ray. 126p. 1981. lib. bdg. 34.50 (*1-56475-210-0*); fiche. write for info. (*1-56475-211-9*) U NV Oral Hist.

N. A. Undercarriage Components Aftermarket: Reexamination of Distribution & Manufacturing Strategies Is Essential for Survival. Frost & Sullivan Staff. 356p. 1996. write for info. (*0-614-15986-5*, 5300) Frost & Sullivan.

***N. A. Wild Exlporation** Maynard Mack. (C). 1999. pap. text. write for info. (*0-393-98038-3*) Norton.

N-Acetyl-L-Cysteine & Its Uses. 1996. lib. bdg. 250.75 (*0-8490-5912-7*) Gordon Pr.

N & N Science Series-Physics. 3rd ed. Nancy A. Moreau. Ed. by Wayne Garnsey. (Science Ser.). (Illus.). 352p. 1998. pap. text 7.95 (*0-935487-55-7*) N & N Pub Co.

N Apocalypse Official Strategy Guide. Brady Games Staff. 112p. 1998. 11.99 (*1-56686-727-4*) Brady Pub.

N-Body Problem in General Relativity. Tullio Levi-Civita. Tr. by Arthur J. Knodel from FRE. 120p. 1965. text 113.00 (*90-277-0106-7*) Kluwer Academic.

N by E. Rockwell Kent. 1976. 23.95 (*0-8488-0760-X*) Amereon Ltd.

N by E. Rockwell Kent. LC 77-13530. (Illus.). 294p. reprint ed. pap. 91.20 (*0-8357-6230-0*, 203466300090) Bks Demand.

N by E. rev. ed. Rockwell Kent. LC 95-45443. (Illus.). 303p. 1996. reprint ed. pap. 15.95 (*0-8195-5292-5*, Wesleyan Univ Pr) U Pr of New Eng.

N. C. High School Record Book. Tim Stevens & Rick Strum. (Illus.). 80p. (Orig.). 1995. pap. 5.00 (*0-935400-23-0*) News & Observer.

N-C Machinability Data Systems. Ed. by Noel R. Parsons. LC 74-153852. (Society of Manufacturing Engineers Numerical Control Ser.). 219p. reprint ed. pap. 67.90 (*0-608-30083-7*, 201599900097) Bks Demand.

N. C. Wyeth. Kate F. Jennings. 48p. 1995. 6.98 (*0-7858-0219-3*) Bk Sales Inc.

N. C. Wyeth. Kate F. Jennings. (Illus.). 112p. 1999. pap. 19.95 (*1-57715-084-8*) Knckerbocker.

N. C. Wyeth: A Biography. David Michaelis. LC 98-6143. (Illus.). 555p. 1998. 40.00 (*0-679-42626-4*) Random.

***N. C. Wyeth: Precious Time.** Daniel E. O'Leary et al. Ed. by Susan L. Ransom. (Illus.). 40p. 2000. pap. write for info. (*0-916857-21-2*) Port Mus Art.

***N. C. Wyeth Paintings.** N. C. Wyeth. (Illus.). 2000. pap. 4.95 (*0-486-41069-2*) Dover.

N. C. Wyeth's Pilgrims. Robert D. San Souci. (Illus.). 40p. (J). (gr. 3-7). 1991. 14.95 (*0-87701-806-5*) Chronicle Bks.

N. C. Wyeth's Pilgrims. Robert D. San Souci. (Illus.). 40p. (J). (gr. 3-7). 1996. pap. 6.95 (*0-8118-1486-6*) Chronicle Bks.

N Celebration of U Black Man. Andrea C. Thomas. pap. text 10.00 (*0-9641425-0-3*) A C Thomas.

***N. Charles Slert Architect: Sketches Drawings Models.** N. Charles Slert. (Illus.). 330p. 1998. 60.00 (*0-9668838-0-2*) C Slert Assocs.

N-Dimensional Nonlinear Psychophysics: Theory & Case Studies. Robert A. Gregson. 320p. 1992. text 69.95 (*0-8058-1143-5*) L Erlbaum Assocs.

N-Dimensional Quasiconformal Mappings. P. Caraman. 554p. 1974. text 146.00 (*0-85626-005-3*) Gordon & Breach.

N. Edd Miller: Presidential Memoir, University of Nevada, Reno, 1965-1973. Intro. by Mary E. Glass. 470p. 1989. lib. bdg. 65.50 (*1-56475-142-2*); fiche. write for info. (*1-56475-143-0*) U NV Oral Hist.

N-Ethylaniline (N-Ethylbenzenamine) Ed. by GDCh-Advisory Committee on Existing Chemicals of E. (BUA Report Ser.: No. 15). 52p. 1993. pap. 32.00 (*3-527-28453-2*, Wiley-VCH) Wiley.

N

N. F. Federov (1828 to 1903) A Study in Russian Eupsychian & Utopian Thought. Stephen Lukashevich. LC 75-29731. 316p. 1977. 39.50 (*0-87413-113-8*) U Delaware Pr.

N. F. S. Grundtvig: An Introduction to His Life & Work. A. M. Allchin. LC 98-107160. 336p. 1997. 39.95 (*87-7288-656-0*, Pub. by Aarhus Univ Pr) David Brown.

N-Factor & Russian Prepositions. S. Hill. (Slavistic Printings & Reprintings Ser.: No. 118). 1977. 103.10 (*90-279-3096-1*) Mouton.

N for Narcissus. Allan Hunt. 1995. per. 12.95 (*0-85449-136-8*, Pub. by Gay Mens Pr) LPC InBook.

N. G. Chernyshevskii. Francis B. Randall. LC 67-19353. (Twayne's World Authors Ser.). 1967. lib. bdg. 20.95 (*0-8057-2212-2*) Irvington.

N-Gons. Friedrich Beckmann & Eckart W. Schmidt. Tr. by Cyril W. Garner. LC 70-185699. (Mathematical Expositions Ser.: No. 18). 207p. reprint ed. pap. 64.20 (*0-608-30880-3*, 201944800011) Bks Demand.

N. H. Real Estate Principles & Practices. 2nd ed. Walter A. Jablonski. LC 89-62236. (Illus.). 408p. 1990. 31.95 (*0-926180-01-0*) PREW.

N. Hawthorne, Sa Vie et Son Oeuvre. L. Dhaleine. LC 77-164828. (BCL Ser. I). reprint ed. 45.00 (*0-404-02122-0*) AMS Pr.

N-Hexane. (Environmental Health Criteria Ser.: No. 122). (ENG, FRE & SPA.). 164p. 1991. pap. text 32.00 (*92-4-157122-5*, 1160122) World Health.

N Is for Naked. Ed Lange. Ed. by Iris Bancroft. (Vintage Nudist Classics Ser.). (Illus.). 64p. (Orig.). 1995. pap. 21.95 (*1-55599-052-5*) Events Unltd.

***N Is for New York.** Mary Bowman-Kruhm. (Alpha Flight Bks.). (Illus.). 60p. (ps-3). 2000. 17.95 (*1-892920-44-1*) G H B Pubs.

N Is for Noose. Sue Grafton. 1999. mass mkt. write for info. (*0-449-00457-0*, Crest) Fawcett.

N Is for Noose. Sue Grafton. LC 99-90100. 290p. 1999. mass mkt. 7.99 (*0-449-22361-2*) Fawcett.

N Is for Noose. Sue Grafton. LC 97-43120. 304p. 1995. 25.00 (*0-8050-3650-4*) H Holt & Co.

N Is for Noose. large type ed. Sue Grafton. LC 98-5566. 576p. 1998. 28.95 (*0-7862-1296-9*) Thorndike Pr.

N Is for Noose. large type ed. Sue Grafton. LC 98-5566. 455p. 2001. 30.00 (*0-7862-1297-7*) Thorndike Pr.

N. J. Title 33: Intoxicating Liquors. 110p. 2000. ring bd. 10.95 (*1-889031-08-9*) Looseleaf Law.

***N. Johnson Rental: Auditing Cases.** 1999. teacher ed. write for info. (*0-13-016935-8*) P-H.

***N. Johnsons Rental: Auditing Cases.** 1999. 4.00 (*0-13-016934-X*) P-H.

N. L. Bowen & Crystallization-Differentiation: The Evolution of a Theory. Davis A. Young. (Monograph Ser.: Vol. 4). 276p. 1998. pap. 16.00 (*0-939950-47-2*) Mineralogical Soc.

N M R Studies of Molecules Oriented in the Nematic Phase of Liquid Crystals. P. Diehl & C. L. Khetrapel. (NMR-Basic Principles & Progress Ser.: Vol. 1). (Illus.). v, 174p. 1970. 35.00 (*0-387-04665-8*) Spr-Verlag.

N. N. Bogolubov: Selected Works, 2. vols., Vol. 2. N. N. Bogolubov. 1990. text 414.00 (*2-88124-771-7*) Gordon & Breach.

N. N. Bogolubov: Selected Works: Dynamical Theory, Vol. 2. Ed. by N. N. Bogolubov. (Classics of Soviet Mathematics Ser.: Vol. 1). x, 386p. 1990. text 211.00 (*2-88124-752-0*) Gordon & Breach.

N. N. Bogolubov Pt. III: Selected Works, Part III: Nonlinear Mechanics & Pure Mathematics, Vol. 2. Ed. by V. S. Vladimirov. (Classics of Soviet Mathematics Ser.). 560p. 1995. text 198.00 (*2-88124-918-3*) Gordon & Breach.

N. N. Bogolubov Pt. IV: Selected Works: Quantum Field, Vol. 2. N. N. Bogolubov, Jr. (Classics of Soviet Mathematics Ser.). 464p. 1995. text 180.00 (*2-88124-926-4*) Gordon & Breach.

N. N. Bogolubov, Selected Works: Quantum & Classical Statistical Mechanics. Ed. by N. N. Bogolubov. (Classics of Soviet Mathematics Ser.: Vol. 2). x, 420p. 1990. text 226.00 (*2-88124-768-7*) Gordon & Breach.

N. N. Bugolubov: Selected Works, 4 vols., Vol. 2. N. N. Bogolubov. 1995. text 785.00 (*2-88449-068-X*) Gordon & Breach.

N, N-Diethylanilin see N, N-Diethylaniline: (N, N-Diethylaminobenzene)

N, N-Diethylaniline: (N, N-Diethylaminobenzene) Ed. by GDCh-Advisory Committee on Existing Chemicals of E. LC 93-2641. (BUA Report Ser.).Tr. of N, N-Diethylanilin. (ENG & GER.). 1993. 32.00 (*1-56081-732-1*, Wiley-VCH) Wiley.

N, N-Diethylaniline: (N, N-Diethylaminobenzene) Ed. by GDCh-Advisory Committee on Existing Chemicals of E. LC 93-2641. (BUA Report Ser.).Tr. of N, N-Diethylanilin. (ENG & GER.). 1993. 25.00 (*0-685-67743-5*, Wiley-VCH) Wiley.

N Nitrogen: Suppl. Vol. B: Compounds with Noble Gases & Hydrogen, Pt. 1. Ed. by Gmelin Institute for Inorganic Chemistry of the Ma. (Gmelin Handbook of Inorganic & Organometallic Chemistry Ser.). (Illus.). xiv, 280p. 1993. 1155.00 (*0-387-93686-6*) Spr-Verlag.

N Nitrogen: Suppl. Vol. B: Compounds with Noble Gases & Hydrogen, Pt. 2. Ed. by Gmelin Institute for Inorganic Chemistry of the Ma. (Gmelin Handbook of Inorganic & Organometallic Chemistry Ser.). (Illus.). xiii, 188p. 1993. 830.00 (*0-387-93672-6*) Spr-Verlag.

N Nitrogen Vol. B6: Compounds with Oxygen. (Gmelin). (Illus.). xv, 377p. 1996. suppl. ed. 1575.00 (*3-540-93729-3*) Spr-Verlag.

N-Nitrosamines. Ed. by Jean-Pierre Anselme. LC 79-12461. (ACS Symposium Ser.: No. 101). 1979. 29.95 (*0-8412-0503-5*) Am Chemical.

N-Nitrosamines. Ed. by Jean-Pierre Anselme. LC 79-12461. (ACS Symposium Ser.: Vol. 101). 214p. 1979. reprint ed. pap. 66.40 (*0-608-03096-1*, 206354900007) Bks Demand.

N-Nitroso Compounds. Ed. by Richard A. Scanlan & Steven R. Tannenbaum. LC 81-19047. (ACS Symposium Ser.: No. 174). 1981. 49.95 (*0-8412-0667-8*) Am Chemical.

N-Nitroso Compounds. Ed. by Richard A. Scanlan & Steven R. Tannenbaum. LC 81-19047. (ACS Symposium Ser.: No. 174). (Illus.). 410p. 1981. reprint ed. pap. 127.10 (*0-608-03240-9*, 206375900007) Bks Demand.

N-Nitroso Compounds Analysis & Formation: Proceedings of a Working Conference Held at the Deutsches Krebsforschungszentrum, Heidelberg, Federal Republic of Germany, 13-15 October 1971. International Agency for Research on Cancer Staff. Ed. by P. Bogovski et al. LC 74-153017. (IARC Scientific Publications: No. 3). 152p. 1972. pap. 47.20 (*0-7837-3990-7*, 204382100011) Bks Demand.

N-Nitroso Compounds, Analysis, Formation, & Occurrence: Proceedings of the 6th International Symposium on N-Nitroso Compounds Held in Budapest, 16-20 October 1979. International Symposium on N-Nitroso Compounds (6t. Ed. by E. A. Walker. LC 81-181190. (IARC Scientific Publications: No. 31). (Illus.). 872p. reprint ed. pap. 200.00 (*0-8357-6452-4*, 203582300097) Bks Demand.

N-Nitroso Compounds in Carcinogenesis: Occurrence & Biological Effects. H. Bartsch. (IARC Scientific Publications: No. 41). (Illus.). 672p. 1986. 75.00 (*0-19-723041-5*) OUP.

N-Nylons: Their Synthesis, Structure & Properties. Shaul M. Aharoni. LC 97-183500. 622p. 1997. 295.00 (*0-471-96068-3*) Wiley.

N-O Spells No! Teddy Slater. LC 92-21422. (Hello Reader! Ser.). (Illus.). 32p. (J). (ps-3). 1993. pap. 3.50 (*0-590-44186-8*) Scholastic Inc.

N-O Spells No! Teddy Slater. (Hello, Reader! Ser.). (J). 1993. 8.70 (*0-606-02781-5*, Pub. by Turtleback) Demco.

N or M? Agatha Christie. 240p. 1986. mass mkt. 5.99 (*0-425-09845-1*) Berkley Pub.

N or M? Agatha Christie. (Agatha Christie Collection). 1998. mass mkt. 3.99 (*0-425-16929-4*) Berkley Pub.

***N or M?** Agatha Christie. (Tommy & Tuppence Mysteries Ser.). 224p. 2000. mass mkt. 5.99 (*0-451-20113-2*, Sig) NAL.

***N-Particle Model.** David Martin Degner. (Illus.). 144p. 2000. pap. text 100.00 (*0-9668628-0-5*) Degner Pr.

N* Physics: Proceedings of the 4th CEBAF/INT Workshop. Ed. by W. Roberts. 300p. 1997. 56.00 (*981-02-3138-5*) World Scientific Pub.

N* Physics & Nonpertubative Quantum Chromodynamics: Proceedings of the Joint ECT*/Jefferson Lab Workshop, May 18-29, 1998, Trento, Italy. Ed. by V. B. Burkert et al. LC 99-15826. (Few-Body Systems Ser.: Vol. 11). 380p. 1999. 99.00 (*3-211-83299-8*) Spr-Verlag.

N. R. I. Investment Policy & Procedure: A Rady Reckoner. Jaynarayan Vyas. (C). 1988. 275.00 (*0-7855-3713-9*) St Mut.

N. S. Trubetzkoy: Studies in General Linguistics & Language Structure. Nikolai Sergeevich Trubetskoi. Ed. & Tr. by Anatoly Liberman. Tr. by Marvin J. Taylor. LC 99-18338. (Sound & Meaning Ser.). 328p. 1999. pap. 24.95 (*0-8223-2299-4*) Duke.

N. S. Trubetzkoy's Letters & Notes. N. S. Trubetzkoy. Ed. by Roman Jakobson et al. (Janua Linguarum, Series Major: No. 47). (Illus.). 1975. 161.55 (*90-279-3181-X*) Mouton.

N Scale Model Railroad That Grows. Kent Wood & Ric LaBan. LC 97-117723. 96p. (Orig.). 1996. pap. 15.95 (*0-89024-223-2*, 12145) Kalmbach.

N Scale Model Railroad Track Plans. Russ Larson. LC 99-196095. (Illus.). 64p. 1969. pap. 10.95 (*0-89024-335-2*) Kalmbach.

***N Scale Model Railroading.** Robert Schleicher. LC 00-102690. (Illus.). 224p. 2000. pap. 23.95 (*0-87341-702-X*, NMRR) Krause Pubns.

N Scale Model Railroading: Getting Started in the Hobby. Marty McGuirk. 1999. pap. text 18.95 (*0-89024-347-6*) Kalmbach.

N Scale Model Railroading Manual. Robert Schleicher. (Illus.). 100p. (Orig.). 1984. pap. text 7.95 (*0-9612692-1-9*) Rocky Mntn Pub Co.

N Scale Product Guide. Ed. by Keith Lyons. 1997. per. 24.95 (*0-945434-26-X*) Hundman Pub.

N. Scott Momaday. Adkins. 1998. 22.95 (*0-8057-4005-8*, Twyne) Mac Lib Ref.

N. Scott Momaday: The Cultural & Literary Background. Matthias Schubnell. LC 85-40479. 338p. 1986. 29.95 (*0-8061-1951-9*) U of Okla Pr.

N-Space. Larry Niven. 704p. 1991. mass mkt. 5.99 (*0-8125-1001-1*, Pub. by Tor Bks) St Martin.

N-Substituted Quaternary Salts of Pyridine & Related Compounds. Wanda Sliwa. LC 91-43348. (Reactivity & Structure Ser.). 1992. write for info. (*0-387-54971-4*); write for info. (*3-540-54971-4*) Spr-Verlag.

'N Sync. Andrews & McMeel Staff. 1999. 4.95 (*0-8362-1648-2*) Andrews & McMeel.

***'N Sync.** John F. Grabowski. LC 99-40636. (Galaxy of Superstars Ser.). (Illus.). 64p. (YA). (gr. 3). 1999. pap. 9.95 (*0-7910-5494-2*) Chelsea Hse.

'N Sync. John F. Grabowski. LC 99-40636. (Galaxy of Superstars Ser.). (Illus.). 64p. 1999. 17.95 (*0-7910-5493-4*) Chelsea Hse.

***'N Sync.** Cynthia Laslo. (High Interest Bks.). (Illus.). (J). 2000. 19.00 (*0-516-23324-6*) Childrens.

***'N Sync.** Cynthia Laslo. LC 00-23321. (High Interest Bks.). (Illus.). 48p. (J). (gr. 4-7). 2000. pap. write for info. (*0-516-23524-9*) Childrens.

***'N Sync.** Lexi Martin & Jessica Davis. LC 00-32923. (Illus.). 96p. 2000. 9.98 (*1-58663-061-X*) M Friedman Pub Grp Inc.

***'N Sync: Chris.** Smithmark Publishing Staff. (Illus.). 48p. (gr. 4-7). 1999. 4.98 (*0-7651-1721-5*) Smithmark.

'N Sync: Get 'n Sync with the Guys. Angie Nichols. (Illus.). 64p. (YA). (gr. 6-12). 1999. pap. 12.95 (*0-8230-8352-7*, Billboard Bks) Watsn-Guptill.

***'N Sync: J. C.** Smithmark Publishing Staff. 48p. 1999. 4.98 (*0-7651-1722-3*) Smithmark.

***'N Sync: Joey.** Smithmark Publishing Staff. (Illus.). 48p. (gr. 4-7). 1999. 4.98 (*0-7651-1723-1*) Smithmark.

***'N Sync: Justin.** Smithmark Publishing Staff. (Illus.). 48p. (gr. 4-7). 1999. 4.98 (*0-7651-1724-X*) Smithmark.

***'N Sync: Lance.** Smithmark Publishing Staff. (Illus.). 48p. (gr. 4-7). 1999. 4.98 (*0-7651-1725-8*) Smithmark.

***'N Sync: No Strings Attached.** Ed. by Triumph Books Staff. (Illus.). 96p. 2000. pap. 9.95 (*1-57243-393-0*) Triumph Bks.

'N Sync: Poster Magazine. Starlog Press Staff. (Superstar Ser.: No. 2). 1998. pap. 2.99 (*0-934551-58-8*) Starlog Grp Inc.

'N Sync: Special Edition. Jasmine Galt. (Illus.). 32p. pap. 7.95 (*0-8230-8355-1*) Watsn-Guptill.

'N Sync: Tearin' up the Charts. Matt Netter. 1998. per. 4.99 (*0-671-03470-7*, Archway) PB.

'N Sync: Tearing up the Charts. Anna Louise Golden. 1999. mass mkt. 4.99 (*0-312-97198-2*, St Martins Paperbacks) St Martin.

'N Sync: The Official Book. 'N Sync. LC 99-165768. 96p. (J). 1998. pap. 9.95 (*0-440-41636-1*) BDD Bks Young Read.

'N Sync & Friends. (Starlog Platinum Ser.). 1998. pap. 4.99 (*0-934551-57-X*) Starlog Grp Inc.

'N Sync & Friends. Ed. by Anne Raso. (Starlog Celebrity Ser.: No. 16). 1999. pap. 4.99 (*0-934551-89-8*, Pub. by Starlog Grp Inc) Kable News Co Inc.

'N Sync Backstage Pass: An Unofficial Scrapbook. Michael-Anne Johns. (Illus.). 48p. (J). (gr. 3-9). 1999. pap. 5.99 (*0-439-07224-7*) Scholastic Inc.

'N Sync Confidential. Angie Nichols. (Illus.). 1999. pap. 16.95 (*0-8230-8353-5*) Watsn-Guptill.

***'N Sync 'n Detail.** Ashley Adams. 64p. 2000. pap. text 12.95 (*0-8256-1801-0*, Amsco Music) Music Sales.

'N Sync with J. C. Nancy E. Krulik. 1999. mass mkt. 4.99 (*0-671-03277-1*) S&S Trade.

'N Sync with Justin. Matt Netter. (Illus.). 123p. (J). (gr. 3-7). 1999. per. 4.99 (*0-671-03276-3*, Archway) PB.

N. T. Church Government. Kenneth Daughters. 1989. pap. 5.50 (*0-937396-82-6*) Walterick Pubs.

N-3 Fatty Acids: Prevention & Treatment in Vascular Disease. Ed. by S. D. Kristensen et al. LC 95-49885. (Current Topics in Cardiovascular Diseases Ser.). (Illus.). 230p. 1996. 110.00 (*3-540-76001-6*) Spr-Verlag.

N-3 Fatty Acids & Vascular Disease: Backgound & Pathophysiology - Hyperlipidaemia - Renal Diseases-Ischaemic Heart Disease. Ed. by R. DeCaterina et al. 166p. 1995. 49.00 (*0-387-19837-7*) Spr-Verlag.

N-Town Play Vol. 1: Introduction & Text, Vol. 1. Ed. by Stephen Spector. (Early English Text Society Ser.: No. 11). (Illus.). 472p. 1992. text 75.00 (*0-19-722411-3*) OUP.

N-Town Play Vol. 2: Commentary & Glossary. Ed. by Stephen Spector. (Early English Text Society - Supplementary Ser.: No. 12). (Illus.). 256p. 1992. text 55.00 (*0-19-722412-1*) OUP.

N-Widths in Approximation Theory. Alan Pinkus. (Ergebnisse der Mathematik und Ihrer Grenzgebiete Ser.: Vol. 7). 300p. 1985. 136.95 (*0-387-13638-X*) Spr-Verlag.

N. Y. C. in 1979. Kathy Acker. (Illus.). 24p. (Orig.). 1981. pap. 3.00 (*0-917061-09-8*) Top Stories.

N. Y. C. Police Department Patrol Guide. 1100p. pap. 29.00 (*0-87526-556-1*) Gould.

N. Y. C. Traffic Rules: With N. Y. Vehicle & Traffic Law. 145p. 1997. pap. 15.95 (*0-87526-545-6*) Gould.

N. Y. Consolidated Laws (NYCU) 1300p. 1998. pap. 35.00 (*0-87526-345-3*); pap. 29.00 (*0-87526-347-X*); ring bd. 39.00 (*0-87526-346-1*); ring bd. 39.00 (*0-87526-348-8*); ring bd. 39.00 (*0-87526-349-6*); ring bd. 39.00 (*0-87526-350-X*); ring bd. 39.00 (*0-87526-351-8*); ring bd. 39.00 (*0-87526-352-6*) Gould.

N. Y. Criminal & Civil Forfeitures: Including Narcotics Eviction Proceedings. annuals rev. ed. Steven L. Kessler. 1000p. pap. 44.95 (*0-87526-543-X*) Gould.

N. Y. Gold: Directory of Photography. 10th ed. (Illus.). 400p. 1996. 49.95 (*0-614-13036-0*) NY Gold.

N. Y. Identification Law: The Wade Hearing - The Trial. annuals rev. ed. Miriam Hibel. Date not set. pap. 44.95 (*0-87526-533-2*) Gould.

N. Y. Indians & the Printup Family. A. D. Printup, II. Ed. by Arvid Harder. LC 83-72027. (Illus.). 99p. 1983. 66.66 (*0-685-07429-3*); pap. 33.33 (*0-685-07430-7*) Clark Inc.

N. Y. Insurance Law. 500p. 1997. pap. 19.95 (*0-87526-539-1*) Gould.

N. Y. Law Enforcement Handbook. 740p. Date not set. pap. 6.95 (*0-87526-510-3*) Gould.

N. Y. S. Memo Book Cards. 2000. 5.95 (*0-930137-19-1*) Looseleaf Law.

N. Y., Understanding the Penal Law. Richard Moriarty. 1998. teacher ed. 25.95 (*0-87526-424-7*) Gould.

Na-beregach Taryni. A. Kondrat'jev. 320p. (Orig.). 1990. reprint ed. 20.00 (*1-878445-52-9*) Antiquary CT.

Na Bregovite na Xadson see On the Edge of the Hudson

Na Fone Kormil'tsa (On the Background of a Provider) Natalya Asenkova. LC 97-6960. (RUS.). 120p. 1997. 9.00 (*1-55779-096-5*) Hermitage Pubs.

***Na Hana a Ka La'i.** Hokulani Cleeland. (HAW., Illus.). 17p. (J). (gr. k). 1999. pap. 6.95 incl. audio (*1-58191-050-9*) Aha Punana Leo.

Na Holoholona Maoli: Native Animals. Wren & Maile. (Keiki's First Bks.). (ENG & HAW., Illus.). 10p. (J). (ps). 1992. bds. 4.95 (*1-880188-27-9*) Bess Pr.

Na Hwa Manhaj Li-Tan Zim Al-Mus Talah Al Shari: Dir Asah Fial-Mak Aniz Wa-Istikhd Am Atiha. Hani M. Atiyyah. LC 97-45666. (Silsilat Al-Manhaj Iyah Al-Islam Iyah Ser.). 1997. write for info. (*1-56564-263-5*) IIIT VA.

Na Kau O Hawai'i Nei. Illus. by 'Umi Kahalio'umi & Kahanano'eau Morita. (HAW.). (J). (gr. k). 1992. 6.95 (*1-58191-039-8*) Aha Punana Leo.

Na Keiki 'Elima. William H. Wilson. (HAW., Illus.). 15p. (J). (gr. k-3). 1992. pap. 6.95 incl. audio (*1-890270-25-3*) Aha Punana Leo.

Na-Khi Religion: An Analytical Appraisal of the Na-Khi Ritual Texts. Anthony Jackson. (Religion & Society Ser.). 1979. text 142.35 (*90-279-7642-2*) Mouton.

Na Ki'i Pohaku. P. F. Kwiatkowski. (Illus.). pap. 19.95 (*0-914916-83-1*) Ku Paa.

***Na Klar! An Introductory German Course.** 3rd ed. 1999. pap., lab manual ed. 24.69 (*0-07-013708-0*) McGrw-H Hghr Educ.

***Na Klar! An Introductory German Course.** 3rd ed. (C). 1999. pap., wbk. ed. 24.69 (*0-07-013707-2*) McGrw-H Hghr Educ.

***Na Klar! An Introductory German Course.** 3rd ed. Robert Di Donato et al. 560p. (C). 1998. pap., student ed. 68.13 incl. audio compact disk (*0-07-230561-4*) McGrw-H Hghr Educ.

***Na Koko O Keia Keiki Hawai'i.** William H. Wilson. (HAW., Illus.). 17p. (J). (gr. k-2). 1999. pap. 6.95 incl. audio (*1-58191-060-6*) Aha Punana Leo.

Na Kraiu Sveta see On the Edge of the World

Na Leo I Ka Makani - Voices on the Wind: Historic Photographs of Hawaiians of Yesteryear. Palani Vaughan. (Illus.). 144p. 1987. boxed set 25.95 (*0-935180-59-1*) Mutual Pub HI.

Na Maka o Halawa: A History of Halawa Ahupua'a, Oahu. P. Christiaan Klieger. 113p. 1995. pap. 29.95 (*0-930897-90-0*) Bishop Mus.

Na Mamo: Hawaiian People Today. Jay Hartwell. pap. 22.95 (*1-883528-04-6*) Ai Pohaku Pr.

Na Mea Kanu: Plants. Wren & Maile. (Keiki's First Bks.). (ENG & HAW., Illus.). 10p. (J). (ps). 1992. bds. 4.95 (*1-880188-28-7*) Bess Pr.

Na Mele Hula: A Collection of Hawaiian Hula Chants. Nona Beamer. LC 87-751437. (Illus.). 96p. (C). 1987. pap. 21.95 incl. audio (*0-939154-58-7*, Pub. by Inst Polynesian) UH Pr.

Na Mele Hula: A Collection of Hawaiian Hula Chants, Vol. 2. Nona Beamer. (Illus.). 96p. 2000. pap. 21.95 incl. audio (*0-939154-57-9*) Inst Polynesian.

Na Mele o Hawai'i Nei: 101 Hawaiian Songs. Compiled by Samuel H. Elbert & Noelani K. Mahoe. (ENG & HAW., Illus.). 120p. (Orig.). 1982. pap. 7.95 (*0-87022-219-8*) UH Pr.

Na Mele Welo: Songs of Our Heritage. Mary K. Pukui. 238p. 1995. pap. 21.95 (*0-930897-87-0*) Bishop Mus.

***Na Moku Kaulana.** Keiki Kawai'ae'a. (HAW., Illus.). 19p. (J). (gr. k). 1999. pap. 6.95 incl. audio (*1-58191-078-9*) Aha Punana Leo.

Na Momi Ho'omana'o: Pearls to Remember, Vol. 2. Barbara S. McDonagh. Ed. by Harold H. Teves. (Illus.). 48p. (YA). (gr. 4 up). 1997. 21.95 (*0-9643781-1-6*) Liko Pubng.

Na Mo'olelo Hawai'i O Ka Wa Kahiko: Stories of Old Hawaii. Roy K. Alameida. LC 99-205062. (Illus.). 128p. 1997. pap. 12.95 (*1-57306-026-7*); pap., teacher ed. 8.95 (*1-57306-065-8*) Bess Pr.

Na 'Olelo Hawaii: Words. Wren & Maile. (Keiki's First Bks.). (ENG & HAW., Illus.). 10p. (J). (ps). 1992. bds. 4.95 (*1-880188-29-5*) Bess Pr.

Na Plus Activated & K Plus Channel in Cardiac Cells. L. Hsiang-Ning. No. 59. 150p. (Orig.). 1993. pap. 39.50 (*90-6186-530-1*, Pub. by Leuven Univ) Coronet Bks.

Na Plus-H Plus Exchange, 1 vols. Ed. by Sergio Grinstein. 376p. 1988. lib. bdg. 248.00 (*0-8493-4701-7*, QH604) CRC Pr.

Na Pule Kahiko: Ancient Hawaiian Prayers. June Gutmanis. Ed. & Illus. by Esther T. Mookini. LC 83-82056. 124p. 1983. 17.50 (*0-9607938-6-0*) Editions Ltd.

Na Rubovima Svijeta: Jedrilicom Hrvatska Cigra od Arktika do Antarktike see Arctic to the Antarctica: Cigra Circumnauigates the Americas

Na To Hoa Aroha: From Your Dear Friend: The Correspondence Between Sir Apirana Ngata & Sir Peter Buck, 1925-50, Vol. 1: 1925-29. Ed. by M. P. Sorrenson. (Illus.). 269p. 1987. 32.00 (*0-19-648035-3*) OUP.

Na Vlastni Kuzi: Dialog Pus Barikadu see Under a Cruel Star: A Life in Prague, 1941-1968

Na Wahi Pana o Ko'olau Poko: Legendary Places of Ko'olau Poko. Anne K. Landgraf. Tr. by Fred K. Meinecke from HAW. LC 94-12427. (Illus.). 176p. (C). 1994. text 34.00 (*0-8248-1578-5*) UH Pr.

***NAA: Fifty Years in the World of Work with 50-Year Cumulative Index.** 738p. 1998. 40.00 (*1-57018-119-5*, 1119) BNA Books.

NAACP: A History of the National Association for the Advancement of Colored People. Charles F. Kellogg. (Illus.). 108.75 (*0-317-20667-2*) Bodmin Bks.

NAACP: A History of the National Association for the Advancement of Colored People. Charles F. Kellogg. LC E 0185.5.K29. 368p. reprint ed. pap. 114.10 (*0-608-12104-5*, 202414500001) Bks Demand.

NAACP & the New Black Agenda. Don Rojas. 1997. write for info. (*0-8129-2687-0*, Times Bks) Crown Pub Group.

NAACP Comes of Age: The Defeat of Judge John J. Parker. Kenneth W. Goings. LC 89-46011. (Blacks in the Diaspora Ser.). 140p. 1990. 8.95 (*0-253-32585-4*) Ind U Pr.

NAACP Never Ending Struggle Will Be Okay, We Can Still Come Out on Top. Tena L. Brown. (Illus.). 30p. (YA). (gr. 5 up). 1997. pap. text 10.00 (*1-890925-23-3*) Stori Tyme.

NAACP's Legal Strategy Against Segregated Education, 1925-1950. Mark V. Tushnet. LC 86-24971. xvi, 222p. (C). 1987. pap. text 15.95 (*0-8078-4173-0*) U of NC Pr.

NAAG 1993-1994 Handbook. 76p. 1994. 15.00 (*0-317-05764-2*, PB01) Natl Attys General.

NAAG Policy Positions. 40p. 1993. 10.00 (*0-317-05765-0*, PB02) Natl Attys General.

Naam or Word. 4th ed. Kirpal Singh. LC 81-51512. (Illus.). 335p. 1982. reprint ed. pap. 10.00 (*0-918224-12-8*) S K Pubns.

NAAO Directory. 107p. 1989. pap. 20.00 (*0-927851-00-8*, 5650) NAAO.

Naaqutet Ataucimek Yaavet Quinum. Betsy Jenkins & Julia K. Egoak. 11.00 (*1-55036-560-6*) Todd Commns.

Na'ar Hayisi: I Was a Child. Aidel Wajngort. 1997. 10.95 (*0-932351-35-2*) B P Marketing.

Na'ar Hayisi: I Was a Child. Aidel Wajngort. (gr. 3 up). 1997. pap. text 8.95 (*0-932351-36-0*) B P Marketing.

NAB Engineering Conference Proceedings, 1993. (Illus.). 512p. 1993. 100.00 (*0-89324-164-4*) Natl Assn Broadcasters.

NAB Guide for Broadcast Station Chief Operators. NAB Staff. 82p. 1991. 60.00 (*0-89324-105-9*) Natl Assn Broadcasters.

NAB Guide to Advanced Television Systems, 1991. 2nd ed. NAB Staff. (Illus.). 150p. (Orig.). 1991. 60.00 (*0-89324-111-3*) Natl Assn Broadcasters.

NAB Guide to AM & FM Radio Performance Measurements. National Association of Broadcasters Staff. 50p. (Orig.). 1990. pap. 60.00 (*0-685-47799-1*) Natl Assn Broadcasters.

NAB Guide to Station Chief Operators. 2nd ed. Harold Hallikainen. 77p. 1996. pap. 75.00 (*0-89324-257-8*, 3838) Natl Assn Broadcasters.

NAB Legal Guide to Broadcast Law & Regulation. 15th ed. William S. Green et al. Ed. by Barry Umansky. 1500p. 1996. 189.95 (*0-89324-254-3*, 3837) Natl Assn Broadcasters.

NAB Legal Guide to Broadcast Law & Regulation - 1993 Supplement. Ed. by William S. Green. 264p. 1993. 125.00 (*0-89324-109-1*) Natl Assn Broadcasters.

NAB 98 Broadcasters Law & Regulation Conference Papers. 693p. 1998. pap. 130.00 (*0-89324-308-6*) Natl Assn Broadcasters.

NAB Proceedings, 1990: 44th Annual Broadcast Engineering Conference. 552p. (Orig.). 1990. pap. 70.00 (*0-89324-086-9*) Natl Assn Broadcasters.

NAB Study Guide: How to Prepare for the Nursing Home Administrator's Examination. 3rd rev. ed. Sorenson & Rock Staff et al. Ed. by James E. Allen. (C). Date not set. pap. 65.00 (*0-9635064-3-9*) Nat Assn Bds Exam.

Nabadwipa: The Hidden Treasure of the Holy Dhama. Bhaktivinoda Thakur. Ed. by Alan Dulfon & Ray Richards. Tr. by Banu Dasa from BEN. (Illus.). 185p. (Orig.). 1993. pap. 9.95 (*1-884295-02-9*) Ananta Prnting.

Nabakov: The Mystery of Literary Structures. Leona Toker. LC 88-47927. 264p. 1988. text 39.95 (*0-8014-2211-6*) Cornell U Pr.

Nabarro Nathanson: Law of the Internet. Clive Gringras. 1997. write for info. (*0-406-00249-5*, LI, MICHIE) LEXIS Pub.

Nabarro Nathanson: Pensions Law. Nabarro Nathanson Pensions Department Members & John Quarrell. 1997. pap. write for info. (*0-406-04933-5*, NNPL, MICHIE) LEXIS Pub.

Nabataean Aramaic Lexicon NABLEX. W. J. Jobling. LC 95-83255. 1996. 39.00 (*1-881265-20-X*) Dunwoody Pr.

Nabataean Tomb Inscriptions of Mada'in Salih: With an Arabic Section Translated by Dr. Solaiman Al-Theeb, King Saud University, Riyadh. Ed. & Tr. by John F. Healey. Tr. by Solaiman Al-Theeb. (Journal of Semetic Studies: Suppl. No. 1). (Illus.). 312p. 1994. text 65.00 (*0-19-922162-6*) OUP.

Nabataeans--Their History, Culture & Archaeology. Philip C. Hammond. (Studies in Mediterranean Archaeology: Vol. XXXVII). (Illus.). 127p. 1973. pap. 39.50 (*91-85058-57-2*) P Astroms.

NABC Drill Book. Ed. by Jerry Krause. LC 98-12624. (Illus.). 224p. (Orig.). 1997. pap. 14.95 (*1-57028-148-3*, 81483H, Mstrs Pr) NTC Contemp Pub Co.

NABC Report 5, Agricultural Biotechnology: A Public Conversation about Risk. Ed. by June F. MacDonald. 135p. 1993. pap. 5.00 (*0-9630907-3-9*) Natl Agri Biotech.

NABC Report 4, Animal Biotechnology: Opportunities & Challenges. Ed. by June F. MacDonald. 181p. 1992. pap. 5.00 (*0-9630907-2-0*) Natl Agri Biotech.

NABC Report 6, Agricultural Biotechnology & the Public Good. Ed. by June F. MacDonald. 213p. 1994. pap. 5.00 (*0-9630907-5-5*) Natl Agri Biotech.

NABC Report 3, Agricultural Biotechnology at the Crossroads: Biological, Social & Institutional Concerns. Ed. by June F. MacDonald. 307p. 1991. pap. 7.00 (*0-9630907-4-7*) Natl Agri Biotech.

NABC Report 3, Agricultural Biotechnology at the Crossroads: Biological, Social & Institutional Concerns. Ed. by June F. MacDonald. 307p. 1992. pap. text 5.00 (*0-685-60015-7*) Natl Agri Biotech.

Nabis: Bonnard, Vuillard & Their Circle. Claire Freches-Thory & Antoine Terrasse. (Illus.). 320p. 39.95 (*2-08-013503-1*, Pub. by Flammarion) Abbeville Pr.

Nabis & Their Period. Charles Chassѐ. LC 73-412171. 136p. 1969. write for info. (*0-85331-074-2*) Lund Humphries.

Nablyudeniya anomal'nykh atmosfernykh yavleniy V S S R see Observations of Anomalous Atmospheric Phenomena in the U. S. S. R., Statistical Analysis: Results of Processing First Sample of Observational Data

Nabobs. Percival Spear. (C). 1991. reprint ed. text 8.50 (*0-8364-2652-5*, Pub. by Rupa) S Asia.

Nabobs: A Study of the Social Life of the English in Eighteenth Century India. Percival Spear. (Oxford India Paperbacks Ser.). (Illus.). 226p. 1998. pap. text 11.50 (*0-19-564381-X*) OUP.

***Nabob's Daughter.** Dawn Lindsey. (Regency Romance Ser.). 224p. 2000. mass mkt. 4.99 (*0-451-20045-4*, Sig) NAL.

Nabob's Nephew. large type ed. Prudence Bebb. (Linford Romance Library). 304p. 1993. pap. 16.99 (*0-7089-7462-7*, Linford) Ulverscroft.

Nabob's Wife. large type ed. Phyllida Barstow. 1991. 27.99 (*0-7089-2401-8*) Ulverscroft.

Nabokov: The Critical Heritage. Ed. by Norman Page. (Critical Heritage Ser.). 400p. 1982. 69.50 (*0-7100-9223-7*, Routledge Thoemms) Routledge.

***Nabokov & His Fiction: New Perspectives.** Ed. by Julian W. Connolly. LC 98-47176. (Studies in Russian Literature). 256p. (C). 1999. write for info. (*0-521-63283-8*) Cambridge U Pr.

Nabokov & the Novel. Ellen Pifer. LC 80-16197. 208p. 1980. 28.50 (*0-674-59840-7*) HUP.

Nabokov at the Limits: Redrawing Critical Boundaries, Vol. 4. Lisa Zunshine. LC 99-36272. (Border Crossings Ser.). 320p. 1999. 70.00 (*0-8153-2895-8*) Garland.

Nabokov Letters. Ed. by Dmitri Nabokov & Matthew J. Bruccoli. 1989. 29.95 (*0-685-26632-X*) Harcourt.

Nabokov, Vian, & Kharms: From Solipsism to Dialogue. Margaret Simonton. LC 94-37759. (Comparative Cultures & Literatures Ser.: 7). 1996. write for info. (*0-8204-2461-7*) P Lang Pubng.

Nabokov's Ada: The Place of Consciousness. Brian Boyd. 255p. 1985. 22.95 (*0-88233-906-0*) Ardis Pubs.

Nabokov's Art of Memory & European Modernism. John B. Foster, Jr. LC 92-24040. 280p. (C). 1993. text 37.50 (*0-691-06971-9*, Pub. by Princeton U Pr) Cal Prin Full Svc.

Nabokov's Blues: The Scientific Odyssey of a Literary Genius. Kurt Johnson & Steven L. Coates. LC 99-23648. (Illus.). 368p. 1999. 27.00 (*1-58195-009-8*, Pub. by Zoland Bks) Consort Bk Sales.

Nabokov's Butterflies: Unpublished & Uncollected Writings. Vladimir Nabokov. Ed. by Brian Boyd & Robert M. Pyle. Tr. by Dmitri Nabokov. LC 98-42846. (Illus.). 800p. 2000. 45.00 (*0-8070-8540-5*) Beacon Pr.

Nabokov's Butterflies: Unpublished & Uncollected Writings. limited ed. Vladimir Nabokov. Ed. by Brian Boyd et al. Tr. by Dmitri Nabokov from RUS. LC 98-42846. (Illus.). 800p. 1999. boxed set 150.00 (*0-8070-8542-1*) Beacon Pr.

Nabokov's Dozen: A Collection of Thirteen Stories. Vladimir Nabokov. LC 82-45237. (Short Story Index Reprint Ser.). 1977. 27.82 (*0-8369-3078-9*) Ayer.

***Nabokov's Gloves & Iona Rain.** Peter Moffatt. 192p. 2000. pap. text 10.95 (*0-413-77180-6*) Methn.

***Nabokov's "Pale Fire" The Magic of Artistic Discovery.** Brian Boyd. LC 99-30682. 303p. 2000. 29.95 (*0-691-00959-7*, Pub. by Princeton U Pr) Cal Prin Full Svc.

Nabonidus & Belshazzar: A Study of the Closing Events of the Neo-Babylonian Empire. Raymond P. Dougherty. LC 78-63559. (Yale Oriental Series: Researches: No. 5). reprint ed. 41.50 (*0-404-60285-1*) AMS Pr.

Naboth's Stone. Sara Lidman. Tr. by Joan Tate from SWE. LC 89-81774. (Norvik Press Series B: No. 7). 262p. (Orig.). 1990. pap. 19.95 (*1-870041-12-7*, Pub. by Norvik Pr) Dufour.

***Naboth's Vineyard: A Novel.** Myra Shofner. 322p. 1999. pap. 17.95 (*1-929228-00-7*) Southern Pub.

Naboth's Vineyard: The Dominican Republic, 1844-1924, 2 vols. Sumner Welles. LC 72-4306. (World Affairs Ser.: National & International Viewpoints). (Illus.). 1112p. 1972. reprint ed. 70.95 (*0-405-04596-4*) Ayer.

Nabozenstvo. 2nd ed. Vladimir Uhri. (SLO.). 48p. (Orig.). 1996. pap. 2.50 (*1-56983-013-4*) New Creat WI.

Nabucodonosor: Dramma Lirico in Four Acts by Temistocle Solera. Giuseppe Verdi. Ed. by Roger Parker. (Works of Giuseppe Verdi: No. 1: Operas, Vol. 3). 736p. 1988. lib. bdg. 300.00 (*0-226-85310-1*) U Ch Pr.

Nabulela. Fiona Moodie. LC 96-27938. (Illus.). 32p. (J). (ps-3). 1997. 15.00 (*0-374-35486-3*) FS&G.

NAC Voters' Guide: The National Action Committee on the Status of Women. Contrib. by National Action Committee on the Status of Women. LC 97-184794. (Illus.). 158p. 1997. pap. 9.95 (*1-55028-552-1*, Pub. by J Lorimer) Formac Dist Ltd.

NACE - Statistical Classification of Economic Activities in the European Community. rev. ed. Eurostat Staff. 200p. 1996. pap. 75.00 (*92-826-8767-8*, CA80-93-436-ENC, Pub. by Comm Europ Commun) Bernan Associates.

NACE Book of Standards. (Illus.). 664p. 1998. 175.00 (*0-915567-62-8*) NACE Intl.

NACE Coating Inspector's Logbook. 3rd ed. (Illus.). 350p. 1996. spiral bd. 52.00 (*1-877914-20-7*) NACE Intl.

NACE Corrosion Engineers Reference Book, 1991. Ed. by R. S. Treseder et al. LC 79-67175. (Illus.). 235p. 1991. 69.00 (*0-915567-82-2*) NACE Intl.

Nace la Esperanza. Larry Jones.Tr. of Beginning of Hope. (SPA.). 140p. 1984. pap. 2.99 (*0-8423-6284-3*, 490242) Editorial Unilit.

Nacer a una Nueva Vida. Billy Graham. Tr. by Rhode Ward from ENG. LC 78-52622.Tr. of How to Be Born Again. (SPA.). 191p. 1978. pap. 8.99 (*0-89922-110-6*) Caribe Betania.

Nach Dem Ende: Posthistoire und die Dramen Thomas Bernhards. Regine Meyer-Arlt. (Germanistische Texte und Studien Ser.: Bd. 56). (GER.). viii, 218p. 1997. 40.00 (*3-487-10480-6*) G Olms Pubs.

Nachalo, Bk. 2. Lubensky. 1996. pap., student ed. 48.75 (*0-07-039040-1*) McGraw.

Nachalo: When in Russia. Lubensky. 1995. audio 11.56 (*0-07-039038-X*) McGraw.

Nachalo: When in Russia. Sophia Lubensky et al. LC 95-41041. 1996. 49.95 (*0-07-038917-9*) McGraw.

Nachalo: When in Russia, Vol. 1. Sophia Lubensky & Gerald L. Ervin. (C). 1996. pap., wbk. ed., lab manual ed. 25.94 (*0-07-038918-7*) McGraw.

Nachalo: When in Russia, Vol. 1, Bk. 1. Sophia Lubensky & Gerald L. Ervin. 368p. (C). 1996. 53.75 (*0-07-912203-5*) McGraw.

Nachalo: When in Russia, Vol. 2. Sophia Lubensky & Gerald L. Ervin. (C). 1996. pap., wbk. ed. 24.69 (*0-07-039042-8*) McGraw.

Nachalo: When in Russia, Vol. 2. Sophia Lubensky & Gerald L. Ervin. 368p. (C). 1997. 53.75 (*0-07-912205-1*) McGraw.

Nachalo: When in Russia Stdt Ca. Lubensky. 1997. audio 11.56 (*0-07-039045-2*) McGraw.

Nachbericht Zur Vierten Abteilung: Richard Wagner in Bayreuth; Menschliches, Allzumenschliches, Baende 1 & 2, Nachgelassene Fragmente, 1875-79 see Nietzsche Werke

Nachdenken Uber Israel, Bibel und Theologie: Festschrift Fur Klaus-Dietrich Schunck Zu Seinem 65. Geburtstag. Ed. by H. Michael Niemann et al. (Beitrage zur Erforschung des Alten Testaments & Antiken Judentums Ser.: Bd. 37). (GER., Illus.). 498p. 1994. 85.95 (*3-631-47033-9*) P Lang Pubng.

Nachemia: German & Jew in the Holocaust. Nachemia Wurman. LC 88-92789. 325p. 1989. 21.95 (*0-88282-046-X*) New Horizon NJ.

Nachexilische JHWH-Gemeinde in Jerusalem: Ein Beitrag Zu Einer Alttestamentlichen Ekklesiologie. Stefan Stiegler. (Beitrage zur Erforschung des Alten Testaments & Antiken Judentums Ser.: Bd. 34). (GER.). 176p. 1994. 35.95 (*3-631-45899-1*) P Lang Pubng.

Nachez Court Records, 1767-1805. May W. McBee. 635p. 1994. pap. 47.50 (*0-8063-1452-4*, 3490) Clearfield Co.

Nachfragemacht der Automobilindustrie: Eine Analyse unter den Gesichtspunkten Kartellrecht, AGB-Recht & Konzernrecht. Holger Kessen. (GER.). 207p. 1996. 42.95 (*3-631-30619-9*) P Lang Pubng.

Nachgelassene Fragmente: Herbst, 1887 Bis Maerz, 1888 see Nietzsche Werke

Nachgelassene Fragmente, 1872-1873 see Nietzsche Werke

Nachgelassene Fragmente, 1869-1872 see Nietzsche Werke

Nachgelassene Schriften, 4 vols. Johann C. Lavater. Ed. by George Gessner. (GER.). lvi, 1652p. 1993. reprint ed. write for info. (*3-487-09697-8*) G Olms Pubs.

Nachgelassene Schriften, 5 vols., Set. Abraham Geiger. Ed. by Steven Katz. LC 79-7132. (Jewish Philosophy, Mysticism & History of Ideas Ser.). 1980. reprint ed. lib. bdg. 189.95 (*0-405-12255-1*) Ayer.

Nachgelassene Schriften, 5 vols., Vol. 1. Abraham Geiger. Ed. by Steven Katz. LC 79-7132. (Jewish Philosophy, Mysticism & History of Ideas Ser.). 1980. reprint ed. lib. bdg. 63.95 (*0-405-12256-X*) Ayer.

Nachgelassene Schriften, 5 vols., Vol. 2. Abraham Geiger. Ed. by Steven Katz. LC 79-7132. (Jewish Philosophy, Mysticism & History of Ideas Ser.). 1980. reprint ed. lib. bdg. 63.95 (*0-405-12257-8*) Ayer.

Nachgelassene Schriften, 5 vols., Vol. 3. Abraham Geiger. Ed. by Steven Katz. LC 79-7132. (Jewish Philosophy, Mysticism & History of Ideas Ser.). 1980. reprint ed. lib. bdg. 63.95 (*0-405-12228-4*) Ayer.

Nachgelassene Schriften Auswahl und Nachlese, 2 vols., Set. Ludwig Tieck. Ed. by Rudolf Koepke. 369p. (C). 1974. reprint ed. 107.70 (*3-11-002352-0*) De Gruyter.

Nachgelassene Schriften Physikalischen, Mechanischen und Technischen Inhalts. Gottfried Wilhelm Leibniz. 1995. reprint ed. write for info. (*3-487-09855-5*) G Olms Pubs.

Nachgelassene Werke, 3 Vols, Set. Johann G. Fichte. Ed. by Immanuel H. Fichte. (C). 1962. reprint ed. 153.85 (*3-11-005101-X*) De Gruyter.

Nachhaltige Entwicklung und Religion: Gesellschaftsvisionen unter Religionsverdacht und die Frage der Religiosen Bedingungen Okologischen Handelns. Matthias B. Lauer. (GER.). 1998. text 24.00 (*3-927120-48-0*, 30) Ugarit-Verlag.

***Nachhaltiges Wirtschaften Mit Nicht-Erneuerbaren Ressourcen: Die Vier Ebenen einer Nachhaltigen Materialnutzung Am Beispiel von Kupfer und Seinen Substituten.** Frank Messner. (Europaische Hochschulschriften Ser.: Bd. 2533). 680p. 1999. 79.95 (*3-631-35121-6*) P Lang Pubng.

***Nachhaltigkeit: Bilanz und Ausblick.** Wolf Dieter Grossmann et al. xxii, 236p. 1999. 42.95 (*3-631-35190-9*) P Lang Pubng.

Nachhaltigkeit Leben: Orientierung und Bibliographie. Ed. by Wolfgang Eisenberg & Klaus Vogelsang. (GER., Illus.). 190p. 1997. 42.95 (*3-631-30650-4*) P Lang Pubng.

Nachiketas. Torkom Saraydarian. LC 94-61087. 74p. 1994. pap. 5.00 (*0-929874-43-9*) TSG Pub Found.

Nachlass zu Lebzeiten see Posthumous Papers of a Living Author

Nachman Krochmal: Guiding the Perplexed of the Modern Age. Jay M. Harris. (Modern Jewish Masters Ser.). 356p. (C). 1991. text 55.00 (*0-8147-3477-4*) NYU Pr.

Nachman Krochmal: Guiding the Perplexed of the Modern Age. Jay M. Harris. (Modern Jewish Masters Ser.). 356p. (C). 1993. pap. text 19.00 (*0-8147-3508-8*) NYU Pr.

Nachrepublikanische Finanzsystem: Fiscus und Fisci in der Fruehen Kaiserzeit. Michael Alpers. (Untersuchungen zur Antiken Literatur und Geschichte Ser.: No. 45). (GER.). 359p. (C). 1995. lib. bdg. 152.30 (*3-11-014562-6*) De Gruyter.

***Nachrichten und Interviews: Linguistische Studien zu franzosischen Rundfunktexten.** Marion Eiche. 2000. 29.95 (*3-631-35843-1*) P Lang Pubng.

Nachrichten Von der Pferdezucht der Araber und Den Arabischen Pferden. Karl W. Ammon. (Documenta Hippologica Ser.). (Illus.). xvi, 408p. 1983. reprint ed. 55.00 (*3-487-08004-4*) G Olms Pubs.

Nachrichten von Ontario. Deutschsprachige Literaturvon Kanada. H. Froeschle. (GER.). 290p. 1981. pap. 27.80 (*3-487-08223-3*) G Olms Pubs.

Nachrichtenubertragung & Datenverarbeitung im Telekommunikationsrecht: Eine Vergleichende Untersuchung Telekommunikationsrechtlicher Regelungsmodelle. Joachim Scherer. (Law & Economics of International Telecommunications Ser.). (GER.). 200p. 1987. 58.00 (*3-7890-1479-6*, Pub. by Nomos Verlags) Intl Bk Import.

Nachrichtenwesen des Altertums Mit Besonderer Rucksicht Auf die Romer. Wolfgang Riepl. xiv, 478p. 1972. reprint ed. write for info. (*3-487-04218-5*) G Olms Pubs.

Nachthymnen. Connie Fox, pseud. 32p. (Orig.). 1986. pap. 8.00 (*0-930012-46-1*) J Mudfoot.

Nachtjagd. Theo Boiten. (Illus.). 256p. 1997. 44.95 (*1-86126-086-5*, Pub. by Crolwood) Motorbooks Intl.

Nachtrage Zu A. Ottos "Sprichworten und Sprichwortlichen Redensarten der Romer" Reinhard Haussler. xii, 324p. 1968. write for info. (*0-318-71139-7*) G Olms Pubs.

Nachtrage zur Plautinischen Prosodie. C. F. Muller. (GER.). xvi, 159p. 1973. reprint ed. write for info. (*0-318-70442-0*) G Olms Pubs.

Nachtrage Zur Plautinischen Prosodie. Carl F. Wilhelm Muller. xvi, 159p. 1973. reprint ed. write for info. (*0-318-71181-8*) G Olms Pubs.

Nachtragliche Werbungskosten - Zu Spate Aufwendungen? Steffen G. Rauch. (GER.). LXXVI, 132p. 1996. 42.95 (*3-631-30069-7*) P Lang Pubng.

Nachume Miller. Donald Kuspit. (Illus.). 10p. (Orig.). 1988. pap. 10.00 (*0-913263-20-6*) Exit Art.

***Nachweis der Schmerzlinderung Durch die Gasteiner Heilstollenkur: Ergebnisse einer Psychologischen und Neuroendokrinologischen Evaluierung.** Antony Grafton & Bernd Minnich. (Berichte des Forschungsinstituts Gastein-Tauernregion. Ser.: Bd. 2). 248p. 1999. 37.95 (*3-631-34363-9*) P Lang Pubng.

Nachweis des Versicherungsfalls. Alexander Hopfner. (GER.). XXX, 166p. 1996. 42.95 (*3-631-30610-5*) P Lang Pubng.

Nacimiento. Gene Edwards.Tr. of Birth. (SPA.). 127p. 1990. pap. 4.99 (*1-56063-400-6*, 498551) Editorial Unilit.

Nacimiento de Jesucristo: Promesas y Profecias bL-Alumno. Daniel Roeda. (SPA.). 1991. pap. 1.00 (*1-55955-134-8*) CRC Wrld Lit.

Nacimiento de Jesucristo: Promesas y Profecias bL-Maestro. Jeff Stam. (SPA.). 1991. pap. 1.50 (*1-55955-135-6*) CRC Wrld Lit.

Nacimiento de Jesucristo: Promesas y Profecias C-Alumno. Daniel Roeda. (SPA.). 1991. pap. 1.00 (*1-55955-130-5*) CRC Wrld Lit.

Nacimiento de Jesucristo: Promesas y Profecias C-Maestro. Jeff Stam. (SPA.). 1991. pap. 1.50 (*1-55955-131-3*) CRC Wrld Lit.

N

Nacimiento de Jesucristo: Promesas y Profecias Db-Alumno. Daniel Roeda. (SPA.). 1991. pap. 1.00 (*1-55955-132-1*) CRC Wrld Lit.

Nacimiento de Jesucristo: Promesas y Profecias Db-Maestro. Jeff Stam. (SPA.). 1991. pap. 1.50 (*1-55955-133-X*) CRC Wrld Lit.

Nacimiento de un Nino. (Serie Pensamientos de Vida - Thoughts of Life Ser.).Tr. of On the Birth of a Child. (SPA.). 24p. 1984. pap. write for info. (*0-614-27085-5*) Editorial Unilit.

Nacimiento de un Nino - On the Birth of a Child. (Serie Pensamientos de Vida - Thoughts of Life Ser.: No. 1). (SPA.). 24p. 1984. write for info. (*0-614-24382-3*) Editorial Unilit.

Nacimiento Especial Libro para Colorear. A. Hudson.Tr. of Special Birthday Coloring Book. (SPA.). (J). 1.69 (*0-7899-0535-3*, 498798) Editorial Unilit.

Nacimos para Triunfar. Swami Guru Devanand & Saraswati J. Maharaj. (SPA., Illus.). 226p. 1993. pap. write for info. (*1-893261-02-6*) USA Dev Yoga.

Nacion Cubana: Esencia y Existencia. Jose I. Rasco et al. LC 99-60995. (Coleccion Felix Varela Ser.: Vol. 9). (SPA.). 103p. 1999. pap. 9.95 (*0-89729-897-7*) Ediciones.

Nacion Puertorriquena: Ensayos en Torno a Pedro Albizu Campos. Ed. by Juan M. Carrion et al. (SPA.). 284p. 1993. pap. 12.50 (*0-8477-0203-0*) U of PR Pr.

Nacionalidades del Estado Espanol: Una Problematica Cultural. Ed. by Cristina Duplaa & Gwendolyn Barnes. LC 86-60528. (ENG & SPA.). 254p. (Orig.). 1986. pap. text 8.95 (*0-910235-11-2*) Prisma Bks.

Nacionalismo Economico e Interdependencia Internacional: El Costo Mundial de las Opciones Nacionales. Peter G. Peterson. LC HC0106.8.P37. (Conferencia Per Jacobsson de 1984 Ser.). (SPA.). 97p. reprint ed. pap. 30.10 (*0-608-08769-6*, 206940800004) Bks Demand.

NaCl Transport in Epithelia. Ed. by R. Greger. (Advances in Comparative & Environmental Physiology Ser.: Vol. 1). (Illus.). 340p. 1988. 141.95 (*0-387-18700-6*) Spr-Verlag.

Nacodoches Archives, 1835 Entrance Certificates. Betty F. Burr. 1982. 8.95 (*0-911619-02-X*) B F Burr.

Nacogdoches - Gateway to Texas: A Biographical Directory, 1850-1880, Vol. II. Carolyn R. Ericson. LC 74-75203. 505p. 1986. lib. bdg. 35.00 (*0-911317-40-6*) Ericson Bks.

Nacogdoches - Gateway to Texas Vol. I: A Biographical Directory, 1773-1849. rev. ed. Carolyn R. Ericson. LC 74-75203. (Illus.). 525p. 1991. lib. bdg. 37.50 (*0-911317-48-1*) Ericson Bks.

Nacogdoches - Past & Present: A Legacy of Texas Pride. Bill Murchison. Ed. by Cynthia H. Murchison. LC 86-72139. 100p. (Orig.). 1986. pap. 21.95 (*0-9617381-0-3*) B&C Pub Odessa.

Nacogdoches Headrights. Carolyn R. Ericson. LC 77-70246. (Illus.). 132p. (Orig.). 1977. pap. 20.00 (*0-911317-05-8*) Ericson Bks.

Nacogdoches, Texas: A Pictorial History. Archie P. McDonald. LC 96-31218. 1996. write for info. (*0-89865-975-2*) Donning Co.

Nacogdoches, the History of Texas' Oldest City. James G. Partin et al. 308p. 25.00 (*1-878096-39-7*, Epigram Pr) Best E TX Pubs.

Nacoochee. Thomas Holley Chivers. LC 77-24233. 160p. 1977. reprint ed. 50.00 (*0-8201-1295-X*) Schol Facsimiles.

Nacoochee: or The Beautiful Star. Thomas Holley Chivers. (Works of Thomas Holley Chivers Ser.). 1990. reprint ed. lib. bdg. 79.00 (*0-7812-2283-4*) Rprt Serv.

NACUBO Annual Membership Directory. National Association of College & University Busin & National Association of College & University Busin. 415p. 1996. 115.00 (*0-685-48508-0*) NACUBO.

NACUBO Executive Briefing Series, 6 papers. National Association of College & University Busin. Ed. by Deirdre McDonald & Jefferson Reeder. 1991. 37.50 (*0-915164-62-0*); 37.50 (*0-915164-65-5*); 37.50 (*0-915164-66-3*); 37.50 (*0-915164-67-1*) NACUBO.

NACUBO Guide to IRS Audits: A Manual for Colleges & Universities. Laura L. Kalick & Peter K. Scott. LC 94-35227. 1994. 69.95 (*0-915164-96-5*) NACUBO.

NACUBO Guide to Issuing & Managing Debt. George A. King et al. LC 94-7163. 1994. 45.00 (*0-915164-93-0*) NACUBO.

***Nad: Understanding the Raga Music.** Sandeep Bagchee. LC 98-903071. (Illus.). 1998. 498.00 (*81-86982-08-6*, Pub. by Business Pubns); pap. 198.00 (*81-86982-07-8*, Pub. by Business Pubns) St Mut.

Nada. Carmen Laforet. 286p. (Orig.). 1958. pap. text 21.95 (*0-19-500942-8*) OUP.

Nada. Carmen Laforet. Tr. by Glafyra Ennis from SPA. LC 92-31936. (Catalan Studies: Vol. 8). 250p. (Orig.). (C). 1993. pap. text 29.95 (*0-8204-2064-6*) P Lang Pubng.

Nada. Carmen LaForet. (SPA.). pap. 19.95 (*84-233-0989-4*, Pub. by Destino) Continental Bk.

Nada Brahma: The World Is Sound. Joachim-Ernst Berendt & Fritjof Capra. 240p. 1987. 16.95 (*0-89281-168-4*, Destiny Bks) Inner Tradit.

Nada en el Buzon. Carolyn Ford. Tr. by Raquel Torres. (Books for Young Learners).Tr. of Nothing in the Mailbox. (SPA., Illus.). 12p. (J). (gr. k-2). 1996. pap. text 5.00 (*1-57274-031-0*, A2880) R Owen Pubs.

Nada Locos, los Gemelos. Bertrand Gauthier. (Primeros Lectores Ser.). (SPA., Illus.). 60p. (J). (gr. 5 up). 1994. pap. 5.95 (*958-07-0071-0*) Firefly Bks Ltd.

***Nada Me Detendra/Unstoppable.** Cynthia Kersey. (SPA., Illus.). 208p. 2000. pap. text 12.95 (*970-643-219-1*) Selector.

NADA Official Used Car Guide. Patricia R. Erney. 1998. pap. text 9.95 (*1-881406-24-5*) NADA VA.

NADA Official Used Car Guide, Fall 1998 Edition. Ed. by Patricia R. Erney et al. 1998. pap. 9.95 (*1-881406-26-1*) NADA VA.

NADA Official Used Car Guide, Fall 1999 Edition. Ed. by Patricia R. Erney et al. 1999. pap. 9.95 (*1-881406-30-X*) NADA VA.

NADA Official Used Car Guide, Spring 1999 Edition. Ed. by Patricia R. Erney et al. 1999. pap. 9.95 (*1-881406-28-8*) NADA VA.

NADA Official Used Car Guide, Summer 1998 Edition. Ed. by Patricia R. Erney et al. xiv, 368p. 1998. pap. 9.95 (*1-881406-25-3*) NADA VA.

NADA Official Used Car Guide, Summer 1999 Edition. Ed. by Patricia R. Erney et al. 1999. pap. 9.95 (*1-881406-29-6*) NADA VA.

NADA Official Used Car Guide, Winter 1998 Edition. Ed. by Patricia R. Erney et al. 1998. pap. 9.95 (*1-881406-27-X*) NADA VA.

Nada Review: Anthology. Harry Smith et al. LC 64-9367. (Illus.). 128p. 1973. pap. 10.00 (*0-912292-24-5*) Smith.

Nadador (The Swimmer) Gonzalo Contreras.Tr. of Swimmer. 240p. 1996. pap. 12.50 (*0-679-76549-2*) Random.

Nadanda, the Wordmaker: Hide the Doll. Vivian W. Owens. Ed. by Carolyn Maxwell. LC 93-74671. (Illus.). 248p. (YA). (gr. 5 up). 1994. 14.95 (*0-9623839-3-7*) Eschar Pubns.

Nadar. Maria Morris Hambourg et al. LC 94-44424. 1995. pap. 19.95 (*0-87099-737-8*) Metro Mus Art.

***Nadar--Warhol, Paris--New York: Photography & Fame** Gordon Baldwin et al. LC 99-21007. 1999. write for info. (*0-89236-565-X*) J P Getty Trust.

Nadarin. Leo Lionni. 1998. pap. 5.50 (*84-264-4650-7*) Lectorum Pubns.

Nadarin - Swimmy. Leo Lionni. 1996. 15.95 (*84-264-3527-0*, Pub. by Editorial Lumen) Lectorum Pubns.

***Nadar/Warhol: Paris/New York: Photography & Fame.** Gordon Baldwin & Judith Keller. LC 99-21007. (Illus.). 240p. 1999. 60.00 (*0-89236-560-9*, Pub. by J P Getty Trust) OUP.

Nadas' Pediatric Cardiology. Ed. by Donald C. Fyler. (Illus.). 784p. 1991. text 92.00 (*0-932883-94-X*) Hanley & Belfus.

NADCA Product Specification Standards for Die Castings. rev. ed. LC 94-70763. (Illus.). 130p. (Orig.). 1995. 95.00 (*1-885271-00-X*) Diecasting Develop.

NADE Self-Evaluation Guides: Models for Assessing Learning Assistance - Developmental Education Programs. Ed. by Susan Clark-Thayer. LC 94-73826. (Orig.). 1995. pap. 18.95 (*0-943202-49-3*) H & H Pub.

NADH: The Energizing Coenzyme. Georg Birkmayer. LC 99-163562. (Good Health Guides Ser.). 1998. pap. 3.95 (*0-87983-862-0*, 38620K, Keats Publng) NTC Contemp Pub Co.

Nadia Boulanger. Jerome Spycket. Tr. by M. M. Shriver from FRE. LC 92-25835. (Illus.). 192p. 1993. lib. bdg. 36.00 (*0-945193-38-6*) Pendragon NY.

Nadia Boulanger: A Life in Music. Leonie Rosenstiel. 440p. 1998. pap. 15.95 (*0-393-31713-7*) Norton.

Nadia, Captive of Hope: Memoir of an Arab Woman. Fay A. Kanafani. LC 98-39925. (Foremother Legacies Ser.). (Illus.). 384p. 1999. pap. text 21.95 (*0-7656-0312-8*) M E Sharpe.

Nadia, Captive of Hope: Memoir of an Arab Woman. Fay Afaf Kanafani. LC 98-39925. (Foremother Legacies Ser.). (Illus.). 384p. (C). (gr. 13). 1999. text 62.95 (*0-7656-0311-X*, East Gate Bk) M E Sharpe.

Nadia of the Night Witches. Tom Townsend. Ed. by Myrna Kemnitz. LC 98-226273. 153p. (J). 1998. pap. 9.99 (*0-88092-273-7*, 2737) Royal Fireworks.

Nadia's Hands. Karen English. LC 98-71668. (Illus.). 32p. (J). (ps-3). 1999. 15.95 (*1-56397-667-6*) Boyds Mills Pr.

Nadie Alzaba La Voz see No One Said a Word

Nadie Espera Que Escriba. Elena Montes de Oca. Ed. by Sergio Zapata. (SPA., Illus.). 50p. (Orig.). 1996. pap. write for info. (*0-9654846-3-7*) E M de Oca.

Nadine & Vinson. Patricia Call. LC 95-79653. (Illus.). 189p. 1995. pap. 12.95 (*0-941092-30-5*) Mtn St Pr.

Nadine Gordimer. Dominic Head. (Studies in African & Caribbean Literature: No. 2). 239p. (C). 1994. pap. text 19.95 (*0-521-47549-X*) Cambridge U Pr.

Nadine Gordimer. Judie Newman. (Contemporary Writers Ser.). 96p. 1988. pap. text 9.95 (*0-415-00660-0*) Routledge.

Nadine Gordimer: A Bibliography of Primary & Secondary Sources. Compiled by Dorothy Driver et al. LC 93-37446. (Bibliographical Research in African Literatures Ser.: No. 4). 360p. 1994. 75.00 (*1-873836-26-0*, Pub. by H Zell Pubs) Seven Hills Bk.

Nadine Gordimer Revisited. Thurston. LC 98-55672. 12p. 1999. 22.95 (*0-8057-4608-0*, Twyne) Mac Lib Ref.

***Nadine Gordimer's Fiction & the Irony of Apartheid.** Brighton J. Kamanga. LC 99-59945. 2000. pap. write for info. (*0-86543-828-5*) Africa World.

Nadir Shah: A Critical Study Based Mainly upon Contemporary Sources. Laurence Lockhart. LC 78-180358. reprint ed. 36.00 (*0-404-56290-6*) AMS Pr.

Nadirs. Herta Muller. Tr. by Sieglinde Lug from GER. LC 98-48347. (European Women Writers Ser.). 134p. 1999. 40.00 (*0-8032-3197-0*) U of Nebr Pr.

***Nadirs.** Herta Muller. Tr. by Sieglinde Lug from GER. LC 98-48347. (European Women Writers Ser.). 134p. 1999. pap. 13.00 (*0-8032-8254-0*, Bison Books) U of Nebr Pr.

Nadja. Andre Breton. (FRE.). 1972. pap. 10.95 (*0-8288-3660-4*, F89531) Fr & Eur.

Nadja. Andre Breton. Tr. by Richard Howard from FRE. LC 60-7639. 160p. 1988. pap. 11.00 (*0-8021-5026-8*, Grove) Grove-Atltic.

Nadja. Andre Breton. (Folio Ser.: No. 73). (FRE.). pap. 9.25 (*2-07-036073-3*) Schoenhof.

Nadja Auermann. Karl Lagerfeld. (Illus.). 144p. 1999. 45.00 (*3-8238-1000-6*) te Neues.

Nadya. Pat Murphy. (The Wolf Chronicles). 1996. mass mkt. 6.99 (*0-8125-5188-5*, Pub. by Tor Bks) St Martin.

Nadya Wolf Chronicles. Pat Murphy. LC 96-22939. 384p. 1996. 23.95 (*0-312-86226-1*) St Martin.

Nadya's Quest. Lisette Allen. 256p. (Orig.). 1997. mass mkt. 5.95 (*0-352-33135-6*, Pub. by BLA4) London Brdge.

NAEA Research Agenda Briefing Papers. Contrib. by Enid D. Zimmerman. 90p. 1996. pap. text 10.00 (*0-937652-92-X*, 260) Natl Art Ed.

Naehrstoffbilanz Des Woelfersheimer Sees (Hessen), Eines Durch Abwaerme und Abwassereinleitung Beemflussten Gewaessers. Ilona B. Arndt-Dietrich. (Dissertationes Botanicae Ser.: Band 142). (GER., Illus.). viii, 166p. 1989. pap. 42.00 (*3-443-64051-6*, Pub. by Gebruder Borntraeger) Balogh.

Naehrstoffstress, Stoerung und Konkurrenz in Ihrer Wirkung Auf Ausgewaehlte Arten der Kopfbinsenriede. Dieter Maas. (Dissertationes Botanicae Ser.: Band 254). (Illus.). x, 186p. 1995. pap. 48.00 (*3-443-64166-0*, Pub. by Gebruder Borntraeger) Balogh.

***NAEP Guide (1997 Edition) A Description of the Contents & Methods of the 1997 & 1998 Assessments.** rev. ed. Ed. by J. Calderone et al. (Illus.). 72p. (C). 1999. pap. text 20.00 (*0-7881-8359-1*) DIANE Pub.

***NAEP 1998 Reading Report Card for the Nation & the States.** Patricia L. Donahue. 293p. 1999. per. 25.00 (*0-16-050062-1*) USGPO.

***NAEP 1998 Writing Report Card for the Nation & the States.** Elissa A. Greenwald. 303p. 1999. per. 28.00 (*0-16-050188-1*) USGPO.

NAEP 1994 Geography Report Card, Findings from the National Assessment of Educational Progress. Hilary R. Persky. 134p. 1996. pap. 11.00 (*0-16-048680-7*) USGPO.

NAEP 1994 United States History Report Card: Findings from the National Assessment of Educational Progress. Alexandra S. Beatty. 136p. 1996. pap. 11.00 (*0-16-048645-9*) USGPO.

***NAEP 1997 Arts Report Card: Eighth-Grade Findings from the National Assessment of Educational Progress.** Hilary R. Persky. 240p. 1999. per. 19.00 (*0-16-049863-5*) USGPO.

***NAEP 1996 Mathematics Cross-State Data Compendium for the Grade 4 & Grade 8 Assessment: Findings from the State Assessment in Mathematics of the National Assessment of Educational Progress.** Catherine A. Shaughnessy. LC 98-121707. 212p. 1998. pap. 18.00 (*0-16-049414-1*) USGPO.

NAEP 1996 Mathematics Report Card for the Nation & the States: Findings from the National Assessment of Educational Progress. Clyde M. Reese. LC 97-152431. 169p. 1997. pap. 13.00 (*0-16-049013-8*) USGPO.

***NAEP 1996 Science Cross-State Data Compendium for the Grade 8 Assessment: Findings from the National Assessment of Educational Progress for the State Science Assessment.** Kellie K. Keiser. 119p. 1998. pap. 12.00 (*0-16-049565-2*) USGPO.

NAEP 1996 Science Report Card for the Nation & States: Findings from the National Assessment of Educational Progress. Christine Y. O'Sullivan. 131p. 1997. pap. 14.00 (*0-16-063616-7*) USGPO.

***NAEP 1996 Technical Report.** Nancy L. Allen. 860p. 1999. per. 65.00 (*0-16-050094-X*) USGPO.

***NAEP 1996 Trends in Writing: Fluency & Writing Conventions, Holistic & Mechanics Scores in 1984 & 1996.** Nada Ballator. LC 99-460649. 67p. 1999. pap. 6.00 (*0-16-050042-7*) USGPO.

NAEP Reading, 1994: A First Look: Findings from the National Assessment of Educational Progress. Paul L. Williams et al. (Illus.). 59p. (Orig.). (C). 1995. pap. text 20.00 (*0-7881-2448-X*) DIANE Pub.

NAEP 1994 Trends in Academic Progress: Achievement of United States Students in Science, 1969 to 1994; Mathematics, 1973 to 1994; Reading, 1971 to 1994 & Writing, 1984 to 1994. Jay R. Campbell. 582p. 1996. pap. 46.00 (*0-16-048918-0*) USGPO.

***Naet Guide Book: The Companion to "Say Good-Bye to Illness"** 4th ed. Devi S. Nambudripad. 1999. pap. 12.00 (*0-9658242-3-3*) Delta Pubs.

Naeui Sarang, Naeui Joguk see My Love, My Country

NAEYC Accreditation: A Decade of Learning & the Years Ahead. Ed. by Sue Bredekamp & Barbara Willer. LC 96-68451. 166p. 1996. pap. text 8.00 (*0-935989-74-9*, NAEYC905) Natl Assn Child Ed.

NAFA Guide to Air Filtration. Robert H. Avery. (Illus.). 180p. 1993. 80.00 (*1-884152-00-7*) Nat Air Filtra.

NAFA Guide to Air Filtration. Robert H. Avery. (Illus.). 180p. 1996. 80.00 (*1-884152-01-5*) Nat Air Filtra.

Nafanua: Saving the Samoan Rain Forest. Paul A. Cox. 238p. 1999. pap. text 14.95 (*0-7167-3563-6*) W H Freeman.

Nafanua: Saving the Samoan Rain Forest. Paul Alan Cox. LC 97-37379. 226p. 1997. pap. text 23.95 (*0-7167-3116-9*) W H Freeman.

***NAFC Sales Tax Service.** American Trucking Associations National Accounting. 300p. 1999. ring bd. 215.00 (*0-88711-396-6*) Am Trucking Assns.

NAFC State Tax Guide. American Trucking Association National Accounting. 1100p. 1988. ring bd. 395.00 (*0-88711-021-5*) Am Trucking Assns.

***NAFCU's Auto Lending Program for Credit Unions: Strategies for Auto Lending Success.** Brian J. Pascouau. LC 99-186950. 1998. write for info. (*1-55827-273-9*) Sheshunoff.

NAFCU'S Common Compliance Violations Robert E. Braun. LC 98-213163. 1998. write for info. (*1-55827-164-3*) Sheshunoff.

Nafcu's Contingency Planning, Disaster Recovery & Record Retention for Credit Unions. Aksel G. Pedersen & National Association of Federal Credits Unions Staff. LC 98-213173. 1998. write for info. (*1-55827-251-8*) Sheshunoff.

NAFCU's Internal Auditing Manual for Credit Unions Aksel G. Pedersen. LC 98-207721. 1997. write for info. (*1-55827-240-2*) Sheshunoff.

NAFCU's Marketing & Advertising Regulatory Guide for Credit Unions. Robert E. Braun & National Association of Federal Credit Unions Staff. LC 98-184450. 1995. ring bd. write for info. (*1-55827-183-X*) Sheshunoff.

Nafcu's Risk Management for Credit Unions. James M. Koltveit et al. LC 99-182823. 1998. write for info. (*1-55827-264-X*) Sheshunoff.

NAFCU's Share Drafts & Negotiable Instruments Handbook. Christiane Gigi Hyland & National Association of Federal Credit Unions Staff. LC 98-184444. 1997. ring bd. write for info. (*1-55827-225-9*) Sheshunoff.

NAFSA's Guide to Education Abroad for Advisers & Administrators. 2nd ed. William Hoffa et al. LC 97-125. 1997. 45.00 (*0-912207-75-2*) NAFSA Washington.

***NAFSA's Guide to International Student Recruitment.** Marie O'Hara et al. LC 00-30541. 2000. pap. write for info. (*0-912207-84-1*) NAFSA Washington.

NAFTA: Environmental Issues. 1995. lib. bdg. 250.75 (*0-8490-7536-X*) Gordon Pr.

NAFTA: Honda Motor Company or Free Trade in the Real World. Michael Ryan et al. (Pew Case Studies in International Affairs). 50p. (C). 1995. pap. text 3.50 (*1-56927-718-4*, GU Schl Foreign) Geo U Inst Dplmcy.

NAFTA: Issues, Industry Sector Profiles & Bibliography. Ed. by B. J. Zangari. 207p. (C). 1994. lib. bdg. 115.00 (*1-56072-191-X*) Nova Sci Pubs.

NAFTA: Managing the Cultural Differences. Robert T. Moran & Jeffrey D. Abbott. LC 94-12482. (Managing Cultural Differences Ser.). 160p. 1994. pap. 14.95 (*0-88415-500-5*, 5500) Gulf Pub.

NAFTA: Poverty & Free Trade in Mexico:; Oxfam Insight. Coote Belinda. (Oxfam Insight Ser.). 64p. (C). 1995. pap. 7.50 (*0-85598-302-7*, Pub. by Oxfam Pub) Stylus Pub VA.

NAFTA: Protecting & Enforcing Intellectual Property Rights in North America. Richard B. Neff & Fran Smallson. LC 94-26390. 1994. write for info. (*0-07-172611-X*) Shepards.

NAFTA: The North American Free Trade Agreement, a Guide to Customs Procedures. Government Printing Office Staff. 59p. 1994. pap. 5.00 (*0-16-045046-2*) USGPO.

NAFTA: What Comes Next?, 166. Sidney Weintraub. LC 94-23323. (Washington Papers: Vol. 166). 160p. 1994. 55.00 (*0-275-95118-9*, Praeger Pubs); pap. 15.95 (*0-275-95119-7*, Praeger Pubs) Greenwood.

NAFTA: What You Need to Know Now. (Commercial Law & Practice Course Handbook Ser.). 480p. 1994. pap. 99.00 (*0-614-17143-1*, A4-4466) PLI.

NAFTA: Year Two & Beyond. (Illus.). 121p. (Orig.). (C). 1997. pap. text 35.00 (*0-7881-3702-6*) DIANE Pub.

NAFTA & Beyond: A New Framework for Doing Business in the Americas. Ed. by Joseph J. Norton et al. LC 95-165428. (International Economic Development Law Ser.). 704p. 1995. lib. bdg. 237.00 (*0-7923-3239-3*, KDZ944) Kluwer Academic.

NAFTA & GATT No. 43: Environmental & Economic Issues: A Bibliography. Ed. by Joan Nordquist. (Contemporary Social Issues: A Bibliography Ser.: No. 43). (Orig.). 1996. pap. 20.00 (*0-937855-84-7*) Ref Rsch Serv.

NAFTA & Its Effect on State Environmental Policies. Doug Farquhar. 9p. 1995. 15.00 (*1-55516-091-3*, 7302-2010) Natl Conf State Legis.

NAFTA & Sovereignty: Trade-Offs for Canada, Mexico, & the United States. Ed. by M. Delal Baer et al. (Significant Issues Ser.). 176p. (C). 1997. pap. text 20.00 (*0-89206-322-X*) CSIS.

NAFTA & the Energy Charter Treaty: Compliance with, Implementation & Effectiveness of International Investment Agreements. Mirian Kene Omalu. LC 98-36786. (NAFTA Law & Policy Ser.). xxiv, 295 p. 1999. 105.00 (*90-411-1076-3*) Kluwer Law Intl.

NAFTA & the Environment. Ed. by Terry L. Anderson. LC 93-1031. 1993. pap. write for info. (*0-936488-73-5*) PRIPP.

NAFTA & the Environment. Seymour J. Rubin & Dean C. Alexander. LC 96-40979. (NAFTA Law & Policy Ser.). 1996. 295.00 (*90-411-0033-4*) Kluwer Law Intl.

NAFTA & the Environment: Substance & Process. LC 95-169337. 772p. 1995. pap. 75.00 (*0-89707-961-2*, 521-0099, ABA Intl Law) Amer Bar Assn.

NAFTA & Trade in Medical Services Between the U. S. & Mexico. David C. Warner. LC 96-78430. (U. S. - Mexican Policy Report Ser.: No. 7). 384p. 1997. pap. 21.00 (*0-89940-326-3*) LBJ Sch Pub Aff.

NAFTA & Trade Liberalization in the Americas. Ed. by Elsie Echeverri-Carroll. LC 93-70232. 100p. 1995. pap. 20.00 (*0-87755-333-5*) Bureau Busn TX.

NAFTA As a Model of Development: The Benefits & Costs of Merging High- & Low-Wage Areas. Ed. by Richard S. Belous & Jonathan Lemco. LC 94-23436. 216p. (C). 1995. text 49.50 (*0-7914-2569-X*); pap. text 19.95 (*0-7914-2570-3*) State U NY Pr.

NAFTA As a Model of Development: The Benefits & Costs of Merging High & Low Wage Areas. Ed. by Richard S. Belous & Jonathan Lemco. 192p. (Orig.). 1993. pap. text 10.50 (*0-614-03254-7*, NPA 266) Natl Planning.

NAFTA at Three: A Progress Report. Sidney Weintraub. LC 97-1941. (Significant Issues Ser.). 105p. (C). 1997. pap. text 16.95 (*0-89206-298-3*) CSIS.

An Asterisk (*) at the beginning of an entry indicates that the title is appearing for the first time.

NAFTA Bibliography, 18. Allan Metz. LC 96-32408. (Bibliographies & Indexes in Economics & Economic History: No. 18). 504p. 1996. lib. bdg. 105.00 (*0-313-29463-1*, Greenwood Pr) Greenwood.

NAFTA Business Guide. Ed. by Gary Brown. 250p. 1997. spiral bd. 185.00 (*1-893323-01-3*) WorldTrade Exec.

NAFTA Customs Procedures Manual. 2nd ed. Ed. by Revenue Canada Staff. LC 95-705441. 1995. ring bd. 69.95 (*0-660-16268-7*, Pub. by Canadian Govt Pub) Accents Pubns.

NAFTA Debate: Grappling with Unconventional Trade Issues. Ed. by M. Delal Baer & Sidney Weintraub. LC 93-38663. 211p. 1994. lib. bdg. 49.95 (*1-55587-464-9*) L Rienner.

NAFTA Documentation & Procedures. 145p. 1996. pap. text 88.00 (*1-883006-47-3*) Intl Busn Pubns.

NAFTA Documentation & Procedures. B. J. Nichols. 140p. 1994. pap. text 88.00 (*1-883006-11-2*) Intl Busn Pubns.

NAFTA, GATT & the World Trade Organization: The New Rules of Corporate Conquest. Kristin Dawkins & Jeremy Brecher. (Open Magazine Pamphlet Ser.: No. 29). 21p. 1994. 4.00 (*1-884519-04-0*) Open Media.

NAFTA Handbook. Baker & Mckenzie. LC 95-106721. 276p. 1994. pap. 38.00 (*0-8080-0025-X*, BLS-3384) CCH INC.

NAFTA Handbook. Ed. by Laura M. Brank. 160p. 1994. spiral bd. 125.00 (*1-893323-00-5*) WorldTrade Exec.

NAFTA Handbook for Water Resource Managers & Engineers. Mark W. Kilgore & David J. Eaton. (U.S.-Mexican Special Publication: No. 3). 85p. 1995. pap. 17.00 (*0-89940-323-9*) LBJ Sch Pub Aff.

NAFTA Handbook for Water Resource Managers & Engineers. Mark W. Kilgore & David J. Eaton. 88p. 1995. 21.00 (*0-7844-0086-5*) Am Soc Civil Eng.

***NAFTA Law & Business.** Ralph H. Folsom & W. Davis Folsom. 1999. ring bd. 150.00 (*90-411-9252-2*) Kluwer Law Intl.

NAFTA (North American Free Trade Agreement) - Supplemental Agreements. 100p. (Orig.). (C). 1994. pap. text 50.00 (*0-7881-0704-6*) DIANE Pub.

NAFTA Now! The Changing Political Economy of North America. Ed. by Brenda M. McPhail. 145p. (C). 1995. pap. 19.50 (*0-8191-9702-5*); lib. bdg. 48.00 (*0-8191-9701-7*) U Pr of Amer.

NAFTA on Second Thought: A Plural Evaluation. Ed. by David R. Davila-Villers. LC 98-9552. 152p. 1998. 49.00 (*0-7618-1057-9*); pap. 27.50 (*0-7618-1058-7*) U Pr of Amer.

***Nafta-Past, Present & Future** Peter Coffey. LC 99-13099. (International Handbooks on Economic Integration). xxiv, 187p. 1999. write for info. (*0-7923-8482-2*) Kluwer Academic.

NAFTA Register. 3rd ed. Michael A. Ruccolo. (Illus.). 180p. 1996. pap. 150.00 (*0-9651569-0-7*) Global Contact.

NAFTA Supplemental Agreements: North American Agreement on Environmental Cooperation: North American Agreement on Labor Cooperation. 1994. lib. bdg. 495.00 (*0-8490-8530-6*) Gordon Pr.

NAFTA Text: Including Supplemental Agreements. Greer L. Phillips & John R. Washlick. Ed. by Maureen Schwartz. LC 94-186661. 824p. (Orig.). 1994. pap. 39.50 (*0-8080-0006-3*) CCH INC.

NAFTA, the First Year: A View from Mexico. Ed. by David R. Villers. LC 97-16535. 228p. 1996. lib. bdg. 42.00 (*0-7618-0391-2*) U Pr of Amer.

***NAFTA Works for America: Administration Update on the North American Free Trade Agreement, 1993-1998.** LC 99-235291. 36p. 1999. per. 6.00 (*0-16-050089-3*) USGPO.

Naftali the Storyteller & His Horse, Sus: And Other Stories. Isaac Bashevis Singer. (Sunburst Ser.). (Illus.). 144p. (J). (gr. 4-7). 1987. pap. 3.50 (*0-374-45487-6*) FS&G.

NAFTA's Broken Promises: A Border Betrayed U. S. - Mexico Border Environment & Health Decline in NAFTA's First Two Years. Public Citizen's Global Trade Watch Staff. (SPA., Illus.). 100p. (Orig.). 1996. pap. text 15.00 (*0-937188-03-4*) Pub Citizen.

NAG FORTRAN Library Manual Mark 9. Numerical Algorithms Group Staff. 1981. 35.00 (*0-317-52218-3*, Pub. by Numer Algo) Princeton Bk Co.

NAG FORTRAN PC50 Handbook - Release 1. Numerical Algorithms Group Staff. 324p. 1983. 30.00 (*0-317-52225-6*, Pub. by Numer Algo) Princeton Bk Co.

NAG FORTRAN PC50 Handbook - Release 1. 2nd ed. Numerical ALgorithms Group Staff. 324p. 1984. 30.00 (*0-317-52226-4*, Pub. by Numer Algo) Princeton Bk Co.

NAG Graphical Supplement Mark 1. Numerical Algorithms Group Staff. 1981. 40.00 (*0-317-52228-0*, Pub. by Numer Algo) Princeton Bk Co.

NAG Graphical Supplement Mark 2. Numerical Algorithms Group. 1985. 25.20 (*0-317-52231-0*, Pub. by Numer Algo) Princeton Bk Co.

Nag Hammadi: Codices III, 3-4 & V, 1: Eugnostos & the Sophia of Jesus Christ. Ed. by Douglas M. Parrott. LC 91-19243. (Nag Hammadi Studies: Vol. 27). xxii, 216p. 1991. 108.00 (*90-04-08366-9*) Brill Academic Pubs.

Nag Hammadi: Codices 11, 12, 13. Ed. by Charles W. Hedrick. LC 88-10481. (Nag Hammadi Studies: Vol. 28). xxxiv, 566p. 1990. 282.50 (*90-04-07825-8*) Brill Academic Pubs.

Nag Hammadi Bibliography, 1970-1994. D. M. Scholer. LC 97-18071. (Nag Hammadi & Manichaean Studies: Vol. 32). 500p. 1997. text 165.50 (*90-04-09473-3*) Brill Academic Pubs.

Nag Hammadi Codex VII. Ed. by Birger A. Pearson. (Nag Hammadi & Manichaean Studies: Vol. 30). 1995. 140.50 (*90-04-10451-8*) Brill Academic Pubs.

Nag Hammadi Codex VIII. Ed. by John H. Sieber. (NHS Ser.: No. 31). xxxv, 301p. 1991. 137.50 (*90-04-09477-6*) Brill Academic Pubs.

Nag Hammadi Library after Fifty Years: Proceedings of the 1995 Society of Biblical Literature Commemoration. Ed. by John D. Turner & Anne McGuire. Vol. 44. (Illus.). Xviii, 531p. 1997. text (*90-04-10824-6*) Brill Academic Pubs.

Nag Hammadi Library in English: Revised Edition. rev. ed. Ed. by James M. Robinson. LC 88-45154. 576p. 1990. reprint ed. pap. 21.00 (*0-06-066935-7*, Pub. by Harper SF) HarpC.

Nag Hammadi Texts & the Bible: A Synopsis & Index. Ed. by Craig A. Evans et al. LC 93-29154. (New Testament Tools & Studies: Vol. 18). xxii, 551p. 1993. 171.00 (*90-04-09902-6*) Brill Academic Pubs.

NAG Library: A Beginner's Guide. Jen Phillips. (Illus.). 252p. 1987. text 35.00 (*0-19-853263-6*) OUP.

Nag Mahasaya: A Saintly Householder Disciple of Sri Ramakrishna. Sarat C. Chakravarty. 1978. pap. 3.95 (*81-7120-238-1*) Vedanta Pr.

Nag Sen of Milind Panho. P. K. Kaul. (Illus.). xix, 134p. 1996. 17.00 (*81-86339-18-3*, Pub. by Eastern Bk Linkers) Nataraj Bks.

Naga. Contrib. by Hajime Sorayama. LC 98-144667. (Illus.). 100p. 1997. 55.00 (*4-87893-272-4*, Pub. by Sakuhin-Sha) Bks Nippan.

Naga: Cultural Origins in Siam & the West Pacific. Sumet Jumsai. (Illus.). 216p. 1988. 45.00 (*0-19-588880-4*) OUP.

Naga: Manners & Customs. J. H. Hutton. 1990. reprint ed. 32.00 (*81-85326-33-9*, Pub. by Vintage) S Asia.

Naga Art. Milada Ganguli. (C). 1993. 52.00 (*81-204-0842-X*, Pub. by Oxford IBH) S Asia.

Naga Art. Milada Ganguli. (Illus.). 96p. (C). text 54.00 (*1-881570-19-3*) Science Pubs.

Naga Awakens: Growth & Change in Southeast Asia. Victor R. Savage et al. 360p. 1998. 39.00 (*981-210-123-3*, Pub. by Times Academic); pap. 29.00 (*981-210-115-2*, Pub. by Times Academic) Intl Spec Bk.

***Naga Cultural Attires & Musical Instruments.** Ed. by A. O. Sanu. 1999. 20.00 (*81-7022-793-3*, Pub. by Concept) S Asia.

Naga Varmma's Karnataka Bhasha-Bhushana. Ed. by Lewis Rice. (C). 1985. reprint ed. 12.00 (*0-8364-2407-7*, Pub. by Asian Educ Servs) S Asia.

Nagaika. Joseph Kessel. 1988. pap. 16.95 (*0-7859-3199-6*, 2264011475) Fr & Eur.

Nagajuna's Seventy Stanzas: A Buddhist Psychology of Emptiness. David R. Komito. Tr. by Geshe S. Rinchen & Tenzin Dorjee from TIB. LC 87-9654. 226p. (Orig.). 1999. pap. 16.95 (*0-937938-39-4*) Snow Lion Pubns.

Nagaland Vol. XXXIV: People of India. Ed. by K. S. Singh et al. (C). 1994. 22.50 (*0-614-04143-0*, Pub. by Seagull Bks) S Asia.

Nagaland File: A Question of Human Rights. Luingam Luithui. 1985. 21.00 (*0-8364-1358-X*, Pub. by Lancer India) S Asia.

Naganandа of Harsa. Bak Kun-Bae. (C). 1992. pap. 9.00 (*81-208-1075-9*, Pub. by Motilal Bnarsidass) S Asia.

Nagara & Commandery: Origins of the Southeast Asian Urban Tradition. Paul Wheatley. LC 83-18014. (Research Papers: Nos. 207-208). (Illus.). 472p. (C). 1983. pap. text 29.00 (*0-89065-113-2*) U Ch Pr.

Nagarjuna & the Philosophy of Openness. Nancy McCagney. LC 97-16697. 256p. 1997. 63.00 (*0-8476-8626-4*); pap. 23.95 (*0-8476-8627-2*) Rowman.

Nagarjuna in China: A Translation of the Middle Treatise. Brian Bocking. LC 94-48168. (Studies in Asian Thought & Religion: Vol. 18). 512p. 1995. text 119.95 (*0-7734-8981-9*) E Mellen.

Nagarjuna's Letter to King Gautamiputra. Lozang Jamspal et al. 1978. 9.95 (*0-89684-022-0*, Pub. by Motilal Bnarsidass) S Asia.

Nagarjuna's Philosophy. K. Venkata Ramanan. 409p. (C). 1987. reprint ed. 18.00 (*81-208-0159-8*, Pub. by Motilal Bnarsidass) S Asia.

Nagarjuna's Philosophy of No-Identity: With Philosophical Translations of the Madhyamaka-Karika, Sunyata-Saptati & Vigrahavyavartani. Ram C. Pandeya. (C). 1991. 20.00 (*0-685-63332-2*, Pub. by Eastern Bk Linkers) S Asia.

Nagarjuna's Philosophy of No-Identity: With Philosophical Translations of the Madhyamaka-Karika, Sunyata-Saptati & Vigrahavyavartani. Ram C. Pandeya & Manju. xxvi, 165p. 1991. 18.00 (*0-685-62634-2*, Pub. by Eastern Bk Linkers) Nataraj Bks.

Nagarjuna's Refutation of Logic, Nyaya: Vaidalyapakarana. Fernando Tola. LC 95-904376. (C). 1995. 17.00 (*81-208-0920-3*, Pub. by Motilal Bnarsidass) S Asia.

Nagarjuna's Twelve Gate Treatise. H. L. Cheng. 165p. 1982. text 121.50 (*90-277-1380-4*, D Reidel) Kluwer Academic.

Nagarjunian Disputations: A Philosophical Journey Through an Indian Looking-Glass. Thomas E. Wood. LC 93-35686. (Monographs of the Society for Asian & Comparative Philosophy: No. 11). 1994. pap. text 22.00 (*0-8248-1609-9*) UH Pr.

Nagas: Hill Peoples of Northeast India. Julian Jacobs. LC 90-70288. (Illus.). 300p. 1990. 45.00 (*0-500-97388-1*, Pub. by Thames Hudson) Norton.

Nagas: Hill Peoples of Northeast India. Julian Jacobs et al. LC 90-70288. (Illus.). 360p. 1999. pap. 24.95 (*0-500-97471-3*, Pub. by Thames Hudson) Norton.

Nagas: Problems & Politics. Ashikho D. Mao. (C). 1992. 24.00 (*81-7024-486-2*, Pub. by Ashish Pub Hse) S Asia.

Nagas: Problems & Politics. Ashikho D. Mao. x, 206p. 1992. 19.95 (*1-881338-30-4*) Nataraj Bks.

Nagas Rebel & Insurgency in the North-East. Kiranshankar Maitra. LC 98-901176. 1998. 30.00 (*81-259-0447-6*, Pub. by Vikas) S Asia.

Nagasaki Dust. W. Colin McKay. 99p. 1998. pap. 5.60 (*0-87129-793-0*, N46) Dramatic Pub.

Nagasaki Journey: The Photographs of Yosuke Yamahata, August 10, 1945. Ed. by Rupert Jenkins. (Illus.). 128p. 1998. pap. text 25.00 (*0-7881-5461-3*) DIANE Pub.

Nagasaki, 1945. Tatsuichiro Akizuki. Ed. by Gordon Honeycombe. (Illus.). 168p. 1982. pap. 5.95 (*0-7043-3382-1*, Pub. by Quartet) Charles River Bks.

Nagashino, 1575. Stephen Turnbull. (Campaign Ser.: No. 57). (Illus.). 96p. 1998. pap. 16.95 (*1-85532-619-1*, Pub. by Ospry) Stackpole.

Nagauta: The Heart of Kabuki Music. William P. Malm. LC 73-6260. (Illus.). 344p. 1973. reprint ed. lib. bdg. 49.75 (*0-8371-6900-3*, Greenwood Pr) Greenwood.

Nagel: Sculptures & Works on Paper. Peter Selz. Ed. by Betina T. Hussey. LC 97-61584. (Illus.). 64p. 1997. pap. write for info. (*0-9655319-2-9*) Tasende Gallery.

Nagel's Encyclopedia Guide: Albania. 1992. 39.95 (*0-8442-9791-7*, Passprt Bks) NTC Contemp Pub Co.

Nagel's Encyclopedia Guide: Bolivia. (Illus.). 1991. 39.95 (*0-8442-9727-5*, Passprt Bks) NTC Contemp Pub Co.

Nagel's Encyclopedia Guide: Brazil. (Illus.). 1991. 39.95 (*0-8442-9728-3*, Passprt Bks) NTC Contemp Pub Co.

Nagel's Encyclopedia Guide: Bulgaria. (Illus.). 1991. 39.95 (*0-8442-9729-1*, Passprt Bks) NTC Contemp Pub Co.

Nagel's Encyclopedia Guide: Canada. (Illus.). 1990. 39.95 (*0-8442-9730-5*, Passprt Bks) NTC Contemp Pub Co.

Nagel's Encyclopedia Guide: Central America. (Illus.). 1992. 39.95 (*0-8442-9731-3*, Passprt Bks) NTC Contemp Pub Co.

Nagel's Encyclopedia Guide: Ceylon. (Illus.). 1986. 39.95 (*0-8442-9732-1*, Passprt Bks) NTC Contemp Pub Co.

Nagel's Encyclopedia Guide: China. (Illus.). 1989. 59.95 (*0-8442-9735-6*, Passprt Bks) NTC Contemp Pub Co.

Nagel's Encyclopedia Guide: Czechoslovakia. (Illus.). 1995. 39.95 (*0-8442-9737-2*, Passprt Bks) NTC Contemp Pub Co.

Nagel's Encyclopedia Guide: Denmark - Greenland. (Illus.). 1990. 39.95 (*0-8442-9738-0*, Passprt Bks) NTC Contemp Pub Co.

Nagel's Encyclopedia Guide: Egypt. (Illus.). 1990. 49.95 (*0-8442-9739-9*, Passprt Bks) NTC Contemp Pub Co.

Nagel's Encyclopedia Guide: Finland. (Illus.). 1990. 34.95 (*0-8442-9741-0*, Passprt Bks) NTC Contemp Pub Co.

Nagel's Encyclopedia Guide: France. (Illus.). 1992. 49.95 (*0-8442-9742-9*, Passprt Bks) NTC Contemp Pub Co.

Nagel's Encyclopedia Guide: German Federal Republic. (Illus.). 1990. 49.95 (*0-8442-9745-3*, Passprt Bks) NTC Contemp Pub Co.

Nagel's Encyclopedia Guide: Great Britain. (Illus.). 1991. 49.95 (*0-8442-9746-1*, Passprt Bks) NTC Contemp Pub Co.

Nagel's Encyclopedia Guide: Gulf Emirates. (Illus.). 1992. 39.95 (*0-8442-9749-6*, Passprt Bks) NTC Contemp Pub Co.

Nagel's Encyclopedia Guide: Hungary. 1990. 39.95 (*0-8442-9752-6*, Passprt Bks) NTC Contemp Pub Co.

Nagel's Encyclopedia Guide: Iceland. (Illus.). 1991. 29.95 (*0-8442-9753-4*, Passprt Bks) NTC Contemp Pub Co.

Nagel's Encyclopedia Guide: India & Nepal. (Illus.). 1991. 59.95 (*0-8442-9754-2*, Passprt Bks) NTC Contemp Pub Co.

Nagel's Encyclopedia Guide: Iran. (Illus.). 1995. 39.95 (*0-8442-9756-9*, Passprt Bks) NTC Contemp Pub Co.

Nagel's Encyclopedia Guide: Ireland. (Illus.). 1988. 39.95 (*0-8442-9757-7*, Passprt Bks) NTC Contemp Pub Co.

Nagel's Encyclopedia Guide: Italy. (Illus.). 1987. 59.95 (*0-8442-9759-3*, Passprt Bks) NTC Contemp Pub Co.

Nagel's Encyclopedia Guide: Malta. (Illus.). 1992. 29.95 (*0-8442-9763-1*, Passprt Bks) NTC Contemp Pub Co.

Nagel's Encyclopedia Guide: Mexico. (Illus.). 1991. 49.95 (*0-8442-9765-8*, Passprt Bks) NTC Contemp Pub Co.

Nagel's Encyclopedia Guide: Philippines. (Illus.). 1990. 39.95 (*0-8442-9773-9*, Passprt Bks) NTC Contemp Pub Co.

Nagel's Encyclopedia Guide: Poland. (Illus.). 1991. 39.95 (*0-8442-9774-7*, Passprt Bks) NTC Contemp Pub Co.

Nagel's Encyclopedia Guide: Rumania. 1992. 29.95 (*0-8442-9777-1*, Passprt Bks) NTC Contemp Pub Co.

Nagel's Encyclopedia Guide: Spain. (Illus.). 1990. 49.95 (*0-8442-9780-1*, Passprt Bks) NTC Contemp Pub Co.

Nagel's Encyclopedia Guide: Thailand. (Illus.). 1995. 39.95 (*0-8442-9785-2*, Passprt Bks) NTC Contemp Pub Co.

Nagel's Encyclopedia Guide: Turkey. (Illus.). 1991. 49.95 (*0-8442-9786-0*, Passprt Bks) NTC Contemp Pub Co.

Nagel's Encyclopedia Guide: U. S. A. (FRE., Illus.). 1986. 49.95 (*0-8442-9798-4*, Passprt Bks); 49.95 (*0-8442-9799-2*, Passprt Bks) NTC Contemp Pub Co.

Nagel's Encyclopedia Guide: U. S. A. (Illus.). 1992. 49.95 (*0-8442-9787-9*, Passprt Bks) NTC Contemp Pub Co.

Nagel's Encyclopedia Guide: U. S. S. R. (Illus.). 1990. 49.95 (*0-8442-9788-7*, Passprt Bks) NTC Contemp Pub Co.

Nagel's Guide to Sweden. Nagel. 1991. 39.95 (*0-8442-9782-8*, Passprt Bks) NTC Contemp Pub Co.

"Nagging" Questions: Feminist Ethics in Everyday Life. Ed. by Dana E. Bushnell. LC 94-32590. (New Feminist Perspectives Ser.). 376p. 1995. lib. bdg. 24.95 (*0-8476-8006-1*) Rowman.

"Nagging" Questions: Feminist Ethics in Everyday Life. Ed. by Dana E. Bushnell. LC 94-32590. (New Feminist Perspectives Ser.). 414p. 1995. pap. text 27.95 (*0-8476-8007-X*) Rowman.

NAGNA's CNA Code of Ethics & Federal Regulation Handbook. Lori Porter & Lisa Cantrell. 31p. 1996. wbk. ed. 4.99 (*0-9662101-1-5*) NAGNA.

Nagual in the Garden: Fantastic Animals in Mexican Ceramics. Lenore H. Mulryan. LC 95-49823. (Illus.). 156p. 1996. 50.00 (*0-930741-48-X*); pap. 29.00 (*0-930741-49-8*) UCLA Fowler Mus.

Naguib Mahfouz's Egypt: Existential Themes in His Writings, 38. Haim Gordon. LC 90-36629. (Contributions to the Study of World Literature Ser.: No. 38). 152p. 1990. 49.95 (*0-313-26876-2*, GLP, Greenwood Pr) Greenwood.

Nagus Volleyball Rulebook, 1998. rev. ed. (Illus.). 254p. 1998. pap. 8.95 (*0-88314-810-2*, 303-10066) AAHPERD.

NAGWS Internship Guide. 2nd rev. ed. Orig. Title: NAGWS Internship Guide - Climbing the Ladder. 1998. pap. 20.00 (*0-88314-809-9*, 303-10064) AAHPERD.

NAGWS Internship Guide - Climbing the Ladder see NAGWS Internship Guide

NAGWS Title IX Toolbox. Ed. by Linda J. Carpenter & Vivian Acosta. 217p. (Orig.). 1992. pap. text 16.00 (*0-88314-536-7*, 303-10021) AAHPERD.

Nagy Ferenc Miniszterelnok. Ed. by Istvan Csicsery-Ronay. (HUN., Illus.). 161p. 1995. 15.00 (*963-7871-05-5*) Occidental.

Nagy Imre a Magyar nep Vedelmeben see In Defense of the Hungarian People

Nah Nah Nah! Teasing. Richard L. Biren. LC 96-79863. (Illus.). 72p. (Orig.). (J). (gr. 3-5). 1997. pap. 13.95 (*1-57543-020-7*) Mar Co Prods.

Nahal Qanah Cave: Earliest Gold in the Southern Levant. Avi Gopher & Tsvika Tsuk. (Monograph Series of the Sonia & Marco Nadler Institute of Archaeology: Vol. 12). xii, 250p. 1996. text 50.00 (*965-440-005-7*, Pub. by Friends Archeol Inst) Eisenbrauns.

Nahalat Shafra: A Book of Eulogettes. Victor M. Solomon. pap. 14.95 (*0-88125-356-1*) Ktav.

Nahali: A Comparative Study. F. B. Kuiper. (Mededelingen der Koninklijke Nederlandse Akademie van Wetenschappen, Afd. Letterkunde Ser.: No. 25(5)). 116p. pap. 20.00 (*0-7204-8382-4*) Elsevier.

Nahan Galleries: Thirty Years. (Illus.). 72p. (Orig.). 1989. 30.00 (*0-9624615-2-0*); pap. 15.00 (*0-9624615-1-2*) Nahan Editions.

Nahanni. Dick Turner. (Illus.). 286p. 1975. pap. 11.95 (*0-88839-028-9*) Hancock House.

Nahanni: River of Gold ...River of Dreams. Neil Hartling. (Illus.). 136p. 1999. pap. 21.95 (*1-895465-06-0*) CNR Canoe.

Nahanni Remembered, Vol. 2. A. C. Lewis. (Northwest Passage Ser.). (Illus.). 312p. (Orig.). 1997. pap. 19.95 (*1-896300-18-9*) NeWest Pubs.

***Nahant.** Kenneth Turino & Christopher Mathias. (Images of America Ser.). 1999. pap. 18.99 (*0-7385-0080-1*) Arcadia Publng.

NAHB Thermal Performance Guidelines. National Association of Home Builders Research Fou. 16p. 1983. pap. 8.00 (*0-86718-192-3*) Home Builder.

Nahbosha Jobsite Safety Handdbook. 2nd ed. Association of Home B. National Staff. LC 98-42711. 1998. 10.00 (*0-86718-454-X*) Home Builder.

Nahi'ena'ena: Sacred Daughter of Hawaii. Marjorie Sinclair. (Illus.). 224p. 1995. mass mkt. 4.95 (*1-56647-080-3*) Mutual Pub HI.

Nahjul Balagha. Ali-Ibne-Abu Talib. Tr. by Syded A. Jafery from ARA. LC 84-51778. 691p. (C). 1984. pap. 16.00 (*0-940368-42-0*, 6A); text 24.00 (*0-940368-43-9*, 6) Tahrike Tarsile Quran.

Nahjul Balagha: Peak of Eloquence. Ali I. Talib. 680p. 1996. pap. 12.50 (*0-614-21185-9*, 884) Kazi Pubns.

Nahjul Balagha & Inter-Religious Understanding. Ed. by Shah Mohammad Waseem & S. Ali Mohammad Naqavi. LC 97-902274. xxviii, 302 p. 1997. write for info. (*81-85199-64-7*) Renaiss Publng Hse.

Nahman of Bratslav, the Tales. Arnold Band. LC 78-53433. (Classics of Western Spirituality Ser.). 368p. 1978. pap. 21.95 (*0-8091-2103-4*) Paulist Pr.

Nahrungsfette und-Ole: Handbuch der Lebensmittel-Technologie see Fats & Oils Handbook: Nahrungsfette und Ole

Nahrungssicherungspolitik in Afrika Zwischen Katastrophenhilfe und Strukturanpassung see Food Security Policy in Africa Between Disaster Relief & Structural Adjustment: Reflections on the Conception & Effectiveness of Policies; the Case of Tanzania

Nahuas after the Conquest: A Social & Cultural History of the Indians of Central Mexico. James Lockhart. xx, 650p. 1994. pap. 29.95 (*0-8047-2317-6*) Stanford U Pr.

Nahuas after the Conquest: A Social & Cultural History of the Indians of Central Mexico, Sixteenth Through Eighteenth Centuries. James Lockhart. LC 91-29972. (Illus.). 672p. (C). 1992. 75.00 (*0-8047-1927-6*) Stanford U Pr.

Nahuas & Spaniards: Postconquest Central Mexican History & Philology. James Lockhart. LC 91-9895. 320p. 1991. 47.50 (*0-8047-1953-5*); pap. 18.95 (*0-8047-1954-3*) Stanford U Pr.

Nahuat Myth & Social Structure. 2nd ed. James M. Taggart. LC 98-117997. (The Texas Pan American Ser.). (Illus.). 299p. 1997. reprint ed. pap. 15.95 (*0-292-78152-0*) U of Tex Pr.

Nahuatl-English Dictionary & Concordance to the "Cantares Mexicanos" With an Analytic Transcription & Grammatical Notes. John Bierhorst. LC 82-61070. 760p. 1985. 95.00 (*0-8047-1183-6*) Stanford U Pr.

Nahuatl in Middle Years: Language Contact Phenomena in Texts of the Colonial Period. Frances Karttunen & James Lockhart. LC 76-19945. (U of C Publications in Linguistics: Vol. 85). 158p. reprint ed. 49.00 (*0-8357-9635-3*, 201511000092) Bks Demand.

Nahuatl Practico: Lecciones y Ejercicios Para el Principiante. 2nd ed. Fernando Horcasitas. (SPA.). 99p. 1996. pap. 10.00 (*968-36-1798-0*, UN51, Pub. by Universidad Nacional) UPLAAP.

N

Nahuatl to Rayuela: The Latin American Collection at Texas. Intro. by Dave Oliphant. (Illus.). 160p. 1992. 15.00 (0-87959-128-5) U of Tex H Ransom Ctr.

Nahum B. Zenil: Witness to the Self. Edward J. Sullivan & Clayton C. Kirking.Tr. of Nahum B. Zenil: Testigo del Ser. (Illus.). 80p. (Orig.). (C). 1996. 24.95 (1-880508-05-2) Mexican Museum.

Nahum B. Zenil: Witness to the Self. Edward J. Sullivan & Clayton C. Kirking.Tr. of Nahum B. Zenil: Testigo del Ser. (Illus.). 80p. (Orig.). 1996. pap. 24.95 (0-295-97570-9) U of Wash Pr.

Nahum B. Zenil: Testigo del Ser see Nahum B. Zenil: Witness to the Self

Nahum Goldmann: His Missions to the Gentiles. Raphael Patai. LC 85-24518. (Judaic Studies). 325p. 1987. pap. 100.80 (0-7837-8397-3, 205920800009) Bks Demand.

Nahum, Habakkuk & Zephaniah. O. Palmer Robertson. (New International Commentary on the Old Testament Ser.). 384p. 1990. 34.00 (0-8028-2532-X) Eerdmans.

Nahum, Habakkuk & Zephaniah: A Commentary. J. J. Roberts. LC 90-24082. (Old Testament Library). 224p. 1991. text 24.95 (0-664-21937-3) Westminster John Knox.

Nahum, Habakkuk, Zephaniah. David W. Baker. LC 88-9360. (Tyndale Old Testament Commentary Ser.). 128p. 1989. pap. 12.99 (0-87784-249-3, 249) InterVarsity.

Nahum, Habakkuk, Zephaniah. David W. Baker. LC 88-9360. (Tyndale Old Testament Commentary Ser.: Vol. 23b). 128p. 1989. 19.99 (0-8308-1427-2, 1427) InterVarsity.

Nahum-Malachi. Elizabeth Achtemeier. LC 85-45458. (Interpretation: A Bible Commentary for Teaching & Preaching Ser.). 216p. 1986. 25.00 (0-8042-3129-X) Westminster John Knox.

Nahum Tate's Injur'd Love, or the Cruel Husband & Lewis Theobald's the Fatal Secret. Ed. by James Hogg. 129p. 1999. pap. 18.95 (3-7052-0157-3, Pub. by Poetry Salzburg) Intl Spec Bk.

Nahum, Zephaniah, Habakkuk: Minor Prophets of the Seventh Century B. C. Hobart E. Freeman. 126p. 1967. reprint ed. pap. 3.95 (1-878725-50-5) Faith Fellowship Min.

Nahum/Habakkuk. J. hVernon McGee. 1997. pap. 6.97 (0-7852-0587-X) Nelson.

Nahwa Nizam Naqdi Adil: (Toward a Just Monetary System) rev. ed. Ed. by Muhammad U. Chapra & Muhammad S. Sayed. LC 87-81431. (Silsilat Islamiyat al Ma'rifah Ser.: No. 3). (ARA.). 403p. (C). 1989. pap. text 12.95 (0-912463-41-4) IIIT VA.

Nahwa Nizam Naqdi Adil: (Toward a Just Monetary System) 2nd rev. ed. Ed. by Muhammad U. Chapra. Tr. by Muhammad S. Sayed from ENG. LC 87-81431. (Silsilat Islamiyat al Ma'rifah Ser.: No. 3). (ARA.). 403p. (C). 1989. text 19.95 (0-912463-40-6) IIIT VA.

Naiad Fauna of the Huron River, in Southeastern, Michigan. Henry Van Der Schalie. LC 38-28431. (University of Michigan, Museum of Zoology, Miscellaneous Publications: No. 40). (Illus.). 110p. reprint ed. pap. 34.10 (0-608-07033-5, 206724000009) Bks Demand.

Naiadea to Pycnoscenus: Including Second Edition of Vol. 1, Plagiochila. 2nd ed. Ed. by Patricia Geissler & Helene Bischler. (Index Hepaticarum Ser.: Vol. 11). (GER.). 353p. 1989. 95.00 (3-443-73002-7, Pub. by Gebruder Borntraeger) Balogh.

Naibhu: A Spiritual Odyssey. Valerie V. Hunt. 208p. 1998. 17.95 (0-9643988-4-2) Malibu Pubng.

NAIC Insurance Department Directory. 181p. 1994. ring bd. 25.00 (0-89382-256-6) Nat Assn Insurance.

NAIC Insurance Department Directory. 182p. 1994. ring bd. 25.00 (0-89382-263-9) Nat Assn Insurance.

NAIC Model Laws, Regulations & Guidelines, 5 vols. 15th rev. ed. Carolyn Johnson. 4000p. 1998. reprint ed. ring bd. 295.00i (0-89382-530-1, MDL-ZM) Nat Assn Insurance.

NAIC Report on Receiverships. rev. ed. Ed. by Patti Carli. Orig. Title: Contact Person Report. 672p. (C). 1995. ring bd. 75.00 (0-89382-360-0, CPR-ZB) Nat Assn Insurance.

***NAICS Desk Reference: (The North American Industrial Classification System Desk Reference)** Ed. by Jist Works Staff. LC 00-23827. 2000. 19.95 (1-56370-694-6) JIST Works.

Naikan Psychotherapy: Meditation for Self-Development. David K. Reynolds. LC 82-21862. 184p. 1983. 17.50 (0-226-71029-7) U Ch Pr.

Nail & Other Stories. Pedro A. De Alarcon. Tr. by Robert M. Fedorchek from SPA. LC 97-2143. (Illus.). 136p. 1997. 29.50 (0-8387-5361-2) Bucknell U Pr.

***Nail & Other Stories.** Laura J. Hird. 2000. pap. 13.95 (0-86241-677-9, Pub. by Canongate Books); pap. 13.95 (0-86241-850-X) Canongate Books.

Nail Art, Incl. nail paints. Sherri Haab. (Illus.). 66p. (J). (gr. 1 up). Date not set. 19.95 (1-57054-111-6) Klutz.

***Nail Art: Everything You Need to Know to Create Healthy, Beautiful Nails.** Ra K. Sa. (Illus.). 1999. 12.99 (0-7858-1065-X) Bk Sales Inc.

***Nail Art: The Nail Design Pack.** Pansy Alexander. 2000. pap. 19.95 (1-85868-825-6) Carlton Bks Ltd.

Nail Art & Design. Tammy Bigan. LC 93-28383. (NAILS). 90p. 1993. pap. 41.95 (1-56253-118-2) Thomson Learn.

Nail Art for Kids. Petra Boase. 1999. pap. text 14.95 (1-85868-662-8, Pub. by Carlton Bks Ltd) Natl Bk Netwk.

Nail Biters Anonymous. Suzanne Taylor-Moore. 48p. 1981. pap. 3.00 (0-938758-12-8) MTM Pub Co.

Nail Biting: The Beatable Habit. Frederick H. Smith. LC 80-11687. (Illus.). xv, 112p. (Orig.). 1981. pap. 7.95 (0-8425-1806-1, Friends of the Library) Brigham.

Nail Care: An Illustrated Guide to Beautiful Nails. 1989. write for info. (0-318-66972-2) Briarcliff Pr.

Nail Disorders: Common Presenting Signs, Differential Diagnosis & Treatment. Robert Baran et al. (Illus.). 188p. 1991. text 39.95 (0-443-08800-4) Church.

Nail 'Em: Confronting High-Profile Attacks on Celebrities & Businesses. Eric Dezenhall. LC 99-26828. 250p. 1999. 27.95 (1-57392-719-8) Prometheus Bks.

Nail File. Leo Palladino & June Hunt. (Illus.). 154p. 1992. pap. text 22.95 (0-333-52584-1) Scholium Intl.

Nail in a Sure Place: Inspiring Stories of God's Faithfulness. Margaret Jensen. LC 96-32284. 160p. (Orig.). 1997. pap. 7.99 (1-56507-569-2) Harvest Hse.

Nail in Health & Disease. 2nd ed. Nardo Zaias. (Illus.). 255p. (C). 1992. pap. text 165.00 (0-8385-6645-6, A6645-4, Apple Lange Med) McGraw.

Nail Surgery: Text & Atlas. Edward A. Krull et al. 175p. 1997. text. write for info. (0-7817-0154-6) Lppncott W & W.

Nail Technology: Answer Key. 3rd ed. Milady Inc. Staff. (Cosmetology Ser.). 1992. pap., teacher ed., wbk. ed. 26.95 (1-56253-091-7) Milady Pub.

***Nail Tech's Questions from the Internet.** Margaret Schoon. 1999. pap. 18.50 (1-56253-447-5) Thomson Learn.

***Nail the Boards: Internal Medicine Board Review Syllabus for the ABIM Exam.** Bradley Mittman. LC 00-132303. (Illus.). 336p. 2000. pap. text 225.00 (0-9677025-2-6) Frontrunners.

Nailah's Surprise. Ashley F. Behr. Ed. by Terry O'Neill. (Illus.). 32p. (J). (ps-3). 1998. pap., per. 5.95 (0-9660533-1-1) D J Behr.

***Nailed: A Biography of Jimmy Nail.** Geraint Jones. 1998. pap. 13.95 (0-00-653072-9, Pub. by HarpC) Trafalgar.

Nailed by the Heart. S. Clark. 1995. mass mkt. 13.95 (0-340-62573-2, Pub. by Hodder & Stought Ltd) Trafalgar.

***Nailed by the Heart.** Simon Clark. 400p. 2000. pap. 5.99 (0-8439-4713-6, Leisure Bks) Dorchester Pub Co.

Nailed to the Coffin of Life. Ivan Arguelles. Ed. by Loss P. Glazier. (Oxyura Jamaicensis Rubida Monographs in Poetry: No. 1). (Illus.). 1985. pap. 3.50 (0-910697-03-5) Ruddy Duck Pr.

Nailed to the Wound. Jose Manuel Di Bella. Tr. by Harry Polkinhorn from SPA. (Baja California Literature in Translation Ser.). 162p. 1993. pap. 12.50 (1-879691-14-0) SDSU Press.

Nailer Tom's Diary. Thomas R. Hazard. LC 75-31119. reprint ed. 67.50 (0-404-13603-6) AMS Pr.

Nailing Down a Board: Serving Effectively on the Not for Profit Board. Charles C. Ryrie. LC 98-50471. 1999. pap. 5.99 (0-8254-3649-4) Kregel.

Nailing Hammering Man: An Embarrassment of Large Mass. Selma Waldman. (Illus.). 40p. (C). 1992. 6.00 (0-940880-45-8, Littlebook) Open Hand.

Nailing Jelly to A Tree Jerry Willis & William Danley. LC 82-170067. viii, 244p. 1982. write for info. (0-8306-4334-6, TAB Elctrncs) McGraw-Hill Prof.

Nailing the Shadow. Roger McGough. (Illus.). (J). (gr. 3). 1989. pap. 7.95 (0-14-032390-2, Pub. by Pnguin Bks Ltd) Trafalgar.

***Nails.** Alexander. 1998. mass mkt. 6.95 (1-85626-292-8, Pub. by Cathie Kyle) Trafalgar.

Nails: Therapy, Diagnosis, Surgery. 2nd ed. Richard K. Scher. LC 96-36756. (C). 1997. text 154.00 (0-7216-7026-1) Harcourt.

Nain. Marcel Ayme. (FRE.). 273p. 1977. pap. 10.95 (0-7859-1844-2, 2070369129) Fr & Eur.

Nainsukh of Guler: A Great Indian Painter from a Small Hill-State. B. N. Goswami. (Illus.). 304p. 1999. 65.00 (3-907070-76-3) U of Wash Pr.

***Naipaul's Truth: The Making of a Writer.** Lillian Feder. 256p. 2000. 29.95 (0-7425-0808-0) Rowman.

Nairn Way: Desert Bus to Baghdad. John M. Munro. LC 80-11875. 112p. 1980. 35.00 (0-88206-035-X) Caravan Bks.

Nairobi. George Myers, Jr. LC 77-99271. 1978. pap. 3.00 (0-917976-01-0, White Ewe Pr) Thunder Baas Pr.

Nairobi to Vancouver: The World Council of Churches & the World, 1975-87. Ernest W. Lefever. LC 87-30302. 166p. (Orig.). (C). 1988. pap. text 12.75 (0-89633-118-0); lib. bdg. 31.50 (0-89633-117-2) Ethics & Public Policy.

Nais see Oeuvres Completes de Jean-Philippe Rameau

Nais: Theatre. Marcel Pagnol. (FRE.). 160p. 1990. pap. 13.95 (0-7859-1561-3, 2877060659) Fr & Eur.

Naiskarmyasiddhi of Suresvara: A Monograph. John Grimes. (C). 1992. 24.00 (81-7030-317-6) S Asia.

Naissance de la Cite Grecque see Cults, Territory & the Origins of the Greek City-State

Naissance de la Science: Grece Presocratique, Vol. 2. Andre Pichot. (FRE.). 1991. pap. 26.95 (0-7859-3972-5) Fr & Eur.

Naissance de la Science: Mesopotamie, Egypte, Vol. 1. Andre Pichot. (FRE.). 1991. pap. 22.95 (0-7859-3971-7) Fr & Eur.

Naissance de l'Odyssee see Oeuvres Romanesques

Naissance de l'Odyssee. Victor Hugo. Ed. by A. R. James. (FRE.). 1105p. 1976. 135.00 (0-7859-1179-0, 2252017910) Fr & Eur.

Naissance de Notre Force see Birth of Our Power

Naissance du Chevalier au Cygne. Ed. by Jan A. Nelson & Emanuel J. Mickel. LC 76-30489. (Old French Crusade Cycle Ser.: Vol. 1). 496p. 1977. text 34.50 (0-8173-8501-0) U of Ala Pr.

Naissance du Jour. Sidonie-Gabrielle Colette. (POR.). 24.95 incl. audio (0-685-21218-1); pap. 8.95 (0-685-37283-9) Fr & Eur.

Naissance d'une Population see First French Canadians: Pioneers in the St. Lawrence Valley

Naissances-Births. Philip Cranston. 99p. 35.00 (0-916379-92-2) Scripta.

***Naive & Sentimental Lover.** John Le Carre, pseud. 528p. 2000. reprint ed. per. 7.99 (0-671-04277-7) PB.

Naive Art. Natalia Brodskaya. (Schools & Movements Ser.). (Illus.). 272p. 2000. 55.00 (1-85995-335-2) Parkstone Pr.

Naive Metaphysics: A Theory of Subjective & Objective Worlds. Geoffrey V. Klempner. (Avebury Series in Philosophy). 288p. 1994. 82.95 (1-85628-962-1, Pub. by Avebry) Ashgate Pub Co.

Naive Semantics for Natural Language Understanding. Kathleen Dahlgren. (C). 1988. text 104.50 (0-89838-287-4) Kluwer Academic.

Naive Set Theory. P. R. Halmos. LC 74-10687. (Undergraduate Texts in Mathematics Ser.). 110p. 1994. reprint ed. 37.95 (0-387-90092-6) Spr-Verlag.

Naj Atu Ur-Ra'ld wa-Shar Atu al-Warid Fi al-Mutaradifi. Ibrahim Yaziji. (ARA.). 1970. 29.95 (0-86685-102-X) Intl Bk Ctr.

Najadicola & Unionicola: I. Diagnoses of Genera & Subgenera, II. Key, III. List of Reported Hosts. Malcolm F. Vidrine. LC 96-60324. (Illus.). vi, 180p. (C). 1996. pap. 75.00 (0-9637304-9-5); lib. bdg. 150.00 (0-9637304-2-8) G Q Vidrine Collect.

Najdi Arabic: Central Arabian. Bruce Ingham. LC 94-34957. (London Oriental & African Language Library: No. 1). xvi, 215p. 1994. 62.00 (1-55619-725-X) J Benjamins Pubng Co.

Na/k-Atpase & Related Transport Atpases: The Surface Pumps on Which Every Living Creature Relies. Ed. by Luis A. Beauge et al. LC 97-35157. (Annals of the New York Academy of Sciences Ser.: No. 834). 694p. 1997. 190.00 (1-57331-060-3) NY Acad Sci.

Nakae Ushikichi in China: The Mourning of Spirit. Joshua A. Fogel. (East Asian Monographs: No. 139). 250p. 1989. 32.50 (0-674-59842-3) HUP.

Nakahara: Family Farming & Population in a Japanese Village, 1717-1830. Thomas C. Smith. LC 76-14273. xvi, 183p. 1977. 32.50 (0-8047-0928-9) Stanford U Pr.

Nakajima KI-84 a/b Hayate in Japanese Army Air Force Service. Richard M. Bueschel. LC 96-70490. (Illus.). 64p. 1997. pap. 14.95 (0-7643-0149-7) Schiffer.

Nakajima KI-44 Shokiin Japanese Army Air Force Service. Richard M. Beuschel. (Illus.). 64p. (YA). (gr. 10-13). 1996. pap. 14.95 (0-88740-914-8) Schiffer.

Nakajima KI-49 Donryu in Japanese Army Air Force Service. Richard M. Bueschel. LC 97-66912. 64p. 1997. pap. 14.95 (0-7643-0344-9) Schiffer.

Nakajima KI-43 Hayabusa in Japanese Army Air Force RATF-CAF-IP. Richard M. Bueschel. LC 95-67623. (Illus.). 80p. (Orig.). 1995. pap. 14.95 (0-88740-804-4) Schiffer.

Nakajima Ki.43 "Haybusa" John Stanaway. (World War II Monograph Ser.: No. 297). (Illus.). 50p. 1998. 22.50 (1-57638-142-0, M297-H); pap. 12.50 (1-57638-141-2, M297-S) Merriam Pr.

Nakama, Vol. 1. Makino. (C). Date not set. pap., teacher ed. 11.96 (0-669-27584-0) HM.

Nakama, Vol. 1. Makino. (C). 1998. pap. text, student ed. 32.36 (0-669-27585-9) HM.

Nakama, Vol. 1. Makino. (C). 1998. pap. text 52.36 (0-669-27583-2) HM.

Naked. John V. Aho. (Orig.). 1986. pap. text 5.00 (0-9613629-2-8) Townsend Harbor.

***Naked.** Luigi Pirandello. 96p. 1998. pap. 14.95 (1-85459-339-0) Theatre Comm.

***Naked.** David Saderis. (Orig.). 1998. mass mkt. 13.00 (0-316-19130-2, Back Bay) Little.

Naked. David Sedaris. Ed. by Geoffrey Koske. LC 96-44566. 304p. (gr. 8). 1997. 21.95 (0-316-77949-0) Little.

Naked. David Sedaris. 224p. 1998. pap. 13.95 (0-316-77773-0) Little.

Naked. Shuntaro Tanikawa. Tr. by William I. Elliott & Kazuo Kawamura from JPN. 64p. (Orig.). 1998. pap. 14.95 (1-880656-25-6) Stone Bridge Pr.

Naked. large type ed. David Sedaris. LC 97-34315. (Wheeler Large Print Book Ser.). 1997. 24.95 (1-56895-486-7) Wheeler Pub.

Naked - Nude: A Long Poem. Chuck Taylor. 100p. (Orig.). 1990. pap. 5.95 (0-941720-85-3) Slough Pr TX.

***Naked Against the Rain: The People of the Lower Columbia River, 1770-1830.** Rick Rubin. (Illus.). 448p. (YA). (gr. 10 up). 1999. 29.95 (1-883287-00-6) Far Shore Pr.

***Naked Airport.** Alastair Gordon. 2000. pap. text 30.00 (0-8050-6518-0) St Martin.

***Naked Airport.** Alastair Gordon. 2001. pap. text 16.00 (0-8050-6519-9) St Martin.

Naked & a Prisoner: Captain Edward C. Bernard's Narrative of Shipwreck in Palau, 1832-33. Edward C. Barnard. Ed. by Kenneth R. Martin. LC 80-83347. (Illus.). 60p. (Orig.). 1980. pap. 7.00 (0-937854-01-8) Kendall Whaling.

Naked & Erect: Male Sexuality & Feeling. Joel Ryce-Menuhin. LC 96-25222. 152p. (Orig.). 1996. pap. 14.95 (1-888602-00-7, 007) Chiron Pubns.

Naked & Not Ashamed. T. D. Jakes. LC 95-186671. 156p. (Orig.). 1995. pap. 9.99 (1-56043-835-5, Treasure Hse) Destiny Image.

Naked & Not Ashamed. T. D. Jakes. 56p. (Orig.). 1995. pap., wbk. ed. 7.99 (1-56043-259-4, Treasure Hse) Destiny Image.

Naked & Other Screenplays. Mike Leigh. LC 96-138277. 272p. (Orig.). 1995. pap. 21.95 (0-571-17386-1) Faber & Faber.

Naked & the Dead. Norman Mailer. 1994. lib. bdg. 65.00 (1-56849-421-1) Buccaneer Bks.

Naked & the Dead. Norman Mailer. LC 80-25751. 740p. 1995. pap. 14.95 (0-8050-0521-8, Owl) H Holt & Co.

Naked & the Dead. Norman Mailer. 721p. 1998. 30.00 (0-8050-6018-9); pap. 16.00 (0-8050-6017-0, Owl) H Holt & Co.

***Naked & the Dead.** Norman Mailer. 752p. 2000. pap. 16.00 (0-312-26505-0) St Martin.

Naked & the Dead. limited ed. Norman Mailer. (Classics Ser.). 736p. 1995. 30.00 (0-8050-1273-7) H Holt & Co.

Naked & the Nude. Jill Bart. (Illus.). 32p. (Orig.). (C). 1993. pap. text 5.00 (1-878173-31-6) Birnham Wood.

Naked & the Undead: Feminism, Philosophy & the Appeal of Horror. Cynthia A. Freeland. LC 99-35593. (Thinking Through Cinema Ser.). (Illus.). 336p. 1999. 26.00 (0-8133-6702-6, Pub. by Westview) HarpC.

***Naked & the Veiled: The Photographic Nudes of Erwin Blumenfeld.** Yorick Blumenfeld. LC 98-61830. (Illus.). 144p. 1999. 50.00 (0-500-54230-9, Pub. by Thames Hudson) Norton.

Naked Angels: The Lives & Literature of the Beat Generation. John Tytell. LC 86-45400. 288p. 1991. pap. 12.95 (0-8021-3247-2, Grove) Grove-Atltic.

Naked Anthropologist: Tales from Around the World. Philip R. DeVita. 263p. (C). 1991. 20.00 (0-534-16266-5) Wadsworth Pub.

Naked Ape. Desmond Morris. 208p. 20.95 (0-8488-2684-1) Amereon Ltd.

Naked Ape. Desmond Morris. 256p. 1999. pap. 11.95 (0-385-33430-3) Delta Alpha.

Naked Architecture No. 1: Fragment. (Illus.). 68p. 1997. pap. 18.00 (0-9661352-0-2) Palimpsest.

Naked Artist. Peter Fuller. (Illus.). 245p. 15.95 (0-86316-045-X); pap. 8.95 (0-86316-046-8) Writers & Readers.

***Naked As Eve: Poems.** Rebecca McClanahan. 63p. 2000. pap. 11.00 (0-914278-78-9) Copper Beech.

Naked As Water: Poems by Mario Azzopardi. Mario Azzopardi. Tr. by Grazio Falzon from MLT. (Illus.). xiii, 178p. 1996. pap. 13.00 (1-879378-11-6) Xenos Riverside.

Naked As We Stand. Jeanne Carpenter. LC 96-79571. 165p. 1997. 12.95 (0-9655354-1-X) About Time Pub.

Naked at Gender Gap: A Man's View of the War Between the Sexes. Asa Baber. 224p. 1992. 18.95 (1-55972-114-6, Birch Ln Pr) Carol Pub Group.

Naked at the Feast: The Biography of Josephine Baker. Lynn Haney. (Illus.). 338p. 1999. reprint ed. pap. text 20.00 (0-7881-6119-9) DIANE Pub.

Naked at the Interview: Tips & Quizzes to Prepare You for Your First Real Job. Burton J. Nadler. 230p. 1994. pap. 10.95 (0-471-59449-0) Wiley.

***Naked Awareness: Practical Instructions on the Union of Mahamudra & Dzogchen.** Karma Chagme. Ed. by Linda Steele. Tr. by B. Alan Wallace from TIB. LC 00-23802. 300p. 2000. pap. 19.95 (1-55939-146-4) Snow Lion Pubns.

***Naked Babies.** Nick Kelsh. (Illus.). 2000. pap. 14.95 (0-14-029484-8) Viking Penguin.

Naked Babies. Nick Kelsh & Anna Quindlen. LC 97-117536. (Illus.). 112p. 1996. 24.95 (0-670-86880-9) Penguin Putnam.

Naked Bear. Margaret Robison. LC 77-83730. 70p. 1977. pap. 6.00 (0-89924-011-9) Lynx Hse.

***Naked Before God: The Return of a Broken Disciple.** Bill Williams & Martha Williams. LC 98-11330. 352p. 1998. 19.95 (0-8192-1739-5) Morehouse Pub.

Naked Before the Father: The Renunciation of Francis of Assisi. Richard C. Trexler. (Humana Civilitas Ser.: Vol. 9). (Illus.). XII, 129p. (C). 1989. text 22.95 (0-8204-0931-6) P Lang Pubng.

***Naked Being of God: Making Sense of Love Mysticism.** Blair Reynolds & Patricia Heinicke, Jr. 160p. 2000. 49.00 (0-7618-1703-4) U Pr of Amer.

***Naked Being of God: Making Sense of Love Mysticism.** Blair Reynolds & Patricia Heinicke. LC 00-36445. 160p. 2000. pap. 27.50 (0-7618-1704-2) U Pr of Amer.

Naked Beneath Our Clothing: A Discussion on the Psychological & Metaphysical Benefits of Nudism. John E. Veltheim. (Illus.). 24p. (Orig.). 1994. pap. 10.00 (0-9645944-1-2) Parama LLC.

Naked Blade, Naked Gunn. Axel Kilgore. (They Call Me the Mercenary Ser.: No. 13). 1983. mass mkt. 2.50 (0-686-43977-5, Zebra Kensgtn) Kensgtn Pub Corp.

Naked Call. Davidyne S. Mayleas. 672p. (Orig.). 1991. mass mkt. 5.50 (0-380-75688-9, Avon Bks) Morrow Avon.

Naked Came the Farmer: A round-robin rural romance & murder mystery. Philip Jose Farmer et al. LC 98-65072. 1998. pap. 12.95 (0-9624613-7-7) Mayfly Prodns.

Naked Came the Manatee: A Novel. Dave Barry et al. Ed. by Carl Hiaasen. 208p. 1998. pap. 11.95 (0-449-00124-5, Columbine) Fawcett.

Naked Came the Robot. Barry B. Longyear. 224p. (Orig.). 1988. mass mkt. 3.95 (0-445-20755-8, Pub. by Warner Bks) Little.

Naked Capitalist. W. Cleon Skousen. (Illus.). 144p. (C). 1970. pap. 11.95 (0-910558-05-1) Ensign Pub.

Naked Capitalist. W. Cleon Skousen. 152p. Date not set. 18.95 (0-8488-2662-0) Amereon Ltd.

Naked Capitalist. W. Cleon Skousen. 1993. reprint ed. lib. bdg. 28.95 (0-89968-323-1, Lghtyr Pr) Buccaneer Bks.

***Naked Chef.** Jamie Oliver. LC 99-54555. 256p. 2000. 34.95 (0-7868-6617-9, Pub. by Hyperion) Time Warner.

Naked Chef: An Aphrodisiac Cookbook. Penelope Ashe. LC 70-167722. 1971. 26.95 (0-87949-000-4) Ashley Bks.

Naked Children. Daniel Fader. LC 97-100940. (Innovators in Education Ser.). 219p. 1996. pap. 14.95 (0-86709-397-8, 0397, Pub. by Boynton Cook Pubs) Heinemann.

Naked Church. 3rd rev. ed. Wayne Jacobsen. 256p. (Orig.). 1998. pap. 11.95 (0-9647292-1-0) BodyLife Pub.

Naked City. Arthur F. Weegee, pseud. (Quality Paperbacks Ser.). (Illus.). 246p. 1985. reprint ed. pap. 13.95 (0-306-80241-4) Da Capo.

Naked City: A Screenplay. Malvin Wald & Albert Maltz. Ed. by Matthew J. Bruccoli. LC 79-10826. (Illus.). 148p. 1979. 25.00 (0-8093-0909-2) Boulevard.

An Asterisk (*) at the beginning of an entry indicates that the title is appearing for the first time.

Naked City: Urban Crime Fiction in the U. S. A. Ralph Willet. LC 95-35843. 176p. 1996. text 26.95 (*0-7190-4301-8*, Pub. by Manchester Univ Pr) St Martin.

Naked Civil Servant. Quentin Crisp. 1997. pap. 12.95 (*0-14-118053-6*) Viking Penguin.

Naked Communist. W. Cleon Skousen. 1994. reprint ed. lib. bdg. 32.95 (*1-56849-367-3*) Buccaneer Bks.

***Naked Communist.** 11th ed. W. Cloen Skousen. 408p. 2000. pap. 14.95 (*0-910558-02-7*) Ensign Pub.

Naked Croquet. Doug Melnyk. 1997. pap. 7.95 (*0-88801-122-9*, Pub. by Turnstone Pr) Genl Dist Srvs.

***Naked Detective.** Laurence Shames. LC 99-54472. 240p. 2000. 22.95 (*0-375-50253-X*) Random.

Naked Doom. Ken St. Andre. (Illus.). 1977. 4.95 (*0-940244-04-7*) Flying Buffalo.

Naked Drawings. Lorne Coutts. (Illus.). 80p. 1994. 25.00 (*0-88962-193-4*) Mosaic.

Naked Drawings of Lorne Coutts. Lorne Coutts. (Illus.). 80p. 1995. pap. 9.95 (*0-88962-223-X*) Mosaic.

Naked Dream: And Other Verses, Stories & Snapshots. Suzanne E. Turner. LC 98-84853. 98p. 1998. pap. 10.95 (*0-9640537-5-6*) Monterey Pubng.

Naked Earth. Shawna Vogel. 1996. pap. 11.95 (*0-452-27162-2*, Plume) Dutton Plume.

Naked Emotions. Melba Meyers. 72p. 1984. pap. 6.00 (*0-9612296-0-8*) Williams SC.

Naked Empress: or The Great Medical Fraud. 3rd rev. ed. Hans Ruesch. (Illus.). 202p. 1982. pap. text 10.00 (*3-905280-02-7*, Pub. by Civis) U of Mich Pr.

Naked Eye. William Burrill. 208p. 1998. pap. 13.99 (*1-895837-31-6*) Insomniac.

Naked Eye. Catherine Ennis. LC 98-13223. 192p. 1998. pap. 11.95 (*1-56280-210-0*) Naiad Pr.

Naked Eye: A True Account of A Stripper's Journey. Shay Stephen. Ed. by Antionette Rabaut. 374p. 1998. 22.00 (0-9657072-0-2) Midnght Writ.

The Naked Eye: A True Account of a Stripper's Journey is aimed at anyone who has ever tried to navigate their way through the two weeks between their last job & their first unemployment check & found themselves changed for life. This book is told in the voice of a girl with average morals who stepped across a threshold onto a road less traveled & found stripping to be an inner journey. She examines her own baggage. She explores power trips between men & women, between society & the individual. She looks at the appearance of power & its seemingly different sources. And finally concludes that power is derived from perspective. In the end she identifies point of view as reality's due north. Price $22.00 plus $4.50 shipping. For more information call (510) 525-0298. Order from Midnight Writer. Make checks payable to: Shay Stephen, 1116 Stannage Ave., Albany, CA 94706.
Publisher Paid Annotation.

Naked Face. 1986. mass mkt. 4.95 (*0-446-73324-5*, Pub. by Warner Bks) Little.

Naked Face. 1986. mass mkt. 4.95 (*0-446-73437-3*, Pub. by Warner Bks) Little.

Naked Face. Sidney Sheldon. 320p. 1985. reprint ed. mass mkt. 7.99 (*0-446-34191-6*, Pub. by Warner Bks) Little.

Naked Face: The Essential Guide to Reading Faces. Lailan Young. (Illus.). 272p. (Orig.). 1994. pap. 13.95 (*0-312-11033-2*) St Martin.

Naked First Lady: Bare Facts from Monterey's Past - A Humorous History of the Monterey Peninsula. Gerald Stern. (Illus.). 132p. (Orig.). 1992. pap. 12.95 (*0-9635460-0-7*) Gerald Stern.

Naked Genius. George M. Horton. LC 82-71039. (Illus.). 160p. 1982. reprint ed. pap. 5.95 (*0-940715-06-6*) Chapel Hill Hist.

Naked Ghost, Burp! And Blue Jam. Jennings. (Clipper Fiction Ser.). 1991. pap. text. write for info. (*0-582-87560-9*, Drumbeat) Longman.

Naked Ghosts: Intimate Stories from the Files of a Sex Therapist. Carol G. Wells. 224p. 1992. mass mkt. 4.99 (*0-380-71828-6*, Avon Bks) Morrow Avon.

Naked Glory: The Erotic Art of Frank Stack. Frank Stack. pap. 12.95 (*1-56097-229-7*, Pub. by Fantagraph Bks) Seven Hills Bk.

Naked God Pt. I: Flight. Peter F. Hamilton. LC 99-36275. 992p. 2000. 26.95 (*0-446-52567-7*, Pub. by Warner Bks) Little.

***Naked God Pt. I: Flight.** Peter F. Hamilton. 800p. 2000. mass mkt. 6.99 (*0-446-60897-1*, Aspect) Warner Bks.

***Naked God Pt. 2: Faith.** Peter F. Hamilton. 2000. mass mkt. 6.99 (*0-446-60518-2*, Aspect) Warner Bks.

Naked Gourmet. Carole Marsh. (Naked Gourmet Ser.). (Orig.). 1997. 29.95 (*1-55609-001-3*) Gallopade Intl.

Naked Government. Steve J. Gluckman. 420p. 1997. pap. 9.95 (*0-9668866-0-7*) I S I S Pubg.

Naked Grace. Fred W. Schott. 2000. write for info. (*1-928818-03-X*) EML Bks.

Naked Heart. Victor Di Suvero. 32p. 1996. pap. 12.00 (*0-938631-28-4*) Pennywhistle Pr.

Naked Heart: A Soldier's Journey to the Front. Harold E. Pagliaro. LC D811.P2678 1996. (Illus.). 238p. (C). 1996. pap. 12.00 (*0-943549-41-8*) Truman St Univ.

Naked Heart: Talking on Poetry, Mysticism, & the Erotic. William Everson. LC 92-8016. (Studies in Twentieth-Century American Poetry & Poetics). 264p. (C). 1992. pap. 19.95 (*0-9629172-4-9*) U NM Arts Sci.

Naked Heart: The Bourgeois Experience - Victoria to Freud. Peter Gay. 496p. 1996. pap. 15.00 (*0-393-31515-0*) Norton.

Naked Heart: The Bourgeois Experience from Victoria to Freud. Peter Gay. (Illus.). 463p. 1995. 29.95 (*0-393-03813-0*) Norton.

***Naked Heartland: Itinerant Photography of Los Angeles.** Bruce Bellas. (Illus.). 2000. 49.95 (*3-925443-88-6*) Janssen.

Naked Hearts: The Voice of the People: A National Grassroots Odyssey in Search of America As It Should Be. James Huie. Ed. by Lynn Green. 212p. (Orig.). 1995. pap. 19.95 (*0-9647779-0-8*) A Possible Wrld Pr.

***Naked Hemingway.** Thomas Prosser. LC 99-72165. (Illus.). 218p. 1999. pap. 19.95 (*0-9669614-0-4*) Cappuccino Prodns.

Naked Hollywood. Weegee, pseud. LC 75-4767. (Photography Ser.). (Illus.). 124p. 1975. reprint ed. pap. 6.95 (*0-306-80047-0*); reprint ed. lib. bdg. 25.00 (*0-306-70728-4*) Da Capo.

***Naked Humanity & the Art of Living: What Can Be Learned from Life & Humankind.** T. C. Duong. LC 99-90351. 200p. 1999. 24.95 (*0-9670180-0-5*) Think Pond.

Naked I. Annie Reiner. 90p. (Orig.). 1994. pap. text 9.95 (*1-881168-22-0*) Red Danceflr.

Naked I Came . . . And Naked I Shall Go: The Growth & Ending of an Organization. Tom Peters. 240p. (Orig.). 1992. pap. write for info. (*1-879516-05-5*) Betterpub Pr.

Naked in a Pinstriped Suit. Al Bowers. LC 97-66959. 234p. 1997. 21.95 (*1-889274-02-X*) Posterity Press.

Naked in Cyberspace: How to Find Personal Information Online. Carole A. Lane et al. LC 97-193244. 544p. (Orig.). 1997. pap. 29.95 (*0-910965-17-X*) Info Today Inc.

Naked in Death. J. D. Robb, pseud. 313p. 1995. mass mkt. 6.99 (*0-425-14829-7*) Berkley Pub.

***Naked in Death.** large type ed. J. D. Robb, pseud. LC 99-89075. (Americana Series). 2000. 29.95 (*0-7862-2415-0*) Thorndike Pr.

Naked in Exile: Khalil Hawi's "The Threshing Floors of Hunger" Khalil Hawi. Tr. by Adnan Haydar & Michael Beard. LC 82-40406.Tr. of Bayadir al-ju. (ARA & ENG.). 208p. 1984. reprint ed. 18.00 (*0-89410-366-0*, Three Contnts) L Rienner.

Naked in My Mirror. 2nd ed. Mere Smith. LC 96-183155. 44p. (Orig.). 1995. pap. 3.00 (*1-888431-04-0*) ASGP.

Naked in Paradise. mass mkt. 6.95 (*0-7472-4730-7*, Pub. by Headline Bk Pub) Trafalgar.

Naked in Paradise. Michael Von Graffenried. 112p. (C). 1997. 45.00 (*1-899235-85-X*) Dist Art Pubs.

Naked in the Garden. Karla Andersdatter. LC 88-60408. 210p. 1988. per. 12.95 (*0-911051-46-5*, Pub. by Plain View) In Between.

Naked in the Night. John Nemec. 160p. (Orig.). 1991. pap. 3.49 (*0-9618998-8-3*) Nemec Pub.

Naked in the Streets. James J. Rush. 256p. 1985. 14.95 (*0-8065-0951-1*, Citadel Pr) Carol Pub Group.

Naked in the Twisted Sky. Jon Albertson. Ed. by N. John Hooper & Anne Hooper. (Air Adventure Ser.: Vol. I). 300p. (YA). (gr. 12). 1989. 16.95 (*0-9621448-2-7*) Aeolus Bks.

Naked Instinct: The Unauthorized Biography of Sharon Stone. Frank Sanello. LC 97-1013. (Illus.). 256p. 1997. 19.50 (*1-55972-402-1*, Birch Ln Pr) Carol Pub Group.

Naked Intent. B. Bell. 1997. mass mkt. 6.95 (*0-7472-5442-7*, Pub. by Headline Bk Pub) Trafalgar.

Naked into the Night. Monty Joynes. LC 97-147701. 256p. (Orig.). 1997. pap. 11.95 (*1-57174-055-4*) Hampton Roads Pub Co.

Naked Is the Best Disguise: The Death & Revolution of Sherlock Holmes. Samuel Rosenberg. 22.95 (*0-89190-169-8*) Amereon Ltd.

Naked Island. large type ed. Russell Braddon. 455p. 1982. 27.99 (*0-7089-8024-4*, Charnwood) Ulverscroft.

Naked Jaybird. Stephen P. Byers. LC 98-89522. 375p. 1998. text 25.00 (*0-7388-0205-0*); pap. text 15.00 (*0-7388-0206-9*) Xlibris Corp.

***Naked Jaybird.** 2nd ed. Stephen F. Byers. 282p. 1999. pap. 15.00 (*1-929663-00-5*) Books By Byers.

Naked Justice. William Bernhardt. 1998. mass mkt. 6.99 (*0-449-00087-7*, GM) Fawcett.

Naked Justice. large type ed. William Bernhardt. (Niagara Large Print Ser.). 688p. 1997. 29.50 (*0-7089-5879-6*) Ulverscroft.

Naked Ladies. Alma L. Villanueva. LC 93-30724. 288p. 1994. 27.00 (*0-927534-30-4*); pap. 17.00 (*0-927534-31-2*) Biling Rev-Pr.

Naked Lens: A History of Beat Cinema. Jack Sargeant. (Creation Cinema Collection). (Illus.). 288p. (Orig.). 1997. pap. 19.95 (*1-871592-67-4*) Creation Books.

Naked Letters Encounters & Adventures: The First Two Years. (Illus.). (Orig.). pap. text 19.95 (*1-887895-07-8*) Serengeti Pubng.

***Naked Lies.** Ray Gordon. 2000. mass mkt. 7.95 (*1-56201-201-0*) Blue Moon Bks.

Naked Lies Your Heart. Lincoln Scott. 1995. 15.95 (*0-533-11423-3*) Vantage.

***Naked London.** Greg Friedler. LC 00-21739. (Illus.). 160p. 2000. pap. 22.50 (*0-393-32029-4*, Norton Paperbks) Norton.

Naked Los Angeles. Greg Friedler. LC 98-29146. (Illus.). 144p. 1998. pap. 22.50 (*0-393-31874-5*) Norton.

Naked Lunch. William S. Burroughs. LC 91-22972. 288p. 1992. pap. 11.95 (*0-8021-3295-2*, Grove) Grove-Atltic.

Naked Lunch. William S. Burroughs. 1994. reprint ed. lib. bdg. 29.95 (*1-56849-538-2*) Buccaneer Bks.

Naked Machine: Selected Poems. Matthias Johannessen. Tr. & Intro. by Marshall Brement. LC 87-83425. (Illus.). 74p. 1988. 18.95 (*0-948259-44-2*, Pub. by Forest Bks); pap. 13.95 (*0-948259-43-4*, Pub. by Forest Bks) Dufour.

Naked Madonna. Jan Wiese. 160p. 1998. mass mkt. 10.00 (*1-86046-149-2*) Harvill Press.

Naked Man Vol. 4: Mythologiques. Claude Levi-Strauss. Tr. by John Weightman & Doreen Weightman. LC 79-3399. (Illus.). 746p. 1990. pap. text 25.95 (*0-226-47496-8*) U Ch Pr.

Naked Management: Bare Essentials for Motivating the X-Generation at Work. Marc Muchnick. 152p. 1996. per. 24.95 (*1-57444-061-6*) St Lucie Pr.

***Naked Manager: Developing Open & Authentic Relationships.** Eileen Dowse. LC 98-19059. (Illus.). 130p. 1998. pap. 12.95 (*1-886939-24-1*, Pub. by OakHill Pr VA) ACCESS Pubs Network.

Naked Marketing. Robert Grede. 160p. 1999. pap. text 8.95 (*0-7352-0112-9*) PH Pr.

Naked Marketing: The Bare Essentials. Robert Grede. LC 96-48813. (Illus.). 142p. (C). 1997. 15.95 (*0-13-845322-5*) P-H.

Naked Masks. Luigi Pirandello. 1957. pap. 13.95 (*0-452-01082-9*, Mer) NAL.

Naked Men: Pioneering Male Nudes. David Leddick. (Illus.). 1997. 35.00 (*0-614-28247-0*) Universe.

***Naked Men, Too: Liberating the Male Nude, 1950-2000.** David Leddick. (Illus.). 144p. 2000. text 35.00 (*0-7893-0396-5*, Pub. by Universe) St Martin.

Naked Mole-Rat Mystery: Scientific Sleuths at Work. Gail Jarrow & Paul Sherman. LC 95-13381. (Illus.). (J). 1996. lib. bdg. 23.95 (*0-8225-2853-3*, Lerner Publctns) Lerner Pub.

Naked Mole-Rats. Gail Jarrow. (Illus.). 48p. (ps-3). 1996. pap. text 8.95 (*1-57505-028-5*, Carolrhoda) Lerner Pub.

Naked Mole-Rats. Gail Jarrow & Paul Sherman. LC 95-44979. (J). 1996. lib. bdg. 19.95 (*0-87614-995-6*, Carolrhoda) Lerner Pub.

Naked Nagas: Head-Hunters of Assam in Peace & War. Christoph V. Fuerer-Haimendorf. LC 76-44720. reprint ed. 47.50 (*0-404-15924-9*) AMS Pr.

Naked Nature: Race & the Subject of National Manhood. Dana D. Nelson. LC 98-14396. (New Americanists Ser.). 1998. write for info. (*0-8223-2130-0*) Duke.

Naked Neuron: Evolution of the Languages of the Body & Brain. R. Joseph. LC 93-9076. (Illus.). 350p. (C). 1993. 27.50 (*0-306-44510-7*, Plenum Trade) Perseus Pubng.

Naked New York. Greg Friedler. LC 96-39282. (Illus.). 75p. 1997. pap. 18.95 (*0-393-31646-7*) Norton.

Naked on the Page. Gail Feldman. (Illus.). 40p. 1998. pap. 6.00 (*1-892609-03-7*) Gracie Pub.

Naked Once More. Elizabeth Peters, pseud. 1990. mass mkt. 6.99 (*0-446-36032-5*, Pub. by Warner Bks) Little.

Naked Once More. large type ed. Elizabeth Peters, pseud. (General Ser.). 550p. 1990. lib. bdg. 20.95 (*0-8161-4939-9*, G K Hall Lrg Type) Mac Lib Ref.

Naked Passion Jogs with the Disco Espionage Gang: The Gaussian Verses. Blake Edwards & Sherman Johnson. 78p. 1997. pap. 5.00 (*1-891499-00-9*) Incremental.

Naked Physician. Ed. by Ron Charach. 184p. 1990. pap. 14.95 (*0-919627-77-3*, Pub. by Quarry Pr) LPC InBook.

***Naked Pictures of Famous People.** Jon Stewart. LC 98-38999. (Illus.). 224p. 1998. 24.00 (*0-688-15530-8*, Wm Morrow) Morrow Avon.

***Naked Pictures of Famous People.** Jon Stewart. 176p. 1999. pap. 14.00 (*0-688-17162-1*, Wm Morrow) Morrow Avon.

***Naked Pictures of My Ex-Girlfriends: Romance in the 70's.** Mark Helfrich. (Illus.). 132p. 2000. 32.95 (*0-9656535-3-6*) Consafos Pr.

Naked Plant. H. L. Wickins. 144p. (C). 1989. text 45.00 (*1-872795-40-4*, Pub. by Pentland Pr) St Mut.

Naked Plunder. J. T. Pearce. 1998. pap. text 8.95 (*1-897809-42-5*) Silver Moon.

Naked Poet. Gavin G. Dillard. LC 89-90911. (Illus.). 86p. (Orig.). (C). 1989. pap. 7.95 (*0-944050-02-6*) Bhakti.

Naked Prey. Larry Kane. 1991. mass mkt. 4.50 (*0-8217-3513-6*, Zebra Kensgtn) Kensgtn Pub Corp.

Naked Public Square: Religion & Democracy in America. Richard J. Neuhaus. 292p. 1988. reprint ed. pap. 20.00 (*0-8028-0080-7*) Eerdmans.

Naked Pueblo: Stories. Mark Jude Poirier. LC 99-25267. 224p. 1999. 21.00 (*0-609-60447-3*, Crown) Crown.

***Naked Pueblo: Stories.** Mark Jude Poirier. 208p. 2001. pap. 12.95 (*0-7868-8593-9*, Pub. by Talk Miramax Bks) Time Warner.

***Naked Quack: Exposing the Many Ways Phony Psychics & Mediums Cheat You!** LC 99-80029. 144p. 2000. pap. 16.95 (*0-9677708-0-7*, NQ-2000) Chanworth Global Ent.

Naked Racial Preference: The Case Against Affirmative Action. Carl Cohen. 240p. (C). 1995. 21.95 (*1-56833-053-7*) Madison Bks UPA.

Naked Savages. Fred M. Stewart. LC 99-24482. 1999. 23.95 (*0-312-86790-5*, Pub. by Forge NYC) St Martin.

***Naked Savages.** Fred Mustard Stewart. 2000. mass mkt. 6.99 (*0-8125-6685-8*) Tor Bks.

Naked Science: Anthropological Inquiry into Boundaries, Power & Knowledge. Ed. by Laura Nader. LC 95-23650. 333p. (C). 1996. pap. 23.99 (*0-415-91465-5*) Routledge.

Naked Song: Poems. Coleman Barks. 140p. (Orig.). (C). 1992. pap. 8.00 (*0-9618916-4-5*) Maypop.

Naked Song & Other Stories. Mandla Langa. (Three Continents Ser.). 147p. 1997. pap. 11.95 (*0-89410-855-7*) L Rienner.

Naked Soul. Gwynne Forster. LC 98-206081. (Indigo Love Stories Ser.). 1998. 15.95 (*1-885478-32-1*, Pub. by Genesis Press) BookWorld.

***Naked Soul.** unabridged ed. Gwynne Foster. 284p. 1999. pap. 8.95 (*1-885478-73-9*, Pub. by Genesis Press) BookWorld.

Naked Soul: Astral Travel & Cosmic Relationships. Marlene M. Druhan. LC 98-30546. (Illus.). 216p. 1999. 12.95 (*1-56718-247-X*, K247) Llewellyn Pubns.

Naked Soul: Coping with War. Robert Wolfe. 1997. pap. write for info. (*0-7880-0913-3*, Fairway Pr) CSS OH.

Naked Soul: Poems & Art. Rosette Mines. (Illus.). 48p. 1999. pap. 8.00 (*0-8059-4666-7*) Dorrance.

***Naked Soul of Iceberg Slim.** Robert Beck. 256p. 1998. mass mkt. 6.99 (*0-87067-998-8*) Holloway.

***Naked Spirits: A Journey into Occupied Tibet.** Adrian Abbotts. LC 97-216755. 288p. 1999. pap. 15.00 (*0-86241-617-5*, Pub. by Canongate Books) Interlink Pub.

Naked Strangers. Robert F. Powell. LC 96-96397. (Illus.). 256p. 1996. pap. 7.95 (*0-9651648-0-2*) Debonair Pr.

Naked Sun. Isaac Asimov. 288p. 1991. mass mkt. 6.99 (*0-553-29339-7*) Bantam.

Naked Text: Chaucer's Legend of Good Women. Sheila Delany. LC 92-21191. 1994. 50.00 (*0-520-08119-6*, Pub. by U CA Pr) Cal Prin Full Svc.

Naked Thief. Rane Arroyo. 30p. (Orig.). 1997. pap. 8.00 (*0-932616-57-7*) Brick Hse Bks.

Naked Through the Gate: A Spiritual Autobiography. Joel, pseud. LC 88-16212. 262p. (Orig.). 1988. pap. 11.95 (*0-9620387-0-9*) Ctr Sacred Sciences.

Naked to Love: Letters from a Young American in Panama, 1952-54. Christopher W. Colie. LC 99-24688. 232p. 1999. 19.95 (*1-57178-082-3*, Pub. by Coun Oak Bks) SPD-Small Pr Dist.

Naked to the Bone: Medical Imaging in the Twentieth Century. Bettyann H. Kevles. LC 97-46598. 1998. pap. 18.00 (*0-201-32833-X*) Addison-Wesley.

Naked to the Bone: Medical Imaging in the Twentieth Century. Bettyann H. Kevles. LC 96-2844. (Illus.). 400p. (C). 1997. 35.95 (*0-8135-2358-3*) Rutgers U Pr.

Naked to the Night. rev. ed. K. B. Raul. 176p. 1986. reprint ed. pap. 10.00 (*0-917342-20-8*) Gay Sunshine.

Naked to the Stars & The Alien Way. Gordon Rupert Dickson. 1991. pap. 3.95 (*0-8125-0396-1*, Pub. by Tor Bks) St Martin.

Naked Tree. Pak Wan-So. Tr. by Yu Youngnan from KOR. LC 96-150384. (Cornell East Asia Ser.: Vol. 83). 198p. (C). 1995. 18.70 (*1-885445-73-3*, 83); pap. 11.90 (*1-885445-83-0*, 83) Cornell East Asia Pgm.

Naked Truth. Nicole Dere. 1998. pap. 9.95 (*1-897809-50-6*) Silver Moon.

***Naked Truth.** Natasha Rostova. 2000. mass mkt. 6.95 (*0-352-33497-5*) BLA4.

Naked Truth. Paul Rudnick. 1999. pap. 7.95 (*0-452-27423-0*, Plume) Dutton Plume.

***Naked Truth.** Dani Sinclair. (Temptation Ser.: Vol. 690). 1998. per. 3.75 (*0-373-25790-2*, 1-25790-6) Harlequin Bks.

Naked Truth: Observations of an Iconoclast. Aaron Stern. LC 79-20449. 172p. 1980. 14.95 (*0-916560-03-1*) Renaiss Pubs.

Naked Truth about Gays: A Text Book on the Past, Present & Future of Homosexuality. Art L. Pekarek. 346p. 1993. pap. 7.95 (*0-9639482-0-2*) Lamb Pubns.

Naked Truth about Hedonism II: A Naughty but Nice Guide to Jamaica's All-Inclusive, Very Adult Resort. Chris Santilli. LC 97-91394. (Illus.). 210p. 1998. pap. 19.95 (*0-9662683-1-8*) Scarlett Oh Pub.

Naked Truth & Personal Vision. Bartlett H. Hayes, Jr. (Illus.). 112p. 1955. write for info. (*1-879886-12-X*) Addison Gallery.

***Naked Truth Ii: The Whip Hand.** Nicole Dere. 1999. pap. text 9.99 (*1-897809-63-8*) Silver Moon.

***Naked Truths: Women, Sexuality & Gender in Classical Art & Archaeology.** Ann K. Ostrow. (Illus.). 2000. pap. 27.99 (*0-415-21752-0*) Routledge.

Naked Truths: Women Sexuality & Gender in Classical Art & Archeology. Ed. by Ann O. Kolowski-Ostrow & Claire L. Lyons. LC 96-41228. (Illus.). 336p. (C). 1997. 80.00 (*0-415-15995-4*) Routledge.

***Naked Verses.** Ed. by Bernard J. Loibl. 2000. 29.95 (*0-9636805-3-6*) Events Unltd.

Naked Villainy. Sara Woods. LC 96-8302. 288p. 1988. pap. 3.50 (*0-380-70479-X*, Avon Bks) Morrow Avon.

Naked Warriors, Vol. 1. Francis D. Fane. 1996. mass mkt. 5.99 (*0-312-95985-0*) St Martin.

Naked Warriors: The Story of the U. S. Navy's Frogmen. rev. ed. Francis D. Fane & Don Moore. (Naval Institute Special Warfare Ser.). (Illus.). 320p. 1995. 29.95 (*1-55750-266-8*) Naval Inst Pr.

Naked with the CEO's Daughter: Corporate Environmental & Personal Ethics in Question. T. D. Herod. 140p. (Orig.). 1998. 10.95 (*1-878985-05-1*) Herod Environ Cnslt.

***Naked Woman.** Juan Ramon Jimenez. Tr. by Dennis Maloney from SPA.Tr. of Mujer Desnuda. (Illus.). 40p. 2000. 26.00 (*1-890654-21-3*); pap. 14.00 (*1-890654-20-5*) Wood Work.

***Naked Woman.** aut. ed. Juan Ramon Jimenez. Tr. by Dennis Maloney from SPA.Tr. of Mujer Desnuda. (Illus.). 40p. 2000. 36.00 (*1-890654-22-1*) Wood Work.

Naked Year. Boris Pilnyak. Tr. by Alexander R. Tulloch from RUS. 207p. 1975. pap. 10.95 (*0-88233-078-0*) Ardis Pubs.

Naked Year. Boris Pilnyak. LC 70-174201. reprint ed. 34.50 (*0-404-06778-6*) AMS Pr.

Nakedness of the Fathers: Biblical Visions & Revisions. Alicia S. Ostriker. LC 94-14616. 225p. (Orig.). (C). 1994. 35.00 (*0-8135-2125-4*) Rutgers U Pr.

Nakedness of the Fathers: Biblical Visions & Revisions. Alicia S. Ostriker. LC 94-14616. 225p. (Orig.). (C). 1997. pap. text 16.95 (*0-8135-2447-4*) Rutgers U Pr.

Nakid Entent unto God: A Source-Commentary on the Cloud of Unknowing. Douglas E. Cowan. LC 90-19810. 400p. (C). 1992. text 40.00 (*0-89341-645-2*, Longwood Academic) Hollowbrook.

***Nakshatras: The Lunar Mansions of Vedic Astrology.** Dennis M. Harness. (Illus.). 200p. 2000. pap. 15.95 (*0-914955-83-7*) Lotus Pr.

N

An Asterisk (*) at the beginning of an entry indicates that the title is appearing for the first time.

*Nakshibendis in Western & Central Asia: Change & Continuity. Ed. by Elisabeth Ozdalga. 180p. 1999. pap. (0-7007-1147-3, Pub. by Curzon Pr Ltd) Paul & Co Pubs.
Naktergalen, Vol. 3. 3rd ed. Ed. by Ingrid Lang. Tr. by Sweden Elex. (Listen & Learn Language Audio Ser.: Vol. LL0399).Tr. of Nightingale. (ENG & SWE., Illus.). 32p. 1999. pap. 9.95 (1-892623-05-6) Intl Book.
Naktergalen: The Nightingale, Vol. 3. 3rd unabridged ed. Ed. by Ingrid Lang. Tr. by Sweden Elex. (Listen & Learn Language Audio Ser.: Vol. LL0399). (ENG & SWE., Illus.). 32p. 1999. pap. 15.95 incl. audio (1-892623-04-8) Intl Book.
NALA Manual for Legal Assistants. 3rd ed. NALA Staff. LC 98-23892. (Paralegal Ser.). 425p. 1998. pap., student ed. 77.95 (0-7668-0393-7) Delmar.
NALCO Guide to Boiler Failure Analysis. NALCO Chemical Company Staff. 293p. 1991. 59.00 (0-07-045873-1) McGraw.
NALCO Guide to Cooling-Water System Failure Analysis. NALCO Chemical Company Staff et al. LC 92-22428. 420p. 1993. 60.00 (0-07-028400-8) McGraw.
NALCO Water Handbook. 2nd ed. NALCO Chemical Company Staff. 1120p. 1988. 85.50 (0-07-045872-3) McGraw.
Nalik Language of New Ireland, Papua New Guinea. Craig A. Volker. LC 96-42508. (Berkeley Models of Grammars Ser.: Vol. 4). (Illus.). XVI, 246p. (C). 1998. text 48.95 (0-8204-3673-9) P Lang Pubng.
Nalk-Atpase & Related Transport Atpases: The Surface Pumps on Which Every Living Creature Relies. Ed. by Luis A. Beauge et al. LC 97-35157. (Annals of the New York Academy of Sciences Ser.: No. 834). 694p. 1997. pap. 190.00 (1-57331-061-1) NY Acad Sci.
Naloxone, Flumazenil & Dantrolene As Antidotes. T. J. Meredith et al. LC 93-32098. (IPCS-CEC Evaluation of Antidotes Ser.: No. 1). 114p. (C). 1994. text 47.95 (0-521-45459-X) Cambridge U Pr.
NALS - Manual for the Lawyer's Assistant. 3rd ed. Kaye Aoki. 333p. (C). 1994. pap. text, teacher ed. write for info. (0-314-04912-6); pap. text, student ed. write for info. (0-314-04849-9) West Pub.
NALS - Probate Handbook for the Lawyer's Assistant. National Association of Legal Secretaries Staff et al. 403p. (C). 1993. pap. text. write for info. (0-314-02351-8) West Pub.
NALS - Teacher's Manual to Accompany the Career Legal Secretary. 3rd ed. Kaye Aoki. 363p. 1993. pap. text, teacher ed. 11.95 (0-314-02924-9) West Pub.
NALS - The Career Legal Secretary. 3rd ed. National Association of Legal Secretary Staff & Kaye Aoki. 864p. 1993. text 31.50 (0-314-02353-4) West Pub.
NALS - The Career Legal Secretary: Student Study Guide & Work Project. 3rd ed. Kaye Aoki. 291p. 1993. pap. text 11.95 (0-314-02914-1) West Pub.
NALS-The Career Legal Secretary: Instructor's Manual for Use with Student Study Guide & Work Projects. 4th ed. Virginia DeLay et al. 360p. (C). 1997. pap. text, teacher ed., suppl. ed. write for info. (0-314-22787-3) West Pub.
NALS-The Career Legal Secretary: Student Study Guide & Work Projects. 4th ed. Virginia DeLay et al. (Practice Ser.). 260p. 1997. pap. text, student ed., suppl. ed. write for info. (0-314-22642-7) West Pub.
'Nam. Doug Murray. (Illus.). 96p. 1999. pap. text 14.95 (0-7851-0718-5) Marvel Entrprs.
Nam-Bok, the Liar. Jack London. (Jamestown Classics Ser.). 1995. pap., teacher ed. 7.32 (0-89061-043-6, Jamestwn Pub) NTC Contemp Pub Co.
Nam-Bok, the Liar. Jack London. (Jamestown Classics Ser.). (J). 1995. pap., student ed. 5.99 (0-89061-042-8, Jamestwn Pub) NTC Contemp Pub Co.
Nam Book. I. Kamazi. Ed. by Morningland Publications, Inc. Staff. (Illus.). 164p. (Orig.). 1981. pap. 10.00 (0-935146-57-1) Morningland.
*Nam June Paik. John G. Hanhardt & Jon Ippolito. 300p. 2000. 65.00 (0-8109-6925-4, Pub. by Abrams) Time Warner.
Nam June Paik: Baraoque Laser. Nam J. Paik. 1996. pap. 14.95 (3-89322-295-2, Pub. by Edition Cantz) Dist Art Pubs.
Nam Malacharitham. Unnayi Warrier. Tr. by V. Subramaniam Iyer. 1978. 6.50 (0-8364-0131-X) S Asia.
*Nam Vet: Making Peace with Your Past. Chuck Dean. LC 99-62936. 176p. 1999. pap. 10.99 (1-57921-221-2, Pub. by WinePress Pub) BookWorld.
Nam Vet Vol. 11: Making Peace with Your Past. Chuck Dean. 10.99 (0-9679371-0-8) Selah Pubg.
Nama Japa: Prayer of the Name in the Hindu & Christian Traditions. Vandana. 1985. pap. 10.00 (0-8364-1509-4, Pub. by Bharat Vidya) S Asia.
Namakarana: Naming of the Child. unabridged ed. Angirasa Muni. LC 98-90795. 66 p. 1999. 5.00 (1-893152-09-X) Sacred Bks.
Namako: Sea Cucumber. Linda W. McFerrin. LC 98-21156. 256p. (YA). 1998. pap. 14.95 (1-56689-075-6) Coffee Hse.
Namami Krsnasundaram - Salutations to Lord Krsna. Shrii Shrii Anandamurti. 252p. 1981. pap. 6.95 (0-686-95432-7) Ananda Marga.
Namamiko Monogatari see Tale of False Fortunes
Namaqualand: A Visual Souvenir. Text by Colin Patterson-Jones. LC 98-214705. 1999. 22.95 (1-86872-166-3) Struik Pubs.
Namaqualand: Garden of the Gods. 2nd ed. Freeman Patterson. (Illus.). 128p. 1984. 35.00 (0-919493-37-8) Firefly Bks Ltd.
Namasmarana. Mavinkurva. 1986. pap. 2.50 (1-57836-090-0, BW-110) Sathya Sai Bk Ctr.
Namaste. Robert Kowalczyk. (Asian Photos Ser.). (Illus.). 40p. 1982. pap. 14.95 (0-933704-27-5) Dawn Pr.
Namaste: Initiation & Transformation. Joyce A. Kovelman. Ed. by Susan Remkus. LC 97-25567. 112p. 1998. pap. 12.95 (1-880396-53-X, JP9653-X) Jalmar Pr.
*Namaste America: Indian Immmigrants in an American Metropolis. Padma Rangaswamy. LC 99-30458. 2000. 20.00 (0-271-01981-6) Pa St U Pr.
Namaste Book of Indian Short Stories, Vol. 1. Ed. by Monisha Mukundan. (C). 1992. 14.00 (81-85674-02-7, Pub. by UBS Pubs Dist) S Asia.
Namaste Book of Indian Short Stories, Vol. I. Ed. by Monisha Mukundan. LC 92-901235. (C). 1994. 9.00 (81-85944-85-7, Pub. by UBS Pubs Dist) S Asia.
Namaste Nepal Handicrafts. Prem R. Uprety. 1994. pap. 25.00 (0-7855-2759-1, Pub. by Ratna Pustak Bhandar) St Mut.
Nambe-Year One. Orlando Romero. LC 76-13385. 1976. pap. 5.95 (0-89229-003-X) TQS Pubns.
Nambudiri Veda Recitation. J. F. Staal. (Disputationes Rheno-Trajectinae Ser.: No. 5). (Illus.). pap. 26.15 (90-279-0031-0) Mouton.
Name. June Epstein. LC 92-34161. (Voyages Ser.). (Illus.). (J). 1993. 3.75 (0-383-03643-7) SRA McGraw.
Name. Michal Govrin. Tr. by Barbara Harshav. LC 98-8133. 384p. 1998. 25.95 (1-57322-072-8, Riverhead Books) Putnam Pub Group.
Name. Bruce C. Randall. 168p. mass mkt. 4.99 (1-55197-281-6) Picasso Publ.
*Name. Michal Govrin. Tr. by Barbara Harshav. 1999. reprint ed. pap. 13.00 (1-57322-755-2, Riverhd Trade) Berkley Pub.
Name: Selected Poetry 1973-1983. David Meltzer. LC 84-454. 160p. 1984. pap. 8.50 (0-87685-491-9) Black Sparrow.
Name above All Names. Contrib. by Mosie Lister. 36p. 1989. 5.99 (0-8341-9545-3, MC-69); audio 10.99 (0-685-68464-4, TA-9116C) Lillenas.
Name above Every Name: (P-S) see Names & Titles of Jesus Christ
Name above the Title: An Autobiography. Frank Capra, Jr. 1985. pap. 11.95 (0-394-71205-6) Vin Bks.
Name above the Title: An Autobiography. Frank Capra, Jr. LC 96-47921. (Illus.). 534p. 1997. reprint ed. pap. 18.95 (0-306-80771-8) Da Capo.
Name & Actuality in Early Chinese Thought. John Makeham. LC 93-31922. (SUNY Series in Chinese Philosophy & Culture). 286p. (C). 1994. pap. text 19.95 (0-7914-1984-3) State U NY Pr.
Name & Actuality in Early Chinese Thought. John Makeham. LC 93-31922. (SUNY Series in Chinese Philosophy & Culture). 286p. (C). 1994. text 59.50 (0-7914-1983-5) State U NY Pr.
Name & Destiny & How Can Everybody Improve It? Paul P. Yan. LC 96-84305. (Illus.). ii, 52p. (Orig.). 1996. pap. 4.95 (0-9652277-0-7) BBS Pubns.
Name & Nature of Poetry: And Other Selected Prose. Alfred E. Housman. 204p. (C). 1989. reprint ed. pap. 9.95 (0-941533-61-1, NAB) I R Dee.
Name & Number Checking. (Career Examination Ser.: C-3743). 1994. pap. 27.95 (0-8373-3743-7) Nat Learn.
*Name & Social Structure: Examples from Southeast Europe. Paul Stahl. 224p. 1998. text 31.50 (0-88033-404-5, 506, Pub. by East Eur Monographs) Col U Pr.
Name & Soul. Matityahu Glazerson. LC 99-20747. Date not set. write for info. (0-7657-6104-1) Aronson.
Name & Way of the Lord: Old Testament Themes, New Testament Christology. Carl J. Davis. LC 96-144621. (JSNT Supplement Ser.: No. 129). 227p. 1996. 65.00 (1-85075-604-X, Pub. by Sheffield Acad) CUP Services.
Name & Word Index to Nga Mahi a Nga Tupuna. Ray Harlow. 244p. 1996. pap. 29.95 (0-908569-51-3, Pub. by Univ Otago Pr) Intl Spec Bk.
*Name Book. Michael Cader. 2000. 8.99 (0-517-16217-2) Crown Pub Group.
Name Book. Raymond Freund & Jan Freund. (Illus.). 92p. 1984. pap. 12.95 (0-940808-31-5) Camino E E & Bk.
Name Book. rev. ed. Pierre Le Rouzic. Ed. by Rodney Charles. LC 94-67155. (Illus.). 646p. 1995. pap. 15.95 (0-9638502-1-0) Sunstar Pubng.
Name Book: A Name for a Lifetime. rev. ed. Pierre Le Rouzic. LC 89-50198. 570p. reprint ed. pap. text 14.95 (0-9622069-0-3) Topos Pr.
Name Book: More Than 2000 Names, Their Meanings, Origin & Significance. Dorothea Austin. LC 97-21023. 34p. 1997. pap. 9.99 (1-55661-982-0) Bethany Hse.
Name Calling. Itah Sadu. (Illus.). 32p. (J). pap. 4.95 (0-88961-204-8, Pub. by Womens Pr) LPC InBook.
Name Change: Change Adult or Minors Name. LawPak Staff. 92p. (Orig.). 1994. pap. 15.95 (1-879421-06-2) LawPak.
Name-Changing: A Practical Guide. Nasreen Pearce. 94p. 1990. 55.00 (1-85190-089-6, Pub. by Tolley Pubng) St Mut.
Name Construction in Medieval Japan: A Guidebook to Period Japanese Names. Solveig Throndardottir. LC 94-66956. (Historical Studies Ser.). 330p. 1994. pap. text 37.50 (0-9642082-0-2) Outlaw Pr.
*Name Dropping. Jane Heller. LC 00-28182. 320p. 2000. text 24.95 (0-312-25234-X) St Martin.
*Name Dropping: From FDR On. John Kenneth Galbraith. LC 99-20070. 194p. (YA). (gr. 10-12). 1999. 26.00 (0-395-82288-2) HM.
Name Dropping: Tales from My San Francisco Nightclub. Barnaby Conrad. LC 96-61771. (Illus.). 212p. 1997. pap. 14.95 (0-964970l-4-7) Wild Coconuts.
Name Dropping: The Life & Lies of Alan King. Alan King & Chris Chase. (Illus.). 224p. 1996. 23.00 (0-684-80384-4) S&S Trade.
Name Dropping: The Life & Lies of Alan King. Alan King & Chris Chase. (Illus.). 224p. 1997. per. 12.00 (0-684-83278-X, Touchstone) S&S Trade Pap.
*Name Droppings: It's All about Me, Isn't It. Chris Michie. 128p. 2000. pap. 18.00 (0-7388-2227-2) Xlibris Corp.
Name Encanyoned River: Selected Poems, 1960-1985. Clayton Eshleman. LC 85-26648. 250p. (Orig.). 1986. 20.00 (0-87685-653-9); pap. 12.50 (0-87685-652-0) Black Sparrow.
Name Encanyoned River: Selected Poems, 1960-1985, signed ed. deluxe ed. Clayton Eshleman. LC 85-26648. 250p. (Orig.). 1986. 30.00 (0-87685-654-7) Black Sparrow.

***Name for Kitty. Marcia Trimble. LC 99-96581. (Illus.). 32p. (J). (ps-2). 2000. pap. 15.95 (1-891577-63-8); pap. 7.95 (1-891577-64-6) Images Press.**
Getting & naming a kitten is one of the beloved experiences of childhood. A NAME FOR KITTY is Malinda Martha's experience of getting a kitten & trying out names until Kitty grows into one that fits. Monette's Pet Shop, where Malinda Martha first meets Kitty, symbolizes that special place where pet & owner meet...& fall in love. Although it is love at first sight for Malinda Martha & Kitty, Malinda Martha has to wish...& hope...& wait through a long afternoon before she knows that Kitty has tugged at Mother's heartstrings, too...& before she can take Kitty home, with a shiny clear nametag tucked in her bag. Malinda Martha sees a piece of Kitty's personality every time she tries a different name. Finally she looks to Kitty for a sign of the perfect name & concludes that he will have to grow into a name that fits afterall. Gloria Lapuyade makes a heartwarming debut as an illustrator of children's picture books with a set of watercolor paintings that capture the universal joy of bonding with a kitten & make A NAME FOR KITTY everybody's story. Available through Images Press, Phone: 650-948-8251, Fax: 650-941-6114, e-mail: bugsmom2@aol.com, Baker & Taylor, Ingram Books, Quality Books, Inc. & amazon.com. *Publisher Paid Annotation.*

Name-Game: A Program about Inappropriate Behavior. Timothy G. Ludwig. LC 94-77202. 32p. (J). (gr. 1-4). 1991. 6.95 (1-884063-21-7) Mar Co Prods.
Name Game: Football, Baseball, Hockey & Basketball How Your Favorite Sports Teams Were Named. Michael L. Donovan. (Illus.). 256p. (Orig.). 1997. pap. 12.95 (1-895629-74-8) Warwick Publ.
Name Game: From Oyster Point to Keowee. Claude H. Neuffer. LC 72-76383. (Illus.). 1979. 6.00 (0-87844-009-7) C H Neuffer.
Name Game: The Book of Lost Names. Warithu-Deen Umar. Ed. by Islah W. Umar. 129p. (Orig.). 1991. pap. 7.95 (1-879661-00-4) Muslim Broadcast.
Name Game: Writing/Fading Writer in de Donde Son los Cantantes. Oscar Montero. LC 88-14376. (North Carolina Studies in the Romance Languages & Literatures: No. 231). 152p. reprint ed. pap. 47.20 (0-608-20071-9, 207134300011) Bks Demand.
*Name Games: A Mark Manning Mystery. Michael Craft. 320p. 2000. 23.95 (0-312-24552-1, Minotaur) St Martin.
Name, Hero, Icon: Semiotics of Nationalism Through Heroic Biography. Anna Makolkin. LC 91-48252. (Approaches to Semiotics Ser.: No. 105). xvi, 264p. (C). 1992. lib. bdg. 113.85 (3-11-013012-2) Mouton.
Name I Can't Read: The Rocky Road to Literacy, a Mother's Story. Claudia M. Darkins. Ed. by Marguerite L. Butler & Brenda Willis. LC 97-92290. 200p. 1998. 14.95 (0-9648154-0-0, Cane Pub) Claudia Prodns.
Name in Heaven. Matthew Mead. 132p. 1995. reprint ed. 18.95 (1-57358-030-9) Soli Deo Gloria.
Name in the Window, No. 1. Margaret Demorest. LC 96-9725. (Illus.). x, 200p. 1996. 37.50 (0-9655491-0-0) M Demorest.
Name in the Window, No. 2. Margaret Demorest. LC 96-9725. (Illus.). x, 200p. 1996. pap. 18.95 (0-9655491-1-9) M Demorest.
Name Index for the Centennial Year Book of Alameda County, California. Dan L. Mosier. 59p. 1999. pap. 9.95 (1-889064-06-8) Mines Rd Bks.
Name Index to the Baltimore City Tax Records: 1798-1808 of the Baltimore City Archives. Ed. by Richard J. Cox. 229p. (Orig.). 1981. pap. 6.50 (0-916623-01-7) City Baltimore.
Name Index to the Library of Congress Collection of Mormon Diaries. Merrill Library, Special Collections Dept. Staff. LC 75-636249. (Western Text Society Ser.: Vol. 1, No. 2). 395p. reprint ed. pap. 122.50 (0-8357-6231-9, 203460600090) Bks Demand.
Name into Word. 2nd ed. Eric Partridge. LC 77-117906. (Select Bibliographies Reprint Ser.). 1977. reprint ed. 44.95 (0-8369-5361-4) Ayer.
Name Is Familiar: Who Played Who in the Movies. Robert A. Nowlan & Gwendolyn W. Nowlan. 1016p. 1993. pap. text 99.95 (1-55570-054-3) Neal-Schuman.
Name It & Claim It! Frederick K. Price. 192p. 1992. pap. 8.99 (0-89274-857-5, HH-857) Harrison Hse.
*Name It Game. Janie Haugen & Melissa Britt. 16p. 1999. teacher ed. 39.95i (1-884074-83-9) PCI Educ Pubg.
*Name Jar. Yangsook Choi. LC 00-39103. (Illus.). (J). 2001. lib. bdg. write for info. (0-375-90613-4) Knopf Bks Yng Read.
Name Me, I'm Yours! Joan Wilen & Lydia Wilen. (Illus.). 144p. (Orig.). 1982. pap. 3.95 (0-941298-04-3) M E Pinkham.
*Name Me Nobody. Lois-Ann Yamanaka. 240p. (YA). (gr. 7-12). 2000. pap. 5.99 (0-7868-1466-7) Hypm Ppbks.
Name "Negro" Richard B. Moore. (African Studies). reprint ed. 18.00 (0-938818-97-X) ECA Assoc.
Name "Negro" Its Origin Evil Use. Richard B. Moore. 88p. 1994. reprint ed. pap. 7.00 (1-56411-087-7, 4BBG0095) Untd Bros & Sis.
Name "Negro" - Its Origin & Evil Use. rev. ed. Richard B. Moore. Ed. by W. Burghardt Turner & Joyce M. Turner. LC 91-77147. 110p. 1992. reprint ed. 19.95 (0-933121-36-9); reprint ed. pap. 8.95 (0-933121-35-0) Black Classic.
Name of a Bullfighter. Luis Sepulveda. 21.00 (0-614-22233-8) Harcourt.
Name of a Bullfighter. Luis Sepulveda. 1997. pap. 12.00 (0-15-600548-4, Harvest Bks) Harcourt.
Name of an Angel: An Original Black Lace Novel. Laura Thornton. (Orig.). 1997. mass mkt. 9.95 (0-352-33205-0, Pub. by BLA4) London Brdge.
Name of God & the Angel of the Lord: Samaritan & Jewish Concepts of Intermeditation & the Origin of Gnosticism. Jarl E. Fossum. 400p. 1985. lib. bdg. 110.00 (3-16-144789-1, Pub. by JCB Mohr) Coronet Bks.
Name of God from the Sinai to the American Southwest: An Alphabetic Script & Language Found in Ancient America & Israel. James R. Harris. Ed. & Tr. by Dann W. Hone. (Illus.). xxviii, 254p. 1998. 19.95 (0-9667629-0-8, 004) Harris Hse Pubns.
Name of Hero. Richard W. Seltzer, Jr. LC 81-50329. 290p. 1981. 12.95 (0-87477-187-0) B & R Samizdat.
Name of Jehovah in the Book of Esther. E. W. Bullinger. 24p. 1999. reprint ed. pap. 3.00 (1-880573-76-8) Bible Search Pubns.
Name of Jesus. Irenee Hausherr. Tr. by Charles Cummings. LC 77-10559. (Cistercian Studies: No. 44). 358p. 1978. pap. 13.95 (0-87907-944-4) Cistercian Pubns.
Name of Love: Great Gay Love Poems. Michael Lassell. LC 94-36026. 87p. 1994. text 10.00 (0-312-11863-5, Stonewall Inn) St Martin.
Name of My Beloved: Verses of the Sikh Gurus. Kaur Singh & Nikky Guinder. LC 95-26459. (Illus.). 272p. 1996. 16.00 (0-06-067049-5) Harper SF.
Name of My Beloved: Verses of the Sikh Gurus: Devotional Poetry from the Dasam Granth. Nikky-Guninder K. Singh. (Sacred Literature Ser.). 272p. 1995. pap. 22.95 (0-7619-8990-0) AltaMira Pr.
Name of Salish & Kootenai Nation: The 1855 Hell Gate Treaty & the Origin of the Flathead Indian Reservation. Robert Bigart. LC 96-4730. (Illus.). 180p. 1996. pap. 14.95 (0-295-97545-8) U of Wash Pr.
Name of the Bullfighter. Luis Sepulveda. Tr. by Suzanne Ruta from SPA. LC 96-4008. 224p. 1996. 21.00 (0-15-100193-6) Harcourt.
Name of the Flower: Stories. Kuniko Mukoda. Tr. by Tomone Matsumoto from JPN. LC 93-6309. (Rock Spring Collection). 152p. (Orig.). 1993. pap. 10.95 (1-880656-09-4) Stone Bridge Pr.
Name of the Game. Julie Garratt. (Scarlet Ser.). 1998. mass mkt. 3.99 (1-85487-986-3, Pub. by Scarlet Bks) London Brdge.
Name of the Game: Making a Lasting Connection with Your Kids! Steve Schall. Date not set. 11.99 (0-89221-492-9) New Leaf.
Name of the Game Is Money: The Business of Sports. Jerry Gorman et al. 278p. 1994. 19.95 (0-471-59423-7) Wiley.
Name of the Game Was Murder. Joan Lowery Nixon. 192p. (YA). (gr. 7 up). 1994. mass mkt. 4.99 (0-440-21916-7) Dell.
Name of the Game Was Murder. Joan Lowery Nixon. (J). 1993. 9.09 (0-606-07048-6, Pub. by Turtleback) Demco.
Name of the Game Was Murder. large type ed. Joan Lowery Nixon. LC 93-20596. 247p. (J). 1993. 16.95 (1-56054-775-8) Thorndike Pr.
Name of the King. unabridged ed. Aloysius P. Sharon. LC 99-70122. 304p. (Orig.). 1999. 24.95 (0-9670606-0-5) Patton Hse.
Name of the Poet: Onomastics & Anonymity in the Works of Stephane Mallarme. Charles Temple. LC 96-140560. 176p. 1995. text 59.95 (0-85989-431-2, Pub. by Univ Exeter Pr) Northwestern U Pr.
Name of the Rose. Umberto Eco. Tr. by William Weaver. LC 82-21286. (Helen & Kurt Wolff Bk.). 512p. 1983. 32.00 (0-15-144647-4) Harcourt.
Name of the Rose. Umberto Eco. Tr. by William Weaver. LC 94-13818. (Harvest Book Ser.). (Illus.). 536p. 1994. pap. 14.00 (0-15-600131-4) Harcourt.
Name of the Rose. Umberto Eco. 1995. 29.95 (0-15-100213-4); pap. 10.95 (0-15-600370-8) Harcourt.
Name of the Rose. Umberto Eco. LC 82-21286. 640p. 1988. mass mkt. 6.99 (0-446-35720-0) Warner Bks.
Name of the Rose. Umberto Eco. LC 82-21286. 1994. reprint ed. lib. bdg. 29.95 (1-56849-544-7) Buccaneer Bks.
Name of the Rose. 4th ed. Umberto Eco. LC 82-21286. 640p. 1986. mass mkt. 4.95 (0-446-34410-9, Pub. by Warner Bks) Little.
Name of the Tree: A Bantu Folktale. Illus. by Ian Wallace. LC 89-2430. 36p. (J). (ps-3). 1990. 16.00 (0-689-50490-X) McElderry Bks.
*Name of the World: A Novel. Denise Johnson. LC 99-85970. 144p. 2000. 22.00 (0-06-019248-8) HarpC.
Name of War: King Philiip's War & the Origins of American Identity. Jill Lepore. (Illus.). 337p. 1999. pap. 15.00 (0-375-70262-8) Vin Bks.
Name of War: King Philip's War & the Origins of American Identity. Jill Lepore. LC 97-2820. (Illus.). 337p. 1998. 30.00 (0-679-44686-9) Random.

N

Name of William Shakespeare. J. L. Haney. LC 72-168239. reprint ed. 27.50 (*0-404-03094-7*) AMS Pr.

Name of Your Game: Four Game Plans for Success at Home & at Work. Stuart Atkins. (Illus.). (C). 1982. 17.95 (*0-942532-00-7*); pap. 6.95 (*0-942532-01-5*) Ellis & Stewart Pub.

Name on the Bracelet. Margaret Sutton. 1993. reprint ed. lib. bdg. 16.95 (*1-56849-228-6*) Buccaneer Bks.

***Name on the Quilt: A Story of Remembrance.** Jeannine Atkins. LC 97-42303. (Illus.). 32p. (J). 1999. 16.00 (*0-689-81592-1*) S&S Trade.

Name on the Schoolhouse: An Anecdotal List of Some Historic Names of Schools in Washington State. Intro. by Kenneth L. Calkins. (Illus.). 250p. 1992. pap. 10.00 (*0-9630702-0-7*) WA Ret Teach.

Name Power 101: The Owner's Manual for People Who Have Names. unabridged ed. 1999. pap. 24.95 (*1-887270-10-8*) Weve Got Your Number.

Name, Rank & Number: A POW's Indomitable Will to Survive. Robert W. Calvey. 112p. 1998. 42.50 (*1-85776-207-X*, Pub. by Book Guild Ltd) Trans-Atl Phila.

Name Reactions & Reagents in Organic Synthesis. Bradford P. Mundy & Michael G. Ellerd. LC 88-14915. 560p. 1988. 89.95 (*0-471-83626-5*) Wiley.

Name Thang Baby Name Book: Over 15,000 English Names with Spanish & French Translations. Earl E. Clark. 1997. pap. text 5.95 (*0-9646643-0-5*) New Vis Dist.

Name That Baby. Barbara Turner. (J. Hook Ser.). 1998. mass mkt. 5.99 (*0-425-12715-X*) Berkley Pub.

Name That Baby. Barbara K. Turner. 1988. mass mkt. 5.99 (*0-425-10894-5*) Berkley Pub.

Name That Baby: Every Parents Guide to Names. Jane Bradshaw. LC 98-16140. 512p. 1998. pap. 10.99 (*0-8054-1271-9*) Broadman.

Name That Book! Questions & Answers on Outstanding Children's Books. 2nd ed. Janet Greeson. LC 97-43322. 240p. 1998. pap. 32.50 (*0-8108-3151-1*) Scarecrow.

Name! That Dog. Jane D. Martin & Barbara M. Rumsey. LC 96-94584. (Illus.). 65p. (Orig.). 1996. pap. write for info. (*0-9652923-0-4*) M Rumsey.

Name That Dog: Dogs of Presidents, Kings, Queens, Governors, & Celebrities. Lynne M. Hamer. (Illus.). 92p. 1991. 24.95 (*0-9627934-0-X*) Animal Pr PA.

Name That Flower: The Identification of Flowering Plants. Ian Clarke & Helen Lee. (Illus.). 272p. 1994. reprint ed. pap. 29.95 (*0-522-84335-2*, Pub. by Melbourne Univ Pr) Paul & Co Pubs.

Name That Insect: A Guide to the Insects of Southeastern Australia. Tim R. New. (Illus.). 208p. 1997. pap. text 22.95 (*0-19-553782-3*) OUP.

Name That Portion: Fractions, Percents, & Decimals. Joan Akers et al. Ed. by Catherine Anderson et al. (Investigations in Number, Data, & Space Ser.). (Illus.). 178p. (Orig.). (J). (gr. 5-6). 1996. pap., teacher ed. 22.95 (*0-86651-990-4*, DS21426) Seymour Pubns.

Name That Song. (Piano Fun! Ser.). 40p. 1996. pap. 32.95 (*0-7935-4088-7*) H Leonard.

Name That Song! Music Trivia Game, Blue. 20p. (J). 1996. per. 12.95 (*0-7935-5089-0*, 00330167) H Leonard.

Name That Song! Music Trivia Game, Gold. 20p. (J). 1996. per. 12.95 (*0-7935-5091-2*, 00330169) H Leonard.

Name That Song! Music Trivia Game, Green. 20p. (J). 1996. per. 12.95 (*0-7935-5090-4*, 00330168) H Leonard.

Name That Song! Music Trivia Game, Red. 20p. (J). 1996. per. 12.95 (*0-7935-5085-8*, 00330166) H Leonard.

***Name That Train.** Illus. by John Maggard & Greg LaFever. 10p. (J). (ps-3). 1998. 7.95 (*1-929174-07-1*) Oshkosh BGosh.

Name the Baby. Mark Cirino. LC 97-41134. 224p. 1998. pap. 12.00 (*0-385-49159-X*) Doubleday.

***Name the Baby: Search Through over 3000 Baby Names & Their Meanings in This Charming & Unique Book.** Kerren Barbas. (Illus.). 1999. 9.95 (*0-7667-2977-X*) Gibson.

Name the Nation: More Than 2,000 Questions & Answers from Afghanistan to Zimbabwe. Gilbert W. Davies & Florice M. Frank. LC 95-75157. 138p. (C). 1995. pap. 7.95 (*0-9634413-8-8*) HiSt ink Bks.

Name to Conjure With. Donald Aamodt. 272p. 1989. pap. 3.50 (*0-380-75137-2*, Avon Bks) Morrow Avon.

Name und Sache: Ein Problem im Fruhgriechischen Denken. Manfred Kraus. (Studien zur antiken Philosophie: Vol. 14). v, 258p. (C). 1987. 69.00 (*90-6032-279-7*, Pub. by B R Gruner) Humanities.

Name Was Olney. 2nd ed. Roscoe Sheller. Ed. & Photos by Dorothy Churchill. Photos by Sam Churchill. (Illus.). 173p. 1993. reprint ed. pap. 14.95 (*0-9630536-2-0*) S Dot S.

Name Withheld: A J.p. Beaumont Mystery. J. A. Jance. LC 95-36071. (J. P. Beaumont Mystery Ser.). 392p. 1997. mass mkt. 6.99 (*0-380-71842-1*, Avon Bks) Morrow Avon.

Name Your Baby. rev. ed. Lareina Rule. 256p. (Orig.). 1986. mass mkt. 4.99 (*0-553-27145-8*) Bantam.

***Name Your Passion: A User's Guide to Finding Your Personal Purpose.** Paul L. Kordis & Susan J. Kordis. (Illus.). 471p. (Orig.). 1999. pap. 29.95 (*0-9673183-0-0*, Pub. by Delphinus Pr) Kordis Grp.

Name Your Pet. Gene Boone. 20p. (Orig.). 1986. pap. 2.95 (*0-930865-05-7*) RSVP Press.

Name Your Pet. Alix Palmer. 1996. mass mkt. 4.99 (*1-85782-041-X*, Pub. by Blake Publng) Seven Hills Bk.

***Name Your Pet! Over 3500 Names.** Rob Miller. (Illus.). 160p. 1999. pap. 7.95 (*1-86436-431-9*, Pub. by New Holland) BHB Intl.

Named Awards in the Geosciences. Compiled by Mary W. Scott. 197p. 1998. wbk. ed. 36.00 (*0-922152-47-0*) Am Geol.

Named in Stone & Sky: An Arizona Anthology. Ed. by Gregory McNamee. LC 92-24494. 196p. (Orig.). (C). 1993. pap. 16.50 (*0-8165-1348-1*); lib. bdg. 34.95 (*0-8165-1278-7*) U of Ariz Pr.

Named Nurse in Practice. Rosie Dargan. (Illus.). 110p. 1997. pap. 18.95 (*1-873853-37-8*) Bailliere Tindall.

***Named of the Dragon.** Susanna Kearsley. 1999. mass mkt. 6.99 (*0-425-17345-3*) Berkley Pub.

Named Organic Reactions. Laue. 298p. 1998. 79.95 (*0-471-97142-1*) Wiley.

***Namedropper: A Novel.** Emma Forrest. LC 99-88008. (J). 2000. pap. 12.00 (*0-684-86538-6*) Scribner.

***Namedroppers.** Susan Compo. 200p. 2000. pap. 16.95 (*1-891241-12-5*) Verse Chorus Pr.

Namedropping: Mostly Literary Memoirs. Richard Elman. LC 97-45812. 288p. (C). 1998. text 31.50 (*0-7914-3879-1*) State U NY Pr.

Namedropping: Mostly Literary Memoirs. Richard M. Elman. LC 97-45812. (C). 1999. pap. text 19.95 (*0-7914-3880-5*) State U NY Pr.

***Nameless.** Charlie Buckley. (Illus.). 96p. 2000. pap. 9.95 (*1-886028-04-4*) Savage Pr.

Nameless. Ramsey Campbell. 288p. 1984. pap. 3.50 (*0-671-44489-1*) PB.

Nameless. Ramsey Campbell. 1987. mass mkt. 4.99 (*0-8125-2243-5*) Tor Bks.

***Nameless Breed.** Will C. Brown. 2000. mass mkt. 5.99 (*0-425-17399-2*) Berkley Pub.

Nameless Breed. large type ed. Will C. Brown. LC 98-29044. 1998. 30.00 (*0-7838-0337-0*) Thorndike Pr.

***Nameless Coffin.** large type ed. Gwendoline Butler. LC 99-49108. 2000. pap. 23.95 (*0-7862-2302-2*) Mac Lib Ref.

Nameless Cults. Robert E. Howard. 1998. pap. 12.95 (*1-56882-130-1*) Chaosium.

Nameless Diseases. Terra Ziporyn. LC 91-36660. 288p. 1992. 24.95 (*0-8135-1800-8*) Rutgers U Pr.

Nameless Impressions see Griztanciu Pauksciu Preliudijos: Bevardes Impressijos

Nameless Magery. Delia M. Turner. 231p. 1998. mass mkt. 5.99 (*0-345-42430-1*, Del Rey) Ballantine Pub Grp.

Nameless Nobleman. Jane G. Austin. (Works of Jane (Goodin) Austin). 1989. reprint ed. lib. bdg. 79.00 (*0-7812-1828-4*) Rprt Serv.

***Nameless Organizational Change: No-Hype, Low-Resistance Corporate Transformation.** Glenn Allen-Meyer. LC 99-91251. (Illus.). 224p. 2000. 24.95 (*0-9675079-0-1*) Talwood Craig Pubng.

Nameless Persons: Legal Discrimination Against Non-Marital Children in the United States. Martha T. Zingo & Kevin E. Early. LC 94-8550. 192p. 1994. 59.95 (*0-275-94711-4*, Praeger Pubs) Greenwood.

Nameless Sight: Selected Poems, 1937-1956. Alan Swallow. 74p. 1963. pap. 9.95 (*0-8040-0223-1*) Swallow.

Nameless Sins. limited ed. Nancy A. Collins. (Classics Revisited Ser.). 1994. boxed set 60.00 (*0-9629659-7-9*) Gauntlet.

Nameless Towns: Texas Sawmill Communities, 1880-1942. Thad Sitton & James H. Conrad. LC 97-15563. 276p. 1998. 37.50 (*0-292-77725-6*, SITNAM); pap. 18.95 (*0-292-77726-4*, SITNAP) U of Tex Pr.

Nameless War. A. H. Ramsey. 1978. pap. 5.00 (*0-911038-38-8*, 0309, Noontide Pr) Legion Survival.

Nameless War. unabridged ed. A. H. M. Ramsey. 112p. 1952. reprint ed. pap. 10.00 (*0-945001-85-1*) GSG & Assocs.

Namemaker's Handbook: Creative Selections for Constant Connections. Leonard E. Pruitt. LC 98-90492. xiv, 400p. 1998. lib. bdg. 25.00 (*0-9665145-1-3*) Wordway Pubg Co.

***Namen der Keilschriftzeichen.** Yushu Gong. (Alter Orient und Altes Testament Ser.: Band 268). viii, 228p. 2000. text 46.50 (*3-927120-83-9*, Pub. by Ugarit-Verlag) Eisenbrauns.

Namenforschung - Name Studies - Les Noms Propres: Ein Internationales Handbuch Zur Onoma, 2 vols., Set, incl. index. Ed. by Ernst Eichler et al. (Handbooks of Linguistics & Communication Science: Vol. 11.2). (ENG, FRE & GER.). xxx, 912p. (C). 1996. lib. bdg. 739.25 (*3-11-014879-X*) De Gruyter.

Namenforschung - Name Studies - Les Noms Propres: Ein Internationales Handbuch Zur Onomastik - An International Handbook of Onomastics - Manuel International D'Onomastique. Ed. by Ernst Eichler et al. (Handbooks of Linguistics & Communication Science: Bd. 11-1). (FRE & GER.). xliv, 977p. (C). 1995. lib. bdg. 600.00 (*3-11-011426-7*) De Gruyter.

Namengebungsmotivationen Zeitgenossischer Hamburger Autoren: Eine Empirische Untersuchung Zur Liter. Sabine Hanno-Weber. (Europaische Hochschulschriften Ser.: Reihe 1, Bd. 1598). (GER.). 243p. 1996. 44.95 (*3-631-31092-7*) P Lang Pubng.

Namenkundliche Studien Zum Germanenproblem. Juergen Udolph. (Ergaenzungsbaende zum Reallexikon der Germanischen Alterrumskunde Ser.: Vol. 9). (GER.). xvi, 1036p. (C). 1994. lib. bdg. 353.85 (*3-11-014138-8*) De Gruyter.

Nameplates, Labels & Tags for Control Centers: ISA Standard RP60.6. ISA Staff. 1984. pap. 40.00 (*0-87664-813-8*, RP60.6) ISA.

Names. Don DeLillo. (Vintage Contemporaries Ser.). 1989. pap. 13.00 (*0-679-72295-5*) Vin Bks.

Names. Ed. by Brigitta Geltrich. (Human Interactions Ser.). (Illus.). 84p. 1996. pap. text. write for info. (*0-936945-68-0*) Creat with Wds.

Names. deluxe ed. Michael Mooney. (Treacle Story Ser.: No. 10). 64p. 1979. 12.50 (*0-914232-33-9*) McPherson & Co.

Names: A Memoir. N. Scott Momaday. LC 96-27237. 170p. 1996. 29.95 (*0-8165-1700-2*) U of Ariz Pr.

Names: A Memoir. N. Scott Momaday. LC 87-18785. (Sun Tracks Ser.: Vol. 16). 170p. 1987. reprint ed. pap. 12.95 (*0-8165-1046-6*) U of Ariz Pr.

Names: Names You Just Won't Find in the Other Books. Daniel Narsai David. LC 97-69592. 200p. 1999. pap. 9.95 (*0-88739-173-7*) Creat Arts Bk.

Names, Addresses & Telephone Numbers for Law Schools & Faculty. 148p. 1997. pap. 50.00 (*0-318-13405-5*) Assn Am Law Schls.

Names & American Literature. Paul Schlueter. (International Library of Names). 250p. write for info. (*0-8290-1284-2*) Irvington.

Names & Descriptions. Leonard Linsky. LC 76-8093. 1993. reprint ed. pap. text 4.50 (*0-226-48442-4*, P871) U Ch Pr.

***Names & Faces Made Easy: The Fun & Easy Way to Remember People.** Jerry Lucas. LC 00-104325. (Illus.). 216p. 2000. pap. 17.95 (*1-930853-01-7*) Lucas Ed Systm.

Names & Local Habitations: Selected Poems. Joel Oppenheimer. 1990. 30.00 (*0-912330-66-X*) Jargon Soc.

Names & Name-Days. Ed. by David Attwater. LC 89-43340. xii, 124p. 1991. reprint ed. lib. bdg. 44.00 (*1-55888-877-2*) Omnigraphics Inc.

Names & Naming in Joyce. Claire A. Culleton. LC 94-15380. 160p. 1994. pap. 15.95 (*0-299-14384-8*) U of Wis Pr.

Names & Naming in Joyce. Claire A. Culleton. LC 94-15380. 160p. 1994. 40.00 (*0-299-14380-5*) U of Wis Pr.

Names & Naming Patterns in England, 1538-1700. Scott Smith-Bannister. LC 97-225842. (Oxford Historical Mongraphs). (Illus.). 238p. (C). 1997. text 68.00 (*0-19-820663-1*) OUP.

Names & Numbers; A Slam Book. Havoc Publishing Staff. 1999. write for info. (*1-57977-021-5*) Havoc Pub.

Names &-or Titles of God. 22p. 1992. pap. 4.50 (*1-57277-019-8*) Script Rsch.

Names & Order of the Books of the Old Testament. Ethelbert W. Bullinger. 40p. 1996. reprint ed. pap. 3.00 (*1-880573-30-X*) Bible Search Pubns.

Names & Sketches of the Pioneer Settlers of Madison County, New York. William H. Tuttle. Ed. by Isabel Bracy. LC 84-80104. (Illus.). 304p. 1984. 25.00 (*0-932334-26-1*, NY27030) Hrt of the Lakes.

Names & Stories: Emilia Dilke & Victorian Culture. Kali Israel. LC 98-42855. (Illus.). 384p. 1998. text 47.50 (*0-19-512275-5*) OUP.

Names & Structures of Organic Compounds. Otto Theodor Benfey. LC 82-10012. 228p. (C). 1982. reprint ed. pap. text 18.50 (*0-89874-520-9*) Krieger.

Names & Substance of the Australian Subsection System. C. G. Von Brandenstein. LC 82-4869. (Illus.). 216p. 1982. 24.00 (*0-226-86481-2*) U Ch Pr.

Names & Their Histories. Isaac Taylor. 1972. 250.00 (*0-8490-0702-X*) Gordon Pr.

Names & Their Varieties: A Collection of Essays in Onomastics. Compiled & Pref. by Kelsie B. Harder. LC 85-29638. 324p. (Orig.). (C). 1986. lib. bdg. 56.00 (*0-8191-5232-3*) U Pr of Amer.

Names & Titles of Jesus Christ, 5 vols. Charles J. Rolls. Incl. Vol. 2. World's Greatest Name: (H-K) rev. ed. LC 84-15416. 183p. 1985. pap. 8.99 (*0-87213-732-5*); Vol. 3. Time's Noblest Name: (L-O) rev. ed. LC 84-14825. 192p. 1985. pap. 8.99 (*0-87213-733-3*); Vol. 4. Name above Every Name: (P-S) rev. ed. LC 85-6927. 255p. 1985. pap. 8.99 (*0-87213-734-1*); Vol. 5. His Glorious Name: (T-Z) 2nd ed. LC 85-6926. 267p. 1986. reprint ed. pap. 43.99 (*0-87213-735-X*); 43.99 (*0-87213-736-8*) Loizeaux.

Name's Buchanan. large type ed. Jonas Ward. LC 95-24496. 204p. 1995. 18.95 (*0-7838-1471-2*, G K Hall Lrg Type) Mac Lib Ref.

Names, Dates & Numbers: A System of Numerology. Roy P. Walton. 80p. 1981. pap. 7.00 (*0-89540-104-5*, SB-104) Sun Pub.

Names, Dates & Numbers: What They Mean to You. Roy P. Walton. 86p. 1996. reprint ed. spiral bd. 11.00 (*0-7873-1197-9*) Hlth Research.

Names, Designations, & Appelations see Persian Words in English

Name's Familiar: Mr. Leotard, Barbie, & Chef Boy-ar-dee. Laura Lee. LC 98-56131. 312p. 1999. pap. 14.95 (*1-56554-394-7*) Pelican.

Names First - Rails Later: New England's 700-Plus Railroads & What Happened to Them. L. Peter Cornwall & Carol A. Smith. (Illus.). 124p. (C). 1988. text. write for info. (*0-9621689-0-4*) Arden Valley.

Names for Dipterocarp Timbers & Trees from Asia. J. M. Fundter. (C). 1991. text 395.00 (*0-89771-611-6*, Pub. by Intl Bk Distr) St Mut.

Names for Love. Patrick Deeley. (C). 1990. 23.00 (*0-948268-79-4*, Pub. by Dedalus); pap. 15.00 (*0-948268-78-6*, Pub. by Dedalus) St Mut.

Names for the Cornish. Dyllansow Truran Staff. (C). 1989. 25.00 (*0-907566-94-4*, Pub. by Dyllansow Truran) St Mut.

Names for the Self. Edward Locke. 76p. 1997. pap. 7.00 (*0-9646587-5-5*) Harlequinade.

Names from Africa. Ogonna Chuks-Orji. LC 72-154523. 96p. 1972. pap. 10.95 (*0-87485-046-0*) Johnson Chicago.

Names from East Africa. Harry McKinzie & Issy K. Tindimwebwa. Ed. by Elisabeth Campbell. 42p. (Orig.). (J). 1980. pap. 9.95 (*0-86626-007-2*) AAIMS Pubs.

Names in Current Use for Extant Plant Genera. Ed. by W. Greuter. (Regnum Vegetabile Ser.: Vol. 129). xxvi, 1464p. 1993. 338.30 (*3-87429-351-3*, 053354, Pub. by Koeltz Sci Bks) Lubrecht & Cramer.

Names in Literature: Essays from Literary Onomastics Studies. Ed. by Grace Alvarez-Altman & Frederick M. Burelbach. LC 87-18916. 248p. (Orig.). (C). 1988. pap. text 24.00 (*0-8191-6610-3*); lib. bdg. 47.50 (*0-8191-6609-X*) U Pr of Amer.

Names in Roman Verse: A Lexicon & Reverse Index of All Proper Names of History, Mythology, & Geography Found in the Classical Roman Poets. Donald C. Swanson. LC 67-25942. 445p. reprint ed. pap. 138.00 (*0-7837-1662-1*, 204195900024) Bks Demand.

Names in South Carolina, 1954-65, Vols. I-XII. Claude H. Neuffer. LC 76-29026. 1976. reprint ed. 25.00 (*0-87152-248-9*) C H Neuffer.

Names in South Carolina, 1966-83, Vols. XIII-XXX. Claude H. Neuffer. 1983. 5.00 (*0-686-18734-2*) C H Neuffer.

***Names in Stone: 75,000 Cemetery Inscriptions from Frederick County, Maryland, 2 vols.** Jacob M. Holdcraft. 1371p. 1999. pap. 90.00 (*0-8063-1115-0*) Clearfield Co.

***Names, Names & More Names: Locating Your Dutch Ancestor in Colonial America.** Arthur C. M. Kelly. 320p. 1999. pap. 19.95 (*0-916489-91-4*) Ancestry.

Names, Natures & Things: The Alchemist Jabir ibn Hayyan & His Kitab al-Ahjar (Book of Stones) Syed N. Haq. (Boston Studies in the Philosophy of Science). 304p. (C). 1993. lib. bdg. 122.00 (*0-7923-2587-7*, Pub. by Kluwer Academic) Kluwer Academic.

Names, Natures & Things: The Alchemist Jabir Ibn Hayyan & His Kitab al-Ahjar (Book of Stones) Syed N. Haq. (Boston Studies in the Philosophy of Science: No. 158). 304p. 1995. pap. text 29.00 (*0-7923-3254-7*) Kluwer Academic.

Names of & Variation in Central American Larger Foraminifera, Particularly the Eocene Pseudophragminids- No. 4 see Bulletins of American Paleontology: Vol. 56

Names of Angels. C. Fred Dickason. (Names of Ser.). 160p. 1997. mass mkt. 4.99 (*0-8024-6181-6*, 15) Moody.

Names of Christ. T. C. Horton & Charles E. Hurlburt. Ed. by James Bell, Jr. (Names of Ser.). 190p. mass mkt. 4.99 (*0-8024-6040-2*, 399) Moody.

Names of Comedy. Anne Barton. 239p. 1990. text 37.50 (*0-8020-5657-1*) U of Toronto Pr.

Names of Countries & Their Capital Cities Including Adjectives of Nationality. 10th rev. ed. (Terminology Bulletins Ser.: No. 20). 226p. 1993. pap. 27.00 (*92-5-003347-8*, F33478, Pub. by FAO) Bernan Associates.

Names of Fishes: Chinese/English/Latin. C. Qingtai. (CHI, ENG & LAT.). 296p. 1992. 49.95 (*0-320-00596-8*) Fr & Eur.

Names of God see Nombres de Dios

Names of God, 3 bks. (Names of Ser.). pap. 12.99 (*0-8024-6046-1*, 402) Moody.

Names of God. Marilyn Hickey. 285p. pap. 7.95 (*1-56441-014-5*) M Hickey Min.

Names of God. Nathan Stone. (Names of Ser.). mass mkt. 4.99 (*0-8024-5854-8*, 400) Moody.

Names of God. Lester Sumrall. 143p. 1993. mass mkt. 5.99 (*0-88368-224-9*) Whitaker Hse.

Names of God. 2nd ed. W. Pascoe Goard. 48p. 1989. reprint ed. pap. 4.00 (*0-934666-29-6*) Artisan Pubs.

Names of God: Discovering God as He Desires to Be Known. Andrew Jukes. LC 67-28843. 234p. 1976. pap. 12.99 (*0-8254-2958-7*, Kregel Class) Kregel.

Names of God: Poetic Readings of Biblical Beginnings. Herbert C. Brichto. LC 96-10381. (Illus.). 480p. 1998. text 65.00 (*0-19-510965-1*) OUP.

Names of God's Promises. Mark A. Tabb. LC 99-163216. 1998. mass mkt. 4.99 (*0-8024-6183-2*) Moody.

Names of Herbes: A. D. 1548. Ed. & Intro. by James Britten. (English Dialect Society Publications: No. 34). 1974. reprint ed. pap. 25.00 (*0-8115-0460-3*) Periodicals Srv.

Names of Heroes of the Faith. Mark A. Tabb. (Names of Ser.). 176p. 1997. mass mkt. 4.99 (*0-8024-6180-8*, 16) Moody.

Names of History: On the Poetics of Knowledge. Jacques Ranciere. Tr. by Hassan Melehy. LC 94-7212. (ENG & FRE.). 1994. pap. 16.95 (*0-8166-2403-8*); text 42.95 (*0-8166-2401-1*) U of Minn Pr.

Names of Israel. John Koessler. LC 99-174834. 1998. mass mkt. 4.99 (*0-8024-6182-4*) Moody.

Names of Jesus. C. Mackenzie. Date not set. pap. 1.75 (*0-906731-61-5*, Pub. by Christian Focus) Spring Arbor Dist.

Names of Jesus. Albert B. Simpson. 197p. 1999. pap. text 5.99 (*0-87509-844-4*) Chr Pubns.

***Names of Jesus: An In-Depth Exploration of the Christ.** Rubel Shelly. LC 99-27900. 181p. 1999. 16.99 (*1-58229-058-X*) Howard Pub LA.

Names of Officers, Soldiers & Seamen in Rhode Island Regiments Belonging to the State of Rhode Island & Serving in the Regiments of Other States & in the Regular Army & Navy of the U. S. Who Lost Their Lives in...the Late Rebellion. (Illus.). 32p. 1997. reprint ed. pap. 6.50 (*0-8328-6469-2*) Higginson Bk Co.

Names of Our Lord. Everitt M. Fjordbak. 169p. 1976. pap. text 2.95 (*1-882449-06-1*) Messenger Pub.

Names of Persons. 4th ed. (UBCIM Publications: Vol. 16). xii, 263p. 1996. write for info. (*3-598-11342-0*) K G Saur Verlag.

Names of Persons for Whom Marriage Licenses Were Issued by the Secretary of the Province of New York, Previous to 1784. Ed. by E. B. O'Callaghan. 480p. 1997. reprint ed. lib. bdg. 49.50 (*0-8328-6089-1*) Higginson Bk Co.

Names of Places in the Transferred Sense in English: A Sematological Study. Carl J. Efveraren. 1972. 59.95 (*0-8490-0703-8*) Gordon Pr.

N

An Asterisk (*) at the beginning of an entry indicates that the title is appearing for the first time.

Names of Plants. 2nd ed. David Gledhill. (Illus.). 208p. (C). 1989. pap. text 20.95 (*0-521-36675-5*) Cambridge U Pr.

Names of Snowdonia. I. Jones. (Illus.). 1996. pap. 12.95 (*0-86243-374-6*, Pub. by Y Lolfa) Intl Spec Bk.

Names of Stoves, Ranges, & Furnaces, 1876. Compiled by National Association of Stove Manufacturers Staff. 74p. 1992. reprint ed. pap. 12.50 (*0-9612204-1-4*) Autonomy Hse.

Names of the Believers. John Koessler. (Names of Ser.). 176p. 1997. mass mkt. 4.99 (*0-8024-6179-4*, 17) Moody.

Names of the Dead. Stewart O'Nan. 416p. 1997. pap. 11.95 (*0-14-026309-8*) Viking Penguin.

Names of the Face of Montana. Roberta C. Cheney. LC 83-15401. 320p. (Orig.). 1983. pap. 12.00 (*0-87842-150-5*) Mountain Pr.

Names of the Holy Spirit. Ray Pritchard. (Names of Ser.). mass mkt. 4.99 (*0-8024-6045-3*, 401) Moody.

Names of the Lost: A Novel. Liza Wieland. LC 92-53614. 312p. 1992. 19.95 (*0-87074-337-6*) SMU Press.

Names of the Mountains. large type ed. Reeve Lindbergh. LC 93-18466. 344p. 1993. reprint ed. lib. bdg. 21.95 (*1-56054-695-6*) Thorndike Pr.

Names of the Mountains: A Novel. Reeve Lindbergh. 224p. 1992. 19.00 (*0-671-73148-3*) S&S Trade.

Names of the Rapids. Jonathan Holden. LC 85-8751. 64p. (Orig.). 1985. pap. 9.95 (*0-87023-502-8*); lib. bdg. 16.00 (*0-87023-501-X*) U of Mass Pr.

Names of the Survivors. Linda Allardt. LC 79-25878. 49p. 1979. 4.00 (*0-87886-108-4*, Greenfld Rev Pr) Greenfld Rev Lit.

Names of Things: Life Language, & Beginning in the Egyptian Desert. Susan Brind Morrow. 240p. 1998. pap. 13.00 (*1-57322-680-7*, Riverhead Books) Putnam Pub Group.

Names of Time. Mary A. Waters. LC 99-231558. 76p. 1998. 20.00 (*1-881090-29-9*) Confluence Pr.

***Names of Washington, D. C.** Dex Nilsson. LC 98-90927. (Illus.). 176p. 1999. pap. 14.95 (*0-9629170-5-2*) Twinbrook Comms.

Names of Women of the Bible. Julie-Allyson Ieron. LC 98-206636. (Names of Ser.). 176p. 1998. mass mkt. 4.99 (*0-8024-6188-3*) Moody.

Names on the Gates of Pearl: Who but God Could Do Such a Thing? C. H. Waller. 154p. 1997. reprint ed. pap. 8.95 (*1-882701-32-1*) Uplook Min.

Names on Trees: Ariosto into Art. Rensselaer W. Lee. LC 76-3270. (Princeton Essays on the Arts Ser.: No. 3). (Illus.). 125p. reprint ed. pap. 38.80 (*0-608-06422-X*, 206663500008) Bks Demand.

Name's Phelan: The First Part of the Autobiography of Jim Phelan. Jim Phelan. 298p. 1993. pap. 11.95 (*0-85640-504-3*, Pub. by Blackstaff Pr) Dufour.

Names Project. Larry D. Brimner. LC 98-49434. (Cornerstones to Freedom Ser.). 32p. (J). (gr. 4-6). 1999. 20.00 (*0-516-20999-X*) Childrens.

***Names Project.** Larry Dane Brimner. (Cornerstones to Freedom Ser.). (J). 2000. pap. text 5.95 (*0-516-26517-2*) Childrens.

Names, Reference & Correctness in Platos Cratylus. Michael D. Palmer. (American University Studies: Philosophy: Ser. 5, Vol. 55). XX, 207p. 1988. 34.40 (*0-8204-0708-9*) P Lang Pubng.

Names Still Charlie. Donna Sharp. (YA). 1993. pap. 16.95 (*0-7022-2471-5*, Pub. by Univ Queensland Pr) Intl Spec Bk.

Names, Synonyms, & Structures of Organic Compounds: A CRC Reference Handbook. David R. Lide, Jr. & G. W. Milne. 3104p. 1994. boxed set 656.95 (*0-8493-0405-9*, 405) CRC Pr.

Names That Sell: How to Create Great Names for Your Company, Product, or Service. Fred Barrett. LC 94-79374. 224p. (Orig.). 1995. pap. 14.95 (*0-9636614-7-7*) Alder Pr OR.

Names They Give Them. J. B. Faulconer. Ed. by Jim Bolus & Suzanne Bolus. LC 99-165384. 128p. 1998. 19.95 (*0-9663511-0-X*) J B Faulconer.

Names Through the Ages. Teresa Norman. (Orig.). 1999. pap. 15.00 (*0-425-16877-8*) Berkley Pub.

Names We Call Home: Autobiography on Racial Identity. Ed. by Becky Thompson & Sangeeta Tyagi. LC 95-539. (Illus.). 320p. (C). (gr. 13). 1995. pap. 23.99 (*0-415-91162-1*) Routledge.

Names We Call Home: Autobiography on Racial Identity. Ed. by Becky Thompson & Sangeeta Tyagi. LC 95-539. (Illus.). 320p. (C). (gr. 13). 1996. 75.00 (*0-415-91161-3*) Routledge.

Names We Go By. John Bennett. LC 93-70640. 208p. 1993. pap. 20.00 (*0-913204-29-3*) December Pr.

Names You Gave It: Poems. fac. ed. Wayne Dodd. LC 80-14240. 79p. 1980. reprint ed. pap. 30.00 (*0-7837-7730-2*, 204748600007) Bks Demand.

Namesake. Michael Goldberg. LC 82-50443. 212p. reprint ed. pap. 65.80 (*0-7837-5301-2*, 208027000004) Bks Demand.

Namesakes, 1956-1980. John O. Greenwood. 1981. 24.75 (*0-912514-15-9*) Freshwater.

Namesakes, 1910-1919. John O. Greenwood. Ed. by Michael J. Dills. (Illus.). 523p. 1986. 24.75 (*0-912514-31-0*) Freshwater.

Namesakes, 1930-1955. enl. rev. ed. John O. Greenwood. 1995. 24.75 (*0-912514-19-1*) Freshwater.

Namesakes, 1920-1929. John O. Greenwood. LC 84-80858. (Illus.). 376p. 1984. 23.00 (*0-912514-27-2*) Freshwater.

***Namesakes 2000.** John O. Greenwood. (Illus.). 250p. 2000. 24.00 (*0-912514-98-1*) Freshwater.

NameTags Plus: Games You Can Play When People Don't Know What to Say. Deborah Shouse. Ed. by Kelly Scanlon. LC 95-69806. (Illus.). 84p. (Orig.). 1995. pap. 12.95 (*1-57294-002-6*, 12-0019) SkillPath Pubns.

***Namfax: Comprehensive Procedures Manual for Programming Cellular Handset & Nam Programmable Phones.** 10th ed. Mark Schnur & Luke Geisler. (Illus.). 1254p. 1999. pap. 179.00 (*0-9671371-0-1*) Curtis Electro.

Namgyal Rinpoche: Unfolding Through Art. Open Path Staff. Ed. by Karma C. Wongmo. (Illus.). 157p. (Orig.). (C). 1982. text 75.00 (*0-9602722-2-4*); pap. text 25.00 (*0-685-07078-6*) Open Path.

Namib Sand Sea: Dune Forms, Processes & Sediments. Nicholas Lancaster. 192p. (C). 1989. text 110.00 (*90-6191-697-6*, Pub. by A A Balkema) Ashgate Pub Co.

Namibia. Insight Guides Staff. (Insight Guides). 1998. pap. text 22.95 (*0-88729-718-8*) Langenscheidt.

***Namibia.** New Holland Publishing Staff. (Globetrotter Travel Packs Ser.). 2000. pap. 14.95 (*1-85974-248-3*) New5 Holland.

Namibia. Bill Revilio. Ed. by Globetrotter Staff. (Globe Trotter Travel Guides Ser.). (Illus.). 128p. 1996. pap. 30.00 (*1-85368-364-7*, Pub. by New5 Holland) Globe Pequot.

Namibia. Stanley Schoeman & Elna Schoeman. (World Bibliographical Ser.: No. 53). 186p. 1985. lib. bdg. 50.00 (*0-903450-90-9*) ABC-CLIO.

Namibia see Enchantment of the World Series

***Namibia.** 2nd ed. New Holland Publishing Staff. (Globetrotter Travel Guides Ser.). 2000. pap. 10.95 (*1-85974-200-9*) New5 Holland.

Namibia. 2nd rev. ed. Stanley Schoeman & Elna Schoeman. LC 98-182751. (World Bibliographical Ser.: Vol. 53). 332p. 1997. lib. bdg. 85.00 (*1-85109-278-1*) ABC-CLIO.

***Namibia: A Country Study Guide.** Global Investment & Business Center, Inc. Staff. (World Country Study Guides Library: Vol. 120). (Illus.). 350p. 2000. pap. 59.00 (*0-7397-2418-5*) Intl Business Pubns.

Namibia: A Violation of Trust. Susanna Smith. 100p. (C). 1986. pap. text 30.00 (*0-85598-076-1*, Pub. by Oxfam Pubns) St Mut.

Namibia: Africa's Harsh Paradise. Ed. by BHB International Staff. 1997. pap. text 49.95 (*1-85368-094-X*, Pub. by New5 Holland) Sterling.

Namibia: Africa's Harsh Paradise. BHB International Staff & Robert T. Teske. 1997. pap. text 49.95 (*1-86825-381-3*, Pub. by New5 Holland) BHB Intl.

Namibia: Apartheid's Forgotten Children. Caroline Moorehead. (C). 1986. pap. text 35.00 (*0-85598-111-3*, Pub. by Oxfam Pubns) St Mut.

Namibia: Kolonialisme, Apartheid Og Frigjeringskamp i Det Serlige Afrika. Tore L. Eriksen. 251p. 1982. write for info. (*91-7106-201-7*, Pub. by Nordic Africa) Transaction Pubs.

Namibia: Photographies. Revue Noire Editions Staff. (Illus.). 1996. pap. text 19.95 (*2-909571-12-2*, Pub. by Revue Noire) Dist Art Pubs.

Namibia: Profile of Agricultural Potential. K. Davies. 1993. pap. 35.00 (*0-85954-363-3*, Pub. by Nat Res Inst) St Mut.

Namibia: The Bradt Travel Guide. Chris McIntyre. LC 98-35300. (Illus.). 300p. 1998. pap. 18.95 (*1-898323-64-X*, 862132Q, Pub. by Bradt Pubns) Globe Pequot.

Namibia: The Independent Traveler's Guide. Scott Bradshaw & Lucinda Bradshaw. (Illus.). 313p. (Orig.). 1994. pap. 16.95 (*0-7818-0254-7*) Hippocrene Bks.

Namibia: The Nation after Independence. Donald L. Sparks. 1992. 46.50 (*0-8133-1023-7*) Westview.

Namibia: The Struggle for Liberation. Alfred T. Moleah. 341p. (Orig.). 1983. 22.95 (*0-913255-00-9*); pap. 12.95 (*0-913255-01-7*) Disa Press Inc.

Namibia: Women in War. M. Wallace & T. Cleaver. LC 89-48794. (Illus.). 172p. (C). 1990. pap. 15.00 (*0-86232-901-9*, Pub. by Zed Books); text 49.95 (*0-86232-900-0*, Pub. by Zed Books) St Martin.

Namibia - A Country Study Guide: Basic Information for Research & Pleasure. Global Investment Center, USA Staff. (World Country Study Guide Library: Vol. 120). (Illus.). 350p. 1999. pap. 59.00 (*0-7397-1517-8*) Intl Business Pubns.

Namibia & External Resources: The Case of Swedish Development Assistance. Henning Melber et al. LC 95-129814. (Research Reports: Vol. 96). 122p. 1994. pap. text 16.95 (*91-7106-351-X*) Transaction Pubs.

Namibia & Southern Africa: Regional Dynamics of Decolonization, 1945-1990. Ronald Dreyer. LC 93-14190. (Publication of the Graduate Institute of International Studies, Geneva). 300p. 1994. 76.50 (*0-7103-0471-4*) Routledge.

Namibia & the Nordic Countries. Ed. by Hans-Otto Sano. 44p. 1981. write for info. (*91-7106-198-3*, Pub. by Nordic Africa) Transaction Pubs.

***Namibia Business Intelligence Report, 190 vols.** Global Investment & Business Center, Inc. Staff. (World Business Intelligence Library: Vol. 120). (Illus.). 350p. 2000. pap. 99.95 (*0-7397-2618-8*) Intl Business Pubns.

***Namibia Business Law Handbook, 190 vols.** Global Investment & Business Center, Inc. Staff. (Global Business Law Handbooks Library: Vol. 120). (Illus.). 350p. 2000. pap. 99.95 (*0-7397-2018-X*) Intl Business Pubns.

***Namibia Business Opportunity Yearbook.** Global Investment & Business Center, Inc. Staff. (Global Business Opportunity Yearbooks Library: Vol. 120). (Illus.). 2000. pap. 99.95 (*0-7397-2218-2*) Intl Business Pubns.

***Namibia Business Opportunity Yearbook: Export-Import, Investment & Business Opportunities.** International Business Publications, U. S. A. Staff & Global Investment Center, U. S. A. Staff. (Global Business Opportunity Yearbooks Library: Vol. 120). (Illus.). 350p. 1999. pap. 99.95 (*0-7397-1318-3*) Intl Business Pubns.

***Namibia Country Review 2000.** Robert C. Kelly et al. (Illus.). 60p. 1999. pap. 39.95 (*1-58310-544-1*) CountryWatch.

***Namibia Foreign Policy & Government Guide.** Contrib. by Global Investment & Business Center, Inc. Staff. (Global Inv: Vol. 116). (Illus.). 350p. 1999. pap. 99.00 (*0-7397-3614-0*) Intl Business Pubns.

***Namibia Foreign Policy & Government Guide.** Global Investment & Business Center, Inc. Staff. (World Foreign Policy & Government Library: Vol. 116). (Illus.). 350p. 2000. pap. 99.95 (*0-7397-3818-6*) Intl Business Pubns.

Namibia Globetrotter Travel Atlas. Globetrotter Staff. (Illus.). 1996. pap. text 12.95 (*1-85368-519-4*, Pub. by New5 Holland) Globe Pequot.

Namibia Handbook. Sebastian Ballard. (Illus.). 240p. 1997. 19.95 (*0-8442-4905-X*) NTC Contemp Pub Co.

***Namibia Handbook.** 2nd ed. Sebastian Ballard. LC 98-68295. (Footprint Handbooks Ser.: Vol. 2). (Illus.). 352p. 1999. pap. text 21.95 (*0-8442-2133-3*, 21333, NTC Business Bks) NTC Contemp Pub Co.

***Namibia Investment & Business Guide.** Global Investment & Business Center, Inc. Staff. (Global Investment & Business Guide Library: Vol. 120). (Illus.). 2000. pap. 99.95 (*0-7397-1818-5*) Intl Business Pubns.

***Namibia Investment & Business Guide: Export-Import, Investment & Business Opportunities.** International Business Publications, USA Staff & Global Investment Center, USA Staff. (World Investment & Business Guide Library-99: Vol. 120). (Illus.). 350p. 1999. pap. 99.95 (*0-7397-0315-3*) Intl Business Pubns.

Namibia, the Broken Shield: Anatomy of Imperialism & Revolution. Kaire Mbuende. 213p. (Orig.). 1986. 19.95 (*91-40-05156-0*, Pub. by Nordic Africa) Transaction Pubs.

Namibia, the Last Colony. Ed. by Reginald H. Green et al. LC 80-40465. 320p. reprint ed. pap. 99.20 (*0-608-13196-2*, 202524900043) Bks Demand.

Namibia under German Rule: Studies on African History. Helmut Bley. 352p. 1997. pap. text 22.95 (*3-89473-225-3*) Transaction Pubs.

Namibia under South African Rule: Mobility & Containment, 1915-1946. Ed. by Patricia Hayes et al. LC 98-11463. 321p. 1998. text 44.95 (*0-8214-1244-2*); pap. text 22.95 (*0-8214-1245-0*) Ohio U Pr.

Namibian Herero: A History of Their Psychosocial Disintegration & Survival. Karla O. Poewe. LC 85-2991. (African Studies: Vol. 1). (Illus.). 364p. 1985. lib. bdg. 99.95 (*0-88946-176-7*) E Mellen.

Namibia's Liberation Struggle: The Two-Edged Sword. Colin T. Leys & John S. Saul. LC 94-8024. (Eastern African Studies). (Illus.). 224p. (C). 1994. text 44.95 (*0-8214-1103-9*); pap. text 19.95 (*0-8214-1104-7*) Ohio U Pr.

Namibia's Post-Apartheid Regional Institutions Vol. 4: The Founding Year, 1993. Joshua B. Forrest. LC 98-42485. (Rochester Studies in African History & the Diaspora: Vol. 1092-5228). 384p. 1998. 75.00 (*1-58046-028-3*) Univ Rochester Pr.

***Naming: Choosing a Meaningful Name.** Caroline Sherwood. (Illus.). 288p. 1999. pap. text 14.99 (*1-869890-56-6*, Pub. by Hawthorn Press) Anthroposophic.

Naming & Believing. G. W. Fitch. 228p. 1986. text 107.50 (*90-277-2349-4*, D Reidel) Kluwer Academic.

Naming & Identity: A Cross-Cultural Study of Personal Naming Practices. Richard D. Alford. LC 86-80925. (Comparative Studies). 190p. 1988. pap. 20.00 (*0-87536-117-X*) HRAFP.

Naming & Necessity. Saul A. Kripke. 172p. 1980. pap. 17.50 (*0-674-59846-6*) HUP.

Naming & Necessity. Saul A. Kripke. 172p. 1980. 27.00 (*0-674-59845-8*) HUP.

Naming & Reference. R. J. Nelson. LC 91-45969. (Problems of Philosophy Series: Their Past & Present). (Illus.). 304p. (C). (gr. 13). 1992. 80.00 (*0-415-00939-1*, A1619) Routledge.

Naming & Referring: The Semantics & Pragmatics of Singular Terms. David Schwarz. (Foundations of Communication & Cognition Ser.). 194p. (C). 1979. text 65.40 (*3-11-007610-1*) De Gruyter.

Naming & Structuring Guidelines for X.500 Directory Pilots. Paul Barker et al. 26p. (Orig.). (C). 1995. pap. text 15.00 (*0-7881-1953-2*) DIANE Pub.

Naming & Unnaming: On Raymond Queneau. Jordan Stump. LC 98-5632. (Stages Ser.). vii, 192p. 1998. text 40.00 (*0-8032-4268-9*) U of Nebr Pr.

Naming Canada: Stories about Place Names from Canadian Geographic. Alan Rayburn. (Illus.). 300p. 1994. pap. 16.95 (*0-8020-6990-8*); text 55.00 (*0-8020-0569-1*) U of Toronto Pr.

Naming Gem Garnets. W. W. Hanneman. (Illus.). 1999. pap. 15.00 (*0-9669063-1-4*) Hanneman Gem.

Naming God. Ed. by Robert P. Scharlemann. LC 85-9327. (Contemporary Discussion Ser.). 188p. (Orig.). (C). 1986. 22.95 (*0-913757-22-5*) Paragon Hse.

Naming God. Ed. by Robert P. Scharlemann. LC 85-9327. (Contemporary Discussion Ser.). 188p. (Orig.). (C). 1986. pap. 12.95 (*0-913757-23-3*) Paragon Hse.

Naming Grace: Preaching & the Sacramental Imagination. Mary C. Hilkert. LC 72-79934. 256p. (C). 1997. pap. 19.95 (*0-8264-1060-X*) Continuum.

Naming in Paradise: Milton & the Language of Adam & Eve. John Leonard. 318p. (C). 1990. 75.00 (*0-19-812958-0*) OUP.

Naming Inorganic Compounds. Marcia L. Gillette & H. Anthony Neidig. (Modular Laboratory Program in Chemistry Ser.). 8p. (C). 1995. pap. text 1.50 (*0-87540-459-6*, MISC 459-6) Chem Educ Res.

Naming Jesus: Titular Christology in the Gospel of Mark. Edwin K. Broadhead. (JSNTS Ser.: Vol. 175). 193p. 1999. 57.50 (*1-85075-929-4*, Pub. by Sheffield Acad) CUP Services.

Naming New World. Calvin Baker. 128p. 1998. pap. 9.95 (*0-312-18140-X*) St Martin.

***Naming New York: Manhattan Places & How They Got Their Names.** Sanna Feirstein. (Illus.). 2001. 45.00 (*0-8147-2711-5*); pap. 16.95 (*0-8147-2712-3*) NYU Pr.

Naming of Animals: An Appellative Reference to Domestic, Work & Show Animals Real & Fictional. Adrian Room. LC 92-56684. 244p. 1993. lib. bdg. 42.50 (*0-89950-795-6*) McFarland & Co.

Naming of Femi's Brother. Kiser D. Barnes. (Illus.). 32p. 1987. pap. 4.95 (*0-85398-232-5*) G Ronald Pub.

Naming of Parts: An Analytical Study of Henry Reed. James S. Beggs. 190p. 1998. pap. 19.95 (*0-85958-671-5*, Pub. by Univ of Hull Pr) Paul & Co Pubs.

Naming of the Soul. Margaret Stetler. (Illus.). 16p. 1980. pap. 3.00 (*0-939622-05-X*) Four Zoas Night Ltd.

Naming Organic Compounds: A Systematic Instruction Manual. 2nd ed. Edward W. Godly. LC 94-27486. (Ellis Horwood Series in Chemical Information Science). 280p. (C). 1995. 100.00 (*0-13-103623-8*) P-H.

Naming Our Ancestors: An Anthology of Hominid Taxonomy. W. Eric Meikle & Sue T. Parker. (Illus.). 254p. (C). 1994. pap. text 15.95 (*0-88133-799-4*) Waveland Pr.

Naming Our Destiny: New & Selected Poems. June Jordan. (Poetry Ser.). 224p. 1989. pap. 12.95 (*0-938410-84-9*, Thunders Mouth) Avalon NY.

Naming Our Truth: Stories of the Sisters of Loretto. Ed. by Ann P. Ware. (Illus.). 289p. (Orig.). 1995. pap. 14.50 (*0-9620222-4-1*) Chardon Pr.

Naming Properties: Nominal Reference in Travel Writings by Basho & Sora, Johnson & Boswell. Earl R. Miner. LC 96-8830. 344p. (C). 1996. text 49.50 (*0-472-10699-6*, 10699) U of Mich Pr.

Naming Silenced Lives: Personal Narratives & the Process of Educational Change. Ed. by Daniel McLaughlin & William G. Tierney. LC 93-20361. 224p. (C). 1993. pap. 19.99 (*0-415-90517-6*, A6581) Routledge.

Naming the Antichrist: The History of an American Obsession. Robert C. Fuller. 240p. 1995. 35.00 (*0-19-508244-3*) OUP.

Naming the Antichrist: The History of an American Obsession. Robert C. Fuller. 240p. 1996. reprint ed. pap. 11.95 (*0-19-510979-1*) OUP.

Naming the Cat. Laurence P. Pringle. LC 97-443. (Illus.). 32p. (J). (ps-3). 1997. lib. bdg. 16.85 (*0-8027-8622-7*) Walker & Co.

Naming the Cat. Laurence P. Pringle. LC 97-443. (Illus.). 32p. (J). (gr. k-3). 1999. 15.95 (*0-8027-8621-9*) Walker & Co.

***Naming the Cat.** Laurence Pringle. (Illus.). 32p. (J). (gr. k-3). 1999. reprint ed. pap. 6.95 (*0-8027-7565-9*) Walker & Co.

Naming the Darkness. Jane E. Glasser. Ed. by Joseph D. Adams. LC 91-61039. (Illus.). xii, 68p. (Orig.). 1991. pap. 9.95 (*1-880016-05-2*) Road Pubs.

Naming the Eastern Sierra. Marguerite Sowaal. LC 85-19502. (Illus.). 125p. (C). 1986. pap. 11.75 (*0-912494-38-7*) Commun Print.

***Naming the Enemy: Anti-corporate Social Movements Confront Glob.** Amory Starr. 2000. pap. 27.50 (*1-85649-765-8*, Pub. by Zed Books); text 69.95 (*1-85649-764-X*, Pub. by Zed Books) St Martin.

***Naming the Father: Legacies, Genealogies & Explorations of Fatherhood in Modern & Contemporary Literature.** Ed. by Eva P. Bueno et al. LC 99-48890. 352p. 2000. 75.00 (*0-7391-0091-2*); pap. 25.95 (*0-7391-0092-0*) Lxngtn Bks.

***Naming the Hills & Hollows of Broome County.** Carol LeVan Thomas. LC 99-76096. (Illus.). 128p. 1999. pap. 12.95 (*0-9675799-0-2*) C LeVan Thomas.

Naming the Island. Judith Neeld. 64p. (Orig.). 1988. pap. 5.95 (*0-939395-08-8*) Thorntree Pr.

Naming the Jungle. Antoine Volodine. Tr. by Linda Coverdale from FRE. (International Fiction Ser.). 167p. 1996. 18.95 (*1-56584-274-X*, Pub. by New Press NY) Norton.

Naming the Light: Familiar Essays, a Week of Years. Rosemary Deen. LC 96-4529. (Creative Nonfiction Ser.). (Illus.). 168p. 1996. 14.95 (*0-252-06572-7*) U of Ill Pr.

Naming the Mind: How Psychology Found Its Language. Kurt Danziger. 224p. 1997. 45.00 (*0-8039-7762-X*); pap. 14.99 (*0-8039-7763-8*) Sage.

Naming the Moons. limited large type ed. Colette Inez. Ed. by John Wheatcroft. (Bucknell University Fine Editions: Series in Contemporary Poetry). (Illus.). 60p. 1994. pap. 150.00 (*0-916375-18-8*) Press Alley.

Naming the Multiple: Poststructuralism & Education. Michael Peters. LC 97-22754. (Critical Studies in Education & Culture). 1998. pap. write for info. (*0-08-989549-5*, Bergin & Garvey) Greenwood.

Naming the Multiple: Poststructuralism & Education. Ed. by Michael Peters. LC 97-22754. (Critical Studies in Education & Culture Ser.). 288p. 1998. 69.50 (*0-89789-485-5*, Bergin & Garvey); pap. 22.95 (*0-89789-549-5*, Bergin & Garvey) Greenwood.

Naming the New World. Calvin Baker. LC 96-29347. 128p. 1997. text 18.95 (*0-312-15178-0*) St Martin.

Naming the Organic Compounds PB. 2nd ed. James E. Banks. LC 75-291. (C). 1976. pap. text 34.50 (*0-7216-1536-8*, W B Saunders Co) Harcrt Hlth Sci Grp.

Naming the Other: Images of the Maori in New Zealand Film & Television. Martin Blythe. LC 94-495. (Illus.). 342p. 1994. 45.00 (*0-8108-2741-7*) Scarecrow.

Naming the Powers: The Language of Power in the New Testament. Walter Wink. LC 83-48905. (Power Ser.: Vol. 1). 198p. 1984. pap. 18.00 (*0-8006-1786-X*, 1-1786, Fortress Pr) Augsburg Fortress.

Naming the Rainbow: Colour Language, Colour Science, & Culture. Don Dedrick. LC 98-30408. (Synthese Library). 215p. 1998. 97.00 (*0-7923-5239-4*) Kluwer Academic.

Naming the Shadows: A New Approach to Individual & Group Psychotherapy for Adult Survivors of Childhood Incest. Susan Roth & Ronald Batson. LC 97-1617. 1997. 29.95 (*0-684-83704-8*) Free Pr.

***Naming the Unnameable.** Jennifer Taylor. 112p. 2000. spiral bd. 14.95 (*0-9679887-0-5*) Embug.

Naming the Unnamed: Interdisciplinary Discussion of Freud's Female Homosexual. Ed. by Ronnie Lesser & Erica Schoenberg. LC 98-41836. 288p. (C). (gr. 13). 1999. 65.00 (*0-415-91670-4*) Routledge.

Naming Your Baby. Patrick Hanks & Flavia Hodges. LC 93-28730. (Oxford Minireference Ser.). 366p. 1995. pap. 2.99 (*0-19-211647-9*) OUP.

Naming Your Boat. Joe Kilgore. 116p. 1997. pap. text 8.95 (*1-884778-22-4*) Old Mountain.

Naming Your Business & Its Products & Services: How to Create Effective Trade Names, Trademarks, & Service Marks to Attract Customers, Protect Your Good Will & Reputation, & Stay Out of Court. Phillip Williams. LC 90-3434. (Small Business Bookshelf Ser.: Vol. 2). 96p. (Orig.). 1991. pap. 19.95 (*0-936284-10-2*) P Gaines Co.

Naming Your Child Prophetically: A Dictionary of South African Names. Vuyo Matanda & Gcotyelwa Matanda. (Illus.). 128p. 1998. mass mkt. 15.95 (*0-9664988-0-1*) Herald Commn.

NAMJAM Pt. 1: Orpheophrenia. 59p. (Orig.). 1996. pap. 5.00 (*0-917455-27-4*) Big Foot NY.

Nampally Road. Meena Alexander. LC 90-5849. 128p. 1991. 15.95 (*0-916515-82-6*); pap. 9.95 (*0-916515-90-7*) Mercury Hse Inc.

Nampeyo & Her Pottery. Barbara Kramer. LC 96-3950. (Illus.). 224p. 1996. 39.95 (*0-8263-1718-9*) U of NM Pr.

Namt: National Advanced Manufacturing Testbed, Toward 21st Century Information-Based Manufacturing. M. A. Bello. 24p. 1997. pap. 2.50 (*0-16-054726-1*) USGPO.

Namu see Books for Young Explorers

Namu: Quest for the Killer Whale. Ted Griffin. 1982. 14.95 (*0-943482-00-3*) Gryphon West Pubs.

Nan: The Life of an Irish Travelling Woman. rev. ed. Sharon Gmelch. (Illus.). 239p. (C). 1991. reprint ed. pap. text 12.50 (*0-88133-602-5*) Waveland Pr.

Nan & the Man. Alan M. Hofmeister et al. (Reading for All Learners Ser.). (Illus.). (J). pap. write for info. (*1-56861-086-6*) Swift Lrn Res.

Nan-Ching - The Classic of Difficult Ideas. Paul U. Unschuld. LC 84-28049. (Comparative Studies of Health Systems & Medical Care: Vol. 18). 700p. 1986. 95.00 (*0-520-05372-9*, Pub. by U CA Pr) Cal Prin Full Svc.

Nan Chronicle. Ed. & Tr. by David K. Wyatt from THA. (Studies on Southeast Asia: No. 16). (Illus.). 158p. (Orig.). (C). 1994. pap. text 14.00 (*0-87727-715-X*) Cornell SE Asia.

Nan Goldin. Elisabeth Sussman. LC 96-17659. 1996. write for info. (*0-87427-102-9*) Whitney Mus.

Nan Goldin: The Other Side. Nan Goldin. (Illus.). 144p. 1993. 39.95 (*1-881616-03-7*, Pub. by Scalo Pubs) Dist Art Pubs.

Nan-Mei-Su Girls of Emerald Hill Sin Tub Goh. LC 90-940655. (Research Monograph). 183 p. 1989. write for info. (*9971-64-199-2*) Miscell Pubs.

***Nan of Music Mountain.** Frank H. Spearman. (Illus.). 2000. pap. 19.95 (*1-889439-09-6*) Paper Tiger NJ.

Nan of Music Mountain. unabridged ed. Frank H. Spearman. (Illus.). 430p. 1996. reprint ed. 34.95 (*1-889439-03-7*) Paper Tiger NJ.

Nan Pyle: Payson's Unhappy Millionaire. Gordon A. Sabine. 144p. (Orig.). 1993. lib. bdg. write for info. (*1-879286-06-8*) AZ Bd Regents.

Nan Shan. Mark Dunster. 1977. pap. 4.00 (*0-89642-007-8*) Linden Pubs.

Nan Sits. Alan M. Hofmeister et al. (Reading for All Learners Ser.). (Illus.). (J). pap. write for info. (*1-56861-092-0*) Swift Lrn Res.

Nana. Emile Zola. Ed. by Henri Mitterand. 500p. 1977. write for info. (*0-318-63492-9*) Fr & Eur.

Nana. Emile Zola. (Coll. Diamant). (FRE.). 442p. 1982. pap. 10.95 (*0-7859-1423-4*, 2080701940) Fr & Eur.

Nana. Emile Zola. Tr. & Intro. by Douglas Parmee. (Oxford World's Classics Ser.). 462p. 1999. pap. 6.95 (*0-19-283670-6*) OUP.

Nana. Emile Zola. Ed. by Henri Mitterand. (Folio Ser.: No. 956). (FRE.). 500p. 1977. pap. 9.95 (*2-07-036956-0*) Schoenhof.

Nana. Emile Zola. Tr. by George Holden. (Classics Ser.). 470p. 1972. pap. 7.95 (*0-14-044263-4*, Penguin Classics) Viking Penguin.

Nana. unabridged ed. Emile Zola. (FRE.). pap. 7.95 (*2-87714-158-6*, Pub. by Bookking Intl) Distribks Inc.

Nana Gets a Cat. Joan B. Barsotti. (Apple Hill Ser.: No. 2). (Illus.). 24p. (Orig.). (J). (ps-2). 1994. pap. 5.99 (*0-9642112-1-1*) Barsotti Bks.

Nana, Grampa & Tecumseh. Richard M. Wainwright. LC 97-5. (Illus.). 64p. (J). 1997. 19.00 (*0-9619566-7-4*) Family Life.

Nana Hannah's Piano. Barbara Bottner. LC 94-39159. (Illus.). 32p. (J). (ps-3). 1996. 15.95 (*0-399-22656-7*, G P Putnam) Peng Put Young Read.

Nana I Ke Kumu, Vol. 1. Mary K. Pukui et al. LC 72-93779. 1972. pap. 12.00 (*0-9616738-0-X*) Hui Hanai.

Nana I Ke Kumu, Vol. 2. Mary K. Pukui et al. LC 72-93779. 1979. pap. 12.00 (*0-9616738-2-6*) Hui Hanai.

Nana Rescue. Joan Buchanan. LC 93-20803. (Illus.). (J). 1994. 4.25 (*0-383-03740-9*) SRA McGraw.

Nana Says. Nana Y. Dinizulu. 73p. (Orig.). 1987. pap. 10.00 (*0-685-54579-2*) Aims Modzawe.

Nana Upstairs & Nana Downstairs see Abuelita de Arriba y la Abuelita de Abajo

Nana Upstairs & Nana Downstairs. Tomie De Paola. LC 77-26698. (Illus.). 32p. (J). (ps-3). 1987. 14.95 (*0-399-21417-8*, G P Putnam) Peng Put Young Read.

Nana Upstairs & Nana Downstairs. Tomie De Paola. LC 96-31908. (Illus.). 32p. (J). (ps-3). 1998. 15.99 (*0-399-23108-0*, G P Putnam) Peng Put Young Read.

***Nana Upstairs & Nana Downstairs.** Tomie De Paola. (Illus.). 32p. (J). (ps-3). 2000. pap. 5.99 (*0-698-11836-7*, PuffinBks) Peng Put Young Read.

Nana Upstairs & Nana Downstairs. Tomie De Paola. (J). 1973. 10.19 (*0-606-02202-3*, Pub. by Turtleback) Demco.

Nana, Will You Write Me from Heaven? Nancy Bestmann. LC 98-227224. 1998. 12.99 (*0-89900-816-X*) College Pr Pub.

Nanaisk-Russian Dictionary. S. N. Onenko. (RUS.). 1980. 24.95 (*0-8288-1627-1*, F47740) Fr & Eur.

Nanas & the Papas: A Boomer's Guide to Grandparenting. Kathryn Zullo & Allan Zullo. LC 98-24174. x, 209 p. 1998. pap. 10.95 (*0-8362-6787-7*) Andrews & McMeel.

Nana's Birthday Party. Amy Hest. LC 92-10260. (Illus.). 32p. (J). (gr. k up). 1993. 15.95 (*0-688-07497-9*, Wm Morrow) Morrow Avon.

Nana's Garden. large type ed. Mackie. (Illus.). 72p. (Orig.). 1997. pap. 18.95 (*0-922705-92-5*) Quilt Day.

Nana's Gift: Some Things in This World Are Very Expensive, but Others Are Priceless. Janette Oke. LC 96-25352. 144p. 1996. text 12.99 (*1-55661-898-0*) Bethany Hse.

Nana's Gift: Some Things in This World Are Very Expensive, but Others Are Priceless. large type ed. Janette Oke. LC 96-45045. (Inspirational Ser.). 1997. lib. bdg. 23.95 (*0-7838-2019-4*, G K Hall Lrg Type) Mac Lib Ref.

Nana's Hog. Larry D. Brimner. LC 97-40045. (Rookie Readers Ser.). (Illus.). (J). 1998. 17.00 (*0-516-20755-5*) Childrens.

Nana's Hog. Larry Dane Brimner. (Rookie Readers Ser.). (Illus.). 32p. (YA). (gr. k-3). 1999. pap. text 4.95 (*0-516-26412-5*) Childrens.

Nana's New Home: A Comforting Story Explaining Alzheimer's Disease to Children. Kristi Cargill. Ed. by Gwen C. Smith. (Illus.). 32p. (J). (ps-6). 1997. pap. text 11.99 (*0-9660566-0-4*) KrisPer.

Nana's Orchard. large type ed. Carol Gould. (Illus.). 12p. (Orig.). (J). (gr. k-2). 1996. text 4.95 (*1-879835-75-4*) Kaeden Corp.

Nana's Rice Pie. Laurie L. Knowlton. LC 96-35356. (Illus.). 32p. (J). (ps-3). Date not set. 14.95 (*1-56554-234-7*) Pelican.

Nana's Rocking Chair. Thomas. (J). 1995. 15.95 (*0-8050-2265-1*) H Holt & Co.

Nana's Trunk Paperdolls. Norma L. Meehan. (Illus.). 24p. 1995. pap. text 4.95 (*0-87588-438-5*) Hobby Hse.

Nanaue the Shark Man & Other Hawaiian Shark Stories. Emma M. Nakuina. Ed. by Dennis Kawaharada. LC 93-83814. 96p. (Orig.). 1994. pap. 7.95 (*0-9623102-4-7*) Kalamaku Pr.

Nance Museum - A Journey into Traditional Saudi Arabia. Paul J. Nance. Ed. by Ismail I. Nawwab & Robert N. Norberg. (Illus.). 208p. 1999. 39.95 (*0-9671454-5-7*) Nance Mus.

Nanci Griffith: Flyer. Ed. by Jeannette DeLisa. 96p. (Orig.). (YA). 1994. pap. text 16.95 (*0-89724-462-1*, P1086GTX) Wrner Bros.

Nanci Griffith's Other Voices: A Personal History of Folk Music. Nanci Griffith. LC 98-19589. (Illus.). 272p. 1998. pap. 19.95 (*0-609-80307-7*, Crown) Crown Pub Group.

Nancy. Karen Barbour. (Illus.). 30p. (J). (ps-3). 1989. 13.95 (*0-15-256675-9*) Harcourt.

Nancy & Plum. Betty MacDonald. 1993. reprint ed. lib. bdg. 31.95 (*1-56849-017-8*) Buccaneer Bks.

Nancy & Plum. Betty MacDonald. (Illus.). 190p. (YA). (gr. 5 up). 1997. reprint ed. pap. 9.95 (*0-944309-00-3*) J Keil Enterp.

Nancy Ann Storybook Dolls. Marjorie Miller. (Illus.). 232p. 1998. reprint ed. 29.95 (*0-87588-156-4*, 1624) Hobby Hse.

Nancy Astor. large type ed. Derek Marlowe. LC 83-26339. 461 P. ;p. 1984. pap. write for info. (*0-89340-773-9*) Chivers N Amer.

Nancy Astor, Portrait of a Pioneer. John Grigg. LC 83-208728. 192p. 1980. write for info. (*0-283-98631-X*) Sl & J.

Nancy Astor, the Lady from Virginia: A Novel. Derek Marlowe. LC 84-139731. viii, 246 p. 1982. 6.95 (*0-297-77866-8*) Weidenfeld & Nicolson.

Nancy Astor's Canadian Correspondence, 1912-1962. Ed. by Martin Thornton. LC 97-39649. (Illus.). 512p. 1997. text 119.95 (*0-7734-8452-3*) E Mellen.

Nancy Azara: Sacred Dwellings: The Work of Nancy Azara. Flavia Bando & Arlene Raven. (Illus.). 32p. (Orig.). 1994. pap. 10.00 (*1-889523-09-7*) Tweed Mus.

Nancy Blackett: Under Sail with Arthur Ransome. Wardale. 19.95 (*0-224-03754-4*, Pub. by Jonathan Cape) Trafalgar.

Nancy Burson: The Age Machine & Composite Portraits. Dana Friis-Hansen. (Illus.). 12p. (Orig.). 1990. pap. 2.50 (*0-938437-31-3*) MIT List Visual Arts.

Nancy City Plan. (Grafocarte Maps Ser.). 1993. 8.95 (*2-7416-0027-9*, 80027) Michelin.

Nancy Clark's Sports Nutrition Guidebook. 2nd ed. Nancy Clark. LC 96-11313. (Illus.). 464p. (Orig.). 1996. pap. 16.95 (*0-87322-730-1*, PCLA0730) Human Kinetics.

Nancy Crow: Improvisational Quilts. Nancy Crow. (Illus.). 96p. 1995. pap. 18.95 (*1-57120-004-5*, 10126) C & T Pub.

Nancy Crow: Work in Transition. Intro. by Penny McMorris. LC 92-12986. 32p. 1992. pap. 12.95 (*0-89145-995-2*, 3331, Am Quilters Soc) Collector Bks.

Nancy Crow Quilts & Influences. Nancy Crow. 1989. 29.95 (*0-89145-944-8*, 1981, Am Quilters Soc) Collector Bks.

***Nancy Davidson: Breathless.** Judith Tannenbaum. (Illus.). 32p. 1999. pap. 15.00 (*0-88454-093-6*) U of Pa Contemp Art.

Nancy Drew & Company. Ed. by Sherrie A. Inness. LC 96-37500. (Culture, Gender & Girls' Ser.). 193p. 1997. pap. 18.95 (*0-87972-736-5*) Bowling Green Univ Popular Press.

Nancy Drew & Company: Culture, Gender, & Girls' Series. Ed. by Sherrie A. Inness. LC 96-37500. (Culture, Gender & Girls' Ser.). 150p. 1997. 41.95 (*0-87972-735-7*) Bowling Green Univ Popular Press.

Nancy Drew & Hardy Boys. Mitchell. (YA). 1996. 23.95 (*0-8057-8822-0*, Twyne); pap. 13.95 (*0-8057-8823-9*, Twyne) Mac Lib Ref.

Nancy Drew & the Hardy Boys Super Sleuths 2: Seven New Mysteries. Carolyn Keene & Franklin W. Dixon. Ed. by Wendy Barish. (Illus.). 192p. (J). (gr. 3 up). 1984. pap. 2.95 (*0-685-09176-7*) S&S Trade.

Nancy Drew Back to Back Mystery Stories: The Secret of the Old Clock; The Hidden Staircase. Carolyn Keene. (Nancy Drew Mystery Stories Ser.: Nos. 1-2). (Illus.). 360p. (J). (gr. 4-7). 1987. 7.99 (*0-448-09570-X*, G & D) Peng Put Young Read.

Nancy Drew Digest. Carolyn Keene. (J). 1987. boxed set 14.00 (*0-671-91515-0*, Minstrel Bks) PB.

Nancy Drew Digest, 4 vols. Carolyn Keene. (J). 1989. boxed set 14.00 (*0-671-92235-1*) PB.

Nancy Drew Files Boxed Set: Trouble in Tahiti; High Marks for Malice; Danger in Disguise; Vanishing Act; Over the Edge. Carolyn Keene. (Nancy Drew Files: Nos. 31, 32, 33, 34, 36). (YA). (gr. 6 up). 1991. pap., boxed set 17.50 (*0-671-96785-1*) PB.

Nancy Drew Files Collectors Edition: Danger for Hire; Make no Mistake; Poison Pen. Carolyn Keene. (Nancy Drew Files: Nos. 52, 56, 60). (YA). (gr. 6 up). 1998. 4.99 (*0-671-01930-9*, Pocket Books) PB.

Nancy Drew Files Collector's Edition: The Wrong Chemistry; Out of Bounds; Flirting with Danger. Carolyn Keene. (Nancy Drew Files: Nos. 42, 45, 47). (YA). (gr. 6 up). 1998. per. 4.99 (*0-671-01929-5*) PB.

Nancy Drew Files Collector's Edition: The Wrong Track; Nobody's Business; Running Scared. Carolyn Keene. (Nancy Drew Files: Nos. 64, 67, 69). (YA). (gr. 6 up). 1998. 4.99 (*0-671-01931-7*, Archway) PB.

Nancy Drew Files Gift Set: Secrets Can Kill; Heart of Danger; Never Say Die; Circle of Evil; Sisters in Crime. Carolyn Keene. (Nancy Drew Files: Nos. 1, 11, 16, 18, 19). (YA). (gr. 6 up). 1989. pap., boxed set 14.75 (*0-671-92236-X*) PB.

Nancy Drew Ghost Stories. Carolyn Keene. Ed. by Ann Greenberg. (Nancy Drew Mystery Stories Ser.). 160p. (J). (gr. 3-6). 1909. pap. 3.99 (*0-671-69132-5*, Minstrel Bks) PB.

Nancy Drew Ghost Stories. Carolyn Keene. (Nancy Drew Mystery Stories Ser.). (J). (gr. 3-6). 1988. mass mkt. 3.50 (*0-671-67863-9*, Pocket Books) PB.

Nancy Drew Ghost Stories. Carolyn Keene. (Nancy Drew Mystery Stories Ser.). (J). (gr. 3-6). 1983. 9.09 (*0-606-02097-7*, Pub. by Turtleback) Demco.

Nancy Drew Gift Set, 3 vols., Set. Carolyn Keene. (J). boxed set 8.55 (*0-317-12425-0*) S&S Trade.

***Nancy Drew Mystery Stories: The Secret of the Old Clock; The Hidden Staircase; The Bungalow Mystery.** Carolyn Keene. LC 99-20940. (Nancy Drew Mystery Stories Ser.: Nos. 1-3). (Illus.). 560p. (J). (gr. 4-7). 1999. 9.98 (*0-7651-1728-2*) Smithmark.

Nancy Drew Mystery Stories Boxed Set: The Nutcracker Ballet Mystery; Crime in the Queen's Court; The Baby-Sitter Burglaries. Carolyn Keene. (Nancy Drew Mystery Stories Ser.: Nos. 110, 112, 129). (J). (gr. 3-6). 1997. pap., boxed set 15.96 (*0-671-87831-X*, Minstrel Bks) PB.

Nancy Drew Mystery Stories Boxed Set # 1: The Secret of the Old Clock; The Hidden Staircase; The Bungalow Mystery; The Mystery at Lilac Inn; The Secret of Shadow Ranch; The Secret of Red Gate Farm. Carolyn Keene. (Nancy Drew Mystery Stories Ser.: Nos. 1-6). (J). (gr. 3-6). 1997. boxed set 19.98 (*0-448-41674-3*, G & D) Peng Put Young Read.

Nancy Enright's Canadian Herb Cookbook. Nancy Enright. 146p. spiral bd. 12.95 (*0-88862-788-2*, Pub. by J Lorimer) Formac Dist Ltd.

Nancy Graves. Ed. by David Bourdon. LC 91-60299. (Illus.). 32p. (Orig.). 1991. pap. 20.00 (*1-879173-00-X*) Locks Gallery.

Nancy Graves: A Survey 1969 to 1980. Linda L. Cathcart. LC 80-13227. (Illus.). 1980. pap. 15.00 (*0-914782-34-7*) Buffalo Fine-Albrght-Knox.

Nancy Graves: Excavations in Print: a Catalogue Raisonne. Thomas Padon. LC 95-23940. (Illus.). 208p. 1996. 49.50 (*0-8109-3391-8*, Pub. by Abrams) Time Warner.

Nancy Graves: In Memoriam. Kay Larson. (Illus.). 31p. (Orig.). 1996. pap. 20.00 (*1-879173-27-1*) Locks Gallery.

Nancy Graves: Recent Works. E. A. Carmean, Jr. & Robert C. Morgan. 40p. 1993. pap. 15.00 (*0-9624565-3-5*) Univ MD Fine Arts.

Nancy Grossman, Ariane Lopez-Huici, Aura Rosenberg, Carolee Schneemann, Joan Semmel. Robert C. Morgan. (Illus.). 7p. 1989. pap. 2.00 (*0-9624615-6-3*) Nahan Editions.

Nancy Hanks: An Intimate Portrait: The Creation of a National Commitment to the Arts. Michael Straight. LC 88-16956. (Illus.). xiii, 400p. 1988. text 32.95 (*0-8223-0869-X*) Duke.

Nancy Hanks of Wilderness Road: A Story of Abraham Lincoln's Mother. Meridel Le Sueur. 80p. (J). 1997. pap. text 7.95 (*0-930100-73-5*) Holy Cow.

Nancy Kerrigan. Paula Edelson. LC 98-29475. (Female Figure Skating Legends Ser.). (Illus.). 64p. (YA). (gr. 3 up). 1999. lib. bdg. 16.95 (*0-7910-5028-9*) Chelsea Hse.

Nancy Kerrigan. Bob Italia. Ed. by Rosemary Wallner. LC 94-23382. (Illus.). 32p. (J). 1994. lib. bdg. 13.98 (*1-56239-339-1*) ABDO Pub Co.

Nancy Kerrigan: In My Own Words. Nancy Kerrigan. 1996. 9.70 (*0-606-08831-8*, Pub. by Turtleback) Demco.

Nancy Kerrigan: In My Own Words. Nancy Kerrigan & Steve Woodward. LC 95-81906. 80p. (J). (gr. 3-7). 1996. pap. 4.50 (*0-7868-1042-4*, Pub. by Hyprn Ppbks) Little.

Nancy Kerrigan: The Courageous Skater. Jim Spence. LC 95-5362. (Great Comeback Champions Ser.). (Illus.). (J). (gr. 2-6). 1995. 18.60 (*1-57103-008-5*) Rourke Pr.

Nancy Lancaster: Her Life, Her World, Her Art. Robert Becker. LC 95-34170. (Illus.). 416p. 1996. 50.00 (*0-394-56791-9*) Knopf.

Nancy Landon Kassebaum: A Senate Profile. Nancy C. Myers. LC 97-47240. (Contemporary Profiles & Policy Series for the Younger Reader). 70p. (YA). (gr. 8 up). 1998. 20.00 (*0-934272-47-6*); pap. 12.95 (*0-934272-46-8*) J G Burke Pub.

Nancy Lopez's the Complete Golfer. Nancy Lopez & Don Wade. (Illus.). 240p. 1989. reprint ed. pap. 15.95 (*0-8092-4711-9*, 471190, Contemporary Bks) NTC Contemp Pub Co.

Nancy R. Reagan. Jill C. Wheeler & Judith A. Stone. LC 91-73027. (Leading Ladies Ser.). 202p. (J). 1991. lib. bdg. 13.98 (*1-56239-080-5*) ABDO Pub Co.

Nancy Reagan. Kitty Kelley. Ed. by Julie Rubenstein. 720p. 1992. reprint ed. mass mkt. 5.99 (*0-671-64647-8*) PB.

Nancy Reagan: The Unauthorized Biography, Vol. 6. large type ed. Kitty Kelley. (General Ser.). 816p. 1992. pap. 18.95 (*0-8161-5336-1*, G K Hall Lrg Type) Mac Lib Ref.

Nancy Reagan Fashion Paper Dolls. Tom Tierney. (Illus.). 1983. pap. 3.95 (*0-486-24474-1*) Dover.

Nancy Rubins. Kathryn Kanjo & Lisa Liebman. (Illus.). 64p. (Orig.). 1996. pap. text 19.95 (*0-934418-45-4*) Mus Contemp Art.

Nancy Shavick's Tarot Universe. Nancy Shavick. LC 99-36560. 336p. 1999. pap. 15.95 (*1-891661-08-6*, 1086) Snta Monica.

Nancy Shippen: Her Journal. Ed. by Ethel Armes. LC 68-21204. 1972. 24.95 (*0-405-08213-4*, Pub. by Blom Pubns) Ayer.

Nancy Shippen, Her Journal Book: The International Romance of a Young Lady of Fashion of Colonial Philadelphia. Anne H. Livingston. (American Biography Ser.). 348p. 1991. reprint ed. lib. bdg. 79.00 (*0-7812-8248-9*) Rprt Serv.

Nancy Silverton's Breads from the La Brea Bakery. Nancy Silverton & Laurie Ochoa. LC 95-13380. (Illus.). 160p. 1996. 34.95 (*0-679-40907-6*) Villard Books.

Nancy Silverton's Pastries from the La Brea Bakery. Nancy Silverton. LC 99-462216. 288p. 2000. 35.00 (*0-375-50193-2*) Villard Books.

Nancy Spero. Jon Bird et al. (Contemporary Artists Ser.). (Illus.). 160p. (Orig.). 1996. pap. 29.95 (*0-7148-3340-1*, Pub. by Phaidon Press) Phaidon Pr.

Nancy Spero & Leon Golub: Notes in Time. Maurice Berger & Jo A. Isaak. 48p. 20.00 (*0-9624565-6-X*) Univ MD Fine Arts.

***Nancy Swimmer: A Story of the Cherokee Nation.** Clyde Bolton. LC 99-37204. 272p. 1999. 24.95 (*0-9630273-3-6*, Southern Treas) Highland AL.

***Nancy Swimmer: A Story of the Cherokee Nation.** deluxe aut. ed. Clyde Bolton. LC 99-37204. 272p. 1999. lthr. 75.00 (*0-9630273-2-8*, Southern Treas) Highland AL.

Nancy Van Laan Author Biography. (YA). 1997. pap. 13.00 (*0-679-83294-7*) Knopf Bks Yng Read.

Nancy Ward - Dragging Canoe. Pat Alderman. (Illus.). 90p. 1978. pap. 7.95 (*0-932807-05-4*) Overmountain Pr.

Nancy Welch's Four Ingredient Cookbook. Nancy Welch. (Illus.). 108p. (Orig.). 1992. pap. 8.00 (*0-9637213-0-5*) NTW Enter.

Nancy Whiskey. Laurel Ames. 1997. per. 4.99 (*0-373-28978-2*, 1-28978-4) Harlequin Bks.

Nancy Wilson. 145p. 1996. VHS 19.95 (*0-7935-6317-8*) H Leonard.

Nancy's Candy Cookbook: How to Make Candy at Home the Easy Way. Nancy Shipman. (Illus.). 208p. (Orig.). 1996. pap. 14.95 (*1-877810-65-7*, CAND) Rayve Prodns.

Nancy's Easy Filing System. Nancy E. Carlberg. 50p. (Orig.). 1987. pap. 5.00 (*0-944878-01-6*) Carlberg Pr.

Nancy's Mysterious Letter. Carolyn Keene. LC 68-15295. (Nancy Drew Mystery Stories Ser.: No. 8). (Illus.). 174p. (J). (gr. 4-7). 1963. 5.95 (*0-448-09508-4*, G & D) Peng Put Young Read.

Nancy's Mysterious Letter. fac. ed. Carolyn Keene. LC 96-760. (Nancy Drew Mystery Stories Ser.: No. 8). (Illus.). iv, 209p. (J). (gr. 4-7). 1996. reprint ed. 14.95 (*1-55709-162-5*, Pub. by Applewood) Consort Bk Sales.

***Nancy's Story, 1765.** Joan Lowery Nixon. (Colonial Williamsburg Ser.). (YA). 2000. 9.95 (*0-385-32679-3*) Delacorte.

***Nanda Devi: Exploration & Ascent.** Eric Shipton & H. W. Tilman. (Illus.). 288p. 2000. pap. 18.95 (*0-89886-721-5*) Mountaineers.

Nanda Devi: The Tragic Expedition. John Roskelley. 224p. 1988. mass mkt. 4.50 (*0-380-70568-0*, Avon Bks) Morrow Avon.

N

*Nanda Devi: The Tragic Expedition. John Roskelley. LC 00-9288. (Illus.). 240p. 2000. pap. 16.95 (0-89886-739-8) Mountaineers.

Nanda Devi: The Tragic Expedition. John Roskelley. LC 87-9949. (Illus.). 208p. 1987. 16.95 (0-8117-1647-3) Stackpole.

NANDA Nursing Diagnoses: Definitions & Classification, 1999-2001. 136p. (C). 1998. pap. text 12.00 (0-9637042-5-7) N Am Nursing.

NANDA Nursing Diagnoses: Definitions & Classifications, 1995-1996. rev. ed. North American Nursing Diagnosis Association Staff. 124p. (C). 1995. pap. 11.00 (0-9637042-1-4) N Am Nursing.

NANDA Nursing Diagnoses: Definitions & Classifications 1997-1998. NANDA Staff. 120p. (C). 1996. pap. 11.00 (0-9637042-3-0) N Am Nursing.

Nanda Platform of Franklin Bookman. 1998. pap. 69.95 (1-56712-437-2) Franklin Elect.

Nandi's Magic Garden. Ron Matthews. LC 97-11612. (Illus.). (YA). (gr. 3-7). 1997. 16.95 (1-881316-21-1); pap. 7.95 (1-881316-34-3) A&B Bks.

N&W Coal Car Equipment. 24p. 1992. pap. 5.95 (0-911581-26-X) Heimburger Hse Pub.

Nanga Parbat Pilgrimage: The Lonely Challenge. Hermann Buhl. LC 99-201697. (Illus.). 384p. 1998. pap. 16.95 (0-89886-610-3) Mountaineers.

Nanhai Trade: The Early History of Chinese Trade in the South China Sea. Wang Gungwu. LC 98-945545. 134p. 1998. 29.00 (981-210-098-9, Pub. by Times Academic) Intl Spec Bk.

*Nani Arnaq Iqvarta? large type ed. Marie Hoover et al.Tr. of Where Is the Girl Picking Berries?. (ESK., Illus.). 8p. (J). (gr. k-3). 2000. pap. text 6.00 (1-58084-201-1) Lower Kuskokwim.

Nanise: A Navajo Herbal. Vernon O. Mayes. 1990. pap. 27.00 (0-912586-62-1) Dine College Pr.

Nanjing Massacre: A Japanese Journalist Confronts Japan's National Shame. Katsuichi Honda. Ed. by Frank Gibney. Tr. by Karen Sandness. LC 98-40563. (Pacific Basin Institute Book Ser.). (Illus.). 400p. (gr. 13). 1999. pap. text 24.95 (0-7656-0335-7) M E Sharpe.

Nanjing Massacre: A Japanese Journalist Confronts Japan's National Shame. Katsuichi Honda. Ed. by Frank Gibney. Tr. by Karen Sandness. LC 98-40563. (Pacific Basin Insitute Book Ser.). (Illus.). 400p. (C). (gr. 13). 1999. text 65.00 (0-7656-0334-9) M E Sharpe.

N

*Nanjing Massacre in History & Historiography Joshua A. Fogel. LC 99-37864. Vol. 2. 264p. 2000. 15.95 (0-520-22007-2) U CA Pr.

Nanjing Wuxi, Suzhou & Jiangsu Province. Caroline Courtauld. (Illus.). 160p. 1995. pap. 8.95 (0-8442-9818-2, Passprt Bks) NTC Contemp Pub Co.

*Nankering with the Rolling Stones: The Untold Story of the Early Days. James Phelge. LC 99-54413. (Illus.). 305p. 2000. pap. 16.95 (1-55652-373-4) A Cappella Bks.

Nanking Letters, 1949. Knight Biggerstaff. (Cornell East Asia Ser.: No. 23). 114p. 1999. reprint ed. pap. 11.90 (0-939657-23-6) Cornell East Asia Pgm.

Nanna Bijou: The Legend of the Sleeping Giant. Jocelyne Villeneuve. (Illus.). 46p. (J). (ps-8). 1984. 6.95 (0-920806-26-0, Pub. by Penumbra Pr) U of Toronto Pr.

Nannabah's Friend. Mary Perrine. (Illus.). 32p. (J). (gr. k-3). 1989. pap. 5.95 (0-395-52020-7) HM.

Nannie. Angela S. Medearis. LC 95-10360. (Illus.). (J). 1997. 16.00 (0-689-31858-8) Atheneum Yung Read.

Nannie Helen Burroughs. Opal V. Easter. LC 94-23655. (Studies in African American History & Culture). (Illus.). 160p. 1995. text 15.00 (0-8153-1861-8) Garland.

*Nannies, Au Pairs & Babysitters: How to Find & Keep the Right In-Home Childcare for Your Family. Jerri L. Wolfe. LC 00-40709. 2001. write for info. (1-58816-004-1, Hearst) Hearst Commns.

Nannies Grannies & Babysitters: Everything You Need to Know Before Hiring Child Care Providers in Your Home. Theresa R. Anderson. 106p. 1997. pap. 19.95 (0-9657440-1-9); ring bd., wbk. ed. 49.95 (0-9657440-0-0) Lord & Anderson.

Nannies, Maids, & More: The Complete Guide for Hiring Household Help. Linda F. Radke. Ed. by Mary E. Hawkins. LC 89-80249. (Illus.). 113p. 1989. pap. 14.95 (0-9619853-2-1) Five Star AZ.

Nanny Affair: Nanny Wanted! Robyn Donald. (Presents Ser.: Vol. 1980). 1998. per. 3.75 (0-373-11980-1, 1-11980-9) Harlequin Bks.

Nanny & Domestic Help Legal Kit. J. Alexander Tanford & Brian A. Mooij. LC 99-41756. (Legal Survival Guides Ser.). 224p. 1999. pap. 19.95 (1-57248-098-X, Sphinx Pubng) Sourcebks.

Nanny & I. large type ed. Ruth Plant. (Ulverscroft Large Print Ser.). (Illus.). 368p. 1998. 29.99 (0-7089-3919-8) Ulverscroft.

Nanny & the Bodyguard. Mollie Molay. (American Romance Ser.: No. 682). 1997. per. 3.75 (0-373-16682-6, 1-16682-6) Harlequin Bks.

*Nanny & the Iceberg. Ariel Dorfman. LC 98-48371. 353p. 1999. 25.00 (0-374-21898-6) FS&G.

Nanny & the Professor: (Fabulous Fathers) Donna Clayton. (Romance Ser.). 1995. per. 2.99 (0-373-19066-2, 1-19066-9) Silhouette.

Nanny & the Reluctant Rancher. Barbara McCauley. 1997. per. 3.50 (0-373-76066-3, 1-76066-9) Silhouette.

Nanny Angel. Karen T. Whittenburg. (American Romance Ser.). 1995. per. 3.50 (0-373-16572-2, 1-16572-9) Harlequin Bks.

*Nanny Angel. Karen T. Whittenburg. 2000. mass mkt. 4.50 (0-373-82234-0, 1-82234-5) Harlequin Bks.

Nanny Book: The Smart Parent's Guide to Hiring, Firing, & Every Sticky Situation in Between. Susan Carlton & Coco Myers. LC 98-50583. 1999. pap. 14.95 (0-312-19933-3) St Martin.

Nanny Connection: How to Find & Keep a Perfect Nanny. O. Robin Sweet & Mary-Ellen Siegel. LC 86-47701. 224p. (Orig.). 1987. 14.95 (0-689-11820-1) Atheneum Yung Read.

Nanny for Christmas: (Nanny Wanted!) Sara Craven. (Presents Ser.: No. 1999). 1998. per. 3.75 (0-373-11999-2, 1-11999-9) Harlequin Bks.

Nanny for Christmas: (Nanny Wanted!) large type ed. Sara Craven. (Mills & Boon Large Print Ser.). 288p. 1998. 24.99 (0-263-15513-7, Pub. by Mills & Boon) Ulverscroft.

Nanny in the Family. Catherine Spencer. (Presents Ser.). 1998. per. 3.75 (0-373-11950-X, 1-11950-2) Harlequin Bks.

Nanny in the Nick of Time. Donna Clayton. (Single Daddy Club Ser.). 1997. per. 3.25 (0-373-19217-7, 1-19217-8) Silhouette.

Nanny Jake. Lisa Bingham. LC 96-569. 249p. 1995. per. 3.50 (0-373-16602-8, 1-16602-4) Harlequin Bks.

Nanny Kit: Everything You Need to Hire the Right Nanny. Kimberly A. Porrazzo. LC 98-30841. 96p. 1999. pap. 12.95 (0-14-027723-4) Viking Penguin.

Nanny-Mac's Cat. Anne L. MacDonald. (Illus.). 24p. (J). (ps-3). 1996. pap. 5.95 (0-921556-54-3, Pub. by Gynergy-Ragweed) U of Toronto Pr.

*Nanny Manicures. 2nd ed. Diane Gray. (Illus.). 32p. 1998. reprint ed. pap. 5.00 (1-929492-02-2) Stringalong.

Nanny Named Nick. Miranda Lee. (Presents Ser.). 1998. per. 3.75 (0-373-11943-7, 1-11943-7) Harlequin Bks.

Nanny Noony & the Dust Queen. Edward Frascino. (Illus.). 32p. (J). (gr. k-3). 1990. lib. bdg. 15.95 (0-945912-09-9) Pippin Pr.

Nanny Noony & the Magic Spell. Edward Frascino. (Illus.). 32p. (J). (gr. k-3). 1988. 15.95 (0-945912-00-5) Pippin Pr.

*Nanny Proposal. Donna Clayton. (Romance Ser.: Bk. 1477). 2000. mass mkt. 3.50 (0-373-19477-3, 1-19477-8) Silhouette.

Nanny Tax: How to Avoid Tax & Legal Problems When Employing Household Help. Chad R. Turner. LC 97-116543. 356p. 1996. 69.95 (0-471-16249-3) Wiley.

Nanny Training Program: The First At-Home Training Program for Your Child Care Provider & You. Interactive Family Management Staff. LC 97-93826. 1997. 89.95 incl. VHS, disk (0-9663646-0-0) Interact Fmly Mgmt.

Nanny World, Heaven or H . . . ? A Nanny Agency's Perception. H. Olivia Kittrell. LC 96-90491. vii, 185p. (Orig.). 1996. pap. 12.00 (0-9653618-0-2) Water Hill Pr.

*Nanny's Gift: Memories & Poetry. Margaret A. Tyler. Ed. by Toni Ketlen. 128p. 1998. pap. 13.95 (1-886966-13-3, Pub. by In Print) Amazon Com.

Nanny's Helper: The Ultimate Babysitter's Reference Guide. Rose Martin. 75p. 1999. ring bd. 39.99 (0-9643457-1-4) Achieve Publns.

Nanny's Special Gift. Rochelle Potaracke. LC 93-26093. (Illus.). 32p. (Orig.). (J). (gr. 1-4). 1994. pap. 4.95 (0-8091-6615-1) Paulist Pr.

Nano: The Emerging Science of Nanotechnology. Ed Regis. 325p. (C). 1998. pap. text 15.00 (0-7881-5714-0) DIANE Pub.

Nano: The Emerging Science of Nanotechnology. Ed Regis. LC 94-35378. 1995. 23.95 (0-316-73858-1) Little.

Nano: The Emerging Science of Nanotechnology. Ed Regis. 1996. pap. 14.95 (0-614-97755-X) Little.

*Nano-Crystalline & Thin Film Mangnetic Oxides: Proceedings of the NATO Advanced Research Workshop on Ferromagnetic Nano-Crystalline & Thin Film Magnetooptical & Microwave Materials, Sozopol, Bulgaria Sept. 27 - Oct. 3, 1998. NATO Advanced Research Workshop on Ferromagnetic Nano-Crystalline & Thin Film Magnetooptical & Microwave Materials Staff et al. LC 99-37366. (NATO Science Ser. 3). 1999. write for info. (0-7923-5872-4) Kluwer Academic.

Nano Flower. Peter F. Hamilton. LC 97-29860. 1998. text 25.95 (0-312-86580-5) St Martin.

Nano Flower. Peter F. Hamilton. 608p. 1999. mass mkt. 6.99 (0-8125-7769-8, Pub. by Tor Bks) St Martin.

Nanoceramics. (British Ceramics Proceedings Ser.: No. 51). (Illus.). 215p. 1993. 115.00 (0-901716-41-3, Pub. by Inst Materials) Ashgate Pub Co.

Nanocrystalline Semiconductor Materials. Ed. by Prashant V. Kamat & D. Meisel. 1996. write for info. (0-614-17932-7) Elsevier.

Nanofabrication & Biosystems: Integrating Materials Science, Engineering & Biology. Ed. by Harvey C. Hoch et al. (Illus.). 441p. (C). 1996. text 130.00 (0-521-46264-9) Cambridge U Pr.

Nanomagnetism: Proceedings of the NATO Advanced Research Workshop on Nanomagnetic Devices, Miraflores de la Sierra, Madrid, Spain, September 14-19, 1992. Ed. by A. Hernando. LC 93-6202. (NATO Advanced Science Institutes Series C: Mathematical & Physical Sciences). 244p. (C). 1993. text 164.50 (0-7923-2485-4) Kluwer Academic.

*Nanomaterials: Synthesis, Properties & Applications. A. S. Edelstein. LC 98-45669. 1998. pap. 75.00 (0-7503-0578-9) IOP Pub.

Nanomaterials: Synthesis, Properties & Applications. Ed. by A. S. Edelstein & R. C. Cammarata. LC 96-12634. (Illus.). 596p. 1996. 280.00 (0-7503-0358-1) IOP Pub.

*Nanomedicine Vol. 1: Basic Capabilities. Robert A. Freitas, Jr. 600p. 1999. 99.00 (1-57059-645-X) Landes Bioscience.

Nanon. George Sand. (FRE.). 260p. 1989. pap. 29.95 (0-686-54941-4, 2903950172) Fr & Eur.

Nanook's Gift. Michio Hoshino. 36p. 1996. 15.95 (1-56931-147-1, Cadence Bks) Viz Commns Inc.

Nanoparticles & Nanostructured Films: Preparation, Characterization & Applications. Janos H. Fendler. 488p. 1998. 260.00 (3-527-29443-0, Wiley-VCH) Wiley.

Nanoparticles in Solids & Solutions: Proceedings of the NATO Advanced Research Workshop on Nanoparticles in Solid & Solutions - An Integrated Approach to Their Preparation & Characterization, Szeged, Hungary, March 8, 1996. Ed. by Janos H. Fendler. LC 96-49520. (NATO ASI Series: Partnership Sub-Series 3). 596p. (C). 1996. text 323.50 (0-7923-4338-7) Kluwer Academic.

*Nanophase & Nanocomposite Materials III Vol. 581: Materials Research Society Symposium Proceedings. Ed. by Sridhar Komarneni et al. LC 00-28750. (Materials Research Society Symposium Proceedings Ser.). 688p. 2000. text 99.00 (1-55899-489-0) Materials Res.

Nanophase & Nanocomposite Materials II. Ed. by J. C. Parker et al. LC 97-6975. (Materials Research Society Symposium Proceedings Ser.: No. 457). 558p. 1997. text 72.00 (1-55899-361-4) Materials Res.

Nanophase Materials. Ed. by E. Bonetti & D. Fiorani. (Materials Science Forum Ser.: Vol. 195). (Illus.). 240p. 1996. text 106.00 (0-87849-709-9, Pub. by Trans T Pub) Enfield Pubs NH.

Nanophase Materials: The Coming Boom in Catalysts, Cosmetics, Coating & Drugs. John Wiley & Sons. Technical Insights. LC 98-164326. (Illus.). 139p. 1997. write for info. (0-471-25731-1) Wiley.

Nanophase Materials - Synthesis, Properties, Applications: Proceedings of the NATO Advanced Study Institute, Corfu, Greece, June 20-July 2, 1993. Ed. by George C. Hadjipanayis. LC 94-6562. (NATO Advanced Study Institutes Series E, Applied Sciences: Vol. 260). 828p. (C). 1994. text 374.00 (0-7923-2754-3) Kluwer Academic.

Nanophases & Nanocrystalline Structures. Ed. by Robert D. Shull & Juan M. Sanchez. LC 94-75037. (Illus.). 169p. 1993. pap. 52.40 (0-608-04980-8, 2065598000004) Bks Demand.

*Nanoporous Materials. G. Q. Lu. (Illus.). 2000. pap. 48.00 (1-86094-211-3) Imperial College.

Nanoscale Characterization of Surfaces & Interfaces. John N. DiNardo. 174p. 1994. 150.00 (3-527-29247-0, Wiley-VCH) Wiley.

Nanoscale Fluid Dynamics in Physiological Processes: A Review Study. Michele Ciofalo et al. (Advances in Computational Bioengineering Ser.: Vol. 2). (Illus.). 360p. 1999. 149.00 (1-85312-586-5, 5865) Computational Mech MA.

Nanoscale Physiology. Ed. by M. W. Collins. (Advances in Computational Bioengineering Ser.). 250p. 2001. 129.00 (1-85312-670-5, 6705, Pub. by WIT Pr) Computational Mech MA.

Nanoscale Probes of the Solid/Liquid Interface: Proceedings of the NATO Advanced Study Institute, Sophia Antipolis, France, July 10-20, 1993. Ed. by Andrew A. Gewirth. (NATO Advanced Study Institute Ser. Series E: no. 88). 352p. (C). 1995. text 191.50 (0-7923-3454-X) Kluwer Academic.

Nanoscale Science & Technology. N. Garcia et al. LC 98-16259. (NATO ASI Ser.). 1998. 175.00 (0-7923-5048-0) Kluwer Academic.

Nanosources & Manipulation of Atoms under High Fields & Temperatures: Applications. Ed. by Nicholas Garcia et al. LC 93-18976. (NATO Advanced Study Institutes Series E, Applied Sciences: Vol. 235). 1993. text 192.00 (0-7923-2266-5) Kluwer Academic.

Nanostructure Physics & Fabrication. Ed. by Mark A. Reed & Wiley P. Kirk. 544p. 1989. text 108.00 (0-12-585000-X) Acad Pr.

Nanostructured & Nanopatterned Materials. James Hendrick et al. (ACS Symposium Ser). 115.00 (0-8412-3653-4, Pub. by Am Chemical) OUP.

Nanostructured & Non-Crystalline Materials: Proceedings of the IVth International Workshop on Non-Crystalline Solid. M. Vazquez & A. Hernando. 500p. 1995. text 122.00 (981-02-2060-X) World Scientific Pub.

*Nanostructured Films & Coatings: Proceedings of the NATO Advanced Research Workshop on Nanostructured Films & Coatings, Santorini, Greece, June 28-30, 1999. Gan-Moog Chow et al. LC 00-29624. 2000. write for info. (0-7923-6265-9, Kluwer Acad) Kluwer Academic.

Nanostructured Materials: Clusters, Composites & Thin Films, Vol. 679. Vladimir M. Shalaev et al. LC 97-34825. (Acs Symposium Series,). 264p. 1997. text 99.95 (0-8412-3536-8, Pub. by Am Chemical) OUP.

Nanostructured Materials: Science & Technology. Gan-Moog Chow, Gan-Moog & Nina I. Noskova. LC 98-20260. (NATO ASI Series: Partnership Sub-Series 3). 457p. 1998. write for info. (0-7923-5071-5) Kluwer Academic.

Nanostructured Materials in Electrochemistry. P. C. Searson & G. J. Meyer. (Proceedings Ser.: Vol. 95-08). 280p. 1995. pap. 43.00 (1-56677-102-1) Electrochem Soc.

Nanostructures & Quantum Effects: Proceedings of the JRDC International Symposium, Tsukuba, Japan, November 17-18, 1993. H. Sakaki & H. Noge. LC 94-31855. 1994. 89.00 (3-540-58383-1) Spr-Verlag.

Nanosystems: Molecular Machinery, Manufacturing & Computation. K. Eric Drexler. LC 92-30870. 576p. 1992. pap. 54.99 (0-471-57518-6) Wiley.

Nanosystems: Molecular Machinery, Manufacturing & Computation. K. Eric Drexler. LC 92-30870. 576p. 1992. 59.99 (0-471-57547-X) Wiley.

Nanotech. Jack Dann. 1998. mass mkt. 5.99 (0-441-00585-3) Ace Bks.

*Nanotechnology. David Savage. 150p. 1998. pap. 1400.00 (0-471-34891-0) Wiley.

Nanotechnology. Ed. by G. L. Timp. LC 98-4681. (Illus.). 500p. 1998. 70.00 (0-387-98334-1) Spr-Verlag.

Nanotechnology. Gregory Timp. 1997. 90.00 (1-56396-321-3) Spr-Verlag.

Nanotechnology: Integrated Processing Systems for Ultra-Precision & Ultra-Fine Products. Ed. by Norio Taniguchi et al. (Illus.). 422p. 1996. text 175.00 (0-19-856283-7) OUP.

Nanotechnology: Molecular Speculations on Global Abundance. Ed. by B. C. Crandall. (Illus.). 224p. 1996. 35.00 (0-262-03237-6, Bradford Bks); pap. text 18.50 (0-262-53137-2, Bradford Bks) MIT Pr.

Nanotechnology: Molecularly Designed Materials. Ed. by Gan-Moog Chow & Kenneth E. Gonsalves. LC 96-6023. (ACS Symposium Ser.: No. 622). (Illus.). 424p. 1996. text 120.00 (0-8412-3392-6, Pub. by Am Chemical) OUP.

Nanotechnology: Research & Perspectives. Ed. by B. C. Crandall. (Illus.). 480p. 1992. 50.00 (0-262-03195-7) MIT Pr.

Nanotechnology in Medicine & the Biosciences. Richard Coombs & Dennis Robinson. (Developments in Nanotechnology Ser.). 320p. 1996. text 54.00 (2-88449-080-9) Gordon & Breach.

*Nanotechnology Research Directions: Vision for Nanotechnology in the Next Decade. Mihail C. Roco et al. 360p. 2000. 149.00 (0-7923-6220-9) Kluwer Academic.

Nanotime. Bart Kosko. 1998. mass mkt. 6.99 (0-380-79147-1, Avon Bks) Morrow Avon.

Nanowires: Proceedings of the NATO Advanced Research Workshop on Nanowires, Miraflores de la Sierra, Madrid, Spain, September 23-27, 1996. P. A. Serena & N. Garcia. LC 97-20547. (NATO ASI Series, Applied Sciences). 1997. text 234.00 (0-7923-4627-0) Kluwer Academic.

Nan's Nickel. Anne T. Perkins. (Big Books - Mini Bks.). (Illus.). 8p. (J). 1993. 12.00 (1-884204-04-X) Teach Nxt Door.

*Nansen: The Explorer as Hero. Roland Huntford. (Illus.). xiv, 610p. (Orig.). 1999. reprint ed. pap. 19.95 (0-7607-1262-X, Pub. by Barnes & Noble Inc) Bookazine Co Inc.

Nansen: The Point of Departure: The Present Day Awakened One Speaks on the Ancient Masters of Zen. Osho. Ed. by Anand Robin. (Zen Ser.). 206p. 1989. 14.95 (3-89338-067-1, Pub. by Rebel Hse) Oshos.

Nantahla Love Feast. Kathleen Carerra. LC 87-71620. (Gazebo Romance Ser.). 200p. 1987. 15.95 (0-89227-075-6) Commonwealth Pr.

Nanta's Lion: A Search-&-Find Adventure. Susan MacDonald. LC 94-16634. (Illus.). 24p. (J). (ps up). 1995. 15.00 (0-688-13125-5, Wm Morrow) Morrow Avon.

Nantasket Beach Branch, NY, NH & HRR. Bob McGarigle. (Illus.). 76p. 1981. 12.00 (0-910506-21-3) De Vito.

Nantes Cite Urbaine City Plan. (Grafocarte Maps Ser.). 1995. 8.95 (2-7416-0028-7, 80028) Michelin.

Nantes Ville City Plan. (Grafocarte Maps Ser.). 1993. 8.95 (2-7416-0063-5, 80063) Michelin.

*Nantes/Les Sables-d'Olonne/Poitiers Map. 1998. 6.95 (2-06-700067-5, 67) Michelin.

Nantgarw Porcelain Album. Ed. by W. D. John et al. 230p. (C). 1989. 295.00 (0-905928-15-6, Pub. by D Brown & Sons Ltd) St Mut.

Nanticoke & Conoy Indians. Frank G. Speck. LC 76-43843. (Papers of the Historical Society of Delaware. New Ser.: I). reprint ed. 39.50 (0-404-15703-3) AMS Pr.

Nanticoke Community of Delaware. Frank G. Speck. LC 76-43844. (Museum of the American Indian, Heye Foundation Ser.: Vol. 2, No. 4). (Illus.). 88p. 1981. reprint ed. 41.50 (0-404-15695-9) AMS Pr.

Nanticoke Indians. Clinton A. Weslager. LC 82-50259. (Illus.). 350p. 1983. 38.50 (0-87413-179-0) U Delaware Pr.

Nanticoke Indians. Clinton A. Weslager. LC 76-43888. (Pennsylvania Historical & Museum Commission Anthropological Ser.). 1983. reprint ed. 29.50 (0-404-15747-5) AMS Pr.

Nantucket. Robert Gambee. LC 92-22199. (Illus.). 352p. 1993. 45.00 (0-393-03458-5) Norton.

Nantucket. Robert Gambee. (Illus.). 352p. 1996. pap. 29.95 (0-393-31493-6, Norton Paperbks) Norton.

Nantucket: Gardens & Houses. Taylor Lewis & Virginia Heard. (Illus.). 230p. (gr. 8). 1990. 50.00 (0-316-52334-8) Little.

Nantucket: Seasons on the Island. Cary Hazlegrove. LC 94-11554. 120p. 1995. 29.95 (0-8118-0724-X) Chronicle Bks.

Nantucket: The Life of an Island. Edwin P. Hoyt. LC 77-92775. 222p. 1980. 11.95 (0-8289-0325-5) Viking Penguin.

Nantucket, an Island Sketchbook. Gretchen Jaeger. (Illus.). 48p. 1996. 24.95 (0-9650885-0-2) Winter Harbor.

Nantucket & the Angel. Gillian Allnutt. LC 97-171760. 64p. 1997. pap. 15.95 (1-85224-382-1, Pub. by Bloodaxe Bks) Dufour.

Nantucket Book: A Complete Guide. Betty Lowry. LC 97-46095. (Great Destinations Ser.). (Illus.). 320p. 1998. pap. 17.95 (0-936399-95-3) Berkshire Hse.

Nantucket Borders. Laura Hurwitz. (Illus.). 96p. 1998. 24.95 (0-9662257-0-8) Vista Pubns CT.

Nantucket Cats. Dawn L. Watkins. LC 97-41138. (Illus.). 32p. (J). 1998. pap. 5.49 (0-89084-975-7) Bob Jones Univ.

Nantucket Collection. Ole Lokensgard. LC 89-50229. (Illus.). 128p. (Orig.). 1989. pap. 8.95 (0-9622429-0-X) Big Mtn.

Nantucket Diet Murders. Virginia Rich. 288p. 1986. mass mkt. 6.50 (0-440-16264-5) Dell.

An Asterisk (*) at the beginning of an entry indicates that the title is appearing for the first time.

Nantucket Doorways: Thresholds to the Past. Edouard A. Stackpole & Melvin B. Summerfield. LC 92-11136. 1992. pap. 12.95 (*0-8191-8660-0*) Madison Bks UPA.

Nantucket Etcetera. Mary Miles. (Illus.). 196p. (Orig.). 1989. pap. 12.00 (*0-9623188-1-7*) Yesterdays Island.

Nantucket, Fascinating Old Town on the Island in the Sea: Brief Historical Data & Memories of My Boyhood Days in Nantucket. 2nd ed. Joseph E. Farnham. (Illus.). 319p. 1992. reprint ed. lib. bdg. 36.00 (*0-8328-2498-4*) Higginson Bk Co.

Nantucket Gam. Mary Miles. LC 93-71134. 192p. 1993. write for info. (*0-9636885-1-0*); pap. write for info. (*0-9636885-2-9*) Faraway Pub.

Nantucket Genesis. Mary Barnard. LC 88-12133. 80p. 1988. 14.95 (*0-932576-64-8*); pap. 8.95 (*0-932576-65-6*) Breitenbush Bks.

Nantucket Hauntings: Twenty-One Firsthand Encounters with the Supernatural. Blue Balliett. LC 90-81834. 176p. 1990. pap. 10.95 (*0-89272-279-7*) Down East.

***Nantucket Holiday Table.** Susan Simon. LC 99-49719. (Illus.). 2000. 29.95 (*0-8118-2508-6*) Chronicle Bks.

Nantucket in Print. Everett U. Crosby. 225p. 1997. reprint ed. 19.95 (*1-57898-003-8*) Martino Pubng.

Nantucket in the 19th Century. Clay Lancaster. LC 77-75512. (Illus.). 160p. 1979. pap. 12.95 (*0-486-23747-8*) Dover.

Nantucket Inspirations. Claire Murray. 1997. 39.95 (*0-9652613-0-1*) ANB Internatl.

Nantucket Island. Robert Gambee. 1987. pap. 24.95 (*0-393-30398-5*) Norton.

Nantucket Island Guidebook: Definitive Guidebook to Points of Interest, Things to Do, Culture, Entertainment, Shopping & Dining, Nantucket Island, Massachusetts. George G. Trask. LC 94-94217. (Illus.). 127p. (Orig.). 1994. pap. 8.95 (*1-882943-03-1*) Coastal Villages.

Nantucket Lands & Land Owners. Henry B. Worth. (Illus.). 440p. 1992. reprint ed. pap. 30.00 (*1-55613-617-X*) Heritage Bk.

Nantucket Lights: An Illustrated History of the Island's Legendary Beacons. Karen T. Butler. LC 96-94744. 1996. 44.95 (*0-9638910-6-5*) Mill Hill Pr.

Nantucket Lightship Baskets. 5th ed. Katherine Seeler & Edgar Seeler. (Illus.). 130p. 1991. reprint ed. 18.00 (*0-9600596-4-4*) Deermouse.

***Nantucket Musings.** Albert J. Repicci. (Illus.). 60p. 2000. 15.99 (*1-930348-00-2*) KHP Museum.

Nantucket, 1970. Tom Farrell. LC 82-90113. 233p. (Orig.). 1982. pap. 3.95 (*0-943306-00-0*) Pier Pr.

***Nantucket 1, 2, 3.** large type ed. Susan Arciero. LC 99-91977. (Illus.). (J). (ps). 2000. 7.95 (*0-9677548-2-8*) Pigtail Pub MD.

Nantucket Open-House Cookbook. Sarah L. Chase. LC 86-40598. (Illus.). 336p. 1987. pap. 14.95 (*0-89480-465-0*, 1465) Workman Pub.

Nantucket Recipes from the Fog Island Cafe. Mark Dawson & Anne Dawson. (Illus.). 128p. 1996. 14.95 (*0-939218-16-X*) Chapman Billies.

Nantucket Scraps. Jane G. Austin. (Works of Jane (Goodin) Austin). 1989. reprint ed. lib. bdg. 79.00 (*0-7812-1830-6*) Rprt Serv.

Nantucket Skeptic Reads the New Testament: Robert A. di Curcio's Companion Reader to the Gospels. Robert A. Di Curcio. 105p. 1998. pap. 18.00 (*0-917358-12-0*) Aeternium Pubng Co.

Nantucket Solitaire. Roy Flanders. LC 86-8193. 177p. (Orig.). 1986. 25.00 (*0-934219-40-0*); pap. 15.00 (*0-934219-43-5*) Great Point Pr.

Nantucket Solitaire. deluxe limited ed. Roy Flanders. LC 86-8193. 177p. (Orig.). 1986. 18.00 (*0-934219-46-X*) Great Point Pr.

Nantucket Style. Leslie Linsley. (Illus.). 228p. 1994. pap. 29.95 (*0-8478-1830-6*, Pub. by Rizzoli Intl) St Martin.

Nantucket Summers Vol. 1: The Story of a Family & a Very Special Cottage Called Sunycliffe. Katharine S. Abbott. LC 96-67895. (Illus.). 176p. (Orig.). 1996. pap. 20.00 (*0-9651777-0-X*, 96001) Pinniped Pr.

Nantucket Table. Susan Simon. LC 97-30797. 168p. 1998. 29.95 (*0-8118-1472-6*) Chronicle Bks.

Nantucket Weather Book. David Ludlum. Ed. by Lesley Farlow. (Illus.). 195p. (Orig.). 1986. pap. text 17.95 (*0-9607340-4-X*) Nantucket Hist Assn.

Nantucket Wild Flowers. Alice O. Albertson. LC 73-80640. (Illus.). 1973. reprint ed. 10.00 (*0-913728-02-0*) Theophrastus.

Nantucket Yesterday & Today. John W. McCalley. (Illus.). 192p. (Orig.). 1981. pap. 13.95 (*0-486-24059-2*) Dover.

Nantucket's Night Magic. Illus. by Kat Drayton. 32p. (J). (gr. k). 1998. 14.95 (*0-9667090-0-4*) Dionis Bound.

Nantucket's Tried-Out Moby-Dick: Robert A. diCurcio's Companion Reader to Melville's Masterpiece. rev. ed. Robert A. DiCurcio. v, 136p. 1997. reprint ed. spiral bd. 18.00 (*0-917358-11-2*) Aeternium Pubng Co.

***Nanuk.** Ed. by Ellery Queen. LC 97-26670. (Illus.). 32p. (J). (gr. k-4). 1998. 15.99 (*0-8037-2194-3*, Dial Yng Read) Peng Put Young Read.

Nan'yo: The Rise & Fall of the Japanese in Micronesia, 1885-1945. Mark R. Peattie. LC 87-19437. (Pacific Islands Monographs: No. 4). (Illus.). 306p. (Orig.). 1992. reprint ed. pap. text 21.00 (*0-8248-1480-0*) UH Pr.

Naomi. Olive Gurney. 176p. 1992. pap. 9.99 (*0-8341-1439-9*) Beacon Hill.

Naomi. Jun'ichiro Tanizaki. Tr. by Anthony H. Chambers from JPN. 238p. 1990. reprint ed. pap. 12.00 (*0-86547-457-5*) N Point Pr.

Naomi - A First Generation American see Naomi - A First Generation American

***Naomi - A First Generation American.** large type ed. Norma Katzakian. Ed. by Ardis Chidester & Robert A. Folchi. Orig. Title: Naomi - A First Generation American. (Illus.). (J). (gr. 4-7). 2000. pap. 12.95 (*0-9662228-1-4*) Dab Pub Co.

***Naomi & Rut.** Yoseif Yaron. (Illus.). 15p. (J). (gr. 3-6). 2000. pap. 10.00 (*0-9700775-1-3*, Gan Elden Pr) Karaism.com.

Naomi & Ruth. Katy K. Arnsteen. LC 96-27839. (KidScripts Ser.). (Illus.). 24p. (Orig.). (J). (gr. 2-5). 1997. pap. 3.95 (*0-8198-5134-5*) Pauline Bks.

Naomi Campbell. (Black Americans of Achievement Ser.). (Illus.). (YA). (gr. 4 up). 2000. 19.95 (*0-7910-4961-2*) Chelsea Hse.

Naomi in the Living Room & Other Short Plays . . . Christopher Durang. 1998. pap. 9.75 (*0-8222-1448-2*) Dramatists Play.

Naomi Judd's Guardian Angels. Naomi Judd. LC 99-13676. (Illus.). 40p. (J). (ps up). 2000. 15.95 (*0-06-027208-2*) HarpC Child Bks.

Naomi Mitchison. Saltire Society Staff. 34p. 1986. 25.00 (*0-85411-036-4*, Pub. by Saltire Soc) St Mut.

Naomi Mitchison: A Biography. Jill Benton. (Illus.). 216p. 1992. pap. text 15.00 (*0-04-440862-5*) NYU Pr.

Naomi Wants to Know: Letters from a Little Girl to the Big Big World. Naomi Shaven. LC 98-35613. 160p. 1998. pap. 12.95 (*1-57749-076-2*, Pub. by Fairview Press) Natl Bk Netwk.

Nap Land. 1997. pap. 1.75 (*0-8289-1009-X*) Viking Penguin.

Nap Time: The True Story of Sexual Abuse at a Suburban Day Care Center. Lisa Manshel. 1991. mass mkt. 4.95 (*0-8217-3262-5*, Zebra Kensgtn) Kensgtn Pub Corp.

Napa. James Conaway. 560p. 1992. pap. 15.00 (*0-380-71599-6*, Avon Bks) Morrow Avon.

Napa & Sonoma Book: A Complete Guide. 5th ed. Tim Fish & Peg Melnik. LC 99-19457. (Great Destinations Ser.). (Illus.). 352p. 1999. pap. 17.95 (*1-58157-008-2*) Berkshire Hse.

***Napa & Sonoma Counties Street Guide & Directory: 2000 Edition.** (Illus.). 384p. 1999. pap. 27.95 (*1-58174-192-8*) Thomas Bros Maps.

Napa Jack's First Flight. Robert G. Kresko. 28p. (J). (gr. k-4). 1995. text 14.95 (*1-887534-00-8*) NVMC.

Napa Town & Country Fair Red Hot Chili Cook Off. Veronica DiRosa. (Illus.). (Orig.). 1981. pap. 4.95 (*0-935360-04-2*) Napa Cnty Landmarks.

***Napa Valley.** Jeffrey Caldewey & Mildred Howie. (California Wine Tour Ser.). 128p. 2000. pap. 11.95 (*1-891267-08-6*) Wine Appreciation.

***Napa Valley: Land of the Golden Vines.** 2nd ed. Kathleen Hill. (Hill Guides Ser.). 2000. pap. 14.95 (*0-7627-0652-X*) Globe Pequot.

***Napa Valley: Picture Perfect.** Tony Kilgallin. (American Enterprise Ser.). (Illus.). 136p. 2000. 49.95 (*1-58192-013-X*) Community Comm.

Napa Valley: The Ultimate Winery Guide. Antonia Allegra & Richard Gillette. LC 96-3063. 1997. pap. 19.95 (*0-8118-1544-7*) Chronicle Bks.

***Napa Valley: The Ultimate Winery Guide.** 3rd rev. ed. Antonia Allegra. LC 99-86937. (Illus.). 120p. 2000. pap. 19.95 (*0-8118-2858-1*) Chronicle Bks.

***Napa Valley Guide, 2000.** Ed. by Steven Veit-Carey & Cordelia Veit-Carey. 136p. 1999. pap. 5.95 (*0-931973-37-6*) Vintage Pubns.

Napa Valley in a Nutshell: An Insider's Guide to the 100 Best Napa Valley. Mick Winter. 96p. 1997. pap. 5.95 (*0-9659000-0-2*) Westsong Pub.

Napa Valley Mustard Celebration Cookbook. Susan J. Parker. 152p. 1995. pap. text 11.95 (*1-887534-02-4*) NVMC.

Napa Valley Wine Tour. Vintage Image Staff. 176p. 1999. pap. 9.95 (*0-932664-34-2*) Wine Appreciation.

Napa Wine: A History from Mission Days to Present. Charles L. Sullivan. Ed. by Eve Kushner. (Illus.). 460p. 1995. 29.95 (*0-932664-70-9*) Wine Appreciation.

Napa Wine: A History from Mission Days to Present. deluxe limited ed. Charles L. Sullivan. Ed. by Eve Kushner. (Illus.). 416p. 1994. 89.95 (*0-932664-97-0*) Wine Appreciation.

Napa Wine: A History from Mission Days to Present. 2nd rev. ed. Charles L. Sullivan. (Illus.). 460p. 2000. 34.95 (*1-891267-07-8*) Wine Appreciation.

***Napalm & Silly Putty: George Carlin.** George Carlin. 272p. 2001. 21.00 (*0-7868-6413-3*, Pub. by Hyperion) Time Warner.

NAPAW '92: Proceedings of the First North American Process Algebra Workshop, Stony Brook, NY, 28 August 1992. Ed. by Sahasranaman Purushothaman & Amy Zwarico. LC 92-44291. 1993. 69.00 (*0-387-19822-9*) Spr-Verlag.

***Napco.** Kathleen Deel. LC 99-61231. (Illus.). 176p. 1999. pap. 29.95 (*0-7643-0844-0*) Schiffer.

Naperville: Reflections of Community. Jini Clare. (Illus.). 150p. 1997. 34.95 (*1-890291-03-X*) Platinum Pubng.

***Naperville Area Handbook & Guide: An Introduction to the Community.** Jini L. Clare & Kelli M. Clare. 82p. 1999. pap. 9.95 (*0-9676084-0-6*) Clare Commns.

Naphthalene. Ed. by GDCh-Advisory Committee on Existing Chemicals of E. (BUA Report Ser.: No. 39). 155p. 1992. pap. 58.00 (*3-527-28467-2*, Wiley-VCH) Wiley.

Naphthalene to Nuclear Technology see Ullmann's Encyclopedia of Industrial Chemistry

Napier: The Forgotten Chessmaster. John Hilbert. (Great Masters Ser.). (Illus.). 354p. 1997. 42.00 (*0-939433-51-6*) Caissa Edit.

Napier - the First to Wear the Green. David Venables. LC 97-76835. (Illus.). 192p. 1998. 64.95 (*0-85429-989-0*) Motorbooks Intl.

***Napier Powered.** Alan Vessey. (Transport Ser.). 1999. pap. 18.99 (*0-7524-0766-X*) Arcadia Publng.

Napier's Curves: As Used in the Examinations. Brown, Son & Ferguson Ltd. Staff. (C). 1987. 40.00 (*0-7855-6056-4*) St Mut.

Napkin, an Apple & a Head Full of Mush. Jack Snyder & Blake Evans. 11p. (Orig.). 1994. pap. 5.95 (*0-9657455-0-3*) N Sturges.

Napkin Folding: Forty-Four Ways to Turn a Square of Linen into a Work of Art. James A. Ginders. (Illus.). 104p. 1987. pap. 9.95 (*0-517-56632-X*) Harmony Bks.

Napkin Folding for Every Occasion. (Illus.). 64p. 1993. spiral bd. 5.98 (*1-56173-463-2*, 3611100) Pubns Intl Ltd.

Napkin Folds: Beautifully Styled Napkins for Every Occasion. Bridget Jones. (Illus.). 64p. 1997. 9.95 (*1-85967-543-3*, Lorenz Bks) Anness Pub.

Napkin Folds: Beautifully Styled Napkins for Every Occasion. Bridget Jones & Madeleine Brehaut. (Illus.). 64p. 1999. pap. 7.95 (*0-7548-0202-7*, Lorenz Bks) Anness Pub.

Napkin Magic. Rena Neff. Ed. by Karen Pemno. 64p. (Orig.). 1990. pap., per. 3.95 (*0-942320-36-0*) Am Cooking.

Napkin Notes: On the Art of Living. G. Michael Durst. LC 79-50554. (Illus.). 230p. 1988. pap. 15.00 (*0-9602552-0-6*) Train Sys.

Napkins: Lunch Bag Notes from Dad. Courtney Garton. LC 97-76634. 160p. 1998. pap. 14.95 (*1-891043-00-5*) Perry Pubng.

Napkins: Lunch Bag Notes from Dad, 1. Courtney Garton. LC 97-76634. 160p. 1998. pap. 14.95 (*1-56912-070-6*) Wharton Pub.

***NAPL Removal: Surfactants, Foams & Microemulsions.** C. H. Ward. LC 99-86278. 719p. 2000. ring bd. 69.95 (*1-56670-467-7*) Lewis Pubs.

***Naples.** Bonechi. 96p. 1999. pap. text 15.95 (*88-8029-773-2*) Bonechi.

Naples. Deni Bown. LC 97-32279. (Eyewitness Travel Guides Ser.). 192p. 1998. pap. 22.95 (*0-7894-2752-4*) DK Pub Inc.

Naples. Patricia Hewitt. (Illus.). 173p. 1995. 35.00 (*1-885352-12-3*) Community Comm.

Naples. Touring Club of Italy Staff. (Heritage Guides Ser.). (Illus.). 224p. 1999. pap. 16.95 (*88-365-1520-7*) Abbeville Pr.

Naples: An Early Guide. Enrico Bacco et al. Ed. & Tr. by Eileen Gardinar from ITA. LC 89-46222. (Historical Travel Ser.). (Illus.). 272p. (Orig.). 1991. pap. 17.50 (*0-934977-20-8*) Italica Pr.

***Naples & Amalfi.** Ed. by Fodors Travel Publications, Inc. Staff. 304p. 2000. pap. 15.50 (*0-679-00457-2*) Fodors Travel.

Naples & Amalfi Coast Pocket Guide, 1998. rev. ed. Berlitz Editors. (Pocket Guides Ser.). (Illus.). 128p. 1998. pap. 8.95 (*2-8315-6418-2*) Berlitz.

Naples & Pompeii. (Knopf Guide Ser.). 384p. 1996. 25.00 (*0-614-15948-2*) Knopf.

Naples at Table: Cooking in Campania. Arthur Schwartz. LC 98-17628. 528p. 1998. 27.50 (*0-06-018261-X*) HarpC.

Naples, Capri & the Coast. 2nd ed. Insight Guides Staff. (Insight Guides). 1998. pap. text 21.95 (*0-88729-719-6*) Langenscheidt.

Naples-Foggia: The United States Army Campaigns of World War 2. Kenneth V. Smith. 24p. 1994. pap. 2.00 (*0-16-042082-2*) USGPO.

Naples '44: An Intelligence Officer in the Italian Labyrinth. Norman Lewis. LC 94-27642. 88p. 1995. pap. 14.95 (*0-8050-3373-4*) H Holt & Co.

Naples '44: An Intelligence Officer in the Italian Labyrinth. large type ed. Norman Lewis. 264p. 1997. text 20.95 (*1-85695-149-9*, Pub. by ISIS Lrg Prnt) Transaction Pubs.

Naples in Color see Travel Guides in Color

Naples in the Time of Cholera, 1884-1911. Frank M. Snowden. (Illus.). 494p. (C). 1996. text 69.95 (*0-521-48310-7*) Cambridge U Pr.

Naples-Marco Philharmonic League Cookbook: Fantastic Foods of the Philharmonic. Naples-Marco Philharmonic League Staff. 324p. (Orig.). 1989. pap. text 12.50 (*0-685-29164-2*) Naples Marco.

***Naples, Pompei, Capri, Ischia, Sorrento et la Cote Amalfitaine.** Michelin Travel Publication Staff. (In Your Pocket Guides Ser.). 2000. 9.95 (*2-06-658301-4*) Michelin.

***Naples, Pompeii, Capri, Sorrento & the Amalfi Coast.** Michelin Travel Publication Staff. (In Your Pocket Guides Ser.). 2000. 9.95 (*2-06-653301-7*) Michelin.

Napolean. Roger Asprey. 624p. 1998. pap. 18.00 (*0-465-04880-3*) Basic.

Napolean. Geoffrey Ellis. LC 96-26814. (Profiles in Power Ser.). 304p. (C). 1996. pap. 22.26 (*0-582-02547-8*) Addison-Wesley.

Napolean & Pozzo Di Borgo in Corsica & after, 1764-1821: Not Quite a Vendetta. J. M. McErlean. LC 95-48785. (Studies in French Civilization: Vol. 10). 328p. 1996. text 99.95 (*0-7734-8853-7*) E Mellen.

Napolean at Dresden: The Battles of August 1813. George Nafziger. (Ancient Empires Ser.). (Illus.). 48p. (Orig.). 1991. 38.00 (*0-9626655-4-1*, Pub. by Emperors Pr) Combined Pub.

Napoleon. Rene De Chateaubriand. (FRE.). 1969. 10.95 (*0-8288-9094-3*) Fr & Eur.

Napoleon. Roger Dufraisse. 180p. (C). 1991. pap. 16.88 (*0-07-018045-8*) McGraw.

Napoleon. Geoffrey Ellis. LC 96-26814. (Profiles in Power Ser.). (J). 1996. text 55.00 (*0-582-02548-6*) Addison-Wesley.

***Napoleon.** Max Gallo. 1999. 32.95 (*84-08-02692-5*) Planeta.

Napoleon. Proctor Jones. 1993. 500.00 (*0-679-41841-5*) Random.

Napoleon. Nelly Kaplan. LC 95-192423. (BFI Film Classics Ser.). (Illus.). 72p. 1995. pap. 10.95 (*0-85170-466-2*) British Film Inst.

Napoleon. Kim Kennedy. 1999. pap. 4.99 (*0-14-055685-0*) Viking Penguin.

***Napoleon.** Emil Ludwig. 2000. per. 69.90 (*0-671-78259-2*, Pocket Books) PB.

Napoleon. Felix M. Markham. 1966. mass mkt. 7.99 (*0-451-62798-9*) NAL.

Napoleon, 2 vols. Stendhal, pseud. Ed. by Ernest Abravanel & Victor Del Litto. (Illus.). 1970. 9.95 (*0-318-52054-0*) Fr & Eur.

Napoleon. Jean F. Tulard. LC 93-10210. 1993. 49.95 (*1-882516-02-8*); pap. 19.95 (*1-882516-03-6*) Lithograph Pub.

***Napoleon.** David Chandler. 2000. reprint ed. pap. 19.95 (*0-85052-750-3*, Pub. by Pen & Sword) Combined Pub.

Napoleon. F. M. Kircheisen. Tr. by Henry St. Lawrence. LC 72-8400. (Select Bibliographies Reprint Ser.). 1977. reprint ed. 70.95 (*0-8369-6981-2*) Ayer.

Napoleon. Friedrick M. Kircheisen. Tr. by Henry St. Lawrence from FRE. 770p. 1982. reprint ed. lib. bdg. 63.00 (*0-8290-0799-7*) Irvington.

Napoleon. William O. Morris. LC 73-14458. (Heroes of the Nations Ser.). reprint ed. 30.00 (*0-404-58276-1*) AMS Pr.

Napoleon. Richard Tames. Ed. by Malcolm Yapp et al. (World History Program Ser.). (Illus.). (J). (gr. 6-11). 1980. reprint ed. pap. text 5.90 (*0-89908-019-7*) Greenhaven.

Napoleon, 2 vols., Set. Stendhal, pseud. 100.00 (*0-686-55074-9*) Fr & Eur.

***Napoleon: A Biographical Companion.** David Nicholls. LC 99-22535. (Bibliography Ser.). 352p. 1999. lib. bdg. 55.00 (*0-87436-957-6*) ABC-CLIO.

Napoleon: A History of the Art of War, 4 vols. Theodore A. Dodge. reprint ed. 275.00 (*0-404-02160-3*) AMS Pr.

Napoleon: An Intimate Account of the Years of Supremacy, 1800-1814. Proctor P. Jones et al. 1992. 95.00 (*0-679-41458-4*) Random.

Napoleon: An Outline. Colin R. Ballard. LC 76-179503. (Select Bibliographies Reprint Ser.). 1977. reprint ed. 23.95 (*0-8369-6632-5*) Ayer.

Napoleon: How He Did It: The Memoirs of Baron Fain, First Secretary of the Emperor's Cabinet. Proctor Jones. Tr. by Dhyan Raufa from FRE. LC 97-94352. (Illus.). 212p. (C). 1998. 39.95 (*1-885446-02-0*) Proctor Jones.

Napoleon: Man & Meaning. Abbott W. Sherower. Ed. by T. S. Mufarrij-Sherower. (Emperor of the Centuries Ser.: Vol. IV). 448p. (C). 1991. 52.50 (*0-937811-04-1*) Napoleonic Heritage.

Napoleon: The Final Verdict. Philip J. Haythornthwaite. (Illus.). 320p. 1998. pap. 16.95 (*1-85409-467-X*, Pub. by Arms & Armour) Sterling.

Napoleon: The Final Verdict. Philip J. Haythornthwaite et al. LC 97-129127. (Illus.). 320p. 1997. 34.95 (*1-85409-342-8*, Pub. by Arms & Armour) Sterling.

***Napoleon: The Man Who Shaped Europe.** Ben Weider & Emile Gueguen. (Illus.). 288p. 2000. pap. 24.95 (*1-86227-078-3*, Pub. by Spellmnt Pubs) St Mut.

Napoleon & Austerlitz. Scott Bowden. (Illus.). 560p. 1997. 49.95 (*0-9626655-7-6*, Pub. by Emperors Pr) Combined Pub.

Napoleon & English Romanticism. Simon Bainbridge. (Studies in Romanticism: No. 14). (Illus.). 274p. (C). 1995. text 59.95 (*0-521-47336-5*) Cambridge U Pr.

***Napoleon & His Artists.** T. Smith. (Illus.). 306p. 1999. pap. text 24.95 (*0-09-479050-7*, Pub. by Constable & Co) Trafalgar.

Napoleon & His Artists. Timothy Wilson-Smith. (Illus.). 306p. 1996. 45.00 (*0-09-476110-8*, Pub. by Constable & Co) Trafalgar.

Napoleon & His Collaborators. Isser Woloch. 29.95 (*0-393-05009-2*) Norton.

Napoleon & His Marshals: Prion Lost Treasures. A. G. Macdonell. 325p. 1997. pap. 16.95 (*1-85375-222-3*) Prion.

Napoleon & His Times. Frank A. Kafker & James M. Laux. LC 88-661. 356p. (Orig.). (C). 1989. 29.50 (*0-89464-324-X*) Krieger.

Napoleon & His Times: Selected Interpretations. Ed. by Frank A. Kafker & James M. Laux. 360p. (C). 1992. pap. 26.50 (*0-89464-677-8*) Krieger.

Napoleon & History Painting: Antoine-Jean Gros's La Bataille d'Eylau. Christopher Prendergast. (Illus.). 238p. 1998. reprint ed. pap. text 45.00 (*0-19-817422-5*) OUP.

Napoleon & Iberia: The Twin Sieges of Ciudad Rodrigo & Almeida, 1810. Donald D. Howard. 440p. 1994. 40.00 (*1-85367-183-5*, 5434) Stackpole.

Napoleon & Josephine. Evangeline Bruce. 576p. 1996. pap. 16.00 (*1-57566-056-3*, Knsington) Kensgtn Pub Corp.

Napoleon & Josephine: An Improbable Marriage. Evangeline Bruce. 1995. 32.00 (*0-02-517810-5*) S&S Trade.

***Napoleon & Marie-Louise: The Emperor's Second Wife.** Alan Palmer. (Illus.). 288p. 2000. 26.00 (*0-7867-0804-2*, Pub. by Carroll & Graf) Publishers Group.

***Napoleon & Persia: Franco-Persian Relations under the First Empire.** Iradj Amini. 288p. 1999. (*0-7007-1168-6*, Pub. by Curzon Pr Ltd) Paul & Co Pubs.

Napoleon & Persia: Franco-Persian Relations under the First Empire. Iradj Amini. (Illus.). 228p. 1999. 34.95 (*0-934211-58-2*) Mage Pubs Inc.

Napoleon & the Conquest of the World: A Fictional Account of Napoleon's Escape from Russia, Invasion of England, & Conquest of Asia & America. Geoffroy-Chateau Louis-Napoleon & Louis-Napoleon Geoffroy-Chateau. LC 94-72170. (Illus.). 440p. 1994. reprint ed. lib. bdg. 39.95 (*0-9642115-3-X*) Campaign Press.

Napoleon & the French Empire: Mini-Play & Activities. Lawrence Stevens. (World History Ser.). (YA). (gr. 7 up). 1981. 6.50 (*0-89550-340-9*) Stevens & Shea.

N

Napoleon & the Restoration of the Bourbons: The Complete Portion of Macaulay's Projected History of France from the Restoration of the Bourbons to the Accession of Louis Phillipe. Thomas Babington Macaulay. LC 77-7107. 117p. 1977. text 44.00 (*0-231-04376-7*) Col U Pr.

Napoleon & the Szlachta. Christopher Blackburn. 260p. 1998. 36.00 (*0-88033-394-4*, 497, Pub. by East Eur Monographs) Col U Pr.

***Napoleon & the World War of 1813: Lessons in Coalition Warfighting.** J. P. Riley. LC 99-16266. (Illus.). 512p. 2000. 57.50 (*0-7146-4893-0*, Pub. by F Cass Pubs) Intl Spec Bk.

Napoleon & Waterloo: The Emperor's Campaign with the Armee Du Nord, 1815. Archibald F. Becke. LC 95-12756. (Napoleonic Library: Vol. 29). 352p. 1995. write for info. (*1-85367-206-8*, Pub. by Greenhill Bks) Stackpole.

Napoleon & Waterloo: The Emperor's Campaign with the Armee Du Nord 1815, 2 vols, Set. Archibald F. Becke. LC 73-160958. (Select Bibliographies Reprint Ser.). 1977. reprint ed. 72.95 (*0-8369-5825-X*) Ayer.

Napoleon at Bay, 1814. F. Loraine Petre. LC 93-40524. (Illus.). 240p. 1994. 40.00 (*1-85367-163-0*, 5557) Stackpole.

Napoleon at Leipzig: The Battle of Nations 1813. George Nafziger. (Illus.). 368p. 1997. 38.00 (*1-883476-10-0*, Pub. by Emperors Pr) Combined Pub.

Napoleon Bonaparte. Bob Carroll. LC 93-17852. (Importance of Ser.). 112p. (J). (gr. 5-8). 1994. lib. bdg. 22.45 (*1-56006-021-2*) Lucent Bks.

Napoleon Bonaparte. Leslie McGuire. (World Leaders Past & Present Ser.). (Illus.). 120p. (YA). (gr. 5 up). 1987. lib. bdg. 19.95 (*0-87754-554-5*) Chelsea Hse.

Napoleon Bonaparte: A Life. Alan Schom. (Illus.). 944p. 1998. pap. 22.00 (*0-06-092958-8*, Perennial) HarperTrade.

Napoleon Bonaparte Broward: Florida's Fighting Democrat. 2nd ed. Samuel Proctor. LC 92-39694. (Florida Sand Dollar Bk.). (Illus.). 416p. 1993. pap. 17.95 (*0-8130-1191-4*) U Press Fla.

Napoleon Bourassa, l'Homme & l'Artiste. Roger Le Moine. LC 75-3958. (Cahiers du Centre de Recherce en Civilisation Canadienne-Francaise Ser.: Vol. 8). (FRE.). 259p. 1974. reprint ed. pap. 80.30 (*0-608-02186-5*, 206285500003) Bks Demand.

Napoleon Conquers Austria: The 1809 Campaign for Vienna. James R. Arnold. LC 94-44177. 280p. 1995. 55.00 (*0-275-94694-0*, Praeger Pubs) Greenwood.

Napoleon Days: Historical Reenactment Script with Insights for Beginning & Intermediate Creative Writing Student. Anna LeNoir & Melanie Carlson. Ed. by I. Glass. (Illus.). 150p. (Orig.). (J). (gr. 1-6). 1996. write for info. (*0-614-13274-6*) Chldrens Mus Coll.

Napoleon Daze, 2 vols. Anna Lenoir. Ed. by Sherry Roberts. Incl. Vol. 1. Napoleon Daze. 2nd ed. Illus. by Jesse Bilyeu. LC 96-75801. 150p. (J). (gr. 4-6). 1997. reprint ed. lib. bdg. 14.95 (*1-889567-16-7*); Vol. 2. The Adventure Continues. Illus. by Sherry Bilyeu. LC 96-75795. 150p. (J). (gr. 6-9). 1997. lib. bdg. 9.99 (*1-889567-17-5*); 24.99 (*1-889567-18-3*) Chldrens Mus Coll.

Napoleon Hill's a Year of Growing Rich: Fifty-Two Steps to Achieving Life's Rewards. Napoleon Hill. Ed. by Matthew Sartwell & Samuel A. Cypert. LC 93-4361. 128p. 1993. pap. 10.95 (*0-452-27054-5*, Plume) Dutton Plume.

Napoleon Hill's Keys to Positive Thinking: 10 Steps to Health, Wealth & Success. Michael J. Ritt, Jr. & Napoleon Hill. 176p. 1999. pap. 11.95 (*0-452-27905-4*, Plume) Dutton Plume.

Napoleon Hill's Positive Action Plan: 365 Meditations for Making Each Day a Success. Napoleon Hill. 272p. 1997. pap. 11.95 (*0-452-27564-4*, Plume) Dutton Plume.

Napoleon, His Family & His Entourage: Actalog of the Documents from the State Historial Museum, Moscow see Napoleon, Sa Famille & Son Entourage: Catalogue des Documents du Musee Historique d'Etat, Moscou

Napoleon House. Walter L. Schindler. LC 89-34966. 107p. (C). 1989. pap. 16.50 (*0-208-02268-6*, Archon Bks) Shoe String.

Napoleon III. James McMillan. 200p. (C). 1995. pap. text 32.60 (*0-582-49483-4*, 78832) Longman.

Napoleon III: The Modern Emperor. Robert Sencourt. LC 71-38366. (Select Bibliographies Reprint Ser.). 1977. reprint ed. 24.95 (*0-8369-6783-6*) Ayer.

Napoleon III & Mexico: American Triumph over Monarchy. Alfred J. Hanna & Kathryn A. Hanna. LC 72-156761. (Illus.). 373p. reprint ed. pap. 115.70 (*0-7837-3751-3*, 204356800010) Bks Demand.

Napoleon III & the Concert of Europe. fac. ed. William E. Echard. LC 82-12660. 343p. 1983. reprint ed. pap. 106.40 (*0-7837-7765-5*, 204752100007) Bks Demand.

Napoleon III & the French Second Empire. Roger D. Price. LC 98-205522. (Lancaster Pamphlets Ser.). 96p. (C). 1997. pap. 11.99 (*0-415-15433-2*) Routledge.

Napoleon in Captivity: Reports of Count Balmain Russian Commissioner on the Island of St. Helena 1816-1820. Aleksandr Balmain. Ed. & Tr. by Julian Park. LC 72-160955. (Select Bibliographies Reprint Ser.). 1977. reprint ed. 25.95 (*0-8369-5822-5*) Ayer.

Napoleon in Egypt: A Chronicle of the French Occupation, 1788. Abal R. Al-Jabarti. Tr. by S. Moreh from ARA. (Illus.). 196p. (C). 1993. text 39.95 (*1-55876-069-5*); pap. text 16.95 (*1-55876-070-9*) Wiener Pubs Inc.

Napoleon in Exile, 2 vols. Barry E. O'Meara. LC 74-106520. reprint ed. 57.50 (*0-404-00610-8*) AMS Pr.

***Napoleon in the Holy Land.** Nathan Schur. LC 98-43920. 224p. 1999. 34.95 (*1-85367-345-5*, Pub. by Greenhill Bks) Stackpole.

Napoleon in the Making: Heir Imperial. Abbott W. Sherower. Ed. by T. S. Mufarrij-Sherower. (Emperor of the Centuries Ser.: Vol. I). 118p. 1986. 24.95 (*0-937811-01-7*) Napoleonic Heritage.

Napoleon in the Making: The First Exile. Abbott W. Sherower. Ed. by T. S. Maufrrij-Sherower. (Emperor of the Centuries Ser.: Vol. III). 130p. 1988. 24.95 (*0-937811-02-5*) Napoleonic Heritage.

Napoleon in the Making: The First Island. Abbott W. Sherower. Ed. by T. S. Mufarrij-Sherower. (Emperor of the Centuries Ser.: Vol. II). 242p. 1988. 28.50 (*0-937811-03-3*) Napoleonic Heritage.

Napoleon Jackson: The Gentleman of the Plush Rocker. Ruth M. Stuart. LC 72-2069. (Black Heritage Library Collection). (Illus.). 1977. reprint ed. 19.95 (*0-8369-9069-2*) Ayer.

Napoleon Lajoic: Modern Baseball's First Superstar, 1988. Jim Murphy. (Illus.). 88p. 1988. pap. 8.00 (*0-910137-31-5*) Soc Am Baseball Res.

Napoleon Must Die: A Mme. Vernet Investigation. Quinn Fawcett. 256p. (Orig.). 1993. mass mkt. 4.99 (*0-380-76541-1*, Avon Bks) Morrow Avon.

Napoleon Myth. Henry Evans. 1972. 59.95 (*0-8490-0704-6*) Gordon Pr.

Napoleon of Crime: The Life & Times of Adam Worth, Master Thief. Ben Macintyre. 368p. 1998. pap. 12.95 (*0-385-31993-2*) Doubleday.

Napoleon of Crime: The Life & Times of Adam Worth, Master Thief. Ben Macintyre. LC 97-520. 304p. 1997. 24.00 (*0-374-21899-4*) FS&G.

Napoleon of Notting Hill. G. K. Chesterton. (Classics Library). 1998. pap. 3.95 (*1-85326-280-3*, 2803WW, Pub. by Wrdsworth Edits) NTC Contemp Pub Co.

Napoleon of Notting Hill. G. K. Chesterton. (Illus.). 160p. 1991. pap. 5.95 (*0-486-26551-X*) Dover.

Napoleon of the Pacific, Kamehameha the Great. Herbert H. Gowen. LC 75-35193. reprint ed. 32.50 (*0-404-14221-4*) AMS Pr.

Napoleon on the Art of War. Ed. & Tr. by Jay Luvaas from FRE. LC 99-13248. 208p. 1999. 25.00 (*0-684-85185-7*) S&S Trade.

***Napoleon Options: Alternative Decisions of the Napoleonic Wars.** Ed. by John North. 208p. 2000. 34.95 (*1-85367-388-9*, Pub. by Greenhill Bks) Stackpole.

Napoleon, Russia, & the Olympian Gods: The Olympic Service of the Armory Museum in the Kremlin - an Illustrated Guide to Greek Mythology. Albert R. Baca. (Illus.). 80p. (Orig.). (C). 1996. pap. text 12.95 (*0-930437-01-2*) NewTEK Indust.

Napoleon, Sa Famille & Son Entourage: Catalogue des Documents du Musee Historique d'Etat, Moscou. Compiled by F. A. Petrov & A. D. Ianovskii.Tr. of Napoleon, His Family & His Entourage: Actalog of the Documents from the State Historial Museum, Moscow. (FRE.). 265p. 1998. lib. bdg. 100.00 (*0-88354-229-3*) N Ross.

Napoleon Takes Power: Dictatorship & Democracy in France at the Turn of the Nineteenth Century. Malcolm Crook. LC 98-211647. (Past in Perspective Ser.). 128p. 1998. pap. 14.95 (*0-7083-1401-5*, Pub. by Univ Wales Pr) Paul & Co Pubs.

Napoleon the Little. Victor Hugo. LC 92-29403. 1993. lib. bdg. 30.00 (*0-86527-408-8*) Fertig.

Napoleon the Little. Victor Hugo. 1972. 75.00 (*0-8490-0705-4*) Gordon Pr.

***Napoleon the Novelist.** Andy Martin. 2001. 57.95 (*0-7456-2535-5*, Pub. by Polity Pr); pap. 22.95 (*0-7456-2536-3*, Pub. by Polity Pr) Blackwell Pubs.

***Napoleon III: A Life.** Fenton Bresler. (Illus.). 300p. 1999. 25.00 (*0-7867-0660-0*) Carroll & Graf.

***Napoleon III & His Regime: An Extravaganza.** David Baguley. (Modernist Studies). (Illus.). 392p. 2000. 49.95 (*0-8071-2624-1*) La State U Pr.

***Napoleon III & Mexican Silver.** rev. ed. Shirley J. Black. (Illus.). vii, 220p. 2000. write for info. (*0-9676777-0-X*) Ferrell Pubns.

Napoleon Third: A Great Life in Brief. Albert L. Guerard. LC 78-13974. 207p. 1979. reprint ed. lib. bdg. 59.50 (*0-313-21062-4*, GUNA, Greenwood Pr) Greenwood.

Napoleon Third & the Crisis, 1865-1866. Evelyn A. Pottinger. LC 66-18253. (Historical Studies: No. 75). 248p. 1966. 20.00 (*0-674-60050-9*) HUP.

Napoleon Third & the Stoffel Affair. Roger L. Williams. LC 93-77109. 248p. 1993. 27.50 (*1-881019-03-9*) High Plns WY.

***Napoleon 1813.** Yehezkel Shelah. 204p. 2000. 32.00 (*1-85756-463-4*, Pub. by Janus Pubng); pap. 16.95 (*1-85756-496-0*, Pub. by Janus Pubng) Paul & Co Pubs.

***Napoleonic Army Handbook: The British Army & Her Allies.** Michael Oliver & Richard Partridge. (Illus.). 80p. 2000. 75.00 (*0-09-477630-X*, Pub. by Constable & Co) Trafalgar.

Napoleonic Art: Nationalism & the Spirit of Rebellion in France, 1815-1848. Barbara A. Day-Hickman. LC 97-35761. (Illus.). 176p. 1998. 55.00 (*0-87413-615-6*) U Delaware Pr.

Napoleonic Empire: Studies in European History. Ellis. 1996. text 11.95 (*0-333-42047-0*, Pub. by Macmillan) St Martin.

Napoleonic Era Daily Almanac: A Chronology of Important Events from 1769-1821. Pierre R. Beaumier. (Illus.). 455p. (Orig.). (C). 1993. pap. 25.00 (*1-883452-00-7*) Vive LEmpereur.

Napoleonic Exiles in America: A Study in Diplomatic History, 1815-1819. Jesse S. Reeves. LC 78-63910. (Johns Hopkins University. Studies in the Social Sciences. Thirtieth Ser. 1912: 9-10). reprint ed. 32.50 (*0-404-61162-1*) AMS Pr.

Napoleonic Imperialism & the Savoyard Monarchy, 1773-1821: State Building in Piedmont. Ed. by Michael Broers. LC 97-20840. (Studies in French Civilization: Vol. 12). 596p. 1997. text 119.95 (*0-7734-8609-7*) E Mellen.

Napoleonic Plastic Figure Modeling: Bill Ottinger's Masterclass. Bill Ottinger. (Illus.). 128p. 1997. 29.95 (*1-85915-019-5*, Pub. by W & G) Motorbooks Intl.

Napoleonic Revolution. Robert B. Holtman. LC 67-11308. 224p. 1979. pap. text 15.95 (*0-8071-0487-6*) La State U Pr.

***Napoleonic Soldier.** Stephen E. Maughan. LC 99-490336. (Illus.). 144p. 2000. 52.95 (*1-86126-281-7*, 129758AE, Pub. by Cro1wood) Motorbooks Intl.

Napoleonic Source Book. Philip J. Haythornthwaite. (Illus.). 416p. 1997. pap. 24.95 (*1-85409-287-1*, Pub. by Arms & Armour) Sterling.

Napoleonic Uniforms, Vol. 1. John R. Elting. 1993. 140.00 (*0-02-897116-7*) Mac Lib Ref.

Napoleonic Uniforms, Vol. 2. John R. Elting. 1993. 140.00 (*0-02-897117-5*) Mac Lib Ref.

***Napoleonic Uniforms; The Allies: Vassals & Enemies.** John R. Elting. (Illus.). 2000. 250.00 (*1-883476-20-8*, Pub. by Emperors Pr) Combined Pub.

Napoleonic Wars. Gunther E. Rothenberg. (Illus.). 224p. 1999. 29.95 (*0-304-35267-5*, Pub. by Cassell) Sterling.

Napoleonic Wars, Vol. I. Liliane Funcken & Fred Funcken. write for info. (*0-318-58180-9*) P-H.

Napoleonic Wars: Napoleon's Army. Rene Chartrand. (Brassey's History of Uniforms Ser.). (Illus.). 144p. 1996. 31.95 (*1-85753-183-3*, Pub. by Brasseys) Brasseys.

Napoleonic Wars: Napoleon's Army. Rene Chartrand. (Illus.). 144p. 1998. pap. text 21.95 (*1-85753-220-1*, Pub. by Brasseys) Brasseys.

Napoleonic Wars: Role Play Peacegames. David W. Felder. 52p. 1996. pap. text 8.95 (*0-910959-77-3*, B&G 26C) Wellington Pr.

Napoleonic Wars: Wellington's Army. Ian Fletcher. (Illus.). 144p. 1998. pap. text 21.95 (*1-85753-221-X*, Pub. by Brasseys) Brasseys.

Napoleonic Wars: Wellington's Army. Jan Fletcher. (Brassey's History of Uniforms Ser.). (Illus.). 144p. 1996. 31.95 (*1-85753-173-6*, Pub. by Brasseys) Brasseys.

Napoleonic Wars, 1803-1815. David Gates. LC 97-14188. (Modern Wars Ser.). (Illus.). 324p. 1997. pap. text 19.95 (*0-340-61447-1*) OUP.

Napoleon's Army, 1807-1814: As Depicted in the Prints of Aaron Martinet. Guy C. Dempsey. LC 98-113836. (Illus.). 192p. 1997. 34.95 (*1-85409-347-9*, Pub. by Arms & Armour) Sterling.

Napoleon's Battle, Napoleonic Miniatures Rules. R. Craig Taylor. (Illus.). 96p. (YA). (gr. 9 up). 1989. 25.00 (*1-56038-008-X*) Avalon Hill.

Napoleon's Book of Fate. Richard Deacon. Orig. Title: The Book of Fate: Its Origins & Uses. 1977. reprint ed. 10.00 (*0-8065-0564-8*, Citadel Pr); reprint ed. pap. 4.95 (*0-8065-0577-X*, Citadel Pr) Carol Pub Group.

Napoleon's Book of Fate & Oraculum. 191p. 1996. reprint ed. pap. 17.95 (*1-56459-687-7*) Kessinger Pub.

Napoleon's British Visitors & Captives, 1801-1815. John G. Alger. LC 71-113541. reprint ed. 42.50 (*0-404-00324-9*) AMS Pr.

Napoleon's Campaigns in Italy. Philip J. Haythornthwaite. (Men-at-Arms Ser.: No. 257). (Illus.). 48p. pap. 11.95 (*1-85532-281-1*, 9228, Pub. by Osprey) Stackpole.

Napoleon's Conquest of Prussia, 1806. F. Loraine Petre. LC 92-41764. 344p. 1993. 40.00 (*1-85367-145-2*, 5561) Stackpole.

Napoleon's Continental Blockade: The Case of Alsace. Geoffrey Ellis. (Oxford Historical Monographs). (Illus.). 1981. 55.00 (*0-19-821881-8*) OUP.

Napoleon's Cuirassiers & Carabiniers. Emir Bukhari. (Men-at-Arms Ser.: No. 64). (Illus.). 48p. pap. 12.95 (*0-85045-096-9*, 9012, Pub. by Osprey) Stackpole.

Napoleon's Dragoons & Lancers. Emir Bukhari. (Men-at-Arms Ser.: No. 55). (Illus.). 48p. pap. 12.95 (*0-85045-088-8*, 9008, Pub. by Osprey) Stackpole.

Napoleon's Egyptian Empire. Michael Barthorp. (Men-at-Arms Ser.: No. 79). (Illus.). 48p. pap. 11.95 (*0-85045-126-4*, 9207, Pub. by Osprey) Stackpole.

Napoleon's Elite. Raymond Horricks. LC 94-43361. Orig. Title: In Flight with the Eagle. 272p. 1995. 34.95 (*1-56000-209-3*) Transaction Pubs.

Napoleon's Elite Cavalry: Cavalry of the Imperial Guard, 1804-1815. Illus. by Lucien Rousselot. 208p. 1999. 85.00 (*1-85367-371-4*, Pub. by Greenhill Bks) Stackpole.

***Napoleon's Generals of the Glory Years.** Tony Linck. (Illus.). 2000. 38.00 (*1-883476-21-6*, Pub. by Emperors Pr) Combined Pub.

Napoleon's German Allies. Otto Von Pivka. (Men-at-Arms Ser.: No. 44). (Illus.). 48p. pap. 11.95 (*0-85045-211-2*, 9216, Pub. by Ospry) Stackpole.

Napoleon's German Allies Vol. 2: Nassau & Oldenburg. Otto Von Pivka. (Men-at-Arms Ser.: No. 43). (Illus.). 48p. pap. 11.95 (*0-85045-255-4*, 9151, Pub. by Osprey) Stackpole.

Napoleon's German Allies Vol. 3: Saxony. Otto Von Pivka. (Men-at-Arms Ser.: No. 90). (Illus.). 48p. pap. 11.95 (*0-85045-309-7*, 9028, Pub. by Ospry) Stackpole.

Napoleon's German Allies Vol. 4: Bavaria. Otto Von Pivka. (Men-at-Arms Ser.: No. 106). (Illus.). 48p. pap. 11.95 (*0-85045-373-9*, 9039, Pub. by Ospry) Stackpole.

Napoleon's German Allies Vol. 5: Hessen-Darmstadt & Hessen-Kassel. Otto Von Pivka. (Men-at-Arms Ser.: No. 122). (Illus.). 48p. 1982. pap. 11.95 (*0-85045-431-X*, 9055, Pub. by Osprey) Stackpole.

Napoleon's Grand Strategy: New Subtitle. Schneid. 320p. write for info. (*0-8133-3423-3*, Pub. by Westview) HarpC.

Napoleon's Grande Armee' of 1813. Scott Bowden. (Armies of the Napoleonic Wars Research Ser.). (Illus.). 376p. 1990. 34.95 (*0-9626655-1-7*, Pub. by Emperors Pr); lib. bdg. 34.95 (*0-318-50061-2*) Emperors Pr.

Napoleon's Great Adversary: Archduke Charles & the Austrian Army, 1792, 1814. Gunther E. Rothenberg. 240p. 1997. 76.00 (*1-873376-40-5*, Pub. by Spellmnt Pubs) St Mut.

Napoleon's Great Adversary: Archduke Charles & the Austrian Army, 1792-1814. Gunther E. Rothenberg. LC 94-77048. (Illus.). 288p. 1995. reprint ed. 32.95 (*1-885119-21-6*) Sarpedon.

Napoleon's Guard Cavalry. Emir Bukhari. (Men-at-Arms Ser.: No. 83). (Illus.). 48p. pap. 11.95 (*0-85045-288-0*, 9022, Pub. by Ospry) Stackpole.

Napoleon's Guard Infantry. Philip J. Haythornthwaite. (Men-at-Arms Ser.: No. 153). (Illus.). 48p. pap. 11.95 (*0-85045-340-2*, 9085, Pub. by Ospry) Stackpole.

Napoleon's Guard Infantry. Philip J. Haythornthwaite. (Men-at-Arms Ser.: No. 160). (Illus.). 48p. pap. 12.95 (*0-85045-535-9*, 9092, Pub. by Ospry) Stackpole.

Napoleon's Guard Infantry. Philip J. Haythornthwaite. 1984. pap. 12.95 (*0-85045-534-0*) Stackpole.

Napoleon's Hussars. Emir Bukhari. (Men-at-Arms Ser.: No. 76). (Illus.). 48p. pap. 12.95 (*0-85045-246-5*, 9019, Pub. by Ospry) Stackpole.

Napoleon's Imperial Guard. Stephen Maughan. (Illus.). 96p. 1999. pap. 22.95 (*1-86126-290-6*, Pub. by Cro1wood) Motorbooks Intl.

Napoleon's Integration of Europe. Stuart J. Woolf. (Illus.). 320p. (C). (gr. 13). 1991. 70.00 (*0-415-04961-X*, A5688) Routledge.

Napoleon's Invasion of Russia. George F. Nafziger. 704p. 1998. pap. 24.95 (*0-89141-661-7*) Presidio Pr.

Napoleon's Irish Legion. John G. Gallaher. LC 92-18518. 356p. (C). 1993. 41.95 (*0-8093-1825-3*) S Ill U Pr.

Napoleon's Italian & Neapolitan Troops. Otto Von Pivka. (Men-at-Arms Ser.: No. 88). (Illus.). 48p. pap. 11.95 (*0-85045-303-8*, 9026, Pub. by Ospry) Stackpole.

Napoleon's Jailer: Lt. Gen. Sir Hudson Lowe "A Life" Desmond Gregory. LC 95-48146. (Illus.). 240p. 1996. 39.50 (*0-8386-3657-8*) Fairleigh Dickinson.

Napoleon's Last Campaign in Germany, 1813. F. Loraine Petre. 424p. 1992. 37.50 (*1-85367-121-5*) Stackpole.

Napoleon's Last Victory & the Emergence of Modern War. Robert M. Epstein. LC 93-38243. (Modern War Studies). (Illus.). 232p. (Orig.). (C). 1994. 29.95 (*0-7006-0664-5*) U Pr of KS.

Napoleon's Last Victory & the Emergence of Modern War. Robert M. Epstein. LC 93-38243. (Modern War Studies). (Illus.). 232p. (Orig.). (C). 1995. pap. 14.95 (*0-7006-0751-X*) U Pr of KS.

***Napoleon's Legacy: Problems of Government in Restoration Europe.** Ed. by Lucy Riall & David Laven. (Illus.). 256p. 2000. 65.00 (*1-85973-244-5*, Pub. by Berg Pubs); pap. 19.50 (*1-85973-249-6*, Pub. by Berg Pubs) NYU Pr.

Napoleon's Letters. Napoleon Bonaparte. Ed. by J. M. Thompson. (Lost Treasure Ser.). 331p. 1998. pap. 19.95 (*1-85375-269-X*) Prion.

Napoleon's Light Infantry. Philip Haythornthwaite. (Men-at-Arms Ser.: No. 146). (Illus.). 48p. pap. 11.95 (*0-85045-521-9*, 9078, Pub. by Ospry) Stackpole.

Napoleon's Line Cavalry: Recreated in Color Photographs. Stephen Maughan. (Illus.). 1997. pap. text 19.95 (*1-85915-038-1*, Pub. by W & G) Motorbooks Intl.

***Napoleon's Line Cavalry Recreated in Color Photographs: Europa Militaria #10.** Maugham. 96p. 2000. pap. 23.95 (*1-86126-266-3*, Pub. by Cro1wood) Motorbooks Intl.

Napoleon's Line Chasseurs. Emir Bukhari. (Men-at-Arms Ser.: No. 68). (Illus.). 48p. pap. 11.95 (*0-85045-269-4*, 9014, Pub. by Ospry) Stackpole.

Napoleon's Line Infantry. Philip J. Haythornthwaite. (Men-at-Arms Ser.: No. 141). (Illus.). 48p. pap. 11.95 (*0-85045-512-X*, 9073, Pub. by Ospry) Stackpole.

Napoleon's Line Infantry & Artillery: Recreated in Color Photographs. Stephen Maughan. (Illus.). 1997. pap. text 19.95 (*1-85915-053-5*, Pub. by W & G) Motorbooks Intl.

***Napoleon's Line Infantry Recreated in Color Photographs: Europa Militaria #11.** Maugham. 96p. 2000. pap. 23.95 (*1-86126-267-1*, Pub. by Cro1wood) Motorbooks Intl.

***Napoleon's Lost Fleet.** Discovery Communications Staff. 1999. write for info. (*0-8129-3281-1*, Times Bks) Crown Pub Group.

***Napoleon's Lost Fleet: Bonaparte, Nelson & the Battle of the Nile.** Laura Foreman & Ellen Blue Phillips. LC 99-33398. (Illus.). 216p. 1999. 35.00 (*1-56331-831-8*) Discovery.

Napoleon's Love Story. R. McNair Wilson. 1972. 250.00 (*0-8490-0706-2*) Gordon Pr.

Napoleon's Love Story. unabridged ed. R. McNair Wilson. 267p. 1952. reprint ed. pap. 12.00 (*0-945001-84-3*) GSG & Assocs.

Napoleon's Mare. Lou Robinson. 177p. 1991. 18.95 (*0-932511-47-3*); pap. 8.95 (*0-932511-48-1*) Fiction Coll.

Napoleon's Marshals. Emir Bukhari. (Men-at-Arms Ser.: No. 87). (Illus.). 48p. pap. 12.95 (*0-85045-305-4*, 9025, Pub. by Ospry) Stackpole.

Napoleon's Memoirs. Napoleon Bonaparte. Ed. & Tr. by Somerset De Chair from FRE. (Illus.). 605p. 1986. reprint ed. pap. 19.95 (*0-948166-10-X*, Pub. by Soho Bk Co) Dufour.

Napoleon's Military Machine. Philip J. Haythornthwaite. 200p. 1997. 100.00 (*1-873376-46-4*, Pub. by Spellmnt Pubs) St Mut.

An Asterisk (*) at the beginning of an entry indicates that the title is appearing for the first time.

Napoleon's Military Machine. Philip J. Haythornthwaite. (Illus.). 200p. 1995. reprint ed. 37.95 (*1-885119-18-6*) Sarpedon.
Napoleon's Mother. R. McNair Wilson. 1972. 250.00 (*0-8490-0707-0*) Gordon Pr.
Napoleon's Navigation System. Frank E. Melvin. LC 79-135721. reprint ed. 47.50 (*0-404-04288-0*) AMS Pr.
Napoleon's Overseas Army. Rene Chartrand. (Men-at-Arms Ser.: No. 211). (Illus.). 48p. pap. 11.95 (*0-85045-900-1*, 9144, Pub. by Ospry) Stackpole.
***Napoleon's Regiments: Battle Histories of the Regiments of the French Army, 1792-1815.** Digby G. Smith. LC 00-38073. 2000. write for info. (*1-85367-413-3*, Pub. by Greenhill Bks) Stackpole.
Napoleon's Russian Campaign. Philippe P. Segur. Tr. by J. David Townsend from FRE. LC 75-27657. (Illus.). 306p. 1976. reprint ed. lib. bdg. 35.00 (*0-8371-8443-6*, SENR, Greenwood Pr) Greenwood.
Napoleon's Satellite Kingdoms: Managing Conquered Peoples. Owen Connelly. 400p. (C). 1990. reprint ed. 21.50 (*0-89464-416-5*) Krieger.
Napoleon's Sea-Soldiers. Rene Chartrand. (Men-at-Arms Ser.: No. 227). (Illus.). 48p. pap. 11.95 (*0-85045-998-2*, 9185, Pub. by Ospry) Stackpole.
Napoleon's Specialist Troops. Philip J. Haythornthwaite. (Men-at-Arms Ser.: No. 199). (Illus.). 48p. pap. 11.95 (*0-85045-841-2*, 9132, Pub. by Ospry) Stackpole.
Napoleons Traitor. (Illus.). 112p. (Orig.). 1989. write for info. (*0-318-65205-6*) T Giese.
Napoleon's Traitor: The Masons & Marshal Ney's Mysterious Escape. Toby Giese. (Illus.). 77p. (Orig.). 1989. pap. 18.00 (*0-9623241-0-8*) T Giese.
Napoleons's Cavalry & Its Leaders. David Johnson. 192p. 1997. write for info. (*1-86227-047-3*, Pub. by Spellmnt Pubs) St Mut.
Napoli Milionaria. Eduardo DeFilippo. Tr. & Adapted by Tori Haring-Smith. 101p. 1996. pap. 5.95 (*0-87129-601-2*, N35) Dramatic Pub.
Napolo & the Python. Steve Chimombo. (African Writers Ser.). 192p. 1994. pap. 15.95 (*0-435-91199-6*) Heinemann.
***Nappen on New Jersey Gun Law.** Evan F. Nappen. (Illus.). 400p. 1999. pap. 24.95 (*0-9670660-2-6*) Gun Writes Pr Inc.
***Nappily Ever After.** Trisha R. Thomas. LC 00-29440. (Illus.). 256p. (J). 2000. 22.00 (*0-609-60583-6*, Crown) Crown Pub Group.
Napping House. Audrey Wood. LC 83-13035. (Illus.). 32p. (J). (ps-3). 1984. 16.00 (*0-15-256708-9*, Harcourt Child Bks) Harcourt.
***Napping House.** Audrey Wood. (Illus.). 32p. (J). (ps-k). 2000. 5.95 (*0-15-202632-0*, Harcourt Child Bks) Harcourt.
Napping House. Audrey Wood. (Big Bks.). (Illus.). 32p. (J). (ps-3). 1991. reprint ed. pap. 23.95 (*0-15-256711-9*, Harcourt Child Bks) Harcourt.
Napping House: Mini Book. Audrey Wood. 1996. 5.95 (*0-15-201508-6*) Harcourt.
Napping House: Mini Edition. Audrey Wood & Don Wood. LC 89-24598. (Illus.). 32p. (J). 1996. pap. 5.95 (*0-15-201062-9*, Red Wagon Bks) Harcourt.
Napping House & Other Stories Audio. unabridged ed. Audrey Wood. (J). (ps-3). 1987. audio 11.95 (*0-89845-747-5*, CPN 1816, Caedmon) HarperAudio.
Napping House Wakes Up. Audrey Wood. LC 83-13035. (Illus.). 20p. (J). (ps-3). 1994. 17.95 (*0-15-200890-X*, Harcourt Child Bks) Harcourt.
Nappy: Growing up Black & Female in America. Aliona L. Gibson. LC 95-165985. (Illus.). 140p. 1995. 17.95 (*0-86316-322-X*) Writers & Readers.
Nappy: Growing up Black & Female in America. Aliona L. Gibson. 176p. 1998. pap. 13.00 (*0-86316-329-7*) Writers & Readers.
Nappy Edges. Ntozake Shange. 160p. 1991. reprint ed. pap. 10.95 (*0-312-06424-1*) St Martin.
Nappy Hair. Caroivia Herron. LC 99-169943. (J). 1999. pap. 6.99 (*0-679-89445-4*, Pub. by Random Bks Yng Read) Random.
Nappy Hair. Carolivia Herron. (Illus.). (J). 17.00 (*0-614-28301-9*) Knopf.
Nappy Hair. Carolivia Herron. LC 96-2061. (Illus.). (J). (gr. k-3). 1997. 17.00 (*0-679-87937-4*, Pub. by Knopf Bks Yng Read) Random.
Nappy Hair. Carolivia Herron. LC 96-2061. (Illus.). (J). 1997. lib. bdg. 18.99 (*0-679-97937-9*) Random.
***Nappyheaded Blackgirls: A New Aesthetic.** 86p. 1999. pap. 12.00 (*0-9674446-0-8*) IBIS Commns.
Napraforgo see Sunflower
***Naps: The Sound of "N"** Cynthia Fitterer Klingel & Robert B. Noyed. LC 99-20956. (Wonder Books Ser.). (Illus.). 24p. (J). 1999. lib. bdg. 21.41 (*1-56766-697-3*) Childs World.
NAPSAC Directory of Alternative Birth Services. 13th ed. Lee Stewart et al. LC 77-93424. 128p. 1998. pap. 7.95 (*0-934426-83-X*) NAPSAC Reprods.
Napsha, the Miracle Dragon. C. J. Ryce. LC 96-69587. (Illus.). 64p. (Orig.). (J). (gr. 1-5). 1997. per. 13.95 (*0-9653695-2-8*) Spellbound Pub.
Naptime, Laptime. Eileen Spinelli. (Illus.). 24p. (J). 1995. 6.95 (*0-590-48510-5*, Cartwheel) Scholastic Inc.
Naqshbandi Sufi Way: History & Guidebook of the Saints of the Golden Chair. Shaykh H. Al-Kabbani. LC 99-211185. (Illus.). 504p. 1995. 99.00 (*0-934905-34-7*) Kazi Pubns.
Nar Morgondagarna Sjong see When Our Tomorrows Sang: From Forgotten Years
Nara Buddhist Art: Todai-Ji. Takeshi Kobayashi. Tr. by Richard L. Gage from JPN. LC 74-22034. (Heibonsha Survey of Japanese Art Ser.: Vol. 5). Orig. Title: Todai-Ji No Daibutsu. (Illus.). 160p. 1975. 20.00 (*0-8348-1021-2*) Weatherhill.
Nara Encounters. Ed. by Keiko McDonald & J. Thomas Rimer. LC 97-2452. (Illus.). 112p. 1997. pap. 19.95 (*0-8348-0387-9*) Weatherhill.
Narada Bhakti Sutra: The Secrets of Transcendental Love. 2nd ed. A. C. Bhaktivedanta & Prabhupada. 213p. 1991. reprint ed. pap. 7.95 (*0-89213-273-6*) Bhaktivedanta.
Narada Bhakti Sutras: The Gospel of Divine Love. Narada. Tr. by Swami Tyagisananda. 287p. 1949. pap. 4.95 (*81-7120-329-9*) Vedanta Pr.
Narada Easy Piano Sampler. (Easy Play Ser.). 64p. 1994. per. 10.95 (*0-7935-2873-9*, 00222569) H Leonard.
Narada New Age Guitar Sampler. 88p. 1992. otabind 14.95 (*0-7935-1638-2*, 00699349) H Leonard.
Narada Purana, Pt. I. Ed. & Tr. by G. V. Tagare. (Ancient Indian Tradition & Mythology Ser.: Vol. 15). 1980. 26.00 (*0-8364-2495-6*, Pub. by Motilal Bnarsidass) S Asia.
Narada Purana, Pt. II. Ed. & Tr. by G. V. Tagare. (Ancient Indian Tradition & Mythology Ser.: Vol. 16). 1981. 26.00 (*0-8364-2496-4*, Pub. by Motilal Bnarsidass) S Asia.
Narada Purana, Pt. III. Ed. & Tr. by G. V. Tagare. (Ancient Indian Tradition & Mythology Ser.: Vol. 17). 1991. 26.00 (*0-8364-2497-2*, Pub. by Motilal Bnarsidass) S Asia.
Narada Purana, Pt. IV. Ed. & Tr. by G. V. Tagare. (Ancient Indian Tradition & Mythology Ser.: Vol. 18). 1982. 26.00 (*0-8364-2498-0*, Pub. by Motilal Bnarsidass) S Asia.
Narada Purana, Pt. V. Ed. & Tr. by G. V. Tagare. (Ancient Indian Tradition & Mythology Ser.: Vol. 19). 1982. 26.00 (*0-8364-2499-9*, Pub. by Motilal Bnarsidass) S Asia.
Narada's Way of Divine Love: The Bhakti Sutras. Narada. Tr. by Swami Prabhavananda from SAN. LC 75-161488. 177p. 1971. pap. 4.95 (*81-7120-506-2*) Vedanta Pr.
***Narada's Way of Divine Love: The Bhakti Sutras.** Swami Prabhavananda. 192p. 2000. pap. 9.95 (*0-87481-054-X*) Vedanta Pr.
Naradasmrti, Pt. 1. Ed. & Tr. by Richard W. Lariviere from SAN. LC 89-37780. (Studies on South Asia: No. 4). xxx, 328p. 1989. 30.00 (*0-936115-06-8*) U Penn South Asia.
Naradasmrti, Pt. 2. Ed. & Tr. by Richard W. Lariviere from SAN. LC 89-37780. (Studies on South Asia: No. 5). xxxii, 250p. 1989. 30.00 (*0-685-48877-2*) U Penn South Asia.
Naradasmrti, Set. Ed. & Tr. by Richard W. Lariviere from SAN. LC 89-37780. (Studies on South Asia: No. 4). xxx, 328p. 1989. 20.00 (*0-936115-04-1*) U Penn South Asia.
Naradasmrti, Set. Ed. & Tr. by Richard W. Lariviere from SAN. LC 89-37780. (Studies on South Asia: No. 5). xxxii, 250p. 1989. 20.00 (*0-936115-05-X*) U Penn South Asia.
***Naradaw New Age Piano: Sampler 2.** 88p. 1998. otabind 14.95 (*0-7935-9805-2*) H Leonard.
Narahari: A Novel. Vinayak K. Gokak. (C). 1992. reprint ed. 15.00 (*81-7018-710-9*, Pub. by BR Pub) S Asia.
Naranja Maravillosa. Silvina Ocampo.Tr. of Marvelous Orange. (Orig.). (J). (gr. 4-7). 1998. pap. text 9.95 (*84-204-3676-3*) Santillana.
Narayan: A Study in Transcendence. Mary Beatina. LC 93-4941. (Studies of World Literature in English: Vol. 3). XII, 154p. (C). 1994. text 41.95 (*0-8204-2137-5*) P Lang Pubng.
Narayan Datt Tiwari: Life Story. D. P. Nautiyal. LC 95-900085. (C). 1994. write for info. (*81-207-1655-8*) Sterling Pubs.
Narayaneeyam. pap. 5.95 (*0-87481-474-X*, Pub. by Ramakrishna Math) Vedanta Pr.
Narc in the Dark. Daniel Byram. (Illus.). 235p. 1998. pap. 14.95 (*1-892798-01-8*, 9801) Sierra West.
Narcisos Negros. Ivan Silen. LC 97-37407. 1997. pap. 12.95 (*0-8477-0303-7*) U of PR Pr.
Narcissa Whitman: Brave Pioneer. Louis Sabin. LC 81-23066. (Illus.). 48p. (J). (gr. 4-6). 1997. pap. 3.95 (*0-89375-763-2*) Troll Communs.
Narcissa Whitman, Brave Pioneer. Louis Sabin. 1982. 8.70 (*0-606-01687-2*, Pub. by Turtleback) Demco.
Narcissa Whitman on the Oregon Trail. Lawrence Dodd. 19p. 1986. pap. 4.95 (*0-87770-369-8*) Ye Galleon.
Narcissism. Alexander Lowen. 1997. per. 8.00 (*0-684-84299-8*) S&S Trade.
Narcissism: A New Theory. Neville Symington. 160p. 1993. pap. text 26.50 (*1-85575-047-3*, Pub. by H Karnac Bks Ltd) Other Pr LLC.
Narcissism: Artists Reflect Themselves. Reesey Shaw & John Welchman. LC 95-83175. (Illus.). 64p. 1996. pap. write for info. (*1-885088-04-3*) CA Ctr Arts.
Narcissism: Psychoanalytic Essays. Bela Grunberger. 332p. 1990. reprint ed. pap. 24.95 (*0-8236-8155-6*, BN 23491) Intl Univs Pr.
Narcissism: The Self & Society. Reuben Fine. 384p. 1986. text 64.50 (*0-231-05732-6*) Col U Pr.
Narcissism & Character Transformation. Nathan Schwartz-Salant. (Illus.). 192p. 1982. pap. 18.00 (*0-919123-08-2*, Pub. by Inner City Bks) BookWorld.
Narcissism & Death. Mariarosa Sclauzero. LC 84-8852. (Illus.). 112p. (Orig.). 1984. 15.00 (*0-88268-027-7*); pap. 8.50 (*0-88268-028-5*) Open Bk Pubns.
Narcissism & Intimacy: Love & Marriage in an Age of Confusion. Marion F. Solomon. 240p. 1992. pap. 12.95 (*0-393-30916-9*) Norton.
Narcissism & the Interpersonal Self. Ed. by John Fiscalini & Alan L. Grey. LC 92-35506. (Personality, Psychopathology & Psychotherapy: Theoretical & Clinical Perspectives Ser.). (Illus.). 384p. (C). 1993. text 61.50 (*0-231-07010-1*) Col U Pr.
Narcissism & the Literary Libido: Rhetoric, Text, & Subjectivity. Marshall W. Alcorn. (Literature & Psychoanalysis Ser.). 1997. pap. text 20.00 (*0-8147-0665-7*) NYU Pr.
Narcissism & the Literary Libido: Rhetoric, Text, & Subjectivity. Marshall W. Alcorn, Jr. & Marshall W. Alcorn, Jr. 300p. (C). 1993. text 50.00 (*0-8147-0614-2*) NYU Pr.
Narcissism & the Novel. Jeffrey Berman. 320p. (C). 1990. text 50.00 (*0-8147-1132-4*) NYU Pr.
Narcissism & the Novel. Jeffrey Berman. 350p. (C). 1992. pap. text 19.50 (*0-8147-1171-5*) NYU Pr.
Narcissism & the Psychotherapist. Sheila R. Welt & William G. Herron. LC 89-27520. 356p. 1990. lib. bdg. 42.00 (*0-89862-398-7*) Guilford Pubns.
***Narcissism & the Relational World.** William G. Herron. LC 99-41511. 288p. 1999. 54.00 (*0-7618-1496-5*); pap. 34.50 (*0-7618-1497-3*) U Pr of Amer.
Narcissism, Nihilism - Simplicity & Self: Studies in Literature As Psychology. Karl M. Abenheimer. Ed. by Robert R. Calder. (Aberdeen University Press Bks.). 160p. 1991. pap. text 16.91 (*0-08-041405-2*, Pub. by Aberdeen U Pr) Macmillan.
Narcissistic - Borderline Couple: A Psychoanalytic Perspective on Marital Treatment. Joan Lachkar. LC 91-28228. 224p. 1992. text 33.95 (*0-87630-634-2*) Brunner-Mazel.
Narcissistic & Borderline Disorders: An Integrated Developmental Approach. 18th ed. James F. Masterson. LC 81-38540. 260p. 1989. text 38.95 (*0-87630-292-4*) Brunner-Mazel.
Narcissistic Condition: A Fact of Our Lives & Times. Ed. by Marie C. Nelson. LC 76-20724. (Self-in-Process Ser.: Vol. 1). 300p. 1977. 43.95 (*0-87705-250-6*, Kluwer Acad Hman Sci) Kluwer Academic.
Narcissistic Family: Diagnosis & Treatment. Stephanie Donaldson-Pressman. LC 97-16678. 181p. 1997. 25.95 (*0-02-925435-3*) Free Pr.
Narcissistic Family: Diagnosis & Treatment. Stephanie Donaldson-Pressman & Robert M. Pressman. LC 93-40133. 1994. write for info. (*0-02-925434-5*) Free Pr.
Narcissistic Family: Diagnosis & Treatment. Stephanie Donaldson-Pressman & Robert H. Pressman. LC 97-16678. 192p. 1997. pap. 25.95 (*0-7879-0870-3*) Jossey-Bass.
Narcissistic Giving: A Study of People Who Cheat in Relationships. Gerald Alper. LC 94-28831. 130p. 1996. 44.95 (*1-883255-81-3*); pap. 24.95 (*1-883255-80-5*) Intl Scholars.
Narcissistic Narrative: The Metafictional Paradox. Linda Hutcheon. 192p. 1984. pap. 13.95 (*0-416-37140-X*, NO. 4148) Routledge.
Narcissistic Process & Corporate Decay: The Theory of the Organizational Ideal. Howard Schwartz. 166p. (C). 1992. pap. text 18.50 (*0-8147-7938-7*) NYU Pr.
Narcissistic Process & Corporate Decay: The Theory of the Organizational Ideal. Howard S. Schwartz. 224p. (C). 1990. text 50.00 (*0-8147-7913-1*) NYU Pr.
Narcissistic Pursuit of Perfection. 2nd rev. ed. Arnold Rothstein. LC 84-25159. 327p. 1985. 50.00 (*0-8236-3494-9*, 03493) Intl Univs Pr.
Narcissistic Pursuit of Perfection. 2nd rev. ed. Arnold Rothstein. 327p. 1999. pap. 29.95 (*0-8236-8157-2*, 23494) Intl Univs Pr.
Narcissistic States & the Therapeutic Process. Sheldon Bach. LC 85-1440. 250p. 1985. 45.00 (*0-87668-893-8*) Aronson.
Narcissistic Wounds: Clinical Perspectives. Judy Cooper & Nilda Maxwell. LC 95-35828. 280p. 1995. pap. 25.00 (*1-56821-747-1*) Aronson.
Narcissus. Alpha Sigma Alpha Staff. 1987. 14.95 (*0-9616651-0-6*) Alpha Sigma Alpha.
Narcissus. Roma Greth. LC 77-82729. (Scene Award Ser.). 88p. 1978. pap. 8.00 (*0-912292-46-6*) Smith.
Narcissus. Evelyn Scott & Evelyn Scott. Ed. by Elizabeth Hardwick. LC 76-51676. (Rediscovered Fiction by American Women Ser.). 1977. reprint ed. lib. bdg. 29.95 (*0-405-10054-X*) Ayer.
Narcissus: Chinese New Year Flower, Legends & Folklore. William C. Hu. LC 89-81751. (Illus.). 1989. 9.95 (*0-89344-035-3*) Ars Ceramica.
Narcissus & Goldmund. Hermann Hesse. Tr. by Ursule Molinaro. 320p. 1984. mass mkt. 6.50 (*0-553-27586-0*, Bantam Classics) Bantam.
Narcissus & Goldmund. Hermann Hesse. Tr. by Ursule Molinaro from GER. LC 68-17291. 314p. 1969. pap. 12.00 (*0-374-50684-1*) FS&G.
Narcissus & Oedipus: The Children of Psychoanalysis. Vicoria Hamilton. 304p. 1982. 37.50 (*0-7100-0869-4*, Routledge Thoemms) Routledge.
Narcissus & Oedipus: The Children of Psychoanalysis. Victoria Hamilton. 336p. 1993. pap. text 33.00 (*1-85575-062-7*, Pub. by H Karnac Bks Ltd) Other Pr LLC.
Narcissus & the Lover: Mythic Recovery & Reinvention in Sceve's Delie. Deborah L. Baker. (Stanford French & Italian Studies: Vol. 46). 160p. 1987. pap. 56.50 (*0-915838-62-1*) Anma Libri.
Narcissus & the Voyeur: Three Books & Two Films. Robert M. MacLean. (Approaches to Semiotics Ser.: No. 48). 1979. text 60.00 (*90-279-7838-7*) Mouton.
Narcissus Dreaming. Dabney Stuart. LC 90-5745. 64p. 1990. pap. 7.95 (*0-8071-1592-4*); text 15.95 (*0-8071-1591-6*) La State U Pr.
Narcissus from Rubble: Competing Models of Character in Contemporary British & American Fiction. Julius R. Raper. LC 91-32604. 200p. (C). 1992. text 30.00 (*0-8071-1712-9*) La State U Pr.
Narcissus Leaves the Pool: Familiar Essays. Joseph Epstein. LC 98-43791. 321p. 1999. 25.00 (*0-395-94403-1*) HM.
Narcissus Sous Rature: Male Subjectivity in Contemporary American Poetry. Jody Norton. LC 99-24089. (Illus.). 256p. 2000. 43.50 (*0-8387-5356-6*) Bucknell U Pr.
Narcissus Transformed: The Textual Subject in Psychoanalysis & Literature. Gray Kochhar-Lindgren. LC 92-30296. (Literature & Philosophy Ser.). 176p. 1993. 35.00 (*0-271-00907-1*) Pa St U Pr.
Narco-Diplomacy in Colombian-U. S. A. Relations. Juan G. Tokatlian. (C). 1992. pap. text 32.50 (*0-8133-8683-7*) Westview.
Narco-Terrorism & the Cuban Connection. Rachel Ehrenfeld. 1988. 4.00 (*0-685-47388-0*) Cuban Amer Natl Fndtn.
Narcobusiness: Latin America & the Illegal Drug Trade. Colin Harding. 220p. 1999. 53.99 (*1-55164-135-6*); pap. 24.99 (*1-55164-134-8*) Consort Bk Sales.
NarcoDiplomacy: Exporting the U. S. War on Drugs. H. Richard Friman. LC 96-18387. (Illus.). 184p. 1996. text 29.95 (*0-8014-3274-X*) Cornell U Pr.
Narcolepsy: A Funny Disorder That's No Laughing Matter. Marguerite J. Utley. LC 95-90011. (Illus.). 166p. 1995. 18.00 (*0-9643328-1-7*); pap. 12.00 (*0-9643328-0-9*) M J Utley.
Narcolepsy Primer, 1991: A Guide for Physicians, Patients, & Their Families. Meeta Goswami. 18p. 1991. pap. 6.00 (*0-9667122-0-X*) Meeta Goswami.
Narcoleptic Dialectic. 222p. 1998. pap. 15.99 (*0-9669398-1-6*, 001-ND) M W Arenz.
Narcopolis & Other Poems. Ed. by Peggy Nadramia. (Illus.). 64p. (Orig.). (C). 1989. pap. 4.00 (*0-9623286-1-8*) Hells Kitchen.
Narcotic Addiction & American Foreign Policy: Seven Studies, 1924 to 1938, An Original Anthology. Ed. by Gerald N. Grob. LC 80-1207. (Addiction in America Ser.). (Illus.). 1981. lib. bdg. 35.95 (*0-405-13561-0*) Ayer.
Narcotic Agent. Maurice Helbrant. Ed. by Gerald N. Grob. LC 80-1230. (Addiction in America Ser.). 1981. reprint ed. lib. bdg. 30.95 (*0-405-13589-0*) Ayer.
Narcotic Drug: Estimated World Requirements for 1994-Statistics for 1992. 205p. 1994. 40.00 (*92-1-048057-0*, T.94.XI.3) UN.
Narcotic Drug Diseases & Allied Ailments: Pathology, Pathogenesis, & Treatment. George E. Pettey. Ed. by Gerald N. Grob. LC 80-1246. (Addiction in America Ser.). (Illus.). 1981. reprint ed. lib. bdg. 49.95 (*0-405-13616-1*) Ayer.
Narcotic Drug Problem. Ernest S. Bishop. LC 75-17204. (Social Problems & Social Policy Ser.). 1976. reprint ed. 17.95 (*0-405-07476-X*) Ayer.
Narcotic Drugs: Estimated World Requirements. 248p. 38.00 (*92-1-048068-6*) UN.
Narcotic Drugs: Estimated World Requirements for 1990, Statistics for 1988. 184p. 35.00 (*92-1-048045-7*, EFS.89.XI.3) UN.
Narcotic Drugs: Estimated World Requirements for 1991; Statistics for 1989. 1990. 35.00 (*92-1-048047-3*, MU90.XI.4) UN.
Narcotic Drugs: Estimated World Requirements for 1992 - Statistics for 1990. 184p. 1991. 36.00 (*92-1-048050-3*, 91.XI.2) UN.
Narcotic Drugs: Estimated World Requirements for 1995 (Statistics for 1993) 207p. 40.00 (*92-1-048060-0*, T.95.XI.3) UN.
Narcotic Drugs: Estimated World Requirements for 1996 (Statistics for 1994) 212p. 38.00 (*92-1-048061-9*) UN.
Narcotic Drugs: Estimated World Requirements for 1997; Statistics for 1995. International Narcotics Control Board Staff. 227p. 1997. pap., suppl. ed. 48.00 (*92-1-048063-5*) UN.
Narcotic Drugs: Estimated World Requirements for 1998; Statistics for 1996. International Narcotics Control Group Staff. 241p. 1998. pap. 58.00 (*92-1-048065-1*) UN.
Narcotic Drugs & Psychotropic Substances Laws of India. B. V. Kumar. (C). 1989. 300.00 (*0-7855-4793-2*) St Mut.
Narcotic Drugs & Psychotropic Substances Laws of India. B. V. Kumar & R. K. Tewari. xx, 617p. 1989. text 50.00 (*81-220-0151-3*, Pub. by Konark Pubs Pvt Ltd) Advent Bks Div.
***Narcotic Drugs 1999: Estimated World Requirements for 2000 - Statistics for 1998.** International Narcotics Control Board Staff. 236p. 2000. pap. 58.00 (*92-1-048071-6*, Pub. by Intl Narcotics) Balogh.
Narcotic Identification Manual. 1991. lib. bdg. 75.00 (*0-8490-4216-X*) Gordon Pr.
Narcotic Offences. Fiori Rinaldi & Peter Gillies. xxx, 444p. 1991. 87.50 (*0-455-21025-X*, Pub. by LawBk Co) Gaunt.
Narcotic Plants of the Old World, Used in Rituals & Everyday Life: An Anthology of Texts from Ancient Times to the Present. Hedwig Schleiffer. (Illus.). (Orig.). 1979. pap. text 17.50 (*0-934454-00-0*); lib. bdg. 22.50 (*0-934454-01-9*) Lubrecht & Cramer.
Narcotics: Dangerous Painkillers. George Glass. LC 97-44384. (Drug Abuse Prevention Library). (Illus.). 64p. (YA). (gr. 5-9). 1998. 17.95 (*0-8239-2719-9*) Rosen Group.
Narcotics: Lieutenant Byram's Investigative Handbooks. Daniel Byram. (Illus.). 50p. 1999. pap. 5.95 (*1-892798-06-9*) Sierra West.
Narcotics & Crime Control. Michael D. Lyman. (Illus.). 206p. 1987. 45.95 (*0-398-05347-2*); pap. 29.95 (*0-398-06252-8*) C C Thomas.
Narcotics & Drug Abuse - A to Z, 3 vols., Set. 1990. write for info. (*0-318-51463-X*) Croner.
Narcotics & Drug Abuse - A to Z, Vol. 1. LC 78-173860. 1990. write for info. (*0-87514-004-1*) Croner.
Narcotics & Drug Abuse - A to Z, Vol. 2. LC 78-173860. 1990. write for info. (*0-87514-005-X*) Croner.

N

Narcotics & Drug Abuse - A to Z, Vol. 3. LC 78-173860. 1990. write for info. (*0-87514-006-8*) Croner.

Narcotics & Reproduction: A Bibliography. Compiled by Ernest L. Abel. LC 83-13252. 215p. 1983. lib. bdg. 75.00 (*0-313-24052-3*, ABN/, Greenwood Pr) Greenwood.

Narcotics & the Law. 2nd ed. William B. Eldridge. LC 67-25528. 1967. lib. bdg. 17.50 (*0-226-20315-8*) U Ch Pr.

Narcotics Education Assistant. Jack Rudman. (Career Examination Ser.: C-2503). 1994. pap. 29.95 (*0-8373-2503-X*) Nat Learn.

Narcotics Education Specialist. Jack Rudman. (Career Examination Ser.: C-847). 1994. pap. 29.95 (*0-8373-0847-X*) Nat Learn.

Narcotics Identification Manual. 1991. lib. bdg. 69.95 (*0-8490-4942-3*) Gordon Pr.

Narcotics Investigation Techniques. Paul T. Mahoney. (Illus.). 406p. (C). 1992. pap. 49.95 (*0-398-06263-3*); text 72.95 (*0-398-05803-2*) C C Thomas.

Narcotics Investigator. Jack Rudman. (Career Examination Ser.: C-1600). 1994. pap. 34.95 (*0-8373-1600-6*) Nat Learn.

Narcotics Menace. St. Charles. 1952. 5.95 (*0-87505-229-0*) Borden.

Narcotics Security Assistant. Jack Rudman. (Career Examination Ser.: C-1378). 1994. pap. 27.95 (*0-8373-1378-3*) Nat Learn.

Narcotics Trial Manual for New York State. Leonard P. Rienzi. 2000. ring bd. 25.95 (*0-930137-78-7*) Looseleaf Law.

Nard. Mark Dunster. (Poems from Hollywood Ser.). 70p. (Orig.). 1984. pap. 5.00 (*0-89642-114-7*) Linden Pubs.

Narelle Jubelin: Soft Shoulder. Narelle Jubelin. (Illus.). 60p. 1994. pap. 20.00 (*0-941548-30-9*) Ren Soc U Chi.

Naresvarapariksa of Sadyojyotih. Madhusudan Kaul. (C). 1989. 42.50 (*81-7013-063-8*) S Asia.

Narino, Hero of Colombian Independence. Thomas Blossom. LC 66-20661. 241p. reprint ed. pap. 74.80 (*0-608-13685-9*, 205537400017) Bks Demand.

Nariokotome Homo Erectus Skeleton. Ed. by Alan Walker & Richard E. Leakey. LC 92-32985. (Illus.). 480p. (C). 1993. 140.50 (*0-674-60075-4*) HUP.

Narmad: Maari Hakikat. Harish Trivedi. Ed. & Pref. by Ramesh Shukla. (GUJ., Illus.). 144p. 1996. pap. write for info. (*0-614-30438-5*) India Fnd.

Narmad: My Life. Harish Trivedi. 88p. (Orig.). 1997. pap. write for info. (*0-614-30439-3*) India Fnd.

Narmada & Environment: An Assessment. Ed. by Y. K. Alagh. (C). 1995. 62.50 (*0-614-08521-7*, Pub. by Har-Anand Pubns) S Asia.

Narmada Project: Politics of Eco-Development. Pravin Sheth. (C). 1994. 27.00 (*81-241-0115-9*, Pub. by Har-Anand Pubns) S Asia.

Narnia: The Short Musical Version. C. S. Lewis et al. 1995. 5.95 (*0-87129-565-2*, N02) Dramatic Pub.

Narnia - Full Musical. Jules Jasca. Ed. & Contrib. by Thomas Tierney. 1986. pap. 5.95 (*0-87129-381-1*, N01) Dramatic Pub.

***Narnia Atlas.** Potter. 124p. (J). (gr. 3 up). 2000. pap. 18.95 (*0-06-443485-0*) HarpC Child Bks.

Narnia Cookbook: Narnian Food from C. S. Lewis's Chronicles of Narnia. Douglas H. Gresham & C. S. Lewis. LC 98-10657. (Illus.). 128p. (J). (gr. 3 up). 1998. 16.95 (*0-06-027815-3*) HarpC.

Narnia Paper Dolls: The Lion, the Witch & the Wardrobe Collection. Illus. by Mary Collier. (World of Narnia Ser.). 24p. (J). (ps-3). 1998. 7.95 (*0-694-01078-2*) HarpC Child Bks.

Narnia Trivia Book: Inspired by The Chronicles of Narnia by C.S. Lewis. C. S. Lewis. LC 98-56502. (Narnia Ser.). (Illus.). 128p. (J). (gr. 3-7). 1999. pap. 4.95 (*0-06-446212-9*, HarpTrophy) HarpC Child Bks.

Naro, the Ancient Spider. Susan Joyce. LC 90-14156. (Illus.). (J). (gr. 4). 1990. 12.00 (*0-939217-04-X*) Peel Prod.

Narodni Divadlo, Slovnik Umelcu Divadel Vlastenskeho, Stavovskeho, Prozatimniho a Narodniho. Ed. by V. Prochazka. (CZE.). 624p. 1990. 70.00 (*0-317-03839-7*) Szwede Slavic.

Narodniki Women: Russian Women Who Sacrificed Themselves for the Dream of Freedom. Margaret Maxwell. (Athene Ser.). 310p. 1990. text 36.00 (*0-08-037462-X*, Pergamon Pr); pap. text 14.50 (*0-08-037461-1*, Pergamon Pr) Elsevier.

Narodniki Women: Russian Women Who Sacrificed Themselves for the Dream of Freedom. Margaret Maxwell. (Athene Ser.). 360p. (C). 1990. text 36.00 (*0-8077-6247-4*); pap. text 17.95 (*0-8077-6246-6*) Tchrs Coll.

Narodnyi Artist Ego Velichestva. . . Chaliapin. unabridged ed. Joseph Darsky.Tr. of People's Artist of His Majesty. . . Chaliapin. (RUS., Illus.). 250p. 1999. mass mkt. 20.00 (*0-9655131-1-4*) J Stremlin.

Narodowy Atlas Polski. Ed. by Pan Instytut Geografii Staff. (POL., Illus.). 60p. 1978. 220.00 (*0-614-25056-0*) Szwede Slavic.

Naroh's Task. Barrie Anderson. 142p. 1986. 19.95 (*0-7212-0727-8*, Pub. by Regency Pr GBR) St Mut.

Naron: A Bushman Tribe of the Central Kalahari. Dorothea F. Bleek. LC 76-44692. reprint ed. 37.50 (*0-404-15908-7*) AMS Pr.

Narraciones. Jorge Luis Borges. Ed. by Marcos Ricardo Barnatan. (SPA.). pap. 13.95 (*84-376-0235-1*, Pub. by Ediciones Catedra) Continental Bk.

Narraciones. 6th ed. Jorge Luis Borges. (SPA.). 256p. 1988. pap. write for info. (*0-7859-4973-9*) Fr & Eur.

Narraciones de Testimonio en America Latina. Juan R. Duchesne-Winter. 226p. 1992. pap. 11.50 (*0-8477-3622-9*) U of PR Pr.

Narrador Picaro: Guzman de Alfarache. Carlos A. Mator. vi, 132p. 1985. 12.50 (*0-942260-51-1*) Hispanic Seminary.

Narraganett Historical Register Vol. 1: A Magazine. Ed. by James N. Arnold. 333p. 1994. pap. 28.50 (*1-55613-967-5*) Heritage Bk.

Narragansett. Craig A. Doherty & Katherine M. Doherty. LC 93-32669. (Native American People Ser.: Set IV). 32p. (J). (gr. 4-8). 1994. lib. bdg. 22.60 (*0-86625-525-7*) Rourke Pubns.

Narragansett. Sallie W. Latimer. LC 97-208129. (Images of America Ser.). 1997. pap. 16.99 (*0-7524-0268-4*) Arcadia Publng.

***Narragansett AC.** Sallie W. Latimer. (Images of America Ser.). 128p. 2000. pap. 18.99 (*0-7385-0085-2*) Arcadia Publng.

***Narragansett Bay: Its History & Romantic Associations & Picturesque Setting.** Edgar Mayhew Bacon. (Illus.). 391p. 1999. reprint ed. pap. 30.00 (*0-7884-1392-9*, B016) Heritage Bk.

Narragansett Historical Register, Vol. 1. Ed. by James N. Arnold. 336p. (Orig.). 1994. pap. text 26.00 (*0-7884-0141-6*) Heritage Bk.

Narragansett Historical Register, Vol. 3. Ed. by James N. Arnold. (Illus.). 336p. (Orig.). 1994. pap. 25.00 (*0-7884-0098-3*) Heritage Bk.

Narragansett Historical Register, Vol. 5. James N. Arnold. 368p. (Orig.). 1996. reprint ed. pap. 28.00 (*0-7884-0510-1*, A660) Heritage Bk.

Narragansett Historical Register, Vol. 7. Ed. by James N. Arnold. xlvi, 432p. 1996. reprint ed. pap. 25.00 (*0-7884-0535-7*, A662) Heritage Bk.

Narragansett Historical Register, Vol. 8. Ed. by James N. Arnold. xxxiv, 352p. (Orig.). 1996. pap. 28.00 (*0-7884-0536-5*, A663) Heritage Bk.

Narragansett Historical Register, Vol. 9. Ed. by James N. Arnold. iv, 200p. 1996. reprint ed. pap. 18.50 (*0-7884-0537-3*, A664) Heritage Bk.

Narragansett Historical Register Vol. 2: A Magazine Devoted to the Antiquities, Genealogy & Historical Matter Illustrating the History of the State of RI & Providence Plantations. Ed. by James N. Arnold. (Illus.). 339p. 1994. reprint ed. pap. text 25.00 (*0-7884-0026-6*) Heritage Bk.

Narragansett Historical Register (R1) James N. Arnold. 404p. 1996. reprint ed. pap. 30.50 (*0-7884-0511-X*, A661) Heritage Bk.

Narragansett Planters: A Study of Causes. Edward Channing. 23p. 1997. reprint ed. pap. 5.00 (*0-8328-6471-4*) Higginson Bk Co.

***Narragansett Postcards.** Sallie W. Latimer. (Images of America Ser.). 128p. 1999. pap. 18.99 (*0-7385-0086-0*) Arcadia Publng.

Narralogues: Truth in Fiction. Ronald Sukenick. LC 99-39774. 128p. (C). 2000. text 44.50 (*0-7914-4399-X*); pap. text 14.95 (*0-7914-4400-7*) State U NY Pr.

Narrar el Apocalipsis (Writing the Apocapypse) Louis P. Zamorra. (SPA.). 285p. 1994. pap. 13.99 (*968-16-3988-X*, Pub. by Fondo) Continental Bk.

Narrate, uomini, la vostra storia see Operatic Lives

***Narrated Bible.** LaGard F. Smith. 1728p. 1999. 39.99 (*0-7369-0239-2*) Harvest Hse.

Narrated Films: Storytelling Situations in Cinema History. Avrom Fleishman. LC 91-12350. (Illus.). 216p. 1991. text 42.50 (*0-8018-4222-0*) Johns Hopkins.

***Narrateur et Points de Vue dans la Litterature Francaise Medievale: Une Approache Linguistique.** Sophie Marnette. 262p. 1998. 37.95 (*3-906760-92-8*, Pub. by P Lang) P Lang Pubng.

***Narrating Africa: George Henty & the Fiction of Empire.** Mawuena Kossi Logan. LC 99-11196. (Children's Literature & Culture Ser.: Vol. 9). 224p. 1999. 55.00 (*0-8153-3275-0*) Garland.

Narrating Discovery: The Romantic Explorer in American Literature, 1790-1855. Bruce Greenfield. (Social Foundations of Aesthetic Forms Ser.). 256p. 1992. 45.00 (*0-231-07996-6*) Col U Pr.

Narrating History, Developing Doctrine: Friedrich Schleiermacher & Johann Sebastian Drey. Bradford E. Hinze. (American Academy of Religion Academy Ser.). 330p. 1993. 29.95 (*1-55540-874-5*, 010182); pap. 19.95 (*1-55540-875-3*) OUP.

Narrating Mothers: Theorizing Maternal Subjectivities. Ed. by Brenda O. Daly & Maureen T. Reddy. LC 90-27053. 310p. (C). 1991. pap. text 19.50 (*0-87049-706-5*) U of Tenn Pr.

Narrating Postmodern Time & Space. Joseph Francese. LC 96-51476. 203p. (C). 1997. text 53.50 (*0-7914-3513-X*); pap. text 17.95 (*0-7914-3514-8*) State U NY Pr.

Narrating Psychology: How Psychology Gets Made. Mary Vander Goot. LC 87-50856. 280p. (C). 1987. text 32.00 (*1-55605-015-1*); pap. text 20.00 (*1-55605-014-3*) Wyndham Hall.

Narrating Reality: Austen, Scott, Eliot. Harry E. Shaw. LC 99-24817. 1999. 35.00 (*0-8014-3672-9*) Cornell U Pr.

***Narrating the Holocaust.** Andrea Ilse Maria Reiter. LC 00-22678. (Illus.). 2000. pap. write for info. (*0-8264-4737-6*) Continuum.

Narrating the Organization: Dramas of Institutional Identity. LC 96-20954. (New Practices of Inquiry Ser.). 1997. pap. text 15.95 (*0-226-13229-3*) U Ch Pr.

Narrating the Organization: Dramas of Institutional Identity. Barbara Czarniawska-Joerges. LC 96-20954. (New Practices of Inquiry Ser.). 1997. lib. bdg. 45.00 (*0-226-13228-5*) U Ch Pr.

Narrating the Past: Fiction & Historiography in Postwar Spain. David K. Herzberger. LC 94-24973. 192p. 1995. text 49.95 (*0-8223-1582-3*); pap. text 16.95 (*0-8223-1597-1*) Duke.

Narrating the Self: Fictions of Japanese Modernity. Tomi Suzuki. LC 95-11917. 260p. 1996. 45.00 (*0-8047-2552-7*) Stanford U Pr.

Narrating the Self: Fictions of Japanese Modernity. Tomi Suzuki. 260p. 1997. pap. 17.95 (*0-8047-3162-4*) Stanford U Pr.

Narrating the Thirties: A Decade in the Making, 1930 to the Present. John Baxendale & Christopher Pawling. 256p. 1996. text 59.95 (*0-312-12898-3*) St Martin.

Narrating Transgression Vol. II: Representations of the Criminal in Early Modern England. Ed. by Rosamaria Loretelli & Roberto De Romanis. (Anglo-American Studies). 172p. (C). 1999. pap. text 37.95 (*0-8204-3599-6*) P Lang Pubng.

***Narrating Utopia: Ideology, Gender, Form in Utopian Literature.** Chris Ferns. (Science Fiction Texts & Studies: Vol. 19). 240p. 1999. 48.95 (*0-85323-594-5*, Pub. by Liverpool Univ Pr); pap. 21.95 (*0-85323-604-6*, Pub. by Liverpool Univ Pr) Intl Spec Bk.

Narration & Allusion in Archaic Greek Art. Anthony M. Snodgrass. 7.00 (*0-904920-08-9*) David Brown.

Narration & Description in the French Realist Novel: The Temporality of Lying & Forgetting. James H. Reid. LC 92-39126. (Cambridge Studies in French: No. 44). 238p. (C). 1993. text 69.95 (*0-521-42092-X*) Cambridge U Pr.

Narration & Discourse in the Book of Genesis. Hugh C. White. 326p. (C). 1991. text 69.95 (*0-521-39020-6*) Cambridge U Pr.

Narration & Knowledge. Arthur C. Danto. LC 84-29362. 400p. 1985. pap. text 21.00 (*0-231-06117-X*) Col U Pr.

Narration & Therapeutic Action: The Construction of Meaning in Psychoanalytic Social Work. Ed. by Jerrold R. Brandell. LC 96-20074. (Journal of Analytic Social Work: Vol. 3, Nos. 2/3). 202p. 1996. 49.95 (*1-56024-827-0*) Haworth Pr.

Narration As Knowledge: Tales of the Teaching Life. LC 97-41508. 1997. text 26.00 (*0-86709-436-2*, Pub. by Boynton Cook Pubs) Heinemann.

Narration in the Fiction Film. David Bordwell. LC 84-40491. (Illus.). 370p. (C). 1985. reprint ed. pap. 24.95 (*0-299-10174-6*) U of Wis Pr.

Narration in the Mirror. Zhu Xiao Feng. (Selected Works of Zhu Xiao Feng Ser.: Vol. 2). (CHI.). 258p. 1997. 30.00 (*1-891158-01-5*) Am Int Rare Bks.

Narration of Desire: Erotic Transferences & Countertransferences. Harriet K. Wrye & Judith K. Welles. 272p. 1998. 29.95 (*0-88163-298-8*) Analytic Pr.

Narration of Desire: Erotic Transferences & Countertransferences. Harriet K. Wrye & Judith K. Welles. LC 93-46946. 272p. 1994. reprint ed. pap. 29.95 (*0-88163-147-7*) Analytic Pr.

***Narration of My Captivity among the Sioux Indians.** Fanny Kelly. 318p. 1999. reprint ed. 7.98 (*1-56852-244-4*) W S Konecky Assocs.

***Narrativa de Alejandro Morales: Encuentro, Historia y Compromiso Social.** Jesus Rosales. (Wor(l)ds of Change Ser.: Vol. 39). (SPA.). XIII, 190p. 1999. text 46.95 (*0-8204-3995-9*, 39959) P Lang Pubng.

Narrativa de Carlos Fuentes: Afan por la Armonia en la Multiplicidad Antagonica del Mundo. Aida E. Ramirez-Mattei. LC 83-1322. (SPA.). xv, 437p. (Orig.). (C). 1983. pap. 8.50 (*0-8477-3507-9*) U of PR Pr.

Narrativa de Concha Alos: La Texto, Pretexto y Contexto. Genaro J. Perez. (Monagrafias A Ser.: No. 157). (SPA.). 95p. (C). 1994. pap. 51.00 (*1-85566-032-6*, Pub. by Tamesis Bks Ltd) Boydell & Brewer.

Narrativa de Jose Sanchez-Boudy (Tragedia y Folklore) Ed. by Laurentino Suarez. LC 82-71021. (SPA.). 192p. (Orig.). 1984. pap. 15.00 (*0-89729-312-6*) Ediciones.

Narrativa De Marta Brunet. Esther Melon Diaz. (UPREX, Literarios Ser.: No. 41). 272p. (C). 1975. pap. 1.50 (*0-8477-0041-0*) U of PR Pr.

Narrativa de Salvador Garmendia: Mas Alla de la Razon. Yesenia M. Rodriguez. LC 97-40309. 108p. 1997. 59.95 (*0-7734-2215-3*) E Mellen.

Narrativa Hispanoamericana Actual: America y Sus Problemas. Anita Arroyo. LC 79-19468. (Coleccion Mente y Palabra). v, 435p. (C). 1980. 15.00 (*0-8477-0562-5*); pap. 12.00 (*0-8477-0563-3*) U of PR Pr.

Narrativa Indigenista Mexicana del Siglo, No. XX. Sylvia Bigas. 488p. 1990. pap. 25.00 (*0-8477-3647-4*) U of PR Pr.

***Narrativa Posmoderna Espanola: Cronica de un Desengano.** Ana M. Spitzmesser. (Wor(l)ds of Change Ser.: Vol. 40). (SPA.). 152p. 1999. text 39.95 (*0-8204-4024-8*, 40248) P Lang Pubng.

Narrativa y Libertad: Cuentos Cubanos de la Diaspora, 2 vols. Ed. & Intro. by Julio E. Hernandez-Miayres. LC 96-86365. (Coleccion Antologias Ser.). (SPA., Illus.). 1119p. (Orig.). 1996. pap. 69.00 (*0-89729-665-6*) Ediciones.

Narrativas de Representacion Urbana: Un Estudio de Expresiones Culturales de la Modernidad Latinoamericana. Hector D. Fernandez L'Hoeste. (Wor(l)ds of Change Ser.: No. 35). 191p. 1998. 44.95 (*0-8204-3893-6*) P Lang Pubng.

Narrative. John Coyle. 200p. (C). 1998. 50.00 (*0-415-13479-X*) Routledge.

Narrative. J. Edwards. 1957. pap. 1.99 (*1-56632-081-X*) Revival Lit.

Narrative see International Monetary Fund, 1966-1971: The System Under Stress

Narrative: A Critical Linguistic Introduction. Michael Toolan. (Interface Ser.). 288p. 1989. text 39.95 (*0-415-00868-9*) Routledge.

Narrative: A Critical Linguistic Introduction. Michael Toolan. (Interface Ser.). 304p. (C). 1989. pap. 24.99 (*0-415-00869-7*) Routledge.

Narrative - Theory. Ed. by David H. Richter. LC 95-21302. 352p. (C). 1995. pap. 35.66 (*0-8013-1610-3*) Longman.

Narrative Analysis. Martin Cortazzi. (Social Research & Educational Studies: Vol. 12). 224p. 1993. pap. 29.95 (*1-85000-963-5*, Falmer Pr) Taylor & Francis.

Narrative Analysis. Catherine K. Riessman. (Qualitative Research Methods Ser.: Vol. 30). (Illus.). 96p. (C). 1993. text 24.00 (*0-8039-4753-4*); pap. text 10.50 (*0-8039-4754-2*) Sage.

Narrative & Adventures of Henry Bibb. Henry Bibb. (C). 1992. reprint ed. pap. text 21.95 (*0-88143-143-5*) Ayer.

Narrative & Argument. Richard Andrews. 160p. 1989. pap. 33.95 (*0-335-09219-5*) OpUniv Pr.

Narrative & Critical History of America, 8 vols. Ed. by Justin Winsor. LC 13-14102. reprint ed. 700.00 (*0-404-07010-8*) AMS Pr.

Narrative & Desire in Russian Literature, 1822-1849: The Feminine & the Masculine. Joe Andrew. LC 92-33089. 1993. text 39.95 (*0-312-09123-0*) St Martin.

Narrative & Drama (Le Narratif et le Dramatique) Vol. 2: Table Ronde IV. Centre d'Etudes Superieures de la Renaissance Univ. LC 95-167635. (THETA Ser.: Vol. 2). (FRE.). 180p. 1995. 31.95 (*3-906754-30-8*, Pub. by P Lang) P Lang Pubng.

Narrative & Dramatic Sources of Shakespeare, Vol. 8. Geoffrey Bullough. 1975. text 99.00 (*0-231-08898-1*) Col U Pr.

Narrative & Event in Ancient Art. Ed. by Peter J. Holliday. (Cambridge Studies in New Art History & Criticism). (Illus.). 386p. (C). 1993. text 80.00 (*0-521-43013-5*) Cambridge U Pr.

***Narrative & Experience: Innovations in Thirteenth-Century Picture Books.** Kumiko Maekawa. 349p. 2000. text 52.95 (*0-8204-4365-4*) P Lang Pubng.

Narrative & Fantasy in the Post-War German Novel: A Study of Novels by Johnson, Frisch, Wolf, Becker & Grass. Chloe E. M. Paver. LC 98-37706. 239p. 1999. text 70.00 (*0-19-815965-X*) OUP.

Narrative & Freedom: The Shadows of Time. Gary S. Morson. LC 94-7065. 336p. 1994. 35.00 (*0-300-05882-9*) Yale U Pr.

Narrative & Freedom: The Shadows of Time. Gary S. Morson. 336p. 1996. pap. 17.00 (*0-300-06875-1*) Yale U Pr.

Narrative & Genre. Ed. by Mary Chamberlain & Paul R. Thompson. LC 97-13178. 224p. (C). 1998. 75.00 (*0-415-15198-8*) Routledge.

***Narrative & Genre: Key Concepts in Media Studies.** Nick Lacey. LC 99-49754. 2000. pap. 21.95 (*0-312-23013-3*); text 55.00 (*0-312-23012-5*) St Martin.

Narrative & Ideology. Jeremy Tambling. (Open Guides to Literature Ser.). 128p. 1991. 102.50 (*0-335-09355-8*); pap. 27.95 (*0-335-09354-X*) OpUniv Pr.

Narrative & Imagination: Preaching the Worlds That Shape Us. Richard L. Eslinger. LC 95-2307. 192p. 1995. pap. 20.00 (*0-8006-2719-9*, Fortress Pr) Augsburg Fortress.

Narrative & Meaning in Early Modern England: Browne's Skull & Other Histories. Howard Marchitello. (Cambridge Studies in Renaissance Literature & Culture: Vol. 20). (Illus.). 245p. (C). 1997. text 59.95 (*0-521-58025-0*) Cambridge U Pr.

Narrative & Morality: A Theological Inquiry. Paul Nelson. LC 86-43034. 192p. 1987. 35.00 (*0-271-00485-1*) Pa St U Pr.

Narrative & Novelle in Samuel: Studies by Hugo Gressmann & Other Scholars 1906-1923. Hugo Gressmann et al. (Historic Texts & Interpreters Ser.: Vol. 9). 182p. (C). 1991. 57.50 (*1-85075-281-8*, Pub. by Sheffield Acad) CUP Services.

Narrative & Professional Communication. Jane Perkins & Nancy Roundy Blyle. LC 99-19561. (ATTW Contemporary Studies in Technical Communications). 1999. pap. 24.95 (*1-56750-449-3*) Ablx Pub.

Narrative & Psychotherapy. John McLeod. LC 97-61827. 180p. 1997. 66.00 (*0-8039-7685-2*) Sage.

Narrative & Psychotherapy. John McLeod. 192p. 1998. pap. 13.99 (*0-8039-7686-0*) Sage.

Narrative & Representation in the Poetry of Wallace Stevens: A Tune Beyond Us, Yet Ourselves. Daniel R. Schwarz. 256p. 1993. pap. 16.95 (*0-312-09594-5*) St Martin.

Narrative & Rosters, 8th Minnesota Regiment. 1997. reprint ed. pap. 5.00 (*0-915709-48-1*) Pk Geneal Bk.

Narrative & Rosters, 11th Minnesota Regiment. 1997. reprint ed. pap. 5.00 (*0-915709-51-1*) Pk Geneal Bk.

Narrative & Rosters, 5th Minnesota Regiment. 1997. reprint ed. pap. 10.00 (*0-915709-45-7*) Pk Geneal Bk.

Narrative & Rosters, 1st Minnesota Regiment. 1997. reprint ed. pap. 12.00 (*0-915709-40-6*) Pk Geneal Bk.

Narrative & Rosters, 4th Minnesota Regiment. 1997. reprint ed. pap. 10.00 (*0-915709-44-9*) Pk Geneal Bk.

Narrative & Rosters, 9th Minnesota Regiment. 1997. reprint ed. pap. 7.50 (*0-915709-49-X*) Pk Geneal Bk.

Narrative & Rosters, 2nd Minnesota Regiment. 1997. reprint ed. pap. 12.00 (*0-915709-41-4*) Pk Geneal Bk.

Narrative & Rosters, 7th Minnesota Regiment. 1997. reprint ed. pap. 7.50 (*0-915709-47-3*) Pk Geneal Bk.

Narrative & Rosters, 6th Minnesota Regiment. 1997. reprint ed. pap. 10.00 (*0-915709-46-5*) Pk Geneal Bk.

Narrative & Rosters, 10th Minnesota Regiment. 1997. pap. 5.00 (*0-915709-50-3*) Pk Geneal Bk.

Narrative & Rosters, 3rd Minnesota Regiment. 1997. reprint ed. pap. 10.00 (*0-915709-43-0*) Pk Geneal Bk.

Narrative & Social Control: Critical Perspectives. Dennis K. Mumby. (Annual Reviews of Communication Research Ser.: Vol. 21). (Illus.). 304p. (C). 1993. text 58.00 (*0-8039-4931-6*); pap. text 26.00 (*0-8039-4932-4*) Sage.

***Narrative & Stylistic Patterns in the Films of Stanley Kubrick.** Luis M. Garcia Mainar. (Illus.). 267p. 2000. pap. 24.95 (*1-57113-265-1*, Pub. by Camden Hse) Boydell & Brewer.

Narrative & Stylistic Patterns in the Films of Stanley Kubrick. Luis M. Mainar. Ed. by Reingard Nischik. LC 98-32423. (European Studies in the Humanities). (Illus.). 190p. 1999. 55.00 (*1-57113-264-3*) Camden Hse.

An Asterisk (*) at the beginning of an entry indicates that the title is appearing for the first time.

***Narrative & the Cultural Construction of Illness & Healing.** Ed. by Cheryl Mattingly & Linda C. Garro. LC 00-31629. 217p. 2000. 45.00 (*0-520-21824-8*); pap. 17.95 (*0-520-21825-6*, Pub. by U CA Pr) Cal Prin Full Svc.

Narrative & the Natural Law: An Interpretation of Thomistic Ethics. Pamela M. Hall. LC 94-15465. 168p. 1999. pap. text 16.00 (*0-268-01485-X*) U of Notre Dame Pr.

***Narrative & Voice in Post-War Poetry.** Roberts. LC 98-37694. 216p. (C). 1999. 65.95 (*0-582-23352-6*) Addison-Wesley.

Narrative & Voice in Post-War Poetry. John H. Roverts. LC 98-37694. 11p. (C). 1999. pap. 33.53 (*0-582-23350-X*) Addison-Wesley.

Narrative & Writings of Andrew Jackson of Kentucky. Andrew Jackson. LC 75-89403. (Black Heritage Library Collection). 1977. 13.95 (*0-8369-8609-1*) Ayer.

Narrative, Apparatus, Ideology: A Film Theory Reader. Philip Rosen. LC 86-2619. 560p. 1986. pap. text 26.00 (*0-231-05881-0*) Col U Pr.

Narrative Approach in Organization Studies. Barbara Czarniawska-Joerges. LC 97-21225. (Qualitative Research Methods Ser.). 1998. 24.00 (*0-7619-0662-2*); pap. 10.50 (*0-7619-0663-0*) Sage.

***Narrative Approaches to Working with Adult Male Survivors of Childhood Sexual Abuse: The Clients', the Counsellor's & the Researcher's Story.** Kim Etherington. LC 00-28274. 224p. 2000. write for info. (*1-85302-818-5*, Pub. by Jessica Kingsley) P H Brookes.

Narrative Art & Act in the Fourth Gospel. Derek Tovey. LC 98-102101. (JSNT Supplement Ser.: Vol. 151). 296p. 1997. 85.00 (*1-85075-687-2*, Pub. by Sheffield Acad) CUP Services.

Narrative Art & Poetry in the Books of Samuel Vol. 1: King David (II Samuel 9-20 & 1 Kings 1-2) J. P. Fokkelman. (Studia Semitica Neerlandica: Vol. 20). xii, 517p. 1981. text 75.50 (*90-232-1852-3*, Pub. by Van Gorcum) Eisenbrauns.

Narrative Art & Poetry in the Books of Samuel Vol. 2: The Crossing Fates (I Samuel 13-31 & II Samuel 1) J. P. Fokkelman. (Studia Semitica Neerlandica: Vol. 20). xii, 796p. 1986. text 81.50 (*90-232-2175-3*, Pub. by Van Gorcum) Eisenbrauns.

Narrative Art & Poetry in the Books of Samuel Vol. 3: Throne & City (II Sam. 2-8 & 21-24) J. P. Fokkelman. (Studia Semitica Neerlandica: Vol. 27). vi, 441p. 1990. text 57.50 (*90-232-2546-5*, Pub. by Van Gorcum) Eisenbrauns.

Narrative Art & Poetry in the Books of Samuel Vol. 4: Vow & Desire (I Samuel 1-12) J. P. Fokkelman. (Studia Semitica Neerlandica Ser.: Vol. 31). 664p. 1993. text 75.50 (*90-232-2738-7*, Pub. by Van Gorcum) Eisenbrauns.

Narrative Art in Genesis: Specimins of Stylistic & Structural Analysis. 2nd ed. J. P. Fokkleman. (Biblical Seminar Ser.: No. 12). (C). 1991. 22.50 (*1-85075-311-3*, Pub. by Sheffield Acad) CUP Services.

Narrative Art in the Bible. S. Bar-Efrat. (JSOTS Ser.: Vol. 70). 295p. 1989. pap. 19.95 (*1-85075-133-1*, Pub. by Sheffield Acad) CUP Services.

Narrative Art of Peter Hutchinson: A Retrospective, Vol. 2. Christopher Busa et al. LC 94-67733. (Artists Ser.: II). (Illus.). 72p. (Orig.). 1994. pap. text 15.00 (*0-944854-14-1*) Provincetown Arts.

Narrative Art of the Bayeux Tapestry Master. J. Bard McNulty. LC 86-47841. (Studies in the Middle Ages: No. 13). 47.50 (*0-404-61443-4*) AMS Pr.

Narrative Art, Political Rhetoric: The Case of Athalia & Joash. Patricia Dutcher-Walls. (Journal for the Study of the Old Testament Supplement Ser.: No. 209). 198p. 1996. 57.50 (*1-85075-577-9*, Pub. by Sheffield Acad) CUP Services.

Narrative As Communication. Didier Coste. (Theory & History of Literature Ser.: Vol. 80). 370p. (Orig.). 1989. pap. 19.95 (*0-8166-1720-1*) U of Minn Pr.

Narrative As Counter-Memory: A Half-Century of Postwar Writing in Germany & Japan. Reiko Tachibana. LC 97-16929. 288p. (C). 1998. pap. text 21.95 (*0-7914-3664-0*) State U NY Pr.

Narrative As Counter-Memory: A Half-Century of Postwar Writing in Germany & Japan. Reiko Tachibana. LC 97-16929. 288p. (C). 1998. text 65.50 (*0-7914-3663-2*) State U NY Pr.

Narrative As Performance: The Baudelairean Experiment. Marie Maclean & Marie MacLean. 220p. 1988. pap. 14.95 (*0-415-00664-3*); text 49.95 (*0-415-00663-5*) Routledge.

Narrative As Rhetoric: Technique, Audiences, Ethics, Ideology. James Phelan. LC 95-50365. (Theory & Interpretation of Narrative Ser.). 237p. (C). 1996. pap. text 14.95 (*0-8142-0689-1*) Ohio St U Pr.

Narrative As Theme: Studies in French Fiction. Gerald Prince. LC 91-22481. x, 161p. 1992. text 40.00 (*0-8032-3699-9*) U of Nebr Pr.

***Narrative as Virtual Reality: Immersion & Interactivity in Literature & Electronic Media.** Marie-Laure Ryan. (Parallax Ser.). (Illus.). 352p. 2000. 45.00 (*0-8018-6487-9*) Johns Hopkins.

***Narrative as Virtual Reality: Immersion & Interactivity in Literature & Electronic Media.** Marie-Laure Ryan. LC 00-8955. (Parallax Ser.). 2001. pap. write for info. (*0-8018-6488-7*) Johns Hopkins.

Narrative Asides in Luke-Acts. Steven M. Sheeley. (JSNT Supplement Ser.: No. 72). 204p. (C). 1992. 57.50 (*1-85075-352-0*, Pub. by Sheffield Acad) CUP Services.

Narrative, Authority & Law. Robin L. West. (Law, Meaning, & Violence Ser.). 456p. 1993. text 57.50 (*0-472-10365-2*, 10365) U of Mich Pr.

Narrative Based Medicine. Ed. by Trisha Greenhalgh & Brian Hurwitz. 286p. 1998. pap. 34.95 (*0-7279-1223-2*) Login Brothers Bk Co.

Narrative Bibliography of the African-American Frontier: Blacks in the Rocky Mountain West, 1535-1912. Roger D. Hardaway. LC 95-16888. (Studies in American History: Vol. 9). 252p. 1995. 89.95 (*0-7734-8879-0*) E Mellen.

Narrative Body. Eldon Garnet et al. LC 95-20806. (FRE, ENG & DUT., Illus.). 76p. Date not set. 6.00 (*0-936756-99-3*) Autonomedia.

Narrative Chance: Postmodern Discourse on Native American Indian Literatures. Ed. by Gerald R. Vizenor. LC 93-4116. (American Indian Literature & Critical Studies: Vol. 8). 1993. reprint ed. 15.95 (*0-8061-2561-6*) U of Okla Pr.

Narrative Comprehension: A Discourse Perspective. Catherine Emmott. (Illus.). 336p. 1997. text 80.00 (*0-19-823649-2*) OUP.

Narrative Comprehension: A Discourse Perspective. Catherine Emmott. (Illus.). 340p. 1999. pap. text 27.50 (*0-19-823868-1*) OUP.

Narrative Comprehension & Film. Edward Branigan. (Sightlines Ser.). (Illus.). 320p. (C). 1992. pap. 24.99 (*0-415-07512-2*, A7036) Routledge.

Narrative Comprehension, Causality & Coherence: Essays in Honor of Tom Trabasso. Ed. by Susan R. Goldman et al. LC 99-19376. 320p. 1999. 79.95 (*0-8058-3358-7*) L Erlbaum Assocs.

Narrative Con-Texts in Dubliners. Bernard Benstock. LC 93-3377. 170p. 1993. text 34.95 (*0-252-02058-8*) U of Ill Pr.

Narrative Consciousness: Structure & Perception in the Fiction of Kafka, Beckett & Robbe-Grillet. George H. Szanto. LC 78-37648. 216p. 1972. 20.00 (*0-292-75500-7*) Lib Soc Sci.

Narrative Consciousness: Structure & Perception in the Fiction of Kafka, Beckett & Robbe-Grillet. George H. Szanto. LC 78-37648. 226p. reprint ed. pap. 70.10 (*0-608-16222-1*, 202715100054) Bks Demand.

Narrative Corpse. Ed. by Art Spiegelman & R. Sikoryak. (Illus.). 1995. pap. 25.00 (*0-9638129-4-7*) Gates of Heck.

Narrative Counseling in Schools: Powerful & Brief. John Winslade & Gerald Monk. LC 98-25351. (PSFC Ser.). 144p. 1998. 45.95 (*0-8039-6623-7*, 81415); pap. 19.95 (*0-8039-6617-2*, 81416) Corwin Pr.

Narrative Covenant: Transformations of Genre in the Growth of Biblical Literature. David Damrosch. LC 86-43001. 368p. 1990. pap. text 17.95 (*0-8014-9934-8*) Cornell U Pr.

Narrative Descriptions, Vol. I. 1983. write for info. Macmillan.

***Narrative Design: Working with Imagination, Craft & Form.** Madison Smartt Bell. 392p. 2000. pap. text 16.95 (*0-393-32021-9*) Norton.

Narrative Development: Six Approaches. Michael G. Bamberg. LC 97-2352. 1997. 69.95 (*0-8058-2057-4*); pap. 32.50 (*0-8058-2058-2*) L Erlbaum Assocs.

Narrative Discourse: An Essay in Method. Gerard Genette. Tr. by Jane E. Lewin from FRE. LC 79-13499. (Illus.). 288p. 1979. pap. text 14.95 (*0-8014-9259-9*) Cornell U Pr.

Narrative Discourse in Normal Aging & Neurologically-Impaired Adults. Ed. by Hiram H. Brownell & Yves Joanette. LC 93-15128. (Illus.). 354p. (Orig.). (C). 1993. pap. text 65.00 (*1-56593-083-5*, 0388) Thomson Learn.

Narrative Discourse Revisited. Gerard Genette. Tr. by Jane E. Lewin from FRE. LC 88-47730. (Illus.). 168p. 1990. reprint ed. pap. text 11.95 (*0-8014-9535-0*) Cornell U Pr.

Narrative Elements & Religious Meanings. Wesley A. Kort. LC 75-15257. 128p. reprint ed. pap. 39.70 (*0-608-16311-2*, 202687300053) Bks Demand.

Narrative Endings. J. Hillis Miller et al. LC PN3378.N3. (Ninteenth-Century Studies: Vol. 33, No. 1). 160p. reprint ed. pap. 49.60 (*0-608-18291-5*, 203154100075) Bks Demand.

Narrative Enlarging. Verle Waters. 1995. pap. 24.95 (*0-88737-641-X*) Natl League Nurse.

Narrative Ethics. William Ellos. (Avebury Series in Philosophy). 128p. 1994. 61.95 (*1-85628-623-1*, Pub. by Avebury) Ashgate Pub Co.

Narrative Ethics. Adam Z. Newton. LC 94-19710. 352p. 1995. text 47.95 (*0-674-60087-8*, NEWNAR) HUP.

Narrative Ethics. Adam Z. Newton. LC 94-19710. 352p. 1997. reprint ed. pap. 18.50 (*0-674-60088-6*) HUP.

Narrative Exchanges. Ian Reid. 240p. (C). (gr. 13 up). 1992. text 52.95 (*0-415-07234-4*) Routledge.

Narrative Exchanges, Unit B. Deakin University Press Staff. 154p. (C). 1988. 54.00 (*0-7300-0571-2*, Pub. by Deakin Univ) St Mut.

Narrative Exchanges Reader, Unit B. Deakin University Press Staff. 172p. (C). 1988. 60.00 (*0-7300-0572-0*, Pub. by Deakin Univ) St Mut.

Narrative Explanation: A Pragmatic Theory of Discourse. Jon-K Adams. Ed. by Richard Martin & Rudiger Schreyer. LC 96-44830. (Aachen British & American Studies: Vol. 7). 170p. 1996. 38.95 (*3-631-30802-7*) P Lang Pubng.

***Narrative Feminine Identity & the Appearance of Woman in Some of the Shorter Fiction of Goethe, Kleist, Hawthrone & James.** Laura Martin. LC 00-20027. (Women's Studies: Vol. 23). 224p. 2000. text 89.95 (*0-7734-7809-4*) E Mellen.

Narrative Fiction. Griffith. (C). 1993. pap. text, teacher ed. 33.75 (*0-15-500156-6*) Harcourt Coll Pubs.

Narrative Fiction: Contemporary Poetics. Shlomith Rimmon-Kenan. (New Accents Ser.). 136p. (C). 1983. pap. 18.99 (*0-415-04294-1*) Routledge.

Narrative Fiction: Contemporary Poetics. Shlomith Rimmon-Kenan. LC 82-18859. 173p. 1983. pap. 13.95 (*0-416-74230-0*, NO. 3817) Routledge.

Narrative Fiction: Introduction & Anthology. Griffit. LC 92-76097. (C). 1994. pap. text 44.50 (*0-15-500155-8*, Pub. by Harcourt Coll Pubs) Harcourt.

Narrative Form in History & Fiction: Hume, Fielding & Gibbon. Leo Braudy. LC 69-18052. viii, 318 p. 1970. write for info. (*0-691-06168-8*) Princeton U Pr.

Narrative Forms of Southern Community. Scott Romine. LC 99-14905. (Southern Literary Studies). 248p. 1999. text 49.95 (*0-8071-2401-X*); pap. text 24.95 (*0-8071-2527-X*) La State U Pr.

Narrative History of Cotton in Alabama: A Tour of the Old Alabama Town Cotton Gin. Thomas W. Oliver. 4th. (Illus.). 96p. (Orig.). 1992. pap. 8.00 (*0-7012-5775-X*) Landmarks Found.

Narrative History of Dover, Mass., As a Precinct, Parish, District & Town. F. Smith. (Illus.). 354p. 1989. reprint ed. lib. bdg. 40.00 (*0-8328-0822-9*, MA0043) Higginson Bk Co.

Narrative History of Experimental Social Psychology. S. Patnoe. (Recent Research in Psychology Ser.). 295p. 1988. pap. 43.00 (*0-387-96850-4*) Spr-Verlag.

Narrative History of Remsen, N. Y. Millard F. Roberts. 397p. 1993. reprint ed. lib. bdg. 42.50 (*0-8328-2884-X*) Higginson Bk Co.

Narrative Identity & Dementia: A Study of Autobiographical Memories & Emotions. Marie A. Mills. LC 98-70989. (CEDR Ser.). (Illus.). 199p. 1998. text 63.95 (*1-84014-175-1*, Pub. by Ashgate Pub) Ashgate Pub Co.

Narrative Imagery: Artists' Portfolios. Florence B. Helzel. (Illus.). 100p. (Orig.). 1991. pap. 16.95 (*0-943376-46-7*) Magnes Mus.

Narrative Imagination: Comic Tales by Philippe de Vigneulles. Armine A. Kotin. LC 77-76329. (Studies in Romance Languages: No. 18). 152p. reprint ed. pap. 47.20 (*0-7837-5823-5*, 204549000006) Bks Demand.

Narrative in Culture: Storytelling in the Sciences, Philosophy & Literature. Ed. by Cristopher Nash & Christopher Nash. LC 94-18539. (Warwick Studies in Philosophy & Literature). 256p. (C). 1994. pap. 24.99 (*0-415-10344-4*, B4640) Routledge.

Narrative in Drama: The Art of the Euripidean Messenger-Speech. Irene J. De Jong. LC 91-19528. (Supplements to Mnemosyne Ser.: No. 116). ix, 214p. 1991. 74.50 (*90-04-09406-7*) Brill Academic Pubs.

***Narrative in Fiction & Film: An Introduction.** Jakob Lothe. LC 99-58885. 250p. 2000. write for info. (*0-19-875232-6*) OUP.

Narrative in Society: A Performer-Centered Study of Narration. Linda Degh. 372p. 1995. text 45.00 (*0-253-31683-9*) Ind U Pr.

Narrative in Teaching, Learning & Research. Ed. by Hunter McEwan & Kieran Egan. (Critical Issues in Curriculum Ser.). 256p. (C). 1995. text 44.00 (*0-8077-3400-4*); pap. text 21.95 (*0-8077-3399-7*) Tchrs Coll.

***Narrative in the Feminine: Daphne Marlatt & Nicole Brossard.** Susan Knutson. 248p. 2000. text 59.95 (*0-88920-301-6*) Wilfrid Laurier.

Narrative in the Hebrew Bible. David M. Gunn & Danna N. Fewell. LC 92-37426. (Oxford Bible Ser.). 280p. 1993. pap. text 19.95 (*0-19-213245-8*) OUP.

Narrative Innovation & Incoherence: Ideology in Defoe, Goldsmith, Austen, Eliot, & Hemingway. Michael M. Boardman. LC 92-3785. 237p. 1992. text 34.95 (*0-8223-1239-5*) Duke.

Narrative Innovation & Political Change in Mexico. John S. Brushwood. (University of Texas Studies in Contemporary Spanish-American Fiction: Vol. 4). XII, 131p. (C). 1989. text 32.50 (*0-8204-0966-9*) P Lang Pubng.

***Narrative Inquiries: The Use of Storytelling in Qualitative Research.** Jean D. Clandinin & F. Michael Connelly. LC 99-6680. 256p. 1999. 29.95 (*0-7879-4343-6*) Jossey-Bass.

Narrative Inquiry with Children & Youth. Ed. by Julia L. Ellis et al. LC 98-23399. (Critical Education Practice Ser.: Vol. 15). (Illus.). 157p. 1998. 49.00 (*0-8153-1166-4*, SS0876) Garland.

Narrative Inquiry with Children & Youth. Julia L. Ellis. Ed. by Joe Kincheloe & Shirley R. Steinberg. 200p. Date not set. pap. text 18.95 (*0-8153-2310-7*) Garland.

***Narrative Intelligence: Papers from the AAAI Fall Symposium.** Ed. by Michael Mateas & Phoebe Senger. (Illus.). 177p. 1999. spiral bd. 25.00 (*1-57735-103-7*) AAAI Pr.

Narrative Invention in 12th-Century French Romance: The Convention of Hospitality (1160-1200) Matilda T. Bruckner. LC 79-53400. (Edward C. Armstrong Monographs on Medieval Literature: No. 17). 230p. (Orig.). 1980. pap. 13.95 (*0-917058-16-X*) French Forum.

Narrative Irony in Luke-Acts: The Paradoxical Interaction of Prophetic Fulfillment & Jewish Rejection. Jerry L. Ray. LC 95-12483. (Biblical Press Ser.: Vol. 28). 200p. 1996. 79.95 (*0-7734-2359-1*, Mellen Biblical Pr) E Mellen.

Narrative Irony in the Contemporary Spanish-American Novel. Jonathan Tittler. LC 83-21074. 211p. 1984. 37.50 (*0-8014-1574-8*) Cornell U Pr.

Narrative Jesus: A Semiotic Reading of Mark's Gospel. Ole Davidsen. 416p. (Orig.). (C). 1993. 33.00 (*87-7288-423-1*, Pub. by Aarhus Univ Pr) David Brown.

Narrative Journals of Travels from Detroit Northwest Through the Great Chain of American Lakes to the Sources of the Mississippi River, in the Year 1820. Henry R. Schoolcraft. (American Biography Ser.). 419p. 1991. reprint ed. lib. bdg. 89.00 (*0-7812-8342-6*) Rprt Serv.

Narrative Journals of Travels Through the Northwestern Regions of the U. S. Extending from Detroit Through the Great Chain of American Lakes to the Sources of the Mississippi River. Henry R. Schoolcraft. LC 73-125763. (American Environmental Studies). 1974. reprint ed. 26.95 (*0-405-02689-7*) Ayer.

Narrative Knowing & the Human Sciences. Donald E. Polkinghorne. LC 87-17992. (SUNY Series in the Philosophy of the Social Sciences). 232p. (C). 1988. pap. text 19.95 (*0-88706-623-2*) State U NY Pr.

***Narrative Learner: Writing, Reading & Analysis for the New College Student.** Hope Parisi. 152p. (C). 1999. per. 38.95 (*0-7872-6486-5*, 41648601) Kendall-Hunt.

Narrative Life of Frederick Douglass. Frederick Douglass. 1976. 17.95 (*0-8488-0264-0*) Amereon Ltd.

Narrative Life of O Equiano Critical. Olaudah Equiano. pap. text. write for info. (*0-393-97494-4*) Norton.

Narrative, Literacy, & Face in Interethnic Communication. Ron Scollon & Suzanne Scollon. LC 81-14857. (Advances in Discourse Processes Ser.: Vol. 7). 224p. (C). 1981. pap. 42.50 (*0-89391-086-4*); text 78.50 (*0-89391-076-7*) Ablx Pub.

Narrative Logic: A Semantic Analysis of the Historian's Language. Franklin R. Ankersmit. 274p. 1983. text 126.50 (*90-247-2731-6*) Kluwer Academic.

Narrative Magic in the Fiction of Isabel Allende. Patricia Hart. LC 88-46152. 200p. 1989. 38.50 (*0-8386-3351-X*) Fairleigh Dickinson.

Narrative Matrix: Stendhal's "Le Rouge & le Noir" Carol A. Mossman. LC 84-80768. (French Forum Monographs: No. 53). 177p. (Orig.). 1984. pap. 13.45 (*0-917058-53-4*) French Forum.

***Narrative Means to Sober Ends: Treating Addiction & Its Aftermath.** Jonathan Diamond. (Guilford Family Therapy Ser.). 344p. 2000. lib. bdg. 37.95 (*1-57230-566-5*, C0566) Guilford Pubns.

Narrative Means to Therapeutic Ends. Michael James Denham White & David Epston. (C). 1990. 27.00 (*0-393-70098-4*) Norton.

***Narrative Mediation: A New Approach to Conflict Resolution.** Gerald Monk & John Winslade. LC 99-48273. 256p. 2000. 34.95 (*0-7879-4192-1*) Jossey-Bass.

Narrative Methods. Ed. by Peter Abell. 160p. 1993. pap. text 455.00 (*2-88124-626-5*) Gordon & Breach.

Narrative Modes: Techniques of the Short Story. Helmut Bonheim. 208p. (C). 1992. 75.00 (*0-85991-086-5*) Boydell & Brewer.

Narrative Modes in Czech Literature. Lubomir Dolezel. LC 74-190343. 161p. reprint ed. pap. 50.00 (*0-608-16580-8*, 202636000049) Bks Demand.

Narrative Mortality: Death, Closure & New Wave Cinemas. Catherine Russell. LC 94-17542. 288p. 1994. pap. 19.95 (*0-8166-2486-0*); text 49.95 (*0-8166-2485-2*) U of Minn Pr.

Narrative of a Child Analysis. Melanie Klein. (Writings of Melanie Klein Ser.). 496p. (C). 1984. 45.00 (*0-02-918450-9*) Free Pr.

Narrative of a Journey Across the Rocky Mountains to the Columbia River. John Kirk Townsend. LC 99-47898. (Northwest Reprints Ser.). 352p. 1999. pap. 16.95 (*0-87071-525-9*) Oreg St U Pr.

Narrative of a Journey down the Ohio & Mississippi in 1789-90 With a Memoir & Illustrative Notes by Lyman C. Draper. Samuel S. Forman. LC 78-146396. (First American Frontier Ser.). 1971. reprint ed. 13.95 (*0-405-02850-4*) Ayer.

Narrative of a Journey in the Interior of China. Abel & Clarke. (Illus.). 420p. Date not set. 55.95 (*0-405-01711-1*) Arno Press.

Narrative of a Journey Through the Upper Provinces of India, 3 vols., Set. Reginal Heber. (C). 1993. 38.00 (*81-85557-37-3*, Pub. by Low Price) S Asia.

Narrative of a Journey to Morocco. Thomas Hodgkin. (Illus.). 183p. Date not set. 55.95 (*0-405-01713-8*) Arno Press.

Narrative of a Journey to Morocco. Thomas Hodgkin. 7.00 (*0-405-18969-9*, 16884) Ayer.

Narrative of a Journey to Musardu: The Capitol of the Mandingoes. Benjamin Anderson. 172p. 1971. 45.00 (*0-7146-1785-7*, BHA-01785, Pub. by F Cass Pubs) Intl Spec Bk.

Narrative of a Journey to the Shores of the Polar Sea, in the Years 1819 - 1822. John Franklin. LC 68-55187. 786p. 1969. reprint ed. lib. bdg. 95.00 (*0-8371-1447-0*, FRPS, Greenwood Pr) Greenwood.

Narrative of a Mission to Bokhara, in the Years 1843-1845, to Ascertain the Fate of Colonel Stoddart & Captain Conol. Joseph Wolff. LC 79-115599. (Russia Observed, Series I). 1970. reprint ed. 40.95 (*0-405-03072-X*) Ayer.

Narrative of a Mission to Central Africa, 1850-1851, 2 vols., Set. James Richardson. (Illus.). 704p. 1970. reprint ed. 95.00 (*0-7146-1848-9*, BHA-01848, Pub. by F Cass Pubs) Intl Spec Bk.

Narrative of a Pedestrian Journey Through Russia & Siberian Tartary, from the Frontiers of China to the Frozen Sea & Kamtchatka. John D. Cochrane. LC 79-115521. (Russia Observed, Series I). 1970. reprint ed. 41.95 (*0-405-03016-9*) Ayer.

Narrative of a Second Voyage in Search of a North-West Passage, & of a Residence in the Arctic Regions During the Years 1829, 1830,1831, 1833, 2 vols., Set. John Ross. LC 68-55217. 1971. reprint ed. lib. bdg. 75.00 (*0-8371-3860-4*, RONP) Greenwood.

Narrative of a Second Voyage in Search of a North-West Passage, & of a Residence in the Arctic Regions During the Years 1829, 1830,1831, 1833, 2 vols., Vol. 1. John Ross. LC 68-55217. 1971. reprint ed. lib. bdg. 55.00 (*0-8371-1332-6*, RONQ) Greenwood.

Narrative of a Second Voyage in Search of a North-West Passage, & of a Residence in the Arctic Regions During the Years 1829, 1830,1831, 1833, 2 vols., Vol. 2. John Ross. LC 68-55217. 1971. reprint ed. lib. bdg. 45.00 (*0-8371-1333-4*, RONR) Greenwood.

Narrative of a Soldier of the Revolution. Ebenezer Fletcher. LC 72-117874. (Select Bibliographies Reprint Ser.). 1977. 16.95 (*0-8369-5327-4*) Ayer.

N

An Asterisk (*) at the beginning of an entry indicates that the title is appearing for the first time.

Narrative of a Tour from the State of Indiana to the Oregon Territory in the Years 1841-2. Joseph Williams. 63p. 1977. 16.95 (*0-87770-172-5*) Ye Galleon.

Narrative of a Visit to the West Indies in Eighteen Forty & Eighteen Forty-One. George Truman et al. LC 71-38027. (Black Heritage Library Collection). 1977. reprint ed. 20.95 (*0-8369-8993-7*) Ayer.

Narrative of a Voyage to California Ports in 1841-1842. enl. ed. George Simpson. 1988. reprint ed. 29.95 (*0-87770-444-9*) Ye Galleon.

Narrative of a Voyage to Senegal. J. B. Savigny & Alexander Correard. LC 86-60536. 240p. 1986. reprint ed. pap. 11.50 (*0-910395-21-7*) Marlboro Pr.

Narrative of a Voyage to the Spanish Main, in the Ship "Two Friends" The Occupation of Amelia Island. fac. ed. Intro. by John W. Griffin. LC 78-9785. 396p. 1978. reprint ed. pap. 122.80 (*0-608-04470-9*, 206521500001) Bks Demand.

Narrative of a Year's Journey Through Central & Eastern Arabia, 1862-63, 2 vols. William G. Palgrave. (Illus.). xii, 864p. reprint ed. write for info. (*0-318-71549-X*) G Olms Pubs.

Narrative of an Expedition into the Interior of Africa, 2 vols., Set. MacGregor Laird & R. A. Oldfield. (Illus.). 1971. reprint ed. 45.00 (*0-7146-1826-8*, Pub. by F Cass Pubs) Intl Spec Bk.

Narrative of an Expedition to the East Coast of Greenland. Wilhelm A. Graah. LC 74-5842. reprint ed. 32.50 (*0-404-11647-7*) AMS Pr.

Narrative of an Exploring Voyage up to the Rivers Kuora & Binue Commonly Known As the Niger & Tsadda in 1854. W. B. Baikie. 456p. 1966. 57.50 (*0-7146-1788-1*, Pub. by F Cass Pubs) Intl Spec Bk.

Narrative of & Expedition of Five Americans into a Land of Wild Animals. John P. Kennedy. (Notable American Authors Ser.). 1999. reprint ed. lib. bdg. 125.00 (*0-7812-3672-X*) Rprt Serv.

Narrative of Antonio Munoz Molina: Self-Conscious Realism & "El Desencanto" Lawrence Rich. LC 98-4951. (Currents in Comparative Romance Languages & Literatures Ser.: Vol. 78). XII, 135p. (C). 1999. text 38.95 (*0-8204-4080-9*, 40809) P Lang Pubng.

Narrative of Arthur Gordon Pym. Edgar Allan Poe. (Notable American Authors Ser.). 1999. reprint ed. lib. bdg. 125.00 (*0-7812-8752-9*) Rprt Serv.

Narrative of Arthur Gordon Pym: The Abyss of Interpretation. Gerald J. Kennedy. LC 94-3667. (Twayne's Masterwork Studies: No. 135). 128p. 1994. 23.95 (*0-8057-4455-X*, Twyne); pap. 13.95 (*0-8057-9443-3*, Twyne) Mac Lib Ref.

Narrative of Arthur Gordon Pym of Nantucket. Edgar Allan Poe. Ed. & Intro. by Richard Kopley. LC 98-50102. 320p. 1999. pap. 8.95 (*0-14-043748-7*) Viking Penguin.

Narrative of Arthur Gordon Pym of Nantucket & Related Tales. Edgar Allan Poe. Ed. & Intro. by J. Gerald Kennedy. (Oxford World's Classics Ser.). 328p. 1998. pap. 8.95 (*0-19-283771-0*) OUP.

Narrative of Broken Winter. Mark Karlins. 59p. 1988. 7.95 (*1-55643-026-4*) North Atlantic.

Narrative of Captain David Woodard & Four Seamen Who Lost Their Ship While in a Boat at Sea, & Surrendered Themselves up to the Malays in the Island of Celebes (1805) David Woodard. (Illus.). 1969. 79.50 (*0-614-01817-X*) Elliots Bks.

Narrative of Captivity in Abyssinia with Some Account of the Late Emperor Theodore, His Country & People. Henry Blanc. (Illus.). 410p. 1970. reprint ed. 55.00 (*0-7146-1792-X*, Pub. by F Cass Pubs) Intl Spec Bk.

Narrative of Charles Prince of Wales' Expedition to Scotland in the Year 1745. James Maxwell. LC 73-173063. (Maitland Club, Glasgow. Publications: No. 53). reprint ed. 37.50 (*0-404-53035-4*) AMS Pr.

Narrative of Colonel David Fanning. 1981. 25.00 (*0-937684-14-7*) Tradd St Pr.

***Narrative of Colonel Ethan Allen's Captivity.** Ethan Allen. Ed. by Stephen Carl Arch. LC 99-74753. (Emergent Texts in American Literature Ser.). 73p. (C). 2000. pap. text 6.95 (*1-58390-009-8*, Copley Editions) Copley Pub.

Narrative of Colonel Robert Campbell's Experiences in the Rocky Mountain Fur Trade from 1825 to 1835. Robert Campbell. Ed. by Drew A. Holloway. 67p. 1995. pap. 12.95 (*0-87770-510-0*) Ye Galleon.

Narrative of Discovery & Adventure in Africa: From the Earliest Ages to the Present Time. Robert Jameson et al. 1977. text 29.95 (*0-8369-9244-X*, 9098) Ayer.

Narrative of Don Alonso DeCalves, John Van Delure & Capt, James Vanleason. Don A. DeCalves et al. LC 96-27267. 1996. 19.95 (*0-87770-582-8*); pap. 14.95 (*0-87770-583-6*) Ye Galleon.

Narrative of Ebenezer Fletcher, a Soldier of the Revolution. Ebenezer Fletcher. (American Biography Ser.). 86p. 1991. reprint ed. lib. bdg. 59.00 (*0-7812-8132-6*) Rprt Serv.

Narrative of Ethan Allen. Ethan Allen. 124p. 1987. reprint ed. pap. 8.95 (*1-55709-127-7*) Applewood.

Narrative of Frederick Douglas Notes. John Chua. LC 96-136125. (Cliffs Notes Ser.). 72p. 1995. pap. 4.95 (*0-8220-0872-6*, Cliff) IDG Bks.

Narrative of Henry Bird. Henry Bird. 15p. 1973. pap. 6.95 (*0-87770-115-6*) Ye Galleon.

Narrative of Hosea Hudson. Nell I. Painter. (Illus.). 424p. 1993. pap. 12.95 (*0-393-31015-9*) Norton.

Narrative of Hosea Hudson: His Life As a Negro Communist in the South. Nell I. Painter. LC 79-4589. 416p. reprint ed. pap. 129.00 (*0-7837-2308-3*, 205739600004) Bks Demand.

Narrative of James Williams, an American Slave, Who Was for Several Years a Driver on a Cotton Plantation in Alabama. James Williams. (American Biography Ser.). 108p. 1991. reprint ed. lib. bdg. 59.00 (*0-7812-8419-8*) Rprt Serv.

Narrative of Johann Carl Buettner in the American Revolution. Johann C. Buettner. LC 75-180037. 70p. 1972. reprint ed. 18.95 (*0-405-08324-6*, Pub. by Blom Pubns) Ayer.

Narrative of John Blatchford: Detailing His Sufferings in the Revolutionary War. John Blatchford. (American Biography Ser.). 127p. 1991. reprint ed. lib. bdg. 59.00 (*0-7812-8027-3*) Rprt Serv.

Narrative of John Blatchford: Detailing His Sufferings in the Revolutionary War While a Prisoner with the British. John Blatchford. LC 70-140855. (Eyewitness Accounts of the American Revolution Ser.). (Illus.). 1971. reprint ed. 14.95 (*0-405-01216-0*) Ayer.

Narrative of Jonathan Rathbun of the Capture of Fort Griswold with Accurate Accounts of the Capture of Groton Fort, the Massacre That Followed, & the Sacking & Burning of New London, September 6, 1781 by the British Forces Under the Command of the Traitor Benedict Arnold. Jonathan Rathbun. LC 76-140878. (Eyewitness Accounts of the American Revolution Ser.). 1971. reprint ed. 21.95 (*0-405-01217-9*) Ayer.

Narrative of Leading Incidents of the Organization of the First Popular Movement in Virginia in 1865 to Reestablish Peaceful Relations Between the Northern & Southern States. Alexander H. Stuart. LC 71-176461. reprint ed. 29.50 (*0-404-04629-0*) AMS Pr.

Narrative of Liberation: Perspectives on Afro-Caribbean Literature, Popular Culture, & Politics. Patrick Taylor. LC 88-19005. 288p. 1989. text 39.95 (*0-8014-2193-4*) Cornell U Pr.

Narrative of Life. Sue H. Horn. 110p. 1999. pap. 12.95 (*0-9656748-3-5*) Winter Again.

Narrative of Major Abraham Leggett. Abraham Leggett. LC 70-140871. (Eyewitness Accounts of the American Revolution Ser.). 1971. reprint ed. 16.95 (*0-405-01215-2*) Ayer.

Narrative of Matthew Bunn. Matthew Bunn. LC 94-14739. 60p. 1995. pap. 9.95 (*0-87770-531-3*) Ye Galleon.

Narrative of Military Operations During the Civil War. Joseph E. Johnston. (Quality Paperbacks Ser.). (Illus.). 644p. 1990. pap. 17.95 (*0-306-80393-3*) Da Capo.

Narrative of Pilgrimage to El Medina & Mecca, 2 vols., Set. Richard F. Burton. (C). 1994. 72.00 (*81-206-0903-4*, Pub. by Asian Educ Servs) S Asia.

Narrative of Realism & Myth: Verga, Lawrence, Faulkner, Pavese. Gregory L. Lucente. LC 81-2084. 205p. 1981. reprint ed. pap. 63.60 (*0-608-07330-X*, 206755800009) Bks Demand.

Narrative of Riots at Alton. Edward Beecher. LC 70-115858. (Studies in Black History & Culture: No. 54). 1970. reprint ed. lib. bdg. 75.00 (*0-8383-1072-9*) M S G Haskell Hse.

Narrative of Robert Hancock Hunter, 1813-1902. Robert H. Hunter. LC 81-2938. 55p. 1982. reprint ed. pap. text 10.00 (*0-86663-401-0*); reprint ed. lib. bdg. 150.00 (*0-86663-426-6*) Ide Hse.

Narrative of Sojourner. Sojourner Truth. 144p. 1993. pap. 9.00 (*0-679-74035-X*) McKay.

Narrative of Sojourner Truth. Olive Gilbert & Sojourner Truth. LC 97-20938. (Dover Thrift Editions Ser.). (Illus.). 80p. 1997. pap. 1.00 (*0-486-29899-X*) Dover.

Narrative of Sojourner Truth. Sojourner Truth. LC 68-29021. (American Negro: His History & Literature. Series 1). 1974. reprint ed. 31.95 (*0-405-01841-X*) Ayer.

Narrative of Sojourner Truth: A Bondswoman of Olden Time, with a History of Her Labors & Correspondence Drawn from Her "Book of Life" Intro. by Jeffrey Stewart. (Schomburg Library of Nineteenth-Century Black Women Writers). (Illus.). 368p. 1991. 42.00 (*0-19-506638-3*) OUP.

Narrative of Sojourner Truth: A Bondswoman of Olden Time, with a History of Her Labors & Correspondence Drawn from Her Book of Life; Also, a Memorial Chapter. Sojourner Truth et al. LC 98-6496. (Classics Ser.). 352p. 1998. pap. 9.95 (*0-14-043678-2*) Viking Penguin.

Narrative of Some Things of New Spain & of the Great City of Temestitan, Mexico. Tr. by Marshall H. Saville. (Cortes Society Ser.: Vol. 1). 1974. reprint ed. 35.00 (*0-527-19721-1*) Periodicals Srv.

Narrative of Ten Years Residence at Tripoli in Africa. Richard Tully. 400p. 1990. 150.00 (*1-85077-006-9*, Pub. by Darf Pubs Ltd) St Mut.

Narrative of the Adventures of John R. Jewitt: Only Survivor of the Crew of the Ship Boston, During a Captivity of Nearly Three Years among the Savages of Nootka Sound. John R. Jewitt. (American Biography Ser.). 203p. 1992. reprint ed. lib. bdg. 69.00 (*0-7812-8220-9*) Rprt Serv.

Narrative of the Campaign in India Which Terminated the War with Tippo Sultan in 1792. Major Dirom. 1986. reprint ed. 32.00 (*0-8364-1846-8*, Pub. by Usha) S Asia.

Narrative of the Captivity & Restoration of Mrs. Mary Rowlandson. Mary W. Rowlandson. (American Biography Ser.). 96p. 1991. reprint ed. lib. bdg. 59.00 (*0-7812-8332-9*) Rprt Serv.

Narrative of the Captivity & the Restoration of Mrs. Mary Rowlandson. Mary Rowlandson. 96p. 1998. pap. 9.95 (*0-939218-20-8*) Chapman Billies.

Narrative of the Captivity of Isaac Webster. Isaac Webster. 25p. 1988. pap. 4.95 (*0-87770-443-0*) Ye Galleon.

Narrative of the Captivity of Nehemiah How. Nehemiah How. 1973. 59.95 (*0-8490-0708-9*) Gordon Pr.

Narrative of the Capture of Abel Janney by the Indians in 1782. Anno. by Alan Gutchess. LC 97-66236. 21p. 1997. reprint ed. pap. 5.95 (*0-9651039-1-9*) Dresslar Publishing.

Narrative of the Chinese Embassy to the Khan of the Tourgouth Tartars, 1712-1715. Tulisen. Tr. by George L. Staunton from CHI. LC 75-32337. (Studies in Chinese History & Civilization). 330p. 1976. reprint ed. lib. bdg. 72.50 (*0-313-26955-6*, U6955) Greenwood.

Narrative of the Dangers & Sufferings of Robert Eastburn During His Captivity in the Years 1756-1757. Robert Eastburn. LC 96-18849. 1996. 14.95 (*0-87770-594-1*); pap. 8.95 (*0-87770-593-3*) Ye Galleon.

Narrative of the Days of the Reformation. Ed. by John G. Nichols. (Camden Society, London. Publications, First Ser.: No. 77). reprint ed. 85.00 (*0-404-50177-X*) AMS Pr.

Narrative of the Discoveries on the North Coast of America, Effected by the Officers of the Hudson's Bay Company During the Years 1836-39. Thomas Simpson. LC 74-5877. reprint ed. 52.50 (*0-404-11685-X*) AMS Pr.

Narrative of the Early Days & Remembrances of Oceola Nikkanochee, Prince of Econchatti: A Young Seminole Indian. Andrew G. Welch. LC 76-54519. (Floridiana Facsimile & Reprint Ser.). 305p. 1977. reprint ed. 23.95 (*0-8130-0411-X*) U Press Fla.

Narrative of the Excursions & Ravages of the King's Troops under Command of General Gage. Provincial Congress of Massachusetts Colony, 1775. LC 67-29008. (Eyewitness Accounts of the American Revolution Ser.). 1968. reprint ed. 14.95 (*0-405-01119-9*) Ayer.

Narrative of the Expedition of an American Squadron to the China Seas & Japan, 3 vols. Matthew C. Perry. Ed. by Francis L. Hawks. LC 01-4228. (Illus.). reprint ed. write for info. (*0-404-05060-3*) AMS Pr.

Narrative of the Expedition of an American Squadron to the China Seas & Japan Performed in the Years 1852, 1853, & 1854 under the Command of Commodore M. C. Perry, United States Navy, by Order of the Government of the United States, Vol. 1. Matthew C. Perry et al. 1968. 60.95 (*0-405-18940-0*, 17148) Ayer.

Narrative of the Expedition of an American Squadron to the China Seas & Japan Performed in the Years 1852, 1853 & 1854, Under the Command of Commodore M. C. Perry, United States Navy, by Order of the Government of the United States, Vol. 3. Matthew C. Perry et al. 1968. 60.95 (*0-405-18942-7*, 17150) Ayer.

Narrative of the Expedition of an American Squadron to the China Seas & Japan Performed in the Years 1852, 1853, & 1854 under the Command of Commodore M. C. Perry, United States Navy, by Order of the Government of the United States, Vol. 4. Matthew C. Perry et al. 1968. 60.95 (*0-405-18943-5*, 17151) Ayer.

Narrative of the Expedition of an American Squadron to the China Seas & Japan Performed in the Years 1852, 1853, 1854, under the Command of Commodore M. C. Perry, United States Navy, by Order of the Government of the United States, Vol. 2. Matthew C. Perry et al. 1968. 60.95 (*0-405-18941-9*, 17149) Ayer.

***Narrative of the Expedition to the China Seas Japan: 1852-1854.** Matthew C. Perry. 2000. pap. 34.95 (*0-486-41133-8*) Dover.

Narrative of the Expedition to the Source of St. Peter's River: Long's Second Expedition. William H. Keating. (Illus.). 1959. 30.00 (*0-87018-036-3*) Ross.

Narrative of the Field Operations Connected with Zulu War 1879. War Office, Intelligence Branch Staff. 196p. 35.00 (*1-85367-033-2*, 5563) Stackpole.

Narrative of the Incas. Juan De Betanzos. Ed. & Tr. by Roland Hamilton & Dana Buchanan from SPA. (Illus.). 352p. 1996. pap. 17.95 (*0-292-75559-7*); text 40.00 (*0-292-75560-0*) U of Tex Pr.

Narrative of the Late Proceedings & Events in China. John Slade. LC 72-79839. (China Library). 1972. reprint ed. lib. bdg. 17.00 (*0-8420-1356-3*) Scholarly Res Inc.

Narrative of the Life & Adventures of Henry Bibb, an American Slave. Henry Bibb. LC 70-89423. (Black Heritage Library Collection). 1977. 19.98 (*0-8369-8511-7*) Ayer.

Narrative of the Life & Adventures of Major C. Bolin, Alias David Butler. A. A. Sargent. 1996. 22.50 (*0-87770-580-1*); pap. 14.95 (*0-87770-581-X*) Ye Galleon.

Narrative of the Life & Medical Discoveries of Samuel Thomson, Containing an Account of His System of Practice & the Manner of Curing. Samuel Thomson. LC 79-180594. (Medicine & Society in America Ser.). 186p. 1972. reprint ed. 18.95 (*0-405-03976-X*) Ayer.

***Narrative of the Life & Times of Frederick Douglass.** Frederick Douglass. 2000. pap. 8.95 (*1-930097-11-5*) Lushena Bks.

Narrative of the Life of an American Slave. large type ed. Frederick Douglass. LC 97-30820. 148p. 1997. text 22.95 (*1-56000-534-3*) Transaction Pubs.

Narrative of the Life of David Crockett. David Crockett. Ed. by Joseph J. Arpad. 1972. pap. 12.95 (*0-8084-0021-5*) NCUP.

Narrative of the Life of David Crockett. David Crockett. (American Biography Ser.). 373p. 1991. reprint ed. lib. bdg. 79.00 (*0-7812-8094-X*) Rprt Serv.

Narrative of the Life of David Crockett of the State of Tennessee. David Crockett. LC 72-177358. (Tennesseana Editions Ser.). 232p. 1973. pap. 15.95 (*0-87049-533-X*) U of Tenn Pr.

Narrative of the Life of David Crockett of the State of Tennessee. David Crockett. LC 87-16226. lvii, 211p. 1987. reprint ed. pap. 10.95 (*0-8032-6325-2*, Bison Books) U of Nebr Pr.

***Narrative of the Life of Frederick Douglass.** 16p. (C). 1999. text 19.50 (*0-321-07737-7*) Addson-Wesley Educ.

Narrative of the Life of Frederick Douglass. Frederick Douglass. (Thrift Editions Ser.). (Illus.). 96p. 1995. pap. text 1.00 (*0-486-28499-9*) Dover.

Narrative of the Life of Frederick Douglass: An American Slave. Frederick Douglass. LC 97-69696. 127p. (C). 1998. mass mkt. 4.95 (*0-451-52673-2*) Addson-Wesley Educ.

Narrative of the Life of Frederick Douglass: An American Slave. Frederick Douglass. 124p. 1963. pap. 5.95 (*0-385-00705-1*, Anchor NY) Doubleday.

Narrative of the Life of Frederick Douglass: An American Slave. Frederick Douglass. Ed. by Deborah E. McDowell. (Oxford World's Classics Ser.). 176p. 2000. pap. 8.95 (*0-19-283250-6*) OUP.

Narrative of the Life of Frederick Douglass: An American Slave. Frederick Douglass. Ed. & Intro. by Houston A. Baker, Jr. (American Library). 159p. 1981. pap. 11.99 (*0-14-039012-X*, Penguin Classics) Viking Penguin.

Narrative of the Life of Frederick Douglass: An American Slave. large type ed. Frederick Douglass. (Large Print Heritage Ser.). 178p. 1997. lib. bdg. 26.95 (*1-58118-016-0*, 21485) LRS.

Narrative of the Life of Frederick Douglass: An American Slave. Frederick Douglass. (American Biography Ser.). 163p. 1991. reprint ed. lib. bdg. 59.00 (*0-7812-8112-1*) Rprt Serv.

Narrative of the Life of Frederick Douglass: An American Slave. Frederick Douglass. (Notable American Authors Ser.). 1992. reprint ed. lib. bdg. 75.00 (*0-7812-2674-0*) Rprt Serv.

Narrative of the Life of Frederick Douglass: An American Slave, Written by Himself. Frederick Douglass. Ed. by Benjamin Quarles. LC 59-11516. (John Harvard Library). (Illus.). 163p. 1960. pap. 8.95 (*0-674-60101-7*) HUP.

Narrative of the Life of Frederick Douglass: An American Slave, Written by Himself. Frederick Douglass. LC 92-61004. (Books in American History). 163p. (C). 1993. pap. text 11.95 (*0-312-07531-6*) St Martin.

Narrative of the Life of Frederick Douglass: Authoritative Text, Contexts, Criticism. Frederick Douglass. Ed. by William L. Andrews & William S. McFeely. LC 95-47594. (C). 1996. pap. text 6.50 (*0-393-96966-5*) Norton.

Narrative of the Life of Frederick Douglass: Reproducible Teaching Unit. James Scott. 43p. (YA). (gr. 7-12). 1999. ring bd. 29.50 (*1-58049-140-5*, TU103) Prestwick Hse.

***Narrative of the Life of Frederick Douglass, an American Slave.** Frederick Douglass & Harriet A. Jacobs. LC 00-30534. 2000. 10.95 (*0-679-78328-8*) Modern Lib NY.

Narrative of the Life of Mrs. Charlotte Charke. Charlotte C. Charke. LC 70-81365. (Illus.). 316p. 1969. reprint ed. 50.00 (*0-8201-1065-5*) Schol Facsimiles.

Narrative of the Life of Mrs. Charlotte Charke by Charlotte Charke. Charlotte Clarke. Ed. by Robert Rehder. LC 97-47587. (Pickering Women's Classics Ser.). 320p. 1998. text 55.00 (*1-85196-267-0*, Pub. by Pickering & Chatto) Ashgate Pub Co.

Narrative of the Life of Mrs. Mary Jemison. James E. Seaver. Ed. & Intro. by June Namias. LC 91-50871. (Illus.). 208p. 1995. pap. 11.95 (*0-8061-2717-1*) U of Okla Pr.

Narrative of the Life of Mrs. Mary Jemison. James E. Seaver. (Iroquois Bks.). 196p. (YA). 1990. reprint ed. pap. text 14.95 (*0-8156-2491-3*) Syracuse U Pr.

Narrative of the Life of Olaudah Equiano: A Norton Critical Edition. Olaudah Equiano. Ed. by Werner Sollors. (Critical Editions Ser.). pap. write for info. (*0-393-97499-5*) Norton.

Narrative of the Lord's Wonderful Dealings with John Marrant, a Black John Marrant & W. Aldridge. LC 77-27409. (Library of Narratives of North American Indian Captivities). v, 38 p. 1978. write for info. (*0-8240-1641-6*) Garland.

Narrative of the Manner in Which the Campaign Against the Indians in the Year 1791 Was Conducted Under the Command of Major General St. Clair. Arthur St. Clair. LC 79-146419. (First American Frontier Ser.). 1971. reprint ed. 32.95 (*0-405-02883-0*) Ayer.

Narrative of the Military Actions of Colonel Marinus Willett, Taken Chiefly from His Own Manuscript. Ed. by William M. Willett. LC 74-71113. (Eyewitness Accounts of the American Revolution Ser.). (Illus.). 1969. reprint ed. 19.95 (*0-405-01186-5*) Ayer.

Narrative of the Mission of the United Brethren Among the Delaware & Mohegan Indians. John Heckewelder. LC 79-146399. (First American Frontier Ser.). 1979. reprint ed. 37.95 (*0-405-02852-0*) Ayer.

Narrative of the Negro. Leila A. Pendleton. LC 78-178481. (Black Heritage Library Collection). 1977. reprint ed. 22.95 (*0-8369-8930-9*) Ayer.

Narrative of the Negro: African-American Women Writers, 1910-1940 by Pendleton & Wilkes. Leila A. Pendleton & Laura E. Wilkes. 1996. 24.95 (*0-7838-1418-6*, Hall Reference) Macmillan.

Narrative of the Niger, Tshadda & Binine Exploration. Thomas J. Hutchinson. 267p. 1966. reprint ed. 45.00 (*0-7146-1137-9*, BHA-01137, Pub. by F Cass Pubs) Intl Spec Bk.

Narrative of the Residence of Fatalla Sayeghir among the Wandering Arabs of the Great Desert. Tr. & Compiled by M. Alphonse De Lamartine. LC 97-126280. (Folios Archive Library). 216p. 1997. 19.95 (*1-85964-088-5*, Pub. by Garnet-Ithaca) LPC InBook.

An Asterisk (*) at the beginning of an entry indicates that the title is appearing for the first time.

Narrative of the Residence of the Persian Princes in London in 1835 & 1836, 2 vols. James B. Fraser. LC 73-6280. (Middle East Ser.). 1973. reprint ed. 50.95 (*0-405-05336-3*) Ayer.

Narrative of the Riots at Alton: In Connection with the Death of Rev. Elijah P. Lovejoy. Edward Beecher. LC 77-89425. (Black Heritage Library Collection). 1977. 17.95 (*0-8369-8509-5*) Ayer.

Narrative of the Shipwreck, Captivity & Sufferings of Horace Holden & Benj. H. Nute: Who Were Cast Away in the American Ship Mentor, on the Pelew Islands, in the Year 1832 Etc. Horace Holden. 149p. 1984. reprint ed. 14.95 (*0-87770-333-7*) Ye Galleon.

Narrative of the Shipwreck of the Sophia. C. Cochelet. 1973. 59.95 (*0-8490-0709-7*) Gordon Pr.

Narrative of the Spanish Marriage Treaty. Francisco De Jesus. Tr. by Samuel R. Gardiner. LC 72-168133. (Camden Society, London, Publications, First Ser.: No. 101). reprint ed. 82.50 (*0-404-50201-6*) AMS Pr.

Narrative of the Sufferings of Massy: From Indian Barbarity, Giving an Account of Her Captivity, the Murder of Her Two Children, Her Escape with an Infant at Her Breast. Massy W. Harbison. (American Biography Ser.). 192p. 1991. reprint ed. lib. bdg. 59.00 (*0-7812-8167-9*) Rprt Serv.

Narrative of the Sufferings of Seth Hubell & Family, in His Begginning (sic) A Settlement in the Town of Wolcott, in the State of Vermont. Seth Hubell. LC 86-51465. 25p. reprint ed. pap. 4.95 (*0-911853-08-1*) Vermont Herit Pr.

Narrative of the Surveying Voyages of His Majesty's Ships Adventure & Beagle, 3 vols. in 4 pts. Robert Fitz-Roy et al. reprint ed. 425.00 (*0-404-09900-9*) AMS Pr.

Narrative of the Texan Santa Fe Expedition, 2 vols., Set. George W. Kendall. 1993. reprint ed. lib. bdg. 150.00 (*0-7812-5886-3*) Rprt Serv.

Narrative of the Town of Machias, Maine: The Old & the New, the Early & the Late. George W. Drisko. (Illus.). 589p. 1988. reprint ed. lib. bdg. 62.00 (*0-8328-0030-9*, ME0020) Higginson Bk Co.

Narrative of the Uncommon Sufferings & Surprizing Deliverance of Briton Hammon. Briton Hammon. 14p. 1994. pap. 5.95 (*0-87770-537-2*) Ye Galleon.

Narrative of the United States' Expedition to the River Jordan & the Dead Sea. William F. Lynch. Ed. by Moshe Davis. LC 77-70719. (America & the Holy Land Ser.). (Illus.). 1977. reprint ed. lib. bdg. 50.95 (*0-405-10264-X*) Ayer.

Narrative of the War Between the States. Jubal A. Early. (Quality Paperbacks Ser.). (Illus.). 550p. 1991. reprint ed. pap. 16.95 (*0-306-80424-7*) Da Capo.

Narrative of the Wreck & Loss of the Whaling Brig William & Joseph. Elisha Dexter. 56p. 1987. 14.95 (*0-87770-418-X*); pap. 9.95 (*0-87770-417-1*) Ye Galleon.

Narrative of Thomas Brown. Thomas Brown. 24p. 1995. pap. 6.95 (*0-87770-552-6*) Ye Galleon.

Narrative of Travels & Discoveries in Northern & Central Africa, Vol. 1. Denham et al. 432p. 1985. 250.00 (*1-85077-057-3*, Pub. by Darf Pubs Ltd) St Mut.

Narrative of Travels & Discoveries in Northern & Central Africa, Vol. 2. Denham et al. 432p. 1985. 250.00 (*1-85077-058-1*, Pub. by Darf Pubs Ltd) St Mut.

Narrative of Travels & Discoveries in Northern & Central Africa, Vols. 1 & 2. Denham et al. 1985. write for info. (*0-7855-2568-8*, Pub. by Darf Pubs Ltd) St Mut.

Narrative of Travels in Northern Africa in the Years, 1816-1820. G. F. Lyon. 400p. 1990. 135.00 (*1-85077-032-8*, Pub. by Darf Pubs Ltd) St Mut.

Narrative of Travels on the Amazon & Rio Negro. Alfred R. Wallace. LC 68-25280. (World History Ser.: No. 48). 1969. reprint ed. lib. bdg. 75.00 (*0-8383-0251-3*) M S G Haskell Hse.

Narrative of Travels on the Amazon & Rio Negro, with an Account of the Native Tribes, & Observations on the Climate, Geology, & Natural History of the Amazon Valley. Alfred R. Wallace. LC 68-55226. (Illus.). 363p. 1969. reprint ed. lib. bdg. 35.00 (*0-8371-1641-4*, WARN) Greenwood.

Narrative of Two Aerial Voyages. John Jeffries. (Illus.). 60p. Date not set. 45.95 (*0-405-01716-2*) Arno Press.

Narrative of Two Aerial Voyages. John Jeffries. 7.00 (*0-405-18972-9*, 16886) Ayer.

Narrative of Various Journeys in Balochistan, Afghanistan & the Panjab, 1826-1838, 3 vols. Charles Masson. (C). 1997. 125.00 (*81-215-0783-9*, Pub. by M Manoharial) Coronet Bks.

Narrative of Voyages & Excursions on the East Coast & in the Interior of Central America: Describing a Journey up the River San Juan, & Passage Across the Lake of Nicaragua to the City of Leon. Orlando W. Roberts. LC 65-28696. (Latin American Gateway Ser.). 331p. 1965. reprint ed. pap. 102.70 (*0-608-04473-3*, 206521800001) Bks Demand.

Narrative of William Biggs. William Biggs. 34p. 1988. pap. 6.95 (*0-87770-425-2*) Ye Galleon.

Narrative of William Hayden, Containing a Faithful Account of His Travels for a Number of Years, Whilst a Slave, in the South. William Hayden. (American Biography Ser.). 156p. 1991. reprint ed. lib. bdg. 59.00 (*0-7812-8174-1*) Rprt Serv.

***Narrative of William Spavens; A Chatham Pensioner by Himself.** William Spavens. 1999. pap. text 18.95 (*1-86176-084-1*, Chatham Pubg) G Duckworth.

Narrative of William W. Brown. William W. Brown. (American Biography Ser.). 98p. 1991. reprint ed. lib. bdg. 59.00 (*0-7812-8044-3*) Rprt Serv.

Narrative or Journal of Voyages & Travels Through the Northwest Continent in the Years 1789 & 1793. Maclauries. 93p. 1980. 16.95 (*0-87770-231-4*) Ye Galleon.

Narrative Path: The Later Works of Paul Ricoeur. Ed. by T. Peter Kemp & David Rasmussen. 150p. (Orig.). 1989. 22.50 (*0-262-11147-0*); pap. text 10.95 (*0-262-61060-4*) MIT Pr.

Narrative Pattern in Ernest Hemingway's Fiction. Chaman Nahal. 245p. 1975. 27.50 (*0-8386-7795-9*) Fairleigh Dickinson.

Narrative Performances: A Study of Modern Greek Storytelling. Alexandra Georgakopoulou. LC 97-8741. (Pragmatics & Beyond New Ser.: Vol. 46). xvii, 282p. 1997. lib. bdg. 85.00 (*1-55619-808-6*) J Benjamins Pubng Co.

Narrative Perspective in Fiction: A Phenomenological Mediation of Reader, Text, & World. Daniel F. Chamberlain. 272p. 1990. text 45.00 (*0-8020-5838-8*) U of Toronto Pr.

Narrative Picture Scrolls. Hideo Okudaira. Ed. by John Rosenfield. Tr. by Elizabeth Ten Grotenhuis from JPN. LC 73-9619. (Arts of Japan Ser.: Vol. 5). (Illus.). 152p. 1973. 15.00 (*0-8348-2710-7*) Weatherhill.

Narrative Pictures: A Survey of English Genre & Its Painters. Sacheverell Sitwell. LC 72-180039. 1972. reprint ed. 24.95 (*0-405-08978-3*) Ayer.

Narrative Poems. C. S. Lewis. Ed. by Walter Hooper. LC 78-15062. 192p. (C). 1978. pap. 4.95 (*0-15-665327-3*, Harvest Bks) Harcourt.

Narrative Poems. large type ed. William Shakespeare. (Charnwood Large Print Ser.). 1991. pap. 24.95 (*0-7089-4526-0*, Charnwood) Ulverscroft.

Narrative Policy Analysis: Theory & Practice. Emery M. Roe. LC 94-7248. (Illus.). 240p. 1994. text 49.95 (*0-8223-1502-5*); pap. text 17.95 (*0-8223-1513-0*) Duke.

Narrative Preaching: Stories from the Pulpit. David P. Mulder. LC 96-10519. (Illus.). 112p. 1996. 10.99 (*0-570-04861-3*, 12-3352) Concordia.

Narrative Principles in Dostoevskij's Besy: Slavonic Languages & Literatures. Slobodanka B. Vladiv. (European University Studies: Ser. 16, Vol. 10). 182p. 1979. pap. 31.00 (*3-261-03086-0*) P Lang Pubng.

***Narrative Prosthesis: Disability & the Dependencies of Discourse.** Ed. by David T. Mitchell & Sharon L. Snyder. (Corporealities Ser.). (Illus.). 264p. (C). 2000. text 49.50 (*0-472-09748-2*, 09748); pap. text 21.95 (*0-472-06748-6*, 06748) U of Mich Pr.

Narrative Psychology: The Storied Nature of Human Conduct. Ed. by Theodore R. Sarbin. LC 86-8130. 321p. 1986. 65.00 (*0-275-92103-4*, C2103, Praeger Pubs) Greenwood.

Narrative Purpose in the Novella. Judith Leibowitz. (De Proprietatibus Litterarum, Ser. Minor: No. 10). 139p. 1974. pap. text 32.35 (*90-279-3007-4*) Mouton.

***Narrative Reader.** Martin McQuillan. LC 00-32308. 2000. pap. write for info. (*0-415-20533-6*) Routledge.

Narrative Remembering. Barbara DeConcini. LC 89-39653. 308p. (C). 1990. lib. bdg. 49.00 (*0-8191-7632-X*) U Pr of Amer.

Narrative Research: Reading, Analysis & Interpretation. Amia Lieblich et al. LC 98-9071. (Applied Social Research Methods Ser.). 1998. 49.95 (*0-7619-1042-5*); pap. 21.95 (*0-7619-1043-3*) Sage.

Narrative Research Method: Studying Behaviour Patterns of Young People - by Young People: A Guide to Its Use. (ENG & FRE.). 38p. 1993. pap. text 7.20 (*0-614-08011-8*, 1930054) World Health.

Narrative Rhetorical Devices of Persuasion in the Greek Community of Philadelphia. Gregory Gizelis. Ed. by Richard M. Dorson. LC 80-728. (Folklore of the World Ser.). 1981. lib. bdg. 31.95 (*0-405-13315-4*) Ayer.

Narrative Schooling: Experiential Learning & the Transformation of American Education. Richard Hopkins. LC 93-44506. (Advances in Contemporary Educational Thought Ser.: No. 13). 240p. (C). 1994. text 28.00 (*0-8077-3333-4*) Tchrs Coll.

Narrative Secret of Flannery O'Connor: The Trickster as Interpreter. Ruthann K. Johansen. LC 93-30919. 224p. (C). 1994. text 34.95 (*0-8173-0717-6*) U of Ala Pr.

Narrative Semiotics in the Epic Tradition: The Simile. Stephen A. Nimis. LC 87-45323. 223p. reprint ed. pap. 69.20 (*0-7837-3722-X*, 205790000009) Bks Demand.

Narrative Setting & Dramatic Poetry. Mary Kuntz. LC 92-46715. (Mnemosyne, Bibliotheca Classica Batava Ser.: No. 124). ix, 178p. 1993. 67.00 (*90-04-09784-8*) Brill Academic Pubs.

Narrative Singing in Ireland. Hugh Shields. (Illus.). 292p. 1993. pap. 19.50 (*0-7165-2500-3*, Pub. by Irish Acad Pr) Intl Spec Bk.

Narrative Singing in Ireland: Lays, Ballads & Come-All-Yes. Hugh Shields. (Illus.). 292p. (C). 1993. 39.50 (*0-7165-2462-7*, Pub. by Irish Acad Pr) Intl Spec Bk.

Narrative Solutions in Brief Therapy. Joseph B. Eron & Thomas W. Lund. (Family Therapy Ser.). 288p. 1996. lib. bdg. 39.95 (*1-57230-126-0*) Guilford Pubns.

Narrative Solutions in Brief Therapy. Joseph B. Eron & Thomas W. Lund. (Family Therapy Ser.). 288p. 1998. pap. text 21.00 (*1-57230-420-0*) Guilford Pubns.

Narrative Space & Mythic Meaning in Mark. Elizabeth Struthers Malbon. (Biblical Seminar Ser.: No. 13). (Illus.). 212p. (C). 1991. pap. 23.75 (*1-85075-711-9*, Pub. by Sheffield Acad) CUP Services.

Narrative Speaker: Multilingual Speaker. Rajendra Singh. LC 97-31054. (Language & Development Ser.). 226p. 1997. write for info. (*0-7619-9213-8*) Sage.

***Narrative Strategies: Essays on South Asian Literature & Film.** Vasudha Dalmia & Th Damsteegt. LC 99-937585. (Illus.). 1999. write for info. (*0-19-564975-3*) OUP.

Narrative Strategies in Joyce's Ulysses. Dermot Kelly. 138p. 1988. 69.95 (*0-7734-1994-2*) E Mellen.

Narrative Strategies in "La Princesse de Cleves" Donna Kuizenga. LC 76-17258. (French Forum Monographs: No. 2). 160p. (Orig.). 1976. pap. 10.95 (*0-917058-01-1*) French Forum.

Narrative Structure in Wilhelm Raabe's Die Chronik der Sperlingsgasse. Charlotte L. Goedsche. LC 88-13533. (Studies in Modern German Literature: Vol. 9). 260p. (C). 1989. text 34.95 (*0-8204-0440-3*) P Lang Pubng.

Narrative Study of Lives. Ruthellen Josselson & Amia Lieblich. (Advances in Narrative & Life History Ser.: Vol. 1). (Illus.). 232p. (C). 1993. text 52.00 (*0-8039-4812-3*) Sage.

Narrative Study of Lives, Vol. 5. Ed. by Amia Lieblich & Ruthellen Josselson. 244p. 1997. 52.00 (*0-7619-0324-0*); pap. 24.00 (*0-7619-0325-9*) Sage.

Narrative Symbol in Childhood Literature: Explorations in the Construction of Text. Joanne M. Golden. (Approaches to Semiotics Ser.: No. 93). xvi, 270p. (C). 1990. lib. bdg. 103.10 (*3-11-012289-8*) Mouton.

Narrative Syntax & the Hebrew Bible: Papers of the Tilburg Conference, 1996. Ed. by Ellen Van Wolde. LC 97-28704. (Biblical Interpretation Ser.: No. 29). x, 269p. 1997. 95.50 (*90-04-10787-8*) Brill Academic Pubs.

Narrative Techniques in the Novels of Fanny Burney. Tracy E. Daugherty. (Studies in the Romantic Age: Vol. 1). 225p. (C). 1989. text 37.00 (*0-8204-0664-3*) P Lang Pubng.

Narrative Tenses in Chretien de Troyes: A Study in Syntax & Stylistics. Tatiana Fotitch. LC 75-94180. (Catholic University of America. Studies in Romance Languages & Literatures: No. 38). 1969. reprint ed. 37.50 (*0-404-50338-1*) AMS Pr.

Narrative Textbook of Psychoanalysis. Peter L. Giovacchini. LC 87-1495. 382p. 1987. 55.00 (*0-87668-964-0*) Aronson.

Narrative Therapies with Children & Adolescents. Ed. by Craig Smith & David Nylund. LC 97-35905. 469p. 1997. 39.95 (*1-57230-253-4*, C0253) Guilford Pubns.

***Narrative Therapies with Children & Adolescents.** Ed. by Craig Smith & David Nylund. 469p. 2000. pap. 24.95 (*1-57230-576-2*, 0576) Guilford Pubns.

Narrative Therapist & the Arts. Pam B. Dunne. (Illus.). 256p. (Orig.). 1992. pap. 40.00 (*1-888657-06-5*) Drama Thrpy Inst.

***Narrative Therapy.** 2000. 95.00 (*0-205-33216-1*) Allyn.

Narrative Therapy: The Social Construction of Preferred Realities. Jill Freedman & Gene Combs. 305p. 1996. 39.00 (*0-393-70207-3*, RC489) Norton.

Narrative Therapy in Practice. Ed. by Gerald Monk et al. LC 96-16258. (Psychology Ser.). 320p. 1996. 36.95 (*0-7879-0313-2*) Jossey-Bass.

Narrative Thought & Narrative Language. Ed. by B. K. Britton & Anthony D. Pellegrini. 296p. (C). 1989. text 79.95 (*0-8058-0099-9*) L Erlbaum Assocs.

Narrative Transvestism: Rhetoric & Gender in the Eighteenth-Century English Novel. Madeleine Kahn. LC 91-55060. (Reading Women Writing Ser.). 200p. 1991. 35.00 (*0-8014-2536-0*); pap. text 13.95 (*0-8014-9770-1*) Cornell U Pr.

Narrative Truth: Memory in Therapeutic Practice. Christiane Sanderson. 250p. 1996. pap. text 29.95 (*1-85302-348-5*, Pub. by Jessica Kingsley) Taylor & Francis.

Narrative Truth & Historical Truth: Meaning & Interpretation in Psychoanalysis. Donald P. Spence & Robert S. Wallerstein. 320p. 1984. reprint ed. pap. 10.95 (*0-393-30207-5*) Norton.

Narrative Unbound. Donald Ault. (Illus.). 544p. Date not set. pap. 43.00 (*1-886449-75-9*, C9795, Pub. by Barrytown Ltd) Consort Bk Sales.

Narrative Unbound: Re-Visioning Blake's "The Four Zoas" Donald Ault. LC 85-3037. 520p. 1987. 43.00 (*0-88268-011-0*) Station Hill Pr.

Narrative Unity of Luke-Acts Vol. 1: A Literary Interpretation. Robert C. Tannehill. LC 86-45224. (Gospel According to Luke Ser.). 358p. 1991. pap. 22.00 (*0-8006-2557-9*, 1-2557) Augsburg Fortress.

Narrative Unity of Luke-Acts Vol. 2: The Acts of the Apostles: A Literary Interpretation. Robert C. Tannehill. LC 86-45224. 408p. 1989. pap. 23.00 (*0-8006-2558-7*, 1-2558, Fortress Pr) Augsburg Fortress.

Narrative, Violence, & the Law: The Essays of Robert Cover. Ed. by Martha Minow et al. (Law, Meaning, & Violence Ser.). 312p. (C). 1993. text 52.50 (*0-472-09495-5*, 09495) U of Mich Pr.

Narrative, Violence & The Law: The Essays of Robert Cover. Martha Minow. Ed. by Michael Ryan & Austin Sarat. LC 92-30307. (Illus.). 312p. (C). 1995. pap. text 20.95 (*0-472-06495-9*, 06495) U of Mich Pr.

Narrative Voices in Modern French Fiction. Ed. by Michael Cardy et al. LC 97-187106. 258p. 1997. 55.00 (*0-7083-1394-9*, Pub. by Univ Wales Pr) Paul & Co Pubs.

Narrative Works of Gunter Grass: A Critical Interpretation. Noel Thomas. (German Language & Literature Monographs: 12). vi, 370p. 1982. 78.00 (*90-272-4005-1*) J Benjamins Pubng Co.

Narrative Writing. Tara McCarthy. (Teaching Writing Ser.). 48p. (J). (gr. 4-8). 1998. pap. 9.95 (*0-590-20937-X*) Scholastic Inc.

Narrative Writing Vol. 2365: The Writing Teachers Handbook. June Hetzel & Deborah McIntire. Ed. by Joel Kupperstein. 64p. (J). (gr. 4-6). 1998. pap. 7.98 (*1-57471-355-8*) Creat Teach Pr.

Narratives & Adventure of Travellers in Africa. Charles W. Williams. LC 72-5525. (Black Heritage Library Collection). 1977. reprint ed. 32.95 (*0-8369-9152-4*) Ayer.

Narratives & Rosters, Minnesota Mounted Rangers & Cavalry. 1997. reprint ed. pap. 12.00 (*0-915709-53-8*) Pk Geneal Bk.

Narratives & Rosters, Minnesota Sharpshooters. 1997. reprint ed. pap. 4.00 (*0-915709-52-X*) Pk Geneal Bk.

Narratives & Rosters, Minnesota's Heavy & Light Artillery Companies. 1997. reprint ed. pap. 12.00 (*0-915709-54-6*) Pk Geneal Bk.

Narratives & Spaces: Technology & the Construction of American Culture. David Nye. LC 97-28777. (Illus.). 224p. 1998. 47.50 (*0-231-11196-7*) Col U Pr.

Narratives & Spaces: Technology & the Construction of American Culture. David Nye. LC 97-28777. (Illus.). 224p. 1998. pap. 18.50 (*0-231-11197-5*) Col U Pr.

Narratives & Spaces: Technology & the Construction of American Culture. David E. Nye. (Cultural Studies Ser.). (Illus.). 224p. 1998. 70.00 (*0-85989-555-6*, Pub. by Univ Exeter Pr); pap. 22.00 (*0-85989-556-4*) Univ Exeter Pr.

Narratives e Narradores em a Pedra do Reino: Estruturas e Perpectivas Cambiantes. Maria-Odilia Leal-McBride. (American University Studies: Romance Languages & Literature: Ser. II, Vol. 110). IX, 199p. (C). 1989. text 36.50 (*0-8204-1049-7*) P Lang Pubng.

Narratives from America. Richard Ronan. LC 81-67639. 139p. 1982. 12.00 (*0-937872-04-0*); pap. 6.00 (*0-937872-05-9*) Dragon Gate.

Narratives from Criminal Trials in Scotland, 2 vols. in 1. John H. Burton. LC 71-39564. reprint ed. 57.50 (*0-404-09925-4*) AMS Pr.

Narratives from the Crib. Ed. by Katherine Nelson. LC 88-28455. (Illus.). 400p. 1989. 41.50 (*0-674-60118-1*) HUP.

Narratives Illustrative of the Contests in Ireland in 1641 & 1690. Ed. by Thomas C. Croker. (Camden Society, London. Publications, First Ser.: No. 14). reprint ed. 50.00 (*0-404-50114-1*) AMS Pr.

Narratives in Popular Culture, Media, & Everyday Life. Arthur A. Berger. LC 96-25182. 138p. 1996. 44.00 (*0-7619-0344-5*); pap. 18.95 (*0-7619-0345-3*) Sage.

Narrative's Journey: The Fiction & Film Writing of Dorothy Richardson. Susan Gevirtz. LC 94-24565. (Writing about Women Ser.: No. 16). XIII, 232p. (C). 1996. pap. 49.95 (*0-8204-2510-9*) P Lang Pubng.

Narratives of a Vulnerable God: Christ, Theology, & Scripture. William C. Placher. LC 93-47618. 192p. (Orig.). 1994. pap. 17.95 (*0-664-25534-5*) Westminster John Knox.

Narratives of African American Art & Identity: The David C. Driskell Collection. Terry Gips. LC 98-21510. 192p. 1998. pap. 35.00 (*0-7649-0689-5*) Pomegranate Calif.

***Narratives of African American Art & Identity: The David C. Driskell Collection.** Terry Gips. LC 98-21510. 192p. 1998. 50.00 (*0-7649-0722-0*) Pomegranate Calif.

Narratives of African Americans in Kansas, 1870-1992: Beyond the Exodust Movement. Jacob U. Gordon. LC 93-30605. (Illus.). 312p. 1993. text 99.95 (*0-7734-9350-6*) E Mellen.

Narratives of Agency: Self-Making in China, India, & Japan. Ed. by Wimal Dissanayake. 1996. text 54.95 (*0-8166-2656-1*); pap. text 21.95 (*0-8166-2657-X*) U of Minn Pr.

***Narratives of America & the Frontier in Nineteenth-Century German Literature.** Jerry Schuchalter. LC 99-25127. (North American Studies in Nineteenth-Century German Literature: Vol. 25). 312p. (C). 2000. 56.95 (*0-8204-4477-4*) P Lang Pubng.

Narratives of Capek & Chekov: A Typological Comparison of the Authors' World Views. Peter Z. Schubert. LC 95-49592. (Slavic Studies). 256p. 1996. pap. 54.95 (*1-57309-060-3*); text 69.95 (*1-57309-061-1*) Intl Scholars.

Narratives of Colored Americans. Lindley Murray. LC 70-170702. (Black Heritage Library Collection). 1977. reprint ed. 28.95 (*0-8369-8892-2*) Ayer.

Narratives of Desire: 19th-Century Spanish Fiction by Women. Lou Charnon-Deutsch. LC 93-17102. (Studies in Romance Literatures). (Illus.). 224p. (C). 1994. 32.50 (*0-271-01007-X*) Pa St U Pr.

Narratives of Early Carolina, 1650-1708. Alexander S. Salley. (BCL1 - United States Local History Ser.). 388p. 1991. reprint ed. lib. bdg. 89.00 (*0-7812-6298-4*) Rprt Serv.

Narratives of Early Maryland, 1633-1684. Clayton C. Hall. (BCL1 - United States Local History Ser.). 460p. 1991. reprint ed. lib. bdg. 99.00 (*0-7812-6281-X*) Rprt Serv.

Narratives of Early Pennsylvania, West New Jersey & Delaware, 1630-1707. Albert C. Myers. (Illus.). xvi, 476p. 1989. reprint ed. pap. 25.00 (*1-55613-176-3*) Heritage Bk.

Narratives of Early Virginia, 1606-1625. Lyon G. Tyler. (Original Narratives of Early American History Ser.). 478p. 1998. reprint ed. lib. bdg. 89.00 (*0-7812-4795-0*) Rprt Serv.

Narratives of Ecstasy: Romantic Temporality in Modern German Poetry. James Rolleston. LC 87-2020. 244p. 1987. 34.95 (*0-8143-1841-X*) Wayne St U Pr.

Narratives of Enlightenment: Cosmopolitan History from Voltaire to Gibbon. Karen O'Brien. LC 96-36667. (Studies in Eighteenth-Century English Literature & Thought: Vol. 34). 264p. (C). 1997. text 59.95 (*0-521-46533-8*) Cambridge U Pr.

Narratives of ESL Students: The World Is Round. Michael McColly. 1996. mass mkt. write for info. (*0-614-19906-9*) R Dean Pr.

Narratives of Exile & Return. Chamberlain. LC 96-41006. 248p. 1997. text 39.95 (*0-312-16484-X*) St Martin.

Narratives of Gothic Stained Glass. Wolfgang Kemp. Tr. by Caroline Dobson Saltzwedel. (Cambridge Studies in New Art History & Criticism). (Illus.). 277p. 1997. text 69.95 (*0-521-43240-5*) Cambridge U Pr.

N

Narratives of Guilt & Compliance in Unified Germany: STASI Informers & Their Impact on Society Barbara Miller. LC 99-22402. 1999. text. write for info. (0-415-20261-2) Routledge.

Narratives of Human Evolution. Misia Landau. (Illus.). 216p. (C). 1991. 32.50 (0-300-04940-4) Yale U Pr.

Narratives of Human Evolution. Misia Landau. LC 90-45177. 216p. (C). 1993. reprint ed. pap. 16.00 (0-300-05431-9) Yale U Pr.

Narratives of Indian Captivities: The Stories of Robert Eastburn, the Gilbert Family, & Nenemian How. Robert Eastburn et al. 352p. 1997. reprint ed. pap. 26.50 (0-7884-0729-5, E089) Heritage Bk.

Narratives of Indian Captivity among the Indians of North America. Compiled by Edward E. Ayer. 169p. 1991. reprint ed. 65.00 (1-888262-37-0) Martino Pubng.

Narratives of Islamic Origins: The Beginnings of Islamic Historical Writing, Vol. 14. Fred M. Donner. LC 97-36808. (Studies in Late Antiquity & Early Islam). 360p. 1998. lib. bdg. 29.95 (0-87850-127-4) Darwin Pr.

Narratives of Justice: Legislators' Beliefs about Distributive Fairness. Grant Reeher. LC 96-532. 352p. (C). 1996. pap. text 22.95 (0-472-06620-X, 06620) U of Mich Pr.

Narratives of Justice: Legislators' Beliefs about Distributive Fairness. Grant Reeher. LC 96-532. 352p. (C). 1996. text 52.50 (0-472-09620-6, 09620) U of Mich Pr.

***Narratives of Memory & Identity: The Novels of Kazuo Ishiguro.** Mike Petry. (Aachen British & American Studies). ix, 174p. 1999. pap. 35.95 (3-631-35360-X) P Lang Pubng.

***Narratives of Memory & Identity: The Novels of Kazuo Ishiguro.** Mike Petry. LC 99-38711. (Aachen British & American Studies: Vol. 12). ix, 174p. (C). 1999. pap. text 35.95 (0-8204-4372-7) P Lang Pubng.

Narratives of Nation in the South Pacific. Ed. by Ton Otto & Nicholas Thomas. (Studies in Anthropology & History: Vol. 19). 245p. 1997. text 37.00 (90-5702-085-8, Harwood Acad Pubs); pap. text 16.00 (90-5702-086-6, Harwood Acad Pubs) Gordon & Breach.

Narratives of New Netherland, 1609-1664. J. Franklin Jameson. 478p. 1993. reprint ed. lib. bdg. 99.00 (0-7812-5185-0) Rprt Serv.

Narratives of New Netherland, 1609-1664. John F. Jameson. (BCL1 - United States Local History Ser.). 478p. 1991. reprint ed. lib. bdg. 99.00 (0-7812-6273-9) Rprt Serv.

Narratives of Nostalgia, Gender, & Nationalism. Ed. by Suzanne Kehde & Jean Pickering. 320p. (C). 1997. text 50.00 (0-8147-6635-8); pap. text 20.00 (0-8147-6636-6) NYU Pr.

Narratives of Outrages, Committed by the Indians in Their Wars with the White People, 2 vols. Archibald Loudon. Ed. by Dale Van Every. LC 76-106124. (First American Frontier Ser.). 658p. 1971. reprint ed. 85.54 (0-405-02866-0) Ayer.

***Narratives of Remembrance.** Ed. by Marianne Borch. 136p. 2000. pap. 18.00 (87-7838-497-4, Pub. by Odense Univ) Intl Spec Bk.

Narratives of Shipwrecks & Disasters, 1586-1860. Ed. by Keith Huntress. LC 73-12084. 287p. reprint ed. pap. 89.00 (0-608-14887-3, 202614200048) Bks Demand.

Narratives of Sorcery & Magic, from the Most Authentic Sources. Thomas Wright. 2000. reprint ed. 53.00 (1-55888-194-8) Omnigraphics Inc.

Narratives of the Career of Hernando De Soto in the Conquest of Florida As Told by a Knight of Elvas, 2 Vols, Set. Ed. by Edward G. Bourne. Tr. by Buckingham Smith. LC 72-2823. (American Explorers Ser.). (Illus.). reprint ed. 87.00 (0-404-54901-2) AMS Pr.

Narratives of the Coranado Expedition, 1540-1542. Ed. & Tr. by George P. Hammond. LC 75-41126. (Coronado Cuatro-Centennial Publications, 1540-1940: Vol. 2). reprint ed. 57.50 (0-404-14669-4) AMS Pr.

Narratives of the Discovery of America. Ed. by A. W. Lawrence & Jean Young. xiii, 300p. 1987. reprint ed. pap. 17.50 (1-55613-086-4) Heritage Bk.

Narratives of the Expulsion of the English from Normandy, 1449-1450. Ed. by Joseph Stevenson. (Rolls Ser.: No. 32). 1974. reprint ed. 70.00 (0-8115-1080-8) Periodicals Srv.

Narratives of the Insurrections, 1675-1690. Ed. by Charles M. Andrews. (Original Narratives Ser.). 414p. 1967. reprint ed. 33.00 (0-06-480028-8, 06316) B&N Imports.

Narratives of the Sufferings of Lewis & Milton Clarke, Sons of a Soldier of the Revolution. Lewis G. Clarke. LC 73-82186. (Anti-Slavery Crusade in America Ser.). 1978. reprint ed. 21.95 (0-405-00624-1) Ayer.

Narratives of the Wreck of the Whale-Ship Essex. Owen Chase et al. 96p. 1989. pap. 5.95 (0-486-26121-2) Dover.

Narratives of Transmission. Bernard Duyfhuizen. LC 91-58803. 280p. 1992. 36.50 (0-8386-3472-9) Fairleigh Dickinson.

***Narratives on Colonialism, Sugar, Java & the Dutch.** G. Roger Knight. 181p. 2000. lib. bdg. 69.00 (1-56072-814-0) Nova Sci Pubs.

Narratives, Politics & the Public Sphere: Struggles over Political Reform in the Final Transitional Years in Hong Kong (1992-1994) Agnes S. Ku. LC 98-74642. (Social & Political Studies from Hong Kong). 3p. 1999. text 69.95 (1-84014-195-6, Pub. by Ashgate Pub) Ashgate Pub Co.

Narrativity. Aaron Shurin. 20p. 1990. pap. 5.00 (1-55713-108-2) Sun & Moon CA.

Narrativity: Theory & Practice. Philip J. Sturgess. LC 92-12027. 332p. 1992. text 85.00 (0-19-811954-2, Clarendon Pr) OUP.

***Narratologies: New Perspectives in Narrative Analysis.** Ed. by David Herman. LC 99-19802. (Theory & Interpretation of Narrative Ser.). 432p. 1999. text 55.00 (0-8142-0821-5) Ohio St U Pr.

Narratologies: New Perspectives on Narrative Analysis. David Herman. LC 99-19802. 432p. 1999. pap. text 25.00 (0-8142-5024-6) Ohio St U Pr.

Narratology. Johanna Drucker. (Illus.). 40p. 1994. 950.00 (1-887123-00-8) Granary Bks.

Narratology. Susana Onega & Jose A. Landa. (Critical Readers Ser.). 336p. (C). 1996. pap. 31.20 (0-582-25543-0); text 63.00 (0-582-25542-2) Longman.

Narratology: Introduction to the Theory of Narrative. Mieke Bal. 176p. 1985. pap. text 14.95 (0-8020-6557-0) U of Toronto Pr.

Narratology: Introduction to the Theory of Narrative. 2nd ed. Mieke Bal. LC 98-117283. 240p. 1998. text 40.00 (0-8020-0759-7) U of Toronto Pr.

Narratology: Introduction to the Theory of Narrative. 2nd ed. Mike Bal. 240p. 1997. pap. text 16.95 (0-8020-7806-0) U of Toronto Pr.

Narratology & Biblical Narratives: A Practical Guide. Francois Tolmie. LC 98-30867. 326p. 1998. 74.95 (1-57309-333-5) Intl Scholars.

Narratology of the Autobiography: An Analysis of the Literary Devices Employed in Ivan Bunin's "The Life of Arsen'ev" Alexander F. Zweers. LC 96-8412. (Middlebury Studies in Russian Languages & Literature: Vol. 11). X, 190p. (C). 1997. text 45.95 (0-8204-3357-8) P Lang Pubng.

Narrator & Character in "Finnegans Wake" Michael H. Begnal & Grace Eckley. LC 73-4957. 241p. 1975. 34.50 (0-8387-1337-8) Bucknell U Pr.

***Narrators Guide.** Unknown. (Dune Chronicles Ser.). 1999. mass mkt. 16.00 (0-671-03506-1) S&S Trade.

Narrators of Barbarian History (A. D. 550-800) Jordanes, Gregory of Tours, Bede, & Paul the Deacon. Walter A. Goffart. LC 87-7358. 507p. reprint ed. pap. 157.20 (0-608-06337-1, 206669800008) Bks Demand.

***Narrator's Toolkit.** Last Unicorn Games Staff. (Illus.). 1999. pap. 16.00 (0-671-04015-4) S&S Childrens.

Narrenschiff. Sebastian Brant. Ed. by Karl Von Goedeke. LC 71-181916. (BCL Ser. II). reprint ed. 39.50 (0-404-01064-4) AMS Pr.

Narrenschneiden: A "Fastnachtspie" Mari Gras Play. Hans Sachs. Tr. by I. E. Clark. (Illus.). 25p. 1967. pap. 3.00 (0-88680-134-6) I E Clark.

Narrenschneiden: Director's Script. Hans Sachs. Tr. by I. E. Clark. (Illus.). 25p. 1967. pap. 7.50 (0-88680-135-4) I E Clark.

Narrenshwamme: Psychotrope Pilze in Europa: Herausforderung au Forschung und Wertsystem see Magic Mushrooms Around the World: A Scientific Journey Across Cultures & Time

Narrow Act: Borges' Art of Allusion. Ronald J. Christ. 240p. 1994. pap. 15.00 (0-930829-34-4) Lumen Inc.

Narrow Act: Borges' Art of Allusion. Ronald J. Christ. LC 69-16345. (Studies in Comparative Literature, Vol. 2). 264p. reprint ed. 81.90 (0-8357-9479-2, 201028800068) Bks Demand.

Narrow-Band Phenomena: Influence of Electrons with Both Band & Localized Character. Ed. by J. C. Fuggle et al. LC 88-25250. (NATO ASI Series B, Physics: Vol. 184). (Illus.). 238p. 1988. 79.50 (0-306-43012-6, Plenum Trade) Perseus Pubng.

Narrow Banking Reconsidered: The Functional Approach to Financial Reform. Ronnie J. Phillips. (Public Policy Brief Ser.: Vol. 17). 52p. (Orig.). 1995. pap. 3.00 (0-941276-05-8) J Levy.

Narrow Bridge. Dinah Dubinky. LC 91-43756. (ENG & HEB.). 1992. 16.95 (0-87306-590-5); pap. 13.95 (0-87306-594-8) Feldheim.

Narrow Bridge. large type ed. Kay Winchester. 304p. 1987. 27.99 (0-7089-1734-8) Ulverscroft.

***Narrow Bridge: Beyond the Holocaust.** Isaac Neuman & Michael Palencia-Roth. 224p. 2000. 22.50 (0-252-02561-X) U of Ill Pr.

Narrow Bridge: Jewish Views on Multiculturalism. Ed. by Marla Brettschneider. LC 95-43322. 320p. (C). 1996. text 48.00 (0-8135-2289-7); pap. text 18.95 (0-8135-2290-0) Rutgers U Pr.

Narrow Cage: An American Family Saga. Kathleen S. Ryan & Kathleen S. Ryan. LC 80-687. 320p. 1980. 12.95 (0-672-52655-7, Bobbs) Macmillan.

Narrow Corner. W. Somerset Maugham. 224p. 1993. pap. 13.95 (0-14-018598-4, Penguin Classics) Viking Penguin.

Narrow Corner. large type ed. Basil Copper & W. Somerset Maugham. (Linford Mystery Library). 1989. pap. 16.99 (0-7089-6749-3, Linford) Ulverscroft.

Narrow Corner. W. Somerset Maugham. LC 75-25359. (Works of W. Somerset Maugham). 1977. reprint ed. 23.95 (0-405-07818-8) Ayer.

***Narrow Escapes: Childhood Memories of the Holocaust & Their Legacy.** 2nd rev. ed. Samuel P. Oliner. 238p. 2000. pap. 14.95 (1-55778-792-1) Paragon Hse.

Narrow Escapes Of Davy Crockett. Ariane Dewey. 1993. 10.15 (0-606-05503-7, Pub. by Turtleback) Demco.

***Narrow-Gap Semiconductor Photodiodes.** Antoni Rogalski et al. LC 00-26570. (Press Monographs). (Illus.). 2000. write for info. (0-8194-3619-4) SPIE.

Narrow Gap Semiconductors: Proceedings of the NATO Workshop, 25-27 June 1991, Oslo, Norway. Ed. by S. Lovold & B. Mullin. (Illus.). 144p. 1992. 218.00 (0-7503-0158-9) IOP Pub.

Narrow Gap Semiconductors: Proceedings of the 8th International Conference Shanghai, China 21-24 April, 1997. Ed. by G. Bauer et al. LC 98-199778. 480p. 1998. 110.00 (981-02-3344-2) World Scientific Pub.

Narrow Gap Semiconductors, 1995: Proceedings of the Seventh International Conference on Narrow Gap Semiconductors, Santa Fe, New Mexico, 8-12 January 1995. Ed. by John L. Reno. LC 95-42877. (Institute of Physics Conference Ser.: Vol. 144). 388p. 1995. 200.00 (0-7503-0341-7) IOP Pub.

Narrow Gap Semiconductors, 1992: Proceedings of the 6th International Conference, University of Southampton, U. K., 19-23 July, 1992. Ed. by J. B. Mullin & R. A. Stradling. (Illus.). 455p. 1993. 229.00 (0-7503-0249-6) IOP Pub.

Narrow Gauge & Miniature Railways from Old Picture Postcards. Andrew Neale. 60p. (C). 1987. 35.00 (0-9511108-0-2, Pub. by Picton) St Mut.

Narrow Gauge at War. Keith Taylorson. 56p. (C). 1987. 60.00 (0-9511108-1-0, Pub. by Picton) St Mut.

Narrow Gauge Fun. Ferguson. (J). (ps-12). 1983. pap. 3.95 (0-9613218-0-6) GCBA.

Narrow Gauge Land. Ed. by James S. Eakin. 136p. 1983. pap. 19.95 (0-912113-02-2) Railhead Pubns.

Narrow-Gauge Locomotive: The Baldwin Catalog of 1877. Baldwin-Lima-Hamilton Corporation Staff. LC 67-24619. 57p. reprint ed. pap. 30.00 (0-608-16173-X, 201625200002) Bks Demand.

Narrow Gauge Railways in America. Howard Fleming. 140p. 1985. pap. 8.95 (0-912113-05-7); pap. 8.95 (0-912113-04-9) Railhead Pubns.

Narrow Gauge Railways in Mid-Wales (1850-1970) J. I. Boyd. 304p. (C). 1985. 50.00 (0-85361-024-X) St Mut.

Narrow Gauge Railways in North Caernarvonshire Vol. 1: West. J. I. Boyd. 282p. (C). 1985. 50.00 (0-85361-273-0) St Mut.

Narrow Gauge Railways in North Caernarvonshire Vol. 2: Penrhyn Quarry Railways. J. I. Boyd. 176p. (C). 1985. 50.00 (0-85361-312-5) St Mut.

Narrow Gauge Railways in North Caernarvonshire Vol. 3: Dinorwic Quarries & Others. J. I. Boyd. 240p. (C). 1985. 39.00 (0-85361-328-1) St Mut.

Narrow Gauge Steam Locomotives. Brian Solomon. LC 99-12321. (Enthusiast Color Ser.). (Illus.). 96p. 1999. pap. 13.95 (0-7603-0543-9) MBI Pubg.

Narrow Gauge to No Man's Land. Richard Dunn. (Illus.). 203p. 1990. 38.95 (0-9615467-2-7) Benchmark Ltd.

Narrow Ground: Aspects of Ulster, 1609-1969. A. T. Stewart. LC 97-164843. 208p. 1997. pap. 18.95 (0-85640-600-7, Pub. by Blackstaff Pr) Dufour.

Narrow Home Plan Collection. rev. ed. Ed. by Carol Stratman Shea & Bruce Arant. 308p. 1998. pap. 14.95 (1-892150-03-4) Design Basics.

Narrow House. Evelyn Scott & Evelyn Scott. Ed. by Elizabeth Hardwick. LC 76-51677. (Rediscovered Fiction by American Women Ser.). 1977. reprint ed. lib. bdg. 24.95 (0-405-10055-8) Ayer.

Narrow Land: Folk Chronicles of Old Cape Cod. 1985. 12.50 (0-9615051-0-9) Chatham His Soc.

Narrow-Lot Homes: 250 Designs for Homes up to 50' Wide. LC 99-73183. (Illus.). 256p. 1999. pap. 9.95 (1-881955-58-3) Home Planners.

Narrow Passage to the Deep Light. Kerry S. Keys. 72p. 1996. pap. 10.00 (0-930502-21-3) Pine Pr.

Narrow Path. Francis Selormey. (African Writers Ser.). 184p. (C). 1967. pap. 9.95 (0-435-90580-5, 90580) Heinemann.

Narrow Path: An Intimate Account of an Inner Journey. Janina Szpotko-Greene. LC 94-61454. (Illus.). 80p. (Orig.). 1995. pap. 9.95 (0-944482-15-5) Except Bks NM.

Narrow Road to Oku. Matsu Basho. 1997. pap. 25.00 (4-7700-2028-7, Pub. by Kodansha Int) OUP.

Narrow Road to Renga: A Collection of Renga. Ed. by Jane Reichhold & William J. Higginson. 270p. (Orig.). 1989. pap. 12.95 (0-944676-19-7) AHA Bks.

Narrow Road to the Deep North: A Journey into the Interior of Alaska. Katherine McNamara. 304p. (Orig.). 1998. pap. 15.95 (1-56279-107-9) Mercury Hse Inc.

***Narrow Road to the Deep North: A Journey Into the Interior of Alaska.** Katherine McNamara. (Illus.). 304p. 2001. pap. 15.95 (1-56279-122-2) Mercury Hse Inc.

Narrow Road to the Deep North & Other Travel Sketches. Matsu Basho. Tr. by Nobuyuki Yuasa from JPN. (Classics Ser.). 176p. 1966. pap. 16.99 (0-14-044185-9, Penguin Classics) Viking Penguin.

Narrow Road to the Interior. Matsu Basho. Tr. by Sam Hamill from JPN. LC 91-8574. (Centaur Editions Ser.). (Illus.). 120p. (Orig.). 1991. pap. 10.00 (0-87773-644-8, Pub. by Shambhala Pubns) Random.

***Narrow Road to the Interior: And Other Writings.** Basheo Matsuo & Sam Hamill. LC 00-38786. 2000. pap. 14.95 (1-57062-716-9, Pub. by Shambhala Pubns) Random.

Narrow Roads of Gene Land. Hamilton. Date not set. write for info. (0-7167-4552-6) W H Freeman.

Narrow Roads of Gene Land, Vol. 1. Hamilton. Date not set. write for info. (0-7167-4556-9); text 20.80 (0-7167-4551-8) W H Freeman.

Narrow Roads of Gene Land, Vol. 2. W. D. Hamilton. pap. text. write for info. (0-7167-4543-7) W H Freeman.

Narrow Roads of Gene Land: The Collected Papers of W. D. Hamilton, Vol. 2: W. D. Hamilton. (Illus.). 512p. 2000. pap. 35.00 (0-19-850336-9) OUP.

Narrow Roads of Gene Land Vol. 1: Evolution of Social Behaviour, Vol. 1. W. D. Hamilton. LC 95-16280. (Evolution of Social Behaviour Ser.). (Illus.). 568p. 1998. reprint ed. pap. text 29.95 (0-7167-4530-5) OUP.

Narrow Roads of Gene Land Volume 2: Evolution Of Sex: The Collected Papers of W. D. Hamilton. W. D. Hamilton. (Illus.). 512p. 2000. 85.00 (0-19-850337-7) OUP.

Narrow Rooms. James Purdy. 185p. 1997. reprint ed. pap. 12.95 (0-907040-57-8, Pub. by Gay Mens Pr) LPC InBook.

Narrow Seas, Small Navies & Fat Merchantmen: Naval Strategies for the 1990s. Charles W. Koburger, Jr. LC 90-31579. 184p. 1990. 52.95 (0-275-93557-4, C3557, Praeger Pubs) Greenwood.

Narrow Street. Elliot Paul. (American Autobiography Ser.). 342p. 1995. reprint ed. lib. bdg. 89.00 (0-7812-8610-7) Rprt Serv.

***Narrow Vision.** James Wells, Jr. LC 99-72401. 226p. 1999. pap. 14.95 (1-878647-64-4) APU Pub Grp.

Narrow Walk. Shirley Brinkerhoff. LC 97-24439. (Nikki Sheridan Ser.: Bk. 3). 192p. (YA). (gr. 9-13). 1998. pap. 5.99 (1-56179-539-9) Focus Family.

Narrow Waters: An Artist's Memoir of Sailing Through Sound, Swamp, City, Forest, Marsh & Glade. Dee Carstarphen. LC 97-76110. (Illus.). v, 131p. 1998. pap. 19.95 (0-9607544-4-X) Pen & Ink.

***Narrow Way.** Frwd. by Bob L. Perryman. 89p. 1999. pap. 7.49 (0-9679090-0-7) Lghthse Bapt.

Narrow Way: Examining Both Heaven & Hell & the Message of Salvation in Jesus Christ. William C. Nichols. 115p. 1993. pap. 6.50 (0-9641803-1-6) Internat Outreach.

Narrow Way of Attainment. Hiram E. Butler. 144p. 1998. reprint ed. pap. 16.95 (0-7661-0458-3) Kessinger Pub.

***Narrow Way to Nearby.** David Robertson. (Western Writers Ser: Vol. 141). (C). 1999. pap. 5.95 (0-88430-140-0) Boise St U W Writ Ser.

Narrow Winding Road: A Behind the Scenes Look at Island Life. Shave I. Solomon. LC 93-85867. (Illus.). 128p. (Orig.). 1993. pap. 8.95 (0-9626070-2-9) B Jay Prodns.

Narrowback. Michael S. Ledwidge. LC 98-25649. 240p. 1999. 23.00 (0-87113-716-X) Grove-Atltic.

Narrowbackin', Vol. 1. William Y. Winebrenner. LC 97-91033. (Illus.). 368p. 1997. pap. 10.00 (0-9661033-0-0) Valley Enterp.

Narrowband Land-Mobile Radio Networks. Jean-Paul Linnartz. LC 92-32244. (Artech House Mobile Communication Library). (Illus.). 363p. 1993. reprint ed. pap. 112.60 (0-608-03158-5, 206361100007) Bks Demand.

Narrowing the U. S. Current Account Deficit: A Sectoral Assessment. Allen J. Lenz. LC 92-8778. 627p. 1992. reprint ed. pap. 194.40 (0-7837-9049-X, 204980000003) Bks Demand.

Narrows. Valery Nash. (CSU Poetry Ser.: No. VII). 62p. (Orig.). 1980. pap. 3.50 (0-914946-16-1) Cleveland St Univ Poetry Ctr.

***Narrows.** Ann Petry. LC 99-16611. 464p. 1999. pap. 13.00 (0-618-00710-5, Mariner Bks) HM.

***Nartananirnaya of Panarika Vitthala, Vol. II.** Ed. by R. Sathyanarayana. 491p. 1998. pap. 325.00 (81-208-1218-2, Pub. by Motilal Bnarsidass) St Mut.

Nartananirnaya of Pandarika Vitthala, Vol. 1. Ed. & Tr. by R. Sathyanarayana. (C). 1994. 40.00 (81-208-1217-4, Pub. by Indian Council Cultural Relations) S Asia.

***Nartananirnaya of Pandarika Vitthala, Vol. III.** Ed. by R. Sathyanarayana. 558p. 1998. pap. text 400.00 (81-208-1219-0, Pub. by Motilal Bnarsidass) St Mut.

NARUC Members, Committees, Policy. 105p. 1996. 10.00 (0-317-01621-0) NARUC.

Narvik: Battles in the Fjords. Peter Dickens. LC 96-23431. (Classics of Naval Literature Ser.). (Illus.). 240p. 1996. 32.95 (1-55750-744-9) Naval Inst Pr.

Narwhal: Unicorn of the Sea. Fred Bruemmer. 1993. 24.95 (1-55013-187-7) U of Toronto Pr.

Narwhals. Sarah Palmer. (Whale Discovery Library). (Illus.). 24p. (J). (gr. k-5). 1988. 8.95 (0-685-58328-7) Rourke Corp.

Narwhals. Sarah Palmer. (Whale Discovery Library). (Illus.). 24p. (J). (gr. k-5). 1988. lib. bdg. 14.60 (0-86592-476-7) Rourke Enter.

Narzibmusproblematik im Werk Italo Svevos. Maria F. Gallistl. (Romanistische Texte und Studien: Bd. 4). (GER.). 1993. write for info. (3-487-09702-8) G Olms Pubs.

(NAS) National Aerospace Standards Index, Issue 99-1. Global Engineering Documents Staff. Ed. by Global Staff. 125p. 1999. pap. text 30.00 (1-57053-085-8) Global Eng Doc.

NASA. Jon Eric Hakkila & Adele D. Richardson. LC 98-20888. (Above & Beyond Ser.). (Illus.). 32p. (YA). (gr. 4 up). 1999. lib. bdg. 21.30 (1-58340-050-8) Smart Apple.

NASA: A History of the U. S. Civil Space Program. Roger D. Launius. LC 93-35977. (Anvil Ser.). 286p. (C). 1994. pap. text 16.50 (0-89464-727-X) Krieger.

NASA: A History of the U. S. Civil Space Program. Roger D. Launius. LC 93-35977. 286p. 1994. 19.50 (0-89464-878-0) Krieger.

NASA: The Endless Journey. 2nd rev. ed. Howard Benedict. 190p. 1996. reprint ed. 29.95 (0-9610648-7-0) Graphic Hse.

NASA - NSF Panel Report on Satellite Communications Systems & Technology, 2 vols., Set. Ed. by Burton I. Edelson & Joseph N. Pelton. (WTEC Panel Reports). (Illus.). (Orig.). 1993. pap. write for info. (1-883712-29-7) Intl Tech Res.

NASA - NSF Panel Report on Satellite Communications Systems & Technology, Vol. I: Analytical Chapters. Ed. by Burton I. Edelson & Joseph N. Pelton. (WTEC Panel Reports). (Illus.). xiv, 322p. (Orig.). 1993. pap. write for info. (1-883712-26-2) Intl Tech Res.

NASA & the Challenge of ISDN. (Satellites in an ISDN World Ser.). 1996. 75.00 (0-614-18387-1, 126NAS) Info Gatekeepers.

NASA & the Exploration of Space: With Works from the NASA Art Collection. Roger D. Launius. LC 98-17742. 224p. 1998. 60.00 (1-55670-696-0) Stewart Tabori & Chang.

An Asterisk (*) at the beginning of an entry indicates that the title is appearing for the first time.

NASA & the Space Industry. Joan L. Bromberg. LC 98-44795. (New Series in NASA History). 1999. write for info. (0-8018-6050-4) Johns Hopkins.

***NASA & the Space Industry.** Joan L. Bromberg. (New Series in NASA History). (Illus.). 256p. 2000. pap. 18.95 (0-8018-6532-8) Johns Hopkins.

NASA Atlas of the Solar System. Ronald Greeley & Raymond Batson. (Illus.). 369p. (C). 1996. 159.95 (0-521-56127-2) Cambridge U Pr.

***NASA Case Studies.** braille ed. Ed. by Marco A. V. Bitetto. (YA). 2000. write for info. (1-58578-082-0) Inst of Cybernetics.

NASA Engineers & the Age of Apollo. 1996. lib. bdg. 252.99 (0-8490-5991-7) Gordon Pr.

NASA Engineers & the Age of Apollo. 1997. lib. bdg. 250.99 (0-8490-6195-4) Gordon Pr.

NASA FAR Supplement. National Aeronautics & Space Administration, Lyndo. 1995. ring bd. 167.00 (1-56726-075-6) Mgmt Concepts.

***NASA Historical Data: NASA Space Applications, Aeronautics & Space Research & Technology, Tracking & Data Acquisition/Support Operations, Commercial Programs & Resources, 1979-1988, Vol. 6.** Judy A. Rumerman. 641p. 2000. boxed set 46.00 (0-16-050266-7) USGPO.

NASA Historical Databook, 6 vols., Set. 1994. lib. bdg. 2225.95 (0-8490-6411-2) Gordon Pr.

NASA Innovative Research Program. N. S. Goel. 280p. 1993. pap. text 564.00 (3-7186-5464-4, Harwood Acad Pubs) Gordon & Breach.

NASA Kennedy Space Center's Spaceport U. S. A. Tour Book. NASA Public Affairs Staff. Tr. by Delavega. (FRE, GER, ITA & SPA., Illus.). 48p. (Orig.). 1991. reprint ed. pap. 5.00 (0-9610648-6-2) Graphic Hse.

NASA Mars Conference. Ed. by Duke B. Reiber. (Science & Technology Ser.: Vol. 71). (Illus.). 570p. 1988. 25.00 (0-87703-293-9, Am Astronaut Soc); pap. 15.00 (0-87703-294-7, Am Astronaut Soc) Univelt Inc.

NASA, Nazis & JFK: The Torbitt Document & the Kennedy Assassination. Intro. by Kenn Thomas. (Orig.). 1996. pap. 16.00 (0-932813-39-9) Adventures Unltd.

NASA Patents Available for Licensing from the George C. Marshall Space Flight Center. (Illus.). 150p. (Orig.). (C). 1992. pap. text 85.00 (1-56806-424-1) DIANE Pub.

***NASA Planetary Spacecraft: Galileo, Magellan, Pathfinder & Voyager.** Carmen Bredeson. LC 99-50639. (Countdown to Space Ser.). (Illus.). 48p. (YA). (gr. 4-10). 2000. lib. bdg. 18.95 (0-7660-1303-0) Enslow Pubs.

NASA Pocket Statistics, 1997. Government Printing Office Staff. 212p. 1997. per. 7.50 (0-16-054675-3) USGPO.

NASA Procurement: Challenges Remain in Implementing Improvement Reforms. (Illus.). 46p. (Orig.). (C). 1995. pap. text 20.00 (0-7881-2084-0) DIANE Pub.

NASA Questionnaire Report. (Satellites in an ISDN World Ser.). 1996. 60.00 (0-614-18389-8, 126ST2) Info Gatekeepers.

NASA Space Medals. Evans E. Kerrigan. (Illus.). 68p. (Orig.). 1989. pap. 9.50 (0-9624663-3-6) Medallic Pub.

NASA Space Medals. Evans E. Kerrigan. (Illus.). 72p. (Orig.). (C). 1989. pap. 7.50 (0-685-29069-7) Medallic Pub.

***NASA Space Vehicles: Capsules, Shuttles & Space Stations.** Michael D. Cole. LC 99-35533. (Countdown to Space Ser.). (Illus.). 48p. (gr. 4-10). 2000. lib. bdg. 18.95 (0-7660-1308-1) Enslow Pubs.

NASA Spinoff 1995: Technology Transfer from NASA. 140p. pap. text 50.00 (0-7881-2850-7) DIANE Pub.

NASA Spinoff, 1994: Technology Transfer from NASA. James J. Haggerty. (Illus.). 132p. (C). 1997. reprint ed. pap. text 50.00 (0-7881-3828-6) DIANE Pub.

NASA Spinoff, 1996: Technology Transfer from NASA. (Illus.). 136p. 1996. pap. text 50.00 (1-57979-054-2) DIANE Pub.

NASA Spinoff, 1996: Technology Transfer from NASA. James J. Haggerty. (Illus.). 130p. (Orig.). (C). 1997. pap. text 45.00 (0-7881-3981-9) DIANE Pub.

NASA Spinoff, 1993: Technology Transfer from NASA. James J. Haggerty. (Illus.). 144p. (Orig.). (C). 1994. pap. text 60.00 (0-7881-1016-0) DIANE Pub.

NASA Systems Engineering Handbook. 1996. lib. bdg. 257.95 (0-8490-6374-4) Gordon Pr.

NASA Systems Engineering Handbook. Robert Shishko. 166p. 1995. per. 21.00 (0-16-061848-7) USGPO.

NASA Systems Engineering Handbook. Robert Shishko. (Illus.). 154p. (C). 1998. reprint ed. pap. text 40.00 (0-7881-3295-4) DIANE Pub.

Nasal & Sinus Surgery. Steven C. Marks. (Illus.). 635p. Date not set. text. write for info. (0-7216-7804-1, W B Saunders Co) Harcrt Hlth Sci Grp.

Nasal Drug Delivery (Seminar Notes - Mar. 1995) 1995. ring bd. 89.95 (1-56676-296-0) Technomic.

Nasal Manifestations of Systemic Diseases. Michael Schatz & Robert S. Zeiger. (Illus.). 116p. 1991. text 48.00 (0-936587-03-2) OceanSide Pubns.

Nasal Neoplasia. Dennis H. Kraus & Howard Levine. LC 96-41026. (Rhinology & Sinusology Ser.). 1996. 79.00 (0-86577-655-5) Thieme Med Pubs.

Nasal Plastic Surgery. E. Gaylon McCollough. LC 93-26436. (Illus.). 400p. 1994. text 152.00 (0-7216-4067-2, W B Saunders Co) Harcrt Hlth Sci Grp.

Nasal Polyps: Epidemiology, Pathogenesis & Treatment. Guy A. Settipane et al. LC 96-70568. (Illus.). 200p. 1997. 98.00 (0-936587-09-1) OceanSide Pubns.

Nasal Systemic Drug Delivery. Yie W. Chien et al. (Drugs & the Pharmaceutical Sciences Ser.: Vol. 39). (Illus.). 320p. 1989. text 167.50 (0-8247-8093-0) Dekker.

Nasal Toxicity & Dosimetry of Inhaled Xenibiotics: Implications for Human Health. Ed. by Chemical Industry Institute of Toxicology Staff et al. LC 94-29943. 450p. 1995. 125.00 (1-56032-366-3) Taylor & Francis.

Nasal Tumors in Animals & Man, 3 Vols., Vol. I. Ed. by Sherman F. Stinson & Gerd K. Reznik. 296p. 1983. 162.00 (0-8493-5577-X, RC271, CRC Reprint) Franklin.

Nasal Tumors in Animals & Man, 3 Vols., Vol. II. Ed. by Sherman F. Stinson & Gerd K. Reznik. LC 82-1277. 288p. 1983. 157.00 (0-8493-5578-8, RC280, CRC Reprint) Franklin.

Nasal Tumors in Animals & Man, 3 Vols., Vol. III. Ed. by Sherman F. Stinson & Gerd K. Reznik. LC 82-1277. 280p. 1983. 156.00 (0-8493-5579-6, RC271, CRC Reprint) Franklin.

Nasal Vowel Evolution in Romance. R. Sampson. LC PC91.S25 1999. (Illus.). 430p. 1999. text 105.00 (0-19-823848-7) OUP.

Nasalcrom in Clinical Practice. Robert N. Ross. LC 83-81193. (Illus.). 40p. 1983. write for info. (0-914132-04-0) Fisons Corp.

***Nasalization, Neutral Segments & Opacity Effects.** Rachel Walker. LC 00-26420. (Outstanding Dissertations in Linguistics Ser.). 2000. write for info. (0-8153-3836-8) Garland.

Nasals, Nasalization, & the Velum. Ed. by Marie K. Huffman et al. (Phonetics & Phonology Ser.: Vol. 5). (Illus.). 483p. 1993. text 79.95 (0-12-360380-3) Acad Pr.

Nasamat. Najwa Brax. (ARA & ENG., Illus.). 507p. 1994. 40.00 (0-935359-42-7) Daheshist.

NASA's Financial Reports Are Based on Unreliable Data. 76p. (Orig.). (C). 1993. pap. text 30.00 (1-56806-909-X) DIANE Pub.

NASA's Mission to Planet Earth Program: Hearing Before the Subcommittee on Science, Technology & Space of the Committee on Commerce, Science & Transportation, United States Senate, 104th Congress, 2nd Session, May 16, 1996. USGPO Staff. LC 97-112715. iii, 69p. 1996. write for info. (0-16-053547-6) USGPO.

NASA's Study of Space Solar Power: Hearing Before the Subcommittee on Space & Aeronautics of the Committee on Science, U. S. House of Representatives, 105th Congress, 1st Session, October 24, 1997. USGPO Staff. LC 98-161410. iii, 73 p. 1997. pap. write for info. (0-16-056270-8) USGPO.

NASA/Trek: Popular Science & Sex in America. Constance Penley. LC 97-10902. (Illus.). 280p. (C). 1997. pap. 17.00 (0-86091-617-0, B4283, Pub. by Verso) Norton.

Nasaurluq Nunalinqigtelleq. large type ed. Hilda Olick & Helen Nicori. (ESK., Illus.). 8p. (J). (gr. k-3). 1997. pap. text 6.00 (1-58084-009-4) Lower Kuskokwim.

Nasaurluum Yurallra. large type ed. Rosalie Lincoln.Tr. of What Girls Should Do When Eskimo Dancing. (ESK., Illus.). 16p. (J). (gr. k-3). 1999. pap. text 21.00 (1-58084-065-5) Lower Kuskokwim.

***NASB Life Application Study Bible.** Zondervan Publishing Staff. 2000. pap. 64.99 (0-310-90099-9); pap. 64.99 (0-310-90859-0) Zondervan.

NASB Thinline Bible. large type ed. Thinline Staff. LC 98-61547. 1999. 19.99 (0-310-91796-4, Zondervan Bibles) Zondervan.

NASB Thinline Bible. large type ed. Thinline Staff. 1999. bond lthr. 39.99 (0-310-91798-0, Zondervan Bibles); bond lthr. 39.99 (0-310-91797-2) Zondervan.

Nasby in Exile. David R. Locke. LC 77-104516. (Illus.). reprint ed. lib. bdg. 22.50 (0-8398-1176-2) Irvington.

NASCAR!, 6 bks. Eric Ethan. Incl. Brickyard 400. LC 99-14715. (Illus.). 24p. (YA). (gr. 1 up). 1999. lib. bdg. 18.60 (0-8368-2136-X); Coca-Cola 600. LC 99-14716. (Illus.). (J). 1999. lib. bdg. (0-8368-2137-8); Daytona 500. LC 99-14717. (Illus.). 24p. (J). 1999. lib. bdg. 18.60 (0-8368-2138-6); Miller 400. LC 99-14633. (Illus.). 24p. (J). 1999. lib. bdg. 18.60 (0-8368-2139-4); Southern 500. LC 99-14634. (Illus.). 24p. (YA). (gr. 1 up). 1999. lib. bdg. 18.60 (0-8368-2140-8); Winston 500. LC 99-24779. (Illus.). 24p. 1999. lib. bdg. 18.60 (0-8368-2141-6); (Illus.). (J). (gr. 1 up). Set lib. bdg. 111.60 (0-8368-2135-1) Gareth Stevens Inc.

***Nascar: A Celebration.** Bob Latford. 1999. 24.95 (1-85868-796-9, Pub. by Carlton Bks Ltd) Natl Bk Netwk.

Nascar: Owens, Tom, Game Plan. Thomas Owens. LC 99-10859. (Game Plan Ser.). 64p. (J). (gr. 5-8). 1999. 23.40 (0-7613-1374-5) TFC Bks NY.

***NASCAR: The Definitive History of America's Sport.** Mike Hembree. LC 99-57928. 204p. 2000. 50.00 (0-06-105080-6) HarpC.

Nascar: The Thunder of America. 50th anniversary ed. NASCAR Staff & Joyce L. Vedral. LC 97-50245. (Illus.). 200p. 1998. 45.00 (0-06-105060-1) HarpC.

NASCAR Cooks: The Tabasco/NASCAR 50th Anniversary Cookbook. Nascar Staff. LC 97-11208. (Illus.). 96p. 1998. 17.95 (0-06-105066-0) HarpC.

***Nascar Die-Cast Collector's Value Guide.** (Illus.). 2000. pap. 19.95 (1-58598-069-2) CheckerBee.

NASCAR Encyclopedia. NASCAR Staff. 2000. 40.00 (0-06-105076-8) HarpC.

***NASCAR 50 Greatest Drivers.** Bill Center & Bob Moore. LC 98-12421. (Illus.). 112p. (J). 1998. pap. 20.00 (0-06-107330-X, HarperHorizon) HarpC.

***NASCAR 50 Greatest Drivers.** Center & Moore. 2000. 40.00 (0-06-105125-X) HarpC.

***NASCAR Generations: The Legacy of Family in Motor Sports.** Robert Edelstein. Ed. by Pat Teberg. LC 00-38887. (Illus.). 256p. 2000. 24.95 (0-06-105079-2, HarpEntertain) Morrow Avon.

NASCAR Greatest Races: The 25 Most Exciting Races in NASCAR History. Tom Higgins. LC 99-43464. (Illus.). 144p. 1999. 30.00 (0-06-105152-7, HarpEntertain) Morrow Avon.

NASCAR Pocket - Race Planner. (Illus.). 64p. 1997. pap. 3.99 (1-890929-02-6) Comp Motorsport.

***Nascar Racers: Daredevil, No. 4.** J. E. Bright. (Nascar Racers Ser.: No. 4). 128p. 2000. pap. 4.50 (0-06-107191-9, HarpEntertain) Morrow Avon.

***Nascar Racers: How They Work.** Mel Gilden. (Nascar Racers Ser.). 64p. 2000. 12.99 (0-06-107182-X, HarpEntertain) Morrow Avon.

***Nascar Racers: Lightning Pace: (book & watch combo)** Mel Gilden. 40p. (gr. 1-5). 2000. pap. 12.99 (0-06-107192-7) Morrow Avon.

***Nascar Racers: Official Owner's Manual.** Mel Gilden. 64p. (J). (gr. 1-5). 2000. pap. 7.99 (0-06-107181-1, HarpEntertain) Morrow Avon.

***Nascar Racers: Tundra 2000, No. 3.** John Whitman. (NASCAR Racers Ser.: No. 3). 144p. (gr. 2-6). 2000. mass mkt. 4.50 (0-06-107183-8) HarpC.

***NASCAR Racers Get on Track.** Dalmatian Press Staff. (Illus.). (J). 2000. pap. 2.99 (1-57759-298-0) Dalmatian Pr.

***NASCAR Racers Maximum Performance.** Dalmatian Press Staff. (Illus.). (J). 2000. pap. 2.99 (1-57759-299-9) Dalmatian Pr.

***NASCAR Racers Road Thunder.** Dalmatian Press Staff. (Illus.). (J). 2000. pap. 2.50 (1-57759-344-8) Dalmatian Pr.

Nascar Racing. William P. Mara. LC 98-20865. (Motorsports Ser.). (J). 1998. 19.00 (0-7368-0025-5, Capstone High Low) Capstone Pr.

NASCAR Racing 2: The Champion's Handbook. Mark Walker. LC 96-70601. 216p. 1997. pap., per. 19.99 (0-7615-0949-6) Prima Pub.

***Nascar Stars & Cars.** Lars Anderson. Ed. by Sherie Holder. (Illus.). 32p. (J). (gr. 2-8). 1999. pap. 3.99 (1-886749-78-7) SI For Kids.

***Nascar: The Driving Force.** Michael F. Hembree. 2000. 12.99 (0-8499-5536-X) Word Pubng.

Nascar Thunder of Amer. NASCAR (Association) Staff. LC 97-50245. 2000. lthr. 75.00 (0-06-105075-X) HarpC.

***NASCAR Transporters.** Bill Burt. (Illus.). 96p. 2000. pap. 13.95 (0-7603-0816-0, 130531AP, Pub. by MBI Pubg) Motorbooks Intl.

NASCAR Trials & Triumphs: True Stories of NASCAR Men & Women Who Overcame Tough Obstacles to Find Success. Ed. by Harpercollins Publishers Staff. LC 99-482799. 256p. (Orig.). 1999. mass mkt. 5.99 (0-06-105931-5) HarpC.

Nascar Way: The Business That Drives the Sport. Robert G. Hagstrom, Jr. LC 97-37082. 230p. 1997. 24.95 (0-471-18316-4) Wiley.

Nascar Yearbook & Press Guide. Intro. by Bob Moore & R. J. Reynolds. (Illus.). 110p. (Orig.). 1992. pap. 6.95 (0-318-17137-6) Nat Assn Stock.

***Nascar 2000: Official Strategy Guide.** Prima Development Staff. 1999. pap. 12.99 (0-7615-2290-5) Prima Pub.

Nascida De Novo. Maria Da Graca Hughes. (POR.). 135p. Date not set. pap. 10.00 (0-9668384-0-8) M D Hughes.

Nascido para a Batalha. R. Arthur Matthews. Orig. Title: Born for Battle. (POR.). 192p. 1987. pap. 5.95 (0-8297-1606-8) Vida Pubs.

NASD Manual April, 1998. CCH Incorporated Staff. 1500p. 1998. pap. text 44.00 (0-8080-0279-1) CCH INC.

NASD Manual As of 1/99. CCH Business Law Editors. 1999. pap. text 49.00 (0-8080-0357-7) CCH INC.

NASD Manual, May 1996 (National Association of Securities Dealers, Inc.) 970p. 1996. pap. 44.00 (0-614-26801-X, 04775101) CCH INC.

NASD Series 7. Rita P. Malm. 300p. 1999. pap. text 32.95 (1-884803-16-4) Werbel Pub.

NASD Series 6. Rita Malm. LC 97-62218. 250p. (Orig.). 1999. pap. text 26.95 (1-884803-08-3) Werbel Pub.

NASD Series 63. Rita Malm. LC 97-62219. 65p. (Orig.). 1999. pap. 12.95 (1-884803-09-1) Werbel Pub.

NASD Series 6 Examination: Annuities & Mutual Funds. Jack Rudman. (Admission Test Ser.: Vol. 97). 59.95 (0-8373-5197-9) Nat Learn.

NASD Series 6 Examination: Annuities & Mutual Funds. Jack Rudman. (Admission Test Ser.: ATS-97). 1994. pap. 39.95 (0-8373-5097-2) Nat Learn.

NASD Telephone Hotline: Enhancements Could Help Investors Be Better Informed about Broker's Disciplinary Records. (Illus.). 57p. (Orig.). (C). 1996. pap. text 20.00 (0-7881-3615-1) DIANE Pub.

NASDAQ: A Guide to Information Sources. Lucy Heckman. Ed. by Wahib Nasrallah. (Research & Information Guides in Business, Industry, & Economic Institutions Ser.). 250p. Date not set. text 37.00 (0-8153-2118-X) Garland.

NASDAQ Handbook: A Complete Reference for Investors, Registered Reps., Researchers & Analysts. rev. ed. National Association of Securities Dealers Staff. 525p. 1992. text 40.00 (1-55738-403-7, Irwn Prfssnl) McGraw-Hill Prof.

NASDTEC Manual on Certification & Preparation of Educational Personnel in the U. S. NASDTEC Staff. 456p. 1995. pap. text, per. 74.95 (0-7872-1681-X) Kendall-Hunt.

NASDTEC Manual on the Preparation & Certification of Educational Personnel, 1998-1999. 4th ed. NASDTEC Staff. 456p. 1997. spiral bd. 74.95 (0-7872-4537-2); per. 74.95 (0-7872-4536-4) Kendall-Hunt.

Nasecode IX: Proceedings of the 9th International Conference on the Numerical Analysis of Semiconductors Devices & Integrated Circuits. Ed. by John Miller. 110p. (Orig.). 1993. pap. 75.00 (0-9631678-2-0) Inst Computation.

Nasecode VII: Proceedings of the 7th International Conference on the Numerical Analysis of Semiconductor Devices & Integrated Circuits. Ed. by John Miller. x, 280p. (Orig.). (C). 1991. pap. 95.00 (0-9631678-0-4) Inst Computation.

Nasenplastik und Sonstige Gesichtsplastik nebst Mammaplastik see Jacques Joseph's Rhinoplasty & Facial Plastic Surgery with a Supplement on Mammaplasty

Nash-Allen Genealogy: Zachariah H. Nash, Lawson Allen, & Their Descendants. James H. Nash & Mary F. Nash. LC 83-62562. (Illus.). 1984. 22.00 (0-9612498-0-3) J H Nash.

Nash dom- Moskva see Moscow Does Not Believe in Tears: Reflections of Moscow's Mayor

Nash Family: or Records of the Descendants of Thomas Nash of New Haven, Connecticut, 1640. S. Nash. (Illus.). 304p. 1989. reprint ed. pap. 45.50 (0-8328-0897-0); reprint ed. lib. bdg. 53.50 (0-8328-0896-2) Higginson Bk Co.

Nash Manifolds. M. Shiota. (Lecture Notes in Mathematics Ser.: Vol. 1269). vi, 223p. 1987. 38.95 (0-387-18102-4) Spr-Verlag.

Nash Styling Sketchbook. Patrick R. Foster. LC 97-95111. (Illus.). 88p. 1998. pap. 24.95 (0-9662019-0-6) Olde Milford.

Nashford's New Almoner. large type ed. Quenna Tilbury. (Linford Romance Library). 336p. 1985. pap. 16.99 (0-7089-6108-8, Linford) Ulverscroft.

Nashid Al-Anshad. Dahesh. (ARA & ENG., Illus.). 143p. 1985. 40.00 (0-935359-24-9) Daheshist.

Nashir Unevareh: Songs & Grace after Meals (Kol Haneshamah) Ed. by David A. Teutsch. LC 91-68254. (Illus.). 78p. 1992. pap. 3.00 (0-935457-45-3) Reconstructionist Pr.

***Nashua: In Time & Places.** Hunt Memorial Building Trustees. (Images of America Ser.). 128p. 1999. pap. 18.99 (0-7385-0024-0) Arcadia Publng.

Nashua Experience: History in the Making. Nashua History Committee Staff. LC 78-980. 1978. 15.95 (0-914016-50-4); pap. 8.95 (0-914016-51-2) Phoenix Pub.

Nashville. Amy Lynch. LC 90-41611. (Downtown America Ser.). (Illus.). 60p. (J). (gr. 3 up). 1991. lib. bdg. 13.95 (0-87518-453-7) Silver Burdett Pr.

Nashville. Rand McNally Staff. 1998. 5.95 (0-528-97567-6) Rand McNally.

Nashville: City of Note. John Seigenthaler et al. LC 97-15755. (Urban Tapestry Ser.). (Illus.). 350p. 1997. 44.95 (1-881096-43-2) Towery Pub.

Nashville: Downtown America. Amy Lynch. (Illus.). 64p. (J). (gr. 4-7). 1996. pap. text 7.95 (0-382-24792-2) Silver Burdett Pr.

Nashville: Gateway to the South. Scott Faragher. LC 98-23355. (Illus.). 288p. 1998. pap. 18.95 (1-888952-40-7) Cumberland Hse.

***Nashville: The Pilgrims of Guitar Town.** Photos by Michel Arnaud. LC 99-57641. (Illus.). 176p. 2000. 27.50 (1-55670-989-7) Stewart Tabori & Chang.

Nashville after Sunset: Nashville Nightlife & Southern Bartending. Gwen Boyd. LC 97-163309. (Illus.). 260p. 1997. pap. 9.95 (0-9657643-0-3) After Sunset.

Nashville, Chattanooga & St. Louis. Charles Castner. (Hobby Bks.: No. C87). (Illus.). 100p. 1995. 26.95 (0-911868-87-9, C87) Carstens Pubns.

***Nashville Chronicles.** Stuart. 2000. write for info. (0-684-86543-2) Simon & Schuster.

Nashville, 1864: The Dying of the Light. Madison Jones. LC 96-29800. 150p. 1997. 17.95 (1-879941-35-X) J S Sanders.

Nashville, 1864: The Dying of the Light. Madison Jones. 144p. 1999. pap. 9.95 (0-14-027880-X) Viking Penguin.

***Nashville Entertainment, 2000.** (Illus.). 534p. 1999. pap. 25.00 (1-58553-041-7, 0064) Enter Pubns.

Nashville Family Album: A Country Music Scrapbook. Alan Mayor. (Illus.). 272p. 1999. 27.50 (0-312-24412-6, Thomas Dunne) St Martin.

Nashville Guitar. Arlen Roth. (Illus.). 144p. 1997. pap. 19.95 (0-8256-0172-X, OK63321, Oak) Music Sales.

***Nashville in Vintage Postcards, Tennessee.** Scott Faragher. (Images of America Ser.). (Illus.). 128p. 1999. pap. 18.99 (0-7385-0199-9) Arcadia Publng.

***Nashville Interiors, Tennessee.** Amelia Edwards. (Images of America Ser.). (Illus.). 128p. 1999. pap. 18.99 (0-7385-0220-0) Arcadia Publng.

Nashville Medicine: A History. James Summerville. (Illus.). 175p. 1998. 29.95 (0-9668380-0-9) Assoc Publ.

Nashville Number System. 5th rev. ed. Chas Williams. LC 97-175386. (Illus.). 96p. (Orig.). 1997. pap. text 14.95 (0-9630906-0-7) Nash Number.

Nashville Numbering System. Neal Mathews, Jr. 64p. 1984. pap. 7.95 (0-88188-335-2, HL 00704491) H Leonard.

Nashville of the North: Country Music in Liverpool. Kevin McManus & Institute of Popular Music Staff. LC 98-134103. (Sounds Ser.). 37 p. 1994. write for info. (1-898806-00-4) Univ. of Liverpool, Inst of Popular Music.

Nashville Ratt. William L. McDonald. (Illus.). 32p. (J). 1995. 2.95 (0-9647114-0-0) Two Starz Prods.

Nashville Red Book: The Complete Directory of Nashville's Music & Entertainment Industry 1988-89. Ed. by Larry Pacheco & Alan Post. 108p. 1989. write for info. (0-318-64828-8) Nashvll Red Bk.

Nashville Redbook: The Complete & Unparalleled Source Directory for Nashville's Music & Entertainment, Vol. 1. Larry Pacheco. 1999. pap. 9.99 (0-927089-01-7) Nashvll Red Bk.

Nashville Savvy. Barbara Blumin. LC 88-61371. (Illus.). 84p. (Orig.). 1988. pap. 3.95 (0-685-23212-3) Portobello Bks.

N

An Asterisk (*) at the beginning of an entry indicates that the title is appearing for the first time.

Nashville since the 1920s. Don H. Doyle. LC 85-3562. (Illus.). 352p. 1985. 34.00 (*0-87049-470-8*) U of Tenn Pr.

Nashville Songwriting. Jerry Cupit. (Illus.). 203p. 1995. pap. 19.95 (*0-9649904-0-7*) Cupit Bks.

Nashville Sound: Authenticity, Commercialization, & Country Music. Joli Jensen. LC 97-45428. (Country Music Foundation Pr Ser.). (Illus.). 232p. 1998. 29.95 (*0-8265-1314-X*) Vanderbilt U Pr.

Nashville, Tennessee. Rand McNally Staff. 1997. pap. 5.95 (*0-528-97223-5*) Rand McNally.

***Nashville, Tennessee: From the Collection of Otto & Carl Giers.** James A. Hoobler. (Images of America Ser.). (Illus.). 128p. 1999. pap. 18.99 (*0-7385-0295-2*) Arcadia Publng.

Nashville Wives: Country Music's Celebrity Wives Reveal the Truth about Their Husbands & Marriages. Tom Carter. (Illus.). 320p. 1999. mass mkt. 6.50 (*0-06-103006-6*) HarpC.

Nashville's Mother Church: The History of the Ryman Auditorium. William U. Eiland. LC 92-71670. (Illus.). 94p. (Orig.). 1992. pap. write for info. (*0-9633010-0-4*) Grnd Ole Opry.

Nashville's Tennessee Centennial, 1897. Bobby E. Lawrence. (Images of America Ser.). (Illus.). 128p. 1998. pap. 18.99 (*0-7524-1311-2*) Arcadia Publng.

Nashville's Unwritten Rules: Inside the Business of Country Music. Dan Daley. (Illus.). 352p. 1998. pap. 16.95 (*0-87951-889-8*, Pub. by Overlook Pr) Penguin Putnam.

Nashville's Unwritten Rules: Inside the Business of Country Music. Dan Daley. LC 96-45691. (Illus.). 288p. 1999. 27.95 (*0-87951-770-0*, Pub. by Overlook Pr) Penguin Putnam.

Nasir al-Din al-Tusi's Memoir on Astronomy - AlTadhkira fi Ilm al-Haya. Nasir Tusi. LC 93-10445. (Sources in the History of Mathematics & Physical Sciences Ser.). 1993. 119.95 (*0-387-94051-0*) Spr-Verlag.

Nasir Khosrow on Pleasure. Abbas Hunzai. 1998. pap. 17.00 (*1-883058-25-2*, Nur) Global Pubns.

Nasiri Khusraw. Hunsberger. Date not set. text 39.50 (*1-85043-919-2*) I B T.

***Nasopharyngeal Carcinoma.** 2nd ed. Ed. by C. Andrew Van Hasselt & Alan G. Gibb. 360p. 1999. text 149.50 (*1-84110-037-4*) OUP.

Nasopharyngeal Carcinoma, Etiology & Control: Proceedings of an International Symposium Jointly Supported by IARC, the National Cancer Institute, U. S. A. & the Japan Society for the Promotion of Science, & Help in Kyoto, Japan, 4-6 April 1977. International Agency for Research on Cancer Staff. LC 80-453210. (IARC Scientific Publications: No. 20). 629p. 1978. pap. 195.00 (*0-7837-3998-2*, 204382900011) Bks Demand.

Nasorespiratory Function & Craniofacial Growth. Ed. by J. A. McNamara. (Craniofacial Growth Ser.: Vol. 9). (Illus.). 332p. 1985. reprint ed. 59.00 (*0-929921-06-2*) UM CHGD.

NASPE/CAP Educational Guidelines: Pacing & Electrophysiology. 2nd ed. Ed. by Lois Schurig et al. LC 97-2755. (Illus.). 640p. 1997. 45.00 (*0-87993-672-X*) Futura Pub.

Nassar. Peter N. Woodward. (Profiles in Power Ser.). 167p. (C). 1991. text 43.95 (*0-582-03388-8*, 79213) Longman.

Nassau. (Panorama Bks.). (FRE., Illus.). 3.95 (*0-685-11413-9*) Fr & Eur.

***Nassau.** John Reisinger. 284p. 2000. pap. 14.95 (*0-595-00093-2*, Writers Club Pr) iUniversecom.

Nassau & the Best of the Bahamas Alive! P. Permenter & J. Bigley. (Alive Guides Ser.). 400p. 1999. pap. write for info. (*1-55650-883-2*) Hunter NJ.

Nassau Country Club: The Place to Be. Desmond Tolhurst. Ed. by Raymond G. Auwarter. (Illus.). 192p. 1995. 50.00 (*0-9648180-0-0*) Nassau Country Club.

Nassau County Dine-a-Mate Book. 128p. 1996. pap. text 25.00 (*1-57393-074-1*) Dine-A-Mate.

Nassau County in the Civil War. Arnold Gates. 1963. reprint ed. pap. 1.25 (*0-940591-00-6*) Basin Pub.

Nassau County, Long Island in Early Photographs, 1869-1940. Bette S. Weidman & Linda B. Martin. (Illus.). 144p. (Orig.). 1998. pap. 10.95 (*0-486-24136-X*) Dover.

Nassau Street. Herman Herst, Jr. 308p. 1989. pap. 9.95 (*0-940403-06-4*) Linns Stamp News.

Nassau W. Senior: The Prophet of Modern Capitalism. Samuel L. Levy. 1943. 30.00 (*0-686-17409-7*) R S Barnes.

Nassau W. Senior, 1790-1864: Critical Essayist, Classical Economist & Adviser of Governments. rev. ed. S. Leon Levy. LC 67-30861. 336p. 1970. 45.00 (*0-678-05676-5*) Kelley.

Nasser: The Final Years. Abdel M. Farid. 234p. 1997. pap. 19.95 (*0-86372-211-3*, Pub. by Garnet-Ithaca) LPC InBook.

Nasser & Sadat: Decision Making & Foreign Policy, 1970-1972. Shaheen Ayubi. LC 94-18550. 276p. (C). 1994. reprint ed. pap. text 34.50 (*0-8191-9604-5*); reprint ed. lib. bdg. 57.50 (*0-8191-9603-7*) U Pr of Amer.

Nasserist Ideology: Its Exponents & Critics. Nissim Rejwan. 271p. 1974. boxed set 39.95 (*0-87855-162-X*) Transaction Pubs.

Nasserist Ideology: Its Exponents & Critics. Nissim Rejwan. LC 74-2116. (Shiloah Center for Middle Eastern & African Studies. The Monograph Ser.). 282p. reprint ed. pap. 87.50 (*0-8357-8962-4*, 203358300086) Bks Demand.

Nasser's "Blessed Movement" Egypt's Free Officers & the July Revolution. Joel Gordon. 1997. pap. text 24.50 (*977-424-410-9*, Pub. by Am Univ Cairo Pr) Col U Pr.

Nasser's New Egypt. Keith Wheelock. LC 75-14708. (Foreign Policy Research Institute Ser.: No. 8). (Illus.). 326p. 1975. reprint ed. lib. bdg. 65.00 (*0-8371-8233-6*, WHNE, Greenwood Pr) Greenwood.

Nasson: The Seventy Years. Albert L. Prosser. Ed. by Richard D'Abate. LC 93-25217. (Illus.). 376p. 1993. 30.00 (*0-914659-63-4*) Phoenix Pub.

NASSP Bulletin: 1990-1994 Author & Subject Index. Ed. by Eugenia C. Potter. 64p. (Orig.). (C). 1996. pap. text 7.00 (*0-88210-307-5*) Natl Assn Principals.

NASTD Directors: The Decade of Decisions - Charting the Course. 84p. 1989. write for info. (*0-318-68103-X*, C-131) Coun State Govts.

Nastoiashchee: Poema; Al'vek: Stikhi. Velemir Khlebnikov. (RUS.). 39p. 1982. reprint ed. pap. 4.50 (*0-933884-30-3*) Berkeley Slavic.

Nastovlenie o Sobstvennikh Vsyakovo Khristianina Dolzhnostyakh see Journey to Heaven: Councils on the Particular Duties of Every Christian

Nasty Affair on the Norfolk. large type ed. Freda Bream. (Linford Mystery Library .). 320p. 1995. pap. 16.99 (*0-7089-7732-4*, Linford) Ulverscroft.

Nasty Bit of Business: A Private Eye's Guide to Collecting a Bad Debt. rev. ed. Fay Faron. Orig. Title: Take the Money & Strut. 122p. 1988. pap. 9.95 (*0-9620096-1-X*) Creighton-Morgan.

Nasty Breaks. large type ed. Charlotte Elkins. LC 98-5903. (Cloak & Dagger Ser.). 316p. 1998. 25.95 (*0-7862-1445-7*) Thorndike Pr.

Nasty Dragon Who Became a Nice Puppy: Reincarnation for Young People. Dick Sutphen. (Illus.). 32p. (Orig.). (J). (ps-3). 1992. pap. 10.98 incl. audio (*0-87554-528-9*, B929) Valley Sun.

Nasty Letter-Bombs: 150 Politically-Incorrect Unfit-to-Print Explosive Guided Missives That Shook the St. Petersburg Times. John Bryant. 280p. (Orig.). 1995. pap. 19.95 (*1-886739-26-9*) Socratic Pr.

Nasty Letter-Bombs: 150 Politically-Incorrect Unfit-to-Print Explosive Guided Missives That Shook the St. Petersburg Times, Vol. 1: 1992 & 1993. John Bryant. 133p. (Orig.). 1995. pap. 9.95 (*1-886739-27-7*) Socratic Pr.

Nasty Letter-Bombs: 150 Politically-Incorrect Unfit-to-Print Explosive Guided Missives That Shook the St. Petersburg Times, Vol. 2: 1994. John Bryant. 145p. (Orig.). 1995. pap. 9.95 (*1-886739-28-5*) Socratic Pr.

Nasty Letter Writing for Revenge, Fun & Profit: (The Snitches' Handbook) CWL. LC 89-51054. (Illus.). 65p. 1989. 20.00 (*0-939856-99-9*) Tech Group.

Nasty Marriage. deluxe ed. Betty A. Neels. 1998. per. 3.99 (*0-373-83341-5*) Harlequin Bks.

Nasty Men. Jay Carter. (Illus.). 144p. 1993. pap. 7.95 (*0-8092-3794-6*, 379460, Contemporary Bks) NTC Contemp Pub Co.

Nasty Nature. Nick Arnold. (Horrible Science Ser.). (Illus.). 159p. (YA). (gr. 5-9). 1998. pap. 3.99 (*0-590-21687-2*) Scholastic Inc.

Nasty Nature Trail. (Kake Ser.: No. 4). 1997. pap. 15.00 (*1-879055-39-2*) Tom Finland.

Nasty People. Jay Carter. 96p. (Orig.). 1989. pap. 7.95 (*0-8092-4406-3*, 440630, Contemporary Bks) NTC Contemp Pub Co.

Nasty People: All You Ever Wanted to Know about SOB's but Were Afraid to Ask Them. James J. Carter. (Illus.). 80p. 14.95 (*0-937004-04-9*); pap. 4.95 (*0-937004-05-7*) Unicorn PA.

Nasty Persuasions. Lindsay Welsh. (Orig.). 1996. mass mkt. 5.95 (*1-56333-436-4*, Rosebud) Masquerade.

Nasty Stinky Sneakers. Eve Bunting. (J). 1995. 10.30 (*0-606-07937-8*) Turtleback.

Nasty, Stinky Sneakers. Eve Bunting. LC 93-34641. 112p. (J). (gr. 4-7). 1994. 14.95 (*0-06-024236-1*); lib. bdg. 14.89 (*0-06-024237-X*, J Cotler) HarpC Child Bks.

Nasty, Stinky Sneakers. Eve Bunting. LC 93-34641. 128p. (J). (gr. 4-7). 1995. pap. 4.95 (*0-06-440507-9*, HarpTrophy) HarpC Child Bks.

Nasty Swans see Gadkie Lebedi

Nasty the Snowman. E. W. Leroe. LC 96-7434. (Friendly Corners Ser.: Vol. 4). (Illus.). 128p. (J). (gr. 3-7). 1996. pap. 3.95 (*0-7868-1098-X*, Pub. by Hyprn Ppbks) Little.

NASW Guidelines on the Private Practice of Clinical Social Work. 19p. 1991. pap. 9.95 (*0-685-62912-0*, A66) Natl Assn Soc Wkrs.

NASW Procedures for the Adjudication of Grievances. 3rd ed. LC 94-18820. 1994. pap. 10.00 (*0-87101-243-X*, 243X) Natl Assn Soc Wkrs.

NASW Register of Clinical Social Workers. 7th ed. 1197p. 1993. 60.00 (*0-87101-231-6*) Natl Assn Soc Wkrs.

Nat. Alan M. Hofmeister et al. (Reading for All Learners Ser.). (Illus.). (J). pap. write for info. (*1-56861-093-9*) Swift Lrn Res.

***Nat King Cole.** Daniel Mark Epstein. LC 99-32940. (Illus.). 400p. 1999. 27.00 (*0-374-21912-5*) FS&G.

***Nat King Cole.** Daniel Mark Epstein. (Illus.). 438p. 2000. pap. 17.95 (*1-55553-469-4*) NE U Pr.

Nat King Cole. James Haskins. LC 84-40242. (Illus.). 288p. 1984. pap. 9.95 (*0-8128-8522-8*, Scrbrough Hse) Madison Bks UPA.

***Nat King Cole.** large type ed. Daniel M. Epstein. LC 00-26026. (Core Ser.). 2000. 30.95 (*0-7838-9012-5*, G K Hall Lrg Type) Mac Lib Ref.

***Nat King Cole: An Unforgettable Life of Music.** Daphne Simpkins. (Illus.). 2000. pap. 7.95 (*1-880216-95-7*, Elliott Clark) Black Belt Communs.

Nat King Cole: Singer & Jazz Pianist. Marianne Ruuth. (Black American Ser.). (Illus.). 192p. (YA). 1992. mass mkt. 3.95 (*0-87067-593-1*, Melrose Sq) Holloway.

***Nat King Cole: The Man & His Music.** James Haskins & Kathleen Benson. (Illus.). 204p. 2000. reprint ed. pap. text 20.00 (*0-7881-6891-6*) DIANE Pub.

Nat "King" Cole All Time Greatest Hits. Ed. by John L. Haag. (Illus.). 176p. 1999. pap. 19.95 (*1-56922-012-3*, 07-1034) Creat Cncpts.

Nat King Cole LPs, Vol. 9. CPP Belwin Staff. 1989. pap. text 14.95 (*0-89724-590-3*, TPF0150) Wrner Bros.

Nat "King" Cole Remembered. Dempsey J. Travis. (Illus.). 16p. 1993. pap. 2.75 (*0-941484-15-7*) Urban Res Pr.

Nat, Nat, the Nantucket Cat. Peter W. Barnes & Cheryl S. Barnes. (Illus.). 30p. (J). 1993. 15.95 (*0-9637688-0-8*) Vacation Spot.

Nat-Pwe: Burma's Supernatural Subculture. Yves Rodrigue. (Illus.). 128p. (C). 1995. pap. 25.00 (*1-870838-11-4*, Pub. by Kiscadale) Weatherhill.

***Nat Tate.** William Boyd. 69p. 1998. 15.95 (*1-901785-01-7*, Pub. by Twenty-One) Dist Art Pubs.

Nat Turner: Cry Freedom in America. James T. Baker. LC 97-74389. 160p. (C). 1997. pap. text 25.00 (*0-15-503855-9*, Pub. by Harcourt Coll Pubs) Harcourt.

Nat Turner: Prophet & Slave Revolt Leader. Terry Bisson. (Black American Ser.). (Illus.). 192p. 1989. reprint ed. mass mkt. 4.95 (*0-87067-895-7*, Melrose Sq) Holloway.

Nat Turner: Slave Revolt Leader. Terry Bisson. Ed. by Nathan I. Huggins. (Black Americans of Achievement Ser.). (Illus.). 124p. (YA). (gr. 5 up). 1988. lib. bdg. 19.95 (*1-55546-613-3*) Chelsea Hse.

Nat Turner: Slave Revolt Leader. Terry Bisson. Ed. by Nathan I. Huggins. (Black Americans of Achievement Ser.). (Illus.). 124p. (YA). (gr. 5 up). 1989. pap. 8.95 (*0-7910-0214-4*) Chelsea Hse.

Nat Turner: Slave Revolt Leader. Ann-Marie Henderickson. (Junior Black Americans of Achievement Ser.). (Illus.). 76p. (J). (gr. 3-6). 1995. lib. bdg. 15.95 (*0-7910-2386-9*) Chelsea Hse.

Nat Turner: Southampton Campaign of the Black Liberation Army of 1831. H. Khalif Khalifah et al. 200p. 1998. pap. 12.00 (*1-56411-207-1*) Untd Bros & Sis.

Nat Turner & the Slave Revolt. Tracy Barrett. LC 92-12086. (Gateway Civil Rights Ser.). (Illus.). 32p. (J). (gr. 2-4). 1993. pap. 4.95 (*1-56294-792-3*) Millbrook Pr.

Nat Turner & the Slave Revolt. Tracy Barrett. LC 92-12086. (Gateway Civil Rights Ser.). 1993. 10.15 (*0-606-06609-8*, Pub. by Turtleback) Demco.

***Nat Turner & the Virginia Slave Revolt.** Rivvy Neshama. LC 00-21399. (Illus.). (J). 2000. lib. bdg. write for info. (*1-56766-744-9*) Childs World.

Nat Turner Before the Bar of Judgment: Fictional Treatments of the Southampton Slave Insurrection. Mary K. Davis. LC 98-24707. (Southern Literary Studies). 272p. 1999. text 30.00 (*0-8071-2249-1*) La State U Pr.

***Nat Turner's Slave Rebellion in American History.** Judith Edwards. LC 99-16687. (In American History Ser.). (Illus.). 112p. (J). (gr. 5 up). 2000. lib. bdg. 20.95 (*0-7660-1302-2*) Enslow Pubs.

Nat Turner's Slave Revolt-1831. Compiled by Henry I. Tragle. 39.00 (*1-56696-094-0*) Jackdaw.

***Natacha Merrit: Digital Diaries.** Natacha Merrit. 2000. 29.99 (*3-8228-6398-X*) Taschen Amer.

Natal & Zululand from Earliest Times to 1910: A New History. Bill Guest. Ed. by Andrew Duminy. 520p. 1989. pap. 45.00 (*0-86980-695-5*, Pub. by Univ Natal Pr) Intl Spec Bk.

Natal Astrology: Delineating the Horoscope. C. C. Zain. (Brotherhood of Light Home Study Ser.: Course 10, Pt. 1). 1976. pap. 12.95 (*0-87887-341-4*) Church of Light.

Natal Astrology: Progressing the Horoscope. C. C. Zain. (Brotherhood of Light Home Study Ser.: Course 10, Pt. 2). 1976. pap. 14.95 (*0-87887-342-2*) Church of Light.

Natal Charting: How to Master the Techniques of Birth Chart Construction. John Filbey. LC 84-670142. (Illus.). 192p. (Orig.). 1988. pap. 8.95 (*0-85030-246-3*, Pub. by Aqrn Pr) Harper SF.

Natal Command. Peter M. Sacks. LC 97-5870. (Phoenix Poets Ser.). 80p. 1997. pap. 12.95 (*0-226-73343-2*) U Ch Pr.

Natal Monocline: The Origin & Scenery of Natal. 2nd ed. Lester C. King. (Illus.). 144p. 1982. pap. write for info. (*0-86980-314-X*, Pub. by Univ Natal Pr) Intl Spec Bk.

Natal Papers of 'John Ross' Charles R. Maclean. Ed. & Intro. by Stephen Gray. (Killie Campbell Africana Library Publication: No. 7). 228p. 1992. pap. 35.00 (*0-86980-851-6*, Pub. by Univ Natal Pr) Intl Spec Bk.

Natal Plants, 1898-1912, 6 vols. in 2, Set. J. M. Wood & M. S. Evans. (Illus.). 1970. 320.00 (*3-7682-0671-8*) Lubrecht & Cramer.

Natale Conti's Mythologies: A Select Translation. Anthony DiMatteo. LC 94-13592. (Renaissance Imagination Ser.). (Illus.). 440p. 1994. text 25.00 (*0-8153-1464-7*) Garland.

Natalia. Elizabeth Cantu. Ed. by Jack Goodman. LC 89-36803. (C). 1992. pap. 14.95 (*0-87949-307-0*) Ashley Bks.

***Natalia Ginzburg.** Maja Pflug. (Illus.). 2001. pap. 15.95 (*1-900850-22-2*) Arcadia Bks.

Natalia Ginzburg: Human Relationships in a Changing World. Alan Bullock. LC 90-39079. (Women's Ser.). 269p. 1991. 59.50 (*0-85496-178-X*) Berg Pubs.

Natalie & Nat "King" Cole. Skip Press. LC 94-22429. (J). 1995. lib. bdg. 15.95 (*0-89686-879-6*, Crstwood Hse) Silver Burdett Pr.

Natalie & Nat "King" Cole. Skip Press. (Star Families Ser.). (Illus.). 48p. (YA). (gr. 5 up). 1995. pap. 4.95 (*0-382-24942-9*, Crstwood Hse) Silver Burdett Pr.

Natalie Babbit. Michael Levy. (Twayne's United States Authors Ser.: No. 573). 136p. (C). 1991. 21.95 (*0-8057-7612-5*, Twyne) Mac Lib Ref.

***Natalie Imbruglia: The Official Book.** Virgin Pub. Staff. 1999. pap. 19.95 (*0-7535-0316-6*) Virgin Bks.

***Natalie Merchant: Ophelia.** 80p. 1999. otabind 14.95 (*1-57560-207-5*, Pub. by Cherry Lane) H Leonard.

Natalie Natalia. 2nd rev. ed. Nicholas Mosley. LC 96-132. 278p. 1996. pap. 12.95 (*1-56478-086-4*) Dalkey Arch.

***Natalie Nurse.** Pam Howard. (Illus.). 8p. (J). 2000. pap. text 10.95 (*1-57332-155-9*) HighReach Lrning.

***Natalie Nurse.** large type ed. Pam Howard. (BB Ser.). (Illus.). 8p. (J). 2000. pap. text 10.95 (*1-57332-154-0*) HighReach Lrning.

Natalie on the Street. Ann Nietzke. 190p. 1994. 24.95 (*0-934971-42-0*); pap. 14.95 (*0-934971-41-2*) Calyx Bks.

Natalie Van Vleck: A Life in Nature & Art. Peter H. Falk. (Illus.). 32p. 1992. pap. 12.00 (*0-932087-22-1*) Sound View Pr.

Natalie Years - Sharing Some Success: Municipal Government Improvements & Experiences. Bryan Prim & Natalie F. Prim. 224p. (Orig.). 1996. pap. 19.95 (*0-9650826-0-1*) Martin Hse.

Natalie's New Home. large type ed. Heidi A. Spietz. Ed. by Frances Henderson. (Illus.). 27p. (J). (gr. 1-2). 1998. pap. 5.00 (*0-929487-12-5*) Am Montessori Consult.

Natality & Fecundity: A Contribution to National Demography. C. J. Lewis & J. Norman Lewis. LC 75-38135. (Demography Ser.). 1976. reprint ed. 19.95 (*0-405-07988-5*) Ayer.

Nataraja in Art, Thought & Literature. C. Sivaramamurti. 417p. 1974. 120.00 (*0-318-36273-2*) Asia Bk Corp.

NATARS: Mini Computer Version. 160p. (C). 1986. pap. text 19.50 (*0-935920-32-3*, Ntl Pubs Blck) P-H.

NATARS - Micro Computer Version. 150p. (C). 1986. ring bd. 27.50 incl. disk (*0-935920-31-5*, Ntl Pubs Blck) P-H.

***Natasha.** Mirjam Voloshin. 160p. 2000. mass mkt. 7.95 (*1-56201-182-0*, Pub. by Blue Moon Bks) Publishers Group.

Natasha: Vygotskian Dialogues. Matthew Lipman. LC 95-52526. 168p. (C). 1996. text 44.00 (*0-8077-3517-5*); pap. text 19.95 (*0-8077-3516-7*) Tchrs Coll.

Natasha's Dream. Boolarong Publications Staff. (YA). 1990. pap. 35.00 (*0-7316-3901-4*, Pub. by Boolarong Pubns) St Mut.

Natasha's Words for Families. Natasha Josefowitz. (Illus.). 112p. (Orig.). 1986. mass mkt. 3.95 (*0-446-38297-3*, Pub. by Warner Bks) Little.

Natasha's Words for Lovers. Natasha Josefowitz. (Illus.). 112p. (Orig.). 1986. mass mkt. 3.95 (*0-446-38299-X*, Pub. by Warner Bks) Little.

Natchez see Oeuvres Romanesques et Voyages

Natchez. Pamela Jekel. 1996. mass mkt. 6.99 (*1-57566-026-1*) Kensgtn Pub Corp.

Natchez: The City in History. Lee D. Swinny. Ed. by Mizette A. Hinson. (Illus.). 128p. (Orig.). (C). 1989. pap. 4.95 (*0-924043-00-8*) AVAVA Bks.

Natchez: The Complete Guide. Mary B. Eidt & Joan W. Gandy. (Illus.). 120p. 1986. pap. 5.00 (*0-9609728-6-2*) Myrtle Bank.

Natchez Indian Archaeology: Culture Change & Stability in the Lower Mississippi Valley. Ian W. Brown. (Mississippi Department of Archives & History Archaeological Reports: No. 15). (Illus.). xiv, 304p. (Orig.). 1984. pap. 10.00 (*0-938896-42-3*) Mississippi Archives.

***Natchez, MS: City Streets Revisited.** Joan W. Gandy & Thomas H. Gandy. (Images of America Ser.). (Illus.). 128p. 1999. pap. 18.99 (*0-7385-0325-8*) Arcadia Publng.

***Natchez, MS: Landmarks, Lifestyles & Leisure.** Joan W. Gandy & Thomas H. Gandy. (Images of America Ser.). (Illus.). 128p. 1999. pap. 18.99 (*0-7385-0324-X*) Arcadia Publng.

Natchez Postscripts, 1721-1798. Carol Wells. 77p. (Orig.). 1992. pap. 12.50 (*1-55613-604-8*) Heritage Bk.

Natchez River Rogues! Pirates, Playboys & the Rest of the Cock-O'-the-Walk Crowd under-the-Hill & along the Natchez Trace. Carole Marsh. (Carole Marsh Mississippi Bks.). 1994. 29.95 (*0-7933-7369-7*); pap. 19.95 (*0-7933-7370-0*) Gallopade Intl.

***Natchez Trace.** Linda George & Charles George. LC 00-31468. (Cornerstones of Freedom Ser.). (Illus.). (J). 2001. write for info. (*0-516-22006-3*) Childrens.

Natchez Trace: A Pictorial History. James A. Crutchfield. LC 85-11774. (Illus.). 160p. 1985. pap. 9.95 (*0-934395-03-9*) Rutledge Hill Pr.

Natchez Trace: Two Centuries of Travel. Robert C. Gildart. LC 95-41152. (Illus.). 104p. (Orig.). 1996. pap. 17.95 (*1-56037-092-0*) Am Wrld Geog.

Natchez under-the-Hill. Stan Applegate. LC 98-43051. (Illus.). 186p. (YA). (gr. 3-7). 1999. pap. 8.95 (*1-56145-191-6*, 51916) Peachtree Pubs.

Natchez Victorian Children: Photographic Portraits, 1865-1915. Joan W. Gandy & Thomas H. Gandy. LC 81-47767. (Illus.). 216p. 1981. 25.00 (*0-9606978-0-2*) Myrtle Bank.

Natchez Victorian Children: Photographic Portraits, 1865-1915. limited ed. Joan W. Gandy & Thomas H. Gandy. LC 81-47767. (Illus.). 216p. 1981. 100.00 (*0-9606978-1-0*) Myrtle Bank.

Natchitoches Church Marriages, 1818-1850: Translated Abstracts from the Registers of St. Francois des Natchitoches, Louisiana. Ed. by Elizabeth S. Mills. LC 84-9654. (Cane River Creole Ser.). vii, 216p. (Orig.). 1985. pap. 22.00 (*0-931069-04-1*) Mills Historical.

Natchitoches Neighbors in the Neutral Strip: Land Claims Between the Rio Hondo & the Sabine. Carolyn Ericson. LC 85-82346. (Illus.). 162p. (Orig.). (YA). 1985. reprint ed. pap. 20.00 (*0-911317-39-2*) Ericson Bks.

***NATE.** Philip Lewis. LC 99-79057. 430p. 2000. pap. 15.00 (*0-9671951-0-1*) Back House.

***Nate & the Monster Mess.** Marjorie Weinman Sharmat. 48p. (J). 1999. pap. 4.50 (*0-440-41662-0*, Pub. by BDD Bks Young Read) Random House.

***Nate by Night.** Jessica Swaim. Ed. by Christina Carpenter. (Illus.). 32p. (J). (gr. k-4). 2000. 15.95 (*1-886440-02-6*) Portunus Pubng.

An Asterisk (*) at the beginning of an entry indicates that the title is appearing for the first time.

Nate Saint: On a Wing & a Prayer. Janet Benge & Geoff Benge. LC 98-7287. (Christian Heroes Ser.). 201p. (J). 1998. pap. 8.99 (*1-57658-017-2*) YWAM Pub.

Nate the Great. Marjorie Weinman Sharmat. (Nate the Great Ser.). (Illus.). 64p. (J). (ps-3). 1977. pap. 4.50 (*0-440-46126-X*, YB BDD) BDD Bks Young Read.

Nate the Great. Marjorie Weinman Sharmat. (Nate the Great Ser.). (Illus.). 48p. (J). (gr. 1-4). pap. 4.50 (*0-8072-1351-9*) Listening Lib.

Nate the Great. Marjorie Weinman Sharmat. (Nate the Great Ser.). (Illus.). (J). (gr. 1-4). 1986. 16.99 (*0-399-23239-7*) Putnam Pub Group.

Nate the Great. Marjorie Weinman Sharmat. (Nate the Great Ser.). (Illus.). (J). (gr. 1-4). 1972. 9.19 (*0-606-01256-7*, Pub. by Turtleback) Demco.

***Nate the Great.** Marjorie Weinman Sharmat & Marc Simont. (Nate the Great Ser.). (Illus.). (J). (gr. 1-4). 1999. pap. 1.99 (*0-375-80604-0*) Random.

Nate the Great: A Guide for Using Nate the Great in the Classroom. Mary Bolte. (Literature Unit Ser.). (Illus.). 48p. (J). 1998. pap., teacher ed. 7.95 (*1-57690-346-X*, TCM2346) Tchr Create Mat.

Nate the Great: A Study Guide. Duncan Searl. Ed. by J. Friedland & R. Kessler. (Novel-Ties Ser.). (J). (gr. 1-3). 1996. pap. text 15.95 (*1-56982-602-1*) Lrn Links.

Nate the Great & Me: The Case of the Fleeing Fang. Marjorie Weinman Sharmat. (Nate the Great Ser.). (Illus.). 64p. (J). (ps-3). 2000. pap. 4.50 (*0-440-41381-8*) BDD Bks Young Read.

Nate the Great & Me: The Case of the Fleeing Fang. Marjorie Weinman Sharmat. LC 98-13768. (Nate the Great Ser.). (Illus.). 64p. (J). (gr. 1-4). 1998. 9.95 (*0-385-32601-7*) Delacorte.

Nate the Great & the Boring Beach Bag. Marjorie Weinman Sharmat. LC 86-29074. (Nate the Great Ser.). (Illus.). 48p. (J). (ps-3). 1989. pap. 4.50 (*0-440-40168-2*, YB BDD) BDD Bks Young Read.

Nate the Great & the Boring Beach Bag. Marjorie Weinman Sharmat. (Nate the Great Ser.). (Illus.). (J). (gr. 1-4). 1997. 16.99 (*0-399-23238-9*) Putnam Pub Group.

Nate the Great & the Boring Beach Bag. Marjorie Weinman Sharmat. (Nate the Great Ser.). (Illus.). (J). (gr. 1-4). 1987. 9.19 (*0-606-04281-4*, Pub. by Turtleback) Demco.

Nate the Great & the Crunchy Christmas. Marjorie Weinman Sharmat. LC 95-43575. (Nate the Great Ser.). (Illus.). 48p. (J). (gr. 1-4). 1996. 13.95 (*0-385-32117-1*) Delacorte.

Nate the Great & the Crunchy Christmas. Marjorie Weinman Sharmat. (Nate the Great Ser.). (J). (gr. 1-4). 1997. 9.95 (*0-606-12779-8*) Turtleback.

Nate the Great & the Crunchy Christmas. Marjorie Weinman Sharmat & Craig Sharmat. (Nate the Great Ser.). (Illus.). 48p. (J). (gr. 1-4). 1997. pap. 4.50 (*0-440-41299-4*) BDD Bks Young Read.

Nate the Great & the Fishy Prize. Marjorie Weinman Sharmat. (Nate the Great Ser.). (Illus.). 48p. (J). (ps-3). 1988. pap. 4.50 (*0-440-40039-2*, YB BDD) BDD Bks Young Read.

Nate the Great & the Fishy Prize. Marjorie Weinman Sharmat. (Nate the Great Ser.). (J). (gr. 1-4). 1985. 9.19 (*0-606-03869-8*, Pub. by Turtleback) Demco.

Nate the Great & the Halloween Hunt. Marjorie Weinman Sharmat. LC 88-25612. (Nate the Great Ser.). (Illus.). 48p. (J). (ps-3). 1990. pap. 4.50 (*0-440-40341-3*, YB BDD) BDD Bks Young Read.

Nate the Great & the Halloween Hunt. Marjorie Weinman Sharmat. (Nate the Great Ser.). (Illus.). 48p. (J). (gr. 1-4). pap. 4.50 (*0-8072-1283-0*) Listening Lib.

Nate the Great & the Halloween Hunt. Marjorie Weinman Sharmat. (Nate the Great Ser.). (J). (gr. 1-4). 1989. 9.19 (*0-606-04487-6*, Pub. by Turtleback) Demco.

Nate the Great & the Lost List. Marjorie Weinman Sharmat. (Nate the Great Ser.). (Illus.). 48p. (J). (ps-3). 1991. pap. 4.50 (*0-440-46282-7*, YB BDD) BDD Bks Young Read.

Nate the Great & the Lost List. Marjorie Weinman Sharmat. (Nate the Great Ser.). (Illus.). (J). (gr. 1-4). 1975. 9.19 (*0-606-02204-X*, Pub. by Turtleback) Demco.

Nate the Great & the Missing Key. Marjorie Weinman Sharmat. (Nate the Great Ser.). (Illus.). 48p. (J). (ps-3). 1982. pap. 4.50 (*0-440-46191-X*, YB BDD) BDD Bks Young Read.

Nate the Great & the Missing Key. Marjorie Weinman Sharmat. (Nate the Great Ser.). (Illus.). 48p. (J). (gr. 1-3). pap. 4.50 (*0-8072-1335-7*) Listening Lib.

Nate the Great & the Missing Key. Marjorie Weinman Sharmat. (Nate the Great Ser.). (Illus.). (J). (gr. 1-4). 1981. 9.19 (*0-606-00708-3*, Pub. by Turtleback) Demco.

Nate the Great & the Missing Key: A Study Guide. Alice Sheff. (Novel-Ties Ser.). (J). (gr. 1-3). 1987. pap. text, teacher ed., student ed. 15.95 (*0-88122-070-1*) Lrn Links.

***Nate the Great & the Monster Mess.** Marjorie Weinman Sharmat. LC 98-39039. (Nate the Great Ser.). (Illus.). 45p. (J). (gr. 1-4). 1999. 14.95 (*0-385-32114-7*) Delacorte.

Nate the Great & the Mushy Valentine. Marjorie Weinman Sharmat. (Nate the Great Ser.). (Illus.). 48p. (J). (gr. 1-4). 1995. pap. 4.50 (*0-440-41013-4*) Dell.

Nate the Great & the Mushy Valentine. Marjorie Weinman Sharmat. (Nate the Great Ser.). (Illus.). (J). (gr. 1-4). 1995. 9.95 (*0-606-07938-6*) Turtleback.

Nate the Great & the Musical Note. Marjorie Weinman Sharmat. LC 89-24233. (Nate the Great Ser.). (Illus.). 48p. (J). (gr. 1-4). 1991. pap. 4.50 (*0-440-40466-5*) Dell.

Nate the Great & the Musical Note. Marjorie Weinman Sharmat. (Nate the Great Ser.). (Illus.). (J). (gr. 1-4). 1990. 9.19 (*0-606-04989-4*, Pub. by Turtleback) Demco.

Nate the Great & the Musical Note: A Study Guide. Laurie Diamond. Ed. by J. Friedland & R. Kessler. (Novel-Ties Ser.). (J). (gr. 1-3). 1992. pap. text, student ed. 15.95 (*0-88122-726-9*) Lrn Links.

Nate the Great & the Phony Clue. Marjorie Weinman Sharmat. LC no-na1823. (Nate the Great Ser.). (Illus.). 48p. (J). (ps-3). 1982. pap. 4.50 (*0-440-46300-9*, YB BDD) BDD Bks Young Read.

***Nate the Great & the Phony Clue.** Marjorie Weinman Sharmat. (Illus.). (J). 1999. pap. 11.70 (*0-8085-3753-9*) Econo-Clad Bks.

Nate the Great & the Phony Clue. Marjorie Weinman Sharmat. (Nate the Great Ser.). (Illus.). (J). (gr. 1-4). 1977. 9.19 (*0-606-02205-8*, Pub. by Turtleback) Demco.

Nate the Great & the Pillowcase. Marjorie Weinman Sharmat & Rosalind Weinman. (Nate the Great Ser.). (Illus.). 48p. (J). (gr. 1-4). 1995. pap. 4.50 (*0-440-41015-0*, YB BDD) BDD Bks Young Read.

Nate the Great & the Pillowcase. Marjorie Weinman Sharmat & Rosalind Weinman. (Nate the Great Ser.). (Illus.). (J). (gr. 1-4). 1995. 9.19 (*0-606-08581-5*, Pub. by Turtleback) Demco.

Nate the Great & the Snowy Trail. Marjorie Weinman Sharmat. LC 84-15545. (Nate the Great Ser.). (Illus.). 48p. (J). (ps-3). 1983. pap. 4.50 (*0-440-46276-2*, YB BDD) BDD Bks Young Read.

Nate the Great & the Snowy Trail. Marjorie Weinman Sharmat. (Nate the Great Ser.). (Illus.). (J). (gr. 1-4). 1982. 9.19 (*0-606-02977-X*, Pub. by Turtleback) Demco.

Nate the Great & the Sticky Case. Marjorie Weinman Sharmat. (Nate the Great Ser.). (Illus.). 48p. (J). (gr. 1-4). 1981. pap. 4.50 (*0-440-46289-4*) Dell.

***Nate the Great & the Sticky Case.** Marjorie Weinman Sharmat. (Illus.). (J). 1999. pap. 11.70 (*0-8085-3755-5*) Econo-Clad Bks.

***Nate the Great & the Sticky Case.** Marjorie Weinman Sharmat. (Nate the Great Ser.). (Illus.). (J). (gr. 1-4). 1999. 9.95 (*1-56137-263-3*) Novel Units.

Nate the Great & the Sticky Case. Marjorie Weinman Sharmat. (Nate the Great Ser.). (Illus.). (J). (gr. 1-4). 1978. 9.19 (*0-606-02206-6*, Pub. by Turtleback) Demco.

Nate the Great & the Stolen Base. Marjorie Weinman Sharmat. (Nate the Great Ser.). (Illus.). 48p. (J). (gr. 1-4). 1994. pap. 4.50 (*0-440-40932-2*) Dell.

Nate the Great & the Stolen Base. Marjorie Weinman Sharmat. (Nate the Great Ser.). (Illus.). (J). (gr. 1-4). 1992. 9.19 (*0-606-05950-4*, Pub. by Turtleback) Demco.

Nate the Great & the Tardy Tortoise. Marjorie Weinman Sharmat. (Nate the Great Ser.). (Illus.). (J). (gr. 1-4). 1995. pap. 19.95 (*0-385-31010-2*) BDD Bks Young Read.

Nate the Great & the Tardy Tortoise. Marjorie Weinman Sharmat. (Nate the Great Ser.). (Illus.). (J). (gr. 1-4). 1996. pap. 4.99 (*0-440-91264-4*) BDD Bks Young Read.

Nate the Great & the Tardy Tortoise. Marjorie Weinman Sharmat. LC 94-49607. (Nate the Great Ser.). (Illus.). 48p. (J). (ps-3). 1995. 13.95 (*0-385-32111-2*) Delacorte.

Nate the Great & the Tardy Tortoise. Marjorie Weinman Sharmat. LC 94-49607. (Nate the Great Ser.). (Illus.). 48p. (J). (gr. 1-4). 1996. pap. 4.50 (*0-440-41269-2*) Dell.

Nate the Great & the Tardy Tortoise. Marjorie Weinman Sharmat. (Nate the Great Ser.). (Illus.). (J). (gr. 1-4). 1997. 9.19 (*0-606-10891-2*, Pub. by Turtleback) Demco.

Nate the Great Goes Down in the Dumps. Marjorie Weinman Sharmat. LC 88-491. (Nate the Great Ser.). (Illus.). 48p. (J). (ps-3). 1991. pap. 4.50 (*0-440-40438-X*) Dell.

Nate the Great Goes Down in the Dumps. Marjorie Weinman Sharmat. (Nate the Great Ser.). (Illus.). (J). (gr. 1-4). 1989. 9.19 (*0-606-04990-8*, Pub. by Turtleback) Demco.

Nate the Great Goes Undercover. Marjorie Weinman Sharmat. LC no-na1796. (Nate the Great Ser.). (Illus.). 48p. (J). (ps-3). 1978. pap. 4.50 (*0-440-46302-5*, YB BDD) BDD Bks Young Read.

Nate the Great Goes Undercover. Marjorie Weinman Sharmat. (Nate the Great Ser.). (Illus.). 48p. (J). (gr. 1-4). pap. 4.50 (*0-8072-1284-9*); pap. text 15.98 (*0-8072-0201-0*) Listening Lib.

Nate the Great Goes Undercover. Marjorie Weinman Sharmat. (Nate the Great Ser.). (Illus.). 48p. (J). (gr. 1-4). 1974. 16.95 (*0-399-23234-6*, G P Putnam) Peng Put Young Read.

Nate the Great Goes Undercover. Marjorie Weinman Sharmat. (Nate the Great Ser.). (Illus.). (J). (gr. 1-4). pap. 10.95 (*0-698-20632-0*, Coward) Putnam Pub Group.

Nate the Great Goes Undercover. Marjorie Weinman Sharmat. (Nate the Great Ser.). (Illus.). (J). (gr. 1-4). 1974. 8.19 (*0-606-02563-4*, Pub. by Turtleback) Demco.

Nate the Great Goes Undercover. unabridged ed. Marjorie Weinman Sharmat & Ruth Stiles Gannett. (Nate the Great Ser.). (J). (gr. 1-4). 1997. audio 16.98 (*0-8072-0229-0*, FTR172SP) Listening Lib.

***Nate the Great, San Francisco Detective.** Marjorie Weinman Sharmat & Marc Simont. (Nate the Great Ser.). (Illus.). 48p. (J). (ps-3). 2000. 15.99 (*0-385-90000-7*) Delacorte.

Nate the Great Saves the King of Sweden. Marjorie Weinman Sharmat. (Nate the Great Ser.). (Illus.). 48p. (J). (gr. 1-4). 1999. pap. 4.50 (*0-440-41302-8*) BDD Bks Young Read.

Nate the Great Saves the King of Sweden. Marjorie Weinman Sharmat. LC 96-14727. (Nate the Great Ser.). (Illus.). 48p. (J). (gr. 1-4). 1997. 14.95 (*0-385-32120-1*) Delacorte.

Nate the Great Stalks Stupidweed. Marjorie Weinman Sharmat. LC 85-30161. (Nate the Great Ser.). (Illus.). 48p. (J). (ps-3). 1989. pap. 4.50 (*0-440-40150-X*, YB BDD) BDD Bks Young Read.

Nate the Great Stalks Stupidweed. Marjorie Weinman Sharmat. (Nate the Great Ser.). (Illus.). (J). (gr. 1-4). 1986. 9.19 (*0-606-04282-2*, Pub. by Turtleback) Demco.

Nathalie Dupree Cooks Everyday Meals from a Well-Stocked Pantry: Strategies for Shopping Less & Eating Better. Nathalie Dupree. LC 94-31426. 1995. 22.50 (*0-517-59735-7*) C Potter.

Nathalie Dupree Cooks Quick Meals for Busy Days: 180 Delicious Timesaving Recipes. Nathalie Dupree. 1996. 22.50 (*0-614-96288-9*) C Potter.

Nathalie Dupree's Comfortable Entertaining: At Home with Ease & Grace. Nathalie Dupree. LC 98-19871. (Illus.). 336p. 1998. 29.95 (*0-670-87885-5*) Viking Penguin.

Nathalie Granger. Marguerite Duras. (FRE.). 200p. 1973. 27.95 (*0-8288-9600-3*, 207028915X) Fr & Eur.

Nathalie Sarraute Vol. 13: Metaphor, Fairy-Tale & the Feminine of the Text. John Phillips. LC 93-40239. (Writing about Women Ser.). XIII, 284p. (C). 1995. text 50.95 (*0-8204-2366-1*) P Lang Pubng.

Nathalie Sarraute & Fedor Dostoevsky: Their Philosophy, Psychology, & Literary Techniques. Ruth Levinsky. (Graduate Studies: No. 3). 44p. (Orig.). 1973. pap. 2.00 (*0-89672-010-1*) Tex Tech Univ Pr.

Nathalie Sarraute & the Feminist Reader: Identities in Process. Sarah Barbour. LC 92-52716. 304p. (C). 1993. 46.50 (*0-8387-5235-7*) Bucknell U Pr.

***Nathalie Sarraute, Fiction & Theory: Questions of Difference.** Ann Jefferson. LC 99-48651. 2000. write for info. (*0-521-77211-7*) Cambridge U Pr.

Nathalie Sarraute ou la Recherche de l'Authenticite. Braun Tison. 9.95 (*0-8288-8014-X*, F124520) Fr & Eur.

Nathalie Sarraute ou la Recherche de l'Authenticite. Micheline Tison-Braun. (Coll. Le Chemin). 12.95 (*0-685-36553-0*) Fr & Eur.

Nathan: The Spiritual Journey of an Uncommon Cat. Jacqueline L. Clarke. (Illus.). 120p. 1997. pap. 7.99 (*0-9660596-0-3*) Matou Communs.

Nathan - Mixing Boys: Version 6.9. Nathan A. Smorynski. 370p. 1999. pap. 18.95 (*0-7414-0037-5*) Buy Books.

Nathan & Lou: The Finders. Melanie Fisher. (Illus.). 36p. (Orig.). (J). (gr. k-4). 1995. mass mkt. 4.95 (*0-9649664-0-9*) Jermel Visuals.

Nathan & Oski's Hematology of Infancy & Childhood. 5th ed. David G. Nathan & Stuart H. Orkin. Ed. by Richard Lampert. LC 96-41120. (Illus.). 2096p. 1997. text 295.00 (*0-7216-5951-9*, W B Saunders Co) Harcrt Hlth Sci Grp.

Nathan Appleton, Merchant & Entrepreneur, 1779-1861. Frances W. Gregory. LC 74-31433. 396p. reprint ed. pap. 122.80 (*0-8357-3280-0*, 203950300013) Bks Demand.

Nathan Axelrod Collection Vol. 1: Moledet Productions, 1927-1934. Ed. by Amy Fronish et al. 256p. 1994. 42.50 (*0-8386-3575-X*) Fairleigh Dickinson.

Nathan, Barnett & Brink see Superior Court Practice

Nathan Bedford Forrest: A Biography. Jack Hurst. 1994. pap. 15.00 (*0-679-74830-X*) Vin Bks.

Nathan Boone & the American Frontier. R. Douglas Hurt. LC 97-40306. (Illus.). 272p. 1998. 29.95 (*0-8262-1159-3*) U of Mo Pr.

***Nathan Boone & the American Frontier.** R. Douglas Hurt. (Illus.). 272p. 2000. pap. 19.95 (*0-8262-1318-9*) U of Mo Pr.

Nathan Burke. Mary S. Watts. 1993. reprint ed. lib. bdg. 89.00 (*0-7812-5413-2*) Rprt Serv.

Nathan Cohen: The Making of a Critic. Wayne Edmonstone. (Illus.). 286p. 1977. mass mkt. 5.95 (*0-88780-108-0*, Pub. by Formac Publ Co) Formac Dist Ltd.

Nathan Coulter. Wendell Berry. LC 84-62306. 192p. 1985. 12.00 (*0-86547-184-3*) N Point Pr.

Nathan der Weise. Lessing. (GER.). (C). 1989. 19.95 (*0-8442-2776-5*, X2776-5) NTC Contemp Pub Co.

Nathan der Weise. Gotthold Ephraim Lessing. Ed. by Christoph Schweitzer. LC 83-18169. (Suhrkamp/Insel Ser.). (ENG & GER.). 165p. 1984. pap. 9.00 (*3-518-02974-6*, Pub. by Suhr Verlag) Intl Bk Import.

Nathan der Weise - Minna Von Barnhelm. unabridged ed. Lessing. (World Classic Literature Ser.). (GER.). pap. 5.95 (*3-89507-015-7*, Pub. by Bookking Intl) Distribks Inc.

Nathan Emory Coffin Collection. James T. Demetrion. LC 81-6726. (Illus.). 20p. 1977. pap. 10.95 (*0-614-31044-X*) Edmundson.

Nathan Hale. Loree Lough. (Revolutionary War Leaders Ser.). (Illus.). 80p. (J). (gr. 3 up). 1999. pap. 8.95 (*0-7910-5704-6*) Chelsea Hse.

Nathan Hale. Lori Lough. LC 99-32043. (J). 1999. 16.95 (*0-7910-5361-X*) Chelsea Hse.

Nathan Hale & John Andre: Reluctant Heroes of the American Revolution. Harlan L. Hagman. LC 90-22535. (Illus.). 152p. 1992. 20.00 (*1-55787-077-2*) Hrt of the Lakes.

Nathan Hale Institute Newsletter. Ed. by Lawrence R. Sulc. pap. 1.00 (*0-935067-15-9*) Nathan Hale Inst.

Nathan Jacobson: Collected Works, 3 vols., Set. Nathan Jacobson. (Contemporary Mathematicians Ser.). 1600p. 1990. 316.00 (*0-8176-3362-6*) Birkhauser.

Nathan Jacobson: Collected Works, 3 vols., Vol. 1. Nathan Jacobson. (Contemporary Mathematicians Ser.). 448p. 1989. 115.00 (*0-8176-3410-X*) Birkhauser.

Nathan Jacobson: Collected Works, 3 vols., Vol. 2. Nathan Jacobson. (Contemporary Mathematicians Ser.). 608p. 1990. 115.00 (*0-8176-3411-8*) Birkhauser.

Nathan Jacobson: Collected Works, 3 vols., Vol. 3. Nathan Jacobson. (Contemporary Mathematicians Ser.). 592p. 1989. 115.00 (*0-8176-3446-0*) Birkhauser.

Nathan Lerner: Photographs, 1932-1944. Tom Bamberger & Debra Brehmer. (Illus.). 16p. 1995. pap. 5.00 (*0-944110-54-1*) Milwauk Art Mus.

Nathan Lerner: 50 Years of Photographic Inquiry. Intro. by Harry Bouras. (Illus.). 48p. 1984. 15.00 (*0-932026-14-1*) Columbia College Chi.

Nathan Levy's 100 Hundred Intriguing Questions, Bk. 1. Nathan Levy. (J). (gr. 3 up). 1993. 7.50 (*1-878347-35-7*) NL Assocs.

Nathan Levy's 100 Hundred Intriguing Questions, Bk. 2. Nathan Levy. (J). (gr. 3 up). 1994. 7.50 (*1-878347-36-5*) NL Assocs.

Nathan Levy's 100 Hundred Intriguing Questions, Bk. 3. Nathan Levy. (J). (gr. 3 up). 1994. 7.50 (*1-878347-37-3*) NL Assocs.

Nathan Levy's 100 Intriguing Questions, Bk. 4. Nathan Levy. 52p. 1994. pap. 7.50 (*1-878347-38-1*) NL Assocs.

Nathan Levy's 100 Intriguing Questions, Bk. 5. Nathan Levy. 52p. 1994. pap. 7.50 (*1-878347-40-3*) NL Assocs.

Nathan Levy's 100 Intriguing Questions, Bk. 6. Nathan Levy. 52p. 1994. pap. 7.50 (*1-878347-42-X*) NL Assocs.

Nathan Narratives. Gwilym H. Jones. (JSOT Supplement Ser.: No. 80). 196p. 1990. 57.50 (*1-85075-225-7*, Pub. by Sheffield Acad) CUP Services.

Nathan Oliveira: Figurative Works, 1958-1992. Marvin A. Schenck. (Illus.). 16p. 1992. pap. 9.95 (*1-886091-04-8*) Hearst Art Gal.

Nathan Oliveira: "The Windhover" : Recent Wing Paintings & Related Works Hilarie Faberman et al. LC 97-152173. 16p. 1995. write for info. (*0-937031-04-6*) Stanford Art.

Nathan Roberts: Erie Canal Engineer. Dorris M. Lawson. Ed. by Eric W. Lawson. (Illus.). 96p. 1997. pap. 15.00 (*0-925168-57-2*) North Country.

Nathan, Spiritual Advisor to Bill & Bob: An Adult Parable by Jacqueline L. Clarke. Jacqueline L. Clarke. (Illus.). 128p. 1998. pap. 9.99 (*0-9660596-1-1*) Matou Communs.

Nathan Starr Arms. Bernard P. Prue. Ed. by Bernadette S. Prue. (Illus.). 214p. 1999. lib. bdg. 32.50 (*0-8328-9811-2*) Higginson Bk Co.

***Nathan Starr Arms.** Bernard P. Prue. Ed. by Bernadette S. Prue. (Illus.). 214p. 1999. pap. 22.50 (*0-8328-9812-0*) Higginson Bk Co.

Nathan the Needle & Other Stories by Rabbi Gitin: Children Stories Based on Ethical & Moral Teachings. Michelle Gabriel. (Illus.). 32p. (Orig.). (J). (gr. 3-5). 1994. pap. text 12.00 (*0-9643475-0-4*) Gabriel Pr.

Nathan the Nervous: A One-Act Comedy. O. B. Rozell. (Illus.). 24p. (J). (gr. 6-12). 1977. pap. 3.25 (*0-88680-136-2*) I E Clark.

Nathan the Wise, Minna Von Barnhelm & Other Plays & Writings: Gotthold Ephraim Lessing. Ed. by Peter Demetz. LC 77-3139. (German Library: Vol. 12). 324p. 1991. 39.50 (*0-8264-0706-4*); pap. 19.95 (*0-8264-0707-2*) Continuum.

Nathan Trotter: Philadelphia Merchant, 1787-1853. Elva Tooker. LC 72-5080. (Technology & Society Ser.). (Illus.). 302p. 1972. reprint ed. 21.95 (*0-405-04729-0*) Ayer.

***Nathanael Greene.** Meg Greene. (Revolutionary War Leaders Ser.). 2000. 18.95 (*0-7910-5977-4*) Chelsea Hse.

Nathanael West. Stanley E. Hyman. LC 62-63699. (University of Minnesota Pamphlets on American Writers Ser.: No. 21). 48p. (Orig.). 1962. pap. 30.00 (*0-7837-2879-4*, 205757600006) Bks Demand.

Nathanael West: A Comprehensive Bibliography. William White. LC 74-79149. (Serif Series: Bibliographies & Checklists: No. 32). (Illus.). 224p. reprint ed. pap. 69.50 (*0-8357-5581-9*, 203521000093) Bks Demand.

***Nathanial Morison & His Descendents.** 2nd ed. George Abbot Morison. (Illus.). 248p. 2000. per. write for info. (*0-9654497-9-3*) Transit Pub.

Nathaniel. John Saul. 384p. (Orig.). 1984. mass mkt. 7.50 (*0-553-26264-5*) Bantam.

***Nathaniel Bacon.** Phelan Powell. (Colonial Leaders Ser.). (Illus.). 2000. 18.95 (*0-7910-5960-X*) Chelsea Hse.

Nathaniel Branden Anthology. Nathaniel Branden. 1980. 17.50 (*0-686-65215-0*) HM.

Nathaniel Branden's Self-Esteem Every Day: Reflections on Self-Esteem & Spirituality. Nathaniel Branden. LC 97-45895. 1998. per. 10.00 (*0-684-83338-7*, Fireside) S&S Trade Pap.

***Nathaniel Hawthorne.** Harold Bloom. (Major Short Story Writers Ser.). 2000. 19.95 (*0-7910-5949-9*) Chelsea Hse.

Nathaniel Hawthorne. Ed. by Donald Crowley. (Critical Heritage Ser.). 548p. (C). 1997. 160.00 (*0-415-15930-X*) Routledge.

Nathaniel Hawthorne. Annie Fields. LC 74-7223. (American Literature Ser.: No. 49). 1974. lib. bdg. 75.00 (*0-8383-1859-2*) M S G Haskell Hse.

Nathaniel Hawthorne. Nathaniel Hawthorne. (Modern Critical Views Ser.). 222p. 1986. 29.95 (*0-87754-695-9*) Chelsea Hse.

Nathaniel Hawthorne. Nathaniel Hawthorne. Ed. by Harold Bloom. LC 99-23593. 120p. 1999. 19.95 (*0-7910-5253-2*) Chelsea Hse.

Nathaniel Hawthorne. George E. Woodberry. 1998. 34.95 (*0-7910-4536-6*) Chelsea Hse.

Nathaniel Hawthorne. Mark Van Doren. LC 72-7878. (American Men of Letters Ser.). (Illus.). 285p. 1973. reprint ed. lib. bdg. 65.00 (*0-8371-6552-0*, VANH, Greenwood Pr) Greenwood.

Nathaniel Hawthorne. George E. Woodberry. (BCL1-PS American Literature Ser.). 302p. 1992. reprint ed. lib. bdg. 89.00 (*0-7812-6732-3*) Rprt Serv.

Nathaniel Hawthorne. rev. ed. Terence Martin. (United States Authors Ser.: No. 75). 240p. 1983. 32.00 (*0-8057-7384-3*, Twyne) Mac Lib Ref.

Nathaniel Hawthorne: A Descriptive Bibliography. C. Frazer Clark, Jr. LC 76-50885. (Series in Bibliography). 328p. 1978. 100.00 (*0-8229-3343-8*) U of Pittsburgh Pr.

N

Nathaniel Hawthorne: A Study of the Short Fiction. Nancy Bunge. (Twayne's Studies in Short Fiction). 180p. 1993. 29.00 (*0-8057-0852-9*, Twyne) Mac Lib Ref.

Nathaniel Hawthorne: American Storyteller. Nancy Whitelaw. LC 96-32961. (World Writers Ser.). (Illus.). 112p. (YA). (gr. 5 up). 1996. lib. bdg. 18.95 (*1-883846-16-1*) M Reynolds.

Nathaniel Hawthorne: An Annotated Bibliography of Comment & Criticism Before 1900. Gary Scharnhorst. LC 88-29221. (Author Bibliographies Ser.: No. 82). 416p. 1988. 45.00 (*0-8108-2184-2*) Scarecrow.

Nathaniel Hawthorne: Critical Assessments. Ed. by Brian Harding. 1900p. (C). 1998. 535.00 (*1-873403-35-6*) Routledge.

Nathaniel Hawthorne: Great American Short Stories I. Illus. by James McConnell. LC 94-75013. (Classic Short Stories Ser.). 80p. 1994. pap. 5.95 (*0-7854-0624-7*, 40002) Am Guidance.

Nathaniel Hawthorne: The Contemporary Reviews. Ed. by John L. Idol, Jr. & Buford Jones. LC 93-36158. (American Critical Archives Ser.: No. 4). 560p. (C). 1994. text 115.00 (*0-521-39142-3*) Cambridge U Pr.

Nathaniel Hawthorne: The English Experience, 1853-1864. Raymona E. Hull. LC 79-26616. 322p. 1980. pap. 99.90 (*0-7837-8546-1*, 204936100011) Bks Demand.

Nathaniel Hawthorne: The Introduction of an American Author's Work into Japan. Fumio Ano et al. (Illus.). 109p. 1993. pap. 15.00 (*0-88389-099-2*, PEMP162) Peabody Essex Mus.

***Nathaniel Hawthorne: The Scarlet Letter: Essays - Articles - Reviews.** Ed. by Elmer Kennedy-Andrews. 192p. 2000. text 39.50 (*0-231-12190-3*) Col U Pr.

Nathaniel Hawthorne, a Biography. Randall Stewart. (BCL1-PS American Literature Ser.). 279p. 1993. reprint ed. lib. bdg. 79.00 (*0-7812-6967-9*) Rprt Serv.

Nathaniel Hawthorne, A Modest Man. Mather Jackson. (BCL1-PS American Literature Ser.). 356p. 1993. reprint ed. lib. bdg. 89.00 (*0-7812-6966-0*) Rprt Serv.

Nathaniel Hawthorne, A Modest Man. Edward A. Mather Jackson. LC 77-110834. 356p. 1971. reprint ed. lib. bdg. 35.00 (*0-8371-2594-4*, MANH, Greenwood Pr) Greenwood.

Nathaniel Hawthorne & European Literary Tradition. Jane Lundblad. (BCL1-PS American Literature Ser.). 196p. 1993. reprint ed. lib. bdg. 69.00 (*0-7812-6965-2*) Rprt Serv.

Nathaniel Hawthorne & His Wife: A Biography, 2 vols., Set. Julian Hawthorne. (BCL1-PS American Literature Ser.). 1992. reprint ed. lib. bdg. 150.00 (*0-7812-6727-7*) Rprt Serv.

Nathaniel Hawthorne & His Wife: A Biography, Set. Julian Hawthorne. LC 17-21573. 1969. reprint ed. 39.00 (*0-403-00084-X*) Scholarly.

Nathaniel Hawthorne & His Wife: A Biography, 2 vols., Set. Julian Hawthorne. (Illus.). (C). 1968. reprint ed. 75.00 (*0-208-00672-9*, Archon Bks) Shoe String.

Nathaniel Hawthorne & the Critics: A Checklist of Criticism, 1900-1978. Jeanetta Boswell. LC 81-9398. (Author Bibliographies Ser.: No. 57). 283p. 1982. 29.00 (*0-8108-1471-4*) Scarecrow.

Nathaniel Hawthorne & the Romance of the Orient. Luther S. Luedtke. LC 88-46018. (Illus.). 304p. 1989. 12.95 (*0-253-33613-9*) Ind U Pr.

Nathaniel Hawthorne & the Tradition of Gothic Romance. Jane Lundblad. LC 65-15898. (Studies in Hawthorne: No. 15). 1969. reprint ed. lib. bdg. 75.00 (*0-8383-0589-X*) M S G Haskell Hse.

Nathaniel Hawthorne Encyclopedia. Robert L. Gale. LC 90-47337. 608p. 1991. lib. bdg. 85.00 (*0-313-26816-9*, GNB/, Greenwood Pr) Greenwood.

Nathaniel Hawthorne (In Beacon Biographies) Annie Fields. (Notable American Authors Ser.). 1992. reprint ed. lib. bdg. 75.00 (*0-7812-2828-X*) Rprt Serv.

Nathaniel Hawthorne in His Time. James R. Mellow. LC 98-2623. 684p. 1998. reprint ed. pap. 19.95 (*0-8018-5900-X*) Johns Hopkins.

Nathaniel Hawthorne Journal. Ed. by C. E. Frazer Clark. Incl. Nathaniel Hawthorne Journal: 1974. 1974. 25.00 (*0-910972-50-8*); write for info. (*0-318-51241-6*) Bruccoli.

Nathaniel Hawthorne Journal: 1972. Ed. by C. E. Frazer Clark. 1972. 25.00 (*0-910972-33-8*) Bruccoli.

Nathaniel Hawthorne Journal: 1973. Ed. by C. E. Frazer Clark. 1973. 25.00 (*0-910972-39-7*) Bruccoli.

Nathaniel Hawthorne Journal: 1974 see Nathaniel Hawthorne Journal

***Nathaniel Hawthorne, the Scarlet Letter.** Elmer Kennedy-Andrews. LC 00-26250. (Critical Guides Ser.). 2000. pap. 14.50 (*0-231-12191-1*) Col U Pr.

Nathaniel Hawthorne to Edward FitzGerald see Library of Literary Criticism

Nathaniel Hawthorne to Joseph Holt Ingraham see Bibliography of American Literature

Nathaniel Hawthorne's Tales. Nathaniel Hawthorne. Ed. by James McIntosh. (Critical Editions Ser.). 480p. (Orig.). (C). 1987. pap. text 14.75 (*0-393-95426-9*) Norton.

Nathaniel Hawthorne's The House of the Seven Gables. Linda Corrente. (Barron's Book Notes Ser.). (C). 1985. pap. 2.50 (*0-8120-3519-4*) Barron.

Nathaniel Hawthorne's The Scarlet Letter see Modern Critical Interpretations

Nathaniel Hawthorne's The Scarlet Letter see Bloom's Notes

Nathaniel Hone the Elder. Adrian Le Harivel. (Lives of Irish Artists Ser.). (Illus.). 36p. 1995. 7.95 (*0-948524-36-7*, Pub. by Town Hse) Roberts Rinehart.

Nathaniel Parker Willis. Henry A. Beers. LC 70-89458. (BCL Ser. I). reprint ed. 24.50 (*0-404-00726-0*) AMS Pr.

Nathaniel Parker Willis. Henry A. Beers. (BCL1-PS American Literature Ser.). 365p. 1992. reprint ed. lib. bdg. 89.00 (*0-7812-6906-7*) Rprt Serv.

Nathaniel Smith of Vermont & Some of His Descendants, Circa, 1775-1985. Gary V. Smith. LC 84-73079. xii, 154p. 1985. 15.00 (*0-318-60268-7*) Gary V Smith.

Nathaniel Southgate Shaler & the Culture of American Science. David N. Livingstone. LC 85-28982. (History of American Science & Technology Ser.). 416p. 1987. text 39.95 (*0-8173-0305-7*) U of Ala Pr.

Nathaniel Talking. Eloise Greenfield. (Illus.). 32p. (J). (gr. k-5). 1989. 12.95 (*0-86316-200-2*) Writers & Readers.

Nathaniel Talking. Eloise Greenfield. (Illus.). 32p. (J). (gr. 4-7). 1993. pap. 6.95 (*0-86316-201-0*) Writers & Readers.

Nathaniel Whiting of Dedham MA, 1641, & Five Generations of His Descendants. T. S. Lazell. 80p. 1990. reprint ed. pap. 16.00 (*0-8328-1561-6*); reprint ed. lib. bdg. 24.00 (*0-8328-1560-8*) Higginson Bk Co.

Nathaniel Willy, Scared Silly. Judith Mathews & Fay Robinson. (Illus.). 32p. (J). (gr. k-3). 1999. per. 5.99 (*0-689-82955-8*) Aladdin.

Nathaniel Willy, Scared Silly. Judith Matthews & Fay Robinson. LC 92-4052. (Illus.). 32p. (J). (gr. k-3). 1994. mass mkt. 15.00 (*0-02-765285-8*, Bradbury S&S) S&S Childrens.

***Nathaniel's Nutmeg: Or, the True & Incredible Adventures of the Spice Trader Who Changed the Course of History.** Giles Milton. (Illus.). 400p. 2000. pap. 13.95 (*0-14-029260-8*) Penguin Putnam.

Nathaniel's Violin. Alison Lohans. (Illus.). 32p. (J). (ps-3). 1996. pap. 6.95 (*1-55143-064-9*) Orca Bk Pubs.

Nathan's Fear: Book One of the Creation. Jamie S. Catalfamo. 104p. (Orig.). 1994. pap. 6.95 (*0-9641739-0-5*) J S Catalfamo.

Nathan's Legal Markets, 1994: The Definitive Resource for Advertising to the Legal Profession. Ed. by Sylvia Dolan. 700p. 1993. pap. write for info. (*0-9637775-0-5*) Dolan Media.

Nathan's Legal Markets, 1995 Edition: The Definitive Resource for Marketing to the Legal Profession. rev. ed. Ed. by Sylvia M. Dolan. 425p. 1994. pap. 159.95 (*0-9637775-1-3*) Dolan Media.

Nathan's Legal Markets 1997 Edition. 4th ed. Ed. by Sylvia M. Dolan. (Nathan's Legal Markets Ser.). 688p. 1997. write for info. (*0-614-28420-1*) Dolan Media.

Nathan's Legal Markets 1996 Edition: The Definitive Resource for Marketing to Legal Professionals. rev. ed. Ed. by Sylvia M. Dolan. 500p. 1996. pap. 159.95 (*0-9637775-2-1*) Dolan Media.

Nathan's Run. John Gilstrap. 384p. 1997. mass mkt. 6.99 (*0-446-60468-2*, Pub. by Warner Bks) Little.

***Nathan's Spiritual Legacy, Fred.** Illus. by Charles H. Clarke. (Nathan Trilogy Ser.). 120p. 1999. pap. 9.99 (*0-9660596-2-X*) Matou Communs.

Natick. Anne K. Schaller. LC 98-88061. (Images of America Ser.). (Illus.). 128p. 1998. pap. 16.99 (*0-7524-1255-8*) Arcadia Publng.

Natick: A Town with Character. Florence L. Macewen. Ed. & Compiled by Carol J. Coverly. LC 97-164679. (Illus.). xvi, 193p. (Orig.). 1997. pap. 24.00 (*0-9653848-0-2*) Morse Inst Lib.

Natick Dictionary. James H. Trumbull. (Bureau of American Ethnology Bulletins Ser.). 349p. 1995. lib. bdg. 99.00 (*0-7812-4025-5*) Rprt Serv.

Natiology: Social Science for the Third Millenium. Igor Souzadaltsev. 200p. 1999. 26.00 (*0-9653753-2-3*) R&R Writers.

Nation: The Foundations of Civil Order & Political Life in the United States. Elisha Mulford. LC 71-120327. xiv, 418p. 1971. reprint ed. 49.50 (*0-678-00705-5*) Kelley.

***Nation - State & Global Order: A Historical Introduction to Contemporary Politics.** Walter C. Opello, Jr. & Stephen J. Rosow. LC 98-28937. 290p. 1999. lib. bdg. 55.00 (*1-55587-811-3*) L Rienner.

Nation Against Nation: What Happened to the U. N. Dream & What the U. S. Can Do about It. Thomas M. Franck. 334p. 1985. text 29.95 (*0-19-503587-9*) OUP.

Nation & Commemoration: Creating National Identities in the United States & Australia. Lyn Spillman. (Cambridge Cultural Social Studies). 264p. 1997. text 59.95 (*0-521-57404-8*); pap. text 19.95 (*0-521-57432-3*) Cambridge U Pr.

Nation & Economic Growth: The Philippines & Thailand. Kunio Yoshihara. (South-East Asian Social Science Monographs). (Illus.). 294p. 1995. text 55.00 (*967-65-3054-9*) OUP.

Nation & Gelehrtenrepublik: Supplement to the Lessing Yearbook. Ed. by Wilfried Barner & Albert M. Reh. 363p. 1984. 16.00 (*3-88377-190-2*) Lessing Soc.

Nation & Identity Ross Poole. LC 99-23022. 208p. 1999. pap. 24.99 (*0-415-12623-1*) Routledge.

***Nation & Identity.** Ross Poole. LC 99-23022. (Ideas Ser.). 208p. (C). 1999. text. write for info. (*0-415-12622-3*) Routledge.

Nation & Identity in Contemporary Europe. Ed. by Brian Jenkins & Spyros A. Sofos. LC 95-25786. 304p. (C). 1996. pap. 22.99 (*0-415-12313-5*) Routledge.

Nation & Ideology. Ed. by Ivo Banac et al. (East European Monographs: No. 95). 479p. 1981. text 84.00 (*0-914710-89-3*, Pub. by East Eur Monographs) Col U Pr.

Nation & Its City: Politics, Corruption, & Progress in Washington, D.C., 1861-1902. Alan Lessoff. LC 93-17513. 337p. 1994. 48.00 (*0-8018-4464-9*) Johns Hopkins.

Nation & Its Fragments: Colonial & Postcolonial Histories. Partha Chatterjee. LC 93-15536. (Studies in Culture - Power - History). 264p. 1994. text 55.00 (*0-691-03305-6*, Pub. by Princeton U Pr); pap. text 17.95 (*0-691-01943-6*, Pub. by Princeton U Pr) Cal Prin Full Svc.

Nation & Migration: The Politics of Space in the South Asian Diaspora. Ed. by Peter Van der Veer. (South Asia Seminar Ser.). 256p. (Orig.). (C). 1995. text 37.50 (*0-8122-3259-3*); pap. text 16.95 (*0-8122-1537-0*) U of Pa Pr.

Nation & Narration. Homi K. Bhabha. 352p. (C). (gr. 13). 1990. pap. 20.99 (*0-415-01483-2*) Routledge.

Nation & Race: The Developing Euro-American Racist Subculture. Ed. by Jeffrey Kaplan & Tore Bjorgo. LC 97-39513. 288p. 1998. text 50.00 (*1-55553-332-9*); pap. text 20.00 (*1-55553-331-0*) NE U Pr.

Nation & Religion: Perspectives on Europe & Asia. Peter Van Der Veer & Hartmut Lehmann. LC 98-40357. 1999. 55.00 (*0-691-01233-4*, Pub. by Princeton U Pr); pap. 17.95 (*0-691-01232-6*, Pub. by Princeton U Pr) Cal Prin Full Svc.

Nation & Religion in Central Europe & the Western Balkans - The Muslims in Bosnia, Hercegovina & Sandzak Vol. 1: A Sociological Analysis. Vatro Murvar. 180p. 1990. 30.00 (*0-931633-04-4*); pap. 15.00 (*0-931633-05-2*) Fnd Soc Stdy.

***Nation & Religion in the Middle East.** Fred Halliday. 260p. 2000. pap. 19.95 (*1-55587-935-7*); lib. bdg. 49.95 (*1-55587-910-1*) L Rienner.

***Nation & Religion in the Middle East.** Fred Halliday. 260p. 1999. 60.00 (*0-86356-078-4*, Pub. by Saqi); pap. 27.95 (*0-86356-044-X*, Pub. by Saqi) Intl Spec Bk.

Nation & State in Late Imperial Russia: Nationalism & Russification on the Western Frontier, 1863-1914. Theodore R. Weeks. LC 96-7364. 310p. 1996. lib. bdg. 34.00 (*0-87580-216-8*) N Ill U Pr.

Nation & the Schools. J. A. Keith & William C. Bagley. LC 77-74944. (American Federalism-the Urban Dimension Ser.). (Illus.). 1978. reprint ed. lib. bdg. 33.95 (*0-405-10492-8*) Ayer.

Nation & the States. Harold L. Hodgkinson et al. 100p. 1992. 12.00 (*0-937846-55-4*) Inst Educ Lead.

Nation & the States, Rivals or Partners? William Anderson. LC 73-16640. 263p. 1974. reprint ed. lib. bdg. 69.50 (*0-8371-7210-1*, ANNS, Greenwood Pr) Greenwood.

***Nation & Word, 1770-1850.** Mary Anne Perkins. 400p. 1999. text 68.95 (*1-85928-286-5*, Pub. by Ashgate Pub) Ashgate Pub Co.

Nation Arabe, 1930-1938, 4 vols. (FRE.). 2430p. 1988. reprint ed. lib. bdg. 395.00 (*1-85207-100-1*, Pub. by Archive Editions) N Ross.

Nation As a Local Metaphor: Wurttemberg, Imperial Germany & National Memory, 1871-1918. Alon Confino. LC 96-52039. 296p. (C). (gr. 13). 1997. pap. text 19.95 (*0-8078-4665-1*); lib. bdg. 59.95 (*0-8078-2359-7*) U of NC Pr.

Nation at Last: The Story of Federation. Kathleen Dermody. (Illus.). 1997. pap. 25.95 (*0-644-47536-6*, Pub. by Aust Gov Pub) Accents Pubns.

Nation at Risk: Report of the President's Commission on Critical Infrastructure Protection Hearing Before the Subcommittee on Technology, Terrorism & Government Information of the Committee on the Judiciary, United States Senate, 105th Congress, First Session....November 5, 1997. LC 98-188646. (S. Hrg. Ser.). iii, 72p. 1998. write for info. (*0-16-056531-6*) USGPO.

Nation at Risk: The Full Account. 2nd ed. National Commisssion on Excellence in Education. Ed. by U. S. A. Research, Inc., Staff. (Illus.). 128p. (Orig.). (C). 1994. pap. 12.95 (*0-917191-02-1*) USA Res.

Nation at War. Arthur A. Stein. LC 80-7994. 165p. 1980. pap. 51.20 (*0-7837-7458-3*, 204918000010) Bks Demand.

Nation at War. Peyton C. March. LC 72-109779. 407p. 1970. reprint ed. lib. bdg. 45.00 (*0-8371-4269-5*, MANW, Greenwood Pr) Greenwood.

Nation at War: Australian Politics, Society & Diplomacy during the Vietnam War. Peter Edwards. LC 97-179298. (Illus.). 480p. 1997. 59.95 (*1-86448-282-6*, Pub. by Allen & Unwin Pty) Paul & Co Pubs.

Nation Betrayed. rev. ed. James B. Gritz. (Illus.). 350p. 1989. text 19.95 (*0-9622238-0-8*) Ctr for Action.

Nation Builders: Female Activism in the Nation of Islam. Ed. by Graham Hodges. (Croscurrents in African American History Ser.). 250p. 1999. text 37.00 (*0-8153-2457-X*) Garland.

Nation Building: The Geopolitical History of Korea. Walter B. Jung. LC 98-39911. 1998. write for info. (*0-7618-1273-3*); pap. write for info. (*0-7618-1274-1*) U Pr of Amer.

Nation Building: The U. N. & Namibia. National Democratic Institute for International Af. 130p. 1990. pap. 6.95 (*1-880134-06-3*) Natl Demo Inst.

Nation-Building & Citizenship: Studies of Our Changing Social Order. enl. ed. Reinhard Bendix. 455p. 1996. pap. text 24.95 (*1-56000-890-3*) Transaction Pubs.

Nation Building & Development Assistance in Africa: Different but Equal. Kaoru Ishikawa. LC 98-21908. 192p. 1999. text 69.95 (*0-312-21667-X*) St Martin.

Nation-Building & Development Process. Ed. by L. R. Singh. (C). 1994. text 34.00 (*81-7033-212-5*, Pub. by Rawat Pubns) S Asia.

***Nation Building & Ethnic Integration in Post-Soviet Societies: An Investigation of Latvia & Kazakstan.** Pal Kolsto et al. 360p. 1999. 75.00 (*0-8133-3697-X*, Pub. by Westview) HarpC.

Nation-Building in Africa: Problems & Prospects. Arnold Rivkin. Ed. by John H. Morrow. LC 74-96028. 320p. reprint ed. pap. 99.20 (*0-7837-5681-X*, 205910900005) Bks Demand.

Nation-Building in Central Europe. Ed. by Hagen Schulze. LC 86-33463. (German Historical Perspectives Ser.). 208p. 1987. 29.95 (*0-85496-529-7*) Berg Pubs.

Nation Building in India. R. C. Dutt. 1987. 29.00 (*81-7062-019-8*, Pub. by Lancer India) S Asia.

Nation-Building in the Post-Soviet Borderlands: The Politics of National Identities. Graham Smith. LC 97-32113. (Illus.). 312p. (C). 1998. text 59.95 (*0-521-59045-0*); pap. text 18.95 (*0-521-59968-7*) Cambridge U Pr.

Nation-Building in the U. S. Francis S. Wagner. LC 84-28234. 190p. boxed set 18.00 (*0-912404-12-4*) Alpha Pubns.

Nation by Rights: National Cultures, Sexual Identity Politics, & the Discourse of Rights. Carl F. Stychin. LC 97-32826. (Queer Politics, Queer Theories Ser.). 256p. (C). 1998. text 59.95 (*1-56639-623-9*); pap. text 22.95 (*1-56639-624-7*) Temple U Pr.

Nation, Class & Creed in Northern Ireland. Edward Moxon-Browne. 224p. (Orig.). 1983. 69.95 (*0-566-00607-3*) Ashgate Pub Co.

Nation Collapses: The Italian Surrender of September, 1943. Elena Agarossi. LC 98-45622. 187p. (C). 2000. text 44.95 (*0-521-59199-6*) Cambridge U Pr.

Nation, Culture, Text: Australian Cultural & Media Studies. Ed. by Graeme Turner. LC 92-21154. (Communication & Society Ser.). 272p. (C). 1993. pap. 27.99 (*0-415-08886-0*, B2337) Routledge.

Nation, Culture, Text: Australian Cultural & Media Studies. Ed. by Graeme Turner. LC 92-21154. (Communication & Society Ser.). 272p. (C). (gr. 13). 1993. 75.00 (*0-415-08885-2*) Routledge.

Nation Dedicated to Religious Liberty: The Constitutional Heritage of the Religion Clauses. Arlin M. Adams & Charles J. Emmerich. LC 90-36248. 188p. (C). 1990. pap. text 14.95 (*0-8122-1318-1*) U of Pa Pr.

Nation Divided: Diversity, Inequality, & Community in American Society. Ed. by Phyllis Moen et al. LC 99-15783. 1999. 49.95 (*0-8014-3719-9*) Cornell U Pr.

Nation Divided: Diversity, Inequality & Community in American Society. Ed. by Phyllis Moen et al. LC 99-15783. 1999. pap. 18.95 (*0-8014-8588-6*) Cornell U Pr.

Nation Divided: The War at Home, 1945-1972. Ed. by Robert Manning. (Vietnam Experience Ser.). (Illus.). 192p. 1984. 16.30 (*0-201-11263-9*) Addison-Wesley.

Nation Divided, 1850-1900. Stuart A. Kallen. Ed. by Rosemary Walner. LC 90-82612. (Building of a Nation Ser.). (Illus.). 64p. (J). (gr. 4). 1990. lib. bdg. 13.98 (*0-939179-90-3*) ABDO Pub Co.

Nation Divides: The Civil War (1820-1880) Richard Steins. LC 93-24993. (First Person America Ser.). (Illus.). 64p. (J). (gr. 5-8). 1995. lib. bdg. 18.90 (*0-8050-2583-9*) TFC Bks NY.

Nation, 1865-1990: Selections from the Independent Magazine of Politics & Culture. Katrina Vanden Heuvel. (Illus.). 552p. 1991. pap. 14.95 (*1-56025-023-2*, Thunders Mouth) Avalon NY.

Nation, Empire, Colony: Historicizing Gender & Race. Ed. by Ruth R. Pierson & Nupur Chaudhuri. LC 98-19966. (Illus.). 288p. 1998. 29.95 (*0-253-33398-9*); pap. 14.95 (*0-253-21191-3*) Ind U Pr.

Nation et Voie Africaine du Socialisme. Leopold S. Senghor. pap. 9.50 (*0-685-35640-X*) Fr & Eur.

Nation Formation: Towards a Theory of Abstract Community. Paul James. LC 96-68420. (Politics & Culture Ser.). 240p. 1996. 69.95 (*0-7619-5072-9*); pap. 26.95 (*0-7619-5073-7*) Sage.

***Nation, Governance, & Modernity: Canton, 1900-1927.** Micheal Tsang-Woon Tsin. LC 99-16648. 1999. 45.00 (*0-8047-3361-9*) Stanford U Pr.

Nation in Arms: The Origins of the People's Army of Vietnam. Greg Lockhart. 314p. 1991. 38.95 (*0-04-301294-9*, Pub. by Allen & Unwin Pty); pap. 24.95 (*0-04-324012-7*, Pub. by Allen & Unwin Pty) Paul & Co Pubs.

Nation in Crisis, 1861-1877. David Herbert Donald. LC 74-79169. (Goldentree Bibliographies Series in American History). (C). 1969. pap. text 6.95 (*0-88295-511-X*) Harlan Davidson.

Nation in Crisis, 1828-1865. Ed. by David R. Ross et al. LC 78-101951. (Structure of American History Ser.: Vol. 3). (C). 1970. pap. text 6.95 (*0-88295-757-0*) Harlan Davidson.

Nation in Debt: Economists Debate the Federal Budget Deficit. Ed. by Richard H. Fink & Jack C. High. LC 86-28252. 328p. 1987. pap. 19.95 (*0-313-27074-0*, P7074); lib. bdg. 42.95 (*0-313-27073-2*, U7073) Greenwood.

***Nation in History: Historiographical Debates about Ethnicity & Nationalism.** Anthony D. Smith. LC 00-21080. (Menahem Stern Jerusalem Lectures). 144p. 2000. pap. 14.95 (*1-58465-040-0*); text 35.00 (*1-58465-039-7*) U Pr of New Eng.

Nation in the History of Marxian Thought. Charles C. Herod. 1976. pap. text 59.00 (*90-247-1749-3*) Kluwer Academic.

Nation in the Making: The Philippines & the United States, 1899-1921. Peter W. Stanley. LC 73-82342. (Harvard Studies in American-East Asian Relations: No. 4). 351p. reprint ed. pap. 108.90 (*0-7837-2337-7*, 205742500004) Bks Demand.

Nation in the Schools: Wanted, a Canadian Education. Rowland M. Lorimer. LC 84-215816. (Research in Education Ser.: No. 11). (Illus.). 131p. reprint ed. pap. 40.70 (*0-7837-0555-7*, 204089600019) Bks Demand.

An Asterisk (*) at the beginning of an entry indicates that the title is appearing for the first time.

Nation in Torment: The Great American Depression, 1929-1939. Edward R. Ellis. Ed. by Philip Turner. (Kodansha Globe Ser.). 576p. 1995. pap. 15.00 (*1-56836-113-0*, Kodansha Globe) Kodansha.

Nation in Trouble & Many Didn't Care. William F. Ballhaus. LC 96-28196. (Illus.). 224p. 1996. 24.95 (*0-9653066-0-7*) W F Ballhaus.

Nation in Turmoil: Civil Rights & the Vietnam War (1960-1973) Gene Brown. LC 93-24995. (First Person America Ser.). (Illus.). 64p. (J). (gr. 5-8). 1995. lib. bdg. 18.90 (*0-8050-2588-X*) TFC Bks NY.

Nation in Turmoil: Nationalism & Ethnicity in Pakistan, 1937-1958. Yunas Samad. LC 94-45239. 240p. (C). 1995. 25.00 (*0-8039-9214-9*) Sage.

Nation in Waiting: Indonesia in the 1990s & Beyond. 2nd ed. Adam Schwarz. 400p. 1999. 68.00 (*0-8133-3649-X*) Westview.

Nation in Waiting: Indonesia's Search for Stability. 2nd ed. Schwartz. 400p. 1999. pap. 28.00 (*0-8133-3650-3*, Pub. by Westview) HarpC.

Nation in 2 States. Baker. 2000. 65.00 (*0-8133-6656-9*) Westview.

Nation into State: The Shifting Symbolic Foundations of American Nationalism. Wilbur Zelinsky. LC 88-4211. 366p. 1988. reprint ed. pap. 113.50 (*0-608-08013-6*, 206797800001) Bks Demand.

Nation Is Born: Rebellion & Independence in America (1700-1820) Richard Steins. LC 93-24994. (First Person America Ser.). (Illus.). 64p. (J). (gr. 5-8). 1995. lib. bdg. 18.90 (*0-8050-2582-0*) TFC Bks NY.

Nation Making: Emergent Identities in Postcolonial Melanesia. Ed. by Robert J. Foster. LC 95-8775. 288p. 1995. text 49.50 (*0-472-10558-2*, 10558) U of Mich Pr.

Nation Making: Emergent Identities in Postcolonial Melanesia. Robert J. Foster. 288p. (C). 1997. pap. text 19.95 (*0-472-08427-5*, 08427) U of Mich Pr.

Nation Moving West: Readings in the History of the American Frontier. Ed. by Robert W. Richmond & Robert W. Mardock. LC 66-10446. 376p. reprint ed. pap. 116.60 (*0-7837-6013-2*, 204582400008) Bks Demand.

Nation of Amor. Chris McConnell. LC 93-36291. 187p. 1994. 22.00 (*1-877946-40-0*) Permanent Pr.

Nation of Beggars? Priests, People, & Politics in Famine Ireland, 1846-1852. Donal A. Kerr. LC 94-13314. (Illus.). 384p. 1994. text 69.00 (*0-19-820050-1*, Clarendon Pr) OUP.

Nation of Beggars? Priests, People & Politics in Famine Ireland, 1846-1852. Donal A. Kerr. (Illus.). 384p. 1998. reprint ed. pap. text 38.00 (*0-19-820737-9*) OUP.

Nation of Behavers. Martin E. Marty. LC 76-7997. xii, 256p. 1980. pap. text 12.95 (*0-226-50892-7*, P890) U Ch Pr.

Nation of Enemies: Chile under Pinochet. Pamela Constable & Arturo Valenzuela. 368p. 1993. pap. 15.95 (*0-393-30985-1*) Norton.

***Nation of Extremes: The Pioneers in Twentieth-Century Ireland.** Diarmaid Ferriter. LC 98-46746. 288p. 1999. 52.50 (*0-7165-2623-9*, Pub. by Irish Acad Pr) Intl Spec Bk.

Nation of Fliers: German Aviation & the Popular Imagination. Peter Fritzsche. (Illus.). 283p. (C). 1992. text 27.95 (*0-674-60121-1*) HUP.

Nation of Home Owners. Peter Saunders. 340p. (C). 1990. text 85.00 (*0-04-445488-0*) Routledge.

Nation of Immigrants: Readings in Canadian History, 1840-1960. Franca Iacovetta. LC 98-231289. 512p. 1998. text 60.00 (*0-8020-0466-0*); pap. text 24.95 (*0-8020-7482-0*) U of Toronto Pr.

Nation of Islam: An American Millenarian Movement. Martha Lee. (Studies in Religion & Society: Vol. 21). 163p. 1989. 79.95 (*0-88946-853-2*) E Mellen.

Nation of Islam: An American Millenarian Movement. Martha F. Lee. (C). 1996. pap. 17.95 (*0-8156-0375-4*, LENIP) Syracuse U Pr.

Nation of Lawyers. Paul Williams. (Illus.). 120p. (Orig.). 1990. pap. 6.00 (*0-934558-15-9*) Entwhistle Bks.

Nation of Learners: Building a New Learning America. Douglas M. Brooks. 1995. 69.95 (*0-590-49386-8*) Scholastic Inc.

Nation of Letters Vol. I: A Concise Anthology of American Literature. Ed. by Stephen Cushman & Paul Newlin. (Illus.). 408p. (C). 1998. pap. text 23.97 (*1-881089-89-4*) Brandywine Press.

Nation of Letters Vol. II: A Concise History of American Literature. Ed. by Stephen Cushman & Paul Newlin. (Illus.). 420p. (C). 1998. pap. text 23.97 (*1-881089-90-8*) Brandywine Press.

Nation of Lions . . . Chained. Mohammad T. Mehdi. LC 62-17245. 1963. pap. 15.00 (*0-911026-05-3*) New World Press NY.

Nation of Lords: The Autobiography of the Vice Lords. 2nd ed. David Dawley. (Illus.). 202p. (C). 1992. pap. text 12.50 (*0-88133-628-9*) Waveland Pr.

Nation of Meddlers. Charles Edgley. (C). 1998. pap. 18.50 (*0-8133-3308-3*) Westview.

Nation of Meddlers. Charles Edgley. LC 98-45152. 288p. 1999. text 65.00 (*0-8133-3307-5*, Pub. by Westview) HarpC.

Nation of Millionaires: Unleashing America's Economic Potential. Robert J. Genetski. LC 96-53426. (Illus.). 162p. 1997. pap. 8.95 (*0-9632027-4-X*) Heartland Inst.

Nation of Millionaires: Unleashing America's Economic Potential. Robert J. Genetski. LC 96-53426. 160p. 1997. write for info. (*1-56833-094-4*) Madison Bks UPA.

Nation of Millionaires: Unleashing America's Economic Potential. Robert J. Genetski. LC 96-53426. 192p. 1997. text 16.95 (*1-56833-095-2*) Madison Bks UPA.

Nation of Nations. 4th ed. Davidson. 2000. 55.00 (*0-07-231502-4*) McGraw.

Nation of Nations, Vol. 1. 2nd ed. Davidson. 1994. student ed. 17.50 (*0-07-015636-0*) McGraw.

Nation of Nations, Vol. I. 3rd ed. Davidson. 752p. 1997. pap. 52.50 (*0-07-015796-0*) McGraw.

Nation of Nations, Vol. I. 3rd ed. Davidson. 1997. pap. 18.13 (*0-07-015797-9*) McGraw.

Nation of Nations, Vol. I. 4th ed. Davidson. 2000. 42.00 (*0-07-231507-5*) McGraw.

Nation of Nations, Vol. 2. 2nd ed. Davidson. 1994. student ed. 17.50 (*0-07-015637-9*) McGraw.

Nation of Nations, Vol. II. 3rd ed. Davidson. 816p. 1997. pap. 52.50 (*0-07-015799-5*) McGraw.

Nation of Nations, Vol. II. 3rd ed. Davidson. 1997. pap. 18.13 (*0-07-015800-2*) McGraw.

Nation of Nations, Vol. 2. 4th ed. Davidson. 2000. 42.00 (*0-07-231509-1*) McGraw.

Nation of Nations, vols. 2nd ed. Davidson. 576p. 1998. pap. 25.63 (*0-07-303385-5*) McGraw.

Nation of Nations: A Concise Narrative of the American Republic, Vol. 1. abr. ed. James W. Davidson & William E. Gienapp. (C). 1995. pap. text 16.50 (*0-07-015742-1*) McGraw.

Nation of Nations: A Concise Narrative of the American Republic, Vol. 2. abr. ed. James W. Davidson. 560p. (C). 1995. pap. 25.94 (*0-07-015740-5*) McGraw.

Nation of Nations: A Concise Narrative of the American Republic, Brief Edition, Vol. 1. James W. Davidson et al. (C). 1995. pap., student ed. 15.63 (*0-07-015750-2*) McGraw.

Nation of Nations: A Concise Narrative of the American Republic, Brief Edition, Vol. 2. James W. Davidson et al. (C). 1995. pap., student ed. 15.63 (*0-07-015751-0*) McGraw.

Nation of Nations: A Narrative History of the American Republic. 3rd ed. James W. Davidson. LC 97-1197. 1408p. 1997. pap. 70.31 (*0-07-015794-4*) McGraw.

Nation of Nations: A Narrative History of the American Republic, 2 vols., 1. 2nd ed. James W. Davidson et al. LC 93-30481. (C). 1994. pap. 42.50 (*0-07-015635-2*) McGraw.

Nation of Nations: A Narrative History of the American Republic, 2 vols., Vol. 2. 2nd ed. James W. Davidson et al. LC 93-30481. (C). 1994. text. write for info. (*0-07-015639-5*) McGraw.

***Nation of Nations: With Map Excercises, Vol. 2.** 4th ed. (C). 2000. pap. 18.13 (*0-07-231505-9*) McGraw.

Nation of Nations Vol. 1: A Concise Narrative of the American Republic, Vol. 1. James W. Davidson et al. LC 95-13161. 1104p. (C). 1995. pap. 39.69 (*0-07-015741-3*) McGraw.

Nation of Nations Vol. 1: A Concise Narrative of the American Republic, Vol. 1. James W. Davidson et al. LC 95-13161. 1070p. (C). 1995. 46.25 (*0-07-015738-3*) McGraw.

Nation of Nations Vol. 1: A Concise Narrative of the American Republic, Vol. 1. abr. ed. James W. Davidson. LC 95-13161. 560p. (C). 1995. pap. 25.94 (*0-07-015739-1*) McGraw.

Nation of Nations, a Concise Narrative of the American Republic: A Concise Narrative of the American Republic. 2nd ed. James W. Davidson et al. LC 98-21631. 1120p. 1999. pap. 31.00 (*0-07-303375-8*, McGrw-H College) McGrw-H Hghr Educ.

Nation of Newcomers. J. Joseph Huthmacher. 17.95 (*0-88411-651-4*) Amereon Ltd.

Nation of Nothing but Poetry: Supplementary Poems. Charles Olson. LC 88-36879. 226p. (Orig.). (C). 1989. pap. 12.50 (*0-87685-750-0*) Black Sparrow.

Nation of Oceans. Michael Weber & Richard Tinney. (Illus.). 95p. 1986. pap. 8.95 (*0-9615294-1-5*) Ctr Env Educ.

Nation of Opportunity: Realizing the Promise of the Information Superhighway. (Illus.). 107p. (Orig.). (C). 1996. pap. text 30.00 (*0-7881-3180-X*) DIANE Pub.

Nation of Opportunity: Realizing the Promise of the Information Superhighway. (Orig.). 1997. lib. bdg. 250.95 (*0-8490-6183-0*); lib. bdg. 250.95 (*0-8490-7752-4*) Gordon Pr.

Nation of Opportunity: Realizing the Promise of the Information Superhighway. 107p. 1996. pap. 8.00 (*0-16-060847-3*) USGPO.

Nation of Peoples: A Sourcebook on America's Multicultural Heritage. Ed. by Elliott Robert Barkan. LC 98-41061. 600p. 1999. lib. bdg. 99.50 (*0-313-29961-7*, Greenwood Pr) Greenwood.

Nation of Poets: Poetry from Nicaraguan Workshops. Tr. by Kent Johnson. (Illus.). 118p. (Orig.). 1986. pap. 5.95 (*0-931122-40-6*) West End.

Nation of Provincials: The German Idea of Heimat. Celia Applegate. LC 89-20522. 273p. 1990. 55.00 (*0-520-06394-5*, Pub. by U CA Pr) Cal Prin Full Svc.

Nation of Rogues? Crime, Law & Punishment in Colonial Australia. Ed. by David Philips & Susanne Davies. 224p. 1994. pap. 24.95 (*0-522-84601-7*, Pub. by Melbourne Univ Pr) Paul & Co Pubs.

Nation of Shopkeepers. Bill Evans & Andrew Lawson. 128p. 1994. per. 14.95 (*0-85965-165-7*, Pub. by Plexus) Publishers Group.

Nation of Steel: The Making of Modern America. Thomas J. Misa. LC 94-38681. (Studies in the History of Technology). (Illus.). 392p. 1995. text 49.95 (*0-8018-4967-5*) Johns Hopkins.

Nation of Steel: The Making of Modern America, 1865-1925. Thomas J. Misa. (Johns Hopkins Studies in the History of Technology). (Illus.). 400p. 1998. pap. text 22.50 (*0-8018-6052-0*) Johns Hopkins.

Nation of Strangers. large type ed. Vicki Goldberg & Arthur Ollman. LC 95-76802. (Points of Entry Ser.). (Illus.). 96p. (C). 1995. pap. 24.95 (*1-878062-03-4*) Mus Photo Arts.

Nation of Tzaddikim: Tales of Great Men Based on Pirkei Avos, Vol. 2. G. Sofer. 232p. 1992. 12.95 (*0-944070-47-7*) Targum Pr.

Nation of Victims: The Decay of the American Character. Charles J. Sykes. 304p. 1993. pap. 13.95 (*0-312-09882-0*) St Martin.

Nation on Trial. Jim Dietz. (Illus.). 64p. Date not set. pap. 20.00 (*0-9658694-0-7*) Jolly Roger.

Nation on Trial: Penyberth 1936. Dafydd Jenkins. Tr. by Ann Corkett from WEL. 200p. 1996. 29.95 (*1-86057-001-1*, Pub. by Welsh Acad) Intl Spec Bk.

Nation on Trial: The Goldhagen Thesis & Historical Truth. Norman G. Finkelstein. LC 97-42632. 176p. 1998. 22.95 (*0-8050-5871-0*) H Holt & Co.

Nation on Trial: The Goldhagen Thesis & Historical Truth. Norman G. Finkelstein & Ruth Bettina Birn. LC 97-42632. 176p. 1998. pap. 12.95 (*0-8050-5872-9*, Owl) H Holt & Co.

Nation or Empire? The Debate over American Foreign Policy. Robert W. Tucker. LC 68-9700. (Washington Center of Foreign Policy Research, Studies in International Affairs: Vol. 10). 170p. reprint ed. pap. 52.70 (*0-608-06115-8*, 206644800008) Bks Demand.

Nation Pays Again: The Demise of The Milwaukee Road, 1928-1986. 3rd ed. Thomas H. Ploss. 214p. (C). 1991. 40.00 (*0-9613788-1-6*) T M Ploss.

Nation Reacts to AIDS: A Report from 6 Cities. John Doble. 77p. (Orig.). 1988. pap. 11.50 (*1-889483-28-1*) Public Agenda.

Nation Reconstructed: A Quest for the Cities That Can Be. Ed. by Roger D. Hart & Sheryl L. Cooley. (Illus.). 306p. 1997. 40.00 (*0-87389-409-X*, H0948) ASQ Qual Pr.

Nation Reunited see **Civil War Series**

Nation Reunited. Richard W. Murphy & Time-Life Books Editors. Ed. by Thomas Flaherty. 176p. 1987. lib. bdg. 25.93 (*0-8094-4793-2*) Time-Life.

Nation So Conceived: Reflections on the History of America from Its Early Visions to Its Present Power. Reinhold Niebuhr & Alan Heimert. LC 83-10708. 155p. 1983. reprint ed. lib. bdg. 39.75 (*0-313-23866-9*, NINA, Greenwood Pr) Greenwood.

Nation State: The Neglected Dimension of Class. Carolyn Vogler. 180p. 1985. pap. 41.95 (*0-566-00876-9*) Ashgate Pub Co.

Nation-State & Global Order: A Historical Introduction to Contemporary Politics. Walter C. Opello, Jr. & Stephen J. Rosow. LC 98-28937. 290p. 1999. pap. 19.95 (*1-55587-832-6*) L Rienner.

Nation, State & Integration in the Arab World, 4 vols., Set. Ed. by Giacomo Luciani & Ghassan Salame. 300p. 1988. lib. bdg. 192.50 (*0-317-64358-4*, Pub. by C Helm) Routldge.

Nation, State & Integration in the Arab World: Beyond Coercion - The Durability of the Arab State, 4 vols. Adeed Kawisha et al. 320p. 1987. lib. bdg. 192.50 (*0-7099-4149-8*, Pub. by C Helm) Routldge.

Nation, State & Integration in the Arab World: The Foundation of the Arab State, Vol. I. Ghassan Salame. Ed. by Giacomo Luciani. 272p. (C). 1987. text 90.00 (*0-7099-4143-9*, Pub. by C Helm) Routldge.

Nation, State & Integration in the Arab World Vol. 2: The Rentier State. Gazen Bebuawu & Giacomo Luciani. 256p. 1987. lib. bdg. 57.50 (*0-7099-4144-7*, Pub. by C Helm) Routldge.

Nation, State & Integration in the Arab World Vol. 4: The Politics of Arab Integration. Ed. by Giacomo Luciani et al. 300p. (C). 1988. text 90.00 (*0-7099-4148-X*, Pub. by C Helm) Routldge.

Nation, State & Its Sexual Dissidents. Ed. by David Murray & Richard Handler. 131p. 1996. pap. text 12.00 (*2-88449-242-9*) Gordon & Breach.

Nation State in a Global/Information Era: Policy Challenges. Ed. by Thomas J. Courchene. 375p. 1997. text 55.00 (*0-88911-766-7*, Pub. by McG-Queens Univ Pr); pap. text 24.95 (*0-88911-770-5*, Pub. by McG-Queens Univ Pr) CUP Services.

***Nation-States & Money: Past, Present & Future of National Currencies.** Ed. by Emily Gilbert & Eric Helleiner. LC 99-32332. 240p. (C). 1999. text. write for info. (*0-415-18926-8*) Routledge.

Nation Takes Shape, 1789-1837. Marcus Cunliffe. LC 59-5770. (Chicago History of American Civilization Ser.). 231p. 1960. pap. text 16.00 (*0-226-12667-6*, CHAC3) U Ch Pr.

***Nation, the Law & the King, Reform Politics in England, 1789-1799, Vols. 1 & 2.** Jenny Graham. LC 99-40974. 1422p. 1999. 115.00 (*0-7618-1484-1*) U Pr of Amer.

Nation to Nation: Aboriginal Sovereignty & the Future of Canada. Ed. by Diane Englestad & John Bird. 256p. (Orig.). 1992. pap. 17.95 (*0-88784-533-9*, Pub. by Hse of Anansi Pr) Genl Dist Srvs.

Nation Torn: The Story of How the Civil War Began. Delia Ray. (Illus.). 112p. (YA). (gr. 5 up). 1996. pap. 9.99 (*0-14-038105-8*, PuffinBks) Peng Put Young Read.

Nation Torn, the Story of How the Civil War Began. Delia Ray. LC 90-5533. (Young Readers' History of the Civil War Ser.). (J). 1996. 12.19 (*0-606-09676-0*, Pub. by Turtleback) Demco.

***Nation Transformed by Information: How It Has Shaped the United States from Colonial Times to the Present.** Alfred Dupont Chandler. LC 99-49438. 368p. 2000. 35.00 (*0-19-512701-3*) OUP.

***Nation Transplanted: Collected Poems.** Emil Jacob. Ed. by Christopher Thorton. LC 99-55332. 72p. 2000. pap. 14.95 (*0-7734-2776-7*, Mellen Poetry Pr) E Mellen.

***Nation Und Sprache: Die Diskussion Ihres Verhaltnisses in Geschichte Und Gegenwart.** Herausgegeben von Andreas Gardt. 1999. 87.00 (*3-11-014841-2*) De Gruyter.

***Nation under God? Essays on the Fate of Religion in American Public Life.** Ed. by R. Bruce Douglass & Joshua Mitchell. 290p. 2000. 63.00 (*0-7425-0750-5*, Pub. by AltaMira Pr) Rowman.

***Nation under God? Essays on the Fate of Religion in American Public Life.** Ed. by R. Bruce Douglass & Joshua Mitchell. 290p. 2000. pap. 22.95 (*0-7425-0751-3*) Rowman.

Nation under Lawyers. Mary Ann Glendon. (Illus.). 352p. 1996. pap. 14.95 (*0-674-60138-6*) HUP.

Nation United, 1780-1850. Stuart A. Kallen. Ed. by Rosemary Walner. LC 90-82610. (Building of a Nation Ser.). (Illus.). 64p. (J). (gr. 4). 1990. lib. bdg. 13.98 (*0-939179-89-X*) ABDO Pub Co.

Nation Within: The Story of America's Annexation of the Nation of Hawaii. Tom Coffman. LC 98-71420. 345p. 1998. pap. 20.00 (*1-892122-00-6*, 1) Epicenter.

Nation Within a Nation: Amiri Baraka (LeRoi Jones) & Black Power Politics. Komozi Woodard. LC 98-22833. (Illus.). 352p. 1999. pap. 17.95 (*0-8078-4761-5*); lib. bdg. 45.00 (*0-8078-2457-7*) U of NC Pr.

Nation Within a Nation: Dependency & the Cree. Marie-Anik Gagne. 160p. 1995. 48.99 (*1-55164-013-9*, Pub. by Black Rose); pap. 19.99 (*1-55164-012-0*, Pub. by Black Rose) Consort Bk Sales.

Nation Work: Asian Nationalisms since 1850. Ed. by Timothy Brook & Andre Schmid. LC 99-6574. 280p. 2000. text 49.50 (*0-472-11032-2*, 11032) U of Mich Pr.

National see **Greek Museums**

National. Incl. How. 5.00 (*0-685-69206-X*) OUP.

National: The Theatre & Its Work 1963-97. Simon Callow. (Nick Hern Books, Drama Classics). 1998. pap. 26.95 (*1-85459-323-4*, Pub. by N Hern Bks) Theatre Comm.

National Aboriginal & Torres Strait Islander Survey, 1994: Detailed Findings. Richard Madden & Australian Bureau of Statistics Staff. LC 98-180477. vi, 103 p. 1995. write for info. (*0-642-20735-6*) Aust Inst Criminology.

National Academies & the Progress of Research. George E. Hale. Ed. by I. Bernard Cohen. LC 79-7965. (Three Centuries of Science in America Ser.). 1980. reprint ed. lib. bdg. 17.95 (*0-405-12546-1*) Ayer.

National Academy of Design Exhibition Record, 1861-1900. Ed. by Maria K. Naylor. 1075p. 1973. 110.00 (*0-87920-055-3*) Kennedy Gall.

National Academy of Sciences: The First Hundred Years, 1863-1963. National Academy of Sciences Staff. 694p. 1978. text 39.95 (*0-309-02518-4*) Natl Acad Pr.

National Academy of Western Art: 13th Annual Exhibition. Ed. by Sara Dobberteen. (Illus.). 93p. 1985. pap. 15.00 (*0-932154-16-6*) Natl Cowboy Hall of Fame.

National Academy of Western Art: 7th Annual Exhibition. (Illus.). 88p. 1979. pap. 15.00 (*0-932154-03-4*) Natl Cowboy Hall of Fame.

National Account Marketing Handbook. Ed. by Robert S. Rogers & V. B. Chamberlain. LC 80-25435. 299p. reprint ed. pap. 92.70 (*0-608-15005-3*, 205608900047) Bks Demand.

***National Accounting & Capital.** John M. Hartwick. LC 99-16006. 232p. 2000. 490.00 (*1-84064-206-8*) E Elgar.

***National Accounting & Economic Policy: The United States & the Un Systems.** Nancy D. Ruggles & Richard Ruggles. LC 99-17050. 576p. 1999. 115.00 (*1-85898-992-2*) E Elgar.

National Accounts Vol. I: Main Aggregates, 1960-1995. OECD Staff. 166p. (Orig.). 1997. pap. 43.00 (*92-64-05258-5*, 30-97-02-3, Pub. by Org for Econ) OECD.

National Accounts Vol. I: Main Aggregates, 1960-1996. OECD Staff. 180p. 1998. pap. 38.00 (*92-64-05550-9*, 30-98-01-3-P, Pub. by Org for Econ) OECD.

***National Accounts Vol. 1: Main Aggregates, 1960-1997 (1999 Edition)** OECD Staff. 180p. 1999. pap. 53.00 (*92-64-05840-0*, 30 1999 01 3 P, Pub. by Org for Econ) OECD.

National Accounts Vol. II: Detailed Tables, 1984-1996. OECD Staff. 676p. 1998. pap. 142.00 (*92-64-05770-6*, 30 98 05 3 P, Pub. by European Conference Ministers Transp) OECD.

National Accounts & the Environment. Ed. by Ignazio Musu & Domenico Siniscalco. LC 95-38220. (FEEM/Kluwer International Series on Economics, Energy & Environment: Vol. 6). 300p. (C). 1996. lib. bdg. 136.00 (*0-7923-3741-7*) Kluwer Academic.

National Accounts ESA - Aggregates, 1970-1993. Eurostat Staff. 227p. 1995. pap. 20.00 (*92-827-4007-2*, CA-87-95-2963AC, Pub. by Comm Europ Commun) Bernan Associates.

National Accounts ESA - Aggregates 1970-1995. 257p. 1997. pap. 25.00 (*92-827-9788-0*, CA03-97-272-3AC, Pub. by Comm Europ Commun) Bernan Associates.

National Accounts ESA - Aggregates 1970-1994. Eurostat Staff. 257p. 1996. pap. 25.00 (*92-827-6756-6*, CA94-96-154-3AC, Pub. by Comm Europ Commun) Bernan Associates.

National Accounts ESA - Detailed Tables by Branch, 1970-1994. (Illus.). 173p. 1996. pap. 35.00 (*92-827-8192-5*, CA97-96-233-3AC, Pub. by Comm Europ Commun) Bernan Associates.

National Accounts ESA - Detailed Tables by Branch, 1970-1995. OECD Staff. (E. C. Non Subscription Comp. Multilingual En/Fr Ser.: Vol. 81411000). 173p. 1997. pap. 50.00 (*92-828-1510-2*, CA-08-97-3473AC, Pub. by Comm Europ Commun) Bernan Associates.

National Accounts ESA - Detailed Tables by Sector, 1980-1995. Eurostat Staff. (E. C. Non Subscription Comp. Multilingual En/Fr Ser.: Vol. 81411000). 903p. 1997. pap. 90.00 (*92-828-1530-7*, CA-07-97-668-3A, Pub. by Comm Europ Commun) Bernan Associates.

National Accounts for Bulgaria: Sources, Methods & Estimates. OECD Staff & Bulgarian National Statistical Institute Staff. LC 96-181868. 186p. (Orig.). 1996. pap. 52.00 (*92-64-14819-1*, Pub. by Org for Econ) OECD.

N

An Asterisk (*) at the beginning of an entry indicates that the title is appearing for the first time.

***National Accounts of OECD Countries Vol. 1: Main Aggregates, 1988-1998.** OECD Staff. 316p. 2000. pap. 71.00 (*92-64-05891-5*, 30 2000 03 3 P, Pub. by Org for Econ) OECD.

National Accounts of OECD Countries Vol. II: Detailed Tables 1983-1995. 668p. 1997. pap. 132.00 (*92-64-05532-0*, 30-97-03-3, Pub. by Org for Econ) OECD.

National Accounts Statistics: Analysis of Main Aggregates. 469p. 1989. 45.00 (*92-1-161307-8*) UN.

National Accounts Statistics: Analysis of Main Aggregates, 1982. 565p. 1985. pap. 45.00 (*92-1-161215-2*, E.85.XVII.4) UN.

National Accounts Statistics: Analysis of Main Aggregates, 1983-1984. 401p. 1987. 45.00 (*92-1-161257-8*, E.86.XVII.4) UN.

National Accounts Statistics: Analysis of Main Aggregates, 1985. 420p. 1987. pap. 45.00 (*92-1-161279-9*, E.87.XVII.11) UN.

National Accounts Statistics: Analysis of Main Aggregates, 1987. 30th ed. 280p. 1990. 50.00 (*92-1-161316-7*, 90.XVII.8) UN.

National Accounts Statistics: Analysis of Main Aggregates: 1988-1989. 277p. 1991. 125.00 (*92-1-161341-8*, E.91.XVII.17) UN.

National Accounts Statistics: Compendium of Income Distribution Statistics. (Statistical Papers, Series M: Ser. M, No. 79). 552p. 1985. 45.00 (*92-1-161253-5*, E.85.XVIII.6) UN.

National Accounts Statistics: Government Accounts & Tables, 1982. 393p. 1986. 35.00 (*92-1-161216-0*, E.85.XVII.5) UN.

National Accounts Statistics: Government Accounts & Tables, 1983. 398p. 1986. 35.00 (*92-1-161258-6*, E.86.XVII.5) UN.

National Accounts Statistics: Main Aggregates & Detailed Tables. 1708p. 1982. 85.00 (*92-1-161214-4*) UN.

National Accounts Statistics: Main Aggregates & Detailed Tables. 2051p. 1994. 135.00 (*92-1-161392-2*) UN.

***National Accounts Statistics: Main Aggregates & Detailed Tables.** 700p. 1999. 160.00 (*92-1-161413-9*) UN.

National Accounts Statistics: Main Aggregates & detailed Tables, 1983. 1731p. 1986. 85.00 (*92-1-161255-1*, E.86.XVII.3) UN.

N

National Accounts Statistics: Main Aggregates & Detailed Tables, 1984. 1784p. 1987. 85.00 (*92-1-161278-0*, E.86.XVII26) UN.

National Accounts Statistics: Main Aggregates & Detailed Tables, 1985. 1495p. 1987. pap. 85.00 (*92-1-161286-1*, E.87.XVII.10) UN.

National Accounts Statistics: Main Aggregates & Detailed Tables, 1987. United Nations Staff. 3429p. 1990. 100.00 (*92-1-161312-4*) UN.

National Accounts Statistics: Main Aggregates & Tables. 1988. 100.00 (*92-1-161325-6*, 90.XVII.18) UN.

National Accounts Statistics: Study of Input-Output Tables, 1970-1980. 321p. 1986. 36.00 (*92-1-161268-3*, 86.XVII.15) UN.

National Accounts Statistics Pts. 1-2: Main Aggregates & Detailed Tables, 1989, 2 vols. 1991. 125.00 (*92-1-161339-6*, E.91.XVII.16) UN.

National Accounts Statistics Pts. 1 & 2: Main Aggregates & Detailed Tables, 2 vols. 2141p. 125.00 (*92-1-161351-5*); 135.00 (*92-1-161373-6*, E.95.XVII.4); 135.00 (*92-1-161381-7*) UN.

National Accounts Statistics Pts. 1 & 2: Main Aggregates & Detailed Tables. United Nations. Statistics Division. 2122p. 125.00 (*92-1-161361-2*) UN.

National Accounts Statistics, 1983 Vol. 3: Government Accounts & Tables. 1986. 35.00 (*0-685-31367-0*) Taylor & Francis.

National Accounts Statistics, 1986, Pts. 1 & 2. 1989. pap. 100.00 (*92-1-161305-1*, E.89.XVII.7) UN.

National Accounts Studies of the ESCWA Region. 202p. 26.00 (*92-1-128198-9*) UN.

National Accounts Studies of the ESCWA Region. 200p. 1991. 42.00 (*92-1-128116-4*, 90.II.L.6) UN.

National Accounts Studies of the ESCWA Region. LC 96-482. (Bulletin Ser.: No. 16). 186p. 1997. pap. 45.00 (*92-1-128172-5*) UN.

National Accounts Studies of the ESCWA Region. Economic & Social Commission for Western Asia Staf. LC 97-477. (Bulletin Ser.: No. 17). 188p. 1997. pap. 45.00 (*92-1-128184-9*, DS101) UN.

National Accounts Studies of the ESCWA Region, No. 15. 200p. 45.00 (*92-1-128152-0*) UN.

National Accounts Studies of the ESCWA Region No. 13, No. 13. 189p. 45.00 (*92-1-128139-3*, B.94.II.L.3) UN.

National Action Conference for Civil Rights: April 19-20, 1942. National Federation for Constitutional Liberties Staff. 40p. 1996. pap. 10.00 (*0-88092-196-X*, 196X, Kav Bks) Royal Fireworks.

National Administrative Systems: Selected Readings. Ed. by Dean L. Yarwood. LC 70-159287. 414p. reprint ed. pap. 128.40 (*0-608-30047-0*, 201187900079) Bks Demand.

National Admissions to Substance Abuse Treatment Services: The Treatment Episode Data Set, 1992-1995. Barbara Ray et al. (Illus.). 91p. (C). 1998. pap. text 25.00 (*0-7881-4907-5*) DIANE Pub.

National Adolescent Student Health Survey. American School Health Association Staff et al. (Illus.). 178p. (Orig.). 1989. pap. 5.00 (*0-88314-453-0*, A4530) AAHPERD.

National Adolescent Student Health Survey - Survey Replication. AAHE Staff et al. 71p. (Orig.). Date not set. pap. 7.00 (*0-88314-481-6*, A4816) AAHPERD.

National Adoption Directory. 1992. lib. bdg. 275.00 (*0-8490-5540-7*) Gordon Pr.

National Advisory Council on Migrant Health: 1993 Recommendations. Ed. by Antonio E. Duran. (Illus.). 93p. (C). 1999. reprint ed. pap. text 20.00 (*0-7881-7617-X*) DIANE Pub.

National Aerospace & Electronics Conference - NAECON, 1997. IEEE, Aerospace & Electronic Systems Society Staff. Ed. by Institute of Electrical & Electronics Engineers, I. LC 79-640977. 1000p. 1997. pap. text. write for info. (*0-7803-3725-5*, 97CH36015); lib. bdg. write for info. (*0-7803-3726-3*, 97CB36015); fiche. write for info. (*0-7803-3727-1*, 97CM36015) Inst Electrical.

National Aerospace Standards Set, 8 vols., Set. 1993. ring bd. 875.00 (*0-912702-84-2*) Global Eng Doc.

National Agenda for Geriatric Education: White Papers. Ed. by Susan M. Klein. LC 97-4390. (Illus.). 232p. 1997. 42.95 (*0-8261-9970-4*) Springer Pub.

National Agenda for the Eighties. President's Commission. (Illus.). 225p. 1982. pap. 5.95 (*0-13-609529-1*) P-H.

National Agenda in Materials Science & Engineering - Implementing the MS & E Report, Vol. NMSE. Ed. by R. Abbaschian et al. 52p. 1991. pap. 15.00 (*0-614-95846-6*) Materials Res.

National Aids Strategy: Appendices, 1997. Government Printing Office Staff. LC 96-231309. 124p. 1996. per. 10.00 (*0-16-048775-7*) USGPO.

National AIDS Strategy, 1997. Government Printing Office Staff. LC 96-230963. 40p. 1996. pap. 6.00 (*0-16-048925-3*) USGPO.

National Air & Space Museum. 2nd rev. ed. C. D. Bryan. (Illus.). 1988. 75.00 (*0-8109-1380-1*) Abrams.

National Air & Space Museum: A Visit in Pictures. Donald S. Lopez. (Illus.). 64p. 1990. 6.99 (*0-517-69514-6*) Random Hse Value.

National Air & Space Museum: A Visit in Pictures. Donald S. Lopez. LC 88-36586. (Illus.). 64p. 1989. 6.98 (*0-87474-710-4*) Smithsonian.

National Air Pollutant Emission Trends, 1990-1995. Sharon V. Nizich et al. (Illus.). 64p. (C). 1998. pap. text 20.00 (*0-7881-7438-X*) DIANE Pub.

National Air Quality & Emissions Trends Report, 1995. Willis Beal. (Illus.). 168p. (C). 1998. pap. text 35.00 (*0-7881-4554-1*) DIANE Pub.

***National Airport Terminal.** Oscar Riera Ojeda. (Single Building Ser.). (Illus.). 120p. 2000. pap. 25.00 (*1-56496-545-7*) Rockport Pubs.

National Airspace System: FAA Has Implemented Some Free Flight Initiatives, but Challenges Remain. John H. Anderson. (Illus.). 76p. 1999. text 20.00 (*0-7881-7914-4*) DIANE Pub.

National Ambulatory Medical Care. 1995. lib. bdg. 255.75 (*0-8490-7432-0*) Gordon Pr.

***National Ambulatory Medical Care Survey: 1993.** Cheryl Nelson. 105p. 1998. per. 8.50 (*0-16-061487-2*) USGPO.

***National Ambulatory Medical Care Survey: 1995- 96 Summary.** Susan M. Schappert. 128p. 1999. per. 12.00 (*0-16-050178-4*) USGPO.

National Analysis of Housing Affordability, Adequacy, & Availability: A Framework for Local Housing Strategies. 75p. (Orig.). (C). 1994. pap. text 30.00 (*0-7881-1013-6*) DIANE Pub.

National & Ethnic Identities: Tension & Harmony. Jaroslav Hroch. LC 98-44464. 1998. pap. 17.50 (*1-56518-113-1*) Coun Res Values.

National & Federal Legal Employment Report. Ed. by Richard L. Hermann & Linda P. Sutherland. 416p. 1979. 135.00 (*0-614-04283-6*) Federal Reports Inc.

National & International Bibliographic Databases: Trends & Prospects. Ed. & Intro. by Michael Carpenter. LC 88-15285. (Cataloging & Classification Quarterly Ser.: Vol. 8, Nos. 3 & 4). (Illus.). 277p. 1988. text 49.95 (*0-86656-749-6*) Haworth Pr.

National & International Black Journalist Directory, 1997-98: Print & Broadcast. Ed. by Grace Adams. (Illus.). (Orig.). 1997. pap. 24.95 (*1-877807-75-3*) Grace Pub MI.

***National & International Conflicts, 1945-1995: New Empirical & Theoretical Approaches.** Frank R. Pfetsch & Christoph Rohloff. LC 99-40347. (Advances in International Relations & Politics Ser.). 272p. 2000. 110.00 (*0-415-22344-X*) Routledge.

National & International Law Enforcement Databases, Vol. 2940. Ed. by George Works. LC 96-69890. 188p. 1997. 56.00 (*0-8194-2342-4*) SPIE.

National & International Politics in the Middle East: Essays in Honour of Elie Kedourie. Ed. by Edward Ingram. 304p. 1986. 39.50 (*0-7146-3278-3*, Pub. by F Cass Pubs) Intl Spec Bk.

National & International Records Retention Standards. 2nd ed. Fred E. Guymon. 750p. 1990. ring bd. 225.00 (*0-9617053-1-0*) Eastwood.

***National & International Security.** Sheehan. 488p. 2000. 149.95 (*1-85521-862-3*) Ashgate Pub Co.

National & International Standardization of Radiation Dosimetry, 2 vols. IAEA Staff. (Proceedings Ser.). 1979. pap. 110.00 (*92-0-010478-9*, ISP471-1, Pub. by IAEA); pap. 80.00 (*92-0-010578-5*, ISP471-2, Pub. by IAEA) Bernan Associates.

National & Nationalism since 1780: Programme, Myth, Reality. 2nd ed. Eric J. Hobsbawm. LC 92-14949. (Canto Book Ser.). 214p. (C). 1992. pap. 12.95 (*0-521-43961-2*) Cambridge U Pr.

***National & Permanent: The Federal Organization of the Liberal Party of Australia, 1944-1965.** Ian Hancock. 350p. 2000. 49.95 (*0-522-84873-7*, Pub. by Melbourne Univ Pr) Paul & Co Pubs.

National & Regional Atlases A Bibliographical Survey. Stams. pap. 48.25 (*90-70310-07-4*, Pergamon Pr) Elsevier.

National & Regional Self-Sufficiency Goals: Implications for International Agriculture. Ed. by Fred J. Ruppel & Earl D. Kellogg. LC 90-25593. 254p. 1991. lib. bdg. 45.00 (*1-55587-152-6*) L Rienner.

National & Regional Tourism. World Tourism Organization Staff & Edward Inskeep. (ITBP Textbooks Ser.). 1994. write for info. (*1-86152-579-6*, Pub. by ITBP) Thomson Learn.

National & Regional Tourism Planning: Methodologies & Case Studies. Edward Inskeep. LC 93-45990. (World Tourism Organization Ser.). (Illus.). 252p. (C). 1994. pap. 32.95 (*0-415-10990-6*, B4250) Thomson Learn.

National & Religious Song Reader: Patriotic, Traditional & Sacred Songs from Around the World. William E. Studwell. LC 96-5944. 150p. 1996. 39.95 (*0-7890-0099-7*); pap. 14.95 (*1-56023-892-5*, Harrington Park) Haworth Pr.

National & Social Problems. Frederic Harrison. LC 76-142639. (Essay Index Reprint Ser.). 1977. 26.95 (*0-8369-2051-1*) Ayer.

National & State Banks: A Study of Their Origins. Leonard C. Helderman. Ed. by Stuart Bruchey. LC 80-1149. (Rise of Commercial Banking Ser.). 1981. reprint ed. lib. bdg. 18.95 (*0-405-13652-8*) Ayer.

National & State Population Estimates, 1990 to 1994. Edwin Byerly & Kevin Deardoff. (Illus.). 86p. 1997. reprint ed. pap. text 30.00 (*0-7881-3845-6*) DIANE Pub.

National & University Library, Ljubljana. Jose Plecnik & Mel Gooding. (Architecture in Detail Ser.). (Illus.). 1997. pap. 29.95 (*0-7148-2938-2*, Pub. by Phaidon Press) Phaidon Pr.

National Anthem. Patricia R. Quiri. LC 97-10970. (True Bks.). (Illus.). 48p. (J). (gr. k-4). 1998. lib. bdg. 21.00 (*0-516-20625-7*) Childrens.

National Anthem. Patricia R. Quiri. Ed. by Shari Joffe. (True Bks). (Illus.). 48p. (J). 1998. pap. 6.95 (*0-516-26382-X*) Childrens.

National Anthem of Greece: 158 Verses. Dionysios Solomos. (GRE., Illus.). 48p. 1997. pap. 10.00 (*1-885778-30-9*) Seaburn.

National Anthems, Bk. 1. Kari H. Guthrie. (Illus.). 36p. (Orig.). (YA). (gr. 2-8). 1992. pap. 6.95 (*0-9631333-0-6*) Hi I Que Pub.

National Anthems, Bk. 2. Kari H. Guthrie. (Illus.). 49p. (Orig.). 1993. pap. 6.95 (*0-9631333-1-4*) Hi I Que Pub.

National Anthems, Bk. 3. Kari H. Guthrie. (Illus.). 41p. (Orig.). 1993. pap. 6.95 (*0-9631333-2-2*) Hi I Que Pub.

National Anthems, Bk. 4. Kari H. Guthrie. (Illus.). 38p. (Orig.). 1993. pap. 6.95 (*0-9631333-3-0*) Hi I Que Pub.

National Anthems: The Americas Set, 3 vols. Kari H. Guthrie. Tr. by Dennis McKelvey. Incl. Bk. 7. (Illus.). 54p. (Orig.). (J). (gr. 4-9). 1995. pap. 8.95 (*0-9631333-5-7*); Bk. 8. (Illus.). 50p. (Orig.). (J). (gr. 4-9). 1995. pap. 8.95 (*0-9631333-6-5*); Bk. 9. (Illus.). 74p. (Orig.). (J). (gr. 4-9). 1995. pap. 8.95 (*0-9631333-7-3*); 1995. 24.95 (*0-9631333-8-1*) Hi I Que Pub.

National Anthems: Western & Central Europe, 4 bks., Set. Kari H. Guthrie. (Europe Ser.). (Illus.). 163p. (Orig.). (J). (gr. 4-9). 1993. pap. 24.95 (*0-9631333-4-9*) Hi I Que Pub.

National Anthems for Easy Guitar. 80p. 1996. pap. 12.95 (*0-7935-6639-8*) H Leonard.

National Anthems from Around the World. 104p. 1996. otabind 3.95 (*0-7935-6961-3*) H Leonard.

National Anthems from Around the World. 104p. 1996. 34.95 (*0-7935-6978-8*) H Leonard.

National Anthems of the World. 9th ed. W. L. Reed. Ed. by M. J. Bristow. (Illus.). 608p. 1997. 95.00 (*0-304-34925-9*, Pub. by Cassell) Sterling.

***National Arbitration Laws.** Ed. by Hans Smit & Vratislav Pechota. (Smit's Guides to International Arbitration Ser.: Unit 6). 3100p. 1999. ring bd. write for info. (*1-57823-015-2*) Juris Pubng.

National Architect. George E. Woodward. LC 75-23066. (Architecture & Decorative Art Ser.). (Illus.). 48p. 1975. reprint ed. lib. bdg. 49.50 (*0-306-70748-9*) Da Capo.

National Archives: America's Ministry of Documents, 1934-1968. Donald R. McCoy. LC 78-2314. 447p. reprint ed. pap. 138.60 (*0-7837-3757-2*, 204357400010) Bks Demand.

National Archives Microfilm Resources for Research: A Comprehensive Catalog. rev. ed. National Archives & Records Administration Staff. LC 85-15242. 136p. 1996. pap. 5.00 (*0-911333-34-7*, 200033) National Archives & Recs.

National Archives of Canada, Ottawa & Canadian Jewish Congress, Montreal. Ed. by Harold Troper & Paula Draper. LC 89-16915. (Archives of the Holocaust Ser.: Vol. 15). 512p. 1991. text 138.00 (*0-8240-5497-0*) Garland.

National Art Education Association: Our History Celebrating 50 Years, 1947-1997. Ed. by John Michael. (Illus.). 254p. 1997. pap. 25.00 (*1-890160-00-8*, 267) Natl Art Ed.

National Art Library Catalog of the Victoria & Albert Museum Author Catalog. Victoria & Albert Museum Staff. 1980. 1410.00 (*0-8161-1265-7*, G K Hall & Co) Mac Lib Ref.

***National Arthritis Action Plan: A Public Health Strategy.** Susan B. Toal. Ed. by Phyllis L. Moir. (Illus.). 58p. 2000. pap. text 20.00 (*0-7567-0042-6*) DIANE Pub.

National Assessment Institute Manual para el Manejo de Alimentos Saludables. Rue & Croese. (Illus.). 224p. (C). 1994. pap. text 25.95 (*0-13-135238-5*) P-H.

National Assessment of Achievement & Participation of Women in Mathematics: Final Report. Jane Armstrong. 236p. 1979. write for info. (*0-318-59921-X*, 10-MA-60) Natl Assessment.

National Assessment of College Student Learning: An Inventory f State-Level Assessment Activities, a Report of the Proceedings of the Third Study Design Workshop. Sal Corrallo. 158p. 1996. per. 13.00 (*0-16-048923-7*) USGPO.

National Assessment of Mathematics Participation in the United States: A Survival Analysis Model for Describing Students' Academic Careers. Xin Ma. LC 97-24257. 196p. 1997. text 79.95 (*0-7734-2222-6*) E Mellen.

National Assessment of Particle Removal by Filtration. Nancy E. McTigue. LC 98-8140. 1998. write for info. (*0-89867-964-8*) Am Water Wks Assn.

National Assessment of Structured Sentencing. James Austin et al. (Illus.). 138p. (Orig.). (C). 1996. pap. text 40.00 (*0-7881-3734-4*) DIANE Pub.

National Association for the Protection of the Insane & the Prevention of Insanity, 2 vols. Ed. by Gerald N. Grob. LC 78-22578. (Historical Issues in Mental Health Ser.). 1980. reprint ed. lib. bdg. 17.95 (*0-405-11930-5*) Ayer.

***National Association of Baseball Players, 1857-1870.** Marshall D. Wright. 408p. 2000. per. 45.00 (*0-7864-0779-4*) McFarland & Co.

National Association of College & University Attorneys: Report of the Annual Conference, 1961-1965, 5 vols. 60.00 (*0-8377-9193-6*, Rothman) W S Hein.

National Association of Government Deferred Compensation Administrators: A Compendium of Presentations. 78p. 1989. 20.00 (*0-685-38249-4*, C-172) Coun State Govts.

National Association of Government Deferred Compensation Administrators Survey of 457 Plans, 1989. 73p. 1990. 40.00 (*0-685-38248-6*, C-177) Coun State Govts.

National Association of Hispanic Publications Media Kit. Kirk Whisler. (Marketing Guidepost Ser.). (Illus.). 251p. (Orig.). 1997. pap. 29.95 (*1-889379-02-6*) WPR Pubng.

National Association of Private Schools for Exceptional Children Membership Directory, 1995-97. 250p. 1995. per. write for info. (*0-318-15164-2*) Natl Assoc Priv Sch.

National Association of Real Estate Appraisers National Roster. 201p. pap. 5.00 (*0-318-19539-9*) Natl Assn Real Estate.

National Association of Realtors Membership Profile, 1987. 122p. 1987. 25.00 (*0-685-26515-3*) Natl Assoc Realtors.

National Atlas of Canada. 4th rev. ed. Canada Staff. LC 76-351950. 254p. 1974. write for info. (*0-7705-1198-8*) Trans-Atl Phila.

National Atlas of Sweden, 17 vols. Ed. by Leif Wastenson. 2900p. 1996. 1650.00 (*91-87760-04-5*, Pub. by Almqvist Wiksell) Coronet Bks.

National Atlas of Sweden Vol. 7: Sea & Coast. (Illus.). 128p. 1992. 99.50 (*91-87760-16-9*) Coronet Bks.

National Audubon Society Pocket Guide: Galaxies & Other Deep-Sky Objects. Audubon Staff & Carolyn B. Mitchell. LC 94-41623. (National Audubon Society Pocket Guides). 1995. pap. 7.99 (*0-679-77996-5*) Knopf.

***National Audubon Society: Birder's Handbook.** Stephen W. Kress. LC 99-50061. (Illus.). 176p. 2000. 24.95 (*0-7894-5153-0*, D K Ink) DK Pub Inc.

National Audubon Society: Speaking for Nature: A Century of Conservation. National Audubon Society Staff. Ed. by Les Line. (Illus.). 240p. 1999. 60.00 (*0-88363-799-5*, Pub. by H L Levin) Publishers Group.

National Audubon Society Concise Birdfeeder Handbook. Robert Burton. LC 91-58218. 128p. 1997. pap. 9.95 (*0-7894-1465-1*) DK Pub Inc.

National Audubon Society Field Guide to African Wildlife. Peter Alden et al. LC 95-5543. (Illus.). 992p. 1995. 20.45 (*0-679-43234-5*) Knopf.

National Audubon Society Field Guide to California. Peter Alden & National Audubon Society Staff. LC 97-31243. 447p. 1998. 19.95 (*0-679-44678-8*) Random.

National Audubon Society Field Guide to Florida. Peter Alden & National Audubon Society Staff. LC 97-31242. 447p. 1998. 19.95 (*0-679-44677-X*) Random.

National Audubon Society Field Guide to New England. Peter Alden & National Audubon Society Staff. LC 97-31241. 448p. 1998. 19.95 (*0-679-44676-1*) Random.

National Audubon Society Field Guide to North American Birds: Eastern Region. John Bull & John Farrand, Jr. LC 94-7768. (Illus.). 800p. 1994. 19.00 (*0-679-42852-6*) Knopf.

National Audubon Society Field Guide to North American Birds: Western Region. rev. ed. Miklos D. Udvardy. LC 94-7415. (Illus.). 822p. 1994. 19.00 (*0-679-42851-8*) Knopf.

National Audubon Society Field Guide to North American Mammals. John O. Whitaker. 780p. 1996. 19.00 (*0-679-44631-1*) Knopf.

National Audubon Society Field Guide to the Mid-Atlantic States. National Audubon Society Staff. LC 98-38191. (Illus.). 448p. 1999. 19.95 (*0-679-44682-6*) Knopf.

National Audubon Society Field Guide to the Pacific Northwest. Peter Alden & National Audubon Society Staff. LC 97-31246. 448p. 1998. 19.95 (*0-679-44679-6*) Random.

National Audubon Society Field Guide to the Rocky Mountain States. National Audubon Society Staff. LC 98-38192. (Illus.). 448p. 1999. 19.95 (*0-679-44681-8*) Knopf.

National Audubon Society Field Guide to the Southeastern States: Alabama, Arkansas, Georgia, Kentucky, Lousiana, Mississippi, North Carolina, South Carolina & Tennessee. National Audubon Society Staff. LC 99-27921. 1999. 19.95 (*0-679-44683-4*) Knopf.

An Asterisk (*) at the beginning of an entry indicates that the title is appearing for the first time.

National Audubon Society Field Guide to the Southwestern States: Arizona, New Mexico, Nevada & Utah. National Audubon Society Staff. LC 99-27920. 1999. 19.95 (*0-679-44680-X*) Knopf.

National Audubon Society Field Guide to Tropical Marine Fishes of the Caribbean, Gulf of Mexico, Florida, the Bahamas & Bermuda. C. Lavett Smith & National Audubon Society Staff. LC 97-7690. (Illus.). 720p. 1997. 20.00 (*0-679-44601-X*) Knopf.

National Audubon Society First Field Guide. John L. Behler. LC 98-8332. (Illus.). 160p. (J). (gr. 3-7). 1999. 17.95 (*0-590-05467-8*); pap. 11.95 (*0-590-05487-2*) Scholastic Inc.

National Audubon Society First Field Guide. Brian Cassie & Marjorie Burns. LC 98-21855. (Illus.). 159p. (J). (gr. 3-7). 1999. 17.95 (*0-590-05472-4*); pap. 11.95 (*0-590-05490-2*) Scholastic Inc.

National Audubon Society First Field Guide: Birds. Annette Tison et al. LC 97-17989. (Illus.). 160p. (J). (gr. 3-7). 1979. 1.95 (*0-590-05446-5*) Scholastic Inc.

National Audubon Society First Field Guide: Birds. Scott Weidensaul & National Audubon Society Staff. LC 97-17989. (Illus.). 160p. (J). (gr. 3-7). 1998. vinyl bd. 10.95 (*0-590-05482-1*) Scholastic Inc.

National Audubon Society First Field Guide: Insects. Annette Tison et al. LC 97-17990. (Illus.). 160p. (J). (gr. 3-7). 1979. 1.95 (*0-590-05447-3*) Scholastic Inc.

National Audubon Society First Field Guide: Rocks & Minerals. Edward R. Ricciuti & National Audubon Society Staff. LC 97-17991. (Illus.). 160p. (J). (gr. 3-7). 1998. vinyl bd. 10.95 (*0-590-05484-8*) Scholastic Inc.

National Audubon Society First Field Guide: Rocks & Minerals. Edward R. Ricciuti & National Audubon Society Staff. LC 97-17991. (Illus.). 160p. (YA). (gr. 3-7). 1998. 17.95 (*0-590-05463-5*) Scholastic Inc.

National Audubon Society First Field Guides: Weather. National Audubon Society Staff. LC 98-2938. (Audubon Society First Field Guide Ser.). (Illus.). 160p. (J). (gr. 3-7). 1998. pap. 10.95 (*0-590-05488-0*) Scholastic Inc.

National Audubon Society Interactive CD-Rom Guide to North American Birds. National Audubon Society Staff. 1996. cd-rom 56.95 (*0-679-76016-4*) Knopf.

National Audubon Society North American Birdfeeder Handbook. rev. ed. Robert Burton. (Illus.). 224p. 1995. 24.95 (*0-7894-0337-4*, 6-70523) DK Pub Inc.

National Audubon Society the Bird Garden. Stephen W. Kress. LC 95-6748. (Illus.). 176p. 1995. 24.95 (*0-7894-0139-8*, 6-70475) DK Pub Inc.

National Auto League Touring Unit: Alabama, Georgia. H. M. Gousha Staff. 1993. pap. 0.25 (*0-671-87401-2*, H M Gousha) Prntice Hall Bks.

National Auto League Touring Unit: Alaska, Mexico, Hawaii. H. M. Gousha Staff. 1993. pap. 0.25 (*0-671-87402-0*, H M Gousha) Prntice Hall Bks.

National Auto League Touring Unit: Arizona, New Mexico. H. M. Gousha Staff. 1993. pap. 0.25 (*0-671-87403-9*, H M Gousha) Prntice Hall Bks.

National Auto League Touring Unit: Arkansas, Louisiana, Mississippi. H. M. Gousha Staff. 1993. pap. 0.25 (*0-671-87404-7*, H M Gousha) Prntice Hall Bks.

National Auto League Touring Unit: California. H. M. Gousha Staff. 1993. pap. 0.25 (*0-671-87405-5*, H M Gousha) Prntice Hall Bks.

National Auto League Touring Unit: Colorado, Utah, Nevada. H. M. Gousha Staff. 1993. pap. 0.25 (*0-671-87419-5*, H M Gousha) Prntice Hall Bks.

National Auto League Touring Unit: Delaware, Maryland, Virginia, West Virginia. H. M. Gousha Staff. 1993. pap. 0.25 (*0-671-87406-3*, H M Gousha) Prntice Hall Bks.

National Auto League Touring Unit: Florida. H. M. Gousha Staff. 1993. pap. 0.25 (*0-671-87407-1*, H M Gousha) Prntice Hall Bks.

National Auto League Touring Unit: Idaho, Montana, Wyoming. H. M. Gousha Staff. 1993. pap. 0.25 (*0-671-87408-X*, H M Gousha) Prntice Hall Bks.

National Auto League Touring Unit: Illinois, Iowa, Missouri. H. M. Gousha Staff. 1993. pap. 0.25 (*0-671-87409-8*, H M Gousha) Prntice Hall Bks.

National Auto League Touring Unit: Indiana, Michigan. H. M. Gousha Staff. 1993. pap. 0.25 (*0-671-87410-1*, H M Gousha) Prntice Hall Bks.

National Auto League Touring Unit: Kansas, Oklahoma. H. M. Gousha Staff. 1993. pap. 0.25 (*0-671-87411-X*, H M Gousha) Prntice Hall Bks.

National Auto League Touring Unit: Kentucky, Tennessee, North Carolina, South Carolina. H. M. Gousha Staff. 1993. pap. 0.25 (*0-671-87412-8*, H M Gousha) Prntice Hall Bks.

National Auto League Touring Unit: New England. H. M. Gousha Staff. 1993. pap. 0.25 (*0-671-87413-6*, H M Gousha) Prntice Hall Bks.

National Auto League Touring Unit: New York, New Jersey. H. M. Gousha Staff. 1993. pap. 0.25 (*0-671-87414-4*, H M Gousha) Prntice Hall Bks.

National Auto League Touring Unit: North Dakota, South Dakota, Minnesota, Wisconsin. H. M. Gousha Staff. 1993. pap. 0.25 (*0-671-87415-2*, H M Gousha) Prntice Hall Bks.

National Auto League Touring Unit: Ohio, Pennsylvania. H. M. Gousha Staff. 1993. pap. 0.25 (*0-671-87416-0*, H M Gousha) Prntice Hall Bks.

National Auto League Touring Unit: Oregon, Washington. H. M. Gousha Staff. 1993. pap. 0.25 (*0-671-87417-9*, H M Gousha) Prntice Hall Bks.

National Auto League Touring Unit: Texas. H. M. Gousha Staff. 1993. pap. 0.25 (*0-671-87418-7*, H M Gousha) Prntice Hall Bks.

National Automated Immigration Lookout System (NAILS) Vol. II: Inspection Report. Richard Hankinson. (Illus.). 37p. (Orig.). (C). 1995. pap. text 25.00 (*0-7881-2322-X*) DIANE Pub.

National Avenue: Of Prohibition & Politics. unabridged ed. L. L. Larson. LC 96-92516. 269p. 1997. pap. 15.00 (*0-9654307-0-7*, 1) South Shore Pr.

National Balance of the United States, 1953 to 1980. Raymond W. Goldsmith. LC 82-2746. (National Bureau of Economic Research Monographs). 234p. 1982. lib. bdg. 38.50 (*0-226-30152-4*) U Ch Pr.

National Bank Act & Its Judicial Meaning. Albert S. Bolles. Ed. by Stuart Bruchey. LC 80-1135. (Rise of Commercial Banking Ser.). 1981. reprint ed. lib. bdg. 41.95 (*0-405-13635-8*) Ayer.

National Bank Notes: A Guide with Prices. 3rd ed. (Illus.). 625p. 100.00 (*0-9656255-0-8*) Paper Money.

National Bank of Commerce of Seattle, 1889-1969: Territorial to Worldwide Banking in Eighty Years, Including the Story of the Marine Bancorporation. Elliot Marple & Bruce H. Olson. LC 72-134228. (Illus.). x, 277p. 1972. 24.95 (*0-87015-189-4*) Pacific Bks.

National Bank of Poland: The Road to Indirect Instruments, Vol. 144. LC 96-46847. (Occasional Papers). 1996. write for info. (*1-55775-602-3*) Intl Monetary.

National Bankruptcy Review Commission Report: Hearing Before the Subcommittee on Commercial & Administrative Law of the Committee on the Judiciary, House of Representatives, One Hundred Fifth Congress, First Session ... November 13, 1997. USGPO Staff. LC 98-190674. iii, 54 p. 1997. write for info. (*0-16-057079-4*) USGPO.

National Bar Journal, 1941-1952, 10 vols. 1941. 225.00 (*0-8377-9194-4*, Rothman) W S Hein.

National Benchbook on Psychiatric & Psychological Evidence & Testimony. John Parry et al. LC 99-185195. 1998. write for info. (*1-57073-581-6*) Amer Bar Assn.

National Benefits from National Labs: Meeting Tomorrow's National Technology Needs. J. Bennett Johnston et al. (CSIS Panel Reports). 97p. (Orig.). (C). 1993. pap. text 14.95 (*0-89206-224-X*) CSIS.

National Biases in French & English Drama. Seth D. Riemer. LC 90-44653. (Studies in Comparative Literature). 184p. 1990. reprint ed. 15.00 (*0-8240-5471-7*) Garland.

National Bibliography of Indian Literature, 1901-1953, 4 vols. B. S. Kesavan. Incl. Vol. 1. Assamese-Bengali-English-Gujarati. Ed. by V. Y. Kulkarni. 1978. 40.00 Vol. 2. Hindi-Jannada-Kashmiri-Malayalam. Ed. by Y. M. Mulay. 1978. 40.00 Vol. 3. Marathi-Oriya-Panjabi-Sanskrit. 1978. 40.00 1978. 150.00 (*0-685-02220-X*) Brill Academic Pubs.

National Bicycling & Walking Study: Transportation Choices for a Changing America. 1997. lib. bdg. 250.99 (*0-8490-7631-5*) Gordon Pr.

National Biodiversity Planning: Guidelines Based on Early Experiences Around the World. Kenton R. Miller & Steven M. Lanou. 160p. 1995. pap. 25.00 (*1-56973-025-3*) World Resources Inst.

National Bituminous Coal Commission Administration of the Bituminous Coal Act, 1937-1941. Ralph H. Baker. LC 78-64183. (Johns Hopkins University. Studies in the Social Sciences. Thirtieth Ser. 1912: 3). (Illus.). 360p. reprint ed. 28.50 (*0-404-61291-1*) AMS Pr.

National Black Christian Resource Directory. 176p. 1994. pap. 12.00 (*0-9638582-1-1*) Stud Ninety.

National Black Community Resource Guide: A Key to Success. Babs Ibirogba. (Orig.). reprint ed. pap. 12.00 (*1-56411-142-3*) Untd Bros & Sis.

National Black Drama Anthology: Eleven Plays from America's Leading African-American Theaters. Ed. by Woodie King, Jr. 536p. (C). 1996. pap. 18.95 (*1-55783-219-6*) Applause Theatre Bk Pubs.

National Black Health Leadership Directory: 1992 Edition. Nathaniel Wesley. 200p. 1991. 65.00 (*0-9631990-0-5*) NRW Assocs.

National Black Health Leadership Directory: 1993 Edition. Ed. by Nathaniel Wesley, Jr. 1993. write for info. (*0-9631990-1-3*) NRW Assocs.

National Black Health Leadership Directory, 1996-97. Ed. by Nathaniel Wesley, Jr. 200p. 1996. pap. 75.00 (*0-9631990-3-X*) NRW Assocs.

National Black Independent Political Party. Nan Bailey et al. 32p. pap. 5.00 (*0-87348-690-0*) Pathfinder NY.

National Black Independent Political Party: Political Insurgency or Ideological Convergence? rev. ed. Warren N. Holmes. LC 99-23966. (Studies in African American History & Culture). 184p. 1999. 48.00 (*0-8153-3092-8*) Garland.

National Black Leadership Profiles: Who's Who among America's Outstanding Leaders. Doug McNair & Wallace Y. McNair. 153p. 1994. pap. 85.00 (*0-9627600-7-2*) Wstrn Images.

National Black Sourcebook. Ed. by P. Trish Turner. (Illus.). 150p. 1996. pap. 9.95 (*0-9638582-2-X*) Stud Ninety.

National Board of Censorship (Review) of Motion Pictures, 1909-1922. Charles M. Feldman. 1977. 18.95 (*0-405-09886-3*, 11481) Ayer.

National Board Specialists: Exam Review, Pt. I. Lyndon Van Wagoner & Laura Van Wagoner. 350p. 42.00 (*0-683-30587-5*) Lppncott W & W.

National Boards Examination Review Pt. I: Basic Science (MEPC) 3rd ed. Mark Dershwitz et al. 422p. 1995. pap. text 35.00 (*0-8385-6655-3*, A6655-3, Apple Lange Med) McGraw.

National Bonsai Collection Guidebook. LC 76-57084. (Illus.). 1986. reprint ed. pap. 2.50 (*0-916352-10-2*); reprint ed. lib. bdg. 5.00 (*0-916352-11-0*) Symmes Syst.

National Book Awards: 48 Years of Literary Excellence, Winners & Finalists, 1950-1997. 2nd ed. National Book Foundation Staff. 1998. pap. 10.00 (*1-889099-24-4*) Natl Bk Fnd.

National Book of Lists, 1992. Ed. by Kevin Cronin. 106p. (Orig.). 1992. pap. 19.95 (*0-9632232-0-8*) Local Know.

National Budgeting for Economic & Monetary Union. Ed. by Aaron Wildavsky. 232p. (C). 1993. lib. bdg. 92.00 (*0-7923-2589-3*) Kluwer Academic.

National Building Codes Handbook. Jonathan F. Hutchings. LC 97-23530. (Illus.). 545p. 1997. 69.95 (*0-07-031819-0*) McGraw.

National Building Regulations: An Explanatory Handbook. 2nd ed. C. J. Freeman. 402p. 1990. pap. write for info. (*0-7021-2390-0*, Pub. by Juta & Co) Gaunt.

National Bureau of Economic Research, 44 vols., Set. 1975. 49.95 (*0-405-07572-3*, 487) Ayer.

National Business Employment Weekly Guide to Cover Letters. 3rd ed. Tannee S. Besson & Taunee S. Besson. LC 98-50853. (Illus.). 304p. 1999. pap. 12.95 (*0-471-32261-X*) Wiley.

***National Business Employment Weekly Guide to Interviewing.** 3rd ed. National Business Employment Weekly Staff & Arlene S. Hirsch. LC 98-33164. (National Business Employment Weekly Premier Guides Ser.). (Illus.). 240p. 1999. pap. 12.95 (*0-471-32257-1*) Wiley.

National Business Employment Weekly Interviewing. National Business Employment Weekly Staff & Arlene S. Hirsch. 288p. 1997. pap. 5.99 (*0-471-19118-3*) Wiley.

National Business Employment Weekly Jobs Rated Almanac. Les Krantz. LC 95-879. (National Business Employment Weekly Care Ser.). 352p. 1995. pap. 16.95 (*0-471-05495-X*) Wiley.

National Business Employment Weekly's Guide to Self-Employment. National Business Employment Weekly Staff. LC 95-51321. 266p. 1996. pap. 12.95 (*0-471-10918-5*) Wiley.

National Business Telephone Directory. 1800p. 1989. text 129.95 (*0-86692-050-1*) Trinet.

National Cancer Control Programmes: Policies & Managerial Guidelines. LC 96-117924. (FRE & SPA.). 134p. (C). 1995. pap. 32.00 (*92-4-154474-0*, 1150422) World Health.

National Cancer Institute Economic Conference: Integration of Economic Outcome Measures into NCI-sponsored Therapeutic Trials. 92p. 1995. pap. 6.50 (*0-16-061572-0*) USGPO.

***National Cancer Institute's Management of Radiation Studies: Hearing Before the Permanent Subcommittee on Investigations of the Committee on Governmental Affairs, United States Senate, 105th Congress, 2nd Session, September 16, 1998.** USGPO Staff. LC 99-162067. iv, 894p. 1998. write for info. (*0-16-057682-2*) USGPO.

National Candle Association 1997 Directory of Members. 2nd ed. 100p. 1996. pap. 25.00 (*0-938369-28-8*) Natl Candle Assn.

National Capital Barbecue Battle Cookbook Vol. 2: Great on the Grill. Ed. by Meagan Ulrich. 48p. 1997. pap. 2.95 (*0-9657955-0-0*) American Red Cross.

National Capital Region: Growth & Development. India National Capital Region Planning Board. LC 96-905172. 272 p. 1996. write for info. (*81-241-0426-3*) Har-Anand Pubns.

***National Capitalisms, Global Competition & Economic Performance.** Ed. by Sigrid Quack et al. 264p. 1999. 45.95 (*3-11-016485-X*); pap. 22.95 (*3-11-016068-4*) De Gruyter.

***National Capitalisms, Global Competition & Economic Performance.** Ed. by Sigrid Quack et al. LC 99-51376. (Advances in Organization Studies: Vol. 3). xii, 322p. 2000. 44.95 (*1-55619-746-2*) J Benjamins Pubng Co.

National Casting Guide. Peter Glenn Staff. 1998. 17.95 (*0-87314-154-7*) Peter Glenn.

National Cave & Karst Research Institute & the Aleutian World War II National Historic Areas: Hearing Before the Subcommittee on Parks, Historic Preservation & Recreation of the Committee on Energy & Natural Resources, United Sates Senate, 104th Congress, 2nd Session, on S. 1699, to Establish the National Cave & Karst Research Institute in the State of New Mexico & for Other Purposes, S. 1809, Entitled "Aleutian World War II National Historic Areas Act of 1966 [e.g. 1996]," July 25, 1996. USGPO Staff. LC 96-217864. iii, 15 p. 1996. pap. write for info. (*0-16-053450-X*) USGPO.

National Cemetery System: Opportunities to Expand Cemeteries' Capacities. Donald C. Snyder. (Illus.). 45p. 1998. pap. text 20.00 (*0-7881-7167-4*) DIANE Pub.

***National Center for Military Deployment Health Research.** Institute of Medicine Staff. Ed. by Lyla M. Hernandez et al. 62p. 1999. pap. 18.00 (*0-309-06630-1*) Natl Acad Pr.

National Certification Examination for Professional Massage & Bodywork (PMB) (Admission Test Ser.: ATS-108). pap. 49.95 (*0-8373-5808-6*) Nat Learn.

National Certifying Examination for Physician's Assistants (PA) Jack Rudman. (Admission Test Ser.: ATS-91). 1994. pap. 29.95 (*0-8373-5091-3*) Nat Learn.

National Cervical Screening Programme Policy National Cervical Screening Programme Staff. LC 97-153727. 47p. 1996. write for info. (*0-478-09451-5*, Pub. by Manaaki Whenua) Balogh.

National Chapter Partnership: A Guide for the Chapter Relations Professional. James DeLizia & American Society of Association Executives Staff. 335p. 1992. pap. text 85.95 (*0-88034-058-4*) Am Soc Assn Execs.

National Character: A Psycho-Social Perspective. Alex Inkeles. LC 96-22498. 408p. 1996. text 49.95 (*1-56000-260-3*) Transaction Pubs.

National Character & National Ideology in Interwar Eastern Europe. Created by Ivo Banac & Katherine Verdery. LC 95-679. 1995. write for info. (*0-936586-13-3*, Pub. by Yale Russian) Slavica.

National Cherry Festival. Lawrence M. Wakefield. 1987. 17.00 (*0-9618903-1-2*); pap. 13.50 (*0-9618903-0-4*) L M Wakefield.

National Child Abuse & Neglect Data System: Working Paper 2: 1991 Summary Data Component. (Illus.). 94p. (Orig.). (C). 1994. pap. text 30.00 (*0-7881-0633-3*) DIANE Pub.

***National Childbirth Trust Book of Breastfeeding.** Mary Smale. 1999. pap. 16.95 (*0-09-182569-5*, Pub. by Vermilion) Trafalgar.

National Childcare Directory. Robin Chater. (C). 1990. 300.00 (*1-872838-01-4*, Pub. by IPM Hse) St Mut.

***National Childcare Strategy in Wales: A Consultation Document.** Great Britain. Welsh Office. LC 98-176614. (Illus.). 1998. write for info. (*0-10-139742-9*) Statnry Office.

National Childhood Encephalopathy Study: A 10-Year Follow-Up. Nicola Madge et al. (Illus.). 121p. (C). 1993. pap. text 19.95 (*0-521-45883-8*) Cambridge U Pr.

National Choices & International Processes. Zeev Maoz. (Cambridge Studies in International Relations: No. 8). (Illus.). 627p. (C). 1990. text 85.00 (*0-521-36595-3*) Cambridge U Pr.

National Christian Manifesto, 1990. Ratibor-Ray M. Jurjevich. 96p. (Orig.). 1990. pap. 5.95 (*0-930711-12-2*) Ichthys Bks.

National Civic Review. Date not set. pap. write for info. (*0-614-11394-6*) Nat Civic League.

National Civil Rights Museum Celebrates Everyday People. Alice F. Duncan. LC 94-15831. (Illus.). 64p. (J). (gr. 2-6). 1996. pap. 6.95 (*0-8167-3503-4*, Troll Medallion) Troll Communs.

National Civil Rights Museum Celebrates Everyday People. Alice Faye Duncan. LC 94-15831. (J). 1995. 12.15 (*0-606-09677-9*, Pub. by Turtleback) Demco.

National Claims to Maritime Jurisdiction: Excerpts of Legislation & Table of Claims. (The Law of the Sea Ser.). 145p. pap. 19.50 (*92-1-133421-7*) UN.

***National Climate Policies & the Kyoto Protocol.** OECD Staff. 88p. 1999. pap. 21.00 (*92-64-17114-2*, 971999101P, Pub. by Org for Econ) OECD.

***National Co-Ordination of EU Policy: The Domestic Level.** Ed. by Hussein Kassim et al. 320p. 2000. text 72.00 (*0-19-829664-9*) OUP.

National Code, 1996. National Fire Protection Assoc. Staff. (McGuffey Editions Ser.). 917p. 1995. pap. 54.95 (*0-442-02223-9*, VNR) Wiley.

National Cold Storage Company: New & Selected Poems. Harvey Shapiro. LC 87-20472. (Wesleyan Poetry Ser.). 103p. 1988. pap. 12.95 (*0-8195-1153-6*, Wesleyan Univ Pr) U Pr of New Eng.

National Collaboratories: Applying Information Technology for Scientific Research. Commission on Physical Sciences, Mathematics, & Ap & National Research Council Staff. 118p. (Orig.). (C). 1993. pap. text 29.00 (*0-309-04848-6*) Natl Acad Pr.

***National Collective Identity: Social Constructs & International Systems.** Rodney Hall. LC 98-27127. 392p. 1998. pap. 20.50 (*0-231-11151-7*); lib. bdg. 50.00 (*0-231-11150-9*) Col U Pr.

National Collegiate Athletic Association: A Study in Cartel Behavior. Arthur A. Fleisher, III et al. LC 91-26437. (Illus.). 202p. 1992. 27.95 (*0-226-25326-0*) U Ch Pr.

National Collegiate Championships, 1987-1988. 543p. 1988. pap. 16.00 (*0-318-41471-6*) NCAA.

National Commission on Nursing Implementation Project: Models for the Future of Nursing. 80p. 1988. pap. 14.95 (*0-88737-427-1*, 15-2251) Natl League Nurse.

National Commission on Product Safety: Final Report, Set. U. S. National Commission on Product Safety. LC 76-606753. 1982. reprint ed. lib. bdg. 95.00 (*0-89941-224-6*, 201460) W S Hein.

National Commodity Futures: Questions & Answers. 9th ed. Dearborn Financial Institute, Inc. Editorial Staff. (Passtrak Ser.: Series 3). 1997. pap. 40.00 (*0-7931-2339-9*) Dearborn.

National Communism in Western Europe: A Third Way for Socialism? Ed. by E. Machin. LC 82-24945. 1983. pap. 13.95 (*0-416-73440-5*, NO. 3854) Routledge.

National Compensation Survey. Government Printing Office Staff. 1989. pap. 114.00 (*0-16-014420-5*) USGPO.

National Competency Mathematics: A Worktext. rev. ed. John Allasio. 302p. 1994. pap. 10.95 (*0-937820-69-5*) WestSea Pub.

National Competency Mathematics Answer Key. rev. ed. John Allasio. 20p. 1994. pap. 3.50 (*0-937820-70-9*) WestSea Pub.

National Competitiveness in a Global Economy. Ed. by David P. Rapkin & William P. Avery. LC 94-43543. (International Political Economy Yearbook Ser.: Vol. 8). 235p. 1995. lib. bdg. 52.00 (*1-55587-542-4*) L Rienner.

National Computer Security Conference, 1994 (17th) Proceedings: Communicating Our Discipline Strategies for the Emerging Infrastructures. (Illus.). 785p. (Orig.). (C). 1995. pap. text 75.00 (*0-7881-0125-0*) DIANE Pub.

National Computer Security Conference, 1987 (10th) Proceedings: Computer Security from Principles to Practices. (Illus.). 388p. (Orig.). (C). 1995. pap. text 50.00 (*0-7881-2299-1*) DIANE Pub.

National Computer Security Conference, 1993 (16th) Proceedings: Information Systems Security: User Choices. (Illus.). 541p. (Orig.). (C). 1995. pap. text 95.00 (*0-7881-1924-9*) DIANE Pub.

National Computer Security Conference Proceedings, 1992: Information Systems Security, 2 vols., Set. (Illus.). 802p. 1992. pap. text 75.00 (*0-7881-0221-4*) DIANE Pub.

National Conference of Commissioners on Uniform State Laws Handbook: Proceedings, 1892-1923, Set, Vols. 1-33. 1892. 500.00 (*0-686-89965-2*) W S Hein.

N

An Asterisk (*) at the beginning of an entry indicates that the title is appearing for the first time.

N

National Conference of Commissioners on Uniform State Laws Handbooks, 10 vols., Set. National Conference of CUSL Staff. LC 06-25307. 1982. lib. bdg. 422.50 (*0-89941-317-X*, 302830) W S Hein.

National Conference on Artificial Intelligence: Proceedings, August 1987, 2 vols. American Association for Artificial Intelligence Staff. (Illus.). 1986. pap. text 55.00 (*0-262-51055-3*) AAAI Pr.

National Conference on Artificial Intelligence: Proceedings, 18 August, 1983. Ed. by American Assocation for Artificial Intelligence Staff. (Illus.). 368p. 1983. pap. text 45.00 (*0-262-51052-9*) AAAI Pr.

National Conference on Artificial Intelligence: Proceedings, 18-20 August 1982. American Association for Artificial Intelligence S. (Illus.). 456p. 1982. pap. text 45.00 (*0-262-51051-0*) AAAI Pr.

National Conference on Artificial Intelligence: Proceedings, 18-21 August, 1980. American Association for Artificial Intelligence S. (Illus.). 339p. 1980. pap. text 40.00 (*0-262-51050-2*) AAAI Pr.

National Conference on Artificial Intelligence: Proceedings, 6-10 August, 1984. American Association for Artificial Intelligence S. (Illus.). 386p. 1984. pap. text 45.00 (*0-262-51053-7*) AAAI Pr.

National Conference on Bulk Materials Handling, 1993. Intro. by Dudley Roach. (National Conference Publication Ser.: No. 93-8). (Illus.). 279p. (Orig.). 1993. pap. text 72.00 (*0-85825-578-2*, Pub. by Inst Engrs Aust-EA Bks) Accents Pubns.

National Conference on Bulk Materials Handling, 1996. John Ramage. (National Conference Proceedings Ser.: Vol. 96/12). (Illus.). 417p. 1996. pap. 108.00 (*0-85825-660-6*, Pub. by Inst Engrs Aust-EA Bks) Accents Pubns.

National Conference on Corporate Governance & Accountability in the 1980's. Institutional Staff. 90p. 1981. pap. 7.50 (*0-8318-0412-2*, B412) Am Law Inst.

National Conference on Criminal History Records: Brady & Beyond. (Illus.). 200p. (Orig.). (C). 1995. pap. text 30.00 (*0-7881-2292-4*) DIANE Pub.

National Conference on Criminal Justice Bulletin Board Systems: Proceedings. 77p. (Orig.). (C). 1994. pap. text 30.00 (*0-7881-1473-5*) DIANE Pub.

***National Conference on Drug Abuse Prevention Research 1996: Presentations, Papers & Recommendations.** Ed. by Susan L. David. (Illus.). 182p. 2000. reprint ed. pap. text 35.00 (*0-7567-0050-7*) DIANE Pub.

National Conference on Drug Abuse Research & Practice: An Alliance for the 21st Century: Conference Highlights. 275p. (C). 1996. reprint ed. pap. text 35.00 (*0-7881-3090-0*) DIANE Pub.

National Conference on Engineering Heritage, 6th, 1992: Conserving & Recording Engineering Heritage. Intro. & Pref. by Keith Drewitt. (National Conference Publication Ser.: No. 92-17). (Illus.). 152p. (Orig.). 1992. pap. 77.00 (*0-85825-567-7*, Pub. by Inst Engrs Aust-EA Bks) Accents Pubns.

National Conference on Improving the Quality of Criminal History Records. 95p. (Orig.). (C). 1993. pap. text 325.00 (*1-56806-809-3*) DIANE Pub.

National Conference on Juvenile Detention. Lynn Atkinson & Sally-Anne Gerull. LC 96-172314. (Australian Institute Conference Proceedings Ser.: Vol. 25). 220p. 1994. pap. 35.00 (*0-642-21301-1*, Pub. by Aust Inst Criminology) Advent Bks Div.

National Conference on Juvenile Justice. Ed. by L. Atkinson & Sally-Anne Gerull. (Australian Institute Conference Proceedings Ser.: Vol. 22). 477p. 1993. pap. 45.00 (*0-642-19620-6*, Pub. by Aust Inst Criminology) Advent Bks Div.

***National Conference on Juvenile Justice Records: Appropriate Criminal & Noncriminal Justice Uses.** Ed. by Twyla R. Cunningham. 97p. 1999. pap. text 25.00 (*0-7881-7993-4*) DIANE Pub.

National Conference on Labor, New York University: Proceedings, 1948-1989, 42 vols. 1948. mic. film 2100.00 (*0-318-57446-2*) W S Hein.

National Conference on Labor, New York University: Proceedings, 1948-1989, 42 vols., Set. 1948. 2100.00 (*0-8377-9122-7*, Rothman) W S Hein.

National Conference on Legal Information Issues: Selected Essays. Timothy L. Coggins. LC 96-14889. (AALL Publications Ser.: No. 51). xxvi, 288p. 1996. 57.50 (*0-8377-0148-1*, Rothman) W S Hein.

National Conference on Products Liability Law, 1989 - Panel. 1989. write for info. (*1-55917-597-4*); audio 175.00 (*1-55917-596-6*) Natl Prac Inst.

National Conference on Sanitary Sewer Overflows: Seminar Publication. Ed. by Daniel Murray. (Illus.). 588p. (C). 1998. pap. text 50.00 (*0-7881-4890-7*) DIANE Pub.

National Conference on Setting An Intermodal Transportation Research Framework, Washington, D.c., March 4-5, 1996. National Conference on Setting an Intermodal Transportation Research Framework et al. LC 97-203582. (Conference Proceedings / Transportation Research Board Ser.). 97 p. 1997. 27.00 (*0-309-05968-2*, CP012) Natl Acad Pr.

***National Conference on Sex Offender Registries Proceedings.** Ed. by Sheila J. Barton. 118p. 2000. reprint ed. pap. text 30.00 (*0-7881-8832-1*) DIANE Pub.

National Conference on the Very Fast Train (VFT) Project. Intro. by B. C. Tonkin. (Illus.). 246p. 1990. ring bd. 101.00 (*0-85825-513-8*, Pub. by Inst Engrs Aust-EA Bks) Accents Pubns.

National Conflict in Czechoslovakia: The Making & Remaking of a State, 1918-1987. Carol S. Leff. LC 87-29034. 315p. 1988. reprint ed. pap. 97.70 (*0-608-07646-5*, 205996300010) Bks Demand.

***National Conformity Assessment Schemes: Nontariff Trade Barriers in Information Technology.** William B. Garrison & Peter S. Watson. LC 99-58941. (Report Ser.). 60p. 1999. pap. text 18.95 (*0-89206-361-0*) CSIS.

National Congress of American Indians: The Founding Years. Contrib. by Thomas Cowger. LC 99-17940. (Illus.). 1999. text 45.00 (*0-8032-1502-9*) U of Nebr Pr.

National Consciousness, History, & Political Culture in Early-Modern Europe. Ed. by Orest A. Ranum. LC 74-6837. (Johns Hopkins Symposia in Comparative History Ser.: No. 5). (Illus.). 192p. reprint ed. pap. 59.60 (*0-8357-4328-4*, 203712800007) Bks Demand.

National Consciousness in Eighteenth-Century Russia. Hans J. Rogger. LC 60-8450. (Russian Research Center Studies: No. 38). 327p. 1960. 29.95 (*0-674-60150-5*) HUP.

National Consensus for Development in Nepal. IIDS Staff. 1997. pap. 21.00 (*0-7855-7452-2*, Pub. by Ratna Pustak Bhandar) St Mut.

National Conservation & Preservation Policy for Movable Cultural Heritage. Cultural Ministers Council (Australia) Staff. LC 97-162210. iv, 8 p. 1995. write for info. (*0-642-23354-3*, Pub. by Aust Inst Criminology) Advent Bks Div.

National Constitutions & International Economic Law. Ed. by Meinhard Hilf & Ernst-Ulrich Petersmann. LC 92-38669. (Studies in Transnational Economic Law: Vol. 8). 1992. 163.00 (*90-6544-665-6*) Kluwer Law Intl.

National Constitutions in the Era of Integration. International Association of Constitutional Law Staff. Date not set. 93.00 (*90-411-9696-X*) Kluwer Academic.

National Construction Law Manual. 2nd ed. James Acret. 1999. pap. 64.95 (*1-55701-265-2*) BNI Pubns.

National Consumer Study on Service Quality in Banking, 1992. 120p. 1992. pap. 295.00 (*0-89982-295-9*, 129300) Am Bankers.

National Contingents in United Nations Peace-Keeping Forces. Robert C. Siekmann. 238p. (C). 1991. lib. bdg. 103.50 (*0-7923-1284-8*) Kluwer Academic.

National Conventions & Platforms of All Political Parties, 1789-1900. Thomas H. McKee. LC 77-107183. 1971. reprint ed. 15.00 (*0-403-00356-3*) Scholarly.

National Conventions & Platforms of All Political Parties, 1789-1905. 6th enl. rev. ed. Thomas H. McKee. LC 70-130239. 1970. reprint ed. 16.00 (*0-404-04133-7*) AMS Pr.

National Conventions in an Age of Party Reform, 91. James W. Davis. LC 82-9382. (Contributions in Political Science Ser.: No. 91). 304p. 1983. 65.00 (*0-313-23048-X*, DNC/, Greenwood Pr) Greenwood.

National Correct Coding Manual. 250p. 1999. pap. 250.00 (*1-58383-052-9*) Robert D Keene.

***National Correct Coding Manual, Version 5.2b.** Robert D. Keene. 250p. 2000. pap. 65.95 (*1-58383-109-6*) Robert D Keene.

National Corrections Reporting Program (1990) Craig A. Perkins. (Illus.). 97p. (Orig.). (C). 1993. pap. text 25.00 (*1-56806-490-X*) DIANE Pub.

National Corrections Reporting Program (1991) Craig A. Perkins. (Illus.). 97p. (Orig.). (C). 1995. pap. text 25.00 (*0-7881-2091-3*) DIANE Pub.

National Corrections Reporting Program (1992) Craig A. Perkins. (Illus.). 92p. (Orig.). (C). 1994. pap. text 25.00 (*0-7881-1384-4*) DIANE Pub.

National Costume Reference: U. S. S. R. S. Sichel. (C). 1990. 100.00 (*0-7855-4434-8*, Pub. by Collets) St Mut.

National Costumes of the Old World. Intro. by Fred L. Israel. LC 97-27223. (Looking into the Past). (Illus.). 64p. (YA). (gr. 5 up). 1999. lib. bdg. 16.95 (*0-7910-4684-2*) Chelsea Hse.

National Costumes of the Soviet Peoples. N. Kalashnikova & G. Pluzhnikova. 224p. (C). 1990. 140.00 (*0-569-09273-6*, Pub. by Collets) St Mut.

National Council for Geographic Education: The First 75 Years & Beyond. James W. Vining. (Illus.). 245p. (Orig.). 1990. pap. text 6.00 (*0-9627379-0-9*) NCFGE.

National Council Licensure Examination for Practical Nurses (NCLEX-PN) Jack Rudman. (Admission Test Ser.: ATS-76). 1994. pap. 29.95 (*0-8373-5076-X*) Nat Learn.

National Council Licensure Examination for Registered Nurses (NCLEX-RN) Jack Rudman. (Admission Test Ser.: ATS-75). 300p. 1994. pap. 29.95 (*0-8373-5075-1*) Nat Learn.

National Council of Women: A Centennial History. Dorothy Page. (Illus.). 252p. 1997. pap. 29.95 (*1-86940-154-9*, Pub. by Auckland Univ) Paul & Co Pubs.

National Council Workmen's Compensation Unit Statistical Plan Manual. National Council on Compensation Insurance Staff. (Illus.). 1983. write for info. (*0-318-58248-1*) Natl Comp Ins.

National Counselor Examination (NCE) (Admission Test Ser.: ATS-102). 1994. pap. 39.95 (*0-8373-5802-7*) Nat Learn.

National Counselor Examination (NCE) Jack Rudman. (Admission Test Ser.: Vol. 102). 59.95 (*0-8373-5852-3*) Nat Learn.

National Court Theatre in Mozart's Vienna: Sources & Documents 1783-1792. Dorothea Link. (Illus.). 560p. 1998. text 125.00 (*0-19-816673-7*) OUP.

National Cowboy Hall of Fame Souvenir Book. (Orig.). Date not set. pap. text. write for info. (*1-56944-123-5*) Terrell Missouri.

National Credit Union Administration Rules & Regulations. Government Printing Office Staff. 1990. ring bd. 72.00 (*0-16-017557-7*) USGPO.

National Credit Union Directory. 1991. lib. bdg. 79.95 (*0-8490-4484-7*) Gordon Pr.

National Crime Information Center & You. Ed. by Federal Bureau of Investigation Staff. (FBI Ser.). 1986. lib. bdg. 79.95 (*0-8490-3811-1*) Gordon Pr.

National Crime Surveys: Cities Attitude Sub-Sample, 1972-1975. U. S. Department of Justice, Bureau of Justice Sta. LC 79-126337. 1979. write for info. (*0-89138-970-9*) ICPSR.

National Crime Surveys: Cities, 1972-1975. U. S. Department of Justice, Bureau of Justice Sta. LC 78-71978. 1978. write for info. (*0-89138-992-X*) ICPSR.

National Crime Surveys: National Sample, 1979-1987 (Revised Questionnaire) U. S. Department of Justice, Bureau of Justice Sta. LC 89-83657. 432p. 1989. write for info. (*0-89138-875-3*) ICPSR.

National Crime Surveys: National Sample, 1986-1989 (Near-Term Data) U. S. Department of Justice, Bureau of the Census. LC 90-81635. 496p. 1990. write for info. (*0-89138-870-2*) ICPSR.

National Crime Surveys: National Sample, 1986-1990 (Near-Term Data) U. S. Department of Justice, Bureau of Justice Sta. LC 91-70675. 496p. 1991. write for info. (*0-89138-867-2*) ICPSR.

National Crime Surveys: National Sample, 1986-1991 (Near-Term Data) U. S. Department of Justice, Bureau of Justice Sta. LC 92-81886. 576p. 1992. write for info. (*0-89138-863-X*) ICPSR.

National Crime Surveys: National Sample, 1986-1991 (Near-Term Data Through Calendar Year 1991): Longitudinal File, 1986-1990. U. S. Department of Justice, Bureau of Justice Sta. LC 93-80540. 472p. 1993. write for info. (*0-89138-861-3*) ICPSR.

National Crisis & National Government: British Politics, the Economy & Empire, 1926-1932. Philip Williamson. (Illus.). 587p. (C). 1992. text 95.00 (*0-521-36137-0*) Cambridge U Pr.

National Critical Technologies Panel - Second Biennial Report. 38p. (Orig.). (C). 1994. pap. text 25.00 (*0-7881-1204-X*) DIANE Pub.

National Critical Technologies Report (1995) 197p. (Orig.). (C). 1995. pap. text 45.00 (*0-7881-1978-8*) DIANE Pub.

National Culture & International Management in East Asia. Herbert J. Davis & William D. Schulte. LC 97-16113. 656p. 1997. pap. 24.99 (*1-86152-052-2*) Thomson Learn.

National Culture & New Global System. Frederick Buell. LC 94-2076. (Parallax). 384p. 1994. text 48.50 (*0-8018-4833-4*); pap. text 17.95 (*0-8018-4834-2*) Johns Hopkins.

National Cultures & European Integration: Exploratory Essays on Cultural Diversity & Common Policies. Ed. by Staffan Zetterholm. (Illus.). 192p. 1994. 37.50 (*0-85496-951-9*, Pub. by Berg Pubs); pap. 19.50 (*1-85973-051-5*, Pub. by Berg Pubs) NYU Pr.

***National Cultures at Grass-Root Level.** Antonina Kloskowska. 480p. (C). 2000. 49.95 (*963-9116-83-1*) Ctrl Europ Univ.

National Cultures of the World: A Statistical Reference. Philip M. Parker. LC 96-41974. (Cross-Cultural Statistical Encyclopedia of the World: Vol. 4). 264p. 1997. lib. bdg. 79.50 (*0-313-29770-3*, Greenwood Pr) Greenwood.

National Curriculum & Early Learning: An Evaluation. Ed. by Geva M. Blenkin & A. V. Kelly. 240p. 1994. pap. 25.00 (*1-85396-241-4*, Pub. by P Chapman) Taylor & Francis.

National Curriculum & the Early Years: Challenges & Opportunities. Ed. by Theo Cox. 192p. 1997. pap. 27.95 (*0-7507-0601-5*, Falmer Pr) Taylor & Francis.

National Curriculum Assessment: A Review of Policy, 1987-1994. Richard Daugherty. LC 94-46733. 152p. 1995. 85.00 (*0-7507-0254-0*, Falmer Pr); pap. 29.95 (*0-7507-0255-9*, Falmer Pr) Taylor & Francis.

National Curriculum for Physical Education. Ed. by L. Almond. 256p. 1991. pap. 49.95 (*0-419-17070-7*, A6275, E & FN Spon) Routledge.

National Curriculum for the Early Years. Angela Anning. LC 95-10789. 160p. 1995. 79.95 (*0-335-19432-X*) OpUniv Pr.

National Curriculum for the Early Years. Ed. by Angela Anning. LC 95-10789. 160p. 1995. pap. 23.95 (*0-335-19431-1*) OpUniv Pr.

National Curriculum Mathematics: Target Book 1. M. J. Tipler & K. M. Vickers. (Illus.). 320p. (J). (gr. 6-9). 1998. pap. 25.00 (*0-7487-3546-1*, Pub. by S Thornes Pubs) Trans-Atl Phila.

National Curriculum Mathematics: Target Book 2. M. J. Tipler & K. M. Vickers. (Illus.). 320p. (J). (gr. 6-9). 1998. pap. 22.50 (*0-7487-3547-X*, Pub. by S Thornes Pubs) Trans-Atl Phila.

National Curriculum, 1995: All Eleven Subjects. LC 97-213282. 256p. 1995. pap. 55.00 (*0-11-270894-3*, HM08943, Pub. by Statnry Office) Bernan Associates.

National Daily Press of France. Clyde Thogmartin. LC 98-60273. 384p. 1998. lib. bdg. 49.95 (*1-883479-20-7*) Summa Pubns.

National Dam Safety Program Act: Implementation Plan. Ed. by Barry Leonard. (Illus.). 46p. (C). 1999. text 20.00 (*0-7881-7924-1*) DIANE Pub.

National Data Collection on Police Use of Force. Tom McEwen. 100p. (Orig.). (C). 1996. pap. text 30.00 (*0-7881-3719-0*) DIANE Pub.

National Database & Fourth Generation Language Symposium Workbook & Proceedings. 500p. 1986. pap. 250.00 (*0-318-01070-4*) Software Inst Am.

National Dean's List see National Deans List, 1997-98

National Deans List, 1997-98, 2 vols. Incl. Vol. I. National Dean's List. 21st ed. LC 79-642835. 1998. 49.95 (*1-56244-198-1*); Vol. II. National Dean's List. 21st ed. LC 79-642835. 1998. 49.95 (*1-56244-199-X*); write for info. (*1-56244-197-3*) Educ Comm.

***National Dean's List, 1998-99, 2 vols.** 22nd ed. Incl. Vol. I. 1999. 49.95 (*1-56244-222-8*); Vol. II. 1999. 49.95 (*1-56244-223-6*); LC 79-642835. 1999. write for info. (*1-56244-221-X*) Educ Comm.

***National Dean's List, 2000, 2 vols.** annuals 23rd ed. Incl. Vol. I. Dean's List, 2000. annuals 23rd ed. LC 79-642835. 2000. 52.95 (*1-56244-246-5*); Vol. II. Dean's List, 2000. annuals 23rd ed. LC 79-642835. 2000. 52.95 (*1-56244-247-3*); LC 79-642835. 2000. write for info. (*1-56244-245-7*) Educ Comm.

National Debt. Cass R. Sandak. (Inside Government Ser.). (Illus.). 64p. (J). (gr. 5-8). 1995. lib. bdg. 18.90 (*0-8050-3423-4*) TFC Bks NY.

National Debt. Eric L. Hardgreaves. 303p. 1966. reprint ed. 35.00 (*0-7146-1226-X*, Pub. by F Cass Pubs) Intl Spec Bk.

***National Debt: From FDR (1941) to Clinton (1996)** Robert E. Kelly. LC 99-52888. (Illus.). 287p. 2000. lib. bdg. 39.95 (*0-7864-0622-4*) McFarland & Co.

National Debt Conclusion: Establishing the Debt Repayment Plan. Charles W. Steadman. LC 92-44688. 176p. 1993. 52.95 (*0-275-94360-7*, C4360, Praeger Pubs) Greenwood.

National Debt in Britain, 1850-1930 Jeremy J. Wormell. LC 98-55080. 1999. write for info. (*0-415-19578-0*) Routledge.

National Decade Plans: Eight Questions They Answer. WHO Staff. 18p. 1982. 3.00 (*92-4-156076-2*) World Health.

***National Decisions: Compendium of Judicial Decisions on Matters Related to Environment.** 511p. 1998. 80.00 (*92-807-1762-6*) United Nat Env.

National Deconstruction: Violence, Identity, & Justice in Bosnia. David Campbell. LC 98-17006. 382p. 1998. 62.95 (*0-8166-2936-6*); pap. 24.95 (*0-8166-2937-4*) U of Minn Pr.

National Defense & the Environment. Stephen Dycus. LC 95-20878. 306p. 1996. pap. 22.00 (*0-87451-735-4*); text 50.00 (*0-87451-675-7*) U Pr of New Eng.

National Defense Migration. U. S. House of Representatives Select Committee on. Ed. by Roger Daniels. LC 78-54835. (Asian Experience in North America Ser.). 1979. reprint ed. lib. bdg. 73.95 (*0-405-11293-9*) Ayer.

***National Defense Panel: Hearings Before the Committee on Armed Services, United States Senate, 105th Congress, 2nd Session, January 28 & 29, 1998.** USGPO Staff. LC 99-180306. iii, 87 p. 1998. write for info. (*0-16-057790-X*) USGPO.

National Defense Stockpile: Disposal of Excess Zinc. 52p. pap. text 30.00 (*0-7881-4066-3*) DIANE Pub.

National Democratic Party: Right Radicalism in the Federal Republic of Germany. John D. Nagle. LC 78-101340. 231p. reprint ed. pap. 71.70 (*0-608-15846-1*, 203144300074) Bks Demand.

National Dental Advisory Service: Comprehensive Fee Report 1999. 17th ed. Yale Wasserman, D.M.D. Medical Publishers, Limited. 1999. per. 49.00 (*1-881072-34-7*) Y W DMD Med.

National Dental Advisory Service: Comprehensive Fee Report 2000. 18th ed. Yale Wasserman, D.M.D. Medical Publishers, Limited. 2000. per. 59.00 (*1-881072-38-X*) Y W DMD Med.

National Dental Assistant Boards (NDAB) Jack Rudman. (Admission Test Ser.: Vol. 87). 59.95 (*0-8373-5187-1*) Nat Learn.

National Dental Assistant Boards (NDAB) Jack Rudman. (Admission Test Ser.: ATS-87). 1994. pap. 39.95 (*0-8373-5087-5*) Nat Learn.

National Dental Boards (NDB), 2 vols. in 1. Jack Rudman. (Admission Test Ser.: Vol. 36). 89.95 (*0-8373-5136-7*) Nat Learn.

National Dental Boards (NDB), 2 pts. in 1 vol. Jack Rudman. (Admission Test Ser.: ATS-36). 1996. pap. 69.95 (*0-8373-5036-0*) Nat Learn.

National Dental Boards (NDB), Pt. I. Rudman. (Admission Test Ser.: ATS-36A). 1996. pap. 49.95 (*0-8373-6955-X*) Nat Learn.

National Dental Boards (NDB), Pt. II. Jack Rudman. (Admission Test Ser.: Vol. 36B). 69.95 (*0-8373-6981-9*) Nat Learn.

National Dental Boards (NDB), Pt. II. Jack Rudman. (Admission Test Ser.: ATS-36B). 1994. pap. 49.95 (*0-8373-6956-8*) Nat Learn.

National Dental Hygiene Boards (NDHB) Jack Rudman. (Admission Test Ser.: Vol. 51). 59.95 (*0-8373-5151-0*) Nat Learn.

National Dental Hygiene Boards (NDHB) Jack Rudman. (Admission Test Ser.: ATS-51). 1994. pap. 39.95 (*0-8373-5051-4*) Nat Learn.

National Department & the Polish American Community, 1916-1923. Ed. by Louis J. Zake. LC 90-3507. (European Immigrants & American Society Ser.). 272p. 1990. reprint ed. text 20.00 (*0-8240-0362-4*) Garland.

***National Development: Being More Effective & More Efficient.** Stuart S. Nagel. LC 99-43344. 200p. 2000. write for info. (*1-84014-024-0*) Ashgate Pub Co.

National Development & Local Reform: Political Participation in Morocco, Tunisia, & Pakistan. Douglas E. Ashford. LC 66-14307. (Princeton Studies on the Near East). 451p. 1967. reprint ed. pap. 139.90 (*0-608-03336-7*, 206404800008) Bks Demand.

National Development & the World System: Educational, Economic, & Political Change, 1950-1970. Ed. by John W. Meyer & Michael T. Hannan. LC 78-26986. 1995. lib. bdg. 32.50 (*0-226-52136-2*) U Ch Pr.

National Development & the World System: Educational, Economic, & Political Change, 1950-1970. Ed. by John W. Meyer & Michael T. Hannan. LC 78-26986. 344p. reprint ed. pap. 106.70 (*0-608-09022-0*, 206965700005) Bks Demand.

National Development & Women. S. N. Chaudhary & Pratima Chaudhary. 192p. (C). 1992. 18.95 (*0-7069-5956-6*, Pub. by Vikas) S Asia.

An Asterisk (*) at the beginning of an entry indicates that the title is appearing for the first time.

National Development, Imperialism, & Religion in the Third World. Ed. by Harold Isaacs. (Journal of Third World Studies: Vol. XIII, No. 1). 483p. 1996. pap. 23.00 (*0-931971-23-3*) Assn Third Wld.

National Development Planning in Nigeria, 1900-1992. Pius N. Okigbo. 229p. (C). 1989. text 40.00 (*0-435-08039-3*, 08039) Heinemann.

National Development Policy & Urban Transformation in Singapore: A Study of Public Housing & the Marketing System. Yue-man Yeung. LC 73-79884. (University of Chicago, Department of Geography, Research Paper Ser.: No. 149). 216p. 1973. reprint ed. pap. 67.00 (*0-608-02268-3*, 206290900004) Bks Demand.

National Development, 1877-1885. Edwin E. Sparks. (History - United States Ser.). 378p. 1992. reprint ed. lib. bdg. 89.00 (*0-7812-6190-2*) Rprt Serv.

National Development, 1877-1885. Edwin E. Sparks. Ed. by Albert B. Hart. LC 70-145311. 1971. reprint ed. 59.00 (*0-403-01223-6*) Scholarly.

National Dialogue Conference on National Agenda, 1996. 18th ed. LCPS Staff. 136p. 1998. pap. write for info. (*1-886604-13-4*) Lebanese Ctr.

National Dialogue on Genetics: Congress, College Park, MD., March 1998. Ed. by I. S. Mittman et al. (Community Genetics Ser.: Vol. 1, No. 3 (1998)). (Illus.). 92p. 1999. pap. 34.00 (*3-8055-6836-3*) S Karger.

National Dictionary of French Communes see Dictionnaire National des Communes de France

National Diet & Nutrition Survey: Children Aged 1 & 1/2 to 4 & 1/2 Years. HMSO Staff. 412p. 1995. pap. 85.00 (*0-11-691611-7*, HM16117, Pub. by Statnry Office) Bernan Associates.

National Diet & Nutrition Survey: Children Aged 1 & 1/2 to 4 & 1/2 Years Volume 2. HMSO Staff. 156p. 1995. pap. text 30.00 (*0-11-691612-5*, Pub. by Statnry Office) Bernan Associates.

National Directory for Community Economic Development. 2nd rev. ed. 325p. 1997. pap. 25.00 (*1-889482-03-X*) Nat Congress CED.

National Directory for the Service of Civil Process. Paul D. Lyman. 587p. (Orig.). 1990. pap. 49.95 (*1-878337-24-6*) Knowles Pub Inc.

National Directory of AIDS Care. 6th ed. Nancy Shenker & Shawn D. Phillps. 500p. 1996. pap. 54.90 (*0-925133-46-9*) Volt Directory.

National Directory of Art & Antique Buyers & Specialists, 1988 Edition. 250p. 1988. 75.00 (*0-929697-00-6*); lib. bdg. 75.00 (*0-929697-01-4*) Merit Agencies.

National Directory of Arts Internships: Millenium 7th Edition. 7th rev. ed. Ed. by Warren Christensen. LC 89-659041. 443p. 1998. pap. 65.00 (*0-945941-08-0*) NNAP.

National Directory of Bereavement Support Groups & Services, 1988/99 Edition. 1998. 39.95 (*0-9645608-5-2*) ADM Pub.

National Directory of Bereavement Support Groups & Services, 1996 Edition. rev. ed. Ed. by Mary M. Wong. 496p. 1996. pap. 29.95 (*0-9645608-7-9*) ADM Pub.

National Directory of Brain Injury Rehabilitation Services, 1997. Ed. by Mary S. Reitter. Orig. Title: National Directory of Head Injury Rehabilitation Services. 1997. pap. text 50.00 (*0-614-30066-5*) Brain Injury Assoc.

National Directory of Budget Motels, 1998-1999 Edition. 22nd rev. ed. Pilot Staff. (Well-Prepared Traveler Ser.). 346p. 1998. pap. 12.95 (*0-87576-221-2*) Pilot Bks.

National Directory of CB Radio Channels. ABM Service Corp. Staff. LC 78-12796. 1979. 19.95 (*0-88280-064-7*); pap. 19.95 (*0-88280-065-5*) ETC Pubns.

National Directory of Children, Youth & Families Service, No. 1. 15th ed. Ed. by Penny K. Spencer. 1000p. 1999. pap. 129.00 (*1-885461-06-2*) National Direct.

National Directory of Children, Youth & Families Services. Marion L. Peterson. 900p. 1996. pap. text 90.00 (*1-885461-03-8*) National Direct.

National Directory of Children, Youth & Families Services. 10th ed. Marion L. Peterson. 800p. 1994. pap. text 84.00 (*1-885461-01-1*) National Direct.

National Directory of Children, Youth & Families Services. 13th rev. ed. Marion L. Peterson. 1997. pap. 96.00 (*1-885461-04-6*) National Direct.

National Directory of Church Philanthropy. Phyllis A. Meiners & Greg A. Sanford. (Illus.). 400p. pap. write for info. (*0-9633694-4-X*) CRC Pub CO.

National Directory of Churches, Synagogues, & Other Houses of Worship, 4 Vols. J. Gordon Melton. Ed. by John Krol. 2400p. 1993. 315.00 (*0-8103-8989-4*, 101773) Gale.

National Directory of Churches, Synagogues, & Other 1 Houses of Worship, Vol. 1: Northeastern States. J. Gordon Melton. Ed. by John Krol. 600p. 1993. 89.00 (*0-8103-8990-8*, 101774) Gale.

National Directory of Churches, Synagogues, & Other 1 Houses of Worship, Vol. 2: Midwestern States, Vol. 2. J. Gordon Melton. Ed. by John Krol. 600p. 1993. 89.00 (*0-8103-8991-6*, 101775) Gale.

National Directory of Churches, Synagogues, & Other 1 Houses of Worship, Vol. 3: Southern States, Vol. 3. J. Gordon Melton. Ed. by John Krol. 600p. 1993. 89.00 (*0-8103-8992-4*, 101776) Gale.

National Directory of Churches, Synagogues, & Other 1 Houses of Worship, Vol. 4: Western States, Vol. 4. J. Gordon Melton. Ed. by John Krol. 600p. 1993. 89.00 (*0-8103-8993-2*, 101777) Gale.

National Directory of College Athletics (Men's Edition), 1985-1986. 416p. 14.00 (*0-943976-03-0*) R Franks Ranch.

National Directory of College Athletics (Men's Edition), 1988-1989. National Association of Collegiate Director of Ath. 1988. pap. 15.00 (*0-318-41469-4*) R Franks Ranch.

National Directory of College Athletics (Women's Edition), 1985-1986. 240p. pap. 10.00 (*0-943976-04-9*) R Franks Ranch.

National Directory of College Athletics, 1988-1989: Women's Edition. National Association of Collegiate Director of Ath. 1988. pap. 11.00 (*0-318-41470-8*) R Franks Ranch.

National Directory of Corporate Distress Specialists: A Comprehensive Guide to Firms & Professionals Providing Services in Bankruptcies, Workouts, Turnarounds & Distressed Securities Investing. Ed. by Joel W. Lustig. 720p. 1992. 99.00 (*0-9630173-0-6*) Lustig Data Res.

National Directory of Corporate Giving. 5th ed. L. Victoria Hall & Foundation Center Staff. Ed. by Jeffrey Falkenstein. 1092p. 1997. pap. text 225.00 (*0-87954-722-7*) Foundation Ctr.

***National Directory of Corporate Giving.** 6th ed. Foundation Center Staff. (Illus.). 1999. pap. text 225.00 (*0-87954-888-6*) Foundation Ctr.

National Directory of Corporate Philanthropy for Native Americans. Susan D. Bailey. Ed. by Phyllis A. Meiners. LC 97-65770. (Multicultural Grant Guides: Vol. 5). (Illus.). 275p. (Orig.). 1999. pap. 98.95 (*0-9633694-7-4*) CRC EagleRock.

***National Directory of Corporate Public Affairs, 2000.** 18th ed. Columbia Books Staff. Ed. by J. Valerie Steele. 1277p. 2000. pap. 109.00 (*1-880873-38-9*) Columbia Bks.

National Directory of Creative Talent - Workbook #20. Scott & Daughters Publishing Staff. (Workbook Ser.: 20). 1998. pap. 105.00 (*1-887528-30-X*) Scott & Daughters.

National Directory of Drug Abuse & Alcoholism Treatment & Prevention Programs. 1986. lib. bdg. 200.00 (*0-8490-3508-2*) Gordon Pr.

National Directory of Drug Abuse & Alcoholism Treatment & Prevention Programs. 1991. lib. bdg. 300.00 (*0-8490-4350-6*) Gordon Pr.

National Directory of Drug Abuse & Alcoholism Treatment & Prevention Programs. Government Printing Office Staff. 526p. 1996. pap. text 45.00 (*0-16-048859-1*) USGPO.

National Directory of Drug Abuse & Alcoholism Treatment Programs. 1991. lib. bdg. 300.00 (*0-8490-4955-5*) Gordon Pr.

***National Directory of Drug Abuse & Alcoholism Treatment Programs (1998)** Ed. by Rick Albright & Deborah Trunzo. 550p. (C). 2000. pap. text 60.00 (*0-7567-0165-1*) DIANE Pub.

National Directory of Early Childhood Teacher Preparation Institutions. 4th ed. 1999. 8.00 (*1-879891-05-0*) Council Early Child.

National Directory of Education Libraries & Collections. Compiled by Doris H. Christo. LC 89-13936. 280p. 1990. lib. bdg. 115.00 (*0-313-28051-7*, CNG/, Greenwood Pr) Greenwood.

National Directory of Expert Witnesses, 1996. 208p. (Orig.). 1996. pap. 37.50 (*1-890714-01-1*) Claims Providers.

National Directory of Expert Witnesses, 1997. 264p. (Orig.). 1997. pap. 37.50 (*1-890714-00-3*) Claims Providers.

National Directory of Expert Witnesses, 1998. Claims Provide of America Staff. 384p. 1998. pap. 45.00 (*1-890714-02-X*) Claims Providers.

National Directory of Expert Witnesses, 1999. 384p. 1999. pap. 45.00 (*1-890714-03-8*) Claims Providers.

***National Directory of Expert Witnesses, 2000.** 480p. 2000. pap. 45.00 (*1-890714-04-6*) Claims Providers.

National Directory of Farmworker Services. Association of Farmworker Opportunity Programs Sta. 113p. 1991. pap. text. write for info. (*1-886567-00-X*) Assn Farmwrker.

National Directory of Federal & State Biomass Tax Incentives & Subsidies. Gregory A. Sanderson. 208p. (C). 1996. reprint ed. pap. text 30.00 (*0-7881-3070-6*) DIANE Pub.

National Directory of Foundation Grants for Native Americans. Phyllis A. Meiners. LC 97-65768. (Multicultural Grant Guides: Vol. 4). (Illus.). 224p. (Orig.). 1998. pap. 99.95 (*0-9633694-8-2*) CRC EagleRock.

National Directory of 420 Current Real Estate Periodicals & Professional Real Estate Associations, 1999. John R. Johnsich. 1999. pap. 19.95 (*0-914256-30-0*) Real Estate Pub.

National Directory of Four Hundred Twenty Current Real Estate Periodicals & Professional Real Estate Associations with Complete Addresses. John R. Johnsich. (Orig.). 1995. pap. 19.95 (*0-914256-28-9*) Real Estate Pub.

National Directory of Four Year Colleges, Two Year Colleges, & Post High School Training Programs for Young People with Learning Disabilities. 7th ed. Ed. by P. M. Fielding & John R. Moss. 1994. pap. 29.95 (*0-937660-10-8*) PIP.

National Directory of Geoscience Data Repositories. Ed. by Nicholas H. Claudy. 91p. 1998. pap. 12.50 (*0-922152-41-1*) Am Geol.

National Directory of Grantmaking Public Charities. Foundation Center Staff. 351p. 1998. 115.00 (*0-87954-802-9*, DGPCZ) Foundation Ctr.

National Directory of Head Injury Rehabilitation Services see National Directory of Brain Injury Rehabilitation Services, 1997

National Directory of Health Care Critical Pathways: Fall 1996 Edition. 2nd ed. Ed. by Marilyn Lang. 135p. 1996. pap. text 98.00 (*0-9645360-2-1*) Cor Hlthcare.

National Directory of Home Mortgage Lenders, 1989. Stuart A. Feldstein. 1200p. (Orig.). 1989. pap. 250.00 (*0-9623022-0-1*) SMR Research.

***National Directory of Integrated Healthcare Delivery Systems.** 2nd ed. Gwen B. Lareau. Ed. by Phyllis Harris. 557p. 1999. pap. text 395.00 (*1-882364-31-7*, Amer Busn Pub) Hlth Res Pub.

National Directory of Internships. 9th ed. Ed. by Barbara E. Baker et al. 607p. (Orig.). 1993. write for info. (*0-937883-11-5*) NSEE.

National Directory of Internships: 1996-97 Edition. Ed. by Gita Gulati & Nancy R. Bailey. LC 90-640948. 673p. (Orig.). 1995. per. 29.00 (*0-937883-15-8*) NSEE.

National Directory of Internships, 1998-1999. rev. ed. Ed. by Gita Gulati & Nancy R. Bailey. 720p. (C). 1998. pap. text 29.95 (*0-536-01123-0*) Pearson Custom.

National Directory of Legal Employers. NALP Staff. 1352p. 1996. pap. 49.95 (*0-15-900179-X*) Harcourt Legal.

National Directory of Legal Employers. 2nd ed. Nalp Staff. 1352p. 1997. pap. text 49.95 (*0-15-900225-7*) Harcourt Legal.

***National Directory of Legal Employers: 22,000 Great Job Openings for Law Students & Law Schools.** National Association for Law Placement Staff. 1999. pap. 39.95 (*0-15-900434-9*) Harcourt Legal.

***National Directory of Legal Employers: 22,000 Great Job Openings for Law Students & Law Schools.** National Association for Law Staff. (Illus.). 2000. pap. 39.95 (*0-15-900454-3*) Harcourt.

National Directory of Legal Employers: 32,000 Great Job Openings for Law Students & Law School. Association National For Law Staff. 1999. pap. text 39.95 (*0-15-900435-7*) Harcourt Legal.

National Directory of Magazines, 1998. Oxbridge Staff. 1692p. 1997. pap. 595.00 incl. cd-rom (*0-917460-90-1*) Oxbridge Comm.

National Directory of Managed & Integrated Care Organizations. Ed. by Melanie Jenkins & Robert Henne. 563p. (Orig.). 1996. pap. 325.00 (*1-882364-02-3*) Hlth Res Pub.

***National Directory of Managed Care Organizations.** 2nd ed. Ed. by Gwen B. Lareau & Phyllis Harris. 863p. 1998. pap. text 285.00 (*1-882364-28-7*, Amer Busn Pub) Hlth Res Pub.

***National Directory of Minority-Owned Business Firms.** 10th ed. Thomas D. Johnson. 1384p. 1999. pap. 275.00 (*0-933527-70-5*, 0886-3881) Business Research.

National Directory of Newspaper Op-Ed Pages. Marilyn Ross. 158p. 1994. 19.95 (*0-918880-17-3*) Comm Creat.

National Directory of Nonprofit Oganizations 99, 3 vols. 1998. 485.00 (*1-56995-311-2*, 00157034) Taft Group.

***National Directory of Nonprofit Organizations, Vol. 2.** 11th ed. 1800p. 1999. 240.00 (*1-56995-385-6*) Taft Group.

***National Directory of Nonprofit Organizations 2000, 2.** 11th ed. Taft Group Staff. 1999. 692.75 (*1-56995-381-3*) Taft Group.

National Directory of Nonprofit Organizations, 1990. 1990. 225.00 (*0-914756-70-2*, 00007077) Taft Group.

National Directory of Nonprofit Organizations, 1991, 2 vols. 91st ed. Ed. by William Wade. 1991. 395.00 (*1-879784-04-1*) Taft Group.

National Directory of Nonprofit Organizations, 1991, 2 vols., II. 91st ed. Ed. by William Wade. 1991. 175.00 (*1-879784-02-5*) Taft Group.

National Directory of Nonprofit Organizations, 1991, Vol. 1, 2 Pts. 91st ed. 1991. 269.00 (*1-879784-03-3*, 00000698) Taft Group.

National Directory of Nonprofit Organizations, 1992, 3 vols. 92nd ed. Ed. by Mark W. Scott. 1992. 399.00 (*1-879784-55-6*, 600376) Taft Group.

National Directory of Nonprofit Organizations, 1992, 2 pts., Vol. 1. 92nd ed. Ed. by Mark W. Scott. 1992. 285.00 (*1-879784-59-9*, 600339) Taft Group.

National Directory of Nonprofit Organizations, 1992, Vol. 2. 92nd ed. Ed. by Mark W. Scott. 1992. 175.00 (*1-879784-51-3*, 600340) Taft Group.

National Directory of Nonprofit Organizations 1993, 2 vols., Set. 93rd ed. Ed. by Mark W. Scott. 6000p. 1993. 425.00 (*1-879784-73-4*, 600445) Taft Group.

National Directory of Nonprofit Organizations 1993, 2 vols., Vol. 1. 93rd ed. Ed. by Mark W. Scott. 3000p. 1993. 305.00 (*1-879784-74-2*, 600441) Taft Group.

National Directory of Nonprofit Organizations 1993, 2 vols., Vol. 2. 93rd ed. Ed. by Mark W. Scott. 3000p. 1993. 190.00 (*1-879784-77-7*, 600442) Taft Group.

National Directory of Nonprofit Organizations, 1994, 3 Vols. 94th ed. Ed. by Mark W. Scott. 1993. 450.00 (*1-879784-81-5*) Taft Group.

National Directory of Nonprofit Organizations, 1994, 2 Vols., Vol. 1. 94th ed. Ed. by Mark W. Scott. 1994. 305.00 (*1-879784-82-3*) Taft Group.

National Directory of Nonprofit Organizations, 1994, Vol. 2. 94th ed. Ed. by Mark W. Scott. 1994. 190.00 (*1-879784-83-1*) Taft Group.

National Directory of Nonprofit Organizations, 1995, 3 Vols. 95th ed. 5963p. 1995. 450.00 (*1-879784-86-6*) Taft Group.

National Directory of Nonprofit Organizations, 1995, 2 Vols., Vol. 1. 95th ed. 4206p. 1995. 325.00 (*1-879784-87-4*) Taft Group.

National Directory of Nonprofit Organizations, 1995, Vol. 2. 95th ed. 1700p. 1995. 199.00 (*1-879784-88-2*) Taft Group.

National Directory of Nonprofit Organizations, 1996, 3 Vols. 96th ed. 1996. 470.00 (*1-56995-042-3*) Taft Group.

National Directory of Nonprofit Organizations, 1996, 2 vols., Vol. 1. 96th ed. 3919p. 1996. 305.00 (*1-56995-045-8*, GML00597-600569) Taft Group.

National Directory of Nonprofit Organizations, 1996, Vol. 2. 96th ed. 1957p. 1996. 190.00 (*1-56995-046-6*, GML00597-600570) Taft Group.

National Directory of Nonprofit Organizations, 1997, 3 vols. 5876p. 1996. 470.00 (*1-56995-236-1*, 00109494) Taft Group.

National Directory of Nonprofit Organizations, 1997, 2 pts., Vol. 1. 8th ed. 3919p. 1996. 340.00 (*1-56995-265-5*, 00156616) Taft Group.

National Directory of Nonprofit Organizations, 1997, Vol. 2. 1996. 210.00 (*1-56995-239-6*, 00109497) Taft Group.

National Directory of Nonprofit Organizations, 1998, 3 vols. 1997. 485.00 (*1-56995-240-X*, 00156582) Taft Group.

National Directory of Nonprofit Organizations, 1998, 2 pts., Vol. 1. 1997. 350.00 (*1-56995-241-8*, 00156583) Taft Group.

National Directory of Nonprofit Organizations, 1998, Vol. 2. 1997. 225.00 (*1-56995-244-2*, 00156586) Taft Group.

***National Directory of Nonprofit Organizations 2000, 2 vols.** 11th ed. 4200p. 1999. 370.00 (*1-56995-382-1*) Taft Group.

National Directory of Nonprofit Organizations '96, Pt. 1. 1996. write for info. (*1-56995-043-1*) Taft Group.

National Directory of Nonprofit Organizations '96, Pt. 2. 1996. write for info. (*1-56995-044-X*) Taft Group.

National Directory of Nonprofit Organizations 99, Vol. 1. 1998. 350.00 (*1-56995-312-0*) Taft Group.

National Directory of Nonprofit Organizations 99, Vol. 2. 1998. 225.00 (*1-56995-315-5*) Taft Group.

National Directory of Philanthropy for Native Americans. Greg A. Sanford. Ed. by Phyllis A. Meiners. LC 92-72997. (Multicultural Grant Guides). 160p. 1994. pap. 69.95 (*0-9633694-0-7*) CRC EagleRock.

***National Directory of Physician Organizations.** 2nd ed. Gwen B. Lareau. Ed. by Phyllis Harris. 605p. 1999. pap. text 495.00 (*1-882364-18-X*, Amer Busn Pub) Hlth Res Pub.

National Directory of Private Social Agencies. LC 64-20853. 1990. write for info. (*0-87514-001-7*) Croner.

National Directory of Propane Refilling Stations. 160p. 1996. 5.95 (*0-318-17002-7*) RV Indus Assn.

National Directory of Prosecuting Attorneys, 1987. 1987. 15.00 (*0-318-01201-4*) Natl Dist Atty.

National Directory of Psychotherapy Training Institutes. Ed. by Laurie A. Baum & Bette G. Pounds. LC 93-574. 224p. 1993. pap. 21.95 (*0-87630-720-9*) Brunner-Mazel.

National Directory of Real Estate Financing Sources. Larry L. Sandifar. LC 83-22979. 383p. 1984. 69.95 (*0-13-609438-4*, Busn) P-H.

National Directory of Recognized Alternative & Non-Traditional Colleges & Universities in the United States: National Guide to the Best Alternative Post-Secondary Education Programs in the U.S. 3rd ed. Jean M. De Lafayette & Jean M. De LaFayette. Ed. by Judith Crawford et al. (Lafayette's Encyclopedia of Non-Traditional Higher Education in the United States Ser.). (Illus.). 160p. 1991. pap. 30.00 (*0-939877-16-3*) ACUPAE.

National Directory of Safe Energy Organizations. 8th ed. Critical Mass Energy Project Staff. 80p. (C). 1994. student ed. 30.00 (*0-937188-90-5*) Pub Citizen.

National Directory of Safety Consultants, 1995-1997. 17th ed. 1997. pap. 50.00 (*0-939874-38-5*) ASSE.

National Directory of Seed Money Grants for American Indian Projects. Nevati Joseph. (Multicultural Grant Guides: Vol. 6). 220p. (Orig.). 2000. pap. 109.95 (*0-9633694-9-0*) CRC EagleRock.

National Directory of State Business Licensing & Regulations. 1994. 95.00 (*0-8103-9141-4*, 00009641) Gale.

National Directory of State Business Licensing & Regulations. 2nd ed. Date not set. 89.50 (*0-8103-9505-3*, 00005346) Gale.

National Directory of the Churches of Christ in the United States & Canada. 3rd rev. ed. Dennis C. Kelly. 192p. 1998. pap. 9.95 (*0-9622649-7-0*) Bible Hse.

National Directory of Woman-Owned Business Firms. 9th ed. Thomas D. Johnson. 900p. 1998. pap. 275.00 (*0-933527-64-0*, 070388) Business Research.

***National Directory of Woman-Owned Business Firms.** 10th ed. Thomas D. Johnson. 988p. 1999. pap. 275.00 (*0-933527-71-3*) Business Research.

National Directory of World War One Sources: Manorial Records (Location & Use) (C). 1987. 30.00 (*0-7855-2126-7*, Pub. by Birmingham Midland Soc) St Mut.

National Discovery Trails Act & National Historic Lighthouse Preservation Act: Hearing Before the Committee on Energy & Natural Resources, United States Senate, One Hundred Fifth Congress, Second Session On S. 1069 ... S. 1403 ... February 11, 1998. LC 98-194593. (S. Hrg. Ser.). iii, 65p. 1998. write for info. (*0-16-057022-0*) USGPO.

National Diversity & Global Capitalism. Ed. by Suzanne Berger & Ronald Dore. (Studies in Political Economy). (Illus.). 376p. 1996. pap. text 17.95 (*0-8014-8319-0*) Cornell U Pr.

National Drawing Invitational, 1992. Townsend Wolfe. 66p. 1992. pap. 15.00 (*1-884240-00-3*) Arkansas Art Ctr.

National Drawing Invitational, 1988. Townsend Wolfe. 1988. pap. 15.00 (*0-9612750-3-0*) Arkansas Art Ctr.

National Drawing Invitational, 1986. Townsend Wolfe. 46p. 1986. pap. 15.00 (*0-9612750-2-2*) Arkansas Art Ctr.

National Drawing Invitational, 1994. Townsend Wolfe. 74p. 1994. pap. 15.00 (*1-884240-06-2*) Arkansas Art Ctr.

National Drawing Invitational, 1996. unabridged ed. Townsend Wolfe. (Illus.). 50p. 1996. pap. 18.00 (*1-884240-10-0*) Arkansas Art Ctr.

National Dream Book. Claire Rougemont. 188p. 1996. pap. 15.00 (*0-89540-247-5*, SB-247) Sun Pub.

National Drug Code Directory, 6 vols., Set. 1996. lib. bdg. 6009.99 (*0-8490-6891-6*) Gordon Pr.

N

National Drug Control Policy: Drug Interdiction Effortsin Florida & the Caribbean : Hearing Before the Subcommittee on National Security, International Affairs & Criminal Justice of the Committee on Government Reform & Oversight, House of Representatives, One Hundred Fifth Congress, First Session, July 17, 1997. United States Government. LC 98-156532. iii, 140 p. 1998. write for info. (*0-16-056329-1*) USGPO.

National Drug Control Strategy, 2 vols. 1997. lib. bdg. 602.99 (*0-8490-8224-2*); lib. bdg. 253.75 (*0-8490-6187-3*) Gordon Pr.

*__National Drug Control Strategy: Budget Summary, February 2000.__ 277p. 2000. per. 25.00 (*0-16-050305-1*) USGPO.

*__National Drug Control Strategy: Counterdrug Research & Development Blueprint Update, 2000 Annual Report.__ 2000. per. 6.00 (*0-16-050312-4*) USGPO.

*__National Drug Control Strategy: 2000 Annual Report.__ 168p. 2000. per. 18.00 (*0-16-050355-8*) USGPO.

National Drug Control Strategy, 1997. (Illus.). 120p. 1997. pap. text 50.00 (*1-57979-199-9*) DIANE Pub.

National Drug Control Strategy, 1997. 76p. 1997. pap. 7.50 (*0-16-061869-X*) USGPO.

National Drug Control Strategy, 1996. Barry R. McCaffrey. (Illus.). 101p. (Orig.). 1996. pap. text 35.00 (*0-7881-3196-6*) DIANE Pub.

National Drug Control Strategy (1997) Barry R. McCaffrey. (Illus.). 70p. (Orig.). 1997. pap. text 30.00 (*0-7881-3994-0*) DIANE Pub.

National Drug Control Strategy (1992) A Nation Responds to Drug Use. (Illus.). 214p. (Orig.). (C). 1992. pap. text 30.00 (*0-941375-79-X*) DIANE Pub.

National Drug Control Strategy (1998) A Ten Year Plan, 1998-2007. Barry McCaffrey. (Illus.). 93p. (C). 1999. pap. text 25.00 (*0-7881-7154-2*) DIANE Pub.

*__National Drug Control Strategy, 1999: Budget Summary.__ Government Printing Office Staff. 249p. 1999. pap. text 22.00 (*0-16-049928-3*) USGPO.

*__National Drug Control Strategy 1998: Budget Summary.__ Ed. by Barry R. McCaffrey. (Illus.). 207p. (C). 1999. pap. text 30.00 (*0-7881-8258-7*) DIANE Pub.

National Drug Control Strategy (1994) Reclaiming Our Communities from Drugs & Violence. (Illus.). 135p. (Orig.). (C). 1994. pap. text 35.00 (*0-7881-0705-4*) DIANE Pub.

National Drug Control Strategy (1995) Strengthening Communities' Response to Drugs & Crime. (Illus.). 195p. (Orig.). (C). 1995. pap. text 45.00 (*0-7881-2278-9*) DIANE Pub.

National Drug Policies. (Public Health in Europe Ser.: No. 12). 99p. 1979. 10.00 (*92-9020-131-2*, 1320012) World Health.

*__National E-mail & Fax Directory.__ 2000p. 2000. 140.00 (*0-7876-3439-5*, UXL) Gale.

National Earthquake Hazards Reduction Program: Hearing Before the Subcommittee on Science, Technology & Space of the Committee on Commerce, Science & Transportation, United States Senate, One Hundred Fifth Congress, First Session, April 10, 1997. United States Government. LC 98-144027. (S. Hrg. Ser.). iii, 92 p. 1997. write for info. (*0-16-056040-3*) USGPO.

National Economic Accounts of the United States. Willford I. King et al. Ed. by Wesley C. Mitchell. LC 75-19734. (National Bureau of Economic Research Ser.). (Illus.). 1975. reprint ed. 23.95 (*0-405-07611-8*) Ayer.

National Economic Accounts of the United States: Review, Appraisal, & Recommendations. National Accounts Review Committee. (General Ser.: No. 64). 206p. 1958. reprint ed. 53.60 (*0-87014-063-9*) Natl Bur Econ Res.

National Economic Atlas of China. Ed. by State Statistical Bureau, Institute of Statistics Staff & Chinese Academy of Sciences & State Planning Commi. (Illus.). 326p. 1994. text 375.00 (*0-19-585736-4*) OUP.

National Economic Council: A Work in Progress. I. M. Destler. LC 96-46215. (Policy Analysis in International Economics Ser.: No. 46). (Illus.). 75p. 1996. pap. 11.95 (*0-88132-239-3*) Inst Intl Eco.

National Economic Development Directory, Vol. 1. 144p. 1988. pap. text 24.95 (*0-9621557-0-5*) Natl Econ Dev Direct.

National Economic Planning. Ed. by Max F. Millikan. (Universities-National Bureau Conference Ser.: No. 19). 423p. 1967. 110.00 (*0-87014-310-7*) Natl Bur Econ Res.

National Economic Planning. C. T. Sandford. LC 73-160794. (Studies in the British Economy Ser.). 88p. 1972. write for info. (*0-435-84549-7*) Heinemann.

National Economic Policies, 1. Ed. by Dominick Salvatore. LC 91-178. (Handbook of Comparative Economic Policies Ser.: No. 1). 416p. 1991. lib. bdg. 105.00 (*0-313-26591-7*, SVS/, Greenwood Pr) Greenwood.

National Economic Policies of Chile. Ed. by Gary M. Walton. LC 85-24239. (Contemporary Studies in Economic & Financial Analysis: Vol. 51). 238p. 1986. 78.50 (*0-89232-599-2*) Jai Pr.

*__National Economic Policy of Luang Pradist Manudharm.__ Pridi Banomyong. 2000. pap. 12.00 (*974-7449-23-4*, Pub. by CPNCOCAPB) Lantern Books.

National Economic Review (1st Quarter) Subscription Service: Windows. annuals Wiley-ValuSource Staff. (ValueSource Financial Software Products Ser.). 24p. 1995. 199.00 (*0-471-14639-0*, VA00) Wiley.

National Economic Security: Perceptions, Threats, & Policies. Ed. by Frans A. Alting Von Gesau & Jacques Pelkmans. 253p. 1983. pap. 24.95 (*0-87855-946-9*) Transaction Pubs.

National Economies Europe. David Dyker. 337p. (C). 1992. 108.00 (*0-582-05918-6*) Addison-Wesley.

National Economies of Europe. David Dyker. 337p. (C). 1995. pap. 56.00 (*0-582-05881-3*) Addison-Wesley.

National Economies of Europe. David A. Dyker. LC 92-12829. 1992. pap. text 32.25 (*0-685-72518-9*, 79413) Longman.

National Economy. (Open Learning for Supervisory Management Ser.). 1986. pap. text 19.50 (*0-08-034178-0*, Pergamon Pr) Elsevier.

National Economy. (Open Learning for Supervisory Management Ser.). 1986. pap. text 19.50 (*0-08-070094-2*, Pergamon Pr) Elsevier.

*__National Edition, 2001-2002.__ Millennium Books Editors. (Pets Welcome Ser.). 516p. 2000. pap. 19.95 (*1-888820-11-X*, Pub. by Millennium Calif) Andrews & McMeel.

National Education: 1836 Edition, 2 vols. Frederic Hill. Ed. & Intro. by Jeffrey Stern. (Classics in Education Ser.). 616p. 1996. reprint ed. 164.00 (*1-85506-288-7*) Bks Intl VA.

National Education Goals: The AACTE Member Response. 1992. 5.00 (*0-614-00936-7*) AACTE.

National Education Goals Report: Building a Nation of Learners (1995) (Illus.). 173p. (Orig.). 1996. pap. text 35.00 (*0-7881-2673-3*) DIANE Pub.

National Education Goals Report: Building a Nation of Learners (1996) 6th ed. Cynthia Prince & Leslie Lawrence. (Illus.). 161p. 1997. pap. text 40.00 (*0-7881-3747-6*) DIANE Pub.

National Education Goals Report: Building a Nation of Learners, 1997. 357p. 1997. pap. 23.00 (*0-16-049234-3*) USGPO.

National Education Goals Report: Building a Nation of Learners, 1997. Ed. by James B. Hunt, Jr. (Illus.). 338p. 1998. pap. text 50.00 (*0-7881-4990-3*) DIANE Pub.

*__National Education Goals Report: Building a Nation of Learners, 1998.__ 82p. 1998. pap. 9.00 (*0-16-063676-0*) USGPO.

National Education Goals Report: Building a Nation of Learners (1998) Leslie Lawrence & Cynthia Price-Cohen. 78p. (C). 1999. pap. text 20.00 (*0-7881-7623-4*) DIANE Pub.

*__National Education Goals Report: Building a Nation of Learners 1999.__ Ed. by Ken Nelson. 88p. 2000. pap. text 20.00 (*0-7881-8834-8*) DIANE Pub.

National Education Goals Report: Summary, 1997, Mathematics & Science Achievement For The 21st Century. 45p. 1997. pap. 4.50 (*0-16-063644-2*) USGPO.

National Education Goals Report, Executive Summary: Commonly Asked Questions about Standards & Assessments. (Illus.). 40p. (Orig.). 1997. pap. text 20.00 (*0-7881-3766-2*) DIANE Pub.

National Education Goals Report Summary, 1997: Mathematics & Science Achievement for the 21st Century. Ed. by Ken Nelson. (Illus.). 48p. 1998. pap. text 20.00 (*0-7881-7175-5*) DIANE Pub.

National Education Longitudinal Study Methodology Report. 1997. lib. bdg. 251.95 (*0-8490-6206-3*) Gordon Pr.

National Educational Institute Resource Notebook, 1988: Successful Job Transitions. 200p. 1988. 23.00 (*0-318-36403-4*) A A A C E.

*__National Educational Technology Standards for Students.__ NETS Standards Development Team Staff. (Illus.). 19p. 1998. pap. 5.00 (*1-56484-164-2*) Intl Society Tech Educ.

*__National Educational Technology Standards for Students: Connecting Curriculum & Technology.__ NETS Project Staff. (Illus.). 378p. (YA). (gr. 5-12). 1999. spiral bd. 29.95 (*1-56484-150-2*) Intl Society Tech Educ.

National/800 - 900 Telephone Service Code Book. Kenneth Sperry. 80p. (Orig.). 1992. pap. 9.95 (*0-939780-15-1*) CRB Res.

National Elderly Explanatory Directory of Services (NEEDS) 1991. 27.50 (*0-685-39167-1*) Graduate Group.

National Elections & the Autonomy of the American State Party Systems. James Gimpel. LC 95-53044. (Pitt Series in Policy & Institutional). 241p. (C). 1996. pap. 19.95 (*0-8229-5597-0*); text 45.00 (*0-8229-3940-1*) U of Pittsburgh Pr.

National Elections in Paraguay, 1993. National Democratic Institute for International Af. 200p. pap. 10.95 (*1-880134-24-1*) Natl Demo Inst.

National Electric Code Handbook, 1996. Mark W. Earley et al. 1016p. 1996. 98.50 (*0-87765-405-0*, SP1099) Natl Fire Prot.

National Electric Code, 1996. Mark W. Earley et al. (SPA.). 992p. 1997. pap. 98.50 (*0-87765-435-2*, 70-965SBE) Natl Fire Prot.

National Electric Code Reference Book. 84th ed. Garland. 1984. 27.95 (*0-13-609545-3*) P-H.

National Electrical Code. Incl. 1978. pap. 1981. 1984. 32.50 (*0-685-73729-2*, 70-87) Natl Fire Prot.

National Electrical Code. (Seventy Ser.). 1975. pap. 5.50 (*0-685-57560-8*, 70) Natl Fire Prot.

National Electrical Code Blueprint Reading Based on the 1996 NEC. R. T. Miller. 192p. 1995. pap. 27.96 (*0-8269-1558-2*) Am Technical.

National Electrical Code Blueprint Reading Based on 1981 Code. 8th ed. Kenneth L. Gebert. LC 80-67345. 200p. reprint ed. pap. 62.00 (*0-608-14641-2*, 202320300032) Bks Demand.

National Electrical Code Illustrated Changes Deskbook, 1993. Gregory P. Bierals. LC 93-9555. 1993. write for info. (*0-88173-171-4*) Fairmont Pr.

National Electrical Code Illustrated Changes Deskbook, 1993. Gregory P. Bierals. (C). 1993. 58.00 (*0-13-605932-5*); text 43.50 (*0-685-66612-3*) P-H.

*__National Electrical Code 1999.__ National Fire Protection Agency Staff. (Illus.). 1998. pap. 51.50 (*0-87765-433-6*) Natl Fire Prot.

*__National Electrical Code 1999.__ National Fire Protection Agency Staff. 775p. (C). 1998. pap. 51.50 (*0-87765-432-8*) Thomson Learn.

National Electrical Code, 1993. 1992. pap. 32.50 (*0-87765-383-6*, 70-93SB) Natl Fire Prot.

National Electrical Code, 1996. NFPA Staff. (Electrical Trades Ser.). 1070p. (C). 1995. pap. 51.50 (*0-87765-402-6*, 70-96) Natl Fire Prot.

National Electrical Code: 1999 Handbook. 3rd ed. National Fire Protection Agency Staff. Ed. by Mark W. Earley. LC 77-93950. (Electrical Trades Ser). (Illus.). 1074p. (C). 1999. pap. 98.50 (*0-87765-437-9*, 70HB99) Thomson Learn.

National Electrical Code Questions & Answers, 1984. J. D. Garland. 144p. (C). 1985. pap. 15.95 (*0-13-609553-4*); text 24.00 (*0-13-609561-5*) P-H.

National Electrical Code Study Guide. Don Singleton. 213p. (C). 1994. 30.79 (*1-56870-151-9*) RonJon Pub.

National Electrical Safety Code, ANSI C2-1990. rev. ed. American National Standards Committee. (Illus.). 432p. 1989. pap. 38.00 (*1-55937-011-4*, SH12641) IEEE Standards.

National Electrical Safety Code Handbook: A Discussion of the Grounding Rules, General Rules, & Pts. 1, 2, 3, & 4 of the 3rd 1920-1990 Editions of the National Electrical Safety Code American National Standard C2. Ed. by Allen L. Clapp. LC 91-12657. (Illus.). 436p. (Orig.). 1991. pap. 55.00 (*1-55937-081-5*, SP00018) IEEE Standards.

National Electrical Safety Code Handbook: A Discussion of the Grounding Rules, General Rules, & Pts. 1, 2, 3, & 4 of the 3rd 1920-1990 Editions of the National Electrical Safety Code American National Standard C2. 3rd ed. Ed. by Allen L. Clapp. LC 92-18434. (Orig.). 1992. write for info. (*1-55937-211-7*) IEEE Standards.

National Electrical Safety Code Handbook (NESC) A Discussion of the Grounding Rules, General Rules, & Parts 1, 2, 3, & 4 of the 3rd (1920) Through 1977 Editions of the National Electrical Safety Code, American National Standard C2. 4th ed. Allen L. Clapp & American National Standards Institute Staff. LC 96-9505. 456p. 1997. pap. 89.00 (*1-55937-724-0*, SP1105) IEEE Standards.

National Electrical Safety Code Interpretations, 1994-1996: Interim Collection. 6th ed. 38.00 (*1-55937-712-7*, SH94403) IEEE Standards.

National Electrical Safety Code (NESC) & NESC Handbook: 1997 Editions, 2 vols. 1997. 137.00 (*1-55937-731-3*, SH94419) IEEE Standards.

National Electronic Library: A Guide to the Future for Library Managers. Ed. by Gary M. Pitkin. LC 95-40028. (Greenwood Library Management Collection). 208p. 1996. lib. bdg. 57.95 (*0-313-29613-8*, Greenwood Pr) Greenwood.

National Electronic Packaging & Production Conference, 1984 West: Proceedings of the Technical Program, Anaheim CA, February 28, 29, & March 1, 1984. National Electronic Packaging & Production Confere. LC TK7872.. 529p. 1984. reprint ed. pap. 164.00 (*0-608-11869-9*, 202306000031) Bks Demand.

National Electronic Packaging & Production Conference, 1985 East: Proceedings of the Technical Program, Boston, MA, June 19-21, 1985. National Electronic Packaging & Production Confere. LC TK7872.. 541p. 1985. reprint ed. pap. 167.80 (*0-608-16876-9*, 202768700056) Bks Demand.

National Electronic Packaging & Production Conference, 1985 West: Proceedings of the Technical Program, Anaheim CA, February 26-28, 1985. National Electronic Packaging & Production Confere. LC TK7872.. 973p. 1985. reprint ed. pap. 200.00 (*0-608-13005-2*, 202509000042) Bks Demand.

National Electronic Packaging & Production Conference, 1986 East: Proceedings of the Technical Program, Boston, MA, June 10-12, 1986. National Electronic Packaging & Production Confere. LC TK7872.. 452p. 1986. reprint ed. pap. 140.20 (*0-608-15440-7*, 202936600060) Bks Demand.

National Electronic Packaging & Production Conference, 1986 West: Proceedings of the Technical Program, Anaheim, CA, February 25-27, 1986, 2 vols., 1. National Electronic Packaging & Production Confere. LC TK7872.. 536p. 1986. reprint ed. pap. 166.20 (*0-608-16870-X*, 202768600001) Bks Demand.

National Electronic Packaging & Production Conference, 1986 West: Proceedings of the Technical Program, Anaheim, CA, February 25-27, 1986, 2 vols., 2. National Electronic Packaging & Production Confere. LC TK7872.. 486p. 1986. reprint ed. pap. 150.70 (*0-608-16871-8*, 202768600002) Bks Demand.

National Electronic Packaging & Production Conference, 1987 West: Proceedings of the Technical Program, February 24-26, 1987, 2 vols., 1. National Electronic Packaging & Production Confere. LC TK7872.. (Illus.). 596p. 1987. pap. 184.80 (*0-608-17396-7*, 203023700001) Bks Demand.

National Electronic Packaging & Production Conference, 1987 West: Proceedings of the Technical Program, February 24-26, 1987, 2 vols., 2. National Electronic Packaging & Production Confere. LC TK7872.. (Illus.). 487p. 1987. pap. 151.00 (*0-608-17397-5*, 203023700002) Bks Demand.

National Electronic Packaging & Production Conference, 1988 East: Proceedings of the Technical Program, June 13-16, 1988, Boston, MA. National Electronic Packaging & Production Confere. LC TK7872.. (Illus.). 515p. 1988. reprint ed. pap. 159.70 (*0-608-18186-2*, 203291400081) Bks Demand.

National Electronic Packaging & Production Conference, 1988 West: Proceedings of the Technical Program, February 22-25, 1988. National Electronic Packaging & Production Confere. LC TK7872.. 947p. reprint ed. pap. 200.00 (*0-608-18184-6*, 203291100081) Bks Demand.

National Electronic Packaging & Production Conference, 1989 West: Proceedings of the Technical Program; NEPCON West '89, Anaheim, CA, March 6-9, 1989, Vol. 1. National Electronic Packaging & Production Confere. LC TK7870.N3. (Illus.). 978p. 1989. reprint ed. pap. 200.00 (*0-8357-6738-8*, 203539400001) Bks Demand.

National Electronic Packaging & Production Conference, 1989 West: Proceedings of the Technical Program; NEPCON West '89, Anaheim, CA, March 6-9, 1989, Vol. 2. National Electronic Packaging & Production Confere. LC TK7870.N3. (Illus.). 1010p. 1989. reprint ed. pap. 200.00 (*0-8357-6739-6*, 203539400002) Bks Demand.

National Electronic Packaging & Production Conference, 1990 Vol. 1: Proceedings of the Technical Program, Anaheim, CA, February 26-March 1, 1990. National Electronic Packaging & Production Confere. LC TK7870.N33. 984p. 1990. 200.00 (*0-7837-0145-4*, 204043500001) Bks Demand.

National Electronic Packaging & Production Conference, 1990 East: Proceedings of the Technical Program, Boston, MA, June 11-14, 1990. National Electronic Packaging & Production Confere. LC TK7870.N33. 1056p. 1990. pap. 200.00 (*0-7837-0148-9*, 204043700016) Bks Demand.

National Electronic Packaging & Production Conference, 1990 West Vol. 2: Proceedings of the Technical Program, Anaheim, CA, February 26-March 1, 1990. National Electronic Packaging & Production Confere. LC TK7870.N33. 929p. 1990. 200.00 (*0-7837-0146-2*, 204043500002) Bks Demand.

National Electronic Packaging & Production Conference, 1991 West: Proceedings of the Technical Program, Anaheim CA, February 24-28, 1991, Vol. 1. National Electronic Packaging & Production Confere. LC TK7870.N33. 782p. 1991. pap. 200.00 (*0-7837-0149-7*, 204043800001) Bks Demand.

National Electronic Packaging & Production Conference, 1991 West: Proceedings of the Technical Program, Anaheim CA, February 24-28, 1991, Vol. 2. National Electronic Packaging & Production Confere. LC TK7870.N33. 705p. 1991. pap. 200.00 (*0-7837-0150-0*, 204043800002) Bks Demand.

National Electronic Packaging & Production Conference, 1991 West: Proceedings of the Technical Program, Anaheim CA, February 24-28, 1991, Vol. 3. National Electronic Packaging & Production Confere. LC TK7870.N33. 923p. 1991. pap. 200.00 (*0-7837-0151-9*, 204043800003) Bks Demand.

National Electronic Packaging & Production Conference, 1992 East: Proceedings of the Technical Program, Boston, MA, June 15-18, 1992. National Electronic Packaging & Production Confere. LC TK7874.N35. 467p. 1992. reprint ed. pap. 144.80 (*0-7837-2688-0*, 204306600006) Bks Demand.

National Electronic Packaging & Production Conference, 1992 West: Proceedings of the Technical Program, Anaheim CA, February 23-27, 1992, Vol. 1. National Electronic Packaging & Production Confere. LC TK7874.N35. (Illus.). 464p. 1992. reprint ed. pap. 143.90 (*0-7837-3073-X*, 204306500001) Bks Demand.

National Electronic Packaging & Production Conference, 1992 West: Proceedings of the Technical Program, Anaheim CA, February 23-27, 1992, Vol. 2. National Electronic Packaging & Production Confere. LC TK7874.N35. (Illus.). 663p. 1992. reprint ed. pap. 200.00 (*0-7837-3074-8*, 204306500002) Bks Demand.

National Electronic Packaging & Production Conference, 1992 West: Proceedings of the Technical Program, Anaheim CA, February 23-27, 1992, Vol. 3. National Electronic Packaging & Production Confere. LC TK7874.N35. (Illus.). 805p. 1992. reprint ed. pap. 200.00 (*0-7837-3075-6*, 204306500003) Bks Demand.

National Electronic Packaging & Production Conference, 1993 East: Proceedings of the Technical Program, Bayside Exposition Center, Boston, Massachusetts, June 14-17, 1993. National Electronic Packaging & Production Confere. LC TK7874.N35. (Illus.). 600p. 1993. reprint ed. pap. 186.00 (*0-7837-7035-9*, 204685000004) Bks Demand.

National Electronic Packaging & Production Conference, 1993 West: Proceedings of the Technical Program, Anaheim CA, February 7-11, 1993, Vol. 1. National Electronic Packaging & Production Confere. LC TK7874.N35. (Illus.). 562p. 1993. reprint ed. pap. 174.30 (*0-7837-7036-7*, 204685100001) Bks Demand.

National Electronic Packaging & Production Conference, 1993 West: Proceedings of the Technical Program, Anaheim CA, February 7-11, 1993, Vol. 2. National Electronic Packaging & Production Confere. LC TK7874.N35. (Illus.). 579p. 1993. reprint ed. pap. 179.50 (*0-7837-7037-5*, 204685100002) Bks Demand.

National Electronic Packaging & Production Conference, 1993 West: Proceedings of the Technical Program, Anaheim CA, 1993, Vol. 3. National Electronic Packaging & Production Confere. LC TK7874.N35. (Illus.). 974p. 1993. reprint ed. pap. 200.00 (*0-7837-7038-3*, 204685100003) Bks Demand.

National Electronic Packaging & Production Conference, 1994 West: Proceedings of the Technical Program, Anaheim CA, February 27-March 4, 1994, Vol. 1. National Electronic Packaging & Production Confere. LC TK7874.N35. (Illus.). 840p. 1994. reprint ed. pap. 200.00 (*0-7837-7039-1*, 204685200001) Bks Demand.

National Electronic Packaging & Production Conference, 1994 West: Proceedings of the Technical Program, Anaheim CA, February 27-March 4, 1994, Vol. 2. National Electronic Packaging & Production Confere. LC TK7874.N35. (Illus.). 852p. 1994. reprint ed. pap. 200.00 (*0-7837-7040-5*, 204685200002) Bks Demand.

An Asterisk (*) at the beginning of an entry indicates that the title is appearing for the first time.

National Electronic Packaging & Production Conference, 1994 West: Proceedings of the Technical Program, Anaheim CA, February 27-March 4, 1994, Vol. 3. National Electronic Packaging & Production Confere. LC TK7874.N35. 878p. 1993. reprint ed. pap. 200.00 (*0-7837-7041-3*, 204685200003) Bks Demand.

National Electronics Conference: Proceedings, Marriott Oak Brook Hotel, Oak Brook, Illinois, October 24, 25 & 26, 1983, Vol. 37. Ed. by Edward C. Bertnolli & William H. Tranter. LC TK0005.N37. 550p. reprint ed. pap. 170.50 (*0-608-13460-0*, 202275800037) Bks Demand.

National Electronics Conference: Proceedings: Regency Hyatt O'Hare, Chicago, Illinois, October 6-8, 1975, Vol. 30. National Electronics Conference Staff. Ed. by William H. Tranter. LC TK0005.M37. 369p. reprint ed. pap. 114.40 (*0-608-16741-X*, 202680600030) Bks Demand.

National Electronics Conference: Proceedings: The Conrad Hilton Hotel, Chicago, Illinois, December 8-10, 1969, Vol. 25. National Electronics Conference Staff. LC TK0005.N37. 972p. reprint ed. pap. 200.00 (*0-608-16728-2*, 202680500025) Bks Demand.

National Elevator Manufacturing Industry's Installation Manual: Basic Field Practices for Installation of Elevators & Escalators. (Illus.). 505p. 1989. reprint ed. 40.00 (*1-886536-19-8*) Elevator Wrld.

National Emergency Training & Information Guide. Patrick Lavalla & Robert C. Stoffel. (Illus.). 350p. 1992. ring bd. 30.00 (*0-913724-35-1*) Emerg Response Inst.

National Employment Screening Directory, 1987: A Guide to Background Investigations. National Employment Screening Services Staff. (National Employment Screening Directory Ser.). (Illus.). 320p. 1987. pap. 95.00 (*0-941233-14-6*) Source Okla.

National Endowment for Democracy: A Foreign Policy Branch Gone Awry. Beth Sims. 93p. 1990. pap. 8.95 (*0-911213-28-7*) Interhemisp Res Ctr.

***National Endowment for the Arts, 1997 Annual Report.** 128p. 1998. per. 13.00 (*0-16-061858-4*) USGPO.

National Endowment for the Arts, 1965-1995: A Brief Chronology of Federal Involvement in the Arts. LC 95-44670. 1995. write for info. (*0-614-09508-5*) Natl Endow Arts.

***National Endowment for the Humanities Annual Report, 1997.** 76p. 1998. pap. 6.50 (*0-16-061857-6*) USGPO.

National Endowments: A Critical Symposium. Ed. by Laurence Jarvik et al. 108p. 1995. pap. 6.95 (*1-886442-02-9*, Sec Thght Bks) Ctr Study Popular.

National Energy Modeling System. 1996. lib. bdg. 250.95 (*0-8490-5973-9*) Gordon Pr.

National Energy Modeling System. National Research Council Staff. LC 93-205713. 164p. 1992. pap. text 19.00 (*0-309-04634-3*) Natl Acad Pr.

***National Energy Modeling System: Overview, 1998.** 72p. 1998. pap. 5.00 (*0-16-063526-8*) USGPO.

National Energy Planning & Management in Developing Countries. Ed. by H. Neu & D. Bain. 1983. text 199.50 (*90-277-1589-0*) Kluwer Academic.

National Energy Strategy: Powerful Ideas for America. 1993. lib. bdg. 262.95 (*0-8490-8922-0*) Gordon Pr.

National Energy Strategy: Powerful Ideas for America. 1996. lib. bdg. 255.95 (*0-8490-5974-7*) Gordon Pr.

National Engineering Conference, 1995: Engineering Design - the Keys to Australia's Future Prosperity. LC 96-165609. (National Conference Proceedings 95 Ser.: Vol. 2). (Illus.). 93p. 1995. pap. 43.50 (*0-85825-625-8*, Pub. by Inst Engrs Aust-EA Bks) Accents Pubns.

National Engineering Conference, 1996: The Darwin Summit - Engineering Tomorrow Today. Geoffrey R. Medley. (National Conference Proceedings Ser.: Vol. 96/03). (Illus.). 510p. 1996. pap. 96.00 (*0-85825-647-9*, Pub. by Inst Engrs Aust-EA Bks) Accents Pubns.

National Engineering Management Conference, 1991: Managing in a Changing Future. Intro. by James Pretsell. (Illus.). 202p. (Orig.). 1991. pap. 57.75 (*0-85825-541-3*, Pub. by Inst Engrs Aust-EA Bks) Accents Pubns.

National Entrepreneurship Education Agenda for Action. Novella Ross et al. 114p. 1984. 9.50 (*0-318-22156-X*, LT66) Ctr Educ Trng Employ.

National Environmental Engineering Conference, 1995: Towards a Sustainable Future: Challenges & Responses. Contrib. by Sven Eriksson. (Illus.). 232p. 1995. pap. 120.00 (*0-85825-623-1*, Pub. by Inst Engrs Aust-EA Bks) Accents Pubns.

National Environmental Health Programmes: Proceedings of the WHO Expert Committee on National Environmental Health Programmes & Their Planning, Organization & Administration, Geneva, 1969. WHO Staff. (Technical Reports: No. 439). 56p. 1970. pap. text 5.00 (*92-4-120439-7*, 1100439) World Health.

National Environmental Impact Assessment: Guidelines 1993. IUCN Staff. 1994. pap. 25.00 (*0-7855-0464-8*, Pub. by Ratna Pustak Bhandar) St Mut.

National Environmental Policies: A Comparative Study of Capacity-Building: With a Data Appendix, International Profiles of Change Since 1970. Ed. by Martin Janicke et al. LC 96-30956. (Illus.). 338p. 1997. 79.95 (*3-540-61519-9*) Spr-Verlag.

National Environmental Policies: A Comparative Study of Capacity-Building: With a Data Appendix, International Profiles of Change Since 1970. Martin Janicke et al. LC 96-30956. 1996. write for info. (*0-387-61519-9*) Spr-Verlag.

National Environmental Policy Act: An Agenda for the Future. Lynton K. Caldwell. LC 98-38666. 272p. 1998. text 29.95 (*0-253-33444-6*) Ind U Pr.

National Environmental Policy ACT: Readings from the Environmental Professional. John Lemons. LC 96-125265. 1995. write for info. (*0-86542-462-4*) Blackwell Sci.

National Environmental Policy (NEPA) Process. Keshava S. Murthy. 224p. 1988. 130.00 (*0-8493-6746-8*, KF3775, CRC Reprint) Franklin.

National Environmental Protection Act. Hickok. (Paralegal Ser.). (C). 2001. pap. 19.95 (*0-8273-7987-0*) Delmar.

National Epics. Kate M. Rabb. LC 76-84355. (Granger Index Reprint Ser.). 1977. 21.95 (*0-8369-6059-9*) Ayer.

National Erectors' Association & the International Association of Bridge & Structural Ironworkers: The United States Commission on Industrial Relations. Luke Grant. LC 72-156414. (American Labor Ser., No. 2). 1971. reprint ed. 16.95 (*0-405-02922-5*) Ayer.

National Estuary Program after Four Years: A Report to Congress. U. S. Environmental Protection Agency Staff. (Illus.). 112p. 1997. reprint ed. 19.00 (*0-89904-598-7*, Bear Meadows Resrch Grp); reprint ed. 19.00 (*0-89904-597-9*, Ecosytems Resrch) Crumb Elbow Pub.

National Ethics Bodies. (Bioethics Ser.). 1993. 15.00 (*92-871-2225-3*, Pub. by Council of Europe) Manhattan Pub Co.

National Evaluation of the Supportive Housing Demonstration Program: Final Report. Mark L. Matulef et al. (Illus.). 300p. (Orig.). (C). 1995. pap. text 45.00 (*0-7881-1994-X*) DIANE Pub.

National Evils & Practical Remedies, with the Plan of a Model Town. James S. Buckingham. LC 73-21. (Illus.). xxx, 512p. 1973. reprint ed. lib. bdg. 65.00 (*0-678-00786-1*) Kelley.

***National Exam & Self-Study Guide for Assisted Living Administration: The Knowledge Base.** James E. Allen. LC 00-22374. 2000. pap. write for info. (*0-8261-1354-0*) Springer Pub.

National Excellence: A Case for Developing America's Talent. 1994. lib. bdg. 250.00 (*0-8490-8586-1*) Gordon Pr.

National Excellence: A Case for Developing America's Talent. Pat O'Connell Ross. 41p. 1993. pap. 3.25 (*0-16-042928-5*) USGPO.

National Excellence: The Case for Developing America's Talent. (Illus.). 65p. (Orig.). (C). 1994. pap. text 20.00 (*0-7881-0439-X*) DIANE Pub.

National Exhibition Centre: Shop Window for the World. Edward D. Mills. (Illus.). 120p. 1976. pap. 14.95 (*0-8464-0667-5*) Beekman Pubs.

***National Expenditures for Mental Health, Alcohol & Other Drug Abuse Treatment (1996)** Tami Mark. (Illus.). 75p. (C). 1999. pap. text 20.00 (*0-7881-7901-2*) DIANE Pub.

National Experience. 8th ed. John M. Blum. (C). 1993. text 75.50 (*0-15-500366-6*, Pub. by Harcourt Coll Pubs) Harcourt.

National Experience. 8th ed. Morgan. (C). 1993. pap. text 33.50 (*0-15-500734-3*, Pub. by Harcourt Coll Pubs) Harcourt.

National Experience, No. 2. 8th ed. Judith M. Walter. (C). 1993. pap. text, student ed. 22.50 (*0-15-500733-5*, Pub. by Harcourt Coll Pubs) Harcourt.

National Experience, Pt. 1. 8th ed. John M. Blum et al. (Illus.). 885p. (C). 1993. pap. text 61.00 (*0-15-500730-0*, Pub. by Harcourt Coll Pubs) Harcourt.

National Experience, Vol. 1. 8th ed. John Blum. (C). 1993. pap. text, student ed. 22.50 (*0-15-500732-7*, Pub. by Harcourt Coll Pubs) Harcourt.

National Experience: A History of the United States. 7th ed. John M. Blum et al. 920p. (C). 1988. student ed. write for info. (*0-318-64537-8*); write for info. (*0-318-64538-6*); disk. write for info. (*0-318-64539-4*) Harcourt Coll Pubs.

National Experience: A History of the United States since 1865, Pt. 2. 7th ed. John M. Blum et al. 560p. (C). 1989. disk. write for info. (*0-318-64536-X*) Harcourt Coll Pubs.

National Experience: A History of the United States to 1877, Pt. 1. 7th ed. John M. Blum et al. 450p. (C). 1989. disk. write for info. (*0-318-64531-9*) Harcourt Coll Pubs.

National Experience in the Use of Community Health Workers: A Review of Current Issues & Problems. V. Ofosu-Amaah. (WHO Offset Publications: No. 71). 49p. 1983. 8.00 (*92-4-170071-8*) World Health.

National Export Strategy. 1997. lib. bdg. 250.95 (*0-8490-6240-3*) Gordon Pr.

National Export Strategy-Toward the Next American Century: A United States Strategic Response to Foreign Competitive Practices. 1998. lib. bdg. 253.75 (*0-8490-9099-7*) Gordon Pr.

National Export Strategy, Toward the Next American Century: A United States Strategic Response to Foreign Competitive Practices, 4th Annual Report to the United States Congress. 232p. 1996. per. 20.00 (*0-16-048825-7*) USGPO.

National Exposure Registry: Policies & Procedures Manual. rev. ed. 44p. (C). 1995. pap. text 25.00 (*0-7881-1981-8*) DIANE Pub.

National Express Group PLC & Central Trains Limited: A Report on the Merger SI Monopolies & Mergers Commission Report, Command Paper 3774. (Command Papers (All) Ser.: No. 81011068). 1998. 35.00 (*0-10-137742-8*, HM77428, Pub. by Statnry Office) Bernan Associates.

National Express Group PLC & Scotrail Railways Limited: A Report on the Merger Monopolies & Mergers Commission Report, Command Paper 3773. (Command Papers (All) Ser.: No. 81011068). 1998. 35.00 (*0-10-137732-0*, HM77320, Pub. by Statnry Office) Bernan Associates.

***National Faculty Directory.** 31st ed. 2000. 301.00 (*0-7876-3379-8*, UXL) Gale.

National Faculty Directory, 2000, 3 vols. 29th ed. 4000p. 1999. 770.00 (*0-7876-2280-X*, GML00299-111802, Gale Res Intl) Gale.

***National Faculty Directory 2001, 3 vols.** 31st ed. 4000p. 2000. 770.00 (*0-7876-3371-2*) Gale.

National Faculty Dirtectory: Supplement. Date not set. 301.00 (*0-7876-2285-0*) Gale.

National Faculty Salary Survey by Discipline & Rank in Private Colleges & Universities. Ed. by College & University Personnel Assoc. Staff. 1995. 40.00 (*1-878240-45-5*) Coll & U Personnel.

National Faculty Salary Survey by Discipline & Rank in Private Colleges & Universities, 1994-95. Ed. by College & University Personnel Assoc. Staff. 1995. 40.00 (*1-878240-44-7*) Coll & U Personnel.

National Faculty Salary Survey by Discipline & Rank in Private Four-Year Colleges & Universities, 1995-96. 1996. pap. 80.00 (*1-878240-51-X*) Coll & U Personnel.

National Faculty Survey by Discipline & Rank in Public Four-Year Colleges & Universities, 1995-96. 1996. 80.00 (*1-878240-52-8*) Coll & U Personnel.

National Fair Housing Summit: Final Report. 150p. (Orig.). (C). 1994. pap. text 40.00 (*0-7881-0806-9*) DIANE Pub.

National Faith of Japan: A Study in Modern Shinto. Daniel C. Holtom. LC 95-17251. (Kegan Paul Japan Library: Vol. 1). (Illus.). 340p. 1996. 110.00 (*0-7103-0521-4*, Pub. by Kegan Paul Intl) Col U Pr.

National Family Policies: Their Relationship to the Role of the Family in the Development Process. (The Family Ser.: No. 3). 56p. pap. 10.00 (*92-1-130121-1*) UN.

***National Farm Survey 1941-43: State Surveillance & the Countryside in England & Wales in the Second World War.** Brian Short et al. LC 99-33180. (CABI Publishing Ser.). 264p. 2000. 70.00 (*0-85199-389-3*) OUP.

***National Fax Directory: 2000 Edition.** 2000th ed. Gale Group Staff. 2000p. 1999. 130.00 (*0-7876-2450-0*) Gale.

National Fictions: Literature, Film & the Construction of Australian Narrative. 2nd ed. Graeme Turner. 184p. 1995. pap. 22.95 (*1-86373-504-6*, Pub. by Allen & Unwin Pty) Paul & Co Pubs.

National Fine Center: Progress Made but Challenges Remain for Criminal Debt System. (Illus.). 37p. (Orig.). (C). 1996. pap. text 25.00 (*0-7881-3441-8*) DIANE Pub.

National Fire Alarm Code Handbook. 3rd ed. Ed. by Wayne D. Moore & Merton W. Bunker. LC 96-87464. 1997. 88.00 (*0-87765-410-7*) Natl Fire Prot.

***National Fire Alarm Code Handbook, 1, 3.** 3rd ed. Merton W. Bunker, Jr. & Wayne D. Moore. LC 99-75955. 422p. 2000. 18.00 (*0-87765-445-X*, 72HB99) Natl Fire Prot.

National Fire Codes, 10 vols. Incl. Vol. 1. 720p. Vol. 2. 640p. Vol. 3. 720p. Vol. 4. 736p. Vol. 5. 720p. Vol. 6. 656p. Vol. 7. 624p. 720p. Vol. 9. 592p. Vol. 10. 624p. write for info. (*0-318-59528-1*) Natl Fire Prot.

National Fire Codes, 16 vols. 1976. 90.00 (*0-685-68873-9*) Natl Fire Prot.

National Fire Codes, 16 vols. LC 38-27236. (Illus.). 1979. pap. 95.00 (*0-87765-140-X*, FC-SET) Natl Fire Prot.

***National Fire Gas Code Handbook, 4, 1.** 3rd ed. Theodore C. Lemoff. LC 99-75206. (Illus.). 422p. 2000. 18.00 (*0-87765-446-8*, 54HB99) Natl Fire Prot.

National Firefighters Coloring Book. Louis A. DePasquale. (Illus.). 26p. (J). 1997. pap. write for info. (*0-9635356-1-7*) All Hands.

National Firefighters Recipe Book. 3rd ed. Louis A. DePasquale et al. Ed. by Iris H. DePasquale. LC 93-71381. (Illus.). 270p. 1993. reprint ed. spiral bd. 15.00 (*0-9635356-0-9*) All Hands.

***National Five-Digit Zip Code & Post Office Directory, 1999, Vols. 1-2.** 3210p. 1999. per. 25.00 (*0-16-061866-5*) USGPO.

***National Five-Digit Zip Code & Post Office Directory, 2000, 2, Vol. 1-2.** 3245p. 2000. per. 25.00 (*0-16-058963-0*) USGPO.

National Flag of Nepal: An Introductory. D. R. Shrestha. 1998. pap. 22.00 (*0-7855-7453-0*, Pub. by Ratna Pustak Bhandar) St Mut.

National Flags. Intro. by Fred L. Israel. LC 97-28951. (Looking into the Past). (Illus.). 64p. (YA). (gr. 5 up). 1999. lib. bdg. 16.95 (*0-7910-4686-9*) Chelsea Hse.

National Fluid Power Association Directory & Member Guide, 1997-98. National Fluid Power Association Staff. 208p. 1997. 100.00 (*0-942220-39-0*) Natl Fluid Power.

National Food Survey: Annual Report on Household Food Consumption & Expend, 1996. 110p. 1997. pap. 60.00 (*0-11-243031-7*, HM30317, Pub. by Statnry Office) Bernan Associates.

National Food Survey - Annual Report on Household Food Consumption & Expend, 1997. 110p. 1998. pap. 65.00 (*0-11-243044-9*, HM30449, Pub. by Statnry Office) Bernan Associates.

National Foreclosure Catalog: Nationwide Access to Foreclosed Real Estate. 3rd ed. Consumer Information Services Incorporated Staff. LC 99-175992. 128 p. 1996. write for info. (*0-9647365-1-9*) Public Infor Servs.

National Forest Planning: A Conservationist's Guide. 2nd ed. V. Alaric Sample & Peter C. Kirby. write for info. (*0-318-58978-8*) Wilderness Soc.

***National Front & France: Ideology, Discourse, & Power.** Peter Davies. LC 98-42868. 278p. 1999. 90.00 (*0-415-15866-4*) Routledge.

National Front & French Politics: The Resistible Rise of Jean-Marie Le Pen. Jonathan Marcus. LC 95-12259. 212p. (C). 1995. text 50.00 (*0-8147-5534-8*) NYU Pr.

National Front & French Politics: The Resistible Rise of Jean-Marie Le Pen. Jonathan Marcus. LC 95-12259. 212p. (C). 1996. pap. text 19.50 (*0-8147-5535-6*) NYU Pr.

National Frontiers & International Scientific Cooperation. Zhores A. Medvedev. (Medvedev Papers: Vol. 1). 296p. (Orig.). 1975. pap. 28.50 (*0-85124-127-1*, Pub. by Spokesman) Coronet Bks.

National Fuel Gas Code Handbook. 3rd ed. Theodore C. Lemoff et al. LC 97-81708. xiii, 547p. 1997. 78.00 (*0-87765-409-3*) Natl Fire Prot.

National Galleries of Scotland. Text by Keepers of the Galleries. (Illus.). 128p. 1990. 30.00 (*1-870248-30-9*) Scala Books.

National Gallery. National Gallery Staff. (Academy Architecture Ser.). (Illus.). 96p. 1986. pap. 19.95 (*0-312-55953-4*) St Martin.

National Gallery - London. Homan Potterton. LC 88-51948. (Illus.). 216p. 1989. pap. 14.95 (*0-500-20161-7*, Pub. by Thames Hudson) Norton.

National Gallery Book of Days. Ed. by Maureen McNeil. (Museum Gift Bks.). (Illus.). 160p. (Orig.). 1982. 10.00 (*0-939456-05-2*) Galison.

National Gallery Companion Guide. enl. rev. ed. Erika Langmuir. (National Gallery Publications). (Illus.). 344p. 1998. pap. 20.00 (*0-300-07481-6*) Yale U Pr.

National Gallery Complete Illustrated Catalogue. Baker. (C). 1995. 160.00 (*0-300-06362-8*) Yale U Pr.

National Gallery Complete Illustrated Catalogue. Baker. (Illus.). (C). 1995. 80.00 (*0-300-06359-8*) Yale U Pr.

National Gallery, London. Michael Wilson. (Illus.). 144p. (Orig.). 1984. pap. 15.00 (*0-935748-57-1*) Scala Books.

National Gallery of Art. LC 90-71649. (World of Art Ser.). (Illus.). 288p. 1993. pap. 14.95 (*0-500-20251-6*, Pub. by Thames Hudson) Norton.

National Gallery of Art. rev. ed. John Walker. (Illus.). 696p. 1984. 75.00 (*0-8109-1370-4*) Abrams.

National Gallery of Art Activity Book. Maura A. Clarkin. (Illus.). 112p. 1994. pap. 16.95 (*0-8109-2595-8*, Pub. by Abrams) Time Warner.

National Gallery of Art Heritage Address Book. Ed. by Maureen McNeil. (Illus.). 208p. 1982. 10.95 (*0-939456-02-8*) Galison.

National Gallery of Art, Washington. rev. ed. National Gallery of Art (U. S.) Staff. LC 95-1028. (Illus.). 696p. 1995. pap. 39.98 (*0-8109-8148-3*, Pub. by Abrams) Time Warner.

National Gallery of Art, Washington: Ten Centuries of Art. Martha Richler. LC 97-61688. (Illus.). 224p. 1998. 40.00 (*1-85759-176-3*) Scala Books.

***National Gallery of Australia: An Introduction to the Collection.** National Gallery of Australia Staff. LC 00-272597. 1998. write for info. (*0-642-13093-0*, Pub. by Natl Gallery) U of Wash Pr.

National Gallery of Ireland. Raymond Keaveney et al. (Illus.). 128p. 1991. 25.00 (*1-870248-58-9*) Scala Books.

National Gallery Technical Bulletin. Ed. by Nicoll. (National Gallery Publications: Vol. 19). (Illus.). 96p. 1998. pap. 30.00 (*0-300-07573-1*) Yale U Pr.

***National Gallery Technical Bulletin.** Yale University Press Staff. Vol. 20. (Illus.). 104p. 2000. 30.00 (*0-300-08394-7*) Yale U Pr.

National Gallery Technical Bulletin, Vol. 14. (Illus.). 96p. 1993. pap. 30.00 (*0-300-06717-8*) Yale U Pr.

National Gallery Technical Bulletin, Vol. 15. (Illus.). 104p. 1994. pap. 30.00 (*0-300-06780-1*) Yale U Pr.

National Gallery Technical Bulletin, Vol. 16. (Illus.). 96p. 1995. pap. 30.00 (*0-300-06779-8*) Yale U Pr.

National Gallery Technical Bulletin, Vol. 17. (Illus.). 104p. 1996. pap. 30.00 (*0-300-06777-1*) Yale U Pr.

National Gallery Technical Bulletin, Vol. 18. (Illus.). 112p. 1997. pap. 30.00 (*0-300-07163-9*) Yale U Pr.

***National Gallery Technical Bulletin 20.** Yale University Press Staff. Vol. 20. (Illus.). 112p. 1999. pap. text 30.00 (*0-300-07888-9*) Yale U Pr.

***National Game.** 2nd ed. Alfred H. Spink. LC 99-46257. (Writing Baseball Ser.). (Illus.). 424p. 2000. pap. 19.95 (*0-8093-2304-4*) S Ill U Pr.

***National Game: Baseball & American Culture.** John P. Rossi. LC 99-53674. (Illus.). 256p. 2000. text 25.00 (*1-56663-287-0*, Pub. by I R Dee) Natl Bk Netwk.

***National Gang Survey (1996) Summary.** Ed. by Shay Bilchik. (Illus.). 75p. 1999. pap. text 20.00 (*0-7881-8453-9*) DIANE Pub.

National Gangs Resource Handbook: An Encyclopedic Reference. George W. Knox. 254p. 1995. 40.00 (*1-55605-257-X*) Wyndham Hall.

National Garden Book: For the U.S. & Southern Canada. Sunset Staff. LC 96-61519. (Illus.). 656p. 1997. pap. text 34.95 (*0-376-03860-8*) Sunset Books.

National Gem Collection. National Museum of Natural History Staff & Jeffrey E. Post. LC 97-7633. (Illus.). 144p. 1997. 39.95 (*0-8109-3690-9*, Pub. by Abrams) Time Warner.

National Genealogy Directory, 1985. (C). 1987. 50.00 (*0-7855-2069-4*, Pub. by Birmingham Midland Soc) St Mut.

National Geographic: Spanish Edition. Taschen Staff. (SPA.). 1997. 39.99 (*3-8228-8537-1*, Pub. by Benedikt Taschen) Bks Nippan.

National Geographic: The Photographs. National Geographic Editors. (Illus.). 1994. pap. 46.95 (*0-87044-987-7*) Natl Geog.

National Geographic: The Photographs. National Geographic Staff. (Illus.). 400p. 1994. per. 50.00 (*0-87044-986-9*) Natl Geog.

National Geographic Action Books, Set. Ed. by Donald J. Crump. Incl. Amazing Monkeys. Judith E. Rinard. 1985. Hide & Seek. Toni Eugene. 1985. (Illus.). 1985. 21.95 (*0-87044-597-9*) Natl Geog.

***National Geographic Animal Encyclopedia.** National Geographic Society (U. S.) Staff. LC 99-48020. 2000. write for info. (*0-7922-7180-7*) Natl Geog.

***National Geographic Atlas of Natural America.** 2000. 40.00 (*0-7922-7955-7*) Natl Geog.

N

National Geographic Atlas of the World. National Geographic Staff. (n). (Illus.). 90p. 1997. per. 25.00 (*0-7922-7120-3*) Natl Geog.

National Geographic Atlas of the World. 2nd ed. National Geographic Society Staff. LC 95-19579. 1995. 100.00 (*0-7922-3038-8*) Natl Geog.

National Geographic Atlas of the World. 2nd rev. ed. National Geographic Society (U. S.) Staff. LC 95-19579. 1995. pap. text. write for info. (*0-7922-3036-1*) Natl Geog.

National Geographic Atlas of the World. 2nd rev. ed. National Science Resource Center Staff. LC 95-19579. 1995. text. write for info. (*0-7922-3040-X*) Natl Geog.

National Geographic Atlas of the World. 6th deluxe rev. ed. National Geographic Society Staff. LC 92-27845. (Special Publications Series 26). (Illus.). 412p. 1993. 100.00 (*0-87044-835-8*) Natl Geog.

National Geographic Atlas of the World. 7th ed. National Geographic Society. LC 99-27026. (Illus.). 280p. 1999. per. 125.00 (*0-7922-7528-4*) Natl Geog.

National Geographic Atlas of the World, Series 26. 6th rev. ed. Ed. by National Geographic Society Staff. (Special Publications). (Illus.). 1990. 65.00 (*0-87044-834-X*) Natl Geog.

National Geographic Atlas of World History. Noel Grove & National Geographic Society Staff. LC 97-28731. 1997. denim. write for info. (*0-7922-7023-1*) Natl Geog.

***National Geographic Beginner's World Atlas: A First Atlas For Beginning Explorers.** National Geographic Society Staff. LC 99-34652. (Illus.). 64p. (J). (gr. k-3). 1999. per. 17.95 (*0-7922-7502-0*) Natl Geog.

***National Geographic Book of Mammals.** National Geographic Society Staff. (Illus.). 608p. (YA). (gr. 5 up). 1998. per. 34.45 (*0-7922-7141-6*, Pub. by Natl Geog) Publishers Group.

National Geographic Desk Reference. LC 99-23549. 699p. 1999. per. 40.00 (*0-7922-7082-7*) Natl Geog.

National Geographic Desk Reference: A Geographical Reference with Hundreds of Photographs, Maps, Charts & Graphs. National Geographic Society Staff. LC 99-23549. (Illus.). 1999. write for info. (*0-7922-7083-5*) Natl Geog.

National Geographic Destinations: American Southwest. J. Paige & B. Dale. 200p. 1999. per. 15.00 (*0-7922-7452-0*, Pub. by Natl Geog) S&S Trade.

National Geographic Destinations: The Sierra, Nevada. N. Grove & Schermeister. 200p. 1999. per. 15.00 (*0-7922-7453-9*) Natl Geog.

National Geographic Destinations-Antartic. Kim Heacox. 1999. pap. 15.00 (*0-7922-7454-7*) Natl Geog.

National Geographic Driving Guide - California. Ed. by National Geographic Staff. 1998. pap. 14.95 (*0-7922-7365-6*) Natl Geog.

National Geographic Driving Guide - Canada. Ed. by National Geographic Staff. 160p. 1998. per. 14.95 (*0-7922-7366-4*) Natl Geog.

National Geographic Driving Guide - Florida. Ed. by National Geographic Staff. 160p. 1998. per. 14.95 (*0-7922-7368-0*) Natl Geog.

National Geographic Driving Guide - New York. Ed. by National Geographic Staff. 1998. pap. 14.95 (*0-7922-7369-9*) Natl Geog.

National Geographic Driving Guide to America. National Geographic Society Staff. 1999. pap. 14.95 (*0-7922-7422-9*); pap. 14.95 (*0-7922-7423-7*); per. 14.95 (*0-7922-7421-0*, Pub. by Natl Geog) S&S Trade.

National Geographic Driving Guide to America Southwest. Mark Miller et al. LC 96-32384. (National Geographic's Driving Guides to America Ser.). 160p. 1997. pap. 14.95 (*0-7922-3425-1*, Pub. by Natl Geog) S&S Trade.

National Geographic Driving Guide to Pacific Northwest. Ed. by National Geographic Staff. 160p. 1998. per. 14.95 (*0-7922-7367-2*) Natl Geog.

National Geographic Europe: Continent Maps. National Geographic Society Staff. 1997. pap. 9.95 (*1-57262-150-8*); pap. 14.95 (*1-57262-151-6*) MapQuest.

***National Geographic Expeditions Atlas.** National Geographic Society (U. S.) Staff. LC 99-86883. 2000. write for info. (*0-7922-7617-5*) Natl Geog.

***National Geographic Expeditions Atlas.** National Geographic Society Staff. LC 99-86883. (Illus.). 304p. 2000. per. 39.50 (*0-7922-7616-7*, Pub. by Natl Geog) S&S Trade.

***National Geographic Eyewitness to the 20th Century.** National Geographic Staff. LC 98-22756. (Destinations Ser.). (Illus.). 400p. (YA). (gr. 5-8). 1998. per. 40.00 (*0-7922-7049-5*) Natl Geog.

National Geographic Eyewitness to the 20th Century. deluxe ed. National Geographic Society Staff. LC 98-22756. 1998. write for info. (*0-7922-7025-8*) Natl Geog.

***National Geographic Family Adventure Vacations: Animal Encounters Cultural Explorations & Learning Escapes in the US & Coastline Evolution of the Upper Adriatic Sea Due to Sea Level Rise & Natural Anthropogenic Land Subsidence.** National Geographic Staff. LC 99-462106. 320p. 2000. per. 25.00 (*0-7922-7590-X*) Natl Geog.

National Geographic Guide to America's Bird Watching: Sites West. Mel White. LC 99-13552. (Illus.). 224p. 1999. per. 21.00 (*0-7922-7450-4*) Natl Geog.

National Geographic Guide to America's Great Houses. Henry Wiencek. LC 98-53013. 320p. 1999. per. 25.00 (*0-7922-7424-5*) Natl Geog.

National Geographic Guide to America's Hidden Corners. National Geographic Society Staff. LC 98-4637. (Illus.). 384p. 1999. pap. 25.00 (*0-7922-7211-0*) Natl Geog.

National Geographic Guide to America's Hidden Corners deluxe ed. National Geographic Society (U. S.) Staff. LC 98-4637. 384 p. 1998. write for info. (*0-7922-7210-2*) Natl Geog.

National Geographic Guide to America's Historic Places. Thomas Schmidt & Michael Lewis. LC 96-38536. 1996. write for info. (*0-7922-3415-4*) Natl Geog.

National Geographic Guide to America's Historic Places. Thomas Schmidt & Michael Lewis. LC 96-38536. 250p. 1997. pap. 24.00 (*0-7922-3414-6*) Natl Geog.

National Geographic Guide to America's Public Gardens. May Z. Jenkins. LC 98-4722. 1998. pap. 25.00 (*0-7922-7152-1*) Natl Geog.

National Geographic Guide to Birdwatching Sites. National Geographic Society Staff. LC 98-53023. 320p. 1999. pap. 21.00 (*0-7922-7374-5*) Natl Geog.

***National Geographic Guide to 100 Easy Hikes: Washington DC, Virginia, Maryland, Delaware.** National Geographic Staff. LC 99-462358. 224p. 2000. per. 15.00 (*0-7922-7588-8*, Pub. by Natl Geog) S&S Trade.

***National Geographic Guide to Small Town Escapes.** National Geographic Staff. LC 00-35144. (Illus.). 352p. 2000. per. 25.00 (*0-7922-7589-6*, Pub. by Natl Geog) S&S Trade.

National Geographic Guide to State Parks. Ed. by National Geographic Staff. 384p. 1998. per. 24.00 (*0-7922-7364-8*) Natl Geog.

National Geographic Guide to the Civil War: National Battlefield Parks. National Geographic Editors. (Illus.). 160p. 1993. per. 12.00 (*0-87044-878-1*) Natl Geog.

National Geographic Guide to Watching Wildlife. National Geographic Staff. LC 97-46750. 1998. pap. 25.00 (*0-7922-7130-0*) Natl Geog.

***National Geographic Italy: Country & Region Map.** National Geographic Society Staff. 1998. pap. 13.95 (*1-57262-368-3*) MapQuest.

***National Geographic Japan: Country & Region Maps: County & Region Maps.** National Geographic Society Staff. 1998. pap. 27.95 (*1-57262-369-1*) MapQuest.

National Geographic Magazine, 10 vols., Set. 1990. reprint ed. 750.00 (*1-57588-336-8*, 306440) W S Hein.

National Geographic on Assignment U. S. A. Priit Vesilind. LC 97-29891. 336p. 1997. per. 50.00 (*0-7922-7010-X*) Natl Geog.

National Geographic on Assignment U. S. A. Priit Vesilind & National Geographic Society (U. S.) Staff. LC 97-29891. 1997. write for info. (*0-7922-7011-8*) Natl Geog.

National Geographic Park Profiles: Canada's National Parks. Ed. by National Geographic Staff. 200p. 1998. per. 15.00 (*0-7922-7355-9*) Natl Geog.

National Geographic Park Profiles: Canyon Country Parklands. Scott Thybony. 200p. 1998. per. 15.00 (*0-7922-7353-2*) Natl Geog.

***National Geographic Photographs: The Milestones: A Visual Legacy of the World.** National Geographic Society Staff. LC 99-29397. (Illus.). 1999. write for info. (*0-7922-7521-7*) Natl Geog.

***National Geographic Photographs: Then & Now.** National Geographic Staff. 1998. 50.00 (*0-676-57897-7*) Random.

***National Geographic Photography Field Guide: Secrets to Making Great Pictures.** Peter Burian & Robert Caputo. LC 99-23595. 352p. 1999. per. 24.95 (*0-7922-7498-9*, Pub. by Natl Geog) S&S Trade.

***National Geographic Photography Field Guide: Secrets to Making Great Pictures.** Peter K. Burian et al. LC 99-23595. (Illus.). 1999. write for info. (*0-7922-7496-2*) Natl Geog.

National Geographic Picture Atlas of Our Fifty States. National Geographic Society Staff. Ed. by Margaret Sedeen. LC 91-28084. (Illus.). 264p. 1994. 25.00 (*0-87044-859-5*) Natl Geog.

National Geographic Picture Atlas of Our Universe. rev. ed. Roy A. Gallant. Ed. by Margaret Sedeen. LC 86-8775. (Illus.). 284p. 1994. lib. bdg. 23.95 (*0-7922-2956-8*) Natl Geog.

National Geographic Picture Atlas of Our World. rev. ed. National Geographic Society Staff. LC 93-4514. (Illus.). 256p. 1993. lib. bdg. write for info. (*0-87044-964-8*) Natl Geog.

National Geographic Picture Atlas of Our World. rev. ed. National Geographic Society Staff. LC 93-4514. (Illus.). 256p. 1994. 25.00 (*0-87044-960-5*) Natl Geog.

National Geographic Road Atlas & Travel Planner. National Geographic Staff. (Illus.). 124p. 1998. pap. 6.95 (*1-57262-414-0*, N3012) MapQuest.

National Geographic Society: 100 Years of Adventure & Discovery. C. D. Bryan. (Illus.). 480p. 1990. 55.00 (*0-8109-1376-3*) Abrams.

National Geographic Society: 100 Years of Adventure & Discovery. rev. enl. ed. C. D. Bryan. LC 97-10714. (Illus.). 528p. 1997. 49.50 (*0-8109-3696-8*, Pub. by Abrams) Time Warner.

***National Geographic Standard Road Atlas, 2000.** (Illus.). 144p. 1999. pap. 10.97 (*1-57262-478-7*, Ntl Geog Maps) MapQuest.

***National Geographic Traveler: Sydney.** Evan McHugh. LC 99-40370. 272p. 1999. per. 22.95 (*0-7922-7435-0*) Natl Geog.

***National Geographic Traveler: The Caribbean.** Nick Hannah & Emma Stanford. LC 99-44267. 400p. 1999. per. 27.95 (*0-7922-7434-2*, Pub. by Natl Geog) S&S Trade.

***National Geographic Traveler Australia.** Rolf Martin Smith. LC 99-40297. (Illus.). 400p. 1999. per. 22.95 (*0-7922-7431-8*, Pub. by Natl Geog) S&S Trade.

National Geographic Traveler Britian. National Geographic Society Staff. LC 99-11700. 400p. 1999. pap. 27.95 (*0-7922-7425-3*) Natl Geog.

National Geographic Traveler Canada. National Geographic Society Staff. LC 99-10549. 1999. pap. 27.95 (*0-7922-7427-X*) Natl Geog.

***National Geographic Traveler Florida.** Kathy Arnold & Paul Wade. LC 99-39976. 272p. 1999. per. 22.95 (*0-7922-7432-6*) Natl Geog.

National Geographic Traveler France. National Geographic Society. LC 98-54974. 400p. 1999. per. 27.95 (*0-7922-7426-1*, Pub. by Natl Geog) S&S Trade.

National Geographic Traveler London. National Geographic Society Staff. LC 99-12613. 272p. 1999. pap. 22.95 (*0-7922-7428-8*, Pub. by Natl Geog) S&S Trade.

***National Geographic Traveler Miami & the Keys.** Mark Miller. LC 99-40354. 271p. 1999. per. 22.95 (*0-7922-7433-4*) Natl Geog.

***National Geographic United States Atlas for Young Explorers: A Complete Reference Guide to the United States.** National Geographic Society Staff. (Illus.). 176p. (J). (gr. 2-6). 1999. 24.95 (*0-7922-7115-7*) Natl Geog.

***National Geographic United States Physical.** National Geographic Society Staff. (Reference Maps Ser.). 1998. pap. 12.95 (*1-57262-329-2*) MapQuest.

National Geographic United States Political. National Geographic Society Staff. (Reference Maps Ser.). 1997. pap. 12.95 (*1-57262-249-0*) MapQuest.

***National Geographic United States Political.** National Geographic Society Staff. 1998. pap. 9.95 (*1-57262-374-8*) MapQuest.

National Geographic World Atlas for Young Explorers: A Complete World Reference for Adventurous Minds. National Geographic Society Staff. LC 98-18366. (National Geographic Ser.). (Illus.). 176p. (J). (gr. 3-7). 1998. per. 24.95 (*0-7922-7341-9*) Natl Geog.

***National Geographic World Physical/Ocean Floor.** National Geographic Society Staff. 1998. pap. 59.95 (*1-57262-332-2*) MapQuest.

***National Geographic World Physical/Ocean Floor.** National Geographic Society Staff. 1998. pap. 34.95 (*1-57262-278-4*) MapQuest.

***National Geographic World Political.** National Geographic Society Staff. (Reference Maps Ser.). 1998. pap. 9.95 (*1-57262-373-X*) MapQuest.

***National Geographic World Satellite.** National Geographic Society Staff. 1998. pap. 15.95 (*1-57262-377-2*); pap. 25.95 (*1-57262-378-0*) MapQuest.

***National Geographical Deluxe Road Atlas, 2000.** (Illus.). 168p. 1999. pap. 16.99 (*1-57262-477-9*, Ntl Geog Maps) MapQuest.

National Geographics Birder's Journal. National Geographic Staff. 464p. 1999. per. 14.95 (*0-7922-7456-3*, Pub. by Natl Geog) S&S Trade.

National Geographic's Driving Guides to America. Jerry C. Dunn et al. LC 96-37340. 1996. write for info. (*0-7922-3427-8*) Natl Geog.

National Geographic's Driving Guides to America. National Geographic Society Staff. LC 96-29758. 1997. write for info. (*0-7922-3428-6*) Natl Geog.

National Geographic's Guide to America's Historic Places. 1996. write for info. (*0-7922-3416-2*) Natl Geog.

***National Geographic's Guide to National Parks of the United States.** 3rd ed. 2001. 25.00 (*0-7922-7028-2*) Natl Geog.

National Geographic's Guide to Scenic Highways & Byways. National Geographic Society Book Division Staff. LC 95-16166. (Illus.). 352p. 1996. per. 21.95 (*0-7922-2950-9*) Natl Geog.

National Geographic's Guide to Scenic Highways & Byways. deluxe ed. National Geographic Society Book Division Staff. LC 95-16166. (Illus.). 1995. write for info. (*0-7922-2951-7*) Natl Geog.

National Geographic's Guide to the Lewis & Clark Trail. Thomas Schmidt. LC 98-8482. 160p. 1998. per. 14.00 (*0-7922-7156-4*) Natl Geog.

National Geographic's Guide to the National Parks of the United States. National Geographic Staff & Elizabeth L. Newhouse. LC 97-168279. (Illus.). 448p. 1997. per. 24.00 (*0-7922-7016-9*) Natl Geog.

National Geographic's Guide to the State Parks of the United States. National Geographic Society Staff. LC 97-14297. 1997. write for info. (*0-7922-7050-9*); pap. write for info. (*0-7922-7051-7*) Natl Geog.

National Geographic's Guide to the State Parks of the United States. National Geographic Society Staff. LC 97-14297. 384p. 1998. 30.00 (*0-7922-7024-X*) Natl Geog.

National Geographic's Guide to Wildlife Watching: 100 of the Best Places in America to See Animals in Their Natural Habitats. Glen Martin & National Geographic Society Staff. LC 97-46750. 1998. 21.95 (*0-7922-7131-9*) Natl Geog.

National Geographic's Hide & Seek. Toni Eugene. LC 98-16367. (Action Book Ser.). (Illus.). 12p. (YA). (ps-12). 1999. 16.00 (*0-7922-7102-5*, Pub. by Natl Geog) Publishers Group.

***National Geographic's How Things Work: Everyday Technology Explained.** John Langone. LC 99-11776. (Illus.). 272p. 1999. 34.50 (*0-7922-7150-5*, Pub. by Natl Geog) S&S Trade.

National Geographic's How Things Work: Everyday Technology Explained. John Langone & National Science Resource Center Staff. LC 99-11776. 1999. write for info. (*0-7922-7151-3*) Natl Geog.

National Geographic's Last Wild Places. National Geographic Society (U. S.) Staff. LC 96-22973. 1997. 35.00 (*0-7922-3500-2*) Natl Geog.

***National Geographic's Ultimate Adventure Sourcebook.** McMenamin. 384p. 2000. per. 30.00 (*0-7922-7591-8*, Pub. by Natl Geog) S&S Trade.

National Geomagnetic Initiative. National Research Council, Commission on Geoscienc. 264p. (Orig.). (C). 1993. pap. text 28.00 (*0-309-04977-6*) Natl Acad Pr.

***National Geotechnical Experimentation Sites.** Jean Benoit & A. J. Lutenegger. LC 00-22935. (Geotechnical Special Publications). 2000. write for info. (*0-7844-0484-4*) Am Soc Civil Eng.

National Government. Barbara Snilberdick Feinberg. LC 92-25915. (First Bks.). 64p. (J). 1993. lib. bdg. 22.00 (*0-531-20155-4*) Watts.

National Government & Public Health. J. A. Tobey. LC 77-74961. (American Federalism-the Urban Dimension Ser.). (Illus.). 1978. lib. bdg. 36.95 (*0-405-10503-7*) Ayer.

National Government & Social Welfare: What Should Be the Federal Role? Ed. by John E. Hansan & Robert Morris. LC 97-1468. 216p. 1997. 59.95 (*0-86569-266-1*, Auburn Hse) Greenwood.

National Government & the Natural Gas Industry, 1946-56: A Study in the Making of a National Policy. Kenneth K. Marcus. Ed. by Stuart Bruchey. LC 78-22697. (Energy in the American Economy Ser.). (Illus.). 1979. lib. bdg. 91.95 (*0-405-12000-1*) Ayer.

National Government 1931-1940. Smart. LC 99-12190. 1999. text 59.95 (*0-312-22329-3*) St Martin.

National Grain Policies. annuals Incl. 2. 1975-1976., **2 Vols.** pap. 30.00 (*92-5-100001-8*, F296); (Orig.). write for info. (*0-318-60480-9*) Bernan Associates.

National Growth & Economic Change in the Upper Midwest. James Henderson & Anne O. Krueger. LC 65-17015. 245p. reprint ed. pap. 76.00 (*0-608-14637-4*, 205587500039) Bks Demand.

National Guard Almanac. Sol Gordon. 252p. 1998. 6.75 (*1-888096-60-8*) Uniformed Srvs.

National Guard & National Defense: The Mobilization of the Guard in World War II. Robert B. Sligh. LC 91-28770. 208p. 1992. 55.00 (*0-275-94056-X*, C4056, Praeger Pubs) Greenwood.

National Guard in Politics. Martha Derthick. LC 65-11588. (Harvard Political Studies). 210p. reprint ed. pap. 65.10 (*0-7837-2251-6*, 205733900004) Bks Demand.

National Guard of the United States: A Half Century of Progress. Elbridge Colby. 369p. 1977. pap. text 46.95 (*0-89126-037-4*) MA-AH Pub.

National Guard Support in the Fight Against Illegal Drugs: Hearing Before the Subcommittee on National Security, International Affairs & Criminal Justice of the Committee on Government Reform & Oversight, House of Representatives, 105th Congress, 1st Session, May 14, 1997. USGPO Staff. LC 98-160067. iii, 81 p. 1998. pap. write for info. (*0-16-056256-2*) USGPO.

National Guide to Educational Credit for Training Programs, 1988. American Council on Education Staff. 639p. (C). 1988. text 39.95 (*0-02-900021-1*) Free Pr.

***National Guide to Educational Credit for Training Programs, 2000.** 10th ed. Ed. by American Council on Education Staff. (Ace/Oryx Series on Higher Education). 1200p. 2000. pap. 90.00 (*1-57356-281-5*) Oryx Pr.

National Guide to Funding for Children, Youth, & Families. 4th ed. Foundation Center Staff. 1095p. 1997. pap. text 150.00 (*0-87954-711-1*) Foundation Ctr.

***National Guide to Funding for Children, Youth & Families.** 5th ed. 1095p. 1999. 150.00 (*0-87954-877-0*) Foundation Ctr.

National Guide to Funding for Community Development. 2nd ed. Foundation Center Staff. 808p. 1998. 135.00 (*0-87954-769-3*) Foundation Ctr.

***National Guide to Funding for Elementary & Secondary Education.** Foundation Center Staff. 1999. pap. 140.00 (*0-87954-880-0*) Foundation Ctr.

National Guide to Funding for Elementary & Secondary Education. 4th ed. 725p. 1997. pap. 140.00 (*0-87954-715-4*) Foundation Ctr.

National Guide to Funding for Information Technology. 414p. 1997. 115.00 (*0-87954-709-X*, FIT) Foundation Ctr.

National Guide to Funding for Information Technology. 2nd ed. Foundation/Center staff. 414p. 1999. pap. text 115.00 (*0-87954-879-7*) Foundation Ctr.

National Guide to Funding for Libraries & Information Services. 4th ed. Foundation Center Staff. LC 97-178445. 234p. 1997. pap. 95.00 (*0-87954-716-2*) Foundation Ctr.

***National Guide to Funding for Libraries & Information Services.** 5th ed. CENTER Foundation Center Staff. 234p. 1999. pap. 95.00 (*0-87954-878-9*) Foundation Ctr.

National Guide to Funding for the Environment & Animal Welfare. 4th ed. Ed. by Liz Rich et al. 527p. 1998. 95.00 (*0-87954-770-7*, FIE4) Foundation Ctr.

National Guide to Funding for Women & Girls. 4th ed. Foundation Center Staff. 414p. 1997. pap. text 115.00 (*0-87954-712-X*) Foundation Ctr.

***National Guide to Funding for Women & Girls.** 5th ed. 414p. 1999. 115.00 (*0-87954-881-9*) Foundation Ctr.

***National Guide to Funding in Aids.** 206p. 1999. 75.00 (*0-87954-882-7*) Foundation Ctr.

National Guide to Funding in Arts & Culture. 5th ed. Foundation Center Staff. 1138p. 1998. 145.00 (*0-87954-768-5*) Foundation Ctr.

National Guide to Funding in Health. 5th ed. Foundation Center Staff. 1195p. 1997. pap. text 150.00 (*0-87954-710-3*) Foundation Ctr.

***National Guide to Funding in Health.** 6th ed. 1195p. 1999. 150.00 (*0-87954-876-2*) Foundation Ctr.

National Guide to Funding in Higher Education. 5th ed. Foundation Center Staff. 1275p. 1998. 145.00 (*0-87954-771-5*, HIED5) Foundation Ctr.

National Guide to Funding in Religion. 4th ed. 865p. 1997. pap. 140.00 (*0-87954-714-6*) Foundation Ctr.

***National Guide to Funding in Religion.** 5th ed. 865p. 1999. 140.00 (*0-87954-875-4*) Foundation Ctr.

National Guide to Funding in Substance Abuse: 600+ Grantmakers Included! 2nd ed. 238p. 1998. 95.00 (*0-87954-773-1*, FSA2) Foundation Ctr.

An Asterisk (*) at the beginning of an entry indicates that the title is appearing for the first time.

National Guide to Guest Homes. Maxine Coplin. (Illus.). (Orig.). 1981. pap. 4.95 (0-686-29699-0, 0-96057804) Home on Arrange.

***National Guidelines for Death Investigation.** Stephen C. Clark. (Illus.). 48p. (C). 1999. reprint ed. pap. text 25.00 (0-7881-7896-2) DIANE Pub.

National Guild of Community Schools of Music Observations & Recommendations. Max Kaplan. 103p. 1966. 20.00 (0-318-21721-X) NGCSA.

National Guns First: Training for Law Enforcement Officers to Help Reduce Illegal Trafficking of Firearms. rev. ed. PERF (Police Executive Research Forum) Staff & BJA (Bureau of Justice Assistance) Staff. 1999. pap. 20.00 (1-878734-63-6) Police Exec Res.

National Health & Safety Performance Standards: Guidelines for Out-of-Home Child Care Programs. (Illus.). 410p. (Orig.). (C). 1996. pap. text 45.00 (0-7881-2650-4) DIANE Pub.

National Health Care: An Annotated Guide to the Current Literature. annot. ed. Ed. by N. G. Arashvili. 204p. 1994. pap. text 95.00 (1-56072-113-8) Nova Sci Pubs.

National Health Care: Issues & Background. Ed. by C. J. Spreding. 290p. (C). 1993. lib. bdg. 135.00 (1-56072-109-X) Nova Sci Pubs.

National Health Care: Law, Policy, Strategy. Donald L. Westerfield. LC 92-40184. 224p. 1993. 55.00 (0-275-94474-3, C4474, Praeger Pubs) Greenwood.

National Health Care: Lessons for the United States & Canada. Ed. by Jonathan Lemco. 304p. 1994. text 54.50 (0-472-10440-3, 10440) U of Mich Pr.

National Health Development Networks in Support of Primary Health Care. (WHO Offset Publications: No. 94). 53p. 1986. pap. text 10.00 (92-4-170094-7, 1120094) World Health.

National Health Directory, 1997. Aspen Reference Group. 250p. 1997. 99.00 (0-8342-0903-9, 20903) Aspen Pub.

National Health Directory, 1996 Edition. Ed. by Aspen Reference Group Staff. 496p. 1996. 99.00 (0-8342-0800-8) Aspen Pub.

National Health Directory, 1995. Aspen Reference Group Staff. (Illus.). 624p. 1995. text 99.00 (0-8342-0596-3) Aspen Pub.

National Health Directory, 1998. Aspen Staff. 472p. 1998. 99.00 (0-8342-1057-6, 10576) Aspen Pub.

National Health Education Standards: Achieving Health Literacy. AAHE Staff et al. 79p. (Orig.). 1995. pap. 3.00 (0-88314-611-8, 301-10035) AAHPERD.

National Health Insurance: Benefits, Costs, & Consequences. Karen Davis. LC 77-91832. (Studies in Social Economics). 182p. 1975. 29.95 (0-8157-1760-1); pap. 10.95 (0-8157-1759-8) Brookings.

National Health Insurance: What Now, What Later, What Never? Ed. by Mark V. Pauly. LC 80-22761. (AEI Symposia Ser.: No. 80C). 399p. reprint ed. pap. 123.70 (0-8357-4513-9, 203737100008) Bks Demand.

National Health Insurance & Health Resources: The European Experience. Jan Blanpain et al. LC 77-25818. 320p. 1978. 29.95 (0-674-26955-1) HUP.

***National Health Interview Survey: Research for the 1995-2004 Redesign.** LC 99-15863. (Vital & Health Statistics Ser.). 1999. write for info. (0-8406-0557-9) Natl Ctr Health Stats.

***National Health Interview Survey: Research for the 1995-2004 Redesign.** David Judkins. 127p. 1999. pap. 12.00 (0-16-050096-6) USGPO.

National Health Planning in Developing Countries: Report of a WHO Expert Committee, 1967. (Technical Report Ser.). 40p. 1967. pap. text 6.00 (92-4-120350-1, 1100350) World Health.

National Health Program Book: A Source Guide for Advocates. David Himmelstein & Steffie Woolhandler. 1994. pap. 11.95 (1-56751-018-3); lib. bdg. 29.95 (1-56751-019-1) Common Courage.

National Health Service? The Restructuring of Health Care in Britain since 1979. John Mohan. LC 94-22962. 1995. text 59.95 (0-312-12410-4) St Martin.

National Health Service & the Labour Market. J. A. Stilwell & R. A. Wilson. 322p. 1992. 77.95 (1-85628-390-9, Pub. by Avebry) Ashgate Pub Co.

National Health Service Corps: Opportunities to Stretch Scarce Dollars & Improve Provider Placement. (Illus.). 59p. (Orig.). (C). 1996. pap. text 20.00 (0-7881-3106-0) DIANE Pub.

National Health Service Management in the 1980s. Steve Harrison. 206p. 1994. 66.95 (1-85628-663-0, Pub. by Avebry) Ashgate Pub Co.

National Health Systems & Their Reorientation Towards Health for All Guidance for Policy-Making. B. Kleczkowski et al. (Public Health Papers: No. 77). 120p. 1984. pap. text 11.00 (92-4-130077-9, 1110077) World Health.

National Health Systems of the World, Vols. I & II. Milton I. Roemer. (Illus.). 1056p. 1993. 140.00 (0-19-508623-6) OUP.

National Health Systems of the World: The Issues, Vol. 2. Milton I. Roemer. 368p. 1993. text 59.50 (0-19-507845-4) OUP.

National Health Systems of the World Vol. 1: Countries, Vol. 1. Milton I. Roemer. (Illus.). 688p. 1991. text 89.50 (0-19-505320-6) OUP.

National Healthlines Directory (TM), 1994: Toll-Free 800 Numbers. rev. ed. Herner & Company Staff. LC 92-71167. viii, 194p. 1994. pap. 30.00 (0-87815-065-X) Info Resources.

National Heat Transfer Conference: Fundamental Experimental Techniques in Heat Transfer, Thermal Hydraulics of Advanced Nuclear Reactors, Heat & Mass Transfer in Supercritical Liquid Proceedings, National Heat Transfer Conference (32nd, 1997, Baltimore, Maryland. Ed. by Donald E. Beasley et al. LC 97-74086. (HTD Ser.: Vol. 350). 255p. 1997. pap. 100.00 (0-7918-1817-9) ASME.

National Heat Transfer Conference: Fundamentals of Convection, Turbulent Heat Transfer, & Mixed Convection Heat Transfer Proceedings, National Heat Transfer Conference (32nd, 1997, Baltimore, Maryland) Ed. by P. H. Oosthuizen et al. LC 97-74082. (HTD Ser.: Vol. 346). 195p. 1997. pap. 90.00 (0-7918-1813-6) ASME.

National Heat Transfer Conference, Atlanta, GA, August 8-11, 1993. 418p. 1994. 50.00 (0-89448-187-8, 700194) Am Nuclear Soc.

National Heat Transfer Conference, Houston, TX, Jul. 24-27, 1988. 460p. 1988. 45.00 (0-89448-140-1, 700133) Am Nuclear Soc.

National Heat Transfer Conference, 1991, Minneapolis, MN, July 28-31, 1991. 356p. 1991. 40.00 (0-89448-162-2, 700161) Am Nuclear Soc.

National Heat Transfer Conference, 1985: Proceedings in Denver, CO August 4-7, 1985. 504p. 75.00 (0-89448-120-7, 700101) Am Nuclear Soc.

National Heat Transfer Conference, Philadelphia, PA, August 6-9, 1989. 320p. 1989. 40.00 (0-89448-149-5, 700143) Am Nuclear Soc.

National Heat Transfer Conference, Pittsburgh, PA: Aug. 9-12, 1987. 1987. 26.00 (0-89448-134-7, 700124) Am Nuclear Soc.

National Heat Transfer Conference Proceedings, San Diego, CA, Aug. 10-12, 1992. 417p. 2000. 50.00 (0-89448-177-0, 700181) Am Nuclear Soc.

National Herbart Society Yearbooks One to Five, 1895-1899, 5 vols., Set. National Herbart Society Staff. LC 70-89209. (American Education: Its Men, Institutions & Ideas, Ser. 1). 1978. reprint ed. 47.95 (0-405-01448-1) Ayer.

National Heroes. Reg Green. (Illus.). 192p. 1997. 35.00 (1-85158-922-8, Pub. by Mainstream Pubng) Trafalgar.

National Heroes & Heroines. 25.95 (0-382-40693-1) Cobblestone Pub Co.

National Highway Program in Poland: A Strategic Entry Report, 1996. Compiled by Icon Group International Staff. (Country Industry Report). (Illus.). 182p. 1999. ring bd. 1820.00 incl. audio compact disk (0-7418-0590-1) Icon Grp.

National Highway Traffic Safety Administration Emergency Medical Dispatch: National Standard Curriculum, Manager's Guide. Government Printing Office Staff. 162p. 1996. ring bd. 13.00 (0-16-048548-7) USGPO.

National Highway Traffic Safety Administration Reauthorization Act of 1997: Hearing Before the Subcommittee on Telecommunications, Trade & Consumer Protection of the Committee on Commerce, House of Representatives, 105th Congress, 1st Session, on H. R. 2691, October 29, 1997. USGPO Staff. LC 98-139002. iii, 42 p. 1997. pap. write for info. (0-16-055866-2) USGPO.

National Highway Traffic Safety Administration's Truck Operator Qualification Examination (NTSATOQ) Jack Rudman. (Admission Test Ser.: ATS-96). 1994. pap. 29.95 (0-8373-5096-4) Nat Learn.

National Hispanic Readership Profile. Leo Estrada. 120p. 1998. pap. 19.95 (1-889379-03-4) WPR Pubng.

National Historic Mechanical Engineering Landmarks. Ed. by R. S. Hartenberg. (Illus.). (Orig.). 1979. 15.00 (0-685-96308-X, H00140) ASME.

National Historic Preservation Act Amendments of 1991: Hearings Before the Subcommittee on Public Lands, National Parks & Forests of the Committee on Energy & Natural Resources, United States Senate, 102nd Congress, 1st Session, on S. 684 ... Macon, GA, September 5, 1991; Augusta, GA, September 6, 1991, 2 Vols. USGPO Staff. LC 92-165699. 1992. write for info. (0-16-038751-5) USGPO.

National History As Cultural Process: A Survey of the Interpretations of Ukraine's Past in Polish, Russian & Ukranian Historical Writing from the Earliest Times to 1914. Stephen Velychenko. LC 91-91238. (Illus.). xxvi, 283p. 24.95 (0-920862-75-6) Ukrainian Acad.

National History in the Heroic Poem: A Comparison of the Aeneid & the Fairie Queen. Nancy P. Pope. LC 90-42002. (Studies in Comparative Literature). 208p. 1990. reprint ed. 15.00 (0-8240-5472-5) Garland.

National History of France, 10 vols. in 11. Ed. by Frantz Funck-Brentano. LC 74-168076. reprint ed. 495.00 (0-404-50790-5) AMS Pr.

National Holidays. Helen Frost. Ed. by Gail Saunders-Smith. (Illus.). 24p. 39.80 (0-7368-0562-1, Pebble Bks) Capstone Pr.

National Home & Hospice Care Survey: 1992 Summary. National Center for Health Statistics Staff. LC 94-1779. (Vital & Health Statistics Ser.: Series 13, No. 117). 110p. 7.00 (0-614-02910-4, 017-022-01271-5) Natl Ctr Health Stats.

National Home & Hospice Care Survey: 1994 Summary. Adrienne Jones. 130p. 1997. per. 12.00 (0-16-061454-6) USGPO.

***National Home & Hospice Care Survey: 1996 Summary.** Barbara J. Haupt. 248p. 1999. per. 23.00 (0-16-050112-1) USGPO.

National Home Mortgage Qualification Kit: How to Qualify for & Obtain the Mortgage Money You Need - Guaranteed! Benji O. Anosike. (Illus.). 220p. (Orig.). 1997. pap. 24.95 (0-932704-41-7) Do It Yourself Legal Pubs.

National Honor Society Handbook. rev. ed. 1997. pap. 15.00 (0-88210-051-3, 7319708) Natl Assn Student.

National Honours & Awards of Australia. Michael Maton. (Illus.). 136p. 1995. 42.50 (0-86417-679-1, Pub. by Kangaroo Pr) Seven Hills Bk.

National Hospital Ambulatory Medical Care Survey: 1992 Emergency Department Summary. Susan M. Schappert. 114p. 1997. per. 13.00 (0-16-061458-9) USGPO.

National Hospital Discharge Survey: Annual Summary, 1988 PHS 91-1767. (Vital & Health Statistics Ser.: Series 13, No. 106). 55p. 1991. 3.25 (0-685-61579-0, 017-022-01142-5) Natl Ctr Health Stats.

National Hospital Discharge Survey: Annual Summary, 1992. National Center for Health Statistics Staff. LC 94-1779. (Vital & Health Statistics Ser.: Series 13, No. 119). 63p. 4.75 (0-614-02912-0, 017-022-01274-0) Natl Ctr Health Stats.

National Hospital Discharge Survey: Annual Summary, 1993. Edmund J. Graves. 67p. 1995. pap. 6.00 (0-16-061437-6) USGPO.

National Hospital Discharge Survey: Annual Summary, 1994. Edmund J. Graves. 56p. 1997. pap. 12.00 (0-16-061459-7) USGPO.

***National Hospital Discharge Survey: Annual Summary, 1995.** Brenda Gillum. 56p. 1998. pap. 5.00 (0-16-049424-9) USGPO.

***National Hospital Discharge Survey, Annual Summary, 1996.** Edmund J. Graves. 50p. 1999. pap. 7.00 (0-16-049868-6) USGPO.

National Household Education Survey: A Guide to Using Data from the National Household Education Survey (NHES) Mary A. Collins. 69p. (Orig.). 1997. pap. 5.00 (0-16-049200-9) USGPO.

National Household Education Survey: An Overview of the National Household Education Survey. Mary Jo Nolin. LC 97-191495. 34p. 1997. pap. 4.25 (0-16-049076-6) USGPO.

National Household Education Survey: NHES. Mary A. Collins. 97p. 1997. pap. 10.00 (0-16-049201-5) USGPO.

National Household Education Survey of 1996: Data File User's Manual. Mary A. Collins. 160p. 1997. pap. 14.00 (0-16-049195-9) USGPO.

National Household Education Survey of 1996: Data File User's Manual, Vol. 4. Mary A. Collins. 98p. 1997. pap. 10.00 (0-16-049198-3) USGPO.

National Household Education Survey of 1996: Data File User's Manual, Household & Library Data File, Vol. 2. Mary A. Collins. 174p. 1997. pap. 15.00 (0-16-049196-7) USGPO.

National Household Education Survey of 1996: Data File User's Manual, Parent & Family Involvement in Education & Civic Involvement, Parent Data File, Vol. 3. Mary A. Collins. 188p. 1997. pap. 15.00 (0-16-049197-5) USGPO.

National Household Education Survey of 1996: Data Files User's Manual. Mary A. Collins. 68p. 1997. pap. 5.00 (0-16-049199-1) USGPO.

National Household Survey on Drug Abuse. (Illus.). 121p. (Orig.). (C). 1992. pap. text 30.00 (1-56806-135-8) DIANE Pub.

National Household Survey on Drug Abuse: Main Findings (1992) (Illus.). 310p. (Orig.). (C). 1996. pap. text 45.00 (0-7881-2857-4) DIANE Pub.

National Household Survey on Drug Abuse: Main Findings, (1993) Wai Choy et al. (Illus.). 330p. (C). 1998. reprint ed. pap. text 45.00 (0-7881-4285-2) DIANE Pub.

National Household Survey on Drug Abuse: Main Findings, 1996. Angela Brittingham et al. (Illus.). 328p. (C). 1998. pap. text 45.00 (0-7881-7419-3) DIANE Pub.

National Household Survey on Drug Abuse: Main Findings, 1997. 364p. 1999. per. 30.00 (0-16-042766-5) USGPO.

National Household Survey on Drug Abuse: Population Estimates, 1992. (Illus.). 125p. (Orig.). (C). 1994. pap. text 30.00 (0-7881-0818-2) DIANE Pub.

National Household Survey on Drug Abuse: Population Estimates, 1996. Joseph Gfroerer et al. (Illus.). 123p. (C). 1998. pap. text 30.00 (0-7881-7075-9) DIANE Pub.

***National Household Survey on Drug Abuse: Population Estimates (1997)** Teresa R. Davis. (Illus.). 123p. (C). 1999. pap. text 30.00 (0-7881-8223-4) DIANE Pub.

***National Household Survey on Drug Abuse: Population Estimates (1998)** Teresa R. Davis. (Illus.). 125p. 2000. pap. text 30.00 (0-7881-8745-7) DIANE Pub.

National Household Survey on Drug Abuse: Preliminary Results (1996) Joseph Gfroerer. (Illus.). 114p. (C). 1999. reprint ed. pap. text 30.00 (0-7881-7074-0) DIANE Pub.

National Household Survey on Drug Abuse: Race/Ethnicity, Socioeconomic Status & Drug Abuse (1991) Robert L. Flewelling et al. 81p. (C). 1996. reprint ed. pap. text 30.00 (0-7881-3154-0) DIANE Pub.

National Household Survey on Drug Abuse: Summary of Findings (1998) 128p. pap. text. write for info. (0-7881-8744-9) DIANE Pub.

National Housing Directory for People with Disabilities. Ed. by Leslie Mackenzie et al. 1429p. (Orig.). 1993. pap. 150.00 (0-939300-13-3) Grey Hse Pub.

National Human Exposure Assessment Survey (NHEXAS) Ed. by Edo Pellizzari. (Journal of Exposure Analysis & Environmental Epidemiology Ser.: Vol. 5, No. 3). (Illus.). 1995. pap. text. write for info. (0-911131-72-8) Specialist Journals.

National Human Rights Institutions: A Handbook on the Establishment & Strengthening of National Institutions for the Promotion & Protection of Human Rights. LC 96-108741. (Professional Training Ser.: No. 4). 55p. pap. 19.00 (92-1-154115-8) UN.

National Hydrology Workshop Proceedings. Ed. by Dan Neary et al. (Illus.). 210p. (Orig.). (C). 1997. pap. text 50.00 (0-7881-3982-7) DIANE Pub.

National Idea & American Federalism. Samuel Hutchison Beer. LC 92-12077. 1993. write for info. (0-674-60212-9) HUP.

National Idea in Eastern Europe: The Politics of Ethnic & Civic Community. Ed. by Gerasimos Augustinos. 211p. (C). 1996. pap. text 18.76 (0-669-39626-5) HM Trade Div.

National Ideals & Problems. Ed. by Maurice G. Fulton. LC 68-54346. (Essay Index Reprint Ser.). 1977. 23.95 (0-8369-0113-4) Ayer.

National Identities & Ethnic Minorities in Eastern Europe: Selected Papers from the 5th World Congress of Central & East European Studies. Ray Taras. LC 97-44223. 228p. 1998. text 65.00 (0-312-21346-8) St Martin.

National Identities & Post-Americanist Narratives. Ed. by Donald E. Pease. LC 93-49689. (New Americanists Ser.). 352p. 1994. text 49.95 (0-8223-1477-0); pap. text 17.95 (0-8223-1492-4) Duke.

***National Identities & Socio-Political Changes in Latin America.** Antonio Gomez-Moriana. (Hispanic Issues Ser.). (Illus.). 2000. pap. 22.95 (0-8153-3908-9) Garland.

***National Identities & Travel in Victorian Britain.** Marjorie Morgan. LC 00-41511. (Illus.). 2000. write for info. (0-333-71999-9, Macmillan UK) Sl & J.

National Identity. Anthony D. Smith. LC 92-31386. (Ethnonationalism in Comparative Perspective Ser.). 240p. (C). 1993. reprint ed. pap. text 13.95 (0-87417-204-7) U of Nev Pr.

National Identity & Adult Education: Challenge & Risk. Ed. by Franz Poggeler. LC 95-22939. (Illus.). 305p. 1995. 57.95 (3-631-48353-8) P Lang Pubng.

National Identity & Democratic Prospects in Socialist China. Edward Friedman. LC 94-42257. 372p. (gr. 13). 1995. text 77.95 (1-56324-433-0, East Gate Bk); pap. text 29.95 (1-56324-434-9, East Gate Bk) M E Sharpe.

National Identity & Foreign Policy: Nationalism & Leadership in Poland, Russia & Ukraine. Ilya Prizel. LC 97-44352. (Russian, Soviet & Post-Soviet Studies: No. 103). 460p. (C). 1998. text 54.95 (0-521-57157-X); pap. text 24.95 (0-521-57697-0) Cambridge U Pr.

National Identity & Geopolitical Visions: Maps of Pride & Pain. Gertjan Dijkink. (Illus.). 200p. (C). 1997. 75.00 (0-415-13934-1); pap. 24.99 (0-415-13935-X) Routledge.

***National Identity & Political Thought in Germany: Wilhelmine Depictions of the French Third Republic, 1890-1914.** Mark Hewitson. 272p. 2000. text 70.00 (0-19-820858-8) OUP.

***National Identity & Regional Cooperation: Experiences of European Integration & South Asian Perceptions.** Ed. by H. S. Chopra et al. 1999. 48.00 (81-7304-233-0, Pub. by Manohar) S Asia.

National Identity & Weimar Germany: Upper Silesia & the Eastern Border, 1918-1922. T. Hunt Tooley. LC 96-34613. (Illus.). xv, 332p. 1997. text 60.00 (0-8032-4429-0) U of Nebr Pr.

National Identity As an Issue of Knowledge & Morality: Georgian Philosophical Studies I. Ed. by N. V. Chavchavadze & Ghia Nodia. LC 93-11929. (Cultural Heritage & Contemporary Change Series IVA: Vol. 7). 110p. 1994. 45.00 (1-56518-052-6); pap. 17.50 (1-56518-053-4) Coun Res Values.

National Identity in Canada & Cosmopolitan Community. H. Raymond Samuels, II. LC 98-101822. 349p. 1997. pap. write for info. (0-9681906-0-X) Agora Publ.

National Identity in Eastern Germany: Inner Unification or Continued Separation? Andreas Staab. LC 97-35135. 192p. 1998. 57.95 (0-275-96177-X, Praeger Pubs) Greenwood.

National Identity in Indian Popular Cinema, 1947-1987. Sumita S. Chakravarty. Ed. by Thomas G. Schatz. LC 93-16985. (Film Studies). (Illus.). 368p. (Orig.). 1994. text 50.00 (0-292-75551-1) U of Tex Pr.

National Identity in Times of Crisis: Argentina & the United Kingdom in the Falklands War. Nora A. Femenia. 237p. (C). 1994. lib. bdg. 115.00 (1-56072-196-0) Nova Sci Pubs.

***National Identity of Romanians in Transylvania.** Sorin Mitu. 450p. (C). 2000. 55.95 (963-9116-95-5) Ctrl Europ Univ.

National Ideology under Socialism: Identity & Cultural Politics in Ceausescu's Romania. Katherine Verdery. LC 90-47727. (Societies & Culture in East-Central Europe Ser.: No. 7). (Illus.). 406p. 1991. 45.00 (0-520-07216-2, Pub. by U CA Pr) Cal Prin Full Svc.

National Ideology under Socialism: Identity & Cultural Politics in Ceausescu's Romania. Katherine Verdery. LC 90-47727. (Societies & Culture in East-Central Europe Ser.: Vol. 7). (Illus.). 406p. 1995. pap. 18.95 (0-520-20358-5, Pub. by U CA Pr) Cal Prin Full Svc.

National Ignition Facility. (Illus.). 42p. (Orig.). (C). 1995. pap. text 35.00 (0-7881-2493-5) DIANE Pub.

National Images & International Systems. K. E. Boulding. (Reprint Series in Social Sciences). (C). 1993. reprint ed. pap. text 5.00 (0-8290-3216-9, PS-30) Irvington.

National Implementation of the Future Chemical Weapons Convention. Ed. by Thomas Stock & Ronald Sutherland. (SIPRI Chemical & Biological Warfare Studies: No. 11). (Illus.). 186p. 1990. pap. text 39.95 (0-19-827837-3) OUP.

National Income: A Summary of Findings. Simon Smith Kuznets. LC 75-19719. (National Bureau of Economic Research Ser.). (Illus.). 1975. reprint ed. 19.95 (0-405-07598-7) Ayer.

National Income: A Summary of Findings. Simon Smith Kuznets. (Twenty-Fifth Anniversary Ser.: No. 1). 154p. 1946. reprint ed. 41.40 (0-87014-113-9) Natl Bur Econ Res.

N

An Asterisk (*) at the beginning of an entry indicates that the title is appearing for the first time.

National Income & Capital Formation, 1919-1935: A Preliminary Report. Simon Smith Kuznets. LC 75-19720. (National Bureau of Economic Research Ser.). (Illus.). 1975. reprint ed. 16.95 (*0-405-07599-5*) Ayer.

National Income & Capital Formation, 1919-1935. Simon Smith Kuznets. (General Ser.: No. 32). 101p. 1937. reprint ed. 26.30 (*0-87014-031-0*) Natl Bur Econ Res.

National Income & Its Composition, 1919-1938, Vol. 1. Simon Smith Kuznets et al. (General Ser.: No. 40). 417p. 1941. reprint ed. 108.50 (*0-87014-039-6*) Natl Bur Econ Res.

National Income & Its Purchasing Power. Willford I. King & Lillian Epstein. (General Ser.: No. 15). 394p. 1930. reprint ed. 102.50 (*0-87014-014-0*) Natl Bur Econ Res.

National Income & Nature: Externalities, Growth & Steady State. Ed. by Jacob J. Krabbe. 248p. 1992. lib. bdg. 173.50 (*0-7923-1529-4*) Kluwer Academic.

National Income & Outlay. Colin Clark. 304p. 1965. reprint ed. 35.00 (*0-7146-1216-2*, Pub. by F Cass Pubs) Intl Spec Bk.

National Income & Product Accounts of the U. S. Vol. 1: 1929-58. 236p. (Orig.). (C). 1995. pap. text 50.00 (*0-7881-2113-8*) DIANE Pub.

National Income & Product Accounts of the U. S. Vol. 2: 1959-88. (Illus.). 396p. (Orig.). (C). 1995. pap. text 60.00 (*0-7881-2428-5*) DIANE Pub.

National Income & Product Accounts of the United States. 1995. lib. bdg. 625.99 (*0-8490-6864-9*) Gordon Pr.

*__National Income & Product Accounts of the United States.__ 2 Bks. (815p. 1998. per. 64.00 (*0-16-060907-0*) USGPO.

National Income & Product Accounts of the United States Vol. 2: 1959-88, Vol. 2. 1996. per. 32.50 (*0-16-038108-8*) USGPO.

National Income & Product Accounts of the United States, 1929-1958, 2 vols. 1994. lib. bdg. 699.95 (*0-8490-9050-4*) Gordon Pr.

National Income & Product Accounts of the United States, 1929-1958, 1959-1988, 2 vols. 1997. lib. bdg. 600.00 (*0-8490-7762-1*) Gordon Pr.

National Income & Product Accounts of the United States, 1929-1982. 1992. lib. bdg. 90.00 (*0-8490-5488-5*) Gordon Pr.

National Income & Product Accounts of the United States, 1929-94, Vol. 1. (Illus.). 1998. pap. write for info. (*0-16-049604-7*) USGPO.

National Income & Product Accounts of the United States, 1929-94, Vol. 2. (Illus.). 1998. pap. write for info. (*0-16-049607-1*) USGPO.

National Income in the United States, 1799-1938. Robert F. Martin. LC 75-22827. (America in Two Centuries Ser.). 1976. reprint ed. 18.95 (*0-405-07699-1*) Ayer.

National Income, 1924-1931. Colin Clark. 180p. 1965. reprint ed. 35.00 (*0-7146-1215-4*, Pub. by F Cass Pubs) Intl Spec Bk.

National Income, 1924 to 1931. Colin Clark. LC 67-33571. (Reprints of Economic Classics Ser.). x, 167p. 1965. reprint ed. 32.50 (*0-678-05161-5*) Kelley.

*__National Income of India in the Twentieth Century.__ Ed. by S. Sivasubramonian. 470p. 2000. text 29.95 (*0-19-565050-6*) OUP.

National Income, 1919-1938. Simon Smith Kuznets. (Occasional Papers: No. 2). 32p. 1941. reprint ed. 20.00 (*0-87014-317-4*) Natl Bur Econ Res.

National Index of American Imprints Through 1800: The Short-Title Evans, 2 vols. Clifford K. Shipton & James E. Mooney. LC 69-11248. 1076p. 1969. 85.00 (*0-8271-6908-6*, 7042) Oak Knoll.

National Index of Recognized & Unrecognized Alternative & Non-Traditional Colleges & Universities in the United States: The Best & Worst Non-Traditional & Alternative Schools in America. 3rd ed. Nasacu Group Staff & Marna R. Wells. (Non-Traditional Higher Education in the U. S. Ser.). (Illus.). 164p. 1991. pap. 30.00 (*0-939877-32-5*) ACUPAE.

National Industrial Security Program: Operating Manual. 140p. (Orig.). 1995. pap. text 40.00 (*1-57979-058-5*) DIANE Pub.

National Industrial Security Program: Operating Manual. 130p. (Orig.). (C). 1995. pap. text 35.00 (*0-7881-2135-9*) DIANE Pub.

National Industrial Security Program January 1995: Operating Manual. 160p. 1995. pap. 12.00 (*0-16-045560-X*) USGPO.

National Information Infrastructure: Access to Information Technologies & Moving to a Global Information Infrastructure. 1996. lib. bdg. 253.75 (*0-8490-5922-4*) Gordon Pr.

National Information Infrastructure Initiatives: Vision & Policy Design. Brian Kahin & Ernest Wilson. (Illus.). 300p. 1996. 55.00 (*0-262-11219-1*) MIT Pr.

National Information Infrastructure Initiatives: Vision & Policy Design. Brian Kahin et al. 663p. 1996. pap. text 27.50 (*0-262-61125-2*) MIT Pr.

National Information Policies: Strategies for the Future. David R. Bender et al. LC 92-129033. (SLA Occasional Papers Ser.: No. 2). 70p. reprint ed. pap. 30.00 (*0-608-20000-X*, 207127700010) Bks Demand.

National Information Systems Security Conference Proceedings (19th) Ed. by Shukri A. Wakid & John C. Davis. (Illus.). 896p. (C). 1998. pap. text 95.00 (*0-7881-7151-8*) DIANE Pub.

National Information Systems Security Conference, 1996 (19th) Organized Crime in the 21st Century. (Illus.). xxx, 896p. 1996. pap. text 100.00 (*1-57979-235-9*) DIANE Pub.

National Information Systems Security '95 (18th) Proceedings: Making Security Real, 2 vols., Set. (Illus.). 760p. (Orig.). 1996. pap. text 75.00 (*0-7881-2852-3*) DIANE Pub.

National Innovation Systems. Ed. by Richard R. Nelson. (Illus.). 560p. 1993. pap. text 39.95 (*0-19-507617-6*) OUP.

National Inpatient Profile 1997: Diagnoses. 1998. ring bd. write for info. (*1-880678-63-2*) HCIA.

National Inpatient Profile 1997: Diagnoses & Procedures. 1998. ring bd. write for info. (*1-880678-78-0*) HCIA.

National Inpatient Profile 1997: Procedures. 1998. ring bd. write for info. (*1-880678-74-8*) HCIA.

National Insecurity: U. S. Intelligence after the Cold War. Ed. by Craig Eisendrath. LC 99-23807. (Illus.). 296p. 1999. 34.50 (*1-56639-744-8*) Temple U Pr.

*__National Insecurity: U. S. Intelligence after the Cold War.__ Ed. by Craig Eisendrath. 296p. 2000. reprint ed. pap. 21.95 (*1-56639-848-7*) Temple U Pr.

*__National Institute of Senior Centers' Senior Center Self-Assessment & National Accreditation Manual.__ National Institute of Senior Centers Staff. 159p. 1999. ring bd. 125.00 (*0-910883-94-7*) Natl Coun Aging.

National Institute on Disability & Rehabilitation Research: Program Directory, Fiscal Year 1996. Katherine D. Seelman. 316p. 1997. pap. 19.00 (*0-16-048999-7*) USGPO.

National Institute on Real Estate Taxation. Ed. by Bernard Goodman. 430p. 1991. ring bd. 125.00 (*1-56423-008-2*) Ntl Ctr Tax Ed.

National Institute on Real Estate Taxation Proceedings Book, 1993. Ed. by Bernard B. Goodman. 263p. 1993. ring bd. 125.00 (*1-56423-034-1*) Ntl Ctr Tax Ed.

National Institute on State & Local Taxation. Ed. by Bernard B. Goodman. 240p. 1991. ring bd. 125.00 (*1-56423-006-6*) Ntl Ctr Tax Ed.

National Institute on State & Local Taxation Proceedings Book, 1993. Ed. by Bernard B. Goodman. 267p. 1993. ring bd. 125.00 (*1-56423-030-9*) Ntl Ctr Tax Ed.

National Institutes of Health, 2 vols. 1994. lib. bdg. 395.00 (*0-8490-8433-4*) Gordon Pr.

National Institutes of Health Consensus Conference on Cervical Cancer: Conference Held at the National Institutes of Health, Bethesda, Maryland, April 1-3, 1996. 168p. 1996. per. 14.00 (*0-16-061576-3*) USGPO.

*__National Insurance Fund Long Term Financial Estimates: Report by the Government Actuary on the Quinquennial Review for the Period Ending 5 April 1995 under Section 166 of the Social Security Administration Act 1992 : Social Security Administration Act 1992.__ LC 99-235928. 1999. write for info. (*0-10-144062-6*) Statnry Office.

National Integration & Indian Constitution. 1986. 27.50 (*0-8364-1939-1*, Pub. by Deep & Deep Pubns) S Asia.

National Integration & Local Integrity: The Miri of the Nuba Mountains in the Sudan. Gerd Baumann. (Illus.). 232p. 1988. text 62.00 (*0-19-823401-5*) OUP.

*__National Integration & Local Power in Japan.__ Yasuo Takao. 270p. 1999. text 74.95 (*0-7546-1056-X*, Pub. by Ashgate Pub) Ashgate Pub Co.

National Integration & the Law: Burning Issues & Challenges. Mohan K. Vyas. (C). 1993. text 26.00 (*81-7100-586-1*, Pub. by Deep & Deep Pubns) S Asia.

National Integration of Italian Return Migration, 1870-1929. Dino Cinel. (Interdisciplinary Perspectives on Modern History Ser.). 288p. (C). 1991. text 64.95 (*0-521-40058-9*) Cambridge U Pr.

National Integration of Sindhis. Subhadra Anand. LC 95-911165. (C). 1996. 27.00 (*0-7069-9970-3*, Pub. by Vikas) S Asia.

National Integration Through Socialist Planning. Steven L. Sampson. 1984. text 68.50 (*0-88033-040-6*, 148, Pub. by East Eur Monographs) Col U Pr.

*__National Intelligence Machinery.__ Ed. by Cabinet Office Staff. 2000. 25.00 (*0-11-430171-9*, Pub. by Statnry Office) Balogh.

National Intelligence Newspaper Abstracts, 1824-1826, Vol. 7. Joan M. Dixon. 520p. 1999. 39.50 (*0-7884-1086-5*, D403) Heritage Bk.

National Intelligencer & Washington Advertiser Newspaper Abstracts, 1800-1805. Joan M. Dixon. ii, 309p. 1996. pap. 26.00 (*0-7884-0392-3*, D395) Heritage Bk.

National Intelligencer & Washington Advertiser Newspaper Abstracts, 1806-1810, Vol. 2. Joan M. Dixon. vi, 275p. (Orig.). 1996. pap. 22.00 (*0-7884-0596-9*, D397) Heritage Bk.

National Intelligencer & Washington Advertiser Newspaper Abstracts 1811-1813. Joan M. Dixion. vi, 370p. 1997. pap. 22.50 (*0-7884-0658-2*, D398) Heritage Bk.

National Intelligencer & Washington Advertiser Newspaper Abstracts, 1814-1817. Joan M. Dixon. vi, 382p. 1997. pap. 28.50 (*0-7884-0707-4*, D400) Heritage Bk.

*__National Intelligencer Newspaper Abstracts: 1830-1831.__ Joan M. Dixon. 160p. 1999. pap. 37.50 (*0-7884-1309-0*, D399) Heritage Bk.

National Intelligencer Newspaper Abstracts, 1818-1820. Joan M. Dixon. 429p. 1998. pap. 30.00 (*0-7884-0830-5*, D401) Heritage Bk.

National Intelligencer Newspaper Abstracts, 1821-1823. Joan M. Dixon. 523p. 1998. pap. 40.00 (*0-7884-0948-4*, D402) Heritage Bk.

*__National Intelligencer Newspaper Abstracts, 1832-1833.__ Joan M. Dixon. 567p. 2000. pap. 34.00 (*0-7884-1428-3*, 1428) Heritage Bk.

National Interest: Rhetoric, Leadership, & Policy. Ed. by W. David Clinton & Kenneth W. Thompson. LC 87-29605. (Exxon Education Foundation Series on Rhetoric & Political Discourse: Vol. 13). 122p. (Orig.). (C). 1988. pap. text 17.00 (*0-8191-6734-7*); lib. bdg. 38.00 (*0-8191-6733-9*) U Pr of Amer.

National Interest - National Honor: The Diplomacy of the Falklands Crisis. Douglas Kinney. LC 88-29271. 392p. 1990. 62.95 (*0-275-92425-4*, C2425, Praeger Pubs) Greenwood.

National Interest & Global Goals. Ed. by George C. McGhee et al. LC 89-36331. (Exxon Education Foundation Series on Rhetoric & Political Discourse: Vol. 16). 224p. 1989. pap. text 24.00 (*0-8191-7543-9*, Pub. by White Miller Center); lib. bdg. 46.00 (*0-8191-7542-0*, Pub. by White Miller Center) U Pr of Amer.

National Interests & Local Government. Ed. by Ken Young. (NIESR-PSI-RIIA Joint Studies in Public Policy: No. 7). viii, 172p. 1983. text 72.95 (*0-435-83947-0*) Ashgate Pub Co.

National Interests & the Military Use of Space. Ed. by William J. Durch. 286p. 1984. text 34.95 (*0-88410-974-7*, HarpBusn) HarpInfo.

National Interests in an Age of Global Technology. National Academy of Engineering, Committee on Engi. Ed. by Thomas H. Lee & Proctor R. Reid. (Prospering in a Global Economy Ser.). 176p. 1991. pap. 29.95 (*0-309-04329-8*) Natl Acad Pr.

National Interests in International Society. Martha Anne Finnemore. (Studies in Political Economy). (Illus.). 176p. 1996. text 37.50 (*0-8014-3244-8*); pap. text 13.95 (*0-8014-8323-9*) Cornell U Pr.

National Interests, Morality & International Law. Raino Malnes. 156p. (C). 1994. 20.00 (*82-00-21968-2*, Pub. by Scand Univ Pr) IBD Ltd.

National Interests of the United States in Foreign Policy: Seven Discussions at the Wilson Center December 1980 - February 1981. Ed. by Prosser Gifford. LC 81-40792. 204p. (Orig.). 1981. lib. bdg. 36.00 (*0-8191-1786-2*) U Pr of Amer.

National Issues in Education: Community Service & Student Loans. Ed. by John F. Jennings. LC 94-65876. 192p. 1995. pap. 18.00 (*0-87367-466-9*) Phi Delta Kappa.

National Issues in Education: Elementary & Secondary Education Act. Ed. by John F. Jennings. LC 95-68412. 167p. 1995. pap. 18.00 (*0-87367-479-0*) Phi Delta Kappa.

National Issues in Education: Goals 2000 & School-to-Work. Ed. by John F. Jennings. LC 94-61364. 202p. 1995. pap. 18.00 (*0-87367-471-5*) Phi Delta Kappa.

National Issues in Education: The Past Is Prologue. Ed. by John F. Jennings. LC 93-83803. 261p. 1995. pap. 18.00 (*0-87367-460-X*) Phi Delta Kappa.

National Issues in Science & Technology, 1993. Institute of Medicine Staff et al. 96p. (Orig.). (C). 1993. pap. text 26.00 (*0-309-04882-6*) Natl Acad Pr.

*__National Jail & Adult Detention Directory, 1999-2001.__ 430p. 1999. pap. 70.00 (*1-56991-115-0*) Am Correctional.

National Job Hotline Directory: The Job Finder's Hot List, 1999-2001. Sue A. Cubbage & Marcia Williams. LC 98-65912. (Illus.). 376p. 1999. pap. text 16.95 (*1-884587-12-7*) Planning Comns.

*__National JobBank, 2000 Edition.__ Adams Media Corporation Staff. LC 90-640981. (JobBank Two Thousand Ser.). 1152p. 1999. 370.00 (*1-58062-226-7*) Adams Media.

*__National JobBank, 2001.__ (JobBank Ser.). 1152p. 2000. 395.00 (*1-58062-406-5*) Adams Media.

National Journal of Legal Education, 1937-1940, 3 vols. 1937. 27.50 (*0-8377-9211-8*, Rothman) W S Hein.

National Judicial Reporting Program (1990) Patrick L. Langan & Richard Solari. (Illus.). 51p. (Orig.). (C). 1995. pap. text 20.00 (*0-7881-2422-6*) DIANE Pub.

National Junior Honor Society Handbook. rev. ed. 1998. pap. 15.00 (*0-88210-058-0*, 8319808) Natl Assn Student.

National Juvenile Custody Trends, 1978-1989. Barry Krisberg et al. (Illus.). 142p. (Orig.). (C). 1994. pap. text 25.00 (*0-7881-0325-3*) DIANE Pub.

National Juvenile Justice Program Collaboration: Auxiliary Appendixes. Genevieve Burch. 164p. (Orig.). 1978. pap. 10.00 (*1-55719-053-4*) U NE CPAR.

National Juvenile Justice Program Collaboration: Evaluation Report. Genevieve Burch. 175p. (Orig.). 1978. pap. 11.00 (*1-55719-038-0*) U NE CPAR.

National Labor Relations Act. 40p. 1997. pap. 2.50 (*0-16-061838-X*) USGPO.

*__National Labor Relations Act.__ 40p. 2000. pap. 2.50 (*0-16-050336-1*) USGPO.

National Labor Relations Acts (NLRA) Wagner Act, 2 vols. in 4. U. S. National Labor Relations Board Staff. LC 49-45500. 1984. reprint ed. 95.00 incl. fiche (*0-89941-194-0*, 201300) W S Hein.

National Labor Relations Board. Cornell University Staff. Ed. by Wahib Nasrallah. (Research & Information Guides in Business, Industry, & Economic Institutions Ser.). 300p. Date not set. text 40.00 (*0-8153-0382-3*) Garland.

National Labor Relations Board Annual Report, 1991. Government Printing Office Staff. 228p. 1994. per. 11.00 (*0-16-043181-6*) USGPO.

National Labor Relations Board Annual Report, 1992. Government Printing Office Staff. 189p. 1994. per. 9.00 (*0-16-045156-6*) USGPO.

National Labor Relations Board Annual Report, 1993. Government Printing Office Staff. 179p. 1995. pap. text 9.00 (*0-16-045420-4*) USGPO.

National Labor Relations Board Annual Report, 1996. Government Printing Office Staff. 170p. 1997. pap. text 12.00 (*0-16-049173-8*) USGPO.

*__National Labor Relations Board Annual Report, 1997.__ Government Printing Office Staff. 174p. 1998. per. 8.00 (*0-16-049520-2*) USGPO.

*__National Labor Relations Board Casehandling Manual Pt. 2: Representation Proceedings, August 1999.__ 324p. 1999. ring bd. 34.00 (*0-16-050177-6*) USGPO.

National Labor Relations Board Election Statistics. BNA PLUS Staff. 1989. write for info. (*1-55871-077-9*) BNA PLUS.

*__National Labor Relations Board Rules & Regulations & Statements of Procedure: National Labor Relations Act & Labor Management Relations Act.__ 302p. 1998. ring bd. 18.00 (*0-16-061843-6*) USGPO.

National Laboratories: Are Their R&D Activities Related to Commercial Product Development? 97p. (Orig.). pap. text 20.00 (*0-7881-2634-2*) DIANE Pub.

National Laboratories: Are Their R&D Activities Related to Commercial Product Development? (Illus.). 97p. (Orig.). (C). 1995. pap. text 35.00 (*0-614-07001-5*) DIANE Pub.

National Laboratories & Public Research Organizations in Japan. (Illus.). 222p. (Orig.). (C). 1994. pap. text 95.00 (*0-7881-1385-2*) DIANE Pub.

National Laboratories & Public Research Organizations in Japan. Ed. by Barry Leonard. (Illus.). 264p. (C). 1998. pap. text 50.00 (*0-7881-7369-3*) DIANE Pub.

National Lampoon Presents True Facts: The Big Book. Compiled by John Bendel & Jason Ward. LC 95-23509. 1995. pap. 103.60 (*0-8092-3245-6*) NTC Contemp Pub Co.

National Lampoon Presents True Facts: The Big Book. John Bendel & Jason Ward. (Illus.). 272p. 1995. pap. 12.95 (*0-8092-3559-5*) NTC Contemp Pub Co.

National Land Code. 2nd ed. Judith E. Sihombing. 1992. boxed set 280.00 (*0-409-99614-9*, ASIA, MICHIE) LEXIS Pub.

National Landmarks, America's Treasures: The National Park Foundation's Complete Guide to National Historic Landmarks. S. Allen Chambers & National Park Foundational Staff. LC 99-31114. 560p. 1999. pap. 29.95 (*0-471-19764-5*) Wiley.

National Law Library, 6 vols., Set. Ed. by Roscoe Pound. LC 39-8999. 1980. reprint ed. lib. bdg. 285.00 (*0-89941-262-9*, 200730) W S Hein.

National Lawyers Guild Quarterly: 1937-1940, Set, Vols. 1-3. 1937. 90.00 (*0-685-42627-0*) W S Hein.

National Lawyers Guild Quarterly: 1937-1940, Vols. 1-3. 1937. mic. film 90.00 (*0-318-57447-0*) W S Hein.

National Leaders of American Conservation. rev. ed. Ed. by Richard H. Stroud. LC 84-600245. 432p. 1985. pap. text 29.95 (*0-87474-867-4*, STLAP) Smithsonian.

National Leaders on Communalism. S. M. Chand. 1985. 24.95 (*0-318-36589-8*) Asia Bk Corp.

National Leadership & Foreign Policy: A Case Study in the Mobilization of Public Support. James N. Rosenau. LC 63-7160. 427p. reprint ed. pap. 132.40 (*0-608-17851-9*, 203263700080) Bks Demand.

National League Baseball Card Classics. Bert R. Sugar. 1982. pap. 4.95 (*0-486-24308-7*) Dover.

National League for Nursing Accrediting Commission Accreditation Manual for Post-Secondary, Baccalaureate & Higher Degree Programs in Nursing, 1997. NLNAC Staff. 100p. 1997. 13.95 (*0-88737-754-8*, 18-7548, NLN Pr) Natl League Nurse.

National Legal Bibliography see Catalog of Current Law Titles

National Legal Bibliography Annual see Lawyer's Monthly Catalog Annual

National Legislation & Regulations Relating to Transnational Corporations, Vol. IV. 241p. 1986. 23.00 (*92-1-104169-4*, E.85.II.A.14) UN.

National Legislation & Regulations Relating to Transnational Corporations, Vol. V. 245p. 1986. 23.00 (*92-1-104176-7*, E.86.II.A.3) UN.

National Legislation & Regulations Relating to Transnational Corporations, Vol. VI. 450p. 1987. pap. 45.00 (*92-1-104201-1*) UN.

National Legislation & Regulations Relating to Transnational Corporations, Vol. VI. UN Centre on Transnational Corporations Staff. (C). 1988. lib. bdg. 122.00 (*0-86010-943-7*, Pub. by Graham & Trotman) Kluwer Academic.

National Legislation & Regulations Relating to Transnational Corporations, Vol. VII. 320p. 36.00 (*92-1-104316-6*, E.89.II.A.9) UN.

National Legislation & Regulations Relating to Transnational Corporations, Vol. VIII. 400p. 60.00 (*92-1-104439-1*, E.94.II.A.18) UN.

National Legislation on Territorial Sea, Right of Innocent Passage & the Contiguous Zone. Division of Ocean Affairs & the Law of the Sea Off. LC 95-209391. (The Law of the Sea Ser.). 440p. 48.00 (*92-1-133486-1*) UN.

National Legislation on the Continental Shelf, Vol. 5. (The Law of the Sea Ser.). 302p. 30.00 (*92-1-133318-0*, E.89.V.5) UN.

National Legislation on the Exclusive Economic Zone. (The Law of the Sea Ser.). 403p. 45.00 (*92-1-133449-7*) UN.

National Legislation, Regulation & Supplementary Documents on Marine, Scientific Research in Areas under National Jurisdiction. (The Law of the Sea Ser.). 306p. 32.00 (*92-1-133322-9*, E.89.V.9) UN.

National Legislation on the Exclusive Economic Zone, the Economic Zone & the Exclusive Fishery Zone, Vol.10. (The Law of the Sea Ser.). 337p. 35.00 (*92-1-133272-9*, E.85.V.10) UN.

National Liberation. Nigel Harris. 350p. 1991. text 59.50 (*1-85043-295-3*, Pub. by I B T) St Martin.

National Liberation. Nigel Harris. LC 93-20376. (Ethnonationalism in Comparative Perspective Ser.). 320p. (C). 1993. reprint ed. pap. text 13.95 (*0-87417-209-8*) U of Nev Pr.

N

An Asterisk (*) at the beginning of an entry indicates that the title is appearing for the first time.

National Liberation Struggle in South Africa: A Case Study of the United Democratic Front, 1983-1987. Gregory F. Houston. LC 99-72657. (Democracy & Governance in the New South Africa Ser.). 320p. 1999. text 61.95 (1-84014-955-8, Pub. by Ashgate Pub) Ashgate Pub Co.

National Library of Healthcare Indicators: Health Plan & Network Edition. Joint Commission on Accreditation of Healthcare Organizations. (Illus.). 439p. 1997. pap. 25.00 (0-86688-504-8, NLHI-96) Joint Comm Hlthcare.

National Library of Medicine Classification: A Scheme for the Shelf Arrangement of Library Materials in the Field of Medicine & its Related Sciences. 552p. 1995. boxed set 42.00 (0-16-045228-7) USGPO.

National Library of Medicine Current Catalog: 1993. 2 Bks. (2841p. 1994. boxed set 88.00 (0-16-061581-X) USGPO.

National Library of Medicine's (Atlas of the Visible Human Male) Victor M. Spitzer & David G. Whitlock. LC 97-16572. (Life Science Ser.). (Illus.). 544p. 1997. pap. 74.95 (0-7637-0347-8) Jones & Bartlett.

National Library of Wales MS. 20541E: The Penpont Antiphonal. Ed. by Owain Edwards. (Facsimiles of Mediaeval Musical Manuscripts: Vol. 22). (ENG & LAT.). 612p. 1997. 400.00 (1-896926-06-1) Inst Mediaeval Mus.

National Link Study. 1993. write for info. (1-880678-86-1) HCIA.

National Link Study, 1997. 1998. ring bd. write for info. (1-880678-38-1) HCIA.

National List of Plant Species That Occur in Wetlands: National Summary. Porter B. Reed. 250p. 1988. pap. 15.00 (0-16-003585-6, S/N 024-010-00682-0) USGPO.

National Listing of Medicare Providers Furnishing Kidney Dialysis & Transplant Services. (Orig.). 1994. lib. bdg. 250.00 (0-8490-9053-9) Gordon Pr.

National Listing of Medicare Providers Furnishing Kidney Dialysis & Transplant Services. (Orig.). 1996. lib. bdg. 253.95 (0-8490-6929-7) Gordon Pr.

National Listing of Medicare Providers Furnishing Kidney Dialysis & Transplant Services. (Orig.). 1997. lib. bdg. 300.00 (0-8490-6218-7) Gordon Pr.

National Listing of Medicare Providers Furnishing Kidney Dialysis & Transplant Services. Ed. by Barry Leonard. 234p. 1999. pap. text 30.00 (0-7881-7566-1) DIANE Pub.

National Listing of Medicare Providers Furnishing Kidney Dialysis & Transplant Services, January 1997. 224p. 1997. per. 16.00 (0-16-049080-4) USGPO.

***National Listing of Medicare Providers Furnishing Kidney Dialysis & Transplant Services, January 1999.** 262p. 1999. per. 24.00 (0-16-050134-2) USGPO.

National Literacy Campaigns: Historical & Comparative Perspectives. R. F. Arnove & H. J. Graff. LC 87-10873. (Illus.). 332p. (C). 1987. 69.50 (0-306-42458-4, Plenum Trade) Perseus Pubng.

***National Literacy Trust's International Annotated Bibliography of Books of Literacy.** Ann Finlay. 1999. 39.95 (1-85856-202-3, Trentham Bks) Stylus Pub VA.

National Livestock, Poultry & Aquaculture Waste Management: Proceedings National Workshop, July 1991. LC 92-81342. 414p. 1991. pap. 61.25 (0-929355-27-X, P0392) Am Soc Ag Eng.

National-Local Linkages: The Interrelationship of Urban & National Polities in Latin America. Ed. by Francine F. Rabinovitz & Felicity M. Trueblood. LC 72-98042. (Latin American Urban Research Ser.: Vol. 3). 312p. reprint ed. pap. 96.80 (0-608-14198-4, 202194100026) Bks Demand.

National Long Term Care Survey: Instructor's Manual. James L. Peterson et al. (Gerontology Research Toolkit Ser.). 85p. (Orig.). 1994. pap. text, teacher ed. 30.00 (0-8018-5042-8) Johns Hopkins.

National Long Term Care Survey: Student Workbook. Elinore E. Lurie et al. (Gerontology Research Toolkit Ser.). 206p. (Orig.). 1994. pap. text, student ed. 49.00 (0-8018-5041-X) Johns Hopkins.

National Lyrics. John Greenleaf Whittier. LC 79-170707. (Black Heritage Library Collection). (Illus.). 1977. reprint ed. 17.95 (0-8369-8894-9) Ayer.

***National Mall.** Brendan January. LC 99-52349. (Cornerstones to Freedom Ser.). (YA). 2000. 20.50 (0-516-21616-3) Childrens.

National Managed Care Leadership Directory: Key Contacts in Today's Leading Managed Care Organization. 11th rev. ed. Brad Bangerter. Ed. by Laura Bangerter & Mirid Weidner. 426p. 1999. pap. 185.00 (0-9639238-3-8) HlthQuest Pubs.

National Manhood: Capitalist Citizenship & the Imagined Fraternity of White Men. Dana D. Nelson. LC 98-14396. (New Americanists Ser.). 1998. pap. 17.95 (0-8223-2149-1) Duke.

***National Maternal & Infant Health Survey, 1988: Methods & Response Characteristics.** Maureen Sanderson. 45p. 1998. pap. 4.00 (0-16-061488-0) USGPO.

National Math Project, 1. (C). 1985. text. write for info. (0-201-16700-X) Addison-Wesley.

National Math Project, 2. (C). 1985. text. write for info. (0-201-16705-0) Addison-Wesley.

National Meaori Language Survey (Te Mahirangahau Reo Meaori) LC 98-199524. 96 p. 1996. write for info. (0-478-09138-9) Manaaki Whenua.

National Measurement System for Radiometry, Photometry, & Pyrometry Based Upon Absolute Detectors. A. C. Parr. 36p. 1996. pap. 5.00 (0-16-053383-X) USGPO.

National Mechanical Estimator. 23rd ed. Victor B. Ottaviano. LC 93-17560. 1993. write for info. (0-88173-186-2) Fairmont Pr.

National Mechanical Estimator. 23rd ed. Victor B. Ottaviano. 1993. pap. 85.00 (1-878656-04-X) Ottaviano Tech Serv.

National Mechanical Estimator. 24th ed. Victor B. Ottaviano. LC 95-37046. 950p. 1995. 98.50 (0-88173-235-4) Fairmont Pr.

National Mechanical Estimator. 24th ed. Victor B. Ottaviano. (Illus.). 850p. 1995. pap. 95.00 (1-878656-05-8) Ottaviano Tech Serv.

National Mechanics Liens Handbook. James Acret. 1998. pap. text 70.00 (1-55701-259-8) BNI Pubns.

National Medals of the United States. Richard M. McSherry. LC 72-14409. (Maryland Historical Society. Fund-Publications: No. 25). reprint ed. write for info. (0-404-57625-7) AMS Pr.

National Media Guide for Emergency & Disaster Incidents. Bob Riha, Jr. & David Handschuh. (Illus.). 81p. 1998. pap. text 30.00 (0-7881-3911-8) DIANE Pub.

National Medical Ambulatory Medical Care Survey, 1991: Summary. National Center for Health Statistics Staff. LC 94-1777. (Vital & Health Statistics Ser.: Series 13, No. 116). 110p. 6.50 (0-614-02909-0, 017-022-01288-3) Natl Ctr Health Stats.

National Medical Boards (NMB), 2 vols. in 1. Jack Rudman. (Admission Test Ser.: Vol. 23). 89.95 (0-8373-5123-5) Nat Learn.

National Medical Boards (NMB), 2 pts. in 1 vol. Jack Rudman. (Admission Test Ser.: Vol. ATS-23). 1994. pap. 69.95 (0-8373-5023-9) Nat Learn.

National Medical Boards (NMB), Pt. I. Jack Rudman. (Admission Test Ser.: Vol. 23A). 69.95 (0-8373-6975-4) Nat Learn.

National Medical Boards (NMB), Pt. I. Jack Rudman. (Admission Test Ser.: ATS-23A). 1994. pap. 49.95 (0-8373-6950-9) Nat Learn.

National Medical Boards (NMB), Pt. II. Jack Rudman. (Admission Test Ser.: Vol. 23B). 69.95 (0-8373-6976-2) Nat Learn.

National Medical Boards (NMB), Pt. II. Jack Rudman. (Admission Test Ser.: Vol. ATS-23B). 1994. pap. 49.95 (0-8373-6951-7) Nat Learn.

National Medical Directory. Jean Carper. (Orig.). 1985. pap. 11.95 (0-671-49974-2) PB.

National Mental Health Association: Eighty Years of Prevention. Ed. by Robert E. Hess & Jean DeLeon. LC 89-19799. (Prevention in Human Services Ser.: Vol. 6, No. 2). (Illus.). 306p. 1989. text 9.95 (0-86656-943-X) Haworth Pr.

National Military Establishments & the Advancement of Science & Technology: Studies in 20th Century History. Ed. by Paul Forman & Jose M. Sanchez-Ron. LC 95-17492. (Boston Studies in the Philosophy of Science: Vol. 180). 1996. lib. bdg. 180.50 (0-7923-3541-4, Pub. by Kluwer Academic) Kluwer Academic.

National Military Strategy of the United States of America: Shape, Respond, Prepare Now, a Military Strategy for a New Era, Dated 1997. 32p. 1997. pap. 4.50 (0-16-061127-X) USGPO.

National Minimum Wage. John Philpott. (Issues Ser.: No. 13). 1996. pap. 60.00 (0-85292-663-4, Pub. by IPM Hse) St Mut.

National Minorities: An International Problem. Inis L. Claude. LC 78-90486. 248p. 1969. reprint ed. lib. bdg. 49.75 (0-8371-2283-X, CLMN, Greenwood Pr) Greenwood.

National Minorities: Who Are They? Nicola Girasoli. LC 96-103570. 112p. 1995. pap. 100.00 (963-05-6866-7, Pub. by Akade Kiado) St Mut.

***National Minorities & Citizenship Rights in Lithuania, 1988-1993.** Vesna Popovski. LC 00-33297. (Studies in Russia & East Europe). (Illus.). 2000. write for info. (0-312-23697-2) St Martin.

National Minorities & the European Nation-States System. Jennifer Jackson Preece. LC 98-29538. 208p. 1999. text 55.00 (0-19-829437-9) OUP.

National Minorities in Rumania: Change in Transylvania. Elemer Illyes. (East European Monographs: No. 112). 355p. 1983. text 48.00 (0-88033-005-8, Pub. by East Eur Monographs) Col U Pr.

National Minority Health Conference: Environmental Contamination. B. L. Johnson et al. (Illus.). 244p. (Orig.). 1992. text 40.00 (0-911131-86-8) Specialist Journals.

***National Missile Defense & Prospects for U. S.-Russia ABM Treaty Accomodation: Congressional Hearing.** Ed. by Thad Cochran. 144p. (C). 1999. reprint ed. pap. text 25.00 (0-7881-8304-4) DIANE Pub.

National Missile Defense & the ABMTreaty: Hearing Before the Subcommittee on International Security, Proliferation & Federal Services of the Committee on Governmental Affairs, United States Senate, One Hundred Fifth Congress, First Session, May 1, 1997. United States Government. LC 98-133554. (S. Hrg. Ser.). iii, 22 p. 1997. write for info. (0-16-055705-4) USGPO.

National Mitigation Strategy: Partnerships for Building Safer Communities. James L. Witt. (Illus.). 51p. (C). 1997. reprint ed. pap. text 30.00 (0-7881-4026-4) DIANE Pub.

National Mod. Frank Thompson. 1985. 45.00 (0-86152-050-5, Pub. by Acair Ltd) St Mut.

National Monetary Policies & the Internation Financial System. Ed. by Robert Z. Aliber. LC 74-75610. (Midway Reprint Ser.). (Illus.). 339p. reprint ed. pap. 105.10 (0-608-09374-2, 205411900004) Bks Demand.

National Monetary Policies & the International Finance System. Ed. by Robert Z. Aliber. LC 74-75610. (Midway Reprint Ser.). (Illus.). 339p. Date not set. reprint ed. pap. 105.10 (0-608-20981-3, 205450900003) Bks Demand.

National Monuments Record of Scotland Jubilee: Guide to Collections, 1941-91. 96p. 1991. pap. 50.00 (0-11-494125-4, HM2154, Pub. by Statnry Office) Bernan Associates.

National Moot Court Competition, 1950-1999: Association of the Bar of the City of New York, 49 bks., Set. 1983. lib. bdg. 3695.00 (0-89941-185-1, 302490) W S Hein.

***National Mortality Profile of Active Duty Personnel in the U. S. Armed Forces, 1980-1993.** Ed. by Stephen C. Joseph & Linda Rosenstock. (Illus.). 51p. 1999. reprint ed. pap. text 20.00 (0-7881-7996-9) DIANE Pub.

National Mortgage Escrow Audit Kit: How to Audit Your Mortgage Escrow Account for Overcharges. Benji O. Anosike. (Illus.). 110p. (Orig.). 1996. pap. 17.95 (0-932704-40-9) Do It Yourself Legal Pubs.

National Mortgage Reduction Kit: How to Cut Your Mortgage Debt in Half & Own Your Home Fast, Free & Clear Like Magic. Benji O. Anosike. LC 99-44611. (Illus.). 200p. (Orig.). 2000. pap. 24.95 (0-932704-42-5) Do It Yourself Legal Pubs.

National Motor Carrier Directory. Transportation Technical Services Staff. 1841p. 1999. pap. text 295.00 (1-880701-05-7) Trans Tech Srvs.

National Movements & National Identity among the Crimean Tatars, 1905-1916. Hakan Kirimli. (Ottoman Empire & Its Heritage Ser.: Vol. 7). xiv, 242p. 1996. 96.50 (90-04-10509-3) Brill Academic Pubs.

National Movements & World Peace. Tuomo Melasuo. 189p. 1990. text 72.95 (1-85628-079-9, Pub. by Avebry) Ashgate Pub Co.

National Movements in Africa & the Middle East: The Domestic Characteristics of Political Mobilization. Ed. by Bruce E. Stanley. 200p. (C). 1991. pap. text 27.50 (0-8133-7334-4) Westview.

National Movements in the Baltic Countries During the 19th Century. Ed. by Aleksander Loit. (Studia Baltica Stockholmiensia). 572p. (Orig.). 1985. pap. 53.00 (91-22-00776-8) Coronet Bks.

National Municipal Gazetteer: New York, 1990 Volume. 500p. 1990. 95.00 (1-878684-00-0) Target Exchange.

National Municipal Gazetteer: New York, 1991 Volume. Ed. by Henry G. McComb. (Illus.). 600p. (Orig.). 1990. pap. 95.00 (1-878684-01-9) Target Exchange.

National Municipal Gazetteer: New York, 1992 Volume. 3rd ed. Ed. by Henry G. McComb. (Illus.). 529p. 1992. pap. 95.00 (1-878684-02-7) Target Exchange.

National Municipal Gazetteer: New York, 1993 Volume. 4th ed. Ed. by Henry G. McComb. (Illus.). 525p. 1993. pap. 95.00 (1-878684-03-5) Target Exchange.

National Municipal Gazetteer: New York, 1994 Volume. 5th rev. ed. Ed. by Henry G. McComb. (Illus.). 525p. (C). 1994. pap. 95.00 (1-878684-04-3) Target Exchange.

National Municipal Gazetteer: New York, 1995 Volume. Ed. by Henry G. McComb. (Illus.). 525p. (C). 1995. pap. 95.00 (1-878864-05-X) Target Exchange.

National Municipal Gazetteer: New York, 1996 Volume. 7th ed. Ed. by Henry G. McComb. (Illus.). 550p. 1996. pap. 95.00 (1-878684-06-X) Target Exchange.

National Municipal Gazetteer: New York, 1997 Volume. 8th unabridged ed. Ed. by Henry G. McComb. (Illus.). 550p. 1997. pap. 95.00 (1-878684-08-6) Target Exchange.

***National Municipal Gazetteer Vol. 10: New York 1999 Volume.** 10th ed. Ed. by Henry G. McComb. (Illus.). 650p. 1999. pap. 95.00 incl. cd-rom (1-878684-09-4) Target Exchange.

National Museum of American Art. National Museum of American Art, Smithsonian Insti. (Illus.). 280p. 1995. 40.00 (0-8212-2216-3, Pub. by Bulfinch Pr) Little.

National Museum of American Art Descriptive Catalog of Painting & Sculpture in the National Museum of American Art IV. 1983. 170.00 (0-8161-0408-5, G K Hall & Co) Mac Lib Ref.

National Museum of American Art, Smithsonian Institution. Frwd. by Elizabeth Broun. LC 94-37723. 1995. pap. write for info. (0-937311-20-0); text. write for info. (0-937311-24-3) Natl Mus Amer Art.

National Museum of American History, 10 bks. (Smithsonian Postcard Bks.). 1989. pap. 49.50 (0-87474-758-9) Smithsonian.

National Museum of Denmark Catalogue of Ancient Sculptures No. 1: Aegean, Cypriote, & Graeco-Phoenician. P. J. Riis et al. (Illus.). 115p. (C). 1989. pap. 27.00 (87-89438-01-9, Pub. by Aarhus Univ Pr) David Brown.

National Museum of Natural History: 75 Years in the Natural History Building. Ellis L. Yochelson. Ed. by Mary Jarrett. LC 85-600180. (Illus.). 216p. (C). 1991. reprint ed. pap. text 19.95 (0-87474-989-1) Smithsonian.

National Museum of Wales: A Companion Guide to the National Art. Mark Evans. (Illus.). 132p. (C). 1993. pap. 35.00 (0-85331-642-2, Pub. by Lund Humphries) Antique Collect.

***National Museum of Wildlife Art: Highlights from the Collection.** Leslie Greene Bowman. Ed. by Ponteir Sackrey & William Kerr. (Illus.). 60p. 1999. pap. write for info. (0-9674644-0-4) Museum of Wildlif.

National Museum of Women in the Arts. LC 86-28672. (Illus.). 256p. 1987. 45.00 (0-8109-1373-9); pap. 29.95 (0-940979-00-4) Natl Museum Women.

National Museum of Women in the Arts. Intro. by Alessandra Comini. (Illus.). 256p. 1987. 39.95 (0-685-43792-2) Abrams.

National Museum, Stockholm. Ulf Abel. LC 96-110230. (Museum Ser.). (Illus.). 145p. 1995. 30.00 (1-85759-048-1) Scala Books.

National Music. Ralph Vaughan Williams. LC 83-45481. reprint ed. 22.50 (0-404-20274-8) AMS Pr.

National Music & Other Essays. 2nd ed. Ralph V. Williams. LC 95-42483. (Illus.). 328p. 1996. pap. text 22.95 (0-19-816593-5, Clarendon Pr) OUP.

***National Nancys.** Fred Hunter. 240p. 2000. text 22.95 (0-312-25233-1) St Martin.

***National Needs in Ionizing Radiation Measurements & Standards: Second Report.** Ed. by Katy Nardi. (Illus.). 106p. (C). 2000. reprint ed. pap. text 35.00 (0-7881-8517-9) DIANE Pub.

National Negotiating Styles. Ed. by Hans A. Binnendijk. 147p. (Orig.). (C). 1995. pap. text 30.00 (0-7881-1570-7) DIANE Pub.

National Negotiating Styles: China, Russia, Japan, France, Egypt & Mexico. 1994. lib. bdg. 259.95 (0-8490-6444-9) Gordon Pr.

National New Age Yellow Pages: The Complete Directory of Consciousness-Raising Services, Products & Organizations. 2nd ed. Ed. by Marcia G. Ingenito. 256p. 1988. pap. 12.95 (0-943083-08-7) NNAYP.

National Newborn Screening Report (1991) Final Report. (Illus.). 110p. (Orig.). (C). 1996. pap. text 25.00 (0-7881-2680-6) DIANE Pub.

National NLG Referral Directory. 1989. 15.00 (0-685-14956-0) Natl Lawyers Guild.

National Nonpartisan League Debate: An Original Anthology. Ed. by Dan C. McCurry & Richard E. Rubenstein. LC 74-30645. (American Farmers & the Rise of Agribusiness Ser.). (Illus.). 1975. 29.95 (0-405-06815-8) Ayer.

National Nursing Home License Exam Study Guide: A Comprehensive Preparation Guide for Administrators & Directors of Nursing. Melissa Tracey & Kenneth M. Bowman. LC 96-22260. 216p. 1996. text 80.00 (0-7863-0973-3, Irwn Prfssnl) McGraw-Hill Prof.

***National Nursing Home Survey: 1995.** 89p. 2000. pap. 8.75 (0-16-050328-0) USGPO.

National Objects Invitational, 1993. Alan DuBois. 50p. 1993. pap. 16.00 (1-884240-02-X) Arkansas Art Ctr.

***National Occupational Exposure Survey Vol. III: Analysis of Management Interview Responses.** Ed. by David H. Pederson & William Karl Sieber. (Illus.). 720p. (C). 1999. reprint ed. pap. text 60.00 (0-7881-8385-0) DIANE Pub.

National Occupational Projections for Voc. Ed. Planning. Neal H. Rosenthal & Michael Pilot. 26p. 1983. 3.25 (0-318-22159-4, IN252) Ctr Educ Trng Employ.

***National Ocean Conference: Oceans of Commerce, Oceans of Life.** Ed. by D. James Baker & John Graykowski. (Illus.). 240p. 2000. reprint ed. pap. text 50.00 (0-7881-8871-2) DIANE Pub.

National of Fliers: German Aviation & the Popular Imagination. Peter Fritzsche. 283p. (C). 1994. pap. text 14.95 (0-674-60122-X) HUP.

National Office Machine Dealers Association Service Report. 54p. (Orig.). (C). 1993. pap. text 20.00 (1-56806-982-0) DIANE Pub.

National Oil Companies. Leslie E. Grayson. LC 80-41436. (Illus.). 277p. reprint ed. pap. 85.90 (0-8357-4560-0, 203746200008) Bks Demand.

***National Online Meeting: Proceedings of the 19th National Online Meeting, May 12-14, 1998.** Ed. by Martha E. Williams. 400p. 1998. pap. 59.00 (1-57387-059-5) Info Today Inc.

***National Online Meeting Proceedings: A Collection of the Papers by Experts in All Facets of the Online & Electronic Publishing Field Presented at the Largest Conference & Exhibition of Its Kind in North America.** Ed. by Martha E. Williams. 53p. 1999. 59.00 (1-57387-084-6) Info Today Inc.

National Open Hearth & Basic Oxygen Steel Conference, 60th: Proceedings, Pittsburgh Meeting, April 17-20, 1977. Iron & Steel Society of AIME Staff. LC TS0300.. (Illus.). 484p. reprint ed. pap. 150.10 (0-7837-6110-4, 204564500060) Bks Demand.

National Open Hearth & Basic Oxygen Steel Conference, 63rd: Proceedings, Washington, DC Meeting, March 23-26, 1980. Iron & Steel Society of AIME Staff. LC TS0300.. (Illus.). 370p. reprint ed. pap. 114.70 (0-7837-6111-2, 204564600063) Bks Demand.

National Operations Security Conference & Exhibition ('97) Proceedings. (Illus.). 86p. 1998. pap. text 30.00 (0-7881-3804-9) DIANE Pub.

National Organ Transplant Act of 1984: A Legislative History of Pub. Law No. 98-507, 3 vols., Set. Ed. by Bernard D. Reams, Jr. LC 89-83919. (Federal Health Law Ser.: Part 1). 2466p. 1990. lib. bdg. 225.00 (0-89941-691-8, 305920) W S Hein.

National Organic Directory, 1999. 16th rev. ed. Community Alliance Staff & Family Farmers Staff. (Illus.). 396p. 1999. pap. 47.95 (1-891894-03-X) Commun Alliance.

National Organic Directory, 1997. 14th rev. ed. Compiled by Community Alliance with Family Farmers Staff. (Illus.). xiii, 388p. 1997. pap. 24.95 (1-891894-00-5) Commun Alliance.

National Organic Directory, 1998, Vol. 15. 15th rev. ed. Compiled by Community Alliance with Family Farmers Staff. (Illus.). 1998. pap. 44.95 (1-891894-01-3) Commun Alliance.

National Organizations Concerned with Mental Health, Housing, & Homelessness. 49p. 1998. pap. text 20.00 (0-7881-4854-0) DIANE Pub.

National Organizations of the U. S., 3 vols. 35th ed. Ed. by Margaret Fisk et al. LC 76-46129. 4000p. 1999. 505.00 (0-7876-2229-X, GML00299-111749, Gale Res Intl) Gale.

National Outdoor Guides Directory. Ed. by Robert A. Mills & Olin R. Haines. (Illus.). 434p. (Orig.). 1987. 12.95 (0-944080-00-6) Prof Guides Pub.

National Outdoor Leadership School's Wilderness Guide. Peter Simer & John Sullivan. 352p. 1985. pap. 10.95 (0-671-61821-0, Fireside) S&S Trade Pap.

N

An Asterisk (*) at the beginning of an entry indicates that the title is appearing for the first time.

National Outdoor Leadership School's Wilderness Guide: The Classic Wilderness Guide. rev. ed. Mark Harvey. LC 99-21875. 272p. 1999. pap. 14.00 (*0-684-85909-2*, Fireside) S&S Trade Pap.

National Overview on Crime Prevention. Ed. by Sandra McKillop & J. Vernon. (Australian Institute Conference Proceedings Ser.: Vol. 15). 310p. 1992. pap. 25.00 (*0-642-18452-6*, Pub. by Aust Inst Criminology) Advent Bks Div.

National Pacifism Germany's New Temptation. Mark Almond. (C). 1991. 35.00 (*0-907967-26-4*, Pub. by Inst Euro Def & Strat) St Mut.

National Pageant. Cherie Bennett. (Pageant Ser.: No. 5). 176p. (YA). 1998. pap. 4.50 (*0-425-16621-X*, JAM) Berkley Pub.

National Palace Museum in Photographs Taipei. Tung Min. (Illus.). 192p. 1987. 59.50 (*957-562-026-7*) Heian Intl.

National Palace, Sintra. Jose Custudio. (Illus.). 128p. 1998. 35.00 (*1-85759-181-X*) Scala Books.

National Paralegal Reporter Magazine (Quarterly) 1995. pap. 10.00 (*0-614-04579-7*) Natl Fed Para.

National Park Activist Guide: A Manual for Citizen Action. 1993. 5.95 (*0-614-10450-5*, L116) Natl Parks & Cons.

National Park Activist Guide: A Manual for Citizen Action. National Parks & Conservation Association Staff. 1993. write for info. (*0-318-72303-4*) Natl Parks & Cons.

National Park & America's Wit. National Flag Foundation Staff & James V. Murfin. (Illus.). 432p. 1992. 19.95 (*0-317-91090-6*, 34526) Interp Mktg Prods.

National Park & Northwest National Park & Forest Wit. William Gibson & James V. Murfin. (Illus.). 432p. 1992. 19.95 (*0-685-34940-3*, 34523) Interp Mktg Prods.

National Park & Yellowstone Teton Wit. William Gibson & James V. Murfin. (Illus.). 432p. 1992. 19.95 (*0-685-45428-2*, 34524) Interp Mktg Prods.

National Park Concession Management: Hearing Before the Subcommittee On National Parks, Historic Preservation, & Recreation of the Committee On Energy & Natural Resources, United States Senate, One Hundred Fifth Congress, First Session ... July 30, 1997. United States. LC 98-138701. iii, 71 p. 1997. write for info. (*0-16-055911-1*) USGPO.

National Park Concessions Measures: Hearing Before the Subcommittee on National Parks & Public Lands of the Committee on Interior & Insular Affairs, House of Representatives, 102 Congress, 1st Session, on H.R. 542... H.R. 294... H.R. 571... H.R. 943... H. Con. Res. 14... H. Con. Res. 20... Hearing Held in Washington, DC, June 11, 1991. USGPO Staff. LC 94-111817. iv, 279 p. 1992. write for info. (*0-16-039607-7*) USGPO.

National Park Cookbook. Judy Giddings. 128p. 1995. 12.00 (*0-9628165-6-6*, Park Pr) J J Collect.

National Park Geology. Bass. (Earth Science Ser.). 2001. 37.00 (*0-534-51702-1*) Wadsworth Pub.

National Park Guide. Michael Frome. (Illus.). 248p. (Orig.). 1988. pap. 12.95 (*0-528-88260-0*) S&S Trade.

National Park Guide. Ed. by Pocket Books Staff. 1988. 12.95 (*0-671-88260-0*) PB.

National Park Guide, 1995-1996 Edition. Frome. 1995. pap. 17.00 (*0-671-87994-4*) S&S Trade.

National Park Guide, 1994. Frome. 1994. pap. 16.00 (*0-671-88418-2*, P-H Travel) Prntice Hall Bks.

National Park Service: A Seventy-Fifth Anniversary Album. Ed. by Linda Griffin & William Sontag. (Illus.). 128p. 1991. 30.00 (*0-911797-92-0*) Roberts Rinehart.

National Park Service: A Seventy-Fifth Anniversary Album. Paul D. Schullery & William H. Sontag. (Illus.). 128p. 1991. pap. 16.95 (*0-911797-93-9*) Roberts Rinehart.

National Park Service: Activities & Adventures for Kids. Bill Hallett & Jane Hallett. (Illus.). 32p. (Orig.). (J). (gr. 3-8). 1991. student ed. 3.95 (*1-877827-07-X*) Look & See.

National Park Service: Efforts to Link Resources to Results Suggest Insights for Other Agencies. Michael J. Curro. (Illus.). 54p. (C). 1999. pap. text 20.00 (*0-7881-7830-X*) DIANE Pub.

National Park Service: Its History, Activities & Organization. Jenks Cameron. LC 72-3024. (Brookings Institution. Institute for Government Research. Service Monographs of the U. S. Government: No. 11). reprint ed. 25.00 (*0-404-57111-5*) AMS Pr.

***National Park Service: The Condition of Lodging Facilities Varies among Selected Parks.** Lynne L. Goldfarb. (Illus.). 63p. (C). 2000. pap. text 20.00 (*0-7881-8723-6*) DIANE Pub.

National Park Service: The Story Behind the Scenery. Horace M. Albright et al. LC 86-81514. (Illus.). 96p. 1987. 17.50 (*0-88714-009-2*); pap. 7.95 (*0-88714-010-6*) KC Pubns.

National Park Service Concessions Policy Reform Act of 1991: Hearings Before the Subcommittee on Public Lands, National Parks & Forests of the Committee on Energy & Natural Resources, United States Senate, 102 Congress, 2nd Session, on S. 1755... March 3 & 5, 1992. USGPO Staff. LC 92-232197. (S. Hrg. Ser.). iii, 214 p. 1992. write for info. (*0-16-038980-1*) USGPO.

National Park Service Concessions Policy Reform Act of 1993: Hearing Before the Subcommittee on Public Lands, National Parks & Forests of the Committee on Energy & Natural Resources, United States Senate, 103 Congress, 1st Session, on S. 208... June 24, 1993. USGPO Staff. LC 94-132574. (S. Hrg. Ser.). iii, 71 p. 1993. write for info. (*0-16-041727-9*) USGPO.

National Park Service Legislation: Hearing Before the Subcommittee on National Parks, Forests & Lands of the Committee on Resources, House of Representatives, 104th Congress, 1st Session, on H. R. 2025, H. R. 2067, H. R. 2464, H.R. 2465, October 26, 1995--Washington, D. C. USGPO Staff. LC 96-120436. iv, 211 p. 1996. pap. write for info. (*0-16-052176-9*) USGPO.

National Park Service Photographs: Ansel Adams. (Illus.). 30p. 1995. pap. 7.95 (*1-55859-922-3*) Abbeville Pr.

***National Park Service Uniforms: In Search of an Identity 1872-1920.** R. Bryce Workman. (Illus.). 90p. 2000. reprint ed. pap. text 25.00 (*0-7881-8791-0*) DIANE Pub.

National Park System Additions: Hearing Before the Subcommittee on National Parks, Historic Preservation, & Recreation of the Committee on Energy & Natural Resources, United States Senate, One Hundred Fifth Congress, First Session ... July 24, 1997. United States. LC 98-208176. 39 p. 1997. write for info. (*0-16-055837-9*) USGPO.

National Park System in Alaska: An Economic Impact Study. Pamela E. Rich & Arlon R. Tussing. LC 73-620004. (ISER Reports: No. 35). (Illus.). 88p. 1973. pap. 2.00 (*0-88353-008-2*) U Alaska Inst Res.

National Park System User Fees: Hearing Before the Subcommittee on National Parks, Historic Preservation & Recreation of the Committee on Energy & Natural Resources, United States Senate, One Hundred Fifth Congress, First Session . . . June 19, 1997. United States Government. LC 98-114498. (S. Hrg. Ser.). iii, 66 p. 1997. write for info. (*0-16-055683-X*) USGPO.

National Park Tours in the Southwest. Roseann Hanson & Jonathan Hanson. LC 99-15488. (Illus.). 64p. 1999. pap. 7.95 (*1-877856-94-0*) SW Pks Mnmts.

National Park Vacation: America's Best. Liberty Publishing Staff. 1991. pap. 9.95 (*0-89709-191-4*) Liberty Pub.

National Park Wit. William Gibson et al. (Illus.). 864p. 1992. boxed set 34.95 (*0-685-21655-1*, 34581) Interp Mktg Prods.

National Park Wit, No. 1. William Gibson & James V. Murfin. LC 85-81843. (Illus.). 216p. 1992. 6.98 (*0-936023-00-7*, 34501) Interp Mktg Prods.

National Parks. Amoco Pathfinder Staff. 1992. pap. 2.25 (*0-671-84030-4*) S&S Trade.

National Parks. Reader's Digest Editors. LC 92-35785. (Explore America Ser.). (Illus.). 144p. 1993. 16.98 (*0-89577-447-X*, Pub. by RD Assn) Penguin Putnam.

National Parks: A Postcard Folio Book. Ansel Adams. (Illus.). 64p. 1995. 10.95 (*0-8212-2181-7*, Pub. by Bulfinch Pr) Little.

National Parks: Camping Guide. 1994. lib. bdg. 250.00 (*0-8490-6474-0*) Gordon Pr.

National Parks: Conservation or Cosmetics. Ann MacEwen & Malcolm MacEwan. (Resource Management Ser.). 1982. pap. text 24.95 (*0-04-719004-3*) Routledge.

National Parks: Difficult Choices Need to be Made about the Future of the Parks. (Illus.). 52p. (Orig.). (C). 1996. pap. text 30.00 (*0-7881-2735-7*) DIANE Pub.

National Parks: Eastern United States. Insight Guides Staff. (Insight Guides). 1998. pap. text 21.95 (*0-88729-720-X*) Langenscheidt.

National Parks: Lesser Known Areas. 49p. 1995. pap. 3.00 (*0-16-061669-7*) USGPO.

National Parks: The American Experience. 3rd ed. Alfred E. Runte. LC 96-37399. (Illus.). xxiii, 379p. 1997. pap. 16.00 (*0-8032-8963-4*) U of Nebr Pr.

National Parks: Western United States. Insight Guides Staff. (Insight Guides). 1998. pap. text 23.95 (*0-88729-721-8*) Langenscheidt.

***National Parks & Other Wild Places of Indonesia.** Janet Cochrane & Gerald Cubitt. (Illus.). 176p. 2000. 49.95 (*1-85974-193-2*, Pub. by New Holland) BHB Intl.

***National Parks & Other Wild Places of Malaysia.** W W F Malaysia Staff. (Illus.). 176p. 2000. 49.95 (*1-85368-626-3*, Pub. by New Holland) BHB Intl.

***National Parks & Other Wild Places of Southern Africa.** Brian Johnson-Barker et al. (Illus.). 176p. 2000. 49.95 (*1-86872-212-0*, Pub. by New Holland) BHB Intl.

National Parks & Protected Areas: Keystones to Conservation & Sustainable Development. Ed. by James G. Nelson & Rafal Serafin. LC 97-37830. (NATO ASI Series G: Vol. 40). (Illus.). ix, 292p. 1997. text 109.00 (*3-540-63527-0*) Spr-Verlag.

National Parks & Protected Areas: Their Role in Environmental Protection. Ed. by R. Gerald Wright & John Lemons. LC 96-8572. (Illus.). 470p. 1996. pap. text 61.95 (*0-86542-496-9*) Blackwell Sci.

***National Parks & Rural Development: Practice & Policy in the United States.** Ed. by Gary E. Machus & Donald R. Field. (Illus.). 296p. 2000. 55.00 (*1-55963-814-1*, Shearwater Bks); pap. 27.50 (*1-55963-815-X*, Shearwater Bks) Island Pr.

National Parks & Seashores of the East. 3rd ed. Fodors Travel Publications, Inc. Staff. 352p. 1998. pap. 17.00 (*0-679-03508-7*) Fodors Travel.

National Parks & the Common Good: A Communitarian Perspective. Francis N. Lovett. LC 97-39380. (Rights & Responsibilities Ser.). 144p. 1998. 53.00 (*0-8476-8977-8*); pap. 21.95 (*0-8476-8978-6*) Rowman.

National Parks & the Women's Voice: A History. Polly W. Kaufman. LC 95-32469. (Illus.). 312p. 1996. pap. 18.95 (*0-8263-1870-3*) U of NM Pr.

National Parks, Conservation, & Development: The Role of Protected Areas in Sustaining Society. Ed. by Jeffrey A. McNeely & Kenton R. Miller. LC 84-600007. (Illus.). 848p. 1984. pap. text 35.00 (*0-87474-663-9*, MCNPP) Smithsonian.

***National Parks Deluxe.** 1998. pap. 12.99 (*0-7631-1430-8*) BrownTrout Pubs Inc.

National Parks for the Twenty-First Century: The Vail Agenda. National Park Service Staff. LC 92-60471. (Illus.). 160p. (Orig.). 1991. pap. 14.95 (*0-9603410-7-2*) Natl Pk Found.

National Parks in Crisis. Ed. by Eugenia H. Connally. 220p. 1982. 13.95 (*0-318-17829-X*) Natl Parks & Cons.

National Parks in Crisis. Pref. by Eugenia H. Connally. LC 82-81269. 220p. (C). 1982. 13.95 (*0-940091-11-9*) Natl Parks & Cons.

National Parks in Crisis. National Parks & Conservation Association Staff. 17p. 1993. write for info. (*0-318-72304-2*) Natl Parks & Cons.

National Parks in Urban Areas. William C. Lienesch. Ed. by Marjorie Corbett. 29p. (Orig.). 1986. pap. 4.50 (*0-940091-17-8*) Natl Parks & Cons.

National Parks in Urban Areas: An Annotated Bibliography. Kathleen Fahey. (CPL Bibliographies Ser.: No. 90). 67p. 1982. 10.00 (*0-86602-090-X*, Sage Prdcls Pr) Sage.

National Parks Index. 1995. lib. bdg. 251.75 (*0-8490-7428-2*) Gordon Pr.

National Parks Index. 1997. lib. bdg. 250.99 (*0-8490-8123-8*); lib. bdg. 252.95 (*0-8490-6204-7*) Gordon Pr.

National Parks Index, 1995. (Illus.). 127p. 1996. pap., per. 4.25 (*0-16-003574-0*, 024-005-01160-9) USGPO.

National Parks: Index 1997-1999, Revised to Include the Actions of the 104th Congress Ending December 31, 1996. Department of Interior, National Park Service, Off. (Illus.). 128p. 1997. per. 6.50 (*0-16-054883-7*) USGPO.

National Parks of Alaska. Marj Dunmire. (Illus.). 48p. (YA). (gr. 2 up). 1991. pap. 4.95 (*0-942559-07-X*) Pegasus Graphics.

National Parks of America. Photos by David Meunch. (Illus.). 208p. 1993. 50.00 (*1-55868-124-8*) Gr Arts Ctr Pub.

National Parks of America. Donald Young. 1998. 16.98 (*1-880908-09-3*) Todtri Prods.

***National Parks of Canada.** Kevin McNamee. (Illus.). 224p. 1998. pap. 26.95 (*1-55013-985-1*, Pub. by Key Porter) Firefly Bks Ltd.

National Parks of Madhya Pardesh: State of Bio Diversity & Human Infringement. S. K. Tiwari. LC 98-908787. xvi, 286p. 1998. write for info. (*81-7024-950-3*) APH Pubng.

National Parks of Montana & Wyoming Souvenir Book. pap. write for info. (*1-56944-045-X*) Terrell Missouri.

National Parks of North America. National Geographic Society Book Division Staff. LC 95-10989. 336p. 1996. 40.00 (*0-7922-2954-1*) Natl Geog.

National Parks of North America. deluxe ed. National Geographic Society Book Division Staff. LC 96-34242. (Illus.). 336p. 1995. write for info. (*0-7922-2955-X*) Natl Geog.

National Parks of the American West. 1990. 34.98 (*1-55521-671-4*) Bk Sales Inc.

***National Parks of the American West.** Frommer's Staff. 464p. 1998. 21.95 (*0-02-862067-4*, Pub. by Macmillan) S&S Trade.

National Parks of the Rocky Mountains: Rocky Mountain, Grand Teton, Yellowstone, Glacier-Waterton Lakes. Kent Dannen & Donna Dannen. (Illus.). 120p. 1986. 14.95 (*0-930487-20-6*) Rocky Mtn Nature Assn.

National Parks of the West. 4th ed. Fodors Travel Publications, Inc. Staff. 464p. 1998. pap. 17.50 (*0-679-03509-5*) Fodors Travel.

National Parks Projects. Mike Graf. 1993. pap. 11.99 (*0-86653-934-4*) Fearon Teacher Aids.

***National Parks Restoration Plan: Congressional Hearing.** Ed. by Craig Thomas. 177p. (C). 2000. reprint ed. pap. text 30.00 (*0-7881-8703-1*) DIANE Pub.

National Parks West. 2nd ed. (Insight Guides Ser.). (Illus.). 1999. pap. 23.95 (*0-88729-028-0*) Langenscheidt.

***National Parks with Kids.** Paris Permenter & John Bigley. 360p. 1999. pap. 14.95 (*1-892975-06-8*) Open Rd Pub.

National Parliaments & the European Union. Ed. by Philip Norton. LC 95-24867. (Journal of Legislative Studies). 204p. 1995. 45.00 (*0-7146-4691-1*, Pub. by F Cass Pubs) Intl Spec Bk.

National Parliaments & the European Union. Ed. by Philip Norton. 204p. (C). 1997. pap. 19.50 (*0-7146-4330-0*, Pub. by F Cass Pubs) Intl Spec Bk.

National Parliaments As Cornerstones of European Integration. Ed. by Eivind Smith. LC 96-7501. 195p. 1996. 77.00 (*90-411-0898-X*) Kluwer Law Intl.

National Party Chairmen & Committees: Factionalism at the Top. Ralph M. Goldman. LC 89-70272. 672p. (gr. 13). 1990. text 95.95 (*0-87332-636-9*) M E Sharpe.

National Party Conventions, 1831-1996. Congressional Quarterly, Inc. Staff. LC 97-20443. viii, 312p. (YA). 1997. 37.95 (*1-56802-280-8*) Congr Quarterly.

National Party Platforms, 2 vols., Set. 6th rev. ed. Compiled by Donald B. Johnson. Incl. Vol. 1. 1840-1956. 612p. 1978. 54.95 (*0-252-00687-9*); Vol. 2. 1960-1976. 462p. 1978. 44.95 (*0-252-00688-7*); 1074p. 1978. Set text 64.95 (*0-252-00692-5*) U of Ill Pr.

National Party Platforms, 1960-1976, Vol. 2. rev. ed. Donald B. Johnson. LC 78-17373. 468p. 1978. reprint ed. pap. 145.10 (*0-7837-8072-9*, 204782500008) Bks Demand.

National Party Platforms of 98. Compiled by Donald B. Johnson. LC 82-11448. 240p. 1982. pap. text 19.95 (*0-252-00923-1*) U of Ill Pr.

National Past-Times: Narrative, Representation, & Power In Modern China. Ann S. Anagnost. LC 96-6609. (Body, Commodity, Text Ser.). (Illus.). 272p. 1997. pap. text 16.95 (*0-8223-1969-1*); lib. bdg. 49.95 (*0-8223-1961-6*) Duke.

National Pastime. 88p. 1982. 5.00 (*0-317-36194-5*) Soc Am Baseball Res.

National Pastime. Ed. by Peter C. Bjarkman. (Illus.). 96p. 1993. pap. 7.95 (*0-910137-48-X*) Soc Am Baseball Res.

National Pastime. Ed. by John B. Holway. (Illus.). 88p. 1992. pap. 7.95 (*0-910137-46-3*) Soc Am Baseball Res.

National Pastime. Ed. by John Thorn. (Illus.). 88p. 1985. pap. 6.00 (*0-910137-19-6*) Soc Am Baseball Res.

National Pastime. Ed. by John Thorn. 288p. 1987. mass mkt. 3.95 (*0-446-34727-2*, Pub. by Warner Bks) Little.

National Pastime. Ed. by Robert L. Tiemann. (Illus.). 88p. 1990. pap. 8.00 (*0-910137-40-4*) Soc Am Baseball Res.

National Pastime, No. 13. Mark Alvarez. 1993. pap. 7.95 (*0-910137-52-8*) Soc Am Baseball Res.

National Pastime, No. 15. Ed. by Mark Alvarez. 1995. pap. 9.95 (*0-910137-62-5*) LPC InBook.

National Pastime, No. 16. Ed. by Mark Alvarez. 1996. pap. 9.95 (*0-910137-64-1*) Soc Am Baseball Res.

***National Pastime Vol. 19: A Review of Baseball History.** Ed. by Mark Alvarez. (Illus.). 116p. 1999. pap. 12.00 (*0-910137-77-3*, Pub. by Soc Am Baseball Res) U of Nebr Pr.

National Pastime, 1984: Pictorial Edition. Ed. by John Thorn. (Illus.). 88p. (Orig.). 1984. 7.00 (*0-910137-09-9*) Soc Am Baseball Res.

National Pastime, 1984: Regular Edition. Ed. by John Thorn. (Illus.). 88p. 1985. pap. 6.00 (*0-910137-11-0*) Soc Am Baseball Res.

National Pastime, 1987. Ed. by John Thorn. (Illus.). 88p. 1987. pap. 6.00 (*0-910137-25-0*) Soc Am Baseball Res.

National Pastime, 1982. 2nd ed. Ed. by John Thorn. (Illus.). 88p. 1983. pap. 5.00 (*0-685-10048-0*) Soc Am Baseball Res.

National Pastime, 1994, No. 14. Mark Alvarez. 1994. pap. 9.95 (*0-910137-56-0*) Soc Am Baseball Res.

National Pastime, 1997, Vol. 17. Ed. by Mark Alvarez. 1997. pap. 9.95 (*0-910137-68-4*) Soc Am Baseball Res.

National Pastime Pictorial: Dead Ball Era. Ed. by John Thorn & Mark Rucker. (Illus.). 88p. 1986. pap. 8.00 (*0-910137-22-6*) Soc Am Baseball Res.

National, Patriotic & Typical Airs of All Lands. John P. Sousa. LC 76-52480. (Music Reprint Ser.). 1977. reprint ed. lib. bdg. 42.50 (*0-306-70861-2*) Da Capo.

National Patterns of R & D Resources (1992) John E. Jankowski, Jr. (Illus.). 84p. (Orig.). (C). 1993. pap. text 25.00 (*1-56806-483-7*) DIANE Pub.

National Patterns of R & D Resources (1994) John E. Jankowski, Jr. & John R. Gawalt. (Illus.). 105p. 1996. reprint ed. pap. text 40.00 (*0-7881-3324-1*) DIANE Pub.

National Performance Indicators for Hospital Materials Management Operations: 1987. 60p. 1987. 205.00 (*0-318-35035-1*, 142814) AHRMM.

National Performance Review: Creating a Government That Works Better & Costs Less, Department of Defense. Al Gore, Jr. (Illus.). 95p. (C). 1996. reprint ed. pap. text 25.00 (*0-7881-3149-4*) DIANE Pub.

National Performance Review: From Red Tape to Results: Creating a Government That Works Better & Costs Less. Al Gore, Jr. 168p. (Orig.). (C). 1994. pap. text 35.00 (*0-7881-0693-7*) DIANE Pub.

National Performance Review: From Red Tape to Results: Creating a Government That Works Better & Costs Less (Status Report, September, 1994) Al Gore, Jr. (Illus.). 127p. (Orig.). (C). 1994. pap. text 30.00 (*0-7881-1794-7*) DIANE Pub.

National Performance Review - Creating a Government That Works Better & Costs Less: Intelligence Community - From Red Tape to Results. Al Gore, Jr. 38p. (C). 1996. reprint ed. pap. text 20.00 (*0-7881-3403-5*) DIANE Pub.

National Performance Standards for Residential Care: A Policy Initiative from Father Flanagan's Boys' Home. Daniel L. Daly & Val J. Peter. 25p. 1996. pap. 4.99 (*1-889322-10-5*, 19-208) Boys Town Pr.

National Period in the History of the New World: An Outline & Commentary. Charles C. Griffin. LC 88-12630. 280p. 1990. reprint ed. lib. bdg. 85.00 (*0-313-23888-X*, GRPH, Greenwood Pr) Greenwood.

National Perspect New Regional. Inotai Hettne. LC 99-29990. Vol. 2. 304p. 1999. text 69.95 (*0-312-22683-7*) St Martin.

***National Perspectives on the New Regionalism in the South.** Contrib. by Bjorn Hettne et al. LC 99-48280. (New Regionalism Ser.). 2000. text 69.95 (*0-312-22772-8*) St Martin.

National Pharmacy Boards (NPB) Jack Rudman. (Admission Test Ser.: Vol. 47). 69.95 (*0-8373-5147-2*) Nat Learn.

National Pharmacy Boards (NPB) Jack Rudman. (Admission Test Ser.: ATS-47). 1994. pap. 49.95 (*0-8373-5047-6*) Nat Learn.

National Plan for American Forestry, 2 vols., Set. U. S. Senate Staff. Ed. by Stuart Bruchey. LC 78-53554. (Development of Public Land Law in the U. S. Ser.). (Illus.). 1979. reprint ed. lib. bdg. 119.95 (*0-405-11389-7*) Ayer.

National Plan for Research on Child & Adolescent Mental Disorders. (Illus.). 80p. 1990. pap. 4.25 (*0-16-021851-9*, S/N 017-024-01395-1) USGPO.

***National Plan for Research on Child & Adolescent Mental Disorders.** Ed. by Lewis L. Judd. 64p. (C). 2000. pap. text 20.00 (*0-7881-8941-7*) DIANE Pub.

National Plan of Integrated Airport Systems 1993-1997: Report to Congress. 161p. 1995. pap. 14.00 (*0-16-062375-8*) USGPO.

National Planning Considerations for the Acquisition of Strong Ground-Motion Data. R. D. Borcherdt et al. 55p. 1984. pap. 10.00 (*0-685-14409-7*) Earthquake Eng.

National Playwrights Directory. 2nd ed. Ed. by Phyllis J. Kaye. LC 81-14097. 1982. 35.00 (*0-9605160-0-X*) E ONeill.

National Plumbing Codes Handbook. R. Dodge Woodson. 285p. 1992. pap. 44.95 (*0-07-071769-9*) McGraw.

N

An Asterisk (*) at the beginning of an entry indicates that the title is appearing for the first time.

National Plumbing Codes Handbook. 2nd rev. ed. R. Dodge Woodson. LC 97-34404. (Illus.). 352p. 1997. 49.95 (*0-07-071854-7*) McGraw-Hill Prof.

National Plumbing Estimator. 8th ed. Victor B. Ottaviano. (Illus.). 792p. 1992. pap. 85.00 (*1-878656-01-5*) Ottaviano Tech Serv.

National Poetry Month, 1998. Ed. by Michale Amato. 32p. 1998. pap. 3.00 (*1-929123-02-7*, MA0498P) No Exit Press.

National Police Custody Survey. David McDonald. LC 98-201071. 64p. 1999. pap. 25.00 (*0-642-24038-8*, Pub. by Aust Inst Criminology) Advent Bks Div.

National Police Selection Test (POST) (Career Examination Ser.: C-3596). 1994. pap. 29.95 (*0-8373-3596-5*) Nat Learn.

National Policies & Agricultural Trade: Finland. OECD Staff. 168p. (Orig.). 1989. pap. text 15.00 (*92-64-13240-6*, 51-89-04-1) OECD.

National Policy & Naval Strength. RICHMOND. 400p. 1993. 73.95 (*0-7512-0122-7*) Ashgate Pub Co.

National Policy & the Wheat Economy. Vernon C. Fowke. LC 58-551. (Social Credit in Alberta: Its Background & Development Ser.: No. 7). 322p. reprint ed. pap. 99.90 (*0-608-16591-3*, 202636400049) Bks Demand.

National Policy Approaches to the Lack of Available Homeowners' Insurance in Disaster-Prone Areas: Field Hearing Before the Subcommittee on Housing & Community Opportunity of the Committee on Banking & Financial Services, House of Representatives, One Hundred Fifth Congress, First Session, August 25, 1997. United States Government. LC 98-139063. iii, 84 p. 1997. write for info. (*0-16-055858-1*) USGPO.

National Policy for Radio Broadcasting. Cornelia B. Rose, Jr. LC 71-161172. (History of Broadcasting: Radio to Television Ser.). 1977. reprint ed. 26.95 (*0-405-03580-2*) Ayer.

National Policy for the Environment: NEPA & Its Aftermath. Richard A. Liroff. LC 75-28910. 284p. reprint ed. pap. 88.10 (*0-608-17408-4*, 205642900067) Bks Demand.

National Policy on Education: Towards an Enlightened & Humane Society. Digumarti Bhaskara Rao. LC 98-908225. 1998. 62.00 (*81-7141-426-5*, Pub. by Discovery Pub Hse) S Asia.

National Politics & International Technology: Nuclear Reactor Development in Western Europe. Henry R. Nau. LC 73-19344. 304p. 1974. reprint ed. pap. 94.30 (*0-608-04059-2*, 206479500011) Bks Demand.

National Politics in a Global Economy: The Domestic Sources of U. S. Trade Policy. Philip A. Mundo. LC 99-18788. (Essential Texts in American Government). 288p. (Orig.). 1999. 65.00 (*0-87840-743-X*); pap. 22.95 (*0-87840-744-8*) Georgetown U Pr.

National Polity & Local Power: The Transformation of Late Imperial China. Ed. by Philip A. Kuhn & Timothy Brook. LC 87-36474. (Harvard-Yenching Institute Monographs: No. 27). 316p. 1990. 26.00 (*0-674-60225-0*) HUP.

National Pool - Waterpark Life - CPR - Training. Jeff Ellis et al. (Emergency Care Ser.). 120p. 1994. pap., teacher ed. 15.00 (*0-86720-995-X*) Jones & Bartlett.

National Pool & Waterpark Lifeguard - CPR Training. Jeffrey L. Ellis & Jill E. White. LC 94-6167. 1993. pap. 28.75 (*0-86720-848-1*) Jones & Bartlett.

***National Pool & Waterpark Lifeguard CPR Training.** 2nd ed. Jeff Ellis. (Illus.). 104p. (C). 1998. pap. text, teacher ed. 30.00 (*0-7637-0983-2*) JB Pubns.

National Pool & Waterpark Lifeguard CPR Training. 2nd ed. Jeff Ellis et al. LC 98-21019. 212p. 1999. 30.00 (*0-7637-0793-7*) Jones & Bartlett.

National Popular Politics in Early Independent Mexico, 1820-1847. Torcuato S. Di Tella. 384p. 1996. 55.00 (*0-8263-1673-5*) U of NM Pr.

National Population Censuses, 1945-1976: Some Holding Libraries. Compiled by Doreen S. Goyer. LC 79-4232. 44p. (Orig.). 1979. pap. 8.00 (*0-933438-00-1*, SP 1) APLIC Intl.

National Population Forecasting in Industrialized Countries. Nico W. Keilman & Harry Cruijsen. (NIDI-CBGS Publications, Population & Family Study Center Ser.: Vol. 24). xiv, 370p. 1992. pap. 55.00 (*90-265-1304-6*) Swets.

National Population Policies: Population Studies. 456p. 45.00 (*92-1-151329-4*) UN.

National Portrait Gallery, 10 bks. (Postcard Bks.). 12p. 1988. pap. text 49.50 (*0-87474-771-6*) Smithsonian.

National Portrait Gallery. Charles S. Smith. (Illus.). 248p. 1997. 50.00 (*1-85514-214-7*, Pub. by Natl Port Gall) Antique Collect.

National Portrait Gallery of Distinguished Americans, 4 vols. James Herring & James B. Longacre. LC 73-103814. 1970. reprint ed. 76.95 (*0-405-02500-9*, 17147) Ayer.

National Portrait Gallery Permanent Collection Illustrated Checklist: 25th Anniversary Edition. rev. ed. Compiled by Dru Dowdy. (Illus.). 480p. 1978. 29.95 (*0-87474-674-4*) Smithsonian.

National Powder Metallurgy Conference Proceedings, 1972. National Powder Metallurgy Conference, Chicago IL. LC TN0695.N3. (Progress in Powder Metallurgy Ser.: No. 28). (Illus.). 322p. reprint ed. pap. 99.90 (*0-7837-1741-5*, 205727200024) Bks Demand.

National Powder Metallurgy Conference Proceedings, 1974. National Powder Metallurgy Conference Staff. Ed. by Gaylord D. Smith. LC TN0695.N3. (Progress in Powder Metallurgy Ser.: No. 31). 312p. reprint ed. pap. 96.80 (*0-8357-6991-7*, 205707500009) Bks Demand.

National Powder Metallurgy Conference Proceedings, 1975. National Powder Metallurgy Conference Staff. Ed. by Richard F. Halter. LC TN0695.N3. (Progress in Powder Metallurgy Ser.: No. 30). 213p. reprint ed. pap. 66.10 (*0-8357-6990-9*, 205707400009) Bks Demand.

National Powder Metallurgy Conference Proceedings, 1977: Sponsored by the Metal Powder Industries Federation & the American Powder Metallurgy Institute, May 24-25, 1977, Detroit Plaza Hotel, Detroit, Michigan. National Powder Metallurgy Conference Staff. Ed. by Stanley Mocarski & Thomas W. Pietrocini. LC TN0695.N3. (Progress in Powder Metallurgy Ser.: No. 33). 283p. reprint ed. pap. 87.80 (*0-7837-3165-5*, 204281300006) Bks Demand.

National Powder Metallurgy Conference Proceedings, 1978: April 24-26, 1978, Los Angeles, CA & the 1979 National Powder Metallurgy Conference, June 4-6, 1979, Cincinnati, OH. National Powder Metallurgy Conference Staff. Ed. by James Hoffman et al. LC TN0695.N3. (Progress in Powder Metallurgy Ser.: Vol. 34-35). (Illus.). 439p. reprint ed. pap. 136.10 (*0-7837-1556-0*, 204184900024) Bks Demand.

National Powder Metallurgy Conference Proceedings, 1982: Sponsored by the Metal Powder Industries Federation & the American Powder Metallurgy Institute, May 24-27, 1982, Westin Bonaventure Hotel, Montreal, Quebec, Canada. National Powder Metallurgy Conference Staff. Ed. by James G. Bewley & Sherwood W. McGee. LC TN0695.N3. (Progress in Powder Metallurgy Ser.: No. 38). 283p. reprint ed. pap. 87.80 (*0-7837-3164-7*, 204281400006) Bks Demand.

National Preparedness for Response Exercise Program Guidelines. 1996. lib. bdg. 252.75 (*0-8490-6872-X*) Gordon Pr.

National Preparedness for Response Exercise Program Guidelines: Oil Pollution. 1997. lib. bdg. 250.95 (*0-8490-7622-6*) Gordon Pr.

National Priciples of Anatomy & Physiology. 8th ed. Gerard J. Tortora. 1996. 106.95 (*0-471-36737-0*) Wiley.

National Product in Wartime. Simon Smith Kuznets. LC 75-19721. (National Bureau of Economic Research Ser.). (Illus.). 1975. reprint ed. 19.95 (*0-405-07600-2*) Ayer.

National Product in Wartime. Simon Smith Kuznets. (General Ser.: No. 44). 174p. 1945. reprint ed. 45.30 (*0-87014-043-4*) Natl Bur Econ Res.

National Product since 1869. Simon Smith Kuznets. LC 75-19722. (National Bureau of Economic Research Ser.). (Illus.). 1975. reprint ed. 25.95 (*0-405-07601-0*) Ayer.

National Product since 1869. Simon Smith Kuznets et al. (General Ser.: No. 46). 256p. 1946. reprint ed. 66.90 (*0-87014-045-0*) Natl Bur Econ Res.

National Product, War & Prewar. Simon Smith Kuznets. (Occasional Papers: No. 17). 56p. 1944. reprint ed. 20.00 (*0-87014-332-8*) Natl Bur Econ Res.

National Profile of Community Colleges: Trends & Statistics. 3rd ed. Date not set. pap. 45.00 (*0-87117-278-X*) Comm Coll Pr Am Assn Comm Coll.

National Profile of Local Boards of Health. Charles F. Bacon. (Illus.). 54p. (C). 1998. pap. text 20.00 (*0-7881-7316-2*) DIANE Pub.

National Psychology Boards (NPsyB) Jack Rudman. (Admission Test Ser.: Vol. 89). 69.95 (*0-8373-5189-8*) Nat Learn.

National Psychology Boards (NPsyB) Jack Rudman. (Admission Test Ser.: ATS-89). 1994. pap. 49.95 (*0-8373-5089-1*) Nat Learn.

National Psychology in International Relations. Franz E. Winkler. 35p. 1976. reprint ed. pap. 1.50 (*0-913098-10-8*) Orion Society.

National Public & Private EC Lobbying. Ed. by M. P. Van Schendelen. LC 93-18108. 301p. 1993. 78.95 (*1-85521-368-0*, Pub. by Dartmth Pub) Ashgate Pub Co.

National Public Employee Reporter. LRP Publications Staff. text. write for info. (*0-934753-10-5*) LRP Pubns.

National Public Employment Reporter: Tables. LRP Publications Staff. text 475.00 (*0-934753-09-1*) LRP Pubns.

National Public Radio: The Cast of Characters. Mary Collins. LC 92-34825. (Illus.). 150p. 1993. text 19.95 (*0-929765-19-2*) Seven Locks Pr.

National Purity Congress, Its Papers, Addresses, Portraits. Aaron M. Powell. LC 75-17238. (Social Problems & Social Policy Ser.). (Illus.). 1976. reprint ed. 39.95 (*0-405-07507-3*) Ayer.

National Quarter Horses. Jack McBryde. LC 97-50619. Date not set. 99.95 (*1-879984-03-2*) Loshadt Publishing.

National Question: Nationalism, Ethnic Conflict, & Self-Determination in the Twentieth Century. Ed. by Berch Berberoglu. LC 95-11672. (Orig.). (C). 1995. pap. text 24.95 (*1-56639-343-4*) Temple U Pr.

National Question: Nationalism, Ethnic Conflict, & Self-Determination in the Twentieth Century. Ed. by Berch Berberoglu. LC 95-11672. 327p. (Orig.). (C). 1995. lib. bdg. 69.95 (*1-56639-342-6*) Temple U Pr.

National Question: Selected Writings by Rosa Luxemburg. Rosa Luxemburg. Ed. by Horace B. Davis. LC 74-2148. 318p. 1976. reprint ed. pap. 98.60 (*0-7837-3913-3*, 204376100010) Bks Demand.

National Question Again. Ed. by John Osmond. 323p. (C). 1985. pap. 20.00 (*0-86383-132-X*, Pub. by Gomer Pr) St Mut.

National Question in Europe in Historical Context. Ed. by Mikulas Teich & Roy Porter. (Illus.). 363p. (C). 1993. pap. text 24.95 (*0-521-36713-1*) Cambridge U Pr.

National Question in Marxist-Leninist Theory & Strategy. Walker Connor. LC 83-43067. 633p. reprint ed. pap. 196.30 (*0-8357-3699-7*, 203642300003) Bks Demand.

National Question in Yugoslavia: Origins, History, Politics. Ivo Banac. LC 83-45931. (Illus.). 456p. 1984. pap. text 19.95 (*0-8014-9493-1*) Cornell U Pr.

National Quotation Bureau Bond Summary. annuals National Quotation Bureau Staff. (Orig.). 115.00 (*1-57447-001-9*) Nat Quot Bur.

National Quotation Bureau Stock Summary. annuals National Quotation Bureau Editorial Staff. (Orig.). 120.00 (*1-57447-000-0*) Nat Quot Bur.

National Radio Pleasure. Tim Dearman. (Illus.). 176p. (Orig.). 1996. pap. 9.95 (*0-9655724-0-4*) Natl Radio Pleasure.

National Rating & Rank Order of Colleges & Universities in the U. S. Profile & Rating of Leading American Colleges & Universities. Jean M. De LaFayette. Ed. by Judith Crawford et al. (Illus.). 154p. 1990. 30.00 (*0-939877-09-0*) ACUPAE.

National Reading Conference Yearbook. Ed. by Timothy Shanahan & Flora Rodriguez Brown. (National Reading Conference Yearbook Ser.: Vol. 47). 556p. 1998. 60.00 (*1-893591-00-X*) Nat Reading Conf.

***National Reading Conference Yearbook, Vol. 48.** Ed. by Timothy Shanahan & Flora Rodriguez-Brown. 512p. 1999. 60.00 (*1-893591-01-8*) Nat Reading Conf.

National Real Estate Directory. 2nd rev. ed. Thomas J. Lucier. Ed. by Barbara V. Lucier. 150p. 1992. per. 39.95 (*0-945343-01-9*) Home Eq.

National Real Estate Examination Study Guide. Richard Beals. 1982. pap. text 10.95 (*0-89764-002-0*) Lincolns Leadership.

National Recovery Administration. Leverett S. Lyon et al. LC 71-171386. (FDR & the Era of the New Deal Ser.). 1972. reprint ed. lib. bdg. 95.00 (*0-306-70385-8*) Da Capo.

National Redeemer: Owain Glyndwr in Welsh Tradition. Elissa Henken. x, 250p. 1996. pap. write for info. (*0-7083-1290-X*, Pub. by Univ Wales Pr) Paul & Co Pubs.

National Redeemer: Owain Glyndwr in Welsh Tradition. Elissa R. Henken. 264p. 1996. text 47.50 (*0-8014-3268-5*); pap. text 19.95 (*0-8014-8349-2*) Cornell U Pr.

***National Register of Apparel Manufacturers: Men & Boy's Wear.** 4th rev. ed. (Illus.). 567p. 1999. pap. 135.00 (*1-930512-02-3*) Marche Pubng.

***National Register of Apparel Manufacturers, Women & Children's Wear.** 5th rev. ed. (Illus.). 800p. 1999. pap. 159.00 (*1-930512-00-7*) Marche Pubng.

National Register of Big Trees. annuals 7.95 (*0-317-59271-8*) Am Forests.

National Register of Historic Places 1966 to 1994. 2nd ed. National Park Service Staff & Preservation Press Staff. (Illus.). 926p. 1995. pap. 98.00 (*0-471-14403-7*) Wiley.

***National Register of Independent Sales Reps: Apparel & Accessories.** 3rd rev. ed. (Illus.). 442p. 2000. pap. 135.00 (*1-930512-01-5*) Marche Pubng.

***National Register of Psychotherapists 1999.** 240p. 1999. pap. 75.00 (*0-415-20405-4*) Routledge.

National Register of Social Prestige & Academic Ratings of American Colleges & Universities. Jean M. De LaFayette. Ed. by Aurele Naffah et al. (Illus.). 136p. 1990. 28.00 (*0-939877-05-8*) ACUPAE.

***National Register of the Apparel Marketplace.** (Illus.). 368p. 1999. pap. 129.00 (*1-930512-03-1*) Marche Pubng.

National Register Properties: Williamson County, Tennessee. Jeri M. Hasselbring. LC 95-80483. (Illus.). 200p. 1995. 29.95 (*1-881576-56-6*, Hillsboro Pr) Providence Hse.

National Registry of Community Mental Health Services. 3rd ed. 158p. 1991. pap. 29.50 (*1-883066-04-2*) Natl Comm Mental.

***National Release Guide: A Comprehensive Guide to the Release of Real Estate Mortgage Documents, 4 vols.** rev. ed. Ed. by Carl R. Ernst & Michael Duckworth. Incl. Vol. 1. National Release Guide: A Comprehensive Guide to the Release of Real Estate Mortgage Documents. rev. ed. 2000. Not sold separately (*1-881627-10-1*); Vol. 2. National Release Guide: A Comprehensive Guide to the Release of Real Estate Mortgage Documents. rev. ed. 2000. Not sold separately (*1-881627-11-X*); Vol. 3. National Release Guide: A Comprehensive Guide to the Release of Real Estate Mortgage Documents. rev. ed. 2000. Not sold separately (*1-881627-12-8*); Vol. 4. National Release Guide: A Comprehensive Guide to the Release of Real Estate Mortgage Documents. rev. ed. 2000. Not sold separately (*1-881627-13-6*); 2000p. 2000. 495.00 (*1-881627-09-8*) Ernst Pub Co.

National Release Guide: A Comprehensive Guide to the Release of Real Estate Mortgage Documents see National Release Guide: A Comprehensive Guide to the Release of Real Estate Mortgage Documents

National Religions & Universal Religions. Abraham Kuenen. LC 77-27169. (Hibbert Lectures: 1882). reprint ed. 44.00 (*0-404-60403-X*) AMS Pr.

National Renal Diet: Renal Dietitians Dietetic Practice Group of the American Dietetic. LC 93-27161. 1993. write for info. (*0-88091-116-6*) Am Dietetic Assn.

National Report on Romania: Black Sea Environmental Priorities Study. Price not set. (*92-1-129503-3*) UN.

National Report on Turkey: Black Sea Environmental Priorities Study. Price not set. (*92-1-126093-0*) UN.

National Report on Ukraine: Black Sea Environmental Priorities Study. Price not set. (*92-1-126094-9*) UN.

National Reporting, 1941-1986: From Labor Conflicts to the Challenger Disaster. Ed. by Heinz-Dietrich Fischer & Erika J. Fischer. (Pulitzer Prize Archive Ser.: Vol. 2). 400p. 1989. lib. bdg. 82.00 (*3-598-30172-3*) K G Saur Verlag.

National Reports of EIFAC Member Countries for the Period January 1984-December 1985. FAO Staff. 138p. 1986. 17.00 (*92-5-002417-7*, F2925, Pub. by FAO) Bernan Associates.

National Representation for the District of Columbia. Judith A. Best & Orrin G. Hatch. LC 83-21721. 85p. 1984. lib. bdg. 59.95 (*0-313-27083-X*, U7083, Greenwood Pr) Greenwood.

National Research & Education Network (NREN) Research & Policy Perspectives. Charles R. McClure et al. Ed. by Peter Hernon. (Information Management, Policies & Services Ser.). 760p. (C). 1991. pap. 125.00 (*0-89391-813-X*) Ablx Pub.

National Resource Guide for the Placement of Artists: An Annotated Guide to Organizations & Publications Essential to Artists. Warren Christensen. Ed. by Cheryl Slean. 249p. (Orig.). pap. 45.00 (*0-945941-04-8*) NNAP.

National Review College Guide: America's Top Liberal Arts Schools. Ed. by Charles Sykes & Brad Miner. 272p. 1993. pap. 13.00 (*0-671-79801-4*, Fireside) S&S Trade Pap.

National Review of Asia in American Textbooks in 1993-Secondary Level: World History, World Cultures, World Geography. Compiled by Columbia University, National Project on Asian in. LC 93-27198. 139p. (Orig.). 1993. pap. 15.00 (*0-924304-16-2*) Assn Asian Studies.

National Review of Scholastic Achievement in General Education: How Are We Doing & Why Should We Care. Steven J. Osterlind. Ed. by Jonathan D. Fife. (ASHE-ERIC Higher Education Reports: Vol. 25-8). 100p. 1997. pap. 24.00 (*1-878380-80-X*) GWU Grad Schl E&HD.

National Review's Politically Incorrect Reference Guide: Your Handbook for the RIGHT Information. John J. Virtes et al. 320p. (Orig.). 1993. pap. text 19.95 (*0-9627841-1-7*) Natl Review.

National Riding Standards. rev. ed. Ed. by Affiliated National Riding Commission. 73p. 1981. pap. text 3.00 (*0-88314-154-X*, 303-10018) AAHPERD.

National Road. Ed. by George F. Thompson & Karl B. Raitz. LC 95-40321. (Road & American Culture Ser.). (Illus.). 424p. (C). 1996. 34.95 (*0-8018-5155-6*) Johns Hopkins.

National Road Race Encyclopedia. Michael Weddington & Barry Perilli. (Weddington's Running Ser.). (Illus.). 456p. (Orig.). 1997. pap. 24.95 (*1-882180-73-9*) Griffin CA.

National Romanticism in Norway. Oscar J. Falnes. LC 68-54263. (Columbia University. Studies in the Social Sciences: No. 386). reprint ed. 32.50 (*0-404-51386-7*) AMS Pr.

National Safety Council - First Aid - CPR I-III: Instructor's Manual. 2nd ed. National Safety Council Staff. 216p. 1993. pap. text 15.00 (*0-86720-795-7*) Jones & Bartlett.

National Saving & Economic Performance. Ed. by B. Douglas Bernheim & John B. Shoven. (Illus.). 396p. 1991. 54.95 (*0-226-04404-1*) U Ch Pr.

National School Boards Association: Reflections on the Development of an American Idea. Thomas A. Shannon. 242p. 1997. pap. 25.00 (*0-88364-211-5*) Natl Sch Boards.

National School of Golf Design. George Bahto. (Illus.). 288p. Date not set. 85.00 (*1-886947-20-1*) Sleepng Bear.

National School Policy: Major Issues in Education Policy for Schools in England & Wales, 1979 Onwards. Ed. by Jim Docking. LC 96-223579. (Roehampton Text Ser.). 176p. 1996. pap. text 27.95 (*1-85346-396-5*, Pub. by David Fulton) Taylor & Francis.

National Schools of Singing: English, French, German & Italian Techniques of Singing Revisited. Richard Miller. LC 96-35557. 1997. 39.00 (*0-8108-3237-2*) Scarecrow.

National Science & Technology Strategies in a Global Context: Report of an International Symposium. National Academy of Sciences Staff. 54p. 1998. pap. text 15.00 (*0-309-06132-6*) Natl Acad Pr.

National Science Education Standards. (Illus.). 262p. (Orig.). (C). 1997. pap. text 50.00 (*0-7881-4281-X*) DIANE Pub.

National Science Education Standards. National Research Council Staff. 272p. 1995. pap. 19.95 (*0-309-05326-9*) Natl Acad Pr.

National Science Foundation: Better Use of Existing Resources Could Improve Program Administration. (Illus.). 95p. (Orig.). (C). 1994. pap. text 30.00 (*0-7881-1496-4*) DIANE Pub.

National Science Foundation & Technology Administration Fiscal Year 1998 Budgets: Hearing Before the Subcommittee on Science, Technology & Space of the Committee on Commerce, Science & Transportation, United States Senate, One Hundred Fifth Congress, First Session, May 7, 1997. USGPO Staff. LC 98-106712. (S. Hrg. Ser.). iii, 80 p. 1997. write for info. (*0-16-055193-5*) USGPO.

National Science Foundations Science & Technology Centers: Building an Interdisciplinary Research Parallism. unabridged ed. 128p. 1995. pap. 15.00 (*1-57744-009-9*) Nat Acad Public Admin.

***National Science Policy Study Pts. 1-7: Hearings Before the Committee on Science, U.S. House of Representatives, One Hundred Fifth Congress, Second Session, March 4, 11, & 25, April 1 & 22, May 14, & June 10, 1998.** United States Congress House Committee on Science. LC 99-172685. 1080p. 1998. write for info. (*0-16-057531-1*) USGPO.

National Search & Rescue Manual. 1991. lib. bdg. 79.95 (*0-8490-4138-4*) Gordon Pr.

National Search & Rescue Manual. 1992. lib. bdg. 350.00 (*0-8490-8873-9*) Gordon Pr.

National Seashores: The Complete Guide to America's Scenic Coastal Parks. 2nd rev. ed. Ruthe Wolverton & Walter Wolverton. LC 94-65085. (Illus.). 302p. (Orig.). 1994. pap. 13.95 (*1-879373-86-6*) Roberts Rinehart.

N

N

National Seashores: The Story Behind the Scenery. Connie Toops. LC 87-81535. (Illus.). 48p. (Orig.). 1987. pap. 7.95 (*0-88714-015-7*) KC Pubns.

National Security. 4th ed. Snow. LC 97-65172. 336p. 1997. pap. text 35.95 (*0-312-14828-3*) St Martin.

National Security. 5th ed. Snow. Date not set. pap. text. write for info. (*0-312-18287-2*) St Martin.

National Security. 5th ed. Snow. 2000. pap. text. write for info. (*0-312-18268-6*) St Martin.

National Security: Case Studies in Policy Making & Implementation, Vol. I. Ed. by R. Allan Ricketts & Richard J. Norton. LC 94-18039. (Illus.). (C). 1994. pap., teacher ed. write for info. (*1-884733-02-6*) Naval War Coll.

National Security: Impact of China's Military Modernization in the Pacific Region. (Illus.). 50p. (Orig.). (C). 1995. pap. text 25.00 (*0-7881-2489-7*) DIANE Pub.

National Security: Perspective Policy & Planning. Ravi Nanda. (C). 1991. text 32.00 (*81-7095-026-0*, Pub. by Lancer International) S Asia.

National Security: Perspectives on Worldwide Threats & Implications for U.S. Forces. 57p. pap. text 25.00 (*0-7881-2856-6*) DIANE Pub.

National Security: The Economic & Environmental Dimension. Michael Renner. 1989. pap. write for info. (*0-916468-90-9*) Worldwatch Inst.

***National Security: The Israeli Experience.** Yisrael Tal. LC 99-36593. 216p. 2000. write for info. (*0-275-96812-X*) Greenwood.

National Security Act, 1980. Vijay Malik. (C). 1991. 110.00 (*0-89771-688-4*) St Mut.

National Security Act, 1980 along with Other Laws on Preventive Detention - Past & Present. Vijay Malik. (C). 1991. text 110.00 (*0-89771-496-2*) St Mut.

National Security Affairs Theoretical Perspectives & Contemporary Issues. Ed. by Thomas B. Trout & James E. Harf. 320p. 1982. pap. 24.95 (*0-87855-900-0*) Transaction Pubs.

National Security & Confidence-Building in the Asia-Pacific Region. (Disarmament Topical Papers: No. 13). 168p. pap. 13.50 (*92-1-142194-2*, E.93.IX.9) UN.

National Security & Defence Policy of the Lithuanian State. LC 96-215985. (UNIDIR Research Papers: No. 26). 66p. pap. 15.00 (*92-9045-091-6*, E.GV.94.0.11) UN.

National Security & Democracy in Israel. Ed. by Avner Yaniv. LC 92-21085. (Israel Democracy Institute Policy Study Ser.). 257p. 1993. pap. text 16.95 (*1-55587-394-4*); lib. bdg. 38.00 (*1-55587-324-3*) L Rienner.

National Security & Individual Freedom. Harold D. Lasswell. LC 71-139193. (Civil Liberties in American History Ser.). 1971. reprint ed. lib. bdg. 32.50 (*0-306-70085-9*) Da Capo.

***National Security & International Environmental Cooperation in the Arctic: The Case of the Northern Sea Route.** Ed. by Willy Ostreng. LC 98-49748. (Environment & Policy Ser.: Vol. 16). 367p. 1999. 198.00 (*0-7923-5528-8*) Kluwer Academic.

National Security & Nuclear Strategy. 1983. pap. 12.95 (*0-614-04175-9*) Acad Poli Sci.

National Security & Our Individual Freedom: A Statement on National Policy by the Research & Policy Committee of the Committee for Economic Development. Committee for Economic Development. LC 50-2569. 50p. reprint ed. pap. 30.00 (*0-608-30726-2*, 200700100060) Bks Demand.

***National Security & Self-Determination: United States Policy in Micronesia (1961-1972)** Howard P. Willens & Deanne C. Siemer. LC 99-88508. 312p. 2000. 65.00 (*0-275-96914-2*, C6914, Praeger Pubs) Greenwood.

National Security & the First Amendment. American Bar Association, Standing Commission on L & American Bar Association, Standing Committee on En. LC 84-7106. 34p. 1984. pap. 3.00 (*0-89707-142-5*, 355-0002) Amer Bar Assn.

National Security & the Nuclear Dilemma: An Introduction to the American Experience. 3rd ed. Richard Smoke. LC 92-31500. 368p. (C). 1992. pap. 33.44 (*0-07-059352-3*) McGraw.

National Security & the U. S. Constitution: The Impact of the Political System. Ed. by George C. Edwards, III & Wallace E. Walker. LC 88-655. 352p. 1988. reprint ed. pap. 109.20 (*0-608-05954-4*, 206629100008) Bks Demand.

National Security & United States Policy Toward Latin America. Lars Schoultz. LC 87-2287. 398p. 1987. reprint ed. pap. 123.40 (*0-608-07177-3*, 206740200009) Bks Demand.

National Security Concepts of States: Argentina. (UNIDIR Research Papers). 131p. 20.00 (*92-9045-061-4*, E.GV.92.0.9) UN.

National Security Constitution: Sharing Power after the Iran-Contra Affair. Harold H. Koh. 336p. (C). 1990. pap. 20.00 (*0-300-04493-3*) Yale U Pr.

National Security in the Nineteen Eighties: From Weakness to Strength. Ed. by W. Scott Thompson. LC 80-80648. 524p. 1980. text 39.95 (*0-87855-398-3*); pap. text 24.95 (*0-917616-38-3*) Transaction Pubs.

National Security Issues. Murray Feshbach. 1987. lib. bdg. 108.00 (*90-247-3553-X*, Pub. by M Nijhoff) Kluwer Academic.

National Security Law. Robert F. Turner et al. Ed. by John N. Moore et al. LC 89-81043. 1290p. 1990. lib. bdg. 75.00 (*0-89089-367-5*) Carolina Acad Pr.

National Security Law. 2nd ed. Stephen Dycus et al. 916p. 1997. teacher ed., boxed set 58.00 (*0-316-09335-1*, 93351) Aspen Law.

National Security Law & the Power of the Purse. William Banks & Peter Raven-Hansen. 272p. 1994. text 60.00 (*0-19-508538-8*) OUP.

National Security Law Documents. John N. Moore et al. LC 94-72699. 994p. (C). 1995. lib. bdg. 75.00 (*0-89089-854-5*) Carolina Acad Pr.

National Security Leaks: Is There a Legal Solution? LC 86-218298. 52p. 1986. pap. 5.00 (*0-89707-224-3*, 355-0013) Amer Bar Assn.

National Security, Merger & Anti-Trust Policy & International Co-operation in the Defence Industry. Ulf Oberg. 87p. (C). 1998. pap. text 25.00 (*0-7881-4797-8*) DIANE Pub.

National Security of Developing States: Lessons from Thailand. Muthiah Alagappa. LC 86-17497. 288p. (C). 1986. 55.00 (*0-86569-152-5*, Auburn Hse) Greenwood.

National Security of Small States in a Changing World. Ed. by Efraim Inbar & Gabriel Sheffer. LC 97-1487. 232p. (C). 1997. 49.50 (*0-7146-4786-1*, Pub. by F Cass Pubs); pap. 24.50 (*0-7146-4339-4*, Pub. by F Cass Pubs) Intl Spec Bk.

National Security Policy for the 1980's. Ed. by Robert L. Pfaltzgraff, Jr. (Annals of the American Academy of Political & Social Science Ser.: Vol. 457). 250p. 1981. 26.00 (*0-8039-1705-8*); pap. 17.00 (*0-8039-1704-X*) Sage.

National Security Policy Formulation: Institutions, Processes, & Issues. Dixon, James H., & Associates Staff. 246p. (Orig.). (C). 1985. pap. text 25.00 (*0-8191-4935-7*) U Pr of Amer.

National Security Strategy: Choices & Limits. Ed. by Stephen J. Cimbala. LC 84-6845. (Foreign Policy Issues: A Foreign Policy Research Institute Ser.). 371p. 1984. 49.95 (*0-275-91138-1*, C1138, Praeger Pubs) Greenwood.

***National Security Strategy for a New Century.** 63p. 1998. pap. 8.00 (*0-16-061885-1*) USGPO.

National Security Strategy of Engagement & Enlargement. 29p. (Orig.). (C). 1994. pap. text 25.00 (*0-7881-1553-7*) DIANE Pub.

National Security Strategy of Engagement & Enlargement. (Orig.). 1997. lib. bdg. 251.99 (*0-8490-6160-1*) Gordon Pr.

National Security Strategy of Engagement & Enlargement, 1995-1996. William J. Clinton, II. (Association of the U. S. Army Book Ser.). 156p. 1995. 16.00 (*1-57488-021-7*) Brasseys.

National Security Strategy of the U. S.(1993) 21p. (C). 1996. reprint ed. pap. text 20.00 (*0-7881-2949-X*) DIANE Pub.

National Security Strategy of the United States: 1994-1995 - Engagement & Enlargement. William J. Clinton. (Association of the U. S. Army Book Ser.). 136p. 1995. 15.00 (*0-02-881050-3*) Brasseys.

National Self-Determination & Secession. Margaret Moore. 296p. 1998. text 65.00 (*0-19-829384-4*) OUP.

National Seminar on Social Statistics, India, 2 vols., 2. 1978. write for info. (*0-8364-0239-1*) S Asia.

National Senior Citizens Survey, 1968. Kermit Schooler. LC 79-84673. 1979. write for info. (*0-89138-969-5*) ICPSR.

National Service: A Promise to Keep. Donald J. Eberly. LC 88-92043. 247p. 1989. 17.95 (*0-9605818-3-9*) John Alden Bks.

National Service: Pro & Con. Ed. by Williamson Evers. (Publication Ser.: No. 393). 270p. (C). 1990. pap. text 14.95 (*0-8179-8932-3*) Hoover Inst Pr.

National Service: Social, Economic, & Military Impacts. Ed. by Michael W. Sherraden & Donald J. Eberly. LC 81-19954. (Policy Studies on Social Policy). 256p. 1982. 64.00 (*0-08-027531-1*, K125, Pergamon Pr) Elsevier.

National Service & AmeriCorps: An Annotated Bibliography, 26. Compiled by Allan Metz. LC 96-41280. (Bibliographies & Indexes in Law & Political Science: Vol. 26). 288p. 1997. lib. bdg. 72.95 (*0-313-30267-7*, Greenwood Pr) Greenwood.

National Service As Credited Service for Public Retirement: Issues & Discussion. Linda Katsuki. 144p. (Orig.). (C). 1994. pap. text 30.00 (*0-7881-1182-5*) DIANE Pub.

National Service, Citizenship, & Political Education. Eric B. Gorham. LC 91-23388. (SUNY Series in Political Theory: Contemporary Issues). 282p. (C). 1992. text 64.50 (*0-7914-1075-7*); pap. text 21.95 (*0-7914-1076-5*) State U NY Pr.

National Service Corps: A State-by-State Guide. (Career Dollar Ser.: Vol. 1). 294p. 1994. ring bd. 50.00 (*1-884669-03-4*) Conway Greene.

National Service Programs: Americorps U. S. A. - Early Program Resource & Benefit Information. (Illus.). 71p. 1996. reprint ed. pap. text 20.00 (*0-7881-3208-3*) DIANE Pub.

National Sheepdog Champions of Britain & Ireland. Barbara Carpenter. (Illus.). 338p. 1994. text 49.95 (*0-85236-282-X*, Pub. by Farming Pr) Diamond Farm Bk.

National Shellfish Sanitation Program Pt. 1: Sanitation of Shellfish Growing Areas. 185p. (C). 1995. pap. text 45.00 (*0-7881-2423-4*) DIANE Pub.

National Shellfish Sanitation Program Pt. 2: Sanitation of the Harvesting, Processing & Distribution of Shellfish. 210p. (C). 1995. pap. text 50.00 (*0-7881-2424-2*) DIANE Pub.

National Skeet Shooting Association Record Annual. 320p. 9.00 (*0-318-15868-X*) Natl Skeet Shoot.

National Socialism: Vanguard of the Future. 136p. 1993. pap. 15.00 (*87-87063-40-9*, Pub. by Nordland Forlag) Aryan Free Pr.

National Socialism & Gypsies in Austria. Erika Thurner. Tr. by Gilya G. Schmidt. LC 98-8880. 216p. 1998. text 34.95 (*0-8173-0924-1*) U of Ala Pr.

National Socialism & the Roman Catholic Church. Nathaniel Micklem. LC 78-63696. (Studies in Fascism: Ideology & Practice). (Illus.). 280p. reprint ed. 31.00 (*0-404-16957-0*) AMS Pr.

***National Socialism & the Sciences.** Margit Szollosi-Janze. (Illus.). 256p. 2001. 65.00 (*1-85973-416-2*, Pub. by Berg Pubs); pap. 19.50 (*1-85973-421-9*, Pub. by Berg Pubs) NYU Pr.

National Socialist Cultural Policy. Ed. by Glenn R. Cuomo. 320p. 1995. text 55.00 (*0-312-09094-3*) St Martin.

National-Socialist Extermination Policies: Contemporary German Perspectives & Controversies. Ed. by Ulrich Herbert. LC 99-25765. (War & Genocide Ser.: Vol. 2). 288p. 1999. 59.95 (*1-57181-750-6*); pap. 19.95 (*1-57181-751-4*) Berghahn Bks.

National Socialist Germany. Louis L. Snyder. LC 83-9392. (Anvil Ser.). 210p. 1984. pap. text 13.50 (*0-89874-636-1*) Krieger.

National Socialist Leadership & Total War, 1941-45. Eleanor Hancock. LC 91-31201. 288p. 1992. text 49.95 (*0-312-07202-3*) St Martin.

National Society for the Study of Education 78th Yearbook, Pts. 1 & 2. Incl. Part II. Classroom Management. Daniel L. Duke. 1982. pap. text 8.00 (*0-226-60096-3*); Pt. I. Education for the Gifted & Talented. A. Harry Passow. 1996. pap. text 13.00 (*0-226-60095-5*); 1979. write for info. (*0-318-56065-8*) U Ch Pr.

National Soft Drink Association: A Tradition of Service. Cheryl H. Lofland. (Illus.). 136p. 1986. 24.95 (*0-87491-840-5*) Natl Soft Drink.

National Solar Energy Convention, 1986: Proceedings. Solar Energy Society of India. 1987. 28.00 (*0-8364-2124-8*, Pub. by Allied Pubs) S Asia.

National Sovereignty & International Organizations. Magdalena M. Martinez. LC 96-4898. (Legal Aspects of International Organization Ser.: No. 25). 376p. 1996. 108.50 (*90-411-0200-0*) Kluwer Law Intl.

National Space Engineering Symposium, 8th, 1993. Intro. by Sam F. Asokanthan. (National Conference Publication Ser.: No. 93-7). (Illus.). 356p. (Orig.). 1993. pap. 48.00 (*0-85825-577-4*, Pub. by Inst Engrs Aust-EA Bks) Accents Pubns.

National Space Engineering Symposium, 9th, 1994: Satellite Communications. Contrib. by Gordon Pike. (National Conference Proceedings 94 Ser.: Vol. 7). (Illus.). 230p. 1994. pap. 38.50 (*0-85825-605-3*, Pub. by Inst Engrs Aust-EA Bks) Accents Pubns.

National Space Engineering Symposium, 1992 (7th), & a Short Course on Spacecraft Engineering: International Co-Operation - Regional Space Opportunities. Intro. by T. E. Stapinski. (Illus.). 271p. (Orig.). 1992. pap. 66.00 (*0-85825-556-1*, Pub. by Inst Engrs Aust-EA Bks) Accents Pubns.

National Space Transportation Policy: Issues for Congress. (Illus.). 114p. (Orig.). (C). 1995. pap. text 35.00 (*0-7881-2506-0*) DIANE Pub.

National Speedway Directory. Ed. by Allan E. Brown & Nancy L. Brown. 532p. 1999. pap. 8.00 (*0-931105-52-8*) Slideways Pubns.

National Speedway Directory, Vol. 18. rev. ed. Ed. by Nancy L. Brown. 464p. 1997. pap. 8.00 (*0-931105-48-X*) Slideways Pubns.

National Speedway Directory, Vol. 19. 19th rev. ed. Allan E. Brown & Nancy L. Brown. 496p. 1998. pap. 8.00 (*0-931105-50-1*) Slideways Pubns.

National Sports & Recreation Frequency Directory. Richard Barnett. 160p. 1994. pap. 13.95 (*0-939430-30-4*) Scanner Master.

National Sports Policies: An International Handbook. Ed. by Laurence Chalip et al. LC 95-25327. 456p. 1996. lib. bdg. 105.00 (*0-313-28481-4*, Greenwood Pr) Greenwood.

National Sprint Car Annual. rev. ed. Allan E. Brown & Nancy L. Brown. 64p. 1999. pap. text 5.00 (*0-931105-51-X*) Slideways Pubns.

National Square Dance Directory, 1992. Ed. by Gordon J. Goss. 232p. 1992. pap. 15.00 (*0-944351-06-9*) N S D Products.

National Square Dance Directory, 1997. Gordon J. Goss. 152p. 1997. 15.95 (*0-944351-12-3*) N S D Products.

National Square Dance Directory, 1981. 3rd ed. Gordon J. Goss. 168p. 1981. pap. 8.50 (*0-9605494-2-0*) N S D Products.

National Square Dance Directory, 1983. 4th ed. Ed. by Gordon J. Goss. 256p. 1983. 11.00 (*0-9605494-3-9*) N S D Products.

National Square Dance Directory, 1984. 5th ed. Ed. by Gordon J. Goss. 304p. 1984. pap. 11.00 (*0-9605494-4-7*) N S D Products.

National Square Dance Directory, 1985. 6th ed. Ed. by Gordon J. Goss. 288p. 1985. pap. 12.00 (*0-9605494-5-5*) N S D Products.

National Square Dance Directory, 1986. 7th ed. Ed. by Gordon J. Goss. 284p. 1986. pap. 12.00 (*0-9605494-6-3*) N S D Products.

National Square Dance Directory, 1987. 8th ed. Ed. by Gordon J. Goss. 276p. 1987. pap. 12.00 (*0-9605494-7-1*) N S D Products.

National Square Dance Directory, 1988. 9th ed. Ed. by Gordon J. Gross. 276p. 1988. pap. 13.00 (*0-9605494-8-X*) N S D Products.

National Square Dance Directory, 1989. 10th ed. Ed. by Gordon J. Goss. 244p. 1989. pap. 13.00 (*0-944351-01-8*) N S D Products.

National Square Dance Directory, 1990. 11th ed. Ed. by Gordon J. Goss. 232p. 1990. pap. 14.00 (*0-944351-02-6*) N S D Products.

National Square Dance Directory, 1991. 12th ed. Ed. by Gordon J. Goss. 232p. 1991. pap. 15.00 (*0-944351-05-0*) N S D Products.

National Square Dance Directory, 1993. 14th ed. Gordon J. Goss. 204p. 1993. pap. 15.00 (*0-944351-07-7*) N S D Products.

National Square Dance Directory, 1994. 15th ed. Gordon J. Goss. 204p. 1994. pap. text 15.00 (*0-944351-08-5*) N S D Products.

National Square Dance Directory, 1995. 16th ed. Gordon J. Goss. 184p. 1995. pap. 15.00 (*0-944351-09-3*) N S D Products.

National Square Dance Directory, 1996. 17th ed. Gordon J. Goss. 184p. 1996. pap. 15.95 (*0-944351-10-7*) N S D Products.

National Stage: Theatre & Cultural Legitimation in England, France, & America. Loren Kruger. LC 91-23859. (Illus.). 256p. 1992. pap. text 14.95 (*0-226-45497-5*); lib. bdg. 39.50 (*0-226-45496-7*) U Ch Pr.

***National Standardized Love Test.** Annie Pigeon. LC 99-46340. 144p. 1999. pap. 6.95 (*1-58062-167-8*) Adams Media.

National Standardized Mom Test. Annie Pigeon. 144p. 1998. pap. 5.95 (*1-55850-837-6*) Adams Media.

National Standards: A Catalyst for Reform. Robert C. Lafayette. LC 96-220759. (ACTFL Foreign Language Education Ser.). 230p. 1996. pap. 16.90 (*0-8442-9395-4*) NTC Contemp Pub Co.

National Standards: From Vision to Reality. Paul R. Lehman & Music Educators National Conference Staff. 4p. 1994. pap. 6.75 (*1-56545-064-7*, 1606) MENC.

National Standards & Testing. 12p. 1992. 4.00 (*0-317-05348-5*) NASBE.

National Standards & the Science Curriculum. BSCS Staff & Diane Pyper-Smith. LC 97-127280. 184p. (C). 1996. pap. text, per. 17.90 (*0-7872-2589-4*) Kendall-Hunt.

National Standards for Arts Education: What Every Young American Should Know & Be Able to Do in the Arts. LC 94-193083. 148p. 1994. 20.00 (*1-56545-036-1*, 1605) MENC.

National Standards for Athletic Coaches: Quality Coaches, Quality Sports. NASPE Staff. 128p. (Orig.). 1995. pap. 22.00 (*0-7872-1282-2*, 304-10084) Kendall-Hunt.

National Standards for Business Education: What America's Students Should Know & Be Able to Do in Business. LC 96-125259. 157p. 1997. pap. 20.00 (*0-933964-44-7*) Natl Busn Ed Assoc.

National Standards for Civics & Government. 179p. (Orig.). 1994. pap. 12.00 (*0-89818-155-0*) Ctr for Civic Educ.

National Standards for History. National Center for History in the Schools Staff et al. LC 97-152950. ix, 225p. 1996. write for info. (*0-9633218-4-6*) Natl Ctr Hist.

***National Standards for History for Grades K-4: Expanding Children[0012]s World in Time & Space (rev. ed.)** rev. ed. Ed. by Charlotte A. Crabtree & Gary B. Nash. (Illus.). 78p. (C). 2000. pap. text 25.00 (*0-7567-0001-9*) DIANE Pub.

National Standards for Total System Balance. 5th ed. Lynn Wray & Leo Meyer. 1989. 50.00 (*0-910289-00-X*) Assoc Air Bal.

National Standards for United States History: Exploring the American Experience. National History Standards Task Force Staff. (National History STandards Project Ser.). (Illus.). 310p. (Orig.). (C). 1994. pap. text 24.95 (*0-9633218-1-1*) Natl Ctr Hist.

National Standards for World History: Exploring Paths to the Present. National History Standards Task Force Staff. (National History STandards Project Ser.). (Illus.). 310p. (Orig.). (C). 1994. pap. text 24.95 (*0-9633218-2-X*) Natl Ctr Hist.

National Standards in American Education: A Citizen's Guide. Diane Ravitch. 223p. (C). 1995. 38.95 (*0-8157-7352-8*) Brookings.

National Standards in American Education: A Citizen's Guide. Diane Ravitch. 223p. 1996. pap. 16.95 (*0-8157-7351-X*) Brookings.

National State & Local Government in the United States. 624p. (C). 1996. text 62.00 (*0-536-59488-0*) Pearson Custom.

National State & Violence: Vol. 2 of a "Contemporary Critique of Historical Materialism" Anthony Giddens. 1985. pap. 19.95 (*0-520-06039-3*, Pub. by U CA Pr) Cal Prin Full Svc.

National State of Child Care Regulation, 1986. Gwen G. Morgan. 250p. 1987. write for info. (*0-9618201-0-1*) Work Family Direct.

National State Papers of the United States: Texts of Documents, 1789-1801: Administration of George Washington, 1789-1797, 35 vols. LC 84-27904. 1985. 2800.00 (*0-89453-154-9*, 31549G) Scholarly Res Inc.

National State Papers of the United States: Texts of Documents, 1789-1801: Administration of John Adams, 1797-1801, 24 vols., Set. LC 80-65406. 1980. 1920.00 (*0-89453-155-7*, 31557G) Scholarly Res Inc.

***National Statecraft & European Integration, 1979-1997: The Conservative Government & the European Union.** Jim Buller. LC 00-21790. 208p. 2000. write for info. (*1-85567-588-9*, Pub. by P P Pubs) Continuum.

National Stewardship Incentives: Conservation Strategies For U.S. Landowners Sara Vickerman & Defenders of Wildlife Staff. LC 99-167490. iii, 109 p. 1998. write for info. (*0-926549-03-0*) Defend Wildlife.

National Storytelling Directory, 1996. National Storytelling Association Staff. Date not set. pap. 11.95 (*0-614-13750-0*) Natl Storytlng Network.

***National Strategic Plan: Modeling & Data Systems for Wildland Fire & Air Quality.** David V. Sandberg. (Illus.). 60p. (C). 2000. pap. text 20.00 (*0-7881-8526-8*) DIANE Pub.

National Strategic Planning & Practice. Hossain. 65.95 (*0-7546-1006-3*) Ashgate Pub Co.

National Strategies for Protection of Flora, Fauna & Their Habitats. (Environmental Ser.: No. 2). 43p. 1988. 14.00 (*92-1-116414-1*, E.88.II.E.2) UN.

An Asterisk (*) at the beginning of an entry indicates that the title is appearing for the first time.

National Strategy for Prevention of Drug Abuse & Drug Trafficking. 1986. lib. bdg. 200.00 (*0-8490-3505-8*) Gordon Pr.

National Study of Charter Schools: Second-Year Report, 1998. Paul Berman et al. LC 98-214737. (Education Department Publication SAI 98 Ser.: Vol. 3033). (Illus.). 130p. 1998. pap. 12.00 (*0-16-049752-3*) USGPO.

***National Study of Charter Schools, Executive Summary, 1998.** Government Printing Office Staff. 16p. 1998. pap. 2.25 (*0-16-049751-5*) USGPO.

National Study of Chemical Residues in Fish. 3rd ed. Ruth Yender et al. (Illus.). 500p. (C). 1996. pap. text 60.00 (*0-7881-3257-1*) DIANE Pub.

National Study of Health & Growth. Roberto J. Rona & Susan Chinn. LC 99-14303. (Illus.). 144p. 1999. text 98.50 (*0-19-262919-0*) OUP.

National Study of Instructional Practices & Perceptions of Elementary School Teachers about Typewriting-Keyboarding: A Report on the National Elementary Keyboarding Research Study of Delta Pi Epsilon. Carolee Sormunen et al. 65p. (Orig.). (C). 1989. pap. text 10.00 (*0-9603064-8-X*) Delta Pi Epsilon.

National Study on the Permanent Diaconate of the Catholic Church in the United States 1994-1995. United States Catholic Conference Staff. 152p. (Orig.). 1996. pap. text 11.95 (*1-55586-087-7*) US Catholic.

National Styles of Humor, 18. Ed. by Avner Ziv. LC 87-23635. (Contributions to the Study of Popular Culture Ser.: No. 18). 256p. 1988. 65.00 (*0-313-24992-X*, ZHW/, Greenwood Pr) Greenwood.

National Styles of Regulation: Environmental Policy in Great Britain & the United States. David Vogel. LC 85-21332. (Cornell Studies in Political Economy). 328p. 1986. text 52.50 (*0-8014-1658-2*) Cornell U Pr.

National Summary of State Medicaid Managed Care Programs: Program Descriptions as of June 30, 1995. Anna Meyers. 182p. 1996. pap. 13.00 (*0-16-048860-5*) USGPO.

National Summary of State Medicaid Managed Care Programs 1998. 422p. 1999. per. 35.00 (*0-16-049972-0*) USGPO.

***National Summary of State Medicaid Managed Care Programs, 1997: Program Descriptions as of June 30, 1997.** Government Printing Office Staff. 280p. 1998. pap. 16.00 (*0-16-049568-7*) USGPO.

National Summary Report on State Financial Incentives for Renewable Energy. Chris Larsen et al. (Illus.). 140p. (Orig.). 1997. pap. 50.00 (*0-9660039-0-X*) NC Solar Ctr.

National Summary Report on State Regulatory Incentives for Renewable Energy. Chris Larsen et al. 170p. 1997. pap. 50.00 (*0-9660039-1-8*) NC Solar Ctr.

National Summit on Racial Justice: Role Play Peacegame. David W. Felder. 52p. 1997. pap. text 8.95 (*1-57501-106-9*, 13D) Wellington Pr.

National Summit on Women Veterans' Issues: Proceedings, 1996. Ed. by Joan Furey. (Illus.). 111p. 1998. pap. text 25.00 (*0-7881-2620-2*) DIANE Pub.

National Supported Work Demonstration. Ed. by Robinson G. Hollister, Jr. et al. LC 83-40266. 360p. 1984. reprint ed. pap. 111.60 (*0-608-01883-X*, 206253500003) Bks Demand.

National, Supranational & International Tort Law: Scope of Protection - Cases, Materials & Text. Walter Van Gerven et al. (Casebooks for the Common Law of Europe Ser.). 480p. 1998. pap. 60.00 (*1-901362-73-6*) Hart Pub.

National Supremacy: Treaty Power vs. State Power. Edward S. Corwin. 1965. 16.50 (*0-8446-1127-1*) Peter Smith.

National Survey Automated Correctional Information Systems - Illinois. 7.00 (*0-318-20313-8*) Natl Coun Crime.

National Survey of American Jews, 1984: Political & Social Outlooks. Steven M. Cohen. iv, 60p. (Orig.). 1985. pap. 4.00 (*0-87495-069-4*) Am Jewish Comm.

National Survey of Black Americans, 1979-1980. James S. Jackson & Gerald Gurin. LC 87-80741. 1214p. 1987. write for info. (*0-89138-881-8*) ICPSR.

National Survey of Corporate Law Compensation & Organization Practices, Set. 11th ed. Association of the Bar of the City of New York, Co et al. (Illus.). 1988. 475.00 (*0-317-00876-5*) Assn Bar NYC.

National Survey of Family Growth, Cycle IV: Evaluation of Linked Design. LC 93-24687. (Vital & Health Statistics Ser.: Series 2, No. 117). 1993. write for info. (*0-8406-0482-3*) Natl Ctr Health Stats.

National Survey of Fishing, Hunting & Wildlife-Associated Recreation (1996) Ed. by Jamie Rappaport Clark. (Illus.). 169p. (C). 1999. reprint ed. pap. text 25.00 (*0-7881-7889-X*) DIANE Pub.

National Survey of Indian Health Service Employees & the Development of a Model Job Training Demonstration Project: Identifying Work Opportunities for American Indians & Alaska Natives with Disabilities. C. A. Marshall et al. 16p. 1994. pap. text. write for info. (*1-888557-17-6*, 100085) No Ariz Univ.

National Survey of Problems & Competencies among Four- to Sixteen-Year Olds. Thomas M. Achenbach et al. (Child Development Monographs: No. 225, Vol. 56, No. 3). (Illus.). 136p. 1992. pap. text 15.00 (*0-226-00221-7*) U Ch Pr.

National Survey of Public Libraries & the Internet: Progress & Issues. 1997. lib. bdg. 250.99 (*0-8490-7739-7*) Gordon Pr.

National Survey of State Laws. 3rd ed. 673p. 1999. 80.00 (*0-7876-0068-7*, 00108717) Gale.

National Survey of State Laws, Vol. 1. 2nd ed. Richard A. Leiter. 605p. 1996. 75.00 (*0-8103-9052-3*) Gale.

National Survey of State Medicaid Managed Care Programs. 1997. lib. bdg. 250.95 (*0-8490-8246-3*) Gordon Pr.

National Survey of the Aged, 1975. Ethel Shanes. LC 82-80683. 1982. write for info. (*0-89138-938-5*) ICPSR.

National Survey of the Aged (United States), 1957. Ethel Shanas. LC 85-60723. 1985. write for info. (*0-89138-890-7*) ICPSR.

National Survey of the Aged (United States), 1962. Ethel Shanas. 1985. write for info. (*0-89138-888-5*) ICPSR.

National Survey of Veterans. 1997. lib. bdg. 252.95 (*0-8490-6166-0*) Gordon Pr.

National Survey of Veterans. 308p. 1995. per. 23.00 (*0-16-062479-7*, Veterans Affairs) USGPO.

National Survey of Women & Men Engineers: A Study of the Members of 22 Engineering Societies. Ed. by Richard Ellis. (Illus.). 44p. 1993. pap. text 40.00 (*0-9625750-1-1*) Soc Women Eng.

National Survey of Worksite Health Promotion Activities, 1992. Lisa Kanner. (Illus.). 383p. (Orig.). (C). 1995. pap. text 40.00 (*0-7881-1558-8*) DIANE Pub.

National Survey Results on Drug Use: Secondary School Students, College Students & Young Adults, 2 vols. 1997. lib. bdg. 600.95 (*0-8490-8242-0*) Gordon Pr.

***National Survey Results on Drug Use from the Monitoring the Future Study, 1975-1995, College Students & Young Adults, Vol. 2.** Lloyd D. Johnston. LC 97-125427. 202p. 1998. pap. text 18.00 (*0-16-049314-5*) USGPO.

National Survey Results on Drug Use from the Monitoring The Future Study, 1975-1995, V. I, Secondary School Students. Lloyd D. Johnston. 399p. 1996. per. 36.00 (*0-16-061512-7*) USGPO.

National Survey Results on Drug Use from the Monitoring the Future Study, 1975-1997 Vol. 1: Secondary School Students. Lloyd D. Johnston. (DHHS Publication Ser.: Vol. 98-4345). (Illus.). 455p. 1998. pap. 36.00 (*0-16-049705-1*) USGPO.

***National Survey Results on Drug Use from the Monitoring the Future Study, 1975-1997, College Students & Young Adults, Vol. 2.** Lloyd D. Johnston. 218p. 1998. pap. text 13.00 (*0-16-049728-0*) USGPO.

***National Survey Results on Drug Use from the Monitoring the Future Study, 1975-1998: College Students & Young Adults, 2.** Johnston. 232p. 1999. per. 24.00 (*0-16-050142-3*) USGPO.

***National Survey Results on Drug Use from the Monitoring the Future Study, 1975-1998: Secondary School Students, 1.** Lloyd D. Johnston. 441p. 1999. per. 40.00 (*0-16-050143-1*) USGPO.

National Symbols of St. Martin: A Primer. enl. rev. ed. Ed. by Lasana M. Sekou. (Illus.). 173p. 1997. 30.00 (*0-913441-30-9*) Hse of Nehesi.

National Symphony Orchestra: The NSO History. Ted Libbey. (Illus.). 152p. (Orig.). Date not set. 39.95 (*0-9649554-0-7*); pap. 29.95 (*0-9649554-1-5*) Devon Jacklin.

National Symphony Orchestra Cookbook. Patty P. Andringa. Ed. by Lonie Landfield. LC 84-82184. (Illus.). 320p. pap. 11.95 (*0-9613672-0-2*) Natl Symp Orches.

***National Symposium on Medical & Public Health: Response to Bioterrorism.** Ed. by Joseph E. McDade. (Illus.). 76p. 2000. pap. text 25.00 (*0-7881-8531-4*) DIANE Pub.

National Symposium on Sentencing: The Judicial Response to Crime Report & Policy Guide. Kathleen M. Sampson. LC 98-73872. 112p. 1998. pap. 25.00 (*0-938870-87-4*, 874) Am Judicature.

National Symposium on the Use of Recycled Materials in Engineering Construction, 1996. Michael J. Thom. (National Conference Proceedings Ser.: Vol. 96/06). (Illus.). 217p. 1996. pap. 90.00 (*0-85825-651-7*, Pub. by Inst Engrs Aust-EA Bks) Accents Pubns.

National Symposium on Violent Offenders: Summary & Resources. Barbara Krauth. 59p. (C). 1999. reprint ed. pap. text 20.00 (*0-7881-7856-3*) DIANE Pub.

National System Planning for Protected Areas. Adrian G. Davey et al. LC 98-173115. (Best Practice Protected Area Guidelines Ser.). x, 71 p. 1998. write for info. (*2-8317-0399-9*, Pub. by IUCN) Island Pr.

National Systems for Financing Innovation. OECD Staff. 120p. (Orig.). 1995. pap. 40.00 (*92-64-14627-X*, Pub. by Org for Econ) OECD.

National Systems of Innovation: Toward a Theory of Innovation & Interactive Learning. Ed. by Lundvall Bengt-Ake. LC 92-5781. 1992. text 59.00 (*1-85567-063-1*) St Martin.

National Systems of Innovation: Towards a Theory of Innovation & Interactive Learning. Bengt-Ake Lundvall. 1995. pap. 29.95 (*1-85567-338-X*) St Martin.

National Tax Journal Quarterly. Ed. by Joel Slemeod & Mary Ceccanese. 1996. pap. 60.00 (*0-318-15875-2*) Natl Tax.

National Tax Rebate: A New America with Less Government. Leonard Greene. LC 98-17074. 132p. 1998. 15.95 (*0-89526-351-3*) Regnery Pub.

***National Tax Reform: Options & Consequences for the Nation's State & Local Governments.** 36p. 1999. pap. 10.00 (*1-886152-62-4*, 3550) Natl League Cities.

National Taxation for Property Management & Valuation. A. MacLeary. 240p. 1990. pap. write for info. (*0-419-15320-9*, E & FN Spon) Routledge.

National Teacher Examination (Core Battery) (NTE) Jack Rudman. (Admission Test Ser.: Vol. 15). 47.95 (*0-8373-5115-4*) Nat Learn.

National Teacher Examination (Core Battery) (NTE) Combined Edition. Jack Rudman. (Admission Test Ser.: ATS-15). 300p. 1994. pap. 27.95 (*0-8373-5015-8*) Nat Learn.

National Teacher Examination Passbook Series. Jack Rudman. (Entire Ser.). 1994. pap. write for info. (*0-8373-8400-1*) Nat Learn.

National Technology Initiative: Summary Proceedings. (Illus.). 59p. (Orig.). (C). 1993. pap. text 20.00 (*1-56806-200-1*) DIANE Pub.

National Television Broadcast & Cable Sales Representative. Richard Williams. 129p. (C). 1998. pap. text 16.50 (*1-891877-01-1*) Sheron Ent.

National Television Violence Study. LC 96-219968. 551p. 1996. pap. 32.95 (*0-7619-0802-1*) Sage.

National Television Violence Study. Wilson. pap. 39.95 (*0-7619-1088-3*) Sage.

National Television Violence Study, Vol. 1. LC 96-219968. 568p. 1996. 69.95 (*0-7619-0801-3*) Sage.

National Television Violence Study, Vol. 2. LC 96-219968. 424p. 1997. 75.00 (*0-7619-1087-5*) Sage.

National Television Violence Study, Vol. 3. Ed. by Center for Communication & Social Policy Staff. 368p. 1998. 79.95 (*0-7619-1653-9*) Sage.

National Tests: What Other Countries Expect Their Students to Know. (Illus.). 116p. (Orig.). (C). 1993. pap. text 30.00 (*1-56806-894-8*) DIANE Pub.

National Textbook Company Beginner's Spanish & English Dictionary. Regina M. Qualls & L. Sanchez. LC 97-39061. (SPA & ENG., Illus.). 488p. 1995. 12.95 (*0-8442-7698-7*, 76987, Natl Textbk Co) NTC Contemp Pub Co.

National Textbook Company Dictionary of Grammar Terminology. Richard A. Spears. (Illus.). 224p. 1995. pap. 12.95 (*0-8442-5129-1*, Natl Textbk Co) NTC Contemp Pub Co.

National Textbook Company's Beginner's French & English Dictionary. National Textbook Company Staff et al. (FRE & ENG.). 512p. 1995. pap. 7.95 (*0-8442-1476-0*, 14760, Natl Textbk Co) NTC Contemp Pub Co.

National Textbook Company's New College French & English Dictionary (Plain Edge) National Textbook Company Staff. (FRE & ENG., Illus.). 600p. 1994. pap. 19.06 (*0-8442-1481-7*, 14817, Natl Textbk Co) NTC Contemp Pub Co.

National Textbook Company's New College French & English Dictionary (Thumb Index) National Textbook Company Staff. LC 97-47251. (FRE & ENG., Illus.). 600p. 1994. 19.95 (*0-8442-1480-9*, 14809, Natl Textbk Co) NTC Contemp Pub Co.

National Textbook Company's New College Greek & English Dictionary. Paul Nathaniel. (GRE & ENG., Illus.). 560p. 1994. 29.95 (*0-8442-8473-4*, 84734, Natl Textbk Co) NTC Contemp Pub Co.

National Textbook's Dictionary of American Slang & Colloquial Expressions. Richard A. Spears. 1994. pap. 12.95 (*0-8442-5460-6*, Natl Textbk Co) NTC Contemp Pub Co.

National Theater in Northern & Eastern Europe, 1746-1900. Ed. by Laurence Senelick. (Theatre in Europe: a Documentary History Ser.). (Illus.). 510p. (C). 1991. text 119.95 (*0-521-24446-3*) Cambridge U Pr.

***National Therapeutics for Infants & Children: Workshop Summary.** Sumner J. Yaffe. 136p. 2000. pap. 30.75 (*0-309-06937-8*) Natl Acad Pr.

National Threat Perceptions in the Middle East. United Nations Institute for Disarmament Research. (UNIDIR Research Papers: No. 37). 115p. 23.00 (*92-9045-107-6*) UN.

National Toll-Free 800 Guide to Real Estate Publications & Publishers, 1995. John R. Johnsich. (Orig.). 1995. pap. 19.95 (*0-914256-29-7*) Real Estate Pub.

National Toll-Free 800 Guide to Real Estate Publications & Publishers, 1999. John R. Johnsich. 1999. pap. 19.95 (*0-914256-32-7*) Real Estate Pub.

National Toxicology Chemical Data Compendium, Vol. 3. Keith. 832p. 1991. boxed set 204.95 (*0-87371-717-1*) CRC Pr.

National Toxicology Program: Fiscal Year, 1994 Annual Plan. 214p. (Orig.). (C). 1995. pap. text 40.00 (*0-7881-2138-3*) DIANE Pub.

National Toxicology Program: Review of Current DHHS, DOE & EPA Research Related to Toxicology. 310p. (Orig.). (C). 1995. pap. text 50.00 (*0-7881-2137-5*) DIANE Pub.

National Toxicology Program Chemical Data Compendium, Vol. 1. Keith. 992p. 1991. boxed set 204.95 (*0-87371-715-5*) CRC Pr.

National Toxicology Program Chemical Data Compendium, Vol. 2. Keith. 1664p. 1991. boxed set 278.95 (*0-87371-716-3*) CRC Pr.

National Toxicology Program Chemical Data Compendium, Vol. 4. Keith. 896p. 1991. boxed set 278.95 (*0-87371-718-X*) CRC Pr.

National Toxicology Program Chemical Data Compendium, Vol. 5. Lawrence H. Keith. 1216p. 1992. boxed set 278.95 (*0-87371-719-8*) CRC Pr.

National Toxicology Program Chemical Data Compendium, Vol. 6. Keith. 1472p. 1991. boxed set 278.95 (*0-87371-720-1*) CRC Pr.

National Toxicology Program Chemical Data Compendium, Vol. 7. Keith. 1440p. 1991. boxed set 278.95 (*0-87371-721-X*) CRC Pr.

National Toxicology Program Chemical Data Compendium, Vol. 8. Keith. 880p. 1991. boxed set 194.95 (*0-87371-722-8*) CRC Pr.

National Toxicology Program's Chemical Database, 8 vols., Set. Lawrence H. Keith & Douglas B. Walters. 1991. 1995.00 incl. 5.25 hd (*0-87371-695-7*) Lewis Pubs.

National Toxicology Program's Chemical Database, Vol. 1: Chemical Names & Synonyms. Lawrence H. Keith & Douglas B. Walters. 1991. 235.00 (*0-87371-687-6*, L687) Lewis Pubs.

National Toxicology Program's Chemical Database, Vol. 1: Chemical Names & Synonyms. Lawrence H. Keith & Douglas B. Walters. 288p. 1993. lib. bdg. 65.00 (*0-87371-703-1*) Lewis Pubs.

National Toxicology Program's Chemical Database, Vol. 2: Chemical & Physical Properties. Lawrence H. Keith & Douglas B. Walters. 1991. 235.00 (*0-87371-688-4*, L688) Lewis Pubs.

National Toxicology Program's Chemical Database, Vol. 3: Standards & Regulations. Lawrence H. Keith & Douglas B. Walters. 1991. 199.00 (*0-87371-689-2*, L689) Lewis Pubs.

National Toxicology Program's Chemical Database, Vol. 4: Medical Hazards & Symptoms of Exposure. Lawrence H. Keith & Douglas B. Walters. 1991. 220.00 (*0-87371-690-6*, L690) Lewis Pubs.

National Toxicology Program's Chemical Database, Vol. 5: Medical First Aid. Lawrence H. Keith & Douglas B. Walters. 1991. 199.00 (*0-87371-691-4*, L691) Lewis Pubs.

National Toxicology Program's Chemical Database, Vol. 5: Medical First Aid. Lawrence H. Keith & Douglas B. Walters. 94p. 1992. lib. bdg. 335.00 incl. 3.5 hd (*0-87371-707-4*) Lewis Pubs.

National Toxicology Program's Chemical Database, Vol. 6: Personal Protective Equipment. Lawrence H. Keith & Douglas B. Walters. 1991. 220.00 (*0-87371-692-2*, L692) Lewis Pubs.

National Toxicology Program's Chemical Database, Vol. 7: Hazardous Properties & Uses. Lawrence H. Keith & Douglas B. Walters. 1991. 220.00 (*0-87371-693-0*, L693) Lewis Pubs.

National Toxicology Program's Chemical Database, Vol. 7: Hazardous Properties & Uses. Lawrence H. Keith & Douglas B. Walters. 84p. 1992. lib. bdg. 359.00 (*0-87371-709-0*) Lewis Pubs.

National Toxicology Program's Chemical Database, Vol. 8: Shipping Classifications & Regulations. Lawrence H. Keith & Douglas B. Walters. 1991. 220.00 incl. 5.25 hd (*0-87371-694-9*, L694) Lewis Pubs.

National Toxicology Program's Chemical Solubility Compendium. Lawrence H. Keith & Douglas B. Walters. 448p. 1991. lib. bdg. 185.00 (*0-87371-653-1*, L653) Lewis Pubs.

National Toxicology Program's Chemical Solubility Database. Lawrence H. Keith & Douglas B. Walters. 32p. 1991. lib. bdg. 260.00 incl. 3.5 hd, 5.25 hd (*0-87371-652-3*, L652) Lewis Pubs.

National Toxicology Program's First Response Expert System. Virginia Keith. 20p. 1992. lib. bdg. 189.00 (*0-87371-862-3*, L862) Lewis Pubs.

National Trade & Professional Associations of the U. S., 1996. 31st ed. 450p. 1996. 85.00 (*0-685-55411-2*) B Klein Pubns.

***National Trade & Professional Associations, 2000.** 35th ed. Ed. by Columbia Books Staff & Buck Downs. 959p. 2000. pap. 99.00 (*1-880873-37-0*) Columbia Bks.

National Trade & Tariff Service, 2 vols. 1993. ring bd. 565.00 (*0-409-85510-3*, MICHIE) LEXIS Pub.

National Trade Estimate Report on Foreign Trade Barriers. 1995. lib. bdg. 299.99 (*0-8490-5860-0*) Gordon Pr.

***National Trade Estimate Report on Foreign Trade Barriers: 2000.** 447p. 2000. per. 40.00 (*0-16-050340-X*) USGPO.

National Trade Estimate Report on Foreign Trade Barriers, 1992. 267p. (Orig.). (C). 1993. pap. text 55.00 (*1-56806-700-3*) DIANE Pub.

National Trade Estimate Report on Foreign Trade Barriers, 1996. 11th ed. Derek Wolff. (Illus.). 357p. (C). 1996. pap. text 50.00 (*0-7881-3540-6*) DIANE Pub.

***National Trade Estimate Report on Foreign Trade Barriers, 1998.** 420p. 1998. per. 32.00 (*0-16-061895-9*) USGPO.

***National Trade Estimate Report on Foreign Trade Barriers (1998)** Ed. by Gregory C. Gerdes. 416p. (C). 1999. pap. text 55.00 (*0-7881-8232-3*) DIANE Pub.

***National Trade Estimate Report on Foreign Trade Barriers, 1999.** Government Printing Office Staff. 445p. 1999. per. 37.00 (*0-16-049979-8*) USGPO.

National Trade Policies. Dominick Salvatore. (Studies in Comparative Economic Policies: Vol. 2). 574p. 1992. 139.50 (*0-444-89300-8*, North Holland) Elsevier.

National Trade Policies No. 2: Handbook of Comparative Economic Policies, 2. Ed. by Dominick Salvatore. LC 91-11332. 592p. 1992. lib. bdg. 125.00 (*0-313-26489-9*, SIO/, Greenwood Pr) Greenwood.

National Traditions in European Community Law: Margarine & Marriage. Elies Steyger. LC 96-52035. 304p. 1997. text 82.95 (*1-85521-948-4*, Pub. by Dartmth Pub) Ashgate Pub Co.

National Traditions in Sociology. Ed. by Nikolai Genov. (International Sociology Ser.: Vol. 36). 248p. (C). 1989. text 45.00 (*0-8039-8197-X*) Sage.

National Trail Companion, 1997. Stilwell Publishing Staff. 1997. pap. text 17.95 (*1-900861-00-3*, Pub. by Stilwell Pubng) Seven Hills Bk.

National Trail Companion, 1998. annuals Tim Stilwell. (Stilwell's Bed & Breakfasts 1998 Ser.). (Illus.). 400p. 1998. pap. 17.95 (*1-900861-05-4*, Pub. by Stilwell Pubng) Seven Hills Bk.

National Training Resource Catalogue. 2nd ed. 163p. 1987. 15.00 (*0-317-03736-6*, 42,550) NCLS Inc.

National Transportation Statistics (1997) Marilyn Gross & Richard Feldman. (Illus.). 352p. (C). 1998. pap. text 45.00 (*0-7881-7504-1*) DIANE Pub.

National Transportation Planning. Ed. by Adib Kanafani & Daniel Sperling. 1982. lib. bdg. 94.00 (*90-247-2636-0*) Kluwer Academic.

National Transportation Policy. Lande. 224p. 1992. boxed set 97.00 (*0-409-89721-3*, MICHIE) LEXIS Pub.

National Transportation Policy. Charles L. Dearing & Wilfred Owen. LC 79-28670. (Illus.). 459p. 1980. reprint ed. lib. bdg. 85.00 (*0-313-22301-7*, DENT, Greenwood Pr) Greenwood.

***National Transportation Safety Board Annual Report To Congress, 1996.** 127p. 1999. per. 11.00 (*0-16-062336-7*) USGPO.

***National Transportation Safety Board Annual Report to Congress, 1997.** 95p. 1999. pap. 8.75 (*0-16-050123-7*) USGPO.

National Transportation Strategic Planning Study, 2 vols. 1995. lib. bdg. 600.00 (*0-8490-6510-0*) Gordon Pr.

National Transposition Measures Situation at 1st January, 1998. European Commission. Directorate-General for Employment, Industrial Relations, and Social Affairs. LC 98-195927. 1998. 20.00 (*92-828-2747-X*, CE-10-97-097ENC, Pub. by Comm Europ Commun) Bernan Associates.

National Trauma & Collective Memory: Major Events in the American Century. Arthur G. Neal. LC 97-46625. 240p. (C). (gr. 13). 1998. text 65.95 (*0-7656-0286-5*) M E Sharpe.

***National Trauma & Collective Memory: Major Events in the American Century.** Arthur G. Neal. LC 97-46625. 240p. (C). (gr. 13). 1998. pap. text 27.95 (*0-7656-0287-3*) M E Sharpe.

***National Treasure.** Peter Bleed. LC 00-130486. (Antiquity Alive Ser.). 309p. 2000. pap. 19.95 (*0-9675798-1-3*) RKLOG Pr.

National Treatment Study, 1998. 532p. 1999. pap. 43.00 (*0-16-049857-0*) USGPO.

***National Tree: A Novel.** David Kranes. 370p. 1999. 23.95 (*0-929712-48-X*) Huntington Pr.

National Trends for Persons in Juvenile Corrective Institutions & Adult Prisons, 1981-1992. D. Daguer & S. Mulcherjee. LC 96-145367. 25p. 1994. pap. 12.00 (*0-642-20067-X*, Pub. by Aust Inst Criminology) Advent Bks Div.

National Trends in Higher Adult Education. A. A. Liveright. 1960. 2.50 (*0-87060-020-6*, OCP 2) Syracuse U Cont Ed.

National Truck Equipment Association, 1997 Membership Roster & Product Directory. Composed by Diane Publishing Staff. 180p. 1998. pap. text 40.00 (*0-7881-4493-6*) DIANE Pub.

National Trust: The First Hundred Years. Merlin Waterson. (Illus.). 288p. 1997. pap. 22.95 (*0-7078-0238-5*, Pub. by Natl Trust) Trafalgar.

National Trust: The First Hundred Years. Merlin Waterson. (Illus.). 288p. 1995. 29.95 (*0-563-37066-1*, BBC-Parkwest) Parkwest Pubns.

National Trust: The Next Hundred Years. Howard Newby. 192p. 1996. 39.95 (*0-7078-0190-7*, Pub. by Natl Trust); pap. 22.95 (*0-7078-0231-8*, Pub. by Natl Trust) Trafalgar.

National Trust Book of Fish Cookery. Sara Paston-Williams. (Illus.). 160p. 1988. 17.95 (*0-7078-0093-5*, Pub. by Natl Trust) Trafalgar.

National Trust Book of Picnics. Margaret Willes & Kate Crookenden. (Illus.). 160p. 1993. 17.95 (*0-7078-0158-3*, Pub. by Natl Trust) Trafalgar.

National Trust Book of Tea-Time Recipes. Jane Pettigrew. (Illus.). 160p. 1991. 17.95 (*0-7078-0128-1*, Pub. by Natl Trust) Trafalgar.

National Trust Centenary Souvenir. Margaret Willes. LC 95-212066. (Illus.). 48p. 1995. pap. 6.95 (*0-7078-0265-2*, Pub. by Natl Trust) Trafalgar.

National Trust Countryside Handbook. Celia Spouncer. (Illus.). 288p. 1992. pap. 8.95 (*0-7078-0143-5*, Pub. by Natl Trust) Trafalgar.

National Trust Desk Diary, 1998. Margaret Willes. (Illus.). 144p. 1997. 19.95 (*0-7078-0248-2*, Pub. by Natl Trust) Trafalgar.

National Trust Desk Diary, 1999. Margaret Willes. (Illus.). 144p. 1998. 19.95 (*0-7078-0254-7*, Pub. by Natl Trust) Trafalgar.

National Trust Family Handbook. Ed. by Gillian Osband. (Illus.). 204p. 1993. pap. 8.95 (*0-7078-0171-0*, Pub. by Natl Trust) Trafalgar.

National Trust Gardens Handbook. Ed. by Alison Honey. (Illus.). 176p. 1993. pap. 8.95 (*0-7078-0200-8*, Pub. by Natl Trust) Trafalgar.

National Trust Guide. Lydia Greeves & Michael Trinick. LC 97-108464. (Illus.). 440p. 1997. 39.95 (*0-8109-6335-3*, Pub. by Abrams) Time Warner.

National Trust Guide: Miami & South Florida. Beth Dunlop. (Illus.). 316p. 1999. pap. text 19.95 (*0-471-18018-1*) Wiley.

National Trust Guide: San Francisco: America's Guide for Architecture & History Travelers. Peter B. Wiley. (Illus.). 296p. 1999. pap. 19.95 (*0-471-19120-5*) Wiley.

National Trust Guide to Art Deco in America. David Gebhard. LC 96-19948. (Illus.). 278p. 1996. pap. 19.95 (*0-471-14386-3*) Wiley.

National Trust Guide to Great Opera Houses in America. Karyl L. Zietz. LC 96-4081. (Illus.). 240p. 1996. pap. 29.95 (*0-471-14421-5*) Wiley.

National Trust Guide to Historic Bed & Breakfast, Inns & Small Hotels. 4th ed. National Trust for Historic Preservation Staff. LC 96-908. 561p. 1996. pap. 18.95 (*0-471-14973-X*) Wiley.

National Trust Guide to Historic Bed & Breakfast, Inns & Small Hotels. 5th ed. National Trust for Historic Preservation Staff. LC 99-12461. 592p. (C). 1999. pap. 22.95 (*0-471-33257-7*) Wiley.

National Trust Guide to New Orleans. Roulhac B. Toledano. LC 95-42538. 272p. 1996. pap. 17.95 (*0-471-14404-5*) Wiley.

National Trust Guide to Savannah. Roulhac B. Toledano. LC 96-43875. 256p. 1997. pap. 24.95 (*0-471-15568-3*) Wiley.

National Trust Guide/Seattle: America's Guide for Architecture & History Travelers. Walt Crowley. LC 97-34627. (Illus.). 288p. 1998. pap. 19.95 (*0-471-18044-0*) Wiley.

National Trust Handbook. Merlin Waterson. 1998. pap. 9.95 (*0-7078-0229-6*, Pub. by Natl Trust) Trafalgar.

***National Trust Handbook 2000.** National Trust Staff. (Illus.). 336p. 2000. pap. 9.95 (*0-7078-0296-2*, Pub. by Natl Trust) Trafalgar.

National Trust Historic Houses Handbook. Adrian Tinniswood. (Illus.). 256p. 1993. pap. 9.95 (*0-7078-0161-3*, Pub. by Natl Trust) Trafalgar.

National Trust Historical Atlas of Britain: Prehistoric & Medieval. Nigel Saul. (Illus.). 224p. (Orig.). 1997. pap. 26.95 (*0-7509-1679-6*, Pub. by Sutton Pub Ltd) Intl Pubs Mktg.

National Trust Meeting Planner's Guide to Historic Places. National Trust for Historic Preservation Staff. LC 97-7478. (Illus.). 369p. 1997. 69.95 (*0-471-17891-8*) Wiley.

National Trust Old Postcard Album. Geoffrey Sowerby. 112p. (C). 1989. text 50.00 (*1-872795-88-9*, Pub. by Pentland Pr) St Mut.

National Trust Recipes. Sarah Edington. (Illus.). 160p. 1996. 19.95 (*0-7078-0251-2*, Pub. by Natl Trust) Trafalgar.

National Tuberculosis Association, 1904-1954: A Study of the Voluntary Health Movement in the United States. Richard H. Shryock. Ed. by Barbara G. Rosenkrantz. LC 76-40645. (Public Health in America Ser.). (Illus.). 1977. reprint ed. lib. bdg. 35.95 (*0-405-09831-6*) Ayer.

***National Uncanny: Indian Ghosts & American Subjects.** Renee L. Bergland. LC 99-35382. (Reencounters with Colonialism Ser.). 211p. 2000. 40.00 (*0-87451-943-8*); pap. 19.95 (*0-87451-944-6*) U Pr of New Eng.

National Union Catalog: A Cumulative Author List, 1958-62. Library of Congress Staff. Incl. Pt. 1. Music & Phonorecords - Authors List. 40.00 (*0-87471-731-0*); Pt. 2. Music & Phonorecords - Subject Index. 40.00 (*0-87471-732-9*); Vol. 53. Motion Pictures & Film Strips Pt. 2: Titles. 40.00 (*0-87471-733-7*); Vol. 54. Motion Pictures & Film Strips Pt. 2: Subject Index. 40.00 (*0-87471-734-5*); write for info. (*0-318-55560-3*) Rowman.

National Union of Mineworkers & British Politics, 1944-1995. Andrew J. Taylor. (Studies in Modern British History). 256p. 1998. 55.00 (*0-7509-1236-7*, Pub. by Sutton Pub Ltd) Intl Pubs Mktg.

National Unity & Regionalism in Eight African States: Nigeria, Niger, the Congo, Gabon, Central African Republic. Gwendolen M. Carter. LC 66-12113. 581p. reprint ed. pap. 180.20 (*0-608-11575-4*, 200545700054) Bks Demand.

National Unity & Religious Minorities. M. M. Sankhdher & K. K. Wadhwa. (C). 1990. 29.50 (*81-85060-36-3*, Pub. by Gitanjali Prakashan) S Asia.

National University: Enduring Dream of the U. S. A. David Madsen. LC 66-22036. 179p. reprint ed. pap. 55.50 (*0-608-16645-6*, 202768300055) Bks Demand.

National Urban Mass Transportation Statistics. 1990. lib. bdg. 79.95 (*0-8490-4016-7*) Gordon Pr.

National Urban Policies in the European Union. Ed. by Leo Van der Berg et al. LC 98-72626. (European Institute for Comparative Urban Research Ser.). 464p. 1998. text 80.95 (*1-84014-360-6*, Pub. by Ashgate Pub) Ashgate Pub Co.

National Urban Policy: Problems & Prospects. Ed. by Harold Wolman & Elizabeth J. Agius. 206p. (Orig.). (C). 1996. pap. 22.95 (*0-8143-2543-2*) Wayne St U Pr.

National Value of Art. 6th ed. Sri Aurobindo. 27p. 1994. pap. 1.50 (*81-7058-228-8*, Pub. by SAA) E-W Cultural Ctr.

National Values & International Differences: Moral Visions in Japan & the U. S. Robert N. Bellah & Hayao Kawai. (Mansfield American-Pacific Lectures). 140p. 1992. write for info. (*0-9635265-1-0*) U MT Mansfld.

National Variations in Jewish Identity: Implications for Jewish Education. Ed. by Steven M. Cohen & Gabriel Horenczyk. LC 99-19029. 288p. (C). 1999. text 65.50 (*0-7914-4371-X*, Suny Pr); pap. text 21.95 (*0-7914-4372-8*, Suny Pr) State U NY Pr.

National Velvet. Enid Bagnold. 272p. (J). 1991. mass mkt. 4.99 (*0-380-71235-0*, Avon Bks) Morrow Avon.

***National Velvet.** Enid Bagnold. 272p. (J). 1999. mass mkt. 4.99 (*0-380-81056-5*, Avon Bks) Morrow Avon.

National Velvet. Enid Bagnold. 1991. 9.60 (*0-606-12446-2*, Pub. by Turtleback) Demco.

National Velvet. Enid Bagnold. 320p. (J). 1981. reprint ed. lib. bdg. 35.95 (*0-89966-359-1*); reprint ed. lib. bdg. 18.95 (*0-89967-033-4*, Harmony Rain) Buccaneer Bks.

National Veterinary Boards (NBE) (NVB), 3 pts. in 1 vol. Rudman. (Admission Test Ser.: ATS-50). pap. 69.95 (*0-8373-5050-6*) Nat Learn.

National Veterinary Boards (NBE) (NVB) Anatomy, Physiology, Pathology, Pt. 1. Rudman. (Admission Test Ser.: ATS-50A). pap. 39.95 (*0-8373-6960-6*) Nat Learn.

National Veterinary Boards (NBE) (NVB) Pt. II: Pharmacology, Therapeutics, Parasitology, Hygiene. Jack Rudman. (Admission Test Ser.: Vol. 50B). 59.95 (*0-8373-6986-X*) Nat Learn.

National Veterinary Boards (NBE) (NVB) Pt. II: Pharmacology, Therapeutics, Parasitology, Hygiene, Pt. 2. Jack Rudman. (Admission Test Ser.: ATS-50B). 1994. pap. 39.95 (*0-8373-6961-4*) Nat Learn.

National Veterinary Boards (NBE) (NVB) Pt. III: Physical Diagnosis, Medicine, Surgery, Pt. 3. Jack Rudman. (Admission Test Ser.: ATS-50C). 1994. pap. 39.95 (*0-8373-6962-2*) Nat Learn.

National Veterinary Boards (NBE) (NVE) Pt. III: Physical Diagnosis, Medicine, Surgery. Jack Rudman. (Admission Test Ser.: Vol. 50C). 59.95 (*0-8373-6987-8*) Nat Learn.

National Visual Arts Standards. Cynthia Colbert & Martha Taunton. 36p. (Orig.). 1994. pap. 14.00 (*0-937652-65-2*, 216) Natl Art Ed.

National Vitality, Its Wastes & Conservation. Irving Fisher. LC 75-17221. (Social Problems & Social Policy Ser.). 1976. reprint ed. 15.95 (*0-405-07492-1*) Ayer.

National VLA Directory, 1997. Robert A. Wallace. 1997. pap. 15.00 (*0-614-05460-5*) Vol Lawyers Arts.

National Voluntary Laboratory Accreditation Program (1996 Directory) Ed. by Vanda R. White. 189p. 1998. pap. text 30.00 (*0-7881-4309-3*) DIANE Pub.

National Voluntary Laboratory Accreditation Program, 1997 Directory. Ed. by Vanda R. White. 225p. 1998. pap. text 30.00 (*0-7881-4936-9*) DIANE Pub.

National Voluntary Laboratory Accreditation Program, 1997 Directory. Vanda R. White. 232p. 1997. per. 20.00 (*0-16-054497-1*) USGPO.

***National Voluntary Laboratory Accreditation Program, 1998 Directory.** Vanda R. White. 302p. 1998. per. 25.00 (*0-16-060875-9*) USGPO.

National War Labor Board: Stability, Social Justice, & the Voluntary State in World War I. Valerie J. Conner. LC 82-13362. (Supplementary Volumes to the Papers of Woodrow Wilson). 247p. reprint ed. pap. 76.60 (*0-7837-2464-0*, 204261700005) Bks Demand.

National Water Conference. Ed. by T. Al Austin. 606p. 1989. pap. text 8.00 (*0-87262-714-4*, 714) Am Soc Civil Eng.

National Water Master Plans for Developing Countries. Ed. by Asit K. Biswas et al. (Water Resources Management Ser.: No. 6). (Illus.). 288p. 1998. text 27.50 (*0-19-564061-6*) OUP.

National Water Master Plans for Developing Countries. Asit K. Biswas & International Workshop on the Intercomparison of National Water Master Plans. LC 97-906437. (Illus.). 1997. write for info. (*0-19-564366-6*) OUP.

National Water-Quality Assessment (NAWQA) Program: Biblio. 40p. pap. text 30.00 (*0-7881-1597-9*) DIANE Pub.

National Water Quality Inventory: 1992 Report to Congress. Ed. by Barry Burgan. (Illus.). 375p. (C). 1996. reprint ed. pap. text 60.00 (*0-7881-3545-7*) DIANE Pub.

National Water Resources Regulation: Where is the Environment Pendulum Now?: Proceedings of the Conference, Georgetown University Conference Center, Washington, D. C., January 1-February 1, 1994. Ed. by Howard Holme. LC 94-30075. 280p. 1994. 28.00 (*0-7844-0045-8*) Am Soc Civil Eng.

National Water Summary, 1987, Hydrologic Events & Water Supply & Use. Jerry E. Carr. 565p. 1994. per. 49.00 (*0-16-061618-2*) USGPO.

National Water Summary, 1988-89: Hydrologic Events & Floods & Droughts. Richard W. Paulson. 601p. 1992. per. 52.00 (*0-16-061614-X*) USGPO.

***National Water Summary on Wetland Resources.** Ed. by Judy D. Fretwell et al. (Illus.). 431p. (C). 2000. reprint ed. pap. text 60.00 (*0-7881-8935-2*) DIANE Pub.

National Waterway: A History of the Chesapeake & Delaware Canal, 1769-1985. 2nd ed. Ralph D. Gray. LC 88-28321. (Illus.). 372p. 1989. pap. text 16.95 (*0-252-06066-0*) U of Ill Pr.

National Wealth of the United States in the Postwar Period. Raymond W. Goldsmith. LC 75-19714. (National Bureau of Economic Research Ser.). (Illus.). 1975. reprint ed. 37.95 (*0-405-07594-4*) Ayer.

National Wealth of the United States in the Postwar Period. Raymond W. Goodsmith. (Studies in Capital Formation & Financing: No. 10). 466p. 1962. reprint ed. 121.20 (*0-87014-108-2*) Natl Bur Econ Res.

***National Weather Service Staff Reductions Proposed for Fiscal Year 1997 & Projected for Fiscal Year 1998: Hearing Before the Subcommittee on Science, Technology & Space of the Committee on Commerce, Science & Transportation, United States Senate, One Hundred Fifth Congress, First Session, May 15, 1997.** United States Government. LC 98-156802. iii, 164 p. 1998. write for info. (*0-16-056292-9*) USGPO.

National Welfare & Economic Interdependence: The Case of Sweden's Foreign Trade Policy. Ebba Dohlman. (Illus.). 264p. 1989. text 65.00 (*0-19-827558-7*) OUP.

National Wilderness Preservation System Database: Key Attributes & Trends, 1964 Through 1998. Peter Landres & Shannon Meyer. (Illus.). 97p. (C). 1999. pap. text 25.00 (*0-7881-7885-7*) DIANE Pub.

National Wildlife Federation Guide to Gardening for Wildlife: How to Create a Beautiful Backyard Habitat for Birds, Butterflies & Other Wildlife. Craig Tufts & Peter H. Loewer. (Illus.). 192p. 1995. text 29.95 (*0-87596-675-6*) Rodale Pr Inc.

National Wildlife Federation Ocean Exploration Kit. (Nature Scope Ser.). (J). (gr. 4-8). 1994. bds. 19.95 (*0-9641742-2-7*) Pequot Pubng.

National Wildlife Federation Rain Forest Exploration Kit. (Nature Scope Ser.). (J). (gr. 4-8). 1994. bds. 19.95 (*0-9641742-1-9*) Pequot Pubng.

National Wildlife Refuge System Improvement Act of 1997: Hearing Before the Committee on Environment & Public Works, United States Senate, 105th Congress, 1st Session on S. 1059... July 30, 1997. USGPO Staff. LC 98-160170. iii, 55 p. 1997. pap. write for info. (*0-16-056015-2*) USGPO.

National Wildlife Refuges: Visitor's Guide. 1997. pap. 1.50 (*0-16-061699-9*) USGPO.

National Wildlife Research Center Highlights Report, Fiscal Year 1996. Ed. by M. L. Avery. (Illus.). 45p. (C). 1997. pap. text 15.00 (*0-7881-3948-7*) DIANE Pub.

National Wiretap Report (1994) 175p. (Orig.). 1996. pap. text 30.00 (*0-7881-2988-0*) DIANE Pub.

National Wiretap Report (1995) (Illus.). 171p. (Orig.). 1996. pap. text 30.00 (*0-7881-3061-7*) DIANE Pub.

National Wiretap Report (1992) (Illus.). 170p. (Orig.). 1992. pap. text 35.00 (*0-941375-46-3*) DIANE Pub.

National Wiretap Report (1996) Leonidas R. Mecham. (Illus.). 193p. (Orig.). (C). 1997. pap. text 40.00 (*0-7881-4527-4*) DIANE Pub.

National Wiretap Report, 1997. Ed. by Leonidas R. Mecham. (Illus.). 207p. (C). 1998. pap. text 35.00 (*0-7881-7318-9*) DIANE Pub.

National Wiretap Report (1993) 208p. pap. text 40.00 (*0-7881-4456-1*) DIANE Pub.

National Women's Directory. Loulou Brown. 384p. 1999. pap. 19.95 (*0-304-70192-0*) Continuum.

National Women's Directory: Of Alcohol & Drug Abuse Treatment & Prevention Programs. Ed. by Margaret Dickson. 80p. 1988. pap. text 19.95 (*0-943519-07-1*, D1907) Sulzburger & Graham Pub.

National Women's Information Exchange Directory. Ed. by Jill Lippitt. LC 93-41914. 192p. (Orig.). 1994. pap. 10.00 (*0-380-77570-0*, Avon Bks) Morrow Avon.

National Workshop on Advances in Hydrological Instrumentation, October 25-26, 1994. V. C. Goyal & National Institute of Hydrology (India) Staff. LC 97-905198. xivi, 245 p. 1997. write for info. (*81-7023-657-6*) Allied Pubs.

***National Writer's Union Freelance Writer's Guide.** 2nd ed. National Writers Union Staff. 2000. pap. 24.95 (*0-9644208-1-3*, Pub. by Natl Writ Union) F & W Pubns Inc.

National Writers Union Guide to Freelance Rates & Standard Practice. National Writers Union Staff. 200p. 1995. pap. 19.95 (*0-9644208-0-5*) Natl Writ Union.

National Youth Administration, Vol. 9. Palmer O. Johnson & Oswald L. Harvey. LC 74-1687. (Children & Youth Ser.). 134p. 1974. reprint ed. 17.95 (*0-405-05964-7*) Ayer.

***National Youth Gang Survey, 1996: Summary.** Ed. by Shay Bilchik. (Illus.). 75p. (C). 2000. pap. text 20.00 (*0-7881-8795-3*) DIANE Pub.

National Youth Policies in Developing Countries. 27p. 1986. 5.00 (*92-1-130102-5*, E.85.IV.7) UN.

National Youth Summit on HIV Prevention & Education: Summary Report & Recommendations. 2nd ed. NASBE Staff. 43p. 1995. pap. 10.00 (*1-58434-013-4*) NASBE.

Nationale Identitatsbestrebungen und Antispanische Polemik im Englischen Pamphlet, 1558-1630. Martina Mittag. (Europaische Hochschulschriften, Reihe 14: No. 261). (Illus.). 261p. 1993. 48.80 (*3-631-45942-4*) P Lang Pubng.

Nationale Six. Jean-Jacques Bernard. Ed. by Alexander Y. Kroff & Karl G. Bottke. (FRE., Illus.). (Orig.). 1961. pap. text 12.95 (*0-89197-312-5*) Irvington.

Nationales Wirtschaftsrecht & Internationale Wirtschaftsordnung: Anwendungsgrenzen Nationalen Rechts bei Internationalen Sachverhalten. Joachim Kaffanke. (GER.). 352p. 1990. pap. 71.00 (*3-7890-1796-5*, Pub. by Nomos Verlags) Intl Bk Import.

Nationalisation Beyond the Slogans. Keith Coleman. 191p. (Orig.). (C). 1992. pap. text 19.95 (*0-86975-413-0*, Pub. by Ravan Pr) Ohio U Pr.

Nationalisation of the Indian Army, 1885-1947. Gautam Sharma. LC 97-901385. (C). 1996. 26.00 (*81-7023-555-3*, Pub. by Allied Pubs) S Asia.

***Nationalising & Denationalising European Border Regions, 1800-2000: Views from Geography & History.** Hans Knippenberg & Jan Markusse. LC 99-56031. (Geojournal Library). (Illus.). 1999. write for info. (*0-7923-6066-4*) Kluwer Academic.

Nationalism. Peter Alter. 176p. 1989. pap. 12.95 (*0-7131-6519-7*, Pub. by E A) Routldge.

Nationalism. Craig Calhoun. LC 97-30511. (Concepts in Social Thought Ser.). 144p. 1998. pap. 14.95 (*0-8166-3121-2*); text 37.95 (*0-8166-3120-4*) U of Minn Pr.

Nationalism. Ernest Gellner. LC 97-33629. 128p. 1997. text 18.50 (*0-8147-3113-9*) NYU Pr.

Nationalism. Kramer. LC 98-28089. 160p. 1998. 33.00 (*0-8057-8610-4*, Twyne) Mac Lib Ref.

Nationalism. O'Leary. 129.95 (*1-85521-387-7*) Ashgate Pub Co.

Nationalism. Ed. by Anthony Smith & John Hutchinson. (Oxford Readers Ser.). 388p. (C). 1995. pap. text 22.95 (*0-19-289260-6*) OUP.

Nationalism. Rabindranath Tagore. 82p. 1985. 4.50 (*0-318-36929-X*) Asia Bk Corp.

Nationalism. enl. ed. Elie Kedourie. 176p. 1993. pap. text 22.95 (*0-631-18885-1*) Blackwell Pubs.

Nationalism. Rabindranath Tagore. LC 72-9088. 159p. 1973. reprint ed. lib. bdg. 55.00 (*0-8371-6571-7*, TANA, Greenwood Pr) Greenwood.

Nationalism. 2nd ed. Peter Alter. LC 94-223681. 160p. 1995. pap. text 18.95 (*0-340-60061-6*, B3542, Pub. by E A) OUP.

Nationalism. 2nd rev. ed. Ed. by Bruno Leone. LC 86-324. (Isms Ser.). (Illus.). 150p. (YA). (gr. 9-12). 1986. lib. bdg. 26.20 (*0-89908-387-0*) Greenhaven.

Nationalism: Critical Concepts in Political Science John Hutchinson & Anthony D. Smith. LC 99-20802. 2000. write for info. (*0-415-21756-3*) Routledge.

Nationalism: Essays in Honor of Louis L. Snyder, 65. Ed. by Michael Palumbo & William O. Shanahan. LC 81-6501. (Contributions in Political Science Ser.: No. 65). 219p. 1981. 57.95 (*0-313-23176-1*, PNA/, Greenwood Pr) Greenwood.

Nationalism: Five Roads to Modernity. Liah Greenfeld. (Illus.). 576p. 1992. 57.00 (*0-674-60318-4*) HUP.

N

An Asterisk (*) at the beginning of an entry indicates that the title is appearing for the first time.

Nationalism: Five Roads to Modernity. Liah Greenfeld. 600p. 1993. pap. 24.50 (*0-674-60319-2*) HUP.
Nationalism: Its Meaning & History. Hans Kohn. LC 82-163. (Anvil Ser.). 192p. (C). 1982. reprint ed. pap. text 11.50 (*0-89874-479-2*) Krieger.
Nationalism & Antisemitism in Modern Europe, 1815-1945. Shumel Almog. (Studies in Antisemitism). (Illus.). 186p. 1990. 59.95 (*0-08-037254-6*, Prgamon Press) Buttrwrth-Heinemann.
Nationalism & Archaeology in Europe. Timothy C. Champion. Ed. by Margarita Diaz-Andreu. (C). 1996. pap. 75.00 (*0-8133-3051-3*, Pub. by Westview) HarpC.
Nationalism & Capitalism in Peru: A Study in Neo-Imperialism. Anibal Quijano. Tr. by Helen R. Lane. LC 78-163117. 128p. reprint ed. pap. 39.70 (*0-608-13927-0*, 201925500011) Bks Demand.
***Nationalism & Civilisation in the Asia Pacific.** Wang Gungwu. 1999. write for info. (*981-210-139-X*, Pub. by Times Academic) Intl Spec Bk.
Nationalism & Colonialism in Modern India. B. Chanra. 395p. 1979. 19.95 (*0-318-36595-2*) Asia Bk Corp.
Nationalism & Communal Politics in India. Mushirul Hasan. (C). 1991. 23.00 (*81-7304-072-9*, Pub. by Manohar) S Asia.
Nationalism & Communal Politics in India. Hasan Mushiru. 1979. 18.50 (*0-8364-0198-0*) S Asia.
Nationalism & Communism in East Asia. William M. Ball. LC 75-30044. (Institute of Pacific Relations Ser.). reprint ed. 39.50 (*0-404-59502-2*) AMS Pr.
Nationalism & Communism in Eastern Europe & the Soviet Union: A Basic Contradiction? Walter A. Kemp. LC 98-38456. 1999. text 69.95 (*0-312-21799-4*) St Martin.
Nationalism & Communism in Eastern Europe & the Soviet Union: A Basic Contradictions? Walter A. Kemp. LC 98-38456. xvii, 292p. 1999. write for info. (*0-333-74157-9*, Pub. by Macmillan) St Martin.
Nationalism & Communism in Macedonia: Civil Conflict, Politics of Mutation, National Identity. 2nd ed. Evangelos Kofos. (Hellenism: Ancient, Mediaeval, Modern Ser.: No. 12). xxi, 336p. (C). 1993. text 40.00 (*0-89241-540-1*) Caratzas.
Nationalism & Cultural Practice in the Postcolonial World. Neil Lazarus. LC 98-38084. (Cultural Margins Ser.: No. 6). 240p. (C). 1999. text 57.95 (*0-521-62410-X*); pap. text 19.95 (*0-521-62493-2*) Cambridge U Pr.
Nationalism & Culture. Rudolf Rocker. 592p. 1997. 57.99 (*1-55164-095-3*, Pub. by Black Rose); pap. 28.99 (*1-55164-094-5*, Pub. by Black Rose) Consort Bk Sales.
Nationalism & Culture. Rudolf Rocker. Tr. by Ray E. Chase from GER. LC 78-5960. 1978. 20.00 (*0-9602574-1-1*) M E Coughlin.
Nationalism & Desire in Early Historical Fiction. Dennis. 210p. 1997. text 49.95 (*0-312-17244-3*) St Martin.
Nationalism & Development in Africa: Selected Essays. James S. Coleman. Ed. by Richard L. Sklar. LC 93-25774. (C). 1994. 60.00 (*0-520-08374-1*, Pub. by U CA Pr); pap. 20.00 (*0-520-08376-8*, Pub. by U CA Pr) Cal Prin Full Svc.
Nationalism & Education in Modern China. Cyrus H. Peake. LC 72-80580. 1970. reprint ed. 35.00 (*0-86527-138-0*) Fertig.
Nationalism & Empire: The Habsburg Monarchy & the Soviet Union. Ed. by Richard L. Rudolph & David A. Good. 320p. 1992. text 49.95 (*0-312-06892-1*) St Martin.
Nationalism & Ethnic Conflict. Ed. by Michael E. Brown et al. LC 96-52337. (IS Reader Ser.). (Illus.). 452p. 1997. pap. text 20.00 (*0-262-52224-1*) MIT Pr.
Nationalism & Ethnic Conflict. Ed. by Charles P. Cozic. LC 93-19854. (Current Controversies Ser.). 288p. (YA). 1994. pap. 16.20 (*1-56510-079-4*); lib. bdg. 26.20 (*1-56510-080-8*) Greenhaven.
***Nationalism & Ethnic Conflict: Philosophical Perspectives.** Ed. by Nenad Miscevic. LC 00-29856. 300p. 2000. 39.95 (*0-8126-9415-5*) Open Court.
Nationalism & Ethnic Conflict: Threats to European Security. Stephen I. Griffiths. (SIPRI Pubns.: Vol. 5). 144p. 1993. pap. text 28.00 (*0-19-829162-0*) OUP.
Nationalism & Ethnicity: An Interpretation of Tamil Cultural History & Social Order. Jacob Pandian. 1987. 27.00 (*0-86132-136-7*, Pub. by Popular Prakashan) S Asia.
Nationalism & Ethnicity in a Hindu Kingdom: The Politics & Culture of Contemporary Nepal. Ed. by David Gellner et al. LC 97-190530. (Studies in Anthropology & History: Vol. 20). 570p. 1997. text 49.00 (*90-5702-089-0*, Harwood Acad Pubs) Gordon & Breach.
Nationalism & Ethnicity Is a Hindu Kingdom: The Politics of Culture in Contemporary Nepal. Gellner & Whelpton. 1997. pap. 384.00 (*0-7855-7454-9*, Pub. by Ratna Pustak Bhandar) St Mut.
***Nationalism & Ethnicity Terminologies: An Encyclopedic Dictionary & Research Guide.** Thomas Spira. 757p. 1999. 125.00 (*0-87569-205-2*) Academic Intl.
Nationalism & Ethnoregional Identities in China. William Safran. LC 98-26002. (Nationalism & Ethnicity Ser.). 224p. 1998. 52.50 (*0-7146-4921-X*, Pub. by F Cass Pubs); pap. 22.50 (*0-7146-4476-5*, Pub. by F Cass Pubs) Intl Spec Bk.
Nationalism & Federalism in Australia. Winston G. McMinn. 324p. 1995. pap. text 35.00 (*0-19-553667-3*) OUP.
Nationalism & Federalism in Yugoslavia, 1962-1991. 2nd ed. Sabrina P. Ramet. LC 91-23623. 365p. 1992. reprint ed. pap. 113.20 (*0-608-01072-3*, 205938000001) Bks Demand.
Nationalism & Federalism in Yugoslavia, 1963-1983. Pedro Ramet. LC 83-49055. 319p. reprint ed. pap. 98.90 (*0-8357-6685-3*, 205686400094) Bks Demand.
***Nationalism & Historiography: The Case of Nineteenth-Century Lithuanian Historicism.** Virgil Krapauskas. 244p. 2000. text 30.00 (*0-88033-457-6*) Col U Pr.
Nationalism & Hybridity in Mongolia. Uradyn E. Bulag. LC 97-39268. (Oxford Studies in Social & Cultural Anthropology). (Illus.). 318p. 1998. text 75.00 (*0-19-823357-4*) OUP.
Nationalism & Identity: Culture & Imagination in a Caribbean Diaspora. Stefano Harney. LC 50-40974. 192p. (C). 1996. text 59.95 (*1-85649-375-X*, Pub. by Zed Books) St Martin.
Nationalism & Independence: Selected Essays on Modern Irish History. Nicholas Mansergh. LC 97-146037. 320p. 1997. 64.95 (*1-85918-105-8*, Pub. by Cork Univ); pap. 24.95 (*1-85918-106-6*, Pub. by Cork Univ) Intl Spec Bk.
Nationalism & International Society. James Mayall. (Cambridge Studies in International Relations: No. 10). 181p. (C). 1990. pap. text 18.95 (*0-521-38961-5*) Cambridge U Pr.
Nationalism & Internationalism: Belonging. Boyd C. Shafer. LC 81-17166. (Anvil Ser.). 278p. (Orig.). 1982. pap. 14.50 (*0-89874-260-9*) Krieger.
Nationalism & Internationalism: Design in the Twentieth Century. Jeremy Aynsley. (Illus.). 72p. 1993. pap. 14.95 (*1-85177-121-2*, Pub. by V&A Ent) Antique Collect.
Nationalism & Internationalism: European & American Perspectives. Erich Hula. LC 84-13094. (American Values Projected Abroad Ser.: Vol. XI). 326p. (Orig.). 1984. pap. text 27.00 (*0-8191-3705-7*) U Pr of Amer.
Nationalism & Internationalism in Science, 1880-1939: Four Studies of the Nobel Population. Elisabeth Crawford. (Illus.). 169p. (C). 1992. text 54.95 (*0-521-40386-3*) Cambridge U Pr.
***Nationalism & Internationalism in the Post-Cold War Era.** Kell Goldmann et al. LC 00-32827. (Illus.). 2000. pap. write for info. (*0-415-23891-9*) Routledge.
***Nationalism & Internationalism in the Post-Cold War Era.** Kjell Goldmann. 1999. pap. text 24.95 (*0-8153-3409-5*) Garland.
Nationalism & Language in Kurdistan, 1918-1985: The Language Factor in National Development. Amir Hassanpour. LC 92-5916. 488p. 1992. lib. bdg. 109.95 (*0-7734-9816-8*) E Mellen.
Nationalism & Liberty: The Swiss Example. Hans Kohn. LC 77-28360. 133p. 1978. reprint ed. lib. bdg. 49.75 (*0-313-20233-8*, KONL, Greenwood Pr) Greenwood.
Nationalism & Literature: English-Language Writing from the Philippines & Singapore. Shirley G. Lim. 186p. (Orig.). 1994. pap. 15.00 (*971-10-0525-5*, Pub. by New Day Pub) Cellar.
Nationalism & Literature: The Politics of Culture in Canada & the United States. Sarah M. Corse. LC 96-14151. (Cambridge Cultural Social Studies). 225p. (C). 1996. text 59.95 (*0-521-57002-6*) Cambridge U Pr.
Nationalism & Literature: The Politics of Culture in Canada & the United States. Sarah M. Corse. LC 96-14151. (Cultural Social Studies). 224p. (C). 1997. pap. text 19.95 (*0-521-57912-0*) Cambridge U Pr.
Nationalism & Marxism in India: Quest for People & Power, 1920-1940. Bibekbrata Sarkar. 207p. 1990. 18.00 (*81-85163-09-X*, Pub. by Kalinga) Nataraj Bks.
Nationalism & Modernism: A Critical Survey of Recent Theories of Nations & Nationalism. Anthony D. Smith. LC 98-18648. 288p. (C). 1998. 85.00 (*0-415-06340-X*); pap. 25.99 (*0-415-06341-8*) Routledge.
Nationalism & Modernity: A Mediterranean Perspective. Ed. by Joseph Alpher. LC 86-11222. 151p. 1986. 49.95 (*0-275-92137-9*, C2137, Praeger Pubs) Greenwood.
Nationalism & National Integration. Anthony H. Birch. LC 88-31365. 272p. (C). (gr. 13). 1989. text 76.00 (*0-04-320180-6*) Routledge.
Nationalism & Nationalities in the New Europe. Ed. by Charles A. Kupchan. 280p. 1995. pap. text 15.95 (*0-8014-8276-3*) Cornell U Pr.
***Nationalism & Politics: The Political Behavior of Nation States.** Martha L. Cottam & Richard W. Cottam. 330p. 2000. lib. bdg. 59.95 (*1-55587-919-5*) L Rienner.
Nationalism & Postcommunism: A Collection of Essays. Ed. by Aleksandar Pavkovic et al. LC 95-8908. 192p. 1995. 77.95 (*1-85521-625-6*, Pub. by Dartmth Pub) Ashgate Pub Co.
Nationalism & Progress in Free Asia. Ed. by Philip W. Thayer et al. LC 56-9414. 412p. reprint ed. pap. 127.80 (*0-608-11710-2*, 202054200018) Bks Demand.
Nationalism & Racism in the Liberal Order. Ed. by Bob Brecher et al. LC 98-70988. (Avebury Series in Philosophy). 244p. 1998. text 63.95 (*1-84014-148-4*, Pub. by Ashgate Pub) Ashgate Pub Co.
Nationalism & Rationality. Ed. by Albert Breton et al. (Illus.). 341p. (C). 1995. text 59.95 (*0-521-48098-1*) Cambridge U Pr.
Nationalism & Realism, 1852-1879. Hans Kohn. (Anvil Ser.). 192p. 1968. pap. 11.50 (*0-442-00096-0*) Krieger.
Nationalism & Regionalism in a Colonial Context: Minahasa in the Dutch East Indies. David Henley. LC 96-180708. (KITLV Verhandelingen Ser.: Vol. 168). 186p. (Orig.). 1996. pap. 33.50 (*90-6718-080-7*, Pub. by KITLV Pr) Cellar.
Nationalism & Religion in America: Concepts of American Identity & Mission. Winthrop S. Hudson. 1990. 16.50 (*0-8446-0711-8*) Peter Smith.
Nationalism & Sectionalism in South Carolina, 1852-1860. Harold S. Schultz. LC 70-84190. (American Scene, Comments & Commentators Ser.). 1969. reprint ed. lib. bdg. 32.50 (*0-306-71646-1*) Da Capo.
Nationalism & Self-Determination in the Horn of Africa. Ed. by I. M. Lewis. (Illus.). 229p. (Orig.). 1984. pap. 19.95 (*0-685-08758-1*) Evergreen Dist.
Nationalism & Separatism in Bengal. Sumitra De. (C). 1992. 32.50 (*0-7069-5964-7*, Pub. by Vikas) S Asia.
Nationalism & Sexuality: Respectability & Abnormal Sexuality in Modern Europe. George L. Mosse. 1997. reprint ed. pap. 13.95 (*0-86527-429-0*) Fertig.
Nationalism & Sexuality: Respectabilty & Abnormal Sexuality in Modern Europe. George L. Mosse. LC 84-6082. (Illus.). 256p. 1985. 40.00 (*0-86527-350-2*) Fertig.
Nationalism & Socialism: Marxist & Labor Theories of Nationalism to 1917. Horace B. Davis. LC 67-19255. 258p. 1973. pap. 12.00 (*0-85345-293-8*, PB-2938, Pub. by Monthly Rev) NYU Pr.
***Nationalism & Territory: Constructing Group Identity in Southeastern Europe.** George W. White. LC 99-39940. (Geographical Perspectives on the Human Past Ser.). 320p. 2000. 69.00 (*0-8476-9808-4*); pap. 29.95 (*0-8476-9809-2*) Rowman.
Nationalism & the Color Line in George W. Cable, Mark Twain, & William Faulkner. Barbara Ladd. LC 96-21711. (Southern Literary Studies). 232p. 1996. text 32.50 (*0-8071-2065-0*) La State U Pr.
Nationalism & the Construction of Korean Identity. Hyung Pai. LC 98-37408. 1999. pap. 18.00 (*1-55729-062-8*) IEAS.
Nationalism & the Crises of Ethnic Minorities in Asia, 34. Ed. by Tai S. Kang. LC 78-19295. (Contributions in Sociology Ser.: No. 34). (Illus.). 148p. 1979. 55.00 (*0-313-20623-6*, KNA/, Greenwood Pr) Greenwood.
***Nationalism & the Crowd in Liberal Hungary, 1848-1914.** Alice Freifeld. (Illus.). 2000. write for info. (*0-8018-6462-3*) Johns Hopkins.
***Nationalism & The Drive for Sovereignty in Tatarstan, 1988-92: Origins & Development.** Sergei Kondrashov. LC 99-14836. 1999. text 65.00 (*0-312-22237-8*) St Martin.
Nationalism & the Genealogical Imagination: Oral History & Textual Authority in Tribal Jordan. Andrew Shryock. LC 95-39809. (Comparative Studies on Muslim Societies: Vol. 23). (Illus.). 363p. (C). 1997. 50.00 (*0-520-20100-0*, Pub. by U CA Pr); pap. 22.50 (*0-520-20101-9*, Pub. by U CA Pr) Cal Prin Full Svc.
Nationalism & the International Labor Movement: The Idea of the Nation in Socialist & Anarchist Theory. Michael Forman. LC 97-7117. 1998. 35.00 (*0-271-01726-0*); pap. 17.95 (*0-271-01727-9*) Pa St U Pr.
Nationalism & the Nation in the Iberian Peninsula: Competing & Conflicting Identities. Ed. by Clare Mar-Molinero & Angel Smith. 256p. 1996. 49.50 (*1-85973-180-5*, Pub. by Berg Pubs); pap. 19.50 (*1-85973-175-9*, Pub. by Berg Pubs) NYU Pr.
Nationalism & the National Question. Nicole Arnaud & Jacques Dofny. Tr. by Penelope Williams from FRE. 133p. 1977. 38.99 (*0-919618-46-4*, Pub. by Black Rose); pap. 9.99 (*0-919618-45-6*, Pub. by Black Rose) Consort Bk Sales.
Nationalism & the Nordic Imagination: Swedish Art of the 1890s. Michele Facos. LC 97-29346. 250p. 1998. 50.00 (*0-520-20626-6*, Pub. by U CA Pr) Cal Prin Full Svc.
Nationalism & the Politics of Culture in Quebec. Richard Handler. LC 87-40362. (New Directions in Anthropological Writing Ser.). (Illus.). 240p. (C). 1988. pap. text 19.95 (*0-299-11514-3*) U of Wis Pr.
Nationalism & the State. John Breuilly. LC 85-8601. x, 422p. 1985. reprint ed. pap. text 13.95 (*0-226-07412-9*) U Ch Pr.
Nationalism & the State. 2nd ed. John Breuilly. LC 93-33180. 407p. 1993. pap. text 18.95 (*0-226-07414-5*) U Ch Pr.
Nationalism & Transnationalism: The National Conflict in Ireland & European Union Integration. James Goodman. LC 96-84406. 376p. 1996. 82.95 (*1-85972-396-9*, Pub. by Avebry) Ashgate Pub Co.
Nationalism & Unionism: Conflict in Ireland, 1885-1921. 2nd ed. Ed. by Peter Collins. LC 94-193877. (Illus.). 206p. 1996. reprint ed. pap. 19.95 (*0-85389-495-7*, Pub. by Inst Irish Studies) Irish Bks Media.
Nationalism & Unionism: Ireland & British Politics in the Late 19th & Early 20th Centuries. Eilis Brennan et al. (Irish History in Perspective Ser.). (Illus.). 80p. (C). 1996. pap. 13.95 (*0-521-46605-9*) Cambridge U Pr.
Nationalism & Violence. Ed. by Christopher Dandeker. LC 97-30500. 1997. text 34.95 (*1-56000-339-1*) Transaction Pubs.
Nationalism & War in the Near East. Ed. by Courtney. LC 79-135800. (Eastern Europe Collection). 1971. reprint ed. 28.95 (*0-405-02742-7*) Ayer.
Nationalism, Anti-Semitism, & Fascism in France. Michel Winock. Tr. by Jane M. Todd from ENG. LC 98-11298. 366p. 1998. 55.00 (*0-8047-3286-8*); pap. write for info. (*0-8047-3287-6*) Stanford U Pr.
Nationalism As Political Paranoia in Burma: An Essay on the Historical Practice of Power. Mikael Gravers. (NIAS Reports: Vol. 11). 168p. 1998. text 35.00 (*0-7007-0980-0*, Pub. by Curzon Pr Ltd); pap. text 16.95 (*0-7007-0981-9*, Pub. by Curzon Pr Ltd) UH Pr.
Nationalism, Capitalism, & Colonization in Nineteenth-Century Quebec: The Upper Saint Francis District. J. I. Little. 336p. (C). 1989. text 55.00 (*0-7735-0699-3*, Pub. by McG-Queens Univ Pr) CUP Services.
Nationalism, Colonialism, & Literature. Terry Eagleton et al. 120p. (C). 1990. pap. 12.95 (*0-8166-1863-1*) U of Minn Pr.
Nationalism, Communism & Canadian Labour: The CIO, the Communist Party, & the Canadian Congress of Labour, 1935-1956. Irving M. Abella. LC 72-80712. 268p. reprint ed. pap. 83.10 (*0-608-13727-8*, 202044800018) Bks Demand.
Nationalism, Communism, Marxist-Humanism & the Afro-Asian Revolutions. 3rd ed. Raya Dunayevskaya. 48p. 1984. pap. 1.25 (*0-914441-06-X*) News & Letters.
Nationalism, Democracy & Development: State & Politics in India. Bose Sugata. (Oxford India Paperbacks Ser.). 206p. 1999. pap. text 10.95 (*0-19-564442-5*) OUP.
Nationalism, Democracy & Security in the Balkans. James F. Brown. 300p. 1992. 73.95 (*1-85521-316-8*, Pub. by Dartmth Pub) Ashgate Pub Co.
Nationalism Eastern Europe. Peter F. Sugar & Ivo John Lederer. LC 74-93026. 465p. 1994. pap. 25.00 (*0-295-97342-0*) U of Wash Pr.
Nationalism, Ethnic Identity & Conflict Management in Russia Today. Ed. by Gail W. Lapidus & Renee De Wevers. LC 96-164644. 98p. 1995. pap. 15.00 (*0-935371-37-0*) CFISAC.
***Nationalism, Ethnicity & Cultural Identity in Europe.** Ed. by Keebet Von Benda-Beckmann & Maykel Verkuyten. (Research in Migration & Ethnic Relations Ser.). 208p. 1999. pap. 20.95 (*90-75719-01-9*, Pub. by Europ Res Centre) Ashgate Pub Co.
Nationalism, Ethnicity, & Identity: Cross National & Comparative Perspectives. Ed. by Russell F. Farnen. LC 93-45994. 538p. (C). 1994. 49.95 (*1-56000-158-5*) Transaction Pubs.
Nationalism, Ethnicity & Political Development in South Asia. Ed. by Diethelm Weidemann. (C). 1991. 22.50 (*81-85425-30-2*, Pub. by Manohar) S Asia.
Nationalism, Ethnocentrism, & Personality: Social Science & Critical Theory. Hugh D. Forbes. LC 85-1202. x, 272p. 1996. lib. bdg. 33.00 (*0-226-25703-7*) U Ch Pr.
Nationalism in Asia & Africa. Ed. by Elie Kedourie. 496p. 1974. 57.50 (*0-7146-3046-2*, Pub. by F Cass Pubs); pap. 24.50 (*0-7146-3045-4*, Pub. by F Cass Pubs) Intl Spec Bk.
Nationalism in Belgium: Shifting Identities, 1780-1995. Kas Deprez & Louis Vos. LC 97-38683. 281p. 1998. write for info. (*0-333-65737-3*) St Martin.
Nationalism in Contemporary Japan. Bruce Stronach. (Politics in Asia & the Pacific). 1996. text 34.95 (*0-8133-8583-0*) Westview.
Nationalism in Contemporary Japan. Bruce Stronach. (Politics in Asia & the Pacific Ser.). (C). 1996. pap. text 19.95 (*0-8133-2334-7*) Westview.
Nationalism in Education. Ed. by Klaus Schleicher. LC 93-34557. (Illus.). 336p. 1993. 51.00 (*3-631-46017-1*) P Lang Pubng.
Nationalism in Europe: A Reader. Ed. by Stuart Woolf. LC 95-8993. 224p. (C). 1995. pap. 20.99 (*0-415-12564-2*) Routledge.
Nationalism in Europe, 1789-1945. Timothy Baycroft. LC 99-174434. (Perspectives in History Ser.). 104p. 1999. pap. 11.95 (*0-521-59871-0*) Cambridge U Pr.
Nationalism in France: Class & Nation since 1789. Brian Jenkins. 256p. (C). 1990. text 70.50 (*0-389-20943-0*) B&N Imports.
Nationalism in Iran: Updated Through 1978. Richard W. Cottam. LC 78-12302. 384p. (C). 1979. pap. 17.95 (*0-8229-5299-8*) U of Pittsburgh Pr.
Nationalism in Ireland. 3rd ed. D. George Boyce. LC 94-48350. 512p. (C). 1995. pap. 25.99 (*0-415-12776-9*) Routledge.
***Nationalism in Russia & Central Asian Republics: Unfinished Democratic Revolution.** Shams Ud-Din. 1999. 44.00 (*81-7095-070-8*, Pub. by Lancer India) S Asia.
Nationalism in South India: Its Economic & Social Background, 1885-1918. C. M. Naidu. 216p. (C). 1988. 31.00 (*81-7099-043-2*, Pub. by Mittal Pubs Dist) S Asia.
***Nationalism in Sri Lanka: Genesis & Evolution.** Krishan Gopal. 2000. 30.00 (*81-87644-04-4*, Pub. by Kalinga) S Asia.
Nationalism in the Age of the French Revolution. Ed. by O. Dann & John R. Dinwiddy. 472p. 1988. 55.00 (*0-907628-97-4*) Hambledon Press.
Nationalism in the Balkans. Gale Stokes. LC 82-49160. 264p. 1983. text 20.00 (*0-8240-9161-2*) Garland.
Nationalism in the Contemporary World: Political & Sociological Perspectives. T. V. Sathyamurthy. 258p. (C). 1983. text 50.00 (*0-86598-117-5*) Rowman.
Nationalism in the Middle Ages. Ed. by C. L. Tipton. LC 76-169900. (European Problem Studies). 128p. 1976. reprint ed. pap. 11.50 (*0-03-084157-7*) Krieger.
Nationalism in the Sixteenth Century. E. D. Marcu. LC 75-39172. 1975. lib. bdg. 25.00 (*0-913870-08-0*) Abaris Bks.
Nationalism in the Soviet Union. Hans Kohn. LC 71-181940. reprint ed. 20.00 (*0-404-03738-0*) AMS Pr.
Nationalism in the 20th Century. Smith. (Australian National University Press Ser.). 1996. write for info. (*0-08-033006-1*, Pergamon Pr) Elsevier.
Nationalism in the Twentieth Century. Anthony D. Smith. LC 78-71404. (C). 1979. pap. text 16.00 (*0-8147-7803-8*) NYU Pr.
Nationalism in the Visual Arts. Richard A. Etlin. (Illus.). 1992. 35.00 (*0-89468-176-1*) Natl Gallery Art.
Nationalism in the Visual Arts. Ed. by Richard A. Etlin. 1996. 35.00 (*0-300-07707-6*) Yale U Pr.
Nationalism, Industrialization, & Democracy, 1815-1914: A Documenatary History of Modern Europe, Vol. III. Ed. by Thomas G. Barnes & Gerald D. Feldman. LC 80-5383. 331p. 1980. pap. text 17.00 (*0-8191-1079-5*) U Pr of Amer.
Nationalism, Islam & Marxism. Pres I. Sukarno. Tr. by Karel H. Warouw et al. LC 71-11689. (Cornell University, Modern Indonesia Project, Monograph Ser.). 66p. reprint ed. pap. 30.00 (*0-608-11688-2*, 202167600022) Bks Demand.
Nationalism, Islam & Marxism, Vol. 48. 2nd ed. Soekarno. (Modern Indonesia Project Ser.). 62p. 1984. reprint ed. pap. 4.00 (*0-87763-012-7*) Cornell Mod Indo.
Nationalism, Islam & Pakistan. A. H. Hashmi. 1989. pap. 14.95 (*1-56744-168-8*) Kazi Pubns.

An Asterisk (*) at the beginning of an entry indicates that the title is appearing for the first time.

Nationalism, Labour & Ethnicity 1870-1939. Ed. by Stefan Berger & Angel Smith. 256p. 1999. 79.96 (*0-7190-5052-9*, Pub. by Manchester Univ Pr) St Martin.

Nationalism, Liberalism, & Progress: The Rise & Decline of Nationalism. Ernst B. Haas. LC 96-48439. (Cornell Studies in Political Economy). 360p. 1996. text 39.95 (*0-8014-3108-5*) Cornell U Pr.

Nationalism, Marxism, & Modern Central Europe: A Biography of Kazimierz Kelles-Krauz (1872-1905) Timothy Snyder. LC 98-112178. (Harvard Papers in Ukrainian Studies). (Illus.). 351p. 1997. pap. text 18.00 (*0-916458-84-9*) Harvard Ukrainian.

Nationalism, Minorities, & Diasporas: Identity & Rights in the Middle East. Ed. by Colm Campbell et al. 266p. 1996. text 65.00 (*1-86064-052-4*, Pub. by I B T) St Martin.

***Nationalism, National Identity & Democratization in China.** Baogang He & Yingjie Guo. 248p. 1999. text 65.95 (*1-84014-780-6*, Pub. by Ashgate Pub) Ashgate Pub Co.

Nationalism (1917) Rabindranath Tagore. 166p. 1998. reprint ed. pap. 17.95 (*0-7661-0646-2*) Kessinger Pub.

Nationalism, Politics & the Practice of Archaeology. Ed. by Philip L. Kohl & Clare Fawcett. LC 97-723. 341p. (C). 1996. text 64.95 (*0-521-48065-5*) Cambridge U Pr.

Nationalism, Politics & the Practice of Archaeology. Ed. by Philip L. Kohl & Clare Fawcett. 341p. (C). 1996. pap. text 23.95 (*0-521-55839-5*) Cambridge U Pr.

Nationalism Question. Tani E. Barlow. 1994. pap. 12.00 (*0-8223-6411-5*) Duke.

Nationalism, Racism & the Rule of Law. Ed. by Peter Fitzpatrick. LC 94-28025. 248p. 1995. 82.95 (*1-85521-554-3*, Pub. by Dartmth Pub) Ashgate Pub Co.

Nationalism Reader. Ed. by Omar Dahbour & Micheline Ishtay. LC 94-12537. 376p. (C). 1995. pap. 18.50 (*0-391-03867-2*) Humanities.

Nationalism Reframed: Nationhood & the National Question in the New Europe. Rogers Brubaker. 213p. (C). 1996. pap. text 17.95 (*0-521-57649-0*) Cambridge U Pr.

Nationalism, Secularism & Communalism. Sarto Esteves. 1996. 42.00 (*81-7433-015-1*, Pub. by S Asia Pubs) S Asia.

Nationalism, Self-Determination & Political Geography. Ed. by R. J. Johnston et al. 240p. 1988. lib. bdg. 59.50 (*0-7099-1480-6*, Pub. by C Helm) Routldge.

Nationalism, Terrorism, Communalism: Essays in Modern India History. Peter Heehs. LC 98-909290. 184p. 1998. text 22.50 (*0-19-564313-5*) OUP.

Nationalism Without a Nation in India. G. Aloysius. 278p. 1998. text 22.95 (*0-19-564104-3*) OUP.

Nationalism Without a Nation in India. G. Aloysius. 280p. (J). 1999. pap. 13.95 (*0-19-564653-3*) OUP.

Nationalism Without Walls: The Unbearable Lightness of Being Canadian. Richard Gwyn. LC 96-112676. 320p. 1996. 29.99 (*0-7710-3717-1*) McCland & Stewart.

Nationalism Without Walls: The Unbearable Lightness of Being Canadian. 2nd ed. Richard Gwyn. 304p. 1997. pap. text 16.95 (*0-7710-3720-1*) McCland & Stewart.

Nationalisme Economique et Independance Internationale: Les Choix Nationaux et Leurs Couts pour l'Economie Mondiale. Peter G. Peterson. LC HC0106.8.P37. (Foundation Per Jacobsson Conference de 1984 Ser.). (FRE.). 100p. reprint ed. pap. 31.00 (*0-608-08770-X*, 206940900004) Bks Demand.

Nationalismo Catalan see Catalan Nationalism: Past & Present

Nationalisms: The Nation-State & Nationalism in the Twentieth Century. Montserrat Guibernau. LC 95-37329. (C). 1996. pap. text 27.95 (*0-7456-1402-7*, Pub. by Polity Pr) Blackwell Pubs.

Nationalisms & Sexualities. Ed. by Andrew Parker et al. (Illus.). 384p. (C). (gr. 13). 1991. pap. 23.99 (*0-415-90433-1*, A5731) Routledge.

Nationalisms Old & New. Kevin J. Brehony. LC 98-49907. 245p. 1999. text 68.00 (*0-312-22052-9*) St Martin.

Nationalist & Unionist: Ireland Before the Treaty. Trevor Gray. LC 90-106243. 89p. 1989. write for info. (*0-216-92663-7*) Penguin Books.

Nationalist Conscience: M. A. Ansari, the Congress & the Raj. Hasan Mushirul. (C). 1987. 25.00 (*81-85054-17-7*, Pub. by Manohar) S Asia.

Nationalist Ideology & Antisemitism: The Case of Romanian Intellectuals in the 1930s. Leon Volovici. (Studies in Antisemitism: No. 13). 226p. 1991. 57.95 (*0-08-041024-3*, Prgamon Press) Buttrwrth-Heinemann.

Nationalist Movement in Puerto Rico. Ed. by Raoul Gordon. 1976. lib. bdg. 59.95 (*0-8490-0713-5*) Gordon Pr.

Nationalist Movements in the Maghrib: A Comparative Approach. Hassan S. Suliman. (Research Report Ser.: No. 78). 87p. 1987. 6.95 (*91-7106-266-1*, Pub. by Nordic Africa) Transaction Pubs.

Nationalist Muslim & Indian Politics. Ed. by V. N. Datta & B. E. Gleghorn. LC 75-902114. 352p. 1974. 14.00 (*0-333-90023-5*) S Asia.

Nationalist Revolutionaries in Ireland, 1858-1928. Tom Garvin. 192p. 1988. text 48.00 (*0-19-820134-6*) OUP.

Nationalist Thought & the Colonial World: A Derivative Discourse. Partha Chatterjee. 190p. (C). 1993. pap. 16.95 (*0-8166-2311-2*) U of Minn Pr.

Nationalistes Hindous see Hindu Nationalist Movement in India

Nationalistic Ideologies: Their Policy Implications & the Struggle for Democracy in African Politics. Tukumbi Lumumba-Kasongo. LC 91-27345. (African Studies: Vol. 23). 148p. 1991. lib. bdg. 69.95 (*0-7734-9696-3*) E Mellen.

Nationalists & Nomads. Miller. LC 98-33698. 1999. lib. bdg. 46.00 (*0-226-52803-0*) U Ch Pr.

Nationalists & Nomads. Miller. LC 98-33698. (Illus.). 248p. 1999. pap. text 19.00 (*0-226-52804-9*) U Ch Pr.

***Nationalists, Cosmopolitans & Popular Music in Zimbabwe.** Thomas Turino. LC 00-8067. (Studies in Ethnomusicology). 1999. pap. text 22.00 (*0-226-81702-4*) U Ch Pr.

Nationalists Myths & Ethnic Identities: Indigenous Intellectuals & the Mexican State. Contrib. by Natividad Gutierrez. LC 99-10550. (Illus.). 1999. text 50.00 (*0-8032-2177-0*); pap. text 25.00 (*0-8032-7078-X*) U of Nebr Pr.

Nationalities Question: Lenin's Approach. Ed. by Collet's Holdings, Ltd. Staff. (Library of Political Knowledge). 190p. 1983. 25.00 (*0-317-39517-3*) St Mut.

Nationalities Question in the Post-Soviet States. Graham Smith. 320p. (C). 1991. pap. text 28.50 (*0-582-03955-X*, 78610) Longman.

Nationalities Question in the Post-Soviet States. 2nd ed. Ed. by Graham Smith. 448p. (C). 1996. 76.00 (*0-582-21808-X*, 77002) Longman.

Nationalities Question in the Soviet Union. Graham Smith. 320p. (C). 1991. text 67.00 (*0-582-03953-3*, 78598) Longman.

Nationalities Question in the Soviet Union. 2nd ed. Ed. by Graham Smith. 524p. (C). 1995. pap. 33.53 (*0-582-21809-8*, 77001) Longman.

Nationality & Citizenship Handbook. Ed. by Robert A. Mautino & Gary Endelman. 130p. 1996. 49.00 (*1-878677-95-0*, 52.40) Amer Immi Law Assn.

***Nationality & Citizenship in Revolutionary France: The Treatment of Foreigners 1789-1799.** Michael Rapport. 280p. 2000. text 70.00 (*0-19-820845-6*) OUP.

Nationality & International Law in Asian Perspective. Ed. by Ko Swan Sik. (C). 1990. lib. bdg. 202.50 (*0-7923-0876-X*) Kluwer Academic.

Nationality & Planning in Scotland & Wales. Ed. by Roderick Macdonald & Huw Thomas. LC 97-187097. 312p. 1997. 65.00 (*0-7083-1398-1*, Pub. by Univ Wales Pr) Paul & Co Pubs.

Nationality & Society in Hobsburg & Ottoman Europe. Peter F. Sugar. LC 96-29908. (Collected Studies: No. CS566). 304p. 1997. 97.95 (*0-86078-629-3*, Pub. by Variorum) Ashgate Pub Co.

Nationality & Statelessness in International Law. rev. ed. P. Weis. 400p. 1979. lib. bdg. 145.00 (*90-286-0329-8*) Kluwer Academic.

Nationality Groups & Social Stratification: A Study of the Socioeconomic Status & Mobility of Selected European Nationality Groups in America. Charles B. Nam. Ed. by Francesco Cordasco. LC 80-882. (American Ethnic Groups Ser.). 1981. lib. bdg. 30.95 (*0-405-13443-6*) Ayer.

Nationality in Modern History. John H. Rose. 1977. 13.95 (*0-8369-6989-8*, 7866) Ayer.

Nationality Issue in the Hungary of 1848-49. Gy Spira. (Illus.). 255p. (C). 1992. 96.00 (*963-05-6296-0*, Pub. by Akade Kiado) St Mut.

Nationality Laws in the European Union = Le Droit de la Nationalitbe Dans l'Union Europbeenne. Bruno Nascimbene. LC 97-123863. xv, 771p. 1996. write for info. (*88-14-06139-4*) Giuffre.

Nationality, Migration Rights & Citizenship of the Union. Stephen Hall. LC 95-1061. 1995. lib. bdg. 99.50 (*0-7923-3400-0*, Pub. by M Nijhoff) Kluwer Academic.

***Nationality of Her Own: Woman, Marriage, & the Law of Citizenship.** Candice L. Bredbenner. LC 97-20734. 308p. 1998. 45.00 (*0-520-20650-9*, Pub. by U CA Pr) Cal Prin Full Svc.

Nationality, Patriotism, & Nationalism. Ed. by Roger Michener. LC 93-36087. 256p. (C). 1994. pap. text 14.95 (*0-943852-66-8*) Prof World Peace.

Nationality, Patriotism & Nationalism. Ed. by Roger Michener. LC 93-36087. 256p. 1994. text 24.95 (*0-943852-65-X*) Prof World Peace.

Nationality Question in the Soviet Union. Ed. by Gail W. Lapidus. LC 92-3618. (Articles on Russian & Soviet History, 1500-1991 Ser.: Vol. 11). 920320p. 1992. text 68.00 (*0-8153-0568-0*) Garland.

Nationality Question in the Soviet Union & Russia. Helene C. d' Encausse. (Norwegian Nobel Institute Lecture Ser.: Vol. 2). 74p. 1995. pap. 18.00 (*82-00-22432-5*) Scandnvan Univ Pr.

Nationality Rooms Book. 4th ed. E. Maxine Bruhns. 60p. 1994. pap. 6.50 (*0-9634096-0-3*) U Pitt Nat Rms & IEP.

Nationality Rooms Recipe Book. Women's International Club Staff. 250p. 1988. pap. 12.50 (*0-9634098-0-8*) Womens Int Club.

Nationalization: A Study in the Protection of Alien Property in International Law. Isi Foighel. LC 82-6263. 136p. 1982. reprint ed. lib. bdg. 59.50 (*0-8371-7675-1*, FONA, Greenwood Pr) Greenwood.

Nationalization of Civil Liberties & Civil Rights. Herbert Wechsler. LC 70-628296. (Quarterly Ser.). 1970. 8.00 (*0-87959-076-9*) U of Tex H Ransom Ctr.

Nationalization of Electric Power. fac. ed. Paul Sauriol. Tr. by Kina Buchanan. LC 64-39385. (French Canadian Renaissance Ser.: No. 3). 95p. pap. 30.00 (*0-7837-7545-8*, 204692400005) Bks Demand.

Nationalization of Hindu Traditions: Bharatendu Harishchandra & Nineteenth-Century Banaras. Vasudha Dalmia. 502p. 1999. pap. text 16.50 (*0-19-564856-0*) OUP.

Nationalization of Liberty. Frederick P. Lewis. 82p. (Orig.). (C). 1990. pap. text 13.50 (*0-8191-7763-6*) U Pr of Amer.

Nationalization of Railways in Japan. Toshiharu Watarai. LC 73-76696. (Columbia University. Studies in the Social Sciences: No. 152). 1969. reprint ed. 32.50 (*0-404-51152-X*) AMS Pr.

Nationalization of the Masses: Political Symbolism & Mass Movements in Germany, from the Napoleonic Wars Through the Third Reich. George L. Mosse. LC 91-55260. (Illus.). 272p. 1991. pap. text 16.95 (*0-8014-9978-X*) Cornell U Pr.

Nationalization of the Masses: Political Symbolism & Mass Movements in Germany, from the Napoleonic Wars Through the Third Reich. George L. Mosse. (Illus.). xiv, 272p. 2000. pap. 13.95 (*0-86527-431-2*) Fertig.

Nationalization of the Social Sciences. Ed. by Samuel Z. Klausner & Victor M. Lidz. LC 85-29630. 305p. 1986. text 52.50 (*0-8122-8015-6*) U of Pa Pr.

Nationalizing Blackness: Afrourbanismo & Artistic Revolution in Havana, 1920-1940. Robin D. Moore. LC 97-21045. (Illus.). 312p. 1997. pap. 19.95 (*0-8229-5645-4*); text 45.00 (*0-8229-4040-X*) U of Pittsburgh Pr.

Nationalizing Femininity: Culture, Sexuality & Cinema in World War Two Britain. Ed. by Christine Gledhill & Gillian Swanson. (Illus.). 288p. 1996. text 79.95 (*0-7190-4259-3*, Pub. by Manchester Univ Pr) St Martin.

Nationalizing Government: Public Policies in America. Ed. by Theodore J. Lowi & Alan Stone. LC 78-19848. (Illus.). 455p. reprint ed. pap. 141.10 (*0-8357-8493-2*, 203476700091) Bks Demand.

***Nationalizing Mortgage Risk: The Growth of Fannie Mae & Freddie Mac.** Peter J. Wallison & Bert Ely. 53p. 2000. pap. 9.95 (*0-8447-7146-5*, Pub. by Am Enterprise) Pub Resources Inc.

***Nationalizing Science: Adolphe Wurtz & the Battle for French Chemistry.** Alan J. Rocke. (Transformations Studies on the History of Science & Technology). (Illus.). 448p. (C). 2001. 39.95 (*0-262-18204-1*) MIT Pr.

Nationalizing Social Security in Europe & America. Ed. by Douglas E. Ashford et al. LC 85-23214. (Monographs in Organizational Behavior & Industrial Relations: Vol. 4). 291p. 1986. 78.50 (*0-89232-555-0*) Jai Pr.

Nationalokonomie: Theorie des Handelns und Wirtschaftens. Ludwig Von Mises. (International Carl Menger Library). xvi, 756p. 1980. reprint ed. pap. 65.00 (*3-88405-023-0*) Philosophia Pr.

Nationalokonomie an den Universitaten Freiburg, Heidelberg & Tubingen 1918-1945: Eine Institutionenhistorische, Vergleichende Studie der Wirtschaftswissenschaftlichen Fakultaten & Abteilungen Sudwestdeutscher Universitaten. Klaus-Rainer Brintzinger. (GER.). 401p. 1996. 63.95 (*3-631-49965-5*) P Lang Pubng.

***Nationals & Expatriates: Population & Labour Dilemmas for the Gulf Cooperation Countries.** Andrzej Kapiszewski. 252p. 2000. 62.00 (*0-86372-275-X*, Pub. by Garnet-Ithaca) LPC InBook.

Nationalsim & Culture Vol. 11: Gabriele D'Annunzio & Italy after the Risorgimento. Jared M. Becker. LC 93-16377. (Studies in Italian Culture: Vol. 11). 226p. (C). 1995. text 46.95 (*0-8204-2085-9*) P Lang Pubng.

Nationalsozialismus. Studien zur Ideologie und Herrschaft. Ed. by Wolfgang Benz et al. (GER.). 272p. 1993. pap. 22.50 (*3-596-11984-7*, Pub. by Fischer Tasch) Intl Bk Import.

Nationalsozialistische Massent Otungen Durch Giftgas see Nazi Mass Murder by Poison Gas: A Documentary Account

Nationbuilding & the Politics of Nationalism: Essays on Austrian Galicia. Ed. by Andrei S. Markovits & Frank E. Sysyn. LC 80-53800. (Harvard Ukrainian Research Institute Monograph). 345p. 1990. pap. text 18.00 (*0-674-60312-5*) Harvard Ukrainian.

Nationhood & Political Theory. Margaret Canovan. LC 95-31939. 168p. 1996. 75.00 (*1-85278-852-6*) E Elgar.

***Nationhood & Political Theory.** Margaret Canovan. 168p. 1998. pap. 20.00 (*1-84064-011-1*) E Elgar.

Nationhood from the Schoolbag: A Historical Analysis of the Development of Secondary Education in Trinidad & Tobago. Michael H. Alleyne. LC 95-50786. (Coleccion INTERAMER Ser.: No. 63). 1995. write for info. (*0-8270-3591-8*) OAS.

Nations: A Simulation Game in International Politics. Michael Herzig & David Skidmore. (Pew Case Studies in International Affairs). 50p. (C). 1995. text 3.50 (*1-56927-169-0*) Geo U Inst Dplmcy.

***Nations: Nationality & the European Revolutions of 1848.** Robert J. Bezucha. 2001. pap. 10.95 (*0-312-17217-6*) St Martin.

Nations Africaines et Solidarite Mondiale see African Nations & World Solidarity

Nations Against State: A New Approach to Ethnic Conflicts, the Decline of Sovereignty, & the Dilemmas of Collective Security. Gidon Gottlieb. 148p. 1993. pap. 14.95 (*0-87609-156-7*) Coun Foreign.

***Nations & Cultures in European Higher Education: Universities Remembering Europe.** Ed. by Francis Crawley et al. LC 99-45863. 256p. 2000. 69.95 (*1-57181-957-6*) Berghahn Bks.

Nations & Governments. 2nd ed. Thomas M. Magstadt. 1994. pap. text, teacher ed. 5.00 (*0-312-09557-0*) St Martin.

Nations & Governments. 3rd ed. Thomas M. Magstadt. LC 97-65173. 608p. 1997. pap. text 56.95 (*0-312-15396-1*) St Martin.

Nations & Men: An Introduction to International Politics. 3rd ed. Ivo D. Duchacek. LC 81-40916. 608p. 1982. reprint ed. pap. text 39.00 (*0-8191-2260-2*) U Pr of Amer.

Nations & Nationalism. Ernest Gellner. LC 83-71199. 170p. 1983. pap. text 11.95 (*0-8014-9263-7*) Cornell U Pr.

Nations & Nationalism in a Global Era. Anthony D. Smith. 160p. (C). 1996. pap. text 20.95 (*0-7456-1019-6*, Pub. by Polity Pr) Blackwell Pubs.

***Nations & States, set of 4, 4.** Diagram Group Staff. (Timelines on File Ser.). 249p. 2000. 125.00 (*0-8160-4307-8*) Facts on File.

Nations & States: A Geographic Background to World Affairs. Thomas M. Poulsen. LC 94-13925. 480p. 1994. text 41.80 (*0-13-678913-7*) P-H.

Nations & States: An Enquiry into the Origins of Nations & the Politics of Nationalism. Hugh Seton-Watson. 563p. 1977. pap. text 99.90 (*0-89158-227-4*) Westview.

Nations & States in Southeast Asia. Nicholas Tarling. LC 97-29973. (Illus.). 146p. (C). 1998. text 59.95 (*0-521-62245-X*); pap. text 17.95 (*0-521-62564-5*) Cambridge U Pr.

Nations & the United Nations. Robert M. MacIver. LC 74-7382. (National Studies on International Organization-Carnegie Endowment for International Peace). (Illus.). 186p. 1974. reprint ed. lib. bdg. 55.00 (*0-8371-7535-6*, MANU) Greenwood.

Nations Are Built of Babies: Saving Ontario's Mothers & Children, 1900-1940. Cynthia R. Comacchio. (Illus.). 360p. 1993. 60.00 (*0-7735-0991-7*, Pub. by McG-Queens Univ Pr) CUP Services.

"Nations Are Built of Babies" Saving Ontario's Mothers & Children, 1900-1940. Cynthia R. Comacchio. (Illus.). 352p. 1998. pap. text 22.95 (*0-7735-1770-7*, Pub. by McG-Queens Univ Pr) CUP Services.

Nations at Dawn. 6th ed. John G. Stoessinger. LC 93-30898. 336p. (C). 1994. 30.31 (*0-07-061626-4*) McGraw.

Nations at Risk: The Impact of the Computer Revolution. Edward Yourdon. LC 85-22618. (Illus.). 500p. 1986. 19.95 (*0-917072-04-9*, Yourdon) P-H.

Nations at the Crossroads: Unification Policies for Germany, Korea & China. Diane D. Pikcunas. LC 92-47227. (Journal of Social, Political & Economic Studies: No. 22). 96p. (C). 1993. pap. text 10.00 (*0-930690-51-6*) Coun Soc Econ.

Nations at War: A Scientific Study of International Conflict. Daniel S. Geller & J. David Singer. LC 97-10267. (Studies in International Relations: No. 58). 260p. (C). 1998. text 59.95 (*0-521-62119-4*); pap. text 18.95 (*0-521-62906-3*) Cambridge U Pr.

Nations Before Nationalism. John A. Armstrong. LC 81-12988. 447p. reprint ed. pap. 138.60 (*0-7837-0287-6*, 204060800018) Bks Demand.

Nations Behind the Iron Curtain: A History of Eastern Europe. rev. ed. Henry Bogdan. Ed. by Istvan Fehervary. Tr. by Jean P. Fleming from FRE. (Illus.). 420p. (Orig.). (C). 1988. 20.50 (*0-317-93036-2*); pap. 16.00 (*0-317-93037-0*) Pro Libertate Pub.

Nations Best Schools, 2 vols. write for info. (*0-8108-3784-6*) Scarecrow.

Nation's Best Schools Vol. 1: Blueprints for Excellence: Elementary & Middle Schools. Evelyn H. Ogden & Vito Germinario. LC 94-60605. 365p. 1998. 44.95 (*1-56676-148-4*) Scarecrow.

Nation's Best Schools Vol. 2: Blueprints for Excellence: Middle & Secondary Schools. Evelyn H. Ogden & Vito Germinario. LC 94-60605. 445p. 1995. text 44.95 (*1-56676-278-2*) Scarecrow.

Nation's Children, 3 vols. in 1. Ed. by Eli Ginzberg. 750p. 1987. pap. 29.95 (*0-88738-676-8*) Transaction Pubs.

Nations, Cultures & Markets: Papers in Applied Psychology. Ed. by Paul Gilbert & Paul Gregory. (Avebury Series in Philosophy). 192p. 1994. 72.95 (*1-85628-695-9*, Pub. by Avebry) Ashgate Pub Co.

Nation's Diet: The Social Science of Food Choice. Anne Murcott. LC 98-11982. 1998. write for info. (*0-582-30285-4*) Addison-Wesley.

Nation's Families: 1960-1990. George Masnick & Mary J. Bane. LC 80-20531. (Illus.). 181p. (Orig.). (C). 1980. 29.95 (*0-86569-050-2*, Auburn Hse); pap. 21.95 (*0-86569-051-0*, Auburn Hse) Greenwood.

Nation's Favourite: The True Adventures of Radio One. Simon Garfield. (Illus.). 240p. 1999. pap. 11.95 (*0-571-19435-4*, Pub. by Faber & Faber) Penguin Books.

***Nation's Favourite Comic Poems: A Selection of Humorous Verse, Vol. 1.** Griff Rhys Jones. 176p. 1999. pap. 9.95 (*0-563-38451-4*, BBC-Parkwest) Parkwest Pubns.

Nation's Future Materials Needs: International SAMPE Technical Conference, 19th, Hyatt Hotel, Crystal City, Virginia, October 13-15, 1987. International SAMPE Technical Conference Staff et al. Ed. by Ted Lynch. LC 88-112891. (International SAMPE Technical Conference Ser.: No. 19). 788p. reprint ed. pap. 200.00 (*0-7837-1293-6*, 204143400020) Bks Demand.

Nation's Great Library: Herbert Putnam & the Library of Congress. Jane A. Rosenberg. LC 92-37287. 256p. (C). 1993. text 39.95 (*0-252-02001-4*) U of Ill Pr.

Nation's Hangar: The Aircraft Study Collection of the National Air & Space Museum. Robert Van der Linden. (Illus.). 176p. Date not set. 39.95 (*1-57427-084-2*) Howell Pr VA.

***Nation's Health.** Philip R. Lee & Carroll L. Estes. LC 00-22254. 2000. write for info. (*0-7637-1286-8*) Jones & Bartlett.

Nation's Health. 3rd ed. Philip R. Lee & Carroll L. Estes. 576p. 1990. pap. 37.50 (*0-86720-428-1*) Jones & Bartlett.

Nation's Health. 4th ed. Ed. by Philip R. Lee & Carroll L. Estes. LC 93-41200. 432p. 1994. pap. 46.25 (*0-86720-840-6*) Jones & Bartlett.

Nation's Health. 5th ed. Philip R. Lee et al. LC 97-5162. (Health Science Ser.). 448p. 1997. pap. 52.00 (*0-7637-0405-9*) Jones & Bartlett.

Nation's Health: A Strategy for the 1990s. Ed. by Alwyn Smith & Bobbie Jacobsen. 352p. 1988. pap. 29.95 (*0-19-724647-8*) OUP.

Nations, Identities, Cultures. V. Y. Mudimbe. 1995. pap. text 10.00 (*0-8223-6428-X*) Duke.

Nations, Identities, Cultures. Ed. by V. Y. Mudimbe. LC 97-20054. 240p. 1997. pap. text 15.95 (*0-8223-2065-7*); lib. bdg. 45.95 (*0-8223-2052-5*) Duke.

Nations, Identity, Power. George Schopflin. LC 98-24516. 320p. 1999. text 38.00 (*0-8147-8117-9*) NYU Pr.

An Asterisk (*) at the beginning of an entry indicates that the title is appearing for the first time.

Nations in Alliance: The Limits of Interdependence. George Liska. LC 62-14359. 313p. reprint ed. pap. 97.10 (*0-8357-8242-5*, 203414600088) Bks Demand.

Nations in Deutero-Isaiah: A Study on Composition & Structure. Andrew Wilson. LC 86-21790. (Ancient Near Eastern Texts & Studies: Vol. 1). 360p. 1986. lib. bdg. 99.95 (*0-88946-086-8*) E Mellen.

Nations in Prophecy. John F. Walvoord. 1967. pap. 7.70 (*0-310-34101-9*, 12159P) Zondervan.

Nations in Public. Gerald Burns. LC PS3552.B8. (Salt Lick Samplers Ser.). 12p. 1975. reprint ed. pap. 30.00 (*0-7837-9158-5*, 204985800003) Bks Demand.

***Nations in Transit 1998: Civil Society, Democracy & Markets in East Central Europe & the Newly Independent States.** Adrian Karatnycky et al. LC 98-50279. 4p. 1999. write for info. (*0-7658-0623-1*) Transaction Pubs.

Nations in Transit, 1997: Civil Society, Democracy & Markets in East Central Europe & the Newly Independent States. Ed. by Adrian Karatnycky et al. LC 97-13779. 418p. 1997. pap. 49.95 (*0-7658-0411-5*) Transaction Pubs.

Nation[0012]s Investment in Cancer Research: A Budget Proposal for Fiscal Years 1997/98. 80p. pap. text. write for info. (*0-7881-8995-6*) DIANE Pub.

***Nation's Library: The Library of Congress.** Alan Bisbort & Linda Barrett Osborne. (Illus.). 144p. 2000. pap. 16.95 (*1-85759-235-2*, Pub. by Scala Books) Antique Collect.

***Nation's Library: The Library of Congress, Washington, D.C.** Library of Congress Staff et al. LC 00-24286. 2000. write for info. (*0-8444-1014-4*) Lib Congress.

Nations Mightier & More Numerous. Edwin C. Hostetter. LC 95-34936. (Dissertation Ser.: Vol. 3). 192p. 1995. pap. 12.95 (*0-941037-36-3*, BIBAL Press) D & F Scott.

Nations, Nationalities Peoples: A Study of the Nationality Policies of the Communist Party in Soviet Moldavia. Michael Bruchis. 230p. 1984. text 55.50 (*0-88033-057-0*, Pub. by East Eur Monographs) Col U Pr.

Nation's Navy: In Quest of Canadian Naval Identity. Ed. by Michael L. Hadley et al. LC 98-123953. (Illus.). 496p. 1992. 49.95 (*0-7735-1506-2*, Pub. by McG-Queens Univ Pr) CUP Services.

Nations Not Obsessed with Crime. Freda Adler. (Wayne State University Law School Comparative Criminal Law Project Publications Ser.: Vol. 15). xx, 204p. 1983. 32.50 (*0-8377-0216-X*, Rothman) W S Hein.

Nations of Africa. Diagram Group Staff. LC 96-38734. (Peoples of Africa Ser.). (Illus.). 112p. (YA). (gr. 6-12). 1997. 19.95 (*0-8160-3488-5*) Facts on File.

Nations of Immigrants: Australia, the United States & International Migration. Ed. by Gary P. Freeman & James Jupp. 264p. (C). 1993. pap. text 19.95 (*0-19-553483-2*, 14368) OUP.

Nations of the Earth Report: United Conference on Environment & Development, Vol. I. 285p. (Orig.). 50.00 (*92-1-100483-7*) UN.

Nations of the Earth Report: United Conference on Environment & Development, Vol. II. 285p. (Orig.). 50.00 (*92-1-100484-5*) UN.

Nations of the Earth Report: United Conference on Environment & Development, Vol. III. 518p. (Orig.). 50.00 (*92-1-100485-3*) UN.

***Nations of the Night.** Oliver Johnson. LC 98-24273. (Lightbringer Trilogy Ser.). 416p. 1998. pap. 16.95 (*0-451-45566-5*) NAL.

***Nations of the Night.** Oliver Johnson. (Lightbringer Trilogy Ser.: Vol. 2). 2000. mass mkt. 6.99 (*0-451-45644-0*, ROC) NAL.

***Nations of the World.** Raintree Steck-Vaughn Publishing Staff. 2000. 31.40 (*0-8172-5787-X*) Raintree Steck-V.

Nations Oil: A Story of Control. G. Corti & F. Frazer. 237p. 1983. lib. bdg. 64.50 (*0-86010-437-0*) G & T Inc.

Nation's Party Concept. Jack W. Boone. 229p. 1993. pap. 9.95 (*1-880719-01-0*) Grafco Prods.

Nation's Physician Workforce: Options for Balancing Supply & Requirements. Institute of Medicine Staff. Ed. by Kathleen N. Lohr et al. 1996. pap. text 22.00 (*0-309-05431-1*) Natl Acad Pr.

Nations Remembered: An Oral History of the Cherokees, Chickasaws, Choctaws, Creeks. Theda Perdue. LC 92-50726. (Illus.). 246p. 1993. pap. 14.95 (*0-8061-2523-3*) U of Okla Pr.

Nations Remembered: An Oral History of the Five Civilized Tribes, 1865-1907, 1. Theda Perdue. LC 79-6828. (Contributions in Ethnic Studies: No. 1). 221p. 1980. 55.00 (*0-313-22097-2*, PFN/, Greenwood Pr) Greenwood.

Nations Rise & Fall: Why? S. Abul Ala Maududi. 36p. (Orig.). 1985. pap. 3.00 (*1-56744-345-1*) Kazi Pubns.

Nation's Shame: Fatal Child Abuse & Neglect in the U. S. (Illus.). 308p. 1995. pap. text 55.00 (*1-57979-200-6*) DIANE Pub.

Nation's Shame: Fatal Child Abuse & Neglect in the U. S. Jill Stewart. (Illus.). 248p. 1996. reprint ed. pap. text 40.00 (*0-7881-3326-8*) DIANE Pub.

Nation's Shame: Fatal Child Abuse & Neglect in the United States. 1997. lib. bdg. 250.99 (*0-8490-8245-5*) Gordon Pr.

Nations That Know Thee Not: Ancient Jewish Attitudes Towards Other Religions. Robert Goldenberg. (Biblical Seminar Ser.: Vol. 52). 215p. 1998. pap. 23.75 (*1-85075-842-5*, Pub. by Sheffield Acad) CUP Services.

***Nation's Tortured Body: Violence, Representation & the Formation of a Sikh "Diaspora"** Brian Keith Axel. LC 00-29399. (Illus.). 376p. 2000. pap. write for info. (*0-8223-2615-9*) Duke.

***Nation's Tortured Body: Violence, Representation, & the Formation of a Sikh "Diaspora"** Brian Keith Axel. LC 00-29399. (Illus.). 376p. 2000. lib. bdg. 64.95 (*0-8223-2607-8*) Duke.

Nations Unbound: Transnational Projects, Postcolonial Predicaments, & Deterritorialized Nation-States. Linda Basch et al. LC 93-28765. 344p. 1993. text 55.00 (*2-88124-607-9*); pap. text 27.00 (*2-88124-630-3*) Gordon & Breach.

Nation's Voice. Timmerman. (C). 1994. pap. text, teacher ed. 33.75 (*0-15-502188-5*) Harcourt Coll Pubs.

Nation's Voice: An Anthology of American Short Fiction. Ed. by John Timmerman. LC 94-19007. 864p. (Orig.). (C). 1994. pap. text 39.00 (*0-15-501220-7*, Pub. by Harcourt Coll Pubs) Harcourt.

Nations Within: Aboriginal-State Relations in Canada, the United States & New Zealand. Jean L. Elliott & Augie Fleras. (Illus.). 224p. 1992. pap. text 24.00 (*0-19-540754-7*) OUP.

Nations Within: The Past & Future of American Indian Sovereignty. rev. ed. Vine Deloria, Jr. & Clifford M. Lytle. LC 97-33718. 296p. 1998. pap. 12.95 (*0-292-71598-6*, DELNAP) U of Tex Pr.

Nations Within a Nation: Historical Statistics of American Indians. Paul Stuart. LC 86-33618. 261p. 1987. lib. bdg. 62.95 (*0-313-23813-8*, SNA/, Greenwood Pr) Greenwood.

Nations Without Nationalism. Julia Kristeva. Ed. by Lawrence D. Kritzman & Richard Wolin. Tr. by Leon S. Roudiez from FRE. LC 92-23568. (European Perspectives Ser.).Tr. of Lettre Ouverte a Harlem Desir. 112p. (C). 1993. 21.50 (*0-231-08104-9*) Col U Pr.

Nations Without States: A Historical Dictionary of Contemporary National Movements. James Minahan. LC 95-6626. 720p. 1996. lib. bdg. 99.50 (*0-313-28354-0*, Praeger Pubs) Greenwood.

***Nations Without States: Political Communities in a Global Age.** Montserrat Guibernau. LC 99-22431. 208p. (C). 1999. pap. text 26.95 (*0-7456-1801-4*, Pub. by Polity Pr) Blackwell Pubs.

Nations Without States: Political Communities in a Global Age. Montserrat Guibernau. LC 99-22431. 208p. 1999. text 59.95 (*0-7456-1800-6*, Pub. by Polity Pr) Blackwell Pubs.

Nationwide Competition for Votes. McAllister. 1992. text 42.50 (*0-86187-383-1*) St Martin.

Nationwide Medical Transcription Service Directory, 1998: The Most Comprehensive Published Listing of Medical Transcription Service Professionals in the United States. Compiled by Denise M. Schultheis. 448p. 1998. pap. 24.95 (*1-877810-67-3*) Rayve Prodns.

***Nationwide Personal Transportation Survey Symposium Proceedings.** Ed. by Gloria J. Jeff. (Illus.). 239p. (C). 1999. pap. text 45.00 (*0-7881-8309-5*) DIANE Pub.

Nationwide Survey of Civil Engineering Related R&D: Prepared by the Civil Engineering Research Foundation. Civil Engineering Research Foundation. LC 93-5108. 64p. 1993. 7.00 (*0-87262-970-8*) Am Soc Civil Eng.

Nationwide Television Studies David Morley & Charlotte Brunsdon. LC 99-20335. (Research in Cultural & Media Studies). ix, 326 p. 1999. write for info. (*0-415-14879-0*) Routledge.

Native. William H. Henderson. LC 93-45423. 256p. 1994. pap. 9.95 (*0-452-27139-8*, Plume) Dutton Plume.

Native Accounts of Nootka Ethnography. Edward Sapir & Morris Swadesh. LC 74-7999. reprint ed. 55.00 (*0-404-11892-5*) AMS Pr.

Native Administration in Nigeria. Margery F. Perham. LC 74-15078. reprint ed. 32.50 (*0-404-12127-6*) AMS Pr.

Native Air. large type ed. Sarah Woodhouse. 1991. 27.99 (*0-7089-8604-8*, Charnwood) Ulverscroft.

Native Ameican Religon. Joel W. Martin. LC 98-50155. 160p. (YA). 1999. lib. bdg. 22.00 (*0-19-511035-8*) OUP.

Native America. Insight Guides Staff. (Insight Guides). 1998. pap. text 21.95 (*0-88729-722-6*) Langenscheidt.

Native America: Arts, Traditions, & Celebrations. Christine Mather. (Illus.). 1990. 40.00 (*0-517-57436-5*) C Potter.

Native America: Portrait of a People. Duane Champagne. (Illus.). 786p. 1994. 18.95 (*0-8103-9452-9*, 089204) Visible Ink Pr.

Native America & the Evolution of Democracy: A Supplementary Bibliography, 40. Compiled by Bruce E. Johansen. LC 98-33136. (Bibliographies & Indexes in American History Ser.: Vol. 40). 184p. 1999. lib. bdg. 65.00 (*0-313-31010-6*) Greenwood.

Native America in the Twentieth Century: An Encyclopedia. Ed. by Mary B. Davis. LC 94-768. (Illus.). 832p. 1994. text 100.00 (*0-8240-4846-6*, 452) Garland.

Native America in the Twentieth Century: An Encyclopedia. Ed. by Mary B. Davis. LC 94-768. (Illus.). 832p. 1996. pap. text 29.95 (*0-8153-2583-5*) Garland.

Native America Medicine: Indians of North America. Chelsea House Publishing Staff. LC 97-11427. (Indians of North America Ser.). 120p. (YA). (gr. 5 up). 1997. pap. 9.95 (*0-7910-4464-5*) Chelsea Hse.

***Native America on the Eve of Conquest.** Suzanne Strauss Art. (Story of the First Americans Ser.: Vol. 2). (Illus.). 232p. (YA). (gr. 6-9). 2000. 12.95 (*0-9656557-9-2*) Pemblewick Pr.

***Native America Today: A Guide to Community Politics & Culture.** Barry M. Pritzker. LC 99-52306. 453p. 1999. lib. bdg. 75.00 (*1-57607-077-8*) ABC-CLIO.

***Native American, 4 bks.** Incl. Indians of the Great Plains: Tradition, History, Legends & Life. Lisa Sita. LC 99-58217. (Illus.). 64p. (J). (gr. 5). 2000. lib. bdg. 23.93 (*0-8368-2645-0*); Indians of the Northeast: Traditions, History, Legends & Life. Lisa Sita. LC 99-58218. (Illus.). 64p. (YA). (gr. 5 up). 2000. lib. bdg. 23.93 (*0-8368-2646-9*); Indians of the Northwest: Traditions, History, Legends & Life. Petra Press. 64p. (J). 1999. lib. bdg. 23.93 (*0-8368-2647-7*); Indians of the Southwest: Traditions, History, Legends & Life. Lisa Sita. LC 99-58220. 64p. (J). 2000. lib. bdg. 23.93 (*0-8368-2648-5*); (Illus.). (YA). (gr. 5 up). 1999. Set lib. bdg. 95.72 (*0-8368-2644-2*) Gareth Stevens Inc.

Native American: Bright Eyes. Lynell Johnson. (Graphic Learning Multicultural Literature Program Ser.). (ENG & SPA., Illus.). (J). (gr. k-5). 1994. teacher ed. 45.00 (*0-87746-437-5*) Graphic Learning.

Native American: How the Hopi Stopped the Wind. Retold by K. Hollenbeck. (Graphic Learning Multicultural Literature Program Ser.). (ENG & SPA., Illus.). (J). (gr. k-5). 1994. teacher ed. 45.00 (*0-87746-446-4*) Graphic Learning.

Native American: Strong Wind & Gentle Maiden. Retold by K. Hollenbeck. (Graphic Learning Multicultural Literature Program Ser.). (ENG & SPA., Illus.). (J). (gr. k-5). 1994. teacher ed. 45.00 (*0-87746-443-X*) Graphic Learning.

Native American: When Coyote Stole Fire. Retold by Beth Lyons. (Graphic Learning Multicultural Literature Program Ser.). (ENG & SPA., Illus.). (J). (gr. k-5). 1994. teacher ed. 45.00 (*0-87746-440-5*) Graphic Learning.

Native American Activity Book: Arts, Crafts, Cooking & Historical Aids. abr. ed. Linda Milliken. Ed. by Kathy Rogers. (Illus.). 48p. 1980. pap., wbk. ed. 6.95 (*1-56472-000-4*) Edupress Inc.

Native American Affairs & the Department of Defense. Donald Mitchell & David Rubenson. LC 95-52248. 80p. (Orig.). 1996. pap. text 15.00 (*0-8330-2351-9*, MR-630-OSD) Rand Corp.

Native American Aliens: Disloyalty & the Renunciation of Citizenship by Japanese Americans During World War II, 32. Donald E. Collins. LC 84-25239. (Contributions in Legal Studies: No. 32). (Illus.). 218p. 1985. 62.95 (*0-313-24711-0*, CNA/) Greenwood.

Native American Almanac. 353p. 1999. 14.95 (*0-02-863003-3*, Pub. by Macmillan) S&S Trade.

Native American Anarchism. Eunice M. Schuster. LC 75-155100. reprint ed. 37.50 (*0-404-05624-5*) AMS Pr.

Native American Anarchism. Eunice M. Schuster. LC 79-98688. (American Scene, Comments & Commentators Ser.). 1970. reprint ed. lib. bdg. 27.50 (*0-306-71838-3*) Da Capo.

Native American Ancestors: Eastern Tribes. Arlene H. Eakle & Linda E. Brinkerhoff. 50p. 1996. pap. 16.50 (*0-940764-69-5*) Genealog Inst.

Native American & Spanish Colonial Experience in the Greater Southwest, Vol. 1: Introduction to the Documentary Records. Ed. by David H. Snow. LC 92-15904. (Spanish Borderlands Sourcebooks Ser.: Vol. 9). 512p. 1992. text 30.00 (*0-8240-0989-4*) Garland.

Native American & Spanish Colonial Experience in the Greater Southwest, Vol. 2: Introduction to Research. Ed. by David H. Snow. LC 92-15904. (Spanish Borderlands Sourcebooks Ser.: Vol. 10). 528p. 1992. text 35.00 (*0-8240-0779-4*) Garland.

Native American Animal Stories. Joseph Bruchac. LC 92-53040. (Illus.). 140p. 1992. pap. 12.95 (*1-55591-127-7*) Fulcrum Pub.

Native American Animal Stories. Joseph Bruchac. LC 92-53040. 1992. 18.05 (*0-606-06610-1*, Pub. by Turtleback) Demco.

Native American Answer Book. Ed. by Reed Ueda & Sandra Stotsky. (Ethnic Answer Bks.). (Illus.). 136p. (YA). (gr. 5 up). 1999. pap. 8.95 (*0-7910-4792-X*); lib. bdg. 17.95 (*0-7910-4791-1*) Chelsea Hse.

Native American Anthology. Power. 1997. 15.95 (*0-8050-5092-2*) H Holt & Co.

Native American Antiquities & Linguistics. Justin Winsor. Ed. by Henry Paolucci & Anne A. Paolucci. (Review of National Literatures Ser.: Vol. 19). 256p. 1995. pap. 14.95 (*0-918680-49-2*) Griffon House.

Native American Architecture. Peter Nabokov & Robert Easton. (Illus.). 432p. 1988. 65.00 (*0-19-503781-2*) OUP.

Native American Architecture. Peter Nabokov & Robert Easton. (Illus.). 432p. 1990. pap. 35.00 (*0-19-506665-0*) OUP.

Native American Archives: An Introduction. John A. Fleckner. 72p. (Orig.). 1985. pap. text 7.00 (*0-931828-66-X*) Soc Am Archivists.

***Native American Art.** William C. Ketchum. (Illus.). 1998. 16.95 (*1-57717-036-9*) Todtri Prods.

Native American Art. National Museum of American Indian Art Staff. 1997. 8.95 (*0-88363-945-9*) H L Levin.

Native American Art. David W. Penney & George C. Longfish. (Illus.). 320p. 1999. 40.00 (*0-88363-479-1*) H L Levin.

***Native American Art: The Collections of the Ethnological Museum Berlin.** Peter Bolz & Hans-Ulrich Sanner. (Illus.). 240p. 2000. pap. 40.00 (*0-295-97954-2*) U of Wash Pr.

Native American Art & the New York Avante-Garde: A History of Cultural Primitivism. W. Jackson Rushing. Ed. by William H. Goetzmann. LC 94-14250. (American Studies). (Illus.). 288p. (C). 1995. text 39.95 (*0-292-75547-3*) U of Tex Pr.

Native American Art in the Twentieth Century. W. Jackson Rushing. LC 98-48803. (Illus.). 1999. 85.00 (*0-415-13747-0*) Routledge.

Native American Art in the Twentieth Century: Makers, Meanings & Histories. Ed. by W. Jackson Rushing. LC 98-48803. (Illus.). 214p. 1999. pap. 29.99 (*0-415-13748-9*) Routledge.

Native American Art Look Book: An Activity Book from the Brooklyn Museum. Dawn Weiss. LC 95-36245. 1996. 15.95 (*1-56584-022-4*, Pub. by New Press NY) Norton.

Native American Art Masterpieces. David W. Penney. LC 97-140157. (Illus.). 120p. 1996. 35.00 (*0-88363-496-1*) S&S Trade.

Native American Art of the Southwest. Linda B. Eaton. (Illus.). 160p. 1993. 24.95 (*1-56173-279-6*, 3311900) Pubns Intl Ltd.

Native American Art, Selections from the Torrence Collection. James T. Demetrion. LC 84-70388. (Illus.). 47p. 1984. pap. 10.00 (*0-614-31045-8*) Edmundson.

***Native American Arts & Crafts.** Colin F. Taylor. (Illus.). 2000. 14.99 (*0-7858-1204-0*) Bk Sales Inc.

Native American Arts & Culture. Mary Connors & Dona Herweck. (Illus.). 1994. 14.95 (*1-55734-619-4*) Tchr Create Mat.

Native American Arts & Cultures. Anne D'Alleva. LC 93-73931. (Arts & Cultures Ser.). (Illus.). 136p. 1994. 25.95 (*0-87192-248-7*) Davis Mass.

***Native American Arts & Cultures: Grades 4-8.** Ellen L. Kronowitz & Barbara Wally. (Illus.). 96p. 2000. pap., teacher ed. 11.95 (*1-57690-590-X*, TCM 2590) Tchr Create Mat.

Native American Astronomy. Ed. by Anthony F. Aveni. LC 78-53569. 302p. reprint ed. pap. 93.70 (*0-608-17843-8*, 203260500080) Bks Demand.

Native American Autobiography: An Anthology. Ed. by Arnold Krupat. LC 93-39068. (Wisconsin Studies in American Autobiography). (Illus.). 560p. 1994. 49.95 (*0-299-14020-2*); pap. 23.95 (*0-299-14024-5*) U of Wis Pr.

Native American Basketry. Sarah P. Turnbaugh. (Illus.). 1992. pap. 20.00 (*0-9628074-2-7*) Hurst Gal.

Native American Basketry: An Annotated Bibliography, 10. Compiled by Frank W. Porter, III. LC 87-37570. (Art Reference Collection Ser.: No. 10). 249p. 1988. lib. bdg. 55.00 (*0-313-25363-3*, PBY/, Greenwood Pr) Greenwood.

Native American Basketry of Central California see Basketry of the Indians of California

Native American Basketry of Southern California see Basketry of the Indians of California

Native American Basketry of the Seneca & Tlingit. Ed. by Richard C. Schneider. (Illus.). 120p. 1995. reprint ed. pap. 8.95 (*0-936984-14-7*) Schneider Pubs.

Native American Beaded Friendship Bracelets. Troll Associates Staff. (J). 1995. pap. 6.95 (*0-8167-3834-3*) Troll Communs.

Native American Beadwork. Georg J. Barth. LC 91-60320. (Illus.). 219p. (Orig.). 1993. 27.95 (*0-936984-13-9*); pap. 19.95 (*0-936984-12-0*) Schneider Pubs.

Native American Biographies, 6 vols. (Illus.). (YA). (gr. 6 up). 1997. lib. bdg. 113.70 (*0-89490-965-7*) Enslow Pubs.

Native American Biography. Globe. 1994. text, teacher ed. write for info. (*0-8359-0615-9*) Globe Fearon.

Native American Book of Change. White. (Native American Legends Ser.). 1992. 10.05 (*0-606-05504-5*, Pub. by Turtleback) Demco.

Native American Book of Change. White Deer of Autumn Staff. LC 92-17001. (Native People, Native Ways Ser.: Vol. 3). (Illus.). 96p. 1992. pap. 5.95 (*0-941831-73-6*) Beyond Words Pub.

Native American Book of Knowledge. White Deer of Autumn Staff. Ed. by Michelle Roehm. (Native People, Native Ways Ser.: Vol. I). (Illus.). 88p. (J). (gr. 5-7). 1992. pap. 5.95 (*0-941831-42-6*) Beyond Words Pub.

Native American Book of Life. White Deer of Autumn Staff. Ed. by Michelle Roehm & Shonto W. Begay. (Native People, Native Ways Ser.: Vol. II). (Illus.). 85p. (J). (gr. 5-7). 1992. pap. 5.95 (*0-941831-43-4*) Beyond Words Pub.

Native American Book of Wisdom. White Deer of Autumn. LC 92-17002. (Native People, Native Ways Ser.: Vol. 4). (Illus.). 96p. (YA). (gr. 5 up). 1992. pap. 5.95 (*0-941831-74-4*) Beyond Words Pub.

Native American Bows. 2nd ed. T. M. Hamilton. LC 82-81155. (Special Publications: No. 5). 1982. reprint ed. pap. 10.00 (*0-943414-00-8*) MO Arch Soc.

Native American Chiefs & Warriors. Deanne Durrett & Stuart A. Kallen. LC 99-13227. (History Makers Ser.). (Illus.). 112p. (YA). (gr. 4 up). 1999. lib. bdg. 17.96 (*1-56006-364-5*) Lucent Bks.

Native American Collectibles: Identification & Price Guide. Dawn E. Reno. 538p. (Orig.). 1994. pap. 17.00 (*0-380-77069-5*, Avon Bks) Morrow Avon.

Native American Colleges: Progress & Prospects. Corporate Publication Staff. LC 97-13002. 100p. (Orig.). 1997. pap. 10.00 (*0-931050-63-4*) Carnegie Fnd Advan Teach.

Native American Communities in Wisconsin, 1600-1960. Robert E. Bieder. LC 94-24314. (Illus.). 272p. (C). 1995. pap. text 18.95 (*0-299-14524-7*); lib. bdg. 39.95 (*0-299-14520-4*) U of Wis Pr.

***Native American Costumes Paper Dolls.** Charlotte Whatley. (Illus.). 32p. 1999. 4.95 (*0-87588-369-9*) Hobby Hse.

Native American Courtship & Marriage Traditions. Leslie Gourse. LC 99-55832. 160p. 1999. 22.50 (*0-7818-0768-9*) Hippocrene Bks.

Native American Coyote Stories. Michael Lacapa. 1996. 12.00 incl. audio (*0-9666415-0-7*, SBP001) Sage Prod AZ.

Native American Craft Inspirations. Janet D'Amato & Alex D'Amato. LC 92-35721. (Illus.). 224p. 1992. pap. 11.95 (*0-87131-707-9*) M Evans.

Native American Crafts. Suzanne McNeill. 1997. write for info. (*0-8069-9952-7*) Sterling.

***Native American Crafts & Skills.** David Montgomery. (Illus.). 2000. pap. 14.95 (*1-58574-070-5*) Lyons Pr.

Native American Crafts Directory: A Guide for Locating Craft Shops & Craft Suppliers. 2nd ed. Diane L. McAlister. LC 98-16036. 1998. 9.95 (*1-57067-058-7*) Book Pub Co.

Native American Crafts of California, the Great Basin, & the Southwest. Judith Hoffman-Corwin. LC 98-31449. 1999. write for info. (*0-531-11339-6*) Watts.

N

***Native American Crafts of the Northwest Coast, the Arctic & the Subarctic.** Judith Hoffman-Corwin. LC 98-31471. 1999. Price not set. (*0-531-11340-X*) Watts.

Native American Crafts Workshop. Bonnie Bernstein & Leigh Blair. LC 81-82041. (Crafts Workshop Ser.). (J). (gr. 3-8). 1982. pap. 11.99 (*0-8224-9784-0*) Fearon Teacher Aids.

Native American Cross Stitch. Julie Hasler. (Illus.). 128p. 1999. 27.95 (*0-7153-0770-3*, Pub. by D & C Pub) Sterling.

***Native American Cultural & Religious Freedoms.** John R. Wunder. LC 99-55731. 400p. 1999. pap. 26.95 (*0-8153-3630-6*) Garland.

Native American Cultural & Religious Freedoms. Ed. by John R. Wunder. LC 96-34652. (Native Americans & the Law Ser.: Vol. 5). 392p. 1996. reprint ed. text 75.00 (*0-8153-2489-8*) Garland.

Native American Cultures: A Study Unit to Promote Critical & Creative Thinking. Rebecca Stark. 80p. 1991. student ed. 12.95 (*0-685-59122-0*) Educ Impress.

Native American Cultures: Book & Poster. Rebecca Stark. 80p. (J). (gr. 4-8). 1998. student ed. 12.95 (*0-910857-92-X*) Educ Impress.

Native American Cultures in Indiana: Proceedings of the First Minnestrista Council for Great Lakes Native American Studies. Ed. by Ronald Hicks. LC 91-68350. (Illus.). vi, 133p. 1992. pap. 15.00 (*0-9623291-3-4*) Minnetrista.

Native American Dance: Ceremonies & Social Traditions. Ed. by Charlotte Heth. LC 92-34969. (Illus.). 208p. 1993. pap. 29.95 (*1-56373-021-9*) Fulcrum Pub.

Native American Demography in the Spanish Borderlands. Clark S. Larsen. LC 90-22357. (Spanish Borderlands Sourcebooks Ser.: Vol. 2). 478p. 1991. reprint ed. text 30.00 (*0-8240-0781-6*) Garland.

Native American Designs: Collected Edition. Caren Caraway. (International Design Library). (Illus.). 240p. (Orig.). 1993. pap. 27.95 (*0-88045-125-4*) Stemmer Hse.

Native American Designs for Quilting. Joyce Mori. LC 98-27956. 80p. 1998. pap. 15.95 (*1-57432-710-0*) Collector Bks.

Native American Directory: Alaska, Canada & U. S. Ed. by Fred Synder. 366p. (Orig.). 1982. pap. text 21.95 (*0-9610334-0-1*) Natl Native.

Native American Directory: Alaska, Canada & U. S. Ed. by Native American Cooperative Staff & Fred Synder. (Illus.). 880p. 1996. reprint ed. pap. 59.95 (*0-9610334-5-2*); reprint ed. lib. bdg. 125.00 (*0-9610334-3-6*) Natl Native.

Native American Directory: Vital Records of Maine, Massachusetts, Rhode Island, Connecticut, New York & Wisconsin. Lorraine Henry. LC 98-179258. 131p. 1998. pap. 15.00 (*0-7884-0896-8*, H154) Heritage Bk.

Native American Doctor: The Story of Susan Laflesche Picotte. Jeri Ferris. (Trailblazers Ser.). (Illus.). 80p. (J). (gr. 4-7). 1991. lib. bdg. 22.60 (*0-87614-443-1*, Carolrhoda) Lerner Pub.

Native American Doctor: The Story of Susan Laflesche Picotte. Jeri Ferris. (Illus.). 88p. (J). (gr. 4-7). 1991. pap. 6.95 (*0-87614-548-9*, Carolrhoda) Lerner Pub.

Native American Dolls & Cradleboards. Judi Johnson. (Handbook of Collections: No. 4). (Illus.). 64p. (Orig.). 1983. pap. 4.00 (*0-89792-095-3*) Ill St Museum.

***Native American Edition School Accreditation Manual: A Comprehensive Guide to the Accreditation Process.** ACSI Staff. 106p. 2000. 9.60 (*1-58331-045-2*) Assn Christ Sch.

***Native American Encyclopedia: History, Culture, & Peoples.** Ed. by Barry M. Pritzker. (Illus.). 576p. 2000. 45.00 (*0-19-513897-X*) OUP.

Native American Estate: The Struggle over Indian & Hawaiian Lands. Linda S. Parker. LC 89-4892. 256p. 1996. pap. text 16.00 (*0-8248-1807-5*) UH Pr.

Native American Ethnobotany. Daniel E. Moerman. LC 97-32877. (Illus.). 928p. 1998. 79.95 (*0-88192-453-9*) Timber.

Native American Experience. Lelia Wardwell. (American Historical Images on File Collection). (Illus.). 295p. 1991. ring bd. 165.00 (*0-8160-2228-3*) Facts on File.

Native American Expressive Culture. Ed. by Jose Barreiro. 176p. (Orig.). Date not set. pap. 12.00 (*0-614-29683-8*) Akwe Kon Pr.

Native American Expressive Culture. National Museum of the American Indian (NMAI) Staf & Akwe:kon Press Staff. (Illus.). 176p. 1995. pap. 17.95 (*1-55591-301-6*) Fulcrum Pub.

Native American Fashion: Modern Adaptations of Traditional Designs. 2nd rev. ed. Margaret Wood. (Illus.). 128p. 1997. pap. 21.95 (*0-9659293-0-2*, 001) Nat Amer Fashions.

***Native American Feast.** Lucille R. Penner. (Illus.). 99p. 1999. reprint ed. text 15.00 (*0-7881-6557-7*) DIANE Pub.

Native American Fetish Carvings of the Southwest. Kay Whittle. LC 97-81266. 160p. 1998. pap. 14.95 (*0-7643-0429-1*) Schiffer.

Native American Folklore in Nineteenth Century Periodicals. Ed. by William M. Clements. LC 86-5409. 250p. 1985. text 29.95 (*0-8040-0872-8*) Swallow.

Native American Foods. Raven Hail. Orig. Title: Foods the Indians Gave Us. (Illus.). 21p. (Orig.). 1986. pap. 3.95 (*0-9617696-0-2*) Raven Hail.

Native American Foods & Cookery. Tom Taylor & Eloise F. Potter. (Illus.). 16p. 1986. 1.50 (*0-917134-11-7*) NC Natl Sci.

***Native American Games.** James Bruchac & Joseph Bruchac. (Illus.). 64p. (J). 2000. pap. 12.95 (*1-55591-979-0*) Fulcrum Pub.

Native American Gardening: Stories, Projects & Recipes for Families. Michael J. Caduto & Joseph Bruchac. (Keepers of the Earth Ser.). (Illus.). 176p. (Orig.). 1996. pap. 15.95 (*1-55591-148-X*) Fulcrum Pub.

Native American Genealogical Sourcebook. Ed. by Paula K. Byers. (Genealogical Sourcebook Ser.). 250p. 1995. 75.00 (*0-8103-9229-1*) Gale.

Native American Grapes. Hudson Cattell & Lee S. Miller. (Wines of the East Ser.). (Illus.). 28p. (Orig.). 1981. pap. 2.75 (*0-911301-03-8*) L&H Photojrnl.

Native American Guide to Traditional Beadwork. Joel Monture. LC 93-12101. (Illus.). 112p. 1993. pap. 14.00 (*0-02-066430-3*) Macmillan.

Native American Heritage. 3rd rev. ed. Merwyn S. Garbarino & Robert F. Sasso. (Illus.). 557p. (C). 1994. pap. text 26.95 (*0-88133-773-0*) Waveland Pr.

Native American Higher Education in the United States. Cary M. Carney. LC 99-14822. 226p. 1999. 32.95 (*1-56000-417-7*) Transaction Pubs.

Native American History. Calloway. LC 98-87523. 574p. 1999. pap. text 42.95 (*0-312-15003-2*) St Martin.

Native American History: A Chronology of the Vast Achievements of a Culture & Their Links to World Events. Judith Nies. 384p. 1997. pap. 13.95 (*0-345-39350-3*) Ballantine Pub Grp.

Native American History & Tribes, 13 bks. (Indians of North America Ser.). (YA). (gr. 5 up). 1996. pap. 129.35 (*0-7910-3833-5*) Chelsea Hse.

Native American Housing: Information on HUD's Funding of Indian Housing Programs. Carol Anderson-Gutherie. (Illus.). 63p. (C). 1999. pap. text 20.00 (*0-7881-7755-9*) DIANE Pub.

Native American Housing Assistance: Joint Hearing Before the Committee on Indian Affairs & the Committee on Banking. Composed by Diane Publishing Staff. (Illus.). 246p. (C). 1998. pap. text 45.00 (*0-7881-4917-2*) DIANE Pub.

Native American Humor. Ed. by James R. Aswell. LC 76-117753. (Essay Index Reprint Ser.). 1977. 28.95 (*0-8369-1862-2*) Ayer.

Native American Identities: From Stereotype to Archetype in Art & Literature. Scott B. Vickers. LC 98-9993. 194p. 1998. 40.00 (*0-8263-1931-9*) U of NM Pr.

Native American Identities: From Stereotype to Archetype in Art & Literature. Scott B. Vickers. LC 98-9993. (Illus.). 194p. 1998. pap. 19.95 (*0-8263-1886-X*) U of NM Pr.

Native American in American Literature: A Selectively Annotated Bibliography, 3. Compiled by Roger O. Rock. LC 84-27972. (Bibliographies & Indexes in American Literature Ser.: No. 3). 211p. 1985. lib. bdg. 59.95 (*0-313-24550-9*, RKN/, Greenwood Pr) Greenwood.

Native American in Long Fiction: An Annotated Bibliography. Joan Beam & Barbara Branstad. LC 95-5636. (Native American Bibliography Ser.: No. 18). 384p. 1996. 56.00 (*0-8108-3016-7*) Scarecrow.

Native American Indian Artist Directory. Robert Painter. LC 98-96874. 300p. 1999. pap. 19.95 (*0-9668806-0-9*) First Nations Art.

Native American (Indian) Directory: Alaska, Canada, U. S. rev. ed. Ed. by Fred Synder. (Illus.). 880p. 1996. 125.00 (*0-9610334-1-X*); pap. 59.95 (*0-9610334-2-8*) Natl Native.

Native American Information Directory. 2nd ed. 1998. 95.00 (*0-8103-9116-3*) Gale.

Native American Interactions: Multiscalar Analyses & Interpretations in the Eastern Woodlands. Ed. by Michael S. Nassaney & Kenneth E. Sassaman. LC 94-18772. (Illus.). 414p. (C). 1995. text 40.00 (*0-87049-895-9*) U of Tenn Pr.

Native American Internet Guide. 2nd ed. Ed. by Martha Crow. 110p. 2000. pap. 50.00 (*0-915344-88-2*) Todd Pubns.

Native American Issues: A Reference Handbook. LC 96-19539. (Contemporary World Issues Ser.). 288p. 1996. 39.50 (*0-87436-828-6*) ABC-CLIO.

Native American Law & Colonialism, Before 1776 to 1903. Ed. by John R. Wunder. LC 96-30772. (Native Americans & the Law Ser.: Vol. 1). (Illus.). 352p. 1996. reprint ed. text 70.00 (*0-8153-2485-5*) Garland.

Native American Leaders. Janet Hubbard-Brown. LC 98-31352. (Illus.). 64p. (YA). (gr. 5 up). 1999. lib. bdg. 16.95 (*0-7910-5209-5*) Chelsea Hse.

Native American Leaders of the Wild West Series, 7 bks., Set. William R. Sanford. (Illus.). (J). (gr. 4-10). 1994. lib. bdg. 105.65 (*0-89490-567-8*) Enslow Pubs.

Native American Legends, 6 bks., Set. Terri Cohlene. (Illus.). 288p. (J). (gr. 4-8). 1990. lib. bdg. 119.58 (*0-86593-000-7*); lib. bdg. 89.70 (*0-685-46445-8*) Rourke Corp.

Native American Legends: The Southeast. 2nd ed. George Lankford. 1998. pap. 14.95 (*0-87483-518-6*) August Hse.

Native American Legends & Lore Library, 1. Troll Books Staff. 1999. pap. text 59.40 (*0-8167-4715-6*) Troll Communs.

***Native American Legends of the Great Lakes & the Mississippi Valley.** Katherine B. Judson. LC 99-52766. 200p. 2000. pap. 38.00 (*0-87580-250-8*, 250-8) N Ill U Pr.

***Native American Legends of the Great Lakes & the Mississippi Valley.** rev. ed. Katharine Berry Judson. LC 99-52766. (Illus.). 200p. 2000. pap. 18.00 (*0-87580-581-7*, 581-7) N Ill U Pr.

Native American Liberation Theology: Healing for Both the Oppressed & the Oppressor. Roy I. Wilson. 1997. pap. write for info. (*0-7880-0912-5*, Express Pr) CSS OH.

Native American Literature see Junior Library of American Indians

Native American Literature. Katherine Gleason. LC 95-40562. (Junior Library of American Indians). (Illus.). (J). 1996. pap. 7.95 (*0-7910-2478-4*) Chelsea Hse.

Native American Literature. Gerald R. Vizenor. Ed. by Ishmael Reed. (Literary Mosiac Ser.). 400p. (C). 1997. pap. 19.69 (*0-673-46978-6*) Addson-Wesley Educ.

Native American Literature. Andrew Wiget. (United States Authors Ser.: No. 467). 168p. 1985. 21.95 (*0-8057-7408-4*, Twyne) Mac Lib Ref.

Native American Literature: An Anthology. Lawana Trout. LC 98-38987. 544p. 1997. pap. 32.50 (*0-8442-5985-3*, 59853) NTC Contemp Pub Co.

Native American Literature: An Anthology. Lawana Trout. 1998. pap., teacher ed. 32.66 (*0-8442-5986-1*) NTC Contemp Pub Co.

Native American Literatures: An Encyclopedia of Works, Characters, Authors & Themes. Kathy J. Whitson. LC 98-49251. (Illus.). 295p. (YA). (gr. 9 up). 1999. lib. bdg. 65.00 (*0-87436-932-0*) ABC-CLIO.

***Native American Look Book: Art & Activities for Kids.** Brooklyn Museum Staff. 2000. pap. 12.95 (*1-56584-604-4*, Pub. by New Press NY) Norton.

***Native American Mandalas.** Klaus Holitzka. 2000. pap. 10.95 (*0-8069-2881-6*) Sterling.

Native American Masks: Create 5 Genuine Native American Designs. Pace Products Staff & Raymond Miller. (Illus.). 16p. (Orig.). (J). 1996. pap. 10.95 (*0-8362-2201-6*) Andrews & McMeel.

Native American Mathematics. Michael P. Closs. (C). 1996. pap. text 19.95 (*0-292-71185-9*) U of Tex Pr.

Native American Medicine: Indians of North America. Nancy Bonvillain. LC 97-11427. 120p. (YA). (gr. 5 up). 1997. lib. bdg. 19.95 (*0-7910-4041-0*) Chelsea Hse.

Native American Monuments. Brian Innes. LC 98-13150. (Unsolved Mysteries Ser.). (J). 1999. 24.26 (*0-8172-5482-X*) Raintree Steck-V.

***Native American Monuments** Brian Innes. LC 98-13150. (Unsolved Mysteries Ser.). 48 p. 1999. pap. write for info. (*0-8172-4279-1*) Raintree Steck-V.

Native American Music Directory. Rough Guides Staff. 1999. audio compact disk 14.95 (*1-85828-372-8*) Penguin Putnam.

Native American Music Directory. 2nd ed. Greg Gombert. LC 97-23729. 176p. 1997. 12.95 (*1-57067-043-9*) Book Pub Co.

Native American Myth & Legend: An A-Z of People & Places. Mike Dixon-Kennedy. 288p. 1996. 27.95 (*0-7137-2623-7*, Pub. by Blandford Pr) Sterling.

Native American Myth & Legend: An A-Z of People & Places. Mike Dixon-Kennedy. (Illus.). 304p. 1998. pap. 17.95 (*0-7137-2669-5*) Blandford Pr.

Native American Myths & Mysteries. rev. ed. Vincent H. Gaddis. LC 91-76082. 183p. 1991. reprint ed. pap. 12.95 (*0-945685-10-6*) Borderland Sciences.

***Native American Oral Tradition: Voices of the Spirit & Soul.** Lois J. Einhorn. LC 99-45989. 192p. 2000. 55.00 (*0-275-95790-X*, Praeger Pubs) Greenwood.

Native American Painters of the Twentieth Century: The Works of 61 Artists. Robert Henkes. LC 95-16637. (Illus.). 239p. 1995. lib. bdg. 45.00 (*0-7864-0092-7*) McFarland & Co.

Native American Pedagogy & Cognitive-Based Mathematics Instruction. Judith T. Hankes. (Native Americans). xv, 151p. 1998. 50.00 (*0-8153-3113-4*) Garland.

Native American People, 6 bks., Reading Level 4. Barbara Brooks et al. (Illus.). 192p. (J). (gr. 5-8). 1989. lib. bdg. 71.70 (*0-685-58768-1*) Rourke Corp.

Native American People, 6 bks., Set. Barbara Brooks et al. (Illus.). 192p. (J). (gr. 5-8). 1989. lib. bdg. 95.64 (*0-86625-375-0*) Rourke Pubns.

Native American People, 6 bks., Set. Rita D'Apice et al. (Illus.). 192p. (J). (gr. 5-8). 1990. lib. bdg. 71.70 (*0-685-36385-6*) Rourke Corp.

Native American People, 6 bks., Set. Rita D'Apice et al. (Illus.). 192p. (J). (gr. 5-8). 1990. lib. bdg. 95.64 (*0-86625-383-1*) Rourke Pubns.

Native American Periodicals & Newspapers, 1828-1982: Bibliography, Publishing Record, & Holdings. Ed. by James P. Danky. LC 83-22579. (Illus.). 532p. 1984. lib. bdg. 85.00 (*0-313-23773-5*, DNP/, Greenwood Pr) Greenwood.

Native American Perspectives on Literature & History. Ed. by Alan R. Velie. LC 95-16724. (American Indian Literature & Critical Studies Ser.: Vol. 19). 136p. 1995. pap. 12.95 (*0-8061-2785-6*) U of Okla Pr.

Native American Perspectives on the Hispanic Colonization of Alta California. Ed. by Edward D. Castillo. LC 91-45780. (Spanish Borderlands Sourcebooks Ser.: Vol. 26). 520p. 1992. text 30.00 (*0-8240-2348-X*) Garland.

Native American Photo Fun Activities. Deneen Celecia. Ed. by Linda Milliken. (Illus.). 8p. (J). (gr. 3-6). 1994. pap. 6.95 (*1-56472-042-X*) Edupress Inc.

Native American Place Names in New York City. Robert S. Grumet. (Illus.). 79p. 1981. 10.00 (*0-89062-110-1*); pap. 4.95 (*0-89062-109-8*); pap. 4.95 (*0-614-05717-5*) Mus City NY.

***Native American Place Names of Connecticut.** R. A. Douglas-Lithgow. 96p. 2000. pap. 9.95 (*1-55709-540-X*) Applewood.

***Native American Place Names of Maine, New Hampshire & Vermont.** R. A. Douglas-Lithgow. 2000. pap. 9.95 (*1-55709-541-8*) Applewood.

***Native American Place Names of Massachusetts.** R. A. Douglas-Lithgow. 2000. pap. 9.95 (*1-55709-542-6*) Applewood.

***Native American Place Names of Rhode Island.** R. A. Douglas-Lithgow. 2000. pap. 9.95 (*1-55709-543-4*) Applewood.

Native American Poetry: Native American Anthology of Poetry. Ed. by Louis Hooban. 100p. 1998. pap. 19.95 (*1-884710-07-7*) Indian Heritage.

Native American Political Systems & the Evolution of Democracy: An Annotated Bibliography, 32. Compiled by Bruce E. Johansen. LC 96-5541. (Bibliographies & Indexes in American History Ser.). 184p. 1996. lib. bdg. 67.95 (*0-313-30010-0*, Greenwood Pr) Greenwood.

Native American Portraits: 1865-1918. Nancy Hathaway. (Illus.). 120p. 1990. 29.95 (*0-87701-766-2*); pap. 16.95 (*0-87701-757-3*) Chronicle Bks.

Native American Postcolonial Psychology. Eduardo Duran & Bonnie Duran. LC 94-13400. (SUNY Series in Transpersonal & Humanistic Psychology). 227p. (C). 1995. pap. text 20.95 (*0-7914-2354-9*) State U NY Pr.

Native American Profiles. Gene Machamer. LC 95-95329. (Illus.). 170p. (Orig.). 1996. pap. 10.00 (*0-9627369-3-7*) Carlisle Pr.

***Native American Prophecies: History, Wisdom & Startling Predictions.** 2nd expanded rev. ed. Scott Peterson. LC 98-45314. 304p. (Orig.). 1999. pap. 15.95 (*1-55778-748-4*) Paragon Hse.

Native American Reader. Arlene B. Hirschfelder. 1995. pap. 15.00 (*0-671-86491-2*) S&S Trade.

Native American Reader: Speeches, Poems & Stories of the American Indian. Jerry Blanche. 302p. (Orig.). 1990. pap. 25.00 (*0-938737-20-1*) Denali Press.

Native American Reflections. Sally A. Denno. LC 93-83036. 52p. 1993. pap. 9.95 (*0-916809-60-9*) Scott Pubns MI.

Native American Religion see Indians of North America

Native American Religion & Black Protestantism see Modern American Protestantism & Its World

Native American Religions. Paula Hartz. LC 96-39201. (World Religions Ser.). (Illus.). 128p. (J). (gr. 4-9). 1997. 19.95 (*0-8160-3578-4*) Facts on File.

Native American Religions: A Geographical Survey. John J. Collins. LC 90-33942. (Native American Studies: Vol. 1). 394p. 1991. lib. bdg. 99.95 (*0-88946-483-9*) E Mellen.

Native American Religions: An Introduction. Denise L. Carmody & John T. Carmody. LC 93-15547. 288p. 1993. pap. 14.95 (*0-8091-3404-7*) Paulist Pr.

Native American Religions: An Introduction. Sam D. Gill. 192p. (C). 1981. 22.00 (*0-534-00973-5*) Wadsworth Pub.

Native American Religions: North America. Intro. by Lawrence E. Sullivan. (Readings from the Encyclopedia of Religion Ser.). (Orig.). (C). 1989. 15.95 (*0-02-897402-6*) Macmillan.

Native American Religious Identity: Unforgotten Gods. Ed. by Jace Weaver. LC 97-35474. 280p. (Orig.). 1998. pap. 18.00 (*1-57075-181-1*) Orbis Bks.

Native American Renaissance. Kenneth Lincoln. LC 82-17450. 320p. 1983. pap. 17.95 (*0-520-05457-1*, Pub. by U CA Pr) Cal Prin Full Svc.

Native American Renaissance. Kenneth Lincoln. LC 82-17450. (Illus.). 323p. reprint ed. pap. 100.20 (*0-7837-4752-7*, 204449900003) Bks Demand.

Native American Research Information Service. William Carmack et al. LC 83-70626. (American Indian Handbook & Manual Ser.). 275p. 1983. pap. 15.00 (*0-935626-11-5*) U Cal AISC.

Native American Resurgence & Renewal: A Reader & Bibliography. Robert N. Wells, Jr. LC 93-39199. (Native American Resources Ser.: No. 3). 671p. 1993. 68.50 (*0-8108-2784-0*) Scarecrow.

Native American Rights. Ed. by Tamara L. Roleff. LC 97-37078. (Current Controversies Ser.). 208p. (J). (gr. 5-12). 1997. pap. 16.20 (*1-56510-684-9*); lib. bdg. 26.20 (*1-56510-685-7*) Greenhaven.

Native American Rights Movement. Mark Grossman & ABC-Clio Companion Staff. LC 96-36782. (Illus.). 498p. 1998. lib. bdg. 65.00 (*0-87436-822-7*) ABC-CLIO.

Native American Rock Art: A Petroglyph Stamp Kit for All Ages. Judith Dupre. (Illus.). 64p. (J). 1997. 24.95 (*0-8118-1611-7*) Chronicle Bks.

Native American Rock Art: Messages from the Past. Yvette La Pierre. LC 94-13659. (Illus.). 48p. 1994. 16.95 (*1-56566-064-1*) Lickle Pubng.

Native-American Scientists see Short Biographies

Native American Scientists. Jetty St. John. (Scientists & Inventors Ser.). (Illus.). 48p. (J). (gr. 3-7). 1996. lib. bdg. 19.00 (*0-516-20104-2*) Childrens.

Native American Shipwrecks James P. Delgado. LC 99-25886. (Watts Library Ser.). 2000. 24.00 (*0-531-20379-4*) Watts.

***Native American Shipwrecks.** James P. Delgado. (Shipwrecks Library). (Illus.). (YA). 2000. pap. 8.95 (*0-531-16473-X*) Watts.

Native American Sign Language. Madeline Olsen. LC 98-106314. (Illus.). 32p. (J). (gr. 3-7). 1998. pap. 4.95 (*0-8167-4509-9*) Troll Communs.

Native American Songs & Poems: An Anthology. Ed. by Brian Swann. LC 96-24331. (Thrift Editions Ser.). 64p. (Orig.). 1996. pap. text 1.00 (*0-486-29450-1*) Dover.

Native American Songs for Piano Solo. Gail Smith. 48p. 1995. pap. 6.95 (*0-7866-0442-5*, 95451) Mel Bay.

Native American Songs for Piano Solo. Gail Smith. 48p. 1997. pap. 21.95 incl. audio compact disk (*0-7866-2847-2*, 95451CDP) Mel Bay.

Native American Sourcebook. John Bacheller. (C). 1997. pap. 28.13 (*0-07-289901-8*) McGrw-H Hghr Educ.

***Native American Sovereignty.** John R. Wunder. (Native Americans & the Law Ser.). 1999. pap. 26.95 (*0-8153-3629-2*) Garland.

Native American Sovereignty. Ed. by John R. Wunder. LC 96-34704. (Native Americans & the Law Ser.: Vol. 6). (Illus.). 392p. 1996. reprint ed. text 77.00 (*0-8153-2490-1*) Garland.

***Native American Spirituality: A Critical Reader.** Ed. by Lee Irwin. LC 00-28664. 424p. 2000. pap. 24.95 (*0-8032-8261-3*, Bison Books) U of Nebr Pr.

Native American Stories. John Bierhorst. LC 97-29253. (Illus.). 160p. (J). (gr. 5-9). 1998. 16.00 (*0-688-14837-9*, Wm Morrow) Morrow Avon.

An Asterisk (*) at the beginning of an entry indicates that the title is appearing for the first time.

Native American Stories. Joseph Bruchac. LC 90-85267. (Illus.). 160p. 1991. pap. 12.95 (*1-55591-094-7*) Fulcrum Pub.

Native American Stories. Joseph Bruchac. LC 90-85267. 1991. 18.05 (*0-606-06611-X*, Pub. by Turtleback) Demco.

Native American Struggle for Equality. Ron Querry. LC 92-7474. (Discrimination Ser.). 112p. (J). 1992. lib. bdg. 18.95 (*0-86593-179-8*) Rourke Corp.

Native American Struggle for Equality. Ron Querry. LC 92-7474. (YA). 1992. 16.95 (*0-685-59320-7*) Rourke Corp.

Native American Studies: New Native American Storytellers. Ed. by Clifford E. Trafzer. 496p. (Orig.). 1996. pap. 14.95 (*0-385-47952-2*, Anchor NY) Doubleday.

Native American Style. Elmo Baca & M. J. Van Deventer. LC 97-7802. (Illus.). 144p. 1998. 39.95 (*0-87905-789-0*) Gibbs Smith Pub.

Native American Sun Dance Religion & Ceremony: An Annotated Bibliography, 37. Compiled by Phillip M. White. LC 98-15332. (Bibliographies & Indexes in American History Ser.: Vol. 37). 144p. 1998. lib. bdg. 55.00 (*0-313-30628-1*, Greenwood Pr) Greenwood.

Native American Sweat Lodge: History & Legends. Joseph Bruchac. (Illus.). 146p. 1993. pap. 12.95 (*0-89594-636-X*) Crossing Pr.

Native American Tales - Coyote. Richard Erdoes. 1992. write for info. (*0-679-41194-1*) McKay.

Native American Tales & Activities: Creative Kids. Mari L. Robbins. (Creative Kids Ser.). (Illus.). 160p. (J). (gr. 2 up). 1996. pap., wbk. ed. 14.95 (*1-55734-677-1*) Tchr Create Mat.

Native American Talking Signs. Michael Kelly. LC 97-26194. (Looking into the Past). (Illus.). 64p. (YA). (gr. 5 up). 1999. lib. bdg. 16.95 (*0-7910-4681-8*) Chelsea Hse.

Native American Tarot Deck & Book Set, Vol. 1. Magda W. Gonzalez. (Illus.). 206p. 1992. pap. 26.00 (*0-88079-533-6*, NAS99) US Games Syst.

Native American Tarot Interpreted. Dona Shaw. (Illus.). 272p. (Orig.). 1993. pap. 20.00 (*1-884776-00-0*) Lazuli Prods.

Native American Tarot Interpreted. 2nd ed. Dona Shaw. (Illus.). 272p. (Orig.). 1993. reprint ed. pap. 20.00 (*1-884776-03-5*) Lazuli Prods.

***Native American Testimony: A Chronicle of Indian-White Relations from Prophecy to the Present, 1492-2000.** rev. ed. Peter Nabokov. (Illus.). 512p. 1999. pap. 16.95 (*0-14-028159-2*, Penguin Bks) Viking Penguin.

Native American Told Us So: Student Book. Melvin Berger. Ed. by Natalie Lunis. (Ranger Rick Science Spectacular Ser.). (Illus.). 16p. (Orig.). (J). (gr. 2-4). 1996. pap. 3.95 (*1-56784-236-4*) Newbridge Educ.

Native American Tradition. Arthur Versluis. 1994. pap. 19.95 (*1-85230-572-X*, Pub. by Element MA) Penguin Putnam.

Native American Traditions. Arthur Versluis. (Element Library). (Illus.). 96p. 1995. pap. 14.95 (*1-85230-719-6*, Pub. by Element MA) Penguin Putnam.

Native American Tribes, 5 bks. (Indians of North America Ser.). (YA). (gr. 5 up). 1990. 99.75 (*0-7910-3829-7*) Chelsea Hse.

Native American Tribes. Norman B. Hunt. (Illus.). 96p. 1997. 12.98 (*0-7858-0840-X*) Bk Sales Inc.

Native American Truths: Philosophy of Good Medicine. H. M. Byron. (Illus.). 72p. 1999. pap. 10.00 (*0-8059-4595-4*) Dorrance.

Native American Use of Non-Quarry Obsidian in Northern Sonoma County: A Preliminary Assessment. Sunshine Psota. 198p. (C). 1994. pap. text 21.25 (*1-55567-111-X*) Coyote Press.

Native American Verbal Art: Texts & Contexts. William M. Clements. LC 96-10026. 252p. 1996. 19.95 (*0-8165-1659-6*); pap. 45.00 (*0-8165-1658-8*) U of Ariz Pr.

Native American Voices: A History & Anthology. Ed. by Steven Mintz. (Illus.). 240p. (C). 1995. pap. text 22.92 (*1-881089-25-8*) Brandywine Press.

***Native American Voices: A History & Anthology.** rev. ed. Ed. by Steven Mintz. (Illus.). 240p. (C). 1998. pap. text 18.50 (*1-881089-38-X*) Brandywine Press.

***Native American Voices: A History & Anthology.** 2nd ed. Ed. by Steven Mintz. 256p. (C). 2000. pap. text 18.50 (*1-881089-59-2*) Brandywine Press.

Native American Voices: A Reader. Ed. by Susan Lobo. LC 97-23820. 448p. (C). 1997. pap. 39.80 (*0-321-01131-7*, Prentice Hall) P-H.

Native American Voices: Native American Health Educators Speak Out. Ed. by Audrey M. Koertvelyessy. 1997. 29.95 (*0-88737-677-0*, 14-6770, NLN Pr) Natl League Nurse.

Native American Voluntary Organizations. Ed. by Armand S. La Potin. LC 86-25764. (Ethnic American Voluntary Organizations Ser.). 204p. 1987. lib. bdg. 49.95 (*0-313-23633-X*, LAN/, Greenwood Pr) Greenwood.

Native American Way of Life. Ed. by SPPTS the Rock Staff. 28p. 1997. pap. 1.50 (*0-89992-109-4*) Coun India Ed.

Native American Wisdom. Ed. by Kristen M. Cleary. 64p. 1996. 4.98 (*1-889461-00-8*) DoveTail Bks.

Native American Wisdom. Ed. by Kristen M. Cleary. (Illus.). 64p. 1996. 4.98 (*0-614-29841-5*) DoveTail Bks.

Native American Wisdom. Compiled by Kent Nerburn & Louise Mengelkoch. LC 91-21315. (Classic Wisdom Collection). 128p. 1991. 15.00 (*0-931432-78-2*) New Wrld Lib.

Native American Wisdom, 3 bks. Terry P. Wilson. (Native American Wisdom Ser.). (Illus.). 192p. 1994. boxed set 29.95 (*0-8118-0427-5*) Chronicle Bks.

Native American Women see Junior Library of American Indians

Native American Women: A Biographical Dictionary. Ed. by Gretchen M. Bataille. LC 92-19990. (Biographical Directories of Minority Women Ser.: Vol. 1). (Illus.). 360p. 1993. text 20.00 (*0-8240-5267-6*, SS649) Garland.

***Native American Women - Social, Economic & Political Aspects: A Bibliography.** Ed. by Joan Nordquist. (Contemporary Social Issues: Vol. 56). 72p. 1999. pap. 20.00 (*1-892068-10-9*) Ref Rsch Serv.

Native American Women Writers. Ed. by Harold Bloom. LC 97-40088. (Women Writers & Their Works Ser.). (Illus.). 180p. (YA). (gr. 10 up). 1998. 29.95 (*0-7910-4479-3*); pap. 16.95 (*0-7910-4495-5*) Chelsea Hse.

***Native American Women's Writing: An Anthology c. 1800-1924.** Ed. by Karen Kilcup. (Anthologies Ser.). 484p. 2000. text 74.95 (*0-631-20517-9*); pap. text 36.95 (*0-631-20518-7*) Blackwell Pubs.

Native American Words. John M. Gogol. 1973. 1.50 (*0-932191-07-X*) Mr Cogito Pr.

Native American Writers. Ed. by Stanley H. Barkan & Joseph Bruchac. 1991. boxed set 75.00 (*0-89304-912-3*); boxed set 50.00 (*0-685-49058-0*) Cross-Cultrl NY.

Native-American Writers. Ed. by Harold Bloom. LC 97-51447. (Modern Critical Views Ser.). 300p. (YA). 1999. 34.95 (*0-7910-4785-7*) Chelsea Hse.

Native American Writing in the Southeast: An Anthology, 1875-1935. Daniel F. Littlefield, Jr. LC 95-18038. 232p. 1995. 40.00 (*0-87805-827-3*); pap. 16.95 (*0-87805-828-1*) U Pr of Miss.

Native American Youth & Alcohol: An Annotated Bibliography, 16. Michael L. Lobb & Thomas D. Watts. LC 88-32345. (Bibliographies & Indexes in Sociology Ser.: No. 16). 210p. 1989. lib. bdg. 55.00 (*0-313-25618-7*, WNY/, Greenwood Pr) Greenwood.

Native Americans. (Time Travel Activity Bks.). 48p. (J). (ps up). 1992. 1.95 (*0-88679-918-X*) Educ Insights.

Native Americans, 10 vols. (Illus.). 800p. (YA). (gr. 5-10). 1999. lib. bdg. 325.00 (*0-7172-9395-5*) Grolier Educ.

Native Americans. John Artman. (Illus.). 16p. (J). (gr. 5-8). 1997. teacher ed. 15.95 (*1-56490-032-0*) G Grimm Assocs.

Native Americans. Norman Bancroft-Hunt. 1998. pap. 12.99 (*0-7858-0880-9*) Bk Sales Inc.

Native Americans. Ed. by William Dudley. LC 97-38334. (Opposing Viewpoints Ser.). (Illus.). (YA). (gr. 5-12). 1997. pap. 16.20 (*1-56510-704-7*); lib. bdg. 26.20 (*1-56510-705-5*) Greenhaven.

Native Americans. Ute Fuhr et al. LC 97-20107. (First Discovery Book). (Illus.). 24p. (J). (ps-2). 1998. 11.95 (*0-590-38153-9*) Scholastic Inc.

Native Americans. Dona Herweck & Mari L. Robbins. (Interdisciplinary Units Ser.). (Illus.). 1994. 14.95 (*1-55734-607-0*) Tchr Create Mat.

***Native Americans.** Jason Hook. (People Who Made History in Ser.). (Illus.). (J). 2000. 27.11 (*0-7398-2750-2*) Raintree Steck-V.

Native Americans. Frederick E. Hoxie & Harvey Markowitz. (Magill Bibliographies Ser.). 324p. 1991. 42.00 (*0-8108-2790-5*) Scarecrow.

Native Americans. N. B. Hunt. 1996. 19.98 (*0-7858-0598-2*) Bk Sales Inc.

Native Americans. Jay Miller. (New True Books Ser.). (Illus.). 48p. (J). (gr. 2-4). 1993. pap. 5.50 (*0-516-41192-6*) Childrens.

Native Americans. Jay Miller. LC 93-3442. (New True Books Ser.). (Illus.). 48p. (J). (ps-3). 1993. lib. bdg. 21.00 (*0-516-01192-8*) Childrens.

Native Americans. Norris & Davis. (Illus.). 48p. (J). (gr. 1-3). 1996. pap., teacher ed. 9.95 (*1-55799-575-3*, 561) Evan-Moor Edu Pubs.

Native Americans. Scholastic, Inc. Staff. 1992. pap. 15.95 (*0-590-49151-2*) Scholastic Inc.

Native Americans. Illus. by Jeff Sinclair. (BipQuiz 100 Questions & Answers Ser.). 64p. (J). 1996. pap. 2.95 (*0-8069-4229-0*) Sterling.

Native Americans. David H. Thomas & Lorann Pendleton. LC 95-12101. (Nature Company Discoveries Library). (Illus.). 64p. (J). (gr. 3 up). 1999. 16.00 (*0-7835-4759-5*) Time-Life.

Native Americans. James Wilson. LC 93-36059. (Threatened Cultures Ser.). (Illus.). 48p. (J). (gr. 5-9). 1994. lib. bdg. 24.26 (*1-56847-150-5*) Raintree Steck-V.

Native Americans. Polly Zane & John Zane. LC 76-5579. (J). (gr. 1-12). 1982. teacher ed. 32.00 (*0-935070-01-X*) Proof Pr.

Native Americans, Vol. 7. Ed. by Robert Adkinson. LC 96-60181. (Sacred Symbols Ser.). (Illus.). 80p. 1996. 10.00 (*0-500-06025-8*, Pub. by Thames Hudson) Norton.

***Native Americans: A History in Pictures.** Arlene B. Hirschfelder. LC 99-49061. 192p. 2000. 24.95 (*0-7894-5162-X*, D K Ink) DK Pub Inc.

Native Americans: A Resource Guide. (Illus.). 55p. (Orig.). (C). 1993. pap. text 25.00 (*1-56806-793-3*) DIANE Pub.

Native Americans: A Thematic Unit. Leigh Hoven. (Thematic Units Ser.). (Illus.). 80p. (gr. 3-5). 1990. student ed. 9.95 (*1-55734-285-7*) Tchr Create Mat.

Native Americans: A Thematic Unit. Leigh Severson. (Thematic Units Ser.). (Illus.). 80p. (Orig.). 1991. student ed. 9.95 (*1-55734-276-8*) Tchr Create Mat.

Native Americans: Akwe: Icon's Journal of Indigenous Issues. Ed. by Jose Barreiro. (Illus.). 64p. (Orig.). Date not set. mass mkt. 20.00 (*0-614-29686-2*) Akwe Kon Pr.

Native Americans: An Encyclopedia of History, Culture & Peoples, 2 vols., Vols. I & II. Barry Pritzker. LC 98-21718. (Illus.). 868p. 1998. lib. bdg. 175.00 (*0-87436-836-7*, FN-1644) ABC-CLIO.

Native Americans: An Integrated Unit. Kathy Rogers. (Primary Thematic Units Ser.). (Illus.). 80p. (Orig.). 1993. pap. 12.95 (*0-944459-74-9*) ECS Lrn Systs.

Native Americans: From the Arctic to the Rainforest. Ed. by Marilyn Courtot. (Illus.). 44p. (Orig.). (J). 1996. pap. 14.95 (*1-890920-04-5*) Childrens Lit.

Native Americans: Projects Grade K-3. 1995. pap., teacher ed. 12.95 (*0-8167-3268-X*) Troll Communs.

Native Americans: Projects Grade 4-6. 1995. pap., teacher ed. 12.95 (*0-8167-3334-1*) Troll Communs.

Native Americans: Social, Economic & Political Aspects - A Bibliography. Joan Nordquist. LC 99-196376. (Contemporary Social Issues: Vol. 50). 72p. 1998. pap. 20.00 (*0-937855-98-7*) Ref Rsch Serv.

Native Americans: The Indigenous People of North America. William Sturtevant. Ed. by Colin Taylor. LC 99-27563. 256p. 1999. 24.98 (*1-57145-209-5*, Thunder Bay) Advantage Pubs.

Native Americans: The New Indian Resistance. William Meyer. LC 71-163221. (Little New World Paperbacks Ser.). 96p. reprint ed. pap. 30.00 (*0-608-13783-9*, 202063500018) Bks Demand.

Native Americans: The People & How They Lived. Eloise F. Potter & John B. Funderburg. LC 86-61434. (Illus.). 80p. (gr. 4-12). 1986. 5.00 (*0-917134-09-5*); lib. bdg. 14.95 (*0-917134-10-9*) NC Natl Sci.

Native Americans: Their Enduring Culture & Traditions. Trudy Griffin-Pierce. 192p. 1996. 24.98 (*1-56799-389-3*, MetroBooks) M Friedman Pub Grp Inc.

Native Americans: Twenty-three Indian Biographies. Roger W. Axford. (Illus.). 128p. 1981. pap. 5.00 (*0-935648-02-X*) Halldin Pub.

Native Americans: A Portrait: The Art & Travels of Charles Bird King, George Catlin, & Karl Bodmer. Robert J. Moore, Jr. LC 97-8563. (Illus.). 280p. 1997. 60.00 (*1-55670-616-2*) Stewart Tabori & Chang.

Native Americans along the Oregon Trail. Joy Stickney. (Illus.). 24p. (Orig.). (J). (gr. 4-6). 1993. pap. 4.50 (*1-884563-02-3*) Canyon Creat.

Native Americans & Archaeologists: Stepping Stones to Common Ground. Ed. by Nina Swidler et al. LC 97-4593. 290p. 1997. 65.00 (*0-7619-8900-5*); pap. 24.95 (*0-7619-8901-3*) AltaMira Pr.

Native Americans & Black Americans see Indians of North America

Native Americans & Black Americans. Kim Dramer. LC 96-51521. (Indians of North America Ser.). 120p. (YA). (gr. 5 up). 1997. pap. 9.95 (*0-7910-4462-9*, Chelsea Juniors) Chelsea Hse.

Native Americans & Christianity. Steve Klots. LC 96-44647. (Indians of North America Ser.). 120p. (YA). (gr. 5 up). 1996. 19.95 (*0-7910-4553-6*) Chelsea Hse.

Native Americans & Christianity. Steve Klots. LC 96-44647. (Indians of North America Ser.). 120p. (YA). (gr. 5 up). 1997. pap. 9.95 (*0-7910-4463-7*) Chelsea Hse.

Native Americans & Early Settlers: The Meeting of Cultures, 1780's-1980's: a History of Indian Wars in Western Ohio, & Later Settlement. Phillip Shriver et al. Ed. by Joyce L. Alig. (Illus.). vi, 42p. 1989. pap. 10.00 (*1-891095-06-4*, 5362-6) Mercer Cty Hist.

Native Americans & Mesa Verde. Hazel M. Martell. LC 92-27758. (Hidden Worlds Ser.). (Illus.). 32p. (YA). (gr. 5 up). 1993. lib. bdg. 13.95 (*0-87518-540-1*, Dillon Silver Burdett) Silver Burdett Pr.

Native Americans & Nixon: Presidential Politics & Minority Self Determination, 1969-1972. 2nd ed. Jack D. Forbes. LC 81-14997. (Native American Politics Ser.). 148p. 1984. pap. 12.00 (*0-935626-06-9*) U Cal AISC.

Native Americans & Public Policy. Ed. by Fremont J. Lyden & Lyman H. Legters. (Orig.). 1988. pap. 15.00 (*0-944285-02-3*) Pol Studies.

Native Americans & the Early Republic. Ed. by Frederick E. Hoxie et al. (Illus.). 2000. pap. 17.50 (*0-8139-1913-4*) U Pr of Va.

Native Americans & the Early Republic. Frederick Hoxie et al. LC 98-39823. (Perspectives on the American Revolution Ser.). 370p. 2000. 49.50 (*0-8139-1873-1*) U Pr of Va.

Native Americans & the Law: A Dictionary. Gary A. Sokolow. (Contemporary Legal Issues Ser.). 310p. 2000. lib. bdg. 55.00 (*0-87436-877-4*) ABC-CLIO.

Native Americans & the Law: Contemporary & Historical Perspectives on American Indian Rights, Freedoms & Sovereignty, 6 vols. Ed. & Intro. by John R. Wunder. 1997. 406.00 (*0-8153-2448-0*) Garland.

Native Americans & the New Deal: The Office Files of John Collier, 1933-1945 Robert Lester & University Publications of America (Firm). LC 94-9017. 18 p. 1993. write for info. (*1-55655-491-5*) U Pubns Amer.

Native Americans & the Reservation in American History. Anita L. McCormick. LC 96-12266. (In American History Ser.). (Illus.). 128p. (YA). (gr. 5 up). 1996. lib. bdg. 20.95 (*0-89490-769-7*) Enslow Pubs.

Native Americans & the Spanish. Therese De Angelis. LC 97-7498. (Indians of North America Ser.). (Illus.). 10p. (YA). (gr. 5-13). 1997. pap. 9.95 (*0-7910-4465-3*) Chelsea Hse.

Native Americans & the Spanish. Therese DeAngelis. Ed. by Frank W. Porter, 3rd. LC 97-7498. (Indians of North America Ser.). (Illus.). 120p. (YA). (gr. 5 up). 1997. lib. bdg. 19.95 (*0-7910-2654-X*) Chelsea Hse.

Native Americans & Wage Labor: Ethnohistorical Perspectives. Ed. by Alice Littlefield & Martha C. Knack. LC 95-31899. (Illus.). 368p. 1996. 32.95 (*0-8061-2816-X*) U of Okla Pr.

Native Americans As Shown on the Stage, 1753-1916. Eugene H. Jones. LC 87-16121. 219p. 1988. 30.00 (*0-8108-2040-4*) Scarecrow.

Native Americans at Mission Santa Cruz, 1791-1834: Interpreting the Archaeological Record. Rebecca Allen. LC 98-36326. (Perspectives in California Archaeology Ser.: No. 5). (Illus.). 1998. pap. text 25.00 (*0-917956-92-3*) UCLA Arch.

Native Americans Before 1492: The Moundbuilding Centers of the Eastern Woodlands. Lynda N. Shaffer. LC 92-28230. (Sources & Studies in World History). 149p. (C). (gr. 13). 1992. pap. text 27.95 (*1-56324-030-0*) M E Sharpe.

Native Americans Before 1492: The Moundbuilding Centers of the Eastern Woodlands. Lynda Norene Shaffer. LC 92-28230. (Sources & Studies in World History). 149p. (C). (gr. 13). 1992. text 64.95 (*1-56324-029-7*) M E Sharpe.

Native Americans in Children's Literature. Jon C. Stott. LC 95-6547. 264p. 1995. pap. 26.50 (*0-89774-782-8*) Oryx Pr.

Native Americans in Fiction: A Guide to 765 Books for Librarians & Teachers, K-9. Vicki Anderson. LC 94-6271. 180p. 1994. lib. bdg. 31.50 (*0-89950-907-X*) McFarland & Co.

Native Americans in Florida. Kevin McCarthy. LC 99-22521. 1999. pap. 18.95 (*1-56164-182-0*) Pineapple Pr.

***Native Americans in Florida.** Kevin McCarthy. 1999. pap., teacher ed. 4.00 (*1-56164-188-X*) Pineapple Pr.

Native Americans in Florida. Kevin McCarthy. LC 99-22521. 200p. (YA). (gr. 6-8). 1999. 25.95 (*1-56164-181-2*) Pineapple Pr.

Native Americans in the News: Images of Indians in the Twentieth Century Press, 49. Mary A. Weston. LC 95-37334. (Contributions to the Study of Mass Media & Communications Ser.: Vol. 49). 200p. 1996. 59,95 (*0-313-28948-4*, Greenwood Pr) Greenwood.

Native Americans in the Saturday Evening Post. LC 99-33113. (Illus.). 464p. 1999. 70.00 (*0-8108-3675-0*) Scarecrow.

Native Americans in the Twentieth Century. James S. Olson & Raymond Wilson. (Illus.). 248p. 1986. text 29.95 (*0-252-01286-0*); pap. text 14.95 (*0-252-01285-2*) U of Ill Pr.

Native Americans of California, 4 bks. (Indians of North America Ser.). (YA). (gr. 5 up). 1990. 79.80 (*0-7910-3822-X*) Chelsea Hse.

Native Americans of California & Nevada, Vol. 1. rev. ed. Jack D. Forbes. LC 82-7906. (Illus.). 240p. 1982. pap. 10.95 (*0-87961-119-7*) Naturegraph.

Native Americans of North America: A Bibliography Based on Collections in the Libraries of California State University, Northridge. David Perkins & Norman Tanis. (Illus.). 1975. 29.00 (*0-8108-0878-1*) Scarecrow.

Native Americans of North America: Basin Region: Northern Paiute. Mary N. Boule. Ed. by Virginia Harding. (Illus.). 64p. (J). (gr. 3-6). 1999. text 7.95 (*1-877599-55-7*) Merryant Pubs.

Native Americans of North America: Northwest Coastal Tribes: Tlingit. Mary Null Boule. LC 98-125191. (Illus.). 68p. (J). (gr. 3-5). 1996. pap. 7.95 (*1-877599-50-6*) Merryant Pubs.

Native Americans of North America: NW Coastal Tribes: Salish. Mary Null Boule. LC 98-125194. (Illus.). 68p. (J). (gr. 3-5). 1996. pap. text 7.95 (*1-877599-51-4*) Merryant Pubs.

Native Americans of North America: Plateau Tribes: Cayuse, Walla Walla & Umatilla People. Mary N. Boule. Ed. by Virginia Harding. (Illus.). 64p. (J). (gr. 3-6). 1999. pap. text 7.95 (*1-877599-54-9*) Merryant Pubs.

Native Americans of North America: Plateau Tribes: Nez Perce People. Mary Null Boule. (Illus.). 64p. (J). (gr. 3-6). 1999. pap. text 7.95 (*1-877599-53-0*) Merryant Pubs.

Native Americans of North America: Plateau Tribes: Yakama Nation. Mary Null Boule. LC 98-125193. (Illus.). 64p. (J). (gr. 3-5). 1996. pap. 7.95 (*1-877599-52-2*) Merryant Pubs.

Native Americans of Texas. Sandra L. Myres. (Texas History Ser.). (Illus.). 46p. 1981. pap. text 9.95 (*0-89641-083-8*) American Pr.

Native Americans of the Frontier. Charles W. Sundling. LC 98-5175. (Frontier Land Ser.). (Illus.). 32p. (J). 2000. lib. bdg. 19.93 (*1-57765-042-5*, ABDO & Dghtrs) ABDO Pub Co.

Native Americans of the Great Lakes, 4 bks. (Indians of North America Ser.). (YA). (gr. 5 up). 1990. 79.80 (*0-7910-3827-0*) Chelsea Hse.

***Native Americans of the Great Lakes (North America)** Stuart A. Kallen. LC 99-23523. (Indigenous Peoples Ser.). (Illus.). 144p. (YA). (gr. 6-9). 2000. lib. bdg. 23.70 (*1-56006-568-0*) Lucent Bks.

Native Americans of the Great Plains, 6 bks. (Indians of North America Ser.). (YA). (gr. 5 up). 1995. pap. 59.70 (*0-7910-3830-0*) Chelsea Hse.

Native Americans of the Great Plains. (Indians of North America Ser.). (YA). (gr. 5 up). 1999. 219.45 (*0-7910-3824-6*) Chelsea Hse.

Native Americans of the Northeast, 8 bks. (Indians of North America Ser.). 1992. 159.60 (*0-7910-3826-2*) Chelsea Hse.

***Native Americans of the Northeast (North America)** Stuart A. Kallen. LC 99-43151. (Indigenous Peoples Ser.). (Illus.). 144p. (YA). (gr. 6-9). 2000. lib. bdg. 23.70 (*1-56006-629-6*) Lucent Bks.

Native Americans of the Northwest, 5 bks. (Indians of North America Ser.). 1990. 99.75 (*0-7910-3825-4*) Chelsea Hse.

Native Americans of the Pacific Coast. Vinson Brown. LC 76-30677. (Illus.). 272p. 1985. pap. 9.95 (*0-87961-135-9*) Naturegraph.

***Native Americans of the Pacific Northwest.** Veda Boyd Jones. LC 00-8053. (Indigenous Peoples of North America Ser.). 2000. write for info. (*1-56006-691-1*) Lucent Bks.

N

*Native Americans of the Plains (North America) Lucille Wood-Peoples. LC 99-43153. (Indigenous Peoples Ser.). (Illus.). 144p. (YA). (gr. 6-9). 2000. lib. bdg. 23.70 (1-56006-627-X) Lucent Bks.

Native Americans of the Southeast, 7 bks. (Indians of North America Ser.). (YA). (gr. 5 up). 1990. 139.65 (0-7910-3823-8) Chelsea Hse.

*Native Americans of the Southeast. Christina M. Girod. LC 00-8654. (Indigenous Peoples of North America Ser.). (Illus.). 2000. write for info. (1-56006-610-5) Lucent Bks.

Native Americans of the Southeast & the Northeast, 8 bks. (Indians of North America Ser.). (YA). (gr. 5 up). 1990. pap. 79.60 (0-7910-3832-7) Chelsea Hse.

Native Americans of the Southwest, 11 bks. (Indians of North America Ser.). (YA). (gr. 5 up). 1990. 219.45 (0-7910-3821-1) Chelsea Hse.

*Native Americans of the Southwest. Stuart A. Kallen. LC 99-50218. (Indigenous Peoples of North America Ser.). 144p. (YA). (gr. 4-12). 2000. lib. bdg. 18.96 (1-56006-681-4) Lucent Bks.

Native Americans of the Southwest: The Serious Traveler's Introduction to Peoples & Places. Zdenek Salzmann. LC 97-701. (C). 1997. pap. 17.00 (0-8133-2279-0, Pub. by Westview) HarpC.

Native Americans of the Southwest & the West, 9 bks. (Indians of North America Ser.). (YA). (gr. 5 up). 1995. pap. 89.55 (0-7910-3831-9) Chelsea Hse.

Native Americans of the West: A Sourcebook on the American West. Ed. by Carter Smith. LC 91-31128. (American Albums from the Collections of the Library of Congress). (Illus.). 96p. (J). (gr. 5-8). 1996. pap. 8.95 (0-7613-0154-2) Millbrook Pr.

Native Americans I. 41.95 (0-382-40674-5) Cobblestone Pub Co.

Native Americans Reference Collections: Documents Collected by the Office of Indian Affairs, Pt. 1. LC 94-42745. 1994. 3695.00 (1-55655-408-7) U Pubns Amer.

Native Americans Today: A Resource Book for Teachers, Grades 4-8. Arlene Hirschfelder & Yvonne Beamer. LC 99-16299. 225p. 1999. pap. 25.00 (1-56308-694-8) Libs Unl.

Native Americans Told Us So. Melvin Berger. Ed. by Natalie Lunis. (Ranger Rick Science Spectacular Ser.). 16p. (J). (gr. 2-4). 1994. pap. 16.95 (1-56784-211-9) Newbridge Educ.

Native Americans Told Us So: Thee Pack. Melvin Berger. Ed. by Natalie Lunis. (Ranger Rick Science Spectacular Ser.). (Illus.). (Orig.). (J). (gr. 2-4). 1996. pap. 36.90 (1-56784-275-5) Newbridge Educ.

Native Americans II. 41.95 (0-382-40675-3) Cobblestone Pub Co.

Native & Christian: Indigenous Voices on Religious Identity in the United States & Canada. Ed. by James Treat. LC 95-10863. 248p. (C). 1996. pap. 19.99 (0-415-91374-8) Routledge.

Native & Christian: Indigenous Voices on Religious Identity in the United States & Canada. Ed. by James Treat. LC 95-10863. 248p. (C). (gr. 13). 1996. 75.00 (0-415-91373-X) Routledge.

Native & Cultivated Conifers of Northeastern North America: A Guide. Edward A. Cope. LC 85-24338. (Illus.). 224p. 1986. text 47.50 (0-8014-1721-X); pap. text 18.95 (0-8014-9360-9) Cornell U Pr.

Native & Foreign Virtuosos: Selected Works of Zimmerman, Alkan, Franck, & Contemporaries. Ed. by Jeffrey Kallberg. LC 92-21232. (Piano Music of the Parisian Virtuosos, 1810-1860 Ser.: Vol. 10). 292p. 1993. text 40.00 (0-8153-0856-6) Garland.

Native & Introduced Earthworms from Selected Chaparral, Woodland, & Riparian Zones in Southern California. Hulton B. Wood & Samuel W. James. (Illus.). 30p. 1998. reprint ed. pap. 4.00 (0-89904-931-1, Wildlife Resrch Grp) Crumb Elbow Pub.

Native & Naturalized Leguminosae (Fabaceae) of the United States: Exclusive of Alaska & Hawaii. Duane Isely. xii, 1007p. 1998. text 60.00 (0-8425-2396-0, Friends of the Library) Brigham.

Native & Naturalized Plants of Nantucket. Frank C. MacKeever. Ed. by Harry E. Ahles. LC 68-19673. 160p. 1968. 22.50 (0-87023-037-9) U of Mass Pr.

Native & Naturalized Woody Plants of Austin & the Hill Country. Daniel Lynch. Ed. by Jane Mosely. LC 80-53737. (Illus.). 180p. (Orig.). 1981. pap. 7.95 (0-938472-00-3) St Edwards Univ.

Native & Newcomer: Making & Remaking a Japanese City. Jennifer Robertson. (Illus.). 252p. (C). 1994. pap. 16.95 (0-520-08655-4, Pub. by U CA Pr) Cal Prin Full Svc.

Native Animals of Hawaii Coloring Book. Patrick Ching. (Illus.). 32p. (Orig.). (J). (ps-6). 1988. pap. 4.95 (0-935848-55-X) Bess Pr.

Native Aquatic Bacteria: Enumeration, Activity & Ecology - STP 695. Ed. by J. W. Costerton & R. R. Colwell. 219p. 1979. 25.00 (0-8031-0526-6, STP695) ASTM.

Native Argosy. Morley Callaghan. LC 70-106255. (Short Story Index Reprint Ser.). 1977. 20.95 (0-8369-3292-7) Ayer.

Native Artists of Europe. Reavis Moore. LC 94-11128. (Rainbow Warrior Artists Ser.). (Illus.). 48p. (J). (gr. 4-7). 1994. 14.95 (1-56261-158-5, J Muir) Avalon Travel.

Native Artists of Europe. Reavis Moore. (Illus.). 48p. 1995. pap. text 9.95 (1-56261-230-1) Avalon Travel.

Native Artists of North America. Reavis Moore. LC 93-16254. (Rainbow Warrior Artists Ser.). (Illus.). 48p. (J). (gr. 4-7). 1993. 14.95 (1-56261-105-4) Avalon Travel.

Native Arts Network: A Special Report, 1986. Ed. by Erin Younger. 20p. 1986. pap. 3.00 (1-881388-01-8) Atlatl.

Native Arts Network, a Special Report: Issues in Contemporary American Indian Art: a Report on a Symposium. Alyce Sadongei et al. 26p. 1990. pap. text 3.00 (1-881388-03-4) Atlatl.

Native Arts of North America. George A. Corbin. LC 87-45606. (Illus.). 352p. 1988. pap. 38.00 (0-06-430174-5, IN-174, Icon Edns) HarpC.

Native Arts of North America. Christian F. Feest. (World of Art Ser.). (Illus.). 216p. 1985. 19.95 (0-500-18179-9, Pub. by Thames Hudson) Norton.

Native Arts of North America. David W. Penney. (Illus.). 208p. 1998. pap. text 27.50 (2-87939-190-3, Pub. by Pierre Terrail) Rizzoli Intl.

Native Arts of North America. 2nd ed. Christian F. Feest. (World of Art Ser.). (Illus.). 216p. 1992. pap. 14.95 (0-500-20262-1, Pub. by Thames Hudson) Norton.

Native Arts of the Columbia Plateau: Selections from the Doris Swayze Bounds Collection. Susan E. Harless & High Desert Museum (Bend, OR) Staff. LC 97-43827. (Illus.). 176p. 1998. pap. 29.95 (0-295-97673-X) U of Wash Pr.

Native Astronomy in the Central Carolinas. Ward H. Goodenough. LC 53-2124. (University of Pennsylvania, University Museum, Anthropological Publications). 52p. reprint ed. pap. 30.00 (0-608-15077-0, 202610600048) Bks Demand.

Native Australian Plants: Horticulture & Uses. Margaret Burchett & Krystyna Johnson. 424p. 1996. 59.95 (0-614-25732-8, Pub. by New South Wales Univ Pr) Intl Spec Bk.

Native Basketry of Western North America. Joan M. Jones. (Handbook of Collections: No. 3). (Illus.). 63p. 1978. pap. 2.00 (0-89792-075-9) Ill St Museum.

Native Brotherhoods: Modern Inter-Tribal Organizations on the Northwest Coast. Philip Drucker. reprint ed. 59.00 (0-403-03657-7) Scholarly.

Native Brotherhoods: Modern Intertribal Organizations. Philip Drucker. (Bureau of American Ethnology Bulletins Ser.). 194p. 1995. lib. bdg. 79.00 (0-7812-4168-5) Rprt Serv.

Native Brotherhoods: Modern Intertribal Organizations on the Northwest Coast. Philip Drucker. (Bureau of American Ethnology Ser.). 200p. 1992. reprint ed. pap. text 39.00 (1-878592-27-0); reprint ed. lib. bdg. 59.00 (1-878592-28-9) Native Amer Bk Pubs.

Native Brotherhoods: Modern Intertribal Organizations on the Northwest Coast. Philip Drucker. 1988. reprint ed. lib. bdg. 79.00 (0-7812-0755-X) Rprt Serv.

Native Cacti of California. Lyman D. Benson. 1969. 10.95 (0-8047-0696-4) Stanford U Pr.

Native Cacti of California. Lyman D. Benson. LC 69-13176. (Illus.). xii, 243p. 1969. pap. 22.50 (0-8047-1526-2) Stanford U Pr.

Native California Guide: Weaving the Past & Present. Dolan H. Eargle, Jr. (Illus.). 306p. 2000. pap. write for info. (0-937401-10-2) Trees Co Pr.

Native Canadian Anthropology & History: A Selected Bibliography. rev. ed. Shepard Krech, III. LC 93-37591. 224p. 1994. 34.95 (0-8061-2617-5) U of Okla Pr.

Native Canadiana: Songs from the Urban Rez. Gregory Scofield. 125p. 1996. pap. write for info. (1-896095-74-7) Polstar Bk.

Native Carolinians: The Indians of North Carolina. Theda Perdue. (Illus.). xiv, 73p. 1995. reprint ed. pap. 8.00 (0-86526-217-9) NC Archives.

*Native Category - Formation of the Aggadah: The Earlier Midrash-Compilations. Ed. by Jacob Neusner. (Studies in Ancient Judaism : Vol. II). 336p. 2000. 52.50 (0-7618-1618-6) U Pr of Amer.

*Native Category - Formations of the Aggadah: The Later Midrash-Compilations. Jacob Neusner. (Studies in Ancient Judaism : Vol. I). 208/p. 2000. 47.50 (0-7618-1616-X) U Pr of Amer.

Native Cemeteries & Forms of Burial East of the Mississippi. David I. Bushnell, Jr. (Bureau of American Ethnology Bulletins Ser.). 160p. 1995. lib. bdg. 79.00 (0-7812-4071-9) Rprt Serv.

Native Cemeteries & Forms of Burial East of the Mississippi. David I. Bushnell. 1988. reprint ed. lib. bdg. 49.00 (0-7812-0095-4) Rprt Serv.

Native Claims & Political Development. Thomas A. Morehouse. (Occasional Papers: No. 18). (Illus.). 28p. 1987. 2.00 (0-88353-039-2) U Alaska Inst Res.

Native College Success in the 70's: Trends at the University of Alaska at Fairbanks. Judith Kleinfeld et al. (Occasional Papers: No. 15). 24p. 1982. pap. 2.00 (0-88353-031-7) U Alaska Inst Res.

*Native Crafts. Maxine Trottier. (Illus.). (J). 2000. 11.40 (0-606-18228-4) Turtleback.

*Native Crafts: Inspired by North America's First People. unabridged ed. Maxine Trottier. (Do it Ser.). (Illus.). 40p. (YA). (gr. 3 up). 2000. 12.95 (1-55074-854-8, Pub. by Kids Can Pr) Genl Dist Srvs.

*Native Crafts: Inspired by North America's First People. unabridged ed. Maxine Trottier. (Do it Ser.). (Illus.). 40p. (YA). (gr. 4-7). 2000. pap. 5.95 (1-55074-549-2, Pub. by Kids Can Pr) Genl Dist Srvs.

Native Creative Process: A Collaborative Discourse. Douglas J. Cardinal & Jeannette C. Armstrong. (Illus.). 128p. 1991. pap. 21.95 (0-919441-26-2, Pub. by Theytus Bks) Orca Bk Pubs.

Native Culture of the Marquesas. E. S. Handy. (BMB Ser.: No. 9). 1974. reprint ed. 50.00 (0-527-02112-1) Periodicals Srv.

Native Culture of the Southwest. fac. ed. A. L. Kroeber. (University of California Publications in American Archaeology & Ethnology: Vol. 23: 9). 26p. (C). 1928. reprint ed. pap. text 3.13 (1-55567-265-5) Coyote Press.

Native Cultures of Alaska: Traditions Through Time. L. J. Campbell. Ed. by Penny Rennick. LC 72-92087. (Alaska Geographic Ser.: Vol. 23-2). (Illus.). 112p. (Orig.). 1996. pap. 19.95 (1-56661-031-1) Alaska Geog Soc.

Native Cultures of the Pacific Islands. Douglas L. Oliver. LC 88-20625. (Illus.). 184p. (C). 1989. pap. text 15.00 (0-8248-1182-8) UH Pr.

*Native Dancer. Eva Jolene Boyd. (Thoroughbred Legends Ser.: Vol. 6). 144p. 2000. 24.95 (1-58150-048-3, Pub. by Blood-Horse) IPG Chicago.

Native Dawta: Poems. Ivy Claudette Armstrong. LC 98-194521. 63 p. 1995. write for info. (976-625-072-3) Kingston Pub.

Native Education & Culture-Contact in New Guinea, a Scientific Approach. William Groves. LC 75-32819. reprint ed. 34.00 (0-404-14123-4) AMS Pr.

Native Education Directory: Organizations & Resources for Educators of Native Americans, 1997. 2nd ed. Compiled by Patricia C. Hammer & Heather Beasley. 102p. 1997. pap. 12.00 (1-880785-17-X) ERIC-CRESS.

Native Encounters: A Look at Oklahoma UFO Sighting & Abduction Reports. Richard Seifried & Scott Carter. (Illus.). 94p. 1994. per. 15.00 (0-9642461-0-4) High Plains OK.

Native Ethnography: A Mexican Indian Describes His Culture. Harvey R. Bernard & Jesus S. Pedraza. LC 88-18628. (Illus.). 649p. 1989. pap. 200.00 (0-608-05177-2, 205259800001) Bks Demand.

Native Faces: Indian Cultures in American Art from the Collection of the Los Angeles Athletic Club & the Southwest Museum. Patricia Trenton & Patrick Houlihan. LC 84-81186. (Illus.). 116p. 1984. pap. 15.95 (0-685-10167-3) Southwest Mus.

Native Faces: Winold Reiss. Ed. by Peter Riess & Thomas Nygard. (Illus.). 67p. (Orig.). 1997. pap. 25.00 (0-9620327-5-1) Nygard Pub.

Native Florida Plants: Low Maintenance Landscaping & Gardening. Robert G. Haehle et al. LC 98-44073. 360p. 1999. pap. 24.95 (0-88415-425-4, 5425) Gulf Pub.

Native Forest Birds of Guam. J. Mark Jenkins. 61p. 1983. 15.00 (0-943610-38-9) Am Ornithologists.

Native Gardens: How to Create an Australian Native Landscape. Bill Molyneux & Ross MacDonald. (Illus.). 136p. (Orig.). 1993. pap. 12.95 (0-86417-462-4, Pub. by Kangaroo Pr) Seven Hills Bk.

Native Gardens in Miniature. Bill Molyneux & Sue Forrester. (Illus.). 136p. (Orig.). 1993. pap. 12.95 (0-86417-463-2, Pub. by Kangaroo Pr) Seven Hills Bk.

Native Hawaiian Garden: How to Grow & Care for Island Plants. John L. Culliney & Bruce P. Koeble. LC 99-15190. (Illus.). 176p. 1999. pap. 24.95 (0-8248-2176-9) UH Pr.

Native Healer. Medicine Grizzlybear Lake. 1993. pap. 5.50 (0-685-66342-6, Harp PBks) HarpC.

Native Healer: Initiation into an Ancient Art. Lake Medicine Grizzly Bear. 1991. pap. 13.00 (0-8356-0667-8, Quest) Theos Pub Hse.

Native Heart: An American Indian Odyssey. Gabriel Horn. LC 92-46448. 304p. 1993. pap. 15.95 (1-880032-07-4) New Wrld Lib.

Native Heritage: Images of the Indian in English-Canadian Literature. Leslie Monkman. 208p. 1981. text 35.00 (0-8020-5537-0) U of Toronto Pr.

Native Heritage: Personal Accounts by American Indians, 1790 to the Present. Ed. by Arlene Hirschfelder. (Illus.). 298p. 1998. pap. text 15.00 (0-7881-5252-1) DIANE Pub.

Native Heritage: Personal Accounts of American Indians, 1790 to the Present. Ed. by Arlene B. Hirschfelder. LC 94-42494. (Illus.). 320p. 1995. 15.00 (0-02-860412-1) Macmillan.

Native Heritage: Personal Accounts of American Indians, 1790 to the Present. Ed. by Arlene B. Hirschfelder. LC 94-42494. 1995. 15.00 (0-02-860090-8) Macmillan.

Native Imprint: The Contribution of First Peoples to Canada's Character. Olive Patricia Dickason. LC 97-200355. 1996. write for info. (0-919737-30-7) Athabasca Univ Pr.

Native in a Strange Land: Trials & Tremors. Wanda Coleman. LC 96-32027. 292p. (Orig.). 1996. pap. 15.00 (1-57423-022-0) Black Sparrow.

Native Indian Wild Game, Fish & Wild Foods Cookbook. D. Hunt. 281p. 1996. 9.98 (0-7858-0707-1) Bk Sales Inc.

Native Indian Wild Game, Fish & Wild Foods Cookbook: 340 Mouthwatering Recipes from Native Cooks. Lovesick Lake Native Women's Association Staff. Ed. by David Hunt. 222p. 1992. 24.95 (1-56523-008-6) Fox Chapel Pub.

Native Indian Wild Game, Fish & Wild Foods Cookbook: 340 Mouthwatering Recipes from Native Cooks. 2nd rev. ed. Lovesick Lake Native Women's Association Staff. Ed. by David Hunt. (Illus.). 222p. 1996. pap. 14.95 (1-56523-077-9) Fox Chapel Pub.

Native Informant: Essays on Film, Fiction, & Popular Culture. Leo Braudy. 1990. 35.00 (0-685-38918-9) OUP.

Native Informant & Other Stories: Six Tales of Defiance from the Arab World. Ramzi M. Salti. 101p. (Orig.). 1994. pap. 12.00 (0-89410-788-7, Three Contnts) L Rienner.

Native Is Restless. unabridged ed. Mary Barnes. (Illus.). 20p. 1996. spiral bd. 6.00 (1-929326-35-1) Hal Bar Pubg.

*Native Justice. George Moss. LC 99-93632. 1999. pap. 10.95 (0-533-13094-8) Vantage.

Native Land. Nadja Tesich. LC 97-17844. 320p. (Orig.). 1997. pap. 15.95 (1-57129-042-7, Lumen Eds) Brookline Bks.

Native Land. Mary A. Wells. LC 94-18460. (Illus.). 256p. 1995. pap. 15.95 (0-87805-734-X); text 45.00 (0-87805-733-1) U Pr of Miss.

Native Land & Foreign Desires: Pehea la E Pono Ai. Lilikala Kame'eleihiwa. 424p. 1992. pap. 34.95 (0-930897-59-5) Bishop Mus.

Native Land (Preservation Copy) limited ed. Lowell Jaeger. 53p. 1988. pap. 20.00 (0-944754-10-4) Pudding Hse Pubns.

Native Lands. Ed. by Dodson. 1991. pap. text. write for info. (0-582-86831-9, Pub. by Addison-Wesley) Longman.

*Native Lands: Indians & Georgia. Sarah Hill & Sue Evans Vrooman. (Illus.). iv, 49p. 1999. pap. 15.00 (1-883828-01-5) Atlanta Hist.

Native Landscapes: An Anthology of Caribbean Short Stories. Elizabeth Nunez-Harrell et al. Ed. by Velta J. Clarke. 131p. (Orig.). (YA). (gr. 7-12). 1989. pap. 7.50 (1-878433-03-2) Caribbean Diaspora Pr.

Native Landscaping from El Paso to L. A. Sally Wasowski & Andy Wasowski. 208p. Date not set. pap. 22.95 (0-8092-2511-5, 251150, Contemporary Bks) NTC Contemp Pub Co.

Native Latin American Cultures Through Their Discourse. Janet W. Hendricks et al. Ed. by Ellen B. Basso et al. (Special Publications of the Folklore Institute: No. 1). (Illus.). 176p. (Orig.). (C). 1992. 29.95 (1-879407-01-9); pap. 12.00 (1-879407-00-0) IN Univ Folk Inst.

Native Law & the Church in Medieval Wales. Huw Pryce. LC 92-25903. (Oxford Historical Monographs). (Illus.). 306p. 1993. text 75.00 (0-19-820362-4, Clarendon Pr) OUP.

Native Law in Sabah & Sarawak. M. B. Hooker. xii, 91p. 1980. 20.00 (9971-70-008-5, MICHIE) LEXIS Pub.

Native Liberty, Crown Sovereignty: The Existing Aboriginal Right of Self-Government in Canada. Bruce Clark. (McGill-Queen's Native & Northern Ser.). 288p. (C). 1990. text 65.00 (0-7735-0767-1, Pub. by McG-Queens Univ Pr) CUP Services.

Native Liberty, Crown Sovereignty: The Existing Aboriginal Right of Self-Government in Canada. Bruce Clark. (McGill-Queen's Native & Northern Ser.). 288p. (C). 1992. pap. 24.95 (0-7735-0946-1, Pub. by McG-Queens Univ Pr) CUP Services.

Native Libraries: Cross-Cultural Conditions in the Circumpolar Countries. Gordon H. Hills. LC 96-48793. (Illus.). 464p. 1997. 59.50 (0-8108-3138-4) Scarecrow.

Native Life in South Africa: Before & since the European War & the Boer Rebellion. Sol T. Plaatje. LC 90-24402. (Ravan Writers Ser.). 450p. 1996. pap. 14.95 (0-86975-466-1, Pub. by Ravan Pr) Ohio U Pr.

Native Life in South Africa: Before & since the European War & the Boer Rebellion. Solomon T. Plaatje. LC 90-24402. 450p. (Orig.). (C). 1991. pap. text 13.95 (0-8214-0986-7, Pub. by Ravan Pr) Ohio U Pr.

Native Life in South Africa, Before & since the European War & the Boer Rebellion. 2nd ed. Solomon T. Plaatje. LC 76-78585. (Illus.). 352p. 1970. lib. bdg. 35.00 (0-8371-1420-9, PLN&) Greenwood.

Native Life in Travancore. Samuel Mateer. 1991. reprint ed. text 34.00 (81-206-0514-4, Pub. by Asian Educ Servs) S Asia.

Native Literature in Canada: From the Oral Tradition to the Present. Ed. by Penny Petrone. (Illus.). 240p. 1990. pap. text 22.00 (0-19-540796-2) OUP.

Native Meso-American Spirituality. Ed. by Miguel Leon-Portilla. Tr. by Arthur J. Anderson et al. LC 80-80821. (Classics of Western Spirituality Ser.). 320p. 1980. pap. 17.95 (0-8091-2231-6) Paulist Pr.

Native Music of the Tuamotus. E. G. Burrows. (BMB Ser.: No. 109). 1974. reprint ed. 25.00 (0-527-02215-2) Periodicals Srv.

Native Names of New England Towns & Villages: Translating 199 Names Derived from Native American Words. rev. ed. C. Lawrence Bond. 84p. 1993. pap. 5.00 (0-9638180-1-5) A B Bond.

*Native Names of New England Towns & Villages: Translating 199 Names Derived from Native American Words. 3rd rev. ed. C. Lawrence Bond. Ed. by Alan B. Bond. (Illus.). 88p. 2000. mass mkt. 9.50 (0-9638180-2-3) A B Bond.

Native Nations: First Americans As Seen by Edward S. Curtis. Christopher Cardozo. Ed. by Antoinette White. (Illus.). 160p. 1993. 75.00 (0-8212-2052-7, Pub. by Bulfinch Pr) Little.

*Native Nations: Journeys in American Photography. Ed. by Booth-Clibborn Editions Staff. (Illus.). 2000. 39.95 (1-86154-073-6) Booth-Clibborn.

Native New England Cooking. 9th ed. Dale Carson. (Illus.). 139p. (Orig.). 1980. reprint ed. pap. 5.95 (0-933614-05-5) Inst Amer Indian.

*Native North America. Larry J. Zimmerman & Brian Leigh Molyneaux. (Illus.). 184p. 2000. pap. 12.95 (0-8061-3286-8) U of Okla Pr.

*Native North America: Critical & Cultural Perspectives. Ed. by Renee Hulan. LC 99-460620. 280p. 1999. pap. 21.95 (1-55022-376-3) ECW.

Native North American Alamanac, 2 vols. Ed. by Cynthia Rose & Duane Champagne. LC 96-150840. 341p. (J). 1994. text 67.00 (0-8103-9820-6, UXL) Gale.

Native North American Art. Janet Catherine Berlo. LC 99-177938. (Illus.). 302p. 1998. 39.95 (0-19-284266-8) OUP.

Native North American Art. Janet Catherine Berlo & Ruth Phillips. LC 99-177938. (Oxford History of Art Ser.). (Illus.). 302p. 1998. pap. 16.95 (0-19-284218-8) OUP.

Native North-American Biography, 2 vols. Simon Glickman & Sharon Malinowski. 400p. 1995. text 63.00 (0-8103-9821-4, UXL) Gale.

Native North American Chronology. LC 97-124879. 185p. 1995. 39.00 (0-8103-9818-4, GML00597-107501, Pub. by EurP) Gale.

Native North American Firsts. Karen Gayton Swisher. 1997. 16.95 (0-7876-0520-4, 00152839) Visible Ink Pr.

Native North American Firsts. Karen Gayton Swisher & AnCita Benally. Ed. by Melissa W. Doig. LC 97-22999. (Illus.). 263p. 1997. 55.00 (*0-7876-0518-2*, GML00198-109559) Gale.

Native North American Firsts, Vol. 14. 450p. 1997. text 60.00 (*0-7876-0953-6*, GML00597-109559) Gale.

Native North American Flutes. Lew P. Price. (Illus.). 1990. pap. 5.00 (*0-917578-07-4*) L Paxton Price.

Native North American Literature: Biographical & Critical Information on Native Writers & Orators from the United States & Canada from Historical Times to the Present. Ed. by Janet Witalec et al. LC 94-32397. 706p. 1994. 105.00 (*0-8103-9898-2*) Gale.

Native North American Music & Oral Data: A Catalogue of Sound Recordings, 1893-1976. Dorothy S. Lee. LC 78-20337. 477p. 1979. reprint ed. pap. 147.90 (*0-7837-9656-0*, 205928900005) Bks Demand.

Native North American Reference Library, 6 vols. 1994. text 184.00 (*0-8103-9813-3*, 00100501, UXL) Gale.

Native North American Reference Library: Cumulative Index. 1997. 5.00 (*0-7876-1881-0*) Gale.

Native North American Shamanism: An Annotated Bibliography, 38. Compiled by Shelley Anne Osterreich. LC 98-28015. (Bibliographies & Indexes in American History: Vol. 38). 128p. 1998. lib. bdg. 55.00 (*0-313-30168-9*, Greenwood Pr) Greenwood.

Native North American Spirituality of the Eastern Woodlands: Sacred Myths, Dreams, Vision Speeches, Healing Formulas, Rituals & Ceremonials. Ed. by Elisabeth Tooker. LC 79-66573. (Classics of Western Spirituality Ser.). 320p. 1979. pap. 24.95 (*0-8091-2256-1*) Paulist Pr.

***Native North American Tribes, 4 vols.** Ed. by Sharon Malinowski et al. LC 98-54353. (J). 1998. text 99.00 (*0-7876-2838-7*, 00158642, UXL) Gale.

Native North American Voices. Deborah A. Straub. 160p. 1996. text 39.00 (*0-8103-9819-2*, UXL) Gale.

Native North Americans: An Ethnohistorical Approach. 2nd ed. Ed. by Molly R. Mignon & Daniel L. Boxberger. LC 97-71354. 508p. (C). 1997. pap. 42.95 (*0-7872-3607-1*) Kendall-Hunt.

Native North Americans in Doctoral Dissertations, 1971-1975: A Classified & Indexed Research Bibliography, No. 1232. Gifford S. Nickerson. 1977. 7.50 (*0-686-19688-0*, Sage Prdcls Pr) Sage.

Native of Winby & Other Tales. Sarah Orne Jewett. LC 70-113679. (Short Story Index Reprint Ser.). 309p. 1977. reprint ed. 19.95 (*0-8369-3408-3*) Ayer.

Native of Winby & Other Tales. Sarah Orne Jewett. (Collected Works of Sarah Orne Jewett). 1988. reprint ed. lib. bdg. 59.00 (*0-7812-1311-8*) Rprt Serv.

Native Orchids of Belize. I. McLeish et al. (Illus.). 340p. (C). 1995. text 123.00 (*90-5410-609-3*, Pub. by A A Balkema) Ashgate Pub Co.

Native Orchids of North America North of Mexico. Donovan S. Correll. LC 78-62270. (Illus.). xvi, 400p. 1950. 55.00 (*0-8047-0999-8*) Stanford U Pr.

***Native Orchids of the Southern Appalachian Mountains.** Stanley L. Bentley. LC 99-87675. (Illus.). 272p. 2000. 39.95 (*0-8078-2563-8*); pap. 24.95 (*0-8078-4872-7*) U of NC Pr.

Native People, Native Lands: Canadian Indians, Inuit & Metis. Ed. by Bruce A. Cox. 300p. 1988. pap. 18.95 (*0-88629-062-7*) OUP.

Native People of Alaska. 3rd rev. ed. Steve J. Langdon. Ed. by Edward Bovy. (Illus.). 96p. (Orig.). 1994. pap. text 8.95 (*0-936425-17-2*) Greatland Graphics.

Native People of Southern New England, 1500-1650. Kathleen J. Bragdon. LC 95-42067. (Civilization of the American Indian Ser.: Vol. 221). (Illus.). 328p. (C). 1996. 28.95 (*0-8061-2803-8*, 2803) U of Okla Pr.

Native People of Southern New England, 1500-1650, Vol. 221. Kathleen J. Bragdon. 1999. pap. text 16.95 (*0-8061-3126-8*) U of Okla Pr.

***Native People of the Northwest: A Traveler's Guide to Land, Art & Culture.** 2nd ed. Jan Halliday et al. (Illus.). 320p. 2000. pap. 18.95 (*1-57061-241-2*) Sasquatch Bks.

Native Peoples. (Illus.). 336p. 196.00 (*0-7368-0136-7*) Capstone Pr.

Native Peoples. Robert Livesey. (Discovering Canada Ser.). (Illus.). 90p. (J). (gr. 3-6). 1993. pap. (*0-7737-5602-7*) STDK.

Native Peoples & Cultures of Canada. 2nd rev. ed. Alan I. McMillan. LC 95-187910. (Illus.). 376p. 1997. pap. 19.95 (*1-55054-150-1*, Pub. by DGL) Orca Bk Pubs.

Native Peoples of Alaska: A Traveler's Guide to Land, Art, & Culture. Jan Halliday & Patricia Petrivelli. 320p. 1998. pap. 17.95 (*1-57061-100-9*) Sasquatch Bks.

Native Peoples of Eritrea. Alberto Pollera. Tr. by Linda Lappin from ITA. LC 99-15794. 384p. 1998. 79.95 (*1-56902-094-9*) Red Sea Pr.

Native Peoples of Eritrea. Alberto Pollera. Tr. by Linda Lappin from ITA. LC 99-15794. 1998. pap. 24.95 (*1-56902-095-7*) Red Sea Pr.

***Native Peoples of North America: A Reader.** Loretta Fowler. 148p. (C). 1999. per. 40.95 (*0-7872-6262-5*, 41626201) Kendall-Hunt.

Native Peoples of North America: Diversity & Development. Susan Edmonds. LC 93-27297. (Cambridge History Programme Ser.). 63p. (J). 1993. pap. 13.95 (*0-521-42846-7*) Cambridge U Pr.

Native Peoples of North America: Diversity & Development. Susan Edmonds. (Cambridge History Programme Ser.). (Illus.). 64p. (C). 1993. pap. 8.95 (*0-685-70449-1*) Cambridge U Pr.

Native Peoples of the Great Plains. McCollough et al. 240p. (C). 1997. pap. text 70.95 (*0-7872-3801-5*, 41380101) Kendall-Hunt.

Native Peoples of the Northwest: A Traveler's Guide to Land, Art, & Culture. Jan Halliday & Gail Chehak. 282p. (Orig.). 1996. pap. 16.95 (*1-57061-056-8*) Sasquatch Bks.

***Native Peoples of the Southwest.** Trudy Griffin-Pierce. LC 00-8872. 2000. write for info. (*0-8263-1907-6*) U of NM Pr.

Native Peoples of the Southwest. Ed. by Susan L. Shaffer. (Illus.). (Orig.). 1987. pap., teacher ed. 1472.15 (*0-934351-00-7*) Heard Mus.

Native Peoples Series, 10 bks. Bill Lund. Incl. Apache Indians. LC 97-6396. (Illus.). 24p. (J). (gr. 2-3). 1998. lib. bdg. 13.75 (*1-56065-561-5*, Bridgestone Bks); Cherokee Indians. LC 96-39767. (Illus.). 24p. (J). (gr. 2-3). 1997. lib. bdg. 13.75 (*1-56065-477-5*, Bridgestone Bks); Chumash Indians. LC 97-6395. (Illus.). 24p. (J). (gr. 2-3). 1998. lib. bdg. 13.75 (*1-56065-562-3*, Bridgestone Bks); Comanche Indians. LC 96-39766. (Illus.). 24p. (J). (gr. 2-3). 1997. lib. bdg. 13.75 (*1-56065-478-3*, Bridgestone Bks); Iroquois Indians. LC 96-51504. (Illus.). 24p. (J). (gr. 2-3). 1997. lib. bdg. 13.75 (*1-56065-480-5*); Ojibwa Indians. LC 96-39765. (Illus.). 24p. (J). (gr. 2-3). 1997. lib. bdg. 13.75 (*1-56065-481-3*, Bridgestone Bks); Pomo Indians. LC 96-39763. (Illus.). 24p. (J). (gr. 2-3). 1997. lib. bdg. 13.75 (*1-56065-479-1*, Bridgestone Bks); Seminole Indians. LC 96-39764. (Illus.). 24p. (J). (gr. 2-3). 1997. lib. bdg. 13.75 (*1-56065-482-1*, Bridgestone Bks); Sioux Indians. LC 97-6394. (Illus.). 24p. (J). (gr. 2-3). 1998. lib. bdg. 13.75 (*1-56065-563-1*, Bridgestone Bks); Wampanoag Indians. LC 97-6397. (Illus.). 24p. (J). (gr. 2-3). 1998. lib. bdg. 13.75 (*1-56065-564-X*, Bridgestone Bks); (J). Set lib. bdg. 137.50 (*1-56065-659-X*, Bridgestone Bks) Capstone Pr.

Native Perennials: North American Beauties. Ed. by Nancy Beaubaire. (21st-Century Gardening Ser.). (Illus.). 112p. (Orig.). 1996. pap. 9.95 (*0-945352-92-1*) Bklyn Botanic.

Native Place, City & Nation: Regional Networks & Identities in Shanghai, 1853-1937. Bryna Goodman. LC 94-24416. (Illus.). 367p. 1995. 50.00 (*0-520-08917-0*, Pub. by U CA Pr) Cal Prin Full Svc.

Native Plant Stories. Joseph Bruchac. 1995. 18.05 (*0-606-12780-1*, Pub. by Turtleback) Demco.

Native Plant Stories. Michael J. Caduto et al. (Illus.). 140p. 1995. pap. 12.95 (*1-55591-212-5*) Fulcrum Pub.

Native Planters of Old Hawaii: Their Life, Lore & Environment. E. S. Handy et al. LC 78-119560. (Bulletin Ser.: No. 233). (Illus.). 641p. 1972. pap. 49.95 (*0-910240-11-6*) Bishop Mus.

Native Plants for Southwestern Landscapes. Judy Mielke. LC 93-12092. (Illus.). 384p. (Orig.). (C). 1993. pap. 24.95 (*0-292-75147-8*); text 39.95 (*0-292-75553-8*) U of Tex Pr.

Native Plants of Southeast Alaska. Judy K. Hall. LC TX 4-39-673. (Illus.). 285p. (Orig.). 1995. pap., spiral bd. 24.95 (*0-9658726-0-2*) Windy Ridge.

Native Plants of the Sydney District: An Identification Guide. Alan Fairley & Phillip Moore. (Illus.). 432p. 1991. 65.00 (*0-86417-261-3*, Pub. by Kangaroo Pr) Seven Hills Bk.

Native Plants Used As Medicine in Hawaii. Beatrice H. Krauss. pap. 4.50 (*0-681-02810-6*) Booklines Hawaii.

Native Population of the Americas in 1492. 2nd ed. Ed. by William M. Denevan. LC 91-40042. (Illus.). 398p. (C). 1992. reprint ed. pap. 19.95 (*0-299-13434-2*) U of Wis Pr.

Native Queen. Michael A. Sawyers. 150p. 1996. pap. 10.95 (0-87012-560-5) McClain.

This book is for the avid hunter & fisherman. It is full of adventure in the outdoors. The author adds humor with each story he tells about experiences he has had through the years with hunting & fishing. If you love nature & enjoy hunting & fishing, this book is for you. Since 1979, Michael Sawyers has published his weekly newspaper column, "Hunting & Fishing" in the Cumberland (MD) TIMES-NEWS. Through 1995 it has won ten awards from the Maryland-Delaware-DC Press Association & two prestigious Mark Twain Awards from the Associated Press. ***Publisher Paid Annotation.***

***Native Races Pt. 1: Wile Tribes.** Hubert Howe Bancroft. (Works of Hubert Howe Bancroft: Vol. 1). 1999. reprint ed. lib. bdg. 90.00 (*0-7812-7801-5*) Rprt Serv.

***Native Races Pt. 2: Civilized Nations.** Hubert Howe Bancroft. (Works of Hubert Howe Bancroft: Vol. 2). 818p. 1999. reprint ed. lib. bdg. 90.00 (*0-7812-7802-3*) Rprt Serv.

***Native Races Pt. 3: Myths & Languages.** Hubert Howe Bancroft. (Works of Hubert Howe Bancroft: Vol. 3). 808p. 1999. reprint ed. lib. bdg. 90.00 (*0-7812-7803-1*) Rprt Serv.

***Native Races Pt. 4: Antiquities.** Hubert Howe Bancroft. (Works of Hubert Howe Bancroft: Vol. 4). 1999. reprint ed. lib. bdg. 90.00 (*0-7812-7804-X*) Rprt Serv.

***Native Races Pt. 5: Primative History.** Hubert Howe Bancroft. (Works of Hubert Howe Bancroft: Vol. 5). 1999. reprint ed. lib. bdg. 90.00 (*0-7812-7805-8*) Rprt Serv.

Native Races & Their Rulers: Sketches & Studies of Official Life & Administrative Problems in Nigeria. Charles L. Temple. (Illus.). 352p. 1968. reprint ed. 57.50 (*0-7146-1727-X*, Pub. by F Cass Pubs) Intl Spec Bk.

***Native Races of America: A Copious Selection of Messages for the Study of Social Anthropology.** James George Frazer. (LC History-America-E). 351p. 1999. reprint ed. lib. bdg. 89.00 (*0-7812-4253-3*) Rprt Serv.

Native Races of the Empire see British Empire

Native Races of the Indian Archipelago: Papuans. George W. Earl. LC 75-32814. (Illus.). reprint ed. 26.00 (*0-404-14118-8*) AMS Pr.

***Native Races of the Pacific States of North America, 5 vols.** Hubert Bancroft. (LC History-America-E). 1999. reprint ed. lib. bdg. 450.00 (*0-7812-4233-9*) Rprt Serv.

Native Realm: A Search for Self-Definition. Czeslaw Milosz. Tr. by Catherine S. Leach. 1981. pap. 16.95 (*0-520-04474-6*, Pub. by U CA Pr) Cal Prin Full Svc.

Native Religions & Cultures of Central & South America: Anthropology of the Sacred. Ed. by Lawrence E. Sullivan. LC 73-84598. (Illus.). 286p. Date not set. 35.00 (*0-8264-1119-3*) Continuum.

Native Religions & Cultures of North America: Anthropology of the Sacred. Ed. by Lawrence Sullivan. LC 79-6148. 250p. 2000. 35.00 (*0-8264-1084-7*) Continuum.

Native Religions of Mexico & Peru: Hibbert Lectures. Albert D. Reville & Philip H. Wicksteed. LC 77-27167. 224p. (C). 1983. reprint ed. 45.00 (*0-404-60405-6*) AMS Pr.

Native Religions of North America: The Power of Visions & Fertility. Ake Hultkrantz. (Illus.). 144p. (C). 1997. reprint ed. pap. text 10.95 (*0-88133-985-7*) Waveland Pr.

Native Resistance & the Pax Colonial in New Spain. Ed. by Susan Schroeder. LC 97-35833. (Illus.). 200p. 1998. text 50.00 (*0-8032-4266-2*); pap. text 22.00 (*0-8032-9249-X*) U of Nebr Pr.

Native Roads: The Complete Motoring Guide to the Navajo & Hopi Nations. Fran Kosik. Ed. by George Hardeen. LC 95-68277. (Illus.). 292p. 1995. reprint ed. pap. 19.95 (*0-9645417-9-3*) Creat Solut Pub.

***Native Roads: The Complete Motoring Guide to the Navajo & Hopi Nations.** Fran Kosik. (Illus.). 292p. 1999. reprint ed. pap. 16.95 (*1-887896-16-3*, Rio Nuevo) Treas Chest Bks.

Native Rock: The Geology of Acadia National Park & Mount Desert Island, Maine, with Field Guide & Atlantis Comparison. J. Power Chaplin. LC 96-230324. (Illus.). 96p. (Orig.). 1996. pap. 12.95 (*0-9654411-0-5*) GEOGuide.

Native Roots: How the Indians Enriched America. Jack M. Weatherford. 320p. 1992. pap. 11.00 (*0-449-90713-9*, Columbine) Fawcett.

Native Science: Natural Laws of Interdependence. Gregory Cajete. LC 99-54279. (Illus.). 256p. 1999. 24.95 (*1-57416-035-4*); pap. 14.95 (*1-57416-041-9*) Clear Light.

Native Shrubs & Woody Vines of the Southeast: Landscaping Uses & Identification. Leonard E. Foote & Samuel B. Jones, Jr. (Illus.). 255p. 1998. pap. 19.95 (*0-88192-416-4*) Timber.

Native Shrubs for Landscaping. Sally L. Taylor et al. (Connecticut College Arboreium Ser.: Bulletin No. 30). 40p. 1987. pap. 5.00 (*1-878899-02-3*) CT Coll Arboretum.

Native Shrubs of Southern California. Peter H. Raven. (California Natural History Guides Ser.: No. 15). (Illus.). 1966. pap. 11.95 (*0-520-01050-7*, Pub. by U CA Pr) Cal Prin Full Svc.

Native Shrubs of the San Francisco Bay Region. Roxana S. Ferris. (California Natural History Guides Ser.: No. 24). (Illus.). 1968. pap. 9.95 (*0-520-00405-1*, Pub. by U CA Pr) Cal Prin Full Svc.

Native Society & Disease in Colonial Ecuador. Suzanne A. Alchon. (Cambridge Latin American Studies: No. 71). (Illus.). 165p. (C). 1992. text 57.95 (*0-521-40186-0*) Cambridge U Pr.

Native Soil: Photographs by Jack Spencer. Photos by Jack Spencer. LC 99-27319. (Illus.). 163p. 1999. 65.00 (*0-8071-2475-3*) La State U Pr.

***Native Son.** (YA). 1999. 9.95 (*1-56137-623-X*) Novel Units.

Native Son. Ed. by Barron's Educational Staff. (Barron's Book Notes Ser.). 134p. 1986. pap. 2.95 (*0-8120-3529-1*) Barron.

Native Son. Ed. by Chelsea House Publishing Staff. 1998. pap. text 4.95 (*0-7910-4139-5*) Chelsea Hse.

***Native Son.** Gloria Levine. 44p. (YA). 1999. 11.95 (*1-56137-624-8*) Novel Units.

***Native Son.** Hayley R. Mitchell. (Literary Companion Ser.). 224p. (YA). 2000. 17.45 (*0-7377-0320-2*) Greenhaven.

***Native Son.** Hayley R. Mitchell. LC 99-53746. (Literary Companion to American Literature Ser.). 224p. (YA). 2000. pap. 13.96 (*0-7377-0319-9*) Greenhaven.

Native Son. Wright. (C). 1997. 7.40 (*0-06-502366-8*) Addison-Wesley.

Native Son. Richard Wright. 371p. Date not set. 26.95 (*0-8488-2577-2*) Amereon Ltd.

Native Son. Richard Wright. 594p. 1997. 49.95 (*1-56849-694-X*) Buccaneer Bks.

Native Son. Richard Wright. LC 98-28838. 528p. 1998. pap. 12.00 (*0-06-092980-4*) HarpC.

Native Son. abr. ed. Richard Wright. LC 86-45710. 398p. 1987. mass mkt. 6.50 (*0-06-080977-9*) HarpC.

Native Son: A Unit Plan. Mary B. Collins. 158p. 1994. teacher ed., ring bd. 26.95 (*1-58337-050-1*) Teachers Pet Pubns.

***Native Son: Reproducible Teaching Unit.** James Scott. 57p. (YA). (gr. 7-12). 1999. ring bd. 29.50i (*1-58049-182-0*, TU125) Prestwick Hse.

Native Son: The Emergence of a New Black Hero. Robert Butler. LC 91-8827. (Twayne's Masterwork Studies: No. 77). 168p. (C). 1991. 25.95 (*0-8057-8086-6*, Twyne); per. 14.95 (*0-8057-8148-X*, Twyne) Mac Lib Ref.

Native Son & How "Bigger" Was Born. Richard Wright. 1993. 12.10 (*0-606-01128-5*, Pub. by Turtleback) Demco.

Native Son Notes. Lola J. Amis. (Cliffs Notes Ser.). 56p. 1971. pap. 4.95 (*0-8220-0874-2*, Cliff) IDG Bks.

Native Son Presidential Candidate: The Carter Vote in Georgia. Hanes Walton, Jr. LC 91-37747. 224p. 1992. 52.95 (*0-275-94118-3*, C4118, Praeger Pubs) Greenwood.

Native Song: Songbook for Nursery & Kindergarten. Olena Klymyshyn.Tr. of Ridna Pisnia. 81p. 1972. pap. 3.00 (*0-317-36112-0*) UNWLA.

***Native Sons in "No Man's Land" Rewriting Afro-American Manhood in Novels of James Baldwin, Alice Walker, John Edgar Wideman, & Ernest Gaines.** Philip Auger. (Studies in African American History & Culture). 250p. 1999. 50.00 (*0-8153-3060-X*) Garland.

Native Sources of Japanese Industrialization, 1750-1920. Thomas C. Smith. (Philip E. Lilienthal Imprint Ser.: No. 1). (C). 1988. pap. 17.95 (*0-520-06293-0*, Pub. by U CA Pr) Cal Prin Full Svc.

Native Sources of Japanese Industrialization, 1750-1920. Thomas C. Smith. LC 87-27470. (Illus.). 288p. reprint ed. pap. 89.30 (*0-7837-4688-1*, 204443500003) Bks Demand.

Native South American Discourse. Ed. by Joel Sherzer & Greg Urban. viii, 356p. 1986. lib. bdg. 123.10 (*0-89925-060-2*) Mouton.

Native South American Discourse. Ed. by Greg Urban & Scherz. viii, 347p. 1986. 123.10 (*3-11-010511-X*) Mouton.

Native South Americans: Ethnology of the Least Known Continent. Patricia J. Lyon. (Illus.). 433p. (C). 1985. reprint ed. pap. text 19.95 (*0-88133-133-3*) Waveland Pr.

Native Speaker. Chang-Rae Lee. 384p. 1996. pap. 12.95 (*1-57322-531-2*, Riverhd Trade) Berkley Pub.

Native Speaker: Teach English & See the World. Elizabeth Reid. 96p. 1996. per. 5.00 (*1-881791-06-8*) In One EAR.

Native Speaker in Applied Linguistics. Alan Davies. 192p. 1992. pap. text 18.00 (*0-7486-0296-8*, Pub. by Edinburgh U Pr) Col U Pr.

Native Speaker Is Dead! An Informal Discussion of a Linguistic Myth. Thomas M. Paikeday. 120p. (C). 1985. pap. 16.00 (*0-920865-00-3*) Lexicography.

Native-Speaker Reactions to Swedish Pronunciation Errors in English. Pia Norell. (Stockholm Studies in English: No. LXXXIX). 181p. (Orig.). 1991. pap. 49.00 (*91-22-01435-7*) Coronet Bks.

N

Native Speech. Eric Overmyer. 96p. 1984. pap. 5.95 (*0-88145-017-0*) Broadway Play.

Native Stock. Arthur Pound. LC 70-90674. (Essay Index Reprint Ser.). 1977. 23.95 (*0-8369-1373-6*) Ayer.

Native Stories of the Origin of People see Des Os Dans un Panier

Native Sulfur: Developments in Geology & Exploration. Ed. by M. A. Alspaugh & R. O. Bailey. LC 95-73103. (Illus.). 150p. (Orig.). 1996. pap. 49.00 (*0-87335-113-4*, 138-X) SMM&E Inc.

Native Texas Gardens. Andy Wasowski & Sally Wasowski. 186p. 1997. 39.95 (*0-88415-513-7*, 5513) Gulf Pub.

Native Texas Plants. 2nd ed. Andy Wasowski & Sally Wasowski. LC 96-52029. 408p. 1997. 45.00 (*0-88415-506-4*, 5506) Gulf Pub.

***Native Texas Plants: Landscaping Region by Region.** 2nd ed. Sally Wasowski & Andy Wasowski. LC 99-88970. (Illus.). 2000. 24.95 (*0-89123-077-7*, Lone Star Books) Gulf Pub.

Native Timber Harvests in Southeast Alaska. Gunnar Knapp. 54p. 1997. reprint ed. pap. 8.40 (*0-89904-646-0*, Ecosytems Resrch) Crumb Elbow Pub.

***Native Time: A Historical Time Line of Native America.** Lee Francis. (Illus.). 356p. 2000. reprint ed. pap. 20.00 (*0-7881-9360-0*) DIANE Pub.

Native Time: An Historical Timeline of Native America. Lee Francis. (Illus.). 356p. 1996. 35.00 (*0-312-13129-1*) St Martin.

Native Title. LC 94-150401. 232p. 32.95 (*0-644-32986-6*, Pub. by Aust Gov Pub) Accents Pubns.

***Native Tongue.** Suzette Haden Elgin. 2000. 32.00 (*1-55861-255-6*); pap. 14.95 (*1-55861-246-7*) Feminist Pr.

Native Tongue. Carl Hiaasen. (Florida Mysteries Ser.). 1992. mass mkt. 5.99 (*0-449-22118-0*, Crest) Fawcett.

Native Tongue. large type ed. Carl Hiaasen. LC 96-19338. (Large Print Bks.). 1996. pap. 21.95 (*1-56895-344-5*) Wheeler Pub.

Native Tongue & the Word: Developments in English Prose Style, 1380-1580. Janel Mueller. LC 83-15817. 512p. 1994. 27.50 (*0-226-54562-8*) U Ch Pr.

***Native Tours: The Anthropology of Travel & Tourism.** Erve Chambers. 137p. (C). 1999. pap. 10.95 (*1-57766-089-7*) Waveland Pr.

Native Traditions in the Postconquest World: A Symposium at Dumbarton Oaks, 2nd Through 4th October 1992. Ed. by Elizabeth H. Boone & Tom Cummins. LC 96-11704. (C). 1998. 30.00 (*0-88402-239-0*) Dumbarton Oaks.

Native Trees & Shrubs of the Florida Keys: A Field Guide. 3rd rev. ed. J. Paul Scurlock. Ed. by Mary-Alice Herbert. (Illus.). 220p. (Orig.). 1996. reprint ed. pap. 37.95 (*0-9619155-3-6*) Laurel & Herbert.

Native Trees & Shrubs of the Hawaiian Islands: A Guide. Samuel H. Lamb. LC 80-19715. 160p. 1981. pap. 14.95 (*0-913270-91-1*) Sunstone Pr.

Native Trees of the Bahamas. Jack Patterson & George B. Stevenson. (Illus.). 1977. pap. 5.95 (*0-916224-42-2*) Banyan Bks.

Native Trees of the San Francisco Bay Region. Woodbridge Metcalf. (California Natural History Guides Ser.: No. 4). (Orig.). 1959. pap. 10.00 (*0-520-00853-7*, Pub. by U CA Pr) Cal Prin Full Svc.

Native Trees, Shrubs, & Vines for Urban & Rural America. Gary L. Hightshoe. LC 87-18911. (Illus.). 832p. 1988. text 89.95 (*0-442-23274-8*, VNR) Wiley.

Native Trees, Shrubs, & Vines for Urban & Rural America: A Planting Design Manual for Environmental Designers. Gary L. Hightshoe. 832p. 1987. 125.00 (*0-471-28879-9*, VNR) Wiley.
Native Tribes Map. Alfred L. Kroeber. 1966. pap. 10.95 (*0-520-00668-2*, Pub. by U CA Pr) Cal Prin Full Svc.
Native Tribes of Eastern Bolivia & Western Matto Grosso. Ed. by Alfred Metraux. (Bureau of American Ethnology Bulletins Ser.). 182p. 1995. lib. bdg. 79.00 (*0-7812-4134-0*) Rprt Serv.
Native Tribes of Old Ohio. Helen C. Tregillis. (Illus.). 137p. (Orig.). 1993. pap. text 15.50 (*1-55613-925-X*) Heritage Bk.
Native Tribes of South-East Australia. Alfred W. Howitt. LC 78-67718. (Folktale Ser.). reprint ed. 92.50 (*0-404-16095-6*) AMS Pr.
Native Trout of Western North America. R. J. Behnke. LC 92-72941. (AFS Monograph Ser.: No. 6). 275p. 1992. pap. 40.00 (*0-913235-78-4*, 520.06P) Am Fisheries Soc.
Native Trout Project, 1994. Ed. by D. V. Buchanan et al. (Illus.). 44p. 1997. reprint ed. pap. 5.40 (*0-89904-645-2*, Cascade Geog Soc) Crumb Elbow Pub.
Native Trout Project, 1991. D. V. Buchanan et al. (Illus.). 52p. 1998. reprint ed. 11.20 (*0-89904-864-1*, Cascade Geog Soc); reprint ed. pap. 6.20 (*0-89904-865-X*, Cascade Geog Soc) Crumb Elbow Pub.
Native Use of Fish in Hawaii. 2nd ed. Margaret Titcomb. 188p. 1972. pap. 11.95 (*0-8248-0592-5*) UH Pr.
Native Vegetation of Nebraska. John E. Weaver. LC 65-13259. (Illus.). 192p. 1965. reprint ed. pap. text 59.60 (*0-608-05048-2*, 205970900005) Bks Demand.
Native Villages & Village Sites East of the Mississippi. Ed. by David I. Bushnell, Jr. (Bureau of American Ethnology Bulletins Ser.). 111p. 1995. lib. bdg. 79.00 (*0-7812-4069-7*) Rprt Serv.
Native Villages & Village Sites East of the Mississippi. David I. Bushnell, Jr. 1988. reprint ed. lib. bdg. 49.00 (*0-7812-0092-X*) Rprt Serv.
Native Visions: Evolution in Northwest Coast Art, from the 18th Through the 20th Century. Steven C. Brown. LC 97-30413. (Illus.). 244p. 1998. 70.00 (*0-295-97657-8*) U of Wash Pr.
Native Visions: Evolution in Northwest Coast Art, from the 18th Through the 20th Century. Steven C. Brown. LC 97-30413. (Illus.). 228p. 1998. pap. 70.00 (*0-295-97658-6*) U of Wash Pr.
Native Voices. Solomon I. Omo-Osagie, II. 108p. 1995. pap. 6.50 (*0-9647217-0-8*) S I Omo-Osagie.
***Native vs. Settler: Ethnic Conflict in Israel/Palestine, Northern Ireland & South Africa, 200.** Thomas G. Mitchell. LC 00-21075. (Contributions in Military Studies: Vol. 200). 272p. 2000. 64.00 (*0-313-31357-1*, GM1357, Greenwood Pr) Greenwood.
Native Ways: California Indian Stories & Memories. Malcolm Margolin & Yolanda Montijo. (Illus.). 128p. (J). (gr. 4-6). 1995. pap. 8.95 (*0-930588-73-8*) Heyday Bks.
Native Wisdom. Ed. by Joseph Bruchac. LC 94-29472. 112p. 1994. pap. 11.00 (*0-06-251172-6*, Pub. by Harper SF) HarpC.
Native Wisdom: Perceptions of the Natural Way. Ed McGaa Eagle Man. Ed. by Sharon Diotte. (Illus.). 260p. (Orig.). 1995. pap. 15.00 (*0-9645173-1-0*) Four Dir Pub.
Native Wisdom for White Minds: Daily Reflections Inspired by the Native Peoples of the World. Anne W. Schaef. LC 94-96757. 384p. (Orig.). 1995. pap. 10.00 (*0-345-39405-4*) Ballantine Pub Grp.
Native Women. Charles L. Convis. (True Tales of the Old West Ser.: Vol. 3). (Illus.). ii, 62p. (Orig.). 1996. pap. 7.95 (*0-9651954-3-0*) Pioneer Pr NV.
Native Writers & Canadian Writing. Ed. by William H. New. 352p. 1991. pap. 22.95 (*0-7748-0371-1*) U of Wash Pr.
Native Writing. Don Scheese. 1996. 33.00 (*0-8057-0964-9*, Twyne) Mac Lib Ref.
Native Writings in Massachusett. Ives Goddard & Kathleen Bragdon. LC 87-72874. (Memoirs Ser.: Vol. 185). (Illus.). 838p. (C). 1988. 60.00 (*0-87169-185-X*, M185-GOI) Am Philos.
Natives: Animals of the Sonoran Desert. Photos by Herbert R. Stratford, 4th. (Illus.). 1993. pap. text 14.95 (*0-9635608-0-8*) Stratford AZ.
Natives & Academics: Research & Writing about American Indians. Ed. by Devon A. Mihesuah. LC 97-30298. xi, 213p. 1998. pap. text 15.00 (*0-8032-8243-5*) U of Nebr Pr.
Natives & Newcomers: Canada's 'Heroic Age' Reconsidered. Bruce G. Trigger. 448p. 1986. pap. 22.95 (*0-7735-0595-4*, Pub. by McG-Queens Univ Pr) CUP Services.
Natives & Newcomers: Ethnic Southerners & Southern Ethnics. George B. Tindall. LC 94-5970. (Georgia Southern University Jack N. & Addie D. Averett Lecture Ser.: No. 3). 64p. 1994. 18.00 (*0-8203-1655-5*) U of Ga Pr.
***Natives & Newcomers: The Cultural Origins of North America.** James Axtell. LC 99-56089. (Illus.). 416p. 2000. text 59.95 (*0-19-513770-1*); pap. text. write for info. (*0-19-513771-X*) OUP.
Natives & Newcomers: The Making of Irish Colonial Society 1534-1641. Ed. by Ciaran Brady & Raymond Gillespie. 260p. 1986. 35.00 (*0-7165-2378-7*, Pub. by Irish Acad Pr) Intl Spec Bk.
Natives & Newcomers: The Ordering of Opportunity in Mid-Nineteenth-Century Poughkeepsie. Clyde Griffen & Sally Griffen. (Studies in Urban History). 320p. 1978. 37.95 (*0-674-60325-7*) HUP.
Natives & Newcomers: The Way We Lived in North Carolina before 1770. Elizabeth Fenn & Peter H. Wood. Ed. by Sydney Nathans. LC 82-20128. 111p. 1983. reprint ed. pap. 34.50 (*0-7837-9033-3*, 204978400003) Bks Demand.
Natives & Settlers: Indian & Yankee Culture in Early California: The Collections of Charles P. Wilcomb. Ed. by Melinda Y. Frye. (Museum Treasures Ser.). (Illus.). 88p. 1988. pap. text 26.50 (*0-8026-0022-0*) Univ Pub Assocs.
Natives & Strangers: A Multicultural History of Americans. 3rd ed. Leonard Dinnerstein et al. (Illus.). 384p. (C). 1996. reprint ed. pap. text 23.95 (*0-19-509084-5*) OUP.
Natives Are Restless. Idries Shah. 224p. 1988. 22.00 (*0-86304-044-6*, Pub. by Octagon Pr) ISHK.
Natives Bills (1935) & Native Views on the Native Bills (1935) G. Heaton Nicholls & Davidson D. Jabavu. (Colin Webb Natal & Zululand Ser.: No. 8). (Illus.). 84p. 1995. pap. 19.00 (*0-86980-913-X*, Pub. by Univ Natal Pr) Intl Spec Bk.
Native's Guide to Chicago's Northern Suburbs. Jason Fargo. LC 98-85576. (Illus.). 1999. pap. 12.95 (*0-9642426-8-0*) Lake Claremont.
Native's Guide to Chicago's Northwest Suburbs. Martin Bartels. LC 99-62508. (Illus.). 1999. pap. 12.95 (*1-893121-00-3*) Lake Claremont.
Native's Guide to Chicago's South Suburbs. Christina Bultinck & Christy Johnston-Czarnecki. LC 98-85577. (Illus.). 1999. pap. 12.95 (*0-9642426-1-3*) Lake Claremont.
Native's Guide to Chicago's Western Suburbs. Laura M. Toops & John Toops. LC 99-62507. (Illus.). 1999. pap. 12.95 (*0-9642426-6-4*) Lake Claremont.
Native's Guide to New York. 4th rev. ed. Richard Laermer. LC 97-47585. 320p. 1998. pap. 15.00 (*0-393-31810-9*) Norton.
Native's Guide to New York: 750 Ways to Have the Time of Your Life in the City. 2nd rev. ed. Richard Laermer. (Illus.). 336p. 1991. pap. 12.95 (*1-55958-114-X*) Prima Pub.
Native's Guide to New York: 750 Ways to Have the Time of Your Life in the City. 3rd rev. ed. Richard Laermer. LC 95-1533. (Illus.). 416p. 1995. pap. 16.95 (*0-7615-0020-0*) Prima Pub.
Natives of My Person. George Lamming. (Ann Arbor Paperbacks Ser.). 300p. (C). 1991. reprint ed. pap. 17.95 (*0-472-06467-3*, 06467); reprint ed. text 49.50 (*0-472-09467-X*, 09467) U of Mich Pr.
Natives of Northern India. W. Crooke. (C). 1995. 36.00 (*81-206-1110-1*, Pub. by Asian Educ Servs) S Asia.
Natives of Note: Biographies. Ellen S. Savage. (Illus.). 40p. 1994. pap. 6.95 (*1-878051-41-5*) Circumpolar Pr.
Natives of Sarawak & British North Borneo, 2 vols., Set. Henry L. Roth. LC 77-87510. reprint ed. 75.00 (*0-404-16780-2*) AMS Pr.
Natives of the Far North: Alaska's Vanishing Culture in the Eye of Edward Sheriff Curtis. Shannon Lowry. (Illus.). 160p. 1994. 29.95 (*0-8117-1102-1*) Stackpole.
Natives Preferred. Caroline Dormon. 1965. 25.00 (*0-87511-026-6*) Claitors.
Native's Return. Louis Adamic. LC 74-34412. 358p. 1975. reprint ed. lib. bdg. 65.00 (*0-8371-7965-3*, ADNR, Greenwood Pr) Greenwood.
Native's Return: An American Immigrant Visits Yugoslavia & Discovers His Old Country. Louis Adamic. (American Biography Ser.). 370p. 1991. reprint ed. lib. bdg. 79.00 (*0-7812-8003-6*) Rprt Serv.
Native's Return, 1945-1988. William L. Shirer. (Twentieth Century Journey Ser.: Vol. 3). 1990. 24.95 (*0-685-31432-4*) Little.
Natives Were Friendly. Noel Barber. 2.95 (*0-86072-021-7*, Pub. by Quartet) Charles River Bks.
Natividad. rev. ed. Tr. by Alma F. Ada. LC 93-46976.Tr. of Nativity. (SPA., Illus.). 32p. (J). (ps up). 1994. pap. 4.95 (*0-15-200184-0*) Harcourt.
Nativism & Slavery: The Know-Nothing Party in the Northern United States. Tyler G. Anbinder. (Illus.). 352p. 1992. text 75.00 (*0-19-507233-2*) OUP.
Nativism & Slavery: The Northern Know Nothings & the Politics of the 1850s. Tyler G. Anbinder. (Illus.). 352p. 1994. pap. text 19.95 (*0-19-508922-7*) OUP.
Nativism in a Metropolis: Shiv Sena in Bombay. 1983. 21.00 (*0-8364-0955-8*, Pub. by Manohar) S Asia.
Nativism Overseas: Contemporary Chinese Women Writers. Ed. by Hsin-sheng C. Kao. LC 92-14643. (SUNY Series, Women Writers in Translation). 282p. (C). 1993. pap. text 21.95 (*0-7914-1440-X*) State U NY Pr.
Nativism Overseas: Contemporary Chinese Women Writers. Ed. by Hsin-sheng C. Kao. LC 92-14643. (SUNY Series, Women Writers in Translation). 282p. (C). 1993. text 65.50 (*0-7914-1439-6*) State U NY Pr.
Nativist Movement. Bruno Knobel. 1995. 26.95 (*0-8057-9712-2*, Twyne) Mac Lib Ref.
Nativities & Passions. Martin L. Smith. 191p. 1995. pap. 10.95 (*1-56101-116-9*) Cowley Pubns.
Nativity see Natividad
Nativity. Arnoul Greban. Tr. by Shelley Sewall. LC 90-33187. (Illus.). 128p. (C). 1991. 26.95 (*0-8093-1646-3*) S Ill U Pr.
***Nativity.** John-Marc Grob. (Bible Kingdom Ser.). 2000. pap. 1.99 (*0-8054-0981-5*) Broadman.
Nativity. Roberta Letwenko & Edward Letwenko. (Jeremy the Bible Bookworm Ser.). (Illus.). 32p. (J). 3.95 (*0-614-22061-0*) Regina Pr.
Nativity. Bonnie L. Line. LC 97-60778. 80p. 1997. pap. 8.95 (*1-57921-029-5*) WinePress Pub.
Nativity. Ed. by San Francisco Harper Staff. (Illus.). 64p. 1984. 20.45 (*0-86683-852-X*, 8464) Harper SF.
Nativity. Julie Vivas. LC 87-23795. (Illus.). 32p. (J). (ps up). 1988. 13.95 (*0-15-200535-8*, Gulliver Bks) Harcourt.
Nativity. Julie Vivas. LC 87-23795. (Illus.). 32p. (J). (ps up). 1994. pap. 6.00 (*0-15-200117-4*, Gulliver Bks) Harcourt.
Nativity. Illus. by Juan Wijngaard. LC 96-14041. 32p. (Orig.). (J). (gr. k-5). 1996. pap. 5.99 (*1-56402-981-6*) Candlewick Pr.
Nativity. Winston Press Editorial Staff. (Illus.). 64p. 1985. 9.95 (*0-86683-726-4*, 8304) Harper SF.
Nativity: Mary Remembers. Laurie L. Knowlton. LC 97-77913. (Illus.). 32p. (J). (gr. 1-4). 1998. 14.95 (*1-56397-714-1*) Boyds Mills Pr.
Nativity & Dramatic Monologues for Today. Lasana M. Sekou. LC 88-80155. (Illus.). 84p. (Orig.). 1988. pap. text 9.00 (*0-913441-04-X*) Hse of Nehesi.
Nativity House. (Illus.). (J). (ps-1). 1992. 34.99 (*1-888074-45-0*) Pckts Lrning.
Nativity of Christ see Rozhdestvo Khristovo
Nativity of Our Lord: The Birth of the Messiah. Euphemia Briere. (Illus.). (J). (gr. 1-3). 1993. pap. 5.00 (*0-913026-38-7*) St Nectarios.
Nativity of the Holy Mother of God see Rozhdestvo Presvjatia Bogoroditsi
***Nativity Poems.** Joseph Brodsky. 2000. text. write for info. (*0-374-21940-0*) FS&G.
Nativity Press Out Model. I. Ashman & Stephen Cartwright. (Illus.). 32p. (J). (gr. 2-7). 1992. text 11.95 (*0-7460-1319-1*, Usborne) EDC.
Nativity Scene. Eduardo De Filippo. Tr. by Anthony Molino & Paul Feinberg from ITA. LC 97-136703. (Drama Ser.: No. 8). 150p. 1992. pap. 12.00 (*0-920717-80-2*) Guernica Editions.
Nativity Stories: Featuring the Art of Fontanini. Gail Cohen & Grace Dumelle. (Illus.). 80p. 1996. text 22.50 (*0-937739-30-8*) Roman IL.
Nativity Story. Gabriele. (J). 1985. pap. 1.95 (*0-911211-75-6*) Penny Lane Pubns.
Nativsm Reborn? The Official English Language Movement in the American States. Raymond Tatalovich. 336p. 1995. text 32.50 (*0-8131-1918-9*) U Pr of Ky.
Natnl Fund Nrsg/ CC+ Comm. A. Kozier. 1995. text 61.88 (*0-201-30253-5*) Addison-Wesley.
***NATO: A History.** Peter Duignan. LC 00-29567. 2000. write for info. (*0-8179-9782-2*) Hoover Inst Pr.
NATO: An Annotated Bibliography. Ed. by Phil Williams. LC 93-42578. (International Organizations Ser.: Vol. 8). 330p. (C). 1994. 69.95 (*1-56000-154-2*) Transaction Pubs.
NATO: From Berlin to Bosnia - Trans-Atlantic Security in Transition. S. Nelson Drew. 49p. (Orig.). (C). 1996. reprint ed. pap. text 25.00 (*0-7881-3680-1*) DIANE Pub.
NATO: Our Guarantee of Peace. H. Hanning. 60p. 1986. pap. 4.95 (*0-08-033604-3*, T130, P130, K125, Pergamon Pr) Elsevier.
NATO after Forty Years. Ed. by Lawrence S. Kaplan et al. LC 90-8817. 293p. 1990. 45.00 (*0-8420-2366-6*); pap. text 17.95 (*0-8420-2367-4*) Scholarly Res Inc.
NATO After Thirty Years. Lawrence S. Kaplan & Robert W. Clawson. LC 80-53885. 262p. (C). 1981. lib. bdg. 40.00 (*0-8420-2172-8*) Scholarly Res Inc.
NATO Airpower: Organizing for Uncertainty. Willard E. Naslund. LC 93-38717. 1994. pap. 9.00 (*0-8330-1474-9*, MR-215-AF) Rand Corp.
NATO Alliances Negotiations over the Soviet Pipeline Sanctions. Beverly Crawford. (Pew Case Studies in International Affairs). 50p. (C). 1993. pap. text 3.50 (*1-56927-101-1*) Geo U Inst Dplmcy.
NATO & American Security. Ed. by Klaus E. Knorr. LC 83-22882. 342p. 1984. reprint ed. lib. bdg. 69.50 (*0-313-24376-X*, KNNA, Greenwood Pr) Greenwood.
NATO & Caspian Security: A Mission Too Far? Richard Sokolsky & Tanya Charlick-Paley. LC 99-31661. (Illus.). xvii, 117p. 1999. pap. 15.00 (*0-8330-2750-6*, MR-1074-AF) Rand Corp.
NATO & Germany: A Study in the Sociology of Supranational Relations. Stanford M. Lyman. LC 95-12243. Vol. 4. (Illus.). 384p. 1995. text 40.00 (*1-55728-389-3*) U of Ark Pr.
***NATO & Southeastern Europe: Security Issues for the Early 21st Century.** Ed. by Dimitris Keridis & Robert L. Pfaltzgraff, Jr. 2000. pap. 26.95 (*1-57488-289-9*) Brasseys.
NATO & the Changing World Order: An Appraisal by Scholars & Policymakers. Ed. by Kenneth W. Thompson. (Miller Center Series on a New World Order: Vol. IV). (Illus.). 252p. (C). 1996. pap. text 24.50 (*0-7618-0203-7*); lib. bdg. 49.50 (*0-7618-0202-9*) U Pr of Amer.
NATO & the Defense of the West. Prince H. Loewenstein & Volkmar Von Zuhlsdorff. Tr. by Edward Fitzgerald from GER. LC 74-20276. 383p. 1975. reprint ed. lib. bdg. 69.50 (*0-8371-7855-X*, LONA, Greenwood Pr) Greenwood.
NATO & the European Union: Confronting the Challenges of European Security & Enlargement. Ed. by S. Victor Papacosma & Pierre H. Laurent. pap. 12.50 (*1-882160-04-5*) Kent St U L L Lemnitzer.
NATO & the European Union Movement. M. Margaret Ball. LC 74-9319. (Library of World Affairs, London, Institute of World Affairs Ser.: No. 45). (Illus.). 486p. 1974. reprint ed. lib. bdg. 79.50 (*0-8371-7642-5*, BANA, Greenwood Pr) Greenwood.
NATO & the Future of European Security. Sean Kay. LC 98-18649. 208p. 1998. 59.00 (*0-8476-9000-8*); pap. 19.95 (*0-8476-9001-6*) Rowman.
NATO & the Mediterranean. Ed. by Lawrence S. Kaplan et al. LC 84-16055. 263p. (C). 1985. 45.00 (*0-8420-2221-X*) Scholarly Res Inc.
NATO & the New Technologies. David Hobbs. LC 88-39010. (NATO Ser.). 164p. (Orig.). (C). 1989. pap. text 17.00 (*0-8191-7324-X*) Atl Coun US.
NATO & the Nuclear Revolution: A Crisis of Credibility, 1966-67. rev. ed. Helga Haftendorn. (Nuclear History Program Ser.). 460p. 1996. text 85.00 (*0-19-828003-3*) OUP.
NATO & the United States: The Enduring Alliance. Lawrence S. Kaplan. LC 93-47497. (Twayne's International History Ser.: Vol. 13). 240p. 1994. 33.00 (*0-8057-7926-4*, Twyne); pap. 20.00 (*0-8057-9221-X*, Twyne) Mac Lib Ref.
NATO Armies Today. Nigel Thomas. (Elite Ser.: No. 16). (Illus.). 64p. pap. 12.95 (*0-85045-822-6*, 9416, Pub. by Osprey) Stackpole.
NATO Deterrence Doctrine: No Way Out. Richard K. Betts. (CISA Working Papers: No. 51). 78p. (Orig.). 1985. pap. 15.00 (*0-86682-064-7*) Ctr Intl Relations.
NATO Enlargement. Jeffrey Simon. 1997. pap. text 15.00 (*1-57906-025-0*) NYU Pr.
NATO Enlargement: Illusions & Reality. Ed. by Ted G. Carpenter & Barbara Conry. 284p. 1998. 21.95 (*1-882577-58-2*); pap. 11.95 (*1-882577-59-0*) Cato Inst.
NATO Enlargement & Central Europe: A Study in Civil-Military Relations. Jeffrey Simon. 333p. 1997. per. 18.00 (*0-16-061194-6*) USGPO.
NATO Enlargement Debate, 1990-1997: Blessings of Liberty, 174. Gerald B. Solomon. LC 97-50393. (Praeger/CSIS the Washington Papers: Vol. 174). 208p. (C). 1998. 49.95 (*0-275-96289-X*, Praeger Pubs); pap. 18.95 (*0-275-96290-3*, Praeger Pubs) Greenwood.
***NATO Enlargement During the Cold War: Strategy & System in the Western Alliance.** Mark Smith. LC 00-33352. 2000. write for info. (*0-312-23606-9*) St Martin.
NATO Expansion. Ed. by Kenneth W. Thompson. LC 98-171072. (Miller Center Series on a New World Order: Vol. VI). 208p. (C). 1998. 44.00 (*0-7618-1079-X*); pap. 24.50 (*0-7618-1080-3*) U Pr of Amer.
Nato from Berlin to Bosnia: Trans-Atlantic Security in Transition. S. Nelson Drew. 53p. 1995. pap. 3.00 (*0-16-061174-1*) USGPO.
NATO from Berlin to Bosnia: Transatlantic Security in Transition, 2 vols. 1997. lib. bdg. 600.75 (*0-8490-6164-4*) Gordon Pr.
NATO in the Balkans: Voice of Opposition. Ramsey Clark et al. LC 97-42683. (Illus.). 220p. 1998. pap. 15.95 (*0-9656916-2-4*) Intl Action Ctr.
NATO in the Fifth Decade. Ed. by Keith Dunn & Stephen J. Flanagan. 242p. (C). 1992. pap. text 40.00 (*0-941375-53-6*) DIANE Pub.
NATO in the New European Order. Fergus Carr & Kostas Ifantis. 270p. 1996. text 65.00 (*0-312-15815-7*) St Martin.
NATO in the 1980's: Challenges & Responses. Ed. by Linda P. Brady & Joyce P. Kaufman. LC 85-6474. 286p. 1985. 55.00 (*0-275-90065-7*, C0065, Praeger Pubs) Greenwood.
NATO in the Post-Cold War Era: Does It Have a Future? Ed. by S. Victor Papacosma & Mary A. Heiss. (Illus.). 384p. 1995. text 55.00 (*0-312-12130-X*) St Martin.
***NATO in the 21st Century What Purpose? What Mission?** Ivo H. Daalder. 1999. pap. text 11.95 (*0-8157-1695-8*) Brookings.
***NATO Looking Ahead: Report of the European Institute on Defense Industry Cooperation & the Economics of Enlargement.** Ed. by Charles Barry & Peter S. Rashish. LC 99-61100. 70p. 1999. pap. 15.00 (*1-886607-13-3*) European Inst.
NATO Looks East. Ed. by Piotr J. Dutkiewicz & Robert Jackson. LC 98-6823. 208p. 1998. 55.00 (*0-275-96059-5*, Praeger Pubs) Greenwood.
***NATO Looks South: New Challenges & New Strategies in the Mediterranean.** Ian O. Lesser. LC 99-87790. xv, 66p. 2000. pap. 12.00 (*0-8330-2810-3*, MR-1126-AF) Rand Corp.
NATO Major Combat Aircraft. Ed. by Michael Taylor. (Illus.). 200p. 1990. 19.95 (*1-85488-001-2*) Howell Pr VA.
NATO Major Warships - Europe. Eric J. Grove. (Illus.). 200p. 1990. 19.95 (*1-85488-006-3*) Howell Pr VA.
NATO Major Warships - U. S. A. & Canada. Eric J. Grove. (Illus.). 200p. 1990. 19.95 (*1-85488-020-9*) Howell Pr VA.
***NATO Meets the Post-Strategic Condition: Political Vicissitudes & Theoretical Puzzles in the Alliance's First Wave of Adaptation, 1990-1997.** Alexander Siedschlag. 144p. 1999. pap. text 26.95 (*3-8258-3853-6*, Pub. by CE24) Transaction Pubs.
NATO Negotiations on the Intermediate-Range Nuclear Forces, 1977-1979. Don R. Drenth. (Pew Case Studies in International Affairs). 50p. (C). 1993. pap. text 3.50 (*1-56927-305-7*) Geo U Inst Dplmcy.
NATO, 1997: Year of Change. Lawrence R. Chalmer et al. LC 98-39243. 1998. write for info. (*1-57906-013-7*) Natl Defense.
NATO on the Brink of a New Millennium: The Battle for Consensus. Rob De Wijk & Nicholas Sherwen. LC 97-23309. (Atlantic Commentaries Ser.). 176p. 1998. 39.95 (*1-85753-258-9*, Pub. by Brasseys) Brasseys.
***NATO Opposition.** Frederick Parkins. 132p. 2000. pap. 9.95 (*0-595-00535-7*, Writers Club Pr) iUniversecom.
NATO Strategy & Nuclear Defense, 69. Carl H. Amme. LC 87-17746. (Contributions in Military Studies Ser.: No. 69). (Illus.). 202p. 1988. 49.95 (*0-313-26037-0*, ANS/, Greenwood Pr) Greenwood.
NATO Summit & Beyond: Consensus Report of the CSIS Senior NATO Policy Group. Alexander Haig & Harold Brown. Ed. by Simon Serefaty. LC 93-48961. (CSIS Panel Reports). 23p. (Orig.). (C). 1994. pap. 14.95 (*0-89206-262-2*) CSIS.
NATO, the Engangling Alliance. Robert E. Osgood. LC 62-8348. 428p. reprint ed. pap. 132.70 (*0-608-30717-3*, 200727800063) Bks Demand.
***Nato The War Machine of The Revived Roman Empire: Where Leads The Road to Kosovo.** Noah W. Hutchings. 1999. pap. text 9.95 (*1-57558-043-8*) Hearthstone OK.

N

An Asterisk (*) at the beginning of an entry indicates that the title is appearing for the first time.

NATO Today: Curing Self-Inflicted Sounds. Angelo Codevilla. (C). 1990. 35.00 (*0-907967-00-0*, Pub. by Inst Euro Def & Strat) St Mut.

NATO Transformed: The Alliance's New Roles in International Security. David S. Yost. (Illus.). 432p. 1998. pap. 19.95 (*1-878379-81-X*) US Inst Peace.

NATO, Turkey, & the Southern Flank: A Mideastern Perspective. Ihsan Gurkan. 67p. 1980. pap. text 14.95 (*0-87855-825-X*) Transaction Pubs.

NATO 2000: A Political Agenda for a Political Alliance, No. 3. Jamie Shea. Ed. by Nicholas Sherwen. (Brassey's Atlantic Commentaries Ser.). 120p. 1990. pap. 16.50 (*0-08-040727-7*, Pub. by Brasseys) Brasseys.

Natoma's Low-Fat Home-Style Cooking. Natoma Riley. LC 95-103480. 260p. 1994. spiral bd. 16.95 (*1-886246-00-9*) Alpha LifeSpan.

Natoma's Low-Fat Lifestyle Cooking: Down-Home Cooking at It's Best. Natoma Riley. Ed. by Frank Riley. 264p. (Orig.). 1997. pap. 15.95 (*1-886246-08-4*) Alpha LifeSpan.

Natoma's 28 Days to a Low-Fat Lifestyle: A Guide to Better Health & Weight Loss. rev. ed. Natoma Riley. Ed. by Frank Riley. (Healthy Living Ser.). 110p. 1997. pap. 12.95 (*1-886246-06-8*) Alpha LifeSpan.

NATO's Anxious Birth: The Prophetic Vision of the 1940's. Ed. by Andre De Staercke. LC 84-40609. (Illus.). 220p. 1985. 29.95 (*0-685-10522-9*) St Martin.

NATO's Conventional Defenses. Stephen J. Flanagan. 200p. 1988. pap. 34.95 (*0-88730-327-7*, HarpBusn); pap. text 14.95 (*0-88730-328-5*, HarpBusn) HarpInfo.

***NATO's Empty Victory: A Postmortem on the Balkan War.** Ed. by Ted G. Carpenter. 152p. 2000. pap. 9.95 (*1-882577-86-8*, Pub. by Cato Inst) Natl Bk Netwk.

Nato's Future: Beyond Collective Defense. Stanley R. Sloan. 81p. 1996. per. 3.75 (*0-16-061181-4*) USGPO.

NATO's Future: Beyond Collective Defense. Stanley R. Sloan. 73p. (C). 1996. reprint ed. pap. text 30.00 (*0-7881-3681-X*) DIANE Pub.

***NATO's Future: Implications for U. S. Military Capabilities & Posture.** David A. Ochmanek. LC 99-86504. xiii, 31p. 2000. 7.50 (*0-8330-2809-X*, MR-1162-AF) Rand Corp.

NATO's Future: Toward a New Transatlantic Bargain. Stanley R. Sloan. (Illus.). 243p. (Orig.). (C). 1995. pap. text 40.00 (*0-7881-2155-3*) DIANE Pub.

NATO's Mediterranean Initiative: Policy Issues & Dilemmas. Stephen F. Larrabee et al. LC 98-14140. (Illus.). 107p. 1998. pap. 15.00 (*0-8330-2605-4*, MR-957-IMD) Rand Corp.

NATO's Military in the Age of Crisis Management. Edward Foster. LC 95-224561. (RUSI Whitehall Paper Ser.). 73p. 1995. write for info. (*0-85516-099-3*) Royal United Services Inst for Defence Studies.

NATO's Northern Allies: The National Security Policies of Belgium, the Netherlands, Norway & Denmark. Ed. by Gregory Flynn. (Atlantic Institute for International Affairs Research Ser.). 320p. 1985. 71.50 (*0-8476-7444-4*) Rowman.

NATO's Nuclear Dilemmas. David N. Schwartz. LC 83-11911. 270p. 1983. 32.95 (*0-8157-7772-8*); pap. 12.95 (*0-8157-7771-X*) Brookings.

NATO's Reserve Forces, No. 5. Ed. by Sjouke De Jong. (Brassey's Atlantic Commentaries Ser.). 114p. 1992. pap. 16.50 (*0-08-041340-4*, Pub. by Brasseys) Brasseys.

NATO's Role in European Stability. Ed. by Stephen A. Cambone. LC 95-16089. (CSIS Panel Reports). 70p. (C). 1995. pap. text 14.95 (*0-89206-324-6*) CSIS.

***NATO's Role, Missions & Futures.** Ed. by A. M. Babkina. 147p. 1999. lib. bdg. 59.00 (*1-56072-667-9*) Nova Sci Pubs.

NATO's Strategic Options: Arms Control & Defense. Ed. by David S. Yost. (Policy Studies on International Politics). (Illus.). 275p. 1981. 72.00 (*0-08-027184-7*, Pergamon Pr) Elsevier.

NATO's Strategy: A Case of Outdated Priorities? Patrick Cosgrave & George Richey. (C). 1990. 45.00 (*0-907967-40-X*, Pub. by Inst Euro Def & Strat) St Mut.

NATO'S Theater Nuclear Force Modernization Program: The Real Issues. Jeffrey Record. LC 81-84988. (Special Reports). 102p. 1981. 11.95 (*0-89549-038-2*) Inst Foreign Policy Anal.

NATO's Transformation: The Changing Shape of the Atlantic Alliance. Ed. by Philip H. Gordon. LC 96-36787. 306p. 1996. reprint ed. 63.00 (*0-8476-8386-9*); reprint ed. pap. 20.95 (*0-8476-8385-0*) Rowman.

Natosi: Strong Medicine. Peter Roop. 32p. (J). (gr. 3-8). 1984. pap. 4.95 (*0-89992-090-X*) Coun India Ed.

Natriuretic Peptides in Health & Disease. Ed. by Willis K. Samson & Ellis Levin. LC 97-18996. (Contemporary Endocrinology Ser.: Vol. 3). (Illus.). 352p. 1997. 125.00 (*0-89603-453-4*) Humana.

Natrual Resources see Alaska Administrative Code 4/99 Supplement

***Natrual Resources: Applications in Biology & Chemistry.** 2nd ed. Cord. 1998. pap. 7.25 (*1-57837-085-X*) Thomson Learn.

Natrue's Patterns Student Book. Lisa Trumbauer. Ed. by Stephanie Pliakas. (Early Science Ser.). 16p. (J). (ps-2). 1998. pap. text, student ed. 3.33 (*1-56784-979-2*) Newbridge Educ.

Nats'ahts'a' Ch'adhah' Ahkhii: How I Tan Hides. Katherine Peter.Tr. of How I Tan Hides. (ESK., Illus.). 22p. 1980. pap. 6.50 (*1-55500-012-6*) Alaska Native.

Natsu No Yami see Darkness in Summer

Natter & Other German Rocket Jet Projects. (Illus.). 48p. 1994. pap. 9.95 (*0-88740-682-3*) Schiffer.

Nattergalen see Nightingale

Nattergalen see Emperor & the Nightingale

Nattergalen see Dom Deluise's the Nightingale

Nattergalen see Nightingale

Nattergalen see Emperor & the Nightingale

Nattergalen, Vol.103B. 3rd ed. Ed. & Tr. by Janne Lillestol. (Listen & Learn Language Audio Ser.: Vol. LL0399).Tr. of Nightingale. (ENG & NOR., Illus.). 32p. 1999. pap. 15.95 (*1-892623-11-0*) Intl Book.

Nattergalen: The Nightingale, Vol. 103. 3rd unabridged ed. Ed. & Tr. by Janne Lillestol. (Listen & Learn Language Ser.: Vol. LL0399). (ENG & NOR., Illus.). 32p. 1999. pap. 15.95 incl. audio (*1-892623-10-2*) Intl Book.

Nattering on the Net: Women, Power & Cyberspace. Dale Spender. LC 95-215316. 304p. 1996. pap. 19.95 (*1-875559-09-4*, Pub. by SpiniFex Pr) LPC InBook.

Natterjack Toad. Trevor J. Beebee. (Illus.). 1983. 24.95 (*0-19-217709-5*) OUP.

***Natter's New York City Education Bluebook, 1999-2000.** Irving Natter. 58p. 1999. pap. 4.50 (*0-936143-14-2*) Natter Pub.

***Natter's New York City Education Bluebook, 2002-01.** 58p. 2000. pap. 4.50 (*0-936143-15-0*) Natter Pub.

Nattie Witch. Ruth Rosner. LC 89-2135. (Illus.). 32p. (J). (ps-3). 1989. 11.95 (*0-06-025098-4*) HarpC Child Bks.

Natuerlich, Technisch, Chemisch: Verhaeltnisse zur Natur Am Beispiel der Chemie. Ed. by Peter Janich & Christoph Ruechardt. (Philosophie & Wissenschaft - Transdisziplinaere Studien: Vol. 11). (GER., Illus.). x, 194p. (C). 1996. text 37.60 (*3-11-015013-1*, 105/96) De Gruyter.

Natuerliche Habichtskraut-Traubeneichenwaelder. O. Denz. (Dissertationes Botanicae Ser.: Band 229). (Illus.). 160p. 1994. pap. 56.00 (*3-443-64143-1*, Pub. by Gebruder Borntraeger) Balogh.

Natuerliche und Synthetische Rubine: Eigenschaften und Bestimmung. K. Schmetzer. vi, 132p. 1986. 23.00 (*3-510-65125-1*, Pub. by E Schweizerbartsche) Balogh.

Natufian Chipped Lithic Assemblage from Sunakh Near Petra, Southern Jordan. Charlott H. Petersen. (Carsten Niebuhr Institute Publications (CNI): No. 18). (Illus.). 100p. 1994. 45.00 (*87-7289-281-1*, Pub. by Mus Tusculanum) Paul & Co Pubs.

Natufian Culture in the Levant. Ed. by Ofer Bar-Yosef & Francois R. Valla. (Archaeological Ser.: No. 1). (Illus.). vi, 644p. (Orig.). 1991. pap. 55.00 (*1-879621-01-0*); lib. bdg. 75.00 (*1-879621-03-7*) Intl Mono Prehstry.

Natufian Encampment No. 1: Excavations at Beidha. Ed. by Brian F. Byrd. (Jutland Archaeological Society Publications: No. 23). (Illus.). 126p. (C). 1989. 29.00 (*87-7288-054-6*, Pub. by Aarhus Univ Pr) David Brown.

Natumaleza Cubana. Carlos Wotzkow. LC 98-84029. (Coleccion Cuba y sus Jueces). (SPA., Illus.). 300p. 1998. pap. 19.00 (*0-89729-866-7*) Ediciones.

***Natuna - Development Plan, Opportunities in Indonesia: A Strategic Entry Report, 1996.** Compiled by Icon Group International Staff. (Illus.). 160p. 1999. ring bd. 1600.00 incl. audio compact disk (*0-7418-1343-2*) Icon Grp.

Natur - Vernunft - Freiheit: Philosophische Analyse der Konzeption "Schopferischer Vernunft" in der Zeitgenossischen Moraltheologie. Andrzej Szostek. (Europaische Hochschulschriften Ser.: Reihe 23, Bd. 447). (GER.). VI, 296p. 1992. 50.80 (*3-631-43861-3*) P Lang Pubng.

Natur- und Landschaftsdarstellungen in der Etruskischen und Unteritalischen Wandmalerei. Ivo Zanoni. (Europaische Hochschulschriften Ser.: Reihe 38, Band 71). (GER.). 377p. 1998. pap. 52.95 (*3-906760-14-6*) P Lang Pubng.

Natur Als Schopfung: Studien Zum Verhaltnis von Naturbegriff und Schopfungsverstandnis Bei Gunter Altner, Sigurd M. Daecke, Hermann Dembowski und Christian Link. Elisabeth Hartlieb. (Darmstadter Theologische Beitrage Zu Gegenwartsfragen Ser.: Bd. 2). (GER.). 296p. 1996. 57.95 (*3-631-49957-4*) P Lang Pubng.

Natur der Sprache: Die Dynamik der Prozesse des Sprechens und Verstehens. Helmut Schnelle. (Foundations of Communication & Cognition Ser.). (GER.). xii, 671p. (C). 1996. pap. text 72.60 (*3-11-015171-5*) De Gruyter.

Natur der Sprache: Die Dynamik der Prozesse Sprechens & Verstehens. Helmut Schnelle. (Grundlagen der Kommunikation & Kognition (Foundations of Communication & Cognition) Ser.). (GER.). 671p. (C). 1991. lib. bdg. 198.50 (*3-11-012704-0*) De Gruyter.

Natur Und Begriff: Fachdidaktische Studien Uber Den Assoziationsraum Biologischer Begriffe Mit Besonderem Schwerpunkt Auf Ordnung Und Chaos. Helmut Hasse. (Illus.). 636p. 1998. 85.95 (*3-631-31235-0*) P Lang Pubng.

Natur und Idee. Carl G. Carus. (GER.). 1997. reprint ed. 108.00 (*3-487-05724-7*) G Olms Pubs.

Natur und Schopfung - Die Realitat Im Prozeb: A. N. Whiteheads Philosophie Als Paradigma Einer Fundamentaltheologie Kreativer Existenz. Hans-Joachim Sander. (Wurzburger Studien Zur Fundamentaltheologie Ser.: Bd. 7). (GER.). XIII, 424p. 1991. 65.80 (*3-631-44126-6*) P Lang Pubng.

Natur und Sittlichkeit Bei Fichte. Max H. Boehm. (Abhandlungen Zur Philosophie und Ihrer Geschichte Ser.: Bd. 46). (GER.). 40p. 1981. reprint ed. write for info. (*3-487-06793-5*) G Olms Pubs.

Natur und Technik in der Literatur des Fruhen Expressionismus. Klaus-Dieter Bergner. (Europaische Hochschulschriften Ser.: Reihe 1, Bd. 1679). 348p. 1998. pap. 51.95 (*3-631-33328-5*) P Lang Pubng.

Natura Naturans, Natura Naturata; Sobranie Stikhov. Aleksandr M. Dobroliubov. (Modern Russian Literature & Culture, Studies & Texts: Vol. 10). (RUS.). 211p. 1981. pap. 10.00 (*0-933884-20-6*) Berkeley Slavic.

Natura Physician. R. S. Clymer. 300p. 1932. 15.00 (*0-916285-52-9*) Humanitarian.

Natural. Bernard Malamud. 336p. (YA). (gr. 8 up). 1999. pap. 13.50 (*0-380-72084-1*, Avon Bks) Morrow Avon.

Natural. Bernard Malamud. 1995. 8.95 (*0-606-01688-0*, Pub. by Turtleback) Demco.

***Natural.** Bernard Malamud. (Perennial Classics Ser.). 2000. pap. 13.00 (*0-06-095829-4*) HarpC.

Natural. large type ed. 312p. 1998. 30.00 (*0-7838-0350-8*, G K Hall Lrg Type) Mac Lib Ref.

Natural: And Other Stories about Contemporary Hawaiians. Leialoha A. Perkins. 43p. 1995. reprint ed. pap. write for info. (*1-892174-07-3*) Kamalu uluolele.

Natural: Short Stories of Contemporary Hawaiians. Leialoha A. Perkins. iv, 43p. 1979. pap. write for info. (*1-892174-08-1*) Kamalu uluolele.

Natural M. Bernard Malamud. 217p. 1980. mass mkt. 6.99 (*0-380-50609-2*, Avon Bks) Morrow Avon.

Natural Acts: A Collection of Poems by Bobbi Murrow. Bobbi Murrow. Ed. by Peter Helfrich. LC 94-90413. (Illus.). (Orig.). (YA). 1994. pap. 18.00 (*0-938055-00-3*) Emerald People.

Natural Acts: A Sidelong View of Science & Nature. David Quammen. 240p. 1996. pap. 12.00 (*0-380-71738-7*, Avon Bks) Morrow Avon.

Natural Acts: Reconnecting with Nature to Recover Community, Spirit, & Self. Amy E. Dean. LC 97-2199. (Illus.). 160p. 1997. 15.00 (*0-87131-821-0*) M Evans.

***Natural Advantage: Renew Yourself.** Alan Heeks. LC 00-20318. 2000. write for info. (*1-85788-261-X*) Nicholas Brealey.

***Natural Adventures in the Mountains of North Georgia.** Mary Ellen Hammond & Jim Parham. (Illus.). 144p. 2000. pap. 12.95 (*1-889596-09-4*) Milestone NC.

Natural Adventures in the Mountains of Western North Carolina. Jim Parham & Mary Ellen Hammond. LC 99-13487. (Illus.). 144p. 1999. pap. 12.95 (*1-889596-06-X*) Milestone NC.

Natural Affection. William Inge. 1963. pap. 5.25 (*0-8222-0805-9*) Dramatists Play.

Natural Affinities. Erica Funkhouser. LC 82-74512. 68p. (C). 1983. 6.95 (*0-914086-43-X*); pap. 9.95 (*0-914086-42-1*) Alice James Bks.

Natural Agency: An Essay on the Causal Theory of Action. John Bishop. (Cambridge Studies in Philosophy). 223p. (C). 1990. text 80.00 (*0-521-37430-8*) Cambridge U Pr.

Natural Aggregate: Building America's Future: Public Issues in Earth Science. William H. Langer & V. M. Glanzman. (Illus.). 39p. (Orig.). (C). 1995. pap. text 20.00 (*0-7881-1942-7*) DIANE Pub.

Natural Alchemy: Evolution of Life, Lessons 124-32. C. C. Zain. (Brotherhood of Light Home Study Ser.: Course 12, Pt. 1). (Illus.). 1997. pap. 16.95 (*0-87887-358-9*) Church of Light.

Natural Alchemy: Evolution of Religion. C. C. Zain. (Brotherhood of Light Home Study Ser.: Course 12, Pt. 2). (Illus.). 1996. pap. 16.95 (*0-87887-346-5*) Church of Light.

Natural Alien: Humankind & Environment. Neil Evernden. 176p. 1985. pap. text 18.95 (*0-8020-6639-9*) U of Toronto Pr.

Natural Alien: Humankind & Environment. 2nd ed. Neil Evernden. LC 93-93066. 172p. 1993. text 40.00 (*0-8020-2962-0*); pap. text 18.95 (*0-8020-7785-4*) U of Toronto Pr.

Natural Allies? Canadian & Mexican Perspectives on International Security, Vol. 2. Ed. by H. P. Klepak. LC 96-900376. 208p. pap. 22.95 (*0-88629-277-8*, Pub. by McG-Queens Univ Pr) CUP Services.

Natural Allies: Women's Associations in American History. Anne F. Scott. (Women in American History Ser.). (Illus.). 272p. (Orig.). (C). 1992. pap. text 15.95 (*0-252-06320-1*) U of Ill Pr.

Natural Alternatives for Weight Loss. Michael T. Murray. 1996. 20.00 (*0-688-14685-6*, Wm Morrow) Morrow Avon.

Natural Alternatives for Weight Loss. Michael T. Murray. 176p. 1997. reprint ed. pap. 10.00 (*0-688-15385-2*, Quil) HarperTrade.

Natural Alternatives (O T C) to Over-The-counter & Prescription Drugs. Michael T. Murray. LC 93-14152. 383p. 1994. 25.00 (*0-688-12358-9*, Wm Morrow) Morrow Avon.

Natural Alternatives (O T C) to Over-The-counter & Prescription Drugs. Michael T. Murray. 384p. 1999. reprint ed. pap. 13.00 (*0-688-16627-X*, Quil) HarperTrade.

Natural Alternatives (p Rozac) to Prozac. Michael T. Murray. 240p. 1999. pap. 10.00 (*0-688-16628-8*, Quil) HarperTrade.

Natural Alternatives (p Rozac) to Prozac. Michael T. Murray. LC 95-47489. 192p. 1996. 20.00 (*0-688-14684-8*, Wm Morrow) Morrow Avon.

Natural Alternatives to Antibiotics. Ray C. Wunderlich, Jr. (Good Health Guides Ser.). 47p. 1995. pap. 3.95 (*0-87983-684-9*, 36849K, Keats Publng) NTC Contemp Pub Co.

Natural Alternatives to Antibiotics: Using Nature's Pharmacy to Help Fight Infections. John McKenna. LC 98-26253. 176p. 1999. pap. 12.95 (*0-89529-839-2*, Avery) Penguin Putnam.

***Natural Alternatives to Viagra: How to Recharge Your Sexual Performance Without Surgery or Prescription.** John Byington. LC 99-41828. 1999. write for info. (*1-55972-527-3*) Carol Pub Group.

Natural America. T. H. Watkins & National Geographic Society (U. S.), Staff. LC 97-45239. 1998. write for info. (*0-7922-7060-6*); pap. write for info. (*0-7922-7064-9*) Natl Geog.

Natural Analogue Studies in the Geological Disposal of Radioactive Wastes. William Miller et al. LC 93-45535. (Studies in Environmental Science: Vol. 57). 412p. 1994. 191.50 (*0-444-81755-7*) Elsevier.

Natural Analogues in Radioactive Waste Disposal. Ed. by B. Come & Neil A. Chapman. (C). 1988. lib. bdg. 287.50 (*1-85333-105-8*, Pub. by Graham & Trotman) Kluwer Academic.

Natural & Anthropogenic Hazards in Development Planning. Frederic R. Siegel. (Environmental Intelligence Unit Ser.). 300p. 1996. text 79.00 (*0-12-641940-X*) Landes Bioscience.

Natural & Anthropogenic Influences in Fluvial Geomorphology. Ed. by John E. Costa et al. LC 95-19002. (Geophysical Monograph Ser.: Vol. 89). 1995. 50.00 (*0-87590-046-1*) Am Geophysical.

Natural & Artificial Control of Hearing & Balance. Ed. by J. H. Allum et al. LC 93-11042. (Progress in Brain Research Ser.: Vol. 97). 452p. 1993. 273.50 (*0-444-81252-0*) Elsevier.

Natural & Artificial Ecosystems. R. D. MacElroy et al. (Advances in Space Research (RJ) Ser.: Vol. 18). 288p. 1995. 194.50 (*0-08-042668-9*, Pergamon Pr) Elsevier.

Natural & Artificial Harmonics for the Guitar. David Winters. 57p. 1983. pap. 6.95 (*0-9616283-0-8*) D Winters.

Natural & Artificial Harmonics for the Guitar. rev. ed. David Winters. 100p. 1985. pap. 15.00 (*0-9616283-1-6*) D Winters.

Natural & Artificial Intelligence New Expanded Edition: Misconceptions about Brains & Neural Networks. enl. ed. Armand M. De Callatay. LC 92-12713. 560p. 1992. pap. 108.50 (*0-444-89502-7*, North Holland) Elsevier.

Natural & Artificial Minds. Ed. by Robert G. Burton. LC 92-35020. (SUNY Series, Scientific Studies in Natural & Artificial Intelligence). 245p. (C). 1993. text 64.50 (*0-7914-1507-4*); pap. text 21.95 (*0-7914-1508-2*) State U NY Pr.

Natural & Artificial Parallel Computation. Michael A. Arbib et al. Ed. by J. Alan Robinson. 1990. 44.00 (*0-262-01120-4*) MIT Pr.

Natural & Artificial Parallel Computation: Proceedings of the Fifth NEC Symposium. Ed. by David L. Waltz. LC 95-48918. (Proceedings in Applied Mathematics Ser.: No. 79). viii, 202p. 1996. 41.50 (*0-89871-357-9*, PR79) Soc Indus-Appl Math.

Natural & Artificial Playing Fields: Characteristics & Safety Features, STP 1073. Ed. by Roger C. Schmidt et al. LC 90-33013. (Special Technical Publication (STP) Ser.). (Illus.). 187p. 1990. text 43.00 (*0-8031-1296-3*, STP1073) ASTM.

Natural & Conceptual Design: Radical Confusion in Critical Theory. Joseph M. Ditta. LC 84-47541. (American University Studies: English Language & Literature: Ser. IV, Vol. 9). 202p. (C). 1984. text 30.00 (*0-8204-0119-6*) P Lang Pubng.

Natural & Divine Law: Reclaiming the Tradition for Christian Ethics. Jean Porter. 320p. 1999. pap. 28.00 (*0-8028-4697-1*) Eerdmans.

Natural & Engineered Pest Management Agents. Ed. by Paul A. Hedin et al. LC 93-41197. (Symposium Ser.: Vol. 551). 550p. 1994. text 120.00 (*0-8412-2773-X*, Pub. by Am Chemical) OUP.

Natural & Healthy Childhood. Jessie R. Thomson. (Orig.). pap. 12.95 (*0-8464-4257-4*) Beekman Pubs.

***Natural & Herb Treatments for Carpal Tunnel Syndrome.** Norma Pasekoff Weinberg. LC 00-37549. (Country Wisdom Bulletin Ser.). (Illus.). 2000. pap. write for info. (*1-58017-304-7*) Storey Bks.

Natural & Herbal Family Remedies. Cynthia Black. LC 96-53552. (Storey Publishing Bulletin Ser.: Vol. A-168). 1997. pap. 2.95 (*0-88266-716-5*) Storey Bks.

***Natural & Herbal Remedies for Indigestion.** Kathleen Brown. LC 00-32223. (Country Wisdom Bulletin Ser.). 2000. pap. write for info. (*1-58017-320-9*) Storey Bks.

Natural & Hot Springs: An Index & Travel Planners Workbook. rev. ed. Alpha Pyramis Research Division Staff. (Illus.). 70p. 1995. pap. text, wbk. ed. 25.95 (*0-913597-07-4*) Prosperity & Profits.

Natural & Human Resources of Rajasthan. T. S. Chouhan. 503p. 1993. pap. 425.00 (*81-7233-068-5*, Pub. by Scientific Pubs) St Mut.

Natural & Human Resources of Rajasthan. T. S. Chouhan. 1993. pap. 240.00 (*81-7233-062-6*, Pub. by Scientific Pubs) St Mut.

Natural & Human Resources of Rajasthan. T. S. Chouhan. 1996. pap. 60.00 (*81-7233-146-0*, Pub. by Scientific Pubs) St Mut.

Natural & Laboratory Testing Monograph. 60p. 1985. 50.00 (*0-915414-81-3*) IEST.

Natural & Living Biomaterials. Ed. by Garth W. Hastings & Paul Ducheyne. 192p. 1984. 105.00 (*0-8493-6264-4*, QP88, CRC Reprint) Franklin.

Natural & Man-Made Hazards. Ed. by M. I. El-Sabh & T. S. Murty. (C). 1988. text 399.50 (*90-277-2524-1*) Kluwer Academic.

Natural & Mesmeric Clairvoyance: With the Practical Application of Mesmerism in Surgery & Medicine. James Esdaile. LC 75-7378. (Perspectives in Psychical Research Ser.). 1975. reprint ed. 26.95 (*0-405-07028-4*) Ayer.

Natural & Political Observations Mentioned in a Following Index, & Made Upon the Bills of Mortality. John Graunt. LC 74-25754. (European Sociology Ser.). 110p. 1975. reprint ed. 16.95 (*0-405-06508-6*) Ayer.

Natural & Prescribed Fire in Pacific Northwest Forests. Ed. by John D. Walstad et al. LC 89-36338. (Illus.). 336p. 1990. text 32.95 (*0-87071-359-0*) Oreg St U Pr.

Natural & Selected Synthetic Toxins: Biological Implications. Anthony T. Tu & William Gaffield. LC 99-43789. (ACS Symposium Ser.: No. 745). (Illus.). 464p. 1999. text 140.00 (*0-8412-3630-5*, Pub. by Am Chemical) OUP.

N

Natural & Shoeless Joe: Curriculum Unit. Bernard Malamud & W. P. Kinsella. (Novel Ser.). 79p. (YA). (gr. 9-12). 1992. spiral bd. 18.95 (*1-56077-236-0*) Ctr Learning.

Natural & Supernatural: A History of the Paranormal. Brian Inglis. 500p. (Orig.). (C). 1992. pap. 18.95 (*1-85327-074-1*, Pub. by Prism Pr) Assoc Pubs Grp.

Natural & Synthetic Neurotoxins. Ed. by Alan L. Harvey. (Neuroscience Perspectives Ser.). (Illus.). 386p. 1993. text 83.00 (*0-12-329870-9*) Acad Pr.

Natural & Synthetic Polymers: An Introduction. Henry I. Bolker. LC 72-97483. (Illus.). 706p. reprint ed. pap. 200.00 (*0-7837-0816-5*, 204113100019) Bks Demand.

Natural & Technological Disasters: Causes, Effects & Preventive Measures. Ed. by Shyamal K. Majumdar et al. (Illus.). x, 561p. (C). 1992. 45.00 (*0-945809-06-9*) Penn Science.

Natural & the Artefactual: The Implications of Deep Science & Deep Technology for Environmental Philosophy. Keekok Lee. LC 99-20325. 288p. 1999. 49.00 (*0-7391-0061-0*) Lxngtn Bks.

Natural & the Normative: Theories of Spatial Perception from Kant to Helmholtz. Gary Hatfield. 380p. 1991. 45.00 (*0-262-08086-9*, Bradford Bks) MIT Pr.

***Natural & the Social: Uncertainty, Risk, Change.** Steve Hinchliffe & Kathleen Woodward. LC 00-32841. (Introduction to the Social Sciences Ser.). 2000. pap. write for info. (*0-415-22290-7*) Routledge.

Natural & the Supernatural. John W. Oman. LC 79-39696. (Select Bibliographies Reprint Ser.). 1977. reprint ed. 22.95 (*0-8369-9941-X*) Ayer.

Natural Antidepressants. Syd Baumel. (Good Health Guides Ser.). 48p. 1998. pap. 3.95 (*0-87983-900-7*, 39007K, Keats Publng) NTC Contemp Pub Co.

Natural Antimicrobial Systems & Food Preservation. Ed. by V. M. Dillon & R. G. Board. LC 97-181222. (Illus.). 300p. 1994. text 105.00 (*0-85198-878-4*) OUP.

Natural Antioxidants: Chemistry, Health. Ed. by Feridoon Shahibi. (Illus.). 432p. 1997. lib. bdg. 105.00 (*0-935315-77-2*, PC111) Am Oil Chemists.

***Natural Antioxidants & Anticarcinogens in Nutrition, Health & Disease.** Ed. by J. T. Kumpulainen & J. T. Salonen. (Special Publication Ser.: Vol. 240). 482p. 1999. 160.00 (*0-85404-793-X*, Pub. by Royal Soc Chem) Spr-Verlag.

Natural Antioxidants in Human Health & Disease. Ed. by Balz Frei. (Illus.). 588p. 1994. text 104.00 (*0-12-266975-4*) Acad Pr.

***Natural Aphrodisiacs.** Fiona Marshall. 2000. pap. 10.95 (*1-86204-577-1*, Pub. by Element MA) Penguin Putnam.

Natural Approach: Language Acquisition in the Classroom. Stephen D. Krashen & Tracy D. Terrell. 191p. 1999. 20.95 (*0-13-609934-3*) P-H.

Natural Approach to Attention Deficit Disorder (ADD) Drug-Free Ways to Treat the Roots of This Childhood Epidemic. Ronald L. Hoffman. LC 98-184502. (Good Health Guides Ser.). 48p. 1997. reprint ed. pap. 3.95 (*0-87983-779-9*, 37799K, Keats Publng) NTC Contemp Pub Co.

Natural Approach to Reading for Suzuki Piano Students. Peggy Swingle. (Illus.). (Orig.). (C). 1988. pap. text 12.95 (*0-317-93507-0*) Tolo Pr.

Natural Approaches to Reading & Writing. Ed. by Patricia Antonacci & Carolyn N. Hedley. 216p. (C). 1994. text 73.25 (*0-89391-750-8*); pap. text 39.50 (*0-89391-922-5*) Ablx Pub.

Natural Approch Theory & Practice. McGraw Hill Staff. 1997. VHS 25.94 (*0-07-079620-3*) McGraw.

Natural Aquarium. S. Yoshino & D. Kobayashi. (Illus.). 128p. 1993. 23.95 (*0-86622-629-X*, TS195) TFH Pubns.

Natural Aquarium World, Bk. 1. Talsashi Amano. (Illus.). 192p. 1993. 35.95 (*0-7938-0089-7*, TS206) TFH Pubns.

Natural Arches of Rattlesnake Canyon. Chris Moore. (Illus.). 32p. 2000. pap. 1.95 (*1-891858-12-2*, 4015) Arch Hunter Bks.

***Natural Arches of the Big South Fork: A Guide to Selected Landforms.** Arthur McDade. LC 99-6687. (Outdoor Tennessee Ser.). (Illus.). 144p. 2000. pap. 12.95 (*1-57233-074-0*) U of Tenn Pr.

Natural Arches of the Moab Area. Chris Moore. (Illus.). 125p. 2001. mass mkt. 12.95 (*1-891858-15-7*, 4052) Arch Hunter Bks.

Natural Areas Facing Climate Change. Ed. by George P. Malanson. (Illus.). viii, 92p. 1989. pap. 30.00 (*90-5103-030-4*, Pub. by SPB Acad Pub) Balogh.

Natural Areas of Oregon & Washington. John Perry & Jane G. Perry. LC 82-16937. (Guides to the Natural Areas of the United States Ser.). (Illus.). 360p. 1983. pap. 12.00 (*0-87156-334-7*, Pub. by Sierra) Random.

Natural Areas of the San Juan Islands. rev. ed. Terry Domico. (Illus.). 172p. 2000. pap. 19.95 (*1-883385-00-8*) Turtleback Bks.

Natural Areas Project: A Summary of Data to Date. J. Arthur Herrick. (Informative Circular Ser.: No. 1). 1974. pap. text 2.00 (*0-86727-070-5*) Ohio Bio Survey.

Natural Aristocracy: History, Ideology, & the Production of William Faulkner. Kevin Railey. LC 98-58100. 213p. 1999. 29.95 (*0-8173-0956-X*) U of Ala Pr.

Natural Art Forms: 120 Classic Photographs. Karl Blossfeldt. (Illus.). 128p. 1998. pap. 10.95 (*0-486-40003-4*) Dover.

Natural Art of Louisa Atkinson. Elizabeth Lawson. (Illus.). 144p. 1995. 65.00 (*0-7305-8927-7*, Pub. by Univ Queensland Pr) Intl Spec Bk.

Natural Artistry of Dreams: Creative Ways to Bring the Wisdom of Dreams to Waking Life. Jill Mellick. (Illus.). 256p. 1996. pap. 14.95 (*1-57324-019-2*) Conari Press.

Natural Asthma & Allergy Management. Celeste White. LC 96-95414. iv, 114p. (Orig.). 1997. pap. 8.95 (*0-9653024-1-5*) Keswick Hse.

Natural Attenuation: Chlorinated & Recalcitrant Compounds. Godage B. Wickramanayake & Robert E. Hinchee. LC 98-25122. 392p. 1998. 79.95 (*1-57477-058-6*) Battelle.

***Natural Attenuation Considerations & Case Studies: Remediation of Chlorinated & Recalcitrant Compounds (C2-3)** Ed. by Godage B. Wickramanayake et al. 242p. 2000. 69.95 (*1-57477-097-7*) Battelle.

***Natural Attenuation for Groundwater Remediation.** National Research Council U. S. Staff. LC 00-8896. 2000. pap. write for info. (*0-309-06932-7*) Natl Acad Pr.

***Natural Attenuation of Chlorinated Solvents, Petroleum Hydrocarbons & Other Organic Compounds.** Ed. by Bruce C. Alleman & Andrea Leeson. LC 99-23401. 378p. 1999. 65.00 (*1-57477-074-8*) Battelle.

Natural Attenuation of Fules & Chlorinated Soivents in the Subsurface. Todd H. Wiedemeier et al. LC 98-45799. 632p. 1999. 89.95 (*0-471-19749-1*) Wiley.

Natural Attenuation of Hazardous Waste: CERCLA, RBCA's, & the Future of Environmental Remediation. Patrick V. Brady et al. LC 97-19742. 245p. 1997. lib. bdg. 65.00 (*1-56670-302-6*) Lewis Pubs.

Natural Attraction. Marisa Carroll. (Men Made in America Ser.). 1994. per. 3.59 (*0-373-45179-2*, 1-45179-8) Harlequin Bks.

Natural Audiences: Qualitative Research of Media Uses & Effects. Ed. by Thomas R. Lindlof & Melvin J. Voigt. LC 86-17425. (Communication & Information Science Ser.). 288p. 1987. text 73.25 (*0-89391-341-3*) Ablx Pub.

Natural Auto Antibodies: Their Physiologocal Role & Regulatory Significance. Yehuda Shoenfeld. 368p. 1992. lib. bdg. 219.00 (*0-8493-5501-X*, QR186) CRC Pr.

Natural BabyCare: Pure & Soothing Recipes & Techniques for Mothers & Babies. Colleen K. Dodt. LC 96-46122. 144p. (Orig.). 1997. pap. 12.95 (*0-88266-953-2*) Storey Bks.

Natural Background of Meaning. Arda Denkel. LC 98-42961. (Boston Studies in the Philosophy of Science). 1p. 1998. write for info. (*0-7923-5331-5*) Kluwer Academic.

***Natural Background Radiation.** Jill Sutcliffe. 1999. 56.00 (*1-86094-174-5*) World Scientific Pub.

Natural Basketry. Carol Hart & Dan Hart. (Illus.). 160p. 1976. pap. 14.95 (*0-8230-3155-1*) Watsn-Guptill.

Natural Baskets: Create over Twenty Unique Baskets with Materials Gathered in Gardens, Fields, & Woods. Ed. by Maryanne Gillooly & Gwen Steege. LC 91-51126. (Illus.). 160p. 1992. pap. 18.95 (*0-88266-793-9*, Garden Way Pub) Storey Bks.

***Natural Beauty.** Anness Publishing Staff. 2000. pap. 19.95 (*1-84215-179-7*) Anness Pub.

Natural Beauty. Aldo Facetti. (Illus.). 144p. (Orig.). 1992. per. 16.00 (*0-671-74691-X*, Fireside) S&S Trade Pap.

Natural Beauty: A Step-by-Step Guide. Amanda Watson. LC 99-17660. (In a Nutshell Ser.). (Illus.). 64p. 1999. 7.95 (*1-86204-235-7*, Pub. by Element MA) Penguin Putnam.

Natural Beauty: Making & Using Pure & Simple Beauty Products. Gail Duff. LC 97-31659. (Illus.). 128p. 1998. 19.95 (*0-7621-0032-X*, Pub. by RD Assn) Penguin Putnam.

Natural Beauty: Making & Using Simple Beauty Products. Gail Duff. LC 97-31659. 1998. pap. write for info. (*0-7621-0033-8*) RD Assn.

***Natural Beauty & Bath Book.** Casey Kellar. 2000. pap. 14.95 (*1-57990-178-6*, Pub. by Lark Books) Sterling.

Natural Beauty & Bath Book: Nature's Luxurious Recipes for Body & Skin Care. Casey Kellar. Ed. by Leslie Dierks. LC 97-16341. (Illus.). 128p. 1997. 24.95 (*1-887374-48-5*, Pub. by Lark Books) Random.

Natural Beauty & Bath Book & Kit: Nature's Luxurious Recipes for Body & Skin Care. Casey Kellar. LC 97-16341. 1997. 49.95 (*1-57990-007-0*, Pub. by Lark Books) Random.

Natural Beauty at Home. Janice Cox. 1995. pap. 15.95 (*0-8050-3313-0*) H Holt & Co.

***Natural Beauty Care with Flowers & Plants: A Magna Colour Guide.** B. Hlava et al. (Illus.). 232p. 1999. reprint ed. text 25.00 (*0-7881-6595-X*) DIANE Pub.

Natural Beauty for All Seasons: 250 Simple Recipes & Gift Giving Ideas for Year-Round Beauty. Janice Cox. (Illus.). 288p. 1995. pap. 16.95 (*0-8050-4655-0*) H Holt & Co.

Natural Beauty from the Garden: More Than 200 Do-It-Yourself Beauty Recipes & Garden Ideas. Janice Cox. LC 98-19042. (Natural Beauty Ser.: Bk. 3). (Illus.). 274p. 1999. pap. 16.95 (*0-8050-5781-1*, Pub. by H Holt & Co) VHPS.

Natural Beauty Kit: Simple Recipes for Healthy Skin, Beautiful Hair & Vibrant Looks. Joanna Sheen. LC 96-37956. (Illus.). 128p. 1997. 26.95 (*1-885203-46-2*) Jrny Editions.

Natural Beauty of America. Patricia Pingry. (Illus.). 160p. 1995. pap. 12.95 (*0-8249-4076-8*) Ideals.

Natural Behavior in Humans & Animals. American Psychological Association Staff. (Human Behavior Curriculum Project Ser.). 55p. (Orig.). 1981. teacher ed. 9.95 (*0-8077-2614-1*); pap. text 3.95 (*0-8077-2613-3*) Tchrs Coll.

***Natural Birth.** Toi Derricotte. 88p. 2000. pap. 10.95 (*1-56341-120-2*, Pub. by Firebrand Bks); lib. bdg. 22.95 (*1-56341-121-0*, Pub. by Firebrand Bks) LPC InBook.

Natural Birth Control Book. 6th rev. ed. Art Rosenblum. (Illus.). 168p. 1984. reprint ed. pap. 6.00 (*0-916726-03-7*, 84-70295) Aquarian Res.

Natural Blonde. Liz Smith. (Illus.). 464p. 2000. 25.95 (*0-7868-6325-0*, Pub. by Hyperion) Time Warner.

***Natural Blonde.** large type ed. Liz Smith. 2000. 24.95 (*0-375-43081-4*) Random.

Natural Blues & Country Western Harmonica. Jon Gindick. (Illus.). 130p. 1978. pap. 8.95 (*0-685-01278-6*) Cross Harp.

Natural Blues & Country Western Harmonica. Jon Gindick. (Illus.). 142p. 1984. pap. 7.95 (*0-8256-9923-1*, CS10002) Music Sales.

Natural Body Basics: Making Your Own Cosmetics. Dorie Byers. LC 96-94319. 1996. pap. 7.95 (*0-9652353-0-0*) Gooseberry.

Natural Body Care Products: A Glossary of Terms & Ingredients. Feather River Company Staff. 72p. (Orig.). 1996. pap. 2.95 (*0-914955-99-3*) Lotus Pr.

Natural Bodycare: Creating Aromatherapy Cosmetics for Health & Beauty. C. Julia Meadows. LC 98-7385. (Illus.). 128p. 1998. 24.95 (*0-8069-4245-2*) Sterling.

***Natural Bodycare: Recipes for Health & Beauty.** Julia Meadows. (Illus.). 128p. 1999. pap. 14.95 (*0-8069-2487-X*) Sterling.

***Natural Born Caadesigners: Young American Architects.** Christian Pongraz & Maria Rita Perbellini. (IT Revolution in Architecture Ser.). (Illus.). 96p. 2000. pap. write for info. (*3-7643-6246-4*) Birkhauser.

Natural Born Daddy. Sherryl Woods. 1996. per. 3.75 (*0-373-24007-4*, 1-24007-6) Silhouette.

***Natural Born Killers: Britain's Eight Deadliest Murderers Tell Their Own True Stories.** Kate Kray. 2000. mass mkt. 6.99 (*1-85782-382-6*) Blake Publng.

Natural Born Killers: The Original Screenplay. Quentin Tarantino. 128p. 2000. pap. 13.00 (*0-8021-3448-3*, Pub. by Grove-Atltic) Publishers Group.

Natural Born Lawman: And Baby Makes Three: The Next Generation. Sherryl Woods. (Special Edition Ser.: No. 1216). 1998. per. 4.25 (*0-373-24216-6*, 1-24216-3) Silhouette.

Natural Born Trouble: And Baby Makes Three: The Next Generation. Sherryl Woods. (Special Edition Ser.: No. 1156). 1998. per. 4.25 (*0-373-24156-9*, 1-24156-1) Silhouette.

Natural Born Winner. George Mair. LC 97-97155. 1998. mass mkt. 5.99 (*0-345-42419-0*) Ballantine Pub Grp.

Natural Bridges. Debbie L. McCampbell. LC 96-19007. 246p. 1997. 24.00 (*1-877946-79-6*) Permanent Pr.

Natural Brilliance: Move from Feeling Stuck to Achieving Success. Paul R. Scheele. 208p. 1997. pap. 6.95 (*0-925480-51-7*) Learn Strategies.

Natural Business Year & Thirteen Other Themes. Elijah W. Sells. LC 75-18484. (History of Accounting Ser.). (Illus.). 1979. reprint ed. 25.95 (*0-405-07566-9*) Ayer.

Natural by Design: Beauty & Balance in Southwest Gardens. Judith Phillips. (Illus.). 208p. 1995. 45.00 (*0-89013-276-3*); pap. 35.00 (*0-89013-277-1*) Museum NM Pr.

Natural Capital & Human Economic Survival 2nd ed. Thomas Prugh & Robert Costanza. LC 99-12121. 1999. 39.95 (*1-56670-398-0*) Lewis Pubs.

Natural Capital & Human Economics Survival. Thomas Prugh. LC 95-78332. 1995. 24.95 (*1-887490-01-9*) Int Soc Ecol.

Natural Capital & Human Economics Survival. Thomas Prugh et al. 216p. 1995. 18.95 (*1-887490-02-7*) Int Soc Ecol.

Natural Capitalism: Creating the Next Industrial Revolution. Paul Hawken et al. LC 99-24067. 416p. 1999. 26.95 (*0-316-35316-7*, Back Bay) Little.

***Natural Capitalism: Creating the Next Industrial Revolution.** Paul Hawken et al. 416p. 2000. pap. 17.95 (*0-316-35300-0*, Back Bay) Little.

Natural Care of Pets. Donald I. Ogden. 65p. 1993. reprint ed. spiral bd. 10.50 (*0-7873-0640-1*) Hlth Research.

***Natural Cat.** Lisa Newman. LC 99-37385. (Crossing Press Pocket Ser.). 96p. 1999. pap. 6.95 (*1-58091-001-7*) Crossing Pr.

Natural Cat: Understanding Your Cat's Needs & Instincts. Helga Hofmann. Tr. by Wanda Boeke from GER. LC 94-11132.Tr. of Katzen Richtig Verstehen. (Illus.). 176p. 1994. 14.95 (*0-89658-255-8*) Voyageur Pr.

Natural Cat Care. Bruce Fogel. LC 98-31107. 160p. 1999. 24.95 (*0-7894-4123-3*) DK Pub Inc.

Natural Cat Care: A Complete Guide to Holistic Health Care for Cats. Celeste Yarnall. (Illus.). 320p. 1998. pap. 16.95 (*1-885203-63-2*) Jrny Editions.

***Natural Cat Care: A Complete Guide to Holistic Health Care for Cats.** Celeste Yarnell. 2000. 9.99 (*0-7858-1124-9*) Bk Sales Inc.

Natural Cats. Chris Madsen. LC 96-30487. 128p. 1997. 14.95 (*0-87605-679-6*) Howell Bks.

Natural Causes. Michael Palmer. 496p. 1994. mass mkt. 7.50 (*0-553-56876-0*) Bantam.

Natural Causes see Henry Cecil Reprint Series

Natural Causes: Death & Disease for the Serious Consumer. Stephen A. Berger. 398p. 1992. 19.95 (*965-229-056-4*, Pub. by Gefen Pub Hse) Gefen Bks.

Natural Causes: Essays in Ecological Marxism. James O'Connor. LC 97-42398. 350p. 1997. pap. text 19.95 (*1-57230-273-9*); lib. bdg. 39.95 (*1-57230-279-8*, C0273) Guilford Pubns.

Natural Change & Human Impact in Madagascar. Ed. by Steven M. Goodman & Bruce D. Patterson. LC 96-44170. (Illus.). 448p. 1997. text 75.00 (*1-56098-682-4*); pap. text 35.00 (*1-56098-683-2*) Smithsonian.

Natural Chelating Polymers. Riccardo A. Muzzarelli. 260p. 1973. 124.00 (*0-08-017235-0*, Pub. by Pergamon Repr) Franklin.

Natural Chemicals in Sediments. Sharon Mason & James Dragun. 204p. (Orig.). (C). 1996. pap. 39.95 (*1-884940-04-8*) Amherst Sci Pubs.

Natural Childbirth after Cesarean: A Practical Guide. Karis Crawford & Johanne Walters. (Illus.). 218p. (Orig.). 1996. pap. 14.95 (*0-86542-490-X*) Blackwell Sci.

Natural Childbirth & the Christian Family see Joy of Natural Childbirth: Fifth Edition of Natural Childbirth & the Christian Family

Natural Childbirth Self-Taught. Chan Thomas. 111p. (Orig.). 1993. otabind 7.95 (*1-884600-00-X*) Bengal Tiger.

Natural Childbirth the Bradley Way. rev. ed. Susan McCutcheon & Peter Rosegg. LC 96-333. (Illus.). 256p. 1996. pap. 17.95 (*0-452-27659-4*, Plume) Dutton Plume.

Natural Childbirth the Bradley Way. rev. ed. Susan McCutcheon & Peter Rosegg. 256p. 1999. pap. 16.95 (*0-452-27658-6*, Plume) Dutton Plume.

Natural Childhood: The First Practical & Holistic Guide for Parents of the Developing Child. Ed. by John Thompson & Tim Kahn. LC 94-23147. (Illus.). 352p. 1995. per. write for info. (*0-02-020739-5*) Macmillan.

Natural Choices for Menopause. Marilyn Glenville. 256p. 1999. mass mkt. 5.99 (*0-312-97013-7*) St Martin.

Natural Church Development: A Guide to Eight Essential Qualities of Healthy Churches. Christian Schwarze. (Illus.). 128p. 1996. 19.95 (*1-889638-00-5*) ChurchSmart.

Natural Circulation Phenomena in Nuclear Reactor Systems: Proceedings: International Mechanical Engineering Congress & Exposition (1994: Chicago, IL) Ed. by F. B. Cheung & E. V. McAssey. LC 94-78960. (HTD Ser.: Vol. 281). 67p. 1995. pap. 40.00 (*0-7918-1386-X*, G00881) ASME Pr.

Natural Classical Guitar: Principles of Effortless Playing. Lee F. Ryan. (Illus.). 291p. 1990. reprint ed. pap. 27.95 (*0-933224-40-0*, T037) Bold Strummer Ltd.

Natural Classicism: Essays on Literature & Science. Frederick J. Turner. 304p. (C). 1992. reprint ed. pap. text 16.50 (*0-8139-1391-8*) U Pr of Va.

Natural Classroom: A Directory to Field Courses, Programs, & Expeditions in the Natural Sciences. Jack R. Edelman. 288p. 1996. lib. bdg. 32.50 (*1-55591-923-5*) Fulcrum Pub.

***Natural Classroom Assessment: Designing Seamless Instruction & Assessment.** Jeffrey K. Smith et al. LC 00-8997. (Experts on Assessment Kit Ser.). 2000. pap. write for info. (*0-7619-7587-X*) AltaMira Pr.

Natural Cleaning for Your Home: 95 Pure & Simple Recipes. Casey Kellar. LC 98-7016. 128p. 1998. 24.95 (*1-57990-054-2*, Pub. by Lark Books) Random.

Natural Climate Variability on Decade-to-Century Time Scales. National Research Council, Climate Research Commit. LC 96-67828. 700p. (Orig.). 1996. text 59.00 (*0-309-05449-4*) Natl Acad Pr.

Natural Cold/Flu Defense. Woodland Publishing Staff. (Woodland Health Ser.). 1997. pap. text 3.95 (*1-885670-90-7*) Woodland UT.

Natural Collection. Steven C. Wilson. LC 81-65683. (Illus.). 220p. (Orig.). (C). 1981. 19.95 (*0-939750-00-7*) Entheos.

***Natural Color Palettes.** Ellen M. Plante. LC 99-49515. (For Your Home Ser.). (Illus.). 72p. 2000. write for info. (*1-56799-918-2*, Friedman-Fairfax) M Friedman Pub Grp Inc.

***Natural Compounds in Cancer Therapy.** John C. Boik. (Illus.). 685p. 2000. pap. 28.00 (*0-9648280-1-4*) OR Med Pr.

Natural Computation: Selected Readings. Ed. by Whitman A. Richards. 571p. (Orig.). 1988. pap. text 30.00 (*0-262-68055-6*, Bradford Bks) MIT Pr.

Natural Conception Through Personal Hormone Monitoring. Ed. by J. Bonnar. (Illus.). 68p. 1996. 25.00 (*1-85070-718-9*) Prthnon Pub.

***Natural Conflict Resolution.** Ed. by Filippo Aureli & Frans B. M. De Waal. LC 99-43046. (Illus.). 424p. 2000. 65.00 (*0-520-21671-7*, Pub. by U CA Pr) Cal Prin Full Svc.

***Natural Conflict Resolution.** Filippo Aureli & F. B. M. Waal. LC 99-43046. (Illus.). 424p. 2000. pap. 24.95 (*0-520-22346-2*, Pub. by U CA Pr) Cal Prin Full Svc.

Natural Connections: Perspectives on Community-Based Conservation. Ed. by R. Michael Wright et al. LC 94-38977. 480p. 1994. pap. text 32.00 (*1-55963-346-8*) Island Pr.

Natural Connections: Photographs by Paula Chamlee. Paula Chamlee & Estelle Jussim. (Illus.). 1994. 200.00 (*0-9605646-7-5*) Lodima.

Natural Connections: Photographs by Paula Chamlee. Estelle Jussim. LC 94-78796. (Illus.). 1994. 60.00 (*0-9605646-6-7*) Lodima.

Natural Construct Study Guide. Ed. by Dennis Hamilton. 340p. 1995. pap. 65.00 (*1-878960-23-7*) WH&O Intl.

Natural Construct Tips & Techniques. Stanley Weinrank & Shaun Achmad. 1995. pap. 75.00 (*1-878960-22-9*) WH&O Intl.

Natural Construct User's Guide. D. D. Hamilton. Ed. by A. John Gangluff et al. 375p. (Orig.). 1992. pap. 65.00 (*1-878960-11-3*) WH&O Intl.

Natural Contract. Michael Serres. Tr. by Elizabeth MacArthur & William Paulson. LC 95-2685. 136p. 1995. pap. 16.95 (*0-472-06549-1*, 06549); text 44.50 (*0-472-09549-8*, 09549) U of Mich Pr.

Natural Convection: Fundamentals & Applications. Ed. by Sadik Kakac et al. LC 84-28987. (Illus.). 1181p. 1985. text 260.00 (*0-89116-405-7*) Hemisp Pub.

Natural Convection Heat & Mass Transfer. Yogesh Jaluria. LC 79-41176. (HMT Ser.). (Illus.). 400p. 1980. 154.00 (*0-08-025432-2*, Pub. by Pergamon Repr) Franklin.

Natural Convection in Enclosures. Ed. by I. Catton & K. E. Torrance. (HTD Ser.: Vol. 26). 113p. 1983. pap. text 24.00 (*0-317-02635-6*, H00270) ASME.

An Asterisk (*) at the beginning of an entry indicates that the title is appearing for the first time.

Natural Convection in Enclosures: Presented at the 19th National Heat Transfer Conference, Orlando, Florida, July 27-30, 1980. National Heat Transfer Conference Staff. Ed. by K. E. Torrance & I. Catton. LC 80-65786. (HTD Ser.: Vol. 8). (Illus.). 128p. reprint ed. pap. 39.70 (*0-8357-2814-5*, 203905300010) Bks Demand.

Natural Cooking. Elizabeth Cornish. 128p. 1995. write for info. (*1-57215-058-0*) World Pubns.

Natural Coumarins: Occurrence, Chemistry & Biochemistry. Robert D. Murray et al. LC 81-14776. 714p. reprint ed. pap. 200.00 (*0-608-18412-8*, 203042900069) Bks Demand.

Natural Counterpoint. Paul Oehler & William Minor. (Illus.). 64p. (Orig.). 1985. pap. 4.95 (*0-9612914-1-9*) Betty's Soup.

Natural Crafts: Seventy-Two Easy Projects. Marilyn T. Oliver. (Illus.). 245p. 1994. pap. 16.95 (*0-8117-2564-2*) Stackpole.

Natural Crafts from America's Backyards: Decorate Your Home with Wreaths, Arrangements & Wall Decorations Gathered from Nature's Harvest. Ellen Spector Platt. LC 96-53570. (Illus.). 224p. 1997. text 27.95 (*0-87596-763-9*) Rodale Pr Inc.

Natural Creation & the Formative Mind. John Davidson. (Illus.). 240p. 1992. pap. 16.95 (*1-85230-197-X*, Pub. by Element MA) Penguin Putnam.

Natural Creation or Natural Selection? John Davidson. (Illus.). 240p. 1992. pap. 16.95 (*1-85230-240-2*, Pub. by Element MA) Penguin Putnam.

Natural Creativity: Exploring & Using Nature's Raw Material. Amy Dean. LC 98-4716. 160p. 1998. pap. 14.95 (*0-87131-852-0*) M Evans.

Natural Cuba/Cuba Natural: A Natural History - Una Historia Natural. Alfonso Silva Lee. LC 96-35385. (ENG & SPA., Illus.). 192p. (Orig.). 1996. 32.95 (*0-9630180-2-7*) Pangaea Pub.

Natural Cuba/Cuba Natural: A Natural History - Una Historia Natural. Alfonso Silva Lee. LC 96-35385. (ENG & SPA., Illus.). 192p. (Orig.). 1997. pap. 24.95 (*0-9630180-0-0*) Pangaea Pub.

Natural Cure for Asthma & Allergies see Curacion Natural del Asma y las Alergias

Natural Cure for Rupture. Barnarr Macfadden. 125p. 1996. reprint ed. spiral bd. 11.50 (*0-7873-0578-2*) Hlth Research.

Natural Cures: More Than 1,000 Remedies from the World of Alternative Medicine. Prevention Health Books Editors. Ed. by Abel Delgado. (Spanish E. P. Ser.).Tr. of Curas Naturales. (SPA.). 1999. pap. 12.95 (*1-57954-015-5*) Rodale Pr Inc.

***Natural Cures & Gentle Medicines: That Work Better Than Dangerous Drugs or Risky Surgery.** FC&A Staff. 368p. 2000. pap. 9.99 (*1-890957-36-4*) FC&A Pub.

***Natural Cures & Gentle Medicines: That Work Better Than Dangerous Drugs or Risky Surgery.** FC&A Staff. 368p. 2000. 27.96 (*1-890957-35-6*) FC&A Pub.

Natural Cures for the Common Cold: Powerful, Drug-Free Remedies Proven to Work. Carol Turkington. LC 98-35534. (Health Ser.). (Illus.). 216p. 1999. pap. 11.95 (*0-936197-38-2*, Pub. by Harbor Pr) Natl Bk Netwk.

Natural Curiosity. Margaret Drabble. 1990. mass mkt. 6.95 (*0-7710-2866-0*) McCland & Stewart.

Natural Curiosity: Taffy's Search for Self. Catherine Peebles & Denzil Edge. LC 87-36882. (Illus.). (Orig.). (J). 1988. pap. 6.95 (*0-939991-01-2*) Learning KY.

Natural Death. Ruthe Furie. 288p. (Orig.). 1996. mass mkt. 4.99 (*0-380-77979-X*, Avon Bks) Morrow Avon.

Natural Death with Dignity: Protecting Your Right to Refuse Medical Treatment. Lee R. Kerr & Delnetta J. Kerr. 170p. (Orig.). 1991. 29.95 (*0-9628237-1-6*); pap. 19.95 (*0-9628237-0-8*) Kerr Pubns.

Natural Decor: The Arranger's Garden & Project Book. Norma Coney. LC 97-31825. (Illus.). 176p. 1998. 30.00 (*1-55821-664-2*); pap. 19.95 (*1-55821-541-7*) Lyons Pr.

Natural Decorating. Elizabeth Wilhide et al. (Illus.). 144p. 1995. 29.95 (*0-7892-0065-1*) Abbeville Pr.

Natural Dental Wellness. Soaring Bear. (Illus.). 90p. (Orig.). 1980. pap. 9.95 (*0-9607518-0-7*) Dental-Info.

Natural Depravity of Mankind: Observations on the Human Condition. Ferdinand Lundberg. LC 93-40407. 1994. 15.95 (*1-56980-003-0*) Barricade Bks.

Natural Depth in Man. Wilson Van Dusen. LC 72-78055. 203p. 1972. pap. 8.95 (*0-87785-165-4*) Swedenborg.

Natural Desire for God. William R. O'Connor. (Aquinas Lectures). 1948. 15.00 (*0-87462-113-5*) Marquette.

Natural Detox. Marie Farquharson. LC 99-10028. 144p. 1999. pap. 10.95 (*1-86204-333-7*, Pub. by Element MA) Penguin Putnam.

***Natural Detoxification: The Complete Guide to Clearing Your Body of Toxins.** 2nd rev. ed. Jacqueline Krohn & Frances Taylor. 400p. 2000. pap. 24.95 (*0-88179-187-3*) Hartley & Marks.

Natural Developers Handbook. Ed. by D. D. Hamilton. 476p. (Orig.). 1991. pap. 65.00 (*1-878960-01-6*) WH&O Intl.

Natural Disaster Experiences: Preparing Environmental Facilities for the Worst. Ed. by William C. Anderson. LC 95-15285. (Illus.). 88p. 1995. pap. 5.95 (*1-883767-09-1*) Am Acad Environ.

***Natural Disaster Management for Wastewater Treatment Facilities.** Water Environment Federation Staff. LC 99-26919. (Special Publication Ser.). 1999. 75.00 (*1-57278-154-8*) Water Environ.

Natural Disaster Mazes. Roger Moreau. (Illus.). 64p. (J). (gr. 3-7). Date not set. 5.95 (*0-8069-5727-1*) Sterling.

Natural Disaster Reduction: Proceedings of the 1996 International Conference & Exposition Natural Disaster Reduction. Ed. by George W. Housner & Riley M. Chung. LC 96-1806. 432p. 1996. 49.00 (*0-7844-0153-5*) Am Soc Civil Eng.

Natural Disaster Reduction in the Caribbean. 30p. (Orig.). (C). 1993. pap. text 20.00 (*1-56806-974-X*) DIANE Pub.

Natural Disasters. (Eyes on Adventure Ser.). 32p. (J). (gr. 1). pap. write for info. (*1-882210-64-6*) Action Pub.

***Natural Disasters, 3 Vols.** (Illus.). 1024p. 2000. 315.00 (*0-89356-071-5*) Salem Pr.

Natural Disasters. Patrick L. Abbott. 400p. (C). 1995. text. write for info. (*0-697-25493-3*, WCB McGr Hill) McGrw-H Hghr Educ.

Natural Disasters. Patrick L. Abbott. 448p. (C). 1997. per. write for info. (*0-07-114020-4*, WCB McGr Hill) McGrw-H Hghr Educ.

Natural Disasters. H. Frater. 5p. 1997. pap. 64.95 incl. cd-rom (*3-540-14609-1*) Spr-Verlag.

***Natural Disasters, 4 vols.** Terry Jennings. (Illus.). 32p. (J). 1999. lib. bdg. 63.80 (*1-929298-48-X*, Pub. by Thameside Pr) Smart Apple.

Natural Disasters. Clare Oliver. (Totally Amazing Ser.). 32p. 1999. pap. 5.99 (*0-307-20165-1*) Gldn Bks Pub Co.

***Natural Disasters.** Ed. by Random House Value Publishing Staff. (Illus.). 128p. 1999. 12.99 (*0-517-16144-3*) Random Hse Value.

Natural Disasters. Reader's Digest Editors. LC 97-22869. (Earth, Its Wonders, Its Secrets Ser.). 1997. 19.95 (*0-89577-915-3*, Pub. by RD Assn) Penguin Putnam.

Natural Disasters. Jenny Vaughan. LC 99-15237. (Fast Forward Ser.). 1999. 26.00 (*0-531-14583-2*) Watts.

Natural Disasters. Jenny Vaughan. (Fast Forward Ser.). (Illus.). 32p. (gr. 4-8). 1999. pap. text 9.95 (*0-531-15434-3*) Watts.

Natural Disasters. Tim Wood. LC 93-8525. (World's Disasters Ser.). 48p. (J). 1993. 5.00 (*1-56847-085-1*) Raintree Steck-V.

Natural Disasters. 2nd ed. Patrick L. Abbott. LC 98-23748. 416p. 1998. pap. 55.94 (*0-697-37439-4*) McGraw.

***Natural Disasters: Protecting the Public's Health.** (Scientific Publication Ser.: Vol. 575). 130p. 2000. pap. 22.00 (*92-75-11575-3*) PAHO.

Natural Disasters: Protecting Vulnerable Communities. Ed. by P. A. Merriman & C. W. Browitt. 600p. 1993. 134.00 (*0-7844-1936-1*) Am Soc Civil Eng.

Natural Disasters: Protecting Vulnerable Communities: Proceedings of the Conference Held in London, October 13-15, 1993. Ed. by P. A. Merriman & C. W. Browitt. 600p. 1993. 134.00 (*0-7277-1936-X*) Am Soc Civil Eng.

Natural Disasters: Two Related Short Plays. Jack Heifner. 1985. pap. 5.25 (*0-8222-0806-7*) Dramatists Play.

Natural Disasters: Unleashing the Fury of Nature. Martin Holden & Karen Holden. (Illus.). 71p. 1998. text 20.00 (*0-7881-5850-3*) DIANE Pub.

Natural Disasters & Public Policy. Ed. by Linda Nilson. 200p. (Orig.). 1985. pap. 15.00 (*0-918592-75-5*) Pol Studies.

***Natural Disasters: Floods: A Reference Handbook.** E. Willard Miller & Ruby M. Miller. LC 00-21512. 200p. 2000. lib. bdg. 45.00 (*1-57607-058-1*) ABC-CLIO.

Natural Disasters Hurricanes: A Reference Book. Robert J. Fitzpatrick. LC 99-40280. (Contemporary World Issues Ser.). 280p. 1999. lib. bdg. 45.00 (*1-57607-071-9*) ABC-CLIO.

Natural Disasters Study Guide. David Alexander. 196p. (C). 1994. pap. text, spiral bd. 28.95 (*0-8403-9511-6*, 40951101) Kendall-Hunt.

***Natural Disease Control: A Common-Sense Approach to Plant First Aid.** Ed. by Beth Hanson. (Twenty-First Century Gardening Ser.: Vol. 164). 112p. 2000. pap. 9.95 (*1-889538-17-5*, Pub. by Bklyn Botanic) IPG Chicago.

Natural Disturbance: The Patch Dymanics Perspective. Ed. by Steward T. Pickett & P. S. White. (C). 1985. text 55.00 (*0-12-554520-7*) Acad Pr.

***Natural Dog.** Lisa Newman. LC 99-37371. (Crossing Press Pocket Ser.). 96p. 1999. pap. 6.95 (*1-58091-000-9*) Crossing Pr.

Natural Dog: A Complete Guide for Caring Owners. Mary L. Brennan & Norma Eckroate. LC 93-3938. (Illus.). 352p. 1994. pap. 17.95 (*0-452-27019-7*, Plume) Dutton Plume.

Natural Dog Care. Bruce Fogle. LC 98-31210. 160p. 1999. 24.95 (*0-7894-4124-1*) DK Pub Inc.

***Natural Dog Care.** John Hoare. (Illus.). 2000. 17.95 (*0-7548-0480-1*, Lorenz Bks) Anness Pub.

***Natural Dog Care: A Complete Guide to Holistic Health Care for Dogs.** Celeste Yarnall. (Illus.). 2000. 9.99 (*0-7858-1123-0*) Bk Sales Inc.

Natural Dog Care: A Complete Guide to Holistic Health Care for Dogs. Celeste Yarnall. LC 98-8453. (Illus.). 320p. 1998. pap. 16.95 (*1-885203-47-0*) Jrny Editions.

Natural Dogs. Chris Madsen. LC 97-31267. 128p. 1998. 17.95 (*0-87605-585-4*) Howell Bks.

Natural Draught Cooling Towers: Proceedings of the 4th International Symposium. Universitat Kaiserslautern, Germany, 29-31 May 1996. Ed. by U. Wittek & W. B. Kratzig. (Illus.). 480p. (C). 1996. text 155.00 (*90-5410-812-6*, Pub. by A A Balkema) Ashgate Pub Co.

Natural Dualities for the Working Algebraist. David M. Clark & Brian A. Davey. LC 97-46777. 368p. 1999. text 64.95 (*0-521-45415-8*) Cambridge U Pr.

Natural Dyes. Hermine Lathrop-Smit. 72p. 1978. 14.95 (*0-88862-227-9*, Pub. by J Lorimer) Formac Dist Ltd.

Natural Dyes & Home Dyeing. Rita J. Adrosko. (Illus.). 160p. 1971. reprint ed. pap. 5.95 (*0-486-22688-3*) Dover.

***Natural Dyes for Natural Fibers: A Beginner's Handbook of Dyeing Wool & Mohair with Plants.** Bobbi A. Chukran. (Illus.). 52p. 1999. pap. 18.95 (*0-944577-07-5*) Limestone.

Natural Dyestuffs & Industrial Culture in Europe, 1750-1880. Ed. by Robert Fox & Augusti Nieto-Galan. LC 98-55519. (European Studies in Science History & the Arts: No. 2). (Illus.). 26p. 1999. write for info. (*0-88135-273-X*, Sci Hist) Watson Pub Intl.

***Natural Earth: The English Standard Reference on Herbal Substances.** Gary Lockhart. (Illus.). 280p. 1999. pap. 29.95 (*1-890693-02-2*) Earthpulse Pr.

Natural Ease for Work: Can You Move to Get the Job Done? Osa Jackson-Wyatt. LC 94-90572. (Natural Ease Ser.). (Illus.). 103p. (Orig.). (C). 1994. pap. 14.95 (*0-9643200-0-2*, 875) Phys Therapy.

***Natural Eating: Nutritional Anthropology: Eating in Harmony with Our Genetic.** Geoffrey C. Bond. (Illus.). 256p. 2000. pap. 19.95 (*1-58000-054-1*) Griffin CA.

Natural Economy: A Study of a Marvellous Order in Human Affairs. John Young. 148p. 1997. pap. 18.95 (*0-85683-166-2*, Pub. by Shepheard-Walwyn Pubs) Paul & Co Pubs.

Natural Economy of Laos. Joel M. Halpern. (Laos Project Papers: No. 17). 85p. 1990. pap. 10.50 (*0-923135-18-9*) Dalley Bk Service.

Natural Education. rev. ed. Stan Padilla. LC 94-5479. (Illus.). 80p. (YA). (gr. 7-12). 1994. pap. text 8.95 (*0-913990-14-0*) Book Pub Co.

Natural Electromagnetic Phenomena below 50 Kc-s: Processing of a NATO Advanced Study Institute Held in Bad Homburg, Germany, July 22-August 2, 1963. International Conference on Nondestructive Evaluat. Ed. by D. F. Bleil. LC 64-25831. 480p. reprint ed. pap. 148.80 (*0-608-16931-5*, 205614400050) Bks Demand.

Natural Elements of Political Economy. Richard Jennings. LC 68-56236. (Reprints of Economic Classics Ser.). 275p. 1969. reprint ed. 39.50 (*0-678-00562-1*) Kelley.

Natural Eloquence: Women Reinscribe Science. Ed. by Barbara T. Gates & Ann B. Shteir. LC 96-43668. (Science & Literature Ser.). (Illus.). 280p. 1997. 45.00 (*0-299-15480-7*); pap. 19.95 (*0-299-15484-X*) U of Wis Pr.

Natural Emphasis: English Versification from Chaucer to Dryden. Susanne Woods. LC 84-28854. 310p. 1985. 18.00 (*0-87328-085-7*) Huntington Lib.

Natural Enemies. Carolyn Keene. (Nancy Drew Files: No. 121). (YA). (gr. 6 up). 1997. per. 3.99 (*0-671-56879-5*, Archway) PB.

***Natural Enemies.** Carolyn Keene. (Nancy Drew Files : No. 121). (YA). (gr. 6 up). 1999. per. write for info. (*0-671-50396-0*) S&S Trade.

Natural Enemies. Carolyn Keene. (Nancy Drew Files: No. 121). (YA). (gr. 6 up). 1997. 9.09 (*0-606-11666-4*, Pub. by Turtleback) Demco.

Natural Enemies. T. Weed. 146p. 1993. mass mkt. write for info. (*0-9658584-1-3*) Free Rad Pr.

Natural Enemies: The Notre Dame-Michigan Football Feud. John Kryk. LC 94-22284. (Illus.). 312p. 1994. 18.95 (*0-8362-8072-5*) Andrews & McMeel.

Natural Enemies: The Population Biology of Predators, Parasites & Diseases. M. J. Crawley. (Illus.). 584p. 1992. pap. 75.00 (*0-632-02698-7*) Blackwell Sci.

***Natural Enemies: The United States & the Soviet Union in the Cold War, 1917-1991.** Robert C. Grogin. 368p. 2000. 80.00 (*0-7391-0139-0*) Lxngtn Bks.

Natural Enemies Handbook: The Illustrated Guide to Biological Pest Control. Mary L. Flint. (Illus.). 154p. 1999. pap. 35.00 (*0-520-21801-9*, Pub. by U CA Pr) Cal Prin Full Svc.

Natural Enemies Handbook: The Illustrated Guide to Biological Pest Control. Ed. by Mary Louise Flint et al. LC 97-62438. (Illus.). pap. 35.00 (*1-879906-41-4*) ANR Pubns CA.

***Natural Enemies of Terrestrial Mulluscs.** Ed. by G. Barker. (CABI Publishing Ser.). 320p. 1999. text 90.00 (*0-85199-319-2*) OUP.

Natural Enemies of Vegetable Insect Pests. Mike Hoffmann & Anne Frodsham. (Illus.). 64p. 1993. pap. 14.95 (*1-57753-252-X*, 139NVP) Corn Coop Ext.

Natural Enemy Databank. J. M. Fry. 192p. (Orig.). 1989. pap. text 45.00 (*0-85198-653-6*) OUP.

Natural Energy: A Consumer's Guide to Legal, Mind-Altering & Mood-Brightening Herbs & Supplements. Mark Mayell. LC 97-24045. 304p. 1998. pap. 15.00 (*0-517-88812-2*) Harmony Bks.

Natural Energy: From Tired to Terrific in Ten Days. Carol Colman & Erika Schwartz. LC 98-38124. 256p. 1999. 22.95 (*0-399-14461-7*) Putnam Pub Group.

***Natural Energy: From Tired to Terrific in 10 Days.** Erika Schwartz & Carol Colman. 1999. reprint ed. pap. 12.95 (*0-425-17158-2*) Berkley Pub.

Natural Energy & Vernacular Architecture: Principles & Examples with Reference to Hot Arid Climates. Hassan Fathy. LC 85-24691. (Illus.). xxiv, 200p. 1986. 32.00 (*0-226-23917-9*); pap. 11.95 (*0-226-23918-7*) U Ch Pr.

Natural Energy Boosters. Carlson Wade. (C). 1993. pap. text 12.95 (*0-13-025215-8*) P-H.

Natural Environment: Interdisciplinary Views. Ed. by Kevin L. Hickey & Demetri Kantarelis. xiv, 368p. (Orig.). 1996. pap. 30.00 (*0-9654033-0-0*) Assumption Coll.

Natural Environment: Wastes & Control. R. Christman et al. LC 74-18363. 256p. reprint ed. pap. 79.40 (*0-608-11590-8*, 200775500064) Bks Demand.

Natural Environment & Constitution of India. P. R. Trivedi et al. vii, 491p. 1994. 57.00 (*81-7024-640-7*, Pub. by Ashish Pub Hse) Nataraj Bks.

Natural Environment & the Biogeochemical Cycles. Contrib. by G. G. Choundhry et al. (Handbook of Environmental Chemistry Ser.: Vol. I, Pt. C). (Illus.). 250p. 1984. 142.95 (*0-387-13226-0*) Spr-Verlag.

Natural Environment & The Biogeochemical Cycles. Ed. by O. Hutzinger. (Handbook of Environmental Chemistry Ser.: Vol. 1, Pt. F). (Illus.). 200p. 1992. 128.95 (*0-387-55255-3*) Spr-Verlag.

Natural Environment & the Biogeochemical Cycles. Ed. by O. Hutzinger. (Handbook of Environmental Chemistry Ser.: Vol. 1, Pt. D). (Illus.). 260p. 1985. 192.95 (*0-387-15000-5*) Spr-Verlag.

Natural Environment & the Biogeochemical Cycles. Ed. by O. Hutzinger. (Handbook of Environmental Chemistry Ser.: Vol. 1, Pt. E). (Illus.). 208p. 1989. 119.95 (*0-387-15548-1*) Spr-Verlag.

Natural Environmental Change. Antoinette M. Mannion. LC 98-25877. (Introductions to Environment Ser.). 1999. 65.00 (*0-415-13932-5*); pap. 20.99 (*0-415-13933-3*) Routledge.

Natural Environments: Studies in Theoretical & Applied Analysis. Ed. by John V. Krutilla. LC 72-4441. (Resources for the Future Ser.). 360p. 1973. 27.50 (*0-8018-1446-4*) Johns Hopkins.

Natural Environments: Studies in Theoretical & Applied Analysis. Ed. by John V. Krutilla. LC 72-4441. (Illus.). 363p. reprint ed. pap. 112.60 (*0-608-18091-2*, 203215700078) Bks Demand.

Natural Estrogen Book: A Natural Treatment for the Symptoms of Menopause. Lana Liew. 1998. pap. text 11.95 (*0-7318-0702-2*) Simon & Schuster.

Natural Estrogen Diet: Healthy Recipes for Perimenopause & Menopause. Lana Liew & Linda Ojeda. LC 98-52737. (Illus.). 224p. 1999. reprint ed. pap. 13.95 (*0-89793-246-3*) Hunter Hse.

Natural Experiments with Decreased Availability of Alcoholic Beverages: Finnish Alcohol Strikes in 1972 & 1985. E. Osterberg & S. L. Saila. (Finnish Foundation for Alcohol Studies: Vol. 40). 1991. pap. 35.00 (*951-9192-49-2*) Rutgers Ctr Alcohol.

***Natural Extracts Using Supercritical Carbon Dioxide.** Mamata Mukhopadhyay. LC 00-39733. (Illus.). 2000. pap. write for info. (*0-8493-0819-4*) Auerbach.

Natural Eye Care: An Encyclopedia: Complementary Treatments for Improving & Saving Your Eyes. Marc Grossman & Glen Swartwout. LC 98-55416. 208p. 1999. pap. 16.95 (*0-87983-704-7*, 37047K, Keats Publng) NTC Contemp Pub Co.

Natural Fabrics: Simple & Stylish Soft Furnishings. Ian Mankin. (Illus.). 128p. 1998. 27.50 (*0-09-182020-0*, Pub. by Ebury Pr) Trafalgar.

***Natural Fabrics: Simple & Stylish Soft Furnishings.** Ian Mankin & Moore. (Illus.). 128p. 1999. reprint ed. pap. 22.95 (*0-09-186891-2*, Pub. by Ebury Pr) Trafalgar.

Natural Face Lift. Juliette Kando. (Illus.). 176p. 1998. 16.00 (*0-7225-3679-8*) Thorsons PA.

Natural Facts. Melanie Neilson. 68p. 1996. pap. 11.00 (*0-937013-57-9*) Potes Poets.

Natural Family Living: The Mothering Magazine Guide to Parenting. Peggy O'Mara & Jane L. McConnell. LC 99-89667. (Illus.). 384p. 2000. per. 17.95 (*0-671-02744-1*, PB Trade Paper) PB.

Natural Family Planning: A Guide to Provision of Services. WHO Staff. 88p. 1988. 16.00 (*92-4-154241-1*) World Health.

Natural Family Planning: Why It Succeeds. Herbert F. Smith. 64p. 1995. pap. 2.95 (*0-8198-5115-9*) Pauline Bks.

Natural Father. Robert Lacy. Ed. by C. W. Truesdale. LC 97-65063. (Minnesota Voices Project Ser.: Vol. 81). 200p. (Orig.). 1997. pap. 14.95 (*0-89823-176-0*) New Rivers Pr.

Natural Features of Indiana. A. A. Lindsey. 1976. 18.00 (*1-883362-06-7*) IN Acad Sci.

Natural Fertility Awareness. John Davidson. 108p. 1994. pap. 11.95 (*0-85207-175-2*, Pub. by C W Daniel) Natl Bk Netwk.

Natural Fertility Awareness. rev. ed. John Davidson & Lucie Davidson. (Illus.). 136p. 1994. pap. 17.95 (*0-8464-4337-6*) Beekman Pubs.

Natural Fibers: Nature's Ancient Gifts for a Modern World History & Uses of the Common & Uncommon. 3rd rev. ed. Phyllis L. Friesen. (Illus.). 200p. (YA). (gr. 6-12). 1995. pap. text 24.50 incl. disk (*0-9645295-0-5*) Arbidar.

Natural Fibers Fact Book, 1998. Natural Fibers Research & Information Center Staff. (Illus.). 50p. 1995. pap. 15.00 (*0-87755-329-7*) Bureau Busn TX.

Natural Fibers Information Guide: Information, History & Uses of Natural Fibers. 2nd ed. Phyllis L. Friesen. LC 95-94270. (Illus.). 157p. 1995. pap., student ed. 17.95 (*0-9645295-1-3*) Arbidar.

Natural Fictions: George Chapman's Major Tragedies. A. R. Braunmuller. LC 89-40764. 192p. 1992. 36.50 (*0-87413-404-8*) U Delaware Pr.

Natural First Aid. Brigitte Mars. LC 99-32307. 144p. 1999. pap. 12.95 (*1-58017-147-8*) Storey Bks.

Natural Fission Reactors. IAEA Staff. (Panel Proceedings Ser.). (Illus.). 754p. 1978. pap. 155.00 (*92-0-051078-7*, ISP475, Pub. by IAEA) Bernan Associates.

Natural Fitness. Bob Paris. 288p. (Orig.). 1996. mass mkt. 14.99 (*0-446-67029-4*, Pub. by Warner Bks) Little.

Natural Flower Arranging. Tricia Guild & Nonie Niesewand. 1999. pap. 21.95 (*1-85732-833-7*) Millers Pubns.

Natural Flowers. Ed. by Wolfgang Hageney. (ENG, FRE, GER, ITA & SPA., Illus.). 96p. 1985. pap. 21.95 (*88-7070-041-0*) Belvedere USA.

***Natural Focusing & Fine Structure of Light: Caustics & Wave Dislocations.** J. F. Nye. LC 99-11442. 8p. 1999. 50.00 (*0-7503-0610-6*) IOP Pub.

N

*Natural Food Antimicrobial Systems. A. S. Naidu. LC 00-36053. 832p. 2000. boxed set 149.95 (0-8493-2047-X) CRC Pr.
Natural Food Colorants. G. Hendry. 1991. text 99.95 (0-442-31464-7) Chapman & Hall.
Natural Food Colors: Emphasizing European Technology & Markets. Contrib. by U. Marz. 130p. 1995. 2750.00 (1-56965-110-8, GA-089) BCC.
Natural Food Cookbook. Hannan. (Runner's World Ser.). 1981. pap. 9.95 (0-02-499570-3, Macmillan Coll) P-H.
Natural Food Cookery. Eleanor Levitt. Orig. Title: The Wonderful World of Natural-Food Cookery. (Illus.). 320p. 1979. reprint ed. pap. 6.95 (0-486-23851-2) Dover.
Natural Food Garden: Growing Vegetables & Fruits Chemical-Free. Patrick Lima & John Scanlan. (Illus.). 160p. 1992. pap. 19.95 (1-55958-202-2) Prima Pub.
Natural Food of Man. Hereward Carrington. 286p. 1996. reprint ed. spiral bd. 20.00 (0-7873-0153-1) Hlth Research.
Natural Food of Man: Being an Attempt to Prove That the Original, Best, & Natural Diet of Man Is Fruits & Nuts. Hereward Carrington. 286p. 1996. reprint ed. pap. 18.95 (1-56459-683-4) Kessinger Pub.
Natural Foods: The Safe Way to Health. Otto Carque. (Illus.). 350p. 1998. reprint ed. pap. text 35.00 (0-87556-858-0) Saifer.
Natural Foods & Good Cooking. Kathy Cituk & John Finnegan. (Illus.). 128p. (Orig.). 1989. pap. 8.00 (0-927425-01-7) Elysian Arts.
Natural Foods & Nutrition: A Report. Center for Self-Sufficiency, Research Division Sta. 50p. 1983. ring bd. 25.95 (0-910811-67-9) Ctr Self Suff.
Natural Foods & Products. Chandler. 1996. write for info. (0-8050-5268-2) H Holt & Co.
Natural Foods Cookbook. Mary Estella. (Illus.). 160p. (Orig.). 1985. pap. 19.95 (0-87040-583-7) Japan Pubns USA.
*Natural Foods Market: A National Survey of Strategies for Growth. Nessa J. Richman. (Policy Studies Report: No. 12). (Illus.). 87p. 1999. pap. 150.00 (1-893182-19-3) H A Wallace Inst.
Natural Foods, the Safe Way to Health. Otto Carque. 359p. 1996. reprint ed. spiral bd. 20.00 (0-7873-0149-3) Hlth Research.
Natural Foot Care. Stephanie Tourles. LC 98-19917. (Illus.). 192p. 1998. pap. 14.95 (1-58017-054-4, Storey Pub) Storey Bks.
Natural for DB2 Developers Handbook. Ed. by Greg Resnick. 560p. 1991. pap. 65.00 (1-878960-06-7) WH&O Intl.
Natural for DB2 Study Guide. Ed. by D. D. Hamilton. 475p. (Orig.). 1991. pap. 65.00 (1-878960-08-3) WH&O Intl.
Natural Fragrances: Outdoor Scents for Indoor Uses. Gail Duff. LC 89-45219. (Illus.). 160p. 1989. 16.95 (0-88266-554-5, Garden Way Pub) Storey Bks.
Natural Fragrances: Outdoor Scents for Indoor Uses. Gail Duff. LC 89-45219. (Illus.). 160p. 1991. pap. 16.95 (0-88266-683-5, Garden Way Pub) Storey Bks.
Natural Fun: The Naturelink Family Activity Book. Gary Soucie. (Illus.). 60p. (Orig.). (J). 1996. pap. write for info. (0-945051-61-1) Natl Wildlife.
Natural Functions Algebras. Charles E. Rickart. (Universitext Ser.). 240p. 1979. 69.95 (0-387-90449-2) Spr-Verlag.
Natural Gaits. Pierre Alferi. Tr. by Cole Swensen from FRE. (Sun & Moon Classics Ser.: Vol. 95). 56p. 1995. pap. 10.95 (1-55713-231-3) Sun & Moon CA.
Natural Garden. Ken Druse. 1988. 40.00 (0-517-55046-6) C Potter.
Natural Garden Book: A Holistic Approach to Gardening. Peter Harper & Jeremy Light. LC 93-19439. 1994. 35.00 (0-671-74487-9, Fireside); pap. 25.00 (0-671-74323-6, Fireside) S&S Trade Pap.
*Natural Garden Book: Gardening in Harmony with Nature. Peter Harper. (Illus.). 286p. 2000. reprint ed. pap. 24.95 (1-85675-056-6, Pub. by Gaia Bks) Trafalgar.
Natural Gardening see Nature Company Guides Series
*Natural Gardening A-Z. Donald Trotter. LC 98-55188. 156p. 1999. text 19.95 (1-56170-594-2) Hay House.
*Natural Gardening A-Z. Donald W. Trotter. (Illus.). 156p. 2001. pap. 11.95 (1-56170-791-0, L472) Hay House.
Natural Gardens of North Carolina, with Keys & Descriptions of the Herbaceous Wild Flowers Found Therein. Bertram W. Wells. LC 68-12515. 478p. reprint ed. pap. 148.20 (0-8357-3859-0, 203659200004) Bks Demand.
Natural Gas: A Catalyst for Regional Economic Development in the Border Region. Ed. by Patricia A. Sullivan. 40p. (Orig.). (C). 1994. pap. text 10.00 (0-685-75218-6) Waste-Mgmt Educ.
Natural Gas: Executive Outlook. Richard K. Miller & Christy H. Gunter. (Market Research Survey Ser.: No. 325). 50p. 1997. pap. 200.00 (1-55865-347-3) Future Tech Surveys.
Natural Gas: Executive Outlook. Richard K. Miller & Marcia E. Rupnow. (Survey on Technology & Markets Ser.: No. 204). 50p. 1993. pap. text 200.00 (1-55865-235-3) Future Tech Surveys.
Natural Gas: Factors Affecting Approval Times for Construction of Natural Gas Pipelines. (Illus.). 40p. (Orig.). (C). 1993. pap. text 25.00 (1-56806-567-1) DIANE Pub.
Natural Gas: Private Sector Participation & Market Development. (Private Sector Ser.). 100p. 1999. pap. 50.00 (0-8213-4485-4, 14485) World Bank.
Natural Gas: Production Processing, Transport. Ed. by Alexandre Rojey & Claude Jaffret. 420p. 1995. pap. 425.00 (2-7108-0693-2, Pub. by Edits Technip) Enfield Pubs NH.
Natural Gas & Alternative Fuels for Engines, Vol. 21. Ed. by S. R. Bell & R. Sekar. LC 93-74680. 108p. 1994. pap. 35.00 (0-7918-1185-9) ASME.
Natural Gas & Alternative Fuels for Engines: 1995: Proceedings: The ASME Internal Combustion Engine Division Spring Meeting (1995: Marietta, Ohio) Ed. by Frank Aboujaoude et al. LC 93-74680. (ICE Ser.: Vol. 24). 111p. 1995. pap. 70.00 (0-7918-1304-5, H00936) ASME.
Natural Gas & Economic Security. Hanns W. Maull. (Atlantic Papers: No. 43). 60p. (Orig.). 1981. pap. text 10.50 (0-86598-082-9) Rowman.
Natural Gas & Electric Power in Nontechnical Language. Ann Chambers. LC 99-13897. 258p. 1999. 64.95 (0-87814-761-6) PennWell Bks.
Natural Gas Annual. 1994. lib. bdg. 256.95 (0-8490-5827-9) Gordon Pr.
Natural Gas Annual. 1995. lib. bdg. 250.00 (0-8490-6496-1) Gordon Pr.
Natural Gas Annual, 1992, 2 vols., Set. (Illus.). 562p. (Orig.). (C). 1994. pap. text 95.00 (0-7881-0493-4) DIANE Pub.
Natural Gas Annual, 1992, Vol. 2. 293p. (Orig.). 1993. per. 21.00 (0-16-063465-2) USGPO.
Natural Gas Annual (1993) Supplement: Company Profiles. 198p. pap. text 60.00 (0-7881-2922-8) DIANE Pub.
Natural Gas Annual, 1996. 259p. 1997. per. 24.00 (0-16-063493-8) USGPO.
*Natural Gas Annual, 1997. 261p. 1998. per. 21.00 (0-16-063547-0) USGPO.
Natural Gas Applications for Air Pollution Control. American Gas Association Staff. Ed. by Nelson Hay. LC 85-45879. 359p. 1986. text 58.00 (0-88173-013-0) Fairmont Pr.
Natural Gas by Sea: The Development of a New Technology. Roger Ffooks. 250p. (C). 1993. 175.00 (1-85609-052-3, Pub. by Witherby & Co) St Mut.
Natural Gas Clauses in Petroleum Arrangements. (UNCTC Advisory Studies: No. 1). 54p. 20.00 (92-1-104198-8, E.87.11.A.3) UN.
*Natural Gas Competition: The Deregulation of Georgia. Ed. by L. Dennis Smith et al. 108p. 2000. spiral bd. 250.00 (1-891790-31-5) Chartwell Inc.
Natural Gas Contracting. Arthur J. Wright. LC 98-38590. 1998. write for info. (1-57073-604-9, ABA Natl Res) Amer Bar Assn.
Natural Gas Conversion: Proceedings of the Symposium, Oslo, Norway, Aug. 12-17, 1990. Ed. by A. Holmen et al. (Studies in Surface Science & Catalysis: No. 61). 572p. 1991. 281.50 (0-444-88735-0) Elsevier.
Natural Gas Conversion V: Proceedings of the 5th International Natural Gas Conversion Symposium, Giardini Naxos-Taormina, Italy, September 20-25, 1998. A. Parmaliana. LC 98-42600. (Studies in Surface Science & Catalysis). 1998. write for info. (0-444-82967-9) Elsevier.
Natural Gas Conversion II: Proceedings of the Third Natural Gas Conversion Symposium, Sydney, July 4-9, 1993. Ed. by H. E. Curry-Hyde & R. F. Howe. LC 94-10953. (Studies in Surface Science & Catalysis: Vol. 81). 594p. 1994. 272.50 (0-444-89535-3) Elsevier.
Natural Gas Conversion IV: Proceedings of the 4th International Natural Gas Conversion Symposium, Kruger Park, South Africa, November 19-23, 1995, Vol. 107. M. De Pontes et al. LC 97-327. (Studies in Surface Science & Catalysis). 600p. 297.00 (0-444-82352-2) Elsevier.
Natural Gas Cooling. Richard K. Miller et al. (Market Research Survey Ser.: No. 239). 50p. 1996. 200.00 (1-55865-270-1) Future Tech Surveys.
Natural Gas Distribution Study: Focus on Western Europe. IEA Staff. LC 99-177209. 336p. 1998. pap. 150.00 (92-64-16182-1, 61 98 19 1 P, Pub. by Org for Econ) OECD.
Natural Gas Energy Measurement. Ed. by A. Attari & D. L. Klass. 482p. 1987. 75.00 (0-910091-61-7) Inst Gas Tech.
Natural Gas Hydrates. Ed. by E. Dendy Sloan et al. LC 94-9630. (Annals Ser.: Vol. 715). 580p. 1994. 160.00 (0-89766-847-2); pap. 160.00 (0-89766-848-0) NY Acad Sci.
Natural Gas in Central Asia: Industries, Markets & Export Options of Kazakstan, Turkmenistan & Uzbekistan. Akira Miyamoto. 80p. 1998. pap. 15.95 (1-86203-012-X, Pub. by Royal Inst Intl Affairs) Brookings.
Natural Gas in Developing Countries: Evaluating the Benefits to the Environment. John Homer. LC 92-43481. (Discussion Paper Ser.: No. 190). 49p. 1993. pap. 22.00 (0-8213-2329-6, 12329) World Bank.
Natural Gas in Nontechnical Language. Rebecca L. Busby & Institute of Gas Technology Staff. LC 99-14115. 200p. 1999. 64.95 (0-87814-738-1) PennWell Bks.
Natural Gas in the Internal Market: A Review of Energy Policy. Ed. by Ernst J. Mestmacker. (International Energy & Resources Law & Policy Ser.). (C). 1993. lib. bdg. 145.50 (1-85333-795-1) Kluwer Academic.
Natural Gas in the U. K. Options to the Year 2000. 2nd ed. Jonathan Stern. (Energy Policy Studies). 64p. 1986. text 66.95 (0-566-05018-8, Pub. by Dartmth Pub) Ashgate Pub Co.
Natural Gas in the World: Outlook to 2000. Ed. by Association Technique de l'Industrie du Gaz en Fra. 200p. (C). 1989. 300.00 (2-7108-0571-5, Pub. by Edits Technip) Enfield Pubs NH.
Natural Gas in Western Europe: Structure, Strategies, & Politics. Gregory F. Treverton et al. LC 87-81459. viii, 68p. (Orig.). 1987. pap. 16.50 (0-942781-01-5) Harvard EEPC.
Natural Gas Industry: Evolution, Structure, & Economics. Arlon Tussing & Bob Tippee. 1995. 84.95 (0-87814-447-1) PennWell Bks.
*Natural Gas Information: 1998 Edition. IEA Staff. 580p. 1999. pap. 150.00 (92-64-17088-X, 61 1999 12 1 P, Pub. by Org for Econ) OECD.
Natural Gas Information, 1996: 1997 Edition. IEA Staff. 496p. 1997. pap. 89.00 (92-64-15592-9, 61-97-15592-9, Pub. by Org for Econ) OECD.
Natural Gas, Issues & Trends. 1995. lib. bdg. 250.00 (0-8490-6495-3) Gordon Pr.
Natural Gas Market Outlook, 1993. 174p. pap. text 40.00 (0-7881-4453-7) DIANE Pub.
Natural Gas Markets after Deregulation: Methods of Analysis & Research Needs. Harry G. Broadman et al. LC 83-42907. 96p. 1983. pap. 11.00 (0-8018-3125-3) Resources Future.
Natural Gas Measurement & Control: A Guide for Operators & Engineers. Lohit Datta-Barua. 205p. 1991. 75.00 (0-07-015608-5) McGraw.
Natural Gas Monthly. Government Printing Office Staff. pap. 77.00 (0-16-012582-0) USGPO.
Natural Gas, 1996: Issues & Trends. Ed. by Joan E. Heinkel. (Illus.). 174p. (Orig.). (C). 1997. pap. text 40.00 (0-7881-4503-7) DIANE Pub.
Natural Gas Price Deregulation: A Case of Trickle up Economics. 27p. 1982. 30.00 (0-318-23872-1) Consumer Energy Coun.
Natural Gas Pricing in Competitive Markets. IEA Staff. LC 99-177193. 184p. 1998. pap. 110.00 (92-64-16955-5, 61 98 30 1 P, Pub. by Org for Econ) OECD.
Natural Gas Producer Regulation & Taxation: Interaction Between Federal Producer Regulation & State Severance Taxation. Milton Russell & Laurence Toenjes. LC 78-635475. (MSU Public Utilities Papers: Vol. 1971). (Illus.). 95p. reprint ed. pap. 30.00 (0-608-20511-7, 207176300002) Bks Demand.
Natural Gas Production Engineering. Chi U. Ikoku. LC 91-21121. 538p. (C). 1992. reprint ed. text 71.50 (0-89464-639-7) Krieger.
Natural Gas Productive Capacity for the Lower 48 States. 1995. lib. bdg. 250.00 (0-8490-6497-X) Gordon Pr.
Natural Gas Productive Capacity for the Lower 48 States: 1985 Through 1997. James N. Hicks et al. (Illus.). 98p. (C). 1997. reprint ed. pap. text 25.00 (0-7881-4259-3) DIANE Pub.
Natural Gas Purchasing Handbook. John M. Studebaker. 270p. 1994. 79.00 (0-87814-645-8) PennWell Bks.
Natural Gas Research & Technology Conference: Proceedings, 1st, February 28-March 3, 1971. 850p. 1971. pap. 10.00 (0-910091-38-2) Inst Gas Tech.
Natural Gas Research & Technology Conference, 3rd: Proceedings, Dallas, Texas, March 6-8, 1974. 430p. 1974. pap. 15.00 (0-910091-40-4) Inst Gas Tech.
Natural Gas Reservoir Engineering. Chi U. Ikoku. 526p. (C). 1992. reprint ed. text 69.50 (0-89464-640-0) Krieger.
Natural Gas Sector in Poland: A Strategic Entry Report, 1997. Compiled by Icon Group International Staff. (Illus.). 188p. 1999. ring bd. 1880.00 incl. audio compact disk (0-7418-0875-7) Icon Grp.
Natural Gas Statistics Sourcebook. 6th ed. 1999. 295.00 (0-318-72980-6) PennWell Bks.
Natural Gas Supplements by Cyclic-Regenerative Hydrogasification of Oils. J. M. Reid et al. (Research Bulletin Ser.: No. 28). iv, 78p. 1960. pap. 25.00 (1-58222-031-X) Inst Gas Tech.
Natural Gas Technologies: A Driving Force for Market Development. IEA Staff. LC 98-103794. 1188p. 1997. pap. 116.00 (92-64-15485-X, 61-97-10-1, Pub. by Org for Econ) OECD.
Natural Gas, the Best Energy Choice. Ernest J. Oppenheimer. LC 89-63205. 188p. 1990. 30.00 (0-9603982-7-9) Pen & Podium.
Natural Gas Trade in North America & Asia. Jonathan Stern. 260p. 1985. text 77.95 (0-566-00948-X) Ashgate Pub Co.
Natural Gas Trade in Transition. Ed. by Bijan Mossavar-Rahmani. LC 87-81051. (International Energy Studies: No. 1). x, 91p. (Orig.). 1987. pap. 16.50 (0-942781-00-7) Harvard EEPC.
Natural Gas Transport in the U. S. S. R. Esfir Rayker. Ed. by Maureen Young. 103p. (Orig.). 1983. pap. text 75.00 (1-55831-039-8) Delphic Associates.
Natural Gas Underground Storage. M. Rasin Tek. LC 96-32399. 1996. 99.95 (0-87814-614-8) PennWell Bks.
Natural Gas Users' Handbook. Stephen A. Herman et al. LC 76-27247. 128p. reprint ed. pap. 39.70 (0-608-14111-9, 202430100036) Bks Demand.
Natural Gas Vehicles. John G. Ingersoll. LC 95-38382. 461p. 1995. 78.00 (0-88173-218-4) Fairmont Pr.
Natural Gas Vehicles. Richard K. Miller & Christy H. Gunter. (Market Research Survey Ser.: No. 327). 50p. 1997. pap. 200.00 (1-55865-349-X) Future Tech Surveys.
Natural Gas Vehicles. Richard K. Miller & Marcia E. Rupnow. (Survey on Technology & Markets Ser.: No. 205). 50p. 1993. pap. text 200.00 (1-55865-236-1) Future Tech Surveys.
Natural Gas Vehicles: A National Security Perspective: a Report. CSIS Energy & Strategic Resources Program Staff. LC 84-23293. (Significant Issues Ser.: Vol. 6, No. 16). (Illus.). 79p. reprint ed. pap. 30.00 (0-8357-6639-X, 203530600094) Bks Demand.
Natural Gas Vehicles Trainer's Manual. West Virginia University Press Staff. 688p. 1997. teacher ed. write for info. (0-8273-7902-1) Delmar.
Natural Gases of North America: A Symposium, Vol. 1. Ed. by B. W. Beebe et al. LC 68-15769. (American Association of Petroleum Geologists. Memoir Ser.: No. 9). 1236p. reprint ed. pap. 200.00 (0-608-11197-X, 205002500057) Bks Demand.
Natural Gases of North America: A Symposium, Vol. 2. Ed. by B. W. Beebe et al. LC 68-15769. (American Association of Petroleum Geologists. Memoir Ser.: No. 9). 1253p. reprint ed. pap. 200.00 (0-608-11198-8, 205002500058) Bks Demand.
Natural Genesis, 2 vols. Gerald Massey. (Illus.). 1087p. 1998. reprint ed. 84.95 (1-57478-010-7); reprint ed. pap. 49.95 (1-57478-009-3) Black Classic.
Natural Genesis. Gerald Massey. (African Studies). reprint ed. 75.00 (0-938818-80-5) ECA Assoc.
Natural Genesis: The Lost Origins of Myths & Mysteries, Types & Symbols, Religion & Language, with Egypt As the Mouthpiece & Africa As the Birthplace, 2 vols., Set. Gerald Massey. 1991. lib. bdg. 119.95 (0-8490-4297-6) Gordon Pr.
Natural Genesis: or, The Second Part of a Book of the Beginnings, Set, Vols. 1[00ad]2. Gerald Massey. 1087p. 1992. reprint ed. pap. 70.00 (1-56459-151-4) Kessinger Pub.
Natural Geography of Plants. Henry Allan Gleason & Arthur Cronquist. LC 64-15448. (Illus.). 420p. (YA). (gr. 9 up). 1964. text 112.00 (0-231-02668-4) Col U Pr.
Natural Golf. Peter Fox & John Burrill. 1997. pap. 14.95 (0-614-27665-9, Mstrs Pr) NTC Contemp Pub Co.
Natural Golf. Seve Ballesteros & John Andrisani. (Illus.). 240p. 1991. reprint ed. pap. 16.95 (0-02-048361-9) Macmillan.
Natural Golf: A Lifetime of Better Golf. unabridged ed. Peter Fox. Ed. & Illus. by Golf Digest Productions Staff. 1998. mass mkt. 19.95 (0-9663524-0-8) Natural Golf.
Natural Golf: Golf Reform Is at Hand. Peter Fox & John Burn, II. LC 96-53512. (Illus.). 160p. 1997. pap. 14.95 (1-57028-125-4, 81254H, Mstrs Pr) NTC Contemp Pub Co.
Natural Golf Swing. George Knudson & Lorne Rubenstein. 1992. reprint ed. pap. 14.95 (1-881108-00-7) Kirsh & Baum.
Natural Goodness of Man: On the System of Rousseau's Thought. Arthur M. Melzer. 368p. 1998. pap. text 22.50 (0-226-51979-1) U Ch Pr.
Natural Goodness of Man: On the System of Rousseau's Thought. Arthur M. Melzer. LC 89-20587. 328p. reprint ed. pap. 101.70 (0-608-09480-3, 205428000005) Bks Demand.
Natural Goodness of Man: The Study of Behavior Without a Goal. Arthur M. Melzer. 368p. 1996. lib. bdg. 61.50 (0-226-51978-3) U Ch Pr.
Natural Goodness of Man: The Study of Behavior Without a Goal. Norman R. Maier. LC 81-20092. (Illus.). 264p. 1982. reprint ed. lib. bdg. 65.00 (0-313-23340-3, MAFRU, Greenwood Pr) Greenwood.
Natural Gourmet: Delicious Recipes for Healthy, Balanced Eating. Annemarie Colbin. 336p. 1991. pap. 12.50 (0-345-37028-7) Ballantine Pub Grp.
Natural Grace. Matthew Fox. 224p. 1997. pap. 12.95 (0-385-48359-7) Doubleday.
Natural Grasslands. R. T. Coupland. (Ecosystems of the World Ser.: Vol. 8A). xiv,470p. 1992. 265.50 (0-444-88264-2) Elsevier.
Natural Grasslands: Eastern Hemisphere & Resume. Ed. by R. T. Coupland. (Ecosystems of the World Ser.: Vol. 8B). xvi,556p. 1993. 276.50 (0-444-89557-4) Elsevier.
Natural Great Perfection: Dzogchen Teachings & Vajra Songs. Nyshul K. Rinpoche. Ed. by Surya Das. LC 95-15875. 204p. 1995. 14.95 (1-55939-049-2) Snow Lion Pubns.
Natural Groundwater Flow. Wouter Zijl & Marek Nawalany. 336p. 1993. lib. bdg. 95.00 (0-87371-868-2, L868) Lewis Pubs.
Natural Guide to Better Health. Petie Clapper. 1990. 19.95 (0-685-29021-2) Orange Bl Pr.
Natural Guide to Colon Health. Louise Tenney. 1997. pap. text 12.95 (1-885670-45-1) Woodland UT.
Natural Guide to Good Health: Nutritional Balance for a Life Time. Mark Curley & Sandra Curley. LC 90-70943. 185p. (Orig.). 1990. pap. 14.95 (0-9626875-9-6) Supreme Pub.
Natural Guide to Treating High Blood Pressure. S. Streicher-Lankin. 1998. pap. 9.99 (0-7615-1554-2) Prima Pub.
Natural Guide to Women's Health. Lynda Wharton. 270p. 1996. 6.98 (1-56731-095-8, MJF Bks) Fine Comms.
*Natural Habitat: Contemporary Wildlife Artists of North America. William H. Gerdts et al. (Illus.). 104p. 1998. 65.00 (0-945936-18-4) Spanierman Gallery.
Natural Habitat Garden. Ken Druse & Margaret Roach. LC 93-12558. 1994. 40.00 (0-517-58989-3) C Potter.
Natural Hair Care Specialist Braiding Book. Diane Bailey. LC 97-25161. (HAIR). 256p. 1997. pap. 37.95 (1-56253-316-9) Thomson Learn.
Natural Hand Care. Norma Weinberg. LC 98-4409. (Illus.). 160p. 1998. pap. 14.95 (1-58017-053-6, Storey Pub) Storey Bks.
Natural Harvest. Blackbirch Graphics Staff. LC 96-15565. (J). 1996. lib. bdg. 16.98 (0-8050-4623-2) H Holt & Co.
Natural Hazard Mitigation: Recasting Disaster Policy & Planning. David Godschalk & Timothy Beatley. LC 98-34884. 450p. 1998. pap. text 45.00 (1-55963-602-5) Island Pr.
Natural Hazard Mitigation Grantees Workshop. (Illus.). 145p. (Orig.). (C). 1996. pap. text 30.00 (0-7881-2677-6) DIANE Pub.
Natural Hazard Phenomena & Mitigation. Ed. by S. J. Chang. 135p. 1996. pap. text 70.00 (0-7918-1777-6, TS283) ASME Pr.
Natural Hazard Phenomena & Mitigation: Proceedings of the Pressure Vessels & Piping Conference, Minneapolis, MN, 1994. Ed. by C. W. Lin. LC 94-71661. (PVP Ser.: Vol. 271). 163p. 1994. pap. 50.00 (0-7918-1194-8) ASME.

N

An Asterisk (*) at the beginning of an entry indicates that the title is appearing for the first time.

Natural Hazard Phenomena & Mitigation - 1995. Ed. by C. W. Lin et al. LC 94-71661. (Proceedings of the 1995 ASME/JSME Pressure Vessels & Piping Conference Ser.: PVP-Vol. 308). 464p. 1995. 140.00 (*0-7918-1339-8*, H00971) ASME.

Natural Hazard Policy Setting: Identifying Supporters & Opponents of Nonstructural Hazard Mitigation. Elliott Mittler. (Program on Environment & Behavior Monograph Ser.: No. 48). 282p. (C). 1989. pap. 20.00 (*0-685-28122-1*) Natural Hazards.

Natural Hazard Risk Assessment & Public Policy: Anticipating the Unexpected. A. A. Atkisson & William J. Petak. (Environmental Management Ser.). (Illus.). 489p. 1982. 108.00 (*0-387-90645-2*) Spr-Verlag.

Natural Hazards. David Chapman. (Meridian Australian Geographical Perspectives Ser.). (Illus.). 192p. (C). 1995. pap. text 19.95 (*0-19-553564-2*) OUP.

Natural Hazards: An Integrative Framework for Research & Planning. Risa Palm. LC 89-45490. 200p. reprint ed. pap. 62.00 (*0-608-08799-8*, 206943800004) Bks Demand.

Natural Hazards: Explanation & Integration. Graham A. Tobin & Burrell E. Montz. LC 97-1191. 388p. 1997. pap. text 30.00 (*1-57230-062-0*, C0062); lib. bdg. 47.95 (*1-57230-061-2*, 0061) Guilford Pubns.

Natural Hazards: Monitoring & Assessment Using Remote Sensing Technique. Ed. by R. P. Singh & R. Furrer. (Advances in Space Research (RJ) Ser.). 162p. 1995. pap. 97.75 (*0-08-042619-0*, Pergamon Pr) Elsevier.

Natural Hazards: Threat, Disaster, Effect Response. Edward Bryant. (Illus.). 312p. (C). 1991. text 85.00 (*0-521-37295-X*); pap. text 30.95 (*0-521-37889-3*) Cambridge U Pr.

Natural Hazards Data Resources Directory. Compiled by Leaura M. Hennig. (Special Publications: No. 21). 150p. (Orig.). (C). 1989. pap. 20.00 (*1-877943-01-0*) Natural Hazards.

Natural Hazards in the Urban Habitat: Proceedings of the Golden Jubilee Year Conference, Central Building Research Institute, Roorkee, New Delhi, November 10-11, 1997 R. N. Iyengar. LC 99-932918. xii, 204 p. 1997. write for info. (*0-07-463188-8*) McGrw-H Intl.

Natural Hazards of the Texas Coastal Zone, SR0002. L. F. Brown, Jr. et al. (Illus.). 13p. 1974. pap. 3.00 (*0-317-05185-7*, SR0002) Bur Econ Geology.

Natural Hazards Policy Setting: Identifying Supporters & Opponents of Nonstructural Hazard Mitigation. Elliott Mittler. (Program on Environment & Behavior Monograph Ser.: No. 48). 282p. 1989. 20.00 (*0-685-62420-X*) Natural Hazards.

Natural Healing. Eric Scott Kaplan. LC 98-86020. (Alternative Health for the Medically-Inept Ser.: No. 1). (Illus.). 352p. 1998. pap. 16.95 (*0-914984-10-1*, Pub. by Starburst) Natl Bk Netwk.

Natural Healing: Alternative/Complementary Resources for Total Health. S. Jeanne Gunn. LC 98-72445. (Illus.). 288p. 1999. pap. 19.95 (*1-58151-013-6*) BookPartners.

***Natural Healing: Homeopathy, Herbalism, Relaxation, Stress Relief.** Sue Hawkey & Robin Hayfield. (Illus.). 192p. 2000. 19.95 (*1-84038-228-7*) Hermes Hse.

Natural Healing: The Total Health & Nutritional Program. Jack Soltanoff. 304p. 1989. reprint ed. mass mkt. 11.99 (*0-446-39022-4*, Pub. by Warner Bks) Little.

Natural Healing & Herbs: A Reference Guide in the Proper Dosage of Herbal Preparations. 1991. lib. bdg. 250.00 (*0-8490-5105-3*) Gordon Pr.

Natural Healing & Prevention Secrets. James Robinson & Nancy Nielson. pap. 19.95 (*0-9638596-1-7*) Amer Pubng.

***Natural Healing Companion: Using Alternative Medicines:What to Buy, How to Take, & When to Combine for Best Results.** Deborah Wiancek. (Illus.). 480p. 2000. pap. 19.95 (*1-57954-245-X*) Rodale Pr Inc.

Natural Healing for Babies & Children. Aviva J. Romm. (Illus.). 256p. (Orig.). 1996. pap. text 16.95 (*0-89594-786-2*) Crossing Pr.

Natural Healing for Children: An A-Z Guide to Easy Home Remedies. Winifred Conkling. 1997. mass mkt. 6.99 (*0-312-96044-1*) St Martin.

***Natural Healing for Depression: Solutions from the World's Great Health Traditions & Practitioners.** Ed. by James Strohecker & Nancy S. Strohecker. LC 99-34778. 338p. 1999. pap. 15.95 (*0-399-52537-8*, Perigee Bks) Berkley Pub.

Natural Healing for Dogs. Susanne Bonisch. LC 96-19222. (Illus.). 96p. 1996. pap. 10.95 (*0-8069-8120-2*) Sterling.

***Natural Healing for Dogs A-Z.** Cheryl Schwartz. (Illus.). 156p. 2001. pap. 11.95 (*1-56170-793-7*, L478) Hay House.

Natural Healing for Dogs & Cats. Diane Stein. (Illus.). 190p. 1993. pap. 16.95 (*0-89594-614-9*) Crossing Pr.

Natural Healing for Dogs & Cats A-Z. Cheryl Schwartz. LC 99-45845. (Illus.). 144p. 2000. 19.95 (*1-56170-666-3*, L454) Hay House.

Natural Healing for Headaches: High-Powered Cures for Ending Pain. Eva Urbaniak. LC 98-45868. (Harbor Health Ser.). (Illus.). 112p. 2000. pap. 14.95 (*0-936197-41-2*) Harbor Pr.

Natural Healing for Parasites. Anne L. Gittleman. 16p. 1995. pap. 2.95 (*0-9647080-0-0*) Healing Wisdom.

Natural Healing for Schizophrenia: A Compendium of Nutritional Methods. Eva Edelman. LC 96-83505. (Illus.). 208p. (Orig.). (C). 1996. pap. 24.95 (*0-9650976-2-5*) Borage Bks.

Natural Healing for Schizophrenia: A Compendium of Nutritional Methods see Natural Healing for Schizophrenia & Other Common Mental Disorders

Natural Healing for Schizophrenia & Other Common Mental Disorders. 2nd rev. ed. Eva Edelman. LC 98-92417. Orig. Title: Natural Healing for Schizophrenia: A Compendium of Nutritional Methods. (Illus.). 256p. 1998. pap. 24.95 (*0-9650976-6-8*) Borage Bks.

Natural Healing for the Pregnant Woman. Elizabeth Burch & Judith Sachs. LC 96-43824. 336p. 1997. pap. 14.00 (*0-399-52308-1*, Perigee Bks) Berkley Pub.

Natural Healing for Women: Caring for Yourself with Herbs, Homeopathy, & Essential Oils. Susan Curtis & Romy Fraser. 304p. 1995. pap. 15.00 (*0-614-10599-4*) Harper SF.

Natural Healing for Women: Caring for Yourself with Herbs, Homeopathy & Essential Oils. Susan Curtis & Romy Fraser. 422p. 1992. pap. 16.00 (*0-04-440645-2*, Pub. by Pandora) Routldge.

Natural Healing from Head to Toe: Traditional Macrobiotic Remedies. Cornellia Aihara & Herman Aihara. LC 93-4659. 464p. pap. 14.95 (*0-89529-496-6*, Avery) Penguin Putnam.

Natural Healing Handbook: Get Back to Health . . . Naturally. 2nd ed. Beth M. Ley. 328p. 1995. pap. 14.95 (*0-9642703-1-5*) B L Pubns.

Natural Healing in Gynecology: A Manual for Women. Rina Nissim. 220p. 1986. pap. 9.95 (*0-86358-069-6*, Pub. by Pandora) Harper SF.

Natural Healing Perspective. Susan Stockton. 44p. 1997. pap. 4.95 (*0-9640539-4-2*, 127) Natures Pubng.

Natural Healing Secrets: An A to Z Guide to the Best Home Remedies. Random House Value Publishing Staff. 176p. 1998. 7.99 (*0-517-16046-3*) Random Hse Value.

Natural Healing Through Ayurveda. Subhash Ranade. 238p. 1993. pap. 14.95 (*1-878423-13-4*) Morson Pub.

Natural Healing Through Cell Salts. Skye Weintraub. 1996. pap. text 12.95 (*1-885670-29-X*) Woodland UT.

Natural Healing Through Macrobiotics. Michio Kushi. LC 79-1959. (Illus.). 1979. pap. 19.95 (*0-87040-457-1*) Japan Pubns USA.

Natural Healing with Aromatherapy. Gisela Bulla. LC 99-20262. (Healthful Alternatives Ser.). (Illus.). 96p. 1999. pap. 14.95 (*0-8069-4221-5*) Sterling.

Natural Healing with Aromatherapy. PH Editorial Staff. (C). 1996. pap. text 5.95 (*0-13-258963-X*) P-H.

Natural Healing with Chinese Herbs. Hong-yen Hsu. 1993. 30.00 (*0-941942-05-8*) Orient Heal Arts.

Natural Healing with Cider Vinegar. Margot Hellmiss. LC 98-3590. (Illus.). 96p. 1998. 10.95 (*0-8069-6167-8*) Sterling.

Natural Healing with Enzymes. Dicqie Fuller. 292p. (C). 1997. 24.95 (*0-13-238601-1*) P-H.

Natural Healing with Herbs. Humbart Santillo. Ed. by Subhuti Dharmananda. LC 84-553. (Illus.). 408p. 1993. reprint ed. pap. 16.95 (*0-934252-08-4*, Pub. by Hohm Pr) SCB Distributors.

Natural Healing with Tibb Medicine: Medicine of the Prophet. Muhammad Al-Akili. 320p. 1996. pap. 16.95 (*0-614-21556-0*, 888) Pearl Pub Hse.

Natural Healing with Tibb Medicine: Medicine of the Prophet. Ibn A. Al-Jawziyya. Tr. by Muhammad M. Al-Akili. LC 92-85137. 384p. (Orig.). (C). 1994. pap. 16.95 (*1-879405-07-5*) Pearl Pub Hse.

***Natural Health Bible: From the Most Trusted Source in Health Information.** Steven Bratman & David Kroll. LC 99-23813. (Natural Pharmacist Ser.). 495p. 2000. pap. 19.95 (*0-7615-2082-1*) Prima Pub.

Natural Health Care for Your Bird. Bernard Dorenkamp. LC 98-72210. (Illus.). 128p. 1998. pap. 8.95 (*0-7641-0124-2*, 835902Q) Barron.

Natural Health Care for Your Cat. Rudolf Deiser. LC 97-15620. 128p. 1997. pap. text 8.95 (*0-7641-0123-4*) Barron.

Natural Health Care for Your Dog. Petra Stein. LC 97-13990. 128p. 1997. pap. text 8.95 (*0-7641-0122-6*) Barron.

Natural Health Cat Care Manual. Quintet Books Staff. 1993. 12.98 (*1-55521-970-5*) Bk Sales Inc.

Natural Health Cookbook: More than 150 Recipes to Sustain & Heal the Body. Natural Health Magazine Editors & Dana Jacobi. LC 95-8. 272p. 1995. 24.00 (*0-684-80398-4*) S&S Trade.

Natural Health First-Aid Guide: The Definitive Handbook of Natural Remedies for Treating Minor Emergencies. Natural Health Magazine Editors & Mark Mayeell. LC 93-11906. 558p. 1994. pap. 14.00 (*0-671-79273-3*) PB.

***Natural health First-Aid Guide: The Definitive Handbook of Natural Remedies for Treating Minor Emergencies.** Ed. by Mark Mayell. 544p. 2000. reprint ed. text 24.00 (*0-7881-6986-6*) DIANE Pub.

Natural Health for African Americans: The Physician's Guide. Marcellus A. Walker & Kenneth B. Singleton. LC 98-24371. 368p. 1999. mass mkt. 14.99 (*0-446-67369-2*, Pub. by Warner Bks) Little.

Natural Health Guide to Beating Supergerms: Use Vitamins & Nutrients to Turn Your Body into the Ultimate Germ Killer. Richard P. Huemer & Jack J. Challem. LC 96-29498. 1997. per. 14.00 (*0-671-53764-4*) PB.

Natural Health Guide to Headache Relief. Ed. by Peter Maas. LC 97-144755. 304p. 1997. per. 14.00 (*0-671-51899-2*, PB Trade Paper) PB.

Natural Health, Natural Medicine. Houghton Mifflin Company Staff. 1998. pap. 13.00 (*0-395-91155-9*) HM.

Natural Health Product Compendium: The Consumer's Guide to Dietary Supplements, Nutrition, Herbs, Homeopathy & Other Natural Products. 176p. 1997. 14.95 (*0-920470-72-6*) Alive Bks.

Natural Health Secrets from Around the World. Jean Barilla. Ed. by Glenn W. Geelhoed. LC 97-13973. 112p. 1997. pap. 19.95 (*0-87983-805-1*, 38051K, Keats Publng) NTC Contemp Pub Co.

***Natural Health Secrets from Around the World.** Glenn W. Geelhoed & Jean Barilla. 1999. 29.95 (*0-13-014961-6*) P-H.

Natural Health Therapies for the Cosmetology Professional: Para-Medical Cosmetology. Claudette M. Hill. LC 98-91669. 61 p. 1998. pap. 10.00 (*0-9666190-0-5*) Alternative Hlth.

Natural Healthcare for Women. Belinda Grant Viagas. LC 99-43490. 256p. 1999. pap. 12.95 (*1-55561-198-2*) Fisher Bks.

Natural Healthcare for Your Child: Trustworthy Information on the Prevention, Causes & Treatment of the Diseases & Ailments Which are Common from Birth Through the Teenage Years. Phylis Austin et al. (Illus.). 268p. (Orig.). 1990. pap. 9.95 (*1-878726-01-3*) Fam Hlth Pubns.

Natural Helping Networks: A Strategy for Prevention. Alice H. Collins & Diane L. Pancoast. LC 76-10027. 144p. reprint ed. pap. 44.70 (*0-7837-6541-X*, 204567800007) Bks Demand.

Natural Heritage: Classification, Inventory, & Information. Albert E. Radford et al. LC 80-23087. xxi, 485p. 1981. 59.95 (*0-8078-1463-6*) U of NC Pr.

Natural Heritage of Indiana. Marion T. Jackson. LC 96-29850. 1997. 39.95 (*0-253-33074-2*) Ind U Pr.

***Natural Hierarchies: The Historical Sociology of Race & Caste.** Chris Smaje. LC 99-87488. (Illus.). 304p. 2000. text 62.95 (*0-631-20948-4*); pap. text 27.95 (*0-631-20949-2*) Blackwell Pubs.

Natural High. John P. Wiley, Jr. LC 92-56912. 128p. 1993. pap. 12.95 (*0-87451-624-2*) U Pr of New Eng.

Natural Histories: Mary Frank's Sculpture, Prints & Drawings. Hayden Herrera & Stella Kramrisch. LC 87-73549. (Illus.). 80p. (Orig.). (C). 1988. pap. 18.00 (*0-945506-00-7*) DeCordova Mus.

Natural Histories of Discourse. Ed. by Michael Silverstein & Greg Urban. LC 95-49852. (Illus.). 304p. (C). 1996. pap. text 19.95 (*0-226-75770-6*) U Ch Pr.

Natural Histories of Discourse. Ed. by Michael Silverstein & Greg Urban. LC 95-49852. (Illus.). 338p. (C). 1996. lib. bdg. 50.00 (*0-226-75769-2*) U Ch Pr.

Natural History. John F. Healey. 448p. 1991. pap. 13.95 (*0-14-044413-0*, Penguin Classics) Viking Penguin.

Natural History. Maureen Howard. (Illus.). 393p. 1999. pap. 12.95 (*0-7867-0632-5*) Carroll & Graf.

Natural History, 1. Pliny. Ed. by E. H. Warmington. (Loeb Classical Library: No. 330, 352-353, 370-371). 372p. 1938. text 19.95 (*0-674-99364-0*) HUP.

Natural History, 2. Pliny. Ed. by E. H. Warmington. (Loeb Classical Library: No. 330, 352-353, 370-371). 674p. 1942. text 19.95 (*0-674-99388-8*) HUP.

Natural History, 3. Pliny. Ed. by E. H. Warmington. (Loeb Classical Library: No. 330, 352-353, 370-371). 626p. 1940. text 19.95 (*0-674-99389-6*) HUP.

Natural History, 4. Pliny. Ed. by E. H. Warmington. (Loeb Classical Library: No. 330, 352-353, 370-371). 564p. 1945. text 19.95 (*0-674-99408-6*) HUP.

Natural History, 5. Pliny. Ed. by E. H. Warmington. (Loeb Classical Library: No. 330, 352-353, 370-371). 562p. 1950. text 19.95 (*0-674-99409-4*) HUP.

Natural History, 6. Tr. by W. H. Jones. (Loeb Classical Library: No. 392-394, 418-419). 558p. 1951. text 18.95 (*0-674-99431-0*) HUP.

Natural History, 7. Pliny. (Loeb Classical Library: No. 392-394, 418-419). 576p. 1956. text 18.95 (*0-674-99432-9*) HUP.

Natural History, 8. Pliny. (Loeb Classical Library: No. 392-394, 418-419). 604p. 1963. text 19.95 (*0-674-99460-4*) HUP.

Natural History, 9. Tr. by H. Rackham. (Loeb Classical Library: No. 392-394, 418-419). 430p. 1952. text 18.95 (*0-674-99433-7*) HUP.

Natural History, 10. Pliny. (Loeb Classical Library: No. 392-394, 418-419). 362p. 1962. text 19.95 (*0-674-99461-2*) HUP.

Natural History see Final Report of the New Melones Archeological Project, California

Natural History Activity Book. (Illus.). (J). (ps-6). pap. 2.95 (*0-565-00857-9*, Pub. by Natural Hist Mus) Parkwest Pubns.

Natural History & Behavior of North American Beewolves. Howard E. Evans & Kevin M. O'Neill. LC 87-25073. (Illus.). 288p. 1988. text 57.50 (*0-8014-1839-9*); pap. text 25.00 (*0-8014-9513-X*) Cornell U Pr.

Natural History & Behavior of the California Sea Lion. Richard S. Peterson & George A. Bartholomew. (ASM Special Publications: No. 1). (Illus.). ix, 79p. 1967. 6.00 (*0-943612-00-4*) Am Soc Mammalogists.

Natural History & Evolution of Cryptopecten. Itaru Hayami. 170p. 1984. 52.50 (*0-86008-359-4*, Pub. by U of Tokyo) Col U Pr.

Natural History & Evolution of Paper-Wasps. Ed. by Stefano Turillazzi & Mary J. West-Ebergard. (Illus.). 414p. (C). 1996. text 115.00 (*0-19-854947-4*) OUP.

Natural History & Resources of Western Massachusetts. Stan Freeman. (Illus.). 80p. (Orig.). (J). (gr. 5-9). 1994. pap. text 14.95 (*0-9636814-1-9*) Hampshire House.

Natural History & the American Mind. William M. Smallwood & Mabel S. Smallwood. LC 41-16864. reprint ed. 21.50 (*0-404-06116-8*) AMS Pr.

Natural History & the New World, 1524-1770: An Annotated Bibliography of Printed Materials in the Library of the American Philosophical Society. Anita Guerrini. LC 86-71010. (American Philosophical Society Library Publication Ser.: No. 11). 95p. reprint ed. pap. 30.00 (*0-8357-3410-2*, 203966700013) Bks Demand.

Natural History Atlas to the Cays of the U. S. Virgin Islands. Arthur E. Dammann & David W. Nellis. LC 92-23127. (Illus.). 160p. 1992. pap. 29.95 (*1-56164-022-0*) Pineapple Pr.

Natural History Collections. (C). Date not set. write for info. (*0-415-08374-5*) Routledge.

Natural History Collections. Swinney. (C). Date not set. write for info. (*0-415-08375-3*) Routledge.

Natural History from A to Z: A Terrestrial Sampler. Tim Arnold. LC 88-26879. (Illus.). 64p. (J). (gr. 5-9). 1991. lib. bdg. 15.95 (*0-689-50467-5*) McElderry Bks.

Natural History, General & Particular: An Original Anthology, 2 vols., Set. Ed. by Frank N. Egerton, 3rd. LC 77-74206. (History of Ecology Ser.). (Illus.). 1978. lib. bdg. 108.95 (*0-405-10376-X*) Ayer.

Natural History Handbook Series. (Illus.). (Orig.). pap. write for info. (*0-937207-14-4*) GSMNH.

Natural History in Shakespeare's Time. Herbert W. Seager. LC 79-160134. reprint ed. 49.50 (*0-404-05667-9*) AMS Pr.

Natural History Investigations in South Carolina from Colonial Times to the Present. Albert E. Sanders & William D. Anderson. LC 98-40208. 288p. 1998. 45.00 (*1-57003-278-5*) U of SC Pr.

Natural History Museum Book of Dinosaurs. Tim Gardom & Angela Milner. (Illus.). 128p. 1999. pap. 14.95 (*1-56649-018-9*) Welcome Rain.

Natural History Museums. Paisley S. Cato & Clyde Jones. 200p. 1990. 25.00 (*0-89672-240-6*) Tex Tech Univ Pr.

Natural History Museums Vol. 1: An Illustrated Guide to Over 350 Museums in the Eastern United States. G. W. Bates. 1992. pap. 12.95 (*0-9629759-5-8*) Batax Mus.

Natural History Notebook of North American Animals. National Museum of Natural History, Canada Staff. write for info. (*0-318-59594-X*) S&S Trade.

Natural History of a Delinquent Career. Clifford R. Shaw. LC 68-56042. (Illus.). 280p. 1969. reprint ed. lib. bdg. 65.00 (*0-8371-0654-0*, SHDC, Greenwood Pr) Greenwood.

Natural History of a Delinquent Career. Clifford R. Shaw & Maurice E. Moore. LC HV9069.S475. 296p. reprint ed. pap. 91.80 (*0-608-12603-9*, 202406600034) Bks Demand.

Natural History of a Mountain Year: Four Seasons in the Wasatch Range. Claude T. Barnes. (Illus.). 400p. (C). 1996. reprint ed. pap. 16.95 (*0-87480-474-4*) U of Utah Pr.

Natural History of a Savant. Charles Richet. Tr. by Oliver J. Lodge from FRE. LC 74-26288. (History, Philosophy & Sociology of Science Ser.). 1975. reprint ed. 23.95 (*0-405-06614-7*) Ayer.

Natural History of a Sumac Tree, with an Emphasis on the Entomofauna. David G. Furth. LC 86-114074. (Transactions Ser.: Vol. 46, Pt. 4). (Illus.). 97p. 1985. pap. 22.50 (*0-208-02094-2*) CT Acad Arts & Sciences.

Natural History of Alaska's Prince William Sound & How to Enjoy It. Peter G. Mickelson. (Illus.). 210p. (Orig.). (C). 1989. pap. 9.95 (*0-317-93866-5*) AK Wild Wings.

Natural History of Alcoholism. George E. Vaillant. LC 82-11696. (Illus.). 384p. 1983. 32.00 (*0-674-60375-3*) HUP.

Natural History of Alcoholism: Causes, Patterns, & Paths to Recovery. George E. Vaillant. 384p. 1985. pap. text 14.95 (*0-674-60376-1*) HUP.

Natural History of Alcoholism Revisited. George E. Vaillant. LC 94-41749. (Illus.). 384p. 1995. text 44.50 (*0-674-60377-X*, VAINAR); pap. text 17.50 (*0-674-60378-8*, VAINAY) HUP.

Natural History of Amphibians. Robert C. Stebbins. 332p. 1995. pap. text 19.95 (*0-691-10251-1*, Pub. by Princeton U Pr) Cal Prin Full Svc.

***Natural History of an Arctic Oil Field.** Truett. 402p. 1999. 79.95 (*0-12-701235-4*) Morgan Kaufmann.

Natural History of Ano Nuevo. Ed. by Burney LeBoeuf & Stephanie Kaza. (Illus.). (Orig.). 1985. reprint ed. pap. 14.95 (*0-910286-77-9*) Otter B Bks.

Natural History of Ants from an Unpublished Manuscript in the Archives of the Academy of Sciences of Paris. Rene A. De Reaumur. Ed. by Frank N. Egerton, 3rd. Tr. by Morton Wheeler. LC 77-74211. (History of Ecology Ser.). 1978. reprint ed. lib. bdg. 25.95 (*0-405-10382-4*) Ayer.

Natural History of Associations: A Study in the Meaning of Community, Vol. 1. Richard M. Bradfield. LC 73-5577. 428p. 1973. 62.50 (*0-8236-3495-7*) Intl Univs Pr.

Natural History of Associations: A Study in the Meaning of Community, Vol. 2. Richard M. Bradfield. LC 73-5577. 596p. 1973. 87.50 (*0-8236-3496-5*) Intl Univs Pr.

Natural History of Australia. Tim M. Berra. LC 97-42820. (Illus.). 256p. (C). 1998. text 44.95 (*0-12-093155-9*) Morgan Kaufmann.

Natural History of Badgers. Ernest G. Neal. LC 85-29248. (Illus.). 264p. reprint ed. pap. 81.90 (*0-7837-6690-4*, 204630700011) Bks Demand.

Natural History of Barbados. Griffith Hughes. LC 71-141086. (Research Library of Colonial Americana). (Illus.). 1972. reprint ed. 42.95 (*0-405-03285-4*) Ayer.

Natural History of Big Sur. Paul Henson. 1993. 40.00 (*0-520-07466-1*, Pub. by U CA Pr) Cal Prin Full Svc.

Natural History of Big Sur. Paul Henson & Donald J. Usner. (California Natural History Guides Ser.: Vol. 57). (Illus.). 416p. (C). 1996. pap. 19.95 (*0-520-20510-3*, Pub. by U CA Pr) Cal Prin Full Svc.

Natural History of Blackflies. Roger W. Crosskey. LC 90-12453. 722p. 1990. 560.00 (*0-471-92755-4*) Wiley.

Natural History of British Fishes: Scientific & General Descriptions of the Most Interesting Species, 2 vols., Set. Edward Donovan. Ed. by Keir B. Sterling. LC 77-81091. (Biologists & Their World Ser.). (Illus.). 1978. reprint ed. lib. bdg. 68.95 (*0-405-10668-8*) Ayer.

An Asterisk (*) at the beginning of an entry indicates that the title is appearing for the first time.

Natural History of British Fishes: Scientific & General Descriptions of the Most Interesting Species, 2 vols., Vol. 1. Edward Donovan. Ed. by Keir B. Sterling. LC 77-81091. (Biologists & Their World Ser.). (Illus.). 1978. reprint ed. lib. bdg. 34.95 (*0-405-10669-6*) Ayer.

Natural History of British Fishes: Scientific & General Descriptions of the Most Interesting Species, 2 vols., Vol. 2. Edward Donovan. Ed. by Keir B. Sterling. LC 77-81091. (Biologists & Their World Ser.). (Illus.). 1978. reprint ed. lib. bdg. 34.95 (*0-405-10670-X*) Ayer.

Natural History of California. Allan A. Schoenherr. 1992. 50.00 (*0-520-06921-8*, Pub. by U CA Pr) Cal Prin Full Svc.

Natural History of California. Allan A. Schoenherr. (California Natural History Guides Ser.: Vol. 56). (Illus.). 772p. 1995. pap. 27.50 (*0-520-06922-6*, Pub. by U CA Pr) Cal Prin Full Svc.

Natural History of Camden & Rockport. Elizabeth C. Parker. LC 99-491482. (Illus.). 152p. (J). (gr. k-12). 1984. reprint ed. pap. 16.00 (*0-9669907-0-6*) E C Parker.

Natural History of Cerebral Palsy. Bronson Crothers & Richmond S. Paine. (Classics in Developmental Medicine Ser.: No. 2). (Illus.). 300p. (C). 1991. text 19.95 (*0-521-41327-3*, Pub. by Mc Keith Pr) Cambridge U Pr.

Natural History of Connemara. Tony Whilde. 256p. (C). 1995. 81.00 (*0-907151-91-4*, Pub. by IMMEL Pubng) St Mut.

Natural History of Coronary Atherosclerosis. Constantin Velican & Doina Velican. LC 88-8128. 416p. 1989. 242.00 (*0-8493-6935-5*, RC685, CRC Reprint) Franklin.

Natural History of Creation: Biblical Evolutionism & the Return of Natural Theology. M. A. Corey. 460p. (Orig.). (C). 1995. pap. text 42.00 (*0-8191-9923-0*); lib. bdg. 67.50 (*0-8191-9922-2*) U Pr of Amer.

Natural History of Deer. Rory Putman. LC 88-22856. (Comstock Bk.). (Illus.). 224p. 1989. text 32.50 (*0-8014-2283-3*) Cornell U Pr.

***Natural History of Domesticated Mammals.** 2nd ed. Juliet Clutton-Brock. (Illus.). 232p. (C). 1999. 90.00 (*0-521-63247-1*); pap. 39.95 (*0-521-63495-4*) Cambridge U Pr.

Natural History of Eastern Massachusetts. Stan Freeman & Mike Nasuti. LC 98-71823. (Illus.). 128p. (J). (gr. 4-10). 1998. pap. 14.95 (*0-9636814-3-5*) Hampshire House.

Natural History of El Malpais National Monument. Compiled by Ken Mabery. (Bulletin Ser.: No. 156). (Illus.). 186p. 1997. pap. 24.95 (*1-883905-01-X*) NM Bureau Mines.

Natural History of Gower. Mary E. Gillham. 352p. (C). 1989. 100.00 (*0-905928-00-8*, Pub. by D Brown & Sons Ltd) St Mut.

Natural History of H. G. Wells. John R. Reed. LC 81-11261. 304p. 1982. lib. bdg. 30.00 (*0-8214-0628-0*) Ohio U Pr.

Natural History of Homosexuality. Francis M. Mondimore. LC 96-16191. (Illus.). 275p. 1996. pap. 15.95 (*0-8018-5440-7*); text 35.00 (*0-8018-5349-4*) Johns Hopkins.

Natural History of Ifaluk Atoll. J. I. Tracey, Jr. et al. (BMB Ser.: No. 222). 1961. 25.00 (*0-527-02330-2*) Periodicals Srv.

Natural History of Inbreeding & Outbreeding: Theoretical & Empirical Perspectives. Ed. by Nancy W. Thornhill. LC 92-38497. (Illus.). 584p. (C). 1993. pap. text 34.95 (*0-226-79855-0*); lib. bdg. 88.00 (*0-226-79854-2*) U Ch Pr.

Natural History of Insects. Rod Preston-Mafham & Ken Preston-Mafham. (Illus.). 160p. 1996. 35.00 (*1-85223-964-6*, Pub. by Cro1wood) Trafalgar.

***Natural History of Ireland.** David Cabot. LC 99-176159. 1999. 60.00 (*0-00-220079-1*, Pub. by HarpC) Trafalgar.

Natural History of Lake County, Ohio. Ed. by Rosemary N. Szubski. (Illus.). 108p. (Orig.). 1994. pap. text 9.45 (*1-878600-06-0*) Cleve Mus Nat Hist.

Natural History of Lakes. Mary J. Burgis & Pat Morris. (Illus.). 224p. 1987. text 39.95 (*0-521-30793-7*) Cambridge U Pr.

Natural History of Living Mammals. William Voelker. 313p. 1986. 29.95 (*0-937548-08-1*) Plexus Pub.

Natural History of Loch Lomond. Picton Publishing Staff. 1987. 30.00 (*0-7855-2181-X*, Pub. by Picton) St Mut.

Natural History of Love. Diane Ackerman. 1995. pap. 13.00 (*0-679-76183-7*) Vin Bks.

Natural History of Make-Believe: Tracing the Literature of Imagination for Children. John Goldwaite. 400p. 1996. 30.00 (*0-19-503806-1*) OUP.

Natural History of Man. John K. Brierley. 184p. 1975. 28.50 (*0-8386-7819-X*) Fairleigh Dickinson.

Natural History of Mania, Depression, & Schizophrenia. George Winokur & Ming T. Tsuang. 336p. 1996. text 44.50 (*0-88048-726-7*, 8726) Am Psychiatric.

***Natural History of Medicinal Plants.** Judith Sumner. LC 99-76555. (Illus.). 248p. 2000. 24.95 (*0-88192-483-0*) Timber.

Natural History of Mexican Rattlesnakes. Barry L. Armstrong & James B. Murphy. Ed. by Joseph T. Collins. (Special Publications: No. 5). (Illus.). 88p. (Orig.). 1979. pap. 6.00 (*0-89338-010-5*) U KS Nat Hist Mus.

Natural History of Moles. Martyn L. Gorman & David Stone. LC 89-25225. (Natural History of Mammals Ser.). (Illus.). 208p. 1990. text 35.00 (*0-8014-2466-6*) Cornell U Pr.

Natural History of Monitor Lizards. Harold F. De Lisle. LC 95-3063. 240p. 1996. 53.50 (*0-89464-897-7*) Krieger.

Natural History of Monterey Bay National Marine Sanctuary. Ed. by Michael A. Rigsby. LC 97-7956. (Illus.). 300p. 1999. pap. 19.95 (*1-878244-11-6*) Monterey Bay Aquarium.

Natural History of Moths. Mark Young. (Poyser Natural History Ser.). (Illus.). 304p. 1996. text 49.95 (*0-85661-103-4*) Morgan Kaufmann.

Natural History of Mount le Conte. Kenneth Wise & Ronald H. Petersen. LC 97-33836. 1998. pap. write for info. (*0-15-723301-4*) Harcourt Coll Pubs.

Natural History of Mount le Conte. Kenneth Wise & Ronald H. Petersen. LC 97-33836. (Illus.). 168p. 1998. pap. 15.95 (*1-57233-010-4*) U of Tenn Pr.

Natural History of Native Fishes in the Death Valley System. David L. Soltz & Robert J. Naiman. (Science Ser.: No. 30). (Illus.). 76p. 1978. 15.00 (*0-938644-10-6*) Nat Hist Mus.

Natural History of Nature Writing. Frank Stewart. LC 94-29330. 320p. 1994. pap. 17.95 (*1-55963-279-8*) Island Pr.

Natural History of Nautilus. Peter D. Ward. (Illus.). 192p. text 65.00 (*0-04-500036-0*) Routledge.

Natural History of Negation. Laurence R. Horn. 336p. 1989. lib. bdg. 75.00 (*0-226-35337-0*) U Ch Pr.

Natural History of Negation. Laurence R. Horn. 336p. 1995. pap. text 42.00 (*0-226-35338-9*) U Ch Pr.

Natural History of New Mexican Mammals. James S. Findley. LC 86-30834. (New Mexico Natural History Ser.). 192p. reprint ed. pap. 59.60 (*0-7837-5861-8*, 204558000006) Bks Demand.

Natural History of New York City. 2nd ed. John Kieran. LC 59-7703. (Illus.). xiii, 428p. 1982. pap. 18.50 (*0-8232-1086-3*) Fordham.

Natural History of North America. Edward Ricciuti. (Illus.). 224p. 1997. 17.99 (*1-85833-757-7*, Pub. by CLib Bks) Whitecap Bks.

***Natural History of North America.** Edward Ricciuti. (Illus.). 224p. 2000. reprint ed. 30.00 (*0-7881-9357-0*) DIANE Pub.

Natural History of Northeastern San Salvador Island: A "New World" Where the New World Began. Paul J. Godfrey et al. (Illus.). 28p. (Orig.). (C). 1994. pap. text 6.00 (*0-935909-51-6*) Bahamian.

Natural History of Orkney. 2nd ed. R J Berry. 320p. 1999. 45.00 (*0-85661-104-2*, Pub. by Poyser) Acad Pr.

Natural History of Orthopaedic Disease: A Gatekeeper's Guide. Ed. by Lewis Cozen. (Illus.). 600p. (Orig.). 1993. 20.00 (*0-9637929-0-3*) Dr L Cozen Pub.

Natural History of Oviparous Quadrupeds & Serpents: Arranged & Published from the Papers & Collections of the Count De Buffon, 4 vols., Set. Georges L. Buffon. Ed. by Keir B. Sterling. Tr. by Robert Kerr. LC 77-81119. (Biologists & Their World Ser.). (Illus.). 1978. reprint ed. lib. bdg. 145.95 (*0-405-10710-2*) Ayer.

Natural History of Oviparous Quadrupeds & Serpents: Arranged & Published from the Papers & Collections of the Count De Buffon, 4 vols., Vol. 1. Georges L. Buffon. Ed. by Keir B. Sterling. Tr. by Robert Kerr. LC 77-81119. (Biologists & Their World Ser.). (Illus.). 1978. reprint ed. lib. bdg. 72.95 (*0-405-10711-0*) Ayer.

Natural History of Oviparous Quadrupeds & Serpents: Arranged & Published from the Papers & Collections of the Count De Buffon, 4 vols., Vol. 2. Georges L. Buffon. Ed. by Keir B. Sterling. Tr. by Robert Kerr. LC 77-81119. (Biologists & Their World Ser.). (Illus.). 1978. reprint ed. lib. bdg. 72.95 (*0-405-10712-9*) Ayer.

Natural History of Parenting. Susan Allport. LC 97-32812. 256p. 1998. pap. 13.00 (*0-609-80182-1*, Crown) Crown Pub Group.

Natural History of Peace. Ed. by Thomas Gregor. LC 95-39462. (Illus.). 346p. 1996. 39.95 (*0-8265-1272-0*); pap. 19.95 (*0-8265-1280-1*) Vanderbilt U Pr.

Natural History of Plants, 2 vols., Set. Ed. by F. W. Oliver. (C). 1988. text 800.00 (*0-7855-3156-4*, Pub. by Scientific) St Mut.

Natural History of Plants: An Illustrated Botanical Primer for Naturalists, Gardeners & Artists. Jorie Hunken. LC 86-471. (Phalarope Bk.). (Illus.). 160p. 1986. text 15.95 (*0-13-610155-0*) P-H.

Natural History of Pliny the Elder. (LAT., Illus.). (C). 1999. pap. 19.95 (*0-9628450-7-8*) P L Chambers.

Natural History of Pollination. Michael Proctor et al. LC 96-198390. (Illus.). 487p. 1996. pap. 27.95 (*0-88192-353-2*) Timber.

Natural History of Puget Sound Country. Arthur R. Kruckeberg. LC 90-12368. (Weyerhaeuser Environmental Classics Ser.). (Illus.). 488p. (C). 1995. reprint ed. pap. 40.00 (*0-295-97477-X*) U of Wash Pr.

Natural History of Rabies. 2nd ed. Ed. by George M. Baer. 640p. 1991. lib. bdg. 375.00 (*0-8493-6760-3*, QR201) CRC Pr.

***Natural History of Rape: Biological Bases of Sexual Coercion.** Randy Thornhill & Craig T. Palmer. LC 99-31685. (Illus.). 243p. 2000. 29.95 (*0-262-20125-9*) MIT Pr.

Natural History of Religion. David Hume. Ed. by H. E. Root. 80p. 1957. reprint ed. pap. 8.95 (*0-8047-0333-7*) Stanford U Pr.

Natural History of Revolution. Lyford P. Edwards. Ed. by Janowitz. LC 77-127821. (Heritage of Sociology Ser.). 1970. pap. text 2.25 (*0-226-18491-9*) U Ch Pr.

Natural History of Rivers. Ron Freethy. 216p. (C). 1988. 70.00 (*0-86138-045-2*, Pub. by T Dalton) St Mut.

Natural History of Seals. Nigel Bonner. (Natural History Ser.). (Illus.). 240p. 1990. 29.95 (*0-8160-2336-0*) Facts on File.

Natural History of Selborne. Gilbert White. 1994. 19.75 (*0-8446-6724-2*) Peter Smith.

Natural History of Selborne. Gilbert White. LC 97-3630. (Nature Classics Ser.). 320p. 1997. pap. 8.95 (*0-14-026486-8*, Penguin Bks) Viking Penguin.

Natural History of Selborne. Gilbert White. Ed. by Richard Mabey. 272p. 1993. pap. 6.95 (*0-460-87269-9*, Everyman's Classic Lib) Tuttle Pubng.

Natural History of Sensibility. Louis I. Bredvold. LC 62-10322. 113p. reprint ed. pap. 35.10 (*0-7837-3645-2*, 204351400009) Bks Demand.

Natural History of Sharks. Thomas H. Lineaweaver, III & Richard H. Backus. LC 97-132421. (Illus.). 256p. 1986. pap. 14.95 (*0-8052-0766-X*) Lyons Pr.

Natural History of Shells. Geerat J. Vermeij. (Science Library). 232p. 1993. pap. text 16.95 (*0-691-00167-7*, Pub. by Princeton U Pr) Cal Prin Full Svc.

Natural History of Shells. Geerat J. Vermeij. LC 92-35371. (Illus.). 232p. 1993. text 47.50 (*0-691-08596-X*, Pub. by Princeton U Pr) Cal Prin Full Svc.

Natural History of Shrews. Sara Churchfield. LC 90-2521. (Natural History of Mammals Ser.). (Illus.). 192p. 1991. text 39.95 (*0-8014-2595-6*) Cornell U Pr.

Natural History of Soils. Berman D. Hudson. 1998. write for info. (*0-89089-794-8*) Carolina Acad Pr.

Natural History of Southern New Zealand. Ed. by Ewan Fordyce et al. (Illus.). 1998. pap. 69.95 (*1-877133-51-5*, Pub. by Univ Otago Pr) Intl Spec Bk.

Natural History of Specific Birth Defects. Ed. by Daniel Bergsma. (Alan R. Liss Ser.: Vol. 13, No. 3c). 1977. 42.00 (*0-686-23122-8*) March of Dimes.

Natural History of Spiders. Ken Preston-Mafham & Rod Preston-Mafham. (Illus.). 160p. 1997. 35.00 (*1-85223-966-2*, Pub. by Cro1wood) Trafalgar.

Natural History of the American Lobster. Francis H. Herrick. Ed. by Frank N. Egerton, 3rd. LC 77-74228. (History of Ecology Ser.). (Illus.). 1978. reprint ed. lib. bdg. 25.95 (*0-405-10398-0*) Ayer.

Natural History of the Antarctic Peninsula. Sanford Moss. (Illus.). 256p. 1990. pap. text 21.50 (*0-231-06269-9*) Col U Pr.

Natural History of the Ballet Girl. Albert Smith. (Illus.). 104p. 1996. reprint ed. 12.95 (*1-85273-046-3*, Pub. by Dance Bks) Princeton Bk Co.

Natural History of the Black Hills & Badlands. rev. ed. Sven G. Froiland & Ronald R. Weedon. LC 90-1996. 200p. (C). 1990. pap. 13.95 (*0-931170-47-8*) Ctr Western Studies.

Natural History of the Burren. Gordon D'Arcy. (Illus.). 168p. (C). 1990. 110.00 (*0-907151-64-7*, Pub. by IMMEL Pubng) St Mut.

Natural History of the Burren. Gordon D'Arcy & John Hayward. 168p. 1995. 60.00 (*0-907151-23-X*, Pub. by IMMEL Pubng) St Mut.

Natural History of the Colorado Plateau & Great Basin. Ed. by Kimball T. Harper. 1998. pap. 22.50 (*0-87081-511-3*) Univ Pr Colo.

Natural History of the Dog. Ed. by Hugh H. Genoways & Marion A. Burgwin. (Illus.). 62p. (Orig.). 1984. pap. 3.00 (*0-911239-11-1*) Carnegie Mus.

Natural History of the Doucs & Snub-Nosed Monkeys. 450p. 1997. text 44.00 (*981-02-3131-8*) World Scientific Pub.

Natural History of the Ducks, 2 vols., 1. John C. Phillips. 1920p. 1986. reprint ed. 50.00 (*0-486-25141-1*) Dover.

Natural History of the Ducks, 2 vols., 2. John C. Phillips. 1920p. 1986. reprint ed. 50.00 (*0-486-25142-X*) Dover.

Natural History of the European Seas. Edward Forbes & Robert Godwin-Austen. Ed. by Frank N. Egerton, 3rd. LC 77-74221. (History of Ecology Ser.). 1978. reprint ed. lib. bdg. 26.95 (*0-405-10392-1*) Ayer.

Natural History of the Fishes of Massachusetts. Jerome V. Smith. (Illus.). 400p. 1970. boxed set 10.75 (*0-88395-002-2*) Freshet Pr.

Natural History of the German People. Wilhelm H. Riehl. Ed. & Tr. by David J. Diephouse from GER. LC 89-12900. (Studies in German Thought & History: Vol. 13). 392p. 1990. lib. bdg. 99.95 (*0-88946-789-7*) E Mellen.

Natural History of the Gorilla. A. F. Dixson. LC 81-57. 236p. reprint ed. pap. 73.20 (*0-7837-0425-9*, 204074800018) Bks Demand.

Natural History of the Hawaiian Islands: Selected Readings II. Ed. by E. Alison Kay. LC 94-6318. 1994. pap. text 25.00 (*0-8248-1659-5*) UH Pr.

Natural History of the Islands of California. Allan A. Schoenherr et al. LC 97-43756. (California Natural History Guides Ser.). 1999. 45.00 (*0-520-21197-9*, Pub. by U CA Pr) Cal Prin Full Svc.

Natural History of the Lewis & Clark Expedition. Ed. by Raymond D. Burroughs. 1995. pap. 19.95 (*0-87013-389-6*) Mich St U Pr.

Natural History of the Long Expedition to the Rocky Mountains (1819-1820) Howard E. Evans. (Illus.). 288p. 1997. pap. 15.95 (*0-19-511185-0*); text 35.00 (*0-19-511184-2*) OUP.

Natural History of the Mammalia. George R. Waterhouse. Ed. by Keir B. Sterling. LC 77-83843. (Biologists & Their World Ser.). (Illus.). 1978. reprint ed. lib. bdg. 93.95 (*0-405-10739-0*) Ayer.

Natural History of the Mind: New Views on the Relatedness of Life. Contrib. by William R. Sickles. LC 97-40891. 236p. 1998. 49.00 (*1-56072-516-8*) Nova Sci Pubs.

Natural History of the Minocki of the Lakeland Region of Wisconsin. Richard C. Schneider. (Illus.). 255p. 1980. 9.95 (*0-936984-03-1*) Schneider Pubs.

Natural History of the National Parks of Hungary Vol. 1: The Fauna of the Hortobagy National Park. Ed. by S. Mahunka. 415p. 1981. 155.00 (*963-05-2519-4*, Pub. by Akade Kiado) St Mut.

Natural History of the National Parks of Hungary Vol. 2: The Fauna of the Hortobagy National Park. Ed. by S. Mahunka & L. Zombort. 489p. 1983. 155.00 (*963-05-3198-4*, Pub. by Akade Kiado) St Mut.

Natural History of the National Parks of Hungary Vol. 4: The Fauna of the Kisjunsag National Park. Ed. by S. Mahunka. 490p. 1986. 150.00 (*963-05-3875-X*, Pub. by Akade Kiado) St Mut.

Natural History of the National Parks of Hungary Vol. 5: The Fauna of the Kisjunsag National Park. Ed. by S. Mahunka. 479p. 1987. 165.00 (*963-05-4352-4*, Pub. by Akade Kiado) St Mut.

Natural History of the Point Reyes Peninsula. rev. ed. Jules G. Evens. Ed. by Nancy F. Adess. LC 92-84085. (Illus.). 230p. (Orig.). 1993. pap. 14.95 (*0-911235-05-1*) Pt Reyes Natl.

Natural History of the Primates. J. R. Napier & P. H. Napier. (Illus.). 200p. 1994. pap. text 21.00 (*0-262-64033-3*) MIT Pr.

Natural History of the Senses. Diane Ackerman. LC 91-50048. 352p. 1991. pap. 13.00 (*0-679-73566-6*) Vin Bks.

Natural History of the Senses. Diane Ackerman. 1995. pap. 12.00 (*0-394-26953-5*) Vin Bks.

Natural History of the Sonoran Desert. Arizona-Sonora Desert Museum Staff. LC 99-33675. 650p. 1999. 55.00 (*0-520-22029-3*, Pub. by U CA Pr) Cal Prin Full Svc.

***Natural History of the Sonoran Desert.** Arizona-Sonora Desert Museum Staff. LC 99-33675. 650p. 1999. pap. 24.95 (*0-520-21980-5*, Pub. by U CA Pr) Cal Prin Full Svc.

Natural History of the Soul in Ancient Mexico. Jill L. Furst. 240p. 1997. pap. text 16.00 (*0-300-07260-0*) Yale U Pr.

Natural History of the Soul in Ancient Mexico. Jill L. McKeever-Furst. LC 95-16961. 240p. 1996. 28.50 (*0-300-06225-7*) Yale U Pr.

Natural History of the Southern Short-Tailed Shrew: Blarina Carolinensis. Hugh H. Genoways & Jerry R. Choate. LC 97-51389. (Occasional Papers). (Illus.). 43p. 1998. pap. 2.00 (*1-879824-04-3*) U of NM Mus Biol.

Natural History of the Traditional Quilt. John Forrest & Deborah Blincoe. (Illus.). 288p. (Orig.). 1995. pap. 22.95 (*0-292-72497-7*); text 45.00 (*0-292-70809-2*) U of Tex Pr.

Natural History of the Universe. Colin A. Ronan. 200p. 1991. 45.00 (*0-385-25327-3*) Doubleday.

***Natural History of the Unnatural World: Discover What Gryptozoology Can Teach Us about Over One Hundred Fabulous & Legendary Creatures That Inhabit Earth, Sea & Sky.** Joel Levy & The Cryptozoological Society of London Staff. (Illus.). 224p. 2000. text 25.95 (*0-312-20703-4*, Thomas Dunne) St Martin.

Natural History of the Waterfowl. Frank S. Todd. 504p. 1996. reprint ed. 80.00 (*0-934797-11-0*) Ibis Pub CA.

Natural History of the White-Inyo Range, Eastern California. Ed. by Clarence A. Hall, Jr. (California Natural History Guides Ser.: No. 55). (Illus.). 560p. 1991. pap. 30.00 (*0-520-06896-3*, Pub. by U CA Pr) Cal Prin Full Svc.

Natural History of the Wild Cats. Andrew Kitchener. (Illus.). 280p. 1997. pap. text 19.95 (*0-8014-8498-7*) Cornell U Pr.

Natural History of Trees of Eastern & Central North America. Donald C. Peattie. (Illus.). 624p. 1991. pap. 19.95 (*0-395-58174-5*) HM.

Natural History of Vacant Lot. Mathew F. Vessel & Herbert H. Wong. LC 85-1073. (California Natural History Guides Ser.: No. 50). (Illus.). 320p. 1988. pap. 12.95 (*0-520-05390-7*, Pub. by U CA Pr) Cal Prin Full Svc.

Natural History of Vampire Bats. Ed. by Arthur M. Greenhall & Uwe Schmidt. LC 87-24622. 272p. 1988. 147.00 (*0-8493-6750-6*, QL737, CRC Reprint) Franklin.

Natural History of Varicella-Zoster Virus. Ed. by Richard W. Hyman. 224p. 1987. 131.00 (*0-8493-6584-8*, RC125, CRC Reprint) Franklin.

Natural History of Viruses. Christopher Andrewes. (World Naturalist Ser.). (Illus.). (C). 1967. 14.00 (*0-393-06277-5*) Norton.

Natural History of Vision. Nicholas J. Wade. LC 97-22697. (Illus.). 486p. 1998. 55.00 (*0-262-23194-8*, Bradford Bks) MIT Pr.

***Natural History of Vision.** Nicholas J. Wade. (Illus.). 488p. 2000. reprint ed. pap. 29.50 (*0-262-73129-0*) MIT Pr.

Natural History of Weasels & Stoats. Carolyn King. LC 89-17316. (Natural History of Mammals Ser.). (Illus.). 272p. 1990. text 35.00 (*0-8014-2428-3*) Cornell U Pr.

Natural History of Western Trees. Donald C. Peattie. (Illus.). 768p. 1991. pap. 19.95 (*0-395-58175-3*) HM.

Natural-History Paintings from Rajasthan. J. J. White et al. (Illus.). 44p. 1994. pap. 5.00 (*0-913196-61-4*) Hunt Inst Botanical.

Natural History Prose Writings of John Clare. John Clare. Ed. by Margaret Grainger. (Illus.). 460p. 1984. text 100.00 (*0-19-818517-0*) OUP.

Natural History Reader in Animal Behavior. Ed. by Howard Topoff. LC 86-26848. (Illus.). 1987. pap. text 22.50 (*0-231-06159-5*) Col U Pr.

Natural History, Rehabilitation & Medicine of the California Towhee (Pipilo Crissalis) Astrid Kasper. (Illus.). 52p. (C). 1999. pap. 10.00 (*0-9660923-2-5*) Wldlfe Pubns.

Natural History, Social Behavior, Reproduction, Vocalizations, Prehension see Gibbon & Siamang: A Series of Volumes on the Lesser Apes

Natural History Southern: First Edition (Hardcover Book) Ed. by G. Dennis Ancinec. (C). 1997. text 72.00 (*0-321-01236-4*) Addison-Wesley.

Natural Home Gardening: A Practical Guide to Growing Vegetables for Macrobiotic & Natural Foods Cooking. Masato Mimura. (Illus.). 96p. (Orig.). 1996. pap. 8.95 (*1-882984-15-3*) One Peaceful World.

N

An Asterisk (*) at the beginning of an entry indicates that the title is appearing for the first time.

***Natural Home Pharmacy: A Concise Reference Guide to Natural Therapies & Self-Help Treatments.** Keith Scott. 144p. 1999. pap. text 17.95 (*1-85368-789-8*) New Holland.

***Natural Home Pharmacy: A Concise Reference Guide to Natural Therapies & Self-Help Treatments.** Keith Scott. 2000. pap. 17.95 (*1-85974-293-9*) New5 Holland.

Natural Home Physician. Powell. 164p. 1975. 11.95 (*0-85032-092-5*, Pub. by C W Daniel) Natl Bk Netwk.

Natural Home Physician. Eric F. Powell. 288p. pap. 17.95 (*0-8464-4316-3*) Beekman Pubs.

Natural Home Remedies: A Step-by-Step Guide. Karen Hurrell. LC 97-18373. (In a Nutshell Ser.). 64p. 1997. 7.95 (*1-86204-108-3*, Pub. by Element MA) Penguin Putnam.

Natural Home Schooling: A Parent-Teacher's Guidebook to Natural Learning in the Home. Kerri B. Williamson. LC 94-46770. 108p. (C). 1995. text 34.95 (*0-398-05977-2*); pap. text 20.95 (*0-398-05978-0*) C C Thomas.

Natural Home Spa: Recreate the Luxurious Beauty Treatments of a Professional Spa in Your Own Home. Sian Rees. LC 99-33940. 1999. 24.95 (*0-8069-6813-3*) Sterling.

***Natural Hormone Balance for Women.** Uzzi Reiss & Martin Zucker. 2001. 24.95 (*0-7434-0665-6*, PB Hardcover) PB.

Natural Hormone Replacement: For Women over 45. Jonathan V. Wright & John Morgenthaler. LC 97-65916. (Illus.). 128p. 1997. pap. 9.95 (*0-9627418-0-9*) Smart Pubns CA.

Natural Hormone Solution: Using Plant Hormones to Overcome Menopausal & PMS-related Symptoms. Duane E. Townsend et al. 303p. 1999. pap. text 14.95 (*1-58054-044-9*) Woodland UT.

Natural Horse. Audrey Townley. (Illus.). 192p. 1993. 34.95 (*1-85223-742-2*, Pub. by Crolwood) Trafalgar.

Natural Horse: Foundations for Natural Horsemanship. 2nd ed. Jaime Jackson. LC 97-62094. (Illus.). 172p. 1997. reprint ed. pap. 24.95 (*0-9658007-0-9*) Star Ridge.

Natural Horse-Man-Ship. Pat Parelli & Kathy Kadash. (Illus.). 223p. (Orig.). 1993. pap. 14.95 (*0-911647-27-9*) Western Horseman.

***Natural House: A Complete Guide to Healthy, Energy Independent, Environmental Homes.** Daniel Chiras. (Illus.). 400p. 2000. pap. 35.00 (*1-890132-57-8*) Chelsea Green Pub.

Natural House Catalog: Everything You Need to Create an Environmentally Friendly Home. David Pearson. LC 95-25220. (Illus.). 288p. 1996. per. 23.00 (*0-684-80198-1*, Fireside) S&S Trade Pap.

Natural Hybridization & Evolution. Michael L. Arnold. LC 96-26496. (Oxford Series in Ecology & Evolution). (Illus.). 232p. 1997. text 75.00 (*0-19-509974-5*); pap. text 40.00 (*0-19-509975-3*) OUP.

Natural Hygiene: The Pristine Way of Life. 2nd ed. Herbert M. Shelton. LC 94-79570. 648p. 1994. reprint ed. pap. 15.95 (*0-914532-37-5*) Amer Natural Hygiene.

Natural Hygiene Diet. Ed. by James M. Lennon & Susan Taylor. 128p. 1999. pap. 10.95 (*0-914532-44-8*, ANHS 254) Amer Natural Hygiene.

Natural Hygiene Handbook. Ed. by James M. Lennon & Susan Taylor. LC 96-86830. 128p. (Orig.). 1996. pap. 10.95 (*0-914532-40-5*, ANHS 0238) Amer Natural Hygiene.

Natural Images in Economic Thought: Markets Read in Tooth & Claw. Philip Mirowski. 634p. 1994. pap. text 34.95 (*0-521-47884-7*) Cambridge U Pr.

Natural Images in Economic Thought: Markets Read in Tooth & Claw. Ed. by Philip Mirowski. (Historical Perspectives on Modern Economics Ser.). (Illus.). 624p. (C). 1994. pap. 29.95 (*0-521-47877-4*); text 95.00 (*0-521-44321-0*) Cambridge U Pr.

Natural Immunity. David Nelson. 844p. 1990. text 132.00 (*0-12-514555-1*) Acad Pr.

Natural Immunity & Biological Response International Symposium, Honolulu, Nov. 1985. Ed. by Eva Lotzova. (Journal: Natural Immunity & Cell Growth Regulation: Vol. 4, No. 5, 1985). 64p. 1985. pap. 28.00 (*3-8055-4243-7*) S Karger.

Natural Immunity, Cancer & Biological Response Modification. Ed. by Eva Lotzova. (Illus.). xii, 324p. 1986. 191.50 (*3-8055-4412-X*) S Karger.

Natural Immunity to Normal Hemopoietic Cells. Bent Rolstad. 256p. 1993. lib. bdg. 189.00 (*0-8493-4837-4*, QR185) CRC Pr.

Natural Ingredients in Cosmetics. Ed. by M. Grievson et al. (Illus.). viii, 120p. 1993. 35.00 (*0-9608752-6-3*) Micelle Pr.

Natural Ingredients in Cosmetics, Vol. II. Petrina Fridd. (Illus.). 194p. 1996. text 40.00 (*1-870228-13-8*) Micelle Pr.

Natural Inheritance. fac. ed. Francis Galton. LC 96-77793. 271p. 1996. 34.95 (*0-9653362-3-9*) Genetics Heritage.

Natural Inheritance. Francis Galton. LC 72-1633. 1989. reprint ed. 40.00 (*0-404-08129-0*) AMS Pr.

Natural Insect Control: The Ecological Gardener's Guide to Foiling Pests. Brooklyn. 1995. pap. text 6.95 (*0-945325-28-2*) Perf Pr OR.

Natural Insect Control: The Ecological Gardener's Guide to Foiling Pests. Ed. by Warren Schultz. LC 94-235450. (21st Century Gardening Ser.). (Illus.). 112p. 1990. pap. 9.95 (*0-945352-83-2*) Bklyn Botanic.

Natural Insect Repel for Pets. Storey/. 1997. pap. 7.95 (*0-676-57062-3*) Random.

Natural Insect Repellents for Pets, People, & Plants. Janette Grainger & Connie Moore. (Illus.). 152p. (Orig.). 1991. pap. text 6.95 (*0-9629712-0-0*) Herb Bar.

***Natural Instability of Capitalism: Expectations, Increasing Returns & the Collapse of Capitalism.** Michael Perelman. LC 98-48413. 188p. 1999. 39.95 (*0-312-22121-5*) St Martin.

Natural Intelligence: Body-Mind Intergration & Human Development. Susan Aposhyan. 196p. 1998. pap. 19.95 (*0-683-30599-9*) Lppncott W & W.

Natural Intelligence Meets Artificial Stupidity. Ed. by Chris Bigum. (C). 1987. 35.00 (*0-7300-0524-0*, Pub. by Deakin Univ) St Mut.

Natural Intelligencer Newspaper Abstracts, 1827-1929. Joan M. Dixon. 572p. 1999. pap. 43.50 (*0-7884-1185-3*, D404) Heritage Bk.

***Natural Interiors, 1vol.** Ann Mcardle. 2000. pap. text 19.99 (*1-56496-609-7*) Rockport Pubs.

Natural Justice: Principles & Practical Application. 2nd ed. Geoffrey A. Flick. 205p. 1984. boxed set 71.00 (*0-409-49123-3*, Austral, MICHIE) LEXIS Pub.

Natural Kansas. Ed. by Joseph T. Collins. LC 85-7542. (Illus.). xiv, 290p. 1985. 25.00 (*0-7006-0258-5*) U Pr of KS.

Natural Killer Cell & Its Interaction with Immune & Non-Immune Cell: Second Meeting of the Society for Natural Immunity, Taormina, May 1994. Ed. by A. Santoni & C. Riccardi. (Journal: Natural Immunity: Vol. 13, No. 4, 1994). (Illus.). 70p. 1994. pap. 38.50 (*3-8055-5999-2*) S Karger.

Natural Killer Cell Protocols: Cellular & Molecular Methods. Ed. by Kerry S. Campbell & Marco Colonna. LC 99-12944. (Methods in Molecular Biology Ser.: Vol. 121). (Illus.). 408p. 2000. 99.50 (*0-89603-683-9*) Humana.

Natural Killer Cells: Biology & Clinical Application, Sixth International Natural Killer Cell Workshop, Goslar, July 1989. Ed. by R. E. Schmidt. (Illus.). xii, 318p. 1990. 257.50 (*3-8055-5200-9*) S Karger.

Natural Killer Cells: Their Definition, Functions, Lineage & Regulation. Ed. by Eva Lotzova. (Journal: Natural Immunity: Vol. 12, Nos. 4-5, 1993). (Illus.). 128p. 1993. pap. 40.00 (*3-8055-5875-9*) S Karger.

Natural Killer Cells & Host Defense. Ed. by Edwin W. Ades & C. Lopez. (Illus.). xiv, 302p. 1989. 256.75 (*3-8055-4791-9*) S Karger.

Natural Killers. Marshall Goldberg. (Orig.). 1976. 23.95 (*0-8488-0804-5*) Amereon Ltd.

Natural Kinds. T. E. Wilkerson. 192p. 1995. 66.95 (*1-85972-131-1*, Pub. by Avebry) Ashgate Pub Co.

Natural Kinds, Laws of Nature & Scientific Methodology. Ed. by Peter J. Riggs. LC 96-35782. (Australasian Studies in History & Philosophy of Science: Vol. 12). 272p. (C). 1996. text 137.50 (*0-7923-4225-9*) Kluwer Academic.

***Natural Kitchen.** Suzanne Havala. 2000. pap. 7.50 (*0-425-17307-0*) Berkley Pub.

Natural Kitchen: Soy! Dana Jacobi. LC 96-27634. (Illus.). 256p. 1996. pap. 14.00 (*0-7615-0478-8*) Prima Pub.

Natural Knowledge in Preclassical Antiquity. Mott T. Greene. LC 91-26952. (Illus.). 112p. 1991. text 38.50 (*0-8018-4292-1*) Johns Hopkins.

Natural Knowledge in Social Context: The Journals of Thomas Archer Hirst FRS, 1845-1892. W. Brook & R. MacLeod. 1980. 500.00 incl. fiche (*0-7201-0373-8*) Continuum.

Natural Landscape Amenities & Suburban Growth: Metropolitan Chicago, 1970-1980. Christopher Mueller-Wille. LC 90-10818. (Geography Research Papers: Vol. 230). (Illus.). xii, 154p. 2000. pap. text 14.00 (*0-89065-136-1*) U Ch Pr.

Natural Landscapes. 5th ed. James Henry & Joann Mossa. 416p. (C). 1995. pap. text, per. 58.95 (*0-7872-0533-8*, 41053301) Kendall-Hunt.

Natural Landscaping: Working with Nature to Create a Backyard Paradise. Sally Roth. LC 96-5912. (Illus.). 256p. 1997. text 29.95 (*0-87596-704-3*) Rodale Pr Inc.

Natural Language & Graphics Interface: Results & Perspectives from the ACORD Project. Ed. by G. C. Bes & T. Guillotin. (Research Reports ESPRIT: Vol. 1). vii, 188p. 1992. 39.00 (*0-387-55675-3*) Spr-Verlag.

Natural Language & Logic: International Scientific Symposium Hamburg, FRG, May 9-11, 1989 Proceedings. Ed. by R. Studer & Joerg H. Siekmann. (Lecture Notes in Computer Science, Lecture Notes in Artificial Intelligence Ser.: Vol. 459). vii, 252p. 1990. 37.00 (*0-387-53082-7*) Spr-Verlag.

Natural Language & Speech: Symposium Proceedings, Brussels, November 20, 1991. Ed. by E. Klein & F. Veltman. (ESPRIT Basic Research Ser.). viii, 192p. 1992. 40.95 (*0-387-54988-9*) Spr-Verlag.

Natural Language & Voice Processing. Richard K. Miller & Terri C. Walker. LC 89-17105. 259p. 1989. pap. text 95.00 (*0-88173-102-1*) Fairmont Pr.

Natural Language & Voice Processing. Richard K. Miller & Terri C. Walker. 269p. (C). 1989. pap. text 95.00 (*0-13-610734-6*, Macmillan Coll) P-H.

Natural Language at the Computer. Ed. by A. Blaser. (Lecture Notes in Computer Science Ser.: Vol. 320). iii, 176p. 1988. 30.00 (*0-387-50011-1*) Spr-Verlag.

Natural Language Communication with Pictorial Information Systems. Ed. by Leonard Bolc. (Symbolic Computation - Artificial Intelligence Ser.). (Illus.). 340p. 1984. 71.95 (*0-387-13478-6*) Spr-Verlag.

Natural Language Computing: An English Generative Grammar in Prolog. Ray C. Dougherty. 400p. (C). 1994. pap. 39.95 (*0-8058-1526-0*); text 69.95 (*0-8058-1525-2*) L Erlbaum Assocs.

Natural Language Generation. Ed. by Gerard Kempen. 1987. text 273.50 (*90-247-3558-0*) Kluwer Academic.

Natural Language Generation in Artificial Intelligence & Computational Linguistics. Ed. by Cecile L. Paris et al. (C). 1990. text 147.50 (*0-7923-9098-9*) Kluwer Academic.

Natural Language Generation Systems. Ed. by D. D. McDonald & Leonard Bolc. (Symbolic Computation - Artificial Intelligence Ser.). (Illus.). 389p. 1988. 72.95 (*0-387-96691-9*) Spr-Verlag.

Natural Language Information Processing: A Computer Grammmar of English & Its Applications. Naomi Sager. 1981. text 37.50 (*0-201-06769-2*) Addison-Wesley.

***Natural Language Information Retrieval** Tomek Strzalkowski. LC 99-22755. (Text, Speech & Language Technology Ser.). 1999. write for info. (*0-7923-5685-3*) Kluwer Academic.

Natural Language Interface for Computer-Aided Design. Tariq Samad. 1986. text 100.50 (*0-89838-222-X*) Kluwer Academic.

Natural Language Parsing & Linguistic Theories. Ed. by Uwe Reyle & C. Rohrer. 1988. lib. bdg. 143.50 (*1-55608-055-7*) Kluwer Academic.

Natural Language Parsing Systems. Leonard Bolc. (Symbolic Computation Ser.). (Illus.). 335p. 1987. 77.95 (*0-387-17537-7*) Spr-Verlag.

Natural Language Processing. Ed. by Fernando C. Pereira & Barbara J. Gross. LC 93-39575. (Artificial Intelligence Special Issues Ser.). (Illus.). 537p. 1994. pap. text 39.00 (*0-262-66092-X*, Bradford Bks) MIT Pr.

Natural Language Processing. Harry Tennant. (Illus.). 1981. pap. text 19.95 (*0-89433-100-0*) Petrocelli.

Natural Language Processing see Courant Computer Science Symposia

Natural Language Processing: EAIA '90: Proceedings of the 2nd Advanced School in Artificial Intelligence Guarda, Portugal, October 8-12, 1990. Ed. by Miguel Filgueiras et al. (Lecture Notes in Artificial Intelligence: Vol. 476). vii, 253p. 1991. 33.00 (*0-387-53678-7*) Spr-Verlag.

Natural Language Processing: The PLNLP Approach. Ed. by Karen Jensen et al. LC 92-30803. (International Series in Engineering & Computer Science, VLSI, Computer Architecture, & Digital Screen Processing: Vol. 196). (C). 1992. text 125.00 (*0-7923-9279-5*) Kluwer Academic.

***Natural Language Processing - NLP 2000: Proceedings of the 2nd International Conference, Patras, Greece, June 2-4, 2000.** International Conference on Natural Language Processing Staff & Dimitrios Christodoulakis. LC 00-41040. (Lecture Notes in Computer Science Ser.). 2000. pap. write for info. (*3-540-67605-8*) Spr-Verlag.

***Natural Language Processing & Knowledge Representation: Language for Knowledge & Knowledge for Landscape.** Lucja M. Iwanska & Stuart C. Shapiro. LC 99-87360. (AAAI Press Ser.). (Illus.). 350p. 2000. pap. 40.00 (*0-262-59021-2*) MIT Pr.

Natural Language Processing for Prolog Programmers. Michael A. Covington. 348p. (C). 1993. 51.00 (*0-13-629213-5*) P-H.

Natural Language Processing for the World Wide Web: Papers from the 1997 Spring Symposium. Ed. by Kavi Mahesh. (Technical Reports). (Illus.). 158p. 1997. spiral bd. 25.00 (*1-57735-025-1*) AAAI Pr.

Natural Language Processing in the 1980s: A Bibliography. Gerald Gazdar et al. LC 87-71618. (CSLI Lecture Notes Ser.: No. 12). 240p. 1987. 54.95 (*0-937073-26-1*); pap. 16.95 (*0-937073-28-8*) CSLI.

Natural Language Processing in Pop-11. Gerard Gazdar. 1989. text 36.75 (*0-201-17448-0*) Addison-Wesley.

Natural Language Processing Technologies in Artificial Intelligence: The Science & Industry Perspective. Klaus K. Obermeier. (Artificial Intelligence Ser.). 1989. text 39.95 (*0-470-21528-3*) P-H.

Natural Language Processing with ThoughtTreasure. Erik T. Mueller. 343p. 1997. spiral bd. 120.00 (*0-9660746-0-2*) Signiform.

Natural Language Understanding. James Allen. 550p. (C). 1988. text 59.25 (*0-8053-0330-8*) Benjamin-Cummings.

Natural Language Understanding. Richard K. Miller & Terri C. Walker. LC 88-81661. (Survey on Technology & Markets Ser.: No. 70). 50p. 1989. pap. text 200.00 (*1-55865-069-5*) Future Tech Surveys.

Natural Language Understanding. 2nd ed. James Allen. (C). 1994. 62.81 (*0-8053-0334-0*) Benjamin-Cummings.

Natural Law. Barbara H. Hyett. (Salt River Poetry Ser.). 88p. (Orig.). 1989. pap. 9.95 (*1-882021-17-7*) Summer.

Natural Law. Heinrich A. Rommen. Ed. by J. P. Mayer. LC 78-67382. (European Political Thought Ser.). 1980. reprint ed. lib. bdg. 23.95 (*0-405-11732-9*) Ayer.

Natural Law, I. Ed. by John Finnis. (International Library of Essays in Law & Legal Theory). 800p. (C). 1991. lib. bdg. 125.00 (*0-8147-2603-8*) NYU Pr.

Natural Law, II. Ed. by John Finnis. (International Library of Essays in Law & Legal Theory). 800p. (C). 1991. lib. bdg. 125.00 (*0-8147-2604-6*) NYU Pr.

Natural Law, Set. Ed. by John Finnis. (International Library of Essays in Law & Legal Theory). 800p. (C). 1991. lib. bdg. 250.00 (*0-8147-2605-4*) NYU Pr.

Natural Law: A Study in Legal & Social History & Philosophy. Heinrich A. Rommen. Tr. by Thomas R. Hanley from GER. LC 97-26334.Tr. of Ewige Wiederkehr des Naturrechts. 1998. 15.00 (*0-86597-160-9*); pap. 8.50 (*0-86597-161-7*) Liberty Fund.

Natural Law: An Introduction to Legal Philosophy. Alexander P. D'Entreves. LC 92-37171. 226p. (C). 1994. pap. text 24.95 (*1-56000-673-0*) Transaction Pubs.

***Natural Law: The Scientific Ways of Treating Natural Law, Its Place in Moral Philosophy.** G. W. Helga. 2000. 29.95 (*0-8122-7693-0*) U of Pa Pr.

Natural Law: Universal in Scope, Moral in Design. Stanley W. Paher. 72p. 1996. pap. 4.95 (*0-913814-93-8*) Nevada Pubns.

Natural Law & Contemporary Public Policy. Ed. by David F. Forte. LC 98-13260. 416p. 1998. 65.00 (*0-87840-692-1*) Georgetown U Pr.

Natural Law & Human Dignity. Ernst Bloch. Tr. by Dennis J. Schmidt from GER. (Studies in Contemporary German Social Thought). 408p. 1986. 32.50 (*0-262-02221-4*) MIT Pr.

Natural Law & Human Dignity. Ernst Bloch. Tr. by Dennis J. Schmidt from GER. (Studies in Contemporary German Social Thought). 408p. 1987. pap. text 24.00 (*0-262-52129-6*) MIT Pr.

Natural Law & Justice. Lloyd L. Weinreb. 336p. 1990. pap. 19.50 (*0-674-60426-1*) HUP.

Natural Law & Modern Society. Center for the Study of Democratic Institutions St. LC 73-156626. (Essay Index Reprint Ser.). 1977. reprint ed. 19.95 (*0-8369-2388-X*) Ayer.

Natural Law & Moral Inquiry: Ethics, Metaphysics, & Politics in the Work of Germain Grisez. Ed. by Robert P. George. LC 97-37975. 281p. 1998. 55.00 (*0-87840-673-5*); pap. 24.95 (*0-87840-674-3*) Georgetown U Pr.

Natural Law & Moral Philosophy: From Grotius to the Scottish Enlightenment. Knud Haakonssen. 396p. (C). 1996. text 64.95 (*0-521-49686-1*); pap. text 23.95 (*0-521-49802-3*) Cambridge U Pr.

Natural Law & Natural. John Finnis. (Clarendon Law Ser.). 442p. 1980. pap. text 29.95 (*0-19-876110-4*) OUP.

Natural Law & Political Ideology in the Philosophy of Hegel. Tony Burnes. LC 95-83286. (Avebury Series in Philosophy). 208p. 1996. 72.95 (*1-85972-040-4*, Pub. by Avebry) Ashgate Pub Co.

Natural Law & Practical Reason: A Thomist View of Moral Autonomy. Martin Rhonheimer. Tr. by Gerald Malsbary. LC 99-89242. (Moral Philosophy & Theology Ser.: Vol. 1). 540p. 1999. 45.00 (*0-8232-1978-X*, Pub. by Fordham) BookMasters.

Natural Law & Practical Reason: A Thomist View of Moral Autonomy. Martin Rhonheimer. Tr. by Gerald Malsbary. LC 99-89242. (Moral Philosophy & Theology Ser.: Vol. 1). 540p. 2000. pap. 19.95 (*0-8232-1979-8*, Pub. by Fordham) BookMasters.

***Natural Law & Public Reason.** Ed. by Robert P. George & Christopher Wolfe. LC 99-38853. 160p. 2000. text 39.95 (*0-87840-765-0*); pap. text 17.95 (*0-87840-766-9*) Georgetown U Pr.

Natural Law & the Theory of Property: Grotius to Hume. Stephen Buckle. 340p. (C). 1993. pap. text 24.95 (*0-19-824094-5*) OUP.

Natural Law Ethics, 72. Philip E. Devine. LC 99-25006. (Contributions in Philosophy Ser.: No. 72). 216p. 2000. 59.95 (*0-313-30702-4*, GM702, Greenwood Pr) Greenwood.

Natural Law in English Renaissance Literature. R. S. White. 305p. (C). 1996. text 59.95 (*0-521-48142-2*) Cambridge U Pr.

Natural Law in Judaism. David Novak. LC 97-50609. 208p. (C). 1998. text 54.95 (*0-521-63170-X*) Cambridge U Pr.

Natural Law in the Spiritual World. Henry Drummond. 371p. 1981. pap. 32.00 (*0-89540-082-0*, SB-082) Sun Pub.

Natural Law, Liberalism, & Morality: Contemporary Essays. Ed. by Robert George. 324p. 1996. text 80.00 (*0-19-825984-0*) OUP.

Natural Law of Race Relations. Laszlo Thomay. 160p. 1993. pap. 15.00 (*1-878465-07-4*) Scott-Townsend Pubs.

Natural Law Party. Robert Roth. LC 98-23739. 272p. 1998. 23.95 (*0-312-19304-1*, Thomas Dunne) St Martin.

***Natural Law Theories in the Early Enlightenment.** T. J. (Tim J.) Hochstrasser. LC 99-59885. 2000. write for info. (*0-521-66193-5*) Cambridge U Pr.

Natural Law Theory. Ed. by Robert P. George. 1992. 33.75 (*0-8446-6928-8*) Peter Smith.

Natural Law Theory: Contemporary Essays. Ed. by Robert P. George. 382p. 1994. pap. text 21.00 (*0-19-823552-6*) OUP.

Natural Lawn & Alternatives. Ed. by Margaret Roach. (Illus.). 96p. 1993. pap. 7.95 (*0-945352-80-8*) Bklyn Botanic.

***Natural Laws in Scientific Practice.** Marc Lange. LC 99-38157. 368p. 2000. write for info. (*0-19-513148-7*) OUP.

Natural Laws of Husbandry. Justus Von Liebig. LC 72-2852. (Use & Abuse of America's Natural Resources Ser.). 392p. 1972. reprint ed. 28.95 (*0-405-04541-7*) Ayer.

Natural Laxative Cookbook. Karin Cadwell & Edith White. LC 95-1230. (Illus.). 160p. 1995. pap. 10.95 (*0-8069-1344-4*) Sterling.

Natural Learning: The Life History of an Environmental Schoolyard. Robin C. Moore & Herbert H. Wong. LC 96-39184. (Illus.). (Orig.). 1997. pap. text 29.95 (*0-944661-24-6*) MIG Comns.

Natural Learning & Mathematics. Rex Stoessiger & Joy Edmunds. LC 91-46271. 113p. (C). (gr. k). 1992. pap. text 18.50 (*0-435-08328-7*, 08328) Heinemann.

Natural Learning from A-Z: Thematic Activities & Phonemic Awareness for Letters & Letter Sounds. Mary Jo Ayres. Ed. by Janie Allen-Bradley. LC 97-75610. (Illus.). 160p. (Orig.). 1997. pap. 19.95 (*0-9661298-0-6*) Natural Lrning.

Natural Learning Rhythms: Discovering How & When Your Child Learns. Josette Luvmour & Sambhava Luvmour. 320p. 1997. pap. 16.95 (*0-89087-840-4*) Celestial Arts.

Natural Legacy. 2nd ed. Recher & Lunney. 1986. text 52.00 (*0-08-029864-8*, Pergamon Pr); pap. text 26.00 (*0-08-029863-X*, Pergamon Pr) Elsevier.

Natural Liberation: Padmasambhava's Teachings in the Six Bardos. Padmasambhava. Tr. by B. Alan Wallace. LC 97-2608. 272p. 1997. pap. 16.95 (*0-86171-131-9*) Wisdom MA.

Natural Life. Humphrey Bower. (Orig.). pap. 14.95 (*0-86819-555-3*, Pub. by Currency Pr) Accents Pubns.

Natural Lifestyle Cooking. Ernestine Finley & Mark Finley. Ed. by Nancy Pardeiro. (Illus.). 80p. 1990. pap. text 5.95 (*0-9625343-1-5*) Creation Enter Intl.

N

Natural Lifestyles Library, Vol. 2, 4 pts., Vol. 2, Pt. 4. S. Freeman. 80p. 1974. pap. 30.00 (*0-677-16005-4*) Gordon & Breach.

Natural Light. Carol Soucek King. LC 98-2959. 1998. write for info. (*0-86636-685-7*); pap. write for info. (*0-86636-686-5*) PBC Intl Inc.

Natural Light & the Italian Piazza: Siena, As a Case Study. Sandra D. Lakeman. LC 93-206345. (Illus.). 110p. 1995. pap. 24.95 (*0-295-97418-4*) U of Wash Pr.

Natural Limitations of Youth: The Predispositions That Shape the Adolescent Character. John J. Mitchell. LC 97-40928. (Developments in Clinical Psychology Ser.). 1998. 73.25 (*1-56750-372-1*); pap. 39.50 (*1-56750-373-X*) Ablx Pub.

Natural Limits to Biological Change. Lane P. Lester & Raymond G. Bohlin. 160p. 1984. pap. 10.95 (*0-310-44511-6*, 12211P) Zondervan.

Natural Limits to Biological Change. 2nd ed. Lane P. Lester & Raymond G. Bohlin. LC 89-70041. (Illus.). 207p. 1989. reprint ed. pap. 12.99 (*0-945241-06-2*) Probe Bks.

Natural Liver Therapy: Herbs & Other Natural Remedies for a Healthy Liver. Christopher Hobbs. Ed. by Michael Miovic & Beth Baugh. (Illus.). 53p. (Orig.). 1986. pap. text 4.95 (*1-884360-00-9*) Botanica CA.

Natural Lives, Modern Times: People & Places of the Delaware River. Bruce Stutz. LC 98-10523. (Pennsylvania Paperbacks Ser.). 400p. 1998. pap. 18.50 (*0-8122-1658-X*) U of Pa Pr.

Natural Lizard Activity. B. J. Freedman. LC 98-89518. 375p. 1998. text 25.00 (*0-7388-0213-1*); pap. text 15.00 (*0-7388-0214-X*) Xlibris Corp.

Natural Logic & the Greek Moods. David Lightfoot. (Janua Linguarum, Series Practica: No. 230). 149p. 1975. pap. text 46.95 (*90-279-3061-9*) Mouton.

Natural Logic, Judicial Proof & Objective Facts. Wan Wells. LC 94-238014. 87p. 1994. 54.00 (*1-86287-150-7*, Pub. by Federation Pr) Gaunt.

Natural Lunchbox. Judy Brown. LC 96-18107. 192p. 1996. pap. text 12.95 (*1-57067-026-9*) Book Pub Co.

Natural Magic. Doreen Valiente. (Illus.). 184p. 1985. reprint ed. pap. 11.50 (*0-919345-80-8*) Phoenix WA.

N

***Natural Magic: Inside the Well-Stocked Witch's Cupboard,** Sally Dubats. 1999. pap. 12.00 (*1-57566-461-5*, Knsington) Kensgtn Pub Corp.

***Natural Magic: Potions & Powers from the Magical Garden.** John M. Greer. LC 00-21538. (Illus.). 312p. 2000. pap. write for info. (*1-56718-295-X*) Llewellyn Pubns.

Natural Male: Photographs by Sherwin Carlquist. Photos by Sherwin Carlquist. (Illus.). 220p. 1999. 42.00 (*0-9648861-3-8*) Pinecone Press.

***Natural Man.** Gary Soto. LC 99-18353. 71p. 1999. pap. 13.95 (*0-8118-2518-3*) Chronicle Bks.

Natural Man. Henry David Thoreau. Ed. by Robert Epstein & Sherry Phillips. LC 77-18122. 119p. 1978. pap. 8.00 (*0-8356-0503-5*, Quest) Theos Pub Hse.

Natural Man. Ed McClanahan. LC 93-77697. 240p. 1993. reprint ed. pap. 13.50 (*0-917788-56-7*) Gnomon Pr.

Natural Man: A Record from Borneo. Charles Hose. LC 77-86984. reprint ed. 32.50 (*0-404-16730-6*) AMS Pr.

Natural Man: Photographs by Sherwin Carlquist. Sherwin Carlquist. (Illus.). 256p. 1991. 35.00 (*0-9648861-2-X*) Pinecone Press.

Natural Man: The True Story of John Henry. Steve Sanfield. (J). 1986. 15.15 (*0-606-04488-4*, Pub. by Turtleback) Demco.

Natural Masques: Gender & Identity in Fielding's Plays & Novels. Jill Campbell. LC 94-33011. 378p. (C). 1994. pap. 16.95 (*0-8047-2520-9*) Stanford U Pr.

Natural Masques: Gender & Identity in Fielding's Plays & Novels. Jill Campbell. LC 94-33011. i , 326p. 1995. 45.00 (*0-8047-2391-5*) Stanford U Pr.

Natural Materials. Erica Burt. (Craft Projects Ser.). (Illus.). 32p. (J). (gr. 2-6). 1990. lib. bdg. 11.95 (*0-685-46442-3*) Rourke Corp.

Natural Materials: Creative Activities for Children. Susan C. Thompson. (Illus.). 200p. (Orig.). (J). (ps-5). 1992. pap. 13.95 (*0-673-36033-4*, GoodYrBooks) Addson-Wesley Educ.

Natural Meals in Minutes: Whole Grains, Beans, Seeds, Sprouting, Powdered Milk Cheeses. Rita Bingham. Orig. Title: Introduction to Natural Foods, Sprouting, Powdered Milk Cheeses. (Illus.). 200p. 1997. reprint ed. student ed. 14.95 (*1-882314-09-3*) Nat Meals Pub.

***Natural Medicine.** Shaykh Nazim Al-Naqshbandi. 64p. (C). 2000. pap. 7.50 (*1-898863-10-5*, Pub. by Zero Prods) Kazi Pubns.

Natural Medicine. Ed. by Joseph E. Pizzorno. (C). Date not set. text 195.00 Church.

***Natural Medicine: A Practical Guide to Family Health.** Beth MacEoin. 512p. 2000. 35.00 (*0-7475-3023-8*, Pub. by Blmsbury Pub) Trafalgar.

Natural Medicine & Medicare: How to Solve the Medicare Crisis & Improve Our Health Care. Joseph E. Pizzorno. 1997. pap. text 16.00 (*1-880831-18-X*) Aletheia Pr.

Natural Medicine Chest: Natural Medicines to Keep You & Your Family Thriving into the Next Millennium. Eugene R. Zamperion & Ellen Kamhi. LC 99-18419. (Illus.). 256p. 1999. pap. 19.95 (*0-87131-882-2*, Pub. by M Evans) Natl Bk Netwk.

Natural Medicine Chest & Home Remedies Handbook. Ed. by Denise Domb. LC 94-220557. 72p. 1994. pap. 4.95 (*0-9636334-8-1*) AlternMed Bks.

Natural Medicine Childre. Julian Scott. LC 89-63649. 192p. 1990. pap. 15.00 (*0-380-75876-8*, Avon Bks) Morrow Avon.

Natural Medicine for Allergies: The Best Alternative Methods for Quick Relief. Glenn S. Rothfeld & Suzanne LeVert. 288p. 1996. pap. 13.95 (*0-87596-286-6*) Rodale Pr Inc.

Natural Medicine for Arthritis: The Best Alternative Methods for Relieving Pain & Stiffness: from Food & Herbs to Acupuncture & Homeopathy. Glenn S. Rothfeld & Suanne LeVert. 288p. 1996. pap. 13.95 (*0-87596-287-4*) Rodale Pr Inc.

Natural Medicine for Back Pain. large type ed. Glenn S. Rothfeld & Suzanne LeVert. LC 96-39213. (Spec-Hall Ser.). 328p. 1997. lib. bdg. 23.95 (*0-7838-2026-7*, G K Hall Lrg Type) Mac Lib Ref.

Natural Medicine for Back Pain: The Best Alternative Methods for Banishing Backache from Acupressure & Chiropractic to Nutrition & Yoga. Glenn Rothfeld & Suzanne LeVert. LC 95-31025. (Illus.). 224p. (Orig.). 1996. pap. 11.95 (*0-87596-288-2*) Rodale Pr Inc.

Natural Medicine for Colds & Flu. Nancy Pauline Bruning. LC 98-179265. (Natural Medicine Library). 240p. 1998. mass mkt. 5.99 (*0-440-22523-X*) Dell.

Natural Medicine for Heart Disease: The Best Alternative Methods to Prevent & Treat High Cholesterol, High Blood Pressure, Stroke, Chest Pain, & Other Circulatory Problems. Glenn Rothfeld et al. LC 95-24445. 233p. (Orig.). 1996. pap. 11.95 (*0-87596-289-0*) Rodale Pr Inc.

Natural Medicine for PMS. Mitchell. LC 98-179226. 240p. 1998. mass mkt. 5.99 (*0-440-22526-4*) Dell.

Natural Medicine for Prostate Problems. Ron Falcone. LC 98-179266. 208p. 1998. mass mkt. 5.99 (*0-440-22524-8*) Dell.

Natural Medicine for Superimmunity. Deborah Mitchell. LC 98-179245. (Natural Medicine Library). 256p. 1998. mass mkt. 5.99 (*0-440-22525-6*) Dell.

Natural Medicine for the Prostate. Rita Elkins. 1996. pap. text 3.95 (*1-885670-17-6*) Woodland UT.

Natural Medicine for Weight Loss. Unknown. LC 98-179224. 240p. 1998. mass mkt. 5.99 (*0-440-22522-1*) Dell.

Natural Medicine vs. Orthodox Medicine. Karen Bradstreet. (The Woodland Health Ser.). 1997. pap. text 3.95 (*1-58054-014-7*) Woodland UT.

Natural Medicine Works!!! Timothy Yeh et al. (Illus.). 400p. 1997. pap. 39.95 (*0-9652967-1-7*) Yehs Ctr Nat Med.

Natural Medicines & Cures Your Doctor Never Tells You About. FC&A Staff. 370p. 1998. 27.96 (*0-915099-81-0*) FC&A Pub.

Natural Medicines & Cures Your Doctor Never Tells You About. FC&A Staff. 366p. (C). 1999. pap. 9.99 (*0-915099-76-4*) FC&A Pub.

***Natural Medicines Comprehensive Database.** Therapeutic Research Faculty Staff. 164p. 1999. pap. 92.00 (*0-9676136-0-4*) Theraptc Res.

***Natural Medicines Comprehensive Database.** 2nd rev. ed. Therapeutic Research Faculty Staff. 1999. pap. 92.00 (*0-9676136-2-0*) Theraptc Res.

***Natural Medicines Reference Manual: Ayurveda, Siddha, Unani, Homoeopathy.** LC 99-933242. 1999. 40.00 (*81-900181-3-2*, Pub. by Eastern Pubs) S Asia.

Natural Menopause. Miriam Stoppard. LC 97-48453. (DK Healthcare Ser.). 96p. 1998. pap. 7.95 (*0-7894-3090-8*) DK Pub Inc.

Natural Menopause: The Complete Guide. 2nd rev. ed. Susan Perry & Katherine O'Hanlon. Ed. by James Broll. 272p. 1997. pap. 15.00 (*0-201-47987-7*) Addison-Wesley.

Natural Menopause: The Complete Guide to a Woman's Most Misunderstood Passage. Susan Perry & Katherine A. O'Hanlan. (Illus.). 224p. 1993. pap. 10.95 (*0-201-62477-X*) Addison-Wesley.

***Natural Mental Health: How to Take Control of Your Own Emotional Health.** Carla Wills-Brandon. LC 00-25650. 272p. 2000. pap. 13.95 (*1-56170-727-9*, 5028) Hay House.

Natural Methods for Equine Health. Mary W. Bromiley. (Illus.). 256p. 1995. pap. 28.95 (*0-632-03818-7*, Pub. by Blckwll Scitfc UK) Blackwell Sci.

Natural Michigan: A Guide to 288 Natural Attractions. expanded rev. ed. Tom Powers. (Illus.). 260p. 1995. pap. 14.95 (*0-923756-13-2*) Friede Pubns.

***Natural Microporous Materials in Environmental Technology.** P. Misaelides. LC 99-38161. (NATO Science Ser.). 1999. write for info. (*0-7923-5888-0*, Kluwer Plenum) Kluwer Academic.

Natural Mind: An Investigation of Drugs & Higher Consciousness. Andrew Weil. LC 98-28464. 240p. 1998. pap. 14.00 (*0-395-91156-7*) HM.

Natural Monopoly & Its Regulation. Richard A. Posner. LC 99-22490. 115p. 1999. 8.95 (*1-882577-81-7*) Cato Inst.

Natural Morning. Jeanette Pelton. Ed. by Dan Pelton. (Illus.). 100p. (Orig.). (J). (gr. 5-7). 1993. pap. 6.00 (*1-879564-06-8*) Long Acre Pub.

Natural Mother. Cathy Williams. (Presents Ser.: Bk. 2076). 186p. 2000. per. 3.75 (*0-373-12076-1*, 1-12076-5) Harlequin Bks.

Natural Mothering: A Guide to Holistic Therapies for Pregnancy, Birth, & Early Childhood. Nicky Wesson. LC 97-10399. (Illus.). 240p. 1997. pap. 14.95 (*0-89281-733-X*) Inner Tradit.

Natural Mysticism: Towards a New Reggae Aesthetic. Kwame Dawes. 216p. 1998. pap. 24.95 (*1-900715-22-8*, Pub. by Peepal Tree Pr) Paul & Co Pubs.

Natural Nidality of Diseases & Questions of Parasitology. Ed. by Norman D. Levine. Tr. by Frederick K. Plous, Jr. LC 68-11027. (Illus.). 495p. reprint ed. 153.50 (*0-8357-9691-4*, 201903100010) Bks Demand.

Natural Nidality of Transmissible Diseases: With Special Reference to the Landscape Epidemiology of Zooanthroponoses. Evgeny N. Pavlovsky. Ed. by Norman D. Levine. LC 66-11023. 275p. reprint ed. pap. 85.30 (*0-608-13741-3*, 202024400016) Bks Demand.

Natural Nursery. Louis Pottkotter. 384p. 1994. pap. 16.95 (*0-8092-3766-0*, 376600, Contemporary Bks) NTC Contemp Pub Co.

Natural Nursery: The Parent's Guide to Ecologically Sound, Nontoxic, Safe, & Healthy Baby Care. Louis Pottkotter. 366p. 1998. pap. text 15.00 (*0-7881-5689-6*) DIANE Pub.

Natural Nutrition for Dogs & Cats: The Ultimate Diet. Kymythy R. Schultze. LC 99-23629. 96p. (Orig.). 1999. pap. 8.95 (*1-56170-636-1*, 598) Hay House.

Natural Object Recognition. Thomas M. Strat. LC 92-1511. (Perception Engineering Ser.). (Illus.). 176p. 1992. 102.95 (*0-387-97832-1*) Spr-Verlag.

Natural Objects. Kathy Carre & Mir Tamim Ansary. LC 96-39409. (Cool Collections). (J). 1998. (*1-57572-115-5*) Heinemann Lib.

Natural Obsessions: Striving to Unlock the Deepest Secrets of the Cancer Cell. Natalie Angier. LC 99-18104. 394p. 1999. pap. 15.00 (*0-395-92472-3*) HM.

Natural Operators in Differential Geometry. Peter W. Michor et al. LC 92-45829. 1993. 111.95 (*0-387-56235-4*) Spr-Verlag.

Natural Options: A Natural Healthcare Guide. Barbara H. Sharp. (Illus.). 112p. (Orig.). 1995. pap. 12.95 (*0-9649166-4-9*, 1) Nat Hlth Res.

Natural Order: The Experience of Landscape in Contemporary Sculpture. Barbara Bloemink. (Illus.). 44p. (Orig.). 1990. pap. 7.50 (*0-943651-23-9*) Hudson Riv.

***Natural Order of Things.** Antonio Lobo Antunes. Tr. by Richard Zenith. LC 99-40063. 320p. 2000. 25.00 (*0-8021-1658-2*, Pub. by Grove-Atltic) Publishers Group.

Natural Order of Things. Antonio Lobo Antunes. Tr. by Richard Zenith. Date not set. pap. 14.00 (*0-8050-5761-7*, Owl) H Holt & Co.

Natural Order of Things. Antonio Lobo Antunes. Tr. by Richard Zenith. 1998. 25.00 (*0-8050-5760-9*) H Holt & Co.

Natural Organic Hair & Skin Care. Aubrey Hampton. LC 86-61883. 441p. (Orig.). 1987. pap. 17.95 (*0-939157-01-2*) Organica Pr.

Natural Organic Hair & Skin Care. 2nd rev. ed. Aubrey Hampton. (Illus.). 441p. (Orig.). 1990. pap. 17.95 (*0-939157-06-3*) Organica Pr.

Natural Organic Materials & Related Synthetic Products, 8 vols., Vol. 5. Intro. by John J. McKetta, Jr. (Illus.). 898p. 1972. 68.50 (*0-06-491106-3*) B&N Imports.

***Natural Organic Matter & Disinfection By-Products: Characterization & Control in Drinking Water.** Ed. by Sylvia E. Barrett et al. (ACS Symposium Ser.). (Illus.). 416p. 2000. text 135.00 (*0-8412-3676-3*, Pub. by Am Chemical) OUP.

Natural Organic Matter in Drinking Water: Origin, Characterization, & Removal. (Illus.). 252p. 1994. pap. 76.00 (*0-89867-753-X*, 90671) Am Water Wks Assn.

***Natural Organic Matter in Drinking Water: Recommendations to Water Utilities.** Billy H. Kornegay et al. LC 00-44159. 2000. write for info. (*1-58321-032-6*) Am Water Wks Assn.

Natural Ornaments for Your Christmas Tree. Betty Wendt. (Illus.). 76p. 1995. pap. 10.95 (*0-9648620-0-X*) B Wendt.

Natural Pain Relief: A Practical Handbook for Self-Help. Jan Sadler. LC 96-43238. 1997. pap. 10.95 (*1-85230-924-5*, Pub. by Element MA) Penguin Putnam.

Natural Pain Relief: Techniques for Miraculous Healing. Scott Lux. ix, 112p. 1997. pap. 10.95 (*0-9609324-1-0*) Wisdom of Pain.

Natural Palette: Hudson River Artists & the Land. Albany Institute of History & Art Staff. Ed. by Jenny Fiore & Stevie Mack. (J). (gr. 4-12). 1997. teacher ed. 94.95 incl. VHS (*0-945666-60-8*) Crizmac.

Natural Parenting: A Practical Guide for Fathers & Mothers: Conception to Age 3. Peter Walker & Fiona Walker. LC 87-35775. (Illus.). 144p. 1988. reprint ed. 17.95 (*0-940793-14-8*); reprint ed. pap. 12.95 (*0-940793-13-X*) Interlink Pub.

Natural Particulars: Nature & the Disciplines in Renaissance Europe. Anthony Grafton & Nancy Siraisi. LC 99-30932. (Dibner Institute Studies in the History of Science & Technology). 448p. 1999. 50.00 (*0-262-07193-2*) MIT Pr.

Natural Patagonia - Patagonia Natural: Argentina & Chile. Marcelo D. Beccaceci. LC 97-28419. (ENG & SPA., Illus.). 136p. 1998. pap. 24.95 (*0-9630180-3-5*) Pangaea Pub.

Natural Patagonia - Patagonia Natural: Argentina & Chile. Marcelo D. Beccaceci. Ed. by Bonnie J. Hayskar. LC 97-28419. (ENG & SPA., Illus.). 136p. 1998. 32.95 (*0-9630180-4-3*) Pangaea Pub.

Natural Pathways of New Jersey. Millard C. Davis. LC 98-106742. (Illus.). 272p. (Orig.). 1997. pap. 19.95 (*0-937548-35-9*) Plexus Pub.

Natural Pattern Forms. Richard L. Dube. (Landscape Architecture Ser.). 1997. pap. 42.95 (*0-442-02286-7*, VNR) Wiley.

Natural Pattern Forms: A Practical Sourcebook for Landscape Design. Richard L. Dube. 229p. 1996. 54.95 (*0-471-28768-7*, VNR) Wiley.

Natural Patterns of Human Bonding: A Message to Women from a Concerned Man. Chester D. Shupe. 600p. (Orig.). 1989. 29.99 (*0-9622853-0-7*); pap. 18.50 (*0-9622853-1-5*) Spiritual Freedom.

Natural Penis Enlargement Vol. 8: Advanced Techniques for Liberated Lovers. (Sex Masters Collection). (Illus.). 60p. (Orig.). 1997. pap. write for info. (*1-890677-07-8*) Delphi Pr.

Natural Perfume Book: Simple, Sensual, Personal Aromatherapy Recipes. Mindy Green. LC 99-24391. 1999. pap. 12.95 (*1-883010-62-4*) Interweave.

Natural Perspective: The Development of Shakespearean Comedy & Romance. Northrop Frye. 176p. (C). 1995. pap. 15.00 (*0-231-08271-1*) Col U Pr.

Natural Perspective: The Development of Shakespearean Comedy & Romance. Northrop Frye. LC 65-17458. 180p. 1969. reprint ed. pap. 6.95 (*0-15-665414-8*, Harvest Bks) Harcourt.

Natural Pest Control: Alternatives to Chemicals for the Home & Garden. 2nd rev. ed. Andrew Lopez. (Illus.). 158p. Date not set. pap. 19.95 (*0-9629768-4-9*) Harmonious Tech.

Natural Pest Control Agents: A Symposium. American Chemical Society, Division of Agricultura. LC 66-22355. (Advances in Chemistry Ser.: No. 53). (Illus.). 152p. 1966. reprint ed. pap. 47.20 (*0-608-03271-9*, 206379000007) Bks Demand.

Natural Pet Cures: Dog & Cat Care the Natural Way. John Heinerman. (Illus.). 352p. 1998. pap. 14.00 (*0-7352-0036-X*) PH Pr.

Natural Pet Cures: The Definitive Guide to Natural Remedies for Dogs & Cats. John Heinerman. LC 98-18803. 1998. 26.95 (*0-13-258484-0*) P-H.

***Natural Pharmacist.** Prima Pub Staff. 1999. text 491.32 (*0-7615-9016-1*) Prima Pub.

***Natural Pharmacist.** 8th rev. ed. Steven Bratman. (Natural Pharmacist Ser.). (Illus.). 2000. pap. 19.99 (*0-7615-2448-7*) Prima Pub.

***Natural Pharmacist: Discover Natural.** Prima. 176p. 1999. pap. 9.99 (*0-7615-2462-2*, Prima Health); pap. 9.99 (*0-7615-2463-0*, Prima Health); pap. 9.99 (*0-7615-2465-7*, Prima Health); pap. 9.99 (*0-7615-2467-3*, Prima Health); pap. 9.99 (*0-7615-2469-X*, Prima Health); pap. 9.99 (*0-7615-2471-1*, Prima Health) Prima Pub.

Natural Pharmacist: Ginko & Memory. Stephen Dentali. LC 98-50708. (Illus.). 164p. 2000. pap. 6.99 (*0-7615-1552-6*) Prima Pub.

Natural Pharmacist: Saw Palmetto & the Prostrate. Anna Barton. LC 98-49607. 208p. 2000. pap. 6.99 (*0-7615-1559-3*) Prima Pub.

***Natural Pharmacist: St John's Wort & Depression.** Stephen Bratman. LC 98-17492. (Illus.). 179p. 2000. pap. 6.99 (*0-7615-1553-4*) Prima Pub.

***Natural Pharmacist: Your Complete.** Prima. 1999. pap. 9.99 (*0-7615-2476-2*, Prima Health) Prima Pub.

***Natural Pharmacist: Your Complete Guide.** S. Fulder & B. Tabachnik. 1999. pap. 6.99 (*0-7615-1757-X*) Prima Pub.

Natural Pharmacist: Your Natural Health Guide to Diabetes. Kathi Head, M.D. LC 98-49613. (Natural Pharmacist Ser.). 192p. 2000. pap. 6.99 (*0-7615-1755-3*) Prima Pub.

Natural Pharmacist Guide to Antioxidants. Lisa Chavis. 1999. pap. 9.99 (*0-7615-1561-5*) Prima Pub.

Natural Pharmacist Guide to Creatine & Sports Performance. Edmund Burke. LC 98-48204. 208p. 1999. pap. 6.99 (*0-7615-1614-X*) Prima Pub.

Natural Pharmacist Guide to Osteoporosis. Sheila Dunn-Merritt & Judy L. Patrick. LC 98-33112. 208p. 1999. per. 6.99 (*0-7615-1618-2*) Prima Pub.

Natural Pharmacy: An Illustrated Guide to Natural Medicine. Miriam Polunin & Christopher Robbins. (Illus.). 144p. 1992. pap. 18.95 (*0-02-036041-X*) Macmillan.

Natural Pharmacy: From the Top Experts in the Field, Your Essential Guide to Vitamins, Herbs, Minerals & Homeopathic Remedies. rev. ed. Skye W. Lininger et al. LC 99-56624. 480p. 1999. pap. 24.95 (*0-7615-1967-X*) Prima Pub.

Natural Pharmacy Products: A Guide. 1991. lib. bdg. 77.95 (*0-8490-5118-5*) Gordon Pr.

Natural Pharmacy Products Guide. (Alternative Medicine Ser.). 1994. lib. bdg. 255.95 (*0-8490-9020-2*) Gordon Pr.

Natural Phenomena: Their Meaning, Depiction & Description in the Ancient Near East. Ed. by D. J. Meijer. 316p. pap. 53.25 (*0-444-85759-1*, North Holland) Elsevier.

Natural Philosophy of Albrecht Von Haller. Ed. by Shirley A. Roe & I. Bernard Cohen. LC 80-2109. (Development of Science Ser.). (Illus.). 1981. lib. bdg. 44.95 (*0-405-13874-1*) Ayer.

***Natural Philosophy of Chu Hsi (1130-1200)** Yung Sik Kim. LC 99-37252. (Memoirs of the American Philosophical Society Ser.: Vol. 235). 2000. 30.00 (*0-87169-235-X*) Am Philos.

Natural Philosophy of James Clerk Maxwell. P. M. Harman. LC 97-35703. (Illus.). 246p. (C). 1998. text 64.95 (*0-521-56102-7*) Cambridge U Pr.

Natural Philosophy of Leibniz. Ed. by Kathleen Okruhlik & James R. Brown. 352p. 1985. text 160.00 (*90-277-2145-9*, D Reidel) Kluwer Academic.

Natural Philosophy of Time. 2nd ed. G. J. Whitrow. (Illus.). 410p. 1981. pap. text 37.50 (*0-19-858215-3*) OUP.

Natural Philosophy Through the 18th Century & Allied Topics. Ed. by A. Ferguson. 172p. 1972. 33.00 (*0-85066-055-6*) Taylor & Francis.

Natural Phonology: The State of the Art. Societas Linguistica Europaea Staff. Ed. by Bernhard Hurch & Richard A. Rhodes. LC 96-20774. (Trends in Linguistics Ser.: Vol. 92). xii, 348p. 1996. lib. bdg. 124.45 (*3-11-014795-5*) Mouton.

Natural Physical Sources of Underwater Sound Sea Surface Sound (2) Proceedings of the Conference on "Natural Physical Sources of Underwater Sound", Cambridge, U.K., July 3-6, 1990. Ed. by B. R. Kerman. LC 92-39158. 768p. (C). 1993. text 392.50 (*0-7923-2071-9*) Kluwer Academic.

Natural Physician: Your Health Guide for Common Ailments. 2nd ed. Mark Stengler. 230p. 1997. pap. 12.95 (*0-920470-46-7*) Alive Bks.

Natural Places of the Gulf Coast from Florida to Texas: A Traveler's Guide to the Culture . . . Fraser Bridges. (Illus.). 352p. 1996. pap. text 18.00 (*0-7615-0570-9*) Prima Pub.

An Asterisk (*) at the beginning of an entry indicates that the title is appearing for the first time.

Natural Places of the Northwest. Donald Stone. (Natural Places Ser.). (Illus.). 400p. 1996. pap. 17.95 (*0-7615-0159-2*) Prima Pub.

Natural Places of the Southwest. Fraser Bridges. (Natural Places Ser.). (Illus.). 432p. 1996. pap. 17.95 (*0-7615-0158-4*) Prima Pub.

Natural Plant Growth Inhibitors & Phytohormones. V. I. Kefeli. (Illus.). 1978. text 141.50 (*90-6193-580-6*) Kluwer Academic.

Natural Plant Hydrocoleoids in Chemistry. S. Stoloff. (C). 1991. text 350.00 (*0-89771-660-4*, Pub. by Intl Bk Distr) St Mut.

Natural Plant Hydrocolloids: A Collection of Papers Comprising the Symposium of Natural Plant Hydrocolloids, Presented Before the Divisions of Colloid Chemistry & Agricultural & Food Chemistry at the 122nd Meeting of the American Chemical Society, Atlantic City, NJ, September 1952. American Chemical Society Staff. LC 55-367. (Advances in Chemistry Ser.: Vol. 11). (Illus.). 107p. 1954. reprint ed. pap. 33.20 (*0-608-06908-6*, 206711600009) Bks Demand.

Natural Power Builders: A Pro & Con Look at Natural Steroids. Winifred Conkling. 1999. mass mkt. 5.99 (*0-312-97103-6*) St Martin.

Natural Power Builders Clip Strip. Winifred Conkling. 1998. 71.88 (*0-312-97105-2*) St Martin.

Natural Prayers. Chet Raymo. LC 99-72103. 212p. 1999. 22.00 (*1-886913-29-3*, Pub. by Ruminator Bks) Consort Bk Sales.

*__Natural Prayers.__ Chet Raymo. 2000. pap. 15.00 (*1-886913-45-5*) Ruminator Bks.

*__Natural Pregnancy A-Z.__ Carolle Jean-Murat. (Illus.). 156p. 2001. pap. 11.95 (*1-56170-794-5*, L479) Hay House.

*__Natural Pregnancy A-Z.__ Carolle Jean Murat. LC 99-45797. (Illus.). 156p. 2000. 19.95 (*1-56170-709-0*, L461) Hay House.

Natural Pregnancy Book: Herbs, Nutrition, & Other Holistic Choices. Aviva J. Romm. LC 97-11514. (Illus.). 304p. 1997. pap. 19.95 (*0-89594-819-2*) Crossing Pr.

Natural Premises: Ecology & Peasant Life in the Western Himalaya, 1800-1950. Chetan Singh. LC 97-914021. (Illus.). 272p. (C). 1998. text 27.95 (*0-19-564276-7*) OUP.

Natural Prescriptions: Dr. Giller's Natural Treatments & Vitamin Therapies for More Than 100 Common Ailments. Robert M. Giller & Kathy Matthews. 400p. 1995. pap. 14.00 (*0-345-37408-8*) Ballantine Pub Grp.

Natural Prescriptions for Women. Robert M. Giller & Kathy Matthews. LC 94-34330. 400p. 1997. 29.98 (*0-941683-38-9*) Instant Improve.

Natural Prescriptions for Women: What to Do - & When to Do It - to Solve Dozens of Female Health Problems - Without Drugs. For Women Editors & Susan Berg. LC 98-10112. (Illus.). 512p. 1998. 29.95 (*0-87596-433-8*) Rodale Pr Inc.

Natural Prescriptions for Women: What to Do - And When to Do It - To Solve More Than 100 Female Problems. Ed. by Prevention Health Books Staff & Susan Berg. LC 98-10112. (Illus.). 576p. 2000. pap. 17.95 (*0-87596-434-6*) Rodale Pr Inc.

Natural Procreation Alternatives: For Men with Low Sperm Counts in Childbearing Efforts. Howard W. Gabriel, III. 16p. 1987. 14.95 incl. audio (*0-936997-14-1*, T87-12) M & H Enter.

Natural Product Chemistry: A Mechanistic & Biosynthetic Approach to Secondary Metabolism. Kurt B. Torssell. LC 82-2045. 413p. reprint ed. pap. 128.10 (*0-7837-0199-3*, 204049500017) Bks Demand.

Natural Product Medicine: A Scientific Guide to Foods, Drugs, Cosmetics. Ara H. Der Marderosian & Lawrence E. Liberti. LC 85-62568. (Illus.). 400p. 1988. reprint ed. pap. 124.00 (*0-608-05868-8*, 20598350007) Bks Demand.

Natural Products. J. Mann. (C). 1994. pap. text 44.50 (*0-582-06009-5*, Pub. by Addison-Wesley) Longman.

Natural Products: A Laboratory Guide. 2nd ed. Raphael Ikan. (Illus.). 360p. 1991. text 65.00 (*0-12-370551-7*) Acad Pr.

Natural Products: Rapid Utilization of Sources for Drug Discovery & Development. Ed. by Nancy Mulford. (Biomedical Library). 352p. 1995. pap. 795.00 (*1-57936-009-2*) IBC USA.

Natural Products As Antiviral Agents. C. K. Chu & H. G. Cutler. LC 92-27287. (Illus.). 288p. (C). 1993. text 95.00 (*0-306-44346-5*, Kluwer Plenum) Kluwer Academic.

Natural Products Chemistry, Vol. III. Koji Nakanishi et al. LC 74-6431. (Illus.). 700p. 1984. 90.00 (*0-935702-14-8*) Univ Sci Bks.

Natural Products Drug Discovery: New Technologies to Increase Efficiency & Speed. Ed. by Wendy Mori. (Illus.). (Orig.). 1997. pap. write for info. (*1-57936-044-0*) IBC USA.

Natural Products from Plants. Peter B. Kaufman. LC 97-49038. 368p. 1998. boxed set 139.95 (*0-8493-3134-X*) CRC Pr.

Natural Products Isolation: Methods & Protocols. Ed. by Richard J. P. Cannell. LC 98-16651. (Methods in Biotechnology Ser.: No. 4). (Illus.). 480p. 1998. 89.50 (*0-89603-362-7*) Humana.

Natural Products Isolation: Spearation Methods for Antimicrobials, Antivirals, & Enzyme Inhibitors. Ed. by G. H. Wagman & R. Cooper. (Journal of Chromatography Library: No. 43). 620p. 1988. 255.75 (*0-444-87147-0*) Elsevier.

Natural Products of Woody Plants. Ed. by J. W. Rowe. (Wood Science Ser.). (Illus.). 1280p. 1990. 645.95 (*0-387-50300-5*) Spr-Verlag.

Natural Products Synthesis through Pericyclic Reactions. Ed. by Giovanni Desimoni et al. LC 83-12303. (ACS Monograph: No. 180). 456p. 1983. text 110.00 (*0-8412-0757-7*, Pub. by Am Chemical) OUP.

*__Natural Progesterone: The Multiple Roles of a Remarkable Hormone.__ 4th rev. ed. John R. Lee. (Illus.). VIII, 156p. 2000. pap. 12.00 (*0-9643737-3-4*) BLL Pubng.

Natural Progesterone: The Natural Way to Alleviate Symptoms of Menopause, PMS & Other Hormone-Related Problems. Anna Rushton & Shirley Bond. 1999. pap. 15.00 (*0-7225-3766-2*) Thorsons PA.

Natural Progesterone Cream. C. Norman Shealy. (Good Health Guides Ser.). 48p. 1998. pap. 3.95 (*0-87983-889-2*, 38892K, Keats Publng) NTC Contemp Pub Co.

Natural Protectants & Natural Toxicants in Food, Vol. 1. Ed. by Wayne R. Bidlak & Stanley T. Omaye. LC 94-61655. 137p. 1994. pap. text 39.95 (*1-56676-206-5*) Technomic.

Natural Prozac: Leaning to Release Your Body's Own Anti-Depressants. Joel C. Robertson & Tom Monte. LC 96-33513. 240p. 1998. pap. 13.00 (*0-06-251354-0*, Pub. by Harper SF) HarpC.

Natural Prozac Program: How to Use St. John's Wort, the Anti-Depressant Drug. Jonathan Zuess. LC 97-8064. 1997. pap. 10.00 (*0-609-80152-X*) Harmony Bks.

Natural Psychology & Human Transformation. rev. ed. Na'im Akbar. 65p. 1995. pap. 8.00 (*0-935257-04-7*) Mind Prods Assocs.

Natural Puerto Rico - Puerto Rico Natural. Alfonso Silva Lee. LC 97-28419. (ENG & SPA., Illus.). 128p. 1998. pap. 18.95 (*0-9630180-6-X*) Pangaea Pub.

Natural Radiation Environment: International Symposium on the Natural Radiation Environment, 1963 Houston, Texas. Ed. by Wayne M. Lowder. LC 64-12256. (Rice University Semicentennial Publications). 1083p. pap. 200.00 (*0-8357-8963-2*, 205676500085) Bks Demand.

Natural Radiation Environment III: Proceedings, 2 vols. Ed. by Thomas F. Gesell et al. LC 80-607130. (DOE Symposium Ser.). 1789p. 1980. fiche 5.00 (*0-87079-458-2*, CONF-780422) DOE.

Natural Radiation Environment III: Proceedings, 2 vols., Set. Ed. by Thomas F. Gesell et al. LC 80-607130. (DOE Symposium Ser.). 1789p. 1980. pap. 52.75 (*0-87079-129-X*, CONF-780422) DOE.

Natural Reality & Abstract Reality: An Essay in Trialogue Form (1919-1920) Piet Mondrian. Tr. by Martin James from DUT. LC 94-38785. 144p. 1995. pap. 14.95 (*0-8076-1372-X*, Pub. by Braziller) Norton.

Natural Reason: Essays in Honor of Joseph Norio Uemura. Ed. by Duane L. Cady & Ronald E. Beanblossom. LC 92-72687. 192p. (Orig.). 1992. text. write for info. (*0-9633686-1-3*); pap. text. write for info. (*0-9633686-0-5*) Hamline Univ.

Natural Reasons: Personality & Polity. S. L. Hurley. (Illus.). 480p. 1992. reprint ed. pap. text 29.95 (*0-19-508012-2*) OUP.

Natural Rebels: A Social History of Enslaved Women in Barbados. Hilary M. Beckles. LC 89-10767. 224p. (Orig.). (C). 1990. text 40.00 (*0-8135-1510-6*); pap. text 16.00 (*0-8135-1511-4*) Rutgers U Pr.

Natural Recipes for the Good Life: Using Wholesome Ingredients for Better Health. Hedi Levine. LC 96-50005. (Illus.). 256p. 1997. pap. 16.95 (*1-882606-74-4*) Peoples Med Soc.

Natural Reef Aquariums: Simplified Approaches to Creating Living Saltwater Microcosms. John H. Tullock. (Illus.). 288p. 1992. pap. 24.95 (*1-57630-024-2*, Chapters Bks) HM.

Natural Reef Aquariums: Simplified Approaches to Creating Living Saltwater Microcosms. John H. Tullock. (Illus.). 288p. 1996. 35.00 (*1-57630-003-X*, Chapters Bks) HM.

Natural Reef Aquariums: Simplified Approaches to Creating Living Saltwater Microcosms. John H. Tullock. Ed. by James Lawrence. LC 97-1440. (Illus.). 336p. 1997. 39.95 (*1-890087-01-7*); pap. 29.95 (*1-890087-00-9*) Microcosm Ltd.

Natural Regeneration in Two Central Idaho Grand Fir Habitat Types. Kathleen Geier-Hayes. (Illus.). 24p. 1998. reprint ed. pap. 3.40 (*0-89904-900-1*, Ecosytems Resrch) Crumb Elbow Pub.

Natural Regeneration of Douglas Fir in the Black Forest see Naturverjuengung der Douglasie Im Schwarzwald Inventur und Analyse Von Umwelt und Konkurrenzfaktoren Sowie Eine Naturschutzfachliche Bewertung

Natural Relations? Ecology, Animal Rights & Social Justice. Ted Benton. 280p. (C). 1993. pap. 19.00 (*0-86091-590-5*, A9732, Pub. by Verso) Norton.

Natural Relief for Your Child's Asthma: A Guide to Controlling Asthma & Reducing Your Child's. Steven J. Bock et al. LC 98-43771. (Illus.). 304p. 1999. pap. 13.95 (*0-06-095289-X*) HarpC.

Natural Relief from Constipation. Donna Dimarco. (Good Health Guides Ser.). 48p. 1999. pap. 3.95 (*0-87983-958-9*, 39589K, Keats Publng) NTC Contemp Pub Co.

Natural Relief from Headaches, Insomnia & Stress. David Hoffmann. LC 99-25559. 240p. 1999. pap. 14.95 (*0-87983-982-1*, 39821K, Keats Publng) NTC Contemp Pub Co.

Natural Relief from Tinnitus. Paul Yanick. (Good Health Guides Ser.). 50p. 1995. pap. 3.95 (*0-87983-655-5*, 36555K, Keats Publng) NTC Contemp Pub Co.

Natural Religion. Friedrich M. Mueller. LC 73-18810. (Gifford Lectures: 1888). reprint ed. 49.50 (*0-404-11450-4*) AMS Pr.

Natural Religion & Christian Theology: First & Second Series, 2 vols., Set. Charles E. Raven. LC 77-27176. (Gifford Lectures: 1951-52). reprint ed. 37.50 (*0-404-60540-0*) AMS Pr.

Natural Religion & the Nature of Religion. Peter Byrne. 272p. 1989. 62.00 (*0-415-04104-X*, A3564) Routledge.

*__Natural Remediation of Environmental Contaminants: Its Role in Ecological Risk Assessment & Risk Management.__ Charles M. Swindoll et al. (Illus.). 2000. write for info. (*1-880611-33-3*, SETAC Pr) SETAC.

*__Natural Remedies.__ 208p. 1998. pap. 16.95 (*0-14-019543-2*, Pub. by Pnguin Bks Ltd) Trafalgar.

Natural Remedies. Day. (Threshold Picture Guide Ser.: No. 35). (Illus.). 24p. 1996. pap. 12.00 (*1-872082-79-3*) Half Halt Pr.

Natural Remedies. Norman Ford. 1995. 8.98 (*0-88365-901-8*) Galahad Bks.

Natural Remedies: A Manual. Phylis Austin et al. 171p. (Orig.). 1983. reprint ed. pap. 6.95 (*1-878726-14-5*) Fam Hlth Pubns.

Natural Remedies: Nondrug Healing Strategies That Work Best. Prevention Health Books for Women Staff. LC 99-19847. (Women's Edge Health Enhancement Guides). 1999. write for info. (*1-57954-103-8*) Rodale Pr Inc.

*__Natural Remedies & Supplements: All-in-One Guide to Vitamins, Minerals, Enzymes, Amino Acids, Fats, Herbs, Aromatherapy, Flower Remedies, Phytochemicals, Nutraceticals.__ Elvis Ali et al. LC 99-41819. 392p. 2000. pap. 9.95 (*1-886508-28-3*, Pub. by Adi Gaia Esalen) Genl Dist Srvs.

Natural Remedies for a Healthy Heart: Remarkable Breakthroughs for Lowering Cholesterol, Lessening Blood Pressure, & Reversing Cardiovascular Disease. David Heber. LC 98-154518. (Illus.). xi, 196p. 1997. pap. 9.95 (*0-89529-808-2*, Avery) Penguin Putnam.

Natural Remedies for a Healthy Heart: Remarkable Breakthroughs for Lowering Cholesterol, Lessening Blood Pressure, & Reversing Cardiovascular Disease. David Heber. 1999. mass mkt. 6.95 (*0-89529-901-1*, Avery) Penguin Putnam.

*__Natural Remedies for Allergies: Safe Self-Help Measures for Treating a Wide Range of Modern Allergies.__ Paul Morgan. 128p. 1999. reprint ed. text 25.00 (*0-7881-6783-9*) DIANE Pub.

Natural Remedies for Better Health. 2nd rev. ed. Ingrid Sherman. LC 90-39261. (Illus.). 224p. 1994. pap. 8.95 (*0-87961-213-4*) Naturegraph.

Natural Remedies for Common Ailments. Constance Mellor. 134p. 1980. 17.95 (*0-8464-1073-7*) Beekman Pubs.

Natural Remedies for Common Ailments Handbook. Celeste White. LC 96-94470. ii, 63p. (Orig.). 1996. pap. 7.95 (*0-9653024-0-7*) Keswick Hse.

Natural Remedies for Dogs & Cats. C. J. Puotinen. LC 99-26191. 244p. 1998. pap. 14.95 (*0-87983-827-2*, 38272K, Keats Publng) NTC Contemp Pub Co.

*__Natural Remedies for Hayfever: Self-Help Measures for Treating the Symptoms of Hayfever Naturally.__ Paul Morgan. (Illus.). 128p. 2000. text 27.00 (*0-7881-6983-1*) DIANE Pub.

Natural Remedies for Pet Ailments. John Heinerman. (C). 1998. pap. 12.95 (*0-13-258476-X*, Macmillan Coll) P-H.

Natural Remedies for Stress. Judith Sachs. 528p. (C). 1996. text 22.95 (*0-13-243338-9*) P-H.

Natural Remedies from the Chinese Cupboard: Healing Foods & Herbs. Fang Jing Pei. LC 98-34671. 128p. 1998. pap. 10.95 (*0-8348-0459-X*) Weatherhill.

Natural Remedies from the Japanese Kitchen. Hiroko Fukuhara & Yasuko Takahata. LC 98-18624. (Illus.). 160p. 1998. pap. 14.95 (*0-8348-0414-X*) Weatherhill.

Natural Remedy Bible: Everyone's Guide to the Natural of Healing. John B. Lust & Michael Tierra. Ed. by Paul McCarthy. 384p. 1990. reprint ed. mass mkt. 6.99 (*0-671-66127-2*) PB.

Natural Remedy Book for Dogs & Cats. Diane Stein. LC 94-22084. (Illus.). 341p. 1994. pap. 16.95 (*0-89594-686-6*) Crossing Pr.

Natural Remedy Book for Women. Diane Stein. (Illus.). 348p. (Orig.). 1992. pap. 16.95 (*0-89594-525-8*) Crossing Pr.

Natural Resistance of Plants to Pests: Roles of Allelochemicals. Ed. by Maurice B. Green & Paul A. Hedin. LC 85-28748. (ACS Symposium Ser.: No. 296). (Illus.). x, 256p. 1986. 49.95 (*0-8412-0950-2*) Am Chemical.

Natural Resistance of Plants to Pests: Roles of Allelochemicals. Ed. by Maurice B. Green & Paul A. Hedin. LC 85-28748. (ACS Symposium Ser.: Vol. 296). 256p. 1986. reprint ed. pap. 79.40 (*0-608-03923-3*, 206437000009) Bks Demand.

Natural Resistance to Tumors & Viruses. Ed. by O. Haller. (Current Topics in Microbiology & Immunology Ser.: Vol. 92). (Illus.). 200p. 1981. 59.00 (*0-387-10732-0*) Spr-Verlag.

Natural Resource & Environmental Economics. Tony Prato. LC 97-25983. (Illus.). 358p. 1997. 49.95 (*0-8138-2938-0*) Iowa St U Pr.

Natural Resource & Environmental Economics. 2nd ed. Roger Perman. LC 99-21560. 1999. pap. text. write for info. (*0-582-36876-6*) Addison-Wesley.

Natural Resource Base Development. Ed. by N. S. Rahtore & M. L. Sukhadia. (C). 1991. 250.00 (*0-7855-6761-5*, Pub. by Scientific Pubs) St Mut.

Natural Resource Commodities: A Century of Statistics, Prices, Output, Consumption, Foreign Trade & Employment in the U. S., 1870-1973. Robert S. Manthy. LC 78-8429. (Resources for the Future Ser.). 1978. text 25.00 (*0-8018-2142-8*) Johns Hopkins.

Natural Resource Commodities: A Century of Statistics: Prices, Output, Consumption, Foreign Trade, & Employment in the United States, 1870-1973. Robert S. Manthy. Ed. by Joan R. Tron. LC 78-8429. 254p. reprint ed. pap. 78.80 (*0-8357-4682-8*, 203762900008) Bks Demand.

Natural Resource Conservation: Management for a Sustainable Future. 7th ed. Oliver S. Owen & Daniel D. Chiras. LC 97-7765. 594p. (C). 1997. 90.00 (*0-13-840133-0*) P-H.

Natural Resource Damages. Preston, Thorgrimson, Shidler, Gates & Ellis Staff et al. 234p. 1993. pap. 79.00 (*0-86587-340-2*) Gov Insts.

Natural Resource Development & Social Impact in the North. James S. Frideres & Joseph E. DiSanto. (American University Studies: Anthropology & Science: Ser. XI, Vol. 42). (Illus.). 222p. (C). 1990. text 48.95 (*0-8204-0913-8*) P Lang Pubng.

Natural Resource Economics. Field. 496p. 2000. pap. 45.00 (*0-07-231677-2*) McGraw.

Natural Resource Economics: Notes & Problems. Jon M. Conrad & Colin W. Clark. (Illus.). 254p. 1987. text 85.00 (*0-521-33188-9*); pap. text 26.95 (*0-521-33769-0*) Cambridge U Pr.

Natural Resource Economics: Selected Papers of Allen V. Kneese. Allen V. Kneese. LC 95-7200. (New Horizons in Environmental Economics Ser.). 512p. 1995. 110.00 (*1-85898-173-5*) E Elgar.

Natural Resource Information for Economic Development. Orris C. Herfindahl. LC 69-15762. (Resources for the Future Ser.). (Illus.). 227p. 1969. 19.50 (*0-8018-1026-4*) Johns Hopkins.

Natural Resource Management & Institutional Change. Diana Carney & John Farrington. LC 97-44290. 136p. (C). 1998. 60.00 (*0-415-18604-8*) Routledge.

Natural Resource Policy & Income Distribution. Adam Rose et al. LC 87-2788. (Illus.). 158p. reprint ed. pap. 49.00 (*0-608-06134-4*, 206646700008) Bks Demand.

Natural Resource Policymaking in Developing Countries: Environment, Economic Growth, & Income Distribution. William L. Ascher & Robert G. Healy. LC 90-2743. 239p. (Orig.). (C). 1990. pap. text 19.95 (*0-8223-1049-X*) Duke.

Natural Resource Pricing in China: Water Supply, Coal & Timber. LI Yining & Jeremy J. Warford. (Illus.). 150p. 1998. pap. text 20.00 (*0-9669004-0-5*) MRM Intl Pr.

Natural Resource Taxation: Cases & Materials. Richard A. Westin. LC 87-62536. 484p. (C). 1987. pap. text 35.00 (*0-916081-07-9*) J Marshall Pub Co.

*__Natural Resource Valuation & Policy in Brazil.__ Peter May. 352p. 1999. 55.00 (*0-231-10826-5*) Col U Pr.

Natural Resource Valuation & Policy in Brazil: Methods & Cases. Peter H. May. LC 99-25861. (Methods & Cases in Conservation Science Ser.). 352p. 1999. pap. 28.00 (*0-231-10827-3*) Col U Pr.

Natural Resources see Alaska Administrative Code--Register 151 Supplement (October 1999)

Natural Resources see Alaska Administrative Code--Register 150 Supplement (July 1999)

Natural Resources, 3 vols. Ed. by Craig Allin & Mark Coyne. LC 97-43364. (Illus.). 978p. 1998. lib. bdg. 315.00 (*0-89356-912-7*) Salem Pr.

Natural Resources. Damian Randle. LC 93-25195. (Young Geographer Ser.). (Illus.). 32p. (J). 1993. lib. bdg. 21.40 (*1-56847-056-8*) Raintree Steck-V.

Natural Resources, Binder 5, Title 11. write for info. (*0-327-06376-9*) LEXIS Pub.

Natural Resources: Cases & Materials. Barlow Burke. 398p. (C). 1998. 44.95 (*0-87084-108-4*) Anderson Pub Co.

Natural Resources: Defense & Interior Can Better Manage Land Withdrawn for Military Use. (Illus.). 57p. (Orig.). (C). 1995. pap. text 30.00 (*0-7881-2238-X*) DIANE Pub.

*__Natural Resources: Ecology, Economics, & Policy.__ Holechek. LC 99-55590. 730p. (C). 1999. 89.00 (*0-13-896077-1*, Macmillan Coll) P-H.

Natural Resources & Conflicts in the Changing International System: Three Studies on Imperialism. Jyrki Kakonen. 251p. 1988. text 69.95 (*0-566-05548-1*, Pub. by Dartmth Pub) Ashgate Pub Co.

Natural Resources & Development: An Annotated Bibliography. William James & David Short. LC 87-81840. xii, 297p. 1987. lib. bdg. 45.00 (*0-89941-577-6*, 305290) W S Hein.

Natural Resources & Economic Growth: Papers Presented at a Conference, Ann Arbor, Michigan, April 7-9, 1960. Ed. by Joseph J. Spengler. LC 77-86411. (Resources for the Future Ser.). 320p. reprint ed. 57.50 (*0-404-60344-0*) AMS Pr.

*__Natural Resources & Environmental Administrative Law & Procedure.__ (Mineral Law Ser.). 600p. 1999. ring bd. 125.00 (*0-929047-84-2*) Rocky Mtn Mineral Law Found.

Natural Resources & Environmental Litigation, No. II. (Mineral Law Ser.: No. 4). 500p. 1996. text 125.00 (*0-929047-61-3*) Rocky Mtn Mineral Law Found.

Natural Resources & Natural Development in Arid Lands: Case Studies from Sudan. 84p. 1986. pap. 15.00 (*92-808-0504-5*, E.85.III.A.5) UN.

Natural Resources & Social Conflicts in the Sahel: Proceedings of the 5th Sahel Workshop 4-6 January 1993. Ed. by Leon Brimer et al. (Illus.). 232p. (C). 1994. pap. 25.00 (*87-984671-0-7*, Pub. by Aarhus Univ Pr) David Brown.

Natural Resources & the Environment: Community Development Issues. Ed. by Ntam Baharanyi et al. LC 97-60977. 336p. 1997. pap. write for info. (*1-891196-00-6*) Tuskegee U CAENS.

Natural Resources & the Macroeconomy. Ed. by J. Peter Neary & Sweder Van Wijnbergen. 336p. 1986. 40.00 (*0-262-14041-1*) MIT Pr.

N

Natural Resources Base Development. N. S. Rathore. (C). 1992. pap. 45.00 (*81-7233-032-4*, Pub. by Scientific Pubs) St Mut.

*__Natural Resources Development & Environmental Regulation in Indian Country.__ (Mineral Law Ser.: No. 3). 600p. 1999. ring bd. 125.00 (*0-929047-81-8*, IL2M) Rocky Mtn Mineral Law Found.

Natural Resources Development in the Sahel: The Role of the United Nations Systems. 95p. pap. 10.00 (*92-808-0422-7*, E.86.III.A.3) UN.

Natural Resources Economics. Wilfred H. Pine. 1977. pap. 4.00 (*0-686-00368-3*) AG Pr.

Natural Resources Economics & Policy Applications: Essays in Honor of James A. Crutchfield. Ed. by Edward L. Miles et al. 448p. 1986. 30.00 (*0-295-96345-X*) U of Wash Pr.

Natural Resources, Energy, & Environmental Law, 1995: The Year in Review. 352p. 1996. pap. 39.95 (*1-57073-283-3*, 535-0049, ABA Natl Res) Amer Bar Assn.

Natural Resources for the Twenty-First Century. Ed. by R. Neil Sampson & Dwight Hair. LC 89-19946. 347p. (Orig.). 1989. pap. text 25.00 (*1-55963-002-7*) Island Pr.

Natural Resources for U. S. Growth: A Look Ahead to the Year 2000. Hans H. Landsberg. LC 64-24348. 269p. reprint ed. pap. 83.40 (*0-7837-3120-5*, 204286700006) Bks Demand.

Natural Resources, Growth & Development: Economics, Ecology & Resource-Scarcity. Clement A. Tisdell. LC 90-42118. 200p. 1990. 57.95 (*0-275-93479-9*, C3479, Greenwood Pr) Greenwood.

Natural Resources in Colorado & Wyoming. Ed. by Duane A. Smith. (Illus.). 71p. (Orig.). 1982. pap. text 15.00 (*0-89745-038-8*) Sunflower U Pr.

Natural Resources in European History: A Conference Report. Ed. by Antoni Maczak & William N. Parker. LC 78-24688. (RFF Research Paper Ser.: No. R-13). 238p. pap. 73.80 (*0-8357-4683-6*, 203763000008) Bks Demand.

Natural Resources in Latin American Development. Joseph Grunwald & Philip Musgrove. LC 77-108381. 512p. reprint ed. pap. 158.80 (*0-608-12534-2*, 202379800034) Bks Demand.

N

Natural Resources in U. S.-Canadian Relations: Patterns & Trends in Resource Supplies & Policies, Vol. 2. Ed. by Carl E. Beigie & Alfred O. Hero, Jr. 1980. pap. text 14.50 (*0-89158-878-7*) Westview.

Natural Resources in U. S.-Canadian Relations: Patterns & Trends in Resource Supplies & Policies, Vol. 2. Ed. by Carl E. Beigie & Alfred O. Hero, Jr. 1980. text 43.00 (*0-89158-555-9*) Westview.

Natural Resources in U. S.-Canadian Relations: The Evolution of Policies & Issues, Vol. 1. Ed. by Carl E. Beigie & Alfred O. Hero, Jr. (Illus.). 362p. 1980. text 42.00 (*0-89158-554-0*) Westview.

Natural Resources Law: Cases & Materials. Jan G. Laitos. LC 85-13787. (American Casebook Ser.). 283p. (C). 1985. teacher ed. write for info. (*0-314-95851-7*) West Pub.

Natural Resources Law: Cases & Materials, Vols. 1-2. W. Jack Grosse. Ed. by Helen B. Brinker. 1482p. (C). 1993. ring bd. 149.95 (*0-9637695-0-2*) Gatewy Pub.

Natural Resources Law Handbook. Donald C. Baur et al. 363p. 1991. pap. text 79.00 (*0-86587-243-0*) Gov Insts.

Natural Resources Law in Australia: A Macro-Legal System in Operation. D. E. Fisher. li, 551p. 1987. pap. 84.00 (*0-455-20769-0*, Pub. by LawBk Co) Gaunt.

Natural Resources Law Manual. LC 95-77118. 512p. 1995. pap. 80.00 (*1-57073-212-4*, 535-0051, ABA Natl Res) Amer Bar Assn.

*__Natural Resources Management Practices: A Primer.__ Peter Ffolliott et al. (Illus.). 296p. 2000. 39.95 (*0-8138-2541-5*) Iowa St U Pr.

Natural Resources of the Garifuna of Orinoco, Nicaragua. Ed. by Virginia Nickerson & Doreen White. (Illus.). 108p. (Orig.). pap. 7.00 (*0-9637982-4-3*) Orang-Utan Pr.

Natural Resources Policy & Law: Trends & Directions. Ed. by Lawrence J. MacDonnell & Sarah F. Bates. LC 93-8388. 280p. 1993. text 45.00 (*1-55963-245-3*); pap. text 25.00 (*1-55963-246-1*) Island Pr.

Natural Resources, Sections 8-101 to End see Michie's Annotated Code of Maryland, 1998 Supplement

Natural Resources, Sections 1-101 - 7-909 see Michie's Annotated Code of Maryland, 1998 Supplement

Natural Rhythms. Joan M. Giusto. Ed. by William D. Moser. (Mechiah Ser.). 50p. (Orig.). (J). (ps). 1994. pap. 6.95 (*0-9633307-2-1*) Poets Farm Pr.

Natural Rider: A Right-Brain Approach to Riding. Mary Wanless. (Illus.). 320p. 1996. reprint ed. pap. 13.95 (*1-57076-038-1*, Trafalgar Sq Pub) Trafalgar.

Natural Right & History. Leo Strauss. 335p. 1965. pap. 16.00 (*0-226-77694-8*, P195) U Ch Pr.

Natural Right & Political Right: Essays in Honor of Harry W. Jaffa. Ed. by Thomas B. Silver & Peter W. Schramm. LC 84-70180. 444p. 1985. reprint ed. lib. bdg. 35.00 (*0-89089-279-2*) Carolina Acad Pr.

Natural Right & the American Imagination: Political Philosophy in Novel Form. Catherine H. Zuckert. LC 89-34917. 284p. (C). 1990. lib. bdg. 52.50 (*0-8476-7611-0*) Rowman.

Natural Right & the American Imagination: Political Philosophy in Novel Form. Catherine H. Zuckert. 284p. 1991. pap. 16.95 (*0-8476-7696-X*) Rowman.

Natural Right in the American Founding: Essays in the Theory & Practice of American Politics. Edward J. Erler. 170p. 1991. pap. 36.95 (*0-8448-1608-6*, Crane Russak) Taylor & Francis.

Natural Rights: An Update to the Soul of Liberty. Fred E. Foldvary. 32p. (Orig.). (C). 1985. pap. 5.00 (*0-9603872-7-7*) Gutenberg.

Natural Rights & Natural Law: The Legacy of George Mason. Ed. by Robert P. Davidow. (George Mason Lectures). (Illus.). 270p. (Orig.). 1986. pap. text 21.25 (*0-8026-0001-8*); lib. bdg. 46.50 (*0-8026-0000-X*) Univ Pub Assocs.

Natural Rights & the New Republicanism. Michael P. Zuckert. LC 94-5498. 422p. 1994. text 49.50 (*0-691-03463-X*, Pub. by Princeton U Pr); pap. text 18.95 (*0-691-05970-5*, Pub. by Princeton U Pr) Cal Prin Full Svc.

Natural Rights Republic: Studies in the Foundation of the American Political Tradition. Michael P. Zuckert. LC 96-9756. 305p. 1999. pap. text 23.00 (*0-268-01487-6*) U of Notre Dame Pr.

Natural Rights Theories: Their Origin & Development. Richard Tuck. LC 78-73819. 193p. 1982. pap. text 19.95 (*0-521-28509-7*) Cambridge U Pr.

Natural Risk & Civil Protection. Ed. by Tom Horlick-Jones et al. (Illus.). 576p. (C). 1995. 135.00 (*0-419-19970-5*, E & FN Spon) Routledge.

Natural Roots of Morality: Observations from the Science of Hermeneutics. Carl R. Selnes. 200p. mass mkt. 12.95 (*1-55197-288-3*) Picasso Publ.

Natural Rose Gardener. Storey Publishing Staff. 1997. pap. 17.95 (*0-676-57122-0*) Random.

Natural Rose Gardener. Lance Walheim. Ed. by Scott Millard. LC 94-75792. (Illus.). 160p. 1994. pap. 17.95 (*0-9628236-3-5*) Ironwood AZ.

Natural Rubber: Biology, Cultivation, & Technology. Ed. by M. R. Sethuraj & N. M. Mathew. LC 92-28340. (Developments in Crop Science Ser.: Vol. 23). 610p. 1992. 264.25 (*0-444-88329-0*) Elsevier.

Natural Rubber Market: Review, Analysis, Policies & Outlook. Kees et al. (Rubber Trade in NY Ser.). 368p. 1997. pap. 710.00 (*1-85573-321-8*, Pub. by Woodhead Pubng) Am Educ Systs.

Natural Salvation: The Message of Science, Outlining the First Principles of Immortal Life on the Earth. Charles A. Stephens. Ed. by Robert J. Kastenbaum. LC 76-19588. (Death & Dying Ser.). 1977. reprint ed. lib. bdg. 21.95 (*0-405-09583-X*) Ayer.

Natural Science: Bridging the Gaps. 3rd ed. Charles M. Wynn & Arthur W. Wiggins. 196p. (C). 1994. text 45.00 (*0-536-58564-4*) Pearson Custom.

Natural Science: Bridging the Gaps. 4th ed. Charles M. Wynn & Arthur W. Wiggins. LC 98-114320. 196p. (C). 1997. text 34.00 (*0-536-00756-X*) Pearson Custom.

Natural Science: Study Guide (Custom Edition) 2nd ed. Ed. by Frola. (C). 1997. text, student ed. 15.94 (*0-321-01286-0*) Addison-Wesley.

Natural Science & Religion. Asa Gray. (Notable American Authors Ser.). 1992. reprint ed. lib. bdg. 75.00 (*0-7812-2949-9*) Rprt Serv.

Natural Science Biology. Frola. 1998. student ed. 6.50 (*0-07-154036-9*) McGraw.

Natural Science Centers Conference, 1974, Nashville, Tennessee: Proceedings. Natural Science Centers Conference Staff. Ed. by John F. Gardner. (Illus.). (Orig.). 1975. 5.00 (*0-916544-04-4*) Natural Sci Youth.

Natural Science Education in the German Elementary School. Lois M. Shoemaker. LC 77-177788. (Columbia University. Teachers College. Contributions to Education Ser.: No. 445). reprint ed. 37.50 (*0-404-55445-8*) AMS Pr.

Natural Science Laboratory Manual. John B. Curtis et al. (Illus.). 87p. (C). 1996. pap. text, lab manual ed. 9.80 (*1-889766-01-1*) Columbus State Bks.

Natural Science 097: An Introduction to a Scientific Inquiry Student Activities. Michael Mimnaugh. 240p. (C). 1996. ring bd. 35.95 (*0-7872-2440-5*, 41244001) Kendall-Hunt.

Natural Science of the Ancient Hindus. Surendranath Dasgupta. Ed. by Debiprasad Chattopadhyaya. 99p. (C). 1987. 9.50 (*81-208-0329-9*, Pub. by Motilal Bnarsidass) S Asia.

Natural Science of the Human Species: An Introduction to Comparative Behavioral Research: the "Russian Manuscript", 1944-1948. Konrad Lorenz. Ed. by Agnes Von Cranach. Tr. by Robert D. Martin. LC 94-48788.Tr. of Naturwissenschaft vom Menschen. (ENG & GER., Illus.). 384p. 1995. 37.50 (*0-262-12190-5*) MIT Pr.

Natural Science of the Human Species: An Introduction to Comparative Behavioral Research the Russian Manuscript 1944-1948. Konrad Lorenz. (Illus.). 384p. 1997. reprint ed. pap. text 18.00 (*0-262-62120-7*) MIT Pr.

Natural Science 1. John B. Curtis et al. (Illus.). 270p. (C). 1996. pap. text 15.72 (*1-889766-00-3*) Columbus State Bks.

Natural Sciences. Jack Rudman. (College Level Examination (CLEP) Ser.: Vol. ATS-9D). 43.95 (*0-8373-5298-3*) Nat Learn.

Natural Sciences. Jack Rudman. (College-Level Examination Series (General Examinations): ATS-9D). 1994. pap. 23.95 (*0-8373-5248-7*) Nat Learn.

Natural Sciences. Bernhard Bavink. LC 74-26248. (History, Philosophy & Sociology of Science Ser.). 1975. reprint ed. 58.95 (*0-405-06578-7*) Ayer.

*__Natural Sciences.__ 17th ed. ETS Staff. (Official GRE/CGS Directory of Graduate Programs Ser.: Vol. A). 2000. pap. 20.00 (*0-446-39661-3*) Warner Bks.

Natural Sciences & American Scientists in the Revolutionary Era: A Bibliography, 17. Compiled by Katalin Harkanyi. LC 90-45084. (Bibliographies & Indexes in American History Ser.: No. 17). 520p. 1990. lib. bdg. 85.00 (*0-313-26547-X*, HMN, Greenwood Pr) Greenwood.

Natural Sciences & Human Thought. Ed. by Robert Zwilling. LC 94-34410. 1995. write for info. (*3-540-57518-9*) Spr-Verlag.

Natural Sciences & Human Thought. Ed. by Robert Zwilling. LC 94-34410. 1995. 86.95 (*0-387-57518-9*) Spr-Verlag.

Natural Sciences & the Arts: Aspects of Interaction from the Renaissance to the 20th Century. James S. Ackerman. (Illus.). 178p. 1985. pap. text 47.50. (*91-554-1658-6*) Coronet Bks.

Natural Sciences & the Social Sciences: Some Critical & Historical Perspectives. Ed. by I. Bernard Cohen. LC 93-3226. (Boston Studies in the Philosophy of Science: Vol. 150). 448p. 1993. lib. bdg. 214.50 (*0-7923-2223-1*, Pub. by Kluwer Academic) Kluwer Academic.

Natural Sciences in America, 58 vols., Set. Ed. by Keir B. Sterling. 1974. 2800.00 (*0-405-05700-8*) Ayer.

Natural Sciences Know Nothing of Evolution: AW004. A. E. Wilder-Smith. 185p. 1981. pap. 6.99 (*0-89051-062-8*) Word for Today.

Natural Selection. Frederick Barthelme. 212p. 1990. 18.95 (*0-685-46943-3*, Viking) Viking Penguin.

Natural Selection. Gini Savage. 32p. (Orig.). 1997. pap. 8.00 (*1-887853-12-X*) Radiolarian.

Natural Selection: Domains, Levels, & Challenges. George C. Williams. (Oxford Series in Ecology & Evolution). (Illus.). 224p. 1992. pap. text 35.00 (*0-19-506933-1*) OUP.

Natural Selection, Heredity & Eugenics. J. H. Bennett. (Illus.). 316p. 1983. text 49.95 (*0-19-858177-7*) OUP.

Natural Selection in the Wild. John A. Endler. LC 85-42683. (Monographs in Population Biology: No. 21). (Illus.). 240p. 1985. pap. text 25.95 (*0-691-08387-8*, Pub. by Princeton U Pr) Cal Prin Full Svc.

Natural Selection of Autonomy. Bruce N. Waller. LC 97-37753. (SUNY Series in Philosophy & Biology). 224p. (C). 1998. text 54.50 (*0-7914-3819-8*); pap. text 17.95 (*0-7914-3820-1*) State U NY Pr.

Natural Selection of the Chemical Elements: The Environment & Life's Chemistry. R. J. Williams & J. J. Frausto Da Silva. LC 95-24776. (Illus.). 672p. 1996. text 80.00 (*0-19-855843-0*) OUP.

Natural Selection of the Chemical Elements: The Environment & Life's Chemistry. Illus. by R. J. P. Williams. 672p. 1997. pap. text 55.00 (*0-19-855842-2*) OUP.

Natural Selections. Jeff Worley & Lance Olsen. 28p. (Orig.). 1992. pap. 5.00 (*1-877801-21-6*) Still Waters.

Natural Selections: A Year of Egypt's Wildlife. Richard Hoath. (Illus.). 160p. 1993. pap. 25.00 (*977-424-281-5*, Pub. by Am Univ Cairo Pr) Col U Pr.

Natural Sex see Challenge to Love

Natural Sex: How to Use Natural & Ancient Techniques to Create a More Passionate Love Life. Elena Oumano. LC 98-42311. 1999. pap. 13.95 (*0-452-28048-6*, Plume) Dutton Plume.

Natural Shade Garden. Ken Druse. 288p. 1992. 40.00 (*0-517-58017-9*) C Potter.

Natural Sinks of COB2S: Proceedings, Palmas Del Mar, Puerto Rico, 24-27 February 1992. Ed. by Joe Wisniewski & Ariel E. Lugo. LC 92-11240. 400p. (C). 1992. text 189.00 (*0-7923-1805-6*) Kluwer Academic.

Natural Skin Care: All You Need to Know for Healthy Skin. Cherie Dehaas. 1987. pap. 8.95 (*0-907061-94-X*, Pub. by Prism Pr) Assoc Pubs Grp.

Natural Skin Care: Alternative & Traditional Techniques. 2nd ed. Joni Loughran. LC 95-18914. (Illus.). 250p. (C). 1996. reprint ed. pap. 16.95 (*1-883319-75-7*) Frog Ltd CA.

Natural, Slag, Soda & Starch Blasting Abrasives. Dennis M. Zogbi. 98p. (Orig.). 1993. pap. 995.00 (*0-929717-19-8*) Paumanok Pubns.

Natural Soap Book: Making Herbal & Vegetable-Based Soaps. Susan M. Cavitch. (Illus.). 144p. 1995. pap. 14.95 (*0-88266-888-9*, Storey Pub) Storey Bks.

*__Natural Soapmaking.__ Marie Browning. (Illus.). 128p. 1999. pap. 14.95 (*0-8069-6289-5*) Sterling.

Natural Solutions: A Guide to a Better Complexion. Cecelia Phillips. 30p. (Orig.). 1989. pap. 6.95 (*0-9618870-1-X*) L C Ellsworth.

*__Natural Solutions for PMS.__ Angela Stengler & Mark Stengler. 1999. pap. 3.95 (*1-890694-13-4*) IMPAKT Communs.

*__Natural Solutions for Sexual Enhancement.__ large type ed. Howard Peiper & Nina Anderson. LC 98-61668. (Illus.). 88p. 1999. pap. 9.95 (*1-884820-42-5*) SAFE GOODS.

Natural Speaker. 3rd ed. Ed. by Allyn & Bacon Incorporated Staff. 48p. (C). 1999. write for info. (*0-205-30759-0*) Allyn.

Natural Speaker. 3rd ed. Randy Fujishin. LC PN4121.F77 2000. 168p. (C). 1999. pap. text 25.00 (*0-205-29575-4*, Longwood Div) Allyn.

Natural Spectacles. Debra B. Balken. (Illus.). 30p. 1996. 16.00 (*0-933519-33-8*) D W Bell Gallery.

*__Natural Spirituality: Recovering the Wisdom Tradition in Christianity.__ Joyce Rockwood Hudson. LC 99-95304. (Illus.). xx, 310p. 2000. pap. 16.95 (*1-893383-55-5*) JRH Pubns.

Natural Sportsman. Michael Biddulph & Deryck Murray. 87p. 1999. 60.00 (*1-897676-63-8*, Pub. by Nottingham Univ Pr) St Mut.

Natural Spring. Judy Gilley. Ed. by Sandra A. Stephens. (Illus.). 88p. (Orig.). 1984. pap. 5.97 (*0-9616013-0-2*) Midwest Media.

Natural State: A Literary Anthology of California Nature Writing. Steven Gilbar. LC 97-19119. 381p. 1998. 45.00 (*0-520-21208-8*, Pub. by U CA Pr) Cal Prin Full Svc.

Natural State: A Literary Anthology of California Nature Writing. Ed. by Steven Gilbar. LC 97-19119. 381p. 1998. pap. 15.95 (*0-520-21209-6*, Pub. by U CA Pr) Cal Prin Full Svc.

Natural State: Essays on Texas. Stephen Harrigan. LC 93-38793. (Illus.). 1994. reprint ed. pap. 12.95 (*0-292-73087-X*) U of Tex Pr.

Natural Step for Business: Wealth, Ecology, & the Evolutionary Corporation. Brian Naijrass & Mary Altomare. (Illus.). 222p. 1999. pap. 16.95 (*0-86571-384-7*, Pub. by New Soc Pubs) Consort Bk Sales.

Natural Stone: A Guide to Selection. Studio Marmo Staff. LC 98-7480. (Illus.). 288p. 1998. 85.00 incl. cd-rom (*0-393-73028-X*) Norton.

Natural Stonescapes: The Art & Craft of Stone Placement. Richard L. Dube & Frederick C. Campbell. LC 98-31046. 1999. pap. 24.95 (*1-58017-092-7*) Storey Bks.

Natural Study Guide. Ed. by D. D. Hamilton. 402p. (Orig.). 1991. pap. 65.00 (*1-878960-00-8*) WH&O Intl.

Natural Style: Contemporary Soft Furnishings from Cotton, Linen, Silk & Wool. Margot Richardson. (Illus.). 128p. 1997. 27.95 (*0-7063-7582-3*, Pub. by WrLock) Sterling.

Natural Style: Decorating Approaches for a Pure, Simple Home. Tessa Evelegh. 160p. 1998. 30.00 (*1-85967-592-1*, Lorenz Bks) Anness Pub.

Natural Style for Gardens. Francesca Greenoak. LC 98-29370. (Illus.). 160p. 1998. 35.00 (*1-57959-033-0*, SOMA) BB&T Inc.

Natural Sulfur Compounds: Novel Biochemical & Structural Aspects. International Meeting on Low Molecular Weight Sulf. Ed. by Doriano Cavallini et al. LC 79-28239. (Illus.). 568p. 1980. reprint ed. pap. 176.10 (*0-608-05433-X*, 206590200006) Bks Demand.

Natural Superiority of the Left-Hander. James T. de Kay. LC 79-15824. (Illus.). 128p. 1979. pap. 3.95 (*0-87131-307-3*) M Evans.

*__Natural Superiority of Women.__ 5th ed. Ashley Montagu. 300p. 1998. 62.00 (*0-7619-8981-1*); pap. 19.95 (*0-7619-8982-X*) AltaMira Pr.

Natural Supernaturalism: Tradition & Revolution in Romantic Literature. Meyer H. Abrams. 550p. 1973. reprint ed. pap. 17.95 (*0-393-00609-3*) Norton.

*__Natural Superwoman: The Survival Guide for Women Who Have Too Much to Do.__ Rosamund Richardson. (Illus.). 208p. 2000. pap. 17.95 (*0-89087-981-8*) Celestial Arts.

Natural Supplements for Your Cat. Shawn Messonnier. (Pet Care Naturally Ser.). 64p. 1998. pap. 4.95 (*0-87983-914-7*, Keats Publng) NTC Contemp Pub Co.

Natural Supplements for Your Dog. Shawn Messonnier. (Pet Care Naturally Ser.). 64p. 1998. pap. 4.95 (*0-87983-913-9*, Keats Publng) NTC Contemp Pub Co.

*__Natural Supports Foundation for Employment.__ John S. Trach & Debra L. Shelden. LC 99-16284. (Innovations Ser.). 1999. write for info. (*0-940898-65-9*) Am Assn Mental.

Natural Supports in Action: Strategies to Facilitate Employer Supports of Workers with Disabilities. Dale DiLeo et al. LC 95-36639. 81p. (Orig.). 1995. pap. 25.00 (*1-883302-10-2*) Trning Res.

Natural Supports in School, at Work, & in the Community for People with Severe Disabilities. Ed. by Jan Nisbet. LC 92-9855. 368p. 1992. pap. text 30.00 (*1-55766-101-4*) P H Brookes.

Natural Symbols: Explorations in Cosmology. 2nd ed. Mary Douglas. LC 96-203. 224p. (C). 1996. reprint ed. 80.00 (*0-415-13825-6*); reprint ed. pap. 22.99 (*0-415-13826-4*) Routledge.

Natural System of House Design. Charles G. Woods. LC 96-48319. (Illus.). 219p. 1997. 59.95 (*0-07-071736-2*) McGraw.

Natural Systems Digest. 200p. 1993. pap. 55.00 (*1-881369-31-5*, P0038) Water Environ.

Natural Systems for Wastewater Treatment. Water Pollution Control Federation Staff. LC 89-51687. (MOP Ser.; No. FD-16). (Illus.). 268p. (Orig.). 1989. pap. text 40.00 (*0-943244-31-5*) Water Environ.

Natural Technics in Piano Mastery. Jacob Eisenberg. 236p. 1991. reprint ed. lib. bdg. 79.00 (*0-7812-9352-9*) Rprt Serv.

Natural Tennis. David J. Staniford & John K. Boaz. (Illus.). 150p. (C). 1993. pap. text 12.95 (*0-87563-451-6*) Stipes.

Natural Theology. William Paley. 1986. reprint ed. pap. 33.95 (*0-935005-62-5*); reprint ed. lib. bdg. 50.95 (*0-935005-61-7*) Lincoln-Rembrandt.

Natural Theology. George G. Stokes. LC 77-27232. (Gifford Lectures: 1891). reprint ed. 39.00 (*0-404-60452-8*) AMS Pr.

Natural Theology, Poems. Kelly Cherry. LC 87-12479. 64p. (C). 1988. pap. 7.95 (*0-8071-1431-6*) La State U Pr.

Natural Theology vs. Theology of Nature - Natuerliche Theologie vs. Theologie der Natur? Tillich's Thinking As Impetus for a Discourse among Theology, Philosophy & Natural Sciences. Ed. by Gert Hummel. (Theologische Bibliothek Toepelmann Ser.: Vol. 60). (ENG & GER.). xiv, 286p. 1993. lib. bdg. 106.15 (*3-11-013926-X*) De Gruyter.

Natural Therapeutics, Vol. II. Henry Lindlahr. 108p. 1981. 17.95 (*0-85207-148-5*, Pub. by C W Daniel) Natl Bk Netwk.

Natural Therapeutics, Vol. III. Henry Lindlahr. 108p. 1983. 12.95 (*0-85207-155-8*, Pub. by C W Daniel) Natl Bk Netwk.

Natural Therapeutics, Vol. IV. Henry Lindlahr. 108p. 1985. pap. 17.50 (*0-85207-171-X*, Pub. by C W Daniel) Natl Bk Netwk.

Natural Therapeutics: Iridiagnosis, Vol. 4. Henry Lindlahr. 284p. pap. 26.95 (*0-685-71020-3*) Beekman Pubs.

Natural Therapeutics Vol. 1: Philosophy. Henry Lindlahr. 354p. (Orig.). pap. 35.95 (*0-8464-4258-2*) Beekman Pubs.

Natural Therapeutics Vol. 2: Practice. Henry Lindlahr. 328p. 26.95 (*0-8464-4259-0*) Beekman Pubs.

Natural Therapeutics Vol. 3: Natural Dietics. Henry Lindlahr. 184p. 19.95 (*0-8464-4260-4*) Beekman Pubs.

An Asterisk (*) at the beginning of an entry indicates that the title is appearing for the first time.

Natural Therapeutics Vol. 4: Iridiagnosis. Henry Lindlahr. 284p. pap. 26.95 (*0-8464-4261-2*) Beekman Pubs.

Natural Therapeutics Vol. 6: Iridiagnosis & Other Diagnostic Methods. 5th ed. Henry Lindlahr. 327p. 1996. reprint ed. spiral bd. 22.00 (*0-7873-0563-4*) Hlth Research.

Natural Therapies for Mitral Valve Prolapse. Ronald L. Hoffman. (Good Health Guides Ser.). 48p. (Orig.). 1997. pap. 3.95 (*0-87983-765-9*, 37659K, Keats Publng) NTC Contemp Pub Co.

Natural Therapy for Your Arthritic Cat. Shawn Messonnier. (Pet Care Naturally Ser.). 64p. 1998. pap. 4.95 (*0-87983-880-9*, Keats Publng) NTC Contemp Pub Co.

Natural Therapy for Your Arthritic Dog. Shawn Messonnier. (Pet Care Naturally Ser.). 64p. 1998. pap. 4.95 (*0-87983-879-5*, Keats Publng) NTC Contemp Pub Co.

Natural Things: Collected Poems, 1969-1998. Constance Hunting. LC 99-45722. (Collected Poems Ser.). 300p. 1999. 49.95 (*0-943373-59-X*, Pub. by Natl Poet Foun); pap. 19.95 (*0-943373-60-3*, Pub. by Natl Poet Foun) U Pr of New Eng.

Natural Things: Poems. Hugh Ogden. LC 98-19112. 23p. 1998. pap. 7.00 (*0-916897-35-4*) Andrew Mtn Pr.

Natural Tips & Techniques. James T. Wisdom. 210p. (Orig.). 1997. pap. 75.00 (*1-878960-02-4*) WH&O Intl.

Natural to Magnesium Compounds see Ullmann's Encyclopedia of Industrial Chemistry

Natural Touch: Reaching Others for Christ. Kim Swithinbank. 128p. 1989. pap. 5.95 (*0-310-55721-6*, 19099P) Zondervan.

Natural Toxicants in Feeds, Forages, & Poisonous Plants. Peter R. Cheeke. LC 97-937. 496p. 1997. pap. 58.75 (*0-8134-3128-X*) Interstate.

Natural Toxicants in Food. Sheffield Academic Press Staff. LC 98-2751. 320p. 1998. ring bd. 139.95 (*0-8493-9734-0*) CRC Pr.

Natural Toxins: Proceedings of the 6th International Symposium on Animal, Plant & Microbial Toxins, Uppsala, August, 1979. D. Eaker. Ed. by Torkel Wadstrom. LC 80-40898. (Illus.). 704p. 1980. 323.00 (*0-08-024952-3*, Pub. by Pergamon Repr) Franklin.

Natural Toxins: Toxicology, Chemistry, & Safety. N. Bhushan Mandava et al. 370p. (C). 1992. pap. text 79.15 (*1-880293-01-3*) Alaken.

Natural Toxins Vol. 2: Structure, Mechanism of Action & Detection, Vol. 391. Ed. by B. R. Singh & Anthony T. Tu. LC 96-3810. (Advances in Experimental Medicine & Biology Ser.: No. 391). (Illus.). 548p. (C). 1996. text 139.50 (*0-306-45289-8*, Kluwer Plenum) Kluwer Academic.

Natural Treasures Field Guide for Kids. Elizabeth Biesiot. (Illus.). 64p. (Orig.). (J). (gr. 3-6). 1996. pap. 12.95 (*1-57098-082-9*) Roberts Rinehart.

Natural Treatment of Carpal Tunnel Syndrome. Ray C. Wunderlich, Jr. (Good Health Guides Ser.). (Illus.). 48p. (Orig.). 1993. pap. 3.95 (*0-87983-609-1*, 36091K, Keats Publng) NTC Contemp Pub Co.

Natural Treatment of Fibroid Tumors & Endometriosis. Susan M. Lark. (Good Health Guides Ser.). 48p. 1995. pap. 3.95 (*0-87983-690-3*, 36903K, Keats Publng) NTC Contemp Pub Co.

Natural Treatments & Remedies: For Over 400 of the World's Most Common Ailments. Global Health Research, Staff. (Illus.). 192p. 1995. pap. 9.95 (*0-921202-11-3*, Pub. by Gloh) BookWorld.

Natural Treatments for Depression: Using St. John's Wort, 5-HTP & Other Therapies, 1. C. M. Hawken. 1998. pap. 3.95 (*1-58054-040-6*) Woodland UT.

Natural Treatments for Hyperactivity. Skye Weintraub. 1996. pap. text 10.95 (*1-885670-36-2*) Woodland UT.

Natural Treatments for Infertility. Karen Bradstreet. (The Woodland Health Ser.). 1997. pap. text 3.95 (*1-58054-002-3*) Woodland UT.

***Natural Treatments for Insomnia.** Marian Broida. (Natural Pharmacist Ser.). 2000. pap. 9.99 (*0-7615-3011-8*) Prima Pub.

***Natural Treatments for Osteoporosis.** Sheila Dunn-Merritt. (Natural Pharmacist Ser.). 2000. pap. 9.99 (*0-7615-3010-X*) Prima Pub.

***Natural Treatments for Urinary Incontinence: Using Butterbur & Other Natural Supplements to Treat Bladder-Control Problems.** Rita Elkins. (Woodland Health Ser.). 32p. 2000. pap. 3.95 (*1-58054-085-6*) Woodland UT.

***Natural Treatments for Varicose Veins.** Richard Conant. (Natural Pharmacist Ser.). 2000. pap. 9.99 (*0-7615-3012-6*) Prima Pub.

Natural Trigonometric Functions to Seven Decimal Places for Every Ten Seconds of Arc Together with Miscellaneous Tables. 2nd ed. Howard C. Ives. LC 42-22096. 376p. reprint ed. pap. 116.60 (*0-608-30874-9*, 201648000004) Bks Demand.

Natural Turf for Sport & Amenity: Science & Management. W. A. Adams & R. J. Gibbs. 420p. 1994. pap. text 50.00 (*0-85198-720-6*) OUP.

Natural U. Learning from Nature. Charles J. Caes. 256p. (Orig.). (C). 1995. pap. text 32.00 (*0-8191-9754-8*); lib. bdg. 52.00 (*0-8191-9753-X*) U Pr of Amer.

Natural Uranium & Thorium Series Disequilibrium: New Approaches to Geochemical Problems, Vol.1. J. K. Osmond & J. B. Cowart. (Nuclear Science Applications Ser.: Section B). 50p. 1982. pap. text 98.00 (*3-7186-0131-1*) Gordon & Breach.

Natural Value. Friedrich von Wieser. Ed. by William Smart. Tr. by Christian A. Malloch. LC 87-17245. (Reprints of Economic Classics Ser.). xlv, 243p. 1989. reprint ed. 37.50 (*0-678-00821-3*) Kelley.

Natural Variations: Photographs by Colonel Stuart Wortley. Katherine DiGiulio. (Illus.). 48p. 1994. pap. 6.95 (*0-87328-148-9*) Huntington Lib.

Natural Vegetation of North America: An Introduction. John L. Vankat. LC 92-25565. 272p. (C). 1992. reprint ed. lib. bdg. 52.00 (*0-89464-782-2*) Krieger.

Natural Vegetation of Oregon & Washington. Jerry F. Franklin & C. T. Dyrness. (Illus.). 464p. 1988. reprint ed. pap. text 29.95 (*0-87071-356-6*) Oreg St U Pr.

Natural Ventilating Systems for Livestock Housing. Midwest Plan Service Engineers Staff. Ed. by Midwest Plan Service Personnel Staff. LC 89-14544. (Illus.). 32p. 1989. pap. 5.00 (*0-89373-074-2*, MWPS-33) MidWest Plan Serv.

Natural Vision Improvement. rev. ed. Janet Goodrich. 230p. 1971. pap. 18.95 (*0-89087-839-0*) Celestial Arts.

Natural Visions: Creative Tips for Wildlife Photography. Heather Angel. (Illus.). 144p. 1999. pap. 24.95 (*0-8174-4992-2*) Watsn-Guptill.

Natural Washington: A Nature-Lover's Guide to Parks, Wildlife Refuges, Trails, Gardens, Zoos, Forests, Aquariums & Arboreums Within a Day's Trip of the Nation's Capital. 4th rev. ed. Richard L. Berman & Deborah McBride. LC 98-38069. (Illus.). 352p. 1999. pap. 14.95 (*1-889324-15-9*, EPM) Howell Pr VA.

Natural Water Garden: Pools, Ponds, Marshes & Bogs for Backyards Everywhere. Ed. by C. Colston Burrell. (Twenty-First Century Gardening Ser.). 1997. pap. 9.95 (*1-889538-01-9*) Bklyn Botanic.

Natural Watercolours. Taylor. LC 98-177128. (Illus.). 128p. 1998. 27.95 (*0-7153-0699-5*, Pub. by D & C Pub) Sterling.

***Natural Waterways of Ireland: A Traveler's Guide to Rental Boating.** Michael Murphy & Laura Murphy. (Illus.). 2000. pap. 15.00 (*1-56656-381-X*) Interlink Pub.

***Natural Way: Acne: Your Guide To: Complementary Therapies, Alternative Techniques, Conventional Treatments.** Elizabeth Holmes. (Illus.). 2001. pap. 5.95 (*1-86204-746-4*) Element MA.

Natural Way: Allergies: Your Guide to Complementary Therapies, Alternative Techniques & Conventional Treatments. Moira Crawford. LC 97-45049. (Natural Way Ser.). (Illus.). 128p. 1998. pap. 5.95 (*1-86204-114-8*, Pub. by Element MA) Penguin Putnam.

***Natural Way: An Inquiry into Happiness.** James Sloman. 232p. 1999. pap. 14.00 (*1-886779-17-1*) OceanBlue Pub.

Natural Way: Arthritis & Rheumatism. Pat Young. (Natural Way Ser.). 128p. 1995. pap. 5.95 (*1-85230-629-7*, Pub. by Element MA) Penguin Putnam.

Natural Way: Asthma; A Comprehensive Guide to Gentle, Safe & Effective Treatment. Roy Ridgeway. (Natural Way Ser.). 128p. 1994. pap. 5.95 (*1-85230-492-8*, Pub. by Element MA) Penguin Putnam.

Natural Way: Back Pain. Helena Bridge. 128p. 1995. pap. 5.95 (*1-85230-581-9*, Pub. by Element MA) Penguin Putnam.

Natural Way: Cancer. Pat Young. (Natural Way with Ser.). 128p. 1996. pap. 5.95 (*1-85230-799-4*, Pub. by Element MA) Penguin Putnam.

Natural Way: Chronic Fatigue Syndrome: Your Guide to Complementary Therapies, Alternative Techniques & Conventional Treatments. Gill Jacobs. LC 97-45058. (Natural Way Ser.). (Illus.). 128p. 1998. pap. 5.95 (*1-86204-113-X*, Pub. by Element MA) Penguin Putnam.

Natural Way: Colds & Flu. Penny Davenport. 128p. 1995. pap. 5.95 (*1-85230-630-0*, Pub. by Element MA) Penguin Putnam.

Natural Way: Diabetes: A Comprehensive Guide to Effective Treatment. Catherine Steven. (Natural Way Ser.). 128p. 1995. pap. 5.95 (*1-85230-705-6*, Pub. by Element MA) Penguin Putnam.

Natural Way: Eczema: A Comprehensive Guide to Gentle, Safe & Effective Treatment. Sheena Meredith. (Natural Way Ser.). 128p. 1994. pap. 5.95 (*1-85230-493-6*, Pub. by Element MA) Penguin Putnam.

Natural Way: Heart Disease: A Comprehensive Guide to Effective Treatment. Richard Thomas. (Natural Way Ser.). 128p. 1994. pap. 5.95 (*1-85230-494-4*, Pub. by Element MA) Penguin Putnam.

Natural Way: Irritable Bowel Syndrome: A Comprehensive Guide to Gentle, Safe & Effective Treatment. Nigel Howard. 128p. 1995. pap. 5.95 (*1-85230-583-5*, Pub. by Element MA) Penguin Putnam.

Natural Way: Migraine: A Comprehensive Guide to Gentle, Safe & Effective Treatment. Eileen Herzberg. (Natural Way Ser.). 128p. 1994. pap. 5.95 (*1-85230-495-2*, Pub. by Element MA) Penguin Putnam.

Natural Way: Multiple Sclerosis - A Comprehensive Guide to Effective Treatment. Richard Thomas. (Natural Way Ser.). (Illus.). 128p. 1995. pap. 5.95 (*1-85230-715-3*, Pub. by Element MA) Penguin Putnam.

Natural Way: Premenstrual Syndrome. Jane Sullivan. (Natural Way Ser.). 128p. 1996. pap. 5.95 (*1-85230-805-2*, Pub. by Element MA) Penguin Putnam.

Natural Way: Psoriasis. Hilary Bower. LC 96-2737. (Natural Way Ser.). 128p. 1996. pap. 5.95 (*1-85230-832-X*, Pub. by Element MA) Penguin Putnam.

Natural Way - Cystitis: A Comprehensive Guide to Effective Treatment. Jacqueline C. Young. LC 97-3508. 128p. 1997. pap. 5.95 (*1-85230-889-3*, Pub. by Element MA) Penguin Putnam.

***Natural Way for Dogs & Cats: Natural Treatments & Remedies for Your Pet.** Midi Fairgrieve. (Illus.). 1999. pap. 13.95 (*1-85158-973-2*) Mainstream Pubng.

Natural Way HIV & AIDS: A Comprehensive Guide to Effective Treatment. Julie-Anne Ryan. LC 99-19663. 128p. 1999. pap. 5.95 (*1-85230-854-0*, Pub. by Element MA) Penguin Putnam.

Natural Way Infertility: A Comprehensive Guide to Effective Treatment. Belinda Whitworth. LC 96-42371. (Natural Way Ser.). 128p. 1997. pap. 5.95 (*1-85230-925-3*, Pub. by Element MA) Penguin Putnam.

Natural Way of Shin Buddhism. Shoji Matsumoto & Ruth Tabrah. LC 93-43084. 176p. (Orig.). (C). 1993. pap. 9.95 (*0-938474-14-6*) Buddhist Study.

Natural Way of Zen Shiatsu. David Sergel. (Illus.). 1998. pap. 23.00 (*0-87040-901-8*) Japan Pubns USA.

***Natural Way to a Healthy Heart: A Layman's Guide to Preventing & Treating Cardiovascular Disease.** Stephen Holt. 320p. 1999. 19.95 (*0-87131-889-X*, Pub. by M Evans) Natl Bk Netwk.

Natural Way to a Healthy Prostate. Michael B. Schachter. (Good Health Guides Ser.). 48p. 1995. pap. 3.95 (*0-87983-650-4*, 36504K, Keats Publng) NTC Contemp Pub Co.

Natural Way to Beat the Common Cold & Flu: A Holistic Approach for Prevention & Relief. Richard Trubo. LC 99-176660. 176p. 1998. pap. 6.50 (*0-425-16625-2*) Berkley Pub.

Natural Way to Beauty. Family Circle Editors & Marie T. Walsh. 1947. 12.95 (*0-405-12054-0*) Ayer.

Natural Way to Better Babies see Healthy Parents, Better Babies: A Couple's Guide to Pre-Conception Health Care

Natural Way to Better Golf. Jack Burke. 1997. pap. 11.00 (*0-684-84255-6*) S&S Trade.

***Natural Way to Digestive Health: A Layman's Guide to Preventing & Treating Stomach Disease.** Steven Holt. 330p. 2000. 19.95 (*0-87131-909-8*) M Evans.

Natural Way to Draw: A Working Plan for Art Study, 001. Kimon Nicolaides. (Illus.). 1975. pap. 8.95 (*0-395-20548-4*) HM.

Natural Way to Draw: A Working Plan for Art Study. Kimon Nicolaides. 240p. 1990. pap. 15.00 (*0-395-53007-5*) HM.

Natural Way to Paint: Rendering the Figure in Watercolor Simply & Beautifully. Charles Reid. LC 94-28590. (Illus.). 144p. 1994. 29.95 (*0-8230-3158-6*) Watsn-Guptill.

***Natural Way to Paint: Rendering the Figure in Watercolor Simply & Beautifully.** Charles Reid. (Illus.). 144p. 2000. pap. 19.95 (*0-8230-3173-X*) Watsn-Guptill.

Natural Way to Sexual Health. Henry G. Bieler & Sarah Nichols. Ed. by Jerome Fried. LC 72-83312. 231p. 1972. text 12.95 (*0-912880-03-1*) Charles Pub.

Natural Way to Vibrant Health. rev. ed. N. W. Walker. 132p. 1995. pap. 6.95 (*0-89019-035-6*) Norwalk Pr.

Natural Ways to Lower Blood Pressure, Cholesterol & Stress. Greg Tyler & Christian Tyler. 402p. 1997. 24.95 (*1-884350-61-5*) Alpha Pubng.

Natural Ways to Lower Your Cholesterol: Safe, Drug-Free Ways to Cut Cholesterol Levels up to 30 Points. Norman D. Ford. 288p. 1997. 7.99 (*0-88365-978-6*) Galahad Bks.

Natural Ways to Relieve the Common Discomforts of Pregnancy. Carl Jones. Ed. by Phyllis Herman. (Good Health Guides Ser.). 48p. 1996. pap. 3.95 (*0-87983-699-7*, 36997K, Keats Publng) NTC Contemp Pub Co.

Natural Wealth of Nations: Harnessing the Market for Environmental Protection & Economic Strength. David M. Roodman. LC 98-228480. 303p. 1998. pap. 13.00 (*0-393-31852-4*) Norton.

Natural Weight Loss Miracles: 20 Wonder Pills, & Supplements to Burn Fat & Shed Pounds Naturally. Maggie Greenwood-Robinson. LC 98-43495. 224p. 1999. pap. 14.00 (*0-399-52479-7*, Perigee Bks) Berkley Pub.

***Natural Well Woman: A Complete Guide to Health & Well-Being for Life.** Penny Stanway. 2000. pap. 24.95 (*1-86204-791-X*, Pub. by Element MA) Penguin Putnam.

Natural Woman. 128p. 1997. otabind 12.95 (*0-7935-7881-7*) H Leonard.

Natural Woman, Natural Menopause. Marcus Laux. 272p. 1998. pap. 13.00 (*0-06-092894-8*, Perennial) HarperTrade.

Natural Woman, Natural Menopause. Marcus Laux & Christine Conrad. LC 96-30096. (Illus.). 272p. 1997. 24.00 (*0-06-017341-6*) HarpC.

Natural Women, Cultured Men: A Feminist Perspective on Sociological Theory. Rosalind A. Sydie. 266p. (C). 1994. pap. text 19.00 (*0-8147-7997-2*) NYU Pr.

Natural Women, Cultured Men: A Feminist Perspective on Sociological Theory. Rosalind A. Sydie. 280p. 1987. pap. 13.99 (*0-335-15512-X*) OpUniv Pr.

Natural Women's Health: A Guide to Healthy Living for Women of Any Age. Lynda Wharton. LC 94-73921. 274p. 1995. pap. 13.95 (*1-57224-007-5*) New Harbinger.

Natural Wonders. Reader's Digest Editors. LC 96-38845. (Explore America Ser.). 1997. write for info. (*0-89577-950-1*) RD Assn.

Natural Wonders. Ed. by Reader's Digest Editors. LC 96-38845. (Explore America Ser.). 1997. write for info. (*0-89577-904-8*) RD Assn.

Natural Wonders, Level 1. Robert Gogan. Ed. by Jean A. McConochie. (Regents Readers Ser.). 52p. (gr. 7-12). 1982. pap. text 2.75 (*0-88345-451-3*, 20709) Prentice ESL.

Natural Wonders: Super Coloring Book. Golden Books Staff. (Precious Moments Ser.). 70p. 1999. pap. text 2.29 (*0-307-28025-X*) Gldn Bks Pub Co.

Natural Wonders: The John & Alice Woodson Forester Miniature Collection. Ed. by Marcia M. Theel. 48p. (Orig.). 1993. pap. 8.00 (*0-945529-08-2*) Le Yawkey.

Natural Wonders & Disasters. Billy Goodman. (Illus.). (J). (gr. 3-7). 1991. 17.95 (*0-316-32016-1*) Little.

Natural Wonders of Alaska. Kent Sturgis. LC 93-444492. (Natural Wonders of... Ser.). (Illus.). 140p. (Orig.). 1994. pap. 9.95 (*1-56626-045-0*, 60450, Cntry Rds Pr) NTC Contemp Pub Co.

Natural Wonders of Connecticut & Rhode Island. Carol Henshaw. LC 94-37491. (Natural Wonders of... Ser.). (Illus.). 180p. (Orig.). 1995. pap. 9.95 (*1-56626-079-5*, 60795, Cntry Rds Pr) NTC Contemp Pub Co.

***Natural Wonders of Connecticut & Rhode Island: Exploring Wild & Scenic Places.** Carol Henshaw. LC 99-59312. (Natural Wonders Ser.). (Illus.). 192p. 2000. pap. 14.95 (*0-658-00240-6*, 002406, Cntry Rds Pr) NTC Contemp Pub Co.

Natural Wonders of Florida. Marty Klinkersberg & Elizabeth Leach. LC 93-70211, (Natural Wonders of... Ser.). (Illus.). 200p. 1994. pap. 9.95 (*1-56626-025-6*, 60256, Cntry Rds Pr) NTC Contemp Pub Co.

Natural Wonders of Idaho. Bill London & Charles Powell. LC 93-44679. (Natural Wonders of... Ser.). (Illus.). 144p. (Orig.). 1994. pap. 9.95 (*1-56626-059-0*, 60590, Cntry Rds Pr) NTC Contemp Pub Co.

***Natural Wonders of Kentucky: Exploring Wild & Scenic Places.** 2nd ed. Ardi Lawrence. LC 98-25114. (Natural Wonders of... Ser.). (Illus.). 400p. 1999. pap. 15.95 (*1-56626-139-2*, 61392) NTC Contemp Pub Co.

Natural Wonders of Massachusetts. 2nd ed. Nancy Prajzner. 1999. pap. 14.95 (*0-8442-4623-9*) NTC Contemp Pub Co.

Natural Wonders of Massachusetts: A Guide to Parks, Preserves & Wild Places. Nancy Prajzner. LC 94-18860. (Natural Wonders Ser.). (Illus.). 130p. 1994. pap. 9.95 (*1-56626-108-2*, Cntry Rds Pr) NTC Contemp Pub Co.

Natural Wonders of Michigan: A Guide to Parks, Preserves & Wild Places. Tom Carney. (Natural Wonders Ser.). (Illus.). 180p. (Orig.). 1995. pap. 9.95 (*1-56626-078-7*, Cntry Rds Pr) NTC Contemp Pub Co.

***Natural Wonders of Michigan: Exploring Wild & Scenic Places.** 2nd ed. Tom Carney. LC 98-50001. (Natural Wonders of... Ser.). 192p. 1999. pap. 14.95 (*0-658-00176-0*, 001760, Cntry Rds Pr) NTC Contemp Pub Co.

Natural Wonders of Minnesota. Martin Hintz. (Natural Wonders of... Ser.). (Illus.). 192p. 1996. pap. 12.95 (*1-56626-162-7*, 61627, Cntry Rds Pr) NTC Contemp Pub Co.

***Natural Wonders of Minnesota: Exploring Wild & Scenic Places.** Martin Hintz. LC F604.3.H565 2000. (Natural Wonders Ser.). (Illus.). 192p. 2000. pap. 14.95 (*0-658-00241-4*, 002414, Cntry Rds Pr) NTC Contemp Pub Co.

N

Natural Wonders of New Hampshire: A Guide to Parks, Preserves & Wild Places. Suki Casanave. LC 93-37652. (Natural Wonders Ser.). (Illus.). 200p. (Orig.). 1994. pap. 9.95 (*1-56626-043-4*, Cntry Rds Pr) NTC Contemp Pub Co.

***Natural Wonders of New Hampshire: Exploring Wild & Scenic Places.** 2nd ed. Suki Casanave. LC 98-25158. (Natural Wonders of... Ser.). (Illus.). 256p. (Orig.). 1998. pap. 14.95 (*1-56626-140-6*, 61406) NTC Contemp Pub Co.

Natural Wonders of New Jersey. 2nd ed. Hope Gruzlovic. (Natural Wonders of... Ser.). 144p. 1999. pap. 14.95 (*0-658-00187-6*, 001876, Cntry Rds Pr) NTC Contemp Pub Co.

Natural Wonders of New Jersey: A Guide to Parks, Preserves & Wild Places. Hope Gruzlovic & Amy Cradic. LC 93-43698. (Natural Wonders Ser.). (Illus.). 140p. (Orig.). 1994. pap. 9.95 (*1-56626-052-3*, Cntry Rds Pr) NTC Contemp Pub Co.

Natural Wonders of New York: A Guide to Parks, Preserves & Wild Places. Debbie Williams. (Natural Wonders Ser.). (Illus.). 180p. (Orig.). 1995. pap. 9.95 (*1-56626-080-9*, Cntry Rds Pr) NTC Contemp Pub Co.

Natural Wonders of North America. Catherine O'Neill. Ed. by Donald J. Crump. LC 84-16614. (Books for World Explorers Series 6: No. 1). (Illus.). 104p. (J). (gr. 3-8). 1984. 8.95 (*0-87044-514-6*); lib. bdg. 12.50 (*0-87044-519-7*) Natl Geog.

Natural Wonders of Northern California: A Guide to Parks, Preserves & Wild Places. Will Kiester. (Natural Wonders Ser.). (Illus.). 180p. 1996. pap. 12.95 (*1-56626-176-7*, Cntry Rds Pr) NTC Contemp Pub Co.

Natural Wonders of Ohio: A Guide to Parks, Preserves & Wild Places. Janet Groene & Gordon Groene. LC 93-41108. (Natural Wonders Ser.). (Illus.). 200p. (Orig.). 1994. pap. 9.95 (*1-56626-053-1*, Cntry Rds Pr) NTC Contemp Pub Co.

Natural Wonders of Ohio: Exploring Wild & Scenic Places. 2nd ed. Gordon Groene & Janet Groene. LC 98-24276. (Natural Wonders of... Ser.). (Illus.). 224p. 1998. pap. 14.95 (*1-56626-201-1*, 62011, Cntry Rds Pr) NTC Contemp Pub Co.

Natural Wonders of Oregon. 2nd rev. ed. Archie Satterfield. (Natural Wonders of... Ser.). (Illus.). 150p. (Orig.). 1996. pap. 12.95 (*1-56626-150-3*, 61503, Cntry Rds Pr) NTC Contemp Pub Co.

Natural Wonders of Southern California. Anne Z. Cooke. LC 94-19459. (Natural Wonders of... Ser.). (Illus.). 180p. 1994. pap. 9.95 (*1-56626-115-5*, 61155, Cntry Rds Pr) NTC Contemp Pub Co.

Natural Wonders of Tennessee: A Guide to Parks, Preserves & Wild Places. H. Lea Lawrence & Ardi Lawrence. LC 94-20920. (Natural Wonders Ser.). (Illus.). 140p. 1994. pap. 9.95 (*1-56626-110-4*, Cntry Rds Pr) NTC Contemp Pub Co.

Natural Wonders of Tennessee: Exploring Wild & Scenic Places. 2nd ed. Ardi Lawrence & H. Lea Lawrence. LC 98-39698. (Natural Wonders of... Ser.). (Illus.). 304p. 1999. pap. 14.95 (*1-56626-196-1*, 61961, Cntry Rds Pr) NTC Contemp Pub Co.

Natural Wonders of Texas. Paul Cooke & Sunita Cooke. LC 94-32680. (Natural Wonders of... Ser.). (Illus.). 180p. (Orig.). 1995. pap. 9.95 (*1-56626-109-0*, 61090, Cntry Rds Pr) NTC Contemp Pub Co.

Natural Wonders of the Florida Keys. Deborah Straw. (Natural Wonders Ser.). (Illus.). 176p. (Orig.). 1994. pap. 14.95 (*1-56626-047-7*, 60477, Cntry Rds Pr) NTC Contemp Pub Co.

*__Natural Wonders of the World.__ Robert J. Moore, Jr. (Illus.). 2000. 59.95 (*0-7892-0667-6*) Abbeville Pr.

Natural Wonders of the World. Joyce Robins. 1992. 16.98 (*1-55521-760-5*) Bk Sales Inc.

Natural Wonders of Vermont. Barbara R. Rogers & Stillman Rogers. (Natural Wonders of... Ser.). (Illus.). 180p. (Orig.). 1996. pap. 12.95 (*1-56626-145-7*, 61457, Cntry Rds Pr) NTC Contemp Pub Co.

Natural Wonders of Virginia. Deane Winegar & Garvey Winegar. LC 94-19186. (Natural Wonders of... Ser.). (Illus.). 160p. 1994. pap. 9.95 (*1-56626-106-6*, 61066, Cntry Rds Pr) NTC Contemp Pub Co.

Natural Wonders of Washington: A Guide to Parks, Preserves & Wild Places. 2nd rev. ed. Archie Satterfield. (Natural Wonders Ser.). (Illus.). 150p. (Orig.). 1996. pap. 12.95 (*1-56626-151-1*, Cntry Rds Pr) NTC Contemp Pub Co.

Natural Wonders of Wisconsin. 2nd ed. Don Davenport. LC 99-462599. (Natural Wonders of... Ser.). 160p. 1999. pap. 14.95 (*1-56626-091-4*, 60914) NTC Contemp Pub Co.

Natural Wonders of Wisconsin: A Guide to Parks, Preserves & Wild Places. Don Davenport. (Natural Wonders Ser.). (Illus.). 180p. 1995. pap. 9.95 (*1-56626-081-7*, Cntry Rds Pr) NTC Contemp Pub Co.

Natural Woodlands. George Peterken. LC 94-20760. (Illus.). 536p. (C). 1996. text 135.00 (*0-521-36613-5*); pap. text 47.95 (*0-521-36792-1*) Cambridge U Pr.

Natural Work of Art: The Experience of Romance in Shakespeare's Winter's Tale. John A. Williams. LC 67-14346. (LeBaron Russell Briggs Prize Honors Essays in English Ser.). 55p. 1967. pap. 3.25 (*0-674-60450-4*) HUP.

*__Natural World.__ Reg Cox. (Wonders of the World Ser.). (Illus.). (J). 2000. 16.95 (*0-7910-6049-7*) Chelsea Hse.

Natural World. Ford. LC 98-72029. 1998. pap. text 8.07 (*0-395-86802-5*) HM.

*__Natural World.__ Raintree Steck-Vaughn Publishing Staff. (Illus.). (J). 2000. 154.14 (*0-7398-2776-6*) Raintree Steck-V.

*__Natural World.__ Ed. by Raintree Steck-Vaughn Publishing Staff. (Illus.). (J). 2000. 102.76 (*0-7398-2772-3*) Raintree Steck-V.

Natural World. Time-Life Books Editors. (Time Frame Ser.). (Illus.). 176p. 1991. lib. bdg. write for info. (*0-8094-6492-6*) Time-Life.

Natural World. L. Watts. (Illustrated Encyclopedia Ser.). (Illus.). 96p. (YA). (gr. 5-9). 1995. text 18.95 (*0-7460-1689-1*, Usborne) EDC.

*__Natural World Book Set.__ Raintree Steck-Vaughn Publishers Staff. (Illus.). 2000. write for info. (*0-7398-1059-6*) Raintree Steck-V.

Natural World of Jackson Hole: An Ecological Primer. rev. ed. Tim W. Clark. Ed. & Illus. by Denise Casey. Illus. by Lawrence Ormsby. 79p. 1999. pap. 16.95 (*0-931895-51-0*) Grand Teton NHA.

Natural World of the California Indians. Robert F. Heizer & Albert B. Elsasser. LC 79-65092. (California Natural History Guides Ser.: No. 46). (Illus.). 1980. pap. 15.95 (*0-520-03896-7*, Pub. by U CA Pr) Cal Prin Full Svc.

Natural World of the Texas Big Thicket. Photos by Blair Pittman. LC 78-6369. (Louise Lindsey Merrick Texas Environement Ser.: No. 2). (Illus.). 100p. 1978. reprint ed. 24.95 (*0-89096-061-5*) Tex A&M Univ Pr.

Natural World of the Texas Big Thicket. Photos by Blair Pittman. LC 78-6369. (Louise Lindsey Merrick Texas Environement Ser.: No. 2). (Illus.). 100p. 1986. reprint ed. pap. 17.95 (*0-89096-303-7*) Tex A&M Univ Pr.

Natural Worlds. Robert Bateman. (Illus.). 192p. 1996. 60.00 (*0-684-82986-X*) S&S Trade.

Natural Year: A Seasonal Guide to Alternative Health & Beauty. Jane Alexander. 416p. 1999. pap. 13.50 (*0-380-73143-6*, Avon Bks) Morrow Avon.

Natural Zeolites. G. Gottardi. Ed. by E. R. Galli. (Minerals & Rocks Ser.: Vol. 18). (Illus.). 390p. 1985. 171.95 (*0-387-13939-7*) Spr-Verlag.

Natural Zeolites: Occurrence, Properties, Use. Ed. by F. A. Mumpton & Leonard B. Sand. LC 77-30439. 546p. 1978. 375.00 (*0-08-021922-5*, Pergamon Pr) Elsevier.

Natural Zeolites: Proceedings of the International Meeting on Zeolites, Sofia. Ed. by G. Girov et al. (Illus.). 330p. 1997. pap. 69.95 (*954-642-015-8*) Intl Scholars.

Naturales Quaestiones, 1, Vol. VII. Lucius Annaeus Seneca. Ed. by E. H. Warmington. (Loeb Classical Library: No. 450). (ENG & LAT.). 328p. 1971. text 18.95 (*0-674-99495-7*) HUP.

Naturales Quaestiones, Two. Lucius Annaeus Seneca. Tr. by Thomas H. Corcoran. (Loeb Classical Library: No. 457). 318p. 1972. text 108.95 (*0-674-99503-1*) HUP.

Naturaleza Baila see Homeplay: La Alegria de Aprender Entre Ninos y Adultos, Series I

Naturaleza de Dios. Fisher Humphreys. Tr. by Arnoldo Canclini from ENG. (Biblioteca de Doctrina Cristiana Ser.).Tr. of Nature of God. (SPA.). 144p. (Orig.). 1987. pap. 6.75 (*0-311-09114-8*) Casa Bautista.

Naturaleza de la Iglesia. Bill J. Leonard. Tr. by Stanley Clark, Jr. from ENG.Tr. of Nature of the Church. (SPA.). 156p. 1989. pap. 6.75 (*0-311-09122-9*) Casa Bautista.

Naturaleza Muerta. Ed. by Taschen Staff. (DUT.). 1996. 24.99 (*3-8228-0670-6*) Benedikt Taschen.

Naturalis Historia, 6 vols. in 3. C. Plinius Secundus. (GER.). 1784p. reprint ed. write for info. (*0-318-70423-4*); reprint ed. write for info. (*0-318-70424-2*); reprint ed. write for info. (*0-318-70425-0*); reprint ed. write for info. (*0-318-70426-9*) G Olms Pubs.

Naturalis Historia Bibliae. Schriften Zur Biblischen Naturkunde Des 16.-18. Jahrhunderts Vol. 1: Hermann Heinrich Frey - Therobiblia. Biblische Thierbuch - Vogelbuch - Fischbuch. fac. ed. Ed. by Heimo Reinitzer & Deutches Bibel-Archiv. (GER., Illus.). 1390p. 1978. reprint ed. 87.00 (*3-201-01042-1*, Pub. by Akademische Druck-und) Balogh.

Naturalis Historia Bibliae. Schriften Zur Biblischen Naturkunde Des 16.-18. Jahrhunderts Vol. 2: Joachim Camerarius - Symbola et Emblemata, 4 vols. fac. ed. Ed. by Heimo Reinitzer & Deutsches Bibel-Archiv. (GER., Illus.). 704p. 1986. reprint ed. 115.00 (*3-201-01309-9*, Pub. by Akademische Druck-und) Balogh.

Naturalisation of Plants in Urban Auckland. A. E. Esler. 1988. 35.75 (*0-477-02539-0*, Pub. by Manaaki Whenua) Balogh.

*__Naturalism: A Critical Analysis.__ William L. Craig & James P. Moreland. LC 00-25324. 2000. write for info. (*0-415-23524-3*) Routledge.

Naturalism: A Critical Appraisal. Ed. by Steven J. Wagner & Richard Warner. LC 91-51119. (C). 1993. text 42.50 (*0-268-01472-8*) U of Notre Dame Pr.

Naturalism: A Critical Appraisal. Ed. by Steven J. Wagner & Richard Warner. LC 91-51119. (C). 1994. reprint ed. pap. text 19.50 (*0-268-01473-6*) U of Notre Dame Pr.

Naturalism & Deontology. Dennis A. Rohatyn. LC 73-92240. (Studies in Philosophy: No. 27). 128p. (Orig.). 1975. pap. text 29.25 (*90-279-3233-6*) Mouton.

Naturalism & Historical Understanding: Essays on the Philosophy of John Hermann Randall, Jr. Peter J. Anton. LC 67-63753. 235p. reprint ed. pap. 72.90 (*0-608-10167-2*, 201095700072) Bks Demand.

Naturalism & Normativity: Proceedings of a Conference Sponsored by Sociedad Filosofica Ibero-Americana. Intro. by Enrique Villanueva. (Philosophical Issues Ser.: No. 4, 1993). viii, 318p. (Orig.). 1993. pap. text 25.00 (*0-924922-17-6*); lib. bdg. 42.00 (*0-924922-67-2*) Ridgeview.

Naturalism & Ontology. Wilfrid Sellars. viii, 182p. (Orig.). (C). 1980. pap. text 15.00 (*0-917930-16-9*); lib. bdg. 27.00 (*0-917930-36-3*) Ridgeview.

Naturalism & Rationality. Ed. by Newton Carver & Peter H. Hare. LC 86-20532. 289p. 1986. 38.95 (*0-87975-350-1*) Prometheus Bks.

*__Naturalism & Religion.__ Kai Nielsen. 350p. 2001. 40.00 (*1-57392-853-4*) Prometheus Bks.

Naturalism & Subjectivism. Marvin Farber. LC 59-11896. 389p. (C). 1959. reprint ed. pap. text 19.95 (*0-87395-036-4*) State U NY Pr.

Naturalism & Symbolism in European Theatre, 1850 to 1918. Ed. by Claude Schumacher. (Theatre in Europe Ser.). (Illus.). 556p. (C). 1996. text 135.00 (*0-521-23014-4*) Cambridge U Pr.

Naturalism & the Troubadour Ethic. Donald K. Frank. (American University Studies: General Literature: Ser. XIX, Vol. 10). 176p. (C). 1988. text 27.95 (*0-8204-0606-6*) P Lang Pubng.

Naturalism in American Fiction: The Classic Phase. John J. Conder. LC 84-8661. 240p. 1984. pap. 16.00 (*0-8131-0169-7*) U Pr of Ky.

Naturalism in English Poetry. Stopford A. Brooke. (BCL1-PR English Literature Ser.). 289p. 1992. reprint ed. lib. bdg. 79.00 (*0-7812-7078-2*) Rprt Serv.

Naturalism in English Poetry. Stopford A. Brooke. 289p. reprint ed. 39.00 (*0-403-03079-X*) Somerset Pub.

Naturalism in Mathematics. Penelope Maddy. LC 97-12665. 264p. (C). 1998. text 35.00 (*0-19-823573-9*) OUP.

*__Naturalism in Mathematics.__ Penelope Maddy. 264p. 2000. pap. 19.95 (*0-19-825075-4*) OUP.

Naturalism in the European Novel: Critical Essays. Ed. by Brian Nelson. LC 91-19724. (European Studies Ser.). 288p. 1992. 19.50 (*0-85496-627-7*) Berg Pubs.

Naturalism Without Foundations. Kai Nielsen. LC 96-8794. 607p. 1996. 49.95 (*1-57392-076-2*) Prometheus Bks.

Naturalisme. Pierre Cogny. 126p. 1968. 9.95 (*0-8288-7414-X*) Fr & Eur.

Naturalisme Francais, 1870-95. Pierre Martino. 206p. 1969. 29.95 (*0-8288-7431-X*) Fr & Eur.

Naturalismus und Heimatkunst Bei Clara Viebig: Darwinistisch-Evolutionare Naturvorstellungen und Ihre Asthetischen Reaktionsformen. Barbara Kraus-Theim. (GER.). 316p. 1992. 58.80 (*3-631-44812-0*) P Lang Pubng.

Naturalist. Jack Rudman. (Career Examination Ser.: C-1379). 1994. pap. 29.95 (*0-8373-1379-1*) Nat Learn.

Naturalist. Edward O. Wilson. LC 94-13111. (Illus.). 352p. 1994. 24.95 (*1-55963-288-7*) Island Pr.

Naturalist. Edward O. Wilson. Ed. by Margaret De Haas. (Illus.). 400p. 1995. mass mkt. 14.95 (*0-446-67199-1*, Pub. by Warner Bks) Little.

Naturalist Afield: J. Alden Loring. William O. Lay. Ed. by Joan Davis. (Illus.). 200p. 1998. pap. 20.00 (*0-9639651-2-3*) Tioga Cnty.

Naturalist along the Jersey Shore. Joanna Burger. LC 95-52724. (Illus.). 287p. (C). 1996. pap. 18.95 (*0-8135-2300-1*); text 40.00 (*0-8135-2299-4*) Rutgers U Pr.

Naturalist amid Tropical Splendor. Alexander F. Skutch. LC 86-25079. (Illus.). 240p. 1987. 29.95 (*0-87745-163-X*) U of Iowa Pr.

Naturalist Buys an Old Farm. Edwin W. Teale. (Illus.). 315p. 1998. reprint ed. pap. 16.95 (*0-939883-02-3*) Bibliopola Pr.

Naturalist Collector: The Best Book on Card Collecting. Jeff Neumann & Romy Ruth. Ed. by Rita Robinson & Alan Frank. LC 94-69480. (Illus.). 128p. (YA). (gr. 9 up). 1994. pap. 14.95 (*0-9643339-0-2*) Romy Pubns.

Naturalist Fiction: The Entropic Vision. David Baguley. (Cambridge Studies in French: No. 28). 295p. (C). 1990. text 69.95 (*0-521-37380-8*) Cambridge U Pr.

Naturalist Image of German Literature: A Study of the German Naturalists - Appraisal of Their Literary Heritage. Warren R. Maurer. 269p. bds. 65.00 (*3-7705-0726-6*) Adlers Foreign Bks.

Naturalist in Alaska. Adolph Murie. LC 89-20671. 302p. 1990. reprint ed. pap. 18.95 (*0-8165-1168-3*) U of Ariz Pr.

Naturalist in Costa Rica. Alexander F. Skutch. (Illus.). 416p. 1992. reprint ed. pap. 17.95 (*0-8130-1148-5*) U Press Fla.

Naturalist in Florida: A Celebration of Eden. Archie Carr. Ed. by Marjorie H. Carr. LC 93-44919. (Illus.). 304p. (C). 1994. 37.00 (*0-300-05589-7*) Yale U Pr.

Naturalist in Florida: A Celebration of Eden. Archie Carr. (Illus.). 304p. 1996. pap. 17.00 (*0-300-06854-9*) Yale U Pr.

Naturalist in Indian Territory: The Journals of S. W. Woodhouse, 1849-1850. S. W. Woodhouse. Ed. by John S. Tomer & Michael J. Brodhead. LC 92-54143. (American Exploration & Travel Ser.: Vol. 72). (Illus.). 288p. 1996. pap. 17.95 (*0-8061-2805-4*) U of Okla Pr.

Naturalist in La Plata. W. H. Hudson. 1988. pap. 8.95 (*0-486-25740-1*) Dover.

Naturalist in La Plata. William Henry Hudson. reprint ed. 64.50 (*0-404-03393-8*) AMS Pr.

Naturalist in New Guinea. Bruce M. Beehler. (Corrie Herring Hooks Ser.: No. 17). (Illus.). 251p. 1991. 29.95 (*0-292-75541-4*) U of Tex Pr.

Naturalist in Nicaragua. Thomas Belt. LC 85-8502. (Illus.). xxxvi, 440p. 1985. reprint ed. pap. 15.95 (*0-226-04220-0*) U Ch Pr.

Naturalist in Nicaragua. Thomas Belt. LC 85-8502. (Illus.). xxxvi, 440p. 1985. reprint ed. lib. bdg. 36.00 (*0-226-04219-7*) U Ch Pr.

Naturalist in North Celebes: A Narrative of Travels in Minahassa, the Sangir & Talaut Islands. Sydney J. Hickson. LC 77-86952. (Illus.). reprint ed. 34.00 (*0-404-16726-8*) AMS Pr.

Naturalist in the Bahamas: October 12, 1861 - June 25, 1891. Ed. by Henry F. Osborn. LC 10-13587. 1910. 24.50 (*0-404-04794-7*) AMS Pr.

Naturalist in Western China, 2 vols. Ernest H. Wilson. LC 76-46620. 1977. reprint ed. write for info. (*0-913728-17-9*) Theophrastus.

Naturalist Intelligence. Karen Roth. LC 98-151321. (Illus.). 36p. 1998. pap. 6.95 (*1-57517-078-7*, 1584A) SkyLght.

Naturalist Novel. Emile Zola. Ed. by Maxwell Geismar. LC 63-21576. (Emulation Bk.). 181p. reprint ed. pap. 56.20 (*0-608-18713-5*, 202777800056) Bks Demand.

Naturalist on Nanticoke: The Natural History of a River on Maryland's Eastern Shore. Robert A. Hedeen. LC 81-18524. (Illus.). 192p. 1982. pap. 14.95 (*0-87033-467-0*, Tidewtr Pubs) Cornell Maritime.

Naturalist on Watch. Alton A. Lindsey. (Illus.). 228p. (Orig.). 1983. 10.00 (*0-913859-00-1*); pap. 4.75 (*0-913859-01-X*) Goshen Coll.

Naturalistic Articulation Carryover Experiences. Nanette C. Dahlke. (Illus.). 1990. student ed. 13.95 (*0-9626939-2-8*) Janelle Pubns.

Naturalistic Decision Making. Ed. by Caroline E. Zsambok & Gary A. Klein. LC 96-27981. (Expertise). 375p. 1996. 89.95 (*0-8058-1873-1*); pap. 45.00 (*0-8058-1874-X*) L Erlbaum Assocs.

Naturalistic Environments in Captivity for Animal Behavior Research. Ed. by Edward F. Gibbons, Jr. et al. LC 92-39108. (SUNY Series in Endangered Species). 387p. (C). 1993. text 67.50 (*0-7914-1647-X*); pap. text 24.95 (*0-7914-1648-8*) State U NY Pr.

Naturalistic Epistemology: A Symposium of Two Decades. Ed. by Abner Shimony & Debra Nails. (Boston Studies in the Philosophy of Science Ser.: No. 100). 372p. 1987. text 176.50 (*90-277-2337-0*) Kluwer Academic.

Naturalistic Evaluation. Ed. by David D. Williams. LC 85-81898. (New Directions for Evaluation Ser.: No. PE 30). (Orig.). 1986. pap. 19.00 (*0-87589-728-2*) Jossey-Bass.

Naturalistic Gardening: Reflecting the Planting Patterns of Nature. Ann Lovejoy. LC 98-6130. (Illus.). 144p. 1998. pap. 21.95 (*1-57061-120-3*) Sasquatch Bks.

Naturalistic Inner-City Novel in America: Encounters with the Fat Man. James R. Giles. LC 95-4340. 221p. 1995. text 34.95 (*1-57003-046-4*) U of SC Pr.

Naturalistic Inquiry. Yvonna S. Lincoln & Egon G. Guba. LC 84-26295. 416p. 1985. 44.00 (*0-8039-2431-3*) Sage.

Naturalistic Inquiry for Library Science: Methods & Applications for Research, Evaluation & Teaching, 64. Constance A. Mellon. LC 89-27276. (Contributions in Librarianship & Information Science Ser.: No. 64). 218p. 1990. 59.95 (*0-313-25653-5*, MNC/) Greenwood.

Naturalistic Novel of the New World: A Comparative Study of Stephen Crane, Aluisio Azevedo, & Federico Gamboa. Joao Sedycias. 314p. (C). 1993. lib. bdg. 54.00 (*0-8191-8941-3*) U Pr of Amer.

Naturalistic Philosophies of Experience: Studies in James, Dewey & Farber Against the Background of Husserl's Phenomenology. D. C. Mathur. LC 79-117613. 192p. 1971. 12.00 (*0-87527-052-2*) Green.

Naturalistic Photography for Students of the Art. Peter H. Emerson. LC 72-9195. (Literature of Photography Ser.). 1973. reprint ed. 23.95 (*0-405-04905-6*) Ayer.

Naturalistic Text Comprehension. Ed. by Herre Van Oostendorp & Rolf A. Zwaan. LC 94-9312. (Advances in Discourse Processes Ser.: Vol. 53). 296p. 1994. pap. 42.50 (*1-56750-125-7*); text 78.50 (*1-56750-099-4*) Ablx Pub.

Naturalistic Tradition in Indian Thought. Dale M. Riepe. LC 82-9185. 308p. 1982. reprint ed. lib. bdg. 65.00 (*0-313-23622-4*, RINA, Greenwood Pr) Greenwood.

Naturalist's Adventure in Nepal: Search for the Spiny Babbler. Dillon S. Ripley. 317p. (C). 1978. 90.00 (*0-89771-109-2*, Pub. by Ratna Pustak Bhandar) St Mut.

Naturalists & the Supernatural: Studies in Horizon & an American Philosophy of Religion. William M. Shea. LC 84-14686. xvi, 242p. 1984. 21.50 (*0-86554-116-7*, MUP/H098) Mercer Univ Pr.

Naturalist's Big Bend. Roland H. Wauer. LC 78-21776. (Illus.). 158p. 1992. pap. 12.95 (*0-89096-070-4*) Tex A&M Univ Pr.

Naturalist's Blue Ridge Parkway. David T. Catlin. LC 83-26003. 234p. 1984. pap. 16.95 (*0-87049-430-9*) U of Tenn Pr.

Naturalists Book of Poetry. Reginald Locke. 64p. 1984. 45.00 (*0-905418-85-9*, Pub. by Gresham Bks) St Mut.

Naturalist's Color Guide, Pt. 1. Frank B. Smithe. 1975. ring bd. 9.00 (*0-913424-03-X*) Am Mus Natl Hist.

Naturalist's Color Guide, Pt. 2. Frank B. Smithe. 1975. ring bd. 9.00 (*0-913424-04-8*) Am Mus Natl Hist.

Naturalists Color Guide, Pt. III. Frank B. Smithe. (Illus.). 1981. pap. 5.00 (*0-913424-05-6*) Am Mus Natl Hist.

Naturalists, Conservationists & Environmentalists. Eileen Lucas. (American Profiles Ser.). (Illus.). 160p. (YA). (gr. 5-12). 1994. 19.95 (*0-8160-2919-9*) Facts on File.

Naturalist's Death Valley. Edmund C. Jaeger. (Illus.). 70p. 1975. 4.95 (*0-936932-04-X*) Death Valley Fortyniners.

Naturalists' Directory & Almanac (International) 47th ed. Ernest Lussier. 400p. 1996. pap. 35.00 (*1-889130-00-1*) Naturalists Dir.

Naturalists Directory & Almanac (International) 48th ed. Ed. by Philip Mallard et al. (Naturalist Directory & Almanac Ser.). (Illus.). 500p. Date not set. pap. 32.50 (*1-889130-01-X*) Naturalists Dir.

Naturalist's Field Guide to Coastal Communities. Vickie Shufer. (Environmental Education Ser.). (Illus.). 48p. 1987. pap. 2.95 (*0-938423-01-0*) Eco Images.

Naturalist's Field Journal: A Manual of Instruction Based on a System Established by Joseph Grinnell. Steven G. Herman. LC 85-73491. (Illus.). 200p. 1986. pap. 19.50 (*0-931130-13-1*) Harrell Bks.

Naturalist's Garden: How to Garden with Plants That Attract Birds, Butterflies & Other Wildlife. 3rd ed. Ruth S. Ernst. LC 95-47935. (Illus.). 288p. 1996. pap. 16.95 (*1-56440-764-0*) Globe Pequot.

*__Naturalist's Guide for Mountain Bikers, Hikers & Drivers to the Seven Mountains.__ Robert Butler & Eva Sonesh Kedar. (Illus.). 152p. 1999. pap. Price not set. (*0-9657934-2-7*) Purple Lizard.

Naturalist's Guide to Chugach State Park. Jenny Zimmerman. 1993. 14.95 (*0-9637309-0-8*) J Zimmerman.

Naturalists' Guide to Fresh-Water Aquarium Fish. J. J. Hoedeman. LC 72-95209. 1152p. 1974. write for info. (*0-8069-3722-X*, Sterling-SIR) Sterling.

Naturalist's Guide to Hiking the Grand Canyon. Stewart Aitchison. LC 84-15035. 172p. 1985. pap. 8.95 (*0-13-610221-2*) P-H.

Naturalist's Guide to Ontario. Ed. by W. W. Judd & J. Murray Speirs. LC 65-3239. (Illus.). 1964. pap. 13.95 (*0-8020-6039-0*) U of Toronto Pr.

Naturalists Guide to Self-Hypnosis. Garry De Young. 1988. pap. 3.00 (*0-936128-10-0*) De Young Pr.

Naturalist's Guide to St. Simons Island. Taylor Schoettle. LC 93-61513. (Illus.). 120p. (Orig.). 1995. pap. text 16.00 (*0-9641038-0-X*) H E T Schoettle.

Naturalist's Guide to the Arctic. E. C. Pielou. LC 94-2555. 344p. 1994. lib. bdg. 57.00 (*0-226-66813-4*) U Ch Pr.

Naturalist's Guide to the Arctic. E. C. Pielou. LC 94-2555. 344p. 1994. pap. 20.00 (*0-226-66814-2*) U Ch Pr.

Naturalist's Guide to the Sacramento River. Mitchell S. Wyss. Tr. by Dover Publications, N. Y. C. Staff. (Illus.). 68p. (Orig.). (C). 1991. pap. text 5.95 (*0-9625847-1-1*) Mango Pubns.

*__Naturalist's Guide to the Southern Blue Ridge Front: Linville Gorge, North Carolina, to Tallulah Gorge, Georgia.__ L. L. Gaddy, Jr. (Illus.). 192p. 2000. pap. 14.95 (*1-57003-372-2*) U of SC Pr.

*__Naturalist's Guide to the Tropics.__ Marco Lambertini. Tr. by John Veneralla. LC 99-32802. (Illus.). 344p. 2000. pap. 25.00 (*0-226-46828-3*) U Ch Pr.

Naturalist's Guide to the Virginia Coast. Curtis J. Badger. LC 96-8192. (Illus.). 96p. 1996. pap., spiral bd. 16.95 (*0-8117-2562-6*) Stackpole.

Naturalists Guide to Tropics. Marco Lambertini. 1997. 55.00 (*0-226-46827-5*) U Ch Pr.

Naturalist's Handbook: Activities for Young Explorers. Lynn Kuntz. LC 95-41122. (Illus.). 64p. (J). (gr. 2-7). 1996. 14.95 (*0-87905-728-9*) Gibbs Smith Pub.

Naturalist's Herb Guide. Sally Ann Berk. 248p. 1996. 9.98 (*1-884822-52-5*) Blck Dog & Leventhal.

Naturalist's Journal: A Book for Records, Notes & Observations. Stephen Kirkpatrick. 32p. 1994. 13.99 (*0-9619353-7-5*) Thy Marvelous Works.

Naturalist's Mexico. Roland H. Wauer. LC 91-33103. (Louise Lindsey Merrick Natural Environment Ser.: No. 12). 336p. 1992. 16.95 (*0-89096-500-5*) Tex A&M Univ Pr.

Naturalists of the Frontier. 2nd enl. rev. ed. Samuel W. Geiser. LC 48-7357. 297p. reprint ed. pap. 92.10 (*0-8357-8964-0*, 203341800086) Bks Demand.

Naturalist's Path: A Handbook for Beginning the Study of Nature. Cathy Johnson. 208p. 1991. pap. 14.95 (*0-8027-7360-5*) Walker & Co.

Naturalist's Shetland. J. Laughton Johnston. (Poyser Natural History Ser.). (Illus.). 300p. (C). 1998. boxed set 49.95 (*0-85661-105-0*) Acad Pr.

Naturalist's View. Sophia G. Schepe. (Illus.). 104p. (Orig.). pap. 7.50 (*0-9615137-1-3*) Galeria Pr.

Naturalist's View of the Healing Arts. Harold E. Buttram. 32p. 1969. pap. 2.00 (*0-916285-53-7*) Humanitarian.

Naturalization in Caldwell County, Texas. Dorothy R. Day. 110p. (Orig.). 1989. pap. 10.50 (*0-9624711-0-0*) D R Day.

An Asterisk (*) at the beginning of an entry indicates that the title is appearing for the first time.

Naturalization of Foreign Protestants in the American & West Indian Colonies, Etc. Montague S. Giuseppi. LC 64-19759. 196p. 1995. reprint ed. pap. 20.00 (*0-8063-0157-0*) Clearfield Co.

***Naturalization of the Soul: Self & Personal Identity in the Birth of Modern Psychology.** Raymond Martin & John Barresi. LC 99-38676. (Studies in 18th Century Philosophy). 216p. 1999. 85.00 (*0-415-21645-1*) Routledge.

Naturalization Records for Oakland County, 1827-1906. Ed. by Ruth S. Kennedy. 122p. (Orig.). 1985. pap. 10.00 (*1-879766-03-5*) OCG Society.

Naturalization Requirements & General Information. (Illus.). 46p. (Orig.). (YA). (gr. 12 up). 1994. pap. text 15.00 (*0-7881-0846-8*) DIANE Pub.

Naturalizations & Declarations of Intention: One Hundred Years, 1784-1884. Ed. by Elizabeth B. Wingo. LC 89-103620. 120p. (Orig.). 1987. pap. 21.50 (*1-878515-82-9*) W S Dawson.

Naturalizations in the Marine Court, New York City, 1827-1835. Kenneth Scott. LC 90-61181. 192p. 1990. 19.95 (*1-877692-01-8*) NY Genealogical & Biographical.

Naturalizations in the Marine Court, New York City, 1834-1840. Kenneth Scott. LC 91-61333. 192p. 1991. 19.95 (*1-877692-03-4*) NY Genealogical & Biographical.

Naturalized Fishes of the World. Christopher Lever. (Illus.). 432p. 1996. text 49.95 (*0-12-444745-7*) Acad Pr.

***Naturalized Terrestrial Stylommatophora: (Mollusca: Gastropoda)** Gary M. Barker. LC 99-488284. (Fauna of New Zealand Ser.: No. 38). (Illus.). 253p. 1999. pap. 72.50 (*0-478-09322-5*, Pub. by Manaaki Whenua) Balogh.

Naturalizing Bulbs. 1996. 35.00 (*0-02-860380-X*) Macmillan.

Naturalizing Bulbs. Rob Proctor. LC 97-1972. (Illus.). 256p. 1995. 35.00 (*0-8050-4631-3*) H Holt & Co.

Naturalizing Epistemology. 2nd ed. Ed. by Hilary Kornblith. LC 93-23976. 488p. 1994. 45.00 (*0-262-11180-2*, Bradford Bks); pap. text 25.00 (*0-262-61090-6*, Bradford Bks) MIT Pr.

Naturalizing Phenomenology: Issues in Contemporary Phenomenology & Cognitive Science. Jean Petitot. LC 99-28716. (Writing Science Ser.). 1999. pap. text 29.95 (*0-8047-3610-3*) Stanford U Pr.

Naturalizing Philosophy of Education: John Dewey in the Postanalytic Period. Jerome A. Popp. LC 97-38677. 1998. 34.95 (*0-8093-2171-8*) S Ill U Pr.

Naturalizing Power: Essays in Feminist Cultural Analysis. Ed. by Sylvia Yanagisako & Carol Delaney. LC 94-3573. 288p. (C). 1994. pap. 21.99 (*0-415-90884-1*) Routledge.

Naturalizing Power: Essays in Feminist Cultural Analysis. Ed. by Sylvia Yanagisako & Carol Delaney. LC 94-3573. 320p. (C). (gr. 13). 1994. 75.00 (*0-415-90883-3*) Routledge.

Naturalizing the Mind. Fred Dretske. LC 95-2229. (Jean Nicod Lectures: Vol. 1995). 1995. 25.00 (*0-262-04149-9*, Bradford Bks) MIT Pr.

Naturalizing the Mind. Fred Dretske. (Jean Nicod Ser.). (Illus.). 232p. 1997. reprint ed. pap. text 12.50 (*0-262-54089-4*, Bradford Bks) MIT Pr.

***Naturalizing Tree of Liberty.** Spary. 1999. lib. bdg. 70.00 (*0-226-76862-7*) U Ch Pr.

Naturally Beautiful: Earth's Secrets & Recipes for Skin, Body & Bath. Dawn Gallagher & Melanie Menagh. (Illus.). 192p. 1999. 29.95 (*0-7893-0353-1*, Pub. by Universe) St Martin.

***Naturally Clean Home: 101 Safe & Easy Herbal Formulas for Non-Toxic Cleansers.** Karyn Siegal-Maier. LC 99-35380. (Tips Ser.). 160p. 1999. pap. 12.95 (*1-58017-194-X*, Random) Storey Bks.

Naturally Creative Candles. Letty Oates. LC 97-73020. 128p. 1997. pap. 19.95 (*0-8019-9045-9*, NACC) Krause Pubns.

Naturally Drawn: Drawings from the Collection. Martina R. Norelli & Jane M. Weinke. (Illus.). 48p. (Orig.). 1992. pap. 5.00 (*0-945529-06-6*) Le Yawkey.

Naturally Fond of Pictures: American Illustration of the 1840s & 1850s. Karen Nipps. (Illus.). 30p. 1989. pap. 6.00 (*0-914076-68-X*) Lib Co Phila.

Naturally Fractured Reservoirs. 2nd ed. Robert Aguilera. LC 95-18164. 720p. 1995. 145.95 (*0-87814-122-7*) PennWell Bks.

Naturally Healing Herbs. Carly Wall. LC 95-52378. (Illus.). 128p. 1996. pap. 12.95 (*0-8069-3801-3*) Sterling.

***Naturally Healthy Babies & Children: A Commonsense Guide to Herbal Remedies.** Aviva Romm. 352p. 2000. pap. 16.95 (*1-58017-285-7*) Storey Bks.

Naturally Healthy Gourmet: Secrets of Quick, Tasty, & Wholesome Cooking. Margaret Lawson & Tom Monte. Ed. by Laurel Ruggles. LC 94-76116. 232p. (Orig.). 1994. pap. 14.95 (*0-918860-53-9*) G Ohsawa.

Naturally Healthy Hair: Herbal Treatments & Daily Care for Fabulous Hair. Mary Beth Janssen. LC 99-33058. (Herbal Body 2). (Illus.). 176p. 1999. pap. 14.95 (*1-58017-129-X*) Storey Bks.

Naturally Healthy Pregnancy: An Essential Guide of Nutritional & Botanical Medicine for the Childbearing Years. Shonda Parker. LC 98-96432. 323 p. 1998. write for info. (*1-892513-10-2*) Naturally Healthy.

***Naturally Healthy Pregnancy: The Essential Guide to Nutritional & Botanical Medicine for the Child Bearing Years.** Shonda Parker. (Illus.). 323p. 2000. pap. 14.99 (*1-929125-12-7*, Pub. by Loyal Pubng) BookWorld.

Naturally Healthy Skin: Tips & Techniques for a Lifetime of Radiant Skin. Stephanie Tourles. LC 99-13151. 208p. 1999. pap. 14.95 (*1-58017-130-3*) Storey Bks.

***Naturally Healthy with Evening Primrose Oil.** Werner Meidinger. 96p. 1999. pap. text 11.95 (*0-8069-2035-1*) Sterling.

Naturally Intelligent Systems. Maureen Caudill & Charles Butler. (Illus.). 320p. 1992. reprint ed. pap. text 17.50 (*0-262-53113-5*, Bradford Bks) MIT Pr.

Naturally, It's Better. Erleen Tilton. (Naturally Cooking with Basic Foods Ser.). (Illus.). 153p. (Orig.). 1983. pap. 12.95 (*0-9613363-0-7*) Bae Pub Co.

Naturally Loving. Catherine Spencer. 1993. per. 2.99 (*0-373-11587-3*, 1-11587-2) Harlequin Bks.

Naturally Loving. large type ed. Catherine Spencer. 1992. lib. bdg. 18.95 (*0-263-13123-8*) Mac Lib Ref.

Naturally, Maine. Dorothy M. Osborne. LC 97-173839. 48p. 1997. pap. 9.95 (*1-885206-46-1*, Iliad Pr) Cader Pubng.

***Naturally Modern: Creating Interiors with Wood, Leather, Stone & Natural Fabrics.** Ros Byman Shaw. (Illus.). 144p. 2000. 27.50 (*0-8109-3668-2*, Pub. by Abrams) Time Warner.

***Naturally Occurring Antimicrobiols in Food, No. 132.** LC 97-33248. (Task Force Report Ser.). (Illus.). 103p. 1998. pap. 28.00 (*1-887383-12-3*) CAST.

Naturally Occurring Antioxidants. Richard A. Larson. LC 97-8169. 224p. 1997. lib. bdg. 89.95 (*0-87371-957-3*) Lewis Pubs.

Naturally Occurring Biological Immunosuppressive Factors & Their Relationship to Disease. Russell H. Neubauer. 304p. 1979. 170.00 (*0-8493-5243-6*, RC268, CRC Reprint) Franklin.

***Naturally Occurring Glysosides.** Ikan. LC 98-39367. 458p. (C). 1999. 240.00 (*0-471-98602-X*) Wiley.

Naturally Occurring 1,2-Dithiolanes & 1,2,3-Trithianes. Chemical & Biological Properties, Vol. 9. L. Teuber. Ed. by Alexander Senning. (Sulfer Reports: Vol. 9, No. 4). 104p. 1989. pap. text 192.00 (*3-7186-5022-3*) Gordon & Breach.

Naturally Occurring Phorbol Esters. Fred J. Evans. 366p. 1986. 182.00 (*0-8493-5117-0*, RS341, CRC Reprint) Franklin.

Naturally Occurring Pyrrolizidine Alkaloids. Abdel-Fattah M. Rizk. (Illus.). 224p. 1990. lib. bdg. 190.00 (*0-8493-4650-9*, QP801) CRC Pr.

Naturally Occurring Quinones. 4th ed. Routledge Chapman Hall, Inc. Staff. 1996. text. write for info. (*0-7514-0248-6*) Kluwer Academic.

Naturally Occurring Radioactive Material: Principles & Practices. Philip Underhill. 160p. 1996. boxed set 64.95 (*1-57444-009-8*) St Lucie Pr.

Naturally Occurring Radioactive Materials (NORM) in Produced Water & Scale from Texas Oil, Gas & Geothermal Wells: Geographic, Geologic & Geochemical Controls. R. S. Fisher. (Geological Circular Ser.: No. 95-3). (Illus.). 43p. (Orig.). 1995. pap. 6.00 (*0-614-11616-3*) Bur Econ Geology.

Naturally Powerful: 200 Simple Actions to Energize Body, Mind, Heart & Spirit. Valerie Wells. LC 98-37291. 224p. 1999. pap. 13.00 (*0-399-52475-4*, Perigee Bks) Berkley Pub.

Naturally Processed Peptides. Ed. by A. Sette. (Chemical Immunology Ser.: Vol. 57). (Illus.). xii, 240p. 1993. 215.75 (*3-8055-5755-8*) S Karger.

Naturally-Produced Organohalogens: Selected & Edited Proceedings of the First Conference on Naturally-Produced Organohalogens. Ed. by Anders Grimvall. (Environment & Chemistry Ser.). 440p. (C). 1995. text 184.00 (*0-7923-3435-3*) Kluwer Academic.

Naturally Reductive Metrics & Einstein Metrics on Compact Lie Groups. J. E. D'Atri & W. Ziller. LC 79-7. (Memoirs Ser.: No. 18/215). 72p. 1982. reprint ed. pap. 21.00 (*0-8218-2215-2*, MEMO/18/215) Am Math.

***Naturally 70's Fabric.** Constance Korosec & Leslie Pina. (Illus.). 112p. 1999. pap. 24.95 (*0-7643-1030-5*) Schiffer.

Naturally Slim & Powerful: The Natural Way to Boost Serotonin Levels Without Drugs. Philip Lipetz. 240p. 1998. pap. text 11.95 (*0-8362-5284-5*) Andrews & McMeel.

***Naturally Slim Without Dieting.** Carter-Scott Cherie. 2000. 12.95 (*0-385-40528-6*, Pub. by Transworld Publishers Ltd) Trafalgar.

Naturally Supernatural. Mark Virkler. 154p. (Orig.). 1994. pap. 9.99 (*1-56043-060-5*) Destiny Image.

Naturally Sweet Baker. Carrie Davis. LC 97-17377. 1997. 25.00 (*0-02-861257-4*) Macmillan.

Naturally Sweet Desserts: The Sugar-Free Dessert Cookbook. David Smither. (Illus.). 264p. (Orig.). pap. 15.95 (*0-89529-443-5*, Avery) Penguin Putnam.

Naturalness of Religious Ideas: A Cognitive Theory of Religion. Pascal Boyer. LC 92-37506. 1994. 45.00 (*0-520-07559-5*, Pub. by U CA Pr) Cal Prin Full Svc.

Naturals: A Guide to Food Organisms of the Trout. Gary A. Borger. LC 79-23099. 224p. 1980. 19.95 (*0-8117-1006-8*) Stackpole.

Nature. (Let's Look Ser.). (Illus.). 96p. (J). 1998. pap. 4.95 (*1-85967-597-2*, Lorenz Bks) Anness Pub.

Nature. 104p. pap. 21.95 (*0-88108-209-0*) Art Dir.

Nature. (Baby's Bk.). (J). 1995. write for info. (*0-7894-0300-5*) DK Pub Inc.

***Nature.** 1999. write for info. (*0-7652-0872-5*) Modern Curr.

Nature. (Encyclopaedia Britannica Fascinating Facts Ser.). (Illus.). 32p. (J). 1993. 8.98 (*1-56173-322-9*); 4.98 (*1-56173-469-1*) Pubns Intl Ltd.

***Nature.** Almuth Bartl. (Eddie's Finger Quiz Bks.). (Illus.). (J). 2000. pap. 4.95 (*0-7641-1609-6*) Barron.

***Nature.** BHB International Staff. (Illus.). 131p. (J). (gr. 1-4). 1999. 9.95 (*2-215-06283-5*, Pub. by CE75) BHB Intl.

Nature. BHB International Staff. 131p. (J). (ps-3). 1999. pap. text 9.95 Editions Herit.

Nature. Boy Scouts of America. (Illus.). 64p. (YA). (gr. 6-12). 1973. pap. 2.90 (*0-8395-3285-7*, 33285) BSA.

Nature. Jennifer Cochrane. LC 92-53091. (World Around Us Ser.). (Illus.). 48p. (J). (gr. 4-7). 1992. pap. 8.95 (*1-85697-813-3*, Kingfisher) LKC.

Nature. Marjorie Eberts. LC 95-49818. (VGM Career Portraits Ser.). (Illus.). 96p. (J). (ps up). 1996. 13.95 (*0-8442-4380-9*, 43809, VGM Career) NTC Contemp Pub Co.

***Nature.** John Farndon. (Concise Encyclopedias Ser.). 192p. (YA). (gr. 5-9). 2000. pap. text 5.95 (*0-7894-6106-4*, D K Ink) DK Pub Inc.

Nature. Ed. by Laura Smith. (Pocket Poems Ser.: No. 2). 36p. 1997. pap. 2.00 (*0-933087-46-2*) Bottom Dog Pr.

Nature. Snapshot Staff. LC 97-143374. (Padded Ser.). (Illus.). 18p. (J). 1997. 4.95 (*0-7894-1548-8*) DK Pub Inc.

Nature. Sterling Staff. (BipQuiz Ser.). (Illus.). 64p. (J). (gr. 4-7). 1995. pap. 2.95 (*0-8069-0939-0*) Sterling.

Nature. Ralph Waldo Emerson. (Notable American Authors Ser.). 1992. reprint ed. lib. bdg. 75.00 (*0-7812-2803-4*) Rprt Serv.

Nature see Encyclopedic Poetique: Anthologie Thematique de la Poesie Francaise Contemporaine

Nature: A Changing Picture Book. Ed. by Intervisual Books Staff. LC 97-158091. (Changing Picture Ser.). (Illus.). 80p. 1997. 4.95 (*0-8362-2679-8*) Andrews & McMeel.

Nature: An Environmental Cosmology. Joseph Grange. LC 96-41494. 272p. (C). 1997. text 59.50 (*0-7914-3347-1*); pap. text 19.95 (*0-7914-3348-X*) State U NY Pr.

Nature: General. Ed. by Bert Hower. (Thematic Anthologies Ser.). (Illus.). 80p. (Orig.). 1995. pap. 11.25 (*0-936945-51-6*) Creat with Wds.

Nature: Literature & its Otherness la Litterature et Son Autre. Ed. by Svend E. Larsen et al. 265p. pap. 30.75 (*87-7838-282-3*, Pub. by Odense Univ) Intl Spec Bk.

***Nature: Poems Old & New.** May Swenson. 240p. 2000. pap. 15.00 (*0-618-06408-7*) HM.

Nature: Stories, Poetry & Education. A. Doyle. (Story Course Ser.). (Illus.). 40p. 1998. pap., wbk. ed. 29.95 (*1-56820-375-6*) Story Time.

Nature: The Beauty & the Wonder. Ariel Books Staff. (Illus.). 80p. 1994. 4.95 (*0-8362-3062-0*, Arie Bks) Andrews & McMeel.

Nature: Western Attitudes since Ancient Times. Peter Coates. LC 99-163024. 256p. 1998. 29.95 (*0-520-21743-8*, Pub. by U CA Pr) Cal Prin Full Svc.

Nature Vol. 2: The Skies. Ed. by Bert Hower. (Illus.). 80p. 1995. pap. write for info. (*0-936945-53-2*) Creat with Wds.

Nature Vol. 3: The Seas, Water & All Associated with It. Ed. by Bert Hower. (Illus.). 66p. 1995. pap. text. write for info. (*0-936945-57-5*) Creat with Wds.

Nature Vol. 4: The Land, Continents/Countries/ Mountains. Ed. by Bert Hower. (Illus.). 64p. 1995. pap. text. write for info. (*0-936945-58-3*) Creat with Wds.

Nature Vol. 5: Woods & Forests; Trees & Shrubs. Ed. by Bert Hower. (Illus.). 64p. 1995. pap. text. write for info. (*0-936945-59-1*) Creat with Wds.

Nature Vol. 7: Seasons. Ed. by Bert Hower. (Illus.). 72p. 1996. pap. text 5.00 (*0-936945-67-2*) Creat with Wds.

***Nature a Day at a Time: A Naturalist's Book of Days.** Cathie Katz. LC 99-86436. (Illus.). 384p. 2000. 20.00 (*1-57805-050-2*, Pub. by Sierra) Random.

Nature Activities for Early Childhood. Janet Nickelsburg. 1976. pap. text 13.85 (*0-201-05097-8*) Addison-Wesley.

Nature Activity Book. Suzanne Ross. (Little Activity Bks.). (Illus.). (J). 1994. pap. 1.00 (*0-486-28036-5*) Dover.

Nature Against Us: The United States & the World Population Crisis, 1965-1980. Peter J. Donaldson. LC 89-38870. 223p. reprint ed. pap. 69.20 (*0-608-10497-3*, 207112600009) Bks Demand.

Nature, Aims, & Policy. Ed. by Adrian M. Dupuis. LC 70-100373. (Readings in the Philosophy of Education Ser.). 358p. reprint ed. pap. 111.00 (*0-608-30917-6*, 202225500026) Bks Demand.

Nature Alberta: An Illustrated Guide to Common Plants & Animals. James Kavanaugh. Ed. by Elaine Butler. 1991. pap. 11.95 (*0-919433-91-X*) Lone Pine.

Nature All Year Long. Clare W. Leslie. LC 90-47866. (Illus.). 56p. (J). (ps up). 1991. 18.00 (*0-688-09183-0*, Grenwillow Bks) HarpC Child Bks.

Nature & Aesthetics of Design. 6th ed. David Pye. (Illus.). 160p. 1995. reprint ed. pap. 22.95 (*0-9643999-1-1*, 9911) Cambium Pr.

Nature & Animals. Quadrillion Media Staff. (Start Me Up Ser.). (J). 1999. pap. text 3.95 (*1-58185-101-4*) Quadrillion Media.

Nature & Art. Elizabeth Inchbald. LC 93-46497. (Revolution & Romanticism, 1789-1834 Ser.). 1994. 65.00 (*1-85477-170-1*) Continuum.

Nature & Art: A Photographic Exploration. Andreas Feininger. (Photography Ser.). 144p. 1984. reprint ed. pap. 10.95 (*0-486-24539-X*) Dover.

Nature & Art by Elizabeth Inchbald: Emily Herbert, or, Perfidy Punish'd. Elizabeth S. Inchbald. Ed. by Shawn L. Maurer. LC 95-21346. (Women's Classics Ser.). 352p. 1997. 55.00 (*1-85196-265-4*, Pub. by Pickering & Chatto) Ashgate Pub Co.

Nature & Art in Renaissance Literature. Edward W. Tayler. LC 64-20484. (Illus.). 1964. text 57.50 (*0-231-02718-4*) Col U Pr.

Nature & Art of Workmanship. rev. ed. David Pye. (Illus.). 144p. 1995. reprint ed. pap. 22.95 (*0-9643999-0-3*, 9903) Cambium Pr.

Nature & Artifice: The Life & Thought of Thomas Hodgskin (1787-1869) David Stack. LC 97-28794. (Royal Historical Society Studies in History: Vol. 0269-2244). 192p. 1997. 60.00 (*0-86193-229-3*, Royal Historical Soc) Boydell & Brewer.

Nature & Causes of Climate Change. Clare Goodness et al. 1992. 83.00 (*0-87371-849-6*, BHL849) Lewis Pubs.

Nature & Causes of Homosexuality. Ed. by Noretta Koertge. LC 81-6960. (Journal of Homosexuality: Vol. 6, No. 4). 100p. 1982. text 39.95 (*0-86656-148-X*) Haworth Pr.

Nature & Character of God. Winkey Pratney. LC 88-19451. 464p. (C). 1988. pap. 15.99 (*1-55661-041-6*) Bethany Hse.

Nature & Consequences of the Multidivisional Structure. Ahmed Riahi-Belkaoui. LC 94-32084. 208p. 1995. 65.00 (*0-89930-904-6*, Quorum Bks) Greenwood.

Nature & Culture: American Landscape & Painting, 1825-1875. rev. ed. Barbara Novak. (Illus.). 476p. 1995. pap. 27.50 (*0-19-510188-X*) OUP.

Nature & Culture in the Andes. Daniel W. Gade. LC 98-49023. 1999. 18.95 (*0-299-16124-2*); write for info. (*0-299-16120-X*) U of Wis Pr.

Nature & Culture in the "Iliad" The Tragedy of Hector. James M. Redfield. LC 93-32349. 336p. 1993. text 54.95 (*0-8223-1409-6*); pap. text 19.95 (*0-8223-1422-3*) Duke.

Nature & Culture in Western Discourses. Stephen Horigan. LC 88-34506. 139p. reprint ed. pap. 43.10 (*0-608-20348-3*, 207160100002) Bks Demand.

Nature & Danger of Gossip. Charles L. Tucker. 20p. 1995. 1.50 (*0-9625516-5-1*) Vision Commns.

Nature & Danger of Infidel Philosophy. Timothy Dwight. (Notable American Authors Ser.). 1992. reprint ed. lib. bdg. 75.00 (*0-7812-2740-2*) Rprt Serv.

Nature & Destiny Vol. 2: Manual, Vol. 2. Reinhold Niebuhr. 1980. pap. text 18.60 (*0-02-387520-8*, Macmillan Coll) P-H.

Nature & Destiny of Man: A Christian Interpretation, 2 vols. Reinhold Niebuhr. (Library of Theological Ethics). 672p. 1996. pap. 32.00 (*0-664-25709-7*) Westminster John Knox.

Nature & Destiny of Man Vol. I: Human Nature. Niebuhr Reunhold. 305p. (C). 1980. pap. text 17.80 (*0-02-387510-0*, Macmillan Coll) P-H.

Nature & Determinants of Disclosure Adequacy: An International Perspective. Ahmed Riahi-Belkaoui. LC 96-26868. 240p. 1997. 69.50 (*1-56720-086-9*, Quorum Bks) Greenwood.

Nature & Development of Decision-Making: A Self-Regulation Model. James P. Byrnes. 1997. write for info. (*0-614-26980-6*) L Erlbaum Assocs.

Nature & Development of Decision Making: A Self-Regulation Model. James P. Byrnes. LC 97-49262. 1998. write for info. (*0-8058-2287-9*) L Erlbaum Assocs.

Nature & Dignity of Love. William of St. Thierry. Ed. by E. R. Elder. Tr. by Thomas X. Davis from LAT. (Cistercian Fathers Ser.: No. 30). Orig. Title: De natura et dignitate amoris. 1981. pap. 13.95 (*0-87907-730-1*) Cistercian Pubns.

Nature & Dignity of Love. William of St. Thierry. Ed. by E. R. Elder. Tr. by Thomas X. Davis from LAT. (Cistercian Fathers Ser.: No. 30). Orig. Title: De natura et dignitate amoris. 1981. 7.95 (*0-87907-330-6*) Cistercian Pubns.

***Nature & Dynamics of Organizational Capabilities.** Ed. by Giovanni Dosi et al. 420p. 2000. text 74.00 (*0-19-829680-0*) OUP.

Nature & Effectiveness of Bilingual Education Programs for the Spanish-Speaking Child in the United States. Solomon H. Flores. Ed. by Francesco Cordasco. LC 77-92296. (Bilingual-Bicultural Education in the U. S. Ser.). 1978. lib. bdg. 23.95 (*0-405-11082-0*) Ayer.

Nature & Elements of Poetry. Edmund C. Stedman. (Notable American Authors Ser.). 1999. reprint ed. lib. bdg. 125.00 (*0-7812-8914-9*) Rprt Serv.

Nature & Evolutionary Status of Herbig Ae/Be Stars, No. 62. P. S. Associates Staff & Edward P. Van Den Heuvel. LC 94-72188. 464p. 1994. 34.00 (*0-937707-81-3*) Astron Soc Pacific.

Nature & Extent of Alcohol Abuse among the Elderly. 1991. lib. bdg. 74.00 (*0-8490-4374-3*) Gordon Pr.

Nature & Extent of Lead Poisoning in Children in the U. S. A Report to Congress. Paul Mushak & Annemarie F. Crocetti. (Illus.). 700p. (Orig.). (C). 1999. reprint ed. pap. text 60.00 (*0-7881-3383-7*) DIANE Pub.

Nature & Function of Art, More Especially of Architecture. Leopold Eidlitz. LC 77-4765. (Architecture & Decorative Art Ser.). 1977. reprint ed. lib. bdg. 55.00 (*0-306-70898-1*) Da Capo.

Nature & Function of Faith in the Theology of John Calvin. Victor A. Shepherd. LC 82-24899. (NABPR Dissertation Ser.: No. 2). viii, 248p. 1983. pap. 17.45 (*0-86554-066-7*, P007) Mercer Univ Pr.

***Nature & Function of Rituals: Fire from Heaven.** Ruth-Inge Heinze. LC 99-33208. 328p. 2000. 75.00 (*0-89789-663-7*, Bergin & Garvey) Greenwood.

Nature & Function of Scientific Theories: Essays in Contemporary Science & Philosophy. Grover Maxwell et al. Ed. by Robert G. Colodny. LC 70-123094. (Pittsburg University Series in Philosophy of Science: Vol. 4). 379p. reprint ed. pap. 117.50 (*0-608-12636-5*, 202543400043) Bks Demand.

***Nature & Function of Syntactic Categories.** Ed. by Robert D. Borsley. (Syntax & Semantics Ser.: Vol. 32). 318p. 1999. 99.00 (*0-12-613532-0*) Acad Pr.

Nature & Functions of Authority. Yves R. Simon. (Aquinas Lectures). 1940. 15.00 (*0-87462-104-6*) Marquette.

Nature & Functions of Law. 4th ed. Berman & Greiner. 1980. text 31.50 (*0-88277-495-6*) Foundation Pr.

Nature & Functions of Law. 5th ed. Harold J. Berman et al. LC 95-47047. (Paralegal). 853p. 1996. text 45.95 (*1-56662-238-7*) Foundation Pr.

Nature & Future of Episcopal Conferences. Legrand et al. LC 88-28555. 410p. 1988. pap. 19.95 (*0-8132-0703-7*) Cath U Pr.

Nature & Grace in Flannery O'Connor's Fiction. Lorine M. Getz. LC 82-22458. (Studies in Art & Religious Interpretation: Vol. 2). 192p. 1982. lib. bdg. 79.95 (*0-88946-550-9*) E Mellen.

Nature & Grace Theol. Occ., No. Betl 127. E. Peters. 1998. 56.95 (*90-6831-832-2*, Pub. by Peeters Pub) Bks Intl VA.

N

An Asterisk (*) at the beginning of an entry indicates that the title is appearing for the first time.

Nature & Growth of Modern Mathematics. E. E. Kramer. 784p. 1982. pap. text 35.00 (0-691-02372-7, Pub. by Princeton U Pr) Cal Prin Full Svc.

Nature & Heaven in the Xunzi: A Study of the Tian Lun. Edward J. Machle. LC 92-31573. (SUNY Series in Chinese Philosophy & Culture). 224p. (C). 1993. text 64.50 (0-7914-1553-8); pap. text 21.95 (0-7914-1554-6) State U NY Pr.

Nature & Her Laws. Paul H. D'Holbach. 1972. 59.95 (0-8490-0714-3) Gordon Pr.

Nature & Hiking Guide to Cape Breton's Cabot Trail. David Lawley. LC 95-208023. (Illus.). 164p. 1995. pap. 14.95 (1-55109-105-4) Nimbus Publ.

Nature & Historical Experience: Essays in Naturalism & the Theory of History. John H. Randall. LC 57-11694. (C). 1962. pap. text 25.50 (0-231-08537-0) Col U Pr.

Nature & History: The Evolutionary Approach for Social Scientists, Vol. 1. Ignazio Masulli. (World Futures General Evolution Studies). 184p. 1990. text 84.00 (2-88124-376-2) Gordon & Breach.

Nature & Human Nature: Essays Metaphysical & Historical. Hartley B. Alexander. LC 75-3018. (Philosophy in America Ser.). reprint ed. 72.00 (0-404-59011-X) AMS Pr.

***Nature & Human Personality: Homeopathic Archetypes.** Catherine Coulter. 250p. 2000. 18.50 (1-57626-117-4) Quality Med Pub.

Nature & Human Society: The Quest for a Sustainable World. National Academy of Sciences Staff et al. Ed. by Peter H. Raven & Tania Williams. LC 99-50565. (Illus.). 500p. 1999. 42.00 (0-309-06555-0) Natl Acad Pr.

Nature & Ideology: Natural Garden Design in the Twentieth Century. Ed. by Joachim Wolschke-Bulmahn. LC 96-46176. (Colloquium on the History of Landscape Architecture Ser.: Vol. 18). (Illus.). 1997. 50.00 (0-88402-246-3, WONA) Dumbarton Oaks.

Nature & Life. Alfred North Whitehead. LC 69-14150. (Illus.). 46p. 1970. reprint ed. lib. bdg. 35.00 (0-8371-0751-2, WHNL, Greenwood Pr) Greenwood.

Nature & Lifeworld: Theoretical & Practical Metaphysics. Ed. by Niels Thomassen & Carsten Bengt-Pedersen. LC 99-189761. 345p. 1998. pap. 32.00 (87-7838-311-0, Pub. by Odense Univ) Intl Spec Bk.

Nature & Limits of Authority. Richard T. De George. LC 85-8128. viii, 312p. 1985. 29.95 (0-7006-0269-0); pap. 14.95 (0-7006-0270-4) U Pr of KS.

Nature & Limits of Political Science. Maurice Cowling. LC 85-12591. 214p. 1985. reprint ed. lib. bdg. 65.00 (0-313-24949-0, CNLI, Greenwood Pr) Greenwood.

Nature & Logic of Capitalism. Robert L. Heilbroner. (Orig.). (C). 1986. reprint ed. pap. 10.95 (0-393-95529-X) Norton.

Nature & Love Poems. Ruth Herschberger. LC 69-15875. 1969. 15.00 (0-87130-009-5) Eakins.

Nature & Madness. Paul Shepard. LC 97-23869. 178p. 1998. pap. 17.95 (0-8203-1980-5) U of Ga Pr.

Nature & Make Believe. Prod. by Zobeida Perez. 16p. (Orig.). (YA). 1991. pap. 17.00 (0-89898-659-1, BMR04065) Wrner Bros.

Nature & Man. Paul Weiss. LC 83-16823. 310p. (C). 1983. reprint ed. pap. text 25.00 (0-8191-3590-9) U Pr of Amer.

Nature & Man: Essays Scientific & Philosophical. William B. Carpenter. LC 78-72791. (Brainedness, Handedness, & Mental Abilities Ser.). reprint ed. 34.50 (0-404-60855-8) AMS Pr.

Nature & Man in the Bible. Yehuda Feliks. (Illus.). 294p. 1981. 30.00 (0-900689-19-6) Soncino Pr.

Nature & Man in the Bible: Chapters in Biblical Ecology. Yehuda Feliks. 1982. 25.00 (1-871055-02-4) Bloch.

Nature & Mission Theology. Joseph C. Ratzinger. LC 94-79301. 130p. 1995. pap. 12.95 (0-89870-538-X) Ignatius Pr.

Nature & Motion in the Middle Ages. James A. Weisheipl. Ed. by William E. Carroll. LC 84-12129. (Studies in Philosophy & the History of Philosophy: No. 11). 304p. 1985. reprint ed. pap. 94.30 (0-7837-9107-0, 204990900004) Bks Demand.

***Nature & Nationalism: Right-wing Ecology & The Politics of Identity in Contemporary Germany.** Jonathan Olsen. LC 99-17474. 1999. text 45.00 (0-312-22071-5) St Martin.

Nature & Necessity of Christ's Church. Michael Richards. LC 83-2596. 142p. 1983. pap. 7.95 (0-8189-0458-5) Alba.

Nature & Nurture During Infancy & Early Childhood. Robert Plomin et al. 368p. 1988. text 69.95 (0-521-34370-4) Cambridge U Pr.

Nature & Nurture in Psychiatry: A Predisposition-Stress Model of Mental Disorders. Joel Paris. 1999. 49.50 (0-88048-781-X, 8781) Am Psychiatric.

Nature & Nuture: An Introduction to Behavioral Genetics. Robert Plomin. LC 89-9725. 150p. (C). 1996. mass mkt. 18.00 (0-534-10768-0) Brooks-Cole.

Nature & Ontogenesis of Meaning. Ed. by Willis F. Overton & David S. Palermo. (Jean Piaget Symposia Ser.). 320p. 1994. text 69.95 (0-8058-1211-3) L Erlbaum Assocs.

Nature & Organization of Retroviral Genes in Animal Cells. D. R. Strayer & D. H. Gillespie. (Virology Monographs: Vol. 17). (Illus.). 117p. 1980. 58.00 (0-387-81563-5) Spr-Verlag.

Nature & Origin of Amyloid Fibrils: Symposium, No. 199. CIBA Foundation Staff. LC 96-2872. (CIBA Foundation Symposium Ser.). 266p. 1996. 128.00 (0-471-96361-5) Wiley.

Nature & Origin of Cordilleran Magmatism. Ed. by J. L. Anderson. (Memoir Ser.: No. 174). (Illus.). 440p. 1990. 40.00 (0-8137-1174-6) Geol Soc.

Nature & Origin of Meteorites. fac. ed. D. W. Sears. LC 79-314881. (Monographs on Astronomical Subjects: No. 5). (Illus.). 197p. 1978. reprint ed. pap. 61.10 (0-7837-8013-3, 204776900008) Bks Demand.

Nature & Origin of the Biological World. E. J. Ambrose. 190p. 1982. text 78.95 (0-470-27513-8); pap. text 38.95 (0-470-27514-6) P-H.

Nature & Origins of Mass Opinion. John R. Zaller. (Illus.). 381p. (C). 1992. text 69.95 (0-521-40449-5); pap. text 20.95 (0-521-40786-9) Cambridge U Pr.

Nature & Origins of Mathematical Skills. Ed. by Jamie I. Campbell. LC 92-18326. (Advances in Psychology Ser.: 91). x,570p. 1992. 185.00 (0-444-89014-9, North Holland) Elsevier.

Nature & Origins of Scientism. John Wellmuth. (Aquinas Lectures). 1944. 15.00 (0-87462-108-9) Marquette.

Nature & Other Mothers: Personal Stories of Women & the Body of Earth. Brenda Peterson. 256p. 1995. pap. 12.00 (0-449-90967-0) Fawcett.

Nature & Other Writings. Ralph Waldo Emerson. Ed. by Peter Turner. LC 94-6183. (Pocket Classics Ser.). 240p. 1994. pap. 6.00 (0-87773-985-4, Pub. by Shambhala Pubns) Random.

Nature & Policy in Iceland, 1400-1800: An Anthropological Analysis of History & Mentality. Kirsten Hastrup. (Illus.). 380p. 1990. text 95.00 (0-19-827728-8) OUP.

Nature & Politics: Liberalism in the Philosophies of Hobbes, Locke, & Rousseau. Andrzej Rapaczynski. LC 87-5451. 312p. (C). 1987. pap. text 16.95 (0-8014-9606-3) Cornell U Pr.

Nature & Power of Mathematics. Donald M. Davis. LC 92-26744. (Illus.). 488p. (C). 1993. pap. text 27.50 (0-691-02562-2, Pub. by Princeton U Pr) Cal Prin Full Svc.

Nature & Practice of Biological Control of Plant Pathogens. R. James Cook & Kenneth F. Baker. LC 83-71224. 539p. 1983. text 58.00 (0-89054-053-5) Am Phytopathol Soc.

Nature & Process of Law: An Introduction to Legal Philosophy. Ed. by Patricia Smith. LC 92-15723. 880p. 1993. text 59.95 (0-19-507697-4) OUP.

Nature & Processes of Preverbal Learning: Implications from Nine Month-Old Infants' Discrimination Problem-Solving. Jeffrey T. Coldren & John Colombo. (Monographs of the Society for Research in Child Development: No. 1). 104p. 1994. pap. text 15.00 (0-226-11327-2) U Ch Pr.

Nature & Properties of Refracting Carbides. G. S. Upadhyaya. 600p. 1997. text 125.00 (1-56072-056-5) Nova Sci Pubs.

Nature & Properties of Semi-Solid Materials: Proceedings of a Symposium Sponsored by the TMS Solidification Committee of the Materials Design & Manufacturing Division, Held During the 1992 Annual Meeting, San Diego, CA, March 1-5, 1992. Ed. by J. A. Sekhar & J. A. Dantzig. LC 91-51051. 299p. 1991. reprint ed. pap. 92.70 (0-608-03822-9, 206278400004) Bks Demand.

Nature & Properties of Soils. 2nd ed. Nyle C. Brady & Ray R. Weil. LC 98-13008. 881p. (C). 1998. 100.00 (0-13-852444-0) P-H.

Nature & Prospects of Bioethics. John C. Fletcher & Franklin G. Miller. 350p. 1999. 44.50 (0-89603-709-6) Humana.

***Nature & Psyche: Radical Environmentalism & the Politics of Subjectivity.** David W. Kidner. (C). 2000. pap. text 24.95 (0-7914-4752-9) State U NY Pr.

***Nature & Psyche: Radical Environmentalism & the Politics of Subjectivity.** David W. Kidner. (C). 2000. text 73.50 (0-7914-4751-0) State U NY Pr.

Nature & Pursuit of Love: The Philosophy of Irving Singer. Ed. by David L. Goicoechea. LC 94-40405. 364p. (C). 1995. 39.95 (0-87975-912-7) Prometheus Bks.

Nature & Religious Imagination: From Edwards to Bushnell. C. Conrad Cherry. LC 79-7374. 254p. reprint ed. pap. 78.80 (0-608-15537-3, 202977000064) Bks Demand.

Nature & Role of Algebra in the K - 14 Curriculum: Proceedings of a National Symposium. National Research Council Staff. LC 99-179839. 206p. (C). 1998. pap. text 36.75 (0-309-06147-4) Natl Acad Pr.

Nature & Salvation in "Piers Plowman" Hugh White. (Piers Plowman Studies: Vol. 6). 136p. 1988. 75.00 (0-85991-271-X, DS Brewer) Boydell & Brewer.

Nature & Science. Joan Bielitz & Marilyn LaPenta. Ed. by Susan Evento. (Macmillan Early Skills Program - Conversion Ser.). 64p. (J). (ps-2). 1995. pap. 9.95 (1-56784-505-3) Newbridge Educ.

Nature & Science of Autumn see Exploring the Science of Nature: New Releases

Nature & Science of Bubbles see Exploring the Science of Nature: Four New Releases

Nature & Science of Color see Exploring the Science of Nature: Four New Releases

Nature & Science of Eggs see Exploring the Science of Nature Series: New Releases

Nature & Science of Energy see Exploring the Science of Nature: Four New Releases

Nature & Science of Flowers see Exploring the Science of Nature Series: New Releases

Nature & Science of Fossils see Exploring the Science of Nature

Nature & Science of Leaves see Exploring the Science of Nature Series

Nature & Science of Mud see Exploring the Science of Nature Series

***Nature & Science of Numbers.** Jane Burton & Kim Taylor. LC 00-32248. (Exploring the Science of Nature Ser.). (Illus.). 2000. lib. bdg. write for info. (0-8368-2193-9) Gareth Stevens Inc.

Nature & Science of Patterns see Exploring the Science of Nature Series: New Releases

Nature & Science of Rain see Exploring the Science of Nature Series

Nature & Science of Rocks see Exploring the Science of Nature: Four New Releases

Nature & Science of Seeds see Exploring the Science of Nature

Nature & Science of Shells see Exploring the Science of Nature

Nature & Science of Spring see Exploring the Science of Nature: New Releases

Nature & Science of Summer see Exploring the Science of Nature: New Releases

Nature & Science of Sunlight see Exploring the Science of Nature Series

Nature & Science of Waste see Exploring the Science of Nature

Nature & Science of Wings see Exploring the Science of Nature Series: New Releases

Nature & Science of Winter see Exploring the Science of Nature: New Releases

Nature & Science Sing: Biophysics in Poems. Ram R. Sharma. LC 86-64034. 88p. (Orig.). 1987. pap. text 8.50 (0-86516-192-5) Bolchazy-Carducci.

Nature & Scientific Method. Ed. by Daniel O. Dahlstrom. LC 89-70817. (Studies in Philosophy & the History of Philosophy: Vol. 22). 328p. 1991. 48.95 (0-8132-0723-1) Cath U Pr.

Nature & Self: A Study of the Poetry of Su Dongpo, with Comparisons to the Poetry of William Wordsworth. Vincent Yang. (American University Studies: Comparative Literature: Ser. III, Vol. 28). 226p. (C). 1989. text 38.50 (0-8204-0939-1) P Lang Pubng.

Nature & Social Power. Lyndsay Farrall. (C). 1982. 45.00 (0-86828-124-7, Pub. by Deakin Univ) St Mut.

Nature & Society: Anthropological Perspectives. Ed. by Philippe Descola & Gisli Palsson. 320p. (C). 1996. 85.00 (0-415-13215-0); pap. 25.99 (0-415-13216-9) Routledge.

Nature & Society in Central Brazil: The Suya Indians of Mato Grasso. Anthony Seeger. LC 80-18682. (Harvard Studies in Cultural Anthropology: No. 4). (Illus.). 294p. (C). 1981. 43.00 (0-674-60485-7) HUP.

Nature & Society in Historical Context. Ed. by Mikulas Teich et al. LC 96-14063. (Illus.). 419p. 1997. text 69.95 (0-521-49530-X); pap. text 27.95 (0-521-49881-3) Cambridge U Pr.

Nature & Sources of the Law. John C. Gray. LC 96-6123. (Classical Jurisprudence Ser.). (Illus.). 250p. 1996. text 78.95 (1-85521-651-5, Pub. by Dartmth Pub) Ashgate Pub Co.

***Nature & Sources of the Law.** John Chipman Gray. LC 99-73248. 332p. 1999. 95.00 (1-56169-535-1) Gaunt.

Nature & Sources of the Law. John C. Gray. Ed. by Bernard D. Reams, Jr. LC 27-15000. (Historical Reprints in Jurisprudence & Classical Legal Literature Ser.). xviii, 348p. 1984. reprint ed. lib. bdg. 47.50 (0-89941-250-5, 303190) W S Hein.

Nature & Sources of the Law. 2nd ed. John C. Gray. 1990. 16.50 (0-8446-2156-0) Peter Smith.

***Nature & Sources of the Law.** 2nd ed. John C. Gray. 2000. reprint ed. 110.00 (1-56169-582-3) Gaunt.

Nature & Spirit: An Essay in Ecstatic Naturalism. Robert S. Corrington. LC 92-361. xiii, 207p. 1992. 30.00 (0-8232-1362-5); pap. 19.95 (0-8232-1363-3) Fordham.

Nature & Spirit in Christianity Today. Joyce Rockwood-Hudson. (Wisdom Ser.: Vol. 1). iii, 36p. 1998. pap. 2.00 (1-893383-01-6) JRH Pubns.

Nature & Status of Ethnobotany. 2nd ed. Ed. & Intro. by Richard I. Ford. LC 95-127278. (Anthropological Papers Ser.: No. 67). (Illus.). xxxii, 428p. (Orig.). 1994. pap. 18.00 (0-915703-38-6) U Mich Mus Anthro.

Nature & Structure of the Islamic World. Ralph Braibanti. LC 95-19136. (Position Papers: No. 1). 1995. write for info. (0-614-32361-4) ISPI.

Nature & Structure of the Islamic World. Ralph Braibanti. 108p. 1996. pap. 10.00 (0-614-21443-2, 1394) Kazi Pubns.

Nature & Structure of the Islamic World. Ralph Braibanti & Javeed Akhter. LC 95-16136. 60p. 1995. write for info. (0-9647204-0-X) ISPI.

Nature & Tasks of a Personalist Psychology. Compiled by James M. Dubois. LC 95-36961. 204p. (Orig.). (C). 1995. pap. text 28.50 (0-7618-0101-4); lib. bdg. 52.50 (0-7618-0100-6) U Pr of Amer.

Nature & Technology of Acoustic Space. Ed. by M. Tohyama et al. (Illus.). 352p. 1995. text 95.00 (0-12-692590-9) Acad Pr.

Nature & the American: Three Centuries of Changing Attitudes. Hans Huth. LC 90-35727. (Illus.). xlviii, 314p. 1990. reprint ed. pap. text 9.95 (0-8032-7247-2, Bison Books) U of Nebr Pr.

Nature & the Crisis of Modernity. Raymond A. Rogers. 187p. 1995. pap. 19.99 (1-55164-014-7, Pub. by Black Rose) Consort Bk Sales.

Nature & the Effect of the Heresy of the Fraticelli. Decima L. Douie. LC 77-84715. reprint ed. 41.50 (0-404-16121-9) AMS Pr.

***Nature & the English Diaspora: Environment & History in the United States, Canada, Australia, & New Zealand.** Thomas Dunlap. (Studies in Environment & History: No. 17). (Illus.). 368p. (C). 1999. 59.95 (0-521-65173-5); pap. 19.95 (0-521-65700-8) Cambridge U Pr.

Nature & the Greeks & Science & Humanism. Erwin Schrodinger. (Canto Book Ser.). (Illus.). 182p. 1996. pap. 10.95 (0-521-57550-8) Cambridge U Pr.

Nature & the Human Spirit: Toward an Expanded Land Management Ethic. Ed. by B. L. Driver et al. LC 96-60358. 497p. 1996. text 39.95 (0-910251-82-7, NHS86) Venture Pub PA.

Nature & the Idea of a Man-Made World: An Investigation into the Evolutionary Roots of Form & Order in the Built Environment. Norman Crowe. LC 94-45594. (Illus.). 296p. 1995. 37.50 (0-262-03222-8) MIT Pr.

Nature & the Idea of a Man-Made World: An Investigation into the Evolutionary Roots of Form & Order in the Built Environment. Norman Crowe. (Illus.). 296p. 1997. reprint ed. pap. text 18.50 (0-262-53146-1) MIT Pr.

***Nature & the Marketplace: Capturing the Value of Ecosystem Services.** Geoffrey Heal. (Illus.). 184p. 2000. 50.00 (1-55963-795-1, Shearwater Bks); pap. 25.00 (1-55963-796-X) Island Pr.

Nature & the Orient: The Environmental History of South & Southeast Asia. Ed. by Richard H. Grove et al. LC 98-902985. (Illus.). 1,056p. 1998. text 75.00 (0-19-563896-4) OUP.

Nature & the Supernatural As Together Constituting the One System of God. Horace Bushnell. LC 70-39569. reprint ed. 52.50 (0-404-01246-9) AMS Pr.

Nature & Treatment of Anxiety Disorders. C. Barr Taylor & Bruce A. Arnow. 368p. 1988. 45.00 (0-02-932981-7) Free Pr.

Nature & Treatment of Capital Gains & Losses. Lawrence H. Seltzer et al. (Fiscal Studies Ser.: No. 3). 576p. 1951. reprint ed. 39.95 (0-87014-119-8) Natl Bur Econ Res.

Nature & Treatment of Depression. Frederic F. Flach & Suzanne C. Draghi. LC 74-28265. 434p. reprint ed. 134.60 (0-8357-9939-5, 205516900011) Bks Demand.

Nature & Treatment of Stuttering. 2nd ed. Richard F. Curlee & Gerald M. Siegel. 452p. 1996. 69.00 (0-205-16336-X) Allyn.

Nature & Treatment of the Stress Response: A Practical Guide for Clinicians. G. S. Everly, Jr. & R. Rosenfeld. (Illus.). 232p. (C). 1981. 42.50 (0-306-40677-2, Plenum Trade) Perseus Pubng.

Nature & Types of Sociological Theory. 2nd ed. Don A. Martindale. (Illus.). 656p. (C). 1988. reprint ed. pap. text 33.95 (0-88133-353-0) Waveland Pr.

Nature & Value of Jurisprudence. 2nd enl. ed. Chan-Toon. xxiv, 187p. 1982. reprint ed. 35.00 (0-8377-0436-7, Rothman) W S Hein.

Nature & Walking. Ralph Waldo Emerson & Henry David Thoreau. LC 85-47940. 144p. 1994. pap. 11.00 (0-8070-1419-2) Beacon Pr.

Nature & Weather see Altabiaa Walmanakn

Nature & Wildlife Photography: A Practical Guide to How to Shoot & Sell. Susan McCartney. LC 93-71919. (Illus.). 256p. (Orig.). 1994. pap. 18.95 (1-880559-12-9) Allworth Pr.

Nature Animated. Michael Ruse. 287p. 1982. lib. bdg. 135.00 (90-277-1403-7, D Reidel) Kluwer Academic.

Nature Aquarium World, Bk. 2. Talsashi Amano. 162p. 1996. 39.95 (0-7938-2077-4, TS-284) TFH Pubns.

Nature Aquarium World, Bk. 3. Talsashi Amano. 1996. 29.95 (0-7938-2078-2, TS-285) TFH Pubns.

Nature Art Anew. Charles Biederman. 218p. 1993. 15.50 (0-9600002-7-5) Art History.

***Nature Art with Chiura Obata.** Michael E. Ross. LC 98-49073. (Naturalist's Apprentice Biographies Ser.). (Illus.). 48p. (J). (gr. 3-6). 2000. 19.93 (1-57505-378-0, Carolrhoda) Lerner Pub.

Nature As a Guide: Using Nature in Counseling, Therapy, & Education. Linda L. Nebbe. LC 95-60563. (Illus.). 256p. (C). 1995. pap. text 14.95 (0-932796-72-9) Ed Media Corp.

Nature as Landscape: Dwelling & Understanding. Kraft E. von Maltzahn. (Illus.). 160p. 1994. 55.00 (0-7735-1233-0, Pub. by McG-Queens Univ Pr) CUP Services.

Nature As Subject: Human Obligation & Natural Community. Eric Katz. (Studies in Social, Political, & Legal Philosophy: No. 70). 290p. 1996. 66.00 (0-8476-8303-6); pap. 25.95 (0-8476-8304-4) Rowman.

Nature at Work: Introducing Ecology. British Museum, Geological Department Staff. LC 78-66795. (Illus.). 96p. (YA). (gr. 7 up). 1978. pap. 12.95 (0-521-29469-X) Cambridge U Pr.

Nature at Your Doorstep: Real World Investigations for Primary Students. Carole G. Basile et al. LC 96-39312. (Illus.). 190p. 1997. pap. text, student ed. 22.00 (1-56308-455-4) Teacher Ideas Pr.

Nature B. C. James Kavanagh. 1993. pap. 14.95 (1-55105-036-6) Lone Pine.

Nature Book to Color. (To Learn & Color Ser.). (Illus.). 96p. (J). (gr. 2-9). 1978. pap. 3.90 (0-7399-0192-3, 2925) Rod & Staff.

Nature Bound Pocket Field Guide. Ron Dawson. 1990. pap. text 13.99 (0-8163-1072-6) Pacific Pr Pub Assn.

Nature by Design. Bruce Brooks. (Knowing Nature Ser.). (Illus.). 80p. (J). (gr. 5 up). 1991. bds. 13.95 (0-374-30334-7) FS&G.

Nature by the Numbers. Lynette Ruschak. (Illus.). 12p. (J). (ps-1). 1994. 12.95 (0-671-88610-X) Litle Simon.

***Nature Call.** Kimon G. Faubion. 100p. 1999. pap. 9.95 (0-7392-0492-0, PO3850) Morris Pubng.

Nature Calls: The History, Lore & Charm of Outhouses. Dottie Booth. LC 97-50323. (Illus.). 86p. 1998. pap. 12.95 (0-89815-990-3) Ten Speed Pr.

***Nature Calls Calendar 2000.** Dottie Booth. (Illus.). 24p. 1999. pap. 9.95 (1-58008-083-9) Ten Speed Pr.

Nature, Change & Agency in Aristotle's Physics: A Philosophical Study. Sarah Waterlow. (Illus.). 280p. 1988. pap. text 22.00 (0-19-824482-7) OUP.

Nature Close Up: A Fantastic Journey into Reality. rev. ed. Andreas Feininger. (Illus.). 160p. 1981. reprint ed. pap. 12.95 (0-486-24102-5) Dover.

Nature Close-Ups, 6 bks. Densey Clyne. Incl. Catch Me If You Can! LC 97-41450. (Illus.). 32p. (YA). (gr. 3 up). 1998. lib. bdg. 21.27 (0-8368-2056-8); Cicada Sing-Song. LC 97-35497. (Illus.). 32p. (YA). (gr. 3 up).

N

An Asterisk (*) at the beginning of an entry indicates that the title is appearing for the first time.

1998. lib. bdg. 21.27 (*0-8368-2057-6*); Flutter by, Butterfly. LC 97-31736. (Illus.). 32p. (YA). (gr. 3 up). 1998. lib. bdg. 21.27 (*0-8368-2058-4*); It's a Frog's Life! LC 97-31734. (Illus.). 32p. (YA). (gr. 3 up). 1998. lib. bdg. 21.27 (*0-8368-2059-2*); Plants of Prey. LC 97-31735. (Illus.). 32p. (YA). (gr. 3 up). 1998. lib. bdg. 21.27 (*0-8368-2060-6*); Spotlight on Spiders. LC 97-31733. (Illus.). 32p. (YA). (gr. 3 up). 1998. lib. bdg. 21.27 (*0-8368-2061-4*); (Illus.). (J). 1998. Set lib. bdg. 127.60 (*0-8368-2055-X*) Gareth Stevens Inc.

Nature, Cognition & System, No. I. Marc E. Carvallo. (C). 1988. lib. bdg. 211.50 (*90-277-2740-6*) Kluwer Academic.

Nature, Cognition & System Two: Current Systems-Scientific Research on Natural & Cognitive Systems, Vol. 2: On Complementarity & Beyond. Ed. by Marc E. Carvallo. (Theory & Decision Library, Series D). 420p. (C). 1992. lib. bdg. 236.00 (*0-7923-1788-2*, Pub. by Kluwer Academic) Kluwer Academic.

Nature Company Guides Series, 8 bks. Incl. Birding. John Forshaw. Ed. by Terence Lindsey. LC 95-8608. (Illus.). 288p. (J). (gr. 3 up). 1999. 24.95 (*0-7835-4752-8*); Natural Gardening. John K. Borin & Young Discoveries Staff. Ed. by R. J. Turner. LC 95-1225. (Illus.). 288p. (gr. 3). 1999. 24.95 (*0-7835-4750-1*); Nature Travel. Dwight Holing. Ed. by Ben Davidson. LC 95-1224. (Illus.). 288p. (J). (gr. 3 up). 1999. 24.95 (*0-7835-4753-6*); Rocks & Fossils. Arthur B. Busbey, 3rd. LC 95-47661. (Illus.). 288p. (gr. 3). 1999. 24.95 (*0-7835-4803-6*); Skywatching. David H. Levy. Ed. by John O'Byrne. LC 95-8609. (Illus.). 288p. (J). (gr. 3 up). 1997. 24.95 (*0-7835-4751-X*); Walker's Companion. Elizabeth Ferber. Ed. by David R. Wallace. LC 95-4551. (Illus.). 288p. (gr. 3). 1999. 24.95 (*0-7835-4754-4*); Weather. William J. Burroughs & Sally Morgan. Ed. by Richard Whitaker. LC 95-20621. (Illus.). 288p. (J). (gr. 4-7). 1999. 24.95 (*0-8094-9374-8*); World Travel: A Guide to International Ecojourneys. Dwight Holing. LC 96-636. (Illus.). 228p. (gr. 3). 1999. 24.95 (*0-7835-4804-4*); 239.60 (*0-7835-8613-2*) Time-Life.

Nature Company 2-in-1 Poster Pack. (Illus.). 14p. (Orig.). (gr. k-7). 1999. pap. 9.95 (*0-7835-4796-X*) Time-Life.

Nature Conservation: Management & Physical Planning in the Wadden Sea Area. Ed. by Bruyns Morzer & W. J. Wolff. 164p. 1983. pap. 71.00 (*90-6191-061-7*, Pub. by A A Balkema) Ashgate Pub Co.

***Nature Conservation 4: The Role of Networks.** Ed. by Surrey Beatty Staff. 696p. 1999. pap. 512.00 (*0-949324-65-5*, Pub. by Surrey Beatty & Sons) St Mut.

***Nature Conservation in Britain: The Formative Years.** John Sheail. 282p. 1998. 45.00 (*0-11-702308-6*, Pub. by Statnry Office) Balogh.

Nature Conservation in Europe: Policy & Practice. P. Bromley. LC 97-189879. (Illus.). 240p. (C). 1998. 60.00 (*0-419-21610-3*, E & FN Spon) Routledge.

Nature Conservation 3: Reconstructed of Fragmented Ecosystems. Ed. by Surrey Beatty Staff et al. 326p. 1999. pap. 328.00 (*0-949324-50-7*, Pub. by Surrey Beatty & Sons) St Mut.

Nature Conservation 2: The Role of Corridors. Ed. by Surrey Beatty Staff. 457p. (C). 1999. pap. 340.00 (*0-949324-35-3*, Pub. by Surrey Beatty & Sons) St Mut.

Nature, Contemplation, & the One: A Study in the Philosophy of Plotinus. 2nd ed. John N. Deck. 152p. 1991. reprint ed. pap. 14.95 (*0-943914-54-X*) Larson Pubns.

***Nature Contested: Environmental History in Scotland & Northern England.** T. C. Smout. 256p. 2000. text 70.00 (*0-7486-1410-9*); pap. text 23.00 (*0-7486-1411-7*) Col U Pr.

Nature Corner: Celebrating the Year's Cycle with a Seasonal Tableau. M. Leeuwen & J. Moeskops. Tr. by Polly Lawson. (DUT., Illus.). 88p. (J). (ps-3). 1990. reprint ed. pap. 12.95 (*0-86315-111-6*, Pub. by Floris Bks) Gryphon Hse.

Nature Craft. Editors at Eaglemoss. (Illus.). 144p. 1993. pap. 16.99 (*0-89134-542-6*, 30531, North Lght Bks) F & W Pubns Inc.

Nature Crafts. Sybil Harp. (Hobby Bks.: No. C-24). (Illus.). 36p. 1972. pap. 4.00 (*0-911868-24-0*, C24) Carstens Pubns.

Nature Crafts. Cynthia Holzschuher. (Illus.). 64p. (J). (gr. k-3). 1997. pap. text 8.95 (*0-88724-395-9*, CD-0973) Carson-Dellos.

Nature Crafts for Children. Wendy Zhorne. (Illus.). 160p. (Orig.). (J). (gr. k-2). 1995. pap. 10.99 (*0-8010-5266-1*) Baker Bks.

Nature Crafts for Christmas: A Step-by-Step Guide to Making Wreaths, Ornaments & Decorations. Dawn Cusick & Carol Taylor. LC 94-15975. 256p. 1994. 27.95 (*0-87596-622-5*) Rodale Pr Inc.

Nature Crafts for Kids: 50 Fantastic Things to Make with Mother Nature's Help. Gwen Diehn & Terry Krautwurst. (Illus.). 144p. (J). 1997. pap. 14.95 (*0-8069-8373-6*) Sterling.

Nature Crafts with a Microwave: Over 80 Projects. Dawn Cusick. (Illus.). 128p. 1995. pap. 14.95 (*0-8069-0667-7*) Sterling.

Nature Crafts Workshop. Will Kirkman. LC 80-84186. (Crafts Workshop Ser.). (J). (gr. 3-8). 1981. pap. 11.99 (*0-8224-9781-6*) Fearon Teacher Aids.

Nature Cross-Section. Moira Butterfield. LC 94-44798. (Illus.). 32p. (J). (gr. 5-8). 1995. 17.95 (*0-7894-0147-9*, 5-70599) DK Pub Inc.

Nature Crossword Puzzles. Suzanne Ross. (Little Activity Bks.). (Illus.). (J). 1995. pap. 1.00 (*0-486-28854-4*) Dover.

Nature, Culture & Gender. Ed. by Carol MacCormack & Marilyn Strathern. (Illus.). 235p. 1980. pap. text 22.95 (*0-521-28001-X*) Cambridge U Pr.

***Nature, Culture & History: The "Knowing" of Oceania.** K. R. Howe. LC 99-87297. 2000. pap. write for info. (*0-8248-2329-X*) UH Pr.

Nature, Culture, Identity. Anne Buttimer & Luke Wallin. LC 99-18814. (Geojournal Library). 1999. write for info. (*0-7923-5651-9*) Kluwer Academic.

Nature, Culture, Imperialism: Essays on the Environmental History of South Asia. Ed. by David Arnold & Ramachandra Guha. (Studies in Social Ecology & Environmental History). (Illus.). 388p. 1997. pap. text 17.95 (*0-19-564075-6*) OUP.

Nature Cure 2000. Henry Lindlahr. Ed. by G. E. Poesnecker. LC 98-227357. 384p. 1998. pap. 15.00 (*0-916285-60-X*) Humanitarian.

Nature de la Connaissance Scientifique: L'Epistemologie Meyersonienne Face a la Critique de Gaston Bachelard. Ndjate-Lotanga Wetshingolo. (Publications Universitaires Europeennes Ser.: Series 20, Vol. 497). (FRE.). xii, 338p. 1996. 50.95 (*3-906754-43-X*, Pub. by P Lang) P Lang Pubng.

***Nature, Design & Science: The Status of Design in Natural Science.** Del Ratzsch. (C). 2001. pap. text 18.95 (*0-7914-4894-0*) State U NY Pr.

***Nature, Design & Science: The Status of Design in Natural Science.** Del Ratzsch. (C). 2001. text 57.50 (*0-7914-4893-2*) State U NY Pr.

Nature Designs Stained Glass Pattern Book. Harry E. Zimmerman. (Stained Glass Ser.). (Illus.). 64p. (Orig.). 1991. pap. 5.95 (*0-486-26732-6*) Dover.

Nature Diary. Illus. by Marjolein Bastin. 128p. 1997. 12.95 (*1-55670-101-2*) Stewart Tabori & Chang.

***Nature Diary.** Marjolein Bastin. (Illus.). 128p. 1999. spiral bd. 14.95 (*1-55670-958-7*) Stewart Tabori & Chang.

Nature Diary. Ruth G. Grierson. Ed. by Janet Strong. LC 92-62343. (Illus.). 140p. 1993. pap. 9.95 (*0-932433-98-7*) Windswept Hse.

Nature Directory: A Guide to Environmental Organizations. Susan D. Lanier-Graham. 304p. 1991. pap. 12.95 (*0-8027-7348-6*) Walker & Co.

Nature Discoveries with a Hand Lens. Richard Headstrom. (Illus.). 412p. 1998. reprint ed. pap. 8.95 (*0-486-24077-0*) Dover.

Nature Discovery Library, Set. Nancy Field et al. (Illus.). (J). (gr. 3-6). 1990. pap. text 63.40 (*0-941042-15-4*) Dog Eared Pubns.

Nature Displayed. Jordonova. LC 98-52908. (C). 1999. text 71.95 (*0-582-30190-4*) Addison-Wesley.

Nature Displayed. Jordonova. LC 98-52908. 272p. (C). 1999. pap. 32.46 (*0-582-30189-0*) Addison-Wesley.

Nature Doctor: A Manual of Traditional & Complementary Medicine. H. C. Vogel. 1991. 29.95 (*0-87983-618-0*, Keats Publng); pap. 18.95 (*0-87983-559-1*, Keats Publng) NTC Contemp Pub Co.

Nature Doctor: A Manual of Traditional & Complementary Medicine. H. C. Vogel. (GER., Illus.). 704p. reprint ed. pap. 29.98 (*0-941683-27-3*) Instant Improve.

Nature Doctors: Pioneers in Naturopathic Medicine. Friedhelm Kirchfeld & Wade Boyle. LC 94-78427. (Illus.). 360p. (Orig.). 1994. pap. text 29.95 (*0-9623518-5-7*) Medicina Bio.

Nature Drawing: A Tool for Learning. Clare W. Leslie. 208p. (C). 1995. pap. text, per. 20.95 (*0-7872-0580-X*) Kendall-Hunt.

Nature Encyclopedia. LC 98-16657. 304p. (J). (gr. 3-9). 1998. 29.95 (*0-7894-3411-3*) DK Pub Inc.

Nature Est un Talisman, Journal I. Jacques De Bourbon Busset. (FRE.). 1978. pap. 10.95 (*0-7859-1866-3*, 2070369943) Fr & Eur.

Nature, Estimation & Management of Political Risk. Janice Monti-Belkaoui & Ahmed Riahi-Belkaoui. LC 98-5287. 176p. 1998. 55.00 (*1-56720-196-2*, Quorum Bks) Greenwood.

Nature Ever New: Essays on the Renewal of Agriculture. George Adams. 1979. pap. 7.50 (*0-916786-40-4*, Saint George Pubns) R Steiner Col.

Nature, Experiment, & the Sciences. Ed. by Trevor H. Levere & William R. Shea. 360p. (C). 1990. lib. bdg. 186.00 (*0-7923-0420-9*, Pub. by Kluwer Academic) Kluwer Academic.

Nature Explorer. Deni Bown. (First Activity Packs Ser.). 24p. (J). (ps-3). 1995. pap. 16.95 (*1-56458-950-1*) DK Pub Inc.

Nature Explorer: A Step-By-Step Guide. Cary Huber. LC 89-27391. (Be the Best! Ser.). (Illus.). 64p. (J). (gr. 4-8). 1990. pap. 3.95 (*0-8167-1954-3*); lib. bdg. 15.85 (*0-8167-1953-5*) Troll Communs.

Nature, Extent, & Proliferation of Federal Law Enforcement: Hearing Before the Committee on the Judiciary, U. S. House of Representatives. Ed. by Bill McCollum. (Illus.). 199p. 1998. reprint ed. pap. text 40.00 (*0-7881-4234-8*) DIANE Pub.

Nature Facts. Dorling Kindersley Staff. LC 97-164285. (Pockets Ser.). (Illus.). 128p. (J). 1997. pap. 6.95 (*0-7894-1494-5*) DK Pub Inc.

Nature Facts & Lists. A. Ganeri. (Facts & Lists Ser.). (Illus.). 144p. (J). (gr. 3-7). 1993. pap. 12.95 (*0-7460-0645-4*, Usborne) EDC.

Nature Fakers: Wildlife, Science & Sentiment. Ralph H. Lutts. LC 89-29521. (Illus.). 272p. 1990. 22.95 (*1-55591-054-8*) Fulcrum Pub.

Nature Fantasy Designs. William Rowe. (Illus.). 48p. 1977. pap. 3.95 (*0-486-23446-0*) Dover.

Nature Flower Essence Therapy. Patricia Kaminski. 1999. pap. 24.00 (*0-609-80513-4*) Harmony Bks.

Nature for the Very Young: A Handbook of Indoor & Outdoor Activities. Marcia Bowden. LC 88-33747. (Illus.). 240p. 1989. pap. 14.95 (*0-471-62084-X*) Wiley.

Nature from Your Back Door. Glenn R. Dudderar. Ed. by Leslie Johnson. (Illus.). 136p. (Orig.). 1991. 14.95 (*1-56525-001-X*, E-2323HC); pap. 9.95 (*1-56525-000-1*, E-2323) MSU Ext.

Nature Go Home. Arthur Zaindenburg. LC 82-45805. 88p. 1984. 9.95 (*0-8453-4753-5*, Cornwall Bks) Assoc Univ Prs.

Nature Got There First. Phil Gates. LC 94-42784. (Illus.). 80p. (J). (gr. 4-7). 1995. 18.95 (*1-85697-587-8*) LKC.

Nature Guide to Jackson Hole. Olaus J. Murie. (Illus.). 60p. (Orig.). (gr. 6-12). 1980. pap. 2.95 (*0-933160-05-4*) Teton Bkshop.

Nature Guide to Ontario. 2nd rev. ed. Ed. by Anne Champagne. (Illus.). 320p. (Orig.). 1992. pap. 19.95 (*0-8020-6802-2*); text 45.00 (*0-8020-2755-5*) U of Toronto Pr.

Nature Guide to the Carolina Coast: Common Birds, Crabs, Shells, Fish, & Other Entities of the Coastal Environment. Peter K. Meyer. LC 90-85396. (Illus.). (Orig.). 1991. pap. 13.95 (*0-9628186-0-7*) Avian Cetacean.

Nature Guide to the Mountains of Southern California by Car & on Foot: Covering the San Gabriel, San Bernardino, San Jacinto, Santa Rosa, Cuyamaca, & Palomar Mountains. unabridged ed. Bill Havert & Gary Gray. LC 96-96310. (Illus.). iv, 140p. (Orig.). 1996. pap. 14.95 (*0-9651760-1-0*) Erth Trails.

Nature-Guided Therapy: Brief Integrative Strategies for Health & Wellbeing. George Burns. LC 97-44772. 250p. 1998. 35.95 (*0-87630-850-7*) Taylor & Francis.

Nature Has a Remedy. Bernard Jensen. 246p. 1979. reprint ed. pap. 12.99 (*0-932615-05-8*) B Jensen.

Nature Heals: The Psychological Essays of Paul Goodman. rev. ed. Paul Goodman. Ed. by Taylor Stoehr. 300p. 1991. pap. 24.95 (*0-939266-11-3*) Gestalt Journal.

Nature Hidden Pictures. S. Ross. (J). (ps-3). 1996. pap. 1.00 (*0-486-29363-7*, 253262Q) Dover.

Nature Hide & Seek: Oceans. John N. Wood. LC 85-73. (Illus.). 24p. (J). (gr. 1-4). 1985. 13.00 (*0-394-87583-4*, Pub. by Knopf Bks Yng Read) Random.

Nature Hike. Abbie Dee & Annie Scott. (Emergent Reader Ser.). 18p. (J). (ps-1). 1991. pap. text 4.25 (*1-56843-076-0*) EMG Networks.

Nature Hike: Big Book. Abbie Dee & Annie Scott. (Emergent Reader Ser.). 18p. (J). (ps-1). 1991. pap. text 21.00 (*1-56843-028-0*) EMG Networks.

Nature Hikes in the White Mountains. Robert Buchsbaum. LC 94-42245. (Nature Walks Guides Ser.). (Illus.). 400p. 1995. pap. text 12.95 (*1-878239-37-6*) AMC Books.

***Nature Hikes in the White Mountains.** 2nd ed. Robert Buchsbaum. (Illus.). 2000. pap. 12.95 (*1-878239-72-4*) AMC Books.

Nature, Human Nature, & Society: Marx, Darwin, Biology, & the Human Sciences, 21. Paul Heyer. LC 82-937. (Contributions in Philosophy Ser.: No. 21). 266p. 1982. 55.00 (*0-313-23161-3*, HNS/, Greenwood Pr) Greenwood.

Nature Illuminated: Flora & Fauna from Court of Emperor Rudolf II. Getty Trust Staff. Ed. by Lee Hendrix & Thea Vignau-Wilberg. LC 97-199200. 64p. 1997. 14.95 (*0-89236-472-6*, Pub. by J P Getty Trust) OUP.

Nature Illustrated: An Address Book. Intro. by Bernard McTigue. (Illus.). 144p. 1990. 17.95 (*0-8109-1389-5*, Pub. by Abrams) Time Warner.

Nature in a Nutshell for Kids: Over 100 Activities You Can do in Ten Minutes or Less. Jean Potter. (Illus.). 144p. (J). (gr. 4). 1995. pap. 12.95 (*0-471-04444-X*) Wiley.

Nature in Art. Anthea Peppin. (YA). 1992. pap. 6.70 (*0-395-64555-7*) HM.

Nature in Art. Anthea Peppin. LC 91-35014. (Millbrook Arts Library). (Illus.). 48p. (J). (gr. 2-6). 1992. lib. bdg. 22.90 (*1-56294-173-9*) Millbrook Pr.

Nature in Art. Anthea Peppin. (Millbrook Arts Library). 1992. 14.15 (*0-606-02804-8*, Pub. by Turtleback) Demco.

Nature in Asian Traditions of Thought: Essays in Environmental Philosophy. Ed. by J. Baird Callicott & Roger T. Ames. LC 88-16003. (SUNY Series in Philosophy & Biology). 335p. (C). 1989. pap. text 22.95 (*0-88706-951-7*) State U NY Pr.

Nature in Cities: The Natural Environment in the Design & Development of Urban Green Space. Ed. by Ian C. Laurie. LC 77-20987. 448p. reprint ed. pap. 138.90 (*0-608-14537-8*, 202480300038) Bks Demand.

Nature in Danger. Rosie Harlow & Sally Morgan. LC 95-6368. (Illus.). 32p. (J). (gr. 2-5). 1995. 12.90 (*1-85697-612-2*, Kingfisher); pap. 7.95 (*1-85697-611-4*, Kingfisher) LKC.

Nature in Danger: Threatened Habitats & Species. Noel Simon. (Illus.). 240p. (YA). 1995. pap. 8.95 (*0-685-20135-X*) OUP.

Nature in Danger: Threatened Habitats & Species. Ed. by Noel Simon. (Illus.). 240p. (YA). 1995. 45.00 (*0-19-521152-9*) OUP.

Nature in Downland. William Henry Hudson. reprint ed. 64.50 (*0-404-03398-9*) AMS Pr.

Nature in Grace: A Study in the Theology of Nature. Claude Y. Stewart, Jr. LC 83-8196. xx, 318p. 1983. pap. 21.50 (*0-86554-068-3*, MUP-P008) Mercer Univ Pr.

Nature in Ireland: A Scientific & Cultural History. John W. Foster & Helena C. Chesney. 1997. 75.00 (*1-874675-29-5*) Dufour.

Nature in Ireland: A Scientific & Cultural History. John W. Foster & Helena C. Chesney. LC 97-164170. 658p. 1998. pap. 39.95 (*1-874675-89-9*) Dufour.

Nature in Ireland: A Scientific & Cultural History. John Wilson Foster & Helena C. G. Chesney. 1998. pap. 34.95 (*0-7735-1817-7*); lib. bdg. 75.00 (*0-7735-1816-9*) McG-Queens Univ Pr.

Nature in Music, & Other Studies in the Tone Poetry of Today. Lawrence Gilman. LC 67-22096. (Essay Index Reprint Ser.). 1977. 18.95 (*0-8369-0475-3*) Ayer.

Nature in the Home, Vol. 1. unabridged ed. David Suzuki. (Nature All Around Ser.). (Illus.). 32p. (J). (ps-4). 1993. pap. 6.95 (*0-7737-5586-1*) STDK.

Nature in the Raw: Erotic Stories from Freshmen Magazine. Ed. by Gerry Kroll. 224p. (Orig.). 1996. pap. 11.95 (*1-55583-363-2*) Alyson Pubns.

Nature in the Urban Landscape: A Study of City Ecosystems. Don Gill & Penelope Bonnett. LC 73-76409. (Illus.). 209p. 1973. 12.00 (*0-912752-03-3*) York Pr.

Nature in the Works of Fray Luis De Granada. Mary B. Brentano. LC 75-94164. (Catholic University of American. Studies in Romance Languages & Literatures: No. 15). reprint ed. 37.50 (*0-404-50315-2*) AMS Pr.

***Nature in Tokyo: A Guide to Plants & Animals in & Around Tokyo.** Kevin Short. (Illus.). 2001. pap. 17.95 (*4-7700-2535-1*) Kodansha.

Nature in Your Backyard: Simple Activities for Children. Cayuga Nature Center Staff & Susan S. Lang. (Illus.). 48p. (J). (gr. 2-4). 1995. pap. 7.95 (*1-56294-893-8*); lib. bdg. 22.90 (*1-56294-451-7*) Millbrook Pr.

Nature Incorporated: Industrialization & the Waters of New England. Theodore Steinberg. (Studies in Environment & History). (Illus.). 302p. (C). 1991. text 54.95 (*0-521-39215-2*) Cambridge U Pr.

Nature Incorporated: Industrialization & the Waters of New England. Theodore Steinberg. LC 94-15035. (Illus.). 304p. (C). 1994. reprint ed. pap. 18.95 (*0-87023-943-0*) U of Mass Pr.

Nature into Art: Cultural Transformations in Nineteenth-Century Britain. Carl R. Woodring. LC 89-31112. (Illus.). 360p. 1989. 46.50 (*0-674-60465-2*) HUP.

Nature Is Busy. Jane Brettle. 1999. 3.98 (*1-57717-103-9*) Todtri Prods.

Nature Is Culture: Indigenous Knowledge & Socio-Cultural Aspects of Trees & Forests in Non-European Cultures. Ed. by Klaus Seeland. LC 98-145195. (Indigenous Knowledge & Development Ser.). 176p. 1998. pap. 30.95 (*1-85339-410-6*, Pub. by Intermed Tech) Stylus Pub VA.

***Nature Is Not Romantic.** Tracy L. Adler & Heidi Z. Jacobson. (Illus.). 16p. 1999. pap. 5.00 (*1-885998-19-8*) Hunter College.

Nature Journal. Ed. by Applewood Books Staff. (Wonderlings Ser.). (Illus.). 32p. (J). (ps up). 1996. pap. 1.50 (*1-55709-377-6*) Applewood.

***Nature Journal.** Joan Germann Lewis. (Illus.). 208p. (C). 2000. 30.00 (*0-9677024-0-2*) J G Lewis.

Nature Journal. Amber Lotus. 112p. 1990. pap. 11.95 (*0-945798-30-X*) Amber Lotus.

Nature Journal. Richard Mabey. (Illus.). 152p. 1992. 24.95 (*0-7011-3507-7*, Pub. by Chatto & Windus) Trafalgar.

Nature Journaling: Learning to Observe & Connect with the World Around You. Clare Walker Leslie et al. LC 98-14497. (Illus.). 192p. 1998. 26.95 (*1-58017-088-9*) Storey Bks.

Nature, Justice, & Rights in Aristotle's Politics. Fred D. Miller, Jr. (Illus.). 442p. 1997. pap. text 24.95 (*0-19-823726-X*) OUP.

Nature Knows No Color Line. J. A. Rogers. 242p. 1952. reprint ed. 13.95 (*0-9602294-5-0*) H M Rogers.

***Nature Lab: The Ultimate Nature Pack.** Josephine Bryan. (Science Lab Ser.). (Illus.). 32p. (J). (ps-3). 2000. 19.95 (*1-57145-407-1*, Silver Dolph) Advantage Pubs.

Nature Log. De Brandt. 1998. pap. 7.95 (*1-885061-54-4*) Adventure Pubns.

Nature Log Kids. DeBrandt. (J). pap. 11.95 (*1-885061-56-0*) Adventure Pubns.

Nature Lost? Natural Science & the German Theological Traditions of the 19th Century. Frederick Gregory. 352p. (C). 1992. 52.00 (*0-674-60483-0*) HUP.

***Nature Lovers.** Charles Potts. 65p. 2000. pap. write for info. (*1-929355-04-1*) Pleasure Boat.

***Nature Lover's Book of Quotations.** Ed. by Tom Crider. (Illus.). xiv, 271p. 2000. 29.00 (*0-9679430-0-0*) Birch Tree Pub.

Nature Lover's Guide to the Big Thicket. Howard Peacock. LC 93-38508. (W. L. Moody, Jr. Natural History Ser.: No. 15). (Illus.). 192p. 1994. pap. 12.95 (*0-89096-596-X*) Tex A&M Univ Pr.

Nature Lover's Guide to the Big Thicket. Howard Peacock. LC 93-38508. (W. L. Moody, Jr. Natural History Ser.: No. 15). (Illus.). 192p. 1994. 29.50 (*0-89096-589-7*) Tex A&M Univ Pr.

Nature Lover's Journal. G. N. Seabright. 1995. pap. 6.35 (*1-895387-64-7*) Creative Bk Pub.

Nature Magick: Psychic Healing & Welsh Witchcraft. Rhuddlwm Gawr. LC 85-73752. (Illus.). 112p. (Orig.). 12.95 (*0-931760-09-7*, CP 10106); pap. 10.95 (*0-931760-06-2*) Camelot GA.

Nature, Man & God. William Temple. LC 77-27190. (Gifford Lectures: 1932-33, 1933-34). 1979. reprint ed. 67.50 (*0-404-60493-5*) AMS Pr.

Nature, Man, & Society in the 12th Century: Essays on New Theological Perspectives in the Latin West. M. D. Chenu. Ed. & Tr. by Jerome Taylor & Lester K. Little. LC 68-15574. (Midway Reprint Ser.). xxii, 362p. 1983. pap. text 21.95 (*0-226-10256-4*) U Ch Pr.

Nature, Man & Society in the 12th Century. 37th ed. M. D. Chenu. (Medieval Academy Reprints for Teaching Ser.). 384p. 1997. reprint ed. pap. text 16.95 (*0-8020-7175-9*) U of Toronto Pr.

Nature, Man & the Indian Economy. Ed. by Tapas Majumdar. (Illus.). 430p. 1994. text 39.95 (*0-19-562915-9*) OUP.

Nature, Man & Woman. Alan W. Watts. LC 90-50166. 224p. 1991. pap. 12.00 (*0-679-73233-0*) Vin Bks.

Nature Mathematized. William R. Shea. 338p. 1982. lib. bdg. 152.00 (*90-277-1402-9*, D Reidel) Kluwer Academic.

N

Nature Mazes. Dave Philips. (Illus.). 48p. 1998. pap. text 2.95 (*0-486-40401-3*) Dover.

Nature Meditations. 2nd ed. Inayat Khan. (Illus.). 80p. (Orig.). 1999. pap. 10.00 (*0-930872-43-6*) Omega Pubns NY.

Nature Medley, Vol. VI. Ed. by Bert Hower. (Nature Ser.). (Illus.). 72p. 1996. pap. text. write for info. (*0-936945-61-3*) Creat with Wds.

Nature Museums: Tools for Learning about, Promoting & Protecting the Natural Heritage of Europe. Council of Europe Staff. (Environmental Encounters Ser.: No. 9). 1990. 15.00 (*92-871-1823-X*, Pub. by Council of Europe) Manhattan Pub Co.

Nature Mysticism (1913) J. Edward Mercer. 273p. 1996. reprint ed. pap. 24.95 (*1-56459-583-8*) Kessinger Pub.

Nature Notes. John F. Kieran. LC 77-84315. (Essay Index Reprint Ser.). 1977. 18.95 (*0-8369-1087-7*) Ayer.

Nature Notes: A Notebook Companion to the Season. Ursula L. Shepherd. LC 89-29529. (Illus.). 136p. (Orig.). 1990. pap. 9.95 (*1-55591-056-4*) Fulcrum Pub.

Nature Notes from Sharer's Creek. Virginia Hoekzema. Ed. by Carol Roberts. (Illus.). 359p. 1995. 15.00 (*1-883228-07-7*) Invictus MI.

Nature, Nurture, & Chance. Peter M. Rinaldo. LC 97-66986. (Illus.). 140p. 1998. 14.95 (*1-890849-01-4*) DorPete Pr.

Nature, Nurture & Psychology. Ed. by Robert Plomin & Gerald E. McClearn. 498p. 1993. pap. 19.95 (*1-55798-396-8*) Am Psychol.

Nature-Nurture Debate: The Essential Readings. Ed. by Steven Ceci. LC 99-16941. (Essential Readings in Developmental Psychology Ser.). 256p. (C). 1999. 59.95 (*0-631-21738-X*) Blackwell Pubs.

Nature-Nurture Debate: The Essential Readings. Ed. by Steven J. Ceci. LC 99-16941. (Essential Readings in Developmental Psychology Ser.). 256p. (C). 1999. pap. 24.95 (*0-631-21739-8*) Blackwell Pubs.

Nature Observed, Nature Interpreted: Nineteenth-Century American Landscape Drawings & Watercolors from the National Academy of Design & Cooper-Hewitt, National Design Museum, Smithsonian Institution. Dita Amory et al. LC 95-5941. 1995. pap. 35.00 (*1-887149-00-7*) Nat Acad of Des.

Nature of a God-Sent Revival. Duncan Campbell. 28p. 1993. pap. 2.50 (*0-942889-05-3*) Christ Life Pubns.

Nature of a Sistuh: Black Women's Lived Experiences in Contemporary Culture. Trevy A. McDonald & T. Ford-Ahmed. LC 98-88954. 335p. 1998. pap. 25.95 (*0-89089-859-6*) Carolina Acad Pr.

Nature of Adolescence. 2nd ed. John Coleman & Leo Hendry. 272p. (C). 1990. pap. 22.99 (*0-415-01485-9*) Routledge.

***Nature of Adolescence.** 3rd ed. John C. Coleman & Leo B. Hendry. LC 99-21503. (Adolescence & Society Ser.). 1999. pap. write for info. (*0-415-19898-4*) Routledge.

***Nature of Adolescence.** 3rd ed. John C. Coleman & Leo B. Hendry. LC 99-21503. (Adolescence & Society Ser.). 232p. (C). 1999. text. write for info. (*0-415-19897-6*) Routledge.

Nature of Aesthetic Experience in Wordsworth. John H. Talbot. (American University Studies: English Language & Literature: Ser. IV, Vol. 83). 292p. 1989. text 43.95 (*0-8204-1008-X*) P Lang Pubng.

Nature of Aesthetic Value. Hugo A. Meynell. LC 85-2742. 158p. (C). 1986. text 29.50 (*0-88706-118-4*) State U NY Pr.

***Nature of Aesthetics.** 2nd rev. ed. Chris Angle. 188p. 1999. pap. 14.99 (*0-9661126-0-1*) Philosophy.

Nature of Alaska: An Introduction to Common Plants & Animals & Natural Attractions. James Kavanagh. (Field Guides Ser.: Vol. 4). (Illus.). 176p. (J). (gr. 3). 1997. pap. 17.95 (*0-9640225-5-9*, Pub. by Waterford WA) Falcon Pub Inc.

Nature of Alcohol & Drug-Related Problems. Ed. by Malcolm H. Lader et al. (Society for the Study of Addiction Monograph Ser.: No. 2). (Illus.). 228p. 1992. text 69.95 (*0-19-262138-6*) OUP.

Nature of Alexander. Mary Renault. LC 74-15152. 288p. 1979. pap. 11.00 (*0-394-73825-X*) Pantheon.

Nature of All Being: A Study of Wittgenstein's Modal Atomism. Raymond Bradley. (Illus.). 272p. 1992. text 60.00 (*0-19-507111-5*) OUP.

Nature of America. Frwd. by Charles Kuralt & Bruce Babbitt. LC 97-11471. (Illus.). 192p. 1997. 49.95 (*0-8174-4994-9*, Amphoto) Watsn-Guptill.

Nature of American Politics. 2nd ed. H. G. Nicholas. 160p. 1986. 29.95 (*0-19-827483-1*); pap. text 14.95 (*0-19-827482-3*) OUP.

***Nature of Animal Healing: The Definitive Holistic Medicine Guide to Caring for Your Dog & Cat.** Martin Goldstein. 368p. 2000. pap. 15.00 (*0-345-43919-8*) Ballantine Pub Grp.

Nature of Animal Healing: The Path to Your Pet's Health, Happiness & Longevity. Martin Goldstein. LC 98-38193. 352p. 1999. 25.00 (*0-679-45500-0*) Knopf.

Nature of Argument. Karel Lambert & William Ulrih. 282p. (C). 1988. reprint ed. pap. text 24.00 (*0-8191-6747-9*) U Pr of Amer.

Nature of Arizona: An Introduction to Common Plants & Animals & Natural Attractions. James Kavanagh. (Field Guides Ser.: Vol. 2). (Illus.). 170p. (YA). (gr. 3). 1996. pap. 17.95 (*0-9640225-8-3*, Pub. by Waterford WA) Falcon Pub Inc.

Nature of Basketry. rev. ed. Ed Rossbach. LC 85-63576. (Illus.). 192p. 1986. reprint ed. pap. 14.95 (*0-88740-059-0*) Schiffer.

Nature of Being Human. Ed. by Marie I. Rasey. LC 58-12082. (Franklin Lectures of 1956-1957 Ser.). 129p. reprint ed. pap. 40.00 (*0-7837-3672-X*, 204354600009) Bks Demand.

Nature of Belief. Martin C. D'Arcy. (Select Bibliographies Reprint Ser.). 1977. reprint ed. 23.95 (*0-8369-5930-2*) Ayer.

Nature of Belief: Fixed Ideas in Post-Industrial America. Bradbury K. Thurlow. LC 89-81127. 382p. 1990. 25.00 (*0-87034-094-8*); pap. 21.00 (*0-87034-087-5*) Fraser Pub Co.

Nature of Birth & Breastfeeding. Michel Odent. LC 91-44076. 160p. 1992. 16.95 (*0-89789-287-9*, H287, Bergin & Garvey) Greenwood.

Nature of Blood. Caryl Phillips. LC 96-49641. 1997. 23.00 (*0-679-45470-5*) Knopf.

Nature of Blood. Caryl Phillips. LC 96-49641. 1998. pap. 12.00 (*0-679-77675-3*) Random.

Nature of Boats: Insights & Esoterica for the Nautically Obsessed. Dave Gerr. (Illus.). 418p. 1995. pap. 21.95 (*0-07-024233-X*) Intl Marine.

Nature of British Local Government. Stewart. LC 99-16307. 1999. text 69.95 (*0-312-22639-X*) St Martin.

Nature of California: An Introduction to Common Plants & Animals & Natural Attractions. 2nd ed. James Kavanagh. (Field Guides Ser.). (Illus.). 176p. (YA). 1998. pap. 17.95 (*0-9640225-4-0*, Pub. by Waterford WA) Falcon Pub Inc.

Nature of Capital: Marx after Foucault. Richard Marsden. LC 99-17994. 288p. 1999. 100.00 (*0-415-19861-5*) Routledge.

Nature of Change in Geographical Ideas. Ed. by Brian J. L. Berry. LC 75-39294. (Perspectives in Geography Ser.: Vol. 3). (Illus.). 167p. 1978. pap. 12.50 (*0-87580-525-6*) N Ill U Pr.

Nature of Change in Geographical Ideas, vol. 3. Ed. by Brian J. L. Berry. LC 75-39294. (Perspectives in Geography Ser.: Vol. 3). (Illus.). 167p. 1978. 28.00 (*0-87580-063-7*) N Ill U Pr.

Nature of Chaos. Ed. by Tom Mullin. LC 92-41598. (Illus.). 344p. 1993. pap. text 29.95 (*0-19-853954-1*, Clarendon Pr) OUP.

Nature of Chaos in Business: Using Complexity to Foster Successful Global Alliances. J. Garrett Ralls. LC 99-20622. (Illus.). 197p. 1999. 21.95 (*0-88415-504-8*, Cashman Dud) Gulf Pub.

Nature of Chicago: A Comprehensive Guide to Natural Sites in & Around the City. Isabel Abrams. LC 96-51835. (Illus.). 272p. 1997. pap. 14.95 (*1-55652-312-2*) Chicago Review.

Nature of Choice & Other Selected Writings. Anita J. Faatz. LC 83-72424. (Studies in Modern Society: Political & Social Issues: No. 18). 1985. 37.50 (*0-404-16043-3*) AMS Pr.

***Nature of Cities: Ecocriticism & Urban Environments.** Ed. by Michael Bennet. LC 99-6284. (Illus.). 312p. 1999. 40.00 (*0-8165-1947-1*) U of Ariz Pr.

***Nature of Cities: Ecocriticism & Urban Environments.** Ed. by Michael Bennett & David Teague. LC 99-6284. (Illus.). 312p. 1999. pap. 19.95 (*0-8165-1949-8*) U of Ariz Pr.

Nature of Civilization: A Psychological Analysis. Paul Rosenfels. LC 86-143005. (Ninth Street Center Monographs). (Orig.). 1977. pap. 3.95 (*0-932961-03-7*) Ninth St Ctr.

Nature of Civilizations. Matthew Melko. LC 69-15527. (Extending Horizons Ser.). (Illus.). 224p. (C). 1969. 4.95 (*0-87558-044-0*) Porter Sargent.

Nature of Co-Operation. John G. Craig. 254p. (Orig.). 1993. text 48.99 (*1-895431-69-7*, Pub. by Black Rose); pap. text 19.99 (*1-895431-68-9*, Pub. by Black Rose) Consort Bk Sales.

Nature of Cognition. Ed. by Robert J. Sternberg. LC 97-47622. (Illus.). 688p. 1998. 60.00 (*0-262-19405-8*, Bradford Bks) MIT Pr.

Nature of Cognition. Ed. by Robert J. Sternberg. LC 97-47622. (Illus.). 688p. 1999. pap. text 35.00 (*0-262-69212-0*, Bradford Bks) MIT Pr.

Nature of Communication Disorders. Orlando L. Taylor. 310p. 1986. text 44.00 (*0-7506-9857-8*) Buttrwrth-Heinemann.

Nature of Community Policing Innovations: Do the Ends Justify the Means? Jihong Zhao & Quint Thurman. LC 96-68261. 28p. (Orig.). (C). 1996. pap. text 6.50 (*1-878734-46-6*) Police Exec Res.

Nature of Compact Objects in Active Galactic Nuclei. Ed. by Andrew Robinson & Roberto J. Terlevich. (Illus.). 455p. (C). 1994. text 74.95 (*0-521-46480-3*) Cambridge U Pr.

Nature of Concepts: Evolution, Structure & Representation. Ed. by Philip Van Loocke. LC 99-185358. (Frontiers of Cognitive Science Ser.: No. 2). (Illus.). viii, 254 p. (C). 1999. 99.99 (*0-415-17963-7*, D6238) Routledge.

Nature of Confession: Evangelicals & Postliberals in Conversation. Ed. by Timothy R. Phillips & Dennis L. Okholm. LC 96-13028. 300p. (Orig.). 1996. pap. 16.99 (*0-8308-1869-3*, 1869) InterVarsity.

Nature of Conscience & Its Religious Significance with Special Reference to John Henry Newman. Ronald Ledek. 130p. 1996. 69.95 (*1-57309-043-3*); pap. 49.95 (*1-57309-042-5*) Intl Scholars.

Nature of Consciousness: Philosophical Debates. Ed. by Ned J. Block et al. LC 96-17500. (Illus.). 608p. 1997. 65.00 (*0-262-02399-7*, Bradford Bks) MIT Pr.

Nature of Consciousness: Philosophical Debates. Ed. by Ned J. Block et al. LC 96-17500. (Illus.). 608p. 1997. pap. text 32.95 (*0-262-52210-1*, Bradford Bks) MIT Pr.

Nature of Creative Activity. Viktor Lowenfeld. 1988. reprint ed. lib. bdg. 69.00 (*0-7812-0376-7*) Rprt Serv.

Nature of Creative Activity. 2nd ed. Viktor Lowenfeld. LC 65-7654. 272p. 1959. reprint ed. 69.00 (*0-686-01428-6*) Somerset Pub.

Nature of Culture. Alfred L. Kroeber. LC 52-12545. (Illus.). 448p. reprint ed. pap. 138.90 (*0-608-18229-X*, 205663700078) Bks Demand.

Nature of Culture. Alfred L. Kroeber. LC 52-12545. viii, 438p. (C). 1992. reprint ed. pap. text 30.00 (*0-226-45425-8*) U Ch Pr.

Nature of Cultures: A Blueprint for a Theory of Culture Genetics. Heiner Muhlmann. LC 96-20113. 160p. 1996. pap. 34.95 (*3-211-82800-1*) Spr-Verlag.

Nature of Dance As a Creative Art Activity. Barbara Mettler. 1980. 12.50 (*0-912536-11-X*) Mettler Studios.

Nature of Deference & Demeanor. Erving Goffman. (Reprint Series in Sociology). (C). 1993. reprint ed. pap. text 2.30 (*0-8290-3926-0*, S-97) Irvington.

Nature of Democracy, Freedom & Revolution. 2nd ed. Herbert Aptheker. LC 67-20076. 128p. 1981. pap. 2.95 (*0-7178-0137-3*) Intl Pubs Co.

Nature of Denali: East Entrance Area Trail Guide. S. Forbes. (Illus.). 42p. 1995. pap. 4.00 (*0-930931-08-4*) Alaska Natural.

Nature of Design: A Quilt Artist's Personal Journal. Joan Colvin. LC 96-3199. (Illus.). 128p. (Orig.). 1996. pap. 29.95 (*1-56477-131-8*, B247, Fiber Studio Pr) Martingale & Co.

Nature of Diamonds. Ed. by George E. Harlow. LC 97-29176. (Illus.). 288p. (C). 1997. pap. 29.95 (*0-521-62935-7*); text 74.95 (*0-521-62083-X*) Cambridge U Pr.

Nature of Disease in Plants. Robert P. Scheffer. LC 96-5231. (Illus.). 334p. (C). 1997. text 69.95 (*0-521-48247-X*) Cambridge U Pr.

Nature of Dividends. Gabriel A. Preinreich. Ed. by Richard P. Brief. LC 77-87286. (Development of Contemporary Accounting Thought Ser.). 1978. reprint ed. lib. bdg. 24.95 (*0-405-10914-8*) Ayer.

Nature of Doctrine: Religion & Theology in a Postliberal Age. George A. Lindbeck. LC 83-27332. 142p. 1984. pap. 19.95 (*0-664-24618-4*) Westminster John Knox.

Nature of Drug Dependence. J. G. Edwards & Malcolm H. Lader. (Society for the Study of Addiction Monograph Ser.: No. 1). (Illus.). 256p. 1990. 59.95 (*0-19-261772-9*) OUP.

Nature of Economic Thought: Essays in Economic Methodology. Johannes J. Klant. Tr. by Trevor S. Preston. LC 93-38551. (Advances in Economic Methodology Ser.). 160p. 1994. 90.00 (*1-85898-018-6*) E Elgar.

***Nature of Economies.** Jane Jacobs. LC 99-41014. 208p. 2000. 21.95 (*0-679-60340-9*) Modern Lib NY.

Nature of Emotion: Fundamental Questions. Paul Ekman & Richard Davidson. (Illus.). 512p. (C). 1994. pap. text 36.95 (*0-19-508944-8*) OUP.

***Nature of Energy.** Walter Russell & Lao Russell. Ed. by Laara Lindo. 40p. 1998. pap. text 6.00 (*1-879605-52-X*) U Sci & Philos.

Nature of Ethics. unabridged ed. Chris Angle. 1997. pap. 14.99 (*0-9661126-1-X*) Philosophy.

Nature of Evil: Considered in a Letter to the Rev. Edward Beecher, D.D. Henry James, Sr. LC 72-920. (Selected Works of Henry James, Sr.: Vol. 6). 1983. reprint ed. 57.50 (*0-404-10086-4*) AMS Pr.

Nature of Existence, 2 vols., Set. John M. McTaggart. 1968. 69.00 (*0-403-00129-3*) Scholarly.

Nature of Expertise. Ed. by Michelene T. Chi et al. 464p. 1988. pap. 49.95 (*0-8058-0404-8*) L Erlbaum Assocs.

Nature of Expertise. Robert Glaser. 20p. 1985. 3.00 (*0-318-20333-2*, OC107) Ctr Educ Trng Employ.

Nature of Expertise in Professional Acting: A Cognitive View. Tony Noice & Helga Noice. LC 97-12571. 200p. 1997. 45.00 (*0-8058-2169-4*); pap. write for info. (*0-8058-2170-8*) L Erlbaum Assocs.

Nature of Faith. Gerhard Ebeling. Ed. by Ronald G. Smith. LC 62-7194. 191p. reprint ed. pap. 59.30 (*0-608-16305-8*, 202687100053) Bks Demand.

Nature of Fascism. Roger Griffin. 1991. text 49.95 (*0-312-07132-9*) St Martin.

Nature of Fascism. Roger Griffin. LC 93-16564. 256p. (C). 1993. reprint ed. pap. 24.99 (*0-415-09661-8*, B2342) Routledge.

Nature of Fife: Scottish Wildlife Trust. Fife Branch & Kinross Branch. 260p. 1997. pap. 30.00 (*1-84017-008-5*) St Mut.

Nature of Florida. John Perry & Jane G. Perry. LC 97-36054. 1998. pap. 17.95 (*0-8203-2008-0*) U of Ga Pr.

Nature of Florida: An Introduction to Common Plants & Animals & Natural Attractions. James Kavanagh. (Field Guides Ser.). (Illus.). 188p. (YA). 1996. pap. 17.95 (*0-9640225-7-5*, Pub. by Waterford WA) Falcon Pub Inc.

Nature of Florida's Beaches: Including Sea Beans, Laughing Gulls & Mermaids' Purses. Cathie Katz. LC 95-81042. (Illus.). 64p. (Orig.). 1996. pap. 9.95 (*1-888025-07-7*) Atlntic Pr.

Nature of Florida's Neighborhoods: Including Bats, Scrub Jays, Lizards & Wildflowers. Cathie Katz. LC 96-84821. (Illus.). 68p. (Orig.). 1997. pap. 8.95 (*1-888025-09-3*) Atlntic Pr.

Nature of Florida's Ocean Life: Including Coral Reefs, Gulf Stream, Sargasso Sea & Sunken Ships. Cathie Katz. LC 97-77819. 72p. 1998. pap. 8.95 (*1-888025-11-5*) Atlntic Pr.

Nature of Florida's Waterways: Including Dragonflies, Cattails & Mangrove Snapper. Cathie Katz. LC 95-81043. (Illus.). 68p. (Orig.). 1996. pap. 8.95 (*1-888025-08-5*) Atlntic Pr.

Nature of Food: Exploring the Roots of Our Ingestible World - From Foraging to Hunting to Haute Cuisine. Susan Allport. LC 99-46244. 288p. 2000. 23.00 (*0-609-60149-0*) Harmony Bks.

Nature of Foxes see World of the Fox

Nature of Frank Lloyd Wright. Ed. by Carol R. Bolon et al. (Illus.). 192p. (C). 1994. 29.95 (*0-226-06351-8*) U Ch Pr.

Nature of Frank Lloyd Wright. Ed. by Carol R. Bolon et al. LC 87-13764. (Illus.). 215p. Date not set. reprint ed. pap. 66.70 (*0-608-20591-5*, 205455600003) Bks Demand.

Nature of Freedom & Other Essays. Colin Stanley. (Colin Wilson Studies: No. 2). 36p. (C). 1990. reprint ed. lib. bdg. 25.00 (*0-8095-6760-1*) Millefleurs.

Nature of Future Conflict. Richard Connaughton. 239p. 1995. 29.95 (*0-85052-460-1*, Pub. by Leo Cooper) Trans-Atl Phila.

***Nature of Gardens.** Ed. by Peter Timms. 312p. 2000. 24.95 (*1-86508-082-9*, Pub. by Allen & Unwin Pty) Paul & Co Pubs.

Nature of Geography: A Critical Survey of Current Thought in the Light of the Past. Richard Hartshorne. LC 76-48691. (Annals of the Association of American Geographers Ser.). 482p. 1978. reprint ed. lib. bdg. 41.50 (*0-8371-9328-1*, HANG) Greenwood.

Nature of God see Naturaleza de Dios

Nature of God. Gerald J. Hughes. LC 94-32685. (Problems of Philosophy Series: Their Past & Present). 232p. (C). 1995. 75.00 (*0-415-10950-7*, C0020); pap. 24.99 (*0-415-12075-6*, C0021) Routledge.

Nature of God. Arthur W. Pink. 347p. 1999. pap. 21.99 (*0-8024-6571-4*) Moody.

Nature of God, Set. Ed. by Frank C. Tribbe. (Spiritual Frontiers Fellowship Thirtieth Anniversary Booklet Ser.: Vol. I. No. 4). 1986. 12.00 (*0-317-68878-2*) Spirit Front Fellow.

Nature of God: An Inquiry into Divine Attributes. Edward Wierenga. LC 88-47929. (Cornell Studies in the Philosophy of Religion). 272p. 1989. text 37.50 (*0-8014-2212-4*) Cornell U Pr.

Nature of God: His Thoughts & Ways. A. Edward Hylton. 133p. 1999. pap. write for info. (*0-7392-0148-4*, PO3088) Morris Pubng.

Nature of Golf Exploring the Beauty of the Game. Tom Stewart. 444p. 1999. 75.00 (*0-9625276-2-9*) T P Stewart Pub.

***Nature of Good & Evil.** Sylvia Browne. (Journey of the Soul Ser.: Vol. 3). 256p. 2001. pap. 13.95 (*1-56170-724-4*, 5027) Hay House.

Nature of Grief: The Evolution & Psychology of Reactions to Loss. John Archer. LC 98-20134. (Illus.). 336p. (C). 1999. 90.00 (*0-415-17857-6*); pap. 31.99 (*0-415-17858-4*) Routledge.

Nature of Harmony & Metre. Moritz Hauptmann. (Music Reprint Ser.). 1990. 49.50 (*0-306-76298-6*) Da Capo.

Nature of Heat see Collected Works of Count Rumford

Nature of Historical Explanation. Patrick L. Gardiner. LC 85-21911. 142p. 1985. reprint ed. lib. bdg. 49.75 (*0-313-24976-8*, GANH, Greenwood Pr) Greenwood.

Nature of Historical Inquiry. Ed. by L. M. Marsak. LC 74-16092. 220p. 1986. reprint ed. 22.00 (*0-88275-221-9*) Krieger.

Nature of Historical Knowledge. Michael Stanford. 208p. 1987. pap. text 30.95 (*0-631-15291-1*) Blackwell Pubs.

Nature of History. 3rd rev. ed. Arthur Marwick. LC 89-2786. 442p. (C). 1989. pap. text 39.95 (*0-925065-00-5*) Lyceum IL.

Nature of Homicide: Trends & Changes - Proceedings of the 1996 Meeting of the Homicide Research Working Group. Ed. by Pamela K. Lattimore & Cynthia A. Nahabedian. (Illus.). 261p. (C). 1999. pap. text 50.00 (*0-7881-7323-5*) DIANE Pub.

Nature of Horses: Basic Training & First Rides. Gene Ulrich. (Illus.). 248p. (Orig.). 1995. write for info. (*0-9646385-2-5*); pap. 15.00 (*0-9646385-3-3*) E Ulrich.

Nature of Horses: Exploring Equine Evolution, Intelligence, & Behavior. Stephen Budiansky. LC 96-47004. (Illus.). 240p. 1997. 29.50 (*0-684-82768-9*) Free Pr.

Nature of Human Feelings: With Exercises in Intimacy. Laurence C. Smith, Jr. 164p. (Orig.). 1990. pap. text 10.95 (*0-9625114-0-4*) BSA Pub.

Nature of Human Nature. abr. ed. Ellsworth Faris. (Midway Reprint Ser.). 1977. pap. text 10.00 (*0-226-23815-6*) U Ch Pr.

***Nature of Human Nature: Instinct & Passion on the Human Spirit.** Melvin Konner. 350p. 2000. pap. text 24.95 (*0-7167-4055-9*) W H Freeman.

Nature of Human Nature & Other Essays in Social Psychology. Ellsworth Faris. LC 69-17575. (Essay Index Reprint Ser.). 1977. 21.95 (*0-8369-0073-1*) Ayer.

Nature of Human Nature & Other Essays in Social Psychology. Ellsworth Faris. (Reprint Series in Sociology). 1971. reprint ed. lib. bdg. 21.00 (*0-697-00217-9*) Irvington.

Nature of Human Speech see Society's Work

Nature of Human Well-Being: The Constructive Conduct of a Society & a Person. John A. Banks. (Conceptual Model of Humanity Ser.: No. 3). 450p. 1995. pap. text 12.00 (*0-9629833-1-4*) Jordan Bk Co.

Nature of Humanity & the State of America: A Unified Theory of the Social World. Craig R. Lundahl. LC 98-49107. 208p. (C). 1998. 49.00 (*0-7618-1304-7*); pap. 29.50 (*0-7618-1305-5*) U Pr of Amer.

Nature of Hypnosis. Paul Schilder. LC 56-5485. 204p. 1956. 30.00 (*0-8236-3500-7*) Intl Univs Pr.

Nature of Hypnosis. Paul Schilder. LC 56-5485. 204p. 1956. pap. 24.95 (*0-8236-8156-4*, 23500) Intl Univs Pr.

Nature of Hypnosis & Suggestion. Milton H. Erickson. Ed. by Ernest L. Rossi. (Collected Papers of Milton H. Erickson on Hypnosis: Vol. I). 570p. (C). 1980. pap. 39.95 (*0-8290-1206-0*); text 59.95 (*0-8290-0542-0*) Ardent Media.

Nature of Hysteria. Niel Micklem. LC 95-18320. 144p. (C). 1995. 45.00 (*0-415-12186-8*) Routledge.

***Nature of Idioms: A Systematic Approach.** Leon Jaeger. 268p. 1999. 38.95 (*3-906763-06-4*, Pub. by P Lang) P Lang Pubng.

An Asterisk (*) at the beginning of an entry indicates that the title is appearing for the first time.

***Nature of Idioms: A Systemic Approach.** Leon Jaeger. LC 99-36883. 268p. (C). 1999. pap. text 38.95 (*0-8204-4605-X*) P Lang Pubng.

Nature of Imagery Analysis & Its Place Beside Intelligence Analysis. Mark G. Marshall & National Tech. Info Service Staff. (Illus.). 300p. (C). 1998. pap. write for info. (*0-9656195-1-6*) Joint Military.

Nature of Information. Paul Young. LC 87-6953. 192p. 1987. 52.95 (*0-275-92698-2*, C2698, Praeger Pubs) Greenwood.

Nature of Information Technology Managerial Work: The Work Life of Five Chief Information Officers. Charlotte S. Stephens. LC 95-809. 232p. 1995. 49.95 (*0-89930-920-8*, Quorum Bks) Greenwood.

Nature of Insight. Ed. by Robert J. Sternberg & Janet Davidson. LC 93-29646. (Illus.). 400p. 1994. 50.00 (*0-262-19345-0*, Bradford Bks) MIT Pr.

Nature of Insight. Ed. by Robert J. Sternberg et al. (Illus.). 640p. 1996. reprint ed. pap. text 27.50 (*0-262-69187-6*, Bradford Bks) MIT Pr.

Nature of Integrative Study. large type ed. Joseph Engelberg. 336p. (Orig.). 1994. pap. 35.95 (*0-913507-51-2*) New Forums.

Nature of Intelligence. Ed. by Lauren B. Resnick. 364p. 1976. text 69.95 (*0-89859-137-6*) L Erlbaum Assocs.

Nature of Intelligence. Louis L. Thurstone. LC 72-13862. (Illus.). 167p. 1973. reprint ed. lib. bdg. 59.50 (*0-8371-6761-2*, THNI, Greenwood Pr) Greenwood.

Nature of "Intelligence" & the Principles of Cognition. Charles E. Spearman. LC 73-2990. (Classics in Psychology Ser.). 1977. reprint ed. 26.95 (*0-405-05163-8*) Ayer.

Nature of Irreversibility. Henry B. Hollinger & Michael J. Zenzen. 352p. 1985. text 147.00 (*90-277-2080-0*, D Reidel) Kluwer Academic.

Nature of Kensington: A Photographic Portrayal. Ted Nelson. LC 98-89962. (Illus.). 112p. 1999. 32.00 (*0-9669880-0-0*) Austin-Carol.

Nature of Knowledge. Alan R. White. LC 81-23450. (American Philosophical Quarterly Library of Philosophy). 142p. (C). 1982. text 31.00 (*0-8476-7073-2*) Rowman.

Nature of Knowledge: Concerning Adaptations, Instinct & the Evaluation of Intelligence. Henry C. Plotkin. LC 93-39328. 1994. write for info. (*0-674-60482-2*) HUP.

***Nature of Leadership.** Stephen R. Covey et al. 1998. 37.95 (*1-883219-90-6*) Franklin Covey.

Nature of Learning Disabilities: Critical Elements of Diagnosis & Classification. Kenneth A. Kavale & Steven R. Forness. 448p. 1995. pap. 39.95 (*0-8058-1607-0*); text 89.95 (*0-8058-1606-2*) L Erlbaum Assocs.

Nature of Life. Monniger & Theodore Taigen. (C). 1992. pap. text, teacher ed. 20.31 (*0-07-003150-9*) McGraw.

Nature of Life. 2nd ed. John H. Postlethwait & Janet L. Hopson. (C). 1991. pap. text, lab manual ed. 26.25 (*0-07-050650-7*) McGraw.

Nature of Life. 3rd ed. John H. Postlethwait & Janet L. Hopson. LC 94-37994. (C). 1995. text 68.00 (*0-07-050750-3*) McGraw.

Nature of Life: Apply & Decide Case Studies. John H. Postlethwait & Janet L. Hopson. (C). 1996. pap. text 7.25 (*0-07-050762-7*) McGraw.

Nature of Life: Critical Thinking Workbook. 2nd ed. John H. Postlethwait & Janet L. Hopson. (C). 1995. pap. text, wbk. ed. 21.87 (*0-07-050666-3*) McGraw.

Nature of Life: Exploring the Living World. Anton E. Lawson. (C). 1995. pap. text, lab manual ed. 23.00 (*0-07-036791-4*) McGraw.

Nature of Life: Preparator's Guide. 2nd ed. John H. Postlethwait & Janet L. Hopson. (C). 1991. text 26.87 (*0-07-050656-6*) McGraw.

Nature of Light & Colour in the Open Air. M. G. Minnaert. (Illus.). 362p. 1954. pap. text 9.95 (*0-486-20196-1*) Dover.

Nature of Literature. Herbert E. Read. LC 74-105034. (Essay Index Reprint Ser.). 1977. 26.95 (*0-8369-1478-3*) Ayer.

Nature of Literature: Its Relation to Science, Language & Human Experiences. Thomas C. Pollock. LC 65-25135. 218p. 1965. reprint ed. 50.00 (*0-87752-086-0*) Gordian.

Nature of Liturgical Prayer in Catechumenate Team Formation. Mary A. Ravizza. LC 97-148989. (Pastoral Ministry Ser.). 80p. (Orig.). 1996. pap. 8.95 (*1-55612-954-8*, LL1954) Sheed & Ward WI.

Nature of Longing. Alyce Miller. 240p. 1995. pap. 10.00 (*0-393-31379-4*, Norton Paperbks) Norton.

Nature of Longing: Stories by Alyce Miller. Alyce Miller. LC 94-7582. (Flannery O'Connor Award for Short Fiction Ser.). 264p. 1994. 19.95 (*0-8203-1674-1*) U of Ga Pr.

Nature of Love, Vol. 3: The Modern World. Irving Singer. xiv, 488p. 1989. pap. text 16.95 (*0-226-76099-5*) U Ch Pr.

Nature of Love, Vol. 1: Plato to Luther. 2nd ed. Irving Singer. LC 84-2554. 352p. 1996. 35.95 (*0-226-76094-4*) U Ch Pr.

Nature of Love, Vol. 1: Plato to Luther. 2nd ed. Irving Singer. LC 84-2554. 396p. 1996. pap. text 19.50 (*0-226-76095-2*) U Ch Pr.

Nature of Love, Vol. 2: Courtly & Romantic. Irving Singer. LC 84-2554. 496p. 1985. 34.95 (*0-226-76096-0*) U Ch Pr.

Nature of Love, Vol. 2: Courtly & Romantic. Irving Singer. LC 84-2554. 528p. 1998. pap. text 17.95 (*0-226-76097-9*) U Ch Pr.

***Nature of Macroeconomics: Instability & Change in the Capitalist System.** Athol Fitzgibbons. LC 99-55246. 192p. 2000. 75.00 (*1-84064-069-3*) E Elgar.

Nature of Magmatism in the Appalachian Orogen. Ed. by A. Krishna Sinha et al. LC 97-7591. (Memoir Ser.: No. 191). 1997. 135.00 (*0-8137-1191-6*) Geol Soc.

Nature of Man. 27p. 1992. pap. 4.00 (*1-930433-00-X*) Liberating Ministries.

Nature of Man. Ed. by Amandus W. Loos. LC 69-18930. (Essay Index Reprint Ser.). 1977. 17.95 (*0-8369-1042-7*) Ayer.

Nature of Man: Series One, Volume I, Series 1, Vol. I. Ed. by Lynchburg College Faculty Staff. LC 82-45158. (Classical Selections on Great Issues, Symposium Readings Ser.). 480p. (Orig.). (C). 1982. pap. text 16.50 (*0-8191-2463-X*) U Pr of Amer.

Nature of Man: Studies in Optimistic Philosophy. Elie Metchnikoff. Ed. by Robert J. Kastenbaum. Tr. by P. Chalmers Mitchell. LC 76-19582. (Death & Dying Ser.). (Illus.). 1977. reprint ed. lib. bdg. 31.95 (*0-405-09578-3*) Ayer.

Nature of Man & the Psychology of the Human Soul. Syed Muhammad Naquib al-Attas. 41p. (C). 1997. pap. 5.00 (*0-934905-92-4*, Library of Islam) Kazi Pubns.

Nature of Man in St. Thomas Aquinas Compared with the Nature of Man in American Sociology. Roberta Snell. 1972. 35.00 (*0-8490-0715-1*) Gordon Pr.

Nature of Man in Theological & Psychological Perspective. Ed. by Simon Doniger. LC 72-10819. (Essay Index Reprint Ser.). 1977. reprint ed. 20.95 (*0-8369-7213-9*) Ayer.

Nature of Man. Regimen in Health. Humours. Amorphisms. Regimen 1-3. Dreams. see Medical Works

Nature of Management. G. J. Cohen. 300p. 1985. pap. text 36.00 (*0-86010-565-2*); lib. bdg. 50.00 (*0-86010-582-2*) G & T Inc.

Nature of Management. G. J. Cohen. 300p. 1985. pap. text, student ed. 25.00 (*0-86010-590-3*) G & T Inc.

Nature of Management. 2nd ed. G. J. Cohen. 300p. 1988. pap. text 36.00 (*1-85333-030-2*) G & T Inc.

Nature of Management Case Studies. Ed. by Bill Braddick. 128p. 1990. pap. 125.00 (*0-85297-147-8*, Pub. by Chartered Bank) St Mut.

Nature of Managerial Work. Henry Mintzberg. (Illus.). 298p. (C). 1997. pap. 62.67 (*0-06-044556-4*) Addson-Wesley Educ.

Nature of Mass Poverty. John Kenneth Galbraith. LC 78-11839. 160p. 1979. 17.95 (*0-674-60533-0*) HUP.

Nature of Mass Poverty. John Kenneth Galbraith. LC 78-11839. 160p. 1980. pap. text 5.95 (*0-674-60535-7*) HUP.

Nature of Mathematical Knowledge. Philip Kitcher. 300p. 1985. pap. text 19.95 (*0-19-503541-0*) OUP.

Nature of Mathematical Modeling. Neil Gershenfeld. LC 98-22029. (Illus.). 400p. (C). 1998. 34.95 (*0-521-57095-6*) Cambridge U Pr.

Nature of Mathematical Thinking. Ed. by Robert J. Sternberg & Talia Ben-Zeev. (Studies in Mathematical Thinking & Reasoning). 330p. 1996. text 69.95 (*0-8058-1798-0*); pap. text 34.50 (*0-8058-1799-9*) L Erlbaum Assocs.

Nature Of Mathematics. 4th ed. Karl J. Smith. LC 83-14455. (Math). 630p. (C). 1984. mass mkt. 31.50 (*0-534-02806-3*) Brooks-Cole.

Nature Of Mathematics. 5th ed. Karl J. Smith. (Math). 674p. (C). 1986. mass mkt. 40.00 (*0-534-06696-8*) Brooks-Cole.

Nature of Mathematics. 6th ed. Karl J. Smith. 800p. (C). 1991. text 55.95 (*0-534-13914-0*) Brooks-Cole.

Nature of Mathematics. 7th ed. Karl J. Smith. LC 94-37364. 900p. 1994. text 63.95 (*0-534-21564-5*) Brooks-Cole.

Nature of Mathematics. 8th ed. Karl J. Smith. LC 97-40528. (Mathematics Ser.). 1998. pap. 79.95 (*0-534-34988-9*) Brooks-Cole.

***Nature of Mathematics.** 9th ed. Smith. 2001. pap. 49.00 (*0-534-36890-5*) Brooks-Cole.

Nature of Mathematics & the Mathematics of Nature. Michael Jacob & Sten Andersson. LC 98-36663. 345p. 1998. 215.50 (*0-444-82994-6*) Elsevier.

***Nature of Meaningfulness: Representing, Powers, & Meaning.** Robert K. Shope. LC 99-16953. (Studies in Epistemology & Cognitive Theory). 352p. 1999. pap. text 22.95 (*0-8476-9287-6*) Rowman.

***Nature of Meaningfulness: Representing, Powers, & Meaning.** Robert K. Shope. LC 99-16953. 352p. 1999. text 65.00 (*0-8476-9286-8*) Rowman.

***Nature of Mediterranean Europe.** A. T. Grove & Oliver Rackham. (Illus.). 352p. 2000. 70.00 (*0-300-08443-9*) Yale U Pr.

***Nature of Melancholy: From Aristotle to Kristeva.** Ed. by Jennifer Radden. LC 99-16828. (Illus.). 352p. 2000. 35.00 (*0-19-512962-8*) OUP.

Nature of Memory. A. Besant & Helena P. Blavatsky. 1935. pap. 4.50 (*81-7059-023-X*, 7647, Quest) Theos Pub Hse.

Nature of Metaphysical Knowledge. Ed. by George F. McLean & Hugo Meynell. LC 88-164. (International Society for Metaphysics Studies in Metaphysics: Vol. IV). 180p. (Orig.). 1988. 45.00 (*0-8191-6926-9*); pap. 17.50 (*0-8191-6927-7*) Coun Res Values.

Nature of Mind. Ed. by David M. Rosenthal. 656p. (C). 1991. pap. text 36.95 (*0-19-504671-4*) OUP.

Nature of Mind: Parapsychology & the Role of Consciousness in the Physical World. Douglas M. Stokes. LC 97-2510. 269p. 1997. lib. bdg. 42.50 (*0-7864-0344-6*) McFarland & Co.

Nature of Miracle. Nahid Angha. 17p. (Orig.). 1993. pap. write for info. (*0-918437-11-3*) Intl Sufism.

Nature of Modern Math. 2nd ed. Smith. (Math). 1976. mass mkt. 16.75 (*0-8185-0171-5*) Brooks-Cole.

Nature of Modern Math. 3rd ed. Smith. (Math). 1980. mass mkt. 24.25 (*0-8185-0352-1*) Brooks-Cole.

Nature of Moral Responsibility. Stephen D. Ross. LC 72-3399. 271p. reprint ed. pap. 84.10 (*0-7837-3628-2*, 204349400009) Bks Demand.

Nature of Morality. Arnold W. Green. LC 93-2205. 176p. (Orig.). (C). 1993. pap. text 24.50 (*0-8191-9210-4*); lib. bdg. 49.50 (*0-8191-9209-0*) U Pr of Amer.

Nature of Morality: An Introduction to Ethics. Gilbert Harman. 180p. (C). 1977. pap. text 20.95 (*0-19-502143-6*) OUP.

Nature of Morality: An Introduction to the Subjectivist Perspective. Ted Trainer. (Avebury Series in Philosophy). 110p. 1991. 77.95 (*1-85628-178-7*, Pub. by Avebry) Ashgate Pub Co.

Nature of Music. Hermann Scherchen. 1988. reprint ed. lib. bdg. 49.00 (*0-7812-0787-8*) Rprt Serv.

Nature of Music. Hermann Scherchen. LC 76-181246. 193p. 1950. reprint ed. 29.00 (*0-403-01671-1*) Scholarly.

Nature of Music. unabridged ed. Karl Signell. 16p. 1993. pap. text 44.50 incl. audio (*0-88432-643-8*, S11300) Audio-Forum.

***Nature of Music: Beauty, Sound & Healing.** Maureen McCarthy Draper. 192p. 2000. 23.95 (*1-57322-170-8*) Putnam Pub Group.

Nature of Music: For the Performing Musician. John Holland. 116p. 1990. pap. 18.50 (*0-9663690-0-9*) Am Sound Pr.

Nature of Narrative. Robert Scholes & Robert Kellogg. 1966. teacher ed. write for info. (*0-318-54907-7*) OUP.

Nature of Narrative. Robert Scholes & Robert Kellogg. 332p. 1968. pap. text 12.95 (*0-19-500773-5*) OUP.

Nature of Natural History. Marston Bates. 336p. 1950. pap. text 16.95 (*0-691-02446-4*, Pub. by Princeton U Pr) Cal Prin Full Svc.

Nature of Natural Languages. Joe E. Pierce. 163p. 1979. pap. 7.95 (*0-913244-20-1*) Hapi Pr.

Nature of Nature: New Essays from America's Finest Writers on Nature. Ed. by William H. Shore. (Illus.). 320p. 1995. pap. 15.00 (*0-15-600245-0*, Harvest Bks) Harcourt.

Nature of Nature from Alpha to Zeta. 2nd ed. Albert E. Fitzwarren, pseud. (Illus.). iv, 54p. 1990. pap. 3.50 (*0-942788-18-4*) Iris Visual.

Nature of Necessity. Alvin Plantinga. (Clarendon Library of Logic & Philosophy). 268p. 1979. pap. text 26.00 (*0-19-824414-2*) OUP.

Nature of New York City. James Kavanagh. (Pocket Naturalist Ser.). (Illus.). 1997. 5.95 (*1-889903-16-7*, Pub. by Waterford WA) Falcon Pub Inc.

Nature of North America: A Handbook to the Continent; Rocks, Plants & Animals. David Rockwell. LC 98-27182. 560p. 1998. 29.95 (*0-425-16587-6*); pap. 15.00 (*0-425-16548-5*) Berkley Pub.

Nature of North Carolina's Southern Coast: Barrier Islands, Coastal Waters & Wetlands. Dirk Frankenberg. LC 96-46448. (Illus.). 272p. (C). 1997. pap. 18.95 (*0-8078-4655-4*) U of NC Pr.

Nature of Nursing: Reflections after 25 Years. 2nd ed. Virginia A. Henderson. (Illus.). 128p. (C). 1991. reprint ed. pap. text 19.95 (*0-88737-494-8*) Natl League Nurse.

Nature of Nursing Work. Alan Pearson. 1996. pap. 40.00 (*0-949823-69-4*, Pub. by Deakin Univ) St Mut.

Nature of Nurture. Theodore D. Wachs. (Individual Differences & Development Ser.: Vol. 3). (Illus.). 160p. (C). 1992. 48.00 (*0-8039-4374-1*); pap. 21.50 (*0-8039-4375-X*) Sage.

Nature of Ornament: Rhythm & Metamorphosis In Architecture. Kent Bloomer. 256p. 1999. 45.00 (*0-393-73036-0*) Norton.

Nature of Our Lives. Christine Doerr. LC 96-96394. (Illus.). vi, 72p. (Orig.). 1996. pap. 8.95 (*0-9652677-0-9*) Doerr Two Dr.

Nature of Our Seeking. N. Sri Ram. 1973. 9.95 (*81-7059-072-8*) Theos Pub Hse.

***Nature of Party Government: A Comparative European Perspective.** Jean Blondel & Maurizio Cotta. LC 00-33337. 2000. write for info. (*0-312-23762-6*) St Martin.

Nature of Peace. Thorstein B. Veblen. LC 97-49871. 367p. 1998. pap. text 24.95 (*1-56000-973-X*) Transaction Pubs.

***Nature of Perception.** John Foster. 264p. 2000. text 55.00 (*0-19-823769-3*) OUP.

Nature of Personal Reality. Jane Roberts. 1993. reprint ed. lib. bdg. 21.95 (*1-56849-244-8*) Buccaneer Bks.

Nature of Personal Reality: Specific, Practical Techniques for Solving Everyday Problems & Enriching the Life You Know. Jane Roberts. LC 94-10677. (Seth Bk.). 480p. 1994. reprint ed. pap. 17.95 (*1-878424-06-8*) Amber-Allen Pub.

Nature of Personality: Selected Papers. Gordon W. Allport. LC 74-2795. 220p. 1975. reprint ed. lib. bdg. 65.00 (*0-8371-7432-5*, ALNP, Greenwood Pr) Greenwood.

Nature of Philosophical Inquiry. Quentin Lauer. LC 88-64165. (Aquinas Lectures). 1989. text 15.00 (*0-87462-156-9*, AQ-53) Marquette.

Nature of Philosophical Inquiry. Ed. by George F. McLean & Valerie Voorhies. (Proceedings of the American Catholic Philosophical Association Ser.: Vol. 41). 1967. pap. 20.00 (*0-918090-01-6*) Am Cath Philo.

Nature of Photographs. Stephen Shore. LC 97-19510. (Illus.). 104p. 1998. pap. 24.95 (*0-8018-5720-1*) Johns Hopkins.

Nature of Photographs. Stephen Shore & Center for American Places, Harrisonburg, Va. Staf. LC 97-19510. (Illus.). 104p. 1998. text 55.00 (*0-8018-5719-8*) Johns Hopkins.

Nature of Physical Existence. Ivor Leclerc. 382p. 1986. reprint ed. pap. text 25.50 (*0-8191-4853-9*) U Pr of Amer.

Nature of Physical Knowledge. Ed. by Lawrence W. Friedrich. LC 60-13219. 156p. 1960. reprint ed. pap. 48.40 (*0-608-04195-5*, 206493000011) Bks Demand.

Nature of Physical Reality: A Philosophy of Modern Physics. Henry Margenau. LC 77-86356. 1977. reprint ed. 35.00 (*0-918024-02-1*); reprint ed. pap. 17.00 (*0-918024-03-X*) Ox Bow.

Nature of Physics: A Physicist's Views on the History & Philosophy of Science. Robert B. Lindsay. LC 68-10642. 220p. reprint ed. 68.20 (*0-608-16567-0*, 202751300055) Bks Demand.

Nature of Politics. Roger D. Masters. LC 88-7652. 320p. (C). 1989. 42.50 (*0-300-04169-1*) Yale U Pr.

Nature of Politics. Roger D. Masters. 315p. 1991. pap. 19.00 (*0-300-04981-1*) Yale U Pr.

Nature of Politics: Selected Essays of Bertrand de Jouvenal. Bertrand De Jouvenel. Ed. by Dennis Hale & Marc K. Landy. 276p. (C). 1992. pap. 24.95 (*1-56000-607-2*) Transaction Pubs.

Nature of Positive Law. John M. Lightwood. xiv, 419p. 1982. reprint ed. 47.50 (*0-8377-0814-1*, Rothman) W S Hein.

Nature of Power. Barry Barnes. 224p. 1988. text 29.95 (*0-252-01582-7*) U of Ill Pr.

Nature of Prejudice. Gordon W. Allport. 1979. pap. 17.00 (*0-201-00179-9*) Addison-Wesley.

Nature of Prejudice: A Philosophical, Sociological, & Biological Evolutionary Inquiry into the Relationship of External Reality & the Human Brain. Barry R. Zeeberg. LC 97-90099. (Illus.). 100p. (Orig.). 1997. pap. 19.95 (*0-9657219-0-6*) B Zeeberg.

Nature of Private Contract. Harold C. Havighurst. (Nineteen Sixty-One Rosenthal Lectures Ser.). ix, 144p. 1981. reprint ed. 45.00 (*0-8377-0638-6*, Rothman) W S Hein.

Nature of Proof. 2nd ed. Erwin P. Bettinghaus. LC 76-173979. (Orig.). 1972. pap. 3.50 (*0-672-61295-X*, SC1, Bobbs) Macmillan.

Nature of Proof: Thirteenth Yearbook. NCTM Staff. Ed. by Harold P. Fawcett. 146p. 1995. reprint ed. pap. 15.95 (*0-87353-402-6*) NCTM.

Nature of Properties: Nominalism, Realism & Trope Theory see Analytical Metaphysics

Nature of Psychodynamic Interpretation. Neil M. Cheshire. LC 75-1391. 241p. reprint ed. pap. 74.80 (*0-608-14532-7*, 202479800038) Bks Demand.

Nature of Psychological Maturity. Paul Rosenfels. LC 86-143042. (Ninth Street Center Monographs). (Orig.). 1978. pap. 3.95 (*0-932961-04-5*) Ninth St Ctr.

Nature of Psychology: A Selection of Papers Essays, & Other Writings. Kenneth J. Craik. LC 65-14851. 204p. reprint ed. pap. 58.20 (*0-608-11273-9*, 2051423) Bks Demand.

Nature of Public Philosophy. Richard Bishirjian. LC 82-20170. 62p. 1983. reprint ed. pap. text 11.50 (*0-8191-2861-9*) U Pr of Amer.

Nature of Quakerism. Howard H. Brinton. (C). 1949. pap. 4.00 (*0-87574-047-2*) Pendle Hill.

Nature of Quantum Paradoxes: Italian Studies in the Foundations & Philosophy of Modern Physics. Ed. by Gino Tarozzi & Alwyn Van Der Merwe. (C). 1988. text 237.50 (*90-277-2703-1*) Kluwer Academic.

Nature of Rationality. Robert Nozick. 232p. 1993. text 42.50 (*0-691-07424-0*, Pub. by Princeton U Pr); pap. text 13.95 (*0-691-02096-5*, Pub. by Princeton U Pr) Cal Prin Full Svc.

Nature of Recreation: A Handbook in Honor of Frederick Law Olmsted. Richard S. Wurman et al. 100p. 1972. pap. text 12.95 (*0-262-73034-0*) MIT Pr.

Nature of Religion. William P. Paterson. LC 77-27202. (Gifford Lectures: 1924-25). reprint ed. 75.00 (*0-404-60476-5*) AMS Pr.

Nature of Religious Experience: Essays in Honor of Douglas Clyde Macintosh. LC 78-152202. (Essay Index Reprint Ser.). 1977. reprint ed. 18.95 (*0-8369-2286-7*) Ayer.

Nature of Religious Knowledge. Norman McLeish. 174p. 1938. 37.95 (*0-567-02193-9*, Pub. by T & T Clark) Bks Intl VA.

Nature of Religious Language: A Colloquium. Ed. by Stanley E. Porter. (Roehampton Institute London Papers: No. 1). 250p. 1996. pap. 24.50 (*1-85075-783-6*, Pub. by Sheffield Acad) CUP Services.

Nature of Religious Language: A Colloquium. Ed. by Stanley E. Porter. LC 96-183330. (Roehampton Institute London Papers: No. 1). 250p. 1996. 70.00 (*1-85075-580-9*, Pub. by Sheffield Acad) CUP Services.

Nature of Religious Man. D. B. Fry. 220p. 1982. 22.00 (*0-900860-67-7*, Pub. by Octagon Pr) ISHK.

Nature of Representation: A Phenomenological Inquiry. Richard Bernheimer. Ed. by H. W. Janson. LC 61-8057. 263p. reprint ed. pap. 81.60 (*0-608-11852-4*, 205026300058) Bks Demand.

***Nature of Risk: Stock Market Survival & the Meaning of Life.** 2nd ed. Justin Mamis. LC 91-14143. 241p. 1999. reprint ed. pap. 18.00 (*0-87034-132-4*) Fraser Pub Co.

Nature of Roman Comedy: A Study in Popular Entertainment. 2nd ed. George E. Duckworth. LC 93-27544. (Illus.). 496p. 1994. pap. 26.95 (*0-8061-2620-5*) U of Okla Pr.

Nature of Roman Poetry. Gordon Williams. 198p. 1984. pap. text 19.95 (*0-19-872115-3*) OUP.

Nature of Russia. John M. Stewart. (Illus.). 192p. 1993. 19.98 (*1-55859-470-1*, Cross Riv Pr) Abbeville Pr.

Nature of San Francisco. James Kavanagh. (Pocket Naturalist Ser.). (Illus.). 1997. 5.95 (*1-889903-17-5*, Pub. by Waterford WA) Falcon Pub Inc.

***Nature of Saving Conversion.** 2nd rev. ed. Solomon Stoddard. Ed. by Don Kistler. 180p. 1999. 18.95 (*1-57358-097-X*) Soli Deo Gloria.

Nature of School Bullying: A Cross-National Perspective. Ed. by Phillip Slee et al. LC 98-24527. (Illus.). xiii, 384 p. (C). 1999. pap. 39.99 (*0-415-17985-8*, D6245) Routledge.

Nature of School Bullying: A Cross-National Perspective. Ed. by Phillip Slee et al. LC 98-24527. (Illus.). 320p. (C). (gr. 13). 1999. 100.00 (*0-415-17984-X*, D6241) Routledge.

N

An Asterisk (*) at the beginning of an entry indicates that the title is appearing for the first time.

Nature of Science. 2nd ed. Frederick Aicken. LC 90-46236. 162p. (C). 1991. pap. text 17.50 (*0-435-08310-4*, 08310) Heinemann.

Nature of Science: Problems & Perspectives. Edwin Hung. LC 96-8979. (Philosophy Ser.). (C). 1996. 67.95 (*0-534-24750-4*) Wadsworth Pub.

***Nature of Science in Science Education: Rationales & Strategies.** William F. McComas. LC 98-20973. (Science & Technology Education Library). 15p. 1998. write for info. (*0-7923-5080-4*) Kluwer Academic.

Nature of Scotland: Landscape, Wildlife & People. Magnus Magnusson & Graham White. (Illus.). 280p. 1998. pap. 25.00 (*0-86241-674-4*, Pub. by Canongate Books) Interlink Pub.

Nature of Selection: Evolutionary Theory in Philosophical Focus. Elliott Sober. xvi, 396p. (C). 1993. pap. text 18.00 (*0-226-76748-5*) U Ch Pr.

Nature of Shamanism: Substance & Function of a Religious Metaphor. Michael Ripinsky-Naxon. LC 92-5415. 289p. (C). 1993. pap. text 21.95 (*0-7914-1386-1*) State U NY Pr.

Nature of Six Sigma Quality. rev. ed. Mikel J. Harry. 25p. 1988. reprint ed. pap. 10.00 (*1-56946-009-4*) Motorola Univ.

Nature of Smoke. Anne Harris. 288p. 1997. text 13.95 (*0-312-86351-9*) St Martin.

Nature of Smoke. Anne Harris. 256p. 1996. 22.95 (*0-312-85286-X*) Tor Bks.

Nature of Smoke. Anne Harris. 1997. pap. 13.95 (*0-614-27320-X*) Tor Bks.

Nature of Social & Educational Inquiry: Empiricism vs. Interpretation. John K. Smith. LC 89-6613. 200p. (C). 1989. text 73.25 (*0-89391-514-9*) Ablx Pub.

***Nature of Social Work in Ireland: A Historical Perspective.** Caroline Skehill. LC 99-11272. 206p. 1999. text 89.95 (*0-7734-8177-X*) E Mellen.

Nature of Solar Prominences. Einar Tandberg-Hanssen. LC 95-10. (Astrophysics & Space Science Library: Vol. 199). 324p. (C). 1995. text 144.00 (*0-7923-3374-8*) Kluwer Academic.

Nature of Solids. Alan Holden. (Illus.). 256p. 1992. reprint ed. pap. 7.95 (*0-486-27077-7*) Dover.

Nature of Soviet Society. Socialist Labor Party Staff. 1978. pap. 0.75 (*0-935534-22-9*) NY Labor News.

***Nature of Space & Time.** Stephen W. Hawking. (Isaac Newton Institute Series of Lectures). (Illus.). 160p. 2000. pap. 14.95 (*0-691-05084-8*) Princeton U Pr.

Nature of Space & Time. Stephen W. Hawking & Roger Penrose. LC 95-35582. (Isaac Newton Institute Series of Lectures). 273p. 1996. text 24.95 (*0-691-03791-4*, Pub. by Princeton U Pr) Cal Prin Full Svc.

Nature of Spirit: And of Man As a Spiritual Being. Chauncey Giles. 212p. 1997. pap. 5.95 (*1-883270-13-8*) Swedenborg Assn.

***Nature of Statistical Learning Theory.** 2nd ed. Vladimir N. Vapnik. LC 99-39803. (Statistics for Engineering & Information Science Ser.). 304p. 1999. pap. 69.95 (*0-387-98780-0*) Spr-Verlag.

Nature of Stuttering. 2nd ed. Charles G. Van Riper. (Illus.). 496p. 1982. text 43.95 (*0-13-610709-5*) P-H.

Nature of Stuttering. 2nd ed. Charles G. Van Riper. (Illus.). 468p. (C). 1992. reprint ed. text 44.95 (*0-88133-677-7*) Waveland Pr.

Nature of Symbiotic Stars. Michael Friedjung. Ed. by Roberto Viotti. 1982. text 141.50 (*90-277-1422-3*) Kluwer Academic.

Nature of Syntactic Representation. Pauline Jacobson & Geoffrey K. Pullum. 498p. 1982. pap. text 65.50 (*90-277-1290-5*, D Reidel); lib. bdg. 182.50 (*90-277-1289-1*, D Reidel) Kluwer Academic.

Nature of System Change: Reform Impact in the Criminal Courts. Raymond T. Nimmer. LC 78-67457. xiv, 225p. 1991. reprint ed. 30.00 (*0-89941-574-1*, 304980) W S Hein.

Nature of System Change: Reform Impact in the Criminal Courts. Raymond T. Nimmer & American Bar Foundation Staff. LC 78-67457. xiv, 225p. 1991. reprint ed. pap. 30.00 (*0-910058-93-8*, 304980) W S Hein.

Nature of Technological Knowledge: Are Models of Scientific Change Relevant? Ed. by Rachel Laudan. 1984. lib. bdg. 84.00 (*90-277-1716-8*) Kluwer Academic.

Nature of Texas: A Feast of Native Beauty from Texas Highways Magazine. Ed. by Howard Peacock. LC 89-20277. (Louise Lindsey Merrick Texas Environement Ser.: No. 11). (Illus.). 144p. 1990. 24.95 (*0-89096-402-5*) Tex A&M Univ Pr.

***Nature of the Atonement.** J. McLeod Campbell. 304p. 1999. pap. 28.00 (*1-57910-320-0*) Wipf & Stock.

Nature of the Beast. Milton Mayer. Ed. by W. Eric Gustafson. LC 74-21243. 376p. 1975. 40.00 (*0-87023-176-6*) U of Mass Pr.

Nature of the Book: Print & Knowledge in the Making. Adrian Johns. LC 97-47252. 1998. 40.00 (*0-226-40121-9*) U Ch Pr.

Nature of the Book: Print & Knowledge in the Making. Adrian Johns. LC 97-47252. (Illus.). 754p. 2000. pap. 22.50 (*0-226-40122-7*) U Ch Pr.

Nature of the Chemical Bond & the Structure of Molecules & Crystals: An Introduction to Modern Structural Chemistry. 3rd ed. Linus Pauling. (George Fisher Baker Non-Resident Lectureship in Chemistry at Cornell University Ser.). (Illus.). 644p. 1960. text 69.95 (*0-8014-0333-2*) Cornell U Pr.

Nature of the Child. Jerome Kagan. 352p. 1994. reprint ed. pap. 17.50 (*0-465-04852-8*, Pub. by Basic) HarpC.

Nature of the Church see Naturaleza de la Iglesia

Nature of the Common Law. Melvin A. Eisenberg. LC 87-31886. 224p. 1988. 37.95 (*0-674-60480-6*) HUP.

Nature of the Common Law. Melvin A. Eisenberg. 224p. 1991. pap. text 18.00 (*0-674-60481-4*) HUP.

Nature of the Crown: A Legal & Political Analysis. Ed. by Maurice Sunkin & Sebastian Payne. LC 98-37677. 394p. 1999. text 85.00 (*0-19-826273-6*) OUP.

Nature of the Cypriot Chronicle of Leontios Makhairas. R. M. Dawkins. 32p. 1980. pap. 6.00 (*0-89005-334-0*) Ares.

Nature of the English Revolution. John Morrill. LC 92-25941. 480p. (C). 1992. text 62.95 (*0-582-08941-7*, 79647) Longman.

Nature of the Environment. 3rd ed. Andrew Goudie. LC 92-15565. 1993. reprint ed. pap. 31.95 (*0-631-18632-8*) Blackwell Pubs.

Nature of the Fifth Dimension: De Revolutionibus Orbium Rotantium. Ian McCrimmon. 512p. (C). 1990. text 195.00 (*0-9514698-0-0*, Pub. by Cosmatom) St Mut.

Nature of the Firm: Origins, Evolution & Development. Ed. by Oliver E. Williamson & Sidney G. Winter. (Illus.). 256p. 1993. reprint ed. pap. text 19.95 (*0-19-508356-3*) OUP.

Nature of the Four Elements. John Rastell. LC 71-133725. (Tudor Facsimile Texts. Old English Plays Ser.: No. 7). reprint ed. 59.50 (*0-404-53307-8*) AMS Pr.

Nature of the Gods. Marcus Tullius Cicero. Tr. & Intro. by Patrick G. Walsh. LC 96-34884. 286p. (C). 1997. text 70.00 (*0-19-815040-7*) OUP.

Nature of the Gods. Marcus Tullius Cicero. Tr. by H. C. McGregor. (Classics Ser.). 280p. 1972. pap. 11.95 (*0-14-044265-0*, Penguin Classics) Viking Penguin.

Nature of the Gods. Marcus Tullius Cicero. Tr. & Intro. by P. G. Walsh. (Oxford World's Classics Ser.). 286p. 1998. reprint ed. pap. 9.95 (*0-19-282511-9*) OUP.

Nature of the Gods & on Divination. Marcus Tullius Cicero. Tr. by C. D. Yonge from GRE. LC 97-34300. 273p. 1997. pap. text 6.95 (*1-57392-180-7*) Prometheus Bks.

***Nature of the International Firm: Nordic Contributions to International Business Research.** Ingmar Bjorkman. LC 98-106378. 1999. 48.00 (*87-16-13359-5*) Mksgaard.

Nature of the Islands: Plants & Animals of the Eastern Caribbean. Virginia Barlow & Chris Doyle. (Illus.). 148p. (Orig.). 1993. pap. 14.95 (*0-944428-13-4*) Cruising Guide.

Nature of the Japanese State: Rationality & Rituality. Brian J. McVeigh. LC 98-34179. (Nissan Institute/Routledge Japanese Studies Ser.). 280p. (C). 1998. 85.00 (*0-415-17106-7*) Routledge.

Nature of the Judicial Process. Benjamin N. Cardozo. (Storrs Lectures). (C). 1960. pap. 14.00 (*0-300-00033-2*, Y21) Yale U Pr.

Nature of the Judicial Process. Benjamin N. Cardozo. 180p. 1997. reprint ed. 55.00 (*1-57588-214-0*, 311210) W S Hein.

Nature of the Judicial Process. 8th ed. Benjamin N. Cardozo. (Storrs Lectures). 180p. 1998. reprint ed. 55.00 (*1-56169-420-7*) Gaunt.

Nature of the Learning Process. Harvey Jackins. 1966. pap. 2.00 (*0-911214-14-3*) Rational Isl.

Nature of the Learning Process: French Translation. Harvey Jackins. 1996. pap. 2.00 (*1-885357-45-1*) Rational Isl.

Nature of the Learning Process: Italian Translation. Harvey Jackins. (ITA.). 1991. pap. 2.00 (*1-885357-70-2*) Rational Isl.

Nature of the Lunar Surface: Proceedings of the 1965 IAU-NASA Symposium, Greenbelt, MD. Conference on the Nature of the Surface of the Moon Staff. Ed. by Wilmot N. Hess et al. LC 65-27671. (Illus.). 328p. reprint ed. pap. 101.70 (*0-608-30224-4*, 200384400037) Bks Demand.

Nature of the Machine. Douglas Davis. Ed. by Lanny Silverman. (Illus.). 32p. (Orig.). 1993. pap. 12.00 (*0-938903-15-2*) Cty of Chicago.

Nature of the Moment. Valentine Ackland. LC 73-84871. 64p. 1974. 5.00 (*0-8112-0517-7*, Pub. by New Directions) Norton.

Nature of the Operations of Modern Armies. V. K. Triandafillov & Jacob W. Kipp. Tr. by William A. Burhans from RUS. LC 92-28919. 234p. 1994. 49.50 (*0-7146-4501-X*, Pub. by F Cass Pubs); pap. 24.50 (*0-7146-4118-9*, Pub. by F Cass Pubs) Intl Spec Bk.

Nature of the Outer Banks: Environmental Processes, Field Sites, & Development Issues, Corolla to Ocracoke. Dirk Frankenberg. LC 95-9913. (Illus.). 174p. (C). 1995. pap. 17.95 (*0-8078-4542-6*) U of NC Pr.

Nature of the Physical World. Arthur S. Eddington. LC 77-27200. (Gifford Lectures: 1927). reprint ed. 27.50 (*0-404-60478-1*) AMS Pr.

Nature of the Place: A Study of Great Plains Fiction. Diane D. Quantic. LC 94-34986. xx, 203p. 1995. text 40.00 (*0-8032-3800-2*) U of Nebr Pr.

Nature of the Place: A Study of Great Plains Fiction. Diane D. Quantic. LC 94-34986. xx, 203p. 1997. pap. text 17.50 (*0-8032-8850-6*, Bison Books) U of Nebr Pr.

Nature of the Psyche: Its Human Expression. Jane Roberts. (Seth Bk.). 256p. 1996. reprint ed. pap. 15.95 (*1-878424-22-X*) Amber-Allen Pub.

Nature of the Right. Roger Eatwell & Noel Sullivan. (Twayne's Themes in Right-Wing Politics & Ideology Ser.: No. 1). 216p. (C). 1990. pap. 16.95 (*0-8057-9551-0*, Twyne); text 30.95 (*0-8057-9550-2*, Twyne) Mac Lib Ref.

Nature of the Right: Feminist Analysis of Order Patterns. Ed. by Gill Seidel. LC 88-339. (Critical Theory Ser.: Vol. 6). ix, 183p. (C). 1988. 59.00 (*1-55619-036-0*); pap. 19.95 (*1-55619-044-1*) J Benjamins Pubng Co.

Nature of the SCEs see Sister Chromatid Exchanges: Twenty-Five Years of Experimental Research

Nature of the Seashore. Michael Glaser. (Illus.). 16p. (J). (gr. 1-6). 1986. pap. 4.99 (*0-911635-02-5*) Knickerbocker.

***Nature of the Self: A Philosophy on Human Nature.** S. K. Leung. 416p. 2000. 32.00 (*1-902835-07-7*, Pub. by Empiricus Bks); pap. 19.95 (*1-902835-03-4*, Pub. by Empiricus Bks) Paul & Co Pubs.

Nature of the Social Sciences: In Relation to Objectives of Instruction. Charles Austin Beard. LC 73-14148. (Perspectives in Social Inquiry Ser.). 256p. 1974. reprint ed. 18.95 (*0-405-05494-7*) Ayer.

Nature of the Social Studies. Robert D. Barr et al. LC 77-2014. (C). 1978. pap. 14.95 (*0-88280-049-3*) ETC Pubns.

Nature of the Soul. Lucille Cedercrans. 614p. pap. text 16.95 (*1-883493-02-1*) Wisdom Impress.

Nature of the Soul. Lucille Cedercrans. 614p. 1993. 3.5 hd 24.95 (*1-883493-03-X*) Wisdom Impress.

Nature of the Soul. Arthur M. Coon. 40p. 1996. reprint ed. pap. 9.00 (*0-7873-1232-0*) Hlth Research.

Nature of the Soviet System. Ed. by Alexander Dallin. LC 91-46445. (Articles on Russian & Soviet History, 1500-1991 Ser.: Vol. 8). 552p. 1992. text 25.00 (*0-8153-0565-6*) Garland.

Nature of the Supervision of Student-Teaching in Universities Using Cooperating Public High Schools & Some Conditioning Factors. Ralph F. Strebel. LC 79-177740. (Columbia University. Teachers College. Contributions to Education Ser.: No. 655). reprint ed. 37.50 (*0-404-55655-8*) AMS Pr.

***Nature of the Transnational Firm.** 2nd ed. Christos N. Pitelis & Roger Sugden. LC 99-53474. 240p. 2000. pap. 32.99 (*0-415-16788-4*) Routledge.

***Nature of the Transnational Firm.** 2nd ed. Ed. by Christos Pitelis & Roger Sugden. LC 99-53474. 240p. (C). 2000. text 100.00 (*0-415-16787-6*) Routledge.

Nature of the Universe. 2nd ed. Proclus & David Felty. LC 97-24982. (Lynchburg College Symposium Readings Ser.). 1997. pap. write for info. (*0-7618-0829-9*) U Pr of Amer.

Nature of the World. Ed. by Patricia Kirkpatrick et al. (Illus.). 176p. (Orig.). 1984. pap. 6.00 (*0-927663-07-4*) COMPAS.

Nature of the World: An Essay in Phenomenalist Metaphysics. Walter T. Stace. LC 69-14093. 262p. 1970. reprint ed. lib. bdg. 49.50 (*0-8371-1039-4*, STNW, Greenwood Pr) Greenwood.

Nature of Their Bodies: Women & Their Doctors in Victorian Canada. Wendy Mitchinson. 512p. 1991. text 60.00 (*0-8020-5901-5*); pap. text 22.95 (*0-8020-6840-5*) U of Toronto Pr.

***Nature of Theoretical Thinking in Nursing.** 2nd ed. Hesook S. Kim. LC 99-54403. (Illus.). 272p. 2000. 39.95 (*0-8261-1306-0*) Springer Pub.

Nature of Things. Tr. by Frank O. Copley. (C). 1977. pap. text 14.00 (*0-393-09094-9*) Norton.

Nature of Things. Francis Ponge. Tr. by Lee Fahnestock from FRE. (French Ser.).Tr. of Parti Pris des Choses. 49p. 1995. 6.95 (*0-87376-080-8*) Red Dust.

Nature of Things. Anthony Quinton. 1978. reprint ed. pap. 19.95 (*0-7100-8903-1*, Routledge Thoemms) Routledge.

Nature of Things: Animals & Habitats. John Tomikel. LC 82-70061. (Illus.). 180p. 1983. pap. 5.00 (*0-910042-44-6*) Allegheny.

***Nature of Things: Emptiness & Essence in the Geluk World.** William Magee. LC 00-22590. 244p. 2000. pap. 19.95 (*1-55939-145-6*) Snow Lion Pubns.

Nature of Things: Secret Life of Inanimate Objects. Lyall Watson. LC 92-19457. 256p. (Orig.). 1992. pap. 12.95 (*0-89281-408-X*, Destiny Bks) Inner Tradit.

Nature of Things on Sanibel. 2nd rev. ed. George R. Campbell. LC 87-36112. (Illus.). 174p. 1988. reprint ed. pap. 16.95 (*0-910923-47-7*) Pineapple Pr.

Nature of Things to Come. Stanley E. Sayers. 1972. 7.95 (*0-88027-013-6*) Firm Foun Pub.

Nature of Thought: Essays in Honor of D. O. Hebb. Ed. by Peter W. Jusczyk & Raymond M. Klein. LC 80-18697. (Illus.). 256p. 1990. text 49.95 (*0-89859-034-5*) L Erlbaum Assocs.

Nature of Time in Schools: Theoretical Concepts, Practitioner Perceptions. Ed. by Miriam Ben-Peretz & Rainer Bromme. LC 90-36416. 320p. 1990. pap. 99.20 (*0-608-05093-8*, 206564900005) Bks Demand.

Nature of Time in Schools: Theoretical Concepts, Practitioner Perceptions. Ed. by Miriam Ben-Peretz & Rainer Bromme. 328p. (C). 1990. text 43.95 (*0-8077-3036-X*); pap. text 22.95 (*0-8077-3035-1*) Tchrs Coll.

Nature of Translation: Essays on the Theory & Practice of Literary Translation. Ed. by James S. Holmes. (Approaches to Translation Studies: No. 1). 1970. text 50.00 (*90-279-1552-0*) Mouton.

***Nature of True Grace.** James Rogers. LC 98-167701. 1998. write for info. (*0-939241-31-5*) Faith Print.

Nature of True Minds. John Heil. (Cambridge Studies in Philosophy). 262p. (C). 1992. text 74.95 (*0-521-41337-0*); pap. text 22.95 (*0-521-42400-3*) Cambridge U Pr.

Nature of True Virtue. Jonathan Edwards. 128p. 1960. pap. text 15.95 (*0-472-06037-6*, 06037, Ann Arbor Bks) U of Mich Pr.

Nature of Trusteeship. John W. Nason. 136p. 1982. 16.00 (*0-318-17378-6*) Assn Gov Bds.

Nature of Trusteeship: The Role & Responsibilities of College & University Boards. John W. Nason. LC 83-174535. 102p. 1982. 9.95 (*0-318-03585-5*) Assn Gov Bds.

Nature of Truth Consciousness & Free Will. Chris Angle. 1997. pap. 14.99 (*0-9661126-2-8*) Philosophy.

Nature of Value: Axiological Investigations. Ramon M. Lemos. LC 95-1079. 240p. 1995. 39.95 (*0-8130-1366-6*) U Press Fla.

Nature of Vermont: Introduction & Guide to a New England Environment. expanded ed. Charles W. Johnson. LC 97-47154. (Illus.). 372p. 1998. pap. 17.95 (*0-87451-856-3*) U Pr of New Eng.

Nature of Violent Storms, 19. Louis J. Battan. LC 80-24986. (Science Study Ser.: No. S19). (Illus.). 158p. 1981. reprint ed. lib. bdg. 35.00 (*0-313-22582-6*, BANV, Greenwood Pr) Greenwood.

Nature of Visual Basic Programs. 2nd ed. 124p. (C). 1999. pap. text 6.14 (*0-536-02512-6*) Pearson Custom.

Nature of Visual Illusion. unabridged ed. Mark Fineman. LC 96-14001. (Illus.). 240p. 1998. reprint ed. pap. text 9.95 (*0-486-29105-7*) Dover.

Nature of Vocabulary Acquisition. Ed. by Margaret G. McKeown & Mary E. Curtis. 208p. 1987. 39.95 (*0-89859-548-7*) L Erlbaum Assocs.

Nature of Wilt Diseases of Plants. C. H. Beckman. LC 87-70385. (Illus.). 182p. 1987. 38.00 (*0-89054-074-8*) Am Phytopathol Soc.

Nature of Woman: An Encyclopedia. Mary A. Warren. LC 79-55299. 736p. 1980. 20.00 (*0-918528-07-0*); pap. 16.00 (*0-918528-06-2*) Edgepress.

***Nature of Woodworking: The Quiet Pleasures of Crafting by Hand.** Rodney Frost. LC 00-37288. (Illus.). 2000. pap. 17.95 (*0-8069-4992-9*) Sterling.

Nature of Work: An Introduction to Debates on the Labour Process. 2nd ed. Paul Thompson. 336p. (C). 1997. text 21.95 (*0-333-49504-7*, Pub. by Macmillan) Humanities.

Nature of Work: Sociological Perspectives. Kai T. Erikson & Steven P. Vallas. 384p. (C). 1990. 50.00 (*0-300-04520-4*) Yale U Pr.

Nature of Work: Sociological Perspectives. Ed. by Kai T. Erikson & Steven P. Vallas. (American Sociological Society Presidential Ser.). 384p. (C). 1992. reprint ed. pap. 19.00 (*0-300-05662-1*) Yale U Pr.

Nature on the Rampage. Harm J. De Blij. LC 94-23115. 224p. 1994. 29.97 (*0-89599-048-2*); pap. text 19.95 (*0-89599-049-0*) Smithsonian Bks.

***Nature on the Rampage.** Harm J. DeBlij. Ed. by David Roland. (Illus.). 224p. 2000. pap. text 20.00 (*0-7881-9101-2*) DIANE Pub.

***Nature on the Rampage.** Ed. by Raintree Steck-Vaughn Publishing Staff. (Illus.). 2000. 136.98 (*0-7398-1799-X*) Raintree Steck-V.

Nature on View: Homes & Gardens Inspired by Japan. Peggy L. Rao & Jean Mahoney. (Illus.). 192p. 1993. 29.95 (*0-8348-0299-6*) Weatherhill.

Nature One & Two. Henry Medwall. LC 71-133709. (Tudor Facsimile Texts. Old English Plays Ser.: No. 17). reprint ed. 59.50 (*0-404-53317-5*) AMS Pr.

Nature Out of Control? 91p. 1994. 2.95 (*1-897647-07-7*) Evang Sisterhood Mary.

***Nature Out of Place: Biological Invasions in the Global Age.** Jason Van Driesche & Roy G. Van Driesche. (Illus.). 352p. 2000. 29.95 (*1-55963-757-9*, Shearwater Bks) Island Pr.

Nature Patterns: Multi-Sized Patterns for Making Cut-Outs, Puppets & Learning Games. Jean Warren. Ed. by Gayle Bittinger. (Mix & Match Pattern Ser.). (Illus.). 128p. (Orig.). (J). (ps-1). 1990. pap. 9.95 (*0-911019-36-7*, WPH 1303) Totline Pubns.

Nature Perfected: Gardens Through History. William Howard Adams. (Illus.). 356p. 1999. pap. text 39.95 (*0-7892-0458-4*) Abbeville Pr.

Nature Photographer's Complete Guide to Professional Field Techniques see John Shaw's Nature Photography Field Guide

Nature Photographer's Complete Guide to Professional Field Techniques. John Shaw. (Illus.). 144p. 1984. pap. 22.50 (*0-8174-5006-8*, Amphoto) Watsn-Guptill.

Nature Photography. Ken Griffiths. (Illus.). 112p. 1998. pap. 29.95 (*0-86840-672-4*, Pub. by New South Wales Univ Pr) Intl Spec Bk.

Nature Photography: A National Audubon Society Guide. Tim Fitzharris. (Illus.). 168p. 1996. pap. text 19.95 (*1-895565-92-8*) Firefly Bks Ltd.

Nature Photography Hot Spots: Where to Find Them When They're at Their Best. How to Approach Them. Tim Fitzharris. LC 96-931984. (Illus.). 144p. 1998. pap. 19.95 (*1-55209-092-2*) Firefly Bks Ltd.

Nature Pictorialized: The View in Landscape History. Gina Crandell. (Illus.). 240p. 1993. text 35.95 (*0-8018-4397-9*) Johns Hopkins.

Nature-Play & Profit in My Garden. Edward P. Roe. (Notable American Authors Ser.). 1999. reprint ed. lib. bdg. 125.00 (*0-7812-8827-4*) Rprt Serv.

Nature Plays for Keeps: Poems. John D. Ogden. 128p. (Orig.). 1996. pap. 9.50 (*1-56474-166-4*) Fithian Pr.

Nature Plays No Favorites: Setting up Oneself for Disappointments in Life. Ricardo Scott. (Ras Cardo Speaks of Life & Reality Ser.). (Illus.). 150p. 1999. pap. write for info. (*1-58470-012-2*, RAS1949) Crnerstone GA.

Nature Poetry for the 21st Century: Whispers of Hope Anthology. Sally P. Hughs. LC 96-95456. (Illus.). 68p. (Orig.). 1997. pap. 5.99 (*1-57502-411-X*, PO1275) Morris Pubng.

Nature, Pregnancy, Sexuality. R. Perkins. 1985. 33.00 (*0-275-91321-X*, C1321, Praeger Pubs) Greenwood.

Nature Printing with Herbs, Fruits, & Flowers. Laura D. Bethmann. Ed. by Deborah Balmuth. (Illus.). 96p. 1996. 24.95 (*0-88266-929-X*, 929-X, Storey Pub) Storey Bks.

***Nature, Production, Power: Towards an Ecological Political Economy.** Fred P. Gale & R. Michael M'Gonigle. LC 00-28846. 2000. write for info. (*1-84064-317-X*) E Elgar.

***Nature Projects for Every Season, 4 vols.** Phyllis S. Busch. (Illus.). 48p. (YA). (gr. 2 up). 2000. boxed set 96.86 (*0-7614-0985-8*, Benchmark NY) Marshall Cavendish.

N

An Asterisk (*) at the beginning of an entry indicates that the title is appearing for the first time.

Nature Projects for Young Scientists. Kenneth G. Rainis. (Projects for Young Scientists Ser.). (J). 1989. pap. 6.95 (*0-531-15135-2*) Watts.

Nature Projects on File. Diagram Group Staff. (Illus.). 288p. (J). (gr. 4-12). 1992. ring bd. 165.00 (*0-8160-2705-6*) Facts on File.

Nature Puzzlers. Lawrence E. Hillman. xiv, 152p. 1989. pap. text 19.50 (*0-87287-778-7*) Teacher Ideas Pr.

Nature Quest. Priscilla M. Tucker & James A. Tucker. LC 94-31780. 1994. 10.99 (*0-8280-0865-5*) Review & Herald.

Nature Quiz. Arup K. Dutta. (Illus.). x, 122p. 1991. 15.95 (*81-220-0237-4*) Advent Bks Div.

Nature Rambles in the Wallowas: Sketches of the Natural History of Northeastern Oregon. Elmo Stevenson. (Illus.). 110p. 1986. reprint ed. pap. 4.95 (*0-918957-01-X*) Pika Oregon.

Nature Reader. Ed. by Daniel Halpern & Dan Frank. 368p. 1998. pap. 16.00 (*0-88001-554-3*) HarpC.

Nature Reader. rev. ed. Ed. by Daniel Halpern & Dan Frank. LC 96-42420. 320p. 1997. 25.00 (*0-88001-491-1*) HarpC.

Nature, Reality, & the Sacred: The Nexus of Science & Religion. Langdon Gilkey. LC 93-14308. (Theology & the Sciences Ser.). 352p. 1993. pap. 25.00 (*0-8006-2754-7*, 1-2754, Fortress Pr) Augsburg Fortress.

***Nature Reborn: The Ecological & Cosmic Promise of Christian Theology.** H. Paul Santmire. LC 00-22295. 144p. 2000. pap. 15.00 (*0-8006-3234-6*, Fortress Pr) Augsburg Fortress.

Nature Recovery, & Enchanting Encounters: A Compilation of Poetry. Linda Garber. 35p. 1998. pap. 9.95 (*1-892218-02-X*) Murlin Pubns.

Nature Rectitude & Divine Law in Aquinas. Oscar J. Brown. xiv, 210p. pap. text 20.57 (*0-88844-055-3*) Brill Academic Pubs.

Nature Religion in America: From the Algonkian Indians to the New Age. Catherine L. Albanese. LC 89-39561. (Chicago History of American Religion Ser.). (Illus.). 284p. 1991. pap. text 17.00 (*0-226-01146-1*) U Ch Pr.

Nature Religion in America: From the Algonkian Indians to the New Age. Catherine L. Albanese. LC 89-39561. (Chicago History of American Religion Ser.). (Illus.). 284p. 1993. 24.95 (*0-226-01145-3*) U Ch Pr.

Nature Reserves: Island Theory & Conservation Practice. Craig L. Shafer. LC 90-96020. (Illus.). 208p. 1991. text 45.00 (*0-87474-805-4*); pap. text 17.95 (*0-87474-384-2*) Smithsonian.

Nature Reserves of Great Britain. Dennis Furnell. (Illus.). 1991. 34.95 (*1-85219-033-7*, Pub. by Bishopsgte Pr) Intl Spec Bk.

Nature, Risk & Responsibility: Discourses of Biotechnology Patrick J. O'Mahony. LC 98-37245. 1999. 80.00 (*0-415-92290-9*); pap. 24.99 (*0-415-92291-7*) Routledge.

Nature Science Adventures, 2 bks. Richard Headstrom. 452p. 1986. reprint ed. pap. 8.90 (*0-486-25145-4*) Dover.

Nature, Science, Realism: A Re-Examination of Programmatic Realism & the Works of Adalbert Stifter & Gottfried Keller. Thomas L. Buckley. LC 92-30111. (Literature & the Sciences of Man Ser.: Vol. 4). VIII, 209p. (C). 1995. text 48.95 (*0-8204-1958-3*) P Lang Pubng.

Nature Smart: A Family Guide to Nature. Stan Tekiela & Karen Shanberg. (Illus.). 300p. 1995. pap. text 17.95 (*1-885061-08-0*) Adventure Pubns.

Nature, Society, Sustainability: On Genes, Greens, Postmodern Georgraphy & Theories of Everything. Gary Sauer-Thompson & Joseph W. Smith. LC 99-86023. (C). 2000. text. write for info. (*1-57524-064-5*) Krieger.

Nature Specialist: A Complete Guide to Program & Activities. Lenore H. Miller. 170p. 1986. pap. 24.95 (*0-87603-087-8*) Am Camping.

Nature Spirits & Elemental Beings: Working with the Intelligence in Nature. Marko Pogacnik. (Illus.). 256p. (Orig.). 1997. pap. 13.95 (*1-899171-66-5*, Pub. by Findhorn Pr) Words Distrib.

Nature Spy. Shelley Rotner & Ken Kreisler. LC 91-38430. (Illus.). 32p. (J). (ps-1). 1992. lib. bdg. 14.95 (*0-02-777885-1*, Mac Bks Young Read) S&S Childrens.

Nature Staged: The Landscape & Still Life Paintings of Levi Wells Prentice. Barbara L. Jones. Ed. by Alice W. Gilborn. LC 92-83836. (Illus.). 164p. (C). 1993. pap. 39.95 (*0-910020-44-2*) Adirondack Mus.

Nature Stencil Designs. Sue Brooks. LC 95-49191. (Illus.). 80p. 1996. pap. 6.95 (*0-486-29092-1*) Dover.

Nature Stories: Depictions of the Environment & Their Effects. James Shanahan & Katherine McComas. LC 98-30187. (Hampton Press Communication Ser.). 246p. (C). 1998. text 45.00 (*1-57273-200-8*); pap. text 21.95 (*1-57273-201-6*) Hampton Pr NJ.

Nature, Structure & Function of the Church of William of Ockham. John J. Ryan. LC 78-2891. (American Academy of Religion. Studies in Religion: No. 16). 69p. reprint ed. pap. 30.00 (*0-7837-5483-3*, 204524800005) Bks Demand.

Nature Studies. John Ryskamp. LC 98-37014. 300p. 1998. pap. 12.95 (*1-57366-039-6*) Fiction Coll.

Nature Study of Belize. Sadie Schrock. (J). (gr. 3). 1991. pap. 2.40 (*0-87813-538-3*) Christian Light.

Nature Talks Back: Surviving in the Nuclear Age. Robert L. Nadeau. LC 84-3574. (Illus.). 128p. (Orig.). 1984. pap. 6.00 (*0-914061-01-1*) Orchises Pr.

Nature, the Exotic, & the Science of French Colonialism. Michael A. Osborne. LC 93-21489. (Science, Technology, & Society Ser.). 244p. 1994. 35.00 (*0-253-34266-X*) Ind U Pr.

Nature, the Exotic & the Science of French Colonialism. Michael A. Osborne. LC 93-21489. (Science, Technology, & Society Ser.). (Illus.). 232p. Date not set. reprint ed. pap. 72.00 (*0-608-20564-8*, 205447800002) Bks Demand.

Nature, the Healer. John T. Richter & Vera M. Richter. 1996. reprint ed. spiral bd. 23.50 (*0-7873-0719-X*) Hlth Research.

Nature, the Soul, & God: A Philosopher's Approach. Ed. by Jean W. Rioux. 152p. (C). 1995. pap. text 14.95 (*0-943025-76-1*) Cummngs & Hath.

Nature Through Science & Art. Susie G. Criswell. (Illus.). 156p. (J). (gr. 3-6). text 22.95 (*0-8306-4575-6*) TAB Bks.

Nature Through Science & Art. Susie G. Criswell. (Illus.). 156p. (J). (gr. 3-6). 1996. pap. 12.95 (*0-8306-4576-4*) TAB Bks.

Nature Through Science & Art. Susie G. Criswell & Judith Gradwohl. LC 93-38579. 1993. 22.95 (*0-07-013782-X*); pap. 12.95 (*0-07-013783-8*) McGraw-Hill Prof.

Nature to Advantage Dress'd. M. J. MacInnes. spiral bd. 3.75 (*0-87018-043-6*) Ross.

Nature Tomorrow. Council of Europe Staff. (Environmental Encounters Ser.: No. 7). 1989. 12.00 (*92-871-1684-9*, Pub. by Council of Europe) Manhattan Pub Co.

Nature Touring: A Guidebook for Travelers & Naturalists. John Brainerd. 224p. 1985. 16.95 (*0-13-610338-3*); pap. 7.95 (*0-13-610320-0*) P-H.

***Nature Trail of Pine View School: Plants of Sarasota County, Florida.** 2nd rev. ed. Bruce K. Holst et al. (Illus.). 27p. (YA). (gr. 5-12). 2000. pap. 14.95 (*0-9701613-0-1*) M Selby.

Nature Trails & Animal Tales. Eileen E. Lantry. LC 96-122228. 96p. (J). 1996. pap. 7.99 (*0-8280-0866-3*) Review & Herald.

Nature Trails Captured in Color. Mary Calvert. (Illus.). iv, 144p. 1983. 18.95 (*0-9609914-2-5*) M Calvert.

Nature Trails of Prince Edward Island. J. Dan McAskill & Kate MacQuarrie. (Island Pathways Ser.). (Illus.). 152p. 1996. spiral bd. 14.95 (*0-921556-58-6*, Pub. by Gynergy-Ragweed) U of Toronto Pr.

Nature Travel see Nature Company Guides Series

Nature Travel. (Nature Company Journals Ser.). (Illus.). 192p. (gr. 3). 1999. 14.95 (*0-8094-9384-5*) Time-Life.

Nature Vivante: The Still Lifes of John La Farge. James L. Yarnall. LC 95-76612. (Illus.). 160p. 1995. 50.00 (*0-614-29362-6*) V Jordan Fine Art.

Nature Walk to Ka'ena Point. Edward Arrigoni. (Illus.). 1978. pap. 1.50 (*0-914916-30-0*) Ku Paa.

Nature Walks: Insight & Advice for Observant Ramblers. Cathy Johnson. (Illus.). 288p. 1994. pap. 16.95 (*0-8117-2561-8*) Stackpole.

Nature Walks & Easy Hikes: A Family Guide to Marin Trails. rev. ed. Tacy Dunham. (Marin Trail Guide Ser.). (Illus.). 56p. 1989. reprint ed. pap. 6.95 (*0-685-27205-2*) Cttnwd Pr.

Nature Walks Around Vancouver. Jean Cousins. LC 96-910831. 1997. pap. write for info. (*1-55054-562-0*) DGL.

Nature Walks in & Around New York City: Discover Great Parks & Preserves Throughout the Tri-State... Sheila Buff. LC 96-9738. (AMC Nature Walks Guides Ser.). (Illus.). 368p. 1996. pap. 12.95 (*1-878239-53-8*) AMC Books.

Nature Walks in & Around Portland: All-Season Exploring in Parks, Forests, & Wetlands. 2nd ed. Karen Whitehill & Terry Whitehill. LC 97-51847. (Illus.). 192p. 1998. pap. 14.95 (*0-89886-563-8*) Mountaineers.

Nature Walks in & Around Seattle: All-Season Exploring in Parks, Forests & Wetlands. 2nd ed. Cathy M. McDonald & Stephen R. Whitney. LC 97-25271. (Illus.). 208p. 1997. pap. text 14.95 (*0-89886-525-5*) Mountaineers.

***Nature Walks in Central & Western Massachusetts.** 2nd ed. Rene Laubach. LC 99-86402. (Illus.). 256p. 2000. pap. 12.95 (*1-878239-95-3*) AMC Books.

Nature Walks in Connecticut. Rene Laubach & Charles Smith. LC 98-54592. (Illus.). 352p. 1999. pap. 14.95 (*1-878239-69-4*) AMC Books.

Nature Walks in Eastern Massachusetts. 2nd rev. ed. Michael Tougias. LC 98-46539. (Illus.). 224p. 1999. pap. 12.95 (*1-878239-71-6*) AMC Books.

Nature Walks in New Jersey: A Collection of Excursions from High Point to Cape May. Glenn Scherer. LC 98-35787. (Illus.). 256p. 1998. pap. 12.95 (*1-878239-68-6*) AMC Books.

Nature Walks in Northern Indiana. Alan McPherson. Ed. by Alfred Strickholm. LC 97-105665. (Illus.). 496p. (Orig.). 1996. pap. 15.95 (*0-9628469-1-0*) Hoosier Chap-Sierra Club.

Nature Walks in Northern Vermont & the Champlain Valley: More Than 40 Scenic Nature Walks. Elizabeth Bassett. LC 98-3375. 1998. pap. text 12.95 (*1-878239-58-9*) AMC Books.

Nature Walks in Orange County. Alan McPherson. (Illus.). 200p. (Orig.). 1990. pap. 9.95 (*0-939919-09-5*) Bear Flag Bks.

Nature Walks in Southern Indiana. Alan McPherson. Ed. by Alfred Strickholm. (Illus.). 416p. (Orig.). 1991. pap. 15.95 (*0-9628469-0-2*) Hoosier Chap-Sierra Club.

Nature Walks in Southern Maine: An AMC Nature Walks Book - Nature Rich Walks along the Maine Coast & Interior Foothills. Jan M. Collins & Joseph E. McCarthy. LC 95-44595. (AMC Nature Walks Guides Ser.). (Illus.). 336p. (Orig.). 1996. pap. 12.95 (*1-878239-46-5*) AMC Books.

Nature Walks in Southern New Hampshire. Julia Older & Steve Sherman. (Nature Walks Guides Ser.). (Illus.). 256p. 1994. pap. 10.95 (*1-878239-35-X*) AMC Books.

Nature Walks in Southern Vermont: Nature-Rich, Easy to Moderate Walks in the Green Mountain State. Mark Mikolas. (AMC Nature Walks Guides Ser.). (Illus.). 384p. 1995. pap. 12.95 (*1-878239-47-3*) AMC Books.

Nature Walks in the Berkshire Hills. Charles W. Smith. LC 96-50396. (Nature Walks Guide Ser.). (Illus.). 320p. (Orig.). 1997. pap. 12.95 (*1-878239-57-0*) AMC Books.

Nature Walks in the New Hampshire Lakes Region. Julia Older & Steve Sherman. LC 97-6637. (Nature Walks Guide Ser.). (Illus.). 336p. (Orig.). 1997. pap. 12.95 (*1-878239-59-7*) AMC Books.

Nature Walks near Philadelphia: Discover Great Parks & Preserves Thoughout the Metro Area... Scott Shalaway & Linda Shalaway. LC 96-30852. (AMC Nature Walks Guide Ser.). (Illus.). 368p. 1996. pap. 12.95 (*1-878239-52-X*) AMC Books.

Nature Walks on the San Luis Coast. Harold Wieman. LC 79-26521. (Illus.). 112p. 1990. pap. 6.95 (*0-939919-19-2*) Bear Flag Bks.

Nature Wars: People vs. Pests. Mark L. Winston. LC 97-17302. 256p. 1997. 24.95 (*0-674-60541-1*) HUP.

Nature Wars: People vs. Pests. Mark L. Winston. 210p. 1999. pap. 15.95 (*0-674-60542-X*) HUP.

Nature Watch. Mick Manning & Brita Granstrom. LC 96-30162. (Illus.). 48p. (J). (gr. 1-4). 1997. 9.95 (*0-7534-5063-1*, Kingfisher) LKC.

Nature Watch. Khushwant Singh. 1997. pap. 14.50 (*81-7476-147-0*, Pub. by UBS Pubs) S Asia.

Nature Watch: Writings from Japan. W. Puck Brecher. (ENG & JPN.). 215p. (Orig.). 1999. pap. 18.50 (*1-55212-228-X*, 98-0047, Pub. by Tra3fford) Trafford Pub.

Nature Watching Kit. Paul Sterry. LC 93-83525. (Illus.). 18p. (J). (gr. 2 up). 1993. 19.95 (*1-56138-213-2*) Running Pr.

Nature Watching Kit. Storey Publishing Staff. 1997. pap. 19.95 (*0-676-57183-2*) Random.

Nature Wells Gray: Volcanoes, Waterfalls, Wildlife, Trails & More. rev. ed. Trevor Goward & Cathie Hickson. (Illus.). 224p. 1996. pap. 11.95 (*1-55105-065-X*) Lone Pine.

Nature! Wild & Wonderful. Laurence Pringle. LC 96-53268. (Meet the Author Ser.). (Illus.). 32p. (J). (gr. 2-5). 1997. 14.95 (*1-57274-071-X*, 718) R Owen Pubs.

Nature, Woman & the Art of Politics. Ed. by Eduardo A. Velasquez. LC 99-48708. 256p. 2000. pap. 23.95 (*0-8476-9247-7*); text 63.00 (*0-8476-9246-9*) Rowman.

Nature Word. R. A. Schwaller De Lubicz. Tr. by Deborah Lawlor & Robert Lawlor from FRE. LC 82-81069. 160p. 1982. pap. 10.95 (*0-89281-036-X*) Inner Tradit.

Nature Word: Verbe Nature. R. A. Schwaller De Lubicz. Tr. by Deborah Lawlor from FRE. 160p. pap. 8.95 (*0-940262-00-2*, 572, Lindisfarne) Anthroposophic.

***Nature Works.** Steve Parker & Jane Parker. (Show Me How Ser.). (Illus.). 40p. (J). 2000. pap. 7.95 (*0-7548-0099-7*, Lorenz Bks) Anness Pub.

Nature Worlds see Exploring Our World: Twenty-Eight Gatefolds of the World's Ecological Zones

Nature Worship: An Account of Phallic Faiths & Practices Ancient & Modern Including the Adoration of the Male & Female Powers in Various Nations & the Sacti Puja of Indian Gnosticism. 108p. 1996. reprint ed. pap. 16.95 (*1-56459-597-8*) Kessinger Pub.

Nature Writing & America: Essays upon a Cultural Type. Peter A. Fritzell. LC 89-15377. (Illus.). 368p. 1990. text 39.95 (*0-8138-0117-6*) Iowa St U Pr.

Nature Writings. John Muir. Ed. by William Cronon. LC 96-9664. (Illus.). 888p. 1997. 35.00 (*1-883011-24-8*, Pub. by Library of America) Penguin Putnam.

NatureCrafts: 50 Extraordinary Gifts & Projects Step by Step. Gillian Souter. (Illus.). 160p. 1996. 18.00 (*0-517-88533-6*) Crown Pub Group.

Nature's Alternatives to Phen-Fen. Rita Elkias. 1996. pap. text 7.95 (*1-58054-015-5*) Woodland UT.

Nature's Amazing Healer Noni: A 2,000 Year Old Tropical Secret That Helps the Body Heal Itself, 1. Neil Solomon. 1998. pap. 7.95 (*1-58054-036-8*) Woodland UT.

Nature's America. rev. ed. Photos by David Muench. (Illus.). 160p. 1995. pap. 24.95 (*1-57098-024-1*) Roberts Rinehart.

Nature's Antiseptics: Tea Tree Oil & Grapefruit Seed Extract. C. J. Puotinen. (Good Health Guides Ser.). (Orig.). 1997. pap. 3.95 (*0-87983-714-4*, 37144K, Keats Publng) NTC Contemp Pub Co.

***Nature's Aphrodisiacs.** Nancy L. Nickell. LC 98-47924. 192p. 1999. pap. 14.95 (*0-89594-890-7*) Crossing Pr.

Nature's Aphrodisiacs. Lynn Sonberg. 224p. 1999. mass mkt. 5.99 (*0-440-23450-6*) Dell.

Nature's Argonaut: Daniel Solander, 1733-1782. Edward Duyker. 400p. 1998. 49.95 (*0-522-84753-6*, Pub. by Melbourne Univ Pr) Paul & Co Pubs.

***Nature's Artistry: There's More to See.** Michael T. Impellizzeri. (Illus.). 184p. 2000. pap. 24.95 (*0-9658427-1-1*) IM Pub.

Nature's Ban: Women's Incest Literature. Ed. by Karen J. McLennan. 384p. 1996. text 45.00 (*1-55553-252-7*); pap. text 16.95 (*1-55553-253-5*) NE U Pr.

Nature's Banquet. Living Springs Retreat Staff & Sherry Weeks. LC 95-61139. 144p. 1997. reprint ed. otabind 12.95 (*1-57258-039-9*) Teach Servs.

Nature's Basic Law of Economics. James Carroll. 92p. 1982. pap. 2.95 (*0-89826-009-4*) Natl Paperback.

Natures Beauty. Bill Huffaker. 44p. 1987. pap. text 6.50 (*1-56770-177-9*) S Scheewe Pubns.

Nature's Beauty Box: Beauty Secrets from Around the World. Laura Sanderford & Amy J. Conway. (Illus.). 88p. (Orig.). 1995. boxed set 19.95 (*0-8048-3033-9*) Tuttle Pubng.

Nature's Beauty Kit: Cosmetic Recipes You Can Make at Home. Deb Carpenter. (Illus.). 148p. (Orig.). (YA). 1995. pap. 9.95 (*1-55591-221-4*) Fulcrum Pub.

Nature's Body: Gender in the Making of Modern Science. Londa Schiebinger. (Illus.). 304p. (C). 1995. pap. 18.00 (*0-8070-8901-X*) Beacon Pr.

Nature's Bounty: Historical & Modern Environmental Perspectives. Anthony N. Penna. LC 98-42514. 320p. 1999. text 70.95 (*0-7656-0187-7*) M E Sharpe.

Nature's Bounty: Historical & Modern Environmental Perspectives. Anthony N. Penna. (Illus.). 320p. 1999. pap. text 29.95 (*0-7656-0188-5*) M E Sharpe.

Nature's Bounty for Your Table. Duane R. Lund. 1982. pap. 8.95 (*0-934860-20-3*) Adventure Pubns.

Nature's Building Codes: Geology & Construction in Colorado. David C. Shelton & Dick Prouty. (Special Publications: No. 12). (Illus.). 72p. (Orig.). 1979. pap. 4.00 (*1-884216-39-0*) Colo Geol Survey.

***Nature's Call.** Janet Oehler. (Illus.). 32p. (J). (gr. 4-6). 2000. 18.00 (*0-9671159-0-6*, Pub. by J Oehler) Booksource.

Nature's Capacities & Their Measurement. Nancy Cartwright. (Illus.). 278p. 1994. reprint ed. pap. text 21.00 (*0-19-823507-0*) OUP.

Nature's Causes. Richard J. Connell. LC 94-22404. (Revisioning Philosophy Ser.: Vol. 21). XX, 324p. (C). 1995. text 61.95 (*0-8204-2597-4*) P Lang Pubng.

Nature's Champion: B. W. Wells, Tar Heel Ecologist. James R. Troyer. LC 92-43554. xii, 244p. (C). 1993. 32.50 (*0-8078-2081-4*) U of NC Pr.

Nature's Chicken: The Story of Today's Chicken Farms. Nigel Burroughs. LC 92-13799. (Illus.). 32p. (J). (gr. 2 up). 1992. pap. 5.95 (*0-913990-92-2*) Book Pub Co.

Nature's Children, 21 vols. (Illus.). 1008p. (J). (gr. k-8). 1997. lib. bdg. 259.00 (*0-7172-7661-9*) Grolier Educ.

Nature's Children. expanded rev. ed. Juliette De Bairacli et al. LC 96-84258. (Herbals by Our Foremothers Ser.). (Illus.). 196p. 1997. reprint ed. pap. 11.95 (*0-9614620-8-6*) Ash Tree.

***Nature's Children, 21 vols., Set 6.** LC 98-33394. (Nature's Children Ser.). (Illus.). (J). (gr. k-8). 1999. lib. bdg. 259.00 (*0-7172-9351-3*) Grolier Educ.

Nature's Children: NC Set #1, 21 vols. (Illus.). 48p. (J). (gr. k-8). 1994. lib. bdg. 259.00 (*0-7172-7274-5*) Grolier Educ.

Nature's Children: NC Set#2, 21 vols. (Illus.). 48p. (J). (gr. k-8). 1994. lib. bdg. 259.00 (*0-7172-7275-3*) Grolier Educ.

Nature's Children: NC Set#3, 21 vols. (Illus.). 48p. (J). (gr. k-8). 1994. lib. bdg. 259.00 (*0-7172-7276-1*) Grolier Educ.

Nature's Children: NC Set#4, 21 vols., (Illus.). 48p. (J). (gr. k-8). 1994. lib. bdg. 259.00 (*0-7172-7277-X*) Grolier Educ.

Nature's Colors: Dyes from Plants. Ida Grae. 1991. 20.00 (*1-56659-002-7*) Robin & Russ.

Nature's Contribution to Aeronautics. Tirrel. 1953. 4.95 (*0-87505-359-9*) Borden.

***Nature's Cornucopia Vol. 148: Our Stake in Plant Diversity.** John Tuxill. Ed. by Jane Peterson. 85p. 1999. pap. 5.00 (*1-878071-50-5*) Worldwatch Inst.

Nature's Covenant: Figures of Landscape in Ruskin. C. Stephen Finley. (Illus.). 304p. 1993. text 38.50 (*0-271-00788-5*) Pa St U Pr.

Nature's Creatures of the Dark: A Pop-Up Glow-in-the-Dark Exploration. (J). pap. text 2.99 (*0-307-05172-2*, 05172) Gldn Bks Pub Co.

Nature's Cures. Michael Castleman. 608p. 1997. mass mkt. 6.99 (*0-553-57696-8*) Bantam.

Nature's Cures: From Acupressure & Aromatherapy to Walking & Yoga--The Ultimate Guide to the Best, Scientifically Proven, Drug-Free Healing Methods. Michael Castleman. 528p. 1995. text 27.95 (*0-87596-301-3*) Rodale Pr Inc.

Nature's Curiosity Shop. Barry E. Zimmerman & David J. Zimmerman. (Illus.). 352p. 1995. pap. 12.95 (*0-8092-3656-7*, 365670, Contemporary Bks) NTC Contemp Pub Co.

Nature's Destiny: How the Laws of Biology Reveal Purpose in the Universe. Michael Denton. LC 98-3295. (Illus.). 480p. 1998. 27.00 (*0-684-84509-1*) S&S Trade.

Nature's Dyepot: A Resource Guide for Spinners, Weavers & Dyers. Bobbi A. McRae. (Illus.). 65p. (Orig.). 1991. pap. 8.95 (*0-944577-02-4*) Limestone.

Nature's Economy: A History of Ecological Ideas. 2nd ed. Donald Worster. LC 93-48248. (Studies in Environment & History). 423p. (C). 1994. pap. text 17.95 (*0-521-46834-5*) Cambridge U Pr.

Nature's Ecosystems. Norris. (Illus.). 32p. (J). (gr. 4-6). 1997. pap., teacher ed. 2.95 (*1-55799-523-0*, 4125) Evan-Moor Edu Pubs.

Nature's Electricity. Charles K. Adams. (Illus.). 176p. 1986. pap. 9.95 (*0-8306-2769-3*, NO. 2769) McGraw-Hill Prof.

Nature's End. 1988. mass mkt. 4.95 (*0-446-73744-5*, Pub. by Warner Bks) Little.

Nature's Endless Pulsations: Poems. Henry P. Pelletier. LC 91-36603. 96p. 1992. pap. 8.95 (*0-86534-168-0*) Sunstone Pr.

Nature's Enigma: The Problem of the Polyp in the Letters of Bonnet, Trembley & Reaumur. Virginia Dawson. LC 86-72886. (Memoirs Ser.: Vol. 174). (Illus.). (C). 1987. 20.00 (*0-87169-174-4*, M174-DAV) Am Philos.

Nature's Eternal Religion. Ben Klassen. Ed. by Rudy Stanko. 489p. 1973. 8.00 (*0-9636094-2-4*, K1) Creativity Bk Pub.

Nature's Everyday Mysteries: A Field Guide to the World in Your Backyard. Sy Montgomery. LC 92-36189. (Curious Naturalist Ser.). (Illus.). 152p. (Orig.). 1993. pap. 9.95 (*0-9631591-9-4*, Chapters Bks) HM.

***Nature's Extremes: Eight Seasons Shape a Southwester Land.** Lawrence W. Cheek. LC 00-100903. (Illus.). 160p. 2000. 34.95 (*1-893860-08-6*) Ariz Hwy.

N

***Nature's Fading Chorus: Classic & Contemporary Writings on Amphibians.** Ed. by Gordon L. Miller. (Illus.). 250p. 2000. 45.00 (*1-55963-793-5*); pap. 19.95 (*1-55963-794-3*) Island Pr.

Nature's Fen Phen. Rita Elkins. 1997. pap. text 3.95 (*1-885670-31-1*) Woodland UT.

Nature's Finer Forces. Rama Prasad. 251p. 1996. reprint ed. spiral bd. 23.00 (*0-7873-1031-X*) Hlth Research.

Nature's Finer Forces: The Science of Breath & the Philosophy of the Tattvas (1894) Rama Prasad. 261p. 1996. reprint ed. pap. 21.95 (*1-56459-803-9*) Kessinger Pub.

Nature's First Law: The Raw-Food Diet. 2nd rev. ed. Stephen Arlin et al. 232p. (Orig.). 1996. pap. 14.95 (*0-9653533-0-3*) Maul Bros.

Nature's Footprints Series, 3 vols., Set. W. J. Pearce & Querida L. Pearce. (Illus.). 96p. (J). (ps-1). 1990. 14.85 (*0-671-94431-2*); lib. bdg. 27.80 (*0-671-94430-4*) Silver Burdett Pr.

Nature's Forms, Nature's Forces: The Art of Alexandre Hogue. Lea R. DeLong. LC 84-60404. (Illus.). 221p. 1984. pap. 22.95 (*0-8061-1917-9*) U of Okla Pr.

Nature's Forms, Nature's Forces: The Work of Alexandre Hogue. Lea DeLong. LC 84-60404. (Illus.). 216p. (Orig.). 1984. pap. 25.00 (*0-86659-005-6*) Philbrook Mus Art.

Nature's Free Herbal Pharmacy - Herbal Healing Using Nature's Wild Foods & Wild Herbs. Ken Larson. (Illus.). 160p. 1997. pap. 10.95 (*0-9642497-3-1*) Rhema Pubng.

***Nature's Fury.** Carole Garbuny Vogel. LC 99-46103. 2000. pap. write for info. (*0-590-11503-0*) Scholastic Inc.

***Nature's Fury: Eyewitness Reports of Natural Disasters.** Carole Garbuny Vogel. LC 99-46103. (Illus.). 128p. (J). (gr. 3-7). 2000. 16.95 (*0-590-11502-2*) Scholastic Inc.

***Nature's Fury: The Power of Weather.** Andrew Gutelle. (Windows on Science Ser.). (Illus.). 16p. (J). (gr. 4-6). 1999. 12.99 (*1-57584-317-X*) Rdrs Digest.

Nature's Gambit: Child Prodigies & the Development of Human Potential. David H. Feldman. (Education & Psychology of the Gifted Ser.: Vol. 9). 284p. (C). 1991. reprint ed. pap. text 18.95 (*0-8077-3143-9*) Tchrs Coll.

Nature's Geography: New Lessons for Conservation in Developing Countries. Karl S. Zimmerer. LC 98-25743. 1999. 60.00 (*0-299-15910-8*); pap. 28.95 (*0-299-15914-0*) U of Wis Pr.

Nature's Golden Treasure. 12.95 (*0-936744-04-9*) Country Bazaar.

***Nature's Government: Science, British Imperialism & the Improvement of the World.** Richard Drayton. LC 99-59158. 416p. 2000. 40.00 (*0-300-05976-0*) Yale U Pr.

Nature's Grace: Essays of H. N. Wieman's Finite Theism. Marvin C. Shaw. LC 94-33887. (American Liberal Religious Thought Ser.: Vol. 2). X, 160p. (C). 1995. pap. text 29.95 (*0-8204-2707-1*) P Lang Pubng.

Nature's Grand Unifying Force Discovered! Robert M. Kopke. (Illus.). 347p. 1991. 24.95 (*0-9630352-0-7*) Kopkean Sci.

Nature's Green Umbrella: Tropical Rain Forests. Gail Gibbons. LC 93-17569. (Illus.). 32p. (J). (gr. 2 up). 1994. 16.00 (*0-688-12353-8*, Wm Morrow) Morrow Avon.

Nature's Green Umbrella: Tropical Rain Forests. Gail Gibbons. LC 93-17569. (Illus.). 32p. (J). (gr. 2 up). 1994. 15.93 (*0-688-12354-6*, Wm Morrow) Morrow Avon.

Nature's Green Umbrella: Tropical Rain Forests. Gail Gibbons. LC 93-17569. (Illus.). 32p. (J). (gr. k-3). 1997. mass mkt. 4.95 (*0-688-15411-5*, Wm Morrow) Morrow Avon.

Nature's Green Umbrella, Tropical Rain Forest. Gail Gibbons. 1997. 10.15 (*0-606-11673-7*, Pub. by Turtleback) Demco.

***Nature's Guide to Healing.** Gary Ross. 176p. 2000. pap. 12.95 (*1-893910-06-7*, 904-006, Pub. by Freedom Pr Inc) BookWorld.

Nature's Harmonic Unity: A Treatise on Its Relation to Proportional Form. Samuel Colman. LC 78-177520. (Illus.). 1972. reprint ed. 27.95 (*0-405-08374-2*) Ayer.

Nature's Harvest: A Produce Reference Guide to Fruits & Vegetables from Around the World. Donald D. Heaton. LC 96-49040. (Illus.). 244p. 1997. 29.95 (*1-56022-865-2*, Food Products) Haworth Pr.

Nature's Healing Agents: The Medicines of Nature. R. S. Clymer. xx, 256p. 1963. lthr. 20.00 (*0-916285-54-5*) Humanitarian.

Nature's Healing Agents: The Medicines of Nature. 4th enl. rev. ed. R. Swinburne Clymer. (Illus.). 230p. 1996. pap. 10.95 (*0-916638-51-0*) Meyerbooks.

Nature's Hidden Terror: Violent Nature Imagery in 18th-Century Literature. Robert H. Brown. (GERM Ser.: Vol. 69). (Illus.). vii, 148p. 1992. 50.00 (*1-879751-06-2*) Camden Hse.

Nature's Holy Realm: Verses for Living in the Natural World. Photos by Pat O'Hara. LC 96-47249. (Illus.). 128p. 1997. 19.95 (*1-55971-598-7*, NorthWord Pr) Creat Pub Intl.

Nature's Ideological Landscape. Kenneth R. Olwig. (London Research Series in Geography: No. 5). (Illus.). 144p. 1984. text 60.00 (*0-04-710002-8*) Routledge.

Nature's Imagination: The Frontiers of Scientific Vision. John Cornwell. (Illus.). 224p. 1995. 25.00 (*0-19-851775-0*) OUP.

Natures Invisible Forces: The Seven Principles or Laws of Nature Analyzed & Expounded (1917) Thos H. Ellis. 272p. 1998. reprint ed. pap. 24.95 (*0-7661-0677-2*) Kessinger Pub.

Nature's Invitation. Bradford Torrey. (Notable American Authors). 1999. reprint ed. lib. bdg. 125.00 (*0-7812-9779-6*) Rprt Serv.

***Nature's Justice: Writings of William O. Douglas.** William O. Douglas & James M. O'Fallon. LC 00-9322. (Northwest Readers Ser.). (Illus.). 320p. 2000. 35.00 (*0-87071-482-1*) Oreg St U Pr.

Nature's Kaleidoscope: The Santa Barbara Botanic Garden. Theodore R. Gardner, 2nd. LC 98-34278. (Illus.). 48p. 1998. pap. 17.00 (*1-888310-03-0*) A A Knoll Pubs.

Nature's Kaleidoscope: The Santa Barbara Botanic Garden. 24th ed. Theodore R. Gardner, 2nd. LC 98-34278. (Illus.). 48p. 1998. 22.00 (*1-888310-02-2*) A A Knoll Pubs.

Nature's Keeper. Peter S. Wenz. LC 95-47189. (Ethics & Action Ser.). 240p. (C). 1996. lib. bdg. 69.95 (*1-56639-427-9*) Temple U Pr.

Nature's Keeper. Peter S. Wenz. LC 95-47189. (Ethics & Action Ser.). 240p. (C). 1996. pap. 19.95 (*1-56639-428-7*) Temple U Pr.

Nature's Keepers: On the Front Lines of the Fight to Save Wildlife in America. Michael Tobias. LC 98-24395. 256p. 1998. 24.95 (*0-471-15728-7*) Wiley.

Nature's Keepers: The New Science of Nature Management. Stephen Budiansky. (Illus.). 310p. 1995. 25.00 (*0-02-904915-6*) Free Pr.

Nature's Kindred Spirits: Aldo Leopold, Joseph Wood Krutch, Edward Abbey, Annie Dillard, & Gary Snyder. James I. McClintock. LC 93-38110. (Illus.). 198p. reprint ed. pap. 61.40 (*0-608-07017-3*, 206722400009) Bks Demand.

Nature's Life Lessons: Everyday Truths from Nature. Jim Carrier & Marc Bekoff. LC 95-49006. (Illus.). 112p. (Orig.). 1996. pap. 10.95 (*1-55591-248-6*) Fulcrum Pub.

Nature's Magic. large type ed. (Illus.). 96p. (J). (ps-1). 1999. write for info. (*1-85854-776-8*) Brimax Bks.

Nature's Magic Formula. Amedeo J. Sorrentino & Ross Robert Olney. (Illus.). 128p. (Orig.). 1985. 16.95 (*0-935131-63-9*); pap. 9.95 (*0-935131-39-6*) Amis Pub.

Nature's Management: Writings on Landscape & Reform, 1822-1852. Edmund Ruffin. Ed. by Jack T. Kirby. LC 99-39150. (Illus.). 424p. 1999. pap. 70.00 (*0-8203-2162-1*) U of Ga Pr.

Nature's Masterpiece at Homosassa. W. Horace Carter. LC 81-69722. (Illus.). 288p. (Orig.). 1984. 9.95 (*0-937866-07-5*) Atlantic Pub Co.

Nature's Masterpieces. Michael Bright. Ed. by Reader's Digest Editors. LC 97-22868. (Earth, Its Wonders, Its Secrets Ser.). (Illus.). 160p. 1997. 19.95 (*0-89577-914-5*, Pub. by RD Assn) Penguin Putnam.

Nature's Materia Medica: A Handy Guide on Prevention & Treatment of Diseases by Rational Methods. J. M. Jussawalla. (C). 1994. 40.00 (*81-7154-560-2*, Pub. by Popular Prakashan) S Asia.

Nature's Mazes: Maze Funbook. Illus. by John Hull. (Troubador Ser.). Orig. Title: MazeCraze 3. 32p. (J). (ps up). 1997. reprint ed. pap. 3.50 (*0-8431-7959-7*, Price Stern) Peng Put Young Read.

***Nature's Medicine: A Chronicle of Mankind's Search for Healing Plants Through the Ages.** Joel L. Swerdlow. LC 99-89037. 2000. write for info. (*0-7922-7587-X*) Natl Geog.

***Nature's Medicine: Plants That Heal.** National Geographic Staff. LC 99-89037. 400p. 2000. per. 34.50 (*0-7922-7586-1*, Pub. by Natl Geog) S&S Trade.

***Nature's Medicine Chest.** Ed. by Reader's Digest Editors. LC 99-39191. 1999. write for info. (*0-7621-0261-6*) RD Assn.

***Nature's Medicine Chest: A Sampler.** Glenn D. Appelt & Jennifer Sinclair. (Illus.). 84p. 2000. pap. 12.95 (*1-930509-00-6*) Lorelei.

***Nature's Medicine Shelf Talker.** Joel Swerdlow. 2000. write for info. (*0-684-01095-X*) S&S Trade.

Nature's Medicines: From Asthma to Weight Gain, from Colds to High Cholesterol-The Most Powerful All-Natural Cures. Gale Malesky et al. LC 99-15694. 704p. 1999. 29.95 (*1-57954-028-7*) Rodale Pr Inc.

Nature's Melody: A Guide to Georgia Wildflowers. Betty L. Benson. Ed. by Thomas S. Patrick. LC 82-74400. (Illus.). 226p. (Orig.). 1994. pap. 25.00 (*0-9612486-1-0*) Garden GA.

Nature's Metropolis: Chicago & the Great West. William Cronon. (Illus.). 592p. 1992. pap. 18.95 (*0-393-30873-1*) Norton.

Nature's Miracle Medicines: Amazing Remedies from Mother Earth. Consumer Guide Editors. 1999. mass mkt. 5.99 (*0-451-19925-1*) NAL.

Nature's Miracle Medicines: Amazing Remedies from Mother Earth. Consumer Guide Editors. LC 98-68003. 256p. 1999. mass mkt. 5.99 (*0-7853-3923-X*) Pubns Intl Ltd.

***Nature's Miracle Medicines: Amazing Remedies from Mother Earth.** Consumer Guide Editors. 2000. mass mkt. 5.99 (*0-7853-4048-3*) Pubns Intl Ltd.

***Natures Mortes.** Pesi Girsch. (Illus.). 112p. 2000. 35.00 (*3-934296-09-2*) G Kehayoff.

***Nature's Museums: Victorian Science & the Architecture of Display.** Carla Yanni. LC 99-34204. 2000. 49.95 (*0-8018-6326-0*) Johns Hopkins.

Nature's Mysteries, 6 vols. Incl. How Bats See in the Dark. Malcolm Penny. LC 96-19940. (Illus.). 32p. (YA). (gr. 3 up). 1996. lib. bdg. 22.79 (*0-7614-0455-4*, Benchmark NY); How Bees Make Honey. Michael Chinery. LC 96-19159. (Illus.). 32p. (YA). (gr. 3 up). 1996. lib. bdg. 22.79 (*0-7614-0453-8*, Benchmark NY); How Birds Fly. N. Williams. LC 96-19939. (Illus.). 32p. (YA). (gr. 3 up). 1996. lib. bdg. 22.79 (*0-7614-0454-6*, Benchmark NY); How Fish Swim. Jill Baily. LC 96-19158. (Illus.). 32p. (YA). (gr. 3 up). 1996. lib. bdg. 22.79 (*0-7614-0451-1*, Benchmark NY); How Plants Grow. Malcolm Penny. LC 96-2827. (Illus.). 32p. (YA). (gr. 3 up). 1996. lib. bdg. 22.79 (*0-7614-0452-X*, Benchmark NY); How Spiders Make Their Webs. J. Bailey. LC 96-19941. (Illus.). 32p. (YA). (gr. 3 up). 1996. lib. bdg. 22.79 (*0-7614-0456-2*, Benchmark NY); (Nature's Mysteries Ser.). (YA). 1996. 136.71 (*0-7614-0450-3*, Benchmark NY) Marshall Cavendish.

Nature's Mysteries. J. Bailey et al. (Illus.). 32p. 91.14 (*0-7614-0856-8*) Marshall Cavendish.

Nature's Mystic Clue (1925) Dwight Goddard. 282p. 1998. reprint ed. pap. 19.95 (*0-7661-0362-5*) Kessinger Pub.

Nature's Nation. Perry G. Miller. LC 67-17316. 314p. 1967. 136.50 (*0-674-60550-0*) Belknap Pr.

Nature's Nation. Opie. 27p. (C). 1998. pap. text 37.00 (*0-15-500219-8*, Pub. by Harcourt Coll Pubs) Harcourt.

Nature's Neighbours. Thomas-Cochran. (What a Wonderful World Ser.). 1991. pap. text. write for info. (*0-582-90952-X*, Drumbeat) Longman.

Nature's New Voices. John A. Murray. LC 92-53030. 256p. (Orig.). 1992. pap. 15.95 (*1-55591-117-X*) Fulcrum Pub.

Nature's Noblemen: The Fortunes of the Independent Collier in Scotland & the American Midwest, 1855-1889. John H. Laslett. (Monograph & Research Ser.: No. 34). 87p. 1984. 6.00 (*0-89215-120-X*) U Cal LA Indus Rel.

Nature's Numbers: Expanding the National Economic Accounts to Include the Environment. National Research Council Staff. Ed. by William D. Nordhaus & Edward C. Kokkelenberg. LC 99-6236. 262p. 1999. text 44.95 (*0-309-07151-8*) Natl Acad Pr.

Nature's Numbers: The Unreal Reality of Mathematical Imagination. Ian Stewart. (Illus.). 176p. 1997. pap. 12.00 (*0-465-07274-7*, Pub. by Basic) HarpC.

Natures of John & William Bartram. Thomas Slaughter. 336p. 1996. 27.50 (*0-679-43045-8*) Knopf.

Natures of John & William Bartram. Thomas Slaughter. 1997. pap. 14.00 (*0-679-78118-8*) Vin Bks.

Natures of Science. Neville McMorris. LC 87-46376. 264p. 1989. 38.50 (*0-8386-3321-8*) Fairleigh Dickinson.

***Nature's Open Secret: Introductions to Goethe's Scientific Writings.** Rudolf Steiner & John Michael Barnes. Tr. by Mado Spiegler. (Illus.). 320p. 2000. pap. 35.00 (*0-88010-393-0*) Anthroposophic.

Nature's Outcasts: A New Look at Living Things We Love to Hate. Des Kennedy. Ed. by Sandra Webb. LC 93-18288. (Illus.). 232p. 1993. reprint ed. pap. 12.95 (*0-88266-868-4*, Garden Way Pub) Storey Bks.

Nature's Own, Vol. 1. Marilyn Kleinhardt. 8p. 1993. pap. 6.00 (*1-884694-01-2*) Wood n Needle.

***Nature's Pain Killers.** Carl Germano. 336p. 2000. pap. 16.00 (*1-57566-527-1*, Knsington) Kensgtn Pub Corp.

***Nature's Pain Killers: Proven New Alternative & Nutritional Therapies for Chronic Pain Relief, Vol. 1.** Carl Germano. 1999. 23.00 (*1-57566-502-6*, Knsington) Kensgtn Pub Corp.

***Nature's Painkillers.** Deborah R. Mitchell. 256p. 2000. mass mkt. 5.99 (*0-312-97315-2*) St Martin.

Nature's Paintbrush: The Patterns & Colors Around You. Susan Stockdale. LC 97-46736. (Illus.). 32p. (J). (ps-3). 1999. 14.00 (*0-689-81081-4*) S&S Bks Yung.

Natures Palette. Carol Binford. 100p. 1992. pap. text 10.50 (*1-56770-248-1*) S Scheewe Pubns.

Nature's Pantry. David A. Wilson. (Illus.). 46p. 1972. pap. 6.00 (*0-934852-08-1*) Lorien Hse.

Nature's Pantry Cookbook. Dick Patricelli. 131p. 1990. spiral bd. 19.95 (*0-9629224-0-4*) Natures Pantry.

***Nature's Path to Supreme Health: A Self-Reliant Guide to Living Supremely Healthy, Full of Energy.** (Illus.). 330p. 1999. pap. write for info. (*0-7392-0495-5*, PO3861) Morris Pubng.

Nature's Patterns: Inspirations & Techniques for Quilt Makers. Joyce R. Becker. LC 95-38016. (Illus.). 176p. 1996. pap. 24.95 (*0-8442-2648-3*, Quilt Dgst Pr) NTC Contemp Pub Co.

Nature's Patterns: Student Book. Lisa Trumbauer. Ed. by Stephanie Pliakas. (Early Science Ser.). 16p. (Orig.). (J). (ps-2). 1998. pap. text, student ed. 3.33 (*1-56784-376-X*) Newbridge Educ.

Nature's Pharmacy: Your Guide to Healing Foods, Herbs, Supplements & Homeopathic Remedies. Gayle Povia Alleman & American Association of Naturopathic Physicians Staff. LC 98-66943. 384 p. 1998. write for info. (*0-7853-2600-6*) Pubns Intl Ltd.

Nature's Places: Photography by Rod Planck. Bert C. Ebbers. Ed. by Kathryn E. Parker. LC 92-73971. (Illus.). 96p. (Orig.). 1993. pap. text 24.95 (*0-9634200-4-6*) Hawk-Owl Pub.

***Nature's Poetic Splendors.** Leta Hartman. 1999. pap. write for info. (*1-58235-278-X*) Watermrk Pr.

Nature's Poisonous Creatures. Nathan Aaseng. (J). 1996. pap. 8.95 (*0-8050-4689-5*) H Holt & Co.

Nature's Poisonous Creatures. Nathan Aaseng. LC 97-8728. (Scientific American Sourcebooks Ser.). 96p. (J). (gr. 5-9). 1997. 22.40 (*0-8050-4690-9*) TFC Bks NY.

Nature's Prescription: Foods, Vitamins & Supplements That Prevent Disease. FC&A Staff. LC 98-230563. (Illus.). 385p. 2000. 27.96 (*1-890957-00-3*); pap. 9.99 (*1-890957-01-1*) FC&A Pub.

Nature's Prozac. Judith Sachs. 1997. 22.95 (*0-614-20668-5*) P-H.

Nature's Prozac. Judith Sachs. (Illus.). 528p. (C). 1997. pap. text 14.95 (*0-13-887654-1*) P-H.

Nature's Purposes: Analyses of Function & Design in Biology. Ed. by Colin Allen et al. LC 97-29290. 576p. 1998. 60.00 (*0-262-01168-9*, Bradford Bks) MIT Pr.

Nature's Purposes: Analysis of Function & Design in Biology. Ed. by Colin Allen et al. LC 97-29290. (Illus.). 576p. 1998. pap. text 30.00 (*0-262-51097-9*, Bradford Bks) MIT Pr.

***Nature's Record-Breakers, 4 bks.** Incl. Animals. Illus. by Francesco Davico. LC 99-26878. 32p. (J). (gr. 3 up). 2000. lib. bdg. 21.27 (*0-8368-2473-3*); Dinosaurs. Francis Davies & Gian P Faleschini. LC 00-25037. (Illus.). 32p. (J). (gr. 3 up). 2000. lib. bdg. 21.27 (*0-8368-2474-1*); Seas & Oceans. Antonella Meucci. LC 00-23897. (Illus.). 32p. (J). (gr. 3 up). 2000. lib. bdg. 21.27 (*0-8368-2475-X*); Universe. Francis Davies. LC 99-26883. (Illus.). 32p. (J). (gr. 3 up). 2000. lib. bdg. 21.27 (*0-8368-2476-8*); (Illus.). (J). (gr. 3 up). 2000. Set lib. bdg. 85.08 (*0-8368-2472-5*) Gareth Stevens Inc.

Nature's Religion. Robert S. Corrington. LC 97-17894. 212p. 1997. 61.00 (*0-8476-8699-X*); pap. 24.95 (*0-8476-8750-3*) Rowman.

Nature's Revenge: The Secrets of Poison Ivy, Poison Oak, & Poison Sumac. Susan C. Hauser. LC 95-44628. (Illus.). 128p. 1996. pap. 13.95 (*1-55821-449-6*) Lyons Pr.

Natures Road to Recovery: Nutritional Supplements for the Social Drinker, Alcoholic & Chemical Dependent. Beth Ley-Jacobs. LC 99-19566. 72p. 1999. pap. text 5.95 (*1-890766-03-8*) B L Pubns.

***Nature's Secret for Health & Beauty.** (Illus.). 24p. 1998. pap. 24.95 (*0-9664814-0-2*) Minoos Skin Co.

Nature's Self: Our Journey from Origin to Spirit. Robert S. Corrington. LC 95-38603. 192p. (C). 1996. pap. text 24.95 (*0-8476-8134-3*); lib. bdg. 58.50 (*0-8476-8133-5*) Rowman.

Nature's Serial Story. Edward P. Roe. (Notable American Authors Ser.). 1999. reprint ed. lib. bdg. 125.00 (*0-7812-8830-4*) Rprt Serv.

Nature's Services: Societal Dependence on Natural Ecosystems. Ed. by Gretchen C. Daily. LC 96-40401. (Illus.). 416p. 1997. pap. text 24.95 (*1-55963-476-6*, Shearwater Bks) Island Pr.

Nature's 7 Doctors: Let Nature Make You Well. H. E. Kirschner. (Illus.). 128p. 1982. pap. 3.95 (*0-88007-153-2*) Woodbridge Pr.

Nature's Silent Music. Philip S. Callahan. LC 91-76335. 194p. 1992. pap. 15.00 (*0-911311-33-5*) Acres USA.

Nature's Simple Plan: A Phase of Radical Thought in the Mid-Eighteenth Century. Chauncey B. Tinker. LC 64-8179. 120p. 1964. reprint ed. 35.00 (*0-87752-112-3*) Gordian.

Nature's Special Moments. Robert Bystrom. Ed. & Illus. by H. Lewis Batts, Jr. Illus. by Marvin Black et al. 80p. 1975. 7.50 (*0-939294-01-X*, QH-71-K3-A7) Beech Leaf.

Nature's Sports Pharmacy: A Natural Approach to Peak Athletic Performance. Frederick C. Hatfield & Frederick C. Hatfield, II. LC 96-1350. (Illus.). 192p. 1999. pap. 14.95 (*0-8092-3221-9*, 322190, Contemporary Bks) NTC Contemp Pub Co.

Nature's Sternest Painter: Five Essays on the Poetry of George Crabbe. Oliver F. Sigworth. LC 64-17262. 204p. reprint ed. pap. 63.30 (*0-608-12767-1*, 202432200037) Bks Demand.

Nature's Super Seven Medicines. John Heinerman. (C). 1997. text 18.95 (*0-13-857731-5*) P-H.

Nature's Symphony: Lessons in Number Vibration. L. Dow Balliett. 127p. 1996. reprint ed. spiral bd. 11.50 (*0-7873-0068-3*) Hlth Research.

Nature's Symphony, 1911: Lessons in Number Vibration. L. Don Balliett. 127p. 1996. reprint ed. pap. 10.95 (*1-56459-649-4*) Kessinger Pub.

Nature's Telling: Anza-Borrego Desert. Jones M. King. LC 96-67887. (Illus.). x, 38p. (Orig.). 1996. pap. 10.95 (*0-9651151-2-7*) Particles to Pots.

Nature's Thumbprint: The New Genetics of Personality. Peter S. Neubauer & Alexander Neubauer. LC 95-37858. 224p. (C). 1996. pap. 18.50 (*0-231-10441-3*) Col U Pr.

Nature's Thumbprint: The Role of Genetics in Human Development. Peter B. Neubauer. 1990. 17.26 (*0-201-09254-9*) Addison-Wesley.

Nature's Timekeeper: The Tree. Gaud Morel. (Young Discovery Library). (Illus.). 40p. (J). (gr. k-6). 1993. lib. bdg. 2.99 (*1-56674-072-X*, HTS Bks) Forest Hse.

Nature's Timekeeper: The Tree. Gaud Morel. Tr. by Vicki Bogard from FRE. LC 92-2710. (Illus.). 38p. (J). (gr. k-5). 1992. 5.95 (*0-944589-43-X*) Young Discovery Lib.

Nature's Tranquility. NorthWord Press Staff. LC 99-21046. (Illus.). 64p. 1999. text 9.95 (*1-55971-711-4*, NorthWord Pr) Creat Pub Intl.

Nature's Treasures Invisibles. Larry Evans. (Funbooks Ser.). (Illus.). 32p. (J). (ps-3). 1995. pap. 2.95 (*0-8431-3886-6*, Price Stern) Peng Put Young Read.

Nature's 12 Magic Healers. Lionel Rolfe & Nigey Lennon. LC 97-31475. 144p. 1997. pap. 12.95 (*0-87983-800-0*, 38000K, Keats Publng) NTC Contemp Pub Co.

***Nature's Virus Killers.** Mark Stengler & Arden Moore. LC 99-53637. 220p. 2000. 19.95 (*0-87131-898-9*) M Evans.

***Nature's Way.** Mark Evans. 128p. 2000. pap. 12.95 (*1-84215-079-0*) Anness Pub.

Nature's Way. David C. Thomas. 1987. 30.00 (*0-7223-2075-2*, Pub. by A H S Ltd) St Mut.

Nature's Way: A Book of Essays about Nature. A. L. Gennaro. 208p. (Orig.). 1996. pap. 11.00 (*0-9648431-0-2*) Marnaric Pr Inc.

Nature's Way Handbook of Skin Care. John Woodruff. (Illus.). x, 170p. 1992. pap. 14.00 (*1-870228-08-1*) Micelle Pr.

Nature's Way on Kiawah: A Barrier Island on the Carolina Coast. Robert W. Cowgill. (Illus.). 150p. 1998. pap. 12.00 (*0-9661595-0-0*) Bobcat Pr.

Nature's Way to a Trouble Free Digestion. Lindsey Berkson. LC 96-52366. 320p. 1997. pap. text 13.95 (*0-13-258724-6*) P-H.

Nature's Way to Nutrition & Vibrant Health. Robert Scrutton. 1977. reprint ed. pap. 3.00 (*0-87980-344-4*) Wilshire.

Nature's Ways: Natural History Essays from Wildlife in North Carolina. Lawrence S. Earley & NC Wildlife Resources Commission. (Illus.). 1998. pap. 30.00 (*1-891097-01-6*) NC Wildlife.

Nature's Web: Rethinking Our Place on Earth. Peter Marshall. LC 96-10481. 523p. (gr. 13). 1996. pap. 29.95 (*1-56324-864-6*) M E Sharpe.

An Asterisk (*) at the beginning of an entry indicates that the title is appearing for the first time.

Nature's Web: Rethinking Our Place on Earth. Peter Marshall. LC 93-17233. 528p. 1993. reprint ed. 24.95 (*1-55778-652-6*) Paragon Hse.

Nature's Weeds, Native Medicines: Native American Herbal Secrets. Marie Miczak. LC 98-75821. 1999. pap. 10.95 (*0-914955-48-9*) Lotus Pr.

Nature's Window - Charles Frace. Bruce H. Davis. Ed. by Elke Frace et al. LC 91-71713. (Illus.). 168p. 1992. 65.00 (*1-880044-00-5*) Am Masters Found.

Nature's Window - Charles Frace. deluxe ed. Bruce H. Davis. Ed. by Elke Frace et al. LC 91-71713. (Illus.). 168p. 1992. 125.00 (*1-880044-01-3*) Am Masters Found.

Nature's Wisdom: A Powerfully Insightful Guide for Exploring Life's Changes. Carol L. McClelland. (Illus.). 80p. 1993. pap. 28.95 (*0-9635123-3-1*) Transition Dyn.

Nature's Wonderful World in Rhyme. William Sheehan. LC 93-15247. (Illus.). 32p. (J). (ps up). 1993. 14.95 (*0-911655-47-6*) Advocacy Pr.

Nature's Wonderlands: National Parks of the World. Ed. by Robert M. Poole. 304p. 1989. 29.95 (*0-87044-766-1*); 39.95 (*0-87044-767-X*) Natl Geog.

Natures Wonders. C. R. Gibson Company Staff. 1997. 6.00 (*0-7852-3719-4*); pap. text 9.99 (*0-7852-3718-6*) Gibson.

***Natures Wonders, 3.** Nelson Publishing Staff. 2000. 35.97 (*0-7852-3712-7*) Nelson.

Nature's Wonders. Sue Strike. LC 98-34728. (Young at Art Coloring Book Ser.). (Illus.). 96p. (J). (gr. 4-7). 1995. pap. 8.95 (*0-8050-4806-5*) H Holt & Co.

Nature's Wonders in Glass: The Art of the Blaschkas. David B. Whitehouse. (Illus.). 12p. 1991. pap. 3.50 (*0-87290-125-4*) Corning.

Nature's Work of Art: The Human Body As Image of the World. Leonard Barkan. LC 74-77067. 301p. reprint ed. pap. 93.40 (*0-8357-8743-5*, 203366600087) Bks Demand.

Nature's Workshop: Renoir's Writings on the Decorative Arts Robert L. Herbert. LC 99-20881. (Illus.). 256p. 2000. 35.00 (*0-300-08136-7*) Yale U Pr.

Nature's World of Wonders. Ed. by Donald J. Crump. LC 82-47842. (Special Publications Series 18: No. 1). 200p. 1983. 12.95 (*0-87044-439-5*) Natl Geog.

Nature's World Records. John R. Quinn. LC 97-39476. (Illus.). 224p. (J). (gr. 3-7). 1997. pap. 12.95 (*0-07-052658-3*, Lrning Triangle) McGraw.

Nature's Yellowstone. Richard A. Bartlett. LC 89-31748. 250p. 1989. reprint ed. pap. 9.95 (*0-8165-1109-8*) U of Ariz Pr.

Naturescaping: A Place for Wildlife. Joanne Hirose et al. 85p. 1992. pap. text 9.95 (*0-9635088-4-9*) OR Fish & Wldlife.

Naturescaping for Kids: Backyard Activities to Attract Wildlife. Robin M. Koontz. LC 97-44445. 64p. (J). 1998. pap. 12.95 (*0-07-037134-2*) McGraw.

Naturespeak. Twintrees. LC 93-84347. 1993. pap. 12.95 (*0-9633084-1-6*) Nu Ink Unltd.

Naturewatch. Adrienne Katz. (Illus.). (J). (ps up). 1986. pap. 11.20 (*0-201-10457-1*) Addison-Wesley.

Naturgemasse Hausapotheke see Home Remedies: Herbal & Homeopathic Treatments for Use at Home

Naturgeschichte und Religion: Eine Theologische Studie Zum Religionsbegriff in der Philosophie Theodor W. Adornos. Ulf Liedke. (Kontexte Ser.: Bd. 21). (GER.). 501p. 1996. 82.95 (*3-631-30937-6*) P Lang Pubng.

***Naturheilkunde In Der Dermatologie.** iv, 36p. 1999. 26.25 (*3-8055-6883-5*) S Karger.

Naturliche Gottesgelahrheit, Vol. 23, 1-5. Christian Wolff. (GER.). 2148p. 1995. reprint ed. write for info. (*3-487-10061-4*) G Olms Pubs.

Naturliche Reitkunst. Otto De La Croix. 1989. write for info. (*3-487-08306-X*) G Olms Pubs.

Naturlized Birds of World. Lever. 1987. pap. text. write for info. (*0-582-46055-7*, Pub. by Addison-Wesley) Longman.

Naturlyrik. Ed. by Gert Vonhoff & Herbert Kraft. (Historisch-Kritische Arbeiten Zur Deutschen Literatur Ser.: Bd. 23). (Illus.). 283p. 1998. pap. 51.95 (*3-631-33148-7*) P Lang Pubng.

Naturnahe Laub- und Nadelwalder Grundwasserferner Standorte Im Niedersaechsischen Tiefland: Gliederung, Standortsbedingungen, Dynamik. Thilo Heinken. (Dissertationes Botanicae Ser.: Band 239). (Illus.). xii, 311p. 1995. pap. 89.00 (*3-443-64151-2*, Pub. by Gebruder Borntraeger) Balogh.

***Naturopathic First Aid.** Karen Barnes. (Illus.). 96p. 1999. pap. 9.95 (*1-55082-248-9*) LPC InBook.

Naturopathic Treatment of Colds & Infectious Diseases. Erich Rauch. Tr. by David M. Fogg from GER. (Illus.). 83p. (Orig.). 1993. pap. 9.95 (*2-8043-4003-1*, Pub. by K F Haug Pubs) Medicina Bio.

Naturopathy: The Art of Drugless Healing. V. M. Kulkarni. 303p. 1986. 29.95 (*0-318-36366-6*) Asia Bk Corp.

Naturopathy: Understanding the Healing Power of Nature. Stewart Mitchell. LC 98-21514. (Health Essentials Ser.). (Illus.). 128p. 1998. 9.95 (*1-86204-303-5*, Pub. by Element MA) Penguin Putnam.

Naturopathy for Horses. Gerd Emich. 320p. 1994. 35.00 (*0-85131-600-X*, Pub. by J A Allen) Trafalgar.

Naturrecht und Liebesethik: Zur Geschichte der Praktischen Philosophie Im Hinblick Auf Christian Thomasius. Werner Schneiders. (Studien und Materialien Zur Geschichte der Philosophie Ser.: Bd. 3). (GER.). 368p. 1971. write for info. (*3-487-04052-2*) G Olms Pubs.

Naturschutz in der Mitverantwortung Von Burgern: Ehrenamtliche Tatigkeiten Im Deutschen Naturschutzrecht. Wolfgang Gerss. 197p. 1998. 28.95 (*3-631-33565-2*) P Lang Pubng.

Naturschutz in Deutschland (Nature Protection in Germany) K. Erdmann et al. (GER.). 200p. 1996. 30.00 (*3-8001-3485-3*, Pub. by Eugen Ulmer) Balogh.

Naturstein-Lexikon: Fur Handwerk und Industrie. 4th ed. Gunther Mehling. (GER.). 668p. 1993. 135.00 (*0-7859-8458-5*, 3766710540) Fr & Eur.

Naturverjuengung der Douglasie Im Schwarzwald Inventur und Analyse Von Umwelt und Konkurrenzfaktoren Sowie Eine Naturschutzfachliche Bewertung. Contrib. by Dietrich Knoerzer. (Dissertationes Botanicae Ser.: Band 306).Tr. of Natural Regeneration of Douglas Fir in the Black Forest. (GER., Illus.). xiv, 306p. 1999. pap. 67.00 (*3-443-64218-7*) Gebruder Borntraeger.

Naturwissenschaft Als Subjektlose Macht? Nietzsches Kritik Physikalischer Grundkonzepte. Klaus Spiekermann. (Monographien und Texte zur Nietzscge-Forschung Ser.: Bd. 24). (GER.). x, 240p. (C). 1991. lib. bdg. 95.40 (*3-11-012832-2*) De Gruyter.

Naturwissenschaft bei den Arabern im 10. Jahrhundert n. Chr. Briefe des Abu l-Fadl Ibn al-'Amid, gest. 360-970, an Adudaddaula. Hans Daiber. LC 92-40571. (Islamic Philosophy, Theology & Science, Studies & Texts Ser.: Vol. 13). (ARA & GER.). vi, 244p. 1993. 60.50 (*90-04-09755-4*) Brill Academic Pubs.

Naturwissenschaft vom Menschen see Natural Science of the Human Species: An Introduction to Comparative Behavioral Research: the "Russian Manuscript", 1944-1948

Natvar Bhavsar: Painting & the Reality of Color. Irving Sandler. (Illus.). 132p. 1998. text 50.00 (*90-5704-061-1*) Gordon & Breach.

Natvar Bhavsar: Twenty Years of Works on Paper. Howard E. Wooden. LC 85-50198. (Illus.). 12p. 1985. pap. 5.00 (*0-939324-18-0*) Wichita Art Mus.

Natwest Markets' Guide to Power in Asia: Financing, Regulation & Development. Asia Law & Practice Staff. 234p. 1997. pap. 140.00 (*962-360-001-1*) Am Educ Systs.

Natwest Markets Handbook of International REPO. Daniel Corrigan et al. 195p. 1995. 100.00 (*1-873440-42-1*, Pub. by IFR Pub) Am Educ Systs.

Natya Sastra of Bharatamuni. Tr. by Board of Scholars Staff from SAN. (Rgarya Natya Ser.: No. 2). 537p. (C). 1996. 34.00 (*81-7030-134-3*, Pub. by Sri Satguru Pubns) S Asia.

Natyasastra: English Translation with Critical Notes. Adya Rangacharya. LC 97-901591. (C). 1997. 45.00 (*81-215-0680-8*, Pub. by M Manoharial) Coronet Bks.

Naty's Parade. Gina Freschet. LC 98-52307. (Illus.). 32p. (J). (ps up). 2000. 16.00 (*0-374-35500-2*) FS&G.

Naufrages du Jonathan: Avec: Socialisme, Communisme et Anarchie. Jules Verne. (FRE.). 442p. 1979. reprint ed. pap. 18.95 (*0-7859-1222-3*, 2010054709) Fr & Eur.

Naufragio: 66 Dias a la Deriva. William B. Salazar. Ed. by Susana B. Lacy.Tr. of Our Last Chance. (SPA., Illus.). 324p. 1993. pap. 14.50 (*0-9632519-3-7*) Exmart Assocs.

Naufragios. Julien Green. Tr. by Emma Calatayud. (Nueva Austral Ser.: Vol. 15). (SPA.). 1991. pap. text 24.95 (*84-239-1815-7*) Elliots Bks.

Naugatuck. Dana J. Blackwell. LC 97-133975. (Images of America Ser.). 1996. pap. 16.99 (*0-7524-0415-6*) Arcadia Publng.

Naugatuck, CT, Congregational Church Records, 1781-1901. Helen S. Ullmann. vi, 143p. (Orig.). 1987. pap. 15.00 (*1-55613-045-7*) Heritage Bk.

Naugatuck Valley: A Rich & Beautiful Prospect: An Illustrated History. Neil Hogan. 1991. 22.95 (*0-89781-384-7*) Am Historical Pr.

Naughties, Nudies & Bathing Beauties. Sharon Weintraub. LC 94-143680. (Illus.). 112p. 1993. pap. 14.95 (*0-87588-401-6*) Hobby Hse.

Naughty Boy & the Strawberry Horse. Geoffrey Patterson. (Illus.). 32p. (J). (gr. 1-3). 1997. 19.95 (*0-09-176547-1*, Pub. by Hutchnson) Trafalgar.

Naughty by Nature. Ed. by John Patrick. LC 96-70306. 564p. 1998. pap. 14.95 (*1-877978-91-4*) FL Lit Foundation.

Naughty by Night. Tiffany White. LC 96-657. (Temptation Ser.). 216p. 1995. per. 3.25 (*0-373-25650-7*, 1-25650-2) Harlequin Bks.

Naughty Crow. Irina Hale. LC 91-39929. (Illus.). 32p. (J). (gr. k-4). 1992. lib. bdg. 14.95 (*0-689-50546-9*) McElderry Bks.

Naughty Games for Lovers. Ed. by Elizabeth Lluch & Alex Lluch. 2000. pap. 17.95 (*1-887169-08-3*) Wedding Solns.

Naughty Games for the Honeymoon... And Beyond. Ed. by Alex Lluch & Elizabeth Lluch. 212p. 1999. pap. 17.95 (*1-887169-06-7*) Wedding Solns.

Naughty Jokes. Bill Stott. Ed. by Helen Exley & Samantha Armstrong. (Joke Bks.). (Illus.). 60p. 1992. reprint ed. 8.50 (*1-85015-261-6*) Exley Giftbooks.

Naughty "Knotty" Wood. Wally Wood. (Illus.). 104p. 1998. pap. 14.95 (*1-56097-319-6*) Fantagraph Bks.

Naughty Ladies of the Old Northwest. Gary Meier & Gloria Meier. (Illus.). 144p. 1990. pap. 12.95 (*0-89288-180-1*) Maverick.

Naughty Lamb. Arlene Blanchard. LC 88-4098. (Illus.). 32p. (J). (ps-1). 1989. 9.95 (*0-8037-0577-8*, Dial Yng Read) Peng Put Young Read.

Naughty Mole. Time-Life Books Editors. (Child's First Library of Values). (Illus.). 30p. 1996. 14.95 (*0-7835-1300-3*) Time-Life.

Naughty Monkey, Level 1. Terence G. Crowther. (Illus.). 32p. 1997. pap. text 3.95 (*0-19-434955-1*) OUP.

Naughty 'n Nice. Linda R. Wisdom. 1997. per. 3.75 (*0-373-16671-0*, 1-16671-9) Harlequin Bks.

***Naughty Nancy.** John S. Goodall. LC 98-85144. (Illus.). 32p. (J). (ps-3). 1999. 8.95 (*0-689-82358-4*) McElderry Bks.

Naughty Nancy Goes to School. John S. Goodall. (Illus.). 32p. (J). (ps-3). 1999. 8.95 (*0-689-82563-3*) McElderry Bks.

Naughty, Naughty. Susan Johnson et al. 1999. pap. 5.99 (*0-312-97174-5*, St Martins Paperbacks) St Martin.

Naughty or Nice. Stephanie Bond. (Love & Laughter Ser.: No. 58). 1998. per. 3.50 (*0-373-44058-8*, 1-44058-5) Harlequin Bks.

***Naughty Parents.** Joy Gosney. LC 99-37398. 32p. (J). (gr. k-1). 2000. 14.95 (*0-7613-1341-9*, Copper Beech Bks); 21.90 (*0-7613-1823-2*) Millbrook Pr.

Naughty Paris: Erotic Photos of the 20's. M. Koetzle. (Illus.). 95p. 1997. pap. 9.99 (*3-8228-8659-9*) Taschen Amer.

Naughty Shakespeare. Michael Macrone. LC 97-2728. (Illus.). 192p. 1997. 16.95 (*0-8362-2757-3*, Cader Bks) Andrews & McMeel.

***Naughty Shakespeare.** Michael Macrone. 2000. 7.99 (*0-517-20960-8*) Random Hse Value.

Naughty Sheep. H. Amery. (Farmyard Tales Ser.). (Illus.). 16p. (J). (ps up). 1989. pap. 3.95 (*0-7460-0470-2*, Usborne) EDC.

Naughty Sheep Sticker Book. Judy Tatchell. (Farmyard Tales Sticker Storybook Ser.). (Illus.). 16p. (J). (ps-3). 1996. text 6.95 (*0-7460-2430-4*, Usborne) EDC.

Naughty Yard. Michael Hemmingson. 104p. (Orig.). 1994. pap. text 5.95 (*1-882633-02-4*) Permeable.

NAUI Advanced Scuba Diver Course Instructor's Guide. (Illus.). 1989. 14.95 (*0-916974-40-5*, 12002) NAUI.

NAUI Course Director Guidelines. 2nd ed. Jim Brown. 280p. 1992. ring bd. 45.00 (*0-916974-52-9*, 14501) NAUI.

NAUI Diving Log Book. National Association of Underwater Instructors Sta. 1973. 8.95 (*0-916974-05-7*, 80034) NAUI.

NAUI Leadership Courses Instructor Guide. 3rd rev. ed. 168p. (Orig.). 1996. pap. 76.95 (*1-57743-006-9*, 12904) NAUI.

NAUI Specialty Course Sample Outlines. 3rd ed. 76p. 1992. pap. text 15.95 (*0-916974-01-4*, 10001) NAUI.

NAUI Textbook, Vol. II. rev. ed. Dennis Graver. (Illus.). 139p. 1995. pap. 29.95 (*0-916974-62-6*, 11505) NAUI.

NAUI Training Record. National Association of Underwater Instructors Sta. 1973. 8.95 (*0-916974-06-5*, 80010) NAUI.

Nauigations into Turkie. Nicolas De Nicolay. Tr. by T. Washington. LC 68-54638. (English Experience Ser.: No. 48). 322p. 1968. reprint ed. 65.00 (*90-221-0048-0*) Walter J Johnson.

Naukar, Rajput & Sepoy: The Ethnohistory of the Military Labour Market of Hindustan, 1450-1850. Dirk H. Kolff. (University of Cambridge Oriental Publications: No. 43). (Illus.). 233p. (C). 1990. text 64.95 (*0-521-38132-0*) Cambridge U Pr.

***Naukratis: Trade in Archaic Greece.** Astrid Moller. LC 99-86587. (Oxford Monographs on Classical Archaeology). (Illus.). 320p. 2000. text 85.00 (*0-19-815284-1*) OUP.

Naukratis I. W. M. Petrie. (IGA VI Ser.: No. 1). (GRE., Illus.). vi, 98p. (C). 1992. text 35.00 (*0-89005-508-4*) Ares.

Naukratis II. E. A. Gardiner. (IGA VI Ser.: No. 2). (GRE., Illus.). vi, 84p. (C). 1992. text 35.00 (*0-89005-509-2*) Ares.

Naum Gabo: Monoprints. L. Williams. (C). 1990. pap. 85.00 (*0-7855-4457-7*, Pub. by Collets) St Mut.

***Naum Gabo: Pioneer of Abstract Sculpture.** Graham Williams. (Illus.). 60p. 1999. pap. write for info. (*1-878283-90-1*) PaceWildenstein.

Naum Gabo: 60 Years of Constructivism. Ed. by Steven A. Nash et al. (Illus.). 272p. 1986. 60.00 (*3-7913-0742-8*, Pub. by Prestel) te Neues.

Naum Slutzky: Meister Am Bauhaus Goldschmied und Designer. Monika Rudolph. (GER., Illus.). 240p. 95.00 (*3-925369-06-6*, Pub. by Arnoldsche Art Pubs) Antique Collect.

Naunton Collection of Japanese Sword Fittings. Ed. by Henri L. Jolly. 4334p. (C). 1988. 375.00 (*0-7855-4038-5*) St Mut.

***Nauru: A Country Study Guide.** Global Investment & Business Center, Inc. Staff. (World Country Study Guides Library: Vol. 121). (Illus.). 350p. 2000. pap. 59.00 (*0-7397-2419-3*) Intl Business Pubns.

Nauru: Environmental Devastation under International Trusteeship. Christopher Weeramantry. (Illus.). 468p. 1992. text 79.00 (*0-19-553289-9*) OUP.

Nauru - A Country Study Guide: Basic Information for Research & Pleasure. Global Investment Center, USA Staff. (World Country Study Guide Library: Vol. 121). (Illus.). 350p. 1999. pap. 59.00 (*0-7397-1518-6*) Intl Business Pubns.

***Nauru Business Intelligence Report, 190 vols.** Global Investment & Business Center, Inc. Staff. (World Business Intelligence Library: Vol. 121). (Illus.). 350p. 2000. pap. 99.95 (*0-7397-2619-6*) Intl Business Pubns.

***Nauru Business Law Handbook, 190 vols.** Global Investment & Business Center, Inc. Staff. (Global Business Law Handbooks Library: Vol. 121). (Illus.). 350p. 2000. pap. 99.95 (*0-7397-2019-8*) Intl Business Pubns.

***Nauru Business Opportunity Yearbook.** Global Investment & Business Center, Inc. Staff. (Global Business Opportunity Yearbooks Library: Vol. 121). (Illus.). 2000. pap. 99.95 (*0-7397-2219-0*) Intl Business Pubns.

***Nauru Business Opportunity Yearbook: Export-Import, Investment & Business Opportunities.** International Business Publications, U. S. A. Staff & Global Investment Center, U. S. A. Staff. (Global Business Opportunity Yearbooks Library: Vol. 121). (Illus.). 350p. 1999. pap. 99.95 (*0-7397-1319-1*) Intl Business Pubns.

***Nauru Country Review 2000.** Robert C. Kelly et al. (Illus.). 60p. 1999. pap. 39.95 (*1-58310-545-X*) CountryWatch.

***Nauru Foreign Policy & Government Guide.** Global Investment & Business Center, Inc. Staff. (World Foreign Policy & Government Library: Vol. 189). (Illus.). 350p. 2000. 99.95 (*0-7397-3819-4*) Intl Business Pubns.

***Nauru Investment & Business Guide.** Global Investment & Business Center, Inc. Staff. (Global Investment & Business Guide Library: Vol. 121). (Illus.). 2000. pap. 99.95 (*0-7397-1819-3*) Intl Business Pubns.

Nauruans. 2nd ed. Solange Petit-Skinner. LC 96-182615. (Illus.). 315p. 1981. pap. 22.80 (*0-9606272-0-0*) Macduff Pr.

Nausea. Jean-Paul Sartre. lib. bdg. 19.95 (*0-8488-2025-8*) Amereon Ltd.

Nausea. Jean-Paul Sartre. Tr. by Lloyd Alexander from FRE. LC 49-8942. 1959. pap. 9.95 (*0-8112-0188-0*, NDP82, Pub. by New Directions) Norton.

Nausea. Jean-Paul Sartre. Tr. by Lloyd Alexander from FRE. LC 79-17598. 1979. reprint ed. lib. bdg. 14.00 (*0-8376-0443-5*) Bentley Pubs.

***Nausea & the Wall.** Jean-Paul Sartre. 352p. 1999. 8.98 (*1-56731-334-5*, MJF Bks) Fine Comms.

***Nausea & Vomiting.** HPNA Staff. 68p. 1999. pap. text 15.00 (*0-7872-6009-6*) Kendall-Hunt.

Nausea & Vomiting: New Perspectives & Practical Treatments. Richard H. Blum. 1998. 80.00 (*1-86156-079-6*) Whurr Pub.

Nausea & Vomiting: Recent Research & Clinical Advances. Walter Kucharczyk. 272p. 1991. lib. bdg. 123.00 (*0-8493-6781-6*, RB150) CRC Pr.

Nausee. Jean-Paul Sartre. (FRE.). (C). 1938. pap. 9.95 (*0-8442-1709-3*, VF1709-3) NTC Contemp Pub Co.

Nausee. Jean-Paul Sartre. (FRE.). 1978. pap. 10.95 (*0-8288-3776-7*) Fr & Eur.

Nausee. Jean-Paul Sartre. (Folio Ser.: No. 805). (FRE.). 1972. pap. 8.95 (*2-07-036805-X*) Schoenhof.

***Nauseous: Sick & Disgusting Tales.** Miklos Hunyedi. (Illus.). 168p. 1999. pap. 14.95 (*1-929471-19-X*) Segregansett Pr.

Nauseous in Paradise. Abby Bee. (Illus.). 40p. (Orig.). 1986. pap. 6.95 (*0-939821-13-3*) HerBooks.

Nauset Light: A Personal History of Nauset Light, the 1875 Lightkeeper's House & the 1892 Oil House. Mary D. VanRoden. (Illus.). 92p. (Orig.). 1995. pap. write for info. (*0-9647864-0-0*) Blackrabbit Pr.

Nausicaa of the Valley of the Wind, Vol. 7. Hayao Miyazaki. (Illus.). 224p. 1997. pap. text 16.95 (*1-56931-197-8*, Viz Comics) Viz Commns Inc.

Nausicaa of the Valley of Wind, Pt. 2, Bk. 1. Hayao Miyazaki. Ed. by Seiji Horibuchi. Tr. by David Lewis & Toren Smith from JPN. (Illus.). 56p. 1989. pap. 2.95 (*0-929279-07-7*) Viz Commns Inc.

Nausicaa of the Valley of Wind, Pt. 2, Bk. 2. Hayao Miyazaki. Ed. by Seiji Horibuchi. Tr. by David Lewis & Toren Smith from JPN. (Illus.). 56p. 1989. pap. 2.95 (*0-929279-08-5*) Viz Commns Inc.

Nausicaa of the Valley of Wind, Pt. 2, Bk. 3. Hayao Miyazaki. Ed. by Seiji Horibuchi. Tr. by David Lewis & Toren Smith from JPN. (Illus.). 56p. 1989. pap. 2.95 (*0-929279-09-3*) Viz Commns Inc.

Nausicaa of the Valley of Wind, Pt. 2, Bk. 4. Hayao Miyazaki. Ed. by Seiji Horibuchi. Tr. by David Lewis & Toren Smith from JPN. (Illus.). 56p. 1989. pap. 2.95 (*0-929279-10-7*) Viz Commns Inc.

Nausicaa of the Valley of Wind, Vol. 1. Hayao Miyazaki. Ed. by Seiji Horibuchi. Tr. by David Lewis & Toren Smith from JPN. (Illus.). 56p. 1988. pap. 2.50 (*0-929279-00-X*) Viz Commns Inc.

Nausicaa of the Valley of Wind, Vol. 1. Hayao Miyazaki. (Illus.). 264p. 1995. pap. 17.95 (*1-56931-096-3*) Viz Commns Inc.

Nausicaa of the Valley of Wind, Vol. 2. Hayao Miyazaki. Ed. by Seiji Horibuchi. Tr. by David Lewis & Toren Smith from JPN. (Illus.). 56p. 1988. pap. 2.50 (*0-929279-01-8*) Viz Commns Inc.

Nausicaa of the Valley of Wind, Vol. 2. Hayao Miyazaki. (Illus.). 284p. 1995. pap. 17.95 (*1-56931-087-4*) Viz Commns Inc.

Nausicaa of the Valley of Wind, Vol. 3. Hayao Miyazaki. Ed. by Seiji Horibuchi. Tr. by David Lewis & Toren Smith from JPN. (Illus.). 56p. 1989. pap. 2.50 (*0-929279-02-6*) Viz Commns Inc.

Nausicaa of the Valley of Wind, Vol. 3. Hayao Miyazaki. (Perfect Collection Ser.). (Illus.). 264p. 1996. pap. text 17.95 (*1-56931-111-0*) Viz Commns Inc.

Nausicaa of the Valley of Wind, Vol. 4. Hayao Miyazaki. Ed. by Seiji Horibuchi. Tr. by David Lewis & Toren Smith from JPN. (Illus.). 56p. 1989. pap. 2.50 (*0-929279-03-4*) Viz Commns Inc.

Nausicaa of the Valley of Wind, Vol. 4. Hayao Miyazaki. Ed. by Seiji Horibuchi. Tr. by David Lewis & Toren Smith from JPN. (Perfect Collection Ser.). (Illus.). 138p. 1990. pap. text 13.95 (*0-929279-61-1*) Viz Commns Inc.

Nausicaa of the Valley of Wind, Vol. 4. Hayao Miyazaki. (Perfect Collection Ser.). (Illus.). 272p. 1997. pap. text 17.95 (*1-56931-211-7*, Viz Comics) Viz Commns Inc.

Nausicaa of the Valley of Wind, Vol. 5. Hayao Miyazaki. Ed. by Seiji Horibuchi. Tr. by David Lewis & Toren Smith from JPN. (Illus.). 56p. 1989. pap. 2.50 (*0-929279-04-2*) Viz Commns Inc.

Nausicaa of the Valley of Wind, Vol. 6. Hayao Miyazaki. Ed. by Seiji Horibuchi. Tr. by David Lewis & Toren Smith from JPN. (Illus.). 56p. 1989. pap. 2.95 (*0-929279-05-0*) Viz Commns Inc.

Nausicaa of the Valley of Wind, Vol. 6. Hayao Miyazaki. (Illus.). 160p. 1995. pap. 15.95 (*1-56931-095-5*) Viz Commns Inc.

Nausicaa of the Valley of Wind, Vol. 7. Hayao Miyazaki. Ed. by Seiji Horibuchi. Tr. by David Lewis & Toren Smith from JPN. (Illus.). 56p. 1989. pap. 2.95 (*0-929279-06-9*) Viz Commns Inc.

N

***Nausicaa of the Valley of Wind, Vols. 1-4.** Hayao Miyazaki. (Perfect Collection Ser.). (Illus.). 2000. pap., boxed set 69.95 (*1-56931-348-2*, Viz Comics) Viz Commns Inc.

Nautical Almanac. 1997. lib. bdg. 259.95 (*0-8490-8249-8*) Gordon Pr.

Nautical Almanac: Tabular Data for Astronomy, Space Sciences, Geodesy, Surveying, Navigation. 1991. lib. bdg. 88.95 (*0-8490-5019-7*) Gordon Pr.

Nautical Almanac for the Year, 1981. U. S. Navy Staff. 316p. 1991. reprint ed. pap. text 33.50 (*0-934114-66-8*, BK-246) Marine Educ.

Nautical Almanac for the Year 1998. 362p. 1997. boxed set 28.00 (*0-16-049028-6*) USGPO.

***Nautical Almanac for the Year 1999.** 355p. 1998. boxed set 27.00 (*0-16-061344-2*) USGPO.

***Nautical Almanac for the Year 2001.** 353p. 2000. pap. 31.00 (*0-16-050301-9*) USGPO.

Nautical Almanac for the Year 2000. H. M. Nautical Almanac Office Staff. (Illus.). xxxv, 358p. 1998. pap. 55.00 (*0-11-887325-3*, HM73253, Pub. by Statnry Office) Balogh.

Nautical Almanac, 1998. TSO Staff. 364p. 1997. pap. 45.00 (*0-11-772848-9*, HM28489, Pub. by Statnry Office) Bernan Associates.

Nautical Almanac, 1999. 360p. 1998. pap. 55.00 (*0-11-772866-7*, HM28667, Pub. by Statnry Office) Bernan Associates.

Nautical Almanac 1997. U. S. Government Staff. 1996. 25.00 (*1-57980-206-0*, NAUT97) Claitors.

Nautical Almanac, 1996. U. S. Government Staff. 1995. 22.00 (*0-614-30804-6*, NAUT96) Claitors.

***Nautical Almanac 2000: European Edition.** Ed. by Neville Featherstone. (Illus.). 900p. 1999. pap. 77.50 (*0-333-72580-8*, Pub. by Macmillan) Trans-Atl Phila.

Nautical Almanac, 1998. 1997. 23.00 (*1-57980-103-X*) Claitors.

Nautical Antiques. Robert W. Ball. LC 94-65429. (Illus.). 240p. 1994. 39.95 (*0-88740-602-5*) Schiffer.

Nautical Antiques & Collectables. Jon Baddeley. (Illus.). 192p. 1993. 70.00 (*0-85667-394-3*, Pub. by P Wilson) Scala Books.

Nautical Charted Designs. Barbara Christopher. (Illus.). 48p. 1990. pap. 3.95 (*0-486-26129-8*) Dover.

Nautical Cyclopedia. Gary Gentile. (Illus.). 136p. 1995. pap. 20.00 (*1-883056-01-2*) GGP.

Nautical Dictionary see Diccionario Nautico

Nautical Dictionary: Over 3,800 Maritime Terms Defined. Joseph P. O'Flynn. (Illus.). 112p. (Orig.). 1992. pap. 11.95 (*0-937360-16-3*) Harbor Hse MI.

Nautical Dictionary in English, Spanish & French. Ed. by Ricardo Ciudad. (ENG, FRE & SPA.). 1992. 150.00 (*0-320-03697-9*) Fr & Eur.

Nautical Dictionary Spanish-English - English-Spanish. J. M. Malagon Ortuondo. (ENG & SPA.). 523p. 1996. pap. 50.00 (*84-283-2254-6*, Pub. by Edit Paraninfon) IBD Ltd.

Nautical Dictionary, Spanish-English/English-Spanish. J. M. Ortuando. (ENG & SPA.). 1996. 50.00 (*0-7859-9689-3*) Fr & Eur.

Nautical Etiquette & Customs. 2nd rev. ed. Lindsay Lord. LC 86-47716. (Illus.). 128p. 1987. pap. 8.95 (*0-87033-356-9*) Cornell Maritime.

***Nautical Knits.** Debbie Bliss. 1998. (*0-316-09386-6*) Little.

Nautical Knits for Kids: 25 Seashore Designs for Children up to Six Years Old. Debbie Bliss. (Illus.). 80p. 1998. 22.95 (*1-57076-107-8*, Trafalgar Sq Pub) Trafalgar.

Nautical Knots & Lines Illustrated. Paul Snyder & Arthur Snyder. LC 96-22142. (Illus.). 96p. 1996. pap. 13.95 (*0-07-059580-1*) McGraw.

Nautical Knowledge. Henry D. Larsen. LC 92-27896. 1992. write for info. (*0-934523-05-3*) Middle Coast Pub.

Nautical Knowledge for Fishermen. A. Simpson. (C). 1987. 60.00 (*0-85174-368-4*) St Mut.

Nautical Motifs. Schein. 1998. pap. 1.00 (*0-486-27669-4*) Dover.

Nautical No-No's. Elyse Katz & Robert Katz. LC 80-50537. (Illus.). 160p. 1993. reprint ed. pap. 20.00 (*0-9604208-0-0*) Shayna Ltd.

Nautical Notes for Writers & Editors. Greg H. Williams. (Illus.). 50p. (Orig.). 1991. pap. 8.50 (*0-911223-02-9*) Star Valley.

Nautical Research Journal Index, Vols. 1-40. Compiled by John M. Barry. LC 96-71037. 216p. (Orig.). 1996. pap. 19.95 (*0-9603456-6-3*) Nautical Res.

Nautical Rules of the Road: The International & Unified Inland Rules. 3rd ed. B. A. Farnsworth & Larry C. Young. LC 89-71243. (Illus.). 238p. 1990. text 20.00 (*0-87033-408-5*) Cornell Maritime.

Nautical Rules of the Road Explained. William F. Conklin. 78p. 1997. pap. 9.95 (*0-9659647-0-1*) BBC Commun.

Nautical Voyages for Quilters. Betty Boyink. 72p. (Orig.). 1990. pap. 14.50 (*0-925623-03-2*) B Boyink.

Nautics an English Reader. M. Luzzatti. 275p. 1976. pap. text 49.95 (*0-8288-5744-X*, M9295) Fr & Eur.

Nautilus. Wanda G. Kachur. LC 97-65269. 175p. (J). (gr. 5-9). 1997. pap. 7.95 (*0-9644271-5-X*) Peytral Pubns.

Nautilus: The Biology & Paleobiology of a Living Fossil. N. H. Landman & W. B. Saunders. LC 87-32725. (Topics in Geobiology Ser.: Vol. 6). (Illus.). 666p. (C). 1988. text 135.00 (*0-306-42709-5*, Kluwer Plenum) Kluwer Academic.

Nautilus: The Story of Man under the Sea. Roy Davies. LC 94-69301. (Illus.). 256p. 1995. 36.95 (*1-55750-615-9*) Naval Inst Pr.

Nautilus Book. rev. ed. Ellington Darden. (Illus.). 344p. 1990. pap. 14.95 (*0-8092-4074-2*, 407420, Contemporary Bks) NTC Contemp Pub Co.

Nauvoo: Kingdom on the Mississippi. Robert B. Flanders. LC 65-19110. (Illus.). 374p. 1975. reprint ed. 15.95 (*0-252-00561-9*) U of Ill Pr.

Nauvoo: The City of Joseph. 2nd ed. David E. Miller & Della S. Miller. (Illus.). 280p. Date not set. reprint ed. pap. 14.95 (*0-9639924-2-2*) Utah Hist Atlas.

Nauvoo Deaths & Marriages. Lyndon Cook. 145p. (C). 1994. 29.95 (*0-910523-08-8*) Grandin Bk Co.

Nauvoo Guide. Federal Writers' Project, Illinois. LC 73-3616. (American Guide Ser.). reprint ed. 14.00 (*0-404-57919-1*) AMS Pr.

Nauvoo in Mormon History: The Kingdom on the Mississippi Revisited. Ed. by Roger D. Launius & John E. Hallwas. LC 95-14673. 280p. 1996. text 36.50 (*0-252-02197-5*); pap. text 16.95 (*0-252-06494-1*) U of Ill Pr.

Nauvoo Poems of Eliza R. Snow. Eliza R. Snow. 76p. 1989. pap. 4.95 (*1-877869-22-8*) Mason Cnty Hist Proj.

Nava Atlas & Chaim Tabak, a Collaborative Exhibition: The Radwaste & Stonehenge Series. Howard D. Spencer. LC 85-50652. (Illus.). 5p. 1985. pap. 3.00 (*0-939324-20-2*) Wichita Art Mus.

Navaho. rev. ed. Clyde Kluckhohn & Dorothea C. Leighton. LC 62-6779. (Illus.). 365p. 1973. pap. text 14.95 (*0-674-60603-5*) HUP.

Navaho Art & Culture. George T. Mills. LC 83-5636. (Illus.). 273p. (C). 1983. reprint ed. lib. bdg. 59.75 (*0-313-24008-6*, MINA, Greenwood Pr) Greenwood.

Navaho Autobiography. (American Autobiography Ser.). 218p. 1995. reprint ed. lib. bdg. 79.00 (*0-7812-8604-2*) Rprt Serv.

Navaho Classification of Their Song Ceremonials. Leland C. Wyman & Clyde Kluckhohn. LC 38-23008. (American Anthropological Association Memoirs Ser.: No. 50). 1938. pap. 15.00 (*0-527-00549-5*) Periodicals Srv.

Navaho Folk Tales. Franc Johson Newcomb. LC 90-39570. (Illus.). 203p. 1990. reprint ed. pap. 11.95 (*0-8263-1231-4*) U of NM Pr.

Navaho Grammar. Gladys A. Reichard. LC 73-15404. (American Ethnological Society Publications: No. 21). reprint ed. 57.50 (*0-404-58171-4*) AMS Pr.

Navaho Indian Myths. Tr. by Aileen O'Bryan. LC 93-9688. (Illus.). 208p. 1993. reprint ed. pap. 6.95 (*0-486-27592-2*) Dover.

Navaho Legends. Tr. & Compiled by Washington Matthews. (Illus.). 320p. 1993. reprint ed. pap. 19.95 (*0-87480-424-8*) U of Utah Pr.

Navaho Magic of Hunting. Elsie Kreischer. 32p. (J). (gr. 4-10). 1988. pap. 4.95 (*0-89992-099-3*) Coun India Ed.

Navaho Myths Prayers & Songs with Texts & Translations. fac. ed. Washington Matthews. Ed. by P. E. Goddard. (University of California Publications in American Archaeology & Ethnology: Vol. 5: 2). 43p. (C). 1907. reprint ed. pap. text 4.69 (*1-55567-170-5*) Coyote Press.

Navaho Religion: A Study of Symbolism. Gladys A. Reichard & Oliver La Farge. (Bollingen Ser.: No. XVIII). 872p. (C). 1950. pap. text 24.95 (*0-691-01906-1*, Pub. by Princeton U Pr) Cal Prin Full Svc.

Navaho Religion: A Study of Symbolism. Gladys A. Reichard. LC 63-14455. (Bollingen Ser.: Vol. 18). 863p. reprint ed. pap. 200.00 (*0-8357-9504-7*, 201488000093) Bks Demand.

Navaho Sandpainting: The Huckel Collection. 2nd ed. Leland C. Wyman. (Illus.). 1971. pap. 5.00 (*0-916537-29-3*, Taylor Museum) CO Springs Fine Arts.

Navaho Symbols of Healing: A Jungian Exploration of Ritual, Image, & Medicine. Donald Sandner. (Illus.). 304p. 1991. reprint ed. pap. 14.95 (*0-89281-434-9*, Heal Arts VT) Inner Tradit.

Navaho Texts. Edward Sapir. LC 73-15405. reprint ed. 79.50 (*0-404-11246-3*) AMS Pr.

Navaho Weaving: Its Technic & History. Charles A. Amsden. (Illus.). 416p. 1991. pap. 12.95 (*0-486-26537-4*) Dover.

Navaho Weaving: Its Technic & History. Charles A. Amsden. (Beautiful Rio Grande Classics Ser.). (Illus.). 460p. 1990. reprint ed. pap. 17.50 (*0-87380-172-5*) Popular E Commerce.

Navaho Witchcraft. Clyde Kluckhohn. 1962. pap. 16.50 (*0-8070-4697-3*) Beacon Pr.

NAVAIR AN 01-85FGD-1 Flight Handbook Navy Models: F9F-6, -6P Aircraft. LC 94-73978. (Illus.). 192p. 1995. pap. 19.95 (*0-88740-778-1*) Schiffer.

NAVAIR 01-245FDD-1 NATOPS Flight Manual Navy Model: F-4J Aircraft. LC 94-62121. (Illus.). 544p. 1995. pap. 39.95 (*0-88740-781-1*) Schiffer.

Navajo see Navajo

***Navajo.** 1999. 7.95 (*5-550-00763-0*) Nairi.

Navajo. Mira Bartok & Christine Ronan. (Ancient & Living Cultures Ser.). 32p. (J). (gr. 3 up). 1996. pap. 9.95 (*0-673-36314-7*, GoodYrBooks) Addson-Wesley Educ.

Navajo. Raymond Bial. LC 97-53248. (Lifeways Ser.). (Illus.). (YA). (gr. 6 up). 1998. lib. bdg. 32.79 (*0-7614-0803-7*, Benchmark NY) Marshall Cavendish.

***Navajo.** Richard Gaines. LC 99-59870. (Native Americans Ser.). 2000. lib. bdg. 21.35 (*1-57765-374-2*) ABDO Pub Co.

Navajo. Alice Osinski. (New True Books Ser.). (Illus.). (J). (gr. 2-4). 1987. pap. 5.50 (*0-516-41236-1*) Childrens.

Navajo. Alice Osinski. LC 86-30978. (New True Books Ser.). (Illus.). 48p. (J). (ps-3). 1987. lib. bdg. 21.00 (*0-516-01236-3*) Childrens.

Navajo. Susan Stan. (Native American People Ser.). (Illus.). 32p. (J). (gr. 5-8). 1989. lib. bdg. 11.95 (*0-685-58580-8*) Rourke Corp.

Navajo. Susan Stan. (Native American People Ser.: Set I). (Illus.). 32p. (J). (gr. 4-8). 1989. lib. bdg. 22.60 (*0-86625-380-7*) Rourke Pubns.

Navajo. Susan Stan. (Pueblos Americanos Nativos Ser.).Tr. of Navajo. (SPA.). 32p. (J). (gr. 5-8). 1990. lib. bdg. 21.27 (*0-86625-455-2*) Rourke Pubns.

Navajo. Terry P. Wilson. (Native American Wisdom Ser.). (Illus.). 64p. 1994. 9.95 (*0-8118-0442-9*) Chronicle Bks.

Navajo. James F. Downs. (Illus.). 136p. 1984. reprint ed. pap. text 10.50 (*0-88133-037-X*) Waveland Pr.

Navajo: A Century of Progress, 1868-1968. Ed. by Martin A. Link. LC 68-15787. (Illus.). 110p. 1968. 6.00 (*0-318-19652-2*) Navajo.

Navajo: Basic Medical. Alan Wilson. 141p. 1992. pap. text 18.95 (*0-88432-535-0*, AFNV94) Audio-Forum.

Navajo: English Mini-Books Set with Audio, 11 bks. Claudia Schwalm. (ENG & NAV., Illus.). (Orig.). (J). (gr. k-6). 1997. pap. 21.95 incl. audio (*0-614-24744-6*) Cultural Cnnect.

Navajo: Tradition & Change in the Southwest. Photos by Helga Teiwes. LC 92-42088. (Illus.). 240p. 1993. 45.00 (*0-8160-2756-0*) Facts on File.

Navajo: Visions & Voices Across the Mesa. Shonto Begay. LC 93-31610. (Illus.). 48p. (J). (ps-3). 1995. 15.95 (*0-590-46153-2*) Scholastic Inc.

***Navajo a Tribal History.** Lana T. Griffin. LC 98-42351. (Illus.). 48p. (ps-3). 1999. 25.69 (*0-8172-5463-3*) Raintree Steck-V.

Navajo ABC: A Dine Alphabet Book. Eleanor Schick & Luci Tapahonso. LC 94-46881. (Illus.). 32p. (J). (ps up). 1995. 16.00 (*0-689-80316-8*, Mac Bks Young Read) S&S Childrens.

Navajo ABC: A Dine Alphabet Book. Luci Tapahonso & Eleanor Schick. LC 94-46881. (Illus.). 32p. (J). 1999. per. 5.99 (*0-689-82685-0*, 076714005990) Aladdin.

Navajo Afterglow. Melvin Eisenstadt. LC 99-62358. 288p. 2000. pap. 15.95 (*0-88739-271-7*) Creat Arts Bk.

Navajo Aging: The Transition from Family to Institutional Support. Stephen J. Kunitz & Jerrold E. Levy. LC 91-3178. (Illus.). 191p. 1991. 39.00 (*0-8165-1260-4*) U of Ariz Pr.

Navajo & His Blanket. Ulysses S. Hollister. LC 72-10567. (Beautiful Rio Grande Classics Ser.). (Illus.). 176p. 1974. reprint ed. lib. bdg. 20.00 (*0-87380-097-4*) Popular E Commerce.

Navajo & Photography: A Critical History of the Representation of an American People. James C. Faris. 1996. 39.95 (*0-614-20396-1*) Tor Bks.

Navajo & Photography: A Critical History of the Representation of an American People. James C. Faris. LC 95-41781. (Illus.). 392p. 1996. 39.95 (*0-8263-1725-1*) U of NM Pr.

Navajo & Pueblo Silversmiths. John Adair. LC 44-7567. (Civilization of the American Indian Ser.: No. 25). (Illus.). 264p. 1989. reprint ed. pap. 15.95 (*0-8061-2215-3*) U of Okla Pr.

Navajo & Tibetan Sacred Wisdom: The Circle of the Spirit. Peter Gold. LC 93-40305. (Illus.). 352p. (Orig.). 1994. pap. 29.95 (*0-89281-411-X*) Inner Tradit.

Navajo Art of Sandpainting. Douglas Congdon-Martin. LC 90-61507. (Illus.). 64p. (Orig.). 1990. pap. 9.95 (*0-88740-271-2*) Schiffer.

Navajo Art of Sandpainting. 2nd rev. ed. Douglas Congdon-Martin. LC 98-89784. (Illus.). 64p. (Orig.). 1999. pap. 9.95 (*0-7643-0810-6*) Schiffer.

Navajo Arts & Crafts. Nancy N. Schiffer. LC 91-60956. (Illus.). 64p. 1991. pap. 12.95 (*0-88740-320-4*) Schiffer.

Navajo Atlas: Environments, Resources, People, & History of the Dine Bikeyah. James M. Goodman. LC 81-40287. (Civilization of the American Indian Ser.: Vol. 157). (Illus.). 120p. 1987. reprint ed. pap. 19.95 (*0-8061-2032-0*) U of Okla Pr.

Navajo Bible. (NAV.). 1987. 15.90 (*0-00-672855-3*) Am Bible.

Navajo Blood. William R. Cox. 240p. 1989. pap. 2.95 (*0-380-70831-0*, Avon Bks) Morrow Avon.

Navajo, Breakthrough: An Introductory Course. Alan Wilson. 234p. pap. text 16.95 (*0-88432-533-4*, AFNV91) Audio-Forum.

Navajo, Breakthrough: An Introductory Course. unabridged ed. Alan Wilson. 1992. pap. text 49.00 incl. audio (*0-88432-447-8*, AFNV10) Audio-Forum.

Navajo Brothers & the Stolen Herd. Maurine Grammer. LC 92-15018. (Illus.). 120p. (J). (gr. 6-8). 1992. pap. 9.95 (*1-878610-23-6*) Red Crane Bks.

Navajo Children. Nancy Armstrong. (Indian Culture Ser.). (J). (gr. 2-6). 1975. pap. 1.95 (*0-89992-037-3*) Coun India Ed.

Navajo Code Talkers. Nathan Aaseng. LC 92-11408. 114p. (J). 1992. 15.95 (*0-8027-8182-9*); lib. bdg. 16.85 (*0-8027-8183-7*) Walker & Co.

Navajo Code Talkers. Doris A. Paul. (Illus.). 176p. (C). 1973. 17.00 (*0-8059-1870-1*) Dorrance.

***Navajo Code Talkers.** Nathan Aaseng. (Illus.). 96p. (J). (gr. 3-6). 2000. reprint ed. pap. 7.95 (*0-8027-7589-6*) Walker & Co.

Navajo Code Talkers: Native American Heroes. Catherine Jones. LC 97-36009. 31p. (J). 1997. pap. 7.95 (*0-936389-52-4*) Tudor Pubs.

Navajo Code Talkers: Native American Heroes. Catherine Jones. LC 97-36009. 31p. (YA). (gr. 6 up). 1997. 12.95 (*0-936389-51-6*) Tudor Pubs.

Navajo Confrontation & Crisis. Floyd A. Pollock. LC 84-3483. 1984. 10.00 (*0-912586-55-9*) Dine College Pr.

Navajo Country: A Geology & Natural History of the Four Corners Region. Donald L. Baars. LC 95-4344. (Illus.). 255p. 1995. pap. 19.95 (*0-8263-1587-9*) U of NM Pr.

Navajo Country Dine Bikeyah: A Geographic Dictionary of Navajo Lands in the 1930's. 2nd ed. A. Richard Van Valkenburgh. Ed. by John McPhee et al. Tr. by Joline Adakai. Orig. Title: Dine Bikeyah - The Navajo Country. (ENG & NAV., Illus.). 140p. 1999. reprint ed. per. 29.95 (*1-892040-02-6*, DB1) Time Trvlr Maps.

Navajo Coyote Tales. William Morgan. Ed. & Tr. by Hildegard Thompson. LC 88-72048. (Illus.). 50p. (J). (gr. 2 up). 1988. reprint ed. pap. 8.95 (*0-941270-52-1*) Ancient City Pr.

Navajo Coyote Tales: The Curly to Aheedliinii Version. Berard Haile. Ed. & Intro. by Karl W. Luckert. LC 83-23462. (American Tribal Religions Ser.: Vol. 8). (Illus.). vi, 146p. 1984. pap. 8.95 (*0-8032-7222-7*, Bison Books) U of Nebr Pr.

Navajo Creation Myth: The Story of Emergence. Hasteen Klah. LC 76-43762. (Museum of Navajo Ceremonial Art. Religion Ser.: Vol. 1). reprint ed. 39.50 (*0-404-15615-0*) AMS Pr.

Navajo Design Book. (J). (gr. 1-6). 1975. pap. 4.95 (*0-918858-04-6*) Fun Pub AZ.

Navajo Dictionary of Diagnostic Terminology. 10.00 (*0-912586-68-0*) Dine College Pr.

Navajo Education, 1948-78, Its Progress & Its Problems. Robert A. Roessel. 340p. 1979. 10.00 (*0-912586-38-9*) Rough Rock Pr.

Navajo-English Dictionary. Davidovic Mladen. (ENG & NAV.). 165p. 1994. pap. 9.95 (*0-7818-0247-4*) Hippocrene Bks.

Navajo Fire (or Corral) Dance. Berard Haile. 1946. pap. 7.50 (*0-318-03030-6*) St Michaels.

Navajo Folk Art: The People Speak. rev. ed. Chuck Rosenak & Jan Rosenak. (Illus.). 176p. 1994. pap. 14.95 (*0-87358-693-X*) Northland AZ.

Navajo Food Practices, Customs, & Holidays. Suzanne Pelican & Karen Bachman-Carter. (Ethnic & Regional Food Practices Ser.). 1992. pap. 10.00 (*0-88091-083-6*, 0867) Am Dietetic Assn.

Navajo Food Practices, Customs, & Holidays. 2nd ed. Karen Bachman-Carter et al. LC 98-30899. (Ethnic & Regional Food Practices Ser.). 1998. 10.00 (*0-88091-170-0*) Am Dietetic Assn.

Navajo Foreign Affairs, 1795-1846. Frank D. Reeve. 54p. 1983. pap. 4.00 (*0-912586-51-6*) Dine College Pr.

Navajo Graves: An Archaeological Reflection of Ethnographic Reality. Albert E. Ward. (Ethnohistorical Report Ser.: No. 2). 1987. 10.00 (*0-932752-04-7*) Ctr Anthrop Studies.

Navajo-Hopi Land Dispute: An American Tragedy. David M. Brugge. (Illus.). 320p. 1999. pap. 18.95 (*0-8263-2156-9*) U of NM Pr.

Navajo Indian Book. (J). (gr. 1-6). 1975. pap. 4.95 (*0-918858-03-8*) Fun Pub AZ.

Navajo Indian Coloring Book. O. T. Branson. 32p. 1983. pap. 3.50 (*0-918080-06-1*) Treas Chest Bks.

Navajo Indian Medical Ethnobotany. Leland C. Wyman & Stuart K. Harris. LC 76-43902. (Univ. of New Mexico Bulletin Anthropological Ser.: Vol. 3, No. 5). reprint ed. 34.50 (*0-404-15761-0*) AMS Pr.

Navajo Indians see Junior Library of American Indians

Navajo Indians. Leigh Hope Wood. (Junior Library of American Indians). (J). 1991. 12.15 (*0-606-07939-4*) Turtleback.

Navajo Indians. Dane Coolidge & Mary R. Coolidge. LC 76-43679. reprint ed. 52.50 (*0-404-15513-8*) AMS Pr.

Navajo Indians & Federal Indian Policy, 1900-1935. Lawrence C. Kelly. LC 66-27381. 231p. reprint ed. pap. 71.70 (*0-608-13684-0*, 205537500017) Bks Demand.

Navajo Infancy: An Ethological Study of Child Development. James S. Chisholm. LC 83-12258. (Evolutionary Foundations of Human Behavior Ser.). 279p. (C). 1983. lib. bdg. 49.95 (*0-202-01169-0*) Aldine de Gruyter.

Navajo Jewelry: A Legacy of Silver & Stone. Lois Essary Jacka. LC 95-16911. (Illus.). 144p. (Orig.). 1995. pap. 14.95 (*0-87358-609-3*) Northland AZ.

Navajo Kinship & Marriage. Gary Witherspoon. LC 74-21340. (Illus.). xii, 138p. 1975. lib. bdg. 6.00 (*0-226-90419-9*) U Ch Pr.

Navajo Kinship & Marriage. Gary Witherspoon. LC 74-21340. xii, 150p. 1986. reprint ed. pap. text 14.50 (*0-226-90417-2*, Midway Reprint) U Ch Pr.

Navajo Kinship & Marriage. Gary Witherspoon. (Native American Studies in Anthropology). (Illus.). xii, 138p. 1996. reprint ed. pap. text 10.95 (*0-226-90418-0*) U Ch Pr.

Navajo Language: A Grammar & Colloquial Dictionary. Robert W. Young & William T. Morgan. LC 79-56812. 1577p. reprint ed. pap. 200.00 (*0-608-12046-4*, 202467600038) Bks Demand.

Navajo Language: A Grammar & Colloquial Dictionary. rev. ed. Robert W. Young & William Morgan, Sr. LC 79-56812. 1521p. 1987. 60.00 (*0-8263-1014-1*) U of NM Pr.

Navajo Laughter: The Navajo Way. unabridged ed. Alan Wilson. 143p. 1992. pap. text 39.00 incl. audio (*0-88432-452-4*, AFNV30) Audio-Forum.

Navajo Long Walk. Nancy Armstrong. 88p. (J). (gr. 4-9). 1983. pap. 5.95 (*0-89992-083-7*) Coun India Ed.

Navajo Long Walk. Nancy Armstrong. (Council for Indian Education Ser.). (Illus.). 128p. (J). (gr. 4-8). 1994. pap. 8.95 (*1-879373-56-4*) Roberts Rinehart.

Navajo Medicine Man Sand Paintings. Gladys A. Reichard. (Illus.). 132p. 1977. reprint ed. pap. 12.95 (*0-486-23329-4*) Dover.

Navajo Missile Project: The Story of the "Know-How" Missile of American Rocketry. James N. Gibson. LC 95-72319. (Illus.). 96p. (C). (gr. 13). 1996. pap. 19.95 (*0-7643-0048-2*) Schiffer.

Navajo Mountain & Rainbow Bridge Religion. Karl W. Luckert. Tr. by Irvy W. Goossen & Harry Bilagody, Jr. LC 77-153661. (American Tribal Religions Ser.: No. 1). 165p. reprint ed. pap. 51.20 (*0-8357-7771-5*, 203613100002) Bks Demand.

Navajo Multi-Household Social Units: Archaeology on Black Mesa, Arizona. Thomas R. Rocek. LC 94-33277. 237p. 1995. 51.00 (*0-8165-1472-0*) U of Ariz Pr.

***Navajo Nation.** Sandra M. Pasqua. LC 99-52187. (Native Peoples Ser.). (Illus.). 24p. (J). (ps-3). 2000. lib. bdg. 15.93 (*0-7368-0499-4*, Bridgestone Bks) Capstone Pr.

N

An Asterisk (*) at the beginning of an entry indicates that the title is appearing for the first time.

Navajo Nation, 3. Peter J. Iverson. LC 80-1024. (Contributions in Ethnic Studies: No. 3). (Illus.). 273p. 1981. 65.00 (*0-313-22309-2*, INN/, Greenwood Pr) Greenwood.

Navajo Nation Employers, 1993 Vol. 1: Development of a Local Labor Market Analysis Model to Identify Employment Opportunities for Persons with Disabilities on Reservations. S. L. Shook et al. 130p. 1994. pap. text. write for info. (*1-888557-19-2*, 100098) No Ariz Univ.

Navajo National Monument. rev. ed. Catherine W. Viele. Ed. by Ronald J. Foreman & Gregory McNamee. LC 92-62471. (Illus.). 24p. 1993. pap. 4.95 (*1-877856-27-4*) SW Pks Mnmts.

Navajo Native Dyes. Nonobah G. Bryan & Stella Young. (Wild & Woolly West Ser.: No. 34). (Illus.). 76p. 1978. reprint ed. pap. 5.00 (*0-910584-57-5*) Filter.

Navajo Native Dyes: Their Preparation & Use. Stella Young. LC 76-43671. reprint ed. 29.50 (*0-404-15504-9*) AMS Pr.

Navajo Nights. Vella Munn. 1995. per. 3.50 (*0-373-27058-5*, 1-27058-6) Silhouette.

***Navajo (North America)** Patricia Cronin Marcello. (Indigenous Peoples Ser.). (Illus.). 144p. (YA). (gr. 6-9). 2000. lib. bdg. 23.70 (*1-56006-619-9*) Lucent Bks.

Navajo of Canyon de Chelly: In Home God's Fields. Rose Houk. Ed. by Sandra Scott. LC 94-69815. (Illus.). 84p. 1995. pap. 9.95 (*1-877856-54-1*) SW Pks Mnmts.

Navajo Oral History, Vol. II. Alfred W. Yazzie. Ed. by Isaac Johnson & Gene Johnson. (ENG & NAV., Illus.). 56p. (Orig.). 1984. write for info. (*0-318-58352-6*) Rough Rock Demonst.

Navajo Pictorial Weaving, 1880-1950. Tyrone Campbell et al. (Illus.). 128p. 1995. pap. 19.95 (*0-8263-1617-4*) U of NM Pr.

Navajo Picture Writing see Study of Navajo Symbolism

Navajo Place Names: An Observer's Guide. Alan Wilson. 100p. (Orig.). 1995. pap. 9.95 (*0-88432-825-2*, AFNV95) Audio-Forum.

***Navajo Places: History, Legend, Landscape.** Laurance D. Linford. 314p. 2000. 60.00 (*0-87480-623-2*) U of Utah Pr.

***Navajo Places: History, Legend, Landscape.** Laurance D. Linford. LC 99-53553. (Illus.). 314p. 2000. pap. 24.95 (*0-87480-624-0*) U of Utah Pr.

***Navajo Political Experience.** David E. Wilkins. 277p. 2000. pap. 24.99 (*0-912586-80-X*) Dine College Pr.

Navajo Progressive in Discourse: A Study in Temporal Semantics. Sally Midgette. (History & Language Ser.: Vol. 6). XIV, 252p. (C). 1995. text 47.95 (*0-8204-2536-2*) P Lang Pubng.

***Navajo Revenge.** Jon Sharpe. (Trailsmen Ser.: Vol. 227). 2000. mass mkt. 4.99 (*0-451-20133-7*, Sig) NAL.

Navajo Roundup: Selected Correspondence of Kit Carson's Expedition Against the Navajo, 1863-1865. Lawrence C. Kelly. LC 71-21754. 220p. reprint ed. pap. 68.20 (*0-8357-8744-3*, AU0037440007) Bks Demand.

Navajo Rug Stik-Withit Notecubes: Multi-Colored Rug Design. 1995. 12.00 (*0-87358-619-0*) Northland AZ.

Navajo Rug Stik-Withit Notecubes: Red & Black Rug Design. Northland School Division No. 61 Staff. 1995. 12.00 (*0-87358-620-4*) Northland AZ.

Navajo Rugs: How to Find, Evaluate, Buy & Care for Them. 2nd rev. ed. Don Dedera. LC 96-10365. (Illus.). 136p. (Orig.). 1996. pap. 14.95 (*0-87358-635-2*) Northland AZ.

Navajo Rugs: Past, Present & Future. Gilbert S. Maxwell. (Illus.). 95p. (Orig.). 1987. reprint ed. pap. 8.95 (*0-918080-35-5*, 20962) Treas Chest Bks.

Navajo Rugs & Blankets Coloring Book. Chuck Mobley & Andrea Mobley. Ed. by Nancie S. Mahan. (Illus.). 32p. (Orig.). (J). (ps up). 1994. pap. 3.50 (*0-918080-76-2*) Treas Chest Bks.

Navajo Sacred Places. Klara B. Kelley & Harris Francis. LC 93-49472. 270p. 1994. 29.95 (*0-253-33116-1*); pap. 14.95 (*0-253-20893-9*) Ind U Pr.

Navajo Sandstone: A Canyon Country Enigma. F. A. Barnes. (Canyon Country Ser.: No. 55). (Illus.). 96p. 1999. pap. 7.00 (*0-925685-37-2*) Canyon Country Pubns.

Navajo Shepherd & Weaver. Gladys A. Reichard. LC 68-25390. (Beautiful Rio Grande Classics Ser.). (Illus.). 280p. 1984. pap. 12.00 (*0-87380-143-1*) Popular E Commerce.

Navajo Skinwalker, Witchcraft, & Related Spiritual Phenomena: Spiritual Clues: Orientation to the Evolution of the Circle. Joanne Teller & Norman Blackwater. LC 96-95314. (Illus.). 256p. (Orig.). 1997. pap. 13.95 (*0-9656014-0-4*) Infinity Horn.

Navajo Speak: Intermediate. Alan Wilson. 180p. 1992. pap. text 16.95 (*0-88432-611-X*, AFVN92) Audio-Forum.

Navajo, Speak: Intermediate. unabridged ed. Alan Wilson. 180p. 1992. pap. text 49.00 incl. audio (*0-88432-451-6*, AFNV20) Audio-Forum.

Navajo Stories of the Long Walk Period. Ruth Roessel. LC 73-78328. 272p. 1973. pap. 15.00 (*0-912586-16-8*) Dine College Pr.

Navajo Summer. Jennifer O. Dewey. LC 97-72770. (Illus.). 136p. (J). (gr. 5-9). 1998. 14.95 (*1-56397-248-4*) Boyds Mills Pr.

***Navajo Summer.** Jennifer Owings Dewey. LC 97-72770. (Illus.). 136p. (YA). (gr. 5 up). 2000. pap. 9.95 (*1-56397-855-5*) Boyds Mills Pr.

Navajo Symbols in Sandpaintings & Ritual Objects see Study of Navajo Symbolism

Navajo Taboos. Ernie Bulow. (Illus.). 216p. 1991. 19.95 (*0-914001-02-7*); pap. 12.95 (*0-914001-01-9*) Buffalo Med.

Navajo Textiles: The William Randolph Hearst Collection. Nancy J. Blomberg. LC 88-4794. (Illus.). 257p. 1994. reprint ed. pap. 36.00 (*0-8165-1467-4*) U of Ariz Pr.

Navajo Texts. Pliny E. Goddard. LC 76-44071. (AMNH. Anthropological Papers: Vol. 34, Pt. 1). reprint ed. 32.50 (*0-404-15775-0*) AMS Pr.

Navajo Trader. Gladwell Richardson. Ed. by Philip R. Rulon. LC 86-11443. (Illus.). 235p. reprint ed. pap. 72.90 (*0-608-08595-2*, 206911800003) Bks Demand.

Navajo Treaty--1868. LC 68-29989. (Illus.). 26p. (Orig.). 1968. pap. 3.00 (*0-88714-087-4*) KC Pubns.

Navajo Tribal Demography, 1983-1986: A Comparative & Historical Perspective. Cheryl Howard. LC 92-39357. (Contemporary Issues in Health Ser.: Vol. 2). 272p. 1993. text 15.00 (*0-8153-0888-4*, SS846) Garland.

Navajo Vengeance. large type ed. John R. Fearn. 400p. 1992. pap. 16.99 (*0-7089-7166-0*, Linford) Ulverscroft.

Navajo Verb: A Grammar for Students & Scholars. Leonard M. Faltz. LC 98-18326. 452p. 1998. 60.00 (*0-8263-1901-7*); pap. 27.95 (*0-8263-1902-5*) U of NM Pr.

***Navajo Verb System: An Overview.** Robert W. Young. LC 99-33790. 2000. 45.00 (*0-8263-2172-0*) U of NM Pr.

Navajo War Dance. Berard Haile. 1946. pap. 6.00 (*0-318-03031-4*) St Michaels.

Navajo Way: Ceremonial Myths of the Navajo. Hausman. 1992. pap. 11.95 (*0-13-613357-6*) P-H.

Navajo Way Postcards. (Illus.). 64p. 1995. pap. text 9.95 (*0-89013-275-5*) Museum NM Pr.

Navajo Weapon. S. McClain. Ed. by Jan Kristiansson. LC 94-72306. (Illus.). 336p. 1994. 29.95 (*1-883862-07-8*) Bks Beyond Brdrs.

Navajo Weavers & Silversmiths. Washington Matthews. LC 70-97218. (Wild & Woolly West Ser.: No. 7). (Illus.). 44p. 1968. pap. 4.00 (*0-910584-07-9*) Filter.

Navajo Weaving: Three Centuries of Change. Kate P. Kent. LC 85-10875. (Studies in American Indian Art). (Illus.). 152p. 1985. pap. 22.95 (*0-933452-13-6*) Schol Am Res.

Navajo Weaving from the Santa Fe Collection. 48p. 1997. pap. text 9.95 (*1-56944-158-8*) Terrell Missouri.

Navajo Weaving, Navajo Ways. Harriet Koenig & Seymour H. Koenig. Ed. by Betty Himmel. LC 86-80248. 56p. 1986. pap. 12.00 (*0-915171-03-1*) Katonah Gal.

Navajo Weaving Today. Nancy N. Schiffer. LC 91-60957. (Illus.). 64p. 1991. pap. 12.95 (*0-88740-319-0*) Schiffer.

Navajo Weaving Tradition: 1650 to the Present. Alice Kaufman & Christopher Selser. (Illus.). 160p. 1999. pap. 29.95 (*1-57178-066-1*) Coun Oak Bks.

Navajo Weaving Way: The Path from Fleece to Rug. Noel Bennett. LC 97-11687. (Illus.). 160p. 1997. pap. text 19.95 (*1-883010-30-6*) Interweave.

Navajo Weavings from the Andy Williams Collection. Ann L. Hedlund & Zoe A. Perkins. Ed. by Mary A. Steiner. LC 97-69559. (Illus.). 72p. 1997. pap. 24.95 (*0-89178-075-0*) St Louis Art Mus.

Navajo Wedding. Suzanne Carey. (Romance Ser.: No. 855). 1992. per. 2.69 (*0-373-08855-8*, 5-08855-4) Silhouette.

Navajo Wedding Day: A Dine Marriage Ceremony. Eleanor Schick. LC 97-42552. (Illus.). 40p. (J). (gr. k-3). 1999. 15.95 (*0-7614-5031-9*, Cav Child Bks) Marshall Cavendish.

Navajoland: Family Settlement & Land Use. Clara B. Kelley & Peter M. Whiteley. 1989. pap. 14.50 (*0-912586-65-6*) Dine College Pr.

Navajoland Plant Catalog. Vernon O. Mayes & James M. Rominger. LC 94-67167. viii, 72p. (Orig.). (C). 1994. pap. 10.00 (*0-9628075-5-9*) Natl Woodlands Pub.

Navajos see Indians of North America

Navajos. Hawk Sneve & Virginia Driving. (Illus.). 32p. (J). (gr. 4-6). 1993. pap. 6.95 (*0-8234-1168-0*) Holiday.

Navajos. Ruth M. Underhill. LC 59-5996. (Civilization of the American Indian Ser.: Vol. 43). (Illus.). 288p. 1983. pap. 15.95 (*0-8061-1816-4*) U of Okla Pr.

Navajos: A First Americans Book. Virginia Driving Hawk Sneve. LC 92-40330. (Illus.). 32p. (J). (ps-3). 1993. lib. bdg. 16.95 (*0-8234-1039-0*) Holiday.

Navajos in 1705: Roque Madrid's Campaign Journal. Ed. by Rick Hendricks & John P. Wilson. (SPA., Illus.). 175p. 1996. pap. 15.95 (*0-8263-1856-8*) U of NM Pr.

Naval Administration & Warfare. Alfred Thayer Mahan. (Notable American Authors Ser.). 1999. reprint ed. lib. bdg. 125.00 (*0-7812-3927-3*) Rprt Serv.

Naval Administration, 1715-1750. Daniel A. Baugh. (C). 1987. 160.00 (*0-7855-3931-X*) St Mut.

Naval Air War, 1939-1945. Nathan Miller. 21.95 (*0-405-13277-8*) Ayer.

Naval & Maritime History: An Annotated Bibliography. 4th rev. ed. Robert G. Albion. LC 73-186863. ix, 370p. 1972. 14.95 (*0-913372-05-6*) Mystic Seaport.

Naval & Military Journal, 1895, Vol. 1. D. Glendinning & Picton Publishing (Chippenham) Ltd. Staff. 188p. 1992. 75.00 (*0-948251-62-X*, Pub. by Picton) St Mut.

Naval & Military Journal, 1895, Vol. 11. D. Glendinning. 186p. 1992. 125.00 (*0-948251-63-8*, Pub. by Picton) St Mut.

Naval & Military Memoirs of Great Britain, from 1727-1783, 6 vols., Set. Robert Beatson. LC 72-8675. (American Revolutionary Ser.). reprint ed. lib. bdg. 398.00 (*0-8398-0189-0*) Irvington.

Naval & Military Memoirs of Great Britain, from 1727-1783, 6 vols., Vol. 1. Robert Beatson. LC 72-8675. (American Revolutionary Ser.). 543p. reprint ed. lib. bdg. 78.00 (*0-8290-1693-7*) Irvington.

Naval & Military Memoirs of Great Britain, from 1727-1783, 6 vols., Vol. 2. Robert Beatson. LC 72-8675. (American Revolutionary Ser.). 464p. reprint ed. lib. bdg. 78.00 (*0-8290-1694-5*) Irvington.

Naval & Military Memoirs of Great Britain, from 1727-1783, 6 vols., Vol. 3. Robert Beatson. LC 72-8675. (American Revolutionary Ser.). 615p. reprint ed. lib. bdg. 78.00 (*0-8290-1695-3*) Irvington.

Naval & Military Memoirs of Great Britain, from 1727-1783, 6 vols., Vol. 4. Robert Beatson. LC 72-8675. (American Revolutionary Ser.). 594p. reprint ed. lib. bdg. 78.00 (*0-8290-1696-1*) Irvington.

Naval & Military Memoirs of Great Britain, from 1727-1783, 6 vols., Vol. 5. Robert Beatson. LC 72-8675. (American Revolutionary Ser.). 131p. reprint ed. lib. bdg. 44.00 (*0-8290-1697-X*) Irvington.

Naval & Military Memoirs of Great Britain, from 1727-1783, 6 vols., Vol. 6. Robert Beatson. LC 72-8675. (American Revolutionary Ser.). 516p. reprint ed. lib. bdg. 73.00 (*0-8290-1698-8*) Irvington.

Naval & Military Vocabulary. A. Guglielmotti. (ITA.). 1991. 195.00 (*0-8288-8445-5*) Fr & Eur.

Naval Architecture for Non-Naval Architects. Harry Benford. (Illus.). 239p. 1991. text 29.50 (*0-939773-08-2*) Soc Naval Arch.

NAVAL ARCHITECTURE FOR NON-NAVAL ARCHITECTS is written in engaging & easily understood terms, this volume concentrates on two aspects of naval architecture: design & analysis. Technical discussions are almost entirely qualitative rather than quantitative & coverage focuses on conventional ships & boats while answering questions about such matters as the proposed vessel's seaworthiness, structural integrity, powering requirements, & functional capability. List $29.50, Members $19.50. The Society of Naval Architects & Marine Engineers, 601 Pavonia Ave., Jersey City, NJ 07306. phone: 201-798-4800. FAX: 201-798-4975. website: http://www.sname.org. *Publisher Paid Annotation.*

Naval Aristocracy of Hellenistic Rhodes. Vincent Gabrielsen. (Studies in Hellenistic Civilization: No. 6). (Illus.). 224p. 1997. 29.95 (*87-7288-430-4*, Pub. by Aarhus Univ Pr) David Brown.

Naval Arms Control. Ed. by Sverre Lodgaard. (International Peace Research Institute Ser.). (Illus.). 288p. (C). 1990. text 49.95 (*0-8039-8387-5*) Sage.

Naval Arms Race. (Study Ser.: No. 16). 100p. 1986. 11.00 (*92-1-142116-0*, E.86.IX.3) UN.

Naval Arms Trade. Ian Anthony. (SIPRI Strategic Issue Papers). (Illus.). 232p. 1990. text 38.00 (*0-19-829137-X*) OUP.

Naval Aviation Guide. 5th ed. Ed. by Richard R. Burgess. (Illus.). 488p. 1996. 27.95 (*1-55750-611-6*) Naval Inst Pr.

Naval Aviation in the First World War: Its Impact & Influence. R. D. Layman. LC 96-69149. (Illus.). 256p. 1996. 37.95 (*1-55750-617-5*) Naval Inst Pr.

Naval Aviation in Vietnam. Van Vleet. 18.95 (*0-405-13278-6*) Ayer.

Naval Aviation News. Government Printing Office Staff. pap. 14.00 (*0-16-010253-7*) USGPO.

***Naval Battle of Guadalcanal: Night Action, 13 November, 1942.** James W. Grace. LC 98-38371. 1999. 32.95 (*1-55750-327-3*) Naval Inst Pr.

Naval Battle of Mobile Bay, August 5, 1864 & Franklin Buchanan on the Tennessee. Francis X. Walter. (Illus.). 72p. (Orig.). 1993. pap. 11.95 (*0-9639140-0-6*) Prester Meridian.

Naval Battle System. Jean Rabe. 1996. 10.95 (*0-7869-0628-6*, Pub. by TSR Inc) Random.

Naval Biography of Great Britain: Consisting of Historical Memoirs of Those Officers of the British Navy Who Distinguished Themselves During the Reign of His Majesty George III, 4 vols., Set. James Ralfe. LC 72-20833. (American Revolutionary Ser.). (Illus.). reprint ed. lib. bdg. 313.00 (*0-8398-1773-8*) Irvington.

Naval Biography of Great Britain: Consisting of Historical Memoirs of Those Officers of the British Navy Who Distinguished Themselves During the Reign of His Majesty George III, 4 vols., Vol. 1. James Ralfe. LC 72-20833. (American Revolutionary Ser.). (Illus.). 456p. reprint ed. lib. bdg. 75.00 (*0-8290-1850-6*) Irvington.

Naval Biography of Great Britain: Consisting of Historical Memoirs of Those Officers of the British Navy Who Distinguished Themselves During the Reign of His Majesty George III, 4 vols., Vol. 2. James Ralfe. LC 72-20833. (American Revolutionary Ser.). (Illus.). 534p. reprint ed. lib. bdg. 80.00 (*0-8290-1851-4*) Irvington.

Naval Biography of Great Britain: Consisting of Historical Memoirs of Those Officers of the British Navy Who Distinguished Themselves During the Reign of His Majesty George III, 4 vols., Vol. 3. James Ralfe. LC 72-20833. (American Revolutionary Ser.). (Illus.). 406p. reprint ed. lib. bdg. 75.00 (*0-685-02674-4*) Irvington.

Naval Biography of Great Britain: Consisting of Historical Memoirs of Those Officers of the British Navy Who Distinguished Themselves During the Reign of His Majesty George III, 4 vols., Vol. 4. James Ralfe. LC 72-20833. (American Revolutionary Ser.). (Illus.). 551p. reprint ed. lib. bdg. 83.00 (*0-8290-1853-0*) Irvington.

Naval Cannon. John Munday. (Album Ser.: No. 312). (Illus.). 32p. 1998. pap. 6.25 (*0-85263-844-2*, Pub. by Shire Pubns) Parkwest Pubns.

Naval Ceremonies, Customs, & Traditions. 5th ed. William P. Mack & Royal W. Connell. LC 79-92236. (Illus.). 386p. 1980. 28.95 (*0-87021-412-8*) Naval Inst Pr.

Naval Chronicle: The Contemporary Record of the Royal Navy at War, Vol. I: 1793-1798. Ed. by Nicholas Tracy. 356p. 1999. 39.95 (*0-8117-1107-2*) Stackpole.

Naval Chronicle: The Contemporary Record of the Royal Navy at War, Vol. II: 1799-1804. Ed. by Nicholas Tracy. 356p. 1999. 39.95 (*0-8117-1108-0*) Stackpole.

***Naval Chronicle: The Contemporary Record of the Royal Navy at War, Vol. III: 1805-1806.** Ed. by Nicholas Tracy. (Illus.). 356p. 1999. 39.95 (*0-8117-1109-9*) Stackpole.

***Naval Chronicle: The Contemporary Record of the Royal Navy at War, Vol. IV: 1807-1809.** Ed. by Nicholas Tracy. (Illus.). 356p. 1999. 39.95 (*0-8117-1110-2*) Stackpole.

Naval Command & Control. W. T. Pakenham. (Sea Power: Naval Vessels Weapon Systems & Technology Ser.: No. 8). 147p. (Orig.). 1989. 40.00 (*0-08-034750-9*, Pub. by Brasseys); 25.00 (*0-08-036254-0*, Pub. by Brasseys) Brasseys.

Naval Command & Control: Policy, Programs, People & Issues. Ed. by Vinny DiGirolamo. LC 91-36822. (Illus.). 396p. 1991. text 29.95 (*0-916159-23-X*) AFCEA Intl Pr.

Naval Confidence-Building Measures. (Disarmament Topical Papers: No. 4). 332p. 27.00 (*92-1-142166-7*) UN.

Naval Documents of the American Revolution, Vol. 9. 1172p. 1996. boxed set 51.00 (*0-16-061330-2*) USGPO.

Naval Documents of the American Revolution Vol. 10: American Theater: October 1, 1777-December 31, 1777; European Theater: October 1, 1777-December 31, 1777. Ed. by Michael J. Crawford. 1374p. 1996. boxed set 61.00 (*0-16-045286-4*, Defense Dept) USGPO.

Naval Electronic Warfare. D. G. Kiely. Ed. by Geoffrey Till. (Sea Power: Naval Vessels Weapon Systems & Technology Ser.: Vol. 5). 122p. 1988. 40.00 (*0-08-034757-6*, Pub. by Brasseys); 25.00 (*0-08-034758-4*, Pub. by Brasseys) Brasseys.

Naval Encyclopedia. 1971. reprint ed. 85.00 (*1-55888-195-6*) Omnigraphics Inc.

Naval Engineering & American Sea Power. 2nd ed. Amer. Soc. of Naval Engineers Staff. 528p. 1998. 49.95 (*0-7872-4838-X*) Kendall-Hunt.

Naval Expeditionary Logistics: Enabling Operational Maneuver from the Sea. National Research Council Staff. 110p. (C). 1999. pap. text 26.25 (*0-309-06429-5*) Natl Acad Pr.

Naval Expeditions: The French Return to Indochina, 1945-1946. Charles W. Koburger. LC 97-2247. 192p. 1997. 57.95 (*0-275-95982-1*, Praeger Pubs) Greenwood.

Naval Fighters No. 20: Grumman AF Guardian. Steven J. Ginter & Bob Kowalski. (Naval Fighters Ser.: No. 20). (Illus.). 82p. (Orig.). 1992. pap. text 14.95 (*0-942612-20-5*) Naval Fighters.

Naval Fighters No. 21: Chance Vought V-173 & XF5U-1 Flying Pancakes. A. Schoni. Ed. by Steven J. Ginter. (Illus.). 34p. 1992. pap. 7.95 (*0-942612-21-3*) Naval Fighters.

Naval Fighters No. 22: North American AJ Savage. Steven J. Ginter. (Illus.). 130p. (Orig.). 1992. pap. text 19.95 (*0-942612-22-1*) Naval Fighters.

Naval Fighters No. 23: Convair XF24-1 & YF24-1 Seadart. B. J. Long. (Illus.). 74p. 1993. pap. 14.95 (*0-942612-23-X*) Naval Fighters.

Naval Fighters No. 28: Ryan FR-1 Fireball & XF2R-1 Darkshadow. Steven J. Ginter. (Naval Fighters Ser.: Vol. 28). (Illus.). 74p. (Orig.). 1995. pap. 14.95 (*0-942612-28-0*) Naval Fighters.

Naval Fighters No. 37: Martin P4M-17-1Q Mercator. Steven J. Ginter. (Naval Fighters Ser.: Vol. 37). (Illus.). 104p. (Orig.). 1996. pap. 17.95 (*0-942612-37-X*) Naval Fighters.

Naval Fighters No. 44: Grumman's Mach-2 International F11F1F Supertiger. Corwin Meyer. Ed. by Steve Ginter. (Illus.). 48p. 1998. pap. 10.95 (*0-942612-44-2*, NF44) Naval Fighters.

Naval Fighters Vol. 34: Convair XP5Y-1 & R3Y-1-2 Tradewind. Steve Ginter. (Illus.). 120p. (Orig.). 1997. pap. 19.95 (*0-942612-34-5*) Naval Fighters.

Naval Fighters Vol. 40: Grumman F11F Tiger. Corwin Meyer & Steve Ginter. (Illus.). 144p. 1998. pap. 22.95 (*0-942612-40-X*, NF40) Naval Fighters.

Naval Fighters Vol. 45, Pt. 1: Douglas A3D Skywarrior: Design/Structures/Testing. Bruce Cunningham. (Illus.). 136p. 1998. pap. 22.95 (*0-942612-45-0*, NF45) Naval Fighters.

***Naval Fighters Number Forty-Eight: Kaiser Fleetwings XRTK-1.** Bob Kowalski. Ed. by Steve Ginter. (Naval Fighters Ser.: Vol. 48). (Illus.). 32p. 1999. pap. 7.95 (*0-942612-48-5*, NF48) Naval Fighters.

Naval Force Levels & Modernization: An Analysis of Shipbuilding Requirements - A Staff Paper. Arnold M. Kuzmack. LC 76-157664. 60p. reprint ed. pap. 30.00 (*0-608-30812-9*, 200570300059) Bks Demand.

Naval Heritage of Portsmouth. John Winton. (C). 1989. 45.00 (*1-85455-002-0*, Pub. by Ensign Pubns & Print) St Mut.

Naval History: The 6th Symposium of the U. S. Naval Academy. Ed. by Daniel M. Masterson. LC 86-29858. (Illus.). 376p. 1987. 65.00 (*0-8420-2278-3*) Scholarly Res Inc.

Naval History: The 7th Symposium of the U. S. Naval Academy. Ed. by William B. Cogar. LC 88-11691. 336p. 1988. 65.00 (*0-8420-2299-6*) Scholarly Res Inc.

***Naval History & Maritime Strategy.** John B. Hattendorf. LC 99-47385. 2000. pap. write for info. (*1-57524-128-5*) Krieger.

***Naval History & Maritime Strategy.** John B. Hattendorf. LC 99-47385. (Illus.). 294p. 2000. text 29.50 (*1-57524-127-7*) Krieger.

Naval History, 1990. Ed. by Paul Stillwell. (Illus.). 320p. 1991. 32.95 (*1-55750-602-7*) Naval Inst Pr.

N

An Asterisk (*) at the beginning of an entry indicates that the title is appearing for the first time.

Naval History, 1994, Vol. 8, 1994, Nos. 1-6. Ed. by Fred L. Schultz. (Illus.). 368p. 1995. 32.95 (*1-55750-610-8*) Naval Inst Pr.

Naval History, 1991. Ed. by Paul Stillwell. (Illus.). 352p. 1992. 32.95 (*1-55750-604-3*) Naval Inst Pr.

Naval History, 1993. Ed. by Paul Stillwell & Fred L. Schultz. (Illus.). 256p. 1994. 32.95 (*1-55750-608-6*) Naval Inst Pr.

Naval History, 1992. Ed. by Paul Stillwell. (Illus.). 352p. 1993. 32.95 (*1-55750-606-X*) Naval Inst Pr.

Naval History of the American Revolution, 2 vols., Set. Gardner W. Allen. (Illus.). 752p. 1995. reprint ed. lib. bdg. 79.95 (*0-8328-4503-5*) Higginson Bk Co.

Naval History of the Civil War. David D. Porter. LC 98-13377. 864p. 1998. pap. 34.95 (*0-486-40176-6*) Dover.

Naval History of the World War, 3 Vols., Set. Thomas G. Frothingham. Incl. Vol. 1. Offensive Operations, 1914-15. LC 70-165633. Vol. 2. Stress of Sea Power, 1915-1916. LC 70-165633. Vol. 3. U. S. in the War, 1917-18. LC 70-165633. LC 70-165633. (Select Bibliographies Reprint Ser.). 1977. reprint ed. 108.95 (*0-8369-5940-X*) Ayer.

Naval History of World War I. Paul G. Halpern. LC 93-24265. 591p. 1994. 55.00 (*0-87021-266-4*) Naval Inst Pr.

Naval History of World War I. Paul G. Halpern. (Illus.). 618p. 1995. pap. 26.95 (*1-55750-352-4*) Naval Inst Pr.

Naval History 1995. Ed. by Fred L. Schultz. (Illus.). 344p. 1996. 32.95 (*1-55750-622-1*) Naval Inst Pr.

Naval Institute Guide to Combat Fleets of the World, 1998: Their Ships, Aircraft & Systems. A. D. Baker, III. (Illus.). 1200p. 1998. 150.00 (*1-55750-111-4*) Naval Inst Pr.

Naval Institute Guide to Combat Fleets of the World, 1998: Their Ships, Aircraft & Systems. A.D. Baker. 1998. 129.95 (*1-55750-112-2*) Naval Inst Pr.

***Naval Institute Guide to Combat Fleets of the World, 2000-2001: Their Ships, Aircraft & Systems.** A. D. Baker, III. (Illus.). 960p. 2000. 175.00 (*1-55750-197-1*) Naval Inst Pr.

Naval Institute Guide to the Ships & Aircraft of the U. S. Fleet. 16th rev. ed. Norman Polmar. (Illus.). 592p. 1996. 79.95 (*1-55750-686-8*) Naval Inst Pr.

Naval Institute Guide to World Military Aviation, 1997-1998. Rene J. Francillon. LC 97-202475. (Naval Institute Guide Ser.). (Illus.). 904p. 1997. 150.00 (*1-55750-265-X*) Naval Inst Pr.

Naval Institute Guide to World Naval Weapons Systems, 1994 Update. Norman Friedman. LC 93-26201. (Illus.). 168p. 1994. 55.00 (*1-55750-259-5*) Naval Inst Pr.

Naval Institute Guide to World Naval Weapons Systems, 1997-1998. Norman Friedman. LC 97-3768. (Naval Institute Guide Ser.). (Illus.). 862p. 1997. 175.00 (*1-55750-268-4*) Naval Inst Pr.

Naval Institute Historical Atlas of the U. S. Navy. Craig L. Symonds. LC 94-22911. (Illus.). 256p. 1995. 49.95 (*1-55750-797-X*) Naval Inst Pr.

Naval Intelligence - Ship Modeler's Guide, 1999. Ed. by Michael C. Benolkin. 1999. pap. write for info. (*1-891344-15-3*) TacAir Pubns.

Naval Law. 2nd ed. USNA (Taylor) Staff. 692p. 1996. per. 29.00 (*0-7872-2310-7*) Kendall-Hunt.

Naval Law: Justice & Procedure in the Sea Services. 3rd ed. Brent G. Filbert & Alan G. Kaufman. LC 97-31042. (Illus.). 400p. 1997. 35.00 (*1-55750-462-8*) Naval Inst Pr.

Naval Leadership: Voices of Experience. Karel Montor. LC 87-10986. (Illus.). 504p. (C). 1987. text 27.95 (*0-87021-325-3*) Naval Inst Pr.

Naval Leadership: Voices of Experience. 2nd ed. Ed. by Karel Montar et al. LC 98-2550. (Illus.). 536p. 1998. 35.00 (*1-55750-596-9*) Naval Inst Pr.

Naval Live Oak Reservation. Virginia Parks & Elizabeth Vickers. (Illus.). 1995. 3.00 (*0-939566-08-7*) Pensacola Hist.

Naval, Marine & Air Force Uniforms of World War 2 Andrew Mollo & Malcolm McGregor. LC 76-361571. 231 p. 1975. 2.75 (*0-7137-0725-9*) A & C Blk.

Naval Mine Warfare Markets. Charles LeMesurier & Marc Arnold. (Special Reports). 1997. 695.00 (*0-7106-1503-5*) Janes Info Group.

Naval Minewarfare: Where the Fleet Goes, We've Been! Turner Publishing Company Staff. LC 95-70461. (Illus.). 104p. Date not set. 39.95 (*1-56311-221-3*) Turner Pub KY.

Naval Navigation Dictionary English-Russian & Russian-English. V. I. Kozlov. (ENG & RUS.). 1995. 95.00 (*0-7859-9228-6*) Fr & Eur.

Naval Nostalgia. W. S. Ainslie. 1985. 40.00 (*0-946270-27-9*, Pub. by Pentland Pr) St Mut.

Naval Occasions, & Some Traits of the Sailorman. Lewis A. Ritchie. LC 70-130070. (Short Story Index Reprint Ser.). 1977. 23.95 (*0-8369-3651-5*) Ayer.

Naval Officer's Guide. 10th ed. William P. Mack & Thomas D. Paulsen. LC 90-22820. (Illus.). 528p. 1991. 25.95 (*0-87021-296-6*) Naval Inst Pr.

Naval Officer's Guide. 11th ed. William P. Mack et al. LC 98-29988. (Illus.). 512p. 1998. 27.95 (*1-55750-645-0*) Naval Inst Pr.

Naval Officers of the American Revolution: A Concise Biographical Dictionary. Charles E. Claghorn. LC 87-35410. (Illus.). 383p. 1988. 58.00 (*0-8108-2096-X*) Scarecrow.

Naval Officers under Hitler: The Story of Crew 34. Eric Rust. LC 90-43918. 248p. 1991. 55.00 (*0-275-93709-7*, C3709, Praeger Pubs) Greenwood.

Naval Operations, Vol. I. Julian S. Corbett. (Great War Ser.: Vol. 55). (Illus.). 528p. 1997. reprint ed. 49.95 (*0-89839-256-X*) Battery Pr.

Naval Operations, Vol. II. Julian S. Corbett. (Great War Ser.: Vol. 56). (Illus.). 460p. 1997. reprint ed. 54.95 (*0-89839-257-8*) Battery Pr.

Naval Operations, Vol. III. 2nd ed. Julian Corbett. (Great War Ser.: No. 41). (Illus.). 486p. 1995. reprint ed. 49.95 (*0-89839-231-4*) Battery Pr.

Naval Operations, Vol. IV. Henry Newbolt. (Great War Ser.: Vol. 53). (Illus.). 456p. 1996. reprint ed. 49.95 (*0-89839-254-3*) Battery Pr.

Naval Operations, Vol. V. Henry Newbolt. (Great War Ser.: Vol. 54). (Illus.). 472p. 1996. reprint ed. 49.95 (*0-89839-255-1*) Battery Pr.

Naval Operations Analysis. 2nd ed. Ed. by U. S. Naval Academy Naval Science Department Staff. LC 77-73342. 372p. 1977. 22.95 (*0-87021-440-3*) Naval Inst Pr.

***Naval Operations Analysis.** 3rd ed. Daniel H Wagner. LC 99-29072. 372p. 1999. 28.95 (*1-55750-956-5*) Naval Inst Pr.

Naval Operations, 1914-1918, 5 vols. Julian S. Corbett. Incl. Vol. 1, Pt. 1. (*0-404-09281-0*); Vol. 1, Pt. 2. (*0-404-09282-9*); Vol. 2. (*0-404-09283-7*); Vol. 3, Pt. 1. (*0-404-09284-5*); Vol. 3, Pt. 2. (*0-404-09285-3*); Vol. 4, Pt. 1. (*0-404-09286-1*); Vol. 4, Pt. 2. (*0-404-09287-X*); Vol. 5, Pt. 1. (*0-404-09288-8*); Vol. 5, Pt. 2. (*0-404-09289-6*); (Illus.). reprint ed. write for info. (*0-404-09280-2*) AMS Pr.

***Naval Operations of the Campaign in Norway, April-June, 1940.** David Brown. LC 00-31708. (Whitehall Histories Ser.). 2000. write for info. (*0-7146-5119-2*, Pub. by F Cass Pubs) Intl Spec Bk.

Naval Petroleum Reserve: Limited Opportunities Exist to Increase Revenues from Oil Sales in California. (Illus.). 46p. (Orig.). (C). 1995. pap. text 20.00 (*0-7881-2235-5*) DIANE Pub.

Naval Power in the Conquest of Mexico. C. Harvey Gardiner. LC 70-94606. 253p. 1970. reprint ed. lib. bdg. 38.50 (*0-8371-2457-3*, GANP, Greenwood Pr) Greenwood.

Naval Power in the 20th Century. Ed. by N. A. Rodger. 318p. 1996. 47.95 (*1-55750-616-7*) Naval Inst Pr.

Naval Prints from the Beverley R. Robinson Collection, 1514-1791, Vol. 1. Compiled by Sigrid Trumpy. LC 90-85801. (Illus.). 400p. 1991. 65.00 (*0-9628260-0-6*) US Naval Acad B R Robinson Collect.

Naval Race or Arms Control in the Indian Ocean? Some Problems for Negotiating Naval Limitations. Alvin J. Cottrell & Walter F. Hahn. 78p. 1978. pap. text 17.95 (*0-87855-799-7*) Transaction Pubs.

***Naval Records for Genealogists.** N.A.M. Rodger. 230p. 1999. pap. 24.95 (*1-873162-58-8*, Pub. by PRO Pubns) Midpt Trade.

Naval Regional Medical Center. (PCI Journal Reprints Ser.). 8p. 1981. pap. 10.00 (*0-686-40150-6*, JR246) P-PCI.

Naval Research Reviews. Government Printing Office Staff. pap. 11.00 (*0-16-010257-X*) USGPO.

Naval Researches. Thomas White. LC 72-10764. (American Revolutionary Ser.). reprint ed. lib. bdg. 43.00 (*0-8398-2180-8*) Irvington.

Naval Reserve Association. Turner Publishing Company Staff. LC 98-88601. (Illus.). 352 p. 1998. 52.50 (*1-56311-381-3*) Turner Pub KY.

Naval Review, 1985. (Illus.). 224p. 1997. 25.00 (*0-87021-451-9*) Naval Inst Pr.

Naval Review, 1984. Ed. by Paul Stillwell. (Illus.). 224p. 1997. 14.00 (*0-87021-518-3*) Naval Inst Pr.

Naval Review, 1989. (Illus.). 224p. 1997. 25.00 (*0-87021-608-2*) Naval Inst Pr.

Naval Review, 1990. (Illus.). 224p. 1997. 25.00 (*1-55750-600-0*) Naval Inst Pr.

Naval Review, 1995. (Illus.). 224p. 1995. 25.00 (*1-55750-612-4*) Naval Inst Pr.

Naval Review, 1994. (Illus.). 224p. 1994. 25.00 (*1-55750-609-4*) Naval Inst Pr.

Naval Review, 1996. (Illus.). 224p. 1997. 25.00 (*1-55750-614-0*) Naval Inst Pr.

Naval Science, Vol. 2. 3rd ed. Rev. by Richard R. Hobbs. LC 91-24950. (Illus.). 327p. (YA). 1992. 17.95 (*1-55750-629-9*) Naval Inst Pr.

Naval Science, Vol. 2. 4th ed. Richard R. Hobbs. (Illus.). 327p. 1997. 17.95 (*1-55750-373-7*) Naval Inst Pr.

Naval Science Vol. 1: An Illustrated Text for the NJROTC Student, 4 vols., Vol. 1. 4th rev. ed. Richard R. Hobbs. (Illus.). 384p. 1996. 17.95 (*1-55750-634-5*) Naval Inst Pr.

Naval Science Vol. 3: An Illustrated Text for the NJROTC Student. 4th ed. Rev. by Richard R. Hobbs. (Illus.). 360p. 1998. pap. 17.95 (*1-55750-636-1*) Naval Inst Pr.

Naval Science Vol. 3: An Illustrated Text for the NJROTC Student, Vol. 3. 3rd ed. Wilbur A. Sundt. LC 91-24950. (Illus.). 320p. 1994. 17.95 (*1-55750-631-0*) Naval Inst Pr.

Naval Science Vol. 4: Selected Readings in Naval Leadership for NJROTC Students. Ed. by Richard R. Hobbs. LC 91-24950. 120p. (YA). 1995. pap. 17.95 (*1-55750-365-6*) Naval Inst Pr.

Naval Shipboard Communications Systems. J. C. Kim & E. I. Muehldorf. LC 94-16309. 450p. (C). 1995. 69.80 (*0-13-613498-X*) P-H.

***Naval Shipbuilders of the World: From the Age of Sail to the Present Day.** Robert J. Winklareth. (Illus.). 192p. 2000. 46.95 (*1-86176-121-X*) Naval Inst Pr.

Naval Shiphandling. 4th ed. R. S. Crenshaw, Jr. LC 74-26360. (Illus.). 479p. 1975. text, suppl. ed. 45.00 (*0-87021-474-8*) Naval Inst Pr.

Naval Stores: Production, Chemistry, Utilization. Ed. by Duane F. Zinkel & James Russell. LC 89-10881. (Illus.). 1060p. 1989. 175.00 (*0-685-30903-7*) Pulp Chem Assn.

Naval Strategy. Alfred Thayer Mahan. LC 74-14359. (Illus.). 475p. 1975. reprint ed. lib. bdg. 99.75 (*0-8371-7802-9*, MANS, Greenwood Pr) Greenwood.

Naval Strategy. Alfred Thayer Mahan. (Notable American Authors Ser.). 1999. reprint ed. lib. bdg. 125.00 (*0-7812-3930-3*) Rprt Serv.

Naval Strategy & National Security: An International Security Reader. Ed. by Steven E. Miller & Stephen Van Evera. LC 87-36108. 401p. reprint ed. pap. 124.40 (*0-8357-2550-2*, 204024100015) Bks Demand.

Naval Strategy & Operations in Narrow Seas. Milan N. Vego. LC 99-18061. (Naval Policy & History Ser.). 344p. 1999. pap. text. write for info. (*0-7146-4425-0*, Pub. by F Cass Pubs) Intl Spec Bk.

***Naval Strategy & Operations in Narrow Seas.** Milan N. Vego. LC 99-18061. (Naval Policy & History Ser.: No. 5). (Illus.). 331p. 1999. 57.50 (*0-7146-4870-1*) F Cass Pubs.

***Naval Strategy & Policy in the Mediterranean: Past, Present & Future.** John B. Hattendorf. LC 99-39158. (Naval Policy & History Ser.: No. 10). (Illus.). 464p. 2000. pap. 29.50 (*0-7146-8054-0*, Pub. by F Cass Pubs) Intl Spec Bk.

***Naval Strategy & Policy in the Mediterranean: Past, Present & Future.** Ed. by John B. Hattendorf. LC 99-39158. (Naval Policy & History Ser.: No. 10). (Illus.). 464p. 2000. 69.50 (*0-7146-4991-0*, Pub. by F Cass Pubs) Intl Spec Bk.

Naval Strategy East of Suez: The Role of Djibouti. Charles W. Koburger, Jr. LC 91-28156. 136p. 1992. 47.95 (*0-275-94116-7*, C4116, Praeger Pubs) Greenwood.

Naval Strategy in Northeast Asia: Geo-Strategic Goals, Policies & Prospects. Duk-Ki Kim. LC 99-23867. (Naval Policy & History Ser.). 256p. 1999. pap. write for info. (*0-7146-8027-3*, Pub. by F Cass Pubs) Intl Spec Bk.

***Naval Strategy in Northeast Asia: Geostrategic Goals, Policies & Prospects.** Duk-Ki Kim. Ed. by Holger Herwig. LC 99-23867. (Naval Policy & History Ser.). (Illus.). 256p. 2000. 57.50 (*0-7146-4966-X*, Pub. by F Cass Pubs) Intl Spec Bk.

Naval Strategy of the World War. Wolfgang Wegener. Ed. by John B. Hattendorf & Wayne P. Hughes, Jr. Tr. & Intro. by Holger H. Herwig. LC 89-3387. (Classics of Sea Power Ser.). 288p. 1989. 34.95 (*0-87021-489-6*) Naval Inst Pr.

Naval Surface Weapons. D. G. Kiely. (Sea Power: Naval Vessels Weapon Systems & Technology Ser.). (Illus.). 116p. 1988. 40.00 (*0-08-036689-9*, Pub. by Brasseys); 25.00 (*0-08-036688-0*, Pub. by Brasseys) Brasseys.

Naval Surgeon: Life & Death at Sea in the Age of Sail. J. Worth Estes. LC 97-31845. 1998. 39.95 (*0-88135-194-6*) Watson Pub Intl.

Naval Surgeon in Yi Korea: The Journal of George W. Woods. Ed. by Fred C. Bohm & Robert R. Swartout, Jr. LC 84-80605. (Korea Research Monographs: No. 10). (Illus.). 137p. (Orig.). 1984. pap. 12.00 (*0-912966-68-8*) IEAS.

Naval Technology & Social Modernization in the 19th Century. Ken J. Hagan et al. 110p. 1976. pap. text 29.95 (*0-89126-025-0*) MA-AH Pub.

Naval Terms Dictionary. 5th ed. John V. Noel, Jr. & Edward L. Beach. LC 88-18657. 336p. 1988. text 24.95 (*0-87021-571-X*) Naval Inst Pr.

Naval Treaty: The Adventures of Sherlock Holmes. Jeremy Paul. (Illus.). 48p. (Orig.). 1991. pap. 11.00 (*0-86025-435-6*, Pub. by I Henry Pubns) Empire Pub Srvs.

***Naval War College.** Lionel Wyld. (Images of America Ser.). 128p. 1999. pap. 18.99 (*0-7385-0290-1*) Arcadia Publng.

Naval War in the Mediterranean: 1940-1943. Jack Greene. 1999. write for info. (*1-885119-61-5*) Sarpedon.

Naval War of 1812. Theodore Roosevelt. Ed. by Caleb Carr. LC 98-48973. (Modern Library War Ser.). 560p. 1999. pap. 15.95 (*0-375-75419-9*) Modern Lib NY.

Naval War of 1812. Theodore Roosevelt. LC 68-24994. (American History & Americana Ser.: No. 47). 1969. reprint ed. lib. bdg. 75.00 (*0-8383-0235-1*) M S G Haskell Hse.

Naval War of 1812: A Documentary History, Vol. 1. Ed. by William S. Dudley & Michael J. Crawford. LC 85-600565. 772p. 1985. 44.00 (*0-16-002042-5*, S/N 008-046-00112-0) USGPO.

Naval War of 1812, or, the History of the United States Navy During the Last War with Great Britain: To Which is Appended an Acount of the Battle of New Orleans. Theodore Roosevelt. LC 98-54660. (Illus.). 512p. 1999. reprint ed. mass mkt. 16.95 (*0-306-80910-9*, Pub. by Da Capo) HarpC.

Naval War of 1812 Vol. 1: 1812: A Documentary History. Ed. by William S. Dudley. (Illus.). 714p. (C). 1985. 34.00 (*0-945274-06-8*) Naval Hist Ctr.

Naval War of 1812 Vol. 2: 1813: A Documentary History. Ed. by William S. Dudley. (Illus.). 779p. (C). 1992. 43.00 (*0-685-71187-0*) Naval Hist Ctr.

Naval War of 1812: or The History of the United States Navy. Theodore Roosevelt. 1988. reprint ed. lib. bdg. 59.00 (*0-7812-0174-8*) Rprt Serv.

Naval War of 1812: or The History of the United States Navy. Theodore Roosevelt. LC 74-108533. (Illus.). 1971. reprint ed. 49.00 (*0-403-00312-1*) Scholarly.

Naval War of 1812. Robert Gardiner. LC 98-68351. 1999. 49.95 (*1-55750-654-X*) Naval Inst Pr.

Naval Warfare: It's Ruling Principles & Practice Historically Treated, 2 vols. Philip Colomb. Ed. by John B. Hattendorf & Wayne P. Hughes. LC 89-13389. (Classics of Sea Power Ser.). (Illus.). 487p. 1990. 69.90 (*0-87021-777-1*) Naval Inst Pr.

***Naval Warfare, 1815-1914.** Lawrence Sondhaus. LC 00-34464. (Warfare & History Ser.). (Illus.). 2000. pap. write for info. (*0-415-21478-5*) Routledge.

Naval Warfare in the Age of Sail. Bernard Ireland. 49.95 (*0-393-04983-3*) Norton.

Naval Warfare in the Baltic, 1939-1945: War in a Narrow Sea. Charles W. Koburger. LC 94-21720. 176p. 1994. 49.95 (*0-275-95027-1*, Praeger Pubs) Greenwood.

Naval Warfare in the Eastern Mediterranean, 1940-1945. Charles W. Koburger, Jr. LC 92-36633. 192p. 1993. 55.00 (*0-275-94465-4*, C4465, Praeger Pubs) Greenwood.

Naval Wargaming: From Ancient Galleys to Modern U-Boats. Paul Haque. (Illus.). 128p. 1992. 29.95 (*1-85260-143-4*, Pub. by J H Haynes & Co) Motorbooks Intl.

Naval Weapons Systems & the Contemporary Law of War. James J. Busuttil. (Oxford Monographs in International Law). 270p. 1998. text 90.00 (*0-19-826574-3*) OUP.

Naval Wrecks of Scapa Flow. Maritime Books Staff. (C). 1986. text 110.00 (*0-7855-5298-7*, Pub. by Maritime Bks) St Mut.

Navalism & the Emergence of American Sea Power, 1882-1893. Mark R. Shulman. LC 94-48539. (Illus.). 256p. 1995. 45.00 (*1-55750-766-X*) Naval Inst Pr.

Navalist & Progressive: The Life of Richmond P. Hobson. Walter E. Pittman, Jr. 235p. 1981. pap. text 37.95 (*0-89126-100-1*) MA-AH Pub.

Navalists & Antinavalists: The Naval Policy Debate in the United States, 1785-1827. Craig L. Symonds. LC 77-92571. 256p. 1980. 36.50 (*0-87413-130-8*) U Delaware Pr.

Navamaga: Actividaded de Entrenamiento para la Integracion de Grupos, Programas de Salud y Generacion de Ingresos. Sujatha Wijetilleke & Dian S. Svendsen. Ed. by Suzanne Kindervatter. LC 86-60931. (SPA.). 176p. 1987. reprint ed. pap. text 15.00 (*0-912917-04-0*) UNIFEM.

Navamaga: Formation Visant a Renforcer les Projets Collectifs, la Sante et les Activites Remuneratrices. Sujatha Wijetilleke & Dian S. Svendsen. Ed. by Suzanne Kindervatter. LC 86-61562. (FRE.). 176p. 1987. reprint ed. pap. text 15.00 (*0-912917-06-7*) UNIFEM.

Navamaga: Training Activities for Group Building, Health & Income Generation. Dian S. Svendsen & Sujatha Wijetilleke. Ed. by Suzanne Kindervatter. LC 83-61078. (Illus.). 156p. (Orig.). 1983. teacher ed. 13.00 (*0-912917-00-8*) UNIFEM.

Navarre Bible: Acts of the Apostles. (ENG & LAT.). 272p. 1989. pap. 14.95 (*1-85182-058-2*) Scepter Pubs.

Navarre Bible: Acts of the Apostles. Members of the Faculty of Theology of the Universi. (Navarre Bible Ser.). (ENG & LAT.). 272p. pap. 14.95 (*1-85182-044-2*, Pub. by Four Cts Pr) Intl Spec Bk.

Navarre Bible: Captivity Epistles. Members of the Faculty of Theology of the Universi & Jose M. Casciaro. Tr. by Michael Adams from SPA. (ENG & LAT., Illus.). 207p. 1991. pap. 14.95 (*1-85182-079-5*) Scepter Pubs.

Navarre Bible: Catholic Epistles. Members of the Faculty of Theology of the Universi & Jose M. Casciaro. Tr. by Michael Adams from SPA. (ENG & LAT., Illus.). 240p. 1991. pap. 14.95 (*1-85182-087-6*) Scepter Pubs.

Navarre Bible: Corinthians. Members of the Faculty of Theology of the Universi & Jose M. Casciaro. Tr. by Michael Adams from SPA. (ENG & LAT., Illus.). 250p. 1990. pap. 14.95 (*1-85182-065-5*) Scepter Pubs.

***Navarre Bible: Gospels & Acts.** 960p. 1999. write for info. (*1-85182-508-8*, Pub. by Four Cts Pr) Intl Spec Bk.

Navarre Bible: Hebrews. Members of the Faculty of Theology of the Universi & Jose M. Casciaro. Tr. by Michael Adams from SPA. (ENG & LAT., Illus.). 198p. 1990. pap. 14.95 (*1-85182-069-8*) Scepter Pubs.

Navarre Bible: Pentateuch. LC 99-23033. (ENG & LAT.). 850p. 1999. 39.95 (*1-889334-21-9*) Scepter Pubs.

Navarre Bible: Revelation. Members of the Faculty of Theology of the Universi & Jose M. Casciaro. Tr. by Michael Adams from SPA. (ENG & LAT., Illus.). 192p. 1992. pap. 14.95 (*1-85182-089-2*) Scepter Pubs.

Navarre Bible: Romans & Galatians. (ENG & LAT.). 212p. 1990. pap. 14.95 (*1-85182-055-8*) Scepter Pubs.

Navarre Bible: St. John. Members of the Faculty of Theology of the Universi. (LAT & ENG.). 247p. 1989. pap. 14.95 (*1-85182-094-9*) Scepter Pubs.

Navarre Bible: St. Luke. (ENG & LAT.). 285p. 1989. pap. 14.95 (*1-85182-072-8*) Scepter Pubs.

Navarre Bible: St. Luke. Members of the Faculty of Theology of the Universi. (Navarre Bible Ser.). (ENG & LAT.). pap. 14.95 (*1-85182-040-X*, Pub. by Four Cts Pr) Intl Spec Bk.

Navarre Bible: St. Mark. (ENG & LAT.). 207p. 1989. pap. 14.95 (*1-85182-096-5*) Scepter Pubs.

***Navarre Bible: The Pentateuch.** 824p. 1999. write for info. (*1-85182-498-7*, Pub. by Four Cts Pr) Intl Spec Bk.

***Navarre Bible in the Revised Standard Version with a Commentary by the Members of the Faculty of Theology of the University of Navarre.** rev. ed. Universidad de Navarra Staff. LC 00-39349. 2000. write for info. (*1-889334-27-8*) Scepter Pubs.

Navarre: or Researches after the Descendants of Robert Navarre. C. Denisson. (Illus.). 418p. 1990. reprint ed. pap. 63.00 (*0-8328-1615-9*); reprint ed. lib. bdg. 71.00 (*0-8328-1614-0*) Higginson Bk Co.

Navassa. Bradd Hopkins. LC 98-189590. Orig. Title: The Navassa Conspiracy. 1998. 24.95 (*1-891954-00-8*) Russell Dean.

***Navassa.** Bradd Hopkins. Orig. Title: The Navassa Conspiracy. 1999. pap. 15.95 (*1-891954-02-4*) Russell Dean.

Navassa. 2nd ed. Bradd Hopkins. Orig. Title: The Navassa Conspiracy. 288p. 1998. 24.95 (*1-891954-01-6*, Four Ravens) Russell Dean.

Navassa Conspiracy see Navassa

N

An Asterisk (*) at the beginning of an entry indicates that the title is appearing for the first time.

Naven: A Survey of the Problems Suggested by a Composite Picture of the Culture of a New Guinea Tribe Drawn from Three Points of View. 2nd ed. Gregory Bateson. (Illus.). xix, 312p. 1958. 45.00 (*0-8047-0519-4*); pap. 16.95 (*0-8047-0520-8*) Stanford U Pr.

Naves Topical Bible. Thomas Nelson Publishers Staff. 1997. 15.97 (*0-7852-0945-X*) Nelson.

Nave's Topical Bible. enl. rev. ed. Orville J. Nave. 1114p. 1969. 29.99 (*0-310-33710-0*, 12246) Zondervan.

Nave's Topical Bible: A Digest of the Holy Scriptures see Supervalue Reference Promotional Superset

Nave's Topical Bible Condensed. Orville J. Nave. mass mkt. 5.99 (*0-8024-0030-2*, 224) Moody.

Naviagatio Sancti Brendani Abbatis. Ed. by Carl Selmer. 128p. 1989. reprint ed. 35.00 (*1-85182-047-7*, Pub. by Four Cts Pr) Intl Spec Bk.

***Navicert System During the World War.** Hugh Ritchie & Carnegie Endowment for International Peace Staff. LC 99-48867. (Carnegie Endowment for International Peace Monograph Ser.: No. 2). viii, 83p. 2000. reprint ed. 37.50 (*1-57588-559-X*, 323910) W S Hein.

Naviculaceae: Neue und Wenig Bekannte Taxa. K. Krammer. (Bibliotheca Diatomologica Ser.: Vol. 9). (GER., Illus.). 232p. 1985. lib. bdg. 71.00 (*3-443-57001-1*, Pub. by Gebruder Borntraeger) Balogh.

Naviculaceae, Neue und Wenig Bekannte Taxa, neue Kombinationan und Synonymer sowie Bemerkungen zu Einigen Gattungen. H. Lange-Bertalot & Kurt Kramer. (Bibliotheca Diamatologica Ser.: No. 9). (Illus.). 250p. 1985. lib. bdg. 78.25 (*3-7682-1437-0*) Lubrecht & Cramer.

***Navidad de Dragon.** Dav Pilkey. (SPA., Illus.). 48p. (J). (gr. 1-3). 1999. pap. 6.95 (*980-257-217-9*, Pub. by Ediciones Ekare) Kane-Miller Bk.

Navidad Salvado. unabridged ed. Walter N. Kuhn, Jr. Ed. by Jean M. Kuhn. Tr. by Norberto Rivera. (Freddy el Grillo y la Ciudad de Corncob Ser.: Vol. 9S). (SPA., Illus.). 20p. (J). (ps-10). 1997. spiral bd. 6.95 (*1-891547-17-8*) Hoppa Prodns.

Navidad y Corpus Christi. (Textos y Estudios Clasicos De las Literaturas Hispanicas Ser.). lxii, 373p. 1983. reprint ed. 95.00 (*3-487-05647-X*) G Olms Pubs.

Navidad/Christmas Story. Ed. by Heather Amery. (Bible Tales Readers Ser.). (Illus.). 16p. (J). (ps up). 1999. 6.95 (*0-7460-3431-8*, Usborne) EDC.

Navidades. Lulu Delacre. (Illus.). 32p. (J). (gr. k-6). 1992. 4.95 (*0-590-43549-3*, Blue Ribbon Bks) Scholastic Inc.

Navidades: Popular Christmas Songs from Latin America. Illus. & Selected by Lulu Delacre. 32p. (J). (ps up). 1990. 13.95 (*0-590-43548-5*, Scholastic Hardcover) Scholastic Inc.

Navidades: Popular Christmas Songs from Latin America. Lulu Delacre. 1990. 10.19 (*0-606-01883-2*, Pub. by Turtleback) Demco.

Navidades Van Asomando en Libro de Cuentas. D. L. O'Neal.Tr. of Christmas Pop-Up Counting Book. (SPA.). (J). 1994. 6.49 (*1-56063-768-4*, 490325) Editorial Unilit.

Navier-Stokes Equations: Theory & Numerical Analysis. 3rd rev. ed. Roger Temam. (Studies in Mathematics & Its Applications: Vol. 2). 526p. 1984. 204.50 (*0-444-87558-1*) Elsevier.

Navier-Stokes Equations: Theory & Numerical Methods. Ed. by Rodolfo Salvi. (Pitman Research Notes in Mathematics Ser.: No. 388). 360p. 1998. pap. 67.50 (*0-582-35643-1*, LM5643, Chap & Hall CRC) Addison-Wesley.

Navier-Stokes Equations: Theory & Numerical Methods: Proceedings of a Conference Held at Oberwolfach, FRG, September 18-24, 1988. Ed. by J. G. Heywood et al. (Lecture Notes in Mathematics Ser.). (Illus.). vii, 238p. 1990. pap. 35.00 (*0-387-52770-2*) Spr-Verlag.

Navier-Stokes Equations & Nonlinear Functional Analysis. 2nd ed. Roger Temam. LC 94-43733. (CBMS-NSF Regional Conference Series in Applied Mathematics: No. 66). (Illus.). xiv, 141p. 1995. pap. 29.00 (*0-89871-340-4*) Soc Indus-Appl Math.

Navier-Stokes Equations & Related Nonlinear Problems: Proceedings of the 3rd International Conference Held in Funchal, Madeira, Portugal, May 21-27, 1994. A. Sequeira. LC 95-35795. (Illus.). 416p. (C). 1995. text 125.00 (*0-306-45118-2*, Kluwer Plenum) Kluwer Academic.

Navier-Stokes Equations in Irregular Domains. L. Stupelis. LC 95-16342. (Mathematics & Its Applications Ser.: Vol. 326). 584p. (C). 1995. text 257.50 (*0-7923-3509-0*) Kluwer Academic.

Navier-Stokes Equations II: Theory & Numerical Methods, Proceedings of a Conference Held in Oberwolfach, Germany, August 18-24, 1991. J. G. Heywood et al. LC 92-37395. 1992. 60.95 (*0-387-56261-3*) Spr-Verlag.

Navier-Strokes Equations. Peter Constantin & Ciprian Foias. (Chicago Lectures in Mathematics). 200p. 1988. pap. text 18.00 (*0-226-11549-6*) U Ch Pr.

Navier-Strokes Equations. Peter Constantin & Ciprian Foias. (Chicago Lectures in Mathematics). 200p. 1996. lib. bdg. 42.00 (*0-226-11548-8*) U Ch Pr.

Navies & Armies: The Anglo Dutch Relationship in War & Peace 1688-1988. G. J. Raven & N. A. Rodger. 128p. (C). 1997. text 50.00 (*0-85976-292-0*, Pub. by J Donald) St Mut.

Navies & Foreign Policy. Ken Booth. LC 79-2254. 1979. 39.95 (*0-8419-0518-5*) Holmes & Meier.

Navies & Global Defense: Theories & Strategy. Ed. by Keith Neilson & Elizabeth J. Errington. LC 95-2239. 256p. 1995. 62.95 (*0-275-94898-6*, Praeger Pubs) Greenwood.

Navies & Men Series, 25 bks., Set. 1980. reprint ed. lib. bdg. 809.50 (*0-405-13030-9*) Ayer.

Navies & Shipbuilding Industries: The Strained Symbiosis. Daniel Todd & Michael Lindberg. LC 96-4848. 216p. 1996. 62.95 (*0-275-95310-6*, Praeger Pubs) Greenwood.

Navies & the American Revolution, 1775-1783. Ed. by Robert Gardiner. (Chatham Pictorial Histories Ser.). (Illus.). 192p. 1997. 49.95 (*1-55750-623-X*) Naval Inst Pr.

Navies in History. Clark G. Reynolds. LC 98-6112. 267p. 1998. pap. 22.95 (*1-55750-715-5*) Naval Inst Pr.

Navies in History. Clark G. Reynolds. LC 98-6112. (Illus.). 304p. 1998. 29.95 (*1-55750-716-3*) Naval Inst Pr.

Navies in the Nuclear Age: Warships since 1945. Ed. by Norman Friedman. (Conway's History of the Ship Ser.). (Illus.). 224p. 1993. 47.95 (*1-55750-613-2*) Naval Inst Pr.

Navies of World War II. Mike Taylor. LC 98-14184. (World War II Ser.). 1998. 14.95 (*1-56239-807-5*) ABDO Pub Co.

Navigate Your Career Transition: Strategies for Nurse Leaders. Ed. by Deborah A. Yancer & Julie K. Moe. LC 96-44580. (Illus.). 162p. (Orig.). 1997. pap. 37.50 (*1-55648-182-9*, 088176) AHPI.

Navigating a Business in the North-East. (China Connection Ser.: No. Q172). 1994. 250.00 (*0-85058-790-5*) Economist Intell.

Navigating a Professional Vision. Purdue University Staff. 144p. (C). 1997. per. 19.95 (*0-7872-4170-9*) Kendall-Hunt.

Navigating ABC Flow Charter 4.0. rev. ed. Vince E. Yokom. (Illus.). 248p. 1995. spiral bd. 29.00 (*1-889231-14-2*) Instrux Ltd.

***Navigating Boundaries: The Rhetoric of Women Governors.** Ed. by Brenda DeVore Marshall & Molly A. Mayhead. LC 99-59513. (Praeger Series in Political Communication). 176p. 2000. 59.95 (*0-275-96778-6*, C6778, Praeger Pubs); pap. 18.95 (*0-275-96779-4*, Praeger Pubs) Greenwood.

Navigating Business Information Sources: A Practical Guide for Information. Maria E. Burke & Hazel Hall. 260p. 1998. pap. 65.00 (*1-85604-258-8*, LAP2588, Pub. by Library Association) Bernan Associates.

Navigating by the Stars. Vernon Fisher. (Illus.). 120p. (Orig.). 1988. write for info. (*0-318-64427-4*) Landfall IL.

Navigating Career Change. John F. McGrew. LC 80-80788. (Illus.). 124p. 1980. pap. 5.00 (*0-936544-00-7*) New Vista.

Navigating Change: How CEO's, Top Teams, & Boards Steer Transformation. Donald C. Hambrick et al. LC 97-19266. 464p. 1998. 35.00 (*0-87584-784-6*, HBS Pr) Harvard Busn.

Navigating Change: How Ceos, Top Teams, & Boards Steer Transformation. Harvard Business School Press Staff. 400p. 1997. 35.00 (*0-07-105066-3*) McGraw.

Navigating Compass Designs. Barbara Caron. LC 98-27957. 1998. pap. text 19.95 (*0-89145-896-4*, 4889, Am Quilters Soc) Collector Bks.

Navigating Complexity: The Essential Guide to Complexity Theory in Business & Management. Ed. by Arthur Battram. 280p. 1998. pap. 18.95 (*1-85835-899-X*, Indust Soc) Stylus Pub VA.

***Navigating Complexity: The Essential Guide to Complexity Theory in Business & Management.** Arthur Battram. (Illus.). 267p. 1999. pap. 19.95 (*1-85835-870-1*, Pub. by Stylus Pub VA) LPC InBook.

Navigating CompuServe. Stanley Schatt. 1985. pap. 12.95 (*0-671-54299-0*) S&S Trade.

Navigating Cross-Cultural Ethics. Morgan. LC 98-37850. xvi, 194p. 1998. 18.95 (*0-7506-9915-9*) Buttrwrth-Heinemann.

Navigating Cultural Hot Spots: Directions for Working with Pregnant & Parenting Teens. Karen Salt. LC 98-72796. 1999. pap. write for info. (*1-888231-65-3*, NCH, Yng Family Pr) For Teen Moms.

Navigating Designer 4.1 T. E. rev. ed. Vince E. Yokom. (Illus.). 330p. 1995. 32.50 (*1-889231-15-0*) Instrux Ltd.

Navigating Differences: Friendships Between Gay & Straight Men. Jammie Price. LC 98-28103. (Illus.). 172p. 1998. pap. 19.95 (*1-56023-952-2*); lib. bdg. 39.95 (*0-7890-0619-7*, Harrington Park) Haworth Pr.

Navigating DOS & Windows v3.x. 1997. write for info. (*1-884486-28-2*) Wave Tech.

Navigating in a Sea of Change. Neil J. Simon & Albert B. Blixt. (Illus.). 237p. 1996. pap. 75.00 (*0-9621241-4-1*) SCIP.

Navigating in Cyberspace: A Guide to the Next Millennium. Frank Ogden. 208p. 1995. text 24.95 (*0-921912-85-4*) MW&R.

***Navigating Islands & Continents: Conversations & Contestations in & Around the Pacific: Selected Essays.** Cynthia G. Franklin et al. LC 00-27717. 2000. write for info. (*0-8248-2365-6*) Coll Lang Ling & Lit.

Navigating Midlife: Using Typology As a Guide. Eleanor Corlett & Nancy Millner. LC 93-4374. 272p. 1993. pap. 17.95 (*0-89106-061-8*, 7394, Davies-Black Pub) Consulting Psychol.

Navigating Modernity: Postcolonialism, Identity & International Relations. Albert J. Paolini. Ed. by Anthony Elliott & Anthony Moran. LC 99-19297. (Critical Perspectives on World Politics Ser.). 240p. 1999. 52.00 (*1-55587-875-X*) L Rienner.

Navigating New Markets Abroad: Charting a Course for International Business. Ed. by David M. Raddock. 272p. (C). 1993. lib. bdg. 62.50 (*0-8476-7843-1*) Rowman.

Navigating Regional Dynamics in the Post-Cold War World: Patterns of Relations in the Mediterranean Area. Stephen C. Calleya. LC 96-43126. (Illus.). 288p. 1997. text 83.95 (*1-85521-850-X*, Pub. by Dartmth Pub) Ashgate Pub Co.

Navigating Research. Langford. 2000. 35.00 (*0-323-00947-6*) Mosby Inc.

Navigating Research. Langford. 2001. text. write for info. (*0-323-01012-1*); text, teacher ed. write for info. (*0-323-01015-6*) Mosby Inc.

Navigating System 7: Understanding the Macintosh Operating System. Jan L. Harrington. LC 94-193069. 386p. 1994. pap. 24.95 incl. mac hd (*1-55828-305-6*, MIS Pr) IDG Bks.

Navigating the AS400. 2nd ed. John Enck & Michael Ryan. LC 97-25872. 512p. (C). 1997. pap. text 49.99 (*0-13-862558-1*) P-H.

Navigating the Deep River: Spirituality in African American Families. Archie Smith, Jr. LC 97-33158. 216p. (Orig.). 1997. pap. 15.95 (*0-8298-1218-0*) Pilgrim OH.

Navigating the Distances: Poems New & Selected. Bruce Bennett. LC 98-50133. 178p. 1999. 24.95 (*0-914061-79-8*) Orchises Pr.

***Navigating the Frenzied World of Work.** (Illus.). 240p. 1999. pap. 19.95 (*1-875680-36-5*) Woodslane.

Navigating the Future. Eni F. Faleomavaega. pap. 12.00 (*0-9644426-1-2*) Kin Pub.

***Navigating the Future.** Tarlow. 1999. write for info. (*0-07-134896-4*) McGraw.

Navigating the Future: A Personal Survival Guide to Achieving Success in the New Millennium. Mikela Tarlow & Philip Tarlow. LC 98-23201. 224p. 1998. pap. 16.95 (*0-07-063364-9*) McGraw.

Navigating the Internet. 3rd ed. Mark Gibbs. (Illus.). 528p. 1995. 22.50 (*0-672-30718-9*) Sams.

***Navigating the Internet: Legal Research on the World Wide Web.** Herbert N. Ramy & Samantha A. Moppett. LC 99-50143. 1999. write for info. (*0-8377-1077-4*, Rothman) W S Hein.

Navigating the Internet with America Online. Wes Tatters. LC 95-68850. 608p. 1995. 29.99 (*0-672-30763-4*) Sams.

Navigating the Internet with Windows 95. Ned Snell. 432p. 1995. 25.00 (*0-672-30765-0*) Sams.

Navigating the Internet with Windows 95, Deluxe. 2nd deluxe ed. Ned Snell. LC 95-72380. 480p. 1995. 29.99 (*1-57521-066-5*) Sams.

Navigating the Internet with Your Macintosh. Ned Snell et al. (Illus.). 360p. 1995. 29.99 (*1-57521-043-6*) Sams.

Navigating the Japanese Market: Business & Socio-Economic Perspectives. Samia El-Badry et al. 284p. (Orig.). 1994. pap. 20.00 (*1-887406-04-2*) ICTwo Inst.

Navigating the Marital Journey: MAP: A Corporate Support Program for Couples. Gary L. Bowen. LC 91-3553. 208p. 1991. 55.00 (*0-275-93423-3*, C3423, Praeger Pubs) Greenwood.

Navigating the Marketplace: Growth Strategies for Your Business. Wayne Lovern & Anna Lovern. LC 98-29049. 300p. 1998. pap. 21.95 (*1-55571-458-7*, NVMPP, Oasis Pr) PSI Resch.

Navigating the Mental Health Internet: An Internet Guided Course. David Lukoff. (Internet Guided Courses Ser.). 1999. pap. 30.00 (*0-9665126-1-8*) Internet Guides.

Navigating the Minefield: Hawkes's Narratives of Perversion. Michaele Whelan. (American University Studies XXIV: Vol. 69). 199p. (C). 1998. text 40.95 (*0-8204-3657-7*) P Lang Pubng.

Navigating the Mortgage Maze: An Interactive High-Tech Guide to Financing Your Home. Andrew E. Turnauer. 192p. (Orig.). 1996. pap. 19.95 (*0-8050-4773-5*, Owl) H Holt & Co.

Navigating the Networks. Ed. by Deborah L. Anderson et al. 255p. 1994. pap. 29.95 (*0-938734-85-7*) Info Today Inc.

Navigating the New Job Market: To Survive & Prosper in the Turbulent 90s. Jo-Ann Vega. LC 92-90080. 160p. (Orig.). 1992. pap. 14.95 (*0-9632161-6-3*) JV Career & Human RCS.

Navigating the NHS: Core Issues for Clinicians. Ed. by Peter Lees. 1996. write for info. (*1-85775-106-X*, Radcliffe Med Pr) Scovill Paterson.

***Navigating the Politics of De-Tracking: Leadership Strategies.** 354p. 2000. write for info. (*1-57517-285-2*) SkyLght.

Navigating the Source. Stanley Schatt. 1985. pap. 12.95 (*0-671-54300-8*) S&S Trade.

***Navigating the Terror.** John Hyatt. (Illus.). 256p. 2000. pap. 15.00 (*1-899858-66-0*, Pub. by Ellipsis) Norton.

***Navigating the Tides of Change: With Stories from Science, the Sacred & a Wise Planet.** David La Chapelle. 256p. 2001. pap. 16.95 (*0-86571-424-X*, Pub. by New Soc Pubs) Consort Bk Sales.

***Navigating the Waters of the Paso del Norte: A People's Guide.** Jurgen Schmandt et al. (U. S. - Mexican Special Publications: Vol. 5). 54p. 1999. pap. 10.00 (*0-89940-332-8*) LBJ Sch Pub Aff.

Navigating the Web. Curt Robbins. Ed. by Susan Alcorn & Holly Nichols. (Illus.). 141p. 1997. pap. text 29.00 (*1-891976-01-X*) NetQuest Pubg.

Navigating the Web: Mastering Internet Hypermedia. DDC Publishing Staff & Curt Robbins. (One-Day Course Ser.). (Illus.). 148p. 1999. pap. 18.00 (*1-56243-828-X*) DDC Pub.

Navigating the Yellow Stream: A Voyage into the Cesspool of Urine Collection for Drug Testing. Paul Crumrine. LC 91-66421. 192p. 1991. pap. 9.95 (*0-9631221-0-X*) Nest Egg Pr.

Navigating Through a Strange Land: A Book for Brain Tumor Patients & Their Families. Tricia A. Roloff. LC 94-25863. (Illus.). 248p. 1995. pap. 16.95 (*0-9641214-1-7*) Indigo Pr AR.

Navigating Through Change. Harry Woodward & Mary B. Woodward. LC 93-48345. 216p. 1994. text 27.50 (*0-7863-0233-X*, Irwn Prfssnl) McGraw-Hill Prof.

***Navigating Toward Home: Charting Your Course Toward Biblical Manhood.** Craig Peters. 192p. 2000. pap. 10.95 (*1-58169-047-9*, Evergrn Pr AL) Genesis Comm Inc.

Navigating Visio Version 4.0. Vince Yokan. Ed. by Hugh Hay-Roe. (Illus.). 204p. (C). 1996. spiral bd. 28.00 (*1-889231-03-7*) Instrux Ltd.

Navigating Windows 95 & Windows NT Workstation v4.0. 1997. write for info. (*1-884486-29-0*) Wave Tech.

***Navigating Your Career: 21 of Americas Leading Headhunters Tell You How It's Done.** Christopher W. Hunt & Scott A. Scanlon. LC 98-8157. 256p. 1998. pap. 16.95 (*0-471-25434-7*) Wiley.

***Navigating Your Way Through the Federal Physician Self-Referral Law.** 3rd rev. ed. Doug Mancino et al. 1998. pap. 169.00 (*0-929156-45-5*) Atlantic Info Services Inc.

Navigatio Sancti Brendani Abbatis: From Early Latin Manuscripts. Ed. by Carl Selmer. LC 58-14184. (University of Norte Dame Publications in Mediaeval Studies: Vol. 16). 184p. reprint ed. pap. 57.10 (*0-608-14232-8*, 202207400024) Bks Demand.

Navigation. (Specialty Diver Ser.). 30p. 1991. teacher ed. 6.95 (*1-880229-03-X*); pap. text 10.95 (*1-880229-02-1*) Concept Sys.

Navigation: Land, Sea, Air & Space. Ed. by Myron Kayton. LC 89-39737. 480p. 1990. 79.95 (*0-87942-257-2*, PC02469) Inst Electrical.

Navigation & Coastal Piloting. Gregory D. Szczurek. (Illus.). 287p. 1988. 49.95 (*0-932889-00-X*) Examco Inc.

Navigation & Control Technologies for Unmanned Systems II. Scott A. Speigle. LC 98-120044. 13p. 1997. pap. 48.00 (*0-8194-2502-8*) SPIE.

Navigation & Direction: The Story of HMS Dryad. Brian B. Schofield. 150p. 1982. 60.00 (*0-85937-087-9*) St Mut.

Navigation & Intelligent Transportation Systems. Ron Jurgen. LC 98-86818. (Automotive Electronic Series). 40p. 1998. 79.00 (*0-7680-0264-8*, PT-72) Soc Auto Engineers.

Navigation & Mobile Telecommunications Technologies for European Road Freight Operations in the Late 1990s. Robert G. Wilfong. (Illus.). 225p. (Orig.). 1996. pap. 57.50 (*90-407-1376-6*, Pub. by Delft U Pr) Coronet Bks.

Navigation at Speed. Tim Bartlett. 64p. (C). 1990. text 65.00 (*0-906754-76-3*, Pub. by Fernhurst Bks) St Mut.

Navigation Control Manual. 2nd ed. A. G. Bole et al. (Illus.). 314p. 1992. pap. 79.95 (*0-7506-0542-1*) Buttrwrth-Heinemann.

Navigation for Masters: A Book Containing up to Date Modern Technical Practices of Seamanship & Navigation. David J. House. 426p. (C). 1995. 120.00 (*1-85609-073-6*, Pub. by Witherby & Co) St Mut.

Navigation for School & College. rev. ed. A. C. Gardner & W. G. Creelman. (C). 1987. 50.00 (*0-85174-236-X*) St Mut.

Navigation in the Age of Discovery: An Introduction. Duane A. Cline. LC 90-91870. (Illus.). 214p. (Orig.). 1990. pap. 17.50 (*0-9627213-0-1*) Montfleury.

Navigation Interieure (Remplace TERM/15) Office des Nations Unies a Geneve. (FRE.). 205p. 1997. pap. 42.00 (*92-1-000058-7*) UN.

Navigation of a Rainmaker: An Apocalyptic Vision of War-Torn Africa. Jamal Mahjoub. (African Writers Ser.). 184p. (Orig.). (C). 1989. pap. 9.95 (*0-435-90560-0*) Heinemann.

Navigation on the High Seas: Analytical Studies of the Law of the Sea Convention - Navigation of the High Seas. (The Law of the Sea Ser.). 91p. pap. 12.00 (*92-1-133315-6*, E.89.V.2) UN.

Navigation Primer for Fishermen. F. S. Howell. 1978. 59.00 (*0-7855-6947-2*) St Mut.

Navigation Primer for Yachtsmen. F. S. Howell. (Illus.). 229p. (C). 1981. 100.00 (*0-85288-071-5*, Pub. by Laurie Norie & Wilson Ltd) St Mut.

Navigation Record Forms. Wilson Ltd. Staff & Imray L. Norie. (C). 1989. 45.00 (*0-7855-5952-3*, Pub. by Laurie Norie & Wilson Ltd) St Mut.

Navigation Rules: International-Inland. (Transportation Ser.). 1991. lib. bdg. 75.00 (*0-8490-5025-1*) Gordon Pr.

Navigation Rules: International-Inland. 1995. lib. bdg. 253.75 (*0-8490-7511-4*) Gordon Pr.

Navigation Rules: International-Inland. 1997. lib. bdg. 251.95 (*0-8490-8132-7*) Gordon Pr.

Navigation Rules: Rules of the Road. 5th rev. ed. Matt Morehouse. 96p. 1999. pap. 8.95 (*0-939837-30-7*) Paradise Cay Pubns.

***Navigation Rules - Rules of the Road: For Inland & International Waters.** 7th rev. ed. Ed. by John M. Morehouse. 104p. 2000. pap. 9.95 (*0-939837-40-4*, Pub. by Paradise Cay Pubns) R Hale & Co.

Navigation Rules, International-Inland. 1996. per. 11.00 (*0-16-048540-1*) USGPO.

***Navigation Rules, International-inland.** 226p. 1999. per. 13.00 (*0-16-050057-5*) USGPO.

Navigation Rules, International-Inland. D. A. Appelbaum. (Illus.). 212p. 1998. pap. text 40.00 (*0-7881-3951-7*) DIANE Pub.

Navigation Rules of the Road. rev. ed. George Trowbridge. (Illus.). 108p. 1995. pap. text 34.95 incl. disk (*1-888116-00-5*) DG Training.

Navigation Rules of the Road, Unit 500. rev. ed. George Trowbridge. (Illus.). 90p. 1996. pap. text 9.34 (*1-888116-05-6*) DG Training.

Navigation, Strategy & Tactics. Stuart Quarrie. 1998. pap. text 34.95 (*0-85265-031-0*) Fernhurst Bks.

Navigational & Surveying Instruments: Industry & Trade Summary. Sundar A. Shetty. (Illus.). 52p. (Orig.). (C). 1994. pap. text 30.00 (*0-7881-0544-2*) DIANE Pub.

N

An Asterisk (*) at the beginning of an entry indicates that the title is appearing for the first time.

Navigational Astronomy: A Non-Technical Step-by-Step Introduction to the Wonders of the Night Sky, Organized for the Seasons of the Year. (Learning Guides Ser.). (Illus.). 60p. Date not set. pap. text 5.79 (*1-891148-09-5*) US Power.

Navigational Guide to the Adriatic. A. Simovic. (Illus.). 152p. (C). 1988. 325.00 (*0-7855-5159-X*, Pub. by Collets) St Mut.

Navigations: One Man Explores the Americas & Discovers Himself. Ted Kerasote. LC 86-5723. (Illus.). 192p. 1986. 16.95 (*0-8117-1013-0*) Stackpole.

Navigator, Vol. 1. Molinsky & Bli. 2001. pap. text, teacher ed. write for info. (*0-13-359605-2*) P-H.

Navigator, Vol. 3. Molinsky & Bli. 2001. pap. text. write for info. (*0-13-359589-7*) P-H.

Navigator, Vol. 4. Molinsky & Bli. 2001. pap. text. write for info. (*0-13-359597-8*) P-H.

Navigator Basic, Vol. 1. Molinsky & Bli. 2001. pap. text 9.27 (*0-13-359555-2*) P-H.

Navigator Bible Study Handbook. rev. ed. Navigators Staff. Ed. by Karen Lee-Thorp. LC 79-87654. (Illus.). 120p. 1994. pap. 7.00 (*0-89109-075-4*) NavPress.

Navigator in the South Seas. Brett Hilder. (Illus.). 1980. pap. 10.00 (*0-936128-44-5*) De Young Pr.

Navigator of the Flood. Mario Brelich. Tr. by John Shepley from ITA. LC 91-61535. 160p. 1991. 25.95 (*0-910395-79-9*) Marlboro Pr.

Navigator of the Flood. Mario Brelich. Tr. & Frwd. by John Shepley. LC 91-61535. 160p. 1994. pap. 10.95 (*0-910395-80-2*) Marlboro Pr.

Navigator 1. Bill Bliss & Steven J. Molinsky. LC 95-514. 176p. 1995. pap. text 9.73 (*0-13-359563-3*) P-H.

Navigator 2. Steven J. Molinsky & Bill Bliss. 160p. 1997. pap. text 9.73 (*0-13-359571-4*) P-H.

Navigators: African American Musicians, Dancers & Visual Artists in Acadame. Theresa Jenoure. LC 99-17224. (SUNY Series, The Social Context of Education). 248p. (C). 1999. text 54.50 (*0-7914-4353-1*, Suny Pr); pap. text 17.95 (*0-7914-4354-X*, Suny Pr) State U NY Pr.

Navigator's Log Book. Wilson Ltd. Staff & Imray L. Norie. (C). 1989. ring bd. 53.00 (*0-7855-5955-8*, Pub. by Laurie Norie & Wilson Ltd); 15.00 (*0-7855-5956-6*, Pub. by Laurie Norie & Wilson Ltd) St Mut.

Navigator's Log of a Tour in Bomber Command. Jack Rodgers. (C). 1989. 35.00 (*0-86303-254-0*) St Mut.

Navigator's Pocket Calculator Handbook. H. Rolf Noer. LC 82-74136. (Illus.). 173p. (Orig.). reprint ed. pap. 53.70 (*0-7837-1212-X*, 204174400023) Bks Demand.

Navigators Supply. William Barlow. LC 76-38150. (English Experience Ser.: No. 430). 100p. 1972. reprint ed. 30.00 (*90-221-0430-3*) Walter J Johnson.

Navigators Tarot of the Mystic Sea. Julia A. Turk. LC 97-34144. 1997. pap. 14.00 (*1-57281-023-8*, BK163) US Games Syst.

Navigators Tarot of the Mystic Sea Deck & Book Set. Julia Turk. 256p. 1997. pap. 30.00 (*1-57281-029-7*, NMS99) US Games Syst.

Navire Argo. Richard Jorif. (FRE.). 344p. 1989. pap. 17.95 (*0-7859-2568-6*, 2070381285) Fr & Eur.

Navire Night. Marguerite Duras. (FRE.). 1989. pap. 10.95 (*0-8288-3639-6*) Fr & Eur.

Navire Night. Marguerite Duras. (Folio Ser.: No. 2009). (FRE.). 1989. pap. 6.95 (*2-07-038097-1*) Schoenhof.

Navire Ou Consolation du Roi Francois 1er a Sasoeur Marguerite: Edition Critique. Marguerite D'Angouleme. Ed. by Robert Marichal. (FRE.). 347p. 1956. pap. 115.00 (*0-7859-5533-X*) Fr & Eur.

***Navohar.** Hilari Bell. 336p. 2000. mass mkt. 6.99 (*0-451-45788-9*, ROC) NAL.

***NAVPAC & Compact Data, 2001-2005: Astro-Navigation Methods & Software for the PC.** Nautical Almanac Office Staff. 125p. 2000. pap. 80.00 incl. cd-rom (*0-11-887311-3*, Pub. by Statnry Office) Balogh.

***Navstar Global Positioning System Surveying.** American Society of Civil Engineers Staff. LC 99-41148. (Technical Engineering & Design Guides Ser.). 2000. write for info. (*0-7844-0353-8*) Am Soc Civil Eng.

Navtex Manual. IMO Staff. (C). 1988. 75.00 (*0-7855-0021-9*, IMO 951E, Pub. by Intl Maritime Org); 65.00 (*0-7855-7076-4*, IMO 952F, Pub. by Intl Maritime Org); 70.00 (*0-7855-7077-2*, IMO 953S, Pub. by Intl Maritime Org) St Mut.

Navtex Manual. International Maritime Organization Staff. 1994. pap. 40.00 (*0-7855-0509-1*, Pub. by Intl Maritime Org) St Mut.

Navy. M. Arthur. text 45.00 (*0-340-68469-0*, Pub. by Hodder & Stought Ltd) Trafalgar.

***Navy.** Ed. by W. J. Holland. (Illus.). 352p. 2000. 75.00 (*0-88363-100-8*) H L Levin.

Navy: 200 Years of the Department of the Navy. Ed. by Robert Yehling & Charles Oldham. (Illus.). 272p. 1998. pap. 12.95 (*0-9644712-9-9*) Faircount Intl.

Navy Acquisition Procedures Supplement. Dept. of the Navy Staff. 96p. 1992. ring bd. 125.00 (*1-56726-064-0*) Mgmt Concepts.

Navy & German Power Politics, 1862-1914. Ivo N. Lambi. 356p. (C). 1984. text 65.00 (*0-04-943035-1*) Routledge.

***Navy & Marine Corps Fire Apparatus: 1866-2000 Photo Gallery.** Bill Killen. (Illus.). 224p. 2000. pap. 24.95 (*1-58388-031-3*, 130634AE, Pub. by Iconografix) Motorbooks Intl.

Navy & Marine Corps Performance Writing Guide. Douglas L. Drewry. (Illus.). 389p. (Orig.). 1986. pap. 23.95 (*0-9623673-7-0*) Prof Mgmt Spectrum.

Navy & You. Dorothy Hole. LC 92-9055. (Armed Forces Ser.). (Illus.). 48p. (J). (gr. 5-6). 1993. lib. bdg. 12.95 (*0-89686-767-6*, Crstwood Hse) Silver Burdett Pr.

Navy Aviation: AV-813 Harrier Remanufacture Strategy Found Not to Be the Most Cost-Effective Option. (Illus.). 15p. (Orig.). (C). 1996. pap. text 20.00 (*0-7881-2859-0*) DIANE Pub.

Navy Aviation: F/A-18E/F Will Provide Marginal Operational Improvement at High Cost. (Illus.). 101p. (Orig.). (C). 1996. pap. text 30.00 (*0-7881-3404-3*) DIANE Pub.

Navy Blue. Watson-Guptill Publications, Inc. Staff. (Watson-Guptill Sketchbooks). 1997. 6.50 (*0-8230-5634-1*) Watsn-Guptill.

Navy Board Ship Models, 1650-1750. John Franklin. LC 88-63546. (Illus.). 192p. 1989. 41.95 (*0-87021-442-X*) Naval Inst Pr.

Navy Carrier Battle Groups: The Structure & Affordability of the Future Force. Norman J. Rabkin et al. (Illus.). 148p. (C). 1997. reprint ed. pap. text 40.00 (*0-7881-4134-1*) DIANE Pub.

Navy Civil Engineer. Government Printing Office Staff. pap. 6.50 (*0-16-010261-8*) USGPO.

Navy Day by Day: Historic Naval Events in Australia & Abroad. Lew Lind. LC 97-114780. (Illus.). 272p. 1997. 42.95 (*0-86417-787-9*, Pub. by Kangaroo Pr) Seven Hills Bk.

***Navy Diver.** David Robbins. (Illus.). (J). 2000. mass mkt. 6.99 (*0-451-40974-4*, Onyx) NAL.

Navy Eternal. Lewis A. Ritchie. LC 72-134977. (Short Story Index Reprint Ser.). 1977. 19.95 (*0-8369-3706-6*) Ayer.

Navy Fighters. David Baker. (Military Aircraft Library). (Illus.). 48p. (J). (gr. 3-8). 1987. 13.95 (*0-685-67594-7*) Rourke Corp.

Navy Football: Gridiron Legends & Fighting Heroes. Jack Clary. LC 97-11916. (Illus.). 280p. 1997. 45.00 (*1-55750-106-8*) Naval Inst Pr.

Navy Gray: Engineering the Confederate Navy on the Chattahoochee & Apalachicola Rivers. Maxine Turner. (Civil War Georgia Ser.). 376p. 1999. pap. 22.00 (*0-86554-642-8*) Mercer Univ Pr.

Navy Hunts the CRG 3070. Lawrence Thompson. 158p. Date not set. 18.95 (*0-8488-2409-1*) Amereon Ltd.

Navy in India 1763-1783. RICHMOND. 448p. 1993. 79.95 (*0-7512-0123-5*) Ashgate Pub Co.

Navy in Newport. Lionel Wyld. (Images of America Ser.). (Illus.). 126p. 1997. pap. 16.99 (*0-7524-0471-7*) Arcadia Publng.

Navy in the Post-Cold War World: The Uses & Value of Strategic Sea Power. Colin S. Gray. 208p. (C). 1994. 37.50 (*0-271-01307-9*); pap. 17.95 (*0-271-01308-7*) Pa St U Pr.

Navy in the War of 1739-1748, Vol. 3. RICHMOND. 968p. 1993. 192.95 (*0-7512-0121-9*) Ashgate Pub Co.

Navy in Toms Drawings. 1997. pap. 10.00 (*1-879055-10-4*) Tom Finland.

***Navy Island: Historic Treasure of the Niagara Heritage - Archaeology - Folklore.** Roland L. Nafus. (Illus.). 168p. 1998. pap. 14.95 (*0-941967-21-2*) Old Fort Niagara Assn.

Navy Laboratories: Plans for Consolidation & Progress Toward Implementation. Richard J. Price et al. (Illus.). 50p. (C). 1997. reprint ed. pap. text 30.00 (*0-7881-4130-9*) DIANE Pub.

Navy League of the United States. Armin Rappaport. LC 62-8227. 284p. reprint ed. pap. 88.10 (*0-7837-3684-3*, 204355800009) Bks Demand.

***Navy List, 1999: Corrected to 12th April 1999.** Ministry of Defence (Navy) Staff. xiv, 302p. 1999. 50.00 (*0-11-772912-4*, Pub. by Statnry Office) Balogh.

Navy List 1997. 415p. 1997. pap. 45.00 (*0-11-772869-1*, Pub. by Statnry Office) Bernan Associates.

Navy List, 1996. annuals 415p. 1996. pap. 40.00 (*0-11-772825-X*, HM2825X, Pub. by Statnry Office) Bernan Associates.

Navy Marriages & Deployment. Elwood Carlson & Ruth Carlson. 114p. (Orig.). 1984. pap. text 18.00 (*0-8191-4159-3*); lib. bdg. 40.00 (*0-8191-4158-5*) U Pr of Amer.

Navy Medicine. Government Printing Office Staff. pap. 11.00 (*0-16-010318-5*) USGPO.

Navy of the American Revolution. Charles Paullin. LC 73-122997. (American History & Americana Ser.: No. 47). 1970. reprint ed. lib. bdg. 75.00 (*0-8383-1130-X*) M S G Haskell Hse.

Navy of the Republic of Texas, 1835-1845. limited ed. Alex Dienst. (Source Texana Ser.: No. 2). 1987. reprint ed. 100.00 (*0-88342-066-X*) Old Army.

Navy Ordinance: Analysis of Business Area Price Increases & Financial Losses. Smith. (Illus.). 50p. 1999. reprint ed. text 20.00 (*0-7881-7939-X*) DIANE Pub.

Navy Pier. Douglas Bukowski. (Illus.). 96p. 1996. text 19.95 (*1-56663-139-4*, Pub. by I R Dee) Natl Bk Netwk.

Navy Pier: A Chicago Landmark. Douglas Bukowski. (Illus.). 96p. 1996. pap. 12.95 (*1-56663-115-7*, Pub. by I R Dee) Natl Bk Netwk.

Navy Poems. Joe McDonald. (Limited Chapbook Ser.). 1998. pap. text 10.00 (*1-56439-073-X*, Pub. by Ridgeway) Partners Pubs Grp.

Navy Publications. 1992. lib. bdg. 288.95 (*0-8490-5588-1*) Gordon Pr.

Navy RDT&E Planning in an Age of Transition: A Survey Guide to Contemporary Literature. Rodney P. Carlisle. LC 97-39907. 1997. write for info. (*0-945274-37-8*) Naval Hist Ctr.

Navy Reader. Ed. by William H. Fetridge. LC 75-134076. (Essay Index Reprint Ser.). 1977. 30.95 (*0-8369-2155-0*) Ayer.

Navy Seal Exercises: Total Body Workout. Mark De Lisle. Ed. by R. J. Wolf. (Illus.). 116p. (Orig.). 1996. reprint ed. pap. text 19.95 (*0-9654093-0-9*) Cutting Edge Fit.

***Navy Seal Nutrition Guide.** 224p. 1998. per. 18.00 (*0-16-058994-0*) USGPO.

Navy Seal Nutrition Guide. Patricia A. Deuster et al. (Illus.). 208p. (Orig.). 1996. reprint ed. pap. text 30.00 (*0-7881-2990-2*) DIANE Pub.

***Navy Seal Physical Fitness Guide.** Frank K. Butler. 298p. 1998. per. 25.00 (*0-16-061339-6*) USGPO.

Navy Seal Physical Fitness Guide. Ed. by Patricia A. Duester. (Illus.). 282p. 1998. pap. text 40.00 (*0-7881-7362-6*) DIANE Pub.

Navy SEAL Workout. Mark De Lisle. LC 97-38946. (Illus.). 160p. 1998. pap. 14.95 (*0-8092-2902-1*, 290210, Contemporary Bks) NTC Contemp Pub Co.

***Navy Seals, Vol. 2.** Mike Murray. 2000. 5.99 (*0-451-19971-5*, Sig) NAL.

Navy Seals: Undersea Commandoes. Marc A. Cerasini. (YA). 1997. pap. write for info. (*0-679-88245-6*, Bullseye Bks) Random Bks Yng Read.

Navy Second to None: The Development of Modern American Naval Policy. George T. Davis. LC 77-110826. (Illus.). 508p. 1971. reprint ed. lib. bdg. 79.50 (*0-8371-3226-6*, DANS, Greenwood Pr) Greenwood.

Navy Song Book. Ed. by Barry Leonard. (Illus.). 216p. 1998. reprint ed. pap. text 25.00 (*0-7881-7468-1*) DIANE Pub.

Navy Spouse's Guide. Laura H. Stavrides. LC 97-26134. (Illus.). 224p. 1997. 26.95 (*1-55750-834-8*) Naval Inst Pr.

Navy Stock List & Publications Index, 2 vols., Set. 1995. lib. bdg. 625.99 (*0-8490-8374-5*) Gordon Pr.

Navy Strike Planes. David Baker. (Military Aircraft Library). (Illus.). 48p. (J). (gr. 3-8). 1989. 13.95 (*0-685-58602-2*) Rourke Corp.

Navy Supply: Improved Material Management Can Reduce Shipyard Costs. (Illus.). 57p. (Orig.). (C). 1995. pap. text 20.00 (*0-7881-2218-5*) DIANE Pub.

Navy Tapestry Leather Binder: With Detachable Shoulder Strap. (Believer's Life System Women's Edition Ser.). 1998. ring bd. 49.99 (*0-8024-6965-5*) Moody.

Navy Times Book of Submarines: A Political, Social & Military History. Brayton Harris. Ed. by Walter J. Boyne. LC 97-38078. 416p. 1997. 31.95 (*0-425-15777-6*) Berkley Pub.

Navy V-12. Turner Publishing Company Staff. (Illus.). 144p. Date not set. 49.95 (*1-56311-189-6*) Turner Pub KY.

Navy V-12 Program: Leadership for a Lifetime. James G. Schneider. 596p. 1996. 29.95 (*0-9636707-0-0*); pap. 19.95 (*0-9636707-1-9*) Marlow Bks.

Navy Was Never Blue! 5 Found It Rosy-Hued! Dorothy T. Holland. 640p. 1992. 20.00 (*1-881118-08-8*) Miramot Pubs.

Navy-Wide Examination Advancement Guide for E-3 - 4 - 5. Harlan E. Flick. (Illus.). 264p. (Orig.). 1989. pap. 21.95 (*0-9623673-8-9*) Prof Mgmt Spectrum.

Navy-Wide Examination Advancement Guide for E-6 - E-7. Harlan E. Flick. (Illus.). 288p. (Orig.). 1990. pap. 21.95 (*0-9623673-6-2*) Prof Mgmt Spectrum.

Navya-Nyaya Doctrine of Negation: The Semantics & Ontology of Negative Statements in Navya-Navya Pgilosophy. Bimal K. Matilal. LC 67-27088. (Oriental Ser.: No. 46). (Illus.). 219p. 1968. 15.00 (*0-674-60650-7*) HUP.

Navya Nyaya System of Logic. D. C. Guha. (C). 1979. pap. 10.00 (*0-8364-2634-7*, Pub. by Motilal Bnarsidass) S Asia.

Navya Nyaya System of Logic. 3rd enl. ed. D. C. Guha. 1979. 18.50 (*0-89684-059-X*, Pub. by Motilal Bnarsidass) S Asia.

Naw-Ruz: New Day: A Compilation. xii, 92 p. 1992. 14.95 (*0-933770-84-7*) Kalimat.

Nawal el Saadawi Reader: Selected Essays, 1970-1996. Nawal El Saadawi. LC 97-25250. 288p. 1997. text 62.50 (*1-85649-513-2*, Pub. by Zed Books); text 22.50 (*1-85649-514-0*, Pub. by Zed Books) St Martin.

NAWDAC Celebrates 70 Years. (Initiatives Ser.: Vol. 49, No. 2). 1986. 15.00 (*0-614-14214-8*) Natl Assn Women.

Naxal Violence. Sachchidanand Pandey. 1985. 18.00 (*81-7001-003-9*, Pub. by Chanakya) S Asia.

Naxalite Movement in India. S. Jawaid. 140p. 1979. 13.95 (*0-318-36621-5*) Asia Bk Corp.

Naxalites & Their Ideology. Rabindra Ray. 262p. 1993. reprint ed. pap. text 10.95 (*0-19-563125-0*) OUP.

Naya Nuki: Shoshoni Girl Who Ran. Kenneth Thomasma. LC 89-143272. (Amazing Indian Children Ser.). (Illus.). 176p. (J). (gr. 4-7). 1983. 9.99 (*0-8010-8869-0*); pap. 5.99 (*0-8010-8868-2*) Baker Bks.

Naya Nuki: Shoshoni Girl Who Ran. Kenneth Thomasma. LC 83-143272. (Amazing Indian Children Ser.). (J). 1991. 12.05 (*0-606-10268-X*, Pub. by Turtleback) Demco.

Naya, the Inuit Cinderella. large type ed. Brittany Marceau-Chenkie. (Illus.). 24p. (J). (ps-3). 1999. pap. 7.95 (*1-894303-05-9*) RRP.

Nayaks of Tanjore. V. Vriddhagirisan. Ed. & Pref. by C. S. Srinivasachariar. (C). 1995. reprint ed. 34.00 (*81-206-0996-4*, Pub. by Asian Educ Servs) S Asia.

Nayantara Sahgal & Doris Lessing: A Feminist Study in Comparison. Neena Arora. 1991. text 25.00 (*81-85218-31-5*, Pub. by Prestige) Advent Bks Div.

Nayantara Sahgal's India: Passion, Politics & History. Ed. by Ralph J. Crane. LC 98-909223. xiv, 178p. 1998. write for info. (*81-207-2009-1*) Sterling Pub.

Nayars of Malabar. F. Fawcett. (Illus.). 144p. 1986. reprint ed. 18.50 (*0-8364-1731-3*, Pub. by Manohar) S Asia.

Naysayer's Yearbook. Sean Miller. 184p. 1997. pap. 16.95 (*0-9658099-0-0*) Presence Pr.

Nazaire et les Mousquetaires. Jasmine Dube. (Novels in the Premier Roman Ser.). (FRE.). 64p. (J). (gr. 2-5). 1995. pap. 8.95 (*2-89021-231-9*, Pub. by La Courte Ech) Firefly Bks Ltd.

Nazare. A. W. Brogger. (C). 1997. pap. text 19.00 (*0-15-504381-1*) Harcourt Coll Pubs.

Nazare: Men & Women in a Prebureaucratic Portuguese Village. Jan Brogger. Ed. by Louise S. Spindler & George D. Spindler. LC 91-32074. (Spindler Ser. (Anthropology)). (Illus.). xii, 135p. (C). 1992. pap. text 13.50 (*0-03-043382-7*) Harcourt Coll Pubs.

Nazarena an American Anchoress. Thomas Matus. LC 98-14691. 208p. 1998. pap. 16.95 (*0-8091-3792-5*, 3792-5) Paulist Pr.

***Nazarene.** Eugenio Zolli. Tr. by Cyril Vollert from ITA. 312p. 1999. pap. 25.00 (*1-892875-90-X*) New Hope Publicatns.

Nazarene. Sholem Asch. 704p. 1996. reprint ed. pap. 15.95 (*0-7867-0379-2*) Carroll & Graf.

Nazarene Jewish Christianity: From the End of the New Testament Period until Its Disappearance in the Fourth Century. Ray A. Pritz. 153p. 1992. 18.00 (*965-223-798-1*, Pub. by Magnes Pr) Gefen Bks.

Nazarenes: A Brotherhood of German Painters in Rome. Keith Andrews. LC 86-81980. (Illus.). 148p. 1989. reprint ed. lib. bdg. 50.00 (*0-87817-306-4*) Hacker.

Nazareth along the Banks of the Ganges, 1947-1990. Eugenia Muething. LC 97-74184. (Illus.). 272p. 1997. write for info. (*1-56469-035-0*); pap. write for info. (*1-56469-036-9*) Harmony Hse Pub.

Nazareth Capitals & the Crusader Shrine of the Annunciation. Jaroslav Folda. LC 86-820. (College Art Association Monographs: Vol. 42). (Illus.). 162p. 1986. 45.00 (*0-271-00430-4*) Pa St U Pr.

Nazareth Hill. Ramsey Campbell. LC 96-6567. 384p. 1997. text 23.95 (*0-312-86344-6*) St Martin.

Nazareth Hill: Gates of Hades. Ramsey Campbell. 1998. mass mkt. 5.99 (*0-8125-3930-3*, Pub. by Tor Bks) St Martin.

Nazarin. Benito Perez Galdos. Tr. by Robert Rudder & Gloria Arjona from SPA. LC 97-17339. (Discoveries Ser.). 200p. 1997. pap. text 15.95 (*0-935480-75-7*) Lat Am Lit Rev Pr.

Nazarin. Benito Perez Galdos. Tr. & Intro. by Jo Labanyi. LC 92-41138. (World's Classics Ser.). (Illus.). 232p. 1993. pap. 9.95 (*0-19-282878-9*) OUP.

Nazariyat al Maqasid 'Inda al Imam al Shatibi: The Theory of the Law's Objectives According to al Shatibi. 2nd ed. Ahmad A. Raysuni. LC 92-8243. (Silsilat al Rasa'il al Jami'iyah Ser.: No. 1). (ARA.). 383p. 1993. 18.00 (*1-56564-036-5*); pap. 12.00 (*1-56564-037-3*) IIIT VA.

Nazariyat al Ma'rifah Bayna al Qur'an Wa'l Falsafah: Epystinology Between the Qur'an & Philosophy. Rajih A. Kurdi. (Silsilat al Rasa'il al Jami'iyah Ser.: No. 2). 828p. (C). 1992. text 25.00 (*0-912463-68-6*) IIIT VA.

Nazariyat Al-siyasah Al-mugarana: Mugaraba Epitemologiat. large type ed. Nasr M. Arif. LC 96-46876. (ARA.). 414p. 1998. pap. text 10.00 (*0-9661494-1-6*) SISS.

Nazariyat Al-siyasah Al-mugarana: Mugaraba Epitimologiat. large type ed. Nasr M. Arif. LC 96-46876. (ARA.). 414p. (C). 1998. 15.00 (*0-9661494-0-8*) SISS.

Nazariyat al Tanmiyah al Siyasiyah al Mu'asirah - Contemporary Theories of Political Development: Dirasah Naqdiyah Muqaranah fi Daw' al Manzur al Hadari al Islami - Islamic Viewpoint. 2nd ed. Nasr M. Arif. LC 91-44547. (Silsilat al Rasa'il al Jami'iyah Ser.: No. 6). (ARA.). 481p. 1992. 18.00 (*1-56564-017-9*); pap. 12.00 (*1-56564-018-7*) IIIT VA.

Nazca Plate: Crustal Formation & Andean Convergence: A Volume Dedicated to George P. Woollard. George P. Woollard. Ed. by LaVerne D. Kulm et al. LC 81-7167. (Geological Society of America Ser.: Vol. 154). (Illus.). 835p. 1981. reprint ed. pap. 200.00 (*0-608-07707-0*, 206779600001) Bks Demand.

Nazca Plate: Crustal Formation & Andean Convergence: A Volume Dedicated to George P. Woollard Supplement. George P. Woollard. Ed. by LaVerne D. Kulm et al. LC 81-7167. (Geological Society of America Ser.: Vol. 154). (Illus.). 113p. 1981. reprint ed. pap. 35.10 (*0-608-07708-9*, 206779600002) Bks Demand.

Nazi among Jews. B. B. Dandekar. Ed. by B. S. Benjamin. 272p. 1990. 14.95 (*0-942387-06-6*) AB Lit Hse.

Nazi Biology & Schools. Anne Baumer-Schleinkofer. LC 95-30154. 252p. 1995. 51.95 (*3-631-48798-3*) P Lang Pubng.

***Nazi Chic? German Politics & Women's Fashion, 1915-1945.** Irene Guenther. 300p. 2001. 65.00 (*1-85973-400-6*, Pub. by Berg Pubs) NYU Pr.

***Nazi Childhood.** Winfried Weiss. 196p. (Orig.). 2000. pap. 15.00 (*0-88962-727-4*, Pub. by Mosaic) Midpt Trade.

Nazi Conquest Through German Culture. Ralph F. Bischoff. LC 78-63651. (Studies in Fascism: Ideology & Practice). reprint ed. 37.50 (*0-404-16906-6*) AMS Pr.

Nazi Conspiracy & Aggression, Set. Office of the United States Chief of Counsel for P. LC 96-79659. 1996. reprint ed. 1195.00 (*1-57588-202-7*, 310890) W S Hein.

Nazi Conspiracy & Aggression: Office of United States Chief of Counsel for Prosecution of Axis Criminality, 8 vols., Suppl. A & B. 12000p. 1999. reprint ed. 2450.00 (*1-56169-440-1*) Gaunt.

Nazi Conspiracy in Spain. LC 77-180418. reprint ed. 24.50 (*0-404-56193-4*) AMS Pr.

Nazi Dictatorship: A Study in Social Pathology & the Politics of Fascism. Frederick L. Schuman. reprint ed. 49.50 (*0-404-56403-8*) AMS Pr.

Nazi Dictatorship: Problems & Perspectives of Interpretation. 2nd ed. Ian Kershaw. 224p. 1989. pap. 15.95 (*0-340-49008-X*, Pub. by E A) Routldge.

Nazi Dictatorship: Problems & Perspectives of Interpretation. 3rd ed. Ian Kershaw. LC 92-47083. 256p. 1995. pap. text 18.95 (*0-340-55047-3*, B0096, Pub. by E A) St Martin.

***Nazi Dictatorship: Problems & Perspectives of Interpretation.** 4th ed. Ian Kershaw. 256p. 2000. pap. text 19.95 (*0-340-76028-1*, Pub. by E A) OUP.

Nazi Doctors & the Nuremberg Code: Human Rights in Human Experimentation. Ed. by George J. Annas & Michael A. Grodin. (Illus.). 400p. 1995. reprint ed. pap. text 24.95 (*0-19-510106-5*) OUP.

An Asterisk (*) at the beginning of an entry indicates that the title is appearing for the first time.

Nazi Economic Recovery 1932-1938. 2nd ed. R. J. Overy. (New Studies in Economic & Social History: No. 27). (Illus.). 84p. (C). 1996. text 34.95 (*0-521-55286-9*); pap. text 10.95 (*0-521-55767-4*) Cambridge U Pr.

Nazi Elite. Ed. by Ronald Smelser & Rainer Zitelmann. LC 92-37036. 260p. (C). 1993. text 42.50 (*0-8147-7950-6*) NYU Pr.

Nazi Family Policy, 1933-1945. Lisa Pine. LC 98-116485. 1997. 60.00 (*1-85973-902-4*, Pub. by Berg Pubs); pap. 18.50 (*1-85973-907-5*, Pub. by Berg Pubs) NYU Pr.

Nazi Germany. Alan F. Wilt. Ed. by Keith Eubank. LC 93-6281. (European History Ser.). 176p. (C). 1994. pap. text 11.95 (*0-88295-910-7*) Harlan Davidson.

Nazi Germany: A New History. Klaus P. Fischer. LC 68-31447. (Illus.). 770p. 1996. pap. 29.95 (*0-8264-0906-7*) Continuum.

Nazi Germany: Its Women & Family Life. Clifford Kirkpatrick. LC 78-63684. (Studies in Fascism: Ideology & Practice). (Illus.). 376p. reprint ed. 49.50 (*0-404-16949-X*) AMS Pr.

Nazi Germany & Its Aftermath in Women Directors' Autobiographical Films of the Late 1970s: In the Murderers' House. Gabriele Weinberger. LC 92-5983. 260p. 1992. 89.95 (*0-7734-9851-6*) E Mellen.

Nazi Germany & the American Germanists: A Study of Periodicals, 1930-1946, Vol. 2. Magda Lauwers-Rech. LC 94-12036. (Literature & the Sciences of Man Ser.: No. 2). X, 222p. (C). 1995. 46.95 (*0-8204-1656-8*) P Lang Pubng.

Nazi Germany & the Jews, 2 vols., Vol. II. Saul Friedlander. LC 96-21915. 416p. 1998. 25.00 (*0-06-019043-4*) HarperTrade.

Nazi Germany & the Jews: The Years of Persecution, 1933-1939, 2 vols., Vol. 1. Saul Friedlander. Vol. 1. 464p. 1998. pap. 16.00 (*0-06-092878-6*) HarpC.

Nazi Germany & WW II. Donald D. Wall. LC 96-32788. 300p. 1996. 37.95 (*0-314-09360-5*) West Pub.

Nazi Germany at War. Martin Kitchen. (C). 1994. text 65.50 (*0-582-07388-X*) Addison-Wesley.

Nazi Germany at War. Martin Kitchen. LC 93-44808. 1995. write for info. (*0-582-07338-3*, Pub. by Addison-Wesley) Longman.

Nazi Germany at War. Martin Kitchen. LC 93-44808. (C). 1995. pap. text 27.19 (*0-582-07387-1*, Pub. by Addison-Wesley) Longman.

Nazi Germany 1933-1945: Faith in the Fuhrer & Pursuit of a War of Annihilation. Jost Dulffer. LC 95-31743. 256p. 1996. pap. text 19.95 (*0-340-61393-9*, Pub. by E A) OUP.

Nazi Germany 1933-1945: Faith in the Fuhrer & Pursuit of a War of Annihilation. Jost Dulffer. Tr. by Dean S. McMurry. LC 95-31743. 288p. 1996. text 49.95 (*0-340-65265-9*, Pub. by E A) St Martin.

Nazi Gold: The Full Story of the 50-Year Swiss-Nazi Conspiracy to Steal Billions from Europe[0012]s Jews & Holocaust Survivors. 381p. text 25.00 (*0-7881-6080-X*) DIANE Pub.

Nazi Gold: The Real Story of How America & Europe Ended up with Jewish Treasures. George Carpozi, Jr. 400p. 1998. 25.95 (*0-88282-167-9*, Pub. by New Horizon NJ) Natl Bk Netwk.

Nazi Gold: U. S. & Allied Efforts to Recover & Restore Gold & Other Assets Stolen or Hidden by Germany During World War II. William Z. Slany. (Illus.). 212p. (Orig.). 1997. pap. text 35.00 (*0-7881-4536-3*) DIANE Pub.

Nazi Gold: U. S. & Allied Efforts to Recover & Restore Gold & Other Assets Stolen or Hidden by Germany During World War II Finding Aids to Records at the National Archives. Greg Bradsher. (Illus.). 277p. (Orig.). (C). 1997. pap. text 35.00 (*0-7881-4537-1*) DIANE Pub.

Nazi Gold - The London Conference. Foreign & Commonwealth Office Staff. LC 98-224572. 834 p. 1998. 55.00 (*0-11-591760-8*, Pub. by Statnry Office) Balogh.

Nazi Gold Report. 1997. lib. bdg. 250.99 (*0-8490-7603-X*) Gordon Pr.

Nazi Holocaust. Ronnie S. Landau. 372p. 1994. pap. 14.95 (*1-56663-052-5*, Elephant Paperbacks); text 27.50 (*1-56663-054-1*) I R Dee.

Nazi Holocaust, 9 vols., Set. Incl. Vol. 1. Perspectives on the Holocaust. Michael R. Marrus. 459p. 1989. 120.00 (*3-598-21551-7*); Vol. 2. Origins of the Holocaust. Michael R. Marrus. 747p. 1989. 120.00 (*3-598-21552-5*); Vol. 3, Pt. 1. Final Solution: Mass Murder. Michael R. Marrus. 366p. 1989. 240.00 (*3-598-21553-3*); Vol. 3, Pt.2. Final Solution: Mass Murder. Michael R. Marrus. 509p. 1989. 120.00 Vol. 4, Pt. 1. Final Solution Outside Germany. Michael R. Marrus. 430p. 1989. 240.00 (*3-598-21555-X*); Vol. 4 Pt. 2. Final Solution Outside Germany. Michael R. Marrus. 389p. 1989. 120.00 Vol. 5, Pt. 1. Public Opinion & Relations to the Jews in Nazi Europe. Ed. by Michael R. Marrus. 462p. 1989. 240.00 (*3-598-21557-6*); Vol. 5, Pt. 2. Public Opinion & Relations to the Jews in Nazi Europe. Michael R. Marrus. 350p. 1989. 120.00 Vol. 6, Pt. 1. Victims of the Holocaust. Ed. by Michael R. Marrus. 562p. 1989. 240.00 (*3-598-21559-2*); Vol. 6, Pt. 2. Victims of the Holocaust. Michael R. Marrus. 721p. 1989. Vol. 7. Jewish Resistance to the Holocaust. Ed. by Michael R. Marrus. 573p. 1989. pap. 120.00 (*3-598-21561-4*); Vol. 8, Pt. 1. Bystanders to the Holocaust. Michael R. Marrus. 488p. 1989. 365.00 (*3-598-21562-2*); Vol. 8, Pt. 1. Bystanders to the Holocaust. Michael R. Marrus. 488p. 1989. Vol. 8, Pt. 1. Bystanders to the Holocaust. Michael R. Marrus. 488p. 1989. Vol. 9. End of the Holocaust. Michael R. Marrus. 744p. 1989. 120.00 (*3-598-21565-7*); 1989. 1630.00 (*3-598-21500-2*) K G Saur Verlag.

Nazi Hunters: The Shocking True Story of the Continuing Search for Nazi War Criminals. Charles Ashman & Robert J. Wagman. 320p. 1990. mass mkt. 4.95 (*0-446-35831-2*, Pub. by Warner Bks) Little.

Nazi Impact on a German Village. Walter Rinderle & Bernard Norling. LC 92-10030. (Illus.). 296p. (C). 1993. text 34.95 (*0-8131-1794-1*) U Pr of Ky.

Nazi Justiz: Law of the Holocaust. Richard L. Miller. LC 94-46176. 248p. 1995. 45.00 (*0-275-94912-5*, Praeger Pubs) Greenwood.

Nazi Legacy: Right-Wing Extremism in West Germany. Rand C. Lewis. LC 90-24277. 208p. 1991. 42.95 (*0-275-93853-0*, C3853, Praeger Pubs) Greenwood.

Nazi Machtergreifung. Ed. by Peter D. Stachura. 208p. (C). 1983. text 60.00 (*0-04-943026-2*) Routledge.

***Nazi Madness - Highlighted at Nuremberg.** Walter T. Schonfeld. (Illus.). 136p. 2000. 21.95 (*0-7541-1012-5*, Pub. by Minerva Pr) Unity Dist.

Nazi Mass Murder by Poison Gas: A Documentary Account. Ed. by Eugen Kogon et al. Tr. by Mary Scott & Caroline Lloyd-Morris from GER. LC 93-13734.Tr. of Nationalsozialistische Massent Otungen Durch Giftgas. (Illus.). 304p. 1994. 40.00 (*0-300-05441-6*) Yale U Pr.

Nazi Menace in Argentina, 1931-1947. Ronald C. Newton. LC 91-20368. (Illus.). 540p. 1992. 52.50 (*0-8047-1929-2*) Stanford U Pr.

Nazi Militaria - Fake or Real? Ray R. Cowdery. (Illus.). 144p. (Orig.). 1992. pap. 10.00 (*0-910667-08-X*) USM.

Nazi Movement in Baden, 1920-1945. Johnpeter H. Grill. LC 82-14483. 734p. reprint ed. pap. 200.00 (*0-7837-3768-8*, 204358500010) Bks Demand.

Nazi Occupation of Crete, 1941-1945. G. C. Kiriakopoulos. LC 95-4290. 264p. 1995. 59.95 (*0-275-95277-0*, Praeger Pubs) Greenwood.

***Nazi Officer's Wife: How One Jewish Woman Survived The Holocaust.** Edith Hahn Beer. 320p. 2000. pap. 14.00 (*0-688-17776-X*, Perennial) HarperTrade.

Nazi Officer's Wife: How One Jewish Woman Survived the Holocaust. Edith Hahn Beer & Susan Dworkin. LC 99-43362. 320p. 1999. 26.00 (*0-688-16689-X*, Wm Morrow) Morrow Avon.

Nazi Olympics. Richard D. Mandell. LC 86-19347. (Sport & Society Ser.). (Illus.). 344p. 1987. pap. text 16.95 (*0-252-01325-5*) U of Ill Pr.

Nazi Olympics: Berlin 1936. Susan D. Bachrach. LC 99-31423. 132p. (YA). 2000. 21.95 (*0-316-07086-6*); pap. 14.95 (*0-316-07087-4*) Little.

Nazi Para-Military Organizations & Their Badges. Ray Cowdery & George C. Robinson. LC 83-60048. (Illus.). 142p. 1985. pap. 20.00 (*0-910667-05-5*) USM.

Nazi Party in Dissolution: Hitler & the Verbotzeit, 1923-25. David Jablonsky. (Cass Series on Politics & Military Affairs in the Twentieth Century). (Illus.). 247p. 1989. text 45.00 (*0-7146-3322-4*, Pub. by F Cass Pubs) Intl Spec Bk.

Nazi Persecution of the Churches, 1933-1945. John S. Conway. 474p. 1997. reprint ed. pap. 29.95 (*1-57383-080-1*) Regent College.

Nazi Persecution of the Gypsies. Ed. by Guenter Lewy. LC 98-52545. (Illus.). 320p. 2000. 30.00 (*0-19-512556-8*) OUP.

***Nazi Policy, Jewish Workers, German Killers.** Christopher R. Browning. (Illus.). 208p. 2000. 49.95 (*0-521-77299-0*); pap. 15.95 (*0-521-77490-X*) Cambridge U Pr.

Nazi Primer: Offical Handbook for Schooling the Hitler Youth. Tr. by Harwood L. Childs from GER. LC 71-180391. reprint ed. 27.50 (*0-404-56107-1*) AMS Pr.

Nazi Prisoners of War in America. Arnold Krammer. (Illus.). 352p. 1996. reprint ed. pap. 17.95 (*0-8128-8561-9*, Scrbrough Hse) Madison Bks UPA.

Nazi Regalia. E. W. Fowler. 106p. 1992. 15.98 (*1-55521-767-2*) Bk Sales Inc.

Nazi-Retro Film: How German Narrative Cinema Remembers the Past. Robert C. Reimer & Carol J. Reimer. LC 92-18054. (Twayne's Filmmakers Ser.). 200p. 1992. pap. 15.95 (*0-8057-9316-X*, Twyne) Mac Lib Ref.

Nazi Revolution: Hitler's Dictatorship & the German Nation. 3rd ed. Ed. by Allan Mitchell. LC 89-80515. (Problems in European Civilization Ser.). 188p. (C). 1990. pap. text 22.36 (*0-669-20880-9*) HM Trade Div.

Nazi Revolution: Hitler's Dictatorship & the German Nation. 4th ed. Allan Mitchell. 208p. (C). 1997. pap. text 22.36 (*0-669-41694-0*) HM Trade Div.

Nazi Rocketeers: Dreams of Space & Crimes of War. Dennis Piszkiewicz. LC 95-10102. 288p. 1995. 24.95 (*0-275-95217-7*, Praeger Pubs) Greenwood.

Nazi Rule & Dutch Collaboration: The Netherlands under German Occupation, 1940-45. Gerhard Hirschfeld. Tr. by Louise Wilmot from GER. LC 87-25594. 360p. 1988. 30.00 (*0-85496-146-1*) Berg Pubs.

Nazi Science: Myth, Truth, & the German Atomic Bomb. Mark Walker. LC 95-6102. (Illus.). 384p. 1995. 28.95 (*0-306-44941-2*) Da Capo.

Nazi Seizure of Power: The Experience of a Single German Town, 1922-1945. rev. ed. William S. Allen. 388p. 1965. pap. 16.95 (*0-531-05633-3*) Watts.

Nazi Spy Conspiracy in America. Leon G. Turrou. LC 72-1433. (Select Bibliographies Reprint Ser.). 1977. reprint ed. 24.95 (*0-8369-6838-7*) Ayer.

Nazi State & New Religions: 5 Case Studies in Non-Conformity. Christine E. King. LC 82-20910. (Studies in Religion & Society: Vol. 4). 350p. 1990. lib. bdg. 99.95 (*0-88946-865-6*) E Mellen.

***Nazi Terror.** Johnson. 2000. pap. 18.00 (*0-465-04908-7*, Pub. by Basic) HarpC.

Nazi Terror: The Gestapo, Jews & Ordinary Germans. Eric Johnson. (Illus.). 600p. 2000. 35.00 (*0-465-04906-0*, Pub. by Basic) HarpC.

Nazi Trials: A Soldier's Story of Terror. James M. Moruzzi. Ed. by Irving J. Klein et al. LC 95-22231. 224p. (Orig.). 1995. pap. 15.95 (*0-938993-23-2*) Coral Gables Pub.

Nazi UFO Secrets & Bases Exposed. Frank E. Stranges. 3034p. 1982. pap. 4.95 (*0-686-37108-9*) Intl Evang.

Nazi Voter: The Social Foundations of Fascism in Germany, 1919-1933. Thomas Childers. LC 83-5924. xvi, 367p. 1986. reprint ed. pap. 18.95 (*0-8078-4147-1*) U of NC Pr.

Nazi War Criminals. Earle Rice, Jr. LC 97-9811. (Holocaust Library). (Illus.). (YA). (gr. 6 up). 1997. lib. bdg. 22.45 (*1-56006-097-2*) Lucent Bks.

Nazi War Criminals in America. Charles R. Allen, Jr. LC 86-110559. 116p. 1985. 6.95 (*0-934215-00-6*) Highgate Hse.

Nazi War Finance & Banking. Otto Nathan. (Occasional Papers). 100p. 1944. reprint ed. 27.60 (*0-87014-335-2*) Natl Bur Econ Res.

***Nazi War on Cancer.** Robert Proctor. (Illus.). 365p. 2000. pap. 16.95 (*0-691-07051-2*) Princeton U Pr.

Nazi War on Cancer. Robert N. Proctor. LC 98-49405. (Illus.). 380p. 1999. 24.95 (*0-691-00196-0*, Pub. by Princeton U Pr) Cal Prin Full Svc.

Nazi Weapons & Munitions Code. Robert D. Pollard. LC 83-6169. 56p. (Orig.). 1983. pap. text 10.00 (*0-86663-986-1*) Ide Hse.

***Nazi Wireless Propaganda: Lord Haw-Haw & British Public Opinion.** Martin Doherty. 256p. 2000. pap. text 25.00 (*0-7486-1363-3*) Col U Pr.

Nazi Years: A Documentary History. Ed. by Joachim Remak. LC 69-11359. 1969. pap. text 5.95 (*0-13-610535-1*, S195, Spectrum IN) Macmillan Gen Ref.

Nazi Years: A Documentary History. Joachim Remak. 178p. (C). 1990. reprint ed. pap. text 10.95 (*0-88133-527-4*) Waveland Pr.

Nazification of an Academic Discipline: Folklore in the Third Reich. Ed. by James R. Dow & Hannjost Lixfeld. LC 93-17205. (Folklore Studies in Translation). 1994. 9.95 (*0-253-31821-1*) Ind U Pr.

Nazification of an Academic Discipline: Folklore in the Third Reich. Ed. by James R. Dow & Hannjost Lixfeld. LC 93-17205. (Folklore Studies in Translation). (Illus.). 374p. Date not set. reprint ed. pap. 116.00 (*0-608-20539-7*, 2054453) Bks Demand.

Nazification of Art: Art, Design, Architecture, Music & Film in the Third Reich. Brandon Taylor. (Illus.). 280p. pap. 24.95 (*0-9506783-9-2*, Pub. by Winchester Schl Art Pr) Paul & Co Pubs.

Nazification of Russia: Antisemitism in the Post-Soviet Era. Semyon Reznik. Ed. by Maureen Martin. LC 96-83319. (Illus.). 276p. 1996. 24.95 (*0-9651360-9-4*); pap. 15.95 (*0-9651360-8-6*) Challenge VA.

Nazir. (ENG & HEB.). 15.00 (*0-910218-69-2*) Bennet Pub.

Nazis. William W. Lace. LC 97-21376. (Holocaust Library). (Illus.). (YA). (gr. 6 up). 1997. lib. bdg. 22.45 (*1-56006-091-3*) Lucent Bks.

Nazis. Piotr Uklanski. 1999. 39.95 (*3-905509-22-9*) Scalo Pubs.

Nazis: A Warning from History. Laurence Rees. (Illus.). 256p. 1998. 25.00 (*1-56584-445-9*, Pub. by New Press NY); pap. 18.95 (*1-56584-551-X*, Pub. by New Press NY) Norton.

Nazis' Last Victims: The Holocaust in Hungary. Ed. by Randolph L. Braham & Scott Miller. LC 97-47721. (Illus.). 224p. 1998. 34.95 (*0-8143-2737-0*) Wayne St U Pr.

Nazis' Literary Grandfather: Adolf Bartels & Cultural Extremism, 1871-1945. Steven N. Fuller. LC 95-11042. (Studies in Modern German Literature: Vol. 62). 261p. (C). 1997. pap. text 32.95 (*0-8204-2329-7*) P Lang Pubng.

***Nazis' March to Chaos: The Hitler Era Through the Lenses of Chaos-Complexity Theory.** Roger Beaumont. LC 99-32027. 224p. 2000. 59.95 (*0-275-96708-5*) Greenwood.

Nazis Seize Power, 1933-1939. Stuart A. Kallen. LC 94-20144. (Holocaust Ser.). (J). 1991. lib. bdg. 14.98 (*1-56239-351-0*) ABDO Pub Co.

Nazis, Women & Molecular Biology: Memoirs of a Lucky Self-Hater. Gunther S. Stent. vi, 338p. 1998. 25.00 (*0-9664563-0-0*) Briones Bks.

Nazism: An Historical & Comparative Analysis. George L. Mosse. 160p. 1998. 32.95 (*0-7658-0684-3*) Transaction Pubs.

Nazism & German Society, 1933-1945. David Crew. LC 93-47053. (Rewriting Histories Ser.). 336p. (C). 1994. pap. 17.95 (*0-415-08240-4*, B4251) Routledge.

Nazism & the Pastors: A Study of the Ideas of Three Deutsche Christian Groups. James A. Zabel. LC 75-30607. (American Academy of Religion, Dissertation Ser.: Vol. 14). 259p. reprint ed. pap. 80.30 (*0-608-08686-X*, 206920900003) Bks Demand.

Nazism & the Working Class in Austria: Industrial Unrest & Political Dissent in the 'National Community' Tim Kirk. LC 95-48269. 204p. (C). 1996. text 49.95 (*0-521-47501-5*) Cambridge U Pr.

Nazism, Fascism & the Working Class. Tim Mason. Ed. by Jane Caplan. 371p. (C). 1995. text 59.95 (*0-521-43212-X*); pap. text 19.95 (*0-521-43787-3*) Cambridge U Pr.

Nazism, Foreign Policy, War & Racial Extermination, 1919-1945. Ed. by Jeremy Noakes & Geoffrey Pridham. (Illus.). 640p. 1995. pap. text 18.95 (*0-85989-474-6*, Pub. by Univ Exeter Pr) Northwestern U Pr.

Nazism in Central Germany: The Brownshirts in 'Red' Saxony. Claus-Christian W. Szejnmann. LC 98-49764. 304p. 1999. 59.95 (*1-57181-942-8*) Berghahn Bks.

Nazism, Liberalism, & Christianity: Protestant Social Conscience in Germany & Great Britain, 1925-1937. Kenneth Barnes. 216p. 1991. text 28.00 (*0-8131-1729-1*) U Pr of Ky.

Nazism, 1919-1945 - A Documentary Reader Vol. 1: The Rise to Power 1919-1934. rev. ed. Ed. by Jeremy Noakes. 220p. 1998. pap. text 15.95 (*0-85989-598-X*, Pub. by Univ Exeter Pr) Northwestern U Pr.

Nazism, 1919-1945 - A Documentary Reader Vol. 4: The German Home Front in World War II. Ed. by Jeremy Naokes. 640p. 1998. pap. text 24.95 (*0-85989-311-1*, Pub. by Univ Exeter Pr) Northwestern U Pr.

Nazism Resistance & Holocaust in World War II: A Bibliography. Vera Laska. LC 84-23586. 205p. 1985. 21.00 (*0-8108-1771-3*) Scarecrow.

Nazism, State, Economy & Society, 1933-39: A Documentary Reader. Ed. by Jeremy Noakes & Geoffrey Pridham. 430p. 1995. pap. text 15.95 (*0-85989-461-4*, Pub. by Univ Exeter Pr) Northwestern U Pr.

Nazism, the Jews & American Zionism, 1933-1988. rev. ed. Aaron Berman. LC 90-11942. (Illus.). 240p. (C). 1992. pap. 16.95 (*0-8143-2232-8*) Wayne St U Pr.

Nazism, the Rise to Power: A Documentary Reader. Ed. by Jeremy Noakes & Geoffrey Pridham. 193p. 1995. pap. text 12.95 (*0-85989-472-X*, Pub. by Univ Exeter Pr) Northwestern U Pr.

Naz's Dictionary of Teen Slang. Ed. by Kenn N. Young. LC 93-27055. (Orig.). 1993. pap. 12.95 (*0-89420-293-6*) Natl Book.

Naz's Underground Dictionary. Kenn N. Young. 327p. (YA). (gr. 7 up). 1993. pap. 19.95 (*0-89420-288-X*, 170550) Natl Book.

NBA. (Bip Quiz Ser.). 256p. (J). 1997. pap. 16.95 (*0-8069-6193-7*) Sterling.

NBA Action from A to Z. Brendan Hanraham. (J). (gr. 1-4). 1997. mass mkt. 3.50 (*0-590-13768-9*) Scholastic Inc.

NBA at 50. Ed. by Mark Vancil. 1996. 50.00 (*0-614-20440-2*) Park Lane Pr.

NBA at 50: The Colorful History of America's Number 1 Pro Sports League. rev. ed. Mark Vancil. 1997. pap. 30.00 (*0-609-80164-3*) Crown Pub Group.

NBA Basketball: An Official Fan's Guide: The NBA's Complete Authorized Guide. 3rd rev. ed. Mark Vancil & Don Jozwiak. (Illus.). 128p. 1997. 19.95 (*1-57243-216-0*) Triumph Bks.

NBA Basketball Basics. Mark Vancil. LC 94-44687. (Illus.). 128p. (J). (gr. 4-7). 1995. 16.95 (*0-8069-0927-7*) Sterling.

NBA Basketball Basics. Mark Vancil. (Illus.). 128p. (J). (gr. 5-8). 1995. pap. 9.95 (*0-8069-0928-5*) Sterling.

NBA Basketball Offense Basics. Mark Vancil. LC 95-49271. (Illus.). 96p. (Orig.). 1996. 16.95 (*0-8069-4892-2*) Sterling.

NBA Basketball Offense Basics. Mark Vancil. (Illus.). 96p. (Orig.). 1996. pap. 9.95 (*0-8069-4893-0*) Sterling.

NBA Book of Big & Little. James Preller. 32p. (J). (ps-2). 1998. pap. text 4.99 (*0-590-37756-6*) Scholastic Inc.

***NBA Book of Opposites.** James Preller. (NBA Ser.). (Illus.). 32p. (J). (ps-2). 2000. pap. 4.50 (*0-439-14075-7*) Scholastic Inc.

NBA by the Numbers. Bruce Brooks. LC 96-27327. (J). 1997. 10.95 (*0-590-97578-1*) Scholastic Inc.

NBA Famous Moments. (BipQuiz NBA Ser.). (Illus.). 64p. (J). 1996. pap. 2.95 (*0-8069-4227-4*) Sterling.

NBA Fun Facts & Trivia Howard Blatt. LC 99-163139. 46p. (J). 1998. write for info. (*0-590-03271-2*) Scholastic Inc.

NBA Game Day: An Inside Look at the NBA. Joe Layden & James Preller. (Illus.). 48p. (J). (gr. 2-7). 1997. pap. 10.95 (*0-590-76742-9*) Scholastic Inc.

NBA Hangtime Players Guide. BradyGames Staff. 96p. 1996. 9.99 (*1-56686-628-6*) Brady Pub.

NBA Hoop Shots: Classic Moments from a Super Era. Photos by Andrew D. Bernstein. (Illus.). 144p. (Orig.). 1996. 34.95 (*0-942627-24-5*); pap. 21.95 (*0-942627-23-7*) Woodford Pubng.

NBA Hot Shots, 1 vol. Joe Layden. LC 99-207568. (Illus.). 24p. (ps-2). 1999. 3.50 (*0-590-06056-2*) Scholastic Inc.

NBA Jam Tournament Edition Official Game Secrets. Carlton. 1995. pap. text 12.95 (*0-7615-0189-4*) Prima Pub.

***NBA Live 2000: Official Strategy Guide.** Prima Development Staff. 1999. pap. 14.99 (*0-7615-2292-1*) Prima Pub.

NBA Map Skills. Ed. by Scholastic, Inc. Staff. (J). 1997. mass mkt. 3.50 (*0-590-06381-2*) Scholastic Inc.

NBA Map Skills. Ed. by Scholastic, Inc. Staff. (gr. 4-7). 1997. mass mkt. 2.95 (*0-590-06380-4*) Scholastic Inc.

NBA Math Skills. Ed. by Scholastic, Inc. Staff. (J). 1997. mass mkt. 2.95 (*0-590-06383-9*) Scholastic Inc.

NBA Math Skills. Ed. by Scholastic, Inc. Staff. (J). 1997. mass mkt. 3.50 (*0-590-06384-7*) Scholastic Inc.

NBA Megastars. Bruce Weber. (J). (gr. 5-7). 1997. mass mkt. 7.99 (*0-590-13769-7*) Scholastic Inc.

***NBA Megastars 99, 1 vol.** Bruce Weber. LC 99-232369. (Illus.). 32p. (gr. 2-5). 1999. 7.99 (*0-590-05468-6*) Scholastic Inc.

NBA Megastars '98. Bruce Weber. (J). 1998. pap. text 7.99 (*0-590-60005-2*) Scholastic Inc.

NBA Power Conditioning. NBCCA Staff. LC 97-19426. (Illus.). 216p. (Orig.). 1997. pap. 17.95 (*0-88011-687-0*) Human Kinetics.

NBA Reading Comprehension for Grades 5-6. Ed. by Scholastic, Inc. Staff. (NBA Skills Bks.). (Illus.). 48p. (J). (gr. 5-7). 1997. pap. 3.50 (*0-590-06388-X*) Scholastic Inc.

NBA Reading Comprehension for Grades 3-4. Ed. by Scholastic, Inc. Staff. (NBA Skills Bks.). (Illus.). 32p. (J). (gr. 2-4). 1997. pap. 2.95 (*0-590-06387-1*) Scholastic Inc.

NBA Records. (BipQuiz NBA Ser.). (Illus.). 64p. (J). 1996. pap. 2.95 (*0-8069-4852-3*) Sterling.

NBA Rules & History. (BipQuiz NBA Ser.). (Illus.). 64p. (J). 1996. pap. 2.95 (*0-8069-4850-7*) Sterling.

N

*__NBA Showtime Official Strategy Guide.__ Brady Games Staff. (Illus.). 128p. 1999. pap. text 12.99 (1-56686-941-2, BradyGAMES) Brady Pub.

*__NBA Slam.__ John Hareas. (NBA Ser.). (Illus.). 32p. (J). (gr. 2-5). 2000. pap. 7.99 (0-439-14070-6) Scholastic Inc.

NBA Slam & Jam Map Skills for Grades 7-8. Joe Layden & James Preller. (NBA Game Day Ser.). (J). (gr. 7-8). 1997. pap. 3.50 (0-590-06382-0) Scholastic Inc.

NBA Slam & Jam Reading Comprehension Skills. Scholastic, Inc. Staff. (Slam & Jam Skills Ser.). (J). (gr. 7-8). 1997. pap. text 3.50 (0-590-29967-0) Scholastic Inc.

NBA Slam & Jam Reading Comprehensive. Scholastic, Inc. Staff. (NBA Slam & Jam Skills Ser.). (gr. 7-12). 1997. pap. text 3.50 (0-590-18846-1) Scholastic Inc.

NBA Slam & Jam Skills Map. Ed. by Scholastic, Inc. Staff. (J). (gr. 8-12). 1997. pap. 3.50 (0-590-18848-8) Scholastic Inc.

NBA Slam & Jam Study Skills for Grades 7-8. Joe Layden & James Preller. (NBA Game Day Ser.). (J). (gr. 7-8). 1997. pap. 3.50 (0-590-29968-9) Scholastic Inc.

NBA Slam Dunk Champ. Joe Layden. (J). (gr. 5-7). 1997. mass mkt. 7.99 (0-590-13770-0) Scholastic Inc.

NBA Superstars. (BipQuiz NBA Ser.). (Illus.). 64p. (J). 1996. pap. 2.95 (0-8069-4851-5) Sterling.

NBA Superstars: A Live Action Look at the Heroes of the NBA. Vince Aversano. (Illus.). 32p. 1994. pap. 6.99 (1-55958-701-6) Prima Pub.

NBA Superstars - NBA Famous Moments. (Bip Quiz Ser.). (J). 1997. pap. 10.95 (0-8069-8185-7) Sterling.

*__NBA 2k Official Strategy Guide.__ BradyGames Inc. Staff. 128p. 1999. pap. 12.99 (1-56686-967-6, BradyGAMES) Brady Pub.

*__NBA Up & Coming: Stars of the New Millennium.__ Joe Layden. (NBA Ser.). (Illus.). 32p. (J). (gr. 2-5). 2000. pap. 7.99 (0-439-14069-2) Scholastic Inc.

NBAA's Tribute to Business Aviation. Robert A. Searles & Robert B. Parke. (Illus.). 180p. 1997. 45.00 (0-9627180-0-9) Natl Busn Aircraft.

*__NBBS: Nuts & Bolts of Body & Soul.__ (Illus.). xv, 270p. 1999. pap. 24.95 (0-9675418-0-8) Easton Facilitator.

NBC: Nuclear, Biological & Chemical Warfare on the Modern Battlefield. Will Fowler & John Norris. LC 97-22122. (Brassey's Modern Military Equipment Ser.). (Illus.). 160p. 1997. 29.95 (1-85753-182-5, Pub. by Brasseys) Brasseys.

NBC News Division & the Economics of Prime Time Access, Washington D. C., September 1973: Proceedings, 2 vols. NBC News Division Staff & Alan Pearce. Ed. by Christopher H. Sterling. LC 78-21730. (Dissertations in Broadcasting Ser.). 1980. lib. bdg. 31.95 (0-405-11768-X) Ayer.

*__NBC Risks: Current Capabilities & Future Perspectives for Protection__ Torsten Sohns & Victor A. Voicu. LC 99-30409. (NATO Science Ser.). 1999. write for info. (0-7923-5802-3) Kluwer Academic.

NBC Video Guide. Ricky Griffin. Ed. by Mary C. McEwing. 34p. 1996. pap. text. write for info. (0-201-56685-0) Addison-Wesley.

NBER Macroeconomics Annual, 1989. Ed. by Oliver J. Blanchard & Stanley Fischer. 320p. (Orig.). 1989. pap. text 20.00 (0-262-52145-8) MIT Pr.

NBER Macroeconomics Annual, 1987. Ed. by Stanley Fischer. (NBER Macroeconomics Ser.). 321p. (Orig.). (C). 1987. pap. text 20.00 (0-262-56040-2) MIT Pr.

NBER Macroeconomics Annual, 1988. Ed. by Stanley Fischer. 320p. (Orig.). 1988. 40.00 (0-262-06119-8); pap. text 20.00 (0-262-56045-3) MIT Pr.

NBER Macroeconomics Annual, 1986. National Bureau of Economic Research Staff. Ed. by Stanley Fischer. LC 87-642897. 417p. reprint ed. pap. 129.30 (0-8357-7930-0, 205233000002) Bks Demand.

NBER Macroeconomics Annual, 1995. Ed. by Ben S. Bernanke & Julio Rotemberg. (NBER Macroeconomics Annual Ser.). (Illus.). 300p. (C). 1996. pap. text 20.00 (0-262-52205-5) MIT Pr.

NBER Macroeconomics Annual, 1996. Ed. by Ben S. Bernanke & Julio Rotemberg. (Illus.). 300p. (C). 1996. 40.00 (0-262-02414-4); pap. text 22.00 (0-262-52222-5) MIT Pr.

NBER Macroeconomics Annual, 1997. Ed. by Ben S. Bernanke & Julio Rotemberg. (Illus.). 300p. 1997. pap. text 20.00 (0-262-52242-X) MIT Pr.

NBER Macroeconomics Annual, 1998. Ed. by Ben S. Bernanke & Julio Rotemberg. (Illus.). 300p. 1999. 45.00 (0-262-02455-1) MIT Pr.

NBER Macroeconomics Annual 1998. Ed. by Ben S. Bernanke & Julio Rotemberg. (Illus.). 300p. 1999. pap. text 25.00 (0-262-52256-X) MIT Pr.

NBER Macroeconomics Annual, 1990. Ed. by Oliver J. Blanchard & Stanley Fischer. 300p. 1990. pap. text 20.00 (0-262-52155-5) MIT Pr.

NBER Macroeconomics Annual, 1991. Ed. by Oliver J. Blanchard & Stanley Fischer. (NBER Macroeconomics Annual Ser.). (Illus.). 350p. 1991. pap. text 20.00 (0-262-52165-2) MIT Pr.

NBER Macroeconomics Annual, 1993. Ed. by Oliver J. Blanchard & Stanley Fischer. (Illus.). 360p. 1993. 40.00 (0-262-02364-4) MIT Pr.

NBER Macroeconomics Annual, 1993. Ed. by Oliver J. Blanchard & Stanley Fischer. (Illus.). 360p. 1993. pap. text 20.00 (0-262-52184-9) MIT Pr.

NBER Macroeconomics Annual, 1992. Ed. by Olivier J. Blanchard et al. 1992. pap. text 20.00 (0-262-52174-1) MIT Pr.

NBER Macroeconomics Annual, 1994. Ed. by Stanley Fischer & Julio J. Rotemberg. 330p. 1994. pap. text 20.00 (0-262-56080-1) MIT Pr.

*__NBER Macroeconomics Annual 1999.__ Ed. by Ben S. Bernanke & Julio Rotemberg. (Illus.). 300p. 2000. 50.00 (0-262-02476-4); pap. 25.00 (0-262-52271-3) MIT Pr.

NBS-NRC Steam Tables. Lester Haar et al. LC 84-663. (Illus.). 400p. 1984. pap. 33.95 (0-89116-353-0) Hemisp Pub.

NC Artist Fellowships. Michael Welzenbach et al. (Illus.). 25p. (Orig.). (YA). 1995. pap. 46.00 (1-885449-02-X) City Gallery Cntmprry Art.

*__NC Compendium: NC Software for Manufacturing Organizations.__ Alan Christman. (Illus.). 200p. 1999. ring bd. 795.00 (1-889760-12-9) CIMdata Inc.

NC Guide: Numerical Control Handbook. 3rd ed. R. Shah. (ENG, FRE & GER.). 346p. 1983. 225.00 (0-8288-0688-8, M6541) Fr & Eur.

NC Machine Tools in Indonesia: A Strategic Entry Report, 1997. Compiled by Icon Group International Staff. (Illus.). 164p. 1999. ring bd. 1640.00 incl. audio compact disk (0-7418-0872-2) Icon Grp.

*__NC Rules of Civil Procedure & Evidence.__ 18p. 1999. Price not set. (0-327-09112-6, 4649116) LEXIS Pub.

*__NC Software Buyer's Guide: The Authoritative Guide to NC Software & Services.__ 5th rev. ed. Alan Christman. (Illus.). 800p. 1998. ring bd. (1-889760-09-9) CIMdata Inc.

NC State Football Mystery. Carole M. Longmeyer. (Sportsmystery Ser.). (Illus.). (Orig.). (J). (gr. 3 up). 1994. pap. 19.95 (0-935326-33-2) Gallopade Intl.

NCA Review for the Clinical Laboratory Sciences. James L. Bender. 315p. 1985. pap. text 19.50 (0-316-08889-7, Little Brwn Med Div) Lppncott W & W.

NCA Review for the Clinical Laboratory Sciences. 2nd ed. NCA Staff. 1989. 32.95 (0-316-59925-5, Little Brwn Med Div) Lppncott W & W.

NCA Review for the Clinical Laboratory Sciences. 3rd ed. Beck. LC 96-16315. 254p. 1996. pap. text 35.00 (0-316-59942-5, Little Brwn Med Div) Lppncott W & W.

NCAA Basketball: The Official 1999 Men's Basketball Records Book. 1998. pap. 15.95 (1-57243-304-3) Triumph Bks.

*__NCAA Basketball: The Official 2000 Men's College Basketball Records Book.__ National Collegiate Athletic Association Staff. 1999. pap. 17.95 (1-57243-311-6) Triumph Bks.

NCAA Basketball's Finest: All-Time Great Men's Players & Coaches. National Collegiate Athletic Association Staff. 1998. pap. 15.95 (1-57243-316-7) Triumph Bks.

NCAA Final Four: The Official 1999 Final Four Records Books. 1998. pap. 13.95 (1-57243-305-1) Triumph Bks.

*__NCAA Final Four: The Official 2000 Final Four Records Book.__ National Collegiate Athletic Association Staff. (Illus.). 204p. 1999. pap. text 15.95 (1-57243-313-2) Triumph Bks.

NCAA Joke Book. Stevie Jay. 50p. 1990. pap. 3.95 (0-9629005-0-8) Theodore Pub.

NCADI's 1995 National Directory of Drug Abuse & Alcoholism Treatment & Prevention Programs That Have a Special Program for American Indians/Alaska Natives. R. Vanderbilt & R. M. Schacht. 55p. 1997. pap. 4.00 (1-888557-68-0) No Ariz Univ.

NCATE Accreditation: A Framework for Preparing Section II of the Institutional Report. James Raths. 1993. 21.00 (0-89333-106-6) AACTE.

NCCD Correctional Population Simulation Model Description. 7.00 (0-318-20312-X) Natl Coun Crime.

NCCLS Collection of ASTM Computerized System Standards. ring bd. 250.00 (1-56238-252-7, SC14-L) NCCLS.

NCE Recovery Boiler Precipitator: Mill Experience & Design Implications. Technical Association of the Pulp & Paper Industry. Ed. by J. S. Henderson. LC TS1176.6.E7. 80p. reprint ed. pap. 30.00 (0-608-12027-8, 202282600030) Bks Demand.

NCFE Handbook to Understanding, Preparing for & Responding to Challenges to Freedom of Artistic Expression. National Campaign for Freedom of Expression. Ed. by Publishing Resources Staff. LC 98-67316. (Illus.). 50p. 1998. pap. 15.00 (0-9666029-0-0) Natl Free Expr.

NCG to Wound Care. 2nd ed. Cathy T. Hess. LC 97-26211. (Illus.). 400p. 1997. 28.95 (0-87434-906-0) Springhouse Corp.

Nchiwana Big River: Mid-Columbia Indians & Their Land. Eugene S. Hunn et al. LC 89-14779. (Illus.). 384p. 1991. reprint ed. pap. 22.50 (0-295-97119-3) U of Wash Pr.

NCLEX: PMIC's Comprehensive Review for the Registered Nurse Licensing Exam. Gisela Nily et al. Ed. by Maureen Lynch & Adrienne DiDonata. LC 98-21936. 600p. (Orig.). 1998. pap. text 34.95 (1-57066-045-X, ME073) Practice Mgmt Info.

NCLEX, 1998. Kaplan Staff. 1997. 34.95 incl. cd-rom (0-684-83684-X) S&S Trade.

NCLEX-PN: A Comprehensive Study Guide. 3rd ed. Joann Zerwekh & Jo Carol Claborn. (C). 1997. student ed. 29.95 (0-9628210-7-1) Nursing Ed Consultants.

*__NCLEX-PN: A Study Guide for Practical Nurses.__ 3rd rev. ed. Jo Ann Zerwekh & Jo Carol Claborn. (Illus.). 500p. (C). 1999. pap. text 29.95 (0-9628210-9-8) Nursing Ed Consultants.

NCLEX Q & A. L.L.C. Lishing. (Princeton Review Ser.). 1999. pap. write for info. (0-375-75188-2) Random.

NCLEX-RN. Research & Education Association Staff. 600p. Date not set. pap. text 24.95 (0-87891-865-5) Res & Educ.

NCLEX-RN: A Comprehensive Study Guide. 3rd ed. JoAnn Zerwekh & Jo Carol Claborn. 700p. 1997. pap., student ed. 29.95 incl. disk (0-9628210-3-9) Nursing Ed Consultants.

*__NCLEX-RN: A Comprehensive Study Guide.__ 4th ed. Jo Ann Zerwekh & Jo Carol Claborn. (Illus.). 675p. (C). 2000. pap. text 34.95 (1-892155-00-1) Nursing Ed Consultants.

NCLEX-RN: A Study for Practical Nursing. 2nd ed. JoAnn Zerwekh & Jo Carol Claborn. LC 96-93049. (Illus.). 550p. (C). 1997. pap., student ed. 24.95 incl. disk (0-9628210-6-3) Nursing Ed Consultants.

*__NCLEX-RN CMAT Review Cards.__ 3rd ed. Acello. (Illus.). 1999. boxed set 33.95 (1-56930-092-5) Skidmore Roth Pub.

*__NCLEX-RN Made Ridiculously Simple.__ Andreas Carl. (Illus.). 379p. 2000. pap. text 24.95 (0-940780-35-6) MedMaster.

NCLEX RN, 1998-99. Kaplan Staff. 336p. 1998. 34.95 incl. cd-rom (0-684-84763-9) S&S Trade.

*__NCLEX-RN Practice: Questions & Answers Made Incredibly Easy.__ Springhouse Corporation Staff. LC 99-37059. 1999. pap. 32.95 (1-58255-017-4) Springhouse Corp.

NCLEX-RN Questions & Answers: More Than 2,000 Quetions & Answers for NCLEX-RN Success. Princeton Review Publishing Staff. 1999. pap. 27.95 (0-375-75291-9) Random.

*__NCLEX-RN Review.__ Springhouse Corporation Staff. LC 99-40804. 1999. pap. 32.95 (1-58255-016-6) Springhouse Corp.

NCLEX-RN 30-Day Planner. Patricia A. Hoefler. Ed. by Judy Laufman. 55p. (C). 1996. 15.95 (1-56533-020-X) M E D S Inc.

NCLEX-RN (TM)-RN 101: How to Pass. 2nd ed. Sylvia Rayfield & Loretta Manning. 264p. (C). 1996. pap. 24.95 incl. disk (0-9643622-1-X) ICAN LA.

*__NCLEX-RN, 2000-2001: National Council Licensure Examination for Registered Nurses.__ Kaplan Staff. 368p. 2000. pap. text 35.00 incl. cd-rom (0-684-87013-4) Kaplan.

*__NCLEX-RN, 1999-2000 ed.__ Kaplan. (Kaplan NCLEX-RN (W/CD) Ser.). 368p. 1999. pap. text 34.95 (0-684-85671-9) S&S Trade.

NCLEX, 2000. SPC Staff. 1997. 44.95 (0-87434-923-0) Springhouse Corp.

NCLEX/CAT-RN: PreTest Self-Assessment & Review. Margaret M. Dahlhauser. (Illus.). 800p. 1996. pap. text 29.00 incl. disk (0-07-912082-2) McGraw-Hill HPD.

NCO Guide. 5th ed. Rev. by Frank Cox. (Illus.). 336p. 1995. pap. 18.95 (0-8117-2563-4) Stackpole.

NCO Guide. 6th ed. Robert L. Rush. LC 98-44321. (Illus.). 336p. 1999. pap. text 18.95 (0-8117-2859-5) Stackpole.

*__NCP Certified Operator: Study Guide.__ Society of the Plastics Industry, Inc. Staff. LC 00-39566. 2000. pap. write for info. (1-56990-304-2) Hanser-Gardner.

*__NCPEA Yearbook 1998.__ 1998. write for info. (1-56676-709-1) Scarecrow.

NCPV Photovoltaics Program Review: Proceedings of the 15th Conference. Ed. by M. Al-Jassim & J. M. Gee. LC 99-60143. (Conference Proceedings Ser.: Vol. 462). 850p. 1999. (1-56396-836-3) Am Inst Physics.

NCR No. 3100 Operator. Jack Rudman. (Career Examination Ser.: C-530). 1994. pap. 19.95 (0-8373-0530-6) Nat Learn.

NCR Stakeholder Essay Competition National Winners, 1988: Creating Value for Stakeholders. NCR Corporation Staff. (Illus.). 73p. (Orig.). 1988. pap. text 11.95 (0-925738-00-X) NCR Law.

NCRA Roofing & Waterproofing Manual. 3rd ed. 800p. 1989. 118.00 (0-934809-04-6) Natl Roofing Cont.

NCRR Reporter. Government Printing Office Staff. 1983. pap. 8.00 (0-16-010572-2) USGPO.

NCS Carreer Assessment Keys. NCS Staff. 1996. pap. text 7.40 (0-13-244559-X) P-H.

NCSA Guide to Enterprise Security: Protecting Information Assets. Michel E. Kabay. (McGraw-Hill Computer Communications Series). 385p. 1996. 50.00 (0-07-033147-2) McGraw.

NCSA Guide to Enterprise Security: Protective Information Assets. Michel E. Kabay. (Illus.). 383p. 1999. reprint ed. text 30.00 (0-7881-6500-3) DIANE Pub.

NCSA Guide to PC & LAN Security. Stephen Cobb. (Illus.). 717p. 1996. 50.00 (0-07-912168-3) McGraw.

NCSA Guide to PC & LAN Security. Stephen Cobb. (Illus.). 717p. 1999. reprint ed. pap. 30.00 incl. disk (0-7881-6537-2) DIANE Pub.

NCSL Glossary of Metrology Terms. unabridged ed. National Conference of Standards Laboratories Glossary Committee. 56p. 1994. 10.00 (1-58464-001-4) Natl Conf Stds Labs.

NCSL State Budget Update: February, 1992. NCSL Fiscal Affairs Staff. (State Legislative Reports: Vol. 17, No. 4). 22p. 1992. pap. text 15.00 (1-55516-276-2, 7302-1704) Natl Conf State Legis.

Ncss Booklet of Social Studies. 10th ed. Jarolimek. 52p. 1997. pap. text. write for info. (0-13-494634-0) P-H.

NCSS in Retrospect. Ed. by O. L. Davis, Jr. LC 95-71964. (Bulletin Ser.: No. 92). 118p. (Orig.). 1996. pap. 14.95 (0-87986-068-5) Nat Coun Soc Studies.

NCSU Physics 205 & 208 Text Pack, 1996-1997. 2nd ed. George Parker. 150p. (C). 1996. pap. text, ring bd. 9.95 (0-7872-2658-0) Kendall-Hunt.

Ncsu Physics 205 & 208 Test Pack: 1998/1999. 4th ed. George Parker. 128p. (C). 1998. spiral bd. 13.95 (0-7872-5469-X, 41546901) Kendall-Hunt.

NCTalk: Instruction Manual. 34p. 1987. write for info. (1-887777-07-5) Datacut Inc.

ND-YAG Laser in Ophthalmology: Principles & Clinical Applications of Photodistribution. Roger F. Steinert & Carmen A. Puliafito. (Illus.). 154p. 1985. text 98.00 (0-7216-1320-9, W B Saunders Co) Harcrt Hlth Sci Grp.

NDA Book, 2 vols., Set. Ed. by FOI Services, Inc. Staff. 1996. pap. 289.00 (1-880626-09-8) FOI Services.

NDA Book, Vol. I. Ed. by FOI Services, Inc. Staff. 1996. pap. write for info. (1-880626-07-1) FOI Services.

NDA Book, Vol. II. Ed. by FOI Services, Inc. Staff. 1996. pap. write for info. (1-880626-08-X) FOI Services.

NDA Pipeline, 1995. 14th ed. (Illus.). xix, 1400p. 1996. 750.00 (0-614-16923-2) F-D-C Reports.

Ndal Sukdu/Gheldzay Sukdu (Crane Story/Moon Story) K. Nicolie. 18p. 1977. pap. 2.50 (0-933769-94-6) Alaska Native.

NDE Education: Training for Engineers. Ed. by D. O. Thompson & W. F. Riley. 78p. 1983. pap. text 20.00 (0-317-02636-4, H00265) ASME.

NDE Engineering Codes & Standards & Materials Characterization. Ed. by J. F. Cook. 95p. 1996. pap. text 70.00 (0-7918-1769-5, TS283) ASME Pr.

NDE for the Energy Industry, 1995 Proceedings: The Energy & Environmental EXPO '95 - the Energy-Sources Technology Conference & Exhibition (1995: Houston, TX) Ed. by Don E. Bray. LC 94-74526. (NDE Ser.: Vol. 13). 91p. 1995. pap. 64.00 (0-7918-1298-7, H00930) ASME.

NDE Handbook: Non-Destructive Examination Methods for Condition Monitoring. Ed. by Knud G. Boving. 432p. 1989. 180.00 (0-408-04392-X, Pub. by Woodhead Pubng) Am Educ Systs.

NDE in Relation to Structural Integrity for Nuclear & Pressurised Components: Proceedings of the 1st International Conference. 1008p. 1999. boxed set 405.00 (1-85573-430-3) Am Educ Systs.

NDE in the Nuclear & Pressure Vessel Industries: 10th International Conference, Glasgow, Scotland, June 11-14, 1990. International Conference on NDE in the Nuclear & P. Ed. by M. John Whittle et al. LC 90-85884. (Illus.). 805p. 1990. reprint ed. pap. 200.00 (0-608-02611-5, 206326900004) Bks Demand.

NDE in the Nuclear Industry: Proceedings of 8th International Conference on Nondestructive Evaluation in the Nuclear Industry, 17-20 November, 1986, Kissimmee, FL, U. S. A. Ed. by David Stahl. LC 87-70227. (Illus.). 695p. reprint ed. pap. 200.00 (0-608-15998-0, 203307000083) Bks Demand.

NDE in the Nuclear Industry & Equipment-Services Exposition: 6th International Conference: 28 November - 2 December 1983, Hotel International, Zurich, Switzerland. LC 84-73247. (Illus.). 839p. reprint ed. pap. 200.00 (0-608-15999-9, 203307100083) Bks Demand.

NDE Near Death Experiences. Lee Nelson. 1994. pap. 12.95 (1-55517-366-7) CFI Dist.

NDE Near Death Experiences. Lee Nelson. 177p. 1995. 14.95 (1-55517-160-5) CFI Dist.

NDE of Cracks in Aircraft. Jacob K. Easter & George A. Matzkanin. (Illus.). 64p. 1998. pap. 75.00 (1-890596-06-X, NTIAC-SR-98-04) TX Res Inst.

*__NDE of Hidden Corrosion.__ George A. Matzkanin & Jacob K. Easter. (Illus.). 61p. 1998. pap. 75.00 (1-890596-05-1, NTIAC-SR-98-03) TX Res Inst.

NDE of Microstructure for Process Control: Proceedings of a Symposium - Sponsored by the Materials Testing & Quality Control Division, Nondestructive Testing Committee of ASM at the ASM Metals Congress, Detroit, MI, September 18-19, 1984. American Society for Metals Staff. Ed. by H. N. Wadley. LC 85-73216. (Illus.). 212p. reprint ed. pap. 65.80 (0-8357-4098-6, 203686400005) Bks Demand.

NDE Performance Demonstration, Planning & Research: Proceedings ASME Pressure Vessels & Piping Conference (1997, Orlando, FL) Ed. by Mohamad M. Behravesh et al. LC 97-73339. (PVP Ser.: Vol. 352, NDE-Vol. 16). 71p. 1997. pap. 84.00 (0-7918-1569-2) ASME.

Ndebele. Elizabeth Schneider. LC 96-20758. (Heritage Library of African Peoples: Set 4). (Illus.). 64p. (YA). (gr. 7-12). 1996. lib. bdg. 16.95 (0-8239-2009-7, D2009-7) Rosen Group.

Ndebele: The Art of an African Tribe. Margaret Courtney-Clark. LC 85-4382. (Illus.). 208p. 1990. 60.00 (0-8478-0685-5, Pub. by Rizzoli Intl) St Martin.

*__Ndebele Beadwork: African Artistry.__ Ann Stalcup. (Crafts of the World Ser.). (Illus.). 24p. (J). (gr. k-4). 1999. 19.33 (0-8239-5336-X) Rosen Group.

*__NDH Pocket Guide to Drug Dosages.__ 2nd ed. Springhouse Publishing Staff. 2000. pap. text 17.95 (1-58255-045-X) Springhouse Corp.

NDI Handbook: How Domestic Organizations Monitor Elections: An A to Z Guide. (ARA., Illus.). 188p. 1997. pap. 14.95 (1-880134-28-4) Natl Demo Inst.

NDI Handbook How Domestic Organizations Monitor Elections: An A to Z Guide. National Democratic Institute for International Af. 160p. 1995. pap. 14.95 (1-880134-17-9) Natl Demo Inst.

NDI Handbook (NDI Manual para la Observacion Nacional de Elecciones) How Domestic Organizations Monitor Elections: An A to Z Guide (Guia de la A a la Z) (SPA., Illus.). 164p. 1997. pap. 14.95 (1-880134-29-2) Natl Demo Inst.

Ndito Runs. Laurie H. Andersen. LC 94-44649. (Illus.). 32p. (J). (ps-2). 1995. 15.95 (0-8050-3265-7) H Holt & Co.

NdjenFerno. Lindsay Hill. 66p. 1998. pap. 8.95 (0-9654877-3-3) Vatic Hum Pr.

NDR, '96. George R. Spratto. (Professional Reference - Nursing Ser.). 1392p. 1996. pap. 26.95 (0-8273-6644-2) Delmar.

Ndroje Balendro: Musiques, Terrain. E. Peters. 1998. 50.00 (90-6831-785-7, Pub. by Peeters Pub) Bks Intl VA.

NDS Design & Implementation. 1999. pap. write for info. (1-884486-04-5) Wave Tech.

NDS for NT. Jeffrey F. Hughes. LC 98-70239. 450p. 1998. pap. 39.99 (0-7645-4551-5) IDG Bks.

NDT Data Fusion. X. E. Gros. LC 96-34010. 256p. 1996. text 94.95 (0-470-23724-4, TA417) Halsted Pr.

NDT Data Fusion. X. E. Gross. 205p. 1997. 89.95 (0-340-67648-5) Wiley.

NDT in the Foundry. Dick Struk. (Illus.). 204p. 1995. pap. 82.00 (0-931403-38-3, 1199) Am Soc Nondestructive.

An Asterisk (*) at the beginning of an entry indicates that the title is appearing for the first time.

NDT Personnel Training, Qualification & Certification Audit Checklist. 24p. (C). 1995. pap. 28.00 (0-931403-24-3, 204) Am Soc Nondestructive.

***Ndugu's Boy.** Peter Dineen. 160p. (YA). 1999. pap. 9.95 (1-893302-06-7) Dandelion Bks.

Ndyuka: A Descriptive Grammar. George L. Hutter & Mary L. Hutter. LC 94-8590. (Descriptive Grammars Ser.). 640p. (C). (gr. 13). 1994. 190.00 (0-415-05992-5, C0451) Routledge.

Ne Delivrer sur Ordonnance. Jean Freustie. (FRE.). 320p. 1974. pap. 10.95 (0-7859-2352-7, 2070366308) Fr & Eur.

Ne Dyshi Bez Menia. Deon Svetlana. LC 98-12666. (RUS.). 128p. 1998. pap. 9.00 (1-55779-108-2) Hermitage Pubs.

Ne Me Casse Pas les Oreilles. Charles M. Schulz. (Peanuts Ser.). (FRE.). (J). 1984. 9.95 (0-8288-4534-4) Fr & Eur.

Ne Nous Enervons Pas! Chester B. Himes. (FRE.). 256p. 1987. pap. 10.95 (0-7859-2537-6, 2070378276) Fr & Eur.

Ne Reveillez Pas Madame see Rendez-Vous de Senlis Suivi de Leocadia

Ne Reveillez Pas Madame. Jean Anouilh. (FRE.). 192p. 1981. pap. 10.95 (0-7859-1940-6, 2070373185) Fr & Eur.

Ne Reveillez Pas Madame. Jean Anouilh. (Folio Ser.: No. 1318). (FRE.). pap. 8.95 (2-07-037318-5) Schoenhof.

NE Symposium on Motivation, 1996: Motivation & Delinquency. Ed. by D. Wayne Osgood. LC 53-11655. (Illus.). xiv, 295p. 1997. text 45.00 (0-8032-3566-6) U of Nebr Pr.

Ne Touchez Pas A Ma Babouche. Gilles Gauthier. (Novels in the Premier Roman Ser.). (FRE.). 64p. (J). (gr. 2-5). 1988. pap. 8.95 (2-89021-083-9, Pub. by La Courte Ech) Firefly Bks Ltd.

Ne vous noyez pas dans une verre d'eau. Tr. of Don't Sweat the Small Stuff,.... (FRE.). pap., boxed set 14.95 incl. audio (2-89517-018-5, Pub. by Coffragants) Penton Overseas.

Ne Zabyt' (Don't Forget) The Tragedy of Jews of Zin'kov. Ilya Abramovich. LC 90-85933. (RUS.). 112p. 1991. pap. text 10.00 (0-911971-62-9) Effect Pub.

NEA: Trojan Horse in American Education. 7th ed. Samuel L. Blumenfeld. LC 84-16546. 284p. (Orig.). 1993. pap. 19.95 (0-941995-07-0) Paradigm ID.

NEA Activities in 1996: 1997 Edition. 72p. 1997. pap. write for info. (92-64-16452-9, Pub. by Org for Econ) OECD.

NEA Series. 5.00 (0-943018-01-3); 5.00 (0-943018-03-X); 5.00 (0-943018-02-1); 5.00 (0-943018-04-8) Backstreet.

Neal A. Maxwell, Set. Neal A. Maxwell. 1992. reprint ed. boxed set 24.95 (0-87579-607-9) Deseret Bk.

Neal A. Maxwell Quote Book. Cory H. Maxwell. 1997. 19.95 (1-57008-325-8) Bookcraft Inc.

Neal Camps Out see Early Phonetic Readers - Set E

***Neal Family.** fac. ed. Emma E. Brigham. 378p. 1999. reprint ed. 67.00 (0-8328-9913-5); reprint ed. pap. 57.00 (0-8328-9914-3) Higginson Bk Co.

Neal Hefti - Anthology. Ed. by Carol Cuellar. 84p. (Orig.). (C). 1988. pap. text 12.95 (0-7692-0735-9, SF0196) Wrner Bros.

Neal McCoy - You Gotta Love That! Ed. by Carol Cuellar. 44p. (Orig.). (YA). 1995. pap. text 14.95 (0-89724-747-7, PF9525) Wrner Bros.

Neal Notes. Iris C. Jones. 155p. (Orig.). 1988. pap. text 14.00 (0-9620067-0-X) Links Geneal Pubns.

Neal R. Amundson: A Special Issue in His Honor - A Special Issue of the Journal Chemical Engineering Communications. Ed. by D. Ramkinshina. 486p. 1987. pap. text 757.00 (2-88124-256-1) Gordon & Breach.

***Neal-Schuman Authoritative Guide to Evaluating Information on the Internet.** Alison Cooke. LC 99-28010. 192p. 1999. pap. 55.00 (1-55570-356-9) Neal-Schuman.

Neal-Schuman Authoritative Guide to Web Search Engines: Policies, Templates & Icons for Library Web Pages; Training Modules for Library Staff & Patrons. Susan Maze et al. LC 97-14805. 178p. 1997. 55.00 (1-55570-305-4) Neal-Schuman.

Neal Schuman Complete Internet Companion for Librarians. Allen C. Benson. LC 97-29536. (Netguides Ser.). 513p. 1997. 65.00 (1-55570-317-8) Neal-Schuman.

Neal-Schuman Directory of Library Technical Services Home Pages. Barbara Stewart. LC 97-25195. 249p. 1997. pap. 59.95 (1-55570-286-4) Neal-Schuman.

Neal-Schuman Guide to Finding Legal & Regulatory Information on the Internet. Yvonne J. Chandler. LC 97-27285. 400p. 1997. 135.00 (1-55570-306-2) Neal-Schuman.

Neal-Schuman Index to Card Games. Compiled by Kay Marke. 125p. (Orig.). 1990. 27.50 (1-55570-052-7) Neal-Schuman.

Neal-Schuman Index to Fingerplays. Kay Cooper. Ed. by Jim Roginski. LC 93-40099. 320p. 1993. 32.95 (1-55570-149-3) Neal-Schuman.

Neal-Schuman Index to Performing & Creative Artists in Collective Biographies. Susan Poorman. 155p. 1991. pap. text 27.50 (1-55570-056-X) Neal-Schuman.

Neal-Schuman Index to Sports Figures in Collective Biographies. Paulette B. Sharkey. 184p. 1991. text 27.50 (1-55570-055-1) Neal-Schuman.

***Neal-Schuman Library Technology Companion: A Basic Guide for Library Staff.** John J. Burke. 250p. 2000. pap. 45.00 (1-55570-398-4) Neal-Schuman.

Neal-Schuman WebMaster: Policies, Templates & Icons for Library WebPages; Training Modules for Library Staff & Patrons. Lisa Champelli & Howard Rosenbaum. LC 97-16026. 182p. 1997. 190.00 incl. cd-rom (1-55570-307-0) Neal-Schuman.

Nealartiyear The Naladiyar, or, Four Hundred Quatrains in Tamil : With Introduction, Translation & Notes Critical, Philological & Explanatory to Which Is Added a Concordance & Lexicon G. U. Pope. LC 98-904958. 440 p. 1997. write for info. (81-206-0023-1) Asian Educ Servs.

Neale: Charter & Records of Neales of Berkley, Yate & Corsham, England. John A. Neale. 263p. 1993. reprint ed. pap. 41.00 (0-8328-3725-3); reprint ed. lib. bdg. 51.00 (0-685-68822-4) Higginson Bk Co.

Neale Donald Walsch on Abundance & Right Livelihood. Neale Donald Walsch. LC 99-95400. 144p. 1999. 14.95 (1-57174-164-X) Hampton Roads Pub Co.

Neale Donald Walsch on Holistic Living. Neale Donald Walsch. LC 99-95398. 112p. 1999. 14.95 (1-57174-165-8) Hampton Roads Pub Co.

Neale Donald Walsch on Relationships. Neale Donald Walsch. 112p. 1999. 14.95 (1-57174-163-1) Hampton Roads Pub Co.

Neale S. Godfrey's Ultimate Kids' Money Book. Neale S. Godfrey. LC 97-35433. (Illus.). 132p. (J). (gr. 3-7). 1998. per. 18.00 (0-689-81717-7) S&S Childrens.

Neal's Common Foot Disorders: Diagnosis & Management. 6th ed. Donald L. Lorimer et al. LC 96-37052. 1997. pap. text 54.95 (0-443-05258-1) Church.

Neal's Homecoming: Sequel to Faded Tracks. Jim L. McAlpin. (Historical Novels on Civil War & Aftermath Ser.). 250p. 1997. pap. 15.95 (0-9658220-1-X) HHI.

Neal's Yard Natural Remedies. Susan Curtis et al. (Illus.). 208p. 1990. pap. 12.95 (0-14-019000-7, Arkana) Viking Penguin.

Neal's Yard Remedies: Essentail Oils. Susan Curtis. (Illus.). 144p. 1996. pap. 14.95 (1-85410-413-6, Pub. by Aurum Pr) London Brdge.

Nealy Way of Knowledge: Twenty Years of Extreme Cartoons. William Nealy. Ed. by Holland Wallace. LC 99-87694. (Illus.). 224p. 2000. pap. 14.95 (0-89732-303-3) Menasha Ridge.

Neanche Dio Puo Stare Solo see Revelation of Love: Scripture, Prayers & Reflections for Eucharistic Adoration

Neander-Thin: A Caveman's Guide to Nutrition. 2nd ed. Raymond V. Audette & Troy Gilchrist. (Illus.). 112p. (Orig.). 1995. pap. 12.00 (0-9646345-1-1) Paleolithic Pr.

Neandertal. John Darnton. 1998. pap. text 11.95 (84-08-02725-5) Planeta.

Neandertals & Modern Humans in Western Asia. Ed. by T. Akazawa et al. LC 98-35581. (Illus.). 552p. (C). 1998. 79.50 (0-306-45924-8, Plenum Trade) Perseus Pubng.

Neanderthal: A Novel. John Darnton. 416p. 1997. mass mkt. 7.99 (0-312-96300-9) St Martin.

Neanderthal: A Novel. large type ed. John Darnton. 1996. 27.95 (0-7862-0824-4) Thorndike Pr.

Neanderthal: A Novel. large type ed. John Darnton. LC PS3554.A727N43 1996b. 609p. 1997. pap. 25.95 (0-7862-0834-1) Thorndike Pr.

Neanderthal: Neanderthal Man & the Story of Human Origins. Paul Jordan. 2000. 34.95 (0-7509-1934-5) Sutton Pub Ltd.

Neanderthal Book & Skeleton. Stephen Cumbaa. LC 97-40108. (Hand in Hand with Nature Ser.). (Illus.). 64p. (J). 1997. pap. 16.95 (0-7611-0904-8) Workman Pub.

Neanderthal Book & Skeleton. Stephen Cumbaa & Kathlyn Stewart. (Illus.). 64p. (J). (gr. 2 up). 1998. pap. 16.95 (1-895897-99-8) Somerville Hse.

Neanderthal Enigma. James Shreeve. 1995. 23.00 (0-06-889407-4) HarpC.

Neanderthal Legacy: An Archaeological Perspective from Western Europe. Paul Mellars. LC 95-4300. 480p. 1995. text 75.00 (0-691-03493-1, Pub. by Princeton U Pr) Cal Prin Full Svc.

Neanderthal Man. Myra L. Shackley. LC 80-497813. x, 149p. 1980. write for info. (0-7156-1429-0) G Duckworth.

Neanderthal Novel 3. J. Robert Sawyer. text. write for info. (0-312-87690-4) St Martin.

Neanderthal Remains from Krapina: A Descriptive & Comparative Study. Fred H. Smith. LC GN0075.C8. (University of Tennessee, Department of Anthropology, Report of Investigations Ser.: No. 15). (Illus.). 391p. reprint ed. pap. 121.30 (0-608-17428-9, 202985000066) Bks Demand.

Neanderthal Tart: The Sexuality of the Dynamic Assertive Woman of Accomplishment & Other Funny Stuff. Jessica Flemming & Bill Tyson. LC 93-83941. (Illus.). 160p. (Orig.). 1993. pap. 12.95 (1-883445-00-0) Plain Brown.

Neanderthals see Extinct Species Collection

Neanderthals: Changing the Image of Mankind. Erik Trinkhaus. LC 93-42583. 1994. pap. 16.00 (0-679-73299-3) Vin Bks.

***Neanderthals, Bandits & Farmers: How Agriculture Really Began.** Colin Tudge. LC 99-15178. 64p. 1999. pap. text 9.95 (0-300-08024-7) Yale U Pr.

***Neanderthals on the Edge: 150th Anniversary Conference of the Forbes' Quarry Discovery, Gibraltar.** Ed. by C. D. Stringer et al. (Illus.). 120p. (C). 2000. pap. 45.00 (1-84217-015-5, Pub. by Oxbow Bks) David Brown.

Neanderthin: Eat Like a Caveman to Achieve a Lean, Strong, Healthy Body. Audette. LC 99-36356. 256p. 1999. text 23.95 (0-312-24338-3) St Martin.

***Neanderthin: Eat Like a Caveman to Achieve a Lean, Strong, Healthy Body.** Raymond V. Audette & Tony Gilchrist. 2000. mass mkt. 6.99 (0-312-97591-0) St Martin.

Neapolitan Festa a Ballo "Delizie Di Posilipo Boscarecce, a Maritime & Selected Instrumental Ensemble Pieces. Francesco Lambardi et al. Ed. by Roland Jackson. (Recent Researches in Music of the Baroque Era Ser.: Vol. RRB25). (Illus.). xx, 69p. 1978. pap. 30.00 (0-89579-093-9, RRB25) A-R Eds.

Neapolitan Memories. 64p. 1984. pap. 7.95 (0-7935-3019-9, 8633) H Leonard.

Neapolitan Painting of the Seicento. Aldo De Rinaldis. LC 75-11055. 1976. reprint ed. lib. bdg. 45.00 (0-87817-177-0) Hacker.

Neapolitan Recipe Collection: Cuoco Napoletano. Terence Scully. LC 98-51414. 264p. 2000. text 47.50 (0-472-10972-3, 10972) U of Mich Pr.

Neaptide. Sarah Daniels. (Royal Court Writers Ser.). 48p. (C). 1988. pap. write for info. (0-413-57800-3, A0182, Methuen Drama) Methn.

Near a Whole City Full. Edward W. Townsend. LC 76-166909. (Illus.). 1971. reprint ed. 29.00 (0-403-01434-4) Scholarly.

Near & Far: Closeness & Distance in Psychotherapy. Martin S. Livingston. LC 91-40451. 225p. 1992. 18.95 (0-944957-34-X) Rivercross Pub.

Near & Middle East see Civilizations of the East

Near & Middle East, 1856-1914, Pt. I see British Documents on Foreign Affairs: Series B: Near & Middle East

Near & the Dear. Dada Mukerjee. (Illus.). 294p. 1996. pap. 12.95 (1-887474-02-1) Hanuman Found.

Near at Hand: Poems. James Whitehead. LC 92-36843. 64p. (C). 1993. pap. 10.95 (0-8262-0878-9); text 18.95 (0-8262-0877-0) U of Mo Pr.

***Near-Birth Experience: A Journey to the Center of Self.** Gerald Bongard. 2000. pap. 13.95 (1-56924-602-5) Marlowe & Co.

Near Breathing: A Memoir of a Difficult Birth. Kathryn Rhett. LC 96-51228. (Emerging Writers in Creative Nonfiction Ser.). 215p. 1997. 24.95 (0-8207-0277-3); pap. text 16.95 (0-8207-0278-1) Duquesne.

Near Changes: Poems. Mona Van Duyn. 1992. pap. 14.00 (0-679-72909-7) Knopf.

NEAR Conference on Missile Aerodynamics, Monterey, CA, Oct. 31-Nov. 2, 1988: Proceedings. Nielsen Engineering & Research, Inc. Staff. 1989. pap. 65.00 (0-9620629-1-X) Nielsen Engineering & Res Inc.

Near Country: Poem of Loss. Glenna Luschei et al. (Illus.). ix, 71p. 1999. pap. 13.00 (0-941490-35-1) Solo Pr.

Near Country: Poem of Loss. aut. limited ed. Glenna Luschei et al. (Illus.). ix, 71p. 1999. 45.00 (0-941490-34-3) Solo Pr.

Near Dead. Stephen R. George. 1992. mass mkt. 4.50 (0-8217-3663-9, Zebra Kensgtn) Kensgtn Pub Corp.

Near Death: A Soul Survivor's Tale. Fred Hughes. 250p. 1998. pap. 15.00 (0-9647568-1-1) Action Acad.

Near Death Vol. 2: Power of the Blood. Nancy Kilpatrick. Ed. by Rebecca Todd. 304p. 1994. mass mkt. 5.50 (0-671-88090-X) PB.

Near Death Vol. 2: Power of the Blood. Nancy Kilpatrick. 281p. 1998. reprint ed. pap. 12.00 (1-901914-17-8, Pub. by Pumpkin Bks) Firebird Dist.

Near Death Experience: A Reader. Ed. by Lee W. Bailey & Jenny Yates. 1996. pap. 19.95 (0-614-97727-4) Routledge.

Near Death Experience: A Reader. Jenny Yates. Ed. by Lee W. Bailey. LC 95-26366. 409p. (C). 1996. 75.00 (0-415-91430-2); pap. 25.99 (0-415-91431-0) Routledge.

Near-Death Experience: An Annotated Bibliography. Terry K. Basford. LC 89-78521. 192p. 1990. text 10.00 (0-8240-6349-X, SS481) Garland.

Near-Death Experience: In the Light of Scientific Research & the Spiritual Science of Rudolf Steiner. Calvert Roszell. LC 91-27842. 96p. 1992. pap. 10.95 (0-88010-360-4) Anthroposophic.

Near-Death Experience: Mysticism or Madness. Judith Cressy. LC 92-74362. 1994. 14.95 (0-8158-0490-3) Chris Mass.

Near-Death Experience: Problems, Prospects, Perspectives. Bruce Greyson & Charles P. Flynn. (Illus.). 304p. 1984. pap. 37.95 (0-398-06362-1); text 50.95 (0-398-05008-2) C C Thomas.

Near-Death Experience, Beliefs about Life after Death, & the Tibetan Book of the Dead. Paul Badham. (ENG & JPN.). 40p. 1990. pap. 3.50 (0-914910-95-7) Buddhist Bks.

Near Death Experience of a Cat. Stefanie Samek. 1999. pap. 8.95 (0-452-27512-1, Plume) Dutton Plume.

Near-Death Experiences. Elaine Landau. (Mysteries of Science Ser.). (Illus.). 48p. (J). (gr. 3-6). 1995. lib. bdg. 20.90 (1-56294-543-2) Millbrook Pr.

Near Death Experiences: Scientific, Philosophical & Religious Perspectives. Douglas W. Shrader. 49p. 1994. 3.00 (0-9633277-9-8, Oneonta Philosophy) Global Pubns.

Near Earth Asteroid Rendezvous Mission. Ed. by C. T. Russell. LC 97-52154. 320p. 1998. 185.00 (0-7923-4957-1) Kluwer Academic.

Near-Earth Objects: The United Nations International Conference, Vol. 822. Ed. by John L. Remo. LC 97-20561. 1997. 140.00 (1-57331-040-9) NY Acad Sci.

Near-Earth Radiation Environment Including Time Variations & Secondary Radiation: Proceedings of Meetings F2.6 & F2.7 of COSPAR Scientific Commission F Which Was Held During the 30th COSPAR Scientific Assembly, Hamburg, Germany, 11-21 July, 1994. Ed. by M. A. Shea et al. (Advances in Space Research Ser.: Vol. 17, No. 2). 184p. 1995. pap. write for info. (0-08-042642-5, Pergamon Pr) Elsevier.

Near East see Supplement to the World Trade Annual, 1983: Trade of the Industrial Nations with Eastern Europe & the Developing Nations

Near East: Archaeology in the 'Cradle of Civilization' Charles K. Maisels. (Experience of Archaeology Ser.). (Illus.). 256p. (C). 1998. pap. 27.99 (0-415-18607-2) Routledge.

Near East since the First World War. M. E. Yapp. (History of the Near East Ser.). (Illus.). 526p. (C). 1990. pap. text 44.00 (0-582-49499-0, 78651) Longman.

Near East under Roman Rule: Selected Papers. Benjamin Isaac. LC 97-40147. (Mnemosyne, Supplements Ser.: No. 177). (Illus.). 225p. 1997. 153.00 (90-04-10736-3) Brill Academic Pubs.

Near Eastern & Aegean Texts. Ed. by A. Bernard Knapp. (Sources for the History of Cyprus Ser.: Vol. II). ix, 99p. (Orig.). 1996. pap. 30.00 (0-9651704-2-X) Greece & Cyprus Res.

Near Eastern & Far Eastern Art. Jay C. Leff. 1966. pap. 4.50 (0-8079-0092-3) October.

Near Eastern Culture & Society. Ed. by T. Cuyler Young. LC 68-29533. 306p. reprint ed. pap. 94.90 (0-608-30406-9, 200113600063) Bks Demand.

Near Eastern Destruction Datings As Sources for Greek & Near Eastern Iron Age Chronology: Archaeological & Historical Studies: The Cases of Samaria (722 B. C.) & Tarsus (696 B. C.) 2nd ed. Stig Forsberg. LC 96-165540. (Uppsala Studies in Ancient Mediterranean & Near Eastern Civilizations: No. 19). (Illus.). 106p. (Orig.). 1995. pap. 42.50 (91-554-3592-0) Coronet Bks.

Near Eastern Numismatics, Iconography, Epigraphy & History: Studies in Honor of George C. Miles. Ed. by Jere L. Bacharach & Dickran K. Kouymjian. 1974. 55.00 (0-8156-6041-3, Pub. by Am U Beirut) Syracuse U Pr.

Near Eastern Policy of the Emperor Napoleon III, Vol. XXV, Nos. 1$2.-- Alyce E. Mange. LC 74-12762. (Illinois Studies in the Social Sciences). 150p. 1975. reprint ed. lib. bdg. 55.00 (0-8371-7742-1, MAEN, Greenwood Pr) Greenwood.

Near Eastern Royalty & Rome, 100-30 B.C. Richard D. Sullivan. (Phoenix Supplementary Volumes Ser.). 556p. 1990. text 125.00 (0-8020-2682-6) U of Toronto Pr.

Near Eastern Seals. Dominique Collon. (Interpreting the Past Ser.). (Illus.). 64p. 1991. pap. 13.95 (0-520-07308-8, Pub. by U CA Pr) Cal Prin Full Svc.

Near Eastern Studies: In Honor of William Foxwell Albright. Ed. by Hans Goedicke. LC 70-142817. 503p. 1971. reprint ed. pap. 156.00 (0-608-00808-7, 206159600010) Bks Demand.

Near Encounters: Festschrift for Richard Martin. Contrib. by Hanjo Berressem & Bernd Herzogenrath. LC 96-150033. xiii, 310p. 1995. 57.95 (3-631-48552-2) P Lang Pubng.

Near Enough to Hear the Words. Geraldine Zetzel. 26p. 1998. pap. 7.95 (0-944754-47-3) Pudding Hse Pubns.

Near-Field Nano-Optics: From Basic Principles to Nano-Fabrication & Nano-Photonics. M. Ohtsu & H. Hori. LC 99-14419. (Lasers, Photonics, & Electro-Optics Ser.). (Illus.). 390p. (C). 1999. write for info. (0-306-45897-7, Plenum Trade) Perseus Pubng.

Near-Field Nano/Atom Optics & Technology. Ed. by M. Ohtsu. LC 98-21851. (Illus.). xiv, 306p. 1998. 74.95 (4-431-70228-8) Spr-Verlag.

Near Field Optics: Proceedings of the NATO Advanced Research Workshop at Arc-et-Senans, Oct. 26-28, 1992. Ed. by Dieter W. Pohl & Daniel Courjon. LC 93-25336. (NATO Advanced Study Institutes Series E, Applied Sciences: No. 242). 1993. text 264.50 (0-7923-2394-7) Kluwer Academic.

Near-Field Optics: Theory, Instrumentation, & Applications. Michael Paesler & Patrick Moyer. LC 95-46171. (Illus.). 355p. 1996. 89.95 (0-471-04311-7, Wiley-Interscience) Wiley.

Near Field Optics & Nanoscopy. J. P. Fillard. 300p. 1996. text 56.00 (981-02-2349-8) World Scientific Pub.

Near Great, Chronicle of the Vice-Presidents. Archibald Laird. (Illus.). 1980. 17.50 (0-8158-0381-8) Chris Mass.

Near Home. Photos by Robert Mitchell. (Illus.). 90p. (Orig.). 1996. pap., per. 14.95 (0-9653279-0-6) Connections Pub.

Near Home. William E. Channing, II. (Works of William Ellery Channing II). 1990. reprint ed. lib. bdg. 79.00 (0-7812-2264-8) Rprt Serv.

Near Infrared Diffuse Reflectance - Transmittance Spectroscopy. J. Hollo. 320p. (C). 1987. 265.00 (0-569-09055-5, Pub. by Collets) St Mut.

Near Infrared Diffuse Reflectance - Transmittance Spectroscopy. J. Hollo et al. 818p. (C). 1987. 114.00 (963-05-4625-6, Pub. by Akade Kiado) St Mut.

Near-Infrared Dyes for High Technology Applications. Siegfried D'Ahne et al. LC 98-7675. (NATO ASI Series: Partnership Sub-Series 3). 458p. 1998. write for info. (0-7923-5101-0) Kluwer Academic.

Near Infrared Photographic Sky Survey: A Field Index. G. S. Rossano & E. R. Craine. (Astronomy & Astrophysics Ser.: Vol. 8). (Illus.). 208p. 1980. 38.00 (0-912918-11-X, 0911) Pachart Pub Hse.

Near-Infrared Spectrometry: Learning the Fundamentals. W. Fred McClure. 350p. 1996. 115.00 (1-56081-690-2, Wiley-VCH) Wiley.

Near-Infrared Spectroscopy. W. F. McClure. 350p. 1997. text. write for info. incl. disk (0-471-18613-9) Wiley.

Near Infrared Spectroscopy in Food Analysis see Practical NIR Spectroscopy: With Applications in Food & Beverage Analysis

Near Infrared Spectroscopy in Pharmaceutical & Medical Applications. E. W. Ciurczak & J. Drennen. (Practical Spectroscopy Ser.). (Illus.). Date not set. text. write for info. (0-8247-9453-2) Dekker.

Near Johannesburg Boy & Other Poems. Gwendolyn Brooks. 1991. 4.00 (0-88378-055-0) Third World.

Near-Life Experiences: Discovering New Powers for Personal Growth. Tom McQueen. LC 97-93191. 126p. 1997. 19.95 (0-9656679-3-6) J E M Pub.

Near Life's End. Ron Delbene. 1988. 5.95 (0-687-60804-X) Abingdon.

Near Life's End: What Family & Friends Can Do. Ron DelBene et al. 24p. 1988. pap. 4.00 (0-8358-0578-6) Upper Room Bks.

N

Near Miss: A Study of Wyndham Lewis (1909-1930) Antonio M. Feijo. LC 97-21533. (Literature & the Visual Arts Ser.: Vol. 11). 217p. (C). 1998. text 46.95 (*0-8204-3681-X*) P Lang Pubng.

Near Miss Haiku. Anselm Hollo. 65p. 1990. 6.95 (*0-916328-20-1*) Yellow Pr.

Near Miss Reporting As a Safety Tool. D. A. Lucas et al. (Illus.). 160p. 1991. 84.95 (*0-7506-1178-2*) Buttrwrth-Heinemann.

Near Misses in Anesthesia. John M. Lewis & Tionette H. Fontrier. 112p. 1988. pap. text 36.50 (*0-409-90111-3*) Buttrwrth-Heinemann.

Near Misses in Cardiac Surgery: Great Saves. Miles E. Lee. 112p. 1992. pap. text 37.50 (*0-7506-9391-6*) Buttrwrth-Heinemann.

***Near Misses in Neuro Anesthesia.** Terri W. Blackburn & Garfield B. Russell. (Illus.). 176p. 2000. pap. 35.00 (*0-7506-7065-7*) Buttrwrth-Heinemann.

Near Misses in Pediatric Anesthesia. Brock-Utne. 128p. 1998. pap. text 35.00 (*0-7506-7018-5*) Buttrwrth-Heinemann.

Near Misses in Pulmonary & Cardiothoracic Critical Care. Joseph Varon. LC 98-54232. 136p. 1999. pap. text 27.50 (*0-7506-7117-3*) Buttrwrth-Heinemann.

Near Net Shape Manufacturing: Proceedings from AMS's, 1993 Conference. LC 93-74722. 200p. 1993. pap. 104.00 (*0-87170-497-8*, 6535U) ASM Intl.

Near Net Shape Manufacturing of Advanced Ceramics. Davison. LC 97-132553. 142p. 1995. 2750.00 (*1-56965-227-9*, GB163) BCC.

Near Occasions of Grace. Richard Rohr. LC 92-33193. 125p. (Orig.). 1993. pap. 12.00 (*0-88344-852-1*) Orbis Bks.

Near-Orbital Rocket: Multi-Stage Capable Altitude Prediction, Drag, Center of Pressure, Plotting Ogive Nose Cones, Trajectory, Reentry. Charles E. Rogers & Jerry Irvine. 60p. 1983. 99.95 (*0-912468-14-9*) CA Rocketry.

Near Planets see Our Solar System

Near Planets. (Voyage Through the Universe Ser.). (Illus.). 144p. 1989. lib. bdg. 24.60 (*0-8094-6871-9*) Time-Life.

Near Planets. Time-Life Books Editors. LC 92-8443. (Voyage Through the Universe Ser.). 144p. 1992. lib. bdg. write for info. (*0-8094-9067-6*) Time-Life.

Near Planets. Time-Life Books Editors. LC 92-8443. (Voyage Through the Universe Ser.). (Illus.). 144p. 1992. write for info. (*0-8094-9066-8*) Time-Life.

Near-Rings & Near-Fields: Proceedings of the Conference on Near-Rings & Near-Fields Fredericton, N. B., Canada, July 18-24, 1993. Ed. by Yuen Fong et al. LC 95-30320. (Mathematics & Its Applications Ser.: Vol. 336). 288p. (C). 1995. text 154.50 (*0-7923-3635-6*) Kluwer Academic.

Near-Shore Sedimentology. William F. Tanner. 300p. 1983. pap. 40.00 (*0-938426-04-4*) FSU Geology.

Near-Sighted Knight & the Far-Sighted Dragon: Musical. Eleanor Harder & Ray Harder. (J). (gr. 1-9). 1977. 6.00 (*0-87602-161-5*) Anchorage.

Near Source Contaminant Mixing in Surface Waters. Steven J. Wright. (C). 1998. 69.33 (*0-13-617556-2*, Macmillan Coll) P-H.

Near Star Planets, 5 vols. Elaine Pageler. Ed. by Betty Lou Kratoville. (Illus.). 48p. (J). 1998. pap. 17.00 (*1-57128-092-8*, 8092-8) High Noon Bks.

***Near Star Planets Reproducible Workbook.** Betty Lou Kratoville. 2000. pap. text 14.00 (*1-57128-149-5*) Acad Therapy.

***Near Surface Disposal of Radioactive Waste: Safety Requirements Safety Standard WS-R-1.** IAEA Staff. (Safety Standards Ser.). 29p. 1999. pap. 17.00 (*92-0-101099-0*, STI/PUB/1073, Pub. by IAEA) Bernan Associates.

Near-Surface Land Disposal. Ed. by J. H. Kittel et al. (Radioactive Waste Management Ser.: Vol. 1). xxx, 440p. 1989. text 184.00 (*3-7186-0486-8*) Gordon & Breach.

Near-Term Electric Vehicle Costs, Oct., 1994. William R. Moomaw et al. (Electric Vehicle Information Ser.: Vol. 14). (Illus.). 126p. 1996. pap. 85.00 (*0-89934-267-1*, BT041); lib. bdg. 135.00 (*0-89934-268-X*, BT941) Bus Tech Bks.

Near the Cathedral. James Snydal. (Illus.). 30p. 1995. pap. 4.95 (*1-883938-22-8*) Dry Bones Pr.

Near the Edge. Pat Bucheister. 1995. mass mkt. 2.95 (*0-553-55035-7*) Bantam.

Near the Far Bamboo. Martin St. Kilda. LC 93-70739. 250p. (Orig.). 1993. pap. 9.99 (*0-87509-510-0*) Chr Pubns.

Near the Fire. Philip K. Jason. LC 83-1488. 1983. pap. 8.95 (*0-931848-55-5*) Dryad Pr.

Near the Greats. Agnes W. Spring. 184p. 1982. 12.95 (*0-939650-31-2*) R H Pub.

Near the Narcotic Sea. Joseph Lisowski. 64p. (Orig.). 1992. pap. 10.00 (*0-9624155-4-5*) Cottage Wordsmiths.

Near the River's Edge. Kathleen Aponick. 34p. 1995. pap. 7.95 (*0-944754-27-9*) Pudding Hse Pubns.

***Near To.** Mark DuCharme. (Poetry New York Pamphlet Ser.: No. 25). 16p. 1999. pap. 5.00 (*0-923389-41-5*) Meet Eyes Bind.

Near to Nature's Heart. Edward P. Roe. (Notable American Authors Ser.). 1999. reprint ed. lib. bdg. 125.00 (*0-7812-8813-4*) Rprt Serv.

Near to the Fire. Kenneth G. Mills. 1979. audio 5.45 (*0-919842-04-6*, KGOC11) Sun-Scape Ent.

Near to the Heart of God: Daily Insights from the Spiritual Classics. Selected by Bernard Bangley. LC 98-24970. 393p. 1998. pap. 11.99 (*0-87788-824-8*, H Shaw Pubs) Waterbrook Pr.

Near to the Heart of God: God's Words of Encouragement for Women. Teery Meeuwsen. LC 97-35181. Orig. Title: He Touched Me. 256p. 1998. pap. 17.99 (*0-7852-7060-4*, J Thoma Bks) Nelson.

***Near to the Heart of God: Scripture Prayer Journal.** Sheila Cragg. 384p. 2000. 14.99 (*1-58134-226-8*) Crossway Bks.

Near to the Wild Heart. Clarice Lispector. Tr. & Afterword by Giovanni Pontiero. LC 90-33455. 192p. 1990. reprint ed. pap. 10.95 (*0-8112-1140-1*, NDP698, Pub. by New Directions) Norton.

Near unto God. James C. Schaap & Abraham Kuyper. LC 97-7877. 235p. 1997. pap. 13.95 (*1-56212-253-3*) CRC Pubns.

Near View: Selected Verse. Dorothy B. Thompson. 131p. 1991. 14.95 (*0-932845-51-7*) Lowell Pr.

Near Visual Acuity Tests. Matthias Sachsenweger. (C). 1987. text 73.50 (*0-85200-664-0*) Kluwer Academic.

Near Wall Turbulence: Proceedings of the International Center for Heat & Mass Tranfer. Ed. by Stephen J. Kline & Naim H. Afgan. 360p. 1989. 198.00 (*0-89116-733-1*) Hemisp Pub.

***Near You: Francis Craig, Dean of Southern Maestros.** Robert W. Ikard. LC 99-66051. (Illus.). 192p. 1999. 36.95 (*1-57736-161-X*, Hillsboro Pr) Providence Hse.

Nearby Eden. Menke Katz. 128p. 1990. pap. 10.95 (*0-912292-90-3*) Smith.

Nearby Faraway: A Personal Journey Through the Heart of the West. David Petersen. LC 97-28206. (Illus.). 240p. 1997. 26.00 (*1-55566-206-4*); pap. 15.00 (*1-55566-187-4*) Johnson Bks.

Nearby Galaxies Catalog. R. Brent Tully & J. Richard Fisher. 224p. 1988. text 74.95 (*0-521-35299-1*) Cambridge U Pr.

Nearby Galaxy Atlas. R. Brent Tully & J. Richard Fisher. LC 87-11689. (Illus.). 29p. 1987. text 95.00 (*0-521-30136-X*) Cambridge U Pr.

Nearby History: Exploring the Past Around You. David E. Kyvig & Myron A. Marty. LC 95-52746. (American Association for State & Local History Book Ser.). (Illus.). 320p. 1982. pap. 24.95 (*0-7619-9158-1*) AltaMira Pr.

***Nearby History: Exploring the Past Around You.** 2nd ed. David E. Kyvig & Myron A. Marty. 320p. 2000. 65.00 (*0-7425-0270-8*); pap. 24.95 (*0-7425-0271-6*) AltaMira Pr.

Nearby Molecular Clouds. Ed. by G. Serra. (Lecture Notes in Physics Ser.: Vol. 237). 242p. 1985. 27.95 (*0-387-15991-6*) Spr-Verlag.

Nearby Stars & the Stellar Luminosity Function. A. G. Davis Philip & Arthur R. Upgren. (IAU Colloquium Ser.: No. 76). 550p. 1983. 32.00 (*0-9607902-5-X*); pap. 32.00 (*0-9607902-4-1*) L Davis Pr.

Nearctic Avian Migrants in the Neotropics: Maps, Appendices, & Bibliography. 2nd ed. T. E. Lovejoy, 3rd et al. Ed. by Sharon Leathery. (Illus.). 325p. 1995. pap. text 12.00 (*0-9638408-5-1*) C & RC Nat Zool.

Nearctic Genera of Chloroperlinae: Plecoptera: Cloroperlidae. Rebecca F. Surdick. LC 84-16284. (Illinois Biological Monographs: No. 54). (Illus.). 160p. 1985. pap. text 14.95 (*0-252-01163-5*) U of Ill Pr.

Nearctic Melanomya & Relatives: Dypeter, Calliphoridae: A Problem in Calyptrate Classification. William L. Downes, Jr. (Bulletin Ser.: No. 460). (Illus.). (Orig.). 1986. pap. 3.00 (*1-55557-000-3*) NYS Museum.

Nearctic Passerine Migrants in South America. Raymond A. Paynter, Jr. (Publications of the Nuttall Ornithological Club: No. 25). (Illus.). 126p. 1995. 13.50 (*1-877973-37-8*, 25) Nuttall Ornith.

Nearer, My God: An Autobiography of Faith. William F. Buckley, Jr. LC 98-16194. 368p. (C). 1998. pap. 14.00 (*0-15-600618-9*, Harvest Bks) Harcourt.

Nearer My God to Thee. A. A. Pennington. LC 98-90133. 1998. pap. 9.95 (*0-533-12708-4*) Vantage.

Nearer Nature. Jim Arnosky. LC 95-43954. (Illus.). 176p. (YA). (gr. 6 up). 1996. 18.00 (*0-688-12213-2*) Lothrop.

***Nearer Than the Sky.** T. Greenwood. LC 00-27852. 288p. 2000. text 23.95 (*0-312-26503-4*) St Martin.

Nearest Active Galaxies. Ed. by J. E. Beckman. 236p. (C). 1993. text 138.50 (*0-7923-2528-1*) Kluwer Academic.

Nearest Far Away Place. abr. ed. Timothy White. 1995. 16.95 incl. audio (*1-882071-55-7*) B&B Audio.

Nearest Faraway Place. Timothy White. Date not set. pap. 15.95 (*0-614-10357-6*) H Holt & Co.

Nearest Faraway Place. Timothy White. 1995. 25.00 (*0-8050-2266-X*) H Holt & Co.

Nearest Faraway Place: Brian Wilson, the Beach Boys, & the Southern California Experience. Timothy White. (Illus.). 432p. 1995. pap. 15.95 (*0-8050-4702-6*, Owl) H Holt & Co.

Nearest in Affection: Towards a Christian Understanding of Islam. Stuart Brown. LC 95-6760. (Pathways Bk.). 136p. (Orig.). 1995. pap. 12.00 (*1-56338-114-1*) TPI PA.

Nearest Living Horizon. Donald Menaker. 64p. (Orig.). 1997. pap. 10.00 (*0-932616-58-5*) Brick Hse Bks.

Nearest Neighbor see Plus Proche Voisin

Nearest Place That Wasn't Ireland: Early Nineteenth Century Irish Labor Migration. Ruth-Ann M. Harris. LC 94-7403. (Illus.). 304p. 1994. reprint ed. pap. 94.30 (*0-608-07137-4*, 206736300009) Bks Demand.

Nearest Star: A Christmas Musical in One-Act. Jerome McDonough. 28p. 1981. pap. 3.25 (*0-88680-137-0*) I E Clark.

Nearing Case: Limitation of Academic Freedom at the Univ. of Penn. by Act of the Board of Trustees, June 14, 1915. Lightner Witmer & Stephen Whitfield. LC 71-122163. (Civil Liberties in American History Ser.). 123p. 1974. reprint ed. lib. bdg. 19.50 (*0-306-71978-9*) Da Capo.

Nearing Case: The Limitation of Academic Freedom at the University of Pennsylvania by Act of the Board of Trustees, June 14, 1915 - A Brief of Facts & Opinions. Lightner Witmer. 144p. 1972. reprint ed. pap. 15.95 (*0-8377-2726-X*, Rothman) W S Hein.

Nearing Notebooks. John Burns & Kerry S. Keys. 36p. 1996. pap. 10.00 (*0-930502-23-X*) Pine Pr.

Nearing of Fall see Osennie Prikoly: Almanakh

Nearing the End in Imperial Russia. George T. Marye. LC 71-115562. (Russia Observed, Series I). 1970. reprint ed. 24.95 (*0-405-03048-7*) Ayer.

Nearing the Year 2000. Edward Hunter-Blair. 114p. (C). 1989. text 40.00 (*0-946270-93-7*, Pub. by Pentland Pr) St Mut.

Nearly a Miner. Einion Evans. 139p. 1994. pap. 17.95 (*0-8464-4660-X*) Beekman Pubs.

Nearly a Miner. Einion Evans. 139p. 1994. pap. 21.00 (*1-85902-064-X*, Pub. by Gomer Pr) St Mut.

Nearly but Not Quite. Paul Rogers. (J). 1997. 19.95 (*0-370-32423-4*, Pub. by Random) Trafalgar.

Nearly but Not Quite. Paul Rogers & John Prater. (Illus.). 32p. (J). (ps-1). 1998. 19.95 (*0-370-32432-3*, Pub. by Bodley Head) Trafalgar.

Nearly Complete Works. Ana Betancourt. (SPA.). 100p. (Orig.). 1991. pap. 8.00 (*0-685-26449-1*) Atabex Collection.

Nearly Departed: Playscript. Vincent D. O'Connor. 1984. pap. 6.00 (*0-88734-212-4*) Players Pr.

Nearly Everybody Read It: Snapshots of the Philadelphia Bulletin. Peter Binzen. LC 97-16200. (Illus.). 192p. 1998. 22.00 (*0-940159-40-6*) Camino Bks.

Nearly Everything Imaginable: The Everyday Life of Utah's Mormon Pioneers. Ed. by Ronald W. Walker & Doris R. Dant. (Illus.). 416p. 1998. 27.95 (*0-8425-2397-9*, BYU Studies) Brigham.

***"nearly Florida"** James Brock. (Florida Poetry Ser.: Vol. 3). xiv, 80p. 2000. pap. 12.00 (*0-938078-67-4*) Anhinga Pr.

Nearly Impossible Brain Bafflers. Tim Sole. LC 98-34853. (Illus.). 96p. 1998. pap. 5.95 (*0-8069-6293-3*) Sterling.

Nearly Integrable Infinite-Dimensional Hamiltonian Systems. Sergej B. Kuksin. LC 93-37172. (Lecture Notes in Mathematics Ser.: Vol. 1556). 1993. 30.95 (*0-387-57161-2*) Spr-Verlag.

Nearly Noodles. Lisa Bruvelaitis. (Annikins Ser.: Vol. 10). (Illus.). 32p. (Orig.). (J). (ps-2). 1990. pap. 0.99 (*1-55037-128-2*, Pub. by Annick) Firefly Bks Ltd.

Nearly Normal, Vol. I. Dustin Beavers. (Illus.). 1994. pap. 5.95 (*0-911505-09-1*) Lifecraft.

Nearly Normal Galaxies. Ed. by S. M. Faber. (Santa Cruz Summer Workshops in Astrophysics Ser.). (Illus.). xxvi, 464p. 1987. 79.95 (*0-387-96521-1*) Spr-Verlag.

Nearly Normal Life: A Memoir. Charles L. Mee. LC 98-25245. 240p. (gr. 8). 1999. 24.00 (*0-316-55852-4*, Back Bay) Little.

Nearly Normal Life: A Memoir. Charles L. Mee. 240p. 2000. pap. 12.95 (*0-316-55836-2*, Back Bay) Little.

***Nearly Normal Life: A Memoir.** large type ed. Charles L. Mee. LC 00-20110. (Americana Series). 2000. 27.95 (*0-7862-2488-6*) Thorndike Pr.

Nearly Out of Heart & Hope: The Puzzle of a Colonial Labourer's Diary. Miles Fairburn. (Illus.). 350p. 1995. pap. 29.95 (*1-86940-118-2*, Pub. by Auckland Univ) Paul & Co Pubs.

Nearly Paradise. Elise Title. (American Romance Ser.: No. 397). 1991. per. 3.25 (*0-373-16397-5*) Harlequin Bks.

Nearly Projective Boolean Algebras. Lutz Heindorf & Leonid B. Shapiro. LC 94-43224. (Lecture Notes in Mathematics Ser.: Vol. 1596). 1994. 43.95 (*3-540-58787-X*); write for info. (*0-387-58787-X*) Spr-Verlag.

Nearly Too Much: The Poetry of J. H. Prynne. N. H. Reeve & Richard Kerridge. 244p. 1997. 34.95 (*0-85323-840-5*, Pub. by Liverpool Univ Pr); pap. 16.95 (*0-85323-850-2*, Pub. by Liverpool Univ Pr) Intl Spec Bk.

Nearly Total Recall: A Guide to a Better Memory at Any Age. Danielle C. Lapp. (Portable Stanford Bks.). 192p. (Orig.). 1992. pap. 12.95 (*0-916318-51-6*) Stanford Alumni Assn.

Nearly-Wed Handbook: How to Survive the Happiest Day of Your Life. Dan Zevin. LC 97-52302. (Illus.). 192p. 2000. 15.00 (*0-380-97555-6*, Avon Bks) Morrow Avon.

Nearness of You. Carolyn Kizer. LC 86-71838. 104p. (Orig.). 1986. 15.00 (*0-914742-96-5*); pap. 10.00 (*0-914742-97-3*) Copper Canyon.

Nearness of You: Students & Teachers Writing On-Line. Ed. by Christopher Edgar & Susan N. Wood. LC 96-7637. 296p. 1996. pap. 16.95 (*0-915924-47-1*) Tchrs & Writers Coll.

Nearrings: Geneses & Applications. James R. Clay. LC 92-30341. (Illus.). 480p. 1992. text 105.00 (*0-19-853398-5*) OUP.

Nearrings, Nearfields & K-Loops: Proceedings of the Conference on Nearrings & Nearfields, Hamburg, Germany, July 30-August 6, 1995. Gerhard Saad & Momme J. Thomsen. LC 97-31470. (Mathematics & Its Applications Ser.). 460p. 1997. text 227.50 (*0-7923-4799-4*) Kluwer Academic.

Nearshore & Estuarine Cohesive Sediment Transport. Ed. by Ashish J. Mehta. (Coastal & Estuarine Studies: Vol. 42). 1993. 54.00 (*0-87590-256-1*) Am Geophysical.

Nearshore Dynamics & Coastal Processes: Theory, Measurement & Prediction Models. Kiyoshi Horikawa. 500p. 1988. 120.00 (*0-86008-418-3*, Pub. by U of Tokyo) Col U Pr.

Nearshore Sediment Dynamics & Sedimentation: An Interdisciplinary Review. Ed. by J. Hails & A. Carr. LC 75-6950. (Illus.). 330p. reprint ed. pap. 102.30 (*0-608-17619-2*, 203047200069) Bks Demand.

Nearshore Sediment Transport. R. J. Seymour. (Illus.). 428p. (C). 1989. 120.00 (*0-306-43157-2*, Plenum Trade) Perseus Pubng.

Nearsighted Naturalist. Ann Zwinger. LC 98-8881. (Illus.). 294p. 1998. 45.00 (*0-8165-1880-7*); pap. text 19.95 (*0-8165-1881-5*) U of Ariz Pr.

Nearsightedness Is Preventable. Emanuel M. Josephson. (Illus.). 35.00 (*0-685-07974-0*); pap. 25.00 (*0-685-07975-9*) Chedney.

Nearsightedness Is Preventable. Emanuel M. Josephson. 1979. 250.00 (*0-318-55527-1*) Revisionist Pr.

Nearsurface Layer of the Ocean. K. N. Fedorov & A. I. Ginzburg. 270p. 1991. 195.00 (*90-6764-136-7*) Coronet Bks.

Neat Feet. Richard Hefter. LC 83-8035. (Stickybear Bks.). (Illus.). (J). (gr. 3-6). 1983. 5.95 (*0-911787-07-0*) Optimum Res Inc.

Neat Plain Modern Stile: Philip Hooker & His Contemporaries, 1796-1836. Ed. by Mary R. Tomlan. LC 94-39001. (Illus.). 344p. (C). 1993. pap. 24.95 (*0-87023-768-3*) U of Mass Pr.

Neat Sheets: The Poetry of James Tiptree, Jr. James Tiptree, Jr. 26p. 1996. 6.50 (*1-892391-02-3*) Tachyon Pubns.

Neate To the Rescue! Debbi Chocolate & Wade Hudson. LC 92-72004. (NEATE Ser.). (Illus.). 112p. (Orig.). (YA). (gr. 5 up). 1992. pap. 3.95 (*0-940975-42-4*) Just Us Bks.

Neater by the Meter: An American Guide to the Metric System. Anton Glaser. LC 73-88193. (Illus.). 112p. (Orig.). 1974. pap. 10.00 (*0-9600324-4-4*) A Glaser.

***Neatest Little Guide to Making Money Online.** Jason Kelly. LC 99-45730. 2000. pap. 12.95 (*0-452-28168-7*, Plume) Dutton Plume.

Neatest Little Guide to Mutual Fund Investing. Jason Kelly. LC 96-25162. 180p. 1996. pap. 11.95 (*0-452-27709-4*, Plume) Dutton Plume.

Neatest Little Guide to Personal Finance. Jason Kelly. LC 98-38220. 176p. 1999. pap. 12.95 (*0-452-28061-3*, Plume) Dutton Plume.

Neatest Little Guide to Stock Market Investing. Jason Kelly. LC 97-34177. 176p. 1998. pap. 12.95 (*0-452-27870-8*, Plume) Dutton Plume.

Neath the Midnight Sun: Alaskan Adventure. abr. ed. Ted H. Leonard. 196p. 1995. pap. 7.95 (*1-56901-407-8*) Alaska Wrd Wrks.

***Neatly Dissected, for the Instruction of Young Ladies & Gentlemen in the Knowledge of Geography: John Spilsbury & Early Dissected Puzzles.** Jill Shefrin. (Children's Library Publications: Vol. 1). (Illus.). 40p. 1999. write for info. (*0-9666084-2-9*); pap. write for info. (*0-9666084-1-0*) Cotsen Occas Pr.

Neatness Counts. Barbara L. McCombs & Linda Brannan. (Skills for Job Success Ser.). (Illus.). 32p. (Orig.). (YA). (gr. 7-12). 1990. teacher ed. 1.95 (*1-56119-046-2*); disk 39.95 (*1-56119-123-X*) Educ Pr MD.

Neatness Counts. Barbara L. McCombs & Linda Brannan. (Skills for Job Success Ser.). (Illus.). 32p. (Orig.). 1990. pap., student ed. 5.95 (*1-56119-045-4*) Educ Pr MD.

Neatness Counts, Set. Barbara L. McCombs & Linda Brannan. (Skills for Job Success Ser.). (Illus.). 32p. (Orig.). (YA). (gr. 7-12). 1990. teacher ed. 54.95 (*1-56119-081-0*) Educ Pr MD.

Neato-Keen Holiday Special. Evan Skolnick. (Tick Ser.). (J). 1997. pap. text 4.50 (*1-57840-163-1*, Pub. by Acclaim Bks) Penguin Putnam.

Nebbadoon's Movie Reviews. Joan Ellis. LC 98-176678. 320p. (Orig.). 1997. pap. 20.00 (*1-891331-06-X*) Nebbadoon Pr.

Nebes Whethlow Ber. Ed. by A. S. Smith. (C). 1989. 22.00 (*0-907566-10-3*, Pub. by Dyllansow Truran) St Mut.

NEBI Yearbook, 1998: North European & Baltic Sea Integration. Ed. by L. Hedegaard & B. Lindstrom. (Illus.). x, 653p. 1998. 109.00 (*3-540-64210-2*) Spr-Verlag.

***NEBI Yearbook 1999: North European & Baltic Sea Integration.** Ed. by L. Hedegaard & B. Lindstrom. (Illus.). xiv, 494p. 2000. 95.00 (*3-540-66407-6*) Spr-Verlag.

Nebojte Sa Pisomnych Prac Z Matematiky (Don't Be Afraid of Mathematical Tests) M. Capova & V. Kolbaska. (SLO.). 216p. 1997. pap. write for info. (*80-08-02433-X*, Pub. by Slov Pegagog Naklad) IBD Ltd.

Nebraska see Official Precancel Catalog, State Sections

Nebraska see Atlas of Historical County Boundaries

Nebraska see One Nation Series

***Nebraska.** (Switched on Schoolhouse Ser.). (Illus.). (J). 2000. pap. 24.95 (*0-7403-0279-5*) Alpha AZ.

Nebraska. Bradley H. Baltensperger. (C). 1996. pap. text 20.00 (*0-86531-471-3*) Westview.

Nebraska. Capstone Press Geography Department Staff. (One Nation Ser.). (Illus.). 48p. (J). (gr. 3-7). 1996. lib. bdg. 19.00 (*0-516-20270-7*) Childrens.

Nebraska. Dennis B. Fradin. LC 95-12951. (Illus.). 64p. (J). (gr. 3-5). 1995. lib. bdg. 26.00 (*0-516-03827-3*) Childrens.

Nebraska. Dennis B. Fradin. (From Sea to Shining Sea Ser.). (J). 1998. pap. text 7.95 (*0-516-26269-5*) Childrens.

Nebraska. Sylvia McNair. LC 97-40704. (America the Beautiful Ser.). 144p. (YA). (gr. 5-8). 1999. 32.00 (*0-516-20689-3*) Childrens.

Nebraska. A. P. Porter. (Hello U. S. A. Ser.). (Illus.). 72p. (J). (gr. 3-6). 1991. lib. bdg. 19.93 (*0-8225-2708-1*, Lerner Publctns) Lerner Pub.

Nebraska. Anne Welsbacher. LC 97-27134. (United States Ser.). (Illus.). 32p. (J). 1998. lib. bdg. 19.93 (*1-56239-887-3*, Checkerboard Library) ABDO Pub Co.

Nebraska. George Whitmore. 153p. 1989. pap. 6.95 (*0-671-67234-7*, WSP) PB.

Nebraska. rev. ed. Kathleen Thompson. LC 87-264855. (Portrait of America Library). 48p. (J). (gr. 4-8). 1996. pap. 5.95 (*0-8114-7453-4*) Raintree Steck-V.

Nebraska. rev. ed. Kathleen Thompson. LC 87-264855. (Portrait of America Library). (Illus.). 48p. (J). (gr. 3-6). 1996. lib. bdg. 22.83 (*0-8114-7347-3*) Raintree Steck-V.

Nebraska: A Guide to the Cornhusker State. Federal Writers' Project Staff. (American Guidebook Ser.). 424p. 1939. reprint ed. 79.00 (*0-403-02177-4*) Somerset Pub.

N

An Asterisk (*) at the beginning of an entry indicates that the title is appearing for the first time.

Nebraska: A Guide to the Cornhusker State. Federal Writers' Project Staff & Writers Program-WPA Staff. (American Guide Ser.). 1989. reprint ed. lib. bdg. 69.00 (*0-7812-1026-7*, 1026) Rprt Serv.

Nebraska: A Photographic Celebration. (Illus.). 120p. 1993. 29.95 (*1-56037-030-0*) Am Wrld Geog.

Nebraska: An Illustrated History. Ed. by Frederick C. Luebke. LC 94-47569. (Great Plains Photography Ser.). (Illus.). xxiv, 407p. 1995. text 45.00 (*0-8032-2902-X*) U of Nebr Pr.

Nebraska: Hello U. S. A. A. P. Porter. (Hello U. S. A. Ser.). (Illus.). 72p. (J). (gr. 3-6). pap. 5.95 (*0-8225-9719-5*, First Ave Edns) Lerner Pub.

Nebraska: No Place Quite Like It! Harold Hamil. LC 85-82088. (Illus.). 200p. 1985. 14.95 (*0-932845-10-X*) Lowell Pr.

Nebraska: Off the Beaten Path: A Guide to Unique Places. 2nd ed. Hannah McNally. LC 99-21462. (Off the Beaten Path Ser.). (Illus.). 225p. 1999. pap. text 12.95 (*0-7627-0459-4*) Globe Pequot.

Nebraska: Stories. Ron Hansen. LC 88-24189. 208p. 1990. pap. 12.00 (*0-87113-349-0*, Atlntc Mnthly) Grove-Atltic.

***Nebraska: Under a Big Red Sky.** Joel Sartore. 144p. 1999. 38.95 (*0-9648992-6-4*) Neb Bk Co.

Nebraska - Collected Works of Federal Writers Project. Federal Writers' Project Staff. 1991. reprint ed. lib. bdg. 98.00 (*0-7812-5653-4*) Rprt Serv.

Nebraska, a Guide to the Cornhusker State. Federal Writer's Project, Nebraska Staff. LC 78-26756. 458p. reprint ed. pap. 142.00 (*0-8357-2693-2*, 204023000015) Bks Demand.

Nebraska Ambush. Jack Aintry. 224p. 1989. mass mkt. 2.95 (*0-8217-2586-6*, Zebra Kensgtn) Kensgtn Pub Corp.

Nebraska & Other State Greats (Biographies) Carole Marsh. (Carole Marsh Nebraska Bks.). (Illus.). (J). (gr. 3 up). 1994. pap. 19.95 (*1-55609-797-2*); lib. bdg. 29.95 (*1-55609-796-4*); disk 29.95 (*1-55609-798-0*) Gallopade Intl.

Nebraska Assessment Battery of Essential Learning Skills (N-ABELS) Jack Rudman. (Admission Test Ser.: Vol. 65). 43.95 (*0-8373-5165-0*) Nat Learn.

Nebraska Assessment Battery of Essential Learning Skills (N-ABELS) Jack Rudman. (Admission Test Ser.: ATS-65). 1994. pap. 23.95 (*0-8373-5065-4*) Nat Learn.

Nebraska Atlas & Gazetteer. David Delorme. LC 99-462944. (Illus.). 1996. pap. 16.95 (*0-89933-256-0*, AA-000019-000) DeLorme Map.

Nebraska Bandits, Bushwackers, Outlaws, Crooks, Devils, Ghosts, Desperadoes & Other Assorted & Sundry Characters! Carole Marsh. (Carole Marsh Nebraska Bks.). (Illus.). (J). (gr. 3 up). 1994. pap. 19.95 (*0-7933-0720-1*); lib. bdg. 29.95 (*0-7933-0721-X*); disk 29.95 (*0-7933-0722-8*) Gallopade Intl.

Nebraska Bandits, Bushwackers, Outlaws, Crooks, Devils, Ghosts, Desperadoes & Other Assorted & Sundry Characters. Carole Marsh. (Carole Marsh Nebraska Bks.). (YA). 1994. student ed. 29.95 (*0-7933-6811-1*) Gallopade Intl.

Nebraska "BIO" Bingo! 24 Must Know State People for Kids to Learn about While Having Fun! Carole Marsh. (Bingo! Ser.). (Illus.). (J). (gr. 2-8). 1998. pap. 14.95 (*0-7933-8603-9*) Gallopade Intl.

***Nebraska Birds.** James Kavanagh. (Pocket Naturalist Ser.). (Illus.). (YA). 1999. 5.90 (*1-58355-002-X*, Pub. by Waterford WA) Falcon Pub Inc.

Nebraska Bookstore Book: A Surprising Guide to Our State's Bookstores & Their Specialties for Students, Teachers, Writers & Publishers. Carole Marsh. (Carole Marsh Nebraska Bks.). (Illus.). 1994. pap. 19.95 (*0-7933-2937-X*); lib. bdg. 29.95 (*0-7933-2936-1*); disk 29.95 (*0-7933-2938-8*) Gallopade Intl.

***Nebraska Business Directory, 2000 Edition.** rev. ed. American Business Directories Staff. 880p. 1999. boxed set 415.00 incl. cd-rom (*0-7687-0174-0*) Am Busn Direct.

Nebraska Carver Alfred Larson. Dave Wooley & Jon Nelson. (Great Plains Art Ser.: No. 1). (Illus.). 32p. 1989. pap. text 10.00 (*0-938932-04-7*) U Nebr CFGPS.

Nebraska Census, 1870. 1988. 95.00 (*0-89593-687-9*, Accel Indexing) Genealogical Srvcs.

Nebraska Census Index, 1880. (Illus.). lib. bdg. write for info. (*0-89593-418-3*, Accel Indexing) Genealogical Srvcs.

Nebraska Census Index, 1885 Mortality Schedule. (Illus.). lib. bdg. write for info. (*0-89593-420-5*, Accel Indexing) Genealogical Srvcs.

Nebraska Census Index, 1880 Mortality Schedule. (Illus.). lib. bdg. 47.00 (*0-89593-419-1*, Accel Indexing) Genealogical Srvcs.

Nebraska Census Index, 1870 Mortality Schedule. (Illus.). lib. bdg. 35.00 (*0-89593-417-5*, Accel Indexing) Genealogical Srvcs.

Nebraska Census Index, 1860 Mortality Schedule. (Illus.). lib. bdg. 35.00 (*0-89593-416-7*, Accel Indexing) Genealogical Srvcs.

Nebraska Census Index 1890 Union Vets: Nebraska Census Index 1890 Vets & Widows. (Illus.). lib. bdg. 90.00 (*0-89593-421-3*, Accel Indexing) Genealogical Srvcs.

Nebraska Championship Season. Ed. by Suzanne Boggs. (Illus.). 160p. pap. text 14.95 (*1-886830-00-2*) Athlon Sports.

Nebraska Classic Christmas Trivia: Stories, Recipes, Activities, Legends, Lore & More! Carole Marsh. (Carole Marsh Nebraska Bks.). (Illus.). (J). (gr. 3 up). 1994. pap. 19.95 (*0-7933-0723-6*); lib. bdg. 29.95 (*0-7933-0724-4*); disk 29.95 (*0-7933-0725-2*) Gallopade Intl.

Nebraska Coastales. Carole Marsh. (Carole Marsh Nebraska Bks.). (J). 1994. lib. bdg. 29.95 (*0-7933-7292-5*) Gallopade Intl.

Nebraska Coastales. Carole Marsh. (Carole Marsh Nebraska Bks.). (Illus.). (J). (gr. 3 up). 1994. pap. 19.95 (*1-55609-791-3*); lib. bdg. 29.95 (*1-55609-790-5*); disk 29.95 (*1-55609-792-1*) Gallopade Intl.

***Nebraska Cornhuskers: Tales, Traditions & Triumphs.** Edson A. Bearg. LC 99-208694. 119p. 1999. write for info. (*1-892902-00-1*) Ramz Pubg.

***Nebraska Crime in Perspective 2000.** Ed. by Kathleen O'Leary Morgan & Scott E. Morgan. 22p. 2000. spiral bd. 19.00 (*0-7401-0326-1*) Morgan Quitno Corp.

Nebraska Crime Perspective, 1998. Ed. by Kathleen O'Leary Morgan & Scott E. Morgan. 20p. 1998. pap. 19.00 (*1-56692-926-1*) Morgan Quitno Corp.

Nebraska Crime Perspectives, 1999. Kathleen O'Leary Morgan. 22p. 1999. spiral bd. 19.00 (*0-7401-0126-9*) Morgan Quitno Corp.

Nebraska Criminal & Traffic Law Manual: 1998 Edition. 1004p. 1998. write for info. (*0-327-06340-8*, 2820113) LEXIS Pub.

***Nebraska Criminal & Traffic Law Manual, 1999 Edition.** 1028p. 1999. 30.00 (*0-327-09672-1*, 2820114) LEXIS Pub.

Nebraska "Crinkum-Crankum" A Funny Word Book about Our State. Carole Marsh. (Carole Marsh Nebraska Bks.). (Illus.). (J). 1994. pap. 19.95 (*0-7933-4890-0*); lib. bdg. 29.95 (*0-7933-4889-7*); disk 29.95 (*0-7933-4891-9*) Gallopade Intl.

Nebraska Cuneiform Texts of the Sumerian Ur III Dynasty. Nels W. Forde. 1972. 12.50 (*0-87291-040-7*) Coronado Pr.

Nebraska Dingbats! Bk. 1: A Fun Book of Games, Stories, Activities & More about Our State That's All in Code! for You to Decipher. Carole Marsh. (Carole Marsh Nebraska Bks.). (Illus.). (J). (gr. 3-12). 1994. pap. 19.95 (*0-7933-3855-7*); lib. bdg. 29.95 (*0-7933-3854-9*); disk 29.95 (*0-7933-3856-5*) Gallopade Intl.

Nebraska Econometric Models: Quarterly & Annual, 1980-2000. James R. Schmidt & Charles L. Bare. 1981. 7.50 (*0-318-42810-5*) Bur Busn Res U Nebr.

Nebraska Economy in the 1980's. Charles L. Bare & Donald E. Pursell. 1982. 7.50 (*0-318-42809-1*) Bur Busn Res U Nebr.

***Nebraska Education Laws: 1999 Edition.** 1063p. 1999. pap. 30.00 (*0-327-09898-8*, 2821211) LEXIS Pub.

Nebraska Education Laws, 1998 Edition. 965p. 1998. write for info. (*0-327-06566-4*, 2821210) LEXIS Pub.

Nebraska Environmental Law Handbook. Kutak, Rock & Campbell Staff. (State Environmental Law Ser.). 274p. 1991. pap. text 79.00 (*0-86587-246-5*) Gov Insts.

Nebraska Facts & Factivities. Carole Marsh. (Carole Marsh State Bks.). (Illus.). (J). (gr. 4-7). 1996. pap., teacher ed. 19.95 (*0-7933-7901-6*, C Marsh) Gallopade Intl.

***Nebraska Facts & Symbols.** Emily McAuliffe. LC 98-7357. (States & Their Symbols Ser.). 24p. (J). 1999. write for info. (*0-7368-0084-0*) Capstone Pr.

***Nebraska Facts & Symbols.** Emily McAuliffe. 1998. 14.00 (*0-531-11608-5*) Childrens.

Nebraska Family Law. Susan Jacobs & Karen B. Flowers. 610p. 1992. ring bd. 95.00 (*1-56257-707-7*, MICHIE) LEXIS Pub.

Nebraska Federal Census Index, 1860. Ronald V. Jackson. (Illus.). 1978. lib. bdg. 68.00 (*0-89593-216-4*, Accel Indexing) Genealogical Srvcs.

Nebraska Festival Fun for Kids! Carole Marsh. (Carole Marsh Nebraska Bks.). (Illus.). (J). (gr. 3-12). 1994. pap. 19.95 (*0-7933-4008-X*); lib. bdg. 29.95 (*0-7933-4007-1*) Gallopade Intl.

Nebraska Festival Fun for Kids! Carole Marsh. (Carole Marsh Nebraska Bks.). (Illus.). (YA). (gr. 3-12). 1994. disk 29.95 (*0-7933-4009-8*) Gallopade Intl.

Nebraska Folklore. Louise Pound. LC 89-32799. x, 245p. 1989. reprint ed. pap. 11.95 (*0-8032-8724-0*, Bison Books) U of Nebr Pr.

Nebraska Football: The Coaches, the Players, the Experience. James F. Sherwood. LC 86-30737. (Illus.). 168p. 1987. reprint ed. pap. 52.10 (*0-608-01706-X*, 206236100002) Bks Demand.

Nebraska Football: The Cornhuskers 1999 Calendar. (Illus.). 1998. boxed set 10.99 (*0-8362-6566-1*) Andrews & McMeel.

Nebraska "GEO" Bingo! 38 Must Know State Geography Facts for Kids to Learn While Having Fun. Carole Marsh. (Bingo! Ser.). (Illus.). 1998. pap. 14.95 (*0-7933-8604-7*) Gallopade Intl.

Nebraska Government & Politics. Ed. by Robert D. Miewald. LC 83-3684. (Politics & Governments of the American States Ser.). xiv, 230p. 1984. text 15.00 (*0-8032-3078-8*); pap. text 12.95 (*0-8032-8113-7*) U of Nebr Pr.

Nebraska Governments Performance Standards, 1990. Ed. by Greg Michels. (Governments Performance Standards Ser.). (Illus.). 150p. 1990. text 125.00 (*1-55507-493-6*) Municipal Analysis.

***Nebraska Health Care in Perspective 2000.** Ed. by Kathleen O'Leary Morgan & Scott E. Morgan. 21p. 2000. spiral bd. 19.00 (*0-7401-0226-5*) Morgan Quitno Corp.

Nebraska Health Care Perspective, 1998. Ed. by Kathleen O'Leary Morgan & Scott E. Morgan. 20p. 1998. pap. 19.00 (*1-56692-826-5*) Morgan Quitno Corp.

Nebraska Health Care Perspective, 1999. Kathleen O'Leary Morgan. 21p. 1999. spiral bd. 19.00 (*0-7401-0076-9*) Morgan Quitno Corp.

Nebraska Highway Archaeological & Historical Investigations, 1969-1975. Gayle F. Carlson & Terry L. Steinacher. (Publications in Archaeology: No. 10). 191p. 1984. 2.00 (*0-933307-09-8*) Nebraska Hist.

Nebraska "HISTO" Bingo! 42 Must Know State History Facts for Kids to Learn While Having Fun! Carole Marsh. (Bingo! Ser.). (Illus.). (J). (gr. 2-8). 1998. pap. 14.95 (*0-7933-8605-5*) Gallopade Intl.

Nebraska Historical Tour Guide. 2nd ed. D. Ray Wilson. LC 88-70028. (Illus.). 314p. 1988. reprint ed. pap. 15.00 (*0-916445-21-6*) Crossroads Comm.

Nebraska History: An Annotated Bibliography, 6. Compiled by Michael L. Tate. LC 95-492. (Bibliographies of the States of the United States Ser.: Vol. 6). 576p. 1995. lib. bdg. 89.50 (*0-313-28249-8*, Greenwood Pr) Greenwood.

Nebraska History! Surprising Secrets about Our State's Founding Mothers, Fathers & Kids! Carole Marsh. (Carole Marsh Nebraska Bks.). (Illus.). (J). (gr. 3-12). 1996. pap. 19.95 (*0-7933-6110-9*); lib. bdg. 29.95 (*0-7933-6109-5*); disk 29.95 (*0-7933-6111-7*) Gallopade Intl.

Nebraska Hot Air Balloon Mystery. Carole Marsh. (Carole Marsh Nebraska Bks.). (Illus.). (J). (gr. 2-9). 1994. 29.95 (*0-7933-2561-7*); pap. 19.95 (*0-7933-2562-5*); disk 29.95 (*0-7933-2563-3*) Gallopade Intl.

Nebraska Hot Zones! Viruses, Diseases, & Epidemics in Our State's History. Carole Marsh. (Hot Zones! Ser.). (Illus.). (J). (gr. 3-12). 1998. pap. 19.95 (*0-7933-8910-0*); lib. bdg. 29.95 (*0-7933-8909-7*) Gallopade Intl.

Nebraska in Perspective, 1998. Ed. by Kathleen O'Leary Morgan & Scott E. Morgan. 24p. 1998. pap. 19.00 (*1-56692-876-1*) Morgan Quitno Corp.

Nebraska in Perspective, 1999. Ed. by Kathleen O'Leary Morgan. 26p. 1999. spiral bd. 19.00 (*1-56692-976-8*) Morgan Quitno Corp.

***Nebraska in Perspective 2000.** Ed. by Kathleen O'Leary Morgan & Scott E. Morgan. 26p. 2000. spiral bd. 19.00 (*0-7401-0276-1*) Morgan Quitno Corp.

Nebraska Indian Dictionary for Kids! Carole Marsh. (Carole Marsh State Bks.). (J). (gr. 2-9). 1996. 29.95 (*0-7933-7725-0*, C Marsh); pap. 19.95 (*0-7933-7726-9*, C Marsh) Gallopade Intl.

Nebraska Indian Wars Reader, 1865-77. Ed. by R. Eli Paul. LC 97-32942. (Illus.). xii, 289p. 1998. pap. 15.00 (*0-8032-8749-6*, Bison Books) U of Nebr Pr.

***Nebraska Investment & Business Guide: Business, Investment, Export-Import Opportunities, 50 vols., Vol. 27.** Global Investment Center, USA Staff. (U. S. Regional Investment & Business Library-99: Vol. 27). (Illus.). 350p. 1999. pap. 59.95 (*0-7397-1126-1*) Intl Business Pubns.

Nebraska Jeopardy! Answers & Questions about Our State! Carole Marsh. (Carole Marsh Nebraska Bks.). (J). 1994. student ed. 29.95 (*0-7933-6810-3*) Gallopade Intl.

Nebraska Jeopardy! Answers & Questions about Our State! Carole Marsh. (Carole Marsh Nebraska Bks.). (Illus.). (J). (gr. 3-12). 1994. pap. 19.95 (*0-7933-4161-2*); lib. bdg. 29.95 (*0-7933-4160-4*); disk 29.95 (*0-7933-4162-0*) Gallopade Intl.

Nebraska "Jography" A Fun Run thru Our State. Carole Marsh. (Carole Marsh Nebraska Bks.). (Illus.). (J). (gr. 3 up). 1994. lib. bdg. 29.95 (*1-55609-778-6*); disk 29.95 (*1-55609-780-8*) Gallopade Intl.

Nebraska Kid's Cookbook: Recipes, How-To, History, Lore & More! Carole Marsh. (Carole Marsh Nebraska Bks.). (Illus.). (J). (gr. 3 up). 1994. pap. 19.95 (*0-7933-0732-5*); lib. bdg. 29.95 (*0-7933-0733-3*); disk 29.95 (*0-7933-0734-1*) Gallopade Intl.

Nebraska Labor & Employment: A Guide to Employment Laws, Regulations, & Practices, Issue 4. Jeffrey L. Hirsh & Lisa D. DeBuse. LC 92-35240. 304p. 1997. ring bd. 89.50 (*0-409-25665-X*, 81971-14, MICHIE) LEXIS Pub.

Nebraska Legal Forms: Bankruptcy. John C. Minahan, Jr. 230p. 1982. ring bd. 69.95 (*0-86678-029-7*, 81974-10, MICHIE); ring bd. 104.95 incl. disk (*1-56257-787-5*, MICHIE) LEXIS Pub.

Nebraska Legal Forms: Bankruptcy. John C. Minahan, Jr. 230p. 1993. suppl. ed. 42.50 (*1-56257-808-1*, MICHIE) LEXIS Pub.

Nebraska Legal Forms: Bankruptcy. John C. Minahan, Jr. & Kevin Ruser. 1982. ring bd. 69.95 (*0-327-00997-7*, 81974-10, MICHIE) LEXIS Pub.

Nebraska Legal Forms: Commercial Real Estate. Peter J. Vaughn. 260p. ring bd. 104.95 incl. disk (*1-56257-788-3*, MICHIE) LEXIS Pub.

Nebraska Legal Forms: Commercial Real Estate. Peter J. Vaughn. 1981. ring bd. 69.95 (*0-327-01003-7*, 81980, MICHIE) LEXIS Pub.

Nebraska Legal Forms: Commercial Real Estate. Peter J. Vaughn. 260p. 1990. ring bd. 69.95 (*0-86678-025-4*, 81980-10, MICHIE) LEXIS Pub.

Nebraska Legal Forms: Commercial Real Estate. Peter J. Vaughn. 260p. 1992. suppl. ed. 32.50 (*1-56257-814-6*, 81983-10, MICHIE) LEXIS Pub.

Nebraska Legal Forms: Creditors' Remedies. Arlen W. Langvardt. 1982. ring bd. 69.95 (*0-327-01001-0*, 81986, MICHIE) LEXIS Pub.

Nebraska Legal Forms: Criminal Law. Donald B. Fiedler. 240p. 1992. ring bd. 69.95 incl. disk (*0-614-05912-7*, Aspen Law & Bus) Aspen Pub.

Nebraska Legal Forms: Criminal Law. Donald B. Fiedler & Deborah R. Pred. 1982. ring bd. 69.95 (*0-327-01005-3*, 81992, MICHIE) LEXIS Pub.

Nebraska Legal Forms: Family Law. Elizabeth S. Borchers. 1982. ring bd. 69.95 (*0-327-01009-6*, 81998, MICHIE) LEXIS Pub.

Nebraska Legal Forms: Family Law. Elizabeth S. Borchers. 310p. 1993. ring bd. 69.95 incl. disk (*0-614-05913-5*, MICHIE) LEXIS Pub.

Nebraska Legal Forms: Personal Injury. John J. Higgins. 1981. ring bd. 69.95 (*0-327-00995-0*, 82004-10, MICHIE) LEXIS Pub.

Nebraska Legal Forms: Personal Injury. John J. Higgins. 200p. 1992. ring bd. 69.95 incl. disk (*0-614-05914-3*, MICHIE) LEXIS Pub.

Nebraska Legal Forms: Residential Real Estate. Norman H. Wright. (Nebraska Legal Forms Ser.). 210p. ring bd. 69.95 (*0-685-70858-6*, MICHIE); ring bd. 104.95 incl. disk (*0-685-49534-5*, MICHIE); ring bd. 69.95 (*0-327-00999-3*, 82009, MICHIE) LEXIS Pub.

Nebraska Legal Forms: Residential Real Estate. Norman H. Wright. (Nebraska Legal Forms Ser.). 1992. ring bd., suppl. ed. 25.00 (*1-56257-746-8*, MICHIE) LEXIS Pub.

Nebraska Legal Forms: Residential Real Estate. Norman H. Wright. 210p. 1993. ring bd. 69.95 incl. disk (*0-614-05915-1*, MICHIE) LEXIS Pub.

Nebraska Legal Forms: Workers' Compensation. Michael P. Cavel. 160p. 1994. ring bd. 69.95 incl. disk (*0-614-05916-X*, MICHIE) LEXIS Pub.

Nebraska Legal Forms with Computer Disk, 8 vols. ring bd. 450.00 incl. disk (*0-86678-944-8*, 81972-10, MICHIE) LEXIS Pub.

Nebraska Library Book: A Surprising Guide to the Unusual Special Collections in Libraries Across Our State for Students, Teachers, Writers & Publishers - Includes Reproducible Mailing Labels Plus Activities for Young People! Carole Marsh. (Carole Marsh Nebraska Bks.). (Illus.). 1994. pap. 19.95 (*0-7933-3087-4*); lib. bdg. 29.95 (*0-7933-3086-6*); disk 29.95 (*0-7933-3088-2*) Gallopade Intl.

Nebraska Limitations Manual, 1989-1990. 2nd ed. Butterworth Staff. 370p. 1992. ring bd. 50.00 (*0-86678-056-4*, MICHIE) LEXIS Pub.

Nebraska Limitations Manual, 1989-1990. 2nd ed. Butterworths Staff. 370p. 1992. suppl. ed. 47.00 (*1-56257-802-2*, MICHIE) LEXIS Pub.

Nebraska Manufacturers Register. 7th rev. ed. Ed. by Frank Lambing. 1999. 67.00 (*1-58202-057-4*) Manufacturers.

Nebraska Math! How It All Adds up in Our State. Carole Marsh. (Carole Marsh Nebraska Bks.). (Illus.). (YA). (gr. 3-12). 1996. pap. 19.95 (*0-7933-6569-4*); lib. bdg. 29.95 (*0-7933-6568-6*) Gallopade Intl.

Nebraska Media Book: A Surprising Guide to the Amazing Print, Broadcast & Online Media of Our State for Students, Teachers, Writers & Publishers - Includes Reproducible Mailing Labels Plus Activities for Young People! Carole Marsh. (Carole Marsh Nebraska Bks.). (Illus.). 1994. pap. 19.95 (*0-7933-3243-5*); lib. bdg. 29.95 (*0-7933-3242-7*); disk 29.95 (*0-7933-3244-3*) Gallopade Intl.

N

Nebraska Medical Directory. rev. ed. Ed. by Jola Publications Staff. 98p. 1999. pap. 16.00 (*1-878373-23-4*) Jola Pubns.

Nebraska Moments: Glimpses of Nebraska's Past. Donald R. Hickey. LC 91-42710. xii, 300p. 1996. pap. 12.95 (*0-8032-7284-7*, Bison Books) U of Nebr Pr.

***Nebraska Motor Vehicle Laws: 1999 Edition.** 466p. 1999. pap. 18.00 (*0-327-09944-5*, 2822511) LEXIS Pub.

Nebraska Motor Vehicle Laws, 1998 Edition. 517p. 1998. pap. write for info. (*0-327-06474-9*, 2822510) LEXIS Pub.

Nebraska Mystery Van Takes Off! Bk. 1: Handicapped Nebraska Kids Sneak off on a Big Adventure. Carole Marsh. (Carole Marsh Nebraska Bks.). (Illus.). (J). (gr. 3-12). 1994. 29.95 (*0-7933-5042-5*); pap. 19.95 (*0-7933-5043-3*); disk 29.95 (*0-7933-5044-1*) Gallopade Intl.

Nebraska National Forest, NE. Ed. by Trails Illustrated Staff. 1994. 8.99 (*1-56695-018-X*) Trails Illustrated.

Nebraska, 1998 Advance Code Service Pamphlet, No. 3. 241p. 1998. pap. write for info. (*0-327-05093-4*, 45258-12) LEXIS Pub.

Nebraska 1999 Advance Annotation Service Pamphlet, No. 3. 209p. 1999. pap. write for info. (*0-327-08652-1*, 45258-13) LEXIS Pub.

***Nebraska 1999 Index.** 930p. 1999. Price not set. (*0-327-09669-1*, 4520514) LEXIS Pub.

Nebraska Ombudsman: Innovation in State Government. Alan J. Wyner. LC 74-8958. 174p. reprint ed. pap. 54.00 (*0-7837-2136-6*, 204242000004) Bks Demand.

Nebraska Pioneer Cookbook. Compiled by Kay Graber. LC 74-77089. (Illus.). ix, 164p. 1974. pap. 7.95 (*0-8032-5801-1*, Bison Books) U of Nebr Pr.

Nebraska Place-Names: Including Selections from the Origin of the Place-Names of Nebraska. Lilian L. Fitzpatrick. LC 60-15471. (Bison Bk.). 238p. reprint ed. pap. 73.80 (*0-7837-1896-9*, 204210000001) Bks Demand.

Nebraska Policy Choices, 1986. Ed. by Jeffrey S. Luke & Vincent J. Webb. (Illus.). 240p. (Orig.). 1986. pap. 9.95 (*1-55719-000-3*) U NE CPAR.

Nebraska Policy Choices, 1987. Ed. by Russell L. Smith. (Illus.). 302p. (Orig.). (C). 1987. pap. 9.95 (*1-55719-178-6*) U NE CPAR.

Nebraska Policy Choices, 1988. Ed. by Russell L. Smith. (Illus.). 191p. (Orig.). (C). 1988. pap. 9.95 (*1-55719-181-6*) U NE CPAR.

Nebraska Policy Choices, 1989: Education. Ed. by Miles T. Bryant et al. (Illus.). 155p. (Orig.). (C). 1989. pap. 9.95 (*1-55719-182-4*) U NE CPAR.

Nebraska Population Projections: State, County, Region & Town, 1975-2020. Vernon Renshaw et al. 232p. (Orig.). 1973. pap. 14.00 (*1-55719-111-5*) U NE CPAR.

Nebraska Population Projections, 1985-2020. Jerome Deichert. (Nebraska Economic & Business Reports: No. 32). 1982. 17.50 (*0-318-02059-9*) Bur Busn Res U Nebr.

Nebraska Portfolio. Robert L. Hanna. LC 92-8308. (Illus.). xxli, 155p. (C). 1992. text 40.00 (*0-8032-2358-7*) U of Nebr Pr.

Nebraska Preschool Child Care, 1990: A Survey of Parents on Access to Quality Child Care. Patricia E. Funk. (Illus.). 80p. 1990. pap. 8.00 (*1-55719-200-6*) U NE CPAR.

Nebraska Program for Technology Transfer: An Operational Framework. Jack J. Ruff. 15p. (Orig.). 1980. pap. 1.50 (*1-55719-034-8*) U NE CPAR.

An Asterisk (*) at the beginning of an entry indicates that the title is appearing for the first time.

Nebraska Question: Some Thoughts on the New Assault upon Freedom in America & the General State of the Country in Relation Thereunto. Theodore Parker. 1977. 12.95 (*0-8369-9191-5*, 9060) Ayer.

Nebraska Quilts & Quiltmakers. Ed. by Patricia C. Crews & Ronald C. Naugle. LC 90-41995. x, 245p. 1991. text 60.00 (*0-8032-1452-9*) U of Nebr Pr.

Nebraska Quiz Bowl Crash Course! Carole Marsh. (Carole Marsh Nebraska Bks.). (Illus.). (J). (gr. 3 up). 1994. pap. 19.95 (*1-55609-794-8*); lib. bdg. 29.95 (*1-55609-793-X*); disk 29.95 (*1-55609-795-6*) Gallopade Intl.

Nebraska Retirement & Relocation Guide. large type ed. (Retirement & Relocation Guides Ser.). (Illus.). 350p. Date not set. pap. 24.95 (*1-56559-146-1*) HGI-Over Fifty.

Nebraska Revised Statutes Annotated Advanced Code Service: 2000 Edition. 44.00 (*0-327-11814-8*) LEXIS Pub.

Nebraska Rollercoasters! Carole Marsh. (Carole Marsh Nebraska Bks.). (Illus.). (J). (gr. 3-12). 1994. pap. 19.95 (*0-7933-5306-8*); lib. bdg. 29.95 (*0-7933-5305-X*) Gallopade Intl.

Nebraska Rollercoasters! Carole Marsh. (Carole Marsh Nebraska Bks.). (Illus.). (YA). (gr. 3-12). 1994. disk 29.95 (*0-7933-5307-6*) Gallopade Intl.

Nebraska Rules of Court Annotated: 1999 Edition. annot. ed. 800p. 1998. write for info. (*0-327-05512-X*, 45250-13) LEXIS Pub.

Nebraska Rules of Court Annotated: 2000 Edition. pap. 65.00 (*0-327-11812-1*) LEXIS Pub.

Nebraska Rules of Court Annotated-1999 Supplement. 80p. 1999. write for info. (*0-327-07969-X*, 45251-13) LEXIS Pub.

*__Nebraska Rules of Court Annotated, 2000 Edition.__ 858p. 1999. Price not set. (*0-327-09673-X*, 4525014) LEXIS Pub.

Nebraska Sand Hills: The Human Landscape. Charles B. McIntosh. LC 95-19845. (Illus.). xvi, 266p. 1996. text 70.00 (*0-8032-3184-9*) U of Nebr Pr.

Nebraska School Trivia: An Amazing & Fascinating Look at Our State's Teachers, Schools & Students! Carole Marsh. (Carole Marsh Nebraska Bks.). (Illus.). (J). (gr. 3 up). 1994. pap. 19.95 (*0-7933-0729-5*); lib. bdg. 29.95 (*0-7933-0730-9*); disk 29.95 (*0-7933-0731-7*) Gallopade Intl.

Nebraska Silly Basketball Sports Mysteries, Vol. I. Carole Marsh. (Carole Marsh Nebraska Bks.). (Illus.). (J). (gr. 3 up). 1994. pap. 19.95 (*0-7933-0726-0*); lib. bdg. 29.95 (*0-7933-0727-9*); disk 29.95 (*0-7933-0728-7*) Gallopade Intl.

Nebraska Silly Basketball Sports Mysteries, Vol. II. Carole Marsh. (Carole Marsh Nebraska Bks.). (Illus.). (J). (gr. 3 up). 1994. pap. 19.95 (*0-7933-1759-2*); lib. bdg. 29.95 (*0-7933-1758-4*); disk 29.95 (*0-7933-1760-6*) Gallopade Intl.

Nebraska Silly Football Sports Mysteries, Vol. I. Carole Marsh. (Carole Marsh Nebraska Bks.). (Illus.). (J). (gr. 3 up). 1994. pap. 19.95 (*1-55609-785-9*); lib. bdg. 29.95 (*1-55609-784-0*); disk 29.95 (*1-55609-786-7*) Gallopade Intl.

Nebraska Silly Football Sports Mysteries, Vol. II. Carole Marsh. (Carole Marsh Nebraska Bks.). (Illus.). (J). (gr. 3 up). 1994. pap. 19.95 (*1-55609-788-3*); lib. bdg. 29.95 (*1-55609-787-5*); disk 29.95 (*1-55609-789-1*) Gallopade Intl.

Nebraska Silly Trivia! Carole Marsh. (Carole Marsh Nebraska Bks.). (YA). 1994. student ed. 29.95 (*0-7933-6809-X*) Gallopade Intl.

Nebraska Silly Trivia! Carole Marsh. (Carole Marsh Nebraska Bks.). (Illus.). (J). (gr. 3 up). 1994. pap. 19.95 (*1-55609-776-X*); lib. bdg. 29.95 (*1-55609-775-1*); disk 29.95 (*1-55609-777-8*) Gallopade Intl.

*__Nebraska Slaying Ground, Vol. 226.__ Jon Sharpe. (Trailsman Ser.). 2000. mass mkt. 4.99 (*0-451-20097-7*) Signet.

Nebraska Sportsman's Atlas. David D. Adams. (Illus.). 1994. spiral bd. 18.75 (*1-56464-686-6*) Universal Map Enterprises Inc.

Nebraska State Constitution: A Reference Guide, 13. Robert D. Miewald & Peter J. Longo. LC 92-21359. (Reference Guides to the State Constitutions of the United States Ser.: No. 13). 240p. 1993. lib. bdg. 75.00 (*0-313-27947-0*, MNG, Greenwood Pr) Greenwood.

Nebraska Symposium on Motivation, 1955. Nebraska Symposium on Motivation Staff. Ed. by Marshall R. Jones. LC 53-11655. (Current Theory & Research in Motivation Ser.: No. 3). 284p. reprint ed. pap. 88.10 (*0-7837-6597-5*, 204616300011) Bks Demand.

Nebraska Symposium on Motivation, 1956. Nebraska Symposium on Motivation Staff. Ed. by Marshall R. Jones. LC 53-11655. (Current Theory & Research in Motivation Ser.: No. 4). 319p. reprint ed. pap. 98.90 (*0-7837-6598-3*, 204616400011) Bks Demand.

Nebraska Symposium on Motivation, 1957. Nebraska Symposium on Motivation Staff. Ed. by Marshall R. Jones. LC 53-11655. (Current Theory & Research in Motivation Ser.: No. 5). 442p. reprint ed. pap. 137.10 (*0-7837-6599-1*, 204616500011) Bks Demand.

Nebraska Symposium on Motivation, 1958. Nebraska Symposium on Motivation Staff. Ed. by Marshall R. Jones. LC 53-11655. (Current Theory & Research in Motivation Ser.: No. 6). 288p. reprint ed. pap. 89.30 (*0-7837-6600-9*, 204616600011) Bks Demand.

Nebraska Symposium on Motivation, 1959. Nebraska Symposium on Motivation Staff. Ed. by Marshall R. Jones. LC 53-11655. (Current Theory & Research in Motivation Ser.: No. 7). 253p. reprint ed. pap. 78.50 (*0-7837-6601-7*, 204616700011) Bks Demand.

Nebraska Symposium on Motivation, 1960. Nebraska Symposium on Motivation Staff. Ed. by Marshall R. Jones. LC 53-11655. (Current Theory & Research in Motivation Ser.: No. 8). 280p. reprint ed. pap. 86.80 (*0-7837-6602-5*, 204616800011) Bks Demand.

Nebraska Symposium on Motivation, 1961. Nebraska Symposium on Motivation Staff. Ed. by Marshall R. Jones. LC 53-11655. (Current Theory & Research in Motivation Ser.: No. 9). 220p. reprint ed. pap. 68.20 (*0-7837-6603-3*, 204616900011) Bks Demand.

Nebraska Symposium on Motivation, 1962. Nebraska Symposium on Motivation Staff. Ed. by Marshall R. Jones. LC 53-11655. (Current Theory & Research in Motivation Ser.: No. 10). 344p. reprint ed. pap. 106.70 (*0-7837-6604-1*, 204617000011) Bks Demand.

Nebraska Symposium on Motivation, 1963. Nebraska Symposium on Motivation Staff. Ed. by Marshall R. Jones. LC 53-11655. (Current Theory & Research in Motivation Ser.: No. 11). 214p. reprint ed. pap. 66.40 (*0-7837-6605-X*, 204617100011) Bks Demand.

Nebraska Symposium on Motivation, 1964. Nebraska Symposium on Motivation Staff. Ed. by David Levine. LC 53-11655. (Current Theory & Research in Motivation Ser.: No. 12). 294p. reprint ed. pap. 91.20 (*0-7837-6606-8*, 204617200011) Bks Demand.

Nebraska Symposium on Motivation, 1965. Nebraska Symposium on Motivation Staff. Ed. by David Levine. LC 53-11655. (Current Theory & Research in Motivation Ser.: No. 13). 356p. reprint ed. pap. 110.40 (*0-7837-6607-6*, 204617300011) Bks Demand.

Nebraska Symposium on Motivation, 1966. Nebraska Symposium on Motivation Staff. Ed. by David Levine. LC 53-11655. (Current Theory & Research in Motivation Ser.: No. 14). 219p. reprint ed. pap. 67.90 (*0-7837-6608-4*, 204617400011) Bks Demand.

Nebraska Symposium on Motivation, 1967. Nebraska Symposium on Motivation Staff. Ed. by David Levine. LC 53-11655. (Current Theory & Research in Motivation Ser.: No. 15). 345p. reprint ed. pap. 107.00 (*0-7837-6609-2*, 204617500011) Bks Demand.

Nebraska Symposium on Motivation, 1968. Nebraska Symposium on Motivation Staff. Ed. by William J. Arnold. LC 53-11655. (Current Theory & Research in Motivation Ser.: No. 16). 347p. reprint ed. pap. 107.60 (*0-7837-6610-6*, 204617800011) Bks Demand.

Nebraska Symposium on Motivation, 1970. Nebraska Symposium on Motivation Staff. Ed. by William J. Arnold & Monte M. Page. LC 53-11655. (Current Theory & Research in Motivation Ser.: No. 18). 302p. reprint ed. pap. 93.70 (*0-7837-6611-4*, 204617600011) Bks Demand.

Nebraska Symposium on Motivation, 1971. Nebraska Symposium on Motivation Staff. Ed. by James K. Cole. LC 53-11655. (Current Theory & Research in Motivation Ser.: No. 19). 316p. reprint ed. pap. 98.00 (*0-7837-6612-2*, 204617700011) Bks Demand.

Nebraska Symposium on Motivation, 1972. Nebraska Symposium on Motivation Staff. Ed. by James K. Cole & Donald D. Jensen. LC 53-11655. (Current Theory & Research in Motivation Ser.: No. 20). 353p. reprint ed. pap. 109.50 (*0-7837-6613-0*, 204617900011) Bks Demand.

Nebraska Symposium on Motivation, 1973. Nebraska Symposium on Motivation Staff. Ed. by James K. Cole & Richard Dienstbier. LC 53-11655. (Current Theory & Research in Motivation Ser.: No. 21). 339p. reprint ed. pap. 105.10 (*0-7837-6614-9*, 204618000011) Bks Demand.

Nebraska Symposium on Motivation, 1974. Nebraska Symposium on Motivation Staff. Ed. by James K. Cole & Theo B. Sonderegger. LC 53-11655. (Current Theory & Research in Motivation Ser.: No. 22). 328p. reprint ed. pap. 101.70 (*0-7837-6615-7*, 204618100011) Bks Demand.

Nebraska Symposium on Motivation, 1996: Alcohol & Addictive Behavior. Ed. by P. Clayton Rivers & Richard A. Dienstbier. LC 53-11655. (Nebraska Symposium on Motivation Ser.: No. 34). 346p. Date not set. text 45.00 (*0-8032-3880-0*); pap. text 25.00 (*0-8032-8925-1*) U of Nebr Pr.

Nebraska Symposium on Motivation, 1979: Beliefs, Attitudes & Values. Nebraska Symposium on Motivation Staff. Ed. by Monte M. Page. LC 53-11655. (Current Theory & Research in Motivation Ser.: No. 27). 377p. reprint ed. pap. 116.90 (*0-7837-6620-3*, 204618600011) Bks Demand.

Nebraska Symposium on Motivation, 1980: Cognitive Processes. Nebraska Symposium on Motivation Staff. Ed. by John H. Flowers. LC 53-11655. (Current Theory & Research in Motivation Ser.: No. 28). 265p. reprint ed. pap. 82.20 (*0-7837-6621-1*, 204618700011) Bks Demand.

Nebraska Symposium on Motivation, 1975: Conceptual Foundations of Psychology. Nebraska Symposium on Motivation Staff. Ed. by William J. Arnold. LC 53-11655. (Current Theory & Research in Motivation Ser.: No. 23). 614p. reprint ed. pap. 190.40 (*0-7837-6616-5*, 204618200011) Bks Demand.

Nebraska Symposium on Motivation, 1989: Cross-Cultural Perspectives. Nebraska Symposium on Motivation Staff. Ed. by John J. Berman & Richard A. Dienstbier. LC 53-11655. (Current Theory & Research in Motivation Ser.: Vol. 37). 375p. reprint ed. pap. 116.30 (*0-608-08689-4*, 206921200003) Bks Demand.

Nebraska Symposium on Motivation, 1978: Human Emotion. Nebraska Symposium on Motivation Staff. Ed. by Richard A. Dienstbier. LC 53-11655. (Current Theory & Research in Motivation Ser.: No. 26). 347p. reprint ed. pap. 107.60 (*0-7837-6619-X*, 204618500011) Bks Demand.

Nebraska Symposium on Motivation, 1993: Integrative View of Motivation, Cognitive, & Emotion. William D. Spaulding. LC 53-11655. xii, 265p. 1994. text 45.00 (*0-8032-4233-6*) U of Nebr Pr.

Nebraska Symposium on Motivation, 1976: Personal Construct Psychology. Nebraska Symposium on Motivation Staff. Ed. by Alvin W. Landfield. LC 53-11655. (Current Theory & Research in Motivation Ser.: No. 24). 379p. reprint ed. pap. 117.50 (*0-7837-6617-3*, 204618300011) Bks Demand.

Nebraska Symposium on Motivation, 1982: Personality - Current Theory & Research. Nebraska Symposium on Motivation Staff. Ed. by Monte M. Page. LC 53-11655. (Current Theory & Research in Motivation Ser.: No. 30). 292p. reprint ed. pap. 90.60 (*0-7837-6623-8*, 204618900011) Bks Demand.

Nebraska Symposium on Motivation, 1995: Perspectives on Anxiety, Panic, & Fear, Vol. 43. Ed. by Debra A. Hope. LC 53-11655. xiii, 351p. 1996. text 45.00 (*0-8032-2382-X*) U of Nebr Pr.

Nebraska Symposium on Motivation, 1981: Response Structure & Organization. Nebraska Symposium on Motivation Staff. Ed. by Daniel J. Bernstein. LC 53-11655. (Current Theory & Research in Motivation Ser.: No. 29). 279p. reprint ed. pap. 86.50 (*0-7837-6622-X*, 204618800011) Bks Demand.

Nebraska Symposium on Motivation, 1977: Social Cognitive Development. Nebraska Symposium on Motivation Staff. Ed. by Charles B. Keasey. LC 53-11655. (Current Theory & Research in Motivation Ser.: No. 25). 373p. reprint ed. pap. 115.70 (*0-7837-6618-1*, 204618400011) Bks Demand.

Nebraska Symposium on Motivation, 1994: The Individual, the Family & Social Good: Personal Fulfillment in Times of Change. Ed. by Gary B. Melton. LC 53-11655. (Nebraska Symposium on Motivation Ser.: No. 42). 200p. Date not set. 45.00 (*0-8032-3185-7*) U of Nebr Pr.

Nebraska Symposium on Motivation, 1994: The Individual, the Family & Social Good: Personal Fulfillment in Times of Change. Ed. by Gary B. Melton. LC 53-11655. (Nebraska Symposium on Motivation Ser.: No. 42). 200p. (C). 1995. pap. text 25.00 (*0-8032-8221-4*) U of Nebr Pr.

Nebraska Symposium on Motivation, 1983: Theories of Schizophrenia & Psychosis. Nebraska Symposium on Motivation Staff. Ed. by William D. Spaulding & James K. Cole. LC 53-11655. (Current Theory & Research in Motivation Ser.: No. 31). 391p. reprint ed. pap. 121.30 (*0-7837-6624-6*, 204619000011) Bks Demand.

Nebraska Symposium on Motivation, 1997 Vol. 45: Gender & Motivation. Ed. by Dan Bernstein. 256p. 1999. text 45.00 (*0-8032-1300-X*) U of Nebr Pr.

Nebraska Symposium on Motivation, 1984: Psychology & Gender. Ed. by Theo B. Sonderegger & Richard A. Dienstbier. LC 53-11655. (Nebraska Symposium on Motivation Ser.: Vol. 32). xx, 326p. 1985. text 45.00 (*0-8032-4152-6*); pap. text 25.00 (*0-8032-9150-7*) U of Nebr Pr.

Nebraska Symposium on Motivation, 1985: The Law as a Behavioral Instrument. Ed. by Gary B. Melbon & Richard A. Denstbier. LC 53-11655. (Nebraska Symposium on Motivation Ser.: Vol. 33). xxvii, 291p. 1986. text 45.00 (*0-8032-3100-8*) U of Nebr Pr.

Nebraska Symposium on Motivation, 1985: The Law as a Behavioral Instrument. Ed. by Gary B. Melton & Richard A. Dienstbier. LC 53-11655. (Nebraska Symposium on Motivation Ser.: Vol. 33). xxvii, 291p. 1986. pap. text 25.00 (*0-8032-8132-3*) U of Nebr Pr.

Nebraska Symposium on Motivation, 1987: Comparative Perspectives in Modern Psychology. Ed. by Daniel W. Leger & Richard Dienstbier. LC 53-11655. (Nebraska Symposium on Motivation Ser.: Vol. 35). xvi, 327p. 1988. text 45.00 (*0-8032-2880-5*); pap. text 25.00 (*0-8032-7926-4*) U of Nebr Pr.

Nebraska Symposium on Motivation, 1988: Socioemotional Development. Ed. by Ross A. Thompson. LC 53-11655. (Nebraska Symposium on Motivation Ser.: Vol. 36). xvi, 492p. 1990. text 45.00 (*0-8032-4421-5*); pap. text 25.00 (*0-8032-9415-8*) U of Nebr Pr.

Nebraska Symposium on Motivation, 1990: Perspectives on Motivation. Ed. by Richard A. Dienstbier. LC 53-11655. (Nebraska Symposium on Motivation Ser.: Vol. 38). xiv, 369p. 1991. text 45.00 (*0-8032-1693-9*) U of Nebr Pr.

Nebraska Symposium on Motivation, 1991: Psychology & Aging. Ed. by Theo B. Sonderegger. LC 53-11655. (Nebraska Symposium on Motivation Ser.: Vol. 39). xiv, 276p. 1991. text 45.00 (*0-8032-4222-0*); pap. text 25.00 (*0-8032-9210-4*, Bison Books) U of Nebr Pr.

Nebraska Symposium on Motivation, 1992: Developmental Perspectives on Motivation. Ed. by Janis E. Jacobs. LC 53-11655. (Nebraska Symposium on Motivation Ser.: Vol. 40). xiii, 299p. 1993. text 45.00 (*0-8032-2575-X*); pap. text 25.00 (*0-8032-7576-5*) U of Nebr Pr.

Nebraska Symposium on Motivation, 1993: Integrative View of Motivation, Cognition, & Emotion. Ed. by William D. Spaulding. LC 53-11655. (Nebraska Symposium on Motivation Ser.: Vol. 41). xii, 265p. 1994. pap. text 25.00 (*0-8032-9221-X*) U of Nebr Pr.

*__Nebraska Symposium on Motivation, 1998 Vol. 46: Motivation & Child Maltreatment.__ Ed. by David J. Hansen. (Nebraska Symposium on Motivation Ser.). (Illus.). 2000. text 45.00 (*0-8032-2401-X*) U of Nebr Pr.

Nebraska Territorial Census Index, 1854, 1855, 1856. Ronald V. Jackson. (Illus.). 1980. lib. bdg. 68.00 (*0-89593-688-7*, Accel Indexing) Genealogical Srvcs.

*__Nebraska Territory Postal History.__ Charles W. Winter. Ed. & Illus. by Leonard H. Hartmann. LC 99-95444. 176p. 1999. 35.00 (*0-917528-16-6*) L H Hartmann.

Nebraska Timeline: A Chronology of Nebraska History, Mystery, Trivia, Legend, Lore & More. Carole Marsh. (Carole Marsh Nebraska Bks.). (Illus.). (J). (gr. 3-12). 1994. pap. 19.95 (*0-7933-5957-0*); lib. bdg. 29.95 (*0-7933-5956-2*); disk 29.95 (*0-7933-5958-9*) Gallopade Intl.

Nebraska Tractor Tests since 1920. Charles H. Wendell. LC 93-7682. (Agricultural Ser.). 548p. 1985. 49.95 (*0-87938-826-9*) MBI Pubg.

Nebraska Trivia. Gabe Parks. LC 98-17242. 192p. 1998. pap. 6.95 (*1-55853-605-1*) Rutledge Hill Pr.

Nebraska 2000! Coming Soon to a Calendar Near You - The 21st Century! - Complete Set of AL 2000 Items. Carole Marsh. (Two Thousand! Ser.). (Illus.). (J). (gr. 3-12). 1998. pap. 75.00 (*0-7933-9363-9*); lib. bdg. 85.00 (*0-7933-9364-7*) Gallopade Intl.

Nebraska 2000! Coming Soon to a Calendar near You--The 21st Century! Carole Marsh. (Two Thousand! Ser.). (Illus.). (J). (gr. 3-12). 1998. pap. 19.95 (*0-7933-8757-4*); lib. bdg. 29.95 (*0-7933-8756-6*) Gallopade Intl.

*__Nebraska 2000 Advance Code Service.__ 60p. 1999. pap. write for info. (*0-327-09834-1*, 4525614) LEXIS Pub.

Nebraska UFO's & Extraterrestrials! A Look at the Sightings & Science in Our State. Carole Marsh. (Carole Marsh Nebraska Bks.). (Illus.). (J). (gr. 3-12). 1997. pap. 19.95 (*0-7933-6416-7*); lib. bdg. 29.95 (*0-7933-6415-9*) Gallopade Intl.

Nebraska, Where Dreams Grow. Dorothy W. Creigh. LC 80-84238. (Illus.). 160p. (Orig.). 1990. reprint ed. pap. 12.95 (*0-934904-15-4*) J & L Lee.

Nebraska Wild Flowers. Robert C. Lommasson. LC 70-188343. (Illus.). 243p. reprint ed. pap. 75.40 (*0-8357-6597-0*, 203599500001) Bks Demand.

Nebraska Wildlife Viewing Guide. Joseph Knue. LC 96-36463. (Illus.). 96p. 1997. pap. 8.95 (*1-56044-512-2*) Falcon Pub Inc.

*__NEBRASKAland Magazine's Wild Game Cookbook.__ (Illus.). 192p. 1999. pap. 12.95 (*0-9625959-4-2*) NE Game & Parks.

*__Nebraska/North Dakota/South Dakota State Credit Directory, 2000 Edition.__ rev. ed. American Business Directories Staff. 384p. 1999. boxed set 125.00 incl. cd-rom (*0-7687-0311-5*) Am Busn Direct.

Nebraskan's Odyssey. Richard E. Hall. LC 98-94188. 1998. pap. 9.95 (*0-9647900-1-7*) Hallgard-Bookman.

Nebraskans Speak Out on Academic Standards: A Public Engagement Report. Will Friedman & Jacqueline Danzberger. 30p. 1997. pap. 5.00 (*1-889483-52-4*) Public Agenda.

Nebraskans' Views on School Standards: A Focus Group Study by Public Agenda. Will Friedman. 37p. 1997. pap. 5.00 (*1-889483-51-6*) Public Agenda.

Nebraska's Five Seasons: The Best of Paul Fell. Paul Fell. (Illus.). 96p. (Orig.). 1991. pap. 8.95 (*0-934904-24-3*) J & L Lee.

Nebraska's Militia: The History of the Army & Air National Guard, 1854-1991. Douglas R. Hartman. LC 93-42035. 1994. write for info. (*0-89865-886-1*) Donning Co.

Nebraska's (Most Devastating!) Disasters & (Most Calamitous!) Castrophies! Carole Marsh. (Carole Marsh Nebraska Bks.). (Illus.). (J). (gr. 3 up). 1994. write for info. (*0-7933-0719-8*); pap. 19.95 (*0-7933-0717-1*); lib. bdg. 29.95 (*0-7933-0718-X*) Gallopade Intl.

Nebraska's Unsolved Mysteries (And Their "Solutions") Includes Scientific Information & Other Activities for Students. Carole Marsh. (Carole Marsh Nebraska Bks.). (Illus.). (J). (gr. 3-12). 1994. pap. 19.95 (*0-7933-5804-3*); lib. bdg. 29.95 (*0-7933-5803-5*); disk 29.95 (*0-7933-5805-1*) Gallopade Intl.

Nebraskaspeak. Paul Fell. LC 82-80300. (Illus.). 76p. 1996. reprint ed. pap. 5.95 (*0-934904-17-0*, 17-0) J & L Lee.

NEBSM Leading Your Team. NEBSM Staff. 96p. 1997. pap. text 36.95 (*0-7506-3311-5*) Buttrwrth-Heinemann.

Nebsm Planning & Controlling. Nebsm. 88p. pap. text. write for info. (*0-7506-3295-X*) Buttrwrth-Heinemann.

NEBSM Support Guide. NEBSM Staff. 64p. 1997. pap. text 34.95 (*0-7506-3704-8*) Buttrwrth-Heinemann.

Nebuchadnezzar & Babylon: The Schweich Lectures of the British Academy 1983. Donald J. Wiseman. (Schweich Lectures on Biblical Archaeology, British Academy). (Illus.). 158p. 1991. reprint ed. pap. text 26.00 (*0-19-726100-0*) OUP.

Nebuchadnezzar's Children: Conventions of Madness in Middle English Literature. Penelope B. Doob. LC 73-86890. 265p. reprint ed. pap. 82.20 (*0-608-14185-2*, 202199400024) Bks Demand.

Nebula: Poetry. Asia A. Czasak. (Illus.). 30p. 1997. pap. 6.00 (*0-9642344-2-4*) A A Czasak.

Nebula Awards No. 4: SFWA's Choices for the Best Science Fiction & Fantasy, 1988. Michael Bishop. 1990. pap. 13.95 (*0-15-665474-1*) Harcourt.

Nebula Awards No. 4: SFWA's Choices for the Best Science Fiction & Fantasy, 1988. Ed. by Michael Bishop. 1990. 22.95 (*0-15-164932-4*) Harcourt.

Nebula Awards No. 21: SFWA's Choices for the Best in Science Fiction & Fantasy 1985. Ed. by George Zebrowski. 320p. 1986. 19.95 (*0-685-14554-9*, Harvest Bks); pap. 8.95 (*0-685-14555-7*, Harvest Bks) Harcourt.

Nebula Awards No. 22: SFWA's Choices for the Best Science Fiction & Fantasy, 1986. Ed. by George Zebrowski. LC 83-647399. 332p. 1988. pap. 11.95 (*0-15-665476-8*, Harvest Bks) Harcourt.

Nebula Awards No. 23: SFWA's choices for the Best Science Fiction & Fantasy 1987. Ed. by Michael Bishop. 352p. 1989. 21.95 (*0-15-164930-8*); pap. 12.95 (*0-15-665475-X*) Harcourt.

Nebula Awards No. 25: SFWA's Choices for the Best Science Fiction & Fantasy of the Year. Michael Bishop. 1991. 24.95 (*0-15-164933-2*) Harcourt.

Nebula Awards No. 25: SFWA's Choices for the Best Science Fiction & Fantasy (1989) Michael Bishop. 346p. 1991. pap. 14.95 (*0-15-665473-3*, Harvest Bks) Harcourt.

Nebula Awards No. 26: SFWA's Choices for the Best Science Fiction & Fantasy of the Year. Ed. by James Morrow. 1992. 24.95 (*0-15-164934-0*, Harvest Bks); pap. 12.95 (*0-15-665472-5*, Harvest Bks) Harcourt.

Nebula Awards No. 27: SFWA's Choices for the Best Science Fiction & Fantasy of the Year. James Morrow. LC 83-647399. 1993. 24.95 (*0-15-164935-9*) Harcourt.

Nebula Awards No. 30: SFWA's Choices for the Best Science Fiction & Fantasy of the Year. Pamela Sargent. 368p. 1996. 25.00 (*0-15-100113-8*, Harvest Bks) Harcourt.

Nebula Awards No. 32: SFWA's Choices for the Best Science Fiction & Fantasy of the Year. Dann. 352p. (J). 1998. pap. 13.00 (*0-15-600552-2*) Harcourt.

Nebula Awards No. 32: SFWA's Choices for the Best Science Fiction & Fantasy of the Year. Jack Dann. 1998. 26.00 (*0-15-100306-8*) Harcourt.

***Nebula Awards Showcase 2000: The Years Best SF & Fantasy Chosen by the Science-Fiction & Fantasy Writers of America.** Gregory Benford. 320p. 2000. 28.00 (*0-15-100479-X*) Harcourt.

***Nebula Awards Showcase 2000: The Year's Best SF & Fantasy Chosen by the Science-Fiction & Fantasy Writers of America.** Gregory Benford. 320p. 2000. pap. text 14.00 (*0-15-600705-3*) Harcourt.

Nebula Awards 33: The Year's Best SF & Fantasy Chosen by the Science-Fiction & Fantasy Writers of America. Ed. by Connie Willis. 288p. 1999. pap. 13.00 (*0-15-600601-4*) Harcourt.

Nebulae & Interstellar Matter. Ed. by Barbara M. Middlehurst & Lawrence H. Aller. LC 66-13879. (Stars & Stellar Systems Ser.: Vol. 7). (Illus.). 1995. lib. bdg. 72.00 (*0-226-45959-4*) U Ch Pr.

Nebulae of Discourse: Interpretation, Textuality, & the Subject. Wojciech Kalaga. LC 97-42237. (Literary & Cultural Theory Ser.). (Illus.). 213p. 1997. write for info. (*0-8204-3289-X*) P Lang Pubng.

***Nec Answers.** Michael A. Anthony. LC 99-35502. 523p. 1999. pap. 34.95 (*0-07-134494-2*) McGraw.

***NEC Changes, 1999.** Mark W. Earley et al. (Illus.). 460p. 1998. pap. 42.25 (*0-87765-438-7*, NEC99CHG) Natl Fire Prot.

NEC Nutrition Manual. Clara L. Gerwick. 116p. (Orig.). 1997. pap. text 25.00 (*0-915187-07-8*) Nutrition Ed.

***NECC 99 Conference Proceedings.** National Educational Computing Conference 1999 Staff. (Illus.). 317p. 1999. spiral bd. 25.00 (*1-56484-151-0*) Intl Society Tech Educ.

***Necco's Sweethearts Be My Valentine Book.** Barbara Barbieri McGrath. 10p. (J). (ps up). 2000. bds. 5.99 (*0-694-01534-2*, HarpFestival) HarpC Child Bks.

Necesidad No. 1 del Creyente. John Osteen.Tr. of Believer's #1 Need. (SPA.). 48p. 1996. mass mkt. 2.00 (*0-912631-71-6*) J O Pubns.

Necesito Ayuda, Soy Lider de un Grupo Pequeno! Gary Teja. (SPA.). 40p. pap. 3.75 (*1-55883-093-6*, 6740-4910C) Libros Desafio.

Necesito Empleo! La Busqueda de Empleo con Historial Penal. Ned Rollo. (Information Ser.). (SPA.). 75p. (Orig.). 1993. pap. 5.95 (*1-878436-13-9*) OPEN TX.

Necesito Esposa (In Need of a Wife) Emma Darcy. (Bianca Ser.).Tr. of I Need a Wife. (SPA.). 1997. per. 3.50 (*0-373-33431-1*, 1-33431-7) Harlequin Bks.

Necessary American Fictions: Popular Literature of the 1950s. William Darby. LC 87-73250. 397p. 1987. 36.00 (*0-87972-389-0*); pap. 17.95 (*0-87972-390-4*) Bowling Green Univ Popular Press.

Necessary & Reasonable Force: The Essential Handbook for Law Enforcement Officers & Security Specialists. Edward F. Sullivan. Ed. by Jenifer H. Baarman. (Illus.). 154p. (Orig.). 1994. pap. 19.95 (*0-9627898-7-9*) Mdrn Bu-Jutsu.

Necessary & Unnecessary Utopias: Socialist Register 2000. Ed. by Leo Panitch & Colin Leys. LC 99-40304. 300p. 1999. pap. 23.00 (*1-58367-021-1*, Pub. by Monthly Rev) NYU Pr.

Necessary Angel. Massimo Cacciari. Tr. by Miguel E. Vatter from ITA. LC 93-50119. (SUNY Series, Intersections: Philosophy & Critical Theory). (Illus.). 124p. (C). 1994. text 14.50 (*0-7914-2189-9*) State U NY Pr.

Necessary Angel. Wallace Stevens. 1965. pap. 9.00 (*0-394-70278-6*) Vin Bks.

Necessary Angels: Tradition & Modernity in Kafka, Benjamin, & Scholem. Robert Alter. LC 90-46478. 160p. 1991. text 22.00 (*0-674-60663-9*, ALTNEC) HUP.

Necessary Blankness: Women in Major American Fiction of the Sixties. Mary Allen. LC 75-38780. 226p. 1976. text 24.95 (*0-252-00519-8*) U of Ill Pr.

***Necessary Boat.** Susan Baran. LC 99-41318. 2000. 12.00 (*1-891305-19-0*) Painted Leaf.

***Necessary but Not Sufficient: The Respective Roles of Single & Multiple Influences on Individual Development.** Theodore D. Wachs. LC 99-37473. 439p. 1999. 49.95 (*1-55798-611-8*) Am Psychol.

Necessary Cat: A Celebration of Cats in Picture & Word. Nicola Bayley. LC 97-46491. (Illus.). 80p. (J). (gr. 3-7). 1998. 17.99 (*0-7636-0571-9*) Candlewick Press.

Necessary Conditions for an Extremum. B. N. Pshenichnyi. (Pure & Applied Mathematics Ser.: Vol. 4). (Illus.). 248p. 1971. text 135.00 (*0-8247-1556-X*) Dekker.

Necessary Dream: A Study of the Novels of Manuel Puig. Pamela Bacarisse. LC 88-23243. 320p. (C). 1988. lib. bdg. 56.00 (*0-389-20809-4*, N8367) B&N Imports.

Necessary Elements. Louis A. Kass. 59p. 1979. pap. 6.00 (*0-87526-242-2*) Gould.

Necessary End. Nathaniel Benchley. LC 75-37105. 208p. (YA). (gr. 7 up). 1976. 13.95 (*0-06-020498-2*) HarpC Child Bks.

Necessary End. Peter Robinson. 320p. 1992. text 19.95 (*0-684-19385-X*, Scribners Ref) Mac Lib Ref.

Necessary End. Peter Robinson. LC 91-24521. (Inspector Banks Mystery Ser.). 352p. 2000. mass mkt. 6.99 (*0-380-71946-0*, Avon Bks) Morrow Avon.

Necessary End. Peter Robinson. pap. write for info. (*0-14-011545-5*) Penguin Putnam.

Necessary End. large type ed. Peter Robinson. 466p. 1992. 25.99 (*0-7505-0343-2*, Pub. by Mgna Lrg Print) Ulverscroft.

***Necessary Ends.** Stanley Middleton. 1999. 27.00 (*0-09-180069-2*, Pub. by Random) Trafalgar.

***Necessary Evil.** Paul DeStefano. 2000. 22.00 (*0-8059-4982-8*) Dorrance.

Necessary Evil. David A. Van Meter. 1996. pap. write for info. (*0-312-95715-7*) St Martin.

Necessary Evil. David A. Van Meter. 1997. mass mkt. 5.99 (*0-312-95924-9*) St Martin.

Necessary Evil. Lindsay Welsh. (Orig.). 1995. mass mkt. 5.95 (*1-56333-277-9*, Rosebud) Masquerade.

***Necessary Evil: A History of America Distrust of Government.** Garry Wills. LC 99-35879. 368p. 1999. 24.50 (*0-684-84489-3*) S&S Trade.

Necessary Evil: Atomic Energy. David R. Marples. (C). 1996. text 49.95 (*0-8133-8858-9*) Westview.

Necessary Evil? Slavery & the Debate over the Constitution. Ed. by John P. Kaminski. (Constitutional Heritage Ser.: Vol. 2). 208p. 1995. text 32.95 (*0-945612-16-8*); pap. text 15.95 (*0-945612-33-8*) Madison Hse.

Necessary Evil? Sports & Violence. William Krieger. (Sports Issues Ser.). 1998. 22.60 (*0-8225-3306-5*) Lerner Pub.

Necessary Excesses. Gene Cler. 32p. 1995. 3.00 (*0-941127-17-6*) Dacotah Terr Pr.

Necessary Fictions. Barbara Croft. LC 98-9033. 224p. 1998. text 22.50 (*0-8229-4078-7*) U of Pittsburgh Pr.

Necessary Fire. Marilyn Johnson. LC 90-85750. 62p. (Orig.). 1996. pap. 9.95 (*1-888219-01-7*) Pearl Edit.

Necessary Fraud: Progressive Reform & Utah Coal. Nancy J. Taniguchi. LC 95-53086. (Legal History of North America Ser.: Vol. 3). (Illus.). 336p. 1996. 39.95 (*0-8061-2818-6*) U of Okla Pr.

Necessary Goods: Our Responsibilities to Meet Others' Needs. Ed. by Gillian Brock. LC 97-45733. (Studies in Social, Political, & Legal Philosophy). 288p. 1998. 63.00 (*0-8476-8818-6*) Rowman.

Necessary Goods: Our Responsibilities to Meet Others' Needs. Ed. by Gillian Brock. LC 97-45733. (Studies in Social, Political, & Legal Philosophy). 288p. 1998. pap. 23.95 (*0-8476-8819-4*) Rowman.

Necessary Heresies: Alternatives to Fundamentalism. Peter Cameron. 175p. 1996. reprint ed. pap. 24.95 (*0-86840-293-1*, Pub. by New South Wales Univ Pr) Intl Spec Bk.

Necessary Hunger. Nina Revoyr. LC 96-32999. 368p. (YA). 1997. 22.50 (*0-684-83234-8*) S&S Trade.

Necessary Hunger. Nina Revoyr. LC 97-50577. 1998. pap. 13.95 (*0-312-18142-6*) St Martin.

Necessary Illusion - Art As "Witness" Resonance & Attunement to Forms & Feelings. Gilbert J. Rose. 148p. 1996. 27.50 (*0-8236-3510-4*) Intl Univs Pr.

Necessary Illusions: Thought Control in Democratic Societies. Noam Chomsky. LC 89-6074. 422p. 1989. 40.00 (*0-89608-367-5*); pap. 22.00 (*0-89608-366-7*) South End Pr.

Necessary Illusions in Becoming a Jew in the Diaspora: Poems by Bernard A. Goldberg. Bernard A. Goldberg. 106p. (Orig.). 1989. pap. 10.00 (*0-9624348-0-9*) B A Goldberg.

***Necessary Journeys.** Nancy Snyderman. (Illus.). 320p. 2001. pap. 14.95 (*0-7868-8432-0*, Pub. by Disney Pr) Time Warner.

Necessary Journeys: Letting Ourselves Learn from Life. Nancy L. Snyderman & Peg Streep. LC 00-29584. 192p. 2000. 19.95 (*0-7868-6513-X*, Pub. by Hyperion) Time Warner.

Necessary Knowledge: Piagetian Perspectives on Constructivism. Leslie Smith. Ed. by Peter Bryant et al. (Essays in Developmental Psychology Ser.). 248p. 1993. 49.95 (*0-86377-270-6*) L Erlbaum Assocs.

Necessary Learning: Liberal Arts & Sciences, Defense & Reform. Intro. by Robert Moynihan. LC 88-26185. 116p. (C). 1988. lib. bdg. 32.00 (*0-8191-7204-9*) U Pr of Amer.

***Necessary Light: Poems of Patricia Fargnoli.** Patricia Fargnoli. LC PS3556.A7144N43 1999. (May Swenson Poetry Award Ser.: Vol. 3). 80p. 1999. pap. 9.95 (*0-87421-284-7*) Utah St U Pr.

Necessary Lives: Biographical Reflections. B. L. Reid. 176p. 1990. 24.95 (*0-8262-0736-7*) U of Mo Pr.

Necessary Losses. Judith Viorst. 1987. mass mkt. 5.95 (*0-449-13206-4*, GM) Fawcett.

Necessary Losses. Judith Viorst. 1996. pap. 12.95 (*0-449-91152-7*) Fawcett.

Necessary Losses. Judith Viorst. 448p. 1998. per. 14.00 (*0-684-84495-8*) S&S Trade.

Necessary Madness. Jenn Crowell. 256p. 1998. mass mkt. 6.99 (*0-446-60606-5*, Pub. by Warner Bks) Little.

Necessary Madness. large type ed. Jenn Crowell. (Niagara Large Print Ser.). 240p. 1997. 29.50 (*0-7089-5889-3*) Ulverscroft.

Necessary Madness: A Novel. Jenn Crowell. 1998. mass mkt. 251.64 (*0-446-16634-0*) Warner Bks.

Necessary Madness: The Humor of Domesticity in Nineteenth-Century American Literature. Gregg Camfield. LC 96-26019. (Illus.). 256p. 1997. text 55.00 (*0-19-510040-9*) OUP.

Necessary Marriage. Sylvia E. Kirk. (Rainbow Romances Ser.). 160p. 1994. 14.95 (*0-7090-5396-7*, 915) Parkwest Pubns.

Necessary Marriage. large type ed. Sylvia E. Kirk. (Linford Romance Library). 272p. 1995. pap. 16.99 (*0-7089-7788-X*, Linford) Ulverscroft.

Necessary Measures. J. M. Barlog. 448p. 1997. pap. 6.99 (*0-9654716-0-8*) BAK Books.

Necessary Motions: Poems. Sam Rasnake. 72p. 1998. pap. 12.00 (*1-885912-10-2*) Sows Ear Pr.

Necessary Parties. Barbara Dana. LC 85-45267. (Charlotte Zolotow Bk.). 352p. (YA). (gr. 7 up). 1986. 14.95 (*0-06-021408-2*) HarpC Child Bks.

***Necessary Ports.** Roger Lee Kenvin & Verna Rudd Kenvin. LC 00-91149. 288p. 2000. pap. 19.95 (*0-9656635-6-6*) July Blue.

***Necessary Power: A Blue Print for Nation Building.** Areeb Malik Shabazz. (Illus.). 76p. 1999. reprint ed. pap. 8.00 (*1-56411-220-9*, Kitabu Pub) Untd Bros & Sis.

Necessary Risk. John F. Bayer. LC 97-43159. 324p. 1998. pap. 12.99 (*0-8054-4016-X*) Broadman.

Necessary Roughness. Jerry Jones. 1999. 23.00 (*0-671-01710-1*) PB.

Necessary Roughness. Marie Lee. LC 96-34185. 176p. (YA). (gr. 7 up). 1996. lib. bdg. 14.89 (*0-06-025130-1*) HarpC Child Bks.

Necessary Roughness. Marie Lee. LC 96-34185. (Illus.). 240p. (YA). (gr. 7 up). 1996. 15.95 (*0-06-025124-7*) HarpC Child Bks.

Necessary Roughness. Marie G. Lee. LC 96-34185. 240p. (J). (gr. 12 up). 1998. pap. 4.95 (*0-06-447169-1*) HarpC Child Bks.

Necessary Roughness. Marie G. Lee. (J). 1998. 10.05 (*0-606-13000-4*, Pub. by Turtleback) Demco.

***Necessary Targets: A Play.** Eve Ensler. 160p. 2001. pap. 12.95 (*0-375-75603-5*) Villard Books.

Necessary Theatre. Ed. by Jorge A. Huerta. LC 89-283. 368p. (C). 1989. pap. 19.95 (*0-934770-95-6*, Pub. by Arte Publico) Empire Pub Srvs.

Necessary Theatre: 6 Plays about the Chicano Experience. Peter Hall. 1999. pap. 10.95 (*1-55936-178-6*, Pub. by Theatre Comm) Consort Bk Sales.

Necessary Toughness: Facing Defenses & Diabetes. Jonathan Hayes & Robert L. Briggs. LC 93-11172. 1993. 7.95 (*0-945448-30-9*, 4807-01) Am Diabetes.

Necessary Virtue: The Pragmatic Origins of Religious Liberty in New England. Charles P. Hanson. LC 97-45092. 288p. 1998. 35.00 (*0-8139-1794-8*) U Pr of Va.

Necessary Wisdom: Meeting the Challenge of a New Cultural Maturity. Charles M. Johnston. 264p. (Orig.). 1995. pap. 14.95 (*0-89087-650-9*) Celestial Arts.

Necessary Woman. Helen Van Slyke. 1983. mass mkt. 3.95 (*0-446-31266-5*, Pub. by Warner Bks) Little.

Necessities: Chicago. 2nd ed. Kathy Kaplan. LC 97-38768. 128p. 1998. pap. 12.95 (*0-8092-3004-6*, 300460, Contemporary Bks) NTC Contemp Pub Co.

Necessities: San Francisco. Kathy Kaplan. LC 98-27484. 128p. 1998. pap. 12.95 (*0-8092-3003-8*, 300380, Contemporary Bks) NTC Contemp Pub Co.

Necessities & Temptations. Junior League of Austin, Texas Staff. LC 86-82853. (Illus.). 1987. pap. 19.95 (*0-9605906-1-7*) Jr League Austin.

Necessities of War: A Study of Thucydides' Pessimism. Peter R. Pouncey. LC 80-16887. 213p. reprint ed. pap. 66.10 (*0-8357-8965-9*, 203359500086) Bks Demand.

Necessity among Us: The Owen Sound General & Marine Hospital, 1891-1985. David Gagan. 180p. 1990. text 30.00 (*0-8020-3462-4*) U of Toronto Pr.

Necessity & Freedom. Rudolf Steiner. Tr. by Pauline Wharle from GER.Tr. of Notwendigkeit und Freiheit im Weltengeschehen und im Menschlichen Handeln. 120p. 1989. 20.00 (*0-88010-259-4*); pap. 9.95 (*0-88010-260-8*) Anthroposophic.

Necessity & Language. Morris Lazerowitz & Alice Ambrose. LC 85-22201. 272p. 1986. text 39.95 (*0-312-56259-4*) St Martin.

Necessity & Possibility: The Metaphysics of Modality see Analytical Metaphysics

Necessity Anti-Semitism. Raphael. LC 97-39682. 1998. text 45.00 (*0-312-21171-6*) St Martin.

Necessity, Cause & Blame: Perspectives on Aristotle's Theory. Richard Sorabji. LC 79-2449. 334p. 1980. pap. 18.95 (*0-8014-9244-0*) Cornell U Pr.

Necessity, Essence, & Individuation: A Defense of Conventionalism. Alan Sidelle. LC 89-7122. 248p. 1989. text 37.50 (*0-8014-2166-7*) Cornell U Pr.

Necessity for Ruins, & Other Topics. J. B. Jackson. LC 79-23212. 136p. (C). 1980. pap. 14.95 (*0-87023-292-4*) U of Mass Pr.

Necessity, Freedom & Transcendence in the Romantic Poets: A Failed Religion. Douglas Kenning. LC 98-22997. (Studies in Art & Religious Interpretation: Vol. 23). 428p. 1998. text 109.95 (*0-7734-8347-0*) E Mellen.

***Necessity Is... The Early Years of Zappa's Mothers of Invention.** Billy James. (Illus.). 2000. pap. 18.95 (*0-946719-14-4*, Pub. by SAF Pub) Interlink Pub.

Necessity Isn't Always the Mother of Invention: True Stories Behind Great Products We Couldn't Live Without. Allyn Freeman & Bob Golden. (Orig.). 1997. pap. 14.95 (*0-614-27639-X*) Wiley.

Necessity of Art. Alan F. Clutton-Brock et al. LC 78-93366. (Essay Index Reprint Ser.). 1977. 19.95 (*0-8369-1364-7*) Ayer.

Necessity of Atheism & Other Essays. Percy Bysshe Shelley. LC 92-40791. (Freethought Library). 96p. 1993. 24.95 (*0-87975-774-4*) Prometheus Bks.

Necessity of Being. Joseph Chiari. LC 73-3338. 168p. 1973. 45.00 (*0-87752-167-0*) Gordian.

Necessity of Choice: 19th Century Political Thought. Louis Hartz. Ed. by Paul Roazen. 228p. (C). 1990. 39.95 (*0-88738-326-2*) Transaction Pubs.

Necessity of Craft: Development & Women's Craft Practices in the Asian-Pacific Region. Ed. by Lorna Kaino. LC 96-147010. 186p. (C). 1995. pap. 24.95 (*1-875560-62-9*, Pub. by Univ of West Aust Pr) Intl Spec Bk.

Necessity of Empty Places. 10th anniversary rev. ed. Paul Gruchow. LC 98-55433. 1999. pap. 13.95 (*1-57131-223-4*) Milkweed Ed.

Necessity of Ethical Absolutes see Measuring Morality: A Comparison of Ethical Systems

Necessity of Ethical Absolutes (CFUC) Erwin W. Lutzer. 112p. (Orig.). 1981. pap. 7.95 (*0-310-35791-8*, 12659P) Zondervan.

Necessity of Experience. Edward S. Reed. LC 96-5980. 200p. 1996. 30.00 (*0-300-06668-6*) Yale U Pr.

Necessity of Friction. Ed. by Nordal Akerman. LC 97-22525. 336p. (C). 1998. pap. 28.00 (*0-8133-3434-9*, Pub. by Westview) HarpC.

Necessity of Friction: 19 Essays on a Vital Force. Ed. by N. Akerman. 336p. 1993. 71.95 (*0-387-91470-6*) Spr-Verlag.

Necessity of Law (1924) John W. Murray. 174p. 1998. reprint ed. pap. 17.95 (*0-7661-0591-1*) Kessinger Pub.

Necessity of Long-Range Goals. Harvey Jackins. 1972. pap. 2.00 (*0-911214-17-8*) Rational Isl.

Necessity of Long-Range Goals: Italian Translation. Harvey Jackins. (ITA.). 1991. pap. 2.00 (*1-885357-72-9*) Rational Isl.

Necessity of Myth: A History of the National Negro Business League, 1900-45. John H. Burrows. LC 82-82259. 236p. (C). 1988. 25.00 (*0-9619848-0-5*) J H Burrows.

***Necessity of Organization: Mary Kenney O'Sullivan & Trade Unionism for Women, 1892-1919.** rev. ed. Kathleen B. Nutter. LC 99-35081. (Studies in the History of American Labor). 232p. 1999. 59.00 (*0-8153-3505-9*) Garland.

Necessity of Prayer. E. M. Bounds. 143p. 1984. mass mkt. 5.99 (*0-88368-139-0*) Whitaker Hse.

***Necessity of Regularity in Quartering Soldiers: The Organization, Material Culture & Quartering of the British Soldier at Michilimackinac.** Brian Leigh Dunnigan. (Illus.). 80p. 1999. pap. 12.95 (*0-911872-72-8*) Mackinac St Hist Pks.

Necessity of Social Control. Istvan Meszaros. (C). 1972. pap. write for info. (*0-85036-153-2*, Pub. by MRLN) Paul & Co Pubs.

Necessity or Contingency? The Master Argument & Its Philosophical Solutions. Jules Vuillemin. (CSLI Lecture Notes Ser.). 296p. (C). 1996. 49.95 (*1-881526-86-0*); pap. 22.95 (*1-881526-85-2*) CSLI.

Necessity or Contingency? The Master Argument & Its Philosophical Solutions. Jules Vuillemin. (CSLI Lecture Notes Ser.). 1996. 49.95 (*0-521-52686-8*); pap. 22.95 (*0-521-52685-X*) Cambridge U Pr.

Necessity, Volition, & Love. Harry B. Frankfurt. LC 98-8081. 200p. (C). 1999. pap. 17.95 (*0-521-63395-8*) Cambridge U Pr.

Necessity, Volition & Love. Harry G. Frankfurt. LC 98-8081. 200p. (C). 1999. text 54.95 (*0-521-63299-4*) Cambridge U Pr.

Necessity's Child: The Story of Walter Hunt, America's Forgotten Inventor. Joseph N. Kane. LC 96-37134. (Illus.). 330p. 1997. boxed set 38.50 (*0-7864-0279-2*) McFarland & Co.

Necessity's Children: Memoirs of an Independent Inventor. Samuel Ruben. LC 89-17290. (Illus.). 160p. 1990. 17.95 (*0-932576-75-3*) Breitenbush Bks.

Nechama & Mendel Get Ready for Moshiach. large type ed. Leah M. Heidingsfeld. (Illus.). 32p. (J). 1995. 9.95 (*1-881400-09-3*) S I E.

Nechemiah. Yosef Rabinowitz. 18.99 (*0-89906-095-1*, NECH); pap. 15.99 (*0-89906-096-X*, NECP) Mesorah Pubns.

Neck see Head & Neck Surgery

Neck Ache & Shoulder Pain. Ian Macnab. (Illus.). 528p. 1994. 69.00 (*0-683-05354-X*) Lppncott W & W.

Neck & Arm Pain. 3rd ed. Rene Cailliet. LC 90-13849. (Pain Ser.). (Illus.). 226p. 1990. pap. 21.95 (*0-8036-1610-4*) Davis Co.

Neck & Back Pain: The Scientific Evidence of Causes, Diagnosis, & Treatment. Alf L. Nachemson & Egon Jonsson. 544p. text 89.00 (*0-7817-2760-X*) Lppncott W & W.

Neck & Neck. large type ed. Leo Bruce. 368p. 1983. 11.50 (*0-7089-0898-5*) Ulverscroft.

Neck & Neck Mark Knopfler Chet Atkins - Guitar Tablature. 128p. 1996. otabind 19.95 (*0-7935-7014-X*) H Leonard.

Neck Bones for Supper. James O. Williams & Otis Williams. vi, 71p. (Orig.). (J). 1996. pap. 6.95 (*0-9654260-0-9*) JOW.

Neck Care. Andrew Cole. (Illus.). 24p. 1999. pap. 1.42 (*0-934230-47-1*) Medic Pub.

***Neck Complaints.** Michael Ronthal. LC 99-37382. (Most Common Complaints Ser.). 152p. 1999. pap. text 25.00 (*0-7506-7156-4*) Buttrwrth-Heinemann.

Neck in a Noose. large type ed. E. X. Ferrars. LC 94-38312. 288p. 1995. pap. 17.95 (*0-7838-1170-5*, G K Hall Lrg Type) Mac Lib Ref.

***Neck Injuries.** Syed M. Babar. LC 99-33583. xii, 148p. 1999. pap. 89.00 (*1-85233-637-4*) Spr-Verlag.

Neck of the Bottle: George W. Goethals & the Reorganization of the U. S. Army Supply System, 1917-1918. Phyllis A. Zimmerman. LC 92-11208. (Military History Ser.: No. 27). 216p. 1992. 41.95 (*0-89096-515-3*) Tex A&M Univ Pr.

Neck Pain. 2nd ed. Henry L. Feffer et al. (Illus.). 456p. 1992. 65.00 (*0-87473-823-7*, 62016-10, MICHIE) LEXIS Pub.

N

An Asterisk (*) at the beginning of an entry indicates that the title is appearing for the first time.

Neck Pain: Medical Diagnosis & Comprehensive Management. David G. Borenstein et al. Ed. by Richard Lampert. 512p. 1996. text 89.00 (*0-7216-5412-6*, W B Saunders Co) Harcrt Hlth Sci Grp.

Neck, Upper Back, Shoulder & Arm Pain. James M. Cox. (Illus.). 11p. (Orig.). (C). 1992. pap. text 2.00 (*0-9616488-9-9*) Alef Bet Comns.

Necker & the Revolution of 1789. Robert D. Harris. LC 86-15881. 816p. (C). 1986. lib. bdg. 78.00 (*0-8191-5602-7*) U Pr of Amer.

Neckerchief Slides You Can Whittle: How to Carve Your Own Slides from Beginner to Expert. Mark Johnson. 48p. 1998. pap. 5.99 (*1-883988-24-1*) RSV Prods.

Necking With Louise. Rick Book. 168p. (YA). (gr. 9-12). 1999. pap. 7.95 (*0-88995-194-2*, Pub. by Red Deer) Genl Dist Srvs.

Necklace. Florence Chard Dacey. LC 87-63131. (Illus.). 64p. (Orig.). 1988. pap. text 5.95 (*0-935697-03-9*) Midwest Villages.

Necklace. Guy de Maupassant. (Illus.). (J). (gr. 4 up). 1992. 26.60 (*1-56846-006-6*, Creat Educ) Creative Co.

Necklace. Guy de Maupassant. 35p. (YA). (gr. 10 up). 1969. pap. 3.50 (*0-87129-853-8*, N10) Dramatic Pub.

Necklace. rev. ed. Guy de Maupassant. Tr. by Mathilde Weissenhorn from FRE. (Read-Along Radio Dramas Ser.). (J). (gr. 6-10). 1993. reprint ed. ring bd. 38.00 (*1-878298-16-X*) Balance Pub.

Necklace: Based on "the Necklace," a Short Story by Guy de Maupassant. Lonnie B. Hewitt et al. LC 94-33729. (Spotlight Ser.). (C). 1994. 7.19 (*0-07-009252-4*) McGraw.

Necklace: From Antiquity to the Present. Daniela Mascetti & Amanda Triossi. LC 96-48107. (Illus.). 224p. 1997. 60.00 (*0-8109-3682-8*, Pub. by Abrams) Time Warner.

Necklace & Calabash: A Chinese Detective Story. Robert H. Van Gulik. LC 92-22803. (Illus.). viii, 143p. 1992. pap. 6.95 (*0-226-84870-1*) U Ch Pr.

Necklace & Other Short Stories. Guy de Maupassant. (Thrift Editions Ser.). Orig. Title: The Works of Guy de Maupassant: Short Stories. 128p. 1992. reprint ed. pap. 1.00 (*0-486-27064-5*) Dover.

Necklace for a Poor Sod. Kusha Petts. (C). 1979. 30.00 (*0-85088-435-7*, Pub. by Gomer Pr) St Mut.

Necklace of Diamonds, 2 vols., 1. Jai P. Bharti. (C). 1989. 12.00 (*81-209-0507-5*, Pub. by Pitambar Pub) St Mut.

Necklace of Diamonds, 2 vols., 2. Jai P. Bharti. (C). 1989. 12.00 (*81-209-0508-3*, Pub. by Pitambar Pub) St Mut.

Necklace of Pearls. Sylvia Lopez-Medina. 320p. 2000. 23.00 (*0-06-017272-X*) HarpC.

Necklace of Stars. unabridged ed. Veronika M. Charles. (Illus.). 32p. (J). (gr. k-4). 1997. 17.95 (*0-7737-2967-4*) STDK.

Necklace of Stories. Moncure D. Conway. (Works of Moncure Daniel Conway). 1990. reprint ed. lib. bdg. 79.00 (*0-7812-2334-2*) Rprt Serv.

Necklace of Words: Short Fiction by Mexican Women. Ed. by Marjorie Agosin & Nancy Hall. (Secret Weavers Ser.: Vol. 12). 148p. (Orig.). 1998. pap. 14.00 (*1-877727-73-3*) White Pine.

Necklace of Wrens. Michael Hartnett. 124p. 1987. 24.95 (*1-85235-009-1*) Dufour.

Necklaces of Gems (Qala'id al-Jawahir) Shaikh Muhammad Ibn Yahya. Tr. by Muhtar Holland from ARA. 603p. 1998. pap. 29.95 (*1-882216-17-2*) Al-Baz Pub.

Necklines: The Art of Jacques-Louis David after the Terror. Ewa Lajer-Burcharth. LC 98-47971. (Illus.). 374p. 1999. 50.00 (*0-300-07421-2*) Yale U Pr.

Necrocorrida. Andrei Codrescu. (Illus.). 80p. (gr. 11 up). 1980. pap. 6.00 (*0-915572-53-2*) Panjandrum.

***Necrofiler II.** Donna Sypchuk. 208p. 2000. pap. 15.99 (*1-895837-53-7*) Insomniac.

Necrology of Graves at the Old Oakland Cemetery. Eric J. Brock. 107p. 1988. pap. 16.50 (*1-57088-055-7*) J&W Ent.

Necrology of the Maryland, New York & New England Provinces of the Society of Jesus. 41p. 1996. pap. 10.95 (*0-87840-332-9*) Georgetown U Pr.

Necromance. Rae Armantrout. (New American Poetry Ser.: No. 7). 56p. 1991. pap. 8.95 (*1-55713-096-5*) Sun & Moon CA.

Necromancer. Gordon Rupert Dickson. 1998. mass mkt. 5.99 (*0-8125-4530-3*, Pub. by Tor Bks) St Martin.

Necromancer: A Romance. George W. Reynolds. Ed. by R. Reginald & Douglas A. Menville. LC 75-46304. (Supernatural & Occult Fiction Ser.). (Illus.). 1976. reprint ed. lib. bdg. 23.95 (*0-405-08164-2*) Ayer.

Necromancer: or Voo-Doo Doctor. Handy N. Brown. LC 77-39544. reprint ed. 29.50 (*0-404-00008-8*) AMS Pr.

Necromancers. Robert H. Benson. LC 75-36826. (Occult Ser.). 1976. reprint ed. 26.95 (*0-405-07939-7*) Ayer.

Necromantic Ritual Book. Leilah Wendell. LC 91-50394. (Illus.). 50p. (Orig.). 1991. pap. 8.50 (*0-944087-03-5*) Westgate Pr.

Necronomian: Workbook of the Necronomicon. Darren Fox. Ed. by Thor Templar. (Illus.). 43p. (Orig.). 1997. text 65.00 (*1-57179-054-3*) Intern Guild ASRS.

Necronomicon. Ed Simon. LC 79-56778. (Illus.). 218p. 1980. mass mkt. 6.99 (*0-380-75192-5*, Avon Bks) Morrow Avon.

Necronomicon: Selected Stories & Essays Concerning the Blasphemous Tome of the Mad Arab. Robert Silverberg et al. Ed. by Robert M. Price. (Call of Cthulhu Fiction Ser.). (Illus.). 352p. (Orig.). 1996. pap. 12.95 (*1-56882-070-4*, 6012) Chaosium.

Necronomicon No. 2: The Journal of Horror & Erotic Cinema. Ed. by Andy Black. (Illus.). 192p. 1998. pap. 17.95 (*1-871592-38-0*) Creation Books.

Necronomicon Vol. 1: The Journal of Horror & Erotic Cinema. Ed. by Andy Black. (Illus.). 192p. (Orig.). 1996. pap. 16.95 (*1-871592-37-2*) Creation Books.

***Necronomicon Files: The Truth Behind the Legend.** limited ed. Daniel Harms & John Wisdom Gonce, III. 332p. (C). 1998. write for info. (*1-892389-00-2*, Pub. by Nght Shde Bks) Brodart.

Necronomicon Files: The Truth Behind the Legend. 2nd rev. ed. Daniel Harms & John Wisdom Gonce, III. 332p. 1999. pap. write for info. (*1-892389-03-7*, Pub. by Nght Shde Bks) Brodart.

Necronomicon Revelations Bk. 1: Guide to the Necronomicon. Tahuti. (Illus.). 80p. 1997. 65.00 (*1-57179-065-9*) Intern Guild ASRS.

Necronomicon Spellbook. Ed. by Simon. (Illus.). 128p. 1998. mass mkt. 6.99 (*0-380-73112-6*, Avon Bks) Morrow Avon.

Necropolis & Songs of Hope: Bilingual Poetry. Nikola Miscevic. 128p. 1996. pap. 12.95 (*0-88962-433-X*) Mosaic.

Necropolis Atlanta. Jennifer Hartshorn. (Illus.). 1994. pap., per. 15.00 (*1-56504-164-X*, 6200) White Wolf.

Necropolis of Hesban: A Typology of Tombs. S. Douglas Waterhouse et al. (Hesban Ser.: Vol. 10). (Illus.). xvi, 207p. 1998. 45.99 (*0-943872-23-5*) Andrews Univ Pr.

Necropolis of Kalorizki. J. L. Benson. (Studies in Mediterranean Archaeology: Vol. XXXVI). (Illus.). 170p. 1973. pap. 52.50 (*91-85058-55-6*) P Astroms.

Necropsy: Procedures & Basic Diagnostic Methods for Practicing Veterinarians. Albert C. Strafuss. (Illus.). 262p. (C). 1988. text 58.95 (*0-398-05375-8*) C C Thomas.

Necropsy Guide: Rodents & the Rabbit. Ed. by Donald B. Feldman & John C. Seely. 176p. 1988. boxed set 208.95 (*0-8493-4934-6*, SF997) CRC Pr.

Necroscope: Deadspawn, Vol. 5. Brian Lumley. 1991. mass mkt. 9.71 (*0-586-20905-0*) HAR3.

Necroscope: Deadspeak, Vol. 4. Brian Lumley. 1990. mass mkt. 8.32 (*0-586-20904-2*) HAR3.

***Necroscope: Defilers.** Brian Lumley. LC 00-23325. 448p. 2000. 25.95 (*0-312-87261-5*, Pub. by Tor Bks) St Martin.

Necroscope: Invaders. 2nd ed. Brian Lumley. LC 99-24562. (Necroscope Ser.: 10). 384p. 1999. 25.95 (*0-312-86814-6*, Pub. by Tor Bks) St Martin.

Necroscope: Resurgence. Brian Lumley. 1997. mass mkt. 6.99 (*0-8125-5364-0*, Pub. by Tor Bks) St Martin.

Necroscope: The Lost Years. Brian Lumley. 1992. mass mkt. 5.99 (*0-8125-2137-4*, Pub. by Tor Bks) St Martin.

Necroscope: The Lost Years. Brian Lumley. 384p. 1994. 23.95 (*0-312-85787-X*, Pub. by Tor Bks) St Martin.

Necroscope: The Lost Years. Brian Lumley. 1996. mass mkt. 6.99 (*0-8125-5363-2*, Pub. by Tor Bks) St Martin.

***Necrotizing Enterocolitis.** Ed. by Brian F. Gilchrist. LC 00-22053. (Medical Intelligence Unit Ser.). 94p. 2000. 99.00 (*1-58706-008-6*) Eurekah.

Nectar. Robert Bove. Ed. by Edward Mycue. (Took Modern Poetry in English Ser.: No. 26). (Illus.). 28p. (Orig.). 1991. pap. 3.00 (*1-879457-27-X*) Norton Coker Pr.

***Nectar & Ambrosia: An Encyclopedia of Food in World Mythology.** Tamra Andrews. 2000. lib. bdg. 65.00 (*1-57607-036-0*) ABC-CLIO.

Nectar & Pollen Plants of China. Xu Wan-lin. (CHI & LAT.). 1992. 198.00 (*0-7855-0528-8*, Pub. by Wanhai Books) St Mut.

Nectar & Pollen Plants of Oregon & the Pacific Northwest: An Illustrated Guide to Plants Used by Honey Bees. enl. rev. ed. D. M. Burgett et al. (Illus.). 151p. (Orig.). (C). 1989. pap. 11.95 (*0-9624785-0-4*) Honeystone Pr.

Nectar at Noon. Sheila Cudahy. 1989. 16.95 (*0-15-152170-0*) Harcourt.

Nectar in a Sieve: A Novel. Kamala Markandaya. 190p. (C). 1998. mass mkt. 5.99 (*0-451-16836-4*, AE2291) NAL.

Nectar in a Sieve: A Novel. Kamala Markandaya. 1982. 11.09 (*0-606-01922-7*, Pub. by Turtleback) Demco.

Nectar in a Sieve & The Woman Warrior: Curriculum Unit. Center for Learning Network Staff. (Novel Ser.). 93p. (YA). (gr. 9-12). 1996. spiral bd. 18.95 (*1-56077-410-X*) Ctr Learning.

Nectar of Devotion: The Complete Science of Bhakti-Yoga. A. C. Bhaktivedanta Swami Prabhupada. LC 78-118082. (Illus.). 521p. 1970. 24.95 (*0-912776-05-6*, NOD) Bhaktivedanta.

Nectar of Immortality: Sri Nisargadatta Maharaj's Discourses on the Eternal. Ed. by Robert Powell. LC 95-44138. 192p. 1996. pap. 14.00 (*1-884997-13-9*) Blue Dove Pr.

Nector of Instruction. A. C. Bhaktivedanta Swami Prabhupada. (Illus.). 130p. 1990. pap. 2.95 (*0-912776-85-4*, NOI) Bhaktivedanta.

Ned. Mark Dunster. LC 74-172084. (Rin Ser.: Pt. 3). 1973. 4.00 (*0-89642-028-0*) Linden Pubs.

Ned & Crow: A Lesson in Diversity. Ron Madison. LC 96-171529. (Ned & Friends Ser.). (Illus.). 12p. (J). (ps-2). 1996. pap. 2.95 (*1-887206-11-6*) Neds Head Prodns.

Ned & Crow Set: Packaged with 8" Doll. Ron Madison. (Ned & Friends Ser.). (Illus.). 12p. (J). (ps-2). 1997. pap. 19.95 incl. audio (*1-887206-13-2*) Neds Head Prodns.

Ned & Fred: A Lesson in Loyalty. Ron Madison. (Ned & Friends Ser.). (Illus.). 12p. (J). (ps-2). 1995. pap. 2.95 (*1-887206-02-7*) Neds Head Prodns.

Ned & Fred Set: Packaged with 8" Doll. Ron Madison. (Illus.). 12p. (J). (ps-2). 1996. pap. 19.95 incl. audio (*1-887206-09-4*) Neds Head Prodns.

Ned & Friends Reading & Rhyming Supplement: Books, Dolls & Cassettes for the Classroom. Ron Madison. (Ned & Friends Ser.). (Illus.). 492p. 1998. pap., spiral bd. 158.00 (*1-887206-14-0*) Neds Head Prodns.

Ned & the Joybaloo. Hiawyn Oram. LC 88-46178. (Illus.). 28p. (J). (ps up). 1989. 11.95 (*0-374-35501-0*) FS&G.

Ned & the Joybaloo. Hiawyn Oram. 26p. (ps-3). 1990. pap. 3.95 (*0-374-45492-2*) FS&G.

Ned Cartledge. Ned Cartledge. 1986. pap. 20.00 (*0-932526-66-7*) Nexus Pr.

Ned Cartledge. Ned Cartledge. 1986. 30.00 (*0-932526-42-X*) Nexus Pr.

Ned Christie's War. Robert J. Conley. LC 91-10260. (Novel of the West Ser.). 180p. 1991. 16.95 (*0-87131-636-6*) M Evans.

Ned Christie's War. Robert J. Conley. Ed. by Doug Grad. 208p. 1993. mass mkt. 3.99 (*0-671-75969-8*) PB.

Ned Crocker. Robin Short. 1968. pap. 5.25 (*0-8222-0807-5*) Dramatists Play.

Ned Feldman, Space Pirate. Daniel Pinkwater. LC 93-40893. (Illus.). 48p. (J). (gr. k-3). 1994. mass mkt. write for info. (*0-02-774633-X*, Mac Bks Young Read) S&S Childrens.

Ned, Fred & Friend: A Lesson in Compassion. Ron Madison. LC 95-237932. (Ned & Friends Ser.). (Illus.). 12p. (J). (ps-2). 1995. pap. 2.95 (*1-887206-03-5*) Neds Head Prodns.

Ned Kelly & the City of the Bees. 2nd ed. Thomas Keneally. LC 94-30951. (Illus.). 128p. (J). (gr. 4-7). 1981. pap. 11.95 (*1-56792-022-5*) Godine.

Ned Kelly Reconstructed. Wendy Morgan. LC 93-48705. 160p. (J). 1995. pap. 21.95 (*0-521-43783-0*) Cambridge U Pr.

Ned Myers. James Fenimore Cooper. (Works of James Fenimore Cooper). 1990. reprint ed. lib. bdg. 79.00 (*0-7812-2391-1*) Rprt Serv.

Ned Myers: A Life Before the Mast. James Fenimore Cooper. Ed. by Jack Sweetman. LC 89-30546. (Classics of Naval Literature Ser.). 320p. 1989. reprint ed. 32.95 (*0-87021-417-9*) Naval Inst Pr.

Ned Newton. Horatio Alger, Jr. (Works of Horatio Alger Jr.). 1989. reprint ed. lib. bdg. 79.00 (*0-685-27576-0*) Rprt Serv.

Ned Rorem: A Bio-Bibliography, 23. Arlys L. McDonald & Donald L. Hixon. LC 89-2139. (Bio-Bibliographies in Music Ser.: No. 23). 294p. 1989. lib. bdg. 49.95 (*0-313-25565-2*, MNR/, Greenwood Pr) Greenwood.

***Ned Ventures: Teenage Life in the 1950s.** Edward Allan Faine. 64p. 2001. pap. write for info. (*0-9654651-7-9*) IM Press.

Ned Ward of Grub Street: A Study of Sub-Literary London in the Eighteenth Century. Howard W. Troyer. (Illus.). 290p. 1968. reprint ed. 28.50 (*0-7146-1523-4*, BHA-01523, Pub. by F Cass Pubs) Intl Spec Bk.

Ned Wayburn & the Dance Routine: From Vaudeville to the Ziegfeld Follies. Barbara Stratyner. LC 96-70657. (Studies in Dance History: Vol. 13). (Illus.). 141p. (Orig.). 1996. pap. 21.95 (*0-9653519-2-0*) Soc Dance Hist.

Nedarim. (ENG & HEB.). 18.00 (*0-910218-68-4*) Bennet Pub.

Neddlework Masterpieces from Winterthur. Hollis Greer Minor. LC 99-171086. (Illus.). 144p. 1998. 29.95 (*0-7153-0705-3*, Pub. by D & C Pub) Sterling.

Neddy Buddy Basil. unabridged ed. Earvin McBride, Jr. (Illus.). 6p. (J). (gr. 7-12). 2000. pap. write for info. (*1-892511-13-4*) E J MacBride.

Neder-Landtsche Gedenck-Clanck. fac. ed. Adrianus Valerius. (Monuments of Music & Music Literature in Facsimile Ser., Series II: Vol. 63). (DUT., Illus.). 314p. 1974. lib. bdg. 60.00 (*0-8450-2263-6*) Broude.

Nederland Trademarks, 1900-1950. John Mendenhall. LC 94-79354. (Illus.). (Orig.). 1995. pap. text 17.95 (*0-88108-150-7*) Art Dir.

Nederlands-Engels Woordenbock Voor Landbouw-Wetenschappen. T. Huitenga. (DUT & ENG.). 66p. 1982. 95.00 (*0-8288-0028-6*, M14226) Fr & Eur.

Nederlandsch Muzikaal Tijdschrift 1839-1848. Ed. by H. Robert Cohen. (Repertoire International de la Presse Musicale Ser.). (DUT.). 284p. 1994. lib. bdg. 145.00 (*0-8357-2329-1*) UMI.

***Nederlandsche Bibliographie van Land- En Volkenkunde.** Pieter Anton Tiele. vii, 288p. 1999. reprint ed. 75.00 (*1-57898-152-2*) Martino Pubng.

Nederlandse Naamlijst Van de Weekdieren (Mollusca) Van Nederland en Belgie. R. H. Bruyne et al. (Illus.). 149p. 1994. pap. 27.00 (*90-73348-33-1*, Pub. by Backhuys Pubs) Balogh.

Nedim & the Poetics of the Ottoman Court: Medieval Inheritance & the Need for Change. Kemal Silay. LC 94-79173. (Turkish Studies: Vol. 13). (Illus.). 198p. (C). 1994. pap. text 16.95 (*1-878318-09-8*) IN Univ Turkish.

Nedjma: Kateb Yacine. Yacine Kateb. Tr. by Richard Howard from FRE. (CARAF: Caribbean & African Literature Ser.). 400p. 1991. pap. 16.50 (*0-8139-1313-6*); text 40.00 (*0-8139-1312-8*) U Pr of Va.

Nedobeck's Alphabet Book. Don Nedobeck. (Illus.). 16p. (J). (gr. 1-8). 1993. reprint ed. 15.00 (*0-944314-00-7*) New Wrinkle.

Nedobeck's Numbers Book. Don Nedobeck. 26p. (J). (gr. 1-8). 1988. 15.00 (*0-944314-01-5*) New Wrinkle.

Nedobeck's Twelve Days of Christmas. Illus. by Don Nedobeck. (J). (gr. 1-8). 1988. reprint ed. lib. bdg. 15.00 (*0-944314-02-3*) New Wrinkle.

Nedoure: Priestess of the Magi. J. T. Betiero & R. Swinburne Clymer. 248p. 1958. 9.95 (*0-932785-34-4*) Philos Pub.

Nedoure: Priestess of the Magi. deluxe ed. J. T. Betiero & R. Swinburne Clymer. 248p. 1958. lthr. 20.00 (*0-932785-96-4*) Philos Pub.

Nedra. George B. McCutcheon. 1976. lib. bdg. 15.75 (*0-89968-063-1*, Lghtyr Pr) Buccaneer Bks.

Ned's Folks: A Lesson in Love. Ron Madison. (Ned & Friends Ser.). (Illus.). 12p. (J). (ps-4). 1996. pap. 2.95 (*1-887206-12-4*) Neds Head Prodns.

Ned's Friend: A Lesson in Friendship. Ron Madison. (Ned & Friends Ser.). (Illus.). 12p. (J). (ps-2). 1995. pap. 2.95 (*1-887206-01-9*) Neds Head Prodns.

Ned's Friend Set: Packaged with 8" Doll. Ron Madison. (Ned & Friends Ser.). (Illus.). 12p. (J). (ps-2). 1996. pap. 19.95 incl. audio (*1-887206-10-8*) Neds Head Prodns.

Ned's Head: A Lesson in Self-Esteem. Ron Madison. (Ned & Friends Ser.). (Illus.). 12p. (J). (ps-2). 1993. pap. 2.95 (*1-887206-00-0*) Neds Head Prodns.

Ned's Head Set: Packaged with 14" Pillow-Doll. Ron Madison. (Ned & Friends Ser.). (Illus.). 24p. (J). (ps-2). 1995. pap. 19.95 incl. audio (*1-887206-04-3*) Neds Head Prodns.

***Ned's Journal.** Fan Brown & Elizabeth Brown. (Illus.). 65p. 2000. 15.95 (*0-9661847-4-2*, Pub. by Tatra Pr) Midpt Trade.

***Ned's Rainbow.** Melanie Walsh. (Toddlers Storybook Ser.). (Illus.). 24p. (ps-k). 2000. pap. 5.95 (*0-7894-5623-0*) DK Pub Inc.

Neecie & the Swarming Germs. Anna P. Barrett. Ed. by Phillip Carmical. (Illus.). 50p. (J). (gr. 2-4). 1998. pap. 9.95 (*0-9661330-0-5*) ORP.

Neecie Celebrates Juneteenth. Anna P. Barrett. Ed. by Lana C. Edwards. (Neecie Books). (Illus.). 49p. (J). (gr. 2-5). 1999. 9.95 (*0-9661330-2-1*) ORP.

Neecie Loves Trouble, Vol. II. Anna P. Barrett. Ed. by Lana C. Edwards. (Neecie Ser.: Vol. 2). (Illus.). 48p. (J). (gr. 2-5). 1999. 9.95 (*0-9661330-1-3*) ORP.

Need. Lawrence David. 1996. mass mkt. 6.99 (*0-312-95922-2*) St Martin.

Need. Alberta T. Turner. 52p. 1971. pap. 6.00 (*0-912592-07-9*) Ashland Poetry.

Need: A Chorale for Black Woman Voices. Audre Geraldine Lorde. (Freedom Organizing Pamphlet Ser.). 20p. 1991. pap. 3.95 (*0-913175-22-6*) Kitchen Table.

Need: A New Federal Policy for Higher Education. Joseph Froomkin. (Policy Paper: No. 6). viii, 88p. 1978. 4.00 (*0-318-14399-2*) Inst Educ Lead.

***Need a Trim, Jim.** Kaye Umansky & Margaret Chamberlain. (Illus.). 32p. 1999. 11.95 (*0-370-32328-9*, Pub. by Bodley Head) Trafalgar.

Need Analysis: Tools for the Human Services & Education. Jack McKillip. (Applied Social Research Methods Ser.: Vol. 10). 160p. 1987. text 42.00 (*0-8039-2647-2*); pap. text 18.95 (*0-8039-2648-0*) Sage.

***Need & Greed: The True Story of the Largest Ponzi Scheme in American History.** Stewart L. Weisman. LC 99-49298. 377p. 1999. 29.95 (*0-8156-0610-9*) Syracuse U Pr.

Need & the Blessing of Prayer. Karl Rahner. Tr. by Bruce W. Gilette. LC 97-7368. 1997. pap. 9.95 (*0-8146-2453-7*) Liturgical Pr.

Need Assessment: A Key to User-Oriented Product Innovation. Knut Holt et al. LC 83-16764. 199p. reprint ed. pap. 61.70 (*0-7837-6384-0*, 204609700010) Bks Demand.

Need for a New Religion in India & Other Essays. Ed. by Khushwant Singh. (C). 1991. 14.00 (*81-85273-65-0*, Pub. by UBS Pubs Dist) S Asia.

Need for a New Religion in India & Other Essays. Khushwant Singh. (C). 1993. 8.00 (*81-85944-53-9*, Pub. by UBS Pubs Dist) S Asia.

Need for a Nurse. large type ed. Lynne Collins. (Linford Romance Library). 304p. 1997. pap. 16.99 (*0-7089-5077-9*, Linford) Ulverscroft.

Need for a Sacred Science. Seyyed Hossein Nasr. 220p. (C). 1993. pap. write for info. (*0-7007-0281-4*, Pub. by Curzon Pr Ltd) Paul & Co Pubs.

Need for a Sacred Science. Seyyed Hossein Nasr. 170p. 1996. pap. 16.95 (*0-614-21605-2*, 892) Kazi Pubns.

Need for a Sacred Science. Seyyed Hossein Nasr. LC 92-26202. (SUNY Series in Religious Studies). 187p. (C). 1993. text 57.50 (*0-7914-1517-1*) State U NY Pr.

Need for a Sacred Science. Seyyed Hossein Nasr. LC 92-26202. (SUNY Series in Religious Studies). 187p. (C). 1993. pap. text 18.95 (*0-7914-1518-X*) State U NY Pr.

Need for a Second Look at Jonestown: Remembering Its People. Ed. by Rebecca Moore & Fielding McGehee, III. (Studies in American Religion: Vol. 41). 248p. 1989. write for info. (*0-88946-649-1*) E Mellen.

Need for an Oxford Science Park. John Glasson et al. (C). 1988. 29.00 (*0-7855-3821-6*, Pub. by Oxford Polytechnic) St Mut.

Need for Better Focus in the Rural Health Care Clinic Program- Part II: Hearing Before the Subcommittee on Human Resources of the Committee on Government Reform & Oversight, House of Representatives, One Hundred Fifth Congress, First Session, September 11, 1997. USGPO Staff. LC 98-167877. iii, 126 p. 1998. write for info. (*0-16-056433-6*) USGPO.

Need for Change: Towards the New International Economic Order. Gamani Corea. LC 80-40800. 350p. 1981. pap. 6.00 (*0-08-028120-6*, Pub. by Pergamon Repr) Franklin.

Need for Civilizational Dialogue. Anwar Ibrahim. (Occasional Papers Ser.). iii, 12p. 1994. pap. 2.95 (*1-929218-11-7*) Georgetwn U Ctr Muslim.

Need for Enemies: A Bestiary of Political Forms. F. G. Bailey. LC 97-38676. 240p. 1998. 39.95 (*0-8014-3470-X*, Comstock Pub); pap. 15.95 (*0-8014-8474-X*, Comstock Pub) Cornell U Pr.

Need for Field Studies to Evaluate Welfare Situations. R. Ewbank. 1981. 30.00 (*0-7855-7558-8*) St Mut.

Need for Food Supplements. 1996. lib. bdg. 250.75 (*0-8490-5885-6*) Gordon Pr.

Need for Healthcare. Rod Sheaff. LC 95-25911. (Social Ethics & Policy Ser.). 240p. (C). 1996. 85.00 (*0-415-10111-5*); pap. 25.99 (*0-415-10112-3*) Routledge.

Need for Logic in Religion among African Americans. Sabir K. Muhammad. (Orig.). 1990. pap. text 5.00 (*0-9627663-0-5*) Designer Comns.

An Asterisk (*) at the beginning of an entry indicates that the title is appearing for the first time.

Need for National Policy for the Use of Underground Space. Compiled by American Society of Civil Engineers Staff. 238p. 1973. pap. 5.00 (*0-87262-102-2*) Am Soc Civil Eng.

Need for Organizational Development in Successful Entrepreneurial Firms. rev. ed. Randel S. Carlock. LC 94-30161. (Garland Studies in Entrepreneurship). (Illus.). 280p. 1994. text 58.00 (*0-8153-1731-X*) Garland.

Need for Roots. 2nd ed. Simone Weil. 304p. (C). 1995. pap. 17.99 (*0-415-11959-6*) Routledge.

***Need for Speed.** Tara Baukus Mello. (Race Car Legends Ser.). (Illus.). (J). 2000. 16.95 (*0-7910-6015-2*) Chelsea Hse.

Need for Speed. unabridged ed. John J. Williams. (Illus.). 16p. 1997. pap. 29.00 (*0-934274-75-4*) Consumertronics.

***Need for Speed: Motor City.** Prima Development Staff. 1999. pap. 19.99 (*0-7615-2322-7*) Prima Pub.

Need for Story: Cultural Diversity in Classroom & Community. Ed. by Anne H. Dyson & Celia Genishi. (Illus.). 259p. (Orig.). 1994. pap. text 22.95 (*0-8141-3300-2*) NCTE.

Need for Story: Cultural Diversity in Classroom & Community. Anne H. Dyson & Celia Genishi. 350p. (Orig.). 1996. pap. text 22.95 (*0-8077-3596-5*) Tchrs Coll.

Need for Understanding: A Handbook of Basic Counseling Information. Bettie P. Mitchell. 190p. (Orig.). 1992. pap. 16.00 (*1-885193-03-3*) Good Samaritan.

Need for Words. Patsy Rodenburg. LC 93-7959. 45.00 (*0-685-65135-5*) Routledge.

Need for Words: Voice & the Text. Patsy Rodenburg. 256p. (gr. 13). 1993. pap. 17.99 (*0-87830-051-1*, Thtre Arts Bks) Routledge.

Need, Greed & Freedom: Business Changes & Personal Choices. John Whitmore. LC 96-49945. 192p. 1997. pap. 19.95 (*1-85230-945-8*, Pub. by Element MA) Penguin Putnam.

Need to Be Versus Hell for Eternity. Melvin Ponder. (Illus.). 141p. 1997. pap. 12.00 (*0-9660742-0-3*) Obedient Faith.

Need to Believe: The Psychology of Religion. Mortimer Ostow & Ben-Ami Scharfstein. 1969. reprint ed. pap. 24.95 (*0-8236-8159-9*, 23520) Intl Univs Pr.

Need to Die. unabridged ed. Robert L. Nessen & Julie Nessen. 170p. 1998. mass mkt. 9.50 (*0-9667170-0-7*) Millenim III Pr.

Need to Fail. Bill Steele. 72p. 1974. pap. text 8.00 (*0-87879-819-6*, Ann Arbor Div) Acad Therapy.

***Need to Feed: With a Mix & Match Salad Section: User Friendly.** Patricia Panozzo. (Illus.). 121p. 1999. spiral bd. 17.95 (*0-9623704-0-1*) Panozzo.

Need to Have Enemies & Allies: From Clinical Practice to International Relationships. Vamik D. Volkan. LC 87-32763. 298p. (C). 1988. 35.00 (*0-87668-999-3*) Aronson.

Need to Hold Still: Poems. Lisel Mueller. LC 79-20965. xii, 68p. 1980. pap. 12.95 (*0-8071-0670-4*) La State U Pr.

Need to Know: The Report of the 20th Century Fund Task Force on Covert Action & American Democracy. Allan E. Goodman & Bruce D. Berkowitz. LC 92-10970. 150p. 1992. 9.95 (*0-87078-331-9*) Century Foundation.

***Need to Know Library: Dealing with Issues, 8 vols.** Incl. Everything You Need to Know about Bipolar Disorder & Manic Depressive Illness. Michael A. Sommers. LC 99-42087. 64p. (YA). (gr. 7-12). 2000. lib. bdg. 17.95 (*0-8239-3106-4*); Everything You Need to Know about Cancer. Francesca Massari. LC 99-39647. (Illus.). 64p. (YA). (gr. 4-6). 1999. lib. bdg. 17.95 (*0-8239-3164-1*); Everything You Need to Know about Deafness. Carol Basinger. (Illus.). 64p. (YA). (gr. 7-12). 2000. lib. bdg. 17.95 (*0-8239-3165-X*); Everything You Need to Know about Epilepsy. Patricia Emanuele. LC 99-88769. (Illus.). 64p. (J). (gr. 4-6). 2000. lib. bdg. 17.95 (*0-8239-3161-7*); Everything You Need to Know about Family Court. Anne Bianchi. LC 99-39557. (Illus.). 64p. (YA). (gr. 4-6). 2000. lib. bdg. 17.95 (*0-8239-3163-3*); Everything You Need to Know about Healing from Rape Trauma. Cheryl Branch Coppin. LC 99-49583. (Illus.). 64p. (J). (gr. 4-6). 2000. lib. bdg. 17.95 (*0-8239-3122-6*); Everything You Need to Know about Media Violence. rev. ed. Kathleen J. Edgar. (Illus.). 64p. (YA). (gr. 4-6). 2000. lib. bdg. 17.95 (*0-8239-3108-0*); Everything You Need to Know about Schizophrenia. Michelle S. Friedman. LC 99-42592. (Illus.). 64p. (YA). (gr. 7-12). 2000. lib. bdg. 17.95 (*0-8239-3091-2*); (Need to Know Library). (Illus.). (J). (gr. 4-6). 2000. Set lib. bdg. 143.60 (*0-8239-9055-9*) Rosen Group.

Need to Know Library: Everyday Issues, 8 vols. Incl. Everything You Need to Know about Being Adopted. Laura Kaminker. LC 98-45629. (Illus.). 64p. (YA). (gr. 4-8). 1999. lib. bdg. 17.95 (*0-8239-2834-9*); Everything You Need to Know about Being HIV-Positive. rev. ed. Amy Shire. (Illus.). 64p. (YA). (gr. 7-12). 1999. lib. bdg. 17.95 (*0-8239-3077-7*); Everything You Need to Know about Dealing with Stalking. Cynthia Wright. LC 99-39556. (Illus.). 64p. (YA). (gr. 7-12). 1999. lib. bdg. 17.95 (*0-8239-2841-1*); Everything You Need to Know about Drug Addiction. Jeanne M. Nagle. (Illus.). 64p. (YA). (gr. 7-12). 1999. lib. bdg. 17.95 (*0-8239-2772-5*, NTDRAD); Everything You Need to Know about Going to the Gynecologist. Shifra N. Diamond. (Illus.). 64p. (YA). (gr. 7-12). 1999. lib. bdg. 17.95 (*0-8239-2839-X*); Everything You Need to Know about Sports Injuries. rev. ed. Lawrence Clayton. (Illus.). 64p. (YA). (gr. 7-12). 1999. lib. bdg. 17.95 (*0-8239-2875-6*); Everything You Need to Know about Staying Safe in Cyberspace. Jennifer Croft. LC 99-16887. (Illus.). 64p. (YA). (gr. 7-12). 1999. lib. bdg. 17.95 (*0-8239-2957-4*); Everything You Need to Know about Teens Who Kill. Jeffrey A. Margolis. LC 98-45103. (Illus.). 64p. (YA). (gr. 4-12). 1999. lib. bdg. 17.95 (*0-8239-2883-7*); (Illus.). (J). (gr. 4-6). Set lib. bdg. 143.60 (*0-8239-9058-3*) Rosen Group.

***Need to Know Library: Facts of Life, 8 vols.** (Need to Know Library). (Illus.). (J). (gr. 4-6). 1999. lib. bdg. 143.60 (*0-8239-9001-X*) Rosen Group.

Need to Know Library: Learning about the World, 8 vols. Incl. Everything You Need to Know about ADD/ADHD (Attention Deficit Disorder/Attention Deficit Hyperactivity Disorder) Eileen J. Beal. LC 97-45149. (Illus.). 64p. (YA). (gr. 7-12). 1998. lib. bdg. 17.95 (*0-8239-2748-2*); Everything You Need to Know about Alcohol. rev. ed. Barbara Taylor. (Illus.). 64p. (YA). (gr. 7-12). 1999. lib. bdg. 17.95 (*0-8239-2952-3*); Everything You Need to Know about an Addictive Personality. Jay Bridges. LC 98-8496. (Illus.). 64p. (YA). (gr. 7-12). 1998. lib. bdg. 17.95 (*0-8239-2777-6*, NTADPE); Everything You Need to Know about Anger. rev. ed. Renora Licata. (Illus.). 64p. (YA). (gr. 7-12). 1999. lib. bdg. 17.95 (*0-8239-2953-1*); Everything You Need to Know about Conflict Resolution. rev. ed. Amy Nathan. (Illus.). 64p. (YA). (gr. 7-12). 1999. lib. bdg. 17.95 (*0-8239-2955-8*); Everything You Need to Know about Dealing with Losses. Millicent K. Brody. LC 98-29092. (Illus.). 64p. (YA). (gr. 7-12). 1998. lib. bdg. 16.95 (*0-8239-2780-6*, NTGRLO); Everything You Need to Know about Dealing with Sexual Assault. Laura Kaminker. LC 98-7048. (Illus.). 64p. (YA). (gr. 7-12). 1998. lib. bdg. 17.95 (*0-8239-2837-3*); Everything You Need to Know about Your Legal Rights. rev. ed. Ken Fox. LC 99-461769. (Illus.). 64p. (YA). (gr. 7-12). 1998. lib. bdg. 17.95 (*0-8239-2872-1*); (Illus.). (J). (gr. 4-6). Set lib. bdg. 143.60 (*0-8239-9059-1*) Rosen Group.

***Need to Know Library: Lessons of Life, 8 vols.** Incl. Everything You Need to Know about Dating & Relationships. Erin M. Hovanec. LC 99-45574. (Illus.). 64p. (YA). (gr. 7-12). 2000. lib. bdg. 17.95 (*0-8239-3081-5*); Everything You Need to Know about Drug Abuse. rev. ed. Arthur Herscovitch. (Illus.). 64p. (YA). (gr. 7-12). 2000. lib. bdg. 17.95 (*0-8239-3036-X*); Everything You Need to Know about Eating Disorders. rev. ed. Rachel Kubersky. (Illus.). 64p. (YA). (gr. 7-12). 2000. lib. bdg. 17.95 (*0-8239-3078-5*); Everything You Need to Know about Looking & Feeling Your Best: A Guide for Girls. Annie Leah Sommers. LC 99-16834. (Illus.). 64p. (YA). (gr. 7-12). 2000. lib. bdg. 17.95 (*0-8239-3079-3*); Everything You Need to Know about Mehndi, Temporary Tattoos & Other Body Art. Stefanie Iris Weiss. LC 99-50355. (Illus.). 64p. (YA). (gr. 4-12). 2000. lib. bdg. 17.95 (*0-8239-3086-6*); Everything You Need to Know about Public Speaking. rev. ed. Rachel Blumstein. (Illus.). 64p. (YA). (gr. 7-12). 2000. lib. bdg. 17.95 (*0-8239-3087-4*); Everything You Need to Know about Self-Confidence. rev. ed. Metthew Ignoffo. (Illus.). 64p. (YA). (gr. 7-12). 2000. lib. bdg. 17.95 (*0-8239-3037-8*); Looking & Feeling Your Best: A Guide for Guys. Michael A. Sommers. (Illus.). 64p. (YA). (gr. 7-12). 2000. lib. bdg. 17.95 (*0-8239-3080-7*); (Illus.). (J). (gr. 4-6). 2000. Set lib. bdg. 143.00 (*0-8239-9056-7*) Rosen Group.

Need to Know Library: Preparing Yourself, 8 vols. Incl. Everything You Need to Know about Being a Baby-Sitter: A Teen's Guide to Responsible Child Care. Aileen Weintraub. LC 99-36045. (Illus.). 64p. (YA). (gr. 7-12). 2000. lib. bdg. 17.95 (*0-8239-3085-8*); Everything You Need to Know about Eating Smart. Aileen Weintraub. LC 99-16802. 64p. (YA). (gr. 7-12). 2000. lib. bdg. 17.95 (*0-8239-3082-3*); Everything You Need to Know about Getting a Job. Carlienne A. Frisch. LC 99-47575. (Illus.). 64p. (J). (gr. 4-6). 2000. lib. bdg. 17.95 (*0-8239-2961-2*); Everything You Need to Know about Hepatitis. Virginia Aronson. (Illus.). 64p. (YA). (gr. 7-12). 2000. lib. bdg. 17.95 (*0-8239-3100-5*); Everything You Need to Know about Living on Your Own. Katherine E. Krohn. LC 99-56219. (Illus.). 64p. (YA). (gr. 7-12). 2000. lib. bdg. 17.95 (*0-8239-3088-2*); Everything You Need to Know about the Art of Leadership: How to Be a Positive Influence in Your Home, School & Community. Holly Cefrey. LC 99-48184. (Illus.). 64p. (YA). (gr. 7-12). 2000. lib. bdg. 17.95 (*0-8239-3217-6*); Everything You Need to Know about the Dangers of Overachieving: A Guide for Relieving Pressure & Anxiety. John Giacobello. LC 99-45580. (Illus.). 64p. (YA). (gr. 4-6). 2000. lib. bdg. 17.95 (*0-8239-3107-2*); Everything You Need to Know about Virginity. Michael A. Sommers & Annie Leah Sommers. LC 99-56218. (Illus.). 64p. (YA). (gr. 7-12). 2000. lib. bdg. 17.95 (*0-8239-3115-3*); (Illus.). (J). (gr. 4-6). Set lib. bdg. 143.60 (*0-8239-9054-0*) Rosen Group.

Need to Know Library: Resources for Healthy Living, 9 vols. Incl. Effective Communication at School & at Work. Annie Leah Sommers. LC 99-56597. (Illus.). 64p. (YA). (gr. 7-12). 2000. lib. bdg. 17.95 (*0-8239-3227-3*); Everything You Need to Know about Cerebral Palsy. Dion Pincus. LC 99-37433. (Illus.). 64p. (YA). (gr. 7-12). 1999. lib. bdg. 17.95 (*0-8239-2960-4*); Everything You Need to Know about Diabetes. Melanie Ann Apel. LC 99-26663. (Illus.). 64p. (YA). (gr. 7-12). 2000. lib. bdg. 17.95 (*0-8239-3090-4*); Everything You Need to Know about Down Syndrome. Ed. by Mary Bowman-Kruhm. LC 99-32465. (Illus.). 64p. (YA). (gr. 7-12). 1999. lib. bdg. 17.95 (*0-8239-2949-3*); Everything You Need to Know about Guns in the Home. Jennifer Croft. LC 99-39555. (Illus.). 64p. (YA). (gr. 7-12). 2000. lib. bdg. 17.95 (*0-8239-3162-5*); Everything You Need to Know about Sexual Identity. Jeff Donaldson Forbes. (Illus.). 64p. (YA). (gr. 7-12). 2000. lib. bdg. 17.95 (*0-8239-3089-0*); Everything You Need to Know about the Dangers of Computer Hacking. John Knittel & Michael Soto. (Illus.). 64p. (YA). (gr. 7-12). 2000. lib. bdg. 17.95 (*0-8239-3034-3*); Everything You Need to Know When a Brother or Sister Is Autistic. Marsha S. Rosenberg. LC 99-26679. (Illus.). 64p. (YA). (gr. 4-6). 1999. lib. bdg. 17.95 (*0-8239-3123-4*); Everything You Need to Know When Someone You Know Has Leukemia. Heather Moehn. LC 99-47210. (Illus.). 64p. (YA). (gr. 7-12). 2000. lib. bdg. 17.95 (*0-8239-3121-8*); (Illus.). (J). (gr. 4-6). Set lib. bdg. 161.55 (*0-8239-9053-2*) Rosen Group.

Need to Know Library: Safety Through Knowledge, 8 vols. Incl. Everything to Know about Grieving. rev. ed. Karen Spies. (Illus.). 64p. (gr. 7-12). 1997. lib. bdg. 17.95 (*0-8239-2623-0*); Everything You Need to Know about Bias Incidents. 2nd rev. ed. Kevin Osborn. LC 99-462461. (Illus.). 64p. (YA). (gr. 7-12). 1997. lib. bdg. 16.95 (*0-8239-2600-1*); Everything You Need to Know about Depression. 2nd rev. ed. Eleanor H. Ayer. LC 94-18822. (Illus.). 64p. (YA). (gr. 7-12). 1997. lib. bdg. 17.95 (*0-8239-2606-0*); Everything You Need to Know about Family Violence. 2nd rev. ed. Evan Stark. (Illus.). 64p. (YA). (gr. 7-12). 1997. lib. bdg. 17.95 (*0-8239-2293-6*); Everything You Need to Know about Teen Marriage. rev. ed. Eleanor H. Ayer. LC 99-462460. (Illus.). 64p. (YA). (gr. 7-12). 2000. lib. bdg. 17.95 (*0-8239-2502-1*); Everything You Need to Know about Teen Motherhood. rev. ed. Jane Hammerslough. (Illus.). 64p. (YA). (gr. 7-12). 1997. lib. bdg. 17.95 (*0-8239-2619-2*); Everything You Need to Know When a Parent Is Out of Work. 3rd rev. ed. Stephanie St. Pierre. (Illus.). 64p. (YA). (gr. 7-12). 1997. lib. bdg. 17.95 (*0-8239-2608-7*, D1655-3); (Illus.). (YA). (gr. 7-12). Set lib. bdg. 143.60 (*0-8239-9063-X*) Rosen Group.

Need to Know Library: Today's Information. Incl. Everything You Need to Know about Being a Vegan. Stefanie I. Weiss. (Illus.). 64p. (YA). (gr. 5-8). 1999. lib. bdg. 17.95 (*0-8239-2958-2*); Everything You Need to Know about Being a Vegetarian. Kim Serafin. LC 99-13244. (Illus.). 64p. (YA). (gr. 5-8). 1999. lib. bdg. 17.95 (*0-8239-2951-5*); Everything You Need to Know about Body Dysmorphic Disorder: Dealing with a Negative Body Image. Pamela Walker. LC 99-16747. (Illus.). 64p. (YA). (gr. 7-12). 1999. lib. bdg. 17.95 (*0-8239-2954-X*); Everything You Need to Know about Learning Disabilities. Mary Bowman-Kruhm & Claudine G. Wirths. LC 99-17084. (Illus.). 64p. (YA). (gr. 7-12). 1999. lib. bdg. 17.95 (*0-8239-2956-6*); Everything You Need to Know about Living with a Single Parent. rev. ed. Richard E. Mancini. (Illus.). 64p. (YA). (gr. 7-12). 1999. lib. bdg. 17.95 (*0-8239-3039-4*); Everything You Need to Know about Teen Pregnancy. rev. ed. Tracy Hughes. (Illus.). 64p. (YA). (gr. 7-12). 1999. lib. bdg. 17.95 (*0-8239-3041-6*); Everything You Need to Know about Teen Suicide. rev. ed. Jay Schleifer. (Illus.). 64p. (YA). (gr. 4-6). 1999. lib. bdg. 17.95 (*0-8239-3038-6*); Everything You Need to Know about Yoga: An Introduction for Teens. Stefanie Iris Weiss. LC 99-30090. (Illus.). 64p. (YA). (gr. 7-12). 1999. lib. bdg. 17.95 (*0-8239-2959-0*); (Illus.). (J). (gr. 4-6). Set lib. bdg. 143.60 (*0-8239-9057-5*) Rosen Group.

***Need to Testify.** Iris Origo. 320p. 2000. pap. 16.95 (*1-885586-51-5*, Pub. by Turtle Point Pr) Dist Art Pubs.

Need Two. Darrell Huckaby. 294p. 1995. 18.95 (*0-9647867-3-7*) St Simons Pr.

Needed: A New Policy for Higher Education. Joseph Froomkin. 96p. 1978. 5.50 (*0-318-03023-3*) Inst Educ Lead.

Needed: A Twenty-First Century Concept of God. George S. Kuntz. LC 98-90121. 106p. 1998. pap. 10.95 (*0-533-12717-3*) Vantage.

Needed: One Dad. Jeanne Allan. 1997. per. 3.25 (*0-373-03456-3*, 1-03456-0) Harlequin Bks.

Needed: One Dad. large type ed. Jeanne Allan. 1997. per. 3.25 (*0-373-15702-9*, 1-15702-3) Harlequin Bks.

Needed: Professional Management in Data Processing. John J. Callahan. (Illus.). 240p. 1983. 40.00 (*0-13-610956-X*) P-H.

Needed Knowledge for Health Care Administrators. Robert W. Haacker. 353p. 149.00 incl. cd-rom (*0-929442-57-1*) Prof Prnting & Pub.

Needed Research in American English. Raven I. McDavid, Jr. (Publications of the American Dialect Society: No. 71). iv, 76p. (Orig.). 1984. pap. 7.60 (*0-8173-0238-7*) U of Ala Pr.

Needed Research in Health & Medical Care: A Bio-Social Approach. Cecil G. Sheps & Eugene E. Taylor. LC 55-160. 228p. reprint ed. pap. 70.70 (*0-8357-3854-X*, 203658700004) Bks Demand.

Needed Words. Ed. by Steele Commager. Incl. Arabic Words in English. Ed. by Logan P. Smith. 1979. B.B.L.'s Recommendations for Pronouncing Doubtful Words. Ed. by Logan P. Smith. 1979. Best English. Ed. by Logan P. Smith. 1979. Bull's Bellow. Ed. by Logan P. Smith. 1979. Colloquial Language in Literature. Ed. by Logan P. Smith. 1979. Index to Tracts XXI-XXIX. Logan P. Smith. 1979. lib. bdg. Oxford English. Logan P. Smith. 1979. lib. bdg. Possibility of a Universal Language. Logan P. Smith. 1979. lib. bdg. Robert Bridges Recollections. Logan P. Smith. 1979. lib. bdg. (Society for Pure English Ser.: Vol. 4). 1979. Set lib. bdg. 46.00 (*0-8240-3668-9*) Garland.

Needful, New & Necessarie Treatise of Chyrugerie. John Banister. LC 73-171732. (English Experience Ser.: No. 300). 276p. 1971. reprint ed. 22.00 (*90-221-0300-5*) Walter J Johnson.

Needful Things. Stephen King. 1992. 13.09 (*0-606-01485-3*, Pub. by Turtleback) Demco.

Needful Things: The Last Castle Rock Story. Stephen King. 752p. 1992. mass mkt. 7.99 (*0-451-17281-7*, Sig) NAL.

Needful Things: The Last Castle Rock Story. large type ed. Stephen King. LC 92-3929. (General Ser.). 1044p. 1992. lib. bdg. 25.95 (*0-8161-5476-7*, G K Hall Lrg Type) Mac Lib Ref.

Needham. Needham Historical Society Staff. (Images of America Ser.). 1997. pap. 16.99 (*0-7524-0578-0*) Arcadia Publng.

Needham Question: Between Mathematics & Sociology, No. I. Ed. by J. Fang. LC 94-92125. (Studies on the Integration of Humanities & Mathematical Knowledge). (Illus.). 250p. (Orig.). (C). 1994. pap. text 19.50 (*0-912490-16-0*) PAIDEIA & PM.

Needle & the Brush - Renaissance Florence: World History Unit for the Middle Grades. rev. ed. Lyn Reese. Ed. by Mary A. Dougherty & Jean B. Wilkinson. (Illus.). 33p. (YA). (gr. 6-9). 1990. spiral bd. 10.00 (*0-9625880-6-7*) Wom Wrld Hist.

Needle & Thread Vol. 1: A Tale of Survival from Bialystok to Poland. Charles S. Zabuski. 196p. (Orig.). 1996. pap. 10.95 (*0-614-21803-9*) Popincourt Pr.

Needle Biopsy of the Thyroid: Current Concepts. J. Martin Miller et al. LC 82-16667. 289p. 1983. 89.50 (*0-275-91403-8*, C1403, Praeger Pubs) Greenwood.

Needle Density, Pith Size & Tracheid Length in Pine. J. L. Ladell. 1963. 50.00 (*0-7855-7181-7*) St Mut.

Needle Exchange & AIDS Prevention: Advances & Controversies in Public Health & Social Policy. Merrill Singer. 134p. 1997. pap. text 18.00 (*90-5699-598-7*) Gordon & Breach.

Needle Exchange Evaluation Report. (Illus.). 57p. (Orig.). (C). 1992. pap. text 25.00 (*1-56806-087-4*) DIANE Pub.

Needle Exchange, Legalization & the Failure of the Swiss Heroin Experiments: Hearing Before the Subcommittee on National Security, International Affairs & Criminal Justice of the Committee on Government Reform & Oversight, House of Representatives, 105th Congress, First Session, September 18, 1997. LC 98-167827. iii, 145p. 1998. write for info. (*0-16-056482-4*) USGPO.

Needle Felts in Gas & Dust Filtration: The Design of Mechanically Bonded Filters. Godwin J. Igwe. 1987. text 61.00 (*0-470-20998-4*) P-H.

Needle in a Haystack: The Exciting Adventures of a Federal Narcotic Agent. William J. Spillard. Ed. by Gerald N. Grob. LC 80-1263. (Addiction in America Ser.). 1981. reprint ed. lib. bdg. 20.95 (*0-405-13618-8*) Ayer.

Needle Lace: Techniques & Inspiration. Jill N. Clark. (Illus.). 144p. 1999. 29.99 (*0-9658248-5-3*) GUILDcom.

***Needle Lace: Techniques & Inspiration.** Jill Nordfors Clark. (Illus.). 144p. 1999. 35.00 (*0-85532-897-5*, 8975, Pub. by Srch Pr) A Schwartz & Co.

Needle Lace & Needleweaving: A New Look at Traditional Stitches. Jill Nordfors. (Illus.). 160p. 1992. reprint ed. pap. 16.95 (*1-879504-00-6*, 400-6) A Schwartz & Co.

Needle Laces: Battenberg, Point & Reticella. 2nd ed. Ed. by Jules Kliot & Kaethe Kliot. 64p. 1988. pap. 8.00 (*0-916896-27-7*) Lacis Pubns.

Needle-Made Lace of Reticella. Ed. by Jules Kliot & Kaethe Kliot. (Illus.). 80p. 1994. pap. 12.00 (*0-916896-57-9*) Lacis Pubns.

Needle-Made Laces & Net Embroideries: Reticella Work, Carrickmacross Lace, Princess Lace & Other Traditional Techniques. Doris C. Preston. (Illus.). 160p. 1984. reprint ed. pap. 5.95 (*0-486-24708-2*) Dover.

Needle Man. Edward McCrorie. (Chestnut Hills Ser.). (Illus.). 80p. 1998. pap. 10.00 (*0-932616-64-X*) Brick Hse Bks.

Needle-Punching. A. T. Purdy. 1986. 75.00 (*0-7855-7206-6*) St Mut.

Needle Sharing among Intravenous Drug Abusers: National & International Perspectives. 1992. lib. bdg. 79.95 (*0-8490-8824-0*) Gordon Pr.

Needle Tatting, 2 vols., Set. rev. ed. Barbara A. Foster. (Illus.). 48p. 1990. pap. 12.00 (*1-883432-00-6*) Handy Hands.

Needle Tatting with Style, Bk. 1. Ed. by Barbara Foster. (Illus.). 32p. 1997. pap. 7.00 (*1-883432-03-0*, T08) Handy Hands.

Needle-Watcher: The Will Adams Story, British Samurai. Richard Blaker. LC 72-89743. 512p. 1973. pap. 16.95 (*0-8048-1094-X*) Tuttle Pubng.

Needlecraft. Susie O'Reilly. (Arts & Crafts Ser.). (Illus.). 32p. (J). 1994. lib. bdg. 21.40 (*1-56847-220-X*) Raintree Steck-V.

***Needlecraft Book.** Lucinda Ganderton. (Illus.). 2000. pap. 14.95 (*0-7548-0467-4*, Lorenz Bks) Anness Pub.

Needlecraft for Fun & Profit. large type ed. (For Fun & Profit Ser.). (Illus.). 350p. (Orig.). Date not set. pap. 24.95 (*1-56559-928-4*) HGI-Over Fifty.

Needlecrafter's Computer Companion: 100s of Easy Ways to Use Your Computer for Sewing, Quilting, Cross-Stitch, Knitting & More! Judy Heim. LC 94-44672. (Illus.). 450p. 1995. pap. 34.95 incl. disk (*1-886411-01-8*) No Starch Pr.

Needlecrafters' Travel Companion: 1999-2001. 2nd ed. Ed. by Audrey Anderson. (Illus.). 192p. 1999. pap. 10.95 (*0-9635290-8-0*) Chalet CO.

Needlecrafts. Family Circle Editors. 1947. 12.95 (*0-405-12056-7*) Ayer.

Needlecrafts: 50 Extraordinary Gifts & Projects, Step by Step. Gillian Souter. LC 97-167774. 160p. 1997. pap. 20.00 (*0-609-80034-5*) Random Hse Value.

***Needlecrafts for Dummies.** Cheryl Fall. (Illus.). 384p. 2000. pap. 19.99 (*0-7645-5201-5*) IDG Bks.

Needled Evergreens for the Midwest. 128p. pap. text. write for info. (*0-7881-8214-5*) DIANE Pub.

***Needlelace & Stumpwork: Contemporary Designs & Techniques for Dimensional Embroidery.** Loretta Holzberger. (Illus.). 100p. 2000. pap. 24.95 (*0-9679454-0-2*) Lorettas Cust Stitch.

Needlelace in Photographs. Cynthia Voysey. 1987. 6.00 (*0-7134-5560-8*) Robin & Russ.

Needlepainting Made Easy. Isabel K. Hobba. (Illus.). 48p. (Orig.). 1982. pap. 3.95 (*0-9609196-0-0*) Wertz Pubns.

***Needlepoint.** Koenemann Inc. Staff. (Illus.). 72p. 2000. pap. text 3.95 (*3-8290-2786-9*) Konemann.

N

Needlepoint: A Dialogue. Ursule Molinaro. LC 87-42543. 24p. 1987. pap. 3.00 (*0-87376-055-7*) Red Dust.

Needlepoint: A Foundation Course. Sandra Hardy. LC 98-226293. (Illus.). 152p. 1998. pap. text 24.95 (*1-86108-082-4*, Pub. by Guild Master) Sterling.

Needlepoint: 20 Classic Projects. Anna Pearson. (Illus.). 128p. 1998. 24.95 (*1-85732-790-X*, Pub. by Mitchell Beazley) Trafalgar.

Needlepoint & Cross-Stitch Directory. Stella Edwards. 1995. 6.98 (*0-7858-0498-6*) Bk Sales Inc.

Needlepoint Book: A Complete Update of the Classic Guide. expanded rev. ed. Jo Ippolito Christensen. LC 98-33812. (Illus.). 448p. 1999. per. 25.00 (*0-684-83230-5*) S&S Trade Pap.

Needlepoint Book: 303 Stitches with Patterns & Projects. Jo I. Christensen. 400p. 1976. pap. 20.00 (*0-671-76662-7*, Fireside) S&S Trade Pap.

Needlepoint Cats. Julie Hasler. LC 98-225089. (Illus.). 128p. 1998. 27.95 (*0-7153-0393-7*, Pub. by D & C Pub) Sterling.

Needlepoint Clock Mystery. Susan W. Younkins. 76p. (Orig.). 1995. pap. 14.95 (*0-9648072-0-3*) S W Younkins.

Needlepoint Designs from the Metropolitan Museum of Art. Erica Wilson. 1991. write for info. (*0-8212-1772-0*) Bulfinch Pr.

Needlepoint Gifts for All Seasons. Judy Clayton & Deborah Dow. (Illus.). 128p. 1996. 24.95 (*0-7153-0317-1*, Pub. by D & C Pub) Sterling.

Needlepoint Home Collection. (Illus.). 1999. pap. 24.95 (*1-85391-641-2*) Tuttle Pubng.

Needlepoint the Sport of Queens. Mary S. De Iturralde. (Illus.). 46p. 1942. pap. 4.95 (*0-87012-066-2*) McClain. Reviews needlepoint for various periods. The author points out the good periods of needlepoint design & discusses ways to incorporate them into patterns prepared today. Second Printing, 1968. *Publisher Paid Annotation.*

Needles: A Memoir. Andie Dominick. LC 98-21415. 224p. 1998. 22.00 (*0-684-84232-7*) Scribner.

*__Needles: A Memoir of Growing up with Diabetes.__ Ed. by Simon & Schuster Staff. 192p. 2000. pap. 13.00 (*0-684-85654-9*) S&S Trade.

Needles: Southern Sierra Rock Climbing. Sally Moser et al. (Southern Sierra Rock Climbing Ser.). (Illus.). 230p. (Orig.). 1992. pap. 20.00 (*0-934641-43-9*) Falcon Pub Inc.

Needles & Needs: Poems. David Shevin. (Midwest Writers Ser.). 80p. (Orig.). 1994. 16.95 (*0-933087-32-2*); pap. 6.95 (*0-933087-30-6*) Bottom Dog Pr.

Needles & Notions: Paper-Pieced Patterns with a Sewing-Room Theme. Jaynette Huff. LC 99-53397. (Illus.). 80p. 2000. pap. 24.95 (*1-56477-289-6*, B411) Martingale & Co.

Needle's Eye. Carol R. Urner. LC 87-62665. (Orig.). 1987. pap. 1.00 (*0-87574-275-0*) Pendle Hill.

Needles Finman , Vol. 2. 5th ed. Needles. 1999. pap. text 8.97 (*0-395-93570-9*) HM.

Needles of Stone. Tom Graves. 1980. reprint ed. pap. 5.95 (*0-586-04965-7*) HarpC.

Needles Solutions to a Problem. Burgess. (C). 1995. pap. text 23.96 (*0-395-72312-4*) HM.

Needles to Portland Bill. Imray, Laurie, Norie & Wilson Ltd. Staff. (Illus.). (C). 1987. text 60.00 (*0-7855-5795-4*, Pub. by Laurie Norie & Wilson Ltd) St Mut.

Needless Casualties of War. John P. Jackson. 176p. 1999. pap. 12.99 (*1-58483-000-X*) Streams Pubns.

Needless Hunger: Voices from a Bangladesh Village. Betsy Hartmann & James K. Boyce. LC 80-142853. 96p. (Orig.). 1979. pap. 6.95 (*0-935028-03-X*) Inst Food & Develop.

*__Needlework & Embroidery Tools.__ Eleanor Johnson. (Illus.). 40p. 1999. pap. 25.00 (*0-7478-0399-4*, Pub. by Shire Pubns) Parkwest Pubns.

Needlework & Fabric, Vol. 3. Vivian C. Kistler. LC 86-72676. (Library of Professional Picture Framing: Vol. 3). (Illus.). 96p. 1998. pap. text 19.00 (*0-938655-02-7*) Columba Pub.

*__Needlework Antique Flowers: With over 25 Charted Designs.__ Elizabeth Bradley. (Illus.). 2000. pap. 19.95 (*0-8069-5579-1*) Sterling.

Needlework Designs for Miniature Projects. 20th ed. Folk. (Dolls, Miniatures Ser.). (Illus.). 48p. pap. 3.95 (*0-486-24660-4*) Dover.

*__Needlework, Patchwork & Quilting.__ Jacqueline Farrell. (Illus.). 2000. 27.95 (*0-600-59488-2*) P HM.

Needlework Tips for the Novice & Expert. Sandy Rodgers. LC 95-90755. 115p. 1995. pap. text 27.95 (*0-9649081-6-6*) Yarn Cellar.

Needlework Tools. Eleanor Johnson. 1989. pap. 25.00 (*0-85263-446-3*, Pub. by Shire Pubns) St Mut.

Needlework Tools. Nerylla Taunton. 1997. 49.50 (*0-614-27835-X*) Antique Collect.

Needs. Steven M. Jacobsen. 1968. pap. 3.25 (*0-8222-0808-3*) Dramatists Play.

Needs. Garrett Thomson. (International Library of Philosophy). 160p. 1987. lib. bdg. 39.95 (*0-7102-1114-7*, Routledge Thoemms) Routledge.

Needs: Of People & Their Communities & the Adult Educator. Ernest E. McMahan. 55p. 1970. 3.00 (*0-88379-004-1*) A A A C E.

Needs - of the People & Their Communities - & the Adult Educator. Ernest E. McMahon. 55p. 1988. 1.95 (*0-318-36408-5*, AEA1-5) A A A C E.

Needs Assessmt & proj Plnn. Connelly. 1999. pap. text 55.00 (*0-536-02353-0*) Pearson Custom.

Needs & Opportunities in the History of the Book: America, 1639-1876. Ed. by David D. Hall & John B. Hench. 284p. 1987. text 35.00 (*0-912296-87-9*) Am Antiquarian.

*__Needs & Prospects for Crime-Fighting Technology: The Federal Role in Assisting State & Local Law Enforcement.__ William Schwabe. LC 99-57290. (Illus.). xi, 50p. 1999. pap. 10.00 (*0-8330-2789-1*, MR-1101-OSTP) Rand Corp.

Needs & Rewards. Nebsm Staff. (Open Learning for Supervisory Management Ser.). 1985. pap. text 19.50 (*0-08-033368-0*, Pergamon Pr) Elsevier.

Needs & Rewards. Nebsm Staff. (Open Learning for Supervisory Management). 1986. pap. text 19.50 (*0-08-033960-3*, Pergamon Pr) Elsevier.

Needs & Wants. Margie Burton et al. Ed. by Susan Evento. (Early Connections Ser.). 16p. (J). (gr. k-2). 1998. pap. 4.25 (*1-892393-48-4*) Benchmark Educ.

Needs & Welfare Provision. Ed. by Alan Ware & Robert E. Goodin. 240p. (C). 1990. text 47.50 (*0-8039-8304-2*); pap. text 19.95 (*0-8039-8305-0*) Sage.

Needs Assessment: A Creative & Practical Guide for Social Scientists. Ed. by Rebecca Reviere et al. LC 96-21821. 233p. 1996. 59.95 (*1-56032-375-2*); pap. 29.95 (*1-56032-376-0*) Taylor & Francis.

Needs Assessment: A Model for Community Planning. Keith A. Neuber et al. (Human Services Guides Ser.: Vol. 14). 107p. 1980. pap. 18.95 (*0-8039-1396-6*) Sage.

Needs Assessment: A User's Guide. Roger Kaufman et al. LC 92-45188. (Illus.). 200p. (Orig.). 1993. pap. 39.95 (*0-87778-258-X*) Educ Tech Pubns.

Needs Assessment: Theory & Methods. Ed. by Donald E. Johnson et al. LC 87-16972. (Illus.). 338p. (Orig.). reprint ed. pap. 104.80 (*0-608-00150-3*, 206093100006) Bks Demand.

Needs Assessment for Agricultural Development: Practical Issues in Informal Data Collection. J. Gilling & J. P. Cropley. 1993. pap. 25.00 (*0-85954-336-6*, Pub. by Nat Res Inst) St Mut.

Needs Assessment of American Indians with Disabilities in the Dallas-Fort Worth Metroplex: Final Report, Phase I. R. M. Schacht et al. 100p. 1993. pap. text. write for info. (*1-888557-04-4*, 100039) No Ariz Univ.

Needs Assessment of American Indians with Disabilities in the Houston Metropolitan Area & Adjacent Rural Counties: Final Report, Phase I. R. M. Schacht et al. 31p. 1994. pap. text. write for info. (*1-888557-05-2*, 100029) No Ariz Univ.

Needs Assessment of Human Problems. Steve Baldwin & Philip Barker. LC 97-41334. (Illus.). 256p. 1998. pap. text 35.00 (*0-7506-2435-3*) Buttrwrth-Heinemann.

Needs Assessment of Older Hispanics in Omaha, Nebraska. David R. DiMartino. 136p. (Orig.). 1979. pap. 9.00 (*1-55719-092-5*) U NE CPAR.

Needs Assessment Strategies for Health Education. 2nd ed. Gary D. Gilmore & Barbara L. Becker. LC 95-81132. 230p. (C). 1995. text 27.04 (*0-697-29229-0*) Brown & Benchmark.

Needs Assessments in Public Policy. Ed. by Janie Percy-Smith. 192p. 1996. 108.95 (*0-335-19596-2*); pap. 29.95 (*0-335-19595-4*) OpUniv Pr.

Needs of a New Age Community: Talks on Spiritual Community & Fourth Way Schools. rev. ed. J. G. Bennett. LC 89-18562. 128p. 1990. reprint ed. pap. 13.00 (*0-9621901-2-8*) Bennett Bks.

Needs of a Woman Book of Poems: Understanding the True Needs of a Woman. Elaine Lockridge. Ed. by Franz Printers. 72p. 1997. pap. 8.00 (*0-9657213-2-9*) Trammella.

Needs of Asia in Primary Education. UNESCO Staff. (Education Studies & Documents: No. 41). 1974. reprint ed. pap. 25.00 (*0-8115-1365-3*) Periodicals Srv.

Needs of Children. 3rd ed. M. K. Pringle. 192p. (C). (gr. 13). 1989. pap. text 19.99 (*0-09-170251-8*) Elsevier Applied Sci.

Needs of Foreign Students from Developing Nations at U. S. College & Universities. Ed. by Motoko Lee. 179p. 1989. reprint ed. 15.00 (*0-912207-27-2*) NAFSA Washington.

Needs of Gifted/Talented Students see Reaching for the Stars Series: A Minicourse for Education of Gifted Students

Needs of Teachers. Ed. by Alan McClelland & Ved P. Varma. LC 95-26740. (Education Ser.). (Illus.). 160p. 1996. pap. 25.95 (*0-304-33335-2*) Continuum.

Needs of Teachers. Ed. by V. Alan McClelland & Ved P. Varma. LC 95-26740. (Education Ser.). (Illus.). 160p. 1996. text 70.00 (*0-304-33334-4*) Continuum.

*__Needs of the Dying: A Guide For Bringing Hope, Comfort, & Love to Life's Final Chapter.__ David Kessler. 224p. 2000. pap. 13.00 (*0-06-095821-9*) HarpC.

Needs of the Elderly in the 21st Century. Sheila R. Zedlewski et al. LC 90-12253. (Reports: No. 90-5). (Illus.). 256p. (Orig.). 1990. pap. text 19.00 (*0-87766-481-1*); lib. bdg. 35.50 (*0-87766-480-3*) Urban Inst.

Needs of the Hour: An Original Rhythmical Message & New Years Greeting (1919) Clara Watson. 50p. 1998. reprint ed. pap. 7.95 (*0-7661-0619-5*) Kessinger Pub.

Needs, Rights & Opportunities. Ed. by Caroline Roaf & Hazel Bines. (Education & Alienation Ser.). 250p. 1989. 65.00 (*1-85000-516-8*, Falmer Pr) Taylor & Francis.

Needs, Rights & the Market. David P. Levine. LC 88-4543. 158p. 1988. lib. bdg. 35.00 (*1-55587-115-1*) L Rienner.

Needs to Know. Harris. (C). 1998. pap. text 35.00 (*0-443-05569-6*, W B Saunders Co) Harcrt Hlth Sci Grp.

Needs, Urges, & Feelings in Early Childhood: Helping Young Children Grow. Erna Furman. 140p. 1998. pap. 24.95 (*0-8236-8160-2*, BN 23515) Intl Univs Pr.

Neef Doff, 1858-1942: A Biography. Evelyne Wilwerth. Tr. by Renee Linkhorn from FRE. LC 96-38727. (Belgian Francophone Library: No. 8). XVIII, 267p. (C). 1997. text 51.95 (*0-8204-3483-3*) P Lang Pubng.

Neekna & Chemai. Barb Marchand & Jeannette C. Armstrong. (Illus.). 44p. (J). (gr. 1-4). 1991. pap. 8.95 (*0-919441-15-7*, Pub. by Theytus Bks) Orca Bk Pubs.

Neel Reid: Of Hentz, Reid & Adler & the Georgia School of Classicists. William R. Mitchell, Jr. (Illus.). 224p. 1997. 50.00 (*0-932958-19-2*) Golden Coast.

*__Neely Jones: The Medusa Pool.__ M. K. Wren. LC 99-22252. 320p. 1999. text 24.95 (*0-312-24223-9*) St Martin.

Neem: A Tree for Solving Problems. National Research Council Staff. 152p. (C). 1992. pap. text 23.00 (*0-309-04686-6*) Natl Acad Pr.

Neem: India's Miraculous Healing Plant. Ellen Norten. LC 99-49948. (Illus.). 96p. 2000. pap. 9.95 (*0-89281-837-9*) Inner Tradit.

*__Neem: The Divine Tree, Azadirachta Indica.__ H. S. Puri. 196p. 1999. text 75.00 (*90-5702-348-2*, Harwood Acad Pubs) Gordon & Breach.

Neem & Environment, 2 vols., Set. Ed. by R. P. Singh. 1000p. 1996. text 149.00 (*1-886106-32-0*) Science Pubs.

Neem in Sustainable Agriculture International Symposium on Allelopathy in Sustainable Agriculture, Forestry & Environment New Delhi 1994. S. S. Narwal et al. LC 97-913999. 1997. pap. 135.00 (*81-7233-167-3*, Pub. by Scientific Pubs) St Mut.

Neem the Half-Boy. Idries Shah. LC 97-6321. (Illus.). 32p. (J). (gr. 4-7). 1998. 17.00 (*1-883536-10-3*, Hoopoe Books) ISHK.

Neem Tree: Sources of Unique Natural Products for Integrated Pest Management & Medicinal, Industrial & Other Purposes. Ed. by H. Schmutterer. 696p. 1995. 152.00 (*3-527-30054-6*, Wiley-VCH) Wiley.

Neena Gathering. Valerie N. Colander. 1988. 2.95 (*0-517-00643-X*) Random Hse Value.

Neeny Coming, Neeny Going. Karen English. LC 95-3624. (Illus.). 32p. (J). (gr. k-3). 1997. 14.95 (*0-8167-3796-7*) BrdgeWater.

Neeny Coming, Neeny Going. Karen English. (Illus.). 32p. (J). (gr. k-4). 1998. pap. 5.95 (*0-8167-3797-5*) Troll Communs.

Neeny Coming, Neeny Going. Karen English. 1998. 11.15 (*0-606-13656-8*, Pub. by Turtleback) Demco.

Ne'er-Do-Well. Rex Ellingwood Beach. (Collected Works of Rex Ellingwood Beach.). 401p. 1998. reprint ed. lib. bdg. 108.00 (*1-58201-545-7*) Classic Bks.

Neerihiinjik: We Traveled from Place to Place: Johnny Sarah Haa Googwandak: The Gwich'in Stories of Johnny & Sarah Frank. Ed. by Craig Mishler. (Illus.). xxx, 690p. 1996. pap. 29.00 (*1-55500-054-1*) Alaska Native.

Neerlandais Sans Peine. Albert O. Cherel. 24.95 (*0-685-11415-5*); audio 125.00 (*0-685-01741-9*) Fr & Eur.

Nees, Values, Truth: Essays in the Philosophy of Value. 3rd ed. DAvid Wiggins. 410p. 1998. pap. text 19.95 (*0-19-823719-7*) OUP.

Neethling's Law of Personality. expanded rev. ed. J. Neethling et al. LC 97-162562. 450p. 1996. pap. write for info. (*0-409-06124-7*, MICHIE) LEXIS Pub.

Neets'aii Gwiindaii: Living in the Chandalar Country. Katherine Peter. Tr. by Adeline Raboff from ENG. (Illus.). xii, 108p. (Orig.). 1992. pap. 14.00 (*0-933769-11-3*) Alaska Native.

Nefazia Visits the Palace. Suzanne Weyn. LC 92-53937. (Little Mermaid Novels Ser.). (Illus.). (J). (gr. 1-4). 1992. pap. 3.25 (*1-56282-247-0*, Pub. by Disney Pr) Time Warner.

*__Nefer the Silent.__ Christian Jacq. (Stone of Light Ser.: Vol. 1). 512p. 2000. per. 16.00 (*0-7434-0346-0*, PB Trade Paper) PB.

Nefertari, Princess of Egypt. Roberta Angeletti. (Illus.). 32p. (YA). 1999. 16.95 (*0-19-521507-9*) OUP.

Nefertiti: Unlocking the Mystery Surrounding Egypt's Most Famous & Beautiful Queen. Joyce A. Tyldesley. LC 98-35469. (Illus.). 232p. 1999. 27.95 (*0-670-86998-8*) Viking Penguin.

*__Nefertiti: Unlocking the Mystery Surrounding Egypt's Most Famous & Beautiful Queen.__ Joyce A. Tyldesley. (Illus.). 272p. 2000. pap. 14.95 (*0-14-025820-5*) Viking Penguin.

Nefertiti & Cleopatra: Queen-Monarchs of Ancient Egypt. Julia Samson. (Illus.). 165p. 1990. pap. 22.95 (*0-948695-18-8*, Pub. by Rubicon Pr) David Brown.

Nefertiti et la Reve de Akhnaton. Andree Chedid. (FRE.). 1988. pap. 12.95 (*0-7859-2994-0*) Fr & Eur.

Nefesh Hayah: Commentary & Interpretation on the Passover Haggadah with the Haggadah Text. P. S. Pollak. (ENG & HEB.). 9.50 (*0-87559-091-8*) Shalom.

Neff-Naf Family History. William A. Neff. LC 91-66144. (Illus.). 480p. 1991. 42.50 (*0-9630457-0-9*) Neff & Assocs.

Nefton. Mark Dunster. 24p. (Orig.). (YA). 1995. pap. 5.00 (*0-89642-288-7*) Linden Pubs.

Negah Az Birun. Daryush Homayun. (PER.). 272p. (Orig.). 1985. pap. 9.00 (*0-936347-02-3*) IBEX.

Negaholics. Scott. 1991. pap. write for info. (*0-7126-4622-1*, Pub. by Random) Random House.

*__Negaholics: How to Overcome Negativity & Turn Your Life Around.__ Carter-Scott Cherie. 272p. 1999. pap. 12.00 (*0-345-43899-X*) Wellspring.

Negara: Theatre-State in 19th Century Bali. Clifford Geertz. LC 80-7520. 256p. 1980. pap. text 17.95 (*0-691-00778-0*, Pub. by Princeton U Pr) Cal Prin Full Svc.

Negation. Gerhard Helbig & Helga Albrecht. 72p. 1990. 13.00 (*3-324-00575-2*) Langenscheidt.

Negation: A Notion in Focus. Ed. by Heinrich Wansing. (Perspektiven der Analytischen Philosophie - Perspectives in Analytical Philosophy Ser.: Vol. 7). vii, 270p. (C). 1996. lib. bdg. 133.35 (*3-11-014769-6*) De Gruyter.

Negation & Clausal Structure: A Comparative Study of Romance Language. Raffaella Zanuttini. LC 96-18432. (Oxford Studies in Comparative Syntax). (Illus.). 216p. 1997. pap. text 45.00 (*0-19-508055-6*) OUP.

Negation & Control in Prology. L. Naish. (Lecture Notes in Computer Science Ser.: Vol. 238). ix, 119p. 1988. 26.00 (*0-387-16815-X*) Spr-Verlag.

*__Negation & Polarity.__ Ed. by Laurence R. Horn & Yasuhiko Kato. LC 99-87825. 304p. 2000. pap. 29.95 (*0-19-823873-8*); text 85.00 (*0-19-823874-6*) OUP.

Negation & Polarity: Syntax & Semantics: Selected Papers from the Colloquium Negation: Syntax & Semantics, Ottawa 11-13 May 1995. Ed. by Danielle Forget et al. LC 97-32234. (Current Issues in Linguistic Theory Ser.: Vol. 155). viii, 367p. 1997. lib. bdg. 83.00 (*1-55619-871-X*) J Benjamins Pubng Co.

Negation & the Comparative Particle in English. Andre Joly. LC 67-6316. (Cahiers de Psychomecanique du Langage Ser.: 9). 44p. reprint ed. pap. 30.00 (*0-608-12045-6*, 202463500038) Bks Demand.

Negation & Theology: With Essays & Replies. Robert P. Scharlemann. LC 91-46593. (Studies in Religion & Culture). 163p. reprint ed. pap. 50.60 (*0-608-08557-X*, 206908000002) Bks Demand.

Negation & Utopia: The German Volksst Uck from Raimund to Kroetz. Calvin N. Jones. LC 93-20110. (Studies in Modern German Literature: Vol. 56). X, 299p. (C). 1993. text 52.95 (*0-8204-2075-1*) P Lang Pubng.

Negation, Critical Theory, & Postmodern Textualtiy. Ed. by Daniel Fischlin. LC 94-13390. 344p. (C). 1994. lib. bdg. 145.50 (*0-7923-2833-7*, Pub. by Kluwer Academic) Kluwer Academic.

Negation in the History of English. Ed. by Ingrid Tieken-Boon Van Ostade et al. LC 98-42858. 1998. 127.75 (*3-11-016198-2*) De Gruyter.

Negation, Subjectivity, & the History of Rhetoric. Victor J. Vitanza. LC 96-3775. 288p. (C). 1996. text 65.50 (*0-7914-3123-1*); pap. text 21.95 (*0-7914-3124-X*) State U NY Pr.

*__Negation, Text Worlds & Discourse.__ Laura Hidalgo-Downing. LC 99-36412. (Advances in Discourse Processes Ser.). 1999. pap. write for info. (*1-56750-475-2*) Ablx Pub.

Negative. Ansel Adams & Robert Baker. (Illus.). 288p. 1995. pap. 22.50 (*0-8212-2186-8*, Pub. by Bulfinch Pr) Little.

Negative Air Ionisation in Buildings. G. Hamilton & J. Kew. (C). 1985. 65.00 (*0-86022-152-0*, Pub. by Build Servs Info Assn) St Mut.

*__Negative Blue: Selected Later Poems.__ Charles Wright. LC 99-36987. 224p. 2000. text 23.00 (*0-374-22020-4*) FS&G.

Negative Burn: Best of Year One. Ed. by Joe Pruett. (Illus.). 128p. 1995. 9.95 (*0-941613-69-0*) Stabur Pr.

Negative Burn: Best of Year Two. Ed. by Joe Pruett. (Illus.). 128p. (Orig.). 1996. pap. 9.95 (*0-941613-84-4*, Caliber Comics) Stabur Pr.

Negative Capability: The Intuitive Approach in Keats. Walter Jackson Bate. LC 75-28991. reprint ed. 27.00 (*0-404-14002-5*) AMS Pr.

Negative Contexts: Collocation, Polarity & Multiple Negation. 2nd ed. Ton Van Der Wouden. LC 96-429. (Studies in Germanic Linguistics). (Illus.). 320p. (C). 1997. 85.00 (*0-415-13849-3*) Routledge.

Negative Criticism & What You Can Do about It. Sidney B. Simon. 121p. 1991. reprint ed. pap. text 5.95 (*1-880424-07-X*) Values.

Negative Cutting, 16mm: Includes Reversal Cutting. Ronald C. Denaro. 106p. (C). 1991. pap. text 14.95 (*0-9630524-3-8*) Split-Reel.

Negative Dialectics. 2nd ed. Theodor W. Adorno. 416p. (J). 1982. pap. 22.95 (*0-8264-0132-5*) Continuum.

Negative Dialectics of a Poodle. Ben Watson. 632p. 1996. pap. 17.95 (*0-312-14124-6*) St Martin.

Negative Differential Resistance & Instabilities in 2-D Semiconductors. N. Balkan et al. LC 93-15664. (NATO ASI Series B, Physics: Vol. 307). (Illus.). 454p. (C). 1993. 125.00 (*0-306-44490-9*, Plenum Trade) Perseus Pubng.

Negative History: Poems. Cathryn Hankla. LC 97-13614. 72p. 1997. pap. 12.95 (*0-8071-2154-1*); text 19.95 (*0-8071-2153-3*) La State U Pr.

Negative Images: A Simple Matter of Black & White: An Examination of 'Race' & the Juvenile Justice System. Bruce Kirk. LC 96-84834. 179p. 1996. 63.95 (*1-85972-119-2*, Pub. by Avebury) Ashgate Pub Co.

Negative Impact of Bankruptcy on Education Funding: Hearing Before the Subcommittee on Administrative Oversight & the Courts of the Committee on the Judiciary, United States Senate, One Hundred Fifth Congress, First Session ... August 1, 1997. United States. LC 98-137760. iv, 110p. 1997. write for info. (*0-16-055780-1*) USGPO.

Negative Man. large type ed. Philip McCutchan. (Dales Large Print Ser.). 274p. 1997. pap. 18.99 (*1-85389-683-7*) Ulverscroft.

Negative Motor Phenomena, No. 67. Ed. by Stanley Fahn et al. (Advances in Neurology Ser.: Vol. 67). (Illus.). 416p. 1995. text 126.00 (*0-7817-0264-X*) Lppncott W & W.

Negative Poetics. Edward Jayne. LC 91-39624. (Illus.). 343p. 1992. text 29.95 (*0-87745-362-4*) U of Iowa Pr.

Negative Political Advertising: Coming of Age. Ed. by K. S. Johnson-Cartee & G. A. Copeland. (Communication Ser.). 328p. (C). 1991. text 69.95 (*0-8058-0834-5*) L Erlbaum Assocs.

An Asterisk (*) at the beginning of an entry indicates that the title is appearing for the first time.

N

Negative Schizophrenic Symptoms: Pathophysiology & Clinical Implications. Ed. by John F. Greden & Rajiv Tandon. LC 90-535. (Progress in Psychiatry Ser.: No. 28). 290p. 1991. text 12.95 (*0-88048-192-7*, 8192) Am Psychiatric.

Negative Sentences in the Languages of Europe: A Typological Approach. Giuliano Bernini & Paolo Ramat. LC 96-15690. (Empirical Approaches to Language Typology Ser.: Vol. 16). xii, 274p. (C). 1996. lib. bdg. 94.80 (*3-11-014064-0*) Mouton.

Negative Space: Manny Farber on the Movies. expanded ed. Manny Farber. LC 98-5486. 416p. 1998. reprint ed. pap. 15.95 (*0-306-80829-3*) Da Capo.

Negative Spring: Crisis Imagery in the Works of Brentano, Lenau, Rilke & T. S. Eliot. David B. Dickens. (Studies in Modern German Literature: Vol. 24). XII, 242p. (C). 1988. text 36.50 (*0-8204-0735-6*) P Lang Pubng.

Negative vs. Positive Schizophrenia. Ed. by Andreas Marneros et al. (Illus.). 464p. 1991. 134.00 (*0-387-54388-0*) Spr-Verlag.

Negative Zone. Victor Appleton. Ed. by Anne Greenberg. (Tom Swift Ser.: No. 2). 176p. (YA). (gr. 7 up). 1991. per. 2.95 (*0-671-67824-8*, Archway) PB.

Negatives & Noun Phrases in Classical Greek: An Investigation Based on the "Corpus Platonicum" Eva-Carin Gero. (Studien zur Klassischen Philologie: Bd. 105). 158p. 1997. pap. 35.95 (*3-631-30677-6*) P Lang Pubng.

Negatives & Noun Phrases in Classical Greek: An Investigation Based on the "Corpus Platonicum" Eva-Carin Gero. LC 97-7556. (Studien zur Klassischen Philologie: Bd. 105). 158p. 1997. pap. 35.95 (*0-8204-3210-5*) P Lang Pubng.

Negatives Through Pictures. Harris Winitz. (Language Through Pictures Ser.). (Illus.). 100p. (YA). (gr. 2-12). 1982. pap. 5.00 (*0-939990-32-6*) Intl Linguistics.

Negatives to Positives. Eileen Curns. (Illus.). 39p. 1982. pap. 10.00 (*0-942968-02-6*) ACCORD IL.

Negativitat des Weltlaufs. Ed. by Klaus-Jurgen Grun et al. (Philosophische Texte und Studien). 150p. 1997. 45.00 (*3-487-10269-2*) G Olms Pubs.

***Negativity & Politics: Dionysus & Dialectics from Kant to Poststructuralism.** Diana Coole. 240p. 2000. 85.00 (*0-415-03176-1*) Routledge.

***Negativity & Politics: Dionysus & Dialectics from Kant to Poststructuralism.** Diana H. Coole. LC 99-52690. 240p. 2000. pap. 25.99 (*0-415-03177-X*) Routledge.

Negativity Trap. Lois Wolfe-Morgan. LC 95-81504. 184p. (Orig.). 1996. pap. 18.00 (*1-879198-19-3*) Knwldg Ideas & Trnds.

Negawatt Power Pt. 3b: Demand-Side Electricity Resources in Western Europe. David Olivier et al. (Energy Policy in the Greenhouse Ser.: Vol. 2). 150p. (Orig.). 1996. pap. 35.00 (*1-883774-04-7*) IPSEP.

Negestanti Sviesa: Mari Jonu Veikla Amerikoje. Pranas Garsva. (LIT., Illus.). 351p. (Orig.). 1964. pap. write for info. (*0-933820-00-3*) Marian Fathers.

Negev: The Challenge of a Desert. 2nd ed. Michael Evenari et al. (Illus.). 456p. 1982. 58.50 (*0-674-60672-8*) HUP.

Negev Bedouin & Livestock Rearing: Social, Economic & Political Aspects. Aref Abu-Rabia. LC 92-32092. 160p. 1994. 47.50 (*0-85496-319-7*, Pub. by Berg Pubs) NYU Pr.

Negev Project. Larry Witham. 301p. 1994. 17.95 (*0-9640428-0-0*) Meridian Bks MD.

Neggar Journeys into Nightmares. Saggittarus. LC 72-96167. 144p. pap. 4.50 (*0-912444-18-5*) DARE Bks.

Neglect & Betrayal: War & Violence in Modern Sociology. David Marsland. (C). 1990. 60.00 (*0-7855-6611-2*, Pub. by Inst Euro Def & Strat) St Mut.

Neglect & Betrayal: War & Violence in Modern Sociology. David Marsland. (C). 1981. pap. 29.00 (*0-907967-65-5*) St Mut.

Neglect of Geologic Data: Sedimentary Strata Compared with Young-Earth Creationist Writings. Daniel E. Wonderly. LC 87-82296. (Illus.). 162p. (C). 1993. pap. 10.95 (*0-944788-00-9*) IBRI.

Neglected & Abused: A Physician's Year in Haiti. Joseph F. Bentivegna. (Illus.). 180p. (Orig.). (C). 1990. pap. 12.95 (*0-9626001-0-5*) Michelle Pub.

Neglected Ape. R. D. Nadler et al. (Illus.). 312p. (C). 1996. 102.00 (*0-306-45213-8*, Plenum Trade) Perseus Pubng.

Neglected Arabia - Arabia Calling, 1892-1962, 8 vols., Set. Archives Research Ltd. Staff. 4600p. (C). 1988. reprint ed. lib. bdg. 995.00 (*1-85207-110-9*, Pub. by Archive Editions) N Ross.

Neglected Aspects of American Poetry: The Greek Independence War & Other Studies. Aaron Kramer. (Studies in the Humanities & the Social Sciences). 396p. (Orig.). (C). 1997. pap. 17.00 (*1-883058-17-1*, Dowling College) Global Pubns.

Neglected Aspects of Foreign Affairs: American Educational & Cultural Policy Abroad. Charles Frankel. LC 65-28724. 168p. reprint ed. pap. 52.10 (*0-608-11990-3*, 202300400030) Bks Demand.

Neglected Aspects of Sufi Study. Idries Shah. 71p. 1977. 18.00 (*0-900860-56-1*, Pub. by Octagon Pr) ISHK.

Neglected Brother: A Study of Henry Kingsley. William H. Scheuerle. LC 77-149955. 195p. reprint ed. pap. 60.50 (*0-7837-5101-X*, 204480000004) Bks Demand.

Neglected Canon: 9 Women Philosophers from the 12th to the 20th Century. Therese B. Dykeman. (New Feminist Perspectives Ser.: No. 67). 384p. 1997. 58.50 (*0-8476-8420-2*); pap. 19.95 (*0-8476-8421-0*) Rowman.

Neglected Cause of Stroke: Occlusion of the Smaller Intracranial Arteries & Their Diagnosis by Cerebral Angiography. B. Albert Ring. LC 68-55659. (Illus.). 220p. 1969. 12.00 (*0-87527-066-2*) Green.

Neglected Challenge: Minority Participation in Higher Education, No. 17. Frank H. Rhodes. 13p. 1987. pap. 2.00 (*0-685-66149-0*) Acad Educ Dev.

Neglected Children: Issues & Dilemmas. Olive Stevenson. LC 97-52985. (Working Together for Children, Young People, & Their Families Ser.). 174p. 1998. write for info. (*0-632-04146-3*) Blackwell Sci.

Neglected Children: Research, Practice & Policy. Howard Dubowitz. LC 98-40296. 288p. 1999. 26.95 (*0-7619-0854-4*) Sage.

***Neglected Children: Research, Practice & Policy.** Ed. by Howard Dubowitz. LC 98-40296. 320p. 1999. 55.00 (*0-7619-0853-6*) Sage.

***Neglected Children: Research, Practice, & Policy.** Howard Dubowitz. LC 98-40296. 320p. 1999. write for info. (*0-7619-1842-6*) Sage.

Neglected Endings: The Significance of the Pauline Letter Closings. Jeffrey A. Weima. LC 94-235078. (Journal for the Study of the New Testament, Supplement Ser.: Vol. 101). 270p. 1994. 75.00 (*1-85075-488-8*, Pub. by Sheffield Acad) CUP Services.

Neglected English Literature. Dorothy L. Latz. LC 98-101782. 130p. 1997. pap. 19.95 (*3-7052-0072-0*, Pub. by Poetry Salzburg) Intl Spec Bk.

Neglected Factors in Pharmacology & Neuroscience Research. Volkert Claassen. LC 94-16419. (Techniques in the Behavioral & Neural Sciences Ser.: Vol. 12). 496p. 1994. 247.50 (*0-444-81871-5*) Elsevier.

Neglected Factors in Pharmacology & Neuroscience Research. Ed. by Volkert Claassen. (Techniques in the Behavioral & Neural Sciences Ser.: Vol. 12). 496p. 1994. pap. 88.50 (*0-444-81907-X*) Elsevier.

***Neglected Few.** Leonard Robinson, Jr. & Thomas Noland. LC 00-130311. 130p. 2000. pap. 24.95 (*0-9678948-0-8*, 1003) Make-Do Prod.

Neglected Generation of American Realist Painters, 1930-1948. Howard E. Wooden. LC 81-51507. (Illus.). 64p. (C). 1981. pap. 15.00 (*0-939324-02-4*) Wichita Art Mus.

Neglected Geological Anomalies: A Catalog of Geological Anomalies. William R. Corliss. LC 90-60568. (Illus.). 333p. (C). 1990. 18.95 (*0-915554-24-0*) Sourcebook.

Neglected Heroes: Leadership & War in the Early Medieval Period. Terry L. Gore. LC 95-13432. 240p. 1995. 59.95 (*0-275-95269-X*, Praeger Pubs) Greenwood.

Neglected History. Charles H. Wesley. (YA). 1990. 5.95 (*0-87498-012-7*) Assoc Pubs DC.

Neglected History: 20th Century American Craft. LC 90-86311. (Illus.). 59p. 1990. 13.50 (*0-88321-062-2*) Am Craft.

Neglected Issue: Some Essays on the Need for Monetary Reform. Duke of Bedford. 1982. lib. bdg. 59.95 (*0-87700-355-6*) Revisionist Pr.

Neglected Majority. Dale Parnell. 1985. pap. 33.00 (*0-87117-154-6*, 1068) Comm Coll Pr Am Assn Comm Coll.

Neglected Majority "Les Camoufleurs," Art History & World War I. Elizabeth L. Kahn. LC 84-13089. (Illus.). 236p. (Orig.). 1984. lib. bdg. 52.00 (*0-8191-4164-X*) U Pr of Amer.

Neglected Northampton Texts of Jonathan Edwards: Edwards on Society & Politics. Richard A. Hall. LC 90-21014. (Studies in American Religion: Vol. 52). 364p. 1990. lib. bdg. 99.95 (*0-88946-593-2*) E Mellen.

Neglected Period of Anti-Slavery in America, 1808-1831. Alice D. Adams. 307p. 1973. reprint ed. 26.95 (*0-87928-034-4*) Corner Hse.

Neglected Period of Anti-Slavery in America, 1808-1831. Alice D. Adams. (History - United States Ser.). 307p. 1992. reprint ed. lib. bdg. 89.00 (*0-7812-6157-0*) Rprt Serv.

Neglected Point in Connection with Crises. Nicholas A. Johannsen. LC 78-129861. (Reprints of Economic Classics Ser.). 194p. 1971. reprint ed. 39.50 (*0-678-00759-4*) Kelley.

Neglected Saints. E. I. Watkin. 230p. (Orig.). 1994. pap. 12.95 (*0-89870-457-X*) Ignatius Pr.

Neglected Stories: The Constitution & Family Values. Peggy C. Davis. (Illus.). 304p. 1998. pap. text 14.00 (*0-8090-1607-9*) Hill & Wang.

Neglected Stories: The Constitution & Family Values. Peggy Cooper Davis. LC 97-3898. 1997. 25.00 (*0-8090-7241-6*) Hill & Wang.

Neglected Treasure: Rediscovering the Old Testament. Dan G. Johnson. LC 89-50312. 1989. pap. 6.95 (*0-917851-28-5*) Bristol Hse.

Neglected Voices. John Indermark. Ed. by Rita Collett. LC 99-19599. 128p. 1999. pap. 10.00 (*0-8358-0891-2*, UR891) Upper Room Bks.

Neglected Voices: Leader's Guide. John Indermark. Ed. by Rita Collett. 48p. 1999. pap., teacher ed. 5.00 (*0-8358-0890-4*, UR890) Upper Room Bks.

Neglected Walt Whitman: Vital Texts. Walt Whitman. Ed. by Sam Abrams. LC 92-42579. 200p. 1993. pap. 12.95 (*0-941423-97-2*) FWEW.

Neglected War: The German South Pacific & the Influence of World War I. Hermann J. Hiery. LC 95-13075. (Illus.). 384p. 1995. text 29.00 (*0-8248-1668-4*) UH Pr.

Neglected Wells: Spirituality & the Arts. Anne Murphy & Eoin Cassidy. LC 97-161612. 144p. 1997. pap. 15.00 (*1-85182-294-1*, Pub. by Four Cts Pr) Intl Spec Bk.

Neglectful Guardian. Anne Ashley. (Historical Ser.: Bk. 21). 1999. per. 4.99 (*0-373-30330-0*, 1-30330-4) Harlequin Bks.

Neglectful Guardian. large type ed. Anne Ashley. (Mills & Boon Large Print Ser.). 350p. 1998. 24.99 (*0-263-15526-9*, Pub. by Mills & Boon) Ulverscroft.

Negligence, All Modern Cases On. 3rd rev. ed. B. Bingham. (C). 1978. 800.00 (*0-7855-4073-3*, Pub. by Witherby & Co) St Mut.

Negligence & Chaos: Bibliographical Access to Persian-Language Materials in the United States. Farideh Tehrani. LC 91-27769. (Illus.). 256p. 1991. 35.00 (*0-8108-2473-6*) Scarecrow.

Negligence at Work. Frederick P. Chambers. 96p. 1995. pap. 30.00 (*1-85811-031-9*, Pub. by CLT Prof) Gaunt.

Negligence Case: Res Ipsa Loquitur, 2 vols., Set. Stuart M. Speiser. LC 72-84856. 1972. 225.00 (*0-685-59914-0*) West Group.

Negligence Charlesworth & Percy On. 7th ed. Witherby & Co. Ltd. Staff. (C). 1983. 1080.00 (*0-7855-4072-5*, Pub. by Witherby & Co) St Mut.

Negligence Clauses in Ocean Bills of Lading: Conflict of Laws & Brussels Convention of 1924: A Comparative Study. Athanassios N. Yiannopoulos. LC 62-10479. 238p. reprint ed. pap. 73.80 (*0-608-14366-9*, 205188400013) Bks Demand.

Negligence in Building Law: Cases & Commentary. Jon Holyoak. LC 92-5670. 1992. 85.00 (*0-632-02078-4*) Blackwell Sci.

Negligence in Law, 2 vols. 4th ed. Thomas Beven. ccxi, 1638p. 1998. reprint ed. 395.00 (*1-56169-407-X*, 15564) Gaunt.

Negligentia: Poems from Hollywood. Mark Dunster. 11p. 1998. pap. 5.00 (*0-89642-614-9*) Linden Pubs.

Negocio de Bienes Raices en Mexico. 2nd ed. Jose M. Septien.Tr. of Real Estate Business in Mexico. (SPA.). 1998. pap. text 21.95 (*0-7931-2903-6*) Dearborn.

Negocios (Spanish-Language Edition of Drown) Junot Diaz. (SPA.). 1997. pap. 11.00 (*0-679-77657-5*) Vin Bks.

Negocios y la Biblia. Tr. of Business by the Book. 1996. pap. text 10.99 (*0-88113-112-1*) Caribe Betania.

***Negocios y Placer (Business & Pleasure) The Bride Means Business.** Anne M. Winston. (Deseo Ser.: No. 186). (SPA.). 156p. 1999. per. 3.50 (*0-373-35316-2*, 1-35316-8) Harlequin Bks.

Negotiability: The Doctrine & Its Application in U. S. Commercial Law. James E. Byrne. 416p. 1995. pap. 45.00 (*1-888870-06-0*) Inst Intl Bnking.

Negotiable Environment: People, White-Collar Work, & the Office. Cecil L. Williams et al. LC 85-10305. (Illus.). 96p. (Orig.). 1985. pap. 15.00 (*0-936658-20-7*) H Miller Res.

Negotiable Instruments. Avtar Singh. (C). 1987. 60.00 (*0-7855-3498-9*) St Mut.

Negotiable Instruments. L. Tager. (Lawsa Student Text Ser.). 146p. 1984. pap. 52.00 (*0-409-04021-5*, SA, MICHIE) LEXIS Pub.

Negotiable Instruments. Avtar Singh. 329p. 1984. reprint ed. 110.00 (*0-7855-1375-2*); reprint ed. pap. 90.00 (*0-7855-1376-0*) St Mut.

Negotiable Instruments. 2nd ed. Steve H. Nickles. LC 92-47440. (Black Letter Ser.). 574p. (C). 1993. pap. 24.50 incl. disk (*0-314-01979-0*) West Pub.

Negotiable Instruments. 2nd ed. L. Tager. (Lawsa Student Text Ser.). 136p. 1996. pap. write for info. (*0-409-02171-7*, MICHIE) LEXIS Pub.

Negotiable Instruments. 4th ed. E. Allan Farnsworth. (University Casebook Ser.). 493p. 1993. text. write for info. (*1-56662-077-5*) Foundation Pr.

Negotiable Instruments: Adaptable to Courses Utilizing Whaley's Casebook on Commercial Law. Casenotes Publishing Co., Inc. Staff. Ed. by Norman S. Goldenberg et al. (Legal Briefs Ser.). 1997. pap. write for info. (*0-87457-108-1*, 1313) Casenotes Pub.

Negotiable Instruments: Under the Uniform Commercial Code & the United Nations Convention on International Bills of Exchange & International Promissory Notes, 3. Louis F. Del Duca et al. LC 93-4774. (Commercial Transactions Ser.: Vols. 2 & 3). 417p. 1993. pap. 45.95 (*0-87084-153-X*) Anderson Pub Co.

Negotiable Instruments Act. K. Khergamwala. (C). 1988. 65.00 (*0-7855-3708-2*) St Mut.

***Negotiable Instruments Act (Act XXVI of 1881) Being an Act to Define & Amend the Law Relating to Promissory Notes, Bills of Exchange & Cheques.** Ed. by M. D. Chalmers. xxxvi, 167p. 1999. reprint ed. 65.00 (*1-56169-565-3*) Gaunt.

Negotiable Instruments Acts. Sanjiva Row. (C). 1988. 150.00 (*0-7855-3546-2*) St Mut.

Negotiable Instruments & Banking. Mata Din. (C). 1989. 350.00 (*0-7855-6034-3*) St Mut.

Negotiable Instruments & Check Collection in a Nutshell. 4th ed. Richard E. Speidel & Steve H. Nickles. (Nutshell Ser.). 544p. (C). 1993. pap. 23.50 (*0-314-02294-5*) West Pub.

Negotiable Instruments & Letters of Credit. Robert J. Jordan & William D. Warren. (University Casebook Ser.). 1992. pap. text 36.00 (*0-88277-985-0*) Foundation Pr.

Negotiable Instruments (In Nutshell) 4th ed. Avtar Singh. (C). 1986. 30.00 (*0-7855-5464-5*) St Mut.

Negotiable Instruments Law: From the Draft Prepared for the Commissioners on Uniformity of Laws, & Enacted in New York, Massachusetts, Rhode Island, Connecticut, Pennsylvania, District of Columbia, Maryland, Virginia, North Carolina, Tennessee, Florida, Wisconsin, North Dakota, Colorado, Utah, Oregon & Washington. 2nd ed. John J. Crawford. xxiv, 173p. 1997. reprint ed. 65.00 (*1-56169-307-3*, 14591) Gaunt.

Negotiable Instruments, Manual for Teacher's to Accompany Cases, Problems & Materials On. 4th ed. Edward Allan Farnsworth. 54p. 1993. write for info. (*0-318-72663-7*) Foundation Pr.

Negotiable Instruments, Payments & Credits. 4th ed. Robert L. Jordan & William D. Warren. (University Casebook Ser.). 456p. 1997. text. write for info. (*1-56662-550-5*) Foundation Pr.

Negotiable Instruments under the U. C. C. Frederick M. Hart. text 490.00 (*0-8205-2121-3*) Bender.

Negotiable Paper & Payment. Donald B. King & Peter Winship. Ed. by Peter Tenen & Norman S. Goldenberg. (Casenote Law Outlines: No. 5720). (Orig.). 1995. pap. write for info. (*0-614-15875-3*) Casenotes Pub.

Negotiate: Winning Strategies for Builders & Developers. David Cash. LC 91-14075. 1991. write for info. (*0-86718-364-0*) Home Builder.

***Negotiate Everything: How to Get the Absolute Best Deal on Any Product or Service You Buy.** Fred Gleeck. 144p. 2000. pap. 14.95 (*0-936965-06-1*) Fast Forwrd.

Negotiate Like the Big Guys: How Small & Mid-Size Companies Can Balance the Power in Dealing with Corporate Giants. Susan Onaitis. 334p. 1998. pap. 29.95 (*1-56343-167-X*) Silver Lake.

Negotiate Like the Pros. John P. Dolan. LC 92-9623. 176p. 1992. pap. 12.00 (*0-399-51775-8*, Perigee Bks) Berkley Pub.

Negotiate Smart. Living Language Staff. 1998. 15.95 incl. audio (*0-609-60152-0*) Liv Lang.

Negotiate Smart. Nicholas R. Schaffzin. 1997. pap. 12.00 (*0-679-77871-3*) Random.

Negotiate Successfully. DK Publishing Staff. LC 97-38889. (Instant Managers Ser.). 1998. 6.95 (*0-7894-2448-7*) DK Pub Inc.

***Negotiate the Raise You Deserve.** Mark Satterfield. (Here's How Ser.). 160p. 2000. pap. 12.95 (*0-658-00389-5*, 003895) NTC Contemp Pub Co.

Negotiate to Close: How to Make More Successful Deals. Gary Karrass. 224p. 1987. pap. 11.00 (*0-671-62886-0*, Fireside) S&S Trade Pap.

Negotiate with Confidence. Ed Brodow. LC 95-83970. (How-to Book Ser.). 97p. (Orig.). 1996. pap. 12.95 (*1-884926-50-9*, NEGOT) Amer Media.

***Negotiate with Feng Shui: Enhance Your Skills in Diplomacy, Business & Relationships.** Jose Armilla. 2001. pap. 12.95 (*1-56718-038-8*) Llewellyn Pubns.

***Negotiate Your Commercial Lease.** Dale R. Willerton. (Business Ser.). 1999. pap. 13.95 (*1-55180-250-3*) Self-Counsel Pr.

Negotiate Your Job Offer: A Step by Step Guide to a Win-Win Situation. Mary Simon. LC 97-26314. 253p. 1997. pap. 14.95 (*0-471-17185-9*) Wiley.

Negotiated Acquisitions. Gordon T. Yamate et al. (Corporate Practice Ser.: No. 61). 1992. ring bd. 95.00 (*1-55871-272-0*) BNA.

Negotiated Acquisitions of Companies, Subsidiaries & Divisions. Lou R. Kling & Eileen N. Simon. 1000p. 1992. ring bd. 90.00 (*0-317-05390-6*, 00617) NY Law Pub.

N

Negotiated Authorities: Essays in Colonial, Political & Constitutional History. Jack P. Greene. LC 93-42238. 1994. pap. text 22.50 (*0-8139-1517-1*) U Pr of Va.

Negotiated Care: The Experience of Family Day Care Providers. Margaret K. Nelson. 400p. 1991. 37.95 (*0-87722-728-4*) Temple U Pr.

***Negotiated Development: Brokers, Knowledge, Technologies.** Ed. by Thomas Bierschenk & Pierre-Yves Le Meur. 174p. 1998. pap. 24.95 (*3-8258-3234-1*, Pub. by CE24) Transaction Pubs.

Negotiated Development & Open Space Preservation: A Case Study of Neighborhood Purchase & Ultimate City Aquisition Involving Partial Development, Betterment Assessments & Federal Tax Benefits. R. Lisle Baker & Norman H. Wolfe. LC HD0266.M37. (Lincoln Institute Monograph: No. 84-1). 66p. reprint ed. pap. 30.00 (*0-7837-5772-7*, 204543700006) Bks Demand.

***Negotiated Empires: Centers & Peripheries in the New World, 1500-1820.** Ed. by Christine Daniels & Leslie Page Moch. 320p. 2000. 80.00 (*0-415-92538-X*); pap. 19.99 (*0-415-92539-8*) Routledge.

Negotiated Evaluation: Involving Children & Parents in the Process. Helen Woodward. LC 94-27613. 92p. 1994. pap. text 15.00 (*0-435-08822-X*, 08822) Heinemann.

Negotiated Interaction in Target Language Classroom Discourse. Jamila Boulima. LC 99-27156. (Pragmatics & Beyond New Ser.: Vol. 51). xiv, 338p. 1999. lib. bdg. 79.00 (*1-55619-813-2*) J Benjamins Pubng Co.

Negotiated Peace. Wayne C. Miller. LC 97-20289. 160p. 1997. pap. text 26.00 (*0-205-27411-0*) P-H.

Negotiated Rulemaking Sourcebook, 3 vols. 1997. lib. bdg. 999.95 (*0-8490-7745-1*) Gordon Pr.

Negotiated Self: The Dynamics of Identity in Francophone Caribbean Narrative. Anne Malena. LC 97-26600. (Francophone Cultures & Literatures Ser.: Vol. 24). X, 192p. (C). 1999. text 47.95 (*0-8204-3887-1*) P Lang Pubng.

***Negotiated Settlement: The Counter-reformation in Upper Austria under the Habsburgs.** Joseph F. Patrouch. LC 99-98004. (Studies in Central European Histories). 2000. write for info. (*0-391-04099-5*) Humanities.

Negotiated World: 3 Centuries of Change in a French Alpine Community. Harriet G. Rosenberg. (Illus.). 256p. 1988. text 35.00 (*0-8020-2640-0*) U of Toronto Pr.

Negotiating. Pilbeam. 1992. pap. text. write for info. (*0-582-06443-0*, Pub. by Addison-Wesley) Longman.

Negotiating: Everybody Wins: A Practical Guide to Negotiation in Your Workplace & Home. Vanessa Helps. (Illus.). 1996. pap. 9.95 (*0-563-36289-8*, BBC-Parkwest) Parkwest Pubns.

Negotiating a Better Deal. Peter Fleming. LC 97-5333. (Self-Development for Managers Ser.). 192p. 1997. pap. 13.99 (*0-415-12567-7*) Thomson Learn.

Negotiating a Book Contract: A Guide for Authors, Agents & Lawyers. Mark L. Levine. 96p. (Orig.). 1988. pap. 12.95 (*0-918825-69-5*) Moyer Bell.

***Negotiating a Complex World: An Introduction to International Negotiation.** Brigid Starkey et al. LC 99-28471. (New Millennium Books in International Studies). 160p. 1999. pap. 16.95 (*0-8476-9045-8*); text 55.00 (*0-8476-9044-X*) Rowman.

An Asterisk (*) at the beginning of an entry indicates that the title is appearing for the first time.

***Negotiating a Good Death: Euthanasia in the Netherlands Foreign Language.** Robert Pool. LC 00-38286. (Illus.). 262p. 2000. pap. 24.95 (*0-7890-1081-X*) Haworth Pr.

***Negotiating a Good Death: Euthanasia in the Netherlands Foreign Language.** Robert Pool. LC 00-38286. (Illus.). 262p. 2000. lib. bdg. 59.95 (*0-7890-1080-1*) Haworth Pr.

Negotiating a Labor Contract: A Management Handbook. 2nd ed. Charles S. Loughran. LC 92-280. 590p. 1992. trans. 58.00 (*0-87179-745-3*, HD6483) BNA Books.

Negotiating a Minerals Regime for Antarctica, 1981-1988. Christopher C. Joyner & William E. Westernmeyer. (Pew Case Studies in International Affairs). 50p. (C). 1993. pap. text 3.50 (*1-56927-134-8*) Geo U Inst Dplmcy.

Negotiating a U. S. - EURATOM Successor Agreement: Finding Common Ground in Nuclear Cooperation. James R. Schlesinger. 33p. (C). 1994. pap. text 9.95 (*0-89206-258-4*) CSIS.

Negotiating Academic Literacies: Readings on Teaching & Learning Across Cultures. Ed. by Vivian Zamel & Ruth Spack. LC 98-13599. 320p. 1998. pap. write for info. (*0-8058-2998-9*) L Erlbaum Assocs.

Negotiating Access to Higher Education: The Discourse of Selectivity & Equity. E. Williams. LC 96-49719. 1997. pap. 35.95 (*0-335-19678-0*) OpUniv Pr.

Negotiating Across Cultures. Robert Greenleaf. (Management Booklets Ser.). Date not set. write for info. (*1-882390-91-1*) Princeton Trng.

Negotiating Across Cultures: International Communication in an Interdependent World. rev. ed. Raymond Cohen. LC 97-45198. 1997. pap. 19.95 (*1-878379-72-0*) US Inst Peace.

***Negotiating Adolescence in Times of Social Change.** Ed. by Lisa J. Crockett & Rainier K. Silbereisen. LC 99-10716. (Illus.). 344p. (C). 1999. 49.95 (*0-521-62389-8*) Cambridge U Pr.

***Negotiating Agreement & Disagreement in Japanese: Connective Expressions & Turn Construction.** Junko Morimoto. LC 99-40505. (Studies in Discourse & Grammar: Vol. 8). xii, 240p. 1999. 75.00 (*1-55619-374-2*) J Benjamins Pubng.

Negotiating Agriculture in the European Union: From Blair House to the Farm House. Richard Grant, Jr. (Pew Case Studies in International Affairs). 50p. (C). 1995. pap. text 3.50 (*1-56927-167-4*, GU Schl Foreign) Geo U Inst Dplmcy.

Negotiating an International Regime to Mine the Deep Seabed. Robert E. Bowen. (Pew Case Studies in International Affairs). 50p. (C). 1992. pap. 3.50 (*1-56927-423-1*) Geo U Inst Dplmcy.

Negotiating & Contracting for Professional Engineering Services. (National Cooperative Highway Research Program Report Ser.: No. 137). 75p. 1988. 9.60 (*0-309-04422-7*) Transport Res Bd.

Negotiating & Documenting Business Acquisitions. David A. Broadwin. LC 97-70290. 374p. 1997. text 189.50 (*0-8318-0690-7*) Am Law Inst.

Negotiating & Drafting Software Consulting Agreements. Raymond L. Ocamps, Jr. et al. 304p. 1996. ring bd. 119.20 incl. disk (*1-888075-52-X*) Glasser LegalWrks.

Negotiating & Influencing Skills: The Art of Creating & Claiming Value. Brad McRae. LC 97-21051. 176p. 1997. 42.00 (*0-7619-1184-7*) Sage.

Negotiating & Influencing Skills: The Art of Creating & Claiming Value. Brad McRae. LC 97-21051. xii, 195 p. 1998. pap. 19.95 (*0-7619-1185-5*) Sage.

Negotiating Arab-Israeli Peace: Patterns, Problems, Possibilities. Laura Z. Eisenberg & Neil Caplan. LC 97-27408. (Indiana Series in Arab & Islamic Studies). (Illus.). 288p. 1998. 35.00 (*0-253-33368-7*); pap. 16.95 (*0-253-21159-X*) Ind U Pr.

Negotiating Arms Control: Missed Opportunities & Limited Successes. Ed. by Kenneth W. Thompson. (W. Alton Jones Foundation Series on Arms Control). 154p. (C). 1991. pap. text 22.50 (*0-8191-8079-3*, Pub. by White Miller Center); lib. bdg. 41.50 (*0-8191-8078-5*, Pub. by White Miller Center) U Pr of Amer.

Negotiating at an Uneven Table: A Practical Approach to Working with Difference & Diversity. Phyllis B. Kritek. (Conflict Resolution Ser.). 361p. 1996. reprint ed. pap. 23.95 (*0-7879-0254-3*) Jossey-Bass.

Negotiating at the Margins: The Gendered Discourse of Power & Resistance. Sue Fisher & Kathy Davis. LC 92-35965. 335p. (C). 1993. text 45.00 (*0-8135-1970-5*); pap. text 17.00 (*0-8135-1971-3*) Rutgers U Pr.

***Negotiating Boundaries of Southern Womanhood: Dealing with the Powers That Be.** Ed. by Janet L. Coryell et al. 256p. 2000. 34.95 (*0-8262-1295-6*) U of Mo Pr.

Negotiating Business Equipment Leases. rev. ed. Richard M. Contino. 320p. 1998. 49.95 (*0-8144-0417-0*) AMACOM.

Negotiating China: Case Studies & Strategies. Carolyn Blackman. LC 97-199211. 224p. 1997. pap. 24.95 (*1-86448-070-X*, Pub. by Allen & Unwin Pty) Paul & Co Pubs.

Negotiating Commercial Leases: How Owners & Corporate Occupants Can Avoid Costly Errors. John B. Wood. LC 98-230532. (Real Estate Law & Practice Course Handbook Ser.). 624 p. 1997. 129.00 (*0-87224-388-5*) PLI.

Negotiating Commercial Leases: Spring, 1993 Action Guide. Misha D. Weidman. Ed. by Marie Hagelstein. 101p. 1993. pap. text 47.00 (*0-88124-631-X*, RE-11651) Cont Ed Bar-CA.

***Negotiating Commercial Real Estate Leases.** rev. ed. Martin I. Zankel. LC 00-103291. 312p. 2000. pap. 19.95 (*0-940352-14-1*) Mesa Hse.

Negotiating Competitiveness. Wever. 1995. 29.95 (*0-07-103622-9*) McGraw.

Negotiating Competitiveness: Employment Relations & Organizational Innovation in Germany & the United States. Kirsten S. Wever. 256p. 1995. 29.95 (*0-87584-554-1*) Harvard Busn.

Negotiating Computer Contracts. 35.00 (*0-317-29492-X*, #CO3670) Harcourt.

Negotiating Conflict: Insights & Skills for Negotiators & Peacemakers. Mark Anstey. 401p. 1991. pap. text 44.00 (*0-7021-2612-8*, Pub. by Juta & Co) Intl Spec Bk.

Negotiating Consent in Psychotherapy. Patrick O'Neill. LC 98-25349. (Qualitative Studies in Psychology Ser.). 200p. 1998. text 55.00 (*0-8147-6194-1*); pap. text 18.50 (*0-8147-6195-X*) NYU Pr.

Negotiating Control: A Study of News Sources. Richard V. Ericson et al. 438p. 1989. 45.00 (*0-335-15867-6*); pap. 16.99 (*0-335-15866-8*) OpUniv Pr.

Negotiating Control: A Study of News Sources. Richard V. Ericson et al. (Illus.). 436p. 1989. pap. 19.95 (*0-8020-6691-7*) U of Toronto Pr.

Negotiating Cooperation: The United States & China, 1969-1989. Robert S. Ross. 1995. 39.50 (*0-8047-2453-9*) Stanford U Pr.

Negotiating Cooperation: The United States & China, 1969-1989. Robert S. Ross. 1997. pap. text 17.95 (*0-8047-2454-7*) Stanford U Pr.

***Negotiating Critical Literacies in the Classroom.** Ed. by Barbara Comber & Anne Simpson. 400p. 2000. pap. write for info. (*0-8058-3794-9*) L Erlbaum Assocs.

***Negotiating Culture & Human Rights: Beyond Universalism & Relativism.** Ed. by Lynda Bell et al. 364p. 2000. text 40.00 (*0-231-12080-X*); pap. text 19.50 (*0-231-12081-8*) Col U Pr.

Negotiating Daily Life in Traditional China: How Ordinary People Used Contracts, 600-1400. Valerie Hansen. LC 94-49177. 285p. 1995. 37.00 (*0-300-06063-7*) Yale U Pr.

Negotiating Democracy: Politicians & Generals in Uruguay. Charles G. Gillespie. (Cambridge Latin American Studies: No. 72). 282p. (C). 1991. text 80.00 (*0-521-40152-6*) Cambridge U Pr.

Negotiating Democracy: Transitions from Authoritarian Rule. Gretchen Casper & Michelle M. Taylor. LC 96-3224. (Pitt Series in Policy & Institutional). 288p. 1996. pap. 19.95 (*0-8229-5588-1*); text 44.95 (*0-8229-3931-2*) U of Pittsburgh Pr.

Negotiating Development: Labour Relations & Development in Southern Asia. Johannes Schregle. vi, 196p. 1982. 36.00 (*92-2-103026-1*) Intl Labour Office.

Negotiating Development Assistance: USAID & the Choice Between Public & Private Implementation in Haiti. Charles Downs. (Pew Case Studies in International Affairs). 50p. (C). 1994. pap. text 3.50 (*1-56927-207-7*) Geo U Inst Dplmcy.

Negotiating Difference. Patricia Bizzell & Bruce Herzberg. 963p. 1995. pap. text 38.95 (*0-312-06846-8*) St Martin.

Negotiating Difference: Race, Gender & the Politics of Positionality. Michael Awkward. (Illus.). 240p. 1995. pap. text 14.95 (*0-226-03301-5*); lib. bdg. 42.50 (*0-226-03300-7*) U Ch Pr.

Negotiating Differences. Bizzell. 1995. pap. text 5.00 (*0-312-11706-X*) St Martin.

Negotiating Different Rules. 3rd ed. Bizzell. 1996. pap. text 31.50 (*0-312-14963-8*) St Martin.

Negotiating Domestic Violence: Police, Criminal Justice & Victims. Carolyn Hoyle. (Clarendon Studies in Criminology). 272p. 1998. text 65.00 (*0-19-826773-8*, Clarendon Pr) OUP.

***Negotiating Domestic Violence: Police, Criminal Justice, & Victims.** Carolyn Hoyle. (Clarendon Studies in Criminology). 266p. 2000. pap. text 29.95 (*0-19-829930-3*) OUP.

Negotiating, Drafting & Enforcing Noncompetition Agreements: Includes Forms on Disk. Laurence H. Reece, III. Ed. by Laurie S. Gill. LC 97-70626. 112p. 1997. pap. text 59.00 incl. disk (*1-57589-063-1*, 97-04.40-QC) Mass CLE.

Negotiating Employee Resignations. 2nd ed. Lee T. Paterson. 120p. 1991. pap. 29.50 (*1-55943-125-3*, MICHIE) LEXIS Pub.

Negotiating Enterprise Agreements in the Federal System. I. Ross. 100p. 1996. pap. write for info. (*0-409-31113-8*, MICHIE) LEXIS Pub.

Negotiating Environmental Agreements: How to Avoid Escalating Confrontation, Needless Costs & Unnecessary Litigation. Lawrence Susskind et al. LC 99-37187. (Illus.). 300p. (C). 2000. pap. 35.00 (*1-55963-633-5*) Island Pr.

***Negotiating Environmental Quality: Policy Implementation in Germany & the U. S.** Markus A. Lehmann. LC 00-37609. (New Horizons in Environmental Economics Ser.). 272p. 2000. text 95.00 (*1-85898-976-0*) E Elgar.

Negotiating Ethnicities in China & Taiwan. Ed. by Melissa Brown. (China Research Monographs: No. 46). (Illus.). 335p. (C). 1995. pap. 20.00 (*1-55729-048-2*) IEAS.

Negotiating Faculty Productivity: The Montana Case. Richard A. Crofts. 1995. 10.00 (*0-614-13552-4*) SHEEO.

***Negotiating Flexibility The Role of the Social Partners & the State.** International Labour Office Staff. 1999. pap. 14.95 (*92-2-110865-1*) Intl Labour Office.

Negotiating Flexible & Compressed Work Schedules. 1997. lib. bdg. 250.75 (*0-8490-7723-0*) Gordon Pr.

Negotiating for Amenities: Zoning & Management Tools That Build Livable Cities, Pt. II: Models & Resources. Clint Page & Penelope Cuff. (Illus.). 80p. (Orig.). 1982. pap. 12.50 (*0-941182-06-1*) Partners Livable.

Negotiating for Business Results. Judith E. Fisher. LC 93-41065. (Business Skills Express Ser.). 96p. 1993. pap. 10.95 (*0-7863-0114-7*, Irwn Prfssnl) McGraw-Hill Prof.

Negotiating for Dummies. Michael Donaldson & Mimi Donaldson. (For Dummies Ser.). 384p. 1996. pap. 19.99 (*1-56884-867-6*) IDG Bks.

***Negotiating for Dummies: A Reference for the Rest of Us!** abr. ed. Michael Donaldson & Mimi Donaldson. 1998. audio 12.00 (*0-694-51917-0*) HarperAudio.

***Negotiating for Dummies/Leadership for Dummies, 2 vols.** IDG Books Staff. (For Dummies Ser.). (Illus.). 2000. pap. 29.99 (*0-7645-8147-3*) IDG Bks.

Negotiating for Entry: The Accession of Greece to the European Community. Iacovos S. Tsalicoglou. 224p. 1995. text 77.95 (*1-85521-227-7*, Pub. by Dartmth Pub) Ashgate Pub Co.

Negotiating for International Development. Russell B. Sunshine. (C). 1990. lib. bdg. 121.50 (*0-7923-0636-8*) Kluwer Academic.

Negotiating for Results. Kandy Kidd. LC 88-72063. 100p. 1988. pap. 9.95 (*0-937751-33-2*) Brendon Hill Pub.

Negotiating for Your Life: New Success Strategies for Women. Nicole Schapiro. 88p. 1995. 22.50 (*0-8050-1383-0*); pap. 12.95 (*0-8050-3554-0*) H Holt & Co.

Negotiating Freer Trade: The United Kingdom, the United States, Canada & the Trade Agreements of 1938. Ian M. Drummond & Norman Hillmer. (Illus.). 200p. (C). 1989. text 35.00 (*0-88920-970-7*) W Laurier U Pr.

Negotiating from Strength: Leverage in U. S.-Soviet Arms Control Negotiations, 113. Robert J. Einhorn. LC 85-3409. (Washington Papers). 136p. 1985. 59.95 (*0-275-90090-8*, C0090, Praeger Pubs) Greenwood.

Negotiating Game. Chester L. Karrass. 272p. 1994. pap. 13.00 (*0-88730-709-4*, HarpBusn) HarpInfo.

Negotiating Graduate School: A Guide for Graduate Students. Mark H. Rossman. LC 95-3258. 160p. 1995. 42.00 (*0-8039-7114-1*); pap. 19.50 (*0-8039-7115-X*) Sage.

Negotiating Health Care: The Social Context of Chronic Illness. Sally E. Thorne. (Illus.). 280p. (C). 1993. text 48.00 (*0-8039-4917-0*); pap. text 22.95 (*0-8039-4918-9*) Sage.

Negotiating Health Insurance in the Workplace: A Basic Guide. Suzanne S. Taylor. LC 92-11190. 346p. 1992. trans. 48.00 (*0-87179-731-3*) BNA Books.

Negotiating Hollywood: The Cultural Politics of Actors' Labor. Danae Clark. LC 94-46538. 1995. text 44.95 (*0-8166-2544-1*); pap. text 17.95 (*0-8166-2545-X*) U of Minn Pr.

Negotiating Identities: Women in the Indian Diaspora. Aparna Rayaprol. LC 97-903275. 180p. 1998. 19.95 (*0-19-564151-5*) OUP.

Negotiating Identity: Catholic Higher Education since 1960. Alice Gallin. LC 99-88281. 280p. 2000. 32.00 (*0-268-01489-2*, Pub. by U of Notre Dame Pr) Chicago Distribution Ctr.

Negotiating Identity: Rhetoric, Metaphor & Social Drama in Northern Ireland. Anthony D. Buckley & Mary C. Kenney. LC 94-47184. 288p. 1995. text 44.50 (*1-56098-520-8*) Smithsonian.

Negotiating Identity in Contemporary Japan: The Case of the Kikokushijo. Ching-Lin Pang. (Japanese Studies Ser.). 220p. 1999. 110.00 (*0-7103-0651-2*, Pub. by Kegan Paul Intl) Col U Pr.

Negotiating in German: A Dual Language Guide. Ulrich Hoffmann & Michael Tobin. (GER.). 136p. 1994. 17.50 (*3-468-42611-9*) Langenscheidt.

Negotiating in Organizations. Ed. by Max H. Bazerman & Roy J. Lewicki. LC 83-10156. 392p. 1983. reprint ed. pap. 121.60 (*0-608-01184-3*, 205948200001) Bks Demand.

Negotiating in Practice. Keith Sisson. 202p. (C). 1977. 50.00 (*0-85292-153-5*, Pub. by IPM Hse) St Mut.

Negotiating in the Public Eye: The Impact of the Press on the Intermediate-Range Nuclear Force Negotiations. Marc A. Genest. LC 94-28866. xiv, 189p. 1995. 32.50 (*0-8047-2439-3*) Stanford U Pr.

***Negotiating in the Real World: Getting the Deal You Want.** Victor Gotbaum. LC 98-50658. 192p. 1999. 24.00 (*0-684-81543-5*) S&S Trade.

***Negotiating in the Real World: Getting the Deal You Want.** Victor Gotbaum. 192p. 2000. per. 13.00 (*0-684-86555-6*) S&S Trade.

***Negotiating India in the 19th Century Media: Negotiating India in the Nineteenth Cent.** David Finkelstein & Douglas M. Peers. LC 00-27823. 2000. write for info. (*0-312-23465-1*) St Martin.

Negotiating International Hotel Chain Management Agreements: A Primer for Hotel Owners in Developing Countries. (UNCTC Advisory Studies: No. 5). 66p. pap. 15.00 (*92-1-104337-9*, E.90.II.A.8) UN.

Negotiating International Joint Venture Agreements Stephen Sayer. LC 98-215879. 1998. write for info. (*0-421-63140-6*) Sweet & Maxwell.

Negotiating International Regimes: Lessons Learned from the U. N. Conference on Environment & Development. Bertram I. Spector. (International Environmental Law & Policy Ser.). 288p. 1994. lib. bdg. 126.50 (*1-85966-077-0*) Kluwer Academic.

***Negotiating Intimacies: Sexualities, Birth Control & Poor Households.** Arna Seal. 2000. 24.00 (*81-85604-29-0*, Pub. by Stree) S Asia.

Negotiating Jerusalem. Jerome M. Segal et al. LC 99-41586. (C). 2000. text 92.50 (*0-7914-4537-2*); pap. text 31.95 (*0-7914-4538-0*) State U NY Pr.

Negotiating Justice: A New Constitution for South Africa. Ed. by Malyn D. D. Newitt & Mervyn Bennum. LC 96-140518. 208p. 1995. pap. text 19.95 (*0-85989-459-2*, Pub. by Univ Exeter Pr) Northwestern U Pr.

Negotiating Language, Constructing Race: Disciplining Difference in Singapore. PuruShotam & Nirmala Srirekam. LC 97-40999. (Contributions to the Sociology of Language Ser.: No. 79). 294p. 1997. 118.65 (*3-11-015679-2*) De Gruyter.

Negotiating Lesbian & Gay Subjects. Ed. by Monica Dorenkamp & Richard Henke. 256p. (C). (gr. 13). 1994. 70.00 (*0-415-90832-9*, B2301); pap. 19.99 (*0-415-90833-7*, B2305) Routledge.

Negotiating Limits on Unitary Taxation in the United States. John M. Kline. (Pew Case Studies in International Affairs). 50p. (C). 1992. pap. 3.50 (*1-56927-402-9*) Geo U Inst Dplmcy.

Negotiating Love: How Men & Women Can Resolve Their Differences. Riki R. Jones. 336p. (Orig.). 1995. pap. 11.00 (*0-345-39061-X*) Ballantine Pub Grp.

Negotiating Managed Care Contracts. 250p. 1998. pap. 75.00 (*1-58383-011-1*, MANCRE9) Robert D Keene.

Negotiating Mineral Industry Agreements & Contracts. (ST-ESCAP Ser.: No. 1267). 323p. 95.00 (*92-1-119673-6*) UN.

Negotiating Mining Agreements: Past, Present & Future Trends. Daniele Barberis. LC 98-30195. (International Energy & Resources Law & Policy Ser.). 288p. 1998. 111.00 (*90-411-9673-0*) Kluwer Academic.

***Negotiating Modernity: Myth in the Theatre of Eliot, O'Neill & Sartre.** Krishna Sen. 1999. 20.00 (*81-85195-94-3*, Pub. by Minerva Assocs) S Asia.

***Negotiating Multiculturalism: Disciplining Difference in Singapore.** Nirmala Purushotam. LC 00-25550. 2000. write for info. (*3-11-015680-6*) De Gruyter.

Negotiating NAFTA: A Mexican Envoy's Account, 173. Hermann Von Bertrab. LC 96-54796. (Washington Papers: Vol. 173). 200p. 1997. 52.95 (*0-275-95934-1*, Praeger Pubs); pap. 15.95 (*0-275-95935-X*, Praeger Pubs) Greenwood.

Negotiating National Identity: Immigrants, Minorities, & the Struggle for Ethnicity in Brazil. Jeff Lesser. LC 98-38238. 1999. 49.95 (*0-8223-2260-9*); pap. 17.95 (*0-8223-2292-7*) Duke.

Negotiating Natural Gas Contracts in the Order 636 Environment. (Mineral Law Ser.). 1993. student ed. 125.00 (*0-929047-40-0*) Rocky Mtn Mineral Law Found.

Negotiating Negotiations. J. Seitz. 1991. teacher ed. 12.81 (*0-07-062579-4*) McGraw.

***Negotiating on the Edge: North Korean Negotiating Behavior.** Scott Snyder. LC 99-48064. 236p. 1999. 37.50 (*1-878379-95-X*); pap. 17.50 (*1-878379-94-1*) US Inst Peace.

***Negotiating Paradox - How You Get More by Giving More.** Bernard H. Zick. LC 99-29258. 270p. 2000. 29.95 (*1-881554-00-7*, Pub. by Skyward Pub) Herveys Bklink.

Negotiating Parent-Adolescent Conflict: A Behavioral-Family Systems Approach. Arthur L. Robin & Sharon L. Foster. LC 87-31502. (Family Therapy Ser.). 338p. 1989. lib. bdg. 39.95 (*0-89862-072-4*) Guilford Pubns.

Negotiating Past & Present: Studies in Spanish Literature for Javier Herrero. Ed. by David T. Gies. LC 96-29466. (Illus.). 300p. 1997. lib. bdg. 49.95 (*1-886365-04-0*) Rookwood Pr.

Negotiating Peace El Salvador: Civil-Military Relations & the Conspiracy to End the War. Juhn. LC 97-50076. 245p. 1998. text 59.95 (*0-312-21060-4*) St Martin.

Negotiating Performance: Gender, Sexuality, & Theatricality in Latin-o America. Ed. by Diana Taylor & Juan Villegas. LC 94-27647. (Illus.). 368p. 1994. text 59.95 (*0-8223-1504-1*); pap. text 18.95 (*0-8223-1515-7*) Duke.

***Negotiating Persuading & Influencing.** Alan Fowler. 96p. 2000. pap. 17.95 (*0-8464-5122-0*) Beekman Pubs.

***Negotiating Physics.** David Manning. 32p. 1999. pap. text 7.95 (*1-884778-59-3*) Old Mountain.

Negotiating Positive Identity in a Group Care Community: Reclaiming Uprooted Youth. Intro. by Zvi Levy. LC 93-34917. (Child & Youth Services Ser.: Vol. 16, No. 2). (Illus.). 141p. 1993. lib. bdg. 39.95 (*1-56024-514-X*) Haworth Pr.

Negotiating Rapture. Ed. by Richard Frances & Sophia Shaw. LC 95-81492. (Illus.). 224p. 1996. pap. 29.95 (*0-933856-40-7*) Mus Art Chicago.

Negotiating Rationally. Max H. Bazerman & Margaret A. Neale. (Illus.). 288p. 1992. 29.95 (*0-02-901985-0*) Free Pr.

Negotiating Rationally. Max H. Bazerman & Margaret A. Neale. (Illus.). 288p. 1994. per. 16.95 (*0-02-901986-9*) Free Pr.

Negotiating Realities: Making Sense of Interaction Between Patients Diagnosed As Neurotic & Nurses. Stephen Tilley. 448p. (C). 1995. text 101.95 (*1-85628-939-7*, Pub. by Avebry) Ashgate Pub Co.

Negotiating Reproductive Right: Women's Perspectives Across Countries & Cultures. Rosalind Petchesky. LC 98-19802. 320p. 1998. text 69.95 (*1-85649-535-3*, Pub. by Manchester Univ Pr) St Martin.

Negotiating Reproductive Right: Women's Perspectives Across Countries & Cultures, Vol. 1. Petchesky. LC 98-19802. 320p. 1998. pap. 25.00 (*1-85649-536-1*, Pub. by Zed Books) St Martin.

Negotiating Responsibility in the Criminal Justice System. Ed. by Jack B. Kamerman. LC 98-5414. (Elmer H. Johnson & Carol Holmes Johnson Ser.). 304p. 1998. 49.95 (*0-8093-2211-0*); pap. 21.95 (*0-8093-2212-9*) S Ill U Pr.

Negotiating Settlements: A Guide to Environmental Mediation. Jane McCarthy & Alice Shorett. LC 84-70963. 120p. 1984. pap. 10.00 (*0-318-43199-8*) Am Arbitration.

***Negotiating Skills.** Astrid French. 96p. 2000. pap. 12.95 (*1-85835-574-5*, Pub. by Stylus Pub VA) LPC InBook.

An Asterisk (*) at the beginning of an entry indicates that the title is appearing for the first time.

Negotiating Skills. Ann Halpern. 120p. (C). 1992. 31.00 (*1-85431-170-0*, Pub. by Blackstone Pr) Gaunt.

Negotiating Skills in Engineering & Construction. Bill Scotts. (C). 1990. text 39.95 (*0-442-30316-5*, VNR) Wiley.

***Negotiating Skills in the Workplace, Set.** (Essential Business Skills Ser.). 1999. pap., wbk. ed. 129.00 incl. audio AMACOM.

***Negotiating Small Truths.** Annette D. Carlozzi. (Illus.). 1999. pap. write for info. (*0-935213-24-4*) J S Blanton Mus.

Negotiating Space: Power Restraint, & Privileges of Immunity in Early Medieval Europe. Barbara H. Rosenwein. LC 98-31501. 328p. 1999. 55.00 (*0-8014-3523-4*); pap. 18.95 (*0-8014-8521-5*) Cornell U Pr.

Negotiating START: Strategic Arms Reduction Talks & the Quest for Strategic Stability. Kerry M. Kartchner. 324p. (C). 1991. text 44.95 (*0-88738-431-5*) Transaction Pubs.

Negotiating Stock Photo Prices, 1997. 4th ed. Jim Pickerell & Cheryl Pickerell. 272p. 1997. pap. 30.00 (*1-886469-04-0*) Stock Connect.

Negotiating Structural Adjustment in Africa. Willem Van Der Geest. LC 94-20204. 230p. 1994. 60.00 (*0-435-08960-9*, 08960) Heinemann.

Negotiating Survival: Four Priorities after Rio. Richard N. Gardner. LC 92-32956. 96p. 1992. reprint ed. pap. 30.00 (*0-608-02001-X*, 206265700003) Bks Demand.

Negotiating Techniques: How to Work Toward a Constructive Agreement. Ross R. Reck & Brian Long. Ed. by Robert F. Guder. 1985. 14.95 (*0-910187-05-3*) Economics Pr.

***Negotiating Techniques in International Commercial Contracts.** 166p. 2000. 69.95 (*0-7546-2031-X*, Pub. by Ashgate Pub) Ashgate Pub Co.

Negotiating Telecommunication Contracts. 35.00 (*0-317-29495-4*, #CO3301) Harcourt.

Negotiating Telecommunications Contracts. annuals 2nd ed. Henry D. Levine & Roger M. Witten. v, 301p. write for info. (*0-318-61625-4*) Harcourt.

Negotiating Telecommunications Contracts: Business & Legal Aspects. Henry D. Levine & David R. Anderson. (Illus.). vi, 457p. write for info. (*0-318-60200-8*) Harcourt.

Negotiating the Boundary: The Response of Kwa Mashu Zionists to a Volatile Political Climate. Matthias Mohr. 288p. 1997. pap. text 38.95 (*3-8258-3015-2*) Transaction Pubs.

Negotiating the Commercial Lease. 1997. 99.00 incl. audio PA Bar Inst.

Negotiating the Constitution: The Earliest Debates over Original Intent. Joseph M. Lynch. LC 98-43447. 1999. 42.50 (*0-8014-3558-7*) Cornell U Pr.

Negotiating the Contract. Duane Beeler. 139p. (Orig.). 1981. pap. 4.95 (*0-317-12243-6*) Union Rep.

Negotiating the Crisis: DRGs & the Transformation of Hospitals. Patricia Geist. 1996. pap. 32.50 (*0-8058-0458-7*) L Erlbaum Assocs.

Negotiating the Curriculum. Ed. by Garth Boomer et al. 224p. 1992. 89.95 (*1-85000-931-7*, Falmer Pr); pap. 29.95 (*1-85000-937-6*, Falmer Pr) Taylor & Francis.

Negotiating the Disability Maze: Critical Knowledge for Parents, Professionals, & Other Caring Persons. 2nd ed. Les Sternberg et al. LC 96-18286. 206p. 1996. text 51.95 (*0-398-06663-9*); pap. text 36.95 (*0-398-06664-7*) C C Thomas.

Negotiating the End of Conflicts II: Namibia & Zimbabwe. (Reports: No. 9). 119p. 1980. 3.50 (*0-937722-14-6*) Intl Peace.

Negotiating the Future: A Labor Perspective on American Business. Barry Bluestone & Irving Bluestone. LC 91-59007. 352p. 1994. pap. 13.00 (*0-465-04918-4*, Pub. by Basic) HarpC.

Negotiating the Game Vol. 1: New Perspectives on Negotiating. unabridged ed. Herb Cohen. 1993. audio 11.00 (*1-55994-711-X*, CPN 1956) HarperAudio.

Negotiating the Glass Ceiling: Careers of Senior Women in the Academic World. Miriam David. 216p. 1998. 85.00 (*0-7507-0837-9*, Falmer Pr) Taylor & Francis.

Negotiating the Gray Maze: The Business of Medicine in Japan. Mark A. Colby & Michael P. Birt. 176p. 1998. 24.95 (*1-891640-00-3*) Float World.

Negotiating the Law of the Sea. James K. Sebenius. LC 83-20163. (Economic Studies: No. 154). (Illus.). 264p. 1984. 24.95 (*0-674-60686-8*) HUP.

Negotiating the Maze of School Reform: How Metaphor Shapes Culture in a New Magnet School. Jean Wincek. 160p. (C). 1995. text 34.00 (*0-8077-3413-6*); pap. text 16.95 (*0-8077-3412-8*) Tchrs Coll.

Negotiating the New Germany: Can Social Partnership Survive? Ed. by Lowell Turner. LC 97-29480. 288p. 1998. pap. 17.95 (*0-8014-8444-8*) Cornell U Pr.

Negotiating the New Germany: Can Social Partnership Survive? Ed. by Lowell Turner. LC 97-29480. (Illus.). 288p. 1998. text 45.00 (*0-8014-3420-3*) Cornell U Pr.

Negotiating the New Ocean Regime. Robert L. Friedheim. LC 92-23764. (Illus.). 431p. 1993. text 49.95 (*0-87249-838-7*) U of SC Pr.

Negotiating the 1988 U. S.-Soviet Long-Term Agreements on Grain Purchases. Charles Benjamin & Charles Powell. (Pew Case Studies in International Affairs). 1988p. (C). 1988. pap. text 3.50 (*1-56927-131-3*) Geo U Inst Dplmcy.

Negotiating the Pacific Century. Roger Bell et al. LC 96-184999. 324p. 1997. pap. text 29.95 (*1-86448-067-X*, Pub. by Allen & Unwin Pty) Paul & Co Pubs.

Negotiating the Past: The Historical Understanding of Medieval Literature. Lee Patterson. LC 87-40144. 253p. 1987. reprint ed. pap. 78.50 (*0-608-01860-0*, 206251100003) Bks Demand.

Negotiating the Past: The Making of National Historic Parks & Sites. C. J. Taylor. 288p. (C). 1990. text 60.00 (*0-7735-0713-2*, Pub. by McG-Queens Univ Pr) CUP Services.

Negotiating the Special Education Maze: A Guide for Parents & Teachers. 3rd ed. Winifred Anderson et al. LC 96-37779. 264p. (Orig.). 1997. pap. 16.95 (*0-933149-72-7*) Woodbine House.

***Negotiating the Therapeutic Alliance: A Relational Treatment Guide.** J. Christopher Muran & Jeremy D. Safran. LC 99-57055. 264p. 2000. lib. bdg. 32.50 (*1-57230-512-6*, CO512) Guilford Pubns.

***Negotiating the World Economy.** John S. Odell. LC 99-55906. (Studies in Political Economy). 288p. 2000. 19.95 (*0-8014-8646-7*) Cornell U Pr.

Negotiating Time: New Scheduling Options in the Legal Profession. Karyn L. Feiden & Linda Marks. LC 86-62234. 80p. (Orig.). 1986. pap. text 14.00 (*0-940173-06-9*) New Ways Work.

Negotiating to Launch Negotiations: Getting Trade in Services onto the GATT Agenda. Jonathan Aronson. (Pew Case Studies in International Affairs). 50p. (C). 1992. pap. text 3.50 (*1-56927-125-9*) Geo U Inst Dplmcy.

Negotiating to Settlement in Divorce. Ed. by Sanford N. Katz. 212p. 1987. ring bd. 75.00 (*0-13-610932-2*) Aspen Law.

Negotiating to Settlement in Divorce. Sanford N. Katz. 35.00 (*0-317-29651-5*, #CO3689) Harcourt.

***Negotiating Water Rights.** Ed. by Bryan Randolph Burns & Ruth S. Meinzen-Dick. 326p. 2000. pap. 25.00 (*1-85339-484-X*, Pub. by Intermed Tech) Stylus Pub VA.

Negotiating Wire Transfer Agreements: A Guide for Treasury Executives, Bankers & Attorneys. Paul S. Turner. 157p. 1996. pap. 152.50 (*0-9614799-5-7*) Treasry Mgmt.

Negotiating with ETA: Obstacles to Peace in the Basque Country, 1975-1988. Robert P. Clark. LC 90-33577. (Basque Ser.). (Illus.). 296p. 1990. text 39.95 (*0-87417-162-8*) U of Nev Pr.

Negotiating with Insight. Michael Lawlor. (C). 1992. 36.00 incl. audio (*0-85171-089-1*, Pub. by IPM Hse) St Mut.

Negotiating with Terrorists: TWA Flight 847. Rodney A. Snyder. (Pew Case Studies in International Affairs). 50p. (C). 1994. pap. text 3.50 (*1-56927-333-2*) Geo U Inst Dplmcy.

Negotiating with the Chinese. Bee C. Goh. (Illus.). 202p. 1996. text 78.95 (*1-85521-889-5*, Pub. by Dartmth Pub) Ashgate Pub Co.

Negotiating with the Russians on Nuclear Arms: Lawyers Making a Difference. John H. Downs. LC 96-49100. 294p. 1997. 64.50 (*0-7618-0649-0*); pap. 41.50 (*0-7618-0650-4*) U Pr of Amer.

Negotiating with the Soviets. Raymond F. Smith. LC 88-46014. 160p. 1989. 31.95 (*0-253-35285-1*); pap. 11.95 (*0-253-20535-2*, MB-535) Ind U Pr.

Negotiating World Order: The Artisanship & Architecture of Global Diplomacy. Ed. by Alan K. Henrikson. LC 86-6544. 265p. 1986. 45.00 (*0-8420-2239-2*) Scholarly Res Inc.

Negotiating Your Contracts. Paul F. Rice. 8p. (Orig.). 1988. 3.95 (*0-9620188-5-6*) Lifestyle Group.

Negotiating Your Salary: How to Make $1000 a Minute. Jack Chapman. LC 96-225201. Orig. Title: How to Make 1000 Dollars a Minute Negotiating Your Salaries & Raises. 130p. (Orig.). 1996. pap. 11.95 (*0-89815-890-7*) Ten Speed Pr.

Negotiation. Roy J. Lewicki & Joseph A. Litterer. 368p. (C). 1985. text 49.95 (*0-256-02633-5*, Irwn McGrw-H) McGrw-H Hghr Educ.

Negotiation. John S. Murray et al. (Paralegal). 236p. 1996. pap. text 13.50 (*1-56662-424-X*) Foundation Pr.

Negotiation. Diana Tribe. Ed. by Julie Macfarlane. (Legal Skills Ser.). 135p. 1994. pap. 28.00 (*1-874241-41-4*, Pub. by Cavendish Pubng) Gaunt.

Negotiation. 2nd ed. Roy J. Lewicki et al. LC 93-40307. 496p. (C). 1994. text 51.95 (*0-256-10163-9*, Irwn McGrw-H) McGrw-H Hghr Educ.

Negotiation: Process, Tactics, Theory. 2nd rev. ed. David Churchman. LC 95-10748. Orig. Title: Negotiation Tactics. 104p. (C). 1995. pap. text 16.00 (*0-8191-9947-8*); lib. bdg. 37.50 (*0-8191-9946-X*) U Pr of Amer.

Negotiation: Readings, Cases & Exercises. 3rd ed. Roy J. Lewicki. LC 99-10103. (Illus.). 528p. (C). 1999. text 59.25 (*0-256-20832-8*, Irwn McGrw-H) McGrw-H Hghr Educ.

Negotiation: Readings, Exercises & Cases. Roy J. Lewicki & Joseph A. Litterer. (C). 1985. pap. text 29.95 (*0-256-02634-3*, Irwn McGrw-H) McGrw-H Hghr Educ.

Negotiation: Readings, Exercises & Cases. 2nd ed. Roy J. Lewicki et al. LC 92-11882. 784p. (C). 1992. text 37.25 (*0-256-10164-7*, Irwn McGrw-H) McGrw-H Hghr Educ.

Negotiation: Readings, Exercises & Cases. 3rd ed. Lewicki. LC 97-44924. 1998. text 29.80 (*0-256-21591-X*, Irwn McGrw-H) McGrw-H Hghr Educ.

***Negotiation: Settling Conflicts & Identifying Opportunities: Papers from the AAAI Workshop.** Ed. by Sandip Sen. (Technical Reports: Vol. WS-99-12). (Illus.). 66p. 1999. spiral bd. 25.00 (*1-57735-096-0*) AAAI Pr.

Negotiation: Skills & Strategies. Alan Fowler. 152p. (C). 1990. 70.00 (*0-7855-4555-7*, Pub. by IPM Hse); 75.00 (*0-7855-5348-7*, Pub. by IPM Hse) St Mut.

Negotiation: Skills & Strategies. Alan Fowler. 192p. 1996. pap. 60.00 (*0-85292-664-2*, Pub. by IPM Hse) St Mut.

Negotiation: Strategies for Mutual Gain. Lavinia Hall. (Illus.). 224p. 1992. 48.00 (*0-8039-4849-2*); pap. 23.50 (*0-8039-4850-6*) Sage.

Negotiation: The Alternative to Hostility. Jimmy Carter. LC 84-10720. (Carl Vinson Memorial Lecture). (Illus.). xxxiii, 57p. 1984. 12.95 (*0-86554-137-X*, MUP/H128) Mercer Univ Pr.

Negotiation: Theories, Strategies & Skills. rev. ed. Wynand Pienaar & Manie Spoelstra. 258p. 1994. reprint ed. text 39.60 (*0-7021-2485-0*, Pub. by Juta & Co) Intl Spec Bk.

Negotiation: Theories, Strategies & Skills. 2nd ed. W. Pienaar. LC 96-220533. 272p. 1996. pap. 40.00 (*0-7021-3578-X*, Pub. by Juta & Co) Gaunt.

Negotiation: Theory & Practice. Ed. by J. William Breslin & Jeffrey Z. Rubin. 460p. (Orig.). (C). 1991. pap. 20.00 (*1-880711-00-1*, Pon Bks) Prog Negot HLS.

Negotiation: Theory & Practice. McCall. (C). 1992. pap. text. write for info. (*0-201-56510-2*) Addison-Wesley.

Negotiation - Dispute Resolution: Module 13, Module 13. Deborah Ancona et al. (GI - Organizational Behavior Ser.). 1995. text 7.95 (*0-538-85893-1*) S-W Pub.

Negotiation Analysis. Ed. by H. Peyton Young. (Illus.). 216p. 1991. pap. text 21.95 (*0-472-08157-8*, 08157) U of Mich Pr.

Negotiation Analysis. Ed. by H. Peyton Young. (Illus.). 216p. 1992. text 65.00 (*0-472-10251-6*, 10251) U of Mich Pr.

Negotiation & Administration of Hotel & Restaurant Management Contracts. James J. Eyster. 221p. 1992. 60.00 (*0-937056-04-9*) Cornell U Sch Hotel.

***Negotiation & Conflict Resolution.** LC 99-28453. (Review Paperback Ser.). 2000. pap. 19.95 (*1-57851-236-0*) Harvard Busn.

Negotiation & Conflict Resolution. Gerald R. Williams. 101p. 1992. pap. text 285.00 (*0-943380-91-X*) PEG MN.

Negotiation & Conflict Resolution. rev. ed. Gerald R. Williams. 107p. 1998. pap. 185.00 incl. audio (*0-943380-35-9*) PEG MN.

Negotiation & Contract Management: Proceedings of a Symposium Sponsored by the Engineering Management Division. Ed. by David C. Johnston. 50p. 1985. 16.00 (*0-87262-454-4*) Am Soc Civil Eng.

Negotiation & Settlement Advocacy: A Book of Readings. Charles B. Wiggins & L. Randolph Lowry. 290p. (C). 1997. pap. 27.50 (*0-314-22586-2*) West Pub.

Negotiation & Social Space: A Gendered Analysis of Changing Kin & Security Networks in South Asia & Sub-Saharan Africa. Ed. by Carla Risseeux & Kamela Ganesh. LC 98-24651. 360p. 1999. 44.95 (*0-7619-9270-7*) Sage.

***Negotiation as a Healing Process.** Gerald R. Williams. 105p. 1999. pap. text 15.95 (*0-943380-92-8*) PEG MN.

Negotiation Basics: Concepts, Skills, & Exercises. Ralph A. Johnson. LC 92-35503. 1993. 42.00 (*0-8039-4051-3*); pap. 17.95 (*0-8039-4052-1*) Sage.

Negotiation Eclectics: Essays in Memory of Jeffrey Z. Rubin. Ed. & Intro. by Deborah M. Kolb, & Associates Staff. 362p. (C). 1998. 25.00 (*1-880711-12-5*, Pon Bks); pap. 20.00 (*1-880711-13-3*, Pon Bks) Prog Negot HLS.

Negotiation for Health & Social Service Professionals. Keith Fletcher. LC 98-150929. 160p. 1997. pap. 26.95 (*1-85302-549-6*, Pub. by Jessica Kingsley) Taylor & Francis.

Negotiation from Strength: A Study in the Politics of Power. Coral Bell. LC 77-1054. 248p. 1977. reprint ed. lib. bdg. 65.00 (*0-8371-9508-X*, BENS, Greenwood Pr) Greenwood.

Negotiation in Dietetic Practice. Darlene Dougherty. (Audio Cassette Ser.). 1990. student ed. 25.00 incl. audio (*0-88091-081-X*, 1213) Am Dietetic Assn.

Negotiation in Its Social Context. Roderick M. Kramer & David M. Messick. 336p. 1995. text 55.00 (*0-8039-5737-8*); pap. text 26.00 (*0-8039-5738-6*) Sage.

Negotiation in Social Conflict. Dean G. Pruitt & Peter J. Carnevale. Ed. by Anthony S. Manstead. (Mapping Social Psychology Ser.). 192p. 1993. 9.00 (*0-335-09866-5*); pap. 30.95 (*0-335-09865-7*) OpUniv Pr.

Negotiation Instruments. 4th ed. Farnsworth. Date not set. pap. text, teacher ed. write for info. (*1-56662-130-5*) Foundation Pr.

Negotiation Literature: A Bibliographic Essay, Citations & Sources. Robert E. Kemper & Danielle R. Kemper. LC 93-33760. 479p. 1994. text 62.00 (*0-8108-2776-X*) Scarecrow.

Negotiation Made Simple. Lynch. 208p. Date not set. pap. text 19.95 (*0-7506-3473-1*) Buttrwrth-Heinemann.

Negotiation, 1998-99. 3rd ed. Susan Blake et al. (Inns of Court School of Law Ser.). 198p. 1998. pap. 42.00 (*1-85431-769-5*) Gaunt.

Negotiation, 1997-98. 2nd ed. Susan Blake et al. (Inns of Court School of Law Ser.). 198p. 1997. pap. 40.00 (*1-85431-671-0*, Pub. by Blackstone Pr) Gaunt.

Negotiation, 1996-97. 186p. 1996. pap. 38.00 (*1-85431-567-6*, Pub. by Blackstone Pr) Gaunt.

Negotiation of Cultural Identity: Perceptions of European Americans & African Americans. Ronald L. Jackson, II. LC 97-50041. 144p. 1999. 49.95 (*0-275-96184-2*, Praeger Pubs) Greenwood.

Negotiation Process & the Resolution of International Conflicts. P. Terrence Hopmann. (Studies in International Relations). (Illus.). 365p. 1998. reprint ed. pap. text 24.95 (*1-57003-293-9*) U of SC Pr.

Negotiation Processes: Modeling Frameworks & Information Technology. Ed. by Melvin F. Shakun. 252p. (C). 1996. lib. bdg. 100.50 (*0-7923-9729-0*) Kluwer Academic.

Negotiation Simulation: Drugs, Books, & Videos--U. S.-Korea Dispute Over Intellectual Property Rights. Michael Ryan et al. (Pew Case Studies in International Affairs). 50p. (C). 1995. pap. text 3.50 (*1-56927-710-9*, GU Schl Foreign) Geo U Inst Dplmcy.

***Negotiation Skills & Strategies.** Alan Fowler. 160p. 2000. pap. 44.95 (*0-8464-5123-9*) Beekman Pubs.

Negotiation Skills for Commercial Lenders. rev. ed. 100p. 1991. teacher ed. 43.00 (*0-685-63173-7*, 630601); pap., student ed. 22.00 (*0-685-63172-9*, 630600); pap., student ed. 35.00 (*0-89982-344-0*, 630600) Am Bankers.

Negotiation Skills for Commercial Lenders: Leader's Guide. rev. ed. 120p. 1991. 28.00 (*0-685-63174-5*, 630601) Am Bankers.

Negotiation Sourcebook. Ed. by Ira G. Asherman & Sandra V. Asherman. 448p. (Orig.). 1989. pap. 49.95 (*0-87425-116-8*) HRD Press.

Negotiation Tactics see Negotiation: Process, Tactics, Theory

Negotiation Techniques You Can Use in the Workplace--Or Anyplace. Ed. by Briefings Publishing Group Staff. 40p. 1998. pap. 12.50 (*1-878604-28-7*) Briefings Pub Grp.

Negotiation the Austrian State Treaty, 1953-1955. Deborah W. Larson. (Pew Case Studies in International Affairs). 50p. (C). 1995. pap. text 3.50 (*1-56927-432-0*) Geo U Inst Dplmcy.

Negotiation Toolkit: How to Get Exactly What You Want in Any Business or Personal Situation. Roger J. Volkema. LC 99-32273. 208p. 1999. pap. 17.95 (*0-8144-8008-X*) AMACOM.

Negotiations. Herman C. Gilbert. 381p. 1983. 14.95 (*0-910671-00-1*) Path Pr Chicago.

Negotiations: A Reader. Judith Summerfield. (C). 1991. text 27.00 (*0-07-062574-3*) McGraw.

Negotiations: Social-Psychological Perspectives. Ed. by Daniel Druckman. LC 76-58353. (Illus.). 416p. reprint ed. pap. 129.00 (*0-8357-8457-6*, 203472200091) Bks Demand.

Negotiations: Varieties, Contexts, Processes, & Social Order. Anselm L. Strauss. LC 78-1156. (Jossey-Bass Social & Behavioral Science Ser.). 293p. reprint ed. pap. 90.90 (*0-7837-6528-2*, 204564000007) Bks Demand.

Negotiations: 6 Steps to Success. Michael A. Walker. 1995. pap. 15.00 (*0-13-125592-4*) P-H.

Negotiations, 1929. abr. ed. Menahem Kaufman. LC 98-165951. 188p. 1998. write for info. (*965-223-987-9*) Gefen Bks.

Negotiation's Behind Closed Doors. Gregory J. Reed. 135p. text 22.00 (*1-882806-07-7*); pap. text 19.00 (*1-882806-08-5*) New Natl Pub.

Negotiations Concerning the Falklands - Maldives Dispute: Breakdown of Negotiations & the Haig Mediation Effort. Don Lipincot & Gregory F. Treverton. (Pew Case Studies in International Affairs). 56p. (C). 1994. pap. text 3.50 (*1-56927-406-1*) Geo U Inst Dplmcy.

Negotiations for a CTBT, 1958-1994: Analysis & Evaluation of American Policy. Thanos P. Dokos. LC 95-16819. 298p. (C). 1995. 44.50 (*0-8191-9985-0*) U Pr of Amer.

Negotiations for a North American Free Trade Agreement. Karen Britto. (State-Federal Issue Brief Ser.: Vol. 4, No. 5). 11p. 1991. pap. text 6.50 (*1-55516-894-9*, 8500-0405) Natl Conf State Legis.

Negotiations for Health Care Materials Manager: A Systematic Approach. Thomas F. Guernsey & Kathe Klare. (Illus.). 106p. (Orig.). 1993. pap. 60.00 (*0-87258-645-6*, 142902) Am Hospital.

Negotiations Game-Options: Communication Skills. Anema. (EC - HS Communication/English Ser.). 1993. pap. 18.95 (*0-538-62516-3*) S-W Pub.

Negotiations Leading to the 1987 Montreal Protocol on Substances That Deplete the Ozone Layer. Allan E. Goodman. (Pew Case Studies in International Affairs). 50p. (C). 1992. pap. text 3.50 (*1-56927-447-9*) Geo U Inst Dplmcy.

Negotiations, 1972-1990. Gilles Deleuze.Tr. of Pourparlers, 1972-1990. 221p. 1997. pap. 17.50 (*0-231-07581-2*) Col U Pr.

Negotiations on Mutual & Balanced Force Reductions: The Search for Arms Control in Central Europe. John G. Keliher. LC 80-16473. (Policy Studies on International Politics). 240p. 1980. 68.00 (*0-08-025964-2*, Pergamon Pr) Elsevier.

Negotiations on the French Withdrawal from NATO. Michael M. Harrison & Mark G. McDonough. (Pew Case Studies in International Affairs). 50p. (Orig.). (C). 1995. pap. text 3.50 (*1-56927-301-4*) Geo U Inst Dplmcy.

Negotiations on Troop Withdrawals from Lebanon: The May 1983 Accord. Robert H. Gromoll. (Pew Case Studies in International Affairs). 50p. (C). 1992. pap. text 3.50 (*1-56927-310-3*) Geo U Inst Dplmcy.

Negotiations Set. Morrison. 508p. 1994. 50.00 (*0-89464-925-6*) Krieger.

Negotiations with Paradox: Narrative Practice & Narrative Form in Bunyan & Defoe. Stuart Sim. 240p. (C). 1990. 65.00 (*0-389-20937-6*) B&N Imports.

Negotiations with the Chill Wind. John Hughes. 64p. 1991. pap. 12.95 (*1-85235-075-X*) Dufour.

***Negotiations without a Loser.** Iwar Unt. 158p. 2000. 34.00 (*87-16-13460-5*, Pub. by Copenhagen Busn Schl) Bks Intl VA.

Negotiator. Frederick Forsyth. 512p. 1990. mass mkt. 7.50 (*0-553-28393-6*) Bantam.

***Negotiator.** Dee Henderson. LC 99-58861. (O'Malley Ser.: Vol. 1). 384p. 2000. pap. 6.99 (*1-57673-608-3*, Pub. by Multnomah Pubs) GL Services.

Negotiator: A Manual for Winners. Royce A. Coffin. LC 73-75768. 174p. reprint ed. pap. 54.00 (*0-608-11093-0*, 202261800028) Bks Demand.

Negotiator's Handbook. George T. Fuller. 288p. (C). 1991. pap. 17.95 (*0-13-612664-2*, Busn) P-H.

***Negotiators Handbook: The Complete Guide to Winning Tactics in Planning & Executing Your Objectives.** George T. Fuller. 304p. 2000. 9.99 (*1-57866-103-X*) Galahad Bks.

N

An Asterisk (*) at the beginning of an entry indicates that the title is appearing for the first time.

*Negotiators Handbook Borders Press Edition. (C). 1999. 4.99 (0-13-017921-3) Addison-Wesley.
Negotiators of Change: Historical Perspectives on Native American Women. Ed. by Nancy Shoemaker. LC 94-15774. 320p. (C). 1994. pap. 20.99 (0-415-90993-7, B3864) Routledge.
Negotiators of Change: Historical Perspectives on Native American Women. Ed. by Nancy Shoemaker. LC 94-15774. 288p. (C). (gr. 13). 1995. 75.00 (0-415-90992-9, B3860) Routledge.
*Negotiator's Pocketbook. Patrick Forsyth. 112p. 2000. pap. 8.95 (1-57922-005-3) Stylus Pub VA.
Negotitating the Past: The Making of Memory in South Africa. Ed. by Sarah Nuttall & Carli Coetzee. LC DT1776.N44 1998. (Illus.). 314p. 1998. pap. text 19.95 (0-19-571503-9) OUP.
*Negotiting Critical Literacies in the Classroom. Ed. by Barbara Comber & Anne Simpson. 400p. 2000. write for info. (0-8058-3793-0) L Erlbaum Assocs.
Negra Angustias (The Black Angustias) 2nd ed. Francisco R. Gonzalez. (SPA.). 222p. 1984. pap. 7.99 (968-16-1625-1, Pub. by Fondo) Continental Bk.
Negre a Paris see African in Paris
Negrero. Alberto. 1996. 9.95 (84-01-46987-2) Plaza.
Negres. Jean Genet. (Folio Ser.: No. 1180). (FRE.). pap. 6.95 (2-07-037180-8) Schoenhof.
Negres, pour Jouer les Negres. Jean Genet. pap. 19.95 (0-685-11416-3) Fr & Eur.
Negres, pour Jouer les Negres. Jean Genet. (FRE.). 1980. pap. 10.95 (0-8288-3649-3, M12667) Fr & Eur.
Negres Precede de pour Jouer les Negres. Jean Genet. (FRE.). 128p. 1980. pap. 10.95 (0-7859-2430-2, 2070371808) Fr & Eur.
Negrito: Negro Dialect Poems of the Southwest. John M. Brewer. LC 78-37585. (Black Heritage Library Collection). (Illus.). 1977. reprint ed. 20.95 (0-8369-8961-9) Ayer.
Negritude: Black Poetry from Africa & the Caribbean. Ed. by Norman R. Shapiro. 1970. 10.00 (0-8079-0149-0); pap. 8.95 (0-8079-0164-4) October.
Negritude & Humanism. Leopold S. Senghor. Tr. by Wendell A. Jeanpierre from FRE. LC 75-508. write for info. (0-89388-197-X) Okpaku Communications.
Negritude & Literary Criticism: The History & Theory of "Negro-African" Literature in French, 178. Belinda E. Jack. LC 95-35714. (Contributions in Afro-American & African Studies: No. 178). 208p. 1996. 59.95 (0-313-29511-5, Greenwood Pr) Greenwood.
Negritude As a Theme in the Poetry of the Portuguese-Speaking World. Richard A. Preto-Rodas. LC 79-107879. (University of Florida Humanities Monographs: No. 31). 98p. reprint ed. pap. 30.40 (0-7837-5082-X, 204478000004) Bks Demand.
Negritude et Nouveaux Mondes: Anthologie de la Poesie Noire: a Africaine, Antillaise, Malgache. Ed. by Peter Thompson. (Illus.). 111p. (YA). (gr. 10-12). 1994. pap. text 6.67 (1-877653-25-X, 28) Wayside Pub.
Negritude Radicale Contre la Negritude Moderee: Radical vs. Moderate Negritude. Afrikadzata Deku. LC 91-72681. (BA. Double Hons Dissertation Ser.). 45p. 2000. write for info. (1-56454-025-1) Cont Afrikan.
Negro: An Anthology. Nancy Cunard. LC 81-70126. (Illus.). 496p. 1996. pap. 39.50 (0-8264-0862-1) Continuum.
Negro: His Rights & Wrongs. Francis J. Grimke. 1972. 59.95 (0-8490-0717-8) Gordon Pr.
Negro - The Southerner's Problem. Thomas N. Page. (Notable American Authors Ser.). 1999. reprint ed. lib. bdg. 125.00 (0-7812-4708-X) Rprt Serv.
Negro a Beast. Charles H. Carroll. LC 74-89419. (Black Heritage Library Collection). 1977. 38.95 (0-8369-8533-8) Ayer.
Negro Almanac: A Reference Work on the Afro-American. 4th ed. Ed. by Harry A. Ploski & James D. Williams. LC 86-72654. (Illus.). 1550p. 1983. text 99.95 (0-685-17467-0) Bellwether Pub.
Negro Almanac: A Reference Work on the Afro-American. 5th ed. Ed. by Harry A. Plosky & James D. Williams. (Illus.). 1989. text 99.95 (0-913144-09-6) Bellwether Pub.
Negro-American Family. Ed. by W. E. B. Du Bois. LC 68-55882. (Illus.). 156p. 1970. reprint ed. lib. bdg. 35.00 (0-8371-1342-3, DUF&) Greenwood.
Negro Americans, What Now? James Weldon Johnson. LC 72-155618. 103p. reprint ed. 27.50 (0-404-00075-4) AMS Pr.
Negro Americans, What Now? James Weldon Johnson. LC 72-8355. 103p. 1973. reprint ed. lib. bdg. 19.50 (0-306-70531-1) Da Capo.
Negro & Apprenticeship. F. Ray Marshall & Vernon M. Briggs, Jr. LC 67-18561. 297p. reprint ed. pap. 92.10 (0-608-14631-5, 202310900032) Bks Demand.
Negro & His Music. Alain L. Locke. LC 69-18592. (American Negro His History & Literature, Ser. 2). 1979. reprint ed. 27.95 (0-88143-078-1) Ayer.
Negro & His Music: Negro Art: Past & Present. Alain L. Locke. Ed. by Ulysses Lee. LC 69-18592. (American Negro: His History & Literature. Series 2). 122p. 1988. pap. 22.95 (0-88143-079-X) Ayer.
Negro & His Needs. Raymond Patterson. LC 74-178480. (Black Heritage Library Collection). 1977. reprint ed. 25.95 (0-8369-8929-5) Ayer.
Negro & His Songs: A Study of Typical Negro Songs in the South. Howard W. Odum & Guy B. Johnson. LC 68-55902. 306p. 1969. reprint ed. lib. bdg. 65.00 (0-8371-0596-X, ODS&) Greenwood.
Negro & Jamaica. Bedford Pim. LC 72-157375. (Black Heritage Library Collection). 1977. 15.95 (0-8369-8813-2) Ayer.
Negro & the Drama: The Direct & Indirect Contribution Which the American Negro Has Made to Drama & the Legitimate Stage. Frederick W. Bond. 26.95 (0-405-18492-1) Ayer.
Negro & the 1st Amendment. Harry Kalven, Jr. LC 66-29115. 1993. pap. text 2.45 (0-226-42315-8, P240) U Ch Pr.
Negro & the Nation. George S. Merriam. LC 75-95441. (Studies in Black History & Culture: No. 54). 1970. reprint ed. lib. bdg. 75.00 (0-8383-0994-1) M S G Haskell Hse.
Negro & the War. Earl L. Brown & George R. Leighton. LC 75-172045. reprint ed. 32.50 (0-404-00194-7) AMS Pr.
Negro & White in a Connecticut Town: A Study in Race Relations. Frank F. Lee. 1961. pap. 15.95 (0-8084-0404-0) NCUP.
"Negro & White, Unite & Fight!" A Social History of Industrial Unionism in Meatpacking, 1930-90. Roger Horowitz. LC 96-35703. (Working Class in American History Ser.). 408p. 1997. text 44.95 (0-252-02320-X); pap. text 17.95 (0-252-06621-9) U of Ill Pr.
Negro Art, Music, & Rhyme. Helen A. Whiting. (Illus.). (J). (gr. 2). 1990. 4.25 (0-87498-005-4) Assoc Pubs DC.
Negro Artists. Harmon Foundation Inc. Staff. LC 72-161262. (Black Heritage Library Collection). (Illus.). reprint ed. 7.50 (0-8369-8821-3) Ayer.
Negro Artists: An Illustrated Review of Their Achievements. Harmon Foundation Inc. Staff. LC 72-161262. (Illus.). 1991. reprint ed. pap. 12.95 (0-88143-142-7) Ayer.
Negro As Capitalist. Epil. by Dempsey J. Travis. 153p. 1992. 21.50 (0-941484-13-0) Urban Res Pr.
Negro As Capitalist. Abram L. Harris. LC 73-117597. (Studies in Negro History & Culture: No. 54). (C). 1970. reprint ed. lib. bdg. 75.00 (0-8383-1030-3) M S G Haskell Hse.
Negro at Home: An Inquiry after His Capacity for Self-Government & the Government of Whites. Lindley Spring. LC 74-149878. (Black Heritage Library Collection). 1977. 21.95 (0-8369-8758-6) Ayer.
Negro at Work During the World War & During Reconstruction. U. S. Department of Labor, Division of Negro Econo. LC 70-88453. (Illus.). 144p. 1970. reprint ed. lib. bdg. 59.50 (0-8371-1909-X, NEW&) Greenwood.
Negro at Work in New York City. George E. Haynes. LC 77-76709. (Columbia University. Studies in the Social Sciences: No. 124). reprint ed. 27.50 (0-404-51124-4) AMS Pr.
Negro at Work in New York City: A Study in Economic Progress. George E. Haynes. LC 68-28999. (American Negro: His History & Literature. Suite 1). 1968. reprint ed. 7.00 (0-405-01818-5) Ayer.
Negro Authors & Composers of the United States. William C. Handy. LC 74-24105. reprint ed. 27.50 (0-404-12953-6) AMS Pr.
Negro Baptist History U. S. A., 1750-1930. Lewis G. Jordan. LC 93-1767. 1993. pap. 12.95 (0-910683-16-6) Townsnd-Pr.
Negro Baptist Pulpit. Ed. by Edward M. Brawley. LC 74-154072. (Black Heritage Library Collection). 1977. 22.95 (0-8369-8783-7) Ayer.
Negro Baseball Leagues. David Fremon. (American Events Ser.). 96p. (J). (gr. 5). 1994. pap. text 7.95 (0-382-24730-2) Silver Burdett Pr.
Negro Baseball Leagues. David Fremon. LC 94-2389. (American Events Ser.). 96p. (YA). (gr. 5 up). 1994. text 14.95 (0-02-835695-0, New Dscvry Bks) Silver Burdett Pr.
Negro Baseball Leagues: A Photographic History. Phil Dixon & Pat Hannigan. (Illus.). 364p. 1992. 39.95 (0-8488-0425-2) Amereon Ltd.
Negro Business & Business Education: Their Present & Prospective Development. J. A. Pierce. LC 95-625. (Plenum Studies in Work & Industry). (Illus.). 368p. (C). 1995. 49.50 (0-306-45073-9, Plenum Trade) Perseus Pubng.
Negro Caravan. Ed. by Sterling A. Brown et al. LC 69-18584. (American Negro: His History & Literature. Series 2). 1969. reprint ed. pap. 4.95 (0-8434-6099-7) Ayer.
Negro Caravan. Ed. by Sterling A. Brown et al. LC 69-18584. (American Negro: His History & Literature. Series 2). 1978. reprint ed. 71.95 (0-405-01852-5) Ayer.
Negro Character in American Literature. John H. Nelson. LC 73-128982. reprint ed. 29.50 (0-404-00203-X) AMS Pr.
Negro Character in American Literature. John H. Nelson. (BCL1-PS American Literature Ser.). 146p. 1992. reprint ed. lib. bdg. 69.00 (0-7812-6616-5) Rprt Serv.
Negro Child Welfare in North Carolina. Wiley B. Sanders. LC 68-55782. (Criminology, Law Enforcement, & Social Problems Ser.: No. 18). (Illus.). 1968. reprint ed. 24.00 (0-87585-018-9) Patterson Smith.
Negro Christianized. Cotton Mather. (Notable American Authors Ser.). 1999. reprint ed. lib. bdg. 125.00 (0-7812-3962-1) Rprt Serv.
Negro Church in America. E. Franklin Frazier & C. Eric Lincoln. LC 72-96201. (Sourcebooks in the Negro History Ser.). 1974. pap. 13.00 (0-8052-0387-7) Schocken.
Negro Churchman, 2 vols., Set. Intro. by Richard Newman. 1990. reprint ed. 190.00 (0-527-66370-0) Periodicals Srv.
Negro Civilization in the South. Charles E. Robert. LC 70-173614. (Black Heritage Library Collection). 1977. reprint ed. 17.95 (0-8369-8906-6) Ayer.
Negro Combat Troops in the World War: The Story of the 371st Infantry. Chester D. Heywood. LC 72-95400. (Illus.). reprint ed. 27.50 (0-404-01947-1) AMS Pr.
Negro Cowboys. Philip Durham & Everett L. Jones. LC 83-6446. (Illus.). x, 278p. 1983. reprint ed. pap. 11.00 (0-8032-6560-3, Bison Books) U of Nebr Pr.
Negro Education: A Study of the Private & Higher Schools for Colored People in the United States. Ed. by Thomas J. Jones. LC 69-18572. (American Negro: His History & Literature. Series 2). 1226p. 1969. reprint ed. 60.95 (0-405-01874-6) Ayer.
Negro Employment in Land & Air Transport: A Study of Racial Policies in the Railroad, Airline, Trucking, & Urban Transit Industries. Herbert R. Northrup et al. LC 70-161216. (Studies of Negro Employment: Vol. 5). 687p. reprint ed. pap. 200.00 (0-8357-3156-1, 203941900012) Bks Demand.
Negro Explorer at the North Pole. Matthew A. Henson. LC 69-18565. (American Negro: His History & Literature. Series 2). 1974. reprint ed. 15.95 (0-405-01868-1) Ayer.
Negro Family: The Case for National Action. U. S. Department of Labor, Office Policy Planning. LC 81-607023. (Illus.). 78p. 1981. reprint ed. lib. bdg. 49.75 (0-313-22853-1, USNF, Greenwood Pr) Greenwood.
Negro Family in the United States. abr. rev. ed. E. Franklin Frazier. LC 66-13868. 1994. pap. text 13.95 (0-226-26141-7) U Ch Pr.
*Negro Family in the United States. rev. ed. Edward F. Frazier. (African American Intellectual Heritage Ser.). 700p. 2001. pap. 24.95 (0-268-03650-0, Pub. by U of Notre Dame Pr); lib. bdg. 48.95 (0-268-03654-3, Pub. by U of Notre Dame Pr) Chicago Distribution Ctr.
Negro Farmer. Carl Kelsey. LC 74-22749. (Labor Movement in Fiction & Non-Fiction Ser.). reprint ed. 29.50 (0-404-58501-9) AMS Pr.
Negro Folk Music U. S. A. Harold Courlander. LC 92-35475. (Illus.). xi, 324p. 1998. reprint ed. pap. text 9.95 (0-486-27350-4) Dover.
Negro Folk Tales. Helen A. Whiting. (Illus.). (J). (gr. 1). 1990. 4.25 (0-87498-006-2) Assoc Pubs DC.
Negro Folktales in Michigan. Richard M. Dorson. LC 73-21099. (Illus.). 245p. 1974. reprint ed. lib. bdg. 49.75 (0-8371-5989-X, DONF, Greenwood Pr) Greenwood.
Negro Freedom: Life Conditions of the American Negro in the Early Years after Emancipation. Henderson H. Donald. LC 70-160846. 1971. reprint ed. lib. bdg. 57.00 (0-8154-0388-7) Cooper Sq.
Negro Freemasonry. D. A. Cass. 18.95 (0-685-22057-5) Wehman.
Negro Freemasonry & Segregation. Don Cass. 17.00 (0-911164-27-8) Powner.
Negro Genius. Benjamin G. Brawley. LC 66-17517. 1966. reprint ed. pap. 27.00 (0-8196-0184-5) Biblo.
Negro History, 1553-1903. Edwin Wolf, II. LC 75-662. (Illus.). v, 83p. (Orig.). 1969. pap. 10.00 (0-914076-66-3) Lib Co Phila.
Negro Housing. President's Conference on Home Building & Home Own. Ed. by John M. Gries & James Ford. LC 79-89053. 282p. 1970. reprint ed. lib. bdg. 45.00 (0-8371-1921-9, NEH&) Greenwood.
Negro Humor & Folk-Lore. James D. Corrothers. LC 72-1047. (Black Cat Club Ser.). (Illus.). reprint ed. 39.00 (0-404-00023-1) AMS Pr.
Negro Illegitimacy in New York City. Ruth Reed. LC 68-57577. (Columbia University. Studies in the Social Sciences: No. 277). reprint ed. 20.00 (0-404-51277-1) AMS Pr.
Negro Immigrant: His Background, Characteristics & Social Adjustment, 1899-1937. Ira D. Reid. LC 68-58615. (Columbia University. Studies in the Social Sciences: No. 449). reprint ed. 20.00 (0-404-51449-9) AMS Pr.
Negro Immigrant: His Background, Characteristics & Social Adjustment, 1899-1937. Ira D. Reid. LC 69-18771. (American Immigration Collectio. Series 1). 1975. reprint ed. 19.95 (0-405-00537-7) Ayer.
Negro in Africa & America. Joseph A. Tillinghast. LC 77-89441. (Black Heritage Library Collection). 1977. 17.95 (0-8369-8667-9) Ayer.
Negro in America: A Bibliography. 2nd enl. rev. ed. Ed. by Elizabeth W. Miller. 373p. (C). 1970. pap. 18.50 (0-674-60702-3) HUP.
Negro in American Fiction. Sterling A. Brown. 1969. reprint ed. 15.00 (0-87266-002-8) Argosy.
Negro in American Fiction. Sterling A. Brown. LC 69-18582. 372p. 1972. reprint ed. 18.95 (0-405-01851-7) Ayer.
Negro in American Life. Jerome Dowd. LC 68-56331. 600p. 1969. reprint ed. lib. bdg. 35.00 (0-8371-0389-4, DON&) Greenwood.
Negro in American Life & Thought see Betrayal of the Negro from Rutherford B. Hayes to Woodrow Wilson: From Rutherford B. Hayes to Woodrow Wilson
Negro in American National Politics. William F. Nowlin. LC 71-173802. reprint ed. 20.00 (0-404-00204-8) AMS Pr.
Negro in Brazil. Artur Ramos. Tr. by Richard Pattee. LC 80-25342. (Perspectives in Latin American History Ser.: No. 3). xx, 203p. 1980. reprint ed. lib. bdg. 35.00 (0-87991-604-4) Porcupine Pr.
Negro in Brazilian Literature. Raymond S. Sayers. (Illus.). x, 240p. 4.75 (0-318-14293-7) Hispanic Inst.
Negro in Business. W. E. B. Du Bois. LC 70-153098. reprint ed. 37.50 (0-404-00153-X) AMS Pr.
Negro in Business. Booker T. Washington & W. E. B. Du Bois. LC 71-144699. (Illus.). reprint ed. 29.50 (0-404-00237-4) AMS Pr.
Negro in Chicago: A Study of Race Relations & a Race Riot. Chicago Commission on Race Relations Editors. LC 68-28990. (American Negro: His History & Literature. Series 1). 1978. reprint ed. 23.95 (0-405-01807-X) Ayer.
Negro in Colonial New England, 1620-1776. Lorenzo J. Greene. (History - United States Ser.). 404p. 1993. reprint ed. lib. bdg. 99.00 (0-7812-4892-2) Rprt Serv.
Negro in Eighteenth-Century Williamsburg. Thad W. Tate. LC 65-26599. 141p. 1985. reprint ed. pap. 9.50 (0-910412-29-4) Colonial Williamsburg.
Negro in Federal Employment: The Quest for Equal Opportunity. Samuel Krislov. LC 67-22017. 167p. reprint ed. pap. 51.80 (0-608-15970-0, 203326500084) Bks Demand.
Negro in Films. Peter Noble. LC 72-124022. (Literature of Cinema, Ser. 1). 1978. reprint ed. 32.95 (0-405-01629-8) Ayer.
Negro in France. Shelby T. McCloy. LC 72-5545. (Studies in Black History & Culture: No. 54). 1972. reprint ed. lib. bdg. 75.00 (0-8383-1601-8) M S G Haskell Hse.
Negro in Greek & Roman Civilization. Grace M. Beardsley. 1979. 22.95 (0-405-10581-9) Ayer.
Negro in Indiana Before 1900: A Study of a Minority. Emma L. Thornbrough. LC 92-46430. 432p. 1993. 31.95 (0-253-35989-9); pap. 17.95 (0-253-35988-0) Ind U Pr.
Negro in Literature & Art in the U. S. Benjamin G. Brawley. 1981. lib. bdg. 59.00 (0-403-00531-0) Scholarly.
Negro in Literature & Art in the U. S. Benjamin G. Brawley. (BCL1 - U. S. History Ser.). 231p. 1991. reprint ed. lib. bdg. 79.00 (0-7812-6087-6) Rprt Serv.
Negro in Literature & Art in the U. S. 3rd ed. Benjamin G. Brawley. LC 75-144586. (BCL Ser. I). reprint ed. 27.50 (0-404-00139-4) AMS Pr.
Negro in Maryland. Jeffrey R. Brackett. LC 69-18529. (Select Bibliographies Reprint Ser.). 1977. 27.95 (0-8369-5000-3) Ayer.
Negro in Maryland: A Study of the Institution of Slavery. Jeffrey R. Brackett. LC 78-64250. (Johns Hopkins University. Studies in the Social Sciences. Thirtieth Ser. 1912: 6). reprint ed. 27.50 (0-404-61354-3) AMS Pr.
Negro in Maryland Politics, 1870-1912. Margaret L. Callcott. LC 69-15395. (Johns Hopkins University Studies in Historical & Political Science: Ser. 87, No. 1). 215p. reprint ed. pap. 66.70 (0-608-14669-2, 202583500046) Bks Demand.
Negro in Mississippi, 1865-1890. Vernon L. Wharton. LC 84-10952. 298p. 1984. reprint ed. lib. bdg. 59.95 (0-313-24568-1, WHNM, Greenwood Pr) Greenwood.
Negro in New Jersey. New Jersey Conference of Social Work Staff. LC 74-78772. (Illus.). 116p. 1969. reprint ed. lib. bdg. 57.50 (0-8371-1411-X, NNJ&) Greenwood.
Negro in North Carolina Politics since Reconstruction. William A. Mabry. LC 75-110130. (Duke University. Trinity College Historical Society. Historical Papers: No. 23). reprint ed. 30.00 (0-404-51773-0) AMS Pr.
Negro in Northern Brazil. Octavio D. Eduardo. (African Heritage Classical Research Studies). 131p. reprint ed. 20.00 (0-938818-53-8) ECA Assoc.
Negro in Northern Brazil: A Study in Acculturation. Octavio D. Eduardo. LC 84-45516. (American Ethnological Society Monographs: No. 15). 1988. reprint ed. 23.00 (0-404-62914-8) AMS Pr.
Negro in Ohio, 1802-1870. Charles T. Hickok. LC 79-169487. reprint ed. 31.50 (0-404-00064-9) AMS Pr.
Negro in Our History. rev. ed. Carter G. Woodson. (YA). 1990. 19.95 (0-87498-080-1); pap. 15.95 (0-87498-081-X) Assoc Pubs DC.
Negro in Pennsylvania: A Study in Economic History. Richard R. Wright, Jr. LC 69-18581. (American Negro: His History & Literature. Series 2). 1969. reprint ed. 20.95 (0-405-01908-4) Ayer.
Negro in Pennsylvania: Slavery - Servitude - Freedom 1639-1861. Edward R. Turner. LC 69-18579. (American Negro: His History & Literature. Series 2). 1969. reprint ed. 27.95 (0-405-01899-1) Ayer.
Negro in South Carolina During the Reconstruction. Alrutheus A. Taylor. LC 70-144693. reprint ed. 29.50 (0-404-00216-1) AMS Pr.
Negro in South Carolina During the Reconstruction. Alrutheus A. Taylor. (BCL1 - U. S. History Ser.). 341p. 1991. reprint ed. lib. bdg. 89.00 (0-7812-6089-2) Rprt Serv.
Negro in Sports. E. B. Henderson. 1990. 25.00 (0-87498-027-5) Assoc Pubs DC.
Negro in Tennessee, 1865-1880. Alrutheus A. Taylor. LC 73-22436. 316p. 1974. reprint ed. 25.00 (0-87152-165-2) Reprint.
Negro in the American Rebellion: His Heroism & His Fidelity. William W. Brown. LC 78-79021. (Black Heritage Library Collection). 1977. 32.95 (0-8369-8518-4) Ayer.
Negro in the American Rebellion: His Heroism & His Fidelity. William W. Brown. 1971. pap. 3.95 (0-8065-0238-X, Citadel Pr) Carol Pub Group.
Negro in the American Revolution. Benjamin Quarles. LC 96-21111. (C). 1996. pap. 15.95 (0-8078-4603-1) U of NC Pr.
Negro in the American Revolution. Benjamin Quarles. LC 61-66795. 250p. 1961. reprint ed. pap. 77.50 (0-7837-9895-4, 206062100006) Bks Demand.
Negro in the Armed Forces: His Value & Status - Past, Present & Potential. Seymour J. Schoenfeld. 1990. 10.00 (0-87498-086-0) Assoc Pubs DC.
Negro in the Caribbean. Eric Williams. LC 71-88421. 119p. 1970. lib. bdg. 35.00 (0-8371-1809-3, WIC&, Greenwood Pr) Greenwood.
Negro in the Caribbean. Eric Williams. 120p. 1993. reprint ed. pap. 9.95 (1-881316-68-8) A&B Bks.
Negro in the Caribbean. Eric E. Williams. LC 74-103458. (Studies in Black History & Culture: No. 54). (C). 1970. reprint ed. lib. bdg. 75.00 (0-8383-1190-3) M S G Haskell Hse.
Negro in the Civil War. Benjamin Quarles. (Quality Paperbacks Ser.). (Illus.). 402p. 1989. pap. 13.95 (0-306-80350-X) Da Capo.

N

An Asterisk (*) at the beginning of an entry indicates that the title is appearing for the first time.

Negro in the District of Columbia. Edward Ingle. LC 78-63818. (Johns Hopkins University. Studies in the Social Sciences. Thirtieth Ser. 1912: 3-4). reprint ed. 27.50 (*0-404-61081-1*) AMS Pr.

Negro in the District of Columbia. Edward Ingle. LC 73-170700. (Black Heritage Library Collection). 1977. reprint ed. 22.95 (*0-8369-8890-6*) Ayer.

Negro in the Making of America. Benjamin Quarles. 400p. 1996. per. 12.00 (*0-684-81888-4*, Touchstone) S&S Trade Pap.

Negro in the Slaughtering & Meat-Packing Industry in Chicago. Alma Herbst. LC 73-156417. (American Labor Ser., No. 2). 1973. reprint ed. 17.95 (*0-405-02925-X*) Ayer.

Negro in the South. Booker T. Washington & W. E. B. Du Bois. 1970. pap. 7.95 (*0-8065-0219-3*, Citadel Pr) Carol Pub Group.

Negro in the South. Booker T. Washington & W. E. B. Du Bois. 1989. pap. 7.95 (*0-8216-0183-0*, Univ Books) Carol Pub Group.

Negro in the South: His Economic Progress in Relation to His Moral & Religious Development. Booker T. Washington & W. E. B. Du Bois. LC 75-177853. reprint ed. 10.00 (*0-404-00219-6*) AMS Pr.

***Negro in the United States.** Dorothy Burnett Porter. LC 99-15293. 313p. 1999. 38.00 (*0-7808-0312-4*) Omnigraphics Inc.

Negro in the United States: A Research Guide. Erwin K. Welsch. LC 84-6547. 142p. 1984. reprint ed. lib. bdg. 55.00 (*0-313-24454-5*, WENU, Greenwood Pr) Greenwood.

Negro in Virginia. Virginia Writers Program Staff. LC 94-31417. 421p. 1994. pap. 12.95 (*0-89587-119-X*) Blair.

Negro in Virginia. WPA Federal Writers' Project Staff. LC 69-18577. (American Negro: His History & Literature. Series 2). 1969. reprint ed. 35.95 (*0-405-01910-6*) Ayer.

Negro in World War II. John D. Silvera. LC 69-18557. (American Negro: His History & Literature. Series 2). 1974. reprint ed. 20.95 (*0-405-01893-2*) Ayer.

Negro-Indian Relationships in the Southeast. Laurence Foster. LC 76-43708. reprint ed. 29.50 (*0-404-15543-X*) AMS Pr.

Negro Intelligence & Selective Migration. Otto Klineberg. LC 74-12884. 66p. 1975. reprint ed. lib. bdg. 35.00 (*0-8371-7771-5*, KLNI, Greenwood Pr) Greenwood.

Negro Is a Man. Wilson S. Armistead. LC 74-89427. (Black Heritage Library Collection). 1977. 44.95 (*0-8369-8505-2*) Ayer.

Negro Kingdom - Three Generations: The Vanished Colony. Loyd M. Barrow. (Illus.). 86p. (Orig.). 1996. pap. 8.95 (*0-9646054-7-3*) Moosehead Communs.

Negro Kinship to the Park. Kimmika Williams. (Illus.). 98p. (Orig.). 1990. pap. 5.00 (*0-9626216-2-5*) Three Goat Pubns.

Negro Labor Unionist of New York. Charles L. Franklin. LC 68-58573. (Columbia University. Studies in the Social Sciences: No. 420). reprint ed. 32.50 (*0-404-51420-0*) AMS Pr.

Negro Lawmakers in the South Carolina Legislature, 1868-1902. Lawrence C. Bryant. 1968. pap. 10.00 (*0-686-05563-2*) L C Bryant.

Negro Leadership in a Southern City. M. Elaine Burgess. 1962. pap. 17.95 (*0-8084-0231-5*) NCUP.

Negro Leagues. Haskins. (J). 1995. 16.95 (*0-8050-2207-4*) H Holt & Co.

Negro Leagues. James A. Riley. LC 95-46411. (African-American Achievers Ser.). 124p. (YA). (gr. 5 up). 1996. pap. 8.95 (*0-7910-2592-6*) Chelsea Hse.

Negro Leagues. James A. Riley. LC 95-46411. (African-American Achievers Ser.). (Illus.). 124p. (YA). (gr. 5 up). 1996. lib. bdg. 19.95 (*0-7910-2591-8*) Chelsea Hse.

Negro Leagues: Autograph Guide. Kevin Keating & Mike Kolleth. (Illus.). 320p. 1998. pap. 24.95 (*0-930625-51-X*, Antique Trader) Krause Pubns.

Negro Leagues: The Story of Black Baseball. Jacob Margolies. (African-American Experience Ser.). (Illus.). 144p. (YA). (gr. 7-12). 1993. lib. bdg. 24.00 (*0-531-11130-X*) Watts.

Negro Leagues: The Story of Black Baseball. Jacob Margolies. (African-American Experience Ser.). (Illus.). 128p. (YA). (gr. 7-12). 1994. pap. 6.95 (*0-531-15694-X*) Watts.

Negro Leagues Book. Clark. Ed. by Lester. 1994. 49.95 (*0-910137-59-5*) Soc Am Baseball Res.

Negro Leagues Book. Dick Clark. 1994. pap. 24.95 (*0-910137-55-2*) Soc Am Baseball Res.

Negro Leagues Book Signed. Clark. Ed. by Lester. 1994. 150.00 (*0-910137-60-9*) Soc Am Baseball Res.

***Negro Leagues Revisited: Conversations with 66 More Baseball Heroes.** Brent Kelley. (Illus.). 399p. 2000. 45.00 (*0-7864-0875-8*) McFarland & Co.

Negro Legislators in South Carolina, 1865-1894. Lawrence C. Bryant. 1966. 15.00 (*0-686-05568-3*); pap. 10.00 (*0-686-05569-1*) L C Bryant.

Negro Legislators in South Carolina, 1868-1902. Lawrence C. Bryant. 1967. 15.00 (*0-686-05564-0*); pap. 10.00 (*0-686-05565-9*) L C Bryant.

Negro Life in the South. Willis D. Weatherford. LC 72-79017. (Black Heritage Library Collection). 1977. 23.95 (*0-8369-8681-4*) Ayer.

Negro-Mania: Examination of the Falsely Assumed Equality of the Various Races of Men. John L. Campbell. LC 79-89420. (Black Heritage Library Collection). 1977. 40.95 (*0-8369-8532-X*) Ayer.

Negro Masonry. William H. Upton. LC 70-144696. reprint ed. 34.50 (*0-404-00218-8*) AMS Pr.

Negro Masonry in the United States. Harold V. Voorhis. 146p. 1996. reprint ed. pap. 16.95 (*1-56459-555-2*) Kessinger Pub.

Negro Migrant in Pittsburgh: A Study in Social Economics. Abraham Epstein. LC 79-92231. (American Negro: His History & Literature. Series 3). 1970. reprint ed. 15.95 (*0-405-01924-6*) Ayer.

Negro Migration, Changes in Rural Organization & Population of the Cotton Belt. Thomas J. Woofter. LC 76-89063. 195p. 1970. reprint ed. lib. bdg. 49.50 (*0-8371-1943-X*, WOK&) Greenwood.

Negro Migration During the War. Emmett J. Scott. LC 69-18555. (American Negro: His History & Literature. Series 2). 1969. reprint ed. 24.95 (*0-405-01891-6*) Ayer.

Negro Militia & Reconstruction. Otis A. Singletary. LC 84-10733. 181p. 1984. reprint ed. lib. bdg. 55.00 (*0-313-24573-8*, SINM, Greenwood Pr) Greenwood.

Negro Mother. Langston Hughes. LC 79-178476. (Black Heritage Library Collection). reprint ed. 10.00 (*0-8369-8925-2*) Ayer.

Negro Mother: And Other Dramatic Recitations. Langston Hughes. LC 79-178476. (Illus.). 24p. 1977. reprint ed. pap. 12.95 (*0-88143-070-6*) Ayer.

Negro Musicians & Their Music. Maud Cuney-Hare. LC 74-4108. (Music Reprint Ser.). 1974. reprint ed. 49.50 (*0-306-70652-0*) Da Capo.

Negro Musicians & Their Music: African-American Women Writers, 1910-1940 by Maud Hare. Maud Hare & Gates. 1996. 30.00 (*0-7838-1417-8*, Hall Reference) Macmillan.

Negro Newcomers in Detroit. George E. Haynes & Sterling A. Brown. LC 76-94132. (American Negro). 1970. reprint ed. 12.95 (*0-405-01926-2*) Ayer.

Negro Novelist: A Discussion of the Writings of American Negro Novelists, 1940-1950. John M. Hughes. LC 67-30218. (Essay Index Reprint Ser.). 1977. 37.44 (*0-8369-0551-2*) Ayer.

Negro Novelist, 1940-1950. Carl M. Hughes. 1970. pap. 7.95 (*0-8065-0006-9*, Citadel Pr) Carol Pub Group.

Negro on the American Frontier. Kenneth W. Porter. LC 77-135872. 1973. reprint ed. 18.95 (*0-405-01983-1*) Ayer.

Negro Orators & Their Orations. Carter G. Woodson. 1990. 50.00 (*0-87498-032-1*) Assoc Pubs DC.

Negro Order see History of the United Brothers of Friendship, & Sisters of the Mysterious Ten

Negro Peasant Turns Cityward. Louise V. Kennedy. LC 68-58597. (Columbia University. Studies in the Social Sciences: No. 329). reprint ed. 20.00 (*0-404-51329-8*) AMS Pr.

Negro Pew. LC 76-149873. (Black Heritage Library Collection). 1977. 15.95 (*0-8369-8753-5*) Ayer.

Negro Playwrights in the American Theatre, 1925-1959. Doris E. Abramson. LC 69-19457. 351p. reprint ed. pap. 108.90 (*0-608-14120-8*, 202428900036) Bks Demand.

Negro Political Participation Study, 1961-1962. 2nd ed. Donald R. Matthews & James W. Prothro. 1975. write for info. (*0-89138-112-0*) ICPSR.

Negro Politicians: The Rise of Negro Politics in Chicago. Harold F. Gosnell. LC 66-30216. 416p. reprint ed. pap. 129.00 (*0-608-10900-2*, 202006700016) Bks Demand.

Negro Population in the United States, 1790-1915. John Cummings. LC 68-28992. (American Negro: His History & Literature. Series 1). 1969. reprint ed. 31.95 (*0-405-01811-8*) Ayer.

Negro Population of Chicago. Otis D. Duncan & Beverly Duncan. LC 57-5271. 399p. reprint ed. 123.70 (*0-8357-9651-5*, 201575400003) Bks Demand.

Negro Potential. Eli Ginzberg et al. LC 80-17250. (Illus.). xvi, 144p. 1980. reprint ed. lib. bdg. 65.00 (*0-313-22389-0*, GINP, Greenwood Pr) Greenwood.

Negro Problem. Booker T. Washington et al. 1970. reprint ed. write for info. (*0-404-00238-2*) AMS Pr.

Negro Problem: A Series of Articles by Representative American Negroes of To-Day. LC 75-79015. (Black Heritage Library Collection). 1977. reprint ed. 17.95 (*0-8369-8636-9*) Ayer.

Negro Problem: A Series of Articles by Representative American Negroes of Today. Booker T. Washington et al. LC 69-18560. (American Negro: His History & Literature. Series 2). 1969. reprint ed. 26.95 (*0-405-01903-3*) Ayer.

Negro Problem Solved: Or, Africa As She Was, As She Is, & As She Shall Be, Her Curse & Her Cure. Hollis Read. LC 77-83874. (Black Heritage Library Collection). 1977. 20.95 (*0-8369-8645-8*) Ayer.

Negro Problems in Cities. Thomas J. Woofter. 1982. 21.95 (*0-8434-0038-2*) McGrath NH.

Negro Professional Class. G. Franklin Edwards. LC 82-11990. 224p. (C). 1982. reprint ed. lib. bdg. 65.00 (*0-313-22330-0*, EDNP, Greenwood Pr) Greenwood.

Negro Protest see King, Malcolm, Baldwin: Three Interviews

Negro Protest Pamphlets: A Compendium. Ed. by Dorothy Porter et al. LC 79-75853. (American Negro: His History & Literature. Series 2). 1969. reprint ed. 11.95 (*0-405-01888-6*) Ayer.

Negro Quarterly Magazine: A Review of Negro Life & Culture, Vols. 1-4. 1969. reprint ed. lib. bdg. 45.00 (*0-8371-1223-0*, NQU&) Greenwood.

Negro Question see Collected Works of George W. Cable

Negro Question. George W. Cable. (Works of George Cable). 1988. reprint ed. 59.00 (*0-685-48942-6*) Rprt Serv.

Negro Salaried Worker. Jack G. Goulay. LC 65-17086. (AMA Research Study Ser.: No. 70). 103p. reprint ed. pap. 32.00 (*0-608-10194-X*, 200010200025) Bks Demand.

Negro Senators & Representatives in the South Carolina Legislature. Lawrence C. Bryant. 1968. 15.00 (*0-686-05566-7*); pap. 10.00 (*0-686-05567-5*) L C Bryant.

Negro Soldiers: These Truly Are the Brave. 2nd ed. Roscoe C. Jamison. LC 73-18582. reprint ed. 20.00 (*0-404-11393-1*) AMS Pr.

Negro Soldiers in World War I: The Human Side. Charles H. Williams. LC 72-126670. Orig. Title: Sidelights on Negro Soldiers. reprint ed. 37.50 (*0-404-06976-2*) AMS Pr.

Negro Spirituals, 2 vols. in 1. Harry T. Burleigh. LC 74-24262. reprint ed. 45.00 (*0-404-12874-2*) AMS Pr.

Negro Spirituals: From Bible to Folk Song. Christa K. Dixon. LC 75-36444. 127p. reprint ed. pap. 39.40 (*0-608-16317-1*, 202687400053) Bks Demand.

Negro Tales. Joseph S. Cotter. LC 75-83923. (Black Heritage Library Collection). 1977. 22.95 (*0-8369-8548-6*) Ayer.

Negro Thought in America, 1880-1915: Racial Ideologies in the Age of Booker T. Washington. August Meier. LC 63-14008. 352p. 1963. text 44.50 (*0-472-64230-8*, 64230); pap. text 22.95 (*0-472-06118-6*, 06118, Ann Arbor Bks) U of Mich Pr.

Negro Traditions. Thomas W. Talley. Ed. by Laura C. Jarman. LC 92-47011. (Illus.). 440p. 1993. pap. 19.50 (*0-87049-925-4*) U of Tenn Pr.

Negro Trail Blazers of California. Delilah L. Beasley. LC 73-88400. 317p. 1969. reprint ed. lib. bdg. 35.00 (*0-8371-1768-2*, BEN&) Greenwood.

Negro Trail Blazers of California: African-American Women Writers, 1910-1940 by Beasley. Gates. LC 97-29612. 1997. 25.00 (*0-7838-1426-7*, Hall Reference) Macmillan.

Negro Troops of Antebellum Louisiana: A History of the Battalion of Free Men of Color. Roland C. McConnell. LC 68-15430. (Louisiana State University Studies: No. 13). 158p. reprint ed. pap. 49.00 (*0-608-30718-1*, 200716400062) Bks Demand.

Negro Vanguard. Richard Bardolph. LC 77-135592. 388p. 1972. reprint ed. lib. bdg. 49.75 (*0-8371-5183-X*, BNV&) Greenwood.

Negro Volunteer Militia Units of the Ohio National Guard, 1870-1954: The Struggle for Military Recognition & Equality in the State of Ohio. Lowell-Dwight Black. 422p. 1976. pap. text 51.95 (*0-89126-031-5*) MA-AH Pub.

Negro Wage Earner. Lorenzo J. Greene & Carter G. Woodson. 1990. 25.00 (*0-87498-029-1*) Assoc Pubs DC.

Negro Wage Earner. Lorenzo J. Greene. (BCL1 - U. S. History Ser.). 388p. 1991. reprint ed. lib. bdg. 89.00 (*0-7812-6088-4*) Rprt Serv.

Negro Wage Earner. Lorenzo J. Greene & Carter G. Woodson. LC 76-126671. reprint ed. 20.00 (*0-404-00163-7*) AMS Pr.

Negro Women of Distinction. C. A. Scruggs. 1973. 69.95 (*0-8490-0718-6*) Gordon Pr.

Negro Workaday Songs. Howard W. Odum & Guy B. Johnson. LC 78-89050. 278p. 1970. reprint ed. lib. bdg. 59.50 (*0-8371-1938-3*, ODW&) Greenwood.

Negro Workaday Songs. Howard W. Odum & Guy B. Johnson. 278p. 1990. reprint ed. lib. bdg. 69.00 (*0-7812-9123-2*) Rprt Serv.

Negro World Series of 1942. James A. Riley. (Orig.). 1989. pap. write for info. (*0-9614023-4-2*) TK Pubs.

Negroes & Negro Slavery: The First an Inferior Race, the Latter Its Normal Condition. John H. Van Evrie. LC 73-83881. (Black Heritage Library Collection). 1977. 31.95 (*0-8369-8674-1*) Ayer.

Negroes & the Great Depression: The Problem of Economic Recovery, 6. Raymond Wolters. Ed. by Stanley E. Kutler. LC 78-95510. (Contributions in American History Ser.: No. 6). 398p. 1970. 39.95 (*0-8371-2341-0*, WON/, Greenwood Pr) Greenwood.

Negroes, Colored People, Blacks, & African Americans in America. Rosie Milligan. 103p. 1992. pap. text 13.95 (*1-881524-03-5*) Milligan Bks.

Negroes for Medicine. Lee Cogan. LC 68-31769. (Josiah Macy Foundation Ser.). 85p. reprint ed. 30.00 (*0-8357-9280-3*, 201568900095) Bks Demand.

Negroes in Michigan History. Ed. by John M. Green. (Illus.). 437p. 1985. 30.00 (*0-935319-00-X*) Hist Res Reposit.

Negroes in Negroland. Hinton R. Helper. (Notable American Authors Ser.). 1992. reprint ed. lib. bdg. 75.00 (*0-7812-3077-2*) Rprt Serv.

Negroes in Science: Natural Science Doctorates, 1876-1969. James M. Jay. LC 74-28394. (Illus.). 87p. 1971. pap. 2.50 (*0-913642-00-2*) Balamp Pub.

Negroes in the United States, 1920-1932. Charles E. Hall. LC 69-18629. (American Negro: His History & Literature. Series 2). 1969. reprint ed. 30.95 (*0-405-01866-5*) Ayer.

Negroes with Guns. Robert F. Williams. LC 98-10737. (African American Life Ser.). (Illus.). 128p. 1998. reprint ed. pap. 14.95 (*0-8143-2714-1*) Wayne St U Pr.

Negroland of the Arabs. rev. ed. W. D. Cooley. 143p. 1966. 35.00 (*0-7146-1799-7*, Pub. by F Cass Pubs) Intl Spec Bk.

***Negrophilia: Avant-Garde Paris & Black Culture in the 1920s.** Petrine Archer-Shaw. LC 99-69806. (Interplay Ser.). (Illus.). 208p. 2000. pap. 24.95 (*0-500-28135-1*, Pub. by Thames Hudson) Norton.

Negrophobia: An Urban Parable. Darius James. 160p. 1992. 15.95 (*0-8065-1293-8*, Citadel Pr) Carol Pub Group.

Negrophobia: An Urban Parable. Darius James. 192p. 1993. pap. 8.95 (*0-312-09350-0*) St Martin.

Negrophobia & Reasonable Racism: The Hidden Costs of Being Black in America. Jody D. Armour. LC 96-51306. (Critical America Ser.). 1997. text 25.00 (*0-8147-0640-1*) NYU Pr.

Negrophobia & Reasonable Racism: The Hidden Costs of Being Black in America. Jody David Armour. 2000. pap. 17.95 (*0-8147-0670-3*) NYU Pr.

***Negros & Human Rights: Promise & Performance.** Claude Emerson Welch. LC 00-33798. (Studies in Human Rights Ser.). (Illus.). 2000. write for info. (*0-8122-3569-X*) U of Pa Pr.

Negros Brujos. Fernando Ortiz. (SPA.). 1995. pap. 19.00 (*0-89729-053-4*) Ediciones.

Negro's Church. Benjamin E. Mays & Joseph W. Nicholson. LC 70-83430. (Religion in America, Ser. 1). 1973. reprint ed. 35.95 (*0-405-00255-6*) Ayer.

Negro's Contribution to Art. Charles C. Seifert. (Illus.). 36p. 1986. reprint ed. pap. 3.00 (*0-933121-11-3*) Black Classic.

Negros Estrangeiros. Carneiro Da Cunha. 1999. pap. text 14.95 (*0-226-09352-2*); lib. bdg. 34.95 (*0-226-09351-4*) U Ch Pr.

Negro's God As Reflected in His Literature. Benjamin E. Mays. LC 69-16578. (Illus.). 269p. 1970. reprint ed. lib. bdg. 59.50 (*0-8371-1139-0*, MAG&) Greenwood.

Negro's Image in the South: The Anatomy of White Supremacy. Claude H. Nolen. LC 67-17843. 252p. reprint ed. 78.20 (*0-8357-9792-9*, 201107100074) Bks Demand.

Negro's Progress in Fifty Years. American Academy of Political & Social Science Sta. LC 71-92737. 266p. 1969. reprint ed. lib. bdg. 59.50 (*0-8371-2187-6*, NEP&) Greenwood.

***NEHA Body Art Code & Guidelines.** National Environmental Health Association Staff. 22p. 1998. pap. text 45.00 (*0-944111-00-9*) Natl Environ Health.

Nehalem Tillamook Tales. Ed. by Melville Jacobs et al. LC 89-16358. (Northwest Reprints Ser.). 276p. 1990. pap. 17.95 (*0-87071-503-8*); text 29.95 (*0-87071-502-X*) Oreg St U Pr.

Nehanda. Yvonne Vera. Date not set. pap. 11.95 (*0-920661-41-6*, Pub. by TSAR Pubns) LPC InBook.

Nehemiah. (BibleTime Bks.). (GAE.). (J). 1995. 2.99 (*0-906731-21-6*, Pub. by Christian Focus) Spring Arbor Dist.

Nehemiah. Alistair Begg. 1999. pap. 16.99 (*0-8024-1719-1*) Moody.

Nehemiah: Becoming a Disciplined Leader. Gene A. Getz. LC 95-1084. 208p. 1995. pap. 10.99 (*0-8054-6165-5*, 4261-65) Broadman.

Nehemiah: Builder for God. N. M. Ross. (BibleTime Bks.). (J). 1995. 2.99 (*0-906731-11-9*, Pub. by Christian Focus) Spring Arbor Dist.

Nehemiah: Man of Radical Obedience. Marie Coody et al. LC 99-25025. (Wisdom of the Word Bible Study Ser.). 88p. 1999. pap. 12.99 (*0-8341-1820-3*) Beacon Hill.

Nehemiah: Rebuilding the Broken Places in Your Life. Marilyn Hickey. Orig. Title: Your Personality Workout. 1989. pap. 7.95 (*1-56441-055-2*) M Hickey Min.

Nehemiah: The Courage to Face Opposition. Don Fields. (LifeGuide Bible Studies). 64p. (Orig.). 1994. pap., wbk. ed. 4.99 (*0-8308-1033-1*, 1033) InterVarsity.

Nehemiah: The Making of a Champion. Lester Sumrall. 63p. (C). 1988. pap. text 10.00 (*0-937580-18-X*) Sumrall Pubng.

Nehemiah: The Wall Builder. John G. Butler. LC 99-180558. 327p. 1998. 18.50 (*1-889773-16-6*) LBC Publns.

Nehemiah & the Dynamics of Effective Leadership. rev. ed. Cyril J. Barber. LC 91-21697. 191p. 1991. pap. 9.99 (*0-87213-026-6*) Loizeaux.

Nehemiah Grew: A Study & Bibliography of His Writings. William LeFanu. 199p. 1990. 36.00 (*0-906795-43-5*) Oak Knoll.

Nehemiah Plan, No. 1. Frank Reid, III. LC 94-200437. Vol. 1. 140p. (Orig.). 1993. pap. 9.99 (*1-56043-766-9*, Treasure Hse) Destiny Image.

Nehemiah Restoring the Breach. Ellen Gould Harmon White. LC 96-61473. 85p. 1996. per. 7.95 (*1-57258-124-7*) Teach Servs.

Nehru. Brown. LC 98-39397. 224p. (C). 1998. pap. 24.60 (*0-582-04284-4*) Longman.

Nehru. Brown. LC 98-39397. (C). 1999. text 63.95 (*0-582-04285-2*) Longman.

Nehru: A Political Biography. Michael Brecher. (Illus.). 704p. 1999. pap. text 29.95 (*0-19-564756-4*) OUP.

Nehru: A Study in Secularism. M. Balasubramanian. 120p. 1980. 14.95 (*0-940500-32-9*) Asia Bk Corp.

Nehru & Administration. Ed. by V. Bhaskara Rao & A. Amruth Rao. (C). 1989. 34.00 (*81-202-0231-7*, Pub. by Ajanta) S Asia.

Nehru & India's Labour Movement. Ed. by M. P. Parekh et al. (C). 1991. text 16.00 (*81-204-0581-1*, Pub. by Oxford IBH) S Asia.

Nehru & Planning in India: Proceedings of the National Seminar on Pandit Jawaharlal Nehru. Planning Commission Staff. (C). 1989. 28.00 (*0-8364-2865-X*, Pub. by Manohar) S Asia.

Nehru & the Language Politics of India. Robert D. King. LC 97-900346. 280p. 1997. text 21.00 (*0-19-563989-8*) OUP.

Nehru & the Language Politics of India. Robert D. King. (Illus.). 280p. 1999. text 10.95 (*0-19-564804-8*) OUP.

Nehru & the People's Movement. Ed. by Jagdish P. Sharma et al. LC 96-906270. xii, 307p. 1997. 39.00 (*81-86562-08-7*, Pub. by Manak Pubns Pvt Ltd) Nataraj Bks.

Nehru & the 20th Century. Ed. by Milton Israel. (C). 1991. 38.00 (*1-895214-04-1*, Pub. by Ctre South Asian); pap. 26.00 (*1-895214-05-X*, Pub. by Ctre South Asian) S Asia.

Nehru Legacy: An Appraisal. Amal Rayed. 1991. 28.00 (*81-204-0556-0*, Pub. by Oxford IBH) S Asia.

Nehru, Man among Men. Raja R. Mehrotra. 1990. 21.50 (*81-7099-196-X*, Pub. by Mittal Pubs Dist) S Asia.

Nehru Memorial Lectures, 1966-1991. Ed. by John Grigg. (Illus.). 290p. (C). 1993. 19.95 (*0-19-563070-X*) OUP.

Nehru on Social Issues. Ed. by S. P. Agrawal & J. C. Aggarwal. (C). 1989. 30.00 (*81-7022-207-9*, Pub. by Concept) S Asia.

Nehru's Foreign Policy. R. C. Hingorani. (C). 1989. 18.00 (*81-204-0431-9*, Pub. by Oxford IBH) S Asia.

Nehwon. Slade. 1993. pap. 9.95 (*0-88038-890-0*) TSR Inc.

N

Nei-Yeh. Hal Roth. 1999. pap. write for info. (0-345-38371-0) Ballantine Pub Grp.

Neiarkaia Zhizn' Sani Kornilova: Stories. Victoria Platova. LC 90-25013. (RUS.). 115p. (Orig.). 1991. pap. 7.50 (1-55779-031-0) Hermitage Pubs.

Neid see Envy: A Theory of Social Behaviour

Neige et la Fleur. Andre Chamson. (FRE.). 448p. 1974. pap. 10.95 (0-7859-2205-9, 207036531X) Fr & Eur.

***Neige Tombait sur les Cedres.** David Guterson. (FRE.). 2000. pap. 14.95 (2-02-032121-1) Editions Seuil.

Neiges D'Antan: Des Contes et des Vers Williams. Curtis Williams. (FRE., Illus.). 81p. 1989. pap. 9.99 (1-878382-00-4) Book Gallery.

Neiges du Kilamandjaro Suivi de Dix Indiens. Ernest Hemingway. (FRE.). 192p. 1982. pap. 10.95 (0-7859-2270-9, 2070361519) Fr & Eur.

***Neigh Neigh Pony.** Tony Potter. 1998. 7.95 (1-902553-11-X) Grimond.

Neighbor. Michael Collier. (Phoenix Poets Ser.). 74p. 1994. pap. 10.00 (0-226-11359-0) U Ch Pr.

Neighbor. Michael Collier. (Phoenix Poets Ser.). 74p. 1995. lib. bdg. 20.00 (0-226-11358-2) U Ch Pr.

Neighbor. Meredith Oakes. (Oberon Bks.). 64p. 1997. pap. 12.95 (1-870259-31-9) Theatre Comm.

Neighbor & Kin: Life in a Tennessee Ridge Community. Elmora M. Matthews. LC 66-15287. 216p. reprint ed. pap. 67.00 (0-8357-3259-2, 203948000013) Bks Demand.

Neighbor Blood. Richard Frost. LC 96-4300. 88p. 1996. 20.95 (0-9641151-4-X); pap. 12.95 (0-9641151-5-8) Sarabande Bks.

Neighbor Jackwood. John T. Trowbridge. LC 68-57556. (Muckrakers Ser.). reprint ed. lib. bdg. 27.50 (0-8398-1974-9) Irvington.

Neighbor Jackwood. John T. Trowbridge. (Notable American Authors). 1999. reprint ed. lib. bdg. 125.00 (0-7812-9793-1) Rprt Serv.

***Neighbor Jackwood: A Domestic Drama in Five Acts.** John Townsend Trowbridge. (Americana Series). 85p. 2000. reprint ed. pap. 4.95 (0-937657-51-4) Feedbk Theabks & Prospero.

Neighbor Law: Fences, Trees, Boundaries, & Noise. 2nd rev. ed. Cora Jordan. Ed. by Mary Randolph. (Illus.). 352p. 1996. pap. 16.95 (0-87337-266-2) Nolo com.

Neighbor Law: Fences, Trees, Boundaries & Noise. 3rd ed. Cora Jordan & Mary Randolph. LC 97-33433. 1998. 24.95 (0-87337-425-8) Nolo com.

Neighbor Next Door see Vecino de al Lado: The Bachelor Next Door

Neighbor vs. Neighbor. 2nd ed. Mark Warda. LC 99-19285. (Legal Survival Guides Ser.). 320p. 1999. pap. 14.95 (1-57248-089-0, Sphinx Pubng) Sourcebks.

Neighborhood. Norbert Blei. (Illus.). 272p. 1998. pap. 14.95 (0-944024-35-1) Ellis Pr.

Neighborhood: A State of Mind. Linda G. Rich et al. LC 81-5992. (Illus.). 152p. 1981. 30.00 (0-8018-2558-X); pap. 16.95 (0-8018-2559-8) Johns Hopkins.

Neighborhood: A Study of Local Life in the City of Columbus, Ohio. Roderick D. McKenzie. LC 71-112560. (Rise of Urban America Ser.). (Illus.). 1974. reprint ed. 19.95 (0-405-02465-7) Ayer.

Neighborhood: My Story of Greenwich House. Mary M. Simkhovitch. 1977. text 21.95 (0-8369-8193-6, 8331) Ayer.

Neighborhood: Social Studies. Harcourt Brace Staff. (J). (gr. 2). 1985. 64.50 (0-15-373209-1) Harcourt Schl Pubs.

Neighborhood: Social Studies. Harcourt Brace Staff. (J). (gr. 2-3). 1985. student ed. 28.75 (0-15-373202-4) Harcourt Schl Pubs.

***Neighborhood No. 18: Cadence of the Numerous: Five Fingers Review.** Ed. by Janice Robles. (Illus.). 224p. (C). 1999. pap. 9.50 (1-880627-08-6) Five Fingers.

Neighborhood Aide. Jack Rudman. (Career Examination Ser.: C-2910). 1994. pap. 23.95 (0-8373-2910-8) Nat Learn.

Neighborhood & Ancestry: Variation in the Spoken Arabic of Maiduguri, Nigeria. Jonathan Owens. LC 98-29002. (Impact: Studies in Language & Society: Vol. 4). xiv, 390p. 1998. 120.00 (1-55619-853-1) J Benjamins Pubng Co.

Neighborhood & Community Environments. I. Altman & J. F. Wohlwill. LC 87-11276. (Human Behavior & Environment Ser.: Vol. 9). (Illus.). 320p. (C). 1987. 65.00 (0-306-42513-0, Plenum Trade) Perseus Pubng.

Neighborhood & Community Histories: Their Value & Suggestions for Their Preparation. R. K. Piper. 33p. (Orig.). 1983. pap. 2.50 (1-55719-031-3) U NE CPAR.

Neighborhood & Community Planning, Vol. 9. (Metropolitan America Ser.). 370p. 1974. 44.95 (0-405-05422-X) Ayer.

Neighborhood & Nation in Tokyo, 1905-1937. Sally A. Hastings. LC 95-14319. (Pitt Series in Policy & Institutional). 274p. 1995. text 39.95 (0-8229-3884-7) U of Pittsburgh Pr.

Neighborhood Bake Shop: Recipes & Reminscences of America's Favorite Bakery Treats. Jill Van Cleave. Ed. by Naomi Glikman. 1997. 23.00 (0-614-30560-8, Wm Morrow) Morrow Avon.

Neighborhood Commercial Revitalization. Sarah Caldes. Ed. by Stephanie Sampson. 32p. (Orig.). 1983. pap. 13.00 (0-317-04851-1) Natl Coun Econ Dev.

***Neighborhood Context & the Development of African American Children.** Maria Loreto Martinez. LC 99-43811. (Children of Poverty Ser.). 1999. write for info. (0-8153-3538-5) Garland.

Neighborhood Cooperative: Economic Democracy in Low-Income Communities. Rodney S. Wead. 95p. 1983. 6.75 (0-318-17932-6, G21B) NASCO.

Neighborhood Crime Watch. Craig Alpaugh. 1995. 5.50 (0-87129-481-8, N26) Dramatic Pub.

Neighborhood Distribution & Consumption of Meat in Pittsburgh: As Related to Other Social & Economic Factors. John H. Cover. LC 75-39353. (Getting & Spending: The Consumer's Dilemma Ser.). 1976. reprint ed. 23.95 (0-405-08017-4) Ayer.

Neighborhood Finds Itself. Julia Abrahamson. 370p. 1972. reprint ed. 30.00 (0-8196-0268-X) Biblo.

***Neighborhood Forager: A\Guide for the Wild Good Gourmet.** Robert Henderson. LC 00-20327. (Illus.). 280p. 2000. pap. 24.95 (1-890132-35-7) Chelsea Green Pub.

Neighborhood Government: The Local Foundations of Political Life. Milton Kotler. LC 69-13097. 1969. pap. 4.50 (0-672-60720-4, Bobbs) Macmillan.

Neighborhood Government: The Local Foundations of Political Life. Milton Kotler. LC 83-5945. 128p. (C). 1983. reprint ed. pap. text 17.00 (0-8191-3187-3) U Pr of Amer.

Neighborhood in Color. Jerry Van Amerongen. (Illus.). 128p. (Orig.). 1989. pap. 8.95 (0-8362-1846-9) Andrews & McMeel.

Neighborhood in Nation-Building: The Running Comment of 30 Years at the South End House. Robert A. Woods. LC 78-112586. (Rise of Urban America Ser.). (Illus.). 1976. reprint ed. 28.95 (0-405-02487-8) Ayer.

Neighborhood Information Centers: A Study & Some Proposals. Alfred J. Kahn et al. 1974. reprint ed. 4.00 (0-942644-01-8) Univ Bk Serv.

Neighborhood Innovations: A Studio for Community Service. Don Hanlon. (Publications in Architecture & Urban Planning: No. R90-2). (Illus.). 118p. (C). 1990. 14.00 (0-938744-71-2) U of Wis Ctr Arch-Urban.

Neighborhood Jobs, Race, & Skills: Urban Unemployment & Commuting. Daniel Immergluck. LC 98-28605. (Studies in the History of American Labor). (Illus.). 156p. 1998. 42.00 (0-8153-3207-6) Garland.

Neighborhood Justice in Capitalist Society: The Expansion of the Informal State, 171. Richard Hofrichter. LC 86-33654. (Contributions in Political Science Ser.: No. 171). 225p. 1987. 59.95 (0-313-25677-2, HNB/, Greenwood Pr) Greenwood.

Neighborhood Law Firms for the Poor: A Comparative Study of Recent Developments in Legal Aid & in the Legal Profession. Bryant Garth. LC 80-51739. 282p. (C). 1980. lib. bdg. 92.50 (90-286-0180-5) Kluwer Academic.

Neighborhood Legal Services Residential Landlord & Tenant Practice Manual. 555p. 1987. 45.00 (0-685-30184-2, 42,670) NCLS Inc.

Neighborhood Mint: Dahlonega in the Age of Jackson. 2nd ed. Sylvia Gailey Head & Elizabeth W. Etheridge. Date not set. text 25.00 (0-9679769-0-1) Gold Rush Gal.

Neighborhood Network Conversations on Nutrition. Ruth L. Cohen. 150p. (Orig.). 1992. pap. 11.50 (0-9633720-0-9) Environ Comms.

Neighborhood Networks for Humane Mental Health Care. Arthur J. Naparstek et al. 238p. 1982. 42.50 (0-306-41051-6, Plenum Trade) Perseus Pubng.

Neighborhood Odes. Gary Soto. LC 91-20710. (Illus.). 80p. (J). (gr. 3-7). 1992. 15.95 (0-15-256879-4, Harcourt Child Bks) Harcourt.

Neighborhood Odes. Gary Soto. 80p. (YA). (gr. 4-7). 1994. pap. 3.50 (0-590-47335-2) Scholastic Inc.

Neighborhood Odes. Gary Soto. 1992. 9.09 (0-606-05951-2, Pub. by Turtleback) Demco.

Neighborhood Organization & Interest-Group Processes. David J. O'Brien. LC 75-3468. 276p. reprint ed. pap. 85.60 (0-8357-8966-7, 203339900085) Bks Demand.

***Neighborhood Organization Starter Guide.** 2nd rev. ed. Guy Ball et al. LC 99-60331. 1999. 19.95 (1-888840-04-8) Wilson-Barnett.

Neighborhood Organizations: Seeds of a New Urban Life, 131. Michael R. Williams. LC 85-9948. (Contributions in Political Science Ser.: No. 131). 278p. 1985. 65.00 (0-313-24749-8, WND/, Greenwood Pr) Greenwood.

Neighborhood Organizer's Handbook. Rachelle Warren & Donald I. Warren. LC 76-640. 1977. pap. 18.00 (0-268-01448-5) U of Notre Dame Pr.

Neighborhood Organizing for Urban School Reform. Michael F. Williams. 192p. 1988. text 30.00 (0-8077-2931-0); pap. text 18.95 (0-8077-2930-2) Tchrs Coll.

Neighborhood-Oriented Policing. (Illus.). 124p. 1994. pap. text 35.00 (1-57979-104-2) DIANE Pub.

Neighborhood-Oriented Policing in Rural Communities: A Program Planning Guide. (Illus.). 117p. (Orig.). (C). 1995. pap. text 35.00 (0-7881-1944-3) DIANE Pub.

Neighborhood Planning: A Guide for Planners & Citizens. Bernie Jones. LC 90-80549. (Illus.). 138p. (Orig.). 1990. pap. 27.95 (0-918286-67-0, Planners Press); lib. bdg. 36.00 (0-918286-68-9, Planners Press) Am Plan Assn.

***Neighborhood Planning & Community-Based Development.** William Peterman. LC 99-50429. (Cities & Planning Ser.). 2000. write for info. (0-7619-1198-7) Sage.

Neighborhood Policing: Proactive Initiatives & Innovations for Urban America. Suman Kakar. 264p. 1998. 74.95 (1-57292-063-7); pap. 54.95 (1-57292-062-9) Austin & Winfield.

Neighborhood Policy & Practice. Ed. by Naomi Carmon. (Orig.). 1987. pap. 15.00 (0-944285-00-7) Pol Studies.

Neighborhood Politics. Matthew A. Crenson. (Illus.). 352p. (C). 1983. 43.00 (0-674-60785-6) HUP.

Neighborhood Politics: Chicago & Sheffield. Larry Bennett. LC 97-17787. (Illus.). 288p. 1997. text 50.00 (0-8153-2112-0) Garland.

Neighborhood Politics: Chicago & Sheffield. Larry Bennett. LC 97-17787. (Illus.). 288p. 1997. pap. text 21.95 (0-8153-2113-9) Garland.

Neighborhood Politics: Residential Community Associations in American Governance. Robert J. Dilger. 220p. (C). 1992. text 45.00 (0-8147-1847-7) NYU Pr.

Neighborhood Poverty: Context & Consequences for Children, Vol. 1. Ed. by Jeanne Brooks-Gunn et al. LC 97-7864. (Illus.). 432p. (C). 1997. 49.95 (0-87154-145-9) Russell Sage.

Neighborhood Poverty: Policy Implications in Studying Neighborhoods, 2 vols., Vol. 2. Ed. by Jeanne Brooks-Gunn et al. LC 97-7864. (Illus.). 288p. (C). 1997. 39.95 (0-87154-146-7) Russell Sage.

Neighborhood Recovery: Reinvestment Policy for the New Hometown. John Kromer. LC 99-28161. 240p. 1999. pap. 22.00 (0-8135-2717-1) Rutgers U Pr.

Neighborhood Recovery: Reinvestment Policy for the New Hometown. John Kromer. LC 99-28161. (Illus.). 240p. 2000. text 55.00 (0-8135-2716-3) Rutgers U Pr.

Neighborhood Reinvestment & Displacement: A Working Paper. Michael H. Schill. LC 80-85160. 60p. 1981. pap. 2.50 (0-685-04191-3) Woodrow Wilson Schl.

Neighborhood Team Policing: Organizational Opportunities & Obstacles. Richard DeParis. LC 97-69038. 60p. 1997. pap. 6.50 (1-878734-51-2) Police Exec Res.

Neighborhood Threat: On Tour with Iggy Pop. Alvin Gibbs. (Illus.). 144p. (Orig.). 1996. pap. text 30.95 (1-899784-10-1, Pub. by Britannia Pr) AK Pr Dist.

Neighborhood Tokyo. Theodore C. Bestor. LC 88-12383. (Illus.). 368p. 1989. 47.50 (0-8047-1439-8); pap. 15.95 (0-8047-1797-4) Stanford U Pr.

Neighborhood Tours: Showcasing Results: A Guide to Giving Neighborhood Tours see Communications Series

Neighborhood Trivia Hunt for Boston's Back Bay. Bettina A. Norton. (Neighborhood Trivia Hunt Ser.). (Illus.). 36p. (Orig.). 1985. pap. 4.95 (0-938357-01-8) BAN Pub Boston.

Neighborhood Trivia Hunt for Boston's Beacon Hill. Bettina A. Norton. (Neighborhood Trivia Hunt Ser.). (Illus.). 36p. (Orig.). 1985. pap. 4.95 (0-938357-00-X) BAN Pub Boston.

Neighborhood Trivia Hunt for Boston's Downtown. Bettina A. Norton. (Neighborhood Trivia Hunt Ser.). (Illus.). 40p. (Orig.). 1986. pap. 5.95 (0-938357-03-4) BAN Pub Boston.

Neighborhood Trivia Hunt for Concord, Massachusetts. Bettina A. Norton. (Neighborhood Trivia Hunt Ser.). (Illus.). 20p. (J). (gr. 7-12). 1985. pap. 4.95 (0-938357-02-6) BAN Pub Boston.

Neighborhood Trivia Hunt for New Haven, Connecticut. Bettina A. Norton. (Illus.). 36p. (Orig.). 1986. pap. 4.95 (0-938357-04-2) BAN Pub Boston.

Neighborhood Trivia Hunt for Providence, R. I. Bettina A. Norton. (Illus.). 36p. (Orig.). 1987. pap. 4.95 (0-938357-06-9) BAN Pub Boston.

Neighborhood Trivia Hunt for Salem, Massachusetts. Bettina A. Norton. (Illus.). 36p. (Orig.). 1986. pap. 4.95 (0-938357-05-0) BAN Pub Boston.

Neighborhood Trivia Hunt on the Salem Heritage Trail for Boys & Girls. Bettina A. Norton. (Neighborhood Trivia Hunt Ser.). (Illus.). 16p. (Orig.). 1986. pap. 1.50 (0-938357-07-7) BAN Pub Boston.

Neighborhood Trucker. Louise Borden. (J). 1997. pap. 3.95 (0-590-46037-4) Scholastic Inc.

Neighborhood Upgrading: A Realistic Assessment. David P. Varady. LC 85-30392. (SUNY Series in Urban Public Policy). 184p. (C). 1986. text 64.50 (0-88706-299-7); pap. text 21.95 (0-88706-300-4) State U NY Pr.

Neighborhood Watch. Andrew Niederman. 336p. 2000. per. 6.99 (0-671-02709-3) PB.

Neighborhood Watch: A Tracer Family Mystery. Jeff Andrus. 288p. 1996. 20.50 (0-684-19706-5) S&S Trade.

Neighborhoods: A Guide to Communities along the Wasatch Front & Beyond. Kent Condon. (Orig.). 1997. pap. 4.95 (0-9656935-0-3) Newspaper Agency.

Neighborhoods & Crime: The Dimensions of Effective Community Control. Robert J. Bursik, Jr. & Harold G. Grasmick. LC 92-29041. 226p. 1992. 37.00 (0-669-24632-8) Lxngtn Bks.

Neighborhoods & Friendship Networks: A Study of 3 Residential Neighborhoods in Jerusalem. Yehoshua S. Cohen & Amnon Shinar. LC 85-21020. (University of Chicago, Department of Geography, Research Paper Ser.: No. 215). 154p. 1985. reprint ed. pap. 47.80 (0-608-02261-6, 206290200004) Bks Demand.

Neighborhoods & Urban Development. Anthony Downs. LC 81-66190. 189p. 1981. 32.95 (0-8157-1920-5); pap. 12.95 (0-8157-1919-1) Brookings.

Neighborhood's Catalogue: Lower East Side Planning & Design File. Diane L. Abbott et al. (Publications in Architecture & Urban Planning: No. R81-5). (Illus.). vi, 117p. 1987. reprint ed. 15.00 (0-938744-18-6) U of Wis Ctr Arch-Urban.

Neighborhoods, Family, & Political Behavior in Urban America: Political Behavior & Orientations. Yvette M. Alex-Assensoh. Ed. by Richard D. Bingham. LC 98-5122. (Contemporary Urban Affairs Ser.). (Illus.). 197p. 1998. 45.00 (0-8153-2381-6) Garland.

Neighborhoods in Transition: The Making of San Francisco's Ethnic & Nonconformist Communities. Brian J. Godfrey. (UC Publications in Geography: Vol. 27). 1988. pap. 22.50 (0-520-09718-1, Pub. by U CA Pr) Cal Prin Full Svc.

Neighborhoods of Brooklyn. Intro. by Kenneth T. Jackson. LC 98-36713. (Illus.). 304p. 1998. 29.95 (0-300-07752-1) Yale U Pr.

Neighborhoods, People, & Community. Roger S. Ahlbrandt, Jr. (Environment, Development, & Public Policy: Public Policy & Social Services Ser.). 256p. 1984. 54.50 (0-306-41542-9, Plenum Trade) Perseus Pubng.

Neighborhoods, Their Place in Urban Life. Howard W. Hallman. LC 83-20024. (Sage Library of Social Research: No. 154). 320p. reprint ed. pap. 99.20 (0-7837-4568-0, 204409700003) Bks Demand.

Neighboring Faiths: A Christian Introduction to World Religions. Winfried Corduan. LC 97-36552. (Illus.). 320p. 1998. 24.99 (0-8308-1524-4, 1524) InterVarsity.

Neighboring Lives. Thomas M. Disch & Charles Naylor. LC 80-19021. 351p. 1981. 25.00 (0-684-16644-5) Ultramarine Pub.

Neighboring Lives. Thomas M. Disch & Charles Naylor. LC 90-25522. 368p. 1991. reprint ed. pap. 13.95 (0-8018-4219-0) Johns Hopkins.

Neighboring on the Air: Cooking with the KMA Radio Homemakers. rev. ed. Evelyn Birkby. LC 91-6304. (Bur Oak Original Ser.). (Illus.). 349p. (Orig.). 1991. pap. 16.95 (0-87745-316-0) U of Iowa Pr.

Neighboring Property Owners. Jacqueline P. Hand & James C. Smith. 450p. 1988. text 115.00 (0-07-026013-3) Shepards.

Neighborly Adversaries. LaRosa & Mora. LC 99-25947. 368p. 1999. text 69.00 (0-8476-9396-1) Rowman.

Neighborly Adversaries: Readings in U. S. - Latin American Relations. Ed. by Michael LaRosa & Frank O. Mora. LC 99-25947. 368p. 1999. pap. 23.95 (0-8476-9397-X) Rowman.

***Neighbors.** Thomas Berger. 288p. 2000. pap. 13.00 (1-58195-023-3) Zoland Bks.

Neighbors. Stephen Emerson. 100p. (Orig.). 1982. pap. 6.00 (0-939180-19-7) Tombouctou.

Neighbors. M. B. Goffstein. LC 78-19491. (Illus.). (J). (ps-3). 1979. 12.95 (0-06-022018-X) HarpC Child Bks.

Neighbors. Glyn Hughes. LC 79-104049. (Illus.). 1970. 15.95 (0-8023-1247-0) Dufour.

Neighbors. Arkady Leokum. 1972. pap. 3.25 (0-8222-0809-1) Dramatists Play.

Neighbors. Jim Pritchard. (Chapbook Ser.). 8p. 1995. pap. 10.00 (0-9652505-0-4) Synaesthesia.

Neighbors. Carol Smith. LC 99-19767. 368p. 1999. 23.95 (0-446-52241-4, Pub. by Warner Bks) Little.

***Neighbors.** Carol Smith. 496p. 2001. mass mkt. write for info. (0-446-60926-9) Warner Bks.

Neighbors: Electric Burro on the Road to Bogota. Scott Hudson. LC 87-72475. (Illus.). 251p. (Orig.). 1988. 16.95 (0-9619198-1-7); pap. 4.95 (0-9619198-0-9); 99.95 (0-9619198-2-5) Breakaway Pub.

Neighbors: "It Seems to Help Me Bear It Better When She Knows about It." Ed. by Maxine Alexander et al. (Southern Exposure Ser.). (Illus.). 72p. (Orig.). (C). 1983. pap. 3.00 (0-943810-69-8) Inst Southern Studies.

Neighbors: Muslims in North America. Elias Mallon. 104p. 1996. pap. 6.50 (0-614-21713-X, 893) Kazi Pubns.

Neighbors: The Social Contract in a Castilian Hamlet. Susan T. Freeman. LC 70-125548. 252p. 1998. lib. bdg. 21.00 (0-226-26169-7) U Ch Pr.

Neighbors Across the Pacific: The Development of Economic & Political Relations Between Canada & Japan, 90. Klaus H. Pringsheim. LC 82-11713. (Contributions in Political Science Ser.: No. 90). 241p. 1983. 59.95 (0-313-23507-4, PRN/) Greenwood.

Neighbors & Family Coloring Book. Peggy A. Moore. (Illus.). 20p. (Orig.). (J). (gr. k up). 1989. pap. 2.50 (0-9613078-4-6) Detroit Black.

Neighbors & Neighborhood in Renaissance Florence: The District of the Red Lion in the Fifteenth Century. Dale Kent & F. W. Kent. LC 82-70335. 1982. 28.00 (0-686-92326-X) J J Augustin.

Neighbors & Strangers: Law & Community in Early Connecticut. Bruce H. Mann. LC 87-6001. (Studies in Legal History). 216p. reprint ed. pap. 67.00 (0-7837-6858-3, 204668700003) Bks Demand.

Neighbors & Strangers: The Fundamentals of Foreign Affairs. William R. Polk. LC 97-2353. 366p. 1997. 24.95 (0-226-67329-4) U Ch Pr.

***Neighbors & Traitors.** Carole Duncan Buckman. LC 99-50724. (Starmaker Books Ser.). 96p. (J). (gr. 6-9). 2000. pap. 5.50 (0-88489-548-3) St Marys.

Neighbors at War: Anthropological Perspectives on Yugoslav Ethnicity, Culture & History. Joel M. Halpern & David A. Kideckel. LC 99-26976. 2000. 85.00 (0-271-01979-4) Pa St U Pr.

***Neighbors at War: Anthropological Perspectives on Yugoslav Ethnicity, Culture & History.** Joel M. Halpern & David A. Kideckel. 2000. pap. 25.00 (0-271-01978-6) Pa St U Pr.

Neighbors Building Community: A Report of the Neighborhood Assistance Act Project. rev. ed. Jenice L. View & Carol E. Wayman. 230p. 1995. pap. 25.00 (1-886949-03-4) Union Inst.

Neighbor's Cats. Can Goknil. Tr. by Eric Van Deventer from DUT. LC 97-25395. 24p. (J). 1998. 10.95 (1-57379-074-5, K1003) High-Scope.

Neighbors, Friends, or Madmen: The Puritan Adjustment to Quakerism in Seventeenth-Century Massachusetts Bay, 14. Jonathan M. Chu. LC 84-29035. (Contributions to the Study of Religion Ser.: No. 14). 205p. 1985. 49.95 (0-313-24809-5, CNE/) Greenwood.

Neighbors Helping Neighbors: A New National Strategy for the Protection of Children. 1994. lib. bdg. 250.00 (0-8490-8431-8) Gordon Pr.

Neighbors Helping Neighbors: A New National Strategy for the Protection of Children. Ed. by Gary B. Melton. 196p. (Orig.). (YA). (gr. 12 up). 1994. pap. text 40.00 (0-7881-0859-X) DIANE Pub.

Neighbors Helping Neighbors: A New Strategy for the Protection of Children. 1996. lib. bdg. 251.95 (0-8490-6908-4) Gordon Pr.

Neighbors in Conflict: The Irish, Germans, Jews & Italians. Ronald H. Bayor. LC 77-14260. (Johns Hopkins University Studies in Historical & Political Science: Ser. 96, No. 1). 249p. reprint ed. pap. 77.20 (0-608-15313-3, 202923900059) Bks Demand.

An Asterisk (*) at the beginning of an entry indicates that the title is appearing for the first time.

Neighbors in Conflict: The Irish, Germans, Jews & Italians of New York City, 1929-41. Ronald H. Bayor. LC 87-19064. 248p. 1988. pap. text 11.95 (0-252-01437-5) U of Ill Pr.
Neighbors in Turmoil see Latin America: History, Politics & U. S. Policy
Neighbors of the Earth. Warren Amster. (Illus.). 87p. (Orig.). 1984. pap. 5.95 (0-86700-012-0) P Walsh Pr.
Neighbors of the U. S. A. Mark Lueckenhoff. (Illus.). 144p. (YA). (gr. 5-8). 1993. pap. text 12.95 (1-58037-046-2, Pub. by M Twain Media) Carson-Dellos.
Neighbors' Wives. John T. Trowbridge. (Notable American Authors). 1999. reprint ed. lib. bdg. 125.00 (0-7812-9796-6) Rprt Serv.
Neighbourhood Guilds: An Instrument of Social Reform. Stanton Coit. LC 73-11917. (Metropolitan America Ser.). 164p. 1974. reprint ed. 17.95 (0-405-05391-6) Ayer.
Neighbourhood Leaders' Participation in Community Development. S. Vasoo. LC 94-942321. 168p. 1994. pap. 17.50 (981-210-026-1, Pub. by Times Academic) Intl Spec Bk.
Neighbourhood Organizations & the Welfare State. David F. Ley & Shlomo Hasson. (Illus.). 472p. (C). 1994. text 65.00 (0-8020-2887-X); pap. text 24.95 (0-8020-7392-1) U of Toronto Pr.
Neighbourhood Regeneration: An International Evaluation. Ed. by Rachelle Alterman & Goran Cars. 240p. 1991. text 110.00 (0-7201-2073-X) Continuum.
***Neighbourhood Threat: On Tour with Iggy Pop.** Alvin Gibbs. (Illus.). 2000. pap. 19.95 (1-899598-17-0) Codex.
Neighbouring Rights: Artists, Producers & Their Collecting Societies. Ed. by Julian Turton & Cees Van Rij. 164p. 1990. pap. 95.00 (90-6215-259-7, Pub. by Maklu Uitgev) Gaunt.
Neighbours. 5th ed. Ed. by Universities Federation for Animal Welfare Staff. 1980. 25.00 (0-7855-1113-X) St Mut.
Neighbours, Bk. 1. large type ed. Sarah A. Shears. (Dales Large Print Ser.). 1995. pap. 18.99 (1-85389-533-4, Dales) Ulverscroft.
Neighbours, Bk. 2. large type ed. Sarah A. Shears. (Dales Large Print Ser.). 1995. pap. 18.99 (1-85389-534-2, Dales) Ulverscroft.
Neighbours: A Story of Every Day Life. 4th ed. Frederika Bremer. Tr. by Mary Howitt from SWE. LC 74-150538. (Short Story Index Reprint Ser.). 1977. reprint ed. 26.95 (0-8369-3835-6) Ayer.
Neighbours: Multicultural Writing of the 1980s. Ed. by R. F. Holt. (Orig.). 1991. pap. 16.95 (0-7022-2318-2, Pub. by Univ Queensland Pr) Intl Spec Bk.
Neighbours: Subdivision Life in England & the United States. H. E. Bracey. LC 64-15877. 220p. 1964. reprint ed. pap. 68.20 (0-7837-9880-6, 206060600006) Bks Demand.
Neighbours Across the Pacific: Canadian-Japanese Relations, 1870-1982. Klaus H. Pringsheim. 242p. 1995. pap. 14.95 (0-88962-216-7) Mosaic.
Neighbours' Children. large type ed. Sarah A. Shears. 555p. 1996. 27.99 (0-7505-0940-6, Pub. by Mgna Lrg Print) Ulverscroft.
Neighbours in a Thicket. 2nd ed. David Malouf. 1980. pap. 12.95 (0-7022-1547-3, Pub. by Univ Queensland Pr) Intl Spec Bk.
Neighbours of the Night: Selected Short Stories. Endre Ady. 176p. 1989. pap. 44.40 (963-13-3901-7, Pub. by Corvina Bks) St Mut.
Neikirk, Newkirk, Nikirk & Related Families. W. N. Hurley, Jr. xx, 401p. (Orig.). 1997. pap. 23.50 (0-7884-0773-2, H868) Heritage Bk.
Neikirk, Newkirk, Nikirk & Related Families, Vol. 1. W. N. Hurley. (Illus.). xv, 348p. 1996. pap. 29.00 (0-7884-0408-3, H868) Heritage Bk.
Neikirk, Newkirk, Nikirk & Related Families, Vol. 2. W. N. Hurley, Jr. (Illus.). 416p. (Orig.). 1996. pap. 28.50 (0-7884-0429-6, H869) Heritage Bk.
***Neil.** D. Delaney. 1998. mass mkt. 6.95 (0-7472-6066-4, Pub. by Headline Bk Pub) Trafalgar.
Neil & Me. Scott Young. LC 96-932532. (Illus.). 288p. 1997. pap. text 15.95 (0-7710-9099-4) McCland & Stewart.
Neil Armstrong see What Would You Ask?
Neil Armstrong. Sean Connolly. LC 98-7465. (Profiles Ser.). (Illus.). (J). 1998. 23.95 (1-57572-692-0) Heinemann Lib.
Neil Armstrong: A Space Biography. Carmen Bredeson. LC 97-25449. (Countdown to Space Ser.). (Illus.). 48p. (YA). (gr. 4-10). 1998. lib. bdg. 18.95 (0-89490-973-8) Enslow Pubs.
Neil Armstrong: The First Man on the Moon. Barbara Kramer. LC 96-45143. (People to Know Ser.). (Illus.). 112p. (YA). (gr. 6 up). 1997. lib. bdg. 20.95 (0-89490-828-6) Enslow Pubs.
Neil Armstrong: Young Flyer. Montrew Dunham. (Illus.). 192p. (J). (gr. 3-7). 1996. per. 4.99 (0-689-80995-6) S&S Trade.
Neil Armstrong, Young Pilot. Montrew Dunham. (Childhood of Famous Americans Ser.). 1996. 10.09 (0-606-11674-5, Pub. by Turtleback) Demco.
Neil Bissondath. Penny Van Toom. (Canadian Author Studies). 55p. 1997. pap. 9.95 (1-55022-323-2, Pub. by ECW) LPC InBook.
Neil Diamond. Diana K. Harvey & Jackson Harvey. (Illus.). 120p. 1996. 19.98 (1-56799-390-7, MetroBooks) M Friedman Pub Grp Inc.
Neil Diamond: Lovescapes. (Piano-Vocal-Guitar Personality Folio Ser.). 96p. (Orig.). 1991. otabind 14.95 (0-7935-1216-6, 00308124) H Leonard.
Neil Diamond: The Christmas Album. (Piano-Vocal-Guitar Ser.). 64p. 1992. per. 14.95 (0-7935-1836-9, 00308164) H Leonard.
Neil Diamond: The Greatest Hits, 1966-1992. 204p. 1992. otabind 17.95 (0-7935-1433-9, 00308134) H Leonard.
Neil Diamond: The Jazz Singer. 64p. 1986. per. 14.95 (0-88188-510-X, 00356454) H Leonard.
Neil Diamond: Up on the Roof. 80p. 1994. otabind 14.95 (0-7935-2951-4, 00308213) H Leonard.
Neil Diamond: 12 Greatest Hits, Vols. 1. 64p. 1984. per. 14.95 (0-7935-9912-1) H Leonard.
Neil Diamond: 12 Greatest Hits, Vol. 2. 72p. 1982. per. 14.95 (0-7935-3633-2, 00356445) H Leonard.
Neil Diamond Collection. 128p. 1985. per. 14.95 (0-7935-2077-0, 00356443) H Leonard.
Neil Diamond Smash Hits. 96p. 1992. pap. 9.95 (0-7935-1290-5, 00702082) H Leonard.
***Neil Finn Once Removed.** Neil Finn. (Illus.). 200p. 2000. pap. 30.00 (1-86074-297-1) Sanctuary Pub.
Neil Gaiman & Charles Vess' Stardust. Neil Gaiman. (Illus.). 224p. 1998. 29.95 (1-56389-431-9, Pub. by DC Comics) Time Warner.
Neil Gaiman & Charles Vess' Stardust. Neil Gaiman. (Illus.). 224p. 1999. pap. text 19.95 (1-56389-470-X, Pub. by DC Comics) Time Warner.
Neil Gaiman's: Midnight People. Neil Gaiman. 160p. 2000. pap. text 17.95 (1-56389-517-X, Pub. by DC Comics) Time Warner.
Neil Gaiman's Wheel of Worlds. Neil Gaiman. 48p. (YA). 1995. write for info. (0-9645175-0-7) Big Enter Inc.
Neil Gaiman's Wheel of Worlds. Bruce Jones. Ed. by Martin Powell & Julie Riddle. (Illus.). 48p. (Orig.). 1996. pap. 3.25 (0-9645175-4-X) Big Enter Inc.
Neil Kinnock: Biography of the Former Leader of the Labour Party. large type ed. Eileen Jones. 24.95 (1-85695-118-9, Pub. by ISIS Lrg Prnt) Transaction Pubs.
Neil M. Gunn: The Fabulous Matter of Fact. Richard Price. (Modern Scottish Writers Ser.). 224p. 1995. pap. 25.00 (0-7486-0536-3, Pub. by Edinburgh U Pr) Col U Pr.
Neil Patrick Harris. (Illus.). 32p. (J). (gr. 3-8). lib. bdg. 19.93 (1-56239-015-5) ABDO Pub Co.
Neil Sedaka's Greatest Hits. 64p. 1985. per. 12.95 (0-7935-1128-3, 00358171) H Leonard.
Neil Simon: A Casebook. Ed. by Gary Konas. LC 96-45084. (Casebooks on Modern Dramatists Ser.: Vol. 21). 256p. 1997. text 52.00 (0-8153-2132-5, H1946) Garland.
Neil Simon Monologues: Speeches from the Works of America's Foremost Playwright. Ed. by Roger Karshner. LC 96-33841. 202p. 1996. pap. 14.95 (0-940669-34-X, D-40) Dramaline Pubns.
Neil Simon's Lost in Yonkers: The Illustrated Screenplay of the Film. Neil Simon. LC 93-7848. (Illus.). 160p. 1993. pap. 15.95 (1-55704-171-7, Pub. by Newmarket) Norton.
Neil Sperry's Complete Guide to Texas Gardening. 2nd ed. Neil Sperry. LC 91-6698. 400p. 1991. 36.95 (0-87833-799-7) Taylor Pub.
***Neil Spiller.** Woods. 128p. 1999. pap. 45.00 (0-471-99870-2) Wiley.
Neil Tofu Luvs Tee-dah Tuna. Akiko Masuda. (Illus.). 32p. (J). (gr. k-8). 1995. pap. write for info. (0-9629842-2-1) Stew & Rice.
Neil Welliver. Deborah E. Scott. Ed. & Intro. by Craig A. Subler. (Illus.). 14p. (Orig.). 1986. pap. text 4.00 (0-914489-03-8) Univ Miss-KC Art.
Neil Welliver Prints, 1973-1995. Neil Welliver. LC 95-23420. (Illus.). 104p. 1996. 37.50 (0-89272-370-X) Down East.
***Neil Young.** Alexis Petridis. Ed. by John Aizlewood. (Illus.). 152p. 2000. pap. 13.95 (1-56025-265-0, Thunders Mouth) Avalon NY.
Neil Young. Johnny Rogan. (Illus.). 176p. (Orig.). 1996. pap. 8.95 (0-7119-5399-6, OP47807) Omnibus NY.
Neil Young. N. Young & J. McDonough. 2000. 25.95 (0-679-42772-4) Villard Books.
Neil Young: Acoustic Classics. Ed. by Colgan Bryan. 120p. (Orig.). (YA). 1996. pap. text 19.95 (1-57623-673-0, PG9618) Wrner Bros.
Neil Young: Don't Be Denied. John Einarson. 224p. 1993. pap. 14.95 (1-55082-044-3, Pub. by Quarry Pr) LPC InBook.
Neil Young: In His Own Words. Neil Young. LC 98-13131. (Illus.). 96p. 1997. 15.95 (0-7119-6161-1, OP 47861) Omnibus NY.
Neil Young: Love to Burn: Thirty Years of Speaking Out, 1966-1996. Paul Williams. 253p. 1997. pap. 19.95 (0-7119-6160-3, OP47860) Omnibus NY.
Neil Young: The Visual Documentary. John Robertson. LC 95-179908. (Illus.). 160p. pap. 21.95 (0-7119-3816-4, OP 47568) Omnibus NY.
Neil Young: Unplugged. 60p. (Orig.). 1993. pap. 19.95 (0-89724-033-2, VF1989) Wrner Bros.
Neil Young - Complete Music, 1966-1969. Ed. by Carol Cuellar. 192p. (Orig.). (C). 1994. pap. text 22.95 (0-7692-0879-7, VF0263) Wrner Bros.
Neil Young - Decade. Ed. by Carole Cuellar. 142p. (Orig.). (C). 1994. pap. text 18.95 (0-7692-0825-8, VF0476) Wrner Bros.
Neil Young - Freedom. Ed. by Carol Cuellar. 60p. (Orig.). (C). 1990. pap. text 14.95 (0-7692-0844-4, VF1611) Wrner Bros.
Neil Young - Harvest. Ed. by Carol Cuellar. 64p. (Orig.). (C). 1972. pap. text 16.95 (0-7692-0852-5, VF0219) Wrner Bros.
Neil Young - Harvest Moon. Ed. by Carol Cuellar. 72p. (Orig.). (C). 1994. pap. text 19.95 (0-7692-0872-X, VF1907) Wrner Bros.
Neil Young - Love to Burn: Thirty Years of Speaking Out, 1966-1996. Paul Williams. 253p. 1998. 39.95 (0-934558-19-1) Entwhistle Bks.
Neil Young - Mirror Ball. Ed. by Carol Cuellar. 56p. (Orig.). (C). 1995. pap. text 18.95 (0-89724-899-6, PF9535) Wrner Bros.
Neil Young - Sleeps with Angels. Ed. by Carol Cuellar. 68p. (Orig.). (C). 1995. pap. text 18.95 (0-7692-0869-X, VF2172) Wrner Bros.
Neil Young - The Rolling Stone Files: The Ultimate Compendium of Interviews, Articles, Facts, & Opinions from the Files of "Rolling Stone" Rolling Stone Editors. LC 94-11012. 320p. (J). 1994. pap. 12.45 (0-7868-8043-0, Pub. by Hyperion) Time Warner.
Neil Young & Crazy Horse - Broken Arrow Songbook. Ed. by Sy Feldman. 84p. (Orig.). (C). 1996. pap. text 22.95 (1-57623-672-2, PG9657); pap. text 18.95 (1-57623-671-4, PF9643) Wrner Bros.
Neil Young & Crazy Horse - Life. Ed. by Carol Cuellar. 72p. (Orig.). (C). 1987. pap. text 12.95 (0-7692-0859-2, VF1418) Wrner Bros.
Neil Young & Crazy Horse - Ragged Glory. Ed. by Carol Cuellar. 64p. (Orig.). (C). 1990. pap. text 16.95 (0-7692-0866-5, VF1688) Wrner Bros.
Neil Young & Crazy Horse - Weld. Ed. by Carol Cuellar. 84p. (Orig.). (C). 1992. pap. text 16.95 (0-7692-0849-5, VF1800) Wrner Bros.
Neil Young & the Blue Notes - This Note's for You. Ed. by Carol Cuellar. 52p. (Orig.). (C). 1988. pap. text 12.95 (0-7692-0828-2, VF1481) Wrner Bros.
Neil Young Complete, Vol. I. 220p. (Orig.). 1994. pap. 22.95 (0-89724-320-X, VF0341) Wrner Bros.
Neil Young Complete, 1974-1979, Vol. I. 232p. (Orig.). 1994. pap. 24.95 (0-89724-178-9, VF1082) Wrner Bros.
Neil Young/Classic, Vol. 2. Ed. by Aaron Stang. 100p. (Orig.). (C). 1993. pap. text 22.95 (0-7692-1347-2, GF0522) Wrner Bros.
Neil Young/Classic Guitar. Ed. by Aaron Stang. 80p. (Orig.). (C). 1991. pap. text 22.95 (0-7692-1337-5, GF0461) Wrner Bros.
Neil Young/Harvest Moon for Guitar. Ed. by Aaron Stang. 92p. (Orig.). (C). 1993. pap. text 24.95 (0-89724-117-7, GF0587) Wrner Bros.
Neil Zurcher's Favorite One Tank Trips: And Tales from the Road. Neil Zurcher. (Illus.). 208p. 1995. pap. 13.95 (1-886228-01-9) Gray & Co Pubs.
***Neil Zurcher's Favorite One Tank Trips: And Tales from the Road.** 2nd ed. Neil Zurcher. (Illus.). 208p. 2000. pap. 13.95 (1-886228-41-8) Gray & Co Pubs.
Neils Bohr - His Heritage & Legacy: An Anti-Realist View of Quantum Mechanics. Jan Faye. 276p. (C). 1991. lib. bdg. 137.50 (0-7923-1294-5, Pub. by Kluwer Academic) Kluwer Academic.
***Neil's Numberless World.** Lucy Coats. LC 99-51676. (Share-a-Story Ser.). (Illus.). 32p. (ps-3). 2000. 5.95 (0-7894-5616-8) DK Pub Inc.
***Neil's Numberless World.** Lucy Coats. (Illus.). 32p. (ps-3). 2000. 9.95 (0-7894-6354-7) DK Pub Inc.
Neilsen: Symphony No. 5. David Fanning. (Cambridge Music Handbooks Ser.). 135p. (C). 1997. text 39.95 (0-521-44088-2); pap. text 13.95 (0-521-44632-5) Cambridge U Pr.
Neisseriae, 1990: Proceedings of the 7th International Neisseria Conference Berlin, Federal Republic of Germany, Sept. 9-14, 1990. Ed. by Mark Achtman et al. (Illus.). xx, 752p. (C). 1991. lib. bdg. 261.55 (3-11-012712-1) De Gruyter.
Neither Angel nor Beast. Francis X. J. Coleman. 1986. pap. 24.95 (0-7102-0693-3, Routledge Thoemms) Routledge.
Neither Ballots nor Bullets: Women Abolitionists & Emancipation During the Civil War. Wendy H. Venet. (Nation Divided: New Studies in Civil War History Ser.). 1991. text 35.00 (0-8139-1342-X) U Pr of Va.
Neither Beasts nor Gods: Civic Life & the Public Good. Francis Kane. LC 97-33188. 208p. 1997. 25.00 (0-87074-422-4) SMU Press.
Neither Beasts nor Gods: Civic Life & the Public Good. Francis Kane. LC 97-33188. 208p. 1998. pap. 14.95 (0-87074-423-2) SMU Press.
Neither Black nor White: Slavery & Race Relations in Brazil & the U. S. Carl N. Degler. LC 86-40780. 328p. 1986. reprint ed. pap. text 17.95 (0-299-10914-3) U of Wis Pr.
Neither Black nor White yet Both: Thematic Explorations of Interracial Literature. Werner Sollors. LC 96-7162. (Illus.). 592p. 1997. 39.95 (0-19-505282-X) OUP.
Neither Black Nor White Yet Both: Thematic Explorations of Interracial Literature. Werner Sollors. 592p. 1999. pap. 19.95 (0-674-60780-5) HUP.
Neither Bond nor Free. George L. Pryor. LC 79-144674. reprint ed. 36.00 (0-404-00208-0) AMS Pr.
Neither Capitalism nor Socialism: Theories of Bureaucratic Collectivism. Ed. by Ernest E. Haberkern & Arthur Lipow. LC 95-35707. 256p. (C). 1996. text 49.95 (0-391-03928-8) Humanities.
Neither Cargo nor Cult: Ritual Politics & the Colonial Imagination in Fiji. Martha Kaplan. LC 94-38508. 248p. 1995. text 49.95 (0-8223-1578-5); pap. text 17.95 (0-8223-1593-9) Duke.
Neither Carpetbaggers Nor Scalawags: Black Officeholders During the Reconstruction of Alabama, 1867-1878. Richard Bailey. (Illus.). 498p. (C). 1991. 29.95 (0-9627218-0-8) R Bailey.
Neither Carpetbaggers Nor Scalawags: Black Officeholders During the Reconstruction of Alabama, 1867-1878. rev. ed. Richard Bailey. (Illus.). 393p. 1997. reprint ed. 21.00 (0-9627218-5-9) R Bailey.
Neither Carpetbaggers nor Scalawags: Black Officeholders During the Reconstruction of Alabama, 1867-1878. 3rd rev. ed. Richard Bailey. (Illus.). 393p. 1995. 39.95 (0-9627218-3-2); pap. 18.95 (0-9627218-4-0) R Bailey.
Neither Cold War nor Detente? Soviet-American Relations in the 1980's. fac. ed. Ed. by Richard A. Melanson. LC 81-16299. 253p. 1982. reprint ed. pap. 78.50 (0-7837-7984-4, 204774000008) Bks Demand.
Neither Confirm nor Deny: The Nuclear Ships Dispute Between New Zealand & the United States. Stuart McMillan. LC 87-15853. 185p. 1987. 57.95 (0-275-92352-5, C2352, Praeger Pubs) Greenwood.
Neither Dies nor Surrenders: A History of the Republican Party in Florida, 1867-1970. Peter D. Klingman. LC 84-7253. 247p. 1984. reprint ed. pap. 76.60 (0-608-04467-9, 206521200001) Bks Demand.
Neither East nor West: Iran, the Soviet Union, & the United States. Nikki R. Keddie & Mark Gsiorowski. 320p. (C). 1990. pap. 20.00 (0-300-04658-8) Yale U Pr.
Neither East nor West: Selected Writings, 1939-1948. Marie L. Berneri. (Centenary Ser.). (Illus.). 192p. (Orig.). 1988. pap. 8.75 (0-900384-42-5) Left Bank.
Neither Escaping nor Exploiting Sex: Women's Celibacy. Janette Gray. 173p. 1996. pap. 39.95 (0-85439-519-9, Pub. by St Paul Pubns) St Mut.
Neither Fife Nor Drum. Henry W. Gurley. 1990. 15.00 (0-938645-39-0) In His Steps.
Neither 5 nor 3. Helen MacInnes. LC 51-1551. 1951. 24.95 (0-15-165069-1) Harcourt.
Neither Friend nor Foe: The European Neutrals. Jerrold M. Packard. 544p. 1992. text 30.00 (0-684-19248-9, Scribners Ref) Mac Lib Ref.
***Neither God nor Devil: Rethinking Our Perception of Wolves.** Eva-Lena Rehnmark. (Illus.). 144p. 2000. 30.00 (0-7649-1338-7, A549) Pomegranate Calif.
Neither Gods nor Emperors: Students & the Struggle for Democracy in China. Craig Calhoun. 1997. pap. text 15.95 (0-520-21161-8, Pub. by U CA Pr) Cal Prin Full Svc.
Neither Here Nor There: A Skeptics Guide to Metaphysics. Robert W. Elkins. (Illus.). 208p. Date not set. pap. 12.95 (0-9660189-0-7) Grand Ideas.
***Neither Here nor There: Travels in Europe.** Bill Bryson. LC 99-59457. (Illus.). 2000. 25.95 (1-56895-831-5, Compass) Wheeler Pub.
***Neither Here Nor There: Travels in Europe.** Bill Bryson. 256p. 1999. pap. 13.50 (0-380-71380-2, Avon Bks) Morrow Avon.
Neither Heroine nor Fool: Anna Ella Carroll of Maryland. Janet L. Coryell. LC 89-24403. (Illus.). 195p. 1990. reprint ed. pap. 60.50 (0-608-07348-2, 206757600009) Bks Demand.
Neither King nor Prelate: Religion & the New Nation, 1776-1826. rev. ed. Edwin S. Gaustad. LC 93-35446. 208p. 1993. pap. text 13.00 (0-8028-0701-1) Eerdmans.
Neither Kingdom nor Nation: The Irish Quest for Constitutional Rights, 1698-1800. Neil L. York. LC 93-633. (Illus.). 280p. 1994. 54.95 (0-8132-0782-7) Cath U Pr.
Neither Left nor Right: The Politics of Individualism in Uwe Johnson's Work. Kurt Fickert. LC 87-3698. (American University Studies: Germanic Languages & Literature: Ser. I, Vol. 59). 188p. (C). 1987. text 28.00 (0-8204-0494-2) P Lang Pubng.
Neither Male nor Female. Q. M. Adams. 1977. per. 6.95 (0-89985-104-5) Christ for the Nations.
Neither Male nor Female. Betty Miller. (Overcoming Life Ser.). 70p. 1994. pap. 5.00 (1-57149-012-4) Christ Unltd.
Neither Male nor Female Workbook. Betty Miller. (Overcoming Life Ser.). 1995. pap. 10.00 (1-57149-013-2) Christ Unltd.
Neither Man nor Beast: Feminism & the Defense of Animals. Carol J. Adams. LC 57-8649. 272p. 1995. pap. 15.95 (0-8264-0803-6) Continuum.
Neither Man nor Woman: The Hijras of India. Serena Nanda. 170p. (C). 1989. mass mkt. 19.25 (0-534-12204-3) Wadsworth Pub.
Neither More nor Less Than Men: Slavery in Georgia. Ed. by Mills Lane. (A Documentary History Ser.). 248p. 1993. 35.00 (0-88322-016-4) Beehive GA.
Neither Nationalisation nor Privatisation. Ed. by Freedom Journal Staff. (Centenary Ser.). 81p. (Orig.). 1989. pap. 5.00 (0-900384-49-2) Left Bank.
Neither Peace nor Honor: The Politics of American Military Policy in Viet-Nam. Robert L. Gallucci. LC 74-24949. (Washington Center of Foreign Policy Research. Studies in International Affairs: No. 24). 200p. reprint ed. pap. 62.00 (0-608-12069-3, 202415100035) Bks Demand.
Neither Poverty nor Riches: A Biblical Theology of Material Possessions. Craig L. Blomberg. LC 99-14691. (New Studies in Biblical Theology). 300p. 1999. pap. 20.00 (0-8028-4401-4) Eerdmans.
***Neither Rain, Nor Snow.** Beverly Vertress. 146p. 2000. 19.95 (0-7541-1189-X, Pub. by Minerva Pr) Unity Dist.
Neither Red nor White: And Other Indian Stories. George A. Boyce. Ed. by Marcia Muth. LC 95-2900. 128p. (Orig.). 1996. pap. 12.95 (0-86534-237-7) Sunstone Pr.
Neither Right nor Left: Fascist Ideology in France. Zeev Sternhell. Tr. by David Maisel. 440p. 1996. pap. text 18.95 (0-691-00629-6, Pub. by Princeton U Pr) Cal Prin Full Svc.
***Neither Separate nor Equal: Congress in the 1790s.** Ed. by Kenneth R. Bowling & Donald R. Kennon. (Perspectives on the History of Congress Ser.: No. 2). (Illus.). 368p. 2000. 44.95 (0-8214-1327-9, Ohio U Ctr Intl) Ohio U Pr.
***Neither Separate Nor Equal: Legislature & Executive in Rhode Island Constitutional History.** Patrick T. Conley. (Illus.). 218p. (C). 1999. 29.95 (0-917012-06-2) RI Pubns Soc.
Neither Separate Nor Equal: Women, Race & Class in the South. Barbara E. Smith. LC 98-40814. (Women in the Political Economy Ser.). (Illus.). 232p. 1999. pap. 19.95 (1-56639-680-8) Temple U Pr.
Neither Separate Nor Equal: Women, Race & Class in the South. Ed. by Barbara E. Smith. LC 98-40814. (Women in the Political Economy Ser.). (Illus.). 232p. 1999. 59.50 (1-56639-679-4) Temple U Pr.

N

An Asterisk (*) at the beginning of an entry indicates that the title is appearing for the first time.

Neither Sharks Nor Wolves: The Men of Nazi Germany's U-Boat Arm, 1939-1945. Timothy Mulligan. LC 98-53659. (Illus.). 340p. 1999. 34.95 (*1-55750-594-2*) Naval Inst Pr.

Neither Slave nor Free: Advice & Encouragement for Women Seeking Equality in the Church. Patricia Gundry. 1995. pap. 11.95 (*1-882169-04-2*) Suitcase Bks.

Neither Socialism nor Monopoly: Theodore Roosevelt & the Decision to Regulate the Railroads. David M. Chalmers. LC 85-18147. 132p. 1985. reprint ed. pap. 9.50 (*0-89874-878-X*) Krieger.

Neither to Laugh nor to Weep: A Memoir of the Amenian Genocide. 2nd ed. Abraham H. Hartunian. Tr. by Vartan Hartunian. LC 86-26464. (Illus.). xx, 206p. 1986. 35.00 (*0-935411-00-3*); pap. 14.95 (*0-935411-01-1*) Natl Assn Arm.

Neither to Laugh nor to Weep: An Odyssey of Faith: Memoir of the Armenian Genocide. 3rd ed. Tr. by Abraham H. Hartunian from ARM. LC 97-40141. (Illus.). 1999. write for info. (*0-935411-13-5*) Natl Assn Arm.

Neither Urban Jungle nor Urban Village: Women, Families, & Community Development. Sara Stoutland. LC 97-33426. (Children of Poverty Ser.). 204p. 1997. text 52.00 (*0-8153-3044-8*) Garland.

Neither Use nor Ornament: A Memoir of Bolton, 1920s. Bill Naughton. 206p. 1996. 45.00 (*1-85224-303-1*, Pub. by Bloodaxe Bks); pap. 19.95 (*1-85224-304-X*, Pub. by Bloodaxe Bks) Dufour.

Neither Victim nor Enemy: Women's Freedom Network Looks at Gender in America. Ed. by Rita J. Simon. (Illus.). 276p. (Orig.). (C). 1995. pap. text 26.50 (*0-7618-0058-1*); lib. bdg. 49.00 (*0-7618-0057-3*) U Pr of Amer.

Neither Victims nor Executioners. Albert Camus. Tr. by Dwight MacDonald. (Modern Classics of Peace Ser.). 1968. pap. 2.95 (*0-912018-04-6*) World Without War.

Neither Voice Not Heart Alone: German Lutheran Theology of Music in the Age of the Baroque. Joyce L. Irwin. LC 92-12085. (American University Studies: Theology & Religion: Ser. VII, Vol. 132). XI, 207p. (C). 1993. text 41.95 (*0-8204-1858-7*) P Lang Pubng.

Neither Wolf Nor Dog: American Indians, Environment & Agrarian Change. David L. Lewis. (Illus.). 256p. 1994. text 45.00 (*0-19-506297-3*) OUP.

Neither Wolf nor Dog: American Indians, Environment & Agrarian Change. David R. Lewis. (Illus.). 256p. 1997. pap. 17.95 (*0-19-511794-8*) OUP.

Neither Wolf nor Dog: On Forgotten Roads with an Indian Elder. Kent Nerburn. LC 94-21558. 308p. 1994. pap. 14.00 (*1-880032-37-6*) New Wrld Lib.

Neither World: Poems. Ralph Angel. LC 95-1768. 1995. 15.95 (*1-881163-12-1*); pap. 9.95 (*1-881163-13-X*) Miami Univ Pr.

Neitzsche - Truth & Redemption: Critique of the Postmodernist Nietzsche. Ted Sadler. LC 94-46838. 200p. (C). 1995. text 85.00 (*0-485-11471-2*, Pub. by Athlone Pr) Humanities.

Neizvestnaia Kniga Sergeia Bobrova: Iz Sobraniia Biblioteki Stenfordskogo Universiteta. M. L. Gasparov. (Stanford Slavic Studies: Vol. 6). (RUS., Illus.). 95p. (Orig.). (C). 1993. pap. 12.00 (*0-933884-83-4*) Berkeley Slavic.

Nek Nechenenawachgissitschik Bambilak Naga Geschiechauchsitpanna Johannessa Elekhangup see Three Epistles of John in Delaware

Nekane, the Lamina & the Bear: A Tale of the Basque Pyrenees. Frank P. Araujo. LC 93-84620. (Toucan Tales Ser.: Vol. 1). (Illus.). 32p. (J). (gr. 1 up). 1993. 16.95 (*1-877810-01-0*, NEKA) Rayve Prodns.

Nekkid Cowboy. 2nd ed. Katie Breeze. LC 82-73110. 216p. 1991. pap. 9.95 (*0-931722-39-X*) Corona Pub.

Neko No Okasan see Mother Cat

Nekomah Creek. Linda Crew. (Illus.). 192p. (J). (gr. 4-7). 1993. pap. 3.99 (*0-440-40788-5*) Dell.

Nekomah Creek. Linda Crew. 1991. 9.09 (*0-606-05506-1*, Pub. by Turtleback) Demco.

Nekomah Creek Christmas. Linda Crew. (Illus.). 160p. (J). (gr. 4-7). 1995. pap. 3.99 (*0-440-41099-1*, YB BDD) BDD Bks Young Read.

Nekomah Creek Christmas. Linda Crew. (J). 1995. 9.34 (*0-606-07940-8*) Turtleback.

***Nekomah Creek Christmas.** Linda Crew. (Illus.). 147p. (YA). (gr. 6-9). 1999. reprint ed. text 15.00 (*0-7881-6628-X*) DIANE Pub.

Nekrasov, Victor: Kira Georgievna. Ed. by M. Greene & H. Blair. (Bristol Russian Texts Ser.). (RUS.). 158p. 1992. pap. 16.95 (*1-85399-293-3*, Pub. by Brist Class Pr) Focus Pub-R Pullins.

Nekrassov see Devil & the Good Lord & Two Other Plays

Nekrassov. Jean-Paul Sartre. (FRE.). 1973. pap. 11.95 (*0-8288-3777-5*, F125461) Fr & Eur.

Nekrassov. Jean-Paul Sartre. (Folio Ser.: No. 431). (FRE.). 1973. pap. 9.95 (*2-07-036431-3*) Schoenhof.

Nekrolog, 28 vols., Set. Ed. by Friedrich Schlichtegroll. reprint ed. write for info. incl. fiche (*0-318-71934-7*) G Olms Pubs.

Nekrolog, Vols. I & II: 1790. Ed. by Friedrich Schlichtegroll. 1984. reprint ed. write for info. (*3-487-05793-X*) G Olms Pubs.

Nekrolog, Vols. III-IV: 1791. Ed. by Friedrich Schlichtegroll. 1984. reprint ed. write for info. (*3-487-05794-8*) G Olms Pubs.

Nekrolog, Vols. V-VI: 1792. Ed. by Friedrich Schlichtegroll. 1984. reprint ed. write for info. (*3-487-05795-6*) G Olms Pubs.

Nekrolog, Vols. VII-VIII. Ed. by Friedrich Schlichtegroll. 1984. reprint ed. write for info. (*3-487-05796-4*) G Olms Pubs.

Nekropole des 6 und 5 Jahrhunderts. Karl Kuebler. (Kerameikos Ser.: Vol. 7, No. 1). (C). 1976. 269.25 (*3-11-004871-X*) De Gruyter.

Nekropole des Spaeten 8. bis Fruehen 6. Jahrhunderts: Text Vol. & Vol. with Plates see Kerameikos: Ergebnisse der Ausgrabungen (Deutsches Archaeologisches Institut)

Nekropole des 10. bis 8. Jahrhunderts see Kerameikos: Ergebnisse der Ausgrabungen (Deutsches Archaeologisches Institut)

Nekropoleis. E. B. Dusenbery. (Samothrace Ser.: Vol. 11). 1252 pages in 2p. 1998. text 500.00 (*0-691-03679-9*, Pub. by Princeton U Pr) Cal Prin Full Svc.

Nekropolen des 12. bis 10 Jahrhunderts see Kerameikos: Ergebnisse der Ausgrabungen (Deutsches Archaeologisches Institut)

***Nekrosius & Lithuanian Theatre.** Ludvika Popenhagen. LC 98-13038. (Artists & Issues in the Theatre Ser.: Vol. 8). 200p. 1999. 43.95 (*0-8204-4062-0*) P Lang Pubng.

Nektarzusammensetzung der Asteridae und Ihre Beziehung Zu Bluetenoekologie und Systematik. Michael Schwerdtfeger. (Dissertationes Botanicae Ser.: Band 264). (Illus.). 95p. 1996. pap. 36.00 (*3-443-64176-8*, Pub. by Gebruder Borntraeger) Balogh.

Nekton. Yu G. Aleyev. (Illus.). 1977. text 191.50 (*90-6193-560-1*) Kluwer Academic.

Nektonic Facteur. Michael Dorian. Ed. by John Bifsso. LC 98-60067. 100p. 1998. pap. 10.95 (*0-9654452-1-6*) Silk City Pr.

Nekudat-Chen see Off the Beaten Track in Israel

Nelchina Gold. Ron Wendt. (Illus.). 68p. 1998. pap. 8.95 (*1-886574-17-0*) Goldstream Pubns.

***Nelda Sees Red: A Murder Mystery.** Helen F. Sheffield. LC 99-91460. 2000. pap. 18.00 (*0-7388-0819-9*) Xlibris Corp.

***Nelda Sees Red: A Murder Mystery.** Helen F. Sheffield. LC 99-91460. 2000. 25.00 (*0-7388-0818-0*) Xlibris Corp.

Nelineinye Nelokalnye Uravneniia v Teorii Voln see Nonlinear Nonlocal Equations in the Theory of Waves

Nelio. Henning Mankell. Tr. by Tiina Nunnally from SWE. Orig. Title: Comedia Infantil. 272p. 1999. pap. 14.00 (*0-940242-72-9*) Fjord Pr.

Nell. Jeanette Baker. 418p. 1999. per. 6.50 (*0-671-01735-7*) S&S Trade.

Nell. Nancy Thayer. 336p. 1986. pap. 3.95 (*0-380-70060-3*, Avon Bks) Morrow Avon.

Nell & Ed. Alan M. Hofmeister et al. (Reading for All Learners Ser.). (Illus.). (J). pap. write for info. (*1-56861-097-1*) Swift Lrn Res.

Nell Blaine. Ed. by Carolyn Harris. (Illus.). 18p. 1995. 10.00 (*0-9626097-6-5*) Fischbach Gal.

Nell Blaine: Her Art & Life. Martica Sawin. LC 98-17813. (Illus.). 156p. 1998. 50.00 (*1-55595-113-9*, Pub. by Hudson Hills) Natl Bk Netwk.

***Nell Dunne: New York City, 1899.** Kathleen Duey. Vol. 15. 2000. 9.85 (*0-606-17903-8*) Turtleback.

***Nell Gwyn.** Derek Parker. (Illus.). 224p. 2000. 29.95 (*0-7509-1992-2*) Sutton Publng.

Nell Gwyn, 1650-1687. Arthur I. Dasent. LC 70-82824. 1972. 24.95 (*0-405-08432-3*, Pub. by Blom Pubns) Ayer.

Nell Nugget & the Cow-Napping Caper. Judith R. Enderle et al. LC 94-10189. (Illus.). 40p. (J). 1996. per. 15.00 (*0-689-80502-0*) S&S Bks Yung.

Nell of Blue Harbor. Marion Doren. LC 84-19816. 160p. (J). (gr. 3-7). 1990. 15.95 (*0-15-256889-1*) Harcourt.

Nell of Branford Hall. William Wise. Ed. by Diane Arico. LC 99-19023. 144p. (YA). (gr. 5-9). 1999. boxed set 16.99 (*0-8037-2393-8*, Dial Yng Read) Peng Put Young Read.

Nell the Nebbish: (The True Adventures of a Mensch in Hiding) Rusty Berkus. Ed. by Alida Allison. (Illus.). 64p. (Orig.). 1988. pap. 7.95 (*0-9609888-4-X*) Red Rose Pr.

Nella Cucina: Traditional Italian Cooking from the Host of Ciao Italia. Mary A. Esposito. LC 92-35623. 1993. 22.00 (*0-688-12151-9*, Hearst) Hearst Commns.

Nella Larsen, Novelist of the Harlem Renaissance: A Woman's Life Unveiled. Thadious M. Davis. LC 93-32515. (Illus.). 520p. (C). 1996. pap. 17.95 (*0-8071-2070-7*) La State U Pr.

Nelle Toroni: 1, 2, 3, 4, 5. (Illus.). 80p. 1990. pap. 30.00 (*90-72191-14-5*, Pub. by Imschoot) Dist Art Pubs.

Nelles Guide: Portugal. Nelles Verlag Staff. 1996. pap. text 14.95 (*3-88618-417-X*, Pub. by Nelles Verlag) Seven Hills Bk.

***Nelles Guide to Bali-Lombok.** 3rd ed. (Nelles Guides Ser.). (Illus.). 256p. 2000. pap. 15.95 (*3-88618-219-3*, Pub. by Nelles Verlag) Hunter NJ.

***Nelles Guide to Cambodia-Laos.** 3rd ed. (Nelles Guides Ser.). (Illus.). 256p. 2000. pap. 15.95 (*3-88618-225-8*, Pub. by Nelles Verlag) Hunter NJ.

***Nelles Guide to Corsica.** 2nd ed. (Nelles Guides Ser.). (Illus.). 256p. 2000. pap. 15.95 (*3-88618-239-8*, Pub. by Nelles Verlag) Hunter NJ.

Nelles Guide to Egypt. Nelles Verlag Staff. (Nelles Guides Ser.). 1996. pap. text 14.95 (*3-88618-107-3*, Pub. by Nelles Verlag) Seven Hills Bk.

***Nelles Guide to Greece: Mainland & Peloponnese.** 2nd ed. (Nelles Guides Ser.). (Illus.). 256p. 2000. pap. 15.95 (*3-88618-217-7*, Pub. by Nelles Verlag) Hunter NJ.

***Nelles Guide to Ireland.** 2nd ed. (Nelles Guides Ser.). (Illus.). 256p. 2000. pap. 15.95 (*3-88618-159-6*, Pub. by Nelles Verlag) Hunter NJ.

***Nelles Guide to Israel.** 2nd ed. (Nelles Guides Ser.). (Illus.). 256p. 2000. pap. 15.95 (*3-88618-223-1*, Pub. by Nelles Verlag) Hunter NJ.

***Nelles Guide to Kenya.** 3rd ed. (Nelles Guides Ser.). (Illus.). 256p. 2000. pap. 15.95 (*3-88618-167-7*, Pub. by Nelles Verlag) Hunter NJ.

***Nelles Guide to Nepal.** 3rd ed. (Nelles Guides Ser.). (Illus.). 256p. 2000. pap. 15.95 (*3-88618-194-4*, Pub. by Nelles Verlag) Hunter NJ.

Nelles Guide to Northern Spain: Pyrenees, Atlantic Coast, Central Spain. Nelles Verlag Staff. (Nelles Guides Ser.). 1997. pap. text 14.95 (*3-88618-400-5*, Pub. by Nelles Verlag) Seven Hills Bk.

Nelles Guide to Norway. Gerhard Lemmer et al. (Illus.). 256p. 1999. pap. 15.95 (*3-88618-048-4*) Hunter NJ.

Nelles Guide to Paris. Nelles Verlag Staff. (Nelles Guides Ser.). 1997. pap. text 14.95 (*3-88618-108-1*, Pub. by Nelles Verlag) Seven Hills Bk.

***Nelles Guide to Paris.** 3rd ed. (Nelles Guides Ser.). (Illus.). 256p. 2000. pap. 15.95 (*3-88618-155-3*, Pub. by Nelles Verlag) Hunter NJ.

***Nelles Guide to Peru.** (Nelles Guides Ser.). (Illus.). 256p. 2000. pap. 15.95 (*3-88618-215-0*, Pub. by Nelles Verlag) Hunter NJ.

Nelles Guide to Sri Lanka. Nelles Verlag Staff. (Nelles Guides Ser.). 1997. pap. text 14.95 (*3-88618-418-8*, Pub. by Nelles Verlag) Seven Hills Bk.

***Nelles Guide to the Canary Islands.** Bernd F. Gruschwitz. (Illus.). 254p. 1999. pap. 15.95 (*3-88618-087-5*) Hunter NJ.

Nelles Guide to the Caribbean: The Greater Antilles, Bermuda, Bahamas. Nelles Verlag Staff. (Nelles Guides Ser.). 1997. pap. text 14.95 (*3-88618-403-X*, Pub. by Nelles Verlag) Seven Hills Bk.

***Nelles Guide to the Philippines.** 3rd ed. (Nelles Guides Ser.). (Illus.). 256p. 2000. pap. 15.95 (*3-88618-222-3*, Pub. by Nelles Verlag) Hunter NJ.

***Nelles Guide to Tuscany.** 2nd ed. (Nelles Guides Ser.). (Illus.). 256p. 2000. pap. 15.95 (*3-88618-209-6*, Pub. by Nelles Verlag) Hunter NJ.

Nellie: A Cat on Her Own. Natalie Babbitt. (Illus.). 32p. (J). (ps up). 1989. 14.00 (*0-374-35506-1*) FS&G.

Nellie: A Cat on Her Own. Natalie Babbitt. 1992. 10.15 (*0-606-07165-2*, Pub. by Turtleback) Demco.

Nellie: A Cat on Her Own. Natalie Babbitt. (Illus.). 32p. (J). (ps-3). 1992. reprint ed. pap. 4.95 (*0-374-45496-5*, Sunburst Bks) FS&G.

Nellie Bishop. Clara Clark. LC 95-76355. (Illus.). 128p. (J). (gr. 7 up). 1997. pap. 7.95 (*1-56397-642-0*) Boyds Mills Pr.

***Nellie Bly: Daredevil Reporter.** Charles Fredeen. LC 98-50519. (Biographies Ser.). 112p. (YA). (gr. 6-9). 1999. 25.26 (*0-8225-4956-5*, Lerner Publctns) Lerner Pub.

Nellie Bly: Making Headlines: A Biography of Nellie Bly. Karen L. Emerson. LC 88-35910. (People in Focus Ser.). (Illus.). 112p. (YA). (gr. 5 up). 1989. lib. bdg. 13.95 (*0-87518-406-5*, Dillon Silver Burdett) Silver Burdett Pr.

Nellie Bly: Reporter for the World. Martha E. Kendall. (J). (gr. 4-7). 1992. pap. 4.80 (*0-395-64538-7*) HM.

Nellie Bly: Reporter for the World. Martha E. Kendall. LC 91-37643. (Gateway Biography Ser.). (Illus.). 48p. (J). (gr. 2-4). 1992. pap. 6.95 (*1-56294-787-7*); lib. bdg. 21.90 (*1-56294-061-9*) Millbrook Pr.

Nellie Bly's Book: Around the World in 72 Days. Ira Peck & Nellie Bly. LC 98-5376. 128p. (YA). (gr. 5 up). 1998. 26.90 (*0-7613-0971-3*) TFC Bks NY.

Nellie Bly's Monkey: His Remarkable Story in His Own Words. Joan W. Blos. LC 95-13713. (Illus.). (J). (ps-3). 1996. 15.00 (*0-688-12677-4*, Wm Morrow) Morrow Avon.

Nellie Brown: or The Jealous Wife, with Other Sketches. Thomas Detter. LC 96-1023. (Blacks in the American West Ser.). xxi, 122p. (C). 1996. text 30.00 (*0-8032-1704-8*) U of Nebr Pr.

Nellie Cashman & the North American Mining Frontier. Don Chaput. (Illus.). 1995. 28.95 (*0-87026-093-6*) Westernlore.

Nellie L. Connie B. Crook. 232p. (Orig.). (YA). (gr. 7-11). 1994. mass mkt. 4.95 (*0-7736-7422-5*) STDK.

Nellie Lou's Hairdos. John Sandford. (Illus.). 32p. (J). 1990. pap. 9.95 (*1-55782-098-8*) Little.

Nellie Mae Rowe. J. Richard Gruber & Xenia Zed. (Illus.). 55p. 1996. pap. 22.95 (*0-9638753-7-X*) Morris Mus Art.

Nellie Melba: A Biography. John Hetherington. 312p. 1996. pap. 19.95 (*0-522-84697-1*, Pub. by Melbourne Univ Pr) Paul & Co Pubs.

Nellie Melba: A Contemporary Review, 5. Compiled by William R. Moran. LC 83-26444. (Contributions to the Study of Music & Dance Ser.: No. 5). (Illus.). 491p. 1985. 69.50 (*0-313-23893-6*, MOM/, Greenwood Pr) Greenwood.

Nellie Stone Johnson: The Life of an Activist. Told to David Brauer. (Illus.). 256p. 2000. 23.00 (*1-886913-35-8*, Pub. by Ruminator Bks) Consort Bk Sales.

Nellie, the Flying Instructor. Robert Ensor. LC 94-61888. (Illus.). 40p. (J). (ps up). 1995. pap. 9.95 (*1-883650-21-6*) Windswept Hse.

Nellie, the Light House Dog. Jane Scarpino. Ed. by Jane Weinberger. LC 93-60463. (Picture Bk.). (Illus.). 40p. (J). (ps up). 1993. pap. 9.95 (*0-932433-23-5*) Windswept Hse.

Nellie Toole & Co. Peter Keveson. 1974. pap. 5.25 (*0-8222-0810-5*) Dramatists Play.

Nellie's Boarding House: A Dual Biography of Nellie Coffman & Palm Springs. Marjorie B. Bright. 1981. 19.95 (*0-88280-068-X*) ETC Pubns.

Nellie's Girl. Marie M. Wilson. LC 35-90247. (Illus.). 200p. (YA). (gr. 5 up). 1993. reprint ed. pap. 5.00 (*0-9615259-0-8*) Pilgrim Way.

Nellie's Girl Two. Marie M. Wilson. (Illus.). 160p. (YA). (gr. 5 up). 1988. 5.00 (*0-9615259-1-6*) Pilgrim Way.

Nellie's Knot. Ken Brown. LC 92-27910. (Illus.). 32p. (J). (ps-1). 1993. lib. bdg. 13.95 (*0-02-714930-7*, Four Winds Pr) S&S Childrens.

Nellie's Quest. Connie B. Crook. 180p. (YA). (gr. 7-12). 1998. pap. 5.95 (*0-7736-7469-1*) Stoddart Publ.

***Nellie's Victory.** Connie B. Crook. (Illus.). 200p. (J). 2000. mass mkt. 5.95 (*0-7736-7481-0*, Stoddart Kids) Stoddart Publ.

Nell's Cowboy. Debbie Macomber. (Promo Ser.: No. 5). 1998. per. 4.50 (*0-373-83346-6*, 1-83346-6) Harlequin Bks.

***Nell's Cowboy.** large type ed. Debbie Macomber. 288p. 1999. 25.99 (*0-263-16173-0*, Pub. by Mills & Boon) Ulverscroft.

Nell's Quilt. Susan Terris. LC 87-12961. 176p. (YA). (gr. 7 up). 1996. pap. 4.95 (*0-374-45497-3*, Sunburst Bks) FS&G.

Nell's Quilt. Susan Terris. 1996. 10.05 (*0-606-10892-0*, Pub. by Turtleback) Demco.

Nell's Story: A Woman from Eagle River. Nell Peters & Robert Peters. LC 94-24164. (Illus.). 172p. (C). 1995. 22.95 (*0-299-14470-4*) U of Wis Pr.

Nell's Story: A Woman from Eagle River. Nell Peters & Robert Peters. LC 94-24164. (Illus.). 172p. 1996. pap. 14.95 (*0-299-14474-7*) U of Wis Pr.

Nelly Custis: Child of Mount Vernon. David L. Ribblett. LC 93-12419. 1993. pap. 7.95 (*0-931917-23-9*) Mt Vernon Ladies.

Nelly Custis Lewis's Housekeeping Book. Eleanor P. Lewis. Ed. by Patricia B. Schmit. LC 82-81038. (Illus.). x, 134p. 1982. 14.95 (*0-917860-09-8*) Historic New Orleans.

Nelly's Silver Mine. Helen H. Jackson. (Notable American Authors Ser.). 1992. reprint ed. lib. bdg. 75.00 (*0-7812-3352-6*) Rprt Serv.

Nels. New Ill. Bible Mann. & Customs. H. F. Vos. LC 99-12227. (Illus.). 608p. 1999. 29.99 (*0-7852-1194-2*) Nelson.

Nelson. Carola Oman. (Illus.). 816p. 1996. 46.95 (*1-55750-618-3*) Naval Inst Pr.

Nelson: A Personal History. Christopher Hibbert. 1995. 30.00 (*0-201-62457-5*) Addison-Wesley.

Nelson: A Personal History. Christopher Hibbert. 446p. 1996. pap. 20.00 (*0-201-40800-7*) Addison-Wesley.

Nelson: A Personal History. Christopher Hibbert. 1996. text 30.00 (*0-07-028658-2*) McGraw.

Nelson: Politics, Economy, Community. Jeffrey Hill. 224p. 1998. pap. 30.00 (*1-85331-216-9*, Pub. by Edinburgh U Pr) Col U Pr.

Nelson: The Essential Hero. Ernie Bradford. 1999. pap. text 12.99 (*1-84022-202-6*) Wrdsworth Edits.

Nelson: The Immortal Memory. Stephen Deuchar et al. (Illus.). 176p. 1995. pap. 24.95 (*1-85669-061-X*, Pub. by Law King Ltd) Trafalgar.

***Nelson: The Immortal Memory.** David Howarth. 1999. pap. text 19.95 (*1-55821-979-X*) Lyons Pr.

Nelson: The Immortal Memory. David Howarth & Stephen Howarth. 1998. 24.95 (*0-85177-720-1*) Brasseys.

Nelson: The Life & Letters of a Hero. Roger Morriss. (Illustrated Letters Ser.). (Illus.). 160p. 1996. 24.95 (*1-85585-274-8*, Pub. by Collins & Br) Trafalgar.

Nelson: The Public & Private Life of Horatio Viscount Nelson. G. Lathom Browne. 762p. 1999. 24.95 (*1-888777-67-2*) Trident Pr Intl.

Nelson - The Life & Letters of a Hero. Roger Morriss. (Illus.). 160p. 1998. pap. 17.95 (*1-85585-299-3*, Pub. by Collins & Br) Trafalgar.

Nelson A. Miles & the Twilight of the Frontier Army. Robert Wooster. LC 92-25510. (Illus.). xvii, 403p. 1993. pap. 18.00 (*0-8032-9775-0*, Bison Books) U of Nebr Pr.

Nelson A. Rockefeller Collection of Mexican Folk Art: A Gift to the Mexican Museum. Carlos Espejel et al. (Illus.). 79p. (Orig.). 1986. 19.95 (*0-9605194-3-2*) Mexican Museum.

Nelson Against Napoleon: From the Nile to Copenhagen, 1798-1801. David Lyon. LC 97-68138. (Chatham Pictorial Histories Ser.). (Illus.). 192p. 1997. 49.95 (*1-55750-642-6*) Naval Inst Pr.

Nelson Algren: A Descriptive Bibliography. Matthew J. Bruccoli. LC 85-1180. (Series in Bibliography). (Illus.). 200p. 1985. text 100.00 (*0-8229-3517-1*) U of Pittsburgh Pr.

Nelson Almanac: A Book of Days Recording Nelson's Life & the Events That Shaped His Era. Ed. by David Harris. LC 98-66111. (Classics of Naval Literature Ser.). (Illus.). 192p. 1998. 38.95 (*1-55750-647-7*) Naval Inst Pr.

Nelson & Helen Glueck Collection of Cypriot Antiquities, Cincinnati. Gisela Walberg. (Studies in Mediterranean Archaeology & Literature: No. 111). (Illus.). 100p. 1992. pap. 23.50 (*91-7081-029-X*, Pub. by P Astroms) Coronet Bks.

Nelson & the Nile: The Naval War Against Bonaparte, 1798. Brian Lavery. (Classics of Naval Literature Ser.). (Illus.). 352p. 1998. 42.95 (*1-55750-640-X*) Naval Inst Pr.

Nelson & Winnie Mandela. John Vail. (World Leaders Past & Present Ser.). 120p. (YA). (gr. 5 up). 1989. pap. 8.95 (*0-7910-0586-0*) Chelsea Hse.

Nelson & Winnie Mandela. John Vail. (World Leaders Past & Present Ser.). (Illus.). 120p. (YA). (gr. 5 up). 1989. lib. bdg. 19.95 (*1-55546-841-1*) Chelsea Hse.

Nelson Artillery Lamkin & Rives Batteries. W. Cullen Sherwood. (Virginia Regimental Histories Ser.). (Illus.). 106p. 1991. 19.95 (*1-56190-019-2*) H E Howard.

Nelson-Atkins Museum of Art: Culture Comes to Kansas City. Kristie C. Wolferman. LC 93-17669. (Illus.). 240p. (C). 1993. 29.95 (*0-8262-0908-4*) U of Mo Pr.

Nelson Augustus Moore: Connecticut Landscape Painter. Moore Picture Trust Staff. (Illus.). 144p. 1994. text 40.00 (*0-9637491-0-2*) Moore Picture.

Nelson Balanced Science: Living World. Roberts. (UK - Science Ser.). 1995. mass mkt. 35.95 (*0-17-438665-6*) S-W Pub.

Nelson Balanced Science: Material World. Holman. (UK - Science Ser.). 1991. mass mkt. 35.95 (*0-17-438666-4*) S-W Pub.

Nelson Balanced Science: Physical World. Dobson. (UK - Science Ser.). 1991. mass mkt. 35.95 (*0-17-438667-2*) S-W Pub.

N

An Asterisk (*) at the beginning of an entry indicates that the title is appearing for the first time.

Nelson Biology. Ritter. (UK - Science Ser.). 1992. pap., teacher ed. 54.95 (*0-17-603861-2*) S-W Pub.

Nelson Biology-Blue: Teacher's Resource Guide. Bob Ritter et al. (Illus.). 288p. (Orig.). pap., teacher ed. 49.75 (*0-17-603871-X*) Thomson Learn.

Nelson Biology Blue Text. Ritter et al. (UK - Science Ser.). 1993. mass mkt. 61.95 (*0-17-603870-1*) S-W Pub.

Nelson Chemistry. Jenkins. (UK - Science Ser.). 1992. mass mkt. 61.95 (*0-17-603863-9*) S-W Pub.

Nelson Chemistry, Blackline Masters. Jenkins. (UK - Science Ser.). 1992. 82.95 (*0-17-603975-9*) S-W Pub.

Nelson Chemistry, Solutions Manual. Jenkins. (UK - Science Ser.). 1993. 68.95 (*0-17-603976-7*) S-W Pub.

Nelson Companion. Colin White. LC 95-68900. (Illus.). 256p. 1995. 35.00 (*1-55750-619-1*) Naval Inst Pr.

***Nelson Complete Books of the Bible.** Thomas Nelson Publishing Staff. 1999. pap. 14.97 (*0-7852-4492-1*) Nelson.

Nelson County, Kentucky, 1850 Census. Rowena Lawson. iv, 88p. (Orig.). 1985. pap. 12.50 (*0-917890-60-4*) Heritage Bk.

Nelson County, Kentucky, Taxpayers, 1793-1799. T.L.C. Genealogy Staff. 100p. (Orig.). 1995. pap., spiral bd. 10.00 (*1-57445-013-1*) TLC Genealogy.

***Nelson County, KY: A Portrait of the Civil War.** Dixie Hibbs. (Civil War History Ser.). 128p. 1999. pap. 18.99 (*0-7385-0261-8*, Tempus Publng) Arcadia Publng.

Nelson County, Virginia Marriages, 1808-1850. John Vogt & T. William Kethley, Jr. 129 p. 1985. pap. 12.95 (*0-935931-09-0*) Iberian Pub.

***Nelson De Mille: A Reader's Checklist & Reference Guide.** CheckerBee Publishing Staff. 1999. pap. text 4.95 (*1-58598-016-1*) CheckerBee.

Nelson, Descendants of John Nelson, Sr. - Mary Toby, Stafford Co., Va., 1740-1959, with Related Families. Olive N. Gibson. (Illus.). 350p. 1993. reprint ed. pap. 54.00 (*0-8328-3587-0*); reprint ed. lib. bdg. 64.00 (*0-8328-3586-2*) Higginson Bk Co.

Nelson Dominguez. Manuel Lopez Oliva. (Illus.). 168p. 1998. text 35.00 (*90-5703-961-3*) Gordon & Breach.

Nelson Eddy: A Bio-Discography. Larry F. Kiner. LC 92-1232. (Illus.). 709p. 1992. 85.00 (*0-8108-2544-9*) Scarecrow.

Nelson Essentials of Pediatrics. 3rd ed. Behrman. 1998. pap. text 32.50 (*0-8089-2052-9*, Grune & Strat) Harcrt Hlth Sci Grp.

Nelson Essentials of Pediatrics. 3rd ed. Richard E. Behrman & Robert M. Kliegman. LC 97-15484. (Illus.). 736p. 1998. pap. text 42.50 (*0-7216-7229-9*, W B Saunders Co) Harcrt Hlth Sci Grp.

Nelson Glueck's 1938-1940 Excavations at Tell El-Kheleifeh: A Reappraisal. Gary D. Pratico. (Archaeological Reports: No. 3). (Illus.). 223p. 1993. reprint ed. 45.00 (*1-55540-883-4*, 85 00 03, Pub. by Am Sch Orient Res) David Brown.

Nelson Goodman's New Riddle of Induction see Philosophy of Nelson Goodman: Selected Essays

Nelson Goodman's Philosophy of Art see Philosophy of Nelson Goodman: Selected Essays

Nelson Goodman's Theory of Symbols & Its Applications see Philosophy of Nelson Goodman: Selected Essays

Nelson Handbook on Pediatric Therapeutics. Richard E. Behrman. (C). 1995. pap. text. write for info. (*0-7216-5018-X*, W B Saunders Co) Harcrt Hlth Sci Grp.

Nelson Illustrated Mysteries & Wonders of the Bible. Ed. by Les Stobbe. 608p. 2000. 29.99 (*0-7852-0968-9*) Nelson.

Nelson in Love. Janice Lee Smith. (Adam Joshua Capers Ser.). (J). 1996. 9.15 (*0-606-08470-3*, Pub. by Turtleback) Demco.

Nelson Island & Seabrook Marsh Sites Pt. 1: Late Archaic, Marine Oriented People on the Central New England Coast. Brian S. Robinson. (Ocassional Publications in Northeastern Anthropology: No. 9). (Illus.). xii, 107p. 15.00 (*0-318-32508-X*) F Pierce College.

Nelson Jackson - Cowboy. Lawanda Randall. (Illus.). (Orig.). (J). (gr. 3-7). 1997. 10.95 (*0-9656838-1-8*) DPSI.

Nelson-Jones & Burton: Medical Negligence Case Law. 2nd ed. Rodney Nelson-Jones & Frank Burton. 1995. write for info. (*0-406-03601-2*, NJBM2, MICHIE) LEXIS Pub.

Nelson Malone Meets the Man from Mush-Nut. Louise Hawes. (J). (gr. 3-7). 1988. pap. 2.50 (*0-380-70508-7*, Avon Bks) Morrow Avon.

Nelson Malone Saves Flight 942. Louise Hawes. 160p. (J). 1990. pap. 2.95 (*0-380-70758-6*, Avon Bks) Morrow Avon.

***Nelson Mandela.** Sean Connolly. LC 99-85742. (Profiles Ser.). (Illus.). 2000. lib. bdg. write for info. (*1-57572-225-9*) Heinemann Lib.

Nelson Mandela. Reggie Finlayson. LC 97-50167. (A&E Biography Ser.). 128p. (J). (gr. 6-9). 1998. 17.95 (*0-8225-4936-0*, Lerner Publctns) Lerner Pub.

Nelson Mandela. Gina Holland. LC 96-4299. 32p. (J). (gr. 1-6). 1997. pap. text 5.95 (*0-8172-6886-3*) Raintree Steck-V.

Nelson Mandela. Gini Holland. LC 96-4299. (First Biographies Ser.). (Illus.). 32p. (J). 1997. lib. bdg. 21.40 (*0-8172-4454-9*) Raintree Steck-V.

Nelson Mandela. Jayne Woodhouse. LC 97-50443. (Lives & Times Ser.). (J). 1998. 12.95 (*1-57572-669-6*) Heinemann Lib.

Nelson Mandela: A Biography. Martin Meredith. LC 97-49351. (Illus.). 596p. 1998. text 29.95 (*0-312-18132-9*) St Martin.

Nelson Mandela: A Biography. Martin Meredith. 608p. 1999. pap. 17.95 (*0-312-19992-9*) St Martin.

Nelson Mandela: A Voice Set Free. Rebecca Stefoff. (Great Lives Ser.). 1990. 10.09 (*0-606-01258-3*, Pub. by Turtleback) Demco.

Nelson Mandela: Determined to Be Free. Jack Roberts. LC 94-21519. (Gateway Biographies Ser.). (Illus.). 48p. (J). (gr. 2-4). 1994. lib. bdg. 21.90 (*1-56294-558-0*) Millbrook Pr.

Nelson Mandela: "No Easy Walk to Freedom" Barry Denenberg. LC 90-8496. 176p. (J). (gr. 4-7). 1991. pap. 3.50 (*0-590-44154-X*) Scholastic Inc.

Nelson Mandela: The Man & the Movement. Mary Benson. 1994. pap. 215.40 (*0-393-31275-5*) Norton.

Nelson Mandela: The Man & the Movement. 2nd ed. Mary Benson. 1994. pap. 10.95 (*0-393-31281-X*, Norton Paperbks) Norton.

Nelson Mandela: Voice of Freedom. Libby Hughes. LC 91-31543. (People in Focus Ser.). (Illus.). 144p. (YA). (gr. 5 up). 1992. lib. bdg. 18.95 (*0-87518-484-7*, Dillon Silver Burdett) Silver Burdett Pr.

Nelson Mandela & Apartheid in South Africa. K. K. Virmani. 1990. 19.00 (*81-85163-20-0*, Pub. by S Asia Pubs) S Asia.

Nelson Mandela: Intensifiquemos la Lucha: Discursos en Africa, Europa y Norteamerica. Nelson Mandela. Ed. & Intro. by Luis Madrid. Intro. by Greg McCartan. LC 90-63059. (SPA., Illus.). 108p. (Orig.). 1990. pap. 13.95 (*0-87348-597-1*); lib. bdg. 35.00 (*0-87348-598-X*) Pathfinder NY.

Nelson Mandela Speaks: Forging a Democratic, Nonracial South Africa. Nelson Mandela. Ed. by Steve Clark. LC 93-85689. (Illus.). 96p. (Orig.). 1993. pap. 18.95 (*0-87348-774-5*); lib. bdg. 50.00 (*0-87348-775-3*) Pathfinder NY.

Nelson Mandela Speeches, 1990: 'Intensify the Struggle to Abolish Apartheid' Nelson Mandela. (Illus.). 74p. (Orig.). (C). 1990. pap. 6.00 (*0-87348-595-5*) Pathfinder NY.

Nelson Mandelamandla. Ed. by Amelia B. House & Cosmo Pieterse. (Illus.). 99p. 1989. pap. 8.00 (*1-57889-028-4*) Passeggiata.

Nelson Mass & Mass in Time of War in Full Score. Joseph Haydn. 208p. pap. 12.95 (*0-486-28108-6*) Dover.

Nelson Music Collection. Newton F. Tolman & Kay Gilbert. pap. 13.95 (*0-89190-952-4*, Rivercity Pr) Amereon Ltd.

Nelson Picture Dictionary English. Ashworth & Clark. Date not set. pap. text. write for info. (*0-17-556454-X*) Addison-Wesley.

Nelson Picture Dictionary French. Ashworth, Clark & Clark. (Illus.). 1993. pap. text. write for info. (*0-17-556452-3*) Addison-Wesley.

Nelson Point: Portrait of a Northern Gold Rush Town. large type ed. David F. Matuszak. LC 92-64297. (Illus.). 270p. (Orig.). 1993. pap. 19.95 (*0-9633582-0-0*) Pacific Sunset.

***Nelson Reference Bible.** 1999. 12.97 (*0-7852-5511-7*) Tommy Nelson.

***Nelson Reference Bible.** Nelson Publishing Staff. 2000. 12.97 (*0-7852-5512-5*) Nelson.

Nelson Reference Bible: Supersaver Edition. 1997. 39.97 (*0-7852-0229-3*); 39.97 (*0-7852-0231-5*) Tommy Nelson.

***Nelson Reference Bible: Supersaver Edition.** 1999. 29.97 (*0-7852-0222-6*) Tommy Nelson.

Nelson Review of Pediatrics. Richard E. Behrman et al. Ed. by Lisette Bralow. 208p. 1996. pap. text 29.00 (*0-7216-5579-3*, W B Saunders Co) Harcrt Hlth Sci Grp.

Nelson Review of Pediatrics. 2nd ed. Richard E. Behrman et al. 315p. (C). 2000. pap. text. write for info. (*0-7216-7785-1*, W B Saunders Co) Harcrt Hlth Sci Grp.

Nelson Rodrigues, the Great Rebel of Brazilian Theatre: The Man & His Plays. Sun L. Yu. LC 91-89711. (Illus.). 272p. 1997. 22.95 (*1-878756-92-3*); pap. 15.95 (*1-878756-93-1*) YCP Pubns.

Nelson Textbook of Pediatrics. 15th ed. Richard E. Behrman. 1997. audio compact disk 240.00 (*0-7216-6361-3*, W B Saunders Co) Harcrt Hlth Sci Grp.

Nelson Textbook of Pediatrics. 15th ed. Richard E. Behrman et al. Ed. by Waldo E. Nelson. LC 95-17879. (Illus.). 2245p. 1995. text 105.00 (*0-7216-5578-5*, W B Saunders Co) Harcrt Hlth Sci Grp.

Nelson Textbook of Pediatrics Pocket Companion. Ed. by Richard E. Behrman. LC 93-9371. (Illus.). 546p. 1993. pap. text 25.00 (*0-7216-3968-2*, W B Saunders Co) Harcrt Hlth Sci Grp.

Nelson the Newsboy. Horatio Alger, Jr. (Works of Horatio Alger Jr.). 1989. reprint ed. lib. bdg. 79.00 (*0-685-27575-2*) Rprt Serv.

Nelson vs. the United States of America: A System in Denial. Marcus Giavanni. (Illus.), 484p. 1998. 49.95 (*0-9660928-0-5*) G & B Pub.

***Nelsonian Reminiscences; A Dramatic Eye-Witness Account of the War at Sea 1795-1810.** G. Parsons. 1999. pap. text 21.95 (*1-86176-083-3*, Chatham Pubg) G Duckworth.

Nelson's Amazing Bible Trivia, Bk. 2. TNP Staff. 2000. pap. 9.99 (*0-7852-4267-8*) Nelson.

***Nelson's Amazing Bible Trivia, Vol. 2.** Nelson Reference Books Staff. 2000. pap. 9.99 (*0-7852-4528-6*) Nelson.

Nelson's Battles: The Art of Victory in the Age of Sail. Nicholas Tracy. LC 96-69150. (Illus.). 224p. 1996. 41.95 (*1-55750-621-3*) Naval Inst Pr.

Nelson's Biographical Dictionary & Historical Reference Book of Erie County: Being a Condensed History of . . . Erie County, & of the Several Cities, Boroughs & Townships in the County. With Biographies. Benjamin Whitman. (Illus.). 922p. 1997. reprint ed. lib. bdg. 92.50 (*0-8328-6410-2*) Higginson Bk Co.

Nelson's Blood. A. J. Pack. 160p. 1987. 45.00 (*0-85937-279-0*, Pub. by K Mason Pubns Ltd) St Mut.

Nelson's Blood: The Story of Naval Rum. James Pack. (Illus.). 208p. 1996. pap. 15.95 (*1-55750-666-3*) Naval Inst Pr.

Nelson's Brand. Diana Palmer. (Silhouette Promo Ser.). 1997. per. 3.99 (*0-373-48361-9*, 1-48361-9) Harlequin Bks.

Nelson's Complete Book of Bible Maps & Charts. expanded rev. ed. (Illus.). 512p. 1996. 19.99 (*0-7852-1154-3*) Nelson.

***Nelson's Directory of Institutional Real Estate, 1999.** Ed. by Marcia Boysen. 2200p. 1998. pap. 335.00 (*1-891851-00-4*) Nelson Info.

Nelson's Directory of Investment Managers, 1997, 2 vols. Ed. by Dan Regusa. 5500p. 1997. pap., per. 495.00 (*0-922460-93-0*) Nelson Info.

***Nelson's Directory of Investment Managers, 1999, 3 vols.** Ed. by Joe Matera. 6000p. 1999. pap. 545.00 (*1-891851-05-5*) Nelson Info.

Nelson's Directory of Investment Research, 1997, 2 vols. Ed. by Marcia Boysen. 4300p. 1996. pap., per. 535.00 (*0-922460-89-2*) Nelson Info.

***Nelson's Directory of Investment Research, 1999, 3 vols.** Ed. by Marcia Boysen. 5000p. 1998. pap. 590.00 (*1-891851-03-9*) Nelson Info.

Nelson's Directory of Pension Fund Consultants, 1997. Ed. by Richard Sinks. 600p. 1997. pap., per. 350.00 (*0-922460-90-6*) Nelson Info.

***Nelson's Directory of Pension Fund Consultants, 1999.** Ed. by Holly DeWaters. 600p. 1999. pap. 350.00 (*1-891851-04-7*) Nelson Info.

***Nelson's Directory of Plan Sponsors, 1999, 3 vols.** Ed. by Holly DeWaters. 5000p. 1998. pap. 545.00 (*1-891851-01-2*) Nelson Info.

Nelson's Directory of Plan Sponsors, 1997, 3 vols. Ed. by Richard Sinks. 5700p. 1996. pap., per. 495.00 (*0-922460-86-8*) Nelson Info.

***Nelson's Electronic Bible Reference Library: Professional Edition.** 1999. 499.99 incl. cd-rom (*0-7852-1238-8*) NelsonElectronic.

Nelson's Favourite: HMS Agamemnon, 1781-1809. Anthony N. Deane. LC 96-68993. (Illus.). 320p. 1996. 44.95 (*1-55750-620-5*) Naval Inst Pr.

Nelson's First Love: Fanny's Story. Patrick Delaforce. 1987. 16.95 (*1-85219-006-X*, Pub. by Bishopsgte Pr) Intl Spec Bk.

Nelson's Illustrated Encyclopedia of Bible Facts. rev. ed. William White, Jr. Ed. by J. I. Packer et al. LC 94-44337. Orig. Title: Bible Almanac. (Illus.). 820p. 1995. 29.99 (*0-8407-1974-4*) Nelson.

Nelson's Illustrated Encyclopedia of the Bible. John W. Drane. LC 98-13164. 34.99 (*0-7852-0985-9*) Nelson.

Nelsons in the Revolutionary War. Lela N. Cooper. LC 94-195484. (Orig.). 1994. pap. text 23.50 (*1-55613-970-5*) Heritage Bk.

Nelson's Last Diary: A Facsimile. Horatio Nelson. Ed. by Oliver Warner. LC 70-165752. 80p. reprint ed. pap. 30.00 (*0-608-14574-2*, 202492400039) Bks Demand.

Nelson's Letters to His Wife & Other Documents. Ed. by G. P. Naish. 1989. 80.00 (*0-7855-1148-2*) St Mut.

Nelson's Navy: English Fighting Ships, 1793-1815. David T. Davies. LC 96-44275. (Illus.). 208p. 1997. 27.95 (*0-8117-1118-8*) Stackpole.

Nelson's Navy: Its Ships, Men & Organization, 1793-1815. Brian Lavery. LC 89-62380. (Illus.). 352p. 2000. 59.95 (*0-87021-258-3*) Naval Inst Pr.

Nelson's Navy, 1793-1815. Philip J. Haythornthwaite. (Elite Ser.). (Illus.). 64p. 1993. pap. 12.95 (*1-85532-334-6*, 9463, Pub. by Ospry) Stackpole.

Nelson's New Illustrated Bible Commentary. Ed. by Radmacher. LC 99-11281. (Illus.). 1200p. 1999. 39.99 (*0-7852-1438-0*) Nelson.

Nelson's New Illustrated Bible Dictionary. rev. ed. Ed. by Ronald F. Youngblood & F. F. Bruce. LC 94-44332. (Illus.). 1344p. 1995. 39.99 (*0-8407-2071-8*) Nelson.

***Nelson's Pocket Reference Bible Concordance.** TNP Staff. LC 99-18408. 624p. 1999. pap. 4.99 (*0-7852-4242-2*) Nelson.

***Nelson's Pocket Reference Bible Dictionary.** TNP Staff. LC 99-18407. 316p. 1999. pap. 4.99 (*0-7852-4241-4*) Nelson.

***Nelson's Pocket Reference Bible Handbook.** TNP Staff. LC 99-18544. 384p. 1999. pap. 4.99 (*0-7852-4243-0*) Nelson.

Nelson's Pocket Reference Bible Maps. LC 99-29102. 384p. 1999. pap. 4.99 (*0-7852-4257-0*) Nelson.

***Nelson's Pocket Reference Bible People.** TNP Staff. LC 99-24254. 384p. 1999. pap. 4.99 (*0-7852-4244-9*) Nelson.

Nelson's Pocket Reference Q&A. 384p. 1999. pap. 4.99 (*0-7852-4258-9*) Nelson.

Nelson's Quick Reference Bible Concordance. Ronald F. Youngblood. LC 92-47033. 416p. 1993. pap. 8.99 (*0-8407-6907-5*) Nelson.

Nelson's Quick-Reference Bible Handbook. LC 92-47032. 1993. 8.99 (*0-8407-6904-0*) Nelson.

Nelson's Textbook of Pediatrics. 15th ed. Behrman. (C). text. write for info. (*0-8089-2154-1*, Grune & Strat) Harcrt Hlth Sci Grp.

Nelson's 3-D Bible Mapbook. Simon Jenkins. LC 94-45223. (Illus.). 128p. 1995. pap. 9.99 (*0-8407-1964-7*) Nelson.

***Nelson's War.** Peter Padfield. (Illus.). 2000. pap. 12.99 (*1-84022-225-5*, Pub. by Wrdsworth Edits) Combined Pub.

Nelson's 2000-2001 Pocket Book of Pediatric Antimicrobial Therapy. 14th ed. John D. Nelson & John S. Bradley. 120p. pap. text 14.95 (*0-7817-2570-4*) Lppncott W & W.

Nely Galan. LC 96-46944. (Contemporary Hispanic Americans Ser.). (Illus.). 48p. (J). 1997. lib. bdg. 24.26 (*0-8172-3991-X*) Raintree Steck-V.

Nemacki Bez Muke. Albert O. Cherel. 24.95 (*0-685-11417-1*); audio 125.00 (*0-685-01742-7*) Fr & Eur.

Nematic Dispersions. Paul S. Drzaic. (Liquid Crystals Ser.: Vol. 2). 200p. 1995. text 48.00 (*981-02-1745-5*) World Scientific Pub.

Nematics: Mathematical & Physical Aspects. Ed. by Jean-Michel Coron et al. (C). 1991. text 208.50 (*0-7923-1113-2*) Kluwer Academic.

Nematoda: Ascaroidea & Strongyloidea. H. A. Baylis. (Fauna of British India Ser.). xxxvi, 416p. 1978. reprint ed. 30.00 (*0-88065-051-6*) Scholarly Pubns.

Nematoda: Filaricidea, Dictophymoidea & Trichinelloidea, Vol. 2. H. A. Baylis. (Fauna of British India Ser.). xxviii, 280p. 1978. reprint ed. 30.00 (*0-88065-052-4*) Scholarly Pubns.

Nematode Caenorhabditis Elegans. Ed. by William B. Wood. LC 87-23916. (Monographs: No. 17). (Illus.). 700p. 1988. pap. 47.00 (*0-87969-433-5*) Cold Spring Harbor.

Nematode Identification & Expert System Technology. Ed. by R. Fortuner. (NATO ASI Series A, Life Sciences: Vol. 162). (Illus.). 396p. 1988. 105.00 (*0-306-43143-2*, Plenum Trade) Perseus Pubng.

***Nematode Parasites of Vertebrates: Their Development & Transmission.** 2nd ed. R. C. Anderson. LC 99-42444. 750p. 2000. 185.00 (*0-85199-421-0*) OUP.

Nematode Vectors of Plant Viruses. C. E. Taylor & D. J. Brown. LC 96-48882. (CAB International Publications). 296p. 1997. text 80.00 (*0-85199-159-9*) OUP.

Nematodes & the Biological Control of Insect Pests. Robin Bedding et al. 178p. 1995. 60.00 (*0-643-05479-0*, Pub. by CSIRO) Accents Pubns.

Nematodes of Plants & Soils. N. I. Sumenkova. LC 88-22299. (Illus.). 1989. 87.00 (*90-04-08921-7*) Brill Academic Pubs.

Nematodes of Plants & Soils. N. I. Sumenkova. (C). 1989. 32.00 (*81-7087-020-8*, Pub. by Oxford IBH) S Asia.

Nematomorpha. Andreas Schmidt-Rhaesa. (Suesswasserfauna von Mitteleuropa Ser.: Band 4, Heft 4). (GER., Illus.). 140p. 1997. pap. 68.00 (*3-437-25428-6*) Gustav Fischer.

Nemea: A Guide to the Site & Museum. Stephen G. Miller. 1990. 45.00 (*0-520-06590-5*, Pub. by U CA Pr); pap. 16.95 (*0-520-06799-1*, Pub. by U CA Pr) Cal Prin Full Svc.

Nemean Odes of Pindar. Peter Pindar. 1890. reprint ed. 19.00 (*0-403-00332-6*) Scholarly.

Nemecko-Slovensky a Slovensko-Nemecky Slovnik. Kovacsova et al. (SLO.). 712p. 1996. write for info. (*80-08-02156-X*, Pub. by Slov Pegagog Naklad) IBD Ltd.

Nemecko-Slovensky Slovnik. Cierna et al. (SLO.). 968p. 1996. write for info. (*80-08-01408-3*, Pub. by Slov Pegagog Naklad) IBD Ltd.

Nemesii Emeseni. Ed. by Morani. (GRE.). 1987. 47.50 (*3-322-00358-2*, T1548, Pub. by B G Teubner) U of Mich Pr.

Nemesis. Isaac Asimov. 432p. 1990. mass mkt. 6.99 (*0-553-28628-5*) Bantam.

Nemesis. Agatha Christie. 256p. 1992. mass mkt. 5.99 (*0-06-100326-3*, Harp PBks) HarpC.

***Nemesis.** Agatha Christie. 2000. mass mkt. 5.99 (*0-451-20018-7*, Sig) NAL.

Nemesis. Agatha Christie. (J). 1992. 11.34 (*0-606-12448-9*) Turtleback.

Nemesis. Scott Ciencin. (Lurker Files Ser.). (YA). (gr. 5 up). 1997. pap. 6.99 (*0-614-28943-2*) Random Bks Yng Read.

Nemesis. Louise Cooper. (Indigo Ser.: No. 1). 1989. pap. write for info. (*0-8125-3401-8*, Pub. by Tor Bks) St Martin.

Nemesis. Lew Daly. 224p. (Orig.). 1991. pap. 8.00 (*0-945926-28-6*) Paradigm RI.

Nemesis. Dorothy S. Darling. 218p. mass mkt. 4.99 (*1-55197-056-2*) Picasso Publ.

Nemesis. Gary Lovisi. (Illus.). 56p. (Orig.). 1988. 4.00 (*0-936071-10-9*) Gryphon Pubns.

Nemesis. Michael Monahan. LC 68-54362. (Essay Index Reprint Ser.). 1977. 20.95 (*0-8369-0712-4*) Ayer.

***Nemesis.** S. D. Perry. (Resident Evil Ser.: No. 5). 288p. 2000. 6.50 (*0-671-78496-X*) PB.

Nemesis. deluxe ed. Lew Daly. 224p. (Orig.). 1991. pap. 20.00 (*0-945926-29-4*) Paradigm RI.

***Nemesis, Vol. 3.** Dan Birlew. (Resident Evil Ser.). 1999. pap. 12.99 (*1-56686-955-2*) Brady Pub.

***Nemesis Bk. II: Masquerade Cycle.** Paul Thompson. LC 98-65591. (Magic the Gathering Ser.: Vol. 2). (Illus.). 320p. 2000. mass mkt. 5.99 (*0-7869-1559-5*) TSR Inc.

Nemesis Affair: A Story of the Death of the Dinosaurs & the Ways of Science. David M. Raup. 240p. 1999. pap. 13.00 (*0-393-31918-0*) Norton.

Nemesis at Potsdam: The Anglo-Americans & the Expulsion of the Germans. rev. ed. Alfred M. De Zayas. LC 98-68071. (Illus.). 320p. 1998. pap. 23.95 (*0-89725-360-4*, 1899) Picton Pr.

Nemesis File: The True Story of an SAS Execution Squad. Paul Bruce. 300p. 1996. 22.95 (*1-85782-135-1*, Pub. by Blake Publng) Seven Hills Bk.

Nemesis in the Mearns: Love, Laughter & Heartache in the Land of Grassic Gibbon. Ed. by Clarke Geddes. 240p. 1990. pap. 30.00 (*1-898218-78-1*) St Mut.

Nemesis Mission. Dean Ing. 480p. 1992. mass mkt. 5.99 (*0-8125-1173-5*, Pub. by Tor Bks) St Martin.

Nemesis of Faith. James A. Froude. (C). 1991. 39.95 (*1-870352-10-6*, Pub. by Libris) Paul & Co Pubs.

***Nemesis of Power: A History of International Relations Theories.** Harald Kleinschmidt. (Globalities Ser.). (Illus.). 280p. 2000. 34.95 (*1-86189-058-3*, Pub. by Reaktion Bks) Consort Bk Sales.

Nemesis of Reform: The Republican Party During the New Deal. Clyde P. Weed. LC 94-6094. (Illus.). 256p. 1994. 44.00 (*0-231-08486-2*) Col U Pr.

N

Nemesis, the Roman State & the Games. Michael B. Hornum. LC 93-726. (Religions in the Graeco-Roman World Ser.: No. 117). (Illus.). xvi, 376p. 1993. 157.50 (*90-04-09745-7*) Brill Academic Pubs.

Nemiah: The Unconquered Country. Photos by Gary Fiegehen et al. (Illus.). 154p. 1992. pap. 19.95 (*0-921586-22-1*, Pub. by New Star Bks) Genl Dist Srvs.

Nemo. Paul Vangelisti. (New American Fiction Ser.: No. 35). 88p. 1995. pap. 11.95 (*1-55713-227-5*) Sun & Moon CA.

Nemrud Dagi: The Hierothesion of Antiochus I of Commagene, 2 vols. Ed. by Donald H. Sanders. Incl. Vol. 1. xl, 520p. 1996. text 125.00 (*0-931464-89-7*); Vol. 2. (Illus.). xxxiv, 334p. 1996. text 125.00 (*0-931464-90-0*); LC 95-45457. Set text 180.00 (*1-57506-015-9*) Eisenbrauns.

Nenagh Castle: Chronology & Architecture. Nancy Murphy. (Illus.). 8p. (Orig.). 1996. pap. 2.00 (*0-946327-10-6*, Pub. by Relay Pubns) Irish Bks Media.

Nenagh Yesterday. Brendan Treacy. (Illus.). 144p. (Orig.). 1995. pap. 20.00 (*0-946327-11-4*, Pub. by Relay Pubns) Irish Bks Media.

Nene. Marion Coste. LC 92-36543. (Illus.). 32p. (J). (gr. 3-6). 1993. 9.95 (*0-8248-1389-8*, Kolowalu Bk) UH Pr.

***Nenets Autonomous Okrug Regional Investment & Business Guide.** Global Investment & Business Center, Inc. Staff. (Russian Regional Investment & Business Guides Ser.: Vol. 50). (Illus.). 350p. 1999. pap. 99.00 (*0-7397-0886-4*) Intl Business Pubns.

***Nenets Autonomous Okrug Regional Investment & Business Guide.** Contrib. by Global Investment & Business Center, Inc. Staff. (Russian Regional Investment & Business Guides Ser.: Vol. 83). (Illus.). 350p. 2000. pap. 99.95 (*0-7397-2998-5*) Intl Business Pubns.

Nenets Autonomous Okrus: Economy, Industry, Government, Business. 2nd rev. ed. Russian Information & Business Center, Inc. Staff. (Russian Regional Business Directories Ser.). (Illus.). 200p. 1997. pap. 99.00 (*1-57751-428-9*) Intl Business Pubns.

Nenets' Song: A Microcosm of a Vanishing Culture. Alla Abramovich-Gomon. (Studies in Ethnomusicology: Vol. 4). (Illus.). 168p. 1999. text 74.95 (*1-84014-603-6*, Pub. by Ashgate Pub) Ashgate Pub Co.

Neng Da: Super Punches. Hei Long. 151p. 1997. pap. 14.95 (*1-880336-13-8*) Turtle CT.

Nenhuma Enfermidade. S. I. McMillen. Orig. Title: None of These Diseases. (POR.). 216p. 1987. pap. 8.95 (*0-8297-0964-9*) Vida Pubs.

N'Enseignez Que L'Amour. Gerard G. Jampolsky. 381p. 1990. 19.95 (*2-920083-42-2*) Edns Roseau.

Nenshu & the Tiger: Parables of Life & Death. Martin Bell. 112p. 1984. 5.95 (*0-8164-2356-3*) Harper SF.

Neo-Adjuvant Chemotherapy: Proceedings of the International Congress on Neo-Adjuvant Chemotherapy, Paris, 1st, November 1985. Ed. by D. Khayat et al. 863p. (Orig.). pap. text 110.00 (*0-318-23805-5*) S M P F Inc.

Neo-African Literature & Culture: Essays in Memory of Jahneinz Jahn. Bernth Lindfors & Ulla Schild. 352p. 1982. text 49.50 (*3-593-32821-6*) Irvington.

Neo-Aramaic Dialect of Kurdistan: Texts, Grammar, & Vocabulary. Georg Krotkoff. (American Oriental Ser.: Vol. 64). xii, 172p. 1982. 21.00 (*0-940490-64-1*) Am Orient Soc.

Neo-Aristotelian & Joycean Theory of Poetic Forms. Thomas E. Connolly. LC 95-7457. (Studies in Comparative Literature: Vol. 6). 1995. 69.95 (*0-7734-8886-3*) E Mellen.

Neo-Aristotelian Theory of Social Justice. Adrian J. Walsh. LC 97-74459. (Series in Philosophy). 206p. 1998. text 64.95 (*1-85972-459-0*, Pub. by Ashgate Pub) Ashgate Pub Co.

Neo-Assyrian Historical Inscriptions & Syria-Palestine. Jeffrey Kah-jin Kuan. (Jian Dao Dissertation Ser.: No. 1). 281p. 1995. 80.00 (*962-7997-09-9*, Pub. by Sheffield Acad); pap. 29.95 (*962-7997-10-2*, Pub. by Sheffield Acad) CUP Services.

Neo-Assyrian Judicial Procedures. Remko Jas. (State Archives of Assyria Ser.: Vol. 5). xx, 138p. (Orig.). 1996. pap. text 29.50 (*951-45-7287-4*, Pub. by Neo-Assyrian Text) Eisenbrauns.

Neo-Avantgarde & Culture Industry: Essays on European & American Art from 1965-1975. Benjamin H. Buchloh. LC 99-59406. (Illus.). 500p. 1999. 50.00 (*0-262-02454-3*) MIT Pr.

Neo-Babylon Ebabbar Temple at Sippar: Its Administration & Its Prosopography. A. C. Bongenaar. LC 97-211764. (Illus.). xvi, 559p. 1997. pap. text 52.25 (*90-6258-081-5*, Pub. by Netherlands Inst) Eisenbrauns.

Neo-Babylonian Letters from Erech. Albert T. Clay. LC 78-63532. (Yale Oriental Series: Babylonian Texts: No. 3). (Illus.). 184p. reprint ed. 35.00 (*0-404-60253-3*) AMS Pr.

Neo-Babylonian Texts in the Yale Babylonian Collection. Maria D. Ellis. (Texts from the Babylonian Collection: Vol. 1). 67p. 1985. pap. 48.00 (*0-9667495-2-9*) Yale Babylonian.

Neo-California. David Henderson. LC 97-47270. 100p. 1998. pap. 20.00 (*1-55643-275-5*) North Atlantic.

Neo-Catechumenal Communities. Ricardo Blazquez. (C). 1988. 39.00 (*0-7855-3222-6*, Pub. by St Paul Pubns) St Mut.

Neo-Catechumenal Communities. Ricardo Blazquez. 110p. (C). 1990. 40.00 (*0-85439-280-7*, Pub. by St Paul Pubns) St Mut.

Neo-Classic Drama in Spain. John A. Cook. LC 74-5771. 576p. 1974. reprint ed. lib. bdg. 85.00 (*0-8371-7518-6*, CONC, Greenwood Pr) Greenwood.

Neo-Classic Post Impressionist Painters: Lives of the Painters, Vol. 3. John Canaday. (C). 1969. 22.25 (*0-393-02417-2*) Norton.

Neo-Classic Theory of Tragedy in England During the 18th Century. Clarence C. Green. LC 65-27913. 1972. 24.95 (*0-405-08578-8*, Pub. by Blom Pubns) Ayer.

Neo-Classical Furniture Designs: A Reprint of Thomas King's "Modern Style of Cabinet Work Exemplified," 1829. unabridged ed. Thomas King. (Illus.). 128p. 1995. pap. text 9.95 (*0-486-28289-9*) Dover.

Neo-Classical Microeconomics, 2 vols., Set. Ed. by Martin Ricketts. (Schools of Thought in Economics Ser.: Vol. 3). 784p. 1989. text 335.00 (*1-85278-115-7*) E Elgar.

Neo-Classical Theory of Distribution & Wealth. H. U. Buhl. (Lecture Notes in Economics & Mathematical Systems Ser.: Vol. 262). v, 146p. 1986. 25.95 (*0-387-16062-0*) Spr-Verlag.

Neo-Classical Theory of Economic Growth. James E. Meade. LC 83-1748. 185p. (C). 1983. reprint ed. lib. bdg. 49.75 (*0-313-23965-7*, MENE, Greenwood Pr) Greenwood.

Neo-Classicism, Style & Motif. Henry Hawley. LC 64-24988. (Illus.). 153p. reprint ed. pap. 47.50 (*0-608-11291-7*, 201449500095) Bks Demand.

Neo-Colonialism in West Africa. Samir Amin. Tr. by Francis McDonagh from FRE. LC 74-7784. 320p. reprint ed. pap. 99.20 (*0-8357-6232-7*, 203435200089) Bks Demand.

Neo-Communist Manifesto: The Andes Christian Islamic Communist Manifesto. Thomas J. Kuna-Jacoby. 27p. 1998. ring bd. 3.12 (*1-878030-35-3*) Assn World Peace.

Neo-Confucian Education: The Formative Stage. William T. De Bary & John W. Chaffee. (Studies on China: Vol. 9). 1989. 90.00 (*0-520-06393-7*, Pub. by U CA Pr) Cal Prin Full Svc.

Neo-Confucian Orthodoxy & the Learning of the Mind-&-Heart. William T. Debary. LC 81-3809. (Neo-Confucian Studies). 267p. 1981. text 57.50 (*0-231-05228-6*) Col U Pr.

Neo-Confucian Orthodoxy & the Learning of the Mind-&-Heart. William T. Debary. LC 81-3809. (Neo-Confucian Studies). 267p. 1986. pap. text 21.00 (*0-231-05229-4*) Col U Pr.

Neo-Confucian Terms Explained: The Pei-hsi Tzu-i. Tr. by Wing-Tsit Chan from CHI. LC 86-5427. (Neo-Confucian Studies). 288p. 1986. text 57.50 (*0-231-06384-9*) Col U Pr.

Neo-Congregationalism. Karl Pruter. LC 85-13416. 90p. 1985. reprint ed. pap. 17.00 (*0-912134-02-X*) Millefleurs.

Neo-Conservatism: Social & Religious Phenomenon. Ed. by Gregory B. Baum & John Coleman. (Concilium Ser.: Vol. 141). 128p. (Orig.). 1981. 6.95 (*0-8164-2308-3*) Harper SF.

Neo-Dada: Redefining Art, 1958-1962. American Federation of Arts Staff & Susan Hapgood. LC 94-7388. (Illus.). 160p. 1994. 42.50 (*0-87663-629-6*, Pub. by Universe) St Martin.

Neo-Dada: Redefining Art, 1958-62. Susan Hapgood. (Illus.). 156p. 1994. 30.00 (*0-917418-98-0*) Am Fed Arts.

Neo-Fascism in Europe. Cheles. 1991. text. write for info. (*0-582-03950-9*, Pub. by Addison-Wesley) Longman.

Neo-Feudalism: The Canadian Dilemma. Gerard S. Vano. 152p. (Orig.). 1981. pap. 7.95 (*0-88784-088-4*, Pub. by Hse of Anansi Pr) Genl Dist Srvs.

Neo-Freudian Social Philosophy. Martin Birnbach. vi, 283p. 1961. 39.50 (*0-8047-0076-1*) Stanford U Pr.

Neo-Freudian Social Philosophy. fac. ed. Martin Birnbach. LC 61-12389. 291p. 1961. reprint ed. pap. 30.00 (*0-7837-7910-0*, 204766600008) Bks Demand.

Neo-Fundamentalism: The Humanist Response. Academy of Humanism Staff. LC 88-61449. 186p. 1988. 32.95 (*0-87975-452-4*) Prometheus Bks.

Neo-Hellenika, II. 373p. 1975. 26.00 (*0-318-12220-0*) Ad Council.

Neo-Hellenika IV. 242p. 1981. 30.00 (*0-932242-01-4*) Ctr Neo Hellenic.

Neo-Hellenika I. 244p. 1970. 26.00 (*0-318-12221-9*, 90-256-0502-8) Ad Council.

Neo-Hellenika I. Adolf M. Hakkert. 1970. 26.00 (*90-256-0502-8*) Ctr Neo Hellenic.

Neo-Hellenika III. Ed. by George G. Arnakis & Costas M. Proussis. 1978. pap. 25.00 (*0-932242-00-6*) Ctr Neo Hellenic.

Neo-Hellenika II. Adolf M. Hakkert. 1975. 26.00 (*90-256-0749-7*) Ctr Neo Hellenic.

Neo-Humanism in a Nutshell, Pt. I. Prabhat Rainjan Sarkar. Tr. by Acarya V. Avadhuta & Acarya M. Avadhuta from BEN. 67p. (Orig.). (C). 1987. pap. 3.95 (*0-88476-027-8*) Ananda Marga.

Neo-Humanism in a Nutshell, Pt. II. Prabhat Rainjan Sarkar. Tr. by Acarya Mantreshwarananda Avadhuta from BEN. (Orig.). (C). 1987. pap. text 3.95 (*0-88476-028-6*) Ananda Marga.

Neo-Humanist Education: Education for a New World. Avadhutika A. Acarya. (Illus.). 160p. (Orig.). 1989. pap. 4.95 (*0-88476-007-3*) Ananda Marga.

Neo-Idealistic Aesthetics: Croce-Gentile-Collingwood. Merle E. Brown. LC 65-20757. 261p. reprint ed. pap. 81.00 (*0-7837-3682-7*, 204355600009) Bks Demand.

Neo-Impressionism & the Search for Solid Ground: Art, Science, & Anarchism in Fin-de-Siecle France. John G. Hutton. LC 93-26334. (Modernist Studies). (Illus.). xxviii, 320p. 1994. text 45.00 (*0-8071-1823-0*) La State U Pr.

***Neo-Impressionist Painters: A Sourcebook on Georges Seurat, Camille Pissarro, Paul Signac, Theo Van Rysselberghe, Henri Edmond Cross, Charles Angrand, Maximilien Luce & Albert Dubois-Pillet, 23.** Russell T. Clement & Annick Houzbe. LC 99-36377. (Art Reference Collection Ser.). 416p. 1999. lib. bdg. 89.50 (*0-313-30382-7*) Greenwood.

Neo-Impressionists & Nabis in the Collection of Arthur G. Altschul. Ed. by Robert L. Herbert et al. LC N 6465.N44H4. (Illus.). 109p. reprint ed. pap. 33.80 (*0-8357-6408-7*, 203576900096) Bks Demand.

***Neo-industrial Organising Renewal By Action & Knowledge Formation in a Project-Intensive Economy.** Eskil Ekstedt. LC 98-31605. 1999. write for info. (*0-415-20334-1*) Routledge.

Neo-Lamarckism & the Evolution Controversy in France, 1870-1920. Stuart M. Persell. LC 98-48633. (Studies in French Civilization: Vol. 14). 300p. 1999. text 89.95 (*0-7734-8275-X*) E Mellen.

Neo-Latin & the Vernacular in Renaissance France. Ed. by Graham Castor & Terence Cave. (Illus.). 1984. 55.00 (*0-19-815780-0*) OUP.

***Neo-Liberalism or Democracy.** Arthur MacEwan. LC 99-51918. 1999. text 69.50 (*1-85649-724-0*) Zed Books.

***Neo-Liberalism or Democracy? Economic Strategy Markets & Alter.** Arthur MacEwan. LC 99-51918. 288p. 1999. pap. 25.00 (*1-85649-725-9*) Zed Books.

Neo-Lineamenta Florae Manshuricae: or Enumeration of the Spontaneous Vascular Plants of Manchuria. Masao Kitagawa. (Flora et Vegetatio Mundi Ser.: No. 4). 1979. lib. bdg. 120.00 (*3-7682-1113-4*) Lubrecht & Cramer.

Neo-Marxism: The Meanings of Modern Radicalism, 77. Robert A. Gorman. LC 81-13404. (Contributions in Political Science Ser.: No. 77). 309p. 1982. 75.00 (*0-313-23264-4*, GON/, Greenwood Pr) Greenwood.

Neo-Melanesian - English Concise Dictionary: New Guinea Pidgin-English Language. Friedrich Steinbauer. 160p. 1998. pap. 11.95 (*0-7818-0656-9*) Hippocrene Bks.

Neo-Mohism. Sheng Liang. (CHI.). 200p. (Orig.). 1995. pap. 20.00 (*0-9642790-2-9*) Sayinga.

Neo-Nazi Movement in Germany: An Eyewitness Documentary Report. Simon Wiesenthal Center Research Staff. (Special Reports). (Illus.). 35p. (Orig.). pap. 4.98 (*0-943058-17-1*) S Wiesenthal Ctr.

Neo-Nazis: A Growing Threat. Kathlyn Gay. LC 96-40872. (Issues in Focus Ser.). (Illus.). 112p. (YA). (gr. 6 up). 1997. lib. bdg. 20.95 (*0-89490-901-0*) Enslow Pubs.

Neo-Nazis & German Unification. Rand C. Lewis. LC 96-2198. 136p. 1996. 49.95 (*0-275-95638-5*, Praeger Pubs) Greenwood.

Neo-Pagan Essence. Otter Zell. 52p. 1994. pap. 5.00 (*1-57353-102-2*) Eschaton Prods.

Neo-Palladianism: Lord Burlington's House & Garden at Chiswick. John Harris. LC 93-49024. 1994. 30.00 (*0-300-05984-1*) Yale U Pr.

Neo-Philobiblon: Ruminations on Manuscript Collecting. James Osborn. LC 72-619565. (Bibliographical Monograph: No. 7). (Illus.). 1973. 10.00 (*0-87959-049-1*) U of Tex H Ransom Ctr.

Neo-Piagetian Theories of Cognitive Development: Implications & Applications for Education. Ed. by Andreas Demetriou et al. LC 94-9764. (Illus.). 320p. (C). 1994. pap. 27.99 (*0-415-11749-6*, B4748) Routledge.

Neo-Platonic Discourse: Being "Against the Gnostics" by Plotinus. Plotinus. Ed. by Early Dodge. Tr. by Roy Elster from GRE. 1997. pap. 8.95 (*1-55818-380-9*) Holmes Pub.

Neo-Platonic Letter to Marcella. Porphyry the Neo-Platonist. Tr. by Alice Zimmern from GRE. 1993. reprint ed. pap. 6.95 (*1-55818-202-0*) Holmes Pub.

Neo-Platonisme Alexandrin: Hierocles d'Alexandrie: Filiations Intellectuelles et Spirituelles d'un Neo-Plantonicien du Ve Siecle. Noel Aujoulat. (Philosophia Antiqua Ser.). x, 461p. 1986. pap. 123.00 (*90-04-07510-0*) Brill Academic Pubs.

Neo-Platonists. Thomas Whittaker. LC 76-114901. (Select Bibliographies Reprint Ser.). 1977. 28.95 (*0-8369-5305-3*) Ayer.

Neo-Platonists: A Study in the History of Hellenism with a Supplement on the Commentaries of Proclus. 4th ed. Thomas Whittaker. xv, 318p. 1987. reprint ed. lib. bdg. 57.20 (*3-487-00244-2*) G Olms Pubs.

Neo-Platonists: 1928 Edition. Thomas Whittaker. 336p. 1996. reprint ed. 58.00 (*1-85506-212-7*) Bks Intl VA.

Neo-Sectarianism & Rainbow Coalitions: Youth & the Drama of Immigration in Contemporary Sweden. Abby Peterson. LC 97-73461. (Research in Ethnic Relations Ser.). 208p. 1997. text 69.95 (*1-85972-700-X*, Pub. by Ashgate Pub) Ashgate Pub Co.

Neo-Slave Narratives: Studies in the Social Logic of a Literary Form. Ashraf H. Rushdy. LC 98-27667. (Race & American Culture Ser.). 296p. 1999. text 45.00 (*0-19-512533-9*) OUP.

Neo-Stalinist State: Class, Ethnicity & Consensus in Soviet Society. rev. ed. Victor Zaslavsky. LC 93-50947. 216p. (C). (gr. 13). 1994. pap. text 35.95 (*1-56324-451-9*) M E Sharpe.

Neo-Sumerian Account Texts from Drehem. Clarence E. Keiser. LC 76-115373. (Babylonia Inscriptions in the Collection of James B. N. Ser.: No. 3). 89p. 1971. 52.50 (*0-300-01296-9*) Yale U Pr.

Neo-Sumerian Account Texts in the Horn Archaeological Museum, Vol. 1. Marcel Sigrist. LC 84-71735. (Institute of Archaeology Publications, Assyriological Ser.: AS Vol. 4; AUCT Vol. 1). (Illus.). 208p. (C). 1984. text 39.99 (*0-943872-25-1*) Andrews Univ Pr.

Neo-Sumerian Account Texts in the Horn Archaeological Museum, Vol. 2. Marcel Sigrist. LC 88-72125. (Assyriological Ser.: AS Vol. 5; AUCT Vol. 2). (Illus.). 122p. (C). 1988. text 39.99 (*0-943872-32-4*) Andrews Univ Pr.

Neo-Sumerian Account Texts in the Horn Archaeological Museum, Vol. 3. Marcel Sigrist & Carney E. Gavin. LC 88-72125. (Assyriological Ser.: AS Vol. 6; AUCT Vol. 3). (Illus.). 224p. (C). 1988. text 39.99 (*0-943872-31-6*) Andrews Univ Pr.

Neo-Sumerian Administrative Texts of the Hirose Collection. Tohru Gomi et al. xlv, 138p. 1990. 48.00 (*0-9620013-2-5*) CDL Pr.

Neo-Sumerian Archival Texts: Primarily from Nippur in the University Museum, the Oriental Institute, & the Iraq Museum. David I. Owen. LC 82-1358. (Illus.). xiii, 85p. 1982. text 50.00 (*0-931464-09-9*) Eisenbrauns.

Neo-Sveshnikov. Jeremy Silman. 113p. (Orig.). 1991. pap. 7.95 (*0-945470-13-4*) Chess Ent.

Neo-Tech - Psychuous Reference Encyclopedia. Frank R. Wallace. LC 81-83436. 480p. 1985. pap. 69.95 (*0-911752-43-9*) Neo-Tech Pub.

Neo-Tech Cures Alcoholism, Drug Abuse, Neurosis. Gary Twitchell. 160p. 1990. pap. 29.95 (*0-911752-63-3*) Neo-Tech Pub.

Neo-Tech Power Letters. Ed. by Drew Ellis. 268p. 1995. pap. 19.95 (*0-911752-76-5*) Neo-Tech Pub.

Neo-Tech Protection Kit, 2 vols. Wallace & Savage. (Illus.). 750p. 1991. pap. 100.00 (*0-911752-65-X*) Neo-Tech Pub.

Neo-Thomists. Gerald McCool. LC 94-42271. (Orig.). (C). 1994. pap. 20.00 (*0-87462-601-3*) Marquette.

Neo Tribes. Ross Winn et al. (Cyberpunk Ser.). (Illus.). 96p. (Orig.). 1995. pap. 12.00 (*0-937279-72-2*, CP3371) Talsorian.

Neo Vao Thien Hoc. 4th ed. Thich Nhat Hahn. (VIE.). 244p. 1990. reprint ed. pap. 9.00 (*1-891667-11-4*) La Boi Soc.

Neo Ve Cua Y. 4th ed. Thich Nhat Hahn. (VIE.). 362p. 1997. reprint ed. pap. 14.00 (*1-891667-45-9*) La Boi Soc.

Neo York: Report on a Phenomenon. Phyllis Plous et al. (Illus.). 72p. (Orig.). 1984. 15.00 (*0-942006-08-9*) U of CA Art.

Neoantology: Management, Procedures, On-Call Problems, Diseases & Drugs. 4th rev. ed. Tricia L. Gomella. (Illus.). 620p. (C). 1999. spiral bd. 34.95 (*0-8385-6687-1*, A-6687-6, Apple Lange Med) McGraw.

Neocarzinostatin: The Past, Present, & Future of an Anticancer Drug. H. Maeda et al. LC 96-47101. 1997. 197.00 (*4-431-70187-7*) Spr-Verlag.

Neocatechumenal Way According to Paul VI & John Paul II. Ezekiel Pasotti. 220p. 1996. pap. 39.95 (*0-85439-520-2*, Pub. by St Paul Pubns) St Mut.

Neocene Spondyli from the Southern United States & Tropical America see Palaeontographica Americana: Vol. 2

Neocheating, the Unbeatable Weapon in Poker, Blackjack, Bridge, & Gin. Frank R. Wallace et al. LC 79-92518. (Illus.). 192p. 1980. pap. 49.95 (*0-911752-29-3*) Neo-Tech Pub.

Neoclassical Economic Theory, 1870 to 1930. Ed. by Warren J. Samuels. (C). 1990. lib. bdg. 102.50 (*0-7923-9038-5*) Kluwer Academic.

Neoclassical Microeconomic Theory: The Founding Austrian Version. A. M. Endres. LC 96-17321. (Foundations of the Market Economy Ser.). 288p. (C). 1997. 85.00 (*0-415-15209-7*) Routledge.

Neoclassical Ornamental Designs. Ed. by Rudolph Ackermann. LC 96-13357. (Pictorial Archive Ser.). (Illus.). 128p. 1996. 9.95 (*0-486-29224-X*) Dover.

Neoclassical Political Economy: The Analysis of Rent-Seeking & DUP Activities. Ed. by David C. Colander. LC 84-11124. 288p. 1984. text 34.95 (*0-88410-999-2*, HarpBusn) HarpInfo.

Neoclassical Theatre: A Historiographical Handbook. Ronald W. Vince. LC 87-17803. 239p. 1988. lib. bdg. 65.00 (*0-313-24445-6*, WNT/, Greenwood Pr) Greenwood.

Neoclassical Theory & Empirical Models of Aggregate Firm Behavior. D. P. Broer. (Advanced Studies in Theoretical & Applied Econometrics). 1986. lib. bdg. 168.00 (*90-247-3412-6*) Kluwer Academic.

Neoclassical Theory of Production & Distribution. Charles E. Ferguson. LC 75-92248. (Illus.). 400p. reprint ed. pap. 114.00 (*0-608-17510-2*, 2030593) Bks Demand.

Neoclassicals in Puerto Rico. Manuel G. Diaz. (Puerto Rico Ser.). 1979. lib. bdg. 59.95 (*0-8490-2975-9*) Gordon Pr.

Neoclassicism. Patricia L. Hollingsworth et al. (Sails - Students' Active Interdisciplinary Learning Ser.: Vol. 5). (Illus.). (YA). (gr. 3-12). 1998. pap. text 20.00 (*1-893413-04-7*) Univ Schl Tulsa.

Neoclassicism. David Irwin. (Art & Ideas Ser.). (Illus.). 448p. 1997. pap. 22.95 (*0-7148-3369-X*, Pub. by Phaidon Press) Phaidon Pr.

Neoclassicism in Music: From the Genesis of the Concept Through the Schoenberg/Stravinsky Polemic. Scott Messing. LC 96-430. 234p. (C). 1996. reprint ed. 65.00 (*1-878822-66-7*) Univ Rochester Pr.

Neoclassicism in the North: Swedish Furniture & Interiors, 1770-1850. 2nd ed. Hakan Groth. LC 98-61443. (Illus.). 204p. 1999. reprint ed. pap. 34.95 (*0-500-28106-8*, Pub. by Thames Hudson) Norton.

Neocolonialism American Style, 1960-2000, 372. William H. Blanchard. LC 95-49673. (Contributions in Political Science Ser.: Vol. 372). 208p. 1996. 57.95 (*0-313-30013-5*, Greenwood Pr) Greenwood.

Neoconservatism: The Autobiography of an Idea. Irving Kristol. 493p. 1995. 24.50 (*0-02-874021-1*) Free Pr.

Neoconservatism: The Autobiography of an Idea. Irving Kristol. LC 98-45126. 516p. 1999. pap. 18.95 (*1-56663-228-5*, Elephant Paperbacks) I R Dee.

Neoconservative Criticism: Norman Podhoretz, Kenneth S. Lynn, & Joseph Epstein. Mark R. Winchell. 196p. 1991. text 22.95 (*0-8057-7617-6*, Twayne) Mac Lib Ref.

Neoconservative Economics in the Southern Cone of Latin America, 1973-1983. Joseph R. Ramos. LC 86-165. (Johns Hopkins Studies in Development). (Illus.). 223p. reprint ed. pap. 69.20 (*0-608-06189-1*, 206652100008) Bks Demand.

Neoconservative Imagination: Essays in Honor of Irving Kristol. DeMuth & Kristol. 150p. 1995. 24.95 (*0-8447-3898-0*) Am Enterprise.

Neoconservative Imagination: Essays in Honor of Irving Kristol. William Kristol & Christopher C. Demuth. 150p. 1995. pap. 12.95 (*0-8447-3899-9*) Am Enterprise.

Neoconservative Mind: Politics, Culture, & the War of Ideology. Gary Dorrien. LC 92-11187. 512p. (C). 1993. 59.95 (*1-56639-019-2*) Temple U Pr.

Neoconservative Mind: Politics, Culture, & the War of Ideology. Gary Dorrien. LC 92-11187. 512p. (C). 1993. pap. 24.95 (*1-56639-144-X*) Temple U Pr.

Neoconservative Vision: From the Cold War to the Culture Wars. Mark Gerson. LC 95-31521. 288p. 1996. 27.95 (*1-56833-054-5*) Madison Bks UPA.

Neoconservative Vision: From the Cold War to the Culture Wars. Mark Gerson. 1997. pap. text 16.95 (*1-56833-100-2*) Madison Bks UPA.

Neocortex: Ontogeny & Phylogeny. Ed. by B. L. Finlay et al. LC 91-21500. (NATO ASI Ser.: Vol. 200). (Illus.). 272p. (C). 1991. text 114.00 (*0-306-43808-9*, Kluwer Plenum) Kluwer Academic.

Neocortical Development. Shirley A. Bayer & Joseph Altman. 272p. 1991. text 150.00 (*0-88167-778-7*) Lppncott W & W.

Neocortical Dynamics & Human EEG Rhythms. Paul L. Nunez. (Illus.). 728p. 1995. text 98.50 (*0-19-505728-7*) OUP.

Neocortical Epilepsies, Vol. 84. Peter D. Williamson et al. 624p. text 149.00 (*0-7817-1872-4*) Lppncott W & W.

Neocortical Grafting to Newborn & Adult Rats: Developmental, Anatomical & Functional Aspects. Afsaneh Gaillard et al. LC 98-3116. (Advances in Anatomy, Embryology & Cell Biology Ser.). (Illus.). 115p. 1998. pap. 99.95 (*3-540-64252-8*) Spr-Verlag.

Neodymium Isotope Geochemistry. D. J. DePaolo. (Minerals & Rocks Ser.: Vol. 20). (Illus.). 200p. 1988. 79.95 (*0-387-18648-4*) Spr-Verlag.

***NeoFax.** 13th ed. Thomas Young. 264p. 2000. spiral bd. 28.00 (*1-888703-13-X*, Pub. by Neofax) Blackwell Sci.

Neofields & Combinatorial Designs. Ed. by Frank D. Hsu. (Advances in Discrete Mathematics & Computer Science Ser.). 401p. 1984. pap. 60.00 (*0-911767-27-4*) Hadronic Pr Inc.

Neofunctionalism & After: Collected Readings. Ed. by Jeffrey C. Alexander. LC 97-8621. (Twentieth-Century Social Theory Ser.). 240p. 1997. text 62.95 (*1-55786-629-5*); pap. text 27.95 (*1-55786-630-9*) Blackwell Pubs.

Neofunctionalist Sociology: Contemporary Statements. Ed. by Paul Colomy. (Schools of Thought in Sociology Ser.: Vol. 4). 396p. 1990. text 190.00 (*1-85278-195-5*) E Elgar.

Neogene Avian Localities of North America. Jonathan J. Becker. LC 87-42557. 200p. (Orig.). (C). 1987. pap. text 19.95 (*0-87474-225-0*) Smithsonian.

Neogene Biostratigraphy of Southern Hispaniola see Bulletins of American Paleontology: Vol. 66

Neogene History of Tropical American Mollusks. Edward J. Petuch. (Illus.). 1988. 64.95 (*0-938415-02-6*) CERF Inc.

Neogene Mollusks from Northwestern Ecuador No. 4: Special Publication. Axel A. Olsson. (Illus.). 258p. 1964. 12.00 (*0-87710-367-4*) Paleo Res.

Neogene Paleontology of the Manonga Valley, Tanzania: A Window into the Evolutionary History of East Africa. T. Harrison. LC 97-14542. (Topics in Geobiology Ser.: Vol. 14). (Illus.). 438p. (C). 1997. text 138.00 (*0-306-45471-8*, Kluwer Plenum) Kluwer Academic.

Neogene-Quaternary Geology of the High Plain of Bogota, Eastern Cordillera, Columbia (Stratigraphy, Paleoenvironments & Landscape Evolution) Karin E. Helmens. (Dissertationes Botanicae Ser.: Band 163). (Illus.). vi, 202p. 1990. pap. 53.00 (*3-443-64075-3*, Pub. by Gebruder Borntraeger) Balogh.

Neogene Smaller Foraminifera from Lau, Fiji. R. M. Kleinpell. (BMB Ser.: No. 211). 1974. reprint ed. 25.00 (*0-527-02319-1*) Periodicals Srv.

Neogene to Recent Displacement & Contact of Sardinian & Tunisian Margins, Central Mediterranean. Maurice G. Gennesseaux & Daniel J. Stanley. LC 83-16647. (Smithsonian Contributions to the Marine Sciences Ser.: No. 23). 24p. reprint ed. pap. 30.00 (*0-608-13989-0*, 202225400026) Bks Demand.

Neoglycoconjugates: Preparation & Applications. Ed. by Y. C. Lee & Reiko T. Lee. (Illus.). 549p. 1994. text 136.00 (*0-12-440585-1*) Acad Pr.

Neoglycoconjugates Pt. A: Synthesis. Ed. by Y. C. Lee et al. (Methods in Enzymology Ser.: Vol. 242). (Illus.). 328p. 1994. text 84.00 (*0-12-182143-9*) Acad Pr.

Neoglycoconjugates Pt. B: Biomedical Applications. Melvin I. Simon. Ed. by Y. C. Lee et al. (Methods in Enzymology Ser.: Vol. 247). (Illus.). 450p. 1994. text 84.00 (*0-12-182148-X*) Acad Pr.

Neogrammarians: A Re-Evaluation of Their Place in the Development of Linguistic Science. Kurt R. Jankowsky. LC 71-189705. (Janua Linguarum, Ser. Minor: No. 116). 275p. (Orig.). (C). 1992. reprint ed. pap. text 44.65 (*3-11-013514-0*) Mouton.

Neohumanism & the Persistence of Pure Mathematics in Wilhelmian Germany. Lewis Pyenson. LC 82-72156. (American Philosophical Society, Memoirs Ser.: No. 150). 148p. reprint ed. pap. 45.90 (*0-7837-4333-5*, 204404400012) Bks Demand.

Neoism, Plagiarism & Praxis. abr. ed. Stewart Home. 208p. (Orig.). 1996. pap. 18.95 (*1-873176-33-3*, AK Pr San Fran) AK Pr Dist.

Neoitaliano: Le Parole Degli Anni Ottanta. S. Vassalli. 55.00 (*0-8288-8024-7*, F63942) Fr & Eur.

Neoitaliano: Le Parole Degli Anni Ottanta. S. Vassalli. 1991. 55.00 (*0-685-49365-2*, F63942) Fr & Eur.

Neoliberalism & Education in Latin America. Adriana Puiggros. LC 98-49326. 224p. 1999. text 69.00 (*0-8133-2909-4*, Pub. by Westview) HarpC.

Neoliberalism & Education in Latin America. Adriana Puiggros. 2000. pap. 20.00 (*0-8133-2910-8*) Westview.

Neolithic Adventures of Taff-Mai Metallu-Mai: How the First Letter Was Written & How the Alphabet Was Made, Just So Stories by Rudyard Kipling. Rudyard Kipling. (Illus.). 55p. (Orig.). 1997. reprint ed. 540.00 (*0-931460-30-1*) Bieler.

Neolithic & Bronze Ages. Sara A. Immerwahr. LC 76-356761. (Athenian Agora Ser.: Vol. 13). (Illus.). xx, 286p. 1971. 40.00 (*0-87661-213-3*) Am Sch Athens.

Neolithic & Early Bronze Age Pottery. Alex Gibson. 1989. pap. 25.00 (*0-85263-755-1*, Pub. by Shire Pubns) St Mut.

Neolithic & Post-Neolithic Cultures. V. Rami Reddy. (C). 1991. text 15.00 (*81-7099-311-3*, Pub. by Mittal Pubs Dist) S Asia.

***Neolithic Britain.** Caroline Malone. (Illus.). 176p. 2000. pap. 24.99 (*0-7524-1442-9*, Pub. by Tempus Pubng) Arcadia Publng.

Neolithic Britain. Joshua Pollard. LC 98-150957. (Archaeology Ser.: No. 75). (Illus.). 64p. 1997. pap. 10.50 (*0-7478-0353-6*, Pub. by Shire Pubns) Parkwest Pubns.

Neolithic Cultures of Western Asia. Singh. 248p. 1974. 117.00 (*0-12-785795-8*) Acad Pr.

***Neolithic Flint Mines in Britain.** Miles Russell. (Illus.). 176p. 2000. 32.50 (*0-7524-1481-X*, Pub. by Tempus Pubng) Arcadia Publng.

Neolithic Houses in North-West Europe & Beyond. Ed. by Timothy Darvill & Julian Thomas. (Monographs in Archaeology: Vol. 57). 213p. 1996. pap. 35.00 (*1-900188-08-2*, Pub. by Oxbow Bks) David Brown.

Neolithic Jades in the National Palace Museum Taipei. 312p. 1990. boxed set 99.50 (*957-562-128-X*) Heian Intl.

Neolithic Levels on the Titelberg, Luxembourg. 2nd ed. Elsebet S. Rowlett et al. LC 76-623772. (Museum Briefs Ser.: No. 18). iii, 61p. 1980. pap. 4.00 (*0-913134-83-X*) Mus Anthro MO.

Neolithic Origins. Purushottam Singh. (C). 1991. text 40.00 (*0-8364-2805-6*, Pub. by Agam Kala Prakashan) S Asia.

***Neolithic Orkney in Its European Context.** Ed. by Anna Ritchie. 300p. (C). 2000. 80.00 (*1-902937-04-X*, Pub. by McDonald Inst) David Brown.

***Neolithic Society in Greece.** Ed. by Paul Halstead. (Studies in Aegean Archaeology: No. 2). 168p. 2000. pap. 24.50 (*1-85075-824-7*, Pub. by Sheffield Acad) CUP Services.

Neolithic Transition & the Genetics of Populations in Europe. Albert J. Ammerman & L. L. Cavalli-Sforza. LC 84-42587. 193p. 1984. reprint ed. pap. 59.90 (*0-608-02931-9*, 206399700008) Bks Demand.

Neolithic Village at Tell El Kowm in the Syrian Desert. Rudolph H. Dornemann. LC 86-70319. (Studies in Ancient Oriental Civilization: No. 43). (Illus.). 89p. 1986. pap. 30.00 (*0-918986-45-1*) Orient Inst.

Neologie Lexicale Berbere. E. Peters. 1998. 46.95 (*90-6831-810-1*, Pub. by Peeters Pub) Bks Intl VA.

Neologisms of the Russian Language: Dictionary Material, 1903. N. Z. Kotelova. (RUS.). 192p. (C). 1987. 95.00 (*0-7855-6667-8*, Pub. by Collets) St Mut.

Neologisms of the Russian Language: Dictionary Material, 1980. N. Z. Kotelova. 286p. (C). 1980. 95.00 (*0-7855-5065-8*, Pub. by Collets) St Mut.

Neologisms of the Russian Language: Dictionary Material, 1980. N. Z. Kotelova. 286p. (C). 1985. 45.00 (*0-7855-2313-8*, Pub. by Collets) St Mut.

Neologisms of the Russian Language: Dictionary Material, 1981. N. Z. Kotelova. 288p. (C). 1986. 65.00 (*0-7855-2312-X*, Pub. by Collets) St Mut.

Neologisms of the Russian Language: Dictionary Material, 1984. Ed. by N. Z. Kotelova. (RUS.). 426p. (C). 1989. 95.00 (*0-7855-6670-8*, Pub. by Collets) St Mut.

Neologisms of the Russian Language: Dictionary Materials, 1981, Vol. 5. N. Z. Kotelova. (RUS.). 288p. (C). 1986. 95.00 (*0-7855-5050-X*, Pub. by Collets) St Mut.

Neomambi. Angel Pardo. LC 89-83445. (Coleccion Espejo de Paciencia). (SPA., Illus.). 94p. (Orig.). 1989. pap. 9.95 (*0-89729-530-7*) Ediciones.

Neon: The Next Generation. Dean Blazek & Michael Blazek. (Illus.). 240p. 1995. pap. 34.95 (*0-944094-07-4*) ST Pubns.

Neon Bible. John Kennedy Toole. LC 88-26074. (Illus.). 176p. 1990. pap. 11.00 (*0-8021-3207-3*, Grove) Grove-Atltic.

Neon Genesis Evangelion. Yoshiyuki Sadamoto. (Illus.). 176p. 1998. pap. 15.95 (*1-56931-294-X*, Cadence Bks) Viz Commns Inc.

***Neon Genesis Evangelion, vol. 3.** Yoshiyuki Sadamoto. 1999. pap. 15.95 (*1-56931-399-7*) Viz Commns Inc.

***Neon Genesis Evangelion, Vol. 4.** Yoshiyuki Sadamoto. (Illus.). 184p. 1999. pap. text 15.95 (*1-56931-434-9*, Pub. by Viz Commns Inc) Publishers Group.

Neon Genesis Evangelion, Volume II. Yoshiyuki Sadamoto. Vol. 2. (Illus.). 168p. 1998. pap. text 15.95 (*1-56931-341-5*) Viz Commns Inc.

Neon Installation Manual: Sign & Outline Lighting. 2nd ed. International Association of Electrical Inspection. Ed. by J. Philip Simmons et al. (Illus.). ii, 67p. 1996. ring bd. 27.95 (*1-890659-06-1*, 365001) Intl Assn Elec Inspect.

Neon Manual de Instalacion: Anuncios y Luces de Neon. Ed. by J. Philip Simmons et al. (SPA., Illus.). ii, 67p. 1994. ring bd. 27.95 (*1-890659-07-X*, 365006) Intl Assn Elec Inspect.

Neon Nevada. Sheila Swan & Peter Laufer. LC 93-23653. (Illus.). 112p. 1994. 39.95 (*0-87417-245-4*) U of Nev Pr.

Neon Noir: Hard-Boiled Film & Fiction from the 1960's to the Present. Woody Haut. 1999. pap. 16.99 (*1-85242-547-4*, Pub. by Serpents Tail) Consort Bk Sales.

Neon Peppers. Tony Moffeit. LC 92-36466. 64p. (Orig.). 1992. pap. 7.00 (*0-916156-90-7*) Cherry Valley.

Neon Principles: The Art of Shaping Light with Neon. Randall L. Caba. Incl. Neon Principles Workbook: A Guide to Shaping Light with Neon. (Illus.). 63p. 1993. pap., student ed. Not sold separately (*0-9634219-1-3*); LC 92-90942. (Illus.). 248p. 1992. Set pap. 39.95 (*0-9634219-0-5*) Neon Pr.

Neon Principles Workbook: A Guide to Shaping Light with Neon see Neon Principles: The Art of Shaping Light with Neon

Neon Rain. James Lee Burke. 288p. 1992. per. 6.99 (*0-671-75644-3*) PB.

Neon Rain. large type ed. James Lee Burke. 377p. 1991. 21.95 (*1-85089-413-2*, Pub. by ISIS Lrg Prnt) Transaction Pubs.

Neon Smile. Dick Lochte. 1995. 20.50 (*0-671-74712-6*) S&S Trade.

Neon Techniques: Handbook of Neon Sign & Cold-Cathode Lighting. 4th rev. ed. Ed. by Wayne Strattman. (Illus.). 233p. 1997. pap. 39.95 (*0-944094-27-9*, 48) ST Pubns.

Neon Trance. Thomas Wiloch. 30p. 1997. pap. 3.00 (*1-57141-034-1*) Runaway Spoon.

Neon Transformers & Power Supplies, UL 2161. (C). 1996. pap. text 135.00 (*1-55989-908-5*) Underwrtrs Labs.

Neon Vernacular: New & Selected Poems. Yusef Komunyakaa. LC 92-56908. (Wesleyan Poetry Ser.). 188p. 1993. pap. 15.95 (*0-8195-1211-7*, Wesleyan Univ Pr) U Pr of New Eng.

Neon Wilderness: 24 Short Stories. Nelson Algren. 1988. 23.95 (*0-8488-0415-5*) Amereon Ltd.

Neon Wilderness: 24 Short Stories. Nelson Algren. Ed. by Dan Simon. LC 96-40151. 304p. 1997. reprint ed. pap. 10.95 (*1-888363-21-5*) Seven Stories.

Neon World. 1924. pap. 29.95 (*0-688-15784-X*, Wm Morrow) Morrow Avon.

Neon World. 1999. 35.00 (*0-688-15358-5*, Wm Morrow) Morrow Avon.

Neon World. D. J. Sprengnagel. (Illus.). 228p. 1998. 39.95 (*0-944094-26-0*, 58) ST Pubns.

Neon World. D. J. Sprengnagel. (Illus.). 172p. 1997. pap. text 34.95 (*0-8230-3162-4*) Watsn-Guptill.

Neonatal & Pediatric Pulmonary Graphics: Principle & Clinical Applications. Ed. by Steven M. Donn. LC 97-39522. (Illus.). 443p. 1997. 85.00 (*0-87993-645-2*). Futura Pub.

***Neonatal & Pediatric Respiratory Care.** 3rd ed. Barbara G. Wilson et al. (Illus.). 576p. (C). 1999. text. write for info. (*0-323-00164-5*) Mosby Inc.

Neonatal & Pediatric Respiratory Care, Vol. 6. Karen Milikowski. (Respiratory Care Workbook Ser.). 24p. (gr. 13). 1995. text, wbk. ed. 8.95 (*0-8151-6309-6*, 26027) Mosby Inc.

Neonatal & Pediatric Ultrasonography. Ed. by Diane S. Babcock. (Clinics in Diagnostic Ultrasound Ser.: Vol. 24). (Illus.). 251p. 1992. text 83.00 (*0-443-08606-0*) Church.

Neonatal & Perinatal Medicine. Arnold J. Rudolph. (Atlas of the Newborn Ser.: Vol. 1). (Illus.). 160p. 1996. boxed set 89.95 incl. cd-rom (*1-55009-031-3*) DEKR.

Neonatal & Perinatal Monitoring Systems Markets. (Market Research Reports: No. 340). (Illus.). 115p. 1992. 795.00 (*0-317-05032-X*) Theta Corp.

Neonatal & Perinatal Screening: The Asian Pacific Perspective. Ed. by Stephen T. Lam & Calvin C. Pang. LC 98-139431. 1997. 34.50 (*962-201-765-7*, Pub. by Chinese Univ) U of Mich Pr.

Neonatal Anesthesia. Ed. by D. Ryan Cook & Joseph H. Marcy. LC 87-27309. 300p. 1988. text 52.50 (*0-941022-10-2*) Davies Pubng.

Neonatal Behavioural Assessment Scale. 3rd ed. Ed. by T. Berry Brazelton & J. Kevin Nugent. (Clinics in Developmental Medicine Ser.: No. 137). (Illus.). 159p. (C). 1995. 33.95 (*1-898683-05-0*, Pub. by Mc Keith Pr) Cambridge U Pr.

Neonatal Care Policy & Procedure Guideline Manual. Mel Pepper & Janet Adams. 260p. 1997. spiral bd. 110.00 (*1-879575-85-X*) Acad Med Sys.

Neonatal Cerebral Ultrasound. Janet M. Rennie. LC 96-13980. (Illus.). 254p. (C). 1997. text 95.00 (*0-521-45079-9*) Cambridge U Pr.

Neonatal Critical Care Nursing: Outline Core Content. AACN (American Association of Critical-Care Nurses) Staff. 1997. pap. write for info. (*0-7216-5898-9*, W B Saunders Co) Harcrt Hlth Sci Grp.

Neonatal Decision Making. Sheldon B. Korones. LC 92-49370. (Clinical Decision Making Ser.). 286p. (C). (gr. 13). 1992. text 74.95 (*1-55664-148-6*) Mosby Inc.

Neonatal Dermatology. Eichenfiel. Date not set. text. write for info. (*0-7216-7810-6*, W B Saunders Co) Harcrt Hlth Sci Grp.

Neonatal Disease & Congenital Disorders: RCP 308 Course. Wojciechowski et al. 270p. (C). 1994. ring bd. 39.95 (*0-933195-75-3*) CA College Health Sci.

Neonatal EEG. American Journal of END Technology Staff. (Illus.). 1998. per. 28.00 (*1-57797-008-X*) ASET.

Neonatal Emergency, No. 1. Charsha. 1997. text, wbk. ed. 16.95 (*0-8151-2377-9*) Mosby Inc.

Neonatal Emergency, No. 2. Charsha. 1997. text, wbk. ed. 16.95 (*0-8151-2378-7*) Mosby Inc.

Neonatal Emergency, No. 3. Charsha. 1997. text, wbk. ed. 16.95 (*0-8151-2380-9*) Mosby Inc.

Neonatal Formulary. Compiled by Northern Neonatal Network Staff. 199p. 1996. pap. text 31.00 (*0-7279-1030-2*, Pub. by BMJ Pub) Login Brothers Bk Co.

Neonatal Group B Streptococcal Infections. Ed. by K. K. Christensen et al. (Antibiotics & Chemotherapy Ser.: Vol. 35). (Illus.). x, 350p. 1985. 215.00 (*3-8055-3953-3*) S Karger.

Neonatal Haematology & Immunology II: Proceedings of the International Symposium, Gottingen, Germany, 13-15 May 1993. Ed. by Marietta Xanthou et al. LC 93-38871. (International Congress Ser.: Vol. 1038). 220p. 1993. 177.25 (*0-444-81656-9*, Excerpta Medica) Elsevier.

Neonatal Heart Disease. R. M. Freedom et al. 912p. 1991. 225.00 (*3-540-19639-0*) Spr-Verlag.

Neonatal Heart Disease. R. M. Freedom et al. (Illus.). 912p. 1991. 361.00 (*0-387-19639-0*) Spr-Verlag.

Neonatal Hematology & Immunology III: Proceedings of the Third Neonatal Hematology & Immunology Symposium, Held in Washington, D. C., U. S. A. on 29 September - 1 October 1996, Vol. 113. Ed. by J. A. Bellanti et al. LC 97-5558. (International Congress Ser.: Vol. 1131). 262p. 1997. 158.00 (*0-444-82573-8*, Excerpta Medica) Elsevier.

Neonatal Immune Thrombocytopenia. Bussell. 1991. write for info. (*0-8493-6469-8*, CRC Reprint) Franklin.

Neonatal Infectious Diseases, No. 2. Charsha. 1997. text, wbk. ed. 16.95 (*0-8151-2368-X*) Mosby Inc.

Neonatal Intensive Care Handbook. 3rd ed. Boyd W. Goetzman & Richard P. Wennberg. LC 98-54475. 1999. write for info. (*0-323-00814-3*) Mosby Inc.

Neonatal Intensive Care Nursing. Rudman. (Certified Nurse Examination Ser.: CN-25). pap. 23.95 (*0-8373-6125-7*) Nat Learn.

Neonatal Kidney & Fluid-Electrolytes. Ed. by Jose Strauss. 1983. text 125.00 (*0-89838-575-X*) Kluwer Academic.

***Neonatal Medications & Nutrition: A Comprehensive Guide.** Karin E. Zenk et al. LC 99-25645. (Illus.). 600p. 1999. pap. 39.95 (*1-887571-03-5*) NICU Ink.

***Neonatal Medications & Nutrition: A Comprehensive Guide.** 2nd ed. Karin E. Zenk et al. LC 99-59774. 2000. pap. 39.95 (*1-887571-07-8*) NICU Ink.

Neonatal Medicine. Ed. by Leo Stern. 1250p. (gr. 13). 1987. 224.50 (*0-89352-229-5*, MA229) Mosby Inc.

Neonatal Meningitis. Pamela A. Davies & P. T. Rudd. (Clinics in Developmental Medicine Ser.: No. 132). (Illus.). 185p. 1995. text 52.95 (*0-901260-96-7*) Cambridge U Pr.

Neonatal Neurology. 2nd ed. Gerald M. Fenichel. LC 85-4227. (Clinical Neurology & Neurosurgery Monographs: No. 2). (Illus.). 356p. reprint ed. pap. 110.40 (*0-8357-4652-6*, 203758300008) Bks Demand.

Neonatal Neurology. 3rd ed. Gerald M. Fenichel. (Illus.). 250p. 1989. pap. text 66.00 (*0-443-08700-8*) Church.

Neonatal Nurse Practitioner. Rudman. (Certified Nurse Examination Ser.: CN-21). pap. 23.95 (*0-8373-6121-4*) Nat Learn.

Neonatal Nursing. Ed. by Doreen Crawford & Maryke Morris. 400p. 1994. pap. 37.50 (*0-412-48730-6*) Chapman & Hall.

Neonatal-Pediatric Respiratory Care. 2nd ed. Koff. (Illus.). 525p. (gr. 13). 1993. text 54.00 (*0-8016-6518-3*, 06518) Mosby Inc.

Neonatal-Perinatal Medicine: Diseases of the Fetus & Infant. 6th ed. Avary A. Fanaroff & Richard J. Martin. LC 96-47141. (Illus.). 1904p. (C). (gr. 13). 1996. text 180.00 (*0-8151-3205-0*, 24740) Mosby Inc.

Neonatal Pig: Development & Survival. Ed. by M. A. Varley. (CAB International Publication). (Illus.). 352p. (C). 1995. text 100.00 (*0-85198-925-X*) OUP.

Neonatal Repiratory Disorders. Anthony Milner et al. (Illus.). 512p. 1996. text 125.00 (*0-340-55242-5*, Pub. by E A) OUP.

Neonatal Seizures. Ed. by Claude G. Wasterlain & Paul Vert. LC 90-8449. (Illus.). 335p. 1990. reprint ed. pap. 103.90 (*0-608-05886-6*, 205985200007) Bks Demand.

Neonatal Skin: Structure & Function. Howard I. Maibach & Edward K. Boisits. (Dermatology Ser.: Vol. 1). (Illus.). 296p. 1982. text 135.00 (*0-8247-1860-7*) Dekker.

Neonatal Surgery of the Cleft Lip & Palate. 400p. 1997. text 44.00 (*981-02-3116-4*) World Scientific Pub.

Neonatal Thyroid Screening. Ed. by Gerard N. Burrow & Jean H. Dussault. LC 79-5320. 332p. 1980. reprint ed. pap. 103.00 (*0-608-00382-4*, 206109600007) Bks Demand.

Neonatal Tumours. Ed. by Prem Puri & Rajendra Surana. LC 96-13126. 150p. 1996. 125.00 (*3-540-19938-1*) Spr-Verlag.

Neonatal Vade-Mecum. 2nd ed. Peter J. Fleming. 448p. (Orig.). pap. text. write for info. (*0-340-53869-4*, Pub. by E A) Routldge.

Neonatal Vade-Mecum. 3rd ed. Ed. by Brian Speidel et al. LC 98-224084. (Arnold Publications). (Illus.). 496p. (Orig.). 1998. pap. text 35.00 (*0-340-69140-9*) OUP.

Neonatal/Pediatric Respiratory Care: A Critical Care Pocket Guide. 3rd ed. Dana Oakes. (Illus.). 320p. 1996. ring bd. 19.95 (*0-932887-08-2*) Health Ed Pubns.

Neonatology. 2nd ed. Thomas. (C). 1998. pap. text 16.95 (*0-443-05885-7*, W B Saunders Co) Harcrt Hlth Sci Grp.

Neonatology. 2nd ed. Roslyn Thomas & David R. Harvey. LC 96-39722. (Colour Guide Ser.). 1997. write for info. (*0-443-05774-5*) Harcrt Hlth Sci Grp.

Neonatology: A Practical Guide. 4th ed. Alistair G. Philip. Ed. by Judy Fletcher. LC 95-9516. (Illus.). 400p. 1996. pap. text 50.00 (*0-7216-4776-6*, W B Saunders Co) Harcrt Hlth Sci Grp.

Neonatology: Pathophysiology & Management of the Newborn. 4th ed. Gordon B. Avery et al. 1,552p. 1993. text 153.00 (*0-397-51101-9*) Lppncott W & W.

Neonatology: Pathophysiology & Management of the Newborn. 5th ed. Ed. by Gordon B. Avery et al. 1999. 145.00 (*0-7817-1210-6*) Lppncott W & W.

Neonatology Word Book. Hazel Tank & Catherine Gilliam. 102p. (Orig.). (C). 1991. pap. text 30.00 (0-935229-10-8) Am Assoc Med.

Neons. Denis Belloc. Tr. by William Rodarmor from FRE. 1991. 18.95 (0-87923-858-5) Godine.

Neopaganismus und Christentum in der Viktorianischen Literatur unter Besonderer Berucksichtigung der Minor Authors. Karin Hagenguth. LC 98-169373. (Studien zur Englischen und Amerikanischen Literatur: No. 18). 440p. 1997. 63.95 (3-631-31986-X) P Lang Pubng.

Neopatriarchy: A Theory of Distorted Change in Arab Society. Hisham B. Sharabi. 224p. 1992. reprint ed. pap. text 18.95 (0-19-507913-2) OUP.

Neoplasia & Cell Differentiation. Ed. by G. V. Sherbet. (Illus.). 1973. 121.75 (3-8055-1581-2) S Karger.

Neoplasia in Infancy & Childhood. Ed. by H. S. Rosenberg & J. Bernstein. (Perspectives in Pediatric Pathology Ser.: Vol. 9). viii, 248p. 1986. 191.50 (3-8055-4373-5) S Karger.

Neoplasia in the Central Nervous System. fac. ed. Ed. by Richard A. Thompson & John R. Green. LC 75-25113. (Advances in Neurology Ser.: No. 15). (Illus.). 394p. pap. 122.20 (0-7837-7514-8, 204699100005) Bks Demand.

Neoplasma & Related Lesions of the Head & Neck: Based on the Proceedings of the 59th Annual Anatomic Pathology Slide Seminar of the American Society of Clinical Pathologists. Stacey E. Mills et al. LC 94-21116. 126p. 1994. 35.00 (0-89189-385-7) Am Soc Clinical.

Neoplasms - Prevention & Control: Index of New Information with Authors, Subjects & Bibliography. Mumford C. Yeatman. 180p. 1993. 47.50 (1-55914-816-0); pap. 44.50 (1-55914-817-9) ABBE Pubs Assn.

Neoplasms--Prevention, Control & Results: Index of New Information for Reference & Research. John C. Bartone. 160p. 1997. 47.50 (0-7883-1666-4); pap. 44.50 (0-7883-1667-2) ABBE Pubs Assn.

***Neoplasms of the Colon, Rectum, & Anus.** Philip H. Gordon & Santhat Nivatvongs. (Illus.). 368p. 2000. text 110.00 (1-57626-124-7) Quality Med Pub.

Neoplasms of the Liver. Kunio Okuda & Kamal G. Ishak. (Illus.). 500p. 1987. 391.00 (0-387-70020-X) Spr-Verlag.

Neoplasms of the Lung: Based on the Proceedings of the 57th Annual Anatomic Pathology Slide Seminar of the American Society of Clinical Pathologists, September 26-27, 1991, New Orleans, Louisiana. LC 93-5551. 1994. 35.00 (0-89189-348-2) Am Soc Clinical.

Neoplasms of the Skin with Sebaceous Differentiation. Charles Steffen & A. Bernard Ackerman. (Illus.). 1000p. 1994. text 150.00 (0-8121-1459-0) Lppncott W & W.

Neoplasms with Eccrine Differentiation. Pascual Abenoza & A. Bernard Ackerman. LC 89-7980. (Illus.). 536p. 1990. text 150.00 (0-8121-1236-9) Lppncott W & W.

Neoplasms with Follicular Differentiation. A. Bernard Ackerman. LC 91-34968. (Illus.). 650p. 1992. text 150.00 (0-8121-1542-2) Lppncott W & W.

***Neoplasms with Follicular Differentiation.** A. Bernard Ackerman et al. LC 99-98185. (Histologic Diagnosis of Neoplastic Skin Diseases Ser.). 2000. write for info. (1-893357-11-2) Ardor Scrib.

Neoplastic Diseases. Ed. by C. Julian Rosenthal. LC 91-62100. 891p. 1991. 129.00 (0-944496-24-5) Precept Pr.

Neoplastic Diseases in Childhood, 2 vol., Set. Ed. by Carl Pochedly et al. LC 93-12664. 1600p. 1995. text 473.00 (3-7186-5340-0) Gordon & Breach.

Neoplastic Diseases of the Blood. 3rd ed. Peter H. Wiernik et al. LC 95-31180. 1240p. 1995. text 235.00 (0-443-07600-6) Church.

Neoplastic Diseases of the Blood, Vol. 1. Ed. by Peter H. Wiernik et al. LC 84-17522. 635p. 1985. pap. 196.90 (0-7837-1374-6, 204152300001) Bks Demand.

Neoplastic Diseases of the Blood, Vol. 2. Ed. by Peter H. Wiernik et al. LC 84-17522. 633p. 1985. pap. 196.30 (0-7837-1375-4, 204152300002) Bks Demand.

Neoplastic Hematopathology. Daniel M. Knowles. (Illus.). 1640p. 1992. 229.00 (0-683-04735-3) Lppncott W & W.

Neoplastic Hematopathology. 2nd ed. Daniel M. Knowles. (Illus.). 1750p. 1998. write for info. (0-683-30246-9) Lppncott W & W.

Neoplastic Transformation in Human Cell Culture: Mechanisms of Carcinogenesis. Ed. by Johng S. Rhim & Anatoly Dritschilo. LC 91-35328. (Experimental Biology & Medicine Ser.: Vol. 25). (Illus.). 408p. 1991. 115.00 (0-89603-227-2) Humana.

Neoplatonic Metaphysics & Epistemology of Anselm of Canterbury. Katherin A. Rogers. LC 97-13027. (Studies in the History of Philosophy: No. 45). 280p. 1997. text 89.95 (0-7734-8622-4) E Mellen.

Neoplatonism. Rich T. Wallis. 224p. (C). 1995. reprint ed. pap. text 16.95 (0-87220-287-9); reprint ed. lib. bdg. 34.95 (0-87220-288-7) Hackett Pub.

Neoplatonism & Christian Thought. Ed. by Dominic J. O'Meara. LC 81-5272. (Studies in Neoplatonism: Ancient & Modern: Vol. 3). 297p. 1981. text 21.50 (0-87395-492-0) State U NY Pr.

Neoplatonism & Indian Thought. Ed. by R. Baine Harris. LC 81-21289. (Studies in Neoplatonism: Ancient & Modern: Vol. 2). 353p. (C). 1981. pap. text 21.95 (0-87395-546-3) State U NY Pr.

Neoplatonism & Islamic Thought. Ed. by Parviz Morewedge. LC 92-388. (Studies in Neoplatonism: Ancient & Modern: Vol. 5). 267p. 1992. text 19.50 (0-7914-1335-7) State U NY Pr.

Neoplatonism & Jewish Thought. Ed. by Lenn E. Goodman. LC 92-8369. (Studies in Neoplatonism: Ancient & Modern: Vol. 7). 454p. (C). 1992. text 27.50 (0-7914-1339-X) State U NY Pr.

Neoplatonists. John Gregory. LC 98-25045. 1999. 65.00 (0-415-18784-2) Routledge.

Neoplatonists. 2nd ed. John Gregory. LC 98-25045. viii, 189 p. 1999. pap. 22.99 (0-415-18785-0) Routledge.

Neopolitan Songs, EFS23. (Illus.). 192p. 1987. pap. 14.95 (0-8256-2023-6, AM40130) Music Sales.

Neopostmodrinism or Dieser Rasen 1st Kein Hundeklo or Gabbertabb, No. 6. Walter S. Hamady. Tr. by Paul H. Duensing. (ENG & GER., Illus.). 118p. 1988. write for info. (0-318-64542-4) Perishable Pr.

Neopseustidae. Don R. Davis. Ed. by John B. Heppner. (Lepidopterorum Catalogus Ser.: Vol. 1: Fasc. 7). (Illus.). 8p. (Orig.). 1997. pap. text 4.50 (0-945417-51-9) Sci Pubs.

Neopterin: Biochemistry-Methods-Applications. H. Wachter et al. (Illus.). xiv, 291p. (C). 1991. lib. bdg. 144.65 (3-11-011790-8, 240-91) De Gruyter.

Neorealism & Its Critics. Ed. by Robert O. Keohane. LC 86-2247. 256p. 1986. pap. text 22.00 (0-231-06349-0) Col U Pr.

Neorealism & Neoliberalism: The Contemporary Debate. Ed. by David A. Baldwin. LC 93-17701. (New Directions in World Politics Ser.). 377p. 1993. pap. 22.00 (0-231-08441-2) Col U Pr.

Neorenaissance in der Deutschen Architektur des 19 Jahrhunderts. Kurt Milde. (GER.). 352p. 1981. 168.00 (0-7855-1598-4) St Mut.

Neosciadiocapsidae, a New Family of Upper Cretaceous Radiolaria see Bulletins of American Paleontology: Vol. 56

Neotectonic Deformation along the East Cache Fault Zone, Cache County, Utah. James P. McCalpin. (Special Study of the Utah Geological Survey Ser.: Vol. 83, No. 5). (Illus.). 37p. (Orig.). 1994. pap. 5.00 (1-55791-202-5, SS83) Utah Geological Survey.

Neotectonics No. 3: Recent Advances. L. A. Owen et al. 118p. 1996. pap. 75.00 (0-471-95702-X) Wiley.

Neotectonics & Active Faulting: Papers Presented at the International Conference on Neotectonics, Recent Advances, London, June 1992. Ed. by Iain Stewart et al. (Zeitschrift fuer Geomorphologie - Annals of Geomorphology Ser.: Supplementband 94). (Illus.). v, 328p. 1993. pap. 116.00 (3-443-21094-5, Pub. by Gebruder Borntraeger) Balogh.

Neotectonics & Resources. Ed. by Mervyn Jones & John Cosgrove. (Illus.). 320p. 1992. 62.95 (1-85293-075-6) CRC Pr.

Neotectonics in Earthquake Evaluation. Ed. by Ellis L. Krinitzsky & D. Burton Slemmons. LC 90-3653. (Reviews in Engineering Geology Ser.: Vol. 8). (Illus.). 164p. 1990. reprint ed. pap. 50.90 (0-608-07765-8, 206785300010) Bks Demand.

Neotectonics in Southern California. Ed. by R. S. Yeats et al. (Illus.). 134p. (Orig.). 1982. pap. 2.00 (1-878861-46-8) Pac Section SEPM.

Neotonics & Resources. Ed. by John Cosgrove & Mervyn Jones. LC 91-14592. 320p. 1994. text 115.00 (0-471-94513-7) Wiley.

Neotraditional Developments: The New Urbanism. Alexander Christoforidis. LC 95-38689. (CPL Bibliographies Ser.: Vol. 322). 30p. 1995. pap. 10.00 (0-86602-322-4, Sage Prdcls Pr) Sage.

***Neotraditionalism in the Russian North: Indigenous Peoples & the Legacy of Perestroika.** Alexander A. Pikayev. LC 99-26273. Vol. 6. (Illus.). 200p. 1999. pap. text 30.00 (0-295-97829-5) U of Wash Pr.

Neotropic Mesochorinae (Hymenoptera - Icheumonidae) Clement E. Dasch. (Memoir Ser.: No. 22). (Illus.). 509p. 1974. 50.00 (1-56665-020-8) Assoc Pubs FL.

Neotropical Bats from Western Mexico. Sydney Anderson. (Museum Ser.: Vol. 14, No. 1). 8p. 1960. pap. 1.00 (0-317-04936-4) U KS Nat Hist Mus.

Neotropical Biodiversity & Conservation. Ed. by Arthur C. Gibson. (Illus.). xxi, 202p. (Orig.). 1996. pap. text 25.00 (0-9655575-0-2) M E Mathias.

Neotropical Birds: Ecology & Conservation. Douglas F. Stotz. LC 95-31571. 536p. 1996. pap. text 37.50 (0-226-77630-1); lib. bdg. 100.00 (0-226-77629-8) U Ch Pr.

Neotropical Companion: An Introduction to the Animals, Plants, & Ecosystems of the New World Tropics. 2nd ed. John C. Kricher. LC 97-9784. 536p. 1997. 29.95 (0-691-04433-3, Pub. by Princeton U Pr) Cal Prin Full Svc.

***Neotropical Companion: An Introduction to the Animals, Plants, & Ecosystems of the New World Tropics.** 2nd expanded rev. ed. John Kricher. 1999. pap. 18.95 (0-691-00974-0, Pub. by Princeton U Pr) Cal Prin Full Svc.

Neotropical Fish Family Chilodontidae: Teleostei: Characiformes: A Phylogenetic Study & a Revision of Caenotropus Gunther. fac. ed. Richard P. Vari et al. LC 95-32787. (Smithsonian Contributions to Zoology Ser.: No. 577). (Illus.). 36p. 1995. reprint ed. pap. 30.00 (0-608-00970-9, 206182400011) Bks Demand.

Neotropical Fish Family Ctenoluciidae (Teleostei, Ostariophysi, Characiformes) Supra & Intrafamilial Phylogenetic Relationships, with a Revisionary Study. Richard P. Vari. LC 94-36338. (Smithsonian Contributions to Zoology Ser.: Vol. 564). 101p. 1995. reprint ed. pap. 31.40 (0-608-00508-8, 206132800008) Bks Demand.

Neotropical Migratory Birds: Natural History, Distribution, & Population Change. Richard M. DeGraaf & John H. Rappole. (Comstock Bk.). (Illus.). 560p. 1995. pap. text 29.95 (0-8014-8265-8) Cornell U Pr.

Neotropical Montane Forests: Biodiversity & Conservation Abstracts from a Symposium at the New York Botanical Garden, June 21 - 26, 1993. Ed. by Henrik Balslev. LC 97-156073. (AAU Reports: No. 31). 112p. (C). 1993. pap. 12.95 (87-87600-40-4, Pub. by Aarhus Univ Pr) David Brown.

Neotropical Ornithology. Ed. by P. A. Buckley et al. (Ornithological Monographs: No. 36). (Illus.). 1041p. 1985. 40.00 (0-943610-44-3) Am Ornithologists.

Neotropical Plant Families: A Concise Guide to Families of Vascular Plants in the Neotropics. Paul J. Maas & Lubbert Y. Westra. (Illus.). vii, 289p. 1992. pap. 34.00 (3-87429-342-4, 049967, Pub. by Koeltz Sci Bks) Lubrecht & Cramer.

Neotropical Rainforest Mammals: A Field Guide. Louise H. Emmons & Francois Feer. LC 89-39353. (Illus.). 296p. 1990. pap. 25.95 (0-226-20718-8); lib. bdg. 54.00 (0-226-20716-1) U Ch Pr.

Neotropical Rainforest Mammals: A Field Guide. 2nd ed. Louise Emmons & Fran C. Feer. LC 96-39088. 380p. 1997. pap. text 26.00 (0-226-20721-8); lib. bdg. 80.00 (0-226-20719-6) U Ch Pr.

Neotropical Toad Genus Atelopus: Checklist - Biology - Distribution. Stefan Lotters. (Illus.). 143p. (Orig.). 1996. pap. 39.95 (3-929449-02-1) Serpents Tale.

Neotropical Wildlife Use & Conservation: With 47 Contributors. Ed. by John G. Robinson & Kent H. Redford. LC 90-44430. (Illus.). 538p. 1991. lib. bdg. 74.50 (0-226-72258-9) U Ch Pr.

Neotropical Wildlife Use & Conservation: With 47 Contributors. Ed. by John G. Robinson & Kent H. Redford. LC 90-44430. (Illus.). 538p. 1997. pap. text 29.95 (0-226-72259-7) U Ch Pr.

Neotropische Okosysteme. Muller. 1976. lib. bdg. 121.50 (90-6193-208-4, Pub. by M Nijhoff) Kluwer Academic.

Neotyphodium & Grass Interactions: Proceedings of the Third International Symposium on Acremonium/ Grass Interactions Held in Athens, Georgia, May 28-31, 1997. Ed. by Charles W. Bacon & Nicholas S. Hill. LC 97-17157. 472p. 1997. 129.50 (0-306-45688-5, Kluwer Plenum) Kluwer Academic.

Nep Formation in Carding. V. Townend. 1983. 65.00 (0-7855-1017-6) St Mut.

Nep Formation in Carding. Wira Staff. (C). 1982. 125.00 (0-900820-16-0, Pub. by British Textile Tech) St Mut.

***NEPA Book: A Step-by-Step Guide to the National Environmental Policy Act.** Ronald E. Bass et al. 2000. pap., wbk. ed. 50.00 (0-923956-67-0) Solano Pr.

NEPA Compliance Manual. 2nd ed. L. Russell Freeman et al. 208p. 1994. pap. text 79.00 (0-86587-413-1) Gov Insts.

NEPA Effectiveness: Mastering the Process. Frederic March. LC 98-27527. 244p. 1998. pap. text 79.00 (0-86587-608-8, 608) Gov Insts.

NEPA in the Courts: A Legal Analysis of the National Environmental Policy Act. Frederick R. Anderson & Robert H. Daniels. 324p. 1973. pap. 23.95 (0-8018-1559-2) Resources Future.

NEPA Law & Litigation. Daniel R. Mandelker. LC 92-24290. 1992. ring bd. 145.00 (0-87632-904-0) West Group.

NEPA Litigation Manual. Mark Squillace & Karin P. Sheldon. LC 98-43800. 1998. pap. write for info. (1-57073-643-X, ABA Litigation) Amer Bar Assn.

***NEPA Planning Process: A Comprehensive Guide with Emphasis on Efficiency.** Charles H. Eccleston. LC 98-26710. 424p. 1999. 65.00 (0-471-25272-7) Wiley.

NEPA Reference Guide. Danny C. Reinke & Lucy Swartz. LC 99-21501. 1999. pap. 45.00 (1-57477-068-3) Battelle.

Nepal see Cultures of the World - Group 3

Nepal see Enchantment of the World Series

Nepal. Connie Bickman. Ed. by Julie Berg. (Through the Eyes of Children Ser.). (J). 1996. lib. bdg. 15.98 (1-56239-549-1) ABDO Pub Co.

Nepal. Ed. by Rajendra S. Khadka. (Travelers' Tales Guides Ser.). 423p. 1997. pap. 17.95 (1-885211-14-7) Trvlers Tale.

Nepal. Mohit Satyanand. 1997. pap. 57.00 (0-7855-7455-7, Pub. by Ratna Pustak Bhandar) St Mut.

Nepal. Nagendra K. Singh. 1997. pap. 68.00 (0-7855-7614-2) St Mut.

Nepal. annuals Ed. by John Whelpton. LC 90-156438. (World Bibliographical Ser.: No. 38). 322p. 1990. lib. bdg. 75.00 (0-903450-68-2) ABC-CLIO.

Nepal. Ed. by Welgang Zeigler. 64p. (C). 1988. 160.00 (81-7002-024-7, Pub. by Himalayan Bks) St Mut.

Nepal. 2nd ed. Insight Guides Staff. (Insight Guides). 1998. pap. text 22.95 (0-88729-723-4) Langenscheidt.

Nepal. 2nd ed. Chris Taylor. (Traveler's Companion Ser.). (Illus.). 256p. 1997. pap. text 22.95 (0-7627-0231-1) Globe Pequot.

Nepal. 3rd ed. Insight Guides Staff. (Insight Guides). 1998. pap. text 12.95 (0-88729-919-9) Langenscheidt.

Nepal, 2 vols., Set. Perceval Landon. (C). 1988. 500.00 (0-7855-0061-8, Pub. by Print Hse) St Mut.

Nepal, 2 vols., Set. Ed. by Perceval Landon. 358p. (C). 1987. 600.00 (0-89771-068-1, Pub. by Ratna Pustak Bhandar) St Mut.

Nepal, 2 vols., Set. Perceval Landon. 1993. 223.00 (0-7855-0263-7, Pub. by Ratna Pustak Bhandar) St Mut.

Nepal, 2 vols., Set. Perceval Landon. (C). 1993. reprint ed. text 70.00 (81-206-0723-6, Pub. by Asian Educ Servs) S Asia.

***Nepal: A Country Study Guide.** Global Investment & Business Center, Inc. Staff. (World Country Study Guides Library: Vol. 122). (Illus.). 350p. 2000. pap. 59.00 (0-7397-2420-7) Intl Business Pubns.

Nepal: A Himalayan Kingdom in Tradisition. P. P. Karan & H. Ishii. 1997. pap. 75.00 (0-7855-7441-7, Pub. by Ratna Pustak Bhandar) St Mut.

Nepal: A Himalayan Kingdom in Transition. 352p. 25.00 (92-808-0924-5) UN.

Nepal: A Pattern of Human Rights Violations. 1987. 4.00 (0-86210-134-4) Amnesty Intl USA.

Nepal: A Study of Socio-Economic & Political Changes. Tulasi R. Vaidya. (C). 1992. 72.00 (0-7855-0198-3, Pub. by Ratna Pustak Bhandar) St Mut.

Nepal: Administration & Social Reforms. Vaidya & Bajracharya. 1996. pap. 75.00 (0-7855-7456-5, Pub. by Ratna Pustak Bhandar) St Mut.

Nepal: Chandra Bahadur Ale's Painting "Simple Living" Jacquiline Touba et al. LC 96-39804. (Young Artists of the World Ser.). (Illus.). 24p. (J). (gr. k-4). 1997. lib. bdg. 15.95 (0-8239-5103-0, PowerKids) Rosen Group.

Nepal: From Kathmandu to Mt. Everest. Marilyn Turkovich et al. 180p. (J). (gr. 6-12). 1983. pap. 10.95 (0-685-55243-8, 5116) World Eagle.

Nepal: Internal Politics & Its Constitutions. S. K. Chaturyedi. (C). 1992. 32.00 (81-210-0315-6, Pub. by Inter-India Pubns) S Asia.

Nepal: Main Ethnic, Caste Groups by Districts Based on Population Census, 1991. H. Gurung. 1994. pap. 25.00 (0-7855-0465-6, Pub. by Ratna Pustak Bhandar) St Mut.

Nepal: Negendra Kr. Singh. Vishnu Latke. 1997. pap. 54.00 (0-7855-7451-4, Pub. by Ratna Pustak Bhandar) St Mut.

Nepal: Nelles Guide. rev. ed. Nelles Verlag Staff. (Nelles Guides Ser.). (Illus.). 256p. (Orig.). 1996. pap. 14.95 (3-88618-046-8, Pub. by Nelles Verlag) Seven Hills Bk.

Nepal: New Horizons. Omar Sattaur. (Oxfam Country Profiles Ser.). (Illus.). 64p. (C). 1996. pap. 9.95 (0-85598-290-X, Pub. by Oxfam Pub) Stylus Pub VA.

Nepal: Off the Beaten Path. Kesar Lall. 1992. 40.00 (0-7855-0280-7, Pub. by Ratna Pustak Bhandar) St Mut.

Nepal: Off the Beaten Path. Kesar Lall. (C). 1992. 30.00 (0-7855-0200-9, Pub. by Ratna Pustak Bhandar) St Mut.

Nepal: Problems of Governance. Lok R. Baral. (Governance in South Asia Ser.). 1993. text 30.00 (81-220-0304-4, Pub. by Konark Pubs Pvt Ltd) Advent Bks Div.

Nepal: Profile of a Himalayan Kingdom. Leo E. Rose & John T. Scholz. LC 79-17857. (Nations of Contemporary Asia Ser.). (Illus.). 156p. 1980. text 32.00 (0-89158-651-2) Westview.

Nepal: Refugee to Ruler, a Militant Race of Nepal. Nagendra K. Singh. LC 97-904203. 250p. 1997. 30.00 (81-7024-847-7, Pub. by APH Pubng) Nataraj Bks.

***Nepal: Tharu & Tarai Neighbours.** S. Skar et al. 1999. pap. 167.00 (0-7855-7615-0) St Mut.

Nepal: The Himalayan Kingdom. M. Lama & A. Thapar. 1997. pap. 110.00 (0-7855-7465-4, Pub. by Ratna Pustak Bhandar) St Mut.

Nepal: The Himalayan Kingdom. Arati Thapa. LC 97-904284. 1998. 19.95 (81-7437-067-6) Heian Intl.

Nepal: The Land of Festivals (Religious, Cultural, Social & Historical Festivals) Trilok C. Majupuria & S. P. Gupta. (Illus.). 152p. 1981. 14.95 (0-940500-83-3) Asia Bk Corp.

***Nepal: The Mountain Kingdom.** Kery Moran. (Illus.). 280p. 2000. reprint ed. pap. text 20.00 (0-7881-9106-3) DIANE Pub.

Nepal - A Country Study Guide: Basic Information for Research & Pleasure. Global Investment Center, USA Staff. (World Country Study Guide Library: Vol. 122). (Illus.). 350p. 1999. pap. 59.00 (0-7397-1519-4) Intl Business Pubns.

Nepal after Democratic Restoration. Y. N. Khanal. 1996. pap. 23.00 (0-7855-7439-5, Pub. by Ratna Pustak Bhandar) St Mut.

Nepal & Bhutan. U. S. Government Staff. (Country Studies). 1994. 23.00 (0-614-30805-4, UNEPAL) Claitors.

Nepal & Bhutan: Country Studies. Andrea Matles Savada. 464p. 1993. boxed set 32.00 (0-16-061154-7) USGPO.

Nepal & Bhutan Country Studies: Area Handbook. Ed. by Andrea M. Savada. LC 93-12226. (Area Handbook Ser.). 1993. 23.00 (0-8444-0777-1) Lib Congress.

Nepal & South Asia: A Study on Continuity & Change. Prem R. Uprety. 1994. pap. 66.00 (0-7855-0462-1, Pub. by Ratna Pustak Bhandar) St Mut.

Nepal & the United Nations, 1956-1996. Mohan P. Lohani. 1996. pap. 27.00 (0-7855-7449-2, Pub. by Ratna Pustak Bhandar) St Mut.

Nepal & the World: A Statistical Profile, 1998. Ratna Pustak Bhandar. 1998. pap. 54.00 (0-7855-7445-X, Pub. by Ratna Pustak Bhandar) St Mut.

Nepal & the World: A Statistical Profits, 1994. P. Subedi. 1994. pap. 40.00 (0-7855-0467-2, Pub. by Ratna Pustak Bhandar) St Mut.

Nepal & Tibet. (Handbooks of the World Ser.). 1996. 24.95 (0-614-97031-8) NTC Contemp Pub Co.

Nepal & Tibet Handbook with Bhutan. Gyurme Dorje. (Handbooks of the World Ser.). (Illus.). 768p. 1996. 24.95 (0-8442-4901-7, Passprt Bks) NTC Contemp Pub Co.

***Nepal Business Intelligence Report, 190 vols.** Global Investment & Business Center, Inc. Staff. (World Business Intelligence Library: Vol. 122). (Illus.). 350p. 2000. pap. 99.95 (0-7397-2620-X) Intl Business Pubns.

***Nepal Business Law Handbook, 190 vols.** Global Investment & Business Center, Inc. Staff. (Global Business Law Handbooks Library: Vol. 122). (Illus.). 350p. 2000. pap. 99.95 (0-7397-2020-1) Intl Business Pubns.

***Nepal Business Opportunity Yearbook.** Global Investment & Business Center, Inc. Staff. (Global Business Opportunity Yearbooks Library: Vol. 122). (Illus.). 2000. pap. 99.95 (0-7397-2220-4) Intl Business Pubns.

***Nepal Business Opportunity Yearbook: Export-Import, Investment & Business Opportunities.** International Business Publications, U. S. A. Staff & Global Investment Center, U. S. A. Staff. (Global Business Opportunity Yearbooks Library: Vol. 122). (Illus.). 350p. 1999. pap. 99.95 (0-7397-1320-5) Intl Business Pubns.

N

An Asterisk (*) at the beginning of an entry indicates that the title is appearing for the first time.

Nepal Cookbook. Association of Nepalis in the Americas Staff. (Illus.). 168p. 1996. 10.95 (*1-55939-060-3*) Snow Lion Pubns.

***Nepal Country Review 2000.** Robert C. Kelly et al. (Illus.). 60p. 1999. pap. 39.95 (*1-58310-546-8*) CountryWatch.

Nepal District Profile: A District-Wise Socio-Techno-Economic Profit along with a Comprehensive National Profit of Nepal, 1997. NRA Staff. 1997. pap. 267.00 (*0-7855-7440-9*, Pub. by Ratna Pustak Bhandar) St Mut.

Nepal Economy & Development. Vaidya & Bajracharya. 1996. pap. 86.00 (*0-7855-7457-3*, Pub. by Ratna Pustak Bhandar) St Mut.

Nepal Encyclopedia. Ed. by Madhu R. Acharya. 1994. pap. 75.00 (*0-7855-0468-0*, Pub. by Ratna Pustak Bhandar) St Mut.

Nepal Environmental Policy & Action Plan. 1994. pap. 27.00 (*0-7855-0469-9*, Pub. by Ratna Pustak Bhandar) St Mut.

Nepal Festivals. D. K. Deep. (C). 1992. 30.00 (*0-7855-0201-7*, Pub. by Ratna Pustak Bhandar) St Mut.

Nepal Festivals. Dhruba K. Deep. 128p. (C). 1982. 40.50 (*0-89771-067-3*, Pub. by Ratna Pustak Bhandar) St Mut.

Nepal Festivals. Dhruba K. Deep. 1992. 30.00 (*0-7855-0261-0*, Pub. by Ratna Pustak Bhandar) St Mut.

***Nepal Foreign Policy & Government Guide.** Global Investment & Business Center, Inc. Staff. (World Foreign Policy & Government Library: Vol. 117). (Illus.). 350p. 2000. pap. 99.95 (*0-7397-3820-8*) Intl Business Pubns.

Nepal Government & Past Politics. Vaidya & Bajracharya. 1996. pap. 75.00 (*0-7855-7460-3*, Pub. by Ratna Pustak Bhandar) St Mut.

Nepal Handbook. Tom Woodhatch. (Footprint Handbks.). (Illus.). 512p. 1997. 19.95 (*0-8442-4924-6*, Passprt Bks) NTC Contemp Pub Co.

***Nepal Handbook.** 2nd ed. Tom Woodhatch. (Footprint Handbooks Ser.). 496p. 1999. pap. 17.95 (*0-658-00016-0*, 000160, NTC Business Bks) NTC Contemp Pub Co.

***Nepal Himalaya.** H. W. Tilman. 1998. pap. 73.00 (*0-7855-7611-8*) St Mut.

Nepal in Pictures. Ed. by Lerner Publications, Department of Geography Staff. (Visual Geography Ser.). (Illus.). 64p. (YA). (gr. 5 up). 1993. lib. bdg. 19.95 (*0-8225-1851-1*, Lerner Publctns) Lerner Pub.

Nepal in the 90's: Versions of the Past, Visions of the Future. Ed. by Michael Hutt. LC 94-903729. (SOAS Studies on South Asia). 184p. 1994. text 15.95 (*0-19-563441-1*) OUP.

Nepal in Transition. M. D. Dharamdasani. 1997. pap. 67.00 (*0-7855-7443-3*, Pub. by Ratna Pustak Bhandar) St Mut.

Nepal India: Democracy in the Making of Mutual Trust. Ed. by Dinesh Bhattarai & Pradip Khatiwada. 320p. 1993. 25.00 (*81-85693-36-6*, Pub. by Nirala Pubns) Nataraj Bks.

Nepal-India Open Border: A Bond of Shaved Aspirations. R. P. Rajbahak. (C). 1992. 48.00 (*0-7855-0199-1*, Pub. by Ratna Pustak Bhandar) St Mut.

Nepal Institutional Man Power Directory, 1994. Thomas Smith. 1994. pap. 60.00 (*0-7855-0473-7*, Pub. by Ratna Pustak Bhandar) St Mut.

Nepal International Perspectives. Vaidya & Bajracharya. 1996. pap. 96.00 (*0-7855-7461-1*, Pub. by Ratna Pustak Bhandar) St Mut.

***Nepal Investment & Business Guide.** Global Investment & Business Center, Inc. Staff. (Global Investment & Business Guide Library: Vol. 122). (Illus.). 2000. pap. 99.95 (*0-7397-1820-7*) Intl Business Pubns.

***Nepal Investment & Business Guide: Export-Import, Investment & Business Opportunities.** International Business Publications, USA Staff & Global Investment Center, USA Staff. (World Investment & Business Guide Library-99: Vol. 122). (Illus.). 350p. 1999. pap. 99.95 (*0-7397-0317-X*) Intl Business Pubns.

Nepal Land of Mystery. Hassoldt Davis. 1997. pap. 92.00 (*0-7855-7616-9*) St Mut.

Nepal Miscellany. Kesar Lall. 1993. 30.00 (*0-7855-0279-3*, Pub. by Ratna Pustak Bhandar) St Mut.

Nepal People & Culture. Vaidya & Bajracharya. 1996. pap. 75.00 (*0-7855-7462-X*, Pub. by Ratna Pustak Bhandar) St Mut.

***Nepal Pocket Guide.** rev. ed. Berlitz Publishing Staff. (Berlitz Pocket Guide Ser.). 144p. 1999. pap. 8.95 (*2-8315-7223-1*, Pub. by Berlitz) Globe Pequot.

Nepal Political Economy of Foreign Aid. M. D. Dharmdasani. 1994. pap. 60.00 (*0-7855-0470-2*, Pub. by Ratna Pustak Bhandar) St Mut.

Nepal Social Demography & Expressions. Harka B. Gurung. 1997. pap. 54.00 (*0-7855-7442-5*, Pub. by Ratna Pustak Bhandar) St Mut.

Nepal Socio-Economic Change & Rural Migration. Poonam Thapa. 1989. 80.00 (*0-7855-0231-9*, Pub. by Ratna Pustak Bhandar) St Mut.

Nepal Socio-Economic Change & Rural Migration. Poonam Thapa. 185p. (C). 1989. 327.00 (*0-89771-042-8*, Pub. by Ratna Pustak Bhandar) St Mut.

***Nepal Struggling for Democracy Big Four the Martyrs Their Revolutionary Stand 1940.** B. B. Mathema. 1998. pap. 50.00 (*0-7855-7612-6*) St Mut.

***Nepal Task Force.** 45p. 1999. pap. 35.00 (*1-882866-64-9*) Pac Asia Trvl.

Nepal, Tibet & Bhutan. Fodors Staff. 368p. 2000. pap. 20.00 (*0-679-00167-0*) Fodors Travel.

Nepal-Tibet Relations, 1850-1930: Years of of Hopes Challenges & Frestrations. Prem R. Uprety. 1998. pap. 47.00 (*0-7855-7444-1*, Pub. by Ratna Pustak Bhandar) St Mut.

Nepal under Amsurvarma (Golden Period) S. L. Joshi. (C). 1993. 72.00 (*0-7855-0195-9*, Pub. by Ratna Pustak Bhandar) St Mut.

Nepal under Amsuvarma (Golden Period) Shankar L. Joshi. 1993. 28.00 (*81-7041-713-9*, Pub. by Anmol) S Asia.

Nepal under the Ranas. Adrian Sever. 1993. 78.00 (*81-204-0770-9*, Pub. by Oxford IBH) S Asia.

Nepal under the Ranas. Adrian Sever. 1993. 240.00 (*0-7855-0262-9*, Pub. by Ratna Pustak Bhandar) St Mut.

Nepal under the Ranas. Adrian Sever. (Illus.). 530p. (C). 1993. 50.00 (*0-948724-31-5*, Pub. by Tricolour Bks); lib. bdg. 49.95 (*0-317-05153-9*, Pub. by Tricolour Bks) Asia Pub Hse.

Nepal under the Ranas. Andrian Sever. (C). 1993. 144.00 (*0-7855-0196-7*, Pub. by Ratna Pustak Bhandar) St Mut.

Nepal Year Book, 1997: Events of the Year 1996. IIDS Staff. 1997. pap. 30.00 (*0-7855-7450-6*, Pub. by Ratna Pustak Bhandar) St Mut.

***Nepal Year Book 1998: Events of the Year 1997.** IIDS Staff. 1998. pap. 43.00 (*0-7855-7613-4*) St Mut.

Nepal Years, 2 vols., Set. Thomas Smith. 1994. pap. 204.00 (*0-7855-0472-9*, Pub. by Ratna Pustak Bhandar) St Mut.

Nepala-Mahatmya of the Skandapurana: Legends on the Sacred Deities of Nepal. Jayaraj Acharya. (Illus.). xvi, 320p. 1992. 33.00 (*81-85693-27-7*, Pub. by Nirala Pubns) Nataraj Bks.

Nepalese: Taxation: A Path for Reform. Donna Addison & Rup B. Khadka. 1994. pap. 147.00 (*0-7855-7466-2*, Pub. by Ratna Pustak Bhandar) St Mut.

Nepalese American Perspectives: Proceedings of the First National Convention of Nepalese & Friends of Nepal in North America. Ed. by Mohan N. Shrestha. 172p. 1995. pap. 15.00 (*0-9647184-0-5*) ANMA.

Nepalese Caitya: 1500 Years of Buddhist Votive Architecture in the Kathmandu Valley. Niels Gutschow. LC 98-202979. (Monograph Ser.). (Illus.). 320p. 1997. 128.00 (*3-930698-75-7*) Dist Art Pubs.

Nepalese Cartoons (Himalayan Humour) R. K. Panday. 1997. pap. 26.00 (*0-7855-7446-8*, Pub. by Ratna Pustak Bhandar) St Mut.

Nepalese Customs & Manners. Ed. by Kesar Lall. 76p. (C). 1990. 35.00 (*0-89771-073-8*, Pub. by Ratna Pustak Bhandar) St Mut.

Nepalese Customs & Manners. Kesar Lall. 1992. 30.00 (*0-7855-0282-3*, Pub. by Ratna Pustak Bhandar) St Mut.

Nepalese Economics. A. M. Shrestha. 1997. pap. 25.00 (*0-7855-7447-6*, Pub. by Ratna Pustak Bhandar) St Mut.

Nepalese Economy & India. S. Singh. 1996. pap. 107.00 (*0-7855-7458-1*, Pub. by Ratna Pustak Bhandar) St Mut.

Nepalese Interviews. Aniruddha Gupta. 1997. pap. 86.00 (*0-7855-7459-X*, Pub. by Ratna Pustak Bhandar) St Mut.

Nepalese National Bibliography (NNR), 1987-1989. Ratna Pustak Bhandar. 1996. pap. 53.00 (*0-7855-7448-4*, Pub. by Ratna Pustak Bhandar) St Mut.

Nepalese Pagoda. Ed. by S. Chand & Co. Ltd. Staff. 334p. 1988. 55.00 (*0-317-52146-2*, Pub. by S Chand & Co) St Mut.

Nepalese Political Behaviour. Borre & Pandey. 1994. pap. 48.00 (*0-7855-0466-4*, Pub. by Ratna Pustak Bhandar) St Mut.

Nepalese Political Behaviour: Comprehensive Study of Nepalese Voters. Ole Borre et al. (Illus.). 240p. (Orig.). (C). 1994. pap. 19.95 (*87-7288-483-5*, Pub. by Aarhus Univ Pr) David Brown.

Nepalese Shaman Oral Texts. Gregory G. Maskannec. LC 98-52681. 707p. 1998. 90.00 (*0-674-60795-3*) HUP.

Nepalese Short Stories. Tr. by Karunakar Vaidya. LC 75-12436. 128p. 1976. lib. bdg. 14.95 (*0-913622-03-6*) Gallery Pr.

Nepalese Textiles. S. Dunsmore. (Illus.). 204p. 1994. pap. 35.00 (*0-7141-2510-5*) U of Wash Pr.

Nepali: A National Language & Its Literature. M. J. Hutt. 1988. 80.00 (*0-7855-0281-5*, Pub. by Ratna Pustak Bhandar) St Mut.

Nepali: A National Language & Its Literature. M. J. Hutt. 252p. (C). 1988. 275.00 (*0-89771-080-0*, Pub. by Ratna Pustak Bhandar) St Mut.

Nepali: A National Language & Its Literature. Michael J. Hutt. (C). 1988. 26.00 (*0-7286-0138-9*, Pub. by Sch Orient & African Stud) S Asia.

Nepali: Language Survival Kit. 3rd ed. Mary-Jo O'Rourke & Bimal Shrestha. (Illus.). 208p. 1996. pap. 5.95 (*0-86442-345-4*) Lonely Planet.

Nepali - English Dictionary. Allora. (ENG & NEP.). 1992. reprint ed. 14.95 (*0-8288-8417-X*) Fr & Eur.

Nepali Community in India. Suman R. Timsina. vi, 113p. 1992. 12.00 (*81-85445-09-5*, Pub. by Manak Pubns Pvt Ltd) Nataraj Bks.

Nepali Congress: An Analysis of the Party's Performance in the General Elections & Its Aftermath. B. C. Upreti. (Illus.). 203p. 1993. 25.00 (*81-85693-33-1*, Pub. by Nirala Pubns) Nataraj Bks.

Nepali Congress: An Analysis of the Party's Performance in the General Elections & Its Aftermath. B. C. Upreti. (C). 1993. 71.00 (*0-7855-0197-5*, Pub. by Ratna Pustak Bhandar) St Mut.

Nepali Dictionary. 2nd ed. Star Publications Staff. (NEP.). 1980. 19.95 (*0-8288-1710-3*, F 27300) Fr & Eur.

Nepali for Trekkers: Ninety Minutes of Phrases & Vocabulary. Contrib. by M. D. Bezruchka. 48p. 1998. pap. 18.95 incl. audio (*0-89886-311-2*) Mountaineers.

Nepali Grammar & Vocabulary. A. Turnbull. (ENG & NEP.). 195p. 1992. 49.95 (*0-8288-8509-5*) Fr & Eur.

Nepali Grammar & Vocabulary. A. Turnbull. Ed. by R. Kilgour. (C). 1982. reprint ed. 15.00 (*0-8364-2402-6*, Pub. by Asian Educ Servs) S Asia.

Nepali Newspaper Reader. 1984. audio 24.00 (*0-931745-10-1*) Dunwoody Pr.

Nepali Newspaper Reader. Champa Jarmul. LC 84-72436. ix, 274p. 1984. text 43.00 (*0-931745-03-9*) Dunwoody Pr.

Nepali Version of the Vetalapancavimsati. Ed. by Theodore Riccardi. (American Oriental Ser.: Vol. 54). ix, 206p. 1971. pap. 17.50 (*0-940490-54-4*) Am Orient Soc.

Nepali Visions, Nepali Dreams: The Poetry of Laxmiprasad Devkota. Tr. by David G. Rubin from NEP. (Modern Asian Literature Ser.). 192p. 1980. text 50.00 (*0-231-05014-3*) Col U Pr.

Nepal's Agricultural Traded in the New World Trading Order. G. H. Gill. 1996. pap. 21.00 (*0-7855-7463-8*, Pub. by Ratna Pustak Bhandar) St Mut.

Nepal's Economic Development Policies: Political Implications. K. N. Sharma. 1994. pap. 54.00 (*0-7855-0471-0*, Pub. by Ratna Pustak Bhandar) St Mut.

Nepal's Who's Who. Ed. by Deepak Aryal. 1997. pap. 130.00 (*0-7855-7464-6*, Pub. by Ratna Pustak Bhandar) St Mut.

Nepantla: Essays from the Land in the Middle. Pat Mora. LC 92-39874. 181p. 1993. 11.95 (*0-8263-1454-6*) U of NM Pr.

***Nepantla: Views from South.** Ed. by Alberto D. Moreiras et al. 286p. 2000. pap. 10.00 (*0-8223-6482-4*) Duke.

Nepenthes. Regina Pagoulatou. Tr. by George Pilitsis from GRE. LC 95-68182.Tr. of Ta Nipenthi. (ENG & GRE.). 63p. (Orig.). 1995. pap. text 10.00 (*0-614-28600-X*) Pella Pub.

Nephelieae Pollen (Sapindaceae) Form, Function, & Evolution. R. W. Van der Ham. (Leiden Botanical Ser.: Vol. 13). (Illus.). 255p. 1990. pap. 47.00 (*90-71236-07-2*, Pub. by Rijksherbarium) Balogh.

Nephew. Mark Dunster. 9p. (Orig.). 1988. pap. 4.00 (*0-89642-161-9*) Linden Pubs.

Nephi & Lehi in Prison. Sherrie Johnson. LC 95-154568. (Steppingstone Ser.). (Illus.). (Orig.). (J). (ps-3). 1994. pap. 4.95 (*0-87579-857-8*) Deseret Bk.

***Nephiad: An Epic in Twelve Books.** Michael R. Collings. 175p. 1999. 30.00 (*1-886405-68-9*, Zarahemla Motets) White Crow Pr.

Nephiad: An Epic Poem in 12 Books. Michael R. Collings. LC 96-61331. 180p. (Orig.). Date not set. pap. 20.00 (*1-886405-52-2*, Zarahemla Motets) White Crow Pr.

Nephilim: The Truth Is Here. L.A. Mazulli. LC 99-35509. 352p. 1999. pap. 12.99 (*0-310-22011-4*) HarpC.

Nephilim Gamemaster Veil. Sam Johnson et al. Ed. & Illus. by Sam Shirley. Illus. by Sam Innabinet. (Nephilim Roleplaying Game Ser.). 22p. (Orig.). 1994. pap. text 14.95 (*1-56882-034-8*, 3101) Chaosium.

Nephilim Gamemaster's Companion: Indispensable Resources for the Nephilim Gamemaster. Shannon Appel et al. (Nephilim Role Playing Game Ser.). (Illus.). 96p. (Orig.). 1996. pap. 14.95 (*1-56882-066-6*, 3106) Chaosium.

Nephrogenesis. Ed. by A. S. Woolf. (Journal Ser.: Vol. 4, No. 2, 1996). (Illus.). 70p. 1996. pap. 45.25 (*3-8055-6294-2*) S Karger.

Nephrolithiasis. Ed. by Fredric L. Coe. LC 80-10326. (Contemporary Issues in Nephrology Ser.: No. 5). (Illus.). 287p. reprint ed. pap. 89.00 (*0-8357-6567-9*, 203594100097) Bks Demand.

Nephrologic Problems of the Newborn. Ed. by J. F. Pascual & P. L. Calcagno. (Contributions to Nephrology Ser.: Vol. 15). (Illus.). 1979. pap. 29.75 (*3-8055-2947-3*) S Karger.

Nephrologie im Kindesalter III. Ed. by O. Oetliker & E. Bern Rossi. (Paediatrische Fortbildungskurse fuer die Praxis Ser.: Bd. 45). (GER., Illus.). 1978. 46.25 (*3-8055-2825-6*) S Karger.

Nephrologie Pediatrique. 3rd ed. P. Royer et al. (Collection Pediatrie Ser.). (FRE., Illus.). 652p. 1983. lib. bdg. 75.00 (*2-257-12397-2*) S M P F Inc.

Nephrology. Laurence Baker. (Medico-Legal Practitioner Ser.). xv, 166p. 1998. 72.00 (*1-85941-025-1*, Pub. by Cavendish Pubng) Gaunt.

Nephrology. M. Legrain. 400p. (gr. 13). 1987. 17.00 (*0-89352-230-9*) Mosby Inc.

Nephrology. Ed. by Rachael Robinson. (Illus.). lv, 1756p. 1984. 367.00 (*0-387-96072-4*) Spr-Verlag.

***Nephrology.** Ed. by Francesco Paolo Schena. (Illus.). 520p. 2000. Price not set. (*0-07-709525-1*) McGraw.

Nephrology. 3rd ed. Ed. by C. Craig Risher & Christopher S. Wilcox. LC 94-27308. (House Officer Ser.). 324p. 1995. pap. 24.95 (*0-683-08277-9*) Lppncott W & W.

Nephrology: Diuretics: Basic, Pharmacological, & Clinical Aspects. Ed. by Vittorio E. Andreucci & Antonio Dal Canton. (Developments in Nephrology Ser.). 640p. (C). 1987. text 208.00 (*0-89838-885-6*) Kluwer Academic.

Nephrology: Proceedings of the International Congress, 5th, Mexico, 1972, 3 vols., Set. Incl. Vol. 1. Morphology & Pathology. International Congress of Nephrology Staff. Ed. by H. Villarreal. 1974. 54.00 (*3-8055-1742-4*); Vol. 2. Physiology. 1974. 54.00 (*3-8055-1743-2*); Vol. 3. Clinic. International Congress of Nephrology Staff. Ed. by H. Villarreal. 1974. 54.00 (*3-8055-1744-0*); 1974. 139.25 (*3-8055-1423-9*) S Karger.

Nephrology: Proceedings of the XIth International Congress of Nephrology, 2 vols., Set. Ed. by M. Hatano. (Illus.). 1800p. 1991. 290.00 (*0-387-70074-9*) Spr-Verlag.

Nephrology & Dialysis Updated. Ed. by G. D'Amico & G. Colasanti. (Contributions to Nephrology Ser.: Vol. 61). (Illus.). vi, 298p. 1988. 29.75 (*3-8055-4673-4*) S Karger.

***Nephrology & Geriatrics Integrated.** D. G. Oreopoulos. LC 00-21825. 2000. write for info. (*0-7923-6181-4*) Kluwer Academic.

***Nephrology & Hypertension.** 4th ed. C. Craig Tisher & Christopher S. Wilcox. LC 99-38983. (House Officer Ser.). (Illus.). 1999. write for info. (*0-7817-2077-X*) Lppncott W & W.

Nephrology & Transplantation, 1986. Jon C. Ransom. 1986. pap. text 24.95 (*0-914899-04-X*) Current Lit Pubns.

Nephrology & Transplantation, 1987. Jon C. Ransom. 340p. 1987. pap. text 24.95 (*0-914899-05-8*) Current Lit Pubns.

Nephrology & Transplantation, 1988. Jon C. Ransom. 436p. 1988. pap. text 29.95 (*0-914899-06-6*) Current Lit Pubns.

Nephrology & Urology. fac. ed. Ed. by Edward B. Breitschwerdt. LC 88-4785. (Contemporary Issues in Small Animal Practice Ser.: No. 4). (Illus.). 294p. 1986. reprint ed. pap. 91.20 (*0-7837-7886-4*, 204764200007) Bks Demand.

Nephrology & Urology for the Pediatrician. Bernard Gauthier et al. 1982. 54.95 (*0-316-30524-3*, Little Brwn Med Div) Lppncott W & W.

Nephrology & Urology in the Aged Patient. Ed. by Dimitrious G. Oreopoulos et al. LC 92-48668. 1993. text 392.50 (*0-7923-2019-0*) Kluwer Academic.

Nephrology for the House Officer. 2nd ed. C. Craig Tisher. LC 92-49487. (Illus.). 336p. 1992. pap. 21.95 (*0-683-08276-0*) Lppncott W & W.

Nephrology Forum. Ed. by J. J. Cohen et al. (Illus.). 376p. 1982. 117.00 (*0-387-90764-5*) Spr-Verlag.

Nephrology Grand Rounds: Clinical Issues in Nephrology. Ed. by Martin Zeier & Eberhard Ritz. LC 98-22539. (Contributions to Nephrology Ser.: Vol. 123). (Illus.). viii, 202p. 1998. 198.25 (*3-8055-6718-9*) S Karger.

Nephrology, 1985. Jon C. Ransom. 337p. 1985. pap. text 24.95 (*0-914899-03-1*) Current Lit Pubns.

Nephrology, 1984. Jon C. Ransom. 338p. (Orig.). 1984. pap. text 24.95 (*0-914899-01-5*) Current Lit Pubns.

Nephrology Nursing. Francine Hekelman & Carol Ostendarp. (Illus.). 1979. text 33.95 (*0-07-027948-9*) McGraw.

Nephrology Secrets: Questions You Will Be Asked on Rounds, in the Clinic, on Oral Exams. Donald E. Hricik et al. LC 99-14494. (Secrets Ser.). (Illus.). 350p. 1999. text 38.00 (*1-56053-309-9*) Hanley & Belfus.

Nephropathy in Type 2 Diabetes. Ed. by Eberhard Ritz. LC 99-26166. (Oxford Clinical Nephrology Ser.). (Illus.). 304p. 1999. text 145.00 (*0-19-262945-X*) OUP.

Nephrotic Syndrome. J. Stewart Cameron & Richard J. Glassock. (Kidney Disease Ser.: Vol. 8). (Illus.). 1080p. 1987. text 299.00 (*0-8247-7361-6*) Dekker.

Nephrotic Syndrome. Ed. by Barry M. Brenner & Jay H. Stein. LC 82-9427. (Contemporary Issues in Nephrology Ser.: No. 9). (Illus.). 320p. reprint ed. pap. 99.20 (*0-7837-2568-X*, 204272700006) Bks Demand.

Nephrotoxicity. J. B. Hook. 86p. 1986. text 119.00 (*2-88124-420-3*) Gordon & Breach.

Nephrotoxicity: Assessment & Pathogenesis: Proceedings of the International Symposium on Nephrotoxicity, University of Surrey, U. K., 7-11 September 1981. International Symposium on Nephrotoxicity (1981: U. Ed. by P. H. Bach et al. LC RC0902.A2. (Monographs in Applied Toxicology: No. 1). 544p. reprint ed. pap. 168.70 (*0-608-15874-7*, 203075200070) Bks Demand.

Nephrotoxicity: In Vitro & in Vivo, Animals to Man. Ed. by Peter H. Bach & E. A. Lock. (Illus.). 788p. 1989. 145.00 (*0-306-43153-X*, Plenum Trade) Perseus Pubng.

Nephrotoxicity: Mechanisms, Early Diagnosis & Therapeutic Management. Ed. by Peter H. Bach et al. 600p. 1991. text 215.00 (*0-8247-8366-2*) Dekker.

Nephrotoxicity in the Experimental & Clinical Situation, Pt. 1. Ed. by Peter H. Bach & E. A. Lock. (Developments in Nephrology Ser.). (C). 1987. lib. bdg. 179.50 (*0-89838-977-1*) Kluwer Academic.

Nephrotoxicity in the Experimental & Clinical Situation, Pt. 2. Ed. by Peter H. Bach & E. A. Lock. (Developments in Nephrology Ser.). (C). 1987. text 195.50 (*0-89838-980-1*) Kluwer Academic.

Nephrotoxicity of Clinically Relevant Drugs. Ed. by William M. Bennett. (Journal: Mineral & Electrolyte Metabolism Ser.: Vol. 2, No. 4, 1994). (Illus.). 76p. 1994. pap. 41.75 (*3-8055-6091-5*) S Karger.

***Neponset - My Home Town.** Mary Solari. 1999. pap. write for info. (*1-58235-279-8*) Watermrk Pr.

Nepos: 3 Lives (Alcibiades, Dion, Atticus) Ed. by R. Roebuck. (Bristol Latin Texts Ser.). (LAT.). 140p. 1993. pap. 18.95 (*0-86292-284-4*, Pub. by Brist Class Pr) Focus Pub-R Pullins.

Nepos, Cornelius. Ed. by Karl Nipperdey & Kurt Witte. iii, 300p. 1967. write for info. (*3-296-12000-9*) G Olms Pubs.

Nepos Dion. Grace S. West. (Latin Commentaries Ser.). 29p. (Orig.). (C). 1985. pap. text 5.00 (*0-929524-44-6*) Bryn Mawr Commentaries.

Nepos Life of Atticus. Cynthia Damon. 40p. (Orig.). 1993. pap. text 5.00 (*0-929524-81-0*) Bryn Mawr Commentaries.

Nepotis, Cornelii. Ed. by Marshall. (LAT.). 1991. 22.95 (*3-8154-1959-X*, T1959, Pub. by B G Teubner) U of Mich Pr.

Neppi Modona Diaries: Reading Jewish Survival Through My Italian Family. Kate Cohen. LC 96-24968. (Illus.). 284p. 1997. 24.95 (*0-87451-783-4*) U Pr of New Eng.

Neprivodimye i Indutsirovannye Predstavleniia i Kopredstavleniia Fedorovoskikh Grupp see Representations of the Crystallographic Space Groups: Irreducible Representations, Induced Representations, & Corepresentations

Nepsy. Kemp. 256p. (C). 2000. pap. 29.95 (*0-471-32690-9*) Wiley.

Nepticulidae: Insecta: Lepidoptera see Fauna of New Zealand Series

Nepticulidae & Opostegidae (Lepidoptera) of North West Europe, 2 pts., Set. R. Johansson et al. LC 89-17459. (Fauna Entomologica Scandinavica Ser.: Vol. 23). (Illus.). 739p. 1990. lib. bdg. 173.50 (*90-04-08698-6*) Brill Academic Pubs.

Nepticulidae of Eastern Europe & Asia. Western, Central & Eastern Parts. R. Puplesis. (Illus.). 552p. 1994. 140.00 (*90-73348-29-3*, Pub. by Backhuys Pubs) Balogh.

Neptune. Larry Dane Brimmer. (True Books: Continents Ser.). 1999. lib. bdg. 6.95 (*0-516-26496-6*) Childrens.

N

Neptune. Larry D. Brimner. LC 98-22039. (Space Ser.). 47p. (J). 1999. 21.50 (0-516-21157-9) Childrens.
Neptune. Elaine Landau. LC 90-13098. (First Bks.). (Illus.). 64p. (J). (gr. 3-5). 1991. lib. bdg. 22.00 (0-531-20014-0) Watts.
*__Neptune.__ Seymour Simon. (Illus.). 1999. pap. 13.35 (0-613-02373-0) Econo-Clad Bks.
Neptune. Seymour Simon. LC 90-13213. (Illus.). 32p. (J). (gr. k up). 1991. 17.93 (0-688-09632-8, Wm Morrow) Morrow Avon.
Neptune. Seymour Simon. LC 90-13213. (Illus.). 32p. (gr. 1-4). 1997. mass mkt. 5.95 (0-688-15277-5, Wm Morrow) Morrow Avon.
Neptune. Seymour Simon. 1997. 11.15 (0-606-11675-3, Pub. by Turtleback) Demco.
*__Neptune.__ Luke Thompson. LC 00-25039. (Illus.). (J). 2000. write for info. (0-8239-5648-2, PowerKids) Rosen Group.
*__Neptune.__ Gregory L. Vogt. LC 99-86979. (Galaxy Ser.). (Illus.). 24p. (J). (ps-3). 2000. lib. bdg. 15.93 (0-7368-0513-3, Bridgestone Bks) Capstone Pr.
Neptune. Gregory L. Vogt. LC 92-30183. (Gateway Solar System Ser.). (Illus.). 32p. (J). (gr. 2-4). 1993. lib. bdg. 19.90 (1-56294-331-6) Millbrook Pr.
Neptune. Elaine Landau. (Illus.). 64p. (J). (gr. 4-6). 1996. reprint ed. pap. 6.95 (0-531-15774-1) Watts.
Neptune & Shark River Hills. Evelyn Stryker Lewis. LC 98-87778. (Images of America Ser.). (Illus.). 128p. 1998. pap. 16.99 (0-7524-0997-2) Arcadia Publng.
Neptune & Surf. Marilyn Jaye Lewis. 1999. pap. text 12.95 (1-58419-001-9) Masq Bks.
Neptune & Triton. Ed. by Dale P. Cruikshank. LC 95-32468. (Space Science Ser.). (Illus.). 1249p. 1996. 110.00 (0-8165-1525-5) U of Ariz Pr.
Neptune Crossing. Jeffrey A. Carver. (Chaos Chronicles). 383p. 1995. mass mkt. 5.99 (0-8125-3515-4, Pub. by Tor Bks) St Martin.
Neptune Expedition. Tom Rothschild. 1995. 15.95 (0-533-11295-8) Vantage.
*__Neptune File: A Story of Mathematical Cunning & the Pioneers of Planet Hunting.__ Tom Standage. (Illus.). 2000. 24.00 (0-8027-1363-7) Walker & Co.
Neptune Fountain: The Apprenticeship of a Renaissance Sculptor. Taylor Morrison. LC 96-41735. (Illus.). 32p. (J). (gr. 4-6). 1997. lib. bdg. 15.95 (0-8234-1293-8) Holiday.
Neptune Slides. Kaufman. (C). 1991. pap. text. write for info. (0-7167-2128-7) W H Freeman.
Neptune's Account. Michael Maffett. 348p. 1995. 23.95 (0-9644618-0-3) Woodvale Pr.
Neptune's Gift: A History of Common Salt. Robert P. Multhauf. LC 77-8688. (Johns Hopkins Studies in the History of Technology; New Ser.: No. 2). (Illus.). 344p. reprint ed. pap. 106.70 (0-8357-4033-1, 203672500005) Bks Demand.
Neptune's Gift: A History of Common Salt. Robert P. Multhauf. (Illus.). 326p. 1996. reprint ed. pap. text 19.95 (0-8018-5469-5) Johns Hopkins.
Neptune's Kingdom. Ivan Mazur & Elena Mazur. Ed. by Stella Freedman. (Ecology for Children Ser.: Vol. 1). (Illus.). 48p. (J). (gr. 2-6). 1998. 11.95 (1-892316-03-X) Rama Pr.
*__Neptune's Militia: The Frigate South Carolina During the American Revolution.__ James A. Lewis. LC 99-20255. (Illus.). 288p. 1999. text 39.00 (0-87338-632-9) Kent St U Pr.
*__Neptune's Nursery.__ Kim Michelle Toft & Allan Sheather. 32p. (J). (ps-3). 2000. 16.95 (1-57091-391-9); pap. 6.95 (1-57091-392-7) Charlesbridge Pub.
Neptune's Table: Cooking the Seafood Exotics. Donald Hubbard. LC 97-8475. (Illus.). 175p. 1997. pap. 17.95 (0-943665-06-X) Sea Eagle Pubns.
Neptunium: Radiation Protection Guidelines. LC 87-11207. (Report Ser.: No. 90). 114p. 1988. pap. text 35.00 (0-913392-87-1) NCRP Pubns.
Neptunium-237 Production & Recovery. Wallace W. Schulz & Glen E. Benedict. LC 72-600249. (AEC Critical Review Ser.). 98p. 1972. pap. 10.50 (0-87079-001-3, TID-25955); fiche 9.00 (0-87079-465-5, TID-25955) DOE.
Neptunus Rex: Naval Stories of the Normandy Invasion, June 6, 1944: Voices of the Navy Memorial. Ed. by Edward F. Prados. LC 98-6151. 304p. 1998. 24.95 (0-89141-648-X) Presidio Pr.
Neqem Ayuqucia Nallunritellruan-qaa... Nega! large type ed. Jim MacDiarmid. Tr. by Joseph Collidge.Tr. of Meet... a Fish!. (ESK., Illus.). 20p. (J). (gr. 3-5). 1999. pap. text 7.00 (1-58084-176-7) Lower Kuskokwim.
Neqengnaqler. large type ed. Margaret Nickerson.Tr. of Gathering Food. (ESK., Illus.). 8p. (J). (gr. k-3). 1999. pap. text 14.50 (1-58084-105-8) Lower Kuskokwim.
Neqliller Pinwaneg Iqallugneg (How to Make Fish Strips) large type ed. Bessie Green. (ESK., Illus.). 12p. (J). (gr. k-3). 1999. pap. text 17.00 (1-58084-107-4) Lower Kuskokwim.
Neqliuryaraq. large type ed. Alice Andrew et al.Tr. of How to Prepare Fish. (ESK., Illus.). 8p. (J). (gr. k-3). 1999. pap. text 6.00 (1-58084-053-1) Lower Kuskokwim.
Neqsulartukut. Tommy Andrew.Tr. of We Fish. (ESK., Illus.). 8p. (J). (gr. k-3). 1998. pap. text 6.00 (1-58084-032-9) Lower Kuskokwim.
Neqsurtek. large type ed. Paul Ilutsik.Tr. of Two Subsistence Fishermen. (ESK., Illus.). 16p. (J). (gr. 3-5). 1999. pap. text 6.00 (1-58084-173-2) Lower Kuskokwim.
Ner Mitzva Vetorah Or. Dov B. Schneur. (HEB.). 543p. reprint ed. 25.00 (0-8266-5496-7) Kehot Pubn Soc.
Neravnovesnye Protsessy v Katalize see Nonequilibrium Processes in Catalysis
Nerd. Larry Shue. 1984. pap. 5.25 (0-8222-0811-3) Dramatists Play.
Nerd No More. Kristine L. Franklin. LC 96-7472. 144p. (J). (gr. 4-7). 1996. 15.99 (1-56402-674-4) Candlewick Pr.
Nerd No More. Kristine L. Franklin. LC 96-7472. 144p. (YA). (gr. 4-7). 1998. pap. 4.99 (0-7636-0487-9) Candlewick Pr.
*__Nerd No More.__ Kristine L. Franklin. 1999. 10.09 (0-606-15653-4, Pub. by Turtleback) Demco.
Nerd Syndrome. Michael Tompkins. (Straight Ahead Management Ser.). 1984. pap. 6.00 (0-931324-03-3) La Grange.
*__Nerdlandia: A Play, 1 vol.__ Gary Soto. LC 98-37093. 96p. (YA). (gr. 7 up). 1999. pap. 5.99 (0-698-11784-0) Putnam Pub Group.
Nerds 2.0.1: A Brief History of the Internet. Stephen Segaller. (Illus.). 400p. 1998. 27.50 (1-57500-106-3, Pub. by TV Bks) HarpC.
*__Nerds 2.0.1: A Brief History of the Internet.__ Stephen Segaller. (Illus.). 400p. 1999. pap. 15.00 (1-57500-088-1, Pub. by TV Bks) HarpC.
Nereis Australis: or Algae of the Southern Ocean, 1847-49. W. H. Harvey. (Illus.). 1965. 128.00 (3-7682-0261-5) Lubrecht & Cramer.
Nereis Boreali-Americana, 1852-1858, 3 parts in 1. W. H. Harvey. (Illus.). 1976. 163.00 (3-7682-1063-4) Lubrecht & Cramer.
Neresheim Abbey Church: Balthasar Neumann. Ed. by Balthasar Neumann. (Opus Ser.). (Illus.). 60p. 1993. 39.95 (3-8030-2706-3, Pub. by E J Wasmuth) Dist Art Pubs.
Nerfertiti: The Mystery Queen. Burnhan Holmes. (Great Unsolved Mysteries Ser.). 1997. pap. 4.95 (0-8114-6863-1) Raintree Steck-V.
Neria Production Notes. Louise Riber. (Illus.). 15p. (Orig.). (C). 1992. pap. text. write for info. (0-936731-26-5) Devel Self Rel.
Nerida Singleton's Romantic Papers. Nerida Singleton. (Illus.). 40p. 1994. pap. 13.95 (1-86351-134-2, Pub. by Sally Milner) Sterling.
Neriglissar - King of Babylon. Ronald H. Sack. (Alter Orient und Altes Testament Ser.: Vol. 236). viii, 270p. 1994. text 65.00 (3-7887-1480-8, Pub. by NeukirchenerV) Eisenbrauns.
Nerilka's Story. Anne McCaffrey. 208p. 1987. mass mkt. 5.99 (0-345-33949-5, Del Rey) Ballantine Pub Grp.
Nerit. Mark Dunster. 48p. (Orig.). 1988. pap. 4.00 (0-89642-159-7) Linden Pubs.
Nernstach - Neurophysiology. Gunther. 1994. 81.25 (0-697-22926-2) McGraw.
Nero. David Shotter. LC 96-14839. (Lancaster Pamphlets Ser.). (Illus.). 128p. (C). 1996. pap. 12.99 (0-415-12931-1) Routledge.
Nero. Gerard Walter. Tr. by Emma Craufurd from FRE. LC 76-45165. 335p. 1977. reprint ed. lib. bdg. 65.00 (0-8371-9302-8, WANER, Greenwood Pr) Greenwood.
*__Nero: The End of a Dynasty.__ Miriam T. Griffin. 2000. pap. 27.99 (0-415-21464-5) Routledge.
*__Nero: The Man Behind the Myth.__ Richard Holland. 2000. 27.95 (0-7509-2447-0, Pub. by Sutton Publng) Intl Pubs Mktg.
*__Nero Ashbury Player's Guide.__ Michael A. Ventrella. (Illus.). 160p. 2000. ring bd. 25.00 (0-9669844-1-2) Nero.
Nero et Agrippina see Cambridge Latin Course
NERO Rule Book. Nero International Holding Company, Inc. Staff. (Illus.). (YA). pap. 10.00 (0-9700563-0-3) N E R O Inter.
Nero Wolf Cook Book. Rex Stout. 20.95 (0-8488-0057-5) Amereon Ltd.
Nero Wolfe Cookbook. Rex Stout. LC 96-42172. (Illus.). 192p. 1996. pap. 16.95 (1-888952-24-5) Cumberland Hse.
Nero Wolfe Omnibus. Rex Stout. lib. bdg. 26.95 (0-8488-1893-8) Amereon Ltd.
Neron Models. S. Bosch et al. (Ergebnisse der Mathematik und Ihrer Grenzgebiete Ser.: Vol. 21). (Illus.). 340p. 1990. 164.95 (0-387-50587-3) Spr-Verlag.
Nerrantsoula-Tsatsa-Minnka-La Famille Perlmutter. Panait Istrati. (FRE.). 448p. 1984. pap. 16.95 (0-7859-2494-9, 2070375943) Fr & Eur.
Neruda. Volodia Teitelboim. (SPA.). 425p. 1984. pap. 13.00 (0-317-46774-3, 3022) Ediciones Norte.
Neruda: An Intimate Biography. Volodia Teitelboim. Tr. by Beverly J. De Long-Tonelli from SPA. (Texas Pan American Ser.). 522p. 1991. 18.95 (0-292-75548-1) U of Tex Pr.
Neruda & Vallejo: Selected Poems. Pablo Neruda & Cesar Vallejo. Ed. & Tr. by Robert Bly. Tr. by John Knoepfle et al. LC 93-10400. (SPA., Illus.). 288p. 1993. pap. 16.00 (0-8070-6489-0) Beacon Pr.
Neruda at Isla Negra. Pablo Neruda. Tr. by Maria Jacketti et al. LC 98-14080. (Illus.). 128p. 1998. pap. text 15.00 (1-877727-83-0) White Pine.
*__Neruda's Ekphrastic Experience: Mural Art & "Canto General"__ Hugo Mendez- Ramirez. LC 98-47708. (Illus.). 248p. 1999. 43.50 (0-8387-5398-1) Bucknell U Pr.
Neruda's Garden: An Anthology of Odes. Pablo Neruda. Ed. by Yvette E. Miller. Tr. by Maria Jacketti from SPA. LC 94-25088. (Discoveries Ser.). (ENG & SPA.). 256p. 1995. pap. 17.95 (0-935480-68-4) Lat Am Lit Rev Pr.
Nerval et la Patrie Perdue. Simone Guers. (American University Studies: Romance Languages & Literature: Ser. II, Vol. 90). X, 223p. (C). 1990. text 54.95 (0-8204-0744-5) P Lang Pubng.
Nerval's Double: A Structural Study. Claire Gilbert. LC 79-4593. (Romance Monographs: No. 34). 199p. 1979. 26.00 (84-499-2818-4) Romance.
Nerval's Magic Alphabet. Phyllis J. Winston. (American University Studies: Romance Languages & Literature: Ser. II, Vol. 102). XVIII, 135p. (C). 1989. text 33.95 (0-8204-0867-0) P Lang Pubng.
Nerve. Dick Francis. 1987. mass mkt. 5.95 (0-449-21266-1) Fawcett.
*__Nerve.__ Marshall Goldberg. 319p. 1999. pap. 16.95 (0-7414-0174-6) Buy Books.
Nerve. Dick Francis. 313p. 1998. reprint ed. mass mkt. 6.99 (0-515-12346-3, Jove) Berkley Pub.
Nerve: Literate Smut. Rufus Griscom & Genevieve Field. LC 98-15141. (Illus.). 288p. 1998. pap. 15.00 (0-7679-0257-2) Broadway BDD.
*__Nerve: The New Nude.__ Ed. by Genevieve Field. LC 00-25782. 2000. 35.00 (0-8118-2957-X) Chronicle Bks.
Nerve & Muscle. 2nd ed. R. D. Keynes & David J. Aidley. (Illus.). 191p. (C). 1992. pap. text 20.95 (0-521-42255-8) Cambridge U Pr.
Nerve & Muscle: Membranes, Cells & Systems. R. B. Stein. LC 80-15028. (Illus.). 274p. 1980. 35.00 (0-306-40512-1, Plenum Trade) Perseus Pubng.
Nerve & Muscle Excitation. 3rd rev. ed. Douglas Junge. LC 91-4994. (Illus.). 263p. (C). 1991. pap. text 29.95 (0-87893-406-5) Sinauer Assocs.
Nerve Block for Common Pain. R. E. Cytowic. (Illus.). viii, 96p. 1991. 30.00 (0-387-97147-5) Spr-Verlag.
Nerve Cells & Animal Behaviour. David G. Young. (Illus.). 248p. 1989. text 69.95 (0-521-30705-8); pap. text 24.95 (0-521-31443-7) Cambridge U Pr.
*__Nerve Cells & Animal Behaviour.__ 2nd ed. Peter J. Simmons & David Young. LC 99-11620. (Illus.). 240p. (C). 1999. 64.95 (0-521-62216-6); pap. 24.95 (0-521-62726-5) Cambridge U Pr.
Nerve Cells & Insect Behavior. Kenneth D. Roeder. LC 98-136606. (Illus.). 256p. 1998. pap. text 16.95 (0-674-60801-1) HUP.
Nerve Cells & Insect Behavior. rev. ed. Kenneth D. Roeder. LC 67-27092. (Books in Biology: No. 4). 91p. 1967. 17.00 (0-674-60800-3) HUP.
Nerve Cells & Nervous Systems: An Introduction to Neuroscience. A. G. Brown. (Illus.). xi, 265p. 1994. 54.95 (0-387-19637-4) Spr-Verlag.
Nerve Conduction Studies. Kathryne Hammer. (Illus.). 166p. 1999. spiral bd. 36.95 (0-398-04519-4) C C Thomas.
Nerve Conduction Studies for the Technologist. American Journal of END Technology Staff. 1999. spiral bd. 25.00 (1-57797-007-1) ASET.
Nerve Conduction Studies from A to Z. Barbara Crout & Charles Flicek. (Illus.). 210p. 1998. spiral bd. 49.95 (1-57797-032-2) ASET.
Nerve Endings. William Martin. 480p. 1996. mass mkt. 6.99 (0-446-36330-8, Pub. by Warner Bks) Little.
Nerve Growth & Guidance. Ed. by C. D. McCaig. (Frontiers in Neurobiology Ser.: No. 2). 188p. (C). 1996. text 110.50 (1-85578-085-2, Pub. by Portland Pr Ltd) Ashgate Pub Co.
Nerve Growth Cone. Ed. by Paul C. Letourneau. 558p. 1991. text 104.00 (0-88167-816-3) Lppncott W & W.
Nerve Growth Cone. Ed. by Paul C. Letourneau et al. LC 91-19165. (Illus.). 557p. reprint ed. pap. 172.70 (0-608-09746-2, 206991500007) Bks Demand.
Nerve Injuries. David G. Kline & Alan R. Hudson. LC 94-12233. (Illus.). 624p. 1995. text 150.00 (0-7216-3264-5, W B Saunders Co) Harcrt Hlth Sci Grp.
Nerve Injuries & Their Repair: A Critical Appraisal. Sydney Sunderland. (Illus.). 538p. 1990. text 210.00 (0-443-04161-X) Church.
Nerve Injury & Repair. Goran Lundborg. (Illus.). 256p. 1988. text 135.00 (0-443-03528-8) Church.
Nerve Membrane: Biochemistry & Function of Channel Proteins. Ed. by Gen Matsumoto & Masao Kontani. LC QP0552.M44N4. 258p. 1981. reprint ed. pap. 80.00 (0-608-01243-2, 206193100001) Bks Demand.
Nerve, Muscle & Synapse. Bernard Katz. (New Biology Ser.). 1966. text. write for info. (0-07-033374-2) McGraw.
Nerve-Muscle Cell Trophic Communication. Ed. by Hugo L. Fernandez & J. Alejandro Donoso. 224p. 1988. 146.00 (0-8493-6660-7, QP364, CRC Reprint) Franklin.
Nerve Storm. Amy Gerstleramy. LC 93-14681. 96p. (Orig.). 1993. pap. 15.95 (0-14-058703-9, Penguin Bks) Viking Penguin.
Nerve Storm. Amy Gerstleramy. (Orig.). 1999. pap. 20.00 (0-670-85100-0) Viking Penguin.
Nerves & Narratives: A Cultural History of Hysteria in 19th-Century British Prose. Peter M. Logan. 241p. 1997. pap. 17.95 (0-520-20775-0, Pub. by U CA Pr) Cal Prin Full Svc.
Nerves & the Gastrointestinal Tract. Ed. by M. V. Singer & H. Goebell. (Falk Symposium Ser.). (C). 1989. lib. bdg. 324.50 (0-7462-0114-1) Kluwer Academic.
Nerves of Some Hangovers. Joseph Manco. LC 97-66422. 310p. (Orig.). 1997. pap. 12.95 (1-890279-00-5) Rising Star MD.
Nerves of State: Taxation & the Financing of the English State, 1558-1714. Michael J. Braddick. (New Frontiers in History Ser.). 256p. 1996. text 79.95 (0-7190-3871-5); text 27.95 (0-7190-3872-3, Pub. by Manchester Univ Pr) St Martin.
Nerves of Steel: Mastering Your Emotions to Beat the Market. Clifford Pistolese. 225p. 1992. 22.95 (1-55738-467-3, Irwn Prfssnl) McGraw-Hill Prof.
Nervilia (Orchidaceae) B. Petterson. Ed. by E. F. De Vogel. (Orchid Monographs: Vol. 5). (Illus.). v, 90p. 1991. pap. 28.00 (90-71236-08-0, Pub. by Rijksherbarium) Balogh.
Nervine Herbs. Rita Elkins. (The Woodland Health Ser.). 1997. pap. text 3.95 (1-885670-32-X) Woodland UT.
Nervous & Hormonal Mechanisms of Integration. Society for Experimental Biology (Great Britain). LC 67-71828. (Symposia of the Society for Experimental Biology Ser.: No. 20). 607p. reprint ed. pap. 188.20 (0-608-16218-3, 201466900093) Bks Demand.
Nervous Christians see Como Vencer la Tension Nerviosa
Nervous Conditions. Tsitsi Dangarembga. LC 89-4076. 210p. 1996. pap. 12.95 (1-878067-77-X) Seal Pr WA.
Nervous Control of Blood Vessels. Terry Bennett & Sheila Gardiner. (Autonomic Nervous System Ser.). 592p. 1996. text 90.00 (3-7186-5139-4, Harwood Acad Pubs) Gordon & Breach.
*__Nervous Control of the Eye.__ Ed. by Geoffrey Burnstock & Adam M. Sillito. (Autonomic Nervous System Ser: Vol. 13). 320p. 2000. text 120.00 (90-5823-018-X, Harwood Acad Pubs) Gordon & Breach.
Nervous Control of the Heart. Ed. by John T. Shepherd & Stephen F. Vatner. (Autonomic Nervous System Ser.). 440p. 1996. text 91.00 (3-7186-5811-9, Harwood Acad Pubs) Gordon & Breach.
Nervous Control of the Urogenital System. Ed. by C. A. Maggi. Vol. 3. 1992. write for info. (0-318-69520-0) Gordon & Breach.
Nervous Dancer. Carol L. Lorenzo. LC 94-13062. (Flannery O'Connor Award for Short Fiction Ser.). 184p. 1995. 22.95 (0-8203-1704-7) U of Ga Pr.
Nervous Disorders & Religion: A Study of Souls in the Making. John G. McKenzie. LC 79-8719. 183p. 1981. reprint ed. lib. bdg. 35.00 (0-313-22192-8, MCND, Greenwood Pr) Greenwood.
Nervous Forces. Jeffrey Gustavson. LC 94-71038. (Series of Poetry & Verse Translation). 48p. 1994. pap. 12.00 (1-882509-02-1) Alef Bks.
Nervous Generation: American Thought, 1917-1930. Roderick Nash. 185p. 1990. pap. text 12.95 (0-929587-21-9, Elephant Paperbacks) I R Dee.
Nervous Hostess Cookbook: A Comforting Guide to Worry-Free Entertaining. Ursula Bacon. LC 96-75459. 272p. 1998. 15.95 (1-885221-09-6, Pub. by BookPartners) Midpt Trade.
Nervous Housewife. Abraham Myerson. LC 72-2616. (American Women Ser.: Images & Realities). 278p. 1974. reprint ed. 21.95 (0-405-04470-4) Ayer.
Nervous Landscapes. Alison D. Nordstrom. 28p. 1994. pap. text 12.00 (1-887040-07-2) SE Mus Photo.
Nervous Laughter. Earl Emerson. 1997. mass mkt. 5.99 (0-345-41407-1) Ballantine Pub Grp.
Nervous Laughter. Earl Emerson. 1986. mass mkt. 4.99 (0-380-89906-X, Avon Bks) Morrow Avon.
Nervous Laughter: Television Situation Comedy & Liberal Democratic Ideology. Darrell Y. Hamamoto. LC 88-30279. (Media & Society Ser.). (Illus.). 189p. 1989. 55.00 (0-275-92861-6, C2861, Praeger Pubs) Greenwood.
Nervous Laughter: Television Situation Comedy & Liberal Democratic Ideology. Darrell Y. Hamamoto. LC 88-30279. (Media & Society Ser.). (Illus.). 192p. 1991. pap. 19.95 (0-275-94050-0, B4050, Praeger Pubs) Greenwood.
*__Nervous Liberals: Propaganda Anxieties from World War I to the Cold War.__ Ed. by Brett Gary. LC 99-31171. 332p. 1999. 50.00 (0-231-11364-1); pap. 20.00 (0-231-11365-X) Col U Pr.
Nervous Man Nervous: Big Jay McNeely & the Rise of the Honking Tenor Sax! Jim Dawson. 160p. 1994. pap. 21.95 (0-936433-17-5) Big Nickel.
Nervous Peace. David McKittrick. 174p. 1996. pap. 22.95 (0-85640-575-2, Pub. by Blackstaff Pr) Dufour.
Nervous People & Other Satires. Mikhail Zoshchenko. Ed. & Tr. by Hugh McLean. Tr. by Maria Gordon. LC 75-9131. 480p. 1975. pap. 17.95 (0-253-20192-6, MB-192) Ind U Pr.
Nervous Songs. Paul Hoover. (Poetry Ser.). 64p. (Orig.). (C). 1986. pap. 8.00 (0-934332-46-0) LEpervier Pr.
Nervous Splendor: Vienna, 1888-1889. Frederic Morton. 340p. 1980. pap. 13.95 (0-14-005667-X, Penguin Bks) Viking Penguin.
Nervous System see Human Body
Nervous System. Thomas Braem. 1994. pap. text 19.95 (1-878576-28-3) Flash Anatomy Inc.
Nervous System. Edward Edelson. (Encyclopedia of Health Ser.). (Illus.). 116p. (YA). (gr. 7 up). 1989. lib. bdg. 19.95 (0-7910-0023-0) Chelsea Hse.
*__Nervous System.__ Helen Frost. (Human Body Systems Ser.). 24p. (J). (ps-2). 2000. lib. bdg. 13.25 (0-7368-0651-2, Pebble Bks) Capstone Pr.
Nervous System. Ed. by R. D. Hunt et al. (Illus.). xvi, 233p. 1988. 210.00 (3-540-19416-9, 194169) Spr-Verlag.
Nervous System. Ed. by R. D. Hunt et al. (Illus.). xvi, 233p. 1988. 256.00 (0-387-19416-9, 194169) Spr-Verlag.
*__Nervous System.__ Walter G. Oleksy. LC 00-9381. (Insider's Guide to the Body Ser.). (Illus.). 2000. lib. bdg. write for info. (0-8239-3341-5) Rosen Group.
Nervous System. Alvin Silverstein et al. (Human Body Systems Ser.). (Illus.). 96p. (J). (gr. 5-8). 1995. lib. bdg. 20.40 (0-8050-2835-8) TFC Bks NY.
Nervous System. Darlene Stille. LC 96-29738. (True Bks.). (Illus.). 48p. (J). (gr. 2-4). 1997. lib. bdg. 21.00 (0-516-20445-9) Childrens.
Nervous System. Darlene R. Stille. (True Bks.). (J). 1998. pap. text 6.95 (0-516-26270-X) Childrens.
Nervous System. Michael Taussig. (Illus.). 256p. (C). (gr. 13). 1991. pap. 20.99 (0-415-90445-5, A5794) Routledge.
Nervous System. 4th ed. Peter E. Nathan. 320p. 1997. pap. 45.00 (1-56593-828-3, 1620) Singular Publishing.
Nervous System: Its Function & Its Interaction with the World. Lloyd D. Partridge & L. Donald Partridge. (Illus.). 593p. 1992. 75.00 (0-262-16134-6, Bradford Bks); pap. text 39.00 (0-262-66079-2, Bradford Bks) MIT Pr.
Nervous System - A Three Volume Work Commemorating the 25th Anniversary of The National Institute of Neurological & Communicative Disorders & Stroke Vol. 1: The Basic Neurosciences. Ed. by Donald B. Tower & Roscoe O. Brady. LC 75-33499. 747p. 1975. reprint ed. pap. 200.00 (0-608-04656-6, 204715500001) Bks Demand.

N

An Asterisk (*) at the beginning of an entry indicates that the title is appearing for the first time.

Nervous System - A Three Volume Work Commemorating the 25th Anniversary of The National Institute of Neurological & Communicative Disorders & Stroke Vol. 2: The Clinical Neurosciences. fac. ed. Ed. by Donald B. Tower. LC 75-33499. (Illus.). 556p. 1975. pap. 172.40 (*0-7837-7380-3*, 204715500002) Bks Demand.

***Nervous System & Behavioral Toxicology, 13 vols.** H. E. Lowndes & K. R. Reuhl. (Comprehensive Toxicology Ser.: Vol. 11). 564p. 1999. 165.00 (*0-08-042976-9*) Elsevier.

Nervous System & Endocrine Glands see Illustrated Human Embryology

Nervous System & the Brain. Muria Bosch Roca & Marta Serrano. (Invisible World Ser.). (Illus.). 32p. (YA). (gr. 4 up). 1995. lib. bdg. 15.95 (*0-7910-3152-7*) Chelsea Hse.

Nervous System & the Heart. Ed. by Gert J. Ter Horst. LC 99-25404. (Illus.). 584p. 1999. 135.00 (*0-89603-693-6*) Humana.

Nervous System Course. Competence Assurance Systems Staff. (Illus.). 1983. pap. text 60.00 (*0-89147-069-7*) CAS.

Nervous System, Muscle & Eyes. 3rd ed. Ed. by R. O. Weller. (Systemic Pathology Ser.: Vol. 4). (Illus.). 776p. 1990. text 220.00 (*0-443-03312-9*) Church.

Nervous System of Invertebrates: An Evolutionary & Comparative Approach. Ed. by O. Breidbach et al. LC 94-35125. Vol. 72. 448p. 1995. 132.00 (*0-8176-5076-8*) Birkhauser.

Nervous System of Invertebrates: An Evolutionary & Comparative Approach, 42. Ed. by O. Breidbach et al. (EXS Ser.). vii, 454p. 1995. 132.00 (*3-7643-5076-8*) Birkhauser.

Nervous Systems in Invertebrates. M. A. Ali. LC 87-25898. (NATO ASI Series A, Life Sciences: Vol. 141). (Illus.). 684p. 1987. 135.00 (*0-306-42770-2*, Plenum Trade) Perseus Pubng.

Nervous Systems Regeneration in the Invertebrates: Invertebrate Neural Regeneration. S. B. Moffett. (Zoophysiology Ser.: Vol. 34). (Illus.). 196p. 1996. 158.00 (*3-540-59454-X*) Spr-Verlag.

Nervousness, Temperament & the Soul. Joseph Massmann. 171p. 1999. reprint ed. 18.95 (*0-912141-75-1*) Roman Cath Bks.

Neryugngaunga Naunerrlugnek (I Can Eat Plants) Elsie Carl. (ESK., Illus.). 16p. (J). (gr. k-3). 1998. pap. text 6.00 (*1-58084-034-5*) Lower Kuskokwim.

Nes Owner's Guide to Whippets. 160p. 12.95 (*0-7938-2770-1*) TFH Pubns.

NESC Interpretations Second Interim Collection, 1991-1993. National Electric Safety Code, ANSI C2 Staff. (Illus.). 68p. (Orig.). 1990. pap. 35.00 (*1-55937-025-4*) IEEE Standards.

NESEA Hymnel. 2nd rev. ed. Jane Wagner & Gary D. McGath. (Illus.). 1997. pap. 13.00 (*1-886778-01-9*, NESFA Pr) New Eng SF Assoc.

NESFA Hymnal, Vol. 1. 2nd ed. Ed. by Joe Ross. vi, 211p. 1979. pap. 18.00 (*0-915368-69-2*) New Eng SF Assoc.

NESFA Index: Science Fiction Magazines & Original Anthologies 1975. New England Science Fiction Association Staff. iv, 36p. 1976. pap. 5.00 (*0-915368-04-8*) New Eng SF Assoc.

NESFA Index: Science Fiction Magazines & Original Anthologies 1976. New England Science Fiction Association Staff. iii, 38p. 1977. pap. 5.00 (*0-915368-05-6*) New Eng SF Assoc.

NESFA Index to Short Science Fiction for 1988. Ed. by Jim Mann. viii, 136p. 1990. 12.00 (*0-915368-43-9*) New Eng SF Assoc.

NESFA Index to Short Science Fiction for 1989. Ed. by Jim Mann. viii, 164p. 1992. 12.00 (*0-915368-48-X*) New Eng SF Assoc.

NESFA Index to Short Science Fiction, 1987. Ed. by Jim Mann. (Index Ser.). vi, 42p. 1989. pap. 12.00 (*0-915368-41-2*) New Eng SF Assoc.

NESFA Index to the Science Fiction Magazines & Original Anthologies, 15 vols., Set. 1989. pap. 71.40 (*0-915368-68-4*) New Eng SF Assoc.

NESFA Index to the Science Fiction Magazines & Original Anthologies, 1971-72. iv, 42p. 1973. pap. 5.00 (*0-915368-06-4*) New Eng SF Assoc.

NESFA Index to the Science Fiction Magazines & Original Anthologies, 1973. ii, 30p. 1974. pap. 5.00 (*0-915368-02-1*) New Eng SF Assoc.

NESFA Index to the Science Fiction Magazines & Original Anthologies, 1974. ii, 44p. 1975. pap. 5.00 (*0-915368-03-X*) New Eng SF Assoc.

NESFA Index to the Science Fiction Magazines & Original Anthologies, 1977-1978. Ed. by Ann A. McCutchen. vi, 74p. 1983. pap. 7.00 (*0-915368-17-X*) New Eng SF Assoc.

NESFA Index to the Science Fiction Magazines & Original Anthologies, 1979-80. Ed. by Ann A. McCutchen. (Index Ser.). viii, 90p. 1982. pap. 7.00 (*0-915368-09-9*) New Eng SF Assoc.

NESFA Index to the Science Fiction Magazines & Original Anthologies, 1981. Ed. by Ann A. McCutchen. (Index Ser.). (Illus.). vi, 60p. 1982. pap. 5.00 (*0-915368-10-2*) New Eng SF Assoc.

NESFA Index to the Science Fiction Magazines & Original Anthologies, 1982. Ed. by Ann A. McCutchen. vi, 64p. 1983. pap. 12.00 (*0-915368-21-8*) New Eng SF Assoc.

NESFA Index to the Science Fiction Magazines & Original Anthologies, 1983. vi, 68p. 1984. pap. 5.00 (*0-915368-23-4*) New Eng SF Assoc.

NESFA Index to the Science Fiction Magazines & Original Anthologies, 1986. Ed. by Jim Mann. (Index Ser.). vi, 82p. 1988. pap. 12.00 (*0-915368-32-3*) New Eng SF Assoc.

NESFA Index to the Science Fiction Magazines, 1966-1970. xiv, 82p. 1971. pap. 10.00 (*0-915368-08-0*) New Eng SF Assoc.

Nesgoraemye Slova. Nikolai Liubimov. 304p. 1983. 50.00 (*0-7855-5985-X*) St Mut.

Neshama the Journey of the Soul. David Sanders. LC 96-96991. (Illus.). 80p. (J). (gr. 3-6). 1996. 19.95 (*0-9653775-0-4*) Blckfire Whitefire.

***Neshanic Station.** Neshanic Station Historical Society Staff. (Images of America Ser.). 128p. 1999. pap. 18.99 (*0-7385-0140-9*) Arcadia Publng.

Nesivos Olam: Nesiv Hatorah. Tr. by Eliakim Willner. 21.99 (*0-89906-032-3*, NETH); pap. 18.99 (*0-89906-033-1*, NETP) Mesorah Pubns.

Neskuchnyi Sad: Poety, Prozaiki, 1980-90-e. Pann Lilya. LC 98-21408. (RUS.). 220p. 1998. pap. 14.00 (*1-55779-110-4*) Hermitage Pubs.

Nesmeshchennye Otsenki I Ikh Primeneniia see Unbiased Estimators & Their Applications, Vol. 1, Univariate Case

Nessa's Fish. Luenn. (J). 1998. pap. 5.99 (*0-87628-954-5*) Ctr Appl Res.

Nessa's Fish. Nancy Luenn. (J). (gr. k-3). 1997. per. 5.99 (*0-689-81465-8*) Aladdin.

Nessa's Fish. Nancy Luenn. LC 89-10548. (Illus.). 32p. (J). (gr. k-3). 1990. 15.00 (*0-689-31477-9*) Atheneum Yung Read.

Nessa's Fish. Nancy Luenn. (Aladdin Picture Bks.). 1997. 11.19 (*0-606-12781-X*, Pub. by Turtleback) Demco.

Nessa's Story (El Cuento de Nessa) Nancy Luenn. Tr. by Alma F. Ada. LC 93-34814. (ENG & SPA., Illus.). 32p. (J). (gr. k-3). 1994. 14.95 (*0-689-31782-4*); 14.95 (*0-689-31919-3*) Atheneum Yung Read.

Nesselrode & the Russian Rapprochement with Britain, 1836-1844. Harold N. Ingle. LC 74-79764. 210p. reprint ed. pap. 65.10 (*0-608-15840-2*, 203143600074) Bks Demand.

Nessie. 2nd ed. Cynthia Todd & Debbie Ziemann. (Sing Me a Song Ser.). (Illus.). 9p. (J). (gr. k-6). 1998. lib. bdg. 15.95 (*1-879056-02-X*) Alpenhorn Pr.

Nessie: Playscript. William Hezlep. LC 98-43011. (J). (gr. 3-12). 1980. reprint ed. pap. 5.00 (*0-88734-401-1*) Players Pr.

***Nessie's Cape Cod Vacation.** Margaret McGarrahan. LC 99-96597. (Illus.). 58p. (J). (gr. 1-3). 2000. pap. 12.50 (*0-9672639-0-5*) Smith Lane Pubs.

Nest. Chris Baines. LC 89-77653. (Ecology Story Book Ser.). (Illus.). 24p. (J). (ps-3). 1990. 7.95 (*0-940793-55-5*, Crocodile Bks) Interlink Pub.

Nest. Bruce Barton. 1987. 2.50 (*0-941127-00-1*) Dacotah Terr Pr.

Nest. G. A. Douglas. 1987. pap. 3.95 (*0-8217-2166-6*) NAL.

Nest. Brian Wildsmith. (Illus.). 16p. (J). (ps-k). 1987. pap. 4.25 (*0-19-272134-8*) OUP.

***Nest: An Artist's Sketchbook.** Illus. & Text by Maryjo Koch. LC 99-22848. 112p. 1999. 35.00 (*1-55670-882-3*) Stewart Tabori & Chang.

Nest Building & Bird Behavior. Nicholas E. Collias & Elsie C. Collias. LC 84-42585. 357p. reprint ed. pap. 110.70 (*0-8357-3435-8*, 203969200013) Bks Demand.

Nest Egg Nightmare. Gibbs Davis. (White House Ghosthunters Ser.: No. 2). (YA). 1997. per. 3.99 (*0-671-56856-6*) PB.

Nest Full of Eggs. Priscilla Belz Jenkins. LC 93-43804. (Let's-Read-&-Find-Out Science Bks.). (Illus.). 32p. (J). (ps-3). 1995. pap. 4.95 (*0-06-445127-5*, HarpTrophy); lib. bdg. 15.89 (*0-06-023442-3*) HarpC Child Bks.

Nest Full of Eggs. Priscilla Belz Jenkins. (Let's Read-&-Find-Out Science Ser.). (J). 1995. 10.40 (*0-606-07941-6*) Turtleback.

Nest in the Gale. unabridged ed. Dave Fullen. LC 93-208563. (Learning Disability Ser.). (Illus.). 72p. (Orig.). (J). (gr. 2-6). 1993. pap. 18.95 incl. audio (*1-881650-01-4*) Mntn Bks.

Nest in the Wind: Adventures in Anthropology on a Tropical Island. Martha C. Ward. (Illus.). 161p. (C). 1989. pap. text 11.50 (*0-88133-405-7*) Waveland Pr.

Nest of Eagles: A Special Plural Presidency. rev. ed. Sally Short & Ralph Short. LC 74-76491. 283p. 1974. 10.00 (*0-915800-01-2*) Short Methods.

Nest of Hooks. Lon Otto. LC 78-16507. (Iowa Short Fiction Award Ser.). 152p. 1978. pap. 3.25 (*0-87745-090-0*) U of Iowa Pr.

Nest of Hornets. Gordon Reid. (Illus.). 1983. 39.95 (*0-19-554358-0*) OUP.

Nest of Ninnies. John Ashbery & James Schuyler. LC 96-42543. 192p. 1997. 21.00 (*0-88001-523-3*) HarpC.

Nest of Ninnies. John Ashbery & James Schuyler. LC 75-28625. 191p. 1976. reprint ed. pap. 5.00 (*0-915990-02-4*) Z Pr.

Nest of Ninnies & Other English Jestbooks of the 17th Century. Ed. by Paul M. Zall. LC 70-88091. 278p. reprint ed. pap. 86.20 (*0-7837-6171-6*, 204589300009) Bks Demand.

Nest of One's Own. Marsha Driscoll. LC 97-94273. 192p. 1997. 18.95 (*0-8034-9267-7*, Avalon Bks) Bouregy.

Nest of Rattlers. large type ed. E. G. Stokoe. (Linford Western Library). 1991. pap. 16.99 (*0-7089-7095-8*, Linford) Ulverscroft.

Nest of Simple Folk. Sean O'Faolain. 1990. 17.95 (*1-55972-041-7*, Birch Ln Pr) Carol Pub Group.

***Nest of Sorrows.** Ruth Hamilton. (J). 2000. pap. 10.95 (*0-552-13755-3*, Pub. by Transworld Publishers Ltd) Trafalgar.

Nest of Sorrows. large type ed. Ruth Hamilton. 1993. 19.95 (*0-7505-0484-6*, Pub. by Mgna Lrg Print) Ulverscroft.

Nest of Traitors: The Petrov Affair. rev. ed. Nicholas Whitlam & John Stubbs. LC 84-28120. (Illus.). 259p. (Orig.). 1985. reprint ed. pap. 16.95 (*0-7022-1857-X*, Pub. by Univ Queensland Pr) Intl Spec Bk.

Nest of Vipers. large type ed. Linda Davies. LC 95-8921. (Large Print Bks.). 1995. 25.95 (*1-56895-222-8*) Wheeler Pub.

Nest of Vultures. large type ed. Bill Knox. (Linford Mystery Library). 336p. 1997. pap. 16.99 (*0-7089-5073-6*, Linford) Ulverscroft.

***Nest of Worlds.** Huberath. 2001. write for info. (*0-15-100602-4*) Harcourt.

Nest on the Porch. Jane F. Babson. LC 88-51084. (Illus.). 32p. (Orig.). (J). (ps up). 1989. pap. 4.95 (*0-940787-01-6*) Winstead Pr.

***Nesta.** large type ed. Marion Harris. 416p. 1999. 31.99 (*0-7505-1335-7*, Pub. by Mgna Lrg Print) Ulverscroft.

Nesta, the Little Witch. Angela McAllister. (Illus.). 32p. (J). (ps-3). 1999. pap. 4.99 (*0-14-054266-3*, PuffinBks) Peng Put Young Read.

Nestandartnye Metody Analiza see Nonstandard Methods of Analysis

Nested Games: Rational Choice in Comparative Politics. George Tsebelis. (California Series on Social Choice & Political Economy: No. 18). (Illus.). 288p. 1991. pap. 17.95 (*0-520-07651-6*, Pub. by U CA Pr) Cal Prin Full Svc.

Nested Games: Rational Choice in Comparative Politics. George Tsebelis. LC 89-33580. (California Series on Social Choice & Political Economy: No. 18). (Illus.). 288p. reprint ed. pap. 89.30 (*0-7837-4684-9*, 204443100003) Bks Demand.

Nested Identities: Nationalism, Territory & Scale. Ed. by Guntram H. Herb & David H. Kaplan. LC 98-28143. 360p. (Orig.). 1998. 73.00 (*0-8476-8466-0*); pap. 29.95 (*0-8476-8467-9*) Rowman.

Nested Relations & Complex Objects in Databases. Ed. by S. Abiteboul et al. (Lecture Notes in Computer Science Ser.: Vol. 361). vi, 323p. 1989. 40.00 (*0-387-51171-7*) Spr-Verlag.

Nested Universal Relation Database Model. M. Levene. Ed. by G. Goos & J. Hartmanis. LC 92-10727. (Lecture Notes in Computer Science Ser.: Vol. 595). x, 177p. 1992. pap. 31.00 (*0-685-59405-X*) Spr-Verlag.

***Nester.** John S. Daniels. 1999. 19.00 (*0-7540-8074-9*, Gunsmoke) Chivers N Amer.

Nesterov, Mikhail. A. Rusakova. 220p. (C). 1990. 118.00 (*0-89771-822-4*, Pub. by Collets) St Mut.

***Nesting: A Celebration of Heart & Home.** large type ed. Lois Wyse. LC 99-48324. (Basic Ser.). 1999. 26.95 (*0-7862-2289-1*) Thorndike Pr.

***Nesting: Tales of Love Life & Real Estate.** Wyse. LC 99-37696. 192p. 1999. 19.45 (*0-684-84494-X*) S&S Trade.

Nesting Biology & Associates of Melitoma (Hymenoptera, Anthophoridae) Earle G. Linsley. LC 80-12433. (University of California Publications in Social Welfare: No. 90). 53p. reprint ed. pap. 30.00 (*0-608-18314-8*, 203158600075) Bks Demand.

Nesting Birds: Eggs & Fledglings. Eric Hosking & W. Winwood Reade. (Illus.). 275p. write for info. (*0-7137-0444-6*) Blandford Pr.

Nesting Birds of the Coastal Islands: A Naturalist's Year on Galveston Bay. John C. Dyes. LC 92-29457. (Corrie Herring Hooks Ser.: No. 22). (Illus.). 163p. 1993. text 24.95 (*0-292-71567-6*) U of Tex Pr.

***Nesting Doll.** Rita Brady Kiefer. LC 99-41313. 64p. 1999. pap. 14.95 (*0-87081-548-2*) Univ Pr Colo.

Nesting Syndrome: Grown Children Living at Home. Valerie Wiener. LC 97-7771. 256p. 1997. pap. text 13.95 (*1-57749-032-0*) Fairview Press.

Nesting Weights, Einsatzgewichte, & Piles a Godets: A Catalog of Nested Cup Weights in the Edward Clark Streeter Collection of Weights & Measures. Ellen Z. Danforth. LC 87-33492. (Transactions Ser.: Vol. 50, Pt. 1). (Illus.). 117p. 1988. pap. 39.50 (*0-208-02220-1*) CT Acad Arts & Sciences.

Nestle Make-It-Simple Entertaining: Fabulous Menus for Festive Celebrations. Better Homes & Gardens. LC 98-164827. (Illus.). 96p. 1996. 12.95 (*0-696-20613-7*, Meredith Pr) Meredith Bks.

***Nestle Toll House Best-Ever Cookies.** Nestle Company Staff. LC 98-66559. (Illus.). 240p. 1999. 24.95 (*0-696-20904-7*) Meredith Bks.

Nestle Toll House Best Loved Cookies. Better Homes & Gardens. 96p. 1996. 12.95 (*0-696-20554-8*) Meredith Bks.

Nestle's Bits & bites. Nancy J. Hill. (Illus.). 32p. (J). (gr. 1-5). 1999. pap. 11.95 (*0-9669436-1-9*) Serenity Press.

Nestlings of a Dark God: Poems: Science Fiction, Fantasy, Myth & Horror - Millennial Collection, 1974-1999. 2nd rev. ed. Michael R. Collings. LC 99-71315. 350p. (C). 1999. 35.00 (*1-886405-64-6*, Zarahemla Motets) White Crow Pr.

Nestlings of a Dark God: Poems, 1974-1996 - Science Fiction, Fantasy, Horror, Myth. Michael R. Collings. LC 96-90726. xii, 302p. (Orig.). 1996. reprint ed. pap. 30.00 (*1-886405-56-5*, Zarahemla Motets) White Crow Pr.

Nestor: Poetic Memory in Greek Epic. Keith Dickson. LC 95-12542. (Albert Bates Lord Studies in Oral Tradition: Vol. 16). (Illus.). 264p. 1995. text 57.00 (*0-8153-2073-6*, H1923) Garland.

Nestorian & Their Rituals, Vol. 1. G. P. Badger. 464p. 1987. 350.00 (*1-85077-166-9*, Pub. by Darf Pubs Ltd) St Mut.

Nestorian & Their Rituals, Vol. 2. G. P. Badger. 1987. 350.00 (*1-85077-167-7*, Pub. by Darf Pubs Ltd) St Mut.

Nestorian Churches. Aubrey R. Vine. LC 78-63173. (Heresies of the Early Christian & Medieval Era Ser.: Second Ser.). reprint ed. 34.50 (*0-404-16188-X*) AMS Pr.

Nestorian Missionary Enterprise. John Stewart. LC 78-63172. (Heresies of the Early Christian & Medieval Era Ser.: Second Ser.). reprint ed. 59.50 (*0-404-16187-1*) AMS Pr.

***Nestorius & His Teachings: A Fresh Examination of the Evidence.** J. F. Bethune-Baker. 252p. 1998. pap. 22.00 (*1-57910-194-1*) Wipf & Stock.

Nestroy & the Critics. W. E. Yates. (LCGERM Ser.). xii, 110p. 1994. 55.00 (*1-879751-97-6*) Camden Hse.

Nests above the Abyss. Isobel Kuhn. 1996. pap. 6.95 (*9971-972-74-3*) OMF Bks.

Nests, Eggs & Nestlings Britain. Colin J. Harrison. 1987. 19.95 (*0-685-43768-X*) Viking Penguin.

Nests, Nests, Nests. Susan Canizares & Mary Reid. LC 97-29198. (Science Emergent Readers Ser.). (Illus.). (J). 1997. pap. 2.50 (*0-590-76183-8*) Scholastic Inc.

***Nestucca: An Oil Spill Turns Creative.** David C. Webster. Ed. by David Starke & Colleen Wasner. LC 99-96154. (Illus.). 300p. 1999. pap. 16.95 (*0-9654023-5-5*) Malamalama Pr.

Nesudte. Vladimir Uhri. (SLO.). 48p. (Orig.). 1996. pap. 2.40 (*1-56983-017-7*) New Creat WI.

Nesuya's Basket. Carol Purdy. (Council of Indian Education Ser.). (Illus.). 110p. (Orig.). (J). (gr. 3-7). 1997. pap. 8.95 (*1-57098-087-X*) Roberts Rinehart.

Net. Sherif Hetata. 304p. (C). 1986. pap. 7.95 (*0-86232-534-X*, Pub. by Zed Books); text 19.95 (*0-86232-533-1*, Pub. by Zed Books) St Martin.

Net. Ilie Nastase. Tr. by Ros Schwartz. 1988. pap. 3.95 (*0-317-70084-7*) St Martin.

Net. large type ed. Edward S. Aarons. 1994. 27.99 (*0-7089-3179-0*) Ulverscroft.

Net. Rex Ellingwood Beach. (Collected Works of Rex Ellingwood Beach). 332p. 1998. reprint ed. lib. bdg. 98.00 (*1-58201-546-5*) Classic Bks.

***Net--Working: Teaching, Learning & Professional Development.** Ed. by Kwok-Wing Lai. 224p. 1999. pap. 39.95 (*1-877133-68-X*, Pub. by Univ Otago Pr) Intl Spec Bk.

Net America: Travel the 50 States on the Information Highway. Gary M. Garfield & Suzanne McDonough. 112p. 1996. teacher ed. 13.99 (*1-56417-852-8*, GA1559) Good Apple.

Net Appeal College Selection Guide: A Winning Game Plan to Help Girls Who Want to Play Sports Choose the Right College. Trudy J. Kaehler. LC 99-167920. (Illus.). 68p. 1998. pap. 8.95 (*0-9664742-0-1*) Kaeland Hse.

Net Assessment & Strategic Analysis. E. Cohen. 1994. 23.99 (*0-02-926911-3*) S&S Trade.

Net Bandits. Michael Coleman. (Internet Detectives Ser.). 128p. (J). (gr. 2-6). 1997. pap. 3.99 (*0-553-48620-9*) Bantam.

Net Bandits, 1. Michael Coleman. (Internet Detectives Ser.). 1997. 9.09 (*0-606-12738-0*, Pub. by Turtleback) Demco.

Net Baseball. Michael Wolff. (Illus.). ix, 400p. (Orig.). 1997. pap. 22.00 (*1-889670-01-4*) Wolff New Media.

***Net Benefit: Guaranteed Electronic Markets: The Ultimate Potential of Online Trade.** Wingham Rowan. 1999. text 35.00 (*0-312-22291-2*) St Martin.

Net Book Agreement: To Break or Not to Break, That Is the Question: Proceedings of a Seminar Organized by the Federation of Local Authority Chief Librarians & the Library Association at the London International Book Fair, 4th April 1989. Ed. by Derek Jones. LC 89-38337. 56p. 1989. reprint ed. pap. 30.00 (*0-7837-9414-2*, 206000800004) Bks Demand.

Net Chick: A Smart-Girl Guide to the Cyberworld. Carla Sinclair. 88p. 1995. pap. 19.95 (*0-8050-4393-4*) H Holt & Co.

Net Curriculum: An Educator's Guide to Using the Internet. Linda C. Joseph. LC 98-43723. 193p. 1999. pap. 29.95 (*0-910965-30-7*, CyberAge Bks) Info Today Inc.

Net Curtains & Closed Doors: Intimacy, Family & Public Life in Dublin. Ed. by Elizabeth A. Throop. LC 98-51217. 192p. 1999. 57.95 (*0-89789-636-X*, Bergin & Garvey) Greenwood.

Net Directory. Ed. by Steven Ewald. 1997. pap. 4.00 (*0-87259-626-5*) Am Radio.

Net Economic Value of Deer Hunting in Idaho. Dennis M. Donnelly & Louis J. Nelson. (Illus.). 36p. 1997. reprint ed. pap. 4.60 (*0-89904-644-4*, Wildlife Resrch Grp) Crumb Elbow Pub.

Net Economic Value of Elk Hunting in Idaho. Cindy F. Sorg & Louis J. Nelson. (Illus.). 32p. 1997. reprint ed. pap. 4.40 (*0-89904-643-6*, Wildlife Resrch Grp) Crumb Elbow Pub.

***Net Effect: School Library Media Centers & the Internet.** Ed. by Lyn Hay & James Henri. LC 99-13789. Orig. Title: A Meeting of the Minds 2: ITEC Virtual Conference '97 Proceedings. (Illus.). 322p. 1999. reprint ed. pap. 36.00 (*0-8108-3601-7*) Scarecrow.

Net Energy Analysis & the Energy Requirements of Energy Systems. Daniel T. Spreng. LC 87-38497. (Illus.). 301p. 1988. 69.50 (*0-275-92796-2*, C2796, Praeger Pubs) Greenwood.

***Net Entrepreneurs Only: 10 Entrepreneurs Tell the Stories of Their Success.** Ernst & Young Staff. 256p. 2000. 24.95 (*0-471-38146-2*) Wiley.

Net Essentials. 2nd ed. Ed. by Microsoft Corporation Staff. 650p. 1998. boxed set 55.00 (*1-57231-909-7*) Microsoft.

Net Ferrets--Electronic Download. 1997. 24.95 (*0-7897-1332-2*, Pub. by Macmillan) S&S Trade.

***Net Flex: 10 Minutes a Day to Better Play.** Paul Frediani. 2000. pap. 9.95 (*1-57826-077-9*, Pub. by Hatherleigh) Norton.

Net Force. Tom Clancy. (Tom Clancy's Net Force Ser.). 384p. (YA). 1999. mass mkt. 7.99 (*0-425-16172-2*) Berkley Pub.

Net Force. Tom Clancy. 384p. write for info. (*0-7278-5511-5*) Severn Hse.

***Net Force.** large type ed. Tom Clancy & Steve Pieczenik. 2000. pap. 11.95 (*1-56895-966-4*) Wheeler Pub.

N

Net Full of Honey. Estelle R. Pinney. (YA). 1996. pap. 12.95 (*0-7022-2744-7*, Pub. by Univ Queensland Pr) Intl Spec Bk.

*Net Future: The 7 Cybertrends That Will Drive Your Business, Create New Wealth, & Define Your Future.** Chuck Martin. 224p. 1998. 24.95 (*0-07-041131-X*) McGraw.

*Net Future: The 7 Cybertrends That Will Drive Your Business, Create New Wealth, & Define Your Future.** Chuck Martin. 1999. pap. write for info. (*0-07-134887-5*) McGraw.

Net Gain: Expanding Markets Through Virtual Communities. John Hagel, 3rd & Arthur G. Armstrong. LC 96-41597. 256p. 1997. 24.95 (*0-87584-759-5*) Harvard Busn.

Net Girl. Michael Wolff & Company, Inc. Staff. 1997. pap. 22.00 (*0-679-77383-5*) Random.

Net Guide, Vol. 3. 3rd ed. Michael Wolff. (Illus.). ix, 752p. 1996. pap. 29.95 (*1-889670-07-3*) Wolff New Media.

Net Impressions. Albert G. Keller. LC 76-117816. (Essay Index Reprint Ser.). 1977. 24.95 (*0-8369-1967-X*) Ayer.

Net in Water: A Selection from the Journals of Mary Casey. Mary Casey. Ed. by J. M. Lang & Louise De Bruin. (Illus.). 229p. (Orig.). 1994. pap. 18.95 (*1-874559-10-4*) S Perennis.

Net Income: Cut Costs, Boost Profits, & Enhance Operations Online. Wally Bock & Jeff Senne. LC 97-216306. 250p. 1997. pap. 29.95 (*0-442-02558-0*, VNR) Wiley.

Net Income: Cut Costs, Boost Profits, & Enhance Operations Online. Wally Bock & Jeff Senne. 320p. 1997. pap. 29.95 (*0-471-28839-X*, VNR) Wiley.

Net Jobs: How to Use the Internet to Land Your Dream Job. Michael Wolff. LC 98-154041. 200p. 1996. pap. 12.95 (*0-679-77032-1*) Random.

Net Kids. Michael Wolff. (Illus.). ix, 208p. (Orig.). (J). (gr. 3-8). 1996. pap. 14.95 (*1-889670-08-1*) Wolff New Media.

Net Law: How Lawyers Use the Internet. Paul Jacobsen. (Computer Science). (Illus.). 232p. (Orig.). 1997. pap. 29.95 (*1-56592-258-1*) Thomson Learn.

Net Lessons: Web-Based Projects for Classroom. Laura P. Roerden. Ed. by Sheryl Avruch. LC 97-1439. (Computer Science). (Illus.). 306p. (Orig.). 1997. pap. 24.95 (*1-56592-291-3*) Thomson Learn.

Net Loss: Fish Jobs & the Marine Environment. Peter Weber. 60p. (Orig.). 1994. pap. 5.00 (*1-878071-21-1*) Worldwatch Inst.

Net Love. Michael Wolff. (Illus.). ix, 400p. (Orig.). 1997. pap. 22.00 (*1-889670-00-6*) Wolff New Media.

Net Mac. Michael Wolff & Co. Staff. 1996. pap. 22.00 (*0-679-77385-1*) Random.

Net of Jewels: A Novel. Ellen Gilchrist. 360p. 1993. pap. 12.95 (*0-316-31432-3*) Little.

*Net of Jewels: A Novel.** Ellen Gilchrist. 1998. pap. text 12.95 (*0-316-18993-6*, Back Bay) Little.

Net of Jewels: Daily Meditations for Seekers of Truth. Ramesh S. Balsekar. Ed. by Gary Starbuck. LC 96-79929. 384p. 1997. 25.00 (*0-929448-15-4*) Advaita Pr CA.

Net of Magic: Wonders & Deceptions in India. Lee Siegel. LC 90-48328. (Illus.). 464p. 1991. pap. 23.95 (*0-226-75687-4*) U Ch Pr.

Net of Magic: Wonders & Deceptions in India. Lee Siegel. LC 90-48328. (Illus.). 464p. 1996. lib. bdg. 69.00 (*0-226-75686-6*) U Ch Pr.

*Net of Nemesis: Studies in Tragic Bond-Age.** August J. Nigro. LC 99-54287. 192p. 2000. 35.00 (*1-57591-036-5*) Susquehanna U Pr.

Net Operating Losses. Jeff Ward. (Ten-Forty Reference Ser.: No. 1). (Illus.). 144p. 1996. ring bd. 55.00 (*0-9652986-1-2*) Aquarian Pr CA.

Net Operating Losses. Jeff Ward. (Ten-Forty Reference Ser.: No. 2). (Illus.). 160p. 1999. ring bd. 60.00 (*0-9652986-2-0*) Aquarian Pr CA.

Net Out. Michael Wolff & Company, Inc. Staff. 400p. 1997. pap. 22.00 (*0-679-77171-9*) Fodors Travel.

Net Profit: How to Invest & Compete in the Real World of Internet Business. Peter S. Cohan. LC 99-6217. 1999. 28.00 (*0-7879-4476-9*) Jossey-Bass.

*Net Profits: How to Win the Internet Game.** Declan Dunn. 2000. cd-rom 17.97 (*1-930336-09-8*) Adnet Intl.

*Net Profits: Winning the Internet Game.** Declan Dunn. 200p. 2000. pap. write for info. (*1-930336-07-1*) Adnet Intl.

*Net Profits: How to Win the Internet Game Pt. 2: Proven Success of the $65,000 Affiliate, the $750,000 Super Affiliate, & the $600,000/6-Week Performance Network, 2 CDs.** Declan Dunn. 200p. 2000. pap. 47.00 incl. cd-rom (*1-930336-10-1*) Adnet Intl.

Net Quest: Exploring A&P. Pendarvis. LC 97-225291. 1997. 5.74 (*0-697-41894-4*, McGrw-H College) McGrw-H Hghr Educ.

Net Quest Exploring Zoology. Pendarvis. 1997. 8.74 (*0-697-38670-8*, WCB McGr Hill) McGrw-H Hghr Educ.

*Net Ready: Strategies for Success in the E-conomy.** Amir Hartman et al. 314p. 1999. 24.95 (*0-07-135242-2*) McGraw.

Net Result: A Working Guide to Recruiting for Student-Athletes. Lynda D. Brill & J. Scott Luster. 119p. (Orig.). (YA). (gr. 7-12). 1996. pap. 13.95 (*0-9653051-0-4*) Classic Kaleidoscope.

Net Results. Kahn. 1988. write for info. (*0-318-63788-X*) Viking Penguin.

Net Results: Web Marketing that Works. Cybernautice Staff. LC 97-72165. 392p. 1998. 29.99 (*1-56830-414-5*) Hayden.

Net Results.2: More Web Marketing that Works. 450p. 1900. 35.00 (*0-7357-1024-4*) New Riders Pub.

Net REXX Language. Michael F. Cowlishaw. LC 96-45703. 208p. (C). 1996. pap. 50.00 (*0-13-806332-X*) P-H.

*Net Security Your Digital Doberman: Sure-Fire Strategies for Wired Businesses.** Michael Alexander. (Illus.). 282p. 1999. reprint ed. pap. text 25.00 (*0-7881-6538-0*) DIANE Pub.

Net Shape Processing of Powder Materials Vol. 216: Proceedings of the ASME International Mechanical Engineering Congress & Exposition, San Francisco, CA, 1995. Ed. by S. Krishnaswami et al. LC 95-81271. (1995 ASME International Mechanical Engineering Congress & Exposition Ser.: AMD-Vol. 216). 172p. 1995. 74.00 (*0-7918-1762-8*, H01044) ASME.

Net Shopping. Michael Wolff. (Illus.). ix, 352p. (Orig.). 1996. pap. 22.00 (*1-889670-09-X*) Wolff New Media.

Net Slaves: True Tales of Working the Web. Bill Lessard & Steve Baldwin. LC 00-687334. 240p. 1999. 19.95 (*0-07-135243-0*) McGraw.

Net Spies: Who's Watching You on the Web? Andrew Gauntlett. 224p. 1999. pap. 14.95 (*1-883319-78-1*) Frog Ltd CA.

*Net Strategy: Charting the Digital Course for Your Company's Growth.** Robert Spiegel. 2000. 27.50 (*0-7931-3866-3*) Dearborn.

Net Success: 24 Leaders in Web Commerce Show You How to Put the Internet to Work for Your Business. Christina Haylock & Len Muscarella. LC 98-51493. (Illus.). 8p. 1999. 24.95 (*1-58062-114-7*) Adams Media.

Net Taxes, 1997. 2nd rev. ed. Michael Wolff. (Illus.). ix, 200p. 1996. pap. 12.95 (*1-889670-04-9*) Wolff New Media.

***Net, the Web & You: All You Really Need to Know about the Internet...& a Little Bit More.** Daniel J. Kurland. 213p. (C). 1995. 19.95 (*0-534-51281-X*) Wadsworth Pub.

Net to Catch Time. Sara H. Banks. (Illus.). (J). 1996. lib. bdg. 17.99 (*0-679-96673-0*) Random.

*Net-Trading: Strategies from the Frontiers of Electronic Day Trading.** Alpesh B. Patel. 256p. 2000. pap. 29.00 (*0-273-64502-1*) F T P H.

Net Trends 2000: Meeting the Challenges of Tomorrow's Networks. Garry Hornbuckle. Ed. by Gary Stein. (Orig.). (C). 1994. pap. 9.95 (*0-9644547-1-8*) Mactivity.

*Net User's Guide to Buying, Selling, & Trading Collectibles.** Randolph J. Gulliver. (Gulliver's Collectibles Ser.). (Illus.). 184p. 2000. pap. 14.95 (*0-7737-6108-X*) Stoddart Publ.

*Net Value: Valuing Dot-Com Companies - Uncovering the Reality Behind the Hype.** Peter J. Clark & Stephen Neill. 2000. 27.95 (*0-8144-0604-1*) AMACOM.

Net Vote. Michael Wolff. LC 98-145103. 1996. pap. 12.95 (*0-679-77028-3*) Random.

*Net-Wit.Com: A Smorgasbord of E-Mail & Internet Wit Blended with Humorous Incidents from the Author's Wild & Woolly Life.** Marv Rubinstein. LC 00-27906. (Illus.). 232p. 2000. pap. 17.50 (*1-887563-52-0*, Pub. by Schreiber Pub) Natl Bk Netwk.

Net Worth: Creating & Maximizing Wealth with the Internet. Edward J. Renehan, Jr. LC 97-155554. 560p. 1996. pap. 49.95 incl. cd-rom (*1-884133-28-2*, Jamsa Press) Gulf Pub.

Net Worth: Shaping Markets When Customers Make the Rules. John Hagel, 3rd & Marc Singer. (Illus.). 313p. 1999. 24.95 (*0-87584-889-3*) Harvard Busn.

NetActivisim: How Citizens Use the Internet. Ed Schwartz. Ed. by Andy Oram. LC 96-228771. (Illus.). 224p. 1996. pap. 24.95 (*1-56592-160-7*) Thomson Learn.

*Netaholics? The Creation of a Pathology.** Carla G. Surrat. LC 99-14712. 243p. 1999. lib. bdg. 34.00 (*1-56072-675-X*) Nova Sci Pubs.

Netaji Vol. 7: Collected Works: Letters to Emilie Schekl 1934-1942. Subhas C. Bose. Ed. by Sisir K. Bose & Sugata Bose. LC 95-128175. (Illus.). 266p. 1995. 32.00 (*0-19-563409-8*) OUP.

Netaji Vol. 8: Collected Works: Letters, Articles, Speeches & Statements 1933-1937. Subhas C. Bose. Ed. by Sisir K. Bose & Sugata Bose. LC 95-182048. (Illus.). 472p. 1995. 32.00 (*0-19-563560-4*) OUP.

Netaji Vol. 9: Collected Works: Congress President: Speeches, Articles, & Letters, January 1938-May 1939. Subhas Chandra Bose. Ed. by Sisir Kumar Bose & Sugata Bose. (Illus.). 332p. 1996. text 15.95 (*0-19-563706-2*) OUP.

Netaji, Azad Hind Fauj & After. K. M. Kasliwal. viii, 78p. 1983. 11.00 (*1-55528-063-3*, Pub. by Today Tomorrow) Scholarly Pubns.

Netaji: Collected Works Vol. 1: An Indian Pilgrim : An Unfinished Autobiography. Subhas C. Bose. Ed. by Sisir K. Bose & Sugata Bose. (Oxford India Paperbacks Ser.). (Illus.). 296p. (Orig.). 1998. pap. text 15.95 (*0-19-564148-5*) OUP.

Netaji Subhas Chandra Bose: Correspondence & Selected Documents. Ed. by Ravindra Kumar. (C). 1992. 48.00 (*0-8364-2817-X*, Pub. by Inter-India Pubns) S Asia.

Netaji Subhas Chandra Bose: Perennial Inspiration to the Indian Youth. S. P. Ruhela & Noor J. Siddiqui. ix, 114p. 1997. 20.00 (*81-7024-908-2*, Pub. by APH Pubng) Nataraj Bks.

*NetAnalyst Reference Guide: The Definitive Resource for the Network Analyst, 10.** 10th rev. ed. Orig. Title: Network Analysis Reference Guide. (Illus.). 197p. (C). 2000. pap. 65.00 (*1-58392-002-1*) Pine Mt.

Netanyahu: The Road to Power. Ben Kaspit & Ilan Kfir. Tr. by Ora Cummings. LC 98-37357. (Illus.). 271p. 1998. 24.95 (*1-55972-453-6*, Citadel Pr) Carol Pub Group.

Netball: Skills of the Game. Betty Galsworthy. (Illus.). 128p. 1997. pap. 19.95 (*1-86126-004-0*, Pub. by Cro1wood) Trafalgar.

Netball: Steps to Success. Wilma Shakespear. LC 97-7790. (Steps to Success Activity Ser.). (Illus.). 160p. (Orig.). 1997. pap. 17.95 (*0-87322-984-3*, PSHA0984) Human Kinetics.

Net.Bargain: The Consumer's Guide to Internet Shopping. Bruce Fries & Karen Porterfield. (Illus.). 224p. 1999. pap. 14.95 (*1-928791-11-5*, 1102) TeamCom.

Netbois Programming. Frank Lusardi. 1990. pap. 45.00 (*5-550-35980-4*) Nairi.

Neteru of Kemet. Tamara Siuda-Legan. LC 95-184445. (Illus.). 80p. 1994. pap. 9.95 (*1-57353-105-7*, Eschaton Bks) Eschaton Prods.

NetFix-It: Your Guide to Creating Your Ideal Home. Michael Wolff. 400p. 1997. 22.00 (*1-889670-23-5*) Wolff New Media.

NetGuide. Michael Wolff. 1997. mass mkt. 7.99 (*0-614-28450-3*) Dell.

NetHealer: Your Guide to Choosing Alternative Health Care. Michael Wolff. 200p. 1997. pap. 12.95 (*1-889670-24-3*) Wolff New Media.

*Nether Scroll.** Lynn Abbey. (Forgotten Realms Ser.). (Illus.). 320p. 2000. mass mkt. 6.99 (*0-7869-1566-8*) Wizards Coast.

Nether Side of New York. Edward Crapsey. LC 69-14919. (Criminology, Law Enforcement, & Social Problems Ser.: No. 46). 1969. reprint ed. 26.50 (*0-87585-046-4*) Patterson Smith.

Nether World. George R. Gissing. Ed. by John Goode. 469p. 24.50 (*0-8386-1543-0*) Fairleigh Dickinson.

Nether World. George R. Gissing. Ed. by Stephen Gill. (Oxford World's Classics Ser.). 438p. 1999. pap. 10.95 (*0-19-283767-2*) OUP.

Nether World: A Novel, 3 vols., Set. George R. Gissing. (BCL1-PR English Literature Ser.). 1992. reprint ed. lib. bdg. 225.00 (*0-7812-7534-2*) Rprt Serv.

Nethercutt Collection: The Cars of San Sylmar. Dennis Adler. (Illus.). 208p. 2000. 35.00 (*1-886768-14-5*) Blue Bk Pubns.

The Nethercutt Collection - The Cars of San Sylmar is the official publication of the famous Nethercutt car collection, a museum located in San Sylmar, CA. Having collected major automotive marques since WW II, Mr. J. P. Nethercutt has amassed one of the world's most important automobile collections. Dennis Adler, an award winning automotive photographer & journalist with over 5,000 articles to his credit, was chosen by the museum to be the writer & photographer for this unique publication. A stunning visual masterpiece with many 2-page color spreads, no expense was spared to make this new 9x12 landscape book an extraordinary literary achievement. Not only are most of the more famous & well-known cars pictured & described, but all the cars are listed in a photo index. Additionally, there is a chapter on mechanical musical instruments, since the Nethercutt Museum also contains one of the world's best collections of these rare & unusual artifacts. Retail $35.00 + $4.00 S/H. Available from Baker & Taylor, Ingram or directly from the publisher by calling 1-800-877-4867, non-domestic 952-854-5229, fax 952-853-1486 or web site: www.bluebookinc.com. *Publisher Paid Annotation.*

Netheril: Empire of Magic. Slade. 1996. 25.00 (*0-7869-0437-2*, Pub. by TSR Inc) Random.

Netherland Yearbook International Law. Nyil. 1995. lib. bdg. 130.00 (*0-7923-3308-X*) Kluwer Academic.

Netherlandic Presence in Ontario: Pillars, Class & Dutch Ethnicity. Frans J. Schryer. LC 98-170661. 424p. 1997. 64.95 (*0-88920-262-1*) W Laurier U Pr.

Netherlandic Presence in Ontario: Pillars, Class & Dutch Ethnicity. Frans J. Schryer. LC 96-931981. (Illus.). 458p. (C). 1998. pap. 39.95 (*0-88920-312-1*) Wilfrid Laurier.

Netherlandic Secular Plays from the Middle Ages: The "Abele Spelen" & the Farces of the Hulthem Manuscript. Ed. & Tr. by Theresia De Vroom. LC 96-901017. (Carleton Renaissance Plays in Translation Ser.: No. 29). 225p. 1997. 28.00 (*1-895537-41-X*, Pub. by Dovehouse); pap. 12.00 (*1-895537-35-5*, Pub. by Dovehouse) Sterling.

*Netherlandish Art, 1400-1600.** Henk Van Os et al. (Illus.). 288p. 2000. 65.00 (*0-300-08746-2*) Yale U Pr.

Netherlandish Drawings of the 15th & 16th Centuries & Flemish Drawings of the 17th & 18th Centuries in the Pierpont Morgan Library. Felice Stampfle et al. (Illus.). 662p. 1991. text 195.00 (*0-691-04063-X*, Pub. by Princeton U Pr) Cal Prin Full Svc.

Netherlandish Paintings in Soviet Museums. Nikolai Nikvlin. (Illus.). 404p. 1990. text 45.00 (*0-7148-2441-0*) Phaidon Pr.

Netherlandish Scrolled Gables of the 16th & Early 17th Centuries. Henry-Russell Hitchcock. LC 77-81905. (College Art Association Monographs: Vol. 34). (Illus.). 176p. 1985. reprint ed. 45.00 (*0-271-00402-9*) Pa St U Pr.

Netherlands see MacDonald Countries

Netherlands see Cultures of the World - Group 10

Netherlands see Countries of the World Series

Netherlands see Festivals of the World

Netherlands. (Baedeker's Ser.). (Illus.). 592p. 1992. pap. 23.00 (*0-13-063611-8*, P-H Travel) Prntice Hall Bks.

Netherlands. (Architecture Guides Ser.). (Illus.). 320p. 1998. pap. 5.95 (*3-89508-624-X*, 520213) Konemann.

Netherlands. Baedeker Staff. (Baedeker's Travel Guide Ser.). 543p. 1995. 24.00 (*0-02-860083-5*, P-H Travel) Prntice Hall Bks.

Netherlands. Jan Dijksma & Martin Hoogendoorn. LC 92-40138. (European Financial Reporting Ser.). 255p. (C). (gr. 13). 1993. pap. 108.95 (*0-415-06316-7*, A9725) Thomson Learn.

Netherlands. Martin Hintz. LC 98-41700. (Enchantment of the World Ser.). 144p. (YA). (gr. 5-9). 1999. 32.00 (*0-516-20962-0*) Childrens.

Netherlands. Peter K. King & Michael Wintle. LC 88-144667. (World Bibliographical Ser.: No.88). 330p. 1988. lib. bdg. 70.00 (*1-85109-041-X*) ABC-CLIO.

Netherlands. Polly Phillimore. (Essential Guides Ser.). (Illus.). 128p. 1994. pap. 7.95 (*0-8442-8924-8*, 89248, Passprt Bks) NTC Contemp Pub Co.

Netherlands. Rand McNally Staff. pap. 16.95 (*0-528-91430-8*) Rand McNally.

Netherlands. Peter Schuler. LC 84-14525. (World Education Ser.). (Illus.). 208p. 1984. pap. text 12.00 (*0-910054-79-7*) Am Assn Coll Registrars.

*Netherlands, No. 908.** 2nd ed. Michelin Staff. 1999. 8.95 (*2-06-090803-5*) Michelin.

*Netherlands: A Country Study Guide.** Global Investment & Business Center, Inc. Staff. (World Country Study Guides Library: Vol. 123). (Illus.). 350p. 2000. pap. 59.00 (*0-7397-2421-5*) Intl Business Pubns.

Netherlands: Major World Nations. Ronald Seth. LC 97-23403. (Major World Nations Ser.). (Illus.). 144p. (YA). (gr. 5 up). 1999. lib. bdg. 19.95 (*0-7910-4745-8*) Chelsea Hse.

*Netherlands: The Politics of Internationalism.** Thomas R. Rochon. LC 99-21633. (Nations of the Modern World Ser.). 288p. 1999. text 65.00 (*0-8133-2880-2*, Pub. by Westview) HarpC.

Netherlands - A Country Study Guide: Basic Information for Research & Pleasure. Global Investment Center, USA Staff. (World Country Study Guide Library: Vol. 123). (Illus.). 350p. 1999. pap. 59.00 (*0-7397-1520-8*) Intl Business Pubns.

Netherlands: a Selective Bibliography of Reference Works see Netherlands & Northern Belgium: A Selective Bibliography of Reference Works

Netherlands & Nazi Genocide: Papers of the 21st Annual Scholars' Conference. Ed. by G. Jan Colijn & Marcia S. Littell. LC 92-8011. (Symposium Ser.: Vol. 32). (Illus.). 560p. 1992. lib. bdg. 119.95 (*0-7734-9516-9*) E Mellen.

Netherlands & Nazi Germany. Louis De Jong. (Erasmus Lectures). 80p. 1990. 19.95 (*0-674-60805-4*) HUP.

Netherlands & Northern Belgium: A Selective Bibliography of Reference Works. rev. ed. Margrit B. Krewson. LC 88-600438. Orig. Title: The Netherlands: a Selective Bibliography of Reference Works. 152p. 1989. 5.50 (*0-8444-0637-6*, 030-020-00014-6) Lib Congress.

Netherlands & the Gold Standard, 1931-1936. Ed. by Richard Griffiths. (C). 1987. pap. text 84.00 (*90-71617-04-1*) Kluwer Academic.

Netherlands & the Rise of Modern Imperialism: Colonies & Foreign Policy, 1870-1902. Maarten Kuitenbrouwer. Tr. by Hugh Beyer from DUT. LC 90-36901. 414p. 1991. 19.50 (*0-85496-681-1*) Berg Pubs.

Netherlands & the World War Vol. 2: Studies in the War History of a Neutral: Manufacturing Industry; Commerce & Navigation; Housing Problem: Food Supply & Agriculture; Cost of Living, Prices, Wages. C. J. Zaalberg et al. (Economic & Social History of the World War Ser.). 1928. 115.00 (*0-317-27525-9*) Elliots Bks.

Netherlands & the World War Vol. 3: Studies in the War History of Neutral: Effect of the War Upon the Colonies. W. De Cock Buning & J. H. Alting. (Economic & Social History of the World War Ser.). 1928. 60.00 (*0-686-83636-7*) Elliots Bks.

Netherlands & the World War Vol. 4: Studies in the War History of a Neutral: Effect of the War upon Banking & Currency-War Finances in the Netherlands, 1918-1922-Costs of the War. H. W. Bordewyk et al. (Economic & Social History of the World War Ser.). 1928. 85.00 (*0-686-83642-1*) Elliots Bks.

Netherlands Antilles & Aruba. Kai Schoenhlas. LC 94-204925. (World Bibliographical Ser.). 184p. 1994. lib. bdg. 50.00 (*1-85109-210-2*) ABC-CLIO.

*Netherlands Antilles Business Law.** Ed. by Dennis E. Cijntje. 624p. 1999. 159.00 (*90-411-1248-0*) Kluwer Law Intl.

Netherlands Arbitration Act, 1986. Pieter Sanders. Ed. by Albert J. Van Den Berg. (ENG, FRE & GER.). 190p. 1987. pap. 51.00 (*90-6544-297-9*) Kluwer Law Intl.

Netherlands Arbitration Law. A. J. Van Den Berg et al. Tr. by B. Ruijsenaars from DUT. LC 93-5971.Tr. of Arbitragerecht. 1993. 109.00 (*90-6544-770-9*) Kluwer Law Intl.

Netherlands Architecture Institute. Text by Kristin Feireiss et al. LC 99-215086. (Illus.). 96p. 1999. pap. 21.50 (*90-5662-088-6*, 910701, Pub. by NAi Uitgevers) Dist Art Pubs.

Netherlands, Belgium & Luxembourg. Fodors Staff. 1999. pap. 18.00 (*0-679-00060-7*) Fodors Travel.

Netherlands, Belgium, Luxembourg: 20th Century. Herman Van Bergeijk & Otokar Macel. LC 98-6331. (Birkhauser Architectural Guides Ser.). (Illus.). 352p. 1998. 35.00 (*3-7643-5766-5*, Pub. by Birkhauser) Princeton Arch.

*Netherlands Business Intelligence Report, 190 vols.** Global Investment & Business Center, Inc. Staff. (World Business Intelligence Library: Vol. 123). (Illus.). 350p. 2000. pap. 99.95 (*0-7397-2621-8*) Intl Business Pubns.

An Asterisk (*) at the beginning of an entry indicates that the title is appearing for the first time.

*Netherlands Business Law Handbook, 190 vols. Global Investment & Business Center, Inc. Staff. (Global Business Law Handbooks Library: Vol. 123). (Illus.). 350p. 2000. pap. 99.95 (0-7397-2021-X) Intl Business Pubns.

*Netherlands Business Legislation. Tr. by Peter Haanappel et al. 1999. ring bd. 210.00 (90-411-0790-8) Kluwer Law Intl.

*Netherlands Business Opportunity Yearbook. Global Investment & Business Center, Inc. Staff. (Global Business Opportunity Yearbooks Library: Vol. 123). (Illus.). 2000. pap. 99.95 (0-7397-2221-2) Intl Business Pubns.

*Netherlands Business Opportunity Yearbook: Export-Import, Investment & Business Opportunities. International Business Publications, U. S. A. Staff & Global Investment Center, U. S. A. Staff. (Global Business Opportunity Yearbooks Library: Vol. 123). (Illus.). 350p. 1999. pap. 99.95 (0-7397-1321-3) Intl Business Pubns.

Netherlands Cookbook. Helen A. Halverbout. 24.50 (0-87559-121-3) Shalom.

*Netherlands Country Review 2000. Robert C. Kelly et al. (Illus.). 60p. 1999. pap. 39.95 (1-58310-547-6) CountryWatch.

*Netherlands Export-Import & Business Directory: Ultimate Directory for Conducting Export-Import Operations in the Country. Largest Exporters & Importers, Strategic Government & Business Contacts, Selected Export-Import Regulations & More. International Business Publications, USA Staff & Global Investment Center, USA Staff. (World Export-Import & Business Library: 23). (Illus.). 250p. 2000. pap. 99.95 (0-7397-3380-X) Intl Business Pubns.

*Netherlands Foreign Policy & Government Guide. Contrib. by Global Investment & Business Center, Inc. Staff. (World Foreign Policy & Government Library: Vol. 118). (Illus.). 350p. 1999. pap. 99.00 (0-7397-3616-7) Intl Business Pubns.

*Netherlands Foreign Policy & Government Guide. Global Investment & Business Center, Inc. Staff. (World Foreign Policy & Government Library: Vol. 118). (Illus.). 350p. 2000. pap. 99.95 (0-7397-3821-6) Intl Business Pubns.

*Netherlands Government & Business Contacts Handbook: Strategic Government & Business Contacts for Conducting Succesful Business, Export-Import & Investment Activity. International Business Publications, USA Staff & Global Investment Center, USA Staff. (World Export-Import & Business Library: 55). (Illus.). 250p. 2000. pap. 99.95 (0-7397-6095-5) Intl Business Pubns.

Netherlands Green Guide: English Edition. Michelin Staff. 1995. pap. 19.95 (0-7859-7190-4, 20600155517) Fr & Eur.

Netherlands in Pictures. (Visual Geography Ser.). 64p. (YA). (gr. 5 up). 1991. lib. bdg. 19.95 (0-8225-1893-7, Lerner Publctns) Lerner Pub.

Netherlands India: A Study of Plural Economy. John S. Furnivall. LC 77-86961. reprint ed. 55.00 (0-404-16712-8) AMS Pr.

Netherlands Indies & Japan. Hurbertus J. Van Mook. LC 77-179226. reprint ed. 27.50 (0-404-54853-9) AMS Pr.

Netherlands International Law Review: Index, Vols. I-XXX. Ed. by Peter A. Morris. (C). 1991. lib. bdg. 135.50 (0-7923-0906-5) Kluwer Academic.

*Netherlands Investment & Business Guide. Global Investment & Business Center, Inc. Staff. (Global Investment & Business Guide Library: Vol. 123). (Illus.). 2000. pap. 99.95 (0-7397-1821-5) Intl Business Pubns.

*Netherlands Investment & Business Guide: Export-Import, Investment & Business Opportunities. International Business Publications, USA Staff & Global Investment Center, USA Staff. (World Investment & Business Guide Library-99: Vol. 123). (Illus.). 350p. 1999. pap. 99.95 (0-7397-0318-8) Intl Business Pubns.

Netherlands Labor & Co-Determination Law in an EEC Perspective. Cornelus De Groot. 312p. 1990. pap. 63.00 (90-6544-525-0) Kluwer Law Intl.

Netherlands Ophthalmological Society, 168th Meeting, Rotterdam, December 1973: Proceedings. (Journal: Ophthalmologica: Vol. 173, No. 3-4). 1976. 52.25 (3-8055-2218-5) S Karger.

Netherlands Reports to the 11th International Congress of Comparative Law. Ed. by H. U. D'Oliveira. 465p. 1982. pap. 34.00 (90-6544-073-9) Kluwer Academic.

Netherlands Securities Trading Act & Securities Trading Decree: With Supplementary Regulations & Official Commentary. H. C. Warendorf & R. L. Thomas. LC 86-21511. 1986. 30.00 (90-6544-277-4) Kluwer Law Intl.

*Netherlands Tax Guide. Global Investment & Business Center, Inc. Staff. (World Tax Guide Library: Vol. 6). (Illus.). 350p. 1999. pap. 99.00 (0-7397-0180-0) Intl Business Pubns.

*Netherlands Travel & Tourism Services A Strategic Entry Report, 1996. Compiled by Icon Group International Staff. (Illus.). 185p. 1999. ring bd. 1850.00 incl. audio compact disk (0-7418-1504-4) Icon Grp.

Netherlands West Indies: A Pictorial Guide to Curacao, Aruba, St. Martin, Bonaire, Saba & St. Eustace. Willem Van De Poll. (Studies in the Caribbean). 1980. lib. bdg. 69.95 (0-8490-3068-4) Gordon Pr.

Netherlands-Wetlands. Ed. by E. P. Best & J. P. Baker. LC 93-20965. (Developments in Hydrobiology Ser.: Vol. 88). 1993. text 267.50 (0-7923-2473-0) Kluwer Academic.

Netherlands Yearbook Index. 1995. lib. bdg. 225.00 (90-411-0093-8) Kluwer Law Intl.

Netherlands Yearbook International Law. Nyil. 1990. lib. bdg. 97.50 (90-247-3481-9, Pub. by M Nijhoff); lib. bdg. 104.50 (90-247-3638-2, Pub. by M Nijhoff) Kluwer Academic.

Netherlands Yearbook of International Law. Ed. by T.M.C. Asser Institute Staff. 532p. (C). 1994. lib. bdg. 111.00 (0-7923-2830-2, Pub. by Graham & Trotman) Kluwer Academic.

Netherlands Yearbook of International Law. Ed. by T.M.C. Asser Institute Staff. (C). 1992. lib. bdg. 107.00 (0-7923-0568-X) Kluwer Academic.

Netherlands Yearbook of International Law, Vol. XXVII 1996. T. M. C. Asser Instituut Staff. 1997. 118.50 (90-411-0403-8) Kluwer Law Intl.

Netherlands Yearbook of International Law, 1988, Vol. XIV. Ed. by T.M.C. Asser Institute Staff. (C). 1991. lib. bdg. 182.00 (0-7923-0104-8) Kluwer Academic.

Netherlands Yearbook of International Law, 1991, Vol. XXI. Ed. by T.M.C. Asser Institute Staff. 570p. (C). 1991. lib. bdg. 107.00 (0-7923-1180-9) Kluwer Academic.

Netherlands Yearbook of International Law, 1991, Vol. 22. Ed. by T.M.C. Asser Institute Staff. 580p. (C). 1992. lib. bdg. 111.00 (0-7923-1721-1) Kluwer Academic.

Netherlands Yearbook of International Law, 1992, Vol. XXIII. T.M.C. Asser Institute Staff. (T. M. C. Asser Instituut Ser.). 646p. (C). 1993. lib. bdg. 117.00 (0-7923-2252-5) Kluwer Academic.

Netherlands Yearbook of International Law, 1995, Vol. 26. Ed. by T. M. C. Asser Instituut Staff. 452p. 1996. 130.00 (90-411-0196-9) Kluwer Law Intl.

*Netherlands Yearbook of International Law 1998, Vol. XXIX. Ed. by T. M. C. Asser Instituut Staff. 373p. 1999. text 117.00 (90-411-1204-9) Kluwer Law Intl.

Netherworld. Kim Elizabeth. LC 94-74564. (Illus.). 192p. (Orig.). 1995. pap. 10.95 (1-886216-00-2) Ghost Girl.

NetInvesting: Your Guide to Making More Money. Michael Wolff. 400p. 1997. 22.00 (1-889670-06-5) Wolff New Media.

Netiquette. Virginia Shea. LC 97-205898. 160p. (Orig.). 1994. pap. 19.95 (0-9637025-1-3) Albion Bks.

Netizens: On the History & Impact of Usenet & the Internet. Michael Hauben & Ronda Hauben. LC 97-5920. 384p. 1997. 28.95 (0-8186-7706-6, BP07706) IEEE Comp Soc.

NetJobs: Your Guide to Getting the Job You Want. 2nd rev. ed. Michael Wolff. (Illus.). ix, 400p. (Orig.). 1997. 22.00 (1-889670-02-2) Wolff New Media.

*Net.Journal Directory: The Catalog of Full Text Periodicals Archived on the World Wide Web, Vol.3, Num.1. 5th rev. ed. Lawrence Krumenaker. 1999. pap. 125.00 (0-9656775-0-8, Pub. by Hermograph) EBSCO Media.

NETL: A System for Representing & Using Real-World Knowledge. Scott E. Fahlman. (Artificial Intelligence Ser.). (Illus.). 298p. 1979. 35.00 (0-262-06069-8) MIT Pr.

Netlaw. Lance Rose. 1997. pap. text 24.99 (0-07-882358-7) McGraw.

Netlaw: Your Rights in the Online World. Lance Rose. Ed. by Joanne Cuthbertson. (Internet Ser.). 432p. 1995. pap. text 19.95 (0-07-882077-4) Osborne-McGraw.

NetLearning: Why Teachers Use the Internet. Melissa Koch & Ferdi Serim. LC 96-171039. (Computer Science). (Illus.). (Orig.). 1996. pap. 24.95 (1-56592-201-8) Thomson Learn.

Netley Abbey: A Gothic Story, 2 vols., Set. Richard Warner. LC 73-2271. 396p. 1975. reprint ed. 79.95 (0-405-06021-1) Ayer.

Netlife: Internet Citizens & Their Communities. Carl G. Surratt. LC 98-25973. 300p. 1998. 39.00 (1-56072-577-X) Nova Sci Pubs.

Netmaking. Percy W. Blandford. (C). 1987. 85.00 (0-85174-197-5) St Mut.

*NETMAX FileServer. 2000. boxed set 99.00 (1-929592-03-5) Cybernet Systems.

*NETMAX WebServer. 2000. boxed set 99.00 (1-929592-02-7) Cybernet Systems.

Netmoney: Your Guide to Personal Finance Solutions. 2nd rev. ed. Michael Wolff. 400p. 1997. pap. 24.95 (1-889670-22-7) Wolff New Media.

NetObjects Fusion Handbook. Timothy Webster. LC 96-77852. 544p. 1996. 50.00 (1-56830-327-0) Hayden.

Netobjects Fusion 3 for Dummies. John San Filippo & Dummies Technical Press Staff. LC 98-84660. 384p. 1998. pap. 24.99 incl. cd-rom (0-7645-0236-0) IDG Bks.

Netochka Nezvanova. Fyodor Dostoyevsky. Tr. & Intro. by Jane Kentish. (Classics Ser.). 192p. 1986. pap. 10.95 (0-14-044455-6, Penguin Classics) Viking Penguin.

Net1000: Your Guide to the Best of Everything on the Net. 400p. 1997. pap. 22.00 (1-889670-29-4) Wolff New Media.

NetOut: Gay Life Online - We're Here, Queer & Wired. Michael Wolff. 400p. 1997. 22.00 (1-889670-05-7) Wolff New Media.

NetPAC. EOS International Staff. (Illus.). 68p. 1996. 35.00 (0-929795-38-5) EOS Intl.

NetPages: The Internationally Renowned Resource Guide to the Internet. 390p. 1996. pap. 9.95 (0-9651670-0-3) Aldea Communs.

*Net.people: The Personalities & Passions Behind the Web Sites. Thomas E. Bleier & Eric C. Steinert. LC 99-42511. (Illus.). 320p. 2000. pap. 19.95 (0-910965-37-4, CyberAge Bks) Info Today Inc.

*NetPolicy.Com: Public Agenda for a Digital World. Leslie David Simon. 2000. 60.00 (1-930365-02-0, Pub. by W Wilson Ctr Pr); pap. 22.95 (1-930365-03-9, Pub. by W Wilson Ctr Pr) Johns Hopkins.

Netrepreneur: The Dimensions of Transferring Your Business Model to the Internet. Joseph Lowery. 1998. pap. 29.99 (0-7897-1725-5) Que.

NetResearch: Finding Information Online. Daniel J. Barrett. 200p. 1997. pap. 24.95 (1-56592-245-X) Thomson Learn.

NetRoots: How You Can Trace Your Family Tree. Michael Wolff. 200p. 1997. pap. 12.95 (1-889670-26-X) Wolff New Media.

Nets & Doors: Shrimping in Southern Waters. Jack Leigh. (Illus.). 96p. 1989. 45.00 (0-941711-12-9) Wyrick & Co.

Nets of Awareness: Urdu Poetry & Its Critics. Frances W. Pritchett. LC 92-43826. 1994. 48.00 (0-520-08194-3, Pub. by U CA Pr); pap. 18.95 (0-520-08386-5, Pub. by U CA Pr) Cal Prin Full Svc.

Nets, Terms & Formulas: Three Views of Concurrent Processes & Their Relationship. Ernst R. Olderog. (Tracts in Theoretical Computer Science Ser.: No. 23). 277p. (C). 1991. text 59.95 (0-521-40044-9) Cambridge U Pr.

Nets to Catch the Wind: Collections of Poems by Writers in Maryland, Virginia & the District of Columbia. Compiled & Pref. by Joseph D. Adams. (Poet's Domain Ser.: Vol. 6). xiv, 80p. (Orig.). 1992. pap. 6.95 (1-880016-10-9) Road Pubs.

*NetSavvy: Building Information Literacy in the Classroom. 2nd ed. Ian Jukes et al. LC 99-50501. (One-Off Ser.). (Illus.). 144p. 2000. pap. 29.95 (0-7619-7565-9); lib. bdg. 65.95 (0-7619-7564-0) Corwin Pr.

Netscape Adventures: Step-by-Step Guide to Netscape Navigator & the World Wide Web. Cynthia B. Leshin. LC 96-18106. 316p. (C). 1996. pap. text 62.00 (0-13-255092-X) P-H.

Netscape & the World Wide Web. Fritz J. Erickson & John A. Vonk. LC 97-150171. 160p. (C). 1997. text 21.00 (0-256-23770-0, Irwn McGrw-H) McGrw-H Hghr Educ.

Netscape & the WWW for Dummies. Paul Hoffman. 384p. 1995. pap. 19.99 (1-56884-373-9) IDG Bks.

Netscape Communicator. O'Leary. 216p. 1998. pap. 27.50 (0-07-012579-1) McGraw.

Netscape Communicator - Windows. Bryan Pfaffenberger. (Illus.). 608p. 1997. pap. text 32.95 (0-12-553164-8) Morgan Kaufmann.

Netscape Communicator & the World Wide Web. Fritz J. Erickson & John A. Vonk. LC 98-2912. 240p. 1998. pap. 28.75 (0-07-303842-3) McGraw.

Netscape Communicator for Busy People. Christian Crumlish & Jeff Hadfield. 320p. 1997. pap. text 24.99 (0-07-882441-9) McGraw.

Netscape Communicator 4 for Dummies. Viraf D. Mohta. LC 96-77276. (Quick Reference Ser.). (Illus.). 224p. 1997. spiral bd. 12.99 (0-7645-0041-4) IDG Bks.

Netscape Communicator 4. Ed. by Ron Pronk. (Illus.). 180p. 1997. pap. 20.00 (1-58264-030-0, 148) ActiveEd.

Netscape Communicator 4 for Dummies. 3rd ed. Paul E. Hoffman. LC 97-70371. (For Dummies Ser.). (Illus.). 384p. 1997. pap. 19.99 (0-7645-0053-8) IDG Bks.

Netscape Communicator 4 for Macintosh: Visual QuickStart Guide. Elizabeth Castro. LC 98-123575. 360p. (C). 1997. pap. text 17.95 (0-201-68886-7, Pub. by Peachpit Pr) Addison-Wesley.

Netscape Communicator 4 for Windows: Visual QuicksSart Guide. Elizabeth Castro. LC 98-104769. 368p. (C). 1997. pap. text 17.95 (0-201-68864-6) Peachpit Pr.

Netscape Communicator 4.5 for Dummies Quick Reference. Viraf D. Mohta. LC TK5105.883.N49M642. (For Dummies). (Illus.). 224p. 1999. spiral bd. 12.99 (0-7645-0325-1) IDG Bks.

Select: Netscape Communicator 4.0 Brief (Projects 1-4) Gillian Hall. (Select Ser.). 112p. (C). 1997. pap. text 19.00 (0-201-31564-5, Prentice Hall) P-H.

Netscape Communicator 4. (Quick Study Computer Ser.). 4p. pap. 3.95 (1-57222-245-X) Barcharts.

Netscape Communicator 4.5 for Dummies. Paul E. Hoffman. LC 98-88794. (For Dummies Ser.). 384p. 1998. pap. 19.99 (0-7645-0324-3) IDG Bks.

*Netscape Devedge Web Developers Library. Dreyfus Editorial Staff. LC 99-46066. 744p. 1999. pap. 34.99 (0-7645-4585-X) IDG Bks.

Netscape Enterprise Server. Allen Wyatt. LC 96-69343. 608p. 1996. per. 40.00 (0-7615-0690-X) Prima Pub.

Netscape Essential. 1997. 18.99 (0-7686-0089-8) Quest Custom.

Netscape Essentials. Que Education & Training Staff. LC 96-68603. (Essentials Ser.). 181p. 1997. pap. text 22.99 (1-57576-367-2) Que Educ & Trng.

Netscape FastTrack Server. Allen Wyatt. LC 96-69344. 528p. 1996. per. 40.00 (0-7615-0691-8) Prima Pub.

Netscape for Macintosh: A Hands-On Configuration & Set-Up Guide for Popular Web Browsers. Richard Raucci. LC 95-47549. (Illus.). 179p. 1996. pap. text 24.95 (0-387-94662-4) Spr-Verlag.

*Netscape for Terrified Teachers. Debi Hooper. (Illus.). 320p. 1999. pap., teacher ed. 24.95 (1-57690-445-8, TCM 2445) Tchr Create Mat.

Netscape for the Macintosh. Richard Raucci. 1996. pap. 24.95 (0-614-12617-7) Spr-Verlag.

Netscape Communicator Essentials. Que Education & Training. 1997. 22.99 (1-57576-827-5) Que Educ & Trng.

Netscape 4 Essentials. Que Education & Training Staff. 1997. 39.99 (1-57576-875-5) Que Educ & Trng.

Netscape Internet Foundation Classes Programming. Arun Rao. LC 97-68572. 350p. 1997. 34.99 (0-7897-1251-2) Que.

Netscape Made Simple. Kennington. 160p. Date not set. pap. text 19.95 (0-7506-3514-2) Buttrwrth-Heinemann.

*Netscape Mozilla Soure Code Guide. Stanek. LC 99-46043. 448p. 1999. pap. 34.99 (0-7645-4588-4) IDG Bks.

Netscape Navigator. (C). 1998. pap. text. write for info. (0-03-023746-7) Harcourt Coll Pubs.

Netscape Navigator: Jumpstart Tutorial. Elisabeth A. Parker. (Illus.). 350p. (Orig.). 1996. pap. 20.95 (1-886801-64-9) Thomson Learn.

Netscape Navigator: Surfing the Web & Exploring the Internet, 2 vols. large type ed. Bryan Pfaffenberger. (Illus.). 430p. 107.50 (0-614-20558-1, L-03801-00 APHB) Am Printing Hse.

Netscape Navigator - Win 95/NT. (Quick Study Computer Ser.). 4p. pap. 3.95 (1-57222-212-3) Barcharts.

Netscape Navigator 4 Guru. Bill Hartman. (Computer Guru Ser.). (Illus.). 20p. 1998. spiral bd. 5.99 (1-58187-029-9) Guru Books.

*Netscape Navigator 4.5: En Preparacion. ENI Publishing Ltd. Staff. (Triunfar Con Ser.). 2000. pap. text 7.95 (2-7460-0757-6) ENI Publng.

Netscape Navigator Gold - Win 95/NT. (Quick Study Computer Ser.). 4p. pap. 3.95 (1-57222-213-1) Barcharts.

Netscape Navigator 6-in-1. Jennifer Fulton & Nat Gertler. LC 96-68586. 624p. 1996. pap. text 29.99 (0-7897-0807-8) Que.

Netscape Navigator 6 Introductory Concepts & Techniques. Gary B. Shelly et al. 168p. per. 22.95 (0-7895-4647-7, Pub. by Course Tech) Thomson Learn.

Netscape Navigator 3 Complete Handbook. John Pivovarnick. LC 96-69520. 312p. 1996. per. 24.99 (0-7615-0852-X) Prima Pub.

Netscape Navigator 3.0. Martin. LC 99-162391. (C). 1998. pap. text 25.00 (0-03-024314-9) Harcourt Coll Pubs.

Netscape Navigator 3.0 (Windows) Bryan Pfaffenberger. (Illus.). 464p. 1996. pap., pap. text 29.95 incl. cd-rom (0-12-553153-2) Morgan Kaufmann.

Netscape Navigator 3 Starter Kit. Mark Brown. LC 96-69457. 560p. 1996. pap. text 34.99 incl. cd-rom (0-7897-0924-4) Que.

Netscape Navigator 3 Starter Kit for Macintosh. Mark Brown. LC 96-77657. 544p. 1996. pap. text 34.99 incl. cd-rom (1-56830-320-3) Hayden.

Netscape Navigator Two Point O: A Jumpstart Tutorial. Elizabeth A. Parker. (Illus.). 317p. (Orig.). 1996. pap. 19.95 (1-886801-16-9) Thomson Learn.

Netscape Navigator 2.0 Jumpstart Tutorial. Elisabeth A. Parker. (Illus.). 317p. 1996. pap. 19.95 (1-886801-46-0) Thomson Learn.

Netscape Navigator 4. Shelly & Cashman. (Shelly-Cashman Ser.). (C). 1997. pap. 22.95 (0-7895-4283-8) Course Tech.

Netscape Navigator 4 Fast & Easy. Rob Tidrow. LC 97-75643. 352p. 1997. pap. 16.99 (0-7615-1382-5) Prima Pub.

Netscape Navigator 5.0. Perry. (Computer Applications Ser.). 1998. mass mkt. 22.00 (0-538-68593-X) S-W Pub.

Netscape ONE Developer's Guide. William R. Stanek. LC 96-67212. 864p. 1997. 49.99 (1-57521-094-0) Sams.

Netscape ONE Sourcebook. Donald Brewer. LC 97-4049. 416p. 1997. pap. 24.99 (0-471-18146-3) Wiley.

Netscape Plug in Developers Kit. Mike Morgan. LC 96-70765. 560p. 1996. pap. text 49.99 incl. cd-rom (0-7897-0844-2) Que.

Netscape Plug-In Field Guide: A Plug-Ins Field Guide. Erica Sadun. (Illus.). 300p. (Orig.). 1997. pap. 35.95 (1-886801-04-5) Thomson Learn.

Netscape Plug-In Power. David Wall. LC 96-78233. 384p. 1996. pap. 34.99 (0-7645-4009-2) IDG Bks.

Netscape Plug-Ins. Abacus Development Group Staff. 1996. pap. text 29.95 incl. cd-rom (1-55755-321-1) Abacus MI.

Netscape Programmer's Guide: Using OLE to Build Componentware Apps. Richard B. Lam. 416p. 1998. pap. 39.95 (0-521-64820-3) Cambridge U Pr.

Netscape Server Programming. 1998. 39.99 (1-57521-114-9) Macmillan.

Netscape Server Survival Guide. Rizwan Virk. LC 96-67956. 528p. 1996. pap. text 49.99 (1-57521-111-4) Sams.

Netscape 3 for Windows: Visual Quickstart Guide. Elizabeth Castro. LC 96-229975. 288p. (C). 1996. pap. text 16.95 (0-201-69409-3) Peachpit Pr.

Netscape Time: The Making of a Billion Dollar Start-Up That Took on Microsoft. Owen Edwards & Jim Clark. LC 98-51609. 276p. 1999. 24.95 (0-312-19934-1) St Martin.

*Netscape Time: The Making of the Billion-Dollar Start-Up That Took on Microsoft. Jim Clark & Owen Edwards. 288p. 2000. pap. 14.95 (0-312-26361-9, St Martin Griffin) St Martin.

Netscape 2 for Windows: Visual QuickStart Guide. Elizabeth Castro. LC 96-167903. (Illus.). 256p. (C). 1996. pap. text 16.95 (0-201-88615-4) Peachpit Pr.

Netscape 2 Unleashed. Neil Randall et al. LC 95-70176. (Illus.). 922p. 1995. 49.99 (1-57521-007-X) Sams.

Netscape Virtuoso. Ellisa Keeler & Robert Miller. 89p. 1995. pap. 24.95 (1-55828-462-1, MIS Pr) IDG Bks.

Netscape Virtuoso. 2nd ed. Ellisa Keeler. 89p. 1996. pap. 24.95 (1-55828-495-8, MIS Pr) IDG Bks.

Net.search. C. Watkins. (Illus.). 387p. (Orig.). 1995. 24.99 (0-7897-0242-8) Que.

Net.Sex: A Discreet Guide to the Adult Side of the Internet. Candi Rose & Dirk Thomas. (Illus.). 243p. (Orig.). 1994. pap. 19.99 (0-672-30702-2) Sams.

Netsilik Eskimo. rev. ed. Asen Balikci. (Illus.). 264p. (C). 1989. reprint ed. pap. text 12.95 (0-88133-435-9) Waveland Pr.

Netsilik Eskimos. Knud J. Rasmussen. LC 76-21685. (Thule Expedition, 5th, 1921-1924 Ser.: No. 8, Pts. 1-2). reprint ed. 105.00 (0-404-58323-7) AMS Pr.

Netsilik Eskimos. Knud Rasmussen. 1998. reprint ed. lib. bdg. 99.00 (0-7812-4788-8) Rprt Serv.

*NetSlaves: True Tales of Working the Web. Bill Lessard. 256p. 2000. pap. 12.95 (0-07-136480-3) McGraw.

N

***Netsmart: A Students Guide.** (C). 1999. 12.00 (*0-8087-6673-2*) Pearson Custom.

***Netspionage: The Global Threats to Information.** William C. Boni & Gerald L. Kovacich. 224p. 2000. pap. 29.95 (*0-7506-7257-9*, Newnes) Buttrwrth-Heinemann.

Netsuccess: Why Realtors Use the Internet. Scott Kersnar. 1996. pap. write for info. (*1-888866-01-2*) Thomson Learn.

NetSuccess: Your Guide to the Best of Everything on the Net. 3rd ed. (Illus.). 400p. 1997. pap. 22.00 (*1-889670-28-6*) Wolff New Media.

Netsuke. Edwin C. Symmes. (Illus.). 200p. 1995. pap. 24.95 (*0-8048-2026-0*) Tuttle Pubng.

Netsuke: A Guide for Collectors. Mary L. O'Brien. LC 65-11837. (Illus.). 246p. 1965. 45.00 (*0-8048-0423-0*, TR84-1) Tuttle Pubng.

Netsuke: Japanese Life & Legend in Miniature. Edwin C. Symmes, Jr. LC 89-51714. (Illus.). 192p. 1991. text 49.95 (*0-8048-1616-6*) Tuttle Pubng.

***Netsuke: The Collection of the Peabody Museum of Salem.** 2nd ed. Lisa A. Edwards & Margie M. Krebs. (Illus.). 160p. 2000. pap. 19.50 (*0-87577-062-2*, PEMP100, Peabody Museum) Peabody Essex Mus.

Netsuke: The Japanese Art of Miniature Carving. Matthew Welch & Sharen Chappell. 204p. 1999. pap. 49.95 (*1-878529-50-1*) Art Media Resources.

Netsuke & Inro Artists, & How to Read Their Signatures. George Lozarnick. LC 81-51945. (Illus.). 1376p. 1982. 295.00 (*0-917064-02-X*) Reed Pubs.

Netsuke & Inro Artists, & How to Read Their Signatures, 2 vols. deluxe ed. George Lazarnick. LC 81-51945. (Illus.). 1376p. 1982. lthr. 950.00 (*0-686-79507-5*) Reed Pubs.

Netsuke Familiar & Unfamiliar: New Principles for Collecting. Raymond Bushell. LC 75-22420. (Illus.). 260p. 1976. 75.00 (*0-8348-0115-9*) Weatherhill.

Netsuke Handbook of Ueda Reikichi. Ueda Reikichi. Tr. by Raymond Bushell. LC 61-8139. (Illus.). 325p. 1961. 45.00 (*0-8048-0424-9*) Tuttle Pubng.

Netsuke Masks. R. Bushell. LC 84-48693. (Illus.). 208p. 1995. reprint ed. 80.00 (*0-8348-0341-0*) Weatherhill.

Nettie Jo's Friends. Pat McKissack. LC 87-14080. (J). 1994. 13.19 (*0-606-06612-8*, Pub. by Turtleback) Demco.

Nettie Jo's Friends. Patricia C. McKissack. (Dragonfly Bks.). (Illus.). 40p. (J). (ps-3). 1994. pap. 7.99 (*0-679-86573-X*, Pub. by Knopf Bks Yng Read) Random.

Nettie Palmer. Nettie Palmer. Ed. by Vivian Smith. LC 88-17606. (UQP Australian Authors Ser.). 548p. (Orig.). 1989. pap. text 16.95 (*0-7022-2130-9*, Pub. by Univ Queensland Pr) Intl Spec Bk.

Nettie's Spaghetti. Roz Rosenbluth. (Illus.). 12p. (J). (ps-2). 1999. pap. 3.75 (*1-880612-88-7*) Seedling Pubns.

Nettie's Trip South. Turner. (J). 1998. pap. 4.95 (*0-87628-955-3*) Ctr Appl Res.

Nettie's Trip South. Ann Turner. LC 86-18135. (Illus.). 32p. (J). 1995. mass mkt. 4.95 (*0-689-80117-3*) Aladdin.

Nettie's Trip South. Ann Turner. LC 86-18135. (Illus.). 32p. (J). (gr. 1-5). 1987. lib. bdg. 16.00 (*0-02-789240-9*, Mac Bks Young Read) S&S Childrens.

Nettie's Trip South. Ann W. Turner. (J). 1989. pap. text 2.95 (*0-590-42721-0*) Scholastic Inc.

Nettie's Trip South. Ann Warren Turner. (J). 1995. 10.40 (*0-606-07942-4*) Turtleback.

Nettie's Vegetarian Kitchen. Nettie Cronish. (Illus.). 200p. 1996. pap. 14.95 (*0-929005-80-5*, Pub. by Sec Story Pr) LPC InBook.

Netting: From Early Sources. Ed. by Jules Kliot & Kaethe Kliot. (Illus.). 80p. 1998. pap. 18.00 (*1-891656-03-1*, LB36) Lacis Pubns.

Netting Materials for Fishing Gear. Gerhard Klust. 1978. 30.00 (*0-7855-6948-0*) St Mut.

Netting the Sun: New & Collected Poems. Phoebe Hesketh. 224p. 1989. reprint ed. 35.00 (*1-870612-40-X*, Pub. by Enitha Pr); reprint ed. pap. 16.95 (*1-870612-35-3*, Pub. by Enitha Pr) Dufour.

Netting Your Ancestors: Genealogical Research on the Internet. Cyndi Howells. LC 97-73445. 173p. 1997. pap. 19.95 (*0-8063-1546-6*) Genealog Pub.

Nettles. Holton Rower. (Illus.). 40p. 1991. pap. 35.00 (*0-9623585-6-8*) Flockophobic Pr.

Nettles. Janice Schofield. LC 98-11561. (Good Herb Guides Ser.). 96p. 1998. pap. 4.95 (*0-87983-840-X*, 3840XK, Keats Publng) NTC Contemp Pub Co.

Nettles. limited ed. Holton Rower. (Illus.). 40p. 1991. 55.00 (*0-9623585-5-X*) Flockophobic Pr.

Nettles: Poems. Betty Adcock. LC 83-726. 60p. 1983. pap. 7.95 (*0-8071-1103-1*) La State U Pr.

Nettles & Balsams. David W. Riggs. 28p. (Orig.). 1995. pap. write for info. (*1-883331-13-7*) Anderie Poetry.

NetTravel: How Travelers Use the Internet. Michael Shapiro. LC 97-164271. 312p. 1997. pap. 24.95 (*1-56592-172-0*) Thomson Learn.

Netu Neter Vol. 2: Anuk Ausar: The Kamitic Initiation System. Ra Un Nefer Amen I. (Illus.). 350p. pap. 14.95 (*1-877662-08-9*) Kamit Pubns.

Netvet: Mosby's Veterinary Guide to the Internet, Vol. 1. Kenneth R. Boschert & Henry James. (Illus.). 275p. (gr. 13). 1997. pap. text 24.95 incl. 3.5 hd (*0-8151-2935-1*, 31825) Mosby Inc.

Netware. (C). 1990. text. write for info. (*0-201-51095-2*) Addison-Wesley.

Netware. Schrieber. (C). 1990. text. write for info. (*0-201-55900-5*) Addison-Wesley.

Netware Answers: Certified Tech Support. James Nadler & Donald Guarnieri. (Certified Tech Support Ser.). 240p. 1994. pap. 16.95 (*0-07-882044-8*) McGraw.

Netware Band 2. (C). 1990. text. write for info. (*0-201-52299-3*) Addison-Wesley.

NetWare Directory Services Troubleshooting. Peter Kuo & Jim Henderson. (Illus.). 400p. (Orig.). 1995. pap. text 40.00 (*1-56205-443-0*) New Riders Pub.

NetWare 5: The Complete Reference. William H. Payne et al. LC 99-229010. (Complete Reference Ser.). 1008p. 1999. 49.99 (*0-07-211882-2*) Osborne-McGraw.

NetWare 5 Administration. 1999. pap. write for info. (*1-884486-01-0*) Wave Tech.

Netware 5 Advanced Administration. write for info. (*1-884486-03-7*) Wave Tech.

NetWare 5 CNE. Michael G. Moncur. LC 99-60004. (Certification NetWare 5 Ser.). 704p. 1999. 44.99 (*0-7821-2389-9*); 39.99 (*0-7821-2390-2*) Sybex.

NetWare 5 CNE. Scott Reeves. LC 98-88910. (Certification NetWare 5 Ser.). 448p. 1999. 39.99 (*0-7821-2388-0*) Sybex.

***NetWare 5 24Seven.** John Hales & Nestor Reyes. 512p. 1999. pap. 34.99 (*0-7821-2593-X*) Sybex.

NetWare for AOS - VS, 5 bks., Set. Rational Data Systems, Inc. Staff. 1992. pap. 375.00 incl. disk (*1-881378-14-4*) Rational Data.

NetWare for AOS - VS Concepts. Rational Data Systems, Inc. Staff. 1992. pap. 75.00 incl. disk (*1-881378-07-1*) Rational Data.

NetWare for AOS - VS Installation. Rational Data Systems, Inc. Staff. 1992. pap. 75.00 incl. disk (*1-881378-10-1*) Rational Data.

NetWare for AOS - VS System Administration. Rational Data Systems, Inc. Staff. 1992. pap. 75.00 incl. disk (*1-881378-09-8*) Rational Data.

NetWare for AOS - VS System Messages. Rational Data Systems, Inc. Staff. 1992. pap. 75.00 incl. disk (*1-881378-11-X*) Rational Data.

NetWare for AOS - VS Utilities. Rational Data Systems, Inc. Staff. 1992. pap. 75.00 incl. disk (*1-881378-08-X*) Rational Data.

NetWare for Dummies. Ed Tittel. (Illus.). 350p. 1993. pap. 19.95 (*1-56884-003-9*) IDG Bks.

Netware for Dummies. 2nd ed. Ed Tittel. 432p. 1995. pap. 19.99 (*1-56884-369-0*) IDG Bks.

Netware 4 Made Easy. Taha & Julius. (C). 2001. pap. text 38.00 (*0-13-244963-3*) P-H.

NetWare 4.1: The Complete Reference. Tom Sheldon. (The Complete Reference Ser.). 1000p. 1995. pap. text 39.95 (*0-07-882172-X*) McGraw.

NetWare 4.1 Supervisor's Guide. John T. McCann. 89p. 1995. pap. 34.95 (*1-55851-402-3*, M&T Bks) IDG Bks.

NetWare 4.1 Survival Guide. Peter Kuo. 1360p. 1992. 49.99 (*0-672-30047-8*) Sams.

Netware 4.1 SmartStart. Que Education & Training Staff. LC 96-68607. (Smartstart Ser.). 330p. 1997. pap. text 29.99 (*1-57576-382-6*) Que Educ & Trng.

Network Press Administration's Handbook to NetWare 4.11. Michael G. Moncur. LC 96-69288. 576p. 1996. pap. text 34.99 (*0-7821-1949-2*) Sybex.

Netware 4.0 for Professionals. Karanjit Siyan. 1424p. 1993. pap. 42.95 (*1-56205-217-9*) New Riders Pub.

NetWare 4.0 SmartStart. Date not set. pap., teacher ed. 39.99 incl. disk (*1-57576-350-8*) Que.

NetWare LANs: Performance & Troubleshooting. 61st ed. I. Theakston. LC 94-1098. (Data Communications & Networks Ser.). 400p. (C). 1995. pap. 44.95 (*0-201-63175-X*) Addison-Wesley.

NetWare Lite. Steve Broadhead. 178p. (C). 1993. pap. text 45.00 (*0-201-63193-8*) Addison-Wesley.

Netware Migration. Richard Hanley. LC 95-48045. 542p. 1996. pap. 34.95 (*0-471-13437-6*) Wiley.

Netware Professional's Toolkit. Gary Araki. 450p. (gr. 10 up). 1999. pap. 39.95 incl. audio compact disk (*1-889671-11-8*) Advice Pr.

Netware Solutions & Shortcuts Batch File Programming for Administrators. Emmett Dulaney. 1995. pap. 39.95 incl. disk (*1-55851-310-8*, M&T Bks) IDG Bks.

Netware Supervisor's Guide. John T. McCann et al. (Illus.). 510p. (Orig.). 1995. pap. 29.95 (*1-55851-111-3*, M&T Bks) IDG Bks.

Netware Supervisor's Guide 4.0. John T. McCann. 1995. pap. 32.95 (*1-55851-284-5*, M&T Bks) IDG Bks.

NetWare TCP - IP Support: For Novell Test No. 50-145; NetWare TCP/IP Transport. 4th rev. ed. Muhammad Zafar. (CNE Training Manual Ser.). (Illus.). 150p. 1996. text 75.00 (*1-57739-007-5*) PC Age.

Netware 386 Programmer's Guide. Ralph Davis. 416p. (C). 1991. pap. 26.95 (*0-201-57709-7*) Addison-Wesley.

NetWare 3.11 - 3.12: Network Administrator, Incl. instr. resource kit, test bank, transparency. Ted L. Simpson. 816p. 1996. text, mass mkt. 35.25 incl. 3.5 ld (*1-56527-282-X*) Course Tech.

NetWare 3.1X to 4.1 Update: For Novell Test No. 50-162; NetWare 3.1x to NetWare 4.1 Update. 4th rev. ed. Muhammad Zafar. (CNE Training Manual Ser.). (Illus.). 262p. 1996. text 100.00 (*1-57739-004-0*) PC Age.

NetWare 3.12 System Administration. Doug Archell. LC 94-67942. 1994. 27.99 (*1-56529-925-6*) Que.

Netware 3.X: A Do-It-Yourself Guide. Charles P. Koontz. (Illus.). 288p. (Orig.). 1992. pap. 24.95 (*1-55958-207-3*) Prima Pub.

***Netware to Internet Gateways (1996)** James E. Gaskin. (Illus.). 532p. 2000. reprint ed. pap. text 30.00 (*0-7881-9189-6*) DIANE Pub.

Netware to Windows NT: Integration & Migration. Arnold Villeneuve & Wayne McKinnon. LC 97-44419. (Illus.). 912p. 1998. pap., pap. text 59.95 incl. cd-rom (*0-07-913171-9*) McGraw.

NetWare Training Guide: CNA Study Guide. New Riders Development Group Staff. LC 94-34769. (Illus.). 876p. (Orig.). 1994. pap. 50.00 (*1-56205-365-5*) New Riders Pub.

Netware Troubleshooting. Michael L. Hader. 624p. 1991. pap. 34.95 (*0-201-57737-2*) Addison-Wesley.

Netware Troubleshooting. Michael L. Hader. (C). 1993. pap. text. write for info. (*0-201-59491-9*) Addison-Wesley.

Netware Troubleshooting: Tips Tricks Tech. (C). 1991. write for info. (*0-201-94741-2*) Addison-Wesley.

***Netware Unleashed.** 3rd ed. Rick Sant'Angelo. 1000p. 1999. 49.99 (*0-672-31708-7*) Sams.

NetWare User's Guide: Versions 3.11 & 3.12. Edward Leibing. LC 93-4987. 1995. pap. 34.95 (*1-55851-318-3*, M&T Bks) IDG Bks.

Netware User's Guide 4.1. J. D. Maryme. 1995. pap. 29.95 (*1-55851-283-7*, M&T Bks) IDG Bks.

Netware 386: Programmer's Guide. Ralph Davis. (C). 1993. pap. text. write for info. (*0-201-59490-0*) Addison-Wesley.

NetWare 4.11 to NetWare 5 Update Exam Cram. Randy Brown Grein & Patrick B. Brown. LC 99-19195. (Exam Cram / Coriolis' Certification Insi Ser.). 346p. 1999. pap. 29.99 (*1-57610-355-2*) Coriolis Grp.

***Netware 5 All-In-One CNA/CNE Certification Exam Guide.** John Mueller. LC 99-38180. 1999. pap. 99.99 (*0-07-134778-X*) Osborne-McGraw.

NetWarriors in C: Programming 3D Multi-Player Games in C. Joe Gradecki. LC 94-44367. 448p. 1995. pap. 34.95 incl. disk (*0-471-11064-7*) Wiley.

Net.Wars. Wendy M. Grossman. LC 97-21214. 232p. 1997. text 22.00 (*0-8147-3103-1*) NYU Pr.

NetWine: Your Guide to Vines, Grapes & Vintages. Michael Wolff. 150p. 1997. pap. 9.95 (*1-889670-25-1*) Wolff New Media.

Netwise Investor: Free Investment Resources on the Internet. Jordan Cohen. LC 97-70478. 1997. pap. 14.95 (*0-9657299-5-8*) Joralis Grp.

Network, Level 5. Parulis. (College ESL Ser.). (J). 1998. mass mkt. write for info. (*0-8384-6972-8*); mass mkt., teacher ed. write for info. (*0-8384-6974-4*) Heinle & Heinle.

Network, Level 6. Parulis. (College ESL Ser.). (J). 1998. mass mkt. write for info. (*0-8384-6936-1*); mass mkt., teacher ed. write for info. (*0-8384-6938-8*) Heinle & Heinle.

Network: Art & the Complex Present. Lawrence Alloway. Ed. by Donald Kuspit. LC 83-24201. (Contemporary American Art Critics Ser.: No. 1). 324p. reprint ed. 100.50 (*0-8357-1519-1*, 207061700007) Bks Demand.

Network: Inside the Tight-Knit World of Black America's Power Brokers. Elizabeth Lesly. 1996. 22.00 (*0-614-15441-3*) McGraw.

Network: Inside the Tight-Knit World of Black America's Power Brokers. Elizabeth Lesly. (Illus.). 304p. 1996. text 22.00 (*0-07-037800-2*) McGraw.

Network Access to Multimedia Information. Chris Adie. 67p. (Orig.). (C). 1995. pap. text 25.00 (*0-7881-1940-0*) DIANE Pub.

***Network Administration.** Steve Wisniewski. 512p. 2001. 90.00 (*0-13-015882-8*) P-H.

Network Administration: For Intel Processors SVR4.2MP. UNIX Staff. (Illus.). 688p. (C). 1994. pap. 51.80 (*0-13-158049-3*) P-H.

***Network Administration Survival Guide.** Sue Plumley. LC 98-30225. 864p. 1998. pap. 49.99 (*0-471-29621-X*) Wiley.

Network Administrator: Microsoft Windows NT 4.0. Michael J. Palmer. 800p. 1997. pap. write for info. (*0-7600-5010-4*) Course Tech.

Network Administrator: NetWare 4.1. Ted L. Simpson et al. 816p. 1997. pap. 51.95 (*0-7600-3299-8*) Course Tech.

Network Administrator: NetWare 4.1. Ted L. Simpson et al. 816p. 1997. teacher ed. 49.95 (*0-7600-3333-1*) Course Tech.

Network Administrator's Reference. Tere Parnell. 1999. pap. text 49.99 (*0-07-882588-1*) Osborne-McGraw.

***Network Administrator's Survival Guide.** Kevin L. Moss. 1999. pap. text 59.99 (*0-07-913786-5*) McGraw.

Network Advisory Committee: Proceedings of the Library of Congress Network Advisory Committee Meeting, December 12-14, 1993. Library of Congress, Network Development Departmen. LC 94-33175. (Network Planning Paper: Vol. 26). 1994. write for info. (*0-8444-0824-7*) Lib Congress.

***Network Algebra.** Gheorghe Stefanescu. LC 00-27501. xvi, 408p. 2000. pap. text 64.00 (*1-85233-195-X*) Spr-Verlag.

Network+ All-In-One Certification Exam Guide. Michael Meyers & Brian Schwarz. 512p. 1999. 54.99 (*0-07-134563-9*) McGraw.

Network Analysis. Gloria H. Cole & Carla E. Chandler. (C). 1989. pap. text 12.00 (*0-13-613191-3*, Macmillan Coll) P-H.

Network Analysis. David Knoke & James H. Kuklinski. (Quantitative Applications in the Social Sciences Ser.: Vol. 28). 88p. 1982. pap. 10.95 (*0-8039-1914-X*) Sage.

Network Analysis. A. K. Walton. (Illus.). 352p. 1987. text 95.00 (*0-521-26459-6*); pap. text 37.95 (*0-521-31903-X*) Cambridge U Pr.

Network Analysis: DC-5510. Randy L. Ratliff. Ed. & Illus. by Michael R. Hall. Illus. by Cathy J. Boulay. (C). 1997. teacher ed., ring bd. 49.95 (*1-884268-94-3*) Marcraft Intl.

Network Analysis: Studies in Human Interaction. Ed. by Jeremy Boissevain & J. Clyde Mitchell. LC 72-77471. (Change & Continuity in Africa Ser.). 1973. 32.35 (*90-279-7187-0*) Mouton.

Network Analysis - ITT Version: DC-5300 ITT. Randy L. Ratliff. Ed. & Illus. by Michael R. Hall. Illus. by Cathy J. Boulay. (C). 1997. teacher ed., ring bd. 35.00 (*1-884268-81-1*); ring bd. 32.95 (*1-884268-82-X*) Marcraft Intl.

***Network Analysis & Troubleshooting.** J. Scott Haugdahl. LC 99-49134. 400p. (C). 1999. pap. text 44.95 (*0-201-43319-2*) Addison-Wesley.

Network Analysis for Management Decisions. S. M. Lee et al. (International Series in Management Science-Operations Research). 1981. lib. bdg. 73.50 (*0-89838-077-4*) Kluwer Academic.

Network Analysis Reference Guide see NetAnalyst Reference Guide: The Definitive Resource for the Network Analyst

***Network Analysis Reference Guide: The Definitive Resource for the Network Analysis.** 9th rev. ed. (Illus.). 104p. 1999. pap. 65.00 (*1-58392-001-3*) Pine Mt.

Network Analysis Techniques. S. K. Bhatnagar. LC 82-23257. 301p. 1987. 28.95 (*0-470-27395-X*) P-H.

***Network Analysis with Applications.** 3rd ed. 1999. teacher ed. write for info. (*0-13-013789-8*) P-H.

Network Analysis with Applications. 3rd ed. William D. Stanley. LC 99-20363. (Illus.). 676p. 1999. 106.00 incl. cd-rom (*0-13-010589-9*) P-H.

Network Analysis with Laplace Transforms for Technology. Frank Tedeschi. (Illus.). 153p. (Orig.). (C). 1988. pap. text 19.00 (*0-929403-02-9*) T&H Pr.

***Network & Certification for Dummies.** Ron Gilster. (For Dummies Ser.). (Illus.). 432p. 1999. pap. 29.99 incl. cd-rom (*0-7645-0545-9*) IDG Bks.

Network & Certification. Syngress Staff. 672p. 1999. student ed. 49.99 (*0-07-211846-6*) McGraw.

***Network & Certification Study Guide.** Joseph F. Byrnes. 384p. 1999. pap. 39.99 (*0-7645-3344-4*) IDG Bks.

***Network & Certification Training.** Patrick T. Lane. Ed. by David Oberman. (Illus.). 1999. pap. write for info. (*1-58143-002-7*, PSG1EUE4) Prosoft I-net.

Network & Certification Training Guide. Charles Brooks. (Training Guides Ser.). 800p. 1999. 89.95 (*0-7357-0077-X*) New Riders Pub.

Network & Discrete Location: Models, Algorithms & Applications. Mark S. Daskin. LC 94-24488. 520p. 1995. 89.95 (*0-471-01897-X*) Wiley.

Network & Distributed Systems Management. Morris Sloman. 688p. (C). 1994. 59.95 (*0-201-62745-0*) Addison-Wesley.

Network & Integration of Facilities Automation Systems Viktor Boed & Ira Goldschmidt. LC 99-15538. 264p. 1999. boxed set 69.95 (*0-8493-0699-X*) CRC Pr.

Network & Internet Security. Vijay Ahuja. (Illus.). 324p. 1999. reprint ed. pap. text 20.00 (*0-7881-6507-0*) DIANE Pub.

Network & Internetwork Security: Principles & Practice. William Stallings. 480p. 1994. 69.95 (*0-7803-1107-8*, PC4614) Inst Electrical.

***Network & Lab Manual.** Tami Evanson. 144p. 1999. pap. 19.99 (*0-7821-2641-3*) Sybex.

Network & NetPlay: Virtual Groups on the Internet. Ed. by Fay Sudweeks et al. LC 97-43441. (AAAI Press Ser.). (Illus.). 333p. 1998. pap. text 35.00 (*0-262-69206-6*) MIT Pr.

Network & Operating System Support for Digital Audio & Video: Proceedings of the Ieee 7th International Workshop on : May 19-21, 1997, Innsbrook Estates Conference Center. LC 96-80423. (Lecture Notes in Computer Science Ser.). 310 p. 1997. write for info. (*0-7803-3800-6*) IEEE Standards.

Network & Operating System Support for Digital Audio & Video: Proceedings of the 4th International Workshop, NOSSDAV '93, Lancaster, U. K., November 3-5, 1993 Proceedings. Ed. by D. Shepherd et al. LC 94-33289. (Lecture Notes in Computer Science Ser.: Vol. 846). 1994. write for info. (*0-387-58404-8*) Spr-Verlag.

Network & Operating System Support for Digital Audio & Video: Proceedings of the 4th International Workshop, NOSSDAV '93, Lancaster, U. K., November 3-5, 1993 Proceedings. Ed. by D. Shepherd et al. LC 94-33289. (Lecture Notes in Computer Science Ser.: Vol. 846). 1994. 44.95 (*3-540-58404-8*) Spr-Verlag.

Network & Operating System Support for Digital Audio & Video: Proceedings, 5th International Workshop, NOSSDAV '95, Durham, New Hampshire, April 19-21, 1995. Ed. by Thomas Little & Riccardo Gusella. LC 95-47131. (Lecture Notes in Computer Science Ser.: No. 1018). 357p. 1995. 62.00 (*3-540-60647-5*) Spr-Verlag.

Network & Operating System Support for Digital Audio & Video: Second International Workshop, Heidelberg, Germany, November 18-19, 1991: Proceedings. Ed. by R. G. Herrtwich et al. LC 92-19698. (Lecture Notes in Computer Science Ser.: Vol. 614). xii, 403p. 1992. 63.95 (*0-387-55639-7*) Spr-Verlag.

Network & Operating System Support for Digital Audio & Video: Third International Workshop, La Jolla, California, U. S. A., November 1992, Proceedings. Ed. by Venkat P. Rangan. LC 93-11825. (Lecture Notes in Computer Science Ser.: Vol. 712). 1993. 61.95 (*0-387-57183-3*) Spr-Verlag.

Network & Practice Tests Exam Cram. Robert Gradante. LC 99-25862. (Exam Cram Ser.). (Illus.). 249p. 1999. pap. 19.99 (*1-57610-484-2*) Coriolis Grp.

***Network Application Programming on Linux/UNIX.** Stephen Heaven. (Illus.). 600p. 2000. pap. text 39.99 (*0-672-31928-4*) Sams.

Network Architecture: Considerations for Design. Ed Taylor. LC 97-34694. 464p. 1998. 89.95 (*0-07-063333-9*) McGraw.

Network Architectures for Distributed Computing. Eduard A. Yakubaitis. Tr. by Martin Morell from RUS. LC 83-70666. x, 415p. 1983. 45.00 (*0-89864-005-9*) Allerton Pr.

Network Auditing: A Control Assessment Approach. Gordon E. Smith. LC 98-51576. 343p. 1999. 75.00 incl. disk (*0-471-17975-2*) Wiley.

Network Bank. Anthony Gandy. 174p. 1999. pap. 500.00 (*0-85297-500-7*, Pub. by Chartered Bank) St Mut.

Network-Based Classrooms: Promises & Realities. Ed. by Bertram Bruce et al. LC 92-31680. (Illus.). 314p. (C). 1993. text 64.95 (*0-521-41636-1*); pap. text 20.95 (*0-521-45702-5*) Cambridge U Pr.

Network-Based Images: A Practical Guide to Acquisition, Storage, Conversion, Compression & Transmission. Gilbert Held. 240p. 1997. text 85.00 (*0-471-97357-2*) Wiley.

Network-Based Language Teaching: Concepts & Practice. Mark Warschauer & Richard Kern. LC 99-12566. (Illus.). 256p. 2000. pap. 22.95 (*0-521-66742-9*) Cambridge U Pr.

***Network-Based Language Teaching: Concepts & Practice.** Mark Warschauer & Richard Kern. (Cambridge Applied Linguistics Ser.). (Illus.). 256p. 2000. 54.95 (*0-521-66136-6*) Cambridge U Pr.

Network-Based Parallel Computing: Communication, Architecture & Applications. A. Sivasubramaniam & M. Lauria. Ed. by G. Goos et al. LC 99-30634. (Lecture Notes in Computer Science Ser.: Vol. 1602). viii, 225p. 1999. pap. 45.00 (*3-540-65915-3*) Spr-Verlag.

Network Cables & Devices. 1999. pap. write for info. (*1-884486-88-6*) Wave Tech.

Network-Centric Computing: Preparing the Enterprise for the Next Millennium. Peter Varhol. LC 97-46547. (Illus.). 189p. 1998. pap. 290.00 (*1-56607-998-5*) Comput Tech Res.

Network Centric Warfare: The Face of Battle in the 21st Century. David S. Alberts et al. LC 98-53271. (CCRP Publication Ser.). 1999. write for info. (*1-57906-019-6*) Natl Defense.

Network+ Certification: Success Guide for Network Administrators. Nancy Cadjan & Dorothy L. Cady. LC 99-12459. (Illus.). 262p. 1999. pap. 24.99 (*0-07-135018-7*) McGraw.

***Network+ Certification Boxed Set.** Media Incorporated Syngress Media Incorporated Staff. 1300p. 1999. 79.99 (*0-07-212033-9*) McGraw.

Network+ Certification Exam Guide. Jonathan Feldman. 500p. 1999. pap. 39.99 (*0-7897-2157-0*) S&S Trade.

***Network+ Certification for Dummies Flash Cards.** Dummies Technical Press Staff. (For Dummies Ser.). 250p. 2000. pap. 24.99 incl. cd-rom (*0-7645-0628-5*) IDG Bks.

Network+ Certification Test Yourself Practice Exams. Syngress Media, Inc. Staff. 749p. 1999. pap. 39.99 (*0-07-212029-0*) McGraw.

Network Communication Technology. Elahi. 2000. 63.95 (*0-7668-1388-6*) Thomson Learn.

Network Communications Manager. (Career Examination Ser.: C-3641). pap. 39.95 (*0-8373-3641-4*) Nat Learn.

Network Competition for European Telecommunications. Oliver Stehmann. (Illus.). 342p. 1996. text 79.00 (*0-19-828925-1*) OUP.

Network Computers vs. High Performance Computers. Dimitris Chorafas. LC 97-185528. 176p. 1997. pap. 28.95 (*0-304-70029-0*) Continuum.

Network Computers vs. High Performance Computers. Dimitris N. Chorafas. LC 97-185528. 1997. 85.00 (*0-304-70028-2*) Continuum.

Network Design: Connectivity & Facilities Location: DIMACS Workshop, April 28-30, 1997. P. M. Panalos & Du Dingzhu. LC 97-45788. (DIMACS Series in Discrete Mathematics & Theoretical Computer Science). 461p. 1998. text 79.00 (*0-8218-0834-6*) Am Math.

Network Design: Management & Technical Perspectives. Teresa C. Rubinson & Kornel Terplan. LC 98-6583. 416p. 1998. boxed set 79.95 (*0-8493-3404-7*) CRC Pr.

***Network Design: Principles & Applications.** Gilbert Held. LC 00-23724. (Best Practices Ser.). 872p. 2000. boxed set 79.95 (*0-8493-0859-3*) CRC Pr.

Network Design & Capacity Planning. Chester Terplan. 1993. 40.00 (*0-07-063637-0*) McGraw.

Network Design, Implementation & Maintenance. 1999. pap. write for info. (*1-884486-92-4*) Wave Tech.

Network Designer's Handbook. Ed. by P. Thompson. (Concurrent Systems Engineering Ser.). 321p. 1998. 76.00 (*90-5199-380-3*) IOS Press.

***Network Developments in Economic Spatial Systems: New Perspectives.** Ed. by Aura Reggiani & Daniele Fabbri. 306p. 1999. text 74.95 (*1-84014-827-6*, Pub. by Ashgate Pub) Ashgate Pub Co.

Network Directory. Granary Pr Ltd Staff. 80p. (C). 1984. 75.00 (*0-86236-022-6*, Pub. by Granary) St Mut.

Network Drafting: An Introduction. Alice Schlein. LC 94-96683. (Illus.). 134p. (C). 1994. pap. text 30.00 (*0-9644474-0-1*) Brdgewater SC.

Network Dynamics in International Marketing. Peter Naude & Peter W. Turnbull. LC 98-8167. (International Business & Management Ser.). xix, 321 p. 1998. 88.50 (*0-08-043358-8*) Elsevier.

Network Economics: A Variational Inequality Approach. Anna Nagurney. LC 92-36524. (Advances in Computational Economics Ser.). 384p. (C). 1992. lib. bdg. 148.50 (*0-7923-9293-0*) Kluwer Academic.

Network Economics: A Variational Inequality Approach. Anna Nagurney. LC 98-45144. 5p. 1999. 150.00 (*0-7923-8350-8*) Kluwer Academic.

***Network+ Exam Cram.** Reeves. (Networking Ser.). (C). 1999. pap. 15.60 (*0-619-01602-7*) Course Tech.

Network+ Exam Cram. Scott Reeves & Kalinda Reeves. LC 99-25789. (Exam Cram (Coriolis' Certification Insider Press) Ser.). (Illus.). 355p. 1999. pap. 29.99 (*1-57610-405-2*) Coriolis Grp.

***Network+ Exam Fast Track.** Glenn Berg. (Fast Track (Hal Leonard) Ser.). (Illus.). 351p. 1999. pap. 29.99 (*0-7357-0904-1*) New Riders Pub.

Network Exchange Theory. Ed. by David Willer. LC 98-56070. 352p. 1999. 75.00 (*0-275-95377-7*, Praeger Pubs); pap. 27.95 (*0-275-95378-5*, Praeger Pubs) Greenwood.

Network File System Version 4. Brent Callaghan. LC 99-56696. 448p. (C). 1999. 49.95 (*0-201-32570-5*) Addison-Wesley.

Network Flow Programming. Paul A. Jensen & J. Wesley Barnes. LC 87-3678. 426p. 1987. reprint ed. lib. bdg. 51.50 (*0-89464-210-3*) Krieger.

Network Flows: Theory, Algorithms, & Applications. Ravindra K. Ahuja et al. 864p. 1993. 105.00 (*0-13-617549-X*) P-H.

Network Flows & Matching: First DIMACS Implementation Challenge. Ed. by David S. Johnson & Catherine C. McGeoch. LC 93-28698. (DIMACS Series in Discrete Mathematics & Theoretical Computer Science: Vol. 12). 592p. 1993. text 96.00 (*0-8218-6598-6*, DIMACS/12) Am Math.

Network Flows & Monotropic Optimization. R. Tyrell Rockafellar. LC 98-72723. 634p. (C). 1998. text 49.50 (*1-886529-06-X*) Athena Scientific.

Network for Effective Transitions to Work: A Transition Coordinator's Handbook. Margo Izzo & Kathryn Shumate. 1991. 25.00 (*0-317-04055-3*, LT72) Ctr Educ Trng Employ.

***Network Infrastructure & the Urban Environment: Advances in Spatial Systems Modelling.** Ed. by L. Lundqvist et al. LC 98-28004. (Advances in Spatial Science Ser.). (Illus.). x, 414p. 1998. 99.00 (*3-540-64585-3*) Spr-Verlag.

Network Infrastructure Design: Mcse Fast Track. 400p. 1900. 29.99 (*0-7357-0985-8*) New Riders Pub.

***Network Inside Out.** Annelise Riles. LC 99-87959. 304p. (C). 1999. text 44.50 (*0-472-11071-3*, 11071) U of Mich Pr.

***Network Instrusion Detection.** 450p. 2000. 45.00 (*0-7357-1008-2*) New Riders Pub.

Network Interface Technical Guide. Ed. by Douglas T. Anderson & Michael Bethany. (Illus.). (Orig.). 1992. pap. 89.95 (*1-880252-21-X*) Micro Hse.

Network Interface Technical Guide, Vol. S-B. rev. ed. Ed. by Douglas T. Anderson & Robert Newkirk, Jr. (Illus.). (Orig.). 1993. write for info. (*1-880252-26-0*) Micro Hse.

Network Interrupts: A Programmer's Reference to Network APIs. Ralf Brown & Jim Kyle. 736p. (C). 1994. pap. 32.95 (*0-201-62644-6*) Addison-Wesley.

Network Intrusion Detection: An Analyst's Handbook. Stephen Northcutt. (Illus.). 267p. 1999. pap. 39.99 (*0-7357-0868-1*) New Riders Pub.

Network Layer Switched Services. Daniel Minoli & Andrew Schmidt. LC 97-31834. 384p. 1998. 49.99 (*0-471-19080-2*) Wiley.

Network Maintenance & Troubleshooting Guide. Neal Allen. Ed. by Joan Good. LC 97-60196. (Illus.). 176p. (Orig.). 1997. pap. text 29.95 (*0-9638650-1-3*) Fluke.

Network Management. Manu Malek-Zavarei. 1999. audio compact disk 250.00 (*0-7803-5309-9*) IEEE Standards.

Network Management: A Practical Perspective. 2nd ed. Allan Leinwand & Karen Fang. Ed. by Tom Stone. LC 95-23029. 352p. (C). 1995. pap. text 39.95 (*0-201-60999-1*) Addison-Wesley.

Network Management: Principles & Practice. Mani Subramanian. LC 99-47374. 644p. (C). 1999. 58.00 (*0-201-35742-9*) Addison-Wesley.

Network Management: Techniques, Tools & Systems. Gilbert Held. LC 91-29940. 250p. 1992. reprint ed. pap. 77.50 (*0-608-04596-9*, 206536600003) Bks Demand.

Network Management & Control, Vol. 1. A. Kershenbaum et al. LC 90-33945. (Illus.). 460p. (C). 1990. 125.00 (*0-306-43587-X*, Plenum Trade) Perseus Pubng.

Network Management & Control, Vol. 2. I. T. Frisch et al. (Illus.). 526p. (C). 1994. 125.00 (*0-306-44807-6*, Plenum Trade) Perseus Pubng.

Network Management Basics. Jack Dempsey. LC 97-73097. 120p. (Orig.). 1997. pap. 29.95 (*0-87288-648-4*) Intertec IL.

Network Management Handbook. Bellcore Technical Personnel. (Illus.). 536p. (C). 1990. 495.00 (*1-878108-10-7*) Telcordia Technologies.

Network Management Markets. 250p. 1992. pap. 2995.00 (*1-56851-004-7*, IGIC-49) Info Gatekeepers.

Network Management Standards: SNMP, CMIP, TMN, MIBs & Object Libraries. 2nd ed. Ulysses D. Black. LC 94-22288. 351p. 1994. 50.00 (*0-07-005570-X*) McGraw.

***Network Management Suites Unraveled: How to Reduce Your Network Management Costs.** Matthew Flint Arnett. 2000. pap. 39.95 (*1-55860-660-2*) Morgan Kaufmann.

Network Management Survival Guide. Fred Engel. 84p. 1998. pap. 3.00 (*0-9668663-0-4*) Concord Commns.

Network Management Systems. Udupa. 1998. 65.00 (*0-07-065834-X*) McGraw.

Network Management with Intel LANDesk Management Suite 6: Managing Nodes Student Manual. Barbara S. Josephson & Brian K. Mason. (Illus.). iv, 243p. 1998. student ed. 79.99 (*1-893854-00-3*) TriTech Ed.

Network Management with Intel LANDesk Management Suite 6 Vol. 2: Installation & Design Student Manual. Barbara S. Josephson & Brian K. Mason. (Illus.). viii, 148p. 1999. student ed. 79.99 (*1-893854-01-9*) TriTech Ed.

Network Manager's Handbook. John M. Lusa. LC 98-2700. 1998. lib. bdg. 175.00 (*0-8493-9958-0*) CRC Pr.

***Network Manager's Handbook.** John M. Lusa. LC 98-46525. 25p. 1998. lib. bdg. 95.00 (*0-8493-9990-4*) CRC Pr.

***Network Manager's Handbook.** 3rd ed. John M. Lusa. LC 99-43797. (Best Practices Ser.). 592p. 1999. boxed set 79.95 (*0-8493-9841-X*) CRC Pr.

Network Marketer's Guide to Success. Jeffrey A. Babener & David Stewart. (Illus.). 240p. 1990. text 24.95 (*0-9628055-0-5*) Forum Network Mktg.

Network Marketing: The Accelerated Game of Life. Randy J. Ward. LC 84-72262. Orig. Title: Winning the Greatest Game of All. (Illus.). 160p. 1998. pap. 12.95 (*0-9613958-7-7*) Prosperity OK.

Network Marketing: The Best of the Best. David Stone & Warren Brookings. 144p. 1995. pap. 11.95 (*0-9648949-0-4*) Sunrise Pr MN.

Network Marketing: The Business of the 90's. Bud Corkin & Mary Averill. Ed. by Andrea Reider. LC 93-73201. (Fifty-Minute Ser.). (Illus.). 78p. (Orig.). 1994. pap. 10.95 (*1-56052-244-5*) Crisp Pubns.

Network Marketing Business Builder Action Pack. Network Action Company Staff. (Illus.). 580p. 1997. ring bd. 124.95 incl. audio, VHS (*0-9664224-0-6*, 02BBAP) Netwrk Action.

***Network Marketing for Christians: A Journey along the King's High Way.** Bill Boylan. 107p. 1999. 11.95 (*0-7414-0166-5*) Buy Books.

***Network Marketing for Dummies.** Zig Ziglar. 384p. 2000. pap. 19.99 (*0-7645-5292-9*) IDG Bks.

Network Marketing Game: Gospel Perspectives on Multi-Level Marketing. Jon M. Taylor. LC 97-93944. (Illus.). 256p. 1997. pap. 12.95 (*0-9657947-0-9*, 01) King Alfred Pr.

Network Modeling Simulation & Analysis. Ricardo F. Garzia. (Electrical Engineering & Electronics Ser.: Vol. 61). (Illus.). 400p. 1990. text 155.00 (*0-8247-7876-6*) Dekker.

***Network Models for Control & Processing.** Ed. by Martin D. Fraser. 192p. 2000. 49.95 (*1-84150-006-2*, Pub. by Intellect) Intl Spec Bk.

Network Models in Optimization & Their Applications in Practice. Nancy V. Phillips et al. LC 91-41110. (Wiley-Interscience Series in Discrete Mathematics & Optimization). 304p. 1992. 109.95 (*0-471-57138-5*) Wiley.

Network Models in Population Biology. E. R. Lewis. LC 77-5873. (Biomathematics Ser.: Vol 7). 1977. 52.95 (*0-387-08214-X*) Spr-Verlag.

Network Models of the Diffusion of Innovations. Thomas W. Valente. Ed. by George Barnett. LC 94-24387. (Communication Series). 192p. 1994. text 45.00 (*1-881303-21-7*); pap. text 21.95 (*1-881303-22-5*) Hampton Pr NJ.

***Network Monitoring & Analysis: A Protocol Approach to Troubleshooting.** Ed Wilson. 350p. 1999. pap. 41.00 (*0-13-026495-4*) P-H.

Network Monitoring Explained. Chiu Dah Ming & Ram Sudama. 207p. (C). 1992. 100.00 (*0-13-614710-0*) P-H.

Network Nation: Human Communication Via Computer. rev. ed. Starr Roxanne Hiltz & Murray Turoff. LC 92-41470. (Illus.). 550p. 1993. pap. text 31.50 (*0-262-58120-5*) MIT Pr.

***Network Nightmare Language Arts.** McGraw-Hill Book Company Staff. (J). (gr. 4). 1999. 19.95 (*1-57768-334-X*) MG-Hill OH.

Network of Champions: What's Right about America - And How to Be a Part of It! Shad Helmstetter. 1995. pap. 12.95 (*0-9645171-1-6*) Chapel & Croft.

Network of Champions: What's Right about America & How to Be a Part of It! Shad Helmstetter. 1995. 19.95 (*0-9645171-0-8*) Chapel & Croft.

Network of Control: State Supreme Courts & State Security Statutes, 1920-1970, 22. Carol E. Jenson. LC 81-6385. (Contributions in Legal Studies: No. 22). 205p. 1982. 57.95 (*0-313-22492-7*, JNE/, Greenwood Pr) Greenwood.

Network of Objects: How to Lower Your Computing Cost & Improve Your Application Memory. Thomas C. Tsai. (VNR Communications Library). 326p. 1994. pap. 41.95 (*0-471-28665-6*, VNR) Wiley.

Network of Objects: How to Lower Your Computing Costs & Improve Application Delivery. Thomas C. Tsai. LC 94-31519. 326p. 1995. pap. 41.95 (*0-442-01933-5*, VNR) Wiley.

Network Operating Systems. 1999. pap. write for info. (*1-884486-90-8*) Wave Tech.

Network Operating Systems. Phillip Hunter. 288p. (C). 1994. pap. text 28.13 (*0-201-62766-3*) Addison-Wesley.

Network Optimization, Vol. 450. Panos M. Pardalos et al. LC 97-642. (Lecture Notes in Economics & Mathematical Systems Ser.). 1997. pap. write for info. (*3-540-62541-0*) Spr-Verlag.

Network Optimization: Continuous & Discrete Models. Dimitri P. Bertsekas. LC 98-70298. 608p. (C). 1998. text 74.00 (*1-886529-02-7*) Athena Scientific.

Network Optimization Problems: Algorithms, Applications & Complexity. D. Z. Du & Panos M. Pardalos. (Series on Applied Mathematics). 416p. 1993. text 109.00 (*981-02-1277-1*) World Scientific Pub.

Network Organizations & Information Technology: A Special Issue of the Journal of Organizational Computing & Electronic Commerce, Vol. 7, Nos. 2 & 3. Ed. by Chee Ching. 210p. 1997. pap. 20.00 (*0-8058-9857-3*) L Erlbaum Assocs.

***Network Performance Baselining.** 500p. 2000. 50.00 (*1-57870-240-2*) Macmillan Tech.

Network Performance Modeling & Simulation. Ed. by Jean Walrand & Kallol Bagchi. 332p. 1998. text 42.00 (*90-5699-596-0*) Gordon & Breach.

Network Planning & Management: Your Personal Consultant. Steve Ringney. 1995. pap. text 24.95 (*1-56276-309-1*, Ziff-Davis Pr) Que.

Network Planning, Procurement, & Management. Nathan J. Muller. (Illus.). 608p. 1996. 75.00 (*0-07-044362-9*) McGraw.

Network + Career Pack. 1999. pap. write for info. (*1-884486-87-8*) Wave Tech.

***Network + Certification.** Kostya Ryvkin et al. LC 99-56523. 500p. 1999. 49.99 (*0-13-016895-5*) P-H.

***Network + Certification Training: Version 2.07.** Patrick T. Lane. Ed. by David Oberman. (CIW Internetworking Professional Track Ser.). (Illus.). 1999. pap. write for info. (*1-58143-052-3*) Prosoft I-net.

Network+ Exam Notes. David Groth & Ben Bergersen. (Network+ Ser.). (Illus.). 411p. 1999. pap. 19.99 (*0-7821-2546-8*) Sybex.

***Network+ Exam Prep.** Melissa Craft et al. LC 99-31053. (Exam Prep (Coriolis' Certification Insider Press) Ser.). (Illus.). 695p. 1999. pap. 44.99 incl. cd-rom (*1-57610-412-5*) Coriolis Grp.

Network + Getting Started: Users Guide. 1999. pap. write for info. (*1-884486-94-0*) Wave Tech.

Network + Study Guide. 1999. pap. write for info. (*1-884486-93-2*) Wave Tech.

***Network+ Study Guide.** David Groth. LC 99-61814. (Network+ Ser.). 736p. 1999. student ed. 49.99 (*0-7821-2547-6*) Sybex.

***Network+ Test Success.** David Groth. (Network+ Ser.). 480p. 1999. pap. text 24.99 (*0-7821-2548-4*) Sybex.

***Network + X: A4, Version 2.07.** Patrick T. Lane. Ed. by David Oberman. (CIW Internetworking Professional Track A4 Ser.). (Illus.). 1999. pap. write for info. (*1-58143-088-4*) Prosoft I-net.

Network Power: Japan in Asia. Peter J. Katzenstein. Ed. by Takashi Shiraishi. LC 96-38802. (Illus.). 416p. 1996. pap. text 22.50 (*0-8014-8373-5*) Cornell U Pr.

Network Power: Japan in Asia. Ed. by Peter J. Katzenstein & Takashi Shiraishi. LC 96-38802. (Illus.). 416p. 1996. text 59.95 (*0-8014-3314-2*) Cornell U Pr.

Network Press Dictionary of Networking. 2nd ed. Peter Dyson. LC 95-70853. 416p. 1995. pap. text 22.99 (*0-7821-1818-6*, Network Pr) Sybex.

Network Press Encyclopedia of Networking. 3rd ed. Werner Feibel. (Network Press Ser.). 1504p. 1999. 84.99 (*0-7821-2255-8*) Sybex.

Network Press QuickPath to Netware 4.11 Networks. 2nd ed. Jeffrey F. Hughes & Blair W. Thomas. LC 96-68706. 480p. 1996. pap. text 29.99 (*0-7821-1883-6*, Network Pr) Sybex.

Network Printing Solutions. Logan Harbaugh. 672p. 1997. pap. text 44.99 incl. cd-rom (*0-7821-2040-7*) Sybex.

Network Program Interface. UNIX System Laboratories Staff. 448p. 1993. pap. text 30.00 (*0-13-177064-0*, Pub. by P-H) S&S Trade.

Network Programming. Katta B. Murty. (C). 1992. text 63.80 (*0-13-615493-X*) P-H.

***Network Programming for Microsoft Windows.** Anthony Jones. LC 99-34581. (Microsoft Programming Ser.). (Illus.). 600p. 1999. pap. 49.99 (*0-7356-0560-2*) Microsoft.

Network Programming in CA-Clipper 5.2. Joe Booth & Greg Lief. (Programming Ser.). (Illus.). 464p. 1993. pap. 29.95 incl. disk (*1-56276-119-6*, Ziff-Davis Pr) Que.

Network Programming in Fox Pro. Joe Booth & Greg Lief. (Programming Ser.). (Illus.). 304p. 1993. pap. 29.95 incl. disk (*1-56276-167-6*, Ziff-Davis Pr) Que.

Network Programming in Windows NT. Alok K. Sinha. (UNIX & Open Systems Ser.). 632p. (C). 1996. pap. 51.95 (*0-201-59056-5*) Addison-Wesley.

Network Programming under VMS DECNet Phases IV & V. Edward B. Toupin. 1993. pap. 39.95 (*0-89435-441-8*) Wiley.

Network Programming under VMS DECNet Phases IV & V. Edward B. Toupin. 320p. 1993. pap. 59.99 (*0-471-60305-8*, GD4418) Wiley.

Network Programming with Microsoft Visual J++ 6.0. Andy Wilson. LC 98-38262. 358p. 49.99 incl. cd-rom (*1-57231-855-4*) Microsoft.

Network Programming with Windows Sockets. Patrice Bonner. LC 95-40773. 512p. (C). 1995. pap. 39.95 incl. disk (*0-13-230152-0*) P-H.

Network Programming with WinSock. Bob Quinn & David K. Shute. LC 95-35247. 656p. (C). 1995. 49.95 (*0-201-63372-8*) Addison-Wesley.

Network Protocals. 1999. pap. write for info. (*1-884486-89-4*) Wave Tech.

Network Protocol Handbook: Signature Edition. 2nd ed. Matthew G. Naugle. LC 98-20249. (Computer Communications Ser.). 650p. 1998. pap. 59.95 (*0-07-046603-3*) McGraw.

***Network Protocols: Proceedings of the 7th International Conference, Toronto, Canada, 1999.** 343p. 1999. 120.00 (*0-7695-0412-4*) IEEE Comp Soc.

Network Re-engineering: The New Technical Imperative. James T. Geier. (McGraw-Hill Computer Communications Series). (Illus.). 319p. 1996. 45.00 (*0-07-023034-X*) McGraw.

Network Reliability: Experiments with a Symbolic Algebra Environment. Darl D. Harms. Ed. by C. J. Colbourn et al. LC 95-16931. (Discrete Mathematics & Its Applications Ser.). 240p. 1995. lib. bdg. 89.95 (*0-8493-3980-4*, 3980) CRC Pr.

Network Remote Access & Mobile Computing: Implementing Effective Remote Access to Networks & E-Mail. Ed. by Melanie McMullen. (Illus.). 230p. 1994. pap. 29.95 (*0-87930-334-4*) Miller Freeman.

Network Revolution: Confession of a Computer Scientist. Jacques Vallee. (Illus.). 210p. (Orig.). 1982. pap. 7.95 (*0-915904-73-X*) And-Or Bks.

Network Routing. Ed. by M. O. Ball et al. LC 95-41879. (Handbooks in Operations Research & Management Science Ser.: Vol. 8). 796p. 1995. 165.00 (*0-444-82141-4*) Elsevier.

Network Scattering Parameters. R. Mavaddat. (Advanced Series on Circuits & Systems). 350p. 1996. text 68.00 (*981-02-2305-6*) World Scientific Pub.

Network Scheduling Techniques for Construction Project Management. Miklos Hajdu. LC 96-37406. (Nonconvex Optimization & Its Applications Ser.). 352p. (C). 1997. lib. bdg. 191.50 (*0-7923-4309-3*) Kluwer Academic.

N

An Asterisk (*) at the beginning of an entry indicates that the title is appearing for the first time.

Network Science, a Decade Later: The Internet & Classroom Learning. Alan Feldman et al. LC 99-38653. 160p. 1999. write for info. (*0-8058-3425-7*); pap. write for info. (*0-8058-3426-5*) L Erlbaum Assocs.

Network, Screen & Page: The Future of Reading in a Digital Age. Interquest Staff & University of Virginia Staff. 120p. 1997. pap. 145.00 (*0-9658790-1-1*) EDSF.

*__Network Security.__ Owen Poole. 208p. 2001. pap. 47.95 (*0-7506-5033-8*) Buttrwrth-Heinemann.

Network Security. Schiller. 2000. text. write for info. (*0-13-227083-8*) P-H.

Network Security: Data & Voice Communications. Fred Simonds. LC 95-30723. (Computers Communications Ser.). 395p. 1995. 60.00 (*0-07-057639-4*) McGraw.

Network Security: Developing & Implementing Effective Enterprise Strategies. Barry Slawter. LC 99-16331. (Illus.). 181p. 1999. pap. 275.00 (*1-56607-074-0*) Comput Tech Res.

Network Security: How to Plan for It & Achieve It. Richard H. Baker. LC 94-20430. 1994. 45.00 (*0-07-005119-4*); pap. 34.95 (*0-07-005141-0*) McGraw.

Network Security: Standards Protocols & Algorithms. Charles Kaufman. 640p. (C). 1995. 63.00 (*0-13-061466-1*) P-H.

*__Network Security & Firewalls: A4, Version 3.07.__ Timothy Crothers & James Stanger. Ed. by Jill McKenna & David Oberman. (CIW Security Professional Track A4 Ser.). (Illus.). 1999. pap. write for info. (*1-58143-089-2*) Prosoft I-net.

*__Network Security & Firewalls: Version 3.07.__ Timothy Crothers & James Stanger. (CIW Security Professional Track Ser.). (Illus.). 1999. pap. write for info. (*1-58143-053-1*) Prosoft I-net.

Network Security & Firewalls Conference 4 (1997) Proceedings. Ed. by Pete Cafarchio. (Illus.). 115p. (C). 1998. pap. text 50.00 (*0-7881-7156-9*) DIANE Pub.

*__Network Security Essentials: Applications & Standards.__ William Stallings. LC 99-45765. 366p. 1999. pap. 41.00 (*0-13-016093-8*) P-H.

Network Security in the 90's: Issues & Solutions for Managers. Thomas W. Madron. LC 92-7427. 304p. 1992. pap. 32.95 (*0-471-54777-8*) Wiley.

Network Security Manager. P. Christmas et al. 138p. 1992. 307.00 (*1-85617-126-4*, Pub. by Elsvr Adv Tech) Elsevier.

Network Security Secrets. Sylvia Moon & David J. Stang. (Illus.). 1200p. 1993. pap. 49.95 (*1-56884-021-7*) IDG Bks.

Network Services Management. CCTA Staff et al. (IT Infrastructure Library Ser.). 200p. 1994. pap. 80.00 (*0-11-330558-3*, Pub. by Statnry Office) Sftware Mgmt Network.

Network Society: Economic Development & International Competitiveness As Problems of Social Governance. Dirk Messner & Deutsches Institute Staff. LC 97-23233. (German Development Institute Ser.). 413p. (C). 1997. pap. 39.95 (*0-7146-4402-1*, Pub. by F Cass Pubs) Intl Spec Bk.

Network Starter Kit. Emmett Dulaney. LC 94-34770. (Illus.). 518p. (Orig.). 1994. pap. 29.99 (*1-56205-403-1*) New Riders Pub.

Network Storage Solutions. 500p. 1900. 50.00 (*1-57870-243-7*) Macmillan Tech.

*__Network+ Sybex E-Trainer.__ K. T. Solutions Staff. 2000. pap. 49.99 (*0-7821-5001-2*) Sybex.

*__Network Systems Design.__ Ed. by Erol Gelenbe et al. 292p. 1999. text 65.00 (*90-5699-635-5*, Harwood Acad Pubs) Gordon & Breach.

*__Network Systems Design & Network Performance Modeling & Simulation Two-Volume Set.__ Ed. by Erol Gelenbe et al. 1998. text 117.00 (*90-5699-653-3*, Harwood Acad Pubs) Gordon & Breach.

Network Systems Tutorial for the IEEE Std. 802.3: Repeater Functions & System Design Topology Considerations for Carrier Sense Multiple Access with Collision Detection (CSMA) Local Area Networks (LANs) Ed. by Tony Peatfield. LC 95-22626. 1995. write for info. (*1-55937-524-8*) IEEE Standards.

Network Technical Guide. Micro House Staff. LC 98-131562. 1997. pap. text 49.95 incl. cd-rom (*1-880252-31-7*) Micro Hse.

Network Television News. Paul Simpson. 1996. pap. 12.00 (*1-880692-08-2*) Legacy Comms.

*__Network Therapy for Alcohol & Drug Abuse.__ Marc Galanter. LC 98-52868. 10p. 1999. pap. text 21.00 (*1-57230-441-3*) Guilford Pubns.

Network Threats: DIMCS Workshop, December, 1996. Rebecca N. Wright & Peter Neumann. LC 97-30683. (DIMACS Series in Discrete Mathematics & Theoretical Computer Science). 110p. 1997. text 29.00 (*0-8218-0832-X*) Am Math.

Network to Home Repair & Decorating Services: Central New Jersey. Ellen Laird et al. 1998. pap. 16.95 (*0-9660791-0-8*) Lairhse Pubns.

Network to Home Repair & Decorating Services: Northern New Jersey Edition. Ellen Laird & Barbara Brunhouse. (Illus.). 250p. 1999. pap. 18.95 (*0-9660791-2-4*, Lairhse Guide); pap. 18.95 (*0-9660791-3-2*) Lairhse Pubns.

Network Toolkit Vol. I: Manufacturing Networks & Competitive Manufacturing. Ed. by Brian Bosworth & Daniel Brown. (Illus.). 267p. (Orig.). (C). 1997. pap. 60.00 (*0-9636927-7-1*) Reg Tech Strat.

Network Toolkit Vol. II: Business Opportunity Networks. Michael Collins. 77p. (Orig.). (C). 1997. pap. 40.00 (*0-9636927-6-3*) Reg Tech Strat.

*__Network Training & Test Preparation Guide.__ Specialized Solutions, Inc. Staff. Ed. by Susan Schmidt. (Illus.). 331p. 1999. pap. text. write for info. (*1-893596-03-6*) Specialized Solns.

N

Network Training Guide: Managing Netware Systems. 3rd ed. Debra Niedermiller-Chaffins. LC 94-28058. 800p. 1994. 70.00 incl. disk (*1-56205-366-3*) New Riders Pub.

Network Training Guide: Networking Technologies. 3rd ed. Debra Niedermiller-Chaffins. LC 94-33319. 1244p. 1994. pap. 70.00 incl. disk (*1-56205-363-9*) New Riders Pub.

Network Troubleshooting. (C). 1996. write for info. (*0-201-41847-9*) Addison-Wesley.

Network Troubleshooting. Taylor. 1999. 74.95 (*0-07-134382-2*) McGraw.

Network Troubleshooting & Repair. Mike Meyers. 1100p. 1999. 59.95 (*0-07-913737-7*) McGraw.

Network Troubleshooting Handbook. Ed Taylor. LC 98-32296. (Taylor Networking Ser.). (Illus.). 909p. 1999. pap. 59.99 (*0-07-134228-1*) McGraw.

*__Network Tutorial: A Complete Introduction to Networks.__ Network Magazine Editors. 480p. 1999. pap. 29.95 (*1-57820-044-X*, Pub. by Telecom Bks) Publishers Group.

Network Version C & C++ Multi. Deitel. 1997. pap. text 790.00 (*0-13-890062-0*) P-H.

Network Your Way to Endless Romance: Secrets to Help You Meet the Mate of Your Dreams. Bob Burg & Laurie S. Brockway. LC 95-94808. 238p. 1997. pap. 9.95 (*0-9650285-1-8*) Samark Pubng.

Network Your Way to Millions: The Definitive Step by Step Guide to Wealth in Network Marketing. Russ Paley. Ed. by Walt Kleine. (Illus.). 280p. Date not set. pap. 14.95 (*0-9672238-0-6*) Wealth Health.

*__Network 2.0 for Dummies.__ Stearns. 384p. 2001. pap. 24.99 incl. cd-rom (*0-7645-0660-9*) IDG Bks.

Networked Applications: A First Course on the New Computing Infrastructure. David G. Messerschmitt. Ed. by Dave Clark. LC 99-44481. (Networking Ser.). 500p. (C). 1999. text 69.95 (*1-55860-537-1*) Morgan Kaufmann.

Networked Applications: A Guide to the New Computing Infrastructure. David G. Messerschmitt. Ed. by David Clark. LC 98-52772. (Networking Ser.). 416p. 1999. pap. text 34.95 (*1-55860-536-3*, Pub. by Morgan Kaufmann) Harcourt.

Networked Business Solutions: A Management Approach. Nigel Hinton. LC 92-13918. 1992. write for info. (*0-07-707661-3*) McGraw.

*__Networked Futures: Trends for Communication Systems Development.__ Bill Whyte. LC 98-48783. 406p. (C). 1999. 79.95 (*0-471-98794-8*) Wiley.

*__Networked Group Communication: Proceedings of the 1st International COST 264 Workshop, NGC'99, Pisa, Italy, November 17-20, 1999.__ rev. ed. Ed. by Luigi Rizzo & Serge Fdida. LC 99-56376. (Lecture Notes in Computer Science Ser.: Vol. 1736). xiii, 339p. 1999. pap. 62.00 (*3-540-66782-2*) Spr-Verlag.

Networked Information & Online Libraries. unabridged ed. Internet Multicasting Services Staff. Ed. by Tim O'Reilly. (Computer Science). 1993. pap. 9.95 (*1-56592-998-5*) Thomson Learn.

Networked Multimedia Systems: Concepts, Architecture & Design. S. V. Raghavan & Satish K. Tripathi. LC 97-27377. 397p. 1997. 71.00 (*0-13-210642-6*) P-H.

Networked Organization: A Resource Based Perspective. Peter S. Ring. (Studia Oeconomiae Negotiorum: Vol. 39). 52p. (Orig.). 1996. pap. 32.50 (*91-554-3685-4*) Coronet Bks.

Networked Protocols, 1997 International Conference on ICNP '97. 155p. 1997. pap. 110.00 (*0-8186-8061-X*) IEEE Comp Soc.

Networked Protocols, 1996 International Conference on ICNP '96. LC 96-77034. 400p. 1996. pap. 80.00 (*0-8186-7453-9*) IEEE Comp Soc.

Networked Virtual Environments: Design & Implementation. Michael Zyda & Sandeep Singhal. LC 99-31315. (Illus.). 352p. (C). 1999. 54.95 (*0-201-32557-8*) Addison-Wesley.

Networker's Practical Reference. Robert Graham. 1994. 50.00 (*0-07-024036-1*) McGraw.

Networker's Practical Reference. Sheldon. 1994. pap. 34.95 (*0-07-024037-X*) McGraw.

Networking. (Illus.). 410p. 1996. pap. 21.95 (*1-55512-256-6*) McGraw.

Networking. Heenehan. LC 97-220317. (Princeton Review Job Notes Ser.). 1997. pap. 4.95 (*0-679-77877-2*) Random.

Networking. Douglass B. Richardson. 224p. 1994. pap. 10.95 (*0-471-31027-1*) Wiley.

*__Networking: A Beginner's Guide.__ Bruce A. Hallberg. 365p. 1999. pap. 29.99 incl. cd-rom (*0-07-212226-9*) McGraw.

Networking: Choosing a LAN Path to Interconnection. Marlyn Kemper. LC 87-12907. (Illus.). 297p. 1987. 39.50 (*0-8108-2031-5*) Scarecrow.

Networking: How to Creatively Tap Your People Resources. Colleen Clarke. xiv, 62p. (Orig.). 1993. pap. 12.95 (*1-878542-41-9*, 12-0011) SkillPath Pubns.

Networking: The Natural Extension of You. John Sexsmith et al. 160p. text 19.95 (*1-882441-51-6*); pap. text 12.95 (*1-882441-52-4*) InANutshell Bks.

Networking - The Skill the Schools Forgot to Teach: What You Need to Know to Get Ahead in Business. Cynthia D'Amour. viii, 120p. (Orig.). 1996. pap. 14.95 (*0-9654600-0-2*) Jump Start Bks.

*__Networking Administration for Netware Versions 4.11 & 5.__ Richard McMahon. 448p. 1999. pap. 46.95 (*0-538-69089-5*) Sth-Wstrn College.

Networking & Communications Desk Reference. Ken Sochats. 1992. 19.95 (*0-672-30096-6*) Sams.

Networking & Community Partnership. 2nd ed. Steve Trevillion. LC 98-52025. 200p. 1999. pap. 39.95 (*1-85742-426-3*) Ashgate Pub Co.

Networking & Data Communications. Ed. by Frances S. Grodzinsky. LC 98-45999. 182p. 1998. pap., lab manual ed. 22.00 (*0-13-011702-1*) P-H.

*__Networking & Internetworking in Belgium: A Strategic Entry Report, 1996.__ Compiled by Icon Group International Staff. (Illus.). 133p. 1999. ring bd. 1330.00 incl. audio compact disk (*0-7418-1471-4*) Icon Grp.

Networking & Telecommunications for Information Systems: An Introduction to Information Networking. Steve Harries. LC 94-7685. 253p. 1993. reprint ed. pap. 78.50 (*0-608-07770-4*, 206785800010) Bks Demand.

*__Networking & the Future of Libraries.__ Richard Heseltine. (Information Landscapes for a Learning Society Ser.: No. 3). 224p. 1999. 75.00 (*1-85604-310-X*, LAP310X, Pub. by Library Association) Bernan Associates.

Networking & the Future of Libraries No. 2: Managing & Intellectual Record. Lorcam Dempsey et al. LC 97-186374. 256p. 1995. pap. text 75.00 (*1-85604-158-1*, LAP1581, Pub. by Library Association) Bernan Associates.

Networking at Writer's Conferences: From Contacts to Contracts. Steven D. Spratt & Lee G. Spratt. LC 94-41639. 179p. 1995. pap. 12.95 (*0-471-05522-0*) Wiley.

Networking Basics. Ciampa. (Computer Applications Ser.). 1999. pap. 12.00 (*0-538-69043-7*) Thomson Learn.

Networking Basics. Ciampa. (Computer Applications Ser.). 1999. pap. 40.95 (*0-538-69042-9*) Thomson Learn.

*__Networking Bible.__ Sue Plumley. 2000. pap. 39.99 (*0-7645-3499-8*) IDG Bks.

*__Networking by Example.__ 450p. 2000. 24.99 (*0-7897-2356-5*) P-H.

*__Networking CD Bookshelf.__ Ed. by O'Reilly & Associates Staff. (Illus.). 456p. 1998. pap. 79.95 incl. cd-rom (*1-56592-523-8*) OReilly & Assocs.

Networking CD-ROMs: The Decision Maker's Guide to Local Area Network Solutions. Ahmed M. Elshami. LC 95-40315. (Illus.). 339p. 1996. pap. 50.00 (*0-8389-0670-2*, 0670-2-2045) ALA.

*__Networking Complete.__ 4th ed. 1008p. 1999. 19.99 (*0-7821-2610-3*) Sybex.

Networking, Connecting Workers in & Between Organizations: Proceedings of Working Conference on Networking, Vienna, Austria, 16-18 June 1993. Ed. by A. Clement et al. LC 93-45315. (IFIP Transactions A: Computer Science & Technology Ser.: Vol. A-38). 264p. 1994. 104.50 (*0-444-81720-4*, North Holland) Elsevier.

Networking Developers Guide with Visual BASIC. 1998. 45.00 (*0-672-30803-7*) Sams.

Networking Device Drivers. Sanjay Dhawan. (B & F - Computer Science Ser.). 398p. 1994. pap. 48.95 (*0-442-01943-2*, VNR) Wiley.

Networking Device Drivers. Sanjay Dhawan. (VNR Communications Library). 416p. 1995. pap. 59.95 (*0-471-28671-0*, VNR) Wiley.

Networking Equipment in Australia: A Strategic Entry Report, 1996. Compiled by Icon Group International Staff. (Illus.). 134p. 1999. ring bd. 1340.00 incl. audio compact disk (*0-7418-1129-4*) Icon Grp.

Networking Essentials. 274p. 1997. pap. write for info. (*1-884486-23-1*) Wave Tech.

*__Networking Essentials.__ ENI Publishing Ltd. Staff. (Preparacion para el Examen MCSE Ser.). 2000. pap. 55.95 (*2-7460-0766-5*) ENI Publng.

Networking Essentials. Michael A. Pastore. LC 97-45352. (Rapid Review Study Guides Ser.). 200p. 1997. pap. 29.95 incl. cd-rom (*1-882419-90-1*, Pub. by News Four-Hund) IPG Chicago.

Networking Essentials. 2nd ed. Microsoft Corporation Staff. LC 97-34595. 800p. 1997. pap. text 99.99 (*1-57231-527-X*) Microsoft.

*__Networking Essentials.__ 3rd ed. Microsoft Corporation Staff. LC 99-41069. 1999. pap. 59.99 (*1-57231-902-X*) Microsoft Pr.

Networking Essentials: Accelerated MCSE Study Guide. Herb Martin & LearnQuick.com Staff. LC 98-36279. (Accelerated MCSE Study Guides Ser.). (Illus.). 320p. 1998. pap. 24.99 (*0-07-067685-2*) McGraw.

Networking Essentials: Concepts & Practice. 200p. 1999. teacher ed. write for info. (*1-58076-200-X*) Que Educ & Trng.

Networking Essentials: Concepts & Practices. 400p. 1998. 59.00 (*1-58076-010-4*) Que Educ & Trng.

Networking Essentials, Deluxe Multimedia Edition. 2nd deluxe ed. Microsoft Corporation Staff. 850p. 199.00 incl. cd-rom (*1-57231-831-7*) Microsoft.

*__Networking Essentials Exam.__ ENI Publishing Ltd. Staff. (Preparation for the MCSE Exam Ser.). 2000. 47.95 (*2-7460-0562-X*) ENI Publng.

Networking Essentials Flashcards. Michael Moncur. Ed. by Tim O'Reilly. 1999. pap. 29.95 (*1-56592-568-8*) OReilly & Assocs.

*__Networking Essentials MCSE Study System.__ Alan R. Carter. 544p. 1999. 49.99 (*0-7645-4604-X*) IDG Bks.

*__Networking Essentials, MS Windows Nt 4.0.__ Barry Meinster et al. LC 98-29340. (Computer Applications Ser.). 1998. pap. 46.95 (*0-538-68477-1*) Thomson Learn.

*__Networking Essentials Study Guide.__ 3rd ed. James Chellis. (MCSE Exam Preparation Guide Ser.). 688p. 1999. pap., student ed. 49.99 (*0-7821-2695-2*) Sybex.

Networking Essentials Study Guide: Exam 70-058 With CDROM. 2nd ed. James Chellis et al. (MCSE Ser.). (Illus.). 683p. 1998. student ed. 54.99 (*0-7821-2220-5*) Sybex.

Networking Europe: Essays on Regionalism & Social Democracy. Ed. by Eberhard Bort & Neil Evans. 400p. 1998. pap. 23.95 (*0-85323-941-X*, Pub. by Liverpool Univ Pr) Intl Spec Bk.

Networking Explained. Michael Gallo & William M. Hancock. LC 99-19218. (Illus.). 481p. 1999. pap. 44.95 (*1-55558-214-1*, Digital DEC) Buttrwrth-Heinemann.

Networking Families in Crisis: Intervention Strategies with Families & Social Networks. Uri Rueveni. LC 78-8024. 162p. 1979. 32.95 (*0-87705-374-X*, Kluwer Acad Hman Sci) Kluwer Academic.

Networking for Building Automation & Control Systems. John J. McGowan. (Illus.). 484p. 79.00 (*0-88173-077-7*, 0205) Fairmont Pr.

Networking for Business Success. Rupert Hart. 1996. pap. 16.95 (*0-949142-09-3*, Pub. by Stirling Pr) Intl Spec Bk.

Networking for Development. Paul Starkey. 96p. 1998. pap. 17.50 (*1-85339-430-0*, Pub. by Intermed Tech) Stylus Pub VA.

Networking for Dummies. Doug Lowe. (For Dummies Ser.). (Illus.). 350p. 1994. pap. 19.95 (*1-56884-079-9*) IDG Bks.

*__Networking for Dummies.__ 4th ed. Doug Lowe. (For Dummies Ser.). 384p. 1999. pap. 19.99 (*0-7645-0498-3*) IDG Bks.

Networking for Everyone: It's Not What You Know, Its Who You Know. L. Michelle Tullier. LC 98-136317. 288p. (Orig.). 1998. pap. 12.95 (*1-56370-440-4*) Park Ave.

Networking for Novices. Susan Shelly. LC 98-27449. (Basics Made Easy...Ser.). 224p. 1998. pap. 13.95 (*1-57685-143-5*) LrningExprss.

Networking for Success. Meredith G. Resnick. (Spotlight on Military Issues Ser.). (Illus.). 8p. 1997. pap. 1.25 (*1-56688-384-9*) Bur For At-Risk.

*__Networking for Success: The NLP Approach to a Key Business & Social Skill.__ Carol Harris. 250p. 2000. pap. 14.95 (*1-86076-161-5*, Pub. by Oak Tr) Midpt Trade.

Networking for the Career-Minded Student. Linda Hewitt. (Lenox Publishing Company Career Materials Ser.). (Illus.). 64p. (Orig.). 1985. pap. 7.00 (*0-917421-02-7*) Lenox Pub.

*__Networking Fundamentals.__ Patrick T. Lane & James Stranger. Ed. by Jill McKenna. (Illus.). 250p. (C). 1999. pap. write for info. (*0-7423-0298-9*) ComputerPREP.

*__Networking Fundamentals: A4, Version 4.07.__ Patrick T. Lane & James Stanger. Ed. by Jill McKenna & David Oberman. (CIW Foundations Track A4 Ser.). (Illus.). 1999. pap. write for info. (*1-58143-062-0*) Prosoft I-net.

*__Networking Fundamentals Using Novell NetWare (4.11)__ Ann Beheler. LC 98-29725. 252p. 1998. pap. 61.00 (*0-13-409806-4*) P-H.

Networking Handbook. Taylor. 1999. write for info. (*0-07-135450-6*) McGraw.

Networking Handbook. Ed Taylor. 896p. 1999. 59.99 (*0-07-135451-4*) McGraw.

Networking Hardware & Software in Poland: A Strategic Entry Report, 1998. Compiled by Icon Group International Staff. (Country Industry Report). (Illus.). 183p. 1999. ring bd. 1830.00 incl. audio compact disk (*0-7418-0154-X*) Icon Grp.

*__Networking Health: Prescriptions for the Internet.__ National Research Council Staff & Commission on Physical Science Staff. 388p. 2000. write for info. (*0-309-06843-6*, Pub. by Natl Acad Pr) World Scientific Pub.

Networking High Performance in New York's Secondary Education: The Regents Curriculum Story. David K. Wiles. 178p. (C). 1996. pap. text 29.50 (*0-7618-0237-1*); lib. bdg. 46.00 (*0-7618-0236-3*) U Pr of Amer.

Networking Home PCs for Dummies. Ivens et al. LC 98-89668. 384p. 1998. pap. 24.99 incl. cd-rom (*0-7645-0491-6*) IDG Bks.

Networking in Brucellosis Research: Report of the United Nations University Brucellosis Research Network. 236p. 35.00 (*92-808-0756-0*, E. 91.III. A. 8) UN.

Networking in International Agriculture Research. Donald L. Plucknett et al. LC 90-31276. (Illus.). 240p. 1990. 37.50 (*0-8014-2384-8*) Cornell U Pr.

Networking in International Agriculture Research. Donald L. Plucknett et al. LC 90-31276. (Food Systems & Agrarian Change Ser.). (Illus.). 240p. reprint ed. pap. 74.40 (*0-608-20933-3*, 207203200003) Bks Demand.

Networking in Japanese Factory Automation, Vol. 2. Ed. by K. Kishimoto. xii, 96p. 1989. pap. text 104.00 (*2-88124-348-7*) Gordon & Breach.

Networking in Multinational Enterprises: The Importance of Strategic Alliances. Bernard M. Gilroy. Ed. by Brian Toyne. LC 92-27434. (Critical Issues Facing the Multinational Enterprise Ser.). (Illus.). 254p. 1993. text 34.95 (*0-87249-845-X*) U of SC Pr.

Networking in New Jersey: A Guide to Professional & Trade Organizations. D. J. Fomby & Tyiana Steptoe. (Illus.). 192p. 1999. pap. 49.95 (*1-883216-22-2*) Res Comns Group.

Networking in Sci-Tech Libraries & Information Centers. Ed. by Ellis Mount. (Science & Technology Libraries: Vol. 1, No. 2). 119p. 1981. pap. text 29.95 (*0-917724-72-0*) Haworth Pr.

Networking in the Music Business. 2nd ed. Dan Kimpel. LC 99-62538. 180p. 1999. pap. text 29.95 (*0-87288-727-8*) Intertec Pub.

Networking in Tokyo: A Guide to English-Speaking Clubs & Societies. Paul Ferguson & Thomas Boatman. 200p. (Orig.). 1995. pap. 9.95 (*0-8048-1946-7*) Tuttle Pubng.

Networking Made Easy. Patty Marler & Jan B. Mattia. LC 97-15798. 96p. 1997. pap. 6.95 (*0-8442-4342-6*, 43426) NTC Contemp Pub Co.

Networking Objects: Building Networks to Access & Distribute Objects. William J. Yarborough. LC 97-34673. 1997. pap. 55.00 (*0-07-072220-X*) McGraw.

Networking Personal Computers with TCP/IP. Craig Hunt. Ed. by Mike Loukides. LC 96-175020. (Illus.). 408p. 1995. pap. 32.95 (*1-56592-123-2*) Thomson Learn.

Networking Security: Hacking. Joel Scambray & Stuart McClure. 484p. 1999. pap. 39.99 (*0-07-212127-0*) McGraw.

An Asterisk (*) at the beginning of an entry indicates that the title is appearing for the first time.

Networking Security & Standards. Weidong Kou. LC 97-5743. (International Series in Engineering & Computer Science, Natural Language Processing & Machine Translation). 224p. (C). 1997. text 96.50 (*0-7923-9890-4*) Kluwer Academic.

Networking Skills That Will Get You the Job You Want. Cherie Kerr. LC 98-43976. 160p. 1999. pap. 14.99 (*1-55870-501-5*, Betrwy Bks) F & W Pubns Inc.

Networking Software & Hardware in Sweden: A Strategic Entry Report, 1998. Compiled by Icon Group International Staff. (Country Industry Report). (Illus.). 100p. 1999. ring bd. 1000.00 incl. audio compact disk (*0-7418-0453-0*) Icon Grp.

Networking Software in Chile: A Strategic Entry Report, 1996. Compiled by Icon Group International Staff. (Illus.). 103p. 1999. ring bd. 1030.00 incl. audio compact disk (*0-7418-1148-0*) Icon Grp.

***Networking Software in Taiwan: A Strategic Entry Report, 1995.** Compiled by Icon Group International Staff. (Illus.). 114p. 1999. ring bd. 1140.00 incl. audio compact disk (*0-7418-1543-5*) Icon Grp.

Networking Spatial Information Systems. Newton et al. 1992. 83.95 (*1-85293-204-X*, Belhaven) Halsted Pr.

Networking Standards: A Guide to OSI, ISDN, LAN, & MAN Standards. William Stallings. 672p. (C). 1993. 60.95 (*0-201-56357-6*) Addison-Wesley.

Networking Starter Kit for Macintosh. Jim Anders. (Illus.). 500p. (Orig.). 1995. pap. text 40.00 (*1-56830-131-6*) Hayden.

Networking Strategies for Information Technology. Bruce R. Elbert. (Telecommunications Library). 257p. 1991. text 65.00 (*0-89006-496-2*) Artech Hse.

Networking Success: How to Turn Business & Financial Relationships into Fun & Profit. Anne Boe. 250p. 1995. pap. 12.95 (*1-55874-365-0*, 3650) Health Comm.

Networking Technologies. Date not set. write for info. (*1-884486-02-9*) Wave Tech.

Networking Technologies: A Guide to Passing the Novell CNE Exam. Andres Forting & Arnold Villeneuve. (Illus.). 560p. 1996. pap. 59.95 incl. cd-rom (*0-07-912312-0*) McGraw.

Networking the Farm: The Social Structure of Cooperation & Competition in Iowa Agriculture. Randy Ziegenhorn. LC 98-74702. 14p. 1999. text 65.95 (*1-84014-869-1*, Pub. by Ashgate Pub) Ashgate Pub Co.

Networking the New Enterprise. Harris Kern & Randy Johnson. 1996. 38.00 (*0-614-20320-1*) P-H.

Networking the Small Office. Patrick T. Campbell. LC 95-72478. 384p. 1995. pap. 29.99 (*0-7821-1790-2*, Network Pr) Sybex.

***Networking the World, 1794-2000.** Armand Mattelart. (Illus.). 2000. pap. 16.95 (*0-8166-3288-X*) U of Minn Pr.

***Networking to Find A Job.** Stuart Schwartz. 1999. 19.93 (*0-516-21792-5*) Capstone Pr.

Networking to Find a Job. Stuart Schwartz & Craig Conley. LC 98-47357. (J). (gr. 3-4). 1999. write for info. (*0-7368-0180-4*) Capstone PC.

Networking Tool. Christina Davis et al. 1993. text 10.95 (*0-9634153-0-1*) Prod Busn Srv.

***Networking 2000: Broadband Communications, High Performance Networking & Performance of Communication Networks: Proceedings of the IFIP-TC6/European Union International Conference, Paris, France, May 14-19, 2000.** Ed. by G. Pujolle et al. (Lecture Notes in Computer Science Ser.: Vol. 1815). xx, 981p. 2000. pap. 129.00 (*3-540-67506-X*) Spr-Verlag.

Networking Using Novell NetWare 3.12. Emilio Ramos et al. LC 95-38018. 274p. (C). 1995. pap. text 93.00 (*0-13-236035-7*) P-H.

***Networking Using Novell Netware 5.0.** Beheler. 304p. 2001. pap. text 45.00 (*0-13-270588-5*) P-H.

Networking Using Novell 3.11: Release 3.11. Emilio Ramos et al. LC 93-30153. (Illus.). 268p. (Orig.). (C). 1993. pap. text 88.00 (*0-02-408025-X*, Macmillan Coll) P-H.

Networking Windows for Workgroups. Barry Nance. 320p. 1993. pap. 22.95 (*0-471-59583-7*) Wiley.

Networking Windows 95. Simon Collin. LC 96-209056. 350p. 1996. pap. 41.95 (*0-7506-2418-3*) Buttrwrth-Heinemann.

Networking Windows 95 with NetWare & NT. Jeff Bankston. 1996. 44.99 incl. cd-rom (*0-614-20335-X*, Network Pr) Sybex.

Networking Windows NT 4.0: Workstation & Server. 3rd ed. John D. Ruley et al. LC 96-46445. 688p. 1997. pap. 34.95 (*0-471-17502-1*) Wiley.

Networking with Microsoft TCP-IP. Drew Heywood. (Illus.). 600p. (Orig.). 1996. pap. 40.00 (*1-56205-520-8*) New Riders Pub.

Networking with Microsoft TCP-IP. 2nd ed. Drew Heywood. LC 97-141512. 600p. (Orig.). 1997. pap. text 44.99 (*1-56205-713-8*) New Riders Pub.

Networking with Microsoft TCP-IP: Certified Administrator's Resourse Edition. Drew Heywood. LC 97-31276. (Orig.). 1997. pap. text 55.00 incl. cd-rom (*1-56205-791-X*) New Riders Pub.

Networking with Microsoft TCP/IP. 3rd ed. Drew Heywood. LC 98-86324. 1998. pap. text 39.99 (*0-7357-0014-1*) New Riders Pub.

Networking with Microsoft Windows NT 5.0. Held Gild. 1998. pap. text 49.95 (*1-55622-591-1*) Wordware Pub.

Networking with NetWare for Dummies. 4th ed. Ed Tittel et al. LC TK5105.8.N65T58 1998. (For Dummies Ser.). 432p. 1998. pap. 19.99 (*0-7645-0281-6*) IDG Bks.

Networking with NetWare for Dummies Quick Reference. Ed Tittel et al. LC TK5105.8.N65T583. (For Dummies). 224p. 1998. spiral bd. 12.99 (*0-7645-0306-5*) IDG Bks.

Networking with the Affluent. Thomas J. Stanley. 288p. 1997. pap. 17.95 (*0-07-061048-7*) McGraw.

Networking with 3 Plus Open. Stanley Schatt. (Illus.). 304p. 1990. 29.95 (*0-8306-9437-4*, 3437); pap. 19.60 (*0-8306-3437-1*) McGraw-Hill Prof.

Networking with Windows NT. Louis Columbus. (Advanced Computer Book Ser.). 280p. (Orig.). 1994. pap. 24.95 incl. disk (*1-55622-421-4*) Wordware Pub.

***Networking with Windows NT5.** Al Emilio & Shroeder Ramos. (C). 2000. pap. text. write for info. (*0-201-61200-3*) Addison-Wesley.

***Networking Your Home.** Mark Speaker & Mark D. Thompson. LC 98-89193. (Illus.). 327p. 1999. pap. write for info. (*0-7897-1963-0*) Que.

Networking Your Way to Success. Ron Sukenick. LC 96-132086. 176p. (C). 1995. pap., per. 20.95 (*0-7872-1703-4*, 41170301) Kendall-Hunt.

***Network+ Accelerated Certification.** Ed. by Kevin C. Dietz & Linea Nigro. (Illus.). 200p. (YA). 2000. pap. write for info. (*0-7423-0445-0*) ComputerPREP.

***Network+ Certification Course.** Tom Hagen. Ed. by Carol Hartwig & Dan Waldo. (Illus.). viii, 228p. 1999. pap. write for info. incl. cd-rom (*1-930894-01-5*) MindWorks PEG.

***Network+ Certification Course Instructor's Guide.** Tom Hagen. Ed. by Carol Hartwig & Dan Waldo. (Illus.). 419p. 1999. pap., teacher ed. write for info. incl. disk (*1-930894-03-1*) MindWorks PEG.

***Network+ Certification Test Study Guide.** Tom Hagen. Ed. by Carol Hartwig & Dan Waldo. (Illus.). 24p. 1999. pap., student ed. write for info. incl. cd-rom (*1-930894-05-8*) MindWorks PEG.

***Network+ Cheat Sheet.** Patrick Grote. 450p. 1999. 24.99 (*0-7897-2177-5*) Que.

Network+ Guide to Networks. Tamara Dean. 800p. per. 61.95 (*0-7600-1145-1*, Pub. by Course Tech) Thomson Learn.

***Network+ Quick Reference Guide.** (Illus.). (YA). 2000. pap. write for info. (*0-7423-0481-7*, NETPLUS00QRG) ComputerPREP.

Networks. Ed. by M. H. Hamza. (Series on Computer Science). 254p. 1995. 95.00 (*0-88986-191-9*, 240) Acta Pr.

Networks. Timothy Ramteke. LC 93-41893. 482p. 1993. 106.00 (*0-13-958059-X*) P-H.

***Networks.** 2nd ed. Ramteke. 720p. 2000. 95.00 (*0-13-901265-6*) P-H.

Networks: Aging of Cell Membranes & Molecules. Ed. by Marguerite M. Kay. (Journal: Gerontology: Vol. 37, Nos. 1-3, 1991). (Illus.). 180p. 1991. pap. 117.50 (*3-8055-5391-9*) S Karger.

***Networks: Proceedings International Conference Brisbane, Australia, 1999.** Ed. by Jadwiga Indulska & Aruna Seneviratne. LC 99-63963. 408p. 1999. 125.00 (*0-7695-0243-1*) IEEE Comp Soc.

Networks: The Deep Structure of Organization. Karen Stephenson. 1998. 69.95 (*0-8493-0490-3*, 490) CRC Pr.

Networks: The Next Millennium. H. K. Pung. Ed. by L. H. Ngoh & J. Biswas. 490p. 1997. text 60.00 (*981-02-3129-6*) World Scientific Pub.

Networks & Algorithms: An Introductory Approach. Alan Dolan & Joan M. Aldous. 556p. 1994. pap. 64.95 (*0-471-93993-5*) Wiley.

Networks & Chaos - Statistical & Probabilistic Aspects. O. E. Barndorff-Nielsen. LC 93-3333. 320p. (gr. 13). 1993. ring bd. 73.95 (*0-412-46530-2*, Chap & Hall CRC) CRC Pr.

Networks & Devices Using Planar Transmission Lines. Franco Di Paolo. 1999. 129.00 (*0-8493-1835-1*, 1835) CRC Pr.

Networks & Imaging Systems in a Windowed Environment. Ed. by Marc R. D'Alleyrand. LC 95-42036. 364p. 1995. 27.00 (*0-89006-654-X*, TA1637) Artech Hse.

Networks & Markets: Pacific Rim Strategies. Ed. by W. Mark Fruin. LC 98-5447. (Japan Business & Economics Ser.). (Illus.). 336p. 1998. text 49.95 (*0-19-511720-4*) OUP.

Networks & Optical Communication '98, 3 vols., Set. Ed. by D. W. Faulkner. Incl. Broadband Access & Network Management Vol. 1: NOC '98 - Networks & Optical Communication. A. L. Harmer. 328p. 1998. pap. 78.00 (*90-5199-400-1*); Long Haul, ATM & Multi-Media Networks Vol. 2: NOC '98 - Networks & Optical Communication. Ed. by A. L. Harmer. LC 98-72433. 1998. pap. 79.00 (*90-5199-401-X*); Technology & Infrastructure Vol. 3: NOC '98 - Networks & Optical Communication. Ed. by A. L. Harmer. LC 98-72433. 290p. 1998. pap. 79.00 (*90-5199-402-8*); 1200p. Set pap. 170.00 (*90-5199-403-6*) IOS Pr.

Networks & Optical Communications, 1996. Ed. by D. W. Faulkner & A. L. Harmer. 1000p. (gr. 12). 1996. pap. 188.00 (*90-5199-274-2*, 274-2) IOS Press.

Networks & Optical Communications, 1997, 3 vols., Set. LC 97-72897. 1000p. (YA). (gr. 12). Date not set. pap. 169.00 (*90-5199-342-0*, 342-0) IOS Press.

Networks & Organizations: Structure, Form & Action. Ed. by Robert G. Eccles & Nitin Nohria. 1993. text 49.95 (*0-07-103374-2*) McGraw.

Networks & Organizations: Structure, Form & Action. Ed. by Nitin Nohria & Robert G. Eccles. LC 92-11442. 560p. 1994. pap. 27.95 (*0-87584-578-9*) Harvard Busn.

Networks & Resource Sharing in the 21st Century: Re-Engineering the Information Landscape. Ed. by Mary Huston-Somerville & Catherine C. Wilt. LC 95-17879. (Resource Sharing & Information Networks Ser.: Vol. 10, Nos. 1 & 2). 139p. 1995. 39.95 (*1-56024-741-X*) Haworth Pr.

Networks & Systems Management: Platforms Analysis & Evaluation. Iosif G. Ghetie. LC 97-4494. 544p. (C). 1997. text 125.00 (*0-7923-9879-3*) Kluwer Academic.

Networks & Telecommunications: Design & Operation. Martin P. Clark. LC 97-9248. 958p. 1997. 175.00 (*0-471-97346-7*) Wiley.

Networks, Exchange & Coercion: The Elementary Theory & Its Applications. David Willer & Bo Anderson. LC 80-21586. (Illus.). 240p. 1981. lib. bdg. 29.95 (*0-444-99078-X*, WNE/) Greenwood.

Networks for Networkers II: Critical Issues for Libraries in the National Network Environment. Ed. by Barbara E. Markuson & Elaine W. Woods. 250p. 1993. 49.95 (*1-55570-128-0*) Neal-Schuman.

Networks for Personal Communications Conference Proceedings, 1994. IEEE, New Jersey Coast Section Staff. Ed. by Institute of Electrical & Electronics Engineers, I. 150p. 1994. pap. write for info. (*0-7803-1913-3*, 94TH0653-6); fiche. write for info. (*0-7803-1914-1*) Inst Electrical.

Networks for Small Businesses. David Norman. (Popular Applications Ser.). 160p. (Orig.). 1995. pap. 15.95 incl. disk (*1-55622-455-9*) Wordware Pub.

Networks for Water Policy: A Comparative Perspective. Ed. by Jeremy J. Richardson et al. 240p. 1995. 45.00 (*0-7146-4642-3*, Pub. by F Cass Pubs) Intl Spec Bk.

Networks in Action: Communication, Economics & Human Knowledge. Ed. by David Batten et al. LC 95-1430. (Illus.). 327p. 1995. 107.00 (*3-540-58944-9*) Spr-Verlag.

Networks in Distributed Computing. Marios Mavronicolas et al. LC 98-37246. (Dimacs Series in Discrete Mathematics & Theoretical Computer Science). 1998. write for info. (*0-8218-0992-X*) Am Math.

Networks in Marketing. Dawn Iacobucci. LC 96-10122. 432p. 1996. 57.00 (*0-7619-0139-6*); pap. 27.95 (*0-7619-0140-X*) Sage.

***Networks in the Global Village: Life in Contemporary Communities.** Ed. by Barry Wellman. 408p. 1999. pap. 34.00 (*0-8133-6821-9*, Pub. by Westview) HarpC.

Networks in Transport & Communications: A Policy Approach. Ed. by Cristina Capineri & Piet Rietveld. LC 97-74509. (Illus.). 368p. 1998. text 83.95 (*1-85972-533-3*, Pub. by Ashgate Pub) Ashgate Pub Co.

Networks in Wordbytes. Edward W. Eckhardt. (Illus.). 100p. (Orig.). 1997. pap. 27.95 (*1-886759-02-2*) IntroTech.

Networks, Infrastructure, & the New Task for Regulation. Werner Sichel & Donald L. Alexander. LC 95-42233. 176p. (C). 1996. text 54.50 (*0-472-10687-2*, 10687) U of Mich Pr.

Networks, Mergers & Partnerships in a Managed Care Environment. David L. Emenhiser et al. LC 97-18559. 1998. pap. 9.95 (*0-87868-686-X*, CWLA Pr) Child Welfare.

Networks, '98: IEEE SICON'98: Proceedings of the 6th IEEE Singapore International Conference. Ed. by A. L. Ananda et al. 492p. 1998. pap. 96.00 (*981-02-3584-4*) World Scientific Pub.

Networks of Americanization: Aspects of the American Influence in Sweden. Ed. by Rolf Lunden & Erik Asard. (Studia Anglistica Upsaliensia Ser.: No. 79). 182p. (Orig.). 1992. pap. 46.00 (*91-554-2981-5*) Coronet Bks.

Networks of Champions: Leadership, Access & Advisory in the U. S. House of Representatives. Christine A. DeGregorio. LC 96-39404. 304p. (C). 1997. text 42.50 (*0-472-10762-3*, 10762) U of Mich Pr.

***Networks of Champions: Leadership, Access & Advocacy in the U.S. House of Representative.** Christine A. DeGregorio. 304p. (C). 1999. pap. text 19.95 (*0-472-08614-6*, 08614) U of Mich Pr.

***Networks of Desire: Gender Sexuality & Computer Culture.** Nina Wakeford. 240p. (C). 1999. pap. 22.99 (*0-415-16971-2*); text 75.00 (*0-415-16970-4*) Routledge.

Networks of Enterprises & Local Development. OECD Staff. LC 97-135359. 256p. (Orig.). 1997. pap. 43.00 (*92-64-15312-8*, 04-96-09-1, Pub. by Org for Econ) OECD.

Networks of Innovation: Vaccine Development at Merck, Sharp & Dohme, & Mulford 1895-1995. Louis P. Galambos. 288p. (C). 1996. text 44.95 (*0-521-56308-9*) Cambridge U Pr.

Networks of Innovation: Vaccine Development at Merck, Sharp & Dohme, & Mulford, 1895-1995. Louis Galambos & Jane E. Sewell. (Illus.). 288p. (C). 1998. reprint ed. pap. text 15.95 (*0-521-62620-X*) Cambridge U Pr.

Networks of Meaning: A Bridge Between Mind & Matter. Christine Hardy. LC 98-14932. 232p. 1998. 57.95 (*0-275-96035-8*, Praeger Pubs) Greenwood.

Networks of Power. Ed. by Robert Perrucci & Harry R. Potter. (Social Institutions & Social Change Ser.). 144p. 1989. pap. text 24.95 (*0-202-30343-8*); lib. bdg. 47.95 (*0-202-30342-X*) Aldine de Gruyter.

Networks of Power: Corporate TV's Threat to Democracy. Dennis W. Mazzocco. 200p. (Orig.). (C). 1994. pap. text 14.00 (*0-89608-472-8*); lib. bdg. 30.00 (*0-89608-473-6*) South End Pr.

Networks of Power: Electrification in Western Society, 1880-1930. Thomas P. Hughes. (Illus.). 488p. 1993. reprint ed. pap. text 34.95 (*0-8018-4614-5*) Johns Hopkins.

Networks, Open Access, & Virtual Libraries: Implications for the Research Library. Ed. by Brett Sutton & Charles H. Davis. LC 92-224886. 161p. reprint ed. pap. 50.00 (*0-7837-6450-2*, 204644900012) Bks Demand.

Networks, Routers & Transputers. M. D. May et al. LC 93-77461. (Transputer & Occam Engineering Ser.: Vol. 32). 221p. (gr. 12). 1993. 80.00 (*90-5199-129-0*, Pub. by IOS Pr) IOS Press.

Networks, Routers & Transputers. P. W. Thompson et al. LC 93-77461. (Transputer & Occam Engineering Ser.: Vol. 32). 221p. (gr. 12). 1994. pap. 50.00 (*90-5199-185-1*) IOS Press.

Networks That Work: A Guide to Dental Networking. Cheryl Maesaka. 100p. 1999. pap. 15.95 (*0-88100-105-8*) Natl Writ Pr.

Networks Trust & Values: Improving Local Human Services. Allan D. Wallis. 1994. 8.00 (*0-916450-52-X*) Nat Civic League.

Networks 2000: Internet, Information Super Highway Multimedia Networks, & Beyond. Ed. by Melanie McMullen. (Illus.). 338p. 1994. pap. 24.95 (*0-87930-335-2*) Miller Freeman.

Networks under Attack. Peter Denning. LC 97-27279. 560p. (C). 1997. pap. text 34.95 (*0-201-30820-7*) Addison-Wesley.

Network/Translation Software Supplier Directories. 1996. 50.00 (*0-318-50036-1*) Uniform Code.

NetWorld: What People Are Really Doing on the Internet & What It Means to You. David Rothman. LC 95-5287. 352p. 1995. 22.95 (*0-7615-0013-8*) Prima Pub.

Networld! What People Are Really Doing on the Internet, & What It Means to You. David H. Rothman. 344p. 1998. text 23.00 (*0-7881-5404-4*) DIANE Pub.

***Networlding.** Melissa Giovagnoli & Jocelyn Carter-Miller. 2000. 25.00 (*0-7879-4819-5*) Jossey-Bass.

Netzwerkprogrammierung Mit Clipper. Mike Becker. (GER.). (C). 1990. text. write for info. (*0-201-55913-7*) Addison-Wesley.

Neu-Aramaischen Handschriften der Koniglichen Bibliothek Zu Berlin. Mark Lidzbarski. (Erganzungshefte Zur Zeitschrift Fur Assyriologie. Semitische Studien: Hefte 4/9, 1-2). (GER.). xliii, 1080p. 1973. reprint ed. write for info. (*3-487-04524-9*) G Olms Pubs.

Neu-Eroffnete Orchestre. Johann Mattheson. (GER.). xviii, 349p. 1993. reprint ed. write for info. (*3-487-09612-9*) G Olms Pubs.

Neuassyrische Glyptik des 8. - 7. Jh. v. Chr. Unter Besonderer Berucksichtigung der Siegelungen Auf Tafeln und Tonverschlussen. Suzanne Herbordt. (State Archives of Assyria Ser.: Vol. 1). (Illus.). xix, 276p. 1992. pap. text 39.50 (*951-45-6047-7*, Pub. by Neo-Assyrian Text) Eisenbrauns.

Neuchatel - Basel - St. Gallen Map. 1997. 8.95 (*2-06-700216-3*, 216) Michelin.

Neue Akquisitionen in der Neonatologie: Nouvelles Acquisitions en Neonatologie. Ed. by E. Bern Rossi. (Paediatrische Fortbildungskurse fuer die Praxis Ser.: Vol. 62). (Illus.). x, 660p. 1988. pap. 34.00 (*3-8055-4742-0*) S Karger.

***Neue Ansatze Zur Robert-Musil-Forschung: Wiener Kolloquium Zum 20-Jahrigen Bestehen der Internationalen Robert-Musil-Gesellschaft.** Marie-Louise Roth. (Musiliana Ser.). 215p. 1999. 35.95 (*3-906762-74-2*, Pub. by P Lang) P Lang Pubng.

Neue Aspekte in der Behandlung der Herzinsuffizienz: Oberrheinisches Kardiologen - Symposium. Ed. by F. Burkhart. (Journal: Cardiology: Vol. 65, Suppl. 1, 1980). (Illus.). 1980. pap. 16.75 (*3-8055-0652-X*) S Karger.

Neue Bibliothek der Schonen Wissenschaften und der Freien Kunste, 72 vols. Ed. by Christian F. Weibe. write for info. incl. fiche (*0-318-71739-5*) G Olms Pubs.

***Neue Bilder Vom Menschen In der Literatur der Europaischen Aufklarung.** Siegfried Juttner. (GER., Illus.). XI, 200p. 1999. 40.00 (*3-631-45662-X*) P Lang Pubng.

Neue Briefstellar. 1999. pap. text 12.50 (*3-8068-0060-X*) Falken Verlag.

***Neue Britische Architektur in Deutschland.** Michael Jenner. (GER., Illus.). 2000. 65.00 (*3-7913-2297-4*) Prestel Pub NY.

Neue Brockhaus, 5 vols. 7th ed. Brockhaus. (GER.). 700p. 1992. boxed set 595.00 (*0-7859-4856-2*) Fr & Eur.

Neue Chinesisch-Deutsche Woertbuch. China Books Staff. (CHI & GER.). 1164p. 1985. 75.00 (*0-7859-8552-2*, 3922373054) Fr & Eur.

Neue Computer-Lexikon Von A-Z. Bernhard Bachmann. (GER.). 280p. 1993. 29.95 (*0-7859-8438-0*, 3572006333) Fr & Eur.

Neue, Curieuse und Vollkommene Artillerie. Christoph F. Von Geissler. (GER.). 177p. 1977. reprint ed. write for info. (*3-487-06131-7*) G Olms Pubs.

Neue Darstellung der Leibnizschen Monadenlehre Auf Grund der Quellen. Eduard Dillmann. (GER.). 1974. reprint ed. write for info. (*3-487-05152-4*) G Olms Pubs.

Neue Darstellung der Logik. Moritz W. Drobisch. (GER.). xxiv, 240p. 1998. reprint ed. write for info. (*3-487-10522-5*) G Olms Pubs.

Neue Deutsche Prosa. Ed. by Erna K. Neuse. LC 68-30796. (GER., Illus.). (Orig.). (C). 1968. pap. text 12.95 (*0-8290-2383-6*) Irvington.

***Neue Entwicklungen Bei der Bilanziellen Behandlung Von Schadstoffelasteten Vermogensgegenstanden.** Christian Depken. 176p. 1998. 39.95 (*3-631-34055-9*) P Lang Pubng.

***Neue Entwicklungen in der Therapie Gynakologischer Malignome.** W. Jonat et al. (Onkologie Ser.). (Illus.). 32p. 1999. 28.00 (*3-8055-7020-1*) S Karger.

Neue Epichorische Schriftzeugnisse Aus Sardis. Roberto Gusmani. (Archaeological Exploration of Sardis Monograph). 176p. (C). 1975. 27.50 (*0-674-60810-0*) HUP.

Neue Epichorische Schriftzeugnisse Aus Sardis. Roberto Gusmani. LC 74-81203. (Archaeological Exploration of Sardis Monograph: No. 3). (GER.). 176p. 1975. text 14.50 (*0-685-02133-5*) HUP.

Neue Erfahrungen Mit Oxazaphosphorinen unter Besonderer Beruecksichtigung des Uroprotektors Uromitexan. Ed. by H. Burkert & G. A. Nagel. (Beitraege Zur Onkologie, Contributions to Oncology Ser.: Band 5). (Illus.). 126p. 1980. pap. 25.25 (*3-8055-1381-X*) S Karger.

***Neue Erziehung: Beitrage zur Internationalitat der Reformpadagogik.** Jurgen Oelkers & Fritz Osterwalder. (Explorationen. Studien zur Erziehungswissenschaft Ser.). (GER.). 418p. 2000. 56.95 (*3-906764-26-5*, Pub. by P Lang Pubng) P Lang Pubng.

N

An Asterisk (*) at the beginning of an entry indicates that the title is appearing for the first time.

Neue Folge. xvi, 352p. 1973. reprint ed. write for info. (3-487-04648-2) G Olms Pubs.

Neue Freunde. Harcourt Brace Staff. (GER.). 1989. pap. text, teacher ed., wbk. ed. 16.75 (0-15-383506-0) Holt R&W.

Neue Freunde. Harcourt Brace Staff. (GER.). 1989. pap. text, teacher ed. 15.25 (0-15-383510-9); pap. text, teacher ed., wbk. ed. 18.00 (0-15-383507-9) Holt R&W.

Neue Freunde: Testbook. Harcourt Brace Staff. (GER.). 1989. pap. text 15.25 (0-15-383508-7) Holt R&W.

Neue Freunde German, 1989, Pt. 1. 89th ed. Harcourt Brace Staff. 1989. text 32.75 (0-15-383490-0) Holt R&W.

Neue Freunde German, 1989, Pt. 2. 89th ed. Harcourt Brace Staff. 1989. text 32.75 (0-15-383491-9) Holt R&W.

Neue Freunde German, 1989, Pt. 3. 89th ed. Harcourt Brace Staff. 1989. text 32.75 (0-15-383492-7, Pub. by Harcourt Coll Pubs) Harcourt.

Neue Freunde-German 1. Harcourt Brace Staff. (Orig.). 1989. text 67.25 (0-15-383501-X) Holt R&W.

Neue Freunds, Level 1. George Winkler. 1989. text 56.50 (0-15-383500-1) Harcourt.

***Neue Galerie New York: Early Twentieth-Century German & Austrian Art.** (Illus.). 2000. 60.00 (1-58567-077-4, Pub. by Overlook Pr) Penguin Putnam.

Neue Gedichte see New Poems

Neue Gelehrte Europa, Als eine Fortsetzung der Dreyen Werke, die Bisher Unter den Auffschriften, Gelehrtes Europa, Geschichte der Gelehrten und Beytrage Zur Historie der Gelahrtheit, Ans Licht Gestellet Worden, 11 vols., Set. Johann C. Strodtmann. reprint ed. write for info. (0-318-71905-3) G Olms Pubs.

Neue Gesamtabenteuer, Band I. Heinrich Niewohner. (GER.). xix, 288p. 1967. write for info. (3-296-20600-0, Pub. by Weidmann) Lubrecht & Cramer.

Neue Grenzen: A German Cultural Reader. Maurice R. Funke. 208p. (C). 1993. pap. 35.00 (0-07-022662-8) McGraw.

***Neue Grunderzeit? Die Wiederentdeckung kleiner Unternehmen in Theorie und Praxis.** D. Bogenhold & D. Schmidt. Vol. 1.Tr. of New Times to Invest? The Rediscovery of Smaller Enterprises in Theory & Practice. (GER.). 304p. 1999. pap. text 35.00 (90-5708-056-7, Verlag Fakultas) Gordon & Breach.

Neue Herder: Lexikon, 14 vols., Set. Herder Staff. (GER.). 1968. 1195.00 (0-8288-6657-0, M-7568) Fr & Eur.

Neue Horizonte: A First Course in German Language & Culture. 2nd ed. David B. Dollenmayer. LC 87-81430. (ENG & GER.). (C). 1988. text 61.16 (0-669-13917-3); student ed. 34.36 (0-669-13919-X); audio 32.76 (0-669-13922-X) HM Trade Div.

Neue Horizonte: A First Course in German Language & Culture. 3rd ed. David B. Dollenmayer & Thomas S. Hansen. (ENG & GER.). 550p. (C). 1992. audio 32.76 (0-669-24249-7) HM Trade Div.

Neue Horizonte: A First Course in German Language & Culture. 3rd annot. ed. David B. Dollenmayer & Thomas S. Hansen. (ENG & GER.). 550p. (C). 1992. text, teacher ed. 56.76 (0-669-24246-2) HM Trade Div.

Neue Horizonte: A First Course in German Language & Culture. 4th ed. David B. Dollenmayer & Thomas S. Hansen. (GER.). 545p. (C). 1996. text 61.16 (0-669-35528-3); pap. text, wbk. ed., lab manual ed. 34.36 (0-669-35530-5) HM Trade Div.

Neue Horizonte: A First Course in German Language & Culture. 4th annot. ed. David B. Dollenmayer & Thomas S. Hansen. (GER.). (C). 1996. text, teacher ed. 56.76 (0-669-35529-1) HM Trade Div.

Neue Klarstellungen see New Elucidations

Neue Kommunikative Grammatik: A Communicative Grammar Worktext with Written & Oral Practice. (GER.). 1997. pap. 8.40 (0-8442-2512-6) NTC Contemp Pub Co.

Neue Kommunikative Grammatik: A Communicative Grammar Worktext with Written & Oral Practice. John Klapper & Trudi McMahon. LC 98-168131. (New Communicative Ser.). (ENG & GER., Illus.). 320p. (C). 1997. pap., wbk. ed. 12.95 (0-8442-2511-8) NTC Contemp Pub Co.

Neue Lexikon der Esoterik. Marc Roberts. (GER.). 461p. 1993. 75.00 (0-7859-8426-7, 3552045015) Fr & Eur.

Neue Lexikon der Musik, 4 vols. (GER.). 1996. 595.00 (0-320-00680-8) Fr & Eur.

Neue Literatur Von Frauen see Literatur und Landeskunde

Neue Mahleriana: Essays in Honour of Henry-Louis de La Grange on His Seventieth Birthday. Ed. by Gunther Weib. LC 98-187569. (Illus.). xxxvi, 447p. 1997. 68.95 (3-906756-95-5, Pub. by P Lang) P Lang Pubng.

***Neue Musik in der Kirche: Visionen Gegen die Zeit: Interdisziplinare Tage Fur Neue Musik und Theologie 11.-14. Juni 1998 - Dokumentation und Auswertung.** Corinna Dahlgrun & Hans Darmstadt. 116p. 1999. 17.95 (3-631-35232-8) P Lang Pubng.

Neue Musikalische Theorien und Phantasien Vol. 2: Der Kontrapunkt. Heinrich Schenker. (GER.). xxiv, 747p. 1991. reprint ed. write for info. (3-487-09519-X) G Olms Pubs.

Neue Nationalgalerie, Berlin. Tr. by John W. Gabriel from GER. LC 97-190. (Museum Guides Ser.). (Illus.). 128p. (Orig.). 1996. pap. 14.95 (3-7913-1732-6, Pub. by Prestel) te Neues.

Neue Oder Bemerkenswerte Arten der Flechtenfamilie Gomphiliaceae in der Neotropis. Klaus Kalb & Antonin Vezda. Ed. by Volkmar Wirth et al. (Bibliotheca Lichenologica: Vol. 29). (GER., Illus.). 112p. 1988. 30.00 (3-443-58008-4, Pub. by Gebruder Borntraeger) Balogh.

Neue Perspektiven. 2nd ed. Manfred Bansleben. (C). Date not set. pap. text, teacher ed., suppl. ed. write for info. (0-15-501101-4) Harcourt Coll Pubs.

Neue Perspektiven. 2nd ed. Manfred Bansleben. (C). 1996. pap. text. write for info. (0-03-072461-9) Harcourt Coll Pubs.

Neue Perspektiven. 2nd ed. Manfred Bansleben. (C). 1997. pap. text, wbk. ed., lab manual ed. write for info. (0-03-072466-X) Harcourt Coll Pubs.

Neue Philologische Untersuchungen, Heft 1. Ocellus Lucanus. xxix, 161p. 1966. write for info. (3-296-14750-0) G Olms Pubs.

Neue Philologische Untersuchungen Heft 2: Monolog und Selbstgesprach. Untersuchungen Zur Formgeschichte der Griechischen Tragodie. Wolfgang Schadewaldt. 270p. 1966. write for info. (3-296-15350-0) G Olms Pubs.

Neue Philologische Untersuchungen Heft 3: Augustin und der Antike Friedensgedanke. Harald Fuchs. viii, 258p. 1965. write for info. (3-296-12710-0) G Olms Pubs.

Neue Philologische Untersuchungen Heft 4: Die Entwicklung der Aristotelischen Logik und Rhetorik. Friedrich Solmsen. viii, 304p. 1975. write for info. (3-296-15590-2) G Olms Pubs.

Neue Philologische Untersuchungen Heft 6: Platos Apologie. Wolff. 103p. write for info. (0-318-70814-0) G Olms Pubs.

Neue Philologische Untersuchungen Heft 8: Antiphonstudien. Friedrich Solmsen. 78p. write for info. (0-318-70815-9) G Olms Pubs.

Neue Philologische Untersuchungen Heft 10: Doxis Epirhysmie. Hermann Langerbeck. 132p. 1967. write for info. (3-296-14190-1) G Olms Pubs.

Neue Pinakothek, Munich. Christian Lenz. (Illus.). 132p. 1989. 30.00 (1-870248-19-8) Scala Books.

Neue Predigten. Abraham A. Sancta Clara. Ed. by Karl Bertsche. (Bibliothek des Literarischen Vereins in Stuttgart Ser.: Vol. 278). (GER.). xxxiv, 232p. 1995. reprint ed. 80.00 (3-487-04435-8) G Olms Pubs.

Neue Schoepfung: Eine Traditionsgeschichtliche und Exegetische Studie zu einem soteriologischen Grundsatz Paulinischer Theologie. Ulrich Mell. (Beiheft zur Zeitschrift fuer die Neuetestamentliche Wissenschaft Ser.: No. 56). (GER.). xv, 436p. (C). 1989. lib. bdg. 119.25 (3-11-011831-9) De Gruyter.

Neue Studien Zur Geschichte der Begriffe, 3 vols. Gustav Teichmuller. xlvii, 1020p. 1965. reprint ed. write for info. (0-318-71048-X); reprint ed. write for info. (0-318-71049-8); reprint ed. write for info. (0-318-71050-1) G Olms Pubs.

Neue Studien Zur Geschichte der Begriffe, 3 vols., Set. Gustav Teichmuller. xlvii, 1020p. 1965. reprint ed. write for info. (0-318-71047-1) G Olms Pubs.

Neue Testament Auf Papyrus: II. Die Paulinischen Briefe, Part1: Roem, 1. Kor., 2 Kor. rev. ed. Intro. by B. Aland. (Arbeiten zur Neutestamentlichen Testforschung Ser.: No. 12). lviii, 418p. (C). 1989. lib. bdg. 119.25 (3-11-012248-0) De Gruyter.

Neue Testament Auf Papyrus II. Die Paulinischen Briefe Tl. 2: Gal, Eph, Phil, Kol, Lu, Two Thess, Lu Two Tim, Tit, Phlm, Hebr. Ed. by Kalus Wachtel & Klaus Witte. (Arbeiten zur Neutestamentlichen Textforschung Ser.: Bd. 22). (GER.). 455p. (C). 1994. lib. bdg. 160.00 (3-11-014612-6) De Gruyter.

Neue Testament in Syrischer Uberlieferung II. Die Paulinsichen Briefe Teil 1: Romer- und 1. Korinthebrief. Ed. by Barbara Aland & Andreas Juckel. (Arbeiten zur Neutestamentlichen Textforschung Ser.: Vol. 14). ix, 644p. 1991. lib. bdg. 315.40 (3-11-011139-X) De Gruyter.

Neue Testament in Syrischer Ueberlieferung II - Die Paulinischen Briefe Teil 2: Korintherbrief, Galaterbrief, Epheserbrief, Philipperbrief und Kolosserbrief. Ed. by Barbara Aland & Andreas Juckel. (Arbeiten zur Neutestamentlichen Textforschung Ser.: Band 23). (GER.). viii, 582p. (C). 1995. lib. bdg. 292.35 (3-11-014613-4) De Gruyter.

Neue Therapeutische Strategien in der Haematologischen Onkologie. Ed. by H. Loeffler. (Beitraege Zur Onkologie, Contributions to Oncology Ser.: Vol. 36). (Illus.). vi, 115p. 1989. 47.00 (3-8055-5046-4) S Karger.

Neue Ullstein Lexikon der Musik. Friedrich Herzfeld. (GER.). 640p. 1989. 75.00 (0-7859-8685-5, 355006523x) Fr & Eur.

Neue Untersuchungen Uber Platon. Constantin Ritter. LC 75-13289. (History of Ideas in Ancient Greece Ser.). (GER.). 1976. reprint ed. 31.95 (0-405-07332-1) Ayer.

Neue Verfassung von Berlin Im Spiegel der Rechtsprechung des Verfassungsgerichtshofs: Eine um Kernaussagen Aus der Rechtsprechung des Verfassungsgerichtshofs Erweiterte Textausgabe. Hans-Joachim Driehaus. viii, 69p. 1996. write for info. (3-11-015131-6) De Gruyter.

Neue Vorschule der Aesthetik: Das Komische Mit Einem Komischen Anhange. Arnold Ruge. (GER.). 274p. 1975. reprint ed. write for info. (3-487-05675-5) G Olms Pubs.

***Neue Wege der Slavistischen Wortbildungsforschung: Tagung der Internationalen Kommission fur Slavische Wortbildung, Magdeburg, 9-11, 10, 97.** Renate Belentschikow. (GER., Illus.). 358p. 1999. 57.00 (3-631-34528-3) P Lang Pubng.

Neue Wege Im Computergestutzten Fremdsprachenunterricht. Ed. by J. Fechner. 240p. 1995. 31.95 (3-468-49451-3) Langenscheidt.

Neuen Leiden des Jungen W., Plenzodorf: Critical Monographs in English. Jurgen Thomaneck. 68p. 1993. pap. 32.00 (0-85261-343-1, Pub. by Univ of Glasgow) St Mut.

Neuer Anzeiger fur Bibliographie und Bibliothekswissenschaft, 31 vols., Set. Ed. by Julius Petzoldt. reprint ed. write for info. incl. fiche (0-318-71731-X) G Olms Pubs.

Neuer Deutscher Bucherschatz. Karl Biltz. viii, 264p. 1967. reprint ed. 75.00 (0-318-71740-9) G Olms Pubs.

Neuer Metrischer Traktat und das Studium der Pindarischen Metrik in der Philologie der Palaologenzeit. Hans-Christian Gunther. (Mnemosyne Ser.: Vol. 180). (GER.). 200p. 1998. 85.50 (90-04-11008-9) Brill Academic Pubs.

Neuer Nekrolog der Deutschen. Ed. by F. A. Schmidt. reprint ed. write for info. incl. fiche (0-318-71935-5) G Olms Pubs.

Neuer Tractat von der Stuterey oder Fohlenzucht. Georg S. Winter Von Adlersflugel. (GER.). xxv, 174p. 1975. write for info. (3-487-08081-8) G Olms Pubs.

Neuer Wettstein Vol. 2: Texte Zum Neuen Testament Aus Griechentum und Hellenismus. Ed. by Georg Strecker & Udo Schnelle. (GER.). xxv, 1831p. (C). 1996. lib. bdg. 368.90 (3-11-014507-3) De Gruyter.

Neuere Alkaios-Papyri Aus Oxyrhynchus. Wilfried Barner. (GER.). viii, 243p. 1967. 50.00 (0-318-70619-9) G Olms Pubs.

Neuere Aspekte der Kinderkardiiology, Set. Ed. by E. Bern Rossi & F. Wyler. (Paediatrische Fortbildungskurse fuer die Praxis Ser.: Vol. 47). (FRE & GER., Illus.). 1978. pap. 32.25 (3-8055-2865-5) S Karger.

Neuere Aspekte der Kinderkardiology. Ed. by F. Stocker et al. (Paediatrische Fortbildungskurse fuer die Praxis Ser.: Vol. 51). (Illus.). vi, 130p. 1980. pap. 50.50 (3-8055-0926-X) S Karger.

Neuere Funktionentheorie see Kontinuum und Andere Monographien

Neuere Musik Agyptens und Muhammad Abdu'l-Wahhab: Eine Musikethnologische Untersuchung. Nour-Al-Din Al-Salihi. (Europaische Hochschulschriften Ser.: Reihe 36, Bd. 180). 215p. 1998. pap. 37.95 (3-631-33032-4) P Lang Pubng.

***Neuere Theorien Zur Inflationsbekampfung und Relevanz Fur Lateinamerika.** Frank Engels. (GER., Illus.). xvi, 315p. 1999. 57.00 (3-631-34332-9) P Lang Pubng.

Neues Allgemeines Deutsches Adels-Lexicon, 9 vols., Set. Ed. by Ernst H. Kneschke. 1973. reprint ed. write for info. (3-487-04549-4) G Olms Pubs.

Neues Bauen in den Alpen: Architekturpreis, 1995. Ed. by Christoph M. Fingerle. (GER & ITA., Illus.). 120p. 1996. pap. text 45.00 (3-7643-5347-3, Pub. by Birkhauser) Princeton Arch.

***Neues Bauen in den Alpen: Architekturpreis, 1995.** Christoph Mayr Fingerle. (Illus.). 42p. 2000. pap. 49.95 (3-7643-6115-8) Birkhauser.

Neues Bauen in der Welt, Rassegna 38. (Illus.). 110p. 1989. pap. 35.00 (88-85322-34-4, Pub. by Birkhauser) Princeton Arch.

Neues Grosses Gartenlexikon. Siebeneil. (GER.). 1973. 65.00 (0-8288-6325-3, M-7567) Fr & Eur.

Neues Lexikon (Color) P. Godecke. (GER.). 800p. 1997. 75.00 (0-320-00110-5) Fr & Eur.

Neues Lexikon der Vornamen. Walter Burkhart. (GER.). 29.95 (0-7859-8328-7, 3404603435) Fr & Eur.

Neues Lexikon der Wirtschaft. Hans-Jurgen Escherle. (GER.). 405p. 1988. 35.00 (0-7859-8503-4, 3817435622) Fr & Eur.

Neues Museum der Philosophie und Literatur, 3 Bande in 1. Ed. by Friedrich Bouterwek. (GER.). v, 935p. 1979. write for info. (3-487-06679-3) G Olms Pubs.

Neues Schulpaedagogisches Woerterbuch. Dieter Hintz. (GER.). 400p. 1993. 49.95 (0-7859-8470-4, 3779910039) Fr & Eur.

Neues Textlinguistisches Instrumentarium: Und Seine Anwendung Im Aufbau der Schreibkompetenz Ungarischer Germanistikstudenten. Ewa Drewnowska-Vargane. (GER.). 300p. 1997. 57.95 (3-631-31460-4) P Lang Pubng.

Neues Urkundenbuch Zur Geschichte der Evangelischen Kirchen-Reformation. Carl E. Forstemann. (GER.). 394p. 1976. reprint ed. write for info. (3-487-06060-4) G Olms Pubs.

Neueste Litteratur Betreffend, 4 vols. Briefe. Ed. by Friedrich Nicolai et al. (GER., Illus.). 4578p. 1974. reprint ed. write for info. (3-487-05074-9) G Olms Pubs.

Neueste Merckwurdigkeiten der Leibnitz-Wolffischen Weltweisheit. Carl G. Ludovici. (GER.). 1973. reprint ed. write for info. (3-487-04749-7) G Olms Pubs.

Neueste Wirtschaftsgeschichte der Juden in Ruphland und Polen. Bernhard Weinryb. xiii, 282p. 1972. reprint ed. write for info. (3-487-04247-9) G Olms Pubs.

Neuf Histoires Vraies de Dauphins see Nine True Dolphin Stories

Neuf lecons sur les notions premieres de la philosophie Morale see Introduction to the Basic Problems of Moral Philosophy

Neufunde aus der Nekropole des 11j. und 10. Jahrhunderts see Kerameikos: Ergebnisse der Ausgrabungen (Deutsches Archaeologisches Institut)

Neugents: Close to Home. 2nd rev. ed. David M. Spear. LC 98-71372. (Illus.). 108p. 1998. 40.00 (0-917788-72-9) Gnomon Pr.

***Neugierigkeit: The Nexis of Creating Innovation.** J. Carl Ficarrotta. 2000. 34.95 (1-55753-209-5) Purdue U Pr.

Neugriechisch ohne Muhe: Greek for German Speakers. Assimil Staff. (GER & GRE.). 28.95 (0-8288-4343-0, F18000) Fr & Eur.

Neugriechisch 1. (Deutsch Konkret Ser.: No. 1). (GER.). 1997. pap. write for info. (3-468-49858-6) Langenscheidt.

Neugriechisch 2. (Deutsch Konkret Ser.: No. 2). (GER.). 32p. 1997. pap. write for info. (3-468-49868-3) Langenscheidt.

Neuhebraische Grammatik Auf Grund Altester Handschriften und Inschriften. Beate Ridzweski. (Heidelberger Orientalistische Studien Ser.: Bd. 21). (GER.). XVIII, 201p. 1992. 44.80 (3-631-43695-5) P Lang Pubng.

Neujahrsrede des Konsuls Claudius Mamertinus Vor Dem Kaiser Julian. Claudius Mamertinus. (Basler Beitrage Zur Geschichtswissenschaft Ser.: No. 10). 254p. 1980. write for info. (3-487-07045-6) G Olms Pubs.

Neukaledonien: Diatomeenflora Einer Tropeninsel. Revision der Collection Maillard & Untersuchung Neuen Materials. Gerd Moser et al. (Bibliotheca Diatomologica Ser.: Vol. 32). (GER., Illus.). 341p. 1995. pap. 140.00 (0-614-97986-2, Pub. by Gebruder Borntraeger) Balogh.

Neuman Systems Model. 3rd ed. Ed. by Betty M. Neuman. LC 94-30479. (C). 1994. pap. text 45.00 (0-8385-6701-0, A6701-5) Appleton & Lange.

***Neuman Systems Model & Nursing Education: Teaching Strategies & Evaluation Outcomes.** Ed. by Lois Lowry. (Monographs). 76p. 1998. pap. text 20.00 (0-9656391-5-0) Sigma Theta Tau.

Neumann Compendium. Ed. by F. Brody & T. Vamos. LC 95-1809. (Series in 20th Century Mathematics: Vol. 1). 850p. 1995. text 86.00 (981-02-2201-7) World Scientific Pub.

Neumann Problem for the Cauchy-Riemann Complex. G. B. Folland & J. J. Kohn. LC 72-1984. (Annals of Mathematics Studies: No. 75). 154p. reprint ed. pap. 47.80 (0-608-06316-9, 206667800008) Bks Demand.

Neumann Systems for the Algebraic AKNS Problem. R. Schilling. LC 92-6951. (Memoirs Ser.: No. 467). 59p. 1992. pap. 23.00 (0-8218-2537-2, MEMO/97/467) Am Math.

Neumann's Problem for Differential Forms on Riemannian Manifolds. P. E. Conner. LC 52-42839. (Memoirs Ser.: No. 1/20). 58p. 1990. reprint ed. pap. 17.00 (0-8218-1220-3, MEMO/1/20) Am Math.

Neumann's Problem for Differential Forms on Riemannian Manifolds. Pierre E. Conner. LC 52-42839. (American Mathematical Society Ser.: Vol. 20). (Illus.). 62p. reprint ed. pap. 30.00 (0-608-09601-6, 205275900007) Bks Demand.

"Neun Stadte" des Mainzer Oberstifts. Norbert Hobelheinrich. iv, 192p. 1994. reprint ed. write for info. (3-487-09838-5) G Olms Pubs.

Neunzehn Briefe uber Judenthum see Nineteen Letters

Neunzehnte Jahrhundert see Geschichte der Deutschen Poetik

Neunzehnte Jahrhundert- Beharrung und Auflosung. Eberhard Fahrenhorst. (GER.). 580p. 1984. write for info. (3-487-07462-1) G Olms Pubs.

Neuordnung der Studienfinanzierung: Eine Kritische Bestandsaufnahme des Heutigen Systems & der Vorliegenden Reformvorschlage. Dieter Dohmen. (GER., Illus.). 239p. 1996. 51.95 (3-631-30903-1) P Lang Pubng.

Neuplatonische Pythagorica in Arabischem Gewande. Hans Daiber. 148p. pap. 37.50 (0-444-85784-2) Elsevier.

Neuplatonische und Gnostische Weltablehnung in der Schule Plotins. Christoph Elsas. (Religionsgeschichtliche Versuche und Vorarbeiten Ser.: Vol. 34). (C). 1975. 123.10 (3-11-003941-9) De Gruyter.

Neural Adaptive Control Technology. Ed. by R. Zbikowski & K. J. Hunt. LC 96-951. (Series in Robotics & Intelligent Systems: Vol. 15). 356p. 1996. write for info. (981-02-2557-1) World Scientific Pub.

Neural Aging & Its Implications in Human Neurological Pathology. fac. ed. Ed. by Robert D. Terry et al. LC 81-19906. (Aging Ser.: No. 18). (Illus.). 269p. pap. 83.40 (0-7837-7211-4, 204708700005) Bks Demand.

***Neural & Adaptive Systems: Fundamentals Through Simulations.** Jose C. Principe et al. LC 99-27794. 658p. 1999. 80.90 incl. cd-rom (0-471-35167-9) Wiley.

Neural & Automata Networks: Dynamical Behavior & Applications. Eric Goles & Servet Martinez. (C). 1990. text 144.00 (0-7923-0632-5) Kluwer Academic.

Neural & Endocrine Peptides & Receptors. Ed. by Terry W. Moody. LC 86-20462. (GWUMC Department of Biochemistry Annual Spring Symposium Ser.). (Illus.). 734p. (C). 1986. text 192.00 (0-306-42300-6, Kluwer Plenum) Kluwer Academic.

Neural & Fuzzy Systems: The Emerging Science of Intelligent Computing. Ed. by Sunanda Mitra et al. LC 94-1640. 1994. 40.00 (0-8194-1566-9, IS12); pap. 40.00 (0-8194-1565-0) SPIE.

Neural & Integrative Animal Physiology: Comparative Animal Physiology, Vol. 2. 4th ed. Ed. by C. Ladd Prosser. LC 90-27164. 786p. 1991. 155.00 (0-471-56071-5) Wiley.

Neural & Intelligent Systems Integration: 5th & 6th Generation Integrated Reasoning Information Systems. Iris Group Staff. Ed. by Branko Soucek. LC 91-26616. (Sixth Generation Computer Technologies Ser.: No. 1880). 688p. 1991. 155.00 (0-471-53676-8) Wiley.

Neural & Neurohumoral Organization of Motivated Behaviour: The 4th Conference in Interbrain Held in Pecs, Hungary, May 19-23, 1975. K. Lissak. 267p. (C). 1978. 60.00 (963-05-1316-1, Pub. by Akade Kiado) St Mut.

Neural & Synergetic Computers. Ed. by H. Haken. (Synergetics Ser.: Vol. 42). (Illus.). viii, 263p. 1988. 70.95 (0-387-50339-0) Spr-Verlag.

Neural Aspects of Human Movement: Implications for Control & Coordination. C. M. Bakker et al. viii, 96p. 1993. pap. 44.00 (90-265-1322-4) Swets.

Neural Aspects of Tactile Sensation. Ed. by J. W. Morley. 1996. write for info. (0-614-17933-5) Elsevier.

Neural Aspects of Tactile Sensation. Ed. by J. W. Morley. LC 98-209962. 366p. 1998. 122.50 (0-444-82282-8) Elsevier.

An Asterisk (*) at the beginning of an entry indicates that the title is appearing for the first time.

Neural Bases of Motor Behaviour: Proceedings of the NATO Advanced Study Institute on Multi-Sensory Control of Movement, Trieste, Italy, 3-12 July 1994. Ed. by Francesco Lacquinniti & Paolo Viviani. (NATO Advanced Science Institutes: Series D, Vol. 85). 356p. (C). 1996. text 180.50 (*0-7923-4009-4*) Kluwer Academic.

Neural Bases of Speech, Hearing, & Language. Ed. by David Kuehn et al. LC 87-2825. (Illus.). 315p. 1989. text 38.00 (*0-316-50491-2*, 1722) PRO-ED.

Neural Bases of Violence & Aggression. William S. Fields & W. H. Sweet. LC 72-13847. (Illus.). 640p. 1975. 37.50 (*0-87527-102-2*) Green.

Neural Basis of Behavior. Ed. by A. L. Beckman. (Illus.). 350p. 1982. text 53.95 (*0-88331-162-3*) R B Luce.

Neural Basis of Behavioral Adaptations: Proceedings of an International Symposium in Honour of Professor Dr. Franz Huber Held in the Evangelische Akademie Tutzing, FRC. Ed. by Klaus Schildberger & Nobert Elsner. LC 93-38296. (Fortschritte der Zoologie Ser.: No. 39). xii, 284p. 1994. 85.00 (*3-437-30680-4*, Pub. by Gustav Fischer) Balogh.

Neural Basis of Consciousness, the Dalai Lama, & a Glorious Piece of Meat: An Interview with Professor Patricia Smith Churchland. Ed. by Meredith Doran. (Living Philosophy Ser.). 52p. 1992. pap. 2.00 (*1-56543-002-6*) Mt SA Coll Philos.

Neural Basis of Elementary Behavior in Stick Insects. U. Bassler. Tr. by C. Strausfeld. (Studies of Brain Function: Vol.10). (Illus.). 180p. 1983. 86.95 (*0-387-11918-3*) Spr-Verlag.

Neural Basis of Feeding & Reward. Ed. by B. G. Hoebel & D. Novin. (Illus.). 575p. (Orig.). 1982. pap. text 39.95 (*0-940090-02-3*) Haer Inst.

Neural Basis of Motor Control. Vernon B. Brooks. (Illus.). 344p. 1986. pap. text 49.50 (*0-19-503684-0*) OUP.

Neural Basis/Visual Function. J. Cronly-Dillon. 1991. 137.00 (*0-8493-7504-5*) CRC Pr.

Neural Blockage in Clinical Anesthesia & Management of Pain. 3rd ed. Ed. by Michael J. Cousins. LC 97-26333. 1,200p. 1997. text 169.00 (*0-397-51159-0*) Lppncott W & W.

Neural Cartography: How Does the CNS Use Sensory Maps? Ed. by Thomas E. Finger. (Journal: Brains, Behavior & Evolution: Vol. 31, No. 1, 1988). 56p. 1987. pap. 85.25 (*3-8055-4724-2*) S Karger.

Neural Cell Culture: A Practical Approach. Ed. by James Cohen & Graham Wilkin. (Practical Approach Ser.: Vol. 165). (Illus.). 268p. (C). 1996. pap. text 55.00 (*0-19-963484-X*) OUP.

Neural Cell Specification: Molecular Mechanisms & Neurotherapeutic Implications: Proceedings of the Third Altschul Symposium Held in Saskatoon, Canada, May 12-14, 1994. Ed. by Bernard H. Juurlink et al. (Altschul Symposia Ser.: Vol. 3). (Illus.). 324p. 1995. 110.00 (*0-306-45185-9*, Kluwer Plenum) Kluwer Academic.

Neural Circuits & Networks. Ed. by V. Torre & J. Nicholls. LC 98-41287. (NATO ASI Ser.: Series F, Vol. 167). ix, 247p. 1999. 74.00 (*3-540-64929-8*) Spr-Verlag.

Neural Codes & Distributed Representations: Foundations of Neural Computation. Ed. by Laurence Abbott & Terrence J. Sejnowski. LC 98-14783. (Computational Neuroscience Ser.). (Illus.). 358p. 1998. pap. 30.00 (*0-262-51100-2*, Bradford Bks) MIT Pr.

Neural Computation & Psychology: Proceedings of the 3rd Neural Computation & Psychology Workshop (NCPW3), University of Stirling, Scotland, 31 August - September 1994. Third Neural Computation & Psychology Workshop Sta. Ed. by L. S. Smith & P. J. Hancock. (Workshops in Computing Ser.). (Illus.). 226p. 1995. 59.00 (*3-540-19948-9*) Spr-Verlag.

Neural Computation in Hopfield Networks & Boltzmann Machines. James P. Coughlin & Robert H. Baran. LC 94-23048. (Illus.). 296p. 1995. 38.50 (*0-87413-464-1*) U Delaware Pr.

Neural Computation of Pattern Motion: Modeling Stages of Motion Analysis in the Primate Visual Cortex. Margaret E. Sereno. (Neural Network Modeling & Connectionism Ser.). (Illus.). 190p. 1993. 28.00 (*0-262-19329-9*, Bradford Bks) MIT Pr.

Neural Computers. Ed. by Rolf Eckmiller & C. Von Der Malsburg. xiii, 566p. 1990. 63.95 (*0-387-50892-9*) Spr-Verlag.

Neural Computers. Ed. by Rolf Eckmiller & Christoph Von Der Maslburg. (NATO Asi Series F: Vol. 41). 566p. 1988. 112.00 (*0-387-18724-3*) Spr-Verlag.

Neural Computing: An Introduction. Russell Beale & T. Jackson. (Illus.). 256p. 1990. pap. 41.00 (*0-85274-262-2*) IOP Pub.

Neural Computing for Structural Mechanics. B. H. V. Topping & A. Bahreininejad. 180p. 1997. 204.00 (*1-874672-02-4*, Pub. by Civil-Comp) St Mut.

Neural Computing Research & Applications: Proceedings of the Second Irish Neural Networks Conference, Queen's University, Belfast, Northern Ireland, 25-26 June, 1992. Ed. by G. A. Orchard. 336p. 1993. 159.00 (*0-7503-0259-3*) IOP Pub.

Neural Connections, Mental Computation. Ed. by Lynn Nadel & Lynn A. Cooper. (Illus.). 368p. 1992. reprint ed. pap. text 27.50 (*0-262-64029-5*, Bradford Bks) MIT Pr.

***Neural Control of Macronutrient Selection: Neural & Metabolic Control of Macronujtrient Intake.** Hans-Rudolf Berthoud & Randy J. Seeley. LC 99-29233. 528p. 1999. boxed set 89.95 (*0-8493-2752-0*, 2752) CRC Pr.

Neural Control of Movement: Proceedings of the 32nd Congress of the International Union of Physiological Sciences (IUPS), Held in Glasgow, Scotland, August 1-6, 1992. Ed. by William R. Ferrell & Uwe Proske. LC 95-8372. (Illus.). 326p. 1995. 95.00 (*0-306-45016-X*, Kluwer Plenum) Kluwer Academic.

Neural Control of Reproduction: Physiology & Behavior. Ed. by Kei-ichiro Maeda et al. LC 97-183208. (Illus.). xii, 254p. 1997. 235.00 (*3-8055-6513-5*) S Karger.

Neural Control of Rhythmic Movements in Vertebrates. Avis H. Cohen et al. LC 87-21573. (Neurobiology Ser.). 500p. 1988. 325.00 (*0-471-81968-9*) Wiley.

Neural Control of Skilled Human Movements. Ed. by F. W. Cody. (Studies in Physiology: Vol. 3). (Illus.). 120p. (Orig.). (C). 1995. pap. text 37.40 (*1-85578-081-X*, Pub. by Portland Pr Ltd) Ashgate Pub Co.

Neural Control of Sweating. Ching-hsi Wang. LC 64-12726. 141p. reprint ed. pap. 43.80 (*0-608-12235-1*, 202371100033) Bks Demand.

Neural Control of the Cardiovascular System & Orthostatic Regulation: Proceedings Basel, 1975. Ed. by H. Denolin et al. (Cardiology Ser.: Vol. 61, Suppl. 1). (Illus.). 250p. 1976. 61.00 (*3-8055-2260-6*) S Karger.

Neural Control of the Respiratory Muscles. Ed. by Alan D. Miller et al. LC 96-8017. 320p. 1996. boxed set 169.95 (*0-8493-4001-2*) CRC Pr.

***Neural Correlates of Consciousness: Empirical & Conceptual Questions.** Thomas Metzinger. LC 99-87947. (Illus.). 367p. 2000. 50.00 (*0-262-13370-9*, Bradford Bks) MIT Pr.

***Neural Crest.** 2nd ed. Nicole M. Le Douarin & Chaya Kalcheim. LC 98-53256. (Developmental & Cell Biology Ser.: No. 36). (Illus.). 480p. (C). 1999. 95.00 (*0-521-62010-4*) Cambridge U Pr.

Neural Crest in Development & Evolution. Brian K. Hall. LC 98-51752. 344p. 1999. 74.95 (*0-387-98702-9*) Spr-Verlag.

Neural Darwinism: The Theory of Neuronal Group Selection. Gerald M. Edelman. LC 87-47744. 416p. 1987. 42.00 (*0-465-04934-6*, Pub. by Basic) HarpC.

Neural Development. Ed. by K. Uyemura et al. LC 98-45347. (Illus.). xxii, 546p. 1999. 189.00 (*4-431-70232-6*) Spr-Verlag.

Neural Development & Plasticity. R. Ranney Mize & Reha S. Erzurumlu. LC 96-41471. (Progress in Brain Research Ser.). 434p. 1996. 247.00 (*0-444-82433-2*) Elsevier.

Neural Development & Regeneration. Ed. by A. Gorio et al. (NATO ASI Series H: Vol. 22). 711p. 1988. 271.00 (*0-387-18553-4*) Spr-Verlag.

Neural Development & Schizophrenia: Theory & Research, No. 275. Ed. by Sarnoff A. Mednick & J. Meggin Hollister. LC 95-3584. (NATO ASI Ser.: Ser. A, Vol. 275). (Illus.). 272p. (C). 1995. text 89.50 (*0-306-44996-X*) Plenum.

***Neural Foundations: What Stimulation Your Baby Needs to Become Smart.** 2nd rev. ed. William H. Staso, (Illus.). 139p. 1999. pap. 19.95 (*0-9644245-2-5*) Great Beginnings.

Neural Function. Michael Wang & Alan Freeman. 208p. 1986. 21.00 (*0-316-92148-3*, Little Brwn Med Div) Lppncott W & W.

Neural Fuzzy Control Systems with Structure & Parameter Learning. Ching-Teng Lin. 150p. 1994. text 39.00 (*981-02-1613-0*) World Scientific Pub.

Neural Geographies: Feminism & the Microstructure of Cognition. Elizabeth A. Wilson. LC 97-28344. 256p. (C). 1998. 75.00 (*0-415-91599-6*); pap. 22.99 (*0-415-91600-3*) Routledge.

Neural Growth & Differentiation. International Symposium on Developmental Neurobiology Staff. Ed. by Esmail Meisami & Mary A. Brazier. LC 79-9646. (International Brain Research Organization Monograph Ser.: No. 5). (Illus.). 546p. reprint ed. pap. 169.30 (*0-7837-7087-1*, 204690100004) Bks Demand.

Neural Hormones & Reproduction: Proceedings of the International Symposium on Brain-Endocrine Interaction, 3rd, Wurzberg, July, 1977. International Symposium on Brain-Endocrine Interac. Ed. by D. E. Scott et al. (Brain-Endocrine Interaction Ser.: Vol. III). (Illus.). 1978. 172.25 (*3-8055-2798-5*) S Karger.

Neural Information Processing & VLSI. Bing J. Sheu & Joongho Choi. Ed. by Robert C. Chang. LC 94-42945. (International Series in Engineering & Computer Science: Vol. 304). 584p. (C). 1995. text 138.00 (*0-7923-9547-6*) Kluwer Academic.

Neural Information Processing Systems. Ed. by Dana Z. Anderson. LC 88-71208. 884p. 1988. lib. bdg. 85.00 (*0-88318-569-5*) Am Inst Physics.

Neural Injury & Regeneration. Ed. by Fredrick J. Seil. LC 92-19861. (Advances in Neurology Ser.: No. 59). 384p. pap. 119.10 (*0-608-05602-2*, 206606000006) Bks Demand.

Neural Logic Networks. Teh H. Heng. 500p. 1995. pap. text 48.00 (*981-02-2419-2*) World Scientific Pub.

Neural Logic Networks. Hoon-Heng Teh. 500p. 1995. text 86.00 (*981-02-1844-3*) World Scientific Pub.

Neural Mechanisms & Cardiovascular Disease: Proceedings of the International Symposium Held in S. Margherita Ligure, Italy, in May 1985. Ed. by A. Malliani et al. (FIDIA Research Ser.). 650p. 1987. 196.00 (*0-387-96454-1*) Spr-Verlag.

Neural Mechanisms in Animal Behavior. Ed. by A. M. Granda & W. N. Hayes. (Illus.). 1972. 39.25 (*3-8055-1558-8*) S Karger.

Neural Mechanisms in Behavior: A Texas Symposium. Ed. by D. McFadden. (Illus.). 350p. 1980. 102.00 (*0-387-90468-9*) Spr-Verlag.

Neural Mechanisms in Cardiac Arrhythmias. Ed. by Peter J. Schwartz et al. LC 77-77962. (Perspectives in Cardiovascular Research Ser.: Vol. 2). 460p. 1978. text 105.00 (*0-89004-209-8*) Lppncott W & W.

Neural Mechanisms in Cardiac Arrhythmias. Ed. by Peter J. Schwartz et al. LC 77-77962. (Perspectives in Cardiovascular Research Ser.: Vol. 2). (Illus.). 460p. reprint ed. pap. 142.60 (*0-608-09742-X*, 206991100007) Bks Demand.

Neural Mechanisms in Disorders of Movement. A. R. Crossman & M. A. Sambrook. (Current Problems in Neurology Ser.: Vol. 9). 224p. 1988. 79.95 (*0-86196-164-1*, Pub. by J Libbey Med) Bks Intl VA.

Neural Mechanisms in Taste. Ed. by Robert H. Cagan. 224p. 1989. lib. bdg. 159.00 (*0-8493-5834-5*, QP456) CRC Pr.

Neural Mechanisms of Conditioning. Ed. by Daniel L. Alkon & Charles D. Woody. (Illus.). 512p. (C). 1985. text 144.00 (*0-306-42041-4*, Kluwer Plenum) Kluwer Academic.

Neural Mechanisms of Salivary Gland Secretion. Ed. by J. R. Garrett et al. (Frontiers of Oral Biology Ser.: Vol. 11). (Illus.). viii, 200p. 1999. 174.00 (*3-8055-6880-0*) S Karger.

***Neural Mechanisms of Salivary Gland Secretion/ Glandular Mechanisms of Salivary Gland Secretion.** Ed. by J. R. Garrett et al. (Frontiers of Oral Biology Ser.: Vols. 10 & 11). (Illus.). xx, 464p. 2000. 283.50 (*3-8055-6964-5*) S Karger.

Neural Mechanisms of Startle Behavior. Ed. by Robert C. Eaton. 398p. 1984. 95.00 (*0-306-41556-9*, Plenum Trade) Perseus Pubng.

Neural Membranes. Ed. by Grace Y. Sun et al. LC 83-6106. (Experimental & Clinical Neuroscience Ser.). (Illus.). 584p. 1983. 120.00 (*0-89603-052-0*) Humana.

Neural Modeling & Neural Networks. Ed. by F. Ventriglia. LC 93-34085. (Studies in Neuroscience). 360p. 1994. 173.00 (*0-08-042277-2*, Pergamon Pr) Elsevier.

Neural Modeling of Brain & Cognitive Disorders. LC 96-35593. 425p. 1996. lib. bdg. 60.00 (*981-02-2879-1*) World Scientific Pub.

Neural Models & Algorithms for Digital Testing. Srimat T. Chakradhar et al. (C). 1991. text 95.00 (*0-7923-9165-9*) Kluwer Academic.

Neural Modulation of Immunity: Proceedings of an International Symposium Held under the Auspices of the Princess Liliane Cardiology Foundation in Brussels, Belgium, October 27 & 28, 1983. Ed. by Roger Guillemin et al. LC 84-24964. (Illus.). 272p. 1985. reprint ed. pap. 84.40 (*0-608-00655-6*, 206124300007) Bks Demand.

Neural Monitoring: The Prevention of Intraoperative Injury. Ed. by Steven K. Salzman. LC 90-4625. (Neurotrauma Ser.). (Illus.). 336p. 1990. 125.00 (*0-89603-189-6*) Humana.

Neural, Morphological & Stochastic Methods in Image & Signal Processing: 10-11 July, 1995, San Diego, California. Edward R. Dougherty & Society of Photo-Optical Instrumentation Engineers. LC 95-68583. vii, 304 p. 1995. write for info. (*0-8194-1927-3*) SPIE.

Neural Net Applications & Products. Richard K. Miller et al. 347p. 1990. pap. 285.00 (*0-89671-107-2*) SEAI Tech Pubns.

Neural Nets: A Systematic Introduction. R. Rojas. 504p. 1996. pap. 35.95 (*3-540-60505-3*) Spr-Verlag.

Neural Nets: A Theory for Brains & Machines, Vol. 638. A. F. Da Rocha. LC 92-31542. (Lecture Notes in Computer Science Ser.). xv, 393p. 1992. 63.95 (*0-387-55949-3*) Spr-Verlag.

Neural Nets: Applications for Geography. Ed. by Bruce C. Hewitson & Robert G. Crane. LC 94-6951. (GeoJournal Library: Vol. 29). 208p. (C). 1994. lib. bdg. 106.00 (*0-7923-2746-2*) Kluwer Academic.

Neural Nets: Proceedings of the 5th Italian Workshop. E. R. Caianiello. LC 92-21204. 384p. 1993. text 100.00 (*981-02-1302-6*) World Scientific Pub.

***Neural Nets - WIRN Vietri-99: Proceedings of the 11th Italian Workshop on Neural Nets, Vietri Sul Mare, Salerno, Italy, 20-22 May, 1999.** Ed. by M. Marinaro & Roberto Tagliaferri. LC 99-42437. (Perspectives in Neural Computing Ser.). (Illus.). 440p. 1999. pap. 94.95 (*1-85233-177-1*, Pub. by Spr-Verlag) Spr-Verlag.

Neural Nets & Chaotic Carriers. Whittle. LC 98-26913. 218p. (C). 1998. 155.00 (*0-471-98541-4*) Wiley.

Neural Nets in Electric Fish. Walter F. Heiligenberg. (Bradford - Computational Neuroscience Ser.). (Illus.). 198p. 1991. 40.00 (*0-262-08203-9*) MIT Pr.

Neural Nets '95: Proceedings of the VII Italian Workshop. 332p. 1996. 67.00 (*981-02-2603-9*) World Scientific Pub.

Neural Nets, Wirn Vietri: Proceedings of the 6th Italian Workshop, 1993. E. R. Caianiello. 420p. 1994. text 109.00 (*981-02-1700-5*) World Scientific Pub.

***Neural Nets, Wirn Vietri-98: Proceedings of the Tenth Italian Workshop on Neural Nets, Vietri Sul Mare, Salerno, 21-23 May 1998.** Italian Workshop on Neural Nets Staff et al. Ed. by M. Marinaro & Roberto Tagliaferri. LC 98-38064. (Perspective in Neural Computing Ser.). x, 390 p. 1999. write for info. (*1-85233-051-1*) Spr-Verlag.

Neural Nets, Wirn Vietri-'97: Proceedings of the 9th Italian Workshop On Neural Nets, Vietri Sul Mare, Salerno, 22-24 May 1997. M. Marinaro & Roberto Tagliaferri. LC 97-26379. (Perspectives in Neural Computing Ser.). 1997. 89.95 (*3-540-76157-8*) Spr-Verlag.

Neural Nets, Wirn Vietri-'96: VIII Italian Workshop on Neural Nets, 23-25 May 1996. M. Marinaro & R. Tagliaferri. (Perspectives in Neural Computing Ser.). (Illus.). 360p. 1996. 89.00 (*3-540-76099-7*) Spr-Verlag.

Neural Network. Richard K. Miller & Marcia E. Rupnow. LC 90-83861. (Survey on Technology & Markets Ser.: No. 154). 50p. 1991. pap. text 200.00 (*1-55865-181-0*) Future Tech Surveys.

Neural Network Analysis, Architectures & Applications. Ed. by Antony Browne. LC 97-31332. 263p. 1997. 63.00 (*0-7503-0499-5*) IOP Pub.

Neural Network Applications: Proceedings of the Second British Neural Network Society Meeting (NCM '91), London, October 1991. Ed. by J. G. Taylor & C. L. Manion. LC 92-2355. (Perspectives in Neural Computing Ser.). x, 157p. 1992. 62.95 (*0-387-19772-9*) Spr-Verlag.

Neural Network Applications in Control. Ed. by Kevin Warwick et al. (IEE Control Engineering Ser.: No. 53). 300p. 1995. boxed set 82.00 (*0-85296-852-3*) INSPEC Inc.

Neural Network Computing. Ramachandran Bharath. 1994. pap. 29.95 incl. disk (*0-8306-4523-3*, Windcrest) TAB Bks.

Neural Network Computing for the Electric Power Industry: Proceedings of the 1992 INNS Summer Workshop. Ed. by Dejan J. Sobajic. 240p. 1993. pap. 49.95 (*0-8058-1467-1*) L Erlbaum Assocs.

Neural Network Control of Robot Manipulators & Non-Linear Systems. F. W. Lewis. LC 99-178266. 1998. 99.00 (*0-7484-0596-8*) Taylor & Francis.

Neural Network Data Analysis Using Simulnet. Edward J. Rzempoluck. LC 97-16666. (Illus.). 216p. 1997. 39.95 incl. cd-rom (*0-387-98255-8*) Spr-Verlag.

Neural Network Design. Beale & Demuth. (Electrical Engineering Ser.). 1996. pap. 37.95 (*0-534-95259-3*) PWS Pubs.

Neural Network Design & the Complexity of Learning. J. Stephen Judd. (Bradford - Network Modeling & Connectionism Ser.). (Illus.). 182p. 1990. 32.00 (*0-262-10045-2*, Bradford Bks) MIT Pr.

Neural Network Dynamics: Proceedings of the Workshop, June 17-21, 1991 at IIASS, Vietri, Italy. Ed. by J. G. Taylor et al. LC 92-24960. (Perspectives in Neural Computing Ser.). xii, 370p. 1992. 89.00 (*0-387-19771-0*) Spr-Verlag.

Neural Network Engineering in Dynamic Control Systems. Ed. by K. J. Hung et al. LC 95-30315. (Advances in Industrial Control Ser.). (Illus.). 296p. 1996. 64.00 (*3-540-19973-X*) Spr-Verlag.

Neural Network Experiments on Personal Computers & Workstations. Granino A. Korn. (Illus.). 264p. 1991. pap. text 45.00 (*0-262-61073-6*, Bradford Bks) MIT Pr.

Neural Network for Optimization & Combinatorics. Yoshiyasu Takefuji & J. Wang. 250p. 1996. text 81.00 (*981-02-1314-X*) World Scientific Pub.

Neural Network Fundamentals with Graphs, Algorithms & Applications. Nirmal K. Bose & Ping Liang. LC 95-16922. (Electrical & Computer Engineering Ser.: Communications & Signal Processing). 512p. (C). 1995. 77.50 (*0-07-006618-3*) McGraw.

Neural Network Guide to Teaching. Justine C. Baker & Francis G. Martin. LC 98-65079. (Fastback Ser.: No. 431). 50p. 1998. pap. 3.00 (*0-87367-631-9*, FB#431) Phi Delta Kappa.

***Neural Network Learning: Theoretical Foundations.** Martin Anthony & Peter Bartlett. LC 98-53260. 416p. (C). 1999. 59.95 (*0-521-57353-X*) Cambridge U Pr.

Neural Network Learning & Expert Systems. Stephen I. Gallant. (Illus.). 364p. 1993. 52.50 (*0-262-07145-2*, Bradford Bks) MIT Pr.

Neural Network Modeling: Statistical Mechanics & Cybernetic Perspectives. Perambur S. Neelakanta & Dolores F. DeGroff. 256p. 1994. boxed set 99.95 (*0-8493-2488-2*, 2488) CRC Pr.

Neural Network Models: An Analysis. Philippe De Wilde. (Lecture Notes in Control & Information Sciences: Vol. 210). 153p. 1995. pap. 44.95 (*3-540-19995-0*) Spr-Verlag.

Neural Network Models: Theory & Projects. 2nd ed. Philippe De Wilde. Ed. by B. W. Dickinson et al. LC 97-14010. (Communications & Control Engineering Ser.). (Illus.). 200p. 1997. pap. 28.00 (*3-540-76129-2*) Spr-Verlag.

Neural Network Models of Cognition: Biobehavioral Foundations. Ed. by J.W. Donahoe. 1996. write for info. (*0-614-17934-3*, North Holland) Elsevier.

Neural-Network Models of Cognition: Biobehavioral Foundations, Vol. 121. John W. Donahoe & Vivian P. Dorsel. LC 97-42861. (Advances in Psychology Ser.: 121). (Illus.). 600p. 1997. 155.00 (*0-444-81931-2*) Elsevier.

Neural Network Parallel Computing. Yoshiyasu Takefuji. (International Series in Engineering & Computer Science, VLSI, Computer Architecture, & Digital Screen Processing). 256p. (C). 1992. text 163.50 (*0-7923-9190-X*) Kluwer Academic.

Neural Network Perception for Mobile Robot Guidance. Dean A. Pomerleau. LC 93-24616. (International Engineering & Computer Science Ser.: SECS 239). 1993. lib. bdg. 99.00 (*0-7923-9373-2*) Kluwer Academic.

Neural Network Simulation Environments. Ed. by Josef Skrzypek. LC 93-41462. (International Series in Engineering & Computer Science, VLSI, Computer Architecture, & Digital Screen Processing). 280p. (C). 1994. text 141.00 (*0-7923-9415-1*) Kluwer Academic.

Neural Network Systems Techniques & Applications, 7 vols. Leondes. 1997. write for info. (*0-12-443860-1*) Acad Pr.

Neural Network Systems Techniques & Applications Vol. 1: Algorithms & Architecture. Ed. by Cornelius T. Leondes. LC 97-80441. (Illus.). 480p. 1997. text 69.95 (*0-12-443861-X*) Morgan Kaufmann.

Neural Network Systems Techniques & Applications Vol. 2: Neural Network Systems, Vol. 2. Ed. by Cornelius T. Leondes. (Neural Network Systems Techniques & Applications Ser.). (Illus.). 398p. 1997. text 69.95 (*0-12-443862-8*) Morgan Kaufmann.

N

Neural Network Systems Techniques & Applications Vol. 3: Implementation Techniques, Vol. 3. Ed. by Cornelius T. Leondes. (Neural Network Systems Techniques & Applications Ser.). (Illus.). 432p. 1997. text 69.95 (0-12-443863-6) Morgan Kaufmann.

Neural Network Systems Techniques & Applications Vol. 4: Industrial & Manufacturing Systems, Vol. 4. Ed. by Cornelius T. Leondes. (Neural Network Systems Techniques & Applications Ser.). (Illus.). 384p. 1997. text 69.95 (0-12-443864-4) Morgan Kaufmann.

Neural Network Systems Techniques & Applications Vol. 5: Image Processing & Pattern Recognition, Vol. 5. Ed. by Cornelius T. Leondes. (Neural Network Systems Techniques & Applications Ser.). (Illus.). 416p. 1997. text 69.95 (0-12-443865-2) Morgan Kaufmann.

Neural Network Systems Techniques & Applications Vol. 6: Fuzzy Logic & Expert Systems Applications, Vol. 6. Ed. by Cornelius T. Leondes. (Neural Network Systems Techniques & Applications Ser.). (Illus.). 384p. 1997. text 69.95 (0-12-443866-0) Morgan Kaufmann.

Neural Network Systems Techniques & Applications Vol. 7: Control & Dynamic Systems, Vol. 7. Ed. by Cornelius T. Leondes. (Neural Network Systems Techniques & Applications Ser.). (Illus.). 438p. 1997. text 69.95 (0-12-443867-9) Morgan Kaufmann.

Neural Network Time Series of. Eitan M. Azoff. LC 93-42336. (Finance Editions Ser.). 212p. 1994. 125.00 (0-471-94356-8) Wiley.

Neural Network Training Using Genetic Algorithms. A. J. Rooij et al. LC 96-49415. (Series in Machine Perception & Artificial Intelligence). 1996. write for info. (981-02-2919-4) World Scientific Pub.

Neural Networks. (C). 1993. write for info. (0-201-59494-3) Addison-Wesley.

***Neural Networks.** Herve Abdi. LC 98-46918. (University Papers Series.). 1999. 13.95 (0-7619-1440-4) Sage.

Neural Networks. Eric Davalo & Patrick Naim. Ed. by F. H. Sumner. Tr. by A. Rawsthorne. (Computer Science Ser.). (Illus.). 157p. (C). 1991. pap. text 35.00 (0-333-54996-1, Pub. by Macmillan Ed) Scholium Intl.

***Neural Networks.** G. David Garson. LC 98-61097. (New Technologies for Social Research Ser.). vi, 194 p. 1998. write for info. (0-7619-5731-6) Sage.

Neural Networks. Giardina. (C). 2002. 53.33 (0-13-616335-1, Macmillan Coll) P-H.

Neural Networks. Richard K. Miller. LC 89-17158. 302p. 1989. pap. text 95.00 (0-88173-100-5) Fairmont Pr.

Neural Networks. Richard K. Miller & Fairmont Press Staff. 312p. (C). 1989. pap. text 95.00 (0-13-615477-8) P-H.

Neural Networks. 2nd ed. Bose. 2001. 59.50 (0-07-232080-X) McGraw.

Neural Networks: A Comprehensive Foundation. Simon Haykin. 1994. 69.95 (0-02-032761-7) Macmillan.

***Neural Networks: A Comprehensive Foundation.** 2nd ed. Simon Haykin. 1999. 86.95 (0-7803-3494-9) IEEE Standards.

Neural Networks: A Comprehensive Foundation. 2nd ed. Simon Haykin. LC 98-7011. 842p. (C). 1998. 105.00 (0-13-273350-1, Prentice Hall) P-H.

Neural Networks: An Introduction. B. Muller & J. Reinhardt. Ed. by E. Domany et al. (Physics of Neural Networks Ser.). (Illus.). xiii, 266p. 1991. reprint ed. text 49.00 incl. 5.25 hd (0-387-52380-4) Spr-Verlag.

Neural Networks: An Introduction. 2nd ed. B. Miller. Ed. by J. L. Van Hemmen et al. LC 95-24948. (Physics of Neural Networks Ser.). 352p. 1995. 39.95 incl. disk (3-540-60207-0) Spr-Verlag.

Neural Networks: Artificial Intelligance & Industrial Applications: Proceedings of the Third Annual SNN Symposium on Neural Networks, Nijmegen, The Netherlands, 14-15 September 1995. Ed. by Bert Kappen & Stan Gielen. LC 95-36463. 398p. 1995. 89.00 (3-540-19992-6) Spr-Verlag.

Neural Networks: Best Practice in Europe: Proceedings of the Stichting Neurale Netwerken Conference 1997, Amsterdam, The Netherlands, 22 May, 1997. Ed. by Bert Kappen & Stan Gielen. LC 97-44641. (Progress in Neural Processing Ser.). 220p. 1997. 58.00 (981-02-3338-8) World Scientific Pub.

Neural Networks: Computers with Intuition. S. Brunak & B. Lautrup. 200p. (C). 1990. text 39.00 (9971-5-0938-5); pap. text 18.00 (9971-5-0939-3) World Scientific Pub.

Neural Networks: Current Applications. P. G. Lisboa. (ITCP-UK Computer Science Ser.). 279p. (C). 1992. mass mkt. 84.95 (0-412-42790-7) Chapman & Hall.

Neural Networks: Current Applications. Ed. by P. G. Lisboa. 288p. 1992. pap. 59.95 (0-442-31564-3) Chapman & Hall.

Neural Networks: Deterministic Methods of Analysis. Steve Ellacott. (Illus.). 250p. 1996. mass mkt. 49.95 (1-85032-244-9) ITCP.

Neural Networks: From Biology to High Energy Physics: Proceedings of the Third Workshop, Elba International Physics Centre, Italy 26 - 30 September 1994. Ed. by Daniel J. Amit et al. 280p. 1995. text 68.00 (981-02-2482-6, RuBnRaPh-P2953) World Scientific Pub.

Neural Networks The Second Generation. Robert Levine. pap. text 24.95 (0-07-037486-4) Gregg-McGraw.

Neural Networks: Theoretical Foundations & Analysis. Clifford Lau. LC 91-39114. (Illus.). 336p. (C). 1991. 69.95 (0-87942-280-7, PC0279-0) Inst Electrical.

Neural Networks Vol. 2: Concepts, Application & Implementations, Vol. 2. Paolo Antognetti. 1991. text 52.60 (0-13-612763-0) P-H.

Neural Networks - The Statistical Mechanics Perspective: Proceedings of the CTP - PBSRI Joint Workshop on Thor Physics. J. H. Oh et al. (Progress in Neural Processing Ser.: Vol. 1). 300p. 1995. text 76.00 (981-02-2324-2) World Scientific Pub.

Neural Networks & a New Artificial Intelligence, Vol. 1. Dorfner. (ITCP-UK Computer Science Ser.). 1996. mass mkt. 39.95 (1-85032-172-8) ITCP.

Neural Networks & Analog Computation: Beyond the Turing Limit. Hava Siegelman. LC 98-29446. (Progress in Theoretical Computer Science Ser.). 200p. 1998. 49.50 (0-8176-3949-7) Birkhauser.

Neural Networks & Artificial Intelligence for Biomedical Engineering. Donna L. Hudson & Maurice E. Cohen. LC 99-30757. 256p. 1999. 89.95 (0-7803-3404-3, PC5675-QOE) Inst Electrical.

Neural Networks & Brain Function. Edmund T. Rolls & Alessandro Treves. LC 97-41669. (Illus.). 432p. 1997. text 115.00 (0-19-852433-1); pap. text 52.50 (0-19-852432-3) OUP.

Neural Networks & Chaos. Amari & Freeman. Ed. by Harold Szu. (INNS Series of Texts, Monographs, & Proceedings). 300p. 1993. write for info. (0-8058-1501-5) L Erlbaum Assocs.

Neural Networks & Combinatorial Optimization in Civil & Structural Engineering. Civil Comp Editors. 1993. pap. text 245.00 (0-948749-18-0, Pub. by Civil-Comp) St Mut.

Neural Networks & Expert Systems in Medicine & Healthcare. Emmanuel Ifeachor. (Artificial Intelligence Ser.). 400p. 1998. 86.00 (981-02-3611-5) World Scientific Pub.

Neural Networks & Fuzzy-Logic Control on Personal Computers & Workstations. Granino A. Korn. 404p. 1995. 57.50 (0-262-11205-1, Bradford Bks) MIT Pr.

Neural Networks & Fuzzy Systems: Theory & Applications. 288p. (C). 1996. text 139.00 (0-7923-9814-9) Kluwer Academic.

Neural Networks & Information Processing. Kunihiko Fukushima. (Computation & Neural Systems Ser.). 208p. (C). 1993. text. write for info. (0-201-52574-7) Addison-Wesley.

Neural Networks & Intellect: Using Model Based Concepts. Leonid Perlovsky. (Illus.). 640p. (C). 2000. pap. 79.00 (0-19-511162-1) OUP.

Neural Networks & Natural Intelligence. Stephen Grossberg. (Bradford Bk.). (Illus.). 656p. 1992. reprint ed. pap. text 42.50 (0-262-57091-2, Bradford Bks) MIT Pr.

Neural Networks & Pattern Recognition. Ed. by Omid Omidvar & Judith Dayhoff. LC 97-25466. (Illus.). 351p. 1997. text 49.95 (0-12-526420-8) Acad Pr.

Neural Networks & Psychopathology: Connectionist Models in Practice & Research. Ed. by Dan J. Stein & Jacques Ludik. LC 98-5826. (Illus.). 386p. (C). 1999. text 85.00 (0-521-57163-4) Cambridge U Pr.

Neural Networks & Qualitative Physics: A Viability Approach. Jean-Pierre Aubin. (Illus.). 298p. (C). 1996. text 54.95 (0-521-44532-9) Cambridge U Pr.

Neural Networks & Simulation Methods. Jian-Kang Wu. LC 93-38085. (Electrical Engineering & Electronics Ser.: Vol. 87). (Illus.). 456p. 1993. text 185.00 (0-8247-9181-9) Dekker.

Neural Networks & Speech Processing. David P. Morgan & Christopher L. Scofield. (International Series in Engineering & Computer Science, VLSI, Computer Architecture, & Digital Screen Processing). 416p. (C). 1991. text 128.00 (0-7923-9144-6) Kluwer Academic.

Neural Networks & Spin Glasses. Ed. by W. K. Theumann et al. 336p. (C). 1990. text 113.00 (981-02-0026-9) World Scientific Pub.

Neural Networks & Their Applications. G. J. Taylor. 322p. 1996. 135.00 (0-471-96282-1) Wiley.

Neural Networks Applications. Ed. by Patrick K. Simpson. LC 96-33928. (IEEE Technology Update Ser.). 970p. 1996. 69.95 (0-7803-2566-4, BR2025) Inst Electrical.

Neural Networks As Cybernetic Systems. Holk Cruse. LC 96-8521. 1996. 105.00 (0-86577-672-5) Thieme Med Pubs.

Neural Networks Finance & Investment: Using Artificial Intelligence to Improve Real-World Performance. 2nd ed. Robert R. Trippi & Efraim Turban. 880p. 1996. 80.00 (1-55738-919-5, Irwn Prfssnl) McGraw-Hill Prof.

Neural Networks for Chemical Engineers. Ed. by A. B. Bulsari. LC 95-9927. (Computer-Aided Chemical Engineering Ser.: Vol. 6). 694p. 1995. 310.50 (0-444-82097-3) Elsevier.

***Neural Networks for Chemists.** Jure Zupan & Johann Gasteiger. 380p. 1999. 90.00 (3-527-29778-2); pap. 45.00 (3-527-29779-0) Wiley.

Neural Networks for Computing. John S. Denker. LC 86-72481. (AIP Conference Proceedings Ser.: No. 151). 464p. 1986. lib. bdg. 70.00 (0-88318-351-X) Am Inst Physics.

Neural Networks for Conditional Probability Estimation: Forecasting Beyond Point Predictions. Dirk Husmeier. Ed. by J. G. Taylor. LC 98-48438. (Perspectives in Neural Computing Ser.). (Illus.). 275p. 1999. pap. 89.95 (1-85233-095-3) Spr-Verlag.

Neural Networks for Control. Ed. by W. Thomas Miller, III & Richard S. Sutton. (Neural Network Modeling & Connectionism). 450p. 1991. 65.00 (0-262-13261-3) MIT Pr.

Neural Networks for Control. Paul J. Werbos. Ed. by W. Thomas Miller & Richard S. Sutton. (Neural Network Modeling & Connectionism). (Illus.). 544p. 1995. pap. text 32.50 (0-262-63161-X, Bradford Bks) MIT Pr.

Neural Networks for Economic & Financial Modelling. Sergio Margarita et al. (Illus.). 224p. 1995. mass mkt. 45.00 (1-85032-169-8) ITCP.

Neural Networks for Financial Forecasting. Edward Gately. LC 95-8998. (Traders' Advantage Ser.). 169p. 1995. 42.95 (0-471-11212-7) Wiley.

Neural Networks for Identification, Control, & Robotics, 1996 International Workshop (NICROSP '96) LC 96-75130. 500p. 1996. 100.00 (0-8186-7456-3) IEEE Comp Soc.

Neural Networks for Identification, Control, & Robotics, 1997 International Workshop (Nicrosp '97) 500p. 1997. pap. 100.00 (0-8186-8022-9) IEEE Comp Soc.

Neural Networks for Identification, Prediction & Control. Duc T. Pham & Liu Xing. LC 95-12935. (Illus.). 240p. 1995. 75.95 (3-540-19959-4) Spr-Verlag.

Neural Networks for Knowledge Representation & Inference. Ed. by Daniel S. Levine & Manuel Aparicio, IV. 512p. 1994. pap. 45.00 (0-8058-1159-1); text 99.95 (0-8058-1158-3) L Erlbaum Assocs.

***Neural Networks for Modelling & Control of Dynamic Systems: A Practitioner's Handbook.** Magnus Norgaard et al. LC 99-49801. (Advanced Textbooks in Control & Signal Processing Ser.). (Illus.). xiv, 246p. 2000. pap. 46.00 (1-85233-227-1) Spr-Verlag.

Neural Networks for Optimization & Signal Processing. A. Cichoki & Rolf Unbehauen. LC 92-46543. 544p. 1993. 220.00 (0-471-93010-5) Wiley.

Neural Networks for Pattern Recognition. Chris Bishop. (Illus.). 500p. 1996. pap. text 49.95 (0-19-853864-2) OUP.

Neural Networks for Pattern Recognition. Albert Nigrin. LC 93-10027. (Illus.). 435p. 1993. 55.00 (0-262-14054-3, Bradford Bks) MIT Pr.

Neural Networks for Pattern Recognition & Their Applications. Ed. by C. H. Chen. 200p. (C). 1994. text 59.00 (981-02-0766-2) World Scientific Pub.

***Neural Networks for RF & Microwave Design.** Q. J. Zhang. (Microwave Library). (Illus.). 2000. write for info. (1-58053-100-8) Artech Hse.

Neural Networks for Robotic Control: Theory & Applications. Ali Zalzala & Allen Morris. 288p. 1995. 80.00 (0-13-119892-0) P-H.

Neural Networks for Vision & Image Processing. Ed. by Gail A. Carpenter & Stephen Grossberg. (Illus.). 504p. 1992. pap. text 59.50 (0-262-53108-9, Bradford Bks) MIT Pr.

Neural Networks from Biology to High Energy Physics: Proceedings of the 2nd Workshop. O. Benhar et al. 356p. 1993. text 121.00 (981-02-1253-4) World Scientific Pub.

Neural Networks in Artificial Intelligence. Matthew Zeidenberg. (Artificial Intelligence Ser.). 1990. text 49.95 (0-470-21660-3) P-H.

Neural Networks in Biomedicine: Proceedings of the Course. F. Masulli & P. G. Morasso. 300p. 1994. text 91.00 (981-02-1744-7) World Scientific Pub.

Neural Networks in Bioprocessing & Chemical Engineering. D. Richard Baughman & Y. A. Liu. LC 95-34841. (Illus.). 488p. 1996. text, boxed set 69.95 incl. disk (0-12-083030-2) Acad Pr.

***Neural Networks in Chemical & Physical Systems.** Jerry A. Darsey. 200p. 2000. 28.00 (981-02-4070-8) World Scientific Pub.

Neural Networks in Computer Intelligence, Set. LiMin Fu. LC 93-45343. (C). 1993. text 51.00 (0-07-911817-8) McGraw.

Neural Networks in Control. D. Elliott. 1997. 59.95 (0-387-94887-2) Spr-Verlag.

Neural Networks in Design & Manufacturing. J. U. Wang & Yoshiyasu Takefuji. 350p. 1993. text 89.00 (981-02-1281-X) World Scientific Pub.

Neural Networks in Financial Engineering: Proceedings of the 3rd International Conference on Neural Networks in the Capital Markets, London, England October 1995. Ed. by Apostolos-Paul Refenes et al. 300p. 1996. text 84.00 (981-02-2480-X, RuaKebMb-P2951) World Scientific Pub.

Neural Networks in Financial Engineering: Proceedings of the 3rd International Conference on Neural Networks in the Capital Markets, London, England, 11-13 October 95. LC 95-51368. (Progress in Neural Processing Ser.). 636p. 1996. pap. write for info. (981-02-2819-8) World Scientific Pub.

Neural Networks in Manufacturing & Robotics. Ed. by Y. C. Shin et al. 172p. 1992. 50.00 (0-7918-1062-3, G00706) ASME.

Neural Networks in QSar & Drug Design. Ed. by James Devillers. (Principles in QSAR & Drug Design Ser.). (Illus.). 304p. 1996. text 99.00 (0-12-213815-5) Acad Pr.

Neural Networks in Robotics. Ed. by George A. Bekey & Kenneth Y. Goldberg. LC 92-27162. (C). 1992. text 210.50 (0-7923-9268-X) Kluwer Academic.

Neural Networks in Telecommunications. Ed. by Ben Yuhas & Nirwan Ansari. LC 93-33665. 384p. (C). 1993. text 157.50 (0-7923-9417-8) Kluwer Academic.

Neural Networks in the Capital Markets. Ed. by Apostolos-Paul Refenes. LC 94-37990. 392p. 1995. 105.00 (0-471-94364-9) Wiley.

Neural Networks in Transport Applications. Ed. by Veli Himanen et al. LC 98-71398. 388p. 1998. text 76.95 (1-84014-808-X, Pub. by Ashgate Pub) Ashgate Pub Co.

Neural Networks in User Modeling & Intelligent Interface: A Special Issue of the International Journal of Human-Computer Interaction, Vol. 9, No. 1. Ed. by Nong Ye. 104p. 1997. pap. 20.00 (0-8058-9862-X) L Erlbaum Assocs.

Neural Networks in Vision & Pattern Recognition. W. Karplus & Joseph Skrzypek. 224p. 1992. text 67.00 (981-02-1014-0) World Scientific Pub.

Neural Networks-Les Reseaux de Neurones: Biological Computers or Electronic Brains- Ordinateurs Biologiques Ou Cervceaux Electroniques. R. Moreau & G. Aubert. (Entretiens de Lyon Ser.). (Illus.). viii, 195p. 1990. 70.95 (0-387-59540-6) Spr-Verlag.

Neural Networks, Neurocomputers & Beyond. BCC Staff. 346p. 1990. 1950.00 (0-89336-719-2, G117) BCC.

Neural Networks, Proceedings of 1993 Workshop. Ed. by Karplus & Padgett. 500p. 1993. pap. 80.00 (1-56555-059-5, WNN-93-1) Soc Computer Sim.

Neural Networks Programming in C++ An Object-Oriented Framework for Building Connectionist Systems. Adam Blum. Ep. 1992. pap. 34.95 (0-471-55202-X) Wiley.

Neural Networks Programming in C++ An Object-Oriented Framework for Building Connectionist Systems. Adam Blum. 224p. 1992. pap., pap. text 69.90 incl. disk (0-471-55201-1) Wiley.

Neural Networks in C++ An Object-Oriented Framework for Building Connectionist Systems. Adam Blum. LC 91-39648. 224p. 1992. pap. 34.95 (0-471-53847-7) Wiley.

Neural Networks Technology & Applications: Theory, Technology & Implementations. IEEE, Technical Activities Board Staff. Ed. by Patrick K. Simpson. LC 95-11170. (IEEE Technology Update Ser.). 1995. write for info. (0-7803-2564-8) Inst Electrical.

Neural, Novel & Hybrid Algorithms for Time Series Prediction. Timothy Masters. LC 95-31203. 544p. 1995. pap. text 59.99 incl. cd-rom, disk (0-471-13041-9) Wiley.

Neural Organization: Structure, Function & Dynamics. Michael A. Arbib et al. LC 96-44543. 328p. 1997. 62.50 (0-262-01159-X, Bradford Bks) MIT Pr.

Neural Peptides & Neuronal Communication. fac. ed. Ed. by Erminio Costa & Marco Trabucchi. LC 79-66738. (Advances in Biochemical Psychopharmacology Ser.: No. 22). (Illus.). 677p. pap. 200.00 (0-7837-7245-9, 204706000005) Bks Demand.

***Neural Plasticity & Regeneration.** Ed. by F. R. Seiler. (Progress in Brain Research Ser.). 2000. write for info. (0-444-50209-2, Excerpta Medica) Elsevier.

Neural Prostheses: Materials, Physiology & Histopathology of Electrical Stimulation of the Nervous System. J. J. Bernstein. (Journal: Brains, Behavior & Evolution: Vol. 14, No. 1-2). (Illus.). 1977. 64.50 (3-8055-2640-7) S Karger.

Neural Prostheses: Replacing Motor Function after Disease or Disability. Richard B. Stein et al. (Illus.). 360p. 1992. text 68.00 (0-19-507216-2) OUP.

Neural Prostheses for Restoration of Sensory & Motor Function. John K. Chapin & Karen A. Moxon. (Methods & New Frontiers in Neuroscience Ser.). 360p. ring bd. 89.95 (0-8493-2225-1) CRC Pr.

Neural Prosthesis & Neurostimulation. Ed. by Philip L. Gildenberg et al. (Applied Neurophysiology Ser.: Vol. 45, No. 1-2). (Illus.). iv, 208p. 1981. pap. 68.00 (3-8055-3500-7) S Karger.

Neural Regeneration. Frederick J. Seil. (Progress in Brain Research Ser.: Vol. 103). 428p. 1994. 272.25 (0-444-81727-1) Elsevier.

Neural Repair, Transplantation & Rehabilitation. Roger A. Baker. 336p. 1999. 54.95 (0-86377-628-0) L Erlbaum Assocs.

Neural Representation of Temporal Patterns: Proceedings of a Symposium Held in Durham, North Carolina, April 29-May 2, 1993. Ed. by Ellen Covey et al. 274p. (C). 1996. text 95.00 (0-306-45199-9, Kluwer Plenum) Kluwer Academic.

Neural Smithing: Supervised Learning in Feedforward Artificial Neural Networks. Russell D. Reed & Robert J. Marks, II. LC 98-13416. (Illus.). 346p. 1999. 47.50 (0-262-18190-8, Bradford Bks) MIT Pr.

Neural Stimulation, 2 vols. Ed. by Joel B. Myklebust et al. 1985. 124.95 (0-318-58963-X, RC350, CRC Reprint) Franklin.

Neural Stimulation, 2 vols., Vol. I. Ed. by Joel B. Myklebust et al. 168p. 1985. 100.00 (0-8493-5253-3, RC350, CRC Reprint) Franklin.

Neural Stimulation, 2 vols., Vol. II. Ed. by Joel B. Myklebust et al. 176p. 1985. 101.00 (0-8493-5254-1, RC350, CRC Reprint) Franklin.

Neural Substrates of Limbic Epilepsy. Makram K. Girgis. (Illus.). 206p. (C). 1981. 42.50 (0-87527-238-X) Green.

Neural Systems: Analysis & Modeling. Ed. by Frank H. Eeckman. (C). 1992. text 194.50 (0-7923-9258-2) Kluwer Academic.

Neural Systems for Control. Ed. by David Elliott & Omid M. Omidvar. LC 96-29556. (Illus.). 358p. 1997. text 49.95 (0-12-526430-5) Morgan Kaufmann.

Neural Systems for Robotics. Ed. by Omid M. Omidvar & Patric Van Der Smagt. LC 96-29555. (Illus.). 346p. 1997. text 49.95 (0-12-526280-9) Morgan Kaufmann.

Neural Tissue Transplantation Research: Proceedings in Life Sciences. Ed. by R. B. Wallace & G. D. Das. (Illus.). 260p. 1983. 152.00 (0-387-90833-1) Spr-Verlag.

Neural Transmission, Learning, & Memory. Ed. by R. Caputto & Cosimo A. Marsan. LC 83-2969. (International Brain Research Organization Monograph Ser.: No. 10). (Illus.). 301p. 1983. reprint ed. pap. 93.40 (0-608-00645-9, 206123300007) Bks Demand.

Neural Transplantation: A Practical Approach. Ed. by Stephen B. Dunnett & Anders T. Bjorklund. (Practical Approach Ser.: Vol. 98). (Illus.). 232p. 1992. 85.00 (0-19-963286-3); pap. text 46.50 (0-19-963285-5) OUP.

Neural Transplantation: An Introduction. William J. Freed. LC 99-20115. (Cellular & Molecular Neuroscience Ser.). (Illus.). 459p. 1999. 55.00 (0-262-06208-9) MIT Pr.

Neural Transplantation, CNS Neuronal Injury & Regeneration. Joe Marwak. 304p. 1994. boxed set 141.95 (0-8493-8683-7, RD124) CRC Pr.

Neural Transplantation in Cerebellar Ataxia. Lazaros C. Triarhou. LC 96-34818. (Neuroscience Intelligence Unit Ser.). 160p. 1996. 99.00 (1-57059-395-7) Landes Bioscience.

***Neural Transplantation Methods.** Ed. by Stephen B. Dunnett et al. (Neuromethods Ser.: No. 36). (Illus.). 576p. 1999. 125.00 (0-89603-793-2) Humana.

Neural Transplants: Development & Function. Ed. by John R. Sladek, Jr. & Don M. Gash. 444p. 1984. 95.00 (0-306-41587-9, Plenum Trade) Perseus Pubng.

Neural Trauma. A. John Popp. LC 78-24627. (Seminars in Neurological Surgery Ser.). 405p. 1979, reprint ed. pap. 125.60 (*0-608-00314-X*, 206103100007) Bks Demand.

Neural Tube Defects, No. 181. CIBA Foundation Staff. (CIBA Foundation Symposium Ser.: Vol. 181). 310p. 1994. 128.00 (*0-471-94172-7*) Wiley.

Neurall Network Design. Howard B. Demuth et al. 736p. 1995. mass mkt. 109.95 (*0-534-94332-2*) Wadsworth Pub.

Neurally Mediated Syncope: Pathophysiology, Investigations & Treatment. Jean-Jacques Blanc et al. (Bakken Research Center Ser.: No. 10). (Illus.). 188p. 1996. 55.00 (*0-87993-644-4*) Futura Pub.

***Neuregelung der Deutschen Rechtschreibung: Beitrage Zu Ihrer Geschichte, Diskussion und Umsetzung.** Burkhard Schaeder. (Forum Angewandte Linguistik Ser.). 125p. 1999. 24.95 (*3-631-35030-9*) P Lang Pubng.

Neuren Algensysteme & Versuch zur Begruendung eines Eigenen Systems der Algen & Florideen. K. Naegeli. (Illus.). 1970. reprint ed. 77.00 (*90-6123-204-X*) Lubrecht & Cramer.

Neuro-Adaptive Process Control: A Practical Approach. Peter M. Mills et al. 228p. 1996. pap. text 170.00 incl. disk (*0-471-95997-9*) Wiley.

Neuro-Anaesthetic Practice. Ed. by Hugo Van Aken. 320p. (Orig.). (C). 1995. pap. text 68.00 (*0-7279-0909-6*, Pub. by BMJ Pub) Login Brothers Bk Co.

Neuro-Control & Its Applications. Sigeru Omatu et al. LC 95-20218. (Advances in Industrial Control Ser.). 272p. 1996. 59.00 (*3-540-19965-9*) Spr-Verlag.

Neuro-Dynamic Programming. Dimitri P. Bertsekas & John N. Tsitsiklis. LC 96-85338. 491p. (C). 1996. text 84.00 (*1-886529-10-8*) Athena Scientific.

Neuro-Fuzzy Modeling & Soft Computing. Jang. LC 96-29050. 614p. 1996. 105.00 (*0-13-261066-3*) P-H.

Neuro-Fuzzy Pattern Recognition: Methods in Soft Computing. Sankar K. Pal. LC 99-24974. 378p. 1999. 89.95 (*0-471-34844-9*) Wiley.

Neuro-Fuzzy Techniques for Intelligent Information Systems. Ed. by N. Kasabov et al. LC 99-22295. (Studies in Fuzziness & Soft Computing: Vol. 300). (Illus.). xii, 449p. 1999. 108.00 (*3-7908-1187-4*) Spr-Verlag.

***Neuro-Genetic Roots of Organizational Behavior.** Daniel A. Silverman. LC 99-47767. 112p. 1999. 21.50 (*0-7618-1540-6*) U Pr of Amer.

Neuro-Immune Endocrine Connection. Ed. by Carl W. Cotman et al. LC 86-26037. (Illus.). 166p. 1987. reprint ed. pap. 51.50 (*0-608-07201-X*, 206742600009) Bks Demand.

***Neuro-Immune Interactions in Neurologic & Psychiatric Disorders.** Ed. by Paul H. Patterson et al. LC 99-36334. (Research & Perspectives in Neurosciences Ser.). (Illus.). xiv, 180p. 1999. 104.00 (*3-540-66013-5*) Spr-Verlag.

Neuro-Immunology for the Clinician. Loren A. Rolek & Yadollah Harati. LC 96-50466. 440p. 1997. text 97.00 (*0-7506-9616-8*) Buttrwrth-Heinemann.

Neuro-Immunology of Fever. Ed. by Tamas Bartfai & David Ottoson. LC 92-48954. (Wenner-Gren International Ser.). 300p. 1992. 178.50 (*0-08-042001-X*, Pergamon Pr) Elsevier.

Neuro-Linguistic Programming, Vol. 1. Robert Dilts et al. LC 80-50147. 1980. 24.95 (*0-916990-07-9*) META Pubns.

Neuro-Linguistic Programming in Alcoholism Treatment. Ed. by Chelly M. Sterman. LC 90-34784. (Addiction Treatment Ser.: Vol. 3). (Illus.). 186p. 1990. 39.95 (*1-56024-002-4*) Haworth Pr.

Neuro-Linguistic Programming in Alcoholism Treatment. Ed. by Chelly M. Sterman. LC 90-34784. 186p. 1996. pap. 19.95 (*0-7890-0081-4*) Haworth Pr.

Neuro-Linguistic Programming Personal Profile. Gregory Engel & Lowell J. Arthur. 24p. 1998. student ed. 5.95 (*1-884180-00-0*) LifeStar.

Neuro-Oncology. Ed. by P. Paoletti et al. (Developments in Oncology Ser.). (C). 1991. text 243.00 (*0-7923-1215-5*) Kluwer Academic.

Neuro Oncology. Ed. by Clifford F. Rose & William S. Fields. (Progress in Experimental Tumor Research Ser.: Vol. 29). (Illus.). xiv, 274p. 1985. 200.00 (*3-8055-4054-X*) S Karger.

Neuro-Oncology, Pt. 1. P. J. Vinken et al. LC 97-50465. (Handbook of Clinical Neurology Ser.). 1997. pap. 247.00 (*0-444-81286-5*) Elsevier.

Neuro-Oncology: Gliomas & Other Primary Tumors of the Brain & Spinal Cord, Pt. II. Ed. by P. J. Vinken et al. 614p. 1998. 258.50 (*0-444-81287-3*) Elsevier.

Neuro-Oncology: Gliomas & Other Primary Tumors of the Brain & Spinal Cord, Pt. III. Ed. by P. J. Vinken et al. 548p. 1997. 247.00 (*0-444-81288-1*) Elsevier.

Neuro-Oncology: Primary Malignant Brain Tumors. Ed. by David G. Thomas. LC 89-8162. (Johns Hopkins Series in Contemporary Medicine & Public Health). (Illus.). 319p. 1990. reprint ed. pap. 98.90 (*0-608-07393-8*, 206762000009) Bks Demand.

***Neuro-Oncology: The Essentials.** Bernstein. (Illus.). 736p. 1999. 149.00 (*0-86577-880-9*) Thieme Med Pubs.

Neuro-oncology For Nurses. Douglas Guerrero. 1998. pap. text 39.95 (*1-86156-087-7*) Whurr Pub.

Neuro-Ophthalmic System. Townsend. LC 98-46226. (Optometric Series). 163p. 1999. spiral bd. 40.00 (*0-7506-9620-6*) Buttrwrth-Heinemann.

Neuro-Ophthalmological Disorders: Diagnostic Work-Up & Management. Ed. by Ronald J. Tusa & Steven A. Newman. (Neurological Disease & Therapy Ser.: Vol. 31). (Illus.). 664p. 1994. text 215.00 (*0-8247-8839-7*) Dekker.

Neuro-Ophthalmology. 3rd ed. Joel S. Glaser. LC 99-24157. 667p. 1999. text 110.00 (*0-7817-1729-9*) Lppncott W & W.

Neuro-Ophthalmology: A Practical Text. Nancy M. Newman. (Illus.). 484p. (C). 1992. pap. text 115.00 (*0-8385-6698-7*, A6698-3, Apple Lange Med) McGraw.

Neuro-Ophthalmology: Clinical Signs & Symptoms. 3rd ed. Thomas J. Walsh. LC 91-14153. (Illus.). 642p. 1991. text 98.50 (*0-8121-1462-0*) Lppncott W & W.

Neuro-Ophthalmology: Clinical Signs & Symptoms. 4th ed. Thomas J. Walsh. LC 96-39631. 600p. 1998. 110.00 (*0-683-08718-5*) Lppncott W & W.

Neuro-Ophthalmology: Diagnosis. Volpe. Date not set. text 100.00 (*0-7216-6533-0*, W B Saunders Co) Harcrt Hlth Sci Grp.

Neuro-Ophthalmology: Section 5. (Basic & Clinical Science Course (1989-90) Ser.). 186p. (C). 1989. pap. text 45.00 (*0-685-26049-6*) Am Acad Ophthal.

Neuro-Ophthalmology Now! 1988. 107.00 (*0-387-17270-X*) Spr-Verlag.

Neuro-Ophthalmology Review Manual. 4th ed. Lanning B. Kline & Frank J. Bajandas. 250p. LC 95-31151. 240p. 1995. pap. 40.00 (*1-55642-255-5*) SLACK Inc.

***Neuro-Ophthalmology Review Manual.** 5th ed. Lanning B. Kline & Frank J. Bajandas. 250p. 2000. pap. text 45.00 (*1-55642-470-1*) SLACK Inc.

***Neuro-Ophthamology.** 2nd ed. Newman. 1999. text 97.00 (*0-8385-6697-9*) Appleton & Lange.

Neuro-Optometric Rehabilitation. 3rd rev. ed. William V. Padula. Ed. by Sally M. Corngold. 212p. 2000. reprint ed. lib. bdg. 29.50 (*0-943599-65-2*) OEPF.

Neuro-Otology & Skull Base Surgery. Paulus Van den Broek et al. (Advances in OtoRhinoLaryngology Ser.: Vol. 34). (Illus.). viii, 280p. 1984. 142.75 (*3-8055-3887-1*) S Karger.

Neuro Rehabilitation. 3rd ed. Darcy P. Umphred. 176p. (gr. 13). 1995. pap. text, student ed. 19.95 (*0-8151-9109-X*, 28572) Mosby Inc.

Neuro-Vision Systems: Principles & Applications. Ed. by Madan M. Gupta & George K. Knopf. LC 93-30009. (Illus.). 576p. 1994. text 89.95 (*0-7803-1042-X*, PC3913) Inst Electrical.

Neuroactive Drugs of Choice in Spinal Cord Injury: A Guide for Using Neurologically Active Medications in Spinal Injured Patients. fac. ed. Lauro S. Halstead & Jacqueline Claus-Walker. LC 81-40858. 95p. pap. 30.00 (*0-7837-7212-2*, 204708600005) Bks Demand.

Neuroanatomica Clinica Hecha Ridiculamente Simple. Stephen Goldberg. (SPA.). 89p. (Orig.). 1985. pap. text 12.95 (*0-940780-03-8*) MedMaster.

***Neuroanatomical Basis of Clinical Neurology.** Orhan Arslan. (Illus.). 350p. 2001. 98.00 (*1-85070-578-X*) Prthnon Pub.

Neuroanatomical Techniques: Insect Nervous System. Ed. by N. J. Strausfeld & T. A. Miller. LC 79-10145. (Experimental Entomology Ser.). (Illus.). 1980. 223.00 (*0-387-90392-5*) Spr-Verlag.

Neuroanatomical Tract-Tracing Methods 2: Recent Progress. L. Heimer & L. Zaborszky. (Illus.). 424p. (C). 1989. text 95.00 (*0-306-43165-3*, Kluwer Plenum) Kluwer Academic.

Neuroanatomy. (National Medical Ser.). 1988. 25.00 (*0-685-75178-3*) Lppncott W & W.

Neuroanatomy. James D. Fix. (Board Review Ser.). 337p. 1991. 19.95 (*0-683-03250-X*) Lppncott W & W.

Neuroanatomy. P. A. Roberts. (Oklahoma Notes Ser.). (Illus.). ix, 84p. (C). 1989. pap. 11.95 (*0-387-96335-9*) Spr-Verlag.

Neuroanatomy. P. A. Roberts. (Oklahoma Notes Ser.). (Illus.). xi, 100p. 1991. pap. 13.95 (*0-387-97477-6*) Spr-Verlag.

Neuroanatomy. 2nd ed. William DeMyer. LC 97-18904. (National Medical Series for Independent Study). (Illus.). 380p. 1997. pap. 27.00 (*0-683-30075-X*) Lppncott W & W.

Neuroanatomy. 2nd ed. James D. Fix. (Board Review Ser.). (Illus.). 428p. 1995. pap. text 21.00 (*0-683-03249-6*) Lppncott W & W.

Neuroanatomy. 3rd ed. P. A. Roberts. (Oklahoma Notes Ser.). (Illus.). 128p. 1992. 13.95 (*0-387-97777-5*) Spr-Verlag.

Neuroanatomy: A Conceptual Approach. C. Romero-Sierra. LC 85-28060. (Illus.). 463p. (Orig.). reprint ed. pap. 143.60 (*0-7837-1609-5*, 204190100024) Bks Demand.

Neuroanatomy: A Functional Atlas of Parts & Pathways. Ray Poritsky. (Illus.). 300p. 1992. pap. text, student ed. 34.00 (*1-56053-008-1*) Hanley & Belfus.

Neuroanatomy: A Programmed Text, Vol. 1. Richard L. Sidman & Murray Sidman. 645p. 1965. spiral bd. 45.95 (*0-316-78985-2*, Little Brwn Med Div) Lppncott W & W.

Neuroanatomy: An Atlas of Structures, Sections & Systems. 3rd ed. Duane E. Haines. (Illus.). 252p. 1991. spiral bd. 27.00 (*0-683-03815-X*) Lppncott W & W.

Neuroanatomy: An Atlas of Structures, Sections & Systems. 5th ed. Duane Haines. LC 99-24992. 264p. 2000. 32.95 (*0-683-30649-9*) Lppncott W & W.

Neuroanatomy: An Illustrated Colour Text. A. R. Crossman & D. Neary. LC 95-6580. (Illus.). 1995. pap. text 28.95 (*0-443-04479-1*) Church.

Neuroanatomy: Basic & Applied. 3rd ed. Fitzgerald. (C). 1996. text 41.00 (*0-7020-1994-1*) Harcourt.

Neuroanatomy: Dissection of the Sheep Brain. Bruce Oakley & Rollie Schafer. (Illus.). 32p. (C). 1980. pap. text 7.95 (*0-472-08691-X*, 08691) U of Mich Pr.

Neuroanatomy: Selected Papers of Walle J. H. Nauta. Walle J. Nauta. LC 93-10358. (Contemporary Neuroscientists Ser.). (Illus.). 614p. 1993. 109.00 (*0-8176-3539-4*) Birkhauser.

***Neuroanatomy: 3D-Stereoscopic Atlas of the Human Brain.** M. C. Hirsch & T. Kramer. LC 99-52139. (Illus.). 350p. 1999. 49.00 incl. cd-rom (*3-540-65998-6*) Spr-Verlag.

Neuroanatomy & Neuropathology: A Clinical Guide for Neuropsychologists. Ralph M. Reitan & Deborah Wolfson. LC 85-61660. (Illus.). 353p. 1985. teacher ed. write for info. (*0-934515-05-0*); text 39.95 (*0-934515-03-4*) Neuropsych Pr.

Neuroanatomy & Physiology of Abdominal Vagal Afferents. Sue Ritter. 336p. 1992. boxed set 127.95 (*0-8493-8881-3*, QM471) CRC Pr.

Neuroanatomy & the Neurologic Exam: A Thesaurus of Synonyms, Similar-Sounding Non-Synonyms, & Terms of Variable Meaning. Terence R. Anthoney. LC 93-13864. 656p. 1993. boxed set 131.95 (*0-8493-8631-4*, QM541) CRC Pr.

Neuroanatomy Atlas. 2nd ed. John H. Martin. 578p. (C). 1996. pap. text 69.95 (*0-8385-6694-4*, A6694-2, Apple Lange Med) McGraw.

Neuroanatomy for Medical Students. 2nd ed. J. S. Wilkinson. (Illus.). 272p. 1992. pap. text 50.00 (*0-7506-1447-1*, Pub. by John Wright) Buttrwrth-Heinemann.

Neuroanatomy for Medical Students. 3rd ed. J. L. Wilkinson. LC 98-9508. 256p. 1998. pap. text 55.00 (*0-7506-3469-3*) Buttrwrth-Heinemann.

Neuroanatomy Laboratory Guide. Jose G. Frontera. 220p. 1970. pap. 5.00 (*0-8477-2310-0*) U of PR Pr.

Neuroanatomy of the Visual Pathways: Their Retinotopic Organization. Cronly-Dillon. 1991. 137.00 (*0-8493-7503-7*) CRC Pr.

Neuroanatomy of the Zebrafish Brain: A Topological Atlas. Mario F. Wullimann et al. 1996. 169.00 (*0-8176-5120-9*) Birkhauser.

Neuroanatomy of the Zebrafish Brain: A Topological Atlas. Mario F. Wullimann et al. (Illus.). 160p. 1996. 169.00 (*3-7643-5120-9*) Birkhauser.

Neuroanatomy Primer: Color to Learn. M. Evelyn McNeill. LC 96-46125. (Illus.). 250p. 1997. write for info. (*0-683-30067-9*) Lppncott W & W.

Neuroanesthesia. Ed. by J. O. Johnson et al. LC 96-6583. (Developments in Critical Care Medicine & Anesthesiology Ser.: Vol. 32). 444p. 1997. text 207.50 (*0-7923-4426-X*) Kluwer Academic.

Neuroanesthesia. 2nd ed. Phillippa Newfield. 458p. 1991. pap. text 71.00 (*0-316-60471-2*, Little Brwn Med Div) Lppncott W & W.

Neuroanesthesia Handbook. rev. ed. David J. Stone et al. LC 95-34090. (Illus.). 496p. (C). 1996. text. write for info. (*0-8151-8145-0*, 25770) Mosby Inc.

Neuroaudiology: Case Studies. Frank E. Musiek et al. LC 93-9066. (Illus.). 320p. (Orig.). (C). 1993. pap. text 65.00 (*1-56593-217-X*, 0577) Thomson Learn.

Neurobehavioral Anatomy. Christopher M. Filley. 227p. 1998. pap. 24.95 (*0-87081-508-3*) Univ Pr Colo.

Neurobehavioral Aspects of Cerebrovascular Disease. Ed. by Robert A. Bornstein & Gregory G. Brown. (Illus.). 384p. 1991. text 68.00 (*0-19-505431-8*) OUP.

Neurobehavioral Aspects of Multiple Sclerosis. Ed. by Stephen M. Rao. (Illus.). 288p. 1990. text 42.50 (*0-19-505400-8*) OUP.

Neurobehavioral Assessment. Robert M. Stowe. (Illus.). 288p. 1999. pap. write for info. (*0-07-061825-9*) McGraw-Hill HPD.

Neurobehavioral Assessment Format (NAF) A Manual for the Clinical Assessment of Patients with Neurologically Related Disorders. Andrew W. Siegal et al. 400p. 1996. lib. bdg. 89.95 (*1-57444-038-1*, SL0381) St Lucie Pr.

Neurobehavioral Consequences of Closed Head Injury. Harvey S. Levin et al. (Illus.). 280p. (C). 1982. text 47.50 (*0-19-503008-7*) OUP.

Neurobehavioral Effects of Sex Steroid Hormones. Ed. by Paul E. Micevych & Ronald P. Hammer, Jr. (Illus.). 464p. (C). 1995. text 90.00 (*0-521-45430-1*) Cambridge U Pr.

Neurobehavioral Plasticity: Learning, Development & Response to Brain Insults. Ed. by Norman E. Spear et al. 488p. 1995. text 99.95 (*0-8058-1425-6*) L Erlbaum Assocs.

Neurobehavioral Problems in Epilepsy. Dennis B. Smith et al. (Advances in Neurology Ser.: Vol. 55). 512p. 1990. text 149.50 (*0-88167-714-0*) Lppncott W & W.

Neurobehavioral Problems in Epilepsy. Ed. by Dennis B. Smith et al. LC 90-9111. (Advances in Neurology Ser.: Vol. 55). (Illus.). 507p. reprint ed. pap. 157.20 (*0-608-09751-9*, 206992400007) Bks Demand.

Neurobehavioral Recovery from Head Injury. Ed. by Harvey S. Levin et al. (Illus.). 446p. 1987. text 49.95 (*0-19-504287-5*) OUP.

Neurobehavioral Toxicology. text. write for info. (*0-7131-4518-8*, Pub. by E A) Routldge.

Neurobehavioral Toxicology. Ed. by Zoltan Annau. LC 86-45452. (Johns Hopkins Series in Environmental Toxicology). (Illus.). 459p. 1986. reprint ed. pap. 142.30 (*0-608-07381-4*, 206760800009) Bks Demand.

Neurobehavioral Treatment of Epilepsy. Ed. by David I. Mostofsky & Yngve Loyning. 352p. 1993. text 69.95 (*0-8058-1106-0*) L Erlbaum Assocs.

***Neurobehavioural Disability & Social Handicap.** Ed. by Rodger L. Wood & Tom McMillan. 288p. 1999. 49.95 (*0-86377-889-5*, Pub. by Psychol Pr) Taylor & Francis.

Neurobehavioural Disorders. Pierre J. Vinken et al. (Handbook of Clinical Neurology Ser.: Vol. 46(2)). 700p. 1985. 400.75 (*0-444-90357-7*) Elsevier.

Neurobiologic Mechanisms in Manipulative Therapy. Ed. by I. M. Korr. LC 78-4667. (Illus.). 488p. (C). 1978. text 125.00 (*0-306-31150-X*, Kluwer Plenum) Kluwer Academic.

Neurobiologic View of Speech Production & the Dysarthrias. Ronald Netsell. (Illus.). 164p. (C). 1991. reprint ed. pap. text 37.95 (*1-879105-25-X*, 0080) Thomson Learn.

Neurobiological & Clinical Consequences of Stress: From Normal Adaptation to Post-Traumatic Stress Disorder. Ed. by Matthew J. Friedman et al. (Illus.). 672p. 1995. text 142.00 (*0-7817-0177-5*) Lppncott W & W.

Neurobiological & Developmental Basis for Psychotherapeutic Intervention. Ed. by Michael Moskowitz et al. LC 97-23572. (Illus.). 288p. 1997. text 50.00 (*0-7657-0097-2*) Aronson.

Neurobiological Approaches to Brain-Behavior Interaction. 1995. lib. bdg. 253.95 (*0-8490-6811-8*) Gordon Pr.

Neurobiological Approaches to Human Disease. Ed. by Dirk Hellhammer et al. LC 87-16813. (Neuronal Control of Bodily Function Ser.: Vol. 2). 451p. (C). 1988. text 69.00 (*0-920887-27-9*) Hogrefe & Huber Pubs.

Neurobiological Basis of Human Locomotion. Ed. by Muneo Shimamura et al. 1991. text 110.00 (*4-7622-4646-8*, Pub. by Busn Ctr Acad) Intl Spec Bk.

Neurobiological Basis of Memory & Behavior. H. Rahmann & M. Rahmann. (Illus.). 272p. 1992. 125.00 (*0-387-97545-4*) Spr-Verlag.

Neurobiological Disorders in Children & Adolescents. Ed. by James W. Howe et al. LC 85-646993. (New Directions for Mental Health Services Ser.: No. MHS 54). 160p. 1992. pap. 25.00 (*1-55542-758-8*) Jossey-Bass.

Neurobiological Issues in Autism. E. Schopler & G. B. Mesibov. (Current Issues in Autism Ser.). (Illus.). 440p. (C). 1987. text 71.00 (*0-306-42451-7*, Kluwer Plenum) Kluwer Academic.

Neurobiological Mechanisms of Adaptation & Behavior. fac. ed. Ed. by Arnold J. Mandell. LC 74-14475. (Advances in Biochemical Psychopharmacology Ser.: No. 13). (Illus.). 314p. pap. 97.40 (*0-7837-7189-4*, 204711000005) Bks Demand.

Neurobiological Mechanisms of Opiate Withdrawal. Rafael Maldonado & Luis Stinus. LC 96-8139. (Neuroscience Intelligence Unit Ser.). 196p. 1996. 99.00 (*1-57059-347-7*) Landes Bioscience.

Neurobiologische Forschung und Psychiatrische Therapie. Ed. by Wolfgang P. Kaschka. (Illus.). viii, 232p. 1996. pap. 121.75 (*3-8055-6310-8*) S Karger.

Neurobiology. Eagles. (Biology Ser.). 2002. mass mkt. 62.95 (*0-534-24216-2*) Wadsworth Pub.

Neurobiology. David Robinson. LC 97-37177. 1997. write for info. (*0-7492-8151-0*) Spr-Verlag.

Neurobiology. Ed. by David Robinson. LC 97-37177. (Illus.). 372p. (C). 1998. pap. 39.95 (*3-540-63546-7*) Spr-Verlag.

Neurobiology. 3rd ed. Gordon M. Shepherd. (Illus.). 784p. (C). 1994. text 85.00 (*0-19-508842-5*); pap. text 57.95 (*0-19-508843-3*) OUP.

Neurobiology: Ionic Channels, Neurons & the Brain. North Atlantic Treaty Organization Staff et al. Ed. by Vincent Torre & Franco Conti. LC 96-29397. (NATO ASI Series A: Vol. 289). (Illus.). 404p. (C). 1997. text 150.00 (*0-306-45480-7*) Plenum.

Neurobiology: Molecules, Cells & Systems. Gary G. Matthews. LC 96-45522. (Illus.). 600p. 1997. pap. 56.95 (*0-86542-404-7*) Blackwell Sci.

***Neurobiology: Molecules, Cells & Systems.** 2nd ed. Gary Matthews. 2000. 75.95 (*0-632-04496-9*) Blackwell Sci.

Neurobiology & Cell Physiology of Chemoreception. P. G. Data et al. (Advances in Experimental Medicine & Biology Ser.: Vol. 337). (Illus.). 466p. (C). 1993. text 135.00 (*0-306-44575-1*, Kluwer Plenum) Kluwer Academic.

Neurobiology & the Human Brain Package. Ed. by D. Robinson & M. Hall. (Illus.). 370p. (C). 1998. pap. 59.95 incl. cd-rom (*3-540-63778-8*) Spr-Verlag.

Neurobiology, Immunology, Cytology see Primatology: Proceedings of the International Congress, 3rd, Zurich, 1970

Neurobiology in the Treatment of Eating Disorders. Hans Hoek et al. LC 97-48993. (Series on Clinical & Neurobiological Advances in Psychiatry). 546p. 1998. 167.50 (*0-471-98102-8*) Wiley.

Neurobiology of Acetylcholine. Ed. by Nae J. Dun & Robert L. Perlman. 590p. 1987. 120.00 (*0-306-42493-2*, Plenum Trade) Perseus Pubng.

Neurobiology of Affect in Language. John Schumann. 350p. 1998. pap. 32.95 (*0-631-21010-5*) Blackwell Pubs.

Neurobiology of Aggression & Impulsivity. Michael Maes & Emil F. Coccaro. LC 98-19062. (Series on Clinical & Neurobiological Advances in Psychiatry). 228p. 1998. 137.95 (*0-471-98101-X*) Wiley.

Neurobiology of Aging: Research on Age-Related Phenomena, Neurodegeneration & Neuropathology. Ed. by Paul D. Coleman. 1989. 65.00 (*0-685-26770-9*, Pergamon Pr) Elsevier.

Neurobiology of Alzheimer's Disease. Ed. by David Dawbarn & Shelley J. Allen. LC 98-138325. (The Molecular & Cellular Neurobiolgy Ser.). (Illus.). 336p. 1998. text 87.00 (*1-872748-14-7*) OUP.

***Neurobiology of Alzheimer's Disease.** 2nd ed. Ed. by David Dawbarn & Shelley J. Allen. (The Molecular & Cellular Neurobiology Ser.). (Illus.). 464p. 2000. pap. text 59.50 (*0-19-852459-5*) OUP.

Neurobiology of Alzheimer's Disease, Vol. 777. Ed. by Richard J. Wurtman et al. LC 95-48168. 439p. 1996. pap. 115.00 (*0-89766-974-6*); text 115.00 (*0-89766-973-8*) NY Acad Sci.

Neurobiology of Amino Acids, Peptides & Trophic Factors. Ed. by James A. Ferrendelli et al. (Topics in Neurosciences Ser.). (C). 1988. text 150.00 (*0-89838-360-9*) Kluwer Academic.

Neurobiology of an Insect Brain. M. Burrows. (Illus.). 698p. 1996. text 125.00 (*0-19-852344-0*) OUP.

Neurobiology of Anxiety: Handbook of Anxiety, Vol. 3. Ed. by G. D. Burrows et al. 496p. 1990. 253.25 (*0-685-54173-8*) Elsevier.

N

Neurobiology of Autism. Margaret L. Bauman. Ed. by Thomas L. Kemper. LC 93-5358. (Johns Hopkins Series in Psychiatry & Neuroscience). 272p. 1997. pap. text 35.00 (*0-8018-5680-9*) Johns Hopkins.

Neurobiology of Behavioral Control in Drug Abuse. 1993. lib. bdg. 261.95 (*0-8490-8504-7*) Gordon Pr.

Neurobiology of Central D1-Dopamine Receptors. Ed. by George R. Breese & Ian Creese. (Advances in Experimental Medicine & Biology Ser.: Vol. 204). 228p. 1986. 69.50 (*0-306-42383-9*, Plenum Trade) Perseus Pubng.

Neurobiology of Central Nervous System Trauma. Steven K. Salzman & Alan I. Faden. (Illus.). 368p. 1994. text 98.00 (*0-19-507230-8*) OUP.

Neurobiology of Cerebrospinal Fluid 2. Ed. by James H. Wood. LC 79-21731. 1002p. 1983. 145.00 (*0-306-40969-0*, Plenum Trade) Perseus Pubng.

Neurobiology of Chemical Transmission. Ed. by Masanori Otsuka & Zach W. Hall. LC 78-24602. 336p. reprint ed. 104.20 (*0-8357-9940-9*, 201571100097) Bks Demand.

Neurobiology of Cholinergic & Adrenergic Transmitters. Ed. by E. Heldman et al. (Monographs in Neural Sciences: Vol. 7). (Illus.). xvi, 200p. 1981. pap. 77.50 (*3-8055-0828-X*) S Karger.

Neurobiology of Cingulate Cortex & Limbic Thalamus: A Comprehensive Handbook. Ed. by Brent A. Vogt & Michael Gabriel. LC 93-18429. (Illus.). 650p. 1993. 219.00 (*0-8176-3568-8*) Birkhauser.

Neurobiology of Cocaine: Cellular & Molecular Mechanisms. Ed. by Ronald P. Hammer, Jr. LC 95-7021. 272p. 1995. boxed set 139.95 (*0-8493-8311-0*, 8311) CRC Pr.

Neurobiology of Cocaine Addiction: From Bench to Bedside. Ed. by Joseph Herman & Barry Stimmel. LC 96-39364. (Journal of Addictive Diseases Monograph Ser.: Vol. 15, No. 4). 129p. (C). 1997. 49.95 (*0-7890-0031-8*); pap. text 19.95 (*0-7890-0300-7*) Haworth Pr.

Neurobiology of Cognition. Ed. by Peter D. Eimas. (Special Issues of Cognition, a Bradford Book Ser.). 256p. 1990. pap. text 24.50 (*0-262-55019-9*) MIT Pr.

Neurobiology of Comparative Cognition. Ed. by David S. Olton & R. Kesner. (Roitblat Bever Olton Ser.). 488p. (C). 1990. pap. 45.00 (*0-8058-0639-3*); text 99.95 (*0-8058-0133-2*) L Erlbaum Assocs.

Neurobiology of Computation: Proceedings of the 3rd Annual Computation & Neural Systems Conference. Conference on Computation & Neural Systems Staff. Ed. by James M. Bower. LC 94-41228. 464p. (C). 1995. text 218.00 (*0-7923-9543-3*) Kluwer Academic.

Neurobiology of Decision-Making. Ed. by A. R. Damasio et al. (Research & Perspectives in Neurosciences Ser.). 192p. 1995. 108.00 (*3-540-60143-0*) Spr-Verlag.

Neurobiology of Disease. Ed. by Alan L. Pearlman & Robert C. Collins. (Illus.). 504p. 1989. text 55.00 (*0-19-505318-4*); pap. text 45.00 (*0-19-505319-2*) OUP.

Neurobiology of Disease: Contributions from Neuroscience to Clinical Neurology. Ed. by H. Bostock et al. LC 95-33564. (Illus.). 462p. (C). 1996. text 125.00 (*0-521-45132-9*) Cambridge U Pr.

Neurobiology of Down Syndrome. Ed. by Charles J. Epstein. LC 86-13098. (Illus.). 272p. 1986. reprint ed. pap. 84.40 (*0-608-00579-7*, 206116600007) Bks Demand.

Neurobiology of Drug Abuse: Learning & Memory. 1992. lib. bdg. 88.75 (*0-8490-8822-4*) Gordon Pr.

Neurobiology of Drug Abuse: Learning & Memory. 1993. lib. bdg. 257.95 (*0-8490-8503-9*) Gordon Pr.

Neurobiology of Drug Use. Ed. by Joe Marwah. (Monographs in Neural Sciences: Vol. 13). (Illus.). viii, 164p. 1987. 128.00 (*3-8055-4561-4*) S Karger.

Neurobiology of Essential Fatty Acids. N. G. Bazan et al. LC 92-16989. (Advances in Experimental Medicine & Biology Ser.: Vol. 318). (Illus.). 454p. (C). 1992. text 135.00 (*0-306-44233-7*, Kluwer Plenum) Kluwer Academic.

Neurobiology of Food & Fluid Intake. E. M. Stricker. (Handbook of Behavioral Neurobiology Ser.: Vol. 10). (Illus.). 576p. (C). 1990. text 125.00 (*0-306-43458-X*, Kluwer Plenum) Kluwer Academic.

Neurobiology of Glycoconjugates. R. U. Margolis & R. K. Margolis. (Illus.). 472p. (C). 1989. text 125.00 (*0-306-43128-9*, Kluwer Plenum) Kluwer Academic.

Neurobiology of Hearing: The Central Auditory System. Ed. by Richard A. Altschuler et al. LC 87-42836. (Neurobiology of Hearing Ser.). (Illus.). 507p. 1991. reprint ed. pap. 157.20 (*0-608-07238-9*, 206746300009) Bks Demand.

Neurobiology of Hearing: The Cochlea. Ed. by Richard A. Altschuler et al. LC 86-22116. 506p. 1986. reprint ed. pap. 156.90 (*0-608-04681-7*, 206540200004) Bks Demand.

Neurobiology of Higher Cognitive Function: UCLA Forum in Medical Science, Number 29. Ed. by Arnold B. Scheibel & Adam F. Wechsler. LC 89-23636. 370p. 1990. lib. bdg. 57.95 (*0-89862-425-8*) Guilford Pubns.

Neurobiology of Histamine. Ed. by George D. Prell. (Illus.). 1999. 125.00 (*0-89603-478-X*) Humana.

Neurobiology of Incontinence - Symposium No. 151. CIBA Foundation Staff. LC 90-12321. (CIBA Foundation Symposium Ser.: No. 151). 346p. 1990. 128.00 (*0-471-92687-6*) Wiley.

Neurobiology of Invertebrates Gastropoda Brain Symposium at Tihany, 8-12 Sept. 1975: Gastropoda Brain Symposium of Tihany 8-12, Sept. 1975. Janos Salanki. 656p. (C). 1976. 123.00 (*963-05-1080-4*, Pub. by Akade Kiado) St Mut.

Neurobiology of Invertebrates Signal Molecules, Networks. J. Salanki. Ed. by K. S. Rozsa & K. Elekes. 1993. pap. 290.00 (*963-05-6443-2*, Pub. by Akade Kiado) St Mut.

Neurobiology of Invertebrates, Transmitters, Modulators & Receptors: Proceedings of the Satellite Symposium of the 2nd World Congress of Neuroscience, Held at the Balaton Limnological Research Institute of Hungarian Academy of Science in Tihany, 22-26 August, 1987. K. Rozsa & Janos Salanki. (Symposia Biologica Hungarica Ser.: No. 36). (Illus.). 768p. (C). 1988. 207.00 (*963-05-4958-1*, Pub. by Akade Kiado) St Mut.

Neurobiology of Invertebrates, Transmitters, Modulators & Receptors: Proceedings of the Satellite Symposium of the 2nd World Congress of Neuroscience, Held at the Balaton Limnological Research Institute of Hungarian Academy of Science in Tihany, 22-26 August, 1987. Janos Salanki. 656p. 1976. 250.00 (*0-569-08369-9*) St Mut.

Neurobiology of Ischemic Brain Damage. Ed. by Bo K. Siesjo et al. (Progress in Brain Research Ser.: Vol. 96). 398p. 1993. 231.50 (*0-444-89603-1*) Elsevier.

Neurobiology of Jawless Fishes: 7th Annual Karger Workshop, San Diego, November 1995. Ed. by Carl M. Rovainen. (Journal Ser.: Vol. 48, No. 5, 1996). (Illus.). 76p. 1996. pap. 45.25 (*3-8055-6404-X*) S Karger.

Neurobiology of Learning & Memory. Grau. (Psychology Ser.). 2001. pap. 28.00 (*0-534-36767-4*) Brooks-Cole.

*__Neurobiology of Learning & Memory.__ Ed. by Joe L. Martinez, Jr. & Raymond P. Desner. LC 98-84370. (Illus.). 456p. 1998. boxed set 69.96 (*0-12-475655-7*) Acad Pr.

Neurobiology of Learning & Memory. G. Shaw et al. (Advanced Series in Neuroscience: Vol. 2). 868p. (C). 1990. reprint ed. text 109.00 (*9971-5-0865-6*); reprint ed. pap. text 55.00 (*9971-5-0868-0*) World Scientific Pub.

Neurobiology of Learning, Emotion, & Affect. John Madden, IV. LC 91-18296. (Illus.). 368p. 1991. reprint ed. pap. 114.10 (*0-608-07190-0*, 206741500009) Bks Demand.

*__Neurobiology of Mastication.__ Ed. by Y. Nakamura & B. J. Sessle. (International Congress Ser.: Vol. 1186). 540p. 1999. 200.50 (*0-444-50113-4*, Excerpta Medica) Elsevier.

Neurobiology of Memory: Concepts, Findings, Trends. Yadin Dudai. (Illus.). 352p. 1989. pap. text 41.95 (*0-19-854229-1*) OUP.

Neurobiology of Mental Illness. Dennis S Charney. LC 98-27421. (Illus.). 984p. 1999. text 150.00 (*0-19-511265-2*) OUP.

Neurobiology of Motivation & Reward. J. R. Stellar & Eliot Stellar. (Illus.). xi, 255p. 1985. 85.95 (*0-387-96092-9*) Spr-Verlag.

Neurobiology of Motor Programme Selection. Jenny Kien et al. (SINS Ser.: Vol. 4). 290p. 1992. 168.00 (*0-08-041986-0*, Pergamon Pr) Elsevier.

Neurobiology of Neural Networks. Ed. by Daniel Gardner. LC 93-9125. (Computational Neuroscience Ser.). (Illus.). 241p. 1993. 45.00 (*0-262-07150-9*, Bradford Bks) MIT Pr.

Neurobiology of Nociceptors. Ed. by C. Belmonte & F. Cervero. (Illus.). 542p. 1996. text 125.00 (*0-19-852334-3*) OUP.

Neurobiology of Opiates. Ed. by Ronald P. Hammer, Jr. Ph.d. 432p. 1992. boxed set 131.95 (*0-8493-7932-6*, RM328) CRC Pr.

Neurobiology of Opioids. Ed. by O. F. Almeida & T. S. Shippenberg. (Illus.). xxii, 456p. 1991. 182.95 (*0-387-50835-X*) Spr-Verlag.

Neurobiology of Primary Dementia. Marshal F. Folstein & Association for Research in Nervous & Mental Disea. LC 97-27523. 440p. 1998. 63.50 (*0-88048-915-4*, 8915) Am Psychiatric.

Neurobiology of Puberty. Ed. by T. M. Plant & P. A. Lee. 368p. 1995. 79.95 (*1-898099-06-5*) Blackwell Sci.

Neurobiology of Reproductive Behavior. Ed. by L. E. Muske. (Journal: Brains, Behavior & Evolution: Vol. 42, No. 4-5, 1993). (Illus.). 84p. 1993. pap. 42.75 (*3-8055-5852-X*) S Karger.

Neurobiology of Saccadic Eye Movements. Ed. by R. H. Wurts et al. (Reviews of Oculomotor Research Ser.: Vol. 3). 472p. 1989. 298.25 (*0-444-81017-X*) Elsevier.

Neurobiology of Sensory Systems. Ed. by R. N. Singh & N. J. Strausfeld. LC 89-22960. (Illus.). 632p. 1989. 140.00 (*0-306-43377-X*, Plenum Trade) Perseus Pubng.

*__Neurobiology of Spinal Cord Injury.__ Ed. by Robert G. Kalb & Stephen M. Strittmatter. LC 99-23563. (Contemporary Neuroscience Ser.). 304p. 1999. 125.00 (*0-89603-672-3*) Humana.

Neurobiology of Stereotyped Behavior. Ed. by Steven J. Cooper & Colin T. Dourish. (Illus.). 320p. 1990. 75.00 (*0-19-852160-X*) OUP.

Neurobiology of Suicide: From the Bench to the Clinic. Ed. by David M. Stoff & J. John Mann. LC 97-43013. (Annals of the New York Academy of Sciences Ser.: No. 836). 365p. 1998. 80.00 (*1-57331-094-8*); pap. 80.00 (*1-57331-095-6*) NY Acad Sci.

Neurobiology of Taste & Smell. Ed. by Thomas E. Finger & Wayne L. Silver. 462p. (C). 1991. reprint ed. lib. bdg. 89.50 (*0-89464-616-8*) Krieger.

*__Neurobiology of Taste & Smell.__ 2nd ed. Thomas E. Finger et al. 448p. 1999. text 109.95 (*0-471-25721-4*) Wiley.

Neurobiology of the Control of Breathing. Ed. by Curt Von Euler & Hugo Lagercrantz. LC 86-26034. (Karolinska Institute Nobel Conference Ser.). (Illus.). 343p. 1987. reprint ed. pap. 106.40 (*0-608-07233-8*, 206745800009) Bks Demand.

Neurobiology of the Inner Retina. Ed. by R. Weiler & Neville N. Osborne. (NATO ASI Series H: Vol. 31). (Illus.). xvi, 529p. 1989. 199.95 (*0-387-50378-1*) Spr-Verlag.

Neurobiology of the Leech. Ed. by Kenneth J. Muller et al. LC 81-68893. (Illus.). 330p. 1981. reprint ed. pap. 102.30 (*0-608-04088-6*, 206482000011) Bks Demand.

Neurobiology of the Locus Coeruleus Vol. 88: Progress in Brain Research. Ed. by C. D. Barnes & O. Pompeiano. 642p. 1991. 323.50 (*0-444-81394-2*) Elsevier.

Neurobiology of the NMDA Receptor: From Chemistry to the Clinic. Alan P. Kozikowski & German Barrinuevo. 253p. 1991. 70.00 (*0-89573-769-8*, Wiley-VCH) Wiley.

Neurobiology of the Nucleus Accumbens. Ed. by R. B. Chronister & J. F. De France. (Illus.). 380p. (Orig.). 1981. pap. 39.95 (*0-940090-00-7*) Haer Inst.

Neurobiology of the Trace Amines. Ed. by Alan A. Boulton et al. LC 84-626. (Illus.). 597p. 1984. 119.50 (*0-89603-063-6*) Humana.

Neurobiology of the Trace Elements Vol. 1: Trace Element Neurobiology & Deficiencies. Ed. by Ivor E. Dreosti & Richard M. Smith. LC 83-8412. (Contemporary Neuroscience Ser.). 374p. 1983. 99.50 (*0-89603-046-6*) Humana.

Neurobiology of the Trace Elements Vol. 2: Neurotoxicology & Neuropharmacology. Ed. by Ivor E. Dreosti & Richard M. Smith. LC 83-8413. (Contemporary Neuroscience Ser.). 323p. 1983. 99.50 (*0-89603-047-4*) Humana.

Neurobiology of Violence. Jan Volavka. 448p. 1995. text 56.00 (*0-88048-543-4*, 8543) Am Psychiatric.

Neurobiology Progression. G. A. Kerkut. (Progress in Neurobiology Ser.: Vol. 14). 1980. pap. 63.00 (*0-08-026048-9*, no. 2, Pergamon Pr) Elsevier.

Neurobiology Progression, ser. vol. 4. G. A. Kerkut. (Progress in Neurobiology Ser.). 1980. pap. 28.00 (*0-08-026042-X*, 1, Pergamon Pr) Elsevier.

Neurobiology Progression, ser. vol. 13. G. A. Kerkut. (Progress in Neurobiology Ser.). 1979. pap. 21.00 (*0-08-024898-5*, no. 3, Pergamon Pr); pap. 18.50 (*0-08-024899-3*, no. 4, Pergamon Pr) Elsevier.

Neurobiology Progression, ser. vol. 14. G. A. Kerkut. (Progress in Neurobiology Ser.). 1980. pap. 29.00 (*0-08-026019-5*, no. 1, Pergamon Pr) Elsevier.

Neuroblastoma: Molecular Genetics in Diagnosis & Therapy. Ed. by M. Sluyser & A. Voue. 168p. 1988. text 49.95 (*0-470-21237-3*) P-H.

Neuroblastoma: Tumor Biology & Therapy. Ed. by Carl Pochedly. 432p. 1990. lib. bdg. 159.00 (*0-8493-0157-2*, RC280) CRC Pr.

Neurocardiology. Ed. by John A. Armour & Jeffrey L. Ardell. LC 93-41500. (Illus.). 456p. (C). 1994. text 75.00 (*0-19-507304-5*) OUP.

Neurocardiology. Richard A. Johnson et al. (Major Problems in Neurology Ser.). (Illus.). 416p. 1985. text 98.00 (*0-7216-1375-6*, W B Saunders Co) Harcrt Hlth Sci Grp.

Neurochemical & Immunologic Components in Schizophrenia. Ed. by Daniel Bergsma & Allan Goldstein. (Alan R. Liss Ser.: Vol. 14, No. 5). 1978. 64.00 (*0-685-03293-0*) March of Dimes.

Neurochemical Aspects of Phospholipid Metabolism. Ed. by Gino Toffano & J. Hawthorne. (FIDIA Research Ser.: Vol. 20). 280p. 1990. 102.00 (*0-387-97060-6*) Spr-Verlag.

Neurochemical Correlates of Cerebral Ischemia Vol. 7: Advances in Neurochemistry. N. G. Bazan et al. (Illus.). 392p. (C). 1992. text 110.00 (*0-306-43944-1*, 441, Kluwer Plenum) Kluwer Academic.

Neurochemical Mechanisms of Opiates & Endorphins. Ed. by Horace H. Loh & David H. Ross. LC 78-24623. (Advances in Biochemical Psychopharmacology Ser.: No. 20). (Illus.). 575p. reprint ed. pap. 178.30 (*0-7837-7129-0*, 204695800004) Bks Demand.

Neurochemical Monitoring in the Intensive Care Unit: Microdialysis, Jugular Venous Oximetry, & Near-Infrared Spectroscopy. Ed. by T. Tsubokawa et al. LC 95-6883. 1995. 134.00 (*4-431-70166-4*) Spr-Verlag.

Neurochemical Pharmacology: A Tribute to B. B. Brodie. Ed. by Erminio Costa. LC 89-3846. (Fidia Research Foundation Symposium Ser.: No. 2). (Illus.). 393p. 1989. reprint ed. pap. 121.90 (*0-608-00677-7*, 206126400007) Bks Demand.

Neurochemical Studies on Monoaminergic Neutotransmitters in the Central Nervous System. Patrick Herregodts. (Illus.). 174p. 1994. pap. 25.00 (*90-70289-93-8*) Paul & Co Pubs.

Neurochemical Techniques in Insect Research. Ed. by H. Breer. (Experimental Entomology Ser.). (Illus.). 310p. 1985. 129.00 (*0-387-13813-7*) Spr-Verlag.

Neurochemistry: A Practical Approach. 2nd ed. Ed. by A. J. Turner & Herman S. Bachelard. LC 96-34313. (The Practical Approach Ser.: No. 172). (Illus.). 322p. 1997. text 130.00 (*0-19-963440-8*); pap. text 60.00 (*0-19-963439-4*) OUP.

Neurochemistry: Cellular, Molecular & Clinical Aspects: Proceedings of the 11th European Society for Neurochemistry Meeting Held in Groningen, The Netherlands, June 15-20, 1996. Ed. by Albert Teelken et al. LC 97-36254. (Illus.). 1190p. (C). 1998. text 294.00 (*0-306-45705-9*, Kluwer Plenum) Kluwer Academic.

Neurochemistry & Clinical Disorders Circuitry of Some Psychiatric & Psychosomatic Syndromes. Ed. by Fuad Lechin & Bertha Van der Dijs. LC 88-19263. 208p. 1989. 139.00 (*0-8493-6595-3*, RC483, CRC Reprint) Franklin.

Neurochemistry in Clinical Application: Proceedings of the International Neuropharmacology Held in Guangzhou, China, November 9-11, 1992, Vol. 363. Ed. by Lily C. Tang & Steven J. Tang. (Advances in Experimental Medicine & Biology Ser.: Vol. 363). (Illus.). 226p. (C). 1995. text 79.50 (*0-306-44836-X*, Kluwer Plenum) Kluwer Academic.

Neurochemistry of Alzheimer's Disease. Bowen. 300p. 1999. write for info. (*0-12-120540-1*) Acad Pr.

Neurochemistry of Drug Dependence: From Molecular Targets to Behavioral Consequences. Ed. by S. Wonnacott & S. S. Lunt. (Biochemical Society Symposium Ser.: Vol. 59). (Illus.). 223p. (C). 1994. text 110.50 (*1-85578-034-8*, Pub. by Portland Pr Ltd) Ashgate Pub Co.

Neurochemistry of Drugs of Abuse: Cocaine, Ibogaine, & Substituted Amphetamines. Ed. by Syed F. Ali. LC 98-3824. (Annals Ser.: Vol. 844). 362p. 1998. pap. 140.00 (*1-57331-146-4*) NY Acad Sci.

Neurochemistry of Drugs of Abuse: Cocaine, Ibogaine, & Substituted Amphetamines. Ed. by Syed F. Ali. LC 98-3824. (Annals of the New York Academy of Sciences Ser.: Vol. 844). 300p. 1998. 140.00 (*1-57331-145-6*) NY Acad Sci.

*__Neurochemistry of Drugs of Abuse: Cocaine, Ibogaine & Substituted Amphetamines.__ Syed F. Ali. (Annals of the New York Academy of Science Ser.). 2000. pap. 24.95 (*0-8018-6546-8*) Johns Hopkins.

Neurochemistry of Hepatic Coma. Ed. by E. E. Polli. (Experimental Biology & Medicine Ser.: Vol. 4). 1971. 30.50 (*3-8055-1187-6*) S Karger.

Neurochemistry of the Vestibular System. Alvin J. Beitz & John H. Anderson. LC 99-38971. 432p. 1999. boxed set 129.95 (*0-8493-7679-3*) CRC Pr.

Neurocognition of Language. Ed. by Colin M. Brown & Peter Hagoort. LC 98-50252. (Illus.). 430p. 1999. text 95.00 (*0-19-852448-X*) OUP.

Neurocomputation in Remote Sensing Data Analysis: Proceedings of Concerted Action Compares (Connectionist Methods for Pre-Processing & Analysis of Remote Sensing Data) Ed. by I. Kanellopoulos et al. LC 97-31283. (Illus.). x, 284p. 1997. 92.95 (*3-540-63316-2*) Spr-Verlag.

Neurocomputational Perspectives: The Nature of Mind & the Structure of Science. Paul M. Churchland. (Illus.). 344p. 1992. pap. text 20.00 (*0-262-53106-2*, Bradford Bks) MIT Pr.

Neurocomputers: An Overview of Neural Networks in VLSI. Manfred Glesner & W. Pochmuller. 304p. 1994. mass mkt. 47.95 (*0-412-56390-8*) Chapman & Hall.

Neurocomputers & Attention, 2 vols., Vol. I: Neurobiology, Synchronisation & Chaos. Ed. by Arun V. Holden & Vitaly I. Kryukov. (Proceedings in Nonlinear Science Ser.). 485p. 1991. text 130.00 (*0-7190-3278-4*, Pub. by Manchester Univ Pr) St Martin.

Neurocomputers & Attention, 2 vols., Vol. II: Connectionism & Neurocomputers. Ed. by Arun V. Holden & Vitaly I. Kryukov. (Proceedings in Nonlinear Science Ser.). 524p. 1991. text 130.00 (*0-7190-3456-6*, Pub. by Manchester Univ Pr) St Martin.

Neurocomputing. Mark Toppan. (C). 1992. pap. text. write for info. (*0-201-55603-0*) Addison-Wesley.

Neurocomputing: Algorithms, Architectures & Applications. Ed. by F. Fogelman Soulie & J. Herault. (NATO ASI Series F: Computer & Systems Sciences, Special Programme AET: Vol. 68). (Illus.). 472p. 1990. 107.95 (*0-387-53278-1*) Spr-Verlag.

Neurocomputing: Foundations of Research. Ed. by James A. Anderson & Edward Rosenfeld. 600p. 1988. 85.00 (*0-262-01097-6*, Bradford Bks) MIT Pr.

Neurocomputing: Foundations of Research. Ed. by James A. Anderson & Edward Rosenfeld. 752p. 1989. reprint ed. pap. text 39.95 (*0-262-51048-0*) MIT Pr.

*__Neurocomputing for Design Automation.__ Hojjat Adeli & Hyo S. Park. LC 98-12674. (Computer-Aided Electronics Ser.). 240p. 1998. boxed set 94.95 (*0-8493-2092-5*) CRC Pr.

Neurocomputing 2: Directions for Research. James A. Anderson et al. (Illus.). 750p. 1993. pap. text 42.50 (*0-262-51075-8*, Bradford Bks) MIT Pr.

Neurocontrol: Learning Control Systems Inspired by Neuronal Architectures & Human Problem Solving Strategies. H. Tolle. Ed. by M. Thoma & A. Wyner. (Lecture Notes in Control & Information Sciences: Vol. 172). x, 211p. 1992. 70.95 (*0-387-55057-7*) Spr-Verlag.

Neurocontrol: Towards Industrial Control Methodology. Tomas Hrycej. LC 96-33490. 380p. 1997. 79.95 (*0-471-17628-1*) Wiley.

Neurocritical Care. Ed. by Thomas P. Bleck. 352p. Date not set. text 65.00 (*0-07-005925-X*) McGraw-Hill HPD.

Neurocritical Care. Ed. by Werner Hacke et al. LC 93-48232. (Illus.). 848p. 1994. 125.00 (*0-387-56443-8*) Spr-Verlag.

Neurocysticercosis: A Clinical Handbook. Oscar H. Brutto et al. LC 98-11617. 1998. 88.00 (*90-265-1513-8*) Swets.

Neurocytochemical Methods. Ed. by A. Calas & D. Eugene. (NATO ASI Series H: Cell Biology: Vol. 58). xvi, 335p. 1991. 216.95 (*0-387-53148-3*) Spr-Verlag.

Neurocytology: Fine Structure of Neurons, Nerve Processes, & Neuroglial Cells. Ennio Pannese. LC 93-18191. 1994. 99.00 (*0-86577-456-0*) Thieme Med Pubs.

Neurocytopathology. John M. Andrews & G. Berry Schumann. (Illus.). 352p. 1992. 125.00 (*0-683-00227-9*) Lppncott W & W.

Neurodegeneration & Neuroprotection in Parkinson's Disease. Charles W. Olanow & Moussa B. Youdim. (Neuroscience Perspectives Ser.). (Illus.). 224p. 1996. text 65.00 (*0-12-525445-8*) Acad Pr.

Neurodegeneration Methods & Protocols. Jean Harry & Hugh A. Tilson. (Methods in Molecular Medicine Ser.: No. 22). 328p. 1999. 89.50 (*0-89603-612-X*) Humana.

*__Neurodegenerative Dementias.__ Ed. by John Q. Trojanowski & Christopher Clark. (Illus.). 1000p. 1999. text 175.00 (*0-07-065093-4*) McGraw-Hill HPD.

Neurodegenerative Diseases. Donald B. Caine. LC 93-13286. (Illus.). 992p. 1994. text 220.00 (*0-7216-4349-3*, W B Saunders Co) Harcrt Hlth Sci Grp.

An Asterisk (*) at the beginning of an entry indicates that the title is appearing for the first time.

Neurodegenerative Diseases. Ed. by G. Jolles & J. M. Stutzman. (Rhone-Poulenc Rorer Round Table Conferences Ser.). (Illus.). 320p. 1994. text 79.00 (*0-12-388185-4*) Acad Pr.

Neurodegenerative Diseases: Molecular & Cellular Mechanisms & Therapeutic Advances. Ed. by Gary Fiskum. LC 96-5688. (GWUMC Department of Biochemistry Annual Spring Symposium Ser.). (Illus.). 467p. (C). 1996. text 162.00 (*0-306-45298-7*, Kluwer Plenum) Kluwer Academic.

Neurodegenerative Disorders: Mechanisms & Prospects for Therapy. Ed. by R. F. Mantoura & J. M. Martin. LC 91-15349. (Dahlem Workshop Reports - Physical, Chemical, Earth Sciences). 320p. 1991. 314.50 (*0-471-92979-4*) Wiley.

Neurodegenerative Disorders: Mechanisms & Prospects for Therapy. D. L. Price et al. (Dahlem Workshop Reports - Life Sciences). 301p. 1991. 165.00 (*0-685-70063-1*, Wiley-Liss) Wiley.

Neurodegenerative Disorders: The Role Played by Endotoxins & Xenobiotics. Ed. by Giuseppe Nappi et al. LC 88-18437. 344p. 1988. reprint ed. pap. 106.70 (*0-608-00304-2*, 206102100007) Bks Demand.

Neurodevelopment, Aging, & Cognition. Ed. by Henryk M. Wisniewski et al. LC 92-396. (Illus.). xiv, 396p. 1992. 127.50 (*0-8176-3599-8*) Birkhauser.

Neurodevelopment & Adult Psychopathology. Ed. by Matcheri S. Keshavan & Robin M. Murray. (Illus.). 298p. (C). 1997. text 120.00 (*0-521-48104-X*); pap. text 47.95 (*0-521-48565-7*) Cambridge U Pr.

Neurodevelopmental Approach to Specific Learning Disorders. Ed. by Kingsley Whitmore & Guy Willems. (Clinics in Developmental Medicine Ser.: Vol. 145). 275p. (C). 1999. text 69.95 (*1-898683-11-5*, Pub. by Mc Keith Pr) Cambridge U Pr.

Neurodevelopmental Basis of Schizophrenia. John Waddington & Peter F. Buckley. LC 95-37078. 177p. 1996. 89.95 (*1-57059-306-X*) Landes Bioscience.

Neurodevelopmental Disorders. Ed. by Helen Tager-Flusberg. LC 98-26850. (Cognitive Neuroscience of Development Ser.). (Illus.). 614p. 1999. 75.00 (*0-262-20116-X*, Bradford Bks) MIT Pr.

Neurodevelopmental Disorders: Diagnosis & Treatment. Randi Jenssen Hagerman. LC 98-54687. (Developmental Perspectives in Psychiatry Ser.). (Illus.). 224p. 1999. text 65.00 (*0-19-512314-X*) OUP.

Neurodevelopmental Problems in Early Childhood: Assessment & Management. Drillien & Drummond. (Illus.). 512p. (gr. 13). 1978. 89.95 (*0-632-00409-6*, B-1475-9) Mosby Inc.

Neurodevelopmental Strategies for Managing Communication Disorders in Children with Severe Motor Dysfunction. Ed. by M. Beth Langley & Linda J. Lombardino. LC 90-9166. 342p. 1991. text 39.00 (*0-89079-422-7*, 1942) PRO-ED.

Neurodynamics. Ed. by F. Pasemann & H. D. Doebner. (Series in Neural Networks: Vol. 1). 240p. (C). 1991. text 83.00 (*981-02-0811-1*) World Scientific Pub.

***Neurodynamics: An Exploration in Mesoscopic Brain Dynamics.** Walter J. Freeman. LC 99-58323. (Perspectives in Neural Computing Ser.). x, 398p. 2000. 99.00 (*1-85233-616-1*) Spr-Verlag.

Neurodynamics & Psychology. Ed. by Michael Oaksford & Gordon Brown. (Illus.). 400p. 1994. text 79.95 (*0-12-523515-1*) Acad Pr.

Neurodynamics of Personality. Jim Grigsby & David Stevens. 436p. Date not set. lib. bdg. 42.50 (*1-57230-547-9*, C0547) Guilford Pubns.

Neurodynamics of the Vertebral Subluxation. 3rd ed. A. E. Homewood. LC 77-85117. 299p. (C). 1981. text 22.00 (*0-685-09073-6*, 605) Parker Chiro.

NeuroDynamix: Computer Models for Neurophysiology. W. Otto Friesen & Jonathan A. Friesen. (Computational Neuroscience Ser.). (Illus.). 224p. (C). 1994. pap. text 38.95 (*0-19-508282-6*) OUP.

Neurodystrophies & Neurolipidoses. George W. Bruyn & Hugo W. Moser. LC 96-51995. (Handbook of Clinical Neurology Ser.). 790p. 1996. 306.25 (*0-444-81285-7*) Elsevier.

Neuroembryology: The Selected Papers of Viktor Hamburger. Viktor Hamburger. 384p. 1990. 87.50 (*0-8176-3459-2*) Birkhauser.

Neuroendocrine - Immune Network. Ed. by Serem Freier. 272p. 1989. lib. bdg. 217.00 (*0-8493-4625-8*, QP356) CRC Pr.

Neuroendocrine Control of the Thymus. Ed. by Savino Wilson. LC 99-203214. (Neuroimmunomodulation Ser.: Vol. 6, Nos. 1-2 (1999)). (Illus.). 144p. 1999. pap. 45.25 (*3-8055-6769-3*) S Karger.

Neuroendocrine Immune Basis of the Rheumatic Disease: The First International Conference. Ed. by H. L. Bradlow. LC 99-26842. 520p. 1999. lib. bdg. 140.00 (*1-57331-215-0*) NY Acad Sci.

***Neuroendocrine Immune Basis of the Rheumatic Diseases** M. Cutolo. LC 99-26842. (Annals Ser.). 1999. pap. write for info. (*1-57331-216-9*) NY Acad Sci.

Neuroendocrine Molecular Biology. Ed. by G. Fink et al. LC 86-4964. (Biochemical Endocrinology Ser.). 510p. 1986. 95.00 (*0-306-42262-X*, Plenum Trade) Perseus Pubng.

Neuroendocrine Neoplasms of the Larynx: Journal: Oto-Rhino-Laryngology, Vol. 53, No. 4, 1991. Ed. by A. Ferlito. (Illus.). 84p. 1991. pap. 55.00 (*3-8055-5445-1*) S Karger.

Neuroendocrine Perspectives, Vol. 6. Ed. by J. A. Wass & M. F. Scanlon. (Illus.). ix, 353p. 1988. 159.00 (*0-387-96636-6*) Spr-Verlag.

Neuroendocrine Perspectives, Vol. 7. (Illus.). xii, 178p. 1989. 93.00 (*0-387-96828-8*) Spr-Verlag.

Neuroendocrine Perspectives, Vol. 8. Ed. by E. E. Muller & R. M. MacLeod. (Illus.). xiv, 182p. 1990. 117.00 (*0-387-97365-6*) Spr-Verlag.

Neuroendocrine Perspectives, Vol. 9. Ed. by E. E. Muller & R. M. MacLeod. (Illus.). xiv, 246p. 1991. 145.00 (*0-387-97524-1*) Spr-Verlag.

Neuroendocrine Regulation & Altered Behavior. Ed. by Pavel D. Hrdina & R. L. Singhal. LC 81-81689. 416p. (C). 1981. 85.00 (*0-306-40840-6*, Kluwer Plenum) Kluwer Academic.

Neuroendocrine Regulation of Behavior. Jay Schulkin. LC 97-41739. (Illus.). 320p. (C). 1999. text 85.00 (*0-521-45385-2*) Cambridge U Pr.

neuroendocrine regulation of behavior. Jay Schulkin. LC 97-41739. (Illus.). x, 323 p. (C). 1999. pap. text 37.95 (*0-521-45985-0*) Cambridge U Pr.

Neuroendocrine Regulation of Fertility: Proceedings. International Symposium on Neuroendocrine Regulation Staff. Ed. by T. C. Anand Kumar. (Illus.). 1976. 133.25 (*3-8055-2199-5*) S Karger.

Neuroendocrine Regulation of Reproduction. Ed. by Samuel S. Yen & Wylie W. Vale. (Serono Symposia, USA Ser.). (Illus.). 368p. (C). 1990. text 65.00 (*1-878601-04-0*) Serono Symposia USA.

Neuroendocrine Research Methods, 2 vols., Vol. 1 & 2. B. Greenstein. xxxxix, 1,040p. 1991. text 515.00 (*3-7186-5101-7*, Harwood Acad Pubs) Gordon & Breach.

Neuroendocrinological Aspects of Neurosurgery. Ed. by J. D. Pickard et al. (Acta Neurochirugica - Supplementum Ser.: Supplement 47). (Illus.). 130p. 1990. 114.95 (*0-387-82160-0*) Spr-Verlag.

Neuroendocrinology. Charles B. Nemeroff. 640p. 1992. lib. bdg. 110.00 (*0-8493-8844-9*, QP356) CRC Pr.

Neuroendocrinology, Vol. V. Warren R. Selman. LC 92-5836. (Concepts in Neurosurgery Ser.). (Illus.). 418p. 1992. 90.00 (*0-683-07665-5*) Lppncott W & W.

Neuroendocrinology: A Clinical Text. Mary L. Forsling & Ashley Grossman. LC 86-7122. 206p. 1986. text 27.95 (*0-914783-14-9*) Charles.

Neuroendocrinology: Retrospect & Perspectives. Ed. by H. W. Korf & K. H. Usadel. LC 97-42699. (Illus.). x, 444p. 1997. 119.00 (*3-540-63629-3*) Spr-Verlag.

Neuroendocrinology & Pituitary Disease see Atlas of Clinical Endocrinology

Neuroendocrinology & Psychiatric Disorder. fac. ed. Ed. by Gregory M. Brown et al. LC 84-4727. (Illus.). 446p. pap. 138.30 (*0-7837-7286-6*, 204702000005) Bks Demand.

Neuroendocrinology in Physiology & Medicine. Ed. by P. Michael Conn & Marc E. Freeman. LC 99-10139. 592p. 1999. 125.00 (*0-89603-725-8*) Humana.

Neuroendocrinology, 1988: 31st International Henri-Pierre Klotz Days of Clinical Endocrinology, Paris, May 1988. Ed. by A. Enjalbert & J. J. Legros. (Journal: Hormone Research Ser.: Vol. 31, Nos. 1-2, 1989). (Illus.). 104p. 1989. pap. 75.75 (*3-8055-5037-5*) S Karger.

Neuroendocrinology of Aging. Ed. by Joseph Meites. LC 83-10937. 400p. 1983. 85.00 (*0-306-41310-8*, Plenum Trade) Perseus Pubng.

Neuroendocrinology of Gastrointestinal Ulceration: Hans Selye Symposia on Neuroendocrinology & Stress; Vol. 2, Vol. 2. Ed. by Sandor Szabo et al. LC 95-14350. (Hans Selye Symposia on Neuroendocrinology & Stress Ser.: Vol. 2). (Illus.). 246p. (C). 1995. text 95.00 (*0-306-44988-9*, Kluwer Plenum) Kluwer Academic.

***Neuroendocrinology of Leptin.** Ed. by U. R. Ehud. LC 99-40628. (Frontiers of Hormone Research Ser.: Vol. 26). (Illus.). x, 130p. 1999. pap. 147.00 (*3-8055-6921-1*) S Karger.

Neuroendocrinology of Reproduction: Physiology & Behavior. Ed. by Norman T. Adler. LC 80-28245. 576p. 1981. 75.00 (*0-306-40600-4*, Plenum Trade); pap. 37.50 (*0-306-40611-X*, Plenum Trade) Perseus Pubng.

Neuroendocrinology of Sex Steroids: Basic Knowledge & Clinical Implications. Ed. by W. G. Rossmanith & W. A. Scherbaum. (New Developments in Biosciences Ser.: No. 6). viii, 222p. (Orig.). (C). 1993. pap. text 98.50 (*3-11-013616-3*) De Gruyter.

Neuroendoscopy. Cohen. Date not set. text. write for info. (*0-7216-7442-9*, W B Saunders Co) Harcrt Hlth Sci Grp.

Neuroendoscopy. Kim H. Manwaring & Kerry R. Crone. 121p. 1991. 40.00 (*0-913113-57-3*) M Liebert.

Neuroepidemiology. Ed. by Devera G. Schoenberg. 384p. 1990. lib. bdg. 195.00 (*0-8493-5237-1*, RC346) CRC Pr.

Neuroepidemiology: Theory & Method. Ed. by Craig Molgaard. (Illus.). 381p. 1993. text 27.00 (*0-12-504220-5*) Acad Pr.

***Neuroepithelial Stem Cells & Progenitors.** Ed. by Steven W. Levinson & Richard S. Nowakowski. (Developmental Neuroscience Ser.: Vol. 22, Nos. 1-2). (Illus.). 178p. 2000. pap. 45.25 (*3-8055-6976-9*) S Karger.

Neuroethology. Jorg-Peter Ewert. (Illus.). 1980. 58.95 (*0-387-09790-2*) Spr-Verlag.

Neuroethology of the Mauthner System, 1991 Vol. 37, No. 5: Journal: Brain, Behavior & Evolution. Ed. by R. C. Eaton. (Illus.). 88p. 1991. pap. 69.75 (*3-8055-5449-4*) S Karger.

Neurofibramatosis. Allen Rubinstein & Bruce R. Korf. (Illus.). 320p. 1990. text 75.00 (*0-86577-154-5*) Thieme Med Pubs.

Neurofibromatosis: Phenotype, Natural History, & Pathogenesis. 2nd rev. ed. Vincent M. Riccardi. (Illus.). 520p. 1992. text 95.00 (*0-8018-4348-0*) Johns Hopkins.

Neurofibromatosis: Phenotype, Natural History & Pathogenesis. 3rd ed. J. M. Friedman. LC 99-27988. 400p. 1999. 99.95 (*0-8018-6285-X*) Johns Hopkins.

***Neurofibromatosis: Trusting God in the Midst of Neurofibromatosis.** Renee Wilson. LC 99-60787. 128p. 1999. pap. 9.95 (*1-57921-217-4*) WinePress Pub.

***Neurofibromatosis Type I: From Genotype to Phenotype.** M. Upadhyaya. (Human Molecular Genetics Ser.). (Illus.). 230p. 1999. 110.00 (*0-12-220443-3*) Acad Pr.

Neurofibromatosis Type 1 in Childhood. Kathryn North. LC 97-181243. (International Review of Child Neurology Ser.). (Illus.). 142p. (C). 1997. 47.95 (*1-898683-13-1*, Pub. by Mc Keith Pr) Cambridge U Pr.

Neurofilaments. Gerry Shaw. LC 98-20271. (Biotechnology Intelligence Unit Ser.). 1998. 179.00 (*1-57059-546-1*) Landes Bioscience.

Neurofilaments. Gerry Shaw. LC 98-20271. (Biotechnology Intelligence Unit Ser.). (Illus.). viii, 287p. 1998. 179.00 (*3-540-64715-5*) Spr-Verlag.

Neurofunctional Systems: 3D Reconstructions with Correlated Neuroimaging. Hans-Joachim Kretschmann et al. LC 97-31484. 1997. write for info. (*3-13-108211-9*) Thieme Med Pubs.

Neurogastroenterology. Ed. by Enrico Corazziari. (Illus.). xix, 410p. (Orig.). (C). 1996. pap. text 91.45 (*3-11-015343-2*) De Gruyter.

Neurogenesis of Central Respiratory Rhythm: Electrophysiological, Pharmacological & Pathological Aspects. Ed. by A. L. Bianchi & M. Denavit-Saubie. 1985. text 322.00 (*0-85200-903-8*) Kluwer Academic.

Neurogenetic Directory see Handbook of Clinical Neurology

Neurogenetics. Ed. by Stefan-M. Pulst. LC 99-22365. (Contemporary Neurology Ser.: No. 57). (Illus.). 488p. 1999. text 110.00 (*0-19-512975-X*) OUP.

Neurogenetics & Neuro-Ophthalmology. Ed. by A. F. Deutman & J. R. Cruysberg. (Documenta Ophthalmologica Proceedings Ser.: No. 17). 1979. text 255.50 (*90-6193-159-2*) Kluwer Academic.

***Neurogenic Communication Disorders: A Functional Approach.** Worrall. (Illus.). 384p. 1999. 49.00 (*0-86577-868-X*) Thieme Med Pubs.

Neurogenic Disorders of Language. Robin. 2001. 40.00 (*1-56593-703-1*) Thomson Learn.

Neurogenic Hypertension: A Synthesis & Review. C. J. Dickinson. 1991. 94.95 (*0-442-31414-0*) Chapman & Hall.

Neurogenic Inflammation. Ed. by Pierangelo Geppetti & Peter Holzer. LC 95-38900. 338p. 1996. boxed set 224.95 (*0-8493-7646-7*) CRC Pr.

Neurogerontology: Aging & the Nervous System. James F. Willott. LC 98-43500. (Illus.). 408p. 1999. 58.95 (*0-8261-1259-5*) Springer Pub.

Neuroglia. Helmut Kettenmann & Bruce R. Ransom. (Illus.). 1104p. 1995. text 195.00 (*0-19-507847-0*) OUP.

Neuroglia, Vol. 1. 1980. 492.00 (*0-387-09430-X*) Spr-Verlag.

Neurohormonal Techniques in Insects. Ed. by T. A. Miller. (Experimental Entomology Ser.). (Illus.). 282p. 1980. 159.00 (*0-387-90451-4*) Spr-Verlag.

Neurohormones in Invertebrates. Ed. by M. C. Thorndyke & Graham J. Goldsworthy. (Society for Experimental Biology Seminar Ser.: No. 33). 336p. 1988. text 90.00 (*0-521-32843-8*) Cambridge U Pr.

Neurohumoral Control of Blood Vessel Tone: Springfield Blood Vessel Symposium. Ed. by T. J. Lee. (Journal: Blood Vessels: Vol. 24, No. 3). (Illus.). 80p. 1987. pap. 42.75 (*3-8055-4604-1*) S Karger.

Neurohumoral Maintenance of Immune Homeostasis. Viktor M. Klimenko & Elenor K. Shkhinek. Ed. by Samuel A. Corson & Elizabeth O. Corson. LC 84-8771. (Illus.). 184p. 1995. lib. bdg. 38.50 (*0-226-45042-2*) U Ch Pr.

Neurohumoral Maintenance of Immune Homeostasis. Elena A. Korneva et al. Ed. & Tr. by Samuel A. Corson & Elizabeth O. Corson. LC 84-8771. (Illus.). 264p. reprint ed. pap. 81.90 (*0-608-09427-7*, 205422700004) Bks Demand.

Neurohumoral Mechanisms of Aging. Ed. by V. V. Frolkis. (Journal: Gerontology: Vol. 34, No. 1-2, 1988). 96p. 1988. pap. 76.75 (*3-8055-4797-8*) S Karger.

Neurohumoral Regulation of Coronary Flow. Ed. by W. H. Van Gilst. (Developments in Cardiovascular Medicine Ser.). 160p. (C). 1993. text 85.50 (*0-7923-2588-5*) Kluwer Academic.

Neurohypophysial Hormones & Similar Polypeptides. Ed. by E. Berde et al. (Handbook of Experimental Pharmacology Ser.: Vol. 23). (Illus.). 1968. 184.00 (*0-387-04149-4*) Spr-Verlag.

Neurohypophysis: Psychological & Clinical Aspects. Ed. by Seymour Reichlin. LC 84-4861. 240p. 1984. 65.00 (*0-306-41642-5*, Kluwer Plenum) Kluwer Academic.

Neurohypophysis: Recent Progress of Vasopressin & Oxytocin Ressearch: Proceedings of the 1st Joint World Congress of Neurohypophysis & Vasopressin, Nasu, Tochigi, Japan, 16-21 July 1995. Ed. by Toshikazu Saito et al. LC 95-44867. (International Congress Ser.: No. 1098). 702p. 1995. 292.00 (*0-444-82231-3*, Excerpta Medica) Elsevier.

Neuroimaging, 5 Vols. William W. Orrison. LC 97-39761. 1999. text. write for info. (*0-7216-6799-6*, W B Saunders Co) Harcrt Hlth Sci Grp.

Neuroimaging: A Companion to Adams & Victor's Principles of Neurology. Ed. by Jack O. Greenberg. LC 93-41639. 614p. 1994. text 125.00 (*0-07-024308-5*) McGraw-Hill HPD.

Neuroimaging: A Companion to Adams, Victor & Ropper's Principles of Neurology. 2nd ed. Jack O. Greenberg. (Illus.). 896p. 1999. 145.00 (*0-07-134615-5*) McGraw-Hill HPD.

Neuroimaging: A Window to the Neurological Foundations of Learning & Behavior in Children. Ed. by G. Reid Lyon & Judith M. Rumsey. 288p. (Orig.). 1996. pap. text 49.95 (*1-55766-256-8*, 2568) P H Brookes.

Neuroimaging: Basic Science. Ed. by Erin D. Bigler. LC 96-29400. (Human Brain Function Ser.: Vol. 1). (Illus.). 334p. (C). 1996. text 75.00 (*0-306-45228-6*, Kluwer Plenum) Kluwer Academic.

Neuroimaging: Clinical & Physical Principles. Ed. by R. A. Zimmerman et al. LC 97-28144. (Illus.). 1232p. 1998. 185.00 (*0-387-94963-1*) Spr-Verlag.

Neuroimaging: Clinical Applications. Ed. by Erin D. Bigler. (Human Brain Function Ser.: Vol. 2). (Illus.). 382p. (C). 1996. text 75.00 (*0-306-45229-4*, Kluwer Plenum) Kluwer Academic.

Neuroimaging & Developmental Neurophysiology in Child Psychiatric Disorders. Bernard Garreau & J. L. Beaulieu. LC 97-42376. 1997. write for info. (*2-287-63634-X*, Pub. by Spl France Editions) Spr-Verlag.

Neuroimaging & the Psychiatry of Late Life. Ed. by David Ames & Edmond Chiu. LC 96-52958. (Illus.). 252p. (C). 1998. text 95.00 (*0-521-49505-9*) Cambridge U Pr.

Neuroimaging Atlas of Radiosurgery. Robert J. Coffey. LC 97-10983. 224p. 1997. text 99.00 (*0-397-51766-1*) Lppncott W & W.

Neuroimaging in Child Neuropsychiatric Disorders. Ed. by B. Garreau. (Illus.). x, 289p. 1998. 149.00 (*3-540-63634-X*) Spr-Verlag.

Neuroimaging in Epilepsy: Principles & Practice. Gregory Cascino & Clifford R. Jack. LC 96-32628. 289p. 1996. text 155.00 (*0-7506-9716-4*) Buttrwrth-Heinemann.

Neuroimmunodegeneration. Paul K. Wong & William S. Lynn. LC 98-23047. (Biotechnology Intelligence Unit Ser.). 1998. write for info. (*1-57059-484-8*) Landes Bioscience.

***Neuroimmunodegeneration.** Ed. by Paul K. Wong & William S. Lynn. LC 98-23047. (Biotechnology Intelligence Unit Ser.). 168p. 1998. 129.00 (*3-540-64712-0*) Spr-Verlag.

Neuroimmunoendocrinology. 3rd enl. rev. ed. Ed. by J. Edwin Blalock. (Chemical Immunology Ser.: Vol. 69, 1997). (Illus.). xiv, 228p. 1997. 194.00 (*3-8055-6524-0*) S Karger.

Neuroimmunological Diseases: Recent Advances in Pathogenesis & Treatment. International Symposium Staff. Ed. by Akihiro Igata. LC RC0346.5.I61. (Japan Intractable Diseases Research Foundation Publication Ser.: No. 26). 429p. 1988. reprint ed. pap. 133.00 (*0-608-01215-7*, 206190400001) Bks Demand.

Neuroimmunology. Ed. by Jeremy Brockes. LC 82-3679. (Current Topics in Neurobiology Ser.). 272p. 1982. 65.00 (*0-306-40955-0*, Plenum Trade) Perseus Pubng.

Neuroimmunomodulation: Molecular Aspects, Integrative Systems, & Clinical Advances. Ed. by Samuel M. McCann et al. LC 98-15845. (Annals of the New York Academy of Sciences Ser.: No. 840). 866p. 1998. 160.00 (*1-57331-072-7*); pap. 160.00 (*1-57331-073-5*) NY Acad Sci.

Neuroimmunomodulation: Proceedings of the 1st International Workshop. Novera H. Spector. xxii, 306p. 1988. pap. text 208.00 (*0-677-21960-1*) Gordon & Breach.

Neuroimmunomodulation - the State of the Art: Proceedings of the 2nd International Congress ISNIM (International Society for Neuroimmunomodulation), Held in Paestum, Salerno, Italy, Sept. 12-17, 1993. Ed. by Nicola Fabris et al. LC 94-39175. (Annals Ser.: Vol. 741). 1994. write for info. (*0-89766-909-6*) NY Acad Sci.

Neuroinflammation: Mechanisms & Management. Ed. by Paul L. Wood. LC 99-207058. (Contemporary Neuroscience Ser.). (Illus.). 392p. 1997. 145.00 (*0-89603-416-X*) Humana.

Neuroinformatics: An Overview of the Human Brain Project. Ed. by Stephen H. Koslow & Michael F. Huerta. (Progress in Neurinformatics Research Ser.). 384p. (C). 1997. text 79.95 (*0-8058-2099-X*) L Erlbaum Assocs.

Neurointervention & Neurosurgery Devices Markets. (Market Research Reports: No. 350). (Illus.). 114p. 1992. 795.00 (*0-317-05033-8*) Theta Corp.

Neurokinesiology. 2nd rev. ed. Arthur Martin. (Illus.). 115p. 1998. pap. 9.95 (*1-891962-07-8*) Personal Trans.

Neurolaryngology. Ed. by Minoru Hirano et al. (Illus.). 304p. (Orig.). (C). 1991. reprint ed. pap. text 65.00 (*1-879105-19-5*, A031) Singular Publishing.

Neurolaw: Brain & Spinal Cord Injuries. J. Sherrod Taylor. LC 97-65755. 1997. write for info. (*0-8366-9003-6*) West Group.

Neuroleptic-Induced Movement Disorders: A Comprehensive Survey. Ed. by Ramzy Yassa et al. (Illus.). 511p. (C). 1996. text 110.00 (*0-521-43364-9*) Cambridge U Pr.

Neuroleptics. Ed. by D. P. Bobon et al. (Modern Problems of Pharmacopsychiatry Ser.: Vol. 5). 1970. 41.00 (*3-8055-0530-2*) S Karger.

Neuroleptics: Neurochemical, Behavioral, & Clinical Perspectives. Ed. by Joseph T. Coyle & Sam J. Enna. LC 81-40892. (Central Nervous System Pharmacology Ser.). (Illus.). 341p. 1983. reprint ed. pap. 105.80 (*0-7837-9519-X*, 206026800005) Bks Demand.

Neurolinguistic Approaches to Stuttering: Proceedings of the International Symposium on Stuttering, Brussels, 1972. International Symposium on Stuttering Staff. Ed. by Y. Lebrun & Richard Hoops. (Janua Linguarum, Series Major: No. 70). (Illus.). 1973. 93.85 (*90-279-2417-1*) Mouton.

Neurolinguistic Aspects of the Japanese Writing System. Michel Paradis & Nancy Hildebrandt. (Perspectives in Neurolinguistics, Neuropsychology & Psycholinguistics Ser.). 1985. text 89.95 (*0-12-544965-8*) Acad Pr.

Neurolinguistics: Historical & Theoretical Perspectives. C. P. Bouton. LC 90-7853. (Applied Psycholinguistics & Communication Disorders Ser.). (Illus.). 286p. (C). 1990. 65.00 (*0-306-43691-4*, Plenum Trade) Perseus Pubng.

Neurolinguistics & Linguistic Aphasiology: An Introduction. David N. Caplan. (Cambridge Studies in Speech Science & Communication). (Illus.). 512p. 1987. text 89.95 (*0-521-32420-3*); pap. text 34.95 (*0-521-31195-0*) Cambridge U Pr.

N

An Asterisk (*) at the beginning of an entry indicates that the title is appearing for the first time.

Neurolinguistics of Bilingualism: An Introduction. Franco Fabbro. 272p. 1999. 49.95 (*0-86377-755-4*) Taylor & Francis.
Neurologia Pediatrica-Princ y. Kenneth F. Swaiman. (C). 1996. text 196.15 (*84-8086-191-6*) Mosby Inc.
Neurologic & Neurosurgical Emergencies. Julio Cruz. Ed. by Richard Zorab. LC 98-7038. (Illus.). 624p. (C). 1998. text 145.00 (*0-7216-6105-X*, W B Saunders Co) Harcrt Hlth Sci Grp.
Neurologic & Psychiatric Diseases, Drugs & Markets, 4 vols. 615p. 1995. spiral bd. 2950.00 (*1-57936-047-5*, 905) IBC USA.
Neurologic Athletic Head & Spinal Injuries. Robert Cantu. (Illus.). 430p. Date not set. text. write for info. (*0-7216-8339-8*, W B Saunders Co) Harcrt Hlth Sci Grp.
***Neurologic Catastrophes in the Emergency Department.** Eelco F. Wijdicks. LC 99-32437. 266p. 1999. text 65.00 (*0-7506-7055-X*) Buttrwrth-Heinemann.
Neurologic Complications in Organ Transplant Recipients. Wijdicks. LC 98-49668. 272p. 1999. text 95.00 (*0-7506-7066-5*) Buttrwrth-Heinemann.
Neurologic Complications of Cancer. Jerome B. Posner. (Contemporary Neurology Ser.: No. 45). (Illus.). 496p. (C). 1995. text 99.00 (*0-8036-0006-2*) OUP.
Neurologic Differential Diagnosis. 2nd ed. Mark Mumenthaler. Tr. by Otto Appenzeller. (GER., Illus.). 192p. (C). 1992. pap. text 47.00 (*0-86577-432-3*) Thieme Med Pubs.
Neurologic Disease in Women. Ed. by Peter W. Kaplan. LC 98-4136. (Illus.). 464p. 1998. 150.00 (*1-888799-15-3*) Demos Medical.
Neurologic Disorders. fac. ed. Ed. by Joe N. Kornegay. LC 88-4803. (Contemporary Issues in Small Animal Practice Ser.: No. 5). (Illus.). 232p. 1986. reprint ed. pap. 72.00 (*0-7837-7882-1*, 204763900007) Bks Demand.
Neurologic Disorders, No. 1. Esther Chipps. (Illus.). 336p. (C). (gr. 13). 1992. text 36.00 (*0-8016-1372-8*, 01372) Mosby Inc.
Neurologic Disorders in Women. Ed. by Merit E. Cudkowicz & Michael C. Irizarry. LC 96-50469. 184p. 1997. text 59.95 (*0-7506-9745-8*) Buttrwrth-Heinemann.
Neurologic Disorders of Ambulatory Patients: Diagnosis & Management. John H. Wagner. LC 88-32599. 303p. reprint ed. pap. 94.00 (*0-7837-2843-3*, 205762900006) Bks Demand.
Neurologic Disorders of the Larynx. Andrew Blitzer et al. (Illus.). 352p. 1992. text 82.00 (*0-86577-400-5*) Thieme Med Pubs.
Neurologic Emergencies. (Emergency Video Ser.). 1991. 36.95 incl. VHS (*0-87434-343-7*) Springhouse Corp.
Neurologic Emergencies: A Symptom Oriented Approach. 2nd ed. Gregory Henry. 1994. text 57.00 (*0-07-029369-4*) McGraw.
Neurologic Emergencies in Infancy & Childhood. 2nd ed. John M. Pellock & Edwin C. Myer. (Illus.). 425p. 1993. text 95.00 (*0-7506-9419-X*) Buttrwrth-Heinemann.
***Neurologic Injury During Cardiac Surgery IV Abstract Booklet: Emerging Consensus.** Ed. by Silent Partners, Inc. Staff. 36p. 1999. pap. write for info. (*1-878353-48-9*) Silent Partners.
Neurologic Localization & Diagnosis. Karl E. Misulis. 217p. 1996. pap. text 33.50 (*0-7506-9636-2*) Buttrwrth-Heinemann.
Neurologic Pearls. Orrin Devinsky et al. (Illus.). 286p. (C). 2000. pap. text 19.95 (*0-8036-0433-5*) Davis Co.
Neurologic Radiology: The Brain, a Practical Approach. Ed. by Burton P. Drayer. 750p. 1999. text 195.00 (*0-7817-0120-1*) Lppncott W & W.
Neurologic Rehabilitation. Bruce H. Dobkin. LC 95-46567. (Contemporary Neurology Ser.: No. 47). (Illus.). 360p. (C). 1996. text 99.00 (*0-8036-0169-7*) OUP.
Neurologic Rehabilitation: A Guide to Diagnosis, Prognosis & Treatment Planning. Virginia M. Mills et al. LC 97-24813. (Illus.). 1995. pap. 49.95 (*0-86542-514-0*) Blackwell Sci.
Neurologic Skills: Examination, History, & Localization for Students & House Officers. Thomas H. Glick. LC 92-49587. (Illus.). 472p. 1993. pap. 46.95 (*0-86542-292-3*) Blackwell Sci.
Neurological Adverse Reactions to Anticancer Drugs. Ed. by J. G. Hildebrand & U. Veronesi. (ESO Monographs). (Illus.). 112p. 1990. 59.00 (*0-387-53263-3*) Spr-Verlag.
Neurological Anatomy in Relation to Clinical Medicine. 3rd ed. Alf Brodal. (Illus.). 1053p. 1981. text 89.00 (*0-19-502694-2*) OUP.
Neurological & Neurosurgical. Nikas. Date not set. text. write for info. (*0-7216-6001-0*, W B Saunders Co) Harcrt Hlth Sci Grp.
Neurological & Neurosurgical Intensive Care. 3rd ed. Ed. by Allan H. Ropper. LC 92-49216. 528p. 1992. text 109.00 (*0-88167-981-X*) Lppncott W & W.
Neurological & Neurosurgical Nursing. write for info. (*0-7131-4521-8*, Pub. by E A) Routldge.
Neurological & Psychiatric Disorders, Neurogenomics No. 1: Drug Discovery, Development & Market Analysis. Stan M. Goldin & Timothy Tankosic. Ed. by Susan C. DiClemente & Laura Carter. (Illus.). 1792p. 1997. spiral bd. write for info. (*1-57936-094-7*, 936, Drug & Market Dev) IBC USA.
Neurological & Psychiatric Disorders, Neurogenomics No. 2: Drug Discovery, Development & Market Analysis - Neurogene Compendium, Market Analysis, Blueprints for Drug Discovery. Stan M. Goldin. Ed. by Susan C. DiClemente & Laura Carter. (Illus.). 700p. 1997. spiral bd. write for info. (*1-57936-092-0*, 936, Drug & Market Dev) IBC USA.
Neurological & Psychiatric Disorders, Neurogenomics No. 3: Drug Discovery, Development & Market Analysis - Company Profiles. Stan M. Goldin & Timothy Tankosic. Ed. by Susan C. DiClemente & Laura Carter. 488p. 1997. spiral bd. write for info. (*1-57936-093-9*, 936, Drug & Market Dev) IBC USA.
Neurological Aspects of Substance Abuse. John C. Brust. (Illus.). 289p. 1993. text 99.95 (*0-7506-9005-4*) Buttrwrth-Heinemann.
Neurological Assessment of the Pre-Term & Full-Term Newborn Infant. Libby Dubowitz & Victor Dubowitz. LC 65-80377. (Clinics in Developmental Medicine Ser.: No. 79). (Illus.). 104p. (C). 1991. text 33.95 (*0-521-41204-8*, Pub. by Mc Keith Pr) Cambridge U Pr.
Neurological Assessment of the Preterm & Full-Term Newborn Infant. 2nd ed. Lilly M. Dubowitz et al. (Clinics in Developmental Medicine Ser.: No. 148). (Illus.). 150p. (C). 2000. text 59.95 (*1-898683-15-8*, Pub. by Mc Keith Pr) Cambridge U Pr.
Neurological Basis of Childhood Psychopathology. George W. Hynd. (Developmental Clinical Psychology & Psychiatry Ser.: Vol. 25). 160p. (C). 1992. text 42.00 (*0-8039-3592-7*); pap. text 18.95 (*0-8039-3593-5*) Sage.
Neurological Complications of Cancer. Ed. by Ronald G. Wiley. LC 94-41748. (Neurological Disease & Therapy Ser.: Vol. 37). (Illus.). 568p. 1995. text 210.00 (*0-8247-8840-0*) Dekker.
Neurological Complications of HIV-AIDS. Said. 1998. text 89.00 (*0-7020-1836-8*) Bailliere Tindall.
Neurological Complications of HIV Infection. Howard E. Gendelman et al. LC 97-9987. 650p. 1997. text 110.00 (*0-412-08631-X*, Pub. by E A) OUP.
***Neurological Development from Birth to Six Years: Guide for Examination & Evaluation.** Claudine Amiel-Tison & Julie Gosselin. LC 00-9626. (Illus.). 2001. pap. write for info. (*0-8018-6564-6*) Johns Hopkins.
Neurological Differential Diagnosis. 2nd ed. John Patten. LC 95-14336. 350p. 1996. 69.00 (*3-540-19937-3*) Spr-Verlag.
Neurological Differential Diagnosis: An Illustrated Approach. J. P. Patten. (Illus.). 292p. 1987. reprint ed. 75.00 (*0-387-90264-3*) Spr-Verlag.
Neurological Disabilities: Assessment & Treatment. Susan Bennett. LC 97-52018. 400p. 1998. text 39.95 (*0-397-55151-7*) Lppncott W & W.
Neurological Disorders: Course & Treatment. Ed. by Thomas Brandt et al. (Illus.). 1150p. 1996. text 159.95 (*0-12-125830-0*) Acad Pr.
Neurological Dysfunction & Nursing Interventions. Joyce Taylor & Sally Ballenger. (Illus.). 1979. text 35.95 (*0-07-063170-0*) McGraw.
Neurological Emergencies. Ed. by R. A. Hughes. 350p. (Orig.). (C). 1994. pap. text 46.00 (*0-7279-0756-5*, Pub. by BMJ Pub) Login Brothers Bk Co.
Neurological Epidemiology: Principles & Clinical Applications. Ed. by Bruce S. Schoenberg. LC 77-72796. (Advances in Neurology Ser.: No. 19). (Illus.). 678p. reprint ed. pap. 200.00 (*0-7837-7104-5*, 204693300004) Bks Demand.
Neurological Evaluation of Infants & Children. Henry W. Baird & Eleanora C. Gordon. LC 65-80419. (Clinics in Developmental Medicine Ser.: Nos. 84-85). (Illus.). 249p. (C). 1991. text 47.95 (*0-521-41205-6*, Pub. by Mc Keith Pr) Cambridge U Pr.
Neurological Evaluation of the Psychogenic Patient. Ed. by W. L. Smith et al. 160p. (C). 1982. text 20.00 (*0-88331-163-1*) R B Luce.
Neurological Examination Made Easy. Geraint Fuller. LC 92-48187. (Illus.). 232p. 1993. pap. text 24.00 (*0-443-04294-2*) Church.
Neurological Examination of the Full-Term Newborn Infant. 2nd ed. Heinz F. Prechtl & David Beintema. (Clinics in Developmental Medicine Ser.: No. 63). (Illus.). 76p. (C). 1991. reprint ed. text 27.95 (*0-521-41199-8*, Pub. by Mc Keith Pr) Cambridge U Pr.
Neurological Examination of the Newborn. N. O'Doherty. 1986. text 124.00 (*0-85200-877-5*) Kluwer Academic.
Neurological Investigations. Ed. by Rac Hughes. 511p. 1997. 85.00 (*0-7279-1080-9*, Pub. by BMJ Pub) Login Brothers Bk Co.
Neurological Manifestations of Systemic Diseases in Children. Avraham Steinberg & Yitzchak Frank. LC 92-49343. (International Review of Child Neurology Ser.). 400p. 1993. reprint ed. pap. 124.00 (*0-608-04740-6*, 206546100004) Bks Demand.
Neurological Organization of Ocular Movement. Ed. by R. Daroff & A. Neetens. LC 90-5225. (Illus.). 562p. 1989. lib. bdg. 146.00 (*90-6299-067-3*, Pub. by Kugler) Kugler Pubns.
Neurological Physiotherapy: A Problem-Solving Approach. Ed. by Susan Edwards. LC 96-1650. 212p. 1996. pap. text 33.00 (*0-443-04887-8*) Church.
Neurological Rehabilitation. Richard Greenwood. LC 97-204472. (Illus.). xiii, 640p. 1997. write for info. (*0-86377-484-9*, Pub. by Psychol Pr) Taylor & Francis.
Neurological Rehabilitation, No. 3. 3rd ed. Darcy A. Umphred. (Illus.). 1056p. (C). (gr. 13). 1995. text 81.00 (*0-8016-7925-7*, 07925) Mosby Inc.
Neurological Side of Neuropsychology. Richard E. Cytowic. LC 95-1528. (Illus.). 529p. 1996. 62.50 (*0-262-03231-7*, Bradford Bks) MIT Pr.
Neurological Surgery: A Comprehensive Reference Guide to the Diagnosis & Management of Neurosurgical Problems. 4th ed. Julian R. Youmans. Ed. by Richard Zorab. LC 94-33455. (Illus.). 3648p. 1995. text 835.00 (*0-7216-5141-0*, W B Saunders Co) Harcrt Hlth Sci Grp.
Neurological Surgery: A Comprehensive Reference Guide to the Diagnosis & Management of Neurosurgical Problems, 3 vols., 1. 2nd ed. Julian R. Youmans. 2600p. 1989. write for info. (*0-7216-9652-X*, W B Saunders Co) Harcrt Hlth Sci Grp.
Neurological Surgery: A Comprehensive Reference Guide to the Diagnosis & Management of Neurosurgical Problems, 3 vols., 2. 2nd ed. Julian R. Youmans. 2600p. 1989. write for info. (*0-7216-9653-8*, W B Saunders Co) Harcrt Hlth Sci Grp.
Neurological Surgery: A Comprehensive Reference Guide to the Diagnosis & Management of Neurosurgical Problems, 3 vols., 3. 2nd ed. Julian R. Youmans. 2600p. 1989. write for info. (*0-7216-9654-6*, W B Saunders Co) Harcrt Hlth Sci Grp.
Neurological Surgery: A Comprehensive Reference Guide to the Diagnosis & Management of Neurosurgical Problems, 4th Edition. 4th ed. Ed. by Julian R. Youmans. (Illus.). 4242p. 1996. write for info. incl. cd-rom (*0-7216-6845-3*, W B Saunders Co); write for info. incl. cd-rom (*0-7216-6846-1*, W B Saunders Co) Harcrt Hlth Sci Grp.
Neurological Surgery of the Ear & Skull Base. Ed. by Derald E. Brackmann. LC 82-5414. (Illus.). 428p. reprint ed. pap. 132.70 (*0-7837-7121-5*, 204695000004) Bks Demand.
Neurological Symptoms in Blood Diseases. Nello D'Eramo. Tr. by John Iliffe. LC 72-1871. 297p. reprint ed. pap. 92.10 (*0-608-12372-2*, 205206900033) Bks Demand.
Neurological Therapeutics. D. L. Davidson & J. A. Lenman. 350p. 1981. pap. 64.95 (*0-8464-1216-0*) Beekman Pubs.
Neurologically-Impaired Child: Doman-Delacato Techniques Reappraised. Robert A. Cummins. 272p. 1988. lib. bdg. 55.00 (*0-7099-4859-X*, Pub. by C Helm) Routldge.
Neurology. Robert C. Collins. Ed. by William Schmitt. LC 96-48724. 224p. 1997. pap. text 36.95 (*0-7216-5992-6*, W B Saunders Co) Harcrt Hlth Sci Grp.
***Neurology.** Crash Course. 1999. text. write for info. (*0-7234-3141-8*) Harcourt.
Neurology. Michael Donaghy. LC 97-11745. (Oxford Core Texts Ser.). (Illus.). 228p. 1997. pap. text 29.50 (*0-19-262795-3*) OUP.
Neurology. Christopher N. Martyn. (Student Notes Ser.). (Illus.). 296p. 1990. pap. text 19.95 (*0-443-03307-2*) Church.
Neurology. 2nd ed. Trend. (C). 1998. pap. text 16.95 (*0-443-05884-9*) Church.
Neurology. 2nd ed. Patrick Trend et al. LC 97-17396. (Colour Guide Ser.). 1997. write for info. (*0-443-05807-5*) Harcrt Hlth Sci Grp.
Neurology. 3rd ed. Mark Mumenthaler. (Flexibook Ser.). (Illus.). 551p. (Orig.). 1990. text 29.90 (*0-86577-317-3*) Thieme Med Pubs.
Neurology. 3rd ed. Elizabeth K. White. LC 92-48848. (Regents - Prentice-Hall Medical Assistant Kit Ser.). 1993. pap. 16.40 (*0-13-036823-7*) P-H.
***Neurology.** 4th ed. Mark Mumenthaler & Heinrich Mattle. (Illus.). 950p. (Orig.). 2000. pap. 39.00 (*0-86577-936-8*) Thieme Med Pubs.
Neurology. 5th ed. Howard L. Weiner & Lawrence P. Levitt. LC 93-12412. (House Officer Ser.). (Illus.). 222p. 1994. 21.95 (*0-683-08906-4*) Lppncott W & W.
Neurology. 6th ed. Howard L. Weiner et al. LC 98-50137. (House Officer Ser.). 1999. pap. text 24.95 (*0-683-30497-6*) Lppncott W & W.
Neurology: A Concise Clinical Text. Michael Swash. (Illus.). 250p. 1989. text 43.50 (*0-7020-1382-X*) Bailliere Tindall.
***Neurology: An Illustrated Collection.** Fuller. (Illus.). 1999. text 31.00 (*0-443-05374-X*) Mosby Inc.
Neurology: Pretest Self-Assessment & Review. 3rd ed. Ed. by Richard Lechtenberg. LC 97-5463. (Pretest Clinical Science Ser.). (Illus.). 200p. 1997. pap. text 18.95 (*0-07-052528-5*) McGraw-Hill HPD.
***Neurology: Pretest Self-Assessment & Review.** 4th ed. Mitchell S. V. Elkind & Steven G. Werdehoff. LC 00-37251. 2000. write for info. (*0-07-136099-9*) McGraw-Hill HPD.
Neurology: Problems in Primary Care. 2nd ed. James L. Bernat & Frederick M. Vincent. Ed. by Melanie C. Karaffa. LC 93-6786. (Problems in Primary Care Ser.). (Illus.). 900p. 1993. pap. text 49.95 (*1-878487-85-X*, 5855M) Practice Mgmt Info.
Neurology: What Shall I Do? 2nd ed. Dayfydd Thomas & Bev Daily. LC 97-178844. 128p. 1996. pap. text 35.00 (*0-7506-3195-3*) Buttrwrth-Heinemann.
Neurology & Clinical Neuroscience. Roger A. Brumback. LC 92-48938. (Oklahoma Notes Ser.). 220p. 1993. 16.95 (*0-387-97959-X*) Spr-Verlag.
Neurology & Clinical Neuroscience. 2nd ed. Roger A. Brumback. Ed. by Rita R. Claudet. LC 96-13784. (Oklahoma Notes Ser.). 186p. 1996. pap. 17.95 (*0-387-94635-7*) Spr-Verlag.
Neurology & General Medicine. 2nd ed. Michael J. Aminoff. 1995. text 140.00 (*0-443-08933-7*) Church.
Neurology & General Medicine: The Neurological Aspects of Medical Disorders. Ed. by Michael J. Aminoff. LC 88-36459. (Illus.). 840p. reprint ed. pap. 200.00 (*0-7837-8752-9*, 204949700012) Bks Demand.
Neurology & Neurosurgery Illustrated. 3rd ed. Kenneth W. Lindsay & Ian Bone. LC 97-16820. 1997. pap. text 45.00 (*0-443-05061-9*) Church.
Neurology & Neurosurgery Two Thousand & Two. Bradley Gibbs. (Illus.). 512p. 2002. text 78.00 (*0-8151-1998-4*, 30639) Mosby Inc.
Neurology & Psychiatry. Plowman. 1987. pap. text 76.00 (*0-471-91450-9*) Wiley.
Neurology & Psychiatry: A Meeting of Minds. Ed. by J. Mueller. (Illus.). xiv, 290p. 1989. 195.00 (*3-8055-4712-9*) S Karger.
Neurology & the Law: Private Litigation & the Public Policy. H. Richard Beresford. LC 97-34794. (Contemporary Neurology Ser.: No. 51). (Illus.). 208p. (C). 1998. text 89.00 (*0-8036-0168-9*) OUP.
Neurology & Trauma. Randolph W. Evans. Ed. by Bill Schmidt. LC 95-42805. (Illus.). 544p. 1996. text 104.00 (*0-7216-4352-3*, W B Saunders Co) Harcrt Hlth Sci Grp.
***Neurology Clinical Practice Online Renewals.** Bradley et al. 2000. 195.00 (*0-7506-9994-9*) Buttrwrth-Heinemann.
Neurology Examination Made Easy. 2nd ed. Geraint Fuller. LC 98-40972. (C). 1998. pap. text 22.95 (*0-443-06166-1*) Church.
Neurology for General Practitioners. Roy Beran. (Illus.). 224p. 1996. text 50.00 (*0-07-470205-X*) McGraw-Hill HPD.
Neurology for Non-Neurologists. 3rd ed. Wiederholt. 368p. 1995. pap. text 43.00 (*0-7216-4191-1*, W B Saunders Co) Harcrt Hlth Sci Grp.
***Neurology for Non-Neurologists.** 4th ed. Wiederholt. 2000. pap. text. write for info. (*0-7216-8874-8*, W B Saunders Co) Harcrt Hlth Sci Grp.
***Neurology for Psychiatrists.** Gin S. Malhi et al. 120p. 2000. pap. 39.95 (*1-85317-922-1*, Pub. by Martin Dunitz) Blackwell Sci.
Neurology for the Boards. James D. Geyer & Janice M. Keating. LC 98-4651. 336p. 1998. pap. text 45.00 (*0-7817-1722-1*) Lppncott W & W.
Neurology for the Non-Neurologist. 2nd ed. William J. Weiner et al. LC 65-10762. (Illus.). 450p. 1988. text 38.50 (*0-397-50911-1*, Lippnctt) Lppncott W & W.
Neurology for the Non-Neurologist. 3rd ed. William J. Weiner. 448p. 1994. pap. text 49.95 (*0-397-51288-0*) Lppncott W & W.
Neurology for the Non-Neurologist. 4th ed. William J. Weiner & Christopher G. Goetz. LC 99-11318. 1999. write for info. (*0-7817-1707-8*) Lppncott W & W.
***Neurology for the Primary Care Physician.** Andrea C. Adams. (Illus.). 300p. 2000. pap. text 35.00 (*0-8036-0538-2*) Davis Co.
Neurology for the Psychiatry Specialty Board Review. Leon A. Weisberg. LC 92-16164. (Continuing Education in Psychiatry Ser.: Vol. 2). 160p. 1992. pap. 21.95 (*0-87630-684-9*) Brunner-Mazel.
Neurology for the Psychiatry Specialty Board Review. 2nd ed. Leon A. Weisberg. LC 97-36014. (Continuing Education in Psychiatry & Psychology Ser.). 162p. 1998. pap. 24.95 (*0-87630-868-X*) Brunner-Mazel.
Neurology for the Psychiatry Specialty Board Review. 2nd ed. Leon A. Weisberg. (Continuing Education in Psychiatry & Psychology Ser.: Vol. 7). 162p. 1998. 69.95 (*0-87630-869-8*) Brunner-Mazel.
Neurology for the Speech-Language Pathologist. 3rd ed. Russell J. Love & Wanda G. Webb. LC 96-20156. 337p. 1996. pap. text 35.00 (*0-7506-9686-9*) Buttrwrth-Heinemann.
***Neurology for the Speech-Language Pathologist.** 4th ed. Russell Love & Rhonda G. Webb. (Illus.). 384p. 2000. pap. 35.00 (*0-7506-7252-8*) Buttrwrth-Heinemann.
***Neurology in Clinical Practice.** 3rd ed. Walter G. Bradley et al. LC 99-31264. 2750p. 1999. text 450.00 (*0-7506-9973-6*) Buttrwrth-Heinemann.
Neurology in Practice. 2nd ed. Y. L. Yu et al. 168p. 1997. pap. 25.00 (*962-209-445-7*) HK Univ Pr.
Neurology in Primary Care. Joseph H. Friedman. 232p. 1998. pap. text 27.50 (*0-7506-7036-3*) Buttrwrth-Heinemann.
Neurology in Science, Medicine & Disease: Index of New Information with Authors & Subjects. Julia M. Knouse. 180p. 1993. 47.50 (*1-55914-884-5*); pap. 44.50 (*1-55914-885-3*) ABBE Pubs Assn.
Neurology Inflammatory Connecti. F. G. Jennekens & L. Kater. (Illus.). 299p. 1998. text. write for info. (*0-7020-2231-4*) W B Saunders.
Neurology of Aphasia. Ed. by H. S. Kirshner & F. R. Freemon. (Neurolinguistics Ser.: Vol. 12). 224p. 1982. 66.75 (*90-265-0409-8*) Swets.
***Neurology of Bladder, Bowel & Sexual Dysfunction.** Clare J. Fowler. LC 99-20093. (Blue Books of Practical Neurology). 416p. 1999. text 95.00 (*0-7506-9959-0*) Buttrwrth-Heinemann.
Neurology of Critical Illness. Eelco F. Wijdicks. LC 94-16409. (Contemporary Neurology Ser.: No. 43). (Illus.). 384p. 1995. text 90.00 (*0-8036-9316-8*) OUP.
Neurology of Eye Movements. 3rd ed. R. John Leigh. LC 98-37880. (Illus.). 656p. 1999. text 120.00 (*0-19-512972-5*) OUP.
Neurology of Eye Movements. 3rd ed. R. John Leigh & David S. Zee. (Contemporary Neurology Ser.). 1999. cd-rom 120.00 (*0-19-512974-1*) OUP.
Neurology of Eye Movements. 3rd ed. R. John Leigh & David S. Zee. (Contemporary Neurology Ser.: No. 55). (Illus.). 656p. 1999. text 195.00 (*0-19-512973-3*) OUP.
Neurology of Hereditary Metabolic Diseases of Children. 2nd ed. Gilles Lyon et al. LC 95-23487. (Illus.). 512p. 1996. text 79.00 (*0-07-000389-0*) McGraw-Hill HPD.
Neurology of the Elderly. Richard Godwin-Austin & M. J. Bendall. (Illus.). xvi, 144p. 1990. 69.00 (*0-387-19593-9*) Spr-Verlag.
Neurology of the Newborn. 3rd ed. Joseph J. Volpe. (Illus.). 876p. 1994. text 97.00 (*0-7216-3690-X*, W B Saunders Co) Harcrt Hlth Sci Grp.
Neurology of the Newborn. 4th ed. Joseph J. Volpe. (Illus.). 995p. Date not set. text. write for info. (*0-7216-8448-3*, W B Saunders Co) Harcrt Hlth Sci Grp.
Neurology of Thinking. D. Frank Benson. LC 93-6521. (Illus.). 328p. (C). 1994. text 59.50 (*0-19-505882-8*) OUP.
Neurology Pearls. Andrew J. Waclawik & Thomas P. Sutula. LC 99-40818. (Pearls Ser.). (Illus.). 250p. 2000. text 39.00 (*1-56053-261-0*) Hanley & Belfus.
Neurology Pearls of Wisdom. Labanowski. (Pearls of Wisdom Ser.). (Illus.). 1998. pap. 88.00 (*1-890369-12-8*) Boston Medical.

N

An Asterisk (*) at the beginning of an entry indicates that the title is appearing for the first time.

Neurology Practical Guidelines. Ed. by Lechtenberg & Schutta. LC 97-36796. (Neurological Disease & Therapy Ser.). (Illus.). 544p. 1997. text 150.00 (*0-8247-0104-6*) Dekker.

Neurology Recall. James Q. Miller & Nathan B. Fountain. LC 97-2668. (Recall Ser.). 340p. 1997. pap. 27.00 (*0-683-18216-1*) Lppncott W & W.

Neurology Resident's Training Program. Epilepsy Foundation of America Staff. 66.95 incl. VHS (*0-916570-16-9*) Epilepsy Foundation of America.

Neurology Secrets: Questions You Will be Asked on Rounds, in the Clinic & on Oral Exams. 2nd ed. Loren A. Rolak. LC 98-21152. 1998. write for info. (*1-56053-251-3*) Hanley & Belfus.

Neurology Short Case. John G. L. Morris. 128p. 1992. pap. text 14.95 (*0-340-54923-8*, Pub. by E A) OUP.

Neuromancer. William Gibson. 271p. 1984. mass mkt. 6.99 (*0-441-56959-5*) Ace Bks.

Neuromancer. William Gibson. 288p. 1994. reprint ed. 21.95 (*0-441-00068-1*) Ace Bks.

***Neuromancer.** William Gibson. 288p. 2000. reprint ed. pap. 13.95 (*0-441-00746-5*) Berkley Pub.

Neuromechanical Basis of Kinesiology. 2nd ed. Roger M. Enoka. LC 93-50146. (Illus.). 480p. 1994. text 55.00 (*0-87322-665-8*, BEN00665) Human Kinetics.

Neuromodulation: The Biochemical Control of Neuronal Excitability. Leonard K. Kaczmarek & Irwin B. Levitan. 295p. 1986. text 33.95 (*0-19-504097-X*) OUP.

Neuromodules & Brain Function. Giovanni Biggio et al. (Advances in the Biosciences Ser.). 460p. 1984. 80.50 (*0-08-030782-5*, Pergamon Pr) Elsevier.

***Neuromonitoring in Brain Injury.** Ed. by Ross Bullock et al. LC 99-46769. (Acta Neurochirurgica Ser.: Suppl. 75'). (Illus.). 80p. 1999. 54.00 (*3-211-83379-X*) Spr-Verlag.

Neuromonitoring in Otology & Head & Neck Surgery. Ed. by Jack M. Kartush & Kenneth R. Bouchard. 272p. 1991. text 84.00 (*0-88167-846-5*) Lppncott W & W.

Neuromorphic Systems: Engineering Silicon from Neurobiology. Leslie S. Smith & Alister Hamilton. LC 98-23904. (Progress in Neural Processing Ser.). 300p. 1998. 58.00 (*981-02-3377-9*) World Scientific Pub.

Neuromorphic Systems Engineering: Neural Networks in Silicon. Tor S. Lande. LC 98-16660. (Series in Engineering & Computer Science). 480p. 1998. 118.00 (*0-7923-8158-0*) Kluwer Academic.

Neuromorphological Plasticity: Proceedings of the Symposium, Dallas, Texas, April 1972. American Association of Anatomists, Cajal Club Mee. Ed. by J. Bernstein & D. C. Goodman. (Brain, Behavior & Evolution Ser.: Vol. 8, Nos. 1-2). (Illus.). 164p. 1973. reprint ed. 42.50 (*3-8055-1703-3*) S Karger.

Neuromorphometry. Weis. 600p. 1998. write for info. (*0-12-742730-9*) Acad Pr.

Neuromotor Speech Disorders: Nature, Assessment, & Management. Michael P. Cannito et al. LC 97-33161. 1997. 44.95 (*1-55766-326-2*) P H Brookes.

Neuromuscular & Skeletal Adaptations to Altered Orofacial Function. James A. McNamara. LC RK0280.. (Craniofacial Growth Monographs: Vol. 1). (Illus.). 194p. reprint ed. pap. 60.20 (*0-608-15983-2*, 205226400083) Bks Demand.

Neuromuscular Block. Stanley Feldman. LC 95-45603. 208p. 1996. text 85.00 (*0-7506-1764-0*) Buttrwrth-Heinemann.

Neuromuscular Block: In Perioperative & Intensive Care. Ed. by David G. Silverman. LC 94-15674. (Illus.). 384p. reprint ed. pap. 119.10 (*0-608-09721-7*, 206988700007) Bks Demand.

Neuromuscular Blockade. David G. Silverman. (Illus.). 320p. 1994. text 54.95 (*0-397-51377-1*) Lppncott W & W.

Neuromuscular Development & Disease. Ed. by Alan M. Kelly & Helen M. Blau. LC 92-9131. (Raven Press Series on Molecular & Cellular Biology: Vol. 2). 400p. 1992. reprint ed. pap. 124.00 (*0-608-04704-X*, 206542500004) Bks Demand.

Neuromuscular Diagnostics & Association. Karen Scotti. 1999. pap. text 45.00 (*0-8385-6709-6*, Medical Exam) Appleton & Lange.

***Neuromuscular Disease.** Ed. by F. S. Deymeer. (Monographs in Clinical Neuroscience: Vol. 18). (Illus.). viii, 200p. 2000. 174.00 (*3-8055-7056-2*) S Karger.

Neuromuscular Diseases. Jaap Bethlem & Charlotte E. Knobbout. Tr. by J. Krabshuis & E. J. Michael. (Illus.). 166p. 1987. pap. 23.95 (*0-19-261586-6*) OUP.

Neuromuscular Diseases. Michael Swash & M. S. Schwartz. (Illus.). 480p. 1988. 245.00 (*0-387-19505-X*) Spr-Verlag.

Neuromuscular Diseases. fac. ed. Ed. by Georges Serratrice et al. LC 83-17159. (Illus.). 630p. pap. 195.30 (*0-7837-7440-0*, 204723400006) Bks Demand.

Neuromuscular Diseases: A Practical Approach to Diagnosis & Management. Michael Swash & M. S. Schwartz. (Illus.). 352p. 1981. 67.00 (*0-387-10548-4*) Spr-Verlag.

Neuromuscular Diseases: A Practical Approach to Diagnosis & Management. 3rd ed. Michael Swash & Martin S. Schwartz. LC 96-39564. xviii, 538p. 1997. write for info. (*3-540-76025-3*) Spr-Verlag.

***Neuromuscular Diseases: Expert Clinicians' Views.** Rahman Pourmand. (Illus.). 520p. 2000. 95.00 (*0-7506-7019-3*) Buttrwrth-Heinemann.

Neuromuscular Diseases During Development. Fernando Cornelio. 168p. 68.00 (*0-86196-541-8*, Pub. by J Libbey Med) Bks Intl VA.

Neuromuscular Disorders: A Guide for Patient & Family. Steven P. Ringel. LC 85-43509. 174p. 1987. reprint ed. pap. 54.00 (*0-608-04667-1*, 206538800004) Bks Demand.

Neuromuscular Disorders: Clinical & Molecular Genetics. Alan E. Emery. LC 97-42637. 590p. 1998. 196.95 (*0-471-97817-5*) Wiley.

***Neuromuscular Disorders in Clinical Practice.** Bashar Katirji & Henry J. Kaminski. (Illus.). 1000p. 2000. 250.00 (*0-7506-7169-6*) Buttrwrth-Heinemann.

Neuromuscular Fatigue: Proceedings of the Symposium, Amsterdam, the Netherlands, 9-11 April 1992. Ed. by A. J. Sargeant & D. Kernell. (Verhandelingen der Koninklijke Nederlandse Akademie van Wetenschappen, Afd. Natuurkunde Ser.: No. 91). 210p. pap. 37.50 (*0-444-85763-X*) Elsevier.

Neuromuscular Maturation of the Human Infant. Myrtle B. McGraw. (Classics in Developmental Medicine Ser.: No. 4). (Illus.). 117p. (C). 1991. text 19.95 (*0-521-41329-X*, Pub. by Mc Keith Pr) Cambridge U Pr.

Neuromuscular Physiology. Bill Garoutte. (Illus.). 500p. (Orig.). 1997. pap. 24.00 (*0-9643644-1-7*) Mill Valley Med.

Neuromuscular Testing with Surface EMG. Gabriel E. Sella. 410p. (C). 1995. pap. text 120.00 (*1-884325-08-4*) G E Sella.

Neuromuscular Transmission: Basic & Applied Aspects. Ed. by Angela Vincent & Dennis Wary. LC 92-23209. 304p. 1992. 168.00 (*0-08-041983-6*, Pergamon Pr) Elsevier.

Neuromuscular Transmission: Basic & Applied Aspects. Ed. by Angela Vincent & D. Wray. (Studies in Neuroscience). 1991. text 90.00 (*0-7190-2598-2*, Pub. by Manchester Univ Pr) St Martin.

Neuromusculoskeletal Examination & Assessment: A Handbook for Therapists. Nicola J. Petty & Ann P. Moore. LC 97-33318. 1998. pap. text 35.00 (*0-443-05980-2*) Church.

Neuron. Cold Spring Harbor Symposia on Quantitative Biolog. LC 34-8174. (Cold Spring Harbor Symposia on Quantitative Biology Ser.: Vol. 17). (Illus.). 337p. 1985. pap. 104.50 (*0-7837-8974-2*, 204975500003) Bks Demand.

Neuron: Cell & Molecular Biology. 2nd ed. Irwin B. Levitan & Leonard K. Kaczmarek. (Illus.). 560p. 1996. pap. text 49.95 (*0-19-510021-2*) OUP.

Neuron, Brain & Behaviour: Proceedings of the Annual Meeting of the European Brain & Behaviour Society, Novi Sad, Yugoslavia, 19th, 23-25 August, 1987. Ed. by M. Bajic. (Advances in the Biosciences Ser.: Vol. 70). 236p. 1988. 94.00 (*0-08-035597-8*, Pergamon Pr) Elsevier.

Neuron-Glia Interrelations During Phylogeny No. 1: Phylogeny & Ontogeny of Glial Cells. Ed. by Antonia Vernadakis & Betty I. Roots. (Contemporary Neuroscience Ser.). 292p. 1995. 125.00 (*0-89603-314-7*) Humana.

Neuron-Glia Interrelations During Phylogeny No. 2: Plasticity & Regeneration. Ed. by Antonia Vernadakis & Betty I. Roots. (Contemporary Neuroscience Ser.). (Illus.). 536p. 1995. 185.00 (*0-89603-316-3*) Humana.

Neuron in Tissue Culture. Haynes. LC 98-22011. 752p. 1999. 395.00 (*0-471-97505-2*) Wiley.

Neuron, Networks & Motor Behavior. Ed. by Paul S. Stein & Douglas G. Stuart. (Computational Neuroscience Ser.). (Illus.). 305p. 1999. reprint ed. pap. 35.00 (*0-262-69227-9*, Bradford Bks) MIT Pr.

Neuronal Acetylcholine Receptors. V. I. Skok et al. (Illus.). 332p. (C). 1989. text 132.00 (*0-306-11019-9*, Kluwer Plenum) Kluwer Academic.

Neuronal Aging & Its Implications in Human Neurological Pathology. (Technical Report Ser.: No. 665). 88p. 1981. pap. text 6.00 (*92-4-120665-9*) World Health.

Neuronal & Extraneuronal Events in Autonomic Pharmacology. fac. ed. Ed. by William W. Fleming et al. LC 84-3410. (Illus.). 280p. pap. 86.80 (*0-7837-7270-X*, 204703500005) Bks Demand.

Neuronal Astrocytic Interactions: Implications for Normal & Pathological CNS Function. Ed. by Albert C. Yu et al. LC 92-23169. (Progress in Brain Research Ser.: Vol. 94). 494p. 1992. 258.75 (*0-444-89537-X*) Elsevier.

Neuronal Bases & Psychological Aspects of Consciousness. Cleo Taddei-Ferretti. LC 99-12883. (Series on Biophysics & Biocybernetics). 1998. 86.00 (*981-02-3597-6*) World Scientific Pub.

Neuronal Cell Lines: A Practical Approach. Ed. by J. N. Wood. (Practical Approach Ser.: Vol. 99). (Illus.). 292p. 1992. 85.00 (*0-19-963346-0*); pap. text 49.95 (*0-19-963345-2*) OUP.

***Neuronal Coding of Perceptual Systems.** Werner G. Backhaus. (Biophysics & Biocybernetics Ser.: Vol. 9). (Illus.). 2000. 86.00 (*981-02-4164-X*) World Scientific Pub.

Neuronal Communications. England-Proceedings of the Kew Chromosome Conference - Jodrell Laboratory Staff. 1984. 91.00 (*0-86961-147-X*) Ashgate Pub Co.

Neuronal Control of Locomotion: From Mollusc to Man. Grigori Orlovsky et al. LC 99-15701. (Illus.). 336p. 1999. text 59.50 (*0-19-852405-6*) OUP.

Neuronal Cooperativity. Ed. by James E. Kruger. (Synergetics Ser.: Vol. 49). (Illus.). 324p. 1991. 123.95 (*0-387-53155-6*) Spr-Verlag.

Neuronal Cytoskeleton. Ed. by Nobutaka Hirokawa. LC 93-29823. (Taniguchi Symposia on Brain Sciences Ser.: No. 16). 1994. 84.95 (*0-8493-7741-2*) CRC Pr.

Neuronal Degeneration & Regeneration: From Basic Mechanisms to Prospects for Therapy. F. W. Van Leeuwen. LC 98-36940. (Progress in Brain Research Ser.). 532p. 1998. 264.50 (*0-444-82817-6*) Elsevier.

Neuronal Development. Ed. by Nicholas C. Spitzer. LC 82-3693. (Current Topics in Neurobiology Ser.). (Illus.). 478p. 1982. 89.50 (*0-306-40956-9*, Plenum Trade) Perseus Pubng.

Neuronal Ensembles: Strategies for Recording & Decoding. Howard B. Eichenbaum & Joel L. Davis. LC 97-28317. 267p. 1998. 119.95 (*0-471-17940-X*) Wiley.

Neuronal Factors. Ed. by Peres. 216p. 1987. 123.00 (*0-8493-5241-X*, QP363, CRC Reprint) Franklin.

Neuronal-Glial Cell Interrelationships. Ed. by T. A. Sears. (Dahlem Workshop Reports: Vol. 20). (Illus.). 375p. 1982. 42.95 (*0-387-11329-0*) Spr-Verlag.

Neuronal Grafting & Alzheimer's Disease. Ed. by F. Gage et al. (Research & Perspectives in Alzheimer's Disease Ser.). (Illus.). 210p. 1989. 86.95 (*0-387-51197-0*) Spr-Verlag.

Neuronal Growth & Plasticity. Ed. by M. Kuno. (Taniguchi Symposia on Brain Sciences Ser.: No. 6). 324p. 1984. lib. bdg. 135.00 (*90-6764-037-9*, Pub. by VSP) Coronet Bks.

Neuronal Growth Cones. Phillip R. Gordon-Weeks. LC 99-34186. (Developmental & Cell Biology Ser.: Vol. 37). (Illus.). 350p. (C). 2000. 90.00 (*0-521-44491-8*) Cambridge U Pr.

Neuronal Information Processing: From Biological Data to Modelling & Application Cargese. P. Combe. (Series in Mathematical Biology & Medicine). 400p. 1999. 88.00 (*981-02-3826-6*) World Scientific Pub.

Neuronal Man: The Biology of the Mind. Jean-Pierre Changeux. Tr. by Laurence Garey. LC 97-209028. 368p. 1983. pap. text 16.95 (*0-691-02666-1*, Pub. by Princeton U Pr) Cal Prin Full Svc.

Neuronal Mechanisms for Generating Locomotor Activity. Ed. by Ole Kiehn et al. (Annals of the New York Academy of Sciences Ser.). 630p. 1998. 160.00 (*1-57331-168-5*); pap. 160.00 (*1-57331-169-3*) NY Acad Sci.

Neuronal Microenvironment. Ed. by Alan A. Boulton et al. LC 87-3668. (Neuromethods Ser.: Vol. 9). (Illus.). 752p. 1988. 139.50 (*0-89603-115-2*) Humana.

Neuronal Morphology of Avian Telencaephalon. Tombol. (SINS Ser.). 1995. write for info. (*0-08-041990-9*, Pergamon Pr) Elsevier.

Neuronal Networks of the Hippocampus. Roger D. Traub & Richard Miles. (Illus.). 301p. (C). 1991. text 49.95 (*0-521-36481-7*) Cambridge U Pr.

Neuronal Nicotinic Receptors: Pharmacology & Therapeutic Opportunities. Ed. by Stephen P. Arneric & Jorge D. Brioni. LC 98-17280. 421p. 1998. 185.00 (*0-471-24743-X*) Wiley.

***Neuronal Nicotinic Receptors: Pharmacology & Therapeutic Opportunities.** Ed. by F. Clementi et al. (Handbook of Experimental Pharmacology Ser.: 144). xvi, 664p. 2000. (*3-540-66123-9*) Spr-Verlag.

Neuronal Operations in the Visual Cortex. Guy A. Orban. (Studies of Brain Function: Vol. 11). (Illus.). 385p. 1984. 101.95 (*0-387-11919-1*) Spr-Verlag.

Neuronal Plasticity. fac. ed. Ed. by Carl W. Cotman. LC 77-72807. 349p. pap. 108.20 (*0-7837-7259-9*, 204704600005) Bks Demand.

Neuronal Plasticity: Building a Bridge from the Laboratory of the Clinic. Jordan Grafman & Yves Christen. LC 98-38384. (Research & Perspectives in Neurosciences Ser.). 180p. 1999. 119.00 (*3-540-64357-5*) Spr-Verlag.

Neuronal Plasticity & Memory Formation. Ed. by Cosimo A. Marsan & H. Matthies. LC 81-21170. (International Brain Research Organization Monograph Ser.: Vol. 9). 681p. 1982. reprint ed. pap. 200.00 (*0-608-00321-2*, 206103800007) Bks Demand.

Neuronal Plasticity & Trophic Factors. Ed. by Giovanni Biggio et al. (FIDIA Research Ser. - Symposia on Neuroscience: Vol. 7). 1988. 75.00 (*0-387-96796-6*) Spr-Verlag.

***Neuronal Processing of Optic Flow.** Markus Lappe. (International Review of Neurobiology Ser.: Vol. 44). (Illus.). 343p. 1999. 99.95 (*0-12-366844-1*) Acad Pr.

Neuronal Receptors, Endogenous Ligands & Biotechnical Approaches. Ed. by M. E. Vartanian. LC 88-13259. 149p. 1989. 35.00 (*0-8236-3558-9*) Intl Univs Pr.

Neuronal Regeneration, Reorganization, & Repair. Ed. by Fredrick J. Seil. (Advances in Neurology Ser.: No. 72). (Illus.). 432p. 1996. text 131.00 (*0-397-51713-0*) Lppncott W & W.

Neuronale Netze. 2nd ed. Ritter. (GER.). (C). 1990. text. write for info. (*0-201-55937-4*) Addison-Wesley.

Neurones Without Impulses. Ed. by Alan Roberts & B. M. Bush. LC 79-42572. (Society for Experimental Biology Seminar Ser.: No. 6). (Illus.). 304p. 1981. pap. text 35.95 (*0-521-29935-7*) Cambridge U Pr.

Neurons: Building Blocks of the Brain. Leonard A. Stevens. LC 74-4399. (Illus.). 128p. (YA). (gr. 7 up). 1974. 12.95 (*0-690-00403-6*) HarpC Child Bks.

Neurons: Directory of Authors of New Medical & Scientific Reviews with Subject Index. Science & Life Consultants Association Staff. 160p. 1995. 47.50 (*0-7883-0598-0*); pap. 44.50 (*0-7883-0599-9*) ABBE Pubs Assn.

Neurons & Interneuronal Connections of the Central Visual System. Ekaterina G. Shkolnik-Iarros. Tr. by Basil Haigh from RUS. LC 69-18115. (Illus.). 303p. 1971. reprint ed. pap. 94.00 (*0-608-05756-8*, 205972000007) Bks Demand.

Neurons & Networks: An Introduction to Neuroscience. John E. Dowling. (Illus.). 447p. (C). 1992. 56.00 (*0-674-60820-8*) HUP.

Neurons & Symbols: The Stuff That Mind Is Made Of. Aleksander Morton & H. Morton. (ITCP-UK Computer Science Ser.). 272p. (C). 1993. mass mkt. 46.95 (*0-412-46090-4*) Chapman & Hall.

Neurons, Networks, & Motor Behavior. Ed. by Paul S. Stein et al. LC 97-1551. (Computational Neuroscience Ser.). (Illus.). 262p. 1997. 60.00 (*0-262-19390-6*, Bradford Bks) MIT Pr.

Neuronuclear Medicine. Ed. by O. Juge & A. Donath. (Progress in Nuclear Medicine Ser.: Vol. 7). (Illus.). viii, 176p. 1981. 135.00 (*3-8055-2319-X*) S Karger.

Neuroophthalmology. Roy W. Beck & Craig H. Smith. (Illus.). 256p. 1987. 64.95 (*0-316-08651-7*, Little Brwn Med Div) Lppncott W & W.

Neuropaediatrie III, III. Ed. by J. Luetschg. (Paediatrische Fortbildungskurse fuer die Praxis Ser.: Vol. 60). (Illus.). xii, 92p. 1986. pap. 47.00 (*3-8055-4232-1*) S Karger.

Neuropaediatrie II. Ed. by F. Vassella. (Paediatrische Fortbildungskurse fuer die Praxis Ser.: Vol. 55). (Illus.). xiv, 190p. 1982. pap. 71.50 (*3-8055-3434-5*) S Karger.

Neuropathic Bladder in Childhood. M. Borzyskowski & A. R. Mundy. (Clinics in Developmental Medicine Ser.: No. 111). (Illuc.). 120p. (C). 1991. text 44.95 (*0-521-41194-7*, Pub. by Mc Keith Pr) Cambridge U Pr.

Neuropathies see Handbook of Clinical Neurology

Neuropathogenic Viruses & Immunity. S. Specter et al. (Infectious Agents & Pathogenesis Ser.). (Illus.). 376p. (C). 1992. text 95.00 (*0-306-43785-6*, Kluwer Plenum) Kluwer Academic.

Neuropathological Diagnostic Criteria for Brain Banking. F. F. Cruz-Sanchez. LC 94-73422. (Biomedical & Health Research Ser.: Vol. 10). 166p. (gr. 12). 1995. 77.00 (*90-5199-208-4*) IOS Press.

Neuropathological Surgery. Spoor. 1992. 105.00 (*0-316-80814-8*, Little Brwn Med Div) Lppncott W & W.

Neuropathology. Ellison. 1997. text 299.00 (*0-7234-2550-7*) Mosby Inc.

Neuropathology: Based on the 1989 IAP Annual Long Course. P. A. Cancilla & F. Stephen Vogel. (Illus.). 160p. 1990. 69.00 (*0-683-01430-7*) Lppncott W & W.

Neuropathology & Basic Neuroscience. Ed. by Roger A. Brumback & Richard W. Leech. LC 94-42193. (Oklahoma Notes Ser.). 289p. 1995. 17.95 (*0-387-94389-7*) Spr-Verlag.

Neuropathology Manual. Fredrich Klutzow. (Illus.). 264p. 1996. 30.00 (*0-89189-358-X*) Am Soc Clinical.

Neuropathology of AIDS. Ed. by Harry V. Vinters & Karl H. Anders. 256p. 1989. lib. bdg. 210.00 (*0-8493-5074-3*, RC607) CRC Pr.

Neuropathology of Dementia. Ed. by Margaret M. Esiri & James H. Morris. LC 96-27783. (Illus.). 454p. (C). 1997. text 150.00 (*0-521-43311-8*) Cambridge U Pr.

Neuropathology of Dementing Disorders. Ed. by William R. Markesbery. (An Arnold Publication). (Illus.). 416p. 1998. text 195.00 (*0-340-59037-8*) OUP.

Neuropathology of Epilepsy. Ed. by F. Scaravilli. LC 97-29351. 300p. 1997. 58.00 (*981-02-3170-9*) World Scientific Pub.

***Neuropathology of Schizophrenia.** Ed. by Paul Harrison & Gareth Roberts. (Illus.). 384p. 2000. text 69.95 (*0-19-262907-7*) OUP.

Neuropathology of Temporal Lobe Epilepsy. C. J. Bruton. (Maudsley Monographs: No. 31). (Illus.). 176p. 1988. 52.50 (*0-19-712155-1*) OUP.

Neuropathology of Vision: An Atlas. Richard Lindenberg et al. LC 73-12319. 510p. reprint ed. pap. 158.10 (*0-608-13665-4*, 205543700022) Bks Demand.

Neuropeptide Cholecystokinin (CCK) Anatomy & Biochemistry, Receptors, Pharmacology & Physiology. John Hughes et al. LC 08-915219. (Ellis Horwood Series in Neuroscience). 1989. text 89.95 (*0-470-21469-4*) P-H.

Neuropeptide Function in the Gastrointestinal Tract. Edwin E. Daniel. 520p. 1990. lib. bdg. 254.00 (*0-8493-6158-3*, QP572) CRC Pr.

Neuropeptide Gene Expression. Ed. by A. J. Turner. (Frontiers in Neurobiology Ser.: Vol. 1). 262p. (C). 1994. text 110.50 (*1-85578-044-5*, Pub. by Portland Pr Ltd) Ashgate Pub Co.

Neuropeptide Protocols. Ed. by G. Brent Irvine & Carvell H. Williams. (Methods in Molecular Biology Ser.: Vol. 73). (Illus.). 400p. 1996. 89.50 (*0-89603-399-6*) Humana.

Neuropeptide Receptors in the CNS. Anders T. Bjorklund et al. (Handbook of Chemical Neuroanatomy Ser.: Vol. 11). xviii,406p. 1992. 293.00 (*0-444-89486-1*) Elsevier.

Neuropeptide Y. Ed. by Viktor Mutt et al. LC 89-10128. (Karolinska Institute Nobel Conference Ser.). (Illus.). 377p. 1989. reprint ed. pap. 116.90 (*0-608-00594-0*, 206118100007) Bks Demand.

Neuropeptide Y & Drug Development. Ed. by Lars Grundemar & Stephen R. Bloom. (Illus.). 224p. 1996. text 75.00 (*0-12-304990-3*) Morgan Kaufmann.

***Neuropeptide Y Protocols.** Ambikaipakan Balasubramaniam. (Methods in Molecular Biology Ser.: Vol. 153). (Illus.). 324p. 2000. 99.50 (*0-89603-662-6*) Humana.

Neuropeptides: Basic & Clinical Advances. Ed. by Jacqueline N. Crawley & Stafford McLean. LC 96-6767. (Annals of the New York Academy of Sciences Ser.: No. 780). 255p. 1996. 100.00 (*0-89766-989-4*) NY Acad Sci.

Neuropeptides: Essential Data. Charles V. Hoyle. LC 96-36017. (Essential Data Ser.). 168p. 1997. pap. 39.95 (*0-471-96442-5*) Wiley.

Neuropeptides: Regulators of Physiological Processes. Fleur L. Strand. LC 97-52765. (Cellular & Molecular Neuroscience Ser.). (Illus.). 670p. 1998. 65.00 (*0-262-19407-4*) MIT Pr.

Neuropeptides & Brain Function. Ed. by G. Telegdy. (Frontiers of Hormone Research Ser.: Vol. 15). (Illus.). viii, 332p. 1987. 256.75 (*3-8055-4500-2*) S Karger.

Neuropeptides & Immunoregulation. Ed. by B. Scharrer et al. LC 93-32233. 1994. 131.00 (*0-387-57188-4*) Spr-Verlag.

Neuropeptides & Stress. Ed. by T. Tache et al. (Hans Selve Symposia on Neuroendocrinology & Stress Ser.). (Illus.). 435p. 1988. 116.00 (*0-387-96748-6*) Spr-Verlag.

Neuropeptides Development & Aging, Vol. 814. Ed. by Bill E. Beckwith et al. LC 97-5944. 1997. 120.00 (*1-57331-066-2*) NY Acad Sci.

Neuropeptides in Development & Aging. Bill E. Beckwith. LC 97-5944. (Annals of the New York Academy of Sciences Ser.). 1997. pap. 120.00 (*1-57331-067-0*) NY Acad Sci.

N

An Asterisk (*) at the beginning of an entry indicates that the title is appearing for the first time.

Neuropeptides in Neurologic & Psychiatric Disease. Ed. by Joseph B. Martin & Jack D. Barchas. LC 85-31183. (Association for Research in Nervous & Mental Disease Research Publications: No. 64). (Illus.). 382p. 1986. reprint ed. pap. 118.50 (0-608-00637-8, 206122500007) Bks Demand.

Neuropeptides in Psychiatric & Neurological Disorders. Charles B. Nemeroff. LC 87-45487. (Johns Hopkins Series in Contemporary Medicine & Public Health). (Illus.). 326p. reprint ed. pap. 101.10 (0-608-08792-0, 206943100004) Bks Demand.

Neuropeptides in Respiratory Medicine. Ed. by Michael A. Kaliner et al. LC 94-5869. (Clinical Allergy & Immunology Ser.: Vol. 4). (Illus.). 720p. 1994. text 245.00 (0-8247-9199-1) Dekker.

Neuropeptides in the CNS, Pt. II. Ed. by M. J. Kuhar et al. xviii,550p. 1990. 349.00 (0-444-81230-X) Elsevier.

Neuropeptides in the Spinal Cord. Ed. by F. Nyberg et al. LC 93-11042. (Progress in Brain Research Ser.: Vol. 104). (Illus.). 438p. 1995. 194.50 (0-444-81719-0) Elsevier.

Neuropharmacological Basis of Reward. Jeffrey M. Liebman & Steven J. Cooper. (Illus.). 448p. 1989. text 75.00 (0-19-852176-6) OUP.

Neuropharmacology. Trevor W. Stone. LC 95-4264. (Biochemical & Medicinal Chemistry Ser.). (Illus.). 160p. (C). 1997. pap. text 27.50 (0-7167-4510-0) OUP.

Neuropharmacology: Clinical Applications. Ed. by Walter B. Essman & L. Valzelli. (Illus.). 500p. 1982. text 60.00 (0-88331-164-X) R B Luce.

Neuropharmacology Methods in Epilepsy Research. Steven L. Peterson & Timothy E. Albertson. LC 98-9863. (Methods in Life Science - Cellular & Molecular Neuropharmacology Ser.). 304p. 1998. per. 129.95 (0-8493-3362-8) CRC Pr.

Neuropharmacology of Epilepsy: Pathophysiology & Drug Mechanisms. Robert A. Gross & Timothy J. Greenamyre. (Illus.). 1999. 125.00 (0-89603-522-0) Humana.

Neuropharmacology of Ethanol: New Approaches. Ed. by Stephen M. Paul et al. 280p. 1991. 69.00 (0-685-48688-5) Spr-Verlag.

Neuropharmacology of Polyamines. Ed. by Chris J. Carter. (Neuroscience Perspectives Ser.). (Illus.). 336p. 1994. text, boxed set 83.00 (0-12-161640-1) Acad Pr.

Neuropharmacology Reviews, Vol. 1. A. V. Valdman. (Soviet Medical Reviews Ser.: Sect. G, Vol 1). xii, 228p. 1990. pap. text 506.00 (3-7186-4884-9) Gordon & Breach.

Neuropharmacology Reviews Vol. 2, Pt. 1.2: Investigation of the Mechanisms of Action of Non-Benzodiazepine Anxiolytics, Vol. 2. I. V. Komissarov. (Soviet Medical Reviews Ser.: Section G). 230p. 1992. pap. text 94.00 (3-7186-5249-8, Harwood Acad Pubs) Gordon & Breach.

Neuropharmacology Reviews Vol. 2, Pt. 2.2: Present-Day Problems in Experimental Psychopharmacology of Nootropic Drugs, Vol. 2. T. A. Voronina. (Soviet Medical Reviews Ser.: Section G). 212p. 1992. pap. text 110.00 (3-7186-5282-X, Harwood Acad Pubs) Gordon & Breach.

Neuropharmacology Reviews Vol. 2, Pt. 3: Blood-Brain Barrier, Vol. 2. S. Borisenko. 78p. 1992. pap. text 80.00 (3-7186-5285-4, Harwood Acad Pubs) Gordon & Breach.

Neurophilosophy: Toward a Unified Science of the Mind-Brain. Patricia S. Churchland. (Illus.). 384p. 1986. 50.00 (0-262-03116-7, Bradford Bks) MIT Pr.

Neurophilosophy: Toward a Unified Science of the Mind-Brain. Patricia S. Churchland. (Illus.). 384p. 1989. pap. text 24.50 (0-262-53085-6, Bradford Bks) MIT Pr.

Neurophilosophy & Alzheimer's Disease. Ed. by Yves Christen & Patricia S. Churchland. (Research & Perspectives in Alzheimer's Disease Ser.). (Illus.). 153p. 1992. 100.00 (0-387-54779-7) Spr-Verlag.

Neurophsiological Correlates of Relaxation & Psychopathology. Ed. by B. Taneli et al. (Advances in Biological Psychiatry Ser.: Vol. 16). (Illus.). vi, 214p. 1987. 143.50 (3-8055-4449-9) S Karger.

Neurophysics. Alwyn C. Scott. LC 77-2762. 352p. reprint ed. 109.20 (0-608-16126-8, 205513600008) Bks Demand.

*__Neurophysics of Human Behavior: Explorations at the Interface of the Brain, Mind & Information.__ Mark E. Furman & Fred Gallo. 376p. 2000. boxed set 79.95 (0-8493-1308-2) CRC Pr.

Neurophysiologic Studies in Tissue Culture. fac. ed. Stanley M. Crain. LC 75-14567. (Illus.). 292p. pap. 90.60 (0-7837-7541-5, 204696300005) Bks Demand.

Neurophysiological & Behavioural Research in Psychiatry: Report of a WHO Scientific Group, 1968. (Technical Report Ser.: No. 381). 33p. 1968. pap. text 5.00 (92-4-120381-1, 1100381) World Health.

Neurophysiological & Clinical Aspects of Vestibular Disorders. Ed. by C. R. Pfaltz. (Advances in OtoRhinoLaryngology Ser.: Vol. 30). (Illus.). xii, 372p. 1983. 171.50 (3-8055-3607-0) S Karger.

Neurophysiological Basis for the Treatment of Cerebral Palsy. 2nd ed. Karel Bobath. (Clinics in Developmental Medicine Ser.: No. 75). (Illus.). 98p. (C). 1991. text 29.95 (0-521-41202-1) Mc Keith Pr.

Neurophysiological Basis of Cerebral Blood Flow. Mraovtich. 424p. 79.00 (0-86196-272-9, Pub. by J Libbey Med) Bks Intl VA.

Neurophysiological Basis of Mind: The Principles of Neurophysiology. John C. Eccles. LC 88-16029. (Genes Cells & Organisms Ser.). 332p. 1988. text 10.00 (0-8240-1377-8) Garland.

Neurophysiological Basis of Movement. Mark L. Latash. LC 97-31920. (Illus.). 280p. 1998. text 45.00 (0-88011-756-7, BLAT0756) Human Kinetics.

Neurophysiological Basis of Patient Treatment: Peripheral Components of Motor Control, Vol. III. Carolyn A. Crutchfield & Marylou R. Barnes. (Illus.). 1984. pap. 35.00 (0-936030-03-8) Stokesville Pub.

Neurophysiological Basis of Patient Treatment: Reflexes in Motor Development, Vol. II. Marylou R. Barnes et al. LC 72-87895. (Illus.). 1978. pap. 35.00 (0-936030-01-1) Stokesville Pub.

Neurophysiological Correlates of Mental Disorders. Ed. by B. Saletu et al. (Advances in Biological Psychiatry Ser.: Vol. 15). (Illus.). vi, 114p. 1985. 74.00 (3-8055-3969-X) S Karger.

Neurophysiological Correlates of Normal Cognition & Psychopathology. Ed. by C. Perris et al. (Advances in Biological Psychiatry Ser.: Vol. 13). (Illus.). viii, 232p. 1984. pap. 85.25 (3-8055-3737-9) S Karger.

Neurophysiological Examination of the Newborn Infant. Ed. by J. A. Eyre. (Clinics in Developmental Medicine Ser.: No. 120). (Illus.). 207p. (C). 1992. text 54.95 (0-521-41276-5) Cambridge U Pr.

Neurophysiological Insights into Teaching. Marion F. Stuart. LC 62-21040. (Illus.). xvi, 125p. (Orig.). 1963. pap. text 14.95 (0-87015-114-2) Pacific Bks.

Neurophysiological Study of Optic Flow Analysis in the Monkey Brain. L. Lagae. No. 47. 189p. (Orig.). 1991. pap. 44.50 (90-6186-479-8, Pub. by Leuven Univ) Coronet Bks.

Neurophysiological Techniques I: Basic Methods & Concepts. Ed. by Alan A. Boulton et al. LC 89-26855. (Neuromethods Ser.: Vol. 14). (Illus.). 408p. 1990. 89.50 (0-89603-160-8) Humana.

Neurophysiological Techniques II: Applications to Neural Systems. Ed. by Alan A. Boulton et al. LC 90-44264. (Neuromethods Ser.: Vol. 15). (Illus.). 391p. 1990. 89.50 (0-89603-185-3) Humana.

Neurophysiology. P. P. Newman. (Illus.). 455p. 1980. text 35.00 (0-88331-165-8) R B Luce.

Neurophysiology. 3rd ed. Roger Carpenter. (Illus.). 322p. 1996. pap. text 43.95 (0-340-60880-3, Pub. by E A) OUP.

Neurophysiology: Applications in the Behavioural & Biomedical Sciences. K. A. Clarke. (Ellis Horwood Series in Eurosciences). 1989. text 59.95 (0-470-21554-2) P-H.

Neurophysiology & Behavior see Hippocampus

Neurophysiology & Emotion. Ed. by David C. Glass. LC 67-31389. (Illus.). 256p. 1967. 13.00 (0-87470-006-X) Rockefeller.

Neurophysiology & Neuropsychology of Motor Development. Ed. by Kevin J. Connolly & Hans Forssberg. LC 98-107760. (Clinics in Developmental Medicine Ser.: No. 143). (Illus.). 350p. (C). 1997. 99.95 (1-898683-10-7, Pub. by Mc Keith Pr) Cambridge U Pr.

Neurophysiology & Neuropsychology of Motor Development. Kevin J. Connolly & Hans Forssberg. LC 98-107760. (Illus.). 1997. write for info. (0-521-01898-6) Cambridge U Pr.

Neurophysiology & Psychophysiology: Experimental & Clinical Applications. Ed. by G. C. Galbraith et al. 416p. 1988. 79.95 (0-89859-946-6) L Erlbaum Assocs.

Neurophysiology & Standards of Spinal Cord Monitoring. Ed. by T. B. Ducker & R. H. Brown. (Illus.). 400p. 1988. 127.00 (0-387-96634-X) Spr-Verlag.

Neurophysiology of Consciousness: Selected Papers of Benjamin Libet. Benjamin Libet. LC 93-16896. (Contemporary Neuroscientists Ser.). (Illus.). 424p. 1993. 109.00 (0-8176-3538-6) Birkhauser.

Neurophysiology of Enlightenment. Robert K. Wallace. (Illus.). 368p. 1997. reprint ed. pap. 12.00 (0-923569-05-7, E03) Maharishi U Mgmt Pr.

Neurophysiology of Ingestion. Ed. by D. A. Booth. LC 93-34148. (Studies in Neuroscience). 186p. 1993. 171.50 (0-08-041988-7, Pergamon Pr) Elsevier.

Neurophysiology of Postural Mechanisms. 2nd ed. Tristan D. Roberts. LC 77-30548. (Illus.). 430p. reprint ed. pap. 133.30 (0-608-18009-2, 205631800058) Bks Demand.

Neurophysiology of the Vestibular System. Ed. by E. Pirodda. (Advances in OtoRhinoLaryngology Ser.: Vol. 41). (Illus.). xii, 244p. 1988. 148.75 (3-8055-4766-8) S Karger.

Neuroplasticity: A New Therapeutic Tool in the CNS Pathology. Ed. by R. Masland et al. (FIDIA Research Ser.: Vol. 12). 230p. 1988. 112.00 (0-387-96620-X) Spr-Verlag.

Neuroplasticity & Repair in the Central Nervous System: Implications for Health Care. WHO Staff. (WHO Offset Publications: No. 73). 56p. 1983. 5.00 (92-4-170073-4) World Health.

Neuropolitique: A New Vision of Neuropolitics. rev. ed. Timothy Leary. LC 88-81431. (Future History Ser.). 208p. 1991. pap. 14.95 (1-56184-012-2) New Falcon Pubns.

Neuroprosthetics: From Basic Research to Clinical Applications:Biomedical & Health Research Program (Biomed) of the European Union, Concerted Action:Restoration of Muscle Activity Through Fes & Associated Technology (Raft) J. Quintern & R. Riener. LC 96-20390. 670p. 1996. 141.00 (3-540-61084-7) Spr-Verlag.

Neuroprotection. Ed. by Peter Rudolf Bar & M. Flint Beal. LC 97-12545. (Illus.). 584p. 1997. text 185.00 (0-8247-9876-7) Dekker.

Neuroprotection. Thomas J. Blanck. 220p. 1997. write for info. (0-683-18328-1) Lppncott W & W.

Neuroprotection in Neurodegeneration. Ed. by M. B. Youdim et al. 1995. 73.00 (0-387-82542-8) Spr-Verlag.

Neuroprotective Agents: Clinical & Experimental Aspects. Ed. by Bruce Trembly & William Slikker, Jr. LC 95-21866. (Annals of the New York Academy of Sciences Ser.: Vol. 765). 1995. write for info. (0-89766-945-2); pap. write for info. (0-89766-946-0) NY Acad Sci.

Neuroprotective Agents: Clinical & Experimental Aspects, 3rd International Conference, Vol. 825. William Slikker, Jr. & Bruce Trembly. LC 97-26504. 1997. 120.00 (1-57331-092-1) NY Acad Sci.

*__Neuroprotective Agents: Fourth International Conference.__ Bruce Trembly & William Slikker. LC 99-47061. 1999. write for info. (1-57331-223-1) NY Acad Sci.

Neuroprotective Agents: 3rd International Conference. Ed. by William Slikker & Bruce Trembly. LC 97-26504. (Annals of the New York Academy of Sciences Ser.). 438p. 1997. pap. 120.00 (1-57331-093-X) NY Acad Sci.

Neuroprotective Signal Transduction. Ed. by Mark P. Mattson. LC 97-37497. (Contemporary Neuroscience Ser.). (Illus.). 360p. 1997. 145.00 (0-89603-473-9) Humana.

Neuroprotective Strategies for Early Intervention in Acute Ischaemic Stroke: Janssen-Cilag Satellite Meeting to the 3rd World Stroke Congress & the 5th European Stroke Conference, Munich, September 1996. Ed. by Werner Hacke. (Journal Ser.: Vol. 7, Supplement 2, 1997). (Illus.). iv, 40p. 1997. pap. 21.75 (3-8055-6463-5) S Karger.

Neuropsychiatric Correlates of Alcoholism. Ed. by Igor Grant. LC 86-10760. (Clinical Insights Ser.). 159p. reprint ed. pap. 48.10 (0-8357-7848-7, 203622400002) Bks Demand.

Neuropsychiatric Dementias. Ed. by Dilip V. Jeste. LC 86-10734. (Clinical Insights Ser.). 153p. reprint ed. pap. 47.50 (0-8357-7837-1, 203621100002) Bks Demand.

Neuropsychiatric Features of Medical Disorders. James W. Jefferson & John R. Marshall. LC 81-2550. (Critical Issues in Psychiatry Ser.). 404p. 1981. 80.00 (0-306-40674-8, Kluwer Plenum) Kluwer Academic.

Neuropsychiatric Guide to Modern Everyday Psychiatry. Michael A. Taylor. LC 92-49025. 1993. 55.00 (0-02-932455-6) Free Pr.

Neuropsychiatric Manifestations of Physical Disease in the Elderly. Ed. by Alvin J. Levenson & Richard C. Hall. LC 79-5420. (Aging Ser.: Vol. 14). 168p. 1981. reprint ed. pap. 52.10 (0-608-00417-0, 206113200007) Bks Demand.

Neuropsychiatric Manifestations of Systemic Lupus Erythemafosus, Vol. 823. Ed. by Patricia M. Moore & Robert G. Lahita. LC 97-28522. (Annals of the New York Academy of Sciences Ser.: No. 823). 336p. 1997. 110.00 (1-57331-080-8) NY Acad Sci.

Neuropsychiatric Manifestations of Systemic Lupus Erythematosus. P. M. Moore & Robert G. Lahita. LC 97-28522. (Annals of the New York Academy of Sciences Ser.: No. 823). 336p. 1997. pap. 110.00 (1-57331-081-6) NY Acad Sci.

Neuropsychiatric Movement Disorders. Ed. by Dilip V. Jeste & Richard J. Wyatt. LC 84-14446. (Clinical Insights Ser.). 160p. reprint ed. pap. 49.60 (0-8357-7816-9, 203618800002) Bks Demand.

Neuropsychiatric Study in Children. Michael Rutter et al. (Clinics in Developmental Medicine Ser.: Vols. 35 & 36). (Illus.). 272p. (C). 1991. text 49.95 (0-521-41198-X, Pub. by Mc Keith Pr) Cambridge U Pr.

Neuropsychiatry. Michael R. Trimble. LC 80-40766. (Illus.). 301p. reprint ed. pap. 93.40 (0-608-16013-X, 203309100083) Bks Demand.

Neuropsychiatry: A Comprehensive Textbook. Barry S. Fogel et al. (Illus.). 1046p. 1996. 139.00 (0-683-03305-0) Lppncott W & W.

Neuropsychiatry & Mental Health Services. Ed. by Fred Ovsiew. 1999. 61.95 (0-88048-730-5, 8730) Am Psychiatric.

Neuropsychiatry & the War: A Bibliography with Abstracts & Supplement I, October, 1918, 2 vols. Ed. by Frankwood E. Williams. LC 75-16690. 1976. reprint ed. 34.95 (0-405-07420-4) Ayer.

Neuropsychiatry in Old Age: An Update. Franz Muller-Spahn. (Psychiatry in Progress Ser.: Vol. 3). 1996. 32.00 (0-88937-137-7) Hogrefe & Huber Pubs.

Neuropsychiatry, Neuropsychology, & Clinical Neuroscience. 2nd rev. ed. R. Joseph. LC 95-38650. (Illus.). 864p. 1996. 69.00 (0-683-04485-0) Lppncott W & W.

Neuropsychiatry of Limbic & Subcortical Disorders. Stephen Salloway et al. LC 97-34481. (Journal of Neuropsychiatry & Clinical Neurosciences). 232p. 1998. 49.50 (0-88048-942-1, 8942) Am Psychiatric.

Neuropsychiatry of Multiple Sclerosis. Anthony Feinstein. LC 98-46888. (Illus.). 200p. (C). 1999. 64.95 (0-521-57274-6) Cambridge U Pr.

Neuropsychiatry of Personality Disorders. John J. Ratey. (Neuropsychiatry Ser.). (Illus.). 352p. 1994. 69.95 (0-86542-293-1) Blackwell Sci.

Neuropsychiatry of Traumatic Brain Injury. Ed. by Jonathan M. Silver et al. LC 93-11646. 832p. 1994. text 82.95 (0-88048-538-8, 8538) Am Psychiatric.

*__Neuropsychological Aging Inventory (NAI)__ W. D. Oswald & U. M. Fleischmann. 300p. 2001. 79.00 (0-88937-215-2) Hogrefe & Huber Pubs.

Neuropsychological Analysis of Problem Solving. A. R. Luria & L. S. Tsvetkova. Tr. by Tichinas Staff from RUS. LC 90-83131. (Classics in Soviet Psychology Ser.). 256p. 1990. boxed set 57.95 (1-878205-10-2) St Lucie Pr.

Neuropsychological & Behavioral Aspects of Diabetes: Contributions to Psychology & Medicine. Ed. by C. S. Holmes. (Illus.). 305p. 1989. 129.00 (0-387-97075-4) Spr-Verlag.

*__Neuropsychological Aspects of Lyme Disease: A Special Issue of "Applied Neuropsychology"__ Ed. by Richard F. Kaplan. 48p. 1999. pap. 20.00 (0-8058-9817-4) L Erlbaum Assocs.

Neuropsychological Assessment. (C). 1999. pap. text 65.33 (0-205-29780-3, Longwood Div) Allyn.

Neuropsychological Assessment. 3rd ed. Muriel D. Lezak. (Illus.). 1056p. 1995. text 72.50 (0-19-509031-4) OUP.

Neuropsychological Assessment & Intervention. Charles J. Golden et al. (Illus.). 314p. 1992. pap. 39.95 (0-398-06353-2) C C Thomas.

Neuropsychological Assessment & Intervention. Charles J. Golden et al. (Illus.). 314p. (C). 1992. 56.95 (0-398-05754-0) C C Thomas.

Neuropsychological Assessment in Clinical Practice: A Guide to Test Interpretation & Integration. Gary Groth-Marnat. LC 99-19227. 653p. 2000. 65.00 (0-471-19325-9) Wiley.

Neuropsychological Assessment of Dementia & Depression in Older Adults: A Clinician's Guide. Ed. by Martha Storandt & Gary R. VandenBos. (Illus.). 219p. 1994. pap. 29.95 (1-55798-437-9) Am Psychol.

Neuropsychological Assessment of Neuropsychiatric Disorders. 2nd ed. Ed. by Igor Grant & Kenneth M. Adams. (Illus.). 672p. 1996. text 76.50 (0-19-509073-X) OUP.

Neuropsychological Bases of God Beliefs. Michael A. Persinger. LC 87-14689. 175p. 1987. 59.95 (0-275-92648-6, C2648, Praeger Pubs) Greenwood.

Neuropsychological Case Histories: A Comparative Analysis. unabridged ed. Ivan G. Ainyette. LC 96-93042. (Illus.). 304p. 1998. text 50.00 (0-9655600-0-7) NY Neurosci Pr.

*__Neuropsychological Differential Diagnosis.__ Konstantine K. Zakzanis et al. LC 99-16397. (Studies on Neuropsychology, Development & Cognition: Vol. 3). 272p. 1999. 79.00 (90-265-1552-9) Swets.

Neuropsychological Differentiation of Dementia Syndrome. M. M. Derix. LC 94-9130. 184p. 1994. 54.00 (90-265-1312-7) Swets.

Neuropsychological Disorders Associated with Subcortical Lesions. Ed. by Guiseppe Vallar et al. (Illus.). 522p. 1992. text 115.00 (0-19-854677-7) OUP.

*__Neuropsychological Effects of the Psychiatric Disorders.__ Simon F. Crowe. 204p. 1998. text 39.00 (90-5702-289-3, Harwood Acad Pubs); pap. text 24.00 (90-5702-377-6) Gordon & Breach.

Neuropsychological Evaluation in Vocational Planning. Jay Uomoto. Ed. by Robert Fraser & David Clemmons. LC 91-73657. (Traumatic Brain Injury Rehabilitation Training Ser.). (Illus.). 120p. 1991. per. 29.95 (1-878205-06-4) St Lucie Pr.

Neuropsychological Evaluation of Head Injury. Lawrence C. Hartlage. Ed. by Harold H. Smith, Jr. LC 89-43626. (Practitioner's Resource Ser.). 68p. 1990. pap. 15.45 (0-943158-47-8, NEHIBP) Pro Resource.

*__Neuropsychological Evaluation of the Older Adult: A Clinician's Guidebook.__ Joanne Green. LC 99-68194. 316p. 2000. 59.95 (0-12-298190-1) Morgan Kaufmann.

Neuropsychological Evaluation of the Spanish Speaker. A. Ardila et al. (Critical Issues in Neuropsychology Ser.). (Illus.). 216p. (C). 1994. text 37.50 (0-306-44149-7, Kluwer Plenum) Kluwer Academic.

Neuropsychological Explorations of Memory & Cognition: Essays in Honor of Nelson Butters. Ed. by Laird S. Cermak. LC 94-41856. (Critical Issues in Neuropsychology Ser.). 352p. 1995. 54.50 (0-306-44983-8, Kluwer Plenum) Kluwer Academic.

Neuropsychological Foundations of Learning Disabilities: A Handbook of Issues, Methods & Practice. John E. Obrzut. 848p. 1996. pap. text 99.00 (0-12-524039-2) Acad Pr.

Neuropsychological Function & Brain Imaging. E. D. Bigler et al. (Critical Issues in Neuropsychology Ser.). (Illus.). 370p. (C). 1989. text 75.00 (0-306-43045-2, Kluwer Plenum) Kluwer Academic.

Neuropsychological Impairments of Short-Term Memory. Ed. by Guiseppe Vallar & Tim Shallice. (Illus.). 538p. (C). 1990. text 80.00 (0-521-37088-4) Cambridge U Pr.

Neuropsychological Outcomes Research. Ed. by Rodney D. Vanderloeg. 56p. 1999. pap. write for info. (0-8058-9810-7) L Erlbaum Assocs.

Neuropsychological Perspectives on Affective & Anxiety Disorders. Richard J. Davidson. LC 98-186024. 224p. 1998. write for info. (0-86377-971-9, Pub. by Psychol Pr) Taylor & Francis.

Neuropsychological Rehabilitation. Ed. by Anne-Lise Christensen & Barbara P. Uzzell. (C). 1988. text 85.50 (0-89838-374-9) Kluwer Academic.

Neuropsychological Rehabilitation. Ed. by Manfred Meier et al. LC 87-154. 468p. 1987. lib. bdg. 57.95 (0-89862-702-8) Guilford Pubns.

Neuropsychological Rehabilitation: Fundamentals, Innovations & Directions. Ed. by Jose Leon-Carrion. (Illus.). 500p. 1997. lib. bdg. 89.95 (1-57444-039-X) St Lucie Pr.

Neuropsychological Studies in Aphasia. Aleksandr R. Luria. (Neurolinguistics Ser.: Vol. 6). 184p. 1977. 52.00 (90-265-0244-3) Swets.

Neuropsychological Studies of Non-Focal Brain Damage. Ed. by H. A. Whitaker. (Neuropsychology Ser.). (Illus.). 290p. 1988. 172.00 (0-387-96605-6) Spr-Verlag.

Neuropsychological Theories of Lashley & Hebb. Jack Orbach. 412p. (C). 1998. 46.00 (0-7618-1165-6) U Pr of Amer.

Neuropsychological Toxicology: Identification & Assessment of Human Neurotoxic Syndromes. 2nd ed. David E. Hartman. LC 87-14795. (Critical Issues in Neuropsychology Ser.). (Illus.). 548p. (C). 1995. text 71.00 (0-306-44922-6, Kluwer Plenum) Kluwer Academic.

Neuropsychological Treatment after Brain Injury. Anne-Lise Christensen. Ed. by David W. Ellis. (Foundations of Neuropsychology Ser.). (C). 1989. text 227.50 (0-7923-0014-9) Kluwer Academic.

Neuropsychological Treatments of Dyslexia. Dirk J. Bakker. (Illus.). 112p. 1990. pap. text 19.95 (0-19-506132-2) OUP.

Neuropsychological Validation of Learning Disability Subtypes. Ed. by Byron P. Rourke. LC 90-3912. 398p. 1990. lib. bdg. 45.00 *(0-89862-446-0)* Guilford Pubns.

Neuropsychology. Ed. by Alan A. Boulton et al. LC 89-26859. (Neuromethods Ser.: Vol. 17). (Illus.). 381p. 1990. 119.50 *(0-89603-133-0)* Humana.

Neuropsychology. Michael S. Gazzaniga. LC 78-21459. (Handbook of Behavioral Neurobiology Ser.: Vol. 2). (Illus.). 586p. (C). 1979. text 125.00 *(0-306-35192-7,* Kluwer Plenum) Kluwer Academic.

Neuropsychology. Ed. by Gerald Goldstein et al. LC 97-42120. (Human Brain Function Ser.). (Illus.). 516p. (C). 1998. text 115.00 *(0-306-45646-X,* Kluwer Plenum) Kluwer Academic.

Neuropsychology. Hynd & Hoope. (JCCP Ser.: Vol. 22, No. 2). 1993. 36.00 *(0-8058-9991-X)* L Erlbaum Assocs.

Neuropsychology. Ed. by Dahlia W. Zaidel. (Handbook of Perception & Cognition Ser.). (Illus.). 342p. 1994. text 64.95 *(0-12-775290-0)* Acad Pr.

Neuropsychology. 2nd ed. Kevin W. Walsh. (Illus.). 429p. 1987. 48.00 *(0-443-03858-9)* Church.

Neuropsychology: The Neural Bases of Mental Function. Marie T. Banich. 640p. (C). 1997. pap. text 61.16 *(0-395-66699-6)* HM.

Neuropsychology & Cognition. Rattihalli N. Malatesha. 1987. lib. bdg. 375.00 *(90-247-2752-9)* Kluwer Academic.

Neuropsychology & Neurolinguistics. Egon Weigl. (Janua Linguarum, Series Major: No. 78). 1980. text 80.80 *(90-279-7956-1)* Mouton.

***Neuropsychology & the Hispanic Patient: A Clinical Handbook.** Marcel O. Pontbon & Jose Leon-Carribon. LC 00-42221. 2000. write for info. *(0-8058-2615-7)* L Erlbaum Assocs.

Neuropsychology & the Law. 1991. 99.95 *(0-387-97471-7)* Spr-Verlag.

Neuropsychology Casebook. D. L. Orsini et al. (Illus.). 300p. 1988. 92.95 *(0-387-96681-1)* Spr-Verlag.

Neuropsychology for Clinical Practice: Etiology, Assessment, & Treatment of Common Neurological Disorders. Ed. by Russell L. Adams et al. LC 95-49944. 546p. 1996. 69.95 *(1-55798-298-8,* 431-7540) Am Psychol.

***Neuropsychology for Lawyers & Health Science Professionals.** 2nd ed. Robert J. Sbordone & Ronald E. Saul. LC 00-23929. 2000. write for info. *(0-8493-0204-8)* CRC Pr.

Neuropsychology for Occupational Therapists: Assessment of Perception & Cognition. June Grieve. LC 93-19447. 176p. 1993. pap. 29.95 *(0-632-03303-7)* Blackwell Sci.

Neuropsychology for the Attorney. 2nd ed. Robert Sbordone. 350p. 1996. lib. bdg. 89.95 *(1-57444-131-0)* St Lucie Pr.

Neuropsychology for the Attorney. 2nd ed. Robert J. Sbordone. LC 91-70189. (Illus.). 392p. 1995. lib. bdg. 95.00 *(1-878205-26-9)* St Lucie Pr.

Neuropsychology Handbook: Foundations & Assessment, Vol. 1. 2nd ed. Ed. by Arthur M. Horton, Jr. et al. LC 97-23192. (Illus.). 544p. 1997. 61.95 *(0-8261-9730-2)* Springer Pub.

Neuropsychology Handbook: Treatment Issues & Special Populations, Vol. 2. 2nd ed. Ed. by Arthur MacNeill et al. (Illus.). 408p. 1997. 52.95 *(0-8261-9731-0)* Springer Pub.

Neuropsychology, Neuropsychiatry & Behavioral Neurology. R. Joseph. LC 89-16319. (Critical Issues in Neuropsychology Ser.). (Illus.). 412p. (C). 1990. text 54.50 *(0-306-43136-X,* Kluwer Plenum) Kluwer Academic.

Neuropsychology of Aggression. Ed. by Joel S. Milner. 208p. (C). 1991. text 147.50 *(0-7923-1245-7)* Kluwer Academic.

Neuropsychology of Aging. Diana S. Woodruff-Pak. (Understanding Aging Ser.). (Illus.). 352p. (C). 1997. text 73.95 *(1-55786-454-3)*; pap. text 34.95 *(1-55786-455-1)* Blackwell Pubs.

Neuropsychology of Alcoholism: Implications for Diagnosis & Treatment. Ed. by Oscar A. Parsons et al. LC 86-29583. 414p. 1987. lib. bdg. 55.00 *(0-89862-696-X)* Guilford Pubns.

Neuropsychology of Alzheimer's Disease & Other Dementias. Ed. by Randolph W. Parks et al. LC 92-49274. (Illus.). 698p. 1993. text 79.00 *(0-19-506612-X)* OUP.

***Neuropsychology of Anxiety: An Inquiry into the Functions of the Septo-Hippocampal System.** 2nd ed. Jeffrey A. Gray & Neil McNaughton. (Oxford Psychology Ser.). (Illus.). 448p. 2000. text 95.00 *(0-19-852270-3)* OUP.

Neuropsychology of Attention. R. A. Cohen. (Critical Issues in Neuropsychology Ser.). (Illus.). 566p. (C). 1993. text 85.00 *(0-306-43953-0,* Kluwer Plenum) Kluwer Academic.

***Neuropsychology of Cardiovascular Disease.** Ed. by Shari R. Waldstein & Merrill F. Elias. 304p. 2000. write for info. *(0-8058-3103-7)* L Erlbaum Assocs.

Neuropsychology of Degenerative Brain Diseases. Robert G. Knight. 360p. 1992. text 69.95 *(0-8058-0927-9)* L Erlbaum Assocs.

Neuropsychology of Developmental Stuttering. Bernard-Thomas Hartman & Stephen F. Austin. LC 94-143. 158p. (C). 1994. pap. text 34.95 *(1-56593-384-2,* 0763) Thomson Learn.

Neuropsychology of Dreams. Mark Solms. LC 96-21693. (Institute for Research in Behavioral Neuroscience Ser.). 304p. 1996. 69.95 *(0-8058-1585-6)* L Erlbaum Assocs.

Neuropsychology of Emotion. Joan C. Borod. (Series in Affective Science). (Illus.). 520p. 2000. text 69.50 *(0-19-511464-7)* OUP.

Neuropsychology of Epilepsy. T. L. Bennett. (Critical Issues in Neuropsychology Ser.). (Illus.). 336p. (C). 1992. text 54.50 *(0-306-43948-4,* Kluwer Plenum) Kluwer Academic.

Neuropsychology of Everyday Life: Assessment & Basic Competencies. Ed. by David E. Tupper & Keith D. Cicerone. (C). 1990. lib. bdg. 132.50 *(0-7923-0671-6)* Kluwer Academic.

Neuropsychology of Everyday Life: Issues in Development & Rehabilitation. Ed. by David E. Tupper & Keith D. Cicerone. (C). 1990. lib. bdg. 132.50 *(0-7923-0847-6)* Kluwer Academic.

Neuropsychology of Eye Movement. Ed. by C. W. Johnston & F. Priozzolo. (Harry Whitaker - Neuropsychology & Neurolinguistics Ser.). 296p. (C). 1988. text 59.95 *(0-89859-796-X)* L Erlbaum Assocs.

Neuropsychology of Face Perception & Facial Expression. Raymond Bruyer. 344p. (C). 1986. text 89.95 *(0-89859-602-5)* L Erlbaum Assocs.

Neuropsychology of High-Level Vision: Collected Tutorial Essays. Ed. by Martha Farah & Graham Ratcliff. (Carnegie Mellon Symposia Ser.). 400p. 1994. pap. 45.00 *(0-8058-0911-2)*; text 79.95 *(0-8058-0910-4)* L Erlbaum Assocs.

Neuropsychology of HIV Infection. Igor Grant & Alex Martin. LC 93-26567. (Illus.). 402p. (C). 1994. text 65.00 *(0-19-507225-1)* OUP.

Neuropsychology of Human Emotion. Ed. by Kenneth M. Heilman & Paul Satz. LC 82-15615. (Advances in Neuropsychology & Behavioral Neurology Ser.: Vol. 1). (Illus.). 251p. 1983. reprint ed. pap. 77.90 *(0-608-07580-9,* 205989500010) Bks Demand.

Neuropsychology of Individual Differences. Ed. by Philip A. Vernon. LC 94-7647. (Illus.). 272p. 1994. text 59.95 *(0-12-718670-0)* Acad Pr.

Neuropsychology of Individual Differences: A Developmental Perspective. Ed. by Lawrence C. Hartlage & Cathy F. Telzrow. (Perspectives on Individual Differences Ser.). (Illus.). 346p. (C). 1985. 84.00 *(0-306-41986-6,* Plenum Trade) Perseus Pubng.

Neuropsychology of Learning Disabilities: Essentials of Subtype Analysis. Ed. by Byron P. Rourke. LC 84-10860. 351p. 1985. lib. bdg. 45.00 *(0-89862-644-7)* Guilford Pubns.

Neuropsychology of Memory. 2nd ed. Ed. by Larry R. Squire & Nelson Butters. 620p. 1992. reprint ed. lib. bdg. 69.95 *(0-89862-881-4)* Guilford Pubns.

Neuropsychology of Memory. 2nd ed. Ed. by Larry R. Squire & Nelson Butters. 620p. 1993. reprint ed. pap. text 42.00 *(0-89862-158-5)* Guilford Pubns.

Neuropsychology of Mental Disorders: A Practical Guide. Leonard F. Koziol & Chris E. Stout. LC 94-2876. (Illus.). 338p. (C). 1994. text 70.95 *(0-398-05905-5)* C C Thomas.

Neuropsychology of Mental Disorders: A Practical Guide. Leonard F. Koziol et al. LC 94-2876. (Illus.). 338p. 1994. pap. 44.95 *(0-398-06213-7)* C C Thomas.

Neuropsychology of Mental Imagery. Ed. by M. Behrmann et al. 258p. 1995. pap. 63.00 *(0-08-042733-2,* Pergamon Pr) Elsevier.

Neuropsychology of Movement Disorders. Ed. by M. Jahanshahi & R. Brown. 1996. write for info. *(0-614-17935-1,* North Holland) Elsevier.

Neuropsychology of Perinatal Complications. Ed. by Jeffrey W. Gray & Raymond S. Dean. 256p. 1990. 39.95 *(0-8261-5890-0)* Springer Pub.

Neuropsychology of Sleep & Dreaming. Ed. by John Antrobus & Mario Bertini. 336p. 1992. text 79.95 *(0-8058-0925-2)* L Erlbaum Assocs.

Neuropsychology of Visual Perception. Ed. by Jason W. Brown. (Institute for Research in Behavioral Neuroscience Ser.). 280p. 1989. 59.95 *(0-8058-0284-3)* L Erlbaum Assocs.

Neuropsychopharmacology: Proceedings of the XVIth C. I. N. P. Congress, Munich, August, 15-19 1988, 2 vols., Set. Ed. by William E. Bunney, Jr. et al. (Illus.). 928p. 1990. 368.00 *(0-387-50252-1)* Spr-Verlag.

Neuropsychopharmacology of the Trace Amines: Experimental & Clinical Aspects. Ed. by Alan A. Boulton et al. LC 85-24904. 510p. 1986. 125.00 *(0-89603-099-7)* Humana.

***Neuropsychotherapy Community Integration: Brain Illness, Emotions & Behavior.** Tedd Judd. LC 99-33665. (Critical Issues in Neuropsychology Ser.). 372p. 1999. 79.95 *(0-306-46170-6,* Kluwer Plenum) Kluwer Academic.

***Neuropsychotic Manifestations of Systematic Lupus Erythematosus.** Patricia M. Moore. 1999. pap. text 22.50 *(0-8018-6216-7)* Johns Hopkins.

Neuroptera, Strepsiptera, Mecoptera, Siphonaptera. Tim R. New et al. (Zoological Catalogue of Australia Ser.: Vol. 28). 230p. 1996. 69.95 *(0-643-05801-X,* Pub. by CSIRO) Accents Pubns.

Neuroradiology. 3rd ed. Ruth G. Ramsey. LC 93-26474. (Illus.). 1056p. 1994. text 175.00 *(0-7216-3657-8,* W B Saunders Co) Harcrt Hlth Sci Grp.

Neuroradiology. 3rd rev. ed. Juan M. Taveras & John Pile-Spellman. LC 95-33623. Orig. Title: Diagnostic Neuroradiology. (Illus.). 1250p. 1996. 189.00 *(0-683-08112-8)* Lppncott W & W.

Neuroradiology, Vol. 1. Edmund H. Burrows & Norman E. Leeds. LC 80-24709. (Illus.). 556p. 1981. reprint ed. pap. 172.40 *(0-7837-3062-4,* 204274400001) Bks Demand.

Neuroradiology, Vol. 2. Edmund H. Burrows & Norman E. Leeds. LC 80-24709. (Illus.). 378p. 1981. reprint ed. pap. 117.20 *(0-7837-3063-2,* 204274400002) Bks Demand.

Neuroradiology: A Pattern Approach. J. Randy Jinkins. LC 97-6721. 800p. 1997. text 199.00 *(0-397-51494-8)* Lppncott W & W.

Neuroradiology: A Study Guide. Ed. by Chi S. Zee & Hervey Segall. (Illus.). 640p. 1995. text 69.00 *(0-07-057128-7)* McGraw-Hill HPD.

Neuroradiology: Applications in Neurology & Neurosurgery. Ed. by Stanley Van den Noort & Elliot M. Frohman. LC 82-642121. 204p. 1988. pap. 24.00 *(0-930195-03-5)* Inst Mind Behavior.

Neuroradiology--The Requisites. Robert I. Gorssman & David M. Yousem. LC 94-229702. (Illus.). 562p. (C). (gr. 13). 1994. text 89.00 *(0-8016-6492-6,* 06492) Mosby Inc.

Neuroradiology of Head & Neck Imaging. Ed. by Jesus Rodriguez-Carbajal. LC 99-19267. 583p. 1998. pap. 80.00 *(0-7817-1447-8)* Lppncott W & W.

Neuroradiology Companion: Methods, Guidelines, & Imaging Fundamentals. Mauricio Castillo. LC 94-34493. (Illus.). 384p. 1994. pap. text 54.00 *(0-397-51472-7)* Lppncott W & W.

Neuroradiology Companion: Methods, Guidelines & Imaging Fundamentals. 2nd ed. Mauricio Castillo. LC 98-26851. 416p. 1998. pap. text. write for info. *(0-7817-1695-0)* Lppncott W & W.

Neuroradiology Test & Syllabus, Vol. 28. Peter E. Weinberg et al. (Professional Self-Evaluation & Continuing Education Program Ser.). (Illus.). 1050p. 1990. 330.00 *(1-55903-028-3)* Am Coll Radiology.

Neuroradiology Test & Syllabus Second Series: Test & Syllabus, Vol. 42, Series 2. Eric J. Russell et al. LC 98-3648. (Professional Self-Evaluation Program Ser.: Vol. 42). (Illus.). 600p. 1998. 220.00 *(1-55903-042-9)* Am Coll Radiology.

Neuroreceptor Mechanisms in the Brain. Ed. by S. Kito et al. (Advances in Experimental Medicine & Biology Ser.: Vol. 287). (Illus.). 510p. (C). 1991. text 174.00 *(0-306-43821-6,* Kluwer Plenum) Kluwer Academic.

Neuroreceptors. Ed. by Ferdinand Hucho. (Illus.). 367p. 1982. 123.10 *(3-11-008855-X)* De Gruyter.

Neuroreceptors: Basic & Clinical Aspects: Based on Symposia Held at the American College of Neuropsychopharmacology Annual Meeting, December, 1979. Ed. by Earl Usdin et al. LC 80-40962. (Illus.). 291p. reprint ed. pap. 90.30 *(0-608-17595-1,* 203044000069) Bks Demand.

Neuroreceptors & Signal Transduction. Ed. by S. Kito et al. (Illus.). 364p. 1988. 95.00 *(0-306-42985-3,* Plenum Trade) Perseus Pubng.

Neuroreceptors in Health & Disease. Ed. by J. Marwaha & W. J. Anderson. (Monographs in Neural Sciences: Vol. 10). (Illus.). viii, 256p. 1984. 129.75 *(3-8055-3715-8)* S Karger.

Neuroregeneration. Ed. by Alfredo Gorio. LC 92-49715. (Illus.). 345p. 1993. reprint ed. pap. 107.00 *(0-608-05856-4,* 205982300007) Bks Demand.

Neuroregulation of Autonomic, Endocrine & Immune Systems. Ed. by R. Frederickson et al. (Topics in the Neurosciences Ser.). 1986. text 208.00 *(0-89838-800-7)* Kluwer Academic.

Neuroregulatory Mechanisms in Aging. Ed. by Maynard H. Makman & George B. Stefano. LC 93-21169. (Studies in Neuroscience). 212p. 1993. 160.50 *(0-08-041989-5,* Pergamon Pr) Elsevier.

Neurorehabilitation. Namerow. Date not set. text. write for info. *(0-7216-5646-3,* W B Saunders Co) Harcrt Hlth Sci Grp.

Neurorehabilitation: A Multisensory Approach. Shereen D. Farber. (Illus.). 282p. 1982. pap. text 47.00 *(0-7216-3571-7,* W B Saunders Co) Harcrt Hlth Sci Grp.

Neuroscience. Ed. by Philip H. Abelson et al. LC 84-24524. (Illus.). 516p. (C). 1986. 54.50 *(0-87168-309-1,* 84-13S) AAAS.

***Neuroscience.** Nikos M. Linardakis. LC 99-31930. (Digging Up the Bones Medical Review Ser.). (Illus.). 130p. 1999. pap. text 18.95 *(0-07-038369-3)* McGraw-Hill HPD.

Neuroscience. Lundy. (C). 1998. text 49.95 *(0-7216-4717-0,* W B Saunders Co) Harcrt Hlth Sci Grp.

Neuroscience. Ed. by Dale Purves et al. LC 96-43031. 562p. (C). 1996. text 62.95 *(0-87893-747-1)* Sinauer Assocs.

Neuroscience. Woolsey. 1999. pap. text. write for info. *(0-7216-4722-7,* W B Saunders Co) Harcrt Hlth Sci Grp.

Neuroscience. Ed. by Philip H. Abelson et al. LC 84-24524. (AAAS Publication: No. 84-13). (Illus.). 467p. reprint ed. pap. 144.80 *(0-8357-6436-2,* 203580700097) Bks Demand.

Neuroscience. 3rd ed. Allan Seigel & Heidi Siegel. LC 98-215429. (Basic Sciences: Pretest Self Assessment & Review Ser.). (Illus.). 1998. pap. text 18.95 *(0-07-052690-7)* McGraw-Hill HPD.

Neuroscience: Exploring the Brain. Mark F. Bear et al. LC 95-13837. (Illus.). 680p. 1996. 49.00 *(0-683-00488-3)* Lppncott W & W.

Neuroscience: Exploring the Brain. 2nd ed. Mark Bear et al. 768p. 52.00 *(0-683-30596-4)* Lppncott W & W.

Neuroscience: From Neural Networks to Artificial Intelligence - Proceedings of a U. S.-Mexico Seminar Held in the City of Xalapa in the State of Veracruz in December 9-11, 1991. Ed. by Pablo Rudomin et al. LC 93-18575. (Research Notes in Neural Computing Ser.: Vol. 4). 1993. 78.95 *(0-387-56501-9)* Spr-Verlag.

Neuroscience: From the Molecular to the Cognitive. Ed. by Floyd E. Bloom. LC 94-12298. (Progress in Brain Research Ser.: Vol. 100). 300p. 1994. 266.00 *(0-444-81678-X)* Elsevier.

Neuroscience: Fundamentals for Rehabilitation. Laurie Lundy-Ekamn. (Illus.). 475p. 1998. pap., teacher ed. write for info. *(0-7216-4718-9,* W B Saunders Co) Harcrt Hlth Sci Grp.

Neuroscience & Behavior: An Introduction. 2nd ed. Ed. by D. M. Atrens & J. S. Curthoys. 214p. 1982. text 55.00 *(0-12-066850-5)* Acad Pr.

Neuroscience & Clinical Science: Toward an Integration. Ed. by Schwartz. (Psychoanalytic Inquiry Ser.: Vol. 12, No. 3). 1992. 20.00 *(0-88163-946-X)* Analytic Pr.

Neuroscience & Connectionist Theory. Ed. by Mark A. Gluck & David E. Rumelhart. (Developments in Connectionist Theory Ser.). 424p. 1990. 125.00 *(0-8058-0504-4)*; pap. 65.00 *(0-8058-0619-9)* L Erlbaum Assocs.

Neuroscience & Endocrinology of Fibromyalgia: 2nd National Institutes of Health Fibromyalgia Conference. Ed. by Stanley R. Pillemer. LC 98-37606. (Journal of Musculoskeletal Pain Ser.: Vol. 6, No. 3). 110p. 1998. 39.95 *(0-7890-0683-9)* Haworth Pr.

***Neuroscience & the Person.** Ed. by Robert John Russell et al. (Scientific Perspectives on Divine Action Ser.). 500p. 2000. pap. 26.95 *(0-268-01490-6,* Pub. by U of Notre Dame Pr) Chicago Distribution Ctr.

Neuroscience Approached Through Cell Culture, Vol. I. Steven E. Pfeiffer. 256p. 1982. 140.00 *(0-8493-6340-3,* QP356, CRC Reprint) Franklin.

Neuroscience Approached Through Cell Culture, Vol. II. Steven E. Pfeiffer. 192p. 1983. 114.00 *(0-8493-6341-1,* QP356, CRC Reprint) Franklin.

***Neuroscience at a Glance.** Roger A. Barker & Stephen Barasi. LC 98-22073. (At a Glance Ser.). (Illus.). 96p. 1999. pap. text 21.95 *(0-86542-869-7)* Blackwell Sci.

Neuroscience Critical Care: Pathophysiology & Patient Management. Marshall et al. (Illus.). 464p. 1990. text 89.00 *(0-7216-2790-0,* W B Saunders Co) Harcrt Hlth Sci Grp.

Neuroscience for Rehabilitation. Ed. by Helen Cohen. LC 92-49041. (Illus.). 480p. 1993. pap. text 42.00 *(0-397-54930-X)* Lppncott W & W.

Neuroscience for Rehabilitation. 2nd ed. Helen Cohen. LC 98-24809. 544p. 1998. text 41.95 *(0-397-55465-6)* Lppncott W & W.

Neuroscience for the Study of Communicative Disorders. Subhash C. Bhatnagar & Orlando Andy. (Illus.). 369p. 1995. pap. text 37.95 *(0-683-00740-8)* Lppncott W & W.

Neuroscience in Medicine. P. Michael Conn. (Illus.). 752p. 1994. text 42.50 *(0-397-51279-1)* Lppncott W & W.

Neuroscience Labfax. Ed. by Marina A. Lynch & Shane M. O'Mara. LC 96-47962. (Labfax Ser.). (Illus.). 288p. 1997. text 59.95 *(0-12-460490-0)* Morgan Kaufmann.

Neuroscience, Memory, & Language. 1996. lib. bdg. 252.95 *(0-8490-6041-9)* Gordon Pr.

Neuroscience, Memory, & Language: Papers Presented at a Symposium Series Cosponsored by the National Institute of Mental Health & the Library of Congress. Ed. by Richard D. Broadwell. LC 94-37346. (Decade of the Brain Ser.: Vol. 1). 1995. pap. write for info. *(0-8444-0847-6)* Lib Congress.

Neuroscience, Memory, & Language: Papers Presented at a Symposium Series Cosponsored by the National Institute of Mental Health & the Library of Congress. Ed. by Richard D. Broadwell. LC 94-37346. (Decade of the Brain Ser.: Vol. 1). (Illus.). 160p. 1995. 26.00 *(0-8444-0815-8)* Lib Congress.

Neuroscience Methods: A Guide for Advanced Students. Ed. by Rosemary Martin. 272p. 1997. text 34.00 *(90-5702-244-3,* Harwood Acad Pubs); pap. text 15.00 *(90-5702-245-1,* Harwood Acad Pubs) Gordon & Breach.

Neuroscience Nursing. Ellen Barker. (Illus.). 848p. (C). (gr. 13). 1994. text 61.95 *(0-8016-6470-5,* 06470) Mosby Inc.

Neuroscience of Animal Intelligence: From the Seahare to the Seahorse. Euan M. Macphail. Ed. by Herbert S. Terrace. LC 92-31167. (Animal Intelligence Ser.). (Illus.). 506p. (C). 1993. text 75.50 *(0-231-06144-7)* Col U Pr.

Neuroscience of Communication. Donald B. Webster. (Singular Textbook Ser.). (Illus.). 326p. (Orig.). (C). 1995. pap. 38.95 *(1-56593-114-9,* 0417) Thomson Learn.

Neuroscience of Communication. 2nd rev. ed. Douglas B. Webster. LC 98-24475. 350p. 1998. pap. 57.95 *(1-56593-985-9,* 1950) Thomson Learn.

Neuroscience of Human Movement: A Primer. Leonard. LC 98-221239. (Illus.). 272p. (gr. 13). 1997. pap. text 25.00 *(0-8151-5371-6,* 26560) Mosby Inc.

Neuroscience of Mental Health. National Institute of Mental Health (U. S.) Staff. LC 84-601129. 94p. reprint ed. pap. 30.00 *(0-8357-7855-X,* 203623200002) Bks Demand.

Neuroscience of Mental Health: A Report on Neuroscience Research. Ed. by Stephen H. Koslow. (Illus.). 182p. (C). 1997. reprint ed. pap. text 45.00 *(0-7881-4694-7)* DIANE Pub.

Neuroscience of Mental Health: A Report on Neuroscience Research, Status & Potential for Mental Health & Mental Illness. Stephen H. Koslow. 196p. 1995. pap. text 16.00 *(0-16-048357-3)* USGPO.

Neuroscience of Perceptual Integration: A Special Issue of the Journal Visual Cognition. Muriel Boucart. 224p. 1999. 49.95 *(0-86377-604-3)* L Erlbaum Assocs.

Neuroscience of the Mind on the Centennial of Freud's "Project for a Scientific Psychology" On the Centennial of Freud's Project for a Scientific Psychology. Ed. by Robert M. Bilder & F. Frank LeFever. LC 98-13652. (Annals of the New York Academy of Sciences Ser.: Vol. 843). 1998. 80.00 *(1-57331-063-8)*; 80.00 *(1-57331-062-X)* NY Acad Sci.

Neuroscience Protocols. Ed. by Floris G. Wouterlood. LC 93-29391. 314p. 1993. 334.00 *(0-444-89539-6)* Elsevier.

Neuroscience Protocols, Module. Floris G. Wouterlood. 196p. 1995. 142.75 *(0-444-81804-9)* Elsevier.

Neuroscience Protocols, Module 2. Ed. by Floris G. Wouterlood. 160p. 1993. ring bd. 136.50 *(0-444-81802-2)* Elsevier.

Neuroscience Protocols, Module 3. Floris G. Wouterlood. 160p. 1994. ring bd. 129.75 *(0-444-81803-0)* Elsevier.

Neuroscience Protocols, Module 6. Floris G. Wouterlood. 122p. 1995. ring bd. 126.75 *(0-444-82342-5)* Elsevier.

N

An Asterisk (*) at the beginning of an entry indicates that the title is appearing for the first time.

Neuroscience Protocols, Module 7. Ed. by Floris G. Wouterlood. 250p. 1996. 136.00 (*0-444-82466-9*) Elsevier.

Neuroscience Protocols, Module 8. Ed. by Floris G. Wouterlood. 156p. 1996. ring bd. 122.00 (*0-444-82512-6*) Elsevier.

Neuroscience Protocols, Modules 1-4. Ed. by Floris G. Wouterlood. 1995. 749.00 (*0-444-82108-2*) Elsevier.

Neuroscience Protocols, Nodule 5. Floris G. Wouterlood. 122p. 1995. ring bd. 126.75 (*0-444-82249-6*) Elsevier.

Neuroscience Protocols Section 5: Neuromophology. 1995. ring bd. 65.00 (*0-444-82109-0*) Elsevier.

Neuroscience Secrets. Ed. by Margaret Wong-Riley. LC 99-34312. (Secrets Ser.). (Illus.). 350p. 1999. pap. text 38.00 (*1-56053-316-1*) Hanley & Belfus.

Neuroscience Year: Encyclopedia of Neuroscience, Supplement 2. Ed. by Barry Smith & George Adelman. (Illus.). xiii, 158p. 1991. 87.50 (*0-8176-3507-6*) Birkhauser.

Neuroscience Year: Supplement 1 to the Encyclopedia of Neuroscience. George Adelman. 200p. 1989. 87.50 (*0-8176-3383-9*) Birkhauser.

Neuroscience Year: Supplement 3. Ed. by Barry Smith & George Adelman. LC 92-49552. (Supplements to the Encyclopedia of Neuroscience Ser.: Vol. 3). (Illus.). 190p. 1993. 109.00 (*0-8176-3592-0*) Birkhauser.

Neurosciences: Paths of Discovery II. Ed. by F. E. Samson. (Illus.). xvi, 352p. 1992. 97.00 (*0-8176-3503-3*) Birkhauser.

Neurosciences: The Basics. Brian A. Curtis. LC 90-5577. 172p. 1990. text 26.00 (*0-8121-1309-8*) Lppncott W & W.

Neurosciences: 2nd Study Program. Ed. by F. O. Schmit. (Illus.). 1069p. 1970. 60.00 (*0-87470-014-0*) Rockefeller.

Neurosciences: 4th Study Program. Ed. by Francis O. Schmitt & Frederic G. Worden. 1201p. 1979. 105.00 (*0-262-19162-8*) MIT Pr.

Neuroscientific Principles of Swallowing & Dysphagia. Arthur J. Miller. LC 98-8532. (Illus.). 300p. 1998. pap. 69.95 (*1-56593-859-3*, 1678) Thomson Learn.

Neurosecretion: Cellular Aspects of the Production & Release of Neuropeptides. Ed. by B. T. Pickering et al. LC 88-12440. (Illus.). 282p. 1988. 75.00 (*0-306-42919-5*, Plenum Trade) Perseus Pubng.

Neurosen - Mythen, Modelle, Fakten: Ein Beitrag zur Genese Neurotischer Stoerungen. H. G. Zapotoczky. Ed. by P. Berner. (Bibliotheca Psychiatrica Ser.: No. 153). (Illus.). 180p. 1976. 38.50 (*3-8055-2310-6*) S Karger.

Neuroses & Character Types: Clinical Psychoanalytic Studies. Helene Deutsch. LC 65-15288. xii, 388p. (Orig.). 1965. 57.50 (*0-8236-3560-0*) Intl Univs Pr.

Neurosis & Human Growth: The Struggle Toward Self-Realization. Karen Horney. 1991. pap. 15.95 (*0-393-30775-1*) Norton.

Neurosis & Narrative: The Decadent Short Fiction of Proust, Lorrain, & Rachilde. Renee A. Kingcaid. LC 91-22156. 240p. (C). 1992. 31.95 (*0-8093-1753-2*) S Ill U Pr.

Neurosis & Treatment: A Holistic Theory. Andras Angyal. (Psychoanalysis: Examined & Re-Examined Ser.). 328p. 1982. lib. bdg. 35.00 (*0-306-79709-7*) Da Capo.

Neurosomatic Addiction Reversal: Permanent Weight Loss & Elimination of Stress & Addictive Behaviors Utilizing Mind-Body Dynamics. Norton Wyner. 150p. 1993. ring bd. 75.00 (*1-884603-00-9*) Beverly Hills Mind.

Neurosonography of the Pre-Term Neonate. Ed. by E. G. Grant. (Illus.). xi, 116p. 1986. 104.00 (*0-387-96219-0*) Spr-Verlag.

Neurosonology. Ed. by Charles H. Tegeler et al. LC 95-32584. (Illus.). 528p. (C). (gr. 13). 1995. text 169.00 (*0-8151-8792-0*, 24076) Mosby Inc.

Neurospeak: Transforms Your Body While You Read. Robert Masters. 124p. 1994. pap. 14.00 (*0-8356-0707-0*, Quest) Theos Pub Hse.

***Neurospora: Contributions of a Model Organism.** Rowland H. Davis. LC 99-42516. (Illus.). 320p. 2000. text 95.00 (*0-19-512236-4*) OUP.

Neurospore Bibliography & Index. Barbara Bachmann & Walter N. Strickland. LC 65-12538. 234p. reprint ed. pap. 72.60 (*0-608-11118-X*, 202197700024) Bks Demand.

Neurospsychological Assessment & Intervention with Children & Adolescents. Lawrence C. Hartlage & Cathy F. Telzrow. LC 86-70324. 192p. (C). 1986. pap. 25.95 (*0-943158-15-X*, NABP) Pro Resource.

Neurosteroids: A New Regulatory Function in the Nervous System. Ed. by Etienne-Emile Baulieu et al. LC 99-10461. (Contemporary Endocrinology Ser.: Vol. 16). (Illus.). 396p. 1999. 135.00 (*0-89603-545-X*) Humana.

***Neurosurgeon's Notebook.** Chris Adams. (Illus.). 19p. 1998. pap. 33.95 (*0-632-05154-X*) Blackwell Sci.

***Neurosurgery.** 3rd rev. ed. Alan Crockard et al. LC 99-28832. (Illus.). 1301p. 2000. 495.00 (*0-632-04838-7*) Blackwell Sci.

Neurosurgery, 3 vols., 1. Ed. by Robert H. Wilkins & Setti S. Rengachary. (Illus.). 2350p. 1985. text. write for info. (*0-07-070307-8*) McGraw-Hill HPD.

Neurosurgery, 3 vols., 2. Ed. by Robert H. Wilkins & Setti S. Rengachary. (Illus.). 2350p. 1985. text. write for info. (*0-07-070308-6*) McGraw-Hill HPD.

Neurosurgery, 3 vols., 3. Ed. by Robert H. Wilkins & Setti S. Rengachary. (Illus.). 2350p. 1985. text. write for info. (*0-07-070309-4*) McGraw-Hill HPD.

Neurosurgery, 3 vols., Set. Ed. by Robert H. Wilkins & Setti S. Rengachary. (Illus.). 2350p. 1985. text 550.00 (*0-07-079790-0*) McGraw-Hill HPD.

Neurosurgery, 3 vols., Set. 2nd ed. Ed. by Robert H. Wilkins & Setti S. Rengachary. Incl. 2nd ed. LC 95-35870. (Illus.). (C). 1995. text (*0-07-070313-2*); 2nd ed. LC 95-35870. (Illus.). (C). 1995. text (*0-07-070314-0*); 2nd ed. LC 95-35870. (Illus.). (C). 1995. text (*0-07-070315-9*); LC 95-35870. (Illus.). 11200p. 1995. Set text 575.00 (*0-07-079991-1*) McGraw-Hill HPD.

Neurosurgery: An Introductory Text. Peter M. Black & Eugene Rossitch. (Illus.). 248p. 1995. text 49.95 (*0-19-504448-7*); pap. text 24.95 (*0-19-504449-5*) OUP.

***Neurosurgery & Medical Ethics.** Ed. by H. A. Van Alphen. LC 99-33462. (Acta Neurochirurgica Ser.: Supplement no. 74). 120p. 1999. 75.00 (*3-211-83348-X*) Spr-Verlag.

Neurosurgery Board Review: Questions & Answers for Self-Assessment. 2nd ed. Cargill H. Alleyne, Jr. & Daniel L. Barrow. LC 96-29700. (Illus.). 254p. 1997. pap. 39.95 (*0-86577-706-3*) Thieme Med Pubs.

Neurosurgery for Spasticity: A Multidisciplinary Approach. Ed. by M. P. Sindou et al. (Illus.). 224p. 1991. 174.00 (*0-387-82225-9*) Spr-Verlag.

Neurosurgery in Transition: The Sociol Economic Transformation of Neurological Surgery. James Bean. 85.00 (*0-683-18345-1*) Lppncott W & W.

Neurosurgery of Complex Tumors & Vascular Lesions. Ed. by S. Kobayashi et al. (Illus.). 480p. 1996. write for info. (*0-443-07870-X*) Church.

Neurosurgery, Ophthalmic Surgery, ENT. Ed. by Gunther O. Schlag et al. LC 94-27186. (Fibrin Sealing in Surgical & Nonsurgical Fields Ser.: Vol. 5). 1994. 68.95 (*0-387-58014-X*) Spr-Verlag.

Neurosurgery Specialty Manual. Association of Surgical Technologists Staff. (Allied Health Ser.). (C). 2002. pap. 40.00 (*0-7668-1209-X*) Delmar.

Neurosurgical & Medical Management of Pain: Trigeminal Neuralgia, Chronic Pain & Cancer Pain. Ed. by Ronald Brisman. (C). 1989. text 145.00 (*0-89838-405-2*) Kluwer Academic.

Neurosurgical Applications of Transcranial Doppler Sonography. A. Harders. (Illus.). 150p. 1986. 47.95 (*0-387-81938-X*) Spr-Verlag.

Neurosurgical Aspects of Epilepsy: Proceedings of the 4th Advanced Seminar in Neurosurgical Research of the European Association of Neurosurgical Societies, May 17-18, 1989, Bressco die Teolo, Padova, Italy. Ed. by J. D. Pickard et al. (Acta Neurochirugica - Supplementum Ser.: No. 50). (Illus.). viii, 144p. 1990. 128.00 (*0-387-82227-5*) Spr-Verlag.

Neurosurgical Care of the Elderly. Ed. by Warren R. Selman & Edward C. Benzel. 95.00 (*1-879284-59-6*) Am Assn Neuro.

Neurosurgical Intensive Care. Ed. by Brian T. Andrews. LC 92-49880. (Illus.). 560p. 1993. text 74.00 (*0-07-001849-9*) McGraw-Hill HPD.

Neurosurgical Management of Pain. Ed. by Robert M. Levy & Richard B. North. LC 95-23662. 376p. 1996. 160.00 (*0-387-94256-4*) Spr-Verlag.

Neurosurgical Operative Atlas, Vol. 1-8. American Association of Neurological Surgeons Staff. 1500p. 500.00 (*0-683-07234-X*) Am Assn Neuro.

Neurosurgical Operative Atlas, Vol. 4. Ed. by Setti S. Rengachary & Robert H. Wilkins. (Illus.). 257p. 1995. ring bd. 165.00 (*1-879284-39-1*) Am Assn Neuro.

Neurosurgical Operative Atlas, Vol. 5. Ed. by Setti S. Rengachary & Robert H. Wilkins. (Illus.). 250p. 1996. ring bd. 165.00 (*1-879284-41-3*) Am Assn Neuro.

Neurosurgical Operative Atlas, Vol. 6. Ed. by Setti S. Rengachary & Robert H. Wilkins. 277p. 1997. 165.00 (*1-879284-50-2*) Am Assn Neuro.

Neurosurgical Operative Atlas, Vol. 7. Ed. by Setti S. Rengachary & Robert H. Wilkins. 267p. 165.00 (*1-879284-56-1*) Am Assn Neuro.

Neurosurgical Operative Atlas, Vol. 8. Ed. by Setti S. Rengachary & Robert H. Wilkins. 276p. 165.00 (*1-879284-67-7*) Am Assn Neuro.

Neurosurgical Procedures: Personal Approaches to Classic Operations. Charles B. Wilson. (Illus.). 288p. 1992. 130.00 (*0-683-09071-2*) Lppncott W & W.

Neurosurgical Review. Christopher D. Sturm & Thomas R. Forget. LC 98-46841. 323p. 1998. 30.00 (*1-57626-115-8*) Quality Med Pub.

Neurosurgical Review Vol. 12, Supplement 1: Advances in Neurotraumatology. Ed. by R. A. Frowein et al. 619p. (C). 1989. pap. text 152.35 (*3-11-011240-X*) De Gruyter.

Neurosurgical Standards, Cerebral Aneurysms, Malignant Gliomas. Ed. by K. Piscol et al. (Advances in Neurosurgery Ser.: Vol. 20). (Illus.). 360p. 1992. pap. 79.00 (*0-387-54838-6*) Spr-Verlag.

Neurosurgical Treatment of Chronic Pain: Physiologica & Pathologic Mechanisms of Human Pain. J. M. Gybels & W. H. Sweet. (Pain & Headache Ser.: Vol. 11). (Illus.). xvi, 444p. 1989. 168.75 (*3-8055-4885-0*) S Karger.

Neurosurgical Treatment of Movement Disorders. Ed. by Isabelle M. Germano. 275p. 95.00 (*1-879284-58-8*) Am Assn Neuro.

Neurosyphilis: Modern Systematic Diagnosis & Treatment Preserved in One Hundred & Thirty-Seven Case Histories. Elmer E. Southard & Harry C. Solomon. LC 73-2418. (Mental Illness & Social Policy; the American Experience Ser.). 1973. reprint ed. 37.95 (*0-405-05228-6*) Ayer.

Neurotheology: Virtual Religion in the 21st Century. Laurence O. McKinney. 172p. (Orig.). 1994. pap. 10.95 (*0-945724-01-2*) Am Inst Mindfulness.

Neurotherapeutics: Emerging Strategies. Ed. by Linda M. Pullan & Jitendra Patel. LC 95-381027. (Contemporary Neuroscience Ser.). (Illus.). 444p. 1995. 125.00 (*0-89603-306-6*) Humana.

Neurotic & Psychotic Language Behavior. Ed. by Ruth Wodak & Pete Van de Craen. 416p. 1987. 99.00 (*0-905028-77-5*, Pub. by Multilingual Matters); pap. 49.00 (*0-905028-76-7*, Pub. by Multilingual Matters) Taylor & Francis.

Neurotic Behavior of Organizations. Uri Merry & George Brown. (Gestalt Institute of Cleveland Press Book Ser.). 300p. 1987. pap. 24.95 (*0-88163-250-3*) Analytic Pr.

Neurotic Child & Adolescent. Ed. by M. Hossein Etezady. LC 89-18246. 440p. 1990. 65.00 (*0-87668-808-3*) Aronson.

Neurotic Constitution. Alfred Adler. LC 74-39684. (Select Bibliographies Reprint Ser.). 1980. reprint ed. 34.95 (*0-8369-9925-8*) Ayer.

Neurotic Disorders in the Elderly. Ed. by James Lindesay. (Illus.). 260p. (C). 1995. text 79.50 (*0-19-262396-6*) OUP.

Neurotic Organization: Diagnosing & Changing Counterproductive Styles of Management. Manfred F. Kets de Vries & Danny Miller. LC 84-5754. (Management Ser.). 259p. 1984. text 34.95 (*0-87589-606-5*) Jossey-Bass.

Neurotic Organization: Diagnosing & Revitalizing Unhealthy Companies. Manfred F. Kets de Vries & Danny Miller. 1991. pap. 14.95 (*0-88730-488-5*, HarpBusn) HarpInfo.

Neurotic Personality of Our Time. Karen Horney. 256p. 1994. pap. 10.95 (*0-393-31097-3*) Norton.

***Neurotic Styles.** David Shapiro. 1999. pap. 22.00 (*0-465-09564-X*, Pub. by Basic) HarpC.

***Neurotic Styles.** David Shapiro. 1999. pap. 20.00 (*0-465-09502-X*, TB5003, Pub. by Basic) HarpC.

Neurotica. Sue Margolis. LC 98-46978. 320p. 1999. 16.95 (*0-553-10984-7*) Bantam.

***Neurotica.** Sue Margolis. 336p. 2000. reprint ed. mass mkt. 6.50 (*0-553-58106-6*) Bantam.

***Neurotica: Jewish Writers on Sex.** Ed. by Melvin J. Bukiet. 368p. 2000. pap. 14.95 (*0-7679-0650-0*) Broadway BDD.

Neurotica: Jewish Writers on Sex. Ed. by Melvin Jules Bukiet. LC 99-27452. 352p. 1999. 26.95 (*0-393-04808-X*) Norton.

Neurotica: The Darkest Art of J. K. Potter. J. K. Potter. LC 96-18136. (Illus.). 128p. 1996. pap. 27.95 (*0-87951-687-9*, Pub. by Overlook Pr) Penguin Putnam.

Neurotic's Handbook. Robert L. McKinley. 131p. (C). 1977. pap. 10.00 (*0-9609644-0-1*) Candle Bks.

Neurotische Gotterhimmel der Griechen: Europa im Falschen Kielwasser? Lore Toman. (Historisch-Anthropologische Studien: Band 3). (GER.). 120p. 1998. 26.95 (*3-631-31088-9*) P Lang Pubng.

Neurotoxic Side Effects of Prescription Drugs. John C. Brust. LC 96-23662. 435p. 1996. pap. text 49.50 (*0-7506-9663-X*) Buttrwrth-Heinemann.

Neurotoxicity: Identifying & Controlling Poisons of the Nervous System. 1992. lib. bdg. 186.96 (*0-8490-8790-2*) Gordon Pr.

Neurotoxicity: Identifying & Controlling Poisons of the Nervous System. U. S. Congress, Office of Technology Assessment Staff. (Illus.). 384p. (C). (gr. 13). 1992. text 64.95 (*0-442-01047-8*) Chapman & Hall.

Neurotoxicity of Excitatory Amino Acids. Alessandro Guidotti. LC 90-8937. (Fidia Research Foundation Symposium Ser.: No. 4). (Illus.). 360p. 1990. reprint ed. pap. 111.60 (*0-608-00678-5*, 206126500007) Bks Demand.

Neurotoxicity of Industrial & Commercial Chemicals, 2 vols., Vol. 1. Ed. by John L. O'Donoghue. LC 84-4261. 232p. 1985. 134.00 (*0-8493-6454-X*, RC347, CRC Reprint) Franklin.

Neurotoxicity of Industrial & Commercial Chemicals, 2 vols., Vol. 2. Ed. by John L. O'Donoghue. LC 84-4261. 224p. 1985. 132.00 (*0-8493-6455-8*, CRC Reprint) Franklin.

Neurotoxicology. M. B. Abou-Donia. 444p. 1989. text 107.00 (*2-88124-406-8*) Gordon & Breach.

Neurotoxicology. Mohammed B. Abou-Donia. 640p. 1992. lib. bdg. 149.00 (*0-8493-8895-3*, RC347) CRC Pr.

Neurotoxicology. Blum & Manzo. (Drug & Chemical Toxicology Ser.: Vol. 3). (Illus.). 704p. 1985. text 255.00 (*0-8247-7283-0*) Dekker.

Neurotoxicology. 2nd ed. Hugh A. Tilson. LC 98-48639. (Target Organ Toxicology Ser.). 1999. 140.00 (*1-56032-720-0*) Taylor & Francis.

Neurotoxicology, Vol. 1, 1977. Ed. by Leon Roizin et al. LC 77-4632. (Illus.). 686p. 1977. reprint ed. pap. 200.00 (*0-608-00631-9*, 206121900001) Bks Demand.

Neurotoxicology: A Clinical Source Book. Peter G. Bernad. LC 98-85162. 1998. text 105.00 (*0-327-00132-1*, 66067-10) LEXIS Pub.

Neurotoxicology: A Clinical Sourcebook, 1999 Supplement. Peter G. Bernad. 72p. 1999. write for info. (*0-327-01487-3*, 66066l0) LEXIS Pub.

Neurotoxicology: Approaches & Methods. Ed. by Louis W. Chang & William Slikker. (Illus.). 851p. 1995. text 149.95 (*0-12-168055-X*) Acad Pr.

Neurotoxins & Their Pharmacological Implications: A Biological Council Symposium. Ed. by Peter Jenner. LC 85-43513. 317p. 1987. reprint ed. pap. 98.30 (*0-608-00326-3*, 206104300007) Bks Demand.

Neurotraining. 1989. 52.95 (*0-387-50489-3*) Spr-Verlag.

Neurotransmission & Hearing Loss: Basic Science, Diagnosis & Management. Charles I. Berlin. LC 97-937. (Illus.). 184p. (Orig.). 1997. 55.00 (*1-56593-834-8*, 1630) Thomson Learn.

Neurotransmitter Actions & Interactions: Proceedings of a Satellite Symposium of the 12th International Society for Neurochemistry Meeting, Algarve, Portugal, April 29-30, 1989. Ed. by M. B. Youdim & Keith F. Tipton. (Journal of Neural Transmission: Suppl. 29). (Illus.). ix, 292p. 1990. 192.00 (*0-387-82142-2*) Spr-Verlag.

Neurotransmitter Actions in the Vertebrate Nervous System. Ed. by Michael A. Rogawski & Jeffrey L. Barker. 536p. 1985. 125.00 (*0-306-41991-2*, Plenum Trade) Perseus Pubng.

Neurotransmitter & Dementia. Ed. by C. G. Gottfries & Joyce Nakamura. (Journal of Neural Transmission: Suppl. 30). 120p. 1990. 56.95 (*0-387-82190-2*) Spr-Verlag.

Neurotransmitter Balances Regulating Behavior. Ed. by E. F. Domino & J. M. Davis. LC 75-21131. (Illus.). 240p. 1975. 30.00 (*0-916182-00-2*) NPP Bks.

Neurotransmitter Enzymes. Ed. by Alan A. Boulton et al. LC 86-10309. (Neuromethods Ser.: Vol. 5). (Illus.). 619p. 1986. 125.00 (*0-89603-079-2*) Humana.

Neurotransmitter Interactions & Cognitive Function. Ed. by Edward D. Levin et al. LC 92-17848. xiv, 362p. 1992. 120.00 (*0-8176-3617-X*) Birkhauser.

Neurotransmitter Interactions in the Basal Ganglia. Ed. by M. Sandler et al. LC 86-26157. 272p. 1987. reprint ed. pap. 84.40 (*0-608-04684-1*, 206540500004) Bks Demand.

Neurotransmitter Methods. Ed. by Richard C. Rayne. LC 96-49802. (Methods in Molecular Biology Ser.: Vol. 72). (Illus.). 288p. 1997. 89.50 (*0-89603-394-5*) Humana.

Neurotransmitter Receptors. Ed. by Ferdinand Hucho. LC 93-2106. (New Comprehensive Biochemistry Ser.: Vol. 24). 386p. 1994. 191.50 (*0-444-89903-0*) Elsevier.

Neurotransmitter Receptors, 2 pts., Pt. 1: Amino Acids, Peptides & Benzodiazepines. Ed. by Sam J. Enna & H. D. Yamamura. (Receptors & Recognition Series B: Vols. 9 & 10). 1980. 49.95 (*0-412-16250-4*, NO. 6399) Chapman & Hall.

Neurotransmitter Receptors, 2 pts., Pt. 2: Biogenic Amines. Ed. by Sam J. Enna & H. D. Yamamura. (Receptors & Recognition Series B: Vols. 9 & 10). 1980. 49.95 (*0-685-42264-X*, 2157) Chapman & Hall.

Neurotransmitter Receptors, 2 pts., Set. Ed. by Sam J. Enna & H. D. Yamamura. (Receptors & Recognition Series B: Vols. 9 & 10). 1980. 105.00 (*0-412-23130-1*, NO. 2178) Chapman & Hall.

***Neurotransmitter Receptors in Actions of Antipsychotic Medications.** Michael S. Lidow. LC 00-25387. (Pharmacology & Toxicology Ser.). 272p. 2000. boxed set 99.95 (*0-8493-0744-9*) CRC Pr.

***Neurotransmitter Release.** Ed. by Hugo Bellen. LC 99-16240. (Frontiers in Molecular Biology Ser.: No. 23). (Illus.). 458p. 1999. text 120.00 (*0-19-963767-9*) OUP.

***Neurotransmitter Release.** Ed. by Hugo Bellen. LC 99-16240. (Frontiers in Molecular Biology Ser.: Vol. 23). (Illus.). 458p. 1999. pap. text 60.00 (*0-19-963766-0*) OUP.

Neurotransmitter Release & Its Modulation: Biochemical Mechanisms, Physiological Function & Clinical Relevance. Ed. by David A. Powis & Stephen J. Bunn. (Illus.). 374p. (C). 1995. text 140.00 (*0-521-44068-8*); pap. text 59.95 (*0-521-44616-3*) Cambridge U Pr.

Neurotransmitter Release & Uptake. Sakire Pogun. LC 97-4076. (NATO ASI Series, Series H, Cell Biology). 1997. 157.00 (*3-540-62479-1*) Spr-Verlag.

Neurotransmitter Revolution: Serotonin, Social Behavior, & the Law. Michael T. McGuire. Ed. by Roger D. Masters. LC 92-49968. 272p. (C). 1993. 41.95 (*0-8093-1792-3*); pap. 21.95 (*0-8093-1801-6*) S Ill U Pr.

Neurotransmitter Transporters: Structure, Function & Regulation. Ed. by Maarten E. A. Reith. LC 96-36600. (Contemporary Neuroscience Ser.). (Illus.). 416p. 1996. 150.00 (*0-89603-372-4*) Humana.

Neurotransmitters & Cortical Function: From Molecules to Mind. Ed. by M. Avoli et al. LC 87-37401. 632p. 1988. 130.00 (*0-306-42729-X*, Plenum Trade) Perseus Pubng.

Neurotransmitters & Epilepsy. Ed. by Phillip C. Jobe & Hugh E. Laird, II. LC 87-27579. (Contemporary Neuroscience Ser.). 390p. 1987. 125.00 (*0-89603-101-2*) Humana.

Neurotransmitters & Pain Control. Ed. by H. Akil & J. W. Lewis. (Pain & Headache Ser.: Vol. 9). (Illus.). x, 306p. 1987. 128.00 (*3-8055-4579-7*) S Karger.

Neurotransmitters & the Cerebral Circulation. E. T. Mackenzie. LC 84-15098. (L. E. R. S. Monograph Ser.: Vol. 2). (Illus.). 270p. 1984. reprint ed. pap. 83.70 (*0-608-00679-3*, 206126600009) Bks Demand.

Neurotransmitters & Their Receptors: Based on a Workshop Sponsored by the European Molecular Biology Organisation & the Weizmann Institute of Science, Rehovot, February, 1980. Ed. by U. Z. Littauer et al. LC 80-41130. (Illus.). 576p. reprint ed. pap. 178.60 (*0-608-17652-4*, 203051000069) Bks Demand.

Neurotransmitters, Comparative Aspects. T. M. Turpaev & Janos Salanki. 514p. (C). 1980. 120.00 (*963-05-2601-8*, Pub. by Akade Kiado) St Mut.

Neurotransmitters in Epilepsy. R. Fariello & G. Avanzini. Ed. by Jerome Engel, Jr. et al. LC 92-18549. (Epilepsy Research Ser.: No. 8). xvi,408p. 1992. 216.50 (*0-444-89710-0*) Elsevier.

Neurotransmitters in Neuronal Plasticity & Psychiatric Disorders: Proceedings of the 10th Workshop on Neurotransmitters & Diseases, Tokyo, Japan, 5 June, 1993. Ed. by M. Toru. (International Congress Ser.: Vol. 1061). 112p. 1994. 136.50 (*0-444-81806-5*, Excerpta Medica) Elsevier.

Neurotransmitters in the Human Brain: Proceedings of a Conference in Honor of Istyan Tork Held in New South Wales, Sydney, February 5, 1994. Ed. by George T. Paxinos et al. (Advances in Behavioral Biology Ser.: Vol. 43). (Illus.). 254p. (C). 1995. text 85.00 (*0-306-44915-3*, Kluwer Plenum) Kluwer Academic.

Neurotransmitters, Receptors, & Drug Action. Ed. by Walter B. Essman. LC 79-23862. (Illus.). 220p. 1980. text 39.50 (*0-88331-166-6*) R B Luce.

N

An Asterisk (*) at the beginning of an entry indicates that the title is appearing for the first time.

Neurotransmitters, Seizures, & Epilepsy, No. II. Ed. by Ruggero G. Fariello et al. LC 84-17997. (Illus.). 391p. 1984. reprint ed. pap. 121.30 (*0-7837-9566-1*, 206031500005) Bks Demand.

Neurotransmitters, Seizures, & Epilepsy III. Ed. by Giuseppe Nistico et al. LC 86-13104. 527p. 1986. reprint ed. pap. 163.40 (*0-608-00397-2*, 206111100007) Bks Demand.

Neurotrauma. Ed. by Raj K. Narayan et al. (Illus.). 1728p. 1996. text 245.00 (*0-07-045662-3*) McGraw-Hill HPD.

Neurotrophic Factors. Ed. by Alan A. Boulton et al. (Neuromethods Ser.: Vol. 25). (Illus.). 440p. 1993. 120.00 (*0-89603-249-3*) Humana.

Neurotrophic Factors. Ed. by Franz F. Hefti. LC 98-27067. (Handbook of Experimental Pharmacology Ser.: Vol. 134). (Illus.). 300p. 1998. 295.00 (*3-540-64614-0*) Spr-Verlag.

Neurotrophic Factors. Ed. by Sandra E. Loughlin & James H. Fallon. (Illus.). 607p. 1992. text 104.00 (*0-12-455830-5*) Acad Pr.

Neurotrophic Factors. Ed. by Yasuzo Tsukada & Eric Shooter. (Taniguchi Symposia on Brain Sciences Ser.: No. 15). 1993. 99.95 (*0-8493-7755-2*, QP552) CRC Pr.

Neurotrophin Protocols. Robert A. Rush. (Methods in Molecular Biology Ser.). 256p. 2000. 89.00 (*0-89603-699-5*) Humana.

Neurovasc Immun: Vasoactive Neurotrans & Modul-Cell Immun. Thomas C. Moore. 480p. 1992. lib. bdg. 199.00 (*0-8493-6894-4*, QP356) CRC Pr.

Neurovascular Compression of the Cranial Nerves in Neurological & Systemic Disease. Ed. by Peter J. Hamlyn. LC 98-47916. 268p. 1998. 215.50 (*0-444-82977-6*) Elsevier.

Neurovascular Neuro-Ophthalmology. M. J. Kupersmith & A. Berenstein. LC 92-49714. 1992. 310.00 (*0-387-55636-2*) Spr-Verlag.

Neurovascular Surgery. Ed. by L. Phillip Carter & Robert F. Spetzler. 1446p. 1994. text 275.00 (*0-07-011020-4*) McGraw-Hill HPD.

Neurovascular Surgery: Specialized Neurosurgical Techniques. Ed. by F. Marguth et al. (Advances in Neurosurgery Ser.: Vol. 7). (Illus.). 420p. 1979. 63.95 (*0-387-09675-2*) Spr-Verlag.

Neurypnology. James Braid. LC 75-16688. (Classics in Psychiatry Ser.). 1976. reprint ed. 23.95 (*0-405-07418-2*) Ayer.

Neusa: 9,000 Anos de Presencia Humana en el Paramo. Sergio Rivera. (SPA., Illus.). 144p. 1992. pap. 8.50 (*1-877812-28-5*, BR026) UPLAAP.

Neuschwanstein. Illus. by Joachim Bunz. (Opus Ser.: Vol. 33). (GER & ENG.). 60p. 1999. 42.00 (*3-930698-33-1*, Pub. by Edition A Menges) Natl Bk Netwk.

Neuses Paedagogisches. 5th ed. Hans H. Groothoff. (GER.). 95.00 (*3-7831-0373-8*, M-7569); 95.00 (*0-8288-7787-4*, M7569) Fr & Eur.

Neusiedlersee: The Limnology of a Shallow Lake in Central Europe. Ed. by H. Loffler. (Monographiae Biologicae: No. 37). (Illus.). x, 559p. 1980. text 310.00 (*90-6193-089-8*) Kluwer Academic.

Neustoychivoe Ravnovesia - Unstable Equilibrium: 8 Russian Poetic Texts. Tomas Venclova. LC 86-50924. (Yale Russian & East European Publications: No. 9). (RUS.). 205p. 1986. 15.00 (*0-936586-09-5*, Pub. by Yale Russian) Slavica.

Neustro Fin de Semana. Roberto M. Cossa. Ed. by Donald A. Yates. (SPA.). (Orig.). 1966. pap. text. write for info. (*0-685-15661-3*) Macmillan.

Neustro Glorioso Dios. Myron J. Houghton et al. Ed. by Richard Meyer. (Adult Sunday School Ser.). (SPA.). 95p. 1995. 4.40 (*1-879892-44-8*) Editorial Bautista.

Neuter Computer: Computers for Girls & Boys. Jo S. Sanders & Antonia Stone. LC 86-8516. 279p. (Orig.). 1986. pap. text 27.50 (*1-55570-006-3*) Neal-Schuman.

Neuter Plural in Latin Iambic & Trochaic Verse. Jessie M. Glenn. (LD Ser.: No. 30). 1939. pap. 25.00 (*0-527-00776-5*) Periodicals Srv.

Neuter Plural in Latin Lyric Verse. Elizabeth G. Zenn. (LD Ser.: No. 42). 1948. pap. 25.00 (*0-527-00788-9*) Periodicals Srv.

Neuter Plural in Vergil. John F. Gummere. (LD Ser.: No. 17). 1934. pap. 25.00 (*0-527-00763-3*) Periodicals Srv.

Neutered Mother, The Sexual Family & Other 20th Century Tragedies. Martha A. Fineman. 256p. (C). 1995. pap. 23.99 (*0-415-91027-7*, B4247) Routledge.

Neutra Houses. Ed. by Molly Siple. 128p. 1999. pap. 35.00 (*1-893329-05-4*) Really Great Bks.

Neutrabas: A Neutral Product Definition Database for Large Multifunctional Systems. Ed. by H. Nowacki et al. (Research Reports ESPRIT: Project 2010, Vol. 1). 214p. 1996. pap. 43.00 (*3-540-59300-4*) Spr-Verlag.

Neutral-Alkaline Papermaking Short Course, 1990: Peabody Hotel, Orlando, FL, October 16-18. Technical Association of the Pulp & Paper Industry. LC TS1118.N5N48. (TAPPI Notes Ser.). (Illus.). 224p. reprint ed. pap. 69.50 (*0-8357-3004-2*, 203927200011) Bks Demand.

Neutral Being Between the Sexes: Samuel Johnson's Sexual Politics. Kathleen N. Kemmerer. LC 97-53298. 160p. 1998. 31.50 (*0-8387-5387-6*) Bucknell U Pr.

Neutral Corner: Boxing Essays. A. J. Liebling. Ed. by Fred Warner & James Barbour. 245p. 1996. pap. text 12.00 (*0-86547-495-8*) N Point Pr.

Neutral Corner: Boxing Essays. A. J. Liebling. Ed. by Fred Warner & James Barbour. 256p. 1990. 19.95 (*0-86547-450-8*) N Point Pr.

Neutral Current Sheets in Plasmas. Ed. by N. G. Basov. Tr. by Dave Parsons from RUS. LC 76-17087. (Proceedings of the P. N. Lebedev Physics Institute Ser.: No. 74). (Illus.). 171p. 1976. reprint ed. pap. 53.10 (*0-608-05533-6*, 206600100006) Bks Demand.

Neutral Currents 20 Years Later: Proceedings of the International Conference. Ed. by U. Nguyen-Khac & A. M. Lutz. LC 95-109334. 500p. 1994. text 109.00 (*981-02-1752-8*) World Scientific Pub.

Neutral Europe Between War & Revolution, 1917-1923. Ed. by Hans A. Schmitt. LC 87-28724. 325p. 1988. text 35.00 (*0-8139-1153-2*) U Pr of Va.

Neutral French: The Exiles of Nova Scotia. Mrs. Williams. LC 99-223813. (Illus.). 416p. 1999. pap. 7.95 (*1-56554-473-0*) Pelican.

Neutral Ground: New Traditionalism & the American Romance Controversy. Ed. by G. R. Thompson & Eric C. Link. LC 98-51112. 256p. 1999. text 47.50 (*0-8071-2351-X*) La State U Pr.

Neutral Ground: The Andre Affair & the Background of Cooper's The Spy, 42. Bruce A. Rosenberg. LC 94-16127. (Contributions to the Study of Popular Culture Ser.: No. 42). 168p. 1994. 52.95 (*0-313-29319-8*, Greenwood Pr) Greenwood.

*__Neutral Heart.__ James McCabe. (Illus.). 192p. 2000. 54.50 (*0-7165-2691-3*, Pub. by Irish Acad Pr); pap. 24.50 (*0-7165-2718-9*, Pub. by Irish Acad Pr) Intl Spec Bk.

Neutral Interfaces in Design, Simulation, & Programming for Robotics. Ed. by I. Bey et al. (Research Reports ESPRIT, Subseries PDT, Project 5109: Vol. 1). xv, 334p. 1994. 50.95 (*0-387-57531-6*) Spr-Verlag.

Neutral Kaons. Radoje Belusevic. LC 99-18463. (Tracts in Modern Physics Ser.). 183p. 1999. 119.00 (*3-540-65645-6*) Spr-Verlag.

Neutral Models in Biology. Ed. by Antoni Hoffman & Matthew H. Nitecki. (Illus.). 176p. 1987. text 40.00 (*0-19-505099-1*) OUP.

Neutral Network Computing. Ramachandran Bharath & James Drosen. LC 94-1199. 1994. pap. 29.95 (*0-07-005145-3*) McGraw-Hill Prof.

Neutral Pion Production in Proton-Proton Collisions Close to the Kinematical Threshold. Anders Mortsell. (Uppsala Dissertations from the Faculty of Science Ser.: No. 6). (Illus.). 102p. 1995. pap. 37.50 (*91-554-3525-4*) Coronet Bks.

Neutral Proteases of Mast Cells. Ed. by L. B. Schwartz. (Monographs in Allergy: Vol. 27). viii, 166p. 1990. 148.00 (*3-8055-5162-2*) S Karger.

*__Neutral Rights & Obligations in the Anglo-Boer War.__ Robert G. Campbell. 149p. 1999. reprint ed. 50.00 (*1-56169-452-5*) Gaunt.

Neutral Sizing: A Literature Review. J. C. Roberts. (Pira Reviews of Pulp & Paper Technology Ser.). 57p. 1995. reprint ed. pap. 95.00 (*0-902799-83-5*, TS1120, Pub. by Pira Internatl) Bks Intl VA.

Neutral States & the European Community. Davis, David, Memorial Institute of International. Ed. by Sheila Harden. 176p. 1994. 49.00 (*1-85753-024-1*, Pub. by Brasseys) Brasseys.

Neutral-Supported Power Cable Assemblies with Weather-Resistant Extruded Insulation, 600 Volts. Date not set. 50.00 (*0-614-18710-9*, S-76-474-1991) Insulated Cable.

Neutral Transplantation & Regeneration. Ed. by R. B. Wallace & G. D. Das. (Proceedings in Life Sciences Ser.). (Illus.). 350p. 1985. 312.00 (*0-387-96160-7*) Spr-Verlag.

*__Neutral Upper Atmosphere.__ S. N. Ghosh. LC 00-42090. (Astrophysics & Space Science Library). 2000. write for info. (*0-7923-6434-1*) Kluwer Academic.

Neutral Zone: Backdoor to the United States. Don C. Marler. 238p. (Orig.). 1995. pap. 15.00 (*1-887745-01-7*) Dogwood TX.

Neutral Zone Campaign. Barth. 1999. per. 15.00 (*0-671-04002-2*) PB.

Neutrale Liquiditat: Zur Theorie & Praktischen Umsetzung. Dirk Lohr & Johannes Jenetzky. (GER., Illus.). 204p. 1996. 42.95 (*3-631-30786-1*) P Lang Pubng.

Neutralism: Theory & Practice. P. K. Dutta. 327p. 1978. 16.95 (*0-318-37249-5*) Asia Bk Corp.

Neutralist Tendency: Defence & the Left in Britain & Germany. Geoffrey L. Williams. (C). 1990. 45.00 (*0-907967-82-5*, Pub. by Inst Euro Def & Strat) St Mut.

Neutrality: Changing Concepts & Practices. Ed. by Alan T. Leonhard & Nicholas Mercuro. LC 88-21755. 164p. (Orig.). (C). 1988. pap. text 18.00 (*0-8191-7141-7*) U Pr of Amer.

Neutrality & International Sanctions: Sweden, Switzerland & Collective Security. John F. Ross. LC 89-32270. 262p. 1989. 59.95 (*0-275-93349-0*, C3349, Praeger Pubs) Greenwood.

Neutrality & Navicerts: Britain, the United States, & Economic Warfare, 1939-1940. Robert W. Matson. LC 93-43702. (Modern American History Ser.). 216p. 1994. text 65.00 (*0-8153-1651-8*) Garland.

*__Neutrality & Peace.__ Nicolas Politis. LC 99-45068. 1999. write for info. (*1-57588-579-4*) W S Hein.

Neutrality & Small States: The European Experience in World War Two & Beyond. Efraim Karsh. 192p. 1988. lib. bdg. 67.50 (*0-415-00507-8*) Routledge.

Neutrality & the Academic Ethic. Robert L. Simon. (Issues in Academic Ethics Ser.). 292p. (C). 1994. pap. text 71.50 (*0-8476-7954-3*); lib. bdg. 27.95 (*0-8476-7955-1*) Rowman.

Neutralization & World Politics. Cyril E. Black et al. LC 68-29388. 216p. reprint ed. pap. 67.00 (*0-8357-8967-5*, 203340000085) Bks Demand.

Neutralization of Waste Water by pH Control. Ralph L. Moore. LC 77-94491. (Instrument Society of America Monographs: No. 1). (Illus.). 177p. reprint ed. pap. 54.90 (*0-7837-6058-2*, 205250400007) Bks Demand.

Neutralized Unification of Korea in Perspective. In K. Hwang. 186p. 1980. boxed set 39.95 (*0-87073-827-5*) Transaction Pubs.

Neutralizing Memory: The Jew in Contemporary Poland. Iwona Irwin-Zarecka. 275p. (C). 1990. 39.95 (*0-88738-227-4*); pap. 24.95 (*0-88738-840-X*) Transaction Pubs.

Neutrals in Europe: Ireland. Ed. by Bo Huldt & Atis Lejins. (Scandinavian Institute of International Affairs Paper Ser.: No. 11). 130p. (Orig.). 1990. pap. 36.50 (*91-7182-937-7*) Coronet Bks.

Neutrino. James S. Allen. LC 57-5464. 178p. 1958. reprint ed. pap. 55.20 (*0-608-02870-3*, 206393400007) Bks Demand.

Neutrino Astrophysics: Proceedings of 10th Jerusalem Winter School for Theoretical Physics. John N. Bahcall et al. 1994. text 72.00 (*981-02-1367-0*) World Scientific Pub.

Neutrino, '88. Ed. by J. Schneps et al. 912p. (C). 1989. pap. 61.00 (*9971-5-0796-X*); text 169.00 (*9971-5-0778-1*) World Scientific Pub.

Neutrino, '86: Sendai, Japan, June 3-8, 1986. Ed. by T. Kitagaki. 840p. 1987. text 164.00 (*9971-5-0166-X*) World Scientific Pub.

Neutrino Interactions with Electrons & Protons. Alfred K. Mann. LC 93-23103. (Key Papers in Physics). 160p. 1993. text 54.95 (*1-56396-228-4*, AIP Pr) Spr-Verlag.

Neutrino Mass & Gauge Structure of Weak Interactions (Telemark, 1982) AIP Conference Proceedings 99, Particles & Fields Subseries 30. Vernon Barger & David Cline. LC 83-71072. 283p. 1983. lib. bdg. 34.50 (*0-88318-198-3*) Am Inst Physics.

Neutrino Mass & Low Energy Weak Interactions: Proc. of the Conference on Neutrino Mass Miniconference. V. Barger & D. B. Cline. 400p. 1985. 75.00 (*9971-5-0069-8*) World Scientific Pub.

Neutrino Mass & Related Topics: Proceedings of the 16th INS International Symposium. Ed. by Shinzi Kato & T. Ohshima. 408p. (C). 1988. text 109.00 (*9971-5-0708-0*) World Scientific Pub.

Neutrino Mass, Dark Matter, Gravitational Waves, Monopole Condensation & Light Cone Quantization: Proceedings of the International Conference on Orbis Scientae 1996 Held in Miami Beach, Florida, January 25-28, 1996. B. N. Kursunoglu et al. LC 96-43713. (Illus.). 416p. (C). 1996. text 132.00 (*0-306-45391-6*, Kluwer Plenum) Kluwer Academic.

Neutrino Masses & Neutrino Astrophysics: Proceedings of the 4th Telemark Workshop, Neutrinos from Supernova 1987. Ed. by V. Barger et al. 544p. (C). 1987. pap. 51.00 (*9971-5-0370-0*); text 137.00 (*9971-5-0367-0*) World Scientific Pub.

Neutrino, '96: Proceedings of the 17th International Conference on Neutrino Physics & Astrophysics, Helsinki, Finland, 13-19 June 1996. Ed. by K. Enqvist et al. 550p. 1998. 98.00 (*981-02-3177-6*) World Scientific Pub.

*__Neutrino Physics.__ Ed. by Klaus Winter. (Cambridge Monographs on Particle Physics, Nuclear Physics & Cosmology). (Illus.). 688p. 2000. write for info. (*0-521-65003-8*) Cambridge U Pr.

*__Neutrino Physics & Astrophysics: Proceedings of the XVIII International Conference on Neutrino Physics & Astrophysics, Takayama, Japan, 4-9 June 1998.__ International Conference on Neutrino Physics & Astrophysics Staff et al. LC 99-36371. 560p. 1999. 111.50 (*0-444-50289-0*, North Holland) Elsevier.

Neutrino Physics & Astrophysics: Proceedings of the 11th International Conference, Dortmund, FRG, June 11-16, 1984. Ed. by K. Kleinknecht & E. A. Paschos. 828p. 1984. 140.00 (*9971-966-70-0*) World Scientific Pub.

Neutrinos. Ed. by H. V. Klapdor. (Graduate Texts in Contemporary Physics Ser.). (Illus.). 350p. 1989. 79.95 (*0-387-50166-5*) Spr-Verlag.

Neutrinos. G. M. Lewis. (Wykeham Science Ser.: No. 12). 132p. 1971. pap. 18.00 (*0-85109-140-7*) Taylor & Francis.

Neutrinos. G. M. Lewis & G. A. Wheatley. LC 73-135382. (Wykeham Science Ser.: No. 12). 132p. (C). 1970. 18.00 (*0-8448-1114-9*, Crane Russak) Taylor & Francis.

Neutrinos & Other Matters: Selected Works of Frederick Reines. Ed. by W. Kropp et al. 616p. (C). 1991. text 99.00 (*981-02-0270-9*) World Scientific Pub.

Neutrinos in Astro, Particle & Nuclear Physics: Proceedings of the International School of Nuclear Physics, Erice, Italy, September 1997. Ed. by A. Faessler. (Progress in Particle & Nuclear Physics Ser.: Vol. 40). 382p. 1998. 373.50 (*0-444-82991-1*) Elsevier.

Neutrinos in Physics & Astrophysics. Chung W. Kim & Aihud Pevsner. LC 93-12385. Vol. 8. xxvi, 429p. 1993. text 80.00 (*3-7186-0566-X*); pap. text 39.00 (*3-7186-0567-8*) Gordon & Breach.

*__Neutrinos in Physics & Astrophysics.__ Paul Langacker. 1999. 179.00 (*981-02-3887-8*) WSC Inst MA Studies.

Neutrinos in Supersymmetry. J. C. Romao & J. W. Valle. 300p. 1997. 78.00 (*981-02-3275-6*) World Scientific Pub.

*__Neutrinos in the Next Millennium: Proceedings of the Johns Hopkins Workshop on Current Problems in Particle Theory 23, Baltimore, 1999, (June 10-12)__ G. Domokos & S. Khovesi-Domokos. LC 00-31993. 2000. write for info. (*981-02-4252-2*) World Scientific Pub.

Neutrinos, 1974: Philadelphia, Pa., 1974, No. 22. American Institute of Physics. Ed. by Charles Baltay. LC 74-82413. (AIP Conference Proceedings Ser.). 1974. 16.00 (*0-88318-121-5*) Am Inst Physics.

Neutron Activation Analysis. Damiaan De Soete et al. LC 73-122343. (Chemical Analysis Ser.: No. 34). (Illus.). 860p. reprint ed. pap. 200.00 (*0-608-17612-5*, 203046200069) Bks Demand.

Neutron Activation Analysis, Vol. I. K. Heydorn. 288p. 1984. 131.00 (*0-8493-5773-X*, QP534, CRC Reprint) Franklin.

Neutron Activation Analysis, Vol. II. K. Heydorn. 224p. 1984. 108.00 (*0-8493-5774-8*, QP534, CRC Reprint) Franklin.

Neutron Activation Analysis Tables: Analyses per Activation. J. C. Leclerc & A. Cornu. LC 74-77710. 72p. reprint ed. pap. 30.00 (*0-608-14048-1*, 202401400035) Bks Demand.

Neutron & Its Applications, 1982: Plenary & Invited Papers from the Conference to Mark the 50th Anniversary of the Discovery of the Neutron Held at Cambridge, 13-17 September 1982. Conference on the Neutron & Its Applications Staff. Ed. by P. Schofield. LC 82-40918. (Conference Ser.: No. 64). 536p. reprint ed. pap. 166.20 (*0-7837-3251-1*, 204327000007) Bks Demand.

Neutron & Synchrotron Radiation for Condensed Matter Studies Vol. I: Theory, Instruments & Methods. Ed. by J. Baruchel et al. 468p. 1993. pap. 59.00 (*0-387-56561-2*) Spr-Verlag.

Neutron & Synchrotron Radiation for Condensed Matter Studies Vol. II: Applications to Soft Condensed Matter & Biology. Ed. by J. Baruchel et al. 310p. 1994. 61.95 (*0-387-57693-2*) Spr-Verlag.

Neutron & Synchrotron Radiation for Condensed Matter Studies Vol. II: Applications to Solid State Physics & Chemistry, Vol. 2. Ed. by J. Baruchel et al. 321p. 1994. 61.95 (*0-387-57691-6*) Spr-Verlag.

Neutron & the Bomb: A Biography of Sir James Chadwick. Andrew Brown. LC 97-200691. (Illus.). 402p. (C). 1997. 35.00 (*0-19-853992-4*) OUP.

Neutron Beam Design, Development & Performance for Neutron Capture. Ed. by O. K. Harling et al. (Basic Life Sciences Ser.: Vol. 52). (Illus.). 364p. (C). 1990. text 132.00 (*0-306-43610-8*, Kluwer Plenum) Kluwer Academic.

Neutron Bomb: Political, Technological & Military Issues. S. T. Cohen. LC 78-63388. (Special Report Ser.). 95p. 1978. 11.95 (*0-89549-009-9*) Inst Foreign Policy Anal.

Neutron Bomb & the Premises of Power: President Carter's Neutron Bomb Decision. Michael Broer et al. (Pew Case Studies in International Affairs). 50p. (C). 1995. pap. text 3.50 (*1-56927-318-9*) Geo U Inst Dplmcy.

Neutron Bomb Controversy: A Study in Alliance Politics. Sherri L. Wasserman. LC 83-6797. (Foreign Policy Issues, a Foreign Policy Research Institute Ser.). 153p. 1983. 45.00 (*0-275-91099-7*, C1099, Praeger Pubs) Greenwood.

Neutron Capture Gamma-Ray Spectroscopy. (Proceedings Ser.). (Illus.). 708p. (Orig.). 1969. pap. 90.00 (*92-0-130369-6*, ISP235, Pub. by IAEA) Bernan Associates.

Neutron Capture Gamma-Ray Spectroscopy & Related Topics, 1981: Proceedings of the Fourth International Symposium on Neutron Capture Gamma-Ray Spectroscopy & Related Topics, Organised by the Institut Laue-Langevin & Held at the Institut des Sciences Nucleaires, Grenoble, France, 7-11 September 1981. International Symposium on Neutron Capture Gamma-R. Ed. by Till Von Egidy et al. LC 82-207144. (Conference Ser.: No. 62). 748p. reprint ed. pap. 200.00 (*0-7837-3250-3*, 204326900007) Bks Demand.

Neutron Contamination from Medical Electron Accelerators. Intro. by Warren K. Sinclair. LC 84-19848. (Report Ser.: No. 79). 132p. 1984. pap. text 35.00 (*0-913392-70-7*) NCRP Pubns.

Neutron Cross Sections Vol. 1, Pt. B: Z - 61-100: Neutron Resonance Parameters & Thermal Cross Sections. Ed. by S. F. Mughabghab et al. 652p. 1984. text 133.00 (*0-12-509711-5*) Acad Pr.

Neutron Diffraction. Ed. by H. Dachs. LC 78-2969. (Topics in Current Physics Ser.: Vol. 6). (Illus.). 1978. 48.95 (*0-387-08710-9*) Spr-Verlag.

Neutron Diffraction of Magnetic Materials. Yu A. Izyumov et al. (Illus.). 350p. (C). 1991. text 110.00 (*0-306-11030-X*, Kluwer Plenum) Kluwer Academic.

Neutron Diffraction Techniques for Nondestructive Evaluation. W. Windsor. 121p. 1991. text 245.00 (*2-88124-785-7*) Gordon & Breach.

Neutron Dynamics & Control: Proceedings. Ed. by David L. Hetrick & Lynn E. Weaver. LC 66-60098. (AEC Symposium Ser.). 611p. 1966. pap. 23.50 (*0-87079-297-0*, CONF-650413); fiche 9.00 (*0-685-01480-0*, CONF-650413) DOE.

*__Neutron Exposure Parameters for Capsule 10. 05 in the Heavy Section Steel Irradiation Program Tenth Irradiation Series.__ I. Remec. 49p. 1998. pap. 4.25 (*0-16-062958-6*) USGPO.

*__Neutron Exposure Parameters for the Dosimetry Capsule in the Heavy Section Steel Irradiation Program Tenth Irradiation Series.__ I. Remec. 47p. 1998. pap. 4.25 (*0-16-062959-4*) USGPO.

Neutron Fluence Measurements. IAEA Staff. (Technical Reports: No. 107). (Illus.). 1970. pap. 35.00 (*92-0-135070-8*, IDC107, Pub. by IAEA) Bernan Associates.

Neutron Fluence, Neutron Spectra & Kerma, No. 13. International Commission on Radiation Units & Meas. LC 75-97639. (Illus.). viii, 57p. 1969. 25.00 (*0-913394-06-8*) Intl Comm Rad Meas.

Neutron Gun. 2nd ed. Ed. by Gerry Reith. (Illus.). 72p. 1987. pap. 4.95 (*0-911627-12-X*) Neither-Nor Pr.

Neutron Induced Reaction. J. Kristiak. 1986. text 221.50 (*90-277-2214-5*) Kluwer Academic.

Neutron Interferometry. Ed. by U. Bonse & H. Rauch. (Illus.). 1980. 69.00 (*0-19-851947-8*) OUP.

*__Neutron Interferometry: Lessons in Experimental Quantum Mechanics.__ Helmut Rauch & Samuel Werner. (Oxford Series on Neutron Scattering in Condensed Matter: Vol. 12). (Illus.). 416p. 2000. text 120.00 (*0-19-850027-0*) OUP.

An Asterisk (*) at the beginning of an entry indicates that the title is appearing for the first time.

Neutron Irradiation Embrittlement of Reactor Pressure Vessel Steels. L. E. Steel. (Technical Reports: No. 163). (Illus.). 235p. 1975. pap. 45.00 (*92-0-155075-8*, IDC163, Pub. by IAEA) Bernan Associates.

Neutron Moisture Gauges. (Technical Reports: No. 112). (Illus.). (Orig.). 1970. pap. 25.00 (*92-0-165070-1*, IDC112, Pub. by IAEA) Bernan Associates.

Neutron Monitoring for Radiation Protection Purposes, Vol. 1. IAEA Staff. (Proceedings Ser.). (Illus.). 1974. pap. 55.00 (*92-0-020173-3*, ISP318-1, Pub. by IAEA) Bernan Associates.

Neutron Monitoring for Radiation Protection Purposes, Vol. 2. IAEA Staff. (Proceedings Ser.). (Illus.). 1974. pap. 75.00 (*92-0-020273-X*, ISP318-2, Pub. by IAEA) Bernan Associates.

Neutron Noise, Waves & Pulse Propagation: Proceedings. Ed. by Robert E. Uhrig. LC 66-60048. (AEC Symposium Ser.). 771p. 1967. pap. 27.75 (*0-87079-290-3*, CONF-660206); fiche 9.00 (*0-87079-291-1*, CONF-660206) DOE.

Neutron Nuclear Data Evaluation. IAEA Staff. (Technical Reports: No. 146). 124p. 1973. pap. 30.00 (*92-0-135173-9*, IDC146, Pub. by IAEA) Bernan Associates.

Neutron-Nucleus Collisions: A Probe of Nuclear Structure: Burr Oak State Park, Ohio, 1984. Ed. by J. Rapaport et al. LC 84-73216. (AIP Conference Proceedings Ser.: No. 124). 548p. 1985. lib. bdg. 52.00 (*0-88318-323-4*) Am Inst Physics.

Neutron Optics: An Introduction to the Theory of Neutron Optical Phenomena & their Applications. Varley F. Sears. (Neutron Scattering in Condensed Matter Ser.: No. 3). (Illus.). 334p. 1989. text 75.00 (*0-19-504601-3*) OUP.

Neutron Physics. G. E. Baron. (Wykeham Science Ser.: No. 2). 256p. 1970. pap. 18.00 (*0-85109-020-6*) Taylor & Francis.

Neutron Physics. Lothar Koester & A. Steyerl. LC 76-52461. (Tracts in Modern Physics Ser.). 135 p. 1977. write for info. (*0-387-08022-8*) Spr-Verlag.

Neutron Radiography. John P. Barton & Peter Von Der Hardt. 1983. text 411.50 (*90-277-1528-9*) Kluwer Academic.

*__Neutron Radiography.__ Harold Berger & Frank Iddings. (Illus.). 80p. 1998. pap. 75.00 (*1-890596-10-8*, NTIAC-SR-98-01) TX Res Inst.

N

Neutron Radiography, No. 3. Ed. by Shigenori Fujine et al. (C). 1990. text 403.00 (*0-7923-0832-8*) Kluwer Academic.

Neutron Radiography: Proceedings of the 2nd World Conference Paris, France, June 16-20, 1986. Ed. by John P. Barton et al. (C). 1987. text 357.00 (*90-277-2495-4*) Kluwer Academic.

Neutron Radiography Handbook. Peter Von Der Hardt & Heinz Rottger. x, 170p. 1981. text 85.50 (*90-277-1378-2*) Kluwer Academic.

Neutron Radiography, Including Radioscopy & Complementary Inspection Methods Using Neutrons: Proceedings of the 4th World Conference, San Francisco, California, U. S. A., May 10-16, 1992. Ed. by John P. Barton. LC 93-25896. 896p. 1993. text 288.00 (*2-88124-624-9*) Gordon & Breach.

Neutron Scattering: Argonne National Laboratory, 1981. American Institute of Physics. Ed. by John Faber, Jr. LC 82-73094. (AIP Conference Proceedings Ser.: No. 89). 397p. 1982. lib. bdg. 35.50 (*0-88318-188-6*) Am Inst Physics.

Neutron Scattering Advances & Applications. Ed. by M. M. Elcombe & T. J. Hicks. (Materials Science Forum Ser.: Vols. 27 & 28). 490p. 1988. text 183.00 (*0-87849-571-1*, Pub. by Trans T Pub) Enfield Pubs NH.

Neutron Scattering by Ferroelectric. V. L. Aksenov et al. 406p. (C). 1989. text 77.00 (*9971-5-0193-7*) World Scientific Pub.

Neutron Scattering for Materials Science Vol. 166: Materials Research Society Symposium Proceedings. Ed. by S. M. Shapiro et al. 499p. 1990. text 17.50 (*1-55899-054-2*) Materials Res.

Neutron Scattering from Hydrogen in Materials. A. Furrer. 264p. 1994. text 61.00 (*981-02-1874-5*) World Scientific Pub.

Neutron Scattering in Layered Copper-Oxide Superconductors. Albert Furrer. LC 98-29278. (Physics & Chemistry of Materials with Low-Dimensional Structures Ser.). 1998. write for info. (*0-7923-5226-2*) Kluwer Academic.

Neutron Scattering in Materials Science II, Vol. 376. Ed. by D. A. Neumann et al. (MRS Symposium Proceedings Ser.). 795p. 1995. 77.00 (*1-55899-278-2*) Materials Res.

Neutron Scattering to Radiation Constants see Encyclopaedic Dictionary of Physics

Neutron Solstice. James Axler. (Deathlands Ser.: No. 3). 256p. 1987. mass mkt. 4.99 (*0-373-63059-X*) Harlequin Bks.

Neutron Solstice. James Axler. 1997. per. 5.99 (*0-373-48597-2*, 1-48597-8) Harlequin Bks.

Neutron Sources: For Applied & Pure Nuclear Research. Ed. by S. W. Cierjacks. (Neutron Physics & Nuclear Data in Science & Technology Ser.: Vol. 2). 370p. 1983. 160.00 (*0-08-029351-4*, Pub. by Pergamon Repr) Franklin.

Neutron Spectroscopy. Yu A. Izyumov & N. A. Chernoplekov. (Illus.). 390p. (C). 1992. text 110.00 (*0-306-11033-4*, Kluwer Plenum) Kluwer Academic.

Neutron Standards & Flux Normalization: Proceedings. Ed. by Alan B. Smith. LC 77-611328. (AEC Symposium Ser.). 539p. 1971. pap. 21.25 (*0-87079-294-6*, CONF-701022); fiche 9.00 (*0-87079-295-4*, CONF-701022) DOE.

Neutron Star. Larry Niven. 1986. mass mkt. 5.99 (*0-345-33694-1*, Del Rey) Ballantine Pub Grp.

Neutron Stars. J. M. Irvine. (Oxford Studies in Physics). (Illus.). 1978. text 45.00 (*0-19-851460-3*) OUP.

Neutron Stars: Theory & Observation. Ed. by Joseph Ventura & David Pines. 600p. (C). 1991. text 264.50 (*0-7923-1397-6*) Kluwer Academic.

Neutron Stars & Their Birth Events: Proceedings of the NATO Advanced Study Institute on "Neutron Stars: Their Birth, Evolution, Radiation & Winds" Held in Erice, Sicily, Italy, September 5-17, 1988. Ed. by Wolfgang Kundt. (C). 1990. text 196.50 (*0-7923-0596-5*) Kluwer Academic.

Neutron Stars, Black Holes & Binary X-Ray Sources. Ed. by H. Gursky & Remo Ruffini. LC 75-15716. (Astrophysics & Space Science Library: No. 48). 441p. (Orig.). 1975. pap. text 88.00 (*90-277-0542-9*); lib. bdg. 182.50 (*90-277-0541-0*) Kluwer Academic.

Neutron Thermalization in Reactor Lattice Cells: An NPY-Project Report. (Technical Reports: No. 68). (Illus.). 131p. 1966. pap. 25.00 (*92-0-155266-1*, IDC68, Pub. by IAEA) Bernan Associates.

Neutron, X-Ray & Light Scattering: Introduction to an Investigative Tool for Colloidal & Polymeric Systems: Proceedings of the European School of Neutron, X-Ray & Light Scattering As an Investigative Tool for Colloidal & Polymeric Systems, Bombannes, Girone, France, 27 May-2 June, 1990. Ed. by P. Lindner & T. Zemb. (North-Holland Delta Ser.). x, 376p. 1991. 131.50 (*0-444-88946-9*, NHD 8, North Holland) Elsevier.

Neutronium Alchemist: Consolidation, 10 vols., Pt. 1. Peter F. Hamilton. 1998. mass mkt. 65.00 (*0-446-16561-1*, Aspect) Warner Bks.

Neutronium Alchemist Pt. 1: Consolidation. Peter F. Hamilton. 608p. 1998. reprint ed. mass mkt. 6.50 (*0-446-60517-4*, Pub. by Warner Bks) Little.

Neutronium Alchemist Pt. 2: Conflict. Peter F. Hamilton. 592p. 1998. mass mkt. 6.50 (*0-446-60546-8*, Pub. by Warner Bks) Little.

Neutrons & Numerical Methods - N2M. Ed. by M. R. Johnson et al. (AIP Conference Proceeding Ser.: No. 479). (Illus.). 256p. 1999. 85.00 (*1-56396-838-X*) Am Inst Physics.

Neutrons in Biology: Proceedings of a Workshop Held in Santa Fe, New Mexico, October 24-28, 1994. Ed. by Benno P. Schoenborn & Robert B. Knott. LC 96-41800. (Basic Life Sciences Ser.: Vol. 64). (Illus.). 462p. 1997. 132.00 (*0-306-45368-1*, Kluwer Plenum) Kluwer Academic.

Neutrons, Nuclei & Matter: An Exploration of the Physics of Slow Neutrons. J. Byrne. LC 95-46493. (Illus.). 788p. 1996. pap. 90.00 (*0-7503-0366-2*) IOP Pub.

Neutrophil. Ed. by J. Gary Wheeler & Jon S. Abramson. LC 92-48202. 336p. 1993. 79.50 (*0-19-963374-6*) OUP.

Neutrophil. Ed. by J. Gary Wheeler & Jon S. Abramson. LC 92-48202. (Illus.). 332p. 1993. pap. text 45.00 (*0-19-963373-8*) OUP.

Neutrophil: Cellular Biochemistry & Physiology. Ed. by Maurice B. Hallett. 288p. 1989. lib. bdg. 239.00 (*0-8493-4808-0*, QR185) CRC Pr.

Neutrophils: New Outlook for Old Cells. Ed. by Dmitry I. Gabrilovich. 280p. 1998. 58.00 (*1-86094-082-X*, Pub. by Imperial College) World Scientific Pub.

Neutrosophy: Neutrosophic Probability, Set & Logic Analytic Synthesis & Synthetic Analysis. Florentin Smarandache. LC 99-189351. (Analytic Synthesis & Synthetic Analysis Ser.). 105p. 1998. write for info. (*1-879585-63-4*) Erhus Univ Pr.

Neutrosophy: Neutrosophic Probability, Set & Logic Analytic Synthesis & Synthetic Analysis. Florentin Smarandache. LC 98-70533. 107p. reprint ed. pap. 33.20 (*0-608-20524-9*, 207177600002) Bks Demand.

Neutrotraumatology: Progress & Perspectives - Proceedings of the International Conference on Recent Advances in Neurotraumatology Porto, Portugal, November 1990. Ed. by A. Martins Da Silva et al. (Acta Neurochirugica - Supplementum Ser.: No. 55). (Illus.). 90p. 1992. 96.95 (*0-387-82378-6*) Spr-Verlag.

Neuva Familia: This Is My Child. Lucy Gordon. (Deseo Ser.). (SPA.). 1996. per. 3.50 (*0-373-35158-5*, 1-35158-4) Harlequin Bks.

Neuva Vida. J. C. Ryle. (SPA.). 220p. 1990. 5.99 (*0-85151-413-8*) Banner of Truth.

Neuve Chapelle: La Bassee. Geoff Bridger. (Battleground Europe Ser.). 1999. pap. text 16.95 (*0-85052-648-5*) Leo Cooper.

Neuvieme Congres International de Stratigraphie et de Geologie du Carbonifere: Compte Rendu: Paleontology, Paleoecology, Paleogeography, Vol. 5. Ed. by J. Thomas Dutro, Jr. & Herman W. Pfefferkorn. LC 83-19147. 556p. 1986. pap. 77.00 incl. 5.25 hd (*0-8093-1172-0*) S Ill U Pr.

Neuvieme Reunion du Sous-Comite Ouest & Centre Africain de Correlation des Sols pour la Mise en Valeur des Terres, Cotonou, 1988. (FRE.). 270p. 1990. 35.00 (*92-5-202922-2*, FF9222, Pub. by FAO) Bernan Associates.

Neuvos Amigo Spanish, 1989, Pt. 2. Harcourt Brace Staff. 1989. text 32.75 (*0-15-388291-3*) Holt R&W.

*__Nevada.__ (Switched on Schoolhouse Ser.). (Illus.). (J). 2000. pap. 24.95 (*0-7403-0280-9*) Alpha AZ.

Nevada. 1995. pap. 2.95 (*0-671-86983-3*) Macmillan.

*__Nevada.__ Alliance for Safe Driving Staff. (Career Education - Licence to Drive Ser.). 2000. 31.50 (*0-7668-2374-1*) Delmar.

Nevada. Dennis B. Fradin. (From Sea to Shining Sea Ser.). (J). 1998. pap. text 7.95 (*0-516-26280-7*) Childrens.

Nevada. Dennis B. Fradin & Judith B. Fradin. LC 95-13419. (Illus.). 64p. (J). (gr. 3-5). 1995. lib. bdg. 26.00 (*0-516-03828-1*) Childrens.

Nevada. Steve Gerber. LC 99-209771. (Illus.). 157p. 1999. pap. text 14.95 (*1-56389-518-8*, Pub. by DC Comics) Time Warner.

Nevada. Paul Joseph. LC 97-16738. (United States Ser.). (Illus.). 32p. (J). 1998. lib. bdg. 19.93 (*1-56239-867-9*, Checkerboard Library) ABDO Pub Co.

Nevada. Patricia K. Kummer. LC 98-3225. (One Nation Ser.). (Illus.). 48p. (J). (gr. 3-7). 1998. 19.00 (*0-7368-0022-0*, Cpstone High Low) Capstone Pr.

*__Nevada.__ Krista McLuskey. (American States Ser.). (Illus.). 32p. (J). (gr. 3-7). 2000. write for info. (*1-930954-60-3*) Weigl Pubs.

Nevada. Karen Sirvaitis. (Illus.). 72p. (J). 1995. pap. text 5.95 (*0-8225-9701-2*) Lerner Pub.

Nevada. Karen Sirvaitis. Ed. by Lerner Geography Department Staff. (Hello U. S. A. Ser.). (Illus.). 72p. (J). (gr. 3-6). 1992. lib. bdg. 19.95 (*0-8225-2719-7*, Lerner Publctns) Lerner Pub.

*__Nevada__ R. Conrad Stein. LC 99-28016. (America the Beautiful Ser.). 2000. 32.00 (*0-516-21041-6*) Childrens.

Nevada. Kathleen Thompson. LC 95-25730. (Portrait of America Library). 48p. (YA). (gr. 4-8). 1996. pap. text 5.95 (*0-8114-7454-2*) Raintree Steck-V.

Nevada. Kathleen Thompson. LC 95-25730. (Portrait of America Library). (Illus.). 48p. (YA). (gr. 3-6). 1996. lib. bdg. 22.83 (*0-8114-7348-1*) Raintree Steck-V.

Nevada. David Thomson. 1998. pap. 14.00 (*0-679-77758-X*) Vin Bks.

Nevada. rev. ed. Dee Lillegard & Wayne Stoker. LC 90-34665. (America the Beautiful Ser.). (Illus.). 144p. (J). (gr. 5-8). 1992. lib. bdg. 28.00 (*0-516-00474-3*) Childrens.

Nevada, 27. Capstone Press Geogra Staff. (One Nation Ser.). (J). 1998. 19.00 (*0-516-21478-0*) Childrens.

Nevada: A Bicentennial History. Robert Laxalt. LC 91-31281. (Illus.). 176p. 1991. reprint ed. pap. 14.95 (*0-87417-179-2*) U of Nev Pr.

Nevada: A Geography. Earl W. Kersten. (Westview Geographies of the United States Ser.). (C). 1996. text 35.00 (*0-89158-988-0*); pap. text 20.00 (*0-86531-482-9*) Westview.

Nevada: A Guide to the Silver State. Federal Writers' Project Staff. (American Guidebook Ser.). 1940. reprint ed. 79.00 (*0-403-02178-2*) Somerset Pub.

Nevada: A Guide to the Silver State. Federal Writers' Project Staff & Writers Program-WPA Staff. (American Guide Ser.). 1989. reprint ed. lib. bdg. 69.00 (*0-7812-1027-5*, 1027) Rprt Serv.

Nevada: An Annotated Bibliography. Stanley W. Paher. (Illus.). 585p. 1980. 95.00 (*0-913814-26-1*) Nevada Pubns.

Nevada: Desert Lows & Mountain Highs. Larry Prosor & Richard Moreno. Ed. by Laurel H. Lippert. (Illus.). 174p. 1994. 39.95 (*1-885515-00-6*) Fineline Productions.

Nevada: Magnificent Wilderness. Photos by Scott T. Smith. (Illus.). 128p. 1996. 14.98 (*1-56579-153-3*) Westcliffe Pubs.

Nevada: Off the Beaten Path: A Guide to Unique Places. 2nd ed. Donna Peck. LC 99-29027. (Off the Beaten Path Ser.). (Illus.). 225p. (Orig.). 1999. pap. text 12.95 (*0-7627-0460-8*) Globe Pequot.

Nevada: The Authorized Edition. Zane Grey. 1976. 26.95 (*0-8488-1026-0*) Amereon Ltd.

Nevada: The Authorized Edition. Zane Grey. LC 95-18179. vii, 367p. (C). 1995. pap. 12.00 (*0-8032-7054-2*, Bison Books) U of Nebr Pr.

Nevada: This Is Our Land. rev. ed. Nancy B. Miluck. (Illus.). 200p. (Orig.). (YA). (gr. 7 up). 1994. reprint ed. pap. 15.00 (*0-9606382-7-X*) Dragon Ent.

Nevada & Other State Greats (Biographies) Carole Marsh. (Carole Marsh Nevada Bks.). (Illus.). (J). 1994. pap. 19.95 (*1-55609-821-9*); lib. bdg. 29.95 (*1-55609-820-0*); disk 29.95 (*1-55609-822-7*) Gallopade Intl.

Nevada & Utah see Atlas of Historical County Boundaries

Nevada Angler's Guide: Fish Tails in the Sagebrush. Richard Dickerson. LC 98-132820. (Illus.). 156p. 1997. pap. 14.95 (*1-57188-100-X*) F Amato Pubns.

Nevada Atlas & Gazetteer. David Delorme. LC 96-675303. (Illus.). 1996. pap. 16.95 (*0-89933-228-5*, AA-000020-000) DeLorme Map.

Nevada Bandits, Bushwackers, Outlaws, Crooks, Devils, Ghosts, Desperadoes & Other Assorted & Sundry Characters! Carole Marsh. (Illus.). (J). 1994. pap. 19.95 (*0-7933-0744-9*); lib. bdg. 29.95 (*0-7933-0745-7*); disk 29.95 (*0-7933-0746-5*) Gallopade Intl.

Nevada "BIO" Bingo! 24 Must Know State People for Kids to Learn about While Having Fun! Carole Marsh. (Bingo! Ser.). (Illus.). (J). (gr. 2-8). 1998. pap. 14.95 (*0-7933-8606-3*) Gallopade Intl.

Nevada Biographical & Genealogical Sketch Index. J. Carlyle Parker & Janet G. Parker. LC 86-12556. 96p. 1986. 23.95 (*0-934153-02-7*, OCLC 13642809) Marietta Pub.

*__Nevada Birds.__ James Kavanagh. (Pocket Naturalist Ser.). (Illus.). 1999. 5.95 (*1-58355-006-2*, Pub. by Waterford WA) Falcon Pub Inc.

*__Nevada Bluff.__ Grant Devereaux. 288p. 2000. 19.95 (*0-9701466-0-4*); pap. 12.95 (*0-9701466-1-2*) Athenean.

Nevada Bookstore Book: A Surprising Guide to Our State's Bookstores & Their Specialties for Students, Teachers, Writers & Publishers. Carole Marsh. (Carole Marsh Nevada Bks.). (Illus.). 1994. pap. 19.95 (*0-7933-2940-X*); lib. bdg. 29.95 (*0-7933-2939-6*); disk 29.95 (*0-7933-2941-8*) Gallopade Intl.

*__Nevada Business Directory, 1999-2000.__ rev. ed. American Business Directories Staff. 752p. 1999. boxed set 375.00 incl. cd-rom (*0-7687-0158-9*) Am Busn Direct.

Nevada Census Index, 1880 Mortality Schedule. (Illus.). lib. bdg. 30.00 (*0-89593-423-X*, Accel Indexing) Genealogical Srvcs.

Nevada Census Index, 1890: Union Veterans. Ronald V. Jackson. (Illus.). lib. bdg. 60.00 (*0-89593-692-5*, Accel Indexing) Genealogical Srvcs.

Nevada Census Index, 1870 Mortality Schedule. (Illus.). lib. bdg. 30.00 (*0-89593-422-1*, Accel Indexing) Genealogical Srvcs.

Nevada Civil Practice Manual. 4th ed. State Bar of Nevada Staff. LC 99-184601. 951p. 1998. 75.00 (*0-327-00761-3*, 6723311) LEXIS Pub.

Nevada Classic Christmas Trivia: Stories, Recipes, Activities, Legends, Lore & More! Carole Marsh. (Carole Marsh Nevada Bks.). (Illus.). (J). 1994. pap. 19.95 (*0-7933-0747-3*); lib. bdg. 29.95 (*0-7933-0748-1*); disk 29.95 (*0-7933-0749-X*) Gallopade Intl.

Nevada Coastales. Carole Marsh. (Carole Marsh Nevada Bks.). (J). 1994. lib. bdg. 29.95 (*0-7933-7293-3*) Gallopade Intl.

Nevada Coastales. Carole Marsh. (Carole Marsh Nevada Bks.). (Illus.). (J). 1994. pap. 19.95 (*1-55609-815-4*); lib. bdg. 29.95 (*1-55609-814-6*); disk 29.95 (*1-55609-816-2*) Gallopade Intl.

Nevada Code Citator 98 Edition. 1600p. 1998. write for info. (*0-327-07058-7*, 4133610) LEXIS Pub.

Nevada Competency-Based High School Diploma Program. Jack Rudman. (Admission Test Ser.: ATS-67). 1994. pap. 23.95 (*0-8373-5067-0*) Nat Learn.

Nevada Competency-Based High School Diploma Program (CHSD) Jack Rudman. (Admission Test Ser.: Vol. 67). 43.95 (*0-8373-5167-7*) Nat Learn.

Nevada Corporation Handbook: Effectively Using Nevada Corporations for Privacy, Asset Protection, & Tax Strategies. 7th ed. Derek G. Rowley. 336p. 1998. pap. 69.95 (*1-886683-01-8*) Strategic NV.

*__Nevada Corporation Handbook: Effectively Using nevada Corporations for Privacy, Asset, Protection & Tax Strategies.__ 8th ed. Derek G. Rowley. (Eighth Edition). 352p. 2000. pap. 69.95 (*1-886683-03-4*) Strategic NV.

Nevada Corporation Law & Practice. Keith P. Bishop. LC 93-39070. (National Corporation Law Ser.). 1993. 110.00 (*0-13-108499-2*) Aspen Law.

Nevada Corporations, Partnerships & Associations Law Annotated, with Cd. 361p. pap. 37.50 (*0-327-10452-X*) LEXIS Pub.

Nevada Corporations, Partnerships & Associations Law, 1993-94 Edition. annot. ed. Amy Gutmann & Dennis Thompson. 422p. 27.50 (*0-614-05917-8*, MICHIE) LEXIS Pub.

Nevada County, California, 1880 History Index. David A. Comstock & Ardis H. Comstock. LC 79-115328. 84p. 1979. pap. 17.50 (*0-933994-00-1*) Comstock Bon.

Nevada County Narrow Gauge. Gerald Best. 216p. 1998. 39.95 (*0-911581-46-4*) Heimburger Hse Pub.

Nevada County Vital Statistics, 1850-1869: Births, Marriages, Separations, Divorces, Naturalizations & Deaths in Nevada County, California. David A. Comstock & Ardis H. Comstock. (Nevada County Pioneers Ser.: No. 1). iv, 104p. (Orig.). 1996. pap. 17.50 (*0-933994-16-8*) Comstock Bon.

Nevada Court Rules Annotated Supplement: NV Court Rules 5-98 Supplement. 100p. 1998. pap. write for info. (*0-327-05006-3*, 45542-151) LEXIS Pub.

Nevada Cowboy Dad: Family Matters. Dorsey Kelley. (Romance Ser.: No. 1371). 1999. per. 3.50 (*0-373-19371-8*, 1-19371-3) Silhouette.

*__Nevada Crime in Perspective 2000.__ Ed. by Kathleen O'Leary Morgan & Scott E. Morgan. 22p. 2000. spiral bd. 19.00 (*0-7401-0327-X*) Morgan Quitno Corp.

Nevada Crime Perspective, 1998. Ed. by Kathleen O'Leary Morgan & Scott E. Morgan. 20p. 1998. pap. 19.00 (*1-56692-927-X*) Morgan Quitno Corp.

Nevada Crime Perspectives, 1999. Kathleen O'Leary Morgan. 22p. 1999. spiral bd. 19.00 (*0-7401-0127-7*) Morgan Quitno Corp.

Nevada Criminal & Traffic Law Manual, 1993 Edition. 27.50 (*0-614-05918-6*, MICHIE) LEXIS Pub.

*__Nevada Criminal & Traffic Manual: 1999-2000 Edition.__ 1101p. 1999. pap. 38.00 incl. cd-rom (*0-327-10176-8*, 2850114) LEXIS Pub.

Nevada "Crinkum-Crankum" A Funny Word Book about Our State. Carole Marsh. (Carole Marsh Nevada Bks.). (Illus.). (J). 1994. pap. 19.95 (*0-7933-4893-5*); lib. bdg. 29.95 (*0-7933-4892-7*); disk 29.95 (*0-7933-4894-3*) Gallopade Intl.

Nevada Desert. Sessions S. Wheeler. LC 72-123581. (Illus.). (Orig.). 1970. pap. 6.95 (*0-87004-205-X*) Caxton.

Nevada Dingbats! Bk. 1: A Fun Book of Games, Stories, Activities & More about Our State That's All in Code! for You to Decipher. Carole Marsh. (Carole Marsh Nevada Bks.). (Illus.). (J). (gr. 3-12). 1994. pap. 19.95 (*0-7933-3858-1*); lib. bdg. 29.95 (*0-7933-3857-3*); disk 29.95 (*0-7933-3859-X*) Gallopade Intl.

Nevada Directory of Maps & Aerial Photo Resources. Mary B. Ansari & Linda P. Newman. LC 83-26068. (Occasional Papers: No. 11). 164p. 1984. pap. 15.00 (*0-939112-13-2*) Western Assn Map.

Nevada Discovery Guide: A Remarkably Useful Travel Companion for Motorists, RVers & Other Explorers. 2nd ed. Don W. Martin & Betty W. Martin. (Discovery Guide Ser.). (Illus.). 416p. 1996. pap. 15.95 (*0-942053-21-4*) Pine Cone Pr NV.

Nevada Drifter. Jackie Merritt. (Desire Ser.). 1994. per. 2.99 (*0-373-05866-7*, 1-05866-8) Silhouette.

Nevada Education: Laying the Groundwork. unabridged ed. Lezlie Porter. Ed. by Elizabeth Sexton. 29p. 1997. 10.00 (*1-886306-14-1*) Nevada Policy.

Nevada Education Law. Richard F. Daugherty & Charles P. Cockerill. 266p. 1998. 32.00 (*1-56534-072-8*) Ed Law Assn.

An Asterisk (*) at the beginning of an entry indicates that the title is appearing for the first time.

Nevada Environmental Law Handbook. 3rd ed. Lionel Sawyer & Collins Staff et al. LC 98-119332. (State Environmental Law Ser.). 351p. 1997. pap. text 89.00 (*0-86587-567-7*) Gov Insts.

Nevada Facts & Factivities. Carole Marsh. (Carole Marsh State Bks.). (Illus.). (J). (gr. 4-7). 1996. pap., teacher ed. 19.95 (*0-7933-7903-2*, C Marsh) Gallopade Intl.

***Nevada Facts & Symbols.** Karen Bush Gibson. LC 00-22774. (States & Their Symbols Ser.). (Illus.). 24p. (J). (ps-3). 2000. lib. bdg. 15.93 (*0-7368-0641-5*, Hilltop Bks) Capstone Pr.

Nevada Federal Census Index, 1880. Ronald V. Jackson. (Illus.). 1979. lib. bdg. 105.00 (*0-89593-691-7*, Accel Indexing) Genealogical Srvcs.

Nevada Federal Census Index, 1870 (Every Name) Ronald V. Jackson. (Illus.). 1979. lib. bdg. 65.00 (*0-89593-690-9*, Accel Indexing) Genealogical Srvcs.

Nevada Federal Census Index, 1860. Ronald V. Jackson. (Illus.). lib. bdg. 60.00 (*0-89593-689-5*, Accel Indexing) Genealogical Srvcs.

Nevada Federal Census Index, 1900. (Illus.). lib. bdg. 120.00 (*0-89593-424-8*, Accel Indexing) Genealogical Srvcs.

Nevada Federal Census Index, 1910. Ronald V. Jackson. (Illus.). lib. bdg. 155.00 (*0-89593-693-3*, Accel Indexing) Genealogical Srvcs.

Nevada Festival Fun for Kids! Carole Marsh. (Carole Marsh Nevada Bks.). (Illus.). (J). (gr. 3-12). 1994. pap. 19.95 (*0-7933-4011-X*); lib. bdg. 29.95 (*0-7933-4010-1*) Gallopade Intl.

Nevada Festival Fun for Kids! Carole Marsh. (Carole Marsh Nevada Bks.). (Illus.). (YA). (gr. 3-12). 1994. disk 29.95 (*0-7933-4012-8*) Gallopade Intl.

Nevada Gaming Law. 2nd ed. Lionel Sawyer & Collins Staff. LC 94-72895. xl, 442p. 1995. write for info. (*0-9644121-0-1*) L Sawyer & Collins.

Nevada "GEO" Bingo! 38 Must Know State Geography Facts for Kids to Learn While Having Fun! Carole Marsh. (Bingo! Ser.). (Illus.). (J). (gr. 2-8). 1998. pap. 14.95 (*0-7933-8607-1*) Gallopade Intl.

Nevada Ghost Town Trails. Mickey Broman. LC 72-94635. 1989. 5.95 (*0-935182-09-8*) Gem Guides Bk.

Nevada Ghost Towns & Mining Camps. Stanley W. Paher. (Illus.). 500p. 1970. 49.95 (*0-913814-04-0*) Nevada Pubns.

Nevada Ghost Towns & Mining Camps: An Illustrated Atlas, 2 vols., Set. Stanley W. Paher. (Illus.). 208p. 1993. 29.95 (*0-913814-11-3*) Nevada Pubns.

Nevada Ghost Towns & Mining Camps: An Illustrated Atlas, Vol. 1. Stanley W. Paher. (Illus.). 104p. 1993. pap. 14.95 (*0-913814-09-1*) Nevada Pubns.

Nevada Ghost Towns & Mining Camps: An Illustrated Atlas, Vol. 2. Stanley W. Paher. (Illus.). 104p. 1993. pap. 14.95 (*0-913814-10-5*) Nevada Pubns.

Nevada Government! The Cornerstone of Everyday Life in Our State! Carole Marsh. (Carole Marsh Nevada Bks.). (Illus.). (J). (gr. 3-12). 1996. pap. 19.95 (*0-7933-6266-0*); lib. bdg. 29.95 (*0-7933-6265-2*); disk 29.95 (*0-7933-6267-9*) Gallopade Intl.

***Nevada Health Care in Perspective 2000.** Ed. by Kathleen O'Leary Morgan & Scott E. Morgan. 21p. 2000. spiral bd. 19.00 (*0-7401-0227-3*) Morgan Quitno Corp.

Nevada Health Care Perspective, 1998. Ed. by Kathleen O'Leary Morgan & Scott E. Morgan. 20p. 1998. pap. 19.00 (*1-56692-827-3*) Morgan Quitno Corp.

***Nevada Health Care Perspective, 1999.** Ed. by Kathleen O'Leary Morgan. 21p. 1999. spiral bd. 19.00 (*0-7401-0077-7*) Morgan Quitno Corp.

***Nevada Heat.** large type ed. Ann Carberry. 416p. 1999. 31.99 (*0-7089-4130-3*) Ulverscroft.

Nevada "HISTO" Bingo! 42 Must Know State History Facts for Kids to Learn While Having Fun! Carole Marsh. (Bingo! Ser.). (Illus.). (J). (gr. 2-8). 1998. pap. 14.95 (*0-7933-8608-X*) Gallopade Intl.

Nevada History! Surprising Secrets about Our State's Founding Mothers, Fathers & Kids! Carole Marsh. (Carole Marsh Nevada Bks.). (Illus.). (J). (gr. 3-12). 1996. pap. 19.95 (*0-7933-6113-3*); lib. bdg. 29.95 (*0-7933-6112-5*); disk 29.95 (*0-7933-6114-1*) Gallopade Intl.

Nevada History Coloring Books: Nevada's Native Americans. Nancy C. Miluck. (Illus.). 48p. (J). (gr. k-5). 1992. pap. text 4.00 (*0-9606382-4-5*) Dragon Ent.

Nevada History Coloring Books: The 1st Settlers. Nancy C. Miluck. (Illus.). 48p. (J). (gr. k-6). 1993. pap. 4.00 (*0-9606382-5-3*) Dragon Ent.

Nevada History Coloring Books: The 20th Century. Nancy C. Miluck. (Illus.). 48p. (Orig.). (J). (gr. k-5). 1992. pap. text 4.75 (*0-9606382-3-7*) Dragon Ent.

Nevada Hot Air Balloon Mystery. Carole Marsh. (Carole Marsh Nevada Bks.). (Illus.). (J). (gr. 2-9). 1994. 29.95 (*0-7933-2570-6*); pap. 19.95 (*0-7933-2571-4*); disk 29.95 (*0-7933-2572-2*) Gallopade Intl.

Nevada Hot Zones! Viruses, Diseases, & Epidemics in Our State's History. Carole Marsh. (Hot Zones! Ser.). (Illus.). (J). (gr. 3-12). 1998. pap. 19.95 (*0-7933-8913-5*); lib. bdg. 29.95 (*0-7933-8912-7*) Gallopade Intl.

Nevada in Perspective, 1998. Ed. by Kathleen O'Leary Morgan & Scott E. Morgan. 24p. 1998. pap. 19.00 (*1-56692-877-X*) Morgan Quitno Corp.

Nevada in Perspective, 1999. Ed. by Kathleen O'Leary Morgan. 26p. 1999. spiral bd. 19.00 (*1-56692-977-6*) Morgan Quitno Corp.

***Nevada in Perspective 2000.** Ed. by Kathleen O'Leary Morgan & Scott E. Morgan. 26p. 2000. spiral bd. 19.00 (*0-7401-0277-X*) Morgan Quitno Corp.

***Nevada in Your Future: The Complete Relocation Guide for Job-Seekers, Retirees & Snowbirds.** Don W. Martin & Betty W. Martin. (Illus.). 256p. 2000. pap. 16.95 (*0-942053-30-3*, Pub. by Pine Cone Pr NV) Publishers Group.

Nevada Indian Dictionary for Kids! Carole Marsh. (Carole Marsh State Bks.). (J). (gr. 2-9). 1996. 29.95 (*0-7933-7728-5*, C Marsh); pap. 19.95 (*0-7933-7729-3*, C Marsh) Gallopade Intl.

***Nevada Investment & Business Guide: Business, Investment, Export-Import Opportunities, 50 vols., Vol. 28.** Global Investment Center, USA Staff. (U. S. Regional Investment & Business Library-99: Vol. 28). (Illus.). 350p. 1999. pap. 59.95 (*0-7397-1127-X*) Intl Business Pubns.

Nevada Jeopardy! Answers & Questions about Our State! Carole Marsh. (Carole Marsh Nevada Bks.). (Illus.). (J). (gr. 3-12). 1994. pap. 19.95 (*0-7933-4164-7*); lib. bdg. 29.95 (*0-7933-4163-9*); disk 29.95 (*0-7933-4165-5*) Gallopade Intl.

***Nevada Jim Lacy: Beyond the Mongolian Rim.** Romer Zane Grey. 224p. 1999. mass mkt. 4.50 (*0-8439-4635-0*, Leisure Bks) Dorchester Pub Co.

Nevada "Jography" A Fun Run Thru Our State! Carole Marsh. (Carole Marsh Nevada Bks.). (Illus.). (J). 1994. pap. 19.95 (*1-55609-803-0*); lib. bdg. 29.95 (*1-55609-802-2*); disk 29.95 (*1-55609-804-9*) Gallopade Intl.

Nevada Kid's Cookbook: Recipes, How-To, History, Lore & More! Carole Marsh. (Carole Marsh Nevada Bks.). (Illus.). (J). 1994. pap. 19.95 (*0-7933-0756-2*); lib. bdg. 29.95 (*0-7933-0757-0*); disk 29.95 (*0-7933-0758-9*) Gallopade Intl.

Nevada Land Surveying Law: Questions & Answers. John E. Keen. 49p. (C). 1995. pap. text 25.00 (*1-56569-033-8*) Land Survey.

Nevada Law of Corporations & Business Organizations. Keith P. Bishop. LC 97-2473. 1000p. 1997. 155.00 (*1-56706-329-2*) Aspen Law.

Nevada Library Book: A Surprising Guide to the Unusual Special Collections in Libraries Across Our State for Students, Teachers, Writers & Publishers - Includes Reproducible Mailing Labels Plus Activities for Young People! Carole Marsh. (Carole Marsh Nevada Bks.). (Illus.). 1994. pap. 19.95 (*0-7933-3090-4*); lib. bdg. 29.95 (*0-7933-3089-0*); disk 29.95 (*0-7933-3091-2*) Gallopade Intl.

***Nevada Light Blue Humor.** Rick Gamble. 240p. 1999. pap. 15.95 (*0-7414-0205-X*) Buy Books.

Nevada Lost Mines & Buried Treasures. Douglas McDonald. (Illus.). 128p. 1981. pap. 7.95 (*0-913814-37-7*) Nevada Pubns.

***Nevada Manufacturers Register 2000.** Ed. by Frances L. Carlsen. 374p. 2000. pap. 61.00 (*1-55600-691-8*) Database Pub Co.

Nevada Math! How It All Adds up in Our State. Carole Marsh. (Carole Marsh Nevada Bks.). (Illus.). (J). (gr. 3-12). 1996. pap. 19.95 (*0-7933-6572-4*); lib. bdg. 29.95 (*0-7933-6571-6*) Gallopade Intl.

Nevada Media Book: A Surprising Guide to the Amazing Print, Broadcast & Online Media of Our State for Students, Teachers, Writers & Publishers - Includes Reproducible Mailing Labels Plus Activities for Young People! Carole Marsh. (Carole Marsh Nevada Bks.). (Illus.). 1994. pap. 19.95 (*0-7933-3246-X*); lib. bdg. 29.95 (*0-7933-3245-1*); disk 29.95 (*0-7933-3247-8*) Gallopade Intl.

Nevada Medicaid Vol. 1: Constructive Reform of the State System. James R. Cantwell & Michael Armitage. 26p. 1996. spiral bd. 10.00 (*1-886306-15-X*) Nevada Policy.

Nevada Mountain Ranges. George Wuerthner. LC 92-5795. (Nevada Geographic Ser.: No. 1). (Illus.). 104p. (Orig.). 1992. pap. 9.95 (*1-56037-014-9*) Am Wrld Geog.

Nevada Mystery Van Takes Off! Bk. 1: Handicapped Nevada Kids Sneak Off on a Big Adventure. Carole Marsh. (Carole Marsh Nevada Bks.). (Illus.). (J). (gr. 3-12). 1994. 29.95 (*0-7933-5045-X*); pap. 19.95 (*0-7933-5046-8*); disk 29.95 (*0-7933-5047-6*) Gallopade Intl.

Nevada Newspaper Days: A History of Journalism in the Silver State. Jake Highton. LC 90-80653. (Illus.). 350p. (C). 1990. 25.00 (*0-9623048-1-6*); text 14.95 (*0-9623048-2-4*) Heritage West.

***Nevada 1999 Replacement Index, 2 vols.** 2270p. 1999. write for info. (*0-327-09945-3*, 4553713) LEXIS Pub.

Nevada Notary Law Primer. 2nd ed. National Notary Association Editors. LC 95-78812. 124p. 1997. pap. 16.00 (*0-933134-94-0*) Natl Notary.

Nevada Pattern Jury Instructions - Civil. State Bar of Nevada Staff. 210p. 1986. pap. 45.00 (*0-87215-976-0*, 68405-10, MICHIE) LEXIS Pub.

Nevada Place Names: A Geographical Dictionary. Helen S. Carlson. LC 74-13877. 296p. 1974. reprint ed. pap. 84.40 (*0-608-01266-1*, 2062015) Bks Demand.

Nevada Place Names: A Geographical Dictionary. Helen S. Carlson. LC 74-13877. (Illus.). 296p. 1974. reprint ed. pap. 21.95 (*0-87417-094-X*) U of Nev Pr.

Nevada Politics & Government: Conservatism in an Open Society. Don W. Driggs & Leonard E. Goodall. LC 95-43756. (Politics & Governments of the American States Ser.). (Illus.). xxviii, 235p. 1996. text 50.00 (*0-8032-1703-X*); pap. text 22.00 (*0-8032-6604-9*) U of Nebr Pr.

Nevada Post Card Album: Photographic Views of Nevada, 1903-1928. Robert Greenwood. (Illus.). xii, 196 p. 1998. pap. 24.95 (*0-9664632-0-X*) F Holabird.

Nevada Post Offices: An Illustrated History. James Gamett & Stanley W. Paher. (Illus.). 160p. 1982. 30.00 (*0-913814-57-1*) Nevada Pubns.

Nevada Printing History: A Bibliography of Imprints & Publications, 1858-1880. Robert D. Armstrong. LC 81-7422. (Illus.). 428p. 1982. 50.00 (*0-87417-063-X*) U of Nev Pr.

Nevada Printing History: A Bibliography of Imprints & Publications, 1881-1890. Robert D. Armstrong. LC 88-33955. (Illus.). 408p. 1982. 50.00 (*0-87417-124-5*) U of Nev Pr.

Nevada Quiz Bowl Crash Course! Carole Marsh. (Carole Marsh Nevada Bks.). (Illus.). (J). 1994. pap. 19.95 (*1-55609-818-9*); lib. bdg. 29.95 (*1-55609-817-0*); disk 29.95 (*1-55609-819-7*) Gallopade Intl.

Nevada Real Estate License Law: Analysis, Interpretation & Sample Questions. 3rd ed. Van Reken. 288p. (C). 1996. pap. 21.73 (*0-13-777418-4*) P-H.

Nevada Revised Statutes, Annotated. 1986. write for info. (*0-87215-973-6*, MICHIE) LEXIS Pub.

Nevada Revised Statutes Annotated: 1998 Replacement, Vol. 1. annot. ed. 707p. 1998. write for info. (*0-327-05037-3*, 45410-11) LEXIS Pub.

Nevada Revised Statutes Annotated: 1998 Replacement, Vol. 19. annot. ed. 1019p. 1998. write for info. (*0-327-05038-1*, 45501-11) LEXIS Pub.

***Nevada Revised Statutes Annotated: 1999 Cumulative Supplement.** 4700p. 1999. pap. write for info. (*0-327-09910-0*, 4553613) LEXIS Pub.

***Nevada Revised Statutes Annotated Vol. 3: 1999 Replacement.** 1000p. 1999. write for info. (*0-327-09911-9*, 4542112) LEXIS Pub.

***Nevada Revised Statutes Annotated Vol. 10: 1999 Replacement.** 1000p. 1999. write for info. (*0-327-09912-7*, 4545611) LEXIS Pub.

Nevada Revised Statutes Annotated, 1998 NRSA Advance Service Pamphlet, No. 3. 40p. 1998. pap. write for info. (*0-327-05441-7*, 45553-13) LEXIS Pub.

Nevada Revised Statutes Annotated, 1998 Advance Service & Interim Supplement Pamphlet, No. 3. annot. ed. Ed. by Karen Walker. 60p. 1998. pap. write for info. (*0-327-05781-5*, 45553-13) LEXIS Pub.

Nevada Revised Statutes Annotated, 1998 Advance Service Pamphlet: 1998 Advance Service Pamphlet, No. 2. 48p. 1998. pap. write for info. (*0-327-05029-2*, 45552-14) LEXIS Pub.

Nevada Revised Statutes Annotated 1999 Advance Service Pamphlet, No. 1. annot. rev. ed. 40p. 1998. pap. write for info. (*0-327-07051-X*, 4555115) LEXIS Pub.

Nevada Revised Statutes Annotated 1999 Replacement Volume, Vol. 15. annot. ed. 800p. 1999. write for info. (*0-327-08649-1*, 45480-12) LEXIS Pub.

***Nevada Revised Statutes Annotated, 1999 NRSA Advance Service, Pamphlet, No. 3.** 120p. 1999. Price not set. (*0-327-08898-2*, 4555315) LEXIS Pub.

Nevada Rollercoasters! Carole Marsh. (Carole Marsh Nevada Bks.). (Illus.). (J). (gr. 3-12). 1994. pap. 19.95 (*0-7933-5309-2*); lib. bdg. 29.95 (*0-7933-5308-4*) Gallopade Intl.

Nevada Rollercoasters! Carole Marsh. (Carole Marsh Nevada Bks.). (Illus.). (YA). (gr. 3-12). 1994. disk 29.95 (*0-7933-5310-6*) Gallopade Intl.

Nevada School Law: Cases & Materials. 4th ed. Gerald Kops. LC 98-67473. 664p. (C). 1998. per. 48.95 (*0-7872-5333-2*) Kendall-Hunt.

Nevada School Trivia: An Amazing & Fascinating Look at Our State's Teachers, Schools & Students! Carole Marsh. (Carole Marsh Nevada Bks.). (Illus.). (J). 1994. pap. 19.95 (*0-7933-0753-8*); lib. bdg. 29.95 (*0-7933-0754-6*); disk 29.95 (*0-7933-0755-4*) Gallopade Intl.

Nevada Silly Basketball Sportsmysteries, Vol. 1. Carole Marsh. (Carole Marsh Nevada Bks.). (Illus.). (J). 1994. pap. 19.95 (*0-7933-0750-3*); lib. bdg. 29.95 (*0-7933-0751-1*); disk 29.95 (*0-7933-0752-X*) Gallopade Intl.

Nevada Silly Basketball Sportsmysteries, Vol. 2. Carole Marsh. (Carole Marsh Nevada Bks.). (Illus.). (J). 1994. pap. 19.95 (*0-7933-1768-1*); lib. bdg. 29.95 (*0-7933-1767-3*); disk 29.95 (*0-7933-1769-X*) Gallopade Intl.

Nevada Silly Football Sportsmysteries, Vol. 1. Carole Marsh. (Carole Marsh Nevada Bks.). (Illus.). (J). 1994. pap. 19.95 (*1-55609-809-X*); lib. bdg. 29.95 (*1-55609-808-1*); disk 29.95 (*1-55609-810-3*) Gallopade Intl.

Nevada Silly Football Sportsmysteries, Vol. 2. Carole Marsh. (Carole Marsh Nevada Bks.). (Illus.). (YA). (J). 1994. pap. 19.95 (*1-55609-812-X*); lib. bdg. 29.95 (*1-55609-811-1*); disk 29.95 (*1-55609-813-8*) Gallopade Intl.

Nevada Silly Trivia! Carole Marsh. (Carole Marsh Nevada Bks.). (Illus.). (J). 1994. pap. 19.95 (*1-55609-800-6*); lib. bdg. 29.95 (*1-55609-799-9*); disk 29.95 (*1-55609-801-4*) Gallopade Intl.

Nevada Silver. Joan Hohl. 256p. 1994. per. 4.99 (*1-55166-002-4*, 1-66002-6, Mira Bks) Harlequin Bks.

Nevada Silver. Joan Hohl. 1994. mass mkt. 4.50 (*0-373-48284-1*, 5-48284-9) Harlequin Bks.

Nevada Silver Rounds, 1964-1989. Dave Andrews & Rusty King. (Illus.). 80p. 1998. pap. 14.95 (*0-932151-03-5*) Gypsyfoot Ent.

Nevada Spelling Bee! Score Big by Correctly Spelling Our State's Unique Names. Carole Marsh. (Carole Marsh Nevada Bks.). (Illus.). (J). (gr. 3-12). 1996. pap. 19.95 (*0-7933-6725-5*) Gallopade Intl.

Nevada Spelling Bee! Score Big by Correctly Spelling Our State's Unique Names. Carole Marsh. (Carole Marsh Nevada Bks.). (Illus.). (YA). (gr. 3-12). 1996. lib. bdg. 29.95 (*0-7933-6724-7*) Gallopade Intl.

Nevada State Census, 1875. 1990. 275.00 (*0-89593-605-4*, Accel Indexing) Genealogical Srvcs.

***Nevada State Children's Home, 1870-1920: Admission Records.** Doreen Robinson. 346p. 2000. pap. 35.00 (*1-58211-229-0*) Quintin Pub RI.

Nevada State Constitution: A Reference Guide, 18. Michael W. Bowers. LC 93-20347. (Reference Guides to the State Constitutions of the United States Ser.: No. 18). 216p. 1993. lib. bdg. 75.00 (*0-313-27977-2*, BNV) Greenwood.

Nevada Statutes. annot. rev. ed. Barbara M. Benedict. write for info. (*0-614-05919-4*, MICHIE) LEXIS Pub.

Nevada Test Site. Geological Society of America, Rocky Mountain Sect. Ed. by Edwin B. Eckel. LC 68-56611. (Geological Society of America, Memoir Ser.: No. 110). 298p. reprint ed. pap. 92.40 (*0-608-15642-6*, 20318120077) Bks Demand.

Nevada Timeline: A Chronology of Nevada History, Mystery, Trivia, Legend, Lore & More. Carole Marsh. (Carole Marsh Nevada Bks.). (Illus.). (J). (gr. 3-12). 1994. pap. 19.95 (*0-7933-5960-0*); lib. bdg. 29.95 (*0-7933-5959-7*); disk 29.95 (*0-7933-5961-9*) Gallopade Intl.

Nevada Tombstone Record Book: Southern Nevada, Vol. I. Richard B. Taylor. 752p. 1986. 35.00 (*0-9616633-1-6*) Beehive NV.

Nevada Towns & Tales: North, Vol. 1. Ed. by Stanley W. Paher. (Illus.). 224p. 1981. 19.95 (*0-913814-41-5*) Nevada Pubns.

Nevada Towns & Tales: South, Vol. 2. Ed. by Stanley W. Paher. (Illus.). 224p. 1982. 19.95 (*0-913814-45-8*) Nevada Pubns.

Nevada Trade Tokens. Len Hoskins et al. 1990. pap. 17.95 (*0-913814-25-3*) Nevada Pubns.

Nevada Treasure Hunter's Ghost Town Guide. Theron L. Fox. (Illus.). 1960. pap. 4.95 (*0-913814-16-4*) Nevada Pubns.

Nevada Trivia. Kenneth A. Bouton & E. Lyn Bouton. LC 99-18326. 192p. 1999. pap. 6.95 (*1-55853-730-9*) Rutledge Hill Pr.

Nevada Trivia Book. 2nd rev. ed. Rich Moreno. LC 98-70069. (Illus.). 220p. 1998. pap. 10.95 (*1-889786-00-4*) Gem Guides Bk.

Nevada 2000! Coming Soon to a Calendar Near You - The 21st Century! - Complete Set of AL 2000 Items. Carole Marsh. (Two Thousand! Ser.). (Illus.). (J). (gr. 3-12). 1998. pap. 75.00 (*0-7933-9365-5*); lib. bdg. 85.00 (*0-7933-9366-3*) Gallopade Intl.

Nevada 2000! Coming Soon to a Calendar near You--The 21st Century! Carole Marsh. (Two Thousand! Ser.). (Illus.). (J). (gr. 3-12). 1998. pap. 19.95 (*0-7933-8760-4*); lib. bdg. 29.95 (*0-7933-8759-0*) Gallopade Intl.

Nevada UFO's & Extraterrestrials! A Look at the Sightings & Science in Our State. Carole Marsh. (Carole Marsh Nevada Bks.). (Illus.). (J). (gr. 3-12). 1997. pap. 19.95 (*0-7933-6419-1*); lib. bdg. 29.95 (*0-7933-6418-3*) Gallopade Intl.

Nevada Vascular Plant Types & Their Collectors. Arnold Tiehm. LC 96-4543. (Memoirs Ser.: No. 77). 1996. 19.50 (*0-89327-401-1*) NY Botanical.

Nevada Wilderness Areas & Great Basin National Park: A Hiking & Backpacking Guide. Michael C. White. LC 97-11921. (Illus.). 325p. (Orig.). 1997. pap. 14.95 (*0-89997-194-6*) Wilderness Pr.

Nevada Wildlife Record Book. 2nd ed. Nevada Wildlife Record Book Committee Staff. (Illus.). 346p. 1990. 29.00 (*0-9622467-0-0*) NV WRBC.

Nevada Wildlife Record Book, 1990. 2nd ed. Nevada Wildlife Record Book Committee Staff. (Illus.). 250p. 1990. write for info. (*0-318-64890-3*) NV WRBC.

Nevada Wildlife Viewing Guide. Jeanne L. Clark. LC 93-17494. (Watchable Wildlife Ser.). (Illus.). 88p. (Orig.). 1993. pap. 6.95 (*1-56044-207-7*) Falcon Pub Inc.

Nevada's Black Rock Desert. Sessions S. Wheeler. LC 76-6648. 1978. pap. 9.95 (*0-87004-258-0*) Caxton.

Nevada's Golden Age of Gambling. Albert W. Moe. LC 96-92834. (Illus.). 120p. (Orig.). 1996. pap. 14.95 (*0-9655215-0-8*) Nevada Collectables.

Nevada's Health: An Analysis of Health Care Options for Nevada's Working Uninsured. Judy Cresanta & Jill B. Ludke. 20p. 1993. 10.00 (*1-886306-04-4*) Nevada Policy.

Nevada's Living Ghost Towns. Richard Moreno. (Illus.). 32p. 1994. pap. 4.95 (*1-890136-03-4*) Nevada Magazine.

Nevada's (Most Devastating!) Disasters & (Most Calamitous!) Castastrophies! Carole Marsh. (Carole Marsh Nevada Bks.). (Illus.). (J). 1994. pap. 19.95 (*0-7933-0741-4*); lib. bdg. 29.95 (*0-7933-0742-2*); disk 29.95 (*0-7933-0743-0*) Gallopade Intl.

Nevada's Northwest Corner: The Black Rock Country of Northern Washoe & Humboldt Counties. Raymond M. Smith. 180p. 1996. pap. 20.00 (*1-883301-06-8*) R M Smith.

***Nevada's Paul Laxalt: A Memoir.** Paul Laxalt. 425p. 2000. 27.50 (*0-930083-09-1*) J Bacon Co.

Nevada's Red Rock Canyon: The Story Behind the Scenery. Cheri C. Madison. LC 88-81169. (Illus.). 48p. (Orig.). 1988. pap. 7.95 (*0-88714-025-4*) KC Pubns.

Nevada's Turbulent '50's: Decade of Political & Economic Change. Mary E. Glass. LC 80-25651. (Wilbur S. Shepperson Series in History & Humanities: No. 15). (Illus.). ix, 152p. (Orig.). 1981. pap. 14.95 (*0-87417-062-1*) U of Nev Pr.

Nevada's Turbulent Yesterday. Don Ashbaugh. LC 63-16925. (Illus.). 349p. 1981. reprint ed. 26.95 (*0-87026-024-3*) Westernlore.

Nevada's Twentieth Century Mining Boom: Tonopah, Goldfield, Ely. Russell R. Elliott. LC 87-35727. (Illus.). 360p. 1988. reprint ed. pap. 12.95 (*0-87417-133-4*) U of Nev Pr.

Nevada's Unsolved Mysteries (And Their "Solutions") Includes Scientific Information & Other Activities for Students. Carole Marsh. (Carole Marsh Nevada Bks.). (Illus.). (J). (gr. 3-12). 1994. pap. 19.95 (*0-7933-5807-8*); lib. bdg. 29.95 (*0-7933-5806-X*); disk 29.95 (*0-7933-5808-6*) Gallopade Intl.

Nevada's Valley of Fire: The Story Behind the Scenery. G. William Fiero. Tr. by Brigitte Morales. LC 75-18136. (GER.). 1996. pap. 8.95 (*0-88714-806-9*) KC Pubns.

Nevada's Valley of Fire: The Story Behind the Scenery. rev. ed. G. William Fiero. LC 84-52882. (Illus.). 48p. 1985. pap. 7.95 (*0-916122-17-4*) KC Pubns.

N

Nevalinna Theory & Complex Differential Equations. Ilpo Laine. LC 92-35852. (Studies in Mathematics: Vol. 15). viii, 341p. (C). 1992. lib. bdg. 92.95 (*3-11-013422-5*) De Gruyter.

*__Neve Campbell.__ Kathleen Tracy. (Illus.). 200p. 2000. pap. 16.95 (*1-55022-401-8*, Pub. by ECW) LPC InBook.

*__Neve Campbell: An Unauthorized Biography.__ Elina Furman. (Illus.). 224p. 2000. pap. text 14.95 (*1-58063-126-6*) Renaissance.

Never . . . Never Give Up. Great Quotations Publishing Staff. 366p. 1995. pap., spiral bd. 6.50 (*1-56245-176-6*) Great Quotations.

Never a Bride. large type ed. Diana Hamilton. (Harlequin Romance Ser.). 1996. 19.95 (*0-263-14356-2*) Thorndike Pr.

Never a Bride: (Bachelor Arms) Joann Ross. LC 95-13564. (Temptation Ser.). 218p. 1995. per. 3.25 (*0-373-25637-X*, 1-25637-9) Harlequin Bks.

Never a Bride (Wedlocked!) Diana Hamilton. LC 96-505. 186p. 1995. per. 3.25 (*0-373-11775-2*) Harlequin Bks.

*__Never a Child (The Beginning) A Different Perspective on the Creation of Heaven & Earth.__ Deborah L. Fisher. 192p. 2000. pap. write for info. (*1-888701-23-4*) Jarrett Pr.

Never a Dad Around. Geoffrey L. Bradley. (Illus.). 14p. (J). (gr. k-4). 1999. pap. 2.99 (*0-9667940-2-8*) World of WISDOM.

Never a Day Off: Surviving Single Parenthood. Elizabeth H. Rigdon. (Christian Living Ser.). 60p. 1990. pap. 3.50 (*0-8341-1376-7*) Beacon Hill.

Never a Dream Come True. Sunny Youngblood. (Illus.). 152p. 1999. pap. 14.00 (*0-8059-4552-0*) Dorrance.

Never a Dull Card. John Carfi & Cliff Carle. (Illus.). 160p. (Orig.). 1992. pap. 5.95 (*0-918259-40-1*) CCC Pubns.

Never a Dull Moment: Bessie & Ray Gibbs. Ed. by Betty L. Gibbs. 176p. 1992. pap. write for info. (*0-943909-09-0*) Gibbs Assocs.

Never a Ho-Hum Day: Stories of a Kentucky Hill Country Veterinarian & His Doctorin' John V. Martin. LC 97-78018. (Illus.). 210p. 1998. 22.95 (*1-57860-052-9*) Guild Pr IN.

Never a Lady. Barbara Dawson Smith. 352p. 1996. mass mkt. 6.99 (*0-312-95936-2*) St Martin.

*__Never a Lady.__ Marlene Suson. 384p. 2000. mass mkt. 5.99 (*0-380-80567-7*) Morrow Avon.

N

*__Never Accept a Gift with Air Holes: Garfield's Holiday Tips & Quips.__ Jim Davis. LC 99-177992. (Illus.). 48p. 1998. 4.95 (*0-8362-5280-2*) Andrews & McMeel.

Never Again. Flora Nwapa. 90p. 1992. 24.95 (*0-86543-318-6*); pap. 9.95 (*0-86543-319-4*) Africa World.

Never Again! Harold Weisberg. 480p. 1995. pap. 15.95 (*0-7867-0206-0*) Carroll & Graf.

Never Again: A Darker Shade of Crimson. Jo-Ann Power. 306p. 1998. mass mkt. 6.50 (*0-671-00899-4*, Pocket Star Bks) PB.

*__Never Again: A History of the Holocaust.__ Martin Gilbert. (Illus.). 192p. 2000. text 29.95 (*0-7893-0409-0*) Universe.

*__Never Again: A Spoken-Word Theatrical Piece.__ 56p. 1999. pap. 7.50 (*0-9675432-0-7*) Nia Bks.

Never Again Good-Bye. Terri Blackstock. LC 96-17275. (Second Chances Ser.: No. 1). 208p. 1996. pap. 8.99 (*0-310-20707-X*) Zondervan.

Never Again Goodbye. large type ed. Terri Blackstock. LC 98-42040. (Christian Fiction Ser.). 1999. 23.95 (*0-7862-1675-1*) Thorndike Pr.

Never Again Once More. Mary B. Morrison. Date not set. write for info. (*0-9674001-6-3*) Booga Bear.

Never Again Scream: Me, Speak? - Eeek! 12 Proven Ways You Can Become a Succesful Speaker. Don Vieweg. 264p. 1998. per. 12.00 (*1-884487-07-6*) Bellman Pubng.

Never Again the Burning Times: Paganism Revived. Loretta Orion. (Illus.). 322p. (C). 1995. pap. text 13.95 (*0-88133-835-4*) Waveland Pr.

Never Alone. 1959. pap. 0.70 (*0-686-23470-7*) Rose Pub MI.

Never Alone. Lyn Cote. (Love Inspired Ser.). 1998. per. 4.50 (*0-373-87030-2*, 1-87030-2) Harlequin Bks.

Never Alone. Albert Krassner. 77p. (Orig.). 1986. pap. 4.95 (*0-912061-10-3*) Veridon Edns.

Never Alone. M. McCoy Smith. (Freestyle Ser.). (J). (gr. 7). 4.99 (*1-85792-020-1*, Pub. by Christian Focus) Spring Arbor Dist.

Never Alone: A Personal Way to God. Joseph F. Girzone. 128p. 1995. pap. 9.95 (*0-385-47683-3*) Doubleday.

Never Alone: Dating from the Biblical Perspective. Harold Davis. 108p. 1993. reprint ed. pap. text 15.00 (*0-9638553-0-1*) KJAC Pubng.

Never Alone: God's Word for Single Adults. Melanie Jongsma. (Friendship Ser.). (Illus.). 48p. (Orig.). 1993. pap. write for info. (*1-882536-18-5*, A100-0058) Bible League.

Never Alone - A True Story: The Amazing Story of a Husband's Love & Devotion from Beyond the Grave. Dinah M. Harrison. LC 97-92284. (Illus.). 144p. 1997. pap. 12.95 (*1-891012-00-2*) DMarie Inc.

Never Always Happens. Emanuel Falzon. 184p. 1998. pap. 14.00 (*0-8059-4489-3*) Dorrance.

*__Never an Island A History of California.__ Ward McAfee. LC 98-46781. (West Coast Studies). 1999. write for info. (*0-89370-808-9*) Millefleurs.

Never an Outbreak: The New Breakthrough Method That Stops the Herpes Virus & Eliminates All Outbreaks. William Fharel. 72p. (Orig.). 1996. pap. 16.95 (*0-9651875-0-0*) Printo Pubng.

*__Never Anything Too Easy: N. A. T. E.__ Nathaniel J. Henry. (Illus.). 128p. 1999. 29.95 (*0-9670584-5-7*, Pub. by NNSJA Pubg) ACCESS Pubs Network.

Never Appear to Choose, but with a Quick Eye, Select the Best. Martha A. Greer. LC 86-91352. (Illus.). 200p. 1986. 12.50 (*0-9617179-0-4*) M A Greer.

Never As Good As the First Time: Love a Second Time Around. 2nd ed. Jonathan M. Hicks. v, 200p. 1996. pap. 12.00 (*0-9655421-1-4*) The Studio Pub.

Never As Strangers. Laini Mataka. LC 88-82280. 60p. (Orig.). 1988. pap. 7.95 (*0-933121-75-X*) Black Classic.

Never Ask a Man the Size of His Spread: A Cowgirl's Guide to Life. Gladiola Montana. LC 92-43920. (Illus.). 144p. 1993. pap. 6.95 (*0-87905-554-5*) Gibbs Smith Pub.

Never Ask Delilah for a Trim . . . And Other Good Advice. Martha Bolton. LC 98-8573. 220p. (YA). 1998. pap. 10.99 (*1-56955-048-4*) Servant.

*__Never Ask Permission: Elisabeth Scott Bocock of Richmond (A Memoir)__ Mary Buford Hitz. LC 00-25951. (Illus.). 256p. 2000. 27.95 (*0-8139-1993-2*) U Pr of Va.

Never at Fault: The Drawings of William Trost Richards. Linda S. Ferber. LC 88-120453. (Illus.). 128p. (Orig.). 1986. pap. 5.00 (*0-943651-08-5*) Hudson Riv.

Never at Rest: A Biography of Isaac Newton. Richard S. Westfall. LC 79-26294. 928p. 1983. pap. text 39.95 (*0-521-27435-4*) Cambridge U Pr.

Never at War: Why Democracies Will Not Fight One Another. Spencer R. Weart. LC 98-2664. 432p. 1998. 35.00 (*0-300-07017-9*) Yale U Pr.

*__Never at War: Why Democracies Will Not Fight One Another.__ Spencer R. Weart. 432p. 2000. pap. 18.00 (*0-300-08298-3*) Yale U Pr.

Never Babysit the Hippopotamuses! Doug Johnson. LC 93-18341. (Illus.). 32p. (J). (ps-2). 1995. 14.95 (*0-8050-1873-5*, Bks Young Read) H Holt & Co.

Never Babysit the Hippopotamuses! Doug Johnson. 1997. pap. 5.95 (*0-8050-5029-9*, Bks Young Read) H Holt & Co.

Never Babysit the Hippopotamuses! Doug Johnson. 1997. 11.15 (*0-606-11676-1*, Pub. by Turtleback) Demco.

Never Balance Your Checkbook on Tuesday: And 300 More Financial Lessons You Can't Afford Not to Know. Nancy Dunnan. LC 98-44042. 256p. (Orig.). 1999. pap. 9.00 (*0-06-273659-0*) HarpC.

Never Be. Lynn Salem & Josie Stewart. (Illus.). 8p. (J). (gr. k-1). 1992. pap. 3.75 (*1-880612-00-3*) Seedling Pubns.

Never Be Afraid: A Jew in the Maquis. Bernard Mednicki & Ken Wachsberger. LC 96-95134. 212p. 1997. pap. 16.00 (*1-879461-04-8*) Azenphony Pr.

Never-Be-Bored Book: Quick Things to Make When There's Nothing to Do. Judith L. Lehne. LC 92-16529. (Illus.). 128p. (J). 1992. 17.95 (*0-8069-1254-5*) Sterling.

Never Be Lied to Again. David J. Lieberman. LC 98-18634. 224p. 1998. text 19.95 (*0-312-18634-7*) St Martin.

Never Be Lied to Again. 2nd ed. David J. Lieberman. 204p. 1999. pap. 12.95 (*0-312-20428-0*) St Martin.

Never Be Short of Cash Again! Richard Starr. (Illus.). 250p. (Orig.). 1994. pap. 39.00 (*1-888221-09-7*) Results Now.

Never Be the Horse. Beckian F. Goldberg. (Akron Series in Poetry). 1999. pap. 13.95 (*1-884836-54-2*) U Akron Pr.

*__Never Be the Horse.__ Beckian F. Goldberg. (Poetry Ser.). 1999. 24.95 (*1-884836-53-4*) U Akron Pr.

Never Be Tired Again! David C. Gardner & Grace J. Beatty. LC 89-45791. (Illus.). 384p. 1990. reprint ed. pap. 13.00 (*0-06-097298-X*, Perennial) HarperTrade.

*__Never Been Here Before? A Genealogists' Guide to the Family Records Centre.__ 2nd rev. ed. Jane Cox. LC 98-161164. 119p. 1999. pap. 10.95 (*1-873162-41-3*) PRO Pubns.

Never Been Kissed. Raymond Crenshaw. 256p. 1999. mass mkt. 5.99 (*0-06-102013-3*) HarpC.

Never Before. Jo-Ann Power. 1998. per. 6.50 (*0-671-00898-6*) PB.

Never Before in History: America's Inspired Birth. Gary Amos & Richard Gardiner. LC 98-72936. (Pandas Publications: A Series about Central Questions). (Illus.). 213p. (YA). (gr. 8-10). 1998. text 27.50 (*0-914513-51-6*) Haughton.

*__Never Before, Never Again: The Autobiography of Eddie Robinson.__ Eddie Robinson & Richard Lapchick. LC 99-36158. 320p. 1999. text 24.95 (*0-312-24224-7*) St Martin.

Never Begin a New Paragraph in the Middle of a Sentence. Gail Shadwell & Caryl Turner. 144p. 1993. pap. 12.00 (*0-9638536-0-0*) Elken Pubng.

*__Never Beyond Hope: How God Touches & Uses Imperfect People.__ J. I. Packer & Carolyn Nystrom. 144p. 2000. 14.99 (*0-8308-2232-1*) InterVarsity.

Never Boil Your Alarm Clock. Cynthia Bentley & Charles Fleming, Jr. 289p. 1990. write for info. (*0-9632511-0-4*) Chase Pubs.

Never Bring a Pigout Home. Date not set. 5.95 (*0-89868-355-6*); pap. 4.95 (*0-89868-410-2*); lib. bdg. 10.95 (*0-89868-354-8*) ARO Pub.

Never Buried. Edie Claire. 256p. 1999. mass mkt. 5.99 (*0-451-19788-7*, Sig) NAL.

Never Call Retreat. Bruce Catton. (Centennial History of the Civil War Ser.: Vol. 3). 572p. 1976. 33.95 (*0-8488-1266-2*) Amereon Ltd.

Never Call Retreat. Bruce Catton. (Centennial History of the Civil War Ser. : Vol. 3). 450p. 1991. reprint ed. lib. bdg. 31.95 (*0-89966-800-3*) Buccaneer Bks.

Never Call Your Broker on Monday: And 300 Other Financial Lessons You Can't Afford Not To Know. Nancy Dunnan. LC 96-3018. 256p. (Orig.). 1997. pap. 8.50 (*0-06-270164-9*, Harper Ref) HarpC.

Never-Ceasing Search. Francis O. Schmitt. LC 89-85487. (Memoirs Ser.: Vol. 188). (Illus.). 400p. (C). 1990. 30.00 (*0-87169-188-4*, M188-SCF) Am Philos.

Never Come Down. Michelle Black. 270p. 1996. pap. 9.95 (*1-57502-210-9*, P0849) Morris Pubng.

Never Come Down. rev. ed. Michelle Black. LC 96-60498. 300p. 1997. pap. 12.00 (*0-9658014-0-3*) WinterSun Pr.

Never Come Morning. Nelson Algren. 1995. 5.60 (*0-87129-597-0*, N40) Dramatic Pub.

Never Come Morning. Nelson Algren. LC 96-14829. 336p. 1987. reprint ed. pap. 10.95 (*1-888363-22-3*) Seven Stories.

*__Never Complain, Never Explain.__ Louise Atherton. 1999. 16.00 (*1-873162-13-8*, Pub. by PRO Pubns) Midpt Trade.

Never Confuse a Memo with Reality: And Other Business Lessons too Simple Not to Know. Richard A. Moran. 96p. 1993. pap. 48.00 (*0-88730-679-9*, HarpBusn) HarpInfo.

Never Confuse a Memo with Reality: And Other Business Lessons Too Simple Not to Know. Richard A. Moran. LC 93-14376. 160p. 1993. pap. 8.00 (*0-88730-669-1*, HarpBusn) HarpInfo.

*__Never Confuse a Memo with Reality: And Other Business Lessons Too Simple Not to Know.__ Richard A. Moran. 1999. pap. 6.95 (*0-06-662033-3*, HarpBusn) HarpInfo.

*__Never Cooked before Gotta Cook Now! A Total Guide for The Beginning Cook, 1.__ Leonard F. Charla. LC 98-93626. 1999. pap. text 15.95 (*0-9664732-0-5*) Countinghse Pr.

Never Cross a Vampire. Stuart M. Kaminsky. (Toby Peters Mystery Ser.). 192p. 1995. mass mkt. 5.50 (*0-446-40190-0*, Mysterious Paperbk) Warner Bks.

*__Never Cross a Vampire.__ Stuart M. Kaminsky. 2000. 12.00 (*0-7434-0713-X*, Pub. by ibooks) S&S Trade.

Never Cry Alone: Someone Somewhere Knows How You Feel, You Are Not Alone. Cynthia D. Grimmett. (Illus.). (YA). (gr. 7-12). 1995. 14.95 (*0-9643303-0-X*) C D Grimmett.

Never Cry "Arp!" And Other Stories of the Great Outdoors. Patrick F. McManus. 160p. (YA). (gr. 6 up). 1995. 15.95 (*0-8050-4662-3*) H Holt & Co.

Never Cry Wolf. Farley Mowat. 19.95 (*0-89190-823-4*) Amereon Ltd.

Never Cry Wolf. Farley Mowat. 176p. 1983. mass mkt. 5.99 (*0-553-27396-5*) Bantam.

Never Cry Wolf. Farley Mowat. 176p. 1985. pap. 6.99 (*0-7704-2137-7*) Bantam.

Never Cry Wolf. Farley Mowat. (J). 1979. 10.60 (*0-606-02207-4*, Pub. by Turtleback) Demco.

Never Cry Wolf. Patricia Rosemoor. (Intrigue Ser.: Vol. 483). 1998. per. 3.99 (*0-373-22483-4*, 1-22483-1) Harlequin Bks.

Never Die Alone. Donald Goines. 224p. 1995. mass mkt. 6.99 (*0-87067-997-X*) Holloway.

*__Never Die Easy: The Autobiography of Walter Payton.__ Walter Payton & Don Yaeger. (Illus.). 288p. 2000. 24.95 (*0-679-46331-3*) Villard Books.

Never Die in January. large type ed. Alan Scholefield. 1994. 27.99 (*0-7089-3157-X*) Ulverscroft.

Never Die Young; or How to Survive ACLS! 2nd ed. David P. Doernbach & Jane Huff. (Illus.). 195p. 1993. pap. text 24.00 (*0-9638043-0-8*) Vital Signs.

Never Dies the Dream. Margaret Landon. lib. bdg. 24.95 (*0-8488-1990-X*) Amereon Ltd.

*__Never Diet Again Workbook.__ Joan Boehm. (Illus.). 146p. 1999. pap. 12.95 (*0-9672084-0-8*, 119) Pers Train Cons.

Never Distrust an Asparagus. Elihu Blotnick. (Complete Blot Ser.). (Illus.). 1979. pap. 4.95 (*0-915090-10-4*) Calif Street.

*__Never Done: A History of American Housework.__ Susan Strasser. LC 00-37023. (Illus.). 384p. 2000. pap. 16.00 (*0-8050-6617-9*, Owl) H Holt & Co.

Never Done Dreamin' Janis Flores. LC 96-306. 299p. 1995. per. 3.75 (*0-373-70662-6*, 1-70662-1) Harlequin Bks.

Never Doubt My Love. large type ed. Daisy Thomson. (Romance Ser.). 1994. pap. 16.99 (*0-7089-7623-9*, Linford) Ulverscroft.

*__. . . Never Dream.__ Scott Charles Adams. Ed. by Carolyn West. 240p. 1999. pap. 15.00 (*0-9673045-0-4*) SC Adams.

Never Drink Coffee from Your Saucer . . . And Other Tips on Socially Correct Dining. Sheila M. Long. 96p. (Orig.). 1996. pap. 7.95 (*0-8362-2169-9*) Andrews & McMeel.

Never Eat Anything Bigger Than Your Head. B. Kliban. LC 75-43837. (Illus.). 160p. (Orig.). 1976. pap. 5.95 (*0-911104-67-4*, 093) Workman Pub.

*__Never Eat In.__ David Leddick. 2000. 24.00 (*1-85242-655-1*) Serpents Tail.

Never Eat More Than You Can Lift, & Other Food Quotes & Quips: 1,500 Notable Quotables about Edibles & Potables. Sharon T. Herbst. LC 96-50017. 384p. 1997. 20.00 (*0-553-06901-2*) Broadway BDD.

Never Eat Your Heart Out. Judith Moore. LC 96-36024. 328p. 1997. 23.00 (*0-374-22073-5*) FS&G.

Never Eat Your Heart Out. Judith Moore. 336p. 1998. pap. text 13.00 (*0-86547-518-0*) N Point Pr.

*__Never Ending.__ Marianne K. Martin. LC 98-48233. 256p. 1999. pap. 11.95 (*1-56280-247-X*) Naiad Pr.

*__Never Ending Cigarettes.__ Scott C. Holstad. 36p. 1999. pap. 5.00 (*1-889289-37-X*) Ye Olde Font Shoppe.

Never-Ending Day. Lissa H. Johnson. LC 97-6251. (China Tate Ser.: Bk. 7). (J). (gr. 6-11). 1997. pap. 5.99 (*1-56179-538-0*) Focus Family.

Never-Ending Greenness. Neil Waldman. 1997. 16.00 (*0-614-27574-1*, Wm Morrow) Morrow Avon.

Never-Ending Greenness. Neil Waldman. LC 96-14844. (Illus.). 40p. (J). 1997. 16.00 (*0-688-14479-9*, Wm Morrow) Morrow Avon.

Never-Ending Greenness. Neil Waldman. LC 96-14844. (Illus.). 40p. (J). 1997. lib. bdg. 15.93 (*0-688-14480-2*, Wm Morrow) Morrow Avon.

Never-Ending Quest: Poetry. Steven Herberts. LC 98-8071. 88p. 1998. text 14.95 (*0-7734-2837-2*) E Mellen.

Never-Ending Search for the Public Interest. Emmette S. Redford. (Reprint Series in Social Sciences). (C). 1993. reprint ed. pap. text 5.00 (*0-8290-3667-9*, PS-236) Irvington.

Never-Ending War: Terrorism in the '80's. Christopher Dobson & Ronald Payne. LC 86-24093. 392p. 1989. reprint ed. pap. 121.60 (*0-608-02854-1*, 206391800007) Bks Demand.

Never Enough. Brian Martin. 1994. 26.95 (*0-7737-2688-8*) Stoddart Publ.

*__Never Enough: Breaking the Spirit of Poverty.__ David Holdaway. LC 99-56751. 2000. pap. 9.99 (*0-8307-2469-9*, Regal Bks) Gospel Lght.

Never Enough Words: How Americans Invented Expressions As Ingenious, Ornery & Colorful As Themselves. Jeffery McQuain. LC 99-12356. 1999. 24.95 (*0-679-45804-2*) Random Ref & Info.

Never, Ever, Serve Sugary Snacks on Rainy Days: The Official Little Instruction Book for Teachers of Young Children. Shirley C. Raines. LC 95-12515. 96p. (Orig.). 1995. pap. 6.95 (*0-87659-175-6*) Gryphon Hse.

*__Never, Ever Shake a Baby.__ large type ed. Jane Scoggins Bauld. (Illus.). 32p. (J). (gr. k-6). 1999. pap. write for info. (*0-9651123-1-4*, Pub. by E W Allen) Any Baby Can.

Never Fade Away: The Kurt Cobain Story. Dave Thompson. 1994. mass mkt. 5.99 (*0-312-95463-8*) St Martin.

Never Far from Water. Rusty Mckenzie. LC 98-96813. 80p. 1998. pap. write for info. (*0-9668455-0-1*) Sand Bottom.

Never Fear, Snake My Dear! Rolf Siegenthaler. Tr. by J. Alison James from GER. LC 98-42991. (Illus.). 32p. (J). (gr. k-3). 1999. 15.95 (*0-7358-1103-2*, Pub. by North-South Bks NYC) Chronicle Bks.

Never Fear, Snake My Dear! Rolf Siegenthaler. Tr. by J. Alison James from GER. LC 98-42991. (Illus.). (J). (gr. k-3). 1999. lib. bdg. 15.88 (*0-7358-1104-0*, Pub. by North-South Bks NYC) Chronicle Bks.

Never Fear the IRS Again: A Defensive Handbook for Dealing with the IRS. Richard E. Clark. 272p. 1997. pap. 29.95 (*0-9666428-0-5*) T Jefferson Pr.

Never Fight Fair! Inside the Legendary U. S. Navy Seals, Their Own True Stories. Orr Kelly. 1996. mass mkt. 6.99 (*0-671-53266-9*) PB.

Never Fight Fair! Navy Seal's Stories of Combat & Adventure. Orr Kelly. (Illus.). 337p. 1998. text 23.00 (*0-7881-5592-X*) DIANE Pub.

Never Final Till Its Vinyl. (Illus.). 224p. 1996. pap. 8.95 (*0-340-60307-0*, Pub. by Hodder & Stought Ltd) Trafalgar.

Never Forget: Christian & Jewish Perspectives on Edith Stein. Ed. by Waltraud Herbstrith. Tr. by Susanne Batzdorff from GER. LC 97-39247. (Carmelite Studies: Vol. VII).Tr. of Erinnere Dich - Vergfs es Nicht: Edith Stein - Christlich-Judische. (Illus.). 330p. 1998. pap. 11.95 (*0-935216-62-6*, C7) ICS Pubns.

Never Forget: Greatest Love Story Ever Told. Ann DeCourt. LC 98-90469. x, 208p. (Orig.). 1998. pap. 14.95 (*0-9664753-1-3*, 1-126) Wabokat Pubg.

Never Forgotten, Always Loved. Roy Lessin. 96p. 1992. pap. 5.95 (*1-884009-00-X*) DaySpring.

Never Forsake: The Story of Amanda Barnes Smith, Legacy of the Massacre at Haun's Mill. Paul W. Hodson. 260p. 1997. 22.95 (*0-9661696-0-3*); pap. 14.95 (*0-9661696-1-1*) Keeban Pubns.

Never Forsaken. Kathleen L. Jacobs. LC 99-20906. 272p. 1999. pap. 10.99 (*1-58134-110-5*) Crossway Bks.

Never Get Naked on Your First Visit: A Patient's Survival Guide. David H. Ellig. LC 90-92333. (Illus.). 310p. (Orig.). 1992. pap. 19.95 (*0-9628311-0-7*) Med Ed Az.

Never Give a Fish an Umbrella. Mike Thaler. (Laffalong Ser.). (Illus.). 32p. (Orig.). (J). (ps-3). 1997. pap. 3.50 (*0-8167-3904-8*, Whistlstop) Troll Communs.

*__Never Give a Heifer a Bum Steer.__ Marshall Trimble. (Illus.). 1999. pap. text 7.95 (*0-916179-98-2*) Ariz Hwy.

*__Never Give a Sucker an Even Break.__ 2000. 22.00 (*0-13-030409-3*) P-H.

Never Give a Sucker an Even Break: W. C. Fields on Business. Ronald Fields & Shaun O'L. Higgins. LC 99-49404. (Illus.). 320p. 2000. 22.00 (*0-7352-0056-4*) PH Pr.

*__Never Give In: Inspirational Quotations for Courageous Living.__ Criswell Freeman. 128p. 2000. pap. 4.95 (*1-58334-073-4*, Pub. by Walnut Gr Pr) Midpt Trade.

Never Give In: The Extraordinary Character of Winston Churchill. Stephen Mansfield. LC 96-32251. (Leaders in Action Ser.). 208p. 1996. 14.95 (*1-888952-19-9*) Cumberland Hse.

Never Give In: The Italian Resistance & Politics. Ed. by Steve Wright & Alistair Davidson. LC 96-7121. (Studies in Modern European History: Vol. 22). 122p. (C). 1998. text 35.95 (*0-8204-3149-4*) P Lang Pubng.

Never Give Up. Dennis A. Cortipassi. LC 90-85169. 1992. 6.95 (*0-8158-0467-9*) Chris Mass.

Never Give Up. E. Evertts. 1986. pap. text, wbk. ed. 14.25 (*0-03-002367-X*) Holt R&W.

Never Give Up. Susanne Starck. 78p. (Orig.). 1994. pap. 7.95 (*1-56245-098-0*) Great Quotations.

Never Give Up, Level 11. E. Evertts. 1983. 40.00 (*0-03-061393-0*) Harcourt Schl Pubs.

Never Give Up, Level 11. E. Evertts. (J). 1983. pap., wbk. ed. 14.75 (*0-03-061436-8*) Harcourt Schl Pubs.

Never Give Up, Level 11. E. Evertts. 1986. 34.25 (*0-03-002362-9*) Harcourt Schl Pubs.

Never Give Up: The Incredible Payoff of Perseverance. Don Hawkins. (Orig.). 1995. 9.95 (*0-8474-1704-2*) Back to Bible.

*__Never Give Up: The Marshall Jones Story__ Cheryl A. Weinstein. LC 99-94096. 74p. 1999. write for info. (*0-9670317-0-2*) Perennial Press.

Never Give up, Never Give In: How to Achieve Your Goals Through the Power of Perseverance. Bryan Drysdale & Julie Blan. LC 93-86783. 200p. 1994. pap. 14.95 (*0-9639506-7-3*) SMD Pubng.

An Asterisk (*) at the beginning of an entry indicates that the title is appearing for the first time.

Never Givin' Up on Love. Margot Dalton. (Crystal Creek Ser.). 1994. per. 3.99 (0-373-82531-5, 1-82531-4) Harlequin Bks.

Never Good Enough. Greta West. 48p. 2000. pap. 8.00 (0-8059-4705-1) Dorrance.

Never Good Enough: Freeing Yourself from the Chains of Perfectionism. Monica Ramirez Basco. LC 98-31575. (Illus.). 273p. 1999. 23.00 (0-684-84963-1) Free Pr.

Never Good Enough: Growing up Imperfect in a "Perfect" Family: How to Break the Cycle of Codependence & Addiction for the Next Generation. Carol Cannon. LC 92-43283. 1993. pap. 11.99 (0-8163-1145-5) Pacific Pr Pub Assn.

Never Good Enough: How to Use Perfectionism to Your Advantage Without Letting It Ruin Your Life. Monica Ramirez Basco. 288p. 2000. per. 12.00 (0-684-86293-X) S&S Trade.

Never Hit a Lady. Fred S. Tobey. LC 84-11043. 190p. (Orig.). 1984. pap. 3.95 (0-918781-00-0) Bay Brewster.

Never in a Hurry: Essays on People & Places. Naomi S. Nye. LC 95-41778. (Illus.). 270p. 1996. pap. 16.95 (1-57003-082-0) U of SC Pr.

***Never in Anger.** Bendell Anthony. 1999. 40.00 (0-7528-1796-5, Pub. by Orion Pubng Grp) Trafalgar.

Never in Anger: Portrait of an Eskimo Family. Jean L. Briggs. LC 75-105368. (Illus.). 379p. 1971. pap. 18.95 (0-674-60828-3) HUP.

Never in Doubt: Remembering Iowa Jima. Edmond B. Bard. Ed. by Lynn S. Kessler. LC 98-47672. (Illus.). 248p. 1999. 32.95 (1-55750-463-6) Naval Inst Pr.

Never Is Late to Love see Nunca Es Tarde para Amar

Never Just a Game: Players, Owners & American Baseball to 1920. Robert F. Burk. LC 93-22719. (Illus.). xviii, 284p. (C). 1994. 45.00 (0-8078-2122-5) U of NC Pr.

***Never Kiss a Duke.** Eileen Putman. 384p. 2000. mass mkt. 5.99 (0-380-80290-2) Morrow Avon.

Never Kiss an Alligator! Colleen Stanley Bare. LC 92-62835. (Illus.). 32p. (J). (ps-3). 1994. pap. 4.99 (0-14-055257-X, PuffinBks) Peng Put Young Read.

Never Kiss an Alligator! Colleen Stanley Bare. LC 92-62835. (Picture Puffin Ser.). (J). 1994. 9.19 (0-606-06614-4, Pub. by Turtleback) Demco.

Never Kiss an Alligator on the Lips! Vol. I: The Life & Trying Times of Boudreaux the Cajun. unabridged ed. Curt Boudreaux. LC 99-160042. (Illus.). 171p. 1998. pap. 20.00 (1-889968-55-2, Pub. by Gestalt Inst Pr) C Boudreaux.

***Never Kiss an Alligator on the Lips! Vol. II: The Life & Trying Times of Boudreaux the Cajun.** Curt Boudreaux. (Illus.). 236p. 1999. pap. 20.00 (1-889968-56-0, Pub. by Gestalt Inst Pr) C Boudreaux.

Never Kneel Down: Drought Development & Liberation in Eritrea. James Firebrace. LC 85-60323. (C). 1985. pap. 9.95 (0-932415-01-6); text 29.95 (0-932415-00-8) Red Sea Pr.

Never Leave Me. Harold Robbins. 224p. 1978. mass mkt. 4.99 (0-380-00179-9, Avon Bks) Morrow Avon.

***Never Leave Me.** Harold Robbins. 2001. text. write for info. (0-312-86610-0) St Martin.

Never Let a Fool Kiss You or a Kiss Fool You: Chiasmus & a World of Quotations That Say What They Mean & Mean What They Say. Ed. by Mardy Grothe. LC 99-18015. (Illus.). 112p. 1999. 17.95 (0-670-87827-8, Viking) Viking Penguin.

Never Let a Skinny Guy Make Sandwiches. Gene Mueller & Bob Denyer. (Illus.). 1994. pap. 14.95 (0-9640419-4-4) B&G MD.

Never Let 'Em Quit: How Scuba Instructors Can Make Confident, Loyal Divers Out of Any Student. Robert A. Clark. 110p. 1997. pap. 29.95 (1-880229-41-2, 2165) Concept Sys.

***Never Let Go.** McCaughrean. 1998. pap. text 11.95 (0-340-68291-4, Pub. by Hodder & Stought Ltd) Trafalgar.

***Never Let Go.** Created by Francine Pascal. (Sweet Valley High Senior Year Ser.: No. 24). (YA). (gr. 7 up). 2000. mass mkt. 4.50 (0-553-49340-X, Sweet Valley) BDD Bks Young Read.

Never Let Go: P. I. Jeeter on Cape Cod. R. Pease. 162p. 1996. per. 12.95 (0-9637154-8-8) Flagg Mtn Pr.

Never Let Her Go. Gayle Wilson. (Intrigue Ser.: No. 490). 1998. per. 3.99 (0-373-22490-7, 0-22490-7) Harlequin Bks.

Never Let Me Down: A Memoir. Susan J. Miller. 244p. 1999. pap. 12.95 (0-8050-6129-0, Pub. by H Holt & Co) VHPS.

Never Let Me Down: A Memoir. Susan J. Miller. LC 97-13690. 1998. text 22.50 (0-8050-4429-9) St Martin.

Never Let Me Go. Tim Kincaid. 416p. 1998. mass mkt. 5.99 (1-57566-341-4) Kensgtn Pub Corp.

Never Let Me Go. Joan Smith. 1994. mass mkt. 3.99 (0-449-22277-2) Fawcett.

Never Let Me Go. large type ed. Joan Smith. LC 97-32440. (Large Print Bk. Ser.). 1997. 21.95 (1-56895-514-6) Wheeler Pub.

***Never Let Me Say, "Why Me?"** 2nd ed. Christy Humphries. Ed. by Lisa M. Lindstrom & Sandi DeFelice. (Illus.). 167p. 2000. reprint ed. pap. 14.99 (0-9650823-1-8, 2, Pub. by Leo Publishing) DDDD Pubns.

Never Let Them See You Cry. Edna R. Buchanan. 336p. 1993. mass mkt. 5.99 (0-425-13824-0) Berkley Pub.

***Never Let You Go: The Circle K Sisters.** Judy Christenberry. (Romance Ser.: Bk. 1453). 2000. per. 3.50 (0-373-19453-6, 1-19453-9) Silhouette.

Never Let Your Cat Make Lunch for You. Lee Harris. LC 98-51999. (Illus.). 24p. (J). (ps-2). 1999. 12.95 (1-883672-80-5) Tricycle Pr.

Never Lick a Frozen Flagpole! More! Humorous Insights That Motivate & Encourage. Marvin Phillips. LC 98-56642. (Illus.). 224p. 1999. pap. 10.99 (1-58229-009-1) Howard Pub LA.

Never Lick a Moving Blender! Humorous Insights That Motivate & Encourage. gif. ed. Marvin Phillips. (Illus.). 215p. 1996. pap. 10.99 (1-878990-58-6) Howard Pub LA.

Never Lie to an Angel. Kate Welsh. (Love Inspired Ser.: Bk. 69). 1999. per. 4.50 (0-373-87069-8, 1-87069-0) Harlequin Bks.

Never Like You Plan. Ed. by Ruth Roston. (Orig.). 1994. pap. 5.00 (0-927663-23-6) COMPAS.

Never Lonely Again. Malcolm Smith. Date not set. 4.99 (1-880089-23-8, AP-923) Albury Pub.

Never Look Back. Judy Baer. LC 97-33842. (Cedar River Daydreams Ser.: No. 27). 144p. (YA). (gr. 7-10). 1997. mass mkt. 4.99 (1-55661-837-9) Bethany Hse.

Never Look Back. Ridley Pearson. 1993. mass mkt. 6.99 (0-312-92975-7, St Martins Paperbacks) St Martin.

Never Look Back. large type ed. Ridley Pearson. (Niagara Large Print Ser.). 397p. 1996. 29.50 (0-7089-5844-3) Ulverscroft.

Never Look Back: A History of World War II in the Pacific. William A. Renzi & Mark D. Roehrs. LC 90-25884. 240p. (gr. 13). 1991. 47.95 (0-87332-808-6) M E Sharpe.

Never Lose. John L. Kline. Ed. by Blandina Rose & J. Thompson Public Relations Staff. (Illus.). 320p. (Orig.). (C). 1996. pap. write for info. (0-9652130-9-9) J Kline Assocs.

Never Lose: A Decade of Sports & Politics in Sacramento. Frank McCormack. LC 89-80370. 200p. (Orig.). 1989. pap. 16.95 (0-9622140-9-4) First Ink Pub Hse.

Never Lose a War: Memoirs & Observations of a National Columnist. Holmes Alexander. LC 83-18964. 158p. 1984. 14.95 (0-8159-6223-1) Devin.

Never Lose Hope. Rabbi Nachman of Breslov. Ed. by Moshe Mykoff. (Illus.). 36p. (J). (gr. 1-4). 1996. 8.00 (0-930213-65-3) Breslov Res Inst.

Never Lose Love. Barbara Cartland. (Camfield Ser.: No. 133). 176p. (Orig.). 1994. mass mkt. 3.99 (0-515-11457-X, Jove) Berkley Pub.

Never Love a Cowboy. Jill Gregory. 416p. 1998. mass mkt. 5.99 (0-440-22439-X) Dell.

***Never Love a Cowboy.** Lorraine Heath. LC 99-96442. 384p. 2000. mass mkt. 6.50 (0-380-80330-5, Avon Bks) Morrow Avon.

Never Love a Cowboy. Kate Hoffmann. LC 96-619. (Temptation Ser.). 216p. 1995. per. 3.25 (0-373-25646-9, 1-25646-0) Harlequin Bks.

Never Love a Stranger. Harold Robbins. 1993. per. 5.99 (0-671-87492-6) PB.

Never Love a Stranger. Harold Robbins. 1995. reprint ed. lib. bdg. 29.95 (1-56849-644-3) Buccaneer Bks.

Never Mail an Elephant. Mike Thaler. LC 93-14395. (Laffalong Bk.). (Illus.). 32p. (J). (ps-3). 1997. pap. 3.50 (0-8167-3019-9) Troll Communs.

Never Mail an Elephant. Mike Thaler. LC 93-14395. (Laffalong Bk.). (Illus.). 32p. (J). (ps-3). 1997. lib. bdg. 16.65 (0-8167-3018-0) Troll Communs.

Never Mail an Elephant. Mike Thaler. LC 93-14395. 1994. 7.70 (0-606-06615-2, Pub. by Turtleback) Demco.

Never Married Women. Barbara L. Simon. (Women in the Political Economy Ser.). 228p. 1989. pap. 19.95 (0-87722-671-7) Temple U Pr.

Never Marry a Girl with a Dead Father: Hysteria in the 19th Century Novel. Helen Hayward. (Illus.). 232p. 1998. pap. 18.95 (1-86064-187-3, Pub. by I B T) St Martin.

Never Marry a Girl with a Dead Father: Hysteria in the 19th Century Novel. Helen Hayward. (Illus.). 232p. 1999. text 55.00 (1-86064-186-5) I B T.

Never Marry in Morocco: A Novel. Virginia Dale. 256p. (Orig.). 1996. pap. 12.95 (1-56474-174-5) Fithian Pr.

Never Met a Man I Didn't Like. Joseph H. Carter. 285p. Date not set. 23.95 (0-8488-2230-7) Amereon Ltd.

Never Met Man Didn't Lik. Joseph H. Carter. LC 92-121146. 275p. 1991. pap. 11.00 (0-380-76808-9, Avon Bks) Morrow Avon.

***Never Mind Nirvana.** Mark Lindquist. LC 99-88358. 256p. 2000. 21.95 (0-679-46302-X) Villard Books.

***Never Mind Nirvana: A Novel.** Mark Lindquist. 256p. 2000. 21.95 (0-375-46302-X) Villard Books.

Never Mind the Bollocks. Composed by Sex Pistols. 56p. 1996. per. 16.95 (0-7935-6334-8) H Leonard.

Never Mind the Bollocks: Here's the Sex Pistols. Clinton Heylin. LC 97-29050. 176p. 1998. 14.95 (0-02-864726-2) Music Sales.

Never Mind What Happened, How Did It End? David Rogers. 104p. 1976. pap. 5.25 (0-87129-103-7, N11) Dramatic Pub.

Never, Never Elephants. Ed Emberley. (Illus.). 48p. (J). 2001. 15.95 (0-316-23638-1) Little.

***Never, Never, Give Up!** Wanda Combs-Moore & Charles F. Queenan. xi, 120p. 1998. pap. 12.95 (0-9675119-0-9) W L Moore Assocs.

Never, Never Give Up. Jack Hartman. 210p. (Orig.). 1995. pap. 9.95 (0-915445-16-6, Lamplight Ministries) Lamplight FL.

Never, Never, Never. Shirley Bassey. 1979. pap. 9.95 (0-686-09062-4, A0038OPX) Wrner Bros.

Never Never Never Will She Stop Loving You. Jolene Durrant. LC 98-91376. (Illus.). 32p. (J). (gr. 3 up). 1998. pap. 9.95 (0-9663567-5-6) JoBiz.

***Never Never Never Will She Stop Loving You: The Adoption Love Story of Angel Annie.** rev. ed. Jolene Durrant. LC 99-72088. (Illus.). 40p. (YA). (gr. k up). 1999. pap. 6.95 (0-9663567-9-9) JoBiz.

Never Never Quit: A Photographic Celebration of Courage in American Sports. Mike Shields. (Illus.). 74p. 1996. 17.95 (1-56245-260-6) Great Quotations.

Never, No Matter What. Maryleah Otto. (Illus.). 24p. (J). (ps-3). pap. 4.95 (0-88961-133-5, Pub. by Womens Pr) LPC InBook.

Never No More. Shirley Seifert. 1976. reprint ed. lib. bdg. 17.95 (0-89190-137-X, Rivercity Pr) Amereon Ltd.

***Never Nosh A Matzo Ball: A Ruby the Rabbi's Wife Mystery.** Sharon Kahn. LC 99-41311. 304p. 2000. 22.00 (0-684-84738-8) Scribner.

Never-Not Sonnets. Barbara L. Greenberg. (University of Central Florida Contemporary Poetry Ser.). 64p. 1989. 17.95 (0-8130-0920-0); pap. 10.95 (0-8130-0939-1) U Press Fla.

Never-Not Sonnets: Poems. Barbara L. Greenberg. LC 88-32425. (Contemporary Poetry Ser.). 61p. 1989. reprint ed. pap. 30.00 (0-608-04483-0, 206522800001) Bks Demand.

Never Off Pay: The Story of the Independent Tanker Union, 1937-1962. John J. Collins. LC 63-16395. 351p. reprint ed. pap. 108.90 (0-7837-0440-2, 204076300018) Bks Demand.

Never Old - The Ultimate Success Story: Secrets of Perpetual Youth, Health & CE Mindpower Revealed. Jesse A. Dawn. (Illus.). 264p. (Orig.). 1995. pap. 9.95 (0-9636589-0-5) Wrld Changing.

Never Open the Bottom of a Circus. Craig Canfield. (Illus.). 55p. (Orig.). 1998. pap. 5.50 (1-880764-15-6) Northwind NJ.

Never Out of Season: A Timeless Guide to Building Your Wealth. David W. Hunter. 1992. 16.95 (0-8191-8549-3) U Pr of Amer.

Never Out of the Hole. Tomasi. LC 99-17534. 1999. pap. 12.95 (0-8050-5938-5, Owl) H Holt & Co.

Never Paint Stranger. Shaw. 1992. mass mkt. (0-8125-0054-7) Tor Bks.

***Never Pay Full Fare Again.** Dave Huetten. 150p. 1999. pap. 19.95 (0-9676277-0-2) D R H Invest.

Never Pay Retail: How to Save 20 Percent to 80 Percent on Everything You Buy. Ed. by Sid Kirchheimer. LC 96-6100. (Illus.). 496p. 1996. pap. 17.95 (0-87596-402-8) Rodale Pr Inc.

Never Pay Retail: How to Save 20 Percent to 80 Percent on Everything You Buy. Ed. by Sid Kirchheimer. LC 96-6100. 496p. 1996. 27.95 (0-87596-302-1) Rodale Pr Inc.

Never Plan Tomorrow. Joseph A. Petak. LC 91-78112. (Illus.). 524p. (Orig.). 1992. pap. 19.95 (0-9631609-6-6) Aquataur.

***Never Preach Past Noon.** Edie Claire. (Leigh Koslow Mysteries Ser.). 2000. mass mkt. 5.99 (0-451-20144-2, Sig) NAL.

Never Question the Miracle. Rose-Mari Toussaint. 336p. 1999. pap. 24.95 (0-449-00526-7) Fawcett.

Never Question the Miracle: A Surgeon's Story. Rose-Marie Toussaint & Anthony E. Santaniello. LC 97-37566. 336p. 1998. 24.95 (0-345-40723-7) Ballantine Pub Grp.

***Never Quit Praying for Your Loved Ones.** Marion H. Price, Sr. 12p. 1999. pap. 1.49 (1-56632-103-4) Revival Lit.

Never Read a Newspaper at Your Desk: The Fundamental Principles of Business. Richard Stiegele. LC 94-16602. 160p. 1994. 7.95 (0-8065-1560-0, Citadel Pr) Carol Pub Group.

Never-Resting Mind: Wallace Stevens & Romantic Irony. Anthony Whiting & Robin G. Schulze. LC 96-2557. 232p. (C). 1996. text 49.50 (0-472-10659-7, 10659) U of Mich Pr.

Never Ride Your Elephant to School. Johnson. (J). 1995. 15.95 (0-8050-4330-6) H Holt & Co.

Never Ride Your Elephant to School. Doug Johnson. (Illus.). 32p. (J). (ps-2). 1995. 15.95 (0-8050-2880-3) H Holt & Co.

Never Satisfied: How & Why Men Cheat. 3rd ed. Michael Baisden. Ed. by Kim Wohlenhaus. LC 94-96628. (Illus.). 254p. (Orig.). 1995. pap. 13.95 (0-9643675-8-0) Legacy Publng.

Never Say Always: Perspectives on Seat Belt Use. J. Peter Rothe & Peter J. Cooper. 192p. 1989. pap. 24.95 (0-88738-775-6) Transaction Pubs.

Never Say Die. Tess Gerritsen. 1996. per. 5.50 (1-55166-176-4, 1-66176-8, Mira Bks) Harlequin Bks.

Never Say Die. Carolyn Keene. (Nancy Drew Files: No. 16). (YA). (gr. 6 up). 1991. pap. 3.50 (0-671-73666-3, Archway) PB.

Never Say Die. Warren Murphy. (Destroyer Ser.: No. 110). 1998. per. 5.99 (0-373-63225-8, 1-63225-6, Wrldwide Lib) Harlequin Bks.

Never Say Die! A Thousand Years of Yiddish in Jewish Life & Letters. Ed. by Joshua A. Fishman. LC 81-3957. (Contributions to the Sociology of Language Ser.: No. 30). 763p. 1981. 73.10 (90-279-7978-2) Mouton.

Never Say Die: Englische Idiome um Den Tod und das Sterben. Heidi Anders. (Europaische Hochschulschriften Ser.: No.14, Vol. 298). (GER.). 324p. 1995. 57.95 (3-631-49351-7) P Lang Pubng.

Never Say Die: The Canadian Air Force Survival Manual. Canadian Government Staff. (Illus.). 208p. 1979. pap. 20.00 (0-87364-112-4) Paladin Pr.

Never Say Diet. 1986. mass mkt. 7.95 (0-446-73363-6, Pub. by Warner Bks) Little.

Never Say Good-Bye. Jana Ellis. LC 89-34376. (Merivale Mall Ser.). 160p. (YA). (gr. 7 up). 1989. pap. text 2.50 (0-8167-1618-8) Troll Communs.

Never Say Good-Bye: An Anthology by New Writers in Prison. Reader's Digest Editors. (New Writers' Voices Ser.). 64p. (Orig.). 1993. pap. text 3.50 (1-56853-005-6, Signal Hill) New Readers.

Never Say Goodbye. Suzanne Carey. (Intimate Moments Ser.: No. 330). 1990. per. 2.95 (0-373-07330-5) Silhouette.

Never Say Goodbye. Claire Lorrimer. 224p. 26.00 (0-7278-5535-2) Severn Hse.

***Never Say Goodbye.** large type ed. Lynne Collins. LC 99-49382. (General Ser.). 2000. pap. 22.95 (0-7862-2307-3) Thorndike Pr.

Never Say "Hi Jack" in an Airport: And 101 Other Life-Saving Travel Tips. Terry Denton & Rocky Denton. LC 93-51042. 128p. (Orig.). 1994. pap. 8.95 (1-56530-104-8) Summit TX.

Never Say Impossible: The Life & Times of an American Entrepreneur. John H. Perry, Jr. LC 96-1882. 1996. write for info. (1-56566-099-4) Thomasson-Grant.

Never Say Lie: How to Beat the Machines, the Interviews, the Chemical Tests. Scott French & Paul Van Houten. (Illus.). 168p. pap. 22.95 (0-87364-639-8) Paladin Pr.

Never Say Moo to a Bull. large type ed. David H. Wilson. (Illus.). (J). 1996. pap. 16.95 (0-7451-4818-2, Galaxy Child Lrg Print) Chivers N Amer.

Never Say Never. Doug Flutie. (J). 1999. 14.95 (0-87833-165-4) Taylor Pub.

Never Say Never. Linda Hill. 224p. 1996. pap. 11.95 (1-56280-126-0) Naiad Pr.

***Never Say Never.** Joan Hohl. 1999. mass mkt. 5.99 (0-8217-6379-2, Zebra Kensgtn) Kensgtn Pub Corp.

Never Say Never. Tina Leonard. 400p. (Orig.). 1997. mass mkt. 3.99 (1-85487-715-1, Pub. by Scarlet Bks) London Brdge.

***Never Say Never.** La Vonda J. McClain. 2000. pap. 7.95 (0-533-13310-6) Vantage.

Never Say Never. Jo-Ann Power. 390p. 1999. mass mkt. 6.50 (0-671-02422-1) S&S Trade.

Never Say Never: The Peter Principal. Catherine G. Swift. Ed. by Neal & Associates Staff. 1994. pap. 5.99 (0-9642159-2-6) Rockwood Pubns.

Never Say No! The Complete Program for a Happier & More Cooperative Dog. Roger Mugford. LC 93-32929. 208p. 1994. pap. 12.00 (0-399-51884-3) Berkley Pub.

Never Say No! The Complete Program for a Happier & More Cooperative Dog. Roger Mugford. LC 93-32929. (Illus.). 224p. 1994. 18.95 (0-399-13947-8, G P Putnam) Peng Put Young Read.

Never Say Quit. Bill Wallace. LC 92-54420. 160p. (J). (gr. 4-6). 1993. 15.95 (0-8234-1013-7) Holiday.

Never Say Quit. Bill Wallace. LC 92-54420. 1993. 8.60 (0-606-06616-0, Pub. by Turtleback) Demco.

Never Say Quit. Bill Wallace. Ed. by Pat MacDonald. 192p. (J). (gr. 3-6). 1994. reprint ed. pap. 3.50 (0-671-88264-3, Minstrel Bks) PB.

Never Send Flowers. John Gardner. 336p. 1994. reprint ed. mass mkt. 5.99 (0-425-14250-7) Berkley Pub.

Never Shake a Family Tree: And Other Heart-Stopping Tales of Murder in New England. Ed. by Billie S. Mosiman & Martin H. Greenberg. LC 98-4799. 224p. 1998. pap. 9.95 (1-55853-577-2) Rutledge Hill Pr.

Never Shake Hands with a Left-Handed Gunman. Benjamin Prado. Tr. by Kristina Cordero from SPA. LC 98-31664. 176p. 1998. text 19.95 (0-312-20084-6) St Martin.

***Never Short a Stock on Wednesday: And 300 More Financial Lessons You Can't Afford Not to Know,** Nancy Dunnan. LC 99-56970. 256p. 2000. pap. 9.50 (0-06-273727-9) HarpC.

"Never Sleep Naked" - Stories & Poems. Dorothy Coe. (Illus.). 1996. pap. 10.00 (0-9661569-1-9) D Coe.

Never Sleep with Strangers. Heather G. Pozzessere. 384p. 1998. mass mkt. 5.99 (1-55166-445-3, Mira Bks) Harlequin Bks.

Never Snap at a Bubble-Small Book. Yvonne Winer & Carol A. McLean-Carr. 8p. (J). 1987. 3.95 (0-88679-541-9) Educ Insights.

Never Snap at a Bubble-Tall Book. Yvonne Winer & Carol A. McLean-Carr. 8p. (J). 1987. 19.95 (0-88679-540-0) Educ Insights.

Never Sniff a Gift Fish. Patrick F. McManus. LC 83-147. 88p. 1995. 17.95 (0-8050-0527-7); pap. 8.95 (0-8050-0031-3, Owl) H Holt & Co.

Never So Pure a Sight - Yr. Eneth Ddisglair Annwyl Morfydd Owen (1891-1918) a Life in Pictures. Rhian Davies. LC 95-128052. 136p. 1994. pap. 27.00 (0-86383-936-3, Pub. by Gomer Pr) St Mut.

Never So Pure a Sight, Morfydd Owen, 1891-1918: A Life in Pictures. Rhian Davies. (Illus.). 136p. 1994. pap. 26.95 (0-8464-4658-8) Beekman Pubs.

***Never Sorry.** Edie Claire. 272p. 1999. mass mkt. 5.99 (0-451-19885-9, Sig) NAL.

Never Sound Retreat. William R. Forstchen. (Lost Regiment Ser.: No. 6). 384p. 1998. mass mkt. 6.99 (0-451-45466-9, ROC) NAL.

"Never Spit on Your Shoes" Denys Cazet. LC 89-35164. (Illus.). 32p. (J). (ps-1). 1990. 16.95 (0-531-05847-6) Orchard Bks Watts.

"Never Spit on Your Shoes" Denys Cazet. LC 89-35164. (Illus.). 32p. (J). (ps-1). 1993. pap. 6.95 (0-531-07039-5) Orchard Bks Watts.

Never Spit on Your Shoes. Denys Cazet. 1993. 12.15 (0-606-05952-0, Pub. by Turtleback) Demco.

Never Stick Your Tongue Out at Mama & Other Life Transforming Revelations. Max Davis. 160p. 1995. pap. 12.50 (0-9648462-0-9) Enhance Pub.

Never Stop Dancing. Illus. by John D. Mahaffy. 184p. 1996. 19.95 (0-9634828-2-3) Pan Pr NY.

Never Stop Running: Allard Lowenstein & the Struggle to Save American Liberalism. William H. Chafe. LC 98-26621. 556p. 1998. pap. text 19.95 (0-691-05973-X, Pub. by Princeton U Pr) Cal Prin Full Svc.

Never Stop Smiling. Jana Ellis. LC 88-12390. (Merivale Mall Ser.). 160p. (YA). (gr. 7 up). 1988. pap. text 2.50 (0-8167-1360-X) Troll Communs.

Never Stop Walking: The Life & Spirit of Saint Alphonsus Liguori. Nancy Fearon. LC 96-13491. 176p. 1996. reprint ed. pap. 8.95 (0-89243-928-9) Liguori Pubns.

Never Street. Loren D. Estleman. 1997. 23.00 (0-614-27892-9) Mysterious Pr.

Never Street. Loren D. Estleman. 1998. mass mkt. write for info. (*0-446-40483-7*, Mysterious Paperbk); mass mkt. 6.99 (*0-446-60596-4*, Pub. by Warner Bks) Little.

Never Such Innocence. large type ed. Daphne Wright. 528p. 1993. 27.99 (*0-7089-8679-X*, Charnwood) Ulverscroft.

Never Swim Alone & This Is a Play: 2 Plays by Daniel Macivor, 2 bks. in 1. Daniel MacIvor. LC 94-173034. 1997. pap. 10.95 (*0-88754-524-6*) Theatre Comm.

Never Take a Pig to Lunch: And Other Poems about the Fun of Eating. Ed. & Illus. by Nadine B. Westcott. LC 93-11801. 64p. (J). (ps up). 1994. 18.95 (*0-531-06834-X*) Orchard Bks Watts.

Never Take a Pig to Lunch: And Other Poems about the Fun of Eating. Nadine B. Westcott. LC 93-11801. (Illus.). 64p. (J). (ps up). 1998. pap. 7.95 (*0-531-07098-0*) Orchard Bks Watts.

Never Take a Pig to Lunch: And Other Poems about the Fun of Eating. Nadine B. Westcott. 1998. 13.15 (*0-606-13657-6*, Pub. by Turtleback) Demco.

Never Take No for an Answer: One Life, One Woman & the Money Mystique. Karen Sheridan. LC 96-86678. 184p. 1996. pap. 14.95 (*1-885221-48-7*) BookPartners.

*__Never Talk to Strangers.__ Irma Joyce. (Family Storytime Ser.). 32p. (J). 2000. 9.95 (*0-307-10231-9*, Goldn Books) Gldn Bks Pub Co.

Never Tell Ben. Diane Namm. (Love Stories Ser.). 192p. (YA). (gr. 7-12). 1996. mass mkt. 3.99 (*0-553-57045-5*) Bantam.

Never the Same. C. Vincent O'Shaughnessy. 134p. 1997. pap. text 9.95 (*1-884920-11-X*) Jubilee Christian Ctr.

Never the Same Again . . . A Young Woman's Story of Life in the Blackstone Valley in the 1820s. Phyllis H. Masso. LC 98-71875. 150p. (YA). (gr. 5-12). 1998. pap. 14.95 (*1-57960-046-8*) Disc Enter Ltd.

Never the Same Again: Encouragement for New & Not-So-New Christians. Shaw Clifton. LC 97-66976. 192p. (Orig.). 1997. pap. 6.00 (*0-9657601-0-3*, Crest Books) SANP.

Never the Same River Twice. Phyllis C. Agins & James A. Freeman. 203p. 1995. 15.95 (*1-883114-05-5*) Waterview Pr.

Never the Sinner: The Leopold & Leob Story. John Logan. LC 98-47733. 142p. 1999. pap. 12.95 (*0-87951-930-4*, Pub. by Overlook Pr) Penguin Putnam.

Never the Twain Shall Meet: Bell, Gallaudet, & the Communications Debate. Richard Winefield. LC 87-1185. (Illus.). 152p. 1987. pap. 19.95 (*1-56368-056-4*) Gallaudet Univ Pr.

Never Tire of Protesting. George Seldes. LC 68-18758. 1968. 6.95 (*0-8184-0060-9*) Carol Pub Group.

*__Never to Be a Mother: A Guide for All Women Who Didn't - Or Couldn't - Have Children.__ Linda Hunt Anton. 197p. 2000. reprint ed. text 18.00 (*0-7881-6945-9*) DIANE Pub.

Never to Be Forgotten: A Young Girl's Holocaust Memoir. Beatrice Muchman. LC 97-8828. 1997. 23.00 (*0-88125-598-X*) Ktav.

Never to Forget: The Jews of the Holocaust. Milton Meltzer. LC 75-25409. (YA). (gr. 7 up). 1976. lib. bdg. 15.89 (*0-06-024175-6*) HarpC Child Bks.

Never to Forget: The Jews of the Holocaust. Milton Meltzer. LC 75-25409. (Trophy Nonfiction Bk.). (Illus.). 240p. (YA). (gr. 7-12). 1991. pap. 7.95 (*0-06-446118-1*, HarpTrophy) HarpC Child Bks.

Never to Forget: The Jews of the Holocaust. Milton Meltzer. 1991. 12.05 (*0-606-01103-X*, Pub. by Turtleback) Demco.

*__Never to Let Go.__ large type ed. Marlene E. McFadden. LC 99-22228. 1999. pap. 19.95 (*0-7838-8656-X*, G K Hall Lrg Type) Mac Lib Ref.

Never to Return. Esther Tusquets. Tr. by Barbara Ichiishi. LC 98-53764. (European Women Writers Ser.). 194p. 1999. text 40.00 (*0-8032-4433-9*) U of Nebr Pr.

*__Never to Return.__ Esther Tusquets. Tr. by Barbara Ichiishi. LC 98-53764. (European Women Writers Ser.). 1999. pap. 15.00 (*0-8032-9438-7*) U of Nebr Pr.

Never to Return: A Modern Quest for Eternal Truth. Sharon Janis. LC 97-44497. 330p. (Orig.). 1998. pap. 16.95 (*1-884997-29-5*) Blue Dove Pr.

*__Never Too Early to Write: Adventures in the K-1 Writing Workshop.__ Bea Johnson. Ed. by Candace Nelson. LC 99-15281. (Illus.). 148p. 1999. pap. text, teacher ed. 12.95 (*0-929895-31-2*) Maupin Hse.

Never Too Late. Judy Baer. (Cedar River Daydreams Ser.: No. 19). 128p. (Orig.). (YA). (gr. 7-10). 1993. mass mkt. 4.99 (*1-55661-329-6*) Bethany Hse.

Never Too Late. Melanie Jongsma. (Friendship Ser.). (Illus.). 48p. (Orig.). 1993. pap. 0.70 (*1-882536-19-3*, A100-0062) Bible League.

Never Too Late. Kathryn Kuhlman. 79p. (Orig.). 1994. mass mkt. 3.99 (*0-88270-720-5*) Bridge-Logos.

Never Too Late. Elizabeth Tettmar. 1996. 22.00 (*0-7278-5190-X*) Severn Hse.

Never Too Late. Angela M. Thirkell. LC 98-53773. 298p. 2000. pap. 12.95 (*1-55921-235-7*) Moyer Bell.

*__Never Too Late.__ Rebecca York. (Intrigue Ser.: Vol. 558). 2000. per. 4.25 (*0-373-22558-X*) Harlequin Bks.

Never Too Late. large type ed. Julia Ashwell. (Large Print Ser.). 336p. 1997. 27.99 (*0-7089-3660-1*) Ulverscroft.

Never Too Late. large type ed. Nancy John. (Romance Ser.). 416p. 1993. 27.99 (*0-7089-2934-6*) Ulverscroft.

Never Too Late. large type ed. Ellen Smith. (Large Print Ser.). 448p. 1996. 27.99 (*0-7089-3562-1*) Ulverscroft.

Never Too Late: My Musical Life Story. John Holt. 256p. 1991. pap. 13.00 (*0-201-56763-6*) Addison-Wesley.

*__Never Too Late: The Prosecutor's Story of Justice in the Medgar Evers Case.__ Bobby DeLaughter. LC 00-30106. 2001. pap. 27.50 (*0-684-86503-3*) Scribner.

Never Too Late for Christmas. Jane M. Choate. LC 97-94271. 192p. 1997. 18.95 (*0-8034-9265-0*, Avalon Bks) Bouregy.

Never Too Late for Love. Warren Adler. 288p. 1995. 22.95 (*0-943972-44-2*); pap. 14.95 (*0-943972-45-0*) Homestead WY.

*__Never Too Late for Love.__ Monica Jackson. 2000. mass mkt. 5.99 (*1-58314-107-3*, Arabesq) BET Bks.

Never Too Late for Love: Like Mother Like Daughter. Marie Ferrarella. 1999. per. 3.50 (*0-373-19351-3*, Harlequin) Harlequin Bks.

Never Too Late to Be Loved: How One Couple under Stress Discovered Intimacy & Joy. Browne Barr. LC 96-19410. 220p. 1996. 19.95 (*1-57249-035-7*, Ragged Edge) White Mane Pub.

Never Too Late to Learn. Bell & Roderick. 1982. pap. text. write for info. (*0-582-49706-X*, Pub. by Addison-Wesley) Longman.

*__Never Too Late to Learn: The Adult Student's Guide to College.__ Vicky Phillips. 304p. 2000. pap. 13.95 (*0-375-75478-4*, Pub. by PRP NY) Random.

Never Too Late to Read: Language Skills for the Adolescent with Dyslexia. Ann C. Tuley. LC 98-45948. 192p. (C). 1998. pap. text 27.50 (*0-912752-47-5*) York Pr.

Never Too Late to Remember: The Politics Behind New York City's Holocaust Museum. Rochelle G. Saidel. (Illus.). 275p. 1996. 30.00 (*0-8419-1367-6*) Holmes & Meier.

Never Too Old for a Lullaby: Death of an Adult Child. Juanita White. LC 97-39271. 1998. 3.95 (*1-56123-097-9*) Centering Corp.

Never Too Old for God. Margaret Cole. 125p. 1987. pap. 3.95 (*0-310-55272-9*, 19027P) Zondervan.

Never Too Old to Have Fun: Seasonal Parties for Seasoned Citizens. Agnes P. Schaller & Annalee Kinney. 128p. (Orig.). 1993. pap. 10.95 (*0-687-27705-1*) Abingdon.

Never Too Old to Play Tennis . . . & Never Too Old to Start. Mansfield Latimer. (Illus.). 176p. (Orig.). 1993. pap. 12.95 (*1-55870-288-1*, Betrwy Bks) F & W Pubns Inc.

Never Too Old to Rock & Roll. Al Blair. 4p. 1988. pap. 3.95 (*0-930366-20-4*) Northcountry Pub.

Never Too Rich. Judith Gould. 560p. 1991. mass mkt. 7.50 (*0-451-40270-7*, Onyx) NAL.

Never Too Small. Robert Wulf. (Illus.). 44p. (J). (ps-3). 1996. 14.95 (*1-883954-01-0*) Milestone.

Never Too Thin. Eva Szekely. 216p. reprint ed. pap. 12.95 (*0-88961-127-0*, Pub. by Womens Pr) LPC InBook.

Never Too Young to Know: Death in Children's Lives. Phyllis R. Silverman. LC 98-50158. 288p. (C). 1999. 45.00 (*0-19-510954-6*) OUP.

Never too Young to Know: Death in Children's lives. Phyllis R. Silverman. LC 98-50158. 288p. (C). 1999. pap. 19.95 (*0-19-510955-4*) OUP.

Never Truly Lost: A Bushwalker's Life. Paddy Pallin. 224p. 1996. reprint ed. pap. 19.95 (*0-86840-194-3*, Pub. by New South Wales Univ Pr) Intl Spec Bk.

Never Trust a Cat Who Wears Earrings. Dan Greenburg. (Zack Files: No. 7). (Illus.). 64p. (J). (gr. 2-5). 1997. pap. 3.95 (*0-448-41340-X*, G & D); lib. bdg. 12.99 (*0-448-41586-0*, G & D) Peng Put Young Read.

Never Trust a Cat Who Wears Earrings. Dan Greenburg. LC 96-52899. (Zack Files: No. 7). (J). (gr. 2-5). 1997. 9.15 (*0-606-12132-3*, Pub. by Turtleback) Demco.

Never Trust a Dead Man. Vivian Vande Velde. LC 98-39885. 208p. (YA). (gr. 7-12). 1999. 17.00 (*0-15-201899-9*) Harcourt.

Never Trust a Flamingo. Devra Newberger Speregen. (Full House Stephanie Ser.: Vol. 19). 144p. (J). (gr. 5-7). 1996. pap. 3.99 (*0-671-56843-4*) PB.

Never Trust a Lady. Kathleen Creighton. 1997. per. 3.99 (*0-373-07800-5*, 1-07800-5) Silhouette.

Never Trust a Man. Anne C. Martens. 1935. 3.50 (*0-87129-443-5*, N12) Dramatic Pub.

Never Trust a Man in Curlers. Tony Lazzarini. xix, 105p. 1997. 14.95 (*1-891555-00-6*); pap. 9.95 (*1-891555-01-4*) Voyager Pub.

Never Trust a Naked Car Salesman: The Most Outrageous Sex Comedy Ever Written. Jim Shier. (Illus.). 329p. 1997. pap. 6.95 (*0-9629048-1-3*) World View FL.

*__Never Trust a One-Eyed Wizard: The Fairie Ring.__ Tom Townsend. (Fairie Ring Ser.: Vol. 2). 171p. (YA). (gr. 8 up). 2000. pap. 9.99 (*0-88092-526-4*) Royal Fireworks.

*__Never Trust a Rake.__ Eileen Putman. 384p. 1999. mass mkt. 5.99 (*0-380-80289-9*, Avon Bks) Morrow Avon.

Never Trust a Sister over Twelve. Stephen Roos. LC 92-34406. (J). 1995. 9.09 (*0-606-09679-5*, Pub. by Turtleback) Demco.

Never Trust a Skinny Cook. Arlene M. Conant. (Illus.). 316p. 1995. spiral bd. 24.95 (*0-9664418-0-X*) A M Conant.

Never Trust a Squirrel. Patrick Cooper. LC 98-23251. (Illus.). (J). (ps-2). 1999. 15.99 (*0-525-46009-8*, Dutton Child) Peng Put Young Read.

Never Trust a White Man: I Am Makah, Son of Whaling Nation. Arlyn Conly. LC 97-76424. (Illus.). 300p. 1998. pap. 16.95 (*1-880222-29-9*) Red Apple Pub.

*__Never Trust Lara.__ Katherine Applegate. LC 99-94488. (Making Out Ser.: No. 20). 176p. (YA). (gr. 7-12). 2000. mass mkt. 3.99 (*0-380-81309-2*, Avon Bks) Morrow Avon.

*__Never Trust the Fall Line.__ Becky Flynn. 336p. 1999. pap. 17.95 (*0-913884-07-3*) Porphyrion Pr.

Never Try to Teach a Pig to Sing: Still More Urban Folklore from the Paperwork Empire. Alan Dundes & Carl R. Pagter. LC 90-28451. (Humor in Life & Letters Ser.). (Illus.). 436p. 1991. pap. 19.95 (*0-8143-2358-8*); text 39.95 (*0-8143-2357-X*) Wayne St U Pr.

Never Try to Teach a Pig to Sing . . . Wit & Wisdom for Leaders. Donald E. Walker. LC 96-94124. 240p. (Orig.). 1996. pap. 12.95 (*0-9651194-2-4*) Lathrop Pr.

Never Turn Back. Erma Robinson. 236p. 1998. pap. 8.00 (*1-57502-772-0*, P02129) Morris Pubng.

Never Turn Back: Father Serra's Mission. James J. Rawls. Ed. by Alex Haley. LC 92-12814. (Stories of America Ser.). (Illus.). 52p. (J). (gr. 2-5). 1993. pap. write for info. (*0-8114-8061-5*); lib. bdg. 24.26 (*0-8114-7221-3*) Raintree Steck-V.

Never Turn Back: The Life of Whitewater Pioneer Walt Blackadar. Ron Watters. LC 94-76564. (Illus.). 320p. 1995. lib. bdg. 31.50 (*1-887625-04-6*) Great Rift.

This fascinating & masterfully written book is considered one of the outdoor world's finest works. The LOS ANGELES DAILY NEWS awarded NEVER TURN BACK their highest rating for a book: "It's the best thing to come across this reviewer's desk in recent memory," wrote Brett Pauly of the NEWS. "Bully for Watters!" said the SAN FRANCISCO CHRONICLE about author Ron Watters' wonderfully told story. William Bushnell of the Library Research Associates called it: "Magnificent...told with sparkling clarity...truly inspirational." NEVER TURN BACK is the unforgettable biography of whitewater sport's most famous personality Dr. Walt Blackadar. Blackadar stunned the outdoor world when he ran the treacherous rapids of Turnback Canyon on the remote & wild Alsek River in Canada & Alaska. What made his solo journey through Turnback Canyon even more remarkable was the fact that he was 49 years old, an age when most athletes are long retired. Blackadar's story is powerful & uplifting. It is the story of the human spirit facing & overcoming great odds. Joining book reviewers in praise for the book are outdoor authorities such as World Whitewater Champion Barb Wright: "A work of art!" Other reviews: "A triumph! I couldn't put it down." "Uncommonly well-written & well-edited." "An inspiring book." Available in paper, hardcover, or library binding from Great Rift Press, 1135 East Bonneville, Pocatello, ID 83201. Toll free information: 800-585-6857. *Publisher Paid Annotation.*

Never Turn Your Back on Kudzu & Other Southern Wisdom. Ed. by Rick Harmon. 244p. (Orig.). pap. 9.95 (*1-882616-02-2*) Advertiser.

Never Underestimate the Power of Cash Deals. Edward E. Sanders. 128p. 1993. pap. 9.95 (*0-9635724-0-7*) Blue Chip Pub.

Never Underestimate the Selling Power of a Woman. Dottie Walters. 1986. pap. 7.00 (*0-87980-416-5*) Wilshire.

Never Underestimate the Selling Power of a Woman. Dottie Walters. 223p. 1983. reprint ed. 13.95 (*0-934344-24-8*) Royal Pub.

Never Victorious, Never Defeated. Taylor Caldwell. 1976. reprint ed. lib. bdg. 32.95 (*0-88411-162-8*) Amereon Ltd.

Never Walk Alone. Delmar Taylor. 1991. pap. 5.95 (*0-86544-062-X*) Salv Army Suppl South.

Never Walk Away: Lessons on Integrity from a Father Who Lived It. Crawford W. Loritts. 1998. pap. 9.95 (*0-8024-2742-1*) Moody.

Never Wear Black Socks or a Plain White T-Shirt While Running: And 501 Other Truths Too Simple Not to Know. Joe Kelly. LC 96-20134. (Illus.). 160p. 1996. pap. 8.95 (*0-9639290-5-4*) Good Times.

Never Were Men So Brave: The Irish Brigade During the Civil War. Susan P. Beller. LC 97-16005. (Illus.). 112p. (YA). (gr. 5-9). 1998. per. 15.00 (*0-689-81406-2*) S&S Childrens.

*__Never Wife.__ Cynthia Hogue. LC 99-65032. 78p. 1999. pap. 12.95 (*0-9666028-4-6*, Pub. by Mammoth Press) SPD-Small Pr Dist.

Never Without a Song: The Years & Songs of Jennie Devlin, 1865-1952. Katharine D. Newman. LC 93-6387. (Music in American Life Ser.). (Illus.). 272p. 1994. text 39.95 (*0-252-02081-2*); pap. text 16.95 (*0-252-06371-6*) U of Ill Pr.

Never Without an Intercessor: The Good News about the Judgment. Morris L. Venden. LC 96-11253. 1996. 10.99 (*0-8163-1349-0*) Pacific Pr Pub Assn.

Never Without Consent: James Bay Crees Stand Against an Independent Quebec. Grand Council of the Crees Staff. LC 98-168927. 200p. 1997. pap. 21.95 (*1-55022-301-1*, Pub. by ECW) Genl Dist Srvs.

Never Without Heroes: Marine Third Reconnaissance Battalion in Vietnam, 1965-70. Lawrence C. Vetter, Jr. (Orig.). 1996. mass mkt. 5.99 (*0-8041-0807-2*) Ivy Books.

Never Without One. Diane Ward. (Roof Bks.). 62p. (Orig.). 1984. pap. 100.00 (*0-937804-13-4*) Segue NYC.

Neverending Nite. Harry Grounds, Jr. 246p. (Orig.). 1995. pap. 14.95 (*0-9643195-0-0*) Park Bks.

Neverending Stories: Toward a Critical Narratology. Ed. by Ann Fehn et al. (Illus.). 268p. 1992. text 42.50 (*0-691-06895-X*, Pub. by Princeton U Pr) Cal Prin Full Svc.

Neverending Story. Michael Ende. Tr. by Ralph Manheim. (Illus.). (YA). (gr. 5 up). 1997. 19.99 (*0-614-28726-X*) NAL.

Neverending Story. Michael Ende. Tr. by Ralph Manheim. LC 96-51187. 448p. (J). 1993. pap. 6.99 (*0-14-038633-5*, PuffinBks) Peng Put Young Read.

Neverending Story. Michael Ende. Tr. by Ralph Manheim. LC 96-49342. (Illus.). 384p. (J). 1997. 21.99 (*0-525-45758-5*, Dutton Child) Peng Put Young Read.

Neverending Story. Michael Ende. 1976. 31.95 (*0-8488-1306-5*) Amereon Ltd.

Neverending Story. Michael Ende. 1985. 10.09 (*0-606-02806-4*, Pub. by Turtleback) Demco.

Neverending Story. Michael Ende. (J). 1997. 11.09 (*0-606-11677-X*, Pub. by Turtleback) Demco.

Neverending Story. Michael Ende. (Illus.). 400p. (J). 1991. reprint ed. lib. bdg. 33.95 (*0-89966-807-0*) Buccaneer Bks.

Neverending Story: Movie Edition. Michael Ende. Tr. by Ralph Manheim. 384p. (gr. 5-9). 1984. pap. 11.95 (*0-14-007431-7*, Penguin Bks) Viking Penguin.

Neverends. Bern Porter. (Illus.). 50p. (Orig.). 1988. pap. 3.00 (*0-926935-03-8*) Runaway Spoon.

Nevereverdrop: A Raindrop's Search for the Meaning of Life. Rodger Stevens. 95p. (Orig.). 1989. pap. 6.95 (*0-9618596-2-8*) TIW.

Neverfield Poem. Nathalie Handal. LC 99-12232. 57p. 1999. pap. 12.00 (*0-942996-35-6*, Pub. by Post Apollo Pr) SPD-Small Pr Dist.

Neverland. Douglas Clegg. (Orig.). 1991. mass mkt. 4.95 (*0-671-31286-3*) PB.

Neverland. Phyllis Nagy. LC 97-150384. 1996. pap. 11.95 (*0-413-70140-9*, Methuen Drama) Methn.

Nevermind: Its Only Rock of Ages. Sal Nudo. 40p. 1999. pap. 8.00 (*0-8059-4662-4*) Dorrance.

Nevermore. William Hjortsberg. 1996. mass mkt. 5.99 (*0-312-95695-9*, Pub. by Tor Bks) St Martin.

Nevermore. Marie Redonnet. Tr. by Jordon Stump. LC 96-1288. (European Women Writers Ser.). vi, 125p. 1996. pap. 12.00 (*0-8032-8959-6*, Bison Books) U of Nebr Pr.

Nevermore. Marie Redonnet. Tr. & Intro. by Jordan Stump. LC 96-1288. (European Women Writers Ser.). vi, 125p. 1996. text 40.00 (*0-8032-3912-2*) U of Nebr Pr.

Nevermore. Harold Schechter. LC 99-14364. 1999. 27.95 (*0-7862-1939-4*) Mac Lib Ref.

Nevermore! Julian Wiles & Edgar Allan Poe. 84p. 1995. pap. 5.50 (*0-87129-612-8*, N41) Dramatic Pub.

Nevermore. Harold Schechter. 480p. 2000. reprint ed. per. 6.99 (*0-671-79856-1*) PB.

Nevermore: A Novel. Harold Schechter. LC 98-50131. 352p. 1999. 23.00 (*0-671-79855-3*, PB Hardcover) PB.

Nevermore: The Hymen & the Loss of Virginity. Deanna Holtzman & Nancy Kulish. LC 96-30401. 1997. pap. 37.50 (*0-7657-0037-9*) Aronson.

*__Nevermore: The Poems of E. A. Poe.__ Ed. by Book Sales Staff. 2000. 8.99 (*0-7858-1213-X*) Bk Sales Inc.

Nevernever. Will Shetterly. LC 93-238. 256p. (YA). (gr. 9 up). 1993. 16.95 (*0-15-257022-5*, Harcourt Child Bks) Harcourt.

Nevernever. Will Shetterly. 288p. 1995. reprint ed. 4.99 (*0-8125-5151-6*, Pub. by Tor Bks) St Martin.

Nevertheless. Bill Panko & Margaret Panko. 100p. (Orig.). Date not set. pap. 9.95 (*1-885342-21-7*) Creative Ways.

An Asterisk (*) at the beginning of an entry indicates that the title is appearing for the first time.

Nevertheless: The Varieties & Shortcomings of Religious Pacifism. 3rd rev. ed. John H. Yoder. LC 93-39633. 192p. 1992. pap. 11.99 (*0-8361-3586-5*) Herald Pr.

Neverwhere. Neil Gaiman. LC 96-53681. 337p. 1997. 24.00 (*0-380-97363-4*, Avon Bks) Morrow Avon.

Neverwhere. Neil Gaiman. LC 96-53681. 388p. 1998. mass mkt. 6.99 (*0-380-78901-9*, Avon Bks) Morrow Avon.

NeverWorld. Erin Laughlin. 1996. boxed set 38.00 (*1-889312-01-0*) ForeverWrld.

NeverWorld: A Life-Time Experience. Erin Laughlin. 304p. 1996. pap. write for info. (*1-889312-00-2*) ForeverWrld.

NeverWorld: GM's Screen. Erin Laughlin. 6p. 1996. pap. write for info. (*1-889312-75-4*) ForeverWrld.

Neveryona: or The Tale of Signs & Cities Part 4: Some Informal Remarks Towards the Modular Calculus. Samuel R. Delany. LC 93-17847. (Return to Neveryon Ser.: Bk. 2). 402p. 1993. pap. 14.95 (*0-8195-6271-8*, Wesleyan Univ Pr) U Pr of New Eng.

Neveu de Rameau. Denis Diderot. Ed. by D'Adam. (Coll. GF). (FRE.). 1966. pap. 10.95 (*0-8288-9958-4*, F46912) Fr & Eur.

Neveu de Rameau - la Reve de d'Alembert... Denis Diderot. (FRE.). 438p. 1978. pap. 11.95 (*0-7859-1818-3*, 2070367614) Fr & Eur.

Neveu de Rameau & le Reve de d'Alembert, Supplement au Voyage de Bougainville, et Autres Dialogues. Denis Diderot. (Folio Ser.: No. 761). (FRE.). (Orig.). pap. 9.95 (*2-07-036761-4*) Schoenhof.

Nevill Mott Festschrift: In Celebration of His Eightieth Birthday, a Special Issue of Philosophical Magazine B, Vol. 52, No. 3. Ed. by E. A. Davis et al. 616p. 1985. 46.00 (*0-85066-972-3*) Taylor & Francis.

***Neville Chamberlain & Appeasement.** Robert J. Caputi. LC 99-23975. 272p. 2000. 45.00 (*1-57591-027-6*) Susquehanna U Pr.

Neville Chamberlain & British Rearmament: Pride, Prejudice & Politics, 71. John Ruggerio. LC 99-14841. (Contributions to the Study of World History Ser.: No. 71). 272p. 1999. 65.00 (*0-313-31050-5*, Greenwood Pr) Greenwood.

Neville Chamberlain, Appeasement & the Road to War. Frank McDonough. LC 97-15519. (New Frontiers in History Ser.). 224p. 1998. pap. 27.95 (*0-7190-4832-X*, Pub. by Manchester Univ Pr); text 69.95 (*0-7190-4831-1*, Pub. by Manchester Univ Pr) St Martin.

***Neville Chamberlain Diary Letters.** Neville Chamberlain & Robert C. Self. LC 00-26601. 2000. write for info. (*1-84014-691-5*, Pub. by Ashgate Pub) Ashgate Pub Co.

***Neville Howse: Australia's First Victoria Cross Winner.** Ed. by Michael B. Tyquin. (Australian Army History Ser.). 256p. 2000. 39.95 (*0-19-551190-5*) OUP.

Neville Site: 8,000 Years at Amoskeag. Dena F. Dincauze. LC 75-40771. (Peabody Museum Monographs: No. 4). (Illus.). 160p. 1976. pap. 12.00 (*0-87365-903-1*) Peabody Harvard.

Neville's Island. Tim Firth. LC 99-205946. 1997. pap. 5.25 (*0-8222-1581-0*) Dramatists Play.

Nevill's Wil Drafting Handbook. 4th ed. W. L. Douglas. 149p. 1988. boxed set 63.00 (*0-409-70222-6*, NZ, MICHIE) LEXIS Pub.

Nevin Genealogica (Some Desc. of Daniel Nevin, Cumberland Valley, Pa., 1770), 2 vols. in 1. John D. Nevin. 435p. 1995. reprint ed. pap. 65.00 (*0-8328-4453-5*); reprint ed. lib. bdg. 75.00 (*0-8328-4452-7*) Higginson Bk Co.

Nevin Shellheap: Burial & Observations, Vol. 9. Douglas S. Byers. 1979. pap. 15.00 (*0-939312-10-7*) Peabody Found.

Nevis: Resource Assessment & Zoning Plan. I. R. Corker. 65p. 1990. pap. 30.00 (*0-85954-271-8*, Pub. by Nat Res Inst) St Mut.

Nevis Mountain Dew. Steve Carter. 1979. pap. 5.25 (*0-8222-0812-1*) Dramatists Play.

New A. L. P. O. Jupiter Handbook. Phillip Budine et al. (Illus.). 181p. (Orig.). (YA). 1990. pap. text 15.00 (*0-9626527-0-9*) Cechoni Prodns.

New A+ Certification Training Guide. Charles J. Brooks. Ed. by Whitney G. Freeman. Tr. by Michael R. Hall & Cathy J. Boulay. (Illus.). 1998. pap. text 59.95 (*1-58122-000-6*); pap. text, teacher ed. 35.00 (*1-58122-002-2*); pap. text, lab manual ed. 59.95 (*1-58122-001-4*) Marcraft Intl.

***New A+ Certification Training Guide.** Charles J. Brooks. LC 99-39274. 2000. write for info. (*0-13-017549-8*) P-H.

New A to Z Horoscope Maker & Delineator. 14th rev. ed. Llewellyn George. Ed. by Marylee Bytheriver. LC 83-80177. (Illus.). 592p. (C). 1999. reprint ed. pap. 14.95 (*0-87542-264-0*) Llewellyn Pubns.

***New A to Z of Women's Health: A Concise Encyclopedia.** 4th ed. Christine Ammer. LC 99-16506. 2000. 19.95 (*0-8160-4002-8*) Facts on File.

New A to Z on Fuchsias. Bill Barnes et al. (Illus.). 1976. 11.95 (*0-686-19065-3*); pap. 9.95 (*0-317-00255-4*) Natl Fuchsia.

New A-Z Book of Women's Health. 3rd rev. ed. Christine Ammer. LC 94-25289. 576p. 1995. 40.00 (*0-8160-3121-5*) Facts on File.

***New A-Z of Babies' Names.** Jacqueline Harrod. 192p. 2000. pap. 8.95 (*0-7160-2039-4*, Pub. by Elliot RW Bks) Midpt Trade.

New A-Z of Managing People. David Freemantle. LC 98-40305. (Adams Critical Skills for Your Business Ser.). 304p. 1999. pap. text 9.95 (*1-58062-075-2*) Adams Media.

New ABC's of Shooting. 2nd ed. Ed. by Colin Willock. (Illus.). 352p. 1994. 39.95 (*0-233-98854-8*, Pub. by Andre Deutsch) Trafalgar.

New Abolitionists: Animal Rights & Human Liberation. rev. ed. B. R. Boyd. (Illus.). 24p. 1987. 1.75 (*0-9616792-1-2*) Taterhill.

New Abrasive Materials. Business Communications Co., Inc. Staff. 236p. 1991. 2650.00 (*0-89336-753-2*, GB-135) BCC.

New Abrasives & Abrasives Products, Technologies, Markets. Edward Giese & Thomas Abraham. LC 97-144903. 129p. 1997. 2950.00 (*1-56965-243-0*, GB-191) BCC.

New Absolutes: How They Are Being Imposed upon Us - How They Are Eroding Our Moral Landscape. William D. Watkins. 32p. 1997. pap. 11.99 (*0-7642-2019-5*) Bethany Hse.

New Academic Generation: A Profession in Transformation. Martin J. Finkelstein et al. LC 97-49368. (Illus.). 176p. 1998. text 32.50 (*0-8018-5886-0*) Johns Hopkins.

New Academic Marketplace, 30. Dolores L. Burke. LC 88-15445. (Contributions to the Study of Education Ser.: No. 30). 208p. 1988. 55.00 (*0-313-26383-3*, BNE/, Greenwood Pr) Greenwood.

New Account Careers. LC 89-91371. (Illus.). 160p. (Orig.). 1989. pap. 8.95 (*0-9623351-1-8*) New Account.

New Account of East India & Persia. S. Fryer. (C). 1985. 750.00 (*81-7136-003-3*, Pub. by Periodical Expert) St Mut.

New Account of Some Parts of Guinea & the Slave Trade. William Snelgrave. 288p. 1971. reprint ed. 57.50 (*0-7146-1898-5*, Pub. by F Cass Pubs) Intl Spec Bk.

New Account of Tales of the World. I-ching Liu. Tr. & Intro. by Richard B. Mather. LC 75-22650. 758p. 1976. reprint ed. pap. 200.00 (*0-608-00792-7*, 205934100010) Bks Demand.

New Account of the East India & Persia Being 9 Years' Travels, 1672-1681, 3 vols., Set. John Fryer. (C). 1992. reprint ed. 72.50 (*81-206-0796-1*, Pub. by Asian Educ Servs) S Asia.

New Accounting Manual: A Guide to the Documentation Process. Athar Murtuza. LC 94-34136. 384p. 1995. 130.00 (*0-471-30370-4*) Wiley.

New Accounting Manual: A Guide to the Documentation Process 1999 Cumulative Supplement. Athar Murtuza. 159p. 1999. pap., suppl. ed. 69.00 (*0-471-29878-6*) Wiley.

New Acoustic Guitar. Tony Rice. 24p. 1996. pap. 19.95 (*0-7935-6048-9*) H Leonard.

New Action Sports, 6 bks. Incl. In-Line Skating Basics. Jackson Jay & Jeff Savage. LC 95-44721. (Illus.). 48p. (J). (gr. 3-4). 1996. lib. bdg. 19.00 (*1-56065-400-7*, Cpstone High Low); Learning Martial Arts. Steve Potts. LC 95-47163. (Illus.). 48p. (J). (gr. 4-7). 1996. lib. bdg. 19.00 (*1-56065-403-1*, Cpstone High Low); Mastering Martial Arts. Steve Potts. LC 95-52010. (Illus.). 48p. (J). (gr. 4-7). 1996. lib. bdg. 19.00 (*1-56065-404-X*, Cpstone High Low); Skateboarding Basics. Jackson Jay. LC 95-44719. (Illus.). 48p. (J). (gr. 3-4). 1996. lib. bdg. 19.00 (*1-56065-374-4*, Cpstone High Low); Snowboarding Basics. Jackson Jay. LC 95-44718. (Illus.). 48p. (J). (gr. 3-4). 1996. lib. bdg. 19.00 (*1-56065-401-5*, Cpstone High Low); Wrestling Basics. Jackson Jay & Jeff Savage. LC 95-44720. (Illus.). 48p. (J). (gr. 3-4). 1996. lib. bdg. 19.00 (*1-56065-402-3*, Cpstone High Low); (Illus.). 48p. 114.00 (*1-56065-654-9*, Cpstone High Low) Capstone Pr.

New Actions of Parathyroid Hormone. Ed. by Shaul G. Massry & T. Fujita. (Illus.). 494p. 1989. 110.00 (*0-306-43418-0*, Plenum Trade) Perseus Pubng.

New Actions of Parathyroid Hormone. Y. Nishizawa & M. Smogorzewski. (Journal: Mineral & Electrolyte Metabolism Ser.: Vol. 21, Nos. 1-3, 1995). (Illus.). 244p. 1995. pap. 129.75 (*3-8055-6195-4*) S Karger.

New Ad Media Reality: Electronic over Print. Barton C. White. LC 93-18242. 264p. 1993. 62.95 (*0-89930-795-7*, WET/, Quorum Bks) Greenwood.

***New Addresses: Poems.** Kenneth Koch. LC 99-53978. 104p. 2000. pap. 23.00 (*0-375-41027-9*) Knopf.

***New Adreana Robbins Novel.** Adreana Robbins. 2000. text 24.95 (*0-312-87280-1*) St Martin.

New Advanced Dry Pilgrimage. Paul Leonard & Nick Walters. (New Adventures Ser.). mass mkt. 5.95 (*0-426-20525-1*, Pub. by Virgin Bks) London Brdge.

New Advanced French Course. Whitmarsh & Jukes. 1971. 6.15 (*0-582-36102-8*, 72365) Longman.

New Advanced French Course. W. H. F. Whitmarsh & Jukes. 1971. pap. text 12.00 (*0-582-36101-X*, 72364) Longman.

New Advances in Absolute Relativistic Space & Time. Ed. by H. E. Wilhelm & Shuoping Wu. (Illus.). 310p. (C). 1997. pap. text 70.00 (*1-57485-040-7*) Hadronic Pr Inc.

New Advances in Computational Structural Mechanics: Proceedings of the European Conference on New Advances in Computational Structural Mechanics, Giens, France, 2-5 April 1991. Ed. by P. Ladeveze & O. C. Zienkiewicz. LC 92-9902. (Studies in Applied Mechanics: Vol. 32). 484p. 1992. 240.75 (*0-444-89057-2*) Elsevier.

New Advances in Computer Graphics. Ed. by Rae A. Earnshaw & B. Wyvill. (Illus.). x, 718p. 1989. 196.95 (*0-387-70045-5*) Spr-Verlag.

New Advances in Distributed Computer Systems: Proceedings of the NATO Advanced Study Institute, Bonas, France, June 15-26, 1981. NATO Advanced Study Institute Staff. Ed. by Kenneth G. Beauchamp. x, 417p. 1982. text 281.50 (*90-277-1379-0*) Kluwer Academic.

New Advances in Diuretic Treatment. Ed. by St. H. Taylor. (Journal: Cardiology: Vol. 84, Suppl. 2, 1994). (Illus.). iv, 172p. 1994. pap. 52.25 (*3-8055-6001-X*) S Karger.

New Advances in Financial Economics. Ed. by Dilip K. Ghosh. LC 94-46677. (International Business & Economics Ser.). 300p. 1995. text 66.50 (*0-08-042408-2*, Pergamon Pr) Elsevier.

New Advances in Histamine Research. Kenji Tasaka. LC 94-39978. 1995. 110.00 (*0-387-70137-0*) Spr-Verlag.

New Advances in Modal Synthesis of Large Structures Non-Linear Damped & Non Deterministic Cases: Proceedings of the International Conference MV2, Lyon, France, 5-6 October 1995. Ed. by Louis Jezequel. (Illus.). 620p. (C). 1997. text 126.00 (*90-5410-859-2*, Pub. by A A Balkema) Ashgate Pub Co.

New Advances in Oriented Plastics: Technical Papers, Regional Technical Conference, September 16-17, 1987, Atlantic City, NJ. Society of Plastics Engineers Staff. LC TA0455.P58. 171p. reprint ed. pap. 53.10 (*0-608-17830-6*, 203250500079) Bks Demand.

New Advances in Polyolefins. T. C. Chung. (Illus.). 256p. (C). 1994. text 89.50 (*0-306-44588-3*, Kluwer Plenum) Kluwer Academic.

New Advances in Renal Ammonia Metabolism. Ed. by A. C. Schoolwerth et al. (Contributions to Nephrology Ser.: Vol. 47). (Illus.). x, 238p. 1985. 29.75 (*3-8055-4009-4*) S Karger.

New Advances in Vascular Biology & Molecular Cardiovascular Medicine: A Society of Cardiovascular Anesthesiologists Monograph. Debra Schwinn. 226p. 68.00 (*0-683-18344-3*) Lppncott W & W.

***New Adventure in Healthy Eating: Tofu.** Susan Ang. 1999. 12.99 (*0-9666322-2-2*) S Ang.

New Adventures. Michael Monahan. LC 77-93363. (Essay Index Reprint Ser.). 1977. 26.95 (*0-8369-1310-8*) Ayer.

New Adventures in Beading Earrings. Laura Reid. Ed. by Monte Smith. (Illus.). 64p. (Orig.). 1989. pap., per. 9.95 (*0-943604-18-4*, BOO/07) Eagles View.

New Adventures of Jasper Woodbury: In the Classroom. Vanderbilt University Staff. 1996. 75.00 incl. vdisk (*1-57004-033-8*) Lrning NJ.

New Adventures of Jasper Woodbury Vol. 1: Journey to Cedar Creek. Vanderbilt University Staff. 1996. 245.00 incl. vdisk (*1-57004-034-6*) Lrning NJ.

New Adventures of Jasper Woodbury Vol. 2: Rescue at Boone's Meadow. Vanderbilt University Staff. 1996. 245.00 incl. vdisk (*1-57004-035-4*) Lrning NJ.

New Adventures of Jasper Woodbury Vol. 3: The Big Splash. Vanderbilt University Staff. 1996. 245.00 incl. vdisk (*1-57004-036-2*) Lrning NJ.

New Adventures of Jasper Woodbury Vol. 4: A Capital Idea. 1996. 245.00 incl. vdisk (*1-57004-037-0*) Lrning NJ.

New Adventures of Jasper Woodbury Vol. 6: The Great Circle Race. 1996. 245.00 incl. vdisk (*1-57004-039-7*) Lrning NJ.

New Adventures of Jasper Woodbury Vol. 7: Get Out the Vote. 1996. 360.00 incl. vdisk (*1-57004-040-0*) Lrning NJ.

New Adventures of Jasper Woodbury Vol. 8: Blueprint for Success. 1996. 360.00 incl. VHS (*1-57004-041-9*) Lrning NJ.

New Adventures of Jasper Woodbury Vol. 9: Bridging the Gap. Vanderbilt University Staff. 1996. 360.00 incl. vdisk (*1-57004-042-7*) Lrning NJ.

New Adventures of Jimmie Lavender. Vincent Starrett. (Vincent Starrett Memorial Library: Vol. 4). (Illus.). x, 242p. 1995. 24.00 (*1-896032-72-9*) Battered Silicon.

New Adventures of Mother Goose: Gemstones Christmas. Rosenberg. (Illus.). 32p. (J). (ps-k). 1999. 9.95 (*0-689-82438-6*) S&S Trade.

New Adventures of Mother Goose: Gentle Rhymes for Happy Times. Illus. by Stephen Carpenter. LC 93-11129. 32p. (J). 1993. 15.00 (*0-88166-201-1*) Meadowbrook.

New Adventures of Mother Goose: Gentle Rhymes for Happy Times. Bruce Lansky. (Illus.). 32p. (J). (ps up). 1993. 15.00 (*1-881662-01-2*) Meadowbrook.

New Adventures of Mother Goose: Gentle Rhymes for Happy Times. Bruce Lansky. (Illus.). 32p. (J). (ps-k). 1993. 15.00 (*0-671-87288-5*) S&S Trade.

New Adventures of Rick O'Shay & Hipshot Bks. 1 & 2: Price of Fame, 2 vols., Set. Stan Lynde. 64p. 1992. pap. text 10.00 (*1-886370-13-3*) Cttnwd Pub.

***New Adventures of Sherlock Holmes.** Ed. by Martin Harry Greenberg & Carol-Lynn Rossel Waugh. (Illus.). 384p. 1999. pap. text 13.95 (*0-7867-0698-8*) Carroll & Graf.

New Adventures of Sherlock Holmes. Stephen King et al. Ed. by Martin H. Greenberg & Carol-Lynn Rossel Waugh. (Illus.). 344p. 1988. pap. 11.95 (*0-88184-435-7*) Carroll & Graf.

New Adventures of Sherlock Holmes: The Strange Case of the Demom Barber & the Mystery of the Headless Monk, Vol. 4. abr. ed. Anthony Boucher & Denis Green. 1989. 9.95 incl. audio (*0-671-68088-9*, Audioworks) PB.

New Adventures of Sherlock Holmes Gift Set, Vol. 4. abr. ed. Anthony Boucher & Denis Green. 1993. audio 25.00 (*0-671-87587-6*) S&S Audio.

New Adventures of Sherlock Holmes, Vol. 1: The Unfortunate Tobacconist & The Paradol Chamber, Vol. 1. abr. ed. Anthony Boucher & Denis Green. 1988. 9.95 incl. audio (*0-671-66076-4*, Audioworks) PB.

New Adventures of Sherlock Holmes, Vol. 2: The Viennese Strangler & The Notorious Canary Trainer, Vol. 2. abr. ed. Denis Green & Anthony Boucher. 1988. 9.95 incl. audio (*0-671-66433-6*, Audioworks) PB.

New Adventures of Sherlock Holmes, Vol. 3: The Aprl Fool's Day Adventure & The Strange Adventure of the Uneasy Easy Chair, Vol. 3. abr. ed. Anthony Boucher & Denis Green. 1989. 9.95 incl. audio (*0-671-67785-3*, Audioworks) PB.

***New Affinities.** 344p. (C). 1999. pap. text 28.00 (*0-536-02300-X*) S&S Trade.

***New Africa: Dispatches from a Changing Continent.** Robert M. Press. LC 99-17517. (Illus.). 358p. 1999. 24.95 (*0-8130-1704-1*) U Press Fla.

New Africa in America Vol. 5: The Blending of African & American Religious & Social Traditions Among Black People in Meridian, Mississippi & Surrounding Counties. Mozella G. Mitchell. LC 93-42526. (Martin Luther King, Jr., Memorial Studies in Religion, Culture, & Social Development: Vol. 5). XII, 240p. (C). 1995. text 39.95 (*0-8204-2425-0*) P Lang Pubng.

New African American Man. Malcolm Kelly. LC 96-95109. 190p. (Orig.). 1997. pap. 15.95 (*0-9656739-0-1*) BYE Pub Servs.

New African American Urban History. Ed. by Kenneth W. Goings & Raymond A. Mohl. LC 95-50234. 330p. (C). 1996. 54.00 (*0-7619-0308-9*) Sage.

New African Americans. Brent Ashabranner. LC 99-31388. (Illus.). 120p. (YA). (gr. 6-12). 1999. 21.00 (*0-208-02420-4*, Linnet Bks) Shoe String.

New African Literature & the Arts, Vol. 3. Ed. by Joseph O. Okpaku. LC 76-109903. 224p. 1973. 29.95 (*0-685-29060-3*); pap. 14.95 (*0-89388-083-3*) Okpaku Communications.

***New African Poetry.** Ed. by Tanure Ojaide & Tijan M. Sallah. LC 99-29889. (Three Continents Ser.). 234p. 2000. 49.95 (*0-89410-879-4*, Three Contnts) L Rienner.

***New African Poetry: An Anthology.** Ed. by Tanure Ojaide & Tijan M. Sallah. 233p. 2000. pap. 17.95 (*0-89410-891-3*, Three Contnts) L Rienner.

New Again! The 28-Day Detox Plan for Body & Soul. Anna Selby. (Illus.). 128p. 1999. pap. 16.95 (*1-56975-190-0*) Ulysses Pr.

New Age see **Nueva Era**

New Age. 2nd ed. Vladimir Uhri. (SLO.). 24p. (Orig.). 1996. pap. 1.40 (*1-56983-012-6*) New Creat WI.

New Age, No. 270. Van Rooyen. 88p. 1993. pap. 8.95 (*0-7935-2726-0*, 00102289) H Leonard.

New Age: A Christian Critique. Ralph Rath. LC 90-80211. viii, 343p. (Orig.). 1990. pap. 6.95 (*0-937779-15-6*) Greenlawn Pr.

New Age: A Cultural Critique. Leslie Shepard. (Occam's Razor Ser.). 1992. pap. 2.00 (*1-56543-008-5*) Mt SA Coll Philos.

New Age: Notes of a Fringe-Watcher. Martin Gardner. LC 87-35967. (Illus.). 273p. (C). 1991. reprint ed. pap. 19.95 (*0-87975-644-6*) Prometheus Bks.

New Age: Problems & Potential. Kenneth R. Pelletier. (Broadside Editions Ser.). 44p. (Orig.). (C). 1985. pap. 4.95 (*0-931191-02-5*) Rob Briggs.

New Age: Religion, Culture & Society in the Age of Post Modernity. Paul Heelas. (Illus.). 232p. (C). 1996. pap. text 25.95 (*0-631-19332-4*) Blackwell Pubs.

New Age Almanac. J. Gordon Melton. 1990. pap. 16.95 (*0-8103-9402-2*) Visible Ink Pr.

New Age American Literature, 2. 5th ed. Nina Baym. 1999. pap. text. write for info. (*0-393-99017-6*) Norton.

New-Age Answers to Age-Old Questions. 2nd ed. Rodger Stevens. (Illus.). 71p. (Orig.). 1987. reprint ed. pap. 6.95 (*0-9618596-0-1*) TIW.

New Age Armageddon - The Goddess or the Gury see **Return of the Dark - Light Goddess: Or New Age Armageddon - Towards a Femenist Vision of the Future**

New Age Astrology, 1994. Milo Kovar. (Astrology Annual Ser.). (Illus.). 64p. (Orig.). 1993. pap. 3.75 (*0-941208-14-1*) Milo Kovar.

New Age Astrology, 1997. Milo Kovar. (Astrology Annual Ser.). (Illus.). 64p. (Orig.). 1996. pap. 3.75 (*0-941208-16-8*) Milo Kovar.

New Age Baby Name Book. Sue Browder. LC 86-40549. (Illus.). 360p. 1987. pap. 7.95 (*0-89480-309-3*, 1309) Workman Pub.

New Age Baby Name Book. rev. ed. Sue Browder. 320p. 1987. mass mkt. 5.99 (*0-446-32004-8*, Pub. by Warner Bks) Little.

New Age Baby Name Book. rev. ed. Sue Browder. 1997. mass mkt. write for info. (*0-446-60391-0*) Warner Bks.

New Age Baby Name Book. rev. ed. Sue Browder. 480p. 1998. mass mkt. 6.99 (*0-446-60607-3*, Pub. by Warner Bks) Little.

New Age Baby Name Book. 3rd ed. Sue Browder. LC 97-53250. 512p. 1998. pap. 9.95 (*0-7611-0232-9*) Workman Pub.

New Age Bible Interpretation, Vol. 1. New Age Bible Interpretation Staff. (Illus.). 496p. 1990. reprint ed. lib. bdg. 29.00 (*0-933963-01-7*) New Age Bible.

New Age Bible Interpretation, Vol. 2. New Age Bible Interpretation Staff. (Illus.). 469p. 1995. reprint ed. lib. bdg. 29.00 (*0-933963-02-5*) New Age Bible.

New Age Bible Interpretation, Vol. 3. New Age Bible Interpretation Staff. Ed. by Frances Paelian. (Illus.). 516p. 1986. reprint ed. text 29.00 (*0-933963-03-3*) New Age Bible.

New Age Bible Interpretation, Vol. 4. New Age Bible Interpretation Staff. 144p. 1994. reprint ed. pap. 22.00 (*0-933963-04-1*) New Age Bible.

New Age Bible Interpretation, Vol. 5. New Age Bible Interpretation Staff. 230p. 1992. reprint ed. lib. bdg. 25.00 (*0-933963-05-X*) New Age Bible.

New Age Bible Interpretation, Vol. 6. New Age Bible Interpretation Staff. (Illus.). 255p. 1992. lib. bdg. 25.00 (*0-933963-06-8*) New Age Bible.

New Age Bible Interpretation, Vol. 7. New Age Bible Interpretation Staff. (Illus.). 298p. 1988. lib. bdg. 25.00 (*0-933963-07-6*) New Age Bible.

New Age Bible Versions: An Exhaustive Documentation of the Message, Men, & Manuscripts Moving Mankind to the Antichrist's One World Religion. 10th ed. Gail A. Riplinger. LC 93-92561. 700p. 1993. pap. 14.95 (*0-9635845-0-2*) A V Pubns.

New Age Brown Rice Cookbook. Gail Pierce. LC 81-84830. (Illus.). 172p. (Orig.). 1982. pap. 9.95 (*0-9607436-0-X*) Sea-Wind Pr.

New Age Business: Community Corporations that Work. Gregory MacLeod. 82p. 1986. pap. 9.95 (*0-88810-354-9*, Pub. by J Lorimer) Formac Dist Ltd.

***New Age Capitalism: Making Money East of Eden.** Kimberly J. Lau. 192p. 2000. pap. text 19.95 (*0-8122-1729-2*) U of Pa Pr.

N

New Age Cat Family Album. Laura Tolchinsky. 84p. (Orig.). 1997. pap. 4.95 (*1-57502-407-1*, PO1265) Morris Pubng.

New Age Christian: My Spiritual Journey. Nancy B. Detweiler. LC 97-93620. (Illus.). 240p. (Orig.). (C). 1997. pap. 24.95 (*0-9658949-0-8*) Bridging Gap.

New Age Christmas. rev. ed. Mike Garson. Ed. by Tom Roed. 56p. (Orig.). (YA). 1992. pap. 14.95 (*0-89898-648-6*, 0085B) Wrner Bros.

New Age Christmas Easy Piano Solo. 56p. 1997. pap. 8.95 (*0-7935-8041-2*) H Leonard.

New Age Community Guidebook. Compiled by Harbin Springs Publishing Staff. (Illus.). 130p. (Orig.). 1989. pap. 7.95 (*0-944202-03-9*) Harbin Springs.

New Age Consciousness & Awareness Poetry, Bk. 1. Alpha Pyramis Research Division Staff. 15p. 1985. pap. 7.95 (*0-913597-59-7*) Prosperity & Profits.

New Age Conversation. Doris C. Doane & Earl H. Cramer. LC 96-152458. 1996. 14.00 (*0-86690-454-9*, D3587-014) Am Fed Astrologers.

New Age Counterfeit: A Study Guide for Individual or Group Use. Johnette S. Benkovic. LC 95-74824. 96p. 1995. pap. 7.50 (*1-877678-36-8*) Queenship Pub.

New Age Cult. Walter Martin. LC 89-6889. 144p. (Orig.). 1989. pap. 7.99 (*1-55661-077-7*) Bethany Hse.

New Age Cults & Religions. Texe Marrs. 1990. pap. 13.95 (*0-9620086-8-0*) Living Truth Pubs.

New Age Dictionary of Mysticism & the Occult. Frederick G. Levine & Peter Israel. LC 90-6744. 1990. write for info. (*0-8022-2575-6*) Philosophical Bk Service.

New Age Directory of Planet Earth: The First International Body-Mind-Spirit Sourcebook, 2 vols. Patti N. Greenwood & Darrell T. Wilson. Incl. Vol. 1. unabridged ed. LC 97-93350. (Orig.). 1997. pap. (*0-9622539-4-4*); Vol. II. unabridged ed. LC 97-93350. (Orig.). 1997. pap. (*0-9622539-6-0*); LC 97-93350. Orig. Title: Holistic Directory of Planet Earth. 48.00 (*0-9622539-3-6*) Mystic Planet.

New Age Directory of Planet Earth: The United States of America. unabridged ed. Patti N. Greenwood & Darrell T. Wilson. 300p. (Orig.). 1997. pap. 29.00 (*0-9622539-9-5*) Mystic Planet.

New Age from a Biblical Viewpoint. M. Basilea Schlink. Orig. Title: New-Aus Biblischer Sicht. 32p. (Orig.). 1988. pap. 0.60 (*3-87209-631-1*) Evang Sisterhood Mary.

New Age Handbook on Death & Dying. Carol E. Parrish-Harra. LC 89-864. 196p. 1982. 10.95 (*0-945027-09-5*) Sparrow Hawk Pr.

New Age Herbalist. Richard Mabey. 1988. per. 21.00 (*0-684-81577-X*) S&S Trade.

New Age Herbalist. Storey Publishing Staff. 1997. pap. 21.00 (*0-676-57192-1*) Random.

New Age Hypnosis. Bruce Goldberg. LC 97-38817. 240p. (Orig.). 1999. pap. 12.95 (*1-56718-320-4*) Llewellyn Pubns.

New Age Hypnosis Workbook: A Technique Manual. Bruce Goldberg. Orig. Title: Past Life Regression/Future Life Progression: A Technique Manual. 66p. Date not set. wbk. ed. 30.00 (*1-885577-00-1*) B Goldberg.

New Age I Ching. Gordon Staff. LC 95-68095. 352p. 1995. pap. 22.00 (*0-89540-254-8*) Sun Pub.

New Age in Physics. 2nd ed. Harrie S. Massey. (Illus.). 1966. 29.95 (*0-8464-0670-5*) Beekman Pubs.

New Age Information Guide to the Federal Government. 593p. 1995. pap. 59.95 (*0-9645986-0-4*) Finkelstein.

New Age Is Dawning. Will Huddleston. 36p. (YA). (gr. 7 up). 1996. pap. 3.00 (*1-57514-192-2*, 1171) Encore Perform Pub.

New Age Is Lying to You. Eldon K. Winker. LC 93-37610. 224p. (Orig.). 1994. pap. 10.99 (*0-570-04637-8*, 12-3217) Concordia.

New Age Jesus see IVP Booklets

***New Age Judaism: Ancient Wisdom for the Modern World.** Melinda Ribner. 200p. 2000. pap. 9.95 (*1-55874-789-3*, Simcha Press) Health Comm.

New Age Judaism: Unlocking the Modern Secrets of Ancient Wisdoms. Melinda Ribner. LC 98-53969. 192p. 1999. 19.95 (*1-55972-511-7*, Birch Ln Pr) Carol Pub Group.

New Age Lies to Women. Texe Marrs & Wanda Marrs. 256p. 1989. 10.95 (*0-9620086-3-X*) Living Truth Pubs.

***New Age Living: A Guide to Principles, Practices & Beliefs.** Paul Roland. 2000. 29.95 (*0-600-59768-7*, Pub. by Hamlyn Publishing Group Ltd) Sterling.

New Age Menace: The Secret War Against the Followers of Christ. David N. Balmforth. 1996. pap. 13.98 (*0-88290-535-X*, 1067) Horizon Utah.

New Age Metaphysics: An Introduction for Young Adults. Paula J. Tyler & Fran Stagg. LC 86-63983. 63p. (YA). 1987. pap. 10.95 (*0-9617920-0-0*) Metaphys Enterp.

New Age Millennium: An Expose of Symbols, Slogans & Hidden Agendas. Grady D. Wilson & Demond Wilson. Ed. by Avaneda D. Hobbs. 217p. 2000. 24.95 (*1-878898-19-1*, Pub. by CAP Pub) ACCESS Pubs Network.

New Age Movement see IVP Booklets

New Age Movement see Nueva Era

New Age Movement. Harold J. Berry. 1996. pap. 1.35 (*0-8474-0827-2*) Back to Bible.

New Age Movement. Philip H. Lochhaas. LC 95-8596. (How to Respond Ser.). 64p. 1995. 3.99 (*0-570-04679-3*, 12-6012) Concordia.

New Age Movement. Ron Rhodes & Alan W. Gomes. (Guide to Cults & Religious Movements Ser.). 64p. 1995. pap. 5.99 (*0-310-70431-6*) Zondervan.

New Age Movement & the Biblical Worldview: Conflict & Dialogue. John P. Newport. 620p. 1998. pap. 35.00 (*0-8028-4430-8*) Eerdmans.

New Age Movement in American Culture. Richard Kyle. 304p. (Orig.). (C). 1995. pap. text 34.50 (*0-7618-0011-5*); lib. bdg. 58.50 (*0-7618-0010-7*) U Pr of Amer.

New Age Music Collection. 184p. (Orig.). (YA). 1994. pap. 16.95 (*0-7692-1052-X*, F3462P9X) Wrner Bros.

New Age Musicians. Ed. by Guitar Player Magazine Editors. 112p. (Orig.). 1989. pap. 14.95 (*0-88188-909-1*, 00183522) H Leonard.

New Age of Communications. John Green. LC 96-46404. 1995. 22.50 (*0-8050-4026-9*, Owl); pap. 10.95 (*0-8050-4027-7*, Owl) H Holt & Co.

New Age of Franklin Roosevelt, 1932-1945. Dexter Perkins. LC 56-11263. (Chicago History of American Civilization Ser.). 202p. 1957. pap. text 12.95 (*0-226-65872-4*, CHAC17) U Ch Pr.

New Age of Franklin Roosevelt, 1932-1945. Dexter Perkins. LC 56-11263. (Chicago History of American Civilization Ser.). 204p. reprint ed. pap. 63.30 (*0-608-10715-8*, 202014200016) Bks Demand.

New Age of Nonprofit Accountabilty. Sally Covington. 24p. 1997. pap. 25.00 (*1-891465-05-8*) Natl Comm Philan.

New Age of the Spirit? A Catholic Response to the New Age Phenomenon. Irish Theological Commission Staff. 80p. 1994. pap. 24.00 (*1-85390-237-3*, Pub. by Veritas Pubns) St Mut.

New Age-Old Path. Ishwar C. Puri. Ed. by Edward D. Scott. 54p. (Orig.). 1985. pap. 3.00 (*0-937067-04-0*) Insti Study Aware.

New Age or Old Lie? Kerry D. McRoberts. LC 89-12831. 138p. 1989. pap. 7.95 (*0-943575-30-3*) Hendrickson MA.

New Age Perspectives in Questions & Answers see World University Insights: With Your Future in Mind

New Age Primer. 206p. (Orig.). 1993. pap. 11.95 (*0-929385-48-9*) Light Tech Pubng.

New Age Reader: Readings for an Educated New Millenium. 2nd ed. Bogus. 536p. 1998. pap. text 41.00 (*0-536-59591-7*) Pearson Custom.

New Age Religion & Western Culture: Esotericism in the Mirror of Secular Thought. Wouter J. Hanegraaff. LC 96-34697. (Studies in the History of Religions). 1996. 146.50 (*90-04-10695-2*); pap. 50.00 (*90-04-10696-0*) Brill Academic Pubs.

New Age Religion & Western Culture: Esotericism in the Mirror of Secular Thought. Wouter J. Hanegraaff. LC 97-37707. (SUNY Series in Western Esoteric Traditions). 593p. (C). 1997. reprint ed. pap. text 24.95 (*0-7914-3854-6*) State U NY Pr.

New Age Resources Directory. Ed. by Erin H. Rado. 225p. (Orig.). 1994. pap. 15.95 (*1-886329-00-1*) Goddess Pr.

New Age-Scale for Humans. Daniel Hershey. (Illus.). 156p. 1998. reprint ed. pap. 25.00 (*0-916961-06-0*) Basal Books.

New Age Secret Plan for World Conquest. Salem Kirban. (Prophecy Studies). 187p. 1976. pap. 7.99 (*0-89957-621-4*) AMG Pubs.

New Age Short Stories: A Collection. Dick Sutphen. LC 97-61408. 136p. 1997. pap. 10.00 (*0-87554-608-0*, B942) Valley Sun.

New Age Tantra Yoga: The Sexual Gateway to Spiritual Fulfillment. 6th ed. Howard J. Zitko. LC 75-3657. 172p. Date not set. pap. 10.95 (*0-941902-00-5*) World Univ AZ.

New Age Tarot: A Workbooks Glossary of Symbols. 3rd ed. James Wanless. (Illus.). 162p. Date not set. pap., wbk. ed. 2.95 (*0-9615079-4-2*) Merrill-West Pub.

New Age Tarot: Guide to the Thoth Deck. James Wanless. 164p. 1988. pap. 10.95 (*0-9615079-1-8*) Merrill-West Pub.

New Age Tarot: Guide to the Thoth Deck. James Wanless. 1997. pap. text 12.95 (*0-88079-591-3*, BK122) US Games Syst.

New Age Thinking: A Psychoanalytic Critique. M. D. Faber. 375p. 1996. 48.00 (*0-7766-0421-X*); pap. 27.95 (*0-7766-0417-1*) Edits Ottawa.

New Age Travellers: Vanloads of Uproarious Humanity Kevin Hetherington. LC 99-26817. 1999. 26.95 (*0-304-33978-4*) Continuum.

New Age Understanding. Donald Curtis. LC 72-92276. 144p. (YA). 1990. reprint ed. pap. 7.95 (*0-941992-23-3*) Los Arboles Pub.

New Age Vegetarian Cookbook. 492p. 1981. text 11.00 (*0-911274-78-2*); pap. text 6.00 (*0-911274-79-0*) Rosicrucian.

New Age Woerterbuch. Elmar Gruber. (GER.). 19.95 (*0-7859-8371-6*, 3451083108) Fr & Eur.

New Age Women. Joyce Carbone & Ana Pine. LC 90-92049. (Illus.). 79p. (Orig.). 1990. pap. 7.95 (*1-878116-02-9*) JVC Bks.

New Age X Factor. Richard Starr. (Illus.). 226p. (Orig.). 1995. pap. 39.00 (*0-9640217-2-2*) Results Now.

New Agenda for Cities. 130p. 1992. 30.00 (*0-933729-75-8*, No. 5701) Natl League Cities.

New Agenda for Global Security: The Cooperating for Peace & Beyond. Ed. by Stephanie Lawson. LC 96-154501. 217p. 1996. pap. 24.95 (*1-86373-974-2*, Pub. by Allen & Unwin Pty) Paul & Co Pubs.

New Agenda for Higher Education: Choices Universities Can Make to Ensure a Brighter Future. K. Edward Renner. (Illus.). 160p. (Orig.). 1995. pap. text. write for info. (*1-55059-113-4*) Detselig Ents.

New Agenda for Interdisciplinary Survey Research Methods: Proceedings of the Casm Li Seminar. CASM Seminar Staff et al. LC 99-11314. 1999. write for info. (*0-8406-0552-8*) Natl Ctr Health Stats.

New Agenda for Medical Missions. Ed. by D. Merrill Ewert. (MAP International Monograph). 136p. (Orig.). 1993. reprint ed. pap. text 6.95 (*1-879148-05-6*) MAP Intl.

***New Agenda for Peace Research.** Ed. by Ho-Won Jeong. LC 98-49093. 382p. 1999. text 105.95 (*1-84014-082-8*, Pub. by Ashgate Pub) Ashgate Pub Co.

New Agenda for Peace Research. Ed. by Ho-Won Jeong. LC 98-49093. 382p. 1999. pap. 43.95 (*1-84014-089-5*) Ashgate Pub Co.

New Agenda for Women's Health & Nutrition. (Development in Practice Ser.). (FRE.). 116p. 1995. pap. 22.00 (*0-8213-3389-5*, 13389) World Bank.

New Agenda for Women's Health & Nutrition. Contrib. by International Bank for Reconstruction & Development Staff. LC 94-29586. (Development in Practice Ser.). 116p. 1994. pap. 22.00 (*0-8213-3009-8*, 13009) World Bank.

New Agendas for Peace Research: Conflict & Security Reexamined. Elise Boulding. LC 91-31610. 199p. 1992. lib. bdg. 38.00 (*1-55587-290-5*) L Rienner.

***New Agendas for Women.** Sylvia Walby. LC 98-53534. 1999. text 69.95 (*0-312-22242-4*) St Martin.

New Aggressive Era in Financial Institutions Mergers & Acquisitions. (Corporate Law & Practice Course Handbook, 1985-86 Ser.). Date not set. pap. 99.00 (*0-614-17214-4*, B4-7135) PLI.

New Aging: Politics & Change in America. Fernando M. Torres-Gil. LC 91-18649. 224p. 1991. 55.00 (*0-86569-035-9*, T035, Auburn Hse); pap. 19.95 (*0-86569-036-7*, R036, Auburn Hse) Greenwood.

***New Agrarian Mind: The Movement Toward Decentralist Thought in 20th Century America.** Allan Carlson. LC 99-56518. 197p. 1999. 29.95 (*1-56000-421-5*) Transaction Pubs.

New Aikido Complete: The Arts of Power & Movement. Yoshimitsu Yamada & Steven Pimsler. LC 80-21543. (Illus.). 212p. 1981. 25.00 (*0-8184-0301-2*) Carol Pub Group.

New Aird's Companion in Surgical Studies. K. C. Burnand & A. E. Young. (Illus.). 1440p. 1993. text 147.00 (*0-443-03831-7*) Church.

***New Aird's Companion in Surgical Studies.** 2nd ed. Ed. by K. G. Burnand & A. E. Young. (Illus.). 1248p. 1998. text. write for info. (*0-443-05326-X*) Church.

New Airedale Terrier. June Dutcher & Janet J. Framke. (Complete Breed Bk.). (Illus.). 256p. 1991. 25.95 (*0-87605-007-0*) Howell Bks.

New Alignment of Life. Ralph W. Trine. 228p. 1997. pap. 20.00 (*0-89540-347-1*, SB-347) Sun Pub.

New Alliance: Continuous Quality & Classroom Effectiveness. Mimi Wolverton. Ed. by Jonathan D. Fife. LC 96-75835. (ASHE-ERIC Higher Education Reports: No. 94-6). (Illus.). 127p. 1996. pap. 24.00 (*1-878380-62-1*) GWU Grad Schl E&HD.

New Alliance for the Next Century: The Future of U. S.-Korean Security Cooperation. Jonathan Pollack & Y. K. Cha. 100p. 1995. pap. text 15.00 (*0-8330-2350-0*, MR-594-OSD) Rand Corp.

New Alliances for Community Education & Technical Assistance in Rural Areas. Glen Pulver. (New Alliances for Rural America Ser.). (Orig.). 1988. pap. text 6.00 (*1-55877-020-8*) Natl Governor.

New Alliances for Rural America. Ed. by DeWitt John et al. 76p. (Orig.). 1988. pap. text 15.00 (*1-55877-011-9*) Natl Governor.

New Alliances in Innovation: A Guide to Encouraging Innovative Applications of New Communication Technologies to Address State Problems. Nancy G. Helme. LC 92-43321. 1992. 15.95 (*0-934842-17-5*) CSPA.

New Alliances in Joyce Studies: "When It's Aped to Foul a Delfian" Ed. by Bonnie K. Scott. LC 86-40607. (Illus.). 256p. 1988. 35.00 (*0-87413-328-9*) U Delaware Pr.

New Altar Guild Book. Betty Sturges & Barbara Gent. LC 96-5655. 128p. 1996. pap. 9.95 (*0-8192-1657-7*, 1354) Morehouse Pub.

New Am Stream Departures, Vol. B. Peter Viney et al. (Illus.). 56p. 1994. pap. text, student ed. 6.50 (*0-19-434842-3*) OUP.

***New Amazons.** Margaret Weis. 2000. mass mkt. 6.99 (*0-88677-887-5*, Pub. by DAW Bks) Penguin Putnam.

New Ambidexterous Universe: Symmetry & Asymmetry from Mirror Reflections to Superstrings. rev. ed. Martin Gardner. LC 89-23610. (Illus.). 1991. pap. 14.95 (*0-7167-2093-0*) W H Freeman.

New Ambitions for Our Country: A New Contract for Welfare. Ed. by Stationery Office Source. LC 98-147314. (Command Papers: No. 3805). 1998. 30.00 (*0-10-138052-6*, HM85026, Pub. by Statnry Office) Bernan Associates.

New America. Poul Anderson. 288p. 1985. pap. 2.95 (*0-8125-3054-3*, Pub. by Tor Bks) St Martin.

New America. Michael A. Smith. LC 98-47003. 352p. 1999. 24.95 (*0-312-86821-9*, Pub. by Forge NYC) St Martin.

New America, 2 vols. William H. Dixon. LC 79-134428. reprint ed. 72.50 (*0-404-08468-0*) AMS Pr.

***New America: Investment Strategies for the New Millennium.** Marion McNair. 202p. 1999. pap. 29.95 (*0-9674946-0-5*) McNair CA.

New America: Prospects for Population & Policy in the 21st Century. Committee for Economic Development Staff. 64p. 1989. pap. 7.50 (*0-87186-345-6*) Comm Econ Dev.

New America Logo. Ed. by Gerry Rosentsweig. (Illus.). 212p. 1994. 37.50 (*0-942604-34-2*) Madison Square.

New American Acupuncture: Acupuncture Osteopathy: The Myofascial Release of the Bodymind's Holding Patterns. Mark Seem. Ed. by Bob Flaws. LC 93-71097. (Illus.). 175p. 1993. pap. 22.95 (*0-936185-44-9*) Blue Poppy Pr.

New American Apartment: Innovations in Residential Design & Construction: 30 Case Studies. Oscar Riera-Ojeda. LC 97-23273. (Illus.). 264p. 1997. 55.00 (*0-8230-3166-7*) Watsn-Guptill.

New American Bartender's Guide. 3rd ed. J. P. Poister. LC 99-212754. 640p. 1999. mass mkt. 6.99 (*0-451-19782-8*, Sig) NAL.

New American Bible: Ecology of Mind, Pt. II. Michael Mathiesen. Ed. by G. O. D. (Collaboration Ser.). 500p. pap. 20.00 (*0-939887-87-8*) Millennium Sta Cruz.

New American Bible for Catholics: Standard Edition. 1394p. 1988. pap. 14.95 (*0-8146-1750-6*) Liturgical Pr.

New American Blues: The Private Life of the Poor. Earl Shorris. LC 97-6384. 576p. 1997. 29.95 (*0-393-04554-4*) Norton.

New American Book of the Dead see Angels Healing Journey

New American Business System. 1991. 49.95 (*0-929586-01-8*) Meridian Learn Systs.

New American Catechism. 1991. pap. text, teacher ed. 1.50 (*0-89942-254-3*, 254/04) Catholic Bk Pub.

New American Center: Mystery of America. Michael K. Winger. (Illus.). 288p. (Orig.). 1994. pap. 11.95 (*1-883564-01-8*) New Lit.

New American Challenge. Marc D. Mont-Joy. LC 85-1445. 1988. pap. 13.95 (*0-87949-263-5*) Ashley Bks.

***New American Cheese: Profiles of America's Great Cheesemakers & Recipes for Cooking with Cheese.** Laura Werlin. LC 99-52588. (Illus.). 280p. 2000. 35.00 (*1-55670-990-0*) Stewart Tabori & Chang.

New American Cinema. Jon Lewis. LC 97-35210. 1998. 59.95 (*0-8223-2087-8*); pap. write for info. (*0-8223-2115-7*) Duke.

New American Circus. Ernest Albrecht. LC 95-2792. (Illus.). 280p. 1995. 29.95 (*0-8130-1364-X*) U Press Fla.

New American City Faces Its Regional Future: A Cleveland Perspective. Ed. by David C. Sweet et al. LC 98-54826. 264p. (Orig.). 1999. pap. 21.95 (*0-8214-1278-7*) Ohio U Pr.

New American Commercial Policy As Evidenced by Section 317 of the Tariff Act of 1922. Wallace M. McClure. LC 70-82240. (Columbia University. Studies in the Social Sciences: No. 255). reprint ed. 37.50 (*0-404-51255-0*) AMS Pr.

New American Community: A Response to the European & Asian Economic Challenge. Jerry M. Rosenberg. LC 91-35038. 200p. 1992. 57.95 (*0-275-94206-6*, C4206, Praeger Pubs) Greenwood.

New American Cottage: Innovations in Small-Scale Residential Architecture. Ed. by James G. Trulove & Il Kim. LC 98-53658. (Illus.). 228p. 1999. pap. text 55.00 (*0-8230-3169-1*) Watsn-Guptill.

New American Crisis: Radical Analyses of the Problems Facing America Today. Ed. by Greg Ruggiero & Stuart Sahulka. 272p. 1996. pap. 13.95 (*1-56584-317-7*, Pub. by New Press NY) Norton.

New American Crossword Puzzle Dictionary. Albert H. Morehead & Loy Morehead. 1986. mass mkt. 6.99 (*0-451-14503-8*, Sig) NAL.

New American Cuisine Pinot Gris Cookbook, Vol. 1. King Estate Winery Staff. Ed. by Stephanie P. Kimmel. LC 95-80581. (Illus.). 132p. 1996. pap. 16.95 (*0-9645500-1-6*) King Estate.

New American Cultural Sociology. Ed. by Philip Smith. LC 98-186670. (Cultural Social Studies). 296p. (C). 1998. text 59.95 (*0-521-58415-9*); pap. text 22.95 (*0-521-58634-8*) Cambridge U Pr.

New American Democracy. (C). 1998. text. write for info. (*0-205-29747-1*, Longwood Div) Allyn.

New American Democracy. (C). 1998. write for info. (*0-205-28505-8*, Macmillan Coll) P-H.

New American Democracy. (C). 1998. write for info. (*0-205-28134-6*, Macmillan Coll) P-H.

New American Democracy. Morris P. Fiorina & Paul E. Peterson. 1999. pap. text 56.45 (*0-205-29291-7*) S&S Trade.

New American Democracy. Fiorina & Peterson. LC 97-34742. 784p. 1997. 77.00 (*0-02-337770-4*) P-H.

New American Democracy. Fiorina & Peterson. 1997. pap. text, student ed. 17.00 (*0-205-27484-6*) P-H.

New American Democracy: Examination Copy. Morris P. Fiorina & Paul E. Peterson. 816p. (C). 1997. write for info. (*0-205-27672-5*) P-H.

New American Democracy: Instructor's Resource Manual. Morris P. Fiorina & Paul E. Peterson. (C). 1998. teacher ed. write for info. (*0-02-337771-2*) P-H.

New American Desk Encyclopedia. Concord Reference Staff. 1999. pap. write for info. (*0-451-17956-0*, Sig) NAL.

New American Desk Encyclopedia. Seafarer Staff. 11.98 (*0-8289-0878-8*) Seafarer Bks.

New American Desk Encyclopedia. 4th ed. Concord Reference Staff. 1424p. 1997. mass mkt. 9.99 (*0-451-19320-2*, Sig) NAL.

New American Destinies: Reader in Contemporary Asian & Latino Immigration. Ed. by Darrell Hamamoto & Rudi Torres. 384p. (C). 1996. 80.00 (*0-415-91768-9*); pap. 28.99 (*0-415-91769-7*) Routledge.

New American Dictionary of Baby Names. Leslie Dunkling & William Gosling. 496p. 1991. mass mkt. 6.99 (*0-451-17107-1*, Sig) NAL.

New American Diet. Sonja L. Connor & William E. Connor. 416p. 1989. pap. 14.00 (*0-671-66375-5*, Fireside) S&S Trade Pap.

New American Dilemma: Liberal Democracy & School Desegregation. Jennifer L. Hochschild. LC 84-40196. (Fastback Ser.: No. 28). 279p. 1984. pap. 17.00 (*0-300-03114-9*, YF-28) Yale U Pr.

New American Emergency Plant Care Guide. Jack Kramer. 1988. pap. 7.95 (*0-452-26161-9*, Plume) Dutton Plume.

New American Eskimo. Nancy J. Hofman & Cathy J. Flamholtz. (Illus.). 224p. 1996. 34.95 (*0-940269-10-4*) OTR Pubns.

An Asterisk (*) at the beginning of an entry indicates that the title is appearing for the first time.

New American Family: Tools for Strengthening Step-Families. Mary A. Artlip et al. LC 92-81392. 272p. 1993. pap. 10.95 (*0-914984-44-6*) Starburst.
New American Family & the Schools. J. Howard Johnston. 42p. (Orig.). (C). 1990. pap. text 9.00 (*1-56090-047-4*) Natl Middle Schl.
New American Furniture: The 2nd Generation of Studio Furnituremakers. Edward S. Cooke, Jr. Ed. by Cynthia M. Purvis. LC 89-63204. (Illus.). 131p. 1989. pap. 24.95 (*0-87846-315-1*) Mus Fine Arts Boston.
New American Garden: Innovations in Residential Landscape Architecture: 60 Case Studies. James G. Trulove. LC 97-51935. 228p. 1998. 55.00 (*0-8230-3168-3*, Whitney Lib) Watsn-Guptill.
New American Ghetto. Camilo J. Vergara. LC 94-45707. (Illus.). 200p. (C). 1995. 49.95 (*0-8135-2209-9*) Rutgers U Pr.
New American Ghetto. Camilo J. Vergara. LC 94-45707. (Illus.). 235p. 1997. pap. 25.95 (*0-8135-2331-1*) Rutgers U Pr.
New American Government. Fiorina. 1998. pap. text. write for info. (*0-02-337774-7*) P-H.
New American Grandparent: A Place in the Family, a Life Apart. Andrew J. Cherlin & Frank F. Furstenberg, Jr. (Illus.). 278p. 1992. pap. 16.95 (*0-674-60838-0*) HUP.
New American Guide to Punctuation. William C. Paxson. 240p. 1996. mass mkt. 5.99 (*0-451-62878-0*, Sig) NAL.
***New American Haggadah.** 3rd rev. ed. Mordecai Menaheim Kaplan et al. Ed. by Gila Gerirtz. LC 77-16803. (Illus.). 1998. pap. 9.95 (*0-87441-675-2*) Behrman.
***New American Handbook of Letter Writing: Plus Other Forms of Correspondence.** 2nd ed. Mary A. Devries. 416p. 2000. mass mkt. 6.99 (*0-451-19931-6*) NAL.
New American Heart Association Cookbook. 6th rev. ed. American Heart Association Staff. LC 99-462584. (Illus.). 698p. 1999. 30.00 (*0-8129-2954-3*, Times Bks) Crown Pub Group.
New American High School. David D. Marsh et al. LC 98-9079. (One-Off Ser.). 240p. 1998. pap. 24.95 (*0-8039-6226-6*); lib. bdg. 55.95 (*0-8039-6225-8*, 2795) Corwin Pr.
New American History. expanded rev. ed. Ed. by Eric Foner. LC 96-52059. (Critical Perspectives on the Past Ser.). 400p. (C). 1997. text 69.95 (*1-56639-551-8*) Temple U Pr.
New American History. expanded rev. ed. Eric Foner & American Historical Association Staff. LC 96-52059. (Critical Perspectives on the Past Ser.). 400p. 1997. pap. 22.95 (*1-56639-552-6*) Temple U Pr.
New American House: Innovations in Residential Design & Construction. Oscar R. Ojeda. (Illus.). 264p. 1995. pap. 55.00 (*0-8230-3163-2*) Watsn-Guptill.
New American House, Architectural Design Competition, 1984: A Catalogue of Winning & Selected Entries. Ed. by Elizabeth Spring & Harvey Sherman. (Illus.). 31p. (Orig.). (C). 1984. pap. 6.00 (*0-9611672-0-3*) Minneapolis Coll Art.
New American House 2: Innovations in Residential Design & Construction: 30 Case Studies. 2nd ed. Ed. by Oscar R. Ojeda. (Illus.). 264p. 1997. 55.00 (*0-8230-3164-0*) Watsn-Guptill.
***New American House 3: Innovations in Residential Design & Construction: 30 Case Studies, No. 3.** Ed. by James Grayson Trulove & Il Kim. (Illus.). 228p. 2000. pap. 55.00 (*0-8230-3192-6*) Watsn-Guptill.
New American Houses: Country, Sea & Cities. LArchivolto Editors. LC 98-164354. 1998. 79.95 (*88-7685-097-X*, Pub. by LArchivolto) Bks Nippan.
New American Ideology. George C. Lodge. 344p. (C). 1986. pap. text 19.00 (*0-8147-5027-3*) NYU Pr.
New American Interventionism. Demetrios Caraley. LC 99-14696. 320p. 1999. pap. 22.50 (*0-231-11849-X*) Col U Pr.
New American Kitchen Garden. Shepherd Ogden. LC 99-216597. (Illus.). 1997. 29.99 (*0-914697-75-7*) N Amer Outdoor Grp.
New American Light Cuisine. Jude W. Theriot. LC 87-32841. 208p. 1988. 12.95 (*0-88289-690-3*) Pelican.
New American Literature, 1890-1930. Fred L. Pattee. (BCL1-PS American Literature Ser.). 507p. 1992. reprint ed. lib. bdg. 99.00 (*0-7812-6622-X*) Rprt Serv.
New American Medical Dictionary & Health Manual. 7th enl. rev. ed. Robert E. Rothenberg. 624p. 1999. mass mkt. 7.99 (*0-451-19720-8*) NAL.
***New American Middle School: Educating Preadolescents in an Era of Change.** 3rd ed. Jon Wiles & Joseph Bondi. LC 00-20675. 400p. 2000. pap. text 56.00 (*0-13-014493-2*) P-H.
New American Navy, 2 vols. John D. Long. Ed. by Richard H. Kohn. LC 78-22386. (American Military Experience Ser.). (Illus.). 1980. reprint ed. lib. bdg. 61.95 (*0-405-11862-7*) Ayer.
New American Neighborhoods: Building Homeownership Zones to Revitalize Our Nation's Communities. (Illus.). 38p. (Orig.). 1997. pap. text 30.00 (*0-7881-3765-4*) DIANE Pub.
New American Painting As Shown in 8 European Countries, 1958-1959. Alfred H. Barr, Jr. LC 70-169297. (Museum of Modern Art Publications in Reprint). (Illus.). 96p. 1972. reprint ed. 21.95 (*0-405-01557-7*) Ayer.
New American Paintings. Ed. by Steven Zevitas. (Illus.). 112p. 1993. pap. 16.95 (*1-883039-00-2*) Open Stud Pr.
New American Paintings Bk. 2: The First Mid-Atlantic Edition, Vol. 2. Steven Zevitas. (New American Paintings Ser.). (Illus.). 112p. (Orig.). 1994. pap. 18.95 (*1-883039-01-0*) Open Stud Pr.
New American Paintings Bk. 3: The First Southeastern Edition. Steven Zevitas. (New American Paintings Ser.: Ser. 3). (Illus.). 112p. (Orig.). 1995. pap. 18.95 (*1-883039-02-9*) Open Stud Pr.
New American Paintings Bk. 4: The First Mid-West Edition. Steven Zevitas. (New American Paintings Ser.: Ser. 4). (Illus.). 112p. (Orig.). 1995. pap. 18.95 (*1-883039-03-7*) Open Stud Pr.
New American Paintings Bk. 5: The First Western Edition. Steven Zevitas. (New American Paintings Ser.: Ser. 5). 112p. (Orig.). 1995. pap. 18.95 (*1-883039-04-5*) Open Stud Pr.
New American Photography. Ed. by Steven Klindt. (Illus.). 48p. 1981. pap. 10.00 (*0-932026-06-0*) Columbia College Chi.
New American Plays 1, No. 1. Richard Strand et al. LC 91-32100. 234p. (C). 1992. pap. 15.95 (*0-435-08604-9*, 08604) Heinemann.
New American Plays 2. Janet Noble et al. LC 91-32100. 291p. (C). 1992. pap. 15.95 (*0-435-08605-7*, 08605) Heinemann.
New American Pocket Medical Dictionary. 2nd ed. Ed. by Nancy Roper. (Illus.). 368p. 1988. pap. text 12.95 (*0-443-08581-1*) Church.
New American Pocket Medical Dictionary. 2nd ed. Nancy Roper. 372p. 1988. pap. 17.00 (*0-684-19031-1*, Scribners Ref) Mac Lib Ref.
New American Poetry, 1945-1960. Donald Allen. 470p. 1999. pap. 16.95 (*0-520-20953-2*, Pub. by U CA Pr) Cal Prin Full Svc.
***New American Poets: A Bread Loaf Anthology.** Ed. by Michael Collier. LC 99-56171. (Bread Loaf Anthology Ser.). (Illus.). 302p. 2000. pap. 19.95 (*0-87451-964-0*); text 50.00 (*0-87451-963-2*) U Pr of New Eng.
New American Poets of the 80's. Ed. by Jack Myers & Roger Weingarten. 480p. 1984. pap. 12.95 (*0-931694-35-3*) Wampeter Pr.
New American Poets of the 90's. Ed. by Jack Myers & Roger Weingarten. 464p. 1991. pap. 19.95 (*0-87923-907-7*) Godine.
New American Political Disorder: An Essay. Robert A. Dahl et al. LC 94-530. 102p. 1994. pap. 10.95 (*0-87772-355-9*) UCB IGS.
New American Political System. 2nd ed. Anthony King. 360p. 1990. pap. 16.50 (*0-8447-3710-0*, AEI Pr) Am Enterprise.
New American Posture Toward Asia. Ed. by James C. Charlesworth & Richard D. Lambert. LC 72-120283. (Annals of the American Academy of Political & Social Science Ser.: No. 390). 1970. 28.00 (*0-685-00183-0*); pap. 18.00 (*0-87761-127-0*) Am Acad Pol Soc Sci.
New American Poverty: Perspectives on Family Homelessness. Institute for Children & Poverty Staff. 1995. pap. 8.00 (*0-9641784-2-7*) Homes Homeless.
New American Practical Navigator. Nathaniel Bowditch. (Works of Nathaniel Bowditch). 1989. reprint ed. lib. bdg. 79.00 (*0-7812-2021-1*) Rprt Serv.
New American Profiles. Lucette R. Kenan. 256p. (C). 1986. pap. text 20.00 (*0-15-565715-1*) Harcourt Coll Pubs.
New American Reality: Who We Are, How We Got Here, Where We Are Going. Reynolds Farley. LC 96-20404. (1990 Census Research Ser.: Vol. 3). 384p. (C). 1996. text 34.95 (*0-87154-237-4*) Russell Sage.
New American Reality: Who We Are, How We Got Here, Where We Are Going. Reynolds Farley. LC 96-20404. (1990 Census Research Ser.: Vol. 3). (Illus.). 385p. (C). 1998. reprint ed. pap. 18.50 (*0-87154-239-0*) Russell Sage.
New American Reference Bible, Vol. 1. large type ed. 1998. lthr. 39.97 (*1-55819-822-9*); lthr. 46.97 (*1-55819-823-7*) Broadman.
New American Rhetoric. Ben W. McClelland. LC 92-15012. 658p. (C). 1993. pap. text 48.00 (*0-673-38605-8*) Addson-Wesley Educ.
New American Rhetoric: Multicultural Approach. (C). 1997. text 13.00 (*0-673-55441-4*, GoodYrBooks) Addson-Wesley Educ.
New American Roget's College Thesaurus. Philip D. Morehead. 1985. pap. 13.95 (*0-452-00977-4*, Plume) Dutton Plume.
New American Roget's College Thesaurus. New American Roget's College Thesaurus Editors. 1986. pap. 3.50 (*0-317-47644-0*) NAL.
New American Roget's College Thesaurus in Dictionary Form. Philip D. Morehead. 1985. 10.09 (*0-606-03348-3*, Pub. by Turtleback) Demco.
New American Roget's College Thesaurus in Dictionary Form, Vol. I. enl. rev. ed. Philip D. Morehead. 656p. (YA). (gr. 9 up). 1957. mass mkt. 5.99 (*0-451-15167-4*, Sig) NAL.
New American Sampler Cookbook. Ed. by Linda Bauer. LC 90-47480. (Illus.). 303p. 1991. reprint ed. pap. 94.00 (*0-608-07345-8*, 2067573) Bks Demand.
New American School: Breaking the Mold. John Hill. LC 91-67674. 150p. 1995. pap. text 39.95 (*0-87762-910-2*) Scarecrow.
New American Schools after Six Years. Thomas Kenneth Glennan, Jr. et al. LC 98-5950. (Illus.). 90p. 1998. pap. 15.00 (*0-8330-2602-X*, MR-945-NAS) Rand Corp.
***New American Spirituality: A Seeker's Guide.** Elizabeth Lesser. LC 98-50310. 352p. 1999. 25.95 (*0-375-50010-3*) Random House.
New American Splendor Anthology. Harvey Pekar. LC 91-2987. (Illus.). 300p. (Orig.). 1991. pap. 18.95 (*0-941423-64-6*) FWEW.
New American Sport History: Recent Approaches & Perspectives. Ed. by Steven W. Pope. LC 96-6137. (Sport & Society Ser.). (Illus.). 440p. 1996. pap. text 19.95 (*0-252-06567-0*) U of Ill Pr.
New American Standard Bible: Giant Print. large type rev. ed. Ed. & Tr. by Lockman Foundation Staff from ARC. 1824p. 1997. im. lthr. 24.99 (*1-885217-90-0*, 1033) Foun Pubns.
New American Standard Bible: Giant Print Bible. large type rev. ed. Ed. & Tr. by Lockman Foundation Staff from ARC. 1824p. 1997. im. lthr. 24.99 (*1-885217-91-9*, 1031) Foun Pubns.
New American Standard Bible: Gift & Award. rev. ed. Ed. & Tr. by Lockman Foundation Staff from ARC. 960p. 1997. im. lthr. 7.99 (*1-885217-70-6*, 931) Foun Pubns.
***New American Standard Bible: Jesus Saves New Testament.** Tr. by Lockman Foundation Staff from GRE. 256p. 1999. mass mkt. 1.25 (*1-58135-077-5*) Foun Pubns.
New American Standard Bible: Readers Pew Bible. 1998. 7.99 (*1-885217-95-1*, 913) Foun Pubns.
New American Standard Bible: Reader's Pew Edition. 2nd rev. ed. Ed. & Tr. by Lockman Foundation Staff from ARC. 960p. 1997. 7.99 (*1-885217-68-4*, 912) Foun Pubns.
New American Standard Bible: Reader's Pew Edition Bible. 2nd rev. ed. Ed. & Tr. by Lockman Foundation Staff from ARC. 960p. 1997. 7.99 (*1-885217-69-2*, 919) Foun Pubns.
New American Standard Bible: Updated Edition Side Column Reference. 1998. lthr. 70.99 (*1-58135-038-4*) Foun Pubns.
New American Standard Bible Update: Side Column Reference Bible. 1998. lthr. 64.99 (*1-885217-96-X*, 869) Foun Pubns.
New American Standard Bible Update: Side Column Reference Bible. 2nd rev. ed. Ed. & Tr. by Lockman Foundation Staff from ARC. 1856p. 1997. bond lthr. 55.99 (*1-885217-80-3*, 841-I) Foun Pubns.
***New American Standard Bible Update Ultrathin.** rev. ed. Ed. & Tr. by Lockman Foundation Staff from ARC. (Illus.). 1184p. 1998. bond lthr. 29.99 (*1-58135-020-1*, 1241); bond lthr. 29.99 (*1-58135-022-8*, 1243); lthr. 39.99 (*1-58135-024-4*, 1261); lthr. 39.99 (*1-58135-026-0*, 1263) Foun Pubns.
***New American Standard Bible Update Ultrathin: Indexed Edition.** rev. ed. Ed. & Tr. by Lockman Foundation Staff from ARC. (Illus.). 1184p. 1998. bond lthr. 35.99 (*1-58135-023-6*, 1243-I); lthr. 45.99 (*1-58135-025-2*, 1261-I); lthr. 45.99 (*1-58135-027-9*, 1263-I) Foun Pubns.
New American Standard Plan of Life: Gospel of John. rev. ed. Ed. & Tr. by Lockman Foundation Staff from GRE. 96p. 1997. pap. 0.75 (*1-885217-88-9*) Foun Pubns.
New American Standard Update: Exhaustive Concordance. Ed. & Tr. by The Lockman Foundation Staff from ARC. 1600p. 1998. 36.99 (*1-58135-046-5*, 109) Foun Pubns.
New American Standard Update: Exhaustive Concordance, Indexed Edition. Ed. & Tr. by The Lockman Foundation Staff from ARC. 1998. 42.99 (*1-58135-047-3*, 109-1) Foun Pubns.
***New American Standard Update: In Touch Ministries Edition.** Ed. & Tr. by Lockman Foundation Staff from HEB. (Illus.). 1568p. 1999. lthr. 149.99 (*1-58135-071-6*, 1473, Pub. by Foun Pubns) Riverside-World.
***New American Standard Update: In Touch Ministries Edition.** 2nd rev. ed. Ed. & Tr. by Lockman Foundation Staff from GRE. (Illus.). 1568p. 1999. 39.99 (*1-58135-073-2*, 1410, Pub. by Foun Pubns) Riverside-World.
***New American Standard Update: In Touch Ministries Edition.** 2nd rev. ed. Ed. & Tr. by Lockman Foundation Staff from HEB. (Illus.). 1568p. 1999. lthr. 149.99 (*1-58135-072-4*, 1479, Pub. by Foun Pubns); lthr. 99.99 (*1-58135-069-4*, 1463, Pub. by Foun Pubns); lthr. 99.99 (*1-58135-068-6*, 1461, Pub. by Foun Pubns); lthr. 149.99 (*1-58135-070-8*, 1471, Pub. by Foun Pubns) Riverside-World.
New American Standard Update Bible. rev. ed. Ed. & Tr. by Lockman Foundation Staff from ARC. 960p. 1997. pap. 4.99 (*1-885217-72-2*, 900) Foun Pubns.
***New American Standard Update (La Biblia de las Americas) Bilingual Bible.** Ed. & Tr. by Lockman Foundation Staff from ARC. (ENG & SPA., Illus.). 1856p. 1998. bond lthr. 41.99 (*1-58135-034-1*, 7341) Foun Pubns.
***New American Standard Update (La Biblia de las Americas) Bilingual Bible.** rev. ed. Ed. & Tr. by Lockman Foundation Staff from ARC. (SPA & ENG., Illus.). 1856p. 1998. 24.99 (*1-58135-028-7*, 7313); bond lthr. 41.99 (*1-58135-036-8*, 7343); im. lthr. 29.99 (*1-58135-030-9*, 7331); im. lthr. 29.99 (*1-58135-032-5*, 7333) Foun Pubns.
New American Standard Update (La Biblia de las Americas) Bilingual Bible - Indexed. Bilingual Staff. (SPA & ENG.). 1998. bond lthr. 47.99 (*1-58135-037-6*) Foun Pubns.
***New American Standard Update (La Biblia de las Americas) Bilingual Bible, Indexed Edition.** rev. ed. Ed. & Tr. by Lockman Foundation Staff from ARC. (SPA & ENG., Illus.). 1856p. 1998. 30.99 (*1-58135-029-5*, 7313-I); bond lthr. 47.99 (*1-58135-035-X*, 7341-I); im. lthr. 35.99 (*1-58135-031-7*, 7331-I); im. lthr. 35.99 (*1-58135-033-3*, 7333-I) Foun Pubns.
***New American Standard Update Ultrathin: Indexed Edition.** rev. ed. Ed. & Tr. by Lockman Foundation Staff from ARC. (Illus.). 1184p. 1998. bond lthr. 35.99 (*1-58135-021-X*, 1241-I) Foun Pubns.
New American Standard UpDate/La Biblia de las Americas: Bilingual Bible. 2nd rev. ed. Ed. & Tr. by Lockman Foundation Staff from HEB. (SPA & ENG., Illus.). 1856p. 1999. lthr. 54.99 (*1-58135-064-3*, 7361); lthr. 54.99 (*1-58135-066-X*, 7363) Foun Pubns.
New American Standard UpDate/La Biblia de las Americas: Bilingual Bible - Indexed Edition. 2nd rev. ed. Ed. & Tr. by Lockman Foundation Staff from HEB. (SPA & ENG., Illus.). 1856p. 1999. lthr. 60.99 (*1-58135-065-1*, 7361-I); lthr. 60.99 (*1-58135-067-8*, 7363-I) Foun Pubns.
New American Start with English, Pt. 1. 2nd ed. D. H. Howe. 80p. 1996. pap. text, teacher ed. 8.50 (*0-19-434014-7*) OUP.
New American Start with English, Pt. 1. 2nd ed. D. H. Howe. (Illus.). 70p. 1996. pap. text, student ed. 8.25 (*0-19-434013-9*) OUP.
New American Start with English, Pt. 1. 2nd ed. D. H. Howe. (Illus.). 64p. 1996. pap. text, wbk. ed. 5.50 (*0-19-434015-5*) OUP.
New American Start with English, Pt. 2. 2nd ed. D. H. Howe. (Illus.). 94p. 1996. pap. text, student ed. 8.25 (*0-19-434017-1*); pap. text, wbk. ed. 5.50 (*0-19-434019-8*) OUP.
New American Start with English, Pt. 2. 2nd ed. D. H. Howe. 136p. 1996. pap. text, teacher ed. 8.50 (*0-19-434018-X*) OUP.
New American Start with English, Pt. 3. 2nd ed. D. H. Howe. (Illus.). 120p. 1996. pap. text, student ed. 8.25 (*0-19-434021-X*); pap. text, wbk. ed. 5.50 (*0-19-434023-6*) OUP.
New American Start with English, Pt. 3. 2nd ed. D. H. Howe. 118p. 1996. pap. text, teacher ed. 8.50 (*0-19-434022-8*) OUP.
New American State: Federal Bureaucracies & Policies since World War II. Ed. by Louis P. Galambos. LC 87-4146. (Symposia in Comparative History Ser.: No. 14). 240p. 1987. pap. text 15.95 (*0-8018-3490-2*) Johns Hopkins.
New American State Papers: Commerce & Navigation, 1789-1860 Subject Set, 47 vols., Set. Ed. by Stephen Salsbury. LC 72-95576. 1973. lib. bdg. 2800.00 (*0-8420-1527-2*) Scholarly Res Inc.
New American State Papers: Naval Affairs, 1789 to 1860, 10 vols., Set. Ed. by K. Jack Bauer. LC 80-53884. 3000p. 1981. lib. bdg. 650.00 (*0-8420-2173-6*) Scholarly Res Inc.
New American State Papers: Public Finance, 1789-1860 Subject Set, 32 vols., Set. Ed. by Sidney Ratner. LC 72-95580. 1973. lib. bdg. 1850.00 (*0-8420-1610-4*) Scholarly Res Inc.
New American State Papers, 1789 to 1860: Military Affairs, 19 vols., Set. Ed. by B. Franklin Cooling, 3rd. LC 79-110. 1979. lib. bdg. 1200.00 (*0-8420-2137-X*) Scholarly Res Inc.
New American Stream Connection, Vol. A. Peter Viney et al. (Illus.). 48p. 1995. pap. text, wbk. ed. 6.50 (*0-19-434830-X*) OUP.
New American Stream Connection, Vol. B. Peter Viney et al. (Illus.). 48p. 1995. pap. text, wbk. ed. 6.50 (*0-19-434838-5*) OUP.
New American Stream Departures. Peter Viney et al. (Illus.). 110p. 1994. pap. text, student ed. 11.95 (*0-19-434825-3*) OUP.
New American Stream Departures, Vol. A. Peter Viney et al. (Illus.). 58p. 1994. pap. text, student ed. 6.50 (*0-19-434841-5*) OUP.
New American Stream Dest. Peter Viney et al. (Illus.). 112p. 1996. pap. text, student ed. 11.95 (*0-19-434833-4*) OUP.
New American Streamline: Connections; An Intensive American-English Series for Intermediate Students' Teachers. Bernard Hartley. (Illus.). 204p. 1995. teacher ed., spiral bd. 16.95 (*0-19-434831-8*) OUP.
New American Streamline: Connections Student Book. Bernard Hartley. LC 95-114115. (Illus.). 106p. 1995. pap. text, student ed. 11.95 (*0-19-434829-6*) OUP.
New American Streamline: Connections Teacher's Book. Bernard Hartley et al. 148p. 1996. pap. text, teacher ed. 16.95 (*0-19-434835-0*) OUP.
New American Streamline: Departures Teacher's Book. Bernard Hartley et al. (Illus.). 114p. 1994. pap. text, teacher ed. 16.95 (*0-19-434827-X*) OUP.
New American Streamline: Destinations, Pt. A: Units 1-40. Bernard Hartley. (Illus.). 64p. 1995. pap. text, student ed. 6.50 (*0-19-434845-8*) OUP.
New American Streamline: Destinations, Pt. B: Units 41-80. Bernard Hartley. (Illus.). 64p. 1996. pap. text, student ed. 6.50 (*0-19-434846-6*) OUP.
New American Streamline Units 1-40: Destinations Workbook A. 2nd ed. Bernard Hartley. (Illus.). 56p. 1996. pap. text 6.50 (*0-19-434834-2*) OUP.
New American Streamline Units 41-80: Destinations Workbook B. 2nd ed. Bernard Hartley. (Illus.). 48p. 1996. pap. text 6.50 (*0-19-434839-3*) OUP.
New American Studies: Essays from "Representations" Ed. by Philip Fisher. (Representation Bks.: No. 5). (Illus.). 390p. 1991. 50.00 (*0-520-07329-0*, Pub. by U CA Pr); pap. 19.95 (*0-520-07330-4*, Pub. by U CA Pr) Cal Prin Full Svc.
New American Style. Mike Strohl. LC 97-22488. 1997. write for info. (*0-86636-510-9*); pap. write for info. (*0-86636-511-7*); pap. write for info. (*0-86636-512-5*) PBC Intl Inc.
New American Style. Mike Strohl. LC 97-22488. (Illus.). 176p. 1997. 34.95 (*0-86636-537-0*) PBC Intl Inc.
New American Town House. Alexander Gorlin. LC 99-23334. (Illus.). 224p. 1999. 60.00 (*0-8478-2141-2*, Pub. by Rizzoli Intl) St Martin.
New American TQM: Four Practical Revolutions in Management. Shoji Shiba et al. Ed. by Diane Asay. LC 93-906. (Illus.). 606p. 1993. text 50.00 (*1-56327-032-3*) Productivity Inc.
New American Trout Fishing. John Merwin. (Illus.). 320p. 1994. 30.00 (*0-02-584382-6*) Macmillan.
New American Vegetable Cookbook. Georgeanne Brennan et al. write for info. (*0-318-59647-4*) S&S Trade.
New American Village. Bob Thall. LC 98-49379. 128p. 1999. 24.95 (*0-8018-6157-8*); pap. 24.95 (*0-8018-6158-6*) Johns Hopkins.

N

An Asterisk (*) at the beginning of an entry indicates that the title is appearing for the first time.

New American Voter. Warren E. Miller & J. Merrill Shanks. LC 96-8079. (Illus.). 640p. 1996. write for info. (*0-674-60840-2*); 45.00 (*0-674-08402-0*); pap. 22.00 (*0-674-60841-0*) HUP.

New American Webster Handy College Dictionary. 3rd ed. Ed. by Philip D. Morehead. 800p. (C). 1995. mass mkt. 5.99 (*0-451-18166-2*) NAL.

New American Workplace: Transforming Work Systems in the United States. Eileen Appelbaum & Rosemary Batt. LC 93-31201. 256p. 1994. pap. text 18.95 (*0-87546-319-3*, ILR Press) Cornell U Pr.

New American World, 5 vols., Set. Ed. by David B. Quinn. (Individual Publications). 1978. lib. bdg. 299.50 (*0-405-10759-5*) Ayer.

New Americana Cookbook: A Heart-Healthy Excursion Through Regional Cuisines. Sherri Eldridge. LC 97-221048. (Illus.). 160p. 1997. pap. 9.95 (*1-886862-06-0*, BK NAC, Coastal New England Pubns) Harv Hill ME.

New Americanism: How the Democratic Party Can Win the Presidency. Steven Jonas. 326p. 1992. pap. 18.95 (*0-912526-56-4*) Lib Res.

New Americans. Arthur H. Marquardt. LC 94-71586. 650p. (Orig.). (YA). (gr. 9-12). 1994. pap. 39.95 (*0-940121-19-0*, P212, Cross Roads Bks) Cross Cultural Pubns.

Authored by a Fulbright scholar who studied both Russian & American youth, this book researched the ways young Americans look at current issues like the economy, religious values & racial or ethnic tensions. This work allows high school students from all over the United States to speak for themselves. Clearly written by a long time high school teacher, this is an unusual look into the minds & hearts of our young people. *Publisher Paid Annotation.*

N

New Americans. Ulli Steltzer. LC 88-61522. (Illus.). 176p. (YA). (gr. 6 up). 1992. pap. 24.95 (*0-939165-07-4*) NewSage Press.

New Americans: Colonial Times, 1620-1689. Betsy C. Maestro. LC 95-19636. (Illus.). 48p. (J). (gr. k up). 1998. 16.00 (*0-688-13448-3*); lib. bdg. 15.93 (*0-688-13449-1*) Lothrop.

New Americans: Economic, Demographic, & Fiscal Effects of Immigration. Ed. by James P. Smith et al. 500p. 1997. 49.95 (*0-309-06356-6*) Natl Acad Pr.

New Americans: The Progress of Asian Indians in America. George P. Alexander. 128p. (Orig.). (C). 1997. pap. text 23.95 (*0-9653688-3-1*) P & P Ent.

New Americans: The Westerner & the Modern Experience in the American Novel. Glen A. Love. LC 80-65717. 288p. 1982. 36.50 (*0-8387-5011-7*) Bucknell U Pr.

New Americans' Legal Guide. City Family Magazine Staff. 1997. pap. 9.95 (*0-8050-4800-6*) H Holt & Co.

New Americans' Medical Guide. City Family Magazine Staff. 1997. pap. 9.95 (*0-8050-4801-4*) H Holt & Co.

***New Amplified Pilgrim's Progress: From This World to That Which Is to Come.** Adapted & Pref. by James Pappas. (Illus.). 348p. 1999. pap. 24.95 (*0-9671269-0-8*) Orions Gate.

New Amsterdam: The Biography of a Broadway Theater. Mary Henderson. LC 97-24154. (Illus.). 192p. (J). 1997. 75.00 (*0-7868-6270-X*, Pub. by Hyperion) Time Warner.

***New Amsterdam City: A Champions RPG Campaign Setting.** Tony W. Digiacomo. (Illus.). 25p. 2000. pap. 10.00 (*1-58265-011-X*, 00011) Orphan Press.

New Analyses in Romance Linguistics: Selected Papers from the Linguistic Symposium on Romance Languages XVII, Urbana-Champaign, April 7-9, 1988. Ed. by Dieter Wanner & Douglas A. Kibbee. LC 90-23247. (Current Issues in Linguistic Theory Ser.: Vol. 69). xviii, 385p. 1991. 112.00 (*90-272-3566-X*) J Benjamins Pubng Co.

New Analysis of Language Learning. Toshiko Chomei. (American University Studies: Linguistics: Ser. XIII, Vol. 15). 190p. (C). 1989. text 32.80 (*0-8204-1105-1*) P Lang Pubng.

New Analysis Techniques for Structural Masonry: Proceedings of a Session Held in Conjunction with Structures Congress '85. Ed. by Subhash Anand. 130p. 1985. 5.00 (*0-87262-481-1*) Am Soc Civil Eng.

New Analytical Greek Lexicon. Ed. by Wesley J. Perschbacher. LC 90-23777. 450p. 1990. 29.95 (*0-943575-33-8*) Hendrickson MA.

New Analytical Methods for Characterizing Fossil Fuels & Derived Products, Direct Coal Liquefaction, Biomass Fuels: Preprints of Papers Presented at the 210th ACS National Meeting, Chicago, IL, August 20-25, 1995. American Chemical Society, Division of Fuel Chemis. LC TP0318.. (American Chemical Society, Division of Fuel Chemistry, Preprints of Papers: Vol. 40, No. 3). 392p. 1995. reprint ed. pap. 121.60 (*0-608-00537-1*, 206141600008) Bks Demand.

New Analytical Techniques for Trace Constituents of Metallic & Metal-Bearing Ores - STP 747. Ed. by A. Javier-Son. 135p. 1981. 15.00 (*0-8031-0743-9*, STP747) ASTM.

New Anatomies. Timberlake Wertenbaker. 1991. pap. 5.95 (*0-87129-089-8*, N33) Dramatic Pub.

New Anchor Book of Counted Thread Embroidery Stitches. Eve Harlow. 1989. pap. write for info. (*0-7153-8862-2*, Pub. by D & C Pub) Sterling.

New & Accurate Description of the Coast of Guinea, 1705. 4th rev. ed. William Bosman. (Illus.). 577p. 1967. 65.00 (*0-7146-1793-8*, Pub. by F Cass Pubs) Intl Spec Bk.

New & Authentic History of the Rosicrucians. Frank Wittemans. 224p. 1996. reprint ed. pap. 19.95 (*1-56459-972-8*) Kessinger Pub.

New & Better Uses of Secondary Resources: Proceedings of the 2nd Recycling World Congress, Philippine International Conventional Center, Manila, March 1979. M. E. Henstock. Ed. by Michael B. Bevin. 278p. 1980. pap. 57.00 (*0-08-026245-7*, Pergamon Pr) Elsevier.

New & Classic Cocktails Without Alcohol. Robert Sutton & Keith Pointing. (Illus.). 128p. 1988. boxed set 9.95 (*0-905743-54-7*, Pub. by Stacey Intl) Intl Bk Ctr.

***New & Classic Tales of Detection, Vol. 3.** Robert J. Randisi. (First Cases Ser.). 288p. 1999. mass mkt. write for info. (*0-451-19892-1*, Sig) NAL.

New & Collected Poems. Ishmael Reed. 256p. 1989. pap. 9.95 (*0-689-12004-4*) Atheneum Yung Read.

***New & Collected Poems.** Wislawa Szymborska. 296p. 2000. pap. 17.00 (*0-15-601146-8*) Harcourt.

New & Collected Poems. Richard Wilbur. 1989. pap. 10.95 (*0-685-44829-0*, Harvest Bks) Harcourt.

New & Collected Poems. Richard Wilbur. 1989. pap. 8.95 (*0-318-42590-4*, Harvest Bks); pap. 15.00 (*0-15-665491-1*) Harcourt.

New & Collected Poems, 1952-1992. Geoffrey Hill. LC 92-5010. 240p. 1994. pap. 17.95 (*0-395-68086-7*) HM.

New & Collected Poems, 1970-1985. David Ignatow. LC 85-15311. (Wesleyan Poetry Ser.). 349p. 1986. pap. 19.95 (*0-8195-6174-6*, Wesleyan Univ Pr) U Pr of New Eng.

New & Collected Poems, 1966-1996. Herbert M. Coursen. LC 96-28680. 155p. 1996. pap. 17.50 (*1-880664-17-8*) E M Pr.

New & Complete Concordance of Shakespeare. John Bartlett. (Works of John Bartlett). 1989. reprint ed. lib. bdg. 198.00 (*0-7812-1905-1*) Rprt Serv.

New & Complete System of Book-Keeping by an Improved Method of Double Entry. William Mitchell. Ed. by Richard P. Brief. LC 77-87279. (Development of Contemporary Accounting Thought Ser.). 1978. reprint ed. lib. bdg. 39.95 (*0-405-10907-5*) Ayer.

New & Critical Plants from Raiatea. John W. Moore. (BMB Ser.: No. 102). 1974. reprint ed. pap. 25.00 (*0-527-02208-X*) Periodicals Srv.

New & Different. Donna Barr. (Desert Peach Ser.: Vol. 27). (Illus.). 64p. 1997. pap. 5.95 (*1-892253-02-X*, Pub. by Fine Line) Last Gasp.

New & Emerging Careers, 6 vols., Set. 98.00 (*0-685-23038-4*, CG363) Ready Ref Pr.

New & Evolving Ocular Infections, Vol. 33. Friedlaen. 1993. 39.00 (*0-316-29399-7*) Little.

New & Expanded Medical Schools, Mid-Century to the 1980s: An Analysis of Changes & Recommendations for Improving the Education of Physicians. James R. Schofield. LC 84-47996. (Jossey-Bass Higher Education Ser.). 492p. reprint ed. pap. 152.60 (*0-8357-4921-5*, 203785100009) Bks Demand.

***New & Exploratory Therapeutic Agents for Asthma.** Ed. by Michael Yeadon & Zuzana Diamant. (Lung Biology in Health & Disease Ser.: Vol. 139). 494p. 2000. 185.00 (*0-8247-7861-8*) Dekker.

New & Full Moons 1001 B. C. to A. D. 1651. Herman H. Goldstine. LC 72-89401. (Memoirs Ser.: Vol. 94). 1973. 25.00 (*0-87169-094-2*) Am Philos.

New & Glorious Life. Michelle Herman. LC 97-77970. (Short Fiction Ser.). 192p. 1998. pap. 15.95 (*0-88748-284-8*) Carnegie-Mellon.

***New &... Improved?, 2 bks. in 1.** Jill Shalvis & Jennifer La Brecque. (Duets 2-in-1 Ser.: Bk. 28). 2000. per. 5.99 (*0-373-44094-4*, 1-44094-0) Harlequin Bks.

New & Improved: The Story of Mass Marketing in America. Harvard Business Staff. 528p. 1996. pap. 17.95 (*0-07-103672-5*) McGraw.

New & Improved: The Story of Mass Marketing in America. Richard S. Tedlow. 528p. (C). 1996. pap. 17.95 (*0-87584-672-6*) Harvard Busn.

New & Improved: The Transformation of American Women's Emotional Culture. John Spurlock & Cynthia Magistro. LC 98-9050. (History of Emotions Ser.). (Illus.). 260p. 1998. text 35.00 (*0-8147-8045-8*) NYU Pr.

New & Improved! 25 Ways to Be More Creative & More Effective. Pam Grout. Ed. by Kelly Scanlon. LC 95-68999. (Illus.). 94p. (Orig.). 1995. pap. 12.95 (*1-878542-78-8*) SkillPath Pubns.

New & Improved 1989 Joint Operating Agreement. LC 91-72727. 294p. 1991. pap. 39.95 (*0-89707-664-8*, 535-0030, ABA Natl Res) Amer Bar Assn.

***New & Improved Pokemon Edition of Blast! Create Your Own Collectable Card Game.** Alexander Gekko & Gille Myotis. 60p. 1999. pap. 13.95 (*1-883573-42-4*) Pride & Imprints.

New & Improved Sarah. Marilyn Kaye. (Camp Sunnyside Friends Ser.: No. 9). 144p. (Orig.). (J). 1990. pap. 2.95 (*0-380-76180-7*, Avon Bks) Morrow Avon.

New & Intense Movements see Modern American Protestantism & Its World

New & Living Way. Jerry V. Roach. (Illus.). 123p. (Orig.). 1993. pap. text 11.95 (*0-943639-16-6*) Anchor Pub Co.

New & Living Way. George A. Turner. 1992. reprint ed. pap. 10.99 (*0-88019-288-7*) Schmul Pub Co.

New & Modified Techniques for Studying Nitrogen-Fixing Bacteria in Small Mammal Droppings. C. Y. Li & Chris Maser. (Illus.). 8p. 1997. reprint ed. pap. 1.30 (*0-89904-650-9*, Wildlife Resrch Grp) Crumb Elbow Pub.

New & Notable Product Design. ID Magazine Staff. (Illus.). 256p. 1991. text 49.99 (*0-935603-86-7*) Rockport Pubs.

New & Notable Product Design 2. 2nd ed. Robert Blaich. (Illus.). 192p. 1994. 39.99 (*1-56496-120-6*) Rockport Pubs.

New & Old in God's Revelation. Benedict Engelzakis. (Studies in Relations Between Spirit & Tradition in the Bible). 128p. 1982. text 12.95 (*0-913836-89-3*) St Vladimirs.

***New & Old Wars: Organized Violence in a Global Era.** Mary Kaldor. LC 98-61601. 192p. 1999. 45.00 (*0-8047-3721-5*); pap. 16.95 (*0-8047-3722-3*) Stanford U Pr.

New & Original Opera Librettos. Ray Leland Caley. LC 83-70679. (Illus.). 283p. (C). 1983. 20.00 (*0-910987-03-3*) Dragons Lair.

New & Rational Treatise of Dowsing According to the Methods of Physical Radiesthesia. Pierre Beasse. 214p. 1996. reprint ed. spiral bd. 18.50 (*0-7873-0083-7*) Hlth Research.

New & Re-Emerging Market for Human Vaccines. Contrib. by Sandra Graham. 187p. 1995. 2750.00 (*1-56965-045-4*, C-171) BCC.

New & Renewable Sources of Energy. Essam E. El-Hinnawi et al. 144p. 1984. 70.00 (*0-907567-58-4*, Tycooly Pub); pap. 40.00 (*0-907567-59-2*, Tycooly Pub) Weidner & Sons.

New & Renewable Sources of Energy for Development. (Energy Resources Development Ser.: No. 30). 101p. 1988. pap. 13.50 (*92-1-119455-5*, 88.II.F.7) UN.

New & Resurgent Infections: Prediction, Detection, & Management of Tomorrow's Epidemics. B. M. Greenwood & Kevin De Cock. LC 97-46506. 236p. 1998. 99.95 (*0-471-98174-5*) Wiley.

New & Revised 1993 Fair Claims Settlement Practices Regulations. 4th rev. ed. Barry Zalma. 200p. 1996. spiral bd. 35.95 (*1-884770-10-X*) ClaimSchool.

New & Selected Poems 1923-85. Robert Penn Warren. 1985. mass mkt. 75.00 (*0-394-54586-9*) Random.

New & Selected Essays. Denise Levertov. LC 92-17887. 256p. 1992. pap. 12.95 (*0-8112-1218-1*, NDP749, Pub. by New Directions) Norton.

New & Selected Poems. Stephen Berg. LC 91-72065. 200p. (Orig.). 1992. 21.00 (*1-55659-044-X*); pap. 12.00 (*1-55659-043-1*) Copper Canyon.

New & Selected Poems. James Bertolino. LC 77-81274. (Poetry Ser.). 1978. pap. 11.95 (*0-915604-14-0*) Carnegie-Mellon.

New & Selected Poems. Yves Bonnefoy. Ed. by John T. Naughton & Anthony Rudolf. 252p. 1995. pap. 14.95 (*0-226-06460-3*) U Ch Pr.

New & Selected Poems. Yves Bonnefoy. Ed. & Tr. by John T. Naughton from FRE. Ed. by Anthony Rudolf. LC 95-10350. 252p. 1995. lib. bdg. 39.00 (*0-226-06458-1*) U Ch Pr.

New & Selected Poems. Paul Carroll. 1978. 7.95 (*0-916328-11-2*); pap. 3.50 (*0-916328-10-4*) Yellow Pr.

New & Selected Poems. Tony Connor. 138p. 1982. pap. 14.95 (*0-85646-069-9*, Pub. by Anvil Press) Dufour.

New & Selected Poems. William Corbett. LC 94-23652. 288p. 1995. pap. 18.75 (*0-944072-54-2*) Zoland Bks.

New & Selected Poems. Lauris Edmond. 216p. 1993. pap. 18.95 (*1-85224-181-0*) Dufour.

New & Selected Poems. Frederick Feirstein. LC 97-33300. 264p. 1997. pap. text 14.00 (*1-885266-51-0*) Story Line.

New & Selected Poems. Ryah Goodman. 79p. 1985. 10.95 (*0-87233-079-6*) Bauhan.

New & Selected Poems. Donald Justice. LC 95-22618. (Illus.). 176p. 1997. pap. 17.00 (*0-679-76598-0*) Knopf.

New & Selected Poems. Anthony Lawrence. LC 98-204375. 1998. pap. 24.95 (*0-7022-2980-6*, Pub. by Univ Queensland Pr) Intl Spec Bk.

New & Selected Poems. Linda Lerner. (Illus.). 90p. 1999. pap. 12.00 (*1-889289-24-8*) Ye Olde Font Shoppe.

New & Selected Poems. Howard Nemerov. LC 60-14236. 122p. 1998. pap. 11.95 (*0-226-57247-1*, PP6) U Ch Pr.

New & Selected Poems. Charles North. (Sun & Moon Classics Ser.: No. 102). 205p. 1998. pap. 13.00 (*1-55713-265-8*, Pub. by Sun & Moon CA) Consort Bk Sales.

New & Selected Poems. Mary Oliver. LC 92-7767. 272p. 1993. 28.50 (*0-8070-6818-7*) Beacon Pr.

New & Selected Poems. Mary Oliver. LC 92-7767. 255p. 1993. pap. 16.00 (*0-8070-6819-5*) Beacon Pr.

New & Selected Poems. Stan Rice. LC 91-43573. 226p. 1992. 24.00 (*0-679-41145-3*) McKay.

New & Selected Poems. Philip Salom. 1998. pap. 22.95 (*1-86368-218-X*, Pub. by Fremantle Arts) Intl Spec Bk.

***New & Selected Poems.** James Scheviil. 144p. 2000. 29.95 (*0-8040-1027-7*); pap. 14.95 (*0-8040-1028-5*) Swallow.

New & Selected Poems. Karl Jay Shapiro. 114p. 1999. pap. 11.95 (*0-226-75033-7*) U Ch Pr.

New & Selected Poems. Sydney B. Smith. LC 84-72521. 91p. 1985. 13.95 (*0-906897-76-9*); pap. 9.95 (*0-906897-75-0*) Dufour.

New & Selected Poems. Gary Soto. LC 94-27081. 192p. 1995. 22.95 (*0-8118-0761-4*); pap. 12.95 (*0-8118-0758-4*) Chronicle Bks.

New & Selected Poems. Eleanor R. Taylor. LC 83-62168. 120p. 1983. 15.00 (*0-913773-02-6*) S Wright.

***New & Selected Poems.** Adam Zagajewski. 2002. text. write for info. (*0-374-22096-4*) FS&G.

New & Selected Poems. Kenneth Fearing. LC 83-12960. 143p. 1983. reprint ed. lib. bdg. 49.50 (*0-313-24175-9*, FENE, Greenwood Pr) Greenwood.

New & Selected Poems. Thomas H. Ferrill. LC 73-104219. 169p. 1982. reprint ed. lib. bdg. 83.50 (*0-8371-3336-X*, AEFESP, Greenwood Pr) Greenwood.

New & Selected Poems. David Waggner. LC 69-16002. 176p. reprint ed. pap. 54.60 (*0-608-17045-3*, 205624400056) Bks Demand.

New & Selected Poems: From the Book of My Life. Edward Field. LC 86-43208. 167p. 1987. 15.95 (*0-935296-68-9*, Pub. by Sheep Meadow) U Pr of New Eng.

New & Selected Poems: The House by Water. Judith Rodriguez. (Illus.). 180p. (Orig.). 1989. pap. text 16.95 (*0-7022-2138-4*, Pub. by Univ Queensland Pr) Intl Spec Bk.

New & Selected Poems, 1956-1996. Philip Appleman. 280p. 1996. 38.00 (*1-55728-419-9*); pap. 22.00 (*1-55728-420-2*) U of Ark Pr.

New & Selected Poems, 1942-1987. Charles E. Eaton. LC 86-71595. 320p. 1987. 28.50 (*0-8453-4807-8*, Cornwall Bks) Assoc Univ Prs.

New & Selected Poems, 1942-1997. John Tagliabue. 388p. 1998. 49.95 (*0-943373-44-1*); pap. 19.95 (*0-943373-45-X*) Natl Poet Foun.

New & Selected Poems, 1974-1994. Stephen Dunn. LC 93-33212. 1994. 22.00 (*0-393-03618-9*) Norton.

New & Selected Poems, 1974-1994. Stephen Dunn. 320p. 1995. pap. 15.00 (*0-393-31300-X*) Norton.

New & Selected Poems, 1975-1995. Thomas Lux. 192p. 1999. pap. 14.00 (*0-395-92488-X*) HM.

New & Selected Poems, 1961-1996. Rochelle Owens. LC 97-70510. 192p. 1997. pap. 20.00 (*1-881523-06-3*) Junction CA.

New & Selected Poems, 1966-1988. Douglas Dunn. (Modern European Poets Ser.). 240p. 1989. 17.95 (*0-88001-177-7*) HarpC.

New & Selected Poems, 1963-1992. Ron Padgett. LC 95-15239. 120p. 1995. 14.95 (*1-56792-038-1*) Godine.

New & Selected Poems, 1962 to 1992. Laurence Lieberman. LC 92-45567. 232p. 1993. 16.95 (*0-252-06314-7*); text 34.95 (*0-252-02010-3*) U of Ill Pr.

New & Selected Poems, 1930-1990. Richard Eberhart. 68p. 1990. pap. 8.95 (*0-929654-91-9*); text 16.95 (*0-929654-95-1*) FoxRock.

New & Selected Poems of Edith Shiffert. Edith Shiffert. 128p. 1979. 7.50 (*0-934834-13-X*) White Pine.

New & Selected Poems of Josephine Young Case. Josephine Y. Case. LC 92-17891. 104p. 1992. 18.00 (*0-915010-37-2*) Sutter House.

New & Selected Poems of Lux. Thomas Lux. LC 97-430. 160p. 1997. 23.00 (*0-395-85832-1*) HM.

New & Selected Poetry. Donald Justice. LC 95-22618. 224p. 1995. 25.00 (*0-679-44173-5*) Random.

New & Simple Theory of Gravity. Donald E. Tyler. 61p. 1970. pap. 10.95 (*1-884981-00-3*) Discov Bks.

***New & Small Business Ventures.** Richard C. Dorf. 178p. 2000. write for info. (*1-58692-021-9*) Copyright Mgmt.

New & the Old Criminology. Ed. by Edith E. Flynn & John P. Conrad. LC 76-14130. (Praeger Special Studies). 350p. 1978. 65.00 (*0-275-90292-7*, C0292, Praeger Pubs) Greenwood.

New & Traditional Styles of Chip Carving: From Classic to Positive Imaging. Wayne Barton. LC 93-43377. (Illus.). 128p. 1994. pap. 12.95 (*0-8069-8574-7*) Sterling.

***New & Untried Course: Woman's Medical College & Medical College of Pennsylvania, 1850-1998.** Steven J. Peitzman. LC 99-45850. 272p. 2000. text 60.00 (*0-8135-2815-1*); pap. text 22.00 (*0-8135-2816-X*) Rutgers U Pr.

***New & Updated Copyright Primer: A Survival Guide to Copyright & the Permissions Process.** rev. ed. AAP Rights & Permissions Advisory Committee. Ed. by Carol Risher & Nisha Tyree. 101p. 2000. pap. 15.00 (*0-933636-37-7*) AAP.

New & Used Poems. Amy J. Schoonover. 105p. 1988. 6.95 (*0-941363-02-3*) Lake Shore Pub.

New & Useful Forms, Stationery & Greetings to Duplicate & Use. Frieda Carrol. 50p. ring bd. 23.95 (*0-939476-84-3*) Prosperity & Profits.

New Andalucia & a Way to the Orient: The American Southeast During the Sixteenth Century. Paul E. Hoffman. LC 89-13492. (Illus.). 392p. 1990. text 57.50 (*0-8071-1552-5*) La State U Pr.

New Anesthetic Agents, Devices & Monitoring Techniques. Theodore H. Stanley & W. Clayton Petty. 1983. text 112.50 (*90-247-2796-0*) Kluwer Academic.

New Angiotherapy. Tai-Ping Fan & Robert Auerbach. 600p. 2000. 150.00 (*0-89603-464-X*) Humana.

New Animal Doctor's Answer Book. rev. ed. Michael W. Fox. LC 84-6973. Orig. Title: The Animal Doctor's Answer Book. (Illus.). 320p. 1989. pap. 14.95 (*1-55704-035-4*, Pub. by Newmarket) Norton.

New Atheneaum - Neues Athenaeum, 1992, Vol. 3. Ed. by Ruth D. Richardson. 226p. 1993. 49.95 (*0-7734-9274-7*) E Mellen.

New Anthology of Contemporary Austrian Folk Plays. Ed. by Richard H. Lawson. (Studies in Austrian Literature, Culture, & Thought). 364p. (Orig.). 1996. pap. 26.50 (*1-57241-020-5*) Ariadne CA.

New Anthology of Orthopaedics. Mercer Rang. 2000. text 79.00 (*0-7216-7141-1*) Harcrt Hlth Sci Grp.

New Anthropomorphism. John S. Kennedy. (Illus.). 204p. (C). 1992. text 59.95 (*0-521-41064-9*); pap. text 19.95 (*0-521-42267-1*) Cambridge U Pr.

New Antibacterial Strategies. Ed. by Harold C. Neu. (Illus.). 340p. (Orig.). 1991. pap. text 87.00 (*0-443-04448-1*) Church.

New Anticancer Drugs. Ed. by S. K. Carter. (Recent Results in Cancer Research Ser.: Vol. 70). (Illus.). 230p. 1980. 66.00 (*0-387-09682-5*) Spr-Verlag.

New Anticancer Drugs: Mitoxantrone & Bisantrene. Ed. by Marcel Rozencweig et al. LC 82-42744. (Monograph Series of the European Organization for Research on Treatment of Cancer: No. 12). (Illus.). 210p. 1983. reprint ed. pap. 65.10 (*0-7837-9553-X*, 206030200005) Bks Demand.

New Anticoagulants for the Cardiovascular Patient. E. Roque Pifarre. LC 96-51845. 1997. text 65.00 (*1-56053-220-3*) Hanley & Belfus.

An Asterisk (*) at the beginning of an entry indicates that the title is appearing for the first time.

New Anticonvulsant Drugs. Brian S. Meldrum & Roger J. Porter. (Current Problems in Epilepsy Ser.: Vol. 4). (Illus.). 350p. 1986. 82.95 (0-86196-063-7, Pub. by J Libbey Med) Bks Intl VA.

New Anticonvulsants: Advances in the Treatment of Epilepsy. Ed. by M. R. Trimble. 176p. 1994. 148.00 (0-471-95122-6) Wiley.

New Antiepileptic Drug Development: Preclinical & Clinical Aspects. Ed. by Jacqueline A. French et al. LC 93-8273. (Epilepsy Research Ser.: Vol. 10). 272p. 1993. 230.50 (0-444-89987-1) Elsevier.

New Antiepileptic Drugs in Psychiatry: Symposium, Schloss Elmau, March 1998, No.38. Ed. by J. Walden & H. Grunze. (Neuropsychobiology Ser.: No.3). (Illus.). 94p. 1998. pap. 29.00 (3-8055-6761-8) S Karger.

New Antiviral Strategies. Ed. by S. R. Norrby. (Frontiers of Infectious Diseases Ser.). (Illus.). 288p. 1989. pap. text 53.00 (0-443-04166-0) Church.

New Antoinette Pope School Cookbook. Pope Staff. 1980. 22.95 (0-02-598060-2) Macmillan.

New Apartment Book. Michele Michael. 1996. pap. 30.00 (0-517-88759-2) C Potter.

*New Apocalypse: The Radical Christian Vision of William Blake. Thomas J. J. Altizer. LC 00-35845. (Series in Philosophical & Cultural Studies in Religion). 2000. write for info. (1-888570-56-3) Davies Grp.

New Apologists for Poetry. Murray Krieger. LC 77-21933. 225p. 1977. reprint ed. lib. bdg. 35.00 (0-8371-9787-2, KRNA, Greenwood Pr) Greenwood.

New Apostolic Churches. C. Peter Wagner. LC 98-11789. 1998. pap. 11.99 (0-8307-2137-1) Gospel Lght.

New Appalachian Trail. Edward Garvey. LC 97-10897. (Illus.). 256p. (Orig.). 1997. pap. 14.95 (0-89732-209-6) Menasha Ridge.

New Appleton's Cuyas English-Spanish & Spanish-English Dictionary. 5th ed. Ed. by Arturo Cuyas Armengol. (ENG & SPA.). 1974. 26.95 (0-13-611749-X) P-H.

New Applications for Copper & Copper Compounds. Midwest Research Institute Staff. 109p. 1974. 16.35 (0-317-34538-9, 229) Intl Copper.

New Applications of Accelerators & Nuclear Detectors to Medical Diagnosis, Vol. 3, No. 2. Ed. by P. Min & Robert Klapisch. (Nuclear Science Applications Ser.: Sec. A, Vol. 3, No. 2). 92p. 1988. text 173.00 (3-7186-4825-3) Gordon & Breach.

New Applications of Analytical Techniques to Fossil Fuels: General Papers Presented at New York, April 13-18, 1986. American Chemical Society, Division of Fuel Chemis. LC TP0319.. (American Chemical Society Division of Fuel Chemistry, Preprints of Papers Ser.: Vol. 31, No. 1). 346p. reprint ed. pap. 107.30 (0-608-18380-6, 202729900055) Bks Demand.

New Applications of Electron Spin Resonance: ESR Dating, Dosimetry & Microscopy. M. Ikeya. 520p. 1993. text 99.00 (981-02-1199-6); pap. text 48.00 (981-02-1200-3) World Scientific Pub.

New Applications of Interpersonal Psychotherapy. Ed. by Gerald L. Klerman & Myrna M. Weissman. 408p. 1993. text 56.00 (0-88048-511-6, 8511) Am Psychiatric.

New Applications of Lasers to Chemistry. Ed. by Gary Hieftje. LC 78-22032. (ACS Symposium Ser.: No. 85). 1978. 31.95 (0-8412-0459-4) Am Chemical.

New Applications of Lasers to Chemistry. Ed. by Gary M. Hieftje. LC 78-22032. (ACS Symposium Ser.: Vol. 85). 254p. 1978. reprint ed. pap. 78.80 (0-608-03946-2, 206439300009) Bks Demand.

New Applications of Plastic Components in Vehicle Design: 1996 International Congress & Exposition. LC 96-207885. (Special Publications). 177p. 1996. pap. 69.00 (1-56091-796-2, SP-1166) Soc Auto Engineers.

New Applications of Zeolite Beta in Selective Catalytic Hydrogenations. Edward J. Creyghton. (Illus.). 157p. (Orig.). 1996. pap. 43.50 (90-407-1382-0, Pub. by Delft U Pr) Coronet Bks.

New Approach for the Derivation of Dynamic Loads of Heavily Loaded (d-e) High Speed Aircraft Gearing. Kayaalp Buyukataman. (Nineteen Eighty-Eight Fall Technical Meeting Ser.: Vol. 88FTM5). (Illus.). 13p. 1988. pap. text 30.00 (1-55589-510-7) AGMA.

New Approach for the Transatlantic Economic Partnership: Report of the European Institute, 8th Annual Transatlantic Seminar on Trade & Investment, November 4-5, 1998. Ed. by Peter S. Raslish. LC 99-72186. 82p. 1999. pap. 15.00 (1-886607-11-7) European Inst.

New Approach in the Treatment of Climacteric Disorders. Ed. by H. P. Schneider & Andrea R. Genazzani. (New Developments in Biosciences Ser.: No. 7). (Illus.). viii, 53p. (Orig.). (C). 1993. pap. text 44.65 (3-11-013471-3) De Gruyter.

New Approach to Continuing Education for Business & the Professions. Philip Nowlen. (ACE-Oryx Series on Higher Education). 304p. 1987. 31.95 (0-02-922740-2) Free Pr.

New Approach to Ear Training. Leo Kraft. (Illus.). (C). 1967. pap. 36.25 (0-393-09764-1) Norton.

New Approach to Ear Training. 2nd ed. Leo Kraft. LC 99-11655. (C). 1999. pap. text. write for info. (0-393-97217-8) Norton.

New Approach to Ear Training w/3 Cd. 2nd ed. Kraft. 1999. pap. text 55.75 (0-393-97412-X) Norton.

*New Approach to Ear Training w/3CD & Caspar Software. 2nd ed. Kraft. 1999. pap. text. write for info. incl. cd-rom (0-393-97415-4) Norton.

New Approach to English Grammar, on Semantic Principles. R. M. Dixon. 416p. 1991. 95.00 (0-19-824272-7) OUP.

New Approach to English Grammar, on Semantic Principles. R. M. Dixon. 416p. 1992. reprint ed. pap. text 29.95 (0-19-824057-0) OUP.

New Approach to Flexibility: Managing the Work - Time Equation. 85p. 1998. 90.00 (0-89584-198-3) Catalyst.

New Approach to Freedom. rev. ed. E. C. Riegel. Ed. by Spencer H. MacCallum. LC 76-24987. (Illus.). 1976. 14.95 (0-9600300-7-7) Heather Foun.

New Approach to Human Psychology. unabridged ed. Ron Dultz. 124p. (Orig.). 1996. mass mkt. 10.00 (0-9601636-8-9) R Dultz.

*New Approach to International Commercial Contracts: The UNIDROIT Principles of International Contracts. Ed. by M. J. Bonell. 456p. 1999. text 138.00 (90-411-1254-5) Kluwer Law Intl.

New Approach to Keyboard Harmony. Allen Brings et al. (Illus.). 181p. (C). 1979. pap. text 23.00 (0-393-95001-8) Norton.

New Approach to Legal Translation. Susan Sarcevic. LC 97-8397. 1997. 175.00 (90-411-0401-1) Kluwer Law Intl.

New Approach to Optimization of Sequencing Decisions see Annual Review in Automatic Programming

New Approach to Play & Defense, Vol. 1. Edwin B. Kantar. 1993. pap. 10.95 (1-882180-07-0) Griffin CA.

New Approach to Play & Defense, Vol. 2. Edwin Kantor. 1994. pap. 10.95 (1-882180-08-9) Griffin CA.

New Approach to Shakespeare's Early Comedies: Theoretical Foundations. William K. Burke. LC 93-95042. (Theoretical Foundations Ser.). 1998. 24.95 (0-533-10933-7) Vantage.

New Approach to Sight-Singing. 4th ed. Sol Berkowitz. (C). 1997. pap. text 36.00 (0-393-96908-8) Norton.

*New Approach to Tax-Emempt Bonds: Infrastructure Financing with the AGIS Bond. Edward V. Regan. (Public Policy Brief Ser.: No. 58). 40p. 1999. pap. write for info. (0-941276-82-1) J Levy.

*New Approach to Tax-Exempt Bonds. Edward V. Regan. (Public Policy Brief Highlights Ser.: No. 58A). 6p. 1999. pap. write for info. (0-941276-83-X) J Levy.

New Approach to the Alexander Technique: Moving Toward a More Balanced Expression of the Whole Self. rev. ed. Glen Park. LC 98-5016. (Illus.). 304p. 1998. pap. 18.95 (0-89594-918-0) Crossing Pr.

New Approach to the Chronology of Biblical History from Abraham to Samuel. Gerald E. Ardsma. LC 95-95068. 112p. 1995. pap. 24.95 (0-9647665-0-7) Aardsma Res & Pub.

New Approach to the Delineation of Hospital Service Areas. H. D. Cherniack & Jerry B. Schneider. (Discussion Papers: No. 16). 1967. pap. 10.00 (1-55869-077-8) Regional Sci Res Inst.

New Approach to the (DOM - 1) Standard Form of Building Subcontract. Glyn P. Jones. LC 83-8356. 207p. reprint ed. pap. 64.20 (0-7837-4026-3, 204385600011) Bks Demand.

New Approach to the Estimation of Low Frequency Floods for Small Watersheds: Eastern Slope, Pennsylvania. Thomas R. Hammer. (Discussion Papers: No. 79). 1975. pap. 10.00 (1-55869-078-6) Regional Sci Res Inst.

New Approach to the ICE (Institution of Civil Engineers) Conditions of Contract, Vol. 1. Glyn P. Jones. LC 76-353979. 203p. reprint ed. pap. 63.00 (0-7837-4027-1, 204385700001) Bks Demand.

New Approach to the ICE (Institution of Civil Engineers) Conditions of Contract, Vol. 2. Glyn P. Jones. LC 76-353979. 124p. reprint ed. pap. 38.50 (0-7837-4028-X, 204385700002) Bks Demand.

New Approach to the JCT Design & Build Contract. Glyn P. Jones. LC 84-16588. 163p. reprint ed. pap. 50.60 (0-7837-4025-5, 204385500011) Bks Demand.

New Approach to the JCT 1980 Standard Form of Nominated Subcontract. Glyn P. Jones. LC TH0425.J65. (New Approach Ser.). 223p. reprint ed. pap. 69.20 (0-7837-4024-7, 204385400011) Bks Demand.

New Approach to the Local Embedding Theorem of CR-Structure for N Greater Than or Equal to 4 (the Local Solvability for the Operator b in the Abstract Sense) T. Akahori. LC 87-1433. (Memoirs of the American Mathematical Society Ser.: No. 67/366). 257p. 1987. pap. 34.00 (0-8218-2428-7, MEMO/67/366) Am Math.

New Approach to the Poetry of Ezra Pound: Through the Medieval Provencal Aspect. Helen M. Dennis. LC 95-18360. 516p. 1996. text 119.95 (0-7734-9010-8) E Mellen.

New Approach to the Prediction of Regional Industrial Growth & a Preliminary Test for the Boston SMSA. Benjamin H. Stevens & Glynnis A. Trainer. (Discussion Papers: No. 87). 1976. pap. 10.00 (1-55869-079-4) Regional Sci Res Inst.

New Approach to the Theory of International Trade. C. J. Rijnvos. 1976. pap. text 78.50 (90-247-1851-1) Kluwer Academic.

New Approach to the Vedas: An Essay in Translation & Exegesis. Ananda K. Coomaraswamy. 126p. (C). 1994. reprint ed. 22.00 (81-215-0630-1, Pub. by M Manoharial) Coronet Bks.

New Approach to Uilleann Piping. H. J. Clarke. (Illus.). 85p. 1999. pap. text 26.95 (1-900428-51-2, OS10968) Ossian.

New Approach to Understanding & Selecting Personnel. Warren C. Trent. LC 83-83330. (Illus.). 206p. 1985. 24.95 (0-9613155-0-4) Gateway Pr TX.

New Approach to Utilitarianism: A Unified Utilitarian Theory & Its Application to Distributive Justice. C. L. Sheng. 592p. (C). 1991. lib. bdg. 278.50 (0-7923-1301-1, Pub. by Kluwer Academic) Kluwer Academic.

New Approach to Winning Complex Litigation: How to Simplify & Dramatize Cases for New Trial Success. Daniel R. Shulman. LC 83-11680. 1983. text 79.50 (0-13-611715-5) P-H.

New Approach to Women & Therapy. 2nd ed. Miriam Greenspan. LC 92-34036. 1993. write for info. (0-8306-4167-X); pap. 12.95 (0-8306-4168-8) McGraw-Hill Prof.

New Approaches & Answers to Aviation Safety: 34th Corporate Safety Seminar: Proceedings, April 19-21, 1989, Hyatt Regency Hotel, Dearborn, Michigan, U. S. Corporate Aviation Safety Seminar, 34th, 1989, Dea. LC TL0722.C6. 177p. reprint ed. pap. 54.90 (0-8357-2646-0, 204013400015) Bks Demand.

New Approaches & Concepts in Turbulence. Ed. by Themistoles A. Dracos & A. Tsinober. LC 93-8949. (Monte Verita Ser.). 1993. 116.00 (0-8176-2924-6) Birkhauser.

New Approaches Design & Economics EHV Transmiss Plant. B. Jones & D. Silverleaf. LC 77-188747. (International Series of Monographs in Electromagnetic Waves: Vol. 4). 1972. 114.00 (0-08-016696-2, Pub. by Pergamon Repr) Franklin.

New Approaches for Antifungal Drugs. Ed. by Prabhavathi B. Fernandes. LC 92-11106. x, 201p. 1992. 87.50 (0-8176-3602-1); write for info. (3-7643-3602-1) Birkhauser.

New Approaches in Cancer Pharmacology: Drug Design & Development. Ed. by P. Workman. LC 94-27065. 1994. write for info. (0-387-58415-3) Spr-Verlag.

New Approaches in Cancer Pharmacology: Drug Design & Development. Ed. by Paul Workman. LC 92-49597. 1993. write for info. (3-540-56089-0); 94.95 (0-387-56089-0) Spr-Verlag.

New Approaches in Cancer Pharmacology: Drug Design & Development II. Ed. by P. Workman. LC 94-27065. (Monographs of the European School of Oncology). 1994. 86.95 (0-387-58153-7) Spr-Verlag.

New Approaches in Cancer Therapy. Ed. by H. Cortes Funes & M. Rozencweig. LC 81-40201. (Monograph Series of the European Organization for Research on Treatment of Cancer: Vol. 11). 203p. 1982. reprint ed. pap. 63.00 (0-608-00337-9, 206105400007) Bks Demand.

New Approaches in Cardiac Mechanics. Ed. by Kazuo Kitamura et al. x, 330p. 1986. text 189.00 (2-88124-126-3) Gordon & Breach.

New Approaches in Chromatography '93. Ed. by H. Kalasz et al. 266p. 1993. pap. 35.00 (963-8254-00-9, Pub. by Akade Kiado) Intl Spec Bk.

New Approaches in Classification & Data Analysis. Ed. by E. Diday et al. (Studies in Classification, Data Analysis, & Knowledge Organization). (Illus.). xii, 693p. 1994. 128.00 (3-540-58425-0) Spr-Verlag.

New Approaches in Coal Chemistry. Ed. by Bernard D. Blaustein et al. LC 81-12740. (ACS Symposium Ser.: No. 169). 1981. 46.95 (0-8412-0659-7) Am Chemical.

New Approaches in Coal Chemistry. Ed. by Bernard D. Blaustein et al. LC 81-12740. (ACS Symposium Ser.: No. 169). (Illus.). 475p. 1981. reprint ed. pap. 147.30 (0-608-03252-2, 206377100007) Bks Demand.

New Approaches in Flaubert Studies. Ed. by Tony Williams & Mary Orr. LC 98-50516. (Studies in French Literature: Vol. 34). 256p. 1999. lib. bdg. 89.95 (0-7734-8197-4) E Mellen.

New Approaches, in Geomagnetism & the Earth's Rotation: Stockholm, Sweden, October 10-12, 1988. Ed. by S. Flodmark. 296p. 1991. text 67.00 (981-02-0359-4) World Scientific Pub.

New Approaches in International Mediation, 223. Ed. by C. R. Mitchell & K. Webb. LC 88-10252. (Contributions in Political Science Ser.: No. 223). 268p. 1988. 65.00 (0-313-25974-7, MNA/, Greenwood Pr) Greenwood.

*New Approaches in Medical Image Analysis. Ed. by Binh Pham et al. 226p. 1999. pap. text 62.00 (0-8194-3229-6) SPIE.

New Approaches in Monetary Policy, No. 4. J. E. Wadsworth & F. Leonard De Juvigny. (Financial & Monetary Policy Studies). 406p. 1979. lib. bdg. 205.00 (90-286-0848-6) Kluwer Academic.

*New Approaches in Nonlinear Analysis. Ed. by Themistocles M. Rassias. 240p. 1999. pap. write for info. (1-57485-042-3) Hadronic Pr Inc.

New Approaches in Pastoral Counseling. Steven K. Kaplan & Lynn A. Schoeneberg. (C). 1988. text 22.95 (0-8290-1806-9) Irvington.

New Approaches in Spectral Decomposition. Ed. by Ridgley Lange & Shengwang Wang. LC 92-6183. (Contemporary Mathematics Ser.: Vol. 128). 273p. 1992. pap. 44.00 (0-8218-5139-X, CONM/128C) Am Math.

New Approaches in the Diagnosis & Management of Cardiovascular Disease: Proceedings of the Conference on Cardiovascular Disease, 9th, Snowmass-at-Aspen, Aspen, Colorado, January, 1978. Conference on Cardiovascular Disease Staff. Ed. by John H. Vogel. (Advances in Cardiology Ser.: Vol. 26). 1979. 71.50 (3-8055-2914-7) S Karger.

*New Approaches in the Elementary Classroom. 3rd ed. Herrold. 400p. 2000. pap. 58.67 (0-13-248550-8) P-H.

New Approaches to Best-Practice: The Role of TNCs & Implications for Developing Countries. 60p. pap. 15.00 (92-1-104342-5, 90.II.A.13) UN.

New Approaches to Breeding for Improved Plant Protein. IAEA Staff. (Panel Proceedings Ser.). (Illus.). 193p. 1969. pap. 25.00 (92-0-111069-3, ISP212, Pub. by IAEA) Bernan Associates.

New Approaches to Chinese Word Formation: Morphology, Phonology, & the Lexicon in Modern & Ancient Chinese. Ed. by Jerome L. Packard. LC 97-33206. (Trends in Linguistics, Studies & Monographs). 304p. 1997. lib. bdg. 137.00 (3-11-015109-X) Mouton.

New Approaches to Comparative Education. Ed. by Philip G. Altbach & Gail P. Kelly. LC 85-24523. vi, 342p. (C). 1986. pap. text 20.50 (0-226-01526-2); lib. bdg. 40.00 (0-226-01525-4) U Ch Pr.

New Approaches to Counseling & Communication: How to Improve Your Skills in Patient Care: Proceedings of the Advances in Patient Care Conference, 4th, 1977. Advances in Patient Care Conference Staff. Ed. by Spring Zoog & Stephen R. Yarnall. 1977. 20.00 (0-917054-14-8) Med Communications.

New Approaches to Developement Co-Operation. (Discussion Papers: No. 7). 96p. pap. 10.00 (92-1-126055-8) UN.

New Approaches to Down Syndrome. Brian Stratford & Pat Gunn. LC 96-223086. (Education Ser.). (Illus.). 448p. 1996. pap. 26.95 (0-304-33350-6) Continuum.

*New Approaches to Drug Development. Pierre Jollaes. LC 00-39811. (Experientia Ser.). 2000. write for info. (0-8176-6129-8) Birkhauser.

New Approaches to Economic & Social Analyses of Discrimination. Ed. by Richard R. Cornwall & Phanindra V. Wunnava. LC 91-15504. 432p. 1991. 65.00 (0-275-93581-7, C3581, Praeger Pubs) Greenwood.

New Approaches to Editing Old English Verse. Ed. by Sarah L. Keefer & Katherine O. O'Keeffe. LC 97-38434. (Illus.). 136p. 1998. 55.00 (0-85991-469-0, DS Brewer) Boydell & Brewer.

New Approaches to Elementary Classroom Music. 2nd rev. ed. Rebecca M. Herrold. 352p. 1991. pap. 76.00 (0-13-611690-6, 650201) P-H.

New Approaches to Employee Management, Vol. 2: Discrimination in Employment. Ed. by David M. Saunders. LC 95-23136. 220p. 1994. 78.50 (1-55938-731-9) Jai Pr.

New Approaches to Employee Management, Vol. 5. Ed. by David M. Saunders. Date not set. 78.50 (0-7623-0311-5) Jai Pr.

New Approaches to Employee Management Vol. 1: Fairness in Employee Selection. Ed. by David M. Saunders. LC 95-23132. (Illus.). 228p. 1993. 78.50 (1-55938-595-2) Jai Pr.

New Approaches to Employee Management Vol. 3: Employee Management in Developing Countries. Ed. by David M. Saunders. LC 95-23137. (Illus.). 255p. 1995. 78.50 (1-55938-930-3) Jai Pr.

New Approaches to Family Pastoral Care. Douglas A. Anderson. LC 79-8898. (Creative Pastoral Care & Counseling Ser.). 96p. (Orig.). reprint ed. pap. 30.00 (0-608-15327-3, 202961400061) Bks Demand.

New Approaches to Family Practice: Confronting Economic Stress. Nancy R. Vosler. LC 96-10083. (Sage Sourcebooks for the Human Services Ser.: Vol. 31). 263p. 1996. 56.00 (0-7619-0032-2); pap. 26.00 (0-7619-0033-0) Sage.

New Approaches to Financing Development in Africa. Ed. by Jean-Claude Berthelemy & Carlos Quenan. 65p. (Orig.). 1996. pap. 8.00 (92-64-15347-0, 41-96-12-1) OECD.

New Approaches to Greek Particles: Proceedings to the Colloquium Held in Amsterdam, January 4-6, 1996, to Honor C. J. Ruigh on the Occasion of His Retirement. Ed. by Albert Rijksbaron. LC 98-139102. (Amsterdam Studies in Greek Philology: Vol. 7). 293p. 1997. 95.00 (90-5063-097-9, Pub. by Gieben) J Benjamins Pubng Co.

New Approaches to Health Education in Primary Health Care: Report of a WHO Expert Committee, 1983. (Technical Report Ser.: No. 690). 44p. 1983. pap. text 5.00 (92-4-120690-X, 1100690) World Health.

New Approaches to Improve Road Safety: Report on a WHO Study Group, 1987. (Technical Report Ser.: No. 781). 62p. 1989. pap. text 8.00 (92-4-120781-7, 1100781) World Health.

New Approaches to Knowledge Acquisition. R. Q. Lu. 360p. 1994. text 58.00 (981-02-1316-6) World Scientific Pub.

New Approaches to Literacy: Helping Students Develop Reading & Writing Skills. Robert J. Marzano & Diane E. Paynter. LC 94-9054. (Psychology in the Classroom Ser.). 143p. (Orig.). 1994. pap. text 17.95 (1-55798-249-X) Am Psychol.

New Approaches to Macroeconomic Modeling: Evolutionary Stochastic Dynamics, Multiple Equilibria, & Externalities As Field Effects. Masanao Aoki. (Illus.). 303p. (C). 1996. text 59.95 (0-521-48207-0) Cambridge U Pr.

New Approaches to Macroeconomic Modeling: Evolutionary Stochastic Dynamics, Multiple Equilibria, & Externalities As Field Effects. Masanao Aoki. (Illus.). 306p. (C). 1998. reprint ed. pap. text 19.95 (0-521-63769-4) Cambridge U Pr.

New Approaches to Medieval Textuality. Ed. by Mikle D. Ledgerwood. LC 95-40414. (Studies on Themes & Motifs in Literature: Vol. 28). VIII, 151p. (C). 1998. text 39.95 (0-8204-3026-9) P Lang Pubng.

New Approaches to Modeling, Specification Selection & Econometric Inference: Proceedings of the 1st International Symposium. Ed. by William A. Barnett et al. (International Symposia in Economic Theory & Econometrics Ser.: No. 1). (Illus.). 490p. (C). 1990. text 89.95 (0-521-38465-6) Cambridge U Pr.

New Approaches to Monitoring Aquatic Ecosystems. Ed. by Terence P. Boyle. LC 86-28666. (Special Technical Publication Ser.: No. 940). (Illus.). 215p. 1987. text 39.00 (0-8031-0939-3, STP940) ASTM.

New Approaches to Old & New Problems in Liquid State Theory: Inhomogeneities & Phase Separation in Simple, Complex, & Quantum Fluids. Carlo Caccamo et al. LC 99-14205. (Nato Science Series, Series C, Mathematical & Physical Sciences). 1999. write for info. (0-7923-5670-5) Kluwer Academic.

New Approaches to Organizational Communication. Ed. by Branislav Kovacic. LC 93-39275. (SUNY Series in Human Communication Processes). 288p. (C). 1994. text 59.50 (0-7914-1917-7); pap. text 21.95 (0-7914-1918-5) State U NY Pr.

N

New Approaches to Other Pasts. Ed. by W. Fred Kinsey, III & Roger W. Moeller. (Illus.). 96p. (C). 1989. pap. text 12.50 (*0-9622320-0-9*) Archaeol Servs.

New Approaches to Pest Control & Eradication: A Symposium Sponsored by the Pesticides Subdivision of the Division of Agricultural & Food Chemistry at the 142nd Meeting. American Chemical Society Staff. Ed. by Stanley A. Hall. LC 63-19396. (American Chemical Society Advances in Chemistry Ser.: No. 41). 86p. reprint ed. pap. 30.00 (*0-608-30177-9*, 201953000013) Bks Demand.

New Approaches to Polymer Materials. Ed. by G. E. Zaikov. 1995. 175.00 (*1-56072-254-1*) Nova Sci Pubs.

***New Approaches to Problem Behavior: Practical Guide to Discipline & Behavior Management for Teachers & Parents.** 2nd ed. Peter Ross. 122p. 1999. pap. 49.95 (*1-884937-55-1*) Manisses Communs.

New Approaches to Public Management: The Case of Michigan. John M. Kost. 50p. 1996. pap. 9.95 (*0-8157-4961-9*) Brookings.

***New Approaches to River Management.** A. J. M. Smits et al. (Illus.). 356p. 2000. pap. 70.00 (*90-5782-058-7*, Pub. by Backhuys Pubs) Balogh.

***New Approaches to Science & Technology Cooperation & Capacity Building.** United Nations Conference on Trade & Development Staff. 417p. 1998. pap. 40.00 (*92-1-112443-3*) UN.

New Approaches to Semiotics & the Human Sciences: Essays in Honor of Roberta Kevelson. Ed. by William A. Pencak & Ralph Lindgren. LC 97-12496. (Semiotics & the Human Sciences Ser.: Vol. 13). XI, 360p. (C). 1998. text 58.95 (*0-8204-3814-6*) P Lang Pubng.

New Approaches to Sex in Marriage. John E. Eichenlaub. 1980. pap. 3.00 (*0-87980-106-9*) Wilshire.

New Approaches to Sight Singing. 4th ed. Sol Berkowitz. (C). 1998. pap. text 45.00 (*0-393-97271-2*) Norton.

New Approaches to Social Problems. Ed. by Irene H. Frieze et al. LC 79-88767. (Jossey-Bass Social & Behavioral Science Ser.). 496p. reprint ed. pap. 153.80 (*0-8357-4975-4*, 203790800009) Bks Demand.

New Approaches to Speciation in the Fossil Record. Ed. by Douglas H. Erwin & Robert L. Anstey. LC 95-7117. 1995. 52.00 (*0-231-08248-7*) Col U Pr.

New Approaches to Stabilisation of Vaccines Potency: WHO Headquarters, May 1995. Ed. by F. Brown. (Developments in Biological Standardization Ser.: Vol. 87). xii, 364p. 1996. pap. 278.25 (*3-8055-6309-4*) S Karger.

New Approaches to Staff Safety (Of Correcitons Officers) Robert L. Thornton & John H. Shireman. (Illus.). 73p. 1999. reprint ed. text 20.00 (*0-7881-7938-1*) DIANE Pub.

New Approaches to the Book of Mormon: Explorations in Critical Methodology. Ed. by Brent L. Metcalfe. LC 92-16269. (Illus.). 460p. 1993. 26.95 (*1-56085-017-5*) Signature Bks.

New Approaches to the Latin American Debt Crisis. Jeffrey D. Sachs. LC 89-10298. (Essays in International Finance Ser.: No. 174). 50p. 1989. pap. text 10.00 (*0-88165-081-1*) Princeton U Int Finan Econ.

New Approaches to the Management of Allergic Diseases: Proceedings of the Collegium Internationale Allergologicum, 12th, New Orleans, LA, Sept. 1978. Collegium Internationale Allergologicum Staff. Ed. by Lawrence M. Lichtenstein & G. J. Gleich. (Monographs in Allergy: Vol. 14). (Illus.). 1979. pap. 126.25 (*3-8055-3039-0*) S Karger.

New Approaches to the State & Peasant in Ottoman History. Ed. by Halil Berktay & Suraiya Faroqhi. 282p. 1992. text 49.50 (*0-7146-3468-9*, Pub. by F Cass Pubs) Intl Spec Bk.

New Approaches to the Study of Central-Local Government Relationships. Ed. by George Jones. 208p. 1980. text 77.95 (*0-566-00332-5*) Ashgate Pub Co.

New Approaches to the Treatment of Leukaemia. Ed. by Emil J. Freireich & U. Veronesi. (ESO Monographs). (Illus.). vii, 193p. 1990. 118.00 (*0-387-52261-1*) Spr-Verlag.

New Approaches to Theodor Fontane: Cultural Codes in Flux. Ed. by Marion Doebeling. (Studies in German Literature, Linguistics & Culture). 213p. 2000. 55.00 (*1-57113-143-4*, Pub. by Camden Hse) Boydell & Brewer.

New Approaches to Undergraduate Engineering Three. Ed. by Patricia Daniels. 380p. 1992. pap. text 50.00 (*0-939204-49-5*) Eng Found.

New Approaches to Understanding Travel Behavior. (National Cooperative Highway Research Program Report Ser.: No. 250). 142p. 1982. 10.00 (*0-309-03420-5*, NR250) Transport Res Bd.

New Approaches to Urban Transportation Needs. 212p. 1971. pap. 3.00 (*0-87262-032-8*) Am Soc Civil Eng.

New Approaches to Welfare Theory. Ed. by Glenn Drover & Patrick Kerans. 336p. 1993. 95.00 (*1-85278-881-X*); pap. 30.00 (*1-85278-981-6*) E Elgar.

New Aquarium Fish Breeding Handbook. Ines Scheurmann. 144p. 1990. pap. 9.95 (*0-8120-4474-6*) Barron.

New Aquarium Fish Handbook. Ines Scheurmann. 144p. 1986. pap. 9.95 (*0-8120-3682-4*) Barron.

New Arabian Nights, The Pavilion on the Links & Other Tales see Works of Robert Louis Stevenson, Valima Edition

New Arabian Studies, Vol. 1. Ed. by R. L. Bidwell et al. 224p. 1994. text 39.95 (*0-85989-408-8*, Pub. by Univ Exeter Pr) Northwestern U Pr.

New Arabian Studies, Vol. 2. Ed. by R. L. Bidwell et al. 245p. 1995. text 39.95 (*0-85989-452-5*, Pub. by Univ Exeter Pr) Northwestern U Pr.

New Arabian Studies, Vol. 3. Ed. by J. R. Smart. (Illus.). 210p. 1996. text 55.00 (*0-85989-479-7*, Pub. by Univ Exeter Pr) Northwestern U Pr.

New Arabian Studies 4. Ed. by J. R. Smart et al. (Arabic Studies). (Illus.). 300p. 1998. 60.00 (*0-85989-552-1*, Pub. by Univ Exeter Pr) Northwestern U Pr.

New Arabic-German, German-Arabic Dictionary, 3 vols., Set. Adolf Wahrmud. (ARA & GER.). 1974. 69.95 (*0-86685-178-X*) Intl Bk Ctr.

New Arabic Grammar of the Written Language. J. A. Haywood & H. M. Nahmad. 696p. (C). 1962. 47.50 (*0-674-60851-8*) HUP.

***New Arabic Grammar of the Written Language.** J. A. Haywood & H. M. Nahmad. 688p. 1999. reprint ed. pap. 40.00 (*0-85331-585-X*) Lund Humphries.

New Archaeology & the Ancient Maya. Jeremy A. Sabloff. LC 89-10927. (Illus.). 193p. 1994. pap. 19.95 (*0-7167-6007-X*) W H Freeman.

New Archetype for Competitive Intelligence. John J. McGonagle, Jr. & Carolyn M. Vella. LC 95-50744. 240p. 1996. 59.95 (*0-89930-973-9*, Quorum Bks) Greenwood.

***New Architects: A Guide To Britains Best Young Architectural Practices,new..** Architecture Foundation Staff. 2000. 39.95 (*1-86154-018-3*) Abrams.

New Architecture. Academy Editions Staff. 1991. pap. 21.95 (*0-312-04521-2*) St Martin.

New Architecture & City Planning. Ed. by Paul Zucker. LC 76-128337. (Essay Index Reprint Ser.). 1977. 46.95 (*0-8369-2035-X*) Ayer.

New Architecture & the Bauhaus. Walter Gropius. (Illus.). 112p. 1965. pap. text 10.95 (*0-262-57006-8*) MIT Pr.

New Architecture Berlin 1990-2000. Martin Kieren. 336p. 1999. pap. text 39.95 (*3-931321-82-7*, Pub. by Jovis Verlags) Dist Art Pubs.

***New Architecture of Learning: Strategies & Solutions in Training & Development.** David Mackey. 240p. 2000. pap. 29.95 (*0-7494-3120-2*, Pub. by Kogan Page Ltd) Stylus Pub VA.

***New Architecture of the International Monetary System.** Paolo Savona. LC 00-36831. 2000. write for info. (*0-7923-7854-7*) Kluwer Academic.

***New Arenas for Community Social Work Practice with Urban Youth: Use of the Arts, Humanities & Sports.** Melvin Delgado. LC 99-86564. (Illus.). 2000. 49.50 (*0-231-11462-1*); pap. 21.50 (*0-231-11463-X*) Col U Pr.

New Arenas for Violence: Homicide in the American Workplace. Michael D. Kelleher. LC 96-16278. 208p. 1996. 55.00 (*0-275-95652-0*, Praeger Pubs) Greenwood.

New Argentine Democracy: The Search for a Successful Formula. Ed. by Edward C. Epstein. LC 92-13658. 296p. 1992. 62.95 (*0-275-93919-7*, C3919, Praeger Pubs) Greenwood.

New Aristotle Reader. Aristotle. Ed. by J. L. Ackrill. 600p. 1987. pap. 18.95 (*0-691-02043-4*, Pub. by Princeton U Pr) Cal Prin Full Svc.

New-Ark. limited ed. Dennis Barone. 44p. (Orig.). 1993. pap. 18.00 (*0-937013-48-X*) Potes Poets.

New Armenian-English Dictionary. Matthias Bedrossian. (ARM & ENG.). 816p. 49.95 (*0-86685-122-4*, LDL1224, Pub. by Librairie du Liban) Intl Bk Ctr.

***New Armenian Kitchen.** St. Andrews Ladies Society Staff. Ed. by Veronica Sarkissian. vi, 248p. 2000. 19.95 (*0-9678382-8-2*, 7413); pap. 15.95 (*0-9678382-5-8*, 7413) St Andrews Ch.

New Arrival: In the Refugee Camp. 2nd ed. Dieter Kuntz. 1990. pap. text 6.25 (*0-13-612342-2*, 640113) P-H.

New Arrival: In the Refugee Camp, Bk. 1. 2nd rev. ed. Laurie Kuntz. Ed. by Helen Munch. (Illus.). 128p. 1988. pap. text 7.25 (*0-88084-261-X*) Alemany Pr.

New Arrival: In the United States, Bk. 2. 2nd rev. ed. Laurie Kuntz. Ed. by Helen Munch. (Illus.). 128p. 1990. pap. text 7.25 (*0-13-612367-8*) Alemany Pr.

New Arrival English. Jane Yeldin & Caroline T. Linse. 128p. (J). 1992. mass mkt. 16.95 (*0-8384-2253-5*) Heinle & Heinle.

New Arrival English. Yeldin & Linse. (J). 1992. mass mkt. 28.95 (*0-8384-2256-X*) Heinle & Heinle.

New Arrival English. Yeldin & Linse. (J). 1992. audio 18.95 (*0-8384-2255-1*) Heinle & Heinle.

New Arrival English. Yeldin & Linse. (J). 1993. mass mkt., teacher ed. 25.95 (*0-8384-2254-3*) Heinle & Heinle.

New Arrivals Vol. 8, No. 4: A Little Magic; Slow Dance; New Year's Baby; Morgan's Child. Rita C. Estrada et al. 1999. mass mkt. 3.50 (*0-373-82746-6*, 1-82746-8, Mira Bks) Harlequin Bks.

New Arrivals, Old Encounters: 12 Stories. Brian W. Aldiss. LC 79-2642. 224p. 1979. 25.00 (*0-06-010055-9*) Ultramarine Pub.

New Art. Roxana Marcoci et al. LC 96-50361. 1997. lib. bdg. write for info. (*0-7172-9090-5*) Abrams.

New Art. Roxana Marcoci et al. LC 96-50361. (Illus.). 160p. 1997. pap. 24.95 (*0-8109-2674-1*, Pub. by Abrams) Time Warner.

New Art - The New Life: The Collected Writings of Piet Mondrian. Piet Mondrian. Ed. & Tr. by Harry Holtzman & Martin S. James from DUT. (Illus.). 440p. 1992. reprint ed. pap. 24.95 (*0-306-80508-1*) Da Capo.

***New Art City.** Perl. 2000. 26.00 (*0-465-05522-2*, Pub. by Basic); pap. 15.00 (*0-465-05523-0*, Pub. by Basic) HarpC.

New Art City. Perl. 1997. 25.00 (*0-684-19575-5*) S&S Trade.

New Art Deco Alphabets. Marcia Loeb. LC 74-29015. (Pictorial Archive Ser.). (Illus.). 75p. (Orig.). 1975. pap. 5.95 (*0-486-23149-6*) Dover.

New Art Deco Borders & Motifs. William Rowe. 80p. 1984. pap. 6.95 (*0-486-24709-0*) Dover.

New Art 8: Profiles in Contemporary Australian Art. Nevill Drury. (Illus.). 204p. 1993. text 37.00 (*976-8097-36-1*) Gordon & Breach.

New Art 5: Profiles in Contemporary Australian Art. Ed. by Nevill Drury. 204p. 1991. text 37.00 (*976-8097-03-5*) Gordon & Breach.

New Art for a New Building. E. John Bullard. LC 93-83952. (Illus.). 44p. 1993. pap. 12.95 (*0-89494-042-2*) New Orleans Mus Art.

New Art 4. Ed. by N. Drury. (Illus.). 230p. 1990. text 30.00 (*0-947131-33-7*) Gordon & Breach.

New Art from Puerto Rico. Text by Hollister Sturges. (SPA., Illus.). 84p. 1990. 12.95 (*0-916746-15-1*) Springfield Lib & Mus.

New Art History. Ed. by A. L. Rees & Frances Borzello. LC 87-2997. 176p. (C). 1988. reprint ed. pap. 17.50 (*0-391-03552-5*) Humanities.

New Art International. Jeremy Sedley. (Illus.). 152p. 1997. pap. 9.95 (*0-9653228-3-1*) Book Art Pr.

New Art International. Jeremy Sedley. (Illus.). 162p. 1998. 19.95 (*0-9653228-5-8*); pap. 9.95 (*0-9653228-4-X*) Book Art Pr.

***New Art International.** 4th ed. G. Alexander Irving. Ed. by Jeremy Sedley. (Illus.). 158p. 1999. 29.95 (*0-9653228-6-6*); pap. 19.95 (*0-9653228-7-4*) Book Art Pr.

New Art International, No. 1. Gary Alexander. Ed. by Jeremy Sedley. (Illus.). 124p. 1996. 39.95 (*0-9653228-0-7*); pap. 19.95 (*0-9653228-1-5*) Book Art Pr.

New Art International, Vol. 3. Jeremy Sedley. (Illus.). 152p. 1997. 19.95 (*0-9653228-2-3*) Book Art Pr.

New Art New World: British Art in Postwar Society. Margaret Garlake. LC 97-51962. (Illus.). 304p. 1998. 50.00 (*0-300-07292-9*) Yale U Pr.

New Art of Aromatherapy. Date not set. 19.95 (*0-8464-4569-7*) Beekman Pubs.

New Art of Autobiography: An Essay on the Life of Giambattista Vico Written by Himself. Donald Phillip Verene. (Illus.). 280p. 1991. text 65.00 (*0-19-823900-9*) OUP.

New Art of Cuba. Luis Camnitzer. LC 92-43116. (Illus.). 448p. (C). 1993. text 45.00 (*0-292-71149-2*) U of Tex Pr.

New Art of Keeping Fit: Modern Methods for Men. rev. ed. Joseph Edmundson. LC 63-13393. (Illus.). 1978. 10.95 (*0-87523-144-6*) Emerson.

New Art of Loving. Mark Fisher. 1989. pap. 9.95 (*1-85230-105-8*, Pub. by Element MA) Penguin Putnam.

New Art of Making Beer. 2nd ed. Stanley F. Anderson & Ken Healey. LC 97-46752. 192p. 1998. pap. 11.95 (*0-452-26939-3*, Plume) Dutton Plume.

***New Art of the Leader.** William A. Cohen. 2000. 23.00 (*0-7352-0166-8*) PH Pr.

New Art on Paper No. 2: Acquired with Funds from the Hunt Manufacturing Co., 1989-1995. Martha Chahroudi et al. LC 96-2426. (Illus.). 92p. 1996. 26.00 (*0-87633-102-9*) Phila Mus Art.

New Art 1: Profiles in Contemporary Australian Art. Nevill Drury. (Illus.). 160p. 1987. 65.00 (*0-947131-02-7*, Pub. by Craftsman House) Gordon & Breach.

New Art 7: Profiles in Contemporary Australian Art. Nevill Drury. (Illus.). 204p. 1992. text 40.00 (*976-8097-18-3*) Gordon & Breach.

New Art 3. Ed. by N. Drury. (Illus.). 224p. 1989. text 37.00 (*0-947131-27-2*) Gordon & Breach.

New Art 2: Profiles in Contemporary Australian Art. Ed. by Nevill Drury. (Illus.). 230p. 1989. text 37.00 (*0-947131-15-9*) Gordon & Breach.

New Arthritis Breakthrough: The Only Medical Therapy Clinically Proven to Produce Long-Term Improvement & Remission: RA, Lupus, Juvenile RA, Fibromyalgia, Scleroderma, Spondyloarthropathy, & Other Inflammatory Forms of Arthritis. Henry Scammell. 256p. 1998. pap. 14.95 (*0-87131-843-1*) M Evans.

New Arthritis Cures: All the Treatments That Work for Your Arthritis Pain. Brenda Adderly & Amal Das. 208p. 1999. 24.95 (*0-89526-332-7*, Pub. by Regnery Pub) Natl Bk Netwk.

New Arthritis Relief Diet: Proven Steps to Stop Inflammation, Prevent Joint Damage, Decrease Medication & Improve the Quality of Your Life. James Scala. LC 97-34927. 272p. 1998. pap. 13.95 (*0-452-27951-8*) NAL.

New Arthurian Encyclopedia. 1991. 91.00 (*1-55862-125-3*, 00005358) St James Pr.

New Arthurian Encyclopedia. Ed. by Norris J. Lacy et al. LC 90-237000. (Illus.). 615p. 1991. text 95.00 (*0-8240-4377-4*, H931) Garland.

New Arthurian Encyclopedia. rev. ed. Ed. by Norris J. Lacy et al. LC 95-36107. (Reference Library of the Humanities: Vol. 931). (Illus.). 656p. 1995. pap. text 32.95 (*0-8153-2303-4*, H931) Garland.

***New Article 9.** Corinne Cooper. LC 99-35859. 1999. write for info. (*1-57073-699-5*) Amer Bar Assn.

***New Article 9.** 2nd ed. Corinne Cooper. LC 00-33219. 2000. pap. write for info. (*1-57073-831-9*) Amer Bar Assn.

New Artists: The Gloria Wilcher Memorial Exhibition. Marilyn F. Hoffman & Michael K. Komanecky. (Illus.). 40p. (Orig.). 1989. pap. 5.00 (*0-929710-01-0*) Currier Gal.

New As a Wave: A Retrospective, 1937-1983. Eve Triem. Ed. by Ethel Fortner. LC 84-4171. 135p. 1984. 16.00 (*0-937872-24-5*); pap. 7.00 (*0-937872-25-3*) Dragon Gate.

New ASBDA Curriculum Guide: A Reference Book for School Band Directors. American School Band Directors Association Staff. Ed. by Thom Proctor. LC 98-101975. 224p. (Orig.). 1997. pap. text 24.95 (*1-57623-997-7*, EL9737) Wrner Bros.

New Asia in Global Perspectives. Myung-Gun Choo. LC 99-22105. 2000. text 69.95 (*0-312-22172-X*) St Martin.

New Asian Architecture: Vernacular Traditions & Contemporary Style. William S. Lim & Tan H. Beng. (Illus.). 176p. 1998. 42.50 (*962-593-302-6*) Tuttle Pubng.

New Asian Corporation: Managing for the Future in Post-Crisis Asia. Michael Alan Hamlin. LC 99-6602. (Illus.). 304p. 1999. text 34.95 (*0-7879-4606-0*) Jossey-Bass.

New Asian Emperors. George Haley. LC 99-164257. 250p. 1998. pap. text 19.95 (*0-7506-4130-4*) Buttrwrth-Heinemann.

New Asian Immigration in Los Angeles & Global Restructuring. Ed. by Edna Bonacich et al. LC 93-49863. (Asian American History & Culture Ser.). 336p. (C). 1994. text 69.95 (*1-56639-217-9*); pap. text 24.95 (*1-56639-218-7*) Temple U Pr.

New Asian Renaissance. Francois Godement. LC 96-20090. 328p. (C). 1997. 90.00 (*0-415-11856-5*); pap. 24.99 (*0-415-11857-3*) Routledge.

***New Aspects in Bioorganic Chemistry.** Ed. by Ulf Diederichsen et al. 468p. 1999. pap. 85.00 (*3-527-29665-4*) Wiley.

New Aspects in Diabetes: Treatment Strategies with Alphaglucosidase Inhibitors. Ed. by P. J. Lefebvre & E. Standl. (Illus.). xii, 306p. (C). 1993. lib. bdg. 98.50 (*3-11-013469-1*) De Gruyter.

New Aspects in Interpolation & Completion Theories. I. Golberg. LC 93-20904. (Operator Theory: Advances & Applications Ser.: Vol. 64). 232p. 1993. 86.00 (*0-8176-2948-3*) Birkhauser.

New Aspects in Physiological Antitumor Substances. Ed. by G. Gillissen & K. E. Theurer. (Illus.). x, 228p. 1985. pap. 35.00 (*3-8055-4002-7*) S Karger.

New Aspects in the Diagnosis & Treatment of Hodgkin's Disease. Ed. by V. Diehl et al. (Recent Results in Cancer Research Ser.: Vol. 17). (Illus.). 305p. 1989. 137.00 (*0-387-51124-5*) Spr-Verlag.

New Aspects in the History & Philosophy of Astronomy see Vistas in Astronomy

New Aspects in the Regulation of Prostatic Function. Ed. by G. Aumuller et al. (Clinical & Experimental Urology Ser.). (Illus.). 186p. 1989. text 61.00 (*3-88603-318-X*, Pub. by W Zuckschwerdt) Scholium Intl.

New Aspects in the Treatment of Failing Heart. Ed. by H. Yasuda & H. Kawaguchi. LC 92-49576. 1992. 139.00 (*0-387-70110-9*) Spr-Verlag.

New Aspects in the Treatment of Pulmonary & Upper Airways Diseases. Ed. by G. Allegra & J. A. Nahkosteen. (Journal: Respiration: Vol. 51, Suppl. 1, 1987). iv, 68p. 1987. pap. 22.75 (*3-8055-4592-4*) S Karger.

New Aspects of Allergic Diseases, Immuno-Regulation & Immunodeficiencies. Ed. by L. A. Hanson et al. (Journal: International Archives of Allergy & Applied Immunology: Vol. 82, No. 3-4, 1987). (Illus.). viii, 332p. 1987. pap. 120.00 (*3-8055-4568-1*) S Karger.

New Aspects of Cochlear Mechanics & Inner Ear Pathophysiology. Ed. by C. R. Pfaltz. (Advances in OtoRhinoLaryngology Ser.: Vol. 44). (Illus.). x, 170p. 1990. 146.25 (*3-8055-5020-0*) S Karger.

New Aspects of Complement Structure & Function. Anna Erdei. 120p. 1994. 99.00 (*1-57059-158-X*, LN9158) Landes Bioscience.

New Aspects of Electromagnetic & Acoustic Wave Diffusion. Ed. by J. Kuhn et al. LC 98-4246. (Tracts in Modern Physics Ser.: Vol. 144). (Illus.). 120p. 1998. 89.95 (*3-540-64137-8*) Spr-Verlag.

New Aspects of Fundamental Problems of Laryngology & Otology. Ed. by C. R. Pfaltz. (Advances in OtoRhinoLaryngology Ser.: Vol. 32). (Illus.). viii, 200p. 1984. 138.50 (*3-8055-3701-8*) S Karger.

New Aspects of Haemophilia Treatment. Ed. by Harold R. Roberts. (Journal Ser.: Vol. 26, No. 1, 1996). (Illus.). vi, 166p. 1996. pap., suppl. ed. 53.25 (*3-8055-6279-9*) S Karger.

New Aspects of High-Energy Proton - Proton Collisions. Ed. by A. Ali. (Ettore Majorana International Science Series, Life Sciences: Vol. 39). (Illus.). 446p. 1988. 120.00 (*0-306-43106-8*, Plenum Trade) Perseus Pubng.

New Aspects of Human Ethology: Proceedings of the 13th Conference of the International Society for Human Ethology Held in Vienna, Austria, August 5-10, 1996. Ed. by Alain Schmitt et al. LC 97-30572. (Illus.). 252p. 1997. 107.00 (*0-306-45695-8*, Kluwer Plenum) Kluwer Academic.

New Aspects of Human Polymorphonuclear Leukocytes. Ed. by Walter H. Horl & P. J. Schollmeyer. (Advances in Experimental Medicine & Biology Ser.). (Illus.). 236p. (C). 1991. text 107.00 (*0-306-43906-9*, Kluwer Plenum) Kluwer Academic.

***New Aspects of Interntional Law: A Series of Lectures Delivered at Columbia University in July 1926.** N. Politis. LC 99-46126. 2000. write for info. (*1-57588-587-5*) W S Hein.

New Aspects of Magellanic Cloud Research: Proceedings of the European Meeting on the Magellanic Clouds, 2nd, Heidelberg, Germany, 1992. Ed. by B. Baschek et al. LC 92-45282. (Lecture Notes in Physics Ser.: Vol. 416). 1993. 96.95 (*0-387-56432-2*) Spr-Verlag.

New Aspects of Nuclear Dynamics. Ed. by J. H. Koch & Huberts De Witt. LC 89-25521. (NATO ASI Series B, Physics: Vol. 209). (Illus.). 238p. 1989. 79.50 (*0-306-43392-3*, Plenum Trade) Perseus Pubng.

New Aspects of Nutritional Status. J. C. Somogyi. (Bibliotheca Nutritio et Dieta Ser.: No. 51). (Illus.). x, 198p. 1994. 213.25 (*3-8055-5988-7*) S Karger.

New Aspects of Organic Chemistry. Ed. by T. Shiba et al. LC 89-22417. (Illus.). 565p. 1990. 135.00 (*3-527-28020-0*, Wiley-VCH) Wiley.

An Asterisk (*) at the beginning of an entry indicates that the title is appearing for the first time.

New Aspects of Pathophysiology & Treatment of Polycycstic Ovary Syndrome: Journal: Hormone Research, Vol. 33. Ed. by Y. Nakamura & Y. Taketani. (Illus.). vi, 50p. 1990. 24.50 (*3-8055-5262-9*) S Karger.

New Aspects of Physiology & Pathology of Luteal Phase: Journal: Hormone Research, Vol. 37, Suppl. 1, 1992. Ed. by H. Mori & A. Miyake. (Illus.). iv, 80p. 1992. pap. 36.75 (*3-8055-5625-X*) S Karger.

New Aspects of Politics. 3rd ed. Charles E. Merriam. LC 77-114809. 1994. lib. bdg. 20.00 (*0-226-52061-7*) U Ch Pr.

New Aspects of Politics. 3rd enl. ed. Charles E. Merriam. LC 77-114809. 1993. pap. text 2.95 (*0-226-52062-5*, P374) U Ch Pr.

New Aspects of Positive-Strand RNA Viruses. Ed. by Margo A. Brinton & Franz X. Heinz. (Illus.). 383p. 1990. 59.00 (*1-55581-022-5*) ASM Pr.

New Aspects of Prolactine in Human Reproductive Physiology: Journal: Hormone Research, Vol. 35, Suppl. 1, 1991. Ed. by T. Aso & S. Kawagoe. (Illus.). iv, 64p. 1991. pap. 29.75 (*3-8055-5470-2*) S Karger.

New Aspects of Renaissance Art. Ricardo Campa. 1998. pap. 24.00 (*1-883058-69-4*) Global Pubns.

New Aspects of Spillover Effect in Catalysis: For Development of Highly Active Catalysts. Ed. by Tomoyuki Inui et al. LC 93-23055. (Studies in Surface Science & Catalysis: Vol. 77). 454p. 1993. 266.75 (*0-444-89964-2*) Elsevier.

New Aspects of Style in the Maxims of La Rochefoucauld. M. Francine Zeller. LC 77-94186. (Catholic University of America. Studies in Romance Languages & Literatures: No. 48). reprint ed. 37.50 (*0-404-50348-9*) AMS Pr.

New Aspects of Thrombolytic Therapy for Acute Myocardial Infarction. Sorin V. Pislaru. (Acta Biomedica Lovaniensia Ser.). (Illus.). 126p. 1998. pap. 45.00 (*90-6186-888-2*, Pub. by Leuven Univ) Coronet Bks.

New Aspects of Time: Its Continuity & Novelties. Milic Capek. (Boston Studies in the Philosophy of Science). 400p. 1991. lib. bdg. 155.50 (*0-7923-0911-1*, Pub. by Kluwer Academic) Kluwer Academic.

New Aspects of Vitreoretinopathology. Ed. by C. Gailloud et al. (Modern Problems in Ophthalmology Ser.: Vol. 20). (Illus.). 1979. 226.25 (*3-8055-3038-2*) S Karger.

New Aspects on Hirudin: Journal: Haemostasis, Vol. 21, Suppl. 1, 1991. Ed. by J. Fareed et al. (Illus.). vi, 174p. 1991. pap. 55.00 (*3-8055-5389-7*) S Karger.

New Aspects on Respiratory Failure. Ed. by E. Rugheimer. (Illus.). xviii, 341p. 1991. 107.00 (*0-387-51445-7*) Spr-Verlag.

New Aspects on Tethyan Cretaceous Fossil Assemblages. Ed. by H. A. Kollmann & H. Zapfe. (Schriftenreihe der Erdwissenschaftlichen Kommissionen Ser.: Bd. 9). (Illus.). vi, 240p. 1992. 94.95 (*0-387-86555-1*) Spr-Verlag.

New Aspects on Thromboembolism. Ed. by U. Hedner. (Journal: Haemostasis: Vol. 23, Suppl. 1, 1993). (Illus.). iv, 228p. 1993. pap. 70.50 (*3-8055-5745-0*) S Karger.

New Astrology. Panisha. 1990. pap. 30.95 (*0-86690-346-1*, 2813-014) Am Fed Astrologers.

New Astrology: A Unique Synthesis of the World's Two Great Astrological Systems: The Chinese & Western. 7th ed. Suzanne White. 698p. 1988. pap. 15.95 (*0-312-01797-9*) St Martin.

New Astrology: The Art & Science of the Stars. Nicholas Campion & Steve Eddy. (Illus.). 288p. 1999. 35.00 (*1-57076-152-3*, Trafalgar Sq Pub) Trafalgar.

New Astronomer. Carole Stott. LC 98-45283. 144p. 1999. 24.95 (*0-7894-4175-6*) DK Pub Inc.

New Astronomy. (Voyage Through the Universe Ser.). 1992. lib. bdg. write for info. (*0-8094-9071-4*) Time-Life.

New Astronomy. (Voyage Through the Universe Ser.). (Illus.). 144p. (gr. 6). 1999. 18.95 (*0-8094-6883-2*) Time-Life.

New Astronomy. Time-Life Books Editors. (Voyage Through the Universe Ser.). (Illus.). 1992. write for info. (*0-8094-9070-6*) Time-Life.

New Astronomy. 2nd ed. Nigel Henbest & Michael Marten. (Illus.). 240p. (C). 1996. pap. 29.95 (*0-521-40871-7*); text 80.00 (*0-521-40324-3*) Cambridge U Pr.

New at the Zoo see Nueva en el Zoologica

New at the Zoo. Frank Edwards. (Illus.). 24p. (J). (gr. k-2). 1998. lib. bdg. 16.95 (*0-921285-70-1*, Pub. by Bungalo Books) Firefly Bks Ltd.

New at the Zoo. Frank B. Edwards. (Illus.). 24p. (J). (gr. k-2). 1998. pap. 5.95 (*0-921285-69-8*, Pub. by Bungalo Books) Firefly Bks Ltd.

New Atalantis. Delarivier Manley. Ed. by Rosalind Ballaster. (Women's Classics Ser.). 600p. (C). 1992. text 55.00 (*0-8147-5478-3*) NYU Pr.

New Atheism & the Erosion of Freedom: How to Recognize & Combat the Hidden Influence of Secular Humanism & Unbelief in Today's Society. Robert A. Morey. 176p. 1994. reprint ed. pap. 8.99 (*0-87552-362-5*) P & R Pubng.

New Athens. Hugh Hood. 226p. (Orig.). 1977. pap. 9.95 (*0-920802-03-6*, Pub. by ECW) Genl Dist Srvs.

New Athens. Hugh Hood. 226p. (Orig.). 1989. pap. 4.95 (*0-7736-7082-3*) Genl Dist Srvs.

New Atlantis see Famous Utopias of the Renaissance

New Atlantis. Francis Bacon. 51p. 1992. reprint ed. pap. 12.00 (*1-56459-230-8*) Kessinger Pub.

New Atlantis & the Great Instauration. rev. ed. Sir Francis Bacon. Ed. by Jerry Weinberger. (Crofts Classics). 128p. 1989. pap. text 4.95 (*0-88295-126-2*) Harlan Davidson.

New Atlantis Continued by R. H. Esquire. Frwd. by Manly P. Hall. 1985. 18.50 (*0-89314-419-3*) Philos Res.

New Atlantis Revisited: Akademgorodok, the Siberian City of Science. Paul R. Josephson. LC 96-45577. 351p. 1997. text 39.50 (*0-691-04454-6*, Pub. by Princeton U Pr) Cal Prin Full Svc.

New Atlas of Breeding Birds in Britain & Ireland, 1988-1991. David W. Gibbons et al. (Poyser Bird Bks.). (Illus.). 536p. 1994. text (*0-85661-075-5*) Poyser.

***New Atlas of Human Anatomy.** Thomas O. McCracken. (Illus.). 240p. 2000. 24.98 (*1-58663-097-0*) M Friedman Pub Grp Inc.

New Atmosphere. Mary A. Dodge. (Notable American Authors Ser.). 1992. reprint ed. lib. bdg. 75.00 (*0-7812-2657-0*) Rprt Serv.

New Attitude: Achieving Personal & Professional Success by Keeping a Positive Mental Outlook. Marian Thomas. LC 98-5751. 128p. 1998. pap. 10.99 (*1-56414-358-9*) Career Pr Inc.

New Audio Program 2 & Spcetrum 2. Byrd. 1994. 160.00 (*0-13-832882-X*) P-H.

New-Aus Biblischer Sicht see New Age from a Biblical Viewpoint

New Austerities. Tito Perdue. 224p. 1993. 20.00 (*1-56145-086-3*) Peachtree Pubs.

New Australia: Citizenship, Radicalism & the First Republic. Bruce Scates. LC 97-26349. (Studies in Australian History). 288p. 1997. pap. text 23.95 (*0-521-57596-6*) Cambridge U Pr.

New Australia: Citizenship, Radicalism & the First Republic. Bruce Scates. LC 97-26349. (Studies in Australian History). (Illus.). 271p. (C). 1997. text 64.95 (*0-521-57296-7*) Cambridge U Pr.

New Australian, a New Australia. Paul Kraus. LC 94-210815. 148p. 1994. pap. 21.00 (*1-86287-144-2*, Pub. by Federation Pr) Gaunt.

New Australian Cinema: Sources & Parallels in British & American Film. Brian McFarlane & Geoff Mayer. (Illus.). 273p. (C). 1992. text 59.95 (*0-521-38363-3*); pap. text 20.95 (*0-521-38768-X*) Cambridge U Pr.

New Australian Parakeet Handbook. Matthew M. Vriends. (New Pet Owner's Handbooks Ser.). (Illus.). 144p. 1992. pap. 9.95 (*0-8120-4739-7*) Barron.

***New Australian Style.** George Mitchell & John Gollings. LC 99-45698. (Illus.). 208p. 1999. 40.00 (*0-8118-2544-2*) Chronicle Bks.

New Austrian Architecture. Frank Dimster & James Steele. LC 95-3185. (Illus.). 224p. 1995. pap. 35.00 (*0-8478-1758-X*, Pub. by Rizzoli Intl) St Martin.

New Austrian Architecture. James Steele & Frank Dimster. LC 95-35427. (Illus.). 224p. 1995. 50.00 (*0-8478-1757-1*, Pub. by Rizzoli Intl) St Martin.

New Authoritarianism in Latin America. Ed. by David Collier et al. LC 79-83982. (Illus.). 467p. reprint ed. pap. 144.80 (*0-608-06356-8*, 206671700008) Bks Demand.

New Automation Technology for Acquisitions & Collection Development. Ed. by Rosann Bazirjian. LC 95-35322. 207p. 1995. 39.95 (*1-56024-732-0*, Z689) Haworth Pr.

New-Automobile Finance Rates, 1924-62. Robert P. Shay. (Occasional Papers: No. 86). 39p. 1963. reprint ed. 20.00 (*0-87014-400-6*) Natl Bur Econ Res.

***New Autonomous House: Design & Planning for Sustainability.** Brenda Vale & Robert Vale. LC 99-66918. (Illus.). 272p. 2000. 31.95 (*0-500-34176-1*, Pub. by Thames Hudson) Norton.

New Avatar & the Destiny of the Soul: The Findings of Natural Science Reduced to Practical Studies in Psychology. Jirah D. Buck. 236p. 1992. reprint ed. pap. 17.00 (*1-56459-196-4*) Kessinger Pub.

New Avengers: Feminism, Feminity & the Rape-revenge Cycle. Jacinda Read. pap. write for info. (*0-7190-5905-4*, Pub. by Manchester Univ Pr); text. write for info. (*0-7190-5904-6*, Pub. by Manchester Univ Pr) St Martin.

New Avenues & Perspectives in the Management of Advanced Prostate Cancer: Paris, September 1996. Ed. by Laurent Boccon-Gibod. (European Urology Ser.: Vol. 31, Suppl. 1997). (Illus.). iv, 40p. 1997. pap. 21.75 (*3-8055-6487-2*) S Karger.

New Aviation Identification Manual for Police Officers: An Aid for Investigating Aviation-Related Crime. rev. ed. Robert Collins & Alan H. Peterson. (Illus.). 100p. 1992. pap. text 75.00 (*1-877858-07-2*, NAIDINVMPO) Amer Focus Pub.

New Ayn Rand Companion. rev. expanded ed. Mimi Reisel Gladstein. LC 98-50226. (Illus.). 176p. 1999. lib. bdg. 45.00 (*0-313-30321-5*, GR0321, Greenwood Pr) Greenwood.

New Babel, a New Pentecost: Communicating the Gospel in a Mass Mediated Culture. Marie J. Hereford & Corrine Thomas. (Illus.). 120p. 1997. pap. 12.95 (*0-8198-5133-7*) Pauline Bks.

New Baby see Aruba Stories Series

New Baby. (Happy Endings Padded Storybooks Ser.). (Illus.). 32p. (J). (ps-1). 1998. pap. write for info. (*0-7666-0153-6*, Honey Bear Bks) Modern Pub NYC.

New Baby. (Little Lessons for Little Learners Ser.). (Illus.). (J). 4.95 (*0-614-22071-8*) Regina Pr.

New Baby. (Little Lessons for Little Learners Ser.). 1996. 4.95 (*0-88271-491-0*) Regina Pr.

New Baby. Baskerville. (J). pap. 4.95 (*0-7136-4111-8*, 93347, Pub. by A & C Blk) Talman.

New Baby. Illus. by Stephen Cartwright. (First Experiences Ser.). 16p. (J). (ps-3). 1994. pap. 4.50 (*0-7460-1271-3*) EDC.

New Baby. Teddy Jam. (Illus.). 32p. 1999. bds. 16.95 (*0-88899-327-7*, Pub. by Gro1undwood-Douglas) Publishers Group.

New Baby. Emily Arnold McCully. LC 87-45294. (Illus.). 32p. (J). (ps-1). 1988. 12.95 (*0-06-024130-6*) HarpC Child Bks.

New Baby. Fred Rogers. LC 84-26210. (Illus.). 32p. (J). (ps-3). 1996. pap. 5.99 (*0-698-11366-7*, PapStar) Peng Put Young Read.

New Baby. Debra M. Zakarin. LC 98-85746. (Look-Look Bks.). 24p. (J). (ps-3). 1998. pap. text 3.29 (*0-307-13154-8*, Goldn Books) Gldn Bks Pub Co.

New Baby. Mercer Mayer. (Look-Look Bks.). (Illus.). 24p. (J). (ps-3). 1985. reprint ed. pap. 3.29 (*0-307-11942-4*, 11942, Goldn Books) Gldn Bks Pub Co.

New Baby: A Coloring Book for Big Sisters & Brothers. Joy Johnson & Marvin Johnson. (Illus.). 24p. (Orig.). (J). (ps). 1981. pap. 1.25 (*1-56123-018-9*) Centering Corp.

New Baby - New Parent. Ed. by Florence Weiner. (Safety Center/Emergency Guide Ser.). (CHI & SPA., Illus.). 50p. (Orig.). 1997. pap. 19.95 (*1-888241-05-5*) Safety Ctr.

New Baby at Koko Bear's House. 2nd ed. Vicki Lansky. (Illus.). 32p. (Orig.). (J). 1991. reprint ed. pap. 5.95 (*0-916773-22-1*) Book Peddlers.

New Baby at Your House. Joanna Cole. LC 85-10653. (Illus.). 48p. (J). (ps-3). 1987. mass mkt. 5.95 (*0-688-07418-9*, Wm Morrow) Morrow Avon.

***New Baby at Your House.** Joanna Cole. LC 97-29267. (Illus.). 48p. (J). (ps-2). 1998. 15.95 (*0-688-13897-7*, Wm Morrow) Morrow Avon.

***New Baby at Your House.** rev. ed. Joanna Cole. LC 97-29267. (Illus.). 48p. (J). (ps-3). 1998. 15.93 (*0-688-13898-5*, Wm Morrow) Morrow Avon.

New Baby at Your House. rev. ed. Joanna Cole. 48p. (J). 1999. mass mkt. 5.95 (*0-688-16698-9*, Wm Morrow) Morrow Avon.

New Baby Book. Ed. by Alice Feinstein. (Illus.). 272p. 1998. 19.95 (*0-696-00069-5*, Better Homes) Meredith Bks.

New Baby Boom. Ed. by Peter Allen. 234p. 1988. 995.00 (*0-941285-21-9*) FIND-SVP.

New Baby Calf. Edith N. Chase. (Illus.). 32p. (J). (ps-3). 1991. pap. 4.99 (*0-590-44776-9*) Scholastic Inc.

New Baby for Us: Sibling Preparation & Activity Book for Big Brothers & Sisters. Lisa Kugler. (Illus.). 32p. (Orig.). (J). (ps-1). 1990. pap. 5.95 (*0-944782-03-5*) Glover Hlth Care.

***New Baby Giraffe.** Laura Gates-Galvin. (Let's Go to the Zoo! Ser.: Vol. 3). (Illus.). 16p. (J). 1999. bds. 5.95 (*1-56899-798-1*) Soundprints.

New Baby Giraffe: Includes Toy. Laura Gates-Galvin. (Let's Go to the Zoo! Ser.: Vol. 3). (Illus.). 16p. (J). 1999. bds. 9.95 (*1-56899-799-X*) Soundprints.

New Baby Knits: 30 Original Designs for 0-3 Year Olds. 2nd ed. Debbie Bliss. (Illus.). 104p. (Orig.). 1991. pap. 19.95 (*0-312-07397-6*) St Martin.

New Baby Therapy. Lisa Engelhardt. LC 97-77583. (Illus.). 88p. 1998. pap. 4.95 (*0-87029-307-9*, 20140) Abbey.

New Baby's Bible. Beverly Larson. (Illus.). 98p. (J). (ps). 1998. bds. 9.99 (*0-7847-0790-1*, 03850) Standard Pub.

New Baby's Bible. Reader's Digest Editors. (First Bible Collection). (Illus.). 8p. (J). (ps-3). 1998. text 10.99 (*1-57584-083-9*, Pub. by Rdrs Digest) Random.

New Baby's Nativity. Kristen Okosky. (First Bible Collection). (Illus.). 8p. (J). (gr. k-3). 1999. 10.99 (*1-57584-329-3*, Pub. by Rdrs Digest) Random.

***New Baby's Nativity.** Standard Publishing Staff. 1999. pap. text 10.99 (*0-7847-0909-2*) Standard Pub.

New Baby's Prayers. Illus. by Yvette Banek. (First Bible Collection). 6p. (J). (gr. k-3). 1999. text 10.99 (*1-57584-279-3*, Pub. by Rdrs Digest) Random.

New Baby's Prayers. Illus. by Yvette Banek. 8p. (J). (ps). 1999. 9.99 (*0-7847-0846-0*, 03499) Standard Pub.

New Bach Flower Body Maps: Treatment by Topical Application. Dietmar Kramer. LC 95-48845. (Illus.). 320p. 1995. pap. 19.95 (*0-89281-531-0*) Inner Tradit.

New Bach Flower Therapies: Healing the Emotional & Spiritual Causes of Illness. Dietmar Kramer. LC 94-49148. 168p. 1995. pap. 12.95 (*0-89281-529-9*, Heal Arts VT) Inner Tradit.

New Bach Reader. Hans T. David. 608p. 1999. pap. 18.95 (*0-393-31956-3*) Norton.

New Bach Reader: A Life of Johann Sebastian Bach in Letters & Documents. Hans David. LC 97-41850. 512p. 1998. 35.00 (*0-393-04558-7*) Norton.

New Back Doctor: The Program or Lifetime Relief from Back Pain. Hamilton Hall. (Illus.). 272p. 1995. pap. 7.99 (*0-7704-2619-0*) Bantam.

New Bacteriology. Sorin Sonea & Maurice Panisset. 140p. 1983. pap. 32.50 (*0-86720-025-1*) Jones & Bartlett.

New Baedeker. Harry T. Peck. (Notable American Authors Ser.). 1999. reprint ed. lib. bdg. 125.00 (*0-7812-8726-X*) Rprt Serv.

New Baja Handbook. enl. rev. ed. James T. Crow. LC 73-81325. (Illus.). 1974. pap. 3.95 (*0-393-60005-X*) Norton.

***New Baking Book.** Ed. by Better Homes & Gardens. LC 98-66245. (Illus.). 384p. 1998. ring bd. 25.95 (*0-696-20799-0*) Meredith Bks.

***New Baking Book.** Better Homes & Gardens. (Better Homes & Gardens Ser.). (Illus.). 416p. 1999. 34.95 (*0-696-20971-3*, Better Homes) Meredith Bks.

New Balanced Anesthesia: Proceedings of the First Congress of the Asian & Oceanic Society for Intravenous Anesthesia, Kyoto, 25-27 February, 1998. Kenjiro Mori & Asian & Oceanic Society for Intravenous Anesthesia Staff. LC 98-38399. (International Congress Ser.). 1998. 184.00 (*0-444-50009-X*) Elsevier.

***New Balanced Diet: Enhance Your Well-Being with Delicious, pH-Balanced Food.** Dagmar Von Cramm. Ed. by Jennifer Newens. (Powerfood Ser.). 64p. 2000. pap. 10.00 (*1-930603-05-3*) Silverback CA.

New Banker: Developing Leadership in a Dynamic Era. James H. Donnelly, Jr. et al. 200p. 1989. text 42.50 (*1-55623-177-6*, Irwn Prfssnl) McGraw-Hill Prof.

New Banking. Jerome R. Corsi. 1996. text 50.00 (*0-8133-0370-2*) Westview.

New Banking Landscape in Central & Eastern Europe: Country Experience & Policies for the Future. Ed. by Eva T. Blommestein. 380p. 1997. pap. 25.00 (*92-64-15683-6*, 14-97-10-1, Pub. by Org for Econ) OECD.

New Banner Book. Betty Wolfe. LC 98-23426. 128p. 1998. pap. 14.95 (*0-8192-1781-6*) Morehouse Pub.

New Bantam-Megiddo Hebrew Dictionary. Edward A. Levenston & Reuven Sivan. (HEB.). 736p. 1984. mass mkt. 6.99 (*0-553-26387-0*) Bantam.

New Baptist Church Manual. rev. ed. 1940. pap. 3.00 (*0-8170-0117-4*) Judson.

***New Barbarian Manifesto: How to Survive the Information Age.** Ian O. Angell. 2000. 24.95 (*0-7494-3151-2*) Kogan Page Ltd.

New Barbarians. Wilbur C. Abbott. LC 75-179499. (Select Bibliographies Reprint Ser.). 1977. reprint ed. 19.95 (*0-8369-6628-7*) Ayer.

New Baseball Catalog. Dan Schlossberg. LC 98-5121. 362p. 1998. 25.95 (*0-8246-0407-5*) Jonathan David.

New Basic Guide to Flying. Paul Fillingham. (Illus.). 1984. 24.95 (*0-13-611815-1*); pap. 9.95 (*0-13-611807-0*) P-H.

***New Basic Skills with Math.** 88p. 1998. write for info. (*0-8359-5728-4*) Globe Fearon.

New Basics Cookbook. Julee Rosso & Sheila Lukins. LC 88-51581. (Illus.). 864p. 1989. 29.95 (*0-89480-392-1*, 1392) Workman Pub.

New Basics Cookbook. Julee Rosso & Sheila Lukins. LC 88-51581. (Illus.). 849p. 1989. pap. 19.95 (*0-89480-341-7*, 1341) Workman Pub.

New Basics, Using Reading Selections to Develop Language Arts Skills. Tom Strelich. 1988. pap. 12.95 (*0-201-07339-0*) Addison-Wesley.

New Basis for Civilization. Simon N. Patten. Ed. by Daniel M. Fox. LC 68-25622. (John Harvard Library). 267p. 1968. 36.50 (*0-674-60901-8*) HUP.

New Basis for Moral Philosophy. Keekok Lee. (International Library of Philosophy). 288p. 1985. 42.50 (*0-7102-0445-0*, Routledge Thoemms) Routledge.

New Basket: A Vessel for the Future. Lucia LaVilla-Havelin. (Illus.). 36p. 1984. pap. 10.00 (*0-942746-06-6*) SUNYP R Gibson.

New Bassett Hound. Margaret S. Walton. LC 93-15114. (Illus.). 224p. 1993. 25.95 (*0-87605-022-4*) Howell Bks.

New Bath Guide: or The Memoirs of the B-R-D Family. Christopher Anstey. iv, 173p. 1989. reprint ed. 50.00 (*3-487-09132-1*) G Olms Pubs.

New Battle over Workplace Privacy: Safe Practices to Minimize Conflict, Confusion & Litigation. William S. Hubbartt. LC 97-38669. 224p. 1998. 27.95 (*0-8144-0357-3*) AMACOM.

New Battlefield: The United States & Unconventional Conflicts, 54. Sam C. Sarkesian. LC 86-3087. (Contributions in Military Studies Ser.: No. 54). (Illus.). 363p. 1986. 69.50 (*0-313-24890-7*, SNB/, Greenwood Pr) Greenwood.

New Battleground for Changing Corporate Control. 35.00 (*0-317-29528-4*, #CO2143) Harcourt.

New Battles over Dixie: The Campaign for a New South. John Slaughter. LC 91-75935. 154p. 1992. pap. text 16.95 (*0-930390-17-2*); lib. bdg. 35.95 (*0-930390-18-0*) Gen Hall.

New Bauhaus - School of Design in Chicago: Photographs, 1937-1944. Ed. by Adam J. Boxer. (Illus.). 56p. (Orig.). 1993. pap. 20.00 (*0-9638522-0-5*) Banning & Assoc.

New Beacon Book of Quotations by Women. Rosalie Maggio. 864p. 1996. 35.00 (*0-8070-6782-2*) Beacon Pr.

New Beacon Book of Quotations by Women. Ed. by Rosalie Maggio & Tisha Hooks. 864p. 1998. pap. 20.00 (*0-8070-6783-0*) Beacon Pr.

New Beadwork. Kathlyn Moss & Alice Scherer. (Illus.). 112p. 1992. 29.95 (*0-8109-3670-4*, Pub. by Abrams) Time Warner.

New Beagle. Judith M. Musladin & Ada Lueke. (Illus.). 288p. 1990. 25.95 (*0-87605-025-9*) Howell Bks.

New Beagle. 2nd ed. Judith Musladin. LC 97-39996. 288p. 1998. 27.95 (*0-87605-028-3*) Howell Bks.

New Bearings in English Poetry: A Study of the Contemporary Situation. Frank R. Leavis. LC 75-30032. reprint ed. 32.50 (*0-404-14035-1*) AMS Pr.

New Beat on an Old Drum. Kurtz Gordon. 1976. pap. 5.25 (*0-8222-0813-X*) Dramatists Play.

New Beatrice: or The Virtue That Counsels. Gratia E. Baldwin. LC 75-160011. reprint ed. 24.50 (*0-404-00469-5*) AMS Pr.

New Beats. Ed. by Jim Villani & Rose Sayre. (Pig Iron Ser.: No. 8). 96p. 1980. pap. 8.95 (*0-917530-16-0*) Pig Iron Pr.

New Beauty. Michelle D. Leigh. Ed. by Meagan Calogeras. (Illus.). 240p. 1995. pap. 18.00 (*4-7700-1869-X*) Kodansha.

New Beauty: 30-Days. Wagner. 1999. pap. 7.95 (*0-312-00056-1*) St Martin.

New Bedding Plant Expert. D. G. Hessayon. (Illus.). 144p. 1996. pap. 12.95 (*0-903505-45-2*, Pub. by Expert Bks) Sterling.

New Bedford. Anthony Mitchell Sammarco. (Images of America Ser.). 1997. pap. 16.99 (*0-7524-0831-3*) Arcadia Publng.

New Bedford, MA, Vol. I. Historical Briefs, Inc. Staff. Ed. by Thomas Antonucci & Michael Antonucci. 176p. 1989. pap. 19.95 (*0-89677-005-2*) Hist Briefs.

New Bedford, MA, Vol. II. Historical Briefs, Inc. Staff. Ed. by Thomas Antonucci & Michael Antonucci. 176p. 1989. pap. 19.95 (*0-89677-012-5*) Hist Briefs.

New Bedford, MA, Vol. III. Historical Briefs, Inc. Staff. Ed. by Thomas Antonucci & Michael Antonucci. 176p. 1989. pap. 19.95 (*0-89677-013-3*) Hist Briefs.

N

New Bedside, Bathtub & Armchair Companion to Agatha Christie. Ed. by Dick Riley & Pam McAllister. 362p. 1986. pap. text 15.95 (*0-8044-6725-0*) F Ungar Bks.

New Beethoven Letters. Ludwig van Beethoven. Tr. by Donald W. MacArdle. LC 57-7331. 628p. reprint ed. pap. 194.70 (*0-608-11008-6*, 201009700068) Bks Demand.

New Beginning. LC 96-45914. (Journals of Corrie & Christopher: No. 2). 24p. 1997. text 14.99 (*1-55661-945-6*) Bethany Hse.

New Beginning. Date not set. pap. text. write for info. (*0-917595-51-3*) Kingdom Pubs.

New Beginning. Veronica Brooks. 70p. 1999. pap. 10.00 (*0-7392-0160-3*, PO3110) Morris Pubng.

New Beginning. Maria De Strakosch. LC 93-71835. (Illus.). 496p. 1994. 29.95 (*0-930422-11-2*) Dennis-Landman.

New Beginning. Gretchen Foy. Ed. by Richard Foy & Gayle Walleen. LC 80-50611. (Illus.). 152p. 1980. pap. 4.95 (*0-89142-036-3*) Sant Bani Ash.

New Beginning. G. A. Members Staff. Ed. by G. A. Literature Committee Staff. 111p. (Orig.). 1989. 7.50 (*0-685-45265-4*); pap. 3.50 (*0-685-45266-2*) Gamblers Anon.

New Beginning. Michael Phillips. LC 96-45914. (Journals of Corrie & Christopher: No. 2). 24p. 1997. pap. 9.99 (*1-55661-933-2*) Bethany Hse.

New Beginning. Helen Steiner Rice. (Thumbprint Bks.). (Illus.). 92p. (gr. 10). 1999. 4.99 (*0-8007-7141-9*) Revell.

New Beginning. Maggie Rubio & Steffi Durnberg. 144p. (C). 1994. pap. text, per. 31.95 (*0-8403-9931-6*, 40993101) Kendall-Hunt.

New Beginning. Rose Toren. LC 96-71339. (Illus.). 1997. 16.95 (*0-88400-196-2*, Shengold Bks) Schreiber Pub.

***New Beginning.** Courtni Wright. (Arabesque Ser.). 2000. mass mkt. 5.99 (*1-58314-189-8*) BET Bks.

***New Beginning, Vol. I.** Ed. by Randi L. Jacobs. LC 00-132312. (So That You May Know... Bks.). 416p. 2000. pap. 19.95 (*0-9700252-3-8*) Fndt Transf.

New Beginning: A Book for Urostomy Patients. Kay Marshall. (Illus.). 1988. pap. text. write for info. (*0-916999-05-X*) HERC Inc.

New Beginning: A Collection of Essays. Dae-Jung Kim. Ed. by George O. Totten, III. Tr. by Young J. Lee & Yong M. Kim from KOR. LC 96-13862. Orig. Title: Saeroun Sijak Eul Wihayeo. (Illus.). xviii, 203p. (Orig.). (C). 1996. 25.00 (*1-884445-19-5*) C Schlacks Pub.

New Beginning: A Survival Guide for Parents of College Freshmen. Kaye B. McGarry. LC 97-91212. (Illus.). 40p. 1998. pap. 9.95 (*0-9661201-0-8*) Survival College.

New Beginning: A Textual Frame Analysis of the Political Campaign Film. Joanne Morreale. LC 90-9904. (SUNY Series in Speech Communication). 154p. (C). 1991. pap. text 18.95 (*0-7914-0609-1*) State U NY Pr.

New Beginning: An ESL Reader. Ann M. Niedermeir et al. (Illus.). 128p. (C). 1988. pap. text 20.80 (*0-13-611849-6*) P-H.

***New Beginning: Design & Adventure.** Golden Books Staff. (Disney Dinosaur Ser.). (Illus.). (J). 2000. pap. 4.99 (*0-307-10471-0*, Goldn Books) Gldn Bks Pub Co.

New Beginning: Foster Family Activity Book. Jim Boulden & Joan Boulden. Ed. by JoAnn Farness. (Illus.). 32p. (Orig.). (J). (gr. 3-4). 1996. pap. 5.95 (*1-878076-76-0*) Boulden Pub.

New Beginning: Handbook for Joyous Survival. Esther W. Hicks & Jerry S. Hicks. 214p. 1988. reprint ed. pap. 15.00 (*0-9621219-3-2*) Crown Intle.

New Beginning: Handbook for Joyous Survival - Abraham Speaks, Vol. V. Jerry S. Hicks & Esther W. Hicks. 165p. (Orig.). (C). 1988. pap. write for info. (*0-9621219-0-8*) Crown Intle.

New Beginning: Stories of Recovery from Relapse. Overeaters Anonymous, Inc. Staff. LC 97-76416. 129 p. 1998. pap. 8.35 (*1-889681-01-6*) Overeaters Anym.

***New Beginning: Tertullian, Cyril & Augustine on Baptism.** Monks of Ampleforth Abbey. 128p. 1999. pap. 6.95 (*0-85244-430-3*, 6117, Pub. by Gra1cewing) Morehouse Pub.

New Beginning: The Jews of Historic Lowell, Massachusetts. Shirley Kolack. LC 96-41811. XI, 101p. (Orig.). (C). 1997. pap. 19.95 (*0-8204-2263-0*) P Lang Pubng.

New Beginning: The World of Poetry. Bilingual Haitian Students of Solomon Lewenberg Mi. Ed. by Lunine P. Jerome. (CRP & ENG.). 181p. (J). (gr. 7-10). 1997. 10.00 (*1-885566-15-8*) Oresjozef.

New Beginning Vol. II: A Personal Handbook to Enhance Your Life, Liberty, & Pursuit of Happiness. Esther W. Hicks & Jerry S. Hicks. 258p. 1991. reprint ed. pap. 15.00 (*0-9621219-1-6*) Crown Intle.

***New Beginning Devotions Workbook.** Ed. by Hal M. Helms. 1999. pap. 19.95 (*1-55725-239-4*) Paraclete MA.

***New Beginning for Pastors & Congregations: Building on the Twelve Keys.** Kennon L. Callahan. LC 99-6345. 228p. 1999. 22.00 (*0-7879-4289-8*) Jossey-Bass.

New Beginning, 1968-1978. Mary Delahoyd. (Illus.). 128p. (Orig.). 1985. pap. 5.00 (*0-943651-19-0*) Hudson Riv.

New Beginnings. Diana Fox. LC 96-97008. 192p. 1996. 18.95 (*0-8034-9181-6*, Avalon Bks) Bouregy.

New Beginnings. Carolyn Keene. (Nancy Drew on Campus Ser.: No. 17). (YA). (gr. 8 up). 1997. per. 3.99 (*0-671-56806-X*) PB.

New Beginnings. Dorothy P. Koger. 100p. 1993. pap. 10.00 (*1-882821-09-2*) DPK Pubns.

New Beginnings. Paul S. McElroy. (Charming Petites Ser.). 80p. 1992. 4.95 (*0-88088-737-0*) Peter Pauper.

New Beginnings. Laura Peyton Roberts. (Clearwater Crossing Ser.). 224p. (YA). (gr. 5-8). 1999. mass mkt. 3.99 (*0-553-49256-X*) BDD Bks Young Read.

***New Beginnings.** Chaya B. Weinfeld. LC 99-33541. 288p. 1999. 13.95 (*1-880582-46-5*) Judaica Pr.

New Beginnings. Brian Wren. Ed. by Jack Schrader. LC 92-74749. 96p. (C). 1993. pap. text 7.95 (*0-916642-51-8*, 742) Hope Pub.

New Beginnings. large type ed. Ann Jennings. (Linford Romance Library). 272p. 1997. pap. 16.99 (*0-7089-5015-9*, Linford) Ulverscroft.

New Beginnings. large type ed. Maisie Mosco. (General Fiction Ser.). 400p. 1992. 27.99 (*0-7089-8657-9*) Ulverscroft.

New Beginnings. rev. ed. Beth A. Haseltine & Lynn Peterson. 1990. 39.95 (*0-914633-18-X*) Rape Abuse Crisis.

New Beginnings: A Creative Writing Guide for Women Who Have Left Abusive Partners. Sharon Doane. LC 96-13790. (New Leaf Ser.). 144p. (Orig.). 1996. pap. 10.95 (*1-878067-78-8*) Seal Pr WA.

New Beginnings: A Guide for Adult Learners & Returning Students. Linda Simon. LC 98-7191. 168p. 1998. pap. text 26.67 (*0-13-849605-6*) P-H.

New Beginnings: A Notebook of Infinite Possibilities. Ed. by Running Press Staff. (Illus.). 96p. (Orig.). 1991. pap. 5.95 (*1-56138-066-0*) Running Pr.

***New Beginnings: A Remarriage Preparation Program Manual: Facilitators Guide.** Ann D. Chidwick. 110p. 1999. ring bd. 50.00 (*0-9697856-0-7*) Manticore Bks.

New Beginnings: A Remarriage Preparation Program Workbook. Ann D. Chidwick. spiral bd., wbk. ed. 50.00 (*0-9697856-1-5*, Pub. by A D Chidwick) Manticore Pubs.

New Beginnings: A Report on the Fost-Opt Program of the San Francisco Department of Social Services. 48p. (Orig.). 1985. 5.00 (*0-936434-16-3*, Pub. by Zellerbach Fam Fund) Intl Spec Bk.

New Beginnings: Celebrating Birth. Anita Ganeri. LC 98-25582. (Life Times Ser.). (Illus.). 32p. (J). (gr. 1). 1999. lib. bdg. 15.95 (*0-87226-286-3*, 62863B, P Bedrick Books) NTC Contemp Pub Co.

New Beginnings: Divorce & Remarriage in the Christian Community. Janice Esh & Stephen Nauta. (Issues in Christian Living Ser.). 1995. pap. 7.75 (*1-56212-132-4*) CRC Pubns.

New Beginnings: Early Modern Philosophy & Postmodern Thought. John Deely. (Studies in Semiotics). 310p. 1994. text 50.00 (*0-8020-0624-8*); pap. text 19.95 (*0-8020-7583-5*) U of Toronto Pr.

New Beginnings: Healing Through Communication. Russ Bedord. LC 94-93982. 272p. (Orig.). 1995. pap. 24.95 (*0-9644918-6-9*) Regenics Pr.

***New Beginnings: More Reflections by Dolly.** Dolly Braida. Ed. by Christina Vaughan. LC 99-95397. (Illus.). 340p. 1999. pap. 18.95 (*0-9658113-4-4*) Jo-Eric.

New Beginnings: Skills for Single Parents & Stepfamily Parents (Parent's Manual) Don Dinkmeyer et al. LC 87-91035. (Illus.). 222p. 1987. pap. text 11.95 (*0-87822-286-3*, 2863) Res Press.

New Beginnings: The Pastorate Start up Workbook. rev. ed. Roy M. Oswald. 90p. 1989. pap. 13.25 (*1-56699-032-7*, AL111) Alban Inst.

New Beginnings: The Skirball Museum Collections & Inaugural Exhibition. Ed. by Grace C. Grossman. LC 96-67646. (Illus.). 208p. 1996. pap. text 24.95 (*0-9651640-1-2*, Pub. by U CA Pr) Cal Prin Full Svc.

New Beginnings: The Skirball Museum Collections & Inaugural Exhibition. Ed. by Grace Cohen Grossman. LC 96-67646. (Illus.). 208p. 1996. 50.00 (*0-9651640-0-4*, Pub. by U CA Pr) Cal Prin Full Svc.

New Beginnings: Your Guide to Retirement & Lifetime Action Planning. DBM Editors. 192p. 1995. pap. 11.95 (*1-880030-41-1*) DBM Pub.

New Beginnings - A Divorce Recovery Handbook see Healing a Broken Heart: A Recovery Handbook for Relationship Loss

New Beginnings in Reading. Bonnie Tivenan. 90p. 1985. pap., teacher ed. 7.20 (*0-8092-5166-3*) NTC Contemp Pub Co.

New Beginnings in Reading, 8 bks, Bk. 1. rev. ed. Bonnie Tivenan. 90p. 1985. pap. 9.60 (*0-8092-5176-0*) NTC Contemp Pub Co.

New Beginnings in Reading, 8 Bks., Bk. 2. rev. ed. Bonnie Tivenan. 90p. 1985. pap. 9.60 (*0-8092-5175-2*) NTC Contemp Pub Co.

New Beginnings in Reading, 8 Bks., Bk. 3. rev. ed. Bonnie Tivenan. 90p. 1985. pap. 9.60 (*0-8092-5174-4*) NTC Contemp Pub Co.

New Beginnings in Reading, 8 Bks., Bk. 4. rev. ed. Bonnie Tivenan. 90p. 1985. pap. 9.60 (*0-8092-5173-6*) NTC Contemp Pub Co.

New Beginnings in Reading, 8 Bks., Bk. 5. rev. ed. Bonnie Tivenan. 90p. 1985. pap. 9.60 (*0-8092-5172-8*) NTC Contemp Pub Co.

New Beginnings in Reading, 8 Bks., Bk. 6. rev. ed. Bonnie Tivenan. 90p. 1985. pap. 9.60 (*0-8092-5170-1*) NTC Contemp Pub Co.

New Beginnings in Reading, 8 Bks., Bk. 7. rev. ed. Bonnie Tivenan. 90p. 1985. pap. 9.60 (*0-8092-5169-8*) NTC Contemp Pub Co.

New Beginnings in Reading, 8 Bks., Bk. 8. rev. ed. Bonnie Tivenan. 90p. 1985. pap. 9.60 (*0-8092-5167-1*) NTC Contemp Pub Co.

New Beginnings in Reading: Groundbreaker Exercises. Bonnie Tivenan. 90p. 1985. pap. 9.60 (*0-8092-5177-9*) NTC Contemp Pub Co.

New Beginnings V2, 2. Marsh. 1982. pap. text 15.95 (*0-7710-5457-2*) McCland & Stewart.

New Belief You Are Seeking. Will Sherburne. LC 98-92932. 420p. 1998. 19.95 (*0-917878-11-6*) Inst Impr Anlt Crtv Abl.

New Believers Station. Touch Publications Staff. 1996. pap. 4.95 (*1-880828-91-X*) Touch Pubns.

New Bells for New Steeples: Communications Strategies. Jay Cormier. LC 90-62651. 160p. (Orig.). (C). 1990. pap. 9.95 (*1-55612-369-8*) Sheed & Ward WI.

New Berceo Manuscript. Ed. by Dutton. (Exeter Hispanic Text Ser.: No. 32). 122p. Date not set. pap. text 17.95 (*0-85989-104-6*, Pub. by Univ Exeter Pr) Northwestern U Pr.

New Bergson. John Mullarkey. 208p. 1999. pap. 29.95 (*0-7190-5553-9*); text 69.95 (*0-7190-5380-3*) Manchester Univ Pr.

New Bernese Mountain Dog. Sharon C. Smith. LC 94-16804. (Illus.). 256p. 1995. 27.95 (*0-87605-075-5*) Howell Bks.

New Best of Big Note (Bradley) 96p. (Orig.). 1994. pap. 12.95 (*0-7692-1128-3*, BP3305B) Wrner Bros.

New Best of Billy Joel. 56p. 1995. pap. 9.95 (*0-7935-3615-4*, 00702087) H Leonard.

New Best of Bob Seger & the Silver Bullet Band. 64p. (Orig.). 1994. pap. 12.95 (*0-89724-355-2*, VF1890) Wrner Bros.

New Best of Bruce Springsteen for Guitar. Ed. by Aaron Stang. (New Best of Ser.). 64p. (Orig.). (YA). 1996. pap. text 12.95 (*1-57623-518-1*, PG9622) Wrner Bros.

New Best of Cole Porter. Ed. by Carol Cuellar. 68p. (Orig.). (C). 1995. pap. text 12.95 (*0-7692-0916-5*, VF1885) Wrner Bros.

New Best of Collective Soul for Guitar. Ed. by Colgan Bryan. 64p. (Orig.). 1996. pap. text 12.95 (*1-57623-551-3*, PG9640) Wrner Bros.

New Best of Creedence Clearwater Revival for Guitar. Ed. by Aaron Stang. 52p. (Orig.). (YA). 1995. pap. text 12.95 (*0-89724-707-8*, PG9522) Wrner Bros.

***New Best of Crosby, Stills, Nash & Young for Guitar.** Warner Brothers Publications Staff. 1999. pap. text 12.95 (*0-89724-839-2*) Warner Bks.

New Best of David Gates. Ed. by Carol Cuellar. 44p. (Orig.). 1994. pap. 12.95 (*0-89724-210-6*, VF1754) Wrner Bros.

New Best of David Lee Roth. Ed. by Carol Cuellar. 64p. (Orig.). (C). 1994. pap. text 12.95 (*0-89724-339-0*, VF2149) Wrner Bros.

New Best of Eagles. Ed. by Sy Feldman. 64p. (Orig.). 1994. pap. 12.95 (*0-89724-165-7*, PG9518) Wrner Bros.

New Best of Eagles for Guitar. Ed. by Aaron Stang. 56p. (YA). 1995. pap. text 12.95 (*0-89724-705-1*, PG9518) Wrner Bros.

New Best of Elton John for Guitar. 56p. 1995. pap. 9.95 (*0-7935-3614-6*, 00702088) H Leonard.

New Best of George Gershwin. Ed. by Carol Cuellar. 68p. (Orig.). (C). 1992. pap. text 12.95 (*0-89724-335-8*, VF1839) Wrner Bros.

New Best of Gin Blossoms. Ed. by Colgan Bryan. 64p. (Orig.). (YA). 1996. pap. text 12.95 (*1-57623-526-2*, PG9639) Wrner Bros.

New Best of Gordon Lightfoot. Ed. by Carol Cuellar. 48p. (Orig.). 1994. pap. 12.95 (*0-89724-430-3*, VF2166) Wrner Bros.

New Best of Jackson Browne. Ed. by Carol Cuellar. 68p. (Orig.). (C). 1994. pap. text 12.95 (*0-89724-293-9*, VF2136) Wrner Bros.

New Best of James Taylor. Ed. by Carol Cuellar. 68p. (Orig.). (C). 1991. pap. text 12.95 (*0-7692-0856-8*, VF1716) Wrner Bros.

New Best of James Taylor for Guitar. Ed. by Colgan Bryan. (New Best of...Ser.). 64p. (Orig.). 1997. pap. text 12.95 (*0-7692-0007-9*) Wrner Bros.

New Best of Jim Croce. Ed. by Carol Cuellar. 68p. (Orig.). (C). 1996. pap. text 12.95 (*0-7692-0279-9*, VF1913) Wrner Bros.

New Best of Joni Mitchell. Ed. by Carol Cuellar. 52p. (Orig.). (C). 1993. pap. text 12.95 (*0-7692-0717-0*, VF1951) Wrner Bros.

New Best of Journey. Ed. by Carol Cuellar. 76p. (Orig.). (C). 1993. pap. text 12.95 (*0-7692-0709-X*, VF1968) Wrner Bros.

New Best of Led Zeppelin. Ed. by Carol Cuellar. 58p. (Orig.). (C). 1982. pap. text 12.95 (*0-7692-0704-9*, VF1798) Wrner Bros.

New Best of Loggins & Messina. Ed. by Sy Feldman. 68p. (Orig.). (C). 1992. pap. text 12.95 (*0-7692-0700-6*, VF1879) Wrner Bros.

New Best of Lynyrd Skynyrd. 112p. 1995. otabind 19.95 (*0-7935-3533-6*, 00694954) H Leonard.

New Best of Melissa Etheridge: Guitar Personality Book. 60p. (Orig.). 1997. pap. 12.95 (*1-57623-908-X*, PG9669) Wrner Bros.

New Best of Michael Franks. Ed. by Carol Cuellar. 76p. (Orig.). (C). 1992. pap. text 12.95 (*0-7692-0459-7*, VF1871) Wrner Bros.

New Best of Moody Blues. Ed. by Carol Cuellar. 52p. (Orig.). (C). 1989. pap. text 12.95 (*0-7692-0719-7*, VF1973) Wrner Bros.

New Best of Neil Young. Ed. by Carol Cuellar. 52p. (Orig.). (C). 1992. pap. text 12.95 (*0-7692-0860-6*, VF1877) Wrner Bros.

New Best of Neil Young for Guitar. Ed. by Colgan Bryan. (Best of...Ser.). 40p. (Orig.). 1996. pap. 12.95 (*1-57623-447-9*, PG9620) Wrner Bros.

New Best of Parteet for Guitars: Guitar Personality Book. Ed. by Colgan Bryan. (New Best of Ser.). 84p. (Orig.). 1997. pap. 12.95 (*1-57623-960-8*, 0052B) Wrner Bros.

New Best of Peter, Paul & Mary. Ed. by Carol Cuellar. 60p. (Orig.). (C). 1991. pap. text 12.95 (*0-7692-0503-8*, VF1778) Wrner Bros.

New Best of Phil Collins. Ed. by Carol Cuellar. 92p. (Orig.). (C). 1994. pap. text 12.95 (*0-89724-302-1*, VF2138) Wrner Bros.

New Best of Roy Orbison. Ed. by Carol Cuellar. 36p. (Orig.). (C). 1993. pap. text 12.95 (*0-7692-0495-3*, VF1944) Wrner Bros.

New Best of Sheryl Crow. Ed. by Bryan Colgan. (Orig.). Date not set. pap. 12.95 (*0-7692-0072-9*, 0067B) Wrner Bros.

New Best of Smashing Pumpkins. Ed. by Colgan Bryan & Aaron Stan. LC 97-3. (New Best of Ser.). 72p. (Orig.). 1997. pap. text 12.95 (*1-57623-756-7*, PG9703) Wrner Bros.

New Best of Stevie Wonder. Ed. by Jeannette DeLisa. 96p. (Orig.). (YA). 1996. pap. text 12.95 (*1-57623-614-5*, PF9646) Wrner Bros.

New Best of the Beach Boys for Guitar. Ed. by Aaron Stang. 68p. (Orig.). (YA). 1995. pap. text 12.95 (*0-7692-0051-6*, PG9528) Wrner Bros.

New Best of the Doobie Brothers. Ed. by Carol Cuellar. (New Best of Ser.). 52p. (Orig.). (C). 1993. pap. text 12.95 (*0-89724-241-6*, PG9663) Wrner Bros.

New Best of Tom Petty for Guitar. Ed. by Aaron Stang. (New Best of Ser.). 48p. (Orig.). (YA). 1996. pap. text 12.95 (*1-57623-428-2*, PG9612) Wrner Bros.

New Best of Toto. Ed. by Carol Cuellar. 52p. (Orig.). (C). 1985. pap. text 12.95 (*0-7692-0848-7*, VF1760) Wrner Bros.

New Best of Van Halen. Ed. by Aaron Stang. 68p. (Orig.). (C). 1995. pap. text 12.95 (*0-89724-710-8*, PG9533) Wrner Bros.

New Best of Van Morrison. Ed. by Carol Cuellar. 60p. (Orig.). (C). 1984. pap. text 12.95 (*0-7692-0770-7*, VF1780) Wrner Bros.

New Best of Vince Gill. Ed. by Aaron Stang. (New Best of Ser.). 56p. (Orig.). 1997. pap. text 12.95 (*1-57623-963-2*, PG9709) Wrner Bros.

New Best of Willie Nelson. 96p. (Orig.). 1993. pap. 12.95 (*0-89724-028-6*, VF1997) Wrner Bros.

***New Best of Willie Nelson.** Warner Brothers Publications Staff. 1999. pap. text 12.95 (*0-7692-7061-1*) Wrner Bros.

New Best of Yes. Ed. by Carol Cuellar. 68p. (Orig.). (C). 1993. pap. text 12.95 (*0-7692-0839-8*, VF1950) Wrner Bros.

New Best of ZZ Top for Guitar. Ed. by Aaron Stang. 60p. (Orig.). (C). 1996. pap. text 12.95 (*1-57623-698-6*, PG9634) Wrner Bros.

New Better Behavior in Dogs: A Guide to Solving All Your Dog's Problems. William E. Campbell. LC 99-10974. (Illus.). 302p. 1999. pap. 16.95 (*1-57779-018-9*) Alpine Pubns.

New Beverly Hills Diet: Born Again Skinny. Judy Mazel. 320p. (Orig.). 1996. 24.00 (*1-55874-431-2*, 4258) Health Comm.

New Beverly Hills Diet: Born Again Skinny. rev. ed. Judy Mazel. 250p. (Orig.). 1996. pap. 12.95 (*1-55874-425-8*, 4258) Health Comm.

New Beverly Hills Diet: Little Skinny Companion. Judy Mazel. LC 97-3330. 64p. 1997. pap. 4.95 (*1-55874-476-2*) Health Comm.

New Beverly Hills Diet: Recipes to Forever. Judy Mazel. LC 97-3323. 200p. 1997. pap. 9.95 (*1-55874-475-4*) Health Comm.

New Beverly Hills Diet Slim Kit, Set. unabridged ed. Judy Mazel. 40p. 1998. 24.95 incl. audio (*1-55874-650-1*) Health Comm.

New Beyond: Psychics - A Global Issue. Norman W. Mathers. 116p. Date not set. pap. 16.95 (*0-9634654-1-4*) ATS Pubns.

New Beyond Peek-a-Boo & Pat-a-Cake: Activities for Baby's First 24 Months. 3rd ed. Evelyn M. Munger & Susan J. Bowdon. LC 93-1421. 256p. 1993. spiral bd. 15.95 (*0-8329-0504-6*) New Win Pub.

New Bible Atlas see Nuevo Atlas Biblico

New Bible Atlas. Ed. by Donald J. Wiseman et al. (Illus.). 132p. 1994. 21.99 (*0-8308-1443-4*, 1443) InterVarsity.

New Bible Commentary see Nuevo Comentario Biblico

New Bible Commentary. 4th enl. rev. ed. J. Alec Motyer & Gordon J. Wenham. LC 94-4076. (Illus.). 1340p. 1994. 39.99 (*0-8308-1442-6*, 1442) InterVarsity.

New Bible Commentary XXI Century see Nuevo Comentario Biblico Siglo XXI

New Bible Companion. Robert B. Hughes & J. Carl Laney. 896p. 1990. 19.99 (*0-8423-4733-X*) Tyndale Hse.

New Bible Dictionary see Nuevo Diccionario Biblico

New Bible Dictionary. 3rd ed. Ed. by Donald J. Wiseman et al. 1298p. 1996. 39.99 (*0-8308-1439-6*, 1439) InterVarsity.

New Bibliography of the Lusophone Literatures of Africa. 2nd rev. ed. Gerald Moser. LC 93-19931. (Bibliographical Research in African Literatures Ser.: No. 2). 432p. 1993. 90.00 (*1-873836-85-6*, Pub. by H Zell Pubs) Seven Hills Bk.

New Bibliography of Writings on Varieties of English, 1984-1992-3. Beat Glauser et al. Ed. by Manfred Gorlach. LC 93-41367. (Varieties of English Around the World (VEAW) Text Ser.: No. G12). 208p. 1993. pap. 47.00 (*1-55619-443-9*) J Benjamins Pubng Co.

New Big Book of Games. B & P Publishing Co. Staff. 1992. 13.00 (*0-394-23520-7*) Random.

***New Big Book of Logos.** David E. Carter. (Illus.). 384p. 2000. 45.00 (*0-688-17890-1*, Hearst) Hearst Commns.

***New Big Book of U. S. Presidents: Fascinating Facts about Each & Every President.** Todd Davis. (Illus.). (J). 2001. 9.98 (*0-7624-0849-9*) Running Pr.

New Big House. Debi Gliori. LC 91-71829. (Illus.). 32p. (J). (ps up). 1992. 13.95 (*1-56402-036-3*) Candlewick Pr.

New Big House. Debi Gliori. LC 91-71829. (Illus.). 32p. (J). (ps up). 1994. pap. 4.99 (*1-56402-371-0*) Candlewick Pr.

New Bike. Marie Vinje. Ed. by Joan Hoffman. (Start to Read! Ser.). (Illus.). 16p. (J). (gr. k-2). 1992. pap. 2.29 (*0-88743-265-4*, 06032) Sch Zone Pub Co.

New Bike. Marie Vinje. Ed. by Joan Hoffman. (Start to Read! Ser.). (Illus.). 32p. (J). (gr. k-2). 1993. pap. 3.99 (*0-88743-426-6*, 06078) Sch Zone Pub Co.

New Bilingualism: An American Dilemma. Martin Ridge. 272p. 1982. 39.95 (*0-88474-104-4*) Transaction Pubs.

An Asterisk (*) at the beginning of an entry indicates that the title is appearing for the first time.

*__New Biography: Performing Femininity in Nineteenth-century France.__ Jo Burr Margadant. LC 99-48288. Vol. 38. (Illus.). 315p. 2001. 48.00 (*0-520-22140-0*, Pub. by U CA Pr); pap. 17.95 (*0-520-22141-9*, Pub. by U CA Pr) Cal Prin Full Svc.

*__New Biological Weapons: Threat, Proliferation & Control.__ Malcolm Dando. 180p. 2000. 49.95 (*1-55587-924-1*) L Rienner.

New Biology. Adrien Hofstetter. (Teilhard Studies: No. 26). 1992. pap. 3.50 (*0-89012-066-8*) Am Teilhard.

New Biology: Discovering the Wisdom in Nature. Robert M. Augros & George N. Stanciu. LC 86-28058. (Illus.). 274p. 1995. reprint ed. 29.95 (*1-889792-00-4*) Principle Source.

New Biology: Law, Ethics, & Biotechnology. G. P. Smith, II. (Illus.). 324p. (C). 1990. 59.50 (*0-306-43187-4*, Plenum Trade) Perseus Pubng.

New Biology & Inherited Diseases. Bakhtaver S Mahjan. (Illus.). 148p. 1999. pap. text 22.95 (*0-19-564769-6*) OUP.

New Biology & Medical Education: Merging the Biological Information & Cognitive Sciences: Report of a Conference. Ed. by Charles P. Friedman & Elizabeth F. Purcell. LC 83-80799. 341p. reprint ed. pap. 105.80 (*0-608-16362-7*, 202669400051) Bks Demand.

New Biomedical Materials. Ed. by D. Chapman & P. I. Haris. LC 97-76731. 209p. 1998. 86.00 (*90-5199-365-X*, 365-X) IOS Press.

New Biopesticide Market. (Report Ser.: No. C-204). 257p. 1996. 2750.00 (*1-56965-358-5*) BCC.

New Biotechnology in Oral Research. Ed. by H. M. Myers. (Illus.). x, 170p. 1989. 128.00 (*3-8055-4916-4*) S Karger.

New Bird Handbook. Matthew M. Vriends. (Illus.). 1989. pap. 9.95 (*0-8120-4157-7*) Barron.

New Birth see Nuevo Nacimiento

New Birth. David K. Bernard. LC 85-106418. 346p. (Orig.). 1984. pap. 9.99 (*0-912315-77-6*) Word Aflame.

New Birth. Kenneth E. Hagin. 1975. pap. 1.00 (*0-89276-050-8*) Faith Lib Pubns.

New Birth. Andy McGowan. 1996. 4.99 (*1-85792-241-7*, Pub. by Christian Focus) Spring Arbor Dist.

New Birth: A Naturalist View of Religious Conversion. Joe E. Barnhart & Mary A. Barnhart. LC 81-9557. xiv, 174p. (C). 1981. 15.50 (*0-86554-009-8*, MUP-H011) Mercer Univ Pr.

New Birth: The Complete Works of Stephen Charnock, B.D., Vol. 3. Stephen Charnock. 534p. 1986. reprint ed. 32.99 (*0-85151-500-2*) Banner of Truth.

*__New Birth & Study Guide for the New Birth.__ David K. Bernard. 506p. 1999. 19.99 (*1-56722-238-2*) Word Aflame.

New Birth of Freedom. Charles L. Black, Jr. LC 98-88790. 175p. 1998. pap. 14.00 (*0-300-07734-3*) Yale U Pr.

New Birth of Freedom: A Theology of Bondage & Liberation. Peter C. Hodgson. LC 75-37145. 384p. reprint ed. pap. 119.10 (*0-608-16287-6*, 202686900053) Bks Demand.

*__New Birth of Freedom: Abraham Lincoln & the Coming of the Civil War.__ Harry V. Jaffa. 750p. 2000. 35.00 (*0-8476-9952-8*) Rowman.

New Birth of Freedom: Human Rights, Named & Unnamed. Charles L. Black, Jr. LC 96-52967. 192p. 1997. 22.95 (*0-399-14230-4*, Grosset-Putnam) Putnam Pub Group.

*__New Birth of Freedom: The Republican Party & Freedom Rights, 1861 to 1866.__ Herman Belz. LC 99-88242. (Reconstructing America Ser.: No. 5). 204p. 2000. reprint ed. pap. 19.95 (*0-8232-2011-7*, Pub. by Fordham) BookMasters.

*__New Birth of Freedom: The Republican Party & Freedom Rights, 1861 to 1866.__ Herman Belz. LC 99-88242. (Reconstructing America Ser.: No. 5). 204p. 2000. reprint ed. 35.00 (*0-8232-2010-9*, Pub. by Fordham) BookMasters.

New Birth Order Book: Why You Are the Way You Are. 2nd rev. ed. Kevin Leman. LC 98-28465. 368p. 1998. pap. 11.99 (*0-8007-5679-7*) Revell.

New Black Middle Class. Bart Landry. 1987. pap. 15.95 (*0-520-06465-8*, Pub. by U CA Pr) Cal Prin Full Svc.

New Black Playwrights: An Anthology. Ed. by William Couch, Jr. LC 68-31137. 282p. reprint ed. pap. 87.50 (*0-608-14359-6*, 201957400013) Bks Demand.

New Blackwell Guide to Recorded Blues. John Cowley & Paul Oliver. (Illus.). 448p. 1996. 55.95 (*0-631-20163-7*); pap. 22.95 (*0-631-19639-0*) Blackwell Pubs.

New Blender Book. Barbara Karoff. (Illus.). 176p. (Orig.). 1993. pap. 8.95 (*1-55867-088-2*, Nitty Gritty Ckbks) Bristol Pub Ent CA.

*__New Blood.__ Ed. by Neil Astley. 240p. 2000. pap. 22.95 (*1-85224-472-0*, Pub. by Bloodaxe Bks) Dufour.

New Blood, 1. Paul Guran. 1999. mass mkt. 7.95 (*1-58419-008-6*) Masq Bks.

*__New Blood From Old Bones.__ large type ed. Sheila Radley. 352p. 2000. 31.99 (*0-7089-4199-0*) Ulverscroft.

New Bloomsday Book: A Guide Through Joyce's Ulysses: The New Text. 2nd rev. ed. Harry Blamires. 288p. 1988. pap. text 14.95 (*0-415-00704-6*) Routledge.

New Bloomsday Book: A Guide Through Ulysses. 3rd ed. Harry Blamires. LC 95-44440. 272p. 1996. pap. 20.99 (*0-415-13858-2*) Routledge.

New Bloomsday Book: A Guide Through Ulysses. 3rd ed. Harry Blamires. LC 95-44440. 272p. (C). 1996. 85.00 (*0-415-13857-4*) Routledge.

New Blue Line: Police Innovation in Six American Cities. Jerome H. Skolnick & David H. Bayley. 246p. 1988. pap. 14.95 (*0-02-929311-1*) Free Pr.

New Blueprint for Marriage. Merrily Neill & Joanne Tangedahl. 256p. 1981. pap. 6.50 (*0-942494-65-2*) Coleman Pub.

New Blueprint Intermediate Student Book. Longman, Inc. Staff. 1995. pap. write for info. (*0-582-25830-8*) Addison-Wesley.

New Blueprints for Gains in Stocks & Grains & One Way Formula for Trading in Stocks & Commodities. William Dunnigan. Ed. by Donald Mack. (Traders Masterclass Ser.). 304p. 1997. 55.00 (*0-273-63096-2*) F T P-H.

*__New Board: Changing Issues, Roles & Relationships.__ Ed. by Nadia Ehrlich Finkelstein & Raymond Schimmer. LC 99-49963. (Residential Treatment for Children & Youth Ser.: Vol. 16, No. 4). 106p. 1999. 39.95 (*0-7890-0834-3*) Haworth Pr.

*__New Boatkeeper: Motorboating & Sailing's Authoritative Guide to Maintenance, Repair & Improvement.__ Motorboating & Sailing Editors. Ed. & Intro. by Bernard Gladstone. LC 99-20867. (Illus.). 305p. 1999. pap. 14.00 (*0-380-79934-0*, Avon Bks) Morrow Avon.

New Bobbin Lace Patterns. Tiny Zwaal-Lint. 1985. 22.50 (*0-7134-4866-0*) Robin & Russ.

New Bobbsey Twins Series Boxed Set, 4 vols. Laura Lee Hope. (New Bobbsey Twins Ser.). (J). (gr. 3-5). 1988. boxed set 11.80 (*0-671-91946-6*) PB.

*__New Body.__ Robert A. Ersek et al. (Illus.). 108p. 2000. pap. 14.95 (*0-9668360-3-0*, 36030) Med Web Wrld.

New Body: Awakening Your Motivational Power to Shape a Perfect Body. Forrest R. Tower. 96p. (Orig.). 1991. pap. 10.00 (*0-9627597-0-8*) F Tower Enter.

New Body in One Day: A Guide to Same-Day Cosmetic Surgery Procedures. Robert Yoho. 1998. pap. 12.95 (*0-9659541-0-2*) R A Yoho.

New Body This Year. Diane Le Clair Sutton. Ed. by Abbey M. Begun. LC 95-80589. (Illus.). 360p. 1996. 17.95 (*0-9649116-0-4*) Bks Benefit.

New Bodytalk: Self-Help for All Your Health Problems. Michael van Straten. (Illus.). 302p. 1994. pap. 13.95 (*0-7472-4156-2*, Pub. by Headline Bk Pub) Trafalgar.

*__New Bones: Contemporary Black Writers in America.__ Kevin Quashie et al. LC 00-22516. 1088p. 2000. pap. 44.00 (*0-13-014127-5*) P-H.

New Book Lover's Guide to Chicagoland: Including Southern Wisconsin. expanded ed. Lane Phalen. LC 95-79486. (Book Lover's Guide Ser.). 320p. 1995. reprint ed. pap. 14.95 (*1-880339-11-0*) Brigadoon Bay.

New Book of American Rankings. rev. ed. Ed. by Ellen Meltzer. 272p. 1997. 50.00 (*0-8160-2878-8*) Facts on File.

*__New Book of Baby & Child Massage.__ Robert Toporek. (Illus.). 2001. pap. 12.95 (*0-7624-0291-1*) Running Pr.

New Book of Boxes: A Stunning Collection of Elegant Gift Boxes. Kunio Ekiguchi. LC 93-34769. (Illus.). 32p. 1994. pap. 19.00 (*4-7700-1773-1*) Kodansha.

New Book of Chinese Lattice Designs. Daniel S. Dye. (Pictorial Archive Ser.). (Illus.). 128p. (Orig.). 1981. pap. 7.95 (*0-486-24128-9*) Dover.

New Book of Dialogues. S. A. Frost. LC 72-8300. (Granger Index Reprint Ser.). 1977. reprint ed. 20.95 (*0-8369-6387-3*) Ayer.

New Book of Dinosaurs. David Unwin. LC 96-38758. (Illus.). 32p. (J). (gr. 4-6). 1997. pap. 9.95 (*0-7613-0589-0*, Copper Beech Bks); lib. bdg. 23.90 (*0-7613-0568-8*, Copper Beech Bks) Millbrook Pr.

*__New Book of El Nino.__ Simon Beecroft. LC 98-55560. 1999. pap. 9.95 (*0-7613-0797-4*) Millbrook Pr.

New Book of El Nino. Simon Beecroft. LC 98-55560. (Illus.). 31p. (J). (gr. 4-6). 1999. lib. bdg. 24.90 (*0-7613-0920-9*) Millbrook Pr.

New Book of Food Combining: A Completely New Approach to Healthy Eating. Jan Dries. 1995. pap. 9.95 (*1-85230-578-9*, Pub. by Element MA) Penguin Putnam.

New Book of Goddesses & Heroines. Patricia Monaghan. LC 97-17471. (Illus.). 384p. 1999. pap. 19.95 (*1-56718-465-0*) Llewellyn Pubns.

New Book of Golden Wedding Songs. Ed. by Carol Cuellar. 152p. (YA). 1994. pap. 14.95 (*0-89898-843-8*) Wrner Bros.

New Book of Health. Frank Osborne & Judy Goldstein. 402p. (Orig.). 1996. pap. 19.95 (*0-9638596-7-6*) Amer Pubng.

*__New Book of Knowledge.__ Grolier, Inc. Staff. LC 00-34718. (Illus.). (J). 2001. write for info. (*0-7172-0532-0*) Grolier Educ.

New Book of Knowledge. Grolier Incorporated Staff. LC 98-29780. (J). 1999. lib. bdg. 659.00 (*0-7172-0530-4*) Grolier Educ.

*__New Book of Knowledge, 21 vols.__ Grolier Incorporated Staff. LC 99-16724. 2000. lib. bdg. 699.00 (*0-7172-0531-2*) Grolier Educ.

New Book of Mars. Nigel Hawkes. LC 97-43126. (Illus.). 32p. (J). (gr. 4-6). 1998. pap. 9.95 (*0-7613-0731-1*, Copper Beech Bks) Millbrook Pr.

New Book of Mars. Nigel Hawkes. LC 97-43126. (Illus.). 32p. (J). (gr. 4-8). 1998. lib. bdg. 23.90 (*0-7613-0811-3*, Copper Beech Bks) Millbrook Pr.

*__New Book of Middle Eastern Food.__ Claudia Roden. (Illus.). 560p. 2000. 35.00 (*0-375-40506-2*) Knopf.

New Book of Nature. Arthur Fabel. (Teilhard Studies: No. 8). 1982. 3.50 (*0-89012-033-1*) Am Teilhard.

New Book of Patience Games. Ruth D. Botterill. 64p. 1995. pap. 6.95 (*0-572-01169-5*, Pub. by Foulsham UK) Assoc Pubs Grp.

New Book of Pharaohs. Anne Millard. LC 98-15579. 32p. (J). (gr. 4-6). 1998. 24.90 (*0-7613-0859-8*, Copper Beech Bks); pap. 9.95 (*0-7613-0778-8*, Copper Beech Bks) Millbrook Pr.

New Book of Popular Science. LC 97-43332. (YA). 1998. 259.00 (*0-7172-1221-1*) Grolier Educ.

*__New Book of Popular Science, 6 vols.__ LC 99-57470. (Illus.). 3100p. (YA). (gr. 6-12). 2000. lib. bdg. 269.00 (*0-7172-1222-X*) Grolier Educ.

New Book of Prime Number Records. 3rd rev. ed. Paulo Ribenboim. LC 95-5441. 541p. 1996. 59.95 (*0-387-94457-5*) Spr-Verlag.

New Book of Revelation: From John, the Disciple of Jesus the Christ, Through James Coyle Morgan. James C. Morgan. 100p. (Orig.). (C). 1991. pap. 9.95 (*1-878555-01-4*) Oakbridge Univ Pr.

New Book of Revelations. Tuella. 160p. pap. 14.00 (*0-938294-85-7*) Inner Light.

New Book of Rights. Comment by Peter B. Ellis et al. (Illus.). 176p. 1998. pap. 30.00 (*0-9654220-4-6*) Gryfons Pubs & Dist.

New Book of Rock Lists: From the Beatles, James Brown & Brand Nubian to Elvis Presley, Prince, Pearl Jam & Public Enemy, All You'd Ever Want to Know about the Music, the People, the Hits & the Misses. Dave Marsh & James Bernard. 624p. 1994. pap. 15.00 (*0-671-78700-4*, Fireside) S&S Trade Pap.

New Book of Saddlery & Tack. Ed. by Carolyn Henderson. LC 98-11565. 1998. 34.95 (*0-87605-289-8*) Howell Bks.

New Book of Sail Trim. Ed. by Ken Textor. (Illus.). 250p. 1995. pap. 17.95 (*0-924486-81-3*) Sheridan.

New Book of Space. Robin Scagell. LC 97-11143. (Illus.). 32p. (J). (gr. 4-6). 1997. pap. 9.95 (*0-7613-0634-X*, Copper Beech Bks); lib. bdg. 23.90 (*0-7613-0619-6*, Copper Beech Bks) Millbrook Pr.

*__New Book of Table Settings: Creative Ideas for the Way We Gather Today.__ Paige Gilchrist & Chris Bryant. LC 00-35227. 128p. 2000. write for info. (*1-57990-169-7*, Pub. by Lark Books) Sterling.

New Book of the Horse: Complete Authoritative Reference for Every Horse Lover. Sarah Haw. LC 92-46211. (Illus.). 208p. 1993. per. 22.95 (*0-87605-974-4*) Howell Bks.

New Book of Treasures under the Ocean. Francis Dipper. LC 97-24313. (Illus.). 32p. (J). (gr. 4-6). 1997. pap. 9.95 (*0-7613-0640-4*, Copper Beech Bks); lib. bdg. 23.90 (*0-7613-0703-6*, Copper Beech Bks) Millbrook Pr.

New Book of Trusts. 2nd ed. Stephan R. Leimberg et al. LC 99-194028. 541p. 1997. pap. 49.95 (*0-9644565-2-4*) Leimberg.

*__New Book of Wedding Etiquette.__ 4th ed. Jan Wilson & Beth Wilson Hickman. 320p. 2000. pap. 16.95 (*0-7615-2541-6*) Prima Pub.

New Book of Whole Grains. Marlene A. Bumgarner. LC 97-5727. (Illus.). 1997. pap. 16.95 (*0-312-15601-4*) St Martin.

New Book on Healing. Hanna Kroeger. LC 98-102067. (Illus.). 155p. 1996. pap. 7.50 (*1-883713-17-X*) Hanna Kroeger.

New Boots. Louis J. Fagan. LC 98-88221. 192p. (Orig.). 1999. pap. 11.95 (*0-9667407-7-7*, Pub. by A-Peak Pubg) North Country.

New Borders & Old Barriers in Spatial Development. Ed. by Peter Nijkamp. LC 94-7287. 272p. 1994. 77.95 (*1-85628-906-0*, Pub. by Avebry) Ashgate Pub Co.

New Borns, 3 bks., Set. Ruth Nierengarten. (Illus.). 96p. 1994. boxed set 12.95 (*0-87839-092-8*) North Star.

New Boss at Birchfields. large type ed. Henrietta Reid. 1991. 27.99 (*0-7089-2524-3*) Ulverscroft.

New Boss Has a Milk Mustache: My Promotion to Motherhood. Leola Floren. LC 96-7097. 120p. (Orig.). 1996. pap. 8.99 (*0-8341-1576-X*) Beacon Hill.

New Bottom Line: Bringing Heart & Soul to Business. John Renesch et al. LC 96-69103. 350p. 1996. 33.95 (*0-9630390-9-1*) New Leaders.

New Bottom Line: Bringing Heart & Soul to Business. John Renesch et al. LC 96-69103. 350p. 1998. reprint ed. pap. 21.95 (*1-886710-04-X*, Pub. by New Leaders) Natl Bk Netwk.

New Boundaries in Old Territory: Forms & Social Rhetoric in Mark. Vernon K. Robbins. LC 93-21579. (Emory Studies in Early Christianity: Vol. 3). XX, 270p. (C). 1994. text 39.95 (*0-8204-1911-7*) P Lang Pubng.

New Boundary Element Formulation in Engineering. T. G. DeFigueiredo. (Lecture Notes in Engineering Ser.: Vol. 68). ix, 198p. 1991. 50.95 (*0-387-54030-X*) Spr-Verlag.

New Boundary Integral Method for Anisotropic Heat Conduction. E. Divo & A. J. Kassab. (Topics in Engineering Ser.). 120p. 1999. 94.00 incl. cd-rom (*1-85312-771-X*, Pub. by WIT Pr) Computational Mech MA.

New Bourgeoisie & the Limits of Dependency: Mining, Class, & Power in "Revolutionary" Peru. David G. Becker. LC 82-61352. 457p. 1983. reprint ed. pap. 141.70 (*0-608-02576-3*, 206322100004) Bks Demand.

New Boxer. Billie McFadden. (Illus.). 256p. 1989. 25.95 (*0-87605-062-3*) Howell Bks.

New Boy. R. L. Stine, pseud. LC 94-131410. (Fear Street Ser.: No. 21). (YA). (gr. 7 up). 1994. mass mkt. 3.99 (*0-671-73869-0*, Archway) PB.

New Boy. R. L. Stine, pseud. (Fear Street Ser.: No. 21). (YA). (gr. 7 up). 1994. 9.09 (*0-606-05953-9*, Pub. by Turtleback) Demco.

New Brahmans: 5 Maharashtrian Families. Dinaker D. Karve. LC 63-11389. 311p. reprint ed. pap. 96.50 (*0-608-15842-9*, 203143800074) Bks Demand.

*__New Brain for Igor.__ Teddy O'Connor. LC 00-38711. (Step into Reading Ser.). (Illus.). (J). 2001. pap. write for info. (*0-375-90626-6*) Random Bks Yng Read.

New Brain Imaging Techniques in Cerebrovascular Disease. Cahn & Lassen. (Current Problems in Neurology Ser.: Vol. 2). 136p. 1985. 54.95 (*0-86196-060-2*, Pub. by J Libbey Med) Bks Intl VA.

New Brainbooster: 6 Hours to Rapid Learning & Remembering. Robert W. Finkel. (Illus.). 204p. 1991. pap. 12.95 (*0-8027-7352-4*) Walker & Co.

New Branch of Mathematics: The Ausdehnungslehre of 1844, & Other Works. Hermann Grassmann. Ed. & Tr. by Lloyd C. Kannenberg. 572p. 1995. pap. 32.95 (*0-8126-9276-4*) Open Court.

New Brand World: Ten Principles for Achieving Brand Leadership in the Twenty-First Century... Scott Bedbury & Stephen Fenichell. 320p. 2000. write for info. (*0-316-08463-8*) Little.

New Braunfels, Comal County, Texas: A Pictorial History. Ed. by Roger Nuhn. LC 93-35505. 1993. write for info. (*0-89865-879-9*) Donning Co.

New Bread Loaf Anthology of Contemporary American Poetry. Ed. by Michael Collier & Stanley Plumly. LC 99-20942. (Bread Loaf Anthology Ser.). 381p. 1999. pap. 19.95 (*0-87451-950-0*); text 45.00 (*0-87451-949-7*) U Pr of New Eng.

New Bread Machine Book. Marjie Lambert. (Illus.). 128p. 1999. 12.99 (*0-7858-1134-6*) Bk Sales Inc.

New Breed. LC 97-69595. 131p. 1997. pap. 12.00 (*0-9659789-0-7*) Southwest Pub.

New Breed. W. E. B. Griffin. (Brotherhood of War Ser.: Bk. 7). 1988. mass mkt. 7.50 (*0-515-09226-6*, Jove) Berkley Pub.

New Breed. Ed. by Jay Kennedy. 128p. 1990. mass mkt. 5.95 (*0-380-76071-1*, Avon Bks) Morrow Avon.

New Breed: Drum. Gary Chester. 48p. 1986. pap. 9.95 (*0-88188-749-8*, 06631619) H Leonard.

New Breed Church: In Your Face. Richard Perinchief. 96p. 1994. pap. 6.00 (*1-879993-18-X*) Albury Pub.

New Breed of Subsea Contractors. T. M. Ehret. 1989. 125.00 (*90-6314-565-9*, Pub. by Lorne & MacLean Marine) St Mut.

New Breed of Subsea Contractors. Ed. by T. M. Ehret. (C). 1989. 95.00 (*0-89771-739-2*, Pub. by Lorne & MacLean Marine) St Mut.

New Breed II: The Sequel - Independence, Inspiration, Innovation. Gary Chester & Chris Adams. (Illus.). 96p. (C). 1990. pap. 14.95 (*0-7935-0004-4*, 00660125) H Leonard.

New Breeze Is Blowing. Trevor M. Phillips. (Illus.). 232p. (Orig.). 1989. text 23.96 (*0-9622708-0-6*) Zubra Pub.

New Breezes: An Anthology of African American Literary Voices. Ed. by Alma Roberts. 51p. 1993. pap. 7.95 (*0-9638191-0-0*) New Breezes.

New Bremen. Mark D. Bernstein. LC 98-4943. (Illus.). 163p. 1998. 19.95 (*1-882203-54-2*) Orange Frazer.

*__New Bremen 2000.__ Mark Bernstein. 96p. 2000. 20.00 (*1-882203-66-6*) Orange Frazer.

New Bretton Woods: Rethinking International Economic Institutions & Arrangements. C. R. Neu. 102p. 1993. pap. 15.00 (*0-8330-1304-1*, MR-116) Rand Corp.

New Brewing Lager Beer: The Most Comprehensive Book for Home- & Microbrewers. Gregory J. Noonan. (Illus.). 387p. 1996. pap. 14.95 (*0-937381-46-2*) Brewers Pubns.

New Bride in Town. Amy Frazier. 1996. per. 3.99 (*0-373-24030-9*, 1-24030-8) Silhouette.

New Bridges. Joan Roig. (Illus.). 192p. 1996. pap. text 60.00 (*84-252-1681-8*) Watsn-Guptill.

New Bridges. Rotovision S. A. Staff. (Illus.). 160p. 1996. pap. text 35.00 (*0-8230-6498-0*) Watsn-Guptill.

New Bridges . . . A Curriculum for Persons with Disabilities Vol. 2: Spring. Ed. by Hilda R. Davis. 72p. 1996. pap. 12.95 (*0-687-71984-4*) Abingdon.

New Bridges . . . A Curriculum for Persons with Disabilities Vol. 2: Winter. Ed. by Hilda R. Davis. 72p. 1996. pap. 12.95 (*0-687-71983-6*) Abingdon.

New Britain. Arlene C. Palmer. (Images of America Ser.). 1995. pap. 16.99 (*0-7524-0209-9*) Arcadia Publng.

New Britain, Vol. II. Arlene C. Palmer. (Images of America Ser.). 1996. pap. 16.99 (*0-7524-0414-8*) Arcadia Publng.

*__New Britain, Vol. III.__ Arlene C. Palmer. (Images of America Ser.). 1999. pap. 16.99 (*0-7385-0025-9*) Arcadia Publng.

New Britain: My Vision of a Young Country. Tony Blair. LC 96-40377. 352p. 1997. 28.00 (*0-8133-3338-5*, Pub. by Westview) HarpC.

New British Design, 1998. Peta Levi. (Illus.). 272p. 1998. 85.00 (*1-84000-099-6*, Pub. by Conran Octopus) Antique Collect.

New British Drama: A Bibliography with Particular Reference to Arden, Bond, Osborne, Pinter, Wesker. Karl-Heinz Stoll. (FAS-A Ser.: Vol. 3). 93p. 1975. pap. 22.00 (*3-261-00966-7*) P Lang Pubng.

New British History, Founding a Modern State, 1500-1707. Burgess. 224p. Date not set. text 59.50 (*1-86064-190-3*, Pub. by I B T) St Martin.

New British Library. Alan E. Day. LC 94-34695. 279p. Date not set. reprint ed. pap. 86.50 (*0-608-20733-0*, 207183100002) Bks Demand.

New British Politics. Budge. 656p. (C). 1998. pap. 33.53 (*0-582-28925-4*) Longman.

New Broadway Songbook. 384p. (Orig.). (YA). 1984. pap. 24.95 (*0-7692-1053-8*, VF1460) Wrner Bros.

New Broadways: Theatre Across America: Approaching a New Millennium. Gerald M. Berkowitz. 2000. pap. 19.95 (*1-55783-412-1*) Applause Theatre Bk Pubs.

New Broadways: Theatre Across America Approaching a New Millennium. rev. ed. Gerald M. Berkowitz. LC 96-37922. 320p. 1997. 24.95 (*1-55783-257-9*) Applause Theatre Bk Pubs.

New Brooms & the Manager in Distress. George Colman. LC 80-14205. 80p. 1980. 50.00 (*0-8201-1353-0*) Schol Facsimiles.

New Bruce Boston Omnibus, 5 bks., Set. Bruce Boston. 210p. 1991. boxed set 39.95 (*0-938075-20-9*) Ocean View Bks.

*__New Brunswick.__ (Canada in the Twenty First Century Ser.). (Illus.). (J). 2000. 18.95 (*0-7910-6064-0*) Chelsea Hse.

New Brunswick. Harry Beckett. LC 97-932. (Journey Across Canada Ser.). 24p. (J). (gr. 3-5). 1997. lib. bdg. 18.60 (*1-55916-202-3*) Rourke Bk Co.

New Brunswick. Kumari Campbell. LC 96-33931. (Hello Canada Ser.). (Illus.). 76p. (J). 1996. lib. bdg. 19.95 (*0-8225-2764-2*, Lerner Publctns) Lerner Pub.

N

*__New Brunswick.__ Campbell Kumari. (Hello Canada Ser.). 1999. pap. 7.95 (*1-55041-268-X*) Fitzhenry & W Ltd.

New Brunswick. Timothy E. Regan. LC 96-208564. (Images of America Ser.). 1996. pap. 16.99 (*0-7524-0430-X*) Arcadia Publng.

New Brunswick: A Colour Guidebook. Marianne Eiselt & H. A. Eiselt. (Illus.). 192p. 1995. pap. 19.95 (*0-88780-270-2*) Formac Dist Ltd.

New Brunswick: A Colour Guidebook. rev. ed. Marianne Eiselt & H. A. Eiselt. (Illus.). 200p. 1996. pap. 16.95 (*0-88780-344-X*, Pub. by Formac Publ Co) Formac Dist Ltd.

New Brunswick & Middlesex County: Hub & the Wheel. Gary Karasik. LC 86-2245. (Illus.). 224p. 1986. 22.95 (*0-89781-188-7*) Am Historical Pr.

New Brunswick in History. William H. Benedict. 391p. 1993. reprint ed. lib. bdg. 42.50 (*0-8328-2856-4*) Higginson Bk Co.

New Brunswick Supreme Court Records, 1825-1928 Vols. 1-54, 54 vols., Set. 1979. 1550.00 (*1-57588-337-6*, 302560) W S Hein.

*__New Buddhism: The Western Transformation of an Ancient Tradition.__ James William Coleman. 256p. 2000. 25.00 (*0-19-513162-2*) OUP.

New Building & Housing Need see Progress in Planning

New Building Contract. E. Finsen. 238p. 1991. pap. 42.50 (*0-7021-2640-3*, Pub. by Juta & Co) Gaunt.

New Building Systems. Warszawski. (Illus.). 464p. (C). 1999. 140.00 (*0-419-20620-5*, E & FN Spon) Routledge.

New Building Today: European Architecture of the 1990's. Ed. by Architektur Z. Wien. LC 95-41155. (Illus.). 288p. 1995. 78.00 (*3-7643-5226-4*, Pub. by Birkhauser) Princeton Arch.

New Building Your Mate's Self-Esteem. expanded ed. Dennis Rainey & Barbara Rainey. 312p. 1995. pap. 12.99 (*0-7852-7824-9*) Nelson.

New Buildings in Historic Settings. John Warren, II et al. LC 98-223556. (Illus.). 192p. 1998. pap. text 69.95 (*0-7506-3738-2*, Butterwrth Archit) Buttrwrth-Heinemann.

New Bulic Speaker, 97. Rodman. (C). 1996. 26.00 (*0-15-505505-4*) Harcourt.

New Bull Terrier. John H. Remer, Jr. (Illus.). 288p. 1989. 25.95 (*0-87605-096-8*) Howell Bks.

*__New Burlington: The Life & Death of an American Village.__ John Baskin. 2000. pap. 14.95 (*0-393-32020-0*) Norton.

*__New Business Card Graphics, Vol. 2.__ Ed. by Pie Books Editorial Staff. (Illus.). 224p. 1999. 65.00 (*4-89444-117-9*, Pub. by Pie Bks) Bks Nippan.

New Business for Ad Agencies. Edward F. Boxton & Susan Fulton. LC 87-81308. 252p. 1989. pap. 35.00 (*0-917168-11-9*) Executive Comm.

New Business Kit & Tax Compliance Guide. rev. ed. Edward Mendlowitz & Peter A. Weitsen. (Illus.). 165p. 1998. pap. 29.95 (*0-9656711-0-0*) Pract Programs.

New Business Landscape: Taking Your Business into the Twenty-First Century. Susan E. Mehrtens. LC 96-92996. 137p. (Orig.). 1997. pap. 15.95 (*1-889919-03-9*) Potlatch Group Inc.

New Business of Banking. Practising Law Institute Staff et al. LC 97-148380. (Corporate Law & Practice Course Handbook Ser.). 832 p. 1996. 39.00 (*0-87224-297-8*) PLI.

New Business of Banking: Surviving & Thriving in Times of Unparalleled Consolidation & Competition. George M. Bollenbacher. 250p. 1992. text 32.50 (*1-55738-331-6*, Irwn Prfssnl) McGraw-Hill Prof.

New Business of Banking: Transforming Challenges into Opportunities in Today's Financial Services Marketplace. George M. Bollenbacher. (Illus.). 278p. 1998. reprint ed. lib. bdg. 35.00 (*0-7351-0038-1*) Replica Bks.

New Business of Banking: Transforming Challenges into Opportunities in Today's Financial Services Marketplace. 2nd rev. ed. George M. Bollenbacher. 250p. 1995. text 35.00 (*1-55738-771-0*, Irwn Prfssnl) McGraw-Hill Prof.

New Business of Banking: What Banks Can Do Now. Melanie L. Fein et al. LC 95-152627. 1000 p. 1995. 39.00 (*0-87224-174-2*) PLI.

New Business of Banking, 1996. (Corporate Law & Practice Course Handbook, 1985-86 Ser.). Date not set. pap. 99.00 (*0-614-17204-7*, B4-7123) PLI.

New Business of Banking, 1995: What Banks Can Do Now. (Corporate Law & Practice Course Handbook, 1985-86 Ser.). 792p. 1994. pap. 99.00 (*0-614-17179-2*, B4-7087) PLI.

New Business of Business: Sharing Responsibility for a Positive Global Future. Ed. by Willis Harman & Maya Porter. LC 97-697. 300p. (Orig.). 1997. pap. 19.95 (*1-57675-018-3*) Berrett-Koehler.

New Business of Design. International Design Conference in Aspen Staff. LC 95-76691. 256p. 1996. pap. 19.95 (*1-880559-38-2*) Allworth Pr.

New Business Opportunities: Getting to the Right Place at the Right Time. Jeffry A. Timmons. LC 89-9721. 160p. 1990. pap. 18.95 (*0-931790-91-3*) Brick Hse Pub.

New Business Opportunities in Latin America: Trade & Investment after the Mexican Meltdown. Louis E. Nevaer. LC 95-38752. 240p. 1996. 62.95 (*1-56720-023-0*, Quorum Bks) Greenwood.

New Business Values for Success in the 21st Century: Improvement, Innovation, Inclusion, Incentives, Information. John Persico, Jr. & Patricia R. Morris. LC 96-51808. 312p. 1997. 49.95 (*0-7890-0155-1*); pap. 24.95 (*0-7890-0239-6*) Haworth Pr.

New Business Ventures. 5th ed. Stevenson. LC 98-8255. 692p. 1998. 82.19 (*0-256-20477-2*) McGraw.

New Business Ventures & the Entrepreneur. 4th ed. Howard H. Stevenson et al. LC 93-24704. 740p. (C). 1993. text 67.25 (*0-256-11030-1*, Irwn McGrw-H) McGrw-H Hghr Educ.

New Businesses, Entrepreneurship, & Rural Development: Building a State Strategy. Mark Popovich. (New Alliances for Rural America Ser.). (Orig.). 1988. pap. text 6.00 (*1-55877-016-X*) Natl Governor.

New Butterfly: My First Look at Metamorphosis. unabridged ed. Pamela Hickman. LC 96-931168. (My First Look at Nature Ser.). (Illus.). 20p. (J). (ps-4). 1997. pap. 6.95 (*1-55074-202-7*, Pub. by Kids Can Pr) Genl Dist Srvs.

New Cabbage Soup Diet. Margaret Danbrot. LC 97-186861. 1997. mass mkt. 4.99 (*0-312-96228-2*) St Martin.

New Cairn Terrier. Betty Marcum. LC 95-13520. (Illus.). 256p. 1995. per. 25.95 (*0-87605-073-9*) Howell Bks.

New Calculus: Analyzing Airpower's Changing Role in Joint Theater Campaigns. Christopher J. Bowie et al. LC 93-16125. 1993. pap. 15.00 (*0-8330-1322-X*, MR-149-AF) Rand Corp.

*__New Caledonia: A Country Study Guide, 110 vols.__ International Business Publications, USA Staff & Global Investment Center, USA Staff. (World Country Study Guides Library Ser.: Vol. 214). (Illus.). 350p. 2000. pap. 69.95 (*0-7397-1037-0*) Intl Business Pubns.

New Caledonia: Issues in Nationalism & Dependency. Ed. by Michael Spencer et al. 253p. (Orig.). (C). 1988. pap. text 32.95 (*0-7022-2126-0*, Pub. by Univ Queensland Pr) Intl Spec Bk.

New Caledonia in Crisis. Michael C. Spencer. LC 87-150825. (Australian Institute of International Affairs, Occasional Paper Ser.: No. 1). 63p. reprint ed. pap. 30.00 (*0-8357-6828-7*, 203551400095) Bks Demand.

New Calendar of the Correspondence of Pierre Simon Laplace. Compiled by Roger Hahn. LC 94-65582. (Berkeley Papers in History of Science: No. 16). 123p. 1994. pap. 10.00 (*0-918102-20-0*) U Cal Hist Sci Tech.

New California: Facing the 21st Century. 2nd ed. Dan Walters. (Illus.). 186p. (C). 1992. pap. text 11.95 (*0-930302-79-6*) Cal Journal.

New California Printmaking: Selections from Northern & Southern California. Mary D. MacNaughton. (Illus.). 20p. 1987. 3.00 (*0-915478-55-2*) Williamson Gallery.

New Call to Holiness. J. Sidlow Baxter. LC 93-13809. 256p. 1993. pap. 11.99 (*0-8254-2170-5*) Kregel.

*__New Call to Mission: Help for Perplexed Churches.__ Alan Neely. LC 99-38748. 1999. 15.00 (*1-57312-296-3*) Smyth & Helwys.

New Cambridge Elementary Statistical Tables. 2nd ed. D. V. Lindley & W. F. Scott. (Illus.). 96p. (C). 1995. pap. text 15.95 (*0-521-48485-5*) Cambridge U Pr.

New Cambridge English Course: Student's Book 1A. 138p. 1990. pap. text, student ed. 9.95 (*0-521-37641-6*) Cambridge U Pr.

New Cambridge GED Program: Exercise Book for Writing Skills, Pt. 2. Prentice-Hall Staff. 1995. pap. 6.95 (*0-13-601204-3*) P-H.

New Cambridge Medieval History Vol. 2: C. 700-c. 900. Ed. by Rosamond McKitterick. (Illus.). 1114p. (C). 1995. text 120.00 (*0-521-36292-X*) Cambridge U Pr.

New Cambridge Medieval History Vol. 3: c. 900 - c. 1024. Ed. by Timothy Reuter. (New Cambridge Medieval History Ser.). (Illus.). 890p. (C). 2000. 110.00 (*0-521-36447-7*) Cambridge U Pr.

New Cambridge Medieval History Vol. 5: C. 1198 - C. 1300. Ed. by David Abulafia. (Illus.). 900p. (C). 1999. text 120.00 (*0-521-36289-X*) Cambridge U Pr.

New Cambridge Medieval History Vol. 6: c. 1300 - c. 1415. Ed. by Michael Jones. (Illus.). 900p. (C). 1999. text 120.00 (*0-521-36290-3*) Cambridge U Pr.

New Cambridge Medieval History c. 1415-c. 1500, Vol. 7. Ed. by Christopher Allmand. (Illus.). 1000p. (C). 1998. text 95.00 (*0-521-38296-3*) Cambridge U Pr.

New Cambridge Modern History, 14 vols. Incl. Vol. 2: The Reformation, 1520-1559. Reformation, 1520-1559. 2nd ed. Ed. by Geoffrey R. Elton. 751p. 1990. text 100.00 (*0-521-34536-7*); Vol. 4: The Decline of Spain & the Thirty Years Wa. Decline of Spain & the Thirty Years War, 1609-59. Ed. by J. P. Cooper. 853p. 1980. pap. 47.95 (*0-521-29713-3*); Vol. 6: The Rise of Great Britain & Russia, 1688-1. Rise of Great Britain & Russia, 1688-1725. Ed. by J. S. Bromley. 972p. 1970. text 160.00 (*0-521-07524-6*); Vol. 7: The Old Regime, 1713-1763. Old Regime, 1713-1763. Ed. by J. O. Lindsay. 646p. 1957. 125.00 (*0-521-04545-2*); Vol. 9. War & Peace in an Age of Upheaval, 1793-1830. Ed. by C. W. Crawley. 762p. 1965. text 150.00 (*0-521-04547-9*); Vol. 13. Companion Volume. Ed. by Peter Burke. 385p. 1979. text 100.00 (*0-521-22128-5*); 775.00 (*0-521-08787-2*) Cambridge U Pr.

New Canaan Inscriptions Copied from Gravestones . . . Arranged with Genealogical Notes & Record of Revolutionary Service. Francis F. Spies. 173p. 1997. reprint ed. pap. 19.50 (*0-8328-5668-1*) Higginson Bk Co.

New Canaan Private in the Civil War: Letters of Justus M. Silliman, Seventeenth Connecticut Volunteers. Ed. by Edward Marcus. (Illus.). 117p. 1984. 7.50 (*0-939958-01-5*) New Canaan.

New Canadian Political Economy. Ed. by Wallace Clement & Glen Williams. 352p. (C). 1989. text 65.00 (*0-7735-0672-1*, Pub. by McG-Queens Univ Pr) CUP Services.

New Canadian Political Economy. Ed. by Wallace Clement & Glen Williams. 344p. (C). 1989. pap. text 24.95 (*0-7735-0681-0*, Pub. by McG-Queens Univ Pr) CUP Services.

New Canary Handbook. Matthew M. Vriends. (New Pet Owner's Handbooks Ser.). (Illus.). 144p. 1992. pap. 9.95 (*0-8120-4879-2*) Barron.

New Cancer Sourcebook. Ed. by Alan R. Cook. LC 95-33730. (Health Reference Ser.: Vol. 12). 1996. lib. bdg. 78.00 (*0-7808-0041-9*) Omnigraphics Inc.

New Cancer Survivors: Living with Grace, Fighting with Spirit. Natalie Davis Spingarn. LC 99-25087. 208p. 1999. 45.00 (*0-8018-6266-3*); pap. 16.95 (*0-8018-6267-1*) Johns Hopkins.

*__New Cancer Therapies: The Patient's Dilemma.__ Penny Williams. (Illus.). 224p. 2000. pap. 16.95 (*1-55209-485-5*) Firefly Bks Ltd.

New Candle Book: Inspirational Ideas for Displaying, Using & Making Candles. Gloria Nicol. (Illus.). 160p. 1995. 30.00 (*1-85967-066-0*, Lorenz Bks) Anness Pub.

New Candle Kit. Gloria Nicol. (Illus.). 160p. 1996. 32.50 (*1-85967-166-7*, Lorenz Bks) Anness Pub.

New Canterbury Tales. Maurice H. Hewlett. LC 72-98575. (Short Story Index Reprint Ser.). 1977. 19.95 (*0-8369-3149-1*) Ayer.

New Capabilities for Strategic Mobility Analysis: Executive Summary. John Schank et al. LC 94-19200. 1994. pap. 7.50 (*0-8330-1547-8*, MR-294-JS) Rand Corp.

New Capabilities for Strategic Mobility Analysis Using Mathematical Programming. Michael G. Mattock et al. LC 94-42766. (Illus.). 103p. 1995. pap. text 15.00 (*0-8330-1610-5*, MR-296-JS) Rand Corp.

New Capitalists. Louis O. Kelso & Mortimer J. Adler. LC 75-14801. 109p. 1975. reprint ed. lib. bdg. 55.00 (*0-8371-8211-5*, KENC, Greenwood Pr) Greenwood.

New Captured Harvest. Storey Publishing Staff. 1997. 29.95 (*0-676-57232-4*) Random.

New Captured Harvest: Creative Crafts from Nature. Terence Moore. (Illus.). 160p. 1995. 29.95 (*1-57076-022-5*, Trafalgar Sq Pub) Trafalgar.

New Captured Harvest: Creative Crafts From Nature. Terence Moore. (Illus.). 160p. Date not set. write for info. (*1-85967-097-0*, Lorenz Bks) Anness Pub.

*__New Car Buying Guide 2000.__ Consumer Reports Books Editors. (Consumer Reports New Car Buying Guide Ser.). (Illus.). 256p. 2000. pap. 9.99 (*0-89043-937-0*) Ed Devel Corp.

New Car Carriers, 1910-1998 Photo Album. Donald F. Wood. LC 98-75272. (Photo Album Ser.). (Illus.). 112p. 1999. pap. 19.95 (*1-882256-98-0*, 10093T) Iconografix.

New Car Cost Guide, 1990. 480p. 1989. 71.00 (*0-13-019068-3*, H M Gousha) Prntice Hall Bks.

New Car Dealers Secret Agenda. Mike Willingham & Chuck Griffin. 64p. (Orig.). (C). 1992. pap. 6.95 (*0-9635541-0-7*) Natl Negot Srvs.

New Car Market in Europe. 1996. 775.00 (*0-85058-898-7*, R339) Economist Intell.

New Car Market in Europe No. R329: 1995 Edition. 1995. 620.00 (*0-85058-839-1*) Economist Intell.

New Car Market in Europe, '97. 1997. write for info. (*0-614-25456-6*) Econ Intel.

New Car Market in Europe: 1997 Edition. 1997. 895.00 (*0-85058-967-3*) Economist Intell.

New Car Price Guide: Retail & Dealer Invoice Prices. Consumer Guide Editors. (Consumer Guide Ser.). 1998. mass mkt. 5.99 (*0-451-19447-0*, Sig) NAL.

New Car Price Guide: 1999 Edition, 1 vol. Consumer Guide Editors. 1999. mass mkt. 5.99 (*0-451-19911-1*) NAL.

New Car Report, 1996. Denis Duquet et al. (Illus.). 428p. 1995. pap. 19.95 (*0-88266-746-7*) Storey Bks.

New Car Reports, 1993. Timothy P. Banse. (Illus.). 1992. pap. 9.95 (*0-934523-04-5*) Middle Coast Pub.

New Carbohydrate Diet Counter. Pat Lear. 64p. 1982. pap. 4.95 (*0-941990-00-1*) Lear.

New Carbohydrate Diet Counter. Lopez-Pereira. 1985. pap. 2.00 (*0-87980-107-7*) Wilshire.

*__New Carbons: Control of Structure & Functions.__ Inagaki. 2000. 200.00 (*0-08-043713-3*, Pergamon Pr) Elsevier.

New Card Games for You to Play. Charles Roberts. 160p. 1995. pap. 7.95 (*0-572-01381-7*, Pub. by Foulsham UK) Assoc Pubs Grp.

New Cardiovascular Drugs, 1987. Ed. by Alexander Scriabine. LC 84-641424. 285p. 1987. reprint ed. pap. 88.40 (*0-608-00329-8*, 206104600007) Bks Demand.

New Cardiovascular Drugs, 1986. Ed. by Alexander Scriabine. LC 84-641424. 286p. 1986. reprint ed. pap. 88.70 (*0-608-00374-3*, 206108700007) Bks Demand.

New Cardiovascular Drugs, 1985. Ed. by Alexander Scriabine. LC 84-641424. (Illus.). 320p. 1985. reprint ed. pap. 99.20 (*0-608-00676-9*, 206126300007) Bks Demand.

New Careers Directory see Jobs You Can Live With: Working at the Crossroads of Science, Technology, & Society

New Careers Directory: Internships & Professional Opportunities in Technology & Social Change. rev. ed. Ed. by Barry S. Lasky. 325p. (Orig.). 1993. pap. 18.00 (*0-9639007-0-6*) Student Pugwash.

New Careers for Older People. Southern Conference on Gerontology Staff. Ed. by Carter C. Osterbind. LC 72-190956. (Institute of Gerontology Ser.: No. 20). 138p. reprint ed. pap. 42.80 (*0-7837-4897-3*, 204456200004) Bks Demand.

New Careers for Therapists. Ronald J. Chenail & Jan Chenail. 224p. (C). 1999. 27.00 (*0-393-70241-3*) Norton.

New Careers Grow Older: A Perspective on the Paraprofessional Experience, 1965-1975. Robert Cohen. LC 76-20036. (Policy Studies in Employment & Welfare: No. 26). 144p. reprint ed. pap. 44.70 (*0-608-11888-5*, 202308900032) Bks Demand.

New Careers in Nursing. Florence Downs & Dorothy A. Brooten. LC 82-18449. (Illus.). 192p. 1985. pap. 12.95 (*0-668-05255-4*, Arco) Macmillan Gen Ref.

New Cargo-Handling Techniques: Implications for Port Employment & Skills. A. D. Couper. xii, 172p. 1986. 36.00 (*92-2-105420-9*); pap. 27.00 (*92-2-105419-5*) Intl Labour Office.

New Caribbean Man, 1972 to 1976: Poems. P. D. Sharma. LC 80-68909. (Illus.). 72p. (Orig.). 1981. pap. 9.95 (*0-936378-00-X*) Carib Hse.

New Caribbean Molluscan Faunas. Edward J. Petuch. (Illus.). 1987. 38.50 (*0-938415-01-8*) CERF Inc.

New Carolingian Modelbook: Counted Embroidery Patterns from Before 1600. Lanthe D'Averoigne. LC 95-70710. 214p. 1995. pap. text 24.95 (*0-9642082-2-9*) Outlaw Pr.

New Carpenter's Guide of 1818. Peter Nicholson. (Illus.). 100p. 1993. reprint ed. pap. 40.00 (*0-87556-826-2*) Saifer.

New Carribean Office. Harrison. 1997. pap. write for info. (*0-582-29301-4*) Longman.

New Cars: American & Imports. Consumer Information Experts Staff. (Edmunds New Car Prices Ser.). 1998. pap. text 8.99 (*0-87759-629-8*) Edmund Pubns.

New Cars: Prices & Reviews, Winter 1999. St. Martin's Press Staff. (Edmund's New Cars: Prices & Reviews Ser.). 560p. 1999. pap. text 8.99 (*0-87759-643-3*) Edmund Pubns.

New Cars Prices & Reviews. Edmunds Publications Staff. (New Car Prices Ser.). (Illus.). 560p. 1999. pap. 8.99 (*0-87759-634-4*) Edmund Pubns.

*__New Cars Prices & Reviews 2000.__ Edmunds Publications Staff. 1999. pap. 8.99 (*0-87759-650-6*) Edmund Pubns.

New Case for the Liberal Arts: Assessing Institutional Goals & Student Development. David G. Winter et al. LC 81-81963. (Jossey-Bass Series in Higher Education). 271p. reprint ed. pap. 84.10 (*0-7837-2523-X*, 204268200006) Bks Demand.

New Casserole. Faye Levy. LC 97-6059. (Illus.). 192p. 1997. 15.00 (*0-02-860993-X*) Macmillan.

New Castle: A Pictorial History. Darrel Radford. (Indiana Pictorial History Ser.). (Illus.). 1994. reprint ed. write for info. (*0-943963-28-1*) G Bradley.

(New Castle County) Records of the Welsh Tract Baptist Meeting, Pencader Hundred, New Castle Co., Dela., 1701-1898, Pts. I & II. (Illus.). 235p. 1998. reprint ed. pap. 25.00 (*0-8328-9591-1*) Higginson Bk Co.

New Castle, Historic & Picturesque: With the Bi-Centennial Souvenir, 1693-1893. John Albee. (Illus.). 205p. 1998. reprint ed. lib. bdg. 29.00 (*0-8328-9725-6*) Higginson Bk Co.

*__New Castle, New Hampshire, Vital Records, 1891-1997.__ Richard P. Roberts. 311p. 2000. pap. 26.00 (*0-7884-1454-2*, 1454) Heritage Bk.

New Cat. Yangsook Choi. LC 97-15668. (Illus.). 32p. (J). (gr. k-3). 1999. 16.00 (*0-374-35512-6*) FS&G.

New Cat Handbook: Everything about the Care, Nutrition, Diseases, & Breeding of Cats. Ulrike Muller. 1984. pap. 9.95 (*0-8120-2922-4*) Barron.

New Catalan Short Story: An Anthology. Albert Porqueras-Mayo et al. LC 82-21927. 278p. (Orig.). 1983. pap. text 25.00 (*0-8191-2900-3*) U Pr of Amer.

New Catalogue of Historical Records, 1898 to 1908-09. Robert Bauer. 494p. 1993. reprint ed. lib. bdg. 99.00 (*0-7812-9702-8*) Rprt Serv.

New Categories for Dancing: The Old Testament. Hal Taussig. (Orig.). 1981. pap. 3.00 (*0-941500-25-X*) Sharing Co.

New Catholic Catechism Workshop Resources. Mary A. Johnston. (Illus.). 60p. (Orig.). 1995. pap. 13.30 (*1-55833-150-6*) Natl Cath Educ.

New Catholic Encyclopedia, 19 vols. 1967. 940.00 (*0-7876-3999-0*) Gale.

*__New Catholic Encyclopedia, 15 Vols. Set.__ 2nd ed. 2001. 995.00 (*0-7876-4004-2*, UXL) Gale.

New Catholic Encyclopedia, 19 vols., Set. Catholic University of America Staff. LC 66-22292. 1989. suppl. ed. 940.00 (*0-07-010235-X*) J Heraty Assocs.

New Catholic Encyclopedia, Vol. 6. 1967. 74.50 (*0-7876-4001-8*) Gale.

New Catholic Encyclopedia, Vol. 11. 1967. 74.50 (*0-7876-4002-6*) Gale.

New Catholic Encyclopedia, Vol. 14. 1967. 74.50 (*0-7876-4000-X*) Gale.

New Catholic Encyclopedia, Vol. 16. 1974. 74.50 (*0-7876-4003-4*) Gale.

New Catholic Encyclopedia, Vol. XVIII, Supplement 1978-1988. Ed. by Berard & L. Marthaler. (Illus.). 599p. 1989. 74.50 (*0-685-26975-2*) J Heraty Assocs.

New Catholic Encyclopedia, Vol. 19. Ed. by Berard L. Marthaler. LC 80-84921. (Illus.). 596p. 1995. text 74.50 (*0-614-10331-2*) J Heraty Assocs.

*__New Catholic Encyclopedia Supplement, Vol. 20.__ 2000. 85.00 (*0-7876-4787-X*, UXL) Gale.

New Catholic Evangelization. Ed. by Kenneth Boyack. LC 91-47721. 256p. 1992. pap. 12.95 (*0-8091-3310-5*) Paulist Pr.

New Catholic Picture Bible. (Illus.). (J). (gr. 1-3). 1997. lthr. 15.95 (*0-89942-433-3*, 435/13BG); lthr. 15.95 (*0-89942-434-1*, 435/13W) Catholic Bk Pub.

New Catholic Schools 1985 to 1995. Tr. by Meitler Consultants, Inc. Staff. LC 97-204552. (Illus.). 120p. 1997. pap. 16.00 (*1-55833-187-5*) Natl Cath Educ.

New Catholic Women: A Contemporary Challenge to Traditional Religious Authority. Mary J. Weaver. LC 85-45371. 288p. 1995. pap. 14.95 (*0-253-20993-5*) Ind U Pr.

New Catholic Women: A Contemporary Challenge to Traditional Religious Authority. Mary Jo. Weaver. LC 95-23295. 288p. 1995. 29.95 (*0-253-32931-0*) Ind U Pr.

New Catholicity: Theology Between the Global & the Local. Robert J. Schreiter. LC 97-1665. (Faith & Culture Ser.). 164p. (Orig.). 1997. pap. 18.00 (*1-57075-120-X*) Orbis Bks.

An Asterisk (*) at the beginning of an entry indicates that the title is appearing for the first time.

*New **Catholics for a New Century: The U. S. Church Today & Where It's Headed.** Arthur Jones. 256p. 2000. 21.95 (0-88347-455-7, Pub. by T More) BookWorld.

New **Caucasus: Armenia, Azerbaijan & Georgia.** Edmund Herzig. (Chatham House Papers). 140p. 1998. 44.95 (1-85567-552-8, Pub. by P P Pubs) Cassell & Continuum.

New **Caucasus: Armenia, Azerbaijan & Georgia.** Edmund Herzig. (Chatham House Papers). 140p. 1999. pap. 15.95 (1-85567-553-6, Pub. by P P Pubs) Cassell & Continuum.

New **Cavalcade, 2 vols., Set.** Arthur P. Davis et al. 1990. pap. 60.00 (0-88258-135-X) Howard U Pr.

New **Cavalcade I: African American Writing.** J. Saunders Redding & Joyce A. Joyce. Ed. by Arthur P. Davis et al. 1991. pap. 32.95 (0-88258-133-3) Howard U Pr.

New **Cavalcade II.** Arthur P. Davis et al. 1992. pap. 32.95 (0-88258-134-1) Howard U Pr.

New **CD Jacket Collection.** Ed. by Pie Books Editorial Staff. (Illus.). 180p. Date not set. pap. 69.96 (4-89444-084-9, Pub. by Pie Bks) Bks Nippan.

New **Cells, New Bodies, New Life! You're Becoming a Fountain of Youth.** Virginia Essene et al. 222p. (Orig.). 1991. pap. 11.95 (0-937147-06-0) SEE Pub Co.

New **Celtic Oracle.** Nigel Pennick & Nigel Jackson. (Orig.). 1997. pap. 22.95 (1-898307-56-3, Pub. by Capall Bann Pubng) Holmes Pub.

New **Censors: Movies & the Culture Wars.** Charles Lyons. LC 96-36587. (Culture & the Moving Image Ser.). 248p. (C). 1997. 69.95 (1-56639-511-9) Temple U Pr.

New **Censors: Movies & the Culture Wars.** Charles Lyons. LC 96-36587. (Culture & the Moving Image Ser.). 248p. (C). 1997. pap. text 17.95 (1-56639-512-7) Temple U Pr.

*New **Central Asia: In Search of Stability: A Report to the Trilateral Commission.** Sherman W. Garnett et al. LC 00-44306. (Triangle Papers). 2000. pap. write for info. (0-930503-79-1) Trilateral Comm.

*New **Central Asia: The Creation of Nations.** Olivier Roy. LC 00-37219. 2000. pap. write for info. (0-8147-7554-3) NYU Pr.

New **Central Europe: Triumphs & Tragedies.** Stephen Borsody. 321p. 1993. 58.50 (0-88033-263-8, 366, Pub. by East Eur Monographs) Col U Pr.

New **Central Europe: Triumphs & Tragedies.** rev. ed. Stephen Borsody. (Illus.). 322p. (C). pap. 20.00 (1-882785-03-7) Matthias Corvinus.

New **Central Texas Gardner.** rev. ed. Cheryl Hazeltine & Barry Lovelace. LC 98-34626. (Illus.). 232p. 1999. 24.95 (0-89096-848-9) Tex A&M Univ Pr.

New **Central Texas Gardner.** 2nd rev. ed. Cheryl Hazeltine & Barry Lovelace. LC 98-34626. (Illus.). 232p. 1999. pap. 14.95 (0-89096-871-3) Tex A&M Univ Pr.

New **Centralization: A Study of Intergovernmental Relationships in the U. S.** G. C. Benson. LC 77-74928. (American Federalism-the Urban Dimension Ser.). 1978. reprint ed. lib. bdg. 19.95 (0-405-10477-4) Ayer.

*New **Centre.** Bodo Hombach. 2000. 59.95 (0-7456-2460-X) Polity Pr.

New **Centurions.** Joseph Wambaugh. 368p. 1972. mass mkt. 6.99 (0-440-16417-6) Dell.

New **Century.** Lynette C. Ross. LC 99-212495. (Illus.). 32p. 1998. pap. 9.95 (0-89672-392-5) Tex Tech Univ Pr.

New **Century Composition-Rhetoric.** Ed. by Edward P. Corbett & Virginia M. Burke. LC 73-150594. (C). 1971. 37.50 (0-8290-2384-4) Irvington.

New **Century Cookbook.** William Connor & Sonja Connor. 1996. 24.00 (0-614-19398-2) S&S Trade.

New **Century Disciple Making: Applying Jesus' Ideas for the Future.** Bill Hull. LC 97-14705. 240p. 1997. pap. 11.99 (0-8007-5641-X, Jesus Christ Di) Revell.

New **Century Family Money Book.** Jonathan Pond. 96p. 1995. pap. 1.11 (0-440-51333-2) Dell.

New **Century for Natural Resources Management.** Ed. by Richard L. Knight & Sarah F. Bates. LC 94-28051. 432p. (C). 1995. pap. text 32.00 (1-55963-262-3) Island Pr.

New **Century Handbook.** (C). 1998. text. write for info. (0-205-29404-9, Longwood Div) Allyn.

*New **Century Handbook.** 48p. 1999. write for info. (0-205-29955-5); cd-rom 32.00 (0-205-29708-0) Allyn.

New **Century Handbook.** 48p. (C). 1999. pap. write for info. (0-205-31637-9) Allyn.

*New **Century Handbook.** Christine A. Hult & Thomas N. Huckin. LC 99-86607. 380p. 2000. pap. text 33.00 (0-205-30928-3) Allyn.

New **Century Handbook: Interactive Edition User's Guide to New Century Reader.** Hult & Huckin. LC 98-43334. 870p. 1998. 39.00 (0-205-27352-1) Allyn.

*New **Century Handbook Brief Edition.** 2000. teacher ed. write for info. (0-205-32699-4) Allyn.

*New **Century Handbook Brief Edition: Exercise Book.** 2000. write for info. (0-205-32914-4) Allyn.

*New **Century Healthcare: Strategies for Providers, Purchasers & Plans.** Russell C. Coile. LC 00-25719. 2000. write for info. (1-56793-123-5) Health Admin Pr.

New **Century of Social Housing.** Ed. by Stuart Lowe & David Hughes. 1991. text 59.00 (0-7185-1353-3) St Martin.

*New **Century Psalter.** Ed. by Burton H. Throckmorton & Arthur G. Clyde. 256p. 1999. 14.95 (0-8298-1361-6) Pilgrim OH.

New **Century Rhetoric.** Ede. 1995. pap. text. write for info. (0-312-20267-9) St Martin.

New **Century Speaker: For School & College.** Henry A. Frink. LC 79-37013. (Granger Index Reprint Ser.). 1977. reprint ed. 23.95 (0-8369-6312-1) Ayer.

New **Century World Atlas.** Hammond Staff. LC 95-9638. 184p. 1995. 29.95 (0-8437-1196-5) Hammond World.

New **Century World of Song: Theory & Practice, Set.** Jeanne F. Wardian & Helen P. Landsverk. (Illus.). 1972. spiral bd. 52.95 incl. lp (0-89197-316-8) Irvington.

*New **Ceramic Design.** Edmund De Waal. (Illus.). 2000. 32.99 (1-880140-44-6) Guild.

New **Ceramics: Trends & Traditions.** 2nd rev. ed. Peter Dormer. LC 94-60277. (Illus.). 232p. 1994. pap. 24.95 (0-500-27775-3, Pub. by Thames Hudson) Norton.

New **Certificate Practical Chemistry.** Samuel O. Acquaah. LC 83-82066. 112p. 1983. write for info. (0-8187-0054-8) Harlo Press.

New **Cezanne.** Charles Biederman. LC 58-10644. 1958. boxed set, bds. 25.00 incl. audio, Apple II (0-9600002-2-4) Art History.

New **Chakra Healing: The Revolutionary 32-Center Energy System.** Cyndi Dale. LC 96-13288. (Illus.). 304p. 1999. pap. 19.95 (1-56718-200-3) Llewellyn Pubns.

New **Challenge of Chemistry.** Philip A. Horrigan. (Illus.). (Orig.). (C). 1997. pap. 38.95 (0-941512-02-9) Marshland Pub.

New **Challenge of Direct Democracy.** Ian Budge. LC 96-28104. (Orig.). 1996. pap. 25.95 (0-7456-1765-4, Pub. by Polity Pr) Blackwell Pubs.

New **Challenges: The Civil Rights Record of the Clinton Administration Mid-Term.** Ed. by Corrine M. Yu & William L. Taylor. 300p. 1995. pap. 20.00 (0-614-04292-5) CCCR.

New **Challenges for ASEAN: Emerging Policy Issues.** Ed. by Amitav Acharya & Richard Stubbs. LC 96-170023. (Canada & International Relations Ser.: Vol. 10). 218p. 1996. 62.00 (0-7748-0521-8, HC441) U of Wash Pr.

New **Challenges for Defense Planning: Rethinking How Much Is Enough.** Ed. by Paul K. Davis. LC 94-9770. 750p. 1994. 35.00 (0-8330-1666-0, MR-400-RC); pap. 20.00 (0-8330-1527-3, MR-400-RC) Rand Corp.

*New **Challenges for Human Resource Management.** Chris Brewster. LC 99-88128. 1999. text 69.95 (0-312-22872-4) St Martin.

New **Challenges for Public Administration in the 21st Century: Efficient Civil Service & Decentralized Public Administration, 4 vols.** Ed. by B. Etien. LC 97-61058. (International Institute of Administrative Sciences Monographs). (Illus.). 200p. 1997. 50.00 (90-5199-350-1, 350-1) IOS Press.

New **Challenges for Teachers & Teacher Education.** Ed. by A. McAlpine et al. vi, 174p. 1988. 31.50 (90-265-0884-0) Swets.

New **Challenges in Organic Electrochemistry.** Ed. by Tetsuo Osa. 384p. 1998. text 59.00 (90-5699-146-9, ECU75) Gordon & Breach.

New **Challenges in Recreation & Tourism Planning.** Ed. by Hubert N. Van Lier & Pat D. Taylor. LC 92-35680. (Developments in Landscape Management & Urban Planning Ser.: No. 6D). 240p. 1992. 150.00 (0-444-89849-2) Elsevier.

*New **Challenges in Surfactant Research: Proceedings of the 15th International Workshop on Surfactant Replacement, Kos, June 2000.** Ed. by C. Papagaroufalis et al. (Biology of the Neonate Ser.: Vol. 77, Suppl. 1 (2000)). (Illus.). iv, 30p. 2000. pap. 25.25 (3-8055-7094-5) S Karger.

New **Challenges, New Strategies: Human Rights & Elected Civilian Governments in Latin America.** Washington Office on Latin America Staff. (Human Rights Reports: No. 1). 28p. 1990. pap. 6.00 (0-929513-08-8) WOLA.

New **Challenges to California State Government's Economic Development Engine.** Gus Koehler. 86p. 1994. pap. write for info. (1-58703-023-3) CA St Libry.

New **Challenges to Documentary.** Ed. by Alan Rosenthal. 1987. pap. 27.50 (0-520-05724-4, Pub. by U CA Pr) Cal Prin Full Svc.

New **Challenges to International Cooperation: Adjustment of Firms, Policies, & Organizations to Global Competition.** Ed. by Peter Gourevitch & Paolo Guerrieri. (Illus.). 309p. 1993. pap. write for info. (0-9637158-0-1) U CA Grad Schl.

New **Challenges to Public Utility Management: Proceedings of the Sixth Annual Conference, 24-25 April, 1973.** Michigan State University, Institute of Public Utilities Staff. LC 74-620096. (MSU Public Utilities Papers: Vol. 1974). (Illus.). 271p. reprint ed. pap. 84.10 (0-608-20505-2, 207175700002) Bks Demand.

New **Challenges to the European Union: Policies & Policy-Making at the End of the Century.** Ed. by Stelios Stavridis et al. LC 96-84762. 624p. 1997. text 91.95 (1-85521-455-5, Pub. by Dartmth Pub) Ashgate Pub Co.

New **Challenges to the European Union: Policies & Policy-Making at the End of the Century.** Stelios Stavridis et al. LC 96-84762. 624p. 1997. pap. 36.95 (1-85521-955-7, Pub. by Dartmth Pub) Ashgate Pub Co.

New **Chameleons Handbook.** Francois Le Berre. (Illus.). 160p. (Orig.). 1995. pap. 9.95 (0-8120-1805-2) Barron.

New **Chapter in United States-Russian Relations Opportunities.** Ed. by Sharyl Cross & Marina A. Oborotova. LC 94-16460. 248p. 1994. 59.95 (0-275-94761-0, Praeger Pubs) Greenwood.

New **Chapters in Greek Art.** Percy Gardner. LC 73-149658. (BCL Ser.: I). reprint ed. 47.50 (0-404-02679-6) AMS Pr.

New **Chapters in the History of Greek Literature.** Ed. by J. U. Powell & E. A. Barber. 1921. 30.00 (0-8196-0286-8) Biblo.

New **Chapters in the History of Greek Literature.** Ed. by J. U. Powell & E. A. Barber. (Second Ser.). 1929. 30.00 (0-8196-0287-6) Biblo.

New **Characterization Techniques for Thin Polymer Films.** Ho-Ming Tong & Luu T. Nguyen. LC 89-22681. (Society of Plastics Engineers Monographs). 368p. 1990. 149.00 (0-471-62346-6) Wiley.

*New **Charges on 800 Number Providers: Congressional Hearing.** Ed. by Conrad Burns. 58p. (C). 2000. reprint ed. pap. text 20.00 (0-7567-0040-X) DIANE Pub.

New **Charles Strouse Songbook.** Ed. by Sy Feldman. 204p. (Orig.). (C). 1996. pap. text 22.95 (1-57623-639-0, PF9638) Wrner Bros.

New **Charter for a Worldwide Organisation?** Ed. by Maurice Bertrand & Daniel M. Warner. LC 96-36769. 288p. 1996. pap. 125.00 (90-411-0286-8) Kluwer Law Intl.

New, **Cheape & Delicate Fire of Cole-Balles.** Hugh Platt. LC 72-7838. (English Experience Ser.: No. 550). 32p. 1972. reprint ed. 15.00 (90-221-0550-4) Walter J Johnson.

New **Checklist of Books Designed by Charles Ricketts & Charles Shannon.** Paul Van Capelleveen. (Illus.). 70p. 1996. pap. 15.00 (1-884718-70-1, 50078) Oak Knoll.

New **Chemical Light Pt. 1: Treatise of Mercury.** Michael Sendivogius. Ed. & Comment by Patrick J. Smith. (Alchemical Studies Ser.: No. 6). (Orig.). 1997. pap. 8.95 (1-55818-361-2, Alchemical) Holmes Pub.

New **Chemical Light Pt. II: Treatise on Sulphur.** Michael Sendivogius. Ed. & Comment by Patrick J. Smith. (Alchemical Studies Ser.: No. 7). (Orig.). 1997. pap. 8.95 (1-55818-362-0, Alchemical) Holmes Pub.

New **Chemical Structure Code for Data Storage & Retrieval in Molecular Spectroscopy.** Leslie C. Thomas. LC 68-20753. (Illus.). 64p. reprint ed. pap. 30.00 (0-8357-8968-3, 203335500085) Bks Demand.

New **Chemical Weapons Convention--Implementation & Prospectus.** Michael Bothe et al. LC 98-42960. 1998. 189.00 (90-411-1099-2) Kluwer Academic.

*New **Chemistry.** Nina Hall. LC 99-16729. 2000. 54.95 (0-521-45224-4) Cambridge U Pr.

New **Chess Computer Book: Chess Computer Book.** 2nd ed. T. D. Harding. LC 84-22719. (Chess Ser.). (Illus.). 312p. 1985. 29.90 (0-08-029769-2, Pub. by PPL) Elsevier.

New **Chicago Photographers.** Ed. by Denise Miller-Clark. (Illus.). 32p. 1984. 10.00 (0-932026-13-3) Columbia College Chi.

New **Chicago Stories: A Multicultural Anthology of Contemporary Short Stories.** Intro. by Fred L. Gardaphe. 198p. (Orig.). 1990. pap. 8.95 (0-9627425-0-3) City Stoop Pr.

New **Chicana - Chicano Writing, No. 3.** Ed. by Charles M. Tatum. 165p. (Orig.). 1993. pap. 15.95 (0-8165-1426-7); lib. bdg. 33.50 (0-8165-1425-9) U of Ariz Pr.

New **Chicana - Chicano Writing 1.** Ed. by Charles M. Tatum. 185p. (Orig.). 1992. pap. 16.95 (0-8165-1307-4); lib. bdg. 40.00 (0-8165-1296-5) U of Ariz Pr.

New **Chicana-Chicano Writing 2.** Ed. by Charles M. Tatum. 152p. (Orig.). 1992. pap. 16.95 (0-8165-1333-3) U of Ariz Pr.

New **Chihuahua.** E. Ruth Terry. (Illus.). 256p. 1990. 25.95 (0-87605-125-5) Howell Bks.

New **Child Health.** Boston Childrens' Hospital Staff. 768p. 1987. pap. 23.95 (0-440-50646-8, Dell Trade Pbks) Dell.

New **Child in the Middle.** Ed. by Michael C. Giammatteo. Orig. Title: The Transescence- The Child in the Middle. (Illus.). 73p. (Orig.). 1980. pap. text 14.95 (0-918428-11-4) Sylvan Inst.

New **Child Protection Team Handbook.** Donald C. Bross et al. LC 88-2542. 658p. 1988. text 30.00 (0-8240-8519-1) Garland.

New **Children's Fables see Nuevas Fabulas Infantiles**

*New **Children's Illustrated Atlas of the World.** Keith Lye. LC 99-75105. (Illus.). 56p. (J). (gr. 4-7). 2000. 9.98 (0-7624-0643-7, Courage) Running Pr.

*New **Children's Party Cakes.** Joanna Farrow. 1998. 19.95 (0-09-186498-4, Pub. by Random) Trafalgar.

New **Chili Cuisine.** Nancy S. Hughes. LC 96-5915. 144p. 1996. pap. 11.95 (0-8092-3191-3, 319130, Contemporary Bks) NTC Contemp Pub Co.

New **China: Intermediate Reader of Modern Chinese.** Chih-Ping Chou. 446p. 1999. pap. text 49.50 (0-691-01045-5, Pub. by Princeton U Pr) Cal Prin Full Svc.

*New **China: Money, Sex, & Power.** Phillippe Massonnet. Tr. by Hannah Taiebr from FRE. LC 99-41591. (Illus.). 240p. 1999. 18.95 (0-8048-2116-X) Tuttle Pubng.

New **Chinatown.** Peter Kwong. (Noonday Ser.). 1988. pap. 9.95 (0-374-52121-2) FS&G.

New **Chinatown.** Peter Kwong. LC 95-47731. 210p. 1996. 13.00 (0-8090-1585-4) Hill & Wang.

New **Chinese Astrology.** Suzanne White. 1996. pap. 15.95 (0-312-15179-9) St Martin.

New **Chinese Cinema.** Kwok-kan Tam & Wimal Dissanayake. (Images of Asia Ser.). (Illus.). 120p. (C). 1998. 16.95 (0-19-590607-1) OUP.

New **Chinese Cinemas: Forms, Identities, Politics.** Ed. by Vivian Sobchack et al. (Illus.). 275p. (C). 1994. text 64.95 (0-521-44409-8) Cambridge U Pr.

New **Chinese Cinemas: Forms, Identities, Politics.** Ed. by Vivian Sobchack et al. (Illus.). 268p. (C). 1996. pap. text 20.95 (0-521-44877-8) Cambridge U Pr.

New **Chinese Criminal Code.** Wei Luo. LC 98-9889. Vol. 1. vii, 341p. 1998. 72.50 (1-57588-398-8, 311580) W S Hein.

New **Chinese-English Dictionary.** Commercial Press Staff. (CHI & ENG.). 718p. 1979. 49.95 (0-8288-4826-2, M9554) Fr & Eur.

New **Chinese Landscape.** American Federation of Arts Staff. (Illus.). (Orig.). 1966. pap. 4.00 (0-8079-0093-1) October.

*New **Chinese Migrants in Europe: The Case of the Chinese Community in Hungary.** Pal Nyiri. (Research in Migration & Ethnic Relations Ser.). 150p. 1999. text 65.95 (0-7546-1154-X, Pub. by Ashgate Pub) Ashgate Pub Co.

New **Chinese Three Hundred.** Beijing Language Institute Staff. 1990. audio 40.00 (0-88727-121-9) Cheng & Tsui.

New **Chinese Three Hundred: A Beginning Language Course.** Language Institute, Beijing Staff. LC 83-73591. (C & T Asian Language Ser.). 355p. (C). 1987. pap. 14.95 (0-88727-001-8) Cheng & Tsui.

New **Chinese Three Hundred: A Beginning Language Course, Set.** unabridged ed. Bejing Language Institute Staff & Beijing Language Institute Staff. (C & T Asian Language Ser.). 355p. 1994. boxed set 49.95 incl. audio (0-88727-002-6) Cheng & Tsui.

*New **Chocolate Classics.** Diana Dalsass. LC 98-31268. (Illus.). 160p. 1999. 14.95 (0-393-31881-8) Norton.

*New **Choices for South Carolina: Preserve, Promote & Protect.** Yon Lambert. Ed. by Kit Smith. (Illus.). 48p. 2000. pap. 6.50 (0-9679016-1-8, Pub. by Palmetto Conservat) Parnassus Bk Dist.

New **Choices in Natural Healing.** Prevention Magazine Staff. 800p. 1997. mass mkt. 6.99 (0-553-57690-9) Bantam.

New **Choices in Natural Healing: Over 1,000 of the Best Self-Help Remedies from the World of Alternative Medicine.** Ed. by Bill Gottlieb. LC 95-15907. (Illus.). 687p. 1997. pap. 18.95 (0-87596-364-1) Rodale Pr Inc.

New **Choices in Natural Healing: Over 1,800 of the Best Self-Help Remedies from the World of Alternative Medicine.** Ed. by Bill Gottlieb. LC 95-15907. (Illus.). 687p. 1995. text 27.95 (0-87596-257-2) Rodale Pr Inc.

New **Choices in Natural Healing for Dogs & Cats.** Prevention Magazine Editors. LC 99-15692. 500p. 1999. 29.95 (1-57954-057-0) Rodale Pr Inc.

New **Choices in Natural Healing for Women: Drug Free Remedies from the World of Alternative Medicine.** (Illus.). 544p. 89.95 (0-87596-515-6) Rodale Pr Inc.

New **Choices in Natural Healing for Women: Drug-Free Remedies from the World of Alternative Medicine.** Sara A. O'Donnell et al. LC 97-2481. (Illus.). 544p. 1997. 29.95 (0-87596-387-0) Rodale Pr Inc.

*New **Choices in Natural Healing for Women: Drug-Free Remedies from the World of Alternative Medicine.** Prevention Magazine Editors. 592p. 1999. pap. 17.95 (1-57954-129-1) Rodale Pr Inc.

New **Choices in Natural Healing for Women: Drug-Free Remedies from the World of Alternative Medicine.** Prevention Magazine Health Books Staff. 640p. 1998. mass mkt. 6.99 (0-553-57980-0) Bantam.

N

New **Chosen People: A Corporate View of Election.** William W. Klein. 368p. 1990. pap. 16.99 (0-310-51251-4) Zondervan.

New **Chosen People: Immigrants in the United States.** Guillermina Jasso & Mark R. Rosenzweig. LC 90-38766. (Population of the United States in the 1980s: A Census Monograph Ser.). (Illus.). 480p. 1990. 49.95 (0-87154-404-0) Russell Sage.

New **Christian Right: Mobilization & Legitimation.** Robert C. Liebman & Robert Wuthnow. (Social Institutions & Social Change Ser.). 264p. 1983. lib. bdg. 44.95 (0-202-30307-1) Aldine de Gruyter.

New **Christian Right: Mobilization & Legitimation.** Ed. by Robert C. Liebman & Robert Wuthnow. (Social Institutions & Social Change Ser.). 264p. (C). 1983. pap. text 23.95 (0-202-30308-X) Aldine de Gruyter.

New **Christian Right: Political & Social Issues.** Martha May & Melvin I. Urofsky. LC 96-24441. 504p. 1996. text 85.00 (0-8153-2581-9) Garland.

New **Christian Right, 1981-1988: Prospects for the Post-Reagan Decade.** Erling Jorstad. LC 87-1636. (Studies in American Religion: Vol. 25). 280p. 1987. lib. bdg. 89.95 (0-88946-669-6) E Mellen.

New **Christianity: or The Religion of the New Age.** Salem G. Bland. LC 73-95815. (Social History of Canada Ser.). 118p. reprint ed. pap. 36.60 (0-8357-8243-3, 203407300088) Bks Demand.

New **Christian's Handbook.** Max Anders. LC 99-11283. 320p. 1999. pap. 10.99 (0-7852-0707-4) Nelson.

New **Christmas Stocking Book.** 32p. (J). 1997. write for info. (0-7459-3391-2, Lion) Chariot Victor.

New **Christology.** Karl Rahner & Wilhelm Thusing. 250p. 1994. 27.00 (0-86012-081-3, Pub. by Srch Pr) St Mut.

New **Chromosomal & Malformation Syndromes.** Ed. by Daniel Bergsma. LC 75-16885. (March of Dimes Ser.: Vol. 11, No.5). 1976. 16.95 (0-686-14573-9) March of Dimes.

New **Church & the New Germany: A Study of Church & State.** Charles S. MacFarland. LC 78-63691. (Studies in Fascism: Ideology & Practice). 224p. reprint ed. 39.50 (0-404-16953-8) AMS Pr.

New **Church Anthem Book: 100 Anthems.** Compiled by Lionel Dakers. 592p. 1992. 43.95 (0-19-353107-0) OUP.

New **Church Anthem Book: 100 Anthems.** Compiled by Lionel Dakers. 592p. 1995. pap. 18.95 (0-19-353109-7) OUP.

New **Church in the New World.** Marguerite Block. LC 67-18752. 502p. 1984. 12.95 (0-87785-126-3) Swedenborg.

New **Church Kneeler Book: A Step-by-Step Guide to Canvaswork Kneelers.** Angela Dewar. 48p. 1997. pap. 11.95 (0-85532-825-8, 8258, Pub. by Srch Pr) A Schwartz & Co.

New **CIM Model: A Blueprint for a Computer-Integrated Manufacturing Enterprise.** Robert M. Thacker. Ed. by Robert E. King & Catherine A. Ploskonka. LC 88-62900. (Illus.). 102p. 1989. reprint ed. pap. 31.70 (0-7837-8187-3, 204789200008) Bks Demand.

New **Circles of Learning: Cooperation in the Classroom & School.** David W. Johnson et al. LC 94-8306. 111p. (Orig.). 1994. pap. 16.95 (0-87120-227-1, 1-94034) ASCD.

*New **Citizen.** Veda Boyd Jones. LC 99-193813. (American Adventure Ser.: No. 31). (J). (gr. 3-6). 1998. pap. 3.97 (1-57748-392-8) Barbour Pub.

New Citizens for a New Society: The Institutional Origins of Mass Schooling in Sweden. J. Boli & P. G. Altbach. LC 88-26571. (Pergamon Comparative & International Education Ser.: Vol. 9). (Illus.). 300p. 1989. 141.00 (*0-08-036461-6*, Pub. by Pergamon Repr) Franklin.

New Citizenship: Origins of Progressivism in Wisconsin, 1885-1900. David P. Thelen. LC 79-158075. 352p. 1972. 35.00 (*0-8262-0111-3*) U of Mo Pr.

New Citizenship: Unconventional Politics, Activism & Service. Craig A. Rimmerman. LC 96-52120. (Dilemmas in American Politics Ser.). 176p. (C). 1997. pap. 17.00 (*0-8133-2267-7*, Pub. by Westview); text 69.00 (*0-8133-2266-9*, Pub. by Westview) HarpC.

*__New Citizenship of the Family: Comparative Perspectives.__ Ed. by Henry Cavanna. 232p. 2000. text 69.95 (*0-7546-1222-8*, Pub. by Ashgate Pub) Ashgate Pub Co.

*__New City.__ Stephen Amidon. LC 99-25619. 464p. 2000. 24.95 (*0-385-49762-8*) Doubleday.

*__New City.__ Stephen Amidon. 2001. reprint ed. pap. 15.00 (*0-385-49763-6*, Anchor NY) Doubleday.

New City: Urban America in the Industrial Age, 1860-1920. Raymond A. Mohl. Ed. by A. S. Eisenstadt & John H. Franklin. LC 84-214170. (American History Ser.). 256p. (C). 1985. pap. text 13.95 (*0-88295-830-5*) Harlan Davidson.

New City Gardener: Natural Techniques & Necessary Skills for a Successful City Garden. Judith Adam. (Illus.). 224p. 1999. pap. 24.95 (*1-55209-313-1*) Firefly Bks Ltd.

New City on the Merrimack: Prints of Lawrence, MA, 1845-1876. Helena Wright. 32p. 1974. pap. 2.00 (*0-614-30320-6*) Am Textile Hist.

New City Republics: Municipal Intervention in Defence. Ed. by David Regan. (C). 1990. 35.00 (*0-907967-87-6*, Pub. by Inst Euro Def & Strat) St Mut.

New City State: Change & Renewal in America's Cities. Tom McEnery. LC 94-66090. (Illus.). 342p. 1994. 24.95 (*1-879373-40-8*) Roberts Rinehart.

New City States. LC 82-82572. 76p. 1982. pap. 5.95 (*0-917582-49-7*) Inst Local Self Re.

*__New Civic Art: Elements of Town Planning.__ Ed. by Andres Duany. (Illus.). 320p. 2000. 75.00 (*0-8478-2186-2*) Rizzoli Intl.

New Civic Atlas: Profiles of Civil Society in 60 Countries. Ed. by CIVICUS Staff. (Illus.). 177p. 1997. pap. 15.00 (*0-9644001-6-2*) CIVICUS.

New Civil Court in Action: The New Civil Court. David Barnard & Mark Houghton. 528p. 1993. pap. text 44.00 (*0-406-00268-1*, UK, MICHIE) LEXIS Pub.

New Civil Military Relations. Ed. by John P. Lovell & Philip S. Kronenberg. LC 72-94547. (Social Policy Ser.). 352p. 1974. 44.95 (*0-87855-075-5*); pap. 24.95 (*0-87855-571-4*) Transaction Pubs.

New Civil War: Government Competition for Economic Development. Douglas J. Watson. LC 94-22005. 144p. 1994. 49.95 (*0-275-94788-2*, Praeger Pubs) Greenwood.

New Civil War: The Lesbian & Gay Struggle for Civil Rights. Diane Silver. (Lesbian & Gay Experience Ser.). 1997. pap. 9.95 (*0-531-15822-5*) Watts.

New Civil War: The Lesbian & Gay Struggle for Civil Rights. Diane Silver. LC 96-6414. (Lesbian & Gay Experience Ser.). 144p. (J). 1997. lib. bdg. 24.00 (*0-531-11290-X*) Watts.

New Civil War: The Psychology, Culture & Politics of Abortion. Ed. by Linda J. Beckman & S. Marie Harvey. LC 98-3553. (Psychology of Women Book Ser.: Div. 35). (Illus.). 432p. 1998. text 49.95 (*1-55798-517-0*) Am Psychol.

*__New Civilization: Liberation from Materialism.__ Frank Strelchun. LC 00-91466. ix, 314p. 2000. pap. 8.95 (*0-9671942-2-9*) Top Tek Corp.

New Class? Ed. by B. Bruce-Briggs. LC 78-62999. 225p. 1979. 39.95 (*0-87855-306-1*) Transaction Pubs.

New Class No. 11: Saved by the Bell. Cruise. 1996. 3.95 (*0-689-80712-0*) S&S Childrens.

*__New Class, Clouds, Birds.__ Aristophanes. LC 98-8446. 1999. 40.00 (*0-8122-3501-0*) U of Pa Pr.

New Class of Renally Active Compounds with Antihypertensive, Diuretic, Uricosuric Properties: Proceedings of the Symposium, Montreal, June 17, 1978. Symposium, Montreal Staff. Ed. by G. Lemieux & T. H. Steele. (Nephron Ser.: Vol. 23 Suppl. 1). (Illus.). 1979. pap. 32.25 (*3-8055-3002-1*) S Karger.

New Class Politics: The Polarization of America & What We Can Do About It. William B. Cannon. 138p. 1987. 7.95 (*0-89758-042-7*) Inst Policy Stud.

New Class Society. Robert Perrucci & Earl Wysong. LC 99-11242. 320p. 1999. 69.00 (*0-8476-9172-1*) Rowman.

New Class Society. Perrucci & Earl Wysong. LC 99-11242. 320p. 1999. pap. 21.95 (*0-8476-9173-X*) Rowman.

New Classic Chinese Cookbook. 2nd rev. ed. Mai L. Thayer. LC 98-11488. (Illus.). 348p. 1998. 26.95 (*1-57178-052-1*) Coun Oak Bks.

New Classic Cocktails. Gary Regan & Mardee H. Regan. LC 96-40035. 144p. 1997. 21.00 (*0-02-861349-X*) Macmillan.

New Classic Deserts. Andrew MacLauchlan. (Illus.). 288p. 1994. text 52.95 (*0-442-01735-9*, VNR) Wiley.

New Classic Quilt Designs. Michall Mussell. LC 99-39939. 112p. 1999. per. 19.95 (*1-57432-735-6*, Am Quilters Soc) Collector Bks.

New Classical King's Indian. John Numn & Graham Burgess. 320p. (Orig.). 1997. pap. 26.95 (*1-879479-48-6*) ICE WA.

New Classical Macroeconomics, 3 vols., Set. Ed. by Kevin D. Hoover. (International Library of Critical Writings in Economics: Vol. 19). 1856p. 1992. write for info. (*1-85278-572-1*) E Elgar.

New Clay: Techniques & Approaches to Jewelry Making. 2nd ed. Nan Roche. Ed. by Seymour Bress. (Illus.). 160p. 1992. pap. 24.95 (*0-9620543-4-8*) Flower Valley Pr.

*__New Cleaning & Cooking Fish.__ Sylvia Bashline. LC 99-18297. (The Freshwater Angler Ser.). (Illus.). 160p. 1999. 19.95 (*0-86573-096-2*) Creat Pub Intl.

New Cleaning Strategies: Environmental Issues & Technological Developments. Ed. by Ron Daniels. LC 95-100492. (Illus.). 190p. (Orig.). 1994. pap. 49.00 (*0-87930-279-8*) Miller Freeman.

New Clear Solution. Alexander Galahad. 28p. (Orig.). 1997. pap. 14.00 (*1-886467-15-3*) WJM Press.

New Clinical & Epidemiological Data on Dipyrone: Yokohama, July 28, 1992. World Conference on Clinical Pharmacology & Therap. Ed. by Kay Brune. LC 93-25354. 1993. 23.50 (*0-8176-2916-5*) Birkhauser.

New Clinical Concepts in Marital Therapy. Ed. by Oliver J. W. Bjorksten. LC 85-11201. (Clinical Insights Ser.). 177p. reprint ed. pap. 54.90 (*0-8357-7828-2*, 203620100002) Bks Demand.

New Cloak, Old Dagger: How Britain's Spies Came in from the Cold. Michael Smith. (Illus.). 288p. 1997. 40.00 (*0-575-06150-2*, Pub. by V Gollancz); pap. 17.95 (*0-575-40104-4*, Pub. by V Gollancz) Trafalgar.

New Clothes from Old Threads: Daily Reflections for Recovering Adults. Sally Hill & Valerie Deilgat. (Illus.). 430p. 1998. pap. text 16.00 (*0-7881-5840-6*) DIANE Pub.

New Coat for Anna. Harriet Ziefert. LC 86-2722. (Dragonfly Bks.). (Illus.). 40p. (ps-3). 1988. pap. 6.99 (*0-394-89861-3*, Pub. by Knopf Bks Yng Read) Random.

New Coat for Anna. Harriet Ziefert. (J). 1986. 12.19 (*0-606-03870-1*, Pub. by Turtleback) Demco.

New Coat for Anna Study Guide. Rebecca Gilleland. 32p. (J). (gr. 1-3). 1994. student ed., ring bd. 9.99 (*1-58609-121-2*) Progeny Pr WI.

New Coat of Leaves. Time-Life Books Editors. (Child's First Library of Values). (Illus.). 30p. 1996. 14.95 (*0-7835-1314-3*) Time-Life.

New Code Environment. (UNCTC Current Studies A: No. 16). 58p. pap. 15.00 (*92-1-104336-0*, E.90.II.A.7) UN.

New Cognitive Neurosciences. 2nd ed. Michael S. Gazzaniga. LC 98-52869. (Illus.). 1276p. 1999. 129.95 (*0-262-07195-9*) MIT Pr.

New Cold Molded Boat Building. Parker. 1989. 29.95 (*0-07-157179-5*) McGraw.

New Cold-Molded Boatbuilding: From Lofting to Launching. Reuel B. Parker. (Illus.). 336p. 1992. pap. 23.95 (*0-87742-358-X*) Intl Marine.

New Cold-Molded Boatbuilding: From Lofting to Launching. Reuel B. Parker. 336p. 1992. pap. 23.95 (*0-07-048578-X*) McGraw.

New Cold War: Moscow vs. Peking. Edward Crankshaw. LC 79-133518. (Select Bibliographies Reprint Ser.). 1980. 18.95 (*0-8369-5550-1*) Ayer.

New Cold War? Religious Nationalism Confronts the Secular State. Mark Juergensmeyer. LC 92-5609. (Comparative Studies in Religion & Society: No. 5). 1993. 45.00 (*0-520-08078-5*, Pub. by U CA Pr) Cal Prin Full Svc.

New Cold War? Religious Nationalism Confronts the Secular State. Mark Juergensmeyer. 292p. (C). 1994. pap. 17.95 (*0-520-08651-1*, Pub. by U CA Pr) Cal Prin Full Svc.

New Collected Poems. Tomas Transtromer & Robin Fulton. LC 98-132204. 220p. 1998. pap. 21.95 (*1-85224-413-5*, Pub. by Bloodaxe Bks) Dufour.

*__New Collected Poems, 1952-1992.__ Geoffrey Hill. 240p. 2000. pap. 18.00 (*0-618-00188-3*, Mariner Bks) HM.

New Collection. Michael Crichton. LC 93-40887. 720p. 1994. 13.99 (*0-517-10135-1*) Random Hse Value.

New Collection of Scintillating Challenges . . . Thomas Middleton. (Simon & Schuster Crostics Treasury Ser.: No. 4). 96p. 1996. per. 8.00 (*0-684-81880-9*) S&S Trade Pap.

New Collection of Three Complete Books. Norman Vincent Peale. LC 95-18750. 528p. 1996. 13.99 (*0-517-14671-1*) Random Hse Value.

New Collection of Three Complete Novels. Rosamunde Pilcher. LC 96-27249. 624p. 1997. 13.99 (*0-517-18237-8*) Wings Bks.

New Collector's Directory. Robert D. Connolly. 56p. 1976. pap. 3.50 (*0-914598-36-8*) Intl Resources.

New Collector's Directory for the 1980's. 2nd rev. ed. Robert D. Connolly. (Illus.). 168p. 1980. pap. 5.95 (*0-914598-38-4*) Intl Resources.

*__New College Course Map & Transcript Files: Changes in Course-taking & Achievement, 1972- 1993, Based on the Postsecondary Records from Two National Longitudinal Studies.__ Clifford Adelman. LC 99-489149. 224p. 1999. per. 21.00 (*0-16-050152-0*) USGPO.

New College Course Map & Transcript Files: Changes in Course-Taking & Achievement, 1972- 1993, Based on the Postsecondary Records from Two National Longitudinal Studies. Clifford Adelman. 294p. 1995. pap. 19.00 (*0-16-063576-4*) USGPO.

New College Dictionary. Langenscheidt Staff. (Insight Guides). 1998. 32.95 (*0-88729-213-5*); 34.95 (*0-88729-216-X*) Langenscheidt.

New College Encyclopedia of Music. 2nd ed. Jack A. Westrup & F. L. Harrison. (Illus.). 768p. 1981. reprint ed. pap. 24.95 (*0-393-00074-5*) Norton.

New College Financial Aid System: Making It Work for You. David Jaffe. 144p. (YA). (gr. 11-12). 1995. pap. 14.95 (*0-933031-82-3*) Coun Oak Bks.

New College German Dictionary. Langenscheidt Editorial Staff. (GER.). (C). 1995. 32.95 (*0-88729-020-5*) Langenscheidt.

New College German Dictionary, Thumb-Indexed. Langenscheidt Editorial Staff. (GER.). (C). 1995. 34.95 (*0-88729-021-3*) Langenscheidt.

New College German-English English-German Dictionary. Incl. New College German-English English-German Dictionary: Thumb-Indexed. (ENG & GER.). 1420p. 31.95 (*0-88729-019-1*); 1420p. 29.95 (*0-88729-018-3*) Langenscheidt.

New College German-English English-German Dictionary: Thumb-Indexed see New College German-English English-German Dictionary

New College on the Prairie: The 1st 25 Years of Southwest State University. Joseph A. Amato. (Illus.). 1991. 18.95 (*0-9614119-3-7*) Crossings Pr.

New College Spanish Dictionary. Langenscheidt Editorial Staff. (SPA.). 1020p. (C). 1995. 32.95 (*0-88729-126-0*) Langenscheidt.

New College Spanish Dictionary, Thumb-Indexed. Langenscheidt Editorial Staff. (SPA.). 1020p. (C). 1995. 34.95 (*0-88729-127-9*) Langenscheidt.

New College Thesaurus. Langenscheidt Staff. (Insight Guides). 1998. 30.95 (*0-88729-214-3*); 32.95 (*0-88729-217-8*) Langenscheidt.

New Colleges for New Students. Laurence Hall. LC 73-10933. (Jossey-Bass Higher Education Ser.). 234p. reprint ed. pap. 72.60 (*0-608-14740-0*, 202571300046) Bks Demand.

New Collie. Collie Club of America Staff. LC 82-19049. (Complete Breed Bk.). (Illus.). 304p. 1982. pap. 25.95 (*0-87605-130-1*) Howell Bks.

New Collie. 4th ed. Collie Club of America Staff. (Illus.). 288p. 1996. 25.95 (*0-87605-127-1*) Howell Bks.

New Color Line: How Quotas & Privilege Destory Democracy. Paul C. Roberts & Lawrence M. Stratton. (Illus.). 247p. 1997. pap. 12.95 (*0-89526-423-4*) Regnery Pub.

New Color Line: How Quotas & Privilege Destroy Democracy. Paul C. Roberts & Lawrence M. Stratton, Jr. 247p. 1995. 24.95 (*0-89526-462-5*) Regnery Pub.

*__New Color of Success.__ Niki Butler Mitchell. LC 99-49381. (Illus.). 268p. 1999. 22.50 (*0-7615-2065-1*) Prima Pub.

New Color Portfolio. Michael Bishop et al. (Illus.). 10p. 1989. 3000.00 (*0-89659-243-X*) Abbeville Pr.

New Colorado: Colorado Holistic Health Series. 3rd rev. ed. M. A. Eckels. (Illus.). 200p. (Orig.). 1997. pap. text 9.95 (*0-9647790-4-8*) Exerbian Pr.

New Colorado History Vol. 1: Ancient Spirits. India Rolling Waters. (Illus.). 450p. (C). 1996. 30.00 (*1-887786-23-6*) Sky & Sage Bks.

New Colored People: The Mixed-Race Movement in America. Jon M. Spencer. pap. text 18.00 (*0-8147-8072-5*) NYU Pr.

New Colored People: The Mixed-Race Movement in America. Jon M. Spencer. LC 96-45791. 1997. text 25.00 (*0-8147-8071-7*) NYU Pr.

New Columbus. Frederick J. Pohl. (Illus.). 262p. 1986. 16.00 (*0-9611422-4-3*) Security Dupont.

New Combinations & New Taxa of Mosses Proposed by Nils Conrad Kindberg. William C. Steere & Howard A. Crum. LC 66-6394. (Memoirs Ser.: Vol. 28, No. 2). 220p. 1977. pap. 15.00 (*0-89327-005-9*) NY Botanical.

*__New Combinatorial Foundation of Homology & Homotopy: Applications to Spaces, Diagrams, Transformation Groups, Compactifications, Differential Algebras, Algebraic Theories, Simplicial Objects & Resolutions: Applications to Spaces, Diagrams, Transformation Groups, Compactifications, Differential Algebras, Algebraic Theories, Simplicial Objects & Resolutions__ Hans J. Baues. LC 98-45574. (Springer Monographs In Mathematics). xv, 362 p. 1998. 99.00 (*3-540-64984-0*) Spr-Verlag.

New Combined Bible Dictionary & Concordance. New Combined Bible Dictionary & Concordance Staff. 456p. (YA). (gr. 10). 1973. pap. 6.99 (*0-8010-6680-8*) Baker Bks.

New Combined Language Handbook. Kenny Joseph & Russell Stellwagon. 520p. 1982. pap. 12.50 (*0-933704-30-5*) Dawn Pr.

New Comedy. Aristophanes. 256p. 1993. pap. 15.95 (*0-413-67180-1*, A0681, Methuen Drama) Methn.

New Comers to America, 1400-1650. Stuart A. Kallen. Ed. by Rosemary Walner. LC 90-82616. (Building of a Nation Ser.). (Illus.). 64p. (J). (gr. 4). 1990. lib. bdg. 13.98 (*0-939179-86-5*) ABDO Pub Co.

*__New Comics & Conversation: Using Humor to Elicit Conversation & Develop Vocabulary.__ Ed. & Intro. by Joan Ashkenas. (Illus.). 30p. 1999. pap. 12.95 (*0-943327-24-5*) JAG Pubns.

New Comics Anthology. Ed. by Bob Callahan. (Illus.). 288p. (Orig.). 1991. pap. 19.95 (*0-02-009361-6*) Macmillan.

New Commandment: Toward a Renewed Rite for the Washing of Feet. Peter Jeffery. 79p. (Orig.). 1992. pap. 4.95 (*0-8146-2004-3*) Liturgical Pr.

New Commentary on the Code of Canon Law. Ed. by John P. Beal et al. LC 98-49546. 1984p. 2000. 89.95 (*0-8091-0502-0*) Paulist Pr.

New Commentary on the Poems of W. B. Yeats. 2nd ed. A. Norman Jeffares. LC 83-40105. xl, 543p. 1984. 55.00 (*0-8047-1221-2*) Stanford U Pr.

*__New Commercial Spaces.__ Carles Broto & Arian Mostaedi. (Illus.). 180p. 2000. 69.95 (*3-931884-55-4*, Pub. by Nippon Shuppan) Bks Nippan.

New Commercial Polymers 2. Hans-George Elias & Friedrich Vohwinkel. xvi, 508p. 1986. text 277.00 (*2-88124-078-X*) Gordon & Breach.

New Commonsense Guide to Mutual Funds. rev. ed. Mary Rowland. LC 98-36088. (Bloomberg Press Ser.). (Illus.). 336p. 1998. pap. 15.95 (*1-57660-063-7*, Pub. by Bloomberg NJ) Norton.

New Commonwealth: From Bureaucratic Corporatism to Socialist Capitalism. Claudiu A. Secara. LC 95-95236. 316p. 1995. pap. 12.95 (*0-9646073-1-X*) Algora Pubng.

New Communication Environments: From Everyday to Virtual. Giuseppe Mantovani. 224p. 1996. 79.95 (*0-7484-0395-7*); pap. 34.95 (*0-7484-0396-5*) Taylor & Francis.

New Communication Technologies in Developing Countries. Jarice Hanson & Uma Narula. (Communication Ser.). 184p. 1990. 45.00 (*0-8058-0846-9*) L Erlbaum Assocs.

New Communication Technology & the Public Interest: Comparative Perspectives on Policy & Research. Ed. by Marjorie Ferguson. (Communications in Society Ser.: Vol. 1). 224p. (C). 1986. pap. text 20.95 (*0-8039-9728-0*) Sage.

New Communications. Frederick Williams. 376p. (C). 1984. pap. write for info. (*0-534-02945-0*) Wadsworth Pub.

New Communications. 2nd ed. Frederick Williams. 355p. (C). 1988. pap. write for info. (*0-534-09378-7*) Wadsworth Pub.

New Communications & Information Technologies. 1979. pap. 5.00 (*0-9603466-1-9*) T R A C.

*__New Communications Landscape: Demystifying Media Globalization.__ Georgette Wang et al. LC 99-56814. (Research in Cultural & Media Studies). 312p. 2000. text 90.00 (*0-415-22325-3*) Routledge.

New Communications Technologies. 3rd ed. Michael M. Mirabito & Barbara L. Morgenstern. LC 97-8134. 304p. 1997. pap. text 34.95 (*0-240-80258-6*, Focal) Buttrwrth-Heinemann.

*__New Communications Technologies.__ 4th ed. Michael M. A. Mirabito & Barbara L. Morgenstern. (Illus.). 304p. 2000. pap. 32.95 (*0-240-80429-5*, Focal) Buttrwrth-Heinemann.

New Communism. Peter Pryer. 108p. 1988. 40.00 (*0-7223-2044-2*, Pub. by A H S Ltd) St Mut.

New Communitarian Thinking: Persons, Virtues, Institutions, & Communities. Ed. by Amitai Etzioni. LC 94-30415. (Constitutionalism & Democracy Ser.). 352p. 1995. text 55.00 (*0-8139-1564-3*); pap. text 19.50 (*0-8139-1569-4*) U Pr of Va.

New Communitarians & the Crisis of Modern Liberalism. Bruce Frohnen. 264p. 1996. 29.95 (*0-7006-0762-5*) U Pr of KS.

New Communities for Urban Squatters: Lessons from the Plan That Failed in Dhaka, Bangladesh. C. L. Choguill. (Urban Innovation Abroad Ser.). (Illus.). 228p. (C). 1987. 79.50 (*0-306-42545-9*, Plenum Trade) Perseus Pubng.

New Communities, New Ministries: The Church Resurgent in Africa, Asia, & Latin America. Michel Bavarel. Tr. by Francis Martin from FRE. LC 82-22318. Orig. Title: Chretienes Du Bout Du Monde. 128p. (Orig.). reprint ed. pap. 39.70 (*0-7837-5506-6*, 204527600005) Bks Demand.

New Comp. A-Z Cross Rev. rev. ed. Compiled by Edy G. Schaffer. LC 95-5897. 1328p. 1996. mass mkt. 6.99 (*0-380-72425-1*, Avon Bks) Morrow Avon.

New Comp Amer. Rhym. Co. Sue K. Young. 624p. 1991. pap. 14.00 (*0-380-71392-6*, Avon Bks) Morrow Avon.

New Compact American Dictionary. 1996. pap. 4.99 (*0-02-861534-4*) Macmillan.

New Compact House Designs: 27 Award-Winning Plans, 1,250 Square Feet Or Less. Don Metz. Ed. by Ben Watson. LC 90-50608. (Illus.). 192p. 1991. 27.95 (*0-88266-667-3*); pap. 19.95 (*0-88266-666-5*) Storey Bks.

New Compacts for Canadian Competitiveness. Joseph R. D'Cruz & Alan M. Rugman. (Illus.). 61p. (C). 1993. pap. text 35.00 (*1-56806-690-2*) DIANE Pub.

New Companion to Homer. B. B. Powell & I. Morris. LC 96-38925. (Mnemosyne, Supplements Ser.: Vol. 163). (Illus.). xviii, 755p. 1997. 250.00 (*90-04-09989-1*) Brill Academic Pubs.

New Companion to Scottish Culture. Ed. by David Daiches. 1993. pap. 12.95 (*0-7486-6148-4*, Pub. by Polygon) Subterranean Co.

*__New Companion to the Literature of Wales.__ Ed. & Composed by Meic Stephens. 841p. 1999. 12.95 (*0-7083-1383-3*, Pub. by Univ Wales Pr) Paul & Co Pubs.

New Comparative Grammar of Greek & Latin. Andrew L. Sihler. LC 93-38929. 720p. 1995. text 60.00 (*0-19-508345-8*) OUP.

New Comparative Syntax. LC 96-39472. (Longman Linguistics Library). 1998. text 69.12 (*0-582-27942-9*) Longman.

New Comparative World Atlas. (Illus.). 96p. 1998. 14.95 (*0-8437-7101-1*, 7101-1) Hammond World.

New Comparative World Atlas. Hammond Incorporated, Staff. (gr. 5 up). 1999. pap. text 10.95 (*0-8437-7100-3*) Hammond World.

New Compass Points: 20th Century Saco (Maine) Roy P. Fairfield. 256p. 1988. 19.95 (*0-9621921-0-4*) Bastille Bks.

New Compendium of Materials Medica (Pharmaceutical Botany & China Medicinal Plants) Ling Yeouruenn. 292p. 1996. 69.00 (*7-03-003789-8*, Pub. by Sci Pr) Lubrecht & Cramer.

*__New Competencies for Volunteer Administrators.__ 15p. 1999. pap. write for info. (*1-58534-029-4*) Points of Light.

New Competition: An Examination of the Conditions Underlying the Radical Change That is Taking Place in the Commercial & Industrial World. Arthur J. Eddy. (Business Enterprises Reprint Ser.). 379p. 1986. reprint ed. lib. bdg. 45.00 (*0-89941-504-0*, 304370) W S Hein.

New Competition: Institutions of Industrial Restructuring. Michael H. Best. LC 90-34371. (Illus.). 304p. 1990. 42.50 (*0-674-60925-5*) HUP.

New Competition: Institutions of Industrial Restructuring. Michael H. Best. (Illus.). 320p. (C). 1993. pap. 21.50 (*0-674-60926-3*) HUP.

New Competitor: Playscript. William-Alan Landes. LC 91-58033. 24p. (Orig.). 1991. pap. 5.00 (*0-88734-121-7*) Players Pr.

New Competitor Intelligence: The Complete Resource for Finding, Analyzing, & Using Information about Your Competitors. 2nd ed. Leonard M. Fuld. LC 94-18292. 512p. 1994. 80.50 (*0-471-58508-4*); pap. 39.95 (*0-471-58509-2*) Wiley.

New Compl. Joy Home Brew. 2nd ed. Charlie Papazian. 416p. 1991. pap. 12.50 (*0-380-76366-4*, Avon Bks) Morrow Avon.

New Complete Afgan Hound. 4th rev. ed. Constance O. Miller & Edward M. Gilbert, Jr. (Illus.). 288p. 1988. pap. 25.95 (*0-87605-001-1*) Howell Bks.

New Complete Akita. Joan M. Linderman & Virginia Funk. (Illus.). 256p. 1994. 25.95 (*0-87605-031-3*) Howell Bks.

New Complete Alaskan Malamute. 2nd ed. Maxwell Riddle & Beth J. Harris. (Illus.). 256p. 1990. 25.95 (*0-87605-008-9*) Howell Bks.

New Complete Babysitter's Handbook. Carol Barkin & Elizabeth James. LC 93-39345. (Illus.). 160p. (J). (gr. 4-8). 1995. 16.95 (*0-395-66557-4*, Clarion Bks); pap. 7.95 (*0-395-66558-2*, Clarion Bks) HM.

New Complete Bloodhound. 2nd rev. ed. Catherine F. Brey & Lena F. Reed. (Illus.). 256p. 1992. 27.95 (*0-87605-077-1*) Howell Bks.

New Complete Book of Bread Machine Baking. Lara Pizzorno. LC 97-29131. 224p. 2000. pap. 12.95 (*0-7615-1125-3*) Prima Pub.

New Complete Book of Bridge. Albert Dormer. 480p. 1996. 29.95 (*0-575-06084-0*, Pub. by V Gollancz) Trafalgar.

New Complete Book of Collectible Cars, 1930-90. R. M. Langworth. 576p. 1989. 19.98 (*1-56173-303-2*) Pubns Intl Ltd.

New Complete Book of Food: A Nutritional, Medical, & Culinary. Carol A. Ringler. LC 99-21200. 448p. 1999. pap. 19.95 (*0-8160-3988-7*, Checkmark) Facts on File.

New Complete Book of Food: A Nutritional, Medical & Culinary Guide. Carol A. Rinzler. LC 99-21200. 464p. 1999. 40.00 (*0-8160-3987-9*, Checkmark) Facts on File.

***New Complete Book of Herbs & Spices.** Carol Ann Rinzler. LC 00-32164. (Illus.). 2001. write for info. (*0-8160-4152-0*) Facts on File.

***New Complete Book of Mexican Cooking,** rev. ed. Elisabeth Lambert Ortiz. 352p. 2000. 30.00 (*0-06-019599-1*) HarpC.

New Complete Brittany. 2nd ed. Maxwell Riddle. LC 87-3891. (Illus.). 304p. 1987. 25.95 (*0-87605-090-9*) Howell Bks.

New Complete Chesapeake Bay Retriever. Janet Horn & Daniel Horn. (Illus.). 256p. 1994. 27.95 (*0-87605-099-2*) Howell Bks.

New Complete Chinese Shar Pei. 1999. 25.00 (*0-87605-123-9*) Howell Bks.

New Complete Chow Chow. 1997. 25.95 (*0-87605-092-5*) Howell Bks.

New Complete Do-It-Yourself Manual. Reader's Digest Editors. LC 90-46830. (Reader's Digest Ser.). (Illus.). 528p. 1991. 30.00 (*0-89577-378-3*, Pub. by RD Assn) Penguin Putnam.

New Complete English Setter. 4th ed. Davis H. Tuck et al. LC 81-20267. (Illus.). 376p. 1981. 29.95 (*0-87605-116-6*) Howell Bks.

New Complete English Springer Spaniel. Julia F. Gasow et al. (Illus.). 288p. 1994. 25.00 (*0-87605-119-0*) Howell Bks.

New Complete German Shepherd Dog. 5th rev. ed. Janet G. Bennett. LC 82-1031. (Illus.). 256p. 1982. 25.95 (*0-87605-151-4*) Howell Bks.

New Complete Golden Retriever. 2nd ed. Gertrude Fischer. LC 84-700. (Complete Breed Bk.). (Illus.). 304p. 1984. 25.95 (*0-87605-185-9*) Howell Bks.

New Complete Great Pyrenees. 2nd ed. Paul Strang. (Illus.). 256p. 1991. 25.95 (*0-87605-188-3*) Howell Bks.

New Complete Guide to Beekeeping. Roger A. Morse. LC 94-3657. (Illus.). 208p. 1994. pap. 17.00 (*0-88150-315-0*, Pub. by Countryman) Norton.

New Complete Guide to Gardening. 2nd ed. Susan A. Roth. Ed. by Cathy Barash. LC 97-71339. (Better Homes & Gardens Ser.). (Illus.). 600p. 1997. 34.95 (*0-696-02573-6*, Better Homes) Meredith Bks.

New Complete Guide to Home Repair & Improvement. 2nd ed. Ed. by Ben Allen. LC 97-71323. (Illus.). 600p. 1997. 34.95 (*0-696-20469-X*) Meredith Bks.

New Complete Guide to Wildlife Photography: How to Get Close & Capture Animals on Film. Joe McDonald. LC 98-18559. 160p. 1998. pap. 24.95 (*0-8174-5009-2*, Amphoto) Watsn-Guptill.

New Complete "How to" Guide to Collegiate Licensing. Jack Revoyr. 139p. (Orig.). 1990. pap. 34.95 (*0-9627106-0-1*) Kent Communs.

New Complete Hoyle: The Authoritative Guide to the Official Rules of All Popular Games of Skill. Albert L. Morehead. 720p. 1991. 27.00 (*0-385-24962-4*) Doubleday.

New Complete Illustrated Guide for Architecture. Larry Evans. (Architecture Ser.). (Illus.). 384p. 1996. pap. 44.95 (*0-442-02239-5*, VNR) Wiley.

New Complete Illustration Guide: The Ultimate Trace File for Architects, Designers, Artists & Students. 4th rev. ed. Larry Evans. (Illus.). 352p. 1996. pap. 49.95 (*0-471-28754-7*, VNR) Wiley.

New Complete International Jewish Cookbook. Evelyn Rose. 736p. 1996. pap. 14.98 (*0-88365-955-7*) Galahad Bks.

New Complete International Jewish Cookbook. Evelyn Rose. 700p. 1998. pap. 24.95 (*1-86105-143-3*, Pub. by Robson Bks) Parkwest Pubns.

New Complete Irish Wolfhound. Joel Samaha. (Illus.). 256p. 1991. 27.95 (*0-87605-171-9*) Howell Bks.

New Complete Italian Greyhound. Ed. by Lilian S. Barber et al. (Illus.). 1993. 21.95 (*0-9611986-2-1*) Ital Greyhnd.

New Complete Job Search. Richard H. Beatty. LC 91-41389. 320p. 1992. pap. 12.95 (*0-471-53494-3*) Wiley.

New Complete Junior Showmanship Handbook: A Complete Book of Instruction on How to Begin, How to Handle & How to Win in Junior Showmanship Classes at Dog Shows. 2nd ed. Bethny H. Mason & Marsha H. Brown. LC 79-25829. (Illus.). 160p. 1980. pap. 16.00 (*0-87605-655-9*) Howell Bks.

New Complete Keeshond. 2nd ed. Ron Cash & Carol Cash. LC 87-3881. (Illus.). 304p. 1987. pap. 25.95 (*0-87605-199-9*) Howell Bks.

New Complete Labrador Retriever. 3rd ed. Helen Warwick. LC 85-27512. (Illus.). 324p. 1986. 27.95 (*0-87605-230-8*) Howell Bks.

New Complete Lhasa Apso. Carolyn Herbel & Norman Herbel. (Illus.). 304p. 1992. 25.95 (*0-87605-233-2*) Howell Bks.

***New Complete Medical & Health Encyclopedia.** Richard J. Wagman & J. G. Ferguson Publishing Company Staff. LC 99-35692. 2000. write for info. (*0-89434-306-8*) Ferguson.

New Complete Mountain Biker. Dennis Coello. LC 96-42439. (Illus.). 240p. 1996. pap. 18.95 (*1-55821-495-X*) Lyons Pr.

New Complete Pembroke Welsh Corgi. Deborah S. Harper. (Illus.). 288p. 1994. 27.95 (*0-87605-249-9*) Howell Bks.

New Complete Poodle Clipping & Grooming Book. Shirlee Kalstone. (Illus.). 192p. 1998. 29.95 (*0-87605-265-0*) Howell Bks.

New Complete Portuguese Water Dog. 2nd ed. Kathryn Braund. (Illus.). 304p. 1997. 27.95 (*0-87605-261-8*) Howell Bks.

New Complete Server. Christopher Heller. LC 96-191602. (Illus.). 63p. 1996. pap. 6.95 (*0-8192-1649-6*) Morehouse Pub.

New Complete Shetland Sheepdog. 2nd ed. Maxwell Riddle. (Illus.). 256p. 1992. 25.95 (*0-87605-333-9*) Howell Bks.

New Complete Siberian Husky. 2nd ed. Michael Jennings. (Illus.). 256p. 1992. 27.95 (*0-87605-339-8*) Howell Bks.

New Complete Van Gogh: Painting, Drawings, Sketches. enl. rev. ed. Jan Hulsker. LC 96-45071. Orig. Title: Catalogue Raisonne. (Illus.). 504p. 1996. lib. bdg. 145.00 (*1-55619-513-3*) J Benjamins Pubng Co.

New Complete Wedding Songbook. (Easy Piano Ser.). 144p. 1985. per. 12.95 (*0-7935-1988-8*, 00364397) H Leonard.

New Complete Works of Josephus. Flavius Josephus. LC 99-18852. 1998. 24.99 (*0-8254-2924-2*) Kregel.

New Complete Works of Josephus, 1. Flavius Josephus. Tr. by William Whiston from GEC. LC 99-18852. 1998. pap. 19.99 (*0-8254-2948-X*) Kregel.

New Complete Yorkshire Terrier. rev. ed. Joan B. Gordon. LC 92-41046. (Illus.). 288p. 1993. 27.95 (*0-87605-361-4*) Howell Bks.

New Comprehensive A-Z Crossword Dictionary. Ed. by Edy G. Schaffer. 1088p. 1976. reprint ed. mass mkt. 4.99 (*0-380-00168-3*, Avon Bks) Morrow Avon.

New Comprehensive A-Z Crossword Dictionary. rev. ed. Ed. by Edy G. Schaffer. 832p. 1995. 21.95 (*0-399-14097-2*, G P Putnam) Peng Put Young Read.

New Comprehensive Russian-Chinese Dictionary of Science & Technology. Science Press Staff. (CHI & RUS.). 1320p. 1986. 95.00 (*0-8288-6945-6*) Fr & Eur.

New Comprehensive Shilo Pocket Dictionary. Zevi Scharfstein. 768p. 1973. pap. 6.75 (*0-88328-012-4*) Shilo Pub Hse.

New Computer Methods for Global Optimization. J. Rokne et al. 200p. 1988. text 52.95 (*0-470-21208-X*) P-H.

New Computer User. 2nd ed. Sullivan. (C). 1996. teacher ed. 29.75 (*0-03-019324-9*) Harcourt Coll Pubs.

New Computer User. 2nd ed. Sullivan. (C). 1996. pap. text 33.50 (*0-03-019199-8*) Harcourt.

New Computer User. 2nd ed. David Sullivan. LC 96-85285. 352p. (C). 1996. pap. text 53.00 (*0-03-018957-8*) Dryden Pr.

New Computing Environments: Microcomputers in Large-Scale Scientific Computing. Ed. by Arthur Wouk. LC 87-60442. (Proceedings in Applied Mathematics Ser.: No. 27). xii, 166p. 1987. 39.75 (*0-89871-210-6*) Soc Indus-Appl Math.

New Computing Environments: Parallel, Vector & Systolic. Ed. by Arthur Wouk. LC 85-63165. (Proceedings in Applied Mathematics Ser.: No. 22). vi, 270p. 1986. text 36.00 (*0-89871-201-7*) Soc Indus-Appl Math.

New Computing Techniques in Physics Research III: Proceedings of the 3rd International Workshop on Software Engineering. K-H. Becks & D. Perret-Gallix. 684p. 1994. text 150.00 (*981-02-1699-8*) World Scientific Pub.

New Computing Techniques in Physics 2. D. Perret-Gallix. 804p. 1992. text 178.00 (*981-02-1122-8*) World Scientific Pub.

New-Concept Development: A Planning Approach for the 21st Century Air Force. Leslie Lewis et al. LC 96-50342. (Illus.). 75p. 1997. pap. 13.00 (*0-8330-2478-7*, MR-815-AF) Rand Corp.

New Concept for Streamlining Up-Front Planning. Glenn A. Kent & David E. Thaler. LC 93-25349. 1993. pap. 13.00 (*0-8330-1415-3*, MR-271-AF) Rand Corp.

New Concept of Art & Popular Culture in Nicaragua since the Revolution in 1979: An Analytical Essay & Compendium of Illustrations. David Craven. LC 88-9350. (Latin American Studies: Vol. 1). (Illus.). 450p. 1988. lib. bdg. 109.95 (*0-88946-489-8*) E Mellen.

New Concept of Cooperative Security. Ashton B. Carter et al. LC 92-74426. 65p. (C). 1993. pap. 8.95 (*0-8157-8145-8*) Brookings.

New Concept of Liberty. Theodore A. Schroeder. 1973. 59.95 (*0-8490-0720-8*) Gordon Pr.

New Concept of Self-Defense. Gong Chen. LC 98-148285. 144p. (C). 1998. per. 38.95 (*0-7872-4350-7*, 41435001) Kendall-Hunt.

New Concept of the Universe: A Brief Treatise on the Russell Cosmogony. Walter Russell. (Illus.). 178p. 1989. reprint ed. pap. text 15.00 (*1-879605-13-9*) U Sci & Philos.

New Conceptions. Perkins. (Educational Psychology Ser.: Vol. 28, No. 1). 1993. 20.00 (*0-8058-9992-8*) L Erlbaum Assocs.

New Conceptions of Matter. Charles Darwin. (Select Bibliographies Reprint Ser.). 1977. reprint ed. 23.95 (*0-8369-6610-4*) Ayer.

New Concepts for Coating Protection of Steel Structures - STP 841. Ed. by Berger & Wint. 135p. 1985. 28.00 (*0-8031-0236-4*, STP841) ASTM.

New Concepts for New Challenges: Professional Development for Teachers of Immigrant Youth. Josue M. Gonzalez & Linda Darling-Hammond. LC 97-27403. (Topics in Immigrant Education Ser.). 1997. pap. write for info. (*1-887744-04-5*) Delta Systems.

New Concepts for Sustainable Management of River Basins. P. H. Nienhuis. Ed. by R. S. Leuven & A. M. Ragas. (Illus.). 400p. 1998. pap. 111.00 (*90-73348-81-1*) Balogh.

***New Concepts for Topical Use of Natural Retinoids: Retinaldehyde in Perspective, Satellite Symposium Held at the 7th EADV Meeting, Nice, October 1998: Proceedings.** Ed. by J. H. Saurat & A. Vahlquist. (Dermatology Ser.: Vol. 199, Suppl. 1). (Illus.). iv, 64p. 1999. pap. 25.25 (*3-8055-6914-9*) S Karger.

New Concepts in AIDS Pathogenesis. Luc Montagnier & Marie-Lise Gougeon. LC 93-4765. (Illus.). 344p. 1993. text 145.00 (*0-8247-9127-4*) Dekker.

New Concepts in Anxiety. M. Briley. Ed. by S. E. File. 1991. 107.00 (*0-8493-7105-8*, QP) CRC Pr.

New Concepts in Blood Formation Cell Generation in Malignant & Benign Tissues: Adult & Embryonic Tissues from Humans & Animals in Chronic Ischemic Conditions, Acute Rhuematic Fever & Coronary Occlusion with Myocardial Infarction. Hemprova G. McDonald. LC 89-90849. (Cardiac Muscle Ser.: Vol. II). (Illus.). 117p. (C). 1995. 90.00 (*0-9627824-1-6*) Diagnostic & Cell.

New Concepts in Dehydrated Food Cookery: Hundreds of New Ideas & Tested Recipes for Enjoying Home Dehydrated Foods. Barbara Densley. LC 79-89357. 191p. 1979. pap. 13.98 (*0-88290-126-5*) Horizon Utah.

***New Concepts in Diabetes & Its Treatment.** Ed. by F. Belfiore & C. E. Mogensen. (Illus.). 2000. 172.25 (*3-8055-6907-6*) S Karger.

New Concepts in Diagnosis & Treatment: Physico Clinical Medicine. Albert Abrams. 414p. 1996. reprint ed. spiral bd. 27.50 (*0-7873-0017-9*) Hlth Research.

New Concepts in Diesel Engine Design, Components, & Technology. 1996. 44.00 (*1-56091-848-9*, SP-1196) Soc Auto Engineers.

New Concepts in Global Tectonics. Sankar Chatterjee & Nicholas Hotton, III. 480p. 1992. 65.00 (*0-89672-269-4*) Tex Tech Univ Pr.

***New Concepts in House Interiors.** Francisco Asensio Cerver. (Illus.). 2000. pap. 24.95 (*84-8185-226-0*) Arco Edit.

***New Concepts in Immunopathology of CNS Infections.** Phillip K. Peterson & Jack S. Remington. (Illus.). 400p. 2000. 99.95 (*0-632-04528-0*) Blackwell Sci.

New Concepts in International Automotive Lighting Technology. 1997. 94.00 (*1-56091-961-2*, SP-1249) Soc Auto Engineers.

New Concepts in Linear Improvisation. Ed. by Larry Clark. (Orig.). (C). 1996. pap. text 24.95 (*1-57623-757-5*, SB32CD) Wrner Bros.

New Concepts in Lipid Research in Honor of Stina & Einar Stenhagen, Vol. 16. Ed. by Ralph T. Holman. (Progress in the Chemistry of Fats & Other Lipids Ser.). 1978. 86.00 (*0-08-022663-9*, Pergamon Pr) Elsevier.

New Concepts in Multi-User Communication. J. K. Skwirzynski. 1981. text 282.00 (*90-286-2771-5*) Kluwer Academic.

New Concepts in Natural Language Generation: Planning, Realization & Systems. Ed. by Helmut Horacek & Michael Zock. 256p. 1993. text 69.00 (*1-85567-084-4*, Pub. by P P Pubs) Cassell & Continuum.

New Concepts in Stroke Pathophysiology & Prevention. Ed. by N. M. Bornstein & A. G. Turpie. (Journal: Cerebrovascular Diseases Ser.: Vol. 4, Suppl. 1, 1994). (Illus.). iv, 48p. 1994. pap. 22.75 (*3-8055-5966-6*) S Karger.

New Concepts in Surgical Correction of Dentofacial Deformities, Vol. 3. William H. Bell. (Illus.). 850p. 1985. text 235.00 (*0-7216-1739-5*, W B Saunders Co) Harcrt Hlth Sci Grp.

New Concepts in the Pathogenesis of NIDDM. C. G. Ostenson et al. LC 93-29031. (Advances in Experimental Medicine & Biology Ser.: Vol. 334). (Illus.). 326p. (C). 1993. text 89.50 (*0-306-44563-8*, Kluwer Plenum) Kluwer Academic.

New Concepts in Transmissions & Controls. 1997. pap. 31.00 (*0-7680-0054-8*) Soc Auto Engineers.

New Concepts in Underground Storage of Natural Gas. American Gas Association Research Committee et al. 342p. 1966. 7.50 (*0-318-12657-5*, L00400) Am Gas Assn.

New Concepts of a Blood-Brain Barrier: Proceedings of a Symposium in Honor of Michael Bradbury Held in London, England, July 4-6, 1994. Ed. by John Greenwood et al. (Illus.). 344p. 1996. 95.00 (*0-306-45204-9*, Kluwer Plenum) Kluwer Academic.

New Concepts of Hypnosis. Bernard C. Gindes. 1974. pap. 15.00 (*0-87980-108-5*) Wilshire.

New Conceptual Aspects of Negative Symptoms: Journal: Psychopathology, 1995, Vol. 28, No. 1. Ed. by H. Gerbaldo & C. Mundt. (Illus.). 64p. 1994. pap. 46.25 (*3-8055-6105-9*) S Karger.

New Conceptual Selling: The Most Effective & Proven Method for Face-to-Face Sales Planning. rev. ed. Stephen E. Heiman et al. LC 99-26832. 1999. mass mkt. 14.99 (*0-446-67449-4*, Pub. by Warner Bks) Little.

New Conceptualism of the Uniform Commercial Code. Donald B. King. 126p. 1968. pap. 20.00 (*0-8377-0726-9*, Rothman) W S Hein.

New Concerete Technologies & Building Design. Ed. by A. M. Nevill & M. Chatterton. LC TA0439.N58. 134p. reprint ed. pap. 41.60 (*0-608-30927-3*, 202098300020) Bks Demand.

New Concise Bible Dictionary. Ed. by Derek Williams. 644p. 1995. reprint ed. pap. 12.99 (*0-8308-1445-0*, 1445) InterVarsity.

New Concise Dictionary of Law for Beginners. Jean M. De LaFayette. Ed. by Oya Akoneck. 226p. 1990. 30.00 (*0-939877-44-9*) ACUPAE.

New Concise English-Japanese-English Computer Dictionary. 2nd ed. Commercial Press Staff. (ENG & JPN.). 254p. 1985. 95.00 (*0-8288-0251-3*, F16070) Fr & Eur.

New Concise Guide to Homeopathy: An Introduction to the Understanding & Use of Homeopathy. Nigel Garion-Hutchings. 1995. pap. 10.95 (*1-85230-634-3*, Pub. by Element MA) Penguin Putnam.

New Concise Handbook. Hans P. Guth. 365p. (C). 1985. pap. write for info. (*0-534-05178-2*) Wadsworth Pub.

New Concise Workbook. Guth. (Illus.). 1984. 11.75 (*0-534-03195-1*) Brooks-Cole.

New Concise Xhosa-English Dictionary. J. McLaren. 193p. 1994. pap. 35.00 (*0-7859-8718-5*) Fr & Eur.

New Concordance of Cranial Chronic Pain. Gelb. 1994. text 155.00 (*0-7234-2041-6*) Wolfe Pubng AZ.

New Concordance of the Bible: Thesaurus of the Language of the Bible - Hebrew & Aramaic - Roots, Words, Proper Names, Phrases & Synonyms. Ed. by Abraham Even-Shoshen. 1244p. 1988. 75.00 (*0-87559-225-2*) Shalom.

New Concordance of the Old Testament: Using the Hebrew & Aramaic Text. 2nd ed. Ed. by Abraham Even-Shoshan. 1255p. 1989. 125.00 (*0-8010-3417-5*) Baker Bks.

New Concordance to the Book of Mormon. rev. ed. Hale Collins & Barbara Collins. 1995. pap. text 25.00 (*0-8309-0637-1*) Herald Pub Hse.

New Concordance to the Doctrine & Covenants. rev. ed. Ed. by Barbara L. Collins. 455p. 1992. pap. text 15.00 (*0-8309-0623-1*) Herald Pub Hse.

New Concrete Technology. 276p. 1993. 59.25 (*0-685-72319-4*, SP-141BOW6) ACI.

New Conference Models for the Information Age. Coleman Lee Finkel. LC 98-28396. (Illus.). x, 211p. 1998. pap. 29.95 (*0-88034-146-7*) Am Soc Assn Execs.

New Confession. William Boyd. 1999. pap. 15.00 (*0-375-70503-1*) Vin Bks.

New Confessors of Russia Vol. I: Nizhny-Novgorod Province. Archimandrite D. Orlovsky. LC 98-86309. (Illus.). 430p. 1998. pap. 19.00 (*1-887904-34-4*) St Herman Pr.

New Conflict Cookbook: A Parent/Teacher Guide for Helping Young People Deal with Anger & Conflict. Thomas Crum et al. Date not set. 15.00 (*1-877803-11-1*) Aiki Works.

New Conformal Absorbing Boundary Condition for Finite Element Meshes & Parallelization of FEMATS. fac. ed. A. Chatterjee et al. LC QC0020.7. (University of Michigan Report: No. 031155-1-T). 72p. 1993. pap. 30.00 (*0-7837-7694-2*, 204745100007) Bks Demand.

New Connecticut. A. Bronson Alcott. 1970. reprint ed. 15.00 (*0-87556-007-5*) Saifer.

New Connecticut. Amos B. Alcott. (Works of Amos Bronson Alcott). 1989. reprint ed. lib. bdg. 79.00 (*0-685-27407-1*) Rprt Serv.

New Connection: A Problem Solving Approach to Chemical Dependency. rev. ed. John Frykman. LC 74-156775. 151p. 1992. pap. 11.95 (*0-916147-04-5*) Regent Pr.

New Connection: Reforming the United Methodist Church. William H. Willimon & Andy Langford. 128p. (Orig.). 1996. pap. 9.95 (*0-687-01542-1*) Abingdon.

New Connections: African American Newcomers & Visitors to the Twin Cities Guide. Black Relocation Assn., Inc. Staff. (Illus.). 108p. (Orig.). 1997. pap. 6.95 (*0-9652905-1-4*) Blck Relocat.

New Connections: African American Newcomers & Visitors to the Twin Cities Guide. Black Relocation Association, Inc., Staff. (Illus.). 108p. (Orig.). 1996. pap. 6.95 (*0-9652905-0-6*) Blck Relocat.

New Connections: Integrated Approach to Literacy. 2nd ed. (C). 1997. 24.00 (*0-673-97903-2*, GoodYrBooks) Addson-Wesley Educ.

New Connoisseurs' Handbook of California Wines. 3rd ed. Norman S. Roby & Charles E. Olken. LC 95-21554. 448p. 1995. 27.50 (*0-679-44486-6*) Knopf.

New Conscience & an Ancient Evil. Jane Addams. LC 76-169367. (Family in America Ser.). 236p. 1977. reprint ed. 24.95 (*0-405-03843-7*) Ayer.

New Conscientious Objection: From Sacred to Secular Resistance. Ed. by Charles C. Moskos, II & John W. Chambers. LC 92-20615. (Illus.). 296p. 1993. pap. text 29.95 (*0-19-507955-8*) OUP.

N

An Asterisk (*) at the beginning of an entry indicates that the title is appearing for the first time.

Concise Dictionary of American Literary Biography: The New Consciousness, 1941-1968. Ed. by Matthew J. Bruccoli. (Concise Dictionary of American Literary Biography Ser.). 539p. 1987. 80.00 (*0-8103-1822-9*) Gale.

New Conservatism: Cultural Criticism & the Historians' Debate. Jurgen Habermas. Ed. & Tr. by Shierry W. Nicholsen. (Studies in Contemporary German Social Thought). 308p. 1989. 35.00 (*0-262-08188-1*) MIT Pr.

New Conservatism: Cultural Criticism & the Historians' Debate. Jurgen Habermas. (Studies in Contemporary German Social Thought). (Illus.). 380p. 1991. pap. text 19.00 (*0-262-58107-8*) MIT Pr.

New Constantines: The Rhythm of Imperial Renewal in Byzantium, 4th-13th Centuries. Ed. by Paul Magdalino. LC 94-5125. (Publications - Society for the Promotion of Byzantine Studies: Vol. 2). 324p. 1994. text 77.95 (*0-86078-409-6*, Pub. by Variorum) Ashgate Pub Co.

New Constellation. Intro. by Gerald R. Ford. LC 76-57294. (Illus.). 32p. 1977. 4.95 (*0-934021-10-4*) Natl Flag Foun.

New Constellation: The Ethical-Political Horizons of Modernity - Postmodernity. Richard J. Bernstein. (Illus.). 360p. 1992. pap. text 22.00 (*0-262-52166-0*) MIT Pr.

New Constellation, 1771-1848. Ed. by Angelus Press Editors. LC 98-124513. (Puritans' Progress Ser.: Vol. 2). 201p. 1996. pap. 7.95 (*0-935952-35-7*) Angelus Pr.

***New Constitution Now.** Henry Hazlitt. xiii, 297p. 2000. 93.00 (*1-56169-581-5*) Gaunt.

New Constitution of India: Being Three Rhodes Lectures. Courtenay Ilbert & Dougall Meston. 212p. 1999. reprint ed. 75.00 (*1-56169-515-7*) Gaunt.

New Constitution of the RCP, U. S. A. see Leadership

New Constitutionalism: Designing Political Institutions for a Good Society. Ed. by Stephen L. Elkin & Karol E. Soltan. LC 92-38703. 250p. (C). 1993. pap. text 15.95 (*0-226-20464-2*) U Ch Pr.

New Constitutionalism: Designing Political Institutions for a Good Society. Ed. by Stephen L. Elkin & Karol E. Soltan. LC 92-38703. 246p. (C). 1993. lib. bdg. 45.00 (*0-226-20463-4*) U Ch Pr.

***New Construction of Homogeneous Quaternionic Manifolds & Related Geometric Structures.** Vicente Cortbes. LC 00-34993. (Memoirs Ser.). 2000. write for info. (*0-8218-2111-3*) Am Math.

New Construction of Single-Family Housing for Infill: A Complete Overview of the Skills & Finance Needed to Run a Successful Program see Program Operations Series

***New Constructions in Cellular Automata.** David Griffeath & Cristopher Moore. (Santa Fe Institute Studies on the Sciences of Complexity). (Illus.). 320p. 2001. text 65.00 (*0-19-513717-5*); pap. text 39.95 (*0-19-513718-3*) OUP.

New Constructions of Functions Holomorphic in the Unit: Ball of C to the N Power. W. Rudin. LC 86-1205. (CBMS Regional Conference Series in Mathematics: No. 63). 78p. 1986. pap. 19.00 (*0-8218-0713-7*, CBMS/63) Am Math.

New Consumer Credit Code. J. Owens et al. LC 94-238078. 260p. 1994. pap. write for info. (*0-409-31089-1*, MICHIE) LEXIS Pub.

New Contents, New Teachers, New Publics. Ed. by Warren C. Born & Thomas H. Geno. 1978. pap. 10.95 (*0-915432-78-1*) NE Conf Teach Foreign.

New Context of World Mission. Bryant L. Myers. LC 97-173725. 60p. 1996. pap. 8.95 (*1-887983-00-7*) MARC.

New Contexts of Canadian Criticism. Ed. by Ajay Heble et al. LC 96-932119. 300p. 1997. pap. 22.95 (*1-55111-106-3*) Broadview Pr.

New Continent Bible Commentary: Acts I see Comentario Biblico Continente Nuevo: Hechos I

New Continent Bible Commentary: Acts II see Comentario Biblico Continente Nuevo: Hechos II

New Continent Bible Commentary: Ephesians see Comentario Biblico Continente Nuevo: Efesios

New Continent Bible Commentary: Ephesians see Commentario Biblico del Continente Nuevo: Efesios

New Continent Bible Commentary: Ephesians see Comentario Biblico Continente Nuevo: Efesios

New Continent Bible Commentary: I Corinthians see Comentario Biblico Continente Nuevo: 1 Corintios

New Continent Bible Commentary: I Corinthians see Comentario Biblico Continente Nuevo: I Corintios

New Continent Bible Commentary: I/II Timothy/Titus see Comentario Biblico Continente Nuevo: Timoteo 1-2, Tito

New Continent Bible Commentary: John see Comentario Biblico Continente Nuevo: Juan

New Continent Bible Commentary: John 1 see Comentario Biblico del Continente Nuevo: Juan 1

New Continent Bible Commentary: John 2 see Comentario Biblico del Continente Nuevo: Juan 2

New Continent Bible Commentary: Marcos see Comentario Biblico del Continente Nuevo: Marcos

New Continent Bible Commentary: Mark see Comentario Biblico Continente Nuevo: Marcos

New Continent Bible Commentary: Matthew see Comentario Biblico Continente Nuevo: Mateo

New Continent Bible Commentary: Philippians see Comentario Biblico Continente Nuevo: Filipenses

New Continent Commentary: Romans see Comentario Biblico Continente Nuevo: Romanos

New Continuous Improvement Tools Handbook. Council for Continuous Improvement Staff. (Illus.). 58p. 1994. pap. text 11.95 (*0-527-76234-2*, 762342) Productivity Inc.

New Contractualism? Glyn Davis et al. LC 98-172799. 270p. 1998. pap. 32.95 (*0-7329-4442-2*, Pub. by Macmill Educ) Paul & Co Pubs.

***New Contributions to Transportation Analysis in Europe.** Ed. by Michel Beuthe & Peter Nijkamp. LC 99-72600. 360p. 1999. 78.95 (*0-7546-1082-9*, Pub. by Ashgate Pub) Ashgate Pub Co.

New Convenant of Peace on Earth 2000 A.D. God's Convenant with the 12 Nations of Israel. Kenna E. Farris. 1996. write for info. (*0-614-14701-8*) Port Love Intl.

New Convenience Foods. 143p. 1992. 2250.00 (*0-89336-879-2*, GA-076) BCC.

New Conventional Weapons & East-West Security. Christopher Bertram. LC 78-78216. (Praeger Special Studies). 97p. 1979. 55.00 (*0-275-90331-1*, C0331, Praeger Pubs) Greenwood.

New Conventional Weapons & Western Defense. Ian Bellany & Tim Huxley. 1987. 35.00 (*0-7146-3310-0*, Pub. by F Cass Pubs) Intl Spec Bk.

***New Conversation: Essays on the Future of Theology & the Episcopal Church.** Robert B. Slocum. LC 99-32379. 1999. write for info. (*0-89869-306-3*) Church Pub Inc.

New Converts to the American Dream? Mobility Aspirations of Young Mexican Americans. Celia S. Heller. 1972. pap. 16.95 (*0-8084-0039-8*) NCUP.

New Cook. Mary Berry & Marlena Spieler. LC 97-11994. 168p. 1997. 24.95 (*0-7894-1996-3*) DK Pub Inc.

New Cook. Donna Hay. (Illus.). 192p. 1997. 19.95 (*0-86411-763-9*) Whitecap Bks.

New Cook Book. 11th ed. Better Homes & Gardens. Ed. by Jennifer Darling. (Illus.). 576p. 1997. boxed set 34.95 (*0-696-20644-7*) Meredith Bks.

New Cook Book. 11th ed. Ed. by Jennifer D. Darling. (Illus.). 544p. 1996. pap. 15.95 (*0-696-20614-5*, Better Homes); ring bd. 26.95 (*0-696-20188-7*, Better Homes) Meredith Bks.

New Cooking of Britain & Ireland: A Culinary Journey in Search of Regional Foods & Innovative Chefs. Gwenda L. Hyman. LC 94-38479. 433p. 1995. pap. 18.95 (*0-471-01279-3*) Wiley.

New Cooks Almost Alone! A Gourmet Survival Manual. Richard T. Calef. (Illus.). 113p. (Orig.). pap. text. write for info. (*0-9634266-0-5*) Calco Pub.

***New Cooks' Catalogue.** Burt Wolf. (Illus.). 576p. 2000. 35.00 (*0-375-40673-5*) Knopf.

***New Cook's Tour of Sonoma: 200 Recipes & the Best of the Region's Food & Wine.** Michele Anna Jordan. 320p. 2000. pap. 21.95 (*1-57061-218-8*) Sasquatch Bks.

New Coptic Texts from the Monastery of Saint Macarius see Monasteries of the Wadi 'n Natrun: Metropolitan Museum of Art Egyptian Expedition Publications

New Core Release for 1998: 1,584 Chemicals. 3548p. 1998. ring bd. 995.00 (*1-56032-725-1*) Hemisp Pub.

New Corinthians Curriculum. Ed. by Judy J. Harris. LC 96-84266. (Illus.). (Orig.). (J). (gr. k-8). 1996. pap. 24.95 (*0-926412-16-7*) Couple to Couple.

New Corporate Bond Market: A Complete & Insightful Analysis of the Latest Trends, Issues. Richard S. Wilson. 1990. 55.00 (*1-55738-128-3*, Irwn Prfssnl) McGraw-Hill Prof.

New Corporate Cultures: Revitalizing the Workplace after Downsizing, Mergers & Reengineering. Terrence E. Deal & Allan A. Kennedy. LC 99-61911. 320p. 1999. text 26.00 (*0-7382-0069-7*, Pub. by Perseus Pubng) HarpC.

***New Corporate Cultures: Revitalizing the Workplace After Downsizing, Mergers & Reengineering.** Allan Kennedy & Terrence Deal. 2000. reprint ed. pap. 16.00 (*0-7382-0380-7*) Perseus Pubng.

New Corporate Finance. 2nd ed. Donald H. Chew, Jr. LC 98-10511. 768p. 1998. pap. 43.44 (*0-07-011675-X*) McGraw.

New Corporate Finance: Where Theory Meets Practice. Donald H. Chew. (C). 1992. text 34.00 (*0-07-011046-8*) McGraw.

New Corporate Performance Measures. Carolyn K. Brancato. (Report / Conference Board Ser.: No. 1118-95-RR). (Illus.). 66p. (Orig.). 1995. pap. text 100.00 (*0-8237-0563-3*) Conference Bd.

New Corporate Strategy. rev. ed. H. Igor Ansoff. LC 87-23266. 288p. 1988. 29.95 (*0-471-62950-2*) Wiley.

New Corporations Law. 2nd ed. Peter Gillies. 750p. 1992. 48.00 (*1-86287-073-X*, Pub. by Federation Pr); pap. 39.95 (*1-86287-072-1*, Pub. by Federation Pr) Gaunt.

New Corpus of Anglo-Saxon Great Square-Headed Brooches. John Hines. LC 98-186777. (Reports of Research Committee: Society of Antiquaries: No. 51). (Illus.). 512p. 1997. 215.00 (*0-85115-679-7*) Boydell & Brewer.

New Cosmetic Science. Ed. by Takeo Mitsui. LC 97-19326. 410p. 1997. 234.50 (*0-444-82654-8*) Elsevier.

***New Cosmic Crystals: The Definitive Guide.** Ronald A. Bonewitz & Lilian Verner-Bonds. 2000. pap. 19.95 (*0-7225-3973-8*, Pub. by Thorsons PA) HarpC.

New Cosmos. Astronomy Magazine Staff. Ed. by Michael Emmerich. LC 92-20538. (Illus.). 160p. (Orig.). 1992. per. 19.95 (*0-913135-15-1*, 18537) Kalmbach.

New Cosmos. 3rd ed. A. Unsold & B. Baschek. Tr. by R. C. Smith et al. (Illus.). 470p. 1985. pap. 44.00 (*0-387-90886-2*) Spr-Verlag.

New Cosmos. 4th rev. ed. A. Unsold & B. Baschek. (Illus.). 460p. 1991. 64.95 (*0-387-52593-9*) Spr-Verlag.

New Cottage Garden. Trevor Nottle. 1998. pap. 14.95 (*0-86417-901-4*, Pub. by Kangaroo Pr) Seven Hills Bk.

New Cottage Home: A Tour of Unique American Dwellings. Jim Tolpin. LC 97-48426. (Illus.). 231p. 1998. 29.95 (*1-56158-229-8*, 070331) Taunton.

***New Cottage Home; A Tour of Unique American Dwellings.** Jim Tolpin. 2000. pap. text 22.95 (*1-56158-355-3*) Taunton.

New Counselor. Diane Muldrow. LC 97-74561. (Super Shape Bks.). (Illus.). 24p. (J). 1998. pap. 3.29 (*0-307-10345-5*, 10345, Goldn Books) Gldn Bks Pub Co.

New Country: Prose & Poetry by the Authors of New Signatures. Ed. by Michael Roberts. LC 78-178457. (Short Story Index Reprint Ser.). 1977. reprint ed. 20.95 (*0-8369-4058-X*) Ayer.

***New Country: Stories from the Yiddish about Life in America.** Henry Goodman. LC 00-34430. (Judaic Traditions in Literature, Music & Art Ser.). 2000. write for info. (*0-8156-0669-9*) Syracuse U Pr.

New Country Music Encyclopedia. Tad Richards. 1993. 25.00 (*0-671-88294-5*) S&S Trade.

New Country Standards. 160p. 1994. per. 12.95 (*0-7935-3748-7*, 00311696) H Leonard.

New Country Western LineDancer's Reference Handbook. Jean Y. Woolman. 90p. 1993. pap. 9.95 (*0-9638125-0-5*) Wild & Wooly.

***New Couple: Why the Old Rules Don't Work & What Does.** Maurice C. Taylor & S. McGee. LC 99-54291. 384p. 2000. 25.00 (*0-06-251633-7*, Pub. by Harper SF) HarpC.

New Course in Algebra: With Answer. Walker. Date not set. pap. text. write for info. (*0-582-31870-X*, Pub. by Addison-Wesley) Longman.

New Course in Arithmetic. Walker. Date not set. pap. text. write for info. (*0-582-31869-6*, Pub. by Addison-Wesley) Longman.

***New Course in Reading Pali: Entering the Word of the Buddha.** James W. Gair & W. S. Karunatillake. 1998. 18.50 (*81-208-1440-1*) Motilal Bnarsidass.

New Course in Reading Peali: Entering the Word of the Buddha. James W. Gair & W. S. Karunatillake. LC 98-902948. xxii, 207 p. 1998. write for info. (*81-208-1441-X*) Motilal Bnarsidass.

New Courts of Industry: Self-Regulation under the Motion Picture Code, Including an Analysis of the Code. Louis Nizer. LC 70-160243. (Moving Pictures Ser.). 344p. 1971. reprint ed. lib. bdg. 41.95 (*0-89198-044-X*) Ozer.

***New Covenant.** Living Stream Ministry Staff. 1999. pap. write for info. (*0-7363-0088-0*) Living Stream Ministry.

New Covenant. Watchman Nee & Witness Lee. 174p. 1981. per. 7.50 (*0-87083-048-1*, 07-007-001) Living Stream Ministry.

New Covenant: Jewish Writers & the American Idea. Sam B. Girgus. LC 83-12458. 234p. reprint ed. pap. 72.60 (*0-7837-7074-X*, 204688600004) Bks Demand.

New Covenant: Poems by Long Island Poets for the Clinton Administration. Ed. by George Wallace. (Illus.). 32p. (Orig.). (C). 1993. pap. text 6.00 (*1-878173-05-7*) Birnham Wood.

New Covenant in Hebrews. Susanne Lehne. (JSNT Supplement Ser.: Vol. 44). 184p. 1990. 57.50 (*1-85075-238-9*, Pub. by Sheffield Acad) CUP Services.

New Covenant of Clinton & Gore. Barela. 1992. pap. 7.95 (*0-9617286-2-0*) Today Bible & You.

New Covenant Passover Haggadah: Remembering the Exodus of Deliverance. Ruth Lascelle. LC 96-80197. (Illus.). 200p. (Orig.). 1997. pap. text 10.00 (*0-9654519-3-3*) Bedrock Pub.

New Covenant Spanish. Watchman Nee. 100p. 1999. per. 6.50 (*0-7363-0064-3*, 07-050-402) Living Stream Ministry.

***New Covenant Unveiled.** David Wilkerson. 2000. 12.00 (*0-9663172-3-8*) Wilkerson Trust.

New Covenant with Nature: Notes on the End of Civilization & the Renewal of Culture. Richard W. Heinberg. 1996. 20.00 (*0-8356-0746-1*, Quest) Theos Pub Hse.

New Cowboy Poetry: A Contemporary Gathering. Ed. & Intro. by Hal Cannon. (Illus.). 176p. (Orig.). 1990. pap. 10.95 (*0-87905-243-0*) Gibbs Smith Pub.

New CRA: What Bankers Need to Know. Francis X. Grady. LC 96-31816. 144p. 1996. 19.95 (*0-7863-1113-4*, Irwn Prfssnl) McGraw-Hill Prof.

New Crafts: Machine Embroidery. Isabel Stanley. (Illus.). 96p. 1996. 14.95 (*1-85967-153-5*, Lorenz Bks) Anness Pub.

New Crafts: Ribbonwork. Christine Kingdom. (Illus.). 96p. 1996. 14.95 (*1-85967-138-1*, Lorenz Bks) Anness Pub.

New Crafts: Wirework. Mary Maguire. (Illus.). 96p. 1996. 15.95 (*1-85967-148-9*, Lorenz Bks) Anness Pub.

New Craftsman Index. Marilyn Fish. (Illus.). (Orig.). 1997. pap. 24.95 (*0-9637896-4-3*) Arts & Crafts.

New Creation. Bill Freeman. 30p. (Orig.). 1992. pap. 1.00 (*0-914271-29-6*) Mnstry Pubns.

New Creation. Phillip G. Goudeaux & Belinda S. Mays. 32p. (Orig.). 1996. pap. 0.25 (*1-889200-00-X*) Calvary Chrstian.

New Creation. Ronald D. Tucker. (Illus.). 34p. (Orig.). 1983. pap. 3.00 (*0-933643-11-X*) Grace Ch-St Louis.

New Creation. Homer G. Rhea. LC 83-62003. 183p. (Orig.). 1997. reprint ed. pap. 9.99 (*0-87148-630-X*) Pathway Pr.

New Creation: America's Contemporary Spiritual Voices. Ed. by Roger S. Gottlieb. 380p. 1990. pap. 18.95 (*0-8245-1042-9*) Crossroad NY.

New Creation: Christian Feminism & the Renewal of the Earth. Catharina J. Halkes. 192p. (Orig.). 1992. pap. 17.95 (*0-664-25288-5*) Westminster John Knox.

***New Creation: Elements of a Liturgical Worldview.** Frank C. Senn. 160p. 2000. pap. 16.00 (*0-8006-3235-4*, Fortress Pr) Augsburg Fortress.

New Creation: John Wesley's Theology Today. Theodore Runyon. LC 97-42936. 288p. 1998. pap. 20.95 (*0-687-09602-2*) Abingdon.

New Creation: Marxist & Christian? Jose M. Gonzalez Ruiz. Tr. by Matthew J. O'Connell. LC 76-10226. 160p. reprint ed. pap. 49.60 (*0-8357-4066-8*, 203675600005) Bks Demand.

New Creation Image. A. L. Gill & Joyce Gill. (KOR.). 165p. 1993. 12.95 (*0-941975-21-5*) Powerhouse.

New Creation Image: Knowing Who You Are in Christ. 116p. 1999. spiral bd. 12.95 (*0-941975-46-0*) Powerhouse.

***New Creation Image: Knowing Who You Are in Christ.** (POR.). 105p. 1999. spiral bd. 12.95 (*0-941975-56-8*) Powerhouse.

New Creation Image: Knowing Who You Are in Christ. A. L. Gill & Joyce Gill. (RUS.). 125p. (Orig.). 1994. spiral bd. 12.95 (*0-941975-27-4*) Powerhouse.

New Creation Image: Knowing Who You Are in Christ. A. L. Gill & Joyce Gill. 112p. (Orig.). 1995. reprint ed. pap. 9.95 (*0-941975-32-0*) Powerhouse.

New Creation Image: Knowing Who You Are in Christ see Imagen de la Nueva Creacion

New Creation in Christ. Bede Griffiths. 112p. 1994. pap. 9.95 (*0-87243-209-2*) Templegate.

New Creation or Eternal Now - Neue Schopfung Oder Ewiges Jetzt: Is There an Eschatology in Paul Tillich's Work? - Hat Paul Tillich eine Eschatologie? Ed. by Gert Hummel. (Theologische Bibliothek Toepelmann Ser.: Vol. 54). (ENG & GER.). xii, 245p. (C). 1991. lib. bdg. 75.40 (*3-11-013002-5*, 222-91) De Gruyter.

New Creation Realities. E. W. Kenyon. 160p. (Orig.). (C). 1945. pap. 10.50 (*1-57770-003-1*) Kenyons Gospel.

New Creation Story: The Creative Spiritituality of Teilhard de Chardin. Donald P. Gray. (Teilhard Studies: No. 2). 1979. pap. 3.50 (*0-89012-014-5*) Am Teilhard.

New Creations. unabridged ed. Joseph S. Medrek. 52p. 1998. pap. 3.98 (*1-58339-175-4*, E11) Triangle Press.

New Creations in the Neighborhood Leonard H. Budd. LC 98-192230. 65 p. 1998. write for info. (*0-7880-0972-9*, Fairway Pr) CSS OH.

New Creative Accounting: How to Make Your Profits What You Want Them to Be. Ian Griffiths. 196p. (Orig.). 1995. pap. 47.50 (*0-333-62865-9*, Pub. by Pan) Trans-Atl Phila.

New Creative Divorce. Mel Krantzler & Patricia B. Krantzler. LC 98-7601. 256p. 1998. 22.95 (*1-58062-054-X*) Adams Media.

New Creative Divorce: How to Create a Happier, More Rewarding Life During & after Your Divorce. Mel Krantzler & Pat Krantzler. LC 99-32368. 256p. 1999. pap. 10.95 (*1-58062-174-0*) Adams Media.

New Creative Serging Illustrated: The Complete Guide to Decorative Overlock Sewing. rev. ed. Pati Palmer et al. LC 93-38107. (Creative Machine Arts Ser.). (Illus.). 176p. 1993. pap. 18.95 (*0-8019-8382-7*) Krause Pubns.

New Creators: A Christian Analysis of Cloning & Genetic Engineering. Noah W. Hutchings. LC 98-191338. 96p. 1997. pap. 9.95 (*1-57558-016-0*) Hearthstone OK.

New Creature. Ed. by Wilfred W. Su. (Curriculum Ser.). 109p. 1997. pap. 5.95 (*1-885216-13-0*) Evan Formosan.

New Creatures. Mordicai Gerstein. LC 90-4128. (Illus.). 32p. (J). (ps-3). 1991. 15.00 (*0-06-022164-X*) HarpC Child Bks.

New Creepy Crawly Collection, 16 bks. Illus. by Tony Gibbons. Incl. Ants. Jenny Vaughan. LC 97-7344. (Illus.). 24p. (J). 1997. lib. bdg. 19.93 (*0-8368-1910-1*); Bees. Enid Fisher. LC 95-54107. (Illus.). 24p. (J). (gr. 2 up). 1996. lib. bdg. 19.93 (*0-8368-1576-9*); Beetles. Enid Fisher. LC 95-54106. (Illus.). 24p. (J). (gr. 2 up). 1996. lib. bdg. 19.93 (*0-8368-1577-7*); Butterflies. Graham Coleman. LC 97-7343. (Illus.). 24p. (J). (gr. 2 up). 1997. lib. bdg. 19.93 (*0-8368-1911-X*); Centipedes. Graham Coleman. LC 95-54108. (Illus.). 24p. (J). (gr. 2 up). 1996. lib. bdg. 19.93 (*0-8368-1578-5*); Cockroaches. Tamara Green. LC 97-7342. (Illus.). 24p. (J). (gr. 2 up). 1997. lib. bdg. 19.93 (*0-8368-1912-8*); Dragonflies. Heather Amery. LC 95-54173. (Illus.). 24p. (J). (gr. 2 up). 1996. lib. bdg. 19.93 (*0-8368-1579-3*); Fleas. Enid Fisher. LC 97-7341. (Illus.). 24p. (J). (gr. 2 up). 1997. lib. bdg. 19.93 (*0-8368-1913-6*); Flies. Tamara Green. LC 97-7335. (Illus.). 24p. (J). (gr. 2 up). 1997. lib. bdg. 19.93 (*0-8368-1914-4*); Grasshoppers. Graham Coleman. LC 97-7334. (Illus.). 24p. (J). (gr. 2 up). 1997. lib. bdg. 19.93 (*0-8368-1915-2*); Mosquitoes. Enid Fisher. LC 97-7333. (Illus.). 24p. (J). (gr. 2 up). 1997. lib. bdg. 19.93 (*0-8368-1916-0*); Scorpions. Tamara Green. (Illus.). 24p. (J). (gr. 2 up). 1996. lib. bdg. 19.93 (*0-8368-1580-7*); Snails. Enid Fisher. LC 95-54171. (Illus.). 24p. (J). (gr. 2 up). 1996. lib. bdg. 18.60 (*0-8368-1581-5*); Spiders. Enid Fisher. (Illus.). 24p. (J). (gr. 2 up). 1996. lib. bdg. 19.93 (*0-8368-1582-3*); Walking Sticks. Tamara Green. LC 97-7332. (Illus.). 24p. (J). (gr. 2 up). 1997. lib. bdg. 19.93 (*0-8368-1917-9*); Worms. Graham Coleman. (Illus.). 24p. (J). (gr. 2 up). 1996. lib. bdg. 19.93 (*0-8368-1583-1*); (Illus.). (J). 1996. Set lib. bdg. 318.93 (*0-8368-1996-9*) Gareth Stevens Inc.

New Creepy Crawly Collection New Titles, 8 bks. Illus. by Tony Gibbons. lib. bdg. 148.80 (*0-8368-1909-8*) Gareth Stevens Inc.

New Creole: Gulf Coast to Pacific Rim. Gerhard W. Brill. Ed. by David C. Barnette & Ashley S. Barnette. 182p. (Orig.). 1998. pap. 12.95 (*1-888769-50-5*) Pub One Hund One.

New Cricket in Town. unabridged ed. Walter N. Kuhn, Jr. & Erika K. Putney. Ed. by Jean M. Kuhn. (Freddy Cricket & the Town of Corncob Ser.: Vol. 6). (Illus.). 20p. (J). (ps-10). 1997. spiral bd. 6.95 (*1-891547-10-0*) Hoppa Prodns.

New Cricket in Town (Un Grillo Nuevo en el Pueblo) unabridged ed. Walter N. Kuhn, Jr. Tr. by Norberto Rivera. (Freddy Cricket & the Town of Corncob Ser.: Vol. 6C). (ENG & SPA., Illus.). 20p. (J). (ps-10). 1997. spiral bd. 6.95 (*1-891547-25-9*) Hoppa Prodns.

An Asterisk (*) at the beginning of an entry indicates that the title is appearing for the first time.

New "Criminal" Classes: Legal Sanctions & Business Managers James V. DeLong. LC 99-165616. 47p. 1997. pap. write for info. (*0-937299-58-8*) Natl Legal Ctr Pub Interest.

New Criminal Type in Jakarta: Counter Revolution Today. James T. Siegel. LC 97-49359. 1998. 49.95 (*0-8223-2212-9*); pap. 17.95 (*0-8223-2241-2*) Duke.

New CRIS Case Studies. Douglas S. Nau. 57p. (J). (gr. 5-12). 1982. pap. 17.50 (*1-881678-03-2*) CSEE.

New Criterion Reader: The First 5 Years. Ed. by Hilton Kramer. 356p. 1988. 35.00 (*0-02-917641-7*) Free Pr.

New Critical Approaches to the Short Stories of Ernest Hemingway. Ed. by Jackson J. Benson. LC 90-3463. 528p. (C). 1991. text 64.95 (*0-8223-1065-1*); pap. text 24.95 (*0-8223-1067-8*) Duke.

New Critical Essays on Caribbean Literature: Caliban's Turn. Carol P. Marsh-Lockett. 224p. 1998. 37.00 (*0-8153-3081-2*, H2082) Garland.

New Critical History of Old English Literature. Stanley B. Greenfield. (C). 1996. pap. text 20.00 (*0-8147-3088-4*) NYU Pr.

New Critical History of Old English Literature. rev. ed. Stanley B. Greenfield & Daniel G. Calder. (Illus.). 372p. (C). 1986. text 55.00 (*0-8147-3002-7*) NYU Pr.

New Critical Perspectives on Martin Walser. Frank Pilipp. LC 94-1979. (GERM Ser.). xii, 196p. 1994. 60.00 (*1-879751-67-4*) Camden Hse.

New Criticism. John Crowe Ransom. LC 78-31133. 339p. 1979. reprint ed. lib. bdg. 65.00 (*0-8371-9079-7*, RANC, Greenwood Pr) Greenwood.

New Criticism & After. fac. ed. Ed. by Thomas D. Young. LC 76-6165. (John Crowe Ransom Memorial Lectures: 1975). 114p. 1976. reprint ed. pap. 35.40 (*0-7837-7985-2*, 204774100008) Bks Demand.

New Criticism & Contemporary Literary Theory: Connections & Continuities. Ed. by William J. Spurlin & Michael Fischer. LC 93-15011. (Wellesley Studies in Critical Theory, Literary History & Culture: Vol. 9). 462p. 1995. text 80.00 (*0-8153-1459-0*, H1780) Garland.

New Criticism in France. Serge Doubrovsky. Tr. by Derek Coltman from FRE. 1995. lib. bdg. 24.00 (*0-226-16040-8*) U Ch Pr.

New Criticism or New Fraud. Raymond Picard. Tr. by Frank Towne. LC 70-5767. 63p. reprint ed. pap. 30.00 (*0-608-18355-5*, 203303600083) Bks Demand.

New Critique of Theoretical Thought Vol. I: The Necessary Presuppositions of Philosophy. Herman Dooyeweerd. Tr. by David H. Freeman & William S. Young from DUT. LC 96-52511. 600p. 1997. reprint ed. text 119.95 (*0-7734-8707-7*) E Mellen.

New Critique of Theoretical Thought Vol. II: The General Theory of the Modal Spheres. Herman Dooyeweerd. Tr. by David H. Freeman & H. De Jongste from DUT. LC 96-52511. 624p. 1997. reprint ed. text 129.95 (*0-7734-8709-3*) E Mellen.

New Critique of Theoretical Thought Vol. III: The Structures of Individuality of Temporal Reality. Herman Dooyeweerd. Tr. by David H. Freeman & H. De Jongste from DUT. LC 96-52511. 816p. 1997. reprint ed. text 139.95 (*0-7734-8711-5*) E Mellen.

New Critique of Theoretical Thought Vol. IV: Index of Subjects & Authors. Herman Dooyeweerd. Tr. by David H. Freeman & Marc Cirigliano from DUT. LC 96-52511. 262p. 1997. reprint ed. text 89.85 (*0-7734-8713-1*) E Mellen.

New Crockery Cooker Cook Book. Better Homes & Gardens. 80p. 1987. 9.95 (*0-696-01740-7*) Meredith Bks.

New Crops. Ed. by Jules Janick. LC 93-17949. 736p. 1993. 180.00 (*0-471-59374-5*) Wiley.

New Crops. Jessop & Wright. 1991. pap. 89.95 (*0-909605-80-7*) Buttrwrth-Heinemann.

New Crops for Food & Industry. Gerald E. Wickens et al. (Illus.). 400p. (C). (gr. 13). 1989. text 87.95 (*0-412-31500-9*) Chapman & Hall.

New Crops, New Uses, New Markets: Industrial & Commercial Products from United States Agriculture. 1996. lib. bdg. 255.99 (*0-8490-6023-0*) Gordon Pr.

New Cross-Country Ski Book. John Caldwell, pseud. (Illus.). 160p. 1987. 9.95 (*0-317-60384-1*, Penguin Bks) Viking Penguin.

New Cross-Country Ski Book. John Caldwell, pseud. 1988. 9.95 (*0-317-67797-7*) Viking Penguin.

***New Cross Stitch Sampler Book: 25 Fabulous Samples & 72 Projects to Stitch from Them.** Helen Philipps. (Illus.). 2000. 24.95 (*0-7153-0797-5*) D & C Pub.

New Crusaders: Christianity & the Far Right in Southern Africa. Gifford. 131p. (C). 37.00 (*0-7453-0456-7*, Pub. by Pluto GBR) Stylus Pub VA.

***New Crusaders: Images of the Crusades in the 19th & Early 20th Centuries.** Elizabeth Siberry. LC 99-49698. (Nineteenth Century Ser.). (Illus.). 256p. 2000. text 78.95 (*1-85928-333-0*, Pub. by Ashgate Pub) Ashgate Pub Co.

New Crusaders: The Corporate Social Responsibility Debate. Douglas J. Uyl. 96p. 1984. pap. 18.95 (*0-912051-03-5*) Transaction Pubs.

New Crusades: Christianity & the Far Right in Southern Africa. Gifford. 131p. (C). pap. 15.95 (*0-7453-0457-5*, Pub. by Pluto GBR) Stylus Pub VA.

New Crusades, the New Holy Land: Conflict in the Southern Baptist Convention, 1969-1991. David T. Morgan. LC 95-12245. 264p. (C). 1996. pap. text 24.95 (*0-8173-0804-0*) U of Ala Pr.

New Crystallographic Detectors: Detectors in Crystallographic Applications. (American Crystallographic Association Program & Abstracts Ser. 2: Vol. 10, 1). 1982. pap. 10.00 (*0-317-02526-0*) Polycrystal Bk Serv.

New Crystallographic Detectors & the Workshop on Crystallographic Detectors at the Nat. Bureau of Standards, Wash. D. C. Ed. by R. C. Hamlin. (Transactions of the American Crystallographic Association Ser.: Vol. 18). 179p. 1982. pap. 25.00 (*0-686-45036-1*) Polycrystal Bk Serv.

***New Cuisine Alternatives Vol. 1: Cream Puff Volcanoes & Chocolate Roller Blades.** Pam Moroso. Ed. by Laura Castellanos. (Illus.). 132p. 2000. pap. 12.95 (*0-9678804-0-8*, Pub. by Buckaroo) I P D.

New Cultural History. Ed. by Lynn A. Hunt. (Studies on the History of Society & Culture: No. 6). 1989. pap. 15.95 (*0-520-06429-1*, Pub. by U CA Pr) Cal Prin Full Svc.

New Curate. Christy Kenneally. 144p. 1998. pap. 10.95 (*1-85635-199-8*, Pub. by Mercier Pr) Irish Amer Bk.

New Currencies in the Former Soviet Union: A Recipe for Hyperinflation or the Path to Price Stability. C. L. Melliss & M. Cornelius. LC HG1076.1. (Bank of England, Economics Division. Working Paper Ser.: No. 26). 99p. reprint ed. pap. 30.70 (*0-608-20164-2*, 207142800011) Bks Demand.

New Currents, Ancient Rivers: Contemporary African Artists in a Generation of Change. Jean Kennedy. LC 90-10314. (Illus.). 208p. 1992. 49.95 (*1-56098-037-0*) Smithsonian.

New Currents in Western Buddhism: The Inner Meaning of the Friends of the Western Buddhist Order. Sangharakshita. 96p. (Orig.). 1996. pap. 6.95 (*0-904766-46-2*) Windhorse Pubns.

New Curriculum for New Times: A Guide to Student-Centered, Problem-Based Learning. Neal A. Glasgow. LC 96-25307. 200p. 1996. 55.95 (*0-8039-6498-6*); pap. 24.95 (*0-8039-6499-4*) Corwin Pr.

New Curriculum Guide to Chile. Ed. by Aaron Tepper. (Latin America Collection Ser.). (Illus.). 175p. 1993. pap. text 16.95 (*0-938305-08-5*) Assn Tchrs Latin Amer.

New Custom. LC 78-133716. (Tudor Facsimile Texts. Old English Plays Ser.: No. 46). reprint ed. 49.50 (*0-404-53346-9*) AMS Pr.

***New Cytokines as Potential Drugs.** Satwant K. Narula & Robert L. Coffman. LC 99-47593. (Progress in Inflammation Research Ser.). 2000. write for info. (*0-8176-5883-1*) Birkhauser.

New Czech Poetry. Jaroslav Cejka et al. LC 88-51309. 64p. 1988. pap. 13.95 (*1-85224-066-0*, Pub. by Bloodaxe Bks) Dufour.

New Czech Republic: Year of Turmoil. George R. Bauer. LC 97-93901. 1997. pap. 9.95 (*0-9658761-0-1*) G R Bauer.

New Dalda Cook Book. Perin Narayan. (Illus.). 200p. 1978. 11.95 (*0-7069-0377-3*) Asia Bk Corp.

New Dalmatian: Coach Dog - Firehouse Dog. 2nd ed. Alfred Treen & Esmerelda Treen. (Illus.). 256p. 1992. 25.95 (*0-87605-134-4*) Howell Bks.

New Dan Coates Easy Piano Encyclopedia. Ed. by Carol Cuellar. 216p. (Orig.). 1995. pap. text 19.95 (*0-89724-942-9*, PF0792A) Wrner Bros.

New Dan Coates Professional Touch Encyclopedia. Ed. by Carol Cuellar. 192p. (Orig.). (J). 1997. pap. text 19.95 (*1-57623-801-6*) Wrner Bros.

New Dan Coates Professional Touch Encyclopedia. rev. ed. Ed. by Carol Cuellar. 192p. (Orig.). 1997. pap. text 19.95 (*0-89724-631-4*, PF0562B) Wrner Bros.

New Dance: Approaches to Nonliteral Choreography. Margery J. Turner & Arlene Zallman. LC 74-134491. (Illus.). 128p. (C). 1976. pap. 12.95 (*0-8229-5269-6*) U of Pittsburgh Pr.

New Danish Fiction. (Review of Contemporary Fiction Ser.: Vol. 15, No. 1). 1995. pap. 8.00 (*1-56478-127-5*) Dalkey Arch.

New Danish Plays. Ed. by Hans Christian Andersen. LC 96-226095. 264p. 1996. pap. 22.95 (*1-870041-32-1*, Pub. by Norvik Pr) Dufour.

New Dare to Discipline see Atrevete a Disciplinar

New Dare to Discipline. James Dobson. 276p. 1992. 18.99 (*0-8423-0507-6*) Tyndale Hse.

New Dare to Discipline. James Dobson. (Christian Growth Self Help Ser.). 276p. 1996. pap. 12.99 (*0-8423-0506-8*) Tyndale Hse.

New Dark Ages. Donald Revell. LC 89-49759. (Wesleyan Poetry Ser.). 72p. 1990. pap. 12.95 (*0-8195-1186-2*, Wesleyan Univ Pr) U Pr of New Eng.

New Darkroom Handbook: A Complete Guide to the Best Design, Construction & Equipment. 2nd ed. Joe Demaio et al. LC 97-24670. (Illus.). 188p. 1997. pap. 29.95 (*0-240-80260-8*, Focal) Buttrwrth-Heinemann.

New Data Challenges in Our Information Age: 13th International CODATA Conference, Beijing, China, October 1992. Ed. by Phyllis S. Glaeser & Michael T. Millword. LC 94-72341. (Proceedings Ser.: Vol. 2). (Illus.). 672p. 1994. 80.00 (*1-884893-04-X*); pap. 50.00 (*1-884893-05-8*) CODATA.

New Data for Lenin's "Imperialism, the Highest Stage of Capitalism." Vladimir Il'ich Lenin. Ed. by E. Varga & L. Mendelsohn. LC 71-121288. reprint ed. 22.75 (*0-404-03965-0*) AMS Pr.

New Data on Rare Element Mineralogy (Authorized Translation from the Russian) Moscow, Vsesoiuznyi Nauchno-issledovatel'skii Inst. Ed. by A. I. Ginzburg. LC 61-18756. 144p. reprint ed. pap. 44.70 (*0-608-11392-1*, 200336800021) Bks Demand.

New Dawn. Osho. LC 97-214025. (Mystery School Ser.). 432p. 1989. 21.95 (*3-89338-023-X*, Pub. by Rebel Hse) Oshos.

New Dawn: Society & Politics in the Light of Initiatic Science, Pt. 1. 2nd ed. Omraam M. Aivanhov. (Complete Works: Vol. 25). (Illus.). 267p. 1990. pap. 14.95 (*2-85566-486-1*, Pub. by Prosveta) Prosveta USA.

New Dawn for America: The Libertarian Challenge. Roger L. Macbride. LC 76-174402. 111p. 1976. 5.95 (*0-916054-03-9*) Jameson Bks.

New Dawn in Guatemala: Toward a Worldwide Health Vision. Ed. by Richard Luecke. (Illus.). 264p. (C). 1993. pap. text 14.95 (*0-88133-734-X*) Waveland Pr.

New Dawn of Liberty: The Story of the American Founding. Gregory Wolfe. 81p. (C). pap. text 2.50 (*0-930783-19-0*) Claremont Inst.

New Dawn on Rocky Ridge. Roger L. MacBride. LC PZ7.M12255Nj 1997. (Little House). (Illus.). 384p. (J). (gr. 3-6). 1997. 15.95 (*0-06-024971-4*) HarpC.

New Dawn on Rocky Ridge. Roger L. MacBride. LC 97-4990. (Little House). (Illus.). 384p. (J). (gr. 3-7). 1997. pap. 4.95 (*0-06-440581-8*, HarpTrophy) HarpC Child Bks.

New Dawn on Rocky Ridge. Roger Lea Macbride. (Little House). (Illus.). (J). (gr. 3-6). 1997. 10.05 (*0-606-11678-8*, Pub. by Turtleback) Demco.

***New Dawn Rising: One Woman's Spiritual Odyssey.** Dawn Kohler. LC 99-93686. 280p. 1999. pap. 15.95 (*0-9670201-0-7*) Zion Publ.

New Dawns. Philip Hubbard. (Illus.). 212p. (Orig.). 1996. pap. 15.95 (*0-87414-105-2*) U IA Pubns Dept.

New Day. Ronald Heuninck. (Illus.). (J). (ps). 1988. bds. 5.50 (*0-86315-052-7*, 20233, Pub. by Floris Bks) Gryphon Hse.

New Day. Margaret Johnson-Hodge. 272p. 1999. pap. text 5.99 (*0-312-96915-5*, Thomas Dunne) St Martin.

New Day. Rod Vickers. 47p. 1984. pap. 0.95 (*0-88144-032-9*) Christian Pub.

New Day: 365 Meditations for Personal & Spiritual Growth. Jack Weiner. 384p. 1988. pap. 9.95 (*0-553-34591-5*) Bantam.

New Day--New Deal: A Bibliography of the Great American Depression, 9. Compiled by David E. Kyvig & Mary-Amm Blasio. LC 87-37568. (Bibliographies & Indexes in American History Ser.: No. 9). 315p. 1988. lib. bdg. 65.00 (*0-313-26027-3*, KNY/) Greenwood.

***New Day, Better You: Navigating the Health Food Maze.** 3rd ed. Dawn Mulkern. Ed. by Misty Purdom. 55p. 1999. pap. 12.95 (*1-929555-38-5*) Mulkern.

New Day Dawning. Judy Miller. 350p. (Orig.). 1989. pap. 10.95 (*0-942341-02-3*) Dawn Pubns TX.

***New Day Dawning: A Portrait of Ireland in 1900.** Daniel Mulhall. LC 99-492098. (Illus.). 248p. 2000. 35.95 (*1-898256-65-9*, Pub. by Collins Press) Irish Bks Media.

New Day for Family Ministry. Richard P. Olson & Joe H. Leonard, Jr. LC 95-83895. 170p. 1996. pap. 15.75 (*1-56699-166-8*, AL170) Alban Inst.

New Day in Babylon: The Black Power Movement & American Culture, 1965-1975. William L. Van Deburg. LC 91-48098. (Illus.). 388p. (C). 1992. 29.95 (*0-226-84714-4*) U Ch Pr.

New Day in Babylon: The Black Power Movement & American Culture, 1965-1975. William L. Van Deburg. LC 91-48098. (Illus.). x, 392p. (C). 1993. pap. text 18.00 (*0-226-84715-2*) U Ch Pr.

New Day in Housing. Louis H. Pink. LC 73-11941. (Metropolitan America Ser.). (Illus.). 262p. 1974. reprint ed. 18.95 (*0-405-05410-6*) Ayer.

New Day Is Dawning: A Powerful New Message from Jesus for Your Life Today & the Future of Our Planet. Diandra. LC 95-82254. 188p. Date not set. pap. text 12.95 (*1-888473-87-8*) Inward Jrney.

New Day Journal: A Journey from Grief to Healing. rev. ed. Maureen O'Brien. LC 99-76612. 96p. 2000. pap. 9.95 (*0-87946-130-6*, 189) ACTA Pubns.

New Day New Church: Evangelism for Mainline Denominations. Ben Johnson. 176p. 1995. pap. 11.95 (*1-885121-15-6*) CTS Press.

New Day Rising. Lauraine Snelling. LC 96-25355. (Red River of the North Ser.: No. 2). 288p. 1996. pap. 9.99 (*1-55661-577-9*) Bethany Hse.

New Deal. Compiled by James V. Compton. 39.00 (*1-56696-023-1*) Jackdaw.

New Deal. Gail B. Stewart. LC 92-41264. (Timestop Bks.). (Illus.). 112p. (YA). (gr. 6 up). 1993. lib. bdg. 14.95 (*0-02-788369-8*, New Dscvry Bks) Silver Burdett Pr.

New Deal. Fiona Venn. 128p. 1999. 35.00 (*1-57958-145-5*) Fitzroy Dearborn.

New Deal. 3rd ed. Paul K. Conkin. Ed. by A. S. Eisenstadt & John H. Franklin. (American History Ser.). (Illus.). 120p. 1992. pap. text 11.95 (*0-88295-889-5*) Harlan Davidson.

***New Deal: America's Response to the Great Depression.** Ronald Edsforth. LC 99-43955. (Problems in American History Ser.). 240p. 1999. 54.95 (*1-57718-142-5*); pap. 22.95 (*1-57718-143-3*) Blackwell Pubs.

New Deal: Government & the Economy. Laurel R. Singleton. (Public Issues Ser.). (Illus.). 68p. (YA). (gr. 10-12). 1989. 3.00 (*0-89994-337-3*); teacher ed. 2.00 (*0-89994-338-1*) Soc Sci Ed.

New Deal: Hope for the Nation. Cheryl Edwards. LC 95-68768. (Perspectives on History Ser.). (Illus.). 68p. (YA). (gr. 8 up). 1995. pap. 6.95 (*1-878668-47-1*) Disc Enter Ltd.

New Deal: Laissez Faire to Socialism. Ed. by Bernard Sternsher. LC 78-73287. 109p. 1979. pap. text 7.95 (*0-88273-212-9*) Forum Pr IL.

New Deal: Revolution or Evolution? rev. ed. Ed. by Edwin C. Rozwenc. (Problems in American Civilization Ser.). 113p. (C). 1959. pap. text 18.36 (*0-669-23838-4*) HM Trade Div.

New Deal: The Depression Years, 1933-1940. Anthony J. Badger. 360p. 1989. pap. 10.95 (*0-374-52174-3*) FS&G.

New Deal: The Historical Debate. Ed. by Richard S. Kirkendall. LC 73-4241. (Problems in American History Ser.). 174p. reprint ed. pap. 54.00 (*0-608-11568-1*, 205513700008) Bks Demand.

New Deal Adobe: The Civilian Conservation Corps & the Reconstruction of Mission la Purisima, 1934-1942. Christine E. Savage. LC 90-14051. (Illus.). 160p. (Orig.). 1991. pap. 9.95 (*0-931832-75-6*) Fithian Pr.

New Deal Agencies & Black America in the 1930s. John B. Kirby et al. LC 86-893395. (Black Studies Research Sources). 25p. 1983. write for info. (*0-89093-656-0*) U Pubns Amer.

New Deal & American Indian Tribalism: The Administration of the Indian Reorganization Act, 1934-45. Graham D. Taylor. LC 79-9178. 219p. 1980. reprint ed. pap. 67.90 (*0-608-01398-6*, 206216100002) Bks Demand.

New Deal & Corporate Power: Antitrust & Regulatory Policies During the Thirties & World War II. Intro. by Robert F. Himmelberg. LC 93-46045. (Business & Government in America since 1870 Ser.: Vol. 7). 416p. 1994. text 83.00 (*0-8153-1409-4*) Garland.

New Deal & Its Critics. Justus D. Doenecke. Date not set. pap. write for info. (*1-57524-083-1*) Krieger.

New Deal & Its Legacy: Critique & Reappraisal, 132. Ed. by Robert Eden. LC 88-37377. (Contributions in American History Ser.: No. 132). 274p. 1989. 69.50 (*0-313-26181-4*, END, Greenwood Pr) Greenwood.

New Deal & Public Policy. Pederson. LC 97-41742. 288p. 1998. text 49.95 (*0-312-17540-X*) St Martin.

New Deal & the Last Hurrah: Pittsburgh Machine Politics. Bruce M. Stave. LC 78-93863. 272p. reprint ed. pap. 84.40 (*0-608-13821-5*, 201786600010) Bks Demand.

New Deal & the Problem of Monopoly: A Study in Economic Ambivalence. Ellis W. Hawley. xxxxii, 525p. 1995. 27.50 (*0-8232-1608-X*); pap. 20.00 (*0-8232-1609-8*) Fordham.

New Deal & the Problem of Monopoly: A Study in Economic Ambivalence. Ellis W. Hawley. LC 65-24273. 542p. reprint ed. pap. 168.10 (*0-8357-2552-9*, 204024300015) Bks Demand.

New Deal & the States: Federalism in Transition. James T. Patterson. LC 80-29606. 226p. 1981. reprint ed. lib. bdg. 55.00 (*0-313-22841-8*, PAND, Greenwood Pr) Greenwood.

New Deal & the Unemployed: The View from New York City. Barbara Blumberg. 332p. 1979. 32.50 (*0-685-19073-0*) Bucknell U Pr.

New Deal & the West. Richard Lowitt. LC 93-15538. 1993. 14.95 (*0-8061-2557-8*) U of Okla Pr.

***New Deal Art in the Land of Enchantment: The War in New Mexico in the 1930s & 1940s.** Kathryn A. Flynn. (Illus.). 224p. 2000. 45.00 (*0-86534-305-5*) Sunstone Pr.

New Deal at the Grassroots: Programs for the People in Otter Tail County, Minnesota. D. Jerome Tweton. (Illus.). x, 205p. 1988. 19.95 (*0-87351-232-4*); pap. 10.95 (*0-87351-233-2*) Minn Hist.

New Deal at Work: Managing the market-Driven Workforce. Cappelli. LC 98-42221. 320p. 1999. 29.95 (*0-87584-668-8*, HBS Pr) Harvard Busn.

New Deal Collective Bargaining Policy. Irving Bernstein. LC 75-8997. (FDR & the Era of the New Deal Ser.). xi, 178p. 1975. reprint ed. lib. bdg. 27.50 (*0-306-70703-9*) Da Capo.

New Deal Days, 1933-1934. Eli Ginzberg. LC 97-2259. 132p. 1997. text 29.95 (*1-56000-331-6*) Transaction Pubs.

***New Deal Fat Cats: Business, Labor & Campaign Finance in the 1936 Presidential Election.** Michael J. Webber. LC 99-48262. 2000. 19.95 (*0-8232-1947-X*) Fordham.

***New Deal Fat Cats: Campaign Finances & the Democratic Party in 1936.** Michael Webber. 208p. 2000. 39.95 (*0-8232-2004-4*, Pub. by Fordham); pap. 19.95 (*0-8232-2005-2*, Pub. by Fordham) BookMasters.

New Deal 50 Years After: A Historical Assessment. Wilbur J. Cohen. LC 84-82347. (Symposia Ser.). 178p. 1984. pap. 10.50 (*0-89940-415-4*) LBJ Sch Pub Aff.

New Deal Fine Arts Projects: A Bibliography, 1933-1992. Martin R. Kalfatovic. LC 93-31116. 577p. 1994. 74.00 (*0-8108-2749-2*) Scarecrow.

New Deal for America: Proceedings from a National Conference on New Deal Communities. Ed. by Bryan Ward. LC 94-79356. 160p. (C). 1995. pap. 12.00 (*1-886351-00-7*) Arthurdale Herit.

New Deal for Art: The Government Art Projects of the 1930s with Examples from New York City & State. Marlene Park & Gerald E. Markowitz. (Illus.). 172p. 1977. 30.00 (*0-934483-00-0*) Gal Assn NY.

New Deal for Blacks: The Emergence of Civil Rights As a National Issue: the Depression Decade. Harvard Sitkoff. LC 78-2633. 412p. 1981. pap. text 23.95 (*0-19-502893-7*) OUP.

New Deal for Social Security. Peter Ferrara & Michael Tanner. LC 98-36656. 262p. 1998. 19.95 (*1-882577-62-0*, Pub. by Cato Inst); pap. 10.95 (*1-882577-63-9*, Pub. by Cato Inst) Natl Bk Netwk.

New Deal for Soft Coal: The Attempted Revitalization of the Bituminous Coal Industry Under the New Deal. James P. Johnson. Ed. by Stuart Bruchey. LC 78-22690. (Energy in the American Economy Ser.). 1979. lib. bdg. 28.95 (*0-405-11993-3*) Ayer.

New Deal for Southeastern Archaeology. Edwin A. Lyon. LC 95-11101. (SPA., Illus.). 304p. (Orig.). (C). 1996. pap. text 29.95 (*0-8173-0791-5*) U of Ala Pr.

New Deal for the American People. Roger Biles. LC 90-27715. 274p. 1991. pap. 15.00 (*0-87580-554-X*); lib. bdg. 32.00 (*0-87580-161-7*) N Ill U Pr.

New Deal for the Arts. Bruce I. Bustard. LC 96-31607. 1997. write for info. (*1-880875-14-4*) Natl Archives VCSG.

New Deal for the Arts. Bruce I. Bustard. LC 96-31607. (Illus.). 144p. 1997. pap. 24.95 (*0-295-97600-4*) U of Wash Pr.

New Deal for the Newcomer: The Federal Transient Service. Helen S. Hawkins. LC 91-32236. (Modern American History Ser.). 544p. 1991. text 35.00 (*0-8240-1902-4*) Garland.

N

New Deal for the World: Eleanor Roosevelt & American Foreign Policy, 1920-1962. Jason Berger. 240p. 1981. text 63.00 (*0-930888-07-3*, SSM1) Col U Pr.

New Deal for Workers' Education: The Workers' Service Program, 1933-42. Joyce L. Kornbluh. LC 86-25048. (Illus.). 188p. 1988. text 24.95 (*0-252-01395-6*) U of Ill Pr.

New Deal for Youth: The Story of the National Youth Administration. Betty Lindley & Ernest K. Lindley. LC 72-172687. (FDR & the Era of the New Deal Ser.). (Illus.). 316p. 1972. reprint ed. lib. bdg. 39.50 (*0-306-70382-3*) Da Capo.

New Deal in Economics. Sanford Fox. LC 80-65256. (Illus.). 144p. (Orig.). 1980. pap. 2.50 (*0-9603854-0-1*) S Fox.

New Deal in Georgia, 36. Michael S. Holmes. LC 74-289. 364p. 1975. 69.50 (*0-8371-7375-2*, HND/, Greenwood Pr) Greenwood.

New Deal in the Urban South. Douglas L. Smith. LC 87-29645. 287p. 1988. text 42.50 (*0-8071-1394-8*) La State U Pr.

New Deal Justice: The Constitutional Jurisprudence of Hugo L. Black, Felix Frankfurter, & Robert H. Jackson. Jeffrey D. Hockett. (Studies in American Constitutionalism). 336p. (C). 1996. lib. bdg. 71.00 (*0-8476-8210-2*) Rowman.

New Deal Justice: The Constitutional Jurisprudence of Hugo L. Black, Felix Frankfurter, & Robert H. Jackson. Jeffrey D. Hockett. (Studies in American Constitutionalism). 336p. (C). 1996. pap. text 26.95 (*0-8476-8211-0*) Rowman.

New Deal Justice: The Life of Stanley Reed of Kentucky. John D. Fassett. 1994. 35.00 (*0-533-10707-5*) Vantage.

New Deal Labor Policy & the American Industrial Economy. Stanley Vittoz. LC 86-24911. 251p. reprint ed. pap. 77.90 (*0-608-06010-0*, 206633800008) Bks Demand.

New Deal Labor Policy & the Southern Cotton Textile Industry, 1933-1941. James A. Hodges. LC 85-20368. (Illus.). 252p. (C). 1986. text 30.00 (*0-87049-496-1*) U of Tenn Pr.

New Deal Medicine: The Rural Health Programs of the Farm Security Administration. Michael R. Grey. LC 98-18240. (Illus.). xvii, 238 p. 1998. 42.50 (*0-8018-5939-5*) Johns Hopkins.

***New Deal Modernism: American Literature & the Invention of the Welfare State.** Michael Szalay. LC 00-29390. (Illus.). 320p. 2000. lib. bdg. 54.95 (*0-8223-2576-4*) Duke.

***New Deal Modernism: American Literature & the Invention of the Welfare State.** Michael Szalay. LC 00-29390. (Post-Contemporary Interventions Ser.). (Illus.). 320p. 2000. write for info. (*0-8223-2562-4*) Duke.

New Deal Planning: The National Resources Planning Board. Marion Clawson. LC 80-8777. 376p. 1981. 32.50 (*0-8018-2595-4*, Pub. by Resources Future) Johns Hopkins.

New Deal Unemployed. (C). 1979. 40.00 (*0-8387-2129-X*) Bucknell U Pr.

***New Dealers War.** Fleming. 2000. 30.00 (*0-465-02464-5*, Pub. by Basic); pap. 16.00 (*0-465-02465-3*, Pub. by Basic) HarpC.

New Deals: Business, Labor, & Politics in America, 1920-1935. Colin Gordon. LC 93-34538. 343p. (C). 1994. pap. text 21.95 (*0-521-45755-6*) Cambridge U Pr.

New Deals: Business, Labor, & Politics in America, 1920-1935. Colin Gordon. LC 93-34538. 343p. (C). 1994. text 69.95 (*0-521-45122-1*) Cambridge U Pr.

New Deal's Black Congressman: A Life of Arthur Wergs Mitchell. Dennis S. Nordin. LC 97-4478. (Illus.). 336p. 1997. spiral bd. 39.95 (*0-8262-1102-X*) U of Mo Pr.

New Debt Collecting Procedures - Die Nuwe Skuldinvorderingsprosedures. 2nd ed. J. M. Fourie. 1981. pap. write for info. (*0-7021-1243-7*, Pub. by Juta & Co) Gaunt.

New Decade of Language Testing Research. Ed. by Dan Douglas & Carol Chapelle. LC 92-62190. 287p. 1993. pap. 29.95 (*0-939791-43-9*) Tchrs Eng Spkrs.

New Decision-Making Tools for Managers: Mathematical Programing As an Aid in the Solving of Business Problems. Ed. by Edward C. Bursk & John F. Chapman. LC 63-11416. (Illus.), 431p. reprint ed. 133.70 (*0-8357-9168-8*, 201775200007) Bks Demand.

New Decorating Book: A Complete Guide. Better Homes & Gardens. LC 96-78792. 408p. 1997. 34.95 (*0-696-20636-6*) Meredith Bks.

***New Decorator.** Julia Barnard. (Living Ser.). (Illus.). 192p. 2000. pap. 13.95 (*0-7894-6146-3*) DK Pub Inc.

New Decorator. Julia Bernard & Nicholas Bernard. LC 98-47710. (Illus.). 10p. 1999. 24.95 (*0-7894-4121-7*) DK Pub Inc.

New Decoupage. Durwin Rice. LC 97-45787. (Illus.). 144p. 1998. 25.00 (*0-517-70560-5*) Random.

New Definitions of Lyric: Theory, Technology, & Culture. Ed. by Mark Jeffreys & William Cain. LC 97-52921. (Wellesley Studies in Critical Theory: Vol. 15). 284p. 1998. 70.00 (*0-8153-1878-2*) Garland.

New Delhi Robert Byron. LC 98-904962. 30 p. 1997. write for info. (*81-206-1286-8*) Asian Educ Servs.

New Delhi Report: The 3rd Assembly of the World Council of Churches, 1961. World Council of Churches Staff. LC BX0006.W77. 454p. reprint ed. pap. 140.80 (*0-7837-5992-4*, 204580200008) Bks Demand.

New Democracies: Global Change & U. S. Policy. Ed. by Brad Roberts. 264p. 1990. 30.00 (*0-262-18137-1*); pap. text 16.50 (*0-262-68062-9*) MIT Pr.

New Democracy: Challenging the Social Order in Industrial Ontario, 1914-1925. James Naylor. 288p. 1992. text 55.00 (*0-8020-5953-8*); pap. text 18.95 (*0-8020-6886-3*) U of Toronto Pr.

New Democratic Federalism for Europe: Functional, Overlapping & Competing Jurisdictions. Bruno S. Frey & Reiner Eichenberger. LC 99-12122. (Studies in Fiscal Federalism & State-Local Finance). 128p. (C). 1999. 65.00 (*1-84064-004-9*) E Elgar.

New Democratic Frontier: A Country by Country Report on Elections in Central & Eastern Europe. Ed. by Larry Garber & Eric Bjornlund. 247p. 1992. pap. 12.95 (*1-880134-09-8*) Natl Demo Inst.

New Denver Airport: Impact of the Delayed Baggage System. (Illus.). 51p. (Orig.). (C). 1994. pap. text 20.00 (*0-7881-1509-X*) DIANE Pub.

New Departures in Linguistics. George Wolf. LC 91-36781. 282p. 1992. text 10.00 (*0-8240-6102-0*, 1406) Garland.

***New Design Berlin: The Edge of Graphic Design.** James Grayson Trulove. (New Design Ser.). 2000. 45.00 (*1-56496-659-3*) Rockport Pubs.

New Design Concepts for High Speed Air Transport. Ed. by H. Sobieczky. (CISM International Centre for Mechanical Sciences Ser.: No. 366). (Illus.). viii, 336p. pap. 83.00 (*3-211-82815-X*) Spr-Verlag.

New Design for Nuclear Disarmament: Pugwash Symposium, Kyoto, Japan, 1975. Ed. by William Epstein & T. Toyoda. 338p. 1977. 62.50 (*0-85124-191-3*, Pub. by Spokesman); pap. 33.50 (*0-85124-192-1*, Pub. by Spokesman) Coronet Bks.

New Design, Los Angeles: The Edge of Graphic Design. Edward M. Gomez. (New Design Ser.). 208p. 1999. 45.00 (*1-56496-559-7*) Rockport Pubs.

***New Design Philosophy: An Introduction to Defuturing.** Tony Fry. (Illus.). 320p. 1999. pap. 39.95 (*0-86840-753-4*, Pub. by New South Wales Univ Pr) Intl Spec Bk.

New Design Portfolio. Home Planners, Inc. Staff. LC 90-124435. 80 p. 1989. 3.95 (*0-918894-76-X*) Home Planners.

New Design Source Book. Penny Spark et al. (Illus.). 224p. 1997. 29.95 (*1-57715-016-3*) Knckerbocker.

New Design Standards for Flexible Couplings: Design Engineering Conference, Chicago, May 10, 1966. Design Engineering Conference. LC TJ0183.A7. 33p. reprint ed. pap. 30.00 (*0-608-11677-7*, 201132400077) Bks Demand.

***New Design,Miami: The Edge of Graphic Design,** Bruce Turkel. (New Design Ser.). (Illus.). 208p. 2000. 45.00 (*1-56496-660-7*) Rockport Pubs.

***New Designs & Operating Experiences with Low-Floor Buses.** Rolland D. King et al. LC 98-61202. (Transit Cooperative Research Program Reports). iv, 68p. 1998. write for info. (*0-309-06308-6*) Transport Res Bd.

New Designs for Machine Patchwork. Higgins. 1980. 15.95 (*0-684-16643-7*, Scribners Ref) Mac Lib Ref.

New Designs for Teaching & Learning: Promoting Active Learning in Tomorrow's Schools. Dennis M. Adams & Mary E. Hamm. (Education Ser.). 366p. 1994. text 32.95 (*0-7879-0020-6*) Jossey-Bass.

New Designs in Raised Embroidery. Barbara Hirst. 1999. 17.95 (*1-85391-578-5*) Merehurst Ltd.

New Design,Tokyo: The Edge of Graphic Design. Edward M. Gomez. (New Design Ser.). 208p. 1999. 45.00 (*1-56496-561-9*) Rockport Pubs.

New Despotism. Gordon Hewart. LC 75-25259. 307p. 1975. reprint ed. lib. bdg. 55.00 (*0-8371-8389-8*, HEND, Greenwood Pr) Greenwood.

New Destinies. Jim Baen. 288p. (Orig.). 1992. per. 4.99 (*0-671-72086-4*) Baen Bks.

New Detectors: Proceedings of the 36th Workshop of the INFN Eloisatron Project Erice, Italy 1-7 November 1997. Ed. by C. Williams & T. Ypsilantis. (Science & Culture Ser.). 500p. 1998. 108.00 (*981-02-3675-1*) World Scientific Pub.

***New Development in Approximation Theory: 2nd International Dortmund Meeting (IDoMAT) '98, February 23-27, 1998.** Ed. by M. W. Muller et al. LC 99-34585. (International Series of Numerical Mathematics: vol. 132). 240p. 1999. 119.00 (*3-7643-6143-3*, Pub. by Birkhauser) Spr-Verlag.

New Development Paradigm: Papers on Institutions, Ngos, Gender & Local Government. S. Akbar Zaida. LC 99-921717. 332p. 1999. 35.00 (*0-19-579041-3*) OUP.

New Developments, Vol. 56. B. Dobias et al. (Structure & Bonding Ser.). (Illus.). 160p. 1984. 66.95 (*0-387-13106-X*) Spr-Verlag.

New Developments & Applications in Composites: Proceedings of a Symposium Fall Meeting in St. Louis, Missouri, October 16-17, 1978. Metallurgical Society of AIME Staff. Ed. by Doris Kuhlmann-Wilsdorf & William C. Harrigan, Jr. LC 79-64414. 377p. reprint ed. pap. 116.90 (*0-8357-2511-1*, 205239100013) Bks Demand.

***New Developments & Applications in Experimental Design.** Ed. by Nancy Flournoy et al. (IMS Lecture Notes - Monographs: Vol. 34). (Illus.). 212p. 1998. pap. 35.00 (*0-940600-46-3*) Inst Math.

New Developments & Applications in Optical Radiometry: Proceedings of the 2nd International Conference Held at the National Physical Laboratory, London, England, 12-13 April 1988. fac. ed. Ed. by N. P. Fox & D. H. Nettleton. LC 88-34771. (Institute of Physics Conference Ser.: No. 92). (Illus.). 214p. 1989. reprint ed. pap. 66.40 (*0-7837-7988-7*, 204774400008) Bks Demand.

New Developments & Directions in Plant Technology & Human Resources: Compilation of Presentations at May 10, 1991 Seminar. 1991. 50.00 (*0-685-50887-0*) Clothing Mfrs.

New Developments & New Applications in Animal Cell Technology. Ed. by Otto-Wilhelm Merten et al. LC 98-2862. 1998. text 345.00 (*0-7923-5016-2*) Kluwer Academic.

New Developments in Anti-Rheumatic Drugs, 2 vols. Ed. by Kim D. Rainsford & G. P. Velo. (Inflammation & Drug Therapy Ser.). 272p. (C). 1989. text 154.00 (*0-7462-0080-3*) Kluwer Academic.

New Developments in Applied Superconductivity. Y. Murakami. (Progress in High Temperature Superconductivity Ser.: Vol. 15). 828p. (C). 1989. pap. 61.00 (*9971-5-0834-6*); text 161.00 (*9971-5-0816-8*) World Scientific Pub.

***New Developments in Approximation Theory: 2nd Internatinal Dortmund Meeting (IDOMAT) '98, Germany, February 23-27, 1998** International Dortmund Meeting Staff & Manfred W. Mhuller. LC 99-34585. (International Series of Numerical Mathematics). 1999. write for info. (*0-8176-6143-3*) Birkhauser.

New Developments in Array Technology & Applications: Proceedings of the 167th Symposium of the International Astronomical Union, Held in the Hague, the Netherlands, August 23-27, 1994. Ed. by A. G. Philip. (International Astronomical Union Symposia Ser.). 420p. (C). 1995. pap. text 95.00 (*0-7923-3640-2*); lib. bdg. 168.00 (*0-7923-3639-9*) Kluwer Academic.

New Developments in Asian Studies: An Introduction. Paul Van der Velde & Alex McKay. LC 97-50216. (Studies from the International Institute for Asian Studies). 300p. 1998. 110.00 (*0-7103-0606-7*, Pub. by Kegan Paul Intl) Col U Pr.

New Developments in Australian Politics. Ed. by Brian Galligan et al. LC 98-220313. 320p. 1998. 74.95 (*0-7329-4304-3*, Pub. by Macmill Educ); pap. 36.95 (*0-7329-4307-8*, Pub. by Macmill Educ) Paul & Co Pubs.

New Developments in Axle, Steering, Suspension, & Chassis Technology: 1995 International Truck & Bus Meeting & Exposition. (Special Publications). 108p. 1995. pap. 36.00 (*1-56091-716-4*, SP-1128) Soc Auto Engineers.

New Developments in Bad Faith & Punitive Damages Litigation: The Exploding Tort. write for info. (*0-318-61921-0*) Harcourt.

New Developments in Behavior Therapy: From Research to Clinical Application. Ed. by Cyril M. Franks. LC 83-26402. (Supplement to Child & Family Behavior Therapy Ser.: No. 1). 589p. 1984. text 89.95 (*0-86656-241-9*); pap. text 39.95 (*0-86656-178-1*) Haworth Pr.

New Developments in Behavioral Research: Theory, Method, & Application: In Honor of Sidney W. Bijou. Ed. by B. C. Etzel et al. 656p. 1977. 59.95 (*0-89859-459-6*) L Erlbaum Assocs.

New Developments in Biosciences: Their Implication for Laboratory Animal Science. Ed. by Anton C. Beynen & H. A. Solleveid. 480p. (C). 1987. text 306.50 (*0-89838-354-4*) Kluwer Academic.

New Developments in Bioseparation. Ed. by Mohammad M. Ataai & Subhas K. Sikdar. LC 92-37375. (AIChE Symposium Ser.: No. 290, Vol. 88). 1992. 35.00 (*0-8169-0577-0*) Am Inst Chem Eng.

New Developments in Biotechnology: Patenting Life. (Illus.). 195p. (Orig.). (C). 1993. pap. text 50.00 (*1-56806-345-8*) DIANE Pub.

New Developments in Biotechnology: Patenting Life. United States Congress, Office of Technology Asses. LC 89-27404. (Illus.). 208p. reprint ed. pap. 64.50 (*0-608-09008-5*, 206964300005) Bks Demand.

New Developments in Cardiac Assist Devices, Vol. 6. Ed. by Safuh Attar. LC 85-6585. (Surgical Science Ser.: No. 6). 222p. 1985. 69.50 (*0-275-91330-9*, C13306, Praeger Pubs) Greenwood.

New Developments in Cardiac Nuclear Imaging. Ed. by Ami E. Iskandrian & Mario S. Verani. LC 97-29167. (Illus.). 288p. 1998. 85.00 (*0-87993-670-3*) Futura Pub.

New Developments in Cervical Cancer Screening & Prevention. Joseph Monsonego & Eduard Franco. LC 96-37506. (Illus.). 464p. 1997. 145.00 (*0-632-04765-8*) Blackwell Sci.

New Developments in Clinical Instrumentation. Ed. by Leroy Hersh. 160p. 1981. 96.00 (*0-8493-5305-X*, RB38, CRC Reprint) Franklin.

New Developments in Computer-Assisted Language Learning. Ed. by Douglas Hainline. 240p. 1986. 45.00 (*0-7099-3780-6*, Pub. by C Helm) Routldge.

New Developments in Construction & Functions of Organic Thin Films. Ed. by Tisato Kajiyama & M. Aizawa. 1996. write for info. (*0-614-17936-X*) Elsevier.

New Developments in Construction & Functions of Organic Thin Films. Tisato Kajiyama & M. Aizawa. LC 96-35751. (Studies in Interface Science: Vol. 4). 370p. 1996. 262.50 (*0-444-81956-8*) Elsevier.

***New Developments in Contact Problems.** Ed. by P. Wriggers et al. (CISM International Centre for Mechanical Sciences Ser.: 384). viii, 246p. 2000. pap. (*3-211-83154-1*) Spr-Verlag.

New Developments in Contemporary German Music. Klaus-Michael Hinz. (Contemporary Music Review Ser.). 138p. 1995. pap. text 17.00 (*3-7186-5423-7*, Harwood Acad Pubs) Gordon & Breach.

New Developments in Design, Manufacturing & Applications of Cylkro-(Face) Gears. G. Basstein & A. Sijtstra. (Nineteen Ninety-Four Fall Technical Meeting Ser.: Vol. 93FTM7). (Illus.). 12p. 1993. pap. text 30.00 (*1-55589-641-3*) AGMA.

New Developments in Diesel Engines & Components: SAE International Congress & Exposition 1994, 9 papers. (Special Publications). 74p. 1994. pap. 29.00 (*1-56091-477-7*, SP-1025) Soc Auto Engineers.

New Developments in Dietary Fiber: Physiological, Physicochemical & Analytical Aspects. Ed. by Ivan Furda & Charles J. Brine. (Advances in Experimental Medicine & Biology Ser.: Vol. 270). (Illus.). 338p. (C). text 114.00 (*0-306-43583-7*, Kluwer Plenum) Kluwer Academic.

***New Developments in Difference Equations & Applications: Proceedings of the Third International Conference on Difference Equations.** Ed. by Sui Sun Cheng et al. 380p. 1999. text 120.00 (*90-5699-669-X*) Gordon & Breach.

New Developments in Differential Geometry: Proceedings of the Colloquium on Differential Geometry, Debrecen, Hungary, July 26-30, 1994. Ed. by L. Tamassy & J. Szenthe. (Mathematics & Its Applications Ser.: Vol. 350). 444p. (C). 1995. text 217.50 (*0-7923-3822-7*) Kluwer Academic.

New Developments in Differential Geometry, Budapest 1996: Proceedings of the Conference on Differential Geometry, Budapest, Hungary, July 27-30, 1996. Conference on Differential Geometry Staff & Jbanos Szenth. LC 98-31137. 1998. write for info. (*0-7923-5307-2*) Kluwer Academic.

New Developments in Electromyography & Clinical Neurophysiology, Set. Ed. by J. E. Desmedt. Incl. Vol. 1. Motor Unit, Neuromuscular Disorders, Electromyographic Kinesiology. (Illus.). x, 700p. 1973. 208.75 (*3-8055-1451-4*); Vol. 2. Pathological Conduction in Nerve Fibers, Electromyography of Sphincter Muscles, Automatic Analysis of Electrogram with Computers. (Illus.). x, 500p. 1973. 156.75 (*3-8055-1452-2*); Vol. 3. Human Reflexes, Pathophysiology of Motor Systems, Methodology of Human Reflexes. (Illus.). x, 850p. 1973. 252.25 (*3-8055-1453-0*); 1973. 521.75 (*3-8055-1409-3*) S Karger.

New Developments in Engine Design & Combustion. American Society of Mechanical Engineers Staff & Teoman Uzkan. LC 98-73768. 1998. write for info. (*0-7918-1581-1*) ASME Pr.

New Developments in Engine Design & Engine Component Technology: SAE International Congress & Exposition 1994, 17 papers. (Special Publications). 195p. 1994. pap. 74.00 (*1-56091-469-6*, SP-1017) Soc Auto Engineers.

New Developments in Engine Management & Driveline Controls. LC 96-71848. 1997. 38.00 (*1-56091-952-3*, SP-1240) Soc Auto Engineers.

New Developments in Event-Related Potentials. Ed. by H. J. Heinze et al. LC 92-39211. xi, 375p. 1992. 82.50 (*0-8176-3669-2*) Birkhauser.

New Developments in Farm Machinery. 1992. 2450.00 (*0-89336-983-7*, GA-073) BCC.

New Developments in Fatty Acid Oxidation: Biochemical & Molecular Aspects of Fatty Acid Oxidation, Held in Philadelphia, Pennsylvania, November 1991. Ed. by Paul M. Coates & Kay Tanaka. (Progress in Clinical & Biological Research Ser.: No. 375). 600p. 1992. 325.00 (*0-471-56144-4*, Wiley-Interscience) Wiley.

New Developments in Fundamental & Applied Radiobiology. Ed. by C. Mothersill & C. Seymour. 460p. 1991. 95.00 (*0-7484-0020-6*, Pub. by Tay Francis Ltd) Taylor & Francis.

New Developments in Group Counseling. Ed. by Samuel T. Gladding. (C). 1997. 18.95 (*1-56109-076-X*) CAPS Inc.

New Developments in Heat Exchangers. Ed. by Naim Afgan et al. 696p. 1996. text 165.00 (*90-5699-512-X*, TJ263) Gordon & Breach.

New Developments in Heat Exchangers for Automotive Design. LC 96-71870. 1997. 49.00 (*1-56091-974-4*, SP-1262) Soc Auto Engineers.

***New Developments in High Temperature Superconductivity: Proceedings of the 2nd Polish - U. S. Conference Held at Wroclaw & Karpacz, Poland, 17-21 August 1998.** Ed. by Jan Klamut et al. LC 00-27987. (Lecture Notes in Physics Ser.: Vol. 545). viii, 275p. 2000. 65.00 (*3-540-67188-9*) Spr-Verlag.

New Developments in Home Care Services for the Elderly: Innovations in Policy, Program, & Practice. Ed. by Lenard W. Kaye. LC 95-48902. 290p. 1995. 45.00 (*1-56024-794-0*) Haworth Pr.

New Developments in Improved Oil Recovery. Ed. by H. J. De Haan. (Geological Society Special Publication Ser.: No. 84). (Illus.). 286p. 1995. 108.00 (*1-897799-22-5*, 231, Pub. by Geol Soc Pub Hse) AAPG.

New Developments in Industrial Polysaccharides. Ed. by V. Crescenzi et al. x, 386p. 1985. text 274.00 (*2-88124-032-1*) Gordon & Breach.

New Developments in Industrial Wastewater Treatment. Ed. by Aysen Turkman & Orhan Uslu. (NATO Advanced Science Institutes Series C: Mathematical & Physical Sciences). (C). 1991. text 155.00 (*0-7923-1070-5*) Kluwer Academic.

New Developments in International Commercial & Consumer Law: Proceedings of the 8th Biennial Conference of the International Academy of Commercial & Consumer Law. Ed. by Jacob Ziegel & Shalom Lerner. LC 98-222386. 388p. 1998. 90.00 (*1-901362-07-8*, Pub. by Hart Pub) Northwestern U Pr.

New Developments in Ion Exchange. M. Abe et al. 636p. 1991. 320.50 (*0-444-98688-X*) Elsevier.

New Developments in Labour Market Information in Nine Asian Countries. 106p. (Orig.). 1981. pap. 11.25 (*92-2-102809-7*) Intl Labour Office.

New Developments in Lie Theory & Their Applications. Ed. by J. Tirao et al. (Progress in Mathematics Ser.: Vol. 105). (Illus.). ix, 228p. 1992. 80.50 (*0-8176-3619-6*) Birkhauser.

New Developments in Lipid-Protein Interactions & Receptor Function. K. W. Wirtz et al. (NATO ASI Ser.: Vol. 246). (Illus.). 328p. (C). 1993. text 110.00 (*0-306-44521-2*, Kluwer Plenum) Kluwer Academic.

An Asterisk (*) at the beginning of an entry indicates that the title is appearing for the first time.

New Developments in Marine Biotechnology: Proceedings of the Fourth International Marine Biotechnology Conference Held in Sorrento, Paestum, Otranto, & Pugnochiuso, Italy, September 22-29, 1997. Ed. by Y. Le Gal & H. O. Halvorson. LC 98-24800. (Illus.). 360p. (C). 1998. text 125.00 (*0-306-45907-8*, Kluwer Plenum) Kluwer Academic.

New Developments in Marine Science & Technology: Economic, Legal & Political Aspects of Change, 22nd Annual Conference Proceedings. Ed. by Lewis M. Alexander et al. 530p. 1989. 42.50 (*0-911189-20-3*) Law Sea Inst.

New Developments in Medical Research: Nih & Patient Groups : Hearing Before the Subcommittee on Health & Environment of the Committee on Commerce, House of Representatives, One Hundred Fifth Congress, Second Session March 26, 1998. USGPO Staff. LC 98-176158. iii, 150p. 1998. write for info. (*0-16-056546-4*) USGPO.

New Developments in Molecular Chirality. Ed. by Paul G. Mezey. 300p. (C). 1991. text 155.50 (*0-7923-1021-7*) Kluwer Academic.

New Developments in Myocardial Imaging: Technetium 99m Tc Sestamibi. Michael N. Maisey et al. 1993. 120.00 (*1-85317-112-3*, M Dunitz) Scovill Paterson.

New Developments in Neural Computing. Ed. by J. G. Taylor & C. L. Mannion. (Illus.). 264p. 1989. 122.00 (*0-85274-193-6*) IOP Pub.

New Developments in Pain Research & Treatment. Ed. by Stephan J. Levitan & Howard L. Berkowitz. LC 84-28254. (Clinical Insights Ser.). 87p. reprint ed. pap. 30.00 (*0-8357-7817-7*, 203618900002) Bks Demand.

New Developments in Plastic Recycling: RETEC, October 30-31, 1989. Society of Plastics Engineers Staff. LC TP1105.N48. (Illus.). 395p. reprint ed. pap. 122.50 (*0-8357-3621-0*, 203632200003) Bks Demand.

***New Developments in Polymer Analytics I.** Ed. by M. Schmidt. (Advances in Polymer Science Ser.: Vol. 150). (Illus.). 200p. 2000. 162.00 (*3-540-66077-1*) Spr-Verlag.

***New Developments in Polymer Analytics II.** Ed. by M. Schmidt. (Advances in Polymer Science Ser.: Vol. 151). (Illus.). 180p. 2000. 135.00 (*3-540-66078-X*) Spr-Verlag.

New Developments in Porous Silicon: Relation with Other Nanostructured Porous Materials: Proceedings of Symposium L on New Developments in Porous Silicon: Relation with Other Nanostructured Porous Materials of the 1996 E-MRS Spring Conference, Strasbourg, France June 4-7, 1996. L. T. Canham & D. Bellet. LC 98-149194. (European Materials Research Society Symposia Proceedings Ser.: Vol. 600). 340p. 1997. 201.00 (*0-444-20508-X*) Elsevier.

New Developments in Productivity Measurement & Analysis. Conference on New Developments in Productivity Mea. Ed. by John W. Kendrick & Beatrice N. Vaccara. LC 79-20399. (Studies in Income & Wealth: No. 44). (Illus.). 726p. reprint ed. pap. 200.00 (*0-8357-8244-1*, 205679600087) Bks Demand.

New Developments in Quantitative Coronary Arteriography. Ed. by Johan H. Reiber & Patrick W. Serruys. (Developments in Cardiovascular Medicine Ser.). (C). 1988. text 226.50 (*0-89838-377-3*) Kluwer Academic.

New Developments in Quantum Field Theory: Proceedings of a NATO ARW Held in Zakopane, Poland, June 14-20, 1997. Ed. by Poul H. Damgaard & Jerzy Jurkiewicz. LC 97-48523. (NATO ASI Ser. Series B, Physics: Vol. 366). (Illus.). 374p. (C). 1998. text 125.00 (*0-306-45816-0*) Kluwer Academic.

New Developments in Refrigeration for Food Safety & Quality. Ed. by William E. Murphy & Margaret M. Barth. LC 96-86512. 318p. 1996. pap. 50.50 (*0-929355-80-6*, P0996) Am Soc Ag Eng.

New Developments in Research on Adult Cognition. Chris Brotherton. (C). 1991. 35.00 (*1-85041-036-4*, Pub. by Univ Nottingham) St Mut.

***New Developments in Science & Technology Policy: Highlights from the SSTI Weekly Digest.** 20p. 2000. pap. 15.00 (*0-9701061-0-6*) State Science.

New Developments in Securitization, 1995. (Commercial Law & Practice Course Handbook Ser.). Date not set. pap. 99.00 (*0-614-17157-1*, A4-4489) PLI.

New Developments in Securitization, 1994. (Commercial Law & Practice Course Handbook Ser.). 600p. 1994. pap. 99.00 (*0-685-66627-1*, A4-4464) PLI.

New Developments in Selective Oxidation II: Proceedings of the 2nd World Congress & Fourth European Workshop Meeting, Benalmadena, Spain, September 20-24, 1993. Ed. by V. Cortes Corberan & S. Vic Bellon. LC 94-10954. (Studies in Surface Science & Catalysis: Vol. 82). 900p. 1994. 316.50 (*0-444-81552-X*) Elsevier.

New Developments in Semiconductor Physics. Ed. by G. Ferenczi & F. Beleznay. (Lecture Notes in Physics Ser.: Vol. 301). 302p. 1988. 48.95 (*0-387-19215-8*) Spr-Verlag.

New Developments in Separation Methods. Symposium on New Methods of Separation Staff. Ed. by Eli Grushka. LC 75-37222. (Illus.). 256p. reprint ed. pap. 79.40 (*0-8357-6233-5*, 205230000090) Bks Demand.

New Developments in Soviet Military Strategy. Andrew C. Goldberg. LC 87-27729. (Significant Issues Ser.: Vol. 9, No. 7). (Illus.). 71p. reprint ed. pap. 30.00 (*0-8357-6641-1*, 203530800094) Bks Demand.

New Developments in Stainless Steel Technology: Conference Proceedings. American Society for Metals Staff. Ed. by R. A. Lula. LC 85-72035. (Illus.). 399p. reprint ed. pap. 123.70 (*0-8357-6234-3*, 203432000089) Bks Demand.

New Developments in Statistics for Psychology & the Social Sciences. Ed. by A. D. Lovie & Frederick Mosteller. 200p. 1986. 57.50 (*0-901715-46-8*, 1020, Pub. by Brit Psychol Soc) Routledge.

New Developments in Statistics for Psychology & the Social Sciences. 2nd ed. A. D. Lovie et al. 256p. (C). 1992. text 70.00 (*1-85433-017-9*, A5028, Pub. by Brit Psychol Soc) Routledge.

New Developments in Sudbury Geology. Ed. by J. V. Guy-Bray. LC 73-155398. (Geological Association of Canada. Special Paper: No. 10). (Illus.). 136p. reprint ed. pap. 42.20 (*0-608-18793-3*, 203031500068) Bks Demand.

New Developments in Systemic Linguistics Vol. 1: Theory & Description. Ed. by M. A. Halliday & Robin P. Fawcett. (Open Linguistics Ser.). 300p. 1987. text 64.00 (*0-86187-636-9*) St Martin.

New Developments in Systemic Linguistics Vol. 2: Theory & Application. Robin P. Fawcett & David G. Young. (Open Linguistics Ser.). 250p. 1988. text 59.00 (*0-86187-637-7*) St Martin.

New Developments in Telemedicine. Feedback Research Services Staff. (Illus.). 200p. 1997. spiral bd. 100.00 (*1-889713-10-4*) Feedback Rsch.

New Developments in the Analysis of Market Structure. Ed. by Joseph E. Stiglitz & G. Frank Mathewson. 672p. (Orig.). 1986. pap. text 22.00 (*0-262-69093-4*, Bradford Bks) MIT Pr.

New Developments in the Chemistry of O- & C- Silicon & Germanium Substituted Oxoderivatives of Small Carbon & Heterocyclic Compounds, Vol. 12. G. S. Zaitseva et al. (Chemistry Reviews Ser.: SSR Sec. B, Vol. 12, Pt. 1). ii, 52p. 1989. pap. text 58.00 (*3-7186-4850-4*) Gordon & Breach.

New Developments in the Chemistry of Packaging Materials. Sarah J. Risch. LC 99-58687. (Illus.). 304p. 1999. text 95.00 (*0-8412-3617-8*, Pub. by Am Chemical) OUP.

New Developments in the Labor Market: Toward a New Institutional Paradigm. Ed. by Katherine Abraham & Robert B. McKersie. 300p. 1990. 39.95 (*0-262-01118-2*) MIT Pr.

New Developments in the Latvian Gambit. Kon Grivainis & John Elburg. (Illus.). 80p. 1998. pap. 6.95 (*0-945470-69-X*) Chess Ent.

New Developments in the Management of Urolithiasis. Ed. by James E. Lingeman & Glenn M. Preminger. LC 95-32960. (Topics in Clinical Urology Ser.). (Illus.). 216p. 1996. 69.50 (*0-89640-287-8*) Igaku-Shoin.

New Developments in the Theory of Knots. Ed. by T. Kohno. (Avanced Series in Mathematical Physics: Vol. 11). 916p. (C). 1990. text 109.00 (*981-02-0162-1*); pap. text 61.00 (*981-02-0163-X*) World Scientific Pub.

New Developments in the Therapy of Allergic Disorders & Asthma. Ed. by S. Z. Langer & Martin K. Church. (International Academy for Biomedical & Drug Research Ser.: Vol. 6). (Illus.). vi, 136p. 1994. 139.25 (*3-8055-5748-5*) S Karger.

New Developments in Theoretical Studies of Proteins. Ron Elber. LC 97-140253. (Advanced Series in Physical Chemistry: Vol. 7). 250p. 1996. text 68.00 (*981-02-2196-7*) World Scientific Pub.

New Developments in Therapeutic Enzyme Inhibitors & Receptor Blockers. 207p. 1996. 3400.00 (*1-56965-353-4*, C-202) BCC.

New Developments in Time Series Econometrics. J. M. Dufour & Baldev Raj. (Studies in Empirical Economics). (Illus.). vi, 250p. 1994. 107.95 (*0-387-91482-X*) Spr-Verlag.

New Developments in Titrimetry. Ed. by Joseph Jordan. LC 73-82701. (Treatise on Titrimetry Ser.: No. 2). (Illus.). 212p. reprint ed. pap. 65.80 (*0-7837-0874-2*, 204118200019) Bks Demand.

New Developments in Transmission & Driveline Design: 1995 International Congress & Exposition Meeting. 192p. 1995. pap. 80.00 (*1-56091-637-0*, SP1087) Soc Auto Engineers.

***New Developments in Understanding Depression & Its Treatment: Proceedings of a Symposium Held During the XXIst CINP Congress.** Jack M. Gorman et al. (Illus.). 34p. 1999. write for info. (*0-9664229-1-0*) Sci Frontiers.

New Developments in X-Ray & Ultraviolet Astronomy: Proceedings of the E1.2 Meeting of the COSPAR Scientific Commission E Which Was Held During the 30th COSPAR Scientific Assembly, Hamburg, Germany, 11-21 July, 1994. Ed. by J. E. Drew. (Advances in Space Research Ser.: Vol. 16). 168p. 1995. pap. 104.00 (*0-08-042623-9*, Pergamon Pr) Elsevier.

New Developments of Integrable Systems & Long-Ranged Interaction Models. M. L. Ge & Y. S. Wu. 300p. 1995. text 99.00 (*981-02-2127-4*) World Scientific Pub.

New Developments of the Aetiogenesis of Chronic Pancreatitis - Implications for Treatment & Disease Prophylaxis: Symposium Held During the World Congresses of Gastroenterology, Vienna, September 1998, Vol.59. Ed. by Joan M. Braganza. (Digestion Ser.: Vol. 59, Suppl. 4). (Illus.). iv, 60p. 1998. pap. 48.00 (*3-8055-6804-5*) S Karger.

New Developments on Fundamental Problems in Quantum Physics. Ed. by Miguel Ferrero & Alwyn Van Der Merwe. LC 97-29301. (Fundamental Theories of Physics Ser.: No. 81). 468p. 1997. text 227.50 (*0-7923-4374-3*) Kluwer Academic.

New Devil's Dictionary: Creepy Cliches & Sinister Synonyms. J. N. Williamson. LC 85-80504. (Illus.). 64p. 1985. 15.00 (*0-932445-13-6*); pap. 5.00 (*0-932445-12-8*) Ganley Pub.

New Devotions. Ruth L. Warrick. (Illus.). 283p. 1997. pap. 25.00 (*1-880994-44-5*) Mt Olive Coll Pr.

New Devotions for Any Occasion! LeNoir Culbertson & Barry Culbertson. 64p. 1997. pap. 6.95 (*0-687-05288-2*) Abingdon.

New Diabetes Without Fear: Take Control of Your Life. rev. ed. Joseph I. Goodman & W. Watts Biggers. LC 94-96769. 176p. 1995. mass mkt. 5.99 (*0-380-77761-4*, Avon Bks) Morrow Avon.

***New Diabetic Cookbook.** (Illus.). 240p. 1999. 24.95 (*0-696-20792-3*) Meredith Bks.

New Diabetic Cookbook. rev. ed. Mabel Cavaiani. 384p. 1989. reprint ed. pap. 14.95 (*0-8092-4251-6*) NTC Contemp Pub Co.

New Diabetic Cookbook. 4th rev. ed. Mabel Cavaiani. 432p. 1996. pap. 14.95 (*0-8092-3164-6*, 316460, Contemporary Bks) NTC Contemp Pub Co.

New Diabetic Cookbook: More than 200 Delicious Recipes for a Low-Fat, Low-Sugar, Low-Cholesterol, Low-Salt, High-Fiber Diet. Mabel Cavaiani. 384p. 1994. pap. write for info. (*0-8092-3547-1*) NTC Contemp Pub Co.

New Diagnostic Methods in Oncology & Hematology. Ed. by D. Huhn. LC 98-22181. (Illus.). 260p. 1998. pap. 59.00 (*3-540-63578-5*) Spr-Verlag.

New Diagnostics in Crop Science. Ed. by J. H. Skerritt & R. Appels. (Biotechnology in Agriculture Ser.: 13). (Illus.). 320p. 1995. text 105.00 (*0-85198-934-9*) OUP.

New Dialectic: Conversational Contexts of Argument. Douglas Walton. LC 98-195109. (Toronto Studies in Philosophy). 256p. 1998. text 55.00 (*0-8020-4143-4*); pap. text 21.95 (*0-8020-7987-3*) U of Toronto Pr.

New Dialogues & Plays, 3 Vols. Binney Gunnison. LC 72-5829. (Granger Index Reprint Ser.). 1977. reprint ed. 34.95 (*0-8369-6372-5*) Ayer.

New Diamond Science & Technology: Proceedings of the 2nd International Conference, Materials Research Society Conference Proceedings, Washington, D. C., U. S. A., September 17-19, 1990, Vol. NDST-2. Ed. by Rustum Roy et al. 1111p. 1991. text 17.50 (*1-55899-111-5*, NDST-2) Materials Res.

New Diary: How to Use a Journal for Self-Guidance & Expanded Creativity. Tristine Rainer. LC 76-62677. 324p. 1979. reprint ed. pap. 13.95 (*0-87477-150-1*, Tarcher Putnam) Putnam Pub Group.

New Diasporas: The Mass Exodus, Dispersal & Regrouping of Migrant Communities. Nicholas Van Hear. LC 98-12125. (Global Diasporas: No. 2). (Illus.). 298p. 1998. pap. text 22.00 (*0-295-97713-2*) U of Wash Pr.

New Dickson Baseball Dictionary. expanded rev. ed. Paul Dickson. LC 98-40700. (Illus.). 592p. 1999. pap. 20.00 (*0-15-600580-8*, Harvest Bks) Harcourt.

New Dickson Baseball Dictionary. expanded rev. ed. Paul Dickson. LC 98-40700. (Illus.). 592p. (C). 1999. 35.00 (*0-15-100380-7*, Harvest Bks) Harcourt.

New Dictionary: Hebrew English - English Hebrew. Y. Lazar. 778p. 1995. pap. 4.95 (*1-888162-00-7*) Kuperand USA.

New Dictionary: Hebrew-English English-Hebrew. Israel Lazar. (HEB & ENG.). 762p. 1998. pap. 6.99 (*1-880880-31-8*) Israeli Trad.

New Dictionary of American History, 10 vols. 3rd ed. Kutler. 2000. 650.00 (*0-684-80533-2*) Mac Lib Ref.

New Dictionary of American History. 3rd ed. Kutler. 100.00 (*0-684-80523-5*) Scribner.

New Dictionary of American History, Vol. 2. 3rd ed. Kutler. 100.00 (*0-684-80524-3*) Scribner.

New Dictionary of American History, Vol. 3. 3rd ed. Kutler. 2000. 100.00 (*0-684-80525-1*) Mac Lib Ref.

New Dictionary of American History, Vol. 4. 3rd ed. Kutler. 2000. 100.00 (*0-684-80526-X*) Mac Lib Ref.

New Dictionary of American History, Vol. 5. 3rd ed. Kutler. 2000. 100.00 (*0-684-80527-8*) Mac Lib Ref.

New Dictionary of American History, Vol. 6. 3rd ed. Kutler. 2000. 100.00 (*0-684-80528-6*) Mac Lib Ref.

New Dictionary of American History, Vol. 7. 3rd ed. Kutler. 2000. 100.00 (*0-684-80529-4*) Mac Lib Ref.

New Dictionary of American History, Vol. 8. 3rd ed. Kutler. 2000. 100.00 (*0-684-80530-8*) Mac Lib Ref.

New Dictionary of American History, Vol. 9. 3rd ed. Kutler. 2000. 100.00 (*0-684-80531-6*) Mac Lib Ref.

New Dictionary of American History, Vol. 10. 3rd ed. Kutler. 2000. 100.00 (*0-684-80532-4*) Mac Lib Ref.

New Dictionary of Americanisms. Sylvia Clapin. 1973. 59.95 (*0-8490-0721-6*) Gordon Pr.

New Dictionary of Astrology. Sepharial. 192p. 1992. pap. 15.00 (*0-89540-204-1*, SB-204, Sun Bks) Sun Pub.

New Dictionary of Catholic Social Thought. Ed. by Judith A. Dwyer. LC 94-4264. 1056p. (Orig.). 1994. 79.50 (*0-8146-5526-2*, M Glazier) Liturgical Pr.

New Dictionary of Catholic Spirituality. Ed. by Michael Downey. 1120p. (Orig.). 1993. 79.50 (*0-8146-5525-4*, M Glazier) Liturgical Pr.

New Dictionary of Christian Ethics & Pastoral Theology. Ed. by David J. Atkinson et al. LC 94-40802. 944p. 1994. 39.99 (*0-8308-1408-6*, 1408) InterVarsity.

New Dictionary of Counted Thread Embroidery Stitches. Rhoda O. Goldberg. LC 97-15954. 192p. 1998. 17.00 (*0-517-88663-4*) Three Rivers Pr.

New Dictionary of Economics & Banking. Codeluppi. (ENG & ITA.). 1466p. 1989. 150.00 (*0-8288-4036-9*, F135525) Fr & Eur.

New Dictionary of Eponyms. Morton S. Freeman. LC 96-32608. (Illus.). 304p. 1997. pap. 14.95 (*0-19-509354-2*) OUP.

New Dictionary of Legal Terms. Irving Shapiro. LC 99-169920. 250p. 1994. pap. 11.95 (*0-930137-01-9*) Looseleaf Law.

New Dictionary of Medical Ethics. Ed. by Kenneth M. Boyd. 285p. 1997. pap. 37.00 (*0-7279-1001-9*, Pub. by BMJ Pub) Login Brothers Bk Co.

New Dictionary of Political Analysis. Geoffrey Roberts & Alistair Edwards. LC 91-26692. 192p. 1995. pap. text 16.95 (*0-340-52860-5*, A6837, Pub. by E A) St Martin.

New Dictionary of Quotations on Historical Principles from Ancient & Modern Sources. Ed. by H. L. Mencken. 1942. 75.00 (*0-394-40079-8*) Knopf.

New Dictionary of Religions. rev. ed. Ed. by John R. Hinnells. LC 94-10302. (Illus.). 672p. 1995. 88.95 (*0-631-18139-3*) Blackwell Pubs.

New Dictionary of Religions, Denominations & Cults see Nuevo Diccionario de Religiones, Denominaciones y Sectas

New Dictionary of Sacramental Worship. Ed. by Peter E. Fink. 1352p. 1990. 69.50 (*0-8146-5788-5*) Liturgical Pr.

New Dictionary of Saints. Donald Attwater. Ed. by John Cumming. 336p. 1994. pap. 27.00 (*0-86012-207-7*, Pub. by Srch Pr) St Mut.

New Dictionary of Saints. Ed. & Rev. by John Cumming. 338p. 1994. pap. 19.95 (*0-8146-2324-7*) Liturgical Pr.

New Dictionary of Scientific & Technical Terms. 5th ed. Ahmed Khatib. (ARA & ENG.). 768p. 1983. 95.00 (*0-8288-0608-X*, M 9968) Fr & Eur.

New Dictionary of Scientific & Technical Terms: English-Arabic. 6th ed. A. S. Al-Khatib. (ARA & ENG.). 751p. Date not set. 125.00 (*0-7859-7136-X*) Fr & Eur.

New Dictionary of Sign Language: Employing the Eshkol-Wachmann Movement Notation System. Enya Cohen et al. (Approaches to Semiotics Ser.: No. 50). 1977. text 113.85 (*90-279-3334-0*) Mouton.

New Dictionary of Spiritual Thought. Carol E. Parrish-Harra. Ed. by Mary B. Marvin & Norma Hallstrom. LC 93-87756. (Illus.). 213p. (Orig.). 1994. pap. 14.95 (*0-945027-11-7*) Sparrow Hawk Pr.

New Dictionary of Statistics: A Complement to the 4th Edition of Mulhall's Dictionary of Statistics. Augustus D. Webb. 1971. reprint ed. 75.00 (*1-55888-196-4*) Omnigraphics Inc.

New Dictionary of the Catalan Dictionary: Nou Diccionari de la Llengua Catalana. 11th ed. Joan B. Parramona. (CAT.). 832p. 1990. 26.95 (*0-7859-4961-5*) Fr & Eur.

New Dictionary of the Italian Language: Novissimo Dizionario della Lingua Italiana. F. Palazzi. Ed. by G. Folena. (ITA.). 1624p. 1981. 150.00 (*0-8288-4673-1*, M9363) Fr & Eur.

New Dictionary of the Social Sciences. Ed. by G. Duncan Mitchell. 244p. 1979. lib. bdg. 49.95 (*0-202-30285-7*) Aldine de Gruyter.

New Dictionary of Theology see Nuevo Diccionario de Teologia

New Dictionary of Theology. Ed. by Mary Collins et al. LC 87-82327. (Illus.). 1120p. (C). 1987. text 69.95 (*0-8146-5609-9*) Liturgical Pr.

New Dictionary of Theology. Ed. by Joseph A. Komonchak & Mary Collins. 1120p. 1995. pap. 49.95 (*0-8146-5633-1*) Liturgical Pr.

New Dictionary of Theology. Ed. by David F. Wright et al. LC 87-30975. (Illus.). 768p. (C). 1988. 37.99 (*0-8308-1400-0*, 1400) InterVarsity.

New Dictionary System. Than M. Anchlia. 1987. write for info. (*0-9621487-0-9*) T M Anchlia.

***New Diesel Engine & Components Applications.** (Special Publications). 96p. 2000. 55.00 (*0-7680-0563-9*, SP-1513) Soc Auto Engineers.

***New Diesel Engines, Components, & Cooling Systems.** (Special Publications). 70p. 1999. 35.00 (*0-7680-0465-9*, SP-1470) Soc Auto Engineers.

New Diet Pills: How to Permanently Lose Weight Based on the Latest Medical Research. Larry S. Hobbs. LC 94-65568. (Illus.). 296p. (Orig.). 1995. pap. 14.95 (*0-9639625-7-4*) Pragmatic CA.

New Dieter's Cookbook: Eat Well, Feel Great, Lose Weight. 2nd ed. Ed. by Kristi Fuller. LC 97-71330. (Illus.). 480p. 1997. 34.95 (*0-696-20714-1*, Better Homes) Meredith Bks.

New Dieter's Guide to Weight Loss During Sex. Richard Smith. LC 94-47003. (Illus.). 160p. 1995. pap. 5.95 (*1-56305-781-6*, 3781) Workman Pub.

New Dimension see Nueva Dimension

New Dimension in Old Testament Study. Sadie Gregory. 103p. (Orig.). 1980. pap. 5.00 (*0-917479-05-X*) Guild Psy.

New Dimension in Public Utility Pricing. Noel D. Uri. LC 81-81648. (Contemporary Studies in Economic & Financial Analysis: Vol. 39). 132p. 1983. 78.50 (*0-89232-239-X*) Jai Pr.

New Dimension in Quantum Chemistry: Analytical Derivative Methods in Ab Initio Molecular Electronic Structure Theory. Yukio Yamaguchi et al. LC 93-31798. (International Series of Monographs on Chemistry: Vol. 29). (Illus.). 496p. 1994. text 100.00 (*0-19-507028-3*) OUP.

New Dimension in Women's Health. Linda Alexander. (Health Science Ser.). 104p. 1994. pap. 10.00 (*0-86720-981-X*) Jones & Bartlett.

New Dimensions. R. O'Neil et al. (Illus.). 1993. pap. text, teacher ed. 18.95 (*0-8013-0921-2*) Longman.

New Dimensions. Terra Parma. (Illus.). 52p. 1996. pap. 12.95 (*0-936459-32-8*) Stained Glass.

New Dimensions, No. 13. Ed. by Marta Randall. (Orig.). 1982. pap. 3.50 (*0-671-44227-9*) PB.

New Dimensions: A Book of Poems. Elinor J. Wolfe. LC 96-31991. 128p. 1997. 15.95 (*0-944957-88-9*) Rivercross Pub.

New Dimensions & Perspectives in Gandhism. V. T. Patil. 1989. 60.00 (*81-210-0230-3*, Pub. by Inter-India Pubns) S Asia.

***New Dimensions for the Cube of Space: The Path of Initiation Revealed by the Tarot upon the Qabalistic Cube.** David Allen Hulse. (Illus.). 176p. 2000. pap. 16.95 (*1-57863-137-8*) Weiser.

New Dimensions in Adult Vocational & Career Counseling. Donald E. Super. 32p. 1985. 3.50 (*0-318-20334-0*, OC106) Ctr Educ Trng Employ.

N

New Dimensions in Aerobic Fitness. Brian J. Sharkey. LC 91-12706. (Current Issues in Exercise Science Ser.). (Illus.). 112p. (Orig.). 1991. pap. text 22.00 (*0-87322-326-8*, BSHA0326) Human Kinetics.

New Dimensions in African History: From the Nile Valley to the New World. Ed. by John Henrik Clarke. LC 91-70616. 49.95 (*0-86543-226-0*); pap. 16.95 (*0-86543-227-9*) Africa World.

New Dimensions in African Linguistics & Languages. Paul A. Kotey. LC 99-21197. (Trends in African Linguistics Ser.). 1999. write for info. (*0-86543-665-7*) Africa World,

New Dimensions in Antimicrobial Therapy. fac. ed. Ed. by Richard K. Root & Merle A. Sande. LC 83-23135. (Contemporary Issues in Infectious Diseases Ser.: No. 1). (Illus.). 360p. 1984. reprint ed. pap. 111.60 (*0-7837-7872-4*, 204762900007) Bks Demand.

New Dimensions in Chinese Ink Painting: Works from the Collection of John & Alice Z. Berninghausen. James Cahill. LC 91-11813. (Illus.). 56p. 1992. pap. 15.00 (*0-9625262-3-1*) Middlebury Coll Mus.

New Dimensions in Classical Guitar for Children. Sonia Michelson. 104p. (J). 1995. spiral bd. 8.95 (*1-56222-115-9*, 94537) Mel Bay.

New Dimensions in Ethnohistory: Papers of the 2nd Laurier Conference on Ethnohistory & Ethnology. Ed. by Barry Gough & Laird Christie. (Mercury Ser.: CES No. 120). (Illus.). 300p. 1991. pap. 19.95 (*0-660-12911-6*, Pub. by CN Mus Civilization) U of Wash Pr.

New Dimensions in Evangelical Thought: Essays in Honor of Millard J. Erickson. Ed. by David S. Dockery. LC 97-50064. 448p. 1998. 34.99 (*0-8308-1517-1*, 1517) InterVarsity.

New Dimensions in Floral Design. Marie S. Miller. (Illus.). 173p. (Orig.). (C). 1981. text 29.95 (*0-9606424-0-4*) M S Miller.

New Dimensions in Healing: Healing & the Future. Torkom Saraydarian. LC 91-75267. 916p. 1992. 50.00 (*0-929874-20-X*); pap. 40.00 (*0-929874-21-8*) TSG Pub Found.

New Dimensions in Healing Yourself. Hanna Kroeger. 150p. (Orig.). 1991. pap. 7.00 (*1-883713-09-9*) Hanna Kroeger.

***New Dimensions in Indian Music, Dance & Drama.** Ed. by L. Annapoorna. LC 98-900588. 1998. 64.00 (*81-7574-004-3*, Pub. by Sandeep Prakas) S Asia.

New Dimensions in Investor Relations: Competing for Capital in the 21st Century. Bruce W. Marcus & Sherwood Wallace. LC 97-3288. 432p. 1997. 69.95 (*0-471-14153-4*) Wiley.

New Dimensions in Manufacturing. Bert P. Erdel. LC 98-26023. 186p. 1998. 52.95 (*1-56990-245-3*) Hanser-Gardner.

New Dimensions in Marketing - Quality of Life Research. M. Joseph Sirgy & A. Coskun Samli. LC 94-37875. 400p. 1995. 75.00 (*0-89930-886-4*, Quorum Bks) Greenwood.

New Dimensions in Mental Health-Psychiatric Nursing. 5th ed. Markian E. Kalkman & Anne B. Davis. 1980. text 31.95 (*0-07-033253-3*) McGraw.

New Dimensions in Military History: An Anthology. Ed. by Russell F. Weigley. 419p. (C). 1998. reprint ed. text 15.00 (*0-7881-5837-6*) DIANE Pub.

New Dimensions in Modern Management. Dibakar Panigrahy. 130p. (C). 1994. pap. 75.00 (*81-85880-24-7*, Pub. by Print Hse) St Mut.

New Dimensions in Monetary Theory. N. N. Shrivastava. 268p. (Orig.). (C). 1986. 150.00 (*81-85009-12-0*, Pub. by Print Hse) St Mut.

***New Dimensions in Photo Imaging.** 3rd ed. Blacklow. (Illus.). 160p. 2000. pap. 36.95 (*0-240-80431-7*, Focal) Buttrwrth-Heinemann.

New Dimensions in Photo Imaging: A Step-by-Step Manual. 2nd ed. Laura Blacklow. LC 94-48311. (Illus.). 112p. 1995. pap. text 37.95 (*0-240-80209-8*, Focal) Buttrwrth-Heinemann.

New Dimensions in Psychiatry: A World Review. Ed. by Silvano Arieti & Gerard Chrzanowski. LC 74-16150. 460p. reprint ed. pap. 142.60 (*0-608-30499-9*, 201195100080) Bks Demand.

New Dimensions in Psychiatry: A World Review, Vol. 2. rev. ed. Ed. by Silvano Arieti & Gerard Chrzanowski. LC 74-16150. 523p. 1977. reprint ed. pap. 162.20 (*0-7837-3423-9*, 205774400008) Bks Demand.

New Dimensions in Public Utility Pricing. Ed. by Harry M. Trebing. LC 76-620036. (MSU Public Utilities Studies: Vol. 1976). (Illus.). 631p. reprint ed. pap. 195.70 (*0-608-20515-X*, 207176700002) Bks Demand.

New Dimensions in Puppet Ministry. Lee Garsee. 1983. pap. 7.75 (*0-89137-607-0*) Quality Pubns.

New Dimensions in Regional Integration. Ed. by Jaime De Melo & Arvind Panagariya. (Illus.). 501p. 1996. pap. text 26.95 (*0-521-55668-6*) Cambridge U Pr.

New Dimensions in School Library Media Service. Mary M. Eble & Jeanne L. Renton. LC 88-4230. (Illus.). 486p. 1988. 55.50 (*0-8108-2115-X*) Scarecrow.

New Dimensions in Self-Directed Learning. Long, Huey B., & Assoc. Staff. 419p. (Orig.). 1995. pap. text 26.95 (*1-885584-00-8*) U OK PMC.

New Dimensions in Tatting. To De Haan-van Beek. 87p. 1994. pap. 14.00 (*0-916896-52-8*) Lacis Pubns.

New Dimensions in the Humanities & Social Sciences. Harry R. Garvin. LC 76-27914. (Bucknell Review Ser.: Vol. 23, No.1). 186p. 1977. 22.00 (*0-8387-1966-X*) Bucknell U Pr.

New Dimensions in Transnational Crime. Donal E. MacNamara & Philip J. Stead. 154p. 1982. lib. bdg. 10.00 (*0-89444-035-7*) John Jay Pr.

New Dimensions in Women's Health. Linda L. Alexander & Judith H. LaRosa. LC 93-50822. (Health Science Ser.). 464p. (C). 1994. 48.75 (*0-86720-777-9*) Jones & Bartlett.

New Dimensions in Women's Health. 2nd ed. Linda Lewis Alexander & Judith H. LaRosa. (Illus.). 440p. (C). 1994. pap. text 51.25 (*0-7637-1083-0*) JB Pubns.

New Dimensions in Women's Health. 2nd ed. Linda Alexander et al. (Nursing Ser.). 1998. 50.00 (*0-7637-0552-7*) Jones & Bartlett.

New Dimensions in Youthwork, Vol. 1. Ed. by Howard P. Galloway. LC 72-96322. 1973. 10.95 (*0-87874-007-4*) Galloway.

New Dimensions in Youthwork: Challenges to Youth Organizations, Vol. 2. Ed. by Howard P. Galloway. LC 74-15245. 224p. 1974. 10.95 (*0-87874-014-7*) Galloway.

New Dimensions of Arms Regulations & Disarmament in the Post-Cold War Era: Report of the Secretary-General. United Nations Secretary General. 53p. pap. 9.95 (*92-1-142192-6*, E.93.IX.8) UN.

New Dimensions of Canadian Federalism. Gregory S. Mahler. LC 85-46013. 192p. 1987. 36.50 (*0-8386-3289-0*) Fairleigh Dickinson.

New Dimensions of Confucian & Neo-Confucian Philosophy. Chung-ying Cheng. LC 89-19655. (SUNY Series in Philosophy). 619p. (C). 1991. text 29.50 (*0-7914-0283-5*) State U NY Pr.

New Dimensions of Deep Analysis: A Study of Telepathy in Interpersonal Relationships. Jan Ehrenwald. LC 75-7377. (Perspectives in Psychical Research Ser.). 1975. reprint ed. 26.95 (*0-405-07027-6*) Ayer.

New Dimensions of Government & Politics of Nepal. Ed. by P. D. Kaushik. LC 96-904368. (C). 1996. 30.00 (*81-7003-203-2*, Pub. by S Asia Pubs) S Asia.

New Dimensions of Human Rights. Zbigniew K. Brzezinski. 22p. (Orig.). 1995. pap. 5.00 (*0-87641-145-6*) Carnegie Ethics & Intl Affairs.

New Dimensions of Market Access. Sylvia Ostry. (Occasional Paper Ser.: No. 49). 32p. (Orig.). 1995. pap. 10.00 (*1-56708-049-9*) Grp of Thirty.

New Dimensions of Peacekeeping. Ed. by Daniel M. Warner et al. LC 95-1338. (Law Specials Ser.: Vol. 9). 1995. pap. text 64.00 (*0-7923-3301-2*) Kluwer Academic.

New Dimensions of Political Economy. Walter W. Heller. LC 66-23467. (Godkin Lectures: 1966). 210p. 1966. 24.00 (*0-674-61100-4*) HUP.

New Dimensions of Spirituality: A Biracial & Bicultural Reading of the Novels of Toni Morrison, 84. Karla F. Holloway & Stephanie Demetrakopoulos. LC 87-8473. (Contributions in Women's Studies: No. 84). 184p. 1987. 57.95 (*0-313-25742-6*, HNF/) Greenwood.

New Dimensions of the Federal-State Partnership in Education. Ed. by Joel D. Sherman et al. 236p. (Orig.). 1983. pap. 8.95 (*0-937846-98-8*) Inst Educ Lead.

New Dimensions of Urban Planning: Growth Controls. James W. Hughes. 246p. 1974. pap. 14.95 (*0-87855-601-X*) Transaction Pubs.

New Dimensions of Warfarin Prophylaxis. Ed. by Stanford Wessler et al. (Illus.). 320p. 1987. 75.00 (*0-306-42588-2*, Plenum Trade) Perseus Pubng.

New Dimensions to Energy Policy. Ed. by Robert Lawrence. (Organization Ser.). 233p. 1979. 15.00 (*0-317-35630-5*) Pol Studies.

New Dinosaur Collection, 30 bks. Illus. by Tony Gibbons. Incl. Ankylosaurus (Cretaceous Period) Mike Brown. LC 93-37055. (Illus.). 24p. (J). (gr. 2 up). 1994. lib. bdg. 19.93 (*0-8368-1083-X*); Apatosaurus/Brontosaurus (Jurassic Period) Graham Coleman. LC 94-36809. (Illus.). 24p. (J). (gr. 2 up). 1995. lib. bdg. 19.93 (*0-8368-1273-5*); Baryonyx (Cretaceous Period) Tamara Green. LC 94-36822. (Illus.). 24p. (J). (gr. 2 up). 1995. lib. bdg. 19.93 (*0-8368-1274-3*); Carnotaurus: A Dinosaur from the Cretaceous Period. Tamara Green. LC 96-41857. (Illus.). 24p. (J). (gr. 2 up). 1997. lib. bdg. 19.93 (*0-8368-1731-1*); Ceratosaurus: A Dinosaur from the Jurassic Period. Mike Brown. LC 94-11523. (Illus.). 24p. (J). (gr. 2 up). 1994. lib. bdg. 19.93 (*0-8368-1138-0*); Chasmosaurus (Cretaceous Period) Heather Amery. LC 95-7211. (Illus.). 24p. (J). (gr. 2 up). 1995. lib. bdg. 19.93 (*0-8368-1345-6*); Coelophysis: A Dinosaur from the Triassic Period. Graham Coleman. LC 94-11524. (Illus.). 24p. (J). (gr. 2 up). 1994. lib. bdg. 19.93 (*0-8368-1139-9*); Deinonychus: A Dinosaur from the Cretaceous Period. Mike Brown. LC 94-16969. (Illus.). 24p. (J). (gr. 2 up). 1994. lib. bdg. 19.93 (*0-8368-1140-2*); Dinosaur Atlas. Tamara Green. LC 97-1055. (Illus.). 24p. (J). (gr. 2 up). 1997. lib. bdg. 19.93 (*0-8368-1791-5*); Diplodocus (Jurassic Period) Graham Coleman. LC 93-37054. (Illus.). 24p. (J). (gr. 2 up). 1994. lib. bdg. 19.93 (*0-8368-1084-8*); Gallimimus: A Dinosaur from the Cretaceous Period. Mike Brown. LC 94-16967. (Illus.). 24p. (J). (gr. 2 up). 1994. lib. bdg. 19.93 (*0-8368-1142-9*); Hypsilophodon: A Dinosaur from the Cretaceous Period. Graham Coleman. LC 96-41851. (Illus.). 24p. (J). (gr. 2 up). 1997. lib. bdg. 19.93 (*0-8368-1732-X*); Maiasaura (Cretaceous Period) Jenny Vaughan. LC 93-37053. (Illus.). 24p. (J). (gr. 2 up). 1994. lib. bdg. 19.93 (*0-8368-1085-6*); Mussaurus. Tamara Green. LC 97-584. (Illus.). 24p. (J). (gr. 2 up). 1997. lib. bdg. 19.93 (*0-8368-1789-3*); New Dinosaur Discoveries. Tamara Green. LC 97-554. (Illus.). 24p. (J). (gr. 2 up). 1997. lib. bdg. 19.93 (*0-8368-1792-3*); Ornitholestes: A Dinosaur from the Jurassic Period. Tamara Green. LC 96-41852. (Illus.). 24p. (J). (gr. 2 up). 1997. lib. bdg. 19.93 (*0-8368-1733-8*); Parasaurolophus (Cretaceous Period) Graham Coleman. LC 93-37052. (Illus.). 24p. (J). (gr. 2 up). 1994. lib. bdg. 19.93 (*0-8368-1086-4*); Plesiosaurus (Jurassic Period) Heather Amery. LC 94-36808. (Illus.). 24p. (J). (gr. 2 up). 1995. lib. bdg. 19.93 (*0-8368-1278-6*); Procompsognatus: A Dinosaur from the Triassic Period. Frances Freedman. LC 96-41853. (Illus.). 24p. (J). (gr. 2 up). 1997. lib. bdg. 19.93 (*0-8368-1734-6*); Protoceratops: A Dinosaur from the Cretaceous Period. Heather Amery. LC 93-5536. (Illus.). 24p. (J). (gr. 2 up). 1993. lib. bdg. 19.93 (*0-8368-1046-5*); Psittacosaurus (Cretaceous Period) Tamara Green. LC 95-7234. (Illus.). 24p. (J). (gr. 2 up). 1995. lib. bdg. 19.93 (*0-8368-1348-0*); Pterodactylus: A Dinosaur from the Jurassic Period. Graham Coleman. LC 94-16966. (Illus.). 24p. (J). (gr. 2 up). 1994. lib. bdg. 19.93 (*0-8368-1143-7*); Spinosaurus (Cretaceous Period) Tamara Green. LC 95-7235. (Illus.). 24p. (J). (gr. 2 up). 1995. lib. bdg. 19.93 (*0-8368-1349-9*); Troodon. Laurence Anthony. LC 97-555. (Illus.). 24p. (YA). (gr. 2 up). 1997. lib. bdg. 19.93 (*0-8368-1790-7*); Tyrannosaurus Rex: A Dinosaur from the Cretaceous Period. Heather Amery. LC 93-28157. (Illus.). 24p. (J). (gr. 2 up). 1993. lib. bdg. 19.93 (*0-8368-1049-X*); Velociropator (Cretaceous Period) Heather Amery. LC 93-37064. (Illus.). 24p. (J). (gr. 2 up). 1994. lib. bdg. 19.93 (*0-8368-1087-2*); Vulcanodon (Jurassic Period) Heather Amery. LC 95-7236. (Illus.). 24p. (J). (gr. 2 up). 1995. lib. bdg. 19.93 (*0-8368-1350-2*); (Illus.). (J). (gr. 2 up). Set lib. bdg. 706.80 (*0-8368-1997-7*) Gareth Stevens Inc.

New Dinosaur Dictionary. Donald F. Glut. (Illus.). 256p. 1982. pap. 14.95 (*0-8065-0918-X*, Citadel Pr) Carol Pub Group.

New Dinosaur Discoveries see New Dinosaur Collection

New Dinosaurs: Skeletons in the Sand. Elaine Pascoe. LC 96-43530. (New Explorers Ser.). (Illus.). 48p. (YA). (gr. 5 up). 1997. lib. bdg. 17.95 (*1-56711-231-5*) Blackbirch.

***New Diplomacy in Italy: American Propaganda & U. S.-Italian Relations, 1917-1919.** Louis John Nigro, Jr. LC 97-32371. (Studies in Modern European History: Vol. 28). XIV, 153p. (C). 1999. text 44.00 (*0-8204-3942-8*) P Lang Pubng.

New Direct Marketing: How to Implement a Profit-Driven Database Marketing Strategy. David Shepard Associates Inc. Staff. 450p. 1990. text 60.00 (*1-55623-317-5*, Irwn Prfssnl) McGraw-Hill Prof.

New Direct Marketing: How to Implement a Profit-Driven Database Marketing Strategy. 2nd ed. Shepard, David, Associates Staff. LC 94-1235. 512p. 1994. text 74.95 (*1-55623-809-6*, Irwn Prfssnl) McGraw-Hill Prof.

New Direct Marketing: How to Implement a Profit-Driven Database Marketing Strategy. 3rd ed. Shepard, David, Associates Staff. (Illus.). 500p. 1998. 114.95 (*0-07-058056-1*) McGraw-Hill Prof.

New Direction. Rod Parsley. 41p. (Orig.). 1994. pap. 1.00 (*1-880244-16-0*) Wrld Harvest Church.

New Direction in American Politics. Ed. by John E. Chubb & Paul E. Peterson. LC 85-71272. 409p. 1985. 39.95 (*0-8157-1406-8*); pap. 18.95 (*0-8157-1405-X*) Brookings.

New Direction in Canadian Poetry. John Robert Colombo. LC 70-865600. (Aspects of English Ser.). 87p. 1971. write for info. (*0-03-923345-6*) Holt R&W.

New Direction in Conflict Resolution. Rubenstein. 1999. text. write for info. (*0-312-10371-9*) St Martin.

New Directions see New Directions in Prose & Poetry

New Directions: Alternatives to the United States Social Welfare System see Human Needs & Social Welfare Curriculum Project: Grades 9-12

New Directions: An Integrated Approach to Reading, Writing & Critical Thinking. Peter S. Gardner. 320p. (C). 1996. pap. text 22.95 (*0-521-65776-8*) Cambridge U Pr.

New Directions: An Integrated Approach to Reading, Writing & Critical Thinking: Instructor's Manual. Peter S. Gardner. 60p. (C). 1996. pap., teacher ed. 6.00 (*0-521-65775-X*) Cambridge U Pr.

New Directions: Media Education Worldwide. Ed. by Cary Bazalgette et al. (Illus.). 256p. (C). 1993. pap. 21.95 (*0-85170-350-X*, Pub. by British Film Inst) Ind U Pr.

New Directions: Stepping Out of Street Life. Patricia E. Kariel. (Illus.). 217p. (Orig.). 1994. pap. 1.50 (*0-614-00622-8*, Pub. by Greenways Pr) Am Youth Wrk Ctr.

New Directions & New Partnerships. James D. Wolfsensohn. (FRE.). 24p. 1996. pap. write for info. (*0-8213-3524-3*, 13524); pap. write for info. (*0-8213-3525-1*, 13525) World Bank.

New Directions Around the Drum. Mark Hamon. (Illus.). 180p. (YA). (gr. 9-12). 1994. pap. 14.95 (*0-931759-81-1*) Centerstream Pub.

New Directions at Madison Park Technical-Vocational High School. Boston Public Schools Staff. 492p. 1993. 30.00 (*0-614-22227-3*) Ctr Law & Ed.

New Directions at the Department of the Interior. Ed. by Law & Business Inc. Staff & Legal Times Seminars Staff. (Seminar Course Handbks.). 1983. pap. 30.00 (*0-686-89377-8*, C00981) Harcourt.

New Directions for Agriculture & Agricultural Research: Neglected Dimensions & Emerging Alternatives. Ed. by Kenneth A. Dahlberg. LC 85-22046. 448p. (C). 1986. 79.50 (*0-8476-7417-7*, R7417); pap. 29.50 (*0-8476-7418-5*, R7418) Rowman.

New Directions for Agriculture, Forestry & Fisheries. FAO Staff. 68p. 1994. 12.00 (*92-5-103586-5*, F35865, Pub. by FAO) Bernan Associates.

New Directions for Biosciences Research in Agriculture: High-Reward Opportunities. National Research Council U. S. Staff. LC 85-60580. 136p. reprint ed. pap. 42.20 (*0-7837-2037-8*, 204230400003) Bks Demand.

New Directions for Child Protective Services Supporting Children, Families & Communities Through Legislative Reform. Stephen M. Christian. LC 97-207221. 58p. 1997. 25.00 (*1-55516-754-3*, 6138) Natl Conf State Legis.

New Directions for Clarinet. rev. ed. Phillip Rehfeldt. (New Instrumentation Ser.: Vol. 4). 1993. pap. 39.95 (*0-520-03379-5*, Pub. by U CA Pr) Cal Prin Full Svc.

New Directions for College Counselors. Charles Warnath et al. LC 73-7150. (Jossey-Bass Higher Education & Behavioral Science Ser.). 350p. reprint ed. pap. 108.50 (*0-608-12178-9*, 202387900034) Bks Demand.

New Directions for Development in Third World Countries: The Failure of U. S. Foreign Policy. J. F. Torres. 107p. 1993. 69.95 (*1-85628-418-2*, Pub. by Avebry) Ashgate Pub Co.

New Directions for Education. Ed. by Lloyd G. Cooper & Gregory P. Maltby. 249p. 1975. pap. text 12.75 (*0-8422-0504-7*) Irvington.

New Directions for Equity in Mathematics Education. Ed. by Walter G. Secada et al. (Illus.). 376p. (C). 1995. text 59.95 (*0-521-47152-4*); pap. text 19.95 (*0-521-47720-4*) Cambridge U Pr.

New Directions for Intelligent Tutoring Systems. Ed. by E. Costa. (NATO ASI Series F: Computer & Systems Science: Vol. 91). x, 396p. 1992. 84.00 (*0-387-55754-7*) Spr-Verlag.

New Directions for Manpower Policy. Barbara Goldman. LC 78-301815. (Special Study of the C. D. Howe Research Institute Ser.). 126p. 1976. reprint ed. pap. 39.10 (*0-608-01382-X*, 206214300002) Bks Demand.

New Directions for Medical Education. Ed. by H. G. Schmidt et al. (Frontiers of Primary Care Ser.). (Illus.). 360p. 1989. 65.00 (*0-387-96390-1*) Spr-Verlag.

New Directions for Men: Using Life's Hard Times to Make Your Life Great. rev. ed. Lee Wotherspoon. 240p. 1994. pap. 14.95 (*0-9620664-3-5*) S A G E.

New Directions for Mental Health Services. Carl A. Taube et al. 325p. 1990. 51.95 (*1-56032-140-7*) Hemisp Pub.

New Directions for NATO: Adapting the Atlantic Alliance to the Needs of the 1990s. Walker et al. (Orig.). 1988. pap. write for info. (*0-945369-02-6*) Inst Resrc & Secur.

New Directions for Organization Theory: Problems & Prospects. Jeffrey Pfeffer. LC 96-33593. (Illus.). 272p. 1997. 38.00 (*0-19-511434-5*) OUP.

New Directions for Placement-Related Research & Practice in the Rehabilitation Process. David Vandergoot et al. LC 79-105250. 44p. 1977. 3.00 (*0-686-38812-7*) Human Res Ctr.

New Directions for Product Testing & Sensory Analysis of Foods. H. R. Moskowitz. 370p. 1985. 73.00 (*0-917678-18-4*) Food & Nut Pr.

New Directions for Social Work Practice Research. Ed. by Miriam Potocky-Tripodi & Tony Tripodi. LC 99-12763. 139p. 1999. 41.95 (*0-87101-305-3*) Natl Assn Soc Wkrs.

New Directions for Teaching Practice & Research. Ed. by Hersholt C. Waxman & Herbert J. Walberg. LC 99-61326. 320p. 1999. 38.00 (*0-8211-2274-6*) McCutchan.

New Directions for Vocational Education at the Secondary Level. James A. Kadamus & Willard R. Daggett. (Eric Information Analysis Ser.). 44p. 1986. 6.00 (*0-318-22357-0*, IN 311) Ctr Educ Trng Employ.

New Directions for Youth Ministry: Practical Strategies to Reach Teenagers. Wayne Rice et al. Ed. by Amy Simpson. LC 98-7059. 128p. 1998. per. 16.99 (*0-7644-2103-4*, Vital Ministry) Group Pub.

New Directions in Action Research. Ed. by Ortrun Zuber-Skerritt. 224p. 1996. 79.95 (*0-7507-0579-5*, Falmer Pr); pap. 27.95 (*0-7507-0580-9*, Falmer Pr) Taylor & Francis.

New Directions in Affective Disorders. Ed. by Bernard Lerer & Samuel Gershon. (Illus.). 625p. 1989. 244.00 (*0-387-96769-9*) Spr-Verlag.

New Directions in African Literature, 1970, 1990. Wright. LC 97-20634. 201p. 1997. 32.00 (*0-8057-4556-4*, Twyne) Mac Lib Ref.

New Directions in AI Planning. Ed. by M. Ghallab. LC 95-7901. (Frontiers in Artificial Intelligence & Applications Ser.: Vol. 31). 400p. (YA). (gr. 12). 1996. 90.00 (*90-5199-237-8*, 237-8) IOS Press.

New Directions in American Architecture. rev. ed. Robert A. Stern. LC 70-81278. (New Directions in Architecture Ser.). 128p. 1969. pap. 11.95 (*0-8076-0527-1*) Braziller.

New Directions in American Indian History. Ed. by Colin G. Calloway. LC 88-5424. (D'Arcy McNickle Center Bibliographies in American Indian History Ser.: Vol. 1). 272p. 1992. pap. text 14.95 (*0-8061-2233-1*) U of Okla Pr.

New Directions in American Intellectual History. Wingspread Conference on New Directions in America. Ed. by Paul K. Conkin & John Higham. LC 78-21563. 265p. reprint ed. pap. 82.20 (*0-8357-8245-X*, 203413100088) Bks Demand.

New Directions in American Religious History. Ed. by Harry S. Stout & Darryl G. Hart. LC 96-10983. 512p. 1998. pap. 19.95 (*0-19-511213-X*); text 55.00 (*0-19-510413-7*) OUP.

New Directions in Analytical Political Economy. Ed. by Amitava K. Dutt. LC 93-50633. 368p. 1994. 95.00 (*1-85898-032-1*) E Elgar.

***New Directions in Anthropological Kinship.** Linda Stone. LC 00-40303. 2000. pap. 27.95 (*0-7425-0108-6*) Rowman.

New Directions in Anti-Cancer Chemotherapy. Ed. by Michel E. Marty. (Journal: Oncology: Vol. 51, Suppl. 1, 1994). (Illus.). iv, 40p. 1994. pap. 19.25 (*3-8055-6080-X*) S Karger.

New Directions in Applied Mathematics: Proceedings. Ed. by Peter J. Hilton & Gail S. Young. (Illus.). 192p. 1981. 69.95 (*0-387-90604-5*) Spr-Verlag.

New Directions in Atomic Physics, 2 vols., Vol. 1: Theory. Ed. by Edward U. Condon & Oktay Sinanoglu. LC 78-140542. (Yale Series in the Sciences). 264p. 1972. reprint ed. pap. 81.90 (*0-608-08433-6*, 201680100001) Bks Demand.

An Asterisk (*) at the beginning of an entry indicates that the title is appearing for the first time.

New Directions in Atomic Physics, 2 vols., Vol. 2: Experiments. Ed. by Edward U. Condon & Oktay Sinanoglu. LC 78-140542. (Yale Series in the Sciences). 179p. 1972. reprint ed. pap. 55.50 (*0-608-08434-4*, 201680100002) Bks Demand.

New Directions in Attitude Measurement. Ed. by Dagmar Krebs & Peter Schmidt. LC 93-22496. xiv, 378p. (C). 1993. lib. bdg. 121.55 (*3-11-013871-9*) De Gruyter.

New Directions in Attribution Research, Vol. 3. Ed. by John H. Harvey et al. 560p. 1981. text 89.95 (*0-89859-098-1*) L Erlbaum Assocs.

New Directions in Attribution Research, Vols. 1 & 2. Incl. Vol. 1. Ed. by J. H. Harvey et al. 467p. 1976. text 89.95 (*0-89859-123-6*); Vol. 2. 416p. 1978. text 89.95 (*0-89859-124-4*); 468p. write for info. (*0-318-56995-7*) L Erlbaum Assocs.

New Directions in Behavioral Development. Ed. by Sidney W. Bijou & Emilio Ribes. (Illus.). 189p. (C). 1996. text 29.95 (*1-878978-24-1*) Context Pr.

New Directions in Biblical Theology Vol. 76: Papers of the Aarhus Conference, 16-19 September, 1993. Ed. by Sigfred Pedersen. LC 94-28789. xiii, 290p. 1994. 116.00 (*90-04-10120-9*) Brill Academic Pubs.

New Directions in British Politics? Essays on the Evolving Constitution. Ed. by Phillip Norton. 208p. 1991. text 80.00 (*1-85278-350-8*) E Elgar.

New Directions in Budget Theory. Ed. by Irene S. Rubin. LC 87-9977. (SUNY Series in Public Administration). 207p. (C). 1988. text 20.50 (*0-88706-624-0*); pap. text 21.95 (*0-88706-625-9*) State U NY Pr.

New Directions in California History: A Book of Readings. James J. Rawls. 399p. (C). 1988. pap. 34.06 (*0-07-051253-1*) McGraw.

New Directions in Cancer Treatment. Ed. by Ian T. Magrath. (Illus.). 610p. 1989. pap. 104.00 (*0-387-19063-5*) Spr-Verlag.

*__New Directions in Career Planning & the Workplace: Practical Strategies for Career Management Professionals.__ 2nd ed. Jean M. Kummerow. LC 00-30855. 368p. 2000. pap. 24.95 (*0-89106-145-2*, Davies-Black Pub) Consulting Psychol.

New Directions in Career Planning & the Workplace: Practical Strategies for Counselors. Ed. by Jean M. Kummerow. LC 91-18206. 216p. 1991. pap. 16.95 (*0-89106-050-2*, 7338, Pub. by Consulting Psychol) Consulting Psychol.

New Directions in Cello Playing: How to Make Playing Easier & Play Without Pain. Victor Sazer. Ed. by Nina S. O'Donnell. (Illus.). 1995. pap. 24.95 (*0-944810-02-0*) Ofnote.

New Directions in Celtic Studies. Ed. by Amy Hale & Philip Payton. (Illus.). 288p. 1999. 80.00 (*0-85989-622-6*); pap. 27.95 (*0-85989-587-4*) Univ Exeter Pr.

New Directions in Chenille. Nannette Holmberg. LC 99-47728. (Illus.). 112p. 2000. pap. 26.95 (*1-56477-275-6*, B394) Martingale & Co.

New Directions in Chicano Scholarship. rev. ed. Ed. by Ricardo Romo & Raymund Paredes. (Monographs in Chicano Studies). 279p. (C). 1977. reprint ed. pap. 18.95 (*0-930929-00-4*) U CA Ctr Chicano Stud.

New Directions in Childhood Psychopathology: Developmental Considerations, Vol. 1. Ed. by Saul I. Harrison & John F. McDermott, Jr. LC 78-70232. (Illus.). xviii, 609p. (C). 1979. 90.00 (*0-8236-3570-8*) Intl Univs Pr.

New Directions in Childhood Psychopathology Vol. 2: Deviations in Development. Ed. by Saul I. Harrison & John F. McDermott, Jr. LC 78-70232. xix, 566p. 1982. 85.00 (*0-8236-3571-6*) Intl Univs Pr.

New Directions in Children's Mental Health. Ed. by Jalal Shamsie. LC 79-17844. 1979. text 25.00 (*0-88331-167-4*) R B Luce.

New Directions in Civil Rights Studies. Ed. by Armstead L. Robinson & Patricia Sullivan. (Carter G. Woodson Institute Series in Black Studies). 240p. 1991. text 29.50 (*0-8139-1319-5*) U Pr of Va.

New Directions in Cognitive Science. Ed. by Theodore Shlechter & Michael Toglia. LC 85-13442. 320p. 1985. text 78.50 (*0-89391-230-1*) Ablx Pub.

New Directions in Cognitive Therapy: A Casebook. Ed. by Gary Emery et al. LC 81-1264. 314p. reprint ed. pap. 97.40 (*0-7837-0690-1*, 204102300019) Bks Demand.

New Directions in Commercial Law. Ed. by R. Cranston & R. M. Goode. LC 92-24004. (Illus.). 450p. 1993. text 95.00 (*0-19-825714-7*, Clarendon Pr) OUP.

New Directions in Composition Research. Ed. by Richard Beach & Lillian S. Bridwell. LC 83-5716. (Perspectives in Writing Research Ser.). (Illus.). 432p. 1984. reprint ed. pap. 134.00 (*0-608-07581-7*, 205989600010) Bks Demand.

New Directions in Computational Economics. Ed. by William W. Cooper & Andrew B. Whinston. LC 93-23548. (Advances in Computational Economics Ser.: Vol. 4). 1994. lib. bdg. 153.00 (*0-7923-2539-7*) Kluwer Academic.

New Directions in Conflict Theory: Conflict Resolution & Conflict Transformation. Raimo Vayrynen. 256p. 1991. 55.00 (*0-8039-8435-9*); pap. 22.50 (*0-8039-8437-5*) Sage.

*__New Directions in Corporate Strategy.__ Ed. by Garry Twite & Michael O'Keeffe. (Illus.). 200p. 2000. pap. 24.95 (*1-86508-207-4*, Pub. by Allen & Unwin Pty) Paul & Co Pubs.

New Directions in Counselling. Ed. by Rowan Bayne et al. 336p. (C). 1996. pap. 29.99 (*0-415-13143-X*) Routledge.

New Directions in Creative & Innovative Management: Bridging Theory & Practice. Ed. by Yuji Ijiri & Robert L. Kuhn. 368p. 1988. pap. 35.00 (*0-88730-365-X*, HarpBusn) HarpInfo.

*__New Directions in Creativity: Mark A.__ M. J. Renzulli et al. 2000. pap. 25.95 (*0-936386-79-7*) Creative Learning.

*__New Directions in Creativity: Mark B.__ L. Smith et al. 2000. pap. 25.95 (*0-936386-80-0*) Creative Learning.

*__New Directions in Creativity: Mark 1.__ Joseph S. Renzulli. 2000. pap. 25.95 (*0-936386-81-9*) Creative Learning.

*__New Directions in Creativity: Mark 2.__ Joseph S. Renzulli. 2000. pap. 25.95 (*0-936386-82-7*) Creative Learning.

*__New Directions in Creativity: Mark 3.__ Joseph S. Renzulli & C. M. Callahan. 2000. pap. 25.95 (*0-936386-83-5*) Creative Learning.

New Directions in Criminological Theory: Advances in Criminological Theory. Ed. by Freda Adler & William S. Laufer. (Advances in Criminological Theory Ser.: Vol. 4). 320p. (C). 1992. 44.95 (*1-56000-046-5*) Transaction Pubs.

New Directions in Current Architecture. (Illus.). 96p. 1989. pap. 19.95 (*0-312-03122-X*) St Martin.

New Directions in Development Economics. Ed. by Amitava K. Dutt & Kenneth P. Jameson. 208p. 1992. text 90.00 (*1-85278-535-7*) E Elgar.

New Directions in Development Economics: Growth, Environmental Concerns, & Government in the 1990s. Ed. by Mats Lundahl & Benno J. Ndulu. LC 95-24256. (Studies in Development Economics: Vol. 3). 472p. (C). 1996. 95.00 (*0-415-12121-3*) Routledge.

New Directions in Dirichlet Forms. Jurgen Jost et al. Ed. by Karl-Theodor Sturm. LC 98-25202. (AMS/IP Studies in Advanced Mathematics: Vol. 8). 277p. 1998. 49.00 (*0-8218-1061-8*) Am Math.

New Directions in Disarmament. Ed. by William Epstein & Bernard Feld. LC 81-4494. 222p. 1981. 67.95 (*0-275-90610-8*, C0610, Praeger Pubs) Greenwood.

New Directions in Discourse Processing. Ed. by Roy O. Freedle. (Advances in Discourse Processes Ser.: Vol. 2). 352p. 1979. text 78.50 (*0-89391-003-1*) Ablx Pub.

New Directions in Dream Interpretation. Ed. by Gayle Delaney. LC 92-33941. (SUNY Series in Dream Studies). 308p. (C). 1993. text 59.50 (*0-7914-1605-4*); pap. text 24.95 (*0-7914-1606-2*) State U NY Pr.

New Directions in Ecological Physiology. Ed. by Martin E. Feder et al. (Illus.). 376p. 1988. pap. text 37.95 (*0-521-34938-9*) Cambridge U Pr.

New Directions in Econometric Modeling of Energy Demand: With Applications to Latin America. Glenn D. Westley. 386p. (C). 1992. pap. text 24.50 (*0-940602-43-1*) IADB.

New Directions in Econometric Modelling & Forecasting in U. S. Agriculture. Rausser. 830p. 1983. 135.00 (*0-444-00736-9*) P-H.

New Directions in Economic Methodology. Ed. by Roger Backhouse. LC 93-37623. (Economics as Social Theory Ser.). 400p. (C). 1994. pap. 29.99 (*0-415-09637-5*, B3179) Routledge.

New Directions in Economic Policy: An Agenda for the 1980's. Everett M. Ehrlich & Raymond C. Scheppach. LC 84-4712. 199p. 1984. 57.95 (*0-275-91148-9*, C1148, Praeger Pubs) Greenwood.

New Directions in Economic Psychology: Theory, Experiment & Application. Stephen E. Lea et al. 304p. 1992. text 95.00 (*1-85278-462-8*) E Elgar.

New Directions in Education: Selections from Holistic Education Review. Intro. by Ron Miller. 400p. (Orig.). (C). 1991. pap. 12.95 (*0-9627232-1-5*) Psychology Pr.

New Directions in Educational Psychology Vol. 2: Behavior & Motivation. Ed. by Nigel Hastings & Josh Schwieso. 285p. 1987. 75.00 (*1-85000-228-2*, Falmer Pr); pap. 39.95 (*1-85000-229-0*, Falmer Pr) Taylor & Francis.

New Directions in Educational Technology. Ed. by Eileen Scanlon & Tim O'Shea. LC 92-31544. (NATO ASI Series F: Computer & Systems Sciences, Special Programme AET: Vol. 96). viii, 251p. 1992. 82.95 (*0-387-55883-7*) Spr-Verlag.

New Directions in Eldercare Services: Cooperation along a Continuum. Ken Dychtwald et al. 1990. pap. 44.95 (*0-685-71203-6*) McGraw.

New Directions in Electroanalytical Chemistry. Ed. by J. Leddy & R. M. Wightman. LC 95-83755. (Proceedings Ser.: Vol. 96-9). (Illus.). 408p. 1996. 59.00 (*1-56677-161-7*) Electrochem Soc.

*__New Directions in Electroanalytical Chemistry II.__ Symposium on New Directions in Electroanalytical Chemistry II et al. Ed. by Johna Leddy et al. LC 99-61130. (Illus.). 268p. 1999. 62.00 (*1-56677-227-3*, PV 99-5) Electrochem Soc.

New Directions in Electrophoretic Methods. Ed. by James W. Jorgenson & Marshall Phillips. LC 87-1777. (ACS Symposium Ser.: No. 335). (Illus.). ix, 284p. 1987. 71.95 (*0-8412-1021-7*) Am Chemical.

New Directions in Electrophoretic Methods. Ed. by James W. Jorgenson & Marshall Phillips. LC 87-1777. (ACS Symposium Ser.: Vol. 335). 288p. 1987. reprint ed. pap. 89.30 (*0-608-03547-5*, 206426600008) Bks Demand.

New Directions in Elementary School Mathematics. Emma E. Holmes. (Illus.). 576p. (C). 1995. pap. text 75.00 (*0-02-356451-2*, Macmillan Coll) P-H.

New Directions in Employability: Reducing Barriers to Full Employment. Ed. by David B. Orr. LC 73-6094. (Special Studies in U. S. Economic, Social & Political Issues). 1973. 42.50 (*0-275-28838-2*) Irvington.

New Directions in Energy Technology. Association of Energy Engineers Staff. LC 84-81176. 500p. 1984. text 45.00 (*0-915586-87-8*); pap. text 38.00 (*0-915586-88-6*) Fairmont Pr.

New Directions in English Language & Literature Teaching in India. S. C. Sood. (C). 1988. 15.00 (*0-8364-2478-6*, Pub. by Ajanta) S Asia.

New Directions in English Language Corpora: Methodology, Results, Software Developments. Ed. by Gerhard Leitner. LC 92-26798. (Topics in English Linguistics Ser.: Vol. 9). (Illus.). ix, 368p. 1992. lib. bdg. 136.95 (*3-11-013201-X*) Mouton.

New Directions in Environmental Participation. David Canter et al. 450p. 1988. text 78.95 (*0-566-05570-8*, Pub. by Avebry) Ashgate Pub Co.

New Directions in Ethics: The Challenge of Applied Ethics. Ed. by Joseph P. DeMarco & Richard M. Fox. 320p. (C). 1986. text 47.50 (*0-7102-0639-9*, Routledge Thoemms) Routledge.

New Directions in European Community Law. Frances G. Snyder. (Law in Context Ser.). 200p. (C). 1994. pap. text 23.95 (*0-297-82031-1*) Northwestern U Pr.

New Directions in European Community Law. Frances G. Snyder. (Law in Context Ser.). xviii, 181p. (C). 1994. 57.50 (*0-297-82030-3*) W S Hein.

New Directions in European Historiography. rev. ed. Georg G. Iggers. LC 83-25975. 280p. 1984. pap. 22.00 (*0-8195-6071-5*, Wesleyan Univ Pr) U Pr of New Eng.

New Directions in European Public Law. Ed. by Jack Beatson & Takis Tridimas. LC 98-196495. 300p. 1998. pap. 60.00 (*1-901362-24-8*, Pub. by Hart Pub) Northwestern U Pr.

New Directions in Failure to Thrive: Implications for Future Research & Practice. Ed. by Dennis Drotar. 398p. 1986. 85.00 (*0-306-42216-6*, Plenum Trade) Perseus Pubng.

New Directions in Federal Indian Policy. University of California, American Indian Studies. (Contemporary American Indian Issues Ser.). 134p. 1979. pap. 10.00 (*0-935626-28-X*) U Cal AISC.

New Directions in Feminist Psychology: Practice, Theory & Research. Ed. by Joan C. Chrisler & Doris Howard. LC 91-5168. (Focus on Women Ser.: Vol. 13). 272p. 1992. 34.95 (*0-8261-7540-6*) Springer Pub.

New Directions in Finance. Ed. by Dilip K. Ghosh & Shahriar Khaksari. LC 94-13587. 400p. (C). (gr. 13). 1995. 130.00 (*0-415-11110-2*, B4641) Routledge.

New Directions in Finance: Strategic Outsourcing. (Research Reports: No. F853). 1995. 295.00 (*0-85058-853-7*) Economist Intell.

New Directions in Greek American Studies. Ed. by Dan Georgakas & Charles C. Moskos. LC 91-61110. 182p. (C). 1991. pap. 12.00 (*0-918618-47-9*) Pella Pub.

New Directions in Guided Wave & Coherent Optics, 2 vols., Set. Ed. by Daniel B. Ostrowsky & E. Spitz. 1984. text 321.50 (*90-247-2938-6*) Kluwer Academic.

New Directions in Health Care: Consequences for the Elderly. Emily Goodman. (Papers: No. 5). 36p. 1986. 5.00 (*0-934459-30-4*) United Hosp Fund.

New Directions in Health Care Policies: Improving Cost Control & Effectiveness. OECD Staff. LC 96-147497. (Health Care Policy Studies: No. 7). 15p. (Orig.). 1995. pap. 34.00 (*92-64-14545-1*, Pub. by Org for Econ) OECD.

New Directions in Health Psychology. Harold E. Schroeder. 1990. 53.95 (*0-89116-925-3*) Hemisp Pub.

New Directions in Hospitality & Tourism: A Worldwide Review. Richard Teare et al. 96p. 1998. pap. 24.95 (*0-304-70394-X*) Continuum.

New Directions in Internal Auditing. Jonathan B. Schiff. (Report: No. 946). (Illus.). viii, 60p. (Orig.). 1990. pap. text 100.00 (*0-8237-0392-4*) Conference Bd.

*__New Directions in International Economic Law: Essays in Honour of John H. Jackson.__ John Howard Jackson et al. LC 00-33089. 2000. write for info. (*90-411-9805-9*) Kluwer Law Intl.

New Directions in International Education. Ed. by Richard D. Lambert. LC 80-65243. (Annals of the American Academy of Political & Social Science Ser.: No. 449). 1980. pap. text 18.00 (*0-87761-251-X*) Am Acad Pol Soc Sci.

*__New Directions in International Environmental Negotiation.__ Ed. by Lawrence E. Susskind & William Moomaw. LC 99-22893. 176p. (C). 1999. pap. 20.00 (*1-880711-14-1*, Pon Bks) Prog Negot HLS.

New Directions in Invertebrate Immunology. Ed. by K. Soderhall et al. LC 95-67854. (Illus.). 494p. (C). 1995. text 95.00 (*0-9625505-9-0*) SOS Pubns NJ.

New Directions in Jewish Theology in America. Arthur Green. (David W. Belin Lectures in American Jewish Affairs). 20p. pap. 2.00 (*1-881759-03-2*) J&S Frankel Ctr.

New Directions in Judicial Review. Ed. by Jeffrey Jowell & Dawn Oliver. (Current Legal Problems Ser.). xiii, 96p. 1988. pap. 40.00 (*0-420-47800-0*) W S Hein.

*__New Directions in Language Development & Disorders.__ Ed. by Michael Perkins & Sara Howard. LC 99-47340. 303p. 1999. write for info. (*0-306-46284-2*) Kluwer Academic.

New Directions in Liability Law. (Proceedings of the Academy of Political Science Ser.: Vol. 37, No. 1). 1988. pap. 12.95 (*0-614-04167-8*) Acad Poli Sci.

New Directions in Library & Information Science Education. Jose-Marie Griffiths & Donald W. King. 467p. 1986. 65.00 (*0-313-25779-5*, Greenwood Pr) Greenwood.

New Directions in Literary History. Ralph Cohen. LC 73-8115. (Illus.). 277p. reprint ed. pap. 85.90 (*0-8357-6743-4*, 203539800095) Bks Demand.

New Directions in Machine Language. Ed. by Dan Maxwell et al. (Distributed Language Translation Ser.). 259p. (C). 1988. 90.80 (*90-6765-377-2*); pap. 61.55 (*90-6765-378-0*) Mouton.

New Directions in Management Science. M. C. Jackson & P. Keys. 150p. 1987. text 75.95 (*0-566-05094-3*) Ashgate Pub Co.

New Directions in Marketing: Business-to-Business Strategies for the 1990s. Aubrey Wilson. (Illus.). 240p. 1992. 29.95 (*0-8442-3364-1*, NTC Business Bks) NTC Contemp Pub Co.

New Directions in Mediation: Communication Research & Perspectives. Ed. by Joseph P. Folger & Tricia S. Jones. LC 93-32784. 288p. (C). 1994. text 56.00 (*0-8039-5550-2*); pap. text 26.00 (*0-8039-5551-0*) Sage.

New Directions in Medicine: A Directory of Learning Opportunities. Raymond F. Rosenthal & James S. Gordon. 1984. pap. 15.95 (*0-931211-00-X*) Aurora Assocs.

New Directions in Memory & Aging: Proceedings of the George A. Talland Memorial Conference. Leonard W. Poon. Ed. by James L. Fozard et al. LC 79-27548. (Illus.). 572p. 1980. text 115.00 (*0-89859-035-3*) L Erlbaum Assocs.

New Directions in MIS Management: A Guide for MIS Practitioners & End Users. Robert J. Thierauf. LC 88-32146. 321p. 1989. 69.50 (*0-89930-409-5*, TGD, Quorum Bks) Greenwood.

New Directions in MIS Management: A Guide for the 1990s. Robert J. Thierauf. LC 88-6735. 257p. 1988. 62.95 (*0-89930-346-3*, TND/, Quorum Bks) Greenwood.

New Directions in Mission & Evangelization No. 2: Theological Foundations. Ed. by James A. Scherer & Stephen B. Bevans. LC 92-1273. 250p. (Orig.). 1994. pap. 22.00 (*0-88344-953-6*) Orbis Bks.

New Directions in Mission & Evangelization 3: Faith & Culture. Ed. by James A. Scherer & Stephen B. Bevans. LC 92-1273. 1992. pap. 25.00 (*0-88344-792-4*) Orbis Bks.

New Directions in Mission & Evangelization 3: Faith & Culture. James A. Scherer & Stephen B. Bevans. 300p. 1999. pap. 25.00 (*1-57075-258-3*) Orbis Bks.

New Directions in Molecular Luminescence - STP 822. Ed. by DeLyle Eastwood. LC 83-70423. 131p. 1983. pap. text 24.00 (*0-8031-0212-7*, STP822) ASTM.

New Directions in Molecular Simulation. Wilfred F. Van Gunsteren. 159p. 1993. pap. text 359.00 (*2-88124-950-7*) Gordon & Breach.

New Directions in Music. 6th ed. David Cope. (Illus.). 399p. (C). 1998. reprint ed. pap. text 38.95 (*0-88133-992-X*) Waveland Pr.

New Directions in New Testament Study. Patrick Henry. LC 79-16267. 300p. reprint ed. pap. 93.00 (*0-7837-2632-5*, 204298200006) Bks Demand.

*__New Directions in Nonlinear Observer Design Vol. 244.__ Ed. by H. Nijmeijer & T. I. Fossen. LC 99-12174. (Lecture Notes in Control & Information Sciences Ser.). (Illus.). xx, 532p. 1999. pap. 119.00 (*1-85233-134-8*, Pub. by Spr-Verlag) Spr-Verlag.

N

New Directions in Old Age Policies. Ed. by Janie S. Steckenrider & Tonya M. Parrott. LC 97-46976. (Illus.). 256p. (C). 1998. pap. text 19.95 (*0-7914-3914-3*) State U NY Pr.

New Directions in Old Age Politics. Ed. by Janie S. Steckenrider & Tonya M. Parrott. LC 97-46976. (Illus.). 256p. (C). 1998. text 59.50 (*0-7914-3913-5*) State U NY Pr.

New Directions in Origami. Steve Biddle & Megumi Biddle. LC 92-2209. 1993. pap. 15.95 (*0-312-08037-9*) St Martin.

New Directions in Parapsychological Research. Joseph H. Rush. LC 64-22612. (Parapsychological Monographs: No. 4). 1964. pap. 5.00 (*0-912328-07-X*) Parapsych Foun.

New Directions in Pediatric Hemotherapy. Ed. by Stephen M. Capon & Linda A. Chambers. (Illus.). 144p. 1996. pap. text 65.00 (*1-56395-064-2*, PC97-960014) Am Assn Blood.

New Directions in Pharmaceutical Tablet Manufacture, No. C-135. Business Communications Co., Inc. Staff. 156p. 1991. 2250.00 (*0-89336-816-4*) BCC.

New Directions in Physical Education, Vol. 1, YN1990. New Directions in Physical Education Staff. Ed. by Neil Armstrong. LC 90-31892. 175p. 1990. reprint ed. pap. 54.30 (*0-608-07115-3*, 206734200001) Bks Demand.

New Directions in Physical Education, Vol. 2, YN1990. New Directions in Physical Education Staff. Ed. by Neil Armstrong. LC 90-31892. 221p. 1990. reprint ed. pap. 68.60 (*0-608-07116-1*, 206734200002) Bks Demand.

New Directions in Physical Education: Change & Innovation. Neil Armstrong. (Cassell Education Ser.). (Illus.). 256p. (Orig.). 1996. pap. 35.00 (*0-304-33449-9*) Continuum.

New Directions in Physical Education Vol. 2: Physical Education Association of Great Britain & Northern Ireland. Ed. by Neil Armstrong. LC 90-31892. (Illus.). 221p. reprint ed. pap. 68.60 (*0-608-20817-5*, 207191600002) Bks Demand.

New Directions in Political Communication: A Resource Book. Ed. by David L. Swanson & Dan Nimmo. LC 89-10711. 413p. 1990. reprint ed. pap. 128.10 (*0-608-03005-8*, 206345500006) Bks Demand.

New Directions in Political Communication: A Resourcebook. Ed. by David L. Swanson & Dan Nimmo. (Illus.). 400p. (C). 1989. 58.00 (*0-8039-3334-7*) Sage.

New Directions in Political Economy: An Approach from Anthropology, 22. Ed. by Madeline B. Leons & Frances A. Rothstein. LC 78-4290. (Contributions in Economics & Economic History Ser.: No. 22). 350p. 1979. 69.50 (*0-313-20414-4*, LND/) Greenwood.

New Directions in Portfolio Assessment: Reflective Practice, Critical Theory & Large-Scale Scoring. Donald Daiker et al. LC 93-43350. 367p. (Orig.). 1994. pap. text 27.50 (*0-86709-338-2*, 0338, Pub. by Boynton Cook Pubs) Heinemann.

New Directions in Post-Keynesian Economics. Ed. by John Pheby. (New Directions in Modern Economics Ser.). 288p. 1989. text 100.00 (*1-85278-013-4*) E Elgar.

*__New Directions in Professional Higher Education.__ Tom Bourner. 2000. pap. text 39.95 (*0-335-20614-X*) OpUniv Pr.

*__New Directions in Progressive Relaxation Training: A Guidebook for Helping Professionals.__ Douglas A. Bernstein et al. LC 99-43100. 176p. 2000. write for info. (*0-275-96318-7*, Praeger Pubs); pap. write for info. (*0-275-96837-5*, Praeger Pubs) Greenwood.

New Directions in Prose & Poetry, Vols. 17-45. Incl. No. 37. New Directions. James Laughlin. LC 37-1751. 1978. 13.95 (0-8112-0695-5, Pub. by New Directions); No. 18. James Laughlin et al. LC 37-1751. 1964. 5.00 (0-8112-0329-8, Pub. by New Directions); No. 19. James Laughlin et al. LC 37-1751. 1966. 6.00 (0-8112-0330-1, Pub. by New Directions); No. 20. James Laughlin et al. LC 37-1751. 1968. 5.00 (0-8112-0331-X, Pub. by New Directions); No. 21. James Laughlin et al. LC 37-1751. 1969. 5.00 (0-8112-0332-8, Pub. by New Directions); No. 22. James Laughlin et al. LC 37-1751. 1970. 6.00 (0-8112-0333-6, Pub. by New Directions); No. 25. James Laughlin et al. LC 37-1751. 192p. 1972. 9.25 (0-8112-0447-2, Pub. by New Directions); No. 27. James Laughlin et al. LC 37-1751. 192p. 1973. pap. 2.95 (0-8112-0485-5, NDP359, Pub. by New Directions); No. 28. James Laughlin et al. LC 37-1751. 192p. 1974. 9.95 (0-8112-0525-8, Pub. by New Directions); No. 29. James Laughlin et al. LC 37-1751. 1974. 9.95 (0-8112-0539-8, Pub. by New Directions); No. 30. James Laughlin et al. LC 37-1751. 192p. 1975. 9.95 (0-8112-0572-X, Pub. by New Directions); No. 31. James Laughlin et al. LC 37-1751. 192p. 1975. 9.95 (0-8112-0587-8, Pub. by New Directions); No. 32. James Laughlin et al. LC 37-1751. 192p. 1976. 8.95 (0-8112-0602-5, Pub. by New Directions); No. 33. James Laughlin et al. LC 37-1751. 1976. 12.00 (0-8112-0616-5, Pub. by New Directions); No. 34. James Laughlin et al. LC 37-1751. 1977. 12.00 (0-8112-0634-3, Pub. by New Directions); No. 35. Ed. by James Laughlin et al. LC 37-1751. 1977. 12.75 (0-8112-0656-4, Pub. by New Directions); No. 36. James Laughlin et al. LC 37-1751. 1978. 12.95 (0-8112-0672-6, Pub. by New Directions); No. 38. James Laughlin et al. LC 37-1751. 1979. 14.95 (0-8112-0710-2, Pub. by New Directions); No. 39. James Laughlin et al. LC 37-1751. 1979. 14.95 (0-8112-0730-7, Pub. by New Directions); No. 40. James Laughlin et al. LC 37-1751. 1980. 15.95 (0-8112-0762-5, Pub. by New Directions); No. 41. James Laughlin et al. LC 37-1751. 1980. 15.95 (0-8112-0770-6, Pub. by New Directions); No. 42. James Laughlin et al. LC 37-1751. 1981. 15.95 (0-8112-0783-8, Pub. by New Directions); No. 43. James Laughlin et al. LC 37-1751. 192p. 1981. 16.95 (0-8112-0811-7, Pub. by New Directions); No. 44. James Laughlin et al. LC 37-1751. 192p. 1982. 16.95 (0-8112-0838-9, Pub. by New Directions); No. 45. James Laughlin et al. LC 37-1751. 1982. 16.95 (0-8112-0844-3, Pub. by New Directions); No. 46. 1983. 17.50 (0-8112-0865-6, Pub. by New Directions); No. 47. J. Laughlin. 1983. 17.50 (0-8112-0878-8, Pub. by New Directions); No. 48. 1984. 17.95 (0-8112-0911-3, Pub. by New Directions); No. 49. 1985. 19.50 (0-8112-0967-9, Pub. by New Directions); No. 51. J. Laughlin et al. 1987. pap. 11.95 (0-8112-1034-0, NDP644, Pub. by New Directions); No. 52. J. Laughlin. 1988. 24.95 (0-8112-1076-6, Pub. by New Directions); No. 53. J. Laughlin. Ed. by Griselda Ohannessian & Peter Glassgold. 1989. pap. 11.95 (0-8112-1107-X, NDP678, Pub. by New Directions); No. 54. J. Laughlin et al. 1990. 24.95 (0-8112-1146-0, Pub. by New Directions); No. 55. J. Laughlin & Griselda Ohannessian. 1991. 24.95 (0-8112-1180-0, Pub. by New Directions); No. 24. James Laughlin et al. LC 37-1751. 224p. 1972. pap. 3.45 (0-8112-0127-9, NDP332, Pub. by New Directions); LC 37-1751. write for info. (0-318-57382-2) New Directions.

New Directions in Prose & Poetry, Vols. 46-55. Incl. No. 37. New Directions. James Laughlin. LC 37-1751. 1978. 13.95 (0-8112-0695-5, Pub. by New Directions); No. 18. James Laughlin et al. LC 37-1751. 1964. 5.00 (0-8112-0329-8, Pub. by New Directions); No. 19. James Laughlin et al. LC 37-1751. 1966. 6.00 (0-8112-0330-1, Pub. by New Directions); No. 20. James Laughlin et al. LC 37-1751. 1968. 5.00 (0-8112-0331-X, Pub. by New Directions); No. 21. James Laughlin et al. LC 37-1751. 1969. 5.00 (0-8112-0332-8, Pub. by New Directions); No. 22. James Laughlin et al. LC 37-1751. 1970. 6.00 (0-8112-0333-6, Pub. by New Directions); No. 25. James Laughlin et al. LC 37-1751. 192p. 1972. 9.25 (0-8112-0447-2, Pub. by New Directions); No. 27. James Laughlin et al. LC 37-1751. 192p. 1973. pap. 2.95 (0-8112-0485-5, NDP359, Pub. by New Directions); No. 28. James Laughlin et al. LC 37-1751. 192p. 1974. 9.95 (0-8112-0525-8, Pub. by New Directions); No. 29. James Laughlin et al. LC 37-1751. 1974. 9.95 (0-8112-0539-8, Pub. by New Directions); No. 30. James Laughlin et al. LC 37-1751. 192p. 1975. 9.95 (0-8112-0572-X, Pub. by New Directions); No. 31. James Laughlin et al. LC 37-1751. 192p. 1975. 9.95 (0-8112-0587-8, Pub. by New Directions); No. 32. James Laughlin et al. LC 37-1751. 192p. 1976. 8.95 (0-8112-0602-5, Pub. by New Directions); No. 33. James Laughlin et al. LC 37-1751. 1976. 12.00 (0-8112-0616-5, Pub. by New Directions); No. 34. James Laughlin et al. LC 37-1751. 1977. 12.00 (0-8112-0634-3, Pub. by New Directions); No. 35. Ed. by James Laughlin et al. LC 37-1751. 1977. 12.75 (0-8112-0656-4, Pub. by New Directions); No. 36. James Laughlin et al. LC 37-1751. 1978. 12.95 (0-8112-0672-6, Pub. by New Directions); No. 38. James Laughlin et al. LC 37-1751. 1979. 14.95 (0-8112-0710-2, Pub. by New Directions); No. 39. James Laughlin et al. LC 37-1751. 1979. 14.95 (0-8112-0730-7, Pub. by New Directions); No. 40. James Laughlin et al. LC 37-1751. 1980. 15.95 (0-8112-0762-5, Pub. by New Directions); No. 41. James Laughlin et al. LC 37-1751. 1980. 15.95 (0-8112-0770-6, Pub. by New Directions); No. 42. James Laughlin et al. LC 37-1751. 1981. 15.95 (0-8112-0783-8, Pub. by New Directions); No. 43. James Laughlin et al. LC 37-1751. 192p. 1981. 16.95 (0-8112-0811-7, Pub. by New Directions); No. 44. James Laughlin et al. LC 37-1751. 192p. 1982. 16.95 (0-8112-0838-9, Pub. by New Directions); No. 45. James Laughlin et al. LC 37-1751. 1982. 16.95 (0-8112-0844-3, Pub. by New Directions); No. 46. 1983. 17.50 (0-8112-0865-6, Pub. by New Directions); No. 47. J. Laughlin. 1983. 17.50 (0-8112-0878-8, Pub. by New Directions); No. 48. 1984. 17.95 (0-8112-0911-3, Pub. by New Directions); No. 49. 1985. 19.50 (0-8112-0967-9, Pub. by New Directions); No. 51. J. Laughlin et al. 1987. pap. 11.95 (0-8112-1034-0, NDP644, Pub. by New Directions); No. 52. J. Laughlin. 1988. 24.95 (0-8112-1076-6, Pub. by New Directions); No. 53. J. Laughlin. Ed. by Griselda Ohannessian & Peter Glassgold. 1989. pap. 11.95 (0-8112-1107-X, NDP678, Pub. by New Directions); No. 54. J. Laughlin et al. 1990. 24.95 (0-8112-1146-0, Pub. by New Directions); No. 55. J. Laughlin & Griselda Ohannessian. 1991. 24.95 (0-8112-1180-0, Pub. by New Directions); No. 24. James Laughlin et al. LC 37-1751. 224p. 1972. pap. 3.45 (0-8112-0127-9, NDP332, Pub. by New Directions); write for info. (0-318-59218-5) New Directions.

New Directions in Psychological Anthropology. Ed. by Theodore Schwartz et al. (Publications of the Society for Psychological Anthropology). 362p. (C). 1993. text 60.00 (0-521-41592-6) Cambridge U Pr.

New Directions in Public Administration: The Federal View. Ed. by Norman Beckman. 209p. 1975. pap. text 24.95 (0-87855-650-8) Transaction Pubs.

New Directions in Public Health Care: A Prescription for the 1980's. Cotton M. Lindsay. 308p. 1980. pap. 24.95 (0-917616-37-5) Transaction Pubs.

New Directions in Public Health Care: A Prescription for the 1980's. 3rd ed. Cotton M. Lindsay. 308p. 1980. 39.95 (0-87855-394-0) Transaction Pubs.

New Directions in Quantitative Comparative Sociology. Wilhelmus A. Arts & Loek Halman. LC 99-21487. (International Studies in Sociology & Social Anthropology Ser.). 1999. write for info. (90-04-11411-4) Brill Academic Pubs.

***New Directions in Quantum Chaos.** Ed. by G. Casati et al. (International School of Physics Enrico Fermi Ser.: Vol. 143). 530p. 2000. 126.00 (1-58603-074-4) IOS Press.

***New Directions in Quantum Chromodynamics.** Ed. by Chueng-Ryong Ji & Dong-Pil Min. (AIP Conference Proceedings Ser.: Vol. 494). 560p. 1999. 150.00 (1-56396-908-4, Pub. by Am Inst Physics) Spr-Verlag.

***New Directions in Reading Instruction.** rev. ed. Bess Hinson. LC 99-56810. 32p. 2000. pap. 7.95 (0-87207-259-2, 259) Intl Reading.

New Directions in Relativity & Cosmology. Ed. by Venzo DeSabbata & T. Singh. (Illus.). 250p. (C). 1998. pap. text 65.00 (1-57485-030-X) Hadronic Pr Inc.

New Directions in Religion & Aging. Ed. by David B. Oliver. 205p. 1987. 39.95 (0-86656-553-1) Haworth Pr.

New Directions in Research with 3rd-Generation Soft X-Ray Sychrotron Radiation Sources. Ed. by A. S. Schlachter & F. J. Wuilleumier. LC 93-38825. 1993. text 267.50 (0-7923-2623-7) Kluwer Academic.

***New Directions in Rough Sets, Data Mining & Granular-Soft Computing: 7th International Workshop, RSFDGrC'99, Yamaguchi, Japan, November 9-11, 1999, Proceedings.** Ning Zhong et al. LC 99-50195. (Lecture Notes In Computer Science: Vol. 1711). xiv, 558p. 1999. pap. 85.00 (3-540-66645-1) Spr-Verlag.

New Directions in Safety. Ed. by Ted S. Ferry. 369p. 1985. 12.95 (0-939874-67-9) ASSE.

New Directions in Satellite Communications: Challenges for North & South. Ed. by Heather E. Hudson. LC 84-73276. (Artech House Telecommunications Library). (Illus.). 325p. reprint ed. pap. 100.80 (0-608-16028-8, 203312700083) Bks Demand.

New Directions in Scandinavian Archaeology. Ed. by Kristian Kristiansen & Carsten Paludan-Muller. (Studies in Scandinavian Prehistory & Early History: No. 1). (Illus.). 270p. (C). 1978. pap. 16.95 (87-480-0150-3, Pub. by Aarhus Univ Pr) David Brown.

New Directions in Second Language Learning, Teaching & Bilingual Education on TESOL 75: Selected Papers from the 9th Annual TESOL Convention, Los Angeles, Calif., March 4-9, 1975. Teachers of English to Speakers of Other Languages. Ed. by Marina K. Burt & Heidi C. Dulay. LC 75-27258. 382p. reprint ed. pap. 118.50 (0-608-14215-8, 202156300022) Bks Demand.

New Directions in Semantics. Ernest LePore. (Cognitive Science Ser.: No. 2). 512p. 1987. text 139.00 (0-12-444040-1) Acad Pr.

New Directions in Sexual Ethics: Moral Theology & the Challenge of AIDS. Kevin Kelly. 241p. 1998. pap. text 17.95 (0-225-66793-2, Pub. by G Chapman) Bks Intl VA.

New Directions in Small Business Research. R. Atkin et al. (Avebury Business School Library). 214p. 1993. 67.95 (1-85628-378-X, Pub. by Avebry) Ashgate Pub Co.

New Directions in Social Work. Ed. by Cora Kasius. LC 68-58800. (Essay Index Reprint Ser.). 1977. 20.95 (0-8369-0121-5) Ayer.

New Directions in Software Management. Capers Jones. 159p. 1994. ring bd. 180.00 (1-56909-009-2) Info Systs Mgmt.

New Directions in Solid State Chemistry. 2nd ed. C. N. Rao & J. Gopalakrishnan. LC 96-37412. (Illus.). 564p. (C). 1997. text 115.00 (0-521-49559-8) Cambridge U Pr.

New Directions in Solid State Chemistry. 2nd ed. C. N. Rao & J. Gopalakrishnan. LC 96-37412. (Illus.). 608p. (C). 1997. pap. text 47.95 (0-521-49907-0) Cambridge U Pr.

New Directions in Soviet History. Ed. by Stephen White. (International Council for Soviet & East European Studies). 226p. (C). 1991. text 69.95 (0-521-41376-1) Cambridge U Pr.

New Directions in Soviet Social Thought: An Anthology. Ed. by Murray Yanowitch. LC 89-31273. 336p. (C). (gr. 13). 1989. text 85.95 (0-87332-495-1) M E Sharpe.

New Directions in Spatial Econometrics. Ed. by Luc Anselin & Raymond Florax. LC 95-31116. (Advances in Spatial Science Ser.). (Illus.). 420p. 1995. 119.00 (3-540-60020-5) Spr-Verlag.

New Directions in Special Needs: Innovation in Mainstream Schools. Alan Dyson et al. LC 97-175377. 208p. 1997. pap. 24.95 (0-304-70024-X) Continuum.

New Directions in Spectrophotometry. Ed. by A. G. Davis Philip et al. 400p. 1988. 32.00 (0-933485-08-5) L Davis Pr.

New Directions in Statistical Data Analysis & Robustness. Ed. by S. Morgenthaler et al. LC 93-8952. (Monte Verita, Proceedings of the Centro Stefano Franciscini Ascona Ser.). 284p. 1993. 79.50 (0-8176-2923-8) Birkhauser.

New Directions in Suspension Design: Making the Fast Car Faster. Colin Campbell. LC 80-24348. (Illus.). 224p. 1981. 21.95 (0-8376-0150-9) Bentley Pubs.

New Directions in Tardive Dyskinesia Research. Ed. by R. H. Belmaker & J. Bannet. (Modern Problems of Pharmacopsychiatry Ser.: Vol. 21). (Illus.). vi, 222p. 1983. 109.75 (3-8055-3735-2) S Karger.

New Directions in Technical Services: Trends & Sources. Ed. by Peggy Johnson. 342p. 1997. 35.00 (0-8389-0700-8) ALA.

New Directions in Telecommunications Policy, 2 vols., Vol. 2. Ed. by Paula R. Newberg. LC 89-1446. (Duke Press Policy Studies). 346p. 1989. pap. text 29.95 (0-8223-0948-3) Duke.

New Directions in Telecommunications Policy, 2 vols., Vol. 2: Information Policy & Economic Policy. Ed. by Paula R. Newberg. LC 89-1446. (Duke Press Policy Studies). 346p. 1989. text 69.95 (0-8223-0923-8) Duke.

New Directions in Terahertz Technology. Ed. by J. M. Chamberlain & R. E. Miles. LC 97-6835. (NATO ASI Series: Vol. 334). 424p. 1997. text 234.00 (0-7923-4537-1) Kluwer Academic.

New Directions in Textual Studies. Ed. by Dave Oliphant & Larry Carver. (Illus.). 185p. 1990. pap. 20.00 (0-87959-111-0) U of Tex H Ransom Ctr.

New Directions in the Applications of Symmetry Principles to Elementary Particle Pyis Walifest-MRST 15. J. Schechter. 316p. 1994. text 86.00 (981-02-1726-9) World Scientific Pub.

New Directions in the Clinical Use of Intravenous Immunoglobulin, Vol. I. Donald Leung. (Illus.). 60p. 1989. write for info. (0-318-65779-1) Health Dimensions.

New Directions in the Clinical Use of Intravenous Immunoglobulin, Vol. II. Arnold I. Levinson. (Illus.). 60p. 1990. write for info. (0-318-65780-5) Health Dimensions.

New Directions in the Clinical Use of Intravenous Immunoglobulin, Vol. III. Stanley Schwartz. (Illus.). 60p. 1990. write for info. (0-318-65781-3) Health Dimensions.

New Directions in the Clinical Use of Intravenous Immunoglobulin, Vol. IV. Stephen H. Polmar. (Illus.). 60p. 1990. write for info. (0-318-65782-1) Health Dimensions.

New Directions in the Clinical Use of Intravenous Immunoglobulin, Vol. V. Harry R. Hill. (Illus.). 60p. 1990. write for info. (0-318-65783-X) Health Dimensions.

New Directions in the Economic Theory of the Environment. Ed. by Carlo Carraro & Domenico Siniscalco. LC 96-40021. 374p. (C). 1998. text 64.95 (0-521-59089-2) Cambridge U Pr.

New Directions in the Law of the Sea: Documents, Series I, 11 vols., Set. Kenneth R. Simmonds & Myron Nordquist. 1973. 495.00 (0-379-00029-6) Oceana.

New Directions in the Law of the Sea: Global Developments, 2 vols. Ed. by Roy S. Lee & Moritaka Hayashi. LC 96-36221. 1996. ring bd. 325.00 (0-379-16552-X, 7910061) Oceana.

New Directions in the Law of the Sea: Regional & National Developments, 2 binders. Roy S. Lee & Moritaka Hayashi. 1995. ring bd. 222.00 (0-379-16551-1) Oceana.

New Directions in the Philosophy of Mathematics. Thomas Tymoczko. 320p. 1986. 62.50 (0-8176-3163-1) Birkhauser.

New Directions in the Philosophy of Mathematics: An Anthology. Thomas Tymoczko. 448p. 1998. pap. text 24.95 (0-691-03498-2, Pub. by Princeton U Pr) Cal Prin Full Svc.

New Directions in the Philosophy of Technology. Ed. by Joseph C. Pitt. (Philosophy & Technology Ser.: Vol. 11). 234p. (C). 1995. text 107.00 (0-7923-3661-5) Kluwer Academic.

New Directions in the Psychological Treatment of Serious Mental Illness. Ed. by Diane T. Marsh. LC 93-23930. 224p. 1993. 67.95 (0-275-94428-X, C4428, Praeger Pubs) Greenwood.

New Directions in the Psychophysiology of Individual Differences: A Symposium of Papers from the 22nd Annual Meeting of the Society for Psychophysiological Research, Minneapolis, 21-24 October 1982. Ed. by R. M. Stelmack. 76p. 1983. pap. 15.25 (0-08-030844-9, Pergamon Pr) Elsevier.

New Directions in the Rehabilitation of Criminal Offenders. Ed. by Susan E. Martin et al. LC 81-11287. 508p. reprint ed. pap. 157.50 (0-8357-3183-9, 203945200012) Bks Demand.

New Directions in the Sociology of Health. Ed. by Pamela Abbott & Geoff Payne. (Explorations in Sociology Ser.: No. 36). 240p. 1990. pap. 34.95 (1-85000-787-X, Falmer Pr) Taylor & Francis.

New Directions in the Study of Foreign Policy. Ed. by Charles W. Kegley, Jr. et al. LC 86-17282. 450p. 1987. text 29.95 (0-04-327093-X) Routledge.

New Directions in the Study of Justice, Law, & Social Control. School of Justice Studies Staff. LC 89-23237. (Critical Issues in Social Justice Ser.). (Illus.). 296p. (C). 1990. 52.50 (0-306-43292-7, Plenum Trade) Perseus Pubng.

New Directions in the Study of Meiji Japan. Ed. by Helen Hardacre & Adam L. Kern. LC 97-18947. (Japanese Studies Library: No. 6). (Illus.). 816p. 1997. 236.50 (90-04-10735-5) Brill Academic Pubs.

New Directions in the Study of Plants & Peoples: Research Contributions from the Institute of Economic Botany. Ed. by Ghillean T. Prance & Michael J. Balick. LC 89-13336. (Advances in Economic Botany Ser.: Vol. 8). (Illus.). 292p. 1990. pap. text 41.25 (0-89327-347-3) NY Botanical.

New Directions in the Study of Social Order. David T. Helm et al. 300p. (C). 1989. text 37.50 (0-8290-1592-2); pap. text 22.95 (0-8290-1593-0) Irvington.

New Directions in Time Series Analysis, Pt. 1. Ed. by David R. Brillinger et al. LC 92-22697. (Mathematics & Its Applications Ser.: Vol. 45). (Illus.). 408p. 1992. 74.95 (0-387-97896-8) Spr-Verlag.

New Directions in Trade Theory. Ed. by Alan V. Deardorff et al. (Studies In International Trade Policy). 424p. 1995. text 60.00 (0-472-10562-0, 10562) U of Mich Pr.

New Directions in Transactional Analysis Counselling: An Explorer's Handbook. David Midgley. (Illus.). 200p. pap. 25.00 (1-85343-429-9) Free Assoc Bks.

***New Directions in Transactional Analysis Counselling: An Explorer's Handbook.** David Midgley. (Illus.). 14p. 1999. 55.00 (1-85343-430-2, Pub. by Free Assoc Bks) Intl Spec Bk.

New Directions in Transportation Fuels, No. E-054R. enl. ed. 208p. 1993. 2550.00 (1-56965-152-3, E054R) BCC.

New Directions in 2-Year College Mathematics. Ed. by Donald J. Albers et al. (Illus.). xxi, 491p. 1985. 65.95 (0-387-96145-3) Spr-Verlag.

New Directions in Understanding Dementia & Alzheimer's Disease. Ed. by T. Zandi & R. J. Ham. LC 90-14297. (Advances in Experimental Medicine & Biology Ser.: Vol. 282). (Illus.). 174p. (C). 1990. text 95.00 (0-306-43728-7, Kluwer Plenum) Kluwer Academic.

New Directions in Urban Public Housing. Ed. by David P. Varady et al. LC 97-29600. (Illus.). 304p. 1998. pap. text 19.95 (0-88285-160-8) Ctr Urban Pol Res.

New Directions in Vestibular Research. Stephen M. Highstein et al. LC 96-1556. (Annals of the New York Academy of Sciences Ser.). 739p. 1996. pap. 145.00 (1-57331-007-7) NY Acad Sci.

New Directions in Water Resources Planning for the U. S. Army Corps of Engineers. National Research Council Staff. 120p. (C). 1999. pap. text 39.00 (0-309-06097-4) Natl Acad Pr.

New Directions of Oceanographic Research & Development. Ed. by N. Nasu & S. Honjo. LC 92-32507. 1993. write for info. (4-431-70113-3) Spr-Verlag.

New Directions of Oceanographic Research & Development. Ed. by N. Nasu & S. Honjo. (Illus.). 232p. 1993. 158.95 (0-387-70113-3) Spr-Verlag.

New Directions 17-55. Ed. by J. Laughlin. LC 37-1751. 1971. 6.75 (0-8112-0300-X, Pub. by New Directions) Norton.

New Directions Through CAD-CAM. W. Beeby & P. Collier. 230p. 1986. 37.00 (0-87263-217-2) SME.

***New Directors for Small Group Ministry.** Carl George et al. LC 99-25742. 160p. 1999. pap. 16.99 (0-7644-2137-9) Group Pub.

New Disaster Relief Handbook. John T. Porter. Ed. by John H. Lionheart. (Illus.). 91p. 1997. pap. 24.95 (0-9666685-0-2) Biggs Pub.

New Discoveries at Karatepe. Julian Obermann. (Connecticut Academy of Arts & Sciences Ser., Trans.: Vol. 38). 1949. pap. 39.50 (0-685-22903-3) Elliots Bks.

New Discoveries in Medicine: Their Effect on the Public Health. Paul R. Hawley. LC 76-37922. (Essay Index Reprint Ser.). 1977. reprint ed. 20.95 (0-8369-2594-7) Ayer.

New Discovery Book of Space. Nick Heathcote et al. (Illus.). 96p. (YA). (gr. 6 up). 1994. lib. bdg. 15.95 (0-02-743506-7, New Dscvry Bks) Silver Burdett Pr.

New Dispensation: As Presented by the Spirit World, Through the Automatic-Writings of Frances Bird. Frances Bird. LC 87-22789. (Automatic Writings Ser.). 400p. 1988. pap. 53.95 incl. audio (1-55768-703-X) LC Pub.

New Diversity in Contemporary Southern Rhetoric. Ed. by Calvin M. Logue & Howard Dorgan. LC 86-21152. 272p. 1987. text 40.00 (0-8071-1312-3) La State U Pr.

New Division of Labour: Emerging Forms of Work Organization in International Perspective. Ed. by W. Littek & T. Charles. LC 95-30413. (Studies in Organization: No. 67). xiv, 514p. (C). 1995. lib. bdg. 98.95 (3-11-013972-3) De Gruyter.

New Doberman Pinscher. 2nd rev. ed. Joanna Walker et al. LC 81-6600. (Illus.). 352p. 1977. 25.95 (0-87605-113-1) Howell Bks.

New Doctor. Elizabeth Seifert. 1974. reprint ed. lib. bdg. 24.95 (0-88411-038-9) Amereon Ltd.

New Dollars & Dreams: American Incomes & Economic Change. rev. ed. Frank Levy. LC 98-20635. (Illus.). 256p. (C). 1998. 39.95 (0-87154-514-4); pap. 16.95 (0-87154-515-2) Russell Sage.

N

An Asterisk (*) at the beginning of an entry indicates that the title is appearing for the first time.

New Dolls' House Do-It-Yourself Book. Venus Dodge. (Illus.). 192p. 1997. pap. 19.95 (*0-7153-0616-2*) Sterling.

New Domestic Agenda: A Strengthened American Family, a Strengthened Economy. Council of State Governments Staff. LC 89-168361. (Publication Ser.: No. C135). 96p. reprint ed. pap. 30.00 (*0-7837-2657-0*, 204301600006) Bks Demand.

New Domestic Detailing. Brenda A. Vale & Robert J. Vale. (Illus.). 144p. Date not set. pap. write for info. (*0-7506-0605-3*) Buttrwrth-Heinemann.

New Domestic Rabbit Cook Book. 222p. 5.00 (*0-318-13129-3*) Am Rabbit Breeders.

New Dominion. Ruth Prawer Jhabvala. LC 73-156517. 218p. 1972. write for info. (*0-7195-2726-0*, Pub. by John Murray) Trafalgar.

***New Don't Blame Mother: Mending the Mother-Daughter Relationship.** Paula Caplan. (Illus.). 320p. 2000. pap. 15.95 (*0-415-92630-0*) Routledge.

New Dosimetry at Hiroshima & Nagasaki & Its Implications for Risk Estimates. LC 88-22727. (Annual Meeting Proceedings Ser.: No. 9). 270p. 1988. pap. 40.00 (*0-913392-98-7*) NCRP Pubns.

New Dostoyevsky Letters. Fyodor Dostoyevsky. Tr. by Samuel S. Koteliansky. LC 73-20335. (Studies in Dostoyevsky: No. 86). 1974. lib. bdg. 75.00 (*0-8383-1824-X*) M S G Haskell Hse.

New Doubleday Cookbook. Jean Anderson & Elaine Hanna. LC 85-16844. (Illus.). 992p. 1990. 35.00 (*0-385-19577-X*) Doubleday.

New Doublespeak: Why No One Knows What Anyone's Saying Anymore. William Lutz. 256p. 1997. pap. 13.00 (*0-06-092839-5*, Perennial) HarperTrade.

New Dow Jones-Irwin Guide to Real Estate Investing. Gaylon Greer. 330p. 1989. 34.00 (*1-55623-085-0*, Irwn Prfssnl) McGraw-Hill Prof.

New Dr. Cookie Cookbook: Dessert Your Way to Health with More Than 150 Scrumptious Cookies, Cakes, & Treats. Marvin A. Wayne & Stephen R. Yarnall. LC 93-2501. 1994. pap. 14.00 (*0-688-12222-1*, Wm Morrow) Morrow Avon.

New Drama: The Liars, by Henry Arthur Jones & the Notorious Mrs. Ebbsmith, by Sir Arthur Wing Pinero. Ed. by Carl Selle. LC 63-21347. (Critical Studies: No. 3). 1968. 19.95 (*0-87024-021-8*) U of Miami Pr.

New Dramatists of Mexico, 1967-1985. Ronald D. Burgess. LC 90-40023. 176p. 1991. text 23.00 (*0-8131-1727-5*) U Pr of Ky.

New Draperies in the Low Countries & England, 1300-1800. Ed. by N. B. Harte. (Pasold Studies in Textile History: No. 10). (Illus.). 348p. 1998. text 67.00 (*0-19-921063-2*) OUP.

New Drawing on the Right Side of the Brain. 2nd expanded rev. ed. Betty Edwards. LC 99-35809. Orig. Title: Drawing on the Right Side of the Brain. (Illus.). 320p. 1999. pap. 16.95 (*0-87477-424-1*, Tarcher Putnam) Putnam Pub Group.

New Drawing on the Right Side of the Brain. 2nd rev. ed. Betty Edwards. LC 99-35809. Orig. Title: Drawing on the Right Side of the Brain. (Illus.). 320p. 1999. 27.95 (*0-87477-419-5*, Tarcher Putnam) Putnam Pub Group.

New Drug Approval in Brazil. Ivo Ferreira. LC 98-148823. (Worldwide Pharmaceutical Regulation Ser.). 62p. (Orig.). 1995. pap. 100.00 (*1-882615-21-2*) Parexel Intl.

New Drug Approval in Canada. Eileen McMahon. (Worldwide Pharmaceutical Regulation Ser.). (Orig.). 1995. pap. 100.00 (*1-882615-20-4*) Parexel Intl.

New Drug Approval in France. Gillian Ivers-Read & Colin Scott. (Worldwide Pharmaceutical Regulation Ser.). 104p. (Orig.). 1996. pap. 100.00 (*1-882615-16-6*) Parexel Intl.

New Drug Approval in Germany. Christian Hinze & Barbara Sickmuller. (Worldwide Pharmaceutical Regulation Ser.). 55p. (Orig.). 1995. pap. 100.00 (*1-882615-15-8*) Parexel Intl.

New Drug Approval in Italy. Guiliana Tabusso & Nadia Peviani. (Worldwide Pharmaceutical Regulation Ser.). 94p. (Orig.). 1995. pap. 100.00 (*1-882615-17-4*) Parexel Intl.

New Drug Approval in Japan. William J. Currie. (Worldwide Pharmaceutical Regulation Ser.). 64p. (Orig.). 1995. pap. 125.00 (*1-882615-14-X*) Parexel Intl.

New Drug Approval in South Korea. Suk C. Lee. (Worldwide Pharmaceutical Regulation Ser.). 92p. (Orig.). 1995. pap. 100.00 (*1-882615-22-0*) Parexel Intl.

New Drug Approval in the European Union. Paul T. Evers. (Worldwide Pharmaceutical Regulation Ser.). 97p. (Orig.). 1995. pap. 150.00 (*1-882615-12-3*) Parexel Intl.

New Drug Approval in the United Kingdom. Paul T. Evers. (Worldwide Pharmaceutical Regulation Ser.). 111p. (Orig.). 1995. pap. 100.00 (*1-882615-18-2*) Parexel Intl.

New Drug Approval in the United States. Mark Mathieu. (Worldwide Pharmaceutical Regulation Ser.). (Orig.). 1995. pap. 100.00 (*1-882615-13-1*) Parexel Intl.

New Drug Approval Process. 2nd expanded rev. ed. Ed. by Richard Guarino. LC 92-23366. (Drugs & the Pharmaceutical Sciences Ser.: Vol. 56). (Illus.). 500p. 1992. text 180.00 (*0-8247-8801-X*) Dekker.

***New Drug Approval Process: The Global Challenge.** 3rd ed. Ed. by Richard A. Guarino. (Drugs & the Pharmaceutical Sciences Ser.: Vol. 100). 471p. 2000. 185.00 (*0-8247-0308-1*) Dekker.

New Drug Development: A Regulatory Overview. 3rd ed. Mark Mathieu. 327p. 1994. 125.00 (*1-882615-01-8*) Parexel Intl.

New Drug Lag: Barriers to the Japanese Pharmaceutical Market. L. G. Thomas. 1998. 29.95 (*0-8447-4048-9*) Am Enterprise.

New Drug Technology Markets. (Market Research Reports: No. 375). 117p. 1993. 795.00 (*0-317-05468-6*) Theta Corp.

New Drugs. Thomas W. Feeley. 1995. 39.00 (*0-316-27684-7*, Little Brwn Med Div) Lppncott W & W.

New Drugs. 2nd ed. Ed. by John Feely. pap. text 29.00 (*0-7279-0297-0*, Pub. by BMJ Pub) Login Brothers Bk Co.

New Drugs. 3rd ed. Ed. by John Feely. 464p. 1994. pap. text 14.00 (*0-7279-0821-9*, Pub. by BMJ Pub) Login Brothers Bk Co.

New Drugs: Discovery & Development. Alan A. Rubin. (Drugs & the Pharmaceutical Sciences Ser.: Vol. 5). (Illus.). 328p. 1978. text 165.00 (*0-8247-6634-2*) Dekker.

New Drugs Annual: Cardiovascular Drugs, Vol. 1, 1983. Ed. by Alexander Scriabine. LC 84-641424. 350p. 1983. reprint ed. pap. 108.50 (*0-7837-9538-6*, 206028700001) Bks Demand.

New Drugs, Concepts & Results in Cancer Chemotherapy. Ed. by Franco M. Muggia. (Cancer Treatment & Research Ser.). 176p. (C). 1991. text 147.50 (*0-7923-1253-8*) Kluwer Academic.

New Drugs for Asthma Therapy Vol. 34: Agents & Actions Supplement. Ed. by I. D. Chapman et al. ix, 548p. 1991. 149.00 (*0-8176-2505-4*) Birkhauser.

New Drugs in Allergy & Asthma. Ed. by Trevor T. Hansel & John Morley. (Agents & Actions Supplements Ser.: Vol. 43). 1993. write for info. (*0-318-70218-5*, Pub. by Birkhauser) Princeton Arch.

New Drugs in Allergy & Asthma. Ed. by Trevor T. Hansel & John Morley. (Agents & Actions Supplements Ser.: Vol. 43). ix, 307p. 1993. 99.50 (*0-8176-2870-3*, Pub. by Birkhauser) Princeton Arch.

New Drugs in Oncology. Ed. by W. Queisser & H. H. Fiebig. (Beitraege Zur Onkologie, Contributions to Oncology Ser.: Vol. 37). (Illus.). 302p. 1989. 68.75 (*3-8055-5047-2*) S Karger.

New Drumbeat. Ron Ferguson. 165p. 1993. pap. 21.00 (*0-86153-165-5*, Pub. by St Andrew) St Mut.

New Duck: My First Look At the Life Cycle of a Bird. Pamela Hickman & Heather Collins. LC 98-93222. (Illus.). 20p. (J). (ps-4). 1999. 6.95 (*1-55074-613-8*, Pub. by Kids Can Pr) Genl Dist Srvs.

New Duck Handbook. Heinz-Sigurd Raethel. (Illus.). 1989. pap. 9.95 (*0-8120-4088-0*) Barron.

***New Dudley Genealogies: The Descendants of William of Guilford.** Gary P. Dudley. 111p. 1999. pap. 23.50 (*0-7884-1293-0*, D814) Heritage Bk.

New Dutch Patent Act #5. 1995. lib. bdg. 45.50 (*90-411-0045-8*) Kluwer Academic.

***New Dutch Swing.** Kevin Whitehead. LC 99-45231. (Illus.). 352p. 2000. pap. write for info. (*0-8230-8348-9*) Watsn-Guptill.

New Dutch Swing: Jazz, Classical Music, Absurdism. Kevin Whitehead. LC 97-46112. 1998. 21.95 (*0-8230-8334-9*, Billboard Bks) Watsn-Guptill.

New Dynamics in the Global Economy. William Beeman & Isaiah Frank. 43p. 1988. pap. 9.50 (*0-87186-248-4*) Comm Econ Dev.

New Dynamics of Emerging Markets Investment: Managing Sub-Investment-Grade Sovereign Risk. Ed. by Jess Ledermann. 1997. 270.00 (*1-85564-546-7*, Pub. by Euromoney) Am Educ Systs.

New Dynamics of Goal Setting: Flextactics for a Fast-Changing Future. Denis Waitley. 192p. 1997. reprint ed. pap. 12.00 (*0-688-15554-5*, Quil) HarperTrade.

New Dynamics of Goal Setting: Flextactics for a Fast-Changing World. Denis E. Waitley. LC 95-52121. 224p. 1996. 25.00 (*0-688-12668-5*, Wm Morrow) Morrow Avon.

New Dynamics of Winn. Denis E. Waitley. 1995. pap. 12.00 (*0-688-14227-3*, Quil) HarperTrade.

New Dynamics of Winning: How to Use Sports Psychology for Winning in Life, Set. Denis Waitley. 1995. 16.00 incl. audio (*0-671-52076-8*) S&S Audio.

New Eagles Complete. Ed. by Aaron Stang. 332p. (YA). 1996. pap. text 26.95 (*0-89724-742-6*, PF9526) Wrner Bros.

New Ears. Anne De Graff. (Tiny Triumphs Ser.). (Illus.). 22p. (J). 1997. pap. text 2.95 (*0-687-07129-1*) Abingdon.

New Ears: A Guide to Education in Audio & the Recording Sciences. Mark Drews. 208p. (Orig.). 1989. pap. 11.95 (*0-9623502-0-6*) New Ear Prodns.

New Ears: The Audio Career & Education Handbook. 2nd rev. ed. Mark Drews. LC 93-92640. 285p. (YA). 1993. pap. 24.95 (*0-9623502-1-4*) New Ear Prodns.

New Earth: Methods, Exercises, Formulas, Prayers. 5th ed. Omraam M. Aivanhov. (Complete Works: Vol. 13). (Illus.). 248p. 1995. pap. 13.95 (*2-85566-622-8*, Pub. by Prosveta) Prosveta USA.

New Earth: The Labor of Language in Pearl, Herbert's Temple, & Blake's Jerusalem. Douglas Thorpe. LC 90-31201. (Illus.). 219p. 1991. text 39.95 (*0-8132-0728-2*) Cath U Pr.

New Earth Book: Our Changing Planet. Melvin Berger. LC 79-7828. (Illus.). 128p. (J). (gr. 5 up). 1980. 12.95 (*0-690-00735-3*) HarpC Child Bks.

New Earth, New Truth: A God-Mind Plan for Saving Planet & Man. Jean K. Foster. LC 88-51918. (God-Mind Bks.: Bk. 5). 225p. (Orig.). 1989. pap. 9.95 (*0-912949-29-5*) Teamup.

"New Earth" of the New Man. Pio Raffaele Angelisanti. Tr. by Bertha De Beracasa Gonzales from SPA. (Illus.). 492p. 1978. student ed. 44.99 (*0-9607590-3-4*) Action Life Pubns.

New Earth Reader: The Best of Terra Nova. Ed. by David Rothenberg & Marta Ulvaeus. LC 99-34983. (Illus.). 208p. 1999. 24.95 (*0-262-18195-9*) MIT Pr.

New East Asian Economic Development: The Interaction of Capitalism & Socialism. Keun Lee. LC 93-19555. 224p. (C). (gr. 13). 1993. text 85.95 (*1-56324-218-4*, East Gate Bk) M E Sharpe.

New East Asian Economic Development: The Interaction of Capitalism & Socialism. Keun Lee. LC 93-19555. 224p. (C). (gr. 13). 1993. pap. text 34.95 (*1-56324-219-2*, East Gate Bk) M E Sharpe.

New Eastern Europe: Social Policy Past, Present & Future. Bob Deacon. 208p. (C). 1992. text 55.00 (*0-8039-8438-3*); pap. text 19.95 (*0-8039-8439-1*) Sage.

New Eastern Europe: Western Responses. J. M. Rollo. LC 90-34197. (Chatham House Papers). 148p. 1990. pap. 14.95 (*0-87609-085-4*) Coun Foreign.

New Easy Basics. Jerry A. Divecchio. LC 96-61701. 192p. 1997. 24.95 (*0-376-02089-X*) Sunset Books.

***New Eating Right for a Bad Gut: The Complete Nutrition Guide to Ileitis, Colitis, Crohn's Disease.** James Scala. LC 99-38609. 2000. pap. 13.95 (*0-452-27976-3*, Plume) Dutton Plume.

***New Ebony Cookbook.** Charlotte Lyons. LC 99-49232. (Illus.). 120p. 1999. 19.95 (*0-87485-090-8*) Johnson Chicago.

New Ecclesial Ministry: Lay Professionals Serving the Church. Zeni Fox. LC 97-33533. 280p. 1997. pap. 16.95 (*1-55612-984-X*, LL1984) Sheed & Ward WI.

New Echota Letters: Contributions of Samuel A. Worcester to the Cherokee Phoenix. Ed. by Jack F. Kilpatrick & Anna G. Kilpatrick. LC 68-55078. 136p. 1968. 14.95 (*0-87074-086-5*) SMU Press.

***New Eco-Order: Economic & Ecological Linkages of the World[0012]s Temperate & Boreal Forest Resources.** James L. McIntire. (Illus.). 122p. 2000. reprint ed. pap. text 35.00 (*0-7881-8953-0*) DIANE Pub.

New Ecological Order. Luc Ferry. Tr. by Carol Volk. LC 94-49333.Tr. of Nouvel Ordre Ecologique. (ENG & FRE.). xxx, 160p. 1995. pap. 15.00 (*0-226-24483-0*) U Ch Pr.

New Ecological Order. Luc Ferry. Tr. by Carol Volk. LC 94-49333.Tr. of Nouvel Ordre Ecologique. (ENG & FRE.). 190p. 1998. lib. bdg. 34.95 (*0-226-24482-2*) U Ch Pr.

New Economic & Social Dictionary: Nouveau Dictionnaire Economique et Social. J. Ibarrola & N. Pasquarelli. (FRE.). 715p. 1981. 57.95 (*0-8288-1266-7*, M14165) Fr & Eur.

New Economic Criticism. Mark Osteen & Martha Woodmansee. LC 98-20146. 320p. (C). 1998. 100.00 (*0-415-14944-4*); pap. 29.99 (*0-415-14945-2*) Routledge.

***New Economic Developments & Their Impact on Arab Economies.** Arhmad Kawweaz. LC 99-36414. 924p. 1999. 139.50 (*0-444-50233-5*, North Holland) Elsevier.

New Economic Disorder. Larry Bates. 1994. pap. text 9.99 (*0-88419-383-7*) Creation House.

New Economic Dynamo. Fong Chan Onn. 270p. (C). 1987. pap. text 24.95 (*0-86861-802-0*) Routledge.

New Economic Health Care: Drugs Case Mix & Patients' Length of Stay. Raymond A. Arons. LC 84-6831. 256p. 1984. 55.00 (*0-275-91421-6*, C1421, Praeger Pubs) Greenwood.

New Economic Initiative for the Former Soviet Republics: A Policy Statement by the NPA Board of Trustees. Vinson Brown & William Willoya. 16p. (Orig.). 1992. pap. text 2.45 (*0-614-03253-9*, NPA 258) Natl Planning.

New Economic Landscape in Europe. Siebert Horst. (Illus.). 160p. 1991. 27.95 (*0-631-18217-9*) Blackwell Pubs.

New Economic Mind. 2nd ed. Paul Webley et al. 300p. (C). 1995. pap. text 43.00 (*0-13-342981-4*) P-H.

New Economic Mind: The Social Psychology of Economic Behavior. Alan Lewis et al. LC 94-31583. 332p. 1995. pap. 42.00 (*0-7450-1325-2*, Pub. by Wheatsheaf Bks) P-H.

New Economic Nationalism. Ed. by Otto Hieronymi. LC 79-93103. 238p. 1980. 59.95 (*0-275-90495-4*, C0495, Praeger Pubs) Greenwood.

New Economic Policy for Britain: Essays on the Development of Industry Keith Cowling & Roger Sugden. LC 90-5573. 217 p. 1990. write for info. (*0-7190-3271-7*) Manchester Univ Pr.

New Economic Policy (NEP) The Closing Stage: The Correlation of Economics & Politics. Ed. by V. P. Dmitrenko et al. LC 99-23935. (Studies in Russian Politics, Sociology, & Economics: Vol. 4). (RUS.). 276p. 1999. text 89.95 (*0-7734-3186-1*) E Mellen.

New Economic Policy of India: Reconstructuring & Liberalising the Economy for 21st Century. Ed. by Ajit K. Sinha. (C). 1994. 52.00 (*81-7100-517-9*, Pub. by Deep & Deep Pubns) S Asia.

New Economic Role of American States: Strategies in a Competitive World Economy. Ed. by R. Scott Fosler. (Illus.). 384p. (C). 1991. pap. text 23.95 (*0-19-506777-0*, 7415) OUP.

New Economic View of American History. 2nd ed. Jeremy Atack. 1994. 35.00 (*0-393-03622-7*) Norton.

New Economic View of American History. 2nd ed. Susan P. Lee et al. (C). 1994. pap. 34.75 (*0-393-96315-2*) Norton.

***New Economics: For Industry, Government, Education.** 2nd ed. W. Edwards Deming. (Illus.). (C). 2000. pap. 19.95 (*0-262-54116-5*) MIT Pr.

New Economics & Its Writing. Ed. by John B. Davis. (History of Political Economy Annual Supplement Ser.). 300p. 1997. lib. bdg. 49.95 (*0-8223-2037-1*) Duke.

New Economics for Industry, Government, Education. 2nd ed. W. Edwards Deming. (Illus.). 247p. (Orig.). (C). 1995. pap. 19.50 (*0-911379-07-X*) MIT Ctr Adv Educ.

New Economics of Human Behaviour. Ed. by Mariano Tommasi & Kathryn Ierulli. (Illus.). 256p. (C). 1995. text 64.95 (*0-521-47420-5*); pap. text 21.95 (*0-521-47949-5*) Cambridge U Pr.

New Economics of India's Green Revolution: Income & Employment Diffusion in Rural Uttar Pradesh. Rita Sharma & Thomas T. Poleman. LC 92-56784. (Food Systems & Agrarian Change Ser.). (Illus.). 296p. (C). 1993. text 52.50 (*0-8014-2806-8*) Cornell U Pr.

New Economics of India's Green Revolution: Income & Employment Diffusion in Uttar Pradesh. Rita Sharma & Thomas T. Poleman. (C). 1994. 30.00 (*0-7069-7595-2*, Pub. by Vikas) S Asia.

New Economics of India's Green Revolution: Income & Employment Diffusion in Uttar Pradesh. Rita Sharma & Thomas T. Poleman. 1995. 28.50 (*0-7069-9243-1*, Pub. by Vikas) S Asia.

New Economics of Sustainable Development. Robertson. LC 99-15905. (Forward Studies Ser.). 184p. 1999. text 39.95 (*0-312-22697-7*) St Martin.

***New Economics of Sustainable Development.** James Robertson. 2000. pap. 22.50 (*0-7494-3093-1*) Kogan Page Ltd.

New Economics of the Less Developed Countries: Changing Perceptions in the North-South Dialogue. Ed. by Nake M. Kamrany. LC 77-14602. (Special Studies in Social, Political, & Economic Development). 1978. text 46.00 (*0-89158-449-8*) Westview.

New Economics One Decade Older. James Tobin. LC 73-16763. (Eliot Janeway Lectures on Historical Economics: 1972). 116p. reprint ed. pap. 36.00 (*0-7837-1422-X*, 204177700023) Bks Demand.

***New Economy?** Doug Henwood. 160p. (C). 2000. 23.00 (*1-85984-768-4*, Pub. by Verso) Norton.

New Ecophysiological. Gindel. 1973. text 85.50 (*90-6193-019-7*) Kluwer Academic.

New Eden. Bonnie Squires. LC 77-20311. (Illus.). 1977. 3.00 (*0-685-88412-0*) D David Pr.

New Eden: For People, Animals & Nature. Michael W. Fox. LC 89-12998. (Illus.). 78p. (Orig.). 1989. pap. 8.95 (*0-941524-46-9*) Lotus Pr.

New Edge of the Anvil: A Resource Book for the Blacksmith. rev. ed. Jack Andrews. (Illus.). 256p. (C). 1994. pap. text 24.95 (*1-879535-09-2*) Skipjack Pr.

New Edition of the Brief History of the Ancient & Accepted Scottish Rite of Freemasonry Together with a Historic Sketch of the So-Called Revival of Freemasonry in 1717. Edwin A. Sherman. 128p. 1997. reprint ed. pap. 16.95 (*0-7661-0026-X*) Kessinger Pub.

New Edition of the Works of T. H. Green, 5 vols. Ed. & Intro. by Peter Nicholson. (Thoemmes Press Idealism Ser.). 2870p. 1997. 625.00 (*1-85506-512-6*) Thoemmes Pr.

N

New Education: A Review of Progressive Education Movements of the Day. Scott Nearing. LC 75-89210. (American Education: Its Men, Institutions, & Ideas. Series 1). 1974. reprint ed. 19.95 (*0-405-01449-X*) Ayer.

New Education for a New Consciousness: Sri Aurobindo & the Mother on Education. 2nd ed. Sri Aurobindo. 246p. 1995. pap. 15.95 (*81-7058-426-4*, Pub. by SAA) Auromere.

New Education in Italy. Howard R. Marraro. LC 78-63692. (Studies in Fascism: Ideology & Practice). reprint ed. 47.00 (*0-404-16954-6*) AMS Pr.

New Education Politics. George Martell. (Our Schools/Our Selves Ser.). 310p. pap. 19.95 (*1-55028-488-6*, Pub. by J Lorimer) Formac Dist Ltd.

New Educational Methods for Increasing Religious Effectiveness. Dean C. Dauw. pap. 1.00 (*0-8199-0389-2*, L38532, Frncscn Herld) Franciscan Pr.

New Educational Pact: Education, Competitiveness & Citizenship in Modern Society. Juan Carlos Tedesco. LC 98-144101. 1998. 25.00 (*92-3-185006-7*, U5006, Pub. by UNESCO) Bernan Associates.

New Educational Programs in Public Policy: The 1st Decade. Ed. by Stuart S. Nagel & John P. Crecine. (Research in Public Policy Analysis & Management Ser.: Suppl. No. 1). 225p. 1983. 73.25 (*0-89232-244-6*) Jai Pr.

***New Educational Technologies & Learning: Empowering Teachers to Teach & Students to Learn in the Information Age.** Ibrahim M. Hefzallah. LC 99-10257. (Illus.). 322p. 1999. text 62.95 (*0-398-06950-6*) C C Thomas.

New Educational Technologies & Learning: Empowering Teachers to Teach & Students to Learn in the Information Age. Ibrahim M. Hefzallah. LC 99-10257. (Illus.). 322p. 1999. pap. 48.95 (*0-398-06951-4*) C C Thomas.

New Effective Public Manager: Achieving Success in a Changing Government. Steven Cohen & William E. Micke. LC 94-44963. (Public Administration Ser.). 307p. 1995. 26.95 (*0-7879-0087-7*) Jossey-Bass.

New 18th Century: Theory, Politics, English Literature. Ed. by Felicity Nussbaum & Laura Brown. 325p. 1987. 35.00 (*0-416-01631-6*, 1191); pap. 13.95 (*0-416-01641-3*, 1196) Routledge.

New El Dorado: or British Columbia. Kinahan Cornwallis. LC 72-9437. (Far Western Frontier Ser.). (Illus.). 442p. 1973. reprint ed. 29.95 (*0-405-04967-6*) Ayer.

New Elect: The Church & New Religious Groups. Martin Tierney. 124p. (Orig.). 1985. pap. 6.95 (*0-86217-186-5*, Pub. by Veritas Pubns) St Mut.

New Electric Power Technologies. 1991. lib. bdg. 75.95 (*0-8490-4975-X*) Gordon Pr.

New Electric Vehicles: A Clean & Quiet Revolution. Michael A. Hackleman. (Illus.). 276p. 1996. pap. text 25.00 (*0-9629588-7-5*) Home Power.

New Electricity 21: Designing a Sustainable Electric System for the Twenty-First Century. IEA Staff. LC 96-218353. 906p. (Orig.). 1996. pap. 147.00 (*92-64-14894-9*, 61-96-16-1, Pub. by Org for Econ) OECD.

New Electronic Media: Innovations in Video Technologies. Homes. 131p. 1989. pap. text 36.95 (*0-240-51731-8*, Focal) Buttrwrth-Heinemann.

New Electronic Pathways: Videotex, Teletex, & Online Databases. Jerome Aumente. LC 87-3354. (Sage Commtext Ser.: No. 17). 159p. 1987. reprint ed. pap. 49.30 (*0-608-01185-1*, 205948300001) Bks Demand.

New Elegant but Easy Cookbook. Marian Burros & Lois Levine. LC 97-46884. 352p. 1998. 24.50 (*0-684-83244-5*) S&S Trade.

New Elementary School Librarian's Almanac: Practical Ideas, Tips, Techniques & Activities for Every Month of the School Year. Barbara F. Bannister. LC 91-252. 256p. 1991. text 32.95 (*0-87628-605-8*) Ctr Appl Res.

New Elementary Teacher's Handbook: (Almost) Everything You Need to Know for Your First Years of Teaching. Kathleen F. Jonson. LC 97-4616. 224p. 1997. pap. 32.95 (*0-8039-6465-X*) Corwin Pr.

New Elementary Teacher's Handbook: (Almost) Everything You Need to Know for Your First Years of Teaching. Kathleen F. Jonson. LC 97-4616. 224p. 1997. 69.95 (*0-8039-6464-1*) Corwin Pr.

New Elements of Mathematics by Charles S. Peirce: Algebra & Geometry, Vol. 2. Ed. by Carolyn Eisele. xxxii, 672p. 1976. text 154.65 (*3-11-000161-6*) Mouton.

New Elements of Mathematics by Charles S. Peirce: Arithmetic, Vol. 1. Carolyn Eisele. xi, 260p. 1976. text 70.80 (*90-279-3025-2*) Mouton.

New Elements of Mathematics by Charles S. Peirce: Mathematical Miscellanea, 2 pts., Set. Ed. by Carolyn Eisele. xi, 1154p. text 284.65 (*90-279-3035-X*) Mouton.

New Elements of Mathematics by Charles S. Peirce: Mathematical Philosophy, Vol. 4. Ed. by Carolyn Eisele. xxviii, 394p. 1976. text 107.70 (*90-279-3045-7*) Mouton.

New Elite in Post-Communist Eastern Europe. Vladimir Shlapentokh et al. LC 99-21472. (Eastern European Ser.). 1999. 44.95 (*0-89096-895-0*) Tex A&M Univ Pr.

New Elites in Old States: Ideologies in Anglo-American Democracies. Neil Nevitte & Roger Gibbins. (Illus.). 352p. 1991. pap. text 29.95 (*0-19-540803-9*) OUP.

New Elites of Tropical Africa: Studies Presented & Discussed at the Sixth International African Seminar at the University of Ibadan, Nigeria, July 1964. International African Seminar - Sixth, Ibadan Staf. LC 66-72756. 400p. reprint ed. pap. 124.00 (*0-7837-0987-0*, 20412930020) Bks Demand.

New Elizabeth. Kate William. (Sweet Valley High Ser.: No. 63). (YA). (gr. 7 up). 1990. 8.09 (*0-606-04489-2*, Pub. by Turtleback) Demco.

New Ellesmere Chaucer Facsimile: The Canterbury Tales. Geoffrey Chaucer. Ed. by Daniel Woodward & Martin Stevens. (Illus.). 1995. write for info. (*0-87328-151-9*) Huntington Lib.

New Elucidations. Hans U. Von Balthasar. Tr. by M. Theresilde Skerry from GER. LC 85-82031. Orig. Title: Neue Klarstellungen. (Illus.). 305p. (Orig.). 1986. pap. text 14.95 (*0-89870-041-8*) Ignatius Pr.

New Embroidery for Beginners. Ondori Publishing Company Staff. (Illus.). 48p. 1986. pap. 11.95 (*0-87040-702-3*) Japan Pubns USA.

New Emergencies: 9th International Seminar on Nuclear War. M. Dardo & K. Goebel. (Science & Culture Ser.). 352p. 1992. text 109.00 (*981-02-1192-9*) World Scientific Pub.

New Emergency Health Kit: Lists of Drugs & Medical Supplies for 10,000 People for Approximately Three Months. (ENG, FRE & SPA.). 44p. 1990. pap. text 7.20 (*0-614-08026-6*, 1930018) World Health.

New Emperors: China... Harrison Salisbury. xvi, 576p. 1993. pap. 14.00 (*0-380-72025-6*, Avon Bks) Morrow Avon.

New Empire. Henry (Brooks) Adams. (Principle Works of Brooks Adams). 1989. reprint ed. lib. bdg. 79.00 (*0-685-27363-6*) Rprt Serv.

*__New Empire.__ Henry (Brooks) Adams. 2000. reprint ed. lib. bdg. 79.00 (*0-7812-2572-8*) Rprt Serv.

New Empire: An Interpretation of American Expansion, 1860-1898. Walter Lafeber. LC 99-160552. 1998. pap. text 16.95 (*0-8014-8595-9*) Cornell U Pr.

New Empire of Diocletian & Constantine. Timothy D. Barnes. LC 81-6569. 324p. reprint ed. pap. 100.50 (*0-7837-2221-4*, 205731100004) Bks Demand.

New Employee: Developing a Productive Human Resource. Gordon F. Shea. LC 80-16346. 1981. 17.95 (*0-201-07137-1*) Addison-Wesley.

New Employee Orientation: A How-to-Do-It Manual for Librarians. H. Scott Davis. LC 93-43416. (How-to-Do-It Manuals for Libraries Ser.: No. 38). 144p. 1994. pap. 45.00 (*1-55570-158-2*) Neal-Schuman.

New Employee Orientation: A Practical Guide for Supervisors. Charles Cadwell. Ed. by Michael G. Crisp. LC 87-73558. (Fifty-Minute Ser.). (Illus.). 76p. 1988. pap. 10.95 (*0-931961-46-7*) Crisp Pubns.

New Employee Orientation: The Standard Manual of Successful Programs. Sue E. Thompson. 1983. ring bd. 25.45 (*1-55645-112-1*) Busn Legal Reports.

New Employment Issues in the Electronic Workplace. Susan E. Culbreath. LC 98-11391. 52p. 1998. spiral bd. 47.00 (*0-925773-42-5*) M Lee Smith.

New Encyclopedia Britannica. Ed. by Robert D. McHenry. (Illus.). 31919p. 1994. 1599.00 (*0-85229-571-5*) Ency Brit Inc.

New Encyclopedia of Agriculture: Organic Material of Soil: Nueva Enciclopedia de Agricultura: Materia Organica del Suelo. M. M. Kanonova. (SPA.). 365p. 1982. 75.00 (*0-8288-1181-4*, S39782) Fr & Eur.

*__New Encyclopedia of American Scandal.__ George Childs Kohn. (Illus.). 448p. 2001. pap. 24.95 (*0-8160-4420-1*, Checkmark); lib. bdg. 65.00 (*0-8160-4225-X*, Checkmark) Facts on File.

New Encyclopedia of Fly Fishing. rev. ed. Conrad V. Bark & Eric Restall. (Illus.). 320p. 1999. 45.00 (*0-7090-6308-3*, Pub. by R Hale Ltd) Seven Hills Bk.

New Encyclopedia of Freemasonry, Set, Vols. I & II. Arthur E. Waite. LC 93-46219. (Illus.). 1024p. 1994. 14.99 (*0-517-19148-2*) Random Hse Value.

New Encyclopedia of Home Repair. rev. ed. Julian Worthington & Bob Pennycook. (Illus.). 300p. 1996. 29.95 (*1-55013-779-4*) Firefly Bks Ltd.

*__New Encyclopedia of Modern Bodybuilding: The Bible of Bodybuilding.__ Arnold Schwarzenegger. LC 99-462453. 832p. 1999. per. 25.00 (*0-684-85721-9*) S&S Trade Pap.

New Encyclopedia of Modern Bodybuilding: The Bible of Bodybuilding. rev. ed. Arnold Schwarzenegger. 1998. 50.00 (*0-684-86223-9*) S&S Trade.

New Encyclopedia of Modern Bodybuilding: The Bible of Bodybuilding. rev. ed. Arnold Schwarzenegger & Bill Dobbins. LC 98-44469. (Illus.). 832p. 1998. 50.00 (*0-684-84374-9*) Simon & Schuster.

New Encyclopedia of Music & Musicians. Waldo S. Pratt. 969p. 1990. reprint ed. lib. bdg. 129.00 (*0-7812-9009-0*) Rprt Serv.

New Encyclopedia of Real Estate Forms. Jerome S. Gross. LC 82-21582. 701p. 1983. 59.95 (*0-686-45921-0*) P-H.

New Encyclopedia of School Letters. Susan Mamchak & Steven R. Mamchak. LC 89-48884. 420p. (C). 1990. pap. text 29.95 (*0-13-612656-1*) P-H.

New Encyclopedia of Social Reform. 3rd ed. Ed. by William D. Bliss & Rudolph M. Binder. LC 77-112524. (Rise of Urban America Ser.). 1970. reprint ed. 72.95 (*0-405-02436-3*) Ayer.

New Encyclopedia of Stage Hypnotism. Ormond McGill. (Illus.). 608p. 1999. reprint ed. 55.00 (*1-899836-02-0*, Pub. by Crown Hse) LPC Group.

New Encyclopedia of the American West. Ed. by Howard R. Lamar. LC 98-6231. (Illus.). 1324p. 1998. 60.00 (*0-300-07088-8*) Yale U Pr.

*__New Encyclopedia of the Dog.__ 2nd ed. Bruce Fogle. LC 00-22642. 2000. 40.00 (*0-7894-6130-7*) DK Pub Inc.

*__New Encyclopedia of Vitamins, Minerals, Supplements & Herbs: A completely cross-referenced user's guide for optimal health.__ Nicola Reavley & Stephen Holt. 794p. 1999. pap. 19.95 (*0-87131-897-0*, Pub. by M Evans) Natl Bk Netwk.

New Encyclopedia of Wine Clarke. 1999. write for info. (*0-15-601068-2*) Harcourt.

New Encyclopedia of Zionism & Israel, 2 vols. 2nd ed. Ed. by Geoffrey Wigoder. (Illus.). 1994. 185.00 (*0-8386-3433-8*) Fairleigh Dickinson.

New Encyclopedic Dictionary of School Law. Richard M. Gatti & Daniel J. Gatti. 312p. 1983. text 39.95 (*0-13-612580-8*, Parker Publishing Co) P-H.

New Endeavour: Selected Political Essays, Letters & Addresses. Frank Scott. 153p. 1986. text 30.00 (*0-8020-5672-5*) U of Toronto Pr.

New Endeavour: Selected Political Essays, Letters, & Addresses. Frank Scott. 153p. 1986. pap. 14.95 (*0-8020-6603-8*) U of Toronto Pr.

*__New Energy Sources.__ Nigel Hawkes. LC 00-34072. (Saving Our World Ser.). (Illus.). (J). 2000. lib. bdg. write for info. (*0-7613-1212-9*, Copper Beech Bks) Millbrook Pr.

New Engagement: Evangelical Political Thought, 1966-1976. Robert B. Fowler. LC 82-11389. 308p. reprint ed. 95.50 (*0-608-16681-2*, 202754300055) Bks Demand.

New Engine Design & Automotive Filtration. 120p. 1998. 59.00 (*0-7680-0182-X*) Soc Auto Engineers.

New Engineer: Management & Professional Responsibility in a Changing World. Sharon Beder. LC 98-185063. 350p. 1998. 84.95 (*0-7329-4675-1*, Pub. by Macmill Educ); pap. 42.95 (*0-7329-4676-X*, Pub. by Macmill Educ) Paul & Co Pubs.

New Engineering & Construction Contract. 2nd rev. ed. Institution of Civil Engineers Staff. LC 95-201737. 65p. 1995. 23.00 (*0-7277-2071-6*) Am Soc Civil Eng.

New Engineering Concepts in Community Development. Jack Newville. LC 67-28256. (Urban Land Institute, Technical Bulletin Ser.: No. 59). 58p. reprint ed. pap. 30.00 (*0-608-10920-7*, 200577600059) Bks Demand.

New Engineering Contract, 10 vols. Institute of Civil Engineers Staff. 580p. 1993. pap. 106.00 (*0-7277-1664-6*, 1664, Pub. by T Telford) RCH.

New Engineering Contract: A Commentary. Brian Eggleston. 432p. 1996. text 89.95 (*0-632-04065-3*) Blackwell Sci.

New Engineer's Guide to Career Growth & Professional Awareness. Ed. by Irving J. Gabelman. LC 96-6440. 296p. 1996. pap. 39.95 (*0-7803-1057-8*, PP4119) Inst Electrical.

New Engines & Power Systems. 80p. 1998. pap. 35.00 (*0-7680-0249-4*, SP-1374) Soc Auto Engineers.

*__New Englad Historical & Genealogical Register, Vol. 65.__ New England Historical Genealogical Society Staff. (Illus.). 537p. 2000. pap. 33.50 (*0-7884-1388-0*, NR65) Heritage Bk.

New England. Colman. (Discover America Ser.). 1985. 6.99 (*0-8442-7473-9*) NTC Contemp Pub Co.

New England. Ted Landphai & Carol M. Highsmith. LC 96-43087. (Photographic Tour Ser.). (Illus.). 128p. 1997. 14.99 (*0-517-18333-1*) Random Hse Value.

*__New England.__ Tanya Lloyd. (America Ser.). (Illus.). 96p. 1999. 14.95 (*1-55110-947-6*) Whitecap Bks.

*__New England.__ Tracey Menges. (Annual Directory of American & Canadian Bed & Breakfasts Ser.: Vol. I). (Illus.). 293p. 2000. pap. 9.95 (*1-57748-771-0*) Barbour Pub.

New England. National Geographic Society U. S. Staff et al. LC 96-24771. (National Geographic's Driving Guides to America Ser.). 160p. 1997. per. 14.95 (*0-7922-3424-3*) Natl Geog.

*__New England.__ National Geographic Staff & Gary Ferguson. (National Geographic Guide to America's Outdoors). (Illus.). 288p. 2000. per. 24.00 (*0-7922-7742-2*) Natl Geog.

New England. Joan D. Norris & Barbara Forsberg. LC 93-49006. (American Food Library). 48p. (J). (gr. 3-6). 1994. lib. bdg. 22.60 (*0-86625-510-9*) Rourke Pubns.

New England. Barbara Paulding-Thrasher. 64p. 1995. write for info. (*1-57215-063-7*) World Pubns.

New England. Rough Guides Staff. 544p. 1999. pap. 17.95 (*1-85828-426-0*, Pub. by Rough Guides) Penguin Putnam.

*__New England.__ Carla Soffritti. (Illus.). 2000. 9.99 (*0-7858-1235-0*) Bk Sales Inc.

*__New England.__ Molly Stevens & Chuck Williams. LC 00-24943. (Williams-Sonoma New American Cooking Ser.). (Illus.). 144p. 2000. 22.95 (*0-7370-2044-X*) Time-Life Educ.

*__New England.__ 2nd ed. Tom Brosnahan et al. (Illus.). 544p. 1999. pap. 19.95 (*0-86442-570-8*) Lonely Planet.

New England. 2nd ed. Laura Purdom. (Traveler's Companion Ser.). (Illus.). 296p. 1999. pap. text 23.95 (*0-7627-0486-1*) Globe Pequot.

New England. 6th ed. Insight Guides Staff. (Insight Guides). 1998. pap. text 22.95 (*0-88729-724-2*) Langenscheidt.

New England. 7th ed. (Insight Guides Ser.). (Illus.). 1999. pap. 22.95 (*0-88729-025-6*) Langenscheidt.

*__New England.__ 9th ed. Michelin Staff. (Green Guide to New England). (Illus.). 1999. 20.00 (*2-06-156909-9*) Michelin.

*__New England.__ 15th ed. Petersons. (Peterson's Colleges in New England Ser.). 139-357p. 1999. pap. 17.95 (*0-7689-0252-5*) Petersons.

New England: A Pictorial Souvenir. Carol M. Highsmith & Ted Landphai. (Pictorial Souvenir Ser.). (Illus.). 64p. 1997. 7.99 (*0-517-20145-3*) Random Hse Value.

New England: Indian Summer, 1865-1915. Van Wyck Brooks. LC 84-8545. xii, 558p. 1985. reprint ed. pap. text 14.95 (*0-226-07578-8*) U Ch Pr.

New England: Land of Scenic Splendor. Ed. by Donald J. Crump. (Special Publications Series 24: No. 2). (Illus.). (YA). 1989. lib. bdg. 12.95 (*0-87044-720-3*) Natl Geog.

New England Adventures: The Driver's Guide. Fraser Bridges. (Illus.). 352p. (Orig.). 1993. pap. 14.95 (*1-883470-01-3*) Amer Traveler.

New England & Foreign Relations, 1789-1850. Paul A. Varg. LC 82-40338. (Illus.). 270p. reprint ed. pap. 83.70 (*0-8357-6522-9*, 203589300097) Bks Demand.

New England & the Middle States see Report on the Social Statistics of Cities

New England & the Sea. Robert G. Albion et al. LC 72-3694. (American Maritime Library: Vol. 5). (Illus.). xiv, 303p. 1972. pap. 18.00 (*0-913372-23-4*) Mystic Seaport.

New England Annals: History & Genealogy, Vol. 1. Ed. by Laird C. Towle. 500p. 1980. 30.00 (*0-917890-19-1*) Heritage Bk.

New England Artists & Writers: In Their Own Words. Brownie Macintosh. (New England Gift Bks.: Vol. 5). (Illus.). 64p. 2000. 4.95 (*1-58066-017-7*, Covered Brdge Pr) Douglas Charles Ltd.

New England at a Glance: Profiles from the 1990 Census. Ed. by Ronald D. Karr. LC 93-72035. 392p. (Orig.). 1993. pap. 39.95 (*0-942147-03-0*) Branch Line Pr.

New England Authors. Eric Tomb. (Illus.). 64p. (J). (gr. 8). 1991. pap. text 4.95 (*0-88388-149-7*) Bellerophon Bks.

New England Autumn. Mimi Lupin. 1988. 9.95 (*0-07-039163-7*) McGraw.

New England Aviators, 1914-1918: Their Portraits & Their Records, Vol. 1. A. Lawrence Lowell. LC 97-66730. (Illus.). 472p. 1997. 49.95 (*0-7643-0345-7*) Schiffer.

New England Aviators, 1914-1918: Their Portraits & Their Records, Vol. 2. A. Lawrence Lowell. LC 97-66730. (Illus.). 480p. 1997. 49.95 (*0-7643-0346-5*) Schiffer.

New England Beach Guide. Ellen Ruggles. Ed. by Andrea Brox & Beverly J. Wood. (Illus.). 336p. (Orig.). 1996. pap. 11.95 (*0-9636123-2-8*) Pleasant St Pr.

New England Berry Book. Bob Krumm. (Illus.). 128p. (Orig.). 1997. pap. 11.95 (*1-56044-525-4*) Falcon Pub Inc.

New England Book of the Dead. James H. Parker. LC 95-4058. (Illus.). 110p. (C). 1995. pap. text 28.50 (*0-8191-9903-6*); lib. bdg. 43.00 (*0-8191-9902-8*) U Pr of Amer.

New England Boyhood. Edward E. Hale. 267p. 1977. reprint ed. lib. bdg. 14.75 (*0-89966-255-2*) Buccaneer Bks.

New England Boyhood. Edward E. Hale. LC 76-104469. 280p. 1976. reprint ed. lib. bdg. 12.00 (*0-8398-0750-3*) Irvington.

New England Boyhood. Edward E. Hale. (BCL1-PS American Literature Ser.). 208p. 1992. reprint ed. lib. bdg. 79.00 (*0-7812-6716-1*) Rprt Serv.

New England Boyhood. Edward E. Hale. (Notable American Authors Ser.). 1992. reprint ed. lib. bdg. 75.00 (*0-7812-2976-6*) Rprt Serv.

New England Boyhood. Edward E. Hale. LC 72-131731. 1970. reprint ed. 49.00 (*0-403-00618-X*) Scholarly.

New England by the Sea. Ed. by Lisa C. Mullins. (Architectural Treasures of Early America Ser.). (Illus.). 245p. 1987. 19.95 (*0-918678-22-6*) Natl Hist Soc.

New England Captives Carried to Canada Between 1677 & 1760 During the French & Indian Wars. Emma L. Coleman. 1977. 48.95 (*0-8369-6970-7*, 7851) Ayer.

New England Charming Small Hotels, 1995. Chris Gill. (Charming Small Hotels Ser.). (Illus.). 224p. (Orig.). 1995. pap. 12.95 (*1-55650-676-7*) Hunter NJ.

New England Christmas. Susie Saunders. 1993. 12.95 (*1-883406-00-5*) Hrt of Byfield.

New England Chronicle News of New England from January 1722-December 1731. Armand F. Lucier. LC 97-190837. vi, 213p. 1997. pap. 19.00 (*0-7884-0634-5*, L816) Heritage Bk.

New England Church Supper Favorites. Dianne L. Bruleigh. (Illus.). 48p. (Orig.). 1989. pap. 3.95 (*0-933050-71-2*) New Eng Pr VT.

New England Clocks & Their Makers. Robert Cheney & Philip M. Zea. LC 92-27611. 1992. pap. 34.95 (*0-913387-03-7*) Old Sturbridge.

New England Coast, a Photographic Tour. C. Highsmith & Landphair. LC 98-35689. 1999. 14.99 (*0-517-20404-5*) Crescent Books.

New England Cookbook: 350 Recipes from Town & Country, Land & Sea, Hearth & Home. Brooke Dojny. LC 99-14393. (Illus.). 512p. 1999. pap. 18.95 (*1-55832-139-X*, Pub. by Harvard Common Pr) Natl Bk Netwk.

*__New England Cookbook: 350 Recipes from Town & Country, Land & Sea, Hearth & Home.__ Brooke Dojny. LC 99-14393. (Illus.). 512p. 1999. text 29.95 (*1-55832-138-1*, Pub. by Harvard Common Pr) Natl Bk Netwk.

*__New England Country Tavern.__ Jack Larkin. (Illus.). iv, 56p. 2000. pap. write for info. (*0-913387-05-3*) Old Sturbridge.

New England Decoys. Shirley Delph & John Delph. LC 81-51445. (Illus.). 159p. 1981. 35.00 (*0-916838-54-4*) Schiffer.

New England Diaries, 1602-1800: A Descriptive Catalogue of Diaries, Orderly Books & Sea Journals. Harriette M. Forbes. 439p. reprint ed. lib. bdg. 65.00 (*0-8328-6571-0*) Higginson Bk Co.

New England Diesels. Dave Albert & George F. Melvin. LC 75-27730. (Illus.). 1977. 28.95 (*0-916160-01-7*) G R Cockle.

New England Dissent, 1630-1833: The Baptists & the Separation of Church & State, 2 vols., Set. William G. McLoughlin. LC 70-131464. (Center for the Study of the History of Liberty in America Ser.). (Illus.). 1346p. 1971. 135.00 (*0-674-61175-6*) HUP.

New England Encounters: Indians & Euroamericans, CA. 1600-1850. Ed. by Alden T. Vaughan. LC 99-28893. 432p. 1999. text 50.00 (*1-55553-404-X*) NE U Pr.

New England Engraved: The Prints of Asa Cheffetz. Intro. by Sinclair Hitchings. LC 84-52226. (Illus.). 158p. 1984. pap. 10.00 (*0-916746-10-0*) Springfield Lib & Mus.

New England Families, Genealogical & Memorial: A Record of the Achievements of Her People in the Making of Commonwealths & the Founding of a Nation, 4 vols. William R. Cutter. (Illus.). 2149p. 1997. reprint ed. pap. 200.00 (*0-8063-4537-3*, 9175, Pub. by Clearfield Co) ACCESS Pubs Network.

New England Families, Genealogical & Memorial: Record of the Achievements of Her People in the Making of Commonwealths & the Founding of a Nation. Ed. by William R. Cutter. (Illus.). 1259p. 1997. reprint ed. lib. bdg. 126.00 (*0-8328-5706-8*) Higginson Bk Co.

*__New England Family Histories: State of Connecticut.__ Lu Verne V. Hall. 262p. 1999. 23.50 (*0-7884-1394-5*, H052) Heritage Bk.

*__New England Family Histories: States of Maine & Rhode Island.__ Lu Verne V. Hall & Donald O. Virdin. 177p. 2000. pap. 19.00 (*0-7884-1431-3*, 1431) Heritage Bk.

*__New England Family Histories & Genealogies: States of New Hampshire & Vermont.__ Lu Verne V. Hall & Donald O. Virdin. 170p. 2000. pap. 18.50 (*0-7884-1451-8*, 1451) Heritage Bk.

New England Family History. Ed. by Henry C. Quinby. (Illus.). 866p. 1992. reprint ed. lib. bdg. 88.00 (*0-8328-2436-4*) Higginson Bk Co.

New England Farm. Thomas Gilson. LC 83-51095. (Illus.). 64p. 1983. pap. 12.95 (*0-685-42660-2*) Wickwire Pr.

New England Farm Vacations. Lisa Rogak. LC 93-37245. (Illus.). 128p. (Orig.). 1994. pap. 9.95 (*1-56626-044-2*, Cntry Rds Pr) NTC Contemp Pub Co.

New England Farmer: or Georgical Dictionary. Samuel Deane. LC 72-5043. (Technology & Society Ser.). 543p. 1972. reprint ed. 36.95 (*0-405-04695-2*) Ayer.

New England Fish Table: Seafood Recipes & Observations of a Way of Life from a Fisherman's Wife. Martha W. Murphy. LC 96-44778. 1995. write for info. (*0-8050-4204-0*) H Holt & Co.

New England Fish Tales. Martha W. Murphy. 1996. pap. 15.95 (*0-8050-4205-9*) St Martin.

New England Fishing Economy: Jobs, Income, & Kinship. Peter B. Doeringer et al. LC 86-7128. (Illus.). 160p. 1987. lib. bdg. 22.50 (*0-87023-535-4*) U of Mass Pr.

New England Foliage Trails. Jay Woodard. (Illus.). 64p. (Orig.). 1988. 14.95 (*0-9618888-2-2*) Anglo-Am TX.

New England Frontier: Puritans & Indians, 1620-1675. Alden T. Vaughan. LC 94-35277. (Illus.). 512p. 1995. pap. 17.95 (*0-8061-2718-X*) U of Okla Pr.

New England Furniture at Williamsburg. Barry A. Greenlaw. LC 73-90536. (Williamsburg Decorative Arts Ser.). 204p. (Orig.). reprint ed. pap. 63.30 (*0-608-13926-2*, 201782900010) Bks Demand.

New England Furniture at Winterthur: Queen Anne & Chippendale Periods. Nancy E. Richards et al. LC 94-46794. (Illus.). 534p. 1997. 85.00 (*0-912724-38-2*) Winterthur.

New England Gazetteer. John Hayward. 623p. 1997. reprint ed. pap. 34.00 (*0-7884-0003-7*, H098) Heritage Bk.

New England Genealogy. rev. ed. Arlene H. Eakle & Linda E. Brinkerhoff. 52p. 1996. pap. 19.50 (*0-940764-36-9*) Genealog Inst.

New England Ghost Files. Charles T. Robinson. LC 95-126. (Illus.). 256p. 1994. pap. 14.95 (*0-924771-48-8*, Covered Brdge Pr) Douglas Charles Ltd.

*__New England Ghost Files Vol. II: The Sequel.__ Charles T. Robinson. (Illus.). 256p. (C). 1999. pap. 14.95 (*1-58066-030-4*, Covered Brdge Pr) Douglas Charles Ltd.

An Asterisk (*) at the beginning of an entry indicates that the title is appearing for the first time.

New England Ghosts. Ed. by Frank McSherry et al. LC 90-43189. (American Ghost Ser.). 214p. (Orig.). 1990. pap. 9.95 (*1-55853-090-8*) Rutledge Hill Pr.

New England Girlhood. Lucy Larcom. 1990. 16.50 (*0-8446-2431-4*) Peter Smith.

New England Girlhood. Lucy Larcom. 274p. 1977. reprint ed. 24.95 (*0-87928-078-6*) Corner Hse.

New England Girlhood: Outlined from Memory. Lucy Larcom. (Illus.). 300p. 1985. reprint ed. pap. text 16.95 (*0-930350-82-0*) NE U Pr.

New England Golf Guide: The Directory for Public Play, 1999 Edition. Leona Curhan et al. 488p. (Orig.). 1998. 17.95 (*0-9624717-5-5*) New Engl Golf.

New England GolfGuide: The Directory for Public Play, 2000 Edition. 11th ed. Leona Curhan & Irwin Garfinkle. 512p. (Orig.). 1999. pap. 17.95 (*0-9624717-6-3*) New Engl Golf.

New England Green Guide. 6th ed. Michelin Staff. 1995. pap. 19.95 (*0-7859-9142-5*) Fr & Eur.

New England Herb Gardener. Patricia Turcotte. (Illus.). 235p. 1990. pap. 13.95 (*0-9623199-2-9*) Dirigo Bks.

New England Herb Gardener: Yankee Wisdom for North American Herb Growers & Users. Patricia Turcotte. LC 91-2132. 256p. 1991. pap. 15.00 (*0-88150-188-3*, Pub. by Countryman) Norton.

New England Historical & Genealogical Register, 1896, Vol. L. NEHGS Staff. 612p. 1998. reprint ed. pap. 29.50 (*0-7884-0865-8*, NR50) Heritage Bk.

New England Historical & Genealogical Register, No. LII. New England Historic Genealogical Society Staff. 551p. 1998. reprint ed. pap. 40.00 (*0-7884-0916-6*, NR52) Heritage Bk.

New England Historical & Genealogical Register, Vol. VII, 1853. New England Historical & Genealogical Society Staf. 388p. (Orig.). 1992. reprint ed. pap. text 25.00 (*1-55613-687-0*) Heritage Bk.

New England Historical & Genealogical Register, Vol. VIII, 1854. New England Historical & Genealogical Society Staf. 388p. (Orig.). 1992. reprint ed. pap. text 25.00 (*1-55613-688-9*) Heritage Bk.

New England Historical & Genealogical Register, Vol. XVI, 1862. New England Historical & Genealogical Society Staf. (Illus.). 397p. (Orig.). 1993. reprint ed. pap. text 25.00 (*1-55613-841-5*) Heritage Bk.

New England Historical & Genealogical Register, Vol. 23. 504p. (Orig.). 1994. pap. text 25.00 (*0-7884-0070-3*) Heritage Bk.

New England Historical & Genealogical Register, Vol. 24. New England Historical & Genealogical Society Staf. 451p. (Orig.). 1994. pap. text 25.00 (*0-7884-0071-1*) Heritage Bk.

New England Historical & Genealogical Register, Vol. XXV. 414p. (Orig.). 1994. pap. text 25.00 (*0-7884-0125-4*) Heritage Bk.

New England Historical & Genealogical Register, Vol. 35. New England Hist. Gen. Soc. Staff. (Illus.). 419p. 1996. pap. 30.00 (*0-7884-0432-6*, NR35) Heritage Bk.

New England Historical & Genealogical Register, Vol. 36. New England Hist. Gen. Soc. Staff. (Illus.). 439p. 1996. pap. 29.50 (*0-7884-0472-5*, NR36) Heritage Bk.

New England Historical & Genealogical Register, Vol. 37. New England Hist. Gen. Soc. Staff. (Illus.). 436p. 1996. pap. 29.50 (*0-7884-0473-3*, NR37) Heritage Bk.

New England Historical & Genealogical Register, Vol. 39. N.E.H.G.S. Staff. (Illus.). 425p. 1996. pap. 29.50 (*0-7884-0498-9*, NR39) Heritage Bk.

New England Historical & Genealogical Register, Vol. 42. New England Historic Genealogical Society Staff. (Illus.). 432p. 1996. reprint ed. pap. 29.50 (*0-7884-0583-7*, NR42) Heritage Bk.

New England Historical & Genealogical Register, Vol. XLIII. New England Historic Genealogical Society Staff. 510p. 1996. reprint ed. pap. 29.50 (*0-7884-0584-5*, NR43) Heritage Bk.

New England Historical & Genealogical Register, Vol. XLIV, 1890. New England Historic Genealogical Soc. Staff. (Illus.). 472p. 1997. reprint ed. pap. 29.50 (*0-7884-0611-6*, NR44) Heritage Bk.

New England Historical & Genealogical Register, Vol. XLV, 1891. New England Historic Genealogical Soc. Staff. (Illus.). 537p. 1997. reprint ed. pap. 29.50 (*0-7884-0610-8*, NR45) Heritage Bk.

New England Historical & Genealogical Register, Vol. 46. New England Historic Genealogical Society Staff. (Illus.). vii, 518p. 1997. reprint ed. pap. 29.50 (*0-7884-0651-5*, NR46) Heritage Bk.

New England Historical & Genealogical Register, Vol. 47. New England Historic Genealogical Society Staff. (Illus.). 595p. 1997. reprint ed. pap. 29.50 (*0-7884-0652-3*, NR47) Heritage Bk.

New England Historical & Genealogical Register, Vol. L VII New England Historical Genealogical Society Staff. (Illus.). 510p. 1999. reprint ed. pap. 35.00 (*0-7884-1076-8*, NR57) Heritage Bk.

New England Historical & Genealogical Register, Vol. 59. New England Historical Society Staff. 512p. 1999. pap. 36.00 (*0-7884-1139-X*, NR59) Heritage Bk.

***New England Historical & Genealogical Register, Vol. 61.** New England Historical Gen. Society Staff. 552p. 1999. reprint ed. pap. 38.50 (*0-7884-1212-4*, NR61) Heritage Bk.

New England Historical & Genealogical Register: Index to Names, Volumes 51 Through 148, 4 vols. Ed. by Jane F. Fiske. 1995. 295.00 (*0-88082-038-1*) New Eng Hist.

New England Historical & Genealogical Register: 1900. New England Historic Genealogical Society Staff. 695p. 1998. reprint ed. pap. 46.50 (*0-7884-1029-6*, NR54) Heritage Bk.

***New England Historical & Genealogical Register Vol. 62: 1908.** New England History & Genealogical Society Staff. 568p. 1999. pap. 39.00 (*0-7884-1313-9*) Heritage Bk.

***New England Historical & Genealogical Register Vol. LXIII: 1909.** New England Historic Genealogical Society Staff. 544p. 1999. reprint ed. pap. 36.00 (*0-7884-1344-9*, NR63) Heritage Bk.

New England Historical & Genealogical Register, 1851, Vol. 5. NEHGS Staff. 486p. 1857. reprint ed. pap. 25.00 (*1-55613-708-7*) Heritage Bk.

New England Historical & Genealogical Register, 1852, Vol. VI. Ed. by NEHGS Staff. 402p. 1852. reprint ed. pap. 25.00 (*1-55613-709-5*) Heritage Bk.

New England Historical & Genealogical Register, 1855, Vol. IX. New England Historical & Genealogical Staff. 388p. (Orig.). 1993. reprint ed. pap. text 25.00 (*1-55613-744-3*) Heritage Bk.

New England Historical & Genealogical Register, 1856, Vol. X. New England Historical & Genealogical Society Staf. 379p. (Orig.). 1993. reprint ed. pap. text 25.00 (*1-55613-745-1*) Heritage Bk.

New England Historical & Genealogical Register, 1857, Vol. XI. New England Historical & Genealogical Society Staf. xii, 380p. 1993. reprint ed. pap. text 25.00 (*1-55613-777-X*) Heritage Bk.

New England Historical & Genealogical Register, 1858, Vol. XII. New England Historical & Genealogical Society Staf. vi, 379p. 1993. reprint ed. pap. text 25.00 (*1-55613-778-8*) Heritage Bk.

New England Historical & Genealogical Register, 1859, Vol. 13. New England Historical & Genealogical Society Staf. iv, 387p. (Orig.). 1993. pap. 22.00 (*1-55613-813-X*) Heritage Bk.

New England Historical & Genealogical Register, 1860, Vol. 14. New England Historical & Genealogical Society Staf. v, 390p. (Orig.). 1993. reprint ed. pap. text 25.00 (*1-55613-814-8*) Heritage Bk.

New England Historical & Genealogical Register, 1861, Vol. 15. New England Historical & Genealogical Society Staf. (Illus.). 375p. 1993. reprint ed. pap. text 25.00 (*1-55613-840-7*) Heritage Bk.

New England Historical & Genealogical Register, 1863, Vol. XVII. New England Historical & Genealogical Society Staf. (Illus.). 387p. (Orig.). 1994. reprint ed. pap. text 25.00 (*1-55613-937-3*) Heritage Bk.

New England Historical & Genealogical Register, 1864, Vol. XVIII. New England Historical & Genealogical Society Staf. (Illus.). 409p. (Orig.). 1994. reprint ed. pap. text 25.00 (*1-55613-938-1*) Heritage Bk.

New England Historical & Genealogical Register, 1865 Vol. XIX, Vol. X. NEHGS Staff. 394p. (Orig.). 1994. pap. 25.00 (*1-55613-976-4*) Heritage Bk.

New England Historical & Genealogical Register, 1866, XX. NEHGS Staff. 398p. (Orig.). 1994. pap. 25.00 (*1-55613-977-2*) Heritage Bk.

New England Historical & Genealogical Register, 1867, Vol. 2. New England Historical & Genealogical Society Staf. 399p. (Orig.). 1994. pap. text 25.00 (*0-7884-0012-6*) Heritage Bk.

New England Historical & Genealogical Register, 1873, Vol. 27. New England Historical & Genealogical Society Staf. 464p. (Orig.). 1995. pap. text 25.00 (*0-7884-0183-1*) Heritage Bk.

New England Historical & Genealogical Register, 1874, Vol. 28. NEHGS Staff. (Illus.). 500p. 1995. reprint ed. pap. text 25.00 (*0-7884-0194-7*) Heritage Bk.

New England Historical & Genealogical Register, 1875, Vol. 29. NEHGS Staff. (Illus.). 513p. (Orig.). 1995. pap. text 25.00 (*0-7884-0195-5*) Heritage Bk.

New England Historical & Genealogical Register, 1876, Vol. 30. New England Historical & Genealogical Society Staf. 497p. 1995. reprint ed. pap. text 27.50 (*0-7884-0239-0*) Heritage Bk.

New England Historical & Genealogical Register, 1877, Vol. 31. New England Historical & Genealogical Society Staf. 468p. 1995. reprint ed. pap. text 27.50 (*0-7884-0240-4*) Heritage Bk.

New England Historical & Genealogical Register, 1878, Vol. 32. New England Historical & Genealogical Society Staf. 464p. 1995. reprint ed. pap. 27.50 (*0-7884-0292-7*) Heritage Bk.

New England Historical & Genealogical Register, 1879, Vol. 33. New England Historical & Genealogical Society Staf. (Illus.). 460p. 1995. reprint ed. pap. 27.50 (*0-7884-0293-5*) Heritage Bk.

New England Historical & Genealogical Register, 1884, Vol. 38. N.E.H.G.S. Staff. (Illus.). 476p. 1996. pap. 29.50 (*0-7884-0497-0*, NR38) Heritage Bk.

New England Historical & Genealogical Register, 1886, Vol. XL. New England Hist. Gen. Soc. Staff. 432p. 1996. reprint ed. pap. 29.50 (*0-7884-0539-X*, NR40) Heritage Bk.

New England Historical & Genealogical Register, 1887, Vol. XLI. New England Hist. Gen. Soc. Staff. 450p. 1996. reprint ed. pap. 29.50 (*0-7884-0540-3*, NR41) Heritage Bk.

New England Historical & Genealogical Register, 1894, Vol. XLVIII. New England Historical & Genealogical Society Staf. 579p. 1998. reprint ed. pap. 29.50 (*0-7884-0814-3*, NR48) Heritage Bk.

New England Historical & Genealogical Register, 1895, Vol. XLIX. New England Historical & Genealogical Society Staf. 576p. 1998. pap. 29.50 (*0-7884-0815-1*, NR49) Heritage Bk.

New England Historical & Genealogical Register, 1897, LI. NEHGS Staff. 575p. 1998. pap. 29.50 (*0-7884-0866-6*, NR51) Heritage Bk.

***New England Historical & Genealogical Register, 1904, Vol. 58.** New England Genealogy Society Staff. (Illus.). 504p. 1999. reprint ed. pap. 35.50 (*0-7884-1087-3*, NR58) Heritage Bk.

***New England Historical & Genealogical Register, 1906.** New England Historical Society Members. (Illus.). 576p. 1999. reprint ed. pap. 39.50 (*0-7884-1191-8*, NR60) Heritage Bk.

New England Historical & Genealogical Registry, 1868, Vol. 2. New England Historical & Genealogical Society Staf. 500p. (Orig.). 1994. pap. text 25.00 (*0-7884-0013-4*) Heritage Bk.

New England Historical & Genealogy Register. New England Historical Genealogy Society. (Illus.). 542p. 1998. reprint ed. pap. 37.50 (*0-7884-1035-0*, NR55) Heritage Bk.

New England Historical Genealogical Register, Vol. LIII. New England Historic Genealogical Society Staff. 522p. 1998. reprint ed. pap. 38.00 (*0-7884-0917-4*, NR53) Heritage Bk.

New England History & Genealogy Reg., 1872, Vol. 26. NEHGS Staff. 464p. 1995. reprint ed. pap. text 25.00 (*0-7884-0126-2*) Heritage Bk.

New England Humor: From the Revolutionary War to the Civil War. Cameron C. Nickels. LC 93-320. (Illus.). 304p. (C). 1993. text 36.00 (*0-87049-804-5*) U of Tenn Pr.

New England Image. Samuel Chamberlain. (Illus.). 192p. 1994. 42.50 (*0-942655-08-7*) Archit CT.

New England in Fiction, 1787-1990: An Annotated Bibliography, 2 vols., 1. Robert B. Slocum. LC 93-47349. 1050p. (C). 1994. lib. bdg. write for info. (*0-933951-55-8*) Locust Hill Pr.

New England in Fiction, 1787-1990: An Annotated Bibliography, 2 vols., 2. Robert B. Slocum. LC 93-47349. 1050p. (C). 1994. lib. bdg. write for info. (*0-933951-56-6*) Locust Hill Pr.

New England in Fiction, 1787-1990: An Annotated Bibliography, 2 vols., Set. Robert B. Slocum. LC 93-47349. 1050p. (C). 1994. lib. bdg. 100.00 (*0-933951-54-X*) Locust Hill Pr.

New England in Focus: The Arthur Griffin Story. Herbert A. Kenny & Damon Reed. 136p. 1994. 49.95 (*0-9642819-0-2*) A Griffin Bk.

New England in the Republic. James T. Adams. 1989. reprint ed. lib. bdg. 79.00 (*0-7812-1507-2*) Rprt Serv.

New England in the Republic, 1776-1850. James T. Adams. (Works of James Truslow Adams). 438p. 1985. reprint ed. lib. bdg. 59.00 (*0-932051-16-2*) Rprt Serv.

New England in the Republic, 1776-1850. James T. Adams. (BCL1 - United States Local History Ser.). 438p. 1991. reprint ed. text 99.00 (*0-7812-6261-5*) Rprt Serv.

New England in the Republic, 1776-1850. James T. Adams. LC 70-144854. reprint ed. 39.00 (*0-403-00821-2*) Scholarly.

New England in U. S. Government Publications, 1789-1849: An Annotated Bibliography, 36. Suzanne M. Clark. LC 98-10085. (Bibliographies & Indexes in American History Ser.: Vol. 36). 616p. 1998. lib. bdg. 125.00 (*0-313-28128-9*, Greenwood Pr) Greenwood.

New England Indian Summer. Van Wyck Brooks. 575p. Date not set. 33.95 (*0-8488-2219-6*) Amereon Ltd.

New England Indians. Chelsea House Publishing Staff. LC 96-41644. (Illus.). 144p. (YA). (gr. 5 up). 1999. 19.95 (*0-7910-4525-0*) Chelsea Hse.

New England Indians. 2nd rev. ed. C. Keith Wilbur. LC 96-21202. (Living History Ser.). (Illus.). 108p. 1996. pap. 16.95 (*1-56440-993-7*) Globe Pequot.

New England Journal of Medicine, Vol. 1, No. 1. deluxe ed. 112p. 1987. 35.00 (*0-910133-20-4*) Mass Med Pub Div.

New England Journal on Criminal & Civil Confinement, 1974-1995, 19 vols. 1978. 90.00 (*0-318-57448-9*) W S Hein.

New England Journal on Criminal & Civil Confinement, 1974-1995, 23 vols., Set. 1974. 805.00 (*0-8377-9118-9*, Rothman) W S Hein.

New England Knight: Enrichment, Advancement & the Life of Sir William Phillips, 1651-1695. Emerson W. Baker. LC 98-204088. (Illus.). 400p. 1998. pap. 19.95 (*0-8020-8171-1*); text 65.00 (*0-8020-0925-5*) U of Toronto Pr.

New England Land Surveying Law: Questions & Answers. John E. Keen. 38p. (C). 1995. pap. text 25.00 (*1-56569-034-6*) Land Survey.

New England Legends & Folk Lore. Samuel A. Drake. 1993. 8.98 (*1-55521-925-X*) Bk Sales Inc.

New England Life in the 18th Century. Clifford K. Shipton. (Illus.). 656p. (Orig.). (C). 1995. pap. text 25.95 (*0-674-61251-5*) Belknap Pr.

New England Life in the 18th Century: Representative Biographies from Sibley's Harvard Graduates. Clifford K. Shipton. LC 63-9562. 654p. 1963. reprint ed. pap. 200.00 (*0-7837-2334-2*, 205742200004) Bks Demand.

***New England Lighthouses.** 1998. pap. 12.99 (*0-7631-1062-0*) BrownTrout Pubs Inc.

***New England Lighthouses: Bay of Fundy to Long Island Sound.** Bruce Roberts & Ray Jones. LC 99-15006. (Illus.). 112p. (YA). (gr. 5 up). 1999. 29.95 (*0-7910-5488-8*) Chelsea Hse.

New England Lighthouses: Bay of Fundy to Long Island Sound. Bruce Roberts & Ray Jones. LC 96-18770. (Lighthouses Ser.). (Illus.). 112p. 1996. pap. 19.95 (*1-56440-944-9*) Globe Pequot.

New England Lighthouses: Postcard Book. Ed. by BrownTrout Publishing Company Staff. (Illus.). 1997. pap. 7.95 (*1-56313-930-8*) BrownTrout Pubs Inc.

New England Literary Culture: From Revolution Through Renaissance. Lawrence Buell. (Cambridge Studies in American Literature & Culture: No. 15). 528p. (C). 1989. pap. text 25.95 (*0-521-37801-X*) Cambridge U Pr.

New England Local Color Literature: A Women's Tradition. Josephine Donovan. LC 72-81713. 168p. 1988. 9.95 (*0-8264-0415-4*) Continuum.

New England Magazine, Set, Vols. 1-9. reprint ed. lib. bdg. 607.50 (*0-404-19535-0*) AMS Pr.

New England Marriages Prior to 1700. Clarence A. Torrey. LC 84-81867. 1009p. 1997. reprint ed. 50.00 (*0-8063-1102-9*) Genealog Pub.

New England Merchants in the 17th Century. Bernard Bailyn. 257p. 1979. pap. 14.95 (*0-674-61280-9*) HUP.

New England Militia. James B. Whisker. LC 97-27189. (American Colonial Militia Ser.: Vol. II). 220p. 1997. text 89.95 (*0-7734-8522-8*) E Mellen.

New England Mill Village, 1790-1860. Ed. by Gary Kulik et al. (Documents in American Industrial History Ser.). (Illus.). 555p. 1982. 60.00 (*0-262-11084-9*) MIT Pr.

New England Milton: Literary Reception & Cultural Authority in the Early Republic. K. P. Van Anglen. 264p. (C). 1993. 45.00 (*0-271-00848-2*) Pa St U Pr.

New England Mind: From Colony to Province. Perry G. Miller. 528p. 1983. pap. 18.50 (*0-674-61301-5*) HUP.

New England Mind: The Seventeenth Century. Perry G. Miller. 540p. 1983. pap. 18.50 (*0-674-61306-6*) HUP.

New England Mind in Transition: Samuel Johnson of Connecticut, 1696-1772. Joseph J. Ellis. LC 73-77149. (Yale Historical Publications: No. 98). 304p. reprint ed. pap. 94.30 (*0-7837-3293-7*, 205769500006) Bks Demand.

New England Natives: A Celebration of People & Trees. Sheila Connor. (Illus.). 312p. 1993. text 39.95 (*0-674-61350-3*) HUP.

New England Natives: A Celebration of People & Trees. Sheila Connor. (Illus.). 312p. (C). 1995. pap. 24.95 (*0-674-61351-1*) HUP.

New England-New Mexico: Artistic Encounters, 1910-1940. Mary Delahoyd. (Illus.). 12p. 1989. 6.00 (*0-915171-12-0*) Katonah Gal.

New England Nun: And Other Stories. Mary E. Wilkins Freeman. (BCL1-PS American Literature Ser.). 468p. 1992. reprint ed. lib. bdg. 99.00 (*0-7812-6714-5*) Rprt Serv.

***New-England Nun & Other Stories.** Mary E. Wilkins Freeman & Sandra A. Zagarell. LC 99-56635. (Penguin Classics). 2000. pap. 12.95 (*0-14-043739-8*) Penguin Putnam.

New England on Land & Sea. (Illus.). 1970. 2.50 (*0-87577-039-8*, PEMP146, Peabody Museum) Peabody Essex Mus.

New England Outpost: War & Society in Colonial Frontier Deerfield. Richard I. Melvoin. 368p. 1992. pap. 14.95 (*0-393-30808-1*) Norton.

New England over the Handlebars: A Cyclist's Guide. Michael Farny. (Illus.). (Orig.). 1975. pap. 12.95 (*0-316-27465-8*) Little.

New England Parks Guide. Barbara Sinotte. (State & National Parks Ser.). (Illus.). 161p. (Orig.). 1996. pap. 11.95 (*1-55650-738-0*) Hunter NJ.

New England Patriots. Bob Italia. LC 95-16471. (Inside the NFL Ser.). (Illus.). 32p. (J). (gr. 3-8). 1996. lib. bdg. 15.98 (*1-56239-467-3*) ABDO Pub Co.

***New England Patriots.** 3rd rev. ed. Julie Nelson. (Pro Football Today Ser.). (Illus.). 32p. (YA). (gr. 3-12). 2000. lib. bdg. 22.60 (*1-58341-050-3*, Creat Educ) Creative Co.

New England Planters in the Maritime Provinces of Canada, 1759-1800: Bibliography of Sources. Compiled by Judith A. Norton. 512p. 1992. text 125.00 (*0-8020-2840-3*) U of Toronto Pr.

New England Poets: A Study of Emerson, Hawthorne, Longfellow, Whittier, Lowell, Holmes. William C. Lawton. LC 72-6941. (Essay Index Reprint Ser.). 1977. reprint ed. 23.95 (*0-8369-7245-7*) Ayer.

New England Political Parties. Josephine F. Milburn & William Doyle. LC 82-17059. (Illus.). 282p. 1983. reprint ed. pap. 87.50 (*0-608-05341-4*, 206504600012) Bks Demand.

New England Politics. Ed. by Josephine F. Milburn & Victoria Schuck. LC 80-14530. (Illus.). 333p. 1986. reprint ed. pap. 103.30 (*0-608-05337-6*, 206504200012) Bks Demand.

New England Primer. Intro. by David Barton. LC 98-119773. (Illus.). 1991. reprint ed. text 6.95 (*0-925279-17-X*) Wallbuilders.

New England Primer: A History of Its Origin & Development. Paul L. Ford. (Notable American Authors Ser.). 1992. reprint ed. lib. bdg. 75.00 (*0-7812-2881-6*) Rprt Serv.

New England Primer, 1996: A Family & Home School Textbook. rev. ed. Richard E. Klenk, Sr. 84p. 1996. reprint ed. pap. text 4.95 (*0-9648958-0-3*) Bizmin Assoc.

New England Primer of 1777. Gary Sanseri & Wanda K. Sanseri. (Illus.). 115p. (J). 1993. reprint ed. 14.95 (*1-880045-10-9*) Back Home Indust.

***New England Quaker Meetinghouses.** Silas Weeks. (Illus.). 128p. 2000. pap. 12.00 (*0-944350-51-8*) Friends United.

New England Quilt Museum Quilts: Featuring the Story of the Mill Girls - Instructions for 5 Heirloom Quilts. Jennifer Gilbert. Ed. by Cyndy Rymer & Sam MacFarland. LC 99-6127. 96p. 1999. pap. 22.95 (*1-57120-075-4*, 10195) C & T Pub.

New England Regional Plan: An Economic Development Strategy. New England Regional Commission. LC 81-50584. 158p. reprint ed. 49.00 (*0-608-16638-3*, 202753300055) Bks Demand.

New England Register, 1880, Vol. 34. New England Hist. Gen. Soc. Staff. (Illus.). 445p. 1996. pap. 33.00 (*0-7884-0431-8*, NR34) Heritage Bk.

New England Revivals, As They Existed at the Close of the Eighteenth & the Beginning of the Nineteenth Centuries Compiled Principally from Narratives First Pub. in the Conn. Evangelical Magazine Revival Library. Bennet Tyler. 378p. (C). 1980. reprint ed. lib. bdg. 15.50 (*0-940033-18-6*) R O Roberts.

N

New England Road Atlas: 1994 Edition. Susan Farewell. 1994. pap. 6.95 (*0-671-88835-8*, H M Gousha) Prntice Hall Bks.
New England Roleplaying Organization Rule Book. 8th ed. Michael A. Ventrella. (Illus.). 134p. 1998. pap. 20.00 (*0-9669844-0-4*) Nero.
New England Rooms (1639-1863) Samuel Chamberlain & Narcissa G. Chamberlain. (Illus.). 192p. 1993. 40.00 (*0-942655-06-0*) Archit CT.
New England Rules of Court (CT, MA, ME, NH, RI, VT), 2 vols., Set. Ed. by Butterworth Staff. 1300p. 1992. ring bd. 140.00 (*1-56257-651-8*, MICHIE) LEXIS Pub.
New England Sampler. Jan Siegrist. (Illus.). 48p. (Orig.). 1987. pap. 3.95 (*0-933050-48-8*) New Eng Pr VT.
New England Scrapbook: A Journey Through Poems, Prose, & Pict. Loretta Krupinski. LC 92-37705. (Illus.). 40p. (J). (gr. 2 up). 1994. 15.95 (*0-06-022950-0*) HarpC Child Bks.
New England Skiing. John B. Allen. (Images of America Ser.). 1999. pap. 16.99 (*0-7524-0494-6*) Arcadia Publng.
New England Snow Country: 701 Ways to Enjoy Winter Whether You Ski or Not. Barbara Radcliffe Rogers. 1999. pap. 14.95 (*0-9652502-6-1*) Williams Hill.
New England Soldiers. Marko Zlatich. (J). (gr. 1-9). 1992. pap. 3.95 (*0-88388-034-2*) Bellerophon Bks.
New England States: People, Politics & Power in the Six New England States. Neal R. Pierce. (Illus.). 1976. 15.95 (*0-393-05558-2*) Norton.
New England Tale. Catharine Maria Sedgwick. LC 78-64096. reprint ed. 37.50 (*0-404-17169-9*) AMS Pr.
New-England Tale: Or, Sketches of New-England Character. Catharine Maria Sedgwick. Ed. by Victoria Clements. (Early American Women Writers Ser.). 208p. 1995. pap. 11.95 (*0-19-509327-5*) OUP.
New England Textiles in the Nineteenth Century: Profits & Investment. Paul F. McGouldrick. LC 68-14267. (Economic Studies: No. 131). (Illus.). 1990. 20.00 (*0-674-61400-3*) HUP.
New England Time Line. 2nd ed. Ron McAdow. LC 92-80179. 96p. 1992. pap. write for info. (*1-880644-01-0*) Nutshell Bks.
New England Time Line: A Concise Guide to the Region's History. Ron McAdow. (McAdow's Time Lines Ser.). 48p. 1991. pap. 4.95 (*1-880644-00-2*) Nutshell Bks.
New England Town: The First Hundred Years. 2nd ed. Kenneth A. Lockridge. (Essays in American History Ser.). 220p. (C). 1985. pap. text 15.50 (*0-393-95459-5*) Norton.
New England Town Affairs. Charles J. Lincoln. 224p. (Orig.). 1995. pap. 12.95 (*0-924771-52-6*, Covered Brdge Pr) Douglas Charles Ltd.
New England Town in Fact & Fiction. Perry D. Westbrook. LC 80-67077. 288p. 1982. 40.00 (*0-8386-3011-1*) Fairleigh Dickinson.
New England Town Meeting: Democracy in Action. Joseph F. Zimmerman. LC 98-31074. 248p. 1999. 59.95 (*0-275-96523-6*, Praeger Pubs) Greenwood.
New England Tragedy. Henry Wadsworth Longfellow. (Notable American Authors Ser.). 1999. reprint ed. lib. bdg. 125.00 (*0-7812-3837-4*) Rprt Serv.
New England Transcendentalism & St. Louis Hegelianism. Henry A. Pochmann. LC 68-55163. (Studies in Comparative Literature: No. 35). 1969. reprint ed. lib. bdg. 75.00 (*0-8383-0610-1*) M S G Haskell Hse.
New England Transcendentalists: Life of the Mind & of the Spirit. Intro. by Ellen Hansen. LC 93-70438. (Perspectives on History Ser.). (Illus.). 64p. (YA). (gr. 5-12). 1993. pap. 6.95 (*1-878668-22-6*) Disc Enter Ltd.
New England Transcendentalists & the DIAL: A History of the Magazine & Its Contributors. Joel Myerson. LC 78-66814. 400p. 1970. 45.00 (*0-8386-2294-1*) Fairleigh Dickinson.
New England Trials. John Smith. LC 70-171793. (English Experience Ser.: No. 416). 1971. reprint ed. 25.00 (*90-221-0416-8*) Walter J Johnson.
New England 2000. Fodors Travel Publications, Inc. Staff. 1999. pap. 19.50 (*0-679-00320-7*) Fodors Travel.
***New England 2001.** Fodor's Staff. 2000. pap. 20.00 (*0-679-00548-X*) Fodors Travel.
New England under Sail: A Guide to Sailing Ships, Ferries & Historic Vessels. Jerry Morris. LC 92-72758. (Under Sail Ser.). (Illus.). 140p. (Orig.). 1993. pap. 12.95 (*1-56626-013-2*, Cntry Rds Pr) NTC Contemp Pub Co.
New England Views: The Photography of Baldwin Coolidge (1845-1928) Susan F. Witzell et al. LC 98-61157. (Illus.). 200p. 1998. 49.95 (*0-961374-5-2*) Woods Hole Hist.
New England Village. Joseph S. Wood. LC 96-27376. (Creating the North American Landscape Ser.). (Illus.). 248p. 1997. text 39.95 (*0-8018-5454-7*) Johns Hopkins.
New England Village Life. Edward M. Chapman. 232p. 1972. 18.95 (*0-405-18115-9*) Ayer.
New England Visionaries: 12 Who Changed America. J. North Conway. 192p. (Orig.). 1998. pap. 12.95 (*0-924771-93-3*, Covered Brdge Pr) Douglas Charles Ltd.
New England Vital Records form the Exeter News-Letter, 1841-1846. Scott L. Chipman. 294p. 1993. 30.00 (*0-89725-145-8*, 1460) Picton Pr.
New England Vital Records from the Exeter News-Letter, 1831-1840. Scott L. Chipman. 288p. 1993. 30.00 (*0-89725-144-X*, 1459) Picton Pr.
New England Vital Records from the Exeter News-Letter, 1847-1852. Scott L. Chipman. 344p. 1994. 30.00 (*0-89725-161-X*, 1513) Picton Pr.
New England Vital Records from the Exeter News-Letter 1853-1858, No. 4. Ed. by Scott L. Chipman. (New Hampshire Society of Genealogists Special Publication Ser.: No. 5). 352p. 1994. 30.00 (*0-89725-189-X*, 1579) Picton Pr.
New England Vital Records from the Exeter News-Letter, 1859-1865. Ed. by Scott L. Chipman. 404p. 1996. 30.00 (*0-89725-261-6*, 1743) Picton Pr.
New England Walks. Gary Ferguson. (Regional Walks Ser.). (Illus.). 304p. 1995. pap. 15.95 (*1-55591-220-6*) Fulcrum Pub.
New England Weather: Poems. Page P. Coulter. LC 97-11767. 68p. 1997. pap. 14.95 (*0-7734-2822-4*, Mellen Poetry Pr) E Mellen.
New England Whaler. Robert F. Baldwin. LC 95-14542. (American Pastfinder Ser.). (Illus.). 48p. (J). (gr. 4-7). 1996. lib. bdg. 19.95 (*0-8225-2978-5*, Lerner Publctns) Lerner Pub.
New England Who, What, When & Where Book. Daniel Ramus. 1994. 9.98 (*0-88365-855-0*) Galahad Bks.
***New England Wild Flower Society Guide to Growing & Propagating Wildflowers of the United States & Canada.** William Cullina. LC 00-20513. 2000. 40.00 (*0-395-96609-4*) HM.
New England Wild Places: Journeys Through the Back Country. Michael J. Tougias. (Illus.). 256p. (Orig.). 1997. pap. 12.95 (*0-924771-88-7*, Covered Brdge Pr) Douglas Charles Ltd.
***New England Wildlife: Habitat, Natural History & Distribution.** Richard M. DeGraaf & Mariko Yamasaki. LC 99-86702. (Illus.). 560p. 2000. pap. 35.00 (*0-87451-957-8*) U Pr of New Eng.
***New England Wildlife: Management of Forested Habitats.** Richard M. DeGraaf. 273p. 1998. per. 28.00 (*0-16-060837-6*, Agriculture Dept) USGPO.
New England Women: In Their Own Words. J. North Conway. (New England Gift Bks.: Vol. 3). (Illus.). 64p. 2000. 4.95 (*1-58066-008-8*, Covered Brdge Pr) Douglas Charles Ltd.
New England Women & Their Families in the 18th & 19th Centuries - Personal Papers, Letters, & Diaries, Pt. 1. Ellen K. Rothman et al. LC 97-46698. (Research Collections in Women's Studies). 1997. 4545.00 (*1-55655-644-6*) U Pubns Amer.
New England Women of Substance: 15 Who Made a Difference. J. North Conway. 176p. (Orig.). 1996. pap. 12.95 (*0-924771-81-X*, Covered Brdge Pr) Douglas Charles Ltd.
New England Working Class & the New Labor History. Ed. by Herbert G. Gutman & Donald H. Bell. LC 85-27095. (Working Class in American History Ser.). 320p. 1987. 37.50 (*0-252-01300-X*) U of Ill Pr.
New England Yankee Cookbook. Imogene Wolcott. 426p. Date not set. 28.95 (*0-8488-2407-5*) Amereon Ltd.
New Englanders in Nova Albion: Some 19th Century Views of California. James D. Hart. 1976. 3.00 (*0-89073-008-3*, 126) Boston Public Lib.
***New Englanders on the Ohio Frontier: Migration & Settlement of Worthington, Ohio.** Virginia E. McCormick. 1999. pap. 19.00 (*0-87338-652-3*) Kent St U Pr.
New Englanders on the Ohio Frontier: Migration & Settlement of Worthington, Ohio. Virginia E. McCormick & Robert W. McCormick. LC 97-36189. 1998. 39.00 (*0-87338-586-1*) Kent St U Pr.
New England's Ancient Mysteries. Robert E. Cahill. (Old New England Ser.: Vol. 5). (Illus.). 88p. (Orig.). 1993. pap. 6.95 (*0-9626162-4-9*) Old Salt Box.
New England's Annoyances: America's First Folk Song. J. A. Lemay. LC 84-40414. (Illus.). 160p. 1985. 29.50 (*0-87413-278-9*) U Delaware Pr.
New England's Best Bed & Breakfasts: New England. 4th ed. Fodors Travel Publications, Inc. Staff. 352p. 1998. pap. 16.00 (*0-679-03435-8*) Fodors Travel.
New England's Best Family Getaways: A Guide to Child-Friendly Inns & B&B's. Dan Laplante & Roberta Laplante. (Illus.). 192p. (Orig.). 1996. pap. 14.95 (*0-924771-73-9*, Covered Brdge Pr) Douglas Charles Ltd.
New England's Best Family Getaways: Country Inns & Bed & Breakfasts. 2nd rev. ed. Dan LaPlante & Roberta LaPlante. LC 94-69865. (Illus.). 300p. (Orig.). 1995. pap. 14.95 (*0-9632294-1-9*) Columbine Pub.
New England's Best-Loved Driving Tours. 3rd ed. Arthur Frommer. (Frommer's Driving Tours Ser.). (Illus.). 168p. 1997. 15.95 (*0-02-861566-2*) Macmillan.
New England's Christmas Memories. Robert E. Cahill. Ed. by Jean H. Cahill. (Old Salt Box Ser.: No. 3B). 48p. (Orig.). 1993. pap. 5.50 (*0-9626162-6-5*) Old Salt Box.
New England's Cooking Secrets: Starring the Best Restaurants & Inns of New England. 2nd rev. ed. Kathleen D. Fish. Ed. by Fred Hernandez. (Illus.). 288p. (Orig.). 1996. pap. text 14.95 (*1-883214-02-5*) Bon Vivant Pr.
New England's Cruel & Unusual Punishments. Robert E. Cahill. Ed. by Keri Cahill. (Old New England Ser.: Vol. 6). (Illus.). 88p. 1994. pap. 6.95 (*0-9626162-9-X*) Old Salt Box.
New England's Disastrous Weather: Hurricanes, Tornadoes, Blizzards, Dark Days, Heat Waves, Cold Snaps ... & the Human Stories Behind Them. Ed. by Benjamin Watson. (Illus.). 240p. 1992. pap. 14.95 (*0-89909-364-7*, 80-552-8) Yankee Bks.
New England's Generation: The Great Migration & the Formation of Society & Culture in the Seventeenth Century. Virginia D. Anderson. 244p. (C). 1992. pap. text 15.95 (*0-521-44764-X*) Cambridge U Pr.
New England's Ghostly Haunts. Robert E. Cahill. (Collectible Classics Ser.: No. 2). (Illus.). 50p. (Orig.). 1983. pap. 3.95 (*0-916787-01-X*) Chandler-Smith.
New England's Gothic Literature: History & Folklore of the Supernatural from the Seventeenth Through the Twentieth Centuries. Faye Ringel. LC 94-34973. 272p. 1995. text 89.95 (*0-7734-9047-7*) E Mellen.
New England's Legacy of Shipwrecks. Henry C. Keatts. (Illus.). 164p. (Orig.). 1988. pap. 16.95 (*0-936849-02-9*) Fathom Pr.
New England's Mad & Mysterious Men. Robert E. Cahill. (Collectible Classics Ser.: No. 4). (Illus.). 50p. (Orig.). 1984. pap. 3.95 (*0-916787-03-6*) Chandler-Smith.
New England's Marvelous Monsters. Robert E. Cahill. (Collectible Classics Ser.: No. 3). (Illus.). 50p. 1983. pap. 3.95 (*0-916787-02-8*) Chandler-Smith.
New England's Memorial. Nathaniel Morton. LC 38-10717. 232p. 1979. reprint ed. 50.00 (*0-8201-1184-8*) Schol Facsimiles.
New England's Memorial: Also Excerpts from Governor Bradford's History of Plymouth Colony & His Dialogue Prince's Chronology, & Governor Winslow's Visit to Massasoit. Nathaniel Morton. xxiv, 515p. 1997. reprint ed. pap. 36.00 (*0-7884-0705-8*, M567) Heritage Bk.
New England's Moral Legislator: A Life of Timothy Dwight, 1752-1817. John R. Fitzmier. LC 98-22498. (Religion in North America Ser.). (Illus.). 272p. 1999. 39.95 (*0-253-33433-0*) Ind U Pr.
New England's Most Intriguing Gangsters, Rascals, Rogues & Thieves. Marc Songini. 256p. (Orig.). 1998. pap. 12.95 (*0-924771-82-8*, Covered Brdge Pr) Douglas Charles Ltd.
New England's Most Intriguing Rascals, Rogues & Thieves. Marc L. Songini. (Illus.). 224p. 1998. pap. 12.95 (*1-58066-019-3*, Covered Brdge Pr) Douglas Charles Ltd.
New England's Most Sensational Murders. Marc Songini. 224p. (Orig.). 1995. pap. 10.95 (*0-924771-53-4*, Covered Brdge Pr) Douglas Charles Ltd.
New England's Mountain Flowers: A High Country Heritage. Jeff Wallner & Mario J. DiGregorio. LC 97-657. (Illus.). 235p. (Orig.). 1997. pap. 17.00 (*0-87842-337-0*) Mountain Pr.
New England's Mountain Madness. Robert E. Cahill. (Collectible Classics Ser.: No. 15). (Illus.). 48p. (Orig.). 1989. pap. 3.95 (*0-916787-14-1*) Chandler-Smith.
New England's Naughty Navy. Robert E. Cahill. (Collectible Classics Ser.: No. 11). (Illus.). 60p. (Orig.). 1987. pap. 4.95 (*0-916787-10-9*) Chandler-Smith.
New England's Notable Dead: A Guide to the Final Resting Places of the Famous & Infamous. Charles T. Robinson. (New England Gift Bks.: Vol. 6). (Illus.). 64p. Date not set. 4.95 (*1-58066-009-6*, Covered Brdge Pr) Douglas Charles Ltd.
New England's Outpost, Acadia the Conquest of Canada. John B. Brebner. (BCL1 - History - Canada Ser.). 291p. 1991. reprint ed. lib. bdg. 79.00 (*0-7812-6367-0*) Rprt Serv.
New England's Pirates & Lost Treasures. Robert E. Cahill. (Collectible Classics Ser.: No. 14). 60p. (Orig.). 1987. pap. 4.95 (*0-916787-13-3*) Chandler-Smith.
New England's Place in the History of Witchcraft. George L. Burr. LC 71-164592. (Select Bibliographies Reprint Ser.). 1977. reprint ed. 18.95 (*0-8369-5876-4*) Ayer.
New England's Plantation. Francis Higginson. LC 76-25635. (English Experience Ser.: No. 256). 24p. 1970. reprint ed. 25.00 (*90-221-0256-4*) Walter J Johnson.
New England's Prospect. William Wood. Ed. & Intro. by Alden T. Vaughan. LC 76-45051. 144p. 1993. reprint ed. pap. text 14.95 (*0-87023-890-6*) U of Mass Pr.
New England's Prospect, 1933. American Geographical Society of New York Staff. Ed. by James T. Adams et al. LC 78-111763. reprint ed. 49.50 (*0-404-00354-0*) AMS Pr.
New-England's Rarities. John Josselyn. 114p. 1986. pap. 7.95 (*0-918222-79-6*) Applewood.
New-Englands Rarities Discovered. John Josselyn. LC 72-192040. (Picture Bks.). 125p. 1972. pap. 10.00 (*0-934909-12-1*) Mass Hist Soc.
New England's Riotous Revolution. Robert E. Cahill. (Collectible Classics Ser.: No. 13). (Illus.). 68p. (Orig.). 1987. pap. 4.95 (*0-916787-12-5*) Chandler-Smith.
New England's Strange Sea Sagas. Robert E. Cahill. (Collectible Classics Ser.: No. 5). (Illus.). 54p. 1984. pap. 3.95 (*0-916787-04-4*) Chandler-Smith.
New England's Things That Go Bump in the Night. Robert E. Cahill. (Collectible Classics Ser.: No. 16). (Illus.). 48p. (Orig.). 1989. pap. 3.95 (*0-916787-15-X*) Chandler-Smith.
New England's Viking & Indian Wars. Robert E. Cahill. (Collectible Classics Ser.: No. 12). (Illus.). 56p. (Orig.). 1986. pap. 3.95 (*0-916787-11-7*) Chandler-Smith.
New England's Visitors from Outer Space. Robert E. Cahill. (Collectible Classics Ser.: No. 8). (Illus.). 54p. (Orig.). 1985. pap. 3.95 (*0-916787-07-9*) Chandler-Smith.
New England's War Wonders. Robert E. Cahill. (Collectible Classics Ser.: No. 7). (Illus.). 50p. (Orig.). 1984. pap. 3.95 (*0-916787-06-0*) Chandler-Smith.
New England's Witches & Wizards. Robert E. Cahill. (Collectible Classics Ser.: No. 1). (Illus.). 50p. (Orig.). 1983. pap. 3.95 (*0-916787-00-1*) Chandler-Smith.
New English Bible: Illustrated Edition. (Illus.). 992p. 1972. 27.00 (*0-19-104716-3*) OUP.
New English Bible Companion to the New Testament: The Gospels. A. E. Harvey. 399p. 1972. pap. text 9.95 (*0-521-09689-8*) Cambridge U Pr.
New English Canaan or New Canaan. Thomas G. Morton. LC 73-141136. (Research Library of Colonial Americana: Personal Narratives & Promotional Literature). 196p. 1972. reprint ed. 23.95 (*0-405-03309-5*) Ayer.
New English-Catalan, Catalan-English Dictionary: Nou Diccionari Angles-Catala-Angles. 4th ed. J. Colomer. (CAT & ENG.). 770p. 1987. 59.95 (*0-8288-0554-7*, S31734) Fr & Eur.
New English-Chinese Dictionary. Commercial Press Staff. (CHI & ENG.). 1252p. 1979. 24.95 (*0-8288-4827-0*, M9290) Fr & Eur.
New English-Chinese Dictionary. deluxe ed. Commercial Press Staff. (CHI & ENG.). 1688p. 1975. 49.95 (*0-8288-5940-X*, M9556) Fr & Eur.
New English-Chinese Dictionary. rev. ed. 1988. reprint ed. 16.95 (*0-8351-1756-1*) China Bks.
New English-Chinese Dictionary. 2nd ed. Yi Li Zheng. (CHI & ENG.). 1613p. 1985. 125.00 (*0-8288-1003-6*, M1598) Fr & Eur.
New English-Chinese Dictionary. 2nd rev. ed. Bang S. Liu et al. 1613p. 1985. pap. 64.95 (*0-471-80897-0*) Wiley.
New English Course, 6 bks. Edwin T. Cornelius, Jr. Incl. Book 1. Illus. by Karl Nicholason. 1979. 4.75 (*0-89285-125-2*); Book 1. Illus. by Karl Nicholason. 1979. 6.95 (*0-89285-137-6*); Book 1. Illus. by Karl Nicholason. 1979. 2.00 (*0-89285-131-7*); Book 1. Illus. by Karl Nicholason. 1979. teacher ed., student ed. 120.00 incl. VHS (*0-89285-119-8*); Book 1. Illus. by Karl Nicholason. 1979. audio 18.00 (*0-89285-113-9*); Book 2. Illus. by Karl Nicholason. 1979. 4.75 (*0-89285-126-0*); Book 2. Illus. by Karl Nicholason. 1979. 6.95 (*0-89285-138-4*); Book 2. Illus. by Karl Nicholason. 1979. 2.00 (*0-89285-132-5*); Book 2. Illus. by Karl Nicholason. 1979. audio 120.00 (*0-89285-120-1*); Eternal We. Illus. by Karl Nicholason. (Orig.). 1979. 4.75 (*0-89285-130-9*); Eternal We. Illus. by Karl Nicholason. (Orig.). 1979. 6.95 (*0-89285-142-2*); Eternal We. Illus. by Karl Nicholason. (Orig.). 1979. 2.00 (*0-89285-136-8*); Eternal We. Illus. by Karl Nicholason. (Orig.). 1979. audio 120.00 (*0-89285-124-4*); Eternal We. Illus. by Karl Nicholason. (Orig.). 1979. audio 18.00 (*0-89285-118-X*); Eternal We. Karl Nicholason. (Orig.). 1979. Book 3. Illus. by Karl Nicholason. 1979. 4.75 (*0-89285-127-9*); Book 3. Illus. by Karl Nicholason. 1979. 6.95 (*0-89285-139-2*); Book 3. Illus. by Karl Nicholason. 1979. 2.00 (*0-89285-133-3*); Book 3. Illus. by Karl Nicholason. 1979. audio 120.00 (*0-89285-121-X*); Book 3. Illus. by Karl Nicholason. 1979. audio 18.00 (*0-89285-115-5*); Book 4. Illus. by Karl Nicholason. 1979. 4.75 (*0-89285-128-7*); Book 4. Illus. by Karl Nicholason. 1979. 6.95 (*0-89285-140-6*); Book 4. Illus. by Karl Nicholason. 1979. 2.00 (*0-89285-134-1*); Book 4. Illus. by Karl Nicholason. 1979. audio 120.00 (*0-89285-122-8*); Book 4. Illus. by Karl Nicholason. 1979. audio 18.00 (*0-89285-116-3*); Book 5. Illus. by Karl Nicholason. 1979. 4.75 (*0-89285-129-5*); Book 5. Illus. by Karl Nicholason. 1979. 6.95 (*0-89285-141-4*); Book 5. Karl Nicholason. 1979. 2.00 (*0-89285-135-X*); Book 5. Illus. by Karl Nicholason. 1979. audio 120.00 (*0-89285-123-6*); Book 5. Illus. by Karl Nicholason. 1979. audio 18.00 (*0-89285-117-1*); 1979. pap. text. write for info. (*0-318-51856-2*) ELS Educ Servs.
New English Dictionary. John Kersey. (Anglistica & Americana Ser.: No. 120). 268p. 1974. reprint ed. 57.20 (*3-487-05349-7*) G Olms Pubs.
New English Firsthand: Developing Communicative Language Skills. M. Helgesen et al. (Illus.). 1995. pap. text 18.60 (*0-582-06851-7*) Addison-Wesley.
New English Firsthand: Developing Communicative Language Skills/Cassette. M. Helgesen et al. (Illus.). 1995. audio 29.79 (*0-582-06853-3*) Addison-Wesley.
New English Firsthand Plus: Expanding Communicative Language Skills. M. Helgesen et al. (Illus.). 1993. pap. text, teacher ed. 16.95 (*0-582-06852-5*) Addison-Wesley.
New English Firsthand Plus: Expanding Communicative Language Skills. M. Helgesen et al. (Illus.). 1993. pap. text, teacher ed. 16.95 (*0-582-06855-X*) Longman.
New English-Gaelic Dictionary. Derick S. Thomson. (GAE.). 210p. 1990. pap. 29.95 (*1-871901-32-4*) Colton Bk.
New English Gaelic Dictionary. Derick S. Thomson. (ENG & GAE.). 211p. 1986. 49.95 (*0-8288-8013-1*, F39190) Fr & Eur.
New English-Greek-English Handy Dictionary. George C. Divry. (ENG & GRE.). 511p. 1978. 12.95 (*0-8288-5256-1*, M9439) Fr & Eur.
New English Handbook. 2nd ed. Hans P. Guth. 554p. (C). 1985. pap. write for info. (*0-534-04830-7*) Wadsworth Pub.
***New English Hymnal.** Morehouse Publishing Staff. 1999. write for info. (*0-907547-51-6*); 15.95 (*1-85311-097-3*) Canterbury Press Norwich.
New English-Italian Dictionary of the Medical Sciences: Nuovo Dizionario Inglese-Italiano delle Scienze Mediche. L. Bussi & M. T. Cognazzo. 864p. 1987. 150.00 (*0-8288-1846-0*, M14387) Fr & Eur.
New English Manual. 2nd ed. Hans P. Guth. 176p. (C). 1985. pap. write for info. (*0-534-04832-3*) Wadsworth Pub.
New English Nine Hundred, Bk. 1. ELS, Inc. Staff. (J). 1977. mass mkt., student ed. 14.95 (*0-8384-3101-1*) Heinle & Heinle.
New English Nine Hundred, Bk. 2. ELS, Inc. Staff. (J). 1978. pap. 22.95 (*0-8384-3105-4*) Heinle & Heinle.
New English Nine Hundred, Bk. 3. ELS, Inc. Staff. (J). 1978. mass mkt., teacher ed. 21.95 (*0-8384-3110-0*) Heinle & Heinle.
New English Nine Hundred, Bk. 3. ELS, Inc. Staff. (J). 1978. pap. 22.95 (*0-8384-3109-7*) Heinle & Heinle.
New English Novel in English: A Study of the 1980s. Viney Kirpal. (C). 1990. 32.00 (*81-7023-256-2*, Pub. by Allied Pubs) S Asia.
New English of the Onitsha Chapbooks. LC 78-630645. (Papers in International Studies: Africa Ser.: No. 1). 24p. reprint ed. pap. 30.00 (*0-608-10967-3*, 200741100063) Bks Demand.
New English-Russian Dictionary, 3 vols., Set. 4th rev. ed. Ed. by E. M. Mednikova & Yuri D. Apresjan. 2496p. (C). 1993. 120.00 (*0-8285-5001-8*) Firebird NY.
New English-Russian Dictionary, Vol. 1. 4th ed. I. Galperin. 1038p. (C). 1988. 210.00 (*0-569-09022-9*, Pub. by Collets) St Mut.

N

An Asterisk (*) at the beginning of an entry indicates that the title is appearing for the first time.

New English-Russian Dictionary, Vol. 2. 4th ed. I. Galperin. 1072p. (C). 1988. 195.00 (*0-569-09096-2*, Pub. by Collets) St Mut.

New English-Russian Dictionary of Legal Terms. Yu F. Berezovenko. (ENG & RUS.). 308p. 1993. 95.00 (*0-7859-9083-6*) Fr & Eur.

New English Workbook. 2nd ed. Guth. 1985. pap. text, wbk. ed. 10.00 (*0-534-04831-5*) Thomson Learn.

New Englishes. John Platt et al. 190p. 1984. pap. 12.95 (*0-7102-0194-X*, Routledge Thoemms) Routledge.

New Englishes: A West African Perspective. Ayo Bamgbosa et al. LC 97-25143. 1997. pap. write for info. (*0-86543-592-8*) Africa World.

New Englishes: A West African Perspective. Ayo Bamgbose et al. LC 97-25143. 1997. write for info. (*0-86543-591-X*) Africa World.

New Englishes: The Case of Singapore. Ed. by Joseph Foley. 234p. 1988. pap. 29.50 (*9971-69-114-0*, Pub. by Sngapore Univ Pr) Coronet Bks.

New Enterprise in the South Pacific: The Indonesian & Melanesian Experience. 1995. lib. bdg. 250.75 (*0-8490-6760-X*) Gordon Pr.

New Entrants to the Full-Time Faculty of Higher Education Institutions. Martin J. Finkelstein. (Education Department Publication Ser.: Vol. 98-252). 121p. 1998. pap. 13.00 (*0-16-049806-6*) USGPO.

***New Entrepreneurs: Making a Living, Making a Life Through Network Marketing.** Rene Reid Yarnell. 300p. 1999. pap. 15.95 (*1-883599-15-6*) Quantum NV.

***New Entrepreneurs: Making a Living, Making a Life Through Network Marketing.** Rene Reid Yarnell. 2000. audio 15.95 (*1-883599-16-4*) Quantum NV.

New Entrepreneur's Guidebook: Leading Your Venture to Business Success. Paul McClure. Ed. by Bill Christopher. LC 97-68248. (Management Library: No. 10). 96p. 1997. pap. 12.95 (*1-56052-441-3*) Crisp Pubns.

New Entries: Learning by Writing & Drawing. Ed. by Ruth Hubbard & Karen Ernst. LC 96-4155. 160p. 1996. pap. text 24.00 (*0-435-07204-8*) Heinemann.

New Environment: Questions for Adult Educators. Robert J. Blakely. (Occasional Papers: No. 23). 1971. pap. text 2.00 (*0-87060-004-4*, OCP 23) Syracuse U Cont Ed.

New Environment for Canadian-American Relations. Canadian-American Committee. LC 72-86374. 80p. 1974. 1.50 (*0-89068-018-3*) Natl Planning.

New Environment in International Accounting: Issues & Practices. Ahmed R. Belkaoui. LC 87-7252. 232p. 1988. 75.00 (*0-89930-267-X*, BDV/, Quorum Bks) Greenwood.

New Environmental Age. Ed. by R. K. Sapru & Shyama Bhardwaj. (C). 1990. 36.00 (*81-7024-339-4*, Pub. by Ashish Pub Hse) S Asia.

New Environments For Working. Duffy. (Illus.). 192p. 1997. pap. write for info. (*0-419-20990-5*, E & FN Spon) Routledge.

New Enzymes for Organic Synthesis: Screening, Supply & Engineering. Ed. by T. Scheper. LC 99-20243. (Desktop Editions in Chemistry Ser.). (Illus.). 250p. 1999. pap. 54.95 (*3-540-65549-2*) Spr-Verlag.

New Epidemics: Proceedings of the International Seminar on Nuclear War & Planetary Emergencies - 21st Session Erice, Italy 19-24 August, 1996. Ed. by K. Goebel. (Science & Culture Ser.). 260p. 1997. 68.00 (*981-02-3232-2*) World Scientific Pub.

New Epidemiology: A Challenge to Health Administration. Ed. by Anne Crichton & Duncan Neuhauser. LC 82-82961. (Illus.). 133p. (Orig.). (C). 1982. pap. text 12.95 (*0-914904-84-1*) AUPHA Pr.

New Epigrams from Martial. Tr. by Richard O'Connell. 1991. pap. 10.00 (*0-685-55466-X*) Atlantis Edns.

New Epigraphic Evidence from the Biblical Period. Robert Deutsch & Michael Heltzer. (Illus.). 116p. 1995. text 48.00 (*965-222-612-2*, Pub. by Archaeol Ctr) Eisenbrauns.

New Episcopal Way: Masters Book. Carl G. Carlozzi. 128p. (J). (gr. 6). 1989. pap. 8.95 (*0-8192-4102-4*) Morehouse Pub.

New Episcopal Way: Students Book. Carl G. Carlozzi. 128p. (J). (gr. 6). 1989. pap. 7.95 (*0-8192-4101-6*) Morehouse Pub.

New Epoch: As Developed by the Manufacture of Power. George S. Morison. LC 72-5064. (Technology & Society Ser.). (Illus.). 148p. 1972. reprint ed. 15.95 (*0-405-04715-0*) Ayer.

New Equine Sports Therapy. Mimi Porter. 1999. 29.95 (*1-58150-015-7*) Blood-Horse.

***New ER Files: The Unauthorized Companion.** John Binns & Mark Jones. (Illus.). 338p. 2000. pap. 13.95 (*0-233-99612-5*, Pub. by Andre Deutsch) Trafalgar.

New Era. Pontifical Council for Social Communications Staff. 48p. 1992. pap. 4.95 (*1-55586-504-6*) US Catholic.

New Era. Charles W. Caryl. LC 78-154432. (Utopian Literature Ser.). (Illus.). 1976. reprint ed. 20.95 (*0-405-03515-2*) Ayer.

New Era & the New Deal, 1920-1940. Robert E. Burke. LC 87-7987. (Goldentree Bibliographies Series in American History). (C). 1981. text 27.95 (*0-88295-537-3*); pap. text 19.95 (*0-88295-581-0*) Harlan Davidson.

New Era Begins: Proceedings of the Conference of Orthodox Bishops, Ligonier, Pennsylvania, 1994. Ed. by George Bedrin & Philip Tamoush. 189p. 1996. per. 7.95 (*1-879038-27-7*) Oakwood Pubns.

New Era Community. (Agni Yoga Ser.). 1978. reprint ed. 12.00 (*0-933574-03-7*) Agni Yoga Soc.

New Era for Irrigation. National Research Council Staff. 225p. 1996. text 39.95 (*0-309-05331-5*) Natl Acad Pr.

New Era in American Poetry. Louis Untermeyer. (BCL1-PS American Literature Ser.). 364p. 1992. reprint ed. lib. bdg. 89.00 (*0-7812-6633-5*) Rprt Serv.

New Era in American Poetry. Louis Untermeyer. LC 76-145334. 1971. reprint ed. 59.00 (*0-403-01245-7*) Scholarly.

New Era in Bioenergetics. Ed. by Yasuo Mukohata. (Illus.). 308p. 1992. text 73.00 (*0-12-509854-5*) Acad Pr.

New Era in Inventory Management: For the Distribution Industry. Charles J. Bodenstab. (Illus.). 133p. 1993. 40.00 (*0-9639358-0-1*) Hilta Pr.

***New Era in Oncology.** Ed. by Seeber. (Onkologie Ser.: Vol. 23, Suppl. 6 (2000)). (Illus.). 48p. 2000. pap. 28.75 (*3-8055-7111-9*) S Karger.

New Era in the Indian Polity: A Study of Atal Bihari Vajpayee & the BJP. G. N. Raghavan. LC 96-906294. (C). 1996. 48.00 (*81-212-0539-5*, Pub. by Gian Publng Hse) S Asia.

New Era in U. S. - EU Relations: The Clinton Administration & the New Transatlantic Agenda. Anthony L. Gardner. 192p. 1997. text 64.95 (*1-85972-530-9*, Pub. by Avebry) Ashgate Pub Co.

New Era of Benefits Communication. Ann Black. Ed. by Mary Jo Brzezinski. LC 96-77776. 1996. pap. 29.00 (*0-89154-505-0*) Intl Found Employ.

New Era of Electronic Composition. N. Edward Berg. LC 79-92190. 188p. reprint ed. pap. 58.30 (*0-7837-0361-9*, 204068300018) Bks Demand.

New Era of Global Competition: State Policy & Market Power. Ed. by Daniel Drache & Meric S. Gertler. 472p. (C). 1991. text 65.00 (*0-7735-0817-1*, Pub. by McG-Queens Univ Pr); pap. text 22.95 (*0-7735-0818-X*, Pub. by McG-Queens Univ Pr) CUP Services.

New Era of Investment Banking: Industry Structure, Trends & Performance. Raymond H. Rupert. 400p. 1993. 75.00 (*1-55738-454-1*, Irwn Prfssnl) McGraw-Hill Prof.

New Era of Lipid-Lowering Drug Alternative: Journal: Cardiology, Vol. 76, Suppl. 1, 1989. Ed. by R. I. Levy. (Illus.). iv, 102p. 1989. pap. 23.25 (*3-8055-5023-5*) S Karger.

New Era of Ocean Politics. Ann L. Hollick & Robert E. Osgood. LC 74-6833. (Studies in International Affairs: No. 22). 144p. 1974. reprint ed. pap. 44.70 (*0-608-04028-2*, 206476400011) Bks Demand.

New Era of Wealth: How Investors Can Profit from the Five Economic Trends Shaping the Future. Stuart A. Wesbury, Jr. & Brian S. Wesbury. LC 99-40337. 199p. 1999. 24.95 (*0-07-135180-9*) McGraw.

New Erie Canal: Travel Guide & History. John R. Fitzgerald. (Illus.). 228p. (Orig.). 1993. pap. 14.95 (*0-9635061-0-2*) J R Fitzgerald.

New Erte Graphics in Full Color. Illus. by Erte. (Fine Art Ser.). 48p. 1984. pap. 8.95 (*0-486-24645-0*) Dover.

New Essays. Oliver Goldsmith. Ed. by Ronald S. Crane. LC 68-57605. 147p. 1969. reprint ed. lib. bdg. 35.00 (*0-8371-0447-5*, GONE, Greenwood Pr) Greenwood.

New Essays. Oliver Goldsmith. (BCL1-PR English Literature Ser.). 147p. 1992. reprint ed. lib. bdg. 69.00 (*0-7812-7356-0*) Rprt Serv.

New Essays: Post-Mao China, Dialectics of Liberation, Trotsky as Theoretician. Raya Dunayevskaya. (Illus.). 50p. (Orig.). 1977. pap. 2.00 (*0-914441-37-X*) News & Letters.

New Essays in Chinese Philosophy. Ed. by Hsueh-li Cheng. LC 95-21520. (Asian Thought & Culture Ser.: Vol. 28). XIII, 256p. (C). 1997. text 48.95 (*0-8204-2875-2*) P Lang Pubng.

***New Essays in Ecofeminist Literary Criticism.** Ed. by Glynis Carr. 192p. 2000. 28.00 (*0-8387-5476-7*) Bucknell U Pr.

New Essays in Hellenistic Poetry. Heather White. (London Studies in Classical Philology: Vol. 13). (Illus.). 136p. (C). 1985. 47.00 (*90-70265-67-2*, Pub. by Gieben) J Benjamins Pubng Co.

New Essays in Informal Logic. Ed. by Ralph H. Johnson & J. Anthony Blair. 164p. 1994. pap. 24.95 (*0-9698755-0-9*) Vale Pr.

New Essays in Metaphysics. Ed. by Robert C. Neville. LC 86-30011. (SUNY Series in Systematic Philosophy). 321p. (C). 1986. pap. text 20.95 (*0-88706-471-X*) State U NY Pr.

New Essays in Religious Naturalism. Ed. by W. Creighton Peden & Larry E. Axel. LC 93-37812. (Highlands Institute Ser.). 1994. pap. 29.95 (*0-86554-426-3*, MUP/H346) Mercer Univ Pr.

New Essays in Technical & Scientific Communications: Theory, Research, & Practice. Ed. by Paul V. Anderson et al. (Baywood Technical Communication Ser.: Vol. 2). 254p. (C). 1983. pap. text 33.95 (*0-89503-036-5*) Baywood Pub.

New Essays in the Philosophy of Sarvepalli Radhakrishnan. Ed. by S. S. Pappu. LC 95-911089. (C). 1995. 64.00 (*81-7030-461-X*, Pub. by Sri Satguru Pubns) S Asia.

New Essays on Bellow's "Seize the Day" Ed. by Michael P. Kramer. LC 97-39145. (American Novel Ser.). 144p. (C). 1999. 49.95 (*0-521-55129-3*); pap. 14.95 (*0-521-55902-2*) Cambridge U Pr.

New Essays on "Call It Sleep" Ed. by Hana Wirth-Nesher. (American Novel Ser.). (Illus.). 200p. (C). 1996. text 32.95 (*0-521-45032-2*) Cambridge U Pr.

New Essays on "Call It Sleep" Ed. by Hana Wirth-Nesher. (American Novel Ser.). (Illus.). 120p. (C). 1996. pap. text 14.95 (*0-521-45656-8*) Cambridge U Pr.

New Essays on Cather's "My Antonia" Ed. by Sharon O'Brien. LC 97-39168. (American Novel Ser.). 144p. (C). 1999. 49.95 (*0-521-45275-9*); pap. text 14.95 (*0-521-45905-2*) Cambridge U Pr.

New Essays on "Daisy Miller" & "The Turn of the Screw" Ed. by Vivian R. Pollak. LC 92-47280. (American Novel Ser.). 165p. 1993. text 32.95 (*0-521-41673-6*) Cambridge U Pr.

New Essays on F. Scott Fitzgerald's Neglected Stories. Ed. by Jackson R. Bryer. 384p. (C). 1996. 49.95 (*0-8262-1039-2*) U of Mo Pr.

New Essays on "Go down, Moses" Ed. by Linda W. Martin. (American Novel Ser.). 167p. (C). 1996. text 29.95 (*0-521-45431-X*); pap. text 15.95 (*0-521-45609-6*) Cambridge U Pr.

New Essays on "Go Tell It on the Mountain" Ed. by Trudier Harris. (American Novel Ser.). 168p. (C). 1996. pap. text 14.95 (*0-521-49826-0*) Cambridge U Pr.

New Essays on "Go Tell It on the Mountain" Ed. by Trudier Harris. (American Novel Ser.). 168p. (C). 1996. text 34.95 (*0-521-49504-0*) Cambridge U Pr.

New Essays on Hamlet. Mark T. Burnett & John Manning. LC 93-4052. (Hamlet Collection: No. 1). 1994. 52.50 (*0-404-62311-5*) AMS Pr.

New Essays on Hemingway's Short Fiction. Ed. & Contrib. by Paul Smith. LC 97-23485. (American Novel Ser.). (Illus.). 154p. (C). 1998. pap. 13.95 (*0-521-55651-1*) Cambridge U Pr.

New Essays On Maternal Voice. Barbara Thaden. 1995. pap. text 18.95 (*0-935061-85-1*) Contemp Res.

New Essays on Performance Practice. Frederick Neumann. LC 89-34600. 267p. (C). 1992. reprint ed. pap. 29.95 (*1-878822-13-6*) Univ Rochester Pr.

New Essays on "Poe's Major Tales" Ed. by Kenneth Silverman. LC 92-14571. (American Novel Ser.). 144p. (C). 1992. pap. text 15.95 (*0-521-42243-4*) Cambridge U Pr.

New Essays on "Rabbit Run" Ed. by Stanley Trachtenberg. LC 93-21806. (American Novel Ser.). 128p. (C). 1993. text 32.95 (*0-521-43337-1*); pap. text 14.95 (*0-521-43884-5*) Cambridge U Pr.

New Essays on Richardson. Samuel Rivero. LC 96-28366. 229p. 1996. text 45.00 (*0-312-12508-9*) St Martin.

New Essays on Shakespeare's Sonnets. Ed. by Hilton J. Landry. LC 71-16167. (Studies in the Renaissance: No. 1). 1976. 34.50 (*0-404-09028-1*) AMS Pr.

New Essays on "Sister Carrie" Ed. by Donald Pizer. (American Novel Ser.). 137p. (C). 1991. text 32.95 (*0-521-38278-5*); pap. text 14.95 (*0-521-38714-0*) Cambridge U Pr.

New Essays on "Song of Solomon" Ed. by Valerie Smith. (American Novel Ser.). 128p. (C). 1995. text 32.95 (*0-521-45440-9*); pap. text 14.95 (*0-521-45604-5*) Cambridge U Pr.

***New Essays on the a Priori.** Ed. by Paul Boghossian & Christopher Peacocke. 400p. 2000. pap. 24.95 (*0-19-924127-9*); text 70.00 (*0-19-924126-0*) OUP.

New Essays on "The American" Ed. by Martha Banta. (American Novel Ser.). 192p. 1987. text 32.95 (*0-521-30730-9*); pap. text 14.95 (*0-521-31449-6*) Cambridge U Pr.

New Essays on the Australian Criminal Codes. R. S. O'Regan. xxii, 125p. 1988. pap. 39.00 (*0-455-20797-6*, Pub. by LawBk Co) Gaunt.

New Essays on "The Country of the Pointed Firs" Ed. by June Howard. (American Novel Ser.). 132p. (C). 1994. text 32.95 (*0-521-41574-8*); pap. text 14.95 (*0-521-42602-2*) Cambridge U Pr.

New Essays on "The Crying of Lot 49" Ed. by Patrick O'Donnell. (American Novel Ser.). 184p. (C). 1992. text 32.95 (*0-521-38163-0*); pap. text 14.95 (*0-521-38833-3*) Cambridge U Pr.

New Essays on the Education of Henry Adams. Ed. by John C. Rowe. LC 95-21110. (American Novel Ser.). 176p. (C). 1996. text 32.95 (*0-521-44551-5*); pap. text 14.95 (*0-521-44573-6*) Cambridge U Pr.

New Essays on "The Great Gatsby" Ed. by Matthew J. Bruccoli. (American Novel Ser.). 128p. 1985. pap. text 14.95 (*0-521-31963-3*) Cambridge U Pr.

***New Essays on "The House of Mirth"** Ed. by Deborah Esch. (The American Novel Ser.). 160p. 2000. write for info. (*0-521-37231-3*); pap. write for info. (*0-521-37833-8*) Cambridge U Pr.

New Essays on "The Last of the Mohicans" Ed. by H. Daniel Peck. (American Novel Ser.). 153p. (C). 1992. text 32.95 (*0-521-37414-6*); pap. text 14.95 (*0-521-37771-4*) Cambridge U Pr.

New Essays on the Maternal Voice in the Nineteenth Century. Ed. by Barbara Thaden. LC 95-34101. (New Essays on English Literature Ser.). 1995. write for info. (*0-935061-78-9*) Contemp Res.

New Essays on the Political Thought of the Huguenots of the Refuge. Ed. by John C. Laursen. LC 94-24939. (Brill's Studies in Intellectual History: Vol. 60). v, 222p. 1994. 75.00 (*90-04-09986-7*) Brill Academic Pubs.

New Essays on "The Portrait of a Lady" Joel Porte. (American Novel Ser.). 176p. (C). 1990. text 32.95 (*0-521-34508-1*); pap. text 14.95 (*0-521-34753-X*) Cambridge U Pr.

***New Essays on the Precritical Kant.** Ed. by Tom Rockmore. 270p. 2001. 59.95 (*1-57392-871-2*) Prometheus Bks.

New Essays on the Psychology of Art. Rudolf Arnheim. (Illus.). 348p. 1986. pap. 18.95 (*0-520-05554-3*, Pub. by U CA Pr) Cal Prin Full Svc.

New Essays on the Rationalists. Ed. by Rocco J. Gennaro & Charles Huenemann. LC 98-30454. (Illus.). 416p. 1999. text 60.00 (*0-19-512488-X*) OUP.

New Essays on "The Rise of Silas Lapham" Ed. by Donald E. Pease. (American Novel Ser.). 142p. (C). 1991. text 32.95 (*0-521-37311-5*) Cambridge U Pr.

New Essays on "The Rise of Silas Lapham" Ed. by Donald E. Pease. (American Novel Ser.). 142p. (C). 1991. pap. text 14.95 (*0-521-37898-2*) Cambridge U Pr.

New Essays on "The Sound & the Fury" Ed. by Noel Polk. LC 93-568. (American Novel Ser.). 192p. (C). 1993. text 34.95 (*0-521-45114-0*); pap. text 15.95 (*0-521-45734-3*) Cambridge U Pr.

New Essays on "The Sun Also Rises" Ed. by Linda Wagner-Martin. (American Novel Ser.). 142p. 1987. pap. text 14.95 (*0-521-31787-8*) Cambridge U Pr.

New Essays on Virginia Woolf. Ed. by Helen M. Wussow. LC 94-13009. (New Essays on English Literature Ser.: No. 2). 1994. 50.00 (*0-935061-77-0*) Contemp Res.

New Essays on "Walden" Ed. by Robert F. Sayre. LC 92-11525. (American Novel Ser.). (Illus.). 127p. (C). 1992. text 32.95 (*0-521-41435-0*); pap. text 15.95 (*0-521-42482-8*) Cambridge U Pr.

New Essays on "White Noise" Ed. by Frank Lentricchia. (American Novel Ser.). 127p. (C). 1991. text 32.95 (*0-521-39291-8*) Cambridge U Pr.

New Essays on "Winesburg, Ohio" Ed. by John W. Crowley. (American Novel Ser.). 141p. (C). 1990. pap. text 14.95 (*0-521-38723-X*) Cambridge U Pr.

New Essays on "Winesburg, Ohio" Ed. by John W. Crowley. (American Novel Ser.). 141p. (C). 1990. text 32.95 (*0-521-38283-1*) Cambridge U Pr.

New Essays on Wise Blood. Michael Kreyling. (American Novel Ser.). 136p. (C). 1995. text 32.95 (*0-521-44550-7*); pap. text 15.95 (*0-521-44574-4*) Cambridge U Pr.

***New Essential Fingerstyle Guitar.** Warner Brothers Publications Staff. (Illus.). 124p. 1999. pap. 14.95 (*0-7692-7810-8*) Wrner Bros.

***New Essential Unplugged Guitar.** Warner Brothers Staff. (Illus.). 121p. 1999. pap. 14.95 (*0-7692-5911-1*) Wrner Bros.

New Estimates of Fertility & Population in the United States: A Study of Annual White Births from 1855 to 1960 & of Completeness of Enumeration in the Censuses from 1880-1960. Ansley J. Coale & Melvin Zelnik. LC 63-9989. 204p. 1963. reprint ed. pap. 63.30 (*0-7837-9320-0*, 206006000004) Bks Demand.

New Estimates of the Effect of Kassebaum-Kennedy's Group-to-Individual Conversion Provision on Premiums for Individual Health Insurance. Jacob A. Klerman. LC 96-19675. 85p. (Orig.). 1996. pap. text 15.00 (*0-8330-2394-2*, MR-766-DOL) Rand Corp.

***New Estrogen Alternative: Natural Hormone Therapy with Botanical Progesterone.** 3rd rev. ed. Raquel Martin & Judi Gerstung. LC 99-89914. 240p. 2000. pap. 14.95 (*0-89281-893-X*, Heal Arts VT) Inner Tradit.

New Ethics for the Public's Health. Ed. by Dan E. Beauchamp & Bonnie Steinbock. LC 99-23617. (Illus.). 400p. 1999. text 67.50 (*0-19-512438-3*); pap. text 39.95 (*0-19-512439-1*) OUP.

New Ethnic Mobs: The Changing Face of Organized Crime in America. William G. Kleinknecht. (Illus.). 320p. 1996. 25.00 (*0-684-82294-6*) Free Pr.

***New Ethnicities, Old Racisms.** Phil Cohen. 2000. text 65.00 (*1-85649-651-1*) St Martin.

***New Ethnicities, Old Racisms.** Phil Cohen. 1999. pap. text 22.50 (*1-85649-652-X*) Zed Books.

New Etiquette. Marjabelle Y. Stewart. 1989. pap. 14.95 (*0-318-41609-3*) St Martin.

New Etiquette. rev. ed. Marjabelle Y. Stewart. LC 97-1094. 1997. pap. 17.95 (*0-312-15602-2*) St Martin.

New Eurasia: A Guide to the Republic of the Former Soviet Union. David T. Twining. LC 92-32670. 240p. 1993. pap. 21.95 (*0-275-94431-X*, B4431, Praeger Pubs) Greenwood.

New Eurasia: A Guide to the Republics of the Former Soviet Union. David T. Twining. LC 92-32228. 240p. 1993. lib. bdg. 69.50 (*0-313-28818-6*, GR8818, Greenwood Pr) Greenwood.

New Europe. (Proceedings of the Academy of Political Science Ser.: Vol. 38, No. 1). 1991. pap. 14.95 (*0-614-04163-5*) Acad Poli Sci.

***New Europe.** Council on Foreign Affairs Staff. 1999. pap. 11.95 (*0-87609-266-0*) Coun Foreign.

New Europe. David Rieff. 2001. 25.00 (*0-684-80977-X*) Simon & Schuster.

New Europe. Ed. by Jonathan Story. LC 92-8606. 1993. pap. 32.95 (*0-631-18613-1*) Blackwell Pubs.

New Europe. Bernard Newman. LC 72-4581. (Essay Index Reprint Ser.). 1977. reprint ed. 31.95 (*0-8369-2963-2*) Ayer.

New Europe: An Introduction to Its Political Geography. Walter Fitzgerald. LC 80-24065. (Illus.). xiii, 298p. 1980. reprint ed. lib. bdg. 75.00 (*0-313-21006-3*, FINE, Greenwood Pr) Greenwood.

New Europe: Economic Developments Towards 2000. Ed. by Euromonitor Staff. 178p. 1990. pap. 795.00 (*0-86338-450-1*, Pub. by Euromonitor PLC) Gale.

New Europe: Economy, Society & Environment. David Pinder. LC 97-31195. 504p. 1998. pap. 49.95 (*0-471-97123-5*) Wiley.

New Europe: Evolving Economic & Financial Systems in East & West. Ed. by Donald E. Fair & Robert Raymond. LC 92-47380. 452p. 1993. lib. bdg. 174.50 (*0-7923-2159-6*) Kluwer Academic.

***New Europe: Transformation & Environmental Issues.** Ed. by Luciano Mariani et al. 424p. 1999. pap. 29.95 (*3-8258-3382-8*) CE24.

New Europe Asserts Itself: A Changing Role in International Relations. Ed. by Beverly Crawford & Peter W. Schulze. LC 90-43505. (Research Ser.: No. 77). x, 448p. (Orig.). (C). 1990. pap. text 19.95 (*0-87725-177-0*) U of Cal IAS.

New Europe at the Crossroads. Ed. by Ursula E. Beitter. XXV, 305p. (C). 1999. text 57.95 (*0-8204-3923-1*) P Lang Pubng.

New Europe for the Old? Ed. by Stephen R. Graubard. LC 98-22054. 276p. 1998. pap. 24.95 (*0-7658-0465-4*) Transaction Pubs.

New Europe in the Changing Global System. Ed. by Richard Falk & Tamas Szentes. 262p. 1997. pap. 25.00 (*92-808-0934-2*, Pub. by UN Univ Pr) Brookings.

N

An Asterisk (*) at the beginning of an entry indicates that the title is appearing for the first time.

New Europe into the 1990s. 4th rev. ed. G. N. Minshull. (Illus.). 348p. 1990. pap. text 27.50 (*0-340-50512-5*, Pub. by Hodder & Stought Ltd) Lubrecht & Cramer.
New European Architecture. Francisco Asensio Cerver. LC 99-198853. (Colour Collection Ser.). 159p. 1997. write for info. (*84-8185-016-0*, Pub. by Arco Edit) Watson Guptill.
New European Architecture. Rotovision S. A. Staff. (Illus.). 160p. 1996. pap. text 35.00 (*0-8230-6491-3*) Watsn-Guptill.
New European Autmobile Industry. Peter Wells & Michael Rawlinson. LC 94-20533. 1994. text 59.95 (*0-312-12238-1*) St Martin.
*__New European Diasporas.__ Michael Mandelbaum. 2000. pap. 19.95 (*0-87609-257-1*) Coun Foreign.
New European Economy Revisited. 3rd ed. Loukas Tsoukalis. LC 96-51593. (Illus.). 320p. 1997. pap. text 19.95 (*0-19-877477-X*) OUP.
New European Economy Revisited. 3rd ed. Loukas Tsoukalis. LC HC240. (Illus.). 320p. 1997. text 81.00 (*0-19-877562-8*) OUP.
New European Furniture Design, 2 vols. , Set. Lorenzo Soledad. (Illus.). 462p. 1999. 89.95 (*84-89861-06-4*, Pub. by Links Inter) Bks Nippan.
New European Landscape. Michael Lancaster. LC 94-15507. (Illus.). 144p. 1995. text 76.95 (*0-7506-1546-X*, Butterwrth Archit) Buttrwrth-Heinemann.
New European Market Place. Ed. by Alfred Steinherr. 1991. pap. text. write for info. (*0-582-08936-0*, Pub. by Addison-Wesley) Longman.
New European Orders, 1919 & 1991. Ed. by Samuel F. Wells, Jr. & Paula B. Smith. (Woodrow Wilson Center Press Ser.). 144p. (C). 1996. text 32.50 (*0-943875-76-5*); pap. text 14.95 (*0-943875-77-3*) W Wilson Ctr Pr.
New European Security Disorder. Simon Duke. LC 94-21686. 1994. text 59.95 (*0-312-12371-X*) St Martin.
New Evaluation Procedures for a New Generation of Water-Related Projects. Ronald Cummings et al. LC 96-39266. (Technical Papers: No. 349). 64p. 1996. pap. 22.00 (*0-8213-3829-3*, 13829) World Bank.
New Evangelicalism: Its History & Its Heart. David W. Cloud. 28p. 1995. pap. 3.00 (*1-58318-019-2*, WOL474B) Way of Life.
New Evangelization: Good News to the Poor. Leonardo Boff. Tr. by Robert R. Barr from POR. LC 91-30804.Tr. of Nova Evangelizacao: Perspectiva dos Oprimidos. 1992. pap. 15.00 (*0-88344-778-9*) Orbis Bks.
New Events & Facts in Diabetes. F. Belfiore. (Frontiers in Diabetes Ser.: Vol. 2). (Illus.). x, 190p. 1982. 99.25 (*3-8055-3541-4*) S Karger.
New Every Morning. D. James Kennedy. LC 96-221309. 365p. 1996. 19.99 (*1-57673-068-9*, Multnomah Bks) Multnomah Pubs.
New Every Morning. large type ed. Ann Purser. LC 97-23293. 1997. pap. 21.95 (*0-7862-1152-0*) Thorndike Pr.
New Every Morning: Meditations from Your Favorite Christian Writers. Compiled by Al Bryant. LC 92-16143. 288p. 1992. reprint ed. pap. 12.99 (*0-8254-2282-5*) Kregel.
*__New Every Morning, a Daily Devotional.__ D. James Kennedy & Jerry Newcombe. 365p. 2000. pap. 14.99 (*1-57673-720-9*) Multnomah Pubs.
*__New Everyday Home Repairs: Simple, Effective Solutions to Your Home's Most Common Problems.__ Creative Publishing International, Inc. Staff. (Home Improvement Library). (Illus.). 160p. 2000. pap. 16.95 (*0-86573-591-3*) Creat Pub Intl.
New Evidence for the Middle School. Paul S. George & Kathy Shewey. 126p. (C). 1994. pap. text 16.00 (*1-56090-084-9*) Natl Middle Schl.
New Evidence That Demands a Verdict, Vol. 1. rev. ed. Josh McDowell. LC 99-47181. 800p. 1999. 29.99 (*0-7852-4219-8*) Nelson.
*__New Evidences of Christ in Ancient America.__ Blaine M. Yorgason et al. (Illus.). 442p. 1999. 24.95 (*0-929753-01-1*, Pub. by Paramount Bks) Granite UT.
New Evil. R. L. Stine, pseud. Ed. by Patricia MacDonald. (Fear Street Cheerleaders Ser.: No.). 192p. (YA). (gr. 7 up). 1994. mass mkt. 3.99 (*0-671-86835-7*, Archway) PB.
New Evil. R. L. Stine, pseud. (Fear Street Cheerleaders Ser.: No. 4). (YA). (gr. 7 up). 1994. 9.09 (*0-606-07057-5*, Pub. by Turtleback) Demco.
New Evolution. Jeffrey Schwartz. 1999. pap. 24.95 (*0-525-94247-5*) NAL.
New Evolutionary Paradigm: Transdisciplinary Studies. Ed. by E. Laszlo. xxvi, 204p. 1991. text 101.00 (*2-88124-375-4*) Gordon & Breach.
New Examples of Frobenius Extensions Lars Kadison. LC 99-25462. (University Lecture Ser.). 13p. 1999. write for info. (*0-8218-1962-3*) Am Math.
*__New Excel Phenomenon.__ 5th ed. James W. Robinson. 2000. 22.00 (*0-7615-2525-4*) Prima Pub.
New Executive Assistant: Advice for Succeeding in Your Career. Melba J. Duncan. LC 96-51841. (Illus.). 256p. 1997. pap. 12.95 (*0-07-018241-8*) McGraw.
*__New Executive Protection Bible.__ M. J. Braunig. (Illus.). 785p. 2000. pap. 89.95 (*0-9640627-3-9*) ESI Educ Dev.
New Exemptions from SEC Regulations. Ed. by Law & Business Inc. Staff & Legal Times Seminars Staff. (Seminar Course Handbks.). 1983. pap. 30.00 (*0-686-89348-4*, C01228) Harcourt.
New Exercises for Runners. Runner's World Editors. LC 78-460. (Illus.). 176p. 1978. pap. 4.95 (*0-89037-151-2*) Anderson World.
*__New Exeter Book of Riddles.__ Ed. by Kevin Crossley-Holland & Lawrence Sail. 96p. 1999. pap. (*1-900564-31-9*, Pub. by Enitha Pr) Dufour.
New Exhibits in Italy. LArchivolto Editors. (Illus.). 260p. 1997. 79.95 (*88-7685-084-8*, Pub. by LArchivolto) Bks Nippan.
New Exiles: American War Resisters in Canada. Roger N. Williams. LC 78-148662. 1971. pap. 3.45 (*0-87140-249-1*, Pub. by Liveright) Norton.
New Exodus see Collected Works of Harold Frederic
New Exodus. Harold Frederic. (Collected Works of Harold Frederic). 1988. reprint ed. lib. bdg. 59.00 (*0-7812-1188-3*) Rprt Serv.
New Exodus: A Study of Israel in Russia. Harold Frederic. LC 71-115538. (Russia Observed, Series I). 1970. reprint ed. 21.95 (*0-405-03027-4*) Ayer.
*__New Exotic Garden: Creating an Exotic-Style Garden in a Temperature Climate.__ Will Giles. (Illus.). 120p. 2000. 24.95 (*1-84000-241-7*) Mitchell Beazley.
New Expanded Bibliography of Jazz Compositions Based on the Chord Progressions of Standard Tunes. Reese Markewich. LC 74-84745. 1974. pap. 4.95 (*0-9600160-5-8*) Markewich.
*__New Expansive Poetry: Theory, Criticism, History.__ 2nd rev. ed. Ed. by R. S. Gwynn. LC 99-21411. Orig. Title: Expansive Poetry: Essays on the New Narrative & the New Formalism. 250p. 1999. pap. 17.95 (*1-885266-69-3*, Pub. by Story Line) Consort Bk Sales.
New Expatriates: Managing Human Resources Abroad. Rosalie L. Tung. LC 87-17835. 216p. 1987. text 29.95 (*0-88730-133-9*, HarpBusn) HarpInfo.
New Expectations: Community Strategies for Responsible Fatherhood. James A. Levine. 230p. 1995. pap. 22.00 (*1-888324-00-7*) Families & Work.
New Experience of the Supersensible. Jesaiah Ben-Aharon. 256p. 1995. 39.95 (*0-904693-67-8*, Pub. by Temple Lodge) Anthroposophic.
New Experimental Modalities in the Control of Neoplasia. Ed. by Prakash Chandra. LC 86-22709. (NATO ASI Series A, Life Sciences: Vol. 102). 414p. 1986. 95.00 (*0-306-42464-9*, Plenum Trade) Perseus Pubng.
New Experimental Techniques for Evaluating Concrete Material & Structural Performance. 335p. 1994. pap. 47.25 (*0-614-02519-2*, SP143BOW6) ACI.
New Experiments in Kalidasa (Plays) Satya V. Shastri. (C). 1994. 34.00 (*81-85133-95-6*, Pub. by Eastern Bk Linkers) S Asia.
New Exploration: A Philosophy of Regional Planning. 3rd ed. Benton MacKaye. 284p. 1991. reprint ed. pap. 8.95 (*0-917953-43-6*) Appalachian Trail.
New Explorations in Italian American Studies: Proceedings of the 25th Annual Conference of the American Italian Historical Association, Washington, D. C., November 12-14, 1992. Ed. by Richard N. Juliani & Sandra P. Juliani. LC 94-32166. 1994. write for info. (*0-934675-31-7*); pap. write for info. (*0-934675-32-5*) Am Italian.
New Explorers. Ed. by Bill Kurtis. (Illus.). 240p. (YA). 1995. pap. write for info. (*0-9647457-0-4*) WTTW Chicago.
New Explorer's Guide to Maps & Compasses. Percy W. Blandford. 160p. 1992. 15.95 (*0-8306-3915-2*); pap. 7.95 (*0-8306-3914-4*) McGraw-Hill Prof.
New Explorers Study Bible for Kids: New Living Testament. New Explorers Sty Kids Staff. 19.97 (*0-7852-0729-5*) Nelson.
New Extragalactic Perspectives in the New South Africa: Proceedings of International Conference on Cold Dust & Galaxy Morphology, Johannesburg, South Africa, 1996. Ed. by David L. Block & J. Mayo Greenberg. LC 96-34039. (Astrophysics & Space Science Library: Vol. 209). 653p. 1996. text 242.50 (*0-7923-4223-2*) Kluwer Academic.
New Eyes for Plants: A Workbook for Plant Observation & Drawing. Margaret Colquttoun & Alex Ewald. (Social Ecology Ser.). (Illus.). 208p. (Orig.). 1996. pap. 24.95 (*1-869890-85-X*, Pub. by Hawthorn Press) Anthroposophic.
New Eyes for Reading: Biblical & Theological Reflections by Women from the Third World. Ed. by John S. Pobee & Barbel Von Wartenberg-Potter. LC 86-211225. 116p. (Orig.). reprint ed. pap. 36.00 (*0-7837-6000-0*, 204581000008) Bks Demand.
New Eyes for the Old: The Quest for Education. Richard McKenna. 1963. 2.50 (*0-87060-019-2*, OCP 7) Syracuse U Cont Ed.
New Eyes to See Inside the Sun & Stars: Pushing the Limits of Helio & Asteroseismology with New Observations from the Ground & from Space: Proceedings of the 185th Symposium of the International Astronomical Union, Held in Kyoto, Japan, August 18-22, 1997. International Astronomical Union Staff et al. LC 98-7555. 1998. 189.00 (*0-7923-5075-8*) Kluwer Academic.
New Fabric Magic. Melanie Paine. (Illus.). 216p. 1995. pap. 25.00 (*0-679-75840-2*) Pantheon.
New Face of Organized Crime. Gregory J. Petrakis. 192p. 1992. per. 34.95 (*0-8403-7411-9*) Kendall-Hunt.
*__New Face of Terriorism: Threats from Weapons of Mass Destruction.__ Nadine Gurr. 2000. pap. 24.50 (*1-86064-460-0*) I B T.
New Face of the Church in Latin America: Between Tradition & Change. Ed. by Guillermo Cook. LC 94-2812. (American Society of Missiology Ser.: No. 18). 250p. (Orig.). 1994. pap. 20.00 (*0-88344-937-4*) Orbis Bks.
New Face of the NHS. 2nd ed. Spurgeon. (C). 1999. pap. text. write for info. (*0-443-05969-1*) Church.
New Face of the Portrait. Intro. by Caroline Graboys. (Orig.). 1994. pap. 10.00 (*0-614-09757-6*) Fuller Mus Art.
*__New Face of the University of California: Undergraduate Admissions in the Aftermath of SP-1.__ Ed. by Tom Hayden & Teresa P. Hughes. 120p. (C). 1999. reprint ed. pap. text 25.00 (*0-7881-8261-7*) DIANE Pub.
New Face of War: Weapons of Mass Destruction & the Revitalization of America's Transoceanic Military Strategy. Robert W. Chandler. LC 97-68443. (Trilogy on Weapons of Mass Destruction & 21st Century Warfare: Vol. 3). 480p. 1998. 33.00 (*0-9650770-2-0*) AMCODA Pr.
New Face on the Countryside: Indians, Colonists, & Slaves in South Atlantic Forests, 1500-1800. Timothy H. Silver. (Studies in Environment & History). (Illus.). 216p. (C). 1990. text 69.95 (*0-521-34374-7*); pap. text 17.95 (*0-521-38739-6*) Cambridge U Pr.
New Faces: An Adventure Resource for over the Edge. Jonathan Tweet. (Over the Edge Ser.). 16p. 1992. pap. 4.95 (*1-887801-03-0*, Atlas Games) Trident MN.
New Faces in Our Schools: Student Generated Solutions to Ethnic Conflicts. Karen Jorgensen & Cynthia S. Brown. 110p. 1992. student ed., ring bd. 20.00 (*0-936434-36-8*, Pub. by Zellerbach Fam Fund) Intl Spec Bk.
New Faces in the Frame: A Guide to Marriage & Parenting in the Blended Family. Dick Dunn. LC 97-220270. 224p. 1997. pap. text 12.95 (*0-8054-9817-6*, LifeWy Press) LifeWay Christian.
New Faces, New Friends. Arleta Richardson. LC 88-34639. (Grandma's Attic Ser.). 160p. (J). (gr. 3-7). 1995. pap. 4.99 (*0-7814-0214-X*, Chariot Bks) Chariot Victor.
New Faces of Europe. 1995. 18.00 (*92-871-2622-4*, Pub. by Council of Europe) Manhattan Pub Co.
New Faces of Liberty: A Curriculum for Teaching about Today's Refugees & Immigrants. Karen Jorgensen-Esmaili. 116p. 1988. ring bd. 20.00 (*0-936434-24-4*) SF Study Ctr.
New Faces of Liberty: Background Essays, 11 vols. 274p. (YA). (gr. 7-12). 1993. teacher ed. 44.00 (*0-936434-48-1*, Pub. by Zellerbach Fam Fund) Intl Spec Bk.
New Faces of 1952. Maxine Chernoff. LC 84-25214. 57p. (Orig.). 1985. pap. 6.00 (*0-87886-124-6*, Greenfld Rev Pr) Greenfld Rev Lit.
New Faces of Poverty: Income Security Needs of Canadian Families. Economic Council of Canada Staff. 70p. (Orig.). 1992. pap. 12.95 (*0-660-14550-2*, Pub. by Canadian Govt Pub) Accents Pubns.
New Faces of the Fur Trade: Selected Papers of the Seventh North American Fur Trade Conference, Halifax, N. S., 1995. Ed. by Jo-Ann Fiske et al. LC 97-51510. (Illus.). 265p. 1998. 39.95 (*0-87013-434-5*) Mich St U Pr.
New Facet of Spin Giant Resonances in Nuclei: SGR 97. Ed. by H. Sakai et al. 480p. 1998. 88.00 (*981-02-3511-9*) World Scientific Pub.
*__New Facets of Financial Federalism.__ S. V. Subrahmanyam. LC 99-931664. xxii, 217p. 1999. (*81-7629-186-2*) Advent Bks Div.
New Facility Start-Up Simulation: Leader's Guide. Cresencio Torres. (Consensus Decision-Making Simulations Ser.). (Orig.). 1995. pap. write for info. (*0-87425-281-4*) HRD Press.
New Facts about Fiber Health Builder, Disease Fighter, Vital Nutrient: How Fiber Supplements Can Enhance Your Health. 6th rev. ed. Betty Kamen. (Illus.). 139p. 1997. pap. 9.95 (*0-944501-05-2*) Nutrition Encounter.
New Facts on Futures: Insights & Strategies for Winning in the Futures Markets. rev. ed. Jacob I. Bernstein. 325p. 1992. 24.95 (*1-55738-422-3*, Irwn Prfssnl) McGraw-Hill Prof.
New Facts on Mental Disorders. Neil A. Dayton. Ed. by Gerald N. Grob. LC 78-22558. (Historical Issues in Mental Health Ser.). (Illus.). 1980. reprint ed. lib. bdg. 37.95 (*0-405-11912-7*) Ayer.
New Facts Regarding the Life of Shakespeare. J. Payne Collier. LC 78-113583. (BCL Ser.: I). 1978. reprint ed. 18.00 (*0-404-01609-X*) AMS Pr.
New Facts Regarding the Life of Shakespeare. John P. Collier. (BCL1-PR English Literature Ser.). 55p. 1992. reprint ed. lib. bdg. 59.00 (*0-7812-7280-7*) Rprt Serv.
New Faculty Member: Supporting & Fostering Professional Development. Robert Boice. LC 91-37579. (Higher & Adult Education Ser.). 396p. (C). 1992. text 38.95 (*1-55542-423-6*) Jossey-Bass.
*__New Faith: A Black Christian Woman's Guide to Reformation, Re-Creation, Rediscovery, Renaissance, Resurrection & Revival.__ Sharon C. Patterson. 2000. pap. 15.00 (*0-8006-3158-7*, Fortress Pr) Augsburg Fortress.
*__New Faith: A "How-To" Guide to Create the Life You Really Want.__ Mark Mangold. LC 99-93940. 1999. pap. 7.95 (*0-533-13203-7*) Vantage.
New Families: Reviving & Creating Meaningful Bonds. C. Margaret Hall. LC 92-44917. 180p. 1994. pap. 19.95 (*1-56023-039-8*, Harrington Park); lib. bdg. 49.99 (*1-56024-422-4*) Haworth Pr.
New Families, New Finances Money Skills for Today's Nontraditional Families. Emily W. Card & Christie W. Kelly. LC 97-37906. (Wiley Personal Finance Solutions Your Family Matters Ser.). 285p. 1998. pap. 14.95 (*0-471-19612-6*) Wiley.
New Families, No Families? The Transformation of the American Home. Frances K. Goldscheider & Linda J. Waite. (Studies in Demography: Vol. 6). 356p. 1991. pap. 17.95 (*0-520-08305-9*, Pub. by U CA Pr) Cal Prin Full Svc.
*__New Family?__ Ed. by Elizabeth Silva & Carol Smart. LC 98-61272. 176p. 1999. 74.50 (*0-7619-5855-X*) Sage.
New Family: Conversion & Ecclesiology in the Early Church with Cross-Cultural Comparisons. Karl O. Sandnes. LC 95-167619. (Studies in the Intercultural History of Christianity: Vol. 91). xi, 222p. 1994. pap. 37.95 (*3-906751-93-7*, Pub. by P Lang) P Lang Pubng.
*__New Family Cookbook: Recipes for Nourishing Yourself & Those You Love.__ Bill Eichner & Julie Alvarez. (Illus.). 208p. 2000. pap. 16.95 (*1-890132-48-9*) Chelsea Green Pub.
*__New Family Cookbook for People with Diabetes.__ American Diabetes Association & American Dietic Association Staff. LC 99-27030. 544p. 1999. pap. 27.50 (*0-684-82660-7*) Simon & Schuster.
*__New Family Homes: Creating the Perfect Home for Today & Tomorrow.__ Jim Tolpin & Mary Lou Lathrop. LC 99-52583. 2000. 34.95 (*1-56158-354-5*) Taunton.
New Family Songbook. Ed. by Tony Esposito. 304p. (Orig.). 1997. pap. text 22.95 (*0-7692-0018-4*) Wrner Bros.
New-Fangled, Old Fashioned Bread Puddings: Sixty Recipes for Delectable Sweet & Savory Puddings, Puffs, Stratas, & Bread Souffles. Linda Hegeman & Barbara Hayford. (Illus.). 144p. (Orig.). 1993. pap. 10.95 (*0-312-10509-6*) St Martin.
New Far Part 15: Course Manual. write for info. (*0-318-61616-5*) Fed Pubns Inc.
New FAR Rules: Implementing the Federal Acquisition Streamlining Act: A Guide. 388p. (Orig.). 1995. pap. 50.00 (*0-9626190-2-7*, OSBO 95 1113) ESI Int.
New Farm Vegetarian Cookbook. Louise Hagler & Dorothy R. Bates. LC 88-26225. (Illus.). 224p. 1988. pap. 9.95 (*0-913990-60-4*) Book Pub Co.
New Farmer's Movements in India. Ed. by Tom Brass. LC 94-31412. 290p. 1994. pap. 19.50 (*0-7146-4134-0*, Pub. by F Cass Pubs) Intl Spec Bk.
New Farmer's Movements in India. Ed. by Tom Brass & T. J. Byres. LC 94-31412. 1994. 45.00 (*0-7146-4609-1*) Intl Spec Bk.
New Fashion Illustrations: How to Draw a Figure. Kojiro Kumagai. (Illus.). 140p. 1997. pap. 39.95 (*4-06-206533-9*, Pub. by Kodansha Ltd) Bks Nippan.
New-Fashioned Grandparenting: Changing America One Grandchild at a Time. Julia Nelson. Ed. by Pamela Allen-Goad. 256p. 1999. pap. 14.95 (*0-9673230-0-2*) Allyn Group Pubns.
New Fat Cats: Members of Congress As Political Benefactors - A Twentieth Century Fund Paper. Ross K. Baker. 92p. 1989. write for info. (*0-87078-301-7*); pap. 8.95 (*0-87078-300-9*) Century Foundation.
New Father Book: What Every New Father Needs to Know to Be a Good Dad. Wade Horn & Jeffrey Rosenberg. Ed. by Alice Feinstein. LC 98-134205. 96p. 1998. pap. 9.95 (*0-696-20617-X*, Better Homes) Meredith Bks.
New Father Boxed Set. Armin Brott. (Illus.). 224p. 1998. pap. 35.00 (*0-7892-0494-0*) Abbeville Pr.
New Father's Baby Guide. Pete Billac. (Illus.). 128p. 1994. per. 9.95 (*0-943629-10-1*) Swan Pub.
New Father's Panic Book. Gene B. Williams. LC 96-39433. 256p. 1997. pap. 12.50 (*0-380-78906-X*, Avon Bks) Morrow Avon.
New Favorite Brand Name Cookie Collection. (Illus.). 224p. 1993. 19.98 (*0-7853-0311-1*, 2017900) Pubns Intl Ltd.
New Fear. R. L. Stine, pseud. (Fear Street Sagas: No. 1). (YA). (gr. 7 up). 1996. mass mkt. 3.99 (*0-671-52952-8*, Archway) PB.
New Fear. R. L. Stine, pseud. (Fear Street Sagas: No. 1). (YA). (gr. 7 up). 1996. 9.09 (*0-606-09270-6*, Pub. by Turtleback) Demco.
New Federal Procedures & Regulations for Document Management. Ed. by Don M. Avedon. 47p. 1997. 100.00 (*0-89258-333-9*, D067) Assn Inform & Image Mgmt.
New Federal State Regulation of Intralata Services. 35.00 (*0-317-29496-2*, #CO2879) Harcourt.
New Federal-State Relationship in the Regulation of Intra-Lata Services. (Illus.). iv, 322p. write for info. (*0-318-60202-4*) Harcourt.
New Federalism: Can the States Be Trusted? Ed. by John A. Ferejohn & Barry R. Weingast. LC 97-16799. (Publication Ser.: No. 443). 170p. 1997. pap. 17.95 (*0-8179-9512-9*) Hoover Inst Pr.
New Federalism: Intergovernmental Reform from Nixon to Reagan. Timothy Conlan. 274p. 1988. 36.95 (*0-8157-1540-4*); pap. 16.95 (*0-8157-1539-0*) Brookings.
New Federalism: The Administration's Approach to Intergovernmental Relations. William L. Dickey. 1970. 1.00 (*1-55614-068-1*) U of SD Gov Res Bur.
*__New Federalism & State Government in Mexico: Bringing the States Back In.__ Ed. by Peter M. Ward et al. LC 99-67871. (U. S. - Mexican Policy Reports: Vol. 9). 206p. (C). 1999. pap. 20.00 (*0-89940-330-1*) LBJ Sch Pub Aff.
New Federalism in Education: State Responses to the 1981 Education Consolidation & Improvement Act. Linda Darling-Hammond & Ellen L. Marks. LC 83-136421. xvii, 86p. 1983. pap. 7.50 (*0-8330-0491-3*, R-3008-ED) Rand Corp.
New Federalist Papers. Ed. by J. Jackson Barlow et al. LC 88-22500. (Illus.). 480p. (Orig.). (C). 1988. pap. text 29.00 (*0-8191-7176-X*); lib. bdg. 63.00 (*0-8191-7175-1*) U Pr of Amer.
New Federalist Papers: Essays. Alan Brinkley et al. LC 96-48355. 1996. write for info. (*0-87078-404-8*) Century Foundation.
New Federalist Papers: Essays in Defense of the Constitution. Alan Brinkley. 192p. 1997. pap. 13.95 (*0-393-31737-4*) Norton.
New Federalist Papers: Essays in Defense of the Constitution. Alan Brinkley et al. 179p. 1997. 23.00 (*0-393-04619-2*) Norton.
New Feet for Old. Barrett Waller. LC 90-21339. (Illus.). 32p. (J). (gr. k-3). 1992. lib. bdg. 13.95 (*0-02-792371-1*, Four Winds Pr) S&S Childrens.

N

An Asterisk (*) at the beginning of an entry indicates that the title is appearing for the first time.

New Feminist Art Criticism: Critical Strategies. Ed. by Katy Deepwell. LC 94-5414. (Illus.). 201p. 1995. text 24.95 (*0-7190-4258-5*, Pub. by Manchester Univ Pr) St Martin.

New Feminist Essays on Virginia Woolf. Ed. by Jane Marcus. LC 80-51823. xx, 272p. 1981. text 50.00 (*0-8032-3070-2*) U of Nebr Pr.

New Feminist Movement. Maren L. Carden. LC 73-83889. 226p. 1974. 35.00 (*0-87154-196-3*) Russell Sage.

New Feminist Tarot. Freer. 1988. 8.95 (*0-85030-563-2*, Pub. by Aqrn Pr) HarpC.

New Fibers. 2nd ed. Tatsuya Hongu & Glyn O. Phillips. 256p. 1997. 159.95 (*1-85573-334-X*) Technomic.

New Fiberworks Sourcebook: Being an Essential Mail-Order Guide to Supplies & Services for the Fiber Arts. Bobbi A. McRae. LC 93-12584. (Illus.). 320p. (Orig.). 1993. pap. 15.95 (*0-944577-06-7*) Limestone.

New Fiction: Interviews with Innovative American Writers. Joe D. Bellamy. LC 74-14841. 225p. 1974. text 24.95 (*0-252-00430-2*); pap. text 11.95 (*0-252-00555-4*) U of Ill Pr.

New Fiction from Indiana. (Chapbook Series I: No. 6). 80p. 1980. pap. 4.00 (*1-880649-06-3*) Writ Ctr Pr.

*__New Fiction in English from Africa: West, East, & South.__ Andre Viola et al. LC 99-171999. (Cross-Cultures Ser.: Vol. 34). 244p. 1998. pap. 19.00 (*90-420-0773-7*) Editions Rodopi.

*__New Fiedler Reader.__ Leslie Fiedler. LC 99-37952. 400p. 1999. pap. 18.95 (*1-57392-746-5*) Prometheus Bks.

New Field Guide to Fungi. Eric Soothill & Alan Fairhurst. (Illus.). 1979. 22.00 (*0-7181-1620-8*) Transatl Arts.

New Field Guide to the U. S. Economy: A Compact & Irreverent Guide to Economic Life in America. Nancy Folbre & Center for Popular Economics Staff. 224p. (Orig.). 1995. pap. 12.95 (*1-56584-153-0*, Pub. by New Press NY) Norton.

New Fields & Other Stones: On a Child's Death. Saul Bennett. LC 98-70021. 97p. 1998. 19.95 (*0-9662299-0-8*) Archer Books.

New 50 Golden Country Hits. 192p. (Orig.). (YA). 1992. pap. 16.95 (*0-7692-1054-6*, VF1819) Wrner Bros.

New 50 Golden Gershwin Classics. 196p. (Orig.). (YA). 1996. pap. 18.95 (*1-57623-276-X*, MF9578) Wrner Bros.

New 50 Golden Jazz Classics. 152p. (Orig.). (YA). 1995. pap. 16.95 (*1-57623-267-0*, MF9574) Wrner Bros.

New 50 Golden Movie Songs. 160p. (Orig.). (YA). 1996. pap. 16.95 (*0-7692-1057-0*, MF9616) Wrner Bros.

New Finance: Regulation & Financial Stability. Franklin R. Edwards. 227p. 1996. 39.95 (*0-8447-3988-X*, AEI Pr); pap. 14.95 (*0-8447-3989-8*, AEI Pr) Am Enterprise.

New Finance: The Case Against Efficient Markets. 2nd ed. Pref. by Robert A. Haugen. LC 98-50818. (Illus.). 144p. 1998. reprint ed. pap. 26.20 (*0-13-010228-8*) P-H.

*__New Financial Architecture: Banking Regulation in the 21st Century.__ Ed. by Benton E. Gup. LC 00-27074. 288p. 2000. 67.00 (*1-56720-341-8*, Q341, Quorum Bks) Greenwood.

New Financial Capitalists: Kohlberg Kravis Roberts & the Creation of Corporate Value. George P. Baker & George D. Smith. LC 98-28007. 240p. (C). 1998. 24.95 (*0-521-64260-4*) Cambridge U Pr.

New Financial Instruments. Cooper et al. 1987. 120.00 (*0-85297-190-7*, Pub. by Chartered Bank) St Mut.

New Financial Instruments. 2nd ed. Julian Walmsley. LC 97-22590. (Series in Financial Engineering). 544p. 1998. 69.95 (*0-471-12136-3*) Wiley.

New Financial Landscape: Forces Shaping the Revolution in Banking, Risk Management & Capital Markets. LC 96-179013. 370p. (Orig.). 1995. pap. 59.00 (*92-64-14650-4*, Pub. by Org for Econ) OECD.

New Financial Metrics: How Leading Companies Measure Success. William L. Simon. LC 97-108350. 272p. (C). 1997. text 30.95 (*0-442-02346-4*, VNR) Wiley.

New Financiers: Profiles of the Industry Leaders Who Are Reshaping Financial Services. Charles B. Wendel. 368p. 1996. 37.50 (*1-55738-908-X*, Irwn Prfssnl) McGraw-Hill Prof.

New Finch Handbook. Christa Koepff. LC 84-14616. 133p. 1984. pap. 9.95 (*0-8120-2859-7*) Barron.

New Findings in Obsessive-Compulsive Disorders. Ed. by Thomas R. Insel. LC 84-2968. (Clinical Insights Ser.). 133p. reprint ed. pap. 41.30 (*0-8357-7824-X*, 203619700002) Bks Demand.

New Findings on Aclarubicin in the Treatment of Acute Myeloid Leukemia. Ed. by W. Hiddemann & R. Mertelsmann. (Illus.). 88p. 1990. 18.95 (*0-387-52613-7*) Spr-Verlag.

New Findings on HSV-Induced Retinitis in the Von Szily Model. H. J. Thiel. LC 95-104225. 100p. 1994. pap. text 63.00 (*0-7506-9588-9*) Buttrwrth-Heinemann.

New Findings on Poverty & Child Health & Nutrition: Summary of a Research Briefing. Institute of Medicine Staff. LC 99-167776. (C). 1998. pap. text 15.00 (*0-309-06085-0*) Natl Acad Pr.

New Findings on the Loading of Plastic Spur Gear Teeth. J. Bessette & Henri Yelle. (Nineteen Ninety-Two Fall Technical Meeting Ser.: Vol. 92FTM11). (Illus.). 8p. 1993. 30.00 (*1-55589-591-3*) AGMA.

New Findings on Welfare & Children's Development: Summary of a Research Briefing. National Research Council Staff & Institute of Medicine Staff. Ed. by Deborah Phillips & Anne Bridgman. LC 97-145038. 32p. (Orig.). 1997. pap. text 10.00 (*0-309-05689-6*, Joseph Henry Pr) Natl Acad Pr.

New Findings with Anxiolytic Drugs: Journal: Psychopathology, Vol. 22, Suppl. 1. Ed. by Samuel Gershon & J. Bruinvels. vi, 78p. 1989. pap. 26.25 (*3-8055-5016-2*) S Karger.

New Fine Points of Furniture: Early American, Good, Better, Best, Superior, Masterpiece. Albert Sack. LC 93-7127. 1993. 50.00 (*0-517-58820-X*, Crown) Crown Pub Group.

New Finnish Architecture. Scott Poole. LC 91-12431. (Illus.). 224p. 1992. pap. 35.00 (*0-8478-1317-7*, Pub. by Rizzoli Intl) St Martin.

New Finnish Fiction. (Review of Contemporary Fiction Ser.: Vol. 16, No. 2). 220p. 1996. pap. 8.00 (*1-56478-098-8*) Dalkey Arch.

New Fire: Renewal of Life in a Precolumbian Spiritual Rhapsody. Edmond B. Szekely. (Illus.). 140p. 1973. pap. 5.95 (*0-89564-028-7*) IBS Intl.

New Fire Is Blazing. Peter Popoff. Ed. by Don Tanner. LC 80-67993. (Illus.). 194p. (Orig.). 1980. pap. 4.95 (*0-938544-02-0*) Faith Messenger.

New Firefighter's Cookbook: Award Winning Recipes from a Firefighting Chef. John Sineno. (Illus.). 256p. 1996. pap. 12.00 (*0-684-81859-0*, Fireside) S&S Trade Pap.

New Firms: An Economic Perspective. Peter Johnson. (Illus.). 224p. (C). 1986. text 55.00 (*0-04-330359-5*) Routledge.

New Firms in the Biotechnology Industry: Their Contribution to Innovation & Growth. Raymond P. Oakey et al. 224p. 1990. text 49.00 (*0-86187-126-X*) St Martin.

New First Chemistry Course. E. N. Ramsden. 192p. (C). 1994. pap. 19.95 (*0-85950-758-0*, Pub. by S Thornes Pubs) Trans-Atl Phila.

New First Mass Book. deluxe ed. (Illus.). 1989. 14.95 (*0-89942-812-6*, 808/82B) Catholic Bk Pub.

New First Mass Book for Boys. deluxe ed. (Illus.). 1989. 4.95 (*0-89942-810-X*, 808/42B) Catholic Bk Pub.

New First Mass Book for Girls. deluxe ed. (Illus.). 1989. 4.95 (*0-89942-811-8*, 808/42W) Catholic Bk Pub.

New First Three Years of Life. Benton L. White. 1995. pap. 13.00 (*0-671-89148-0*, Fireside) S&S Trade Pap.

New First Three Years of Life: The Completely Revised & Updated Edition of the Parenting Classic. rev. ed. Burton L. White. 384p. 1995. per. 14.00 (*0-684-80419-0*) S&S Trade Pap.

New Fiscal & Economic Strategies for Growth in Developing Countries. S. S. Kothari. 328p. (C). 1993. 27.00 (*0-19-562931-0*) OUP.

New Fiscal Federalism & the Social Safety Net: A View from California. James R. Hosek & Robert A. Levine. LC 96-9161. 1996. pap. 15.00 (*0-8330-2411-6*, CF-123) Rand Corp.

New Fish Cookery. 1979. 19.95 (*0-8464-4405-4*) Beekman Pubs.

New Fish Lover's Cookbook. London. 1991. 24.95 (*0-13-613423-8*) S&S Trade.

New Fish Tank Blues: How to Solve That Problem. Kevin Brandt. (Illus.). 1999. pap. write for info. (*1-928813-03-8*) K Brandt.

New Fishes Obtained by the Crane Pacific Expedition. Albert W. Herre. LC 36-1704. (Field Museum of Natural History, Publication 335, Zoological Ser: Vol. 18, No. 12). 57p. 1935. reprint ed. pap. 30.00 (*0-608-03781-8*, 206462800009) Bks Demand.

New Fit or Fat. enl. rev. ed. Covert Bailey. 180p. 1991. pap. 11.00 (*0-395-58564-3*) HM.

New Fitness Formula. Stephen G. Banks et al. (Orig.). 1990. pap. text 7.95 (*0-9627708-0-9*) NordicPress.

New 5-Week Formula for Winning Fabulous Sweepstakes Prizes! How to Win More . . . Mailing Fewer Than 20 Entries. 2nd rev. ed. Ina Collins. (Illus.). 1996. pap. 10.95 (*0-9620910-1-4*) CollinsBooks.

New Fix-It-Yourself Manual: How to Repair, Clean & Maintain Anything & Everything in & Around Your Home. Reader's Digest Editors. LC 96-15189. 448p. 1996. 35.00 (*0-89577-871-8*, Pub. by RD Assn) Penguin Putnam.

*__New Flag.__ Henry Fuller. 2000. reprint ed. lib. bdg. 79.00 (*0-7812-1204-9*) Rprt Serv.

New Flag. Henry B. Fuller. (Collected Works of Henry B. Fuller). 1988. reprint ed. lib. bdg. 59.00 (*0-317-90330-6*) Rprt Serv.

*__New Flatness: Surface Tension in Architecture.__ Alicia Imperiale. (Illus.). 96p. 2000. pap. 12.50 (*3-7643-6295-2*) Birkhauser.

New Flavors from Your Crockery Cooker. Ed. by Better Homes & Gardens. LC 98-66247. (Illus.). 96p. 1998. 15.95 (*0-696-20855-5*, Better Homes) Meredith Bks.

New Flavours: Lighter & Healthier Dining at Home. Elaine Eliot, pseud et al. LC 97-950007. (Maritime Flavours Ser.). (Illus.). 128p. 1997. pap. 21.95 (*0-88780-408-X*, Pub. by Formac Publ Co) Formac Dist Ltd.

New Flexi-Manager. David W. Birchall. LC 96-38885. 152p. 1996. pap., wbk. ed. 12.99 (*0-415-12502-2*) Thomson Learn.

New Flora & Botany of North America, 4 pts. in 1 vol. C. S. Rafinesque. 1946. reprint ed. pap. 20.00 (*0-934454-66-3*) Lubrecht & Cramer.

New Flora of the British Isles. Clive Stace. (Illus.). 1160p. (C). 1997. 89.95 (*0-521-58935-5*) Cambridge U Pr.

New Flora of the British Isles. Clive A. Stace. (Illus.). 1250p. 1991. pap. 49.95 (*0-7131-2966-2*, A6124, Pub. by E A) Routldge.

New Flower Arranger: Contemporary Approaches to Floral Design. Fiona Barnett. (Illus.). 256p. 1995. 32.50 (*1-85967-080-6*, Lorenz Bks) Anness Pub.

New Flower Design. Terence Moore. 1999. 19.98 (*1-84038-208-2*) Hermes Hse.

New Flower Expert. D. G. Hessayon. LC 99-461797. 1999. pap. text 17.95 (*0-903505-52-5*) Expert Bks.

New Flower Gardener. Pippa Greenwood. LC 94-6323. 168p. 1998. 24.95 (*0-7894-3525-X*) DK Pub Inc.

New Fluid Power Applications, Components, & Testing. 1996. 36.00 (*1-56091-844-6*, SP-1192) Soc Auto Engineers.

New Fluorinating Agents in Organic Synthesis. Ed. by L. S. German & S. V. Zenskov. (Illus.). 310p. 1989. 256.95 (*0-387-51160-1*) Spr-Verlag.

New Fluorocarbon Compound Alternatives, No. C-134. Business Communications Co., Inc. Staff. 199p. 1991. 2150.00 (*0-89336-764-8*) BCC.

*__New Food Fast.__ Donna Hay. (Illus.). 192p. 2000. pap. 19.95 (*1-55110-978-6*) Whitecap CAN.

New Food for Thought: A New Era in Vegetarian Cuisine. Jane Stimpson. (Illus.). 190p. 1995. pap. 16.95 (*0-233-98860-2*, Pub. by Andre Deutsch) Trafalgar.

*__New Food Lover's Companion.__ 3rd ed. Sharon Tyler Herbst. LC 00-39809. 2001. write for info. (*0-7641-1258-9*) Barron.

New Food Lover's Companion: Comprehensive Definitions of over 4000 Food, Wine, & Culinary Terms. rev. ed. Sharon T. Herbst. LC 95-15208. (Cooking Guide Ser.). 600p. 1995. pap. 13.95 (*0-8120-1520-7*) Barron.

New Food of Life: Ancient Persian & Modern Iranian Cooking & Ceremonies. Najmieh Khalili Batmanglij. LC TX725.I7 B373 1992. (Illus.). 440p. 1993. 44.95 (*0-934211-34-5*) Mage Pubs Inc.

New Food Product Development: From Concept to Marketplace. Gordon W. Fuller. LC 93-33273. 304p. 1994. boxed set 136.95 (*0-8493-8002-2*) CRC Pr.

New Food Sources. Blackbirch Graphics Staff. LC 96-22659. (J). 1996. lib. bdg. 16.98 (*0-8050-4624-0*) H Holt & Co.

New Foods for Healing: Capture the Powerful Cures of More Than 100 Common Foods. Selene Yeager & Prevention Health Books Editors. 800p. 1999. mass mkt. 7.50 (*0-553-58044-2*) Bantam.

New Force at a New Frontier: Europe's Development in the Space Field in the Light of Its Main Actors, Policies, Law & Activities from Its Beginnings up to the Present. Kevin Madders. LC 96-15202. (Illus.). 628p. (C). 1997. text 155.00 (*0-521-57096-4*) Cambridge U Pr.

New Forces at Work: Industry Views Critical Technologies. Steven W. Popper et al. LC 98-37588. 180p. 2000. pap. 15.00 (*0-8330-2651-8*, MR-1008-OSTP, Pub. by Rand Corp) Natl Bk Netwk.

New Forces in the World Economy. Ed. by Brad Roberts & Ernest Preeg. (Washington Quarterly Reader Ser.). (Illus.). 447p. 1996. pap. text 22.00 (*0-262-68089-0*) MIT Pr.

New Forces in World Politics. Seyom Brown. LC 74-912. 236p. reprint ed. pap. 73.20 (*0-8357-8969-1*, 203358800086) Bks Demand.

New Forces, Old Forces, & the Future of World Politics. Seyom Brown. (C). 1988. pap. text 22.00 (*0-673-39709-2*) Addson-Wesley Educ.

New Forces, Old Forces, & the Future of World Politics. 2nd ed. Seyom Brown. LC 94-9128. 280p. (C). 1997. pap. text 45.00 (*0-673-52210-5*) Addson-Wesley Educ.

New Forest. Insight Guides Staff. (Insight Guides). 1998. pap. text 7.95 (*0-88729-549-5*) Langenscheidt.

New Forest Cookery: Traditional Recipes from a Forest Cabin. Irene Soper. 96p. 1987. 40.00 (*0-907753-06-X*) St Mut.

New Forest of Hope. Winifred Rawlins. 45p. 1996. pap. 4.50 (*0-938875-35-3*) Pittenbruach Pr.

New Forest Walks. Anne-Marie Edwards. 64p. 1987. 35.00 (*0-907753-03-5*) St Mut.

New Forester. Philip O'Keefe & Barry Van Gelder. 128p. (Orig.). 1995. pap. 19.50 (*1-85339-232-4*, Pub. by Intermed Tech) Stylus Pub VA.

New Form of Warfare: The Rise of Non-Lethal Weapons. Malcolm R. Dando. (Illus.). 200p. 1996. 39.95 (*1-85753-127-2*, Pub. by Brasseys) Brasseys.

New Formalism. McPhillips. 1998. 22.95 (*0-8057-4614-5*, Twyne) Mac Lib Ref.

New Formations, New Questions - Asian American Studies: Positions Special Issue, Vol. 5. Ed. by Elaine H. Kim & Lisa Lowe. 200p. 1997. pap. text 19.00 (*0-8223-6450-6*) Duke.

New Forms: The Last 10 Years in Architecture. Philip Jodidio. LC 99-462698. (World Architecture Ser.). 1997. 29.99 (*3-8228-8579-7*) Taschen Amer.

New Forms New Spaces. Toby Lurie. (Illus.). 94p. (Orig.). 1971. reprint ed. pap. 5.95 (*0-945349-03-3*) Journeys Into Language.

*__New Forms of Consumption: Consumers, Culture & Commodification.__ Mark Gottdiener. LC 00-32849. 2000. write for info. (*0-8476-9570-0*) Rowman.

New Forms of Data Communication. 1981. 31.95 (*0-387-10736-3*) Spr-Verlag.

New Forms of Municipal Finance. 35.00 (*0-317-29529-2*, #CO1562) Harcourt.

New Forms of Security: Views from Central, Eastern & Western Europe. Ed. by Andrew J. Williams. 194p. 1995. text 77.95 (*1-85521-621-3*, Pub. by Dartmth Pub) Ashgate Pub Co.

New Forms of Work Organisation Can Europe Realise Its Potential? Results of a Su. OECD Staff. LC 98-125537. 1997. 45.00 (*92-828-1888-8*, SX-09-07-002ENC, Pub. by Comm Europ Commun) Bernan Associates.

New Forms of Work Organization: The Challenge for North American Unions. Tom Rankin. 168p. 1990. text 40.00 (*0-8020-2698-2*) U of Toronto Pr.

New Forms of Work Organization: The Challenge for North American Unions. Tom Rankin. 168p. 1992. pap. text 17.95 (*0-8020-7398-0*) U of Toronto Pr.

New Forms of Work Organization in Europe. Ed. by Peter Grootings et al. 252p. (C). 1991. 49.95 (*0-88738-215-0*) Transaction Pubs.

New Formulation of Particle Mechanics. Reese T. Prosser. LC 52-42839. (Memoirs Ser.: No. 1/61). 57p. 1980. reprint ed. pap. 17.00 (*0-8218-1261-0*, MEMO/1/61) Am Math.

New 40Ar/39Ar Ages of Intrusive Rocks from the Henry & La Sal Mountains, Utah. Stephen T. Nelson et al. (Miscellaneous Publications: 92-2). (Illus.). 24p. 1992. pap. 4.50 (*1-55791-318-8*, MP-92-2) Utah Geological Survey.

New Foster Parents: The First Experience. Patricia W. Cautley. LC 80-10937. 287p. 1980. 45.95 (*0-87705-495-9*, Kluwer Acad Hman Sci) Kluwer Academic.

New Found Facts & Memorabilia about Elvis Presley: A Manual on the Life & Times of Elvis Presley Using Psychographology (Handwriting Analysis) with Related Memorabilia. Stan P. Putnam. (Illus.). 100p. 1987. 20.00 (*0-318-22861-0*); pap. 12.00 (*0-318-22862-9*) Res Improvement Inst.

New Found Land of Stephen Parmenius: The Life & Writings of a Hungarian Poet, Drowned on a Voyage from Newfoundland, 1583. Stephanus Parmenius et al. LC 78-151386. xii, 250 p. 1972. write for info. (*0-8020-0027-4*) U of Toronto Pr.

New Found Lands: Maps in the History of Exploration. Peter Whitfield. LC 97-47767. (Illus.). 208p. (C). (gr. 13). 1998. 40.00 (*0-415-92026-4*) Routledge.

New Found Voices: Women in Nineteenth Century British Music. 3rd ed. Derek Hyde. LC 97-33014. 220p. 1997. text 69.95 (*1-85928-349-7*, Pub. by Ashgate Pub) Ashgate Pub Co.

New Found Worlde, or Antarctike. Andre Thevet. Tr. by T. Hacket. LC 74-174794. (English Experience Ser.: No. 417). 296p. 1971. reprint ed. 28.00 (*90-221-0417-6*) Walter J Johnson.

*__New Foundations: Ireland, 1660-1800.__ rev. ed. David Dickson. LC 99-36787. (Illus.). 264p. 2000. 49.50 (*0-7165-2632-8*, Pub. by Irish Acad Pr); pap. 24.50 (*0-7165-2637-9*, Pub. by Irish Acad Pr) Intl Spec Bk.

New Foundations: The Polish Strike Wave of 1980-81. John Hennig et al. LC 92-192244. (Illus.). 85p. (Orig.). 1981. pap. 5.00 (*0-933522-08-8*) Kent Popular.

New Foundations for a Science of Text & Discourse. Robert De Beaugrande. (Advances in Discourse Processes Ser.: Vol. 61). (Illus.). 300p. 1997. pap. 42.50 (*1-56750-279-2*) Ablx Pub.

New Foundations for a Science of Text & Discourse. Robert De Beaugrande. (Advances in Discourse Processes Ser.: Vol. 61). (Illus.). 300p. 1997. text 78.50 (*1-56750-278-4*) Ablx Pub.

New Foundations for Asian & Pacific Security. Ed. by Joyce E. Larson. 330p. (C). 1980. text 39.95 (*0-87855-413-0*); pap. text 24.95 (*0-87855-845-4*) Transaction Pubs.

New Foundations for Classical Mechanics. David Hestenes. 1986. lib. bdg. 238.00 (*90-277-2090-8*) Kluwer Academic.

New Foundations for Classical Mechanics. 2nd ed. David Hestenes. (Fundamental Theories of Physics Ser.: Vol. 99). Date not set. pap. text 87.00 (*0-7923-5514-8*) Kluwer Academic.

New Foundations for Insurance Law. Ed. by F. D. Rose. (Current Legal Problems Ser.). xvii, 106p. 1987. pap. 48.00 (*0-420-47780-2*) W S Hein.

New Foundations for Insurance Law: Current Legal Problems. F. D. Rose. (C). 1987. 210.00 (*0-7855-4071-7*, Pub. by Witherby & Co) St Mut.

New Foundations for Scientific Social & Behavioral Research: The Heuristic Paradigm. Katherine Tyson. (Illus.). 624p. (C). 1994. 82.00 (*0-02-421901-0*, Macmillan Coll) P-H.

New Foundations for Video Technology: Proceedings. Ed. by Jeffrey Friedman. 250p. (Orig.). 1995. pap. 25.00 (*0-940690-50-0*) Soc Motion Pic & TV Engrs.

New Foundations in Health: Six Stories. Frwd. by Daniel M. Fox et al. 168p. 1999. pap. write for info. (*1-887748-27-X*) Milbank Memorial.

New Foundations in Legal Education. John Goldring et al. xiv, 222p. 1998. pap. 34.00 (*1-876213-26-4*, Pub. by Cavendish Pubng) Gaunt.

New Foundations of Management Accounting. Ahmed Righi-Belkaoui. LC 91-36667. 192p. 1992. 57.95 (*0-89930-700-0*, BKJ/, Quorum Bks) Greenwood.

New Foundations of Ontology. Gustav Bergmann. Ed. by William Heald. LC 91-31693. 488p. (C). 1992. text 55.00 (*0-299-13130-0*) U of Wis Pr.

New Four Rules Decimals. Hesse. Date not set. pap. text. write for info. (*0-582-18036-8*, Pub. by Addison-Wesley) Longman.

New Four Rules Fractions. Hesse. Date not set. pap. text. write for info. (*0-582-18177-1*, Pub. by Addison-Wesley) Longman.

*__New Fourth Army: Communist Resistance along the Yangtze & the Huai, 1938-1941.__ Gregor Benton. LC 99-10875. 800p. 1999. 80.00 (*0-520-21992-9*, Pub. by U CA Pr) Cal Prin Full Svc.

New Fowler's Modern English Usage. 3rd ed. H. W. Fowler. 1010p. 2000. 29.95 (*0-19-860263-4*) OUP.

New Foxe's Book of Martyrs. John Foxe. LC 97-73697. (Illus.). 427p. 1997. pap. 12.99 (*0-88270-672-1*) Bridge-Logos.

New Fragments (1897) John Tyndall. 506p. 1998. reprint ed. pap. 39.95 (*0-7661-0667-5*) Kessinger Pub.

New France. Robert Livesey. LC 99-162686. (Discovering Canada Ser.). (Illus.). (YA). (gr. 3 up). 1990. pap. write for info. (*0-7737-5341-9*) STDK.

New France. Edward R. Tannenbaum. LC 61-8076. 291p. reprint ed. pap. 90.30 (*0-608-30009-8*, 201123600074) Bks Demand.

New France & New England. John Fiske. (Illus.). xxiii, 378p. 1997. reprint ed. pap. 28.50 (*0-7884-0650-7*, F374) Heritage Bk.

New France & New England. John Fiske. (Notable American Authors Ser.). 1992. reprint ed. lib. bdg. 75.00 (*0-7812-2863-8*) Rprt Serv.

New Fred Wiche Lawn & Garden Almanac. Bob Hill & Fred Wiche. Ed. & Illus. by Stephen Sebree. 211p. (Orig.). 1992. pap. 13.95 (*0-9621352-6-7*) Green Thumb Pub.

New Freedom: Individualism & Collectivism in the Social Lives of Americans. William A. Donohue. 296p. (C). 1994. 39.95 (*0-88738-298-3*); pap. 24.95 (*1-56000-789-3*) Transaction Pubs.

***New Freedom of Forgiveness.** David Augsburger. LC 99-86117. 2000. pap. 12.99 (*0-8024-3292-1*) Moody.

New Freedom to the New Deal, 1913-1939. William L. Katz. LC 92-39948. (History of Multicultural America Ser.). (Illus.). 96p. (J). (gr. 6-8). 1993. lib. bdg. 27.11 (*0-8114-6279-X*) Raintree Steck-V.

New Freedom to the New Deal, 1913-1939. William L. Katz. LC 92-39948. 96p. (gr. 7 up). 1995. pap. text 6.95 (*0-8114-2916-4*) Raintree Steck-V.

New French Baker: Perfect Pastries & Beautiful Breads from Your Kitchen. Shelia Linderman. LC 98-26185. (Illus.). 320p. 1998. 35.00 (*0-688-14325-3*, Wm Morrow) Morrow Avon.

New French-Chinese Dictionary: Nouveau Dictionnaire: Francais-Chinois. Commercial Press Staff. (CHI & FRE.). 1499p. 1981. 49.95 (*0-8288-4672-3*, M9372) Fr & Eur.

New French Fiction. Ed. by John O'Brien. (Review of Contemporary Fiction Ser.: Vol. 9, No. 1). 220p. 1989. pap. 8.00 (*1-56478-112-7*) Dalkey Arch.

New French Painting. Text by Jerome Sans. (Illus.). 96p. 1983. pap. 24.00 (*0-905836-40-5*, Pub. by Museum Modern Art) St Mut.

New French Poetry. Tr. by David Kelley & Jean Khalfa from FRE. 224p. 1996. pap. 21.00 (*1-85224-260-4*, Pub. by Bloodaxe Bks) Dufour.

New French-Russian Dictionary. 3rd rev. ed. V. G. Gak & K. A. Ganshina. (FRE & RUS.). 1195p. (C). 1997. 89.95 (*0-8285-5539-7*) Firebird NY.

New French Thought: Political Philosophy. Ed. by Mark Little. LC 94-8848. (New French Thought Ser.). 232p. 1994. text 55.00 (*0-691-03434-6*, Pub. by Princeton U Pr); pap. text 15.95 (*0-691-00105-7*, Pub. by Princeton U Pr) Cal Prin Full Svc.

New French with Ease. Anthony Bulger. 1999. pap. text 29.95 (*2-7005-0229-9*) Assimil USA.

***New French with Ease.** Jean Bulger. 1999. audio 69.95 (*2-7005-2013-0*) Assimil.

New Frequency: And the Music of Annihilation. Tod Thilleman. LC 98-4791. 1998. 12.00 (*0-9661242-0-0*) Maarri.

New Friend: The Story of Paul's Conversion. Patricia L. Nederveld. LC 98-16962. (God Loves Me Ser.). (Illus.). 24p. (J). (ps). 1998. pap. 2.45 (*1-56212-317-3*, 1105-0148) CRC Pubns.

***New Friend, Blue Friend.** Ellen Weiss. LC 98-44158. (Road to Reading Ser.). 32p. (J). 1999. 3.99 (*0-307-26210-3*, Whitman Coin) St Martin.

New Friends. Colleen O. McKenna. (Dr. Quinn, Medicine Woman Ser.: No. 1). (J). 1995. pap. 3.99 (*0-590-60372-8*) Scholastic Inc.

New Friends in a New World: Thanksgiving Story of Children with New Friends. Eugene L. Vickery. (Illus.). 20p. (Orig.). (J). (gr. k-8). 1986. pap. 1.95 (*0-937775-03-7*) Stonehaven Pubs.

***New Friends, True Friends, Stuck-Like-Glue Friends.** Virginia Kroll. LC 94-27557. (Illus.). 32p. (J). 2000. pap. 7.50 (*0-8028-5202-5*) Eerdmans.

New Frog: The Life Cycle of an Amphibian. unabridged ed. Pamela Hickman. (Illus.). 20p. (J). (ps-4). 1999. 6.95 (*1-55074-615-4*, Pub. by Kids Can Pr) Genl Dist Srvs.

New Frontier. Michael Cherkas & John Sabljic. LC 96-121366. 112p. 1994. pap. 12.95 (*1-56163-101-9*) NBM.

New Frontier. Peter David. (Star Trek: Bks. 1-4). 688p. 1998. per. 15.00 (*0-671-01978-3*, Star Trek) PB.

New Frontier: Australia's Rising Northwest. Jeff Carter. LC 76-882106. 90p. 1971. write for info. (*0-207-12146-X*) Consort Bk Sales.

New Frontier: Saga of the Sierras. Brock Thoene. (Saga of the Sierras Ser.). 1998. 12.99 (*0-88486-224-0*) Arrowood Pr.

New Frontier: The National Information Infrastructure: Proceedings from the State-of-the-Art Institute, November 3-4, 1994. Special Libraries Association, State of the Art In. LC 95-192844. (Illus.). 98p. 1995. reprint ed. pap. 30.40 (*0-608-07900-6*, 206788100011) Bks Demand.

New Frontier: The Response of Farmers to Land Degradation: A West African Study. Kojo S. Amanor. (Illus.). 244p. (C). 1994. text 65.00 (*1-85649-241-9*, Pub. by Zed Books) St Martin.

New Frontier for Land Policy: Planning & Growth Management in the States. John M. DeGrove. LC 92-56505. 176p. (Orig.). 1992. pap. 18.95 (*1-55844-121-2*) Lincoln Inst Land.

New Frontiers. Margaret Early. 1983. text 42.25 (*0-15-331260-2*) Harcourt Schl Pubs.

***New Frontiers: Imperialism's New Communities in East Asia, 1842-1953.** Robert Bickers & Christian Henriot. LC 99-54910. 300p. 2000. 74.95 (*0-7190-5604-7*) Manchester Univ Pr.

New Frontiers: Navigational Strategies for Integrating Technology into the School. Contrib. by David Thronburg et al. LC 98-207786. 264p. 1997. pap. 22.00 (*1-55833-195-6*) Natl Cath Educ.

New Frontiers for Worker-Friendly Companies: Report of the Corporate Symposium on Linking Work/Family & Workplace Dinesity. Leslie R. Wolfe & Jennifer Tucker. 24p. 1996. pap. 10.00 (*1-877966-30-4*) Ctr Women Policy.

New Frontiers in Agrochemical Immunoassay. Ed. by David A. Kurtz et al. LC 96-109113. 325p. 1995. pap. 89.00 (*0-935584-58-7*) AOAC Intl.

New Frontiers in Algebras, Groups & Geometries. Grigorios T. Tsagas. (Illus.). 577p. (C). 1996. pap. text 89.00 (*1-57485-009-1*) Hadronic Pr Inc.

New Frontiers in Barnacle Evolution. Ed. by Frederick R. Schram & Jens T. Hoeg. (Crustacean Issues Ser.: No. 10). (Illus.). 350p. (C). 1995. 110.00 (*90-5410-626-3*, Pub. by A A Balkema) Ashgate Pub Co.

New Frontiers in Binary Research. Ed. by K. C. Leung & I. S. Nha. (ASP Conference Series Proceedings: Vol. 38). 471p. 1993. 34.00 (*0-937707-57-0*) Astron Soc Pacific.

New Frontiers in Cancer Causation: Proceedings of the 2nd International Conference on Theories of Carcinogenesis. Ed. by Olav H. Iversen. 432p. 1993. 89.50 (*1-56032-251-9*, Pub. by Tay Francis Ltd) Taylor & Francis.

New Frontiers in Cytology. Ed. by K. Goeritler et al. (Illus.). 510p. 1988. 256.00 (*0-387-19168-2*) Spr-Verlag.

New Frontiers in European Industrial Relations. Ed. by Anthony Ferner. (Industrial Relations in Context Ser.). 448p. 1994. pap. text 43.95 (*0-631-18606-9*) Blackwell Pubs.

New Frontiers in Food Microstructure. Ed. by D. B. Bechtel. LC 83-70795. (Illus.). 392p. 1983. text 76.00 (*0-913250-32-5*) Am Assn Cereal Chem.

New Frontiers in Foreign Language Education. Ed. by Robert DiDonato. (Central States Ser.). pap. 14.21 (*0-8442-9308-3*, VF9308-3) NTC Contemp Pub Co.

New Frontiers in Forensic & Demonstrative Evidence: A Bibliography. Richard A. Leiter. (Legal Bibliography Ser.: No. 29). 27p. (Orig.). 1985. pap. 15.00 (*0-935630-12-0*) U of Tex Tarlton Law Lib.

New Frontiers in Gravitation. Gennadi A. Sardanashvily. LC 96-22397. (Illus.). 360p. (C). 1996. pap. text 75.00 (*0-911767-96-7*) Hadronic Pr Inc.

New Frontiers in Hadronic Mechanics. Ed. by Tepper G. Gill. (Illus.). 416p. (C). 1996. pap. text 75.00 (*1-57485-016-4*) Hadronic Pr Inc.

New Frontiers in Hispanic & Luso-Brazilian Scholarship: Como se Fue el Maestro. Ed. by Trevor Dadson et al. (Illus.). 584p. 1994. text 119.95 (*0-7734-9117-1*) E Mellen.

New Frontiers in Hyperstructures: Conference Proceedings. Thomas Vougiouklis. LC 96-35978. (Series on New Frontiers in Advanced Mathematics). 1996. 70.00 (*1-57485-008-3*) Hadronic Pr Inc.

New Frontiers in Mammary Pathology, 1986. Ed. by K. H. Hollman & J. M. Verley. (Developments in Oncology Ser.). 1986. text 278.50 (*0-89838-852-X*) Kluwer Academic.

New Frontiers in Medical Device Technology. Ed. by Arye Rosen & Harel D. Rosen. LC 94-26892. (Series in Microwave & Optical Engineering). 364p. 1995. 112.00 (*0-471-59189-0*) Wiley.

New Frontiers in Middle East Security. Lenore G. Martin. LC 98-44039. 1998. text 49.95 (*0-312-21414-6*) St Martin.

New Frontiers in Nuclear Physics. S. Homma et al. 264p. 1994. text 81.00 (*981-02-1617-3*) World Scientific Pub.

New Frontiers in Organometallic & Inorganic Chemistry. Ed. by H. Yaozeng et al. LC 85-62529. xxix, 522p. 1985. 59.50 (*0-9608224-1-0*) S P Richards.

New Frontiers in Particle Physics: Proceedings of the 1st Lake Louise Winter Institute, Lake Louise, Canada, February 16-22, 1986. Ed. by J. M. Cameron et al. 650p. 1986. text 124.00 (*9971-5-0135-X*) World Scientific Pub.

New Frontiers in Physics, Vols. I & II. Ed. by Tepper G. Gill. 610p. 1996. 140.00 (*1-57485-018-0*) Hadronic Pr Inc.

New Frontiers in Physics Vol. I: History of Physics, Electrodynamics & Experimental Physics. Ed. by Tepper G. Gill. LC 96-50880. (Illus.). 330p. (C). 1996. pap. text 70.00 (*1-57485-002-4*) Hadronic Pr Inc.

New Frontiers in Physics Vol. II: Foundations of Physics, Quantum Groups, Dynamical Systems. Ed. by Tepper G. Gill. (Illus.). 360p. (C). 1996. pap. text 70.00 (*1-57485-014-8*) Hadronic Pr Inc.

New Frontiers in Psychosocial Occupational Therapy. Ed. by Anne Hiller-Scott. LC 98-36240. 176p. 1998. 29.95 (*0-7890-0652-9*) Haworth Pr.

New Frontiers in Public Sector Management: Trends & Issues in State & Local Government in Europe. Frieder Naschold. Tr. by Andrew Watt. (De Gruyter Studies in Organization: No. 69). xiv, 329p. (C). 1996. text 79.95 (*3-11-015016-6*) De Gruyter.

New Frontiers in Quantum Electrodynamics & Quantum Optics. Ed. by Asim O. Barut. LC 90-7932. (NATO ASI Ser.: Vol. 232). (Illus.). 620p. (C). 1990. text 191.00 (*0-306-43669-8*, Kluwer Plenum) Kluwer Academic.

New Frontiers in Relativities. Ed. by Tepper G. Gill. LC 96-48614. (Series on New Frontiers in Advanced Physics). (Illus.). 450p. 1996. pap. text 75.00 (*1-57485-015-6*) Hadronic Pr Inc.

New Frontiers in Renal Stone Disease: International ASTIF Meeting, Fiuggi, July 1998. Ed. by Vittorio E. Andreucci. (Nephron Ser.: Vol. 81, Supplement 1 (1999)). (Illus.). iv, 104p. 1998. pap. 34.00 (*3-8055-6818-5*) S Karger.

New Frontiers in Screening for Microbial Biocatalysts: Proceedings of an International Symposium Held in Ede, The Netherlands, 15-18, December, 1996. Klaus Kieslich. LC 97-32763. (Studies in Organic Chemistry). 282p. 1997. 216.25 (*0-444-82436-7*) Elsevier.

New Frontiers in Stress Research: Modulation of Brain Function. Ed. by Aharon Levy et al. (Illus.). 320p. 1998. text 80.00 (*90-5702-266-4*, Harwood Acad Pubs) Gordon & Breach.

New Frontiers in Technology Applications: Integration of Emerging & Traditional Technologies. E. U. Von Weitzsacker. (Science & Technology for Development Ser.: Vol. 2). (Illus.). 271p. 1983. 70.00 (*0-907567-66-5*, Tycooly Pub) Weidner & Sons.

New Frontiers in the Archaeology of the Pacific Coast of Southern Mesoamerica. Ed. by Frederick J. Bove & Lynette Heller. LC 88-84021. (Anthropological Research Papers: No. 39). (Illus.). xvii, 292p. (Orig.). 1989. pap. 30.00 (*0-936249-02-1*) AZ Univ ARP.

New Frontiers in the Study of Gene Functions. G. Poste & S. T. Crooke. LC 86-30313. (New Horizons in Therapeutics Ser.). (Illus.). 218p. (C). 1987. text 75.00 (*0-306-42502-5*, Kluwer Plenum) Kluwer Academic.

New Frontiers in Theoretical Biology. Ed. by C. A. Dreismann. (Illus.). 540p. (C). 1996. pap. text 85.00 (*1-57485-012-1*) Hadronic Pr Inc.

New Frontiers in Transport Theory: Selected Papers from the 6th Conference at U. of Ariz, Tuscon, April 1979. Ed. by B. D. Ganapol. 122p. 1980. pap. 45.00 (*0-08-026698-3*, Pergamon Pr) Elsevier.

***New Frontiers in Ultrasonic & Traditional Liposuction.** Elliott Lavey. 1998. 15.00 incl. audio (*1-58111-075-8*) Contemporary Medical.

New Frontiers in Women's Studies: Knowledge, Identity, & Nationalism. Ed. by Mary Maynard & June Purvis. LC 96-10665. 1996. 79.95 (*0-7484-0287-X*); pap. 27.95 (*0-7484-0288-8*) Taylor & Francis.

New Frontiers of Aging. Ed. by Clark Tibbitts et al. LC 79-8666. (Growing Old Ser.). (Illus.). 1980. reprint ed. lib. bdg. 23.95 (*0-405-12808-8*) Ayer.

New Frontiers of Archaeology: Heras Memorial Lectures. S. R. Rao. LC 95-900334. (C). 1994. 20.00 (*81-7154-689-7*, Pub. by Popular Prakashan) S Asia.

New Frontiers of Genetics. Ed. by Shain-Dow Kung. 132p. (C). 1989. text 54.00 (*981-02-0042-0*) World Scientific Pub.

New Frontiers of Information Technology. LC 97-81043. 728p. 1997. pap. 155.00 (*0-8186-8129-2*) IEEE Comp Soc.

New Frontiers of the Mind: The Story of the Duke Experiments. Joseph B. Rhine. LC 71-178080. (Illus.). 275p. 1972. reprint ed. lib. bdg. 49.75 (*0-8371-6279-3*, RHNF, Greenwood Pr) Greenwood.

New Frontiers I. Ed. by Martin H. Greenberg. 1990. mass mkt. 4.50 (*0-8125-8329-9*) Tor Bks.

New Frontiers II. Ed. by Martin H. Greenberg. 1990. mass mkt. 4.50 (*0-8125-8331-0*) Tor Bks.

New Fuck You: Adventures in Lesbian Reading. Eileen Myles & Liz Kotz. 1995. pap. 8.00 (*1-57027-057-0*) Autonomedia.

New Fuels & Advances in Combustion Technologies Symposium, March 1979. 681p. 1979. pap. 60.00 (*0-910091-28-5*) Inst Gas Tech.

New Full Spectrum, Bk. 3. Byrd. 1994. pap., teacher ed. 28.00 (*0-13-830092-5*) P-H.

New Fun-Way Bandsman: C Flute. Edmondson. 1990. 4.95 (*0-685-32116-9*, N081) Hansen Ed Mus.

***New Future Beckoning.** large type ed. Shirley Worrall. 384p. 1999. 31.99 (*0-7089-4140-0*) Ulverscroft.

New Futures for Student Affairs: Building a Vision for Professional Leadership & Practice. Margaret J. Barr et al. LC 90-41464. (Higher Education Ser.). 335p. 1990. text 36.95 (*1-55542-298-5*) Jossey-Bass.

New G. E. Microwave Cookbook. General Electric Company Staff. (Illus.). 1983. 15.95 (*0-394-53151-5*) Random.

New Gambler's Bible: How to Beat the Casinos, the Track, Your Bookie & Your Buddies. Arthur S. Reber. LC 96-219807. 496p. 1996. pap. 18.00 (*0-517-88669-3*) Crown Pub Group.

New Game, New Rules: Jobs, Corporate America & the Information Age. Adele Gray & Gina Alphonso. LC 96-5264. (Studies in the History of American Labor). 232p. 1996. text 61.00 (*0-8153-2463-4*) Garland.

New Games for Information Skills: Ready, Set, Go . . . Eleanor B. Krause & Margaret R. Tassia. 50p. 1996. pap. 18.00 (*0-931510-59-7*) Hi Willow.

New Games for the Whole Family. Dale N. LeFevre. 160p. 1988. pap. 9.95 (*0-399-51448-1*, Perigee Bks) Berkley Pub.

New Garden Apartment: Current Market Realities of an American Housing Form. Carl F. Horowitz. LC 83-7364. 180p. (C). 1983. pap. text 1.00 (*0-88285-093-8*) Ctr Urban Pol Res.

New Garden Book. Better Homes & Gardens. (Better Homes & Gardens Ser.). 384p. 1990. 29.95 (*0-696-00042-3*) Meredith Bks.

New Garden Book. Better Homes & Gardens. (Better Homes & Gardens Ser.). (Illus.). 384p. 1990. pap. 16.95 (*0-696-02557-4*) Meredith Bks.

New Garden Friends Meeting: The Christian People Called Quakers. Hiram H. Hilty. 134p. 1983. pap. 7.00 (*0-614-04685-8*) NC Frnds Hist Soc.

New Gardener. Dorling Kindersley Staff. 1998. pap. 13.95 (*0-7894-3298-6*, D K Ink) DK Pub Inc.

New Gardener: The Practical Guide to Gardening Basics. Pippa Greenwood. LC 94-6323. (Illus.). 176p. 1994. 24.95 (*1-56458-650-2*) DK Pub Inc.

New Garzanti English Dictionary. Tr. of Nuovo Dizionario Inglese Garzanti. (ENG & ITA.). 1088p. 59.95 (*0-7859-8880-7*) Fr & Eur.

New Garzanti English Dictionary. Garzanti. (ENG & ITA.). 1088p. 1984. write for info. (*0-8288-7757-2*, 8811504333) Fr & Eur.

New GATT: Implications for the U. S. Ed. by Susan M. Collins & Barry P. Bosworth. (Integrating National Economies: Promise & Pitfalls Ser.). 128p. (C). 1995. pap. 14.95 (*0-8157-1029-1*) Brookings.

New GATT Round of Multilateral Trade Negotiations: Legal & Economic Problems. Ed. by Meinhard Hilf & Ernst-Ulrich Petersmann. 598p. 1989. 144.00 (*90-6544-365-7*) Kluwer Academic.

New GATT Round of Multilateral Trade Negotiations: Legal & Economic Problems. 2nd rev. ed. Ed. by Ernst-Ulrich Petersmann & Meinhard Hilf. (Studies in Transnational Economic Law: Vol. V). 648p. 1991. 168.00 (*90-6544-518-8*) Kluwer Law Intl.

New GATT Trade Round. Nils Johnson & Charles Pearson. (Pew Case Studies in International Affairs). 59p. (C). 1986. pap. text 3.50 (*1-56927-115-1*) Geo U Inst Dplmcy.

New Gay Book of Lists. 2nd rev. ed. Leigh W. Rutledge. LC 96-19267. 208p. 1996. pap. text 11.95 (*1-55583-359-4*) Alyson Pubns.

New GE: How Jack Welch Revived an American Institution. Robert Slater. LC 92-11676. 304p. 1992. text 29.95 (*1-55623-670-0*, Irwn Prfssnl) McGraw-Hill Prof.

New Gear Shaper Technology. E. Tlaker. (1984 Fall Technical Meeting Ser.: Vol. 84FTM8). 10p. 1984. pap. text 30.00 (*1-55589-090-3*) AGMA.

New GED Interpretin. Long. (Illus.). pap. 9.15 (*0-8428-8704-0*) Cambridge Bk.

New GED Sciences. Long. (Illus.). pap. 9.15 (*0-8428-8703-2*) Cambridge Bk.

New GED Social Sciences. Long. (Illus.). pap. 9.15 (*0-8428-8702-4*) Cambridge Bk.

New GED Tests: An Overview for 1988-1998. (GED Staff Development Videotape Ser.). 307.40 incl. VHS (*0-8092-4755-0*) NTC Contemp Pub Co.

New GED Tests Overview Viewer's Guide. Patricia Reid. (GED Staff Development Videotape Ser.). teacher ed. 9.50 (*0-8092-4932-4*) NTC Contemp Pub Co.

New GED Writing Skills. Aaron Percefull. (Illus.). pap. 9.15 (*0-8428-8701-6*) Cambridge Bk.

New Genealogical Atlas of Ireland. Brian Mitchell. 123p. 1998. reprint ed. pap. 18.95 (*0-8063-1152-5*, 3853) Genealog Pub.

New General Catalogue of the Ants of the World. Barry Bolton. LC 95-12908. 512p. (C). 1995. 140.50 (*0-674-61514-X*) HUP.

New General Collection of Voyages & Travels, 1745-1747, 4 vols., Set. Thomas Astley. (Illus.). 1968. reprint ed. 395.00 (*0-7146-1786-5*, Pub. by F Cass Pubs) Intl Spec Bk.

New General English Dictionary. Thomas W. Dyche. (Anglistica & Americana Ser.: No. 81). 912p. 1972. reprint ed. 154.70 (*3-487-04398-X*) G Olms Pubs.

New General Manager: Confronting the Key Challenge of Today's Organization. Paul Thorne. (Illus.). 224p. 1989. 24.95 (*0-07-707083-6*) McGraw.

New Generation: Poems from China Today. Ed. by Ping Wang et al. Tr. by Anne Waldman et al from CHI. LC 99-17919. 236p. 1999. 16.00 (*1-882413-55-5*) Hanging Loose.

***New Generation: Poems from China Today.** Ed. by Ping Wang et al. Tr. by Anne Waldman et al from CHI. LC 99-17919. 1999. pap. 16.00 (*1-882413-54-7*) Hanging Loose.

New Generation: The Intimate Problems of Modern Parents & Children. Ed. by V. F. Calverton & Samuel D. Schmalhausen. LC 70-165712. (American Education, Ser, No. 2). (Illus.). 1978. reprint ed. 42.95 (*0-405-03701-5*) Ayer.

New Generation & Artistic Modernism in the Ukraine. Myroslava M. Mudrak. LC 86-7043. (Studies in the Fine Arts: The Avant-Garde: No. 50). (Illus.). 294p. reprint ed. pap. 91.20 (*0-8357-1687-2*, 207051400097) Bks Demand.

New Generation Computer: Proceedings of International Symposium on New Generation Computer, Beijing, 7-11 December, 1988. Y. Ci et al. (International Academic Publishers Ser.). 500p. 1989. 145.00 (*0-08-037041-1*, Pergamon Pr) Elsevier.

***New Generation Draws the Line: Kosovo, East Timor & the Standards of the West.** Noam Chomsky. 160p. 2000. 22.00 (*1-85984-789-7*, Pub. by Verso) Norton.

New Generation Drivetrains, No. R332. 1995. 875.00 (*0-85058-847-2*) Economist Intell.

New Generation Engines: 1997 Edition. 1996. 945.00 (*0-614-25450-7*, R342) Econ Intel.

New Generation Engines, 1997. J. R. Daniels. LC 99-186989. (Research Reports: No. R342). xviii, 268p. 1997. 945.00 (*0-85058-935-5*) Economist Intell.

New Generation Floating Production Facility. Tor Naess. 1989. 150.00 (*90-6314-505-5*, Pub. by Lorne & MacLean Marine) St Mut.

New Generation Floating Production Facility. Tor Naess. (C). 1989. 110.00 (*0-89771-732-5*, Pub. by Lorne & MacLean Marine) St Mut.

New Generation Guide to the Birds of Britain & Europe. Christopher M. Perrins. (Corrie Herring Hooks Ser.: No. 8). (Illus.). 320p. 1987. 16.95 (*0-292-75532-5*) U of Tex Pr.

New Generation Guide to the Butterflies & Day-Flying Moths of Britain & Europe. Michael Chinery. Ed. by David Attenborough. (Corrie Herring Hooks Ser.: No. 13). (Illus.). 320p. 1989. 22.95 (*0-292-75539-2*) U of Tex Pr.

New Generation in Meiji Japan: Problems of Cultural Identity, 1885-1895. Kenneth B. Pyle. LC 69-13183. viii, 240p. 1969. 29.50 (*0-8047-0697-2*) Stanford U Pr.

New Generation Jails: An Innovative Approach to an Age-Old Problem. 1990. lib. bdg. 75.00 (*0-8490-4046-9*) Gordon Pr.

New Generation Knowledge Engineering: I. A. K. E. '92 Proceedings. Contrib. by Elias Awad et al. 832p. (Orig.). 1992. pap. 35.00 (*0-938801-06-6*) Systemsware.

An Asterisk (*) at the beginning of an entry indicates that the title is appearing for the first time.

New Generation of Antipsychotic Drugs: Novel Mechanisms of Action. N. Brunello et al. Ed. by G. Racagni et al. (International Academy for Biomedical & Drug Research Ser.: Vol. 4). (Illus.). vi, 150p. 1993. 146.25 (*3-8055-5654-3*) S Karger.

New Generation of Environmental Leadership: Action for the Environment & Economy. Ed. by World Resources Institute Staff. 23p. 1993. pap. 15.00 (*0-915825-92-9*, WRNGP) World Resources Inst.

New Generation of Quinolones. C. Siporin et al. (Infectious Disease & Therapy Ser.: Vol. 5). (Illus.). 368p. 1990. text 155.00 (*0-8247-8224-0*) Dekker.

New Generation of Two-Stroke Engines for the Future (A)? Proceedings of the International Seminar Held in Rueil-Malmaison, France, November 29-30, 1993. Ed. by Pierre Duret. 224p. (C). 1993. pap. 395.00 (*2-7108-0654-1*, Pub. by Edits Technip) Enfield Pubs NH.

New Generation SAT Mathematics Workshop. (Illus.). 98p. 1997. pap. write for info. (*0-9656864-5-0*) J Ghim.

New Generation Vaccines. 2nd ed. Myron M. Levine. LC 97-12541. (Illus.). 1240p. 1997. text 195.00 (*0-8247-0061-9*) Dekker.

New Generation Vaccines: The Role of Basic Immunology. G. Poste et al. (NATO ASI Ser.: Vol. 261). (Illus.). 232p. (C). 1994. text 85.00 (*0-306-44666-9*, Kluwer Plenum) Kluwer Academic.

New Generations Engines, No. R326. 1994. 770.00 (*0-85058-816-2*) Economist Intell.

New Generic Technologies in Developing Countries. M. R. Bhagavan & Sweden. LC 97-11909. 1997. text 79.95 (*0-312-17643-0*) St Martin.

***New Genesis: A Mormon Reader on Land & Community.** Terry T. Williams et al. 304p. 1998. 29.95 (*0-87905-822-6*) Gibbs Smith Pub.

New Genesis: A Mormon Reader on Land & Community. Terry Tempest Williams et al. LC 97-32750. 304p. 1998. pap. 19.95 (*0-87905-843-9*) Gibbs Smith Pub.

New Genesis: Theology & the Genetic Revolution. Ronald Cole-Turner. LC 92-26564. 144p. (Orig.). 1993. pap. 15.95 (*0-664-25406-3*) Westminster John Knox.

New Genesis & the Technoid Movement. Joseph Leonaites. (Illus.). 1977. pap. write for info. (*0-9601272-1-6*) Leonaitis.

New Genesis Poems: A Trilogy: "Word Behind the Word", "Under the Sign of the Cross", "Crossword Church" Sylvester L. Steffen. (Illus.). 392p. (Orig.). (C). 1992. pap. text 11.95 (*0-9633664-0-8*) Word Unltd.

New Genetics. Hipkins. 1990. pap. text. write for info. (*0-582-85881-X*, Pub. by Addison-Wesley) Longman.

New Genetics: Challenges for Science, Faith & Politics. Roger L. Shinn. LC 95-43419. 176p. (Orig.). 1996. text 22.95 (*1-55921-171-7*) Moyer Bell.

***New Genetics: From Research into Health Care: Social & Ethical Implications for Users & Providers.** Ed. by Irmgard Nippert et al. LC 99-31137. (Illus.). viii, 185p. 1999. pap. 109.00 (*3-540-65920-X*) Spr-Verlag.

New Genetics & Clinical Practice. 3rd ed. D. J. Weatherall. (Illus.). 392p. 1991. pap. 35.00 (*0-19-261905-5*) OUP.

***New Geography.** Joel Kotkin. 2000. 22.95 (*0-375-50199-1*) Random.

New Geography of Consumer Spending: A Political Economy Approach. Alan G. Hallsworth. LC 92-24767. 192p. 1993. text 155.00 (*0-471-94630-3*) Wiley.

New Geography of European Migrations. Ed. by Russell King. LC 93-25980. 288p. 1993. 82.95 (*0-471-94700-8*) Halsted Pr.

New Geography of Ghana. Benneh. 1988. pap. text. write for info. (*0-582-58532-5*, Pub. by Addison-Wesley) Longman.

New Geography of Nigeria. Ilaeje. Date not set. pap. text. write for info. (*0-582-60393-5*, Pub. by Addison-Wesley) Longman.

New Geography of Poets. Ed. by Gerald Locklin & Charles Stetler. LC 91-46003. 376p. 1992. 34.00 (*1-55728-240-4*); pap. 22.00 (*1-55728-241-2*) U of Ark Pr.

New Geography of Services & Office Buildings. James W. Hughes et al. LC 92-13237. (Rutgers Regional Report Ser.). 200p. 1992. pap. text 1.00 (*0-88285-140-3*) Ctr Urban Pol Res.

New Geopolitics. Ed. by Michael D. Ward. xii, 187p. 1992. text 80.00 (*2-88124-535-8*) Gordon & Breach.

New Geopolitics of Central Asia. Ed. by Ali Banuazizi & Myron Weiner. LC 94-11996. 288p. 1995. 39.95 (*0-253-31139-X*); pap. 15.95 (*0-253-20918-8*) Ind U Pr.

New Georgia: Space, Society, Politics. Revaz Gachechiladze. Ed. by R. Anthony French. LC 95-42791. (Eastern European Studies: Vol. 3). (Illus.). 236p. 1996. 39.95 (*0-89096-703-2*) Tex A&M Univ Pr.

New Georgia Guide. Contrib. by Mary Hood & James Kilgo. LC 95-46800. 800p. (C). 1996. 39.95 (*0-8203-1798-5*); pap. 19.95 (*0-8203-1799-3*) U of Ga Pr.

New German Architecture. Gerhard Feldmeyer. LC 92-32826. (Illus.). 224p. 1993. 50.00 (*0-8478-1672-9*, Pub. by Rizzoli Intl) St Martin.

New German Cinema. John Sandford. LC 82-8981. (Quality Paperbacks Ser.). (Illus.). 180p. 1982. reprint ed. pap. 16.95 (*0-306-80177-9*) Da Capo.

New German Cookbook: More Than 230 Contemporary & Traditional Recipes. Jean Anderson et al. LC 92-56211. (Illus.). 416p. 1993. 27.50 (*0-06-016202-3*) HarperTrade.

New German Film: The Displaced Image. rev. ed. Timothy Corrigan. LC 93-4971. 1994. pap. 14.95 (*0-253-20841-6*) Ind U Pr.

New German Film: The Displaced Image. rev. ed. Timothy Corrigan. LC 93-4971. (Illus.). 248p. 1994. 35.00 (*0-253-31439-9*) Ind U Pr.

New German Public Sector? Reform, Adaptation & Stability. Ed. by Arthur Benz & Klaus H. Goetz. (Association for the Study of German Politics Ser.). 250p. 1996. text 77.95 (*1-85521-710-4*, Pub. by Dartmth Pub) Ashgate Pub Co.

New German Shorthaired Pointer. 3rd ed. C. Bede Maxwell. LC 74-75758. 12.95 (*0-87605-156-5*) Howell Bks.

New Germany: Literature & Society after Unification. Ed. by Osman Durran et al. 1995. 35.00 (*1-85075-560-4*, Pub. by Sheffield Acad) CUP Services.

New Germany: Social, Political, & Cultural Challenges in Unification. Ed. by Derek Lewis & John R. P. McKenzie. 352p. 1995. pap. text 29.95 (*0-85989-442-8*) Northwestern U Pr.

New Germany: Social, Political, & Cultural Challenges of Unification. Ed. by Derek Lewis & John R. McKenzie. 352p. (C). 1995. text 59.95 (*0-85989-494-0*, Pub. by Univ Exeter Pr) Northwestern U Pr.

New Germany & Migration in Europe. Barbara Marshall. pap. write for info. (*0-7190-4336-0*, Pub. by Manchester Univ Pr) St Martin.

New Germany & the New Europe. Ed. by Paul B. Stares. 406p. (C). 1992. 42.95 (*0-8157-8138-5*); pap. 18.95 (*0-8157-8137-7*) Brookings.

New Germany Votes: Reunification & the Creation of a German Party System. Ed. by Russell J. Dalton. (German Studies). 256p. 1993. text 39.50 (*0-85496-314-6*); pap. text 19.50 (*0-85496-386-3*) Berg Pubs.

New Gesham World Encyclopaedia, 12 vols., Set. Prints India Staff. (C). 1988. 1000.00 (*0-7855-0043-X*, Pub. by Print Hse) St Mut.

New Ghosts, Old Ghosts: Prisons & Labor Reform Camps in China. James D. Seymour & Richard Anderson. LC 97-26806. (Socialism & Social Movements Ser.). (Illus.). 336p. (C). (gr. 13). 1998. 44.95 (*0-7656-0097-8*, East Gate Bk) M E Sharpe.

New Ghosts, Old Ghosts: Prisons & Labor Reform Camps in China. James D. Seymour & Richard Anderson. LC 97-26806. (Socialism & Social Movements Ser.). (Illus.). 336p. 1999. pap. 26.95 (*0-7656-0510-4*, East Gate Bk) M E Sharpe.

New Giant Book of Rock. 448p. (YA). 1997. pap. 19.95 (*1-57623-902-0*, VF1942B) Wrner Bros.

New Giant Book of Rock. Ed. by Carol Cuellar. 448p. (Orig.). (YA). 1997. pap. text 19.95 (*1-57623-277-8*, VF1942B) Wrner Bros.

New Girl. Lois G. Leppard. (Mantlemass Ser.: No. 2). 118p. (J). (gr. 2-5). 1999. pap. 4.50 (*0-553-48660-8*) BDD Bks Young Read.

New Girl. R. L. Stine, pseud. (Fear Street Ser.: No. 1). (YA). (gr. 7 up). 1991. mass mkt. 3.99 (*0-671-74649-9*, Archway) PB.

New Girl. R. L. Stine, pseud. (Fear Street Ser.: No. 1). (YA). (gr. 7 up). 1989. 9.09 (*0-606-04283-0*, Pub. by Turtleback) Demco.

New Girl: Girls' Culture in England, 1880-1915. Sally Mitchell. LC 95-10929. (YA). 1995. 64.00 (*0-231-10246-1*) Col U Pr.

New Girl: Girls' Culture in England, 1880-1915. Sally Mitchell. 1995. pap. text 19.50 (*0-231-10247-X*) Col U Pr.

New Girl in Cabin Six. Marilyn Kaye. (Camp Sunnyside Friends Ser.: No. 4). 128p. (Orig.). (J). 1989. pap. 2.95 (*0-380-75703-6*, Avon Bks) Morrow Avon.

New Girl in Town. Judy Baer. LC 88-71504. (Cedar River Daydreams Ser.: No. 1). 144p. (Orig.). (YA). (gr. 7-10). 1988. mass mkt. 4.99 (*1-55661-022-X*) Bethany Hse.

New Girls. Beth R. Gutcheon. LC 95-54201. 352p. 1996. pap. 13.00 (*0-06-097702-7*, Perennial) HarperTrade.

New Glamour. Alex Larg. (Pro-Lighting Ser.). (Illus.). 160p. 1997. pap. 35.00 (*2-88046-322-X*, Rotovision) Watsn-Guptill.

New Glass Review, No. 3. LC 81-641214. (Illus.). 32p. 1982. pap. 2.50 (*0-87290-106-8*) Corning.

New Glass Review, Vol. 18. Corning Museum of Glass Staff. (Illus.). 72p. (Orig.). 1997. pap. 8.50 (*0-87290-140-8*) Corning.

New Glass Review, Vol. 19. Corning Museum of Glass Staff. (Illus.). 72p. (Orig.). 1998. pap. 8.50 (*0-87290-141-6*) Corning.

New Glass Review, Vol. 20. Corning Museum of Glass Staff. (Illus.). 72p. (Orig.). 1999. pap. 8.50 (*0-87290-145-9*) Corning.

New Glass Review, Vol. 21. Corning Museum of Glass Staff. LC 81-641214. (Annual Compendium of Contemporary Glass Made in Previous Calendar Year Ser.). (Illus.). 104p. (Orig.). 2000. pap. 8.50 (*0-87290-147-5*) Corning.

New Glass Review: Annual Compendium of Contemporary Glass Made in Previous Calendar Year, No. 13. Corning Museum of Glass Staff. LC 81-641214. (Illus.). 56p. 1992. pap. 2.50 (*0-87290-128-9*) Corning.

New Glass Review: Annual Compendium of Contemporary Glass Made in Previous Calendar Year, No. 17. Corning Museum of Glass Staff. LC 81-641214. 72p. 1996. pap. 8.50 (*0-87290-137-8*) Corning.

New Glasses. Houghton Mifflin Company Staff. (Literature Experience 1993 Ser.). (J). 1993. pap. 4.48 (*0-395-62582-3*) HM.

New Glasses. Mary Rogers & Bernada D. Rosario. (Foundations Ser.). 28p. (J). (gr. 1). 1992. pap. text 4.50 (*1-56843-071-X*) EMG Networks.

New Glasses: Big Book. Mary Rogers & Bernada D. Rosario. (Foundations Ser.). 28p. (J). (gr. 1). 1992. pap. text 23.00 (*1-56843-021-3*) EMG Networks.

New Global Banker: What Every U. S. Bank Must Know to Compete Internationally. Hazel J. Johnson. LC 94-161463. 1993. text 37.50 (*1-55738-358-8*, Irwn Prfssnl) McGraw-Hill Prof.

New Global Economy & Developing Countries. Dani Rodrik. LC 98-54766. 10p. 1998. pap. text 13.95 (*1-56517-027-X*) Overseas Dev Council.

New Global Economy & the Developing Countries: Essays in International Economics & Development. Gerald K. Helleiner. (Illus.). 304p. 1990. text 90.00 (*1-85278-329-X*) E Elgar.

New Global Economy & the Developing Countries: Essays in International Economics & Development. Gerald K. Helleiner. LC 93-19989. 304p. 1993. pap. 30.00 (*1-85278-848-8*) E Elgar.

New Global Economy in the Information Age: Reflections on Our Changing World. Martin Carnoy et al. LC 92-33652. 170p. (C). 1993. pap. 15.95 (*0-271-00910-1*) Pa St U Pr.

***New Global Human Order.** Cheddi Jagan & Janet Jagan. 1999. 12.00 (*0-9684059-1-6*) Hrpy.

New Global Leaders: Richard Branson, Percy Barnevik, & David Simon. De Vries Manfred F.R. Kets Staff & Elizabeth Florent-Treacy. LC HD62.4.K484 1999. 224p. 1999. 28.50 (*0-7879-4657-5*) Jossey-Bass.

New Global Oil Market: Understanding Energy Issues in the World Economy. Siamack Shojai. LC 94-25960. 280p. 1995. 69.50 (*0-275-94583-9*, Praeger Pubs) Greenwood.

New Global Order: A World Regional Geography. Michael Bradshaw. LC 96-84098. 624p. (C). 1996. text. write for info. (*0-697-21692-6*, WCB McGr Hill) McGrw-H Hghr Educ.

New Global Order: World Regional Geography. 2nd ed. Michael Bradshaw. 148p. 1999. pap. 22.81 (*0-697-38517-5*); pap. text 52.25 (*0-697-38514-0*) McGraw.

New Global Partnerships: Defining the Burdens & Sharing the Costs. David F. Gordon. (Overseas Development Council Ser.: Vol. 22). 112p. 1998. pap. text 13.95 (*1-56517-025-3*) Johns Hopkins.

New Global Resource Book. 250p. 1993. ring bd. 30.00 (*0-614-03006-4*) Amer Forum.

New Globalism & Developing Countries. Ed. by John H. Dunning & Khalil A. Hamdani. LC 99-490580. 346p. 1997. pap. 29.95 (*92-808-0944-X*, Pub. by UN Univ Pr) Brookings.

New Goals for Old Age. Ed. by George Lawton. LC 76-169390. (Family in America Ser.). 230p. 1972. reprint ed. 17.95 (*0-405-03868-2*) Ayer.

New Goals in Police Management. Ed. by Bruce Smith. LC 75-154580. (Police in America Ser.). 1971. reprint ed. 13.95 (*0-405-03386-9*) Ayer.

New Goat Handbook. Ulrich Jaudas. (Illus.). 1989. pap. 9.95 (*0-8120-4090-2*) Barron.

New Gocco Guide. (Illus.). 245p. 1996. pap. 29.95 (*0-9655387-0-2*) Think Ink WA.

New God-Image: A Study of Jung's Key Letters Concerning the Evolution of the Western God-Image. Edward F. Edinger. LC 95-51642. (Illus.). 206p. (Orig.). 1996. pap. 24.95 (*0-933029-98-5*, 985) Chiron Pubns.

New God, New Nation: Protestants & Self-Reconstruction Nationalism in Korea, 1896-1937. Kenneth M. Wells. LC 90-21320. 224p. (C). 1991. text 34.00 (*0-8248-1338-3*) UH Pr.

New Golden Bough. abr. ed. James George Frazer. Ed. by Theodore H. Gaster. LC 59-6125. 1959. 52.95 (*0-87599-036-3*) S G Phillips.

New Golden Dawn Ritual Tarot: Keys to the Rituals, Symbolism, Magic & Divination. Chic Cicero & Sandra T. Cicero. LC 91-10428. (New Age Tarot Ser.). (Illus.). 256p. (Orig.). 1999. pap. 14.95 (*0-87542-139-3*) Llewellyn Pubns.

New Golden Door to Retirement & Living in Costa Rica: A Guide to Living & Investing in a Tropical Paradise. 11th ed. Christopher Howard. Orig. Title: Golden Door to Retirement & Living in Costa Rica. (Illus.). 300p. 24.95 (*1-881233-37-5*, Pub. by Costa Rica Bks) Sunbelt Pubns.

New Golden Retriever. Marcia R. Schlehr. (Illus.). 288p. 1996. per. 25.95 (*0-87605-187-5*) Howell Bks.

New Golden Rule: Community & Morality in a Democratic Society. Amitai Etzioni. 336p. 1998. pap. 16.00 (*0-465-04999-0*, Pub. by Basic) HarpC.

New Golden Treasury of English Verse. Ed. by Edward Leeson. 506p. (Orig.). 1994. pap. 32.50 (*0-333-61649-9*, Pub. by Papermac) Trans-Atl Phila.

New Golf Mind. Gary Wiren & Richard Coop. 160p. 1985. pap. 9.00 (*0-671-62026-6*) S&S Trade.

New Good Cake Book. Dalsass. 1999. pap. 14.95 (*0-393-31882-6*) Norton.

New Good Cake Book: Over 125 Delicious Recipes That Can Be Prepared in 30 Minutes or Less. large type ed. Diana Dalsass. LC 96-48726. (Spec-Hall Ser.). 361p. 1997. lib. bdg. 26.95 (*0-7838-8050-2*, G K Hall Lrg Type) Mac Lib Ref.

New Good Housekeeping Cookbook. Good Housekeeping Editors et al. Ed. by Mildred Ying et al. LC 86-81549. (Illus.). 832p. 1986. 25.00 (*0-688-03897-2*, Hearst) Hearst Commns.

New Good Housekeeping Cookbook: Revised Edition. Good Housekeeping Editors. 800p. 1999. mass mkt. 7.99 (*0-380-81167-7*, Avon Bks) Morrow Avon.

New Good Old Index. William D. Goodrich. 602p. (Orig.). 1994. pap. 29.95 (*0-938501-20-8*) Wessex.

New Good Ole Boy's Cook Book. (Illus.). viii, 236p. 1999. mass mkt. 14.95 (*0-9667654-0-0*) Jodon Pubg.

New Good Vibrations Guide to Sex: How to Have Fun Safe Sex. 2nd rev. ed. Cathy Winks & Anne Semans. LC 97-2426. (Illus.). 300p. (Orig.). 1997. pap. 21.95 (*1-57344-069-8*) Cleis Pr.

New Gospel: Good News for Christians. Eric Bowes. 88p. 1958. reprint ed. 14.95 (*0-933770-67-7*) Kalimat.

New Gospel Parallels: Mark. 2nd rev. ed. Robert W. Funk. (Illus.). 288p. 1990. 21.95 (*0-944344-12-7*) Polebridge Pr.

New Gospel Parallels: Mark. 3rd ed. Robert W. Funk. (Foundations & Facets: Reference Ser.). (Illus.). 288p. 1990. pap. 19.95 (*0-944344-13-5*) Polebridge Pr.

New Gourmet Light: Simple & Sophisticated Recipes for the Health-Conscious Cook. 3rd ed. Greer Underwood. LC 98-30910. (Illus.). 250p. 1998. pap. 14.95 (*0-7627-0322-9*) Globe Pequot.

New Goverance for Rural America: Creating Intergovernmental Partnerships. Beryl A. Radin et al. LC 95-46677. (Rural America Ser.). 240p. (C). 1996. 29.95 (*0-7006-0770-6*); pap. 17.95 (*0-7006-0771-4*) U Pr of KS.

New Governance: Strategies for an Era of Health Reform. Russell C. Coile, Jr. LC 93-44914. 241p. 1994. text 22.00 (*1-56793-007-7*, 0940) Health Admin Pr.

New Governments West of the Alleghenies Before 1780: Introductory to a Study of the Organization & Admission of New States. George H. Alden. LC 70-106117. (First American Frontier Ser.). (Illus.). 1971. reprint ed. 12.95 (*0-405-02822-9*) Ayer.

New Grab a Pencil Book of Crosswords. Richard B. Manchester. 1998. pap. text 6.95 (*0-88486-227-5*, Bristol Park Bks) Arrowood Pr.

New Grab a Pencil Book of Word Games. Richard B. Manchester. 1998. pap. text 6.95 (*0-88486-228-3*, Bristol Park Bks) Arrowood Pr.

New Graft on the Family Tree. Isabella Alden. (Grace Livingston Hill Library: No. 17). 1997. pap. 5.99 (*0-8423-3193-X*) Tyndale Hse.

New Grammar in Action, Bk. 1. Barbara Foley & Elizabeth Neblett. (Global ESL/ELT Ser.). 200p. (J). 1997. pap., suppl. ed. 21.95 incl. audio (*0-8384-6720-2*) Heinle & Heinle.

New Grammar in Action, Bk. 2. Barbara Foley & Elizabeth Neblett. 200p. (J). 1998. pap. 21.95 incl. audio (*0-8384-6724-5*) Heinle & Heinle.

New Grammar in Action, Bk. 3. Barbara Foley & Elizabeth Neblett. 200p. (J). 1998. pap. 21.95 incl. audio (*0-8384-6729-6*) Heinle & Heinle.

New Grammarians Funeral. Ed. by Brynmill Press Ltd. Staff. 203p. (C). 1989. 110.00 (*0-907839-30-4*, Pub. by Brynmill Pr Ltd) St Mut.

New Grammarian's Funeral. Ian Robinson. LC 75-6009. (Illus.). 190p. 1978. pap. text 21.95 (*0-521-29316-2*) Cambridge U Pr.

New Graphic Communications Trade Customs & Business Practices. 58p. 10.00 (*0-614-25590-2*, 00GM44701) Print Indus Am.

New Graphic Design School. Alan Swann. 1991. text 29.95 (*0-442-30423-4*, VNR) Wiley.

New Graphic Design School. 2nd ed. Alan Swann. LC 97-14317. (Design & Graphic Design Ser.). 1997. pap. 34.95 (*0-442-02549-1*, VNR) Wiley.

New Graphic Design School. 2nd ed. Alan Swann. 192p. 1997. pap. 39.95 (*0-471-28834-9*, VNR) Wiley.

New Gravity: A New Force - A New Mass - A New Acceleration Unifying Gravity with Light. Kenneth G. Salem. (Illus.). 208p. (Orig.). 1994. pap. 12.00 (*0-9625398-1-3*) Salem Bks.

New Great American Brand Name Recipes Cookbook. (Illus.). 384p. 1993. 39.95 (*1-56173-660-0*, 2016900) Pubns Intl Ltd.

New Great Dane. 288p. 1998. 27.95 (*0-87605-167-0*) Howell Bks.

New Great Dutch English Dictionary. 2nd ed. H. Jansonius. 1973. 350.00 (*0-7859-7503-9*, 9061100321) Fr & Eur.

New Great English-Russian Dictionary, 2 vols. 4th rev. ed. I. R. Galperin. 1685p. 1988. 30.00 (*0-8285-0603-5*) Firebird NY.

New Great English-Russian Dictionary, 3 vols., Set. Collets. (C). 1992. 1035.00 (*0-89771-853-4*, Pub. by Collets) St Mut.

New Great Game in Muslim Central Asia. 1997. lib. bdg. 251.95 (*0-8490-6159-8*) Gordon Pr.

New Great Game in Muslim Central Asia. M. E. Ahrari & James Beal. (Illus.). 91p. (C). 2000. reprint ed. pap. text 30.00 (*0-7881-3492-2*) DIANE Pub.

New Great Transformation? Change & Continuity in East-Central Europe. Ed. by Christopher G. Bryant & Edmund Mokrzycki. LC 93-20938. (Illus.). 240p. (C). 1994. pap. 27.99 (*0-415-09250-7*) Routledge.

New Greek-English Interlinear New Testament. 913p. 1993. bond lthr. 44.99 (*0-8423-4565-5*) Tyndale Hse.

New Greek-English Interlinear New Testament. Ed. by J. D. Douglas. Tr. by Robert K. Brown & Philip W. Comfort. 928p. 1990. 39.99 (*0-8423-1213-7*) Tyndale Hse.

New Greek Reader. Ed. by Alston H. Chase & Henry Phillips, Jr. LC 54-12234. (Illus.). 480p. (gr. 10 up). reprint ed. 148.80 (*0-8357-9169-6*, 201672800005) Bks Demand.

New Green Christmas: How to Make This & Every Holiday an Ecological Celebration. 2nd ed. Evergreen Alliance Staff. (Illus.). 128p. 1991. pap. 5.95 (*1-879904-00-4*) Halo Bks.

New Green over Old Green. Mary Kennedy. 1979. pap. 5.95 (*0-910664-48-X*) Gotham.

New Greenland. A. R. Eguiguren. LC 96-67122. 274p. (Orig.). 1996. pap. 11.95 (*1-883378-96-6*) Sun on Earth.

New Gresham Encyclopaedia of the World, 12 vols. Angelo S. Rappoport. 1991. 5500.00 (*81-85484-18-X*, Pub. by Print Hse) St Mut.

***New Grilling Book: Charcoal, Gas, Smokers, Indoor Grills, Rotisseries.** Better Homes & Gardens. 372p. 2000. ring bd. 29.95 (*0-696-21029-0*, Better Homes) Meredith Bks.

New Grolier Children's Encyclopedia. Grolier Educational Staff. LC 98-7378. (J). (gr. 2-6). 1998. lib. bdg. 225.00 (*0-7172-9373-4*) Grolier Educ.

New Grolier Encyclopedia of World War II, 8 vols., Set. (Illus.). (YA). (gr. 5 up). 1995. lib. bdg 235.00 (*0-7172-7508-6*) Grolier Educ.

N

New Ground. Nancy Dilingham. LC 98-8790. 159p. 1998. pap. 9.95 (*1-56664-134-9*) WorldComm.

New Ground: Western American Narrative & the Literary Canon. A. Carl Bredahl, Jr. LC 88-38938. xii, 196p. 1989. 45.00 (*0-8078-1854-2*) U of NC Pr.

New Group Theory for Mathematical Physics Gas Dynamics & Turbulence. Gabriel A. Oyibo. 187p. 1993. lib. bdg. 145.00 (*1-56072-123-5*) Nova Sci Pubs.

New Grove Composer Biography Schubert. Maurice J. Brown. (New Grove Composer Biography Ser.). 1997. pap. 12.95 (*0-393-31586-X*) Norton.

New Grove Dictionary. S. Sadie. 1995. pap. write for info. (*0-312-13656-0*) Shiloh Med.

New Grove Dictionary, Vol. 1. Stanley Sadie. 1999. pap. write for info. (*0-312-13657-9*) St Martin.

New Grove Dictionary, Vol. 2. Stanley Sadie. 1999. pap. write for info. (*0-312-14164-5*) St Martin.

New Grove Dictionary, Vol. 3. Stanley Sadie. 1999. pap. write for info. (*0-312-14165-3*) St Martin.

New Grove Dictionary, Vol. 4. Stanley Sadie. 1999. pap. write for info. (*0-312-14166-1*) St Martin.

New Grove Dictionary, Vol. 5. Stanley Sadie. 1999. pap. write for info. (*0-312-14167-X*) St Martin.

New Grove Dictionary, Vol. 6. Stanley Sadie. 1999. pap. write for info. (*0-312-14168-8*) St Martin.

New Grove Dictionary, Vol. 7. Stanley Sadie. 1999. pap. write for info. (*0-312-14169-6*) St Martin.

New Grove Dictionary, Vol. 8. Stanley Sadie. 1999. pap. write for info. (*0-312-14170-X*) St Martin.

New Grove Dictionary, Vol. 9. Stanley Sadie. 1999. pap. write for info. (*0-312-14171-8*) St Martin.

New Grove Dictionary, Vol. 10. Stanley Sadie. 1999. pap. write for info. (*0-312-14172-6*) St Martin.

New Grove Dictionary, Vol. 11. Stanley Sadie. 1999. pap. write for info. (*0-312-14173-4*) St Martin.

New Grove Dictionary, Vol. 12. Stanley Sadie. 1999. pap. write for info. (*0-312-14174-2*) St Martin.

New Grove Dictionary, Vol. 13. Stanley Sadie. 1999. pap. write for info. (*0-312-14176-9*) St Martin.

New Grove Dictionary, Vol. 14. Stanley Sadie. 1999. pap. write for info. (*0-312-14177-7*) St Martin.

New Grove Dictionary, Vol. 15. Stanley Sadie. 1999. pap. write for info. (*0-312-14178-5*) St Martin.

New Grove Dictionary, Vol. 16. Stanley Sadie. 1999. pap. write for info. (*0-312-14179-3*) St Martin.

New Grove Dictionary, Vol. 17. Stanley Sadie. 1999. pap. write for info. (*0-312-14180-7*) St Martin.

New Grove Dictionary, Vol. 18. Stanley Sadie. 1999. pap. write for info. (*0-312-14181-5*) St Martin.

New Grove Dictionary, Vol. 19. Stanley Sadie. 1999. pap. write for info. (*0-312-14182-3*) St Martin.

New Grove Dictionary, Vol. 20. Stanley Sadie. 1999. pap. write for info. (*0-312-14183-1*) St Martin.

New Grove Dictionary of American Music, 4 Vols. Ed. by H. Wiley Hitchcock & Stanley Sadie. LC 86-404. (Illus.). 2600p. (C). 1986. 725.00 (*0-943818-36-2*) Groves Dictionaries.

New Grove Dictionary of Jazz, 2 vols. Ed. by Barry D. Kernfeld. LC 87-25452. (Illus.). 1600p. 1988. 395.00 (*0-935859-39-X*) Groves Dictionaries.

New Grove Dictionary of Music & Musicians, 20 vol. Stanely Sadie. 1998. 725.00 (*1-56159-229-3*) Groves Dictionaries.

New Grove Dictionary of Music & Musicians, 20 vols. 6th ed. Ed. by Stanley Sadie. LC 79-26207. 18000p. 1980. 2300.00 (*0-333-23111-2*) Groves Dictionaries.

*__New Grove Dictionary of Music & Musicians, 29 vols., Set.__ 2nd rev. ed. Ed. by Stanley Sadie & John Tyrrell. (Illus.). 25000p. 2000. lib. bdg. 4850.00 (*1-56159-239-0*) Groves Dictionaries.

New Grove Dictionary of Musical Instruments, 3 Vols., Set. Ed. by Stanley Sadie. LC 84-9062. (Dictionaries of Music Ser.). (Illus.). 1600p. 1984. 550.00 (*0-943818-05-2*) Groves Dictionaries.

New Grove Dictionary of Opera, 4 vols. Ed. by Stanley Sadie. (Illus.). 5400p. 1998. reprint ed. pap. 275.00 (*1-56159-228-5*) Groves Dictionaries.

New Grove Dictionary of Opera, 4 Vols., Set. Ed. by Stanley Sadie. (Illus.). 5400p. 1992. 850.00 (*0-935859-92-6*) Groves Dictionaries.

New Grove Early Romantic Masters, I: Chopin, Schumann, & Liszt. Nicholas Temperley et al. (New Grove Composer Biography Ser.). 1985. 25.00 (*0-393-01691-9*) Norton.

New Grove Early Romantic Masters, II: Weber, Berlioz, & Mendelssohn. John Warrack et al. (New Grove Composer Biography Ser.). (Illus.). 1985. pap. 9.95 (*0-393-30096-X*) Norton.

*__New Grove Haydn.__ Ed. by James Webster & Georg Feder. (Illus.). 208p. 2000. pap. 16.95 (*0-312-23323-X*, St Martin Griffin) St Martin.

New Grove Modern Masters: Bartok, Stravinsky, Hindemith. Laszlo Somfai et al. Ed. by Stanley Sadie. (New Grove Composer Biography Ser.). 292p. 1984. pap. 9.95 (*0-393-30097-8*) Norton.

*__New Grove Mozart.__ Ed. by Cliff Eisen & Stanley Sadie. (Illus.). 176p. 2000. pap. 12.95 (*0-312-23325-6*, St Martin Griffin) St Martin.

New Grove Mozart. Stanley Sadie. (New Grove Composer Biography Ser.). (Illus.). 1983. pap. 12.95 (*0-393-30084-6*) Norton.

New Grove Mozart. Stanley Sadie. pap. write for info. (*0-393-31593-2*) Norton.

New Grove North European Baroque Masters. Joshua Rifkin et al. (New Grove Composer Biography Ser.). (Illus.). 1985. pap. 9.95 (*0-393-30099-4*) Norton.

New Grove Russian Masters II: Rimsky-Korsakov, Skryabin, Rakhmaninov, Prokofiev, Shostakovich. Gerald E. Abraham et al. (Orig.). 1986. 25.00 (*0-393-02283-8*) Norton.

*__New Grove Stravinsky: The New Grove Composer Biographies.__ Ed. by Stephen Walsh. (Illus.). 112p. 2000. pap. 14.95 (*0-312-23326-4*, St Martin Griffin) St Martin.

New Grove Twentieth Century English Masters. Diana McVeagh. pap. write for info. (*0-393-31595-9*) Norton.

New Grove Twentieth Century English Masters: Elgar, Delius, Vaughan, Tippett, Holst, Williams, Walton & Britten. Diana McVeagh et al. 1986. pap. 16.95 (*0-393-30351-9*) Norton.

New Grove Twentieth Century French. Jean M. Nectoux. pap. write for info. (*0-393-31589-4*) Norton.

New Grove Twentieth Century French Masters. Jean-Michel Nectoux. 1986. 25.00 (*0-393-02284-6*) Norton.

New Grove Twentieth Century French Masters: Faure, Debussy, Satie, Ravel, Poulenc, Messaien. Jean-Michel Nectoux. 1986. pap. 14.95 (*0-393-30350-0*) Norton.

*__New Grove Wagner: The New Grove Composer Biographies.__ Ed. by Barry Millington. (Illus.). 112p. 2000. pap. 12.95 (*0-312-23324-8*, St Martin Griffin) St Martin.

New Growth. Joy Bennett. 30p. 1998. pap. 5.00 (*0-9632649-4-X*) J Bennett.

New Growth No. 2: Contemporary Short Stories by Texas Writers. Ed. by Mark Busby. LC 93-71686. 280p. (Orig.). 1993. pap. 12.95 (*0-931722-96-9*) Corona Pub.

New Growth Theory: An Applied Perspective. Jatikumar Sengupta. LC 98-42877. 256p. 1999. 85.00 (*1-85898-875-6*) E Elgar.

New Grrrl in Town. R. A. Noonan. (Monsterville Ser.). (J). (gr. 3-7). 1996. pap. 3.99 (*0-614-15783-8*) Aladdin.

New Grub Street. George R. Gissing. Ed. & Intro. by John Goode. LC 99-191923. (Oxford World's Classics Ser.). (Illus.). 576p. 1999. pap. 10.95 (*0-19-283658-7*) OUP.

New Grub Street. George R. Gissing. 1997. pap. 9.95 (*0-460-87724-0*, Everyman's Classic Lib) Tuttle Pubng.

New Grub Street. George R. Gissing. Ed. by Bernard Bergonzi. (English Library). 560p. 1976. pap. 12.95 (*0-14-043032-6*, Penguin Classics) Viking Penguin.

New Guardians of the Press: Selected Profiles of America's Women Newspaper Editors. Ed. by Judith G. Clabes. LC 83-71282. 140p. 1983. 18.95 (*0-89730-106-4*) R J Berg.

New Guide for Better Technical Presentations: Applying Proven Techniques with Modern Tools. Ed. by Robert M. Woelfle. (Illus.). 384p. (C). 1992. pap. 39.95 (*0-87942-283-1*, PP0277-4) Inst Electrical.

*__New Guide to Babycare.__ Anness Publishing Staff. 2000. pap. 15.00 (*0-7548-0515-8*) Anness Pub.

New Guide to Bahrain. Peter Vine. (Illus.). 120p. (C). 1995. pap. 50.00 (*0-907151-48-5*, Pub. by IMMEL Pubng) St Mut.

New Guide to Better Fishing. Ralph Bashford. (Illus.). 252p. 1987. pap. 6.00 (*0-9617953-0-1*) Otha Bk.

New Guide to Better Writing see Reference Collection Boxed Set

New Guide to Better Writing. Rudolf Flesch & A. H. Lass. 304p. 1989. mass mkt. 4.50 (*0-446-31504-4*, Pub. by Warner Bks) Little.

New Guide to Capital Cost Estimations. ICHEM Engineers Staff. (Institution of Chemical Engineers Symposum Ser.). 1983. pap. 17.00 (*0-08-031407-4*, Pergamon Pr) Elsevier.

New Guide to Distance Running. rev. ed. Runner's World Editors. (Illus.). 400p. 1983. reprint ed. 11.95 (*0-89037-133-4*); reprint ed. pap. 8.95 (*0-89037-270-5*) Anderson World.

New Guide to Effective Media Relations. Ed. by Nancy S. Raley & Laura Carter. 101p. 1988. 20.00 (*0-89964-255-1*, 24402) Coun Adv & Supp Ed.

New Guide to Fruit. Kate Whiteman. (Illus.). 128p. 1999. pap. 15.95 (*1-85967-895-5*, Lorenz Bks) Anness Pub.

New Guide to Graphic Design. Bob Cotton. 1990. 25.98 (*1-55521-508-4*) Bk Sales Inc.

New Guide to Herbs. Lorenz Staff. Date not set. 14.95 (*1-85967-736-3*) Anness Pub.

New Guide to Horses. Lorenz Staff. 1998. 27.50 (*1-85967-777-0*) Anness Pub.

*__New Guide to Massage: A Guide to Massage Techniques for Health, Relaxation & Vitality.__ Carole McGilvery. (Illus.). 96p. 1998. 16.95 (*1-85967-194-2*, Lorenz Bks) Anness Pub.

New Guide to Mushrooms. Lorenz Staff. 1998. 14.95 (*1-85967-735-5*) Anness Pub.

New Guide to Old Rome. Mary C. Kelley. 400p. 2000. pap. 19.95 (*1-879899-23-X*) Newjoy Pr.

New Guide to Palmistry: The Mystery of Your Palm & How It Affects Your Life. Psychos. 200p. 1995. pap. 6.95 (*0-572-01378-7*, Pub. by Foulsham UK) Assoc Pubs Grp.

New Guide to Reading & Studying the Bible. Wilfrid J. Harrington. 192p. 1989. pap. 30.00 (*0-905092-42-2*, Pub. by Veritas Pubns) St Mut.

New Guide to Sea & Sea. Joe Liburdi & Cara Sherman. LC 98-65719. (Illus.). 320p. 1998. mass mkt. 24.95 (*0-9621111-3-9*) Orca Pubns.

New Guide to Skiing. A. Joseph Heckelman. 144p. 1999. pap. 21.95 (*0-393-31966-0*) Norton.

New Guide to Skiing. Martin Heckelman. (Illus.). 1995. pap. 17.95 (*0-393-30609-7*, Norton Paperbks) Norton.

New Guide to Spices. Sallie Morris. 1998. 12.98 (*1-84038-073-X*) Random.

New Guide to Spirits & Liqueur. Lorenz Staff. 1998. 14.95 (*1-85967-734-7*) Anness Pub.

New Guide to Student Recruitment Marketing. Ed. by Virginia C. Smith & Susan Hunt. (Illus.). 95p. (Orig.). 1986. pap. 8.00 (*0-89964-245-4*, 24501) Coun Adv & Supp Ed.

New Guide to the Collections in the Library of the American Philosophical Society. J. Stephen Catlett. LC 86-71834. (Memoirs Ser.: Vol. 66S). (C). 1987. 20.00 (*0-87169-660-6*, M66S-CAS) Am Philos.

New Guide to the Debate about God. Martin Prozesky. 200p. 1992. pap. write for info. (*0-86980-877-X*, Pub. by Univ Natal Pr) Intl Spec Bk.

New Guide to the English Tongue. Thomas Dilworth. LC 78-14283. (American Linguistics Ser.). 176p. 1978. reprint ed. 50.00 (*0-8201-1322-0*) Schol Facsimiles.

New Guide to Treasure Hunting. H. Glenn Carson. 160p. 1992. 12.95 (*0-941620-45-X*) Carson Ent.

New Guide to Vegetables: A Comprehensive Cook's Guide to Identifying, Choosing & Using the Vegetables. Christine Ingram. (Illus.). 1997. write for info. (*1-901289-87-7*) Hermes Hse.

New Guide to Washington. rev. ed. Michael Prince. (Illus.). 96p. 1998. pap. 6.50 (*1-879295-25-3*) L B Prince.

New Guide to Washington D. C. 8 Tours with 80 Photos - City Maps. Michael B. Prince. (Illus.). 82p. 1990. pap. 5.95 (*1-879295-03-2*) L B Prince.

New Guidelines - A Kestrel for a Knave: Pupils' Booklet. Stanley Thornes. (C). 1988. student ed. 35.00 (*1-85234-049-5*, Pub. by S Thornes Pubs) St Mut.

New Guidelines - Of Mice & Men: Pupils' Booklet. Stanley Thornes. (C). 1990. student ed. 37.50 (*0-7487-0117-6*, Pub. by S Thornes Pubs) Trans-Atl Phila.

New Guidelines - The Crucible: Pupils' Booklet. Stanley Thornes. (C). 1990. student ed. 22.50 (*0-7487-0119-2*, Pub. by S Thornes Pubs) Trans-Atl Phila.

New Guidelines for Diagnosing & Treating Prostate Cancer. 1996. write for info. (*0-614-96417-2*) Hlth Edu Lit.

New Guidelines for Surviving Prostate Cancer. James Lewis, Jr. & E. Roy Berger. LC 95-50596. (Illus.). 460p. 1997. pap. 22.95 (*1-883257-13-1*) Hlth Edu Lit.

New Guidelines for Surviving Prostrate Cancer. James Lewis, Jr. & Roy Berger. 1996. pap. 18.95 (*0-915253-47-X*) Wilkerson Pub Co.

New Guidelines for Wind Turbine Gearboxes. Robert L. Errichello & B. McNiff. (Technical Papers: Vol. 97FTM8). (Illus.). 5p. 1997. pap. text 30.00 (*1-55589-702-9*) AGMA.

New Guinea. William P. Mack. (Destroyer Ser.). 320p. 1993. 22.95 (*1-877853-32-1*) Nautical & Aviation.

New Guinea. 2nd ed. Kal Muller. LC 76-18466. (Regional Guides of Indonesia Ser.). (Illus.). 288p. 1994. pap. 15.95 (*0-8442-9898-0*, Passprt Bks) NTC Contemp Pub Co.

New Guinea: Journey into the Stone Age. 1994. pap. 12.95 (*0-8442-9901-4*, Passprt Bks) NTC Contemp Pub Co.

New Guinea: Journey into the Stone Age. 3rd rev. ed. Kal Muller. (Passport's Regional Guides of Indonesia Ser.). (Illus.). 208p. 1996. pap. 19.95 (*0-8442-8997-3*, 89973, Passprt Bks) NTC Contemp Pub Co.

New Guinea: United States Army Campaigns of World War 2. Edward J. Drea. 31p. 1993. pap. 1.50 (*0-16-061299-3*) USGPO.

New Guinea & Neighboring Areas: A Sociolinguistic Laboratory. Ed. by S. A. Wurm. (Contributions to the Sociology of Language Ser.: No. 24). 1979. text 50.00 (*90-279-7848-4*) Mouton.

New Guinea Art & Crafts: The Charles Rand Penney Collection. Charles R. Penney. (Illus.). 80p. 1988. 25.00 (*0-9620346-0-6*) C R Penney.

New Guinea Expedition, Fly River Area, 1936-1937. Richard Archbold & Austin L. Rand. LC 75-32797. (Illus.). reprint ed. 52.50 (*0-404-14100-5*) AMS Pr.

New Guinea Flatidae (Homoptera) Species Collected on Economic & Other Plants, with Descriptions of New Species. John T. Medler. (Bishop Museum Bulletin in Entomology Ser.: Vol. 2). (Illus.). 79p. (C). 1989. pap. 21.00 (*0-930897-38-2*) Bishop Mus.

New Guinea Impatiens: A Ball Guide. Ed. by Warren Banner & Michael Klopmeyer. LC 95-6865. (Illus.). 288p. 1995. pap. text 56.95 (*1-883052-07-6*, B024) Ball Pub.

New Guinea Skies: A Fighter Pilot's View of World War II. Wayne P. Rothgeb. LC 92-2916. (Illus.). 278p. 1992. 39.95 (*0-8138-0836-7*) Iowa St U Pr.

New Guinea Tapeworms & Jewish Grandmothers: Tales of Parasites & People. Robert S. Desowitz. 224p. 1987. reprint ed. pap. 12.95 (*0-393-30426-4*) Norton.

New Guitar Songbook. Frederick Noad. 160p. 1997. pap. 16.95 (*0-8256-1309-4*, FN 10032) Music Sales.

New Guitar Techniques for Sightreading. Arnie Berle. Ed. by Aaron Stang. 104p. (Orig.). (YA). 1991. pap. text 12.95 (*0-89898-583-8*, F3141GTX) Wrner Bros.

New Gym Shoes. Joe Yukish. (Illus.). 12p. (J). (gr. k-2). 1998. text 4.95 (*1-879835-33-9*, Kaeden) Kaeden Corp.

New Gymnarthrid Microsaur from the Lower Permian of Kansas with a Review of the Tuditanomorph Microsaurs (Amphibia) Hans-Peter Schultze & Brian Foreman. (Occasional Papers: No. 91). 25p. 1981. 1.00 (*0-317-04814-7*) U KS Nat Hist Mus.

*__New Habits: Today's Women Who Choose to Become Nuns.__ Isabel Losada. 195p. 1999. pap. 14.95 (*0-340-72238-X*, Pub. by Hodder & Stought Ltd) Trafalgar.

New Hacienda. Karen Witynski & Joe P. Carr. LC 99-25674. (Illus.). 144p. 1999. 39.95 (*0-87905-909-5*) Gibbs Smith Pub.

New Hacker's Dictionary. 3rd ed. Eric S. Raymond. (Illus.). 569p. 1996. 39.00 (*0-262-18178-9*); pap. text 19.50 (*0-262-68092-0*) MIT Pr.

New Haircuts, Pierced Ears & Braces. Barbara B. Miller. (Illus.). 162p. 1997. pap. 9.95 (*0-9658700-0-6*) B B Miller.

New Ham Survival Guide. Ed. by Rich Moseson. (Illus.). 16p. (Orig.). 1995. mass mkt. 1.00 (*0-943016-12-6*) CQ Commns Inc.

New Hampshire 2000! Coming Soon to a Calendar near You--The 21st Century! Carole Marsh. (Two Thousand! Ser.). (Illus.). (J). (gr. 3-12). 1998. pap. 19.95 (*0-7933-8763-9*); lib. bdg. 29.95 (*0-7933-8762-0*) Gallopade Intl.

New Hampshire see From Sea to Shining Sea

*__New Hampshire.__ (Switched on Schoolhouse Ser.). (Illus.). (J). 2000. pap. 24.95 (*0-7403-0281-7*) Alpha AZ.

New Hampshire. Dottie Brown. LC 92-28662. (Hello U. S. A. Ser.). (Illus.). 72p. (J). (gr. 3-6). 1993. lib. bdg. 19.95 (*0-8225-2730-8*, Lerner Publctns) Lerner Pub.

New Hampshire. Dottie Brown. (Hello U. S. A. Ser.). (Illus.). 72p. (J). (gr. 3-6). 1998. pap. 5.95 (*0-8225-9789-6*) Lerner Pub.

New Hampshire. Dennis B. Fradin. LC 92-9216. (From Sea to Shining Sea Ser.). (Illus.). 64p. (J). (gr. 3-5). 1992. pap. 7.95 (*0-516-43829-8*) Childrens.

New Hampshire. Keith W. Jennison. (Illus.). 102p. 1973. pap. 8.95 (*0-87233-828-2*) Bauhan.

*__New Hampshire.__ Kaiji Kawaguchi. 2000. pap. 6.95 (*1-56931-461-6*, Viz Comics) Viz Commns Inc.

New Hampshire. Sylvia McNair. (America the Beautiful Ser.). 144p. (J). (gr. 5-8). 1991. lib. bdg. 28.00 (*0-516-00475-1*) Childrens.

*__New Hampshire.__ R. Conrad Stein. LC 99-86345. (America the Beautiful Ser.). (J). 2000. 33.00 (*0-516-21071-8*) Childrens.

New Hampshire. Kathleen Thompson. LC 87-26480. (Portrait of America Library). 48p. (J). (gr. 4-8). 1996. pap. 5.95 (*0-8114-7455-0*) Raintree Steck-V.

New Hampshire. Kathleen Thompson. LC 87-26480. (Portrait of America Library). (Illus.). 48p. (YA). (gr. 3-6). 1996. lib. bdg. 22.83 (*0-8114-7349-X*) Raintree Steck-V.

New Hampshire. Anne Welsbacher. LC 97-27135. (United States Ser.). (Illus.). 32p. (J). 1998. lib. bdg. 19.93 (*1-56239-888-1*, Checkerboard Library) ABDO Pub Co.

New Hampshire. 2nd rev. ed. Nancy Elcock et al. (Insiders' Guide Ser.). (Illus.). 498p. 1999. pap. 15.95 (*1-57380-094-5*, The Insiders Guide) Falcon Pub Inc.

New Hampshire, 28. Capstone Press Geogra Staff. (J). 1998. 19.00 (*0-516-21304-0*) Childrens.

New Hampshire, 5 vols., Set. Steven Otfinoski. LC 97-50379. (Celebrate the States Ser.). 144p. (J). 1999. 35.64 (*0-7614-0669-7*, Benchmark NY) Marshall Cavendish.

New Hampshire: A Geography. William H. Wallace. 1996. text 39.50 (*0-86531-340-7*) Westview.

New Hampshire: A Guide to the Granite State. Federal Writers' Project Staff. (American Guidebook Ser.). 559p. 1938. reprint ed. 89.00 (*0-403-02179-0*) Somerset Pub.

New Hampshire: A Guide to the Granite State. Federal Writers' Project Staff & Writers Program-WPA Staff. (American Guide Ser.). 1989. reprint ed. lib. bdg. 79.00 (*0-7812-1028-3*, 1028) Rprt Serv.

New Hampshire: A Living Landscape. Photos by Peter E. Randall. (Illus.). 96p. 1996. 35.00 (*0-914339-56-7*, Pub. by P E Randall Pub) U Pr of New Eng.

New Hampshire: A Scenic Discovery. Clyde H. Smith. Ed. by James B. Patrick. (Scenic Discovery Ser.). (Illus.). 96p. 1983. 15.95 (*0-940078-07-4*) Foremost Pubs.

New Hampshire: An Epitome of Popular Government. Franklin B. Sanborn. LC 72-3768. (American Commonwealths Ser.: No. 16). reprint ed. 37.50 (*0-404-57216-2*) AMS Pr.

New Hampshire: An Explorer's Guide. 4th ed. Christina Tree. LC 98-13752. (Explorer's Guide Ser.). (Illus.). 447p. 1999. pap. 18.00 (*0-88150-450-5*, Pub. by Countryman) Norton.

New Hampshire: Crosscurrents in Its Development. 2nd ed. Nancy C. Heffernan & Ann Page Stecker. LC 96-4614. (Illus.). 238p. 1996. pap. 17.95 (*0-87451-757-5*) U Pr of New Eng.

*__New Hampshire: Drives, Day Trips & Weekend Excursions.__ 3rd ed. Steve Sherman. LC 98-46139. (Country Roads of... Ser.). (Illus.). 256p. (Orig.). 1999. reprint ed. pap. 12.95 (*1-56626-016-7*, 60167, Cntry Rds Pr) NTC Contemp Pub Co.

*__New Hampshire: Off the Beaten Path.__ 4th ed. Barbara Radcliffe Rogers & Stillman Rogers. LC 99-88412. (Off the Beaten Path Ser.). (Illus.). 176p. 2000. pap. 12.95 (*0-7627-0626-0*) Globe Pequot.

*__New Hampshire: The Spirit of America.__ Patricia Harris & David Lyon. LC 99-56048. (Art of the State Ser.). (Illus.). 96p. 2000. 12.95 (*0-8109-5571-7*, Pub. by Abrams) Time Warner.

*__New Hampshire: The Way I See It.__ John Clayton. (Illus.). 172p. 1999. pap. 16.95 (*0-9650684-3-9*) In The City.

New Hampshire: 9 Poems. Richard Eberhart. 11p. (C). 1980. pap. 5.00 (*0-913219-25-8*) Pym-Rand Pr.

New Hampshire - Collected Works of Federal Writers Project. Federal Writers' Project Staff. 1991. reprint ed. lib. bdg. 98.00 (*0-7812-5664-X*) Rprt Serv.

New Hampshire Actions & Proceedings. Ed. by Butterworth Staff. 690p. 1994. pap. 39.50 (*1-56257-148-6*, 21801-10, MICHIE); pap. 35.00 (*0-250-44435-6*, MICHIE) LEXIS Pub.

*__New Hampshire Advance Legislative Service 1999, No. 1.__ 140p. 1999. Price not set. (*0-327-09097-9*, 4564713) LEXIS Pub.

*__New Hampshire Advance Legislative Service 1999, No. 3.__ 300p. 1999. pap. Price not set. (*0-327-09744-2*, 4564913) LEXIS Pub.

New Hampshire & Extraterrestrials! A Look at the Sightings & Science in Our State. Carole Marsh. (Carole Marsh New Hampshire Bks.). (Illus.). (J). (gr. 3-12). 1997. pap. 19.95 (*0-7933-6422-1*); lib. bdg. 29.95 (*0-7933-6421-3*) Gallopade Intl.

New Hampshire & Other State Greats (Biographies) Carole Marsh. (Carole Marsh New Hampshire Bks.). (Illus.). (J). 1994. pap. 19.95 (*1-55609-845-6*); disk 29.95 (*1-55609-846-4*) Gallopade Intl.

N

An Asterisk (*) at the beginning of an entry indicates that the title is appearing for the first time.

New Hampshire & Other State Greats (Biographies) Carole Marsh. (Carole Marsh New Hampshire Bks.). (Illus.). (J). 1997. lib. bdg. 29.95 (*1-55609-844-8*) Gallopade Intl.

New Hampshire Annotation Service. Butterworth Staff. 130p. 1994. pap. 26.00 (*0-614-03163-X*, MICHIE) LEXIS Pub.

New Hampshire As a Royal Province. William H. Fry. LC 73-130938. (Columbia University. Studies in the Social Sciences: No. 79). reprint ed. 42.50 (*0-404-51079-5*) AMS Pr.

New Hampshire As It Is. Edwin A. Charlton. (Illus.). 623p. 1997. reprint ed. pap. 41.00 (*0-7884-0633-7*, C306) Heritage Bk.

***New Hampshire Atlas & Gazetteer.** 12th ed. DeLorme Mapping Staff. (Illus.). 1999. pap. 19.95 (*0-89933-242-0*) DeLorme Map.

New Hampshire Bandits, Bushwackers, Outlaws, Crooks, Devils, Ghosts, Desperadoes & Other Assorted & Sundry Characters! Carole Marsh. (Carole Marsh New Hampshire Bks.). (Illus.). (J). 1994. pap. 19.95 (*0-7933-0768-6*); lib. bdg. 29.95 (*0-7933-0769-4*); disk 29.95 (*0-7933-0770-8*) Gallopade Intl.

***New Hampshire Banks & Banking Laws Annotated, 1999-2000 Edition.** 252p. 1999. pap. 45.00 (*0-327-09959-3*, 2884212) LEXIS Pub.

New Hampshire Banks & Banking, 1998-99. LC 99-462621. 286p. 1998. write for info. (*0-327-07073-0*, 28842-11) LEXIS Pub.

New Hampshire "BIO" Bingo! 24 Must Know State People for Kids to Learn about While Having Fun! Carole Marsh. (Bingo! Ser.). (Illus.). (J). (gr. 2-8). 1998. pap. 14.95 (*0-7933-8609-8*) Gallopade Intl.

New Hampshire Bookstore Book: A Surprising Guide to Our State's Bookstores & Their Specialties for Students, Teachers, Writers & Publishers. Carole Marsh. (Carole Marsh New Hampshire Bks.). (Illus.). 1994. pap. 19.95 (*0-7933-2943-4*); lib. bdg. 29.95 (*0-7933-2942-6*); disk 29.95 (*0-7933-2944-2*) Gallopade Intl.

New Hampshire Branch of the Pease Family, Being the Results of a Search for the Ancestors of Patty Pease Who Married John Pivkering of Barnstead, N. H. L. S. Cox. 64p. 1993. reprint ed. pap. 13.00 (*0-8328-3775-X*); reprint ed. lib. bdg. 23.00 (*0-8328-3774-1*) Higginson Bk Co.

***New Hampshire Business Directory (2000-2001)** American Business Directories Staff et al. 688p. 2000. boxed set 375.00 incl. cd-rom (*0-7687-0229-1*) Am Busn Direct.

***New Hampshire Business Directory, 1999-2000.** American Business Directories Staff. 688p. 1999. boxed set 375.00 incl. cd-rom (*0-7687-0144-9*, 1048-714X) Am Busn Direct.

New Hampshire Census Index, 1880, 2 vols., Set. (Illus.). lib. bdg. write for info. (*0-89593-428-0*, Accel Indexing) Genealogical Srvcs.

New Hampshire Census Index, 1850 Mortality Schedule. (Illus.). lib. bdg. 48.00 (*0-89593-425-6*, Accel Indexing) Genealogical Srvcs.

New Hampshire Census Index, 1890 Union Veterans. Ronald V. Jackson. (Illus.). lib. bdg. 55.00 (*0-89593-696-8*, Accel Indexing) Genealogical Srvcs.

New Hampshire Census Index, 1870, 2 vols., Set. (Illus.). lib. bdg. write for info. (*0-89593-427-2*, Accel Indexing) Genealogical Srvcs.

New Hampshire Census Index, 1860 Mortality Schedule. (Illus.). lib. bdg. write for info. (*0-89593-426-4*, Accel Indexing) Genealogical Srvcs.

New Hampshire City & Town Atlas. Arrow Staff. 1992. 12.95 (*1-55751-441-0*) Arrow Map.

New Hampshire Civil Jury Instructions. 2nd ed. Walter L. Murphy & Daniel C. Pope. 400p. 1992. ring bd. 75.00 (*1-56257-310-1*, MICHIE) LEXIS Pub.

New Hampshire Civil Jury Instructions. 2nd ed. Walter L. Murphy & Daniel C. Pope. 400p. 1993. suppl. ed. 27.00 (*0-685-74472-8*, MICHIE) LEXIS Pub.

New Hampshire Civil Jury Instructions. 3rd ed. Walter L. Murphy. 456p. 1994. spiral bd. 89.00 (*0-250-40748-5*, MICHIE) LEXIS Pub.

New Hampshire Civil Jury Instructions. 3rd ed. Walter L. Murphy & Daniel C. Pope. 89.00 (*0-250-40766-3*) LEXIS Pub.

New Hampshire Civil Jury Instructions, Issue 5. Daniel C. Pope & Walter L. Murphy. LC 92-8094. 50p. 1998. ring bd. write for info. (*0-327-00510-6*, 8202715) LEXIS Pub.

***New Hampshire Civil Jury Instructions, Issue 6.** Walter L. Murphy & Daniel C. Pope. 50p. 1999. ring bd. write for info. (*0-327-01695-7*, 8202716) LEXIS Pub.

New Hampshire Civil Practice & Procedure, 1984-1993, Vols. 4-6. Richard V. Wiebusch. (New Hampshire Practice Ser.). 1700p. 1993. suppl. ed. 45.00 (*0-685-74295-4*, MICHIE) LEXIS Pub.

New Hampshire Classic Christmas Trivia: Stories, Recipes, Activities, Legends, Lore & More! Carole Marsh. (Carole Marsh New Hampshire Bks.). (Illus.). (J). 1994. pap. 19.95 (*0-7933-0771-6*); lib. bdg. 29.95 (*0-7933-0772-4*); disk 29.95 (*0-7933-0773-2*) Gallopade Intl.

New Hampshire Clocks, Silver, & Furniture: A Salute to Charles S. Parsons. Ed. by Michael K. Komanecky. 44p. (Orig.). 1988. pap. 6.00 (*0-929710-00-2*) Currier Gal.

New Hampshire Coastales. Carole Marsh. (Carole Marsh New Hampshire Bks.). (J). 1994. lib. bdg. 29.95 (*0-7933-7294-1*) Gallopade Intl.

New Hampshire Coastales. Carole Marsh. (Carole Marsh New Hampshire Bks.). (Illus.). (J). 1994. pap. 19.95 (*1-55609-839-1*); lib. bdg. 29.95 (*1-55609-838-3*); disk 29.95 (*1-55609-840-5*) Gallopade Intl.

***New Hampshire Code of Administrative Rules Annotated 10/99.** 3850p. 1999. Price not set. (*0-327-09776-0*, 4567513) LEXIS Pub.

New Hampshire Code of Administrative Rules Annotated, 1984-1991, 6 vols. 1994. ring bd., suppl. ed. 125.00 (*0-685-74143-5*, MICHIE) LEXIS Pub.

New Hampshire Code of Administrative Rules Annotated, 1984-1991, 4 vols., Set. annot. ed. Ed. by Butterworth Staff. 1994. ring bd. 275.00 (*0-88063-471-5*, MICHIE) LEXIS Pub.

New Hampshire Code of Administrative Rules, 1998, 4 vols. 2700p. 1998. 275.00 (*0-327-06017-4*, 45675-12) LEXIS Pub.

New Hampshire Code of Administrative Rules 3/99 Supplement. 280p. 1999. pap. write for info. (*0-327-08004-3*, 45687-17) LEXIS Pub.

New Hampshire Colony. Dennis B. Fradin. LC 87-14619. (Thirteen Colonies Ser.). (Illus.). 190p. (J). (gr. 4 up). 1987. lib. bdg. 30.00 (*0-516-00388-7*) Childrens.

New Hampshire Consolidated Index, 1994. Ed. by Butterworth Staff. 380p. 1994. 45.00 (*0-685-74750-6*, MICHIE) LEXIS Pub.

New Hampshire Corporations, Partnerships & Associations. Ed. by Butterworth Staff. 300p. 1994. pap. 30.00 (*0-88063-474-X*, MICHIE); pap. 30.00 (*0-250-44733-9*, MICHIE); pap. 40.00 (*0-250-44766-5*, MICHIE) LEXIS Pub.

New Hampshire Court Rules Annotated. Ernst D. Kuehl. 22p. 1994. ring bd., suppl. ed. write for info. (*0-614-03164-8*, MICHIE) LEXIS Pub.

New Hampshire Court Rules Annotated, 2 vols. annot. ed. Ed. by Butterworth Staff. 1000p. 1993. ring bd. 61.00 (*0-88063-475-8*, 45650-10, MICHIE) LEXIS Pub.

New Hampshire Court Rules Annotated June 1998 Replacement Pages. annot. ed. Ed. by Lexis Law Publishing Staff. 1998. ring bd. write for info. (*0-327-05020-9*, 45657-14) LEXIS Pub.

New Hampshire Court Rules Annotated Rules of Evidence - Desk Copy, 1999. 230p. 1998. write for info. (*0-327-06848-5*, 4566014) LEXIS Pub.

***New Hampshire Court Rules Annotated 2000-2001 Edition.** 1244p. 2000. write for info. (*0-327-11118-6*, 4567011) LEXIS Pub.

New Hampshire Court Rules Annotated 12/98 Replacement Pages. 750p. 1998. write for info. (*0-327-07092-7*, 45657-15) LEXIS Pub.

New Hampshire Court Rules Annotated 1999-2000 Edition. annot. ed. 1200p. 1999. 61.00 (*0-327-08769-2*, 45670-10) LEXIS Pub.

***New Hampshire Court Rules of Evidence--Desk Copy: 1999-2000 Edition.** Publisher's Editorial Staff. 230p. 1999. pap. 45.00 (*0-327-10179-2*, 4566015) LEXIS Pub.

***New Hampshire Crime in Perspective 2000.** Ed. by Kathleen O'Leary Morgan & Scott E. Morgan. 22p. 2000. spiral bd. 19.00 (*0-7401-0328-8*) Morgan Quitno Corp.

New Hampshire Crime Perspective, 1998. Ed. by Kathleen O'Leary Morgan & Scott E. Morgan. 20p. 1998. pap. 19.00 (*1-56692-928-8*) Morgan Quitno Corp.

New Hampshire Crime Perspectives, 1999. Kathleen O'Leary Morgan. 22p. 1999. spiral bd. 19.00 (*0-7401-0128-5*) Morgan Quitno Corp.

New Hampshire Criminal Code. Ed. by Butterworth Staff. 300p. 1994. pap. 33.00 (*0-88063-472-3*, MICHIE); pap. 30.00 (*0-250-44736-3*, MICHIE) LEXIS Pub.

***New Hampshire Criminal Code Advance Legislative Service: 1999 Edition.** 140p. 1999. pap. write for info. (*0-327-09859-7*, 2884612) LEXIS Pub.

New Hampshire Criminal Code Advance Legislative Service, 1998 Edition. 85p. 1998. pap. write for info. (*0-327-06385-8*, 2884611) LEXIS Pub.

New Hampshire Criminal Code, 1998-99 Edition. 366p. 1998. pap. write for info. (*0-327-06508-7*, 2881714) LEXIS Pub.

***New Hampshire Criminal Code, 1999-2000 Edition.** 380p. 1999. Price not set. (*0-327-19725-0*, 2881715) LEXIS Pub.

New Hampshire "Crinkum-Crankum" A Funny Word Book about Our State. Carole Marsh. (Carole Marsh New Hampshire Bks.). (Illus.). (J). 1994. pap. 19.95 (*0-7933-4896-X*); lib. bdg. 29.95 (*0-7933-4895-1*); disk 29.95 (*0-7933-4897-8*) Gallopade Intl.

New Hampshire Dingbats! Bk. 1: A Fun Book of Games, Stories, Activities & More about Our State That's All in Code! for You to Decipher. Carole Marsh. (Carole Marsh New Hampshire Bks.). (Illus.). (J). (gr. 3-12). 1994. pap. 19.95 (*0-7933-3861-1*); lib. bdg. 29.95 (*0-7933-3860-3*) Gallopade Intl.

New Hampshire DWI Manual. John A. Stephen. LC 96-76163. 293p. 1996. 75.00 (*1-55834-326-1*, 67213-10, MICHIE) LEXIS Pub.

New Hampshire DWI Manual. 2nd ed. John A. Stephen. 597p. 1999. pap. 95.00 (*0-327-01326-5*, 6721311) LEXIS Pub.

New Hampshire DWI Manual: 1997 Supplement. John Stephen. 101p. 1997. pap., suppl. ed. 32.50 (*1-55834-570-1*, 67214-10, MICHIE) LEXIS Pub.

New Hampshire DWI Manual: 1998 Cumulative Supplement. John A. Stephen. 170p. 1998. write for info. (*0-327-00226-3*, 67214-11) LEXIS Pub.

New Hampshire Early Census, Vol. 1. Ronald V. Jackson. (Illus.). 1981. lib. bdg. 38.00 (*0-89593-732-8*, Accel Indexing) Genealogical Srvcs.

New Hampshire Education Laws Annotated: 1998-99 Edition. Lexis Law Publishing Staff. 954p. 1998. pap. write for info. (*0-327-06672-5*) LEXIS Pub.

***New Hampshire Education Laws Annotated: 1999-2000 Edition.** annot. ed. 984p. 1999. pap. 50.00 incl. cd-rom (*0-327-10002-8*, 2887013) LEXIS Pub.

New Hampshire Environmental Law. 2nd ed. McLane, Graf, Raulerson & Middleton Staff. LC 94-73602. 341p. 1994. pap. text 89.00 (*0-86587-447-6*) Gov Insts.

New Hampshire Environmental Practice: Regulation & Compliance. Orr & Reno P. A. Staff. Ed. by Thomas C. Platt & Cordell A. Johnston. LC 92-14890. 680p. 1994. ring bd. 95.00 (*1-56257-190-7*, 83350-10, MICHIE) LEXIS Pub.

New Hampshire Environmental Practice: Regulation & Compliance. Orr & Reno P. A. Staff. Ed. by Thomas C. Platt & Cordell A. Johnston. LC 92-14890. 1993. ring bd., suppl. ed. 50.00 (*0-685-74438-8*, MICHIE) LEXIS Pub.

New Hampshire Evidence Manual. Charles G. Douglas, III. 500p. 1992. suppl. ed. 32.50 (*0-685-74457-4*, MICHIE) LEXIS Pub.

New Hampshire Evidence Manual. 2nd rev. ed. Charles G. Douglas, III. 500p. 1994. spiral bd. 75.00 (*1-56257-226-1*, MICHIE) LEXIS Pub.

New Hampshire Evidence Manual. 3rd ed. Charles G. Douglas. 1998. 85.00 (*0-327-00692-7*, 8203111) LEXIS Pub.

New Hampshire Facts & Factivities. Carole Marsh. (Carole Marsh State Bks.). (Illus.). (J). (gr. 4-7). 1996. pap., teacher ed. 19.95 (*0-7933-7905-9*, C Marsh) Gallopade Intl.

***New Hampshire Facts & Symbols.** Muriel L. Dubois. LC 99-53461. (States & Their Symbols Ser.). (Illus.). 24p. (J). (ps-3). 2000. lib. bdg. 15.93 (*0-7368-0524-9*, Hilltop Bks) Capstone Pr.

New Hampshire Family Law, 1992-93, 2 vols., Set, Vols. 3 & 3A. 2nd ed. Charles G. Douglas, III & Caroline G. Douglas. (New Hampshire Practice Ser.: Vol. 3 & 3A). 950p. 1994. 140.00 (*1-56257-316-0*, MICHIE) LEXIS Pub.

New Hampshire Family Law, 1992-93, 2 vols., Vol. 3 & 3A. 2nd ed. Charles G. Douglas, III & Caroline G. Douglas. 1993. ring bd., suppl. ed. 35.00 (*0-685-74469-8*, MICHIE) LEXIS Pub.

New Hampshire Family Records. William Copeley. 834p. (Orig.). 1995. pap. text 50.00 (*0-7884-0068-1*) Heritage Bk.

New Hampshire Federal Census Index, 1810. Ronald V. Jackson. (Illus.). 1976. lib. bdg. 47.00 (*0-89593-695-X*, Accel Indexing) Genealogical Srvcs.

New Hampshire Federal Census Index, 1800. Ronald V. Jackson. LC 77-85979. (Illus.). 1974. lib. bdg. 49.00 (*0-89593-083-8*, Accel Indexing) Genealogical Srvcs.

New Hampshire Federal Census Index, 1820. Ronald V. Jackson. LC 77-85981. (Illus.). 1976. lib. bdg. 55.00 (*0-89593-085-4*, Accel Indexing) Genealogical Srvcs.

New Hampshire Federal Census Index, 1830. Ronald V. Jackson. LC 77-85983. (Illus.). 1977. lib. bdg. 58.00 (*0-89593-086-2*, Accel Indexing) Genealogical Srvcs.

New Hampshire Federal Census Index, 1840. Ronald V. Jackson. LC 77-85984. (Illus.). 1976. lib. bdg. 58.00 (*0-89593-087-0*, Accel Indexing) Genealogical Srvcs.

New Hampshire Federal Census Index, 1850. Ronald V. Jackson. LC 77-86133. (Illus.). lib. bdg. 85.00 (*0-89593-088-9*, Accel Indexing) Genealogical Srvcs.

New Hampshire Federal Census Index, 1860. Ronald V. Jackson. 1992. 110.00 (*0-89593-851-0*, Accel Indexing) Genealogical Srvcs.

New Hampshire Federal Census Index, 1790. Ronald V. Jackson. (Illus.). 1978. lib. bdg. 39.00 (*0-89593-694-1*, Accel Indexing) Genealogical Srvcs.

New Hampshire Festival Fun for Kids! Carole Marsh. (Carole Marsh New Hampshire Bks.). (Illus.). (J). (gr. 3-12). 1994. pap. 19.95 (*0-7933-4014-4*); lib. bdg. 29.95 (*0-7933-4013-6*) Gallopade Intl.

New Hampshire Festival Fun for Kids! Carole Marsh. (Carole Marsh New Hampshire Bks.). (Illus.). (YA). (gr. 3-12). 1994. disk 29.95 (*0-7933-4015-2*) Gallopade Intl.

***New Hampshire Fire Laws: 1999-2000 Edition.** annot. ed. 269p. 1999. pap. 35.00 (*0-327-10001-X*, 2888511) LEXIS Pub.

New Hampshire Fire Laws 1998-99 Edition. 280p. 1999. write for info. (*0-327-07741-7*, 2888510) LEXIS Pub.

New Hampshire Fish & Game Laws. Ed. by Butterworth Staff. (New Hampshire Statutes Ser.). 200p. 1994. pap. 30.00 (*0-250-44734-7*, MICHIE) LEXIS Pub.

***New Hampshire Fish & Game Laws Annotated: 1999-2000 Edition.** 315p. 1999. pap. 37.50 (*0-327-10174-1*, 2886513) LEXIS Pub.

New Hampshire Fish & Game Laws Annotated, 1998-99 Edition. 287p. 1998. write for info. (*0-327-07102-8*, 28865-12) LEXIS Pub.

New Hampshire Fish & Game Laws, 1990-1992. 300p. 1994. pap. 30.00 (*0-88063-477-4*, MICHIE) LEXIS Pub.

New Hampshire for-Profit & Non-Profit Business Laws Annotated with Update Forms, 1998-99 Supplement. 38p. 1999. pap. write for info. (*0-327-07384-5*, 2886110) LEXIS Pub.

***New Hampshire For-Profit Business Laws Annotated with Updated Forms, 1999-2000 Edition.** 345p. 1999. 45.00 (*0-327-09972-0*, 2886012) LEXIS Pub.

New Hampshire Genealogical Record, Vol. 1. 1987. reprint ed. pap. 5.00 (*0-935207-90-2*) Danbury Hse Bks.

New Hampshire Genealogical Record, Vol. 2. 1987. reprint ed. pap. 5.00 (*0-935207-91-0*) Danbury Hse Bks.

New Hampshire Genealogical Record, Vol. 3. 1987. reprint ed. pap. 5.00 (*0-935207-92-9*) Danbury Hse Bks.

New Hampshire Genealogical Record, Vol. 4. 1987. reprint ed. pap. 5.50 (*0-935207-93-7*) Danbury Hse Bks.

New Hampshire Genealogical Record, Vol. 5. 1987. reprint ed. pap. 5.50 (*0-935207-94-5*) Danbury Hse Bks.

New Hampshire Genealogical Record, Vol. 6. 61p. 1987. reprint ed. pap. 7.50 (*0-935207-95-3*) Danbury Hse Bks.

New Hampshire Genealogical Record, Vol. 7. 1987. reprint ed. pap. 5.00 (*0-935207-96-1*) Danbury Hse Bks.

New Hampshire Genealogical Record, Vols. 1-7. 194p. 1987. reprint ed. pap. 30.50 (*0-935207-47-3*) Danbury Hse Bks.

New Hampshire "GEO" Bingo! 38 Must Know State Geography Facts for Kids to Learn While Having Fun! Carole Marsh. (Bingo! Ser.). (Illus.). (J). (gr. 2-8). 1998. pap. 14.95 (*0-7933-8610-1*) Gallopade Intl.

New Hampshire Government! The Cornerstone of Everyday Life in Our State! Carole Marsh. (Carole Marsh New Hampshire Bks.). (Illus.). (J). (gr. 3-12). 1996. pap. 19.95 (*0-7933-6269-5*); lib. bdg. 29.95 (*0-7933-6268-7*); disk 29.95 (*0-7933-6270-9*) Gallopade Intl.

***New Hampshire Health Care in Perspective 2000.** Ed. by Kathleen O'Leary Morgan & Scott E. Morgan. 21p. 2000. spiral bd. 19.00 (*0-7401-0228-1*) Morgan Quitno Corp.

New Hampshire Health Care Perspective, 1998. Ed. by Kathleen O'Leary Morgan & Scott E. Morgan. 20p. 1998. pap. 19.00 (*1-56692-828-1*) Morgan Quitno Corp.

New Hampshire Health Care Perspective, 1999. Kathleen O'Leary Morgan. 21p. 1999. spiral bd. 19.00 (*0-7401-0078-5*) Morgan Quitno Corp.

New Hampshire "HISTO" Bingo! 42 Must Know State History Facts for Kids to Learn While Having Fun! Carole Marsh. (Bingo! Ser.). (Illus.). (J). (gr. 2-8). 1998. pap. 14.95 (*0-7933-8611-X*) Gallopade Intl.

New Hampshire Historical & Biographical Index, Vol. 1. Ronald V. Jackson. LC 78-53707. (Illus.). 1984. lib. bdg. 30.00 (*0-89593-697-6*, Accel Indexing) Genealogical Srvcs.

New Hampshire History! Surprising Secrets about Our State's Founding Mothers, Fathers & Kids! Carole Marsh. (Carole Marsh New Hampshire Bks.). (Illus.). (J). (gr. 3-12). 1996. pap. 19.95 (*0-7933-6116-8*); lib. bdg. 29.95 (*0-7933-6115-X*); disk 29.95 (*0-7933-6117-6*) Gallopade Intl.

New Hampshire Hot Air Balloon Mystery. Carole Marsh. (Carole Marsh New Hampshire Bks.). (Illus.). (J). (gr. 2-9). 1994. 29.95 (*0-7933-2579-X*); pap. 19.95 (*0-7933-2580-3*); disk 29.95 (*0-7933-2581-1*) Gallopade Intl.

New Hampshire Hot Zones! Viruses, Diseases, & Epidemics in Our State's History. Carole Marsh. (Hot Zones! Ser.). (Illus.). (J). (gr. 3-12). 1998. pap. 19.95 (*0-7933-8916-X*); lib. bdg. 29.95 (*0-7933-8915-1*) Gallopade Intl.

New Hampshire House Journal, 1998. 1050p. 1998. write for info. (*0-327-07060-9*, 4578112) LEXIS Pub.

New Hampshire in Perspective, 1998. Ed. by Kathleen O'Leary Morgan & Scott E. Morgan. 24p. 1998. pap. 19.00 (*1-56692-878-8*) Morgan Quitno Corp.

New Hampshire in Perspective, 1999. Ed. by Kathleen O'Leary Morgan. 26p. 1999. spiral bd. 19.00 (*1-56692-978-4*) Morgan Quitno Corp.

***New Hampshire in Perspective 2000.** Ed. by Kathleen O'Leary Morgan & Scott E. Morgan. 26p. 2000. spiral bd. 19.00 (*0-7401-0278-8*) Morgan Quitno Corp.

New Hampshire in the Great Rebellion, Containing Histories of the Several New Hampshire Regiments & Biographical Notices of Many of the Prominent Actors in the Civil War of 1861-5. Otis F. Waite. (Illus.). 608p. 1997. reprint ed. lib. bdg. 65.00 (*0-8328-5968-0*) Higginson Bk Co.

New Hampshire Indian Dictionary for Kids! Carole Marsh. (Carole Marsh State Bks.). (J). (gr. 2-9). 1996. 29.95 (*0-7933-7731-5*, C Marsh); pap. 19.95 (*0-7933-7732-3*, C Marsh) Gallopade Intl.

New Hampshire Insider's Guide. Ron Barracliffe. LC 83-60054. (Illus.). 160p. (Orig.). 1983. pap. 2.95 (*0-9611606-0-8*) New Impressions.

New Hampshire Insurance Laws. Butterworth Staff. 650p. 1993. pap. 35.00 (*1-56257-506-6*, MICHIE) LEXIS Pub.

***New Hampshire Investment & Business Guide: Business, Investment, Export-Import Opportunities, 50 vols., Vol.29.** Global Investment Center, USA Staff. (U. S. Regional Investment & Business Library-99: Vol. 29). (Illus.). 350p. (Orig.). 1999. pap. 59.95 (*0-7397-1128-8*) Intl Business Pubns.

New Hampshire Jeopardy! Answers & Questions about Our State! Carole Marsh. (Carole Marsh New Hampshire Bks.). (Illus.). (J). (gr. 3-12). 1994. pap. 19.95 (*0-7933-4167-1*); lib. bdg. 29.95 (*0-7933-4166-3*); disk 29.95 (*0-7933-4168-X*) Gallopade Intl.

New Hampshire "Jography" A Fun Run Thru Our State! Carole Marsh. (Carole Marsh New Hampshire Bks.). (Illus.). (J). 1994. pap. 19.95 (*1-55609-827-8*); lib. bdg. 29.95 (*1-55609-826-X*); disk 29.95 (*1-55609-828-6*) Gallopade Intl.

New Hampshire Juvenile Laws. Ed. by Butterworth Staff. 500p. 1994. pap. 37.50 (*0-250-44827-0*, MICHIE) LEXIS Pub.

New Hampshire Juvenile Laws: 1998-99 Edition. Lexis Law Publishing Staff. 587p. 1999. write for info. (*0-327-06653-9*) LEXIS Pub.

***New Hampshire Juvenile Laws Advance Legislative Service: 1999 Edition.** 110p. 1999. pap. write for info. (*0-327-09860-0*, 2881012) LEXIS Pub.

New Hampshire Juvenile Laws Advance Legislative Service, 1998 Edition. 110p. 1998. pap. write for info. (*0-327-06386-6*, 2881011) LEXIS Pub.

New Hampshire Juvenile Laws, Annual. Ed. by Butterworth Staff. 500p. 1993. pap. 35.00 (*1-56257-505-8*, MICHIE) LEXIS Pub.

***New Hampshire Juvenile Laws, 1999-2000 Edition.** 454p. 1999. 49.00 incl. audio compact disk (*0-327-09960-7*, 2880915) LEXIS Pub.

New Hampshire Kid's Cookbook: Recipes, How-To, History, Lore & More! Carole Marsh. (Carole Marsh New Hampshire Bks.). (Illus.). (J). 1994. pap. 19.95 (*0-7933-0780-5*); lib. bdg. 29.95 (*0-7933-0781-3*); disk 29.95 (*0-7933-0782-1*) Gallopade Intl.

New Hampshire Land Sales Disclosure & Condominium Laws & Rules. 200p. 1992. pap. 15.00 (*0-88063-479-0*, MICHIE) LEXIS Pub.

N

New Hampshire Landlord & Tenant Law Advance Legislative Service, 1998 Edition. 29p. 1998. pap. write for info. (*0-327-06387-4*, 2884810) LEXIS Pub.

New Hampshire Landlord & Tenant Law Annotated, 1998-99 Edition. 365p. 1998. pap. 45.00 (*0-327-06515-X*, 2881115) LEXIS Pub.

New Hampshire Landlord & Tenant Law, 1990-1994. 100p. 1993. pap. 30.00 (*0-88063-478-2*, MICHIE) LEXIS Pub.

New Hampshire Landlord &Tenant Law Annotated: 1999-2000 Edition. pap. 45.00 (*0-327-10489-9*) LEXIS Pub.

New Hampshire Law Bulletin. Susan E. Marshall & Esquire Editors. 'p. 60.00 (*0-327-01930-1*) LEXIS Pub.

***New Hampshire Law for Bingo & Lucky 7 & Raffles & Games of Chance: 1999 Edition.** 46p. 2000. pap. 10.00 (*0-327-10003-6*, 2885011) LEXIS Pub.

New Hampshire Laws: Laws of the State of New Hampshire, 1997 Regular Session. 715p. 1998. write for info. (*0-327-05387-9*, 45666-13) LEXIS Pub.

New Hampshire Laws of the 1998 Session. 650p. 1999. pap. write for info. (*0-327-08440-5*, 45665-14) LEXIS Pub.

New Hampshire Legal Assistance Food Stamp Advocates' Manual. 64p. 1988. pap. 9.50 (*0-317-02677-1*, 43,890) NCLS Inc.

New Hampshire Library Book: A Surprising Guide to the Unusual Special Collections in Libraries Across Our State for Students, Teachers, Writers & Publishers - Includes Reproducible Mailing Labels Plus Activities for Young People! Carole Marsh. (Carole Marsh New Hampshire Bks.). (Illus.). 1994. pap. 19.95 (*0-7933-3093-9*); lib. bdg. 29.95 (*0-7933-3092-0*); disk 29.95 (*0-7933-3094-7*) Gallopade Intl.

New Hampshire Life. Nackey S. Loeb. (Illus.). 112p. Date not set. write for info. (*0-9648921-0-3*) Union Leader.

New Hampshire Local Government Law. 2nd ed. Peter Loughlin. LC 95-81570. 531p. 1995. text 65.00 (*1-55834-297-4*, 82056-11, MICHIE) LEXIS Pub.

New Hampshire Local Government Law, 1990-93. Peter J. Loughlin. 24p. 1993. ring bd., suppl. ed. 34.50 (*0-614-03165-6*, MICHIE) LEXIS Pub.

New Hampshire Local Government Law, 1990-93, Vols. 13 & 14. Peter J. Loughlin. (NH Practice Ser.). 1500p. 1990. 130.00 (*0-88063-654-8*, MICHIE) LEXIS Pub.

New Hampshire Manual for Notaries Public & Justices of the Peace. Charles G. Douglas, III. 70p. 1991. pap. 25.00 (*0-88063-811-7*, MICHIE) LEXIS Pub.

New Hampshire Manufacturers Register. Ed. by Frank Lambing. 1998. 55.00 (*1-58202-075-2*) Manufacturers.

New Hampshire Math! How It All Adds up in Our State. Carole Marsh. (Carole Marsh New Hampshire Bks.). (Illus.). (YA). (gr. 3-12). 1996. pap. 19.95 (*0-7933-6575-9*); lib. bdg. 29.95 (*0-7933-6574-0*) Gallopade Intl.

New Hampshire Media Book: A Surprising Guide to the Amazing Print, Broadcast & Online Media of Our State for Students, Teachers, Writers & Publishers - Includes Reproducible Mailing Labels Plus Activities for Young People! Carole Marsh. (Carole Marsh New Hampshire Bks.). (Illus.). 1994. pap. 19.95 (*0-7933-3249-4*); lib. bdg. 29.95 (*0-7933-3248-6*); disk 29.95 (*0-7933-3250-8*) Gallopade Intl.

New Hampshire Militia Officers, 1820-1850: Division, Brigade & Regimental Field & Staff Officers. Scott Lanzendorf. 232p. (Orig.). 1995. pap. 21.00 (*0-7884-0299-4*) Heritage Bk.

***New Hampshire Motor Vehicle Laws Advance Legislative Service: 1999 Edition.** 114p. 1999. pap. write for info. (*0-327-09861-9*, 2885512) LEXIS Pub.

New Hampshire Motor Vehicle Laws Advance Legislative Service, 1998 Edition. 69p. 1998. pap. write for info. (*0-327-06361-0*, 2885511) LEXIS Pub.

New Hampshire Municipal Practice Series, 4 vols., Set. Peter J. Loughlin. ring bd. 225.00 (*0-88063-780-3*, MICHIE) LEXIS Pub.

New Hampshire Mystery Van Takes Off! Bk. 1: Handicapped New Hampshire Kids Sneak Off on a Big Adventure. Carole Marsh. (Carole Marsh New Hampshire Bks.). (Illus.). (J). (gr. 3-12). 1994. 29.95 (*0-7933-5048-4*); pap. 19.95 (*0-7933-5049-2*) Gallopade Intl.

New Hampshire Name Changes, 1768-1923. Richard P. Roberts. LC 96-228059. 333p. 1996. pap. 28.00 (*0-7884-0500-4*, R507) Heritage Bk.

New Hampshire Newspapers & the Constitution, 1787-1788. Charles E. Clark. (Illus.). 80p. (Orig.). 1989. pap. 15.00 (*0-317-93998-X*) NH Human Council.

New Hampshire, 1998 Index: New Hampshire Revised Statutes Annotated. (New Hampshire Revised Statutes Annotated Ser.). 1031p. 1998. write for info. (*0-327-06439-0*, 4564114) LEXIS Pub.

New Hampshire 1998 Special Supplement. 5160p. 1998. write for info. (*0-327-07137-0*, 45645-13) LEXIS Pub.

***New Hampshire 1999 Index.** 1039p. 1999. pap. write for info. (*0-327-09916-X*, 4564115) LEXIS Pub.

***New Hampshire 1999 Replacement Titles 15, 16 (Chs. 186 to 202-B)** 732p. 1999. Price not set. (*0-327-09734-5*, 4561311) LEXIS Pub.

New Hampshire Notables. Charles Brereton. (Illus.). 256p. 1986. 5.00 (*0-914339-11-7*) P E Randall Pub.

New Hampshire Notaries Public & Justices of the Peace. 2nd ed. Charles G. Douglas, III. 82p. 1999. pap. 32.50 (*0-327-01361-3*, 8203611) LEXIS Pub.

New Hampshire Objections at Trial. Ronald L. Carlson & Myron H. Bright. 200p. 1992. pap. 39.50 (*0-88063-822-2*, MICHIE) LEXIS Pub.

New Hampshire Personal Injury: Tort & Insurance Practice, 1988-1993. Richard B. McNamara. 190p. 1993. ring bd., suppl. ed. 32.00 (*0-614-03166-4*, MICHIE) LEXIS Pub.

New Hampshire Personal Injury: Tort & Insurance Practice, 1988-1993, Vols. 8 & 9. Richard B. McNamara. (New Hampshire Practice Ser.). 950p. 1988. 140.00 (*0-88063-489-8*, MICHIE) LEXIS Pub.

New Hampshire Photographs: The Portrait & the Environment. Ed. by Robert M. Doty. (Illus.). 72p. (Orig.). 1985. pap. text 10.00 (*0-914339-07-9*) P E Randall Pub.

New Hampshire Planning & Land Use Regulation. Ed. by Butterworth Staff. (New Hampshire Statutes Ser.). 275p. 1994. pap. 30.00 (*0-250-44735-5*, MICHIE); pap. 35.00 (*0-614-05921-6*, MICHIE) LEXIS Pub.

***New Hampshire Planning & Land Use Regulation: 1999-2000 Edition.** 400p. 1999. pap. 41.00 (*0-327-10170-9*, 2882115) LEXIS Pub.

New Hampshire Planning & Land Use Regulation, Annual. 340p. 1994. pap. 30.00 (*0-88063-483-9*, MICHIE) LEXIS Pub.

New Hampshire Planning & Land Use Regulations, 1998-99. 379p. 1998. write for info. (*0-327-06598-2*, 2882114) LEXIS Pub.

New Hampshire Political Troubadour. Library & Archives of New Hampshire's Political Tradition Staff. LC 98-68671. 112p. 1999. pap. 15.00 (*0-9637615-2-8*) Res N Hampshire.

New Hampshire Practice: Consolidated Tables, 1999 Edition. 250p. 1998. write for info. (*0-327-00860-1*, 8205914) LEXIS Pub.

***New Hampshire Practice: Family Law, 1999 Cumulative Supplement.** Charles G. Douglas, 3rd & Caroline Douglas. 300p. 1999. write for info. (*0-327-01572-1*, 8442015) LEXIS Pub.

New Hampshire Practice: Index, 1999 Edition, 22 vols. Ed. by LLP Staff. 550p. 1998. write for info. (*0-327-00721-4*, 8206414) LEXIS Pub.

New Hampshire Practice: Land Use Planning & Zoning, 1998 Cumulative Supplement. Peter J. Loughlin. 90p. 1998. pap. write for info. (*0-327-00583-1*, 8441714) LEXIS Pub.

New Hampshire Practice: Probate Law & Procedure, 1998 Cumulative Supplement (Vols. 10-12) Charles A. Degrandpre. 150p. 1998. pap. 225.00 (*0-327-00571-8*, 8203513) LEXIS Pub.

New Hampshire Practice Vol. 3: Family Law, 1998 Cumulative Supplement. Caroline Douglas & Charles G. Douglas, III. 300p. 1998. write for info. (*0-327-22858-X*, 8442014) LEXIS Pub.

New Hampshire Practice Vol. 3A: Family Law, 1998 Cumulative Supplement. Caroline Douglas & Charles G. Douglas, III. 300p. 1998. write for info. (*0-327-00859-8*, 8442014) LEXIS Pub.

New Hampshire Practice Vol. 4: Civil Practice, 3 vols. 2nd ed. Richard Wiebusch. LC 97-81062. 608p. 1997. text 210.00 (*1-55834-835-2*, 82046-11, MICHIE) LEXIS Pub.

New Hampshire Practice Vol. 4: Civil Practice & Procedure, 1998 Supplement. Richard V. Wiebusch. 70p. 1998. pap. write for info. (*0-327-00758-3*, 8440613) LEXIS Pub.

New Hampshire Practice Vol. 7: Wills, Trusts & Gifts, 1998 Cumulative Supplement. Charles DeGrandpre. 250p. 1998. pap. write for info. (*0-327-00703-6*, 8440914) LEXIS Pub.

New Hampshire Practice Vol. 13: Local Government Law, 1998 Cumulative Supplement. Peter J. Loughlin. 100p. 1998. pap., suppl. ed. write for info. (*0-327-00679-X*, 8441514) LEXIS Pub.

New Hampshire Practice Vol. 14: Local Government Law, 1998 Cumulative Supplement. Peter J. Loughlin. 100p. 1998. pap., suppl. ed. write for info. (*0-327-00680-3*, 8441614) LEXIS Pub.

New Hampshire Practice Vol. 14A: Local Government Law, 1998 Cumulative Supplement. Peter J. Loughlin. 100p. 1998. pap., suppl. ed. write for info. (*0-327-00681-1*, 8442514) LEXIS Pub.

New Hampshire Practice Vol. 16: Municipal Finance & Taxation, 1998 Cumulative Supplement. Peter J. Loughlin. 70p. 1998. pap., suppl. ed. write for info. (*0-327-00702-8*, 8441814) LEXIS Pub.

New Hampshire Practice Vols. 1, 2, 2A: Criminal Practice & Procedure, 1998 Cumulative Supplement, Set. Richard B. McNamara. 800p. 1998. pap., suppl. ed. write for info. (*0-327-00720-6*, 8206313) LEXIS Pub.

New Hampshire Practice, 1997 Vol. 7: Wills & Trusts. 3rd ed. Charles DeGrandpre. LC 97-81025. 875p. 1997. text 70.00 (*1-55834-834-4*, 82049-11, MICHIE) LEXIS Pub.

New Hampshire Practice Series, 16 Volumes, hardbound plus softbound index and tab, Set, Vols. 1-16. 1984. 960.00 (*0-88063-679-3*, 82040-10, MICHIE) LEXIS Pub.

New Hampshire Practice Series: Consolidated Tables, 1997. 1996. pap. 37.50 (*1-55834-306-7*, 82059-12) LEXIS Pub.

New Hampshire Practice Series: Local Government Law, 3 vols., Vols. 13, 14, 14A. 2nd ed. Peter J. Loughlin. 195.00 (*0-327-01018-5*) LEXIS Pub.

New Hampshire Primary & the American Electoral Process. Niall A. Palmer. LC 96-50322. 216p. 1997. 55.00 (*0-275-95569-9*, Praeger Pubs) Greenwood.

***New Hampshire Primary & the American Electoral Process.** Niall A. Palmer. LC 96-50322. 195p. 2000. reprint ed. 22.00 (*0-8133-3777-1*) Westview.

New Hampshire Primer: An Almost Fool-Proof Guide for Winning the New Hampshire Presidential Primary. M. J. Beagle. (Illus.). 64p. (Orig.). 1995. pap. text 9.95 (*0-9642213-4-9*) Moose Cntry.

New Hampshire Public Retirement Laws Annotated, 1998-99. Contrib. by New Hampshire Retirement System Staff. LC 99-172485. v, 112p. 1998. write for info. (*0-327-07116-8*, 28905-10) LEXIS Pub.

New Hampshire Quiz Bowl Crash Course! Carole Marsh. (Carole Marsh New Hampshire Bks.). (Illus.). (J). 1994. pap. 19.95 (*1-55609-842-1*); lib. bdg. 29.95 (*1-55609-841-3*); disk 29.95 (*1-55609-843-X*) Gallopade Intl.

New Hampshire Reports, 63 vols., Set. 1979. 1400.00 (*1-57588-338-4*, 501100) W S Hein.

New Hampshire Reports, Vol. 143. 1000p. write for info. (*0-327-12244-7*, 4575116) LEXIS Pub.

***New Hampshire Reports, Vol. 143** 1127p. 2000. write for info. (*0-327-13597-2*, 4576710) LEXIS Pub.

New Hampshire Reports, Vol. 143, Unit 1. 200p. 1999. pap. write for info. (*0-327-08642-4*, 45753-14) LEXIS Pub.

New Hampshire Reports, Vols. 1-138. Ed. by Butterworth Staff. 900p. 1979. boxed set 41.00 (*0-88063-492-8*, 45750-10, MICHIE) LEXIS Pub.

New Hampshire Reports & Current Case Service. William Crook. 32p. 48.00 (*0-614-03167-2*, MICHIE) LEXIS Pub.

New Hampshire Reports & Current Case Service, Vol. 130. 38.00 (*0-685-67705-2*, MICHIE) LEXIS Pub.

New Hampshire Reports & Current Case Service, Vol. 132. boxed set 40.00 (*0-88063-441-3*, MICHIE) LEXIS Pub.

New Hampshire Reports & Current Case Service, Vol. 133. 42.00 (*1-56257-005-6*, MICHIE) LEXIS Pub.

New Hampshire Reports & Current Case Service, Vol. 134. 45.00 (*1-56257-070-6*, MICHIE) LEXIS Pub.

New Hampshire Reports & Current Case Service, Vol. 135. 46.00 (*1-56257-503-1*, MICHIE) LEXIS Pub.

New Hampshire Reports & Current Case Service, Vol. 136. 48.00 (*1-56257-583-X*, MICHIE) LEXIS Pub.

New Hampshire Reports & Current Case Service, Vols. 130 & 131. 38.00 (*0-685-74144-3*, MICHIE) LEXIS Pub.

New Hampshire Reports Bound Volume, No. 142. 1000p. 1998. write for info. (*0-327-06403-X*, 4576610); write for info. (*0-327-06404-8*, 4575115) LEXIS Pub.

New Hampshire Reports Current Case Service. pap. 50.00 (*0-327-10237-3*) LEXIS Pub.

New Hampshire Reports Current Case Service, Vol. 142, Unit 3. 200p. 1998. pap. 50.00 (*0-327-05872-2*, 45755-13) LEXIS Pub.

New Hampshire Reports Current Case Service, Vol. 142, Unit 4. 1998. pap. write for info. (*0-327-05514-6*, 45757-13) LEXIS Pub.

New Hampshire Reports Current Case Service Vol. 142: Unit 1. 1998. pap. write for info. (*0-327-05094-2*, 45757-13) LEXIS Pub.

New Hampshire Residents, 1633-1699. Jay M. Holbrook. LC 79-88038. 234p. 1979. lib. bdg. 30.00 (*0-931248-01-9*) Holbrook Res.

New Hampshire Retirement & Relocation Guide. large type ed. (Retirement & Relocation Guides Ser.). (Illus.). 350p. Date not set. pap. 19.95 (*1-56559-147-X*) HGI-Over Fifty.

New Hampshire Retirement System Statutory Provisions: 1999-2000 Edition. 120p. pap. 17.00 (*0-327-10173-3*) LEXIS Pub.

New Hampshire Revised Statues Annotated Advance Code Service March 1999. 60p. 1999. pap. write for info. (*0-327-07714-X*, 4566113) LEXIS Pub.

New Hampshire Revised Statutes Annotated, 23 vols. annot. rev. ed. Ed. by Butterworth Staff. 1994. boxed set 500.00 (*0-88063-491-X*, 45605-10, MICHIE) LEXIS Pub.

***New Hampshire Revised Statutes Annotated Advance Code Service, February 2000.** Ed. by LEXIS Law Publishing Editors. 86p. 2000. write for info. (*0-327-11115-1*, 4566114) LEXIS Pub.

New Hampshire Revised Statutes Annotated Replacement Volume Titles 35-37. 800p. 1998. write for info. (*0-327-05315-1*, 45625-11) LEXIS Pub.

New Hampshire Revised Statutes Annotated Replacement Volume Titles 37, 38. 800p. 1998. write for info. (*0-327-05316-X*, 45626-11) LEXIS Pub.

New Hampshire Revised Statutes Annotated, 1998: Advance Legislative Service: Pamphlet 3. Date not set. pap. write for info. (*0-327-06214-2*, 45649-12) LEXIS Pub.

New Hampshire Revised Statutes Annotated, 1998 Pamphlet 2: Advance Legislative Service. annot. ed. Date not set. pap. write for info. (*0-327-06213-4*, 45648-12) LEXIS Pub.

New Hampshire Revised Statutes Annotated 1998 Supplement, Set. 1998. pap. write for info. (*0-327-05171-X*, 45640-14) LEXIS Pub.

New Hampshire Revised Statutes Annotated, 1998 Supplement, Vol. 1, Title 1. 1998. pap., suppl. ed. write for info. (*0-327-05450-6*, 84100-14) LEXIS Pub.

New Hampshire Revised Statutes Annotated, 1998 Supplement, Vol. 2, Titles 1-3. 1998. pap., suppl. ed. write for info. (*0-327-05451-4*, 84101-14) LEXIS Pub.

New Hampshire Revised Statutes Annotated, 1998 Supplement, Vol. 3, Titles 3-5. 1998. pap., suppl. ed. write for info. (*0-327-05452-2*, 84102-14) LEXIS Pub.

New Hampshire Revised Statutes Annotated, 1998 Supplement, Vol. 4, Titles 6-9. 1998. pap., suppl. ed. write for info. (*0-327-05453-0*, 84103-14) LEXIS Pub.

New Hampshire Revised Statutes Annotated, 1998 Supplement, Vol. 5, Title 10. 1998. pap., suppl. ed. write for info. (*0-327-05454-9*, 84129-14) LEXIS Pub.

New Hampshire Revised Statutes Annotated, 1998 Supplement, Vol. 7, Titles 10, 11. 1998. pap., suppl. ed. write for info. (*0-327-05455-7*, 84105-14) LEXIS Pub.

New Hampshire Revised Statutes Annotated, 1998 Supplement, Vol. 8, Titles 12-14. 1998. pap., suppl. ed. write for info. (*0-327-05457-3*, 84106-14) LEXIS Pub.

New Hampshire Revised Statutes Annotated, 1998 Supplement, Vol. 9, Titles 15-16. 1998. pap., suppl. ed. write for info. (*0-327-05458-1*, 84107-14) LEXIS Pub.

New Hampshire Revised Statutes Annotated, 1998 Supplement, Vol. 10, Titles 17-19A. 1998. pap., suppl. ed. write for info. (*0-327-05459-X*, 84108-14) LEXIS Pub.

New Hampshire Revised Statutes Annotated, 1998 Supplement, Vol. 11, Title 20. 1998. pap., suppl. ed. write for info. (*0-327-05460-3*, 84109-14) LEXIS Pub.

New Hampshire Revised Statutes Annotated, 1998 Supplement, Vol. 13, Titles 22, 23. 1998. pap., suppl. ed. write for info. (*0-327-05462-X*, 84111-14) LEXIS Pub.

New Hampshire Revised Statutes Annotated, 1998 Supplement, Vol. 14, Titles 24-27. 1998. pap., suppl. ed. write for info. (*0-327-05463-8*, 84112-14) LEXIS Pub.

New Hampshire Revised Statutes Annotated, 1998 Supplement, Vol. 15, Titles 28-30. 1998. pap., suppl. ed. write for info. (*0-327-05464-6*, 84113-14) LEXIS Pub.

New Hampshire Revised Statutes Annotated, 1998 Supplement, Vol. 16, Title 30. 1998. pap., suppl. ed. write for info. (*0-327-05465-4*, 84127-14) LEXIS Pub.

New Hampshire Revised Statutes Annotated, 1998 Supplement, Vol. 17, Title 31. 1998. suppl. ed. write for info. (*0-327-05466-2*, 84114-14) LEXIS Pub.

New Hampshire Revised Statutes Annotated, 1998 Supplement, Vol. 18, Titles 32-34. 1998. pap., suppl. ed. write for info. (*0-327-05467-0*, 84128-14) LEXIS Pub.

New Hampshire Revised Statutes Annotated, 1998 Supplement, Vol. 19, Title 34A, Art. 1-4. 1998. pap., suppl. ed. write for info. (*0-327-05468-9*, 84115-14) LEXIS Pub.

New Hampshire Revised Statutes Annotated, 1998 Supplement, Vol. 20, Title 34A, Art. 4A-9. 1998. pap., suppl. ed. write for info. (*0-327-05469-7*, 84116-14) LEXIS Pub.

New Hampshire Revised Statutes Annotated, 1998 Supplement, Vol. 21, Titles 35-37. 1998. pap., suppl. ed. write for info. (*0-327-05470-0*, 84117-14) LEXIS Pub.

New Hampshire Revised Statutes Annotated, 1998 Supplement, Vol. 22, Titles 37, 38. 1998. pap., suppl. ed. write for info. (*0-327-05471-9*, 84118-14) LEXIS Pub.

New Hampshire Revised Statutes Annotated, 1998 Supplement, Vol. 23, Titles 39-41. 1998. pap., suppl. ed. write for info. (*0-327-05472-7*, 84119-14) LEXIS Pub.

New Hampshire Revised Statutes Annotated, 1998 Supplement, Vol. 24, Titles 42-47. 1998. pap., suppl. ed. write for info. (*0-327-05473-5*, 84120-14) LEXIS Pub.

New Hampshire Revised Statutes Annotated, 1998 Supplement, Vol. 25, Titles 48-50. 1998. pap., suppl. ed. write for info. (*0-327-05474-3*, 84121-14) LEXIS Pub.

New Hampshire Revised Statutes Annotated, 1998 Supplement, Vol. 26, Titles 51 & 52. 1998. pap., suppl. ed. write for info. (*0-327-05475-1*, 84122-14) LEXIS Pub.

New Hampshire Revised Statutes Annotated, 1998 Supplement, Vol. 27, Titles 53-56. 1998. pap., suppl. ed. write for info. (*0-327-05476-X*, 84123-14) LEXIS Pub.

New Hampshire Revised Statutes Annotated, 1998 Supplement, Vol. 28, Titles 57-61. 1998. pap., suppl. ed. write for info. (*0-327-05477-8*, 84124-14) LEXIS Pub.

New Hampshire Revised Statutes Annotated, 1998 Supplement, Vol. 30, Titles 63-64. 1998. pap., suppl. ed. write for info. (*0-327-05479-4*, 84125-14) LEXIS Pub.

New Hampshire Revised Statutes Annotated, 1998 Supplement, Vol. 31. 1998. pap., suppl. ed. write for info. (*0-327-05480-8*, 84126-14) LEXIS Pub.

New Hampshire Revised Statutes Annotated 1999 Cumulative Supplements. rev. annot. ed. write for info. (*0-327-09846-5*, 45640-15) LEXIS Pub.

New Hampshire Rollercoasters! Carole Marsh. (Carole Marsh New Hampshire Bks.). (Illus.). (J). (gr. 3-12). 1994. pap. 19.95 (*0-7933-5312-2*); lib. bdg. 29.95 (*0-7933-5311-4*) Gallopade Intl.

New Hampshire Rollercoasters! Carole Marsh. (Carole Marsh New Hampshire Bks.). (Illus.). (YA). (gr. 3-12). 1994. disk 29.95 (*0-7933-5313-0*) Gallopade Intl.

New Hampshire Rules of Evidence Deskbook, 1994. Ed. by Butterworth Staff. 150p. 1994. pap. 20.00 (*0-88063-465-0*, 91185-10, MICHIE) LEXIS Pub.

New Hampshire Rules of Professional Conduct. 28p. 1998. pap. write for info. (*0-327-07236-9*, 4567413) LEXIS Pub.

New Hampshire Scenes & Seasons. Photos by Dick Hamilton. LC 89-60636. (Illus.). 72p. (Orig.). 1989. pap. 14.95 (*0-933050-72-0*) New Eng Pr VT.

New Hampshire School Trivia: An Amazing & Fascinating Look at Our State's Teachers, Schools & Students! Carole Marsh. (Illus.). (J). 1994. pap. 19.95 (*0-7933-0777-5*); lib. bdg. 29.95 (*0-7933-0778-3*); disk 29.95 (*0-7933-0779-1*) Gallopade Intl.

New Hampshire Selected Motor Vehicle, Boating & Related Laws Annotated: 1998-99 Edition. Lexis Law Publishing Staff. 487p. 1998. 49.50 (*0-327-06583-4*) LEXIS Pub.

New Hampshire Selected Motor Vehicle, Boating & Related Laws Annotated: 1999-2000 Edition. pap. 49.50 (*0-327-10493-7*) LEXIS Pub.

New Hampshire, 1742 Estate List. Pauline J. Oesterlin. (Illus.). 432p. 1995. text 31.00 (*0-7884-0129-7*) Heritage Bk.

New Hampshire 1790 Census Index: Heads of Families. pap. 20.00 (*1-877677-46-9*) Herit Quest.

An Asterisk (*) at the beginning of an entry indicates that the title is appearing for the first time.

New Hampshire, 1732 Census. Jay M. Holbrook. LC 81-80038. 75p. 1981. lib. bdg. 25.00 (*0-931248-10-8*) Holbrook Res.

New Hampshire Silly Basketball Sportsmysteries, Vol. I. Carole Marsh. (Carole Marsh New Hampshire Bks.). (Illus.). (J). 1994. pap. 19.95 (*0-7933-0774-0*); lib. bdg. 29.95 (*0-7933-0775-9*); disk 29.95 (*0-7933-0776-7*) Gallopade Intl.

New Hampshire Silly Basketball Sportsmysteries, Vol. II. Carole Marsh. (Carole Marsh New Hampshire Bks.). (Illus.). (J). 1994. pap. 19.95 (*0-7933-1777-0*); lib. bdg. 29.95 (*0-7933-1776-2*); disk 29.95 (*0-7933-1778-9*) Gallopade Intl.

New Hampshire Silly Football Sportsmysteries, Vol. 1. Carole Marsh. (Carole Marsh New Hampshire Bks.). (Illus.). (J). 1994. pap. 19.95 (*1-55609-833-2*); lib. bdg. 29.95 (*1-55609-832-4*); disk 29.95 (*1-55609-834-0*) Gallopade Intl.

New Hampshire Silly Football Sportsmysteries, Vol. 2. Carole Marsh. (Carole Marsh New Hampshire Bks.). (Illus.). (J). 1994. pap. 19.95 (*1-55609-836-7*); lib. bdg. 29.95 (*1-55609-835-9*); disk 29.95 (*1-55609-837-5*) Gallopade Intl.

New Hampshire Silly Trivia! Carole Marsh. (Carole Marsh New Hampshire Bks.). (Illus.). (J). 1994. pap. 19.95 (*1-55609-824-3*); lib. bdg. 29.95 (*1-55609-823-5*); disk 29.95 (*1-55609-825-1*) Gallopade Intl.

New Hampshire Spelling Bee! Score Big by Correctly Spelling Our State's Unique Names. Carole Marsh. (Carole Marsh New Hampshire Bks.). (Illus.). (YA). (gr. 3-12). 1996. pap. 19.95 (*0-7933-6728-X*); lib. bdg. 29.95 (*0-7933-6727-1*) Gallopade Intl.

New Hampshire Statues Pertaining to Health & Human Services, 1998-99 Edition. 596p. 1999. ring bd. write for info. (*0-327-07617-8*, 2881914) LEXIS Pub.

New Hampshire Statutes Pertaining to Health & Human Services: 1997-98 Edition. Michie Staff. Date not set. 42.50 (*1-55834-866-2*, 28819-13, MICHIE) LEXIS Pub.

***New Hampshire Statutes Pertaining to Health & Human Services: 1999-2000 Edition.** 610p. 1999. pap. 49.50 (*0-327-10148-2*, 2881915) LEXIS Pub.

New Hampshire Statutes Relating to Surveying & Boundaries: 1996-1997 Edition. 256p. pap. 25.00 (*1-55834-506-X*) LEXIS Pub.

***New Hampshire Sweepstakes Laws: 1999 Edition.** 48p. 2000. 14.00 (*0-327-10000-1*, 2892011) LEXIS Pub.

New Hampshire Sweepstakes Laws, 1998 Edition. 41p. 1998. pap. write for info. (*0-327-05088-8*, 28920-10) LEXIS Pub.

New Hampshire Timeline: A Chronology of New Hampshire History, Mystery, Trivia, Legend, Lore & More. Carole Marsh. (Carole Marsh New Hampshire Bks.). (Illus.). (J). (gr. 3-12). 1994. pap. 19.95 (*0-7933-5963-5*); lib. bdg. 29.95 (*0-7933-5962-7*); disk 29.95 (*0-7933-5964-3*) Gallopade Intl.

New Hampshire Towns & Counties. Michael J. Denis. (New England Towns & Counties Ser.). 27p. (Orig.). 1982. pap. 4.00 (*0-935207-04-X*) Danbury Hse Bks.

New Hampshire 2000! Coming Soon to a Calendar Near You - The 21st Century! - Complete Set of AL 2000 Items. Carole Marsh. (Two Thousand! Ser.). (Illus.). (J). (gr. 3-12). 1998. pap. 75.00 (*0-7933-9367-1*); lib. bdg. 85.00 (*0-7933-9368-X*) Gallopade Intl.

New Hampshire Unclaimed & Abandoned Property Law: 1997-98 Edition. 45p. pap. 7.00 (*1-55834-827-1*) LEXIS Pub.

New Hampshire vs. Vermont: Sibling Rivalry Between the Twin States. Lisa Shaw. 1997. pap. text 11.95 (*0-9652502-0-2*) Williams Hill.

New Hampshire Wildlife Viewing Guide. Judith K. Silverberg. LC 96-37280. (Illus.). 96p. 1997. pap. 8.95 (*1-56044-544-0*) Falcon Pub Inc.

New Hampshire Workers' Compensation Manual. 2nd ed. Richard E. Galway. LC 92-47276. 400p. 1994. spiral bd. 85.00 (*1-56257-347-0*, MICHIE) LEXIS Pub.

New Hampshire Workers Compensation Manual, No. 5. Salafia. 100p. 1998. ring bd. write for info. (*0-327-00793-1*, 8206715) LEXIS Pub.

***New Hampshire 1999 Replacement Titles 22, 23: Chs. 270 to 283.** 620p. 1999. Price not set. (*0-327-08795-1*, 4561711) LEXIS Pub.

***New Hampshire 1999 Replacement Titles 24-27: Chs. 284 to 303.** 504p. 1999. Price not set. (*0-327-08796-X*, 4561811) LEXIS Pub.

***New Hampshire/Maine: An Atlas of New Hampshire & Southern Maine's Greatest Off-Road Bicycle Rides.** Bob Fitzhenry. (Mountain Bike America Guidebks.). (Illus.). 288p. 2000. pap. 17.95 (*0-7627-0700-3*) Globe Pequot.

New Hampshire's First Tourists in the Lakes & Mountains. rev. ed. Charles S. Lane. (Illus.). 207p. 1993. pap. 18.00 (*0-9637214-1-0*) Old Print Barn.

New Hampshire's Living Legacy: The Biodiversity of the Granite State. Ed. by James Taylor et al. (Illus.). vi, 98p. (Orig.). 1996. pap. text 9.95 (*0-9652156-1-X*) NH Fish & Game.

New Hampshire's (Most Devastating!) Disasters & (Most Calamitous!) Catastrophies! Carole Marsh. (Carole Marsh New Hampshire Bks.). (Illus.). (J). 1994. pap. 19.95 (*0-7933-0765-1*); lib. bdg. 29.95 (*0-7933-0766-X*); disk 29.95 (*0-7933-0767-8*) Gallopade Intl.

New Hampshire's Unsolved Mysteries (And Their "Solutions") Includes Scientific Information & Other Activities for Students. Carole Marsh. (Carole Marsh New Hampshire Bks.). (Illus.). (J). (gr. 3-12). 1994. pap. 19.95 (*0-7933-5810-8*); lib. bdg. 29.95 (*0-7933-5809-4*); disk 29.95 (*0-7933-5811-6*) Gallopade Intl.

New Hampshire's White Mountains: Presidential Range - Franconia-Pemigewasett. Ed. by Eugene S. Daniel, III & Jon Burroughs. (Illus.). 1998. pap. 7.95 (*1-878239-61-9*) Applchn Pub.

New Hampshire's White Mountains Map: Carter Range-Evans Notch/Kikenny-Mahoosuc. Larry Garland. (Illus.). 1998. pap. 7.95 (*1-878239-66-X*) Globe Pequot.

New Hampshire's White Mountains Map: Moosilauke-Kinsman/Crawford Notch-Sandwich Range. Larry Garland. (Illus.). 1998. pap. 7.95 (*1-878239-62-7*) Globe Pequot.

New Hamsphire. Patricia K. Kummer & Capstone Press. LC 97-40819. (One Nation Ser.). 1998. lib. bdg. 19.00 (*1-56065-681-6*) Capstone Pr.

New Handbook of Attracting Birds. Thomas P. McElroy, Jr. (Illus.). 258p. 1985. pap. 9.95 (*0-393-30280-6*) Norton.

New Handbook of Basic Writing. 4th ed. Cora L. Robey. (C). 1996. pap. text, teacher ed. 28.00 (*0-15-503693-9*) Harcourt Coll Pubs.

New Handbook of Basic Writing Skills. 4th ed. Cora L. Robey et al. LC 96-75218. 432p. (C). 1996. pap. text 31.00 (*0-15-503694-7*, Pub. by Harcourt Coll Pubs) Harcourt.

***New Handbook of British Pottery & Porcelain Marks.** rev. exp. ed. Geoffrey A. Godden. LC 99-490225. (Illus.). 208p. 2000. pap. 19.95 (*0-09-186580-8*, Pub. by Barrie & Jenkins) Trafalgar.

New Handbook of Christian Theologians. Ed. by Donald W. Musser & Joseph L. Price. LC 96-12801. 528p. 1996. pap. 29.95 (*0-687-27803-1*) Abingdon.

New Handbook of Christian Theology. Ed. by Donald W. Musser & Joseph L. Price. 544p. (Orig.). 1992. pap. 24.95 (*0-687-27802-3*) Abingdon.

New Handbook of Cognitive Therapy Techniques. Rian E. McMullin. LC 99-16390. 480p. 1999. 45.00 (*0-393-70313-4*) Norton.

New Handbook of Health & Preventive Medicine. rev. ed. Kurt Butler & Lynn Rayner. LC 90-32513. (Illus.). 450p. 1990. reprint ed. pap. 21.95 (*0-87975-581-4*) Prometheus Bks.

New Handbook of Living Religions. John R. Hinnells. LC 96-13842. (Illus.). 640p. 1997. 83.95 (*0-631-18275-6*) Blackwell Pubs.

New Handbook of Living Religions. 2nd ed. John R. Hinnells. 912p. 1998. pap. 19.95 (*0-14-051407-4*) Viking Penguin.

***New Handbook of Multicultural Assessment: Social, Psychological & Educational Applications.** Lisa A. Suzuki. 2000. 49.95 (*0-7879-5177-3*) Jossey-Bass.

New Handbook of Political Science. Ed. by Robert E. Goodin & Hans-Dieter Klingemann. (Illus.). 864p. 1998. reprint ed. pap. text 29.95 (*0-19-829471-9*) OUP.

***New Handbook of Psychotherapy & Counseling with Men: A Comprehensive Guide for All Settings.** Gary R. Brooks. 2001. 69.95 (*0-7879-5155-2*) Jossey-Bass.

New Handbook of Stage Lighting Graphics. enl. rev. ed. William Warfel. (Illus.). 128p. (C). 1990. pap. text 22.50 (*0-89676-112-6*, By Design Pr) QSMG Ltd.

New Handbook of Teacher Evaluation: Assessing Elementary & Secondary School Teachers. 2nd ed. Jason Millman & Linda Darling-Hammond. (Illus.). 448p. (C). 1990. pap. 34.95 (*0-8039-4523-X*, 3810) Corwin Pr.

New Handbook of Texas, 6 vols., Set. Ed. by Ron Tyler et al. LC 96-12861. (Illus.). 7000p. 1996. 395.00 (*0-87611-151-7*) Tex St Hist Assn.

New Handbook of the Christian Year. Hoyt L. Hickman et al. LC 92-18473. 304p. (Orig.). 1992. spiral bd. 22.95 (*0-687-27760-4*) Abingdon.

New Hanover County: A Brief History. E. Lawrence Lee. (Illus.). xiv, 124p. 1984. pap. 6.00 (*0-86526-128-8*) NC Archives.

New Hard-Boiled Dicks: Heroes for a New Urban Mythology. 2nd ed. Robert E. Skinner. LC 93-16090. (Brownstone Mystery Guides Ser.: Vol. 2). 192p. 1995. pap. 21.00 (*0-941028-14-3*) Millefleurs.

***New Hard-Boiled Writers, 1970s-1990s.** Leroy L. Panek. LC 00-37889. 2000. pap. 25.95 (*0-87972-820-5*) Bowling Green Univ Popular Press.

New Hard-Boiled Writers, 1970s-1990s. LeRoy L. Panek. 51.95 (*0-87972-819-1*) Bowling Green Univ Popular Press.

New Hardcore Bodybuilding. rev. ed. Robert Kennedy. LC 90-39881. (Illus.). 192p. (Orig.). 1990. pap. 12.95 (*0-8069-7480-X*) Sterling.

New Harlen, Part & Present: The Story of an Amazing Civil Wrong, Now at Last Righted. Carl H. Pierce. (Illus.). 332p. 1997. reprint ed. lib. bdg. 39.50 (*0-8328-6153-7*) Higginson Bk Co.

New Harmonies: Choosing Contemporary Music for Worship. Terri Bocklund McLean. 17.95 (*1-56699-206-0*) Alban Inst.

New Harmony, an Adventure in Happiness: Papers of Thomas & Sarah Pears. Thomas Pears & Sarah Pears. Ed. by Thomas C. Pears, Jr. LC 72-77058. 96p. 1973. reprint ed. lib. bdg. 27.50 (*0-678-00908-2*) Kelley.

New Harmony As Seen by Participants & Travelers Pts. 1-3: Letters of William Pelham; Diary & Recollections of Victor Colin Duclos; Report of a Visit to New Harmony by Karl Bernhard. Ed. by H. Lindley. LC 74-32002. (American Utopian Adventure Ser.). (Illus.). 128p. 1975. reprint ed. lib. bdg. 25.00 (*0-87991-028-3*) Porcupine Pr.

New Harmony Communities. G. Lockwood. 1972. 59.95 (*0-8490-0722-4*) Gordon Pr.

New Harmony Communities. George B. Lockwood. LC 72-134410. reprint ed. 47.50 (*0-404-08456-7*) AMS Pr.

New Harmony, Indiana: Robert Owen's Seedbed for Utopia. Donald F. Carmony & Josephine M. Elliott. (Illus.). 102p. 1999. pap. 5.99 (*0-9640288-7-5*) Univ So IN.

New Harmony Movement. George B. Lockwood. LC 76-134411. reprint ed. 49.50 (*0-404-08457-5*) AMS Pr.

New Harmony Movement. George B. Lockwood. LC 68-56245. (Illus.). vxi, 404p. 1970. reprint ed. 45.00 (*0-678-00667-9*) Kelley.

New Harp of Columbia. M. L. Swan. Ed. by Dorothy D. Horn et al. LC 78-5504. (Tennesseana Editions Ser.). 256p. 1978. pap. 16.95 (*0-87049-624-7*) U of Tenn Pr.

New Harvard Dictionary of Music. Ed. by Don M. Randel. LC 86-4780. (Illus.). 1024p. 1986. text 39.95 (*0-674-61525-5*) Belknap Pr.

New Harvard Guide to Psychiatry. Armand M. Nicholi. LC 87-24115. (Illus.). 864p. 1988. 58.00 (*0-674-61540-9*) Belknap Pr.

New Hat Stories: Banks/Eubanks. Tom Hart. (Illus.). 160p. 1999. pap. 9.95 (*1-891830-10-4*, Pub. by Top Shelf Prodns) LPC InBook.

New Haven: A Guide to Architecture & Urban Design. Elizabeth M. Brown. LC 75-18166. (Illus.). 228p. 1976. pap. 14.00 (*0-300-01993-9*) Yale U Pr.

New Haven: An Illustrated History. Ed. by Floyd Shumway & Richard Hegel. (Illus.). 176p. 1995. pap. 18.85 (*0-89781-033-3*) Am Historical Pr.

New Haven - Middlesex, CT. LC 94-675619. (Streetfinder Ser.). (Illus.). 1994. pap. 14.95 (*0-528-91308-5*) Rand McNally.

New Haven Clocks & Watches - With a Special Section on New Haven Movements. Tran Duy Ly. (Illus.). 520p. 1997. 55.00 (*0-930163-75-3*) Arlington Bk.

New Haven Community Study, 1959. 2nd ed. Robert A. Dahl & William Flanigan. LC 75-38491. 1975. reprint ed. write for info. (*0-89138-024-8*) ICPSR.

***New Haven Entertainment, 2000.** (Illus.). 678p. 1999. pap. 35.00 (*1-58553-042-5*, 00G4) Enter Pubns.

New Haven from the Collection of Charles Rufus Harte. Frederick W. Chesson. (Images of America Ser.). 1995. pap. 16.99 (*0-7524-0212-9*) Arcadia Publng.

New Haven Negroes, a Social History. Robert A. Warner. LC 78-94138. (American Negro: His History & Literature. Series 3). 1970. reprint ed. 23.95 (*0-405-01940-8*) Ayer.

New Haven Poems. Wally Swist. 1977. pap. 2.00 (*0-686-23220-8*) Conn Fireside.

New Haven Poems by Wally Swist. Wally Swist. 1977. pap. 2.00 (*0-686-21245-2*) Fireside Pr.

New Haven Power. Jack Swanberg. LC 87-91339. (Illus.). 608p. 1988. 80.00 (*0-944513-09-3*) Staufer Bks.

New Haven Railroad. Scott Hartley. LC 92-22729. 1992. 49.95 (*0-9621541-5-6*) Railpace Co.

New Haven Railroad along the Shoreline: The Thoroughfare from New York City to Boston. Martin J. McGuirk. LC 99-162124. (Golden Years of Railroading Ser.). (Illus.). 128p. 1998. pap. 18.95 (*0-89024-344-1*, 01088, Kalmbach Books) Kalmbach.

New Haven Railroad in the Streamline Era. Geoffrey H. Doughty. (Illus.). 128p. 1998. 33.95 (*1-883089-33-6*) TLC VA.

***New Haven Railroad's Streamline Passenger Fleet, 1934-1953.** Geoffrey H. Doughty. (Illus.). 160p. 2000. 28.95 (*1-883089-52-2*, 130611AE, Pub. by TLC VA) Motorbooks Intl.

New Haven Trackside withThomas J. Mcnamara. Jeremy F. Plant & Thomas J. MacNamara. LC 98-65133. 127 p. 1998. write for info. (*1-878887-98-X*) Morning NJ.

New Haven's Oyster Industry, 1638-1987. Virginia M. Galpin. (Illus.). 77p. (Orig.). 1989. pap. 5.00 (*0-943143-01-2*) New Haven Col Hist Soc.

New Headway English Course: Intermediate. John Soars & Liz Soars. (Illus.). 160p. 1999. pap. text, student ed. 18.95 (*0-19-470223-5*) OUP.

New Headway English Course: Intermediate. Liz Soars & John Soars. (Illus.). 166p. 1999. pap. text, teacher ed. 10.50 (*0-19-470224-3*) OUP.

New Headway English Course: Intermediate Workbook with Key. John Soars & Liz Soars. (Illus.). 100p. 1999. pap. text 10.50 (*0-19-470225-1*) OUP.

New Healers: The Promise & Problems of Molecular Medicine in the Twenty-First Century. William R. Clark. LC 97-9086. (Illus.). 256p. 1997. 27.50 (*0-19-511730-1*) OUP.

New Healers: The Promise & Problems of Molecular Medicine in the Twenty-First Century. William R. Clark. (Illus.). 256p. 1999. pap. 14.95 (*0-19-513084-7*) OUP.

New Health Care for Profit: Doctors & Hospitals in a Competitive Environment. Ed. by Bradford H. Gray. LC 83-8054. 188p. reprint ed. pap. 58.30 (*0-7837-2040-8*, 204230700003) Bks Demand.

New Health Considerations in Water Treatment. Roger Holdsworth. 109p. 1991. text 64.95 (*1-85628-823-4*, Pub. by Avebry) Ashgate Pub Co.

***New Health Partners: Renewing the Leadership of Physician Practice.** Stephen E. Prather. LC 99-22322. 352p. 1999. 39.95 (*0-7879-4024-0*) Jossey-Bass.

New Healthcare Market: A Guide to PPOs for Purchasers, Payors, & Providers. Ed. by Peter Boland. (Health Care Administration Ser.). 1152p. 1988. 115.00 (*0-87094-534-3*) Aspen Pub.

New Hearing: Living Options in Homiletic Method. Richard L. Eslinger. LC 86-22166. 1987. pap. 13.95 (*0-687-27693-4*) Abingdon.

New Hearing of an Old Prayer: Sermons on the Lord's Prayer. Thomas C. Short. LC 94-36868. 64p. (Orig.). 1995. pap. 7.75 (*0-7880-0323-2*) CSS OH.

New Heart - A New Start: Discovering the Promise of Restoration. Neva Coyle. (Devotional Daybook Ser.: Vol. 2). 16p. (Orig.). 1992. pap. 8.99 (*1-55661-277-X*) Bethany Hse.

New Heart & A New Spirit: A Plan for Renewing Your Church. David S. Young. 128p. 1994. pap. 12.00 (*0-8170-1209-5*) Judson.

New Heart, New Spirit: Biblical Humanism for Modern Israel. Arie L. Eliav. 237p. 1988. 22.50 (*0-8276-0317-7*) JPS Phila.

New Heartland. John Herbers. 228p. 1986. 19.95 (*0-317-53670-2*, Times Bks) Crown Pub Group.

New Heat Transfer. 2nd ed. Eugene T. Adiutori. 434p. 1989. 39.95 (*0-9626220-0-1*) Ventuno Pr.

New Heaven? New Earth? Simon Tugwell et al. 210p. 1977. pap. 5.95 (*0-87243-072-3*) Templegate.

New Heaven & New Earth: Prophecy & the Millennium, Essays in Honor of Anthony Gelston. Ed. by Peter J. Harland & C. T. Hayward. LC 99-30452. (Vetus Testamentum, Supplements Ser.). 310p. 1999. 94.50 (*90-04-10841-6*) Brill Academic Pubs.

New Heaven, New Earth: Practical Essays on the Catholic Worker Program. Richard G. Cleaver. Ed. by Beth Preheim & Michael Sprong. 92p. (Orig.). 1993. pap. 5.95 (*0-9636224-0-4*) Rose Hill Bks.

New Heaven, New Earth: The Visionary Experience in Literature. Joyce Carol Oates. 1978. pap. 2.50 (*0-449-23662-5*, Crest) Fawcett.

New Heaven, New Earth: The Visionary Experience in Literature. Joyce Carol Oates. LC 76-371756. 307 p. 1976. write for info. (*0-575-02076-8*) Trafalgar.

New Heaven on a New Earth: Revelation. Philip Bender. LC 85-81579. (Faith & Life Bible Studies). 106p. 1985. pap. 1.95 (*0-87303-106-7*) Faith & Life.

New Heavens & New Earth: Hope for the Creation in Jewish Apocalyptic & the New Testament. David M. Russell. LC 96-60935. (Studies in Biblical Apocalyptic Literature Ser.: Vol. 1). 266, vip. (Orig.). 1996. pap. 18.00 (*1-896400-17-5*, SBAL-1) Visionary Press.

New Heavens & the New Earth. Gordon Lindsay. (Revelation Ser.: Vol. 16). 1962. 1.95 (*0-89985-049-9*) Christ for the Nations.

New Heavens, New Earth: A Commentary on First & Second Peter. Gordon H. Clark. Ed. & Intro. by John W. Robbins. 250p. 1993. pap. 10.95 (*0-940931-36-2*) Trinity Found.

New Hebrew & Heritage Siddur Program Bk. 1: Script Writing Skills: Step III. Pearl Tarnor & Norman Tarnor. (J). 1995. pap., wbk. ed. 3.95 (*0-87441-501-2*) Behrman.

New Hebrew & Heritage Siddur Program Bk. 1: Step III. Pearl Tarnor & Norman Tarnor. (J). 1995. pap., teacher ed. 16.95 (*0-87441-498-9*); pap., wbk. ed. 4.95 (*0-87441-497-0*); pap. text 6.95 (*0-87441-496-2*) Behrman.

New Hebrew & Heritage Siddur Program Bk. 2: Prayer Reading Concept: Step IV. Pearl Tarnor & Norman Tarnor. (J). 1995. pap., wbk. ed. 4.95 (*0-87441-519-5*) Behrman.

New Hebrew & Heritage Siddur Program Bk. 2: Step IV. Pearl Tarnor & Norman Tarnor. (J). 1995. pap. text 6.95 (*0-87441-506-3*) Behrman.

New Hebrew & Heritage Siddur Program Bk. 2: Step IV, book 2. Pearl Tarnor & Norman Tarnor. (J). 1995. pap., teacher ed. 16.95 (*0-87441-514-4*) Behrman.

New Hebrew & Heritage Siddur Program Bk. 3: Step V. Pearl Tarnor & Norman Tarnor. (J). 1995. pap., teacher ed. 16.95 (*0-87441-535-7*) Behrman.

New Hebrew & Heritage Siddur Program Bk. 3: Step V. rev. ed. Pearl Tarnor & Norman Tarnor. (J). 1995. pap. text 6.95 (*0-87441-588-8*) Behrman.

New Hebrew & Heritage Siddur Program Bk. 3: Torah Skills: Step V. Pearl Tarnor & Norman Tarnor. (J). 1995. pap., wbk. ed. 4.95 (*0-87441-533-0*) Behrman.

New Hebrew & Heritage Siddur Program Bk. 4: Honor Level. Pearl Tarnor et al. (J). 1995. pap. text 7.95 (*0-87441-567-5*) Behrman.

New Hebrew Nation: A Study in Israeli Heresy & Fantasy. Yaacov Shavit. 1987. 47.50 (*0-7146-3302-X*, Pub. by F Cass Pubs) Intl Spec Bk.

New Hedges for the Countryside. Murray MacLean. (Illus.). 288p. 1992. text 34.95 (*0-85236-242-0*, Pub. by Farming Pr) Diamond Farm Bk.

New Hedonics Primer for Economists & Attorneys. 2nd ed. Ed. by John O. Ward & Thomas R. Ireland. LC 96-30657. 547p. 1992. 65.00 (*0-913875-52-X*, 0870-N) Lawyers & Judges.

New Helots: Migrants in the International Division of Labour. Robin Cohen. 250p. 1987. text 78.95 (*0-566-00932-3*, Pub. by Avebry) Ashgate Pub Co.

New Helvetia Diary. John A. Sutter. Ed. by Robert E. Merritt. 200p. 1996. reprint ed. 50.00 (*0-9652821-1-2*) R Merritt.

New Herb & Vegetable Expert. D. G. Hessayon. LC 97-183508. (Illus.). 144p. 1997. 12.95 (*0-903505-46-0*) Sterling.

New Herball, Pt. 1. William Turner. Ed. by George T. Chapman & Marilyn N. Tweddle. 364p. (C). 1996. text 105.00 (*0-521-44548-5*) Cambridge U Pr.

New Herball, Set, Pts. 2-3. William Turner. Ed. by George T. Chapman et al. 1214p. (C). 1996. 265.00 (*0-521-47768-9*); text 200.00 (*0-521-44549-3*) Cambridge U Pr.

New Hermeneutic of Reality: Raimon Panikkar's Cosmotheandric Vision. Anthony S. Raj. LC 98-23702. (Studies in the Intercultural History of Christianity: Vol. 111). 193p. 1998. pap. text 30.95 (*0-8204-3445-0*) P Lang Pubng.

New Herst-Sampson Guide to Nineteenth Century U. S. Cancellations & Postmarks. Ed. by Kenneth L. Gilman, Jr. LC 89-62024. (Illus.). 202p. (Orig.). 1989. pap. 19.95 (*1-877998-00-1*) D G Phillips.

New Hide or Seek: Building Self-Esteem in Your Child. 3rd rev. ed. James Dobson. LC 98-27744. 240p. (C). 1999. 16.99 (*0-8007-1760-0*) Revell.

New High Altitude Cookbook. Beverly M. Anderson & Donna M. Hamilton. LC 80-5287. (Illus.). 320p. 1980. 17.95 (*0-685-04236-7*) Random.

N

New High Priests: Lawyers in Post-Civil War America, 29. Ed. by Gerald W. Gawalt. LC 83-18328. (Contributions in Legal Studies: No. 29). (Illus.). 214p. 1984. 55.00 (*0-313-24021-3*, GNH/, Greenwood Pr) Greenwood.

New High School Spanish, Level 1. Medley. (Secondary Spanish Ser.). (C). 2001. mass mkt., teacher ed. 14.00 (*0-8384-7743-7*) Heinle & Heinle.

New High School Spanish, Level 2. Medley. (Secondary Spanish Ser.). 2002. mass mkt. 15.95 (*0-8384-7907-3*) Heinle & Heinle.

New High School Spanish, Level 3. Medley. (Secondary Spanish Ser.). 2001. text 15.95 (*0-8384-7899-9*); text, teacher ed. 15.95 (*0-8384-7908-1*) Heinle & Heinle.

New High School Spanish Level 1. Medley. (Secondary Spanish Ser.). 2001. pap. text 25.00 (*0-8384-7752-6*) Heinle & Heinle.

New High School Spanish Level 3. Medley. 2001. pap. text, wbk. ed. 15.00 (*0-8384-7996-0*) Heinle & Heinle.

New High-Tech Manager: Six Rules for Success in Changing Times. Kenneth Durham & Bruce Kennedy. LC 97-3746. 201p. 1997. 63.00 (*0-89006-926-3*) Artech Hse.

New High-Yield Bond Market: Investment Opportunities. Ed. by Jess Lederman & Michael P. Sullivan. 400p. 1993. 55.00 (*1-55738-436-3*, Irwn Prfssnl) McGraw-Hill Prof.

New High Yield Market: A Handbook for Portfolio Managers & Analysts. Frank J. Fabozzi. 608p. 1990. 65.00 (*0-88730-430-3*, HarpBusn) HarpInfo.

New Hilton Head Metabolism Diet. Peter M. Miller. 256p. (Orig.). 1996. mass mkt. 6.99 (*0-446-60325-2*, Pub. by Warner Bks) Little.

New Hiscox Guide for Baptist Churches. Everett C. Goodwin. LC 95-5880. 352p. 1995. 23.00 (*0-8170-1215-X*) Judson.

New Hispanics: The New Image for New Leaders. Edward Valdez & Kim Valdez. 112p. (Orig.). 1994. pap. 9.95 (*1-886291-00-4*) CEO Intl.

***New Historians of the 12th-Century Renaissance: Authorising History in the Vernacular Revolution.** Peter Damian-Grint. LC 99-37949. 320p. 1999. 90.00 (*0-85115-760-2*, Suffolk Records Soc) Boydell & Brewer.

New Historical Atlas of Religion in America. 3rd ed. (Illus.). 416p. 2000. text 125.00 (*0-19-509168-X*) OUP.

***New Historical Dictionary of the American Film Industry.** Ed. by Anthony Slide. 256p. 1998. pap. text 55.00 (*1-57958-056-4*) Fitzroy Dearborn.

New Historical Dictionary of the American Film Industry. Anthony Slide. LC 97-35737. 256p. 1998. 55.00 (*0-8108-3426-X*) Scarecrow.

New Historical Literary Study: Essays on Reproducing Texts, Representing History. Ed. by Jeffrey Cox & Larry Reynolds. (Illus.). 344p. (C). 1993. text 57.50 (*0-691-06990-5*, Pub. by Princeton U Pr) Cal Prin Full Svc.

New Historicism. Ed. by Harold Veeser. 288p. 1989. 39.50 (*0-415-90069-7*) Routledge.

New Historicism. Ed. by Harold Veeser. 272p. (C). 1989. pap. 19.99 (*0-415-90070-0*) Routledge.

***New-Historicism: Studies in Renaissance Literature, History & Politics.** Ed. by Robin Headlam Wells et al. (Studies in Renaissance Literature). 256p. 2000. 75.00 (*0-85991-581-6*) Boydell & Brewer.

New Historicism & Cultural Materialism. John Brannigan. LC 97-52610. (Transitions Ser.). 272p. 1998. pap. 19.95 (*0-312-21389-1*) St Martin.

New Historicism & Cultural Materialism. Phillippe Burrin. 480p. text. write for info. (*0-340-65222-5*, Pub. by E A) Routldge.

New Historicism & Cultural Materialism: A Reader. Ed. by Kiernan Ryan. 232p. 1996. 65.00 (*0-340-66307-3*, Pub. by E A) OUP.

New Historicism & Cultural Materialism: A Reader. Kiernan Ryan. 232p. 1996. pap. text 19.95 (*0-340-61458-7*, Pub. by E A) OUP.

New Historicism & Renaissance Drama: Longman Critical Readers. Wilson Wilson & Richard Dutton. 249p. (C). 1992. pap. text 28.50 (*0-582-04554-1*, 79285) Longman.

New Historicism & the Comedia: Poetics, Politics & Praxis. Ed. by Jose A. Madrigal. LC 97-66177. (ENG & SPA.). 236p. 1997. pap. 30.00 (*0-89295-087-0*) Society Sp & Sp-Am.

New Historicism Reader. Ed. by Harold Veeser. 288p. (C). (gr. 13). 1993. pap. 23.99 (*0-415-90782-9*, B0627) Routledge.

New Historicism Renaissance. Wilson Wilson & Richard Dutton. 249p. (C). 1995. 74.00 (*0-582-04562-2*, 79284) Longman.

New History & the Old. Gertrude Himmelfarb. LC 87-327. (Illus.). 224p. 1987. 34.95 (*0-674-61580-8*) HUP.

New History & the Old: Critical Essays & Reappraisals. Gertrude Himmelfarb. 224p. 1989. reprint ed. pap. text 16.00 (*0-674-61581-6*) HUP.

New History & the Social Studies. Harry E. Barnes. (Harry Elmer Barnes Ser.). (Illus.). 624p. 1972. reprint ed. lib. bdg. 300.00 (*0-87700-033-6*) Revisionist Pr.

New History in an Old Museum: Creating the Past at Colonial Williamsburg. Richard Handler & Eric Gable. LC 96-6519. (Illus.). 304p. 1997. pap. 16.95 (*0-8223-1974-8*); lib. bdg. 49.95 (*0-8223-1978-0*) Duke.

New History of American People. Deutsch. (History Ser.). 1919. pap., wbk. ed. 10.00 (*0-534-55019-3*) Wadsworth Pub.

New History of American People. Deutsch. (History Ser.). 1919. 24.00 (*0-534-55021-5*); 50.00 (*0-314-22556-0*) Wadsworth Pub.

New History of American People, Vol. 1. Deutsch. (History Ser.). 1919. 30.00 (*0-534-55017-7*) Wadsworth Pub.

New History of American People, Vol. 2. Deutsch. (History Ser.). 1919. 30.00 (*0-534-55018-5*) Wadsworth Pub.

New History of British Shipping. Ronald Hope. (Illus.). 533p. 1991. 75.00 (*0-7195-4799-7*, Pub. by John Murray) Trafalgar.

***New History of Christianity.** Vivian H. Green. (Illus.). 472p. 2000. pap. text 27.95 (*0-8264-1227-0*) Continuum.

New History of Classical Rhetoric. George A. Kennedy. LC 94-11249. 336p. 1995. pap. text 19.95 (*0-691-00059-X*, Pub. by Princeton U Pr) Cal Prin Full Svc.

New History of Early English Drama. John D. Cox & David S. Kastan. LC 96-29670. 1997. 52.00 (*0-231-10242-9*) Col U Pr.

New History of Early English Drama. John Cox & David Kaston. LC 96-29670. (Illus.). 384p. (C). 1997. 25.00 (*0-231-10243-7*) Col U Pr.

New History of Educational Philosophy, 58. James S. Kaminsky. LC 92-25742. (Contributions to the Study of Education Ser.: No. 58). 304p. 1993. 62.95 (*0-313-28430-X*, KHN, Greenwood Pr) Greenwood.

***New History of England.** Jeremy Black. 288p. 2000. pap. 15.95 (*0-7509-2319-9*) Sutton Publng.

New History of Florida. Ed. by Michael Gannon. LC 95-11055. (Illus.). 492p. (C). 1996. 34.95 (*0-8130-1415-8*) U Press Fla.

New History of French Literature. Denis Hollier. LC 88-27027. (Illus.). 1280p. 1989. 68.00 (*0-674-61565-4*) HUP.

New History of French Literature. Ed. by Denis Hollier. LC 95-139611. (Illus.). 1184p. 1994. pap. text 29.95 (*0-674-61566-2*, HOLNEX) HUP.

New History of India. 6th ed. Stanley Wolpert. LC 99-17705. (Illus.). 528p. (C). 1999. text 49.95 (*0-19-512876-1*) OUP.

New History of India. 6th ed. Stanley A. Wolpert. LC 99-17705. 528p. (C). 1999. pap. text 27.95 (*0-19-512877-X*) OUP.

New History of Ireland Vol. II: Medieval Ireland, 1169-1534. 2nd rev. ed. Ed. by Art Cosgrove. (New History of Ireland Ser.: No. 2). (Illus.). 1,064p. 1993. text 165.00 (*0-19-821755-2*) OUP.

New History of Ireland Vol. V: Ireland under the Union, Pt. 1; 1801-1870. Ed. by W. E. Vaughan. (New History of Ireland Ser.: No. 5). (Illus.). 904p. 1990. text 165.00 (*0-19-821743-9*) OUP.

New History of Ireland Vol. VI: Ireland under the Union II, 1870-1921. Ed. by W. E. Vaughan. (New History of Ireland Ser.: No. II). (Illus.). 974p. 1996. text 165.00 (*0-19-821751-X*) OUP.

New History of Kentucky. Lowell H. Harrison & James C. Klotter. LC 96-35904. (Illus.). 464p. 1997. 34.95 (*0-8131-2008-X*) U Pr of Ky.

New History of Korea. Ki-baik Lee. Tr. by Edward W. Wagner & Edward J. Schultz from KOR. LC 83-246. (Harvard-Yenching Institute Studies). (Illus.). 472p. 1985. 25.00 (*0-674-61575-1*) HUP.

New History of Korea. Ki-baik Lee. Tr. by Edward W. Wagner & Edward J. Schultz from KOR. LC 83-246. (Harvard-Yenching Institute Publications). (Illus.). 472p. 1985. reprint ed. pap. 14.95 (*0-674-61576-X*) HUP.

New History of Medieval India. A. C. Banerjee. 1983. text 23.00 (*0-685-14083-0*) Coronet Bks.

New History of Modern India, 1707-1947. Anil Chandra Banerjee. (C). 1992. reprint ed. 15.00 (*81-7074-122-X*, Pub. by KP Bagchi) S Asia.

New History of Muhlenberg County. Paul Camplin. LC 84-71350. (Illus.). 304p. 1985. 28.95 (*0-9613634-0-1*) Caney Station Bks.

New History of Music: The Middle Ages to Mozart. Henry Prunieres. (Music Book Index Ser.). 413p. 1992. reprint ed. lib. bdg. 99.00 (*0-7812-9465-7*) Rprt Serv.

New History of Old Windsor, Connecticut. Daniel Howard. 428p. 1997. reprint ed. lib. bdg. 45.00 (*0-8328-5701-7*) Higginson Bk Co.

New History of Philosophy, Vol. 1. Wallace I. Matson. (C). 1997. pap. text 32.50 (*0-15-517661-7*) Harcourt.

New History of Philosophy, Vol. 1. 2nd ed. Matson. (C). 1999. text 44.50 (*0-15-507848-8*, Pub. by Harcourt Coll Pubs) Harcourt.

New History of Philosophy, Vol. 1: Ancient & Medieval. Wallace I. Matson. (Illus.). 249p. (C). 1987. pap. text 30.25 (*0-15-565728-3*) Harcourt Coll Pubs.

New History of Philosophy, Vol. 2: Modern. Wallace I. Matson. (Illus.). 236p. (C). 1987. pap. text 38.50 (*0-15-565729-1*, Pub. by Harcourt Coll Pubs) Harcourt.

New History of Photography. Contrib. by Michael Vrizot. (Illus.). 776p. 1998. 39.95 (*3-8290-1328-0*, 520494) Konemann.

***New History of Social Welfare.** 3rd ed. Phyllis J. Day. LC 99-24028. 469p. (C). 1999. 61.00 (*0-205-29691-2*) Allyn.

New History of Spanish Literature. rev. ed. Richard E. Chandler & Kessel Schwartz. LC 91-2667. 479p. 1991. text 67.50 (*0-8071-1699-8*) La State U Pr.

***New History of Spanish Writing, 1939 to the 1990s.** Chris Perriam et al. 240p. 2000. pap. 24.95 (*0-19-871517-X*); text 65.00 (*0-19-871516-1*) OUP.

New History of the American People Map Workbook. Deutsch. (History Ser.). 1919. pap., wbk. ed. 10.00 (*0-534-55020-7*) Thomson Learn.

New History of the Civil War. Bruce Catton. 1996. pap. write for info. (*0-670-78082-0*) Viking Penguin.

New History of the English Public Library: Social & Intellectual Contexts, 1850-1914. Alistair Blackleeds. LC 95-41411. 352p. 1996. 95.00 (*0-7185-0015-6*) Bks Intl VA.

New History of the Italian South: The Mezzogiorno Revisited. Ed. by Robert Lumley & Jonathan Morris. (Illus.). 160p. 1998. pap. text 22.50 (*0-85989-506-8*, Pub. by Univ Exeter Pr) Northwestern U Pr.

New History of the Marathas, 3 vols. Govind S. Sardesai. 1986. 40.00 (*81-215-0067-2*, Pub. by M Manoharial) Coronet Bks.

New History of the Marathas, 3 vols., Vol. 1: Shivaji & His Line, 1600-1707. Govind S. Sardesai. 1986. 40.00 (*81-215-0066-4*, Pub. by M Manoharial) Coronet Bks.

New History of the Marathas, 3 vols., Vol. 3: Sunset over Maharashtra, 1772-1848. Govind S. Sardesai. 1986. 40.00 (*81-215-0068-0*, Pub. by M Manoharial) Coronet Bks.

New History of the Royal Mint. Ed. by C. E. Challis. (Illus.). 830p. (C). 1993. text 175.00 (*0-521-24026-3*) Cambridge U Pr.

***New History of Wales.** Jeremy Black. 256p. 2000. pap. 15.95 (*0-7509-2320-2*) Sutton Publng.

New History of Western Australia. C. T. Stannage. (Illus.). 836p. (C). 1993. pap. 39.95 (*0-85564-181-9*, Pub. by Univ of West Aust Pr) Intl Spec Bk.

New Hobbit. Philip W. Helms & David L. Dettman. 52p. 1991. pap. 5.00 (*1-881799-01-8*) Am Tolkien Soc.

New Holiday Songs for Children: A Creative Approach. Beth R. Mochnick. Ed. by Barbara Davis. (Illus.). iv, 44p. (J). 1988. pap. text 15.95 (*0-916656-25-X*, MFBK 25) Mark Foster Mus.

New Holistic Herbal. 3rd ed. David Hoffmann. 284p. 1991. pap. 16.95 (*1-85230-193-7*, NEHOLP, Pub. by Element MA) Penguin Putnam.

New Holland Journal: Baron Charles von Hugel November 1833-October 1834. Ed. & Tr. by Dymphna Clark. (Miegunyah Press Ser.: No. 1:17). (Illus.). 240p. 1995. 49.95 (*0-522-84474-X*, Pub. by Melbourne Univ Pr) Paul & Co Pubs.

New Holy Office, or Why I Oppose Conscription see Reminiscences of War Resisters in World War I

New Home - Who'll Follow? Glimpses of Western Life. Caroline M. Kirkland. Ed. by William S. Osborne. (Masterworks of Literature Ser.). 1965. pap. 15.95 (*0-8084-0233-1*) NCUP.

New Home Advertising That Works. Richard Elkman. LC 96-21824. 1996. write for info. (*0-86718-418-3*) Home Builder.

New Home & Warranty Inspection Handbook. Joseph Natale, Jr. 40p. 1997. pap. 19.95 (*0-9659999-0-4*) ARCC.

New Home Buyer's Guide. Martin E. Turk. 1994. pap. 14.95 (*0-9632701-1-7*) Groom Bks.

New Home Buyer's Workbook. National Association of Home Builders Staff & Patricia Ratzlaff. Ed. by John Tuttle. 32p. 1995. student ed. 25.00 (*0-86718-402-7*) Home Builder.

New Home Buying Strategy: Solve Your Cash Crunch with Team Buying Power. Marilyn D. Sullivan. LC 96-20702. 416p. 1997. pap. 24.95 (*0-9629239-1-5*) Venture Two.

New Home Decorating Projects Step By Step, 1999. pap. text 24.95 (*0-86573-179-9*) Creative Intl.

***New Home for Fab the Fox.** Eli A. Cantillon. (Illus.). 14p. (J). (ps-1). 1998. 14.98 (*1-58048-043-8*) Sandvik Pub.

New Home for Tiger. Joan Stimson. (Illus.). 40p. (J). 1997. pap. 5.50 (*0-7641-0102-1*) Barron.

New Home Library Vol. 5: PV the Greatest Sons of 1975-1990. CPP Belwin Staff. 1994. pap. text 12.95 (*0-89898-986-8*) Wrner Bros.

New Home Library Vol. 7: PV Movies. 112p. (YA). 1990. pap. 12.95 (*0-7692-1055-4*, THL1007A) Wrner Bros.

New Home Library - Classical Vol. 10: Easy Piano. 144p. (Orig.). 1990. pap. 12.95 (*0-7692-1132-1*, THL2010A) Wrner Bros.

New Home Library - Country, Vol. 9. 112p. (Orig.). 1994. pap. 12.95 (*0-89898-845-4*, THL1009C) Wrner Bros.

New Home Library - Movies Vol. 7: Easy Piano. 112p. (Orig.). 1994. pap. 12.95 (*0-7692-1131-3*, THL2007B) Wrner Bros.

New Home Library, 1960-1975 Vol. 4: Easy Piano. 112p. (Orig.). 1994. pap. 12.95 (*0-7692-1129-1*, THL2004B) Wrner Bros.

***New Home, New School.** Lynne Caluggero. (Illus.). 40p. (J). (ps-3). 2000. 6.50 (*0-9700250-0-9*) L Lemon O'Pea.

New Home Plans for 2000. Garlinghouse Company Staff. LC 98-75666. 1999. pap. text 4.95 (*0-938708-87-2*) L F Garlinghouse Co.

***New Home Plans for 2001.** Garlinghouse Staff. LC 99-76701. (Illus.). 256p. 2000. pap. 4.95 (*0-938708-93-7*) L F Garlinghouse Co.

New Home Sales Management: How to Build & Lead a Winning Team. Bonnie Alfriend & Richard Tiller. 350p. (Orig.). 1996. pap. text 29.95 (*0-9639500-1-0*) Alfriend & Assocs.

New Home Selling Strategies: A Handbook for Success. Nancy Davenport-Ennis. 206p. (Orig.). 1992. pap. 24.95 (*0-7931-0354-1*, 1909-0601, Real Estate Ed) Dearborn.

New Home, Who'll Follow? Caroline M. Kirkland. Ed. by Sandra A. Zagarell. (American Women Writers Ser.). 250p. (C). 1990. text 40.00 (*0-8135-1541-6*); pap. text 16.00 (*0-8135-1542-4*) Rutgers U Pr.

New Homeless & Old: Community & the Skid Row Hotel. Charles Hoch & Robert A. Slayton. (Conflicts in Urban & Regional Development Ser.). 312p. 1990. pap. 22.95 (*0-87722-765-9*) Temple U Pr.

***New Homeowner's Handbook: What to Do after You Move In.** Nehemiah Progressive Housing Development Corporation, Inc. Staff. 2000. pap. 13.95 (*0-7931-3818-3*) Dearborn.

New Homes for Old see Americanization Studies: The Acculturation of Immigrant Groups into American Society

New Homes for Old. Sophonisba P. Breckenridge. LC 99-51436. 365p. 1999. pap. 29.95 (*0-7658-0607-X*) Transaction Pubs.

New Homes in a New Land: German Immigration to Texas, 1847-1861. Ethel H. Geue. (Illus.). 166p. 1999. pap. 21.50 (*0-8063-0980-6*, 2173, Pub. by Clearfield Co) ACCESS Pubs Network.

New Honey & Yogurt Recipes. Rena Cross. 1995. pap. 5.95 (*0-572-01441-4*, Pub. by Foulsham UK) Assoc Pubs Grp.

***New Hope.** Ernest Haycox. 256p. 2000. pap. 4.50 (*0-8439-4721-7*, Leisure Bks) Dorchester Pub Co.

New Hope. George Lucas. (Star Wars Ser.). 272p. 1995. 16.00 (*0-345-40077-1*, Del Rey) Ballantine Pub Grp.

New Hope. Henri Sorensen. LC 94-78939. (Illus.). 32p. (J). (gr. k up). 1995. 15.00 (*0-688-13925-6*); lib. bdg. 14.93 (*0-688-13926-4*) Lothrop.

***New Hope.** Henri Sorensen. 1998. 11.19 (*0-606-13658-4*, Pub. by Turtleback) Demco.

New Hope. Star Wars Staff. LC 97-97054. (Star Wars Ser.). (Illus.). 208p. 1998. pap. 12.00 (*0-345-42069-1*, Del Rey) Ballantine Pub Grp.

New Hope. Larry Weinberg. (Illus.). 1995. pap. 3.99 (*0-679-87203-5*) Random.

New Hope. deluxe ed. George Lucas. LC PN1997.S65943 1998b. (Star Wars Ser.). (Illus.). 192p. 1998. pap. 18.95 (*0-345-42080-2*, Del Rey) Ballantine Pub Grp.

New Hope. limited ed. Christopher Golden. (Choose Your Own Star Wars Adventure Ser.). (Illus.). 128p. (J). (gr. 4-8). 1998. pap. 4.50 (*0-553-48651-9*, Skylark BDD) BDD Bks Young Read.

New Hope. Ruth Suckow. LC 97-43862. (Bur Oak Book Ser.). 358p. 1998. reprint ed. pap. 12.95 (*0-87745-630-5*) U of Iowa Pr.

New Hope: Special Edition. Bruce Jones et al. (Star Wars Ser.). 104p. 1997. pap. 9.95 (*1-56971-213-1*) Dark Horse Comics.

New Hope: The Art of Star Wars. 2nd ed. Carol W. Titelman. LC 96-95204. (Star Wars). 1997. pap. 18.95 (*0-345-40980-9*, Del Rey) Ballantine Pub Grp.

New Hope!!! There Is New Hope for the Drug & Alcohol Abuser - You Too Can Be Healed! Ruth E. Norman. (Illus.). 48p. (Orig.). (C). 1984. pap. 4.00 (*0-932642-96-9*) Unarius Acad Sci.

***New Hope: Western Stories.** Ernest Haycox. LC 99-11208. 1999. 20.95 (*0-7862-1033-8*) Mac Lib Ref.

New Hope: Western Stories. Ernest Haycox. LC 98-10088. 1998. 18.95 (*0-7862-0994-1*) Thorndike Pr.

New Hope: 12 Talks. 2nd ed. Sun Myung Moon. 1982. 4.95 (*0-910621-02-0*) HSA Pubns.

New Hope for Alcoholics. Osmond & Hoffer. 7.50 (*0-8216-0007-9*) Carol Pub Group.

New Hope for Broken Marriages. Dana Hartong & Val Hartong. 1994. 7.00 (*0-9644136-0-4*) New Hope Broken Marriages.

New Hope for Deprived Children. Betty M. Flint. LC 77-16287. 212p. reprint ed. pap. 65.80 (*0-608-16892-0*, 202641200049) Bks Demand.

***New Hope for People with Bipolar Disorder.** Jan Fawcett. 2000. 24.95 (*0-7615-3008-8*) Prima Pub.

New Hope Friends Meeting & the Elroy Community: A History. James K. Thompson. 174p. 1987. pap. 7.50 (*0-942585-15-1*) NC Frnds Hist Soc.

New Hope Series, 10 bks., Set. John Benton. 2004p. (J). (gr. 3-12). 35.00 (*0-9635411-1-0*) J Benton Bks.

New Horizon . . . Myungkark Park. (Illus.). 100p. (Orig.). 1991. pap. write for info. (*1-877974-19-6*) Prompter Pubns.

New Horizon. Dorothy Simpson. 192p. Date not set. 20.95 (*0-8488-2622-1*) Amereon Ltd.

***New Horizon: For the Right Hand Alone.** Randall Hartsell. 1999. mass mkt. 2.50 (*0-7390-0315-1*, 18992) Alfred Pub.

New Horizon English - Japanese Dictionary. Tokyo Shoseki. (JPN., Illus.). 640p. 1980. pap. 14.95 (*4-487-34251-1*) Heian Intl.

New Horizon for Psychotherapy: Autonomy As a Profession. Ed. by Robert R. Holt. LC 77-143391. 418p. 1971. 62.50 (*0-8236-3580-5*) Intl Univs Pr.

New Horizon Ladder Dictionary of the English Language. Signet Staff. 1996. mass mkt. 7.99 (*0-451-18892-6*, Sig) NAL.

New Horizons. (Transactions Ser.: Vol. 12). 500p. 1988. 40.00 (*0-934412-64-2*) Geothermal.

New Horizons? Gwynne. 1990. pap. 25.95 (*0-582-02519-2*, Pub. by Addison-Wesley) Longman.

New Horizons. Ernest Holmes. Ed. by Willis H. Kinnear. 96p. (Orig.). 1973. pap. 5.95 (*0-911336-52-4*) Sci of Mind.

New Horizons. 2nd ed. Baehr. 276p. 1998. pap. text 36.00 (*0-536-02000-0*) Pearson Custom.

New Horizons: A Guide to Sexuality after Spinal Cord Injury. Pam Bieluniss. Ed. by Betty Garee. LC 95-67324. 100p. (Orig.). 1995. pap. 7.95 (*0-915708-42-6*) Cheever Pub.

New Horizons: An AOCS CSMA Detergent Industry Conference. Richard T. Coffey. LC 96-49995. 1996. 60.00 (*0-935315-78-0*) Am Oil Chemists.

New Horizons: Proceedings of the Institute of Environmental Sciences 14th Annual Technical Meeting, St. Louis, 1968. (Illus.). 1968. pap. text 75.00 (*0-915414-08-2*) IEST.

***New Horizons: The Story of Ashland Inc.** Jeffrey L. Rodengen. LC 97-62155. xi, 223 p. 1999. 39.95 (*0-945903-42-1*) Write Stuff Syndicate.

New Horizons: Yesterday's Portraits of Tomorrow. Ed. by August Derleth. LC 98-49573. xv, 299p. 1999. 25.95 (*0-87054-174-9*) Arkham.

New Horizons No. 3: Multiple Organ Failure. Ed. by David Bihari & Frank B. Cerra. 1989. write for info. (*0-936145-52-8*) SCCM Fullerton.

New Horizons Vol. 1: Piano Course for Busy Adults. Walter Noona & Carol Noona. 96p. (Orig.). 1992. pap. 8.95 (*0-89328-109-3*, KM152) Lorenz Corp.

An Asterisk (*) at the beginning of an entry indicates that the title is appearing for the first time.

New Horizons Vol. 2: Piano Course for Busy Adults. Walter Noona & Carol Noona. 96p. (Orig.). 1992. pap. 8.95 (*0-89328-111-5*, KM153) Lorenz Corp.

New Horizons & the Future of Heart Valve Bioprotheses: Is Glutaraldehyde a Villain? Ed. by Shlomo Gabbay & Robert W. Frater. (Illus.). 310p. 1995. write for info. (*1-878353-37-3*) Silent Partners.

New Horizons for Failing Heart Syndrome. Ed. by S. Sasayama. LC 95-44936. 1995. write for info. (*3-540-70151-6*) Spr-Verlag.

New Horizons for Failing Heart Syndrome. Ed. by S. Sasayama. LC 95-44936. 1996. 117.00 (*4-431-70151-6*) Spr-Verlag.

New Horizons for Failing Heart Syndrome. Ed. by S. Sasayama. LC 95-44936. (Illus.). x, 238p. 1996. 117.00 (*0-387-70151-6*) Spr-Verlag.

New Horizons II: Oxygen Transport & Utilization. Ed. by Christopher W. Bryan-Brown & Stephen M. Ayres. 1987. write for info. (*0-318-61520-7*) SCCM Fullerton.

New Horizons in Allergy Immunotherapy: Proceedings of the Second International Conference on the Molecular Biology of Allergens & the Atopic Immune Research Held in Quebec City, Canada, February 18-22, 1995. Ed. by Alec Sehon et al. LC 96-50090. (Advances in Experimental Medicine & Biology Ser.: No. 409). (Illus.). 494p. (C). 1997. text 129.50 (*0-306-45498-X*, Kluwer Plenum) Kluwer Academic.

New Horizons in American Art. Holger Cahill. LC 75-86428. (Museum of Modern Art Publications in Reprint). (Illus.). 1969. reprint ed. 24.95 (*0-405-01533-X*) Ayer.

New Horizons in American Art: 1985 Exxon National Exhibition. Lisa Dennison. (Illus.). 120p. (Orig.). 1985. pap. 15.00 (*0-89207-050-1*) S R Guggenheim.

New Horizons in American Indian Art. (Illus.). 1976. pap. 2.00 (*0-916561-54-2*) Southwest Mus.

New Horizons in American Realism. Christopher R. Young. LC 91-71180. (Illus.). 94p. 1991. pap. 14.95 (*0-939896-11-7*) Flint Inst Arts.

New Horizons in Aquatics: CNCA Twentieth National Aquatic Conference, Town & Country Inn, San Diego, CA, November 13-17, 1978. Council for National Cooperation in Aquatics Staff. Ed. by Bernard E. Empleton. LC GV0770.3.C68. (Illus.). 114p. reprint ed. pap. 35.40 (*0-8357-3835-3*, 203656000004) Bks Demand.

New Horizons in Biological Dosimetry. Barton Gledhill & Francesco Mauro. LC 91-18936. (Progress in Clinical & Biological Research Ser.). 648p. 1991. 369.95 (*0-471-56128-2*, Wiley-Interscience) Wiley.

New Horizons in Carbonyl Chemistry: Reagents for Nucleophilic Acylation. Ed. by O. W. Lever. 29p. 1976. pap. 12.75 (*0-08-021334-0*, Pergamon Pr) Elsevier.

New Horizons in Chinese Linguistics. Ed. by C. T. Huang. (Studies in Natural Language & Linguistic Theory). 400p. (C). 1996. pap. text 69.00 (*0-7923-3868-5*) Kluwer Academic.

New Horizons in Chinese Linguistics. Ed. by C. T. Huang & Y. H. Li. (Studies in Natural Language & Linguistic Theory: Vol. 36). 400p. (C). 1996. text 155.00 (*0-7923-3867-7*) Kluwer Academic.

New Horizons in Construction Materials. Ed. by D. Y. Lee & S. P. Shah. (Session Proceedings Ser.). 96p. 1988. 5.00 (*0-87262-677-6*) Am Soc Civil Eng.

New Horizons in Construction Materials: (International Symposium), Vol. 1. Ed. by Hsai-Yang Fang. LC 76-27387. 682p. 1976. 35.00 (*0-932871-04-6*) Envo Pub Co.

New Horizons in Construction Materials: (International Symposium), Vol. 2. Ed. by Hsai-Yang Fang. LC 76-27397. 152p. 1982. pap. 14.50 (*0-932871-07-0*) Envo Pub Co.

New Horizons in Creative Thinking. Institute for Religious & Social Studies Staff. Ed. by R. M. MacIver. LC 75-26660. (Religion & Civilization Series). 159p. 1976. reprint ed. lib. bdg. 55.00 (*0-8371-8371-5*, MANHC, Greenwood Pr) Greenwood.

New Horizons in East-West Economic & Business Relations. Ed. by Marvin R. Jackson & James D. Woodson. 277p. 1984. text 65.00 (*0-88033-048-1*, Pub. by East Eur Monographs) Col U Pr.

New Horizons in Electric, Magnetic & Gravitation Field Theory. 1987. 22.50 (*0-914119-18-4*) Tesla Bk Co.

New Horizons in Electrochemical Science & Technology. National Research Council Staff. 164p. 1987. pap. text 17.95 (*0-309-03735-2*) Natl Acad Pr.

New Horizons in English. Mellgren. 1980. text 63.07 (*0-201-60403-5*) Addison-Wesley.

New Horizons in English. 2nd ed. Mellgren. 1983. pap. text 20.08 (*0-201-04589-3*) S&S Trade.

New Horizons in English, Bk. 2. 3rd ed. Michael Walker, Jr. 128p. 1991. pap. text, student ed. 12.61 (*0-201-53504-1*); ring bd., wbk. ed. 7.23 (*0-201-53506-8*) Addison-Wesley.

New Horizons in English, Bk. 3. 3rd ed. Michael Walker, Jr. 128p. 1991. pap. text, student ed. 12.61 (*0-201-53508-4*); ring bd., wbk. ed. 7.23 (*0-201-53510-6*) Addison-Wesley.

New Horizons in English, Bk. 4. 3rd ed. Michael Walker, Jr. 1991. pap. text, student ed. 12.61 (*0-201-53512-2*); ring bd., wbk. ed. 7.23 (*0-201-53514-9*) Addison-Wesley.

New Horizons in English, Bk. 5. 3rd ed. Michael Walker, Jr. 1991. pap. text, student ed. 12.61 (*0-201-53516-5*); pap. text, student ed., wbk. ed. 7.23 (*0-201-53518-1*) Addison-Wesley.

New Horizons in English, Bk. 6. 3rd ed. Michael Walker, Jr. 1991. pap. text, student ed. 12.61 (*0-201-53520-3*); ring bd., wbk. ed. 7.23 (*0-201-53522-X*) Addison-Wesley.

New Horizons in English, Vol. 1. 3rd ed. M. Walker. (NHE Ser.). (Illus.). 128p. 1991. pap. text, student ed. 12.61 (*0-201-53500-9*); student ed., ring bd. 7.22 (*0-201-53502-5*) Addison-Wesley.

New Horizons in Facial Nerve Research & Facial Expression. Ed. by Naoaki Yanagihara. (Illus.). x, 610p. 1998. 183.00 (*90-6299-166-1*) Kugler Pubns.

New Horizons in Hermeneutics: The Theory & Practice of Transforming Biblical Reading. Anthony C. Thiselton. 720p. 1997. pap. 29.99 (*0-310-21762-8*) Zondervan.

New Horizons in Human Biology. I. J. Bansal et al. (Illus.). 250p. 1991. 59.00 (*1-55528-254-7*, Pub. by Today Tomorrow) Scholarly Pubns.

New Horizons in International Law. 2nd rev. ed. T. O. Elias. LC 92-21623. 416p. (C). 1992. lib. bdg. 133.50 (*0-7923-1871-4*) Kluwer Academic.

New Horizons in Latin America. John J. Considine. LC 74-93330. (Essay Index Reprint Ser.). 1977. 30.95 (*0-8369-1561-5*) Ayer.

New Horizons in Low Dimensional Electron Systems: A Festschrift in Honour of Professor H. Kamimura. Ed. by A. Aoki et al. 488p. (C). 1992. text 287.50 (*0-7923-1302-X*) Kluwer Academic.

New Horizons in Natural Gas Deregulation. Ed. by Jerry P. Ellig & Joseph P. Kalt. LC 95-11263. 304p. 1996. 65.00 (*0-275-95168-5*, Praeger Pubs) Greenwood.

New Horizons in Neonatal Screening: Proceedings of the Nineth International Neonatal Screening Symposium, & the 2nd Meeting of the International Society for Neonatal Screening, Lille, France, 13-17 September 1993. Ed. by Jean-Pierre Farriaux & Jean-Louis Dhondt. LC 93-46349. (International Congress Ser.: Vol. 1041). 406p. 1994. 205.50 (*0-444-81602-X*) Elsevier.

New Horizons in Neuropsychology: Proceedings of the 9th Tokyo Metropolitan Institute of Neuroscience (TMIN) Symposium 'New Horizons in Neuropsychology', Tokyo, 24-25 November 1993. Tokyo Metropolitan Institute of Neuroscience Sympo. Ed. by Morihiro Sugishita. LC 94-37535. 242p. 1994. 184.75 (*0-444-81757-3*) Elsevier.

New Horizons in Nitrogen Fixation: Proceedings of the 9th International Congress on Nitrogen Fixation, Cancun, Mexico, December 6-12, 1992. Rafael Palacios. (Current Plant Science & Biotechnology in Agriculture Ser.). 808p. (C). 1993. text 289.50 (*0-7923-2207-X*) Kluwer Academic.

New Horizons in Pediatric Exercise Science. Ed. by Cameron J. Blimkie & Oded Bar-Or. LC 95-7588. 264p. 1995. text 40.00 (*0-87322-528-7*, BBLI0528) Human Kinetics.

***New Horizons in Pro-p Groups.** Ed. by D. Segal et al. (Progress in Mathematics Ser.: Vol. 184). (Illus.). 440p. 2000. 64.95 (*0-8176-4171-8*, Pub. by Birkhauser) Spr-Verlag.

New Horizons in Quasicrystals Research & Applications. LC 97-160064. 300p. 1997. 54.00 (*981-02-3033-8*) World Scientific Pub.

New Horizons in Quilting. Doris Carmack. 47p. 1992. pap. 14.95 (*1-883504-03-1*) Sew-Art Int.

New Horizons in Radiation Protection & Shielding Proceedings, Pasco, WA, Apr. 26-May 1, 1992. 652p. 94.00 (*0-89448-168-1*, 700169) Am Nuclear Soc.

New Horizons in Reading: Proceedings of the World Congress on Reading, 5th, Vienna, Austria, 1975. World Congress on Reading Staff. Ed. by John E. Merritt. LC 75-35998. 582p. reprint ed. pap. 180.50 (*0-608-14959-4*, 202596900047) Bks Demand.

New Horizons in Reproductive Medicine. Cristos Coutifaris & Luigi Mastroianni. LC 96-37080. (International Congress, Symposium & Seminar Ser.: Vol. 12). (Illus.). 620p. 1997. text 98.00 (*1-85070-793-6*) Prthnon Pub.

New Horizons in Sephardic Studies. Ed. by Yedida K. Stillman & George K. Zucker. LC 92-13578. (SUNY Series in Anthropology & Judaic Studies). 309p. (C). 1993. text 64.50 (*0-7914-1401-9*); pap. text 21.95 (*0-7914-1402-7*) State U NY Pr.

New Horizons in Sperm Cell Research. Hideo Mohri. xx, 516p. 1987. text 361.00 (*2-88124-254-5*) Gordon & Breach.

New Horizons in Testing: Latent Trait Test & Computerized Adaptive Testing. David J. Weiss. 1983. text 65.00 (*0-12-742780-5*) Acad Pr.

New Horizons in the Pharmaceutical Industry. Business Communications Co., Inc. Staff. 245p. 1990. 2450.00 (*0-89336-566-1*, C-072) BCC.

New Horizons in the Philosophy of Science. Ed. by David Lamb. (Philosophy of Science Ser.). 200p. 1992. 72.95 (*1-85628-296-1*, Pub. by Avebry) Ashgate Pub Co.

New Horizons in the Study of Ancient Syria. Ed. by Mark W. Chavalas & John L. Hayes. LC 92-42733. (Bibliotheca Mesopotamica Ser.: Vol. 25). 1992. 41.00 (*0-89003-324-2*); pap. 31.00 (*0-89003-323-4*) Undena Pubns.

***New Horizons in the Study of Language & Mind.** Noam Chomsky. 256p. 2000. 54.95 (*0-521-65147-6*); pap. 19.95 (*0-521-65822-5*) Cambridge U Pr.

New Horizons Multi Wave. Ed. by Brian J. McLean et al. LC 97-31469. (International Astronomical Union Symposia Ser.: No. 179). 508p. 1997. 182.00 (*0-7923-4802-8*); pap. 90.00 (*0-7923-4803-6*) Kluwer Academic.

New Horizons of Economic Progress. Ed. by Lawrence H. Seltzer. LC 64-13304. (Franklin Memorial Lectures Ser.: No. 12). 169p. reprint ed. pap. 52.40 (*0-7837-3803-X*, 204362300010) Bks Demand.

New Horizons of Quantum Chemistry. Ed. by Per-Olov Lowdin & Bernard Pullman. 1982. text 220.00 (*90-277-1526-2*) Kluwer Academic.

New Horizons of Social Welfare & Policy. Ed. by Brij Mohan. (Illus.). 140p. (Orig.). 1985. 18.95 (*0-87073-158-0*); pap. 13.95 (*0-87073-159-9*) Schenkman Bks Inc.

New Horizons of Soviet Policies. Rajiv Shah. 103p. 1988. text 15.95 (*81-7050-062-1*, Pub. by Patriot Pubs) Advent Bks Div.

New Horizons, Poems' see Uj Egtajak

New Horizons the Complete Guide to Horse Careers. Sue Reynolds. Ed. by Bobette Host. LC 98-65621. 1998. per. 29.95 (*0-9663559-0-3*) New Horizons CO.

New Horizons with Biological Response Modifiers in Haematological Malignancies. Ed. by J. M. Goldman. (Journal: Acta Haematologica: Vol. 89, Suppl. 1, 1993). (Illus.). vi, 34p. 1993. pap. 17.50 (*3-8055-5801-5*) S Karger.

New Horse for Marny. Libby Anderson. (Illus.). 1994. pap. 9.95 (*0-939481-41-3*) Half Halt Pr.

New Hospital: Future Strategies for a Changing Industry. Russell C. Coile, Jr. 220p. 1986. 85.00 (*0-87189-363-0*) Aspen Pub.

New Hospital Supervisor. Nancy L. Diekelmann & Martin M. Broadwell. (Illus.). 1977. pap. text. write for info. (*0-201-00773-8*) Addison-Wesley.

New Hot Discography. Charles Delaunay. 1948. 24.95 (*0-910468-04-4*) Criterion Mus.

New Hotel No. 3: International Hotel & Resort Design. Michael Kaplan. (Illus.). 184p. 1996. 47.50 (*0-86636-396-3*) PBC Intl Inc.

New Hotel No. 3: International Hotel & Resort Design. Michael Kaplan. (Illus.). 184p. 1998. pap. write for info. (*0-86636-490-0*) PBC Intl Inc.

New Hotel Architecture. Meisei Publications Editorial Staff. (Illus.). 400p. 1993. 115.00 (*4-87246-282-3*, Pub. by Meisei Co Ltd) Bks Nippan.

New Hotels. PBC International Staff. 1998. pap. 35.00 (*0-688-15403-4*, Wm Morrow) Morrow Avon.

New House. Joyce Maynard. (Illus.). 32p. (J). (gr. k-3). 1987. 12.95 (*0-15-257042-X*) Harcourt.

New House Book. Terence Conran. 1999. pap. text 24.95 (*1-84091-112-3*) Conran Octopus.

New House Buyer Guide. William Marchiony. LC 86-70558. (Illus.). 120p. (Orig.). 1986. pap. text, student ed. 18.95 (*0-938411-00-4*) Carefree Living.

***New Houses.** Carles Broto & Arian Mostaedi. (Illus.). 180p. 2000. 69.95 (*3-931884-65-1*, Pub. by Nippon Shuppan) Bks Nippan.

***New Houses in Old Buildings.** Links Editors. (Architectural Design Ser.). 1998. 85.00 (*84-89861-01-3*, Pub. by Links Inter) Bks Nippan.

New Housewife's First Cookbook. Leela Naidu. (C). 1992. pap. 16.00 (*81-85846-00-6*, Pub. by UBS Pubs Dist) S Asia.

New Housing Policy for America: Recapturing the American Dream. David C. Schwartz et al. LC 88-1121. 288p. (C). 1988. 44.95 (*0-87722-567-2*); pap. 24.95 (*0-87722-568-0*) Temple U Pr.

New Housing Policy for America: Recapturing the American Dream. David Schwartz et al. 322p. 1988. 20.00 (*0-685-56596-3*) CPA Washington.

New How to Advertise. expanded rev. ed. Kenneth Roman & Jane Maas. (Illus.). 192p. 1992. 22.95 (*0-685-52426-4*) St Martin.

New How to Pick & Strum the Ukulele, Bk. 1. 64p. 1989. pap. 9.95 (*0-917822-24-2*) Heedays.

New How to Sell Your Home Fast! The Only Guide You'll Need for the Successful Sale of Your Home. Bruce L. Hahn. 142p. (Orig.). 1995. pap. 12.95 (*0-940313-12-X*) Am Home Found.

New HR. Jonathan Smilansky. (Bus Press-New). 224p. 1997. pap. 19.99 (*1-86152-112-X*) Thomson Learn.

New Hugo Winners, No. 4. 4th ed. Ed. by Gregory Benford. 544p. 1997. per. 6.99 (*0-671-87852-2*) Baen Bks.

New Human Genetics. Stine. 1988. teacher ed. 14.06 (*0-697-06911-7*) McGraw.

New Human Genetics. Gerald J. Stine. 528p. (C). 1988. text. write for info. (*0-697-03779-7*, WCB McGr Hill) McGrw-H Hghr Educ.

New Human Revolution, Vol. 1. Daisaku Ikeda. (Illus.). 294p. 1995. pap. 10.00 (*0-915678-33-0*) World Tribune Pr.

New Human Revolution, Vol. 2. Daisaku Ikeda. (Illus.). 296p. 1995. pap. 10.00 (*0-915678-34-9*) World Tribune Pr.

New Human Revolution, Vol. 3. Daisaku Ikeda. (Illus.). 288p. 1996. pap. 10.00 (*0-915678-35-7*) World Tribune Pr.

New Human Revolution, Vol. 4. Daisaku Ikeda. (Illus.). 304p. 1996. pap. 10.00 (*0-915678-36-5*) World Tribune Pr.

New Human Revolution, Vol. 5. Daisaku Ikeda. (Illus.). 296p. 1997. pap. 10.00 (*0-915678-37-3*) World Tribune Pr.

***New Human Revolution, Vol. 6.** Daisaku Ikeda. (Illus.). 312p. 1998. pap. 10.00 (*0-915678-38-1*) World Tribune Pr.

New Humanism: The University Addresses of Daisaku Ikeda. Daisaku Ikeda. 224p. 1995. 29.95 (*0-8348-0334-8*) Weatherhill.

New Humanities & Academic Disciplines: The Case of Jewish Studies. Ed. by Jacob Neusner. LC 83-16893. 216p. 1984. reprint ed. pap. 67.00 (*0-7837-9791-5*, 206052000005) Bks Demand.

New Humanity of Intuition (1938) C. Jinarajadasa. 185p. 1998. reprint ed. pap. 19.95 (*0-7661-0271-8*) Kessinger Pub.

***New Hume Debate.** Rupert J. Read & Kenneth Richman. LC 99-86749. 2000. write for info. (*0-415-23884-6*) Routledge.

New Hungarian Agriculture. Lewis A. Fischer & Phillip E. Uren. LC 73-79093. 160p. reprint ed. pap. 49.60 (*0-608-14629-3*, 202384900034) Bks Demand.

New Hungarian Peasants: An East Central European Experience with Collectivization. Marida Hollos & Bela C. Maday. (East European Monographs: No. 134). 341p. 1983. text 63.00 (*0-88033-024-4*, Pub. by East Eur Monographs) Col U Pr.

New Hydroboration Reagent. Clinton F. Lane & George W. Kabalka. 1976. pap. 12.75 (*0-08-021330-8*, Pergamon Pr) Elsevier.

New Hylid Frog of the Genus Plectrohyla from a Cloud Forest in Honduras. James R. McCranie & Larry D. Wilson. (Occasional Papers: No. 92). 7p. 1981. 1.00 (*0-317-04882-1*) U KS Nat Hist Mus.

New Hymnal. rev. ed. Evangelical Formosan Church Commun. Center Staff. 604p. 1994. pap. 14.95 (*0-9631789-9-7*) Evan Formosan.

New Hymnal for Colleges & Schools. Ed. by Jeffery Rowthorn & Russell Schulz-Widmar. LC 91-5026. 512p. (C). 1992. 25.00 (*0-300-05113-1*) Yale U Pr.

New Hymns for the Lectionary: To Glorify the Maker's Name. Thomas H. Troeger. 144p. 1986. pap. text 7.95 (*0-19-385729-4*) OUP.

New Hymns for the Life of the Church: To Make Our Prayer & Music One. 86p. 1992. pap. text 12.95 (*0-19-385865-7*) OUP.

New Hypnosis in Family Therapy. Daniel L. Araoz & Esther Negley-Parker. LC 87-25960. 304p. 1988. text 35.95 (*0-87630-491-9*) Brunner-Mazel.

New Hypnosis in Sex Therapy: Cognitive-Behavioral Methods for Clinicians. Daniel L. Araoz. LC 97-34484. 208p. 1998. pap. 40.00 (*0-7657-0137-5*) Aronson.

New I. D. in America. (Illus.). 120p. 1983. pap. 18.00 (*0-87364-260-0*) Paladin Pr.

New Iberian World: A Documentary History of the Discovery & Settlement of Latin America to the Early 17th. Century, 5 vols. Incl. Caribbean. LC 82-19664. 592p. Vol. I. Conquerors & the Conquered. Ed. by John H. Parry & Robert G. Keith. LC 82-19664. 512p. 1984. Vol III. Central America & Mexico. Ed. by John H. Parry & Robert G. Keith. LC 82-19664. 624p. 1984. Vol. IV. Andes. Ed. by John H. Parry & Robert G. Keith. LC 82-19664. 592p. 1984. Vol. V. Coastlines, Rivers & Forest. Ed. by John H. Parry & Robert G. Keith. LC 82-19664. 592p. 1984. LC 82-19664. (Illus.). 1984. 500.00 (*0-8129-1070-2*, Times Bks) Crown Pub Group.

New Iberian World: A Documentary History of the Discovery & Settlement of Latin America to the Early 17th. Century, 5 vols., Set. Ed. by John Parry & Robert G. Keith. LC 82-19664. (New Iberian World Ser.). 2912p. 1988. text 250.00 (*0-8240-4839-3*) Garland.

New Icelanders: A North American Community. Ed. by David Arnason & Vincent Arnason. (Illus.). 125p. 1997. pap. 14.95 (*0-88801-186-5*, Pub. by Turnstone Pr) Genl Dist Srvs.

New Icons. Peggy Davis. LC 80-5679. (Lucky Heart Bk.). 16p. 1980. reprint ed. pap. 30.00 (*0-7837-9153-4*, 204985300003) Bks Demand.

New Icons? The Art of Television Advertising. Paul Rutherford. (Illus.). 270p. (C). 1994. text 55.00 (*0-8020-2928-0*); pap. text 19.95 (*0-8020-7428-6*) U of Toronto Pr.

***New Icons: Three Japanese Artists Begin in the West: Tetsuji Aono, Kazuhito Kobayashi, Ren Sakurai.** Kate Bonansinga. Ed. by Terri M. Hopkins. (Illus.). 12p. 2000. pap. 5.00 (*0-914435-34-5*) Marylhurst Art.

New I.D. Your New Identity in Christ. Gary Purdy. (Inter Acta Ser.). (Illus.). 6p. (C). 1994. teacher ed., ring bd. 1.25 (*0-9629245-6-3*, 741-003t, Inter Acta); student ed., ring bd. 3.25 (*0-9629245-5-5*, 741-003s, Inter Acta) WSN Pr.

***New Idea Factory: Expanding Technology Companies with University Intellectual Capital.** Clifford M. Gross et al. LC 00-27204. 180p. 2000. pap. 24.95 (*1-57477-090-X*) Battelle.

New Idea for Special Education. (C). 1999. pap. write for info. (*0-13-016315-5*) P-H.

New Ideas about Self-Directed Learning. Long, Huey B., & Assoc. Staff. 246p. (Orig.). 1994. pap. text 26.95 (*0-9622488-9-4*) U OK PMC.

New Ideas Better Government. Patrick Weller & Glyn Davis. LC 96-211180. 360p. 1996. pap. 24.95 (*1-86448-014-9*, Pub. by Allen & Unwin Pty) Paul & Co Pubs.

New Ideas Efforting School Improvement. Ramsay. 250p. 1990. pap. 39.95 (*1-85000-697-0*, Falmer Pr) Taylor & Francis.

New Ideas for a New Building: The Roll Building Project at Kellogg Community College. Christin N. Grant & Karla L. Meima. Ed. by M. K. Joscelyn & Clark Malcolm. LC 86-13466. (Studies in Facility Management). (Illus.). 36p. 1986. pap. 10.00 (*0-936658-21-5*) H Miller Res.

New Ideas for Lap Quilting. Georgia Bonesteel. (Illus.). 160p. 1987. 19.95 (*0-8487-0704-4*) Oxmoor Hse.

New Ideas for Reforming Social Security. Robert Eisner. 62p. 1998. pap. 9.95 (*0-87078-416-1*) Century Foundation.

New Ideas for Teacher Education: A Mathematics Framework. Linda Haggarty. LC 97-130185. (Children, Teachers & Learning Ser.). 160p. 1996. 100.00 (*0-304-33498-7*); pap. 31.95 (*0-304-33499-5*) Continuum.

***New Ideas from Dead Economists: An Introduction to Modern Economic Thought.** rev. ed. Todd G. Buchholz. LC 99-222760. 332p. 1999. pap. 14.95 (*0-452-28052-4*) NAL.

New Ideas in Backgammon. Kit Woolsey & Hal Heinrich. 336p. (Orig.). 1996. pap. 40.00 (*1-880604-08-6*) Gammon Pr.

New Ideas in Chess. unabridged ed. Larry Evans. LC 94-30973. (Illus.). 196p. 1995. pap. text 5.95 (*0-486-28305-4*) Dover.

New Ideas in Environmental Education. Ed. by Salvano Briceno & David Pitt. 256p. 1988. lib. bdg. 59.00 (*0-7099-5042-X*, Pub. by C Helm) Routldge.

New Ideas in Needlepoint Lace. Valerie Grimwood. (Illus.). 128p. 1995. 39.95 (*0-7134-7193-X*) Trafalgar.

N

New Ideas in Psychoanalysis: The Process of Change in a Humanistic Science. Ed. by Calvin F. Settlage & Reed Brockbank. 364p. 1985. text 49.95 (*0-88163-040-3*) Analytic Pr.

New Ideas in the Caro-Kann Defense. Jon Spellman. (Chess Library). 144p. 1992. pap. 14.95 (*0-02-028718-6*) Macmillan.

New Ideas in the Four Knights. John Nunn. (Batsford Chess Library). 128p. 1993. pap. 16.95 (*0-8050-2629-0*, Owl) H Holt & Co.

New Ideas in the Nizmo Indian Defence. Tony Kosten. 1995. pap. write for info. (*0-8050-3286-X*, Pub. by Batsford Chess) H Holt & Co.

New Ideas in the Pirc Defence. John Nunn. 144p. 1995. pap. 16.95 (*0-8050-2939-7*, Pub. by Batsford Chess) H Holt & Co.

New Ideas in the Queen's Gambit Accepted. Glenn Flear. 1995. pap. 19.95 (*0-8050-3577-X*, Pub. by Batsford Chess) H Holt & Co.

New Ideas in Therapy: Introduction to an Interdisciplinary Approach, 10. Ed. by Douglas H. Ruben & Dennis J. Delprato. LC 86-31922. (Contributions in Psychology Ser.: No. 10). (Illus.). 235p. 1987. 59.95 (*0-313-24845-1*, RNI/, Greenwood Pr) Greenwood.

New Ideas in Tokamak Confinement. Marshall N. Rosenbluth. (Research Trends in Physics Ser.). (Illus.). 496p. 1994. boxed set 99.00 (*1-56396-131-8*) Spr-Verlag.

New Ideas on Population: With Remarks on the Theories of Malthus & Godwin. 2nd ed. Alexander H. Everett. LC 65-26364. (Reprints of Economic Classics Ser.). xxii, 125, 52p. 1970. reprint ed. 35.00 (*0-678-00276-2*) Kelley.

New Ideas on the Structure of the Nervous System in Man & Vertebrates. Santiago Ramon Y Cajal. Tr. by Larry W. Swanson & Neely Swanson from FRE. 200p. 1990. 37.95 (*0-262-18141-X*) MIT Pr.

New Ideas with Dough. R. Imoti. (Illus.). 160p. 1997. pap. 19.95 (*0-7063-7565-3*, Pub. by WrLock) Sterling.

New Identities in Europe: Immigrant Ancestry & the Ethnic Identity of Youth. Karmela Liebkind. (Illus.). 1989. text 82.95 (*0-566-05741-7*, Pub. by Gower) Ashgate Pub Co.

New Ideology of Imperialism: Renewing the Moral Imperative. Feredi. LC 93-50843. (C). 44.95 (*0-7453-0845-7*, Pub. by Pluto GBR); pap. 15.95 (*0-7453-0846-5*, Pub. by Pluto GBR) Stylus Pub VA.

New Idioms in Action. George Reeves. (J). 1975. pap. text 22.95 (*0-8384-2652-2*, Newbury) Heinle & Heinle.

New Idols of the Cave: On the Limits of Anti-Realism. Norris. LC 96-46264. 1997. 69.95 (*0-7190-5092-8*, Pub. by Manchester Univ Pr) St Martin.

New Illustrated Atlas of the Bible. (Illus.). 128p. 1997. 12.98 (*0-7858-0660-1*) Bk Sales Inc.

New Illustrated Bible Dictionary see Nuevo Diccionario Ilustrado de la Biblia

New Illustrated Bible Handbook see Nuevo Manual Biblico Ilustrado

New Illustrated Book of Development Definitions. Harvey S. Moskowitz & Carl G. Lindbloom. LC 92-19394. 328p. (C). 1993. pap. 29.95 (*0-88285-144-6*) Ctr Urban Pol Res.

New Illustrated Dictionary of the Spanish Language: Nuevo Diccionario Ilustrado de la Espanola. Sopena Staff. (SPA., Illus.). 1981. 32.50 (*0-8288-2065-1*, S60108) Fr & Eur.

***New Illustrated Encyclopedia of Aircraft: Military & Civil Aviation from the Beginnings to the Present.** Lance Cole. (Illus.). 2000. 24.99 (*0-7858-1164-8*) Bk Sales Inc.

***New Illustrated Encyclopedia of Automobiles.** David Wise. (Illus.). 2000. 24.99 (*0-7858-1106-0*) Bk Sales Inc.

***New Illustrated Encyclopedia of Billiards.** rev. ed. Michael I. Shamos. LC 99-88256. (Illus.). 368p. 1999. 40.00 (*1-55821-797-5*) Lyons Pr.

New Illustrated Encyclopedia of Firearms. Ivan V. Hogg. (Illus.). 320p. 1992. 24.98 (*1-55521-807-5*) Bk Sales Inc.

New Illustrated Encyclopedia of Knowledge. 1986. 17.95 (*0-685-16806-9*, 618796) Random Hse Value.

***New Illustrated Encyclopedia of Motorcycles.** Kevin Nash. (Illus.). 2000. 24.99 (*0-7858-1163-X*) Bk Sales Inc.

New Illustrated Encyclopedia of Motorcycles. Erwin Tragatsch. (Illus.). 1992. 24.98 (*1-55521-809-1*) Bk Sales Inc.

***New Illustrated Encyclopedia of Railroad Locomotives.** Robert Tufnell. (Illus.). 2000. 24.99 (*0-7858-1105-2*) Bk Sales Inc.

New Illustrated Encyclopedia of World's Automobiles. David B. Wise. (Illus.). 352p. 1992. 24.98 (*1-55521-808-3*) Bk Sales Inc.

New Illustrated Family Medical & Health Guide. rev. ed. Consumer Guide Editors. (Illus.). 448p. 1993. 14.98 (*1-56173-600-7*, 3210102) Pubns Intl Ltd.

New, Illustrated Great Controversy. Ellen Gould Harmon White. (Illus.). 719p. 1990. 23.95 (*0-9636975-0-1*) Laymen Relig Lib.

New, Illustrated Great Controversy. deluxe ed. Ellen Gould Harmon White. (Illus.). 719p. 1990. 69.95 (*0-9636975-1-X*) Laymen Relig Lib.

***New Illustrated Guide to Gardening.** rev. ed. Illus. by Reader's Digest Editors. LC 99-49792. 544p. 2000. 35.00 (*0-7621-0276-4*, Pub. by RD Assn) Penguin Putnam.

New Illustrated Hebrew-English Dictionary for Young Readers. Nathan Goldberg. (HEB., Illus.). (J). (gr. 4-7). 1958. pap. 6.95 (*0-87068-830-8*) Ktav.

New Illustrated Medical Encyclopedia. Robert E. Rothenberg. 1990. 19.98 (*0-88365-762-7*) Galahad Bks.

New Illustrated Michaelis English-Portuguese Dictionary: Novo Michaelis Dicionario Ilustrado, Vol. 1. 41st ed. Michaelis. (ENG & POR., Illus.). 1151p. 1986. 95.00 (*0-8288-0494-X*, M14123) Fr & Eur.

New Illustrated Rock Handbook. Mike Clifford. (GER.). 208p. 1992. 25.00 (*3-283-00266-5*) G Olms Pubs.

New Illustrated Science & Invention Encyclopedia: How It Works, 28 vols., Set. LC 85-30973. (Illus.). 1987. 307.44 (*0-87475-450-X*) Websters Unified.

New Illustrated Treasury of Disney Songs: Complete Sheet Music for over 60 Popular Tunes. rev. ed. Hyperion Staff. (Illus.). 256p. (J). 1998. 34.00 (*0-7868-6456-7*, Pub. by Hyperion) Time Warner.

New Illustrations of the Life, Studies, & Writings of Shakespeare, 2 vols., Set. Joseph Hunter. LC 79-169460. reprint ed. 115.00 (*0-404-03455-1*) AMS Pr.

New Image. Claude Bragdon. (Illus.). 198p. 1998. reprint ed. pap. 19.95 (*0-7661-0427-3*) Kessinger Pub.

New Image of Religious Film. John R. May. LC 97-5897. (Communication, Culture & Theology Ser.). (Illus.). 288p. (Orig.). 1997. pap. 24.95 (*1-55612-761-8*, LL1761) Sheed & Ward WI.

New Image of the Common Man. Carl J. Friedrich. LC 84-20511. 382p. 1984. reprint ed. lib. bdg. 75.00 (*0-313-24243-7*, FRNE, Greenwood Pr) Greenwood.

New Image of the Person: The Theory & Practice of Clinical Philosophy, 9. Peter Koestenbaum. LC 77-84764. (Contributions in Philosophy Ser.: No. 9). 540p. 1978. 75.00 (*0-8371-9888-7*, KNI, Greenwood Pr) Greenwood.

New Image Processing Techniques & Applications: Algorithms, Methods & Components II. Ed. by Philippe Refregier & Rolf-Juergen Ahlers. LC 98-125171. (Europto Ser.: Vol. 3101). 352p. 1997. 69.00 (*0-8194-2521-4*) SPIE.

New Images: Adult Children of Dysfunctional Families. rev. ed. Theo Johnson. 106p. 1997. 10.00 (*1-886592-03-9*) Healing Touch.

New Images from Spain. Margit Rowell. Tr. by Lucy Flint. LC 79-92992. (Illus.). 144p. (Orig.). 1980. pap. 8.50 (*0-89207-023-4*) S R Guggenheim.

New Images of Man. Peter H. Selz. LC 59-14221. (Museum of Modern Art Publications in Reprint). (Illus.). 1969. reprint ed. 18.95 (*0-405-01549-6*) Ayer.

New Images of Medieval Women: Essays Toward a Cultural Anthropology. Edelgard E. DuBruck. LC 87-26040. (Studies in Women & Religion). 1988. write for info. (*0-88946-523-1*) E Mellen.

New Images of Medieval Women: Studies Toward a Cultural Anthropology. Ed. by Edelgard E. DuBruck. LC 88-9351. (Medieval Studies: Vol. 1). 330p. 1988. lib. bdg. 99.95 (*0-88946-265-8*) E Mellen.

New Images of Musical Sound. Robert Cogan. (Illus.). 224p. 1984. 36.50 (*0-674-61585-9*) HUP.

New Images of Musical Sound. Robert Cogan. (Illus.). 177p. 1998. reprint ed. pap. 28.00 (*0-9634500-2-6*) Pubn Contact Intl.

New Immigrant Literatures in the United States: A Sourcebook to Our Multicultural Literary Heritage. Ed. by Alpana S. Knippling. LC 95-45211. 408p. 1996. lib. bdg. 79.95 (*0-313-28968-9*, Greenwood Pr) Greenwood.

New Immigrants & Democratic Society: Minority Integration in Western Democracies. Marilyn B. Hoskin. LC 91-10586. 184p. 1991. 52.95 (*0-275-94004-7*, C4004, Praeger Pubs) Greenwood.

New Immigrants in New York. Ed. by Nancy Foner. 324p. 1989. pap. text 20.00 (*0-231-06131-5*) Col U Pr.

***New Immigrants in the United States: Readings for Second Language Educators.** Sandra Lee McKay & Sau-ling Cynthia Wong. LC PE1128.N384 1999. (Cambridge Language Teaching Library). (Illus.). 472p. (C). 1999. 69.95 (*0-521-66087-4*) Cambridge U Pr.

***New Immigrants in the United States: Readings for Second Language Educators.** Sandra Lee McKay & Sau-ling Cynthia Wong. LC PE1128.N384 1999. (Cambridge Language Teaching Library). (Illus.). 472p. (C). 2000. pap. 26.95 (*0-521-66798-4*) Cambridge U Pr.

New Immigrants, Old Unions: Organizing Undocumented Workers in Los Angeles. Hector L. Delgado. LC 92-36423. 200p. (C). 1994. pap. 22.95 (*1-56639-205-5*) Temple U Pr.

New Immigrants to Brooklyn & Queens: Policy Implications, Especially with Regard to Housing. Intro. by Lydio F. Tomasi. LC 83-14400. (CMS Occasional Papers & Documentation Ser.). (Illus.). 165p. (C). 1986. pap. text 35.00 (*0-913256-63-3*) CMS.

New Immigration: A Challenge to American Society. Nathan Glazer. LC 87-32229. (Distinguished Graduate Research Lectures: No. 3). 110p. 1989. pap. 12.50 (*0-916304-81-7*) SDSU Press.

New Immigration: A Study of the Industrial & Social Life of Southeastern Europeans in America. Peter Roberts. LC 79-129411. (American Immigration Collection. Series 2). (Illus.). 1970. reprint ed. 26.95 (*0-405-00565-2*) Ayer.

New Immigration: A Study of the Industrial & Social Life of Southeastern Europeans in America. Peter Roberts. LC 78-145490. (American Immigration Library). xxii, 418p. 1971. reprint ed. lib. bdg. 49.95 (*0-89198-023-7*) Ozer.

New Immigration: Implications for Poverty & Public Assistance Utilization, 10. Leif Jensen. LC 88-25096. (Studies in Social Welfare Policies & Programs: No. 10). 219p. 1989. 52.95 (*0-313-26455-4*, JNI/, Greenwood Pr) Greenwood.

New Immunology: Molecules to Medicine. S. Umlauf. 250p. 1998. text 45.00 (*0-8176-3968-3*) Birkhauser.

New Immunosuppressive Modalities & Antirejection Approaches in Organ Transplantation. Ed. by Jerzy W. Weglinski. LC 94-25392. (Medical Intelligence Unit Ser.). 130p. 1994. 99.00 (*1-57059-136-9*) Landes Bioscience.

***New Imperialism: Crisis & Contradiction in North & South.** Robert Bielak. 2000. text 69.50 (*1-85649-746-1*, Pub. by Zed Books) St Martin.

***New Improved Big 6 Workshop Handbook.** Michael Eisenberg & Robert E. Berkowitz. LC 99-41202. (Professional Growth Ser.). (Illus.). 1999. pap. 36.95 (*0-938865-87-0*) Linworth Pub.

New, Improved! Dykes to Watch Out For. Alison Bechdel. LC 90-3184. (Illus.). 120p. 1990. pap. 10.95 (*0-932379-79-6*); lib. bdg. 22.95 (*0-932379-80-X*) Firebrand Bks.

New Improved Poor Man's James Bond, Vol. 1. 6th rev. ed. Kurt Saxon. (Illus.). 477p. 1988. pap. text 25.00 (*1-881801-01-2*) Atlan Formularies.

New Improved Santa. George F. Sabato. Ed. by William-Alan Landes. LC 96-29750. 55p. (Orig.). (J). (gr. k-7). 1997. pap. 5.00 (*0-88734-457-7*) Players Pr.

New, Improved Wilderness. unabridged ed. David Hoefer. 80p. (Orig.). 1996. pap. 7.95 (*0-9654877-1-7*) Vatic Hum Pr.

New in Chess Yearbook, Vol. 31. Garry Kasparov et al. (Supplement to New in Chess Magazine Ser.). 240p. 1994. 36.00 (*0-917237-56-0*) Chess Combi.

New in Chess Yearbook, Vol. 32. Garry Kasparov et al. (Supplement to New in Chess Magazine Ser.). 240p. 1994. 36.00 (*0-917237-57-9*) Chess Combi.

New in Chess Yearbook, Vol. 33. Garry Kasparov et al. (Supplement to New in Chess Magazine Ser.). 240p. 1994. 36.00 (*0-917237-58-7*) Chess Combi.

New in Chess Yearbook, Vol. 34. Garry Kasparov et al. (Supplement to New in Chess Magazine Ser.). 240p. 1994. 36.00 (*0-917237-59-5*) Chess Combi.

***New in Chess Yearbook: Periodic Analysis of Current Opening Practice, Vol. 28.** Ed. by G. Sosonko. 240p. 1999. lib. bdg. 36.00 (*0-917237-53-6*) Chess Combi.

New in Chess Yearbook: Periodic Analysis of Current Opening Practice, Vol. 29. Ed. by G. Sosonko. 240p. 1993. lib. bdg. 36.00 (*0-917237-54-4*) Chess Combi.

New in Chess Yearbook: Periodic Analysis of Current Opening Practice, Vol. 30. Ed. by G. Sosonko. 240p. 1993. lib. bdg. 36.00 (*0-917237-55-2*) Chess Combi.

New in Chess Yearbook: Periodic Analysis of Current, Opening Practice, Vol. 35. 240p. 1995. 36.00 (*0-917237-60-9*) Chess Combi.

New in Chess Yearbook: Periodic Analysis of Current Opening Practice, Vol. 36. 240p. 1995. 36.00 (*0-917237-61-7*) Chess Combi.

New in Chess Yearbook: Periodic Analysis of Current Opening Practice, Vol. 37. 240p. 1996. 35.00 (*0-917237-62-5*) Chess Combi.

New in Chess Yearbook: Periodic Analysis of Current Opening Practice, Vol. 38. 240p. 1996. 35.00 (*0-917237-63-3*) Chess Combi.

New in Chess Yearbook: Periodic Analysis of Current Opening Practice, Vol. 39. 240p. 1997. 35.00 (*0-917237-64-1*) Chess Combi.

New in Chess Yearbook: Periodic Analysis of Current Opening Practice, Vol. 40. 240p. 1997. 35.00 (*0-917237-65-X*) Chess Combi.

New in Chess Yearbook: Periodic Analysis of Current Opening Practice, Vol. 41. 240p. 1997. 36.00 (*0-917237-66-8*) Chess Combi.

New in Chess Yearbook: Periodic Analysis of Current Opening Practice, Vol. 42. 240p. 1997. 36.00 (*0-917237-67-6*) Chess Combi.

New in Chess Yearbook: Periodic Analysis of Current Opening Practice, Vol. 43. 240p. 1997. 36.00 (*0-917237-68-4*) Chess Combi.

New in Chess Yearbook: Periodic Analysis of Current Opening Practice, Vol. 44. 240p. 1997. 36.00 (*0-917237-69-2*) Chess Combi.

New in Chess Yearbook: Periodic Analysis of Current Opening Practice, Vol. 45. 240p. 1997. 36.00 (*0-917237-70-6*) Chess Combi.

New in Chess Yearbook: Periodic Analysis of Current Opening Practice, Vol. 46. 240p. 1998. 36.00 (*0-917237-71-4*) Chess Combi.

New in Chess Yearbook: Periodic Analysis of Current Opening Practice, Vol. 47. Ed. by G. Sosonko. 240p. 1998. lib. bdg. 36.00 (*0-917237-72-2*) Chess Combi.

***New in Chess Yearbook: Periodic Analysis of Current Opening Practice, Vol. 48.** Ed. by G. Sosonko. 240p. 1998. lib. bdg. 36.00 (*0-917237-73-0*) Chess Combi.

***New in Chess Yearbook: Periodic Analysis of Current Opening Practice, Vol. 49.** Ed. by G. Sosonko. 240p. 1998. lib. bdg. 36.00 (*0-917237-74-9*) Chess Combi.

***New in Chess Yearbook: Periodic Analysis of Current Opening Practice, Vol. 50.** Ed. by G. Sosonko. 240p. 1998. lib. bdg. 36.00 (*0-917237-75-7*) Chess Combi.

***New in Chess Yearbook: Periodic Analysis of Current Opening Practice, Vol. 51.** Ed. by G. Sosonko. 240p. 1999. lib. bdg. 36.00 (*0-917237-76-5*) Chess Combi.

***New in Chess Yearbook: Periodic Analysis of Current Opening Practice, Vol. 52.** Ed. by G. Sosonko. 240p. 1999. lib. bdg. 36.00 (*0-917237-77-3*) Chess Combi.

***New in Chess Yearbook: Periodic Analysis of Current Opening Practice, Vol. 53.** Ed. by G. Sosonko. 240p. 1999. lib. bdg. 36.00 (*0-917237-78-1*) Chess Combi.

***New in Chess Yearbook: Periodic Analysis of Current Opening Practice, Vol. 54.** Ed. by G. Sosonko. 240p. 1999. lib. bdg. 36.00 (*0-917237-79-X*) Chess Combi.

New in Chess Yearbook: Supplement to New in Chess Magazine, Vol. 2. Ed. by Garry Kasparov et al. (International Chess Data System Ser.: Vols. 2-3). 1984. 36.00 (*0-917237-22-6*) Chess Combi.

New in Chess Yearbook: Supplement to New in Chess Magazine, Vol. 3. Ed. by Garry Kasparov et al. (International Chess Data System Ser.: Vols. 2-3). 1984. 36.00 (*0-917237-29-3*) Chess Combi.

New in Chess Yearbook: Supplement to New in Chess Magazine, Vol. 4. Ed. by Garry Kasparov et al. (International Chess Data System Ser.: Vols. 4-6). 1986. 36.00 (*0-917237-25-0*) Chess Combi.

New in Chess Yearbook: Supplement to New in Chess Magazine, Vol. 5. Ed. by Garry Kasparov et al. (International Chess Data System Ser.: Vols. 4-6). 1986. 36.00 (*0-917237-26-9*) Chess Combi.

New in Chess Yearbook: Supplement to New in Chess Magazine, Vol. 6. Ed. by Garry Kasparov et al. (International Chess Data System Ser.: Vols. 4-6). 1986. 36.00 (*0-917237-27-7*) Chess Combi.

New in Chess Yearbook: Supplement to New in Chess Magazine, Vol. 7. Ed. by Garry Kasparov et al. (International Chess Data System Ser.: Vols. 7-10). 1988. 35.00 (*0-917237-32-3*) Chess Combi.

New in Chess Yearbook: Supplement to New in Chess Magazine, Vol. 8. Ed. by Garry Kasparov et al. (International Chess Data System Ser.: Vols. 7-10). 1988. 36.00 (*0-917237-33-1*) Chess Combi.

New in Chess Yearbook: Supplement to New in Chess Magazine, Vol. 9. Ed. by Garry Kasparov et al. (International Chess Data System Ser.: Vols. 7-10). 1988. 36.00 (*0-917237-34-X*) Chess Combi.

New in Chess Yearbook: Supplement to New in Chess Magazine, Vol. 10. Ed. by Garry Kasparov et al. (International Chess Data System Ser.: Vols. 7-10). 1988. 36.00 (*0-917237-35-8*) Chess Combi.

New in Chess Yearbook: Supplement to New in Chess Magazine, Vol. 11. Ed. by Garry Kasparov et al. (International Chess Data System Ser.: Vols. 11-13). 1989. 36.00 (*0-917237-36-6*) Chess Combi.

New in Chess Yearbook: Supplement to New in Chess Magazine, Vol. 12. Ed. by Garry Kasparov et al. (International Chess Data System Ser.: Vols. 11-13). 1989. 36.00 (*0-917237-37-4*) Chess Combi.

New in Chess Yearbook: Supplement to New in Chess Magazine, Vol. 13. Ed. by Garry Kasparov et al. (International Chess Data System Ser.: Vols. 11-13). 1989. 36.00 (*0-917237-38-2*) Chess Combi.

New in Chess Yearbook: Supplement to New in Chess Magazine, Vol. 14. Ed. by Garry Kasparov et al. (International Chess Data System Ser.: Vols. 14-18). 1990. 36.00 (*0-917237-39-0*) Chess Combi.

New in Chess Yearbook: Supplement to New in Chess Magazine, Vol. 15. Ed. by Garry Kasparov et al. (International Chess Data System Ser.: Vols. 14-18). 1990. 36.00 (*0-917237-40-4*) Chess Combi.

New in Chess Yearbook: Supplement to New in Chess Magazine, Vol. 16. Ed. by Garry Kasparov et al. (International Chess Data System Ser.: Vols. 14-18). 1990. 36.00 (*0-917237-41-2*) Chess Combi.

New in Chess Yearbook: Supplement to New in Chess Magazine, Vol. 17. Ed. by Garry Kasparov et al. (International Chess Data System Ser.: Vols. 14-18). 1990. 36.00 (*0-917237-42-0*) Chess Combi.

New in Chess Yearbook: Supplement to New in Chess Magazine, Vol. 18. Ed. by Garry Kasparov et al. (International Chess Data System Ser.: Vols. 14-18). 1990. 36.00 (*0-917237-43-9*) Chess Combi.

New in Chess Yearbook: Supplement to New in Chess Magazine, Vol. 19. Ed. by Garry Kasparov et al. (International Chess Data System Ser.: Vols. 19-20). 1991. 36.00 (*0-917237-44-7*) Chess Combi.

New in Chess Yearbook: Supplement to New in Chess Magazine, Vol. 20. Ed. by Garry Kasparov et al. (International Chess Data System Ser.: Vols. 19-20). 1991. 36.00 (*0-917237-45-5*) Chess Combi.

New in Chess Yearbook: Supplement to New in Chess Magazine, Vol. 21. Ed. by Garry Kasparov et al. (International Chess Data System Ser.: Vols. 21-22). 1992. 36.00 (*0-917237-46-3*) Chess Combi.

New in Chess Yearbook: Supplement to New in Chess Magazine, Vol. 22. Ed. by Garry Kasparov et al. (International Chess Data System Ser.: Vols. 21-22). 1992. 36.00 (*0-917237-47-1*) Chess Combi.

New in Chess Yearbook: Supplement to New in Chess Magazine, Vol. 23. Ed. by Garry Kasparov et al. (International Chess Data System Ser.: Vols. 23- 26). 1992. 36.00 (*0-917237-48-X*) Chess Combi.

New in Chess Yearbook: Supplement to New in Chess Magazine, Vol. 24. Ed. by Garry Kasparov et al. (International Chess Data System Ser.: Vols. 23- 26). 1992. 36.00 (*0-917237-49-8*) Chess Combi.

New in Chess Yearbook: Supplement to New in Chess Magazine, Vol. 25. Ed. by Garry Kasparov et al. (International Chess Data System Ser.: Vols. 23- 26). 1992. 36.00 (*0-917237-50-1*) Chess Combi.

New in Chess Yearbook: Supplement to New in Chess Magazine, Vol. 26. Ed. by Garry Kasparov et al. (International Chess Data System Ser.: Vols. 23- 26). 1992. 36.00 (*0-917237-51-X*) Chess Combi.

New in Chess Yearbook Vol. 27: Periodic Analysis of Current Opening Practice. Ed. by Genna Sosonko. 240p. 1993. 36.00 (*0-917237-52-8*, New Chess) Chess Combi.

New in Town. B. B. Calhoun. (His & Hers Ser.). 128p. (Orig.). (YA). 1997. mass mkt. 3.99 (*0-380-78470-X*, Avon Bks) Morrow Avon.

New Income Tax Inventory Capitalization Rules: A Case Study. John B. Barrack & James D. Edwards. Ed. by Claire Barth. 57p. (Orig.). 1989. pap. 20.00 (*0-86641-176-3*, 89238) Inst Mgmt Account.

New Independent Home: People & Houses That Harvest the Sun, Wind, & Water. Michael Potts. LC 98-7767. (Illus.). 350p. 1999. pap. 30.00 (*1-890132-14-4*) Chelsea Green Pub.

N

An Asterisk (*) at the beginning of an entry indicates that the title is appearing for the first time.

New Independent States & the Baltic Republics: A Directory of Institutions in Armenia, Azerbaijan, Belarus, Estonia, Georgia, Kazakhstan, Kyrgyzstan, Latvia, Lithuania, Moldova, Russian Federation, Tajikistan, Turkmenistan, Ukraine, Uzbekistan. Erika Popovych. (Special Reports). 458p. 1995. 50.00 (*0-929851-70-6*, 5345) Am Assn Coll Registrars.

New Index to Bishop Gregg's History of the Old Cheraws: People & Places, Indians, Slaves. Compiled by Mary C. Moody. LC 86-70106. 100p. (Orig.). 1986. pap. 15.50 (*0-9615836-2-2*) Blackstone Pub.

*__New India.__ Asia Law & Practice Staff. 1999. pap. text 125.00 (*962-936-072-1*, Pub. by Asia Law & Practice) Am Educ Systs.

New India, 1948-1955. Asok Mitra. (C). 1991. 22.50 (*81-7154-691-9*, Pub. by Popular Prakashan) S Asia.

New Indian Cookbook. Neelam Batra. 1997. 25.00 (*0-02-861004-0*) Macmillan.

*__New Indian Home Cooking.__ Madhu Gadia. LC 00-27774. 304p. 2000. pap. 16.95 (*1-55788-343-2*, HP Books) Berkley Pub.

New Indian Sketches. Pierre-Jean De Smet. 146p. 1985. 16.95 (*0-87770-336-1*) Ye Galleon.

New Indian Sketches. P. J. DeSmet. 175p. reprint ed. pap. 10.00 (*0-8466-4049-X*, I49) Shoreys Bkstore.

New Individualism: Personal Change to Transform Society. Richard Botelho. 176p. 1995. 19.95 (*0-9643926-1-5*); pap. 12.95 (*0-9643926-2-3*) Windstream Pubng.

New Individualist Review. New Individualist Review Journal Staff. LC 65-35281. 1024p. 1992. pap. 8.50 (*0-86597-065-3*) Liberty Fund.

*__New Inductive Study Bible.__ Precept Ministries International Staff. 2240p. 2000. 42.99 (*0-7369-0016-0*); 74.99 (*0-7369-0017-9*); lthr. 89.99 (*0-7369-0018-7*) Harvest Hse.

*__New Inductive Study Bible: Indexed.__ Precept Ministries International Staff. 2240p. 2000. 49.99 (*0-7369-0022-5*); lthr. 81.99 (*0-7369-0023-3*); lthr. 96.99 (*0-7369-0024-1*) Harvest Hse.

New Industrial Diamond & Their Products. 100p. 1991. 2950.00 (*0-89336-862-8*, GB-044) BCC.

New Industrial Economics & Experiences from European Merger Control - New Lessons. European Commission. LC 96-118354. 94p. 1995. pap. text 18.00 (*92-827-4343-8*, Pub. by Comm Europ Commun) Bernan Associates.

*__New Industrial Geography: Regions, Regulations & Institutions.__ Trevor J. Barnes & Meric S. Gertler. LC 99-22501. (Studies in the Modern World Economy). 1999. text. write for info. (*0-415-21802-0*) Routledge.

New Industrial Relations in Australia. Ed. by Ian Hunt & Chris Provis. 196p. 1995. pap. 49.00 (*1-86287-172-8*, Pub. by Federation Pr) Gaunt.

New Industrial Revolution. W. Meakin. Ed. by Mira Wilkins. LC 76-29998. (European Business Ser.). 1977. reprint ed. lib. bdg. 25.95 (*0-405-09756-5*) Ayer.

New Industrial Subcontracting in Europe First Results with an Updated Definition. 1997. 25.00 (*92-827-9676-0*, CA-01-96-130ENC, Pub. by Comm Europ Commun) Bernan Associates.

New Industrial Unrest: Reasons & Remedies. Ray S. Baker. LC 78-156402. (American Labor Ser., No. 2). 1977. reprint ed. 19.95 (*0-405-02912-8*) Ayer.

New Industry Emerges: Making Construction Materials from Cellulosic Waste. David Lorenz. 14p. 1995. 15.00 (*0-614-18033-3*) Inst Local Self Re.

New Inequalities: The Changing Distribution of Income & Wealth in the UK. Ed. by John Hills. (Illus.). 419p. (C). 1996. pap. text 28.95 (*0-521-55698-8*) Cambridge U Pr.

New Inequalities: The Changing Distribution of Income & Wealth in the UK. Ed. by John Hills. LC 95-9285. (Illus.). 419p. (C). 1996. text 69.95 (*0-521-55326-1*) Cambridge U Pr.

New Inequality: Creating Solutions for Poor America. Richard B. Freeman. LC 98-37374. (New Democracy Forum Ser.). 80p. 1999. pap. 11.00 (*0-8070-4435-0*) Beacon Pr.

New Inflation: The Collapse of Free Markets. W. David Slawson. LC 81-13805. 437p. 1981. reprint ed. pap. 135.50 (*0-7837-9448-7*, 206019000004) Bks Demand.

New Informants: The Betrayal of Confidentiality in Psychoanalysis & Psychotherapy. Christopher Bollas & David Sundelson. LC 95-14299. 232p. 1995. 35.00 (*1-56821-595-9*) Aronson.

New Information Industry: Regulatory Challenges & the First Amendment. Richard Klingler. 208p. (C). 1996. 36.95 (*0-8157-4944-9*); pap. 16.95 (*0-8157-4943-0*) Brookings.

New Information Infrastructure: Strategies for U. S. Policy. Ed. by William J. Drake. 448p. (C). 1995. pap. 14.95 (*0-87078-366-1*) Century Foundation.

New Information Revolution: A Reference Handbook. Martin K. Gay. LC 96-28832. (Contemporary World Issues Ser.). 249p. 1996. lib. bdg. 45.00 (*0-87436-847-2*) ABC-CLIO.

New Information Technologies & Development: ATAS Bulletin, No. 3. 176p. 1986. 9.00 (*92-1-104173-2*, E.85.II.A.18) UN.

New Information Technologies & Libraries. Ed. by H. Liebaers et al. 1985. text 167.00 (*90-277-2105-X*) Kluwer Academic.

*__New Information Technologies in Organizational Processes: Field Studies & Theoretical Reflections on the Future of Work: IFIP TC8 WG8.2 International Working Conference on New Information Technologies in Organizational Processes: Field Studies & Theoretical Reflections on the Future of Work, August 21-22, 1999, St. Louis, Missouri, USA__ IFIP TC8 WG8.2 International Working Conference on New Information Technologies in Organizational Processes: Field Studies & Theoretical Reflections on the Future of Work Staff & Ojelanki Ngwenyama. LC 99-28492. (International Federation for Information Processing Ser.). 1999. write for info. (*0-7923-8578-0*) Kluwer Academic.

New Information Technologies-New Opportunities: Proceedings of the Clinic on Library Applications of Data Processing, 1981. Ed. by Linda C. Smith. LC 82-10947. 119p. 1982. 15.00 (*0-87845-066-1*) U of Ill Grad Sch.

New Information Technology & Industrial Change: The Italian Case. Ed. by Cristiano Antonelli. (C). 1988. lib. bdg. 130.50 (*90-277-2747-3*) Kluwer Academic.

New Information Technology in Education. David G. Hawkridge. LC LB1028.5.H38. 248p. 1983. reprint ed. pap. 76.90 (*0-608-04024-X*, 206476000011) Bks Demand.

New Infotainment Technologies in the Home: Demand-Side Perspectives. Ed. by Ruby R. Dholakia et al. (LEA's Communication Ser.). 296p. 1996. text 59.95 (*0-8058-1626-7*) L Erlbaum Assocs.

New Infrastructure Tactics 2000: Tactics 2000. 64p. 1998. write for info. (*0-9664652-0-2*) Eloquent Harbor.

*__New Ingredients in Food Processing.__ G. Linden & Denis Lorient. LC 99-32797. 1999. write for info. (*0-8493-0631-0*) CRC Pr.

*__New Ingredients in Food Processing: Biochemistry & Agriculture.__ G. Linden & D. Lorient. 392p. 1999. pap. 207.00 (*1-85573-443-5*) Am Educ Systs.

New Initiatives & Approaches in Health Care Quality. (Illus.). 242p. (C). 1995. pap. text 45.00 (*0-7881-2280-0*) DIANE Pub.

New Initiatives for Africa's Debt. Ed. by Phillip LeBel. 104p. (Orig.). 1989. pap. 9.00 (*0-944572-02-2*) MSU Ctr Econ Res Africa.

New Injection Treatment for Impotence: Medical & Psychological Aspects. Gorm Wagner & Helen S. Kaplan. LC 92-49232. (Illus.). 248p. 1993. text 32.95 (*0-87630-689-X*) Brunner-Mazel.

New Inn. Ben Jonson. (Swan Theatre Plays Ser.). 76p. (C). 1988. pap. 9.95 (*0-413-16630-9*, A0183) Heinemann.

*__New Innovators: Global Patenting Trends in Five Sectors.__ Michael B. Albert. (Illus.). 54p. 2000. pap. text 20.00 (*0-7881-8787-2*) DIANE Pub.

New Innovators: How Canadians Are Shaping the Knowledge-Based Economy. Royer Voyer & Patti Ryan. LC 94-229893. (Illus.). 239p. 29.95 (*1-55028-463-0*, Pub. by J Lorimer) Formac Dist Ltd.

New Inquisition: Irrational Rationalism & the Citadel of Science. rev. ed. Robert A. Wilson. LC 86-83176. 256p. 1991. pap. 14.95 (*1-56184-002-5*) New Falcon Pubns.

New Insecurity: The End of the Standard Job & Family. Jerald Wallulis. LC 97-13598. (SUNY Series in Social & Political Thought). 238p. (C). 1997. text 59.50 (*0-7914-3655-1*); pap. text 19.95 (*0-7914-3656-X*) State U NY Pr.

*__New Insight into Business.__ 2000. teacher ed. (*0-582-33556-6*) Addison-Wesley.

*__New Insight into Business.__ Power Tullis. 2000. pap., wbk. ed. write for info. (*0-582-33557-4*) Addison-Wesley.

*__New Insights in Germanic Linguistics I, Vol. 33.__ Ed. by Irmengard Rauch & Gerald F. Carr. LC 99-23178. 260p. (C). 1999. text 52.95 (*0-8204-3888-X*) P Lang Pubng.

New Insights in Gynecology & Obstetrics: Research & Practice. Ed. by B. Ottesen & A. Tabor. LC 98-15899. (Illus.). 336p. 1998. 125.00 (*1-85070-966-1*) Prthnon Pub.

New Insights in Modern Astrology. 2nd rev. ed. Stephen Arroyo & Liz Greene. Orig. Title: The Jupiter - Saturn Conference Lectures. 212p. 1991. pap. 14.95 (*0-916360-47-4*) CRCS Pubns CA.

New Insights in Vertebrate Kidney Function. Ed. by J. Anne Brown et al. (Society for Experimental Biology Seminar Ser.: No. 52). (Illus.). 403p. (C). 1993. text 130.00 (*0-521-38324-2*) Cambridge U Pr.

*__New Insights into Business.__ Trappe Tullis. 2000. pap., student ed. write for info. (*0-582-33553-1*) Addison-Wesley.

New Insights into Cell & Membrane Transport Processes. Ed. by Stanley T. Crooke & George H. Poste. LC 86-8175. (New Horizons in Therapeutics Ser.). (Illus.). 456p. (C). 1986. text 138.00 (*0-306-42183-6*, Kluwer Plenum) Kluwer Academic.

New Insights into the Clinical Profile of Norfloxacin: Journal: European Urology, Vol. 17, Suppl. 1. Ed. by S. R. Norrby. (Illus.). iv, 52p. 1990. pap. 17.50 (*3-8055-5198-3*) S Karger.

New Insights into the Universe: Proceedings of a Summer School, Held in Valencia, Spain, 23-27 September 1991. Ed. by V. J. Martinez et al. LC 92-27336. (Lecture Notes in Physics Ser.: Vol. 408). xi, 298p. 1992. 70.95 (*0-387-55842-X*); write for info. (*3-540-55842-X*) Spr-Verlag.

New Insights on English Authors from Marvell to Larkin: An English Variety. Roger Sharrock. LC 95-1688. (Salzburger Studien Ser.). (Illus.). 192p. 1995. text 79.95 (*0-7734-1282-4*) E Mellen.

New Insights on Renin-Angiotensin System in the Kidney. Ed. by N. Yanagawa & C. E. Palant. (Journal: Renal Physiology & Biochemistry: Vol. 14, No. 4-5, 1991). (Illus.). 76p. 1991. pap. 72.25 (*3-8055-5378-1*) S Karger.

New Insights to Antiquity: A Drawing Aside of the Veil. Richard Petersen. LC 97-77780. (Illus.). xiv, 336p. 1998. 27.95 (*0-9662134-1-6*) Engwald & Co.

New Institutional Arrangements for the World Economy. Ed. by Hans-Jurgen Vosgerau. (Studies in International Economics & Institutions). (Illus.). 492p. 1989. 94.95 (*0-387-50480-X*) Spr-Verlag.

New Institutional Economics: A Collection of Articles from the Journal of Institutional & Theoretical Economics. Ed. by Eirik G. Furubotn & Rudolf Richter. LC 91-4019. (Economics Ser.: No. 13). 386p. (Orig.). 1992. pap. 37.95 (*0-89096-502-1*) Tex A&M Univ Pr.

New Institutional Economics & Third World Development. Ed. by John Harris & Jane Hunter. 376p. (C). 1997. pap. 29.99 (*0-415-15791-9*) Routledge.

New Institutional Politics: Outcomes & Consequences. Jan-Erik Lane & Svante O. Ersson. LC 99-32334. 304p. 1999. pap. 27.99 (*0-415-18321-9*) Routledge.

*__New Institutional Politics: Outcomes & Consequences.__ Jan-Erik Lane & Svante O. Ersson. LC 99-32334. 304p. (C). 2000. text. write for info. (*0-415-18320-0*) Routledge.

New Institutionalism. Ed. by Karol E. Soltan et al. LC 97-33947. (Illus.). 256p. (C). 1998. text 44.50 (*0-472-10868-9*, 10868) U of Mich Pr.

New Institutionalism in Organizational Analysis. Ed. by Walter W. Powell & Paul DiMaggio. LC 91-9999. (Illus.). 486p. 1991. pap. text 27.50 (*0-226-67709-5*) U Ch Pr.

New Institutionalism in Organizational Analysis. Ed. by Walter W. Powell & Paul DiMaggio. LC 91-9999. (Illus.). 528p. 1993. lib. bdg. 65.00 (*0-226-67708-7*) U Ch Pr.

New Institutionalism in Sociology. Ed. by Mary C. Brinton & Victor Nee. LC 97-37595. 388p. 1998. 45.00 (*0-87154-139-4*) Russell Sage.

New Institutions of Federalism: The Politics of Intergovernmental Relations - 1960-1985. William K. Hall. (Recent American History Ser.: Vol. 1). XIII, 236p. (C). 1989. text 35.95 (*0-8204-0782-8*) P Lang Pubng.

New Instrumentation for Space Astronomy: Proceedings of a Symposium of the 20th Plenary Meeting of COSPAR, Tel Aviv, Israel, June 1977. Ed. by K. Van der Hucht & G. Vaiana. (Advances in Space Exploration Ser.). (Illus.). 416p. 1978. 76.00 (*0-08-022417-2*, Pergamon Pr) Elsevier.

New Instrumentation Technologies for Testing the Bonding of Sensors to Solid Materials. H. M. Hashemian et al. (Illus.). 368p. (Orig.). 1996. pap., per. write for info. (*1-882148-05-3*) Analysis & Measurement.

New Instruments for Environmental Policy. Jonathan Golub. LC 97-47648. (Illus.). 288p. (C). 1998. 85.00 (*0-415-15696-3*) Routledge.

New Insurance Supervisor Workbook. W. F. Simpson & Martin M. Broadwell. 1981. pap. 19.95 (*0-201-00896-3*) Addison-Wesley.

New Insurgencies: Anti-Communist Guerrillas in the Third World. Michael Radu. 300p. 1990. 44.95 (*0-88738-307-6*) Transaction Pubs.

New Integrals. Ed. by P. S. Bullen et al. (Lecture Notes in Mathematics Ser.: Vol. 1419). v, 202p. 1990. pap. 34.80 (*0-387-52322-7*) Spr-Verlag.

New Integrated Direct Marketing. Mike Berry. LC 97-31504. 264p. 1998. 74.95 (*0-566-07960-7*, Pub. by Gower) Ashgate Pub Co.

New Intellectuals. Ed. by Terence P. Logan & Denzell S. Smith. LC 75-38051. (Survey & Bibliography of Recent Studies in English Renaissance Drama). 384p. 1977. reprint ed. pap. 119.10 (*0-608-02378-7*, 206302000004) Bks Demand.

New Intelligence: Artificial Intelligence Ideas & Applications in Financial Services. Jessica A. Keyes. 448p. 1990. 39.95 (*0-88730-441-9*, HarpBusn) HarpInfo.

New Intensive Japanese. Kenji Ogawa. (ENG & JPN.). 340p. 1997. pap. 32.95 (*4-590-00259-0*, Pub. by Hokuseido Pr) Book East.

New Interchange Student's Book: English for International Communication, Bk. 1. Jack C. Richards et al. LC 97-17432. (Illus.). 152p. (C). 1998. pap. text, student ed. 13.50 (*0-521-62881-4*) Cambridge U Pr.

New Interchange Student's Book: English for International Communication, Bk. 2. Jack C. Richards et al. LC 97-27440. (Interchange Ser.). (Illus.). 152p. (C). 1997. pap. text, student ed. 13.50 (*0-521-62862-8*) Cambridge U Pr.

New Interchange Student's Book: English for International Communication, Bk. 3. Jack C. Richards et al. (Illus.). 152p. (C). 1998. pap. text, student ed. 13.50 (*0-521-62844-X*) Cambridge U Pr.

New Interchange Teacher's Edition: English for International Communication, Bk. 1. Jack C. Richards et al. (Illus.). 312p. 1997. pap. text, teacher ed. 26.95 (*0-521-62875-X*) Cambridge U Pr.

New Interchange: English for International Communication, No. 3. Jack C. Richards et al. (Illus.). 226p. (C). 1998. pap. text, teacher ed. 24.95 (*0-521-62838-5*) Cambridge U Pr.

New Interchange: English for International Communication, Vol. 2. Jack C. Richards et al. (Interchange Ser.). (Illus.). 304p. (C). 1998. pap. text, teacher ed. 26.95 (*0-521-62856-3*) Cambridge U Pr.

New Interchange Video Activity Book: English for International Communication, Vol. 1. Jack C. Richards. (Interchange Ser.). (Illus.). 80p. (C). 1998. pap. text 12.95 (*0-521-62864-4*) Cambridge U Pr.

New Interchange Video Activity Book: English for International Communication, Vol. 2. Jack C. Richards. (Interchange Ser.). (Illus.). 72p. (C). 1998. pap. text 12.95 (*0-521-62846-6*) Cambridge U Pr.

New Interchange Video Teacher's Guide: English for International Communication, Vol. 1. Jack C. Richards et al. (Interchange Ser.). (Illus.). 128p. (C). 1997. pap. text, teacher ed. 16.95 (*0-521-62863-6*) Cambridge U Pr.

New Interchange Video Teacher's Guide: English for International Communication, Vol. 2. Jack C. Richards et al. LC 98-141916. (Interchange Ser.). (Illus.). 118p. (C). 1998. pap. text, teacher ed. 16.95 (*0-521-62845-8*) Cambridge U Pr.

New Interchange Workbook: English for International Communication, Level 3. Jack C. Richards et al. (New Interchange Ser.). (Illus.). 100p. (C). 1998. pap. text, wbk. ed. 8.50 (*0-521-62841-5*) Cambridge U Pr.

New Interchange Workbook: English for International Communication, Vol. 2. Jack C. Richards et al. (Interchange Ser.). (Illus.). 100p. (C). 1998. pap. text, wbk. ed. 8.95 (*0-521-62859-8*) Cambridge U Pr.

New Interchange Workbook 1: English for International Communication. Jack C. Richards et al. (Interchange Ser.). (Illus.). 100p. (C). 1997. pap. text, wbk. ed. 8.95 (*0-521-62878-4*) Cambridge U Pr.

New Intercom, Book 3. 2nd rev. ed. R. Yorkey et al. (YA). 1984. mass mkt. 12.95 (*0-8384-1246-7*) Heinle & Heinle.

New Intercom, Book 4. 2nd rev. ed. R. Yorkey et al. (J). 1988. mass mkt. 12.95 (*0-8384-1250-5*) Heinle & Heinle.

New Intercom-student Book 1, Book 1. 2nd ed. R. Yorkey et al. (Global ESL). (J). 1984. pap. 10.95 (*0-8384-1238-6*) Heinle & Heinle.

New Interior Decoration. Dorothy Todd & Raymond Mortimer. LC 77-4444. (Architecture & Decorative Art Ser.). (Illus.). 1977. reprint ed. lib. bdg. 65.00 (*0-306-70899-X*) Da Capo.

*__New International: U. S. Imperialism has Lost the Cold War.__ Jack Barnes. 306p. 1998. pap. 14.00 (*0-87348-796-6*) Pathfinder Pubns.

New International Atlas. 25th deluxe ed. Rand McNally Staff. (Illus.). 560p. 1994. 200.00 (*0-528-83694-3*) Rand McNally.

New International Atlas: Twenty-Fifth Anniversary Edition. 25th anniversary ed. Rand McNally Staff. LC 94-15784. 560p. 1994. 150.00 (*0-528-83693-5*) Rand McNally.

*__New International Bible Concordance: Includes All References of Every Significant Word in the NIV.__ Edward W. Goodrick & John R. Kohlenberger, III. LC 98-33125. 1998. 24.99 (*0-310-22902-2*) Zondervan.

New International Business English. Leo Jones & Richard Alexander. (Illus.). 224p. (C). 1996. pap. text, teacher ed. 19.95 (*0-521-45576-6*) Cambridge U Pr.

New International Business English. Leo Jones & Richard Alexander. (C). 1996. pap., student ed. 36.95 incl. audio (*0-521-45577-4*); pap., wbk. ed. 36.95 incl. audio (*0-521-45578-2*) Cambridge U Pr.

New International Business English. 2nd ed. Leo Jones & Richard Alexander. (Illus.). 176p. (C). 1996. pap. text, student ed. 17.95 (*0-521-45580-4*); pap. text, wbk. ed. 12.95 (*0-521-45579-0*) Cambridge U Pr.

*__New International Carriers: 1999 American Edition; The Guide to International Telecommunications Carriers.__ Ed. by Gregory C. Staple. 371p. 1999. pap. 595.00 (*1-886142-19-X*) TeleGeography.

*__New International Carriers: 1999 Asia Pacific Edition; The Guide to International Telecommunications.__ Ed. by Gregory C. Staple. 235p. 1999. pap. 595.00 (*1-886142-17-3*) TeleGeography.

*__New International Carriers: 1999 Europe Edition; The Guide to International Telecommunications Carriers.__ Ed. by Gregory C. Staple. 377p. 1999. pap. 595.00 (*1-886142-18-1*) TeleGeography.

New International Commentary on the New Testament, 16 vols. F. F. Bruce. 1984. 617.00 (*0-8028-2445-5*) Eerdmans.

New International Commentary on the Old Testament, 18 vols. Ed. by Robert L. Hubbard, Jr. 717.00 (*0-8028-2520-6*) Eerdmans.

New International Dictionary of Acronyms in Library & Information Science. 10th ed. H. Sawoniak. (ENG & GER.). 449p. 1988. lib. bdg. 250.00 (*0-8288-3395-8*, F87121) Fr & Eur.

New International Dictionary of Acronyms in Library & Information Science & Related Fields. 3rd enl. rev. ed. Ed. by Henry K. Sawoniak & Maria Witt. LC 95-154325. 500p. 1994. 145.00 (*3-598-11171-1*) K G Saur Verlag.

New International Dictionary of Biblical Archaeology. Ed. by Edward M. Blaiklock & R. K. Harrison. 1983. 34.99 (*0-310-21250-2*, 9277) Zondervan.

New International Dictionary of Music. Philip D. Morehead. 1999. pap. 7.99 (*0-451-17379-1*, Sig) NAL.

New International Dictionary of New Testament Theology, 4 vols. Ed. by Colin Brown. 1986. 169.99 (*0-310-33238-9*, 11137) Zondervan.

New International Dictionary of Old Testament Theology & Exegesis, 5 vols. Incl. Vol. 1. Ed. by Willem A. Van Gemeren. LC 96-15006. 5760p. 1997. 40.00 (*0-310-48170-8*); Vol. 4. Ed. by William A. Van Gemeren. 950p. 1997. 40.00 (*0-310-20219-1*); Vol. 2. Ed. by William A. Van Gemeren. LC 96-15006. 950p. 1997. 40.00 (*0-310-20217-5*); Vol. 3. Ed. by William A. Van Gemeren. 950p. 1997. 40.00 (*0-310-20218-3*); 1997. 199.99 (*0-310-21400-9*) Zondervan.

New International Dictionary of Old Testament Theology & Exegesis, Vol. 5. Ed. by William A. Van Gemeren. 1997. write for info. (*0-614-20961-7*) Zondervan.

New International Dictionary of Quotations. 2nd ed. Ed. by Hugh N. Rawson. 562p. 1994. mass mkt. 6.99 (*0-451-17597-2*, Sig) NAL.

*__New International Dictionary of Quotations.__ 3rd rev. ed. Margaret Miner. 2000. mass mkt. 6.99 (*0-451-19963-4*, Sig) NAL.

New International Dictionary of Refrigeration. (ENG, FRE, GER, ITA & NOR.). 600p. 1975. 175.00 (*0-8288-0964-X*, M 6432) Fr & Eur.

N

New International Dictionary of the Bible. Ed. by J. D. Douglas & Merrill C. Tenney. 1987. 29.99 (0-88469-214-0) BMH Bks.

New International Dictionary of the Bible, Pictorial Edition. rev. ed. Ed. by J. D. Douglas & Merrill C. Tenney. (Illus.). 1216p. 1987. 29.99 (0-310-33190-0, 6751) Zondervan.

New International Directions in HIV Prevention for Gay & Bisexual Men. Ed. by Michael T. Wright et al. LC 98-27620. 167p. 1998. 49.95 (0-7890-0538-7, Harrington Park) Haworth Pr.

New International Directions in HIV Prevention for Gay & Bisexual Men. Ed. by Michael T. Wright et al. LC 98-27620. 212p. 1998. pap. 22.95 (1-56023-116-5, Harrington Park) Haworth Pr.

New International Economic Order. P. N. Agarwala. (Studies on the New International Economic Order). 350p. 1983. 88.00 (0-08-028823-5, Pergamon Pr) Elsevier.

New International Economic Order. Rachel M. McCleary. (Pew Case Studies in International Affairs). 81p. (C). 1988. pap. text 3.50 (1-56927-149-6) Geo U Inst Dplmcy.

New International Economic Order: A Bibliography. Compiled by Tawfique Nawaz. LC 79-28077. 163p. 1980. lib. bdg. 52.95 (0-313-22111-1, NAI/, Greenwood Pr) Greenwood.

New International Economic Order: A Third World Perspective, 9. Ed. by Pradip K. Ghosh. LC 83-26484. (International Development Resource Bks.: No. 9). (Illus.). 562p. 1984. lib. bdg. 85.00 (0-313-24145-7, GNI/, Greenwood Pr) Greenwood.

New International Economic Order & the Promotion of Human Rights. 50p. 1987. 8.50 (92-1-154049-6, E.85.XIV.6) UN.

New International Economics. Jan S. Hogendorn & Wilson H. Brown. LC 78-67953. (Economics Ser.). (Illus.). 1980. text 38.36 (0-201-02824-7) Addison-Wesley.

New International Encyclopedia of the Bible. Lawrence O. Richards. LC 98-51045. 2000. 24.99 (0-310-22912-X) Zondervan.

New International Fondue Cookbook. Ed. by Coleen Simmons & Bob Simmons. (Illus.). 112p. 1990. pap. 8.95 (1-55867-008-4, Nitty Gritty Ckbks) Bristol Pub Ent CA.

New International Health Order. Charles O. Pannenborg. 476p. 1980. lib. bdg. 72.00 (90-286-0239-9) Kluwer Academic.

New International History of the Spanish Civil War. Michael Alpert. 304p. 1998. pap. 19.95 (0-312-21043-4) St Martin.

New International House. Francisco Cerver. (Illus.). 208p. 55.00 (0-8230-3167-5) Watsn-Guptill.

New International Labour Studies: An Introduction. Ronaldo Munck. LC 88-27566. 256p. (C). 1988. pap. 17.50 (0-86232-587-0, Pub. by Zed Books); text 49.95 (0-86232-586-2, Pub. by Zed Books) St Martin.

New International Lesson Annual, 1999-2000. Ed. by Nan Duerling. 140.00 (0-687-02293-2) Abingdon.

New International Lesson Annual, 1999-2000. Ed. by Nan Duerling. 488p. 1999. pap. 14.00 (0-687-02303-3) Abingdon.

New International Lesson Annual, 1995-96. Nan Duerling. 400p. (Orig.). 1995. pap. 11.95 (0-687-19159-9) Abingdon.

New International Lesson Annual, 1996-97. Ed. by Nan Duerling. 480p. (Orig.). 1996. pap. 12.50 (0-687-00279-6) Abingdon.

New International Lesson Annual, 1997-98. Ed. by Nan Duerling. 488p. 1997. 12.95 (0-687-01523-5) Abingdon.

***New International Money Game.** 6th ed. Robert Z. Aliber. LC 99-55593. 1999. pap. text 27.50 (0-226-01397-9) U Ch Pr.

***New International Money Game.** 6th ed. Robert Z. Aliber. 1999. lib. bdg. 50.00 (0-226-01396-0) U Ch Pr.

New International Perspectives on Telework: From Telecommuting to the Virtual Organisation. Paul J. Jackson & Joseph Van Der Wielen. LC 97-28677. 336p. (C). 1998. 100.00 (0-415-17354-X); pap. 32.99 (0-415-17127-X) Routledge.

New International Politics South Asia. 2nd ed. Hewitt. LC 97-5367. (Regional International Politics Ser.). (Illus.). 272p. 1997. pap. 24.95 (0-7190-5122-3, Pub. by Manchester Univ Pr) St Martin.

New International Role for the Arab World: Lessons from the Japanese Experience. Baher A. Ghosheh. LC 88-72073. 185p. 1998. 24.85 (0-940121-10-7, H111) Cross Cultural Pubns.

New International Status of Civil Defence. B. Jakovljevic. 1982. lib. bdg. 80.00 (90-247-2567-4) Kluwer Academic.

***New International Studies Classroom: Active Teaching, Active Learning.** Ed. by Jeffrey S. Lantis et al. LC 99-56615. 308p. 2000. pap. 26.95 (1-55587-889-X); lib. bdg. 59.95 (1-55587-865-2) L Rienner.

New International Version & the Translation by J. N. Darby. 2nd ed. R. A. Huebner. 44p. 1994. pap. 2.50 (0-9638869-3-2) Pres Truth.

***New International Version 2000-2001.** Standard Publishing Co. Staff. (Lesson Commentary Ser.). 2000. pap. text 14.99 (0-7847-1055-4) Standard Pub.

New International Webster's Compact Dictionary of the English Language: Encyclopedic Edition. rev. ed. Ed. by Sidney Landau. (Illus.). 864p. 1999. 24.95 (1-888777-97-4) Trident Pr Intl.

***New International Webster's Comprehensive Dictionary of the English Language.** 1946p. 1999. 89.95 (1-888777-79-6) Trident Pr Intl.

New International Webster's Concise Dictionary: International Encyclopedic Edition. Ed. by Sidney I. Landau et al. Orig. Title: Webster's Illustrated Contemporary Dictionary - Encyclopedic Edition. (Illus.). 1070p. 1998. reprint ed. 49.95 (1-888777-91-5) Trident Pr Intl.

New International Webster's Concise Dictionary of the English Language: Deluxe Padded Edition. rev. ed. Ed. by Sidney I. Landau. Orig. Title: The Illustrated Contemporary Dictionary-Encyclopedic. (Illus.). 1070p. 1998. 49.95 (1-888777-10-9) Trident Pr Intl.

New International Webster's Concise Dictionary of the English Language: Standard Edition. rev. ed. Ed. by Sidney I. Landau. Orig. Title: The Illustrated Contemporary Dictionary-Encyclopedia. (Illus.). 1070p. 1997. 39.95 (1-888777-09-5) Trident Pr Intl.

New International Webster's Dictionary of the English Language: Encyclopedic Edition. rev. ed. Ed. by S. Stevenson Smith et al. (Illus.). 1946p. 1998. reprint ed. 69.95 (1-888777-82-6) Trident Pr Intl.

New International Webster's Dictionary of the English Language: Encyclopedic Edition. rev. ed. Ed. by S. Stevenson Smith et al. (Illus.). 1946p. 1998. reprint ed. 79.95 (1-888777-80-X) Trident Pr Intl.

New International Webster's Family Dictionary. deluxe rev. ed. Ed. by Sidney Landau. (Illus.). 864p. 1999. 24.95 (1-888777-99-0) Trident Pr Intl.

New International Webster's French & English Dictionary. Roger J. Steiner. Orig. Title: The Bantam New College French & English Dictionary. x, 738p. 1998. reprint ed. 24.95 (1-888777-44-3) Trident Pr Intl.

New International Webster's German & English Dictionary. John C. Traupman. Orig. Title: The Bantam New College German & English Dictionary. x, 752p. 1998. reprint ed. 24.95 (1-888777-45-1) Trident Pr Intl.

New International Webster's Italian & English Dictionary. Robert C. Melzi. Orig. Title: The Bantam New College Italian & English Dictionary. xiii, 719p. 1998. reprint ed. 24.95 (1-888777-46-X) Trident Pr Intl.

New International Webster's Mass Market Reference Library, 8 vols. rev. ed. 2890p. 1998. reprint ed. mass mkt. 39.95 (1-888777-87-7) Trident Pr Intl.

New International Webster's Pocket Desk Reference: Dictionary, Thesaurus, Quotations, Spelling, Business, 5 vols. 1997. 39.99 (1-888777-24-9) Trident Pr Intl.

New International Webster's Pocket Desk Reference: Dictionary, Thesaurus, Quotations, Spelling, Business, 5 vols. 2000p. 1998. 37.95 (1-888777-23-0) Trident Pr Intl.

New International Webster's Pocket Desk Reference: Includes: Dictionary, Thesaurus, Quotations, Spelling, Business, Computer, Medical & First Aid, & Grammar, Speech & Style Dictionaries, 8 vols. 1997. 59.95 (1-888777-42-7) Trident Pr Intl.

***New International Webster's Pocket Reference Library: Desk Reference Set, 5 bks.** 1999. mass mkt., boxed set 24.95 (1-888777-94-X) Trident Pr Intl.

New International Webster's Pocket Reference Library: Includes: Dictionary, Thesaurus, Quotations, Speller, Grammar, Speech & Style, Business, Computer, & Medical & First Aid Dictionaries, 8 vols. 2900p. 1998. 59.95 (1-888777-41-9) Trident Pr Intl.

***New International Webster's Pocket Reference Set: Desk Reference Set, 3 bks.** 1999. mass mkt., boxed set 14.95 (1-58279-040-X) Trident Pr Intl.

New International Webster's Spanish & English Dictionary. Edwin B. Williams. Orig. Title: The Bantam New College Spanish & English Dictionary. xi, 724p. 1997. reprint ed. 24.95 (1-888777-43-5) Trident Pr Intl.

New International Webster's Student Dictionary. rev. ed. Ed. by Sidney I. Landau & Ronald J. Bogus. Orig. Title: Illustrated Contemporary Dictionary-Encyclopedic Edition. (Illus.). 864p. 1998. pap. 14.99 (1-888777-08-7) Trident Pr Intl.

New International Webster's Student Dictionary of the English Language: International Encyclopedic Edition. rev. ed. Ed. by Sidney I. Landau & Ronald J. Bogus. Orig. Title: Illustrated Contemporary Dictionary-Encyclopedic Edition. (Illus.). 864p. 1998. 24.95 (1-888777-01-X, 2495) Trident Pr Intl.

New International World Atlas. 25th anniversary ed. Rand McNally Staff. (Illus.). 560p. 1996. 150.00 (0-528-83808-3) Rand McNally.

New Internationalism. Clark Foreman. LC 71-37342. (Select Bibliographies Reprint Ser.). 1977. reprint ed. 18.95 (0-8369-6689-9) Ayer.

New Internet Business Book. 2nd ed. Jill H. Ellsworth & Matthew V. Ellsworth. LC 95-25740. (Illus.). 499p. 1996. pap. 24.95 (0-471-14160-7) Wiley.

New Internet Design Project: The Best of Graphic Art on the Web Reloaded. Patrick Burgoyne & Liz Faber. (Illus.). 144p. 1999. pap. 29.95 (0-7893-0362-0, Pub. by Universe) St Martin.

New Internships for 1997-1998. 1997. 27.50 (0-938609-12-2) Graduate Group.

New Interpretation of Dreams: Maps for Psychotherapy & the General Reader. (Illus.). 302p. 1997. pap. 30.00 (0-9662185-0-7) J P Gustafson.

New Interpretations. 3rd ed. Dale A. Burk. LC 82-99859. (Illus.). 204p. 1982. reprint ed. pap. 14.95 (0-912299-07-X) Stoneydale Pr Pub.

New Interpretations in Naval History: Selected Papers from the Tenth Naval History Symposium, United States Naval Academy, September 1991. Ed. by Jack Sweetman et al. LC 93-17714. 418p. 1993. 37.50 (1-55750-782-1) Naval Inst Pr.

New Interpretations in Naval History: Selected Papers from the Thirteenth Naval History Symposium. Ed. by William M. McBride. LC 98-38020. 302p. 1998. 37.50 (1-55750-648-5) Naval Inst Pr.

New Interpretations in Naval History: Selected Papers from the Twelfth Naval History Symposium. Ed. by William B. Cogar. LC 97-25160. (Illus.). 400p. 1997. 37.50 (1-55750-624-8) Naval Inst Pr.

New Interpretations of Ape & Human Ancestry. Ed. by Russell L. Ciochon & Robert S. Corruccini. (Advances in Primatology Ser.). 850p. 1983. 165.00 (0-306-41072-9, Plenum Trade) Perseus Pubng.

New Interpretations of Classical American Authors. Ed. by Richard Fleming & Michael Payne. LC 86-48008. (Bucknell Review Ser.: Vol. XXXI, No. 2). 168p. 1988. 22.00 (0-8387-5127-X) Bucknell U Pr.

New Interpreter's Bible Vol. 3: Kings - Esther. 1996. 81.50 (0-687-27816-3) Abingdon.

New Interpreter's Bible Vol. 6: Isaiah - Ezekiel. 1006p. 1996. 81.50 (0-687-27819-8) Abingdon.

New Interpreter's Bible Vol. 10: Acts - Corinthians. 1999. 81.50 (0-687-27823-6) Abingdon.

New Interpreter's Bible Vol. 11: Corinthians - Philippians. 1996. 81.50 (0-687-27824-4) Abingdon.

New Interpreters Handbook. Alex Marquez & Marta Marquez. 116p. (Orig.). (C). 1987. pap. text 20.00 (0-943407-00-1) Iberia Lang.

New, Interpretive Translation of St. Anselm's Monologion & Proslogion. Jasper Hopkins. LC 86-70086. xiv, 343p. 1986. text 25.00 (0-938060-33-3); pap. text 10.00 (0-938060-34-1) Banning Pr.

New Interventionism 1991-1994: United Nations Experience in Cambodia, Former Yugoslavia & Somalia. Ed. by James Mayall. (London School of Economics Monographs in International Studies). 248p. (C). 1996. text 59.95 (0-521-55197-8); pap. text 18.95 (0-521-55856-5) Cambridge U Pr.

New Interventions for Children & Youth: Action-Research Approaches. Robert N. Rapoport. (Illus.). 288p. 1987. text 59.95 (0-521-34122-1) Cambridge U Pr.

New Intimacy. Barbara Cully. LC 96-49453. 80p. 1997. pap. 14.95 (0-14-026480-9) Viking Penguin.

New Intimacy: Discovering the Magic at the Heart of Your Differences. Judith Sherven & James Sniechowski. LC 97-27656. 320p. 1997. pap. 12.95 (1-55874-511-4) Health Comm.

New Introducing Sociology. Peter Worsley et al. 496p. 1987. 7.95 (0-14-022625-7, Penguin Bks) Viking Penguin.

New Introduction to Bibliography. Philip Gaskell. LC 95-23532. (Illus.). 464p. 1996. pap. 29.95 (1-884718-13-2, 18132) Oak Knoll.

New Introduction to Biology. Douglas M. Fambrough. (C). 1997. text. write for info. (0-03-098797-0) Harcourt Coll Pubs.

New Introduction to British Politics. Peter J. Madgwick. 550p. 1994. pap. 37.50 (0-7487-1592-4, Pub. by S Thornes Pubs) Trans-Atl Phila.

New Introduction to British Politics: Analysing a Capitalist Democracy. Ed. by John Dearlove & Peter Saunders. 550p. (C). 1991. pap. 43.95 (0-7456-0600-8) Blackwell Pubs.

New Introduction to British Politics: Analysing a Capitalist Democracy. 2nd ed. Ed. by John Dearlove & Peter Saunders. 550p. (C). 1991. 93.95 (0-7456-0599-0) Blackwell Pubs.

New Introduction to Greek. 3rd enl. rev. ed. Alston H. Chase & Henry Phillips, Jr. LC 61-13748. (Illus.). 235p. 1961. 29.00 (0-674-61600-6) HUP.

New Introduction to Management. Banks. (GC - Principles of Management Ser.). Date not set. text 54.95 (0-538-83380-7) S-W Pub.

New Introduction to Modal Logic. G. E. Hughes & M. J. Cresswell. LC 95-14728. 432p. (C). 1996. pap. 25.99 (0-415-12600-2) Routledge.

New Introduction to Modal Logic. G. E. Hughes & M. J. Criswell. LC 95-14728. 432p. (C). (gr. 13). 1996. 75.00 (0-415-12599-5) Routledge.

New Introduction to Organic Chemistry. Brown. Date not set. pap. text. write for info. (0-582-35128-6, Pub. by Addison-Wesley) Longman.

***New Introduction to Poverty: The Role of Race, Power, & Politics.** Ed. by Louis Kushnick & James Jennings. LC 98-40087. 400p. 1999. text 60.00 (0-8147-4238-6) NYU Pr.

New Introduction to Poverty: The Role of Race, Power & Politics. Ed. by Louis Kushnick & James Jennings. LC 98-40087. 400p. 1999. pap. text 22.50 (0-8147-4239-4) NYU Pr.

New Introduction to Stochastic Processes. 250p. 1997. pap. text 26.00 (957-8981-38-4) World Scientific Pub.

New Introduction to Stochastic Processes. K. L. Chung. (CHI.). 250p. 1997. text 36.00 (981-02-2365-X) World Scientific Pub.

New Invention of Shooting Fireshafts in Long-Bowes. LC 74-80195. (English Experience Ser.: No. 674). 1974. reprint ed. 15.00 (90-221-0674-8) Walter J Johnson.

New Investigations in Modern Chemistry. Harry A. Kranepool. Ed. by Richard M. Plass. (Illus.). 154p. (J). 1989. 5.95 (0-685-74153-2); student ed. 5.95 (0-685-74152-4); student ed. 9.95 (0-685-29318-1) Amer Scholastic.

New Investigations of Marx's Method. Ed. by Fred Moseley & Martha Campbell. LC 96-48493. 212p. (C). 1997. text 45.00 (0-391-04021-9) Humanities.

New Investigations of Marx's Method. Fred Moseley & Martha Campbell. LC 99-10402. 1999. write for info. (1-57392-364-8, Humanity Bks) Prometheus Bks.

New Investors' Bible Vol. 1: Become Wealthy Starting at Any Age. Stanton E. Christie. LC 99-217172. (Illus.). 160p. 1998. pap. 19.95 (0-9664802-0-1) WEALTH Inc.

***New Investors' Bible Vol. 1: Become Wealthy Starting at Any Age.** Stanton E. Christie. (Illus.). 160p. 1998. 23.95 (0-9664802-1-X) WEALTH Inc.

New Invitation Bridges . . . A Curriculum for Persons with Disabilities Vol. 1: Fall. Ed. by Hilda R. Davis. 72p. 1995. pap. 12.95 (0-687-71978-X) Abingdon.

New Invitation Bridges . . . A Curriculum for Persons with Disabilities Vol. 1: Spring. Ed. by Hilda R. Davis. 72p. 1994. pap. 12.95 (0-687-71980-1) Abingdon.

New Invitation Bridges . . . A Curriculum for Persons with Disabilities Vol. 1: Summer. Ed. by Hilda R. Davis. 72p. 1996. pap. 12.95 (0-687-71981-X) Abingdon.

New Invitation Bridges . . . A Curriculum for Persons with Disabilities Vol. 1: Winter. Ed. by Hilda R. Davis. 72p. 1995. pap. 12.95 (0-687-71979-8) Abingdon.

New Invitation Bridges . . . A Curriculum for Persons with Disabilities Vol. 2: Fall. Ed. by Hilda R. Davis. 72p. 1996. pap. 12.95 (0-687-71982-8) Abingdon.

New Invitation Bridges . . . A Curriculum for Persons with Disabilities Vol. 2: Summer. Ed. by Hilda R. Davis. 72p. 1997. pap. 12.95 (0-687-71985-2) Abingdon.

New Invitation Bridges . . . A Curriculum for Persons with Disabilities Vol. 3: July. Ed. by Hilda R. Davis. 72p. 1997. pap. 12.95 (0-687-71986-0) Abingdon.

New Invitation Bridges . . . A Curriculum for Persons with Disabilities Vol. 3: Spring. Ed. by Hilda R. Davis. 72p. 1997. pap. 12.95 (0-687-71988-7) Abingdon.

New Invitation Bridges . . . A Curriculum for Persons with Disabilities Vol. 3: Summer. Ed. by Hilda R. Davis. 72p. 1998. pap. 12.95 (0-687-71989-5) Abingdon.

New Invitation Bridges . . . A Curriculum for Persons with Disabilities Vol. 3: Winter. Ed. by Hilda R. Davis. 72p. 1997. pap. 12.95 (0-687-71987-9) Abingdon.

New IQ Test: Joint Editors of the Mensa UK Puzzle Group Journal. Philip J. Carter & Ken A. Russell. (Illus.). 128p. 1994. pap. 5.95 (0-7063-7229-8, Pub. by WrLock) Sterling.

New IRA Opportunities. Jeffrey A. Hackney & Linda M. Johnson. Ed. by Lawrence M. Norris. LC 98-175019. (Client Care Ser.). 72p. 1998. pap. 7.15 (0-8080-0260-0) CCH INC.

New IRA Opportunities. Linda M. Johnson & Jeffrey A. Hackney. 64p. 1998. pap. text 7.00 (0-8080-0292-9) CCH INC.

New Iraq: The Gulf War & the Implications for U. S. Policy, 133. Frederick W. Axelgard. LC 88-2403. (Washington Papers: No. 133). 139p. 1988. 49.95 (0-275-93013-0, C3013); pap. 18.95 (0-275-93014-9, B3014) Greenwood.

New Ireland: Politics, Peace & Reconciliation. John Hume. Ed. by Jack Van Zandt. LC 95-72789. (Illus.). 192p. 1996. 21.95 (1-57098-066-7) Roberts Rinehart.

New Ireland: Politics, Peace, & Reconciliation. John Hume. LC 96-72311. 192p. 1997. pap. text 13.95 (1-57098-141-8) Roberts Rinehart.

New Ireland: Ritual Arts of Oceania in the Collections of the Barbier-Mueller Museum. Michael Gunn. (Illus.). 224p. 1999. 60.00 (88-8118-207-6, Pub. by Skira IT) Abbeville Pr.

New Ireland Forum. Veritas Publications Staff. 1989. pap. 30.00 (0-86217-171-7, Pub. by Veritas Pubns) St Mut.

New Irish Americans. Ray O'Hanlon. LC 97-52317. (Illus.). 256p. 1998. pap. text 15.95 (1-57098-212-0) Roberts Rinehart.

New Irish Cooking: Recipes from Dublin's Peacock Alley. Conrad Gallagher. (Illus.). 184p. 1997. 39.95 (1-899047-29-8, Pub. by A A Farmar) Irish Bks Media.

New Irish Cooking: Recipes from Dublin's Peacock Alley. Conrad Gallagher. (Illus.). 184p. 1997. pap. 15.95 (1-899047-54-9, Pub. by A A Farmar) Irish Bks Media.

***New Irish Walks & Scrambles 5: The Burren, the Aran Islands, & County Clare.** Barry Keane. (Illus.). 118p. 2000. pap. 13.95 (1-898256-83-7, Pub. by Collins Press) Irish Bks Media.

New Irish Writing. James D. Brophy & Eamon Grennan. 242p. 1988. 28.95 (0-8057-9025-X, Twyne) Mac Lib Ref.

New Irish Writing. Ed. by David Marcus. 3.95 (0-7043-3101-2, Pub. by Quartet) Charles River Bks.

New Ironmaking & Steelmaking Processes: Proceedings of the 7th Process Technology Conference, April 17-20, 1988, Toronto, Ontario. Process Technology Conference Staff. LC 82-197229. (Illus.). 307p. reprint ed. pap. 95.20 (0-8357-5552-5, 203518100093) Bks Demand.

New Is Not Yet Born: Conflict Resolution in Southern Africa. Thomas Ohlson et al. LC 93-51052. 322p. (C). 1994. 44.95 (0-8157-6452-9) Brookings.

New Is Not Yet Born: Conflict Resolution in Southern Africa. Thomas Ohlson et al. LC 93-51052. 322p. (C). 1994. pap. 19.95 (0-8157-6451-0) Brookings.

New Ischemic Syndromes: Beyond Angina & Infarction. Derek M. Yellon & Shahbudin H. Rahimtoola. 254p. 1997. pap. text 49.95 (1-881063-06-2) Lppncott W & W.

New Islamic Dynasties: A Chronological & Genealogical Manual. rev. ed. Clifford E. Bosworth. LC 96-28471. 320p. 1996. 47.50 (0-231-10714-5) Col U Pr.

New Islands & Other Stories. Maria L. Bombal. Tr. by Richard Cunningham & Lucia Cunningham from SPA. LC 88-47764. 112p. 1988. reprint ed. pap. text 10.95 (0-8014-9538-5) Cornell U Pr.

New Israel. Ed. by Gershon Shafir & Yoav Peled. LC 99-41453. 294p. 2000. 65.00 (0-8133-3567-1) HarpC.

New Israeli Architecture. Amiram Harlap. LC 73-8291. (Illus.). 600p. 1983. 65.00 (0-8386-1425-6) Fairleigh Dickinson.

New Israelis: An Intimate View of a Changing People. Yossi Melman. 320p. 1992. 19.95 (1-55972-129-4, Birch Ln Pr) Carol Pub Group.

***New Issues in Audit & Accounting: PPC's Annual Audit & Accounting Update.** Practitioners Publishing Staff. 1999. ring bd. write for info. (0-7646-0763-4) Prctnrs Pub Co.

New Issues in the Economics of Technological Change. Ed. by Christopher Freeman & Luc Soete. 256p. 1987. text 54.00 (0-86187-128-6, Pub. by P P Pubs) Cassell & Continuum.

An Asterisk (*) at the beginning of an entry indicates that the title is appearing for the first time.

New Issues in the Reconstruction of Shakespeare's Theatre: Proceedings of the Conference Held at the Unversity of Georgia, February 16-18, 1990. Ed. by Franklin J. Hildy. LC 90-40573. (Artists & Issues in the Theatre Ser.: Vol. 1). (Illus.). XX, 256p. (C). 1991. text 48.95 (0-8204-1400-X) P Lang Pubng.

New Issues in the Theory of Investment: Modernization & Persistence Effects. M. Savioz. Ed. by Dieter Bos et al. (Studies in Contemporary Economics). (Illus.). xvi, 216p. 1992. 49.95 (0-387-54979-X) Spr-Verlag.

New Issues in the Uruguay Round of Multilateral Trade Negotiations. 55p. 1990. 12.50 (92-1-104344-1, 90.II.A.15) UN.

New Italian - Russian Dictionary. G. F. Zor'ko et al. (ITA & RUS.). 1018p. 1995. 64.95 (0-8285-5382-3) Firebird NY.

***New Italian Architecture.** Ed. by Anna Giuseppe Ciorra. (Library of Architecture). (Illus.). 184p. 2000. pap. text 19.95 (88-8118-654-3, Pub. by Skira IT) Abbeville Pr.

New Italian Fiction. (Review of Contemporary Fiction Ser.: Vol. 12, No. 3). 1992. pap. 8.00 (1-56478-121-6) Dalkey Arch.

New Italian Novel. Zygmunt G. Baranski. (Toronto Italian Studies). 272p. 1997. pap. text 19.95 (0-8020-8080-4) U of Toronto Pr.

New Italian Novel. Ed. by Zygmunt G. Baranski & Lino Pertile. (Writers of Italy Ser.). 300p. (C). 1994. text 60.00 (0-7486-0414-6, Pub. by Edinburgh U Pr) Col U Pr.

New Italian Poets. Ed. by Dana Gioia & Michael Palma. 386p. (Orig.). 1991. pap. 16.95 (0-934257-42-6) Story Line.

New Italian Republic: From the Fall of the Berlin Wall to Berlusconi. Ed. by Stephen Gundle & Simon Parker. LC 95-20748. 352p. (C). 1996. 90.00 (0-415-12161-2); pap. 24.99 (0-415-12162-0) Routledge.

New Italian Women: A Collection of Short Fiction. Tr. by Gloria I. Anzilotti et al from ITA. LC 89-45539. 218p. (Orig.). 1989. pap. 14.95 (0-934977-16-X) Italica Pr.

***New Italy.** Marco Sabellico & Daniele Cernilli. (Illus.). 224p. 2000. 40.00 (88-86961-28-6, Pub. by Mitchell Beazley) Antique Collect.

New Jack Cinema. Steven D. Kendall. LC 92-75983. 209p. 1995. pap. 14.95 (0-9629513-1-5) J L Denser.

New Jackals: Ramzi Yousef, Osama bin Laden, & the Future of Terrorism. Simon Reeve. LC 99-37245. (Illus.). 256p. 1999. 26.95 (1-55553-407-4) NE U Pr.

New Jacobinism: Can Democracy Survive? Claes G. Ryn. LC 91-2774. 102p. (Orig.). 1991. pap. 9.95 (0-932783-03-1) Natl Human Inst.

New Jacoby & Meyers Practical Guide to Everyday Law. Gail J. Koff. LC 93-31638. 320p. 1994. pap. 12.00 (0-671-86903-5, Fireside) S&S Trade Pap.

New Japan: Government & Politics. Harold S. Quigley & John E. Turner. LC 74-10473. (Illus.). 456p. 1974. reprint ed. lib. bdg. 79.50 (0-8371-7689-1, QUNJ, Greenwood Pr) Greenwood.

New Japan Solo. 4th ed. Eiji Kanno. 1998. pap. text 22.00 (4-7700-2187-9, Pub. by Kodansha Intl) Kodansha.

New Japanese-English Dictionary of Economic Terms. (ENG & JPN.). 501p. 1985. 125.00 (0-8288-0116-9, M 9334) Fr & Eur.

New Japanese Photography: APA II. (Illus.). 480p. 1992. 69.99 (1-56496-019-6) Rockport Pubs.

New Japanese Poetry: The 70's & 80's. Ed. by Thomas Fitzsimmons & Yoshimazu Gozo. Tr. by Robert Brady et al from JPN. (Asian Poetry in Translation Ser.: No. 15). (Illus.). 224p. 1993. pap. 25.00 (0-942668-36-7) Katydid Bks.

New Japanese Voices: The Best Contemporary Fiction from Japan. Ed. by Helen Mitsios. LC 90-967. 224p. 1992. pap. 10.95 (0-87113-522-1, Atlntc Mnthly) Grove-Atltic.

New Jerome Bible Handbook. Ed. by Raymond E. Brown et al. LC 92-46508. 416p. 1993. 24.95 (0-8146-2204-6) Liturgical Pr.

New Jerome Biblical Commentary. 3rd ed. Fitzmyer. LC 99-40992. 1475p. 1999. pap. text 56.00 (0-13-859836-3) P-H.

New Jersey see From Sea to Shining Sea

New Jersey see Atlas of Historical County Boundaries

New Jersey see One Nation Series

***New Jersey.** (Switched on Schoolhouse Ser.). (Illus.). (J). 2000. pap. 24.95 (0-7403-0282-5) Alpha AZ.

New Jersey. Capstone Press, Geography Department Staff. (One Nation Ser.). (Illus.). 48p. (J). (gr. 3-7). 1997. lib. bdg. 19.00 (0-516-20930-2) Childrens.

New Jersey. Dennis B. Fradin. LC 92-34601. (From Sea to Shining Sea Ser.). (Illus.). 64p. (J). (gr. 3-5). 1993. pap. 7.95 (0-516-43830-1) Childrens.

New Jersey. Charles Fredeen. LC 92-13363. (Hello U. S. A. Ser.). (Illus.). 72p. (J). (gr. 3-6). 1993. lib. bdg. 19.95 (0-8225-2732-4, Lerner Publctns) Lerner Pub.

***New Jersey.** John Gilman & Robert Heide. LC 99-28807. (Art of the State Ser.). (Illus.). 96p. 1999. 12.95 (0-8109-5566-0, Pub. by Abrams) Time Warner.

New Jersey. Kathleen Thompson. LC 85-9981. (Portrait of America Library). 48p. (J). (gr. 4-8). 1996. pap. text 5.95 (0-8114-7456-9) Raintree Steck-V.

New Jersey. Kathleen Thompson. (Portrait of America Library). (Illus.). 48p. (J). (gr. 3-6). 1996. lib. bdg. 22.83 (0-8114-7375-9) Raintree Steck-V.

New Jersey. Anne Welsbacher. LC 97-34112. (United States Ser.). (Illus.). 32p. (J). 1998. lib. bdg. 19.93 (1-56239-892-X, Checkerboard Library) ABDO Pub Co.

New Jersey. Barbara Westergaard. (Guide to the State Ser.). 400p. 1987. pap. 12.95 (0-8135-1242-5) Rutgers U Pr.

New Jersey. 2nd ed. R. Conrad Stein. LC 97-41839. (America the Beautiful Ser.). (J). 1998. lib. bdg. 32.00 (0-516-20637-0) Childrens.

***New Jersey, 5 vols., Set.** Wendy Moragne. LC 98-43948. (Celebrate the States Ser.). (Illus.). 144p. (J). (gr. 4-7). 2000. lib. bdg. 35.64 (0-7614-0673-5, Benchmark NY) Marshall Cavendish.

New Jersey: A Geography. Charles A. Stansfield, Jr. 240p. 1983. text 61.00 (0-89158-957-0) Westview.

New Jersey: A Guide to Its Present & Past. Federal Writers' Project Staff. (American Guidebook Ser.). 735p. 1939. reprint ed. 95.00 (0-403-02180-4) Somerset Pub.

New Jersey: A Guide to Its Present & Past. Federal Writers' Project Staff & Writers Program-WPA Staff. (American Guide Ser.). 1989. reprint ed. lib. bdg. 89.00 (0-7812-1029-1, 1029) Rprt Serv.

New Jersey: A Guide to the State. 2nd ed. Barbara Westergaard. LC 97-23594. (Illus.). xvii, 372p. 1998. pap. 17.00 (0-8135-2482-2) Rutgers U Pr.

New Jersey: A History. Thomas Fleming. (States & the Nation Ser.). (Illus.). 1984. pap. 11.95 (0-393-30180-X) Norton.

New Jersey: A Mirror on America. John T. Cunningham. 1996. student ed. write for info. (0-89359-012-6) Afton Pub.

New Jersey: A Photographic Celebration. Walter Choroszewski. LC 96-86342. (Illus.). 152p. 1996. 35.00 (0-933605-06-4) Aesthetic Pr.

New Jersey: A Photographic Journey. Walter Choroszewski. LC 87-72222. (Illus.). 136p. 1987. 30.00 (0-933605-01-3) Aesthetic Pr.

New Jersey: A Scenic Discovery. Walter Choroszewski. (Scenic Discovery Ser.). (Illus.). 120p. 1984. 27.50 (0-89909-049-4) Foremost Pubs.

New Jersey: Daytripping, Backroads, Eateries & Funky Attractions. Robert Heide. LC 98-145104. 1998. pap. 16.95 (0-312-18147-7) St Martin.

New Jersey: Environment & Cancer. Eustace A. Dixon. Ed. by V. Eugene Vivian. (Illus.). 410p. (C). 1982. pap. 19.95 (0-942848-01-2) Eureka Pubns.

New Jersey: Hello U. S. A. Charles Fredeen. (Illus.). 72p. (J). (gr. 3-6). 1996. pap. text 5.95 (0-8225-9720-9, First Ave Edns) Lerner Pub.

New Jersey: Index to Military Men of New Jersey 1775-1815. Ronald V. Jackson. LC 77-86053. lib. bdg. 55.00 (0-89593-157-5, Accel Indexing) Genealogical Srvcs.

***New Jersey: Off the Beaten Path.** 5th ed. William G. Scheller & Kay Scheller. LC 99-87863. (Off the Beaten Path Ser.). (Illus.). 176p. 2000. pap. 12.95 (0-7627-0553-1) Globe Pequot.

New Jersey: Off the Beaten Path: A Guide to Unique Places. 4th ed. William Scheller & Kay Scheller. LC 97-52956. (Off the Beaten Path Ser.). (Illus.). 256p. 1998. pap. 12.95 (0-7627-0194-3) Globe Pequot.

New Jersey: The Garden State on the Eve of the 21st Century. Stephen Barr. LC 98-71768. (Illus.). 414p. 1998. 39.95 (1-882933-22-2) Cherbo Pub Grp.

***New Jersey: The Natural State.** Dwight Hiscano. LC 99-43169. (Illus.). 130p. 2000. 39.00 (0-8135-2772-4) Rutgers U Pr.

New Jersey - Collected Works of Federal Writers Project, Vol. 1. Federal Writers' Project Staff. 1991. reprint ed. lib. bdg. 98.00 (0-7812-5668-2) Rprt Serv.

New Jersey - Collected Works of Federal Writers Project, Vol. 2. Federal Writers' Project Staff. 1991. reprint ed. lib. bdg. 98.00 (0-7812-5674-7) Rprt Serv.

New Jersey? What Exit? 300 Questions & Answers about People, Places, & Events in the Garden State. Gerald Tomlinson. LC 95-95079. (Illus.). 128p. (Orig.). 1996. pap. 11.95 (0-917125-05-3) Home Run Pr.

New Jersey African American History Curriculum Guide, Grades 9 to 12. Larry A. Greene & Lenworth Gunther. LC 95-38310. 1995. write for info. (0-89743-082-4) NJ Hist Com.

New Jersey Almanac. Ed. by Donald Linky et al. 369p. 1997. pap. 85.00 (0-9658857-0-4) Pub Affairs Res.

New Jersey, America's Main Road, 1976. John T. Cunningham. 1976. reprint ed. pap. 18.95 (0-89359-007-X) Afton Pub.

New Jersey & Other State Greats (Biographies) Carole Marsh. (Carole Marsh New Jersey Bks.). (Illus.). (J). 1994. pap. 19.95 (1-55609-869-3); lib. bdg. 29.95 (1-55609-868-5); disk 29.95 (1-55609-870-7) Gallopade Intl.

New Jersey & the Rebellion: History of the Services of the Troops & People of New Jersey in Aid of the Union Cause. John Y. Foster. (Illus.). 870p. 1997. reprint ed. lib. bdg. 89.00 (0-8328-6032-8) Higginson Bk Co.

New Jersey & the Revolutionary War. Alfred H. Bill. (New Jersey Historical Ser.). (Illus.). 117p. 1970. reprint ed. pap. 12.95 (0-8135-0642-5) Rutgers U Pr.

New Jersey Anthology. Ed. by Maxine N. Lurie. LC 94-2821. 502p. (Orig.). (C). 1994. pap. 18.95 (0-911020-29-2) NJ Hist Soc.

New Jersey Appellate Handbook. Edward A. Zunz, Jr. & Alan E. Kraus. Ed. by Edward L. Raymond, Jr. & Anne S. Rutland. LC 95-79901. 600p. 1995. text. write for info. (0-7620-0005-8) West Group.

New Jersey Appellate Practice Handbook. 3rd ed. New Jersey Appellate Practice Study Committee. 92p. 1993. ring bd. 65.00 (0-685-65972-0) NJ Inst CLE.

New Jersey Architecture. Susanne C. Hand. LC 95-3371. (New Jersey History Ser.: Vol. 5). 1995. 9.00 (0-89743-081-6) NJ Hist Com.

New Jersey Archives Series 1: Documents Relating to the Colonial, Revolutionary, & Post-Revolutionary History of the State of New Jersey, 42 vols. LC 74-20233. reprint ed. write for info. (0-404-12700-2) AMS Pr.

New Jersey Archives Series 2: Documents Relating to the Revolutionary History of the State of New Jersey, 5 vols., Set. LC 74-20234. reprint ed. 4955.00 (0-404-12744-4) AMS Pr.

New Jersey Arts. Patricia Herold. LC 89-49082. (Illus.). 240p. (Orig.). (C). 1990. pap. 13.95 (0-8135-1554-8) Rutgers U Pr.

New Jersey As a Royal Province, 1738-1776. Edgar J. Fisher. LC 75-168028. (Columbia University. Studies in the Social Sciences: No. 107). reprint ed. 47.50 (0-404-51107-4) AMS Pr.

New Jersey at the Crossroads of Migration. Peter Dunne et al. LC 89-14554. (Illus.). 74p. 1989. pap. 8.00 (0-9624065-0-3) NJ Audubon Soc.

***New Jersey Atlas & Gazetteer: Topo Maps of the Entire State.** DeLorme US Staff. LC 99-464320. 88p. 1999. 16.95 (0-89933-227-7) DeLorme Map.

New Jersey Attorney General Guidelines. Mark Adamson & Daniel Del Bagno. 350p. (C). 1995. ring bd. 39.95 (1-885682-03-4) Princeton Educ.

New Jersey Attorney General Guidelines. 3rd rev. ed. Mark Adamson & Daniel Del Bagno. 418p. 1998. ring bd. 49.95 (1-885682-13-1) Princeton Educ.

New Jersey Automotive Directory. Ed. by T. L. Spelman. 1985. 24.95 (1-55527-022-0) Auto Contact Inc.

New Jersey Bandits, Bushwackers, Outlaws, Crooks, Devils, Ghosts, Desperadoes & Other Assorted & Sundry Characters! Carole Marsh. (Carole Marsh New Jersey Bks.). (Illus.). (J). 1994. pap. 19.95 (0-7933-1789-4); lib. bdg. 29.95 (0-7933-1788-6); disk 29.95 (0-7933-1790-8) Gallopade Intl.

New Jersey Beach Diver: A Diver's Guide to New Jersey Beach Dives. Daniel Berg & Denise Berg. (Illus.). 100p. pap. text. write for info. (0-9616167-8-4) Aqua Explorers.

New Jersey "BIO" Bingo! 24 Must Know State People for Kids to Learn about While Having Fun! Carole Marsh. (Bingo! Ser.). (Illus.). (J). (gr. 2-8). 1998. pap. 14.95 (0-7933-8612-8) Gallopade Intl.

New Jersey Biographical & Genealogical Notes. William Nelson. 222p. 1997. reprint ed. pap. 22.00 (0-8063-0562-2, 4005) Clearfield Co.

New Jersey Birds. James Kavanagh. (Pocket Naturalist Ser.). (Illus.). 1999. 5.95 (1-889903-82-5, Pub. by Waterford WA) Falcon Pub Inc.

New Jersey Book of Lists. Gerald Tomlinson & Ronald A. Mayer. LC 91-66039. (Illus.). 192p. (Orig.). 1992. pap. 11.95 (0-917125-01-0) Home Run Pr.

New Jersey Bookstore Book: A Surprising Guide to Our State's Bookstores & Their Specialties for Students, Teachers, Writers & Publishers. Carole Marsh. (Carole Marsh New Jersey Bks.). (Illus.). 1994. pap. 19.95 (0-7933-2946-9); lib. bdg. 29.95 (0-7933-2945-0); disk 29.95 (0-7933-2947-7) Gallopade Intl.

New Jersey Business Corporations: 1998 Cumulative Supplement see New Jersey Business Corporations, 1998 Cumulative Supplement

New Jersey Business Corporations, 1996, 2 vols. 2nd ed. John Mackay. LC 96-79308. 1996. text 160.00 (1-55834-435-7, 83000-11, MICHIE) LEXIS Pub.

New Jersey Business Corporations, 1998 Cumulative Supplement, 2 vols. 2nd ed. John R. MacKay, II. Incl. Vol. 1. New Jersey Business Corporations: 1998 Cumulative Supplement. 2nd ed. 50p. 1998. 160.00 (0-327-00620-X, 8299611); Vol. 2. New Jersey Business Corporations: 1998 Cumulative Supplement. 2nd ed. 50p. 1998. (0-327-00621-8, 8299711); 50p. 1998. 45.00 (0-327-00576-9, 8299511) LEXIS Pub.

***New Jersey Business Directory, 1999.** American Business Directories Staff. 2992p. 1999. boxed set 520.00 incl. cd-rom (0-7687-0132-5, 1048-7158) Am Busn Direct.

***New Jersey Business Directory (2000)** American Business Directories Staff et al. 2,992p. 2000. boxed set 520.00 incl. cd-rom (0-7687-0217-8) Am Busn Direct.

New Jersey Business Source Book: A Marketing Guidebook to the Business Leaders & Companies. 7th ed. Ed. by Jeanne Graves. 300p. 1998. 149.95 (1-883216-16-8) Res Comns Group.

New Jersey Canals: State Policy & Private Enterprise, 1820-1832. H. Jerome Cranmer. LC 77-14768. (Dissertations in American Economic History Ser.). 1978. 37.95 (0-405-11030-8) Ayer.

New Jersey Census Index, 1850 Mortality Schedule. (Illus.). lib. bdg. 67.00 (0-89593-429-9, Accel Indexing) Genealogical Srvcs.

New Jersey Census Index, 1870 North Federal. lib. bdg. write for info. (0-89593-431-0, Accel Indexing) Genealogical Srvcs.

New Jersey Census Index, 1860 North Federal. LC 99-197972. (Illus.). 1998. lib. bdg. 250.00 (0-89593-430-2, Accel Indexing) Genealogical Srvcs.

New Jersey Census Index 1824-1832 (Patterson City) Ronald V. Jackson. (Illus.). lib. bdg. 50.00 (0-685-42826-5, Accel Indexing) Genealogical Srvcs.

New Jersey Central: Steam Locomotives & Trains 1934 to 1937. Robert K. Durham. LC 95-96119. (Steam of the Thirties Ser.). (Illus.). 52p. 1996. pap. 21.00 (0-9644480-4-1) Durham Publng.

***New Jersey Central/Middlesex Entertainment, 2000.** (Illus.). 807p. 1999. pap. 35.00 (1-880248-44-1, 0048) Enter Pubns.

New Jersey Citations Cases, 6 vols. Shepard's Citations, Inc. Staff. LC 71-1597. 1987. suppl. ed. 720.00 (0-686-89835-4) Shepards.

New Jersey City of (Patterson & Passaic County) Federal Census Index, 1870. 1990. 145.00 (0-89593-616-X, Accel Indexing) Genealogical Srvcs.

New Jersey (City of Trenton & Mercer County) Federal Census Index, 1870. 1990. 145.00 (0-89593-617-8, Accel Indexing) Genealogical Srvcs.

New Jersey Civil Practice & Court Rules: Annual Edition. Gould Editorial Staff. 1020p. (C). ring bd. 21.95 (0-87526-299-6) Gould.

New Jersey Classic Christmas Trivia: Stories, Recipes, Activities, Legends, Lore & More! Carole Marsh. (Carole Marsh New Jersey Bks.). (Illus.). (J). 1994. pap. 19.95 (0-7933-1792-4); lib. bdg. 29.95 (0-7933-1791-6); disk 29.95 (0-7933-1793-2) Gallopade Intl.

New Jersey Coast & Pines. Gustav Kobbe. (Illus.). 144p. (C). 1982. reprint ed. pap. 6.95 (0-915850-07-9) Walking News Inc.

New Jersey Coastales. Carole Marsh. (Carole Marsh New Jersey Bks.). (J). 1994. lib. bdg. 29.95 (0-7933-7295-X) Gallopade Intl.

New Jersey Coastales. Carole Marsh. (Carole Marsh New Jersey Bks.). (Illus.). (J). 1994. pap. 19.95 (1-55609-863-4); lib. bdg. 29.95 (1-55609-862-6); disk 29.95 (1-55609-864-2) Gallopade Intl.

New Jersey Code of Criminal Justice. 440p. 2000. ring bd. 16.95 (0-930137-38-8) Looseleaf Law.

New Jersey Code Research Guide. LC 87-80712. 1987. 90.00 (0-317-03788-9) West Group.

New Jersey Code Research Guide. LC 87-80712. 1991. suppl. ed. 37.50 (0-317-03789-7) West Group.

New Jersey Colony. Dennis B. Fradin. LC 90-22437. (Thirteen Colonies Ser.). (Illus.). 144-190p. (J). (gr. 4 up). 1991. lib. bdg. 30.00 (0-516-00395-X) Childrens.

New Jersey Commercial Real Estate Development. Carleton R. Kemph. 450p. 1991. spiral bd. 159.00 (0-8342-0187-9, MICHIE) LEXIS Pub.

New Jersey Comprehensive Statewide Master Plan for Alcoholism, Tobacco & Other Drug Abuse. Joseph P. Miele. (Illus.). 243p. (C). 1998. pap. text 30.00 (0-7881-4899-0) DIANE Pub.

New Jersey Condominium Law: A Practical Guide to Condominium & Other Common Interest Projects. Wendell A. Smith. (Orig.). 1985. pap. 35.00 (0-933902-11-5) Gann Law Bks.

New Jersey Contemporary Criminal Procedure, 2 vols. Larry E. Holtz. Ed. by D. William Subin. 2000p. (C). 1996. pap. 79.95 (0-87526-369-0) Gould.

New Jersey Cooking. B. Carlson. (Illus.). 160p. 1997. spiral bd. 5.95 (1-57166-090-9) Hearts N Tummies.

New Jersey Copyright Registrations, 1791-1845. Joseph J. Felcone. 64p. 1994. pap. 15.00 (0-944026-57-5) Am Antiquarian.

New Jersey Corporate Forms, 2 vols. Stuart L. Pachman & John L. Conover. 1993. ring bd., suppl. ed. 75.00 (0-685-74626-7, MICHIE) LEXIS Pub.

New Jersey Corporate Forms, 2 vols., Set. Stuart L. Pachman & John L. Conover. 1260p. 1990. ring bd. 250.00 incl. disk (0-8342-0155-0, 82080-10, MICHIE); disk 75.00 (0-685-74627-5, MICHIE) LEXIS Pub.

New Jersey Corporate Practice for the Paralegal: With Forms. Charles P. Nemeth. LC 94-72418. 399p. 1995. ring bd. 89.50 (1-887024-37-9) Bisel Co.

New Jersey Corporation Law & Practice. Laurence R. Reich. (National Corporation Law Ser.). 1466p. 1992. ring bd. 155.00 (0-13-109257-X) Aspen Law.

New Jersey Crags. Paul Nick & Neil J. Sloane. (Classic Rock Climbs Ser.: No. 5). 1996. pap. 12.95 (1-57540-032-4) Falcon Pub Inc.

***New Jersey Crime in Perspective 2000.** Ed. by Kathleen O'Leary Morgan & Scott E. Morgan. 22p. 2000. spiral bd. 19.00 (0-7401-0329-6) Morgan Quitno Corp.

New Jersey Crime Perspective, 1998. Ed. by Kathleen O'Leary Morgan & Scott E. Morgan. 20p. 1998. pap. 19.00 (1-56692-929-6) Morgan Quitno Corp.

New Jersey Crime Perspectives, 1999. Kathleen O'Leary Morgan. 22p. 1999. spiral bd. 19.00 (0-7401-0129-3) Morgan Quitno Corp.

New Jersey Criminal & Traffic Law Manual: 1998 Edition. 1998. pap. write for info. (0-327-05015-2, 29110-11) LEXIS Pub.

***New Jersey Criminal & Traffic Law Manual: 1999 Edition.** 847p. 1999. pap. 35.00 (0-327-08867-2, 2911012) LEXIS Pub.

***New Jersey Criminal & Traffic Law Manual, 2000 Edition.** 852p. 2000. write for info. incl. cd-rom (0-327-10503-8, 2911013) LEXIS Pub.

***New Jersey Criminal Code: Handbook for Law Enforcement Officers.** Anderson Publishing Co. Staff. 360p. 1999. pap. 14.95 (1-58360-036-1) Anderson Pub Co.

New Jersey Criminal Justice Code. annuals Gould Editorial Staff. student ed. 6.00 (0-87526-272-4) Gould.

New Jersey Criminal Justice Code: Annual Edition. annuals Gould Editorial Staff. 950p. (C). ring bd. 18.95 (0-87526-024-1) Gould.

New Jersey Criminal Law & Motor Vehicle Handbook. Ed. by Gould Editorial Staff. 1300p. (C). pap. 29.95 (0-87526-371-2) Gould.

New Jersey Criminal Procedure. Knowlton & Coburn. 1976. text 115.00 (0-327-00966-7, 68890, MICHIE) LEXIS Pub.

New Jersey Criminal Procedure, Vol. 1. Robert E. Knowlton & Daniel R. Coburn. LC 76-27194. 589p. Date not set. text 115.00 (0-317-00455-7, 68890, MICHIE) LEXIS Pub.

New Jersey Criminal Procedure, Vol. 1. Robert E. Knowlton & Daniel R. Coburn. LC 76-27194. 589p. 1993. suppl. ed. 62.50 (0-317-03177-5) West Group.

New Jersey "Crinkum-Crankum" A Funny Word Book about Our State. Carole Marsh. (Carole Marsh New Jersey Bks.). (Illus.). (J). 1994. pap. 19.95 (0-7933-4899-4); lib. bdg. 29.95 (0-7933-4898-6); disk 29.95 (0-7933-4900-1) Gallopade Intl.

New Jersey Day Trips: A Guide to Outings in New Jersey, New York, Pennsylvania & Delaware. 8th rev. ed. Barbara Hudgins. Orig. Title: Trips & Treks. (Illus.). 256p. (Orig.). 1998. pap. 12.95 (0-9607762-7-3) Woodmont Pr.

New Jersey Decoys. Henry A. Fleckenstein, Jr. LC 82-62952. (Illus.). 272p. 1983. text 37.50 (0-916838-75-7) Schiffer.

N

An Asterisk (*) at the beginning of an entry indicates that the title is appearing for the first time.

New Jersey Devils see NHL Today

New Jersey Devils. Jim Stevens. LC 98-24549. (Inside the NHL Ser.). (J). 1999. 16.45 (*1-57765-051-4*) ABDO Pub Co.

New Jersey Dingbats! Bk. 1: A Fun Book of Games, Stories, Activities & More about Our State That's All in Code! for You to Decipher. Carole Marsh. (New Jersey Bks.). (Illus.). (J). (gr. 3-12). 1994. pap. 19.95 (*0-7933-3864-6*); lib. bdg. 29.95 (*0-7933-3863-8*); disk 29.95 (*0-7933-3865-4*) Gallopade Intl.

New Jersey Directory: The Insider Guide to New Jersey Leaders. 5th ed. Ed. by Donald Linky. 578p. 1998. pap. 86.00 (*1-879171-22-8*) Joshua Comns.

New Jersey Directory: The Insider Guide to New Jersey Leaders, 1992-1993 Edition. Ed. by Donald Linky. 456p. 1992. pap. 86.00 (*1-879171-00-7*) Joshua Comns.

New Jersey Directory: The Insider Guide to New Jersey Leaders (1996 Edition) Donald Linky. 506p. Date not set. pap. 86.00 (*1-879171-06-6*) Joshua Comns.

New Jersey Directory, 1993-94: The Insider Guide to New Jersey Leaders. 3rd ed. Ed. by Donald Linky. 486p. pap. 86.00 (*1-879171-02-3*) Joshua Comns.

New Jersey Early Census, Vol. 1. Ronald V. Jackson. (Illus.). 1981. lib. bdg. 55.00 (*0-89593-733-6*, Accel Indexing) Genealogical Srvcs.

New Jersey Early Census, Vol. 1. Ronald V. Jackson. 1992. 50.00 (*0-89593-852-9*, Accel Indexing) Genealogical Srvcs.

New Jersey Early Census, Vol. 2. Ronald V. Jackson. (Illus.). 1981. lib. bdg. 65.00 (*0-89593-584-8*, Accel Indexing) Genealogical Srvcs.

New Jersey Early Census, Vol. 2. Ronald V. Jackson. 1992. 60.00 (*0-89593-853-7*, Accel Indexing) Genealogical Srvcs.

New Jersey Education Laws: 1998 Edition. 563p. 1998. write for info. (*0-327-05111-6*, 29135-10) LEXIS Pub.

***New Jersey Education Laws: 1999 Edition.** 607p. 1999. pap. 40.00 (*0-327-08861-3*, 2913511) LEXIS Pub.

***New Jersey 1870 Census Index, Vols. 1 & 2.** Raeone C. Steuart. LC 99-170098. xix, 1831 p. 1998. 295.00 (*1-877677-94-9*) Herit Quest.

New Jersey, 1860: South. 1988. 240.00 (*0-89593-581-3*, Accel Indexing) Genealogical Srvcs.

New Jersey Environmental Law. C. Zachary Seltzer. LC 97-50502. 1998. 165.00 (*1-57823-024-1*) Juris Pubng.

New Jersey Environmental Law: 1990. Louis Goldshore & Marsha Wolf. 568p. 1990. pap., suppl. ed. 35.00 (*0-685-14653-7*); ring bd. 92.00 (*0-685-14652-9*) NJ Inst CLE.

New Jersey Environmental Law Handbook. 5th ed. Lowenstein, Sandler, Kohl, Fisher & Boylan Staff. LC 98-119096. 420p. 1999. pap. text 95.00 (*0-86587-641-X*) Gov Insts.

New Jersey Estate Planning, Will Drafting & Estate Administration Issue 9, 2 vols. Martin & Borteck. 150p. 1998. ring bd. write for info. (*0-327-00801-6*, 8210214) LEXIS Pub.

New Jersey Estate Planning, Will Drafting & Estate Administration Forms, 2 vols. Alvin C. Martin & Robert D. Borteck. 1993. ring bd., suppl. ed. 82.00 (*0-685-74628-3*, MICHIE) LEXIS Pub.

New Jersey Estate Planning, Will Drafting & Estate Administration Forms, 2 vols., Set. Alvin C. Martin & Robert D. Borteck. 1120p. 1988. spiral bd. 250.00 (*0-87189-072-0*, 82098-10, MICHIE) LEXIS Pub.

New Jersey Estate Planning, Will Drafting & Estate Administration Forms, Set. Alvin C. Martin & Robert D. Borteck. 1994. disk 75.00 (*0-685-74629-1*, MICHIE) LEXIS Pub.

***New Jersey Evidence Courtroom Manual 2000.** rev. ed. Judson Jennings & Glen Weissenberger. 472p. 1999. pap. 55.00 (*1-58360-140-6*) Anderson Pub Co.

New Jersey Evidentiary Foundations. Mark P. Denbeaux et al. LC 95-75584. 364p. 1995. 85.00 (*1-55834-222-2*, 61180-10, MICHIE) LEXIS Pub.

***New Jersey Experience Pocket Guide.** Carole Marsh. (New Jersey Experience! Ser.). (Illus.). (J). 2000. pap. 6.95 (*0-7933-9453-8*) Gallopade Intl.

New Jersey Facts & Factivities. Carole Marsh. (Carole Marsh State Bks.). (Illus.). (J). (gr. 4-7). 1996. pap., teacher ed. 19.95 (*0-7933-7907-5*, C Marsh) Gallopade Intl.

New Jersey Facts & Symbols. Emily McAuliffe. 1999. 15.00 (*0-531-12005-8*) Watts.

***New Jersey Facts & Symbols.** Shelley Swanson Sateren. LC 99-31783. (States & Their Symbols Ser.). (Illus.). 24p. (ps-3). 1999. 14.60 (*0-7368-0379-3*) Capstone Pr.

New Jersey Family Law. Alan M. Grosman. LC 98-89023. 980p. 1999. 99.00 (*0-327-00575-0*, 6887010) LEXIS Pub.

New Jersey Family Law Practice, 3 vols., Set. 6th ed. Laurence Cutler & Gary N. Skoloff. (Illus.). 1302p. 1990. ring bd. 175.00 (*0-685-65973-9*) NJ Inst CLE.

New Jersey Family Law Practice, 1992 Supplement. Gary N. Skoloff & Lawrence J. Cutler. 1992. pap. 23.00 (*0-685-67548-3*) NJ Inst CLE.

New Jersey Federal Census, Hoboken & New Jersey City, 1870. 1990. 130.00 (*0-89593-582-1*, Accel Indexing) Genealogical Srvcs.

New Jersey Federal Census Index, 1800 (Cumberland Edition) Ronald V. Jackson. LC 77-86134. (Illus.). 1977. lib. bdg. 58.00 (*0-89593-089-7*, Accel Indexing) Genealogical Srvcs.

New Jersey Federal Census Index, 1830. Ronald V. Jackson. LC 77-86130. (Illus.). 1981. lib. bdg. 69.00 (*0-89593-092-7*, Accel Indexing) Genealogical Srvcs.

New Jersey Federal Census Index, 1840. Ronald V. Jackson. LC 77-86131. (Illus.). lib. bdg. 68.00 (*0-89593-093-5*, Accel Indexing) Genealogical Srvcs.

New Jersey Federal Census Index, 1850. Ronald V. Jackson. LC 77-86122. (Illus.). 1976. lib. bdg. 125.00 (*0-89593-094-3*, Accel Indexing) Genealogical Srvcs.

New Jersey Federal Census Index, 1870: Newark City, Essex County, 2 vols. 1992. 210.00 (*0-89593-855-3*, Accel Indexing) Genealogical Srvcs.

New Jersey Federal Civil Practice Manual. Ed. by R. Barticus. 900p. 1993. suppl. ed. 99.00 (*0-685-65980-1*) NJ Inst CLE.

New Jersey Federalists. Rudolph J. Pasler & Margaret C. Pasler. LC 73-22570. 256p. 1975. 36.50 (*0-8386-1525-2*) Fairleigh Dickinson.

New Jersey Ferns & Fern-Allies. James D. Montgomery & David E. Fairbrothers. LC 91-40920. (Illus.). 300p. (C). 1992. text 45.00 (*0-8135-1817-2*) Rutgers U Pr.

New Jersey Festival Fun for Kids! Carole Marsh. (Carole Marsh New Jersey Bks.). (Illus.). (J). (gr. 3-12). 1994. pap. 19.95 (*0-7933-4017-9*); lib. bdg. 29.95 (*0-7933-4016-0*) Gallopade Intl.

New Jersey Festival Fun for Kids! Carole Marsh. (Carole Marsh New Jersey Bks.). (Illus.). (YA). (gr. 3-12). 1994. disk 29.95 (*0-7933-4018-7*) Gallopade Intl.

New Jersey Firefighter. 35.00 (*0-576-85069-1*) Gregg Intl.

New Jersey Firsts: The Famous, Infamous & Quirky of the Garden State. Harry Armstrong & Tom Wilk. LC 98-55151. (Illus.). 176p. 1999. pap. 9.95 (*0-940159-45-7*) Camino Bks.

New Jersey Forms - Legal & Business, 11 vols. 1993. suppl. ed. 85.90 (*0-317-03348-4*) West Group.

New Jersey Forms - Legal & Business, 11 vols., Set. LC 79-134917. 1984. 1140.00 (*0-317-01752-7*) West Group.

New Jersey from Colony to State, 1609-1789. Richard P. McCormick. (Classics Ser.). (Illus.). 191p. 1988. pap. 12.95 (*0-911020-02-0*) NJ Hist Soc.

New Jersey Gardener's Guide: The What, Where, When, How & Why of Gardening in New Jersey. Pegi Ballister-Howells. (Illus.). 400p. 1998. pap. 19.95 (*1-888608-47-1*) Cool Springs Pr.

New Jersey "GEO" Bingo! 38 Must Know State Geography Facts for Kids to Learn While Having Fun! Carole Marsh. (Bingo! Ser.). (Illus.). (J). (gr. 2-8). 1998. pap. 14.95 (*0-7933-8613-6*) Gallopade Intl.

New Jersey Government! The Cornerstone of Everyday Life in Our State! Carole Marsh. (Carole Marsh New Jersey Bks.). (Illus.). (J). (gr. 3-12). 1996. pap. 19.95 (*0-7933-6272-5*); lib. bdg. 29.95 (*0-7933-6271-7*); disk 29.95 (*0-7933-6273-3*) Gallopade Intl.

New Jersey Governments Performance Standards, 1990. Ed. by Greg Michels. (Governments Performance Standards Ser.). (Illus.). 150p. 1990. text 125.00 (*1-55507-494-4*) Municipal Analysis.

New Jersey Grants Guide, 1998-1999. Composed by Grants Guide Plus Staff. 800p. 1998. pap. 149.00 (*0-9658306-3-2*) Grantseeker.

New Jersey Guide to Nursing Homes: And Other Care Facilities for the Elderly. Ed. by Roby McClellan. LC 97-77548. 252p. 1997. pap. 19.95 (*0-9661654-0-3*) Guide Inc.

***New Jersey Health Care in Perspective 2000.** Ed. by Kathleen O'Leary Morgan & Scott E. Morgan. 21p. 2000. spiral bd. 19.00 (*0-7401-0229-X*) Morgan Quitno Corp.

New Jersey Health Care Perspective, 1998. Ed. by Kathleen O'Leary Morgan & Scott E. Morgan. 20p. 1998. pap. 19.00 (*1-56692-829-X*) Morgan Quitno Corp.

New Jersey Health Care Perspective, 1999. Kathleen O'Leary Morgan. 21p. 1999. spiral bd. 19.00 (*0-7401-0079-3*) Morgan Quitno Corp.

New Jersey Highlands: Treasures at Risk. Alison E. Mitchell. (Illus.). (Orig.). 1992. pap. 9.95 (*0-913234-10-9*) NJ Cons Foun.

New Jersey "HISTO" Bingo! 42 Must Know State History Facts for Kids to Learn While Having Fun! Carole Marsh. (Bingo! Ser.). (Illus.). (J). (gr. 2-8). 1998. pap. 14.95 (*0-7933-8614-4*) Gallopade Intl.

New Jersey Historical & Biographical Index, Vol. 1. Ronald V. Jackson. LC 78-53708. (Illus.). 1984. lib. bdg. 30.00 (*0-89593-191-5*, Accel Indexing) Genealogical Srvcs.

New Jersey History! Surprising Secrets about Our State's Founding Mothers, Fathers & Kids! Carole Marsh. (Carole Marsh New Jersey Bks.). (Illus.). (J). (gr. 3-12). 1996. pap. 19.95 (*0-7933-6119-2*); lib. bdg. 29.95 (*0-7933-6118-4*); disk 29.95 (*0-7933-6120-6*) Gallopade Intl.

New Jersey Homeowner's Guide to Property Tax Appeals. Robert Appaluccio. Ed. by Mark Vanzini. 35p. 1998. pap. 29.95 (*0-9673269-0-7*) Insight Mktg.

***New Jersey Homeowner's Guide to Property Tax Appeals.** 2nd rev. ed. Robert Appaluccio. Ed. by Mark Vanzini. (Illus.). 48p. 2000. pap. 11.95 (*0-9673269-1-5*) Insight Mktg.

New Jersey Hot Air Balloon Mystery. Carole Marsh. (Carole Marsh New Jersey Bks.). (Illus.). (J). (gr. 2-9). 1994. 29.95 (*0-7933-2588-9*); pap. 19.95 (*0-7933-2589-7*); disk 29.95 (*0-7933-2590-0*) Gallopade Intl.

New Jersey Hot Zones! Viruses, Diseases, & Epidemics in Our State's History. Carole Marsh. (Hot Zones! Ser.). (Illus.). (J). (gr. 3-12). 1998. pap. 19.95 (*0-7933-8919-4*); lib. bdg. 29.95 (*0-7933-8918-6*) Gallopade Intl.

New Jersey House. Helen Schwartz. (Illus.). 238p. 1983. pap. 19.95 (*0-8135-0990-4*) Rutgers U Pr.

New Jersey in History: Fighting to be Heard. Thomas P. Farner. LC 96-19221. (Illus.). 235p. 1996. 26.00 (*0-945582-38-2*) Down the Shore Pub.

New Jersey in Perspective, 1998. Ed. by Kathleen O'Leary Morgan & Scott E. Morgan. 24p. 1998. pap. 19.00 (*1-56692-879-6*) Morgan Quitno Corp.

New Jersey in Perspective, 1999. Ed. by Kathleen O'Leary Morgan. 26p. 1999. spiral bd. 19.00 (*1-56692-979-2*) Morgan Quitno Corp.

***New Jersey in Perspective 2000.** Ed. by Kathleen O'Leary Morgan & Scott E. Morgan. 26p. 2000. spiral bd. 19.00 (*0-7401-0279-6*) Morgan Quitno Corp.

New Jersey in the Colonial Wars. Richard W. Parker. Ed. by Timothy G. Cutler. (New Jersey in the French & Indian Wars Ser.: Vol. 1). 84p. 1997. 7.95 (*1-58057-020-8*, NJCW003B) Digital Antiq.

***New Jersey Index of Wills, Inventories, Etc. In the Office of the Secretary of State Prior to 1901, 3 vols., Set.** New Jersey Department of State Staff. 1452p. 2000. reprint ed. pap. 125.00 (*0-8063-4968-9*, Pub. by Clearfield Co) ACCESS Pubs Network.

New Jersey Indians! A Kid's Look at Our State's Chiefs, Tribes, Reservations, Powwows, Lore & More from the Past & the Present. Carole Marsh. (Carole Marsh State Bks.). (J). (gr. 2-9). 1996. 29.95 (*0-7933-7734-X*, C Marsh); pap. 19.95 (*0-7933-7735-8*, C Marsh); disk 29.95 (*0-7933-7736-6*, C Marsh) Gallopade Intl.

New Jersey Internship Guide, 1999. Tyiana Steptoe et al. 91p. 1999. 24.95 (*1-883216-23-0*) Res Comns Group.

***New Jersey Investment & Business Guide: Business, Investment, Export-Import Opportunities, 50 vols., Vol. 30.** Global Investment Center, USA Staff. (U. S. Regional Investment & Business Library-99: Vol. 30). (Illus.). 30p. (Orig.). 1999. pap. 59.95 (*0-7397-1129-6*) Intl Business Pubns.

***New Jersey Jeopardy.** Carole Marsh. (New Jersey Experience! Ser.). (Illus.). (J). (gr. 2-6). 2000. pap. 7.95 (*0-7933-9522-4*) Gallopade Intl.

New Jersey Jeopardy! Answers & Questions about Our State! Carole Marsh. (Carole Marsh New Jersey Bks.). (Illus.). (J). (gr. 3-12). 1994. pap. 19.95 (*0-7933-4170-1*); lib. bdg. 29.95 (*0-7933-4169-8*); disk 29.95 (*0-7933-4171-X*) Gallopade Intl.

New Jersey JobBank. Adams Media Corporation Staff. Ed. by Steven Graber et al. (Illus.). 352p. 1999. pap. 16.95 (*1-58062-140-6*) Adams Media.

***New Jersey Jography.** Carole Marsh. (New Jersey Experience! Ser.). (Illus.). 2000. pap. 7.95 (*0-7933-9523-2*) Gallopade Intl.

New Jersey "Jography" A Fun Run Thru Our State! Carole Marsh. (Carole Marsh New Jersey Bks.). (Illus.). (J). 1994. pap. 19.95 (*1-55609-851-0*); lib. bdg. 29.95 (*1-55609-850-2*); disk 29.95 (*1-55609-852-9*) Gallopade Intl.

New Jersey Joke Book. Mike Dalton. LC 95-19919. 160p. 1996. pap. 7.95 (*0-8065-1714-X*, Citadel Pr) Carol Pub Group.

New Jersey Kid's Cookbook: Recipes, How-to, History, Lore & More. Carole Marsh. (Carole Marsh New Jersey Bks.). (Illus.). (J). 1994. pap. 19.95 (*0-7933-1804-1*); lib. bdg. 29.95 (*0-7933-1803-3*); disk 29.95 (*0-7933-1805-X*) Gallopade Intl.

***New Jersey Labor & Employment, Issue 7.** Roger B. Jacobs. 100p. 1999. ring bd. write for info. (*0-327-01573-X*, 8212517) LEXIS Pub.

***New Jersey Labor Unions: New Jersey Business Source Book.** Jeanne Graves. (Illus.). 106p. 1999. pap. 49.95 (*1-883216-24-9*) Res Comns Group.

New Jersey Lake Survey Fishing Maps Guide. annuals 5th rev. ed. Ed. & Pref. by Steve Perrone. (Illus.). 132p. 1997. per. 10.95 (*1-887544-01-1*) NJ Sportsmens Guides.

New Jersey Land Use & Environmental Law, 3 vols. S. V. Stoldt. 1300p. 295.00 (*0-8205-1646-5*) Juris Pubng.

New Jersey Law Enforcement Handbook, 2 vols. Larry E. Holtz. 2000p. (C). ring bd. 79.95 (*0-87526-325-9*) Gould.

New Jersey Legal Research Handbook 1984. Paul Axel-Lute. 395p. 1984. 45.00 (*0-318-02062-9*) NJ Inst CLE.

New Jersey Legal Secretaries Handbook: 1987 Cumulative Supplement. New Jersey Association of Legal Secretaries Staff. 1987. ring bd. 50.00 (*0-87215-923-X*, 65154-10, MICHIE) LEXIS Pub.

New Jersey Legal Secretary's Handbook. rev. ed. New Jersey Association Of Legal Secretaries Staff. 570p. 1984. spiral bd. 50.00 (*0-87215-721-0*, MICHIE) LEXIS Pub.

New Jersey Legal Secretary's Handbook. rev. ed. New Jersey Association Of Legal Secretaries Staff. 574p. 1991. ring bd., suppl. ed. 40.00 (*0-87473-859-8*, 65155-10, MICHIE) LEXIS Pub.

New Jersey Library Book: A Surprising Guide to the Unusual Special Collections in Libraries Across Our State for Students, Teachers, Writers & Publishers - Includes Reproducible Mailing Labels Plus Activities for Young People! Carole Marsh. (Carole Marsh New Jersey Bks.). (Illus.). 1994. pap. 19.95 (*0-7933-3096-3*); lib. bdg. 29.95 (*0-7933-3095-5*); disk 29.95 (*0-7933-3097-1*) Gallopade Intl.

New Jersey Library Network: Interlibrary Loan Study. Kenneth J. Bierman & Florence M. Mason. (Illus.). 92p. (Orig.). (C). 1996. pap. text 30.00 (*0-7881-3717-4*) DIANE Pub.

New Jersey Limited Liability Company Forms & Practice Manual, 1995 Supplement. 2nd rev. ed. Lawrence A. Goldman & Alyce C. Halchak. LC 94-21323. 672p. 1994. ring bd. 219.90 (*1-57400-006-3*) Data Trace Pubng.

New Jersey Manufacturers Register. 2nd rev. ed. Ed. by Frank Lambing. 1999. 105.00 (*1-58202-058-2*) Manufacturers.

New Jersey Marriage Records, 1665-1800. William Nelson. LC 67-18088. (Illus.). 804p. 1997. reprint ed. 40.00 (*0-8063-0254-2*) Genealog Pub.

New Jersey Marriages, As Published in "The Christian Intelligencer" of the Reformed Dutch Church, 1830-71. Ray C. Sawyer. (Illus.). 1333p. 1997. reprint ed. lib. bdg. 37.00 (*0-8328-6034-4*) Higginson Bk Co.

New Jersey Math! How It All Adds up in Our State. Carole Marsh. (Carole Marsh New Jersey Bks.). (Illus.). (YA). (gr. 3-12). 1996. pap. 19.95 (*0-7933-6578-3*); lib. bdg. 29.95 (*0-7933-6577-5*) Gallopade Intl.

New Jersey Media Book: A Surprising Guide to the Amazing Print, Broadcast & Online Media of Our State for Students, Teachers, Writers & Publishers - Includes Reproducible Mailing Labels Plus Activities for Young People! Carole Marsh. (Carole Marsh New Jersey Bks.). (Illus.). 1994. pap. 19.95 (*0-7933-3252-4*); lib. bdg. 29.95 (*0-7933-3251-6*); disk 29.95 (*0-7933-3253-2*) Gallopade Intl.

New Jersey Media Guide. 325p. 1998. 94.95 (*1-883216-20-6*) Res Comns Group.

New Jersey Media Guide. Jeanne R. Graves. Ed. by Lauren Dixon & Matt Entswinger. (Illus.). 300p. 1999. pap. 94.95 (*1-883216-26-5*) Res Comns Group.

New Jersey Modern Map Chart Set. 1988. pap. write for info. (*0-89359-008-8*) Afton Pub.

New Jersey Mortgage Foreclosures Handbook. Leonard Zucker et al. 25p. 1992. ring bd., suppl. ed. 60.00 (*0-317-57865-0*) NJ Inst CLE.

New Jersey Motor Vehicle & Traffic Laws. annuals Gould Editorial Staff. 610p. pap. 14.95 (*0-87526-232-5*) Gould.

New Jersey Motor Vehicle & Traffic Laws, Title 39. 480p. 2000. ring bd. 14.95 (*0-930137-49-3*) Looseleaf Law.

New Jersey Motor Vehicle & Traffic Laws: Annual Edition. Gould Editorial Staff. student ed. 6.00 (*0-87526-284-8*) Gould.

New Jersey Motor Vehicles - Condensed Guide. 2000. spiral bd. 5.95 (*0-930137-93-0*) Looseleaf Law.

***New Jersey Municipal Data Book, 2000.** Ed. by Louise L. Hornor. x, 593p. 2000. pap. 89.00 (*0-911273-25-5*) Info Pubns.

New Jersey Municipal Data Book, 1999. 18th rev. ed. Ed. by Edith R. Horner. 608p. 1999. pap. 87.00 (*0-911273-24-7*) Info Pubns.

New Jersey Mystery Van Takes Off! Book 1: Handicapped New Jersey Kids Sneak off on a Big Adventure, Bk. 1. Carole Marsh. (Carole Marsh New Jersey Bks.). (Illus.). (J). (gr. 3-12). 1994. 29.95 (*0-7933-5051-4*); pap. 19.95 (*0-7933-5052-2*); disk 29.95 (*0-7933-5053-0*) Gallopade Intl.

New Jersey Naturally, 1990: A Resource Directory for Natural Living in the Tri-State Area, Including New York & Connecticut. Ed. by Jerome Rubin & Stephen Donaldson. (Orig.). 1990. pap. 4.95 (*0-9622953-2-9*) City Spirit Pubns.

New Jersey, Naturescapes & Detail. Walter Choroszewski. LC 92-70484. (Illus.). 80p. 1995. 20.00 (*0-933605-05-6*) Aesthetic Pr.

New Jersey Nets see Pro Basketball Today

New Jersey Nets. Paul Joseph. LC 96-39615. (Inside the NBA Ser.). (Illus.). 32p. (J). (gr. 3-8). 1997. lib. bdg. 16.95 (*1-56239-766-4*) ABDO Pub Co.

***New Jersey North Bergen Entertainment, 2000.** (Illus.). 788p. 1999. pap. write for info. (*1-880248-45-X*, 0052) Enter Pubns.

***New Jersey North Essex Entertainment, 2000.** (Illus.). 774p. 1999. pap. 35.00 (*1-880248-47-6*, 0026) Enter Pubns.

***New Jersey North Morris Entertainment, 2000.** (Illus.). 776p. 1999. pap. 35.00 (*1-880248-48-4*, 00T5) Enter Pubns.

New Jersey Notary Handbook. 3rd ed. American Society of Notaries Staff. LC 72-97800. 90p. 1997. pap. 9.95 (*0-318-13197-8*) Am Soc Notaries.

New Jersey Notary Law Primer. Ed. by National Notary Association Staff. (Notary Law Primers Ser.). 1998. pap. 16.00 (*0-933134-89-4*) Natl Notary.

New Jersey Objections at Trial. Barry M. Epstein et al. LC 92-39773. 190p. 1992. pap. 39.50 (*1-56257-345-4*, MICHIE) LEXIS Pub.

New Jersey Parks, Forests, & Natural Areas: A Guide. rev. ed. Michael P. Brown. (Illus.). 250p. 1997. pap. 16.00 (*0-8135-2481-4*) Rutgers U Pr.

New Jersey Pleading & Practice Forms, 11 vols. 1991. write for info. (*0-318-57149-8*) West Group.

New Jersey Pleading & Practice Forms, 11 vols., Set. LC 87-82646. 1991. 1495.00 (*0-318-57148-X*) West Group.

New Jersey Poetry Resource Book. 3rd ed. Ed. by Laura Boss & Maria Gillan. 1996. pap. text 5.00 (*0-9621495-0-0*) Poetry Ctr PCCC.

New Jersey Poetry Resource Book. 3rd rev. ed. Maria M. Gillan. Ed. by Laura Boss. 62p. 1996. pap. write for info. (*0-9621495-5-1*) Poetry Ctr PCCC.

New Jersey Polish Cemetery Inscriptions. Ed. by Jonathan D. Shea. LC 91-60070. 786p. (Orig.). 1991. pap. text. write for info. (*0-945440-06-5*) Pol Geneal CT.

New Jersey Political Almanac, 1996-1997. (New Jersey Reporter Ser.: Vol. 25, No. 5). 116p. 1996. pap. 19.95 (*0-943136-23-7*) Ctr Analysis Public Issues.

New Jersey Politics & Government: Suburban Politics Comes of Age. 2nd rev. ed. Barbara G. Salmore & Stephen A. Salmore. LC 98-26753. (Politics & Governments of the American States Ser.). (Illus.). 432p. 1998. pap. 25.00 (*0-8032-9256-2*, SALN2X) U of Nebr Pr.

New Jersey Postal History. John L. Kay & Chester M. Smith. LC 74-47325. 1977. 30.00 (*0-88000-095-3*) Quarterman.

New Jersey Probate Procedures Manual, 2 vols., Set. Walter S. Kane. 800p. 1983. ring bd. 85.00 (*0-317-57867-7*) K Hansen NJ.

New Jersey Products Liability Law, 2 vols. Barry M. Epstein et al. LC 94-30792. 1994. spiral bd. 190.00 (*0-250-40737-X*, 82107-10, MICHIE) LEXIS Pub.

New Jersey Profiles in Public Policy. Ed. by Silvio R. Laccetti. 1990. 22.00 (*0-940390-05-1*) Comwealth Bks NJ.

An Asterisk (*) at the beginning of an entry indicates that the title is appearing for the first time.

New Jersey Property Tax Assessments: A Homeowner's Guided Tour to Understanding Assessments, Appeals, Revluations, & Reassessments. 2nd rev. ed. Joyce Restaino & Judy Keenan. (Illus.). 50p. 1995. 12.95 (*0-9628989-1-0*) Milford Pr.

New Jersey Public Employee Reporter. LRP Publications Staff. text 645.00 (*0-934753-07-5*) LRP Pubns.

New Jersey Public Employee Reporter, Vol. 12. LRP Publications Staff. 1987. write for info. (*0-934753-15-6*) LRP Pubns.

New Jersey Quilts 1777 to 1950: Contributions to an American Tradition. Heritage Quilt Project of New Jersey Staff. LC 92-30177. 176p. 1992. pap. 29.95 (*0-89145-996-0*, 3332, Am Quilters Soc) Collector Bks.

New Jersey Quiz Bowl Crash Course! Carole Marsh. (Carole Marsh New Jersey Bks.). (Illus.). (J). 1994. pap. 19.95 (*1-55609-866-9*); lib. bdg. 29.95 (*1-55609-865-0*); disk 29.95 (*1-55609-867-7*) Gallopade Intl.

New Jersey Real Estate Forms. David S. Gordon et al. 1993. ring bd., suppl. ed. 85.00 (*0-685-74630-5*, MICHIE) LEXIS Pub.

New Jersey Real Estate Forms, Issue 10. Robert C. Schachter & Charles Applebaum. 250p. 1999. ring bd. write for info. incl. disk (*0-327-01514-4*, 8211915) LEXIS Pub.

New Jersey Real Estate Forms, No. 9. Gordon Staff et al. 75p. 1998. ring bd. 324.00 (*0-327-00307-3*, 82119-14) LEXIS Pub.

New Jersey Real Estate Forms, 2 vols., Set. David S. Gordon et al. 1300p. 1988. spiral bd. 260.00 (*0-87189-073-9*, 82115-10, MICHIE); disk 75.00 (*1-56257-355-1*, MICHIE) LEXIS Pub.

New Jersey Real Estate Leasing Forms, 2 vols. Martin E. Dollinger. 1991. disk 75.00 (*1-56257-356-X*, 83011-10, MICHIE) LEXIS Pub.

New Jersey Real Estate Leasing Forms, 2 vols., Set. Martin E. Dollinger. 1040p. 1991. spiral bd. 229.00 (*0-8342-0182-8*, 83007-10, MICHIE) LEXIS Pub.

New Jersey Reapportionment Politics, Strategies & Tactics in the Legislative Process. Alan Shank. LC 69-18908. (Illus.). 308p. 1975. 26.50 (*0-8386-6950-6*) Fairleigh Dickinson.

New Jersey Regulations: Containing Administrative Rules of the New Jersey Insurance Department & Selected Attorney General's Opinions. New Jersey. Dept. of Insurance. LC 97-69282. 1997. write for info. (*0-89246-479-8*); write for info. (*0-89246-480-1*); write for info. (*0-89246-481-X*) NILS Pub.

New Jersey Retirement & Relocation Guide. large type ed. (Retirement & Relocation Guides Ser.). (Illus.). 350p. Date not set. pap. 19.95 (*1-56559-135-6*) HGI-Over Fifty.

New Jersey Road Maps of the Eighteenth Century. Howard C. Rice, Jr. (Illus.). 42p. 1981. pap. 5.00 (*0-87811-024-0*) Princeton Lib.

New Jersey Rollercoasters! Carole Marsh. (Carole Marsh New Jersey Bks.). (Illus.). (J). (gr. 3-12). 1994. pap. 19.95 (*0-7933-5315-7*); lib. bdg. 29.95 (*0-7933-5314-9*) Gallopade Intl.

New Jersey Rollercoasters! Carole Marsh. (Carole Marsh New Jersey Bks.). (Illus.). (YA). (gr. 3-12). 1994. disk 29.95 (*0-7933-5316-5*) Gallopade Intl.

New Jersey Sampler. John T. Cunningham. (Historic Tales of Old New Jersey Ser.). 1977. write for info. (*0-89359-014-2*) Afton Pub.

New Jersey School District Information Summary. Ed. by Catherine K. Flynn. 200p. 1991. 45.00 (*0-9631404-0-X*) Kiernan Pub.

New Jersey School Law. William S. Greenberg. LC 86-131246. 350p. 1985. ring bd. 50.00 (*0-685-14086-5*) NJ Inst CLE.

New Jersey School Trivia: An Amazing & Fascinating Look at Our State's Teachers, Schools & Students! Carole Marsh. (Carole Marsh New Jersey Bks.). (Illus.). (J). 1994. pap. 19.95 (*0-7933-1801-7*); lib. bdg. 29.95 (*0-7933-1800-9*); disk 29.95 (*0-7933-1802-5*) Gallopade Intl.

New Jersey Shore. 1985. 25.00 (*0-87982-504-9*) Art Alliance.

New Jersey Shore: Maps by William N. Canfield. John T. Cunningham. LC 58-6287. 272p. reprint ed. pap. 84.40 (*0-7837-5682-8*, 205911000005) Bks Demand.

New Jersey Shore a Vanishing Splendor. Tova Navarra. LC 84-9337. (Illus.). 112p. 1985. pap. 9.95 (*0-8453-4793-4*, Cornwall Bks) Assoc Univ Prs.

New Jersey Silly Basketball Sportsmysteries, Vol. 1. Carole Marsh. (Carole Marsh New Jersey Bks.). (Illus.). (J). 1994. pap. 19.95 (*0-7933-1795-9*); lib. bdg. 29.95 (*0-7933-1794-0*); disk 29.95 (*0-7933-1796-7*) Gallopade Intl.

New Jersey Silly Basketball Sportsmysteries, Vol. 2. Carole Marsh. (Carole Marsh New Jersey Bks.). (Illus.). (J). 1994. pap. 19.95 (*0-7933-1798-3*); lib. bdg. 29.95 (*0-7933-1797-5*); disk 29.95 (*0-7933-1799-1*) Gallopade Intl.

New Jersey Silly Football Sportsmysteries, Vol. 1. Carole Marsh. (Carole Marsh New Jersey Bks.). (Illus.). (J). 1994. pap. 19.95 (*1-55609-857-X*); lib. bdg. 29.95 (*1-55609-856-1*); disk 29.95 (*1-55609-858-8*) Gallopade Intl.

New Jersey Silly Football Sportsmysteries, Vol. 2. Carole Marsh. (Carole Marsh New Jersey Bks.). (Illus.). (J). 1994. pap. 19.95 (*1-55609-860-X*); lib. bdg. 29.95 (*1-55609-859-6*); disk 29.95 (*1-55609-861-8*) Gallopade Intl.

New Jersey Silly Trivia! Carole Marsh. (Carole Marsh New Jersey Bks.). (Illus.). (J). 1994. pap. 19.95 (*1-55609-848-0*); lib. bdg. 29.95 (*1-55609-847-2*); disk 29.95 (*1-55609-849-9*) Gallopade Intl.

New Jersey Slave Schedule, 1850. Ronald V. Jackson. 1992. 30.00 (*0-89593-854-5*, Accel Indexing) Genealogical Srvcs.

*New Jersey South Entertainment, 2000.** (Illus.). 662p. 1999. pap. 35.00 (*1-880248-49-2*, 0076) Enter Pubns.

New Jersey Spelling Bee! Score Big by Correctly Spelling Our State's Unique Names. Carole Marsh. (Carole Marsh New Jersey Bks.). (Illus.). (YA). (gr. 3-12). 1996. pap. 19.95 (*0-7933-6731-X*); lib. bdg. 29.95 (*0-7933-6730-1*) Gallopade Intl.

New Jersey State Attorney General Guidelines Quizzer. Mark Adamson et al. 1994. 39.95 (*1-885682-00-X*) Princeton Educ.

New Jersey State Constitution: A Reference Guide. Robert F. Williams. LC 97-22831. xlvii, 174p. 1997. pap. 22.00 (*0-8135-2499-7*) Rutgers U Pr.

New Jersey State Constitution: A Reference Guide, 1. Robert F. Williams. LC 89-25912. (Reference Guides to the State Constitutions of the United States Ser.: No. 1). 192p. 1990. lib. bdg. 65.00 (*0-313-26245-4*, WNT/, Greenwood Pr) Greenwood.

*New Jersey State Credit Directory, 2000 Edition.** rev. ed. American Business Directories Staff. 784p. 1999. boxed set 175.00 incl. cd-rom (*0-7687-0312-3*) Am Busn Direct.

New Jersey Statutes Annotated. write for info. (*0-318-57499-3*) West Pub.

New Jersey Studies Program: Activity Book. Sally Isaacs. (Illus.). 156p. (J). (gr. 4). 1996. 6.50 (*0-87746-578-9*) Graphic Learning.

New Jersey Studies Program: Teacher's Manual. Sally Isaacs. (Illus.). 106p. 1996. teacher ed. 125.00 (*0-87746-579-7*) Graphic Learning.

New Jersey Style. Ed. by Craig Carl. (Illus.). 72p. 1991. 29.95 (*0-934590-35-4*) Visual Refer.

New Jersey Survival. Betty L. Hall & Francis J. Gardella. 160p. (Orig.). (gr. 10-12). 1984. pap. text 5.84 (*0-03-046921-X*) Westwood Pr.

New Jersey Tax Handbook. Ernst & Young Staff & Whinney. 328p. 1988. 17.50 (*0-13-614942-1*) P-H.

New Jersey Tax Handbook. Ernst & Young Staff & Whinney. 224p. 1988. 18.95 (*0-13-614876-X*, Busn) P-H.

New Jersey Tax Handbook, 1998. rev. ed. Susan A. Feeney & Michael A. Guariglia. 160p. 1997. pap. text 45.00 (*0-7811-0184-0*) Res Inst Am.

New Jersey Tax Handbook, 1999. rev. ed. Susan A. Feeney & Michael A. Guariglia. 146p. 1998. pap. text 35.75 (*0-7811-0196-4*) Res Inst Am.

New Jersey Tax List, 1772-1822, 4 vols., Series 1. Ronald V. Jackson. (Illus.). lib. bdg. 550.00 (*0-89593-699-2*, Accel Indexing) Genealogical Srvcs.

New Jersey Timeline: A Chronology of New Jersey History, Mystery, Trivia, Legend, Lore & More. Carole Marsh. (Carole Marsh New Jersey Bks.). (Illus.). (J). (gr. 3-12). 1994. pap. 19.95 (*0-7933-5966-X*); lib. bdg. 29.95 (*0-7933-5965-1*); disk 29.95 (*0-7933-5967-8*) Gallopade Intl.

New Jersey Toward the Year 2000: Employment Projections. Connie O. Michaelson & Michael R. Greenberg. 190p. 1978. pap. text 18.95 (*0-88285-051-2*) Transaction Pubs.

New Jersey Toward the Year 2000: Population Projections. Michael R. Greenberg & Nancy Neuman. 230p. 1978. pap. text 18.95 (*0-88285-034-2*) Transaction Pubs.

New Jersey Transaction Guide, 13 vols. E. J. Jennings & Christopher H. Clancy. LC 84-72650. (Illus.). 1984. ring bd. write for info. (*0-8205-1491-8*) Bender.

New Jersey Transfer Inheritance Tax Manual, 2 vols., Set. Walter Kane. 1300p. 1984. ring bd. 95.00 (*0-317-57863-4*) K Hansen NJ.

New Jersey Trivia. Compiled by Al Menendez & Shirley Menendez. LC 93-12564. 192p. (Orig.). 1993. pap. 6.95 (*1-55853-223-4*) Rutledge Hill Pr.

New Jersey Troops in the Gettysburg Campaign. Samuel Toombs. (Illus.). 439p. (C). 1988. reprint ed. 30.00 (*0-944413-11-0*) Longstreet Hse.

New Jersey Trout. John A. Punola. (Illus.). 124p. (Orig.). 1994. pap. 9.95 (*0-939888-18-1*) Outdoors USA.

New Jersey 2C Quizzer. Mark Adamson. 238p. 1999. ring bd. 39.95 (*1-885682-14-X*) Princeton Educ.

New Jersey 2C Quizzer. Mark Adamson & Daniel R. Del Bagno. 218p. (C). 1996. ring bd. 39.95 (*1-885682-06-9*) Princeton Educ.

New Jersey 2000! Coming Soon to a Calendar Near You - The 21st Century! - Complete Set of AL 2000 Items. Carole Marsh. (Two Thousand! Ser.). (Illus.). (J). (gr. 3-12). 1998. pap. 75.00 (*0-7933-9369-8*); lib. bdg. 85.00 (*0-7933-9370-1*) Gallopade Intl.

New Jersey 2000! Coming Soon to a Calendar near You--The 21st Century! Carole Marsh. (Two Thousand! Ser.). (Illus.). (J). (gr. 3-12). 1998. pap. 19.95 (*0-7933-8766-3*); lib. bdg. 29.95 (*0-7933-8765-5*) Gallopade Intl.

*New Jersey 2001.** Ed. by Zagat Publishers Staff. (Illus.). 2000. pap. 10.95 (*1-57006-237-4*) Zagat.

New Jersey UFO's & Extraterrestrials! A Look at the Sightings & Science in Our State. Carole Marsh. (Carole Marsh New Jersey Bks.). (Illus.). (J). (gr. 3-12). 1997. pap. 19.95 (*0-7933-6425-6*); lib. bdg. 29.95 (*0-7933-6424-8*) Gallopade Intl.

New Jersey Veterans Census Index, 1890. Ronald V. Jackson. 1990. 156.00 (*0-89593-823-5*, Accel Indexing) Genealogical Srvcs.

New Jersey vs. T. L. O. Drug Searches in Schools. Deborah A. Persico. LC 97-38667. (Landmark Supreme Court Cases Ser.). (Illus.). 128p. (YA). (gr. 6 up). 1998. lib. bdg. 20.95 (*0-89490-969-X*) Enslow Pubs.

New Jersey Walk Book. New York-New Jersey Trail Conference Staff. LC 98-44411. 1998. 15.95 (*1-880775-05-0*) NY-NJ Trail Confer.

*New Jersey WATERS: A Watershed Approach to Teaching the Ecology of Regional Systems.** Dale A. Rosselet et al. LC 99-56146. (Illus.). 218p. 1999. teacher ed. 30.00 (*0-9624065-3-8*) NJ Audubon Soc.

New Jersey Wildlife Viewing Guide. Karenne Snow. LC 97-6081. 160p. 1998. pap. 10.95 (*1-56044-569-6*) Falcon Pub Inc.

New Jersey Will & Trust Forms Manual, 2 vols. Walter S. Kane. 1200p. 1988. ring bd. 198.00 (*0-317-02015-3*) K Hansen NJ.

New Jersey Wills Index, 1689-1890. Ronald V. Jackson. (Illus.). lib. bdg. 300.00 (*0-89593-750-6*, Accel Indexing) Genealogical Srvcs.

New Jersey Women: A History of Their Status, Roles, & Images. Carmela A. Karnoutsos & New Jersey Historical Commission. LC 97-24147. (New Jersey History Ser.). 1997. 9.00 (*0-89743-086-7*) NJ Hist Com.

New Jersey Women Seventeen Seventy to Nineteen Seventy: A Bibliography. Elizabeth Steiner-Scott & Elizabeth P. Wagle. 167p. 1978. 34.50 (*0-8386-1967-3*) Fairleigh Dickinson.

*New Jerseyans & the Civil War: For Union & Liberty.** William J. Jackson. LC 99-43166. (Illus.). 288p. (C). 2000. text 36.00 (*0-8135-2775-9*) Rutgers U Pr.

New Jersey's Best Shopping: Dozens of Day Trips for the Passionate Shopper. Liz Fuerst. 150p. 1998. pap. 12.00 (*0-9637022-4-6*) Gldn Sun Bks.

New Jersey's Best Shopping: 1996-97 Edition. Liz Fuerst. (New Jersey's Best Ser.). 125p. (Orig.). 1996. pap. 9.95 (*0-9637022-3-8*) Gldn Sun Bks.

*New Jersey's Best Shopping - Millennium Edition.** rev. ed. Liz Fuerst. 240p. 1999. pap. 12.95 (*0-9637022-5-4*) Gldn Sun Bks.

*New Jersey's Big Activity Book.** Carole Marsh. (New Jersey Experience! Ser.). (Illus.). (J). (gr. k-5). 2000. pap. 9.95 (*0-7933-9463-5*) Gallopade Intl.

New Jersey's Coastal Heritage: A Guide. Mark Dilonno. LC 96-26025. (Illus.). 224p. 1997. pap. 16.95 (*0-8135-2342-7*); text 38.00 (*0-8135-2341-9*) Rutgers U Pr.

New Jersey's Contributions to the Chemical Industry & Chemical Education see Science & the Human Imagination: Albert Einstein

New Jersey's Distinguished Restaurants, 1995. Ed. by Larry Lazar. 160p. 1994. pap. 9.95 (*0-9634765-3-X*) Qual Restaurants.

New Jersey's Distinguished Restaurants, 1996. Ed. by Larry Lazar. pap. 9.95 (*0-9634765-4-8*) Qual Restaurants.

New Jersey's Distinguished Restaurants, 1997. Ed. by Larry Lazar. 1997. pap. text 9.95 (*0-9634765-5-6*) Qual Restaurants.

New Jersey's Great Gardens: A Four-Season Guide to 125 Public Gardens, Parks, & Arboretums. Arline Zatz. LC 98-13750. (Illus.). 269p. (Orig.). 1999. pap. 17.00 (*0-88150-356-8*, Pub. by Countryman) Norton.

New Jersey's Jeffersonian Republicans: The Genesis of an Early Party Machine, 1789-1817. Carl E. Prince. LC 67-15103. 282p. reprint ed. pap. 87.50 (*0-8357-3919-8*, 203665400004) Bks Demand.

New Jersey's Money. George W. Wait. Ed. by Dorothy B. Bartle. LC 76-3234. 1977. 14.00 (*0-932828-03-5*) Newark Mus.

New Jersey's (Most Devastating!) Disasters & (Most Calamitous!) Catastrophies! Carole Marsh. (Carole Marsh New Jersey Bks.). (Illus.). (J). 1994. pap. 19.95 (*0-7933-1786-X*); disk 29.95 (*0-7933-1787-8*) Gallopade Intl.

New Jersey's (Most Devastating!) Disasters & (Most Calamitous!) Catastrophies! Carole Marsh. (Carole Marsh New Jersey Bks.). (Illus.). (J). 1997. lib. bdg. 29.95 (*0-7933-1785-1*) Gallopade Intl.

New Jersey's Multiple Municipal Madness. Alan Karcher. LC 98-15606. (Illus.). 320p. (C). 1999. text 49.00 (*0-8135-2565-9*) Rutgers U Pr.

New Jersey's Multiple Municipal Madness. Alan J. Karcher. LC 98-15606. (Illus.). 320p. (C). 1999. pap. text 22.00 (*0-8135-2566-7*) Rutgers U Pr.

New Jersey's Revolutionary War Powder Mill. Fred Bartenstein & Isabel Bartenstein. (Illus.). 194p. 1975. 5.50 (*0-614-29776-1*) M C H S.

New Jersey's Special Places: Scenic, Historic & Cultural Treasures in the Garden State. 2nd rev. ed. Arline Zatz. (Special Places Ser.). (Illus.). 248p. 1994. pap. 15.00 (*0-88150-290-1*, Pub. by Countryman) Norton.

New Jersey's Union College. Donald R. Raichle. LC 83-45027. (Illus.). 272p. 1983. 25.00 (*0-8386-3198-3*) Fairleigh Dickinson.

New Jersey's Unsolved Mysteries (& Their "Solutions") Includes Scientific Information & Other Activities for Students. Carole Marsh. (Carole Marsh New Jersey Bks.). (Illus.). (J). (gr. 3-12). 1994. pap. 19.95 (*0-7933-5813-2*); lib. bdg. 29.95 (*0-7933-5812-4*); disk 29.95 (*0-7933-5814-0*) Gallopade Intl.

New Jerusalem. 24p. (Orig.). 1982. pap. 0.95 (*0-937408-18-2*) GMI Pubns Inc.

New Jerusalem. G. K. Chesterton. 1976. lib. bdg. 59.95 (*0-8490-2339-4*) Gordon Pr.

New Jerusalem. Len Jenkin. (New American Fiction Ser.: No. 3). 216p. (Orig.). 1986. 16.95 (*0-940650-43-6*); pap. 10.95 (*0-685-12126-7*) Sun & Moon CA.

New Jerusalem. James Roache. 217p. (Orig.). 1998. pap. 9.95 (*1-891929-00-3*, Manatee Publng) Four Seasons.

New Jerusalem. Paul L. Tan. LC 78-73221. 1978. pap. text 1.95 (*0-932940-05-6*) Bible Coms.

New Jerusalem. deluxe limited ed. Len Jenkin. (New American Fiction Ser.: No. 3). 216p. (Orig.). 1986. 30.00 (*0-940650-44-4*) Sun & Moon CA.

New Jerusalem: Aspects of Utopianism in the Thought of Kagawa Toyohiko. George B. Bikle, Jr. LC 75-36125. (Monographs: No. 30). v, 343p. 1976. 15.00 (*0-8165-0550-0*) Assn Asian Studies.

New Jerusalem: Aspects of Utopianism in the Thought of Kagawa Toyohiko. fac. ed. George B. Bikle. LC 75-36125. (Association for Asian Studies, Monographs & Papers: No. 30). 351p. 1976. pap. 108.90 (*0-7837-7672-1*, 204742500007) Bks Demand.

New Jerusalem & Its Heavenly Doctrine. Emanuel Swedenborg. Orig. Title: De Nova Hierosolyma et Ejus Doctrina Coelesti. 245p. 1997. 14.95 (*1-883270-10-3*); pap. 9.95 (*1-883270-11-1*) Swedenborg Assn.

New Jerusalem & Its Heavenly Doctrine Parallel Latin-English Edition: De Nova Hierosolyma et Ejus Doctrina Coelesti. Emanuel Swedenborg. Orig. Title: De Nova Nierosolyma et Ejus Doctrina Coelesti. 490p. 1997. 27.50 (*1-883270-12-X*) Swedenborg Assn.

*New Jerusalem Bible: Standard Edition.** Ed. by Henry Wansbrough. 1424p. 1999. 47.50 (*0-385-49658-3*) Doubleday.

*New Jerusalem in the Revelation of John: The City As Symbol of Life with God.** Bruce J. Malina. 112p. 2000. pap. 11.95 (*0-8146-5938-1*) Liturgical Pr.

New Jerusalem Lutheran Church Cemetery Lovettsville, Virginia 1770-1943. Marty Hiatt & Craig R. Scott. 60p. 1995. pap. 10.00 (*1-888265-05-1*) Willow Bend.

New Jerusalem Scroll from Qumran: A Comprehensive Reconstruction. Michael Chyutin. (JSP Supplement Ser.: Vol. 25). 167p. 1997. 52.50 (*1-85075-683-X*, Pub. by Sheffield Acad) CUP Services.

New Jewelry: Trends & Traditions. 2nd rev. ed. Peter Dormer & Ralph Turner. LC 94-60278. (Illus.). 216p. 1994. pap. 24.95 (*0-500-27774-5*, Pub. by Thames Hudson) Norton.

New Jewish Baby Book: Names, Ceremonies & Customs - A Guide for Today's Families. Anita Diamant. LC 93-25870. 336p. (Orig.). 1994. pap. 16.95 (*1-879045-28-1*) Jewish Lights.

New Jewish Catalogue. Michael Strassfeld. 1996. write for info. (*0-8052-4124-8*) Schocken.

New Jewish Cuisine. Elizabeth W. Cohen. 128p. 1993. 12.98 (*1-55521-926-8*) Bk Sales Inc.

New Jewish Encyclopedia. rev. ed. David Bridger & Samuel Wolk. LC 76-15251. (Illus.). 542p. 1976. 24.95 (*0-87441-120-3*) Behrman.

New Jewish Ethics. S. Daniel Breslauer. LC 83-23659. (Symposium Ser.: Vol. 9). 136p. 1983. lib. bdg. 69.95 (*0-88946-700-5*) E Mellen.

New Jewish Holiday Cookbook: An International Collection of Recipes & Customs. rev. ed. Gloria K. Greene. LC 98-55721. (Illus.). 539p. 1999. 27.50 (*0-8129-2977-2*, Times Bks) Crown Pub Group.

New Jewish Quiz Book. Barbara Spector. LC 96-52516. (J). 1997. pap. 9.95 (*0-8276-0594-3*) JPS Phila.

New Jewish Songbook. Compiled by Harry Coopersmith. LC 65-14593. (Illus.). pap. 16.95 (*0-87441-060-6*) Behrman.

New Jewish Teachers Handbook. Ed. by Audrey F. Marcus & Raymond A. Zwerin. LC 94-70560. 480p. (Orig.). 1994. pap. text, teacher ed. 45.00 (*0-86705-033-0*) A R E Pub.

New Jewish Voices: Plays Produced by the Jewish Repertory Theatre. Ed. by Edward M. Cohen. LC 84-8799. (SUNY Series in Modern Jewish Literature & Culture). 260p. (C). 1985. pap. text 21.95 (*0-87395-997-3*) State U NY Pr.

*New Jewish Wedding.** Diamant. 2001. write for info. (*0-7432-0255-4*) S&S Trade.

New Jewish Wedding. Anita Diamant. (Illus.). 272p. 1986. per. 12.00 (*0-671-62882-8*) S&S Trade Pap.

New Job Contract: Economic Justice in an Age of Insecurity. Barbara H. Andolsen. LC 98-35073. 164p. 1998. pap. 15.95 (*0-8298-1272-5*) Pilgrim OH.

New Job Interview. Dinah Tallent. 149p. (YA). (gr. 7-12). 1995. pap. 6.95 (*1-57515-046-8*) PPI Pubng.

New John G. Lake Sermons. Gordon Lindsay. 1971. 3.95 (*0-89985-987-9*) Christ for the Nations.

New Joy of Being Sober: A Book for Recovering Alcoholics & Those who love them. rev. ed. Jack Mumey. LC 94-28358. 240p. 1994. pap. 11.95 (*0-925190-31-4*) Fairview Press.

New Joy of Eating. Renny Darling. 1991. 17.95 (*0-930440-32-3*) Royal Hse.

New Joy of Gay Sex. rev. ed. Charles Silverstein & Felice Picano. LC 92-52594. (Illus.). 240p. 1993. pap. 22.00 (*0-06-092438-1*, Perennial) HarperTrade.

New Joy of Photography: The Classic Guide to the Tools & Techniques of Better Photography. Ed. by Eastman Kodak Company Editors. write for info. (*0-318-59579-6*) Addison-Wesley.

New Joy of Sex: A Gourmet Guide to Lovemaking for the Nineties. rev. ed. Alex Comfort. Ed. by Julie Rubenstein. 256p. 1992. per. 20.00 (*0-671-77859-5*) PB.

New Joy of Sex: The Gourmet Guide to Lovemaking in the '90s. Alex Comfort. (Illus.). 256p. 1991. 32.00 (*0-517-58583-9*, Crown) Crown Pub Group.

New Joy of Sex - Compact Edition: A Gourmet Guide to Lovemaking in the Nineties. Alex Comfort. LC 94-9658. (Illus.). 224p. 1994. 12.00 (*0-517-59910-4*) Crown Pub Group.

New Joy of Sex - More Joy of Sex. Alex Comfort. 1994. pap. text 38.00 (*0-671-90619-4*) PB.

New Joys of Jell-O Brand. (Illus.). 224p. 1993. 19.98 (*0-88176-905-3*, 2003800); spiral bd. 3.50 (*1-56173-363-6*, 2003801) Pubns Intl Ltd.

New Judea: Jewish Life in Modern Palestine & Egypt. Benjamin L. Gordon. Ed. by Moshe Davis. LC 77-70697. (America & the Holy Land Ser.). (Illus.). 1977. reprint ed. lib. bdg. 33.95 (*0-405-10251-8*) Ayer.

New Judiciary: The Effects of Expansion & Activism. Kate Malleson. LC 98-37427. 260p. 1999. text 78.95 (*1-84014-077-1*, Pub. by Ashgate Pub) Ashgate Pub Co.

N

New Junior Cookbook: 77 Easy-to-Make Recipes. 6th ed. Better Homes & Gardens. Ed. by Jennifer Darling. LC 97-71329. (Better Homes & Gardens Test Kitchen Ser.). (Illus.). 112p. (J). (gr. 3-7). 1997. 15.95 (*0-696-20708-7*, Better Homes) Meredith Bks.

***New Junior Craft Book: 52 Cool Projects for Kids to Make.** Better Homes & Gardens. (Illus.). 112p. 2000. 15.95 (*0-696-21021-5*, Better Homes) Meredith Bks.

***New Junior Garden Book.** Felder Rushing. Ed. by Cathy Wilkinson Barash. LC 98-68021. (Illus.). 112p. (J). (ps-3). 1999. 15.95 (*0-696-20849-0*) Meredith Bks.

New Kabuki Encyclopedia: A Revised Adaptation of Kabuki Jiten. rev. ed. Samuel L. Leiter. LC 96-36530. 840p. 1997. lib. bdg. 115.00 (*0-313-29288-4*, Greenwood Pr) Greenwood.

New Kate. Susan Saunders. (Sleepover Friends Ser.: No. 26). (J). (gr. 5-7). 1990. pap. 2.50 (*0-590-44721-1*) Scholastic Inc.

New Kate, No. 26. Susan Saunders. (Sleepover Friends Ser.: 26). (J). 1990. pap. 2.50 (*0-590-43192-7*) Scholastic Inc.

***New Kayak Shop: More Elegant Wooden Kayaks Anyone Can Build.** Chris Kulczycki. (Illus.). 2000. pap. 21.95 (*0-07-135786-6*) McGraw.

New Kent County, Virginia Land Tax Lists, 1782-1790. T.L.C. Genealogy Staff. LC 92-60554. 82p. (Orig.). 1992. pap., spiral bd. 12.00 (*1-886633-96-7*) TLC Genealogy.

New Key to Belize. 3rd rev. ed. Stacy Ritz. LC 97-60638. (New Key Guides Ser.). (Illus.). 232p. (Orig.). 1997. pap. 14.95 (*1-56975-085-8*) Ulysses Pr.

New Key to Costa Rica. 14th ed. Beatrice Blake & Anne Beecher. (New Key Travel Ser.). (Illus.). 512p. 1998. reprint ed. pap. 17.95 (*1-56975-146-3*) Ulysses Pr.

***New Key to Costa Rica.** 15th ed. Beatrice Blake. (Illus.). 2000. pap. 17.95 (*1-56975-219-2*) Ulysses Pr.

New Key to Ecuador & the Galapagos. 3rd rev. ed. David Pearson & David Middleton. (New Key Guides Ser.). (Illus.). 400p. 1997. pap. 16.95 (*1-56975-075-0*) Ulysses Pr.

New Key to Ecuador & the Galapagos. 3rd rev. ed. David Pearson & David Middleton. (New Key Travel Ser.). (Illus.). 480p. 1999. pap. 17.95 (*1-56975-199-4*, Pub. by Ulysses Pr) Publishers Group.

New Key to Guatemala. Richard Harris. LC 95-60708. (New Key Guides Ser.). (Illus.). 272p. (Orig.). 1995. pap. 14.95 (*1-56975-039-4*) Ulysses Pr.

New Key to Wild Flowers. rev. ed. John Hayward. (Illus.). 288p. (C). 1995. pap. text 25.95 (*0-521-48346-8*) Cambridge U Pr.

New Keynesian Economics. Ed. by Roy Rotheim. LC 96-54816. (Routledge Frontiers of Political Economy Ser.: Vol. 9). (Illus.). 408p. (C). 1998. 90.00 (*0-415-12388-7*) Routledge.

New Keynesian Economics Vol. 1: Imperfect Competition & Sticky Prices. Ed. by N. Gregory Mankiw & David Romer. (Illus.). 444p. 1991. pap. text 25.00 (*0-262-63133-4*) MIT Pr.

New Keynesian Economics Vol. 2: Coordination Failures & Real Rigidities. Ed. by N. Gregory Mankiw & David Romer. (Illus.). 340p. 1991. pap. text 25.00 (*0-262-63134-2*) MIT Pr.

New Kid. Chris Economos. (Real Readers Ser.: Level Blue). (Illus.). 32p. (J). (ps-3). 1989. lib. bdg. 21.40 (*0-8172-3512-4*) Raintree Steck-V.

New Kid. Chris Economos. (Real Readers Ser.: Level Blue). (Illus.). 32p. (J). (gr. 1-4). 1989. pap. 4.95 (*0-8114-6715-5*) Raintree Steck-V.

New Kid. Susan Hood. LC 98-10040. (Real Kids Readers Ser.). (Illus.). 32p. (J). (ps-1). 1998. pap. 3.99 (*0-7613-2039-3*); lib. bdg. 16.90 (*0-7613-2014-8*) Millbrook Pr.

New Kid. Uthman Hutchinson. LC 95-80049. (Children Stories Project Ser.). (Illus.). 84p. (Orig.). (YA). (gr. 6 up). 1995. pap. 8.95 (*0-915957-45-0*) amana pubns.

New Kid & the Cookie Thief. Lisa McCourt. LC 98-5111. (Illus.). 32p. (J). 1998. 14.95 (*1-55874-588-2*) Health Comm.

New Kid at School. K. H. McMullan. LC 97-15520. (Dragon Slayers' Academy Ser.: No. 1). (Illus.). 92p. (J). (gr. 2-5). 1997. pap. 3.95 (*0-448-41592-5*, G & D); lib. bdg. 13.89 (*0-448-41727-8*, G & D) Peng Put Young Read.

New Kid at School, 1. K. H. McMullan. (Dragon Slayers' Academy Ser.: No. 1). (Illus.). (J). (gr. 2-5). 1997. 9.05 (*0-606-12921-9*, Pub. by Turtleback) Demco.

New Kid Collection of Six Stories. Uthman Hutchinson. 84p. (J). 1996. pap. 9.95 (*0-614-21037-2*, 1525) Kazi Pubns.

New Kid in School Is a Vampire Bat. George E. Stanley. LC 96-43865. (Scaredy Cats Ser.). (Illus.). 80p. (J). (gr. 1-4). 1997. mass mkt. 3.99 (*0-689-81349-X*) Aladdin.

***New Kid in Town.** Janette Oke. (Oke Children's Classics Ser.). (Illus.). 136p. (Orig.). (J). (gr. 3 up). 1998. pap. 5.99 (*0-934998-16-7*) Bethany Hse.

New Kid on Block. Jack Prelutsky. (J). (gr. 1 up). 1994. pap. 23.75 incl. cd-rom (*1-57135-072-1*) Living Bks.

New Kid on the Block. 1995. 39.95 (*1-57135-073-X*); lib. bdg. 99.95 (*1-57135-074-8*) Living Bks.

New Kid on the Block. Jack Prelutsky. LC 83-20621. (Illus.). 160p. (J). (ps-3). 1984. 17.95 (*0-688-02271-5*, Grenwillow Bks) HarpC Child Bks.

New Kid on the Block. Jack Prelutsky. LC 83-20621. (Illus.). 160p. (J). (ps-3). 1984. 17.89 (*0-688-02272-3*, Grenwillow Bks) HarpC Child Bks.

New Kids. Leah Klein. (B. Y. Times Ser.: No. 10). (J). 1993. pap. 8.95 (*0-944070-91-4*) Targum Pr.

***New Kids Book of Angel Visits.** Anne Adams. (New Kids Junior Reference Ser.). (Illus.). 96p. (J). (gr. k-4). 1999. 6.99 (*0-8010-4435-9*) Baker Bks.

***New Kids Book of Bible Animals.** Anne Adams. (Illus.). 96p. (J). (gr. k-4). 1999. 6.99 (*0-8010-4436-7*) Baker Bks.

***New Kids Book of Bible Facts.** Anne Adams. 192p. (J). (gr. 1-10). 2000. 14.99 (*0-8010-4441-3*, New Kids Media) Baker Bks.

***New Kids Book of Bible Passages.** Anne Adams. 96p. (J). (gr. k-4). 1999. 6.99 (*0-8010-4434-0*) Baker Bks.

***New Kids Book of Bible People.** Anne Adams. (Illus.). 96p. (J). (gr. k-4). 1999. 6.99 (*0-8010-4437-5*) Baker Bks.

New Kids' Cookbook. (Mini Cook Bks.). (Illus.). 64p. 1999. pap. 1.95 (*3-8290-1613-1*) Konemann.

New Kids in Town: Oral Histories of Immigrant Teens. Janet Bode. 128p. (J). 1991. pap. 3.50 (*0-590-44144-2*) Scholastic Inc.

New Kids of the Polk Street School, 6 vols., Set. Patricia Reilly Giff. (J). (gr. 4-7). 1990. pap., boxed set 16.50 (*0-440-36029-3*) Dell.

New Kids on Net: A Tutorial for Teachers, Parents & Students. Sheryl Burgstahler. 214p. 1998. pap. text 24.95 (*0-205-28594-5*) Allyn.

New Kids on the Block: The Whole Story by Their Friends. Robin McGibbon. 1990. pap. 6.95 (*0-380-76344-3*, Avon Bks) Morrow Avon.

New Kids on the Net. Burgstahler. LC 98-172243. 190p. (C). 1997. pap. text 24.95 (*0-205-27698-9*) P-H.

New Kids on the Net: A Tutorial. Sheryl Burgstahler. LC 97-150029. 252p. (C). 1996. pap. text 24.95 (*0-205-19872-4*) Allyn.

New Kids on the Net: Activities for K-12. Sheryl Burgstahler. 199p. (J). (gr. k-12). 1996. pap. text 24.95 (*0-205-19873-2*) Allyn.

***New Kids on the Net: Internet Activities in Elementary Language Arts.** Sheryl Burgstahler. 232p. 1999. pap. text 24.95 (*0-205-30587-3*) Allyn.

New Kids' Question & Answer Book. Owl Magazine Editors. (Illus.). 64p. 1993. pap. 9.95 (*1-895688-05-1*, Pub. by Greey dePencier) Firefly Bks Ltd.

New Kids Say the Darndest Things. Art Linkletter. (Illus.). 180p. 1996. pap. 8.95 (*0-915463-72-5*) Jameson Bks.

New Kind of Communicator see Nou Tip De Profesor: Profesorul de Reevaluare Prin Consiliere

New Kind of Communicator. 5th ed. Harvey Jackins et al. 1993. pap. 4.00 (*0-913937-76-2*) Rational Isl.

New Kind of Country. Dorothy Gilman. 1985. reprint ed. lib. bdg. 23.95 (*0-89966-571-3*) Buccaneer Bks.

New Kind of Doctor: The General Practitioner's Part in the Health of the Community. Julian T. Hart. (C). 1988. pap. write for info. (*0-85036-300-4*, Pub. by MRLN) Paul & Co Pubs.

New Kind of Family: A Separation-Divorce Handbook for Children in Transition. Cynthia D. Schulze. (Illus.). 64p. (Orig.). (J). (gr. 1-6). 1995. pap. 9.95 (*0-9644335-0-8*) Fmly Srv St Croix.

New Kind of Fool: Meditations on St. Francis & His Values. Christopher Coelho. 128p. 1994. pap. 21.00 (*0-86012-184-4*, Pub. by Srch Pr) St Mut.

New Kind of Life: Study Guide. James A. Meek. (Discover Life Ser.). 18p. 1990. pap., student ed. 3.25 (*1-56212-229-0*) CRC Pubns.

New Kind of Love. E. W. Kenyon. 95p. (Orig.). (C). 1942. pap. 8.00 (*1-57770-010-4*) Kenyons Gospel.

***New Kind of Party Animal: How the Young Are Redefining "Politics As Usual"** Michele Mitchell. 224p. 1999. pap. 13.00 (*0-684-85441-4*, Touchstone) S&S Trade Pap.

New Kind of Party Animal: How the Young Are Tearing Up the American Political Landscape. Michele Mitchell. LC 98-10495. 224p. (YA). 1998. 22.00 (*0-684-83697-1*) S&S Trade.

New Kind of Science. Stephen Wolfram. (Illus.). 832p. 1997. 35.00 (*0-684-82290-3*) Free Pr.

***New Kind of Science.** Stephen Wolfram. (Illus.). 992p. 2000. 39.95 (*1-57955-008-8*) Wolfram Media.

New Kind of War. Anthony Price. LC 87-40385. 272p. 1988. 17.95 (*0-89296-281-X*, Pub. by Mysterious Pr) Little.

New Kind of War: America's Global Strategy & the Truman Doctrine in Greece. Howard Jones. (Illus.). 360p. 1997. reprint ed. pap. 24.95 (*0-19-511385-3*) OUP.

New King. Earl B. Lewis. 1999. pap. 4.99 (*0-14-055729-6*) Viking Penguin.

New King. M. P. Shiel. 170p. 1983. pap. 12.00 (*0-317-14708-0*) Reynolds Morse.

New King James Version: In the Great Tradition. Arthur L. Farstad. 172p. 1990. pap. 8.99 (*0-8407-3148-5*) Nelson.

New King James Version Compact Reference Snap Flap Bible Bonded Leather Blue, Supersaver ed. Compact Reference Staff. 1997. 19.97 (*0-7852-0209-9*) Nelson.

New King James Version Giant Print Personal Size Bonded Leather Blue Indexed, Supersaver ed. Personal Reference Group Staff. 1998. 32.97 (*0-7852-0399-0*) Nelson.

New King James Version Giant Print Personal Size Bonded Leather Blue, Supersaver ed. Personal Reference Group Staff. 1998. 24.97 (*0-7852-0397-4*) Nelson.

New King James Version New Testament with Psalms: Father's Day Edition. 1998. bond lthr. 12.97 (*0-7852-0521-7*) Nelson.

New King James Version Spirit Filled Life Personal Size Readers Edition, Supersaver ed. Thomas Nelson Publishing Staff. 1998. write for info. (*0-7852-0480-6*) Nelson.

New Kingdom Egypt. Mark Healy. (Elite Ser.: No. 40). (Illus.). 64p. pap. 12.95 (*1-85532-208-0*, 9455, Pub. by Osprey) Stackpole.

New Kingdom of the Saints: Religious Art of New Mexico, 1780-1907. Larry Frank. LC 92-53884. (Illus.). 336p. 1992. 75.00 (*1-878610-18-X*) Red Crane Bks.

New Kingdom Royal City. Peter Lacovara. LC 96-11773. (Studies in Egyptology). 282p. 1996. 161.50 (*0-7103-0544-3*, Pub. by Kegan Paul Intl) Col U Pr.

New Kitchen Garden. Anna Pavord. LC 95-44070. (DK Living Ser.). 208p. 1999. pap. text 13.95 (*0-7894-4119-5*) DK Pub Inc.

New Kitchen Remodeling. Creative Publishing International Staff. LC 98-49173. (Black & Decker Home Improvement Library). (Illus.). 160p. 1999. pap. text 16.95 (*0-86573-638-3*) Creat Pub Intl.

New Knighthood: A History of the Order of the Temple. Malcolm C. Barber. (Canto Book Ser.). (Illus.). 465p. (C). 1995. pap. 12.95 (*0-521-55872-7*) Cambridge U Pr.

New Knitting Stitch Library. Leslie Stanfield. LC 97-31247. (Illus.). 192p. 1997. pap. 21.95 (*1-57990-027-5*, Pub. by Lark Books) Random.

New Know-Nothings: The Political Foes of the Scientific Study of Human Nature. Morton Hunt. LC 98-28985. 472p. 1998. 59.95 (*1-56000-393-6*); pap. 24.95 (*0-7658-0497-2*) Transaction Pubs.

New Knowledge in the Biomedical Sciences. Ed. by William B. Bondeson et al. 242p. 1982. text 106.00 (*90-277-1319-7*, D Reidel) Kluwer Academic.

New Kobbe's Opera Book. rev. ed. Antony Peattie. Ed. by Earl of Harewood. LC 97-10981. (Illus.). 1008p. 1997. 60.00 (*0-399-14332-7*, G P Putnam) Peng Put Young Read.

New Korean Dictionary. Dong-A. (KOR.). 1988. 59.95 (*0-8288-3953-0*, F117800) Fr & Eur.

New KornShell Command & Programming Language. 2nd ed. Morris Bolsky & David G. Korn. 416p. 1995. pap. 55.00 (*0-13-182700-6*) P-H.

New Kosher Cookbook Trilogy. Ruth Grossman & Bob Grossman. (Illus.). 312p. 1992. 9.99 (*0-88365-704-X*) Galahad Bks.

New Kosher Cuisine for All Seasons. Ed. by Ivy Feuerstadt & Melinda Strauss. LC 93-2373. (Illus.). 368p. 1993. pap. 18.95 (*0-89815-559-2*) Ten Speed Pr.

New Labels. Sara Nephew. (Illus.). 16p. 1998. pap. 6.95 (*0-9621172-8-5*) Clearview Triangle.

***New Labor.** Maurice Mullard. LC 00-40103. 2000. write for info. (*1-56072-824-8*) Nova Sci Pubs.

***New Labor Forum Vol. 5: A Journal of Ideas Analysis & Debate.** (Illus.). 116p. 1999. write for info. (*0-9679672-0-1*) Queens College.

New Labor Movement for the New Century. Ed. by Gregory Mantsios & Dan Georgakas. LC 98-4474. (Labor in America Ser.: Vol. 5). 406p. 1998. 80.00 (*0-8153-2473-1*, SS1126) Garland.

New Labor Movement for the New Century: A Collection of Essays from the Labor Resource Center, Queens College, City University of New York. Gregory Mantsios & Queens College Staff (New York, N.Y.). LC 98-17905. 1998. 24.00 (*0-85345-937-1*, Pub. by Monthly Rev) NYU Pr.

New Labor, New Laws: Public Sector Collective Bargaining Laws. Berkeley Miller & William L. Canak. 200p. (C). 1999. pap. 35.00 (*0-8133-0689-2*) Westview.

New Labor Press: Journalism for a Changing Union Movement. Ed. by Sam Pizzigati & Fred J. Solowey. LC 92-10352. (Illus.). 256p. (Orig.). 1992. text 42.50 (*0-87546-189-1*, ILR Press); pap. text 17.95 (*0-87546-190-5*, ILR Press) Cornell U Pr.

New Labor Radicalism & New York City's Garment Industry: Progressive Labor Insurgents During the 1960s. rev. ed. Leigh David Benin. LC 99-51937. (Studies in the History of American Labor). 336p. 1999. 46.00 (*0-8153-3385-4*) Garland.

New Labour - Polity Press: Politics after Thatcherism. Stephen Driver & Luke Martell. LC 98-16531. 224p. 1998. 59.95 (*0-7456-2050-7*); pap. 29.95 (*0-7456-2051-5*) Blackwell Pubs.

***New Labour & Thatcherism.** Richard Heffernan. LC 99-46780. 2000. text 65.00 (*0-312-22973-9*) St Martin.

***New Labour in Government.** Steve Ludlam & Martin J. Smith. LC 00-42245. 2000. write for info. (*0-312-23743-X*) St Martin.

New Labour in Power. Brian Brivati & Tim Bale. LC 97-30749. 224p. (C). 1998. 70.00 (*0-415-17972-6*); pap. 20.99 (*0-415-17973-4*) Routledge.

New Labour into Power. David Coates. pap. write for info. (*0-7190-5462-1*, Pub. by Manchester Univ Pr); text. write for info. (*0-7190-5461-3*, Pub. by Manchester Univ Pr) St Martin.

New Labour Law: Strikes, Dismissals & the Unfair Labour Practice in South African Law. M. Brassey et al. 510p. 1987. pap. 60.00 (*0-7021-1828-1*, Pub. by Juta & Co) Gaunt.

***New Labour, New Language?** Norman Fairclough. LC 99-46501. 192p. (C). 2000. text. write for info. (*0-415-21826-8*) Routledge.

New Labour Relations Act - The Law after the 1988 Amendments. E. Cameron et al. 305p. 1989. pap. write for info. (*0-7021-2235-1*, Pub. by Juta & Co) Gaunt.

New Labour Triumphs: Britain at the Polls. Anthony King et al. LC 97-33818. (Illus.). 272p. 1997. pap. text 21.95 (*1-56643-057-7*, Chatham House Pub) Seven Bridges.

New Labrador Retriever. Janet I. Churchill. LC 94-24401. (Illus.). 320p. 1995. 27.95 (*0-87605-206-5*) Howell Bks.

New Lagrangian & Hamiltonian Methods in Field Theory. L. Mangiarotti & Gennadi A. Sardanashvily. LC 98-196719. 300p. 1997. text 71.00 (*981-02-1587-8*) World Scientific Pub.

New Lake Poets. Intro. by William Scammell. 160p. (Orig.). 1991. pap. 18.95 (*1-85224-146-2*, Pub. by Bloodaxe Bks) Dufour.

New Lamps for Old. Anatol M. Kotenev. LC 78-171630. reprint ed. 49.50 (*0-404-03776-3*) AMS Pr.

New Lanchester Strategy, Vol. 1. Shinichi Yano. LC 95-77646. 175p. 1995. pap. 17.95 (*1-57321-000-5*) Lanchester Pr.

New Lanchester Strategy: Sales & Marketing Strategy for the Weak, Vol. 2. Shinichi Yano. Ed. by John Schuler. Tr. by Connie Prenor from JPN. LC 96-75197. (Illus.). 190p. (Orig.). 1996. pap. 17.95 (*1-57321-004-8*) Lanchester Pr.

New Lanchester Strategy Vol. 3: Sales & Marketing Strategy for the Strong. Shinichi Yano. LC 96-77528. 178p. 1996. pap. 17.95 (*1-57321-005-6*) Lanchester Pr.

New Land: A First Year on the Prairie. Marilynn Reynolds. LC 96-72452. (Illus.). 32p. (J). (ps-3). 1997. pap. 6.95 (*1-55143-071-1*) Orca Bk Pubs.

New Land! Conscious Experience Beyond Horizons. Kenneth G. Mills. (Illus.). 77p. 1978. pap. 8.95 (*0-919842-01-1*, KGOB2) Sun-Scape Ent.

***New Land Law.** Peter Sparkes. 720p. 1999. 90.00 (*1-84113-012-5*); pap. 45.00 (*1-84113-013-3*) Hart Pub.

New Land New Lives: Scandinavian Immigrants to the Pacific Northwest. Rasmussen. LC 93-22999. (Illus.). 344p. 1993. 24.95 (*0-295-97288-2*) U of Wash Pr.

New Land, New Lives: Scandinavian Immigrants to the Pacific Northwest. Janet E. Rasmussen. (Illus.). 334p. 1998. pap. text 12.95 (*0-295-97711-6*) U of Wash Pr.

***New Landlord & Tenant.** Peter Sparkes. 720p. 2000. 90.00 (*1-84113-022-2*, Pub. by Hart Pub); pap. 45.00 (*1-84113-023-0*, Pub. by Hart Pub) Intl Spec Bk.

New Lands, New Men: America & the Second Great Age of Discovery. William H. Goetzmann. (Fred H. & Ella Mae Moore Texas History Reprint Ser.). (Illus.). 536p. 1995. 24.95 (*0-87611-148-7*) Tex St Hist Assn.

New Landscapes, New Territories. Compiled by Eduard Bru. 209p. 1998. pap. 34.00 (*84-89698-40-6*, 810741, Pub. by Actar) Dist Art Pubs.

New Langton Arts: The First 15 Years. Ed. by Judy Moran. (Illus.). 96p. (Orig.). 1990. pap. 30.00 (*0-9627010-0-9*) New Langton Arts.

New Langton Arts, 1991-1997. Nao Bustamante et al. LC 99-177303. (Illus.). 160p. 1998. pap. 20.00 (*0-9627010-1-7*) New Langton Arts.

New Language Arts Idea Book: Classroom Ideas for Teachers, Grades 1-6. Joanne Schaff. (Illus.). 96p. (Orig.). 1984. pap. 9.95 (*0-673-18081-6*, GoodYrBooks) Addson-Wesley Educ.

New Language for Psychoanalysis. Roy Schafer. LC 75-18185. 432p. 1981. pap. 20.00 (*0-300-02761-3*) Yale U Pr.

New Language for Psychoanalysis. Roy Schafer. LC 75-18185. 408p. reprint ed. pap. 126.50 (*0-8357-8246-8*, 203388200087) Bks Demand.

New Language of Change: Constructive Collaboration in Psychotherapy. Ed. by Steven Friedman. LC 92-49093. 464p. 1993. lib. bdg. 46.95 (*0-89862-145-3*) Guilford Pubns.

New Language of Change: Constructive Collaboration in Psychotherapy. Steven Friedman. 464p. 1997. pap. text 25.00 (*1-57230-282-8*) Guilford Pubns.

New Language of Qualitative Method. Jaber F. Gubrium & James A. Holstein. LC 96-23816. 256p. 1997. pap. text 25.95 (*0-19-509994-X*) OUP.

New Language of Toys: Teaching Communication Skills to Children with Special Needs. 2nd rev. ed. Sue Schwartz & Joan E. Miller. LC 95-47452. (Illus.). 350p. (Orig.). 1996. pap. 16.95 (*0-933149-73-5*) Woodbine House.

New Lao Tzu: A Contemporary Tao Te Ching. Ray Grigg. LC 94-46615. (Illus.). 192p. 1995. 18.95 (*0-8048-3034-7*) Tuttle Pubng.

New Laos, New Challenges. Ed. by Jacqueline Butler-Diaz. (Illus.). xxvii, 356p. (C). 1998. pap. 19.95 (*1-881044-18-1*) ASU Prog SE Asian.

New Large Shining Sea-Torch, 3 vols. Johannes Van Keulen & Gerard Van Keulen. Incl. Vol. 1. LC 75-81728. 1962. reprint ed. lib. bdg. 300.00 (*0-306-77241-8*); Vol. 2. LC 75-81728. 1962. reprint ed. lib. bdg. 300.00 (*0-306-77242-6*); Vol. 3. LC 75-81728. 1962. reprint ed. lib. bdg. 300.00 (*0-306-77243-4*); LC 75-81728. (Science & Medicine Ser.). reprint ed. 750.00 (*0-306-77240-X*) Da Capo.

New Larkins for Old: Critical Essays. Ed. by James Booth. LC 99-16693. 247p. 1999. text 59.95 (*0-312-22669-1*) St Martin.

New Larousse Adonis French-English-French. Jean Mergault. 532p. 1987. pap. 11.95 (*0-7859-4735-3*) Fr & Eur.

New Larousse of Gastronomy: Nouveau Larousse Gastronomique. R. J. Courtine. (ENG & FRE.). 1152p. 1984. 150.00 (*0-8288-0157-6*, M6433) Fr & Eur.

New Larousse of Scrabble & Word Games: Nouveau Larousse du Scrabble, Dictionnaire des Jeux de Letters. M. Pialat. (FRE.). 830p. 1981. pap. 31.95 (*0-8288-2345-6*, M14461) Fr & Eur.

New Late Night Top 10 Lists. David Letterman. 1994. per. 5.99 (*0-671-51144-0*) PB.

New Lateral Thinking Puzzles. Paul Sloane. LC 98-26069. (Illus.). 96p. 1998. 6.95 (*0-8069-6259-3*) Sterling.

New Latin American Cinema: A Continental Project. Zuzana M. Pick. Ed. by Thomas G. Schatz. LC 93-73. (Film Studies). 264p. (C). 1993. text 37.50 (*0-292-76545-2*) U of Tex Pr.

New Latin American Cinema: A Continental Project. Thomas G. Schatz. LC 93-73. (Film Studies). 264p. (C). 1993. pap. 18.95 (*0-292-76549-5*) U of Tex Pr.

New Latin American Cinema: An Annotated Bibliography of English-Languages Sources, 1960-1980. Ed. by Julianne Burton. LC 83-80377. (Orig.). 1983. pap. 4.00 (*0-918266-17-3*) Smyrna.

New Latin American Cinema: Studies of National Cinemas, Vol. 2. Ed. by Michael T. Martin. LC 96-46741. (Contemporary Film & Television Ser.). 480p. 1997. text 49.95 (*0-8143-2706-0*); pap. text 18.95 (*0-8143-2586-6*) Wayne St U Pr.

An Asterisk (*) at the beginning of an entry indicates that the title is appearing for the first time.

New Latin American Cinema: Theory, Practices, & Transcontinental Articulations. Ed. by Michael T. Martin. LC 96-46741. (Contemporary Film & Television Ser.). 336p. 1997. pap. text 15.95 (*0-8143-2585-8*) Wayne St U Pr.

New Latin American Cinema Vol. I: Theory, Practices, & Transcontinental Articulations. Ed. by Michael T. Martin. LC 96-46741. (Contemporary Film & Television Ser.). 336p. 1997. text 39.95 (*0-8143-2705-2*) Wayne St U Pr.

New Latin American Mission History. Ed. by Erick D. Langer & Robert H. Jackson. LC 94-43080. (Latin American Studies). xviii, 215p. 1995. text 45.00 (*0-8032-2911-9*); pap. text 22.00 (*0-8032-7953-1*) U of Nebr Pr.

New Latin Composition. Charles E. Bennett. 304p. 1996. reprint ed. pap. 20.00 (*0-86516-345-6*) Bolchazy-Carducci.

New Latin Grammar. J. H. Allen & J. B. Greenough. Ed. by George L. Kittredge et al. (College Classical Ser.). 490p. 1992. lib. bdg. 37.50 (*0-89241-001-9*) Caratzas.

New Latin Grammar. J. H. Allen & J. B. Greenough. Ed. by George L. Kittredge et al. (College Classical Ser.). 490p. 1995. pap. 22.50 (*0-89241-331-X*) Caratzas.

New Latin-Italian Dictionary: Nuovo Dizionario Latino-Italiano. G. Angelini. (ITA & LAT.). 1981. 45.00 (*0-8288-1030-3*, F43170) Fr & Eur.

New Latin Syntax. E. Woodcock. 291p. 1985. pap. 29.95 (*0-86292-042-6*, Pub. by Brist Class Pr) Focus Pub-R Pullins.

New Latin Syntax. E. C. Woodcock. xxiv, 268p. 1987. reprint ed. pap. 20.00 (*0-86516-126-7*) Bolchazy-Carducci.

New Latina Narrative: The Feminine Space of Postmodern Ethnicity. Ellen McCracken. LC 98-25528. 1999. 40.00 (*0-8165-1940-4*); pap. 19.95 (*0-8165-1941-2*) U of Ariz Pr.

New Latitudes: Theory & English Renaissance Literature. Thomas Healy. LC 91-27514. 160p. 1995. text 16.95 (*0-340-49308-9*, A5366, Pub. by E A) St Martin.

New Latvian Fiction. Ed. by John O'Brien. (Review of Contemporary Fiction Ser.: Vol. 18, No. 1). 256p. 1998. pap. 8.00 (*1-56478-178-X*) Dalkey Arch.

New Laurel's Kitchen. 2nd ed. Laurel Robertson et al. LC 86-14330. (Illus.). 511p. 1986. pap. 19.95 (*0-89815-166-X*) Ten Speed Pr.

New Law & Life: Sixty Practical Questions & Answers on the New Code of Canon Law. Ed. by Elissa Rinere. 103p. (Orig.). 1985. pap. 3.00 (*0-943616-28-X*) Canon Law Soc.

New Law Dictionary & Glossary: Containing Full Definitions of the Principal Terms of the Common & Civil Law, Together with Translations & Explanations of the Various Technical Phrases in Different Languages, Occurring in the Ancient & Modern Reports, & Standard Treatises; Embracing Also All the Principal Common & Civil Law Maxims - Compiled on the Basis of Spelman's Glossary, & Adapted to the Jurisprudence of the United States; Alexander M. Burrill. LC 97-38481. xviii, 1099p. 1997. reprint ed. lib. bdg. 175.00 (*1-886363-32-3*) Lawbk Exchange.

New Law Dictionary & Institute of the Whole Law: For the Use of Students, the Legal Profession, & the Public. Archibald Brown. lxviii, 391p. 1987. reprint ed. 47.50 (*0-8377-1949-6*, Rothman) W S Hein.

New Law Dictionary, Containing Explanations of Such Technical Terms & Phrases As Defined in the Works of Legal Authors, in the Practice of the Courts, & in the Parliamentary Proceedings of the House of Lords & Commons, to Which Is Added an Outline of an Action at Law & of a Suit in Equity... 1847. 2nd ed. Henry J. Holthouse. LC 98-49350. 495p. 1999. reprint ed. 75.00 (*1-886363-67-6*) Lawbk Exchange.

New Law for a New People. Frederick K. Price. 92p. (Orig.). 1993. pap. 6.99 (*1-883798-01-9*) Faith One.

New Law of Arbitration, ADR & Contract in India. Mital. LC 97-8441. 1997. 163.00 (*90-411-0358-9*) Kluwer Law Intl.

New Law of Negotiable Instruments. Wayne K. Lewis & Steven H. Resnicoff. LC 96-76060. 1996. 95.00 (*1-55834-373-3*, 64238, MICHIE) LEXIS Pub.

New Law of Negotiable Instruments, 1998 Supplement. Wayne K. Lewis & Steven H. Resnicoff. 90p. 1998. suppl. ed. 35.00 (*0-327-00342-1*, 6423911) LEXIS Pub.

New Law of the Sea for the Caribbean: An Examination of Marine Law & Policy Issues in the Lesser Antilles. Ed. by Edgar Gold. 276p. 1988. pap. 43.00 (*0-387-96805-9*) Spr-Verlag.

New Law of Trade Marks & Designs. Ed. by Coenraad Visser. LC 96-171410. 1995. pap. 40.00 (*0-7021-3348-5*, Pub. by Juta & Co) Gaunt.

New Law on Inter-Corporate Loans & Inter-Corporate Investments. G. Agarwal. (C). 1989. 75.00 (*0-7855-6131-5*) St Mut.

New Law on Managerial Remuneration (under Company Law & Income Tax Law) D. C. Jain & R. K. Agarwal. (C). 1989. 140.00 (*0-7855-4813-0*) St Mut.

New Lawn Expert. D. G. Hessayon. LC 97-183496. (Illus.). 144p. 1997. 12.95 (*0-903505-48-7*) Sterling.

New Laws for New Forests: Wisconsin's Forest-Fire, Tax, Zoning & County-Forest Laws in Operation. Erling Solberg. LC 60-5661. 636p. reprint ed. pap. 197.20 (*0-608-14628-5*, 202114800021) Bks Demand.

New Laws of the Indies for the Good Treatment & Preservation of the Indians. Ed. by Henry Stevens. LC 79-128422. (ENG., Illus.). reprint ed. 52.50 (*0-404-06159-1*) AMS Pr.

New Laws of the Mines of Spain: Mining in Early New World History. Juan De Onate. Ed. by Homer Milford. LC 99-13096. (SPA.). 96p. 1999. pap. 8.95 (*0-86534-291-1*) Sunstone Pr.

New Leader. Hart. 1996. 22.00 (*0-02-287409-7*) Free Pr.

New Leader: Bringing Creativity & Innovation to the Workplace. Gregory P. Smith. 288p. 1996. boxed set 49.95 (*1-57444-034-9*) St Lucie Pr.

New Leaders: Achieving Corporate Transformation Through Dynamic Leadership. Paul Taffinder. 1997. pap. text 19.95 (*0-7494-2229-7*) Kogan Page Ltd.

New Leaders: Leadership Diversity in America. Ann M. Morrison. (Management Ser.). 352p. 1996. reprint ed. mass mkt. 18.50 (*0-7879-0184-9*) Jossey-Bass.

New Leadership: Managing Participation in Organizations. Victor H. Vroom & Arthur G. Jago. (Illus.). 288p. (C). 1988. text 33.80 (*0-13-615030-6*) P-H.

New Leadership in Health Care Management: The Physician Executive. 2nd ed. Ed. by Wesley Curry. LC 94-72291. 329p. 1994. 45.00 (*0-924674-30-X*) Am Coll Phys Execs.

New Leadership 101: Inspirational Quotes & Insights for Leaders. John C. Maxwell. 160p. 1997. pap. 6.99 (*1-56292-369-2*) Honor Bks OK.

New Leadership Paradigm: Social Learning & Cognition in Organizations. Henry P. Sims, Jr. & Peter Lorenzi. 320p. 1992. text 52.00 (*0-8039-4297-4*); pap. text 24.00 (*0-8039-4298-2*) Sage.

New Leaf. large type ed. Jill Roe. LC 97-23512. 310p. 1997. 22.95 (*0-7862-1070-2*) Thorndike Pr.

New Leaf. large type ed. Jill Roe. (Ulverscroft Large Print Ser.). 368p. 1997. 27.99 (*0-7089-3817-5*) Ulverscroft.

New Leaf Mills. William Dean Howells. (Notable American Authors Ser.). 1992. reprint ed. lib. bdg. 75.00 (*0-7812-3261-9*) Rprt Serv.

New Leafing: A Journey from Grief. Doreen Gandy. LC 85-70002. (Illus.). (Orig.). 1985. pap. 5.95 (*0-9614529-0-0*) Celilo Pubns.

*__New Learning.__ Robert-Jan Simons et al. LC 00-38939. 2000. write for info. (*0-7923-6296-9*, Kluwer Plenum) Kluwer Academic.

New Learning Environment. Harold L. Cohen & James Filipczak. LC 70-151108. (Jossey-Bass Behavioral Science Ser.). 220p. reprint ed. pap. 68.20 (*0-608-14901-2*, 202566800045) Bks Demand.

New Learning Environment: A Case for Learning. Harold L. Cohen & James Filipczak. LC 70-151108. (Illus.). xxviii, 192p. reprint ed. pap. 19.95 (*0-9623311-3-9*) Authors Coop.

New Learning for Older Americans. Roger DeCrow. 1975. 5.75 (*0-88379-011-4*) A A A C E.

New Learning Medicine. 14th ed. Contrib. by Peter Richards & Simon Stockill. 148p. 1997. pap. 19.00 (*0-7279-1155-4*, Pub. by BMJ Pub) Login Brothers Bk Co.

New Learning Tool I for Little Learners: Easy Adding & Subtracting Tables. Art Roberts. (Illus.). (J). (gr. 1-2). 1995. text 7.99 (*1-887252-04-5*) Kids Success Learn.

New Learning Tool II for Young Learners: Easy Multiplying & Dividing Tables. Art Roberts. (Illus.). 2p. (J). (gr. 3-5). 1995. text 7.99 (*1-887252-05-3*) Kids Success Learn.

New Lease on Life: Facing the World after a Suicide Attempt. John A. Chabot. LC 96-35265. 224p. 1997. pap. 14.95 (*1-57749-009-6*) Fairview Press.

New Lease on Life: Landlords, Tenants & Immigrants in Ireland & Canada. Catharine A. Wilson. (McGill-Queen's Studies in Ethnic History). (Illus.). 336p. 1994. 49.95 (*0-7735-1117-2*, Pub. by McG-Queens Univ Pr) CUP Services.

New Lease on Love. Shannon Waverly. (Romance Ser.: No. 204). 1992. per. 2.89 (*0-373-03204-8*, 1-03204-4) Harlequin Bks.

New Leash on Death. Susan Conant. 1990. mass mkt. 5.99 (*0-425-14622-7*) Berkley Pub.

New Leaves: Studies & Translations of Japanese Literature in Honor of Edward Seidensticker. Ed. by Aileen Gatten & Anthony H. Chambers. LC 91-48341. (Michigan Monographs in Japanese Studies: No. 11). x, 283p. (C). 1993. 39.95 (*0-939512-56-4*) U MI Japan.

New Left: A Collection of Essays. Ed. by Priscilla Long. LC 69-15528. (Extending Horizons Ser.). (Illus.). 500p. (C). 1969. 6.00 (*0-87558-042-4*); pap. 3.00 (*0-87558-043-2*) Porter Sargent.

New Left & Labor in the 1960s. Peter B. Levy. LC 93-30844. (Illus.). 328p. 1994. text 49.95 (*0-252-02074-X*); pap. text 16.95 (*0-252-06367-8*) U of Ill Pr.

New Left & the Cultural Revolution of the 1960's: A Reevaluation. L. H. Gunn & Peter Duignan. LC 94-48832. (Hoover Essays Ser.: No. 10). 49p. 1995. pap. 5.00 (*0-8179-3732-3*) Hoover Inst Pr.

New Left Diplomatic Histories & Historians: The American Revisionists. rev. ed. Joseph M. Siracusa. (Topics in Diplomatic History Ser.). 132p. 1993. 21.95 (*0-941690-46-6*); pap. 11.95 (*0-941690-47-4*) Regina Bks.

New Left in Canada. 2nd ed. Dimitrios J. Roussopoulos. LC HN0018.R6. (Black Rose Bks.: Vol. 1). 156p. 1971. reprint ed. pap. 48.40 (*0-608-00457-X*, 206127600007) Bks Demand.

New Left in France: The Unified Socialist Party, 9. Charles Hauss. LC 77-94753. (Contributions in Political Science Ser.: No. 9). (Illus.). 283p. 1978. 65.00 (*0-313-20113-7*, HNL/, Greenwood Pr) Greenwood.

New Left, New Right, & the Legacy of the Sixties. Paul Lyons. LC 96-13397. 256p. (C). 1996. pap. 22.95 (*1-56639-478-3*) Temple U Pr.

New Left, New Right, & the Legacy of the Sixties. Paul Lyons. LC 96-13397. 256p. (C). 1996. 69.95 (*1-56639-477-5*) Temple U Pr.

New Legal Dynamics of European Union. Ed. by Jo Shaw & Gillian More. 376p. 1996. text 70.00 (*0-19-825980-8*) OUP.

*__New Legal Order in Hong Kong.__ Raymond Wacks. 687p. 1999. (*962-209-507-0*) HK Univ Pr.

*__New Legal Order in Hong Kong.__ Ed. by Raymond Wacks. (Law Ser.). 710p. 1999. pap. 45.00 (*962-209-508-9*, Pub. by HK Univ Pr) Coronet Bks.

New Legends. Ed. by Greg Bear. 384p. 1995. 22.95 (*0-312-85930-9*, Pub. by Tor Bks) St Martin.

New Legends. Ed. by Greg Bear. 384p. 1996. pap. 13.95 (*0-312-86201-6*) Tor Bks.

New Leisure Challenges for the Schools. Eugene T. Lies. 1982. 24.95 (*0-8434-0425-6*) McGrath NH.

New Lepidoptera Records for the Blue Mountains of Eastern Oregon. David G. Grimble et al. (Illus.). 16p. 1998. reprint ed. pap. 2.60 (*0-89904-901-X*, Wildlife Resrch Grp) Crumb Elbow Pub.

New Lesbian Criticism: Literary & Cultural Readings. Ed. by Sally Munt. (Between Men - Between Women Ser.). 256p. 1992. pap. 18.50 (*0-231-08019-0*); text 57.50 (*0-231-08018-2*) Col U Pr.

New Lesbian Studies: Into the Twenty-First Century. 2nd ed. Ed. by Bonnie Zimmerman et al. LC 95-50927. 320p. (C). 1996. pap. 17.95 (*1-55861-136-3*) Feminist Pr.

New Lesbian Studies: Into the Twenty-First Century. 2nd ed. Ed. by Bonnie Zimmerman & Toni A. McNaron. LC 95-50927. 320p. (C). 1996. lib. bdg. 35.00 (*1-55861-135-5*) Feminist Pr.

New Lesbian Writing. Margaret Cruikshank. LC 83-22603. 220p. 1984. pap. 7.95 (*0-912516-81-X*) Grey Fox.

New Lessons from Old Projects: The Workings of Rural Development in Northeast Brazil. Operations Evaluation Department Staff, World Bank. LC 93-14543. (Operations Evaluation Studies). 126p. 1993. pap. 22.00 (*0-8213-2512-4*, 12512) World Bank.

New Let There Be Neon. Rudi Stern. (Illus.). 160p. 1996. reprint ed. pap. 29.95 (*0-944094-16-3*) ST Pubns.

New Letter of Notable Contents. Gabriel Harvey. LC 73-26389. (English Experience Ser.: No. 193). 38p. 1969. reprint ed. 15.00 (*90-221-0193-2*) Walter J Johnson.

New Letters. James Russell Lowell. (Notable American Authors Ser.). 1999. reprint ed. lib. bdg. 125.00 (*0-7812-3902-8*) Rprt Serv.

New Letters, 2 vols., Set. Thomas Carlyle. (BCL1-PR English Literature Ser.). 1992. reprint ed. lib. bdg. 150.00 (*0-7812-7487-7*) Rprt Serv.

New Letters, 2 vols., Set. Thomas Carlyle. (Anglistica & Americana Ser.: No. 42). (Illus.). 1969. reprint ed. 150.00 (*0-685-66442-2*, 05102525) G Olms Pubs.

New Letters, Vol. 53, No. 3. James McKinley. (Illus.). 128p. 1987. pap. 4.00 (*0-317-64815-2*) New Letters MO.

New Letters: A Book of Translations. Ed. by David Ray. (New Letters Ser.). (Illus.). 184p. (Orig.). 1985. pap. 4.00 (*0-938652-09-5*) New Letters MO.

New Letters & Memorials of Jane Welsh Caryle, 2 vols., Set. Jane B. Carlyle. Ed. by Alexander Carlyle. LC 78-37672. (Illus.). 1983. reprint ed. 150.00 (*0-404-56724-X*) AMS Pr.

New Letters, Fall, 1985, Vol. 52, No. 1. Ed. by David Ray. (Illus.). 136p. 1985. pap. 4.00 (*0-317-44322-4*) New Letters MO.

New Letters, Fall, 1984, Vol. 51, No. 1. Ed. by David Ray. (Illus.). 1984. pap. 4.00 (*0-317-17179-8*) New Letters MO.

New Letters, Fall, 1987, Vol. 54, No. 1. Ed. by James McKinley et al. (Illus.). 126p. 1987. write for info. (*0-318-62726-4*) New Letters MO.

New Letters, Fall, 1986, Vol. 53, No. 1. James McKinley. (Illus.). 119p. 1986. pap. 4.00 (*0-317-62345-1*) New Letters MO.

New Letters from Hiroshima. Alex Kuo. 1974. 3.00 (*0-912678-14-3*, Greenfld Rev Pr) Greenfld Rev Lit.

New Letters of Abigail Adams, 1788-1801. Abigail S. Adams. (American Biography Ser.). 281p. 1991. reprint ed. lib. bdg. 69.00 (*0-7812-8005-2*) Rprt Serv.

New Letters of Berlioz, 1830-1868. Hector Berlioz. Tr. & Intro. by Jacques Barzun. LC 75-100144. 322p. 1974. reprint ed. lib. bdg. 35.00 (*0-8371-3251-7*, BENL, Greenwood Pr) Greenwood.

New Letters of Thomas Carlyle, 2 vols., Set. Thomas Carlyle. Ed. by Alexander Carlyle. LC 75-108465. (Illus.). 1970. reprint ed. 49.00 (*0-403-00204-4*) Scholarly.

New Letters Reader I: Reader One. Ed. by David Ray. (New Letters Ser.). 288p. (Orig.). 1983. pap. 7.50 (*0-938652-07-9*) New Letters MO.

New Letters Reader II. Ed. by David Ray. (New Letters Ser.). 288p. (Orig.). 1984. pap. 7.50 (*0-938652-08-7*) New Letters MO.

New Letters, Winter, 1986, Vol. 53, No. 2. James McKinley. (Illus.). 126p. 1986. pap. 4.00 (*0-317-62347-8*) New Letters MO.

New Leviathan: Man, Society, Civilization & Barbarism. Robin George Collingwood. LC 84-19284. 387p. 1984. reprint ed. lib. bdg. 55.50 (*0-313-24621-1*, CONL, Greenwood Pr) Greenwood.

New Leviathan: Or Man, Society, Civilization & Barbarism. 2nd rev. ed. R. G. Collingwood. Ed. by David Boucher. 584p. 1999. pap. text 29.95 (*0-19-823880-0*) OUP.

New Leviathan: or Man, Society, Civilization & Barbarism. Robin George Collingwood. LC 83-45423. reprint ed. 40.00 (*0-404-20066-4*) AMS Pr.

New Leviathan: or Man, Society, Civilization & Barbarism. 2nd rev. ed. Robin George Collingwood. LC 92-17771. 586p. 1993. text 95.00 (*0-19-823981-5*, Clarendon Pr) OUP.

New Lexicon Webster's Dictionary of the English Language: Deluxe Encyclopedia Edition. Ed. by Bernard S. Cayne. (Illus.). 2064p. 1987. 14.95 (*0-7172-4546-2*) Lexicon Pubns.

New Lexicon Webster's Dictionary of the English Language: Encyclopedia Edition, 2 vols., Set, Vols. 1 & 2. Ed. by Bernard S. Cayne. (Illus.). 1987. write for info. (*0-7172-4547-0*) Lexicon Pubns.

New Lexicon Webster's Dictionary of the English Language: One Volume Encyclopedia Edition. Ed. by Bernard S. Cayne. (Illus.). 1504p. 1987. write for info. (*0-7172-4535-7*) Lexicon Pubns.

New Liberalism: The Political Economy of J. A. Hobson. John Allett. LC 82-136586. 287p. reprint ed. pap. 89.00 (*0-8357-8247-6*, 203398300088) Bks Demand.

*__New Liberalism: The Rising Power of Citizen Groups.__ Jeffrey M. Berry. LC 98-40248. 4p. 1999. 24.95 (*0-8157-0908-0*) Brookings.

New Libertarian Gospel: Pitfalls of the Theology of Liberation. Juan G. Gutierrez. 109p. 1977. 3.49 (*0-8199-0682-4*, Frncscn Herld) Franciscan Pr.

New Liberty Bell: A Bicentennial Anthology of American Choral Music. Ed. & Intro. by James G. Smith. LC 76-373. (Illus.). 1976. pap. 7.95 (*0-916656-00-4*, MF276) Mark Foster Mus.

New Library: Seventeen Discussion-Reviews of Books, Vol. 3. John P. Cavarnos. Ed. by Constantine Cavarnos. LC 95-75903. (Illus.). 120p. 1995. 15.00 (*1-884729-05-3*); pap. 7.50 (*1-884729-06-1*) Inst Byzantine.

New Library Vol. 1: Reviews & Discussions of Over Fifty Books of Modern Greek, Russian & Other Writers - Ancient, Byzantine & Modern Greek - Eastern Orthodox Christianity, Byzantine Art & Hellenism. Constantine Cavarnos. LC 89-80265. 176p. 1989. 15.00 (*0-914744-81-X*); pap. 7.95 (*0-914744-82-8*) Inst Byzantine.

New Library Vol. 2: Summaries & Discussions of Thirty Books of or about Byzantine & Modern Writers, Greeks & Russians, in the Fields of Philosophy, Literature & Christian Religion. Constantine Cavarnos. LC 89-80265. (Illus.). 211p. 1992. pap. 9.50 (*1-884729-12-6*) Inst Byzantine.

New Library Buildings: 1976 Issue: Years 1973-1974. Ed. by Herbert D. Ward. LC Z 0679.N39. (Illus.). 279p. reprint ed. pap. 86.50 (*0-608-20960-0*, 207183200002) Bks Demand.

New Library Key. 3rd ed. Margaret G. Cook. LC 75-11754. (Illus.). 264p. (C). 1975. pap. 10.00 (*0-8242-0541-3*) Wilson.

New Library Legacy. Ed. by Susan Lee. (New Library Ser.: Vol. 2). 200p. 1998. pap. 59.95 (*1-55570-294-5*) Neal-Schuman.

New Lies for Old. rev. ed. Anatoliy Golitsyn. LC 90-82477. 448p. 1990. reprint ed. pap. 14.95 (*0-9626646-1-8*) Soundview Pubns.

New Lies for Old: An ex-KGB Officer Warns How Communist Deception Threatens Survival of the West. Anatoliy Golitsyn. 420p. 1984. reprint ed. pap. 15.00 (*0-945001-08-8*) GSG & Assocs.

New Lies for Old: An ex-KGB Officer Warns How Communist Deception Threatens Survival of the West. unabridged ed. Anatoliy Golitsyn. 420p. 1984. reprint ed. 23.00 (*0-945001-13-4*) GSG & Assocs.

New Lieutenant. Philip McCutchan. LC 97-10026. 1997. text 20.95 (*0-312-15604-9*) St Martin.

New Lieutenant. large type ed. Philip McCutchan. LC 97-13095. 266p. 1997. pap. 20.95 (*0-7862-1127-X*) Thorndike Pr.

New Life see Vida Nueva: Babes in Arms

New Life. Bernard Malamud. 208p. 1995. pap. 12.95 (*0-14-018681-6*, Penguin Classics) Viking Penguin.

New Life. Orhan Pamuk. Tr. by Guneli Gun. LC 96-45722. 296p. 1997. 24.00 (*0-374-22129-4*) FS&G.

New Life. Orhan Pamuk. Tr. by Guneli Gun. LC 97-35622. 1998. pap. 13.00 (*0-375-70171-0*) Vin Bks.

New Life. Vern Rutsala. LC 97-31167. 1978. pap. 2.00 (*0-932264-20-4*) Trask Hse Bks.

New Life. Wally Swist. LC 97-69739. 72p. 1998. 24.00 (*1-887628-07-X*) Plinth Bks.

New Life. Wally Swist. LC 97-69739. 78p. 1998. pap. 12.00 (*1-887628-06-1*) Plinth Bks.

New Life. Dante Alighieri.Tr. of La/Vita Nuova. 77p. reprint ed. 39.00 (*0-932051-68-5*) Rprt Serv.

New Life. rev. ed. A. R. Knight & Gordon H. Schroeder. 1971. pap. 4.00 (*0-8170-0120-4*) Judson.

New Life: Being a Gay Man in the Era of HIV. Aydin Tozeren. LC 97-5626. 190p. 1997. 48.50 (*0-7618-0716-0*); pap. 28.50 (*0-7618-0717-9*) U Pr of Amer.

New Life: New Room. June Jordan. LC 73-9755. (Illus.). 64p. (J). (gr. 3-5). 1975. lib. bdg. 12.89 (*0-690-00212-2*) HarpC Child Bks.

New Life: Pregnancy, Birth & Your Child's First Year. Ed. by John T. Queenan & Carrie N. Queenan. 1986. 24.95 (*0-316-72892-6*) Little.

New Life: Pregnancy, Birth, & Your Child's First Year - A Comprehensive Guide. 2nd rev. ed. Ed. by John T. Queenan & Carrie N. Queenan. (Illus.). 240p. 1992. 29.45 (*0-316-72878-0*) Lppncott W & W.

New Life: Stories & Photographs from the Suburban South. Alex Harris. (Illus.). 240p. 1996. 29.95 (*0-393-04030-5*) Norton.

*__New Life: The Only Way to Win.__ Eric Ronald Jackson. 72p. 1999. pap. 10.00 (*0-9643374-4-4*) PBLSH.

New Life: The Sunday Paper's Baptism Book. Gretchen W. Pritchard. (Illus.). 80p. (Orig.). (J). (gr. k-6). 1986. pap. 5.75 (*0-9614022-2-9*) Sunday Paper.

New Life - Same Husband. Romaine Wismer. (Illus.). 100p. (Orig.). 1987. pap. 5.95 (*0-9617021-2-5*) R Wismer.

New Life (Adult) 1980. 1.00 (*0-918403-16-2*) Agape Ministries.

New "Life after Death" Religion. Charles R. Smith. 1980. pap. 1.50 (*0-88469-125-X*) BMH Bks.

N

An Asterisk (*) at the beginning of an entry indicates that the title is appearing for the first time.

New Life at Ground Zero: New York, Home Ownership, & the Future of American Cities. Charles J. Orlebeke. LC 97-27654. (Illus.). 300p. 1997. 42.95 (*0-914341-52-9*, Rockefeller Inst Pr); pap. 18.95 (*0-914341-51-0*, Rockefeller Inst Pr) Nelson Rockefeller Inst Govt.

*__New Life Bible: With Salvation Plan.__ New Life Inc. Staff. 2000. pap. 4.99 (*0-8297-2405-2*) Vida Pubs.

New Life Bible Study Series: Grow in Grace & the Knowledge of Our Lord & Saviour Jesus Christ, Vol. 1. Beverly Smith. 63p. 1998. pap. text. write for info. (*0-9669859-0-7*) Beverly Smith.

New Life Community Choir Featuring John P. Kee: Show Up! Ed. by Jeannette DeLisa. 88p. (YA). 1995. pap. text 16.95 (*0-89724-923-2*, PF9531) Wrner Bros.

New Life Cookbook: Based on the Health & Nutritional Philosophy of the Edgar Cayce Readings. Marceline N. Peet. LC 97-31082. 180p. 1998. pap. 12.95 (*0-87604-400-3*, 522) ARE Pr.

New Life for Dying Churches. Rose G. Sims. (SPA.). 1998. pap. text 8.95 (*1-882415-03-5*) New Life Church.

New Life for Dying Churches: It Can Happen Anywhere! 4th rev. ed. Rose G. Sims. LC 89-61121. Orig. Title: The Dream Lives On. 176p. 1992. reprint ed. pap. 10.95 (*0-917851-51-X*) New Life Church.

New Life for Dying Churches: Seminar Guide Book. Rose G. Sims. Ed. by Ken Anderson, Sr. (Illus.). 64p. 1992. pap., student ed. 3.95 (*1-882415-00-0*) New Life Church.

New Life for Dying Churches Seminar: Church Growth Seminar, 5 bks., Set. Rose G. Sims. Ed. by Ken Anderson, Sr. 1992. pap., student ed. 69.95 incl. VHS (*1-882415-01-9*) New Life Church.

New Life for Joanna. large type ed. Iris Bromige. 1986. 15.95 (*0-7089-1538-8*) Ulverscroft.

New Life for Sir Christopher. 2nd ed. Richard M. Wainwright. (Illus.). 48p. 1998. reprint ed. 17.00 (*0-9619566-4-X*) Family Life.

New Life for the College Curriculum: Assessing Achievements & Furthering Progress in the Reform of General Education. 2nd ed. Jerry G. Gaff. LC 91-19068. (Higher & Adult Education Ser.). 293p. 1991. text 36.45 (*1-55542-392-2*) Jossey-Bass.

New Life for the Elderly: God's Vision to a Home Care Provider. Rose Reyes. LC 96-119674. 112p. (Orig.). 1994. pap. 8.00 (*0-9636577-1-2*) Trego-Hill.

New Life for the Old, Old Story: A Guide for Developing Story Sermons. Amanda J. Burr. 150p. 1989. 25.00 (*0-945253-06-0*) Thornsbury Bailey Brown.

New Life for Toby. Nancy F. Rivers. LC 97-73252. 80p. (Orig.). (J). (gr. 3-4). 1997. pap. 9.95 (*1-57736-052-4*, Hillsboro Pr) Providence Hse.

New Life for Women. 2nd ed. Daisy Osborn. (RUS., Illus.). (Orig.). 1995. reprint ed. mass mkt. write for info. (*1-890863-07-6*) Wrld Wide Print.

New Life for Your Sunday School. James H. Robinson. 78p. (Orig.). 1995. pap. 19.99 (*0-8100-0564-6*, 09N0935) Northwest Pub.

New Life in Action. Marilyn Ganskow. 94p. 1973. pap., wbk. ed. 10.00 (*1-928712-09-6*) New Life Series.

New Life in Christ see Instrucciones para una Nueva Vida en Cristo

New Life in Christ. (Discipleship Ser.). 48p. 1992. pap. 5.99 (*0-310-54761-X*) Zondervan.

New Life in Christ. Una Conran. (C). 1988. 60.00 (*0-85439-131-2*, Pub. by St Paul Pubns) St Mut.

New Life in Christ. George B. Eager. LC 86-62669. (Illus.). 163p. 1987. pap. text 5.95 (*0-9603752-6-0*) Mailbox.

New Life in Christ. Adam L. Richardson, Sr. 37p. (Orig.). 1995. pap. text 10.00 (*0-9657431-0-1*) Chrstian Life Bible.

New Life in Christ: Christ My Hope of Glory. Leanna Courtney. 188p. (Orig.). 1997. pap. 10.00 (*1-57502-378-4*, PO1202) Morris Pubng.

New Life in Christ: Study Guide. Forrest L. Bivens & David Vallesky. Ed. by William E. Fischer. (Bible Class Course for Young Adults Ser.). 120p. (Orig.). 1986. pap. text 8.00 (*0-938272-07-1*, 07N2161) WELS Board.

New Life in Christ: Teacher's Guide. Forrest L. Bivens & David Vallesky. (Bible Class Course for Young Adults Ser.). 40p. (Orig.). 1986. pap. text 8.00 (*0-938272-03-9*, 07-2162) WELS Board.

*__New Life in Christ: Workbook for New Believers.__ Jim Starr. (Discipleship Series). 126p. (Orig.). 2000. pap. 2.50i (*1-930264-02-X*) True Jesus.

New Life in Christ Jesus. C. I. Scofield. 1975. pap. 3.25 (*0-915374-41-2*, 41-2) Rapids Christian.

New Life in God's World. Doris Willis. (Bible Board Book Ser.). 1997. pap. 1.19 (*0-687-03125-7*) Abingdon.

New Life in Jesus: Lent. Judi H. Winkowski. (C). 1990. text 40.00 (*0-85439-290-4*, Pub. by St Paul Pubns) St Mut.

New Life in the Neighborhood: How Persons with Retardation & Other Disabilities Can Help Make a Good Community Better. Robert Perske. LC 80-15517. (Illus.). 80p. (Orig.). 1997. pap. 3.59 (*0-687-27800-7*) Abingdon.

New Life Insurance Investment Advisor: Achieving Financial Security for You & Your Family Through Today's Insurance Product, Revised Edition. 2nd rev. ed. Ben G. Baldwin. LC 94-172094. 350p. 1994. text 24.95 (*1-55738-512-2*, Irwn Prfssnl) McGraw-Hill Prof.

New Life Journal: A Pathway to Strength & Serenity. New Life Clinics Staff. 128p. 1998. 14.99 (*0-8407-9702-8*) Nelson.

New Life Manifesto. Seth D. King. 180p. 1994. pap. 14.00 (*0-9640837-0-1*) Vice Press.

New Life Manifesto. 2nd ed. Seth D. King. 214p. 1994. pap. 16.00 (*0-9640837-1-X*) Vice Press.

New Life Manifesto. 3rd ed. Seth D. King. 216p. pap. 15.00 (*0-9640837-2-8*) Vice Press.

New Life Naturally: The Home Guide to Harmonious Health. Margery P. Childs. 152p. 1995. pap. 9.95 (*1-885857-14-4*) Four Wnds Pubng.

New Life, New Land. Ann Crawford. (Illus.). 48p. (J). 1997. 8.95 (*1-57168-004-7*, Eakin Pr) Sunbelt Media.

New Life, New Lifestyle. Green. pap. 7.95 (*0-340-56311-7*, Pub. by Hodder & Stought Ltd) Trafalgar.

New Life of Dante. Stephen Bemrose. 224p. 1999. 75.00 (*0-85989-583-1*, Pub. by Univ Exeter Pr); pap. 22.95 (*0-85989-584-X*) Univ Exeter Pr.

New Life of Virginea: Being the Second Part of Nova Britannia. Robert Johnson. LC 73-17167. (English Experience Ser.: No. 332). 52p. 1971. reprint ed. 20.00 (*90-221-0332-3*) Walter J Johnson.

New Life Source Book. (Pathways Through Science Ser.). 1994. pap. text. write for info. (*0-582-09425-9*, Pub. by Addison-Wesley) Longman.

New Life Tables for Latin American Populations in the Nineteenth & Twentieth Centuries, Vol. 3. Eduardo E. Arriaga. LC 76-4841. (Population Monograph: No. 3). (Illus.). 1976. reprint ed. lib. bdg. 55.00 (*0-8371-8827-X*, ARLT, Greenwood Pr) Greenwood.

New Life (Youth) 1980. 1.00 (*0-918403-18-9*) Agape Ministries.

New Lifestyle for Health & Happiness. Bernard Jensen. 1980. pap. 12.99 (*0-932615-06-6*) B Jensen.

New Lifetime Reading Plan. 4th ed. Clifton Fadiman & John S. Major. LC 96-49838. 400p. 1997. 24.00 (*0-06-270208-4*) HarpC.

New Lifetime Reading Plan: The Classic Guide to World Literature. 4th rev. exp. ed. Clifton Fadiman & John S. Major. LC 97-2975. 400p. 1999. pap. 14.00 (*0-06-272073-2*) HarpC.

New Light & Truth: The Making of the Revised English Bible. Roger Coleman. (Illus.). 96p. 1989. 5.00 (*0-19-101441-9*) OUP.

*__New Light from the Ancient Greek Bible.__ 2nd ed. George Morrish. (GRE.). 297p. 1998. pap. 8.95 (*0-86585-001-1*) Wm Carey Intl.

New Light from the Prophets. Finklestein. Date not set. 14.50 (*0-85303-023-5*, Pub. by M Vallentine & Co) Intl Spec Bk.

*__New Light on Alcoholism: God, Sam Shoemaker & A. A.__ 2nd rev. ed. B., Dick. LC 98-92124. (History of Early A.A.'s Spiritual Roots Ser.: Vol. 9). Orig. Title: New Light on Alcoholism: The A. A. Legacy from Sam Shoemaker. 638p. 1999. pap. 24.95 (*1-885803-27-3*, 996) Paradise Res Inc.

New Light on Alcoholism: The A. A. Legacy from Sam Shoemaker see New Light on Alcoholism: God, Sam Shoemaker & A. A.

New Light on Boswell: Critical & Historical Essays on the Occasion of the Bicentenary of the Life of Johnson. Ed. by Greg Clingham. (Illus.). 255p. (C). 1991. text 69.95 (*0-521-38047-2*) Cambridge U Pr.

New Light on Chaco Canyon. Ed. by David G. Noble. LC 84-10506. (Exploration Ser.). (Illus.). 108p. 1984. pap. 14.95 (*0-933452-10-1*) Schol Am Res.

*__New Light on Dark Stars: Red Dwarfs, Low-Mass Stars, Brown Dwarfs.__ Neill Reid & Suzanne L. Hawley. LC 99-49519. (Praxis Bks.). 415p. 2000. pap. 146.00 (*1-85233-100-3*) Spr-Verlag.

New Light on Delinquency & Its Treatment: Results of a Research Conducted for the Institute of Human Relations, Yale University. William Healy & Augusta F. Bronner. LC 79-90525. 226p. 1969. reprint ed. lib. bdg. 65.00 (*0-8371-2253-8*, HENL) Greenwood.

New Light on Early & Medieval Japanese Historiography: Two Translations & an Introduction. John A. Harrison. LC 60-62605. (University of Florida Monographs: Social Sciences: No. 4). 51p. reprint ed. pap. 30.00 (*0-7837-4986-4*, 204465300004) Bks Demand.

New Light on Early Buddhism. B. G. Gokhale. LC 94-900098. (C). 1994. 22.50 (*81-7154-572-6*, Pub. by Popular Prakashan) S Asia.

New Light on Early Farming. Ed. by Jane Renfrew. 1991. text 95.00 (*0-7486-0131-7*, Pub. by Edinburgh U Pr) Col U Pr.

New Light on Eighteenth-Century Literary Sources: Proceedings of the Eighteenth-Century Tryon Palace Symposium. Ed. by Lynn V. Sadler. (Illus.). (Orig.). 1989. pap. text 5.00 (*1-878304-01-1*) Methodist Coll Pr.

New Light on Galaxy Evolution. Ed. by Ralf Bender & Roger L. Davies. LC 96-246. 482p. 1996. lib. bdg. 179.00 (*0-7923-3975-4*) Kluwer Academic.

New Light on George Fox & Early Quakerism. Ed. by Richard Bailey. LC 92-27477. 368p. 1992. text 99.95 (*0-7734-9829-X*) E Mellen.

New Light on George Fox, 1624-1691. Michael Mullett. 1999. pap. 24.00 (*1-85072-142-4*, Pub. by W Sessions) St Mut.

New Light on Longfellow: With Special Reference to His Relations with Germany. James T. Hatfield. LC 70-114097. (Illus.). 196p. (C). 1970. reprint ed. 50.00 (*0-87752-050-X*) Gordian.

New Light on Medieval Aberdeen. J. S. Smith. 80p. 1986. pap. text 9.95 (*0-08-032449-5*, Pub. by Aberdeen U Pr) Macmillan.

New Light on Old Masters. Ernst H. Gombrich. LC 85-31797. (Illus.). 192p. (C). 1998. 54.00 (*0-226-30219-9*); pap. 25.00 (*0-226-30220-2*) U Ch Pr.

New Light on Tantra: Accounts of Some Tantras, Both Hindu & Buddhist, Alchemy in Tantra, Tantric Therapy, List of Unpublished Tantras, Etc. (C). 1992. 60.00 (*81-85094-56-X*, Pub. by Punthi Pus) S Asia.

New Light on the Early History of the Greater Northwest, 3 vols., Set. Alexander Henry. (BCL1 - History - Canada Ser.). 1991. reprint ed. lib. bdg. 225.00 (*0-7812-6372-7*) Rprt Serv.

New Light on the Gospels. 2nd ed. Omraam M. Aivanhov. (Izvor Collection: Vol. 217). 181p. 1985. pap. 7.95 (*2-85566-339-3*, Pub. by Prosveta) Prosveta USA.

New Light on the Old Testament: Some Factors Shaping Ancient Palestine. Allen H. Godbey. 136p. 1998. reprint ed. spiral bd. 20.00 (*1-885395-74-4*) Book Tree.

New Light on the Renaissance Displayed in Contemporary Emblems. Harold Bayley. LC 67-23851. (Illus.). 288p. 1972. reprint ed. 24.95 (*0-405-08244-4*, Pub. by Blom Pubns) Ayer.

New Light on the Shepherd Psalm. William S. Deal. 1982. pap. 3.95 (*0-317-00334-8*) Crusade Pubs.

New Light on the Strength of Gear Teeth. A. B. Cox. (Technical Papers: Vol. P70A). (Illus.). 36p. 1932. pap. text 30.00 (*1-55589-264-7*) AGMA.

New Light on William Harvey. W. Pagel. (Illus.). 200p. 1975. 78.50 (*3-8055-2209-6*) S Karger.

New Light School. Jan Frichot. 50p. (Orig.). 1993. pap. text. write for info. (*1-879121-00-X*) New Light Prods.

New Lights on Piers Plowman. Allan H. Bright. 1984. reprint ed. 19.00 (*0-403-01320-8*) Scholarly.

New Linguistic & Exegetical Key to the Greek New Testament. Cleon L. Rogers, 3rd & Cleon L. Rogers, Jr. LC 97-45109. 896p. 1998. 39.99 (*0-310-20175-6*) Zondervan.

New Links Between General Education & Business Careers. Russell G. Warren. (Liberal Learning & Careers Ser.). 31p. 1983. pap. 6.00 (*0-911696-15-6*) Assn Am Coll.

New Links with Shakespeare. Etwell A. Barnard. LC 73-153301. reprint ed. 32.50 (*0-404-00655-8*) AMS Pr.

New Literacy: Moving Beyond the 3 Rs. Paul J. Morris & Stephen N. Tchudi. LC 96-25189. 1996. 30.95 (*0-7879-0292-6*) Jossey-Bass.

New Literacy: Moving Beyond the 3Rs. Paul J. Morris, II & Stephen Tchudi. LC 98-33552. 288p. 1998. pap. text 20.00 (*0-9663233-4-3*, 323343) Calendar Islands.

New Literary Continents: Selected Papers of the Fifth Annual NDEA Seminar on Foreign Area Studies Held February, 1981. Rosette C. Lamont et al. (CNL/World Report Ser.: Vol. 1). 68p. 1984. pap. 4.95 (*0-918680-25-5*) Griffon House.

New Literary Criticism & the Hebrew Bible. Ed. by J. Cheryl Exum & David J. Clines. LC 94-992. 276p. (C). 1994. pap. 18.00 (*1-56338-079-X*) TPI PA.

New Literary Criticism & the Hebrew Bible. Ed. by J. Cheryl Exum & David J. A. Clines. (JSOT Supplement Ser.: No. 143). 276p. 1993. 80.00 (*1-85075-424-1*, Pub. by Sheffield Acad) CUP Services.

New Literary Criticism & the New Testament. Ed. by Elizabeth S. Malbon & Edgar V. McKnight. (Journal for the Study of the New Testament, Supplement Ser.: Vol. 109). 276p. 1994. 80.00 (*1-85075-510-8*, Pub. by Sheffield Acad) CUP Services.

New Literary Criticism & the New Testament. Edgar V. McKnight & Elizabeth S. Malbon. LC 94-41734. 400p. 1994. pap. 20.00 (*1-56338-107-9*) TPI PA.

New Literary Histories: New Historicism & Contemporary Criticism. Colebrook. LC 97-11953. 208p. 1997. pap. 27.95 (*0-7190-4987-3*, Pub. by Manchester Univ Pr) St Martin.

New Literary Histories: New Historicism & Contemporary Criticism. Colebrook. LC 97-11953. 208p. 1998. 59.95 (*0-7190-4986-5*, Pub. by Manchester Univ Pr) St Martin.

New Literary History International Bibliography of Literary Theory & Criticism (1984-85) Ed. by Ralph Cohen & Jeffrey M. Peck. LC 88-3016. xix, 188p. 1989. text 32.00 (*0-8018-3687-5*) Johns Hopkins.

New Literary Values. David Daiches. LC 68-54342. (Essay Index Reprint Ser.). 1977. 18.95 (*0-8369-0358-7*) Ayer.

New Literature on Fetal Alcohol Exposure & Effects: A Bibliography, 1983-1988, 4. Compiled by Ernest L. Abel. LC 89-28641. (Bibliographies & Indexes in Medical Studies: No. 4). 245p. 1990. lib. bdg. 65.00 (*0-313-27329-4*, ANL/, Greenwood Pr) Greenwood.

New Literatures in English. Chaman Nahal. 225p. 1986. 24.00 (*81-7023-056-X*, Pub. by Allied Pubs) S Asia.

*__New Little Cabin.__ Maria D. Wilkes. (J). 2001. pap. write for info. (*0-06-442109-0*, HarpTrophy); lib. bdg. write for info. (*0-06-028554-0*) HarpC Child Bks.

New Liturgy, Old Heresy. T. Robert Ingram. LC 81-52116. (Orig.). 1981. pap. 4.50 (*0-686-75087-X*) St Thomas.

*__New Lives for Old.__ Margaret Mead. 2000. pap. 16.00 (*0-06-095806-5*) HarpC.

New Lives in the Valley: Slate Quarries & Quarry Villages in North Wales, New York, & Vermont. Gwilym R. Roberts. (Illus.). x, 470p. 1998. 23.95 (*0-9668292-0-4*) RM Dist.

New Lives, New Loves. Carolyn Keene. (Nancy Drew on Campus Ser.: No. 1). (J). (gr. 8 up). 1995. mass mkt. 3.99 (*0-671-52737-1*, PB Trade Paper) PB.

*__New Living, Hans Richter 1930.__ Arthur Rlegg. (Illus.). 160p. 2000. 60.00 (*3-907078-22-5*) Lars Muller.

New Living Heart. Michael E. Debakey. LC 97-365. (Illus.). xvi, 495 p. 1997. pap. text 18.95 (*1-55850-722-1*) Adams Media.

New Living Heart Diet. rev. ed. Michael E. DeBakey et al. LC 95-40787. (Illus.). 416p. 1996. per. 16.00 (*0-684-81188-X*, Fireside) S&S Trade Pap.

New Living Qabalah. Will Parfitt. 1995. pap. 19.95 (*1-85230-682-3*, Pub. by Element MA) Penguin Putnam.

New Living Spaces. (Home Repair & Improvement Ser.). (Illus.). 136p. 1977. 14.60 (*0-8094-2374-X*); lib. bdg. 20.60 (*0-8094-2375-8*) Time-Life.

New Living Spaces. Time-Life Books Editors. LC 96-152. (Home Repair & Improvement Ser.). (Illus.). 128p. (gr. 11). 1999. spiral bd. 14.95 (*0-7835-3901-0*) Time-Life.

New Living Translation: Gospel of John, 25. John Gospel. 1997. pap. 22.25 (*0-8423-4572-8*) Tyndale Hse.

New Living Translation Pew Bible, Blue. Bible Pew Staff. 1997. 10.99 (*0-8423-3346-0*) Tyndale Hse.

New Living Translation Pew Bible, Burgundy. 1997. 10.99 (*0-8423-3347-9*) Tyndale Hse.

New Local Centers in Centralized States. Ed. by Peter H. Merkl. (Illus.). 356p. (Orig.). 1985. pap. text 29.00 (*0-8191-4536-X*) U Pr of Amer.

New Local Level Politics in East Africa: Studies on Uganda, Tanzania & Kenya. Per Tidemand et al. LC 96-233085. (Research Reports: Vol. 95). 119p. 1994. pap. text 16.95 (*91-7106-348-X*) Transaction Pubs.

New Localism: Comparative Urban Politics in a Global Era. Ed. by Edward G. Goetz & Susan E. Clarke. (Focus Editions Ser.: Vol. 164). (Illus.). 288p. (C). 1993. text 59.95 (*0-8039-4921-9*); pap. text 26.00 (*0-8039-4922-7*) Sage.

*__New Logevity Dier.__ Henry Mallek. 224p. 2001. 23.95 (*0-399-14628-8*) Putnam Pub Group.

New Logos & Trademark Design. Ed. by Pie Editorial Staff. 1998. 69.95 (*4-89444-081-4*, Pub. by Pie Bks) Bks Nippan.

New London. John L. Ruddy. (Images of America Ser.). (Illus.). 128p. 1998. pap. 16.99 (*0-7524-0949-2*) Arcadia Publng.

*__New London Garden.__ George Carter. (Illus.). 208p. 2000. 45.00 (*1-84000-347-2*, Pub. by Mitchell Beazley) Antique Collect.

New London Property Guide, 1998: The Only Guide to Buying & Selling, Renting & Letting Homes in London. Carrie Segrave. 720p. 1998. pap. 25.00 (*1-84000-073-2*, Pub. by Conran Octopus) Antique Collect.

*__New London Property Guide 1999-2000: The Only Guide You Need to Buying & Selling, Renting & Letting Homes in London.__ Carrie Segrave. (Illus.). 672p. 1999. pap. 25.00 (*1-84000-184-4*, Pub. by Mitchell Beazley) Antique Collect.

*__New London Property Guide 2001.__ 672p. 2000. 19.95 (*1-84000-242-5*, Pub. by Mitchell Beazley) Antique Collect.

New London Raid. Walter L. Powell. (Illus.). (C). Date not set. pap. write for info. (*1-57747-059-1*) Thomas Publications.

New Long Poem Anthology. Ed. by Sharon Thesen. LC 92-245261. 384p. 1991. pap. 26.95 (*0-88910-407-7*, Pub. by Talonbks) Genl Dist Srvs.

New Longman Literature: Doctor Faustus. Christopher Marlowe. 1995. pap. text. write for info. (*0-582-25409-4*, Pub. by Addison-Wesley) Longman.

New Look: Design in the Fifties. Lesley Jackson. LC 91-65322. (Illus.). 160p. (Orig.). 1998. reprint ed. pap. 27.50 (*0-500-27644-7*, Pub. by Thames Hudson) Norton.

New Look: The Dior Revolution. Nigel Cawthorne. 1998. 19.99 (*0-7858-0963-5*) Bk Sales Inc.

New Look at an Old Book. Rubin Gorewitz. (Illus.). 16p. (J). (gr. 1-4). 1998. pap. 6.00 (*0-8059-4424-9*) Dorrance.

New Look at Authentic Metals '95. McGraw Hill Staff. 1997. VHS 25.94 (*0-07-079476-6*) McGraw.

New Look at Black Families. 4th ed. Charles V. Willie. LC 90-86405. 272p. 1991. pap. text 16.95 (*0-930390-10-5*); lib. bdg. 36.95 (*0-930390-11-3*) Gen Hall.

*__New Look at Culture & Nature Conservation in Africa.__ Charles J. Kara. LC 99-97495. 2000. pap. 8.95 (*0-533-13399-8*) Vantage.

New Look at Ethics & Fraud: Participant's Workbook. Courtenay M. Thompson, Jr. 31p. 1988. pap. text 25.00 (*0-89413-186-9*, A7329) Inst Inter Aud.

New Look at Ethics & Fraud: Videotape & Discussion Leader's Guide. Institute of Internal Auditors Staff. 17p. 1988. pap. text 695.00 (*0-89413-180-X*, A6558) Inst Inter Aud.

New Look at Grace. Bill Huebsch. LC 87-51566. 160p. 1988. pap. 9.95 (*0-89622-355-8*) Twenty-Third.

New Look at Great Standards: Intermediate Piano. Arranged by Bill Irwin. (Creative Concepts Library). 1998. 14.95 (*1-56922-166-9*, 07-2048) Creat Cncpts.

New Look at Houseplants. Ed. by Tovah Martin. (Illus.). 96p. 1994. pap. 7.95 (*0-945352-81-6*) Bklyn Botanic.

New Look at Leadership: Charting a Course for the 21st Century. LaSalle R. Vaughn. 168p. 1997. 21.95 (*1-886065-01-2*) N Life Christian.

New Look at Love. Elaine Hatfield & G. William Walster. LC 85-17957. (Illus.). 224p. 1985. reprint ed. pap. text 21.00 (*0-8191-4957-8*) U Pr of Amer.

New Look at Porfolio Management. David M. Ahlers. Ed. by Edward I. Altman & Ingo I. Walter. LC 76-10448. (Contemporary Studies in Economic & Financial Analysis: Vol. 5). 250p. 1977. 78.50 (*0-89232-012-5*) Jai Pr.

New Look at Postgraduate Failure. E. Rudd. 144p. 1985. pap. 38.00 (*1-85059-009-5*) Taylor & Francis.

New Look at Prayer: Searching for Bliss. Bill Huebsch. LC 90-71136. 136p. (Orig.). 1991. pap. 7.95 (*0-89622-458-9*) Twenty-Third.

New Look at Preaching, Vol. 7. Walter J. Burghardt et al. 164p. 1989. pap. 24.00 (*0-86217-074-5*, Pub. by Veritas Pubns) St Mut.

New Look at Schools. Daniel Greenberg. 142p. 1992. pap. 10.00 (*1-888947-03-9*) Sudbury Valley.

New Look at Segovia, Vol. 1. Gerard Garno & Graham Wade. LC 98-111173. 508p. 1997. pap. 49.95 (*0-7866-2366-7*, MB95769) Mel Bay.

New Look at Segovia, Vol. 2. Gerard Garno & Graham Wade. LC 98-111173. 504p. 1997. pap. 49.95 (*0-7866-2611-9*, MB96473) Mel Bay.

New Look at Segovia, His Life, His Magic, V2 CD. Gerard Garno & Graham Wade. 1997. 64.95 incl. cd-rom (*0-7866-2800-6*, 96473COP) Mel Bay.

New Look at Segovia, His Life, His Music. Gerard Garno. 508p. 1997. pap. 64.95 incl. cd-rom (*0-7866-2527-9*, 95769CDP) Mel Bay.

New Look at Sixteenth-Century Counterpoint. Margarita Merriman. LC 81-40924. (Illus.). 230p. (Orig.). 1982. lib. bdg. 56.00 (*0-8191-2391-9*) U Pr of Amer.

An Asterisk (*) at the beginning of an entry indicates that the title is appearing for the first time.

New Look at Social Cogniton in Groups: A Special Issue of Basic & Applied Social Psychology. Ed. by Leigh Thompson. 80p. 1998. pap. write for info. (*0-8058-9975-8*) L Erlbaum Assocs.

New Look at Some Old Mechanisms in Human Newborns: Taste & Tactile Determinants of State, Affect, & Action. Elliott M. Blass & Vivian Ciaramitaro. (Monographs of the Society for Research in Child Development: No. 239). 112p. 1994. pap. text 15.00 (*0-226-05699-6*) U Ch Pr.

New Look at the American West: Lessons for Secondary History & Literature Classes. Gloria Eastman & Barbara Miller. 238p. 1995. pap. 22.50 (*0-89994-384-5*) Soc Sci Ed.

New Look at the Commonwealth. A. M. Walker. 1978. 69.00 (*0-08-021823-7*, Pub. by Pergamon Repr) Franklin.

New Look at the Dinosaurs. Alan Charig. 1985. 29.95 (*0-87196-139-3*) Facts on File.

New Look at the Lutheran Confession. Holsten Fagerberg. Tr. by Gene J. Lund. 336p. 1981. pap. 16.95 (*0-570-03223-7*, 15-2121); pap. 21.00 (*0-570-04499-5*, 15-2121) Concordia.

New Look at the Old Earth: What the Creation Institutes Are Not Telling You about Genesis. Don Stoner. 192p. (C). 1992. pap. 9.95 (*1-881446-00-X*) Schroeder Pub.

New Look at the Sacraments. 2nd ed. William J. Bausch. LC 82-74313. 300p. 1983. pap. 12.95 (*0-89622-174-1*) Twenty-Third.

New Look at the Scoring Phenomena of Gears. B. W. Kelley. (Technical Papers: Vol. P219.04). (Illus.). 17p. 1952. pap. text 30.00 (*1-55589-249-3*) AGMA.

New Look at Tumour Immunology. Ed. by A. J. McMichael & W. F. Bodmer. (Cancer Surveys Ser.: Vol. 13). (Illus.). 208p. (C). 1992. text 66.00 (*0-87969-370-3*) Cold Spring Harbor.

New Look at Vegetables. (Illus.). 96p. 1993. pap. 7.95 (*0-945352-78-6*) Bklyn Botanic.

New Look at Vegetarianism. Sukhraj S. Dhillon. 60p. (YA). (gr. 7-12). 1993. pap. 6.95 (*1-57515-029-8*) PPI Pubng.

New Look at Wormgear Hobbing. E. Wildhaber. (Technical Papers: Vol. P129.10). (Illus.). 17p. 1954. pap. text 30.00 (*1-55589-157-8*) AGMA.

New Look for Needlework, Embroidery & Cross Stitch. Ondori Publishing Company Staff. (Illus.). 112p. (Orig.). 1983. pap. 13.95 (*0-87040-568-3*) Japan Pubns USA.

New Look into the Old Book: A Look into the Bible to Be in Health. Ruth Lascelle. 230p. (C). 1998. pap. text 13.00 (*0-9654519-0-9*) Bedrock Pub.

New Look Mercury Retrograde. Robert Wilkinson. LC 97-14603. (Illus.). 224p. 1997. pap. 14.95 (*1-57863-013-4*) Weiser.

New Look of Corporate Performance Measurement. 1994. 495.00 (*0-85058-775-1*) Economist Intell.

New Looks at Italian Opera: Essays in Honor of Donald J. Grout. Ed. by William W. Austin. LC 76-1010. (Illus.). 290p. 1976. reprint ed. lib. bdg. 35.00 (*0-8371-8761-3*, AUNL, Greenwood Pr) Greenwood.

New Loricifera from Southeastern United States Coastal Waters. Robert P. Higgins & Reinhardt M. Kristensen. LC 85-600264. (Smithsonian Contributions to Zoology Ser.: No. 438). 74p. reprint ed. pap. 30.00 (*0-608-17142-5*, 202731200055) Bks Demand.

***New Lots.** John Clarkson. 2001. mass mkt. 6.99 (*0-8125-6476-6*) Tor Bks.

New Lots: A Novel. John Clarkson. LC 98-19395. 320p. 1998. 24.95 (*0-312-85242-8*, Pub. by Forge NYC) St Martin.

New Lottie Moon Story. 2nd ed. Catherine B. Allen. 320p. 1997. pap. text 12.95 (*1-56309-225-5*, W974118) Womans Mission Union.

New Love. Mab G. Hoover. (Serenade Serenata Ser.: No. 34). 1986. pap. 1.49 (*0-310-47212-1*) Zondervan.

New Low-Cholesterol Gourmet. Lynn Fischer & W. Virgil Brown. LC 87-43101. 1988. 18.45 (*0-13-615139-6*) P-H.

New Low-Country Cooking: 125 Recipes for Southern Cooking with Innovative Style. Marvin Woods. LC 99-57545. (Illus.). 240p. 2000. 25.00 (*0-688-17205-9*, Wm Morrow) Morrow Avon.

New Low-Fat Favorites. Ruth Spear. 320p. 1998. pap. 13.95 (*0-316-80686-2*) Little.

New Low Fat This for That: A Cooks Handbook of Savvy Substitutions. Meryl Nelson. (Illus.). 138p. 1998. pap. 7.95 (*0-941090-07-X*) This N That.

New Loyalist Index, Vol. 1. Paul J. Bunnell. 525p. (Orig.). 1989. pap. 38.50 (*1-55613-234-4*) Heritage Bk.

New Loyalist Index, Vol. 2. Paul J. Bunnell. xii, 218p. 1996. pap. 22.00 (*0-7884-0400-8*, B844) Heritage Bk.

New Loyalist Index Vol. 3: Including Cape Cod & Islands, Massachusetts, New Hampshire, New Jersey & New York Loyalists. Paul J. Bunnell. 195p. 1998. pap. 21.00 (*0-7884-0987-5*, B859) Heritage Bk.

New Lyrics. Sarah Lockwood. LC 72-77822. (Living Poets' Library). pap. 2.50 (*0-686-02576-8*) Dragons Teeth.

New Macdesigner's Handbook. 2nd ed. Alastair Campbell. (Illus.). 192p. 1997. spiral bd. 27.50 (*0-7624-0206-7*) Running Pr.

New Machiavelli. H. G. Wells. Ed. by Norman MacKenzie. 320p. 1994. pap. text 7.95 (*0-460-87422-5*, Everyman's Classic Lib) Tuttle Pubng.

New Machiavelli see Works of H. G. Wells

***New Machiavelli: The Art of Politics in Business.** Alistair McAlpine. LC 98-21069. 256p. 1998. 24.95 (*0-471-29564-7*) Wiley.

***New Machiavelli: The Art of Politics in Business.** Alistair McAlpine. 224p. 1999. pap. 16.95 (*0-471-35095-8*) Wiley.

***New Macrame.** Katie DuMont. (Illus.). 2000. 24.95 (*1-57990-163-8*) Lark Books.

***New Macrame: Contemporary Knotted Jewelry & Accessories.** Katie DuMont. LC 99-37032. (Illus.). 128p. 2000. 18.95 (*1-57990-127-1*) Lark Books.

New Macroeconomics: Imperfect Markets & Policy Effectiveness. Ed. by Huw Dixon & Neil Rankin. (Illus.). 402p. (C). 1995. pap. text 25.95 (*0-521-47947-9*) Cambridge U Pr.

New Macrolides, Azalides & Streptogramin in Clinical Practice. Acar et al. Ed. by Harold C. Neu et al. (Infectious Disease & Therapy Ser.: Vol. 18). (Illus.). 568p. 1995. text 190.00 (*0-8247-9311-0*) Dekker.

New Macrolides, Azalides, & Streptogramins: Pharmacology & Clinical Applications. Lowell S. Young et al. Ed. by Harold C. Neu & Stephen H. Zinner. (Infectious Disease & Therapy Ser.: Vol. 8). (Illus.). 256p. 1993. text 155.00 (*0-8247-9038-3*) Dekker.

New Macromolecular Architecture & Functions: Proceedings of the Oums '95 Toyonaka, Osaka, Japan, 2-5 June, 1995. Mikiharu Kamachi & Akira Nakamura. LC 96-43179. 1996. write for info. (*0-387-61473-7*) Spr-Verlag.

New Macromolecular Architecture & Functions: Proceedings of the Oums '95 Toyonaka, Osaka, Japan, 2-5 June, 1995. Mikiharu Kamchi & Akira Nakamura. LC 96-43179. (Illus.). 218p. 1996. 236.00 (*3-540-61473-7*) Spr-Verlag.

New Madrid County, Missouri Court Orders, 1816-1825. T.L.C. Genealogy Staff. 89p. (Orig.). 1991. pap., spiral bd. 11.00 (*1-886633-28-2*) TLC Genealogy.

New Madrid Earthquake. Myron Fuller. (Earthquake Ser.: No. 7). (Illus.). 120p. 1993. reprint ed. pap. 15.95 (*0-934426-49-X*, Gutenberg-Richter) NAPSAC Reprods.

New Madrid Earthquakes. rev. ed. James L. Penick. LC 81-50531. 192p. (C). 1981. pap. 16.95 (*0-8262-0344-2*) U of Mo Pr.

New Madrid Fault Finders Guide: Maps & Directions for a Self-Guided Tour of Earthquake Features Still Visible Today from the New Madrid Quakes of 1811-12. David Stewart & Ray Knox. LC 91-91491. (Earthquake Ser.: No. 4). (Illus.). 180p. (Orig.). 1995. pap. 16.95 (*0-934426-42-2*, Gutenberg-Richter) NAPSAC Reprods.

New Madrid Run. Michael Reisig. 312p. 1998. mass mkt. 5.95 (*0-9651240-1-0*) Clear Creek Pr.

New Magdalen. Wilkie Collins. LC 93-26285. (Pocket Classics Ser.). 1993. pap. 8.95 (*0-7509-0455-0*, Pub. by Sutton Pub Ltd) Intl Pubs Mktg.

New Magic: Bev Doolittle. Bev Doolittle & Elise Maclay. LC 95-15087. 86p. 1995. 30.00 (*0-553-10104-8*) Bantam.

New Magician's Manual. Walter B. Gibson. LC 73-87046. (Illus.). 159p. 1975. reprint ed. pap. 8.95 (*0-486-23113-5*) Dover.

***New Magik Handbook: Simple Spells for a Complex World.** Dragonstar Staff. (Illus.). 150p. 2000. pap. 14.95 (*1-892062-19-4*) Inner Light.

New Magnet Marketing: The Fast-Track Strategy to Put Your Company on Top. rev. ed. John R. Graham. 288p. 1998. pap. 16.95 (*1-886284-24-5*, Pub. by Chandler Hse) Natl Bk Netwk.

New Magus see New Millennium Magic: A Complete System of Self-Realization

New Mahayana: Buddhism for a Post-Modern World. Ryomin Akizuki. Tr. by James W. Heisig & Paul L. Swanson from JPN. LC 90-83802. 208p. 1991. pap. 15.00 (*0-89581-900-7*) Asian Humanities.

New Maine Cooking: The Healthful New Country Cuisine. Jean A. Pollard. (Illus.). 288p. 1996. reprint ed. pap. 15.95 (*0-89272-388-2*) Down East.

New Maine Writing Two. Ed. by Constance Hunting & Lee Sharkey. 124p. 1979. pap. 3.50 (*0-685-04189-1*) Puckerbrush.

New Maintenance Strategies: Organizing, Implementing & Managing Effective Mill Programs. Ed. by Ken L. Patrick. (Illus.). 223p. 1992. pap. 49.00 (*0-87930-189-9*) Miller Freeman.

***New Maiolica: Contemporary Approaches to Colour & Technique.** Matthias Ostermann. (Illus.). 160p. 1999. text. write for info. (*90-5703-562-6*, Pub. by Craftsman House) Gordon & Breach.

***New Maiolica: Contemporary Approaches to Colour & Technique.** Matthias Ostermann. LC 99-20674. 1999. 39.95 (*0-8122-3513-4*) U of Pa Pr.

New Majority: A Look at What the Preponderance of Women in Journalism Education Means to the Schools & to the Professions. Maurine H. Beasley & Kathryn T. Theus. LC 88-2456. 186p. (Orig.). (C). 1988. pap. text 21.00 (*0-8191-6915-3*) U Pr of Amer.

New Majority: Toward a Popular Progressive Politics. Stanley B. Greenberg. 352p. 1999. pap. text 17.95 (*0-300-07862-5*) Yale U Pr.

New Majority: Toward a Popular Progressive Politics. Ed. by Stanley B. Greenberg & Theda Skocpol. LC 97-61147. 352p. 1998. 30.00 (*0-300-07341-0*) Yale U Pr.

New Majority or Old Minority? The Impact of the Republicans on Congress. Ed. by Colton C. Campbell & Nicol C. Rae. LC 98-54157. 256p. 1999. 65.00 (*0-8476-9168-3*); pap. 19.95 (*0-8476-9169-1*) Rowman.

New Making It on Your Own. 2nd rev. ed. Dorothy I. Ansell. Ed. by Samuel M. Cauldwell & Jeannette R. Insley. (Illus.). 92p. (YA). (gr. 7-12). 1995. spiral bd. 25.00 (*1-878848-55-0*, 237) Natl Res Ctr.

New Making of a Cook: The Art, Techniques, & Science of Good Cooking. Madeleine Kamman. Ed. by Pamela Hoenig. LC 96-37452. (Illus.). 832p. 1997. 40.00 (*0-688-15254-6*, Wm Morrow) Morrow Avon.

New Maladies of the Soul. Julia Kristeva. Tr. by Ross M. Guberman from FRE. LC 94-32204. 236p. 1995. 41.50 (*0-231-09982-7*) Col U Pr.

New Maladies of the Soul. Julia Kristeva. 242p. 1997. pap. 17.50 (*0-231-09983-5*) Col U Pr.

New Male Sexuality. rev. ed. Bernie Zilbergeld. LC 99-12946. 432p. 1999. pap. 13.95 (*0-553-38042-7*) Bantam.

***New Mamluks: Egyptian Society & Modern Feudalism.** Amira El Azhary Sonbol. LC 00-35820. (Middle East Studies Beyond Dominant Paradigms). 2000. 19.95 (*0-8156-2845-5*) Syracuse U Pr.

New Mammoth Book of Crossword Puzzles. Richard Manchester. 1997. pap. text 12.95 (*0-88486-173-2*, Bristol Park Bks) Arrowood Pr.

New Mammoth Book of Seek-a-Word. Richard B. Manchester. 416p. 1998. pap. 12.95 (*0-88486-210-0*, Bristol Park Bks) Arrowood Pr.

***New Mammoth Book of Seek-A-Word.** 2nd ed. Richard Manchester. 416p. 2000. pap. 13.95 (*0-88486-279-8*, Bristol Park Bks) Arrowood Pr.

New Mammoth Book of Word Games. Richard Manchester. 1997. pap. text 12.95 (*0-88486-174-0*, Bristol Park Bks) Arrowood Pr.

***New Mammoth Book of Word Games.** 2nd ed. Richard Manchester. 416p. 2000. pap. 13.95 (*0-88486-278-X*, Bristol Park Bks) Arrowood Pr.

New Man. Thomas Merton. 256p. 1999. pap. 13.00 (*0-374-51444-5*) FS&G.

New Man. Thomas Merton. 184p. 1994. pap. 21.00 (*0-7855-2734-6*, Pub. by Srch Pr) St Mut.

New Man: Twenty-Nine Years a Slave, Twenty-Nine Years a Free Man, Recollections of H. C. Bruce. H. C. Bruce. LC 96-9626. (Blacks in the American West Ser.). (Illus.). xxvii, 165p. 1996. pap. 10.00 (*0-8032-6132-2*, Bison Books) U of Nebr Pr.

New Man: 29 Years a Slave, 29 Years a Free Man. Henry C. Bruce. LC 72-89421. (Black Heritage Library Collection). 1977. 18.95 (*0-8369-8526-5*) Ayer.

New Man & Other Stories. Hunter. Date not set. pap. text. write for info. (*0-17-555986-4*) Addison-Wesley.

New Man in Soviet Psychology. Raymond A. Bauer. LC 52-5385. (Harvard University, Russian Research Center Studies: No. 7). 255p. reprint ed. pap. 79.10 (*0-608-30588-X*, 201768300007) Bks Demand.

New Man in Town. Lyn Cote. No. 66. 1999. per. 4.50 (*0-373-87066-3*, 1-87066-6, Harlequin) Harlequin Bks.

New Management. 4th ed. Robert M. Fulmer. 806p. (C). 1987. pap. 61.38 (*0-02-339360-2*, Macmillan Coll) P-H.

New Management: Bringing Democracy & Markets Inside Organizations. William E. Halal. LC 96-7027. 204p. 1998. reprint ed. pap. 19.95 (*1-57675-032-9*) Berrett-Koehler.

New Management: Democracy & Enterprise Are Transforming Organizations. William E. Halal. LC 96-7027. 300p. 1996. 29.95 (*1-881052-53-2*) Berrett-Koehler.

New Management: Readings & Perspectives. Ed. by Rob Paton. LC 95-40497. 304p. 1996. mass mkt. 27.95 (*0-415-13987-2*) Routledge.

New Management: Readings & Perspectives. Ed. by Rob Paton et al. LC 95-40497. 304p. 1996. pap. 79.95 (*0-415-13986-4*) Thomson Learn.

New Management Accounting. William F. Christopher. Ed. by Bill Christopher. LC 97-68250. (Management Library: No. 9). 88p. 1997. pap. 12.95 (*1-56052-444-8*) Crisp Pubns.

New Management Challenge: Information Systems for Improved Performance. Ed. by David Boddy et al. 160p. 1988. lib. bdg. 57.50 (*0-7099-5084-5*) Routledge.

New Management Handbook. xx, 156p. 1997. pap., teacher ed. 20.00 (*1-889236-02-0*) New Mgmt CA.

New Management in Human Services. 2nd ed. Ed. by Paul R. Keys & Leon H. Ginsberg. LC 88-28922. 279p. (C). 1995. 31.95 (*0-87101-251-0*, 2510) Natl Assn Soc Wkrs.

New Management of Life. J. D. De Raadt. LC 97-52027. (Toronto Studies in Theology: Vol. 75). 152p. 1998. text 69.95 (*0-7734-8508-2*) E Mellen.

New Management of Local Government. John Stewart. (Institute of Local Government Studies). 224p. (C). 1987. text 55.00 (*0-04-352232-7*); pap. text 18.95 (*0-04-352233-5*) Routledge.

New Management Paradigm: A Review of Principles & Practices. Arnold S. Levine & Jeff Luck. LC 94-28874. 1994. pap. 13.00 (*0-8330-1571-0*, MR-458-AF) Rand Corp.

New Management Reader. Paton. 1996. pap. write for info. (*1-86152-200-2*) Thomson Learn.

New Management Reader. Rob Paton. 304p. 1996. pap. 27.95 (*1-86152-201-0*) Thomson Learn.

New Manager. Chris Elgood. (Financial Times Management Briefings Ser.). 1997. pap. 89.50 (*0-273-63200-0*) F T P-H.

New Manager. Alfred Tack. 300p. 1988. text 43.95 (*0-566-02754-2*, Pub. by Gower) Ashgate Pub Co.

New Managerial Mentor: Becoming a Learning Leader to Build Communities of Purpose. Patricia J. Fritts. LC 98-25919. 240p. 1998. 27.95 (*0-89106-120-7*, 7793, Pub. by Consulting Psychol) Natl Bk Netwk.

New Managerial Mindsets: Organizational Transformation & Strategy Implementation. Michael A. Hitt. LC 98-28119. 370p. 1999. 60.95 (*0-471-98667-4*) Wiley.

New Managerialism: Administrative Reform in Whitehall & Canberra. Spencer M. Zifcak. LC 94-229. (Public Policy & Management Ser.). 1994. 118.00 (*0-335-19305-6*); pap. 39.95 (*0-335-19304-8*) OpUniv Pr.

New Manager's Guide to Success. James R. Baehler. LC 80-19509. 147p. 1980. 52.95 (*0-275-91684-7*, C1684, Praeger Pubs) Greenwood.

New Manager's Handbook. Brad L. Thompson. LC 94-143. (Briefcase Bks.). 288p. 1994. pap. 13.95 (*0-7863-0206-2*, Irwn Prfssnl) McGraw-Hill Prof.

New Manager's Survival Manual. 2nd ed. Clay Carr. LC 94-34049. 261p. 1995. 69.95 (*0-471-10986-X*); pap. 19.95 (*0-471-10987-8*) Wiley.

New Mandate: Democratic Choices for a Prosperous Economy. Louis A. Ferleger & Jay R. Mandle. LC 93-40157. 168p. 1994. 29.95 (*0-8262-0940-8*) U of Mo Pr.

***New Mannerist Tricycle.** Lisa Jarnot et al. 44p. 2000. write for info. (*0-9667655-5-9*, Pub. by Beautifulswimmer) SPD-Small Pr Dist.

New Manners & Customs of Bible Times see Nuevo Manual de Usos y Costumbres de los Tiempos Biblicos

New Manners & Customs of Bible Times. Ralph Gower & Fred H. Wight. 29.99 (*0-8024-5954-4*, 226) Moody.

***New Manners & Customs of the Bible.** 2nd rev. ed. James M. Freeman. Ed. by Harold J. Chadwick. LC 97-770836. (Illus.). 600p. 1998. pap. 14.99 (*0-88270-745-0*) Bridge-Logos.

New Manual for Managing Dental Office Personnel: A Management Tool for Structuring & Administering Personnel Policies in the Dental Practice. Karen Moawad & Lynne R. Costain. 368p. 1992. 79.95 (*0-87814-372-6*, D4293) PennWell Bks.

New Manual of Astrology. Sepharil. Date not set. pap. text 14.95 (*0-87877-244-8*) Newcastle Pub.

New Manual of Classification. Rita Marcell & Robert Newton. LC 94-172. 304p. 1994. 84.95 (*0-566-07547-4*, Pub. by Gower) Ashgate Pub Co.

New Manual of Interventional Cardiology. unabridged ed. Mark Freed et al. 821p. 1997. text 84.95 (*1-890114-25-1*) Physicians Pr.

New Manual of Interventional Cardiology. 2nd ed. Freed. 1996. 84.95 (*0-9633886-5-7*, F0567) Physicians Pr.

New Manual of Kung Fu. P. Tang. 15.95 (*0-685-63786-7*) Wehman.

New Manufacturing. Harvard Business Review Staff. 150p. 1991. pap. 19.95 (*0-07-103335-1*) McGraw.

New Manufacturing Challenge: Techniques for Continuous Improvement. Kiyoshi Suzaki. 352p. 1987. 40.00 (*0-02-932040-2*) Free Pr.

New Manufacturing Engineer: Coming of Age in an Agile Environment. Michael J. Termini. LC 96-69144. 301p. 1996. text 45.00 (*0-87263-479-5*, 2522) SME.

New Map Graphics in RSAS 5.0. Bruce W. Bennett & Mark C. Hoyer. LC 93-18545. 1993. pap. 9.00 (*0-8330-1337-8*, MR-122-NA) Rand Corp.

New Map of the World: The Poetic Philosophy of Giambattista Vico. Giuseppe Mazzotta. LC 98-26421. 1999. 45.00 (*0-691-00180-4*, Pub. by Princeton U Pr) Cal Prin Full Svc.

New Maps of Hell. Kingsley Amis. LC 74-15944. (Science Fiction Ser.). 161p. 1977. reprint ed. 21.95 (*0-405-06321-0*) Ayer.

New Marine Aquarium: Step-by-Step Setup & Stocking Guide. Michael S. Paletta. Ed. by James Lawrence. LC 98-34407. (Illus.). 144p. 1999. pap. 19.95 (*1-890087-52-1*) Microcosm Ltd.

New Maritimes Seasonal Cooking: Delicious Recipes for Light & Healthy Meals Year Round. Donna Young & Marg Routledge. (Illus.). 294p. 1999. pap. 19.95 (*1-55209-390-5*) Firefly Bks Ltd.

New Market. Don Trosper & Janet Haag. (History of Tumwater Ser.: Vol. 2). (Illus.). 70p. 1987. reprint ed. pap. 6.00 (*1-890717-01-0*) Tumwater Hist.

New Market & Arabia: An Examination of the Descent of Racers & Coursers. Roger D. Upton. (Illus.). xi, 211p. 1987. reprint ed. pap. text 36.00 (*3-487-08283-7*) G Olms Pubs.

New Market Campaign, May 1864. 22.95 (*0-8488-1542-4*, Evergreen NY) Amereon Ltd.

New Market Timing Techniques: Innovative Studies in Markets Rhythm & Price Exhaustion. Thomas R. DeMark. LC 97-19962. (Trading Advantage Ser.). 368p. 1997. 69.95 (*0-471-14978-0*) Wiley.

New Market Wizards: Conversations with America's Top Traders. Jack D. Schwager. LC 95-20314. 512p. 1995. 39.95 (*0-471-13236-5*) Wiley.

New Market Wizards: Conversations with America's Top Traders. Jack D. Schwager. LC 92-52612. 512p. 1994. reprint ed. pap. 15.00 (*0-88730-667-5*, HarpBusn) HarpInfo.

New Market Wizards: Wall Street's Best Advice for Making Money in Tough Times. Jack D. Schwager. LC 92-52612. 448p. 1992. 25.00 (*0-88730-587-3*, HarpBusn) HarpInfo.

New Marketing. Richard Brookes. 200p. 1988. text 65.95 (*0-566-02677-5*, Pub. by Gower) Ashgate Pub Co.

New Marketing Era: Marketing to the Imagination in a Technology-Driven World. Paul Postma. LC 98-34857. 176p. 1998. 19.95 (*0-07-052675-3*) McGraw.

New Marketing Opportunities: The Business & Trade Directory for the New Age - Visionary Marketplace. 7th ed. Ed. by Sophia Tarila. 550p. 1999. pap. text 139.95 (*0-944773-18-4*) New Editions Intl.

New Marketing Paradigm. Don E. Schultz et al. LC 93-44563. (Illus.). 240p. 1995. pap. 19.95 (*0-8442-3452-4*, NTC Business Bks) NTC Contemp Pub Co.

New Marketing Practice: Rules for Success in a Changing World. David Mercer. 304p. 1997. pap. 19.95 (*0-14-024078-0*, Pub. by Pnguin Bks Ltd) Trafalgar.

New Marketing Research Systems: How to Use Strategic Database Information for Better Marketing Decisions. David J. Curry. LC 92-9811. 432p. 1992. 147.50 (*0-471-53058-1*) Wiley.

New Marketing Tool: The Internet. Strauss & Frost. (C). 1997. pap. text 12.40 (*0-13-852469-6*) P-H.

***New Markets: The Untapped Retail Buying Power in America's inner Cities.** 51p. 1999. pap. 5.00 (*0-16-050105-9*) USGPO.

***New Markets, New Opportunities? Economic & Social Mobility in a Changing World.** Nancy Birdsall. LC 99-50451. 1999. pap. 24.95 (*0-8157-0917-X*) Brookings.

N

New Marlboro Stage. Gerald Hausman. (Illus.). 50p. 1972. reprint ed. 15.00 (*0-912846-20-8*); reprint ed. pap. 10.00 (*0-912846-19-4*) Bookstore Pr.

***New Marriage: Transcending the Happily-Ever-After Myth: How to Put Your Relationship Back on Track.** Linda Miles & Robert Miles. 144p. 2000. pap. 19.95 (*1-879384-39-6*) Cypress Hse.

New Marriage, a New Life. Frederic F. Flach. LC 77-27976. xiii, 233 p. 1978. write for info. (*0-07-021250-3*) McGraw.

New Marriage, a New Life: Making Your Second Marriage a Success. rev. ed. Frederic Flach. LC 98-37862. 256p. 1998. pap. 14.95 (*1-57826-017-5*, Pub. by Hatherleigh) Norton.

New Marsupial Frog: Hylidae: Gastrotheca, from the Andes of Ecuador. William E. Duellman & Rebecca A. Pyles. (Occasional Papers: No. 84). 13p. 1980. 1.00 (*0-317-04854-6*) U KS Nat Hist Mus.

New Martinsville Glass, 1900-1944. James Measell. (Illus.). 240p. 1994. pap. 34.95 (*0-915410-85-0*) Antique Pubns.

New Martyrs of the Turkish Yoke. Ed. by St. Nictarios Press Staff. Tr. by Georgia Lizardos et al from GRE. LC 84-50974. 400p. (Orig.). 1985. pap. 17.00 (*0-913026-57-3*) St Nectarios.

New Masonic Music Manual (1907) William H. James. 120p. 1998. reprint ed. pap. 14.95 (*0-7661-0173-8*) Kessinger Pub.

New Masonic Trestle-Board: Adapted to the Work & Lectures As Practiced in the Lodges, Chapters, Councils, & Encampments of Knight Templars in the U. S. A. Charles W. Moore. (Illus.). 207p. 1994. reprint ed. pap. 16.95 (*1-56459-462-9*) Kessinger Pub.

New Mass. Michael Davies. 48p. 1992. reprint ed. pap. text 3.95 (*0-935952-22-5*) Angelus Pr.

New Massage: Total Body Conditioning for People Who Exercise. Gordon Inkeles. LC 92-35864. (Illus.). 192p. 1993. reprint ed. pap. 12.95 (*0-399-51813-4*, Perigee Bks) Berkley Pub.

New Masses: An Anthology of the Rebel Thirties. Joseph North. LC 77-93268. (Illus.). 352p. 1980. pap. 2.25 (*0-7178-0355-4*) Intl Pubs Co.

New Master Course in Hypnotism. Henry Arons. 223p. 1997. pap. 8.95 (*0-87505-420-X*) Borden.

New Masters: Northern Planters During the Civil War & Reconstruction. Lawrence N. Powell. LC 98-30179. (North's Civil War Ser.: No. 9). 300p. 1999. reprint ed. 37.50 (*0-8232-1893-7*); reprint ed. pap. 17.95 (*0-8232-1894-5*) Fordham.

New Materials: Conjugated Double Bond Systems. Ed. by Jan Przyluski & Siegmar Roth. (Materials Science Forum Ser.: Vol. 191). (Illus.). 296p. (C). 1995. 100.00 (*0-87849-695-5*, Pub. by Trans T Pub) Enfield Pubs NH.

New Materials: INDO-Japanese Workshop, 24-26 October 1991, Bangalore, India. Ed. by S. K. Joshi et al. (Illus.). 504p. 1992. 97.95 (*0-387-55290-1*) Spr-Verlag.

New Materials & Profits in Grocery Sacks & Coextrusions: Regional Technical Conference, Holiday Inn, Somerset, New Jersey, March 12-13, 1985. Society of Plastics Engineers Staff. LC TP1185.C6. (Illus.). 215p. reprint ed. pap. 66.70 (*0-608-15131-9*, 202580200046) Bks Demand.

New Materials & Their Applications, 1990: Proceedings of the 2nd International Symposium, University of Warwick, 10-12 April 1990. Ed. by D. Holland. (Institute of Physics Conference Ser.: Vol. 111). (Illus.). 548p. 1990. 247.00 (*0-85498-049-0*) IOP Pub.

New Materials Approaches to Tribology - Theory & Applications Vol. 140: Materials Research Society Symposium Proceedings. Ed. by L. E. Pope et al. (Symposium Proceedings Ser.). 522p. 1989. text 17.50 (*1-55899-013-5*) Materials Res.

New Materials for Advanced Solid-State Lasers Vol. 329: Materials Research Society Symposium Proceedings. Ed. by B. H. Chai et al. LC 94-6659. 299p. 1994. text 30.00 (*1-55899-228-6*) Materials Res.

New Materials for Batteries & Fuel Cells Vol. 575: Materials Research Society Symposium Proceedings. Ed. by D. H. Doughty et al. LC 99-85708. 439p. 2000. text 73.00 (*1-55899-482-3*) Materials Res.

New Materials for Next-Generation Commercial Transports. National Research Council New Materials for Advanc. 98p. (Orig.). 1996. pap. text 29.00 (*0-309-05390-0*) Natl Acad Pr.

New Materials Society: Materials Shifts in the New Society, Vol. 3. (Illus.). 153p. (Orig.). (C). 1994. pap. text 35.00 (*1-56806-656-2*) DIANE Pub.

New Materials Society, Challenges & Opportunities Vol. 1: New Materials Markets & Issues. (Illus.). 150p. (Orig.). (C). 1993. pap. text 45.00 (*0-7881-0146-3*) DIANE Pub.

New Materials Society, Challenges & Opportunities Vol. 2: New Materials Science & Technology. (Illus.). 300p. (Orig.). (C). 1993. pap. text 45.00 (*0-7881-0147-1*) DIANE Pub.

New Math - Or New Myth? Leo Macarow. LC 81-90343. 70p. 1981. pap. text 4.95 (*0-9606994-1-4*) Greenview Pubns.

New Math Workbook for SAT I. 7th ed. Lawrence S. Leff. 1996. pap. 12.95 (*0-8120-9285-6*) Barron.

New Mathematical Diversions. rev. ed. Martin Gardner. LC 95-76293. (MAA Spectrum Ser.). (Illus.). 272p. 1995. reprint ed. pap. 19.95 (*0-88385-517-8*, DIVER) Math Assn.

New Mathematical Framework for the Study of Linkage & Selection. S. Shahshahani. LC 78-23487. (Memoirs of the American Mathematical Society Ser.: No. 211). 34p. 1980. reprint ed. pap. 17.00 (*0-8218-2211-X*, MEMO/17/211C) Am Math.

New Mattheson Studies. Ed. by George J. Buelow & Hans J. Marx. LC 83-5157. 512p. 1984. text 95.00 (*0-521-25115-X*) Cambridge U Pr.

***New Maximarketing.** Rapp. 1999. write for info. (*0-07-134891-3*) McGraw.

New Maximarketing: The New Direction in Advertising, Promotion, & Marketing Strategy. 2nd ed. Stan Rapp & Thomas L. Collins. LC 95-37007. (Illus.). 330p. 1995. 24.95 (*0-07-052033-X*) McGraw.

New Maximarketing Paperback Conversions. Rapp. 1999. 15.95 (*0-07-134251-6*) McGraw.

New Maximize Your Body Potential: Lifetime Skills for Weight Management. 2nd ed. Joyce D. Nash. LC 96-39862. (Illus.). 475p. 1997. pap. text 24.95 (*0-923521-36-4*) Bull Pub.

New Mazal Tov. Rebecca Shore. 1997. 14.95 (*965-229-178-1*, Pub. by Gefen Pub Hse) Gefen Bks.

New McDougall Cookbook. John McDougall. 1997. pap. 13.95 (*0-452-27465-6*, Plume) Dutton Plume.

***New Me.** Amanda Christie. (Seventh Heaven Ser.). (Illus.). 132p. (J). (gr. 4-7). 2000. pap. 3.99 (*0-375-81161-3*, Pub. by Random Bks Yng Read) Random.

***New Me in the New Millennium.** Shawn Dove & Ronald Johnson. iv, 60p. 2000. pap. 5.00 (*0-9678063-0-5*) Dove & Gibbons.

New Meaning of Educational Change. 2nd ed. Michael G. Fullan. 416p. (C). 1991. text 52.00 (*0-8077-3061-0*); pap. text 26.95 (*0-8077-3060-2*) Tchrs Coll.

New Means of Financing International Needs. Eleanor Steinberg et al. LC 77-21275. 270p. reprint ed. pap. 83.70 (*0-608-12601-2*, 202541200043) Bks Demand.

New Measures in Astrology: A Symbolic Basis in Direction. W. Frankland. 132p. 1997. pap. 11.00 (*0-89540-236-X*, SB-236, Sun Bks) Sun Pub.

New Measures of Wage-Earner Compensation in Manufacturing, 1914-57. Albert E. Rees. (Occasional Papers; No. 75). 38p. 1960. reprint ed. 20.00 (*0-87014-389-1*) Natl Bur Econ Res.

New Meatlover's Cookbook: 200 Traditional & Innovative Recipes for Today's Healthy Lifestyle. Janeen A. Sarlin & Diane Porter. LC 96-224739. (Illus.). 320p. 1997. 25.00 (*0-02-860393-1*) Macmillan USA.

New Mecca, New Babylon: Paris & the Russian Exiles, 1920-1945. Robert H. Johnston. 264p. (C). 1988. text 60.00 (*0-7735-0643-8*, Pub. by McG-Queens Univ Pr) CUP Services.

New Media, Vol. 2. Ed. by B. Martin Pedersen. 256p. 1998. 69.95 (*1-888001-42-9*) Graphis US.

New Media: Communication, Research, & Technology. Ronald E. Rice et al. LC 84-3287. (Illus.). 352p. reprint ed. pap. 109.20 (*0-7837-4560-5*, 204408800003) Bks Demand.

***New Media: Dutch Design, 2000 - 2001.** Association of Dutch Design Staff. 152p. 2000. 29.95 (*90-72007-60-3*, Pub. by Bis NLD) Gingko Press.

New Media: Intellectual Property, Entertainment, & Technology Law. James N. Talbott. LC 97-18737. 1997. write for info. (*0-8366-1132-2*) West Group.

New Media & American Politics. Richard Davis & Diana Owen. LC 97-52291. 320p. 1998. 45.00 (*0-19-512060-4*); pap. 19.95 (*0-19-512061-2*) OUP.

New Media & Education: Their Impact on Society. Ed. by Peter H. Rossi & Bruce J. Biddle. LC 66-19580. (Monographs in Social Research: No. 12). 1966. 15.00 (*0-202-09005-1*) Natl Opinion Res.

New Media & Multimedia Developer see CoolCareers.Com

***New Media Companies.** Waterlow Staff. 1000p. 1999. pap. 952.00 (*1-85783-874-2*, Pub. by Waterlow Info Services) Konnect Soft.

New Media for Kids, Vol. 1. Mark H. Cohen. Ed. by Christopher Byrne. 144p. (Orig.). 1997. pap. 24.95 (*0-9655999-0-6*) Market Focus.

New Media Guide to Creative Photography: Image Capture & Printing in the Digital Age. John Carucci. 144p. 1998. pap. 24.95 (*0-8174-5010-6*) Watsn-Guptill.

New Media in Europe: Satellite, Cable, VCR's & Videotex. John Tydeman & Ellen J. Kelm. 272p. 1988. 34.95 (*0-07-084799-1*) McGraw.

New Media in the Late 20th Century Art. Michael Rush. LC 99-70940. (World of Art Ser.). (Illus.). 224p. (Orig.). 1999. pap. 14.95 (*0-500-20329-6*, Pub. by Thames Hudson) Norton.

New Media in the Muslim World: The Emerging Public Sphere. Dale F. Eickelman & Jon W. Anderson. LC 99-12409. (Series in Middle East Studies). 1999. pap. 19.95 (*0-253-21329-0*) Ind U Pr.

New Media New Policies: Media & Communication Strategy for the Future. Richard Collins & Cristina Murroni. LC 96-33130. 233p. (Orig.). 1996. pap. text 25.95 (*0-7456-1786-7*) Blackwell Pubs.

New Media New Policies: Media & Communication Strategy for the Future. Richard Collins & Cristina Murroni. LC 96-33130. 233p. (Orig.). 1996. text 72.95 (*0-7456-1785-9*) Blackwell Pubs.

New Media, New Politics? Fun Satellite Television to the Internet Arab World. Jon B. Alterman. LC 98-44198. (Policy Paper Ser.: No. 48). 1998. pap. 19.95 (*0-944029-28-0*) Wash Inst NEP.

New Media Showcase: The Digital Sourcebook, No. 6. American Showcase Inc. Staff. (Illus.). 266p. 1996. pap. text 29.95 (*0-8230-6516-2*) Watsn-Guptill.

***New Media Showcase 8: The Digital Sourcebook, 1.** American Showcase Inc. Staff. 1998. pap. text 29.95 (*1-887165-24-X*) Am Showcase.

New Media Studies: A Reader. Lisa Taylor & Andrew Willis. 368p. 1999. pap. 32.95 (*0-631-20324-9*) Blackwell Pubs.

New Media Technologies: A Special Issue of the Journal of Mass Media Ethics. Ed. by Clifford G. Christians & Thomas W. Cooper. 72p. 1998. pap. write for info. (*0-8058-9816-6*) L Erlbaum Assocs.

New Media Technology: Cultural & Commercial Perspectives. 2nd ed. John V. Pavlik. LC 97-37599. 450p. 1997. pap. 34.67 (*0-205-27093-X*) Allyn.

***New Media Titles.** Waterlow Staff. 1000p. 1999. pap. 952.00 (*1-85783-869-6*, Pub. by Waterlow Info Services) Konnect Soft.

New Medicaid: Issues & Prospects. Ed. by Frank J. Thompson & John J. DiIulio, Jr. LC 97-45316. 310p. 1997. 36.95 (*0-8157-8450-3*); pap. 14.95 (*0-8157-8451-1*) Brookings.

New Medical Devices: Invention, Development & Use. National Academy of Engineering & the Institute of. 204p. 1988. 34.50 (*0-309-03847-2*); pap. 24.50 (*0-309-03846-4*) Natl Acad Pr.

New Medical Dictionary. 2nd ed. Igakushoin. (ENG & JPN.). 1045p. 1984. 150.00 (*0-8288-1849-5*, F18860) Fr & Eur.

New Medical Encyclopedia: Nueva Enciclopedia Medica, 3 vols. G. Venzmer. (SPA.). 820p. 1980. 150.00 (*0-8288-1880-0*, S34777) Fr & Eur.

New Medical Follies. Morris Fishbein. LC 75-23711. reprint ed. 37.50 (*0-404-13262-6*) AMS Pr.

New Medical Marketplace: A Physician's Guide to Health Care Economics in the 1990s. 2nd rev. ed. Anne M. Stoline et al. 336p. 1993. text 45.00 (*0-8018-4582-3*); pap. text 18.95 (*0-8018-4583-1*) Johns Hopkins.

New Medical Model: A Challenge for Biomedicine? H. Balner. 96p. 1989. pap. 18.00 (*90-265-1067-5*) Swets.

New Medical-Pharmaceutical Dictionary. A. M. Oweida. (ARA & ENG.). 2404p. 1970. 150.00 (*0-8288-6550-7*, M-9766) Fr & Eur.

New Medical Pluralism: Alternative Medicine, Doctors, Patients & the State. Sarah Cant. 1998. 25.95 (*1-85728-511-5*) UCL Pr Ltd.

New Medically Based No-Nonsense Beauty Book. Deborah Chase. 416p. 1990. reprint ed. pap. 8.95 (*0-380-71203-2*, Avon Bks) Morrow Avon.

***New Medications: The Debate over Approval & Access.** Debbie Stanley. LC 00-20571. (Focus on Science & Society Ser.). 2000. 19.95 (*0-8239-3212-5*) Rosen Group.

***New Medications for Drugs of Abuse.** Stanley D. Glick et al. LC 00-30527. (Annals of the New York Academy of Science Ser.). (Illus.). 2000. pap. write for info. (*1-57331-276-2*) NY Acad Sci.

New Medicine. rev. ed. Jeanne Williams. (Illus.). 168p. 1994. 14.95 (*0-937460-90-7*); pap. 8.95 (*0-937460-93-1*) Hendrick-Long.

New Medicine: Reshaping Medical Practice & Health Care Management. Russell C. Coile, Jr. (Health Care Administration Ser.). 420p. 1990. 73.00 (*0-8342-0103-8*) Aspen Pub.

New Medicine & the Old Ethics. Albert R. Jonsen. LC 90-33157. 176p. 1990. 23.50 (*0-674-61725-8*) HUP.

New Medicine & the Old Ethics. Albert R. Jonsen. (Illus.). 192p. (C). 1992. pap. 15.00 (*0-674-61726-6*) HUP.

New Medicine Man: A Different Kind of Health Care for the Elderly. Hugh A. Scott. LC 91-24245. 192p. (Orig.). 1992. pap. 9.95 (*1-56474-004-8*) Fithian Pr.

New Medicine Show. Richard Johnson. 29p. (Orig.). (YA). (gr. 7-12). 1994. pap. 3.00 (*1-57514-154-X*, 3067) Encore Perform Pub.

New Medieval Literatures, Vol. I. Ed. by Wendy Scase et al. (Illus.). 284p. 1998. text 70.00 (*0-19-818389-5*) OUP.

New Medieval Literatures, Vol. II. Ed. by Rita Copeland et al. (Illus.). 290p. 1998. text 82.00 (*0-19-818476-X*) OUP.

***New Medieval Literatures Volume Iii.** Ed. by David Lawton et al. (Illus.). 344p. 2000. text 74.00 (*0-19-818680-0*) OUP.

New Medievalism. Ed. by Marina S. Brownlee et al. LC 91-2927. (Parallax: Re-Visions of Culture & Society Ser.). (Illus.). 312p. 1991. text 50.00 (*0-8018-4171-2*); pap. text 18.95 (*0-8018-4172-0*) Johns Hopkins.

New Mediumship. Grace Cooke. 88p. 1965. pap. 8.95 (*0-85487-068-7*) White Eagle.

New Meeting of the Religions: Interreligious Relationships & Theological Questioning. E. Luther Copeland. LC 99-12735. 195p. 1999. 26.95 (*0-918954-71-1*) Baylor Univ Pr.

New Mellenium: Do You Have the Time? Darlene Dumpit. LC 98-88882. 112p. 1999. pap. 12.95 (*1-56167-464-8*) Am Literary Pr.

New Melville, Vol. 66, No. 1. Cathy N. Davidson. 1994. pap. 10.00 (*0-8223-6407-7*) Duke.

New Member Assimilation: Practical Prevention of Backdoor Loss Through Frontdoor Care. Joel D. Heck. (Orig.). 1988. pap. 8.95 (*0-570-04497-9*, 12-3110) Concordia.

New Members of Congress Almanac: 106th Congress. Hans Johnson et al. (Illus.). 100p. 1998. pap. 19.95 (*1-886222-14-2*, BPD2142) Bernan Pr.

***New Memory Boosters.** Ray Sahelian. 1999. mass mkt. write for info. (*0-312-96909-0*) St Martin.

New Men: Inside the Vatican's Elite School for American Priests. Brian Murphy. LC 97-19620. 320p. 1997. 25.95 (*0-399-14328-9*, Grosset-Putnam) Putnam Pub Group.

New Men: Inside the Vatican's Elite School for American Priests. Brian Murphy. 320p. 1998. pap. 14.00 (*1-57322-699-8*, Riverhd Trade) Berkley Pub.

New Men - Deeper Hungers. Tom Owen-Towle. LC 88-63742. (Illus.). 146p. (Orig.). (C). 1988. pap. 7.95 (*0-931104-25-4*) SunInk Pubn.

New Men, New Cities, New South: Atlanta, Nashville, Charleston, Mobile, 1860-1910. Don H. Doyle. LC 89-34924. (Fred W. Morrison Series in Southern Studies). (Illus.). xxii, 369p. (C). 1990. 65.00 (*0-8078-1883-6*); pap. 19.95 (*0-8078-4270-2*) U of NC Pr.

New Men, New Issues: The Formation of the Republican Party in Maine. Richard R. Wescott. 1986. 15.50 (*0-915592-34-7*) Maine Hist.

New Men of Power: America's Labor Leaders. C. Wright Mills. LC 68-56261. 323p. 1971. reprint ed. 45.00 (*0-678-00715-2*) Kelley.

New Men's Studies: A Selected & Annotated Interdisciplinary Bibliography. 2nd ed. Eugene R. August. xx, 440p. 1995. lib. bdg. 65.00 (*1-56308-084-2*) Libs Unl.

New Mentors & Proteges: How to Succeed with the New Mentoring Partnerships. rev. ed. Linda Phillips-Jones. LC 93-84972. 184p. 1997. pap. 10.00 (*1-890608-00-9*) Coalition Cnsling.

New Merger Game: The Plan & the Players. Donald Gussow. LC 77-28480. 276p. reprint ed. pap. 85.60 (*0-608-12169-X*, 202391800034) Bks Demand.

New Merle Haggard Anthology. (Piano-Vocal-Guitar Ser.). 184p. (Orig.). 1991. otabind 16.95 (*0-7935-0325-6*, 00356853) H Leonard.

***New Messies Manual: The Procrastinator's Guide to Good Housekeeping.** 3rd rev. ed. Sandra Felton. 240p. (gr. 13). 2000. pap. 11.99 (*0-8007-5726-2*) Revell.

New Metaphysical Foundations of Modern Science. Ed. by Willis Harman & Jane Clark. LC 94-6253. 1994. write for info. (*0-943951-11-9*) Inst Noetic Sci.

New Method for Analyzing Gear Tooth Stress as a Function of Tooth Contact Pattern Shape & Position. L. E. Wilcox. (Technical Papers: Vol. P229.25). (Illus.). 8p. 1982. pap. text 30.00 (*1-55589-292-2*) AGMA.

New Method for Designing Worm-Gear. Michel Octrue. (Nineteen Eighty-Eight Fall Technical Meeting Ser.: Vol. 88FTM6). (Illus.). 5p. 1988. pap. text 30.00 (*1-55589-511-5*) AGMA.

New Method for Double Bass, Bk. I. F. Simandl. (Illus.). 88p. (Orig.). 1984. pap. 18.95 (*0-8258-0362-4*, 0492) Fischer Inc NY.

New Method for Double Bass, Bk. II. F. Simandl. 88p. (Orig.). 1984. pap. 14.95 (*0-8258-0363-2*, 03567) Fischer Inc NY.

New Method for the Double Bass, Bk. I. F. Simandl. 136p. 1964. pap. 18.95 (*0-8258-0152-4*, 0492) Fischer Inc NY.

New Method for Valuing Treasury Bond Futures Options. Ehud I. Ronn & Robert R. Bliss, Jr. 1992. pap. text 20.00 (*0-943205-15-8*) RFICFA.

New Method of Chess Notation. John Bartlett. (Works of John Bartlett). 1989. reprint ed. lib. bdg. 79.00 (*0-7812-1903-5*) Rprt Serv.

New Method of Impregnating PEI Sheets for the In-Situ Foaming of Sandwiches. P. W. Kluit. (Series 07-Aerospace Materials: No. 04). (Illus.). 24p. 1998. pap. 14.95 (*90-407-1590-4*, Pub. by Delft U Pr) Coronet Bks.

New Method Supplementary Readers, 10 bks., Stage 5. Incl. Five Famous Fairy Tales. 1988. pap. text 4.46 (*0-582-53521-2*); Great Men & Women. Ed. by D. K. Swan. 1981. pap. text 4.46 (*0-582-53512-3*); Greek Heroes: Nmsr Stage 2. 1985. pap. text 4.46 (*0-582-52677-9*); Legend of Sleepy Hollow & Rip Van Winkle. Washington Irving. 1989. pap. text 4.46 (*0-582-53530-1*); Pirates: New Method Supplementary Series. D. K. Swan. 1989. pap. text 4.46 (*0-582-53541-7*); Secret Garden. Frances Hodgson Burnett. pap. text 4.46 (*0-582-53417-8*); Singing Wind & Other Stories. Ed. by D. K. Swan. 1981. pap. text 4.46 (*0-582-53491-7*); Stories of Mystery & Imagination. Edgar Allan Poe. 1985. pap. text 4.46 (*0-582-53471-2*); White Fang. 1981. pap. text 4.46 (*0-582-53498-4*); (English As a Second Language Bk.). 1981. Set pap. 40.50 (*0-318-54113-0*) Longman.

New Methodologies for Commodity Promotion Economics. Ed. by H. M. Kaiser et al. 1996. pap. write for info. (*0-9649003-1-9*) Nat Inst Commodity.

New Methodology for Assessing Multi-Layer Missile Defense Options. Eric V. Larson & Glenn A. Kent. LC 94-32983. 1994. pap. 13.00 (*0-8330-1579-6*, MR-390-AF) Rand Corp.

New Methods & Results in Non-Linear Field Equations. Ed. by P. Blanchard et al. (Lecture Notes in Physics Ser.: Vol. 347). viii, 133p. 1989. 45.95 (*0-387-51977-7*) Spr-Verlag.

New Methods & Techniques in Education. UNESCO Staff. (Education Studies & Documents: No. 48). 1974. reprint ed. pap. 25.00 (*0-8115-1372-6*) Periodicals Srv.

New Methods & Technologies for Functional Genomics: Drug Discovery from Gene to Screen. Ed. by Susan Gilbert. (Biomedical Library). 1997. pap. write for info. (*1-57936-030-0*) IBC USA.

New Methods for Corrosion Testing of Aluminum Alloys. Ed. by Vinod S. Agarwala & Gilbert M. Ugiansky. LC 91-35946. (Special Technical Publication Ser.: No. 1134). (Illus.). 225p. 1992. text 65.00 (*0-8031-1435-4*, STP1134) ASTM.

New Methods for Old-Age Research. Christine L. Fry et al. LC 85-26792. 325p. (Orig.). 1986. 62.95 (*0-89789-063-9*, Bergin & Garvey); pap. 24.95 (*0-89789-034-5*, Bergin & Garvey) Greenwood.

New Methods for Polymer Synthesis. Ed. by J. R. Ebdon. 320p. 1991. mass mkt. 153.50 (*0-412-02471-3*, A4213, Chap & Hall NY) Chapman & Hall.

New Methods for Polymer Synthesis. W. J. Mijs. (Illus.). 336p. (C). 1992. text 85.00 (*0-306-43871-2*, Kluwer Plenum) Kluwer Academic.

New Methods for Puberty Education. Carolyn Cooperman & Chuck Rhoades. (Illus.). 176p. 1992. pap. 25.00 (*0-9609366-0-2*) Plan Parenthood.

New Methods for Robust Science & Technology Planning. Robert J. Lempert & James L. Bonomo. (Illus.). 50p. 1998. pap. 6.00 (*0-8330-2585-6*, DB-238-DARPA) Rand Corp.

New Methods for the Arbitrage Pricing Theory & the Present Value Model. Jian-Ping Mei. 100p. 1994. text 30.00 (*981-02-1839-7*) World Scientific Pub.

New Methods for the Consolidation of Metal Powders. Ed. by Henry H. Hausner et al. LC 66-22786. (Perspectives in Powder Metallurgy: Fundamentals, Methods, & Applications Ser.: Vol. 1). 263p. reprint ed. pap. 81.60 (*0-608-11501-0*, 201940600011) Bks Demand.

N

An Asterisk (*) at the beginning of an entry indicates that the title is appearing for the first time.

New Methods for the Study of Biomolecular Complexes: Proceedings of the NATO Advances Research Workshop on New Methods for the Study of Molecular Aggregates, the Lodge at Kananaskis Village, Alberta, Canada, June 16-20, 1996. Ed. by Werner Ens et al. LC 98-9441. (NATO Science Series C). 368p. 1998. 154.00 (*0-7923-5003-0*) Kluwer Academic.

New Methods in Business Cycle Research: Proceedings from a Conference. Christopher A. Sims et al. 1977. 1.50 (*0-9603936-1-7*) FRB Minneapolis.

New Methods in College Writing Programs: Theories in Practice. Ed. by Paul Connolly & Teresa Vilardi. LC 86-16259. (Options for Teaching Ser.: No. 9). vii, 167p. 1987. pap. 19.75 (*0-87352-363-6*, J209C) Modern Lang.

New Methods in Dialectology. Ed. by Piet Van Keenen & Bert Schouten. (Publications in Language Sciences). iv, 208p. (Orig.). (C). 1989. pap. 52.35 (*0-685-34767-2*) Mouton.

New Methods in Financial Modeling: Explorations & Applications. Houston H. Stokes & Hugh M. Neuburger. LC 97-48617. 168p. 1998. 65.00 (*1-56720-125-3*, Quorum Bks) Greenwood.

New Methods in Language Processing. Ed. by Daniel B. Jones & Harold Somers. LC 97-198777. (Studies in Computational Linguistics). 400p. 1997. 79.95 (*1-85728-711-8*, Pub. by UCL Pr Ltd) Taylor & Francis.

New Methods in Optimization & Their Industrial Uses. J. P. Penot. (International Series of Numerical Mathematics: No. 87). 240p. 1989. 91.00 (*0-8176-2286-1*) Birkhauser.

New Methods in Peptide Mapping for the Characterization of Proteins: New Methods in Tryptic Mapping. Ed. by W. S. Hancock. (Analytical Biotechnology Ser.). 272p. 1995. boxed set 139.95 (*0-8493-7822-2*, 7822) CRC Pr.

New Methods in Quantum Theory: Proceedings of the NATO Advanced Research Workshop, Halkidiki, Greece, May 14 - 19, 1995. Ed. by Constantinos A. Tsipis et al. LC 96-1798. (NATO Advanced Science Institutes Ser.: No. 3). 564p. (C). 1996. text 291.00 (*0-7923-3960-6*) Kluwer Academic.

New Methods in Social History. Ed. by Larry Griffin & Marcel Van Der Linden. LC 98-40332. (International Review of Social History Supplements Ser.: No. 6). (Illus.). 192p. (C). 1999. pap. text 22.95 (*0-521-65599-4*) Cambridge U Pr.

New Methods in Social Science Research: Policy Sciences & Futures Research. T. Harrell Allen. LC 76-12840. (Praeger Special Studies). 176p. 1978. 42.95 (*0-275-90282-X*, C0282, Praeger Pubs) Greenwood.

New Methods in Transient Analysis. Ed. by P. Smolinski et al. (PVP Ser.: Vol. 246). 156p. 1992. 45.00 (*0-7918-1088-7*, G00732) ASME.

***New Methods, Mechanisms & Models of Vapor Deposition: Materials Research Society Symposium Proceedings, Vol. 616.** Ed. by H. N. G. Wadley et al. 2000. text 77.00 (*1-55899-524-2*) Materials Res.

New Methods of Celestial Mechanics, 3 vols., Set. Henri Poincare. (History of Modern Physics & Astronomy Ser.: Vol. 13). 1600p. 1990. 199.95 (*1-56396-117-2*) Spr-Verlag.

New Methods of Food Preservation. G. W. Gould. 324p. 1994. 95.00 (*0-8342-1341-9*) Aspen Pub.

New Methods of Geostatistical Analysis & Graphical Presentation: Distributions of Populations over Territories. R. Bachi. LC 99-17060. (Illus.). 578p. (C). 1998. text. write for info. (*0-306-45544-7*, Kluwer Plenum) Kluwer Academic.

New Methods of Integrated Computerized Design & Manufacturing of High Speed Gearing. Manfred Hirt & T. Weiss. (Nineteen Eighty-Seven Fall Technical Meeting Ser.: Vol. 87FTM16). (Illus.). 21p. 1987. pap. text 30.00 (*1-55589-492-5*) AGMA.

New Methods of Measuring Marginal Utility. Ragnar Frisch. LC 78-15136. (Illus.). 142p. 1978. reprint ed. lib. bdg. 29.50 (*0-87991-863-2*) Porcupine Pr.

New Methods of Modelling Processes Within Solids & at Their Surfaces. Ed. by C. R. A. Catlow et al. LC 92-42240. (Illus.). 192p. 1994. text 55.00 (*0-19-853988-6*) OUP.

New Methods of Polymer Synthesis. Routledge, Chapman, Hall Ltd Staff. text 189.50 (*0-7514-0142-0*) Routledge.

New Methods of Rectification: Lincoln. T. Patrick Davis. LC 83-71861. 154p. 1985. 16.50 (*0-86690-254-6*, D2440-014) Am Fed Astrologers.

New Methods of Sensory Visual Testing. Ed. by M. Wall & A. A. Sadun. (Illus.). xiv, 138p. 1989. 68.00 (*0-387-96865-2*) Spr-Verlag.

New Methods R. E. Teaching. Hammond. 1990. pap. text. write for info. (*0-05-004303-X*) Addison-Wesley.

New Metrical Psalter. Christopher L. Webber. 260p. 1986. pap. 16.95 (*0-89869-132-X*) Church Pub Inc.

New Metropolis: New York City, 1840-1857. Edward K. Spann. LC 81-91. (Columbia History of Urban Life Ser.). (Illus.). 512p. 1983. pap. text 32.50 (*0-231-05085-2*) Col U Pr.

New Mexican Furniture of the W. P. A. Spanish Colonial Revival in the Great Depression. Kinesley H. Hammett. (Illus.). 114p. 1998. pap. 19.95 (*0-9648256-1-9*, Fleetwd Pr) Fine Additions.

New Mexican Furniture, 1600-1940. Lonn Taylor & Dessa Bokides. (Illus.). 336p. 1987. pap. 45.00 (*0-89013-168-6*) Museum NM Pr.

New Mexican Hispano. Ed. by Carlos E. Cortes. LC 73-14210. (Mexican American Ser.). (Illus.). 510p. 1975. reprint ed. 39.95 (*0-405-05684-2*) Ayer.

New Mexican Spanish Religious Oratory. T. J. Steele. LC 96-10115. (Illus.). 229p. 1997. 65.00 (*0-8263-1768-5*) U of NM Pr.

New Mexico see From Sea to Shining Sea

New Mexico see One Nation Series

New Mexico. Capstone Press, Geography Department Staff. (One Nation Ser.). (Illus.). 48p. (J). (gr. 3-7). 1997. lib. bdg. 19.00 (*0-516-20931-0*) Childrens.

New Mexico. Theresa S. Early. LC 92-13364. (Hello U. S. A. Ser.). (Illus.). 72p. (J). (gr. 3-6). 1993. lib. bdg. 19.95 (*0-8225-2748-0*, Lerner Publctns) Lerner Pub.

New Mexico. Dennis B. Fradin. (From Sea to Shining Sea Ser.). (Illus.). 64p. (J). (gr. 3-5). 1994. pap. 7.95 (*0-516-43831-X*) Childrens.

New Mexico. Paul Joseph. LC 97-16749. (United States Ser.). (Illus.). 32p. (J). 1998. lib. bdg. 19.93 (*1-56239-868-7*, Checkerboard Library) ABDO Pub Co.

New Mexico. Deborah Kent. LC 98-19576. (America the Beautiful Ser.). (Illus.). 144p. (YA). (gr. 4-10). 1999. lib. bdg. 32.00 (*0-516-20690-7*) Childrens.

New Mexico. Rand McNally Staff. 1997. pap. 5.95 (*0-528-97208-1*) Rand McNally.

New Mexico. C. Roberts. LC 87-30086. (Illus.). 220p. 1989. pap. 16.95 (*0-8263-1145-8*) U of NM Pr.

New Mexico. Kathleen Thompson. LC 85-10832. (Portrait of America Library). 48p. (J). (gr. 4-8). 1996. pap. 5.95 (*0-8114-7457-7*) Raintree Steck-V.

New Mexico. Kathleen Thompson. LC 85-10832. (Portrait of America Library). (Illus.). 48p. (J). (gr. 3-6). 1996. lib. bdg. 22.83 (*0-8114-7376-7*) Raintree Steck-V.

New Mexico! large type ed. Dana Fuller Ross. (General Ser.). 397p. 1990. lib. bdg. 21.95 (*0-8161-4771-X*, G K Hall Lrg Type) Mac Lib Ref.

New Mexico. Photos by Margia Keegan. (Illus.). 96p. 1991. reprint ed. 19.95 (*0-940666-02-2*) Clear Light.

New Mexico! 2nd rev. ed. Marc Simmons. 346p. 1997. pap. 30.00 (*0-8263-1788-X*) U of NM Pr.

New Mexico. 3rd ed. Frommer's Staff. (Frommer's Travel Guides Ser.). (Illus.). 300p. 1995. 14.95 (*0-02-860076-2*, P-H Travel) Prntice Hall Bks.

New Mexico. 3rd ed. Nancy Harbert. LC 97-47186. (Compass American Guides Ser.). 344p. 1998. pap. 18.95 (*0-679-00031-3*, Compass Amrcn) Fodors Travel.

New Mexico. 5th ed. Ed. by Macmillan Travel Staff. (Frommer's New Mexico Ser.). 1999. pap. 15.95 (*0-02-862371-1*, Frommer) Macmillan Gen Ref.

New Mexico see Celebrate the States - Group 5

***New Mexico: A Brief Multi-History.** Ruben Salaz-Marquez, pseud. 700p. 1999. pap. 39.95 (*0-932492-05-3*) Cosmic Hse NM.

New Mexico: A Guide to the Colorful State. Federal Writers' Project Staff. (American Guidebook Ser.). 1940. reprint ed. 89.00 (*0-403-02181-2*) Somerset Pub.

New Mexico: A Guide to the Colorful State. Federal Writers' Project Staff & Writers Program-WPA Staff. (American Guide Ser.). 1989. reprint ed. lib. bdg. 79.00 (*0-7812-1030-5*, 1030) Rprt Serv.

New Mexico: An Interpretive History. rev. ed. Simmons. LC 88-21623. 228p. 1988. reprint ed. pap. 10.95 (*0-8263-1110-5*) U of NM Pr.

New Mexico: County Guides, 6 vols. C. K. Stribling. (County Guide Ser.). (Illus.). 1990. pap. 4.95 (*0-944383-13-0*) High-Lonesome.

New Mexico: Hello U. S. A. Theresa S. Early. (Illus.). 72p. (J). 1996. pap. text 5.95 (*0-8225-9736-5*) Lerner Pub.

***New Mexico: Off the Beaten Path: A Guide to Unique Places.** 4th ed. Todd R. Staats. LC 99-44247. (Off the Beaten Path Ser.). 224p. 1999. pap. text 12.95 (*0-7627-0533-7*) Globe Pequot.

New Mexico: The Spirit of America State by State. Cynthia O. Bix. Ed. by Diana Landau. LC 97-12019. (Art of the State Ser.). (Illus.). 86p. 1998. 12.95 (*0-8109-5553-9*, Pub. by Abrams) Time Warner.

New Mexico - Collected Works of Federal Writers Project. Federal Writers' Project Staff. 1991. reprint ed. lib. bdg. 98.00 (*0-7812-5684-4*) Rprt Serv.

New Mexico A to Z. Dorothy H. Weaver. LC 95-41614. (Illus.). 32p. (Orig.). (J). (ps-1). 1996. pap. 6.95 (*0-87358-636-0*, Rising Moon Bks) Northland AZ.

New Mexico Acequias: 1998 Edition. 213p. pap. 10.00 (*1-55834-885-9*) LEXIS Pub.

New Mexico Activity & Coloring Book. Anne M. Eccles. (Illus.). 32p. (J). (ps-8). 1987. pap. 2.95 (*0-9618555-1-7*) Anne M Eccles.

New Mexico Advance Annotation & Rules Service, Pamphlet No. 1. annot. ed. 170p. 1998. pap. write for info. (*0-327-06301-7*, 46184-15) LEXIS Pub.

New Mexico & Arizona State Parks: A Complete Recreation Guide. Don Laine & Barbara Laine. LC 97-43393. (State Parks Ser.). (Illus.). 250p. 1998. pap. 16.95 (*0-89886-559-X*) Mountaineers.

New Mexico & Other State Greats (Biographies) Carole Marsh. (Carole Marsh New Mexico Bks.). (Illus.). (J). 1994. pap. 19.95 (*1-55609-893-6*); lib. bdg. 29.95 (*1-55609-892-8*); disk 29.95 (*1-55609-894-4*) Gallopade Intl.

New Mexico & the Sectional Controversy, 1846-1861. Loomis M. Ganaway. LC 76-8250. (Perspectives in American History Ser.: No. 28). (Illus.). x, 140p. 1976. reprint ed. lib. bdg. 29.50 (*0-87991-352-5*) Porcupine Pr.

New Mexico Appellate Manual. 2nd ed. Michael Schwarz. 710p. Date not set. ring bd. 125.00 (*0-409-25642-0*, 82129, MICHIE) LEXIS Pub.

New Mexico Appellate Manual. 2nd ed. Michael Schwarz. 1993. suppl. ed. 55.00 (*0-685-74468-X*, MICHIE) LEXIS Pub.

***New Mexico Atlas.** 2nd ed. Delorme Publishing Company Staff. (Illus.). 2000. pap. 19.95 (*0-89933-317-6*) DeLorme Map.

New Mexico Atlas & Gazetteer. DeLorme Publishing Staff. LC 99-464319. (Illus.). 1998. pap. 16.95 (*0-89933-229-3*) DeLorme Map.

New Mexico Bandits, Bushwackers, Outlaws, Crooks, Devils, Ghosts, Desperadoes & Other Assorted & Sundry Characters! Carole Marsh. (Illus.). (J). 1994. pap. 19.95 (*0-7933-0792-9*); lib. bdg. 29.95 (*0-7933-0793-7*); disk 29.95 (*0-7933-0794-5*) Gallopade Intl.

New Mexico "BIO" Bingo! 24 Must Know State People for Kids to Learn about While Having Fun! Carole Marsh. (Bingo! Ser.). (Illus.). (J). (gr. 2-8). 1998. pap. 14.95 (*0-7933-8615-2*) Gallopade Intl.

New Mexico Boating Guide. Ron Swartley. (Illus.). 94p. (Orig.). 1997. pap. 9.95 (*1-888571-02-0*) Frontier Image.

New Mexico Bookstore Book: A Surprising Guide to Our State's Bookstores & Their Specialties for Students, Teachers, Writers & Publishers. Carole Marsh. (Carole Marsh New Mexico Bks.). (Illus.). 1994. pap. 19.95 (*0-7933-2949-3*); lib. bdg. 29.95 (*0-7933-2948-5*); disk 29.95 (*0-7933-2950-7*) Gallopade Intl.

New Mexico Boundary Law: Answers Book. John E. Keen. 20p. (C). 1995. pap. text 15.00 (*1-56569-049-4*) Land Survey.

New Mexico Boundary Law: Questions Book. John E. Keen. 225p. (C). 1995. pap. text 60.00 (*1-56569-050-8*) Land Survey.

***New Mexico Business Directory, 1999-2000.** rev. ed. American Business Directories Staff. 816p. 1999. boxed set 375.00 incl. cd-rom (*0-7687-0152-X*) Am Busn Direct.

***New Mexico Campaign Finance Reporting Act, 1999 Edition.** 19p. 1999. 7.00 (*0-327-09740-X*, 2941813) LEXIS Pub.

New Mexico Census Index, 1890 Union Veterans. (Illus.). lib. bdg. 50.00 (*0-89593-435-3*, Accel Indexing) Genealogical Srvcs.

New Mexico Census Index, 1870 Mortality Schedule. (Illus.). lib. bdg. write for info. (*0-89593-434-5*, Accel Indexing) Genealogical Srvcs.

New Mexico Census Index, 1870 (Every Name) Ronald V. Jackson. (Illus.). lib. bdg. 150.00 (*0-89593-751-4*, Accel Indexing) Genealogical Srvcs.

New Mexico Census Index, 1860 Mortality Schedule. (Illus.). lib. bdg. write for info. (*0-89593-433-7*, Accel Indexing) Genealogical Srvcs.

New Mexico Census Index, 1860 (Every Name) Ronald V. Jackson. (Illus.). 1981. lib. bdg. 80.00 (*0-89593-432-9*, Accel Indexing) Genealogical Srvcs.

New Mexico Classic Christmas Trivia: Stories, Recipes, Activities, Legends, Lore & More! Carole Marsh. (Carole Marsh New Mexico Bks.). (Illus.). (J). 1994. pap. 19.95 (*0-7933-0795-3*); lib. bdg. 29.95 (*0-7933-0796-1*); disk 29.95 (*0-7933-0797-X*) Gallopade Intl.

New Mexico Coastales. Carole Marsh. (Carole Marsh New Mexico Bks.). (J). 1994. lib. bdg. 29.95 (*0-7933-7296-8*) Gallopade Intl.

New Mexico Coastales. Carole Marsh. (Carole Marsh New Mexico Bks.). (Illus.). (J). 1994. pap. 19.95 (*1-55609-887-1*); lib. bdg. 29.95 (*1-55609-886-3*); disk 29.95 (*1-55609-888-X*) Gallopade Intl.

***New Mexico Code Annotated 1999 Annotation Citator.** 1500p. 1999. pap. write for info. (*0-327-09878-3*, 4133811) LEXIS Pub.

New Mexico Computer Resources Directory, 1996. Ed. by Cherilyn J. Peay & Mary P. McArthur. vi, 110p. (Orig.). 1996. pap. 7.95 (*0-9655541-0-4*) NMex Computer.

New Mexico Cook Book. Lynn Nusom. LC 90-3391. 144p. (Orig.). 1990. ring bd. 5.95 (*0-914846-48-5*) Golden West Pub.

New Mexico Cooking: Southwestern Flavors of the Past & Present. Clyde Casey. LC 94-8949. (Illus.). 192p. (Orig.). 1994. reprint ed. pap. 12.95 (*1-55561-059-5*) Fisher Bks.

New Mexico Creditor - Debtor Law, 1989-1992. Marian Matthews. 300p. 1993. suppl. ed. 53.50 (*1-56257-976-2*, MICHIE) LEXIS Pub.

New Mexico Creditor - Debtor Law, 1989-1992, Issue 8. rev. ed. David Reynolds. 326p. 1997. ring bd. 60.00 (*0-409-25140-2*, 82135-12, MICHIE) LEXIS Pub.

New Mexico Creditor/Debtor Law. rev. ed. David Reynolds. Date not set. ring bd. 120.00 (*0-327-00951-9*, 82134, MICHIE) LEXIS Pub.

New Mexico Creditor/Debtor Law, Issue 10. Matthews & Reynold. 101p. 1998. ring bd. 120.00 (*0-327-00762-1*, 8213514) LEXIS Pub.

New Mexico Creditor/Debtor Law: 1989 Edition. David Reynolds. 1995. ring bd. 120.00 (*0-409-25395-2*, 82134-10, MICHIE) LEXIS Pub.

***New Mexico Crime in Perspective 2000.** Ed. by Kathleen O'Leary Morgan & Scott E. Morgan. 22p. 2000. spiral bd. 19.00 (*0-7401-0330-X*) Morgan Quitno Corp.

New Mexico Crime Perspective, 1998. Ed. by Kathleen O'Leary Morgan & Scott E. Morgan. 20p. 1998. pap. 19.00 (*1-56692-930-X*) Morgan Quitno Corp.

New Mexico Crime Perspectives, 1999. Kathleen O'Leary Morgan. 22p. 1999. spiral bd. 19.00 (*0-7401-0130-7*) Morgan Quitno Corp.

New Mexico Criminal & Traffic Law Manual: 1998 Edition. 1087p. 1998. write for info. (*0-327-05321-6*, 29402-15) LEXIS Pub.

***New Mexico Criminal & Traffic Law Manual: 1999 Edition.** 1,200p. 1999. pap. 25.00 (*0-327-09103-7*, 2940216) LEXIS Pub.

New Mexico Criminal & Traffic Law Manual, 1994 Edition. 27.50 (*0-614-05923-2*, MICHIE) LEXIS Pub.

***New Mexico Criminal & Traffic Law Manual, 1999 ALS.** 522p. 1999. pap. 12.00 (*0-327-09444-3*, 2940610) LEXIS Pub.

New Mexico "Crinkum-Crankum" A Funny Word Book about Our State. Carole Marsh. (Carole Marsh New Mexico Bks.). (Illus.). (J). 1994. pap. 19.95 (*0-7933-4902-8*); lib. bdg. 29.95 (*0-7933-4901-X*); disk 29.95 (*0-7933-4903-6*) Gallopade Intl.

New Mexico David, & Other Stories, & Sketches of the South-West. Charles F. Lummis. LC 76-90586. (Short Story Index Reprint Ser.). 1977. 19.95 (*0-8369-3069-X*) Ayer.

New Mexico Digest, 1852 to Date. West Publishing Company Editorial Staff. write for info. (*0-318-60694-1*) West Pub.

New Mexico Dingbats! A Fun Book of Games, Stories, Activities & More about Our State That's All in Code! For You to Decipher, Bk. 1. Carole Marsh. (Carole Marsh New Mexico Bks.). (Illus.). (J). (gr. 3-12). 1994. pap. 19.95 (*0-7933-3867-0*); lib. bdg. 29.95 (*0-7933-3866-2*) Gallopade Intl.

New Mexico Directory of Hispanic Culture. 2nd ed. Ed. by Lenore Miner & Carol Guzman. (Illus.). 171p. 1992. pap. 8.95 (*0-944725-02-3*) Hispanic Culture.

New Mexico Discovery Guide: A Remarkably Useful Travel Companion for Motorists, RVers & Other Explorers. Don W. Martin & Betty W. Martin. LC 97-76165. (Discovery Guide Ser.). (Illus.). 416p. 1998. pap. 16.95 (*0-942053-25-7*) Pine Cone Pr NV.

New Mexico Discovery Practice Manual. Adams. 1993. suppl. ed. 45.00 (*0-685-74338-1*, MICHIE) LEXIS Pub.

New Mexico Discovery Practice Manual. Charles W. Adams. 560p. 1994. ring bd. 115.00 (*0-409-25545-9*, MICHIE) LEXIS Pub.

New Mexico Domestic Relations Law & Forms. Thomas C. Montoya & David H. Kelsey. LC 95-79155. 1995. spiral bd. 105.00 (*0-250-47252-X*, 63825, MICHIE) LEXIS Pub.

***New Mexico Driver's Survival Guide for Visitors & Locals: How to Live Long Enough to Enjoy New Mexico's Natural Wonders.** Jim Terr. LC 99-72472. (Illus.). 94p. 1999. pap. 7.95 (*0-929830-02-4*) Blue Canyon Bks.

New Mexico Environmental Law Handbook. 4th ed. Rodey, Dickason, Sloan, Akin & Robb Staff. 443p. 1996. pap. text 95.00 (*0-86587-530-8*) Gov Insts.

New Mexico Experience: 1598-1998: A Confluence of Cultures. Richard E. Peck. (Illus.). 240p. 1998. 29.95 (*0-9661142-0-5*) Sierra Pub.

New Mexico Facts & Factivities. Carole Marsh. (Carole Marsh State Bks.). (Illus.). (J). (gr. 4-7). 1996. pap., teacher ed. 19.95 (*0-7933-7909-1*, C Marsh) Gallopade Intl.

New Mexico Facts & Symbols. Emily McAuliffe. (States & Their Symbols Ser.). 1999. 15.00 (*0-531-12006-6*) Watts.

***New Mexico Facts & Symbols.** Shelley S. Sateren. LC 99-31829. (States & Their Symbols Ser.). 2000. write for info. (*0-7368-0380-7*, Hlltop Bks) Capstone Pr.

New Mexico Federal Census Index, 1850. Ronald V. Jackson. LC 77-86123. (Illus.). 1978. lib. bdg. 58.00 (*0-89593-095-1*, Accel Indexing) Genealogical Srvcs.

New Mexico Festival Fun for Kids! Carole Marsh. (Carole Marsh New Mexico Bks.). (J). (gr. 3-12). 1994. pap. 19.95 (*0-7933-4020-9*); lib. bdg. 29.95 (*0-7933-4019-5*) Gallopade Intl.

New Mexico Festival Fun for Kids! Carole Marsh. (Carole Marsh New Mexico Bks.). (Illus.). (YA). (gr. 3-12). 1994. disk 29.95 (*0-7933-4021-7*) Gallopade Intl.

***New Mexico Financial Disclosure Act, 1999 Edition.** 9p. 1999. Price not set. (*0-327-09741-8*, 2942413) LEXIS Pub.

New Mexico for Kids: A Learning - Activity Guidebook for Young People. Lynnell Diamond. (America for Kids Ser.). (Illus.). 48p. (YA). (gr. 3-6). 1997. pap. 7.95 (*0-9651853-0-3*) Otter Be Reading Bks.

New Mexico Gardener's Guide: The What, Where, When, How & Why of Gardening in New Mexico. Judith Phillips. (Illus.). 400p. 1998. pap. 19.95 (*1-888608-55-2*) Cool Springs Pr.

New Mexico "GEO" Bingo! 38 Must Know State Geography Facts for Kids to Learn While Having Fun! Carole Marsh. (Bingo! Ser.). (Illus.). (J). (gr. 2-8). 1998. pap. 14.95 (*0-7933-8616-0*) Gallopade Intl.

New Mexico Government. 3rd ed. Paul L. Hain et al. LC 93-51054. 320p. (C). 1994. pap. 16.95 (*0-8263-1508-9*) U of NM Pr.

New Mexico Government! The Cornerstone of Everyday Life in Our State! Carole Marsh. (Carole Marsh New Mexico Bks.). (Illus.). (J). (gr. 3-12). 1996. pap. 19.95 (*0-7933-6275-X*); lib. bdg. 29.95 (*0-7933-6274-1*); disk 29.95 (*0-7933-6276-8*) Gallopade Intl.

New Mexico Government & Politics. Maurilio E. Vigil. 206p. (Orig.). (C). 1990. pap. text 22.00 (*0-8191-7790-3*) U Pr of Amer.

***New Mexico Governmental Conduct Act 1999 Edition.** 10p. 1999. 7.00 (*0-327-09737-X*, 2942213) LEXIS Pub.

New Mexico Guide. 2nd ed. Charles L. Cadieux. LC 91-58487. (Illus.). 304p. (Orig.). 1995. pap. 15.95 (*1-55591-219-2*) Fulcrum Pub.

***New Mexico Guide.** 2nd ed. Larry Ludmer. (Illus.). 336p. 1999. pap. 16.95 (*1-892975-11-4*) Open Rd Pub.

New Mexico Haiku. rev. ed. Hank Malone. viii, 100p. (Orig.). 1998. pap. 6.95 (*1-888923-05-9*) Poetic License.

***New Mexico Health Care in Perspective 2000.** Ed. by Kathleen O'Leary Morgan & Scott E. Morgan. 21p. 2000. spiral bd. 19.00 (*0-7401-0230-3*) Morgan Quitno Corp.

New Mexico Health Care Perspective, 1998. Ed. by Kathleen O'Leary Morgan & Scott E. Morgan. 20p. 1998. pap. 19.00 (*1-56692-830-3*) Morgan Quitno Corp.

New Mexico Health Care Perspective, 1999. Kathleen O'Leary Morgan. 21p. 1999. spiral bd. 19.00 (*0-7401-0080-7*) Morgan Quitno Corp.

New Mexico "HISTO" Bingo! 42 Must Know State History Facts for Kids to Learn While Having Fun! Carole Marsh. (Bingo! Ser.). (Illus.). (J). (gr. 2-8). 1998. pap. 14.95 (*0-7933-8617-9*) Gallopade Intl.

N

An Asterisk (*) at the beginning of an entry indicates that the title is appearing for the first time.

New Mexico Historical & Biographical Index, Vol. 1. Ronald V. Jackson. LC 78-53709. (Illus.). 1984. lib. bdg. 30.00 (*0-89593-192-3*, Accel Indexing) Genealogical Srvcs.

New Mexico History! Surprising Secrets about Our State's Founding Mothers, Fathers & Kids! Carole Marsh. (Carole Marsh New Mexico Bks.). (Illus.). (J). (gr. 3-12). 1996. pap. 19.95 (*0-7933-6122-2*); lib. bdg. 29.95 (*0-7933-6121-4*); disk 29.95 (*0-7933-6123-0*) Gallopade Intl.

New Mexico Hot Air Balloon Mystery. Carole Marsh. (Carole Marsh New Mexico Bks.). (Illus.). (J). (gr. 2-9). 1994. 29.95 (*0-7933-2597-8*); pap. 19.95 (*0-7933-2598-6*); disk 29.95 (*0-7933-2599-4*) Gallopade Intl.

New Mexico Hot Zones! Viruses, Diseases, & Epidemics in Our State's History. Carole Marsh. (Hot Zones! Ser.). (Illus.). (J). (gr. 3-12). 1998. pap. 19.95 (*0-7933-8922-4*); lib. bdg. 29.95 (*0-7933-8921-6*) Gallopade Intl.

New Mexico in Perspective, 1998. Ed. by Kathleen O'Leary Morgan & Scott E. Morgan. 24p. 1998. pap. 19.00 (*1-56692-880-X*) Morgan Quitno Corp.

New Mexico in Perspective, 1999. Ed. by Kathleen O'Leary Morgan. 26p. 1999. spiral bd. 19.00 (*1-56692-980-6*) Morgan Quitno Corp.

***New Mexico in Perspective 2000.** Ed. by Kathleen O'Leary Morgan & Scott E. Morgan. 26p. 2000. spiral bd. 19.00 (*0-7401-0280-X*) Morgan Quitno Corp.

New Mexico in 1602. Ed. by George P. Hammond & Agapito Rey. LC 67-24719. (Quivira Society Publications: Vol. 8). 1967. reprint ed. 19.95 (*0-405-00082-0*) Ayer.

***New Mexico in the Nineteenth Century: A Pictorial History** Andrew K. Gregg. LC 99-15815. 2000. 0.00 (*1-57168-338-0*, Eakin Pr) Sunbelt Media.

New Mexico Indian Dictionary for Kids! Carole Marsh. (Carole Marsh State Bks.). (J). (gr. 2-9). 1996. 29.95 (*0-7933-7737-4*, C Marsh); pap. 19.95 (*0-7933-7738-2*, C Marsh) Gallopade Intl.

New Mexico Indian Ruins. Ron Swartley. (Illus.). 44p. (Orig.). 1996. pap. 9.95 (*0-9634309-9-8*) Frontier Image.

***New Mexico Investment & Business Guide: Business, Investment, Export-Import Opportunities, 50 vols., Vol. 31.** Global Investment Center, USA Staff. (U. S. Regional Investment & Business Library-99: Vol. 31). (Illus.). 350p. (Orig.). 1999. pap. 59.95 (*0-7397-1130-X*) Intl Business Pubns.

New Mexico Jeopardy! Answers & Questions about Our State! Carole Marsh. (Carole Marsh New Mexico Bks.). (Illus.). (J). (gr. 3-12). 1994. pap. 19.95 (*0-7933-4173-6*); lib. bdg. 29.95 (*0-7933-4172-8*); disk 29.95 (*0-7933-4174-4*) Gallopade Intl.

New Mexico "Jography" A Fun Run Thru Our State! Carole Marsh. (Carole Marsh New Mexico Bks.). (Illus.). (J). 1994. pap. 19.95 (*1-55609-875-8*); lib. bdg. 29.95 (*1-55609-874-X*); disk 29.95 (*1-55609-876-6*) Gallopade Intl.

New Mexico 7/99 Court Rules Supplement, 3 vols. Incl. Rule Sets 1 to 9. 1999. (*0-327-09439-7*, 51638-16); Rule Sets 10-12, 15-27 & Local Dist. Rules 1-11, 13. 1999. (*0-327-09440-0*, 51639-16); UJI 13, UJI 14 & Local Fed. Rules. 1999. (*0-327-09441-9*, 51640-16); suppl. ed. write for info. (*0-327-09438-9*, 46195-16) LEXIS Pub.

New Mexico Kid's Cookbook: Recipes, How-to, History, Lore & More! Carole Marsh. (Carole Marsh New Mexico Bks.). (Illus.). (J). 1994. pap. 19.95 (*0-7933-0804-6*); lib. bdg. 29.95 (*0-7933-0805-4*); disk 29.95 (*0-7933-0806-2*) Gallopade Intl.

New Mexico, Land of Enchantment Alphabet Book. Jan M. Mike. (Illus.). 32p. (Orig.). (J). (gr. k-5). 1993. pap. 7.95 (*0-918080-55-X*) Treas Chest Bks.

New Mexico Land Surveying Law: Questions & Answers. John E. Keen. 65p. (C). 1995. pap. text 25.00 (*1-56569-035-4*) Land Survey.

New Mexico Library Book: A Surprising Guide to the Unusual Special Collections in Libraries Across Our State for Students, Teachers, Writers & Publishers - Includes Reproducible Mailing Labels Plus Activities for Young People! Carole Marsh. (Carole Marsh New Mexico Bks.). (Illus.). 1994. pap. 19.95 (*0-7933-3099-8*); lib. bdg. 29.95 (*0-7933-3098-X*); disk 29.95 (*0-7933-3100-5*) Gallopade Intl.

***New Mexico Lobbyist Regulation Act, 1999 Edition.** 11p. 1999. Price not set. (*0-327-09742-6*, 2942013) LEXIS Pub.

***New Mexico Local & Federal Rules.** 2nd ed. Ed. by LLP Staff. 894p. 1999. write for info. (*0-327-04917-0*, 8215011) LEXIS Pub.

New Mexico Local & Federal Rules, Issue 59. 100p. 1999. ring bd., suppl. ed. write for info. (*0-327-00922-5*, 8215422) LEXIS Pub.

***New Mexico Local & Federal Rules, Issue 60.** Ed. by LLP Staff. 100p. 1999. ring bd. write for info. (*0-327-01380-X*, 8215423) LEXIS Pub.

New Mexico Local & Federal Rules Handbook, 1976-1992, 2 vols. University of New Mexico School of Law, Institute. 970p. 1993. ring bd. 135.00 (*0-409-25142-9*, 82150-10, MICHIE) LEXIS Pub.

New Mexico Local Federal Rules, 2 Vols. 2nd ed. 145.00 (*0-327-10167-9*) LEXIS Pub.

New Mexico Manufacturers Register. 3rd rev. ed. Ed. by Frank Lambing. 1999. 62.00 (*1-58202-059-0*) Manufacturers.

New Mexico Math! How It All Adds up in Our State. Carole Marsh. (Carole Marsh New Mexico Bks.). (Illus.). (YA). (gr. 3-12). 1996. pap. 19.95 (*0-7933-6581-3*); lib. bdg. 29.95 (*0-7933-6580-5*) Gallopade Intl.

New Mexico Media Book: A Surprising Guide to the Amazing Print, Broadcast & Online Media of Our State for Students, Teachers, Writers & Publishers - Includes Reproducible Mailing Labels Plus Activities for Young People! Carole Marsh. (Carole Marsh New Mexico Bks.). (Illus.). 1994. pap. 19.95 (*0-7933-3255-9*); lib. bdg. 29.95 (*0-7933-3254-0*); disk 29.95 (*0-7933-3256-7*) Gallopade Intl.

New Mexico Military Institute: A Centennial History. William E. Gibbs & Eugene T. Jackman. (Illus.). 450p. 1991. write for info. (*0-9630997-1-X*) NM Military.

New Mexico Mystery Van Takes Off! Book 1: Handicapped New Mexico Kids Sneak Off on a Big Adventure, Bk. 1. Carole Marsh. (Carole Marsh New Mexico Bks.). (Illus.). (J). (gr. 3-12). 1994. 29.95 (*0-7933-5054-9*); pap. 19.95 (*0-7933-5055-7*); disk 29.95 (*0-7933-5056-5*) Gallopade Intl.

New Mexico 1998 Replacement Index: 1998 Edition. rev. ed. 1375p. 1998. pap. write for info. (*0-327-05139-6*, 46181-14) LEXIS Pub.

New Mexico 1999 Advance Legislative Service Set. 2800p. 1999. pap. write for info. (*0-327-08653-X*, 46177-17) LEXIS Pub.

New Mexico 1999 Advance Annotation & Rules Service, No. 2. 220p. 1999. pap. write for info. (*0-327-08410-3*, 46185-15) LEXIS Pub.

New Mexico 1999 Advance Annotation & Rules Service, No. 3. annot. ed. 300p. 1999. pap. write for info. (*0-327-08625-4*, 46186-15) LEXIS Pub.

***New Mexico 1999 Cumulative Supplement, 80 vols.** Incl. Chapter. 1999. ring bd. (*0-327-09372-2*, 5138317); Chapter 8. 1999. ring bd. (*0-327-09303-X*, 5127717); Chapter 18. 1999. ring bd. (*0-327-09311-0*, 5130917); Chapter 11. 1999. ring bd. (*0-327-09306-4*, 5128817); Chapter 50. 1999. ring bd. (*0-327-09337-4*, 5142317); Chapter 58. 1999. ring bd. (*0-327-09347-1*, 5145717); Chapter 55 (Arts. 7-12) 1999. ring bd. (*0-327-09344-7*, 5144617); Chapter 55 (Arts. 3-6) 1999. ring bd. (*0-327-09343-9*, 5144417); Chapter 54. 1999. ring bd. (*0-327-09342-0*, 5143917); Chapter 59A (Arts. 26-56) 1999. ring bd. (*0-327-09349-8*, 5146317); Chapter 59, 59A (Arts. 1-25) 1999. ring bd. (*0-327-09348-X*, 5146017); Chapter 51. 1999. ring bd. (*0-327-09338-2*, 5142617); Chapter 57. 1999. ring bd. (*0-327-09346-3*, 5145217); Chapter 56. 1999. ring bd. (*0-327-09345-5*, 5144917); Chapter 53 (Arts. 11-19) 1999. ring bd. (*0-327-09341-2*, 5143617); Chapter 53 (Arts. 1-10) 1999. ring bd. (*0-327-09340-4*, 5143417); Chapter 52. 1999. ring bd. (*0-327-09339-0*, 5142917); Chapter 5. 1999. ring bd. (*0-327-09300-5*, 5126017); Chapter 48. 1999. ring bd. (*0-327-09336-6*, 5141717); Chapter 45. 1999. ring bd. (*0-327-09333-1*, 5140417); Chapter 44. 1999. ring bd. (*0-327-09332-3*, 5140117); Chapter 41. 1999. ring bd. (*0-327-09329-3*, 5138917); Chapter 47 (Arts. 5-13) 1999. ring bd. (*0-327-09335-8*, 5141417); Chapter 47 (Arts. 1-4) 1999. ring bd. (*0-327-09334-X*, 5141217); Chapter 43. 1999. ring bd. (*0-327-09331-5*, 5139817); Chapter 42. 1999. ring bd. (*0-327-09330-7*, 5139217); Chapter 4 (Arts. 33-62) 1999. ring bd. (*0-327-09249-1*, 5125717); Chapter 14. 1999. ring bd. (*0-327-09309-9*, 5129717); Chapter 9. 1999. ring bd. (*0-327-09304-8*, 5128017); Chapter 19. 1999. ring bd. (*0-327-09312-9*, 5131217); Chapter 1. 1999. ring bd. (*0-327-09244-0*, 5123817); Chapter 7 (Arts. 19-39) 1999. ring bd. (*0-327-09302-1*, 5127417); Chapter 7 (Arts. 1-18A) 1999. ring bd. (*0-327-09301-3*, 5127217); Chapter 17. 1999. ring bd. (*0-327-09310-2*, 5130617); Chapter 70. 1999. ring bd. (*0-327-09360-9*, 5151417); Chapter 75. 1999. ring bd. (*0-327-09368-4*, 5153717); Chapter 74. 1999. ring bd. (*0-327-09367-6*, 5153417); Chapter 71. 1999. ring bd. (*0-327-09361-7*, 5151717); Chapter 76 (Arts. 4-9) 1999. ring bd. (*0-327-09369-2*, 5154417); Chapter 73 (Arts. 14-19) 1999. ring bd. (*0-327-09365-X*, 5152917); Chapter 73 (Arts. 9-13) 1999. ring bd. (*0-327-09364-1*, 5152717); Chapter 73 (Arts. 1-8) 1999. ring bd. (*0-327-09363-3*, 5152517); Chapter 73 (Arts. 20-24) 1999. ring bd. (*0-327-09366-8*, 5153117); Chapter 72. 1999. ring bd. (*0-327-09362-5*, 5152217); Chapter 60 (Arts. 1-2E) 1999. ring bd. (*0-327-09350-1*, 5146817); Chapter 60 (Arts. 13-15) 1999. ring bd. (*0-327-09352-8*, 5147217); Chapter 60 (Arts. 3-12) 1999. ring bd. (*0-327-09351-X*, 5147017); Chapter 65. 1999. ring bd. (*0-327-09353-6*, 5149317); Chapter 69 (Arts. 11-25B) 1999. ring bd. (*0-327-09358-7*, 5150917); Chapter 69 (Arts. 1-10) 1999. ring bd. (*0-327-09357-9*, 5150717); Chapter 69 (Arts. 26-36) 1999. ring bd. (*0-327-09359-5*, 5151117); Chapter 67. 1999. ring bd. (*0-327-09356-0*, 5150117); Chapter 66 (Arts. 1-6) 1999. ring bd. (*0-327-09354-4*, 5149617); Chapter 66 (Arts. 7-12) 1999. ring bd. (*0-327-09355-2*, 5149817); Chapter 10. 1999. ring bd. (*0-327-09305-6*, 5128317); Chapter 13. 1999. ring bd. (*0-327-09308-0*, 5129417); Chapter 30 (Arts. 1-28) 1999. ring bd. (*0-327-09319-6*, 5135017); Chapter 30 (Arts. 29-50) 1999. ring bd. (*0-327-09320-X*, 5135217); Chapter 38. 1999. ring bd. (*0-327-09328-5*, 5138017); Chapter 35. 1999. ring bd. (*0-327-09325-0*, 5136917); Chapter 34. 1999. ring bd. (*0-327-09324-2*, 5136617); Chapter 31 (Arts. 1-16A) 1999. ring bd. (*0-327-09321-8*, 5135517); Chapter 31 (Arts. 17-26) 1999. ring bd. (*0-327-09322-6*, 5135717); Chapter 37. 1999. ring bd. (*0-327-09327-7*, 5137717); Chapter 36. 1999. ring bd. (*0-327-09326-9*, 5137217); Chapter 33. 1999. ring bd. (*0-327-09323-4*, 5136317); Chapter 3 (Arts. 1-7) 1999. ring bd. (*0-327-09246-7*, 5124617); Chapter 3 (Arts. 36-64) 1999. ring bd. (*0-327-09248-3*, 5125217); Chapter 3 (Arts. 23-35) 1999. ring bd. (*0-327-09247-5*, 5125017); Chapter 12. 1999. ring bd. (*0-327-09307-2*, 5129117); Chapter 20. 1999. ring bd. (*0-327-09313-7*, 5131517); Chapter 28. 1999. ring bd. (*0-327-09317-X*, 5134017); Chapter 25. 1999. ring bd. (*0-327-09371-4*, 5133217); Chapter 24. 1999. ring bd. (*0-327-09316-1*, 5132917); Chapter 29. 1999. ring bd. (*0-327-09318-8*, 5134717); Chapter 21. 1999. ring bd. (*0-327-09314-5*, 5132017); Chapter 22, 22A. 1999. ring bd. (*0-327-09315-3*, 5132317); Chapter 2. 1999. ring bd. (*0-327-09245-9*, 5124117); NM Const. 1999. ring bd. (*0-327-09243-2*, 5123217); Tables. 1999. ring bd. (*0-327-09370-6*, 5155617); 1900p. 1999. ring bd. write for info. (*0-327-09197-5*, 4618315) LEXIS Pub.

***New Mexico 1999 Replacement Pamphlets.** 4000p. 1999. ring bd. write for info. (*0-327-09235-1*, 4619813) LEXIS Pub.

***New Mexico 1999 Replacement Index.** 1441p. 1999. Price not set. (*0-327-09509-1*, 4618115) LEXIS Pub.

New Mexico 1999 Session Laws. 1200p. 1999. write for info. (*0-327-08654-8*, 4617617) LEXIS Pub.

***New Mexico, 1999 Session Laws (Hardbound of ALS Contents), Vol. 1.** 1400p. 1999. write for info. (*0-327-08790-0*, 4613813) LEXIS Pub.

***New Mexico 1999 Session Laws, Vol. 2.** 1400p. 1999. Price not set. (*0-327-08791-9*, 4613913) LEXIS Pub.

***New Mexico 1999 Session Laws, Vol. 3.** 1400p. 1999. write for info. (*0-327-09201-7*, 4612710) LEXIS Pub.

New Mexico 98 Supplement & Replacement Redos Pamphlett 94. 1998. write for info. (*0-327-07117-6*, 51469-13) LEXIS Pub.

New Mexico Objections at Trial. Barbara Bergman. 190p. 1992. pap. 39.50 (*0-614-05924-0*, MICHIE) LEXIS Pub.

New Mexico on My Mind. Intro. by Jim Arnholz. LC 90-80038. (America on My Mind Ser.). (Illus.). 120p. 1990. 29.95 (*1-56044-034-1*) Falcon Pub Inc.

New Mexico 100 Hundred Years Ago. Ingersoll et al. (Historical Ser.). (Illus.). 1977. pap. 4.50 (*0-89540-057-X*, SB-057) Sun Pub.

New Mexico Poetry Renaissance. Ed. by Sharon Niederman & Miriam Sagan. LC 94-12905. (Illus.). 216p. 1994. pap. 14.95 (*1-878610-41-4*) Red Crane Bks.

New Mexico Probate Manual. 2nd ed. William Henderson. 1997. ring bd. 120.00 (*0-327-03959-0*, 82157-10, MICHIE) LEXIS Pub.

New Mexico Probate Manual, Issue 3. 2nd ed. William Henderson. 66p. 1997. ring bd. 35.00 (*0-327-03974-4*, 82158-10, MICHIE) LEXIS Pub.

New Mexico Probate Manual, 1978-1992. 2nd ed. William N. Henderson. 290p. Date not set. ring bd. 120.00 (*0-409-25598-X*, 82156, MICHIE) LEXIS Pub.

New Mexico Probate Manual 1978-1992. 2nd ed. William N. Henderson. 1993. suppl. ed. 55.00 (*0-685-74465-5*, MICHIE) LEXIS Pub.

***New Mexico Profundo: Rituals of an Indo-Hispano Homeland.** Photos by Miguel A. Gandert. (Illus.). 2000. 50.00 (*0-89013-348-4*); pap. 29.95 (*0-89013-349-2*) Museum NM Pr.

New Mexico Project Archaeology. Carol J. Ellick. (Statistical Research Public Archaeology Ser.: Vol. 1). 106p. 1995. per. 10.00 (*1-879442-52-3*) Stats Res.

New Mexico Quiz Bowl Crash Course! Carole Marsh. (Carole Marsh New Mexico Bks.). (Illus.). (J). 1994. pap. 19.95 (*1-55609-890-1*); lib. bdg. 29.95 (*1-55609-889-8*); disk 29.95 (*1-55609-891-X*) Gallopade Intl.

New Mexico Register, No. IX. 40p. Date not set. pap. 270.00 (*0-327-05314-3*, 45911-15) LEXIS Pub.

New Mexico Register Vol. IX, No. 7: April 15, 1998. 302p. 1998. pap. write for info. (*0-327-05047-0*, 45919-37) LEXIS Pub.

New Mexico Regulations: Containing Insurance Department Rules, Selected Attorney General's Opinions, & Advice of the General Counsel. New Mexico. Insurance Dept et al. LC 97-67934. (Illus.). 1997. write for info. (*0-89246-476-3*) NILS Pub.

New Mexico Retirement & Relocation Guide. large type ed. Rip Reed et al. (Retirement & Relocation Guides Ser.). (Illus.). 350p. Date not set. pap. 24.95 (*1-56559-108-9*) HGI-Over Fifty.

New Mexico, Rio Grande & Other Essays. Photos by Robert Reynolds & David Muench. (Illus.). 96p. 1992. 27.50 (*1-55868-093-4*) Gr Arts Ctr Pub.

New Mexico Road & Recreation Atlas. Benchmark Maps Staff. LC 96-129084. 96p. 1995. write for info. (*0-929591-26-7*, Benchmark Maps) Map Link.

New Mexico Road & Recreation Atlas. Benchmark Maps Staff. 1997. pap. 18.95 (*0-929591-42-9*) Map Link.

New Mexico Rockhounding: A Guide to Minerals, Gemstones, & Fossils. Stephen M. Voynick. LC 97-10502. 350p. 1997. pap. text 20.00 (*0-87842-360-5*) Mountain Pr.

New Mexico Rocks & Minerals Guide: A Guidebook. Frank S. Kimbler & Robert J. Narsavage, Jr. LC 81-5350. (Illus.). 76p. (Orig.). 1986. pap. 8.95 (*0-913270-97-0*) Sunstone Pr.

New Mexico Rollercoasters! Carole Marsh. (Carole Marsh New Mexico Bks.). (Illus.). (J). (gr. 3-12). 1994. pap. 19.95 (*0-7933-5318-1*); lib. bdg. 29.95 (*0-7933-5317-3*) Gallopade Intl.

New Mexico Rollercoasters! Carole Marsh. (Carole Marsh New Mexico Bks.). (Illus.). (YA). (gr. 3-12). 1994. disk 29.95 (*0-7933-5319-X*) Gallopade Intl.

New Mexico Roots Ltd, 11 vols., Set. Fray A. Chavez. 2308p. 1982. lib. bdg. 120.00 (*0-913630-06-3*) UNM Gen Lib.

New Mexico Rules Annotated. 1998. write for info. (*0-327-07109-5*, 46120-16) LEXIS Pub.

New Mexico Rules Annotated, 3 vols. 3100p. 1998. 81.00 (*0-327-07106-0*, 46182-16) LEXIS Pub.

New Mexico Rules Annotated, Vol. 1. 1998. write for info. (*0-327-07107-9*, 46121-16) LEXIS Pub.

New Mexico Rules Annotated, Vol. 2. 1998. write for info. (*0-327-07108-7*, 46122-16) LEXIS Pub.

New Mexico Rules of Evidence. Murl A. Larkin. 480p. 1994. ring bd. 125.00 (*0-614-05925-9*, MICHIE) LEXIS Pub.

New Mexico Rules of Evidence, 1983, 1986, 1991. rev. ed. Murl A. Larkin. 480p. 1991. ring bd. 125.00 (*0-409-25133-X*, MICHIE) LEXIS Pub.

New Mexico Rules of Evidence, 1983, 1986, 1991. rev. ed. Murl A. Larkin. 1994. ring bd., suppl. ed. 65.00 (*0-685-49752-6*, MICHIE) LEXIS Pub.

New Mexico Santos: Religious Images in the Spanish New World. E. Boyd. (Illus.). 64p. 1995. pap. 12.95 (*0-89013-284-4*) Museum NM Pr.

New Mexico Scenic Drives see Scenic Driving New Mexico

New Mexico School Trivia: An Amazing & Fascinating Look at Our State's Teachers, Schools & Students! Carole Marsh. (Carole Marsh New Mexico Bks.). (Illus.). (J). 1994. pap. 19.95 (*0-7933-0801-1*); lib. bdg. 29.95 (*0-7933-0802-X*); disk 29.95 (*0-7933-0803-8*) Gallopade Intl.

New Mexico Showdown. W. Camp. 1989. pap. 2.95 (*1-55817-194-0*) Kensgtn Pub Corp.

New Mexico Silly Basketball Sportsmystereis, Vol. 1. Carole Marsh. (Carole Marsh New Mexico Bks.). (Illus.). (J). 1994. pap. 19.95 (*0-7933-0798-8*); lib. bdg. 29.95 (*0-7933-0799-6*); disk 29.95 (*0-7933-0800-3*) Gallopade Intl.

New Mexico Silly Basketball Sportsmysteries, Vol. 2. Carole Marsh. (Carole Marsh New Mexico Bks.). (Illus.). (J). 1994. pap. 19.95 (*0-7933-1819-X*); lib. bdg. 29.95 (*0-7933-1818-1*); disk 29.95 (*0-7933-1820-3*) Gallopade Intl.

New Mexico Silly Football Sportsmysteries. Carole Marsh. (Carole Marsh New Mexico Bks.). (Illus.). (J). 1994. pap. 19.95 (*1-55609-881-2*); pap. 19.95 (*1-55609-884-7*); lib. bdg. 29.95 (*1-55609-880-4*); disk 29.95 (*1-55609-882-0*); disk 29.95 (*1-55609-885-5*) Gallopade Intl.

New Mexico Silly Trivia! Carole Marsh. (Carole Marsh New Mexico Bks.). (Illus.). (J). 1994. pap. 19.95 (*1-55609-872-3*); lib. bdg. 29.95 (*1-55609-871-5*); disk 29.95 (*1-55609-873-1*) Gallopade Intl.

New Mexico Spanish Colonial House. Bunny Huffman. 1991. pap. 17.50 (*0-89013-228-3*) Museum NM Pr.

New Mexico Spelling Bee! Score Big by Correctly Spelling Our State's Unique Names. Carole Marsh. (Carole Marsh New Mexico Bks.). (Illus.). (YA). (gr. 3-12). 1996. pap. 19.95 (*0-7933-6734-4*); lib. bdg. 29.95 (*0-7933-6733-6*) Gallopade Intl.

New Mexico State Constitution: A Reference Guide, 23. Chuck Smith. LC 95-46275. (Reference Guides to the State Constitutions of the United States Ser.: Vol. 23). 248p. 1996. lib. bdg. 79.50 (*0-313-29548-4*, Greenwood Pr) Greenwood.

New Mexico State Parks. Barbara McCaig & Boyce. (Illus.). 100p. (Orig.). 1989. pap. text 5.95 (*0-935201-66-1*) Affordable Adven.

New Mexico Statutes. annot. ed. Arlene Eisenberg. write for info. (*0-614-05926-7*, MICHIE) LEXIS Pub.

New Mexico Statutes Annotated, 18. 800.00 (*0-327-11865-2*) LEXIS Pub.

New Mexico Statutes Annotated, 1978 Compilation. 1978. write for info. (*0-87215-224-3*, MICHIE) LEXIS Pub.

New Mexico Statutes Annotated, 1998 Advance Legislative Service Pamphlet, No. 1. annot. ed. 848p. 1998. pap. write for info. (*0-327-05041-1*, 46106-16) LEXIS Pub.

New Mexico Statutes Annotated, 1998 Advance Legislative Service Pamphlet, No. 2. annot. ed. 840p. 1998. pap. write for info. (*0-327-05042-X*, 46107-16) LEXIS Pub.

New Mexico Style: A Sourcebook of Traditional Architectural Details. Nancy H. Warren. (Illus.). 176p. 1995. pap. 35.00 (*0-89013-279-8*) Museum NM Pr.

New Mexico, the Shining Land. John L. Sinclair. LC 80-52271. 221p. reprint ed. pap. 68.60 (*0-608-17832-2*, 203258700080) Bks Demand.

New Mexico Timeline: A Chronology of New Mexico History, Mystery, Trivia, Legend, Lore & More. Carole Marsh. (Carole Marsh New Mexico Bks.). (Illus.). (J). (gr. 3-12). 1994. pap. 19.95 (*0-7933-5969-4*); lib. bdg. 29.95 (*0-7933-5968-6*); disk 29.95 (*0-7933-5970-8*) Gallopade Intl.

New Mexico Trivia. Robert Ellis et al. LC 96-2092. 192p. 1996. pap. text 6.95 (*1-55853-380-X*) Rutledge Hill Pr.

New Mexico II: Photos of David Muench. Photos by David Muench. (Illus.). 160p. 1991. 39.95 (*1-55868-048-9*) Gr Arts Ctr Pub.

***New Mexico 2000.** Fodors Travel Publications, Inc. Staff. (2000 Ser.). (Illus.). 1999. pap. 16.50 (*0-679-00361-4*) Fodors Travel.

New Mexico 2000! Coming Soon to a Calendar Near You - The 21st Century! - Complete Set of AL 2000 Items. Carole Marsh. (Two Thousand! Ser.). (Illus.). (J). (gr. 3-12). 1998. pap. 75.00 (*0-7933-9371-X*); lib. bdg. 85.00 (*0-7933-9372-8*) Gallopade Intl.

New Mexico 2000! Coming Soon to a Calendar near You--The 21st Century! Carole Marsh. (Two Thousand! Ser.). (Illus.). (J). (gr. 3-12). 1998. pap. 19.95 (*0-7933-8769-8*); lib. bdg. 29.95 (*0-7933-8768-X*) Gallopade Intl.

***New Mexico 2000 Advance Annotation & Rules Service No. 1.** 1999. pap. Price not set. (*0-327-09746-9*, 4618416) LEXIS Pub.

***New Mexico 2000 Advance Legislative Service.** 800p. 2000. pap. write for info. (*0-327-11122-4*, 4617718) LEXIS Pub.

New Mexico UFO's & Extraterrestrials! A Look at the Sightings & Science in Our State. Carole Marsh. (Carole Marsh New Mexico Bks.). (Illus.). (J). (gr. 3-12). 1997. pap. 19.95 (*0-7933-6428-0*); lib. bdg. 29.95 (*0-7933-6427-2*) Gallopade Intl.

***New Mexico Unemployment Compensation Laws: 1999 Edition.** 78p. 1999. ring bd. 14.00 (*0-327-09895-3*, 2942612) LEXIS Pub.

***New Mexico Vegetation: Past, Present & Future.** William A. Dick-Peddie. (Illus.). 2000. pap. 24.95 (*0-8263-2164-X*) U of NM Pr.

New Mexico Vegetation: Past, Present, & Future. William A. Dick-Peddie. LC 92-3138. (Illus.). 276p. 1993. reprint ed. pap. 85.60 (*0-608-07284-2*, 206751200009) Bks Demand.

An Asterisk (*) at the beginning of an entry indicates that the title is appearing for the first time.

New Mexico Village Arts. Roland F. Dickey. LC 90-33107. (Illus.). 280p. 1990. reprint ed. pap. 86.80 (0-608-04130-0, 206486300011) Bks Demand.
New Mexico Wildlife. James Kavanagh. (Pocket Naturalist Ser.). (Illus.). 1998. 5.95 (1-889903-25-6, Pub. by Waterford WA) Falcon Pub Inc.
New Mexico Wildlife Viewing Guide. Jane S. MacCarter. LC 93-42965. (Watchable Wildlife Ser.). (Illus.). 96p. 1994. pap. 8.95 (1-56044-213-1) Falcon Pub Inc.
***New Mexico Wildlife Viewing Guide.** 2nd ed. Jane S. MacCarter. LC 99-89042. (Illus.). 2000. 9.95 (1-56044-991-8) Falcon Pub Inc.
New Mexico Worker's Compensation Laws & Regulations Annotated, 2 vols. 32p. 1998. ring bd., suppl. ed. 10.00 (0-327-05855-2, 29412-12) LEXIS Pub.
New Mexico Workers' Compensation Laws & Regulations Annotated: 1997 Edition. 356p. pap. 35.00 (1-55834-671-6) LEXIS Pub.
New Mexico Workers' Compensation Manual, 1996-1997. Carlos G. Martinez. LC 93-27860. 684p. 1997. ring bd. 99.95 (1-57292-048-3); ring bd., suppl. ed. 69.95 (1-57292-047-5) Austin & Winfield.
New Mexico 1998 Cumulative Supplement, 93 vols. 1585p. 1998. write for info. (0-327-05590-1, 46183-14) LEXIS Pub.
New Mexico's Atomic Tour. Ron Swartley. 52p. 1992. pap. 4.95 (0-9634309-0-4) Frontier Image.
New Mexico's Atomic Tour. 2nd ed. Ron Swartley. (Illus.). 62p. 1995. pap. 5.95 (0-9634309-5-5) Frontier Image.
New Mexico's Best. Richard Mahler. (Illus.). 240p. 1996. pap. 15.95 (1-55591-232-X) Fulcrum Pub.
New Mexico's Best Ghost Towns: A Practical Guide. Philip Varney. LC 80-84818. (Illus.). 190p. 1987. reprint ed. pap. 15.95 (0-8263-1010-9) U of NM Pr.
New Mexico's Book World: A Resource Guide. 2nd ed. Ed. by Richard L. Polese. 210p. 1999. pap. text 10.00 (0-943734-37-1) Ocean Tree Bks.
New Mexico's Buffalo Soldiers, 1866-1900. Monroe L. Billington. (Illus.). 278p. 1993. pap. 22.50 (0-87081-346-3) Univ Pr Colo.
New Mexico's Continental Divide Trail: The Official Guide. Bob Julyan. LC 00-23499. (Illus.). 304p. 2000. pap. 24.95 (1-56579-331-5) Westcliffe Pubs.
New Mexico's First Colonists, the 1597-1600 Enlistments for New Mexico, under Juan de Onate, Adelantado & Gobernador. David Snow. (Illus.). 138p. Date not set. 35.00 (0-9652463-0-2) Hispanic Geneal.
New Mexico's Historic Places: The Guide to National & State Register Sites. Ed. by Marci L. Riskin. LC 99-58985. (Adventure Roads Ser.). (Illus.). 160p. 2000. pap. 16.95 (0-943734-40-1, 1HIS) Ocean Tree Bks.
New Mexico's (Most Devastating!) Disasters & (Most Calamitous!) Catastrophies! Carole Marsh. (Carole Marsh New Mexico Bks.). (Illus.). (J). 1994. pap. 19.95 (0-7933-0789-9); lib. bdg. 29.95 (0-7933-0790-2); disk 29.95 (0-7933-0791-0) Gallopade Intl.
New Mexico's Quest for Statehood, 1846-1912. Robert W. Larson. LC 68-23022. 415p. reprint ed. pap. 128.70 (0-608-15463-6, 202931500060) Bks Demand.
New Mexico's Railroads: A Historical Survey. rev. ed. David F. Myrick. LC 89-27309. (Illus.). 276p. 1990. pap. 18.95 (0-8263-1185-7) U of NM Pr.
New Mexico's Royal Road: Trade & Travel on the Chihuahua Trail. Max L. Moorhead. LC 94-35293. (Illus.). 242p. 1995. 14.95 (0-8061-2651-5) U of Okla Pr.
New Mexico's 34 Counties. Illus. by Kate G. Harper. 69p. (J). 1990. student ed. 3.50 (1-879978-00-8) J O Foley.
New Mexico's Timber Production & Mill Residue, 1986. William H. McLain. (Illus.). 24p. 1998. reprint ed. pap. 3.40 (0-89904-932-X, Ecosytems Resrch) Crumb Elbow Pub.
New Mexico's Unsolved Mysteries (& Their "Solutions") Includes Scientific Information & Other Activities for Students. Carole Marsh. (Carole Marsh New Mexico Bks.). (Illus.). (J). (gr. 3-12). 1994. pap. 19.95 (0-7933-5816-7); lib. bdg. 29.95 (0-7933-5815-9); disk 29.95 (0-7933-5817-5) Gallopade Intl.
New Mexico's Wilderness Areas: The Complete Guide. Bob Julyan. LC 98-19238. (Illus.). 264p. 1999. pap. 24.95 (1-56579-291-2) Westcliffe Pubs.
***New Mexico/Utah State Credit Directory, 2000 Edition.** rev. ed. American Business Directories Staff. 368p. 1999. boxed set 115.00 incl. cd-rom (0-7687-0313-1) Am Busn Direct.
New Michaelis Portuguese-English Illustrated Dictionary: Novo Michaelis Dicionario Ilustrado, Vol. 2. 40th ed. Michaelis. (ENG & POR., Illus.). 1327p. 1986. 95.00 (0-8288-0495-8, M14122) Fr & Eur.
***New Microbiotests for Routine Toxicity Screening.** Guido Persoone et al. 210p. 2000. 99.50 (0-306-46406-3, Kluwer Plenum) Kluwer Academic.
New Microsurgical Concepts (Posterior & Anterior Segments) Ed. by J. Draeger & R. Winter. (Developments in Ophthalmology Ser.: Vol. 14). (Illus.). xii, 208p. 1987. 156.75 (3-8055-4545-2) S Karger.
New Microsurgical Concepts II: Cornea, Posterior Segment, External Microsurgery. Ed. by J. Draeger & R. Winter. (Developments in Ophthalmology Ser.: Vol. 18). (Illus.). x, 226p. 1989. 182.75 (3-8055-4922-9) S Karger.
New Mid-Life Crisis: The Reality of Caring for Your Parents. Martha I. Dixon. vi, 110p. 1998. pap. 13.00 (0-9668125-0-6) Revelat Pr Inc.
New Middle Class & the Remaking of the Central City. David Ley. LC 96-11424. (Oxford Geographical & Environmental Studies Series). (Illus.). 400p. (C). 1997. text 85.00 (0-19-823292-6) OUP.
New Middle Classes: Social, Psychological, & Political Issues. Ed. by Arthur J. Vidich. LC 94-7525. (Main Trends of the Modern World Ser.). 320p. (C). 1994. text 50.00 (0-8147-8776-2); pap. text 18.50 (0-8147-8777-0) NYU Pr.
New Middle East. Shimon Peres. 240p. 1995. pap. 14.95 (0-8050-3811-6, Owl) H Holt & Co.
New Middle Jurassic Ammonitina from New Guinea see Bulletins of American Paleontology: Vol. 57
New Midwifery: Reflections on Renaissance & Regulation. Ed. by Farah M. Shroff. 250p. 1997. pap. 16.95 (0-88961-224-2, Pub. by Womens Pr) LPC InBook.
New Migrants in the Marketplace: Boston's Ethnic Entrepreneurs. Ed. by Marilyn Halter. LC 94-24122. (Illus.). 192p. (C). 1995. lib. bdg. 30.00 (0-87023-963-5) U of Mass Pr.
***New Milford.** Frances L. Smith. (Images of America Ser.). (Illus.). 128p. 2000. pap. 18.99 (0-7385-0450-5) Arcadia Publng.
New Milford, CT. Historical Briefs, Inc. Staff. Ed. by Thomas Antonucci & Michael Antonucci. 176p. 1991. pap. 19.95 (0-89677-007-9) Hist Briefs.
New Military & Naval Dictionary. Ed. by Frank Gaynor. LC 70-90512. 295p. 1969. reprint ed. lib. bdg. 59.75 (0-8371-2129-9, GAMN, Greenwood Pr) Greenwood.
***New Military Humanism: Lessons from Kosovo.** Noam Chomsky. LC 99-38488. 208p. (C). 1999. 29.95 (1-56751-177-5); pap. 11.96 (1-56751-176-7, Pub. by Common Courage) LPC InBook.
New Military in Russia: Ten Myths That Shape the Image. Richard F. Staar. LC 95-49877. (Illus.). 272p. 1996. 42.95 (1-55750-798-8); pap. 16.95 (1-55750-740-6) Naval Inst Pr.
New Military Policy in Latin America. Robert Wesson. LC 82-9871. 230p. 1982. 49.95 (0-275-90924-7, C0924, Praeger Pubs) Greenwood.
New Millenium Guide to Managing Your Money. John T. McCarthy. LC 98-174951. (Illus.). 288p. 1998. 27.95 (0-9660577-0-8) Maggie Pub.
***New Millenium School Teachers: Tock 'n Rapsody Rapin.** Mark Stephens. 557p. 2000. pap. 16.95 (1-881524-70-1) Milligan Bks.
***New Millennial Sexstyles.** Carol Siegel. LC 00-35011. 2000. pap. write for info. (0-253-21404-1) Ind U Pr.
***New Millennium, 1 vol.** Mary Engelbreit. 1999. 8.95 (0-7407-0206-8) Andrews & McMeel.
***New Millennium.** Anthony F. Gulotta. LC 99-69940. 59p. 2000. pap. 8.00 (1-886467-51-X) WJM Press.
New Millennium: Under the Cosmic Influences of the Outer Planetary Systems. Trudy Jarno. LC 91-76683. (Illus.). 240p. 1992. pap. 13.95 (0-930422-01-5) Dennis-Landman.
***New Millennium Atlas of the U. S., Canada & the World.** (Illus.). 200p. (J). (gr. 4 up). 1999. lib. bdg. 33.27 (0-8368-2491-1) Gareth Stevens Inc.
New Millennium Catechism. Joao De Deus Gois. LC 98-230806. 32p. 1998. pap. text 1.00 (0-7648-0277-1) Liguori Pubns.
***New Millennium Encyclopedia Reference.** 1999. pap. 7.00 (0-671-04676-4) S&S Trade.
***New Millennium Families: How You Can Soar above the Coming Flood of Change.** Michael C. Blackwell. LC 99-48420. 160p. 2000. pap. 17.95 (1-887905-21-9) Pkway Pubs.
***New Millennium Fullfills Ancient Prophecies.** Mahajan. LC 99-931139. ix, 93 p. 1999. write for info. (81-208-1644-7, Pub. by Motilal Bnarsidass) S Asia.
New Millennium Magic: A Complete System of Self-Realization. expanded rev. ed. Donald Tyson. LC 96-20700. Orig. Title: New Magus. (Illus.). 384p. 1996. pap. text 19.95 (1-56718-745-5) Llewellyn Pubns.
New Millennium Manual: A Once & Future Guide. Robert G. Clouse et al. LC 98-48302. (Illus.). 224p. (C). 1999. pap. 12.99 (0-8010-5848-1, Bridgept Bks) Baker Bks.
New Millennium NASA: International Space Station & 21st Century Space Exploration. Irene K. Brown. LC 98-65118. 116p. 1998. write for info. (1-881547-26-4) Pioneer Pubns.
New Millennium Spiritual Journey: Change Your Life - Develop Your Spritual Priorities with Help from Today's Most Inspiring Spiritual Teachers. SkyLight Paths Editors. LC 99-38669. 144p. 1999. pap. 16.95 (1-893361-05-5) SkyLight Paths.
New Millennium Writings, Vol. 1. Don Williams. 1996. pap. text 7.95 (1-888338-03-2) New Messenger Bks.
New Millennium Writings: Spring & Summer, 1996. Madison Smartt Bell et al. (Illus.). 128p. (Orig.). 1996. pap. 5.95 (1-888338-01-6) New Messenger Bks.
New Millennium Writings: Winter, 1998-1999. Ed. by Don Williams. 160p. pap. 7.95 (1-888338-12-1) New Messenger Bks.
New Millennium Writings Vol. 3: Spring & Summer 1998, Issue 1. 1998. pap. 7.95 (1-888338-11-3) New Messenger Bks.
***New Millionaire's Handbook: A Guide to Contemporary Social Climbing.** Chris Fountain. LC 00-35511. (Illus.). 224p. 2000. pap. 12.95 (0-7407-1167-9) Andrews & McMeel.
***New Millionaires How to Succeed in Network Marketing.** Pete Billac. Ed. by Ken Harris & Bill Jones. LC 99-65295. 93p. 1999. pap. 9.95 (0-943629-41-1) Swan Pub.
New Mime in Europe. Peter Bu. Ed. by Thomas Leabhart. (Mime Journal Ser.). (Illus.). 179p. (Orig.). 1983. pap. 12.00 (0-9611066-7-0) Mime Jour.
New Mime in North America. Lust et al. (Mime Journal Ser.). (Illus.). 183p. (Orig.). 1982. pap. text 12.00 (0-9611066-8-9) Mime Jour.
New Mimesis: Shakespeare & the Representation of Reality. A. D. Nuttall. 232p. (C). 1985. pap. 12.95 (0-416-35870-5, 3947) Routledge.
New Miniature Pinscher. Sari B. Tietjen. (Illus.). 192p. 1988. 27.95 (0-87605-211-1) Howell Bks.
New Miniature Schnauzer. 2nd ed. Dan Kiedrowski. LC 96-30037. 1997. 27.95 (0-87605-241-3) Howell Bks.
New Ministries: The Global Context. William R. Burrows. LC 80-17261. 192p. (Orig.). 1980. reprint ed. pap. 59.60 (0-7837-9818-0, 206054700005) Bks Demand.
New Minority Groups in the Citadel of Europe: (Report on the Multidisciplinary Conference on the Educational & Cultural Aspects of Community Relations - Strasbourg, 1989) 1992. 21.00 (92-871-2051-X, Pub. by Council of Europe) Manhattan Pub Co.
New Mirrors for Travelers. James K. Paulding. (Notable American Authors Ser.). 1999. reprint ed. lib. bdg. 125.00 (0-7812-4747-0) Rprt Serv.
***New Missionaries: Memoirs of a Foreign Advisor in Less-Developed Countries.** Richard D. Mallon. 128p. 2000. pap. 14.95 (0-674-00348-9) HUP.
New Mobility Magazine's Spinal Network: The Total Wheelchair Resource Book. 3rd rev. ed. Ed. & Illus. by Spinal Network Staff. 570p. 1998. pap. 49.95 (0-9661701-1-3) Miramar Commns.
New Model Army, 1645-60. Stuart Asquith. (Men-at-Arms Ser.: No. 110). (Illus.). 48p. pap. 11.95 (0-85045-385-2, 9043, Pub. by Ospry) Stackpole.
New Model Me. John R. Rowe et al. (gr. 8-12). 1983. teacher ed. 13.95 (0-8077-2733-4); text, student ed. 10.95 (0-8077-2732-6) Tchrs Coll.
New Model of Health & Disease. George Vithoulkas. 216p. (Orig.). 1991. pap. 14.95 (1-55643-087-6) North Atlantic.
New Model of the Universe. P. D. Ouspensky. LC 97-6291. 576p. 1997. reprint ed. pap. text 12.95 (0-486-29701-2) Dover.
New Model of the Universe (1931) P. D. Ouspensky. 570p. 1999. reprint ed. pap. 27.50 (0-7661-0822-8) Kessinger Pub.
New Model Seder. Ed. by Sidney Greenberg. pap. 2.75 (0-87677-058-8) Prayer Bk.
New Models & Opportunities: Electronic Publishing '97 Conference Proceedings. Ed. by Fytton Rowland & Jack Meadows. (Illus.). 300p. 1997. 60.00 (1-891365-00-2) ICCC Pr.
New Models for Depression. Ed. by Dieter Ebert & Klaus P. Ebmeier. LC 98-27633. (Advances in Biological Psychiatry Ser.: Vol. 19, 1998). (Illus.). viii, 204p. 1998. 170.50 (3-8055-6698-0) S Karger.
New Models for Higher Education. Ed. by Joel W. Meyerson & Richard Anderson. LC 98-161257. 144p. 1997. 34.95 (1-56079-808-4) Petersons.
New Models in Geography: The Political-Economy Perspective, 1. Ed. by Richard Peet & Nigel J. Thrift. 448p. 1989. text 75.00 (0-685-44712-X) Routledge.
New Models, New Extensions of Attribution Theory: The Third Attribution - Personality Theory Conference, CSPP-LA, 1988. Ed. by S. L. Zelen. (Recent Research in Psychology Ser.). (Illus.). viii, 212p. 1990. 71.95 (0-387-97492-X) Spr-Verlag.
New Models of Social Service Research. Ed. by Edwin J. Thomas. (Journal of Social Service Research: Vol. 2, No. 1). 140p. 1979. pap. text 14.95 (0-917724-71-2) Haworth Pr.
New Modern. Carla Breeze. LC 94-38699. 1995. 47.50 (0-86636-327-0) PBC Intl Inc.
New Modern. Carla Breeze. (Illus.). 160p. 1996. pap. 27.50 (0-86636-437-4) St Martin.
New Modern. PBC International Staff. 1997. pap. 24.95 (0-688-14926-X, Wm Morrow) Morrow Avon.
New Modern: Anything Goes in Today's Decorating. Joan Mackie. (Illus.). 128p. 1998. pap. 19.95 (0-7710-2013-9) McCland & Stewart.
New Modern Furniture Design. ARCO Editorial Board Staff. (Illus.). 208p. 1998. 55.00 (0-8230-7194-4) Watsn-Guptill.
New Modern Times: Factors Reshaping the World of Work. Ed. by David B. Bills. LC 94-1044. (SUNY Series in the Sociology of Work). 319p. (C). 1995. pap. text 21.95 (0-7914-2228-3) State U NY Pr.
New Modern Witch's Dreambook. rev. ed. Sarah L. Morrison. LC 93-43437. Orig. Title: The Modern Witch's Dreambook. 240p. 1994. reprint ed. 8.95 (0-8065-1471-X, Citadel Pr) Carol Pub Group.
New Modernism: Deconstructive Tendencies in Art. (Art & Design Profiles Ser.). (Illus.). 80p. 1988. pap. 21.95 (0-312-02243-3) St Martin.
New Modernist in World Architecture. Patricia M. Snibbe. 288p. 1999. pap., student ed. 79.95 (0-07-059484-8) McGraw.
***New Modernity? Reason & Passion at the Century's End.** Wendy Wheeler. 256p. 1999. pap. 20.00 (0-85315-877-0, Pub. by Lawrence & Wishart) NYU Pr.
New Moderns: Architecture & Design for Living. Jonathan Glancey. (Illus.). 191p. 1998. pap. 25.00 (1-57959-036-5, SOMA) BB&T Inc.
New Modes of Conflict. B. Jenkins. LC 83-3132. 20p. 1983. pap. 4.00 (0-8330-0486-7, R-3009-DNA) Rand Corp.
New Modes of Local Political Organization: Local Government Fragmentation in Scandinavia. Ed. by Peter Bogason. LC 95-48993. (Illus.). 207p. (C). 1996. lib. bdg. 115.00 (1-56072-295-9) Nova Sci Pubs.
New Modes of Particle Acceleration - Techniques & Sources: Proceedings of a Conference Held in Santa Barbara, CA, 1996. Ed. by Zohreh Parsa. LC 97-72977. (AIP Conference Proceedings Ser.: Vol. 396). (Illus.). 201p. 1997. 70.00 (1-56396-728-6) Am Inst Physics.
New Modes of Thought (1901) C. T. Stockwell. 156p. 1998. reprint ed. pap. 17.95 (0-7661-0651-9) Kessinger Pub.
New Moment in the Americas. Ed. by Robert S. Leiken. LC 94-47503. 160p. (C). 1994. pap. 19.95 (1-56000-811-3, Pub. by U Miami N-S Ctr) L Rienner.
New Mom's Bath Book: A Soak for the Maternal Soul, 4 vols. Elizabeth O'Dowd & Cynthia Good. (Floating Bath Book Collection). (Illus.). 10p. 1998. pap. 9.95 (1-56352-458-9) Longstreet.
New Moms' Practical Parenting Tips. Mothers of Pre-Schoolers Int'l Staff. 1997. pap. 6.99 (0-614-28112-1) Zondervan.
New Monetary Order for Europe. Karl O. Pohl. LC HG0930.5.P6. (Per Jacobsson Lecture Ser.: Vol. 1992). 32p. reprint ed. pap. 30.00 (0-608-08739-4, 206937800004) Bks Demand.
New Monetary System. C. S. Norburn & Russell Norburn. 1979. lib. bdg. 59.95 (0-8490-2977-5) Gordon Pr.
New Money for Healthy Communities. Thomas H. Greco, Jr. (Illus.). 216p. (Orig.). 1994. pap. 15.95 (0-9625208-2-9) T H Greco.
New Money for Healthy Communities. 2nd rev. ed. Thomas H. Greco, Jr. (Illus.). 260p. (Orig.). 1999. pap. 18.95 (0-9625208-3-7) T H Greco.
New Money Management: A Framework for Asset Allocation. Ralph Vince. LC 94-31463. (Finance Editions Ser.). 224p. 1995. 65.00 (0-471-04307-9) Wiley.
New Money Masters. John Train. LC 89-45071. 400p. 1994. pap. 16.00 (0-88730-637-3, HarpBusn) HarpInfo.
New Money System. Mary S. Relfe. 272p. 1982. pap. 7.00 (0-9607986-1-7) League Prayer.
New Money System: Electronic Funds Transfer, Cashless Systems & the Elimination of Freedom & Privacy. 1992. lib. bdg. 75.00 (0-8490-5387-0) Gordon Pr.
New Money Workbook for Women. Carole Phillips. LC 87-27657. 160p. (Orig.). 1988. pap. 9.95 (0-931790-82-4) Brick Hse Pub.
New Monologues for Mature Actors. Compiled by Ann McDonough. 190p. 1996. pap. 19.95 (0-87129-715-9, N44) Dramatic Pub.
New Monologues for Reader's Theater. Steven Porter. LC 94-46526. 74p. 1995. pap. 10.00 (0-88734-651-0) Players Pr.
New Monte Carlo Methods with Estimating Derivatives. G. A. Mikhailov. 202p. 1995. 145.00 (90-6764-190-1, Pub. by VSP) Coronet Bks.
New Moon. Richard Grossinger. LC 96-2106. 592p. 1996. 25.00 (1-883319-44-7) Frog Ltd CA.
New Moon. Pegi D. Shea. LC 95-83979. (Illus.). 32p. (J). (ps-k). 1996. 14.95 (1-56397-410-X) Boyds Mills Pr.
***New Moon.** Pegi Deitz Shea. LC 95-83979. (Illus.). 32p. (J). (ps up). 2000. pap. 8.95 (1-56397-922-5) Boyds Mills Pr.
New Moon. Wells. 32p. (J). 2000. 14.45 (0-7868-0396-7, Pub. by Hyperion); lib. bdg. 15.49 (0-7868-2346-1, Pub. by Hyperion) Little.
New Moon: Vocal Selections. Ed. by Carol Cuellar. 36p. (Orig.). (C). 1984. pap. text 10.95 (0-7692-0769-3, SF0118) Wrner Bros.
New Moon - Luna Nueva. Nellie P. Cartwright. LC 70-38. (ENG & SPA.). 85p. (Orig.). 1982. pap. text 5.00 (0-9601482-4-8) N P Cartwright.
New Moon of the Seasons: Prayers from the Highlands & Islands. Tr. & Compiled by Alexander Carmichael. 160p. 1992. reprint ed. pap. 8.95 (0-940262-51-7, Lindisfarne) Anthroposophic.
New Moon Rising. Linda Heron-Wind. 233p. (Orig.). 1995. pap. 13.95 (1-878980-12-2) Delphi IL.
New Moon Rising. Eugenia Price. 320p. 1985. mass mkt. 6.99 (0-553-26848-1) Bantam.
***New Moon Rising.** Eugenia Price. LC 99-57799. 352p. 2000. pap. 14.95 (1-57736-181-4) Providence Hse.
New Moon Rising. Eugenia Price. pap. 12.95 (0-8027-2607-0) Walker & Co.
New Moon Rising. large type ed. Eugenia Price. LC 91-18383. 483p. 1991. reprint ed. lib. bdg. 19.95 (1-56054-184-9) Thorndike Pr.
New Moon with the Old Moon in Her Arms. Ursule Molinaro. 119p. (Orig.). 1993. 22.00 (0-7043-5057-2); pap. 10.00 (0-929701-29-1) McPherson & Co.
New Mormon History: Revisionist Essays on the Past. Ed. by D. Michael Quinn. LC 91-21224. (Essays on Mormonism Ser.: No. 4). 310p. (Orig.). 1991. pap. 18.95 (1-56085-011-6) Signature Bks.
New Mosaics: 40 Projects to Make with Glass, Metal, Paper, Beans, Buttons, Felt, Found Objects & More. Danielle Truscott. LC 99-33046. (Illus.). 128p. 1999. 24.95 (1-57990-138-7, Pub. by Lark Books) Random.
New Moses: A Matthean Typology. Dale C. Allison, Jr. LC 93-18735. 304p. 1994. 30.00 (0-8006-2699-0, 1-2699, Fortress Pr) Augsburg Fortress.
New Most Excellent Dancing Master: The Journal of Joseph Lowe's Visits to Balmoral & Windsor (1852-1860) to Teach Dance to the Family of Queen Victoria. Joseph Lowe. Ed. by Allan Thomas. LC 92-13521. (Dance & Music Ser.: No. 5). 150p. 1992. lib. bdg. 36.00 (0-945193-30-0) Pendragon NY.
New Mother Syndrome. Carol Dix. 320p. 1988. mass mkt. 4.50 (0-671-64485-8) PB.
New Motherhood: Cultural & Personal Transitions in the 1980's. Mira Crouch & Lenore Manderson. 222p. 1993. text 61.00 (2-88124-945-0) Gordon & Breach.
New Mother's Body Book. Jacqueline Shannon. 288p. 1994. pap. 9.75 (0-8092-3795-4, 379540, Contemporary Bks) NTC Contemp Pub Co.
New Mother's Survival Guide: A Primer for the First Year of Motherhood. Elizabeth Wright. LC 97-15828. (Illus.). 224p. (Orig.). 1997. pap. 9.95 (1-888952-54-7) Cumberland Hse.
***New Motor Queen City.** Patricia Seaman. 144p. 1999. pap. 19.95 (1-55245-045-7, Pub. by Coach Hse Bks) SPD-Small Pr Dist.
New Movement in the Theatre. Sheldon W. Cheney. LC 70-88532. 1972. 24.95 (0-405-08356-4, Pub. by Blom Pubns) Ayer.

N

An Asterisk (*) at the beginning of an entry indicates that the title is appearing for the first time.

New Movement in the Theatre. Sheldon W. Cheney. LC 70-95089. 303p. 1971. reprint ed. lib. bdg. 59.75 (*0-8371-3081-6*, CHNT, Greenwood Pr) Greenwood.

New Movement in the Theatre. Compiled by Leon Moussinac. LC 65-19619. (Illus.). 1972. reprint ed. 82.95 (*0-405-08808-6*, Pub. by Blom Pubns) Ayer.

New Mown Hay: Even More Poems about Indiana & Hoosiers. L. D. Gilley. 52p. 1997. pap. 7.50 (*0-9643707-3-5*) L D Gilley.

New Mozart Documents: A Supplement to O. E. Deutsch's Documentary Biography. Cliff Eisen. LC 91-65554. 192p. 1991. 39.50 (*0-8047-1955-1*) Stanford U Pr.

New Mozartiana. Henry G. Farmer & Herbert Smith. LC 74-24077. (Illus.). reprint ed. 37.50 (*0-404-12906-4*) AMS Pr.

New Mrs. Rainier. large type ed. Eva Burfield. 336p. 1987. 27.99 (*0-7089-1581-7*) Ulverscroft.

New Multilateralism in Japan's Foreign Policy. Dennis T. Yasutomo. 288p. 1995. text 45.00 (*0-312-04778-9*) St Martin.

New Multinational Enterprises from Korea & Taiwan: Beyond Export-Led Growth. Roger Van Hoesel. LC 98-41198. (Studies in International Business & the World Economy Ser.). 8p. 1999. write for info. (*0-415-19488-1*) Routledge.

New Munsell Student Color Set. 119p. 1994. ring bd. 40.00 (*1-56367-031-3*) Fairchild.

New Murphy's Law: 10 Unconventional Rules for Making Everything Go Right in Your Life & Work. Emmett C. Murphy. 228p. 1998. 15.95 (*1-886284-19-9*, Pub. by Chandler Hse) Natl Bk Netwk.

New Museology. Peter Vergo. (Illus.). 238p. 1997. pap. text 22.50 (*0-948462-03-5*, Pub. by Reaktion Bks) Consort Bk Sales.

New Museology, Vol. 1. Academy. 1991. pap. 21.95 (*0-312-07141-8*) St Martin.

*__New Museum: Selected Writings.__ John Cotton Dana. Ed. by William A. Peniston. LC 99-44326. 262p. 1999. pap. 28.00 (*0-931201-64-0*) Am Assn Mus.

New Museum Registration Methods. Ed. by Rebecca A. Buck & Jean A. Gilmore. LC 98-16006. 427p. 1998. pap. 55.00 (*0-931201-31-4*) Am Assn Mus.

New Museums. Olivier Bossiere. (Illus.). 160p. 24.95 (*2-7450-0036-5*) Telleri Edit.

New Museums. Joseph M. Montaner. (Illus.). 188p. 1997. 39.95 (*1-85454-600-7*) Chronicle Bks.

New Museums, Vol. 1. 1991. pap. 21.95 (*0-312-07145-0*) St Martin.

New Music. George Dyson. (Select Bibliographies Reprint Ser.). 1977. 19.95 (*0-8369-5231-6*) Ayer.

New Music. George Dyson. 151p. 1990. reprint ed. lib. bdg. 59.00 (*0-7812-9010-4*) Rprt Serv.

New Music: A Trilogy. Reynolds Price. LC 90-48090. 240p. 1990. 22.95 (*1-55936-015-1*); pap. 10.95 (*1-55936-016-X*) Theatre Comm.

New Music: The Avant-Garde since 1945. 2nd ed. Reginald S. Brindle. (Illus.). 224p. 1987. pap. text 27.95 (*0-19-315468-4*) OUP.

New Music & the Claims of Modernity. Alastair Williams. LC 96-45418. 175p. 1997. text 74.95 (*1-85928-368-3*, Pub. by Scolar Pr) Ashgate Pub Co.

New Music for Plucked Strings. James Tenney et al. 117p. (Orig.). (C). 1986. pap. text 15.00 (*0-945996-02-0*) Frog Peak Music.

New Music, 1900-1960. Aaron Copland. 194p. reprint ed. lib. bdg. 39.00 (*0-685-14848-3*) Rprt Serv.

New Music System Especially for Electronic Keyboards: A Quicker & Easier Method for Learning to Play Keyboard Instruments. Robert E. Ross. LC 92-90282. (Illus.). 195p. 1992. write for info. (*0-9630043-2-8*) Keyboard Mus.

*__New Music Therapist's Handbook.__ 2nd ed. Suzanne B. Hanser. (Illus.). 2000. pap. 29.95 (*0-634-00645-2*, Berklee Pr) H Leonard.

New Music Vocabulary: A Guide to Notational Signs for Contemporary Music. Howard Risatti. LC 73-81565. 235p. reprint ed. pap. 72.90 (*0-7837-5743-3*, 204540400006) Bks Demand.

New Musical Figurations: Anthony Braxton's Cultural Critique. Ronald M. Radano. LC 93-1878. (Illus.). 336p. 1993. pap. 16.95 (*0-226-70196-4*); lib. bdg. 55.00 (*0-226-70195-6*) U Ch Pr.

New Musical Resources. Henry Cowell. 195p. (C). 1996. text 59.95 (*0-521-49651-9*); pap. text 21.95 (*0-521-49974-7*) Cambridge U Pr.

New Mutual Fund Investment Advisor: Everything You Need to Know about Investing in No-Loads. Richard C. Dorf. 1991. text 24.95 (*1-55738-157-7*, Irwn Prfssnl) McGraw-Hill Prof.

New My Writing Book. Joyce C. Bumgardner. (Illus.). 72p. (J). (gr. 2-6). 1998. pap. 5.95 (*0-9624260-1-6*) Froggie Pr.

New Mysteries of Paris. Barry Gifford. LC 90-85632. 96p. 1991. pap. 11.95 (*0-944439-31-4*) Clark City Pr.

*__New Mythos Legends.__ Bruce Gehweiler et al. (Illus.). 304p. 1999. 25.00 (*1-892669-06-4*, 07) Marietta Pubg.

New Naked Poetry: Recent American Poetry in Open Forms. Ed. by Stephen Berg & Robert Mezey. LC 75-12999. 1976. pap. write for info. (*0-672-61354-9*) Macmillan.

New Name. Grace Livingston Hill. 303p. reprint ed. lib. bdg. 23.95 (*0-89190-054-3*, Rivercity Pr) Amereon Ltd.

New Name Dictionary. Alfred J. Kolatch. LC 88-25826. 360p. 1994. pap. 19.95 (*0-8246-0376-1*) Jonathan David.

New Name for Nero. John McGahee. LC 96-86364. 1996. mass mkt., spiral bd. 9.95 (*1-889131-03-2*) CasAnanda.

New Name for Peace: International Environmentalism, Sustainable Development, & Democracy. Philip Shabecoff. LC 96-2235. (Illus.). 287p. 1996. 35.00 (*0-87451-688-9*) U Pr of New Eng.

New Names Introduced by H. A. Pilsbry in the Mollusca & Crustacea. William J. Clench & Ruth D. Turner. (Special Publication: No. 4). 218p. (Orig.). 1962. pap. 7.00 (*0-910006-32-6*) Acad Nat Sci Phila.

New Narrative of Mexico: Sub-Versions of History in Mexican Fiction. Kathy Taylor. LC 92-56605. 1994. 33.50 (*0-8387-5266-7*) Bucknell U Pr.

New Nation. Joy Hakim. (History of US Ser.: Vol. 4). (Illus.). 176p. (YA). (gr. 5 up). 1994. text 14.95 (*0-19-507751-2*) OUP.

New Nation. Joy Hakim. (History of Us Ser.). 1993. 16.05 (*0-606-09419-9*, Pub. by Turtleback) Demco.

New Nation. Betsy C. Maestro. 1924. lib. bdg. write for info. (*0-688-16016-6*) Lothrop.

New Nation Bk. 4: The New Nation. John Grenham. 59p. 1994. 4.98 (*0-7858-0083-2*) Bk Sales Inc.

New Nation (1789 - 1850) see History of U. S.

*__New National Accounts: An Introduction to the System of National Accounts 1993 & the European System of Accounts 1995.__ Dudley Jackson. LC 00-29364. 416p. 2000. 110.00 (*1-84064-157-6*) E Elgar.

New National & Post-Colonial Literatures: An Introduction. Bruce King. 328p. 1998. reprint ed. pap. text 21.00 (*0-19-818484-0*) OUP.

*__New National Curriculum Mathematics: Target Book 4.__ M. J. Tipler & K. M. Vickers. (Illus.). 344p. (YA). (gr. 6-10). 2000. pap. 27.50 (*0-7487-3549-6*, Pub. by S Thornes Pubs) Trans-Atl Phila.

*__New National Curriculum Mathematics: Target Book 5.__ M. J. Tipler & K. M. Vickers. (Illus.). 320p. (YA). (gr. 6-10). 2000. pap. 27.50 (*0-7487-3550-X*, Pub. by S Thornes Pubs) Trans-Atl Phila.

*__New National Curriculum Mathematics: Target Teacher's Book 4.__ M. J. Tipler & K. M. Vickers. (Illus.). 192p. (YA). (gr. 5-10). 2000. pap. 110.00 (*0-7487-3554-2*, Pub. by S Thornes Pubs) Trans-Atl Phila.

*__New National Curriculum Mathematics: Target Teacher's Book 5.__ M. J. Tipler & K. M. Vickers. (Illus.). 416p. (YA). (gr. 6-10). 2000. pap. 110.00 (*0-7487-3555-0*, Pub. by S Thornes Pubs) Trans-Atl Phila.

New National Curriculum Mathematics Bk. 2: Targe Teacher's Book. M. J. Tipler & K. M. Vickers. 192p. 1998. pap., teacher ed. 105.00 (*0-7487-3552-6*) St Mut.

New National Gallery: Berlin, 1962-8. Ludwig Mies Van Der Rohe & Maritz Vandenberg. (Architecture in Detail Ser.). (Illus.). 60p. 1998. pap. 29.95 (*0-7148-3763-6*, Pub. by Phaidon Press) Phaidon Pr.

New National Gallery, Martin Luther King Jr. Memorial Library, & Other Buildings & Projects. Ed. by Franz Schulze & George E. Danforth. LC 86-9980. (Mies Van Der Rohe Archive Series: An Illustrated Catalog of the Mies Van Der Rohe Drawing in the Museum of Modern Art, Pt. II, 1938-1967, the American Work: Vol. 19). (Illus.). 496p. 1993. text 330.00 (*0-8153-0120-0*) Garland.

New Nationalisms of the Developed West: Toward Explanation. Ed. by Edward A. Tiryakian & Ronald Rogowski. 300p. 1985. text 55.00 (*0-04-320167-9*) Routledge.

New Nations. Lucy P. Mair. LC 63-20197. (Nature of Human Society Ser.). 1993. lib. bdg. 19.00 (*0-226-50275-9*) U Ch Pr.

New Nations. Lucy P. Mair. LC 63-20917. (Nature of Human Society Ser.). 235p. reprint ed. pap. 72.90 (*0-608-09018-2*, 206965300005) Bks Demand.

New Nations for Old. Kenneth E. Boulding. (C). 1942. pap. 4.00 (*0-87574-017-0*) Pendle Hill.

New Nations Rising: The Fall of the Soviets & the Challenge of Independence. Nadia Diuk & Adrian Karatnycky. LC 92-40195. 304p. (Orig.). 1993. pap. 14.95 (*0-471-58263-8*) Wiley.

New Native. Thomas R. Crowe. LC 93-92609. (Night Sun Trilogy Ser.: Bk. 2). 93p. 1993. pap. 9.95 (*1-883197-02-3*) New Native Pr.

New Native American Drama: Three Plays. Ed. by Hanay Geiogamah. LC 79-4733. (Illus.). 158p. 1980. pap. 13.95 (*0-8061-1697-8*) U of Okla Pr.

New Natural Cat: A Complete Guide for Finicky Owners. Anitra Frazier & Norma Eckroate. 304p. 1990. pap. 17.95 (*0-452-26517-7*, Plume) Dutton Plume.

New Natural Family Doctor: The Authoritative Self-Help Guide to Health & Natural Medicine. 2nd ed. Ed. by Andrew Stanway. LC 97-104458. (Illus.). 352p. 1996. pap. text 19.95 (*1-55643-217-8*) North Atlantic.

*__New Natural Healing Cookbook: A Wellness Program for Optimal Health.__ rev. ed. Bessie Jo Tillman. (Illus.). 2000. pap. write for info. (*0-8069-4474-9*) Sterling.

New Natural House Book. David Pearson. LC 98-228688. 304p. 1998. per. 22.00 (*0-684-84733-7*) S&S Trade Pap.

New Natural Pregnancy: Practical Wellbeing from Conception to Birth. Janet Balaskas. 1999. pap. 15.00 (*1-56656-311-9*) Interlink Pub.

New Natural Selection. Brian Swimme. (Teilhard Studies: No. 10). 1983. pap. 3.50 (*0-89012-036-6*) Am Teilhard.

New Negotiating Edge: How to Use Negotiating Styles & Strategies to Get the Results & Relationships You Want. Gavin Kennedy. (People Skills for Professionals Ser.). 275p. 1998. pap. 17.95 (*1-85788-205-9*) Nicholas Brealey.

New Negro. Alain Locke. 1999. per. 15.00 (*0-684-83831-1*) Simon & Schuster.

New Negro. Mathew H. Ahmann. LC 73-77031. 1969. reprint ed. 30.00 (*0-8196-0232-9*) Biblo.

New Negro: An Interpretation. Ed. by Alain L. Locke. LC 68-29008. (American Negro: His History & Literature. Series 1). 1968. reprint ed. 57.98 (*0-405-01826-6*) Ayer.

*__New Negro Artists in Paris.__ Theresa A. Leininger-Miller. LC 00-24449. 2000. pap. write for info. (*0-8135-2858-5*) Rutgers U Pr.

*__New Negro Artists in Paris: African American Painters & Sculptors in the City of Light, 1922-1934.__ Theresa Leininger-Miller. LC 00-24449. (Illus.). 320p. (C). 2000. text 60.00 (*0-8135-2810-0*); pap. text 32.00 (*0-8135-2811-9*) Rutgers U Pr.

New Negro for a New Century. Booker T. Washington et al. LC 74-172759. reprint ed. 27.50 (*0-404-00197-1*) AMS Pr.

New Negro for a New Century. Booker T. Washington et al. LC 69-18559. (American Negro: His History & Literature. Series 2). 1969. reprint ed. 24.95 (*0-405-01904-1*) Ayer.

New Negro for a New Century: An Accurate & Up-To-Date Record of the Upward Struggles of the Negro Race. Booker T. Washington. LC 79-81134. (Black Heritage Library Collection). 1977. 23.95 (*0-8369-8679-2*) Ayer.

New Negro, His Political, Civil & Mental Status & Related Essays. William Pickens. LC 72-95399. reprint ed. 21.50 (*0-404-00271-4*) AMS Pr.

*__New Negro, Old Left: African-American Writing & Cmmunism Between the Wars.__ William J. Maxwell. LC 98-52487. (Illus.). 10p. 1999. 49.50 (*0-231-11424-9*) Col U Pr.

*__New Negro, Old Left: African-American Writing & Communism Between the Wars.__ William J. Maxwell. LC 98-52487. (Illus.). 272p. 1999. pap. 17.50 (*0-231-11425-7*) Col U Pr.

New Negroes & Their Music: The Success of the Harlem Renaissance. Jon M. Spencer. LC 96-25273. (Illus.). 200p. 1997. pap. text 20.00 (*0-87049-967-X*) U of Tenn Pr.

New Neighbor. Ray Garton. (Illus.). 280p. 1991. 500.00 (*0-927389-02-9*) Charnel Hse.

New Neighbor. limited ed. Ray Garton. (Illus.). 280p. 1991. 125.00 (*0-927389-03-7*) Charnel Hse.

New Neighbor & Other Stories. 2nd ed. David N. Monreal. LC 87-63154. 173p. 1987. pap. 14.95 (*0-944870-09-0*) Pacific Writers Pr.

New Neighborhoods. W. T. Pfefferle. (Illus.). 100p. 1998. pap. 15.00 (*1-57502-724-0*, PO2030) Morris Pubng.

New Neighbors for Nora. Johanna Hurwitz. LC 90-47882. (Illus.). 80p. (J). 1991. reprint ed. lib. bdg. 12.88 (*0-688-09948-3*, Wm Morrow) Morrow Avon.

New Neighbours: A Case Study of Cooperative Housing in Toronto. Matthew Cooper & Margaret C. Rodman. 368p. (Orig.). 1992. text 50.00 (*0-8020-5992-9*); pap. text 19.95 (*0-8020-6925-8*) U of Toronto Pr.

New Nelson Japanese-English Character Dictionary: Based on the Classic Edition by Andrew N. Nelson. Rev. by John H. Haig & Dept. of East Asian Languages & Literatures, Unive. LC 96-60004. 1760p. 1997. 49.95 (*0-8048-2036-8*) Tuttle Pubng.

New Nest. Sue Camm. (Read to Me Ser.). 10p. (J). (ps). 1994. bds. 3.98 (*1-85854-139-5*) Brimax Bks.

New Netherland Roots. Gwenn F. Epperson. LC 93-80320. (Illus.). 176p. 1995. reprint ed. 20.00 (*0-8063-1400-1*, 1685) Genealog Pub.

New Netherlands Civil Code Patrimonial Law: Property, Obligations & Special Contracts. Tr. by Peter P. Haanappel & Ejan Mackaay from DUT. (ENG & FRE.). 528p. 1990. 79.00 (*90-6544-482-3*) Kluwer Law Intl.

New Neuroethology on the Move. Elsner. pap. 59.00 (*0-86577-806-X*) Thieme Med Pubs.

New Neurotic Realism. Text by Dick Price. (Illus.). 208p. 1999. 45.00 (*0-9527453-8-0*, Pub. by Saatchi) Dist Art Pubs.

New New Painting. Donald Kuspit et al. Ed. by Anne G. Low. (Illus.). 96p. (Orig.). (YA). (gr. 7-12). 1996. per. 35.00 (*0-9655443-0-3*) Fine Art Two-Thousand.

New New Thing: A Silicon Valley Story. Michael Lewis. LC 99-43412. 256p. 1999. 25.95 (*0-393-04813-6*) Norton.

*__New New Thing: A Silicon Valley Story.__ Michael Lewis. 2001. pap. 13.00 (*0-14-029646-8*) Penguin Putnam.

New, New York Bartender's Guide. Sally A. Berk. 256p. 1997. 10.98 (*1-57912-005-9*) Blck Dog & Leventhal.

New News Business: A Guide to Writing & Reporting. John Chancellor & Walter R. Mears. 194p. 1999. reprint ed. pap. text 12.00 (*0-7881-6221-7*) DIANE Pub.

New News vs. the Old News: Press & Politics in the 1990s. Ed. by Jay Rosen & Paul Taylor. LC 92-32299. (Perspectives on the News Ser.). (Orig.). 1992. pap. 9.95 (*0-87078-344-0*) Century Foundation.

New NHS Modern - Dependable White Paper, Command Paper 3807. (Command Papers (All) Ser.: No. 81011068). 1998. 30.00 (*0-10-138072-0*, HM80720, Pub. by Statnry Office) Bernan Associates.

New Niagara: Tourism, Technology, & the Landscape of Niagara Falls, 1776-1917. William Irwin. (Illus.). 304p. 1996. pap. 18.95 (*0-271-01593-4*) Pa St U Pr.

New Niagara: Tourism, Technology, & the Landscape of Niagara Falls, 1776-1917. William Irwin. LC 95-48821. (Illus.). 304p. (C). 1996. 50.00 (*0-271-01534-9*) Pa St U Pr.

New Nick Kramer, My Life As a Babysitter. James Howe. LC 95-2148. (Illus.). 128p. (J). (gr. 5-9). 1995. 13.95 (*0-7868-0066-6*, Pub. by Hyprn Child); lib. bdg. 13.89 (*0-7868-2053-5*, Pub. by Hyprn Child) Little.

New Nick Kramer, My Life As a Babysitter. James Howe. LC 95-2148. 128p. (J). (gr. 5-9). 1997. pap. 4.50 (*0-7868-1017-3*, Pub. by Hyprn Ppbks) Little.

New Nietzsche: Contemporary Styles of Interpretation. Ed. by David B. Allison. 302p. 1985. reprint ed. pap. text 19.50 (*0-262-51034-0*) MIT Pr.

*__New Nine: A Pocket Guide to Understanding Collateral & Transaction Types in Article 9 of the UCC.__ William H. Henning. 142p. 2000. pap. 9.95 (*0-943380-32-4*) PEG MN.

*__New Nineteenth-Century: Feminist Readings of Underread Victorian Fiction.__ Ed. by Barbara Harman & Susan Meyer. (Wellesley Studies in Critical Theory, Literary History & Culture). 328p. 1999. pap. 24.95 (*0-8153-3589-X*) Garland.

New Nineteenth-Century: Feminist Readings of Underread Victorian Fiction. Ed. by Barbara L. Harman et al. LC 95-52470. (Wellesley Studies in Critical Theory, Literary History & Culture: No. 10). 328p. 1996. reprint ed. text 70.00 (*0-8153-1292-X*, H1700) Garland.

New '98-'99 Genre Specific Publishers: Reference Book. Kelly O'Donnel. 1998. pap. 39.95 (*1-57532-116-5*) Press-Tige Pub.

New 90-Minute Resume: For Job Hunters Who Want Top-Notch Results - Fast! 2nd rev. ed. Peggy J. Schmidt. 160p. (Orig.). 1996. pap. 15.95 (*1-56079-633-2*) Petersons.

New 90-Minute Resume: For Resume Revisers. Peggy J. Schmidt. LC 91-45722. 128p. 1992. pap. 7.95 (*1-56079-151-9*) Petersons.

New No-Nonsense Landlord: Building Wealth with Rental Properties. 2nd ed. Richard H. Jorgensen. 262p. 1994. pap. 16.95 (*0-07-033040-9*) McGraw.

New No-Pill, No-Risk Birth Control: The Latest Findings on Natural Family Planning, the Method for Postponing Pregnancy Without Using Drugs, Chemicals, IUDs or Barrier Devices. Nona Aguilar. LC 85-42927. (Illus.). 240p. 1985. pap. 12.95 (*0-89256-300-1*, Rawson Assocs) Macmillan.

New Noir: Stories by John Shirley. John Shirley. (Black Ice Bks.). (Illus.). 115p. 1993. pap. 7.00 (*0-932511-55-4*) Fiction Coll.

New Non-Perturbative Methods & Quantization on the Light Cone: Les Houches School, February 24-March 7, 1997. Ed. by P. Grange et al. xviii, 320p. 1998. pap. 79.95 (*3-540-64520-9*) Spr-Verlag.

New North America: Cooperation & Enhanced Interdependence. Ed. by Charles F. Doran & Alvin Drischler. LC 95-40576. 184p. 1996. 55.00 (*0-275-95406-4*, Praeger Pubs); pap. 17.95 (*0-275-95407-2*, Praeger Pubs) Greenwood.

New North American Order: A Win-Win Strategy for U. S.-Mexico Trade. Clyde V. Prestowitz, Jr. et al. 134p. (C). 1991. pap. text 17.50 (*0-8191-8438-1*) U Pr of Amer.

*__New North American Trout Fishing.__ John Merwin. (Illus.). 2000. 9.99 (*0-7858-1192-3*) Bk Sales Inc.

New Northern Gardener. rev. ed. Jennifer Bennett. (Illus.). 256p. 1996. pap. 24.95 (*1-55209-012-4*) Firefly Bks Ltd.

New Norton Guides: Borland C++ Norton. 1991. pap. 5.00 incl. 3.5 hd (*0-13-625054-8*) Macmillan USA.

New Norton Guides: Engine. Norton. 1990. pap. 34.95 (*0-13-617358-6*) P-H.

New Norton Guides: Turbo Pascal 6.0. Norton. 1991. pap. 5.00 incl. 3.5 hd (*0-13-625062-9*) Macmillan USA.

New Norwegian Plays. Ed. by Janet Garton & Henning K. Schmsdorf. LC 89-85272. (Norvik Press Series B: No. 6). 293p. (Orig.). 1990. pap. 25.00 (*1-870041-11-9*, Pub. by Norvik Pr) Dufour.

*__New Nose: For a New Look & a New Outlook.__ Robert A. Ersek. (Illus.). 108p. 1999. pap. 14.95 (*0-9668360-2-2*, 36022) Med Web Wrld.

New Note on the Film. Trisha Curran. Ed. by Garth S. Jowett. LC 79-6671. (Dissertations on Film, 1980 Ser.). 1980. lib. bdg. 12.95 (*0-405-12905-X*) Ayer.

New Novel, New Wave, New Politics: Fiction & the Representation of History in Postwar France. Lynn A. Higgins. LC 95-15226. (Stages Ser.). (Illus.). ix, 260p. 1996. pap. text 15.00 (*0-8032-7309-6*) U of Nebr Pr.

New Novelty Songbook. (Piano-Vocal-Guitar Ser.). 128p. (Orig.). 1989. per. 12.95 (*0-88188-845-1*, HL 00490072) H Leonard.

New Novelty Songbook. (Easy Piano Ser.). 144p. (Orig.). 1990. per. 12.95 (*0-7935-0052-4*, HL00290233) H Leonard.

New Nuclear Physics with Advanced Techniques: Proceedings of the International Conference, Crete, Greece, 23-29 June 1991. Ed. by F. A. Beck et al. 450p. 1992. text 124.00 (*981-02-0861-8*) World Scientific Pub.

New Nucleic Acid Techniques, Vol. 4. Ed. by John M. Walker. LC 84-15696. (Methods in Molecular Biology Ser.). (Illus.). 576p. 1988. 69.50 (*0-89603-127-6*) Humana.

New Nuctemeron: The Twelve Hours of Apollonius of Tyana. Marjorie Livingston. 143p. 1996. reprint ed. pap. 16.95 (*1-56459-522-6*) Kessinger Pub.

New Nukes: India, Pakistan & Global Nuclear Disarmament. Praful Bidwai & Achin Vanaik. LC 99-23965. 2000. 40.00 (*1-56656-318-6*); pap. 17.95 (*1-56656-317-8*) Interlink Pub.

New Number 1 Songs of the 90's. (Decade Ser.). 120p. 1995. otabind 12.95 (*0-7935-4059-3*, 00310018) H Leonard.

*__New Numbers.__ Josie Kearns. 2000. pap. 12.00 (*0-932826-93-8*) WMU Poetry & Prose.

New Numbers. 2nd ed. F. Emerson Andrews. LC 61-5320. 168p. 1944. reprint ed. 12.00 (*0-317-36274-7*) Dozenal.

New Numbers: Poetry by Josie Kearns. Josie Kearns. Ed. by Robert Bixby. 33p. Date not set. pap. 6.00 (*1-882983-40-8*) March Street Pr.

New Nurse. E. Michael Hanton. LC 74-79614. 122p. 1974. 10.00 (*0-914698-01-X*); pap. 6.95 (*0-914698-02-8*) New Nurse.

*__New Nurse at St. Benedict's.__ large type ed. Lilian Chisholm. (Dales Romance Ser.). 352p. 1999. pap. 20.99 (*1-85389-920-8*) Ulverscroft.

New Nurse Manager: A Guide to Management Development. Donna R. Sheridan et al. 328p. (C). 1984. 60.00 (*0-89443-594-9*, 43594) Aspen Pub.

An Asterisk (*) at the beginning of an entry indicates that the title is appearing for the first time.

New Nutrients Against Cancer. Judi Quilici-Timmcke. LC 99-185182. 48p. 1998. pap. 3.95 (*0-87983-890-6*, Keats Publng) NTC Contemp Pub Co.
***New Nutrition: From Antioxidants to Zinc.** Felecia Busch. LC 99-51841. 336p. 2000. pap. 16.95 (*0-471-34793-0*) Wiley.
New Nutrition: Medicine for the Millennium. Michael Colgan. (Your Personal Guide to Health Ser.). (Illus.). 261p. 1995. 24.95 (*0-9624840-6-7*); pap. 14.95 (*0-9624840-7-5*) Colgan Inst.
New Object Lessons: For Children of All Ages. Sheryl Bruinsma. (Object Lessons Ser.). 128p. (YA). (gr. 10). 1980. pap. 6.99 (*0-8010-0775-5*) Baker Bks.
New Observing Modes for the Next Century. Ed. by Todd Boroson et al. (ASP Conference Series Proceedings: Vol. 87). 262p. 1996. 34.00 (*1-886733-08-2*) Astron Soc Pacific.
New Occasions Teach New Duties? Christian Ethics for Today. Ed. by Cyril S. Rodd. 240p. 1996. pap. 29.95 (*0-567-29300-9*, Pub. by T & T Clark) Bks Intl VA.
New of Grateful Dead. Ed. by Carol Cuellar. 76p. (Orig.). (C). 1994. pap. text 12.95 (*0-7692-0727-8*, VF1735) Wrner Bros.
New Office. PBC International Staff. 1998. pap. 34.95 (*0-688-16144-8*, Wm Morrow) Morrow Avon.
New Office: Designs for Corporations, People & Technology. Karin Tetlow. LC 96-16250. (Illus.). 184p. 1997. 47.50 (*0-86636-442-0*) PBC Intl Inc.
New Office: Designs for Corporations, People & Technology. Karin Tetlow. LC 96-16250. 184p. 1998. pap. 39.95 (*0-86636-497-8*) PBC Intl Inc.
New Office: With 20 International Case Studies. Francis Duffy. LC 98-189791. (Illus.). 256p. 1997. 90.00 (*1-85029-891-2*, Pub. by Conran Octopus) Antique Collect.
New Office Technology. Harry J. Otway & Malcolm Peltu. LC 82-24473. 248p. 1983. text 73.25 (*0-89391-198-4*) Ablx Pub.
New Offices in the USA. Larchivolto. 1997. 79.95 (*88-7685-100-3*) LArchivolto.
New Offices in the USA. LArchivolto Editors. 1998. 79.95 (*1-56970-528-3*) US Renditions.
New Official Rules: Maxims for Muddling Through to the 21st Century. Paul Dickson. 1989. pap. 8.95 (*0-685-25284-1*) Addison-Wesley.
New Oil Crisis & Fuel Economy Technologies: Preparing the Light Transportation Industry for the Nineteen Nineties. Deborah L. Bleviss. LC 87-3260. 283p. 1988. 72.95 (*0-89930-311-0*, BVP/, Quorum Bks) Greenwood.
New Oil Stakes. Jean-Marie Chevalier. Tr. by Ian Rock from FRE. 187p. (C). 1973. 22.95 (*0-8464-1182-2*) Beekman Pubs.
New Old-Fashioned Ways: Holidays & Popular Culture. Jack Santino. LC 96-9993. (Illus.). 200p. (C). 1996. pap. 15.95 (*0-87049-952-1*) U of Tenn Pr.
New Older Woman: A Dialogue for the Coming Century. Peggy Downs et al. 196p. 1995. pap. 12.95 (*0-89087-769-6*) Celestial Arts.
New Olefin Resins Via New Polymerization & Compounding, No. P-124. Business Communications Co., Inc. Staff. 129p. 1991. 2150.00 (*0-89336-841-5*) BCC.
New Olympia Reader, 1957-1966: The Best from the First Ten Years of America's Most Provocative, Most Controversial, Most Important Literary Magazine. Ed. by Barney Rosset et al. (Illus.). 356p. 1993. pap. 15.95 (*1-56201-046-8*) Blue Moon Bks.
New 100 Great Rock Songs of the Superstars. rev. ed. 114p. (Orig.). (YA). 1995. reprint ed. pap. text 19.95 (*0-89724-567-9*, GF0548A) Wrner Bros.
***New Online Investor: The Revolution Continues.** 2nd ed. Peter Temple. LC 99-57857. 272p. 2000. pap. 39.95 (*0-471-99877-X*) Wiley.
New Open Bible. large type ed. (Illus.). 1856p. 1993. bond lthr. 97.99 (*0-8407-8598-4*, 16651) Nelson.
New Operational Approaches for Financial Modelling. Ed. by Constantin Zopounidis. LC 97-36996. (Contributions to Management Science Ser.). (Illus.). xii, 454p. 1997. pap. 95.00 (*3-7908-1043-6*) Spr-Verlag.
New Opportunities: Civil Rights at a Crossroads. Ed. by Susan M. Liss & William L. Taylor. LC 92-56191. 300p. 1993. pap. 20.00 (*0-9622865-2-4*) CCCR.
New Opportunities for Entrepreneurship. Ed. by Herbert Griesch. 268p. 1984. lib. bdg. 62.50 (*3-16-344816-X*, Pub. by JCB Mohr) Coronet Bks.
New Opportunities for Military Women: Effects upon Readiness, Cohesion, & Morale. Margaret C. Harrell et al. LC 97-32067. 280p. 1997. pap. 15.00 (*0-8330-2558-9*, MR-896-OSD) Rand Corp.
***New Opportunities for Older Workers: A Statement on National Policy.** Ed. by Scott Morris. 56p. 2000. pap. text 20.00 (*0-7881-8972-7*) DIANE Pub.
New Opportunities for Publishers in the Information Market. (Illus.). 233p. 1996. reprint ed. pap. text 50.00 (*0-7881-2652-0*) DIANE Pub.
New Opportunities for Purchasing Natural Gas. A. Williams. 374p. 1986. 79.00 (*0-13-615154-X*) P-H.
New Opportunities for Purchasing Natural Gas. Anna F. Williams & Len Parent. LC 86-46134. 250p. 1987. text 79.00 (*0-88173-034-3*) Fairmont Pr.
New Opportunities in a New Nation: The Development of New York After the Revolution. Ed. by Manfred Jonas & Robert V. Wells. 158p. 1983. 10.95 (*0-912756-07-1*) Union Coll.
New Opportunity see **Nueva Oportunidad**
New Option in Low-Dose Oral Contraception: Expanding the Gestadene Choice. Ed. by P. Lopes & S. R. Killick. LC 96-33683. (Illus.). 96p. 1996. text 25.00 (*1-85070-739-1*) Prthnon Pub.
***New Option Secret: Volatility: The Weapon of the Professional Trader & the Most Important Indicator in Option Trading.** David L. Caplan. (Illus.). 311p. 2000. pap. text 65.00 (*1-883272-33-5*) Traders Lib.
New Option Secret - Volatility. David Caplan. 310p. 1996. pap. 65.00 (*1-883272-18-1*) Traders Lib.
New Options Advantage: Gaining a Trading Edge over the Markets, Revised Edition. 2nd rev. ed. David L. Caplan. 225p. 1995. text 45.00 (*1-55738-863-6*, Irwn Prfssnl) McGraw-Hill Prof.
New Options for America. Mark Satin. 249p. (Orig.). 1991. pap. 9.95 (*0-912201-24-X*) CSU Pr Fresno.
New Options for America: The Second American Experiment Has Begun. Mark Satin. 240p. (C). 1991. pap. 11.95 (*0-8093-1794-X*) S Ill U Pr.
New Options for Librarians: Finding a Job in a Related Field. Ed. by Dimity S. Berkner & Betty-Carol Sellen. LC 83-22143. 300p. 1984. 39.95 (*0-918212-73-1*) Neal-Schuman.
***New Options Market.** 4th ed. Max G. Ansbacher. (Trading Advantage Ser.). 336p. 2000. text 39.95 (*0-471-34880-5*) Wiley.
New Options, New Talent Vol. 98-14: The Government Manager's Guide to the Flexible Workforce. 141p. 1998. pap. 20.00 (*1-57744-073-0*) Nat Acad Public Admin.
New Optoelectronics Ball Game: The Policy Struggle Between the U. S. & Japan for the Competitive Edge. Philip N. Seidenberg. (Illus.). 144p. (C). 1992. pap. 24.95 (*0-7803-0406-3*, PP0301-2) Inst Electrical.
New Order. (Third Reich Ser.). (Illus.). 192p. 1989. 9.99 (*0-8094-6962-6*) Time-Life.
New Order & Last Orientation, 7. Eric Voegelin. (History of Political Ideas Ser.). 1999. 37.50 (*0-8262-1214-X*) U of Mo Pr.
New Order & the French Economy. Alan S. Milward. (Modern Revivals in Economic & Social History Ser.). (Illus.). 336p. 1993. 77.95 (*0-7512-0146-4*, Pub. by Gregg Revivals) Ashgate Pub Co.
***New Order of Business: Managing & Working in the Information Age.** James W. Cortada. 350p. 2000. pap. 24.00 (*0-13-030569-3*) P-H.
New Order of Jesus, Vol. I. Thomas. Ed. & Tr. by Luiz A. Schiefer from POR. 230p. (Orig.). 1991. pap. 9.50 (*0-9629775-0-0*) New Order Jesus.
New Order of the Ages: Time, the Constitution, & the Making of Modern American Political Thought. Michael Lienesch. 245p. (C). 1988. text 42.50 (*0-691-07779-7*, Pub. by Princeton U Pr) Cal Prin Full Svc.
New Order of the Ages: Time, the Constitution, & the Making of Modern American Political Thought. Michael Lienesch. LC 88-1503. 245p. 1988. reprint ed. pap. 76.00 (*0-608-04576-4*, 206534500003) Bks Demand.
New Order of the Oceans: The Advent of a Managed Environment. Ed. by Giulio Pontecorvo. LC 86-6804. 240p. 1986. text 61.50 (*0-231-05870-5*) Col U Pr.
New Order of Things: Property, Power & the Transformation of the Creek Indians, 1733-1816. Claudio Saunt. LC 99-12567. (Studies in North American Indian History: Vol. 6). (Illus.). 288p. (C). 1999. 49.95 (*0-521-66043-2*) Cambridge U Pr.
New Order of Things: Property, Power & the Transformation of the Creek Indians, 1733-1816. abr. ed. Claudio Staunt. LC 99-12567. (Studies in North American Indian History: No. 6). (Illus.). 288p. (C). 1999. pap. 17.95 (*0-521-66943-X*) Cambridge U Pr.
New Ordinary Cause Rules. William McCulloch & Evelyn Laing. 216p. 1995. pap. 47.00 (*1-85811-027-0*, Pub. by CLT Prof) Gaunt.
New Orelans. Paul Malone. (Majesty Architecture Ser.). (Illus.). 112p. 1998. pap. text 14.95 (*1-56554-377-7*) Pelican.
New Oresteia of Yannis Ritsos. Yannis Ritsos. Tr. by George Pilitsis & Philip Pastras from GRE.Tr. of E Nea Oresteia. 168p. (Orig.). 1990. pap. text 12.00 (*0-918618-45-2*) Pella Pub.
New Organ Principles & Their Interpretation. Terence White. 50p. 1991. reprint ed. 59.00 (*0-7812-9319-7*) Rprt Serv.
New Organic Grower: A Master's Manual of Tools & Techniques for the Home & Market Gardener. 2nd expanded rev. ed. Eliot Coleman. (Illus.). 304p. 1995. pap. 24.95 (*0-930031-75-X*) Chelsea Green Pub.
New Organization - Managing: Module 1. Deborah Ancona et al. (GI - Organizational Behavior Ser.). 1995. mass mkt. 7.95 (*0-538-85877-X*) S-W Pub.
New Organizational Forms Module 8: Managing for the Future. Deborah Ancona et al. (GI - Organizational Behavior Ser.). 1995. mass mkt. 6.25 (*0-538-85882-6*) S-W Pub.
New Organizational Reality: Downsizing, Restructuring, & Revitalization. Ed. by Marilyn K. Gowing et al. LC 97-37722. 278p. 1997. pap. 34.95 (*1-55798-462-X*) Am Psychol.
New Organizational Responses to the Changing Transit Environment. (Special Reports: No. 217). 109p. 1988. 14.00 (*0-309-04663-7*) Transport Res Bd.
New Organizational Wealth: Managing & Measuring Knowledge-Based Assets. Karl E. Sveiby. LC 97-1964. 275p. 1997. 29.95 (*1-57675-014-0*) Berrett-Koehler.
New Organizations from Old: How to Survive & Prosper in a Changing Environment. Derek E. Taylor & Edwin J. Singer. 160p. (C). 1983. 72.00 (*0-85292-328-7*, Pub. by IPM Hse) St Mut.
New Organon: Bacon. Ed. by Fulton H. Anderson. 336p. (C). 1960. pap. text 14.00 (*0-02-303380-0*, Macmillan Coll) P-H.
New Orientation: Lectures Delivered at the Political Study Camp Held at Dehradun from May 8th-18th, 1946. M. N. Roy. 1999. 7.00 (*0-8364-5684-X*) S Asia.
New Orientations in the Teaching of English. Peter D. Strevens. 1978. pap. text 10.95 (*0-19-437076-3*) OUP.
New Original Version of Boscana's Historical Account of the San Juan Capistrano Indians of Southern California, Pt. 4. fac. ed. John P. Harrington. (Smithsonian Institution, Bureau of American Ethnology Ser.: Vol. 92). (Illus.). 69p. (C). 1934. reprint ed. pap. text 8.13 (*1-55567-849-1*) Coyote Press.
New Orleans. 64p. pap. text 9.95 (*88-7009-613-0*, Pub. by Bonechi) Eiron.
New Orleans. (Panorama Bks.). (FRE., Illus.). 3.95 (*0-685-11406-6*) Fr & Eur.
New Orleans. 1969. lib. bdg. 35.00 (*0-8371-0512-9*, Greenwood Pr) Greenwood.
New Orleans. Balliet & Fitzgerald Staff. (Edge Guide to . . . Ser.). 256p. 1999. pap. 14.00 (*1-56352-520-8*) Longstreet.
New Orleans. Richard Bizier. (Illus.). 240p. 1998. pap. text 13.95 (*1-56554-352-1*) Pelican.
***New Orleans.** Eric J. Brock. (Images of America Ser.). (Illus.). 128p. 1999. pap. 18.99 (*0-7385-0223-5*) Arcadia Publng.
New Orleans. Photos by Bernard M. Hermann. LC 80-82900. (Illus.). 160p. 1980. 29.95 (*0-8071-0799-9*) La State U Pr.
New Orleans. Carol M. Highsmith & Ted Landphair. LC 96-29726. (A Photographic Tour Ser.). (Illus.). 128p. 1997. 14.99 (*0-517-18610-1*) Crown Pub Group.
New Orleans. Carol M. Highsmith & Ted Landphair. LC 97-23484. (Pictorial Souvenir Ser.). 64p. 1998. 7.99 (*0-517-18761-2*) Crown Pub Group.
New Orleans. Insight Guides Staff. (Insight Guides). 1998. pap. text 12.95 (*0-88729-293-3*) Langenscheidt.
***New Orleans.** Insight Guides Staff. (Insight Compact Guide). 1999. pap. 7.95 (*0-88729-818-4*) Langenscheidt.
New Orleans. David C. King. LC 97-51203. (Battlefields Across America Ser.). (Illus.). 63p. (J). (gr. 5-8). 1998. lib. bdg. 23.40 (*0-7613-3010-0*) TFC Bks NY.
New Orleans. Joan K. Nichols. LC 88-35915. (Downtown America Ser.). (Illus.). 60p. (J). (gr. 3 up). 1989. lib. bdg. 13.95 (*0-87518-403-0*, Dillon Silver Burdett) Silver Burdett Pr.
New Orleans. G. S. Prentzas. LC 98-22247. (Cities of the World Ser.). (J). 1998. 26.00 (*0-516-20788-1*) Childrens.
New Orleans. G. S. Prentzas. (Cities of the World Ser.). (Illus.). 64p. (YA). (gr. 4-9). 1999. pap. text 9.95 (*0-516-26397-8*) Childrens.
New Orleans. Tripbuilder, Inc. Staff. 1998. pap. text 5.95 (*1-56621-625-7*) TripBuilder.
***New Orleans.** 2nd ed. 400p. 1999. pap. 15.95 (*0-02-863059-9*) Macmillan.
***New Orleans.** 2nd ed. Tom Downs & John T. Edge. (Illus.). 288p. 2000. pap. 15.95 (*0-86442-782-4*) Lonely Planet.
New Orleans. 3rd ed. Access Press Staff. LC 95-659042. (Illus.). 176p. 1997. pap. 19.00 (*0-06-277227-9*, Access Trvl) HarpInfo.
***New Orleans.** 3rd ed. American Map Publishing Staff. (Insight Guides - USA Ser.). 1999. pap. 21.95 (*0-88729-029-9*) Langenscheidt.
New Orleans. 3rd ed. Compass America Staff. LC 97-33361. (Compass American Guides Ser.). 320p. 1997. pap. 18.95 (*0-679-03597-4*, Compass Amrcn) Fodors Travel.
***New Orleans.** 4th ed. Fodor's Staff. 2000. pap. 21.00 (*0-679-00647-8*) Random.
New Orleans. 4th ed. Richard Saul Wurman. 176p. 1999. pap. 20.00 (*0-06-277275-9*, Access Trvl) HarpInfo.
***New Orleans: A Century of Travel Experience in Every Guide.** Mark Miller. (National Geographic Traveler Ser.). (Illus.). 2000. pap. 22.95 (*0-7922-7948-4*) Natl Geog.
New Orleans: A City Guide. Federal Writers' Project Staff. (American Guidebook Ser.). 416p. 1938. reprint ed. 69.00 (*0-403-02203-7*) Somerset Pub.
New Orleans: A Pictorial History. Leonard V. Huber. LC 91-15549. (Illus.). 384p. 1991. 26.00 (*0-88289-868-X*) Pelican.
New Orleans: An Artist's Sketchbook. Steven Lindsley. (Illus.). 86p. 1997. pap. 18.00 (*1-884824-03-X*) Tryon Pubng.
New Orleans: An Illustrated History. John R. Kemp. LC 97-77010. (Illus.). 288p. 1997. 39.95 (*0-9654754-6-8*) Am Historical Pr.
New Orleans: Elegance & Decadence. Photos by Richard Sexton. (Illus.). 224p. 1993. 40.00 (*0-8118-0074-1*) Chronicle Bks.
***New Orleans: Insiders' Guide for Cosmopolitan Travelers.** Dan Levine. (Avant-Guide Bks.). (Illus.). 2000. pap. 19.95 (*1-891603-10-8*) Empire Pr.
New Orleans: Multiple Language Edition - Includes Text for English - Spanish - French - German - Japanese. (ENG, FRE, GER, JPN & SPA.). 32p. 1997. pap. text 2.50 (*1-56944-157-X*) Terrell Missouri.
New Orleans: Now it Like a Native. 2nd ed. Griffin Trade Paperbacks Publishing Staff. (Let's Go Map Guides Ser.). 1999. pap. 8.95 (*0-312-19912-0*) St Martin.
New Orleans: River Region Renaissance. Diana Pinckley et al. LC 96-39345. 288p. 1996. 45.00 (*1-885352-46-8*); write for info. (*1-885352-47-6*) Community Comm.
New Orleans: Rollin' on the River. Angus Lind & Paul F. Stahls. LC 96-36009. (Urban Tapestry Ser.). (Illus.). 256p. 1996. 44.95 (*1-881096-36-X*) Towery Pub.
New Orleans: Sightseeing in 88 Pictures. Lisa D. Hoff. (Cities in Color Pictorial Guidebooks Ser.). (Illus.). 80p. (Orig.). 1991. pap. 10.95 (*0-9617959-5-6*) Cities in Color.
New Orleans: The Making of an Urban Landscape. Peirce F. Lewis. LC 76-4797. (Contemporary Metropolitan Analysis Ser.). (Illus.). 136p. 1976. text 16.95 (*0-88410-433-8*, HarpBusn) HarpInfo.
New Orleans: The Passing Parade. Patsy Sims. LC 80-82442. (Illus.). 132p. 1980. pap. 14.95 (*0-937430-00-5*) Picayune Pr.
New Orleans: The Ultimate Guide. Randolph Delehanty. LC 97-26742. 496p. 1998. pap. 16.95 (*0-8118-0870-X*) Chronicle Bks.
New Orleans - Treasure City. Thomas P. Terry. (Illus.). 36p. (Orig.). 1980. pap. 2.95 (*0-939850-07-9*) Spec Pub.
New Orleans Architecture: The Cemeteries, Vol. 3. Leonard V. Huber et al. (Illus.). 208p. 1997. reprint ed. pap. 22.50 (*1-56554-270-3*) Pelican.
New Orleans Architecture: The University Section, Vol. 8. Friends of the Cabildo Staff. (Illus.). 208p. 1997. 34.95 (*1-56554-235-5*) Pelican.
New Orleans Architecture Vol. I: The Lower Garden District. Samuel Wilson & Bernard Lelmar. (Illus.). 176p. 1991. reprint ed. pap. 22.50 (*0-88289-843-4*) Pelican.
New Orleans Architecture Vol. IV: Creole Faubourgs. Mary Louise Christovich et al. LC 74-16744. (New Orleans Architecture Ser.). (Illus.). 200p. 1974. reprint ed. 32.50 (*0-88289-037-9*) Pelican.
New Orleans Architecture Vol. V: The Esplanade Ridge. Mary Louise Christovich et al. (Illus.). 192p. (Orig.). 1995. pap. 22.50 (*1-56554-072-7*) Pelican.
New Orleans Architecture Vol. VI: Faubourg Treme & the Bayou Road. Roulhac B. Toledano & Mary Louise Christovich. LC 72-172272. (New Orleans Architecture Ser.). (Illus.). 240p. 1980. 34.95 (*0-88289-166-9*) Pelican.
New Orleans Architecture Vol. VII: Jefferson City. Friends of the Cabildo Staff et al. (Illus.). 208p. 1989. 34.95 (*0-88289-668-7*) Pelican.
New Orleans As It Was. Henry C. Castellanos. LC 89-26568. (Illus.). 364p. 1990. pap. 10.95 (*0-88289-787-X*) Pelican.
New Orleans Beat: A Skip Langdon Mystery. Julie Smith. 1995. mass mkt. 5.99 (*0-8041-1336-X*) Ivy Books.
New Orleans Bicycle Book. Louis Alvarez. (Illus.). 168p. (Orig.). 1984. pap. 5.95 (*0-9614451-0-6*) Little Nemo Pr.
New Orleans Cabildo: Colonial Louisiana's First City Government, 1769-1803. Gilbert C. Din & John E. Harkins. LC 95-45715. (Illus.). 376p. (C). 1996. text 45.00 (*0-8071-2042-1*) La State U Pr.
***New Orleans Cemeteries.** Eric J. Brock. (Images of America Ser.). (Illus.). 128p. 1999. pap. 18.99 (*0-7385-0126-3*) Arcadia Publng.
New Orleans Cemeteries: Life in the Cities of the Dead. Robert Florence. Ed. by Ann Cahn. LC 97-70870. (Illus.). 211p. 1997. 29.95 (*0-9657085-1-9*) Batture Pr.
New Orleans' Charity Hospital: A Story of Physicians, Politics, & Poverty. John E. Salvaggio. LC 91-44719. (Illus.). 264p. (C). 1992. text 45.00 (*0-8071-1613-0*) La State U Pr.
New Orleans Chefs Cookbook. Ed. by Phil Johnson. LC 87-7243. (Illus.). 360p. 1988. 18.95 (*0-88289-666-0*) Pelican.
New Orleans Chef's Cookbook. Phil Johnson. 1999. 9.99 (*0-517-20396-0*) Random Hse Value.
New Orleans Cookbook. Rima Collin & Richard Collin. 1987. pap. 17.00 (*0-394-75275-9*) Knopf.
***New Orleans Cuisine.** Ed. by Tom Stumph. (Illus.). 150p. 1999. pap. 7.95 (*1-893350-00-2*) R Hart Mktg.
***New Orleans Dizzy Spit.** Jesse Freeman. 80p. 2000. pap. 12.00 (*1-930259-00-X*) Anabasis.
New Orleans E. R. 18th ed. Robert M. Maughon. Ed. by Curry Copple. 315p. (Orig.). 1999. pap. 14.95 (*0-9650366-0-X*) Cinnamon Moon.
New Orleans Eat Book: The Encyclopedia of New Orleans Restaurants. 13th rev. ed. Tom Fitzmorris. 272p. (Orig.). 1991. pap. 8.95 (*1-878593-25-0*) NO Big Bend & Pacific.
New Orleans, 1815. Tim Pickles. (Campaign Ser.). (Illus.). 96p. 1994. pap. 14.95 (*1-85532-360-5*, 9527, Pub. by Ospry) Stackpole.
***New Orleans Entertainment, 2000.** (Illus.). 582p. 1999. pap. 25.00 (*1-58553-043-3*, 005G) Enter Pubns.
***New Orleans for Dummies.** (For Dummies Ser.). 336p. 2000. pap. 15.99 (*0-7645-6159-6*) IDG Bks.
New Orleans Garden: Gardening in the Gulf South. Charlotte Seidenberg. LC 93-16436. (Illus.). 528p. 1993. pap. 19.95 (*0-87805-637-8*) U Pr of Miss.
***New Orleans Gardens.** Lake Douglas & Jeanette Hardy. LC 00-43013. 2001. write for info. (*0-8118-2421-7*) Chronicle Bks.
New Orleans Getaway: Reading Level 3-4. (Stormy Night Stories Ser.). 16p. 1993. 2.50 (*0-88336-080-2*) New Readers.
New Orleans Ghosts. Victor C. Klein. 132p. 1993. pap. 9.95 (*1-880365-66-9*) Lycanthrope Pr.
New Orleans Ghosts, Vol. II. Victor C. Klein. (Illus.). 1998. pap. 9.95 (*0-9661812-2-0*) Lycanthrope Pr.
New Orleans Guide. Ed. by Penguin Books Staff. (Time Out Travel Guides Ser.). 296p. 1998. pap. 14.95 (*0-14-027448-0*) Viking Penguin.
New Orleans Houses: A House-Watcher's Guide. Lloyd Vogt. LC 84-9541. (Illus.). 176p. 1985. pap. 23.95 (*0-88289-299-1*) Pelican.
New Orleans in the '50's. Mary L. Widmer. LC 91-13824. (Illus.). 176p. 1991. 22.95 (*0-88289-854-X*) Pelican.
New Orleans in the '40's. Mary L. Widmer. LC 90-38100. (Illus.). 192p. 1990. 22.95 (*0-88289-814-0*) Pelican.
New Orleans in the Gilded Age: Politics & Urban Progress, 1880-1896. Joy J. Jackson. LC 70-89828. (Louisiana Historical Association Ser.). 367p. reprint ed. 113.80 (*0-8357-9390-7*, 201363500087) Bks Demand.
New Orleans in the Gilded Age: Politics & Urban Progress, 1880-1896. 2nd ed. Joy J. Jackson. LC 96-84965. (Illus.). 326p. 1998. 25.00 (*1-887366-16-4*) Univ LA Lafayette.
***New Orleans in the Sixties.** Mary Lou Widmer. LC 99-57268. 176p. 2000. 22.95 (*1-56554-718-7*) Pelican.
New Orleans in the '30's. Mary L. Widmer. LC 89-31479. (Illus.). 176p. 1989. 22.95 (*0-88289-736-5*) Pelican.

N

New Orleans in the '20's. Mary L. Widmer. LC 93-13988. (Illus.). 176p. 1993. 22.95 (*0-88289-933-3*) Pelican.

*__New Orleans in Vintage Postcards.__ Scott Faragher. (Postcard History Ser.). (Illus.). 128p. 1999. pap. 18.99 (*0-7385-0206-5*) Arcadia Publng.

New Orleans in Your Pocket Guide. (In Your Pocket Guide Ser.). 1997. per. 9.95 (*2-06-651801-8*, 6518) Michelin.

New Orleans Irish: Famine Exiles. John Finn. LC 97-70593. (Illus.). 683p. 1997. pap. 35.00 (*0-9656878-0-5*) Holy Fmly Church.

New Orleans Jazz: The End of the Beginning. Barry Martyn. LC 98-75089. (Jazzology Press Book #6 Ser.). 200 p. 1998. write for info. (*0-9638890-5-2*) GHB Jazz Fnd.

New Orleans Jazz - A Revised History: The Development of American Music from the Origin to the Big Bands. R. Collins. LC 95-90004. (Illus.). 290p. 1996. 21.95 (*0-533-11427-6*) Vantage.

New Orleans Jazz & Second Line Drumming. Harlin Riley & Johnny Vidacaich. Ed. by Dan Thress. (Illus.). 120p. (Orig.). 1995. pap. text 24.95 (*0-89724-921-6*, MMBK0043CD) Wrner Bros.

New Orleans Jazz Fest: A Pictorial History. Michael P. Smith. LC 90-25055. (Illus.). 208p. 1991. 22.95 (*0-88289-810-8*) Pelican.

New Orleans Knockout. Don Pendleton. (Executioner Ser.: No. 20). 1989. mass mkt. 3.50 (*1-55817-219-X*, Pinncle Kensgtn) Kensgtn Pub Corp.

New Orleans Legacy. Alexandra Ripley. 496p. 1988. mass mkt. 6.99 (*0-446-34210-6*, Pub. by Warner Bks) Little.

New Orleans, Louisiana. Rand McNally Staff. 1997. pap. 5.95 (*0-528-97200-6*) Rand McNally.

New Orleans Mardi Gras Guide, 1981. rev. ed. Arthur Hardy. (Illus.). 80p. 1981. pap. 2.95 (*0-930892-05-4*) A Hardy & Assocs.

New Orleans Mardi Gras Guide, 1980. 4th ed. Arthur Hardy. LC 79-92736. (Illus.). 80p. 1980. pap. 2.95 (*0-930892-04-6*) A Hardy & Assocs.

New Orleans Mardi Gras Guide, 1982. 6th ed. Arthur Hardy. (Illus.). 80p. 1982. pap. 2.95 (*0-930892-06-2*) A Hardy & Assocs.

New Orleans Mardi Gras Guide, 1983. 7th ed. Arthur Hardy. (Illus.). 80p. 1983. pap. 2.95 (*0-930892-07-0*) A Hardy & Assocs.

New Orleans Mardi Gras Guide, 1984. 8th ed. Arthur Hardy. (Illus.). 100p. 1984. pap. 1.95 (*0-930892-08-9*) A Hardy & Assocs.

New Orleans Mardi Gras Guide, 1985. 9th ed. Arthur Hardy. (Illus.). 112p. 1985. pap. 1.95 (*0-930892-09-7*) A Hardy & Assocs.

New Orleans Mardi Gras Guide, 1977. Arthur Hardy. 56p. 1977. pap. 2.95 (*0-930892-01-1*) A Hardy & Assocs.

New Orleans Mardi Gras Guide, 1978. 2nd ed. Arthur Hardy. LC 77-93191. (Illus.). 64p. 1978. pap. 2.95 (*0-930892-02-X*) A Hardy & Assocs.

New Orleans Mardi Gras Guide, 1979. 3rd ed. Arthur Hardy. LC 78-71117. (Illus.). 72p. 1979. pap. 2.95 (*0-930892-03-8*) A Hardy & Assocs.

New Orleans Mint Gold Coins, 1839-1909: A Numismatic History & Analysis. Douglas E. Winter. (Illus.). 216p. (Orig.). 1992. text 31.95 (*0-943161-46-0*); pap. text 19.95 (*0-943161-43-6*) Bowers & Merena.

New Orleans Monastery Cookbook: Recipes from St. Clare's Kitchen. Poor Clares of New Orleans Staff. Ed. by Sister Olivia Wassmer. 184p. 1992. 10.95 (*0-9634521-0-X*) St Clares Monastery.

New Orleans Mourning. Julie Smith. 352p. 1991. mass mkt. 5.99 (*0-8041-0738-6*) Ivy Books.

New Orleans Museum of Art: The First 75 Years. Prescott N. Dunbar. LC 90-6002. (Illus.). 456p. 1990. 24.95 (*0-8071-1604-1*) La State U Pr.

New Orleans, My Darling: The Selected Budget Guide for the Young & Intrepid. Ed. by Barbara Heller. LC 84-828. (Special Ser.: No. 1). 120p. (Orig.). 1984. pap. 4.95 (*0-918786-29-0*) Lost Roads.

*__New Orleans Nocturne: A Novel.__ Jillian McCade. LC 00-190852. 2000. 25.00 (*0-7388-2031-8*); pap. 18.00 (*0-7388-2032-6*) Xlibris Corp.

New Orleans on the Half-Shell: A Native's Guide to the Crescent City. 3rd ed. Alan Graham & James Taylor. LC 94-42798. (Illus.). 160p. (Orig.). 1995. pap. 9.95 (*1-56554-058-1*) Pelican.

New Orleans on the Mississippi River. 32p. 1998. pap. text. write for info. (*1-56944-173-1*) Terrell Missouri.

New Orleans Piano Legends. 104p. 1999. otabind 19.95 (*0-7935-5159-5*, 00310092) H Leonard.

*__New Orleans Pocket Guide.__ Berlitz Editors. (Pocket Guides Ser.). (Illus.). 144p. 2000. pap. 8.95 (*2-8315-7702-0*) Berlitz.

New Orleans Q & A: Trivial Questions, Terrific Answers. Jane Berins & Madilyn Samuels. (Illus.). 96p. (Orig.). 1985. pap. 5.95 (*0-9614929-0-2*) Royale LA.

New Orleans Requiem. D. J. Donaldson. LC 96-2377. (Mystery Ser.). 250p. 1996. per. 3.99 (*0-373-26188-8*, 1-26188-2, Wrldwide Lib) Harlequin Bks.

New Orleans Riots of July 13th, 1866: Proceedings of the House Report No. 16, 39th Congress, 2nd Session, 1866-1867. U. S. House of Representatives Staff. LC 75-170706. (Black Heritage Library Collection). 1977. reprint ed. 33.95 (*0-8369-8896-5*) Ayer.

New Orleans Riots of July 13, 1866: 39th Congress, Second Session, House Report No. 16. U. S. House of Representatives Staff. LC 79-90200. (Mass Violence in America Ser.). 1969. reprint ed. 33.95 (*0-405-01317-5*) Ayer.

New Orleans Saints. Bob Italia. LC 95-40360. (Inside the NFL Ser.). (Illus.). 32p. (J). (gr. 3-8). 1996. lib. bdg. 15.98 (*1-56239-532-7*) ABDO Pub Co.

*__New Orleans Saints.__ 3rd rev. ed. Julie Nelson. (Pro Football Today Ser.). (Illus.). 32p. 2000. lib. bdg. 22.60 (*1-58341-051-1*, Creat Educ) Creative Co.

*__New Orleans Saints Bk. 1: 25 Yearsof Heroic Effort.__ Christian Serpas. 2000. 11.95 (*0-925417-09-2*) Acadian Hse Pub.

New Orleans Scrapbook. Ross Yockey. (Illus.). 206p. 1988. 15.95 (*0-929199-00-6*); pap. 8.95 (*0-929199-01-4*) Plantain Pub.

New Orleans Seafood Cookbook. Andrew Jaeger & John DeMers. LC 99-23378. (Illus.). 165p. 1999. pap. 19.95 (*1-58008-064-2*) Ten Speed Pr.

New Orleans 7th Ward Nostalgia Dictionary, 1938-1965. Darrlyn A. Smith. (Illus.). xii, 117p. (Orig.). 1996. pap. 9.95 (*0-9655353-0-4*) JADA Inc.

New Orleans Souvenir Book. pap. text. write for info. (*1-56944-021-2*) Terrell Missouri.

New Orleans Stories: Great Writers on the City. John Miller. 224p. 1992. pap. 12.95 (*0-8118-0059-8*) Chronicle Bks.

New Orleans Tavern & Bar Guide. Chris Keadle & Rich Dorn. Ed. by Chris Boyce. (Illus.). 100p. (Orig.). 1988. pap. text 4.95 (*0-935201-29-7*) Affordable Adven.

New Orleans Then & Now. Richard Campanella & Marina Campanella. LC 98-47016. (Illus.). 400p. 1999. 39.95 (*1-56554-347-5*) Pelican.

New Orleans Times: Receptionist. 3rd ed. Butler. (Office Procedures Ser.). 1993. text 18.50 (*0-538-60950-8*) S-W Pub.

New Orleans 2000. Fodors Travel Publications, Inc. Staff. (Illus.). 1999. pap. 15.00 (*0-679-00333-9*) Fodors Travel.

New Orleans Uncovered. Larenda L. Roberts. LC 98-22264. 1998. pap. text 16.95 (*1-55622-620-9*) Wordware Pub.

New Orleans Voodoo Tarot-Book with Cards. Louis Martiniez. 1992. pap. text 29.95 (*0-89281-363-6*) Inner Tradit.

New Orleans Voter: A Handbook of Political Description. Tulane University, Urban Life Research Institute Staff et al. LC 56-3785. (Tulane Studies in Political Science: No. 2). 176p. Date not set. reprint ed. pap. 54.60 (*0-608-20662-8*, 207209900003) Bks Demand.

New Orleans Voter: A Handbook of Political Description, Vol. 2. L. Reisman et al. LC 56-3785. 1955. 11.00 (*0-930598-01-6*) Tulane Stud Pol.

New Orleans Weather, 1961-1980: A Climatology by Means of Synoptic Weather Types. R. A. Muller & J. E. Willis. LC 83-80108. (Miscellaneous Publication: No. 83-1). (Illus.). 74p. 1983. pap. 8.00 (*0-938909-29-0*) Geosci Pubns LSU.

New Orleans, Yesterday & Today: A Guide to the City. Walter G. Cowan et al. LC 83-772. (Illus.). xiv, 272p. 1983. 14.95 (*0-8071-1108-2*); pap. 11.95 (*0-8071-1109-0*) La State U Pr.

New Orpheus: Essays on Kurt Weill. Ed. by Kim H. Kowalke. LC 85-29536. 460p. 1986. 42.00 (*0-300-03514-4*) Yale U Pr.

New Orpheus: Essays on Kurt Weill. Ed. by Kim H. Kowalke. 390p. (C). 1990. reprint ed. pap. 22.00 (*0-300-04616-2*) Yale U Pr.

New Otani Hotel & Garden: A Corporate Campaign Case Study. Ron Kipling. (Illus.). 31p. 1998. pap. 12.50 (*0-9667568-1-9*) LPA Inc.

New OTC Drug Strategies/Markets. Barbara Breindel. LC 98-120756. 90p. 1997. 2950.00 (*1-56965-371-2*, B-104) BCC.

New Other Woman: Contemporary Single Women in Affairs with Married Men. Laurel W. Richardson. 288p. (C). 1987. pap. 14.95 (*0-02-926891-5*) Free Pr.

New Ourselves, Growing Older. Paula B. Doress-Worters & Diana L. Siegal. 1996. 28.50 (*0-8446-6844-3*) Peter Smith.

New Ourselves, Growing Older: Revised & Updated. Paula B. Doress-Worters & Diana L. Siegal. 560p. 1994. per. 18.00 (*0-671-87297-4*, Touchstone) S&S Trade Pap.

New Outline of Social Psychology. Martin Gold. LC 96-54814. 287p. 1997. 29.95 (*1-55798-408-5*, 431-6840) Am Psychol.

New Outline of the Roman Civil Trial. Ernest Metzger. 184p. 1998. text 87.00 (*0-19-826474-7*) OUP.

New Owners: The Mass Emergence of Employee Ownership & What It Means to American Business. Joseph R. Blasi. LC 91-58513. 224p. 1991. 27.95 (*0-88730-509-1*, HarpBusn) HarpInfo.

New Owner's Guide to Akitas: AKC Rank #35. Barbara J. Andrews. (New Owner's Guide to Ser.). (Illus.). 160p. 1996. 12.95 (*0-7938-2760-4*, JG-111) TFH Pubns.

New Owner's Guide to Alaskan Malamutes: AKC Rank #44. Al Holabach & Mary J. Holabach. (New Owner's Guide to Ser.). (Illus.). 160p. 1997. 12.95 (*0-7938-2789-2*, JG-140) TFH Pubns.

*__New Owner's Guide to Australian Cattle Dogs.__ Narelle Robertson. LC 99-461780. (New Owner's Guide to Ser.). (Illus.). 160p. 1999. 12.95 (*0-7938-2808-2*) TFH Pubns.

New Owner's Guide to Australian Shepherds: AKC Rank #40. Joseph Hartnagle. (New Owner's Guide to Ser.). (Illus.). 160p. 1997. 12.95 (*0-7938-2767-1*, JG-118) TFH Pubns.

New Owner's Guide to Basset Hounds: AKC Rank #22. Joan Urban. (New Owner's Guide to Ser.). (Illus.). 160p. 1997. 12.95 (*0-7938-2787-6*, JG-138) TFH Pubns.

New Owner's Guide to Beagles. David Arnold. (Illus.). 160p. 1998. 12.95 (*0-7938-2785-X*, JG136) TFH Pubns.

New Owner's Guide to Bichons Frises. Mary E. Mills & Andrew Mills. (Illus.). 160p. 1997. 12.95 (*0-7938-2779-5*, JG130) TFH Pubns.

New Owner's Guide to Boston Terriers. Bob & Elanor Candland. (New Owner's Guide to Ser.). (Illus.). 160p. 12.95 (*0-7938-2802-3*) TFH Pubns.

New Owner's Guide to Boxers: AKC Rank #13. Richard K. Tomita. (New Owner's Guide to Ser.). (Illus.). 160p. Date not set. 12.95 (*0-7938-2752-3*, JG-103) TFH Pubns.

*__New Owner's Guide to Brittanys.__ Beverly Millette. 160p. 2000. 12.95 (*0-7938-2807-4*) TFH Pubns.

New Owner's Guide to Bulldogs. Hank Williams. (Illus.). 160p. 1998. 12.95 (*0-7938-2788-4*, JG139) TFH Pubns.

New Owner's Guide to Cavalier King Charles Spaniels. Meredith Johnson-Snyder. (New Owner's Guide to Ser.). (Illus.). 160p. 12.95 (*0-7938-2804-X*) TFH Pubns.

New Owner's Guide to Chinese Crested: AKC Rank #72. Joseph Rachunas. (New Owner's Guide to Ser.). (Illus.). 160p. 1998. 12.95 (*0-7938-2773-6*, JG-124) TFH Pubns.

New Owner's Guide to Chinese Shar Pei: AKC Rank #31. Karen Kleinhans. (New Owner's Guide to Ser.). (Illus.). 160p. 1996. 12.95 (*0-7938-2761-2*, JG-112) TFH Pubns.

New Owner's Guide to Chow Chows. G. Beauchamp. (Illus.). 160p. 1997. 12.95 (*0-7938-2780-9*, JG131) TFH Pubns.

New Owner's Guide to Cocker Spaniels: AKC Rank #8. Judy Iby. (New Owner's Guide to Ser.). (Illus.). 160p. 1996. 12.95 (*0-7938-2755-8*, JG-106) TFH Pubns.

New Owner's Guide to Collies. Alice Wharton. LC 99-199907. 1998. 12.95 (*0-7938-2800-7*) TFH Pubns.

New Owner's Guide to Dachshunds: AKC Rank #7. Kaye Ladd. (New Owner's Guide to Ser.). (Illus.). 160p. 1996. 12.95 (*0-7938-2759-0*, JG-110) TFH Pubns.

New Owner's Guide to Dalmatians: AKC Rank #15. Helen Shue. (New Owner's Guide to Ser.). (Illus.). 160p. Date not set. 12.95 (*0-7938-2754-X*, JG-105) TFH Pubns.

New Owner's Guide to Doberman Pinschers: AKC Rank #20. Faye Strauss. (New Owner's Guide to Ser.). (Illus.). 160p. 1998. 12.95 (*0-7938-2784-1*, JG-135) TFH Pubns.

New Owner's Guide to Dog Training. Dorman Pantfoeder. LC 99-205928. (New Owner's Guide to Ser.). (Illus.). 160p. 1997. 12.95 (*0-7938-2766-3*, JG-117) TFH Pubns.

New Owner's Guide to English Springer Spaniels: AKC Rank #25. Art Perle. (New Owner's Guide to Ser.). (Illus.). 160p. 1997. 12.95 (*0-7938-2763-9*, JG-114) TFH Pubns.

New Owner's Guide to German Shepherds: AKC Rank #3. Charlotte Schwartz. (New Owner's Guide to Ser.). (Illus.). 160p. Date not set. 12.95 (*0-7938-2751-5*, JG-102) TFH Pubns.

New Owner's Guide to Golden Retrievers: AKC Rank #4. Judy Laureano. (New Owner's Guide to Ser.). (Illus.). 160p. 1996. 12.95 (*0-7938-2757-4*, JG-108) TFH Pubns.

New Owner's Guide to Great Danes: AKC Rank #32. Jill Swedlow. (New Owner's Guide to Ser.). (Illus.). 160p. 1997. 12.95 (*0-7938-2764-7*, JG-115) TFH Pubns.

New Owner's Guide to Italian Greyhounds. 160p. 12.95 (*0-7938-2775-2*) TFH Pubns.

New Owner's Guide to Labrador Retrievers: AKC Rank #1. Mary Feazell. (New Owner's Guide to Ser.). (Illus.). 160p. 1996. 12.95 (*0-7938-2756-6*, JG-107) TFH Pubns.

New Owner's Guide to Maltese: AKC Rank #23. Vicki Abbot. (New Owner's Guide to Ser.). (Illus.). 160p. 1997. 12.95 (*0-7938-2783-3*, JG-134) TFH Pubns.

New Owner's Guide to Miniature Pinschers: AKC Rank #18. Jacqueline O'Neil. (New Owner's Guide to Ser.). (Illus.). 160p. 1997. 12.95 (*0-7938-2768-X*, JG-119) TFH Pubns.

*__New Owner's Guide to Old English Sheepdogs.__ Marilyn Mayfield. 160p. 2000. 12.95 (*0-7938-2795-7*) TFH Pubns.

New Owner's Guide to Pekingese. Ron Deanne & Larry Ulmer. (New Owner's Guide to Ser.). (Illus.). 160p. 12.95 (*0-7938-2806-6*) TFH Pubns.

*__New Owner's Guide to Pomeranians.__ Julie Moreno. 160p. 2000. 12.95 (*0-7938-2794-9*) TFH Pubns.

New Owner's Guide to Poodles. Charlotte Schwartz. (Illus.). 160p. 1997. pap. 12.95 (*0-7938-2778-7*, JG-129) TFH Pubns.

New Owner's Guide to Pugs. 160p. 12.95 (*0-7938-2774-4*) TFH Pubns.

New Owner's Guide to Rottweilers: AKC Rank #2. Urs Ochsenbein. (New Owner's Guide to Ser.). (Illus.). 160p. Date not set. 12.95 (*0-7938-2750-7*, JG-101) TFH Pubns.

New Owner's Guide to Samoyeds. Terry Campbell. (Illus.). 160p. 1998. 12.95 (*0-7938-2790-6*, JG141) TFH Pubns.

New Owner's Guide to Scottish Terriers. Contrib. by Miriam Stamm & Rick Beauchamp. LC 99-205929. 160p. 1998. 12.95 (*0-7938-2786-8*) TFH Pubns.

New Owner's Guide to Shih Tzu: AKC Rank #11. JoAnne Regelman. (New Owner's Guide to Ser.). (Illus.). 160p. Date not set. 12.95 (*0-7938-2753-1*, JG-104) TFH Pubns.

New Owner's Guide to Siberian Huskies: AKC Rank #17. Kathleen Kanzler. (New Owner's Guide to Ser.). (Illus.). 160p. 1996. 12.95 (*0-7938-2776-0*, JG-127) TFH Pubns.

New Owner's Guide to Soft Coated Wheaten Terriers. 160p. 12.95 (*0-7938-2772-8*) TFH Pubns.

New Owner's Guide to Sugar Gliders. Helen O'Reilly. 160p. 1998. 12.95 (*0-7938-2825-2*, JG-200) TFH Pubns.

New Owner's Guide to the American Pit Bull Terrier. Todd Fenstermacher. (New Owner's Guide to Ser.). (Illus.). 160p. 1996. 12.95 (*0-7938-2762-0*, JG-113) TFH Pubns.

New Owner's Guide to Training the Perfect Puppy. Andrew De Prisco. (New Owner's Guide to Ser.). (Illus.). 160p. 1996. 12.95 (*0-7938-2758-2*, JG-109) TFH Pubns.

*__New Owner's Guide to Weimaraners.__ Judythe Coffman. LC 99-205925. (New Owner's Guide to Ser.). (Illus.). 160p. 1998. 12.95 (*0-7938-2805-8*) TFH Pubns.

New Owner's Guide to West Highland White Terriers: AKC Rank #36. Dawn Martin. (New Owner's Guide to Ser.). (Illus.). 160p. 1996. 12.95 (*0-7938-2765-5*, JG-116) TFH Pubns.

New Owner's Guide to Yorkshire Terriers: AKC Rank #9. Janet Jackson. (New Owner's Guide to Ser.). (Illus.). 160p. 1996. 12.95 (*0-7938-2777-9*, JG-128) TFH Pubns.

New Owners's Guide to Bearded Collies. 160p. 12.95 (*0-7938-2791-4*) TFH Pubns.

New Oxford Annotated Bible. (Illus.). 1995. write for info. (*0-19-528435-6*) OUP.

New Oxford Annotated Bible. rev. ed. (Illus.). 1995. write for info. (*0-19-528436-4*) OUP.

New Oxford Bible Maps. Ed. by Oxford University Press Staff. 1996. pap. 49.99 incl. cd-rom (*0-19-528465-8*) OUP.

New Oxford Book of American Verse. Ed. by Richard Ellmann. LC 75-46354. 1128p. 1976. 45.00 (*0-19-502058-8*) OUP.

New Oxford Book of Australian Verse. Ed. by Les A. Murray. 432p. 1986. 39.95 (*0-19-554618-0*) OUP.

New Oxford Book of Carols. Hugh Keyte. Ed. by Andrew Parrott & Clifford Bartlett. 744p. 1992. 145.00 (*0-19-353323-5*) OUP.

New Oxford Book of Carols. Ed. by Hugh Keyte et al. (Illus.). 736p. 1998. pap. text 31.95 (*0-19-353322-7*) OUP.

New Oxford Book of Children's Verse. Ed. by Neil Philip. 410p. (J). 1996. 35.00 (*0-19-214247-X*) OUP.

New Oxford Book of Children's Verse. Ed. by Neil Philip. (Oxford Books of Verse). 408p. 1998. reprint ed. pap. 18.95 (*0-19-288107-8*) OUP.

New Oxford Book of Christian Verse. Ed. by Donald Davie. 368p. 1988. pap. 14.95 (*0-19-282157-1*) OUP.

New Oxford Book of Eighteenth-Century Verse. Ed. by Roger Lonsdale. 912p. 1989. pap. 17.95 (*0-19-282054-0*) OUP.

New Oxford Book of English Prose. John Gross. LC 97-49397. 1054p. 1998. 45.00 (*0-19-214246-1*) OUP.

*__New Oxford Book of English Prose.__ Ed. by John Gross. 1056p. 2000. pap. 19.95 (*0-19-283000-7*) OUP.

New Oxford Book of English Verse, 1250-1950. Ed. by Helen Gardner. 992p. 1972. 45.00 (*0-19-812136-9*) OUP.

New Oxford Book of Food Plants: A Guide to the Fruit, Vegetables, Herbs & Spices of the World. J. G. Vaughan & Catherine Geissler. (Illus.). 264p. 1999. pap. 25.00 (*0-19-850567-1*) OUP.

New Oxford Book of Food Plants: A Guide to the Fruit, Vegetables, Herbs & Spices of the World. John G. Vaughan & Catherine Geissler. LC 97-6803. (Illus.). 260p. 1997. 45.00 (*0-19-854825-7*) OUP.

New Oxford Book of Irish Verse. Ed. & Tr. by Thomas Kinsella from IRI. (Illus.). 454p. 1989. pap. 16.95 (*0-19-282643-3*) OUP.

New Oxford Book of Light Verse. Ed. & Selected by Kingsley Amis. 384p. 1987. pap. 14.95 (*0-19-282075-3*) OUP.

New Oxford Book of Romantic Period Verse. Ed. by Jerome J. McGann. LC 93-32333. (Illus.). 860p. 1994. reprint ed. pap. 18.95 (*0-19-282329-9*) OUP.

New Oxford Book of Seventeenth-Century Verse. Ed. by Alastair Fowler. LC 92-7313. 876p. 1992. pap. 19.95 (*0-19-282996-3*) OUP.

New Oxford Book of Sixteenth Century Verse. Selected by Emrys Jones. (Oxford Books of Verse). 808p. 1992. pap. 22.00 (*0-19-282971-8*) OUP.

New Oxford Book of Sixteenth Century Verse. Ed. by Emyrus Jones. (Oxford Books of Verse). 816p. 1991. 45.00 (*0-19-214126-0*) OUP.

New Oxford Book of Victorian Verse. Ed. by Christopher Ricks. LC 94-273. (Oxford Poets Ser.). 688p. 1990. pap. 17.95 (*0-19-282778-2*) OUP.

New Oxford Companion to Literature in French. Ed. by Peter France. (Illus.). 916p. 1995. 60.00 (*0-19-866125-8*) OUP.

New Oxford Companion to Music, 2 vols., Set. Ed. by Denis Arnold. (Illus.). 2,032p. 1983. 185.00 (*0-19-311316-3*) OUP.

New Oxford English Dictionary. 2nd ed. Ed. by John A. Simpson & Edmund Weiner. 2000. audio compact disk 395.00 (*0-19-521573-7*) OUP.

New Oxford Guide to Writing. Thomas S. Kane. (Illus.). 336p. 1988. text 35.00 (*0-19-504538-6*) OUP.

New Oxford Guide to Writing. Thomas S. Kane. (Illus.). 336p. 1994. reprint ed. pap. text 14.95 (*0-19-509059-4*) OUP.

New Oxford History of Music. Incl. Vol. 1. Ancient & Oriental Music. Ed. by Egon Wellesz. (Illus.). 556p. 1957. text 95.00 (*0-19-316301-2*); Vol. 3. Ars Nova & the Renaissance, Thirteen Hundred to Fifteen Hundred Forty. Ed. by Dom A. Hughes & Gerald Abraham. (Illus.). 586p. 1960. text 95.00 (*0-19-316303-9*); Vol. 4. Age of Humanism, 1540-1630. Ed. by Gerald Abraham. (Illus.). 1,004p. 1968. text 95.00 (*0-19-316304-7*); Vol. 7. Age of Enlightenment, 1745-1790. Ed. by Egon Wellesz & Frederick Sternfeld. (Illus.). 744p. 1974. text 95.00 (*0-19-316307-1*); Vol. 10. Modern Age, 1890 to 1960. Ed. by Martin Cooper. (Illus.). 784p. 1974. text 95.00 (*0-19-316310-1*); write for info. (*0-318-54860-7*) OUP.

New Oxford History of Music, 4 vols. 1990. reprint ed. lib. bdg. 280.00 (*0-7812-9022-8*) Rprt Serv.

New Oxford History of Music Vol. 2: The Early Middle Ages to 1300. 2nd ed. Ed. by Richard Crocker & David Hiley. (Illus.). 816p. 1990. text 105.00 (*0-19-316329-2*) OUP.

New Oxford History of Music Vol. 5: Opera & Church Music, 1630-1750. Ed. by Nigel Fortune & Anthony Lewis. (Illus.). 892p. 1975. 95.00 (*0-19-316305-5*) OUP.

New Oxford History of Music Vol. 6: Concert Music, Sixteen Thirty to Seventeen Fifty, Vol. 6. Ed. by Gerald Abraham. LC 85-2950. (Illus.). 806p. 1986. text 95.00 (*0-19-316306-3*) OUP.

New Oxford History of Music Vol. 8: The Age of Beethoven, 1790-1830. Ed. by Gerald E. Abraham. (Illus.). 768p. 1983. text 95.00 (*0-19-316308-X*) OUP.

New Oxford History of Music Vol. 9: Romanticism (1830-1890), Vol. 9. Ed. by Gerald E. Abraham. (Illus.). 956p. 1990. text 130.00 (*0-19-316309-8*) OUP.

An Asterisk (*) at the beginning of an entry indicates that the title is appearing for the first time.

New Oxford Picture Dictionary. 1993. 9.25 (0-88336-160-4) OUP.

New Oxford Picture Dictionary. Ed. by Oxford University Press Staff. 1988. 6.95 (0-19-434296-4) OUP.

New Oxford Picture Dictionary. E. C. Parnwell. LC 87-23950. (MUL., Illus.). 124p. 1988. pap. 9.95 (0-19-434199-2) OUP.

New Oxford Picture Dictionary. E. C. Parnwell. (ENG & JPN., Illus.). 150p. 1990. pap. text 9.95 (0-19-434356-1) OUP.

New Oxford Picture Dictionary: American English - Spanish. Ed. by E. C. Parnwell. (Illus.). 148p. 1989. pap. text 9.95 (0-19-434355-3) OUP.

New Oxford Picture Dictionary: Beginner's Workbook. 1993. 7.75 (0-88336-162-0) OUP.

New Oxford Picture Dictionary: Beginner's Workbook. E. C. Parnwell. (Illus.). 1988. pap. text, wbk. ed. 7.95 (0-19-434326-X) OUP.

New Oxford Picture Dictionary: Chinese - English. E. C. Parnwell. (ENG & CHI., Illus.). 128p. 1989. pap. text 9.95 (0-19-434357-X) OUP.

New Oxford Picture Dictionary: English-Navajo Edition. E. C. Parnwell. (Illus.). 148p. 1990. pap. text 9.95 (0-19-434362-6) OUP.

New Oxford Picture Dictionary: Intermediate Workbook. 1993. 7.75 (0-88336-163-9) OUP.

New Oxford Picture Dictionary: Intermediate Workbook. E. C. Parnwell. (Illus.). 144p. 1988. pap. text, wbk. ed. 7.95 (0-19-434325-1) OUP.

New Oxford Picture Dictionary: Listening & Speaking Activity Book. Jayme Adelson-Goldstein et al. (Illus.). 206p. 1993. pap. text 19.95 (0-19-434365-0) OUP.

New Oxford Picture Dictionary: Monolingual English. Margot F. Gramer. (Illus.). 130p. 1992. text 16.95 (0-19-434533-5) OUP.

New Oxford Picture Dictionary: Overhead Transparencies (100) E. C. Parnwell. 1993. 199.95 (0-19-434532-7) OUP.

New Oxford Picture Dictionary: Russian - English. E. C. Parnwell. (RUS & ENG., Illus.). 1994. pap. text 9.95 (0-19-434651-X) OUP.

New Oxford Picture Dictionary: Teacher's Guide. 1993. 7.50 (0-88336-161-2) OUP.

New Oxford Picture Dictionary: Teacher's Guide. Margot F. Gramer. (Illus.). 144p. 1988. pap. text, teacher ed. 8.50 (0-19-434330-8) OUP.

***New Oxford Textbook of Psychiatry.** Ed. by Michael Gelder et al. (Illus.). 2064p. 2000. text 225.00 (0-19-262970-0) OUP.

New Oxford Treasury of Children's Poems. Ed. by Michael Harrison & Christopher Stuart-Clark. (Illus.). 174p. (J). (gr. k-5). 1999. reprint ed. pap. 15.95 (0-19-276196-X) OUP.

New Oz: The Wizard Revisited. Richard Marvel. Ed. by Marjorie M. Schuck. 86p. (Orig.). 1992. pap. text 10.00 (0-934616-45-0) Valkyrie Pub Hse.

New Pacific Community: U. S. Strategic Options in Asia. Martin Lasater. LC 96-19487. 192p. (C). 1996. pap. 69.00 (0-8133-8869-4, Pub. by Westview) HarpC.

New Pacific Community in the 1900s. Ed. by Young J. Kim. LC 96-12784. 246p. (C). (gr. 13). 1996. text 76.95 (1-56324-783-6, East Gate Bk) M E Sharpe.

New Pacific Community in the 1990s. Ed. by Young J. Kim. LC 96-12784. 246p. (C). (gr. 13). 1996. pap. text 34.95 (1-56324-784-4, East Gate Bk) M E Sharpe.

New Pacific Literatures: Culture & Environment in the European Pacific. John McLaren. LC 92-1672. 416p. 1993. text 20.00 (0-8153-0496-X, H1054) Garland.

New Package Types - Configurations for Processed Convenience Foods. 201p. 1992. 2450.00 (0-89336-903-9, GA-077) BCC.

New Page. Federico Mayor. (UNESCO Ser.). 128p. 1995. text 51.95 (1-85521-652-3, Pub. by Dartmth Pub) Ashgate Pub Co.

New Pages: News & Reviews of the Progressive Book Trade. 1982. write for info. (0-318-56719-9) New Pages Pr.

New Paint Magic. rev. ed. Jocasta Innes. LC 92-54111. (Illus.). 239p. 1992. pap. 25.00 (0-679-74251-4) Pantheon.

New Painting: Impress, 1874-86. C. Moffett. (Illus.). 510p. (Orig.). 1989. pap. 29.95 (0-295-96883-4) U of Wash Pr.

New Painting: Impressionism 1874-1886. Charles S. Moffett. (Orig.). 1986. 60.00 (0-295-96367-0) U of Wash Pr.

New Painting: Impressionism 1874-1886. Fronia E. Wiseman et al. LC 85-24537. (Illus.). 510p. (Orig.). 1986. pap. 29.95 (0-88401-047-3) Fine Arts Mus.

New Pakistan. Satish Kumar. 387p. 1978. 24.95 (0-318-37272-X) Asia Bk Corp.

New Palauan-English Dictionary. Lewis S. Josephs. LC 90-40948. (PALI Language Texts, Micronesia Ser.). 552p. (C). 1990. text 36.00 (0-8248-1345-6) UH Pr.

New Palestine: An Authoritative Account of Palestine Since the Great War; the Problems, Political, Economic & Racial, That Confront the British Administration. William D. McCrackan. Ed. by Moshe Davis. LC 77-70722. (America & the Holy Land Ser.). (Illus.). 1977. reprint ed. lib. bdg. 47.95 (0-405-10266-6) Ayer.

New Palestinians: The Emerging Generation of Leaders. John Wallach. LC 92-24551. (Illus.). 368p. 1992. 22.95 (1-55958-215-4) Prima Pub.

New Palestinians: The Emerging Generations of Leaders. John Wallach. (Illus.). 1994. pap. 14.95 (1-55958-429-7) Prima Pub.

New Palgrave: A Dictionary of Economics, 4 Vols. Ed. by John Eatwell et al. 4194p. 1998. pap. 225.00 (1-56159-197-1) Groves Dictionaries.

New Palgrave: A Dictionary of Economics, 4 Vols., Set. John Eatwell et al. LC 87-1946. 4194p. (C). 1988. 750.00 (0-935859-10-1, HB61.N49) Groves Dictionaries.

New Palgrave: Econometrics. John Eatwell. (Orig.). 1990. 39.95 (0-393-02731-7) Norton.

New Palgrave: Econometrics. Ed. by John Eatwell et al. (New Palgrave Series in Economics). (Orig.). (C). 1990. pap. 14.95 (0-393-95856-6) Norton.

New Palgrave: Marxian Economics. John Eatwell. (Orig.). 1990. 39.95 (0-393-02735-X) Norton.

New Palgrave: Marxian Economics. John Eatwell. Ed. by Murray Milgate & Peter Newman. (New Palgrave Series in Economics). (Orig.). (C). 1990. pap. 15.95 (0-393-95860-4) Norton.

New Palgrave: Time Series & Statistics. John Eatwell et al. 1991. pap. 18.95 (0-393-95862-0) Norton.

New Palgrave: Utility & Probability. John Eatwell et al. 1990. 39.95 (0-393-02738-4) Norton.

New Palgrave Dictionary of Economics & the Law, 3 vols. Ed. by Peter Newman. 2210p. 1998. 550.00 (1-56159-215-3) Groves Dictionaries.

New Palgrave Dictionary of Money & Finance, 2 Vols., Set. Peter Newman et al. 2621p. 1992. 595.00 (1-56159-041-X) Groves Dictionaries.

New Palgrave Economic Development. John Eatwell. 1989. pap. 15.95 (0-393-95850-7) Norton.

New Palgrave Economic Development. John Eatwell. 1989. 39.95 (0-393-02725-2) Norton.

New Palgrave Finance. John Eatwell. 1989. pap. 14.95 (0-393-95857-4) Norton.

New Palgrave Game Theory. John Eatwell et al. 1989. pap. 14.95 (0-393-95858-2) Norton.

New Palgrave General Equilibrium. John Eatwell et al. 1989. pap. 18.95 (0-393-95853-1) Norton.

New Palgrave General Equilibrium. John Eatwell et al. 1989. 39.95 (0-393-02728-7) Norton.

New Palgrave Money. John Eatwell. 1989. pap. 15.95 (0-393-95851-5) Norton.

New Palgrave Money. John Eatwell. 1989. 39.95 (0-393-02726-0) Norton.

New Palgrave Social Economics. John Eatwell. 1989. pap. 14.95 (0-393-95852-3) Norton.

New Palgrave Social Economics. John Eatwell. 1989. 39.95 (0-393-02727-9) Norton.

New Palladini Tarot Deck & Book Set. Susan Hansson. (Illus.). 218p. 1997. pap. 26.00 (0-88079-998-6, PNS99) US Games Syst.

New Palmistry: How to Read the Whole Hand & Knuckles. Judith Hipskind. 1995. pap. 62.50 (81-7224-425-8, Pub. by Print Hse) St Mut.

New Palmistry: How to Read the Whole Hand & the Knuckles. Judith Hipskind. LC 93-38438. (Illus.). 336p. 1999. pap. 12.95 (1-56718-352-2) Llewellyn Pubns.

New Panorama Bible Study Course see Panorama de la Biblia

New "Panorama" Bible Study Course No. 1: A Plan of the Ages. Alfred Thompson Eade. (Illus.). 28p. (gr. 11). 1993. pap. 16.99 (0-8007-1578-0) Revell.

New "Panorama" Bible Study Course No. 2: The Study of Angelology. Alfred Thompson Eade. (Illus.). 32p. (gr. 11). 1986. pap. 16.99 (0-8007-0222-0) Revell.

New "Panorama" Bible Study Course No. 3: The Second Coming of Christ. Alfred Thompson Eade. (Illus.). 36p. (gr. 11). 1984. pap. 16.99 (0-8007-0223-9) Revell.

New "Panorama" Bible Study Course No. 4: The Book of Revelation. Alfred Thompson Eade. (Illus.). 32p. (gr. 11). 1984. pap. 16.99 (0-8007-0434-7) Revell.

New Papercrafts. Lorenz Pub. 1998. 24.95 (1-85967-752-5) Anness Pub.

New Papyrological Primer. 5th ed. Ed. by P. W. Pestman. (Illus.). xxii, 318p. 1990. pap. 46.50 (90-04-10019-9) Brill Academic Pubs.

***New Parade: Level Starter.** 2nd ed. (C). 1999. student ed. 24.13 (0-201-63140-7) Addison-Wesley.

***New Parade Level 1.** 2nd ed. 112p. (C). 2000. pap., student ed. 7.93 (0-201-62147-9) Addison-Wesley.

***New Parade Level 1.** 2nd ed. (C). 2000. student ed. 100.00 incl. VHS (0-201-70423-4) Addison-Wesley.

***New Parade Level 1.** 2nd ed. (C). 2000. text 40.00 (0-13-030326-7) P-H.

***New Parade Level 1.** 2nd ed. (C). 1999. student ed. 13.33 (0-201-60427-2) Pearson Custom.

***New Parade Level 2.** 2nd ed. 112p. (C). 2000. pap., student ed. 7.93 (0-201-63130-X) Addison-Wesley.

***New Parade Level 2.** 2nd ed. (C). 2000. student ed. write for info. (0-201-70424-2) Addison-Wesley.

***New Parade Level 2.** 2nd ed. (C). 2000. text 40.00 (0-13-030327-5) P-H.

***New Parade Level 2.** 2nd ed. (C). 1999. student ed. 13.33 (0-201-60425-6) Pearson Custom.

***New Parade Level 3.** 2nd ed. 112p. (C). 2000. pap., student ed. 7.93 (0-201-63135-0) Addison-Wesley.

***New Parade Level 3.** 2nd ed. (C). 2000. student ed. 100.00 (0-201-70425-0) Addison-Wesley.

***New Parade Level 3.** 2nd ed. (C). 1999. student ed. 13.33 (0-201-60429-9) Pearson Custom.

***New Parade Level 3.** 2nd ed. (C). 2000. pap., student ed. 40.00 (0-13-026517-9) Pearson Custom.

***New Parade Level 4.** 2nd ed. 112p. (C). 2000. student ed. 7.93 (0-201-63136-9) Addison-Wesley.

***New Parade Level 4.** 2nd ed. (C). 2000. student ed. write for info. (0-201-70426-9) Addison-Wesley.

***New Parade Level 4.** 2nd ed. 2p. (C). 2000. student ed. write for info. (0-13-026518-7) P-H.

***New Parade Level 4.** 2nd ed. (C). 2000. student ed. 13.33 (0-201-60430-2) Pearson Custom.

***New Parade Level 5.** 2nd ed. (C). 2000. student ed. 13.33 (0-201-60431-0) Addison-Wesley.

***New Parade Level 5.** 2nd ed. 112p. (C). 2000. student ed. 7.93 (0-201-63137-7) Addison-Wesley.

***New Parade Level 5.** 2nd ed. (C). 2000. student ed. write for info. (0-201-70427-7) Addison-Wesley.

***New Parade Level 5.** 2nd ed. (C). 2000. student ed. 40.00 (0-13-026515-2) P-H.

***New Parade Level 6.** 2nd ed. 112p. (C). 1999. student ed. 7.93 (0-201-63139-3) Addison-Wesley.

***New Parade Level 6.** 2nd ed. (C). 2000. student ed. 13.33 (0-201-60432-9) Addison-Wesley.

***New Parade Level 6.** 2nd ed. (C). 2000. student ed. write for info. (0-201-70428-5) Addison-Wesley.

***New Parade Level 6.** 2nd ed. (C). 2000. student ed. 40.00 (0-13-026516-0) P-H.

***New Parade Level Starter.** 2nd ed. 112p. (C). 1999. student ed. 7.93 (0-201-62980-1) Addison-Wesley.

***New Parade Level Starter.** 2nd ed. (C). 2000. student ed. write for info. (0-201-70422-6) Addison-Wesley.

***New Parade Level Starter.** 2nd ed. (C). 2000. text. write for info. (0-13-030325-9) P-H.

***New Parade Level Starter.** 2nd ed. (C). 2000. student ed. 13.33 (0-201-60426-4) Pearson Custom.

New Parade Sampler. 12p. (C). 1999. pap. write for info. (0-13-017049-6) S&S Trade.

New Paradigm Cooking: A Tasteful Shift in Healthy Eating. Nancy E. Sandbach et al. LC 96-84940. (Illus.). 176p. 1996. 18.95 (0-9652360-0-5) Favorite Recipes.

New Paradigm for Collaborative Science & Engineering Research. Jay Kayne. 35p. 1996. pap. 15.00 (1-55877-260-X) Natl Governor.

New Paradigm for Informed Consent. Irene S. Switankowsky. LC 97-50149. (Illus.). 160p. 1998. 32.50 (0-7618-1016-1) U Pr of Amer.

New Paradigm in Business: Emerging Strategies for Leadership & Organizational Change. Ed. by Michael Ray & Alan Rinzler. LC 92-26205. 320p. 1993. pap. 15.95 (0-87477-726-7, Tarcher Putnam) Putnam Pub Group.

New Paradigm of Leadership: An Inquiry into Transformational Leadership. Bernard M. Bass. LC 97-18769. 258p. 1997. write for info. (0-8058-2696-3); pap. write for info. (0-8058-2697-1) L Erlbaum Assocs.

New Paradigm of Leadership: Visions of Excellence for 21st Century Organizations. Ed. by Ken Shelton. (Executive Excellence Classics Ser.: Vol. II). (Illus.). 262p. 1997. 20.00 (1-890009-18-0) Exec Excell.

New Paradigm of Productivity Movement in Japan. Japan Productivity Center Staff. 63p. 1989. pap. text 7.50 (92-833-1809-9) Productivity Inc.

New Paradigm of Systemic Competitiveness: Toward More Integrated Policies in Latin America. OECD Staff. 272p. 1994. pap. 29.00 (92-64-14259-2) OECD.

New Paradigms: For Creating Quality Schools. Brad Greene. LC 94-69069. 113p. (Orig.). 1995. pap. 12.00 (0-944337-23-6, 236) New View Pubns.

***New Paradigms, Culture & Subjectivity.** Dora Fried Schnitman & Jorge Schnitman. LC 99-51426. (Advances in Systems Theory, Complexity & the Human Sciences Ser.). 1999. write for info. (1-57273-262-8) Hampton Pr NJ.

New Paradigms for College Teaching. Ed. by William E. Campbell & Karl A. Smith. 285p. (Orig.). 1997. pap. text, teacher ed. 20.00 (0-939603-26-8) Interaction Bk Co.

New Parakeet Handbook. I. Bermelin & A. Wolter. 1986. pap. 9.95 (0-8120-2985-2) Barron.

***New Parallel Algorithms for Direct of Linear Equations.** C. Siva Ram Murthy et al. LC 99-86570. 200p. 2000. text 69.95 (0-471-36165-8) Wiley.

New Parent: The Essential Guide for All First-time Mothers & Fathers. Miriam Stoppard. LC 97-50087. 168p. 1998. 24.95 (0-7894-1997-1) DK Pub Inc.

New Parents for Older Children. A. Rushton et al. (C). 1989. 50.00 (0-903534-79-7, Pub. by Brit Ag for Adopt & Fost) St Mut.

New Parents' Sourcebook: Information, Products, & Services for You & Your Baby. Hilory Wagner. LC 95-26660. 256p. 1996. 12.95 (0-8065-1794-8, Citadel Pr) Carol Pub Group.

New Parish Ministers: Laity & Religious on Parish Staffs. Philip J. Murnion. (Illus.). (Orig.). 1992. pap. 11.95 (1-881307-01-8) Natl Pastoral LC.

New Parish Ministries, Series 2, Series 2. 248p. 1984. 8.95 (0-86683-839-2) Harper SF.

New Parish Prayers. Colquhoun. text 34.95 (0-340-27237-6, Pub. by Hodder & Stought Ltd) Trafalgar.

New Park Street Pulpit, 6. Charles H. Spurgeon. 2424p. 1990. 175.00 (0-8010-8303-6) Baker Bks.

New Park Street Pulpit: Sermons Preached by Charles H. Spurgeon, 6 vols. Charles H. Spurgeon. Incl. Vols. 1 & 2. 1855-1856. 1975. reprint ed. 35.00 (1-56186-001-8); Vols. 3 & 4. 1857-1858. 1975. reprint ed. 35.00 (1-56186-002-6); Vols. 5 & 6. 1858-1859. 1975. reprint ed. 35.00 (1-56186-003-4); reprint ed. 105.00 (1-56186-000-X) Pilgrim Pubns.

New Park Street Pulpit & Metropolitan Tabernacle Pulpit, 1855-1917 Vols. 1-63, Set. Charles H. Spurgeon. reprint ed. 1505.00 (1-56186-004-2) Pilgrim Pubns.

New Park Street Pulpit Index. Charles H. Spurgeon. 1976. pap. 2.00 (1-56186-414-5) Pilgrim Pubns.

New Parliaments of Central & Eastern Europe. Ed. by David M. Olson & Philip Norton. 264p. (C). 1996. 52.50 (0-7146-4715-2, Pub. by F Cass Pubs); pap. 24.50 (0-7146-4261-4, Pub. by F Cass Pubs) Intl Spec Bk.

New Parrot Handbook. Werner Lantermann. (Illus.). 144p. 1986. pap. 9.95 (0-8120-3729-4) Barron.

New Parrot Training Handbook. Jennifer Hubbard. LC 96-92980. 1997. pap. text 14.95 (0-9626724-2-4) Parrot Pr.

New Particles, '85: Proceedings of the Conference on New Particles, Madison, Wisconsin, May 8-11, 1985. Ed. by V. Barger & Francis Halzen. 360p. 1986. text 124.00 (9971-5-0045-0) World Scientific Pub.

New Particulars Regarding the Works of Shakespeare. J. Payne Collier. LC 71-113584. reprint ed. 21.50 (0-404-01614-6) AMS Pr.

New Partnership: A Straight-Talking Guide to Bringing Out the Best in People at Work. Tom Melohn. 265p. 1996. pap. 14.95 (0-471-14738-9) Wiley.

New Partnership: Human Services with Business & Industry. Barbara Feinstein & Edwin G. Brown. 186p. 1982. pap. text 13.95 (0-87073-654-X) Schenkman Bks Inc.

New Partnership for African Development: Issues & Parameters. Ed. by Henock Kifle et al. LC 97-192242. 216p. 1997. 24.95 (91-7106-412-5, Pub. by Nordic Africa) Transaction Pubs.

New Partnerships for Managing Technological Change. Nancy Bancroft. LC 91-16748. 288p. 1991. 128.95 (0-471-54674-7) Wiley.

New Partnerships for Sustainable Agriculture. Ed. by Lori A. Thrupp. (Biodiversity & Sustainable Agriculture Ser.). 148p. 1996. pap. 20.00 (1-56973-102-0) World Resources Inst.

New Passages: Mapping Your Life Across Time. Gail Sheehy. 528p. 1996. pap. 12.95 (0-345-40445-9) Ballantine Pub Grp.

New Passages: Mapping Your Life Across Time. large type ed. Gail Sheehy. LC 95-33650. 842p. 1999. 26.95 (0-7838-1550-6, G K Hall Lrg Type) Mac Lib Ref.

New Passport to Survival: 12 Steps to Self-Sufficient Living. Rita Bingham & Esther Dickey. (Illus.). 240p. 1999. pap. 15.95 (1-882314-24-7) Nat Meals Pub.

New Past, & Other Essays on the Development of Civilization. Ed. by Edward H. Carter. LC 68-8446. (Essay Index Reprint Ser.). 1977. reprint ed. 19.95 (0-8369-0278-5) Ayer.

New Pasta Cuisine: Low-Fat Noodle & Pasta Dishes from Around the World. Aveline Kushi & Wendy Esko. (Illus.). 192p. (Orig.). 1992. pap. 19.00 (0-87040-798-8) Japan Pubns USA.

New Patent Interference Rules. New Patent Editors. 35.00 (0-317-29498-9, #CO3530) Harcourt.

New Patent Interference Rules Implementing Patent Law Amendments Act of 1984. Law & Business Inc. Staff et al. (Illus.). xi, 299p. write for info. (0-318-60203-2) Harcourt.

New Paternalism: Supervisory Approaches to Poverty. Ed. by Lawrence M. Mead. LC 97-33742. 355p. 1997. 42.95 (0-8157-5650-X); pap. 18.95 (0-8157-5651-8) Brookings.

New Path: Undergraduate Libraries at United States & Canadian Universities, 1949-1987, 17. Roland C. Person. LC 87-29553. (New Directions in Information Management Ser.: No. 17). (Illus.). 173p. 1988. 45.00 (0-313-25303-X, PNU/) Greenwood.

New Path from Welfare to Work. Oren M. Levin-Waldman. (Public Policy Brief Highlights Ser.: Vol. 31A). 4p. 1997. pap. write for info. (0-941276-26-0) J Levy.

New Path from Welfare to Work: The New Welfare & the Potential for Workforce Development. Oren M. Levin-Waldman. (Public Policy Briefs Ser.: Vol. 31). (Illus.). 36p. 1997. pap. text 3.00 (0-941276-24-4) J Levy.

New Path to the Waterfall. rev. ed. Raymond Carver. LC 88-34989. 160p. 1998. pap. 10.95 (0-87113-374-1, Atlntc Mnthly) Grove-Atltic.

New Paths in Book Collecting: Essays by Various Hands. Ed. by John Carter. LC 67-30179. (Essay Index Reprint Ser.). 1977. 18.95 (0-8369-0279-3) Ayer.

New Paths in Buddhist Research. Ed. by Anthony K. Warder. LC 82-83594. x, 137p. 1985. 24.95 (0-89386-008-5); pap. 13.95 (0-89386-009-3) Acorn NC.

New Paths in the Use of Nuclear Techniques for Art & Archeology: Trieste, Italy September 30--October 3, 1985. Ed. by G. Furlan et al. 400p. 1986. text 98.00 (9971-5-0195-3) World Scientific Pub.

New Paths Through the Old Testament. Carroll Stuhlmueller. 1989. pap. 5.95 (0-8091-3094-7) Paulist Pr.

New Paths to Democratic Development in Latin America: The Rise of NGO-Municipal Collaboration. Ed. by Charles A. Reilly. LC 94-31381. 376p. 1995. pap. text 29.95 (1-55587-557-2) L Rienner.

New Paths to Mineral Exploration: Proceedings of the 3rd International Symposium, Hannover, Federal Republic of Germany, at the Federal Institute for Geosciences & Mineral Resources, October 27-29, 1982. Ed. by Friedrich Bender. (Illus.). v, 169p. (Orig.). 1983. pap. 35.00 (3-510-65114-6, Pub. by E Schweizerbartsche) Balogh.

New Paths to Power: American Women, 1890-1920 see Young Oxford History of Women in the United States

New Paths to Power: American Women 1890-1920, Vol. 7. Karen M. Smith. (Young Oxford History of Women in the United States Ser.). (Illus.). 144p. (J). 1998. reprint ed. pap. 10.95 (0-19-512405-7) OUP.

***New Paths to Urbanization in China: Seeking More Balanced Patterns.** Yucai Zhu. LC 99-22770. 215p. 1999. lib. bdg. 59.00 (1-56072-681-4) Nova Sci Pubs.

New Pathways: A Dialogue in Christian Higher Education. Ed. by Ben C. Fisher. LC 80-80255. x, 110p. 1980. pap. 4.95 (0-86554-000-4, MUP-P001) Mercer Univ Pr.

New Pathways for Organic Synthesis: Practical Applications of Transition Metals. H. M. Colquhoun et al. LC 83-16085. (Illus.). 468p. (C). 1984. text 135.00 (0-306-41318-3, Kluwer Plenum) Kluwer Academic.

New Pathways in Medical Education: Learning to Learn at Harvard Medical School. Ed. by Daniel C. Tosteson et al. (Illus.). 192p. 1994. pap. text 21.50 (0-674-61739-8, TOSNEX) HUP.

An Asterisk (*) at the beginning of an entry indicates that the title is appearing for the first time.

New Pathways to Medical Education: Learning to Learn to at Harvard Medical School. Ed. by Daniel C. Tosteson et al. LC 94-11196. (Illus.). 192p. 1994. text 39.00 (*0-674-61738-X*, TOSNEW) HUP.

New Patricians. Paterson. LC 97-38224. 168p. 1998. text 55.00 (*0-312-21194-5*) St Martin.

New Patriotism. Ed. by Thomas C. Clark & Esther A. Gillespie. LC 73-108581. (Granger Index Reprint Ser.). 1977. 15.95 (*0-8369-6109-9*) Ayer.

New Pattern for a Tired World. Louis Bromfield. LC 72-174234. (Right Wing Individualist Tradition in America Ser.). 1972. reprint ed. 25.95 (*0-405-00416-8*) Ayer.

New Patterns from Old Architecture. Carol Wagner. LC 95-11618. (Illus.). 72p. 1998. 12.95 (*0-89145-840-9*, No. 3927) Collector Bks.

New Patterns in Global Television: Peripheral Vision. Ed. by John Sinclair et al. (Illus.). 250p. (C). 1996. pap. text 28.00 (*0-19-871123-9*) OUP.

New Patterns in the Sky: Myths & Legends of the Stars. rev. ed. Julius D. Staal. LC 87-92030. (Illus.). xiv, 300p. 1988. 24.95 (*0-939923-10-6*); pap. 18.95 (*0-939923-04-1*) M & W Pub Co.

New Patterns of Adult Learning: A 6-Country Comparative Study. Paul Belanger & Albert Tuijnman. LC 97-30104. 200p. 1997. 78.75 (*0-08-043069-4*, Pergamon Pr) Elsevier.

New Patterns of Collective Labour Law in Central Europe: Czech & Slovak Republics, Hungary, Poland (Nuovi Modelli di Diritto Sindacale Nell'Europa Centrale: Repubbliche Ceca e Slovacca, Ungheria, Polonia) Umberto Carabelli & Silvana Sciarra. LC 99-215182. xiii, 495 p. 1996. write for info. (*88-14-05075-9*, Pub. by Giuffre) IBD Ltd.

New Patterns of Democracy in India. 2nd ed. Vera M. Dean. LC 79-78516. 267p. 1969. 29.00 (*0-674-61751-7*) HUP.

New Patterns of Work. Stanley D. Nollen. (Studies in Productivity: Highlights of the Literature Ser.: Vol. 7). 59p. 55.00 (*0-08-029488-X*, PS7) Work in Amer.

New Patterns of Work. Hugh Ormiston & Donald M. Ross. 144p. (C). 1992. pap. 40.00 (*0-86153-127-2*, Pub. by St Andrew) St Mut.

New Patterns of World Mineral Development. Raymond F. Mikesell. LC 79-90054. (British-North American Committee Ser.). 116p. 1980. 5.00 (*0-89068-049-3*) Natl Planning.

New Pavement Materials. Ed. by E. R. Brown. (Sessions Proceedings Ser.). 112p. 1988. 5.00 (*0-87262-638-5*) Am Soc Civil Eng.

New Pay: Linking Employee & Organizational Performance. Jay R. Schuster. LC 97-180562. 368p. 1996. mass mkt. 18.50 (*0-7879-0273-X*) Jossey-Bass.

New Pay: Linking Employee & Organizational Performance. Jay R. Schuster & Patricia K. Zingheim. 266p. 1992. 25.95 (*0-669-15358-3*) Jossey-Bass.

New Peace Movement. William I. Hull. LC 77-137546. (Peace Movement in America Ser.). xi, 216p. 1972. reprint ed. lib. bdg. 30.95 (*0-89198-074-1*) Ozer.

New Peace Sign. Dennis DeNure. (Illus.). 125p. (Orig.). 1985. 4.95 (*0-915659-04-2*) Video Athlete.

New Peaceful Easy Feeling Songbook. 256p. (Orig.). (YA). 1990. pap. 16.95 (*0-7692-1056-2*, VF1621) Wrner Bros.

New Pearl of Great Price. Petrus of Ferrara Bonus. 441p. 1992. reprint ed. pap. 29.95 (*1-56459-142-5*) Kessinger Pub.

New Pearl of Great Price: Treatise Concerning the Treasure & Most Precious Stone of the Philosophers, Vol. 7. Petrus. LC 74-349. 453p. 1974. reprint ed. 35.95 (*0-405-05911-6*) Ayer.

*****New, Peculiar State: Explorations in Soviet History, 1917-1937.** Andrea Graziosi. LC 99-55220. 296p. 2000. 64.00 (*0-275-96650-X*, C6650, Praeger Pubs) Greenwood.

New Pediatrics: A Profession in Transition. Dorothy Pawluch. (Social Problems & Social Issues Ser.). 187p. 1996. lib. bdg. 41.95 (*0-202-30534-1*) Aldine de Gruyter.

New Pelican Guide to English Literature Vol. 5: From Blake to Byron. Boris Ford. 1990. pap. 17.95 (*0-14-013811-0*, Pub. by Pnguin Bks Ltd) Trafalgar.

New Pencil Pastimes Book of Crosswords. Ed. by Richard Manchester. 256p. 1999. pap. 9.95 (*0-88486-244-5*, Bristol Park Bks) Arrowood Pr.

New Pencil Pastimes Book of Seek-a-Word. Ed. by Richard Manchester. 256p. 1999. pap. 9.95 (*0-88486-245-3*, Bristol Park Bks) Arrowood Pr.

New Pencil Pastime's Book of Word Games. Richard Manchester. 1998. pap. 9.95 (*0-88486-189-9*, Bristol Park Bks) Arrowood Pr.

New Penguin Atlas of Medieval History. enl. rev. ed. Colin McEvedy. (Illus.). 128p. 1992. pap. 13.95 (*0-14-051249-7*, Penguin Bks) Viking Penguin.

New Penguin Book of Scottish Short Stories. Ed. by Ian Murray. 317p. 2000. pap. 15.95 (*0-14-006411-7*, Pub. by Pnguin Bks Ltd) Trafalgar.

New Penguin Dictionary of Geography. 2nd ed. Audrey N. Clark. LC 99-187508. (Penguin Reference Ser.). 464p. 1998. pap. 14.95 (*0-14-051388-4*) Viking Penguin.

New Penguin Dictionary of Geology. Philip Kearey. LC 97-105682. 384p. 1996. pap. 14.95 (*0-14-051277-2*, Penguin Bks) Viking Penguin.

New Penguin Dictionary of Modern History, 1789-1945. Duncan Townson. 960p. 1994. pap. 15.95 (*0-14-051274-8*, Penguin Bks) Viking Penguin.

*****New Penguin Economic History of Britain.** Christopher Dyer. 1999. write for info. (*0-7139-9162-3*, A Lane) Viking Penguin.

New Penguin Russian Course: A Complete Course for Beginners. Nicholas J. Brown. LC 96-232400. 528p. 1996. pap. 15.95 (*0-14-012041-6*, Penguin Bks) Viking Penguin.

New Pentecost? Leon-Joseph Suenens. 256p. 1984. 1.95 (*0-8164-2139-0*) Harper SF.

New People: Miscegenation & Mulattoes in the United States. Joel Williamson. LC 80-65201. (Illus.). 240p. (C). 1995. pap. 16.95 (*0-8071-2035-9*) La State U Pr.

New People in Old Neighborhoods: The Role of New Immigrants in Rejuvenating New York's Communities. Louis Winnick. LC 90-38765. 328p. 1990. text 29.95 (*0-87154-952-2*) Russell Sage.

New People of God: A Study in Salvationism. John R. Rhemick. 261p. (C). 1993. write for info. (*1-883719-00-3*) Salvat Army Supp.

New Peoplemaking. 2nd ed. Virginia M. Satir. 1988. pap. 19.95 (*0-8314-0070-6*) Sci & Behavior.

*****New Perenial Garden.** N. Kingsbury. 160p. 1998. 35.00 (*0-7112-1049-7*, Pub. by F Lincoln) St Mut.

New Perennial Garden. Noel Kingsbury. (Illus.). 160p. 1995. 40.00 (*0-8050-4673-9*) H Holt & Co.

New Perennial Garden. Storey Publishing Staff. 1997. 40.00 (*0-676-57059-3*) Random.

New Perennials: The Latest & Best Perennials. Richard Bird & David Tarrant. (Illus.). 144p. pap. 14.95 (*1-55110-821-6*) Whitecap Bks.

New Perennials Preferred. Helen V. Wilson. (Illus.). 320p. 1992. reprint ed. pap. 15.95 (*0-02-082661-3*) Macmillan.

New Perfect Resume: Breakthrough Resumes for Today's Best Careers. rev. ed. Tom Jackson. 240p. 1996. pap. 11.95 (*0-385-48190-X*) Doubleday.

New Performance Challenge: Measuring Operations for World-Class Competition. J. Robb Dixon et al. 200p. 1990. 47.50 (*1-55623-301-9*, Irwn Prfssnl) McGraw-Hill Prof.

New Persectives on the Internet. Perry. (C). 1998. mass mkt. 21.95 (*0-7600-6973-5*) Course Tech.

New Person to Person, Bk. 2. Jack C. Richards. (Illus.). 128p. 1995. pap. text, student ed. 11.95 (*0-19-434681-1*) OUP.

New Person to Person, Vol. 1. Jack C. Richards et al. (Illus.). 128p. 1995. pap. text, student ed. 11.95 (*0-19-434678-1*) OUP.

New Person to Person: Teacher's Book. Jack C. Richards et al. (Illus.). 150p. 1995. teacher ed., spiral bd. 16.95 (*0-19-434679-X*) OUP.

New Person to Person Pt. 2: Communicative Speaking & Listening Skills. Jack C. Richards. (Illus.). 152p. 1996. teacher ed., spiral bd. 16.95 (*0-19-434682-X*) OUP.

New Personal Media - Outpacing Society? unabridged ed. Anthony T. Green. LC 95-138118. 111p. (Orig.). 1994. pap. text. write for info. (*1-879716-19-4*, I-94-6) Ctr Info Policy.

New Personality Self-Portrait: Why You Think, Work, Love & Act the Way You Do. rev. ed. John M. Oldham & Lois B. Morris. LC 95-12233. Orig. Title: The Personality Self-Portrait. 464p. 1995. pap. 14.95 (*0-553-37393-5*) Bantam.

New Perspective for European Spatial Development Policies. Wolfgang Blaas. LC 97-76941. (Illus.). 172p. 1998. text 59.95 (*1-84014-342-8*, Pub. by Ashgate Pub) Ashgate Pub Co.

New Perspective in Cohesion on Expository Paragraphs. Robin B. Markels. LC 83-14561. (Studies in Writing & Rhetoric). 120p. (Orig.). 1984. pap. text 14.95 (*0-8093-1152-6*) S Ill U Pr.

*****New Perspective, NLP.** Carol Harris. (Illus.). 2000. pap. 9.95 (*1-86204-668-9*, Pub. by Element MA) Penguin Putnam.

New Perspective on Asset Allocation Martin L. Leibowitz & Institute of Chartered Financial Analysts Staff. LC 99-207584. xiv, 75 p. 1987. write for info. (*0-943205-00-X*) RFICFA.

New Perspective on the Strength of Bevel Gear Teeth. W. Coleman. (Technical Papers: Vol. P229.13). (Illus.). 18p. 1969. pap. text 30.00 (*1-55589-280-9*) AGMA.

*****New Perspective on Word 97: Comprehensive Enhanced.** Zimmerman. (C). 1998. 44.95 (*0-7600-7308-2*) Thomson Learn.

New Perspectives. Raintree Steck-Vaughn Publishers Staff. (New Perspectives Ser.). 1998. 151.84 (*0-8172-5022-0*) Raintree Steck-V.

*****New Perspectives.** Ed. by Raintree Steck-Vaughn Publishing Staff. 2000. 244.08 (*0-7398-2793-6*) Raintree Steck-V.

New Perspectives. rev. ed. Gonzalez et al. (New Perspectives: Intermediate English Ser.). (Illus.). 176p. (J). 1985. audio 102.95 (*0-8384-1306-4*) Heinle & Heinle.

New Perspectives for Bank Directors. Ed. by Richard B. Johnson. LC 77-12973. 253p. reprint ed. pap. 78.50 (*0-8357-8970-5*, 203344500086) Bks Demand.

New Perspectives for Energy Savings in Agriculture: Current Progress in Solar Technologies. Ed. by V. Goedseels et al. 1986. text 221.50 (*90-277-2319-2*) Kluwer Academic.

*****New Perspectives for Intercultural Dialogue & an Alternative Economic Order.** Ed. by V. N. Kly. 122p. 1999. per. 9.95 (*0-932863-31-0*, Pub. by Clarity Pr) LPC InBook.

New Perspectives for Reference Service in Academic Libraries, 23. Raymond G. McInnis. LC 77-94742. (Contributions in Librarianship & Information Science Ser.: No. 23). (Illus.). 351p. 1979. 59.95 (*0-313-20311-3*, MNP/, Greenwood Pr) Greenwood.

New Perspectives for Student Affairs Professionals: Evolving Realities, Responsibilities & Roles. Peter H. Garland & Thomas W. Grace. Ed. & Frwd. by Jonathan D. Fife. (ASHE-ERIC Higher Education Reports: No. 93-7). 107p. (Orig.). 1994. pap. 24.00 (*1-878380-28-1*) GWU Grad Schl E&HD.

New Perspectives for U. S.-Asia Pacific Security Strategy: The 1991 Pacific Symposium. Dora Alves. (Illus.). 197p. (Orig.). (C). 1994. pap. text 40.00 (*0-7881-1232-5*) DIANE Pub.

New Perspectives in Algebraic Combinatorics. Ed. by Louis J. Billera et al. LC 99-34738. (Mathematical Sciences Research Institute Publications: Vol. 38). 320p. (C). 1999. 49.95 (*0-521-77087-4*) Cambridge U Pr.

New Perspectives in American Art: Exxon National Exhibition, 1983. Diane Waldman. LC 83-50248. (Illus.). 160p. 1983. 13.00 (*0-89207-043-9*) S R Guggenheim.

New Perspectives in American Jewish Sociology. Nathan Glazer. LC 87-70763. 20p. 1987. pap. 2.00 (*0-87495-087-2*) Am Jewish Comm.

New Perspectives in American Music. Lornell & Anne K. Rasmussen. LC 97-19860. 1997. 35.00 (*0-02-864585-5*) Macmillan.

New Perspectives in American Politics: The National Political Science Review, Vol. 1. Ed. by Lucius J. Barker. 300p. 1989. 39.95 (*0-88738-744-6*) Transaction Pubs.

New Perspectives in Anthropology. S. Seth. Ed. by P. K. Seth. 359p. (C). 1993. pap. 195.00 (*81-85880-19-0*, Pub. by Print Hse) St Mut.

New Perspectives in Anti-Inflammatory Therapies. Ed. by Alan Lewis et al. LC 86-43103. (Advances in Inflammation Research Ser.: Vol. 12). 352p. 1988. reprint ed. pap. 109.20 (*0-608-00434-0*, 206114900007) Bks Demand.

New Perspectives in Astrophysical Cosmology. 2nd ed. Martin Rees. LC 99-21389. (Illus.). 168p. 2000. 24.95 (*0-521-64238-8*) Cambridge U Pr.

New Perspectives in Basin Analysis. Ed. by K. Kleinspehn & C. Paola. (Frontiers in Sedimentary Geology Ser.). (Illus.). 500p. 1988. 161.00 (*0-387-96611-0*) Spr-Verlag.

New Perspectives in Cerebral Localization. Ed. by Richard A. Thompson & John R. Green. LC 81-17910. (Illus.). 264p. 1982. reprint ed. pap. 81.90 (*0-608-00617-3*, 206120400007) Bks Demand.

New Perspectives in Clinical Microbiology. Ed. by William Brumfitt. 1978. text 99.50 (*90-247-2074-5*) Kluwer Academic.

*****New Perspectives in Contraception.** Donald DeMarco. 128p. 1999. pap. 12.00 (*0-9669777-1-8*) One More Soul.

New Perspectives in Criminology: A Reader. John E. Conklin. LC 95-24524. 649p. 1995. pap. text 42.00 (*0-205-18388-3*) Allyn.

New Perspectives in Diagnosis & Treatment of Kidney Disease. Ed. by G. Colasanti & G. D'Amico. (Contributions to Nephrology Ser.: Vol. 55). (Illus.). vi, 258p. 1987. 29.75 (*3-8055-4393-X*) S Karger.

New Perspectives in Early Childhood Teacher Education. Ed. by Stacie Goffin & David Day. (Early Childhood Education Ser.). 240p. (C). 1994. text 32.00 (*0-8077-3381-4*) Tchrs Coll.

New Perspectives in Early Emotional Development. unabridged ed. Ed. by John G. Warhol. (Pediatric Round Table Ser.). (Illus.). 300p. 1998. pap. text 10.00 (*0-931562-19-8*) J & J Consumer Prods.

New Perspectives in Early Greek Art. Diana Buitron-Oliver. 1992. 60.00 (*0-89468-177-X*) Natl Gallery Art.

New Perspectives in Early Greek Art. Ed. by Diana Buitron-Oliver. 1996. 60.00 (*0-300-07699-1*) Yale U Pr.

New Perspectives in German Literary Criticism: A Collection of Essays. Ed. by Richard E. Amacher & Victor Lange. LC 78-12472. 496p. reprint ed. pap. 153.80 (*0-8357-2777-7*, 203990300014) Bks Demand.

New Perspectives in Hemodialysis, Peritoneal Dialysis, Arteriovenous Hemofiltration, & Plasmapheresis. Ed. by Walter H. Horl & P. J. Schollmeyer. LC 89-22951. (Advances in Experimental Medicine & Biology Ser.). (Illus.). 226p. 1989. 69.50 (*0-306-43376-1*, Plenum Trade) Perseus Pubng.

New Perspectives in Histamine Research. Ed. by H. Timmerman & H. Van der Goot. (Agents & Actions Supplements Ser.: Vol. 33). 448p. 1991. 124.00 (*0-8176-2507-0*) Birkhauser.

New Perspectives in Hungarian Geography. A. Kertesz & Zoltan Kovacs. 219p. 1994. 28.00 (*963-05-6572-2*, Pub. by Akade Kiado) Intl Spec Bk.

New Perspectives in Indian Literature. Ed. by P. N. Yaravintelimath et al. (C). 1995. write for info. (*81-207-1757-0*) Sterling Pubs.

New Perspectives in Language, Culture & Personality: Proceedings of the Edward Sapir Centenary Conference (Ottawa, 1-3 October 1984) Ed. by William Cowan et al. LC 86-26834. (Studies in the History of the Language Sciences: No. 41). xiv, 627p. 1986. 110.00 (*90-272-4522-3*) J Benjamins Pubng Co.

New Perspectives in Lung Cancer. Ed. by N. Thatcher & S. Spiro. 203p. 1994. pap. text 16.00 (*0-7279-0786-7*, Pub. by BMJ Pub) Login Brothers Bk Co.

New Perspectives in Molecular & Clinical Management of Gastrointestinaltumors. Ed. by E. D. Kreuser & P. M. Schlag. (Recent Results in Cancer Research Ser.: Vol. 142). 480p. 1996. 157.00 (*3-540-60498-7*) Spr-Verlag.

New Perspectives in Monetary Macroeconomics: Explorations in the Tradition of Hyman P. Minsky. Ed. by Gary Dymski & Robert Pollin. LC 93-45596. 424p. 1994. text 70.00 (*0-472-10472-1*, 10472) U of Mich Pr.

New Perspectives in Music Theory, Vol. 1. Charles E. Van Riper. 112p. 1998. pap. 18.95 (*1-878398-32-6*) Blue Note Pubns.

New Perspectives in Nuclear Medicine. Ed. by Peter H. Cox & E. Touja. (Monographs in Nuclear Medicine: Vol. 2). xxviii, 414p. 1986. text 489.00 (*2-88124-131-X*) Gordon & Breach.

New Perspectives in Nuclear Medicine Vol. 1: Clinical in Vitro Studies. P. H. Cox & E. Touja. xxx, 394p. 1986. write for info. (*2-88124-129-8*) Gordon & Breach.

New Perspectives in Nuclear Medicine Vol. 2: Instrumentation, Laboratory Investigations & in Vitro Studies. P. H. Cox & E. Touja. 1986. write for info. (*2-88124-130-1*) Gordon & Breach.

New Perspectives in Nuclear Structure. A. Covello. 650p. 1996. text 148.00 (*981-02-2359-5*) World Scientific Pub.

New Perspectives in Psychoanalysis. Ed. by Harold Kelman. 1965. 5.00 (*0-393-01028-7*) Norton.

New Perspectives in Quantum Field Theories: Proceedings of the XVI Gift International Seminar on Theoretical Physics, Jaca, Huesca, June 3-8, 1985. Ed. by J. Abad et al. 490p. 1986. pap. 60.00 (*9971-5-0057-4*); text 131.00 (*9971-5-0048-5*) World Scientific Pub.

New Perspectives in Scottish Legal History. Ed. by Albert Kiralfy & Hector L. MacQueen. 124p. 1984. 35.00 incl. sl. (*0-7146-3251-1*, Pub. by F Cass Pubs) Intl Spec Bk.

New Perspectives in Special Educational Needs. Ed. by Meijer. 176p. (C). 1996. pap. 24.99 (*0-415-08337-0*) Routledge.

New Perspectives in Sponge Biology. Ed. by Klaus Rutzler. LC 90-9996. (Illus.). 544p. (C). 1991. text 59.95 (*0-87474-784-8*) Smithsonian.

New Perspectives in the North & South. Kafi B. Hadjor. 1990. text 59.50 (*1-85043-105-1*, Pub. by I B T) St Martin.

New Perspectives in the Physics of Mesoscopic Systems: Quantum-Like Descriptions & Macroscopic Coherence Phenomena Caserta, Italy 18-20 April, 1996. Ed. by S. De Martino et al. 350p. 1997. 78.00 (*981-02-3236-5*) World Scientific Pub.

New Perspectives in the Roman Law of Property: Essays for Barry Nicholas. Ed. by Peter B. H. Birks. (Illus.). 244p. 1989. text 59.00 (*0-19-825614-0*) OUP.

New Perspectives in Theoretical & Applied Statistics. Ed. by Madan L. Puri et al. LC 86-22401. 544p. 1987. 298.00 (*0-471-84800-X*) Wiley.

New Perspectives in Turbulence. Ed. by Lawrence Sirovich. (Illus.). 456p. 1991. 60.95 (*0-387-97559-4*) Spr-Verlag.

New Perspectives in Urban Geography. Ed. by S. B. Singh. LC 96-904993. 168p. 1996. pap. 150.00 (*81-7533-014-7*, Pub. by Print Hse) St Mut.

New Perspectives in Water Supply. Williams Whipple, Jr. LC 93-38815. 240p. 1994. lib. bdg. 85.00 (*1-56670-032-9*, L1032) Lewis Pubs.

New Perspectives in Wood Anatomy. P. Baas. 1982. text 184.00 (*90-247-2526-7*) Kluwer Academic.

New Perspectives in Workers' Compensation. Ed. by John F. Burton, Jr. (Frank W. Pierce Memorial Lectureship & Conference Ser.: No. 7). 176p. 1988. pap. text 14.95 (*0-87546-144-1*, ILR Press) Cornell U Pr.

New Perspectives Internal Functionalism. Ashworth. LC 98-16547. 208p. 1998. text 65.00 (*0-312-21575-4*) St Martin.

New Perspectives, New Directions in Foreign Language Education. Ed. by Michael D. Bush & Robert M. Terry. (ACTFL Foreign Language Education Ser.). 1998. pap. 16.90 (*0-8442-9388-1*, VF9388-1) NTC Contemp Pub Co.

New Perspectives of Surfactant Research: Proceedings of the 12th International Workshop, Stockholm, May 1997. Ed. by Tore Curstedt et al. (Journal: Biology of the Neonate: Vol. 71, Suppl. 1, 1997). (Illus.). iv, 70p. 1997. pap. 22.75 (*3-8055-6528-3*) S Karger.

New Perspectives on Abraham Geiger: An HUC-JIR Symposium. Ed. by Jakob J. Petuchowski. LC 75-19131. 64p. reprint ed. pap. 30.00 (*0-7837-3000-4*, 204294100006) Bks Demand.

New Perspectives on Access 97: Comprehensive Enhanced. Adamski & Hommel. 1998. 44.95 (*0-7600-7309-0*) Course Tech.

New Perspectives on Adolescent Risk Behavior. Ed. by Richard Jesor. LC 97-49944. (Illus.). 450p. (C). 1998. 59.95 (*0-521-58432-9*); pap. 21.95 (*0-521-58607-0*) Cambridge U Pr.

*****New Perspectives on Advaita Vedanta: Essays in Commemoration of Professor Richard De Smet, S. F.** Ed. by Bradley J. Malkovsky. 184p. 2000. 73.00 (*90-04-11666-4*) Brill Academic Pubs.

New Perspectives on American Law: An Introduction to Private Law in Politics & Society. Lief Carter et al. LC 97-69308. 488p. 1997. pap. 29.95 (*0-89089-709-3*) Carolina Acad Pr.

New Perspectives on American Politics. Lawrence Dodd & Calvin Jillson. LC 93-38566. 360p. 1993. 44.95 (*0-87187-882-8*) Congr Quarterly.

New Perspectives on American Politics. Lawrence Dodd & Calvin Jillson. LC 93-38566. 360p. (YA). (gr. 11). 1994. pap. text 32.95 (*0-87187-877-1*) Congr Quarterly.

New Perspectives on Ancient Judaism: Judaic & Christian Interpretation of Texts: Contents & Contexts, Vol. 3. Ed. by Jacob Neusner & Ernest S. Frerichs. 226p. (C). 1987. pap. text 24.00 (*0-8191-6563-8*) U Pr of Amer.

New Perspectives on Ancient Judaism: Religion, Literature, & Society in Ancient Israel, Formative Christianity & Judaism, Vol. II. Ed. by Jacob Neusner et al. LC 87-23027. 184p. (C). 1988. lib. bdg. 44.00 (*0-8191-6597-2*) U Pr of Amer.

New Perspectives on Ancient Judaism Vol. 5: Society & Literature in Analysis. Ed. by Paul V. Flesher. LC 87-16073. (Studies in Judaism). 204p. (C). 1990. lib. bdg. 40.00 (*0-8191-7614-1*) U Pr of Amer.

New Perspectives on Applications Development in Microsoft Access: Advanced. David Paradice & Dirk Baldwin. (New Perspectives Ser.). 600p. 1997. pap. 45.95 (*0-7600-3576-8*) Course Tech.

New Perspectives on Austrian Economics. Ed. by Gerrit Meijer. LC 94-32065. 272p. (C). (gr. 13). 1995. 90.00 (*0-415-12283-X*, C0482) Routledge.

An Asterisk (*) at the beginning of an entry indicates that the title is appearing for the first time.

New Perspectives on Ben Jonson. Ed. by James Hirsh. LC 96-30907. (Illus.). 224p. 1997. 36.50 (*0-8386-3687-X*) Fairleigh Dickinson.

***New Perspectives on Benign Prostatic Hypertrophy (BPH)** Paul D. Miller. (New Perspectives Ser.). (Illus.). 2001. pap. text 19.95 (*1-873413-62-9*) Merit Pub Intl.

New Perspectives on Business Cycles: An Analysis of Inequality & Heterogeneity. Satya Das. 256p. 1993. 95.00 (*1-85278-800-3*) E Elgar.

New Perspectives on Chu Culture During the Eastern Zhou Period. Ed. by Thomas Lawton. (Illus.). 230p. 1991. text 52.50 (*0-691-04095-8*, Pub. by Princeton U Pr) Cal Prin Full Svc.

***New Perspectives on Computer.** 3rd ed. June Parsons et al. 1998. pap. 8.95 (*0-7600-7331-7*) Course Tech.

New Perspectives on Computer Concepts. 2nd ed. June J. Parsons & Dan Oja. (New Perspectives Ser.). 256p. 1996. pap. 19.75 (*0-7600-4312-4*) Course Tech.

***New Perspectives on Computer Concepts.** 4th ed. Parsons & Oja. (New Perspectives Ser.). (C). 1999. text 32.95 (*0-7600-6490-3*) Course Tech.

New Perspectives on Computer Concepts: Brief. 3rd ed. June Parsons & Dan Oja. (New Perspectives Ser.). 304p. (C). 1997. pap. text, mass mkt. 29.95 incl. cd-rom (*0-7600-5796-6*) Course Tech.

New Perspectives on Computer Concepts: Complete, Incl. instr. manual, test manager, labs. 2nd ed. June J. Parsons & Dan Oja. (New Perspectives Ser.). (Illus.). 840p. (C). 1996. pap. 33.50 (*0-7600-3440-0*) Course Tech.

New Perspectives on Computer Concepts: Comprehensive. 3rd ed. June Parsons & Dan Oja. (New Perspectives Ser.). 648p. (C). 1998. pap. text, mass mkt. 36.00 incl. cd-rom (*0-7600-5500-9*) Course Tech.

New Perspectives on Computer Concepts: Introductory. 3rd ed. June Parsons & Dan Oja. (New Perspectives Ser.). 424p. (C). 1997. pap. text, mass mkt. 41.95 incl. cd-rom (*0-7600-5449-5*) Course Tech.

New Perspectives on Computer Concepts: Introductory with Microsoft Office Professional for Windows 3.1 - Illustrated Enhanced Edition. 10th ed. Parsons et al. (New Perspectives Ser.). (Illus.). 944p. (C). 1996. pap. 39.80 (*0-7600-4647-6*) Course Tech.

New Perspectives on Computer Concepts -- Introductory. 4th ed. June Jamrich Parsons & Dan Oja. 472p. per. 42.95 (*0-7600-6491-1*, Pub. by Course Tech) Thomson Learn.

New Perspectives on Computer Concepts - Essentials. (New Perspectives Ser.). (C). 1996. pap. 6.75 (*0-7600-5263-8*) Course Tech.

New Perspectives on Computers, Technology & Society. June J. Parsons & Dan Oja. (New Perspectives Ser.). 560p. 1997. pap. 35.50 (*0-7600-4604-2*) Course Tech.

New Perspectives on Computers, Technology & Society. 2nd ed. June Parsons. 1998. pap. text 48.95 (*0-7600-7022-9*) Course Tech.

New Perspectives on Computers, Technology & Society - Brief. 2nd ed. June Jamrich Parsons et al. 168p. per. 21.95 (*0-7600-7107-1*, Pub. by Course Tech) Thomson Learn.

***New Perspectives on Conceptual Change.** Wolfgang Schnotz et al. LC 99-36628. (Advances in Learning & Instruction Ser.). 322p. 1999. 91.50 (*0-08-043455-X*, Pergamon Pr) Elsevier.

New Perspectives on Corel Presentations 7 for Windows 95: Brief. S. Scott Zimmerman & Beverly Zimmerman. (New Perspectives Ser.). 136p. 1996. pap. 23.95 (*0-7600-4042-7*) Course Tech.

New Perspectives on Corel WordPerfect 7 for Windows 95: Introductory. Beverly B. Zimmerman & S. Scott Zimmerman. (New Perspectives Ser.). 304p. 1996. pap. 37.95 (*0-7600-3539-3*) Course Tech.

New Perspectives on Creating Web Pages with HTML: Brief. Patrick Carey. (New Perspectives Ser.). 64p. 1996. pap. 8.00 (*0-7600-4585-2*) Course Tech.

New Perspectives on Creating Web Pages with HTML -- Comprehensive. Patrick Carey. 512p. per. 44.95 (*0-7600-6484-9*, Pub. by Course Tech) Thomson Learn.

***New Perspectives on Current Sociolinguistic Knowledge with Regard to Language Use, Proficiency & Attitudes among Hispanics in the U. S. The Case of a Rural Northern California Community.** Susana Victoria Rivera-Mills. LC 99-46936. (Studies in Linguistics & Semiotics: Vol. 4). 196p. 1999. text 79.95 (*0-7734-7906-6*) E Mellen.

New Perspectives on Cybernetics: Self-Organization, Autonomy & Connectionism. (Synthese Library). 260p. (C). 1991. lib. bdg. 137.50 (*0-7923-1519-7*, Pub. by Kluwer Academic) Kluwer Academic.

New Perspectives on Dermatological Infections (Handbook) J. Bikowski. 1995. 9.95 (*1-873413-16-5*) Merit Pub Intl.

New Perspectives on Economic Growth & Technological Innovation. F. M. Scherer. 1999. pap. text 16.95 (*0-8157-7795-7*) Brookings.

New Perspectives on Economic Growth & Technological Innovation. F. M. Scherer. LC 99-6202. (Illus.). 167p. 1999. 38.95 (*0-8157-7794-9*) Brookings.

New Perspectives on Encounter Groups. Ed. by Lawrence N. Solomon & Betty Berzon. LC 73-186583. (Jossey-Bass Behavioral Science Ser.). 456p. reprint ed. pap. 141.40 (*0-608-14933-0*, 202567900045) Bks Demand.

New Perspectives on Environmental Education & Research: A Report on the University Colloquium on Environmental Research & Education. Ed. by Charles F. Blackburn. 58p. (Orig.). 1993. pap. 4.00 (*0-914446-05-3*) Sigma Xi.

New Perspectives on Essential Computer Concepts 4th ed. (New Perspectives Ser.). (C). 1999. pap. 8.95 (*0-7600-6372-9*) Course Tech.

***New Perspectives on European Development Cooperation.** Ed. by Marjorie Lister. 172p. 1999. 60.00 (*0-8133-3712-7*, Pub. by Westview) HarpC.

New Perspectives on Evolution. Ed. by Leonard Warren. LC 90-45462. (Wistar Symposium Ser.). 272p. 1991. 125.00 (*0-471-56068-5*) Wiley.

***New Perspectives on Excel for Windows.** Ageloff. (C). 1998. spiral bd. 44.95 (*0-7600-7000-8*) Course Tech.

New Perspectives on Excel 97: Expert Supplement. Parson & Oja. (C). 1997. 10.50 (*0-7600-7211-6*) Thomson Learn.

***New Perspectives on Expressionist Film.** Dietrich Scheunemann. (GERM Ser.). 2001. 55.00 (*1-57113-068-3*) Camden Hse.

***New Perspectives on F. Holland Day.** Thomas G. Boss et al. (Illus.). 1998. 20.00 (*0-9660964-1-X*) Stonehill Coll.

New Perspectives on Fichte. Ed. by Daniel Breazeale & Tom Rockmore. LC 95-570. 256p. (C). 1996. text 55.00 (*0-391-03917-2*) Humanities.

New Perspectives on Financing Small Business in Developing Countries. Ed. by Ernst A. Brugger & Sarath Rajapatirana. LC 95-9273. 194p. 1995. pap. 19.95 (*1-55815-341-1*) ICS Pr.

New Perspectives on Galileo. Ed. by Robert E. Butts & Joseph C. Pitt. (Western Ontario Ser.: No. 14). 278p. 1978. pap. text 58.50 (*90-277-0891-6*, D Reidel); lib. bdg. 112.00 (*90-277-0859-2*, D Reidel) Kluwer Academic.

New Perspectives on Genetic Markers & Diseases among Jewish People. Batsheva Bonne-Tamir. (Illus.). 488p. 1992. text 69.50 (*0-19-506817-3*) OUP.

New Perspectives on Hegel's Philosophy of Religion. Ed. by David Kolb. LC 92-23739. 224p. (C). 1992. text 64.50 (*0-7914-1437-X*); pap. text 21.95 (*0-7914-1438-8*) State U NY Pr.

New Perspectives on Historical Writing. Ed. by Peter Burke. 280p. 1992. text 35.00 (*0-271-00827-X*); pap. text 15.95 (*0-271-00834-2*) Pa St U Pr.

New Perspectives on Human Abortion. Ed. by Thomas W. Hilgers et al. LC 81-51983. 504p. 1981. lib. bdg. 55.00 (*0-313-27079-1*, U7079) Greenwood.

New Perspectives on Human Resource Management. Ed. by John Storey. 224p. (C). 1989. mass mkt. 29.95 (*0-415-01041-1*, A5256) Routledge.

New Perspectives On Human Resource Management. John Storey. 1989. pap. text 32.95 (*1-86152-508-7*) Thomson Learn.

***New Perspectives on Hypertension.** Adrian Brady. (New Perspectives Ser.). 2000. pap. text 24.95 (*1-873413-67-X*) Merit Pub Intl.

New Perspectives on Industrial Disputes. David Metcalf & Simon Milner. 240p. (C). 1993. pap. 77.95 (*0-415-09151-9*) Thomson Learn.

New Perspectives on Integrating Microsoft Office Professional for Windows 95. 10th ed. Joseph Adamski & Judy Adamski. (New Perspectives Ser.). 264p. (C). 1996. pap. 30.95 (*0-7600-4576-3*) Course Tech.

New Perspectives on International Industrial/ Organizational Psychology. P. Christopher Earley. 1997. 70.00 (*0-7879-0936-X*) Jossey-Bass.

New Perspectives on International Marketing. Ed. by Stanley J. Paliwoda. 272p. (C). (gr. 13). 1991. pap. 75.95 (*0-415-05344-7*, A5117) Thomson Learn.

***New Perspectives on Internet.** Sandra Poindexter. 1998. pap. 14.00 (*0-7600-5784-2*) Course Tech.

New Perspectives on Israeli History: The Early Years of the State. Ed. by Laurence J. Silberstein. (New Perspectives on Jewish Studies). 340p. (C). 1991. text 50.00 (*0-8147-7928-X*); pap. text 20.00 (*0-8147-7929-8*) NYU Pr.

New Perspectives on Keynes. Ed. by Allin F. Cottrell & Michael S. Lawlor. 320p. 1995. text 49.95 (*0-8223-1705-2*) Duke.

New Perspectives on Local Economic Development in Texas & Strategies for the South Texas Region. Ed. by Sherman M. Wyman & Ernest J. Gerlach. (Texas Local Economic Development Ser.). 137p. 1994. pap. 7.50 (*0-936440-86-4*) U TX SUPA.

New Perspectives on Margaret Laurence: Poetic Narrative, Multiculturalism & Feminism, 154. Greta M. Coger. LC 95-35711. (Contributions in Women's Studies: No. 154). 264p. 1996. 65.00 (*0-313-29042-3*, Greenwood Pr) Greenwood.

New Perspectives on Microsoft Access 97: Brief Edition. 10th ed. Joseph Adamski et al. (New Perspectives Ser.). 160p. (C). 1997. pap. 21.95 (*0-7600-4552-6*) Course Tech.

New Perspectives on Microsoft Access 2000: Comprehensive Edition. Kathy Finnegan. 1999. pap. text 42.95 (*0-7600-7090-3*) Course Tech.

New Perspectives on Microsoft Access 2000 - Brief. Joseph J. Adamski & Kathy Finnegan. 168p. per. 21.95 (*0-7600-7088-1*, Pub. by Course Tech) Thomson Learn.

New Perspectives on Microsoft Access 2000 - Introductory. Joseph J. Adamski et al. 392p. per. 31.95 (*0-7600-7089-X*, Pub. by Course Tech) Thomson Learn.

New Perspectives on Microsoft Access 97: Introductory Edition. 10th ed. Joseph Adamski et al. (New Perspectives Ser.). 304p. (C). 1997. pap. 31.95 (*0-7600-5253-0*) Course Tech.

New Perspectives on Microsoft Excel. June J. Parsons. 1997. pap. text 46.95 (*0-7600-7261-2*) Course Tech.

New Perspectives on Microsoft Excel for Windows: Advanced. Roy Ageloff & Roger Hayen. 696p. 1996. teacher ed. 18.50 (*0-7600-3971-2*) Course Tech.

New Perspectives on Microsoft Excel 7 for Windows 95: Introduction & Comprehensive. June J. Parsons et al. 624p. 1996. teacher ed. 18.50 (*0-7600-3974-7*) Course Tech.

New Perspectives on Microsoft Excel 2000 Comprehensive Edition. June J. Parsons. 1999. pap. text 44.95 (*0-7600-7087-3*) Course Tech.

New Perspectives on Microsoft Excel 2000 - Brief. June Jamrich Parsons et al. 184p. per. 21.95 (*0-7600-7085-7*, Pub. by Course Tech) Thomson Learn.

New Perspectives on Microsoft Excel 2000 - Introductory. June Jamrich Parsons et al. 432p. per. 31.95 (*0-7600-7086-5*, Pub. by Course Tech) Thomson Learn.

New Perspectives on Microsoft Excel 97: Advanced. Roy Ageloff & Roger Hayen. (New Perspectives Ser.). 600p. 1997. pap. write for info. (*0-7600-5271-9*) Course Tech.

New Perspectives on Microsoft Excel 97: Brief Edition. June J. Parsons et al. (New Perspectives Ser.). 160p. 1997. pap. 21.95 (*0-7600-4553-4*) Course Tech.

New Perspectives on Microsoft Excel 97: Comprehensive Edition. 10th ed. June J. Parsons et al. (New Perspectives Ser.). 552p. (C). 1997. pap. 33.50 (*0-7600-5261-1*) Course Tech.

New Perspectives on Microsoft Excel 97: Introductory Edition. 10th ed. June J. Parsons et al. (New Perspectives Ser.). 304p. (C). 1997. pap. 31.95 (*0-7600-5260-3*) Course Tech.

New Perspectives on Microsoft Frontpage 2000 -- Comprehensive. Jessica Evans & Roger L. Hayen. 568p. per. 44.95 (*0-7600-6472-5*, Pub. by Course Tech) Thomson Learn.

New Perspectives on Microsoft Frontpage 2000 -- Introductory. Roger L. Hayen & Jessica Evans. 416p. per. 31.95 (*0-7600-6471-7*, Pub. by Course Tech) Thomson Learn.

New Perspectives on Microsoft FrontPage 97. Patrick Carey. 336p. (C). 1998. pap. 31.95 (*0-7600-5417-7*) Course Tech.

New Perspectives on Microsoft Internet Explorer 4.0: Introductory. 10th ed. Joan Carey & Sandra Poindexter. (New Perspectives Ser.). 200p. (C). 1998. pap. 21.95 (*0-7600-5785-0*) Course Tech.

New Perspectives on Microsoft Internet Explorer 5 - Brief. Joan Carey & Sandra E. Poindexter. 176p. per. 18.95 (*0-7600-7121-7*, Pub. by Course Tech) Thomson Learn.

New Perspectives on Microsoft Internet Explorer 5 - Introductory. Joan Carey & Sandra E. Poindexter. 272p. per. 21.95 (*0-7600-7122-5*, Pub. by Course Tech) Thomson Learn.

New Perspectives on Microsoft Office Professional for Windows 95: 5-in-1. 10th ed. Zimmerman et al. (New Perspectives Ser.). 1096p. (C). 1996. pap. 61.95 (*0-7600-4649-2*) Course Tech.

New Perspectives on Microsoft Office 2000. June J. Parsons et al. (New Perspectives Ser.). (Illus.). 856p. 1999. pap. 58.95 (*0-7600-6961-1*) Course Tech.

New Perspectives on Microsoft Office 97 Professional. Adamski et al. (New Perspectives Ser.). 824p. (C). 1997. pap. 43.50 (*0-7600-5272-7*) Course Tech.

New Perspectives on Microsoft PowerPoint 2000: Introductory Edition. Beverly B. Zimmerman. 1999. pap. text 21.95 (*0-7600-7092-X*) Course Tech.

New Perspectives on Microsoft Powerpoint 2000 - Brief. Beverly B. Zimmerman & S. Scott Zimmerman. 96p. per. 17.95 (*0-7600-7091-1*, Pub. by Course Tech) Thomson Learn.

New Perspectives on Microsoft PowerPoint 7 for Windows 95 - Brief. Beverly B. Zimmerman & S. Scott Zimmerman. 128p. 1996. teacher ed. write for info. (*0-7600-3780-9*) Course Tech.

New Perspectives on Microsoft PowerPoint 97: Brief. 10th ed. S. Scott Zimmerman & Beverly B. Zimmerman. (New Perspectives Ser.). 80p. (C). 1997. pap. 17.95 (*0-7600-5252-2*) Course Tech.

New Perspectives on Microsoft PowerPoint 97: Brief & Introductory. S. Scott Zimmerman & Beverly B. Zimmerman. 152p. (C). 1997. teacher ed. 18.50 (*0-7600-5284-0*) Course Tech.

New Perspectives on Microsoft PowerPoint 97 - Introduction. Zimmerman. (C). 1997. pap. 21.95 (*0-7600-5276-X*) Course Tech.

New Perspectives on Microsoft Windows 95: Advanced. Harry Phillips. 480p. 1996. teacher ed. 40.00 (*0-7600-3933-X*) Course Tech.

New Perspectives on Microsoft Windows NT Server 4.0. Peter Brierley. 1997. pap. text 49.99 (*0-7600-5604-8*) Course Tech.

New Perspectives on Microsoft Windows NT Workstation 4.0: Comprehensive. 10th ed. June J. Parsons et al. (New Perspectives Ser.). 504p. (C). 1997. pap. 44.95 (*0-7600-5221-2*) Course Tech.

New Perspectives on Microsoft Windows NT Workstation 4.0: Introductory. June J. Parsons et al. (New Perspectives Ser.). 152p. (C). 1996. pap. 13.00 (*0-7600-5218-2*) Course Tech.

New Perspectives on Microsoft Windows NT Workstation 4.0: Introductory & Comprehensive. June J. Parsons et al. 656p. (C). 1997. teacher ed. 18.50 (*0-7600-5223-9*) Course Tech.

New Perspectives on Microsoft Windows NT Workstation 4.0 Comprehensive. June Parsons. 1997. pap. text 39.99 (*0-7600-5611-0*) Course Tech.

New Perspectives on Microsoft Windows NT 4.0 Server. Peter Brierley. 600p. 1997. write for info. (*0-7600-5384-7*) Course Tech.

New Perspectives on Microsoft Windows NT 4.0 Server. 10th ed. Peter Brierley. (New Perspectives Ser.). 600p. (C). 1997. pap. 53.95 (*0-7600-5254-9*) Course Tech.

New Perspectives on Microsoft Windows 2000 Professional - Comprehensive. June Jamrich Parsons et al. 512p. per. 44.95 (*0-7600-7094-6*, Pub. by Course Tech) Thomson Learn.

New Perspectives on Microsoft Windows 98 Brief. June J. Parsons et al. 80p. per. 11.95 (*0-7600-5446-0*, Pub. by Course Tech) Thomson Learn.

New Perspectives on Microsoft Word 7 for Windows 95: Introductory & Comprehensive. Beverly B. Zimmerman & S. Scott Zimmerman. 632p. 1997. teacher ed. 18.50 (*0-7600-4005-2*) Course Tech.

New Perspectives on Microsoft Word 2000: Comprehensive Edition. Ann Shaffer. 1999. pap. text 44.95 (*0-7600-6995-6*) Course Tech.

New Perspectives on Microsoft Word 2000 - Brief. S. Scott Zimmerman et al. 168p. per. 21.95 (*0-7600-6991-3*) Course Tech.

New Perspectives on Microsoft Word 2000 - Introductory. Beverly B. Zimmerman et al. 344p. per. 31.95 (*0-7600-6993-X*, Pub. by Course Tech) Thomson Learn.

New Perspectives on Microsoft Word 97: Brief. S. Scott Zimmerman et al. (New Perspectives Ser.). 168p. 1997. pap. 21.95 (*0-7600-4551-8*) Course Tech.

New Perspectives on Microsoft Word 97: Comprehensive. S. Scott Zimmerman et al. (New Perspectives Ser.). 552p. (C). 1997. pap. 31.50 (*0-7600-5256-5*) Course Tech.

New Perspectives on Microsoft Word 97: Introductory. 10th ed. S. Scott Zimmerman et al. (New Perspectives Ser.). 304p. (C). 1997. pap. 31.95 (*0-7600-5255-7*) Course Tech.

***New Perspectives on Middle English Texts.** Susan Powell. 256p. 2000. 75.00 (*0-85991-590-5*) Boydell & Brewer.

New Perspectives on Modern Russian History: Selected Papers from the Fourth World Congress of Soviet & East European Studies, Harrogate, 1990. Ed. by Robert B. McKean. 300p. 1992. text 55.00 (*0-312-07594-4*) St Martin.

New Perspectives on Ms Project. Johnson. (New Perspectives Modules Ser.). (C). 2000. pap. 31.95 (*0-7600-7076-8*) Course Tech.

New Perspectives on MS Visual Basic 5: Comprehensive. Mike Ekedahl & Bill Newman. (New Perspectives Ser.). 512p. (C). 1997. pap. 46.95 (*0-7600-4668-9*) Course Tech.

***New Perspectives on MS Win 98.** Carey & Oja. (New Perspectives Ser.). (C). 1999. ring bd. 16.50 (*0-7600-6547-0*) Course Tech.

New Perspectives on MS Window 98-Comprehensive. 10th ed. Parsons et al. (New Perspectives Ser.). (C). 1998. pap. 44.95 (*0-7600-5448-7*) Course Tech.

***New Perspectives on Narrative Perspective.** Ed. by Willie Van Peer & Seymour Chatman. LC 00-27694. (C). 2000. pap. text 24.95 (*0-7914-4788-X*) State U NY Pr.

***New Perspectives on Narrative Perspective.** Ed. by Willie Van Peer & Seymour Chatman. LC 00-27694. (C). 2001. text 73.50 (*0-7914-4787-1*) State U NY Pr.

New Perspectives on Nationalism & War. Ed. by John L. Comaroff & Paul Stern. (International Studies in Global Change). 336p. 1995. text 75.00 (*2-88449-165-1*); pap. text 32.00 (*2-88449-166-X*) Gordon & Breach.

New Perspectives on Netscape Communicator 6.0 - Brief. Joan Carey & Sandra E. Poindexter. 160p. per. 18.95 (*0-7600-7133-0*, Pub. by Course Tech) Thomson Learn.

New Perspectives on Netscape Communicator 6.0 - Introductory. Joan Carey & Sandra E. Poindexter. 256p. per. 21.95 (*0-7600-7134-9*, Pub. by Course Tech) Thomson Learn.

***New Perspectives on Nitrogen Cycling in the Temperate & Tropical Americas: Report.** Alan R. Townsend & SCOPE Nitrogen Project Staff. LC 99-23436. 293p. 1999. write for info. (*0-7923-5704-3*) Kluwer Academic.

New Perspectives on Noise-Induced Hearing Loss. Ed. by Roger P. Hamernik et al. LC 80-5540. 550p. 1982. reprint ed. pap. 170.50 (*0-608-04730-9*, 206545100004) Bks Demand.

New Perspectives on Office: 1997 Edition. June Parsons et al. (New Perspectives Ser.). (Illus.). 300p. 1998. pap. 53.95 (*0-7600-5798-2*) Course Tech.

New Perspectives on Office 97. Zimmerman. (C). 1997. pap. 46.75 (*0-7600-7015-6*) Thomson Learn.

New Perspectives on Office 2000 - Second Course. June Jamrich Parsons & Dan Oja. 1016p. per. 62.95 (*0-7600-6433-4*, Pub. by Course Tech) Thomson Learn.

New Perspectives on Old-Time Religion. George N. Schlesinger. 208p. 1988. text 49.95 (*0-19-824986-1*) OUP.

New Perspectives on Organization Theory: An Empirical Reconsideration of the Marxian & Classical Analyses, 1. William L. Zwerman. LC 71-90791. (Contributions in Sociology Ser.: No. 1). (Illus.). 219p. 1970. 35.00 (*0-8371-1851-4*, ZWN/) Greenwood.

New Perspectives on Organizational Effectiveness. Ed. by Paul S. Goodman et al. LC 77-82916. (Jossey-Bass Social & Behavioral Science Ser.). 295p. reprint ed. pap. 91.50 (*0-8357-4976-2*, 203790900009) Bks Demand.

New Perspectives on Personality Development in College Students. Florence B. Brawer. LC 73-7150. (Jossey-Bass Higher Education Ser.). 254p. reprint ed. 78.80 (*0-8357-9338-9*, 201379400087) Bks Demand.

New Perspectives on Poughkeepsie's Past: Essays to Honor Edmund Platt. Ed. by Clyde Griffen. (Dutchess County Historical Society Yearbook, 1987: Vol. 72). (Illus.). 140p. 1988. pap. text 20.00 (*0-944733-00-X*, 1987) Dutchess Hist Soc.

New Perspectives on Problems in Classical & Quantum Physics, Vol. 1. Pier P. Delsanto & Albert W. Saenz. 404p. 1998. text 51.00 (*90-5699-548-0*) Gordon & Breach.

New Perspectives on Problems in Classical & Quantum Physics: A Festschrift in Honor of Herbert Uberall, vols. 2, Set. Pier P. Delsanto & Albert W. Saenz. 743p. 1998. text 96.00 (*90-5699-550-2*) Gordon & Breach.

New Perspectives on Problems in Classical & Quantum Physics: A Festschrift in Honor of Herbert Uberall:Acoustic Propagation & Scattering, Electromagnetic Scattering, Vol. 2, Pt. 2. Pier P. Delsanto & Albert W. Saenz. 440p. 1998. text 55.00 (*90-5699-549-9*) Gordon & Breach.

N

An Asterisk (*) at the beginning of an entry indicates that the title is appearing for the first time.

New Perspectives on Psychotherapy & Homosexualities. Ed. by Christopher Shelley. 275p. 1998. 55.00 (*1-85343-403-5*, Pub. by Free Assoc Bks); pap. 22.50 (*1-85343-404-3*, Pub. by Free Assoc Bks) NYU Pr.

New Perspectives on Robert Graves. Ed. by Patrick J. Quinn. LC 99-19629. 232p. 1999. 39.50 (*1-57591-020-9*) Susquehanna U Pr.

New Perspectives on Security. Ed. by Michael Clarke. 158p. 1993. text 37.00 (*0-08-041790-6*, Pub. by Brasseys) Brasseys.

New Perspectives on Security. Ed. by Michael Clarke. 158p. 1994. pap. 21.00 (*0-08-041789-2*, Pub. by Brasseys) Brasseys.

New Perspectives on Social Class & Socio-Economic Development in the Periphery, 77. Ed. by Nelson W. Keith & Novella Z. Keith. LC 87-25113. (Contributions in Economics & Economic History Ser.: No. 77). 204p. 1988. 55.00 (*0-313-25688-8*, KNR/) Greenwood.

New Perspectives on Solar Prominences, IAU Colloquium 167. Ed. by David F. Webb et al. LC 98-72562. (Conference Series Proceedings: Vol. 150). 515p. 1998. 52.00 (*1-886733-70-8*) Astron Soc Pacific.

New Perspectives on State Socialism in China. Ed. by Timothy Cheek & Tony Saich. LC 97-5272. 422p. (C). (gr. 13). 1997. text 74.95 (*0-7656-0041-2*, East Gate Bk) M E Sharpe.

New Perspectives on State Socialism in China. Ed. by Timothy Cheek & Tony Saich. LC 97-5272. (Illus.). 422p. (C). 1999. pap. text 27.95 (*0-7656-0042-0*, East Gate Bk) M E Sharpe.

New Perspectives on Stellar Pulsation & Pulsating Variable Stars. Ed. by James M. Nemec & Jaymie M. Matthews. (Illus.). 463p. (C). 1993. text 74.95 (*0-521-44382-2*) Cambridge U Pr.

New Perspectives on Teacher Education. Donald J. McCarty. LC 73-1852. (Jossey-Bass Higher Education Ser.). 271p. reprint ed. pap. 84.10 (*0-608-14789-3*, 202566200045) Bks Demand.

***New Perspectives on Teaching & Learning Modern Languages.** Simon Green. LC 99-45550. (Modern Languages in Practice Ser.). 2000. pap. write for info. (*1-85359-471-7*, Pub. by Multilingual Matters) Taylor & Francis.

New Perspectives on Technology & American Culture. Ed. by Bruce Sinclair. LC 86-71782. (American Philosophical Society Library Publication Ser.: No. 12). 91p. reprint ed. pap. 30.00 (*0-8357-3409-9*, 203966600013) Bks Demand.

New Perspectives on the Art of Ceramics in China. Ed. by George Kuwayama. (Illus.). 208p. 1992. pap. text 24.00 (*0-87587-156-9*) LA Co Art Mus.

New Perspectives on the Beatitudes. Ed. by Francis A. Eigo. LC 95-15812. 1995. write for info. (*0-87723-063-3*) Villanova U Pr.

New Perspectives on the Belgian Revolution. John W. Rooney, Jr. et al. 338p. 1994. 35.00 (*0-87291-204-3*); pap. text 17.50 (*0-87291-208-6*) Coronado Pr.

New Perspectives on the Chinese Revolution. Ed. by Tony Saich & hans Van de Ven. LC 94-26985. 436p. (C). (gr. 13). 1994. text 99.95 (*1-56324-428-4*, East Gate Bk) M E Sharpe.

New Perspectives on the Chinese Revolution. Ed. by Tony Saich & Hans Van de Ven. LC 94-26985. 436p. (C). (gr. 13). 1994. pap. text 34.95 (*1-56324-429-2*, East Gate Bk) M E Sharpe.

New Perspectives on the Civil War: Myths & Realities of the National Conflict. John Y. Simon & Michael E. Stevens. LC 98-18909. 180p. 1998. 27.95 (*0-945612-62-1*) Madison Hse.

New Perspectives on the Cultural Revolution. Ed. by William A. Joseph et al. LC 90-20970. (Harvard Contemporary China Ser.: No. 8). (Illus.). 365p. (C). 1991. 35.00 (*0-674-61757-6*); pap. 20.00 (*0-674-61758-4*) HUP.

New Perspectives on the Dead Sea Scrolls: Understanding Their Spiritual Message. Steven A. Fisdel. LC 96-49938. 368p. 1997. 40.00 (*1-56821-973-3*) Aronson.

New Perspectives on the Early Republic: Essays from the Journal of the Early Republic, 1981-1991. Ralph D. Gray. Ed. by Michael A. Morrison. LC 93-5652. 456p. 1994. 42.50 (*0-252-03084-2*); pap. text 16.95 (*0-252-06375-9*) U of Ill Pr.

New Perspectives on the Early Republic: Essays from the Journal of the Early Republic, 1981-1991. Ed. by Ralph D. Gray & Michael A. Morrison. 496p. 1994. text 42.50 (*0-252-02084-7*) U of Ill Pr.

New Perspectives on the Earth's Magnetotail. Ed. by A. Nishida et al. LC 98-38668. (Geophysical Monograph Ser.: Vol. 105). 341p. 1998. 70.00 (*0-87590-088-7*) Am Geophysical.

***New Perspectives on the Fin de Siecle in Nineteenth- & Twentieth-Century France.** Ed. by Kay Chadwick & Timothy Unwin. LC 99-59020. (Studies in French Civilization: Vol. 15). 296p. 2000. text 89.95 (*0-7734-7786-1*) E Mellen.

New Perspectives on the Financial System. Ed. by Laurence Harris et al. 384p. 1988. lib. bdg. 82.50 (*0-7099-3741-5*, Pub. by C Helm) Routldge.

New Perspectives on the History of Life: Essays on Systematic Biology As Historical Narrative. Ed. by Michael T. Ghiselin & Giovanni Pinna. (Memoirs of the California Academy of Sciences Ser.: No. 20). (Illus.). 107p. 1996. 30.00 (*0-940228-43-2*) Calif Acad Sci.

New Perspectives on the Holocaust: A Guide for Teachers & Scholars. Ed. by Rochelle L. Millen et al. (C). 1996. pap. text 19.50 (*0-8147-5540-2*) NYU Pr.

New Perspectives on the Holocaust: A Guide for Teachers & Scholars. Ed. by Rochelle L. Millen et al. 420p. (C). 1996. text 55.00 (*0-8147-5539-9*) NYU Pr.

New Perspectives on the House of Representatives. rev. ed. Ed. by Robert L. Peabody & Nelson W. Polsby. 392p. 1992. pap. text 17.95 (*0-8018-4158-5*) Johns Hopkins.

New Perspectives on the Internet: Comprehensive. James Perry. (C). 1998. pap. 44.95 (*0-7600-7010-5*) Course Tech.

New Perspectives on the Internet Using Netscape Navigator Software: Introductory. Sharon Caswell. (New Perspectives Ser.). 300p. (C). 1997. pap. 31.95 (*0-7600-4078-8*) Course Tech.

New Perspectives on the Internet Using Netscape Navigator Software - Introductory. Sharon Caswell. 300p. 1997. teacher ed. write for info. (*0-7600-4080-X*) Course Tech.

***New Perspectives on the Interstellar Medium, Vol. 168.** Ed. by A. R. Taylor et al. (ASP Conference Series Proceedings). 473p. (C). 1999. text 52.00 (*1-886733-89-9*) Astron Soc Pacific.

New Perspectives on the Irish Diaspora. Charles Fanning. LC 00-25054. 1995. pap. 19.95 (*0-8093-2344-3*) S Ill U Pr.

New Perspectives on the Late Victorian Economy: Essays in Quantitative Economic History, 1860-1914. Ed. by James Foreman-Peck. (Illus.). 369p. (C). 1991. text 69.95 (*0-521-39107-5*) Cambridge U Pr.

New Perspectives on the Life & Art of Richard Crashaw. Ed. by John R. Roberts. LC 84-52264. (Illus.). 248p. 1990. text 32.50 (*0-8262-0739-1*) U of Mo Pr.

New Perspectives on the Northern Ireland Conflict. Adrian Guelke. 224p. 1994. 72.95 (*1-85628-446-8*, Pub. by Avebry) Ashgate Pub Co.

New Perspectives on the Practical PC. Parsons. (New Perspectives Ser.). (C). 1999. pap. 40.95 (*0-7600-7066-0*) Course Tech.

New Perspectives on the Seventeenth-Century English Religious Lyric. Ed. by John R. Roberts. (Illus.). 336p. (C). 1994. text 47.50 (*0-8262-0909-2*) U of Mo Pr.

New Perspectives on the Treatment of Obesity & Redux: A Comprehensive Overview. Ed. by Stylianos Nicolaidis. LC 96-36686. (Illus.). 150p. 1996. pap. text 36.00 (*0-12-518170-1*) Acad Pr.

***New Perspectives on Therapeutics in the Elderly.** Mark T. Kinirons. (New Perspectives Ser.). (Illus.). 128p. 2001. pap. text 19.95 (*1-873413-08-4*) Merit Pub Intl.

New Perspectives on Unemployment. Ed. by Barbara A. Jones. 106p. 1984. pap. 16.95 (*0-87855-978-7*) Transaction Pubs.

New Perspectives on Visual Basic 5.0: Introductory. 10th ed. William Newman & Michael Ekedahl. (New Perspectives Ser.). 316p. (C). 1997. pap. 28.50 (*0-7600-5380-4*) Course Tech.

New Perspectives on Window 98 for Power Users. 10th ed. Carey & Parsons. (New Perspectives Ser.). (C). 1998. pap. 42.95 (*0-7600-7272-8*) Course Tech.

New Perspectives on Women & Comedy. Ed. by Regina Barreca. (Studies in Gender & Culture). xii, 244p. 1992. text 52.00 (*2-88124-533-1*); pap. text 24.00 (*2-88124-534-X*) Gordon & Breach.

New Perspectives on Works 4. Kelly. (New Perspectives Ser.). (C). 1997. spiral bd. 31.50 (*0-7600-7302-3*) Course Tech.

New Perspectives on Works 4.5. 10th ed. Clemens. (New Perspectives Ser.). (C). 1998. pap. 44.95 (*0-7600-7004-0*) Course Tech.

***New Pet.** Dan Yaccarino. 32p. (J). 2001. 14.99 (*0-7868-0579-X*, Pub. by Disney Pr) Time Warner.

New Pharmacological & Epidemiological Data in Analgesics Research. Kay Brune. 60p. 1990. 22.50 (*0-8176-2452-X*) Birkhauser.

New Pharmacological Approaches to the Therapy of Depressive Disorders. Ed. by G. Racagni et al. (International Academy for Biomedical & Drug Research Ser.: Vol. 5). (Illus.). vi, 196p. 1993. 194.00 (*3-8055-5746-9*) S Karger.

New Pharmacotherapy of Schizophrenia. Ed. by Alan Breier. (Clinical Practice Ser.: No. 36). 272p. 1996. text 33.50 (*0-88048-491-8*, 8491) Am Psychiatric.

New Phil Collins Deluxe Anthology. Ed. by Carol Cuellar. 240p. (Orig.). (C). 1993. pap. text 19.95 (*0-7692-0280-2*, VF1909) Wrner Bros.

New Philosophy & the Philosophical Sciences, 2 vols., Set. Apostolos Makrakis. Ed. by Orthodox Christian Educational Society Staff & Denver Cummings. Incl. Vol. 1. Introduction to Philosophy, Psychology, Logic, & Theology. 888p. 1940. Vol. 2. Introduction to Ethics. 745p. 1940. 1940. reprint ed. 44.95 (*0-938366-01-7*) Orthodox Chr.

New Philosophy & Universal Languages in Seventeenth Century England: Bacon, Hobbes, & Wilkins. Robert E. Stillman. LC 94-47467. 360p. 1995. 48.50 (*0-8387-5310-8*) Bucknell U Pr.

New Philosophy (1884) Albert W. Paine. 174p. 1998. reprint ed. pap. 17.95 (*0-7661-0570-9*) Kessinger Pub.

New Philosophy for K-12 Education: A Deming Framework for Transforming America's Schools. James F. Leonard. 330p. 1996. 35.00 (*0-87389-363-8*, H0924) ASQ Qual Pr.

New Philosophy of Social Science: Problems of Indeterminacy. James Bohman. 288p. 1993. pap. text 17.50 (*0-262-52183-0*) MIT Pr.

New Philosophy of History. Ed. by Franklin R. Ankersmit & Hans Kellner. LC 95-11010. 300p. 1995. pap. text 19.95 (*0-226-02100-9*); lib. bdg. 55.00 (*0-226-02099-1*) U Ch Pr.

New Phoebe: Perspectives on Roman Catholic Women & the Permanent Diaconate. Ed. by Virginia K. Ratigan & Arlene A. Swidler. LC 90-60898. 120p. (Orig.). (C). 1990. pap. 7.95 (*1-55612-357-4*) Sheed & Ward WI.

New Phonologies: Developments in Clinical Linguistics. Martin J. Ball. Ed. by Raymond D. Kent. LC 96-53434. 282p. 1997. pap. 49.95 (*1-56593-082-7*, 0387) Thomson Learn.

New Photography: A Guide to New Images, Processes, & Display Techniques for Photographers. Catherine Reeve & Marilyn Sward. (Quality Paperbacks Ser.). (Illus.). xiv, 242p. 1987. reprint ed. pap. 18.95 (*0-306-80295-3*) Da Capo.

New Phrynichus Being a Revised Text of the Ecloga of the Grammarian Phrynichus. Arabius Phrynichos. xi, 539p. 1968. reprint ed. 83.20 (*0-685-66502-X*, 05101885) G Olms Pubs.

New Phrynichus Being a Revised Text of the Ecloga of the Grammarian Phrynichus. Arabius Phrynichos. xi, 539p. 1968. reprint ed. write for info. (*0-318-70998-8*) G Olms Pubs.

New Physical Anthropolgy. Strum & Lindburg. 285p. 1998. 58.00 (*0-13-206517-7*) P-H.

New Physical Problems in Electronic Materials: Proceedings of the 6th ISCMP. M. Borissov et al. 572p. 1991. text 151.00 (*981-02-0474-4*) World Scientific Pub.

New Physician's Guide to Legal Medicine. RiskCare Staff & Chad D. Kollas. 59p. 1997. pap. text 19.00 (*1-893929-06-X*) RiskCare.

New Physics. Ed. by P. C. Davies. (Illus.). 526p. (C). 1992. pap. 38.95 (*0-521-43831-4*) Cambridge U Pr.

New Physics. Chandrasekhara V. Raman. LC 73-128292. (Essay Index Reprint Ser.). 1977. 19.95 (*0-8369-2020-1*) Ayer.

New Physics & a New Theology. Michael Heller. Tr. by George V. Coyne. 103p. 1996. pap. 9.00 (*0-268-01479-5*) U of Notre Dame Pr.

New Physics & the Modern French Novel: An Investigation of Interdisciplinary Discourse. Maureen D. Troiano. LC 93-17012. (Currents in Comparative Romance Languages & Literatures Ser.: Vol. 19). 282p. (C). 1995. text 55.95 (*0-8204-2198-7*) P Lang Pubng.

New Physics with New Experiments. Z. Ajduk et al. 500p. 1994. text 112.00 (*981-02-1684-X*) World Scientific Pub.

New Physiognomy or Signs of Character As Manifested Through Temperament & External Forms & Especially in the Human Face Divine (1876) Samuel R. Wells. 800p. 1998. reprint ed. pap. 50.00 (*0-7661-0357-9*) Kessinger Pub.

New Pianist: A Cognitive Approach, 3 vols., Set. Charlotte L. Warren. 1992. pap. 67.00 (*1-880571-04-8*) Decision Pt.

New Pianist Vol. I: A Cognitive Approach: The Musical Lesson. 2nd ed. Charlotte L. Warren. 58p. 1990. reprint ed. pap. 10.00 (*1-880571-01-3*) Decision Pt.

New Pianist Vol. II: A Cognitive Approach: Getting the Most from Your Practicing. Charlotte L. Warren. 75p. (Orig.). 1989. pap. 12.00 (*1-880571-02-1*) Decision Pt.

New Pianist - A Cognitive Approach Vol. III: Part 1: Dancing at the Keyboard, Part 2: Applied Problem Solving, 2 cass., Set. Charlotte L. Warren. 1991. pap. 45.00 incl. audio (*1-880571-03-X*) Decision Pt.

New Picture Bible. 760p. (J). 1998. write for info. (*0-7814-0307-3*, Chariot Bks) Chariot Victor.

New Pilgrim's Progress. John Bunyan. LC 89-36626. 224p. 1989. pap. 10.99 (*0-929239-13-X*) Discovery Hse Pubs.

New Pilot: Guide to Your First 100 Hours, As Pilot in Command. H. Allen Smith. (Illus.). 113p. 1998. pap. 15.95 (*0-9672190-4-3*) New Pilot.

New Pioneers: The Back-to-the-Land Movement & the Search for a Sustainable Future. Jeffrey Jacob. LC 96-12913. 1997. 26.50 (*0-271-01621-3*) Pa St U Pr.

New Pioneers: The Back-to-the-Land Movement & the Search for a Sustainable Future. Jeffrey Jacob. 278p. 1998. pap. 18.95 (*0-271-01828-3*) Pa St U Pr.

New Pioneers: The Men & Women Who Are Transforming the Workplace & Marketplace. Thomas Petzinger, Jr. LC 98-50132. 304p. 1999. 24.50 (*0-684-84636-5*) S&S Trade.

New Pioneers in Heartland: Among Life. Jo A. Koltyk & Nancy Foner. LC 97-227948. 146p. 1997. pap. 20.00 (*0-205-27412-9*) P-H.

New Place. Ed. by Levi Fox. (Shakespeare Travel Ser.). (Illus.). 20p. (Orig.). 1994. pap. 2.50 (*0-7117-0378-7*) Seven Hills Bk.

New Place for Learning Science: Starting & Running a Science Center. Sheila Grinell. (Illus.). 154p. 1992. pap. 40.00 (*0-944040-30-6*, 62-0) AST Ctrs.

New Place, New Face. Sue Mongredien. 144p. (J). 1997. pap. 6.95 (*0-09-926319-X*, Pub. by Random) Trafalgar.

New Place, Old Ways: Essays on Indian Society & Culture in Modern Singapore. Nilavu Mohdx et al. Ed. by Anthony E. Walker. (C). 1994. 36.00 (*81-7075-027-X*, Pub. by Hindustan) S Asia.

New Planning System in Victoria. Julia Bruce. xxxii, 390p. 1988. pap. 74.50 (*0-455-20792-5*, Pub. by LawBk Co) Gaunt.

New Plant Sources for Drugs & Foods from the New York Botanical Garden Herbarium. Siri V. Von Reis & Frank J. Lipp, Jr. LC 81-6280. (Illus.). 376p. 1982. 45.95 (*0-674-61765-7*) HUP.

New Plantation South: Land, Labor, & Federal Favor in Twentieth-Century Arkansas. Jeannie M. Whayne. (Carter G. Woodson Institute Series in Black Studies). (C). 1996. text 39.50 (*0-8139-1655-0*) U Pr of Va.

New Plants from Fiji-I. John W. Gillespie. (Illus.). pap. 30.00 (*0-527-02180-6*, B074K) Periodicals Srv.

New Plants from Fiji-III, 1932. John W. Gillespie. (Illus.). pap. 18.00 (*0-527-02197-0*, BO91K) Periodicals Srv.

New Plants from Fiji-II, 1931. John W. Gillespie. (Illus.). pap. 18.00 (*0-527-02189-X*, BO83K) Periodicals Srv.

New Plastic Material for Non-Metallic Gears. F. R. Zumstein. (Technical Papers: Vol. P249.03). (Illus.). 25p. 1951. pap. text 30.00 (*1-55589-192-6*) AGMA.

New Plastics Applications for the Automotive Industry. 1997. 61.00 (*1-56091-965-5*, SP-1253) Soc Auto Engineers.

New Platonism & Alchemy. Alexander Wilder. (Secret Doctrine Reference Ser.). 1975. reprint ed. pap. 3.50 (*0-913510-18-1*) Wizards.

New Player's Handbook. 2nd rev. ed. Zeb Cook. (Advanced Dungeons & Dragons, 2nd Edition Ser.). (Illus.). 1995. 29.95 (*0-7869-0329-5*, Pub. by TSR Inc) Random.

New Playing Christmas Music L4. 64p. (Orig.). 1994. pap. 7.95 (*0-7692-1133-X*, BP3322A) Wrner Bros.

New Playing Classical Music L5. 80p. (Orig.). 1994. pap. 8.95 (*0-7692-1138-0*, BP3329A) Wrner Bros.

New Playing Classical Music L4. 64p. (Orig.). 1994. pap. 7.95 (*0-7692-1137-2*, BP3328A) Wrner Bros.

New Playing Classical Music L1. 24p. (Orig.). 1994. pap. 5.95 (*0-7692-1134-8*, BP3325A) Wrner Bros.

New Playing Classical Music L3. 48p. (Orig.). 1994. pap. 6.95 (*0-7692-1136-4*, BP3327A) Wrner Bros.

New Playing Classical Music L2. 32p. (Orig.). 1994. pap. 5.95 (*0-7692-1135-6*, BP3326A) Wrner Bros.

New Playing Popular Music, Level 5. 80p. (YA). 1994. pap. 8.95 (*0-910957-78-9*, BP3317A) Wrner Bros.

New Playmaking: The Latest in the Intergration of the Arts in Education. (Illus.). 160p. 1993. pap. text 20.00 (*0-942345-10-X*, Creat Educ Systs) Dovehaven Pr Ltd.

New Plays. Joyce Carol Oates. LC 97-46802. 284p. 1998. 23.00 (*0-86538-089-9*) Ontario Rev NJ.

***New Plays.** Joyce Carol Oates. LC 97-46802. 284p. 1998. pap. 13.50 (*0-86538-090-2*) Ontario Rev NJ.

New Plays for the Black Theatre. Ed. by Woodie King, Jr. (Orig.). (C). 1988. pap. 14.95 (*0-88378-124-7*) Third World.

New Plays from ACT's Young Conservatory, Vol. I. Ed. by Craig Slaight. (Young Actors Ser.). 256p. (YA). (gr. 9 up). 1993. pap. 14.95 (*1-880399-25-3*) Smith & Kraus.

New Plays from ACT's Young Conservatory, Vol. II. Craig Slaight. (Young Actors Ser.). 256p. (YA). (gr. 9 up). 1995. pap. 14.95 (*1-880399-73-3*) Smith & Kraus.

New Plays from A.C.T.'s Young Conservatory, Vol. III. Ed. by Craig Slaight. 256p. (YA). (gr. 7-12). 1999. pap. 16.95 (*1-57525-122-1*) Smith & Kraus.

New Plays from the Abbey Theatre 1993-1995. Ed. by Christopher Fitz-Simon & Sanford Sternlicht. (Illus.). (C). 1996. pap. 19.95 (*0-8156-0345-2*, FINPP) Syracuse U Pr.

New Plays U. S. A. Four. Ed. by James Leverett et al. 254p. (C). 1988. 24.95 (*0-930452-80-1*); pap. 12.95 (*0-930452-81-X*) Theatre Comm.

New Plays U. S. A. Three. Ed. by James Leverett & M. Elizabeth Osborn. 300p. (Orig.). (C). 1986. pap. 11.95 (*0-930452-54-2*) Theatre Comm.

New Plays U. S. A. Two. Ed. by M. Elizabeth Osborn & Gillian Richards. 396p. 1984. 17.95 (*0-930452-35-6*) Theatre Comm.

New Playwrights: The Best Plays of 1998. Ed. by Marisa Smith. 320p. 1999. pap. 19.95 (*1-57525-171-X*) Smith & Kraus.

New Pleiade: Selected Poems. Fred Chappell et al. LC 98-24404. 232p. 1998. pap. 18.95 (*0-8071-2330-7*); text 39.95 (*0-8071-2329-3*) La State U Pr.

New Pleistocene Conifer Records, Coastal California. 2nd ed. Daniel I. Axelrod. LC 83-6874. (University of California Publications in Geological Sciences: No. 127). 122p. 1983. pap. 37.90 (*0-7837-7466-4*, 204918800010) Bks Demand.

New Pocket Dictionary Armenian-English (Kerbani Nor Pararan Hayeren Ankleren) Mesrob G. Kouyoumjian. (ARM & ENG.). 320p. 1998. pap. 16.00 (*1-58253-008-4*) Shirak.

New Pocket Dictionary, Armenian-English/English-Armenian (Kerbani Nor Pararan Ankleren Heyeren-Hayeren Ankleren) Mesrob G. Kouyoumjian. (ARM & ENG.). 672p. 1998. pap. 30.00 (*1-58253-010-6*) Shirak.

New Pocket Dictionary English-Armenian (Kerbani Nor Pararan Ankleren-Hayeren) Mesrob G. Kouyoumjian. (ARM & ENG.). 352p. 1998. pap. 16.00 (*1-58253-009-2*) Shirak.

New Pocket Hawaiian Dictionary. rev. ed. Mary K. Pukui & Samuel H. Elbert. LC 91-25854. 272p. 1992. pap. 4.95 (*0-8248-1392-8*) UH Pr.

New Pockets of Jewish Energy: A Study of Adults Who Found Their Way Back to Judaism. 32p. 1982. 2.50 (*0-87495-046-5*) Am Jewish Comm.

New Poems. Roy Fuller. LC 68-31827. 1968. 15.95 (*0-8023-1180-6*) Dufour.

***New Poems.** Al Grass. 1999. pap. write for info. (*0-15-601063-1*) Harcourt.

New Poems. D. H. Lawrence. LC 74-6450. (Studies in D. H. Lawrence: No. 20). (C). 1974. lib. bdg. 75.00 (*0-8383-1967-X*) M S G Haskell Hse.

New Poems. Rainer Maria Rilke. Tr. by Stephen Cohn. Orig. Title: Neue Gedichte. (ENG & GER.). 296p. 1997. pap. 18.95 (*1-85754-323-8*, Pub. by Carcanet Pr) Paul & Co Pubs.

New Poems. Robert Browning & Elizabeth Barrett Browning. (BCL1-PR English Literature Ser.). 186p. 1992. reprint ed. lib. bdg. 69.00 (*0-7812-7459-1*) Rprt Serv.

New Poems. George Crabbe. LC 85-30523. (Illus.). 198p. 1986. reprint ed. lib. bdg. 55.00 (*0-313-25046-4*, CRNE, Greenwood Pr) Greenwood.

***New Poems: Bilingual Edition.** Rainer Maria Rilke. Tr. by Stephen Cohn. (European Poetry Classics Ser.). 295p. 1998. pap. text 16.95 (*0-8101-1649-9*) Northwestern U Pr.

New Poems: 1980-1988. John Haines. 114p. 1990. 16.95 (*0-934257-44-2*); pap. 9.95 (*0-934257-45-0*) Story Line.

New Poems by American Poets. Ed. by Rolfe Humphries. LC 70-121924. (Granger Index Reprint Ser.). 1977. 18.95 (*0-8369-6164-1*) Ayer.

New Poems by American Poets, No. 2. Ed. by Rolfe Humphries. LC 70-121924. (Granger Index Reprint Ser.). 1980. 19.95 (*0-8369-6165-X*) Ayer.

An Asterisk (*) at the beginning of an entry indicates that the title is appearing for the first time.

New Poems by James I of England. James First King of England. Ed. by Allan F. Westcott. LC 76-144424. reprint ed. 32.50 (*0-404-06909-6*) AMS Pr.

***New Poems from the Third Coast: Contemporary Michigan Poetry.** Ed. by Michael Delp et al. 480p. 1999. 44.95 (*0-8143-2796-6*); pap. 24.95 (*0-8143-2797-4*) Wayne St U Pr.

New Poems, 1908: The Other Part. Rainer Maria Rilke. Tr. by Edward Snow. LC 86-62835. 224p. 1990. pap. 13.00 (*0-86547-416-8*) N Point Pr.

New Poems, 1907. Rainer Maria Rilke. Tr. by Edward Snow from FRE. LC 84-60683. 224p. 1990. pap. 12.00 (*0-86547-415-X*) N Point Pr.

New Poems of Emily Dickinson. Emily Dickinson. Ed. by William H. Shurr. LC 93-20353. x, 126p. 1993. 24.95 (*0-8078-2115-2*); pap. 12.95 (*0-8078-4416-0*) U of NC Pr.

New Poet: Novelty & Tradition in Spenser's "Complaints" Richard D. Brown. LC 99-494968. 320p. 1998. 45.95 (*0-85323-803-0*, Pub. by Liverpool Univ Pr); pap. 23.95 (*0-85323-813-8*, Pub. by Liverpool Univ Pr) Intl Spec Bk.

New Poetic. Christian K. Stead. LC 78-64053. (Des Imagistes: Literature of the Imagist Movement Ser.). 200p. reprint ed. 37.50 (*0-404-17103-6*) AMS Pr.

New Poetic: Yeats to Eliot. C. K. Stead. LC 97-32310. (Orig.). 1998. pap. 25.00 (*0-485-12137-9*, Pub. by Athlone Pr) Humanities.

New Poetics in Canada & Quebec: From Concretism to Post-Modernism. Caroline Bayard. 374p. 1989. text 45.00 (*0-8020-5726-8*) U of Toronto Pr.

New Poetries: Poetic Form Since Coleridge & Wordsworth. Donald Wesling. LC 82-74493. 400p. 1985. 47.50 (*0-8387-5031-1*) Bucknell U Pr.

New Poetries & Some Old. Richard Kostelanetz. (Crosscurrents-Modern Critiques, Third Ser.). 262p. (C). 1991. 26.95 (*0-8093-1656-0*) S Ill U Pr.

New Poetry: An Anthology. Harriet Monroe. LC 78-64048. (Des Imagistes: Literature of the Imagist Movement Ser.). reprint ed. 49.50 (*0-404-17080-3*) AMS Pr.

New Poetry from a New Spain: The Generation of 1970: A Bilingual Anthology. Ed. by Dave Oliphant et al. Tr. by Constance Sulllivan et al from SPA. (Poiesis Ser.: No. 8). (Illus.). 400p. (C). 1993. 15.95 (*0-934840-15-6*) Studia Hispanica.

New Poetry from California: Dead/Requiem. Ivan Arguelles & Jack Foley. (Illus.). 127p. 1998. pap. 9.95 (*1-880766-16-7*) Pantograph Pr.

New Poets of Los Angeles. Intro. by Jack Grapes. LC 86-73085. 220p. (Orig.). 1989. pap. 12.50 (*0-941017-10-9*) Bombshelter Pr.

New Poker Games. Mike Caro. 156p. 1984. pap. 6.95 (*0-89746-040-5*) Gambling Times.

New Poland. Nevin O. Winter. LC 79-37920. (Select Bibliographies Reprint Ser.). 1977. reprint ed. 42.95 (*0-8369-6757-7*) Ayer.

New Police: Crime, Conflict & Control in Nineteenth-Century England. David Conrad Taylor. LC 96-32187. (New Frontiers in History Ser.). 196p. 1997. pap. 24.95 (*0-7190-4729-3*, Pub. by Manchester Univ Pr); text 74.95 (*0-7190-4728-5*, Pub. by Manchester Univ Pr) St Martin.

New Police Report Manual. 4th ed. Devallis Rutledge. LC 84-70351. (Illus.). 172p. (C). 1996. pap. 14.95 (*0-942728-12-2*) Copperhouse.

New Policies for Part-Time & Contingent Workers. Ed. by New Ways to Work Staff. 67p. 1992. 5.00 (*0-685-66556-9*, G-006) New Ways Work.

New Policies for the Part-Time & Contingent Workforce. Ed. by Virginia L. DuRivage. LC 92-28670. (Economic Policy Institute Ser.). 155p. (C). (gr. 13). 1992. text 70.95 (*1-56324-164-1*); pap. text 36.95 (*1-56324-165-X*) M E Sharpe.

New Policies, New Politics: Government's Response to Government's Growth. Lawrence D. Brown. LC 82-45979. 71p. 1983. pap. 7.95 (*0-8157-1165-4*) Brookings.

New Policy Imperatives for Energy Producers. Ed. by Ragaei E. El Mallakh & Dorothea H. El Mallakh. LC 80-81017. (Illus.). 1980. pap. 16.50 (*0-918714-06-0*) Intl Res Ctr Energy.

New Political Consciousness: A Context for Ecocommunity. Wendell G. Bradley. 176p. (Orig.). 1992. pap. write for info. (*0-9632130-2-4*) Lysander.

New Political Culture. Terry N. Clark. LC 98-159745. (Urban Policy Challenges Ser.). 1998. text 65.00 (*0-8133-2814-4*, Pub. by Westview) HarpC.

New Political Economy of EMU. Ed. by Jeffry Frieden et al. LC 98-24158. (Governance in Europe Ser.). 216p. 1998. 65.00 (*0-8476-9018-0*); pap. 24.95 (*0-8476-9019-9*) Rowman.

New Political Entities in Public & Private International Law: With Special Reference to the Palestinian Entity. Amos Shapira et al. LC 99-10552. 1999. 159.00 (*90-411-1155-7*) Kluwer Law Intl.

New Political Geography of Eastern Europe. John O'Loughlin & Herman Van der Wusten. LC 92-36085. 320p. 1993. 130.00 (*0-471-94812-8*) Wiley.

New Political Parties & Movements in the Soviet Union. Ed. by A. M. Babkina. 160p. (C). 1991. pap. text 125.00 (*1-56072-041-7*) Nova Sci Pubs.

New Political Realities & the Gulf: Egypt, Syria, & Jordan. Mary E. Morris. LC 92-46989. 1993. pap. 13.00 (*0-8330-1315-7*, MR-127-AF) Rand Corp.

New Politicians of Fifth-Century Athens. W. Robert Connor. LC 92-23958. 232p. (C). 1992. reprint ed. pap. text 14.95 (*0-87220-142-2*); reprint ed. lib. bdg. 34.95 (*0-87220-143-0*) Hackett Pub.

New Politics. Ed. by Ferdinand Muller-Rommel & Thomas Poguntke. LC 95-7762. (International Library of Politics & Comparative Government). (Illus.). 612p. 1995. text 199.95 (*1-85521-374-5*) Ashgate Pub Co.

***New Politics: Catholic Social Teaching for the Twenty First Century.** Paul Valley. 1998. pap. 26.00 (*0-334-02748-9*) TPI PA.

New Politics? Continuity & Change under MMP. Jonathan Boston et al. LC 96-173925. 200p. 1996. pap. 24.95 (*1-86940-138-7*, Pub. by Auckland Univ) Paul & Co Pubs.

***New Politics American Science.** Daniel S. Greenberg. 1998. 30.00 (*0-226-30634-8*) U Ch Pr.

New Politics in Trade Unions: Applying Organizational Theory to the Ecological Discourse on Nuclear Energy in Sweden & Germany. Detlef Jahn. 336p. 1993. 77.95 (*1-85521-411-3*, Pub. by Dartmth Pub) Ashgate Pub Co.

New Politics of American Foreign Policy. David A. Deese. 285p. 1993. pap. 31.95 (*0-312-09133-8*) St Martin.

***New Politics of British Local Governance.** Gerry Stoker. LC 99-47267. 2000. text 65.00 (*0-312-22803-1*) St Martin.

New Politics of British Trade Unionism: Union Power & the Thatcher Legacy. David Marsh. (Cornell International Industrial & Labor Relations Reports: No. 20). 288p. (Orig.). 1992. 45.00 (*0-87546-704-0*, ILR Press); pap. 17.95 (*0-87546-705-9*, ILR Press) Cornell U Pr.

New Politics of Class: Social Movements & Cultural Dynamics in Advanced Societies. Klaus Eder. (TCS Ser.: Vol. 23). (Illus.). 224p. 1993. 59.95 (*0-8039-8687-4*); pap. 24.95 (*0-8039-8868-0*) Sage.

***New Politics of Financing the UN.** Anthony McDermott. LC 99-23353. 1999. text 65.00 (*0-312-22224-6*) St Martin.

New Politics of Inequality. Thomas B. Edsall. 288p. 1985. reprint ed. pap. 8.95 (*0-393-30250-4*) Norton.

New Politics of Inequality in Latin America: Rethinking Participation & Representation. Ed. by Douglas A. Chalmers et al. (Oxford Studies in Democratization). (Illus.). 662p. 1997. pap. text 28.00 (*0-19-878183-0*) OUP.

New Politics of Inequaltiy in Latin America: Rethinking Participation & Representation. Ed. by Douglas A. Chalmers et al. LC 96-29002. (Oxford Studies in Democratization). (Illus.). 664p. 1997. text 85.00 (*0-19-878184-9*) OUP.

New Politics of Old Values. 3rd ed. John K. White. LC 98-27175. 306p. 1998. pap. 36.50 (*0-7618-1205-9*) U Pr of Amer.

New Politics of Pornography. Donald A. Downs. LC 89-34968. 290p. 1989. lib. bdg. 49.95 (*0-226-16162-5*) U Ch Pr.

New Politics of Pornography. Donald A. Downs. LC 89-34968. 290p. 1989. pap. text 17.95 (*0-226-16163-3*) U Ch Pr.

New Politics of Poverty: The Nonworking Poor in America. Lawrence M. Mead. LC 91-55458. 368p. 1993. pap. 16.00 (*0-465-05069-7*, Pub. by Basic) HarpC.

New Politics of Public Policy. Ed. by Marc K. Landy & Martin A. Levin. LC 94-24379. 384p. 1995. text 49.95 (*0-8018-4877-6*); pap. text 16.95 (*0-8018-4878-4*) Johns Hopkins.

New Politics of Race & Gender: The 1992 Yearbook of the Politics of Education Association. Ed. by Catherine Marshall. (Education Policy Perspectives Ser.). 230p. 1993. 69.95 (*0-7507-0176-5*, Falmer Pr) Taylor & Francis.

New Politics of Right. Betz. LC 97-50396. 288p. 1998. pap. 18.95 (*0-312-21338-7*); text 55.00 (*0-312-21134-1*) St Martin.

New Politics of Science. David Dickson. (Illus.). 416p. 1988. pap. text 15.95 (*0-226-14763-0*) U Ch Pr.

New Politics of Survival: Grassroots Movements in Central America. Ed. & Intro. by Minor Sinclair. (Illus.). 301p. (Orig.). 1995. pap. 15.00 (*0-85345-951-7*, PB9517, Pub. by Monthly Rev) NYU Pr.

***New Politics of the Budgetary Process.** 4th ed. Aaron Wildavsky & Naomi Caiden. 400p. 2000. pap. text 49.00 (*0-321-04255-7*) Longman.

***New Politics of the National Health Service.** Rudolf Klein. LC 00-39981. 2000. pap. write for info. (*0-13-017737-7*) P-H.

New Politics of the NHS. 3rd ed. Rudolf Klein. LC 95-17177. 265p. (C). 1995. pap. text 28.40 (*0-582-23882-X*) Addison-Wesley.

New Politics of the Old South: An Introduction to Southern Politics. Ed. by Charles S. Bullock, III & Mark J. Rozell. LC 97-36019. 296p. (Orig.). 1998. 63.00 (*0-8476-8612-4*); pap. 19.95 (*0-8476-8613-2*) Rowman.

***New Politics of the Welfare State.** 342p. 2000. text 72.00 (*0-19-829753-X*) OUP.

***New Politics of the Welfare State.** Ed. by Paul Pierson. 342p. 2000. pap. 19.95 (*0-19-829756-4*) OUP.

***New Politics of Tony Blair.** Melanie A. Sully. 128p. 2000. text 24.50 (*0-88033-985-3*) Col U Pr.

New Politics of U. S. Trade Policy see American Trade Politics & Supplement

New Politics of Unemployment: Radical Policy Initiatives in Western Europe. Hugh Compston. LC 96-26288. 240p. (C). 1996. 90.00 (*0-415-15054-X*); pap. 29.99 (*0-415-15055-8*) Routledge.

New Politics of Welfare: An Agenda for the 1990s. Ed. by Michael McCarthy. LC 89-12855. 274p. (Orig.). (C). 1989. pap. text 29.95 (*0-925065-23-4*) Lyceum IL.

***New Politics of Welfare: Social Justice in a Global Context.** Bill Jordan. LC 98-61178. 256p. 1998. 78.00 (*0-7619-6021-X*); pap. 24.95 (*0-7619-6022-8*) Sage.

New Polten: Profile of the Lower Austrian Capital. Otto Kapfinger & Michaela Steiner. (Illus.). 100p. 1997. pap. 30.00 (*3-211-82954-7*) Spr-Verlag.

New Polygamy: The Polyamorous Lifestyle As a Spiritual Descipline. Ed. by Aidan A. Kelly. (Illus.). 300p. 1994. 30.00 (*1-883322-02-2*) Agamemnon Pr.

New Polymeric Materials: Reactive Processes & Physical Properties: Invited Papers Presented at a Symposium, Naples, Italy, June, 1986. Ezio Martuscelli & Carlo Marchetta. 194p. 1987. lib. bdg. 85.00 (*90-6764-091-3*, Pub. by VSP) Coronet Bks.

New Polytechnic Dictionary of the Spanish & English Languages Vol. 1: English-Spanish. F. Beigbeder Atienza. (ENG & SPA.). 1733p. 1988. 395.00 (*0-7859-7141-6*) Fr & Eur.

New Polytechnic Dictionary of the Spanish & English Languages Vol. 1: Nuevo Diccionario Politecnico de las Lenguas English-Spanish. Federico B. Atienza. (ENG & SPA.). 3420p. 1988. 295.00 (*0-7859-0399-2*, M6238) Fr & Eur.

New Polytechnic Dictionary of the Spanish & English Languages Vol. 2: Nuevo Diccionario Politecnico de las Lenguas Espanola - Inglesa. Federico B. Atienza. (ENG & SPA.). 3420p. 1988. 300.00 (*0-8288-0664-0*, M6237) Fr & Eur.

New Polytechnic Dictionary of the Spanish & English Languages Vol. 2: Spanish-English. F. Beigbeder Atienza. (ENG & SPA.). 1662p. 1988. 395.00 (*0-7859-7142-4*) Fr & Eur.

New Pomeranian. Sari B. Tietjen. (Illus.). 192p. 1987. 27.95 (*0-87605-251-0*) Howell Bks.

New Pony. H. Amery. (Farmyard Tales Ser.). (Illus.). 64p. (J). (ps up). 1993. pap. 3.95 (*0-7460-1414-7*) EDC.

New Pony Sticker Book. Alastair Smith. (Farmyard Tales Sticker Storybook Ser.). (Illus.). 18p. (Orig.). (J). (ps up). 1997. pap. 6.95 (*0-7460-3138-6*, Usborne) EDC.

New Populism & The New Europe: New Protest Parties in Sweden in a Comparative Perspective. Paul Taggart. 256p. 1996. text 65.00 (*0-312-16204-9*) St Martin.

New Populist Reader. Karl G. Trautman. LC 97-11072. 264p. 1997. 69.50 (*0-275-96023-4*, Praeger Pubs); pap. 24.95 (*0-275-96024-2*, Praeger Pubs) Greenwood.

New Porcine History of Philosophy & Religion. James C. Taylor. 64p. (Orig.). 1992. pap. 4.95 (*0-687-27866-X*) Abingdon.

New Portable MBA. 2nd ed. Eliza G. Collins & Mary A. Devanna. 441p. 1994. 27.95 (*0-471-08004-7*) Wiley.

New Portfolios. Intro. by Leland D. Rice. (Illus.). 24p. 1976. 2.00 (*0-915478-35-8*) Montgomery Gallery.

New Portugal: Democracy & Europe. Ed. by Richard Herr. LC 92-34235. (Research Ser.: No. 86). 205p. (C). 1992. pap. text 15.50 (*0-87725-186-X*) U of Cal IAS.

New Portuguese Letters. Maria I. Barreno. 326p. 1994. pap. 11.95 (*0-930523-98-9*) Readers Intl.

New Portuguese Letters. Maria I. Barreno et al. Tr. by Helen R. Lane & Faith Gillespie. 326p. 1994. 19.95 (*0-930523-97-0*) Readers Intl.

New Pos Just Say "Yes" Activity Book. Art Fettig. LC 86-83236. (Illus.). 96p. 1994. pap. 6.95 (*0-916927-21-0*) Growth Unltd.

New Positioning: The Latest on the World's #1 Business Strategy. Jack Trout. (Illus.). 173p. 1996. pap. 12.95 (*0-07-065328-3*) McGraw.

New Possibilities for Weight Reduction. Ed. by J. C. Somogyi. (Bibliotheca Nutritio et Dieta Ser.: No. 39). (Illus.). xx, 68p. 1986. 68.75 (*3-8055-4416-2*) S Karger.

New Possibilities in Gear Finishing Using the Form Grinding Method. Gerhard Sulzer. (Technical Papers: Vol. P129.28). (Illus.). 18p. 1982. pap. text 30.00 (*1-55589-520-4*) AGMA.

New Possibilities, New Paradigms? Ed. by Roberta J. Park & Helen M. Eckert. LC 90-23215. (American Academy of Physical Education Papers). 176p. 1991. pap. text 15.00 (*0-87322-313-6*, BPAR0313) Human Kinetics.

***New Postcard Graphics.** Ed. by Pie Books Editorial Staff. (Illus.). 224p. 1999. pap. 89.95 (*4-89444-110-1*, Pub. by Pie Bks) Bks Nippan.

New Pots from Old: A Recycling Tale. Papa Joe. (Step into a Story Book Ser.). 19p. 1996. pap. 3.50 (*1-889238-00-7*) Papa Joes.

New Potty: Gina & Mercer Mayer. Gina Mayer & Mercer Mayer. (Little Look-Look Bks.). (Illus.). 24p. (J). (ps-3). 1992. 1.79 (*0-307-11523-2*, 11523, Goldn Books) Gldn Bks Pub Co.

New Poverty: Families in Postmodern Society. David Cheal. LC 95-50520. 232p. 1999. pap. 22.95 (*0-275-96584-8*, Praeger Pubs) Greenwood.

New Poverty: Families in Postmodern Society, 115. David Cheal. LC 95-50520. (Contributions in Sociology Ser.: No. 115). 232p. 1996. 59.95 (*0-313-29444-5*, Greenwood Pr) Greenwood.

***New Poverty in Canada.** Abdolmohammed Kazemipur & Shiva S. Halli. (Illus.). 250p. 1999. pap. 19.95 (*1-55077-108-6*) Thompson Educ.

New Poverty Row: Independent Filmmakers As Distributors. Fred O. Ray. LC 91-52743. (Illus.). 240p. 1991. lib. bdg. 39.95 (*0-89950-628-3*) McFarland & Co.

***New Power.** Christine Lowther et al. 72p. 1999. pap. 9.75 (*0-921411-94-4*) Genl Dist Srvs.

New PR Client Service Manual: Firm Planning, Growth & Management in the Electronic Age. 3rd ed. Ed. by Tom Gable. (Illus.). 290p. 1997. pap. 125.00 (*0-9639708-8-7*) Gable Grp.

"New" PR Client Service Manual: Managing for Results into the 21st Century. 2nd ed. Ed. by Tom Gable. (Illus.). 1996. pap. 95.00 (*0-9639708-9-5*) Gable Grp.

New Practical Diving: A Complete Manual for Compressed Air Divers. Tom Mount & Akira J. Ikehara. LC 79-52941. (Illus.). 200p. 1980. reprint ed. pap. 19.95 (*0-87024-300-4*) U of Miami Pr.

New Practical English-Chinese Dictionary. (CHI & ENG.). 2410p. 45.00 (*0-686-92368-5*, M-9552) Fr & Eur.

New Practical Guide for Parish Councils. William J. Rademacher & Marliss Rogers. LC 88-50662. 264p. (Orig.). 1988. pap. 12.95 (*0-89622-371-X*) Twenty-Third.

New Practice Handbook: A Guide to Establishing a Successful Medical Practice. Maryann Szostak-Ricardo. 115p. 1994. student ed. 49.95 (*1-57066-029-8*) Practice Mgmt Info.

New Prayer Book Guide to Christian Education. rev. ed. Ed. by Joseph Russell. 225p. (Orig.). 1996. pap. 15.95 (*1-56101-121-5*) Cowley Pubns.

New Prayers. Michel Quoist. 160p. 1990. pap. 12.95 (*0-8245-0983-8*, Pub. by Crossroad NY) Natl Bk Netwk.

New Precast Prestressed System Saves Money in Hawaii Hotel. (PCI Journal Reprints Ser.). 6p. 1973. pap. 10.00 (*0-686-40055-0*, JR128) P-PCI.

New Precious Metals Market: How the Changes in Fundamentals Are Creating Extraordinary Profit Opportunities. Philip Gotthelf. LC 97-35304. 1998. 40.00 (*0-7863-0840-0*, Irwn Prfssnl) McGraw-Hill Prof.

***New Predator: Women Who Kill.** Schurman-Kauflin. 200p. 2000. pap. 22.95 (*1-892941-58-9*, Pub. by Algora Pubng) Midpt Trade.

New Pregnancy & Childbirth. 2nd ed. Elizabeth Palmer. (C). 1993. pap. text. write for info. (*0-201-53932-2*) Addison-Wesley.

New Premium Coin Book. T. Elder. (Illus.). 1935. pap. 10.00 (*0-932106-20-X*) S J Durst.

***New Prescription: Marijuana As Medicine.** 2nd ed. Martin Martinez & Francis Podrebarac. 142p. 2000. pap. text 14.95 (*0-932551-35-1*) Quick Am Pub.

New Prescription Drug Reference Guide. Consumer Guide Editors. (Illus.). 448p. 1993. 14.98 (*1-56173-601-5*, 3210801) Pubns Intl Ltd.

New Prescription for Women's Health: Getting the Best Medical Care in a Man's World. Bernadine Healy. 560p. 1996. pap. 12.95 (*0-14-023727-5*, Penguin Bks) Viking Penguin.

New Presentation of the Prometheus Bound of Aischylos: Wherein is Set Forth the Hidden Meaning of the Myth (1925) James M. Pryse. 209p. 1996. reprint ed. pap. 17.95 (*1-56459-823-3*) Kessinger Pub.

New Presidential Elite: Men & Women in National Politics. Jeane Kirkpatrick. LC 76-1816. 606p. 1976. 55.00 (*0-87154-475-X*) Russell Sage.

New Press Guide to Multicultural Resources for Young Readers. Ed. by Daphne Muse. (Illus.). 700p. 1997. 60.00 (*1-56584-339-8*, Pub. by New Press NY) Norton.

New Pressed Flower Designs. Alison Morrison. 1999. 14.95 (*1-85391-548-3*) Merehurst Ltd.

New Pressure Cooker Cookbook. Pat Dailey. (Illus.). 160p. 1990. pap. 14.95 (*0-8092-4186-2*, 418620, Contemporary Bks) NTC Contemp Pub Co.

New Pressures, New Responses in Religious Life. John P. Dondero & Thomas D. Frary. LC 76-26585. 1979. pap. 5.95 (*0-8189-0332-5*) Alba.

New Prevention of Terrorism Act: The Case for Repeal. Catherine Scorer et al. (C). 1988. 21.00 (*0-946088-13-6*, Pub. by NCCL) St Mut.

New Priest in Conception Bay, 2 vols. Robert T. Lowell. reprint ed. write for info. (*0-318-53718-4*); reprint ed. write for info. (*0-318-53719-2*) Irvington.

New Priest in Conception Bay. Robert T. Lowell. (Notable American Authors Ser.). 1999. reprint ed. lib. bdg. 125.00 (*0-7812-3903-6*) Rprt Serv.

New Priest in Conception Bay, 2 vols., Set. Robert T. Lowell. LC 72-104520. reprint ed. lib. bdg. 40.00 (*0-8398-1173-X*) Irvington.

New Primary Teacher's Guide to Implementing the National Curriculum. Ed. by Kate Ashcroft & David Palacio. LC 97-202456. 240p. 1996. teacher ed. 79.95 (*0-7507-0592-2*, Falmer Pr); pap., teacher ed. 27.95 (*0-7507-0593-0*, Falmer Pr) Taylor & Francis.

***New Primer in Radical Criminology: Critical Perspectives on Crime, Power & Identity.** 3rd rev. ed. Michael J. Lynch et al. LC HV6018.L95 1989. 154p. 2000. pap. text 19.90 (*1-881798-21-6*, Pub. by Willow Tree NY) Lib Res.

***New Prince.** Dick Morris. 256p. 2000. pap. text 15.95 (*1-58063-147-9*) Renaissance.

New Prince: Machiavelli Updated for the 21st Century. Dick Morris. LC 99-21767. 240p. 1999. 21.95 (*1-58063-079-0*) Renaissance.

New Princeton Encyclopedia of Poetry & Poetics. Ed. by Alex Preminger et al. 1400p. 1996. reprint ed. 19.98 (*1-56731-152-0*, MJF Bks) Fine Comms.

New Princeton Handbook of Poetic Terms. Ed. by T. V. Brogan. LC 93-43944. 360p. (C). 1994. text 49.50 (*0-691-03671-3*, Pub. by Princeton U Pr); pap. text 18.95 (*0-691-03672-1*, Pub. by Princeton U Pr) Cal Prin Full Svc.

New Princeton Handbook of Poetic Terms. Terry V. Brogan. LC 93-43944. 355p. 1994. reprint ed. pap. 110.10 (*0-608-07173-0*, 206739800009) Bks Demand.

New Principles in Organic Chemistry: The Discovery & Invention of Chemical Reactions. Ed. by Derek H. Barton. 400p. 1996. text 99.00 (*981-02-1361-1*) World Scientific Pub.

New Principles of Political Economy. Jean C. Simonde De Sismondi. Tr. by Richard Hyse. 780p. 1990. 89.95 (*0-88738-336-X*) Transaction Pubs.

New Pritikin Program. Robert C. Pritikin. Ed. by Julie Rubenstein. 464p. 1991. reprint ed. per. 6.99 (*0-671-73194-7*) PB.

New Private International Law of Contract of the European Community. Peter Kaye. 560p. 1993. 115.95 (*1-85521-276-5*, Pub. by Dartmth Pub) Ashgate Pub Co.

New Probe by the Workers League Against the Communist Movement: Record of an Antilabor Outfit, from the Gelfand Harassment Case to the Campaign Against Mark Curtis. 30p. 1995. pap. 5.00 (*0-87348-825-3*) Pathfinder NY.

New Problems in Astronomy: Proceedings of the I.A.U. Symposium, No. 61, Perth, Western, Australia, Aug. 13-17, 1973. International Astronomical Union Staff. Ed.

N

An Asterisk (*) at the beginning of an entry indicates that the title is appearing for the first time.

by W. Gliese et al. LC 73-94453. (Symposia of the International Astronomical Union Ser.: No. 61). 280p. 1974. lib. bdg. 141.50 (*90-277-0444-9*) Kluwer Academic.

New Problems in Differential Geometry. M. Rahuler. (Series on Soviet & East European Mathematics: Vol. 8). 200p. (C). 1993. text 44.00 (*981-02-0819-7*) World Scientific Pub.

New Problems, Methods & Techniques in Quantum Field Theory & Statistical Mechanics. Ed. by M. G. Rasetti. 232p. (C). 1990. text 61.00 (*981-02-0225-3*); pap. text 33.00 (*981-02-0226-1*) World Scientific Pub.

New Procedures in Nuclear Medicine. Ed. by Richard P. Spencer. LC 88-26260. 224p. 1989. 134.00 (*0-8493-4592-8*, R895, CRC Reprint) Franklin.

***New Proclamation: Advent to Holy Week, 2000-2001 Series C.** Marshall D. Johnson & K. C. Hanson. 2000. pap. 25.00 (*0-8006-4243-0*, Fortress Pr) Augsburg Fortress.

New Proclamation: Easter to All Saints. Robin Mattison et al. LC 99-210103. (Proclamation: Aids for Interpreting the Church Year, 1999, Series A). 224p. 1998. pap. 24.99 (*0-8006-4240-6*, 1-4240) Augsburg Fortress.

***New Proclamation Series B: 2000 Easter to All Saints.** Ed. by Neil Elliott et al. 304p. 1999. pap. 25.00 (*0-8006-4242-2*, Fortress Pr) Augsburg Fortress.

***New Proclamation Year c. 2000-2001: Advent Through Holy Week.** Richard S. Ascough. LC 00-35467. 2000. 25.00 (*0-8006-4244-9*, Fortress Pr) Augsburg Fortress.

New Product & Brand Management: Marketing Engineering Applications. Gary Lilien. 144p. (C). 1998. pap. text 33.00 (*0-321-04643-9*, Prentice Hall) P-H.

New Product Development. Barclay et al. 196p. pap. 65.95 (*0-7506-4998-4*) Buttrwrth-Heinemann.

New Product Development. Jones Staff. LC 97-126064. 240p. 1996. pap. text 39.95 (*0-7506-2427-2*) Buttrwrth-Heinemann.

***New Product Development.** Robert M. Monczka. LC 99-47759. 2000. write for info. (*0-87389-468-5*) ASQ Qual Pr.

New Product Development. Thomas. (C). Date not set. text. write for info. (*0-395-82495-8*) HM.

New Product Development: A Practical Workbook for Improving Performance. I. Barclay et al. 192p. Date not set. text 170.00 (*1-85573-447-8*, Pub. by Woodhead Pubng) Am Educ Systs.

New Product Development: A Reader. Hart. 1998. pap. 21.99 (*1-86152-441-2*) Thomson Learn.

New Product Development: Design & Analysis. Ronald E. Kmetovicz. LC 91-28941. (New Dimensions in Engineering Ser.). 352p. 1992. 120.00 (*0-471-55536-3*) Wiley.

New Product Development: Its Marketing Research & Management. A. J. Oswald & S. J. Mascarenhas. (C). 1987. 17.50 (*81-204-0231-6*, Pub. by Oxford IBH) S Asia.

New Product Development: Managing & Forecasting for Strategic Success. Robert J. Thomas. LC 93-15395. (Portable MBA Ser.). 368p. 1993. 39.95 (*0-471-57226-8*) Wiley.

New Product Development: Responding to Market Demands. 2nd ed. George Gruenwald. 1995. VHS 59.95 (*0-8442-3350-1*, NTC Business Bks) NTC Contemp Pub Co.

New Product Development: Responding to Market Demands. 2nd ed. George Gruenwald. (Illus.). 480p. 1995. 39.95 (*0-8442-3352-8*, NTC Business Bks) NTC Contemp Pub Co.

New Product Development & Marketing: A Practical Guide. Italo S. Servi. LC 89-70956. 200p. 1990. 55.00 (*0-275-93403-9*, C3403, Greenwood Pr) Greenwood.

New Product Development Checklists. George Gruenwald. LC 90-43722. (Illus.). 128p. 1994. pap. 22.95 (*0-8442-3217-3*, NTC Business Bks) NTC Contemp Pub Co.

***New Product Diffusion Models.** Vijay Mahajan et al. LC 00-24639. (International Series in Quantitative Marketing). 2000. write for info. (*0-7923-7751-6*) Kluwer Academic.

New Product Introduction. J. David Viale. (Crisp 50-Minute Ser.). (Illus.). 96p. 1998. pap. 10.95 (*1-56052-492-8*) Crisp Pubns.

***New Product Management.** 6th ed. Crawford. LC 99-34882. 560p. 1999. 86.25 (*0-07-027552-1*) McGraw.

New Product Planning Management of the Marketing-R & D Interface: An Annotated Bibliography. Douglas W. Mellott, Jr. LC 76-57928. (American Marketing Association Bibliography Ser.: No. 26). 51p. reprint ed. pap. 30.00 (*0-608-11938-5*, 202335300032) Bks Demand.

New Product Programs: Their Planning & Control. David H. Uman. LC 72-78604. 159p. reprint ed. pap. 49.30 (*0-608-16192-6*, 205615700052) Bks Demand.

New Product Screening: A Step-Wise Approach. William C. Lesch & David Rupert. LC 93-15579. (Illus.). 116p. 1994. lib. bdg. 39.95 (*1-56024-404-6*) Haworth Pr.

New Product Shakeout. Robert McMath. write for info. (*0-8129-2698-6*, Times Bks) Crown Pub Group.

New Product Shots: A Guide to Professional Lighting Techniques. Alex Larg. (Pro-Lighting Ser.). 100p. 1999. pap. 35.00 (*2-88046-371-8*, Rotovision) Watsn-Guptill.

New Product Success Stories: Lessons from Leading Innovators. Ed. by Robert J. Thomas. LC 94-26557. 352p. 1994. 29.95 (*0-471-01320-X*) Wiley.

New Production of Knowledge: The Dynamics of Science & Research in Contemporary Societies. Michael Gibbons et al. 192p. 1994. 65.00 (*0-8039-7793-X*); pap. 24.95 (*0-8039-7794-8*) Sage.

New Products: The Key Factors in Success. Robert G. Cooper & Elko J. Kleinschmidt. LC 90-49464. 52p. 1990. pap. text 20.00 (*0-87757-213-5*) Am Mktg.

New Products & Applications in Surfactant Technology: Annual Surfactants Review. Ed. by David R. Karsa. 248p. 1998. write for info. (*1-85075-872-7*, Pub. by Sheffield Acad) CUP Services.

New Products Management. 3rd ed. C. Merle Crawford. 592p. (C). 1990. text 66.95 (*0-256-08207-3*, 09-1566-03, Irwn McGrw-H) McGrw-H Hghr Educ.

New Products Management. 4th ed. C. Merle Crawford. LC 93-20131. (Marketing Ser.). (Illus.). 528p. (C). 1993. text 69.95 (*0-256-12152-4*, Irwn McGrw-H) McGrw-H Hghr Educ.

New Products Management, International. 3rd ed. C. Merle Crawford. (C). 1991. text, student ed. 30.95 (*0-256-11406-4*, Irwn McGrw-H) McGrw-H Hghr Educ.

New Products, New Profits: Company Experiences in New Product Planning. American Management Association, Research Developm. Ed. by Elizabeth Marting. LC 64-12772. 303p. reprint ed. pap. 94.00 (*0-608-12964-X*, 202391900034) Bks Demand.

New Profession, Old Order: Engineers & German Society, 1815-1914. C. W. Gispen. (Illus.). 367p. (C). 1990. text 74.95 (*0-521-37198-8*) Cambridge U Pr.

New Professional Chef. 5th ed. Culinary Institute of America Staff. (Illus.). 848p. 1991. pap., teacher ed. 23.95 (*0-442-00831-7*, VNR) Wiley.

New Professional Chef. 5th ed. Culinary Institute of America Staff. 869p. 1991. 49.95 (*0-471-29372-5*, VNR) Wiley.

New Professional Chef. 5th ed. Culinary Institute of America Staff. 1992. 49.95 (*0-471-29367-9*, VNR) Wiley.

New Professional Chef. 6th ed. Culinary Institute of America, Inc., Staff. LC 95-35590. (Culinary Arts Ser.). (Illus.). 1216p. 1996. text 59.95 (*0-442-01961-0*, VNR) Wiley.

New Professional Chef. 6th ed. Culinary Institute of America Staff. (Illus.). 1190p. 1997. 64.95 (*0-471-28679-6*, VNR) Wiley.

New Professional Chef: Academy Edition. 5th ed. CIA Staff. 1997. 54.95 (*0-442-01143-1*, VNR) Wiley.

New Professional Image: From Corporate Casual to the Ultimate Power Look, How to Tailor Your Appearance. Susan Bixler. LC 97-6553. 1997. pap. text 12.95 (*1-55850-729-9*) Adams Media.

"New" Professional Touch. 2nd ed. Eve Cappello. 128p. 1988. pap. 10.00 (*0-8403-4910-6*) Eve Cappello.

New Professionalism: Connecting Science & Spirit to Empower Professional (& Other) Relationships. Illus. by Humberto Lopez. 152p. 1998. pap. 16.95 (*0-9661864-0-0*) Harmony-Quest.

New Professionals: Managing Today's High-Technology Employees. Mary A. Von Glinow. 224p. 1988. text 32.95 (*0-88730-271-8*, HarpBusn) HarpInfo.

New Professionals: The Rise of Network Marketing as the Next Major Profession. Rene R. Yarnell & Charles King. 304p. 2000. pap. 15.00 (*0-7615-1966-1*) Prima Pub.

New Professor's Handbook: A Guide to Teaching & Research in Engineering & Science. Cliff I. Davidson & Susan A. Ambrose. 216p. (C). 1994. pap. text 24.95 (*1-882982-01-0*) Anker Pub.

New Proficiency English, Bk. 3. Fowler. Date not set. pap. text. write for info. (*0-17-555607-5*) Addison-Wesley.

New Program for Democratic Socialism: Lessons from the Market-Planning Experience in Austria. Leland G. Stauber. 412p. 1987. 35.00 (*0-9620720-0-1*) Four Willows Pr.

New Program of the Communist Party, U. S. A: A Draft. LC 66-19254. 1966. pap. 0.95 (*0-87898-006-7*) New Outlook.

New Programme & New Constitution of the Revolutionary Communist Party, U. S. A. Revolutionary Communist Party, U S A. Staff. 128p. (Orig.). (C). 1981. pap. 3.00 (*0-89851-037-6*) RCP Pubns.

New Programmed Instruction in Braille. 2nd ed. Samuel C. Ashcroft et al. 386p. 1994. spiral bd. 49.00 (*0-9634229-3-6*) SCALARS Pub.

New Progress in China's Special Economic Zones. Sun Xiuping et al. 229p. 1997. pap. 9.95 (*7-119-00523-5*, Pub. by Foreign Lang) China Bks.

New Progress in Mathematics, Grade 8, Workbook. rev. ed. Rose Anita McDonnell et al. (New Progress in Mathematics Ser.: Vol. 2). (Illus.). 208p. (YA). (gr. 8-9). 1993. pap., wbk. ed. 9.75 (*0-8215-1728-7*) Sadlier.

New Progress in Mathematics, Grade 8, Workbook, Teacher's Edition. rev. ed. Rose Anita McDonnell et al. (New Progress in Mathematics Ser.: Vol. 2). (Illus.). 208p. 1993. pap., teacher ed., wbk. ed. 13.95 (*0-8215-1758-9*) Sadlier.

New Progress in Mathematics, Grade 8, Student Test Booklet, Free Response. rev. ed. Rose Anita McDonnell et al. (New Progress in Mathematics Ser.: Vol. 2). (Illus.). 44p. (YA). (gr. 8-9). 1994. pap. write for info. (*0-8215-1748-1*) Sadlier.

New Progress in Mathematics, Grade 8, Student Test Booklet, Standardized. rev. ed. Rose Anita McDonnell et al. (New Progress in Mathematics Ser.: Vol. 2). (Illus.). 44p. (YA). (gr. 8-9). 1994. pap. 35.73 (*0-8215-1768-6*) Sadlier.

New Progress in Mathematics, Grade 8, Student Text: An Innovative Approach Including Two Options: Pre-Algebra, Algebra. rev. ed. Rose Anita McDonnell et al. (New Progress in Mathematics Ser.: Vol. 2). (Illus.). 578p. (YA). (gr. 8-9). 1996. pap. text 40.50 (*0-8215-1708-2*) Sadlier.

New Progress in Mathematics, Grade 8, Teacher's Edition: An Innovative Approach Including Two Options: Pre-Algebra, Algebra. rev. ed. Rose Anita McDonnell et al. (New Progress in Mathematics Ser.: Vol. 2). (Illus.). 704p. 1996. pap., teacher ed. 67.50 (*0-8215-1718-X*) Sadlier.

New Progress in Mathematics, Grade 7, Workbook, Teacher's Edition. rev. ed. Rose Anita McDonnell et al. (New Progress in Mathematics Ser.: Vol. 2). (Illus.). 176p. 1994. pap., teacher ed., wbk. ed. 13.95 (*0-8215-1757-0*) Sadlier.

New Progress in Mathematics, Grade 7, Workbook. rev. ed. Rose Anita McDonnell et al. (New Progress in Mathematics Ser.: Vol. 2). (Illus.). 178p. (YA). (gr. 7-8). 1993. pap., wbk. ed. 9.75 (*0-8215-1727-9*) Sadlier.

New Progress in Mathematics, Grade 7, Student Test Booklet, Free Response. rev. ed. Rose Anita McDonnell et al. (New Progress in Mathematics Ser.: Vol. 2). (Illus.). 44p. (YA). (gr. 7-8). 1994. pap. write for info. (*0-8215-1747-3*) Sadlier.

New Progress in Mathematics, Grade 7, Student Test Booklet, Standardized. rev. ed. Rose Anita McDonnell et al. (New Progress in Mathematics Ser.: Vol. 2). (Illus.). 44p. (YA). (gr. 7-8). 1994. pap. 35.73 (*0-8215-1767-8*) Sadlier.

New Progress in Mathematics, Grade 7, Student Text: With Pre-Algebra Readiness. rev. ed. Rose Anita McDonnell et al. (New Progress in Mathematics Ser.: Vol. 2). (Illus.). 516p. (YA). (gr. 7-8). 1996. text 40.50 (*0-8215-1707-4*) Sadlier.

New Progress in Mathematics, Grade 7, Teacher's Edition: With Pre-Algebra Readiness. rev. ed. Rose Anita McDonnell et al. (New Progress in Mathematics Ser.: Vol. 2). (Illus.). 632p. 1996. pap., teacher ed. 67.50 (*0-8215-1717-1*) Sadlier.

New Progress to First Certificate. 208p. 1996. pap. text 17.95 (*0-521-49985-2*) Cambridge U Pr.

New Progress to First Certificate. Leo Jones. 1997. teacher ed. 18.95 (*0-521-49986-0*); student ed. 17.95 (*0-521-49988-7*) Cambridge U Pr.

***New Progressive Era: Toward a Fair & Deliberative Democracy.** Peter Levine. LC 99-45647. 304p. 2000. pap. 19.95 (*0-8476-9574-3*); text 65.00 (*0-8476-9573-5*) Rowman.

New Project Management: Tools for the Age of Rapid Change, Corporate Reengineering & Other Business Realities. J. Davidson Frame. (Business-Management Ser.). 352p. 1994. 32.95 (*1-55542-662-X*) Jossey-Bass.

New Project Management: Winning Through the Competitive Advantage. 2nd ed. Deborah S. Kezsbom & Katherine A. Edward. LC 99-45548. 512p. 2000. text 89.99 (*0-471-25494-0*) Wiley.

***New Projects.** ARCO Editorial Board Staff. 2000. pap. 39.95 (*84-8185-235-X*) Arco Edit.

New Promise of American Life. William A. Schambra et al. Ed. by Chester E. Finn, Jr. & Lamar Alexander. LC 96-206261. 400p. (Orig.). 1995. pap. 12.95 (*1-55813-053-5*) Hudson Instit IN.

New Promising Electrochemical Systems for Rechargeable Batteries: Proceedings of the NATO Advanced Research Workshop, Puscha Voditsa Near Kiev, Ukraine, May 14 - 17, 1995. Ed. by V. Barsukov & F. Beck. LC 96-1342. (NATO Advanced Science Institutes Ser.: No. 3). 536p. (C). 1996. text 291.00 (*0-7923-3948-7*) Kluwer Academic.

New Pronouncing Dictionary of Plant Names. 64p. 1964. pap. 2.95 (*1-887632-50-6*) Amer Nurseryman Pub.

New Prosperity: Investment Opportunities in Long-Wave Economic Cycles. Jacob I. Bernstein. 1988. 19.95 (*0-317-03945-8*) NY Inst Finance.

New Protectionism: Protecting the Future Against Free Trade. Tim Lang & Colin Hines. LC 93-28024. 208p. 1993. pap. 11.95 (*1-56584-135-2*, Pub. by New Press NY) Norton.

New Protein Foods in Human Health: Nutrition, Prevention & Therapy. F. H. Steinke et al. (Illus.). 232p. 1991. lib. bdg. 129.00 (*0-8493-6904-5*, TX558) CRC Pr.

New Protein Techniques, Vol. 3. Ed. by John M. Walker. LC 84-15696. (Methods in Molecular Biology Ser.). (Illus.). 540p. 1988. 69.50 (*0-89603-126-8*) Humana.

New Protein Technologies. Business Communications Co., Inc. Staff. 313p. 1991. 2850.00 (*0-89336-769-9*, C-117) BCC.

New Provencal Cuisine: Innovative Recipes from the South of France. Louisa Jones. (Illus.). 168p. 1995. 29.95 (*0-8118-0800-9*) Chronicle Bks.

New Providence. Joan Gonazlik & Jane Coddington. LC 98-86140. (Images of America Ser.). (Illus.). (Orig.). 1998. pap. 16.99 (*0-7524-1369-4*) Arcadia Publng.

New Providence: A Changing Cityscape. Renata Von Tscharner & Ronald L. Fleming. (Illus.). 26p. (J). (ps up). 1987. 10.95 (*0-15-200540-4*, Gulliver Bks) Harcourt.

New Provinces: Poems of Several Authors. LC 76-45350. (Literature of Canada Ser.: 20). xxxii, viii, 77p. 1976. write for info. (*0-8020-2246-4*) U of Toronto Pr.

New Provinces: Poems of Several Authors. Intro. by Michael Gnarowski. LC 76-45350. (Literature of Canada Ser.: No. 20). 120p. reprint ed. pap. 37.20 (*0-7837-4292-4*, 204398400012) Bks Demand.

New Psalms for New Moms: A Keepsake Journal. Linda A. Olson. LC 98-53387. (Illus.). 1999. 15.00 (*0-8170-1298-2*) Judson.

New Psy-Cosmetologist. Donald W. Scoleri & Lewis E. Losoncy. (Illus.). 137p. (Orig.). 1985. pap. text 12.95 (*0-9615591-0-1*) People Media.

New Psychiatry. Wilbur. 1994. 23.99 (*0-02-933220-6*) S&S Trade.

New Psychiatry: The Essential Guide to State-of-the-Art Therapy, Medication, & Emotional Health. Jack M. Gorman. (Illus.). 389p. 1998. text 27.00 (*0-7881-5563-6*) DIANE Pub.

New Psychology: Its Message, Principles & Practice (1909) William W. Atkinson. 200p. 1998. reprint ed. pap. 18.95 (*0-7661-0265-3*) Kessinger Pub.

New Psychology Complete: Mind the Builder & Scientific Man Building (1922) A. A. Lindsay. 446p. 1998. reprint ed. pap. 29.95 (*0-7661-0553-9*) Kessinger Pub.

New Psychology of Language: Cognitive & Functional Approaches to Language Structure. Ed. by Michael Tomasello. LC 98-11415. 300p. 1998. write for info. (*0-8058-2576-2*); pap. 29.85 (*0-8058-2577-0*) L Erlbaum Assocs.

New Psychology of Men. Ed. by Ronald Levant & William Pollack. LC 94-41028. 352p. 1995. pap. 42.00 (*0-465-08656-X*, Pub. by Basic) HarpC.

New Psychology of Women: Gender, Culture & Ethnicity. Hilary M. Lips. LC 98-19271. xviii, 413p. 1999. pap. text 40.00 (*1-55934-334-6*, 334-6) Mayfield Pub.

New Psychology of Women: Instructor's Manual. Hilary M. Lips. (C). 1999. pap. text. write for info. (*0-7674-1047-5*, 1047-5) Mayfield Pub.

New Psychometrics: Science, Psychology, & Measurement. Paul Kline. LC 98-13276. 208p. (C). 1998. 85.00 (*0-415-18751-6*) Routledge.

***New Psychotherapy for Men.** William S. Pollack & Ronald F. Levant. LC 98-5652. 318p. 1998. 64.50 (*0-471-17772-5*) Wiley.

New Psychotherapy for Traditional Men. Gary R. Brooks. LC 97-45455. 288p. 1998. 36.95 (*0-7879-4123-9*) Jossey-Bass.

New Public: Professional Communication & the Means of Social Influence. Leon H. Mayhew. LC 96-49355. (Cultural Social Studies). 344p. (C). 1997. text 59.95 (*0-521-48146-5*) Cambridge U Pr.

New Public: Professional Communication & the Means of Social Influence. Leon H. Mayhew. LC 96-49355. (Cultural Social Studies). 332p. (C). 1997. pap. 22.95 (*0-521-48493-6*) Cambridge U Pr.

New Public Architecture. Jeremy Myerson. (Illus.). 240p. 1996. 65.00 (*1-85669-083-0*, Pub. by L King Pubng) Bks Nippan.

New Public Health. John Ashton & Howard Seymour. 160p. 1988. 110.00 (*0-335-15555-3*); pap. 37.95 (*0-335-15550-2*) OpUniv Pr.

New Public Health. Tulchinsky. (Illus.). 450p. (C). 1999. pap. 69.95 (*0-12-703350-5*) Acad Pr.

New Public Health. Hibbert W. Hill. Ed. by Barbara G. Rosenkrantz. LC 76-40630. (Public Health in America Ser.). (Illus.). 1977. reprint ed. lib. bdg. 20.95 (*0-405-09823-5*) Ayer.

New Public Health: Health & Self in the Age of Risk. Alan Petersen & Deborah Lupton. 224p. (C). 1997. 69.95 (*0-7619-5403-1*, 54031); pap. 25.95 (*0-7619-5404-X*, 5404X) Sage.

New Public Health Redesigning Care for Social Responsiblity. Ed. by Rosemarie Rowney & Stephen Holzemer. (Council of Community Health Services Monograph Ser.: Vol. II). 150p. 1997. 23.95 (*0-88737-747-5*, 19-7475, NLN Pr) Natl League Nurse.

***New Public Management: Improving Research & Policy Dialogue.** Michael Barzelay. LC 00-55168. 2001. write for info. (*0-520-22443-4*) U CA Pr.

New Public Management Canada in Comparative. Peter Aucoin. 280p. 1996. pap. 19.95 (*0-88645-180-9*, Pub. by Inst Res Pub) Ashgate Pub Co.

New Public Management in Action. Ewan Ferlie. (Illus.). 298p. 1996. pap. text 35.00 (*0-19-828903-0*) OUP.

New Public Personnel Administration. 4th ed. Felix A. Nigro & Lloyd G. Nigro. LC 92-61962. 328p. (C). 1993. boxed set 50.00 (*0-87581-374-7*, NPPA4) F E Peacock Pubs.

New Public Policy for Neighborhood Preservation. Roger S. Ahlbrandt, Jr. et al. LC 79-12363. 276p. 1979. 65.00 (*0-275-90327-3*, C0327, Praeger Pubs) Greenwood.

New Public Sector Marketing. David Chapman & Theo Cowdell. 336p. 1998. pap. 62.50 (*0-273-62347-8*, Pub. by Pitman Pub) Trans-Atl Phila.

New Public Speaker. George Rodman. (C). 1997. pap. text, teacher ed. 17.75 (*0-15-503159-7*) Harcourt Coll Pubs.

New Public Speaker. George Rodman & Ronald B. Adler. LC 95-81786. 496p. (C). 1996. pap. text 46.50 (*0-15-502708-5*, Pub. by Harcourt Coll Pubs) Harcourt.

New Publications for Planning Libraries: List No. 16, No. 903. Mary Vance. 1975. 6.00 (*0-686-20372-0*, Sage Prdcls Pr) Sage.

New Publications for Planning Libraries: List No. 20, No. 928. Mary Vance. 1975. 7.00 (*0-686-20377-1*, Sage Prdcls Pr) Sage.

New Publications for Planning Libraries: List No. 21, No. 955. Mary Vance. 1976. 8.00 (*0-686-20383-6*, Sage Prdcls Pr) Sage.

New Publications for Planning Libraries: List No. 23, No. 988. Veronica Walker & Mary Vance. 1976. 5.00 (*0-686-20389-5*, Sage Prdcls Pr) Sage.

New Publications for Planning Libraries: List No. 30, No. 1152. Veronica Walker & Mary Vance. 1976. 5.00 (*0-686-20414-X*, Sage Prdcls Pr) Sage.

New Publications for Planning Libraries: List No. 34. Veronica Walker & Mary Vance. 1977. 3.00 (*0-686-19122-6*, 1245, Sage Prdcls Pr) Sage.

New Publications for Planning Libraries: List No. 35. Veronica Walker & Mary Vance. 1977. 2.50 (*0-686-19103-X*, 1267, Sage Prdcls Pr) Sage.

New Publications for Planning Libraries: List No.19, No. 927. Mary Vance. 1975. 6.00 (*0-686-20376-3*, Sage Prdcls Pr) Sage.

New Publications for Planning Libraries: Urban & Regional Planning, No. 905. Mary Vance. 1975. 5.00 (*0-686-20373-9*, Sage Prdcls Pr) Sage.

New Publications of the U. S. Geological Survey, List 1034. U. S. Geological Survey Staff. (Illus.). 58p. 1998. reprint ed. 11.80 (*0-89904-728-9*, Cascade Geog Soc); reprint ed. pap. 6.80 (*0-89904-729-7*, Cascade Geog Soc) Crumb Elbow Pub.

An Asterisk (*) at the beginning of an entry indicates that the title is appearing for the first time.

New Publications of the U. S. Geological Survey, List 1035. U. S. Geological Survey Staff. (Illus.). 54p. 1998. reprint ed. 6.40 (*0-89904-786-6*, Cascade Geog Soc); reprint ed. pap. 11.40 (*0-89904-787-4*, Cascade Geog Soc) Crumb Elbow Pub.

New Publications of the U. S. Geological Survey, List 1039. U. S. Geological Survey Staff. (Illus.). 84p. 1998. reprint ed. 14.40 (*0-89904-721-1*); reprint ed. pap. 9.40 (*0-89904-722-X*) Crumb Elbow Pub.

New Publications of the U. S. Geological Survey, Lists 1050-1055. U. S. Geological Survey Staff. (Illus.). 136p. 1997. reprint ed. 20.00 (*0-89904-713-0*, Cascade Geog Soc); reprint ed. pap. 14.60 (*0-89904-714-9*, Cascade Geog Soc) Crumb Elbow Pub.

New Publications of the U. S. Geological Survey, Lists 1056-1061. U. S. Geological Survey Staff. (Illus.). 160p. 1997. 12.40 (*0-89904-540-5*, Cascade Geog Soc); spiral bd. 7.40 (*0-89904-541-3*, Cascade Geog Soc) Crumb Elbow Pub.

New Publications of the U. S. Geological Survey, Lists 1056-1061. U. S. Geological Survey Staff. (Illus.). 160p. 1997. reprint ed. 22.00 (*0-89904-711-4*, Cascade Geog Soc); reprint ed. pap. 17.00 (*0-89904-712-2*, Cascade Geog Soc) Crumb Elbow Pub.

New Publications of the U. S. Geological Survey, Lists 1065-1067. U. S. Geological Survey Staff. (Illus.). 60p. 1998. reprint ed. 12.00 (*0-89904-770-X*, Cascade Geog Soc); reprint ed. pap. 7.00 (*0-89904-771-8*, Cascade Geog Soc) Crumb Elbow Pub.

New Publicity Kit. Jeanette Smith. LC 94-41429. 352p. 1995. pap. 19.95 (*0-471-08014-4*) Wiley.

New Pug. Shirley Thomas. (Illus.). 288p. 1990. 25.95 (*0-87605-264-2*) Howell Bks.

***New Pup on the Block.** Susan Saunders. (All-American Puppies Ser.: No. 1). (J). 2001. pap. write for info. (*0-06-440884-1*) Morrow Avon.

New Puppy: Big Book. Mary Rogers. (Foundations Ser.). 35p. (J). (gr. k). 1992. pap. text 23.00 (*1-56843-012-4*); pap. text 4.50 (*1-56843-062-0*) EMG Networks.

New Purchase: Or, Seven & a Half Years in the Far West. Baynard R. Hall. LC 75-101. (Mid-American Frontier Ser.). 1975. reprint ed. 51.95 (*0-405-06869-7*) Ayer.

New Puritanism: During the Semi-Centennial Celebration of Plymouth Church, N.Y., 1847-1897. Lyman Abbott et al. LC 70-39672. (Essay Index Reprint Ser.). 1977. 21.95 (*0-8369-2732-X*) Ayer.

***New QDRO Handbook: How to Divide Erisa, Military & Civil Service Pensions & Collect Child Support from Employee Benefit Plans.** David Clayton Carrad. LC 00-30619. 2000. pap. write for info. (*1-57073-798-3*) Amer Bar Assn.

***New Quantitative Approach to Powder Technology.** Yoshimoto Wanibe & Takashi Itoh. LC 97-41821. 280p. 1999. 210.00 (*0-471-98154-0*) Wiley.

New Queries in Aesthetics & Metaphysics: Time, Historicity, Art, Culture, Metaphysics, the Transnatural. Ed. by Anna-Teresa Tymieniecka. (Analecta Husserliana Ser.). 480p. (C). 1991. lib. bdg. 182.00 (*0-7923-1195-7*, Pub. by Kluwer Academic) Kluwer Academic.

New Question Box: Catholic Life in a New Century. 11th rev. ed. John J. Dietzen. LC 83-18540. 574p. 1997. pap. 15.95 (*0-940518-08-2*) Guildhall Pubs.

New Questions & Answers about Dinosaurs. Seymour Simon. LC 88-36226. (Illus.). 48p. (J). (gr. k up). 1990. 16.00 (*0-688-08195-9*, Wm Morrow) Morrow Avon.

New Questions of British Cinema Vol. 2: Working Papers. Ed. by Duncan Petrie. (Illus.). 128p. (C). 1993. pap. 16.95 (*0-85170-322-4*, Pub. by British Film Inst) Ind U Pr.

New Quests for Corvo. Cecil Woolf & Brocard Sewell. 1961. 6.95 (*0-8023-9061-7*) Dufour.

New Quests for Corvo: A Collection of Essays. Ed. by Cecil Woolf & Brocard Sewell. 1961. 6.95 (*0-685-09185-6*); pap. 3.00 (*0-685-09186-4*) Dufour.

New Quick Job-Hunting Map. rev. ed. Richard Nelson Bolles. 64p. 1985. pap. 4.95 (*0-89815-387-5*) Ten Speed Pr.

New Quilt: Quilt National, 1989. Ed. by Nancy Roe. LC 88-63933. (Illus.). 96p. 1989. pap. 14.95 (*0-88740-157-0*) Schiffer.

New Quilt Two, No. 2. Dairy Barn Quilt National Staff. Ed. by Christine Timmons. (Illus.). 96p. 1993. pap. 21.95 (*1-56158-056-2*) Taunton.

New Quilting by Machine. Creative Publishing International Staff. LC 98-49890. (Singer Sewing Reference Library). (Illus.). 128p. 1999. pap. text 16.95 (*0-86573-335-X*) Creat Pub Intl.

New Qumran Texts & Studies: Proceedings of the First Meeting of the International Organization for Qumran Studies, Paris, 1992. Ed. by George J. Brooke & Florentino G. Martinez. LC 94-18402. (Studies on the Texts of the Desert of Judah: Vol. 15). ix, 328p. 1994. 109.00 (*90-04-10093-8*) Brill Academic Pubs.

New Quotable Woman. rev. ed. Elaine Partnow. 736p. 1992. 40.00 (*0-8160-2134-1*) Facts on File.

New Rabbit Handbook. Lucia Vriends-Parent. (Illus.). 144p. 1989. pap. 9.95 (*0-8120-4202-6*) Barron.

***New Racer's Tax Guide.** rev. ed. Steve Smith. LC 99-161878. 80p. 1999. 17.95 (*0-936834-17-X*) S S Autosports.

New Racism in Europe: A Sicilian Ethnography. Jeffrey Cole. LC 97-4075. (Studies in Social & Cultural Anthropology: Vol. 107). (Illus.). 170p. (C). 1998. text 54.95 (*0-521-58493-0*) Cambridge U Pr.

New Radiance Metaphysical & Holistic Florida Directory. Barbara Casey. 1997. pap. 7.95 (*1-889131-35-0*) CasAnanda.

***New Radiance Metaphysical & Holistic Florida Directory: Millennium Edition.** 6th rev. ed. Ed. by Barbara Casey & Brenda Dupas. 208p. 1999. pap. 11.95 (*0-9645702-3-8*) New Radiance Dir.

New Radical Theatre Notebook. expanded rev. ed. Arthur Sainer. LC 97-12185. (Illus.). 512p. 1996. pap. 19.95 (*1-55783-168-8*) Applause Theatre Bk Pubs.

New Radicalism & Other Essays. Amlan Datta. (C). 1989. 11.00 (*81-85195-22-6*, Pub. by Minerva) S Asia.

New Radicalism in America, 1889-1963: The Intellectual As a Social Type. Christopher Lasch. 384p. 1997. pap. 14.95 (*0-393-31696-3*) Norton.

New Radicals in the Multiversity: A 1968 Manifesto of Students for a Democratic Society. Carl Davidson. (Sixties Ser.). 64p. (Orig.). 1990. reprint ed. pap. 9.00 (*0-88286-177-8*); reprint ed. lib. bdg. 24.95 (*0-88286-178-6*) C H Kerr.

New Radiotracers in Cardiac Imaging: Principles & Approach. Raymond Taillefer. 224p. 1999. 150.00 (*0-8385-6749-5*, Apple Lange Med) McGraw.

New Ragazzini, Biagi Concise Italian-English, English-Italian Dictionary: Il Nuovo Ragazzini - Biagi Concise Dizionario Inglese-Italiano Italiano-Inglese. 2nd ed. Giuseppe Ragazzini & Adele Biagi. (ENG & ITA.). 1200p. 1986. lib. bdg. 85.00 (*0-8288-3332-X*, F10010) Fr & Eur.

New Ragazzini English-Italian, Italian-English Dictionary: Il Nuovo Ragazzini Dizionario Inglese-Italiano: Italiano-Inglese. 2nd ed. Giuseppe Ragazzini. (ENG & ITA.). 2144p. 1989. lib. bdg. 150.00 (*0-8288-3331-1*, F9072) Fr & Eur.

New Raiments of Self: African American Clothing in the Antebellum South. Helen B. Foster. LC 97-202428. (Illus.). 320p. 1997. 55.00 (*1-85973-184-8*, Pub. by Berg Pubs); pap. 19.95 (*1-85973-189-9*, Pub. by Berg Pubs) NYU Pr.

New Rain, Vol. 1. Ed. by Gary Johnston & C. D. Grant. 60p. (Orig.). 1981. pap. 4.00 (*0-940738-02-3*) Blind Beggar.

New Rain, Vol. 2. Ed. by Gary Johnston & C. D. Grant. 1982p. (Orig.). 1982. pap. 4.25 (*0-940738-04-X*) Blind Beggar.

New Rain, Vol. 3. Ed. by Gary Johnston & C. D. Grant. (Illus.). 60p. (Orig.). 1984. pap. 4.00 (*0-940738-05-8*) Blind Beggar.

New Rain, Vol. 4. Ed. by C. D. Grant. (Illus.). 80p. (Orig.). 1984. pap. 5.00 (*0-940738-06-6*) Blind Beggar.

New Rain, Vol. 5. Ed. by Gary Johnston & C. D. Grant. (Illus.). 88p. (Orig.). 1985. pap. 5.00 (*0-940738-07-4*) Blind Beggar.

New Rain, Vol. 6. Ed. by Gary Johnston & C. D. Grant. (Illus.). 100p. (Orig.). 1986. pap. 6.95 (*0-940738-09-0*) Blind Beggar.

New Rain, Vols. 7 & 8. Ed. by Judy D. Simmons. (Illus.). 200p. 1990. pap. 9.95 (*0-940738-12-0*) Blind Beggar.

***New Rank & File.** Staughton Lynd & Alice Lynd. LC 00-9146. 2000. pap. write for info. (*0-8014-8676-9*) Cornell U Pr.

***New Rank & File.** Ed. by Staughton Lynd & Alice Lynd. 2000. pap. 15.95 (*0-8014-3806-3*, ILR Press) Cornell U Pr.

New Rapture Scenario: It's Not Like Your Daddy Pictured It. Ed J. MacWilliams. 1995. pap. 7.95 (*1-878897-01-2*) Blueprint Pubns.

New Rating Guide to Life in America's Small Cities. Kevin Heubusch. LC 97-35830. 527p. 1997. 34.95 (*1-57392-170-X*); pap. 18.95 (*1-57392-192-0*) Prometheus Bks.

New Rational Manager. Charles H. Kepner & Benjamin B. Tregoe. LC 80-84367. 220p. 1981. 17.50 (*0-936231-01-7*) Kepner-Tregoe.

New Reactions & Chemicals Based on Sulfur & Acetylene, Vol. 3. B. A. Trofimov. 38p. 1983. pap. text 123.00 (*3-7186-0175-3*) Gordon & Breach.

New Reader of the Old South: Major Stories, Tales, Slave Narratives, Diaries, Essays, Travelogues, Poetry & Songs 1820-1920. Ed. by Ben Forkner & Patrick Samway. 704p. 1991. 34.95 (*1-56145-019-7*); pap. 19.95 (*1-56145-020-0*) Peachtree Pubs.

New Reader's Guide to African Literature. 2nd ed. Ed. by Hans M. Zell et al. LC 83-15472. (Illus.). 300p. (C). 1983. text 45.95 (*0-8419-0639-4*, Africana); pap. text 29.50 (*0-8419-0640-8*, Africana) Holmes & Meier.

New Reading the Landscape: Fieldwork in Landscape History. Richard Muir. (Illus.). 288p. 1999. 80.00 (*0-85989-579-3*); pap. 29.95 (*0-85989-580-7*) Univ Exeter Pr.

New Reading vs. Old Plays: Recent Trends in the Reinterpretation of English Renaissance Drama. Richard L. Levin. LC 78-10695. 292p. reprint ed. pap. 90.60 (*0-608-09463-3*, 205426300005) Bks Demand.

***New Readings in John: Literary & Theological Perspectives Essays from the Scandinavian Conference on the Fourth Gospel in Aarhus 1997.** Ed. by Johannes Nissen & Sigfred Pedersen. (JSNTS Ser.: Vol. 182). 289p. 1999. 85.00 (*1-85075-974-X*, Pub. by Sheffield Acad) CUP Services.

New Readings of Late Medieval Love Poems. Ed. by David Chamberlain. LC 92-32018. 204p. (Orig.). (C). 1993. pap. text 26.00 (*0-8191-8912-X*); lib. bdg. 49.50 (*0-8191-8911-1*) U Pr of Amer.

New Readings of Spiritual Narrative from the Fifteenth to the Twentieth Century: Secular Force & Self-Disclosure. Ed. by Phebe Davidson. LC 95-6141. (Studies in Religion & Society: Vol. 31). 132p. 1995. 69.95 (*0-7734-8878-2*) E Mellen.

New Readings of the American Novel: Narrative Theory & Its Application. Peter B. Messent. LC 98-21410. 336p. 1998. pap. text 24.95 (*0-8173-0958-6*) U of Ala Pr.

New Readings on Women in Old English Literature. Ed. by Helen Damico & Alexandra Hennessey Olsen. LC 88-45459. (Illus.). 330p. 1990. 39.95 (*0-253-33413-6*); pap. 15.95 (*0-253-20547-6*) Ind U Pr.

New Readings on Women in Old English Literature. Ed. by Helen Damico & Alexandra Hennessey Olsen. LC 88-45459. 329p. Date not set. reprint ed. pap. 102.00 (*0-608-20536-2*, 205445000002) Bks Demand.

New Readings vs. Old Plays. Richard Levin. LC 78-10695. xiv, 278p. (C). 1994. pap. text 8.95 (*0-226-47521-2*) U Ch Pr.

New Readings vs. Old Plays: Recent Trends in the Reinterpretation of English Renaissance Drama. Richard Levin. LC 78-10695. 1994. lib. bdg. 24.00 (*0-226-47520-4*) U Ch Pr.

New Real Book, Vol. 1. Ed. by Charles Sher. (Illus.). 438p. 1988. spiral bd. 38.00 (*0-9614701-4-3*) Sher Music.

New Real Book, Vol. 2. Ed. by Chuck Sher & Bob Bauer. (Illus.). 484p. (Orig.). (C). 1991. pap. text 38.00 (*0-9614701-7-8*) Sher Music.

New Real Book, Vol. 3. Ed. by Chuck Sher. 437p. (Orig.). 1995. pap. text 38.00 (*1-883217-03-2*) Sher Music.

New Realism. Cox. LC 96-17550. 304p. 1997. text 55.00 (*0-312-16234-0*) St Martin.

***New Realism, New Barbarism: The Crisis of Capitalism.** Boris Kagarlitsky. LC 99-35172. 1999. write for info. (*0-7453-1556-9*, Pub. by Pluto GBR) Stylus Pub VA.

***New Realism, New Barbarism: The Crisis of Capitalism.** Boris Kagarlitsky. LC 99-35172 . 1999. pap. 18.95 (*0-7453-1551-8*) Pluto GBR.

***New Realities.** Peter F. Drucker. 1999. pap. 13.50 (*0-06-662027-9*, HarpBusn) HarpInfo.

New Realities. Peter F. Drucker. LC 89-1192. 288p. 1994. reprint ed. pap. 14.00 (*0-88730-617-9*, HarpBusn) HarpInfo.

New Realities for Stockholder-Management Relations. John D. Martin & John W. Kensinger. LC 94-70909. 70p. (Orig.). 1994. pap. text 25.00 (*0-910586-91-8*, 094-01) Finan Exec.

New Reality: How to Make Change Your Competitive Advantage. Karl G. Schoemer. 34p. 1995. 7.95 (*1-929037-00-7*) KGS Inc.

New Realm of the Buddhaking. Sheng-Yen Lu. LC 98-52714. 1999. pap. write for info. (*1-881493-07-5*) Purple Lotus Soc.

New Rebellion. Kristine Kathryn Rusch. LC 96-8073. (Star Wars Ser.: 1). 400p. 1996. 22.95 (*0-553-10093-9*, Spectra) Bantam.

New Rebellion. Kristine Kathryn Rusch. (Star Wars Ser.). 1996. 22.95 (*0-614-20653-7*) Bantam.

New Rebellion. Kristine Kathryn Rusch. LC 96-8073. (Star Wars Ser.). 532p. 1997. mass mkt. 5.99 (*0-553-57414-0*, Spectra) Bantam.

New Rebellion. Kristine Kathryn Rusch. (Star Wars Ser.). 1997. 11.09 (*0-606-11894-2*, Pub. by Turtleback) Demco.

New Recipes from Moosewood Restaurant. Moosewood Collective Staff. (Illus.). 320p. 1987. pap. 21.95 (*0-89815-208-9*) Ten Speed Pr.

New Recipes from Moosewood Restaurant. Moosewood Collective Staff. (Illus.). 302p. 1987. 19.95 (*0-89815-209-7*) Ten Speed Pr.

***New Recipes from Moosewood Restaurant.** rev. ed. Moosewood Collective Staff. 320p. 2000. pap. 19.95 (*1-58008-148-7*) Ten Speed Pr.

New Recipes from Quilt Country: More Food & Folkways from the Amish & Mennonites. Marcia Adams. LC 97-22620. 304p. 1997. 30.00 (*0-517-70562-1*) C Potter.

New Reckoning: Capitalism, States & Citizens. David Marquand. LC 97-39516. 272p. (C). 1998. pap. 26.95 (*0-7456-1745-X*, Pub. by Polity Pr) Blackwell Pubs.

New Reckoning: Capitalism, States & Citizens. David Marquand. LC 97-39516. 272p. (C). 1998. 57.95 (*0-7456-1744-1*, Pub. by Polity Pr) Blackwell Pubs.

New Recording Studio Handbook. rev. ed. John Woram & Alan P. Kefauver. LC 88-80009. (Illus.). 550p. 1989. lib. bdg. 44.50 (*0-914130-04-8*) Elar Pub Co.

New Records for Illinois Vascular Plants. Ed. by Glen S. Winterringer & Robert A. Evers. (Scientific Papers: Vol. XI). 135p. 1960. pap. 3.25 (*0-89792-020-1*) Ill St Museum.

New Rector. large type ed. Rebecca Shaw. 432p. 1996. 27.99 (*0-7089-3493-5*) Ulverscroft.

New Red Bed. Sindy McKay. LC 98-61797. (We Both Read Ser.). (Illus.). 48p. (J). (gr. k-1). 1999. 7.99 (*1-891327-12-7*); pap. 3.99 (*1-891327-16-X*) Treas Bay Inc.

New Red Legions: A Survey Data Source Book, Vol. 2. Richard A. Gabriel. LC 79-24458. (Contributions in Political Science Ser.: No. 44). (Illus.). 252p. 1980. 59.95 (*0-313-21497-2*, GAP/, Greenwood Pr) Greenwood.

New Red Legions: An Attitudinal Portrait of the Soviet Soldier, 2 vols., Set. Richard A. Gabriel. LC 79-8956. (Contributions in Political Science Ser.: No. 44). (Illus.). xiv, 246p. 1980. 115.00 (*0-313-21495-6*, GAN/) Greenwood.

New Red Legions: An Attitudinal Portrait of the Soviet Soldier, 2 vols., Vol. 1. Richard A. Gabriel. LC 79-8956. (Contributions in Political Science Ser.: No. 44). (Illus.). 246p. 1980. 69.50 (*0-313-21496-4*, GAO/) Greenwood.

***New Red Lion Inn Cookbook.** rev. ed. Suzi Forbes Chase. LC 99-87036. (Illus.). 224p. 2000. pap. 23.95 (*1-58157-012-0*, Pub. by Berkshire Hse) Natl Bk Netwk.

New Red Negro: The Literary Left & African American Poetry. James E. Smethurst. LC 98-17128. (Race & American Culture Ser.). 304p. 1999. text 45.00 (*0-19-512054-X*) OUP.

New Reference: Grammar of Modern Spanish. John Butt & Carmen Benjamin. 448p. 1989. pap. 32.95 (*0-7131-6612-6*, Pub. by E A) Routldge.

New Reference Grammar of Modern Spanish. 2nd ed. Carmen Benjamin & John Butt. (Reference Grammar of Ser.). (Illus.). 536p. 1995. pap. 32.95 (*0-8442-7088-1*, 70881, Natl Textbk Co) NTC Contemp Pub Co.

New Reference Grammar of Modern Spanish. 2nd ed. John Butt & Carmen Benjamin. 1994. write for info. (*0-340-58390-8*, Pub. by E A) Routldge.

***New Reference Grammar of Modern Spanish.** 3rd ed. John Butt & Carmen Benjamin. LC 99-47014. 540p. 2000. pap. 32.95 (*0-658-00873-0*, 008730) NTC Contemp Pub Co.

New Reflections on Speechreading. Ed. by Carol L. De Filippo & Donald G. Sims. LC HV2471.. (Volta Review: Vol. 90, No. 5, Sept. 1988). 319p. 1988. reprint ed. pap. 98.90 (*0-7837-9094-5*, 204984400003) Bks Demand.

New Reflections on Terrorism & Terrorism in America: International Connections. Fernando P. Pizarro. Tr. by Joseph Serio & George Samaniego from SPA.Tr. of Nuevas Reflexiones Respecto Al Terrorismo Y el Terrorismo En America (Conexiones Internacionales). (Illus.). 66p. (C). 1989. pap. 7.95 (*0-942511-09-3*) OICJ.

New Reflections on Women: By the Marchioness de Lambert. Anne T. Lambert. Tr. by Ellen M. Hine from FRE. (Writing about Women Ser.: Vol. 17). 90p. (C). 1995. text 33.95 (*0-8204-2705-5*) P Lang Pubng.

New Reformation: From Physical to Spiritual Realities. Michael Pupin. 300p. 1998. reprint ed. pap. 19.95 (*0-7661-0414-1*) Kessinger Pub.

New Reformation: Returning the Ministry to the People of God. Greg Ogden. 1990. 14.95 (*0-310-31020-2*) Zondervan.

New Reformation: Returning the Ministry to the People of God. Greg Ogden. 224p. 1991. pap. 12.99 (*0-310-31021-0*) Zondervan.

New Reformation: Tomorrow Arrived Yesterday. Lyle E. Schaller. (Third Millennium Ser.). 176p. (Orig.). 1996. pap. 12.95 (*0-687-01474-3*) Abingdon.

New Reformed Catechism: A Shorter Catechism for Today. John C. Bush. 64p. 1997. pap. 4.99 (*1-882547-14-4*, Viaticum) Kash Literary.

New Refrigerants for Air. David M. Wylie. LC 96-23417. 346p. (C). 1996. 79.00 (*0-13-268715-1*) P-H.

New Refrigerants for Air Conditioning & Refrigeration Systems. David M. Wylie & James W. Davenport. LC 96-23417. 315p. 1996. 79.00 (*0-88173-224-9*) Fairmont Pr.

N

New Regents High School Graduation Requirements: Curricular & Instructional Implications & Estimates of Resources Necessary to Meet the New Standards. Contrib. by Gary Natriello. 86p. 1998. 15.00 (*0-88156-252-1*) Comm Serv Soc NY.

New Regime: Transformations of the French Civic Order, 1789-1820s. Isser Woloch. 536p. 1995. pap. 16.95 (*0-393-31397-2*, Norton Paperbks) Norton.

New Regime for Foreign Direct Investment. Sylvia Ostry. (Occasional Paper Ser.: No. 53). 30p. 1997. pap. 10.00 (*1-56708-102-9*) Grp of Thirty.

New Regime for the Oceans see Trilateral Commission Task Force Reports

New Regional Economies: The U. S. Common Market & the Global Economy. William R. Barnes & Larry C. Ledebur. LC 97-4751. (Cities & Planning Ser.: Vol. 2). 192p. 1997. text 42.00 (*0-7619-0938-9*); pap. text 19.95 (*0-7619-0939-7*) Sage.

New Regional Map of Europe. Tony Champion et al. 70p. 1996. pap. text 102.50 (*0-08-042906-8*, Pergamon Pr) Elsevier.

New Regionalism, Vol. 3. Ed. by Lawrence W. Speck & Wayne Attoe. (Illus.). 128p. 1987. pap. 22.00 (*0-8478-5453-1*) Ctr for Amer Archit.

New Regionalism: Essays & Commentaries. Robert L. Dorman. Ed. by Charles R. Wilson. LC 97-9367. (Chancellor's Symposium Ser.). 184p. 1998. text 40.00 (*1-57806-013-3*) U Pr of Miss.

***New Regionalism & the Future of Security & Development.** Bjorn Hettne. (New Regionalism Ser.). 2000. text 69.95 (*0-312-22773-6*) St Martin.

New Regionalism in Trade Policy. Jaime De Melo & Arvind Panagariya. LC 92-39285. 32p. 1993. pap. 22.00 (*0-8213-2294-X*, 12294) World Bank.

New Regionalism in Western Europe: Territorial Restructuring & Political Change. Michael Keating. LC 97-47520. 272p. 1998. 85.00 (*1-85898-527-7*) E Elgar.

***New Regionalism in Western Europe: Territorial Restructuring & Political Change.** Michael Keating. LC 97-47520. 256p. 2000. pap. 30.00 (*1-84064-486-9*) E Elgar.

***New Regulation of the Financial Industry.** Contrib. by Dimitris N. Chorafas. LC 99-50145. 2000. text 65.00 (*0-312-22899-6*) St Martin.

New Regulations for Uniform, Laces, Badges, etc. to Be Worn by the British Army: (Regulars & Militia) 21p. (C). 1987. pap. 40.00 (*0-948251-10-7*, Pub. by Picton) St Mut.

New Regulations on Indulgences. Winfrid Herbst. 47p. 1992. pap. 2.50 (*0-89555-103-9*) TAN Bks Pubs.

New Regulatory & Management Strategies in a Changing Market Environment: Proceedings of the Institute of Public Utilities Eighteenth Annual Conference, Williamsburg, VA, 1986. Michigan State University, Institute of Public Utilities Staff. Ed. by Harry M. Trebing & Patrick C. Mann. LC 87-73267. (MSU Public Utilities Papers: Vol. 1987). (Illus.). 661p. reprint ed. pap. 200.00 (*0-608-20499-4*, 207175100002) Bks Demand.

New Reign of Terror in the Slaveholding States, for 1859-1860. William L. Garrison. LC 76-82192. (Anti-Slavery Crusade in America Ser.). 1976. reprint ed. 22.95 (*0-405-00631-4*) Ayer.

New Relatedness for Man & Woman in Christ: A Mirror of the Divine. V. Norskov Olsen. LC 93-13440. 1993. pap. 9.95 (*1-881127-01-X*) LLU Ctr Christ Bio.

New Relation of Gaspesia: With the Customs & Religion of the Gaspesian Indian, Vol. 5. Chretien Le Clercq. Ed. by William F. Ganong. LC 68-28600. 452p. 1969. reprint ed. lib. bdg. 75.00 (*0-8371-5044-2*, LERG, Greenwood Pr) Greenwood.

New Relations: The Refashioning of British Poetry, 1980-1994. David Kennedy. LC 96-220019. 256p. 1997. 45.00 (*1-85411-162-0*, Pub. by Seren Bks); pap. 22.95 (*1-85411-163-9*, Pub. by Seren Bks) Dufour.

***New Relationship: Human Capital in the American Corporation.** Margaret M. Blair. LC 99-50476. 2000. pap. 22.95 (*0-8157-0901-3*) Brookings.

***New Relationship: Human Capital in the American Corporation.** Ed. by Margaret M. Blair & Thomas A. Kochan. LC 99-50476. 395p. 1999. 49.95 (*0-8157-0902-1*) Brookings.

New Relationships. Shari Jae. 58p. (Orig.). 1985. pap. 6.95 (*0-87418-008-2*, 149) Coleman Pub.

New Relationships in the Organized Professions: Managers, Professionals & Knowledge Workers. Ed. by Robin Fincham. (Stirling School of Management Ser.). 304p. 1996. text 77.95 (*1-85972-451-5*, Pub. by Avebry) Ashgate Pub Co.

New Religion & Relativity. Dicksen T. Lau. LC 83-62038. 138p. (Orig.). 1983. pap. 5.95 (*0-9612000-0-6*) Magnolia Bks.

***New Religion of Life in Every Speech.** Don Cupitt. 1998. pap. 16.00 (*0-334-02763-2*) TPI PA.

New Religions America. Eck. 2000. pap. 14.00 (*0-06-062159-1*) HarpC.

***New Religions America.** Diana Eck. 2000. 25.00 (*0-06-062175-3*); pap. 16.00 (*0-06-062176-1*) HarpC.

New Religions & Mental Health: Understanding the Issues. Ed. by Herbert W. Richardson. (Symposium Ser.: Vol. 5). 177p. (Orig.). (C). 1988. lib. bdg. 89.95 (*0-88946-910-5*) E Mellen.

New Religions & New Religiosity. Ed. by Margit Warburg & Eileen Barker. (Renner Studies on New Religions: Vol. 4). 309p. 1998. pap. 24.95 (*87-7288-552-1*, Pub. by Aarhus Univ Pr) David Brown.

New Religions & the New Europe. Ed. by Robert Towler. (Renner Studies on New Religions: Vol. 1). 256p. 1995. pap. 27.00 (*87-7288-433-9*, Pub. by Aarhus Univ Pr) David Brown.

New Religions & the Theological Imagination in America. Mary F. Bednarowski. LC 88-46038. (Religion in North America Ser.). 192p. 1989. text 25.00 (*0-253-31137-3*) Ind U Pr.

New Religions & the Theological Imagination in America. Mary F. Bednarowski. LC 88-46038. (Religion in North America Ser.). 192p. 1995. pap. 12.95 (*0-253-20952-8*) Ind U Pr.

New Religions As Global Cultures: Making the Human Sacred. Irving Hexham & Karla O. Poewe. LC 96-51758. (Explorations Ser.). 208p. (C). 1997. pap. text 24.00 (*0-8133-2508-0*, Pub. by Westview) HarpC.

***New Religions in a Postmodern World.** Ed. by Reender Kranenborg & Mikael Rothstein. (Renner Studies on New Religions: Vol. 5). 248p. 2000. pap. 24.95 (*87-7288-748-6*, Pub. by Aarhus Univ Pr) David Brown.

New Religions Movements: Challenge & Response. Bryan R. Wilson. LC 98-30970. 1999. write for info. (*0-415-20049-0*); pap. 24.99 (*0-415-20050-4*) Routledge.

New Religions of Africa. Ed. by Bennetta Jules-Rosette. LC 78-16925. (Modern Sociology Ser.). (Illus.). 248p. (C). 1979. text 73.25 (*0-89391-014-7*) Ablx Pub.

New Religions of Japan. Harry Thomsen. LC 77-13846. (Illus.). 269p. 1978. reprint ed. lib. bdg. 35.00 (*0-8371-9878-X*, THNR, Greenwood Pr) Greenwood.

New Religious America. Eck. 25.00 (*0-06-062158-3*) HarpC.

New Religious Consciousness. Ed. by Charles Y. Glock & Robert N. Bellah. LC 75-17295. 409p. reprint ed. pap. 126.80 (*0-7837-4810-8*, 204445700003) Bks Demand.

New Religious Humanists. Gregory Wolfe. LC 97-37196. 1997. 24.50 (*0-684-83254-2*) S&S Trade.

New Religious Image of Urban America: The Shopping Mall As Ceremonial Center. 2nd rev. ed. Ira G. Zepp, Jr. LC 96-51780. (Illus.). 176p. 1997. pap. 27.50 (*0-87081-436-2*) Univ Pr Colo.

New Religious Movements. Ed. by Gregory B. Baum & John Coleman. (Concilium Ser.: Vol. 161). 128p. (Orig.). 1983. 6.95 (*0-8164-2441-1*) Harper SF.

New Religious Movements: A Perspective for Understanding Society. Ed. by Eileen Barker. LC 82-8263. (Studies in Religion & Society: Vol. 3). 398p. (C). 1982. lib. bdg. 99.95 (*0-88946-864-8*) E Mellen.

New Religious Movements & Rapid Social Change. Ed. by James A. Beckford. 272p. (C). 1987. text 47.50 (*0-8039-8003-5*); pap. text 19.95 (*0-8039-8591-6*) Sage.

New Religious Movements in Nigeria. Ed. by Rosalind I. Hackett. LC 86-31080. (African Studies: Vol. 5). 245p. 1987. lib. bdg. 89.95 (*0-88946-180-5*) E Mellen.

New Religious Movements in the United States & Canada: A Critical Assessment & Annotated Bibliography, 5. Compiled by Diane Choquette. LC 85-9964. (Bibliographies & Indexes in Religious Studies: No. 5). 235p. 1985. lib. bdg. 69.50 (*0-313-23772-7*, CRM/) Greenwood.

New Religious Movements in Western Europe: An Annotated Bibliography, 41. Elisabeth B. Arweck & Peter Clarke. LC 96-44066. (Bibliographies & Indexes in Religious Studies: Vol. 41). 328p. 1997. lib. bdg. 95.00 (*0-313-24324-7*, Greenwood Pr) Greenwood.

New Religious Movements, Mass Suicide & Peoples Temple: Scholarly Perspectives on a Tragedy. Ed. by Rebecca Moore & Fielding M. McGehee, III. LC 88-34382. (Studies in American Religion). 256p. 1989. lib. bdg. 89.95 (*0-88946-680-7*) E Mellen.

New Religious Right: Piety, Patriotism & Politics. Walter H. Capps. LC 90-39818. 253p. 1990. pap. 15.95 (*0-87249-741-0*) U of SC Pr.

New Relocating Spouse's Guide to Employment: Options & Strategies in the U. S. & Abroad. 4th ed. Francis Bastress. 352p. 1993. 32.95 (*0-942710-57-6*) Impact VA.

New Remediation Technology in the Changing Environmental Arena. Ed. by B. J. Scheiner et al. LC 94-69212. (Illus.). 244p. 1995. pap. 59.50 (*0-87335-131-2*, 131-2) SMM&E Inc.

New Remodeling Book: Your Complete Guide to Planning Your Dream Project. Ed. by Better Homes & Gardens. LC 98-66254. (Illus.). 360p. 1998. 34.95 (*0-696-20740-0*, Better Homes) Meredith Bks.

New Renaissance: Computers & the Next Level of Civilization. Douglas S. Robertson. LC 97-31239. 208p. 1998. 25.00 (*0-19-512189-9*) OUP.

New Representationalisms: Essays in the Philosophy of Perception. Ed. by Edmond Wright. LC 93-1819. (Avebury Series in Philosophy). 304p. 1993. 72.95 (*1-85628-356-9*, Pub. by Avebry) Ashgate Pub Co.

New Reproductive Techniques: A Legal Perspective. Douglas J. Cusine. (Medico-Legal Issues Ser.). 280p. 1988. text 87.95 (*0-566-05410-8*, Pub. by Dartmth Pub) Ashgate Pub Co.

New Reproductive Techniques: A Legal Perspective. Douglas J. Cusine. (Medico-Legal Issues Ser.). 1990. pap. 39.95 (*1-85521-007-X*, Pub. by Dartmth Pub) Ashgate Pub Co.

***New Reproductive Technologies, Women's Health & Autonomy: Freedom or Dependency.** Jyotsna Agnihotri Gupta. LC 00-23510. (Indo-Dutch Studies on Development Alternatives). 2000. write for info. (*0-7619-9431-9*) Sage.

New Republic: A Commentary on Book I of More's "Utopia" Showing Its Relation to Plato's "Republic". Colin Starnes. 152p. (C). 1990. text 29.95 (*0-88920-978-2*) W Laurier U Pr.

New Republic: A Discourse of the Prospects, Dangers, Duties & Safeties of the Time. Thomas L. Harris. LC 76-42801. (Communal Societies in America Ser.). reprint ed. 31.50 (*0-404-60071-9*) AMS Pr.

New Republic: A Voice of Modern Liberalism. David Seideman. LC 85-30776. 220p. 1986. 57.95 (*0-275-92015-1*, C2015, Praeger Pubs) Greenwood.

New Republic: Or, Culture, Faith & Philosophy in an English Country House. William H. Mallock. LC 75-30033. 376p. reprint ed. 47.50 (*0-404-14036-X*) AMS Pr.

***New Republic: The United States of America, 1789-1815.** Reginald Horsman. LC 99-40529. (History of the United States of America Ser.). 275p. 2000. pap. 24.33 (*0-582-29287-5*) Addison-Wesley.

New Republic Guide to the Issues: The '96 Campaign. Michael Lind. LC 96-24671. 272p. 1996. pap. 12.00 (*0-465-05086-7*, Pub. by Basic) HarpC.

New Republic of Childhood: A Critical Guide to Canadian Children's Literature in English. 3rd ed. Sheila A. Egoff & Judith Saltman. (Illus.). 392p. 1990. pap. text 26.00 (*0-19-540576-5*) OUP.

New Republican Coalition: The Reagan Campaigns & White Evangelicals. Bruce Nesmith. LC 92-40964. (American University Studies, X, Political Science: Vol. 41). (Illus.). VIII, 182p. (C). 1994. text 39.95 (*0-8204-2138-3*) P Lang Pubng.

New Research & Child Witnesses Pt. I: A Special Issue of Applied Developmental Science. Ed. by Michael Lamb. 72p. 1999. pap. 20.00 (*0-8058-9800-X*) L Erlbaum Assocs.

New Research Center. 21st ed. Anthony L. Gerring. 1996. 340.00 (*0-8103-4948-5*) Taft Group.

***New Research Centers.** 25th ed. 125p. 1999. 375.00 (*0-7876-2194-3*) Gale.

New Research Frontiers of Communications Policy. LC 96-47837. 286p. 1996. 125.00 (*0-444-82251-8*) Elsevier.

New Research in Moral Development, Vol. 5. Ed. by Bill Puka. LC 94-462. (Moral Development: a Compendium Ser.: No. 5). (Illus.). 448p. 1994. reprint ed. text 85.00 (*0-8153-1552-X*) Garland.

New Research in Psychiatry. rev. ed. Ed. by H. Hafner & E. M. Wolpert. LC 96-931354. (Illus.). 190p. 1996. text 38.00 (*0-88937-174-1*) Hogrefe & Huber Pubs.

New Research on Child Witnesses Pt. II: A Special Issue in Applied Developmental Science. Ed. by Michael E. Lamb. 80p. 1999. pap. 20.00 (*0-8058-9795-X*) L Erlbaum Assocs.

New Research on Current Philosophical Systems. 36p. 1982. pap. 9.00 (*0-86304-016-0*, Pub. by Octagon Pr) ISHK.

New Research on the Aetiology & Surgery of Retinal Detachment: Proceedings of the Jules Gorin Club, 9th Meeting, La Baule, May 1974. Gorin, Jules, Club Staff. Ed. by E. B. Streiff. (Modern Problems in Ophthalmology Ser.: Vol. 15). (Illus.). xiv, 338p. 1975. 132.75 (*3-8055-2141-3*) S Karger.

***New Resonance: Emerging Voices in English-Language Haiku.** Ed. by Jim Kacian & Dee Evetts. 208p. 1999. pap. 14.95 (*1-893959-03-1*) Red Moon Pr.

New Resource for Welfare Reform: The Poor Themselves. Hope H. Pressman. LC 75-2399. 140p. reprint ed. pap. 43.40 (*0-7837-2138-2*, 204242400004) Bks Demand.

New Resource Wars: Native & Environmental Struggles Against Multinational Corporations. Al Gedicks. LC 93-22108. 272p. 1993. 35.00 (*0-89608-463-9*) South End Pr.

New Resource Wars: Native Struggles Against Multinational Corporations. Al Gedicks. 250p. write for info. (*1-55164-001-5*); pap. write for info. (*1-55164-000-7*) Black Rose.

New Response: Contemporary Painters of the Hudson River. John Yau. LC 85-73133. (Illus.). 80p. 1985. pap. 12.95 (*0-939072-05-X*) Albany Hist & Art.

New Restaurants in U. S. A. & East Asia. LArchivolto Editors. LC 99-174810. 1998. 79.95 (*88-7685-098-8*, Pub. by LArchivolto) Bks Nippan.

New Results & New Trends in Computer Science: Graz, Austria, June 20-21, 1991 Proceedings. Ed. by H. A. Maurer. (Lecture Notes in Computer Science Ser.: Vol. 555). viii, 403p. 1991. 48.00 (*0-387-54869-6*) Spr-Verlag.

New Results in High Energy Physics, 1978: Proceedings of the 3rd International Conference, Vanderbilt Univ., Mar. 1978. Ed. by R. S. Panvini & S. E. Csorna. LC 78-67196. (AIP Conference Proceedings Ser.: No. 45). (Illus.). 1978. lib. bdg. 20.25 (*0-88318-144-4*) Am Inst Physics.

New Results in Operator Theory & Its Applications: The Israel M. Glazman Memorial Volume. I. M. Glazman et al. LC 97-28595. (Operator Theory, Advances, & Applications Ser.). 1997. write for info. (*0-8176-5775-4*) Birkhauser.

New Results in Operator Theory & Its Applications: The Israel M. Glazman Memorial Volume. I. M. Glazman et al. LC 97-28595. (Operator Theory, Advances, & Applications Ser.). 264p. 1997. write for info. (*3-7643-5775-4*) Birkhauser.

New Results in the Theory of Topological Classification of Integrable Systems. Ed. by A. T. Fomenko. (Proceedings of the Steklov Institute of Mathematics Ser.: Vol. 205). 186p. 1996. 163.00 (*0-8218-0480-4*, STEKLO/205C) Am Math.

***New Retail.** Rasshied Din. (Illus.). 250p. 2000. 80.00 (*1-84091-042-9*, Pub. by Conran Octopus) Antique Collect.

***New Retail Power & Muscle: Remarkable Weapon to Win the War at the Point of Sale.** Thomas E. Austin. LC 00-131367. 64p. 2000. mass mkt. 12.95 (*0-9661144-5-0*, Pub. by BRG Pub) Baker & Taylor.

***New Retirement.** Dian Cohen. 320p. 1999. pap. 12.95 (*0-385-25786-4*, Pub. by Doubleday) Random House.

***New Retirement: Financial Strategies for Life after Work.** Dian Cohen. 320p. 1999. 23.50 (*0-385-25746-5*, Pub. by Doubleday) Random House.

***New Retirement: How to Secure Finanical Freedom & Live Out Your Dreams.** Dan Benson. 210p. 2000. pap. 14.99 (*0-8499-4248-9*) Word Pub.

New Revelation. Arthur Conan Doyle. 122p. 1983. pap. 10.00 (*0-89540-103-7*, SB-103) Sun Pub.

New Reversible Mao-R Inhibitor. 1989. 38.95 (*0-387-82133-3*) Spr-Verlag.

New Review of Mammillaria Names. D. Hunt. 128p. 1987. reprint ed. pap. 20.00 (*0-902099-14-0*, Pub. by Royal Botnic Grdns) Balogh.

New Revised Cambridge GED Program: Comprehensive Book. 2nd ed. Cambridge Staff. 912p. (C). 1992. pap. text 9.45 (*0-13-388752-9*) P-H.

New Revised Cambridge GED Program: Exercise Book for Mathematics. Cambridge University Publishing Staff. LC 93-7573. (Illus.). 160p. (C). 1994. pap. text 5.55 (*0-13-701897-5*) P-H.

New Revised Cambridge GED Program: Social Studies Workbook. rev. ed. Cambridge Staff. 1995. pap. 6.95 (*0-13-702101-1*) P-H.

New Revised Cambridge GED Program: Writing. 2nd ed. Cambridge Staff. 1993. pap. text 7.65 (*0-13-116963-7*) P-H.

New, Revised Restaurateur's Easy Guide to Do-It-Yourself Public Relations. rev. ed. Katherine D. Bessell & Cynthia Traina. 45p. 1985. pap. 18.50 (*0-9629953-0-4*) Bessell Pub.

New Revised Sixth & Seventh Books of Moses & the Magical Use of the Psalms. Ed. by M. Gonzalez Wippler. 219p. 1985. pap. 8.95 (*0-942272-02-1*) Original Pubns.

New Revolution: Cultural Conservatism & Moral Values. Wilbur M. Savidge. 240p. 1995. pap. text 14.95 (*1-884848-07-9*) Praxis Music.

New Revolution: The Impact of Computers on Society. Barrie Sherman. LC 84-5200. (Wiley Series in Information Processing). 412p. reprint ed. pap. 127.80 (*0-7837-4014-X*, 204384400011) Bks Demand.

New Rhetoric. O'Dell. pap. text. write for info. (*0-312-24508-4*) St Martin.

New Rhetoric: A Treatise on Argumentation. Chaim Perelman & L. Olbrechts-Tyteca. Tr. by John Wilkinson & Purcell Weaver. LC 68-20440. (C). 1969. pap. text 23.00 (*0-268-00446-3*) U of Notre Dame Pr.

New Rhetoric of Chaim Perelman: Statement & Response. Ed. by Ray D. Dearin. LC 88-31489. 266p. (Orig.). (C). 1989. pap. text 24.00 (*0-8191-7309-6*) U Pr of Amer.

New Rhymes about Animals. Bruce Lansky. (Illus.). 16p. (J). (gr. k up). 1995. lib. bdg. 4.95 (*0-671-51980-8*) Meadowbrook.

New Rhymes about Animals: The New Adventures of Mother Goose Board Book Collection. Bruce Lansky. (Illus.). 1995. bds. 4.95 (*0-88116-228-0*) Meadowbrook.

New Rhymes for Bedtime. Bruce Lansky. (Illus.). 16p. (J). (gr. k up). 1995. lib. bdg. 4.95 (*0-671-51978-6*) S&S Trade.

New Rhymes for Bedtime: The New Adventures of Mother Goose Board Book Collection. Bruce Lansky. (Illus.). (J). 1995. bds. 4.95 (*0-88116-226-4*) Meadowbrook.

New Rhymes for Mealtime. Bruce Lansky. (Illus.). 16p. (J). (gr. k up). 1995. lib. bdg. 4.95 (*0-671-51979-4*) S&S Trade.

New Rhymes for Mealtime: The New Adventures of Mother Goose Board Book Collection. Bruce Lansky. (Illus.). (J). 1995. bds. 4.95 (*0-88116-225-6*) Meadowbrook.

New Rhymes for Playtime. Bruce Lansky. (Illus.). 16p. (J). (gr. k up). 1995. lib. bdg. 4.95 (*0-671-51977-8*) S&S Trade.

New Rhymes for Playtime: The New Adventures of Mother Goose Board Book Collection. Bruce Lansky. (Illus.). (J). 1995. bds. 4.95 (*0-88116-227-2*) Meadowbrook.

New Rhyming Dictionary & Poets' Handbook. Burges Johnson. LC 57-9585. 480p. 1991. reprint ed. pap. 16.00 (*0-06-272014-7*, Harper Ref) HarpC.

New Ribbon Embroidery: Innovative, Easy Techniques for Embellishing Ribbon Embroidery with Creativity. Victoria A. Brown. LC 97-19403. (Illus.). 144p. 1997. pap. text 24.95 (*0-8230-3171-3*) Watsn-Guptill.

New Rich in Asia. Richard Robison. LC 96-178419. 224p. (C). 1996. pap. 24.99 (*0-415-11336-9*) Routledge.

New Rich, New Poor, New Russia: Winners & Losers on the Russian Road to Capitalism. Bertram Silverman & Murray Yanowitch. LC 97-6665. 176p. (gr. 13). 1997. pap. text 26.95 (*1-56324-705-4*) M E Sharpe.

New Rich, New Poor, New Russia: Winners & Losers on the Russian Road to Capitalism. Bertram Silverman & Murray Yanowitch. LC 97-6665. 176p. (C). (gr. 13). 1997. text 72.95 (*1-56324-704-6*) M E Sharpe.

***New Rich, New Poor, New Russia: Winners & Losers on the Russian Road to Capitalism.** 2nd expanded ed. Bertram Silverman & Murray Yanowitch. LC 99-462036. (Illus.). 216p. 2000. text 69.95 (*0-7656-0523-6*) M E Sharpe.

***New Rich, New Poor, New Russia: Winners & Losers on the Russian Road to Capitalism.** 2nd rev. ed. Bertram Silverman & Murray Yanowitch. (Illus.). 216p. 2000. reprint ed. pap. text 24.95 (*0-7656-0524-4*) M E Sharpe.

New Riddle Book. Charles Keller. LC 00-22279. (Illus.). 96p. (J). (gr. 3-7). 2000. write for info. (*0-8069-1361-4*) Sterling.

New Riders Companion. Emma Callery. 1994. 19.98 (*0-7858-0165-0*) Bk Sales Inc.

New Riders' Official Internet & World Wide Web Directory. 7th ed. 1100p. 1998. 29.99 (*1-56205-881-9*) New Riders Pub.

New Riders' Official Internet & World Wide Web Yellow Pages. 7th ed. Macmillan Development Team. 1998. pap. text 29.99 (*1-56205-874-6*) New Riders Pub.

New Riders Official Internet Directory. rev. ed. New Riders Publishing Staff. LC 96-174598. 1997. pap. text 29.99 (*1-56205-643-3*) New Riders Pub.

New Riders' Official Internet Directory. 6th ed. LC 98-216422. 1997. 29.99 (*1-56205-793-6*) New Riders Pub.

New Riders' Official Internet Yellow Pages. 2nd ed. Christine Maxwell & Czeslaw J. Grycz. LC 94-34785. 802p. 1994. pap. 29.99 (*1-56205-408-2*) New Riders Pub.

New Riders Official Internet Yellow Pages, 1996. rev. ed. Point Communications Staff. 700p. 1996. pap. text 29.99 (*1-56205-623-9*) New Riders Pub.

New Rider's Official World Wide Web Directory. New Riders Development Group Staff. 1024p. 1995. pap. 29.99 (*1-56205-485-6*) New Riders Pub.

New Riders Official World Wide Web Directory, 1997. New Riders Publishing Staff. 1996. pap. text 34.99 incl. cd-rom (*1-56205-677-8*) New Riders Pub.

New Rider's Official World Wide Web Yellow Pages. abr. ed. Marcia Layton. LC 98-85921. 1998. pap. 19.99 (*0-7357-0005-2*) Que.

New Riders' Official World Wide Web Yellow Pages. 5th ed. 1997. pap. 34.99 incl. cd-rom (*0-614-28477-5*, New Riders Sftwre) MCP SW Interactive.

New Riders' Official World Wide Web Yellow Pages. 5th ed. New Riders Development Group Staff. 1176p. 1997. 34.99 (*1-56205-742-1*) New Riders Pub.

New Riders Official World Wide Web Yellow Pages. 6th ed. 1997. 34.99 (*1-56205-794-4*) New Riders Pub.

New Riders' Official World Wide Web Yellow Pages: 1996 Edition. New Riders Development Group Staff. (Illus.). 1024p. (Orig.). 1995. pap. 29.99 (*1-56205-536-4*) New Riders Pub.

New Rider's Official WWW Directory. rev. ed. Jay Forlini. 1997. pap. text 29.99 (*1-56205-644-1*) New Riders Pub.

New Riders Official WWW International Pages. New Riders Development Staff. 1997. 34.99 (*1-56205-744-8*) New Riders Pub.

New Riders Reference Guide to AutoCAD Release 12. New Riders Publishing Staff. (Illus.). 577p. (Orig.). 1992. pap. 19.95 (*1-56205-058-3*) New Riders Pub.

New Riders Reference Guide to AutoCAD Release 13. 784p. 1995. 25.00 (*1-56205-237-3*) New Riders Pub.

New Right & the Constitution: Turning Back the Legal Clock. Bernard Schwartz. LC 90-39468. 352p. 1990. text 45.00 (*1-55553-082-6*) NE U Pr.

New Right Discourse on Race & Sexuality: Britain, 1968-1990. Anna M. Smith. LC 93-42801. (Cultural Margins Ser.: Vol. 1). 297p. (C). 1995. text 64.95 (*0-521-45297-X*); pap. text 20.95 (*0-521-45921-4*) Cambridge U Pr.

New Right Humanitarians. Tom Barry et al. 66p. (Orig.). 1986. pap. 5.95 (*0-911213-07-4*) Interhemisp Res Ctr.

New Right in Britain: An Introduction to Theory & Practice. Hayes. LC 94-20614. (Pluto Perspectives Ser.). (C). 49.95 (*0-7453-0904-6*, Pub. by Pluto GBR); pap. 14.95 (*0-7453-0903-8*, Pub. by Pluto GBR) Stylus Pub VA.

***New Right in Chile 1973-1997.** Pollack. LC 99-21776. 214p. 1999. text 65.00 (*0-312-22278-5*) St Martin.

New Right in the States: The Groups, the Issues, & the Strategies. Mike Bohannon et al. 92p. 1983. 7.95 (*0-89788-079-X*) CPA Washington.

New Right, New Racism: Race & Reaction in the United States & Great Britain. Amy Ansell. LC 97-14583. 352p. (C). 1998. text 40.00 (*0-8147-0656-8*) NYU Pr.

New Risks: Issues & Management. L. A. Cox. Ed. by Paolo F. Ricci. LC 90-7162. (Advances in Risk Analysis Ser.: Vol. 6). (Illus.). 728p. (C). 1990. text 210.00 (*0-306-43537-3*, Kluwer Plenum) Kluwer Academic.

An Asterisk (*) at the beginning of an entry indicates that the title is appearing for the first time.

*New Risks, New Welfare: Signposts for Social Policy. Ian Shaw. (Broadening Perspectives on Social Policy Ser.). 160p. 2000. pap. text. write for info. (0-631-22042-9) Blackwell Pubs.

New Rite: Conservative Catholic Organizations & Their Allies. Steve Askin. 91p. (Orig.). 1994. pap. text 15.00 (0-915365-23-5) Cath Free Choice.

New River. Gail Peck. (Harperprints Chapbook Competition Ser.). 24p. 1993. 5.00 (0-9624274-9-7) NC Writers Network.

New River: A Legal History. Bernard Rudden. (Illus.). 1985. 39.00 (0-19-825497-0) OUP.

New River: A Photographic Essay. 2nd ed. Ed. by Arnout Hyde, Jr. (Illus.). 96p. reprint ed. pap. 17.00 (0-9623153-4-6) Cannon Graphics.

New River Company: Mining Coal & Making History, 1906-1976. Robert Craig. (Illus.). 111p. 1991. reprint ed. pap. 10.00 (1-881413-06-3) Thomas In-Prints.

New River Early Settlement. Patricia G. Johnson. LC 83-81157. (Illus.). 232p. (YA). (gr. 6 up). 1991. reprint ed. 20.00 (0-9614765-3-2) Walpa Pub.

New River Gorge. Eugenia M. Horstman. LC 93-77187. (Illus.). 44p. (Orig.). 1993. pap. 6.95 (0-936478-16-0) Interpretive Pubns.

*New River Gorge & Summersville Lake Rock Climbers' Guidebook. 2nd rev. ed. Steve Cater. (Illus.). 200p. 1999. 19.95 (0-9678270-1-9) King Coal.

New River Gorge NRA, WV. 1997. 8.99 (1-56695-013-9) Trails Illustrated.

New River Gorge Select Rock Climbs. Steve Cater. (Illus.). 86p. 1997. 11.95 (0-9678270-0-0) King Coal.

*New River Gorge Trail Guide. 2nd ed. Steve Cater. (Illus.). 2000. 11.95 (0-9678270-2-7) King Coal.

New River Heritage, 4 vols., Vol. 1. William Sanders. (Illus.). 350p. 1991. 35.00 (0-9625273-1-9) McClain. Volume I reveals the history of the west side of the New River from Pearisburg, West Virginia, to Pipestem, West Virginia. Volume II recites the history of the Pipestem & Bluestone benches of Flat Top Mountain. Volume III backtracks New River settlers with various maps, photos & family history. Volume IV traces the areas of Flat Top & Camp Creek, West Virginia, with the help of select stories by Barty Wyatt. All volumes depict the author's research & personal experiences of the New River-Bluestone areas of the original Mercer County settlement. William Sanders efforts of retrieving colorful history of this area shall be used in forming a basis for the preservation of the natural beauty in a setting of scenic byways for future generations to enjoy. Each book contains over 300 pages plus over 50 illustrations. *Publisher Paid Annotation.*

New River Heritage, 4 vols., Vol. II. William Sanders. 350p. 1991. 35.00 (0-9625273-2-7) McClain. Volume I reveals the history of the west side of the New River from Pearisburg, West Virginia, to Pipestem, West Virginia. Volume II recites the history of the Pipestem & Bluestone benches of Flat Top Mountain. Volume III backtracks New River settlers with various maps, photos & family history. Volume IV traces the areas of Flat Top & Camp Creek, West Virginia, with the help of select stories by Barty Wyatt. All volumes depict the author's research & personal experiences of the New River-Bluestone areas of the original Mercer County settlement. William Sanders efforts of retrieving colorful history of this area shall be used in forming a basis for the preservation of the natural beauty in a setting of scenic byways for future generations to enjoy. Each book contains over 300 pages plus over 50 illustrations. *Publisher Paid Annotation.*

New River Heritage, Vol. III. 1992. write for info. (0-318-69360-7) W Sanders.

New River Heritage, 4 vols., Vol. III. William Sanders. 300p. 1994. 35.00 (0-9625273-4-3) McClain. Volume I reveals the history of the west side of the New River from Pearisburg, West Virginia, to Pipestem, West Virginia. Volume II recites the history of the Pipestem & Bluestone benches of Flat Top Mountain. Volume III backtracks New River settlers with various maps, photos & family history. Volume IV traces the areas of Flat Top & Camp Creek, West Virginia, with the help of select stories by Barty Wyatt. All volumes depict the author's research & personal experiences of the New River-Bluestone areas of the original Mercer County settlement. William Sanders efforts of retrieving colorful history of this area shall be used in forming a basis for the preservation of the natural beauty in a setting of scenic byways for future generations to enjoy. Each book contains over 300 pages plus over 50 illustrations. *Publisher Paid Annotation.*

New River Heritage, 4 vols., Vol. IV. William Sanders. 300p. 1994. 35.00 (0-9625273-5-1) McClain. Volume I reveals the history of the west side of the New River from Pearisburg, West Virginia, to Pipestem, West Virginia. Volume II recites the history of the Pipestem & Bluestone benches of Flat Top Mountain. Volume III backtracks New River settlers with various maps, photos & family history. Volume IV traces the areas of Flat Top & Camp Creek, West Virginia, with the help of select stories by Barty Wyatt. All volumes depict the author's research & personal experiences of the New River-Bluestone areas of the original Mercer County settlement. William Sanders efforts of retrieving colorful history of this area shall be used in forming a basis for the preservation of the natural beauty in a setting of scenic byways for future generations to enjoy. Each book contains over 300 pages plus over 50 illustrations. *Publisher Paid Annotation.*

New River Rock: Rock Climbs in West Virginia's New River Gorge. Rick Thompson. (Illus.). 200p. (Orig.). 1987. pap. 19.95 (0-9618386-0-4) Etched Stone.

New River Rock: Rock Climbs in West Virginia's New River Gorge. 2nd rev. ed. Richard Thompson. (Illus.). 250p. (Orig.). 1997. pap. 30.00 (1-57540-015-4) Falcon Pub Inc.

New Road! Gail Gibbons. LC 82-45917. (Illus.). 32p. (J). (gr. k-4). 1983. lib. bdg. 15.89 (0-690-04343-0) HarpC Child Bks.

New Road. Gail Gibbons. LC 82-45917. (Trophy Nonfiction Bk.). (Illus.). 32p. (J). (gr. k-4). 1987. reprint ed. pap. 4.95 (0-06-446059-2, HarpTrophy) HarpC Child Bks.

New Road for France. Jacques Soustelle. 1965. 15.00 (0-8315-0047-6) Speller.

New Roadmaps from APA. write for info. (0-318-58203-1) P-H.

New Roads to Development, 64. Raanan Weitz. LC 85-21979. (Contributions in Economics & Economic History Ser.: No. 64). (Illus.). 278p. 1986. 37.95 (0-313-25177-0, WNR/, Greenwood Pr) Greenwood.

New Roadside America: The Modern Traveler's Guide to the Wild & Wonderful World of America's Tourist Attractions. Doug Kirby et al. (Illus.). 288p. (Orig.). 1992. per. 13.00 (0-671-76931-6) S&S Trade Pap.

*New Roberts Rules of Order. Mary Ann De Vries. 1999. pap. 14.55 (0-613-17400-3) Econo-Clad Bks.

New Roberts Rules of Order: The Essential Reference. 2nd ed. Mary A. Devries. 272p. 1998. mass mkt. 6.99 (0-451-19517-5, Sig) NAL.

*New Roger Caras Treasury of Great Cat Stories. Roger A. Caras. 512p. 2000. 11.99 (1-57866-098-X) Galahad Bks.

New Roget Thesaurus. 416p. 1994. pap. write for info. (1-884907-04-0) Paradise Pr FL.

New Roget's Thesaurus. 416p. (Orig.). 1989. pap. 6.95 (0-938261-40-1) PSI & Assocs.

New Roget's Thesaurus: In Dictionary Form. Norman Lewis. 1978. 10.09 (0-606-01133-1, Pub. by Turtleback) Demco.

New Roget's Thesaurus in Dictionary Form. Norman Lewis. 512p. 1986. mass mkt. 5.99 (0-425-09975-X) Berkley Pub.

New Roget's Thesaurus in Dictionary Form. Dean R. None. 1992. pap. 5.99 (0-425-12714-1) Berkley Pub.

New Roget's Thesaurus in Dictionary Form. rev. ed. Norman Lewis. LC 77-24457. 552p. 1981. 13.95 (0-399-12678-3, G P Putnam); 15.95 (0-399-12679-1, G P Putnam) Peng Put Young Read.

New Roget's Thesaurus in Dictionary Form: Student Edition. Paul Roget. 1990. mass mkt., student ed. 5.99 (0-425-12361-8) Berkley Pub.

New Roget's Thesaurus in Dictionary Form (Student Edition) pap., student ed. 5.99 (0-425-13008-8) Berkley Pub.

New Role of Employee Ownership in Corporate Acquisition. 35.00 (0-317-29541-1, #CO3624) Harcourt.

New Role of National Parliaments in Pan-European Construction Proceedings: National Assembly (Paris, 28-29 March, 1996) (Parliamentary Assembly Ser.). (ENG & FRE.). 1996. 18.00 (92-871-3049-3, Pub. by Council of Europe) Manhattan Pub Co.

New Role of the Academies of Sciences in the Balkan Countries. Charalampos Proukakes & N. Katsaros. LC 97-34490. (NATO ASI Ser.). 237p. 1997. lib. bdg. 144.00 (0-7923-4773-0) Kluwer Academic.

New Roles for Educational Fundraising & Institutional Advancement. Ed. by Melvin C. Terrell & James A. Gold. LC 85-644751. (New Directions for Student Services Ser.: No. SS 63). 116p. (Orig.). 1993. pap. 22.00 (1-55542-680-8) Jossey-Bass.

*New Roles for Leaders: A Step-by-Step Guide to Competitive Advantage. Tom Hornsby & Larry Warkaczeski. LC 00-101334. (Illus.). 320p. 2000. pap. 22.95 (1-57736-184-9, Hillsboro Pr) Providence Hse.

New Roles for Psychiatrists in Organized Systems of Care. Ed. by Jeremy A. Lazarus & Steven S. Sharfstein. LC RC465.5.N49 1998. 271p. 1998. pap. text 38.00 (0-88048-758-5, 8758) Am Psychiatric.

New Roles of Parliamentary Committees. Ed. by Lawrence D. Longley & Roger H. Davidson. LC 98-13228. (Library of Legislative Studies). 264p. 1998. 52.50 (0-7146-4891-4, Pub. by F Cass Pubs); pap. 22.50 (0-7146-4442-0, Pub. by F Cass Pubs) Intl Spec Bk.

New Rolling Stone Encyclopedia of Rock & Roll. Ed. by Patricia Romanowski et al. 1120p. pap. 25.00 (0-7866-2588-0, MB96454) Mel Bay.

New Rolling Stone Encyclopedia of Rock & Roll. rev. ed. Ed. by Jon Pareles et al. LC 95-35045. (Illus.). 1136p. 1995. per. 25.00 (0-684-81044-1, Fireside) S&S Trade Pap.

New Romagnolis' Table: Classic & Contemporary Italian Family Recipes Designed for Today's Faster Pace & Lighter Palate. Margaret Romagnoli & G. Franco Romagnoli. LC 87-22871. (Illus.). 320p. 1988. pap. 15.95 (0-87113-214-1, Atlntc Mnthly) Grove-Atltic.

New Romance. David McFadden. 1979. pap. 3.00 (0-916696-10-3) Cross Country.

New Romanized English-Japanese Dictionary: With Japanese-English Dictionary & Most Useful Expressions. Eizo Fujikake. 512p. 1995. pap. 19.95 (0-9647040-0-5) Book East.

New Romanticism. 1989. pap. 21.95 (0-312-03065-7) St Martin.

*New Romanticism: American Fiction since 1950. Ed. by Eberhard Alsen. 380p. 2000. 85.00 (0-8153-3547-4); pap. 29.95 (0-8153-3548-2) Garland.

New Romanticisms: Theory & Critical Practice. Ed. by David L. Clark & Donald C. Coellnicht. (Theory - Culture Ser.). 144p. 1994. text 55.00 (0-8020-2890-X) U of Toronto Pr.

New Roof for My House: Un Techo Nuevo para Mi Casa. Marjory A. Ulm. Tr. by Elizabeth Z. Vigil. (ENG & SPA., Illus.). 20p. (Orig.). (J). (gr. 2-3). 1996. pap. 7.00 (0-9644678-3-6) Biling Publ.

New Room. David Keller. (QRL Poetry Bks.: Vol. XXVII). 1987. 35.00 (0-614-06422-8) Quarterly Rev.

*New Room for William. Sally Grindley. (Illus.). 32p. (J). (ps-3). 2000. 15.99 (0-7636-1196-4) Candlewick Pr.

New Root Formation in Plants & Cuttings. Ed. by Micheal B. Jackson. (Developments in Plant & Soil Sciences Ser.). 1986. text 186.00 (90-247-3260-3) Kluwer Academic.

New Roots: Institutionalizing Environmental Mechanisms in Africa. Clement Dorm-Adzobu. LC 95-45485. 57p. 1995. 20.00 (1-56973-037-7) World Resources Inst.

New Roots for Agriculture: New Edition. Wes Jackson. LC 84-25694. xvi, 151p. 1985. reprint ed. pap. 9.95 (0-8032-7562-5, Bison Books) U of Nebr Pr.

New Rose Expert. D. G. Hessayon. LC 97-131399. (Illus.). 144p. 1997. 12.95 (0-903505-47-9) Sterling.

New Rose Garden of Mystery & Book of Slaves. Muhammad Iqbal. Tr. by M. Hadi Hussain. 66p. (Orig.). 1985. pap. 6.50 (1-56744-348-6) Kazi Pubns.

New Rottweiler. Joan R. Klem & Susan C. Rademacher. LC 96-46188. 1996. 25.95 (0-87605-296-0) Howell Bks.

New Router Handbook. Patrick Spielman. LC 93-25637. (Illus.). 384p. 1993. pap. 17.95 (0-8069-0518-2) Sterling.

New Routes to English, Bk. 3. Sampson. 1980. 9.95 (0-685-59491-2) Heinle & Heinle.

New Royal Court. large type ed. Brian Hoey. (Illus.). 254p. 1992. 22.95 (1-85089-407-8, Pub. by ISIS Lrg Prnt) Transaction Pubs.

New Royal Hindustani & Hindustani English Dictionary. Chitamber Carven. (ENG & HIN.). 706p. 1992. 95.00 (0-8288-8427-7) Fr & Eur.

New Royal Horticultural Society Dictionary of Gardening, 4 Vols. Ed. by Anthony Huxley et al. (Illus.). 3000p. 1999. 795.00 (1-56159-001-0) Groves Dictionaries.

*New Royal Horticultural Society Dictionary of Gardening, 4 vols. Ed. by Anthony Huxley & Mark Griffiths. (Illus.). 3000p. 1999. reprint ed. pap. 250.00 (1-56159-240-4) Groves Dictionaries.

New Rubaiyat of Stanley Berne, Vol. 1. Stanley Berne. LC 73-77094. (Archives of Post-Modern Literature Ser.). 111p. 1973. pap. 25.00 (0-913844-00-4) Am Canadian.

New Rulers in the Ghetto: The Community Development Corporation & Urban Poverty, 28. Harry E. Berndt. LC 76-47888. (Contributions in Afro-American & African Studies: No. 28). (Illus.). 161p. 1977. 47.95 (0-8371-9399-0, BNL/, Greenwood Pr) Greenwood.

New Rules: How to Succeed in Today's Post-Corporate World. John P. Kotter. 1995. 25.00 (0-02-917586-0) Free Pr.

New Rules: Regulation, Markets, & the Quality of American Health Care. Troyen A. Brennan & Donald M. Berwick. (Health Ser.). 416p. 1995. text 40.95 (0-7879-0149-0) Jossey-Bass.

New Rules for a New Economy: Employment & Opportunity in Postindustrial America. Stephen Herzenberg et al. LC 98-18220. (Illus.). 240p. 1998. text 26.50 (0-8014-3524-2, ILR Press) Cornell U Pr.

*New Rules for a New Economy: Employment & Opportunity in Postindustrial America. Stephen Herzenberg et al. 2000. pap. 17.95 (0-8014-8658-0) Cornell U Pr.

New Rules for Classic Games. R. Wayne Schmittberger. LC 91-22386. 256p. 1992. pap. 9.95 (0-471-53621-0) Wiley.

New Rules for Financial Success: 25 Myths You've Got to Avoid If You Want to Manage Your Money. Jonathan Clements. LC 97-30430. 1998. 22.50 (0-684-83982-2) S&S Trade.

New Rules for Fund Raising. Larry Entwistle et al. (Defining Moments Ser.: Vol. 12). audio 12.99 (0-310-24629-6) Zondervan.

New Rules for Fund Raising. Willow Creek Resources Staff & Willow Creek Resources Staff. (Defining Moments Ser.: Vol. 5). 1994. audio 12.99 (0-310-21019-4) Zondervan.

New Rules for the New Economy: 10 Radical Strategies for a Connected World. Kevin Kelly. LC 98-36917. (Illus.). 179p. 1998. 19.95 (0-670-88111-2) Viking Penguin.

*New Rules for the New Economy: 10 Radical Strategies for a Connected World. Kevin Kelly. 192p. 1999. pap. 12.95 (0-14-028060-X, Penguin Bks) Viking Penguin.

New Rules For the New World: Cautionary Tales For the New World Manager. Eddie Obeng. 1998. 24.65 (1-900961-15-6) Capstone Pub NH.

New Rules for Victims of Armed Conflict. M. Bothe et al. 1982. lib. bdg. 342.50 (90-247-2537-2) Kluwer Academic.

New Rules of Corporate Conduct: Rewriting the Social Charter. Ian Wilson. LC 99-33204. 240p. 2000. 65.00 (1-56720-249-7) Greenwood.

New Rules of Golf. Tom Watson & Frank Hannigan. 1984. pap. 7.95 (0-685-08080-3) Random.

New Rules of Healthcare Marketing: 23 Strategies for Success. Arthur C. Sturm. LC 97-42425. 1998. pap. 33.00 (1-56793-074-3) Health Admin Pr.

*New Rules of Internet Marketing: Industry Experts Reveal the Secrets to Marketing, Advertising. eBrandedBooks.com Staff. (Inside the Minds Ser.). 224p. 2000. pap. 27.95 (1-58762-002-2) ebrandedbookscom.

New Rules of Marketing: How to Use One-to-One Relationship Marketing to Be the Leader in Your Industry. Frederick Newell. LC 97-9622. 1997. 27.95 (0-7863-1228-9, Irwn Prfssnl) McGraw-Hill Prof.

New Rules of Measurement: What Every Psychologist & Educator Should Know. Ed. by Susan E. Embretson & Scott L. Hershberger. LC 98-24513. 272p. 1999. 69.95 (0-8058-2860-5) L Erlbaum Assocs.

*New Rules of Money: Edelman,&Ric. abr. ed. Ric Edelman. 1998. audio 18.00 (0-694-51929-4, CPN2718) HarperAudio.

New Rules of Money: 88 Simple Strategies for Financial Success Today. Ric Edelman. LC 97-42402. (Illus.). 320p. 1999. pap. 14.00 (0-06-272074-0, Harper Ref) HarpC.

New Rules of Money: 88 Strategies for Financial Success Today. Ric Edelman. LC 97-42402. (Illus.). 320p. 1998. 25.00 (0-06-270219-X, Harper Ref) HarpC.

New Rules of Professional Conduct: The Impact on Ethical Practice in Massachusetts. James S. Bolan & Massachusetts Continuing Legal Education, Inc. Sta. LC 97-76381. xxii, 508p. 1998. write for info. (1-57589-076-3) Mass CLE.

New Rules of Sociological Method. 2nd ed. Anthony Giddens. LC 93-83809. 200p. (C). 1993. 37.50 (0-8047-2225-0); pap. 14.95 (0-8047-2226-9) Stanford U Pr.

New Rules of the Game: The Four Key Experiences Managers Must Have to Thrive in the Non-Hierarchical 90s & Beyond. James R. Emshoff & Teri E. Denlinger. LC 91-58516. 240p. 1992. reprint ed. pap. 11.00 (0-88730-532-6, HarpBusn) HarpInfo.

New Rules of the Ratings Game. Robert Balon. 156p. 1995. pap. 59.95 (0-89324-227-6, 3792) Natl Assn Broadcasters.

New Rural America. Ed. by Frank Clemente & Richard D. Lambert. LC 76-27028. (Annals Ser.: No. 429). 1977. pap. 18.00 (0-87761-209-9) Am Acad Pol Soc Sci.

New Russia. John Gillies. LC 93-25380. (Discovering Our Heritage Ser.). (Illus.). 128p. (YA). (gr. 5 up). 1994. lib. bdg. 14.95 (0-87518-481-2, Dillon Silver Burdett) Silver Burdett Pr.

New Russia: A Political Risk Analysis. LC 94-226115. (Research Reports: No. M213). 1994. 325.00 (0-85058-798-0) Economist Intell.

New Russia: Between the First & Second Five-Year Plans. Ed. by Jerome Davis. LC 68-22909. (Essay Index Reprint Ser.). 1977. 19.95 (0-8369-0365-X) Ayer.

*New Russia: Economic Transition Reconsidered. Lawrence R. Klein & Marshall I. Pomer. LC 00-34443. 2000. pap. write for info. (0-8047-4165-4) Stanford U Pr.

New Russia: Journey from Riga to the Crimea, by Way of Kiev. Mary Holderness. LC 75-115547. (Russia Observed, Series I). 1970. reprint ed. 20.95 (0-405-03035-5) Ayer.

New Russia: Troubled Transformation. Ed. by Gail W. Lapidus. 320p. (C). 1994. pap. 28.00 (0-8133-2077-1, Pub. by Westview) HarpC.

New Russian Art: Paintings from the Christian Keesee Collection. Photos by Jon Burris. (Illus.). 138p. 1995. 35.00 (1-55670-435-6) Stewart Tabori & Chang.

New Russian-Chinese Dictionary of Mathematical Terms. Science Press Staff. (CHI & RUS.). 766p. 1988. lib. bdg. 75.00 (0-7859-3660-2, 7030004620) Fr & Eur.

New Russian Diaspora: Russian Minorities in the Former Soviet Republics. Ed. by Vladimir Shapentokh et al. LC 94-727. 248p. (gr. 13). 1994. pap. text 39.95 (1-56324-336-9) M E Sharpe.

New Russian Diaspora: Russian Minorities in the Former Soviet Republics. Ed. by Vladimir Shlapentokh et al. LC 94-727. 248p. (gr. 13). 1994. text 85.95 (1-56324-335-0) M E Sharpe.

New Russian Nationalism, 16. John B. Dunlop. (Washington Papers: Vol. 16). 1985. 47.95 (0-275-90191-2, Praeger Pubs) Greenwood.

New Russian Nationalism, 16. John D. Dunlop. (Washington Papers: No. 116). 192p. 1985. pap. 11.95 (0-275-91665-0, B1665, Praeger Pubs) Greenwood.

New Russian Poets. Ed. & Tr. by George Reavey. 320p. 1981. pap. 9.95 (0-7145-2715-7) M Boyars Pubs.

New Russian Poets. Ed. by George Reavey. 1966. 15.00 (0-8079-0095-8); pap. 7.95 (0-8079-0096-6) October.

New Russians. rev. ed. Hedrick Smith. 656p. 1991. pap. 12.50 (0-380-71651-8, Avon Bks) Morrow Avon.

New Ryan: The ST's & SC's. Ev Cassagneres. 195p. 1995. pap. 24.95 (0-911139-20-6) Flying Bks.

New S Language. Becker. 1988. lib. bdg. 64.95 (0-412-74150-4) Chapman & Hall.

N

New S Language: A Programming Environment for Data Analysis & Graphics. Richard A. Becker et al. 702p. (C). (gr. 13). 1988. per. 69.95 (*0-534-09193-8*, Chap & Hall CRC) CRC Pr.

New S Language: A Programming Environment for Data Analysis & Graphics. Richard A. Becker et al. (Wadsworth & Brooks-Cole Statistics-Probability Ser.). 702p. (C). 1988. mass mkt. 44.50 (*0-534-09192-X*) Chapman & Hall.

New Sabin, 6. Lawrence S. Thompson. LC 73-85960. 1980. 25.00 (*0-87875-159-9*) Whitston Pub.

New Sabin: Entries, Vol. 7. Lawrence S. Thompson. 345p. 1980. 25.00 (*0-87875-182-3*) Whitston Pub.

New Sabin: Entries 5803-8443, Vol. 3. Lawrence S. Thompson. LC 73-85960. 1976. 25.00 (*0-87875-103-3*) Whitston Pub.

New Sabin Vol. 4: Entries 8444-11221. Lawrence S. Thompson. LC 73-85960. 1977. 25.00 (*0-87875-134-3*) Whitston Pub.

New Sabin Vol. 9: Entries 21753-23828. Ed. by Lawrence S. Thompson. LC 73-85960. 362p. 1983. 30.00 (*0-87875-262-5*) Whitston Pub.

New Sabin Vol. 10: Entries 23829-25946. Ed. by Lawrence D. S. Thompson. LC 73-85960. 319p. 1984. 30.00 (*0-87875-287-0*) Whitston Pub.

New Sailboard Book. 2nd ed. Jake Grubb. 1990. pap. 16.95 (*0-393-30682-8*) Norton.

*****New Saint Bernard.** George G. Williams. (Illus.). 176p. 2000. 29.95 (*1-58245-168-0*) Howell Bks.

New Saint Joseph Baltimore Catechism. rev. ed. Bennet Kelley. (Official Baltimore Catechism Ser.: No. 1). (Illus.). (J). (gr. 3-5). 1976. pap., student ed. 2.75 (*0-89942-241-1*, 241/05) Catholic Bk Pub.

New Saint Joseph Baltimore Catechism. rev. ed. Bennet Kelley. (Official Baltimore Catechism Ser.: No. 2). (Illus.). (J). (gr. 6-8). 1976. pap. 3.25 (*0-89942-242-X*, 242/05) Catholic Bk Pub.

New St. Joseph Children's Missal for Boys. (Illus.). 1977. 4.95 (*0-89942-804-5*, 806/42B) Catholic Bk Pub.

New Saint Joseph Children's Missal for Girls. (Illus.). 1977. 4.95 (*0-89942-803-7*, 806/42W) Catholic Bk Pub.

First Book of Saints. Lawrence G. Lovasik. (Illus.). 96p. (J). 1987. 5.75 (*0-89942-133-4*, 133/22) Catholic Bk Pub.

New Saint Joseph First Communion Catechism. rev. ed. Bennet Kelley. (Official Baltimore Catechism Ser.: No. 0). (Illus.). (J). (gr. 1-2). 1976. pap. 2.25 (*0-89942-240-3*, 240/05) Catholic Bk Pub.

New Saint Joseph Sunday Missal & Hymnal. (Illus.). 1586p. 1986. 15.50 (*0-89942-820-7*, 820/09); 16.95 (*0-89942-819-3*, 820/22GN); 16.95 (*0-89942-818-5*, 820/22-B); 17.95 (*0-89942-817-7*, 820/10-BR) Catholic Bk Pub.

*****New St. Martin's Handbook.** Andrea Lunsford & Connors. 1999. pap. text 32.95 (*0-312-25101-7*) St Martin.

New St. Martin's Handbook. 4th ed. Andrea Lunsford. LC 98-84406. 1998. pap. text 36.95 (*0-312-16744-X*) St Martin.

New Salad Cookbook. (Illus.). 64p. 1988. pap. 3.95 (*0-8249-3074-6*) Ideals.

New Sales Force. Stowell. Date not set. 25.00 (*0-02-874004-1*) Free Pr.

New Sales Manager: Challenges for the 21st Century. Walter Vieira. LC 97-11577. 1997. pap. 14.95 (*0-8039-9385-4*) Sage.

*****New Sales Speak.** Terri L. Sjodin. 240p. 2000. pap. 18.95 (*0-471-39570-6*) Wiley.

New Salmagundi Reader. Ed. by Robert Boyers & Peggy Boyers. LC 96-8965. (C). 1996. pap. 24.95 (*0-8156-0384-3*, BOSRP); text 49.00 (*0-8156-2704-1*, BOSR) Syracuse U Pr.

New Saltwater Aquarium Handbook. George Blasiola. 144p. 1991. pap. 9.95 (*0-8120-4482-7*) Barron.

New Samisch. Andrew Martin. 1997. pap. 19.95 (*1-85744-065-X*) S&S Trade.

*****New Sammy Cahn Song Book.** Sammy Cahn. (Illus.). 1999. pap. 24.95 (*1-57623-763-X*) Wrner Bros.

New Samoyed. 3rd ed. Robert Ward & Dolly Ward. LC 97-20503. 302p. 1997. 27.95 (*0-87605-701-6*) Howell Bks.

New Sampler Quilt. Diana Leone. Ed. by Maura McAndrew. LC 95-83398. (Illus.). 144p. 1993. reprint ed. 24.95 (*1-57120-011-8*, 10135) C & T Pub.

New San Francisco at Your Feet. 3rd rev. ed. Margot P. Doss. LC 79-6170. (Illus.). 256p. 1990. pap. 12.95 (*0-8021-1145-9*, Grove) Grove-Atltic.

New Saroyan Reader: A Connoisseur's Anthology of the Writings of William Saroyan. William Saroyan. Ed. by Brian Darwent. LC 83-73533. 350p. 1984. 17.95 (*0-916870-80-4*); pap. 11.50 (*0-916870-81-2*) Creat Arts Bk.

New SAT in Ten Easy Steps. 2nd ed. Raymond Karelitz. LC 94-8686. 252p. 1994. pap. 9.95 (*1-55850-362-5*) Adams Media.

New Savory Wild Mushroom. 3rd enl. rev. ed. Margaret McKenny & Daniel E. Stuntz. (Illus.). 264p. 1987. pap. 19.95 (*0-295-96480-4*) U of Wash Pr.

New Saxa Loquuntur. J. J. Hondius. Ed. by M. C. J. Miller. 300p. 2000. reprint ed. 30.00 (*0-89005-116-X*) Ares.

New SBC: Fundamentalism's Impact on the Southern Baptist Convention. Grady C. Cothen. LC 95-2441. 232p. 1995. pap. 18.00 (*1-57312-025-1*) Smyth & Helwys.

New Scholarship - New Serials: Proceedings of the North American Serials Interest Group, Inc., 8th Annual Conference, June 10-13, 1993, Brown University, Providence, R.I. Ed. by Gail McMillan & Marilyn L. Norstedt. LC 94-6729. (Serials Librarian Ser.: Vol. 24, Nos. 3-4). (Illus.). 290p. 1994. lib. bdg. 39.95 (*1-56024-685-5*) Haworth Pr.

New Scholarship from BFI Research. Duncan Petrie. LC 96-139034. 1996. pap. text 19.95 (*0-85170-520-0*, Pub. by British Film Inst) Ind U Pr.

New Scholarship on Dewey. Ed. by Jim Garrison. LC 95-8387. 238p. (C). 1995. pap. text 44.00 (*0-7923-3446-9*, Pub. by Kluwer Academic) Kluwer Academic.

New School: 1809 Edition. Thomas Bernard. Ed. & Intro. by Jeffrey Stern. (Classics in Education Ser.). 120p. 1996. reprint ed. 65.00 (*1-85506-271-2*) Bks Intl VA.

New School Acting: Taking It to the Next Level. Jeremy Whelan. 201p. (Orig.). 1996. pap. 17.00 (*0-9650908-0-9*) Whelan Intl.

New School Health Handbook 1997: A Ready Reference for School Nurses & Educators. 3rd ed. Jerry Newton et al. LC 97-7189. 388p. (C). 1997. text 34.95 (*0-13-614652-X*) P-H.

New Schoolhouse. Ed. by W. M. Chramosta et al. (Illus.). 260p. 1997. 58.00 (*3-211-82814-1*, Pub. by Birkhauser) Princeton Arch.

New Schoolma'am: A Summer in North Sparta. Horatio Alger, Jr. 140p. 1976. reprint ed. 24.00 (*0-686-37020-1*) G K Westgard.

New Schools for a New Century: A Leader's Guide to High School Reform. Kenneth J. Tewel. LC 94-46301. 248p. 1995. boxed set 54.95 (*1-884015-38-7*) St Lucie Pr.

New Schools for a New Century: The Redesign of Urban Education. Diane Ravitch. 336p. 1999. pap. text 15.95 (*0-300-07874-9*) Yale U Pr.

New Schools for a New Century: The Redesign of Urban Education. Diane Ravitch & Joseph P. Viteritti. LC 96-39929. 320p. 1997. 30.00 (*0-300-07046-2*) Yale U Pr.

New Schoonmaker Ency Win. exp. rev. ed. Alexis Bespaloff. LC 88-5270. (Illus.). 544p. 1988. 25.00 (*0-688-05749-7*, Wm Morrow) Morrow Avon.

*****New Science.** Giambattista Vico. Tr. by David Marsh. (Penguin Classics Ser.). 560p. 1999. pap. 20.99 (*0-14-043569-7*, Penguin Classics) Viking Penguin.

New Science: Poems. J. T. Barbarese. LC 88-26080. (Contemporary Poetry Ser.). 96p. 1989. pap. 14.95 (*0-8203-1117-0*) U of Ga Pr.

New Science: Self-Esteem Psychology. Robert N. Campbell. LC 84-5085. 354p. (Orig.). 1984. lib. bdg. 52.00 (*0-8191-3892-4*) U Pr of Amer.

New Science: The Breakdown of Connections & the Birth of Sociology. Bruce H. Mazlish. 352p. 1989. text 70.00 (*0-19-505846-1*) OUP.

New Science: The Breakdown of Connections & the Birth of Sociology. Bruce Mazlish. LC 93-3773. 348p. 1993. reprint ed. pap. 18.95 (*0-271-01092-4*) Pa St U Pr.

New Science - New Architecture? Maggie Toy. (Architectural Design Ser.: Vol. 129). 112p. 1997. pap. 29.95 (*1-85490-498-1*) Academy Ed UK.

New Science Library, 6 vols. Peter Lafferty & George Fryer. LC 95-21537. (Illus.). (J). 1995. write for info. (*0-89434-160-X*) Ferguson.

New Science New Architecture. Maggie Toy. 112p. 1998. pap. 39.95 (*0-471-97739-X*, Wiley-Interscience) Wiley.

New Science, New World. Denise Albanese. LC 95-47757. (Illus.). 264p. 1996. pap. text 16.95 (*0-8223-1768-0*); lib. bdg. 49.95 (*0-8223-1759-1*) Duke.

New Science of Asset Allocation. Warren E. Bitters. (Glenlake Business Monographs). 320p. 1998. 55.00 (*1-884964-70-2*) Fitzroy Dearborn.

New Science of Asset Allocation. Warren E. Bitters. 320p. 1998. 55.00 (*1-888998-02-4*) Glenlake Pub.

New Science of Color. B. Irwin. Date not set. pap. text 9.95 (*0-87877-246-4*) Newcastle Pub.

New Science of Drowning: The Perspectives on Intervention & Prevention. Sports Aid International Inc. Staff. LC 98-55090. 314p. 1998. 59.95 (*1-57444-223-6*, SL2236) St Lucie Pr.

New Science of Elocution. S. S. Hamill. LC 72-37014. (Granger Index Reprint Ser.). 1977. reprint ed. 23.95 (*0-8369-6313-X*) Ayer.

New Science of Giambattista Vico: Unabridged Translation of the Third Edition (1744) with the Addition of "Practice of the New Science" unabridged ed. Giambattista Vico. Tr. by Thomas G. Bergin & Max H. Fisch from ITA. LC 68-16393. (Illus.). xlv, 445p. 1984. pap. text 17.95 (*0-8014-9265-3*) Cornell U Pr.

New Science of Healing: The Doctrine of the Unity of Diseases. Louis Kuhne. 460p. 1993. reprint ed. spiral bd. 25.00 (*0-7873-0518-9*) Hlth Research.

New Science of Investing: Managing Your Money in the Twenty First Century. Eric Kirzner. 1996. 50.00 (*0-7863-0003-5*, Irwn Prfssnl) McGraw-Hill Prof.

New Science of Life: The Hypothesis of Morphic Resonance. Rupert Sheldrake. LC 94-44869. (Illus.). 272p. 1995. pap. 14.95 (*0-89281-535-3*, Park St Pr) Inner Tradit.

New Science of Marketing: State-of-the-Art Tools for Anticipating & Tracking the Market Forces that will Shape Your Company's Future. Vithala R. Rao & Joe H. Steckel. LC 96-195518. 250p. 1995. text 42.50 (*1-55738-539-4*, Irwn Prfssnl) McGraw-Hill Prof.

New Science of Organizations: A Reconceptualization of the Wealth of Nations. Alberto G. Ramos. 224p. 1984. pap. 17.95 (*0-8020-6561-9*) U of Toronto Pr.

New Science of Organizations: A Reconceptualization of the Wealth of Nations. Alberto G. Ramos. LC 81-178962. 224p. reprint ed. pap. 69.50 (*0-608-16236-1*, 202646900049) Bks Demand.

New Science of Politics: An Introduction. Eric Voegelin. LC 52-13531. xiv, 211p. 1987. pap. text 14.95 (*0-226-86114-7*) U Ch Pr.

New Science of Politics: An Introduction. Eric Voegelin. 1997. pap. text 9.00 (*0-226-86112-0*) U Ch Pr.

New Science of Stock Market Investing: How to Predict Stock Price Movements. Gerald H. Rosen. 224p. 1989. 18.95 (*0-88730-393-5*, HarpBusn) HarpInfo.

New Science of Strong Materials. J. E. Gordon. 1991. pap. 16.95 (*0-14-013597-9*, Pub. by Pnguin Bks Ltd) Trafalgar.

New Science of Strong Materials or Why You Don't Fall Through the Floor. J. E. Gordon. LC 83-43103. (Illus.). 287p. 1984. reprint ed. pap. text 14.95 (*0-691-02380-8*, Pub. by Princeton U Pr) Cal Prin Full Svc.

New Science of Swimming. 2nd ed. James E. Counsilman & Brian E. Counsilman. LC 93-29229. 432p. 1994. pap. text 53.00 (*0-13-099888-5*) P-H.

New Science of Technical Analysis. Thomas R. DeMark. (Wiley Finance Editions Ser.). 264p. 1994. 59.95 (*0-471-03548-3*) Wiley.

New Science of Technical Analysis: Using the Statistical Techniques of Neuroscience. Clifford J. Sherry. 300p. 1994. text 60.00 (*1-55738-502-5*, Irwn Prfssnl) McGraw-Hill Prof.

New Science out of Old Books: Studies in Manuscripts & Early Printed Books in Honour of A. I. Doyle. Richard Beadle. Ed. by A. J. Piper. (Illus.). 467p. 1995. 121.95 (*1-85928-003-X*, Pub. by Scolar Pr) Ashgate Pub Co.

New Science Strategy for Space Astronomy & Astrophysics. National Research Council Staff. LC 97-193223. 92p. (C). 1997. pap. text 15.00 (*0-309-05827-9*) Natl Acad Pr.

*****New Science Teacher: Cultivating Good Practice** Deborah J. Trumbull. LC 99-33355. (Ways of Knowing in Science Ser.). 144p. 1999. pap. text 18.95 (*0-8077-3874-3*) Tchrs Coll.

*****New Science Teacher: Cultivating Good Practice.** Deborah J. Trumbull. LC 99-33355. (Ways of Knowing in Science Ser.). 144p. 1999. write for info. (*0-8077-3875-1*) Tchrs Coll.

*****New Sciences for Public Administration & Policy: Connections & Reflections.** Ed. by Goktug Morcol & Linda F. Dennard. LC 99-50556. x, 314p. 2000. pap. 24.95 (*1-57420-070-4*) Chatelaine.

New Scientific Applications of Geometry & Topology. Ed. by De Witt L. Sumners et al. LC 92-26335. (Proceedings of Symposia in Applied Mathematics Ser.: Vol. 45). 250p. 1992. text 36.00 (*0-8218-5502-6*, PSAPM/45) Am Math.

*****New Scofield Readers Edition Study Bible.** Scofield Study Bible Staff. 1760p. 1998. 44.99 (*0-19-528142-X*) OUP.

*****New Scofield Reader's Study Bible.** SCF STDY OLD. 1760p. 1998. pap. 39.99 (*0-19-528145-4*) OUP.

*****New Scofield Study Bible.** 1760p. 1998. 79.99 (*0-19-528167-5*) OUP.

*****New Scofield Study Bible.** New Scofield Study Staff. 1760p. 1998. 44.99 (*0-19-528144-6*) OUP.

*****New Scofield Study Bible: Supersaver Edition.** (Illus.). 1998. 54.99 (*0-19-528150-0*) OUP.

New Scofield Study Pocket Bible. 1760p. 1998. 44.99 (*0-19-528134-9*) OUP.

*****New Scotland Township: New York.** New Scotland Historical Association Staff. LC 00-101909. (Images of America Ser.). (Illus.). 128p. 2000. pap. 18.99 (*0-7385-0420-3*) Arcadia Publng.

New Scots. Bashir Maan. 200p. (C). 1996. pap. 30.00 (*0-85976-357-9*, Pub. by J Donald) St Mut.

New Scottish Terrier. Cindy Cooke. LC 95-47430. (Illus.). 256p. 1996. per. 25.95 (*0-87605-307-X*) Howell Bks.

*****New Scratchboard.** Charles Ewing. (Illus.). 144p. 2000. pap. 29.95 (*0-8230-4658-3*) Watsn-Guptill.

New Screenwriter Looks at the New Screenwriter. William Froug. LC 91-48355. 369p. (Orig.). 1991. pap. 15.95 (*1-879505-04-5*) Silman James Pr.

New Screenwriter's Workshop. Christopher Keane. 320p. (Orig.). (C). 1995. pap. 18.95 (*0-9647922-0-6*) ME Photog Workshops.

New Script of Life: A Relationship Textbook. Loy Young. Ed. by Kathryn Hall. 238p. (Orig.). 1994. pap. 14.95 (*1-882888-01-4*) Aquarius Hse.

*****New Scriptwriter's Journal.** Mary Johnson. (Illus.). 288p. 2000. pap. 16.95 (*0-240-80384-1*, Focal) Buttrwrth-Heinemann.

*****New Scrooge Investing: The Bargain Hunter's Guide to Thrifty Investments, Super Discounts, Special Privileges & Other Money-Saving Tips.** Mark Skousen. LC 99-54988. 2000. 22.95 (*0-07-135500-6*, McGrw-H College) McGrw-H Hghr Educ.

New Sculpture. Susan Beattie. LC 83-42876. (Studies in British Art). (Illus.). 240p. 1985. reprint ed. pap. 30.00 (*0-300-03359-1*, Y-517) Yale U Pr.

New Sculpture: Profiles in Contemporary Australian Sculpture. Nevill Drury. (Illus.). 186p. 1993. text 35.00 (*976-8097-72-8*) Gordon & Breach.

New Sculpture: Robert Gober, Jeff Koons, Haim Steinbach. Robert Gober et al. (Illus.). 10p. 1986. pap. 3.00 (*0-941548-11-2*) Ren Soc U Chi.

New SDR Allocation? John Williamson. LC 84-3731. (Policy Analyses in International Economics Ser.: No. 7). 64p. (Orig.). reprint ed. pap. 30.00 (*0-7837-4217-7*, 204390600012) Bks Demand.

*****New Seasons of Happiness: The Ultimate Dimension of Life.** John M. Oxley. LC 99-90597. 1999. 25.00 (*0-7388-0488-6*); pap. 18.00 (*0-7388-0489-4*) Xlibris Corp.

New Seattle. FASA Corp. Staff. (Shadowrun Ser.). 176p. 1998. pap. 18.00 (*1-55560-342-4*, 03424F, Pub. by FASA Corp) NTC Contemp Pub Co.

New SEC Reform Proposals: The "Aircraft Carrier"; Regulation of Takeovers. Ed. by Ted Trautmann. 600p. 1998. pap. text 20.00 (*0-8080-0336-4*) CCH INC.

New Second Generation. Ed. by Alejandro Portes. 316p. (C). 1996. text 45.00 (*0-87154-683-3*); pap. text 19.95 (*0-87154-684-1*) Russell Sage.

New Secondary French, Level 1. Bragger. (Miscellaneous/Catalogs Ser.). 2000. pap., wbk. ed., lab manual ed. 17.95 (*0-8384-7357-1*) Brooks-Cole.

New Secondary French, Level 1. Bragger. (Miscellaneous/Catalogs Ser.). 2000. pap. 47.95 (*0-8384-7339-3*) Heinle & Heinle.

New Secondary French, Level 2. Bragger. (Miscellaneous/Catalogs Ser.). 2002. mass mkt., student ed. 48.95 (*0-8384-7338-5*) Heinle & Heinle.

New Secret of Effective Natural Stress Weight Management: Using Rhodiola Rosea & Rhododendron Caucasirum. Zakir Ramazanov et al. LC 99-71262. (Illus.). 88p. 1999. pap. 8.95 (*1-884820-45-X*) SAFE GOODS.

New Secretary: How to Handle People As Well As You Handle Paper. Dianna D. Booher. LC 85-15864. 352p. 1985. reprint ed. pap. 109.20 (*0-608-02820-7*, 206388700007) Bks Demand.

New Secrets for Acquiring Wealth - & Keeping It! It's Your Personality, Stupid! Maxx Robinson. LC 97-69566. (Illus.). 256p. (Orig.). 1999. mass mkt. 19.95 (*1-891014-03-X*) Cardinal Books.

New Secrets of a Corporate Headhunter. John Wareham. LC 94-3986. 176p. 1994. 20.00 (*0-88730-650-0*, HarpBusn) HarpInfo.

New Secrets of Charisma. Doe Lang. LC 98-38352. (Illus.). 336p. 1999. pap. 14.95 (*0-8092-2826-2*, 282620, Contemporary Bks) NTC Contemp Pub Co.

New Security Agenda in the Asia-Pacific Region. Denny Roy. LC 97-11429. 256p. 1997. text 59.95 (*0-312-17371-7*) St Martin.

New Security Challenges. Peters. LC 96-17549. 216p. 1996. text 59.95 (*0-312-16262-6*) St Martin.

New Seed & Old Laws: Regulatory Reform & the Diversification of National Seed Systems. Robert Tripp. 208p. 1998. pap. 24.95 (*1-85339-415-7*, Pub. by Intermed Tech) Stylus Pub VA.

New Seed Starter's Handbook. Nancy Bubel. LC 87-27698. 416p. 1988. pap. 15.95 (*0-87857-752-1*) Rodale Pr Inc.

New Seeds & Poor People. Michael Lipton & Richard Longhurst. LC 88-23079. (Johns Hopkins Studies in Development). 489p. reprint ed. pap. 151.60 (*0-608-06082-8*, 206641400008) Bks Demand.

New Seeds in Old Soil: A Study of the Land Reform in Western Wollega, Ethiopia, 1975-1976. Michael Stahl. (Research Report Ser.: No. 40). 90p. 1981. write for info. (*91-7106-112-6*, Pub. by Nordic Africa) Transaction Pubs.

New Seeds of Contemplation. rev. ed. Thomas Merton. LC 61-17869. 297p. 1974. pap. 10.95 (*0-8112-0099-X*, NDP337, Pub. by New Directions) Norton.

New Select Committees: A Study of the 1979 Reforms. 2nd ed. Gavin Drewry. (Illus.). 496p. 1989. pap. write for info. (*0-19-822784-1*) OUP.

New Select Committees: A Study of the 1979 Reforms. 2nd ed. Gavin Drewry. (Illus.). 496p. 1989. 85.00 (*0-19-822835-7*) OUP.

New Selected Odes of Pindar. Eleanor Dickey & Richard Hamilton. (Bryn Mawr Greek Commentaries Ser.). 112p. (Orig.). (C). 1991. pap. text 8.00 (*0-929524-72-1*) Bryn Mawr Commentaries.

New Selected Poems. Ted Hughes. LC 80-8207. 256p. 1982. pap. 17.00 (*0-06-090925-0*, CN925, Perennial) HarperTrade.

*****New Selected Poems.** Galway Kinnell. LC PS3521.I582A6 2000. 176p. 2000. 25.00 (*0-618-02187-6*) HM.

New Selected Poems. Philip Levine. 1992. pap. 20.00 (*0-679-74056-2*) McKay.

New Selected Poems. Stevie Smith. LC 88-1428. (Illus.). 160p. 1988. 18.95 (*0-8112-1067-7*, Pub. by New Directions); pap. 9.95 (*0-8112-1068-5*, NDP659, Pub. by New Directions) Norton.

New Selected Poems, 1970-1985. Jerome Rothenberg. LC 86-5388. 160p. 1986. pap. 8.95 (*0-8112-0997-0*, NDP625, Pub. by New Directions) Norton.

New Selected Poems, 1970-1985. Jerome Rothenberg. LC 86-5388. 160p. 1986. 23.50 (*0-8112-0996-2*, Pub. by New Directions) Norton.

New Self: Self Therapy with Transactional Analysis. Muriel James & Louis M. Savary. LC 76-55632. (Illus.). 1977. pap. 8.61 (*0-201-03463-8*) Addison-Wesley.

New Self-Directed Work Teams: Mastering the Challenge. 2nd ed. Jack Orsburn et al. LC 99-30690. (Illus.). 416p. 1999. 45.00 (*0-07-043414-X*) McGraw.

New Self-Hypnosis. Paul Adams. 1978. pap. 10.00 (*0-87980-233-2*) Wilshire.

*****New Sensations for Horse & Rider.** Tex Larrigan. 2000. 35.00 (*0-85131-767-7*, Pub. by J A Allen) Trafalgar.

New Sense of Destiny from Ancient Symbols: Renewal of Vision Through the Lost Language. George W. Fisk. (Illus.). 126p. (Orig.). 1988. pap. 9.95 (*0-9620507-0-9*) Cosmic Concepts Pr.

New Sensor for Measurement of Low Air Flow Velocity. H. M. Hashemian & E. T. Riggsbee. (Illus.). (Orig.). 1995. pap. write for info. (*1-882148-03-7*) Analysis & Measurement.

New Sensual Massage. 2nd rev. ed. Gordon Inkeles. LC 92-20126. (Illus.). 176p. 1998. pap. 17.95 (*0-9669149-0-2*) Arcata Arts.

New Sentence. Ron Silliman. LC 85-63543. (Roof Bks.). 200p. (Orig.). 1987. pap. 15.00 (*0-937804-20-7*) Segue NYC.

New Separator Design for Floating Production Facilities. John A. Endacott. 1989. 150.00 (*90-6314-501-2*, Pub. by Lorne & MacLean Marine) St Mut.

New Serge in Wearable Art. Ann Boyce. LC 95-23435. (Illus.). 128p. 1995. pap. 18.95 (*0-8019-8396-7*) Krause Pubns.

New Series see **Southern Literary Journal & Monthly Magazine**

New Series of Blackfoot Texts. Christianus C. Uhlenbeck. LC 76-44083. (Verhandelingen der Koninklijke Akademie Van Wetenschappen Te Amsterdam. Afdeeling Letterkunde. Nieuwe Reeks, Deel Ser.: 13, No. 1). reprint ed. 55.00 (*0-404-15798-X*) AMS Pr.

An Asterisk (*) at the beginning of an entry indicates that the title is appearing for the first time.

New Series on Home Mortgage Yields since 1951. Jack M. Guttentag & Morris Beck. (General Ser.: No. 92). 377p. 1971. reprint ed. 98.10 (*0-87014-213-5*) Natl Bur Econ Res.

*__New Sermon Slot: All Age Worship: Year B.__ Sharon Swain. 1999. pap. text 21.95 (*0-281-05186-0*) Society Prom Christ Know.

New Servants of Power: A Critique of the 1980s School Reform Movement. Ed. by Christine M. Shea et al. LC 90-30213. (Illus.). 216p. 1990. pap. 19.95 (*0-275-93602-3*, B3602, Praeger Pubs) Greenwood.

New Servants of Power: A Critique of the 1980s School Reform Movement, 28. Ed. by Christine M. Shea et al. LC 88-15490. (Illus.). 216p. 1989. 55.00 (*0-313-25475-3*, Greenwood Pr) Greenwood.

New Service Economy. Gershuny. (C). 1992. text 45.00 (*0-86187-314-9*) St Martin.

New Service Society. Russell Lewis. LC 74-169688. 187p. reprint ed. pap. 58.00 (*0-608-10744-1*, 200588700056) Bks Demand.

New Settlement Cookbook: The First Classic Collection of American Ethnic Recipes. rev. ed. Charles Pierce. (Illus.). 832p. 1997. 12.98 (*0-7651-9310-8*) Smithmark.

New Settlement Cookbook: The First Collection of American Ethnic Recipes. rev. ed. Ed. by Charles L. Pierce. (Illus.). 640p. 1991. 25.00 (*0-671-69336-0*) S&S Trade.

New Settlement of Old Scores. John Brunner. LC 83-62071. (Illus.). 68p. 1983. pap. 8.00 (*0-915368-22-6*); ring bd. 8.00 (*0-915368-26-9*) New Eng SF Assoc.

*__New Settler Interviews: Boogie on the Brink.__ Beth Bosk. LC 00-26896. (Illus.). 320p. 2000. pap. 22.95 (*1-890132-39-X*) Chelsea Green Pub.

*__New Sex over 40.__ Saul H. Rosenthal. LC 99-56740. 1999. 24.95 (*1-56895-802-1*) Wheeler Pub.

New Sex over 40. Saul M. Rosenthal. LC 99-16285. 288p. 1999. 23.95 (*0-87477-998-7*, Tarcher Putnam) Putnam Pub Group.

New Sex Therapy: Active Treatment of Sexual Dysfunctions. Helen S. Kaplan. LC 73-7729. 554p. 1974. text 45.95 (*0-87630-083-2*) Brunner-Mazel.

New Sexual Agendas. Lynne Segal. LC 96-46014. 1997. text 45.00 (*0-8147-8076-8*); pap. text 19.00 (*0-8147-8075-X*) NYU Pr.

New Shakespeare Society, London. Transactions, Nos. 1-2. (New Shakespeare Society, London, Ser.: No. 1). 1974. reprint ed. pap. 80.00 (*0-8115-0227-9*) Periodicals Srv.

New Shakespeare Society, London: Transactions, Nos. 3-4. (New Shakespeare Society, London, Ser.: No. 1). 1974. reprint ed. pap. 80.00 (*0-8115-0228-7*) Periodicals Srv.

New Shakespeare Society, London: Transactions, Nos. 5-7. (New Shakespeare Society, London, Ser.: No. 1). 1974. reprint ed. pap. 100.00 (*0-8115-0229-5*) Periodicals Srv.

New Shakespeare Society, London: Transactions, Nos. 8-10. (New Shakespeare Society, London, Ser.: No. 1). 1974. reprint ed. pap. 100.00 (*0-8115-0230-9*) Periodicals Srv.

New Shakespeare Society, London: Transactions, Nos. 11-14. (New Shakespeare Society, London, Ser.: No. 1). 1974. reprint ed. pap. 80.00 (*0-8115-0231-7*) Periodicals Srv.

New Shakespearean Dictionary. Richard J. Cunliffe. 1977. lib. bdg. 69.95 (*0-8490-2340-8*) Gordon Pr.

New Shakespearean Dictionary. Richard J. Cunliffe. LC 76-39872. reprint ed. 52.50 (*0-404-01377-5*) AMS Pr.

New Shakespeareana, Set, Vols. 1-10. reprint ed. lib. bdg. 625.00 (*0-404-19537-7*) AMS Pr.

New Shalom Seders. New Jewish Agency Staff. 1985. pap. 12.95 (*0-915361-22-1*) Lambda Pubs.

New Shamans. Piers Vitebsky. 500p. 1999. 24.95 (*0-670-86151-0*, Viking) Viking Penguin.

New Shell Book of Firsts. Patrick Robertson. (Illus.). 674p. 1996. pap. 19.95 (*0-7472-7818-0*, Pub. by Headline Bk Pub) Trafalgar.

New Shoe. Arthur W. Upfield. 192p. 1983. pap. 4.95 (*0-684-18020-0*, Scribners Ref) Mac Lib Ref.

New Shoes for Silvia. Johanna Hurwitz. LC 92-40868. (Illus.). 32p. (J). (ps-3). 1993. 16.00 (*0-688-05286-X*, Wm Morrow) Morrow Avon.

New Shoes for Silvia. Johanna Hurwitz. LC 92-40868. (Illus.). 32p. (J). (ps up). 1993. 15.93 (*0-688-05287-8*, Wm Morrow) Morrow Avon.

New Shoes for Silvia. Johanna Hurwitz. 32p. (J). 1999. mass mkt. 4.95 (*0-688-17115-X*, Wm Morrow) Morrow Avon.

*__New Shoes, Red Shoes.__ Susan Rollins. LC 99-48058. (Illus.). 32p. (J). (ps-1). 2000. 15.95 (*0-531-30268-7*) Orchard Bks Watts.

New Shop Floor Management: Empowering People for Continuous Improvement. Kiyoshi Suzaki. LC 92-42559. 256p. 1993. 37.50 (*0-02-932265-0*) Free Pr.

New Shops in Italy. LArchivolto Editors. 1998. 79.95 (*1-56970-529-1*) Bks Nippan.

New Shops in Italy, Vol. 4. LArchivolto Editors. 79.95 (*88-7685-096-1*, Pub. by LArchivolto) Bks Nippan.

New Shops in Italy, Vol. 5. Ed. by L'Archivolto Editorial Staff. (Illus.). 240p. 79.95 (*88-7685-101-1*, Pub. by LArchivolto) Bks Nippan.

New Short Story Theories. Ed. by Charles E. May. LC 94-7037. 363p. (Orig.). (C). 1994. pap. text 16.95 (*0-8214-1087-3*) Ohio U Pr.

New Short Textbook of Chemical Pathology. write for info. (*0-340-37686-4*, Pub. by E A) Routldge.

New Short Textbook of Psychiatry. write for info. (*0-340-40543-0*, Pub. by E A) Routldge.

New Shorter Oxford English Dictionary. Oxford University Press Staff. 1997. disk 110.00 (*0-19-268302-0*) OUP.

New Shorter Oxford English Dictionary, 2 vols., Set. Ed. by Lesley Brown. 3840p. (C). Date not set. pap., boxed set. write for info. (*0-19-863142-1*) OUP.

New Shorter Oxford English Dictionary on Historical Principles, 2 vols. 4th ed. Ed. by Lesley Brown. 3,836p. (C). 1993. 135.00 (*0-19-861271-0*, 6036) OUP.

New Shortwave Propagation Handbook. George Jacobs et al. (Illus.). 176p. (Orig.). 1995. pap. 19.95 (*0-943016-11-8*) CQ Commns Inc.

New Siam in the Making: A Survey of the Political Transition in Siam, 1932-1936. M. Sivaram. LC 77-87066. reprint ed. 41.50 (*0-404-16869-8*) AMS Pr.

New Sicilian - Italian Dictionary. M. Vincenzo. (ITA.). 1220p. 1990. 250.00 (*0-8288-7342-9*) Fr & Eur.

New Sights on the Gita. Som P. Ranchan. (C). 1987. 11.00 (*81-202-0184-1*, Pub. by Ajanta) S Asia.

New Signet World Atlas. rev. ed. Hugh Rawson. (C). 1998. mass mkt. 8.99 (*0-451-19732-1*) NAL.

New Significance: Re-Envisioning the History of the American West. Clyde A. Milner, 2nd. (Illus.). 320p. 1996. pap. 21.00 (*0-19-510048-4*); text 60.00 (*0-19-510047-6*) OUP.

New Silk Flower Book: Making Stylish Arrangements, Wreaths & Decorations. Laura D. Doran. LC 97-3614. (Illus.). 128p. 1997. 24.95 (*1-887374-41-8*); pap. 16.95 (*1-57990-010-0*, Pub. by Lark Books) Random.

New Silk Road: Secrets of Business Success in China Today. John Stuttard & PricewaterhouseCoopers Staff. LC 99-88514. 160p. 2000. text 24.95 (*0-471-37722-8*) Wiley.

New Silk Road & the Global Counterculture. Kiichi Mochizuki. Ed. by Katherine Mueller. 176p. 1999. 39.00 (*1-883223-14-8*) Pacific NY.

New Silk Roads: East Asia & World Textile Markets. Ed. by Kym Anderson. (Trade & Development Ser.). (Illus.). 271p. (C). 1992. text 59.95 (*0-521-39278-0*) Cambridge U Pr.

New Simpler French Course. Whitmarsh. Date not set. pap. text. write for info. (*0-582-36093-5*, Pub. by Addison-Wesley) Longman.

New Singing Theatre. Michael Bawtree. (Illus.). 270p. 1991. pap. text 22.95 (*0-19-385867-3*) OUP.

New Single Mothers. Catherine Whitney. 1994. pap. 20.00 (*0-8217-4709-6*) NAL.

New Single Woman. Barbara Schoichet. 276p. 1995. pap. 12.95 (*1-56565-218-5*) Lowell Hse.

New Single Woman: Discovering a Life of Her Own. Barbara Schoichet. LC 93-41993. 276p. 1994. 22.95 (*1-56565-128-6*) Lowell Hse.

New Sites for Shakespeare: Theatre, the Audience, & Asia. John R. Brown. LC 98-29630. 18p. 1998. 65.00 (*0-415-19449-0*); pap. 21.99 (*0-415-19450-4*) Routledge.

*__New Sivananda Companion to Yoga: A Complete Guide to the Physical Postures, Breathing Exercises, Diet, Relaxation & Meditation Techniques of Yoga.__ Sivananda Yoga Center Staff. LC 99-56087. 192p. 2000. pap. 16.00 (*0-684-87000-2*) S&S Trade.

New Siwalik Primates: Their Bearing on the Question of Evolution of Man & the Anthropoidea. G. E. Pilgrim. LC 77-86436. (India Geological Survey: Records of the Geological Survey of India Ser.: Vol. 45). reprint ed. 15.00 (*0-404-16675-X*) AMS Pr.

New Sjogren's Syndrome Handbook. Sjogren's Syndrome Foundation Staff. Ed. by Steven Carsons & Elaine K. Harris. LC 97-44421. (Illus.). 256p. 1998. 25.00 (*0-19-511724-7*) OUP.

New Skepticism: Inquiry & Reliable Knowledge. Paul Kurtz. LC 92-28358. 371p. (C). 1992. 27.95 (*0-87975-766-3*) Prometheus Bks.

New Skete Communities: An Introduction. Monks of New Skete. 32p. 1985. pap. 2.00 (*0-9607924-9-X*) Monks of New Skete.

New Skills for Frazzled Parents: The Instruction Manual That Should Come with Your Child. Daniel G. Amen. 129p. 2000. pap. 29.95 (*1-886554-02-1*, 499-005, Pub. by MindWrks) BookWorld.

*__New Skills for New Futures: Higher Education Guidance & Counselling Services in the European Union.__ Ed. by A. G. Watts & Raoul Van Esbroeck. 152p. 1999. pap. 17.00 (*90-5487-199-7*, Pub. by VUB Univ Pr) Paul & Co Pubs.

New Skills for New Schools: Preparing Teachers in Family Involvement. Angela M. Shartrand et al. (Illus.). 76p. 1998. pap. text 20.00 (*0-7881-7196-8*) DIANE Pub.

New Slant on Bargello Quilts. Marge Edie. Ed. by Christine Barnes. LC 98-4510. (Illus.). 96p. 1998. pap. 21.95 (*1-56477-227-6*, B339, That Patchwrk Pl) Martingale & Co.

New Slant on Life. L. Ron Hubbard. 286p. 1989. 22.00 (*0-88404-153-0*) Bridge Pubns Inc.

New Slave Ship. Melvin Farmer. LC 98-169583. 109p. 1998. pap. 10.00 (*1-881524-18-3*) Milligan Bks.

New Slave Song. Lonzie Symonette. (Illus.). 162p. (Orig.). 1992. pap. 11.95 (*0-9633078-9-4*) LMS Pubs.

*__New Slavery: A Reference Handbook.__ Kevin Bales. 2000. lib. bdg. 45.00 (*1-57607-239-8*) ABC-CLIO.

New Slavic Language Is Born: The Rusyn Literary Language of Slovakia. Ed. by Paul R. Magocsi. LC 95-61203. (East European Monographs: No. CDXXXIV). 68p. 1996. 28.00 (*0-88033-331-6*, 434, Pub. by East Eur Monographs) Col U Pr.

New Small Garden: Plans & Plants That Make Every Inch Count. Peter H. Loewer. (Illus.). 192p. 1994. pap. 19.95 (*0-8117-2568-5*) Stackpole.

New Small Temples of the Church of Jesus Christ of Latter-day Saints: Counted Cross-stitch Patterns for Current & Future Small Temples. Jean D. Crowther. (Illus.). 24p. pap. 8.98 (*0-88290-682-8*) Horizon Utah.

New Smaller Zingarelli Vocabulary of the Italian Language (Il Nuovo Zingarelli Minore Vocabolario) della Lingua Italiana. 11th ed. Nicola Zingarelli. (ITA Ser.). 1186p. 1987. lib. bdg. 75.00 (*0-8288-3336-2*, M14535) Fr & Eur.

New Smyrna: An Eighteenth Century Greek Odyssey. 2nd ed. Epaminodes P. Panagopoulos. LC 77-16303. (Illus.). 207p. 1978. reprint ed. 14.95 (*0-916586-13-8*, Pub. by Holy Cross Orthodox) BookWorld.

*__New Snow.__ Bill Martin, Jr. 28p. 1999. 5.00 (*0-938711-62-8*) Tecolote Pubns.

New (So-Called) Magdeburg Experiments of Otto von Guericke. Otto von Guericke. LC 93-5121. (Archives Internationales d'Histoire des Idees (International Archives of the History of Ideas) Ser.). 412p. (C). 1994. lib. bdg. 237.50 (*0-7923-2399-8*, Pub. by Kluwer Academic) Kluwer Academic.

New Soaring Pilot. 3rd ed. Anne Welch & Frank Irving. (Illus.). 412p. 1990. reprint ed. 28.95 (*0-7195-3302-3*) Knauff.

New Social Atlas of Britain. Daniel Dorling. 286p. 1995. 125.00 (*0-471-94868-3*) Wiley.

New Social Contract: America's Journey from a Welfare State to a Police State. Joseph D. Davey. LC 95-3326. 208p. 1995. 65.00 (*0-275-95123-5*, Praeger Pubs); pap. 18.95 (*0-275-95239-8*, Praeger Pubs) Greenwood.

New Social Contract: An Inquiry into Modern Contractual Relations. Ian R. Macneil. LC 80-5395. 180p. reprint ed. pap. 55.80 (*0-7837-6218-6*, 208022000004) Bks Demand.

*__New Social Democracy.__ Ed. by Andrew Gamble & Tony Wright. LC 99-44981. (Political Quarterly Book Ser.). 196p. 1999. pap. write for info. (*0-631-21765-7*) Blackwell Publishers.

New Social Marketplace: Notes on Effecting Social Change in America's 3rd Century. Hewitt D. Crane. LC 80-11674. (Communication & Information Science Ser.). (Illus.). 136p. 1980. text 73.25 (*0-89391-063-5*) Ablx Pub.

New Social Movements: From Ideology to Identity. Ed. by Enrique Larana et al. LC 93-37495. 384p. (C). 1994. text 59.95 (*1-56639-186-5*); pap. text 22.95 (*1-56639-187-3*) Temple U Pr.

New Social Movements in the South. Ed. by Ponna Wignaraja. LC 92-29103. 320p. (C). 1993. text 65.00 (*1-85649-107-2*, Pub. by Zed Books) St Martin.

New Social Movements in Western Europe: A Comparative Analysis. Hanspeter Kriese et al. (Social Movements, Protest & Contention Ser.: Vol. 5). 344p. 1995. pap. 21.95 (*0-8166-2671-5*); text 54.95 (*0-8166-2670-7*) U of Minn Pr.

New Social Order in China. Leang-Li T'Ang. LC 75-32331. (Studies in Chinese History & Civilization). 282p. 1976. reprint ed. lib. bdg. 59.95 (*0-313-26966-1*, U6966, Greenwood Pr) Greenwood.

New Social Philosophy. Werner Sombart. Ed. by Karl F. Geiser. LC 69-14085. 295p. 1969. reprint ed. lib. bdg. 65.00 (*0-8371-1042-4*, SONP, Greenwood Pr) Greenwood.

*__New Social Question: Rethinking the Welfare State.__ Pierre Rosanvallon. Tr. by Barbara Harshav from FRE. LC 99-37483. (New French Thought Ser.). 139p. 2000. 22.95 (*0-691-01640-2*, Pub. by Princeton U Pr) Cal Prin Full Svc.

New Social Risks. Date not set. text 150.00 (*90-411-0464-X*) Kluwer Law Intl.

New Social Sciences, 18. Ed. by Baidya N. Varma. LC 75-35358. (Contributions in Sociology Ser.: No. 18). 277p. 1976. 59.95 (*0-8371-8591-2*, VSS/, Greenwood Pr) Greenwood.

New Social Security Guide. 1991. lib. bdg. 75.00 (*0-87700-987-2*) Revisionist Pr.

New Social Security Guide. Ed. by Fred W. Evicci. 112p. 1987. pap. 6.95 (*0-942271-00-9*) Capital Pubns.

New Social Security Guide. 2nd ed. 1988. 7.95 (*0-942271-01-7*) Capital Pubns.

New Social Strategies & the Criminal Justice System. Council of Europe Staff. (Collected Studies in Criminological Research: Vol. XXIX). 1994. 15.00 (*92-871-2024-2*, Pub. by Council of Europe) Manhattan Pub Co.

New Society: The Anatomy of Industrial Order. Peter F. Drucker. 365p. (C). 1993. pap. text 24.95 (*1-56000-624-2*) Transaction Pubs.

New Socioeconomic Order. P.K. Geevarghese. (C). 1996. pap. 5.00 (*0-536-00004-2*) Pearson Custom.

*__New Sociotech: Graffiti on the Long Wall.__ Ed. by Elayne Coakes et al. LC 99-50084. (Computer Supported Cooperative Work Ser.). 225p. 2000. pap. 69.95 (*1-85233-040-6*, Pub. by Spr-Verlag) Spr-Verlag.

New Soft Furnishings. Tricia Guild. 1999. pap. 17.95 (*1-85029-802-5*) Conran Octopus.

New Softbill Handbook. Werner Steinigeweg. (Illus.). 104p. 1988. pap. 9.95 (*0-8120-4075-9*) Barron.

New Software Development Paradigms. Harald Gall. 1999. 49.95 (*0-387-98714-2*) Spr-Verlag.

New Software Engineering. Sue A. Conger. 800p. 1994. pap. 55.95 (*0-534-17143-5*) Course Tech.

New Software Technologies: Future Directions & Market Implications. Chirag Desai & Fred Y. Phillips. 116p. 1993. pap. 30.00 (*1-887406-00-X*) ICTwo Inst.

New Solar Electric Home: The Photovoltaics How-To Handbook. Joel Davidson. (Illus.). 416p. 1987. pap. 18.95 (*0-937948-09-8*) aatec Pubns.

New Solar Home Book. 2nd ed. Bruce Anderson & Michael Riordan. LC 86-23214. (Illus.). 204p. (Orig.). 1996. pap. 20.00 (*0-931790-70-0*) Brick Hse Pub.

New Solar Physics. Ed. by John A. Eddy. 1978. 23.50 (*0-89158-444-7*) Westview.

New Solar Return Book of Prediction. rev. ed. Raymond A. Merriman. 160p. 1998. pap., per. 15.95 (*0-930706-34-X*) Seek-It Pubns.

New Solar System. Ed. by J. Kelly Beatty et al. (Illus.). 432p. 1998. pap. 39.95 (*0-521-64587-5*) Cambridge U Pr.

New Solar System. Ed. by J. Kelly Beatty et al. (Illus.). 432p. 1999. text 59.95 (*0-521-64183-7*) Cambridge U Pr.

New Solar System. 3rd ed. Ed. by J. Kelly Beatty & Andrew Chaikin. LC 89-38040. (Illus.). 336p. 1990. 24.95 (*0-933346-55-7*) Sky Pub.

New Solar System. 4th rev. ed. Ed. by Kelly J. Beatty et al. LC 98-34472. (Illus.). 422p. (C). 1997. pap. 39.95 (*0-933346-86-7*, 46867) Sky Pub.

New Solid Acids & Bases. K. Tanabe et al. (Studies in Surface Science & Catalysis: Vol. 51). 370p. 1989. 304.50 (*0-444-98800-9*) Elsevier.

New Solutions to the Problems of the Present Day: A Plan for International Prosperity & World Peace. John Stahl. 48p. (Orig.). 1992. pap. 4.00 (*0-945303-13-0*) Evanescent Pr.

New Song. Alice I. Cravens. 1988. pap. 3.85 (*0-89137-445-0*) Quality Pubns.

New Song. Jan Karon. LC 99-25693. (Mitford Years Ser.: Vol. 5). 1999. 28.95 (*1-57490-190-7*, Beeler LP Bks) T T Beeler.

New Song. Jan Karon. LC 98-55141. (Mitford Years Ser.). (Illus.). 400p. 1999. 24.95 (*0-670-87810-3*) Viking Penguin.

*__New Song.__ Jan Karon. LC 98-55141. (Illus.). 400p. 2000. pap. 12.95 (*0-14-027059-0*, Penguin Bks) Viking Penguin.

New Song: Celibate Women in the First Three Christian Centuries. Jo A. McNamara. LC 83-10852. (Women & History Ser.: Nos. 6 & 7). 154p. 1983. text 39.95 (*0-86656-249-4*) Haworth Pr.

New Song: Celibate Women in the First Three Christian Centuries. Jo A. McNamara. LC 85-8505. (Women & History Ser.: Nos. 6 & 7). 154p. 1985. reprint ed. pap. 11.95 (*0-918393-17-5*, Harrington Park) Haworth Pr.

New Song: Temple Emanuel Songbook. 130p. 1995. write for info. (*0-9648766-0-4*) Temp Emanuel.

New Song & Dance from the Central Pacific: Creating & Performing the Fatele of Tokelau in the Islands & in New Zealand. Thomas Allen. (Dance & Music Ser.: No. 9). 180p. 1996. 54.00 (*0-945193-77-7*) Pendragon NY.

New Song for the Lord. Joseph C. Ratzinger. LC 96-33184. 144p. 1996. pap. 24.95 (*0-8245-1536-6*) Crossroad NY.

New Song in the Andes see Canto Nuevo en los Andes

New Song in the Andes. John Maust. LC 89-35170. (Illus.). 173p. (Orig.). 1992. pap. 9.95 (*0-87808-219-0*, WCL219-0) William Carey Lib.

New Song to the Lord. Charles J. Healey. LC 91-11350. 99p. (Orig.). 1991. pap. 5.95 (*0-8189-0590-5*) Alba.

New Songs of Rejoicing. Ed. by David P. Schaap. 224p. 1994. pap. 12.00 (*0-9622553-9-4*, 125-010) Selah Pub Co.

N

New Sopena Illustrated Dictionary of the Spanish Language (Nuevo Diccionario Ilustrado Sopena de: Nuevo Diccionario Ilustrado Sopena de la Espanola. Sopena Staff. (SPA., Illus.). 1270p. 1981. 75.00 (*0-8288-2023-6*, S122227) Fr & Eur.

New Soul Food Cookbook: Healthier Recipes for Traditional Favorites. Wilbert Jones. LC 95-19248. (Illus.). 128p. 1995. 14.95 (*1-55972-317-3*, Birch Ln Pr) Carol Pub Group.

New Sound of Indo-European: Essays on Phonological Reconstruction. Ed. by Theo Vennemann. (Trends in Linguistics, Studies & Monographs: No. 41). xvi, 300p. (C). 1989. lib. bdg. 111.55 (*0-89925-521-3*) Mouton.

New Source of Project Finance Capital Through Energy Derivatives. Peter C. Fusaro. 22p. 1993. pap. 10.00 (*0-918714-37-0*) Intl Res Ctr Energy.

New Source Selection Rules. 170p. (Orig.). 1997. pap., per. write for info. (*0-9626190-9-4*) ESI Int.

New Sourcebook for Teaching Reasoning & Problem Solving in Elementary School. Stephen Krulik & Jesse A. Rudnick. 368p. 1995. pap. text 33.00 (*0-205-14826-3*, Longwood Div) Allyn.

New Sourcebook for Teaching Reasoning & Problem Solving in Junior & Senior High School. Stephen Krulik. LC 95-48956. 337p. 1996. pap. text 33.00 (*0-205-16520-6*) Allyn.

New Sources of Early Chinese History: An Introduction to the Reading of Inscriptions & Manuscripts. Edward L. Shaughnessy. LC 97-19807. (Early China Speical Monographic Ser.). 1997. 35.00 (*1-55729-058-X*) IEAS.

New South. Carl Schurz. (Notable American Authors Ser.). 1999. reprint ed. lib. bdg. 125.00 (*0-7812-8872-X*) Rprt Serv.

New South - New Law: Legal Foundations of Credit & Labor Relations in the Postbellum Agricultural South. Harold D. Woodman. LC 94-31543. 144p. 1995. text 22.50 (*0-8071-1941-5*) La State U Pr.

*__New South Africa.__ Guy Arnold. LC 00-33322. 2000. write for info. (*0-312-23517-8*) St Martin.

New South Africa. Toase. LC 97-48684. 212p. 1998. text 65.00 (*0-312-21325-5*) St Martin.

New South Africa: Business Prospects & Corporate Strategies. (Research Reports: No. P404). 1994. 375.00 (*0-85058-801-4*) Economist Intell.

New South Africa: The Dawn of Democracy: Report of a Mission on Behalf of the International Commission of Jurists & the American Association for the International Commission of Jurists. William J. Butler. LC 94-21392. 1994. 20.00 (*0-916265-06-4*) Am Assn Intl Comm Jurists.

New South Africa & the Socialist Vision: Positions & Perspectives Toward a Post-Apartheid Society. Thomas K. Ranuga. LC 95-18539. (Revolutionary Studies). 168p. (C). 1995. text 49.95 (*0-391-03926-1*) Humanities.

Bridging the Rift: The New South Africa in Africa. David R. Black. Ed. by Larry A. Swatuk. LC 96-49701. 260p. (C). 1997. text 75.00 (*0-8133-2752-0*, Pub. by Westview) HarpC.

New South & Other Addresses. Henry W. Grady. 1972. 250.00 (*0-87968-024-5*) Gordon Pr.

New South & Other Addresses. Henry W. Grady. LC 68-24979. (American History & Americana Ser.: No. 47). (C). 1969. reprint ed. lib. bdg. 59.00 (*0-8383-0948-8*) M S G Haskell Hse.

New South & Other Addresses. Henry W. Grady. (BCL1 - United States Local History Ser.). 136p. 1991. reprint ed. lib. bdg. 69.00 (*0-7812-6289-5*) Rprt Serv.

New South & Other Addresses. Henry W. Grady. (Notable American Authors Ser.). 1992. reprint ed. lib. bdg. 75.00 (*0-7812-2937-5*) Rprt Serv.

New South Carolina Cookbook. Ed. & Compiled by South Carolina Family & Community Leaders Staff. LC 96-9972. (Illus.). 280p. 1997. pap. 16.95 (*1-57003-112-6*) U of SC Pr.

New South Comes to Wiregrass Georgia, 1860-1910. Mark V. Wetherington. LC 93-30287. 416p. 1994. text 42.00 (*0-87049-826-6*) U of Tenn Pr.

New South Investigated. David A. Straker. 1977. 17.95 (*0-8369-9254-7*) Ayer.

New South Investigated. David A. Straker. LC 72-11348. (American South Ser.). 1973. reprint ed. 18.95 (*0-405-05064-X*) Ayer.

New South, 1945-1980. Numan V. Bartley. LC 95-19542. (A/History of the South Ser.: Vol. XI). 1995. 39.95 (*0-8071-1944-X*) La State U Pr.

New South, 1945-1980. Numan V. Bartley. (A/History of the South Ser.: Vol. XI). (Illus.). 545p. 1995. 39.95 (*0-8071-2038-3*) La State U Pr.

New South, 1945-1980. Numan V. Bartley. LC 95-19542. (History of the South Ser.: Vol. XII). 548p. 1996. pap. text 19.95 (*0-8071-2122-3*) La State U Pr.

New South Rebellion: The Battle Against Convict Labor in the Tennessee Coalfields, 1871-1896. Karin A. Shapiro. LC 97-39125. (Fred W. Morrison Series in Southern Studies). (Illus.). 352p. (C). 1998. pap. 22.50 (*0-8078-4733-X*); lib. bdg. 55.00 (*0-8078-2423-2*) U of NC Pr.

New South Wales Police Law Handbook. J. Oxley-Oxland. 1988. pap. 33.00 (*0-409-49319-8*, A.T., MICHIE) LEXIS Pub.

New Southern Basics: Traditional Southern Food for Today. Martha P. Stamps. LC 96-49094. (Illus.). 256p. 1997. 20.95 (*1-888952-26-1*) Cumberland Hse.

New Southern Cook. John M. Taylor. 352p. 1997. pap. 16.95 (*0-553-37806-6*) Bantam.

New Southern Harmonies: Four Emerging Fiction Writers. Rosa Shand et al. (Illus.). 176p. 1998. 50.00 (*1-891885-06-5*); pap. 14.95 (*1-891885-00-6*) Hub City Writers.

New Sovereignty: Compliance with International Regulatory Agreements. Abram Chayes & Antonia H. Chayes. LC 95-21960. (Illus.). 368p. (C). 1996. text 56.00 (*0-674-61782-7*) HUP.

New Sovereignty: Compliance with International Regulatory Agreements. Abram Chayes & Antonia H. Chayes. 432p. 1998. pap. 22.95 (*0-674-61783-5*) HUP.

New Soviet Constitution of 1977. Ed. by Robert Sharlet. 1978. pap. 9.00 (*0-89139-024-3*) Kings Court.

New Soviet Elite: How They Think & What They Want. Jeffrey Klugman. LC 88-27510. 247p. 1989. 24.95 (*0-275-93155-2*, C3152, Praeger Pubs) Greenwood.

New Soviet Thinking & U. S. Nuclear Policy. David B. Myers. 304p. 1990. 49.95 (*0-87722-710-1*) Temple U Pr.

New Soy Cookbook: Delicious Ideas for Soybeans, Soy Milk, Tofu, Tempeh, Miso & Soy Sauce. Lorna J. Sass. LC 97-34151. 120p. 1998. pap. 17.95 (*0-8118-1682-6*) Chronicle Bks.

New Space Markets: Symposium Proceedings, International Symposium, 26-28 May 1997, Strasbourg, France. G. Haskell & Michael J. Rycroft. LC 98-14452. (Space Studies Ser.). 1998. write for info. (*0-7923-5027-8*) Kluwer Academic.

New Spaces: Poems, 1975-1983. Joel Oppenheimer. LC 85-9060. 151p. (Orig.). 1985. pap. 8.50 (*0-87685-640-7*) Black Sparrow.

New Spaces/New Faces: An Artist of the Region Invitational Exhibition. Helen A. Harrison et al. LC 87-80695. (Illus.). 27p. 1987. pap. 5.00 (*0-933793-05-7*) Guild Hall.

New Spain: The First Complete Guide to Contemporary Spanish Wine. John Radford. LC 99-236908. (Illus.). 224p. 1998. 40.00 (*1-85732-254-1*, Pub. by Mitchell Beazley) Antique Collect.

New Spain's Far Northern Frontier: Essays on Spain in the American West, 1540-1821. Ed. & Intro. by David J. Weber. LC 88-42631. (Illus.). 344p. (C). 1988. reprint ed. pap. text 13.95 (*0-87074-280-9*) SMU Press.

New Spaniards. John Hooper. 480p. 1995. pap. 13.95 (*0-14-013191-4*, Penguin Bks) Viking Penguin.

New Spanish, Level 1. Medley. (Secondary Spanish Ser.). 2001. pap. text, wbk. ed. 15.95 (*0-8384-7898-0*) Heinle & Heinle.

New Spanish for Travelers. Alberto H. Lozano & John R. Petrovsky. 36p. 1998. pap. text 16.95 (*0-940935-01-5*) Vista Press.

New Special Relationship: Free Trade & U. S.-Canada Economic Relations in the . . . Peter Morici. 153p. 1991. pap. 23.95 (*0-88645-132-9*, Pub. by Inst Res Pub) Ashgate Pub Co.

New Specially Selected Jokes & Stories for All Occasions. 2nd ed. Al Schock. 180p. Date not set. pap. 8.99 (*1-887526-01-3*) Nordica Enter.

New Species: Gender & Science in Science Fiction. Robin Roberts. LC 92-25385. (Illus.). 200p. (C). 1993. text 29.95 (*0-252-01983-0*); pap. text 12.95 (*0-252-06284-1*) U of Ill Pr.

New Species & Novel Aspects in Ecology & Physiology of Lichens: In Honour of O. L. Lange. Ed. by L. Kappen. (Bibliotheca Lichenologica Ser.: Vol. 67). (Illus.). xviii, 309p. 1997. 94.40 (*3-443-58046-7*, Pub. by Gebruder Borntraeger) Balogh.

New Species of Coronula (Cirripedia) from the Lower Pliocene of Venezuela see Bulletins of American Paleontology: Vol. 60

New Species of Criticism: Eighteenth-Century Discourse on the Novel. Joseph F. Bartolomeo. LC 93-29770. 1994. 36.50 (*0-87413-488-9*) U Delaware Pr.

New Species of Devonian Fossils from Western Tennessee. Carl O. Dunbar. (Connecticut Academy of Arts & Sciences Ser., Trans.: Vol. 23). 1920. pap. 49.50 (*0-685-22834-7*) Elliots Bks.

New Species of Frogs (Leptodactylidae Eleutherodactylus) from the Pacific Versant of Ecuador. John D. Lynch. (Occasional Papers: No. 55). 33p. 1976. pap. 1.00 (*0-686-80372-8*) U KS Nat Hist Mus.

New Species of Liolaemus: Sauria: Iguanidae, from the Andean Mountains of the Southern Mendoza Volcanic Region of Argentina. Jose M. Cei. (Occasional Papers: No. 76). 6p. 1978. 1.00 (*0-317-04841-4*) U KS Nat Hist Mus.

New Species of Man: The Poetic Persona of W. B. Yeats. Gale C. Schricker. LC 81-65860. 216p. 1982. 32.50 (*0-8387-5033-8*) Bucknell U Pr.

New Species of Peromyscus: Rodentia: Cricetidae, & a New Specimen of P. Simulatus from Southern Mexico, with Comments on Their Ecology. Paul B. Robertson & Guy G. Musser. (Occasional Papers: No. 47). 8p. 1976. pap. 1.00 (*0-317-04909-7*) U KS Nat Hist Mus.

New Species of Steamer-Duck (Tachyeres) from Argentina. Phillip S. Humphrey & Max C. Thompson. (Occasional Papers: No. 95). 12p. 1981. pap. 1.00 (*0-317-04596-2*) U KS Nat Hist Mus.

New Species of Tropidurus (Sauria, Iguanidae) from the Arid Chacoan & Western Regions of Argentina. Jose M. Cei. (Occasional Papers: No. 97). 10p. 1982. 1.00 (*0-317-04843-0*) U KS Nat Hist Mus.

New Species of Trouble: The Human Experience of Modern Disasters. Kai T. Erikson. 272p. 1995. pap. 12.00 (*0-393-31319-0*, Norton Paperbks) Norton.

New Species Syndrome in Indian Pteriodology & Ferns of Nepal. Jenkins Fraser. 403p. 1997. pap. 1000.00 (*81-7089-252-X*, Pub. by Intl Bk Distr) St Mut.

New Spectrum, Bk. 4. Byrd. 1994. pap. text, teacher ed. 28.00 (*0-13-830175-1*) P-H.

New Spectrum, Bk. 5. Byrd. 1994. pap., teacher ed. 28.00 (*0-13-830217-0*) P-H.

***New Spellaway, Bk. 1.** Lynn Goss & Helen Donaldson. (J). (gr. 2-6). 1999. pap. 20.00 (*0-7217-0768-8*, Pub. by Schofield) St Mut.

***New Spellaway, Bk. 2.** Lynn Goss & Helen Donaldson. (J). (gr. 2-6). 1999. pap. 20.00 (*0-7217-0769-6*, Pub. by Schofield) St Mut.

***New Spellaway, Bk. 3.** Lynn Goss & Helen Donaldson. (J). (gr. 2-6). 1999. pap. 20.00 (*0-7217-0770-X*, Pub. by Schofield) St Mut.

***New Spellaway, Bk. 4.** Lynn Goss & Helen Donaldson. (J). (gr. 2-6). 1999. pap. 20.00 (*0-7217-0771-8*, Pub. by Schofield) St Mut.

New Spelling: Orthographic Structuralism. Raymond E. Laurita. 192p. (Orig.). 1981. pap. 14.95 (*0-914051-00-8*) Leonardo Pr.

New Spiders from New England. James H. Emerton. (Connecticut Academy of Arts & Sciences Ser., Trans.: Vol. 20, No. 11). 1915. pap. 39.50 (*0-685-22847-9*) Elliots Bks.

New Spies. James Adams. pap. 22.95 (*0-7126-7410-1*, Pub. by Random) Trafalgar.

New Spinoza. Ed. by Warren Montag & Ted Stolze. LC 97-27337. (Theory Out of Bounds Ser.: Vol. 11). 512p. 1997. pap. 24.95 (*0-8166-2541-7*); text 62.95 (*0-8166-2540-9*) U of Minn Pr.

New Spirit: Modern Architecture in Vancouver, 1938-1963. Rhodri W. Liscombe. LC 96-37595. (Illus.). 208p. 1997. pap. 35.00 (*0-262-62115-0*) MIT Pr.

New Spirit in Arab Lands. Habeeb I. Katibah. LC 76-180352. reprint ed. 34.50 (*0-404-56284-1*) AMS Pr.

New Spirit in the Cinema. Huntly Carter. 1972. 59.95 (*0-8490-0724-0*) Gordon Pr.

New Spirit in the Cinema. Huntly Carter. LC 76-112580. (Literature of Cinema, Ser. 1). 1970. reprint ed. 21.95 (*0-405-01605-0*) Ayer.

New Spirit in the Russian Theatre 1917-1928. Huntly Carter. LC 77-112583. (Literature of Cinema, Ser. 1). 1970. reprint ed. 19.95 (*0-405-01606-9*) Ayer.

New Spirit Within You. Mollie H. Sorensen. (Illus.). v, 109p. 1984. pap. 4.95 (*0-9659261-2-5*) Sun W Publ.

New Spiritual Homes: Religion & Asian Americans. Ed. by David K. Yoo. LC 98-35976. (Intersections Ser.). 323p. 1999. pap. 22.00 (*0-8248-2072-X*) UH Pr.

New Spirituality: And the Christ Experience of the Twentieth Century. Rudolf Steiner. 127p. 1987. 20.00 (*0-88010-212-8*, 1280); pap. 9.95 (*0-88010-213-6*, 1279) Anthroposophic.

New Spirituality - Beyond Religion: With Personal Growth That Leads to Spiritual Growth - The Human Being Becomes a Spiritual Being. Patty Paul. LC 94-79198. 208p. 1995. pap. 12.95 (*0-9642726-7-9*) IMDEX Pub.

New Spirituality, Self & Belonging: How New Agers & Neo-Pagans Talk about Themselves. Jon P. Bloch. LC 97-27929. (Religion in the Age of Transformation Ser.). 144p. 1998. 55.00 (*0-275-95957-0*, Praeger Pubs) Greenwood.

New Splined Shaft Configurations for Naval Aircraft Accessories. F. Hall et al. (Technical Papers: Vol. P109.39). (Illus.). 18p. 1977. pap. text 30.00 (*1-55589-209-4*) AGMA.

New Spoon Rivers. Edgar Lee Masters. (Collected Works of Edgar Lee Masters). 324p. 1999. reprint ed. lib. bdg. 98.00 (*1-58201-772-7*, c0772) Classic Bks.

***New Spouse: For Better or for Worse.** Susan U. Dikas. LC 99-93827. 1999. pap. 10.95 (*0-533-13160-X*) Vantage.

New Springtime. Robert Silverberg. 1991. mass mkt. 4.95 (*0-446-36172-0*, Pub. by Warner Bks) Little.

***New St. Martin's Guide to Teaching Writing** Robert J. Connors & Cheryl Glenn. LC 98-86514. xi, 548p. 1999. pap. text 19.95 (*0-312-19762-4*) St Martin.

***New St Martin's Handbook.** 4th ed. Andrea Lunsford & Connors. 1999. pap. text 36.95 (*0-312-25117-3*) St Martin.

New St Martins Handbook Answers Exercise, Vol. 1. Andrea Lunsford. 1998. pap. text 5.00 (*0-312-18976-1*) St Martin.

***New St Martins Handbook Assign Respond & Evaluate.** 3rd ed. Andrea Lunsford & White. 1998. pap. text 19.95 (*0-312-19732-2*) St Martin.

New St Martins Handbook Online, Vol. 1. Andrea Lunsford. 1999. pap. text 31.95 (*0-312-18973-7*) St Martin.

New St. Petersburg: The First Five Years, 1991-1996. John Slade. LC 98-90987. 106p. 1999. pap. 9.95 (*1-893617-01-7*) Woodgate Intl.

***New Stage for a City: Developing the New Jersey Performing Arts Center.** (Illus.). 128p. 1999. 39.95 (*1-875498-91-5*, Pub. by Images Publ) Antique Collect.

***New Standard Bible.** Contrib. by Lockman Foundation Staff. (Illus.). 960p. 1999. 7.99 (*1-58135-075-9*) Foun Pubns.

***New Standard Bible: Gospel of John.** Tr. by Lockman Foundation Staff. 96p. 1999. pap. 0.75 (*1-58135-074-0*) Foun Pubns.

New Standard Bible, N. T. Ed. by P. R. Johnson. 231p. 1987. 8.95 (*0-685-19216-4*) Paul R Johnson.

New Standard Documentary Credit Forms for the UCP 500. rev. ed. International Chamber of Commerce Staff. Ed. by Charles Del Busto. 88p. 1993. pap. 29.95 (*92-842-1160-3*, 516) ICC Pub.

New Standard Encyclopedia. Ferguson, J. G., Publishing Co. Staff. LC 98-48966. 1999. write for info. (*0-87392-103-8*) Ferguson.

New Standard Encyclopedia. Ferguson Publishing Co. Staff. LC 96-20729. 1997. write for info. (*0-87392-102-X*) Ferguson.

***New Standard Encyclopedia, 20 vols.** J. G. Ferguson Publishing Company Staff. LC 99-57814. 1999. 479.00 (*0-87392-104-6*) Ferguson.

New Standard English-Serbian, Serbian-English Dictionary. Branislav Grujic. (ENG & SER.). 826p. 1992. 95.00 (*0-8288-0505-9*, M 14515) Fr & Eur.

New Standard English-Serbocroatian & Serbocroatian-English Dictionary. Branislav Grujic. (ENG & SER.). 826p. (C). 1990. 275.00 (*0-569-09282-5*, Pub. by Collets) St Mut.

New Standard Jewish Encyclopedia. 7th rev. ed. Geoffrey Wigoder. LC 92-18351. (Illus.). 1008p. 1992. 59.95 (*0-8160-2690-4*) Facts on File.

New Standard San Francisco Bartenders Workbook, No. 1. Charles T. Davis. Ed. by Robert L. Walter. (Illus.). 270p. (Orig.). (C). 1998. pap. text 26.50 (*0-9621628-0-9*, 6969) Fubar Pr.

New Standardization: Keystone of Continuous Improvement in Manufacturing. Shigehiro Nakamura. Tr. by Bruce Talbot from JPN. (Illus.). 286p. 1993. 50.00 (*1-56327-039-0*) Productivity Inc.

***New Standards.** Leonard, Hal, Corporation Staff. 176p. 1998. otabind 12.95 (*0-7935-9284-4*) H Leonard.

New Standards for Evaluating Technological Innovation in the U. S. S. R. The Petro-Chemical Machine-Building Industry. Ninel Kogan. Ed. by Steven Jones. (Illus.). 103p. (Orig.). 1985. pap. text 75.00 (*1-55831-023-1*) Delphic Associates.

New Standards in Advanced Cardiac Life Support (ACLS) for the Adult Patient & Pediatric ACLS Algorithms: Synopsis & Commentary. 3rd ed. Ed. by Andrew D. Weinberg & James L. Paturas. 60p. 1993. pap. text 8.00 (*1-887272-04-6*) Amer Med Pub.

New Star. Taffy Davies. (Illus.). 32p. (J). (gr. k). 1997. 12.95 (*0-687-08750-3*) Abingdon.

New Star Chamber & Other Essays. Edgar Lee Masters. (Collected Works of Edgar Lee Masters). 213p. 1999. reprint ed. lib. bdg. 88.00 (*1-58201-779-4*, c0779) Classic Bks.

New Star Papers. Henry W. Beecher. (Works of Henry Ward Beecher). 1989. reprint ed. lib. bdg. 79.00 (*0-685-44799-5*) Rprt Serv.

New Star Wars Campaign Pack. (Star Wars Ser.). 1991. 12.00 (*0-87431-119-5*, 40048) West End Games.

New Starlight Express. Andrew Lloyd Webber. 56p. 1994. per. 12.95 (*0-7935-3367-8*, 00312500) H Leonard.

New Starr of the North, Shining upon the King of Sweden. Alexander Gil. LC 76-57383. (English Experience Ser.: No. 801). 1977. reprint ed. lib. bdg. 15.00 (*90-221-0801-5*) Walter J Johnson.

New Starting Right with Bees. rev. ed. Ed. by Kim Flottum & Diana Sammataro. 136p. 1990. pap. 7.99 (*0-936028-02-5*) A I Root.

New State. Victor Pradera. Tr. by B. Malley. LC 79-180421. reprint ed. 36.00 (*0-404-56196-9*) AMS Pr.

New State: Etatization of Western Societies. Szymon Chodak. LC 88-18552. 355p. 1989. lib. bdg. 55.00 (*1-55587-107-0*) L Rienner.

New State: Group Organization the Solution of Popular Government. Mary P. Follett. LC 98-16949. 1998. 49.50 (*0-271-01825-9*); pap. 18.95 (*0-271-01826-7*) Pa St U Pr.

New States in the Modern World. Ed. by Martin L. Kilson. LC 75-4560. (Center for International Affairs Ser.). 331p. 1975. 43.00 (*0-674-62261-8*) HUP.

New States, New Politics: Building the Post-Soviet Nations. 2nd ed. Ed. by Ian Bremmer & Raymond C. Taras. 764p. (C). 1996. text 74.95 (*0-521-57101-4*); pap. text 29.95 (*0-521-57799-3*) Cambridge U Pr.

New Statesman: Portrait of a Political Weekly, 1913-1931. Adrian Smith. 272p. 1995. 39.50 (*0-7146-4659-8*, Pub. by F Cass Pubs); pap. 24.00 (*0-7146-4188-X*, Pub. by F Cass Pubs) Intl Spec Bk.

New Statesman: Portrait of a Political Weekly, 1913-1931. Ed. by Adrian Smith. LC 95-21578. (Illus.). 368p. (C). 1996. 42.50 (*0-7146-4645-8*, Pub. by F Cass Pubs); pap. text 24.00 (*0-7146-4169-3*, Pub. by F Cass Pubs) Intl Spec Bk.

New Statesmanship. New Statesman Staff. Ed. by E. Hyams. LC 72-128281. (Essay Index Reprint Ser.). 1977. 23.95 (*0-8369-1891-6*) Ayer.

New Statistical Analysis of Data. T. W. Anderson & Jeremy D. Finn. LC 95-44885. 712p. (C). 1996. text 59.95 (*0-387-94619-5*) Spr-Verlag.

New Statistical Methods in Longitudinal Research Vol. 1: Principles & Structuring Change. Ed. by Alexander Von Eye. (Statistical Modeling & Decision Science Ser.). 256p. 1990. text 100.00 (*0-12-724960-5*) Acad Pr.

New Statistical Methods in Longitudinal Research Vol. 2: Time Series & Categorical Longitudinal Data. Ed. by Alexander Von Eye. 314p. 1990. pap. text 48.00 (*0-12-724963-X*) Acad Pr.

New Statistical Procedures for the Social Sciences: Modern Solutions to Basic Problems. Randy Wilcox. 442p. 1987. 89.95 (*0-89859-936-9*) L Erlbaum Assocs.

New Statistical Thinking. V. V. Shvyrkov. LC 94-60038. (Illus.). 204p. (C). 1994. pap. text 35.55 (*0-942004-58-2*) Throwkoff Pr.

New Statistics. 2nd ed. V. V. Shvyrkov. LC 96-60011. (Illus.). 140p. 1996. pap. text 37.55 (*0-942004-64-7*) Throwkoff Pr.

New Steel Products & Processing for Automotive Applications: 1996 International Congress & Exposition. LC 96-207877. (Special Publications). 181p. 1996. pap. 49.00 (*1-56091-802-0*, SP-1172) Soc Auto Engineers.

New Steinbeck Bibliography, 1971-1981. Tetsumaro Hayashi. LC 82-24077. (Author Bibliographies Ser.: No. 64). 169p. 1983. 21.00 (*0-8108-1610-5*) Scarecrow.

***New Stencil Book: With over 40 Stencil Motifs to Use.** Simone Smart. (Illus.). 128p. (J). 1999. pap. 19.95 (*1-55209-299-2*) Firefly Bks Ltd.

New Steps in Religious Education, Bk. 1. Michael Keene. (Illus.). 96p. 1997. pap. 20.00 (*0-7487-3079-6*, Pub. by S Thornes Pubs) Trans-Atl Phila.

New Steps in Religious Education, Bk. 2. Michael Keene. (Illus.). 96p. 1997. pap. 20.00 (*0-7487-3078-8*, Pub. by S Thornes Pubs) Trans-Atl Phila.

New Steps in Religious Education, Bk. 3. Michael Keene. (Illus.). 96p. 1997. pap. 20.00 (*0-7487-3077-X*, Pub. by S Thornes Pubs) Trans-Atl Phila.

New Steps to Service: Common-Sense Advice for the School Library Media Specialist. Ann Wasman & Mildred L. Nickel. LC 98-16248. 256p. 1998. 20.00 (*0-8389-3483-8*) ALA.

New Stereo Soundbook. F. Alton Everest & Ron Streicher. 296p. 1992. 29.95 (*0-8306-3904-7*); pap. 18.95 (*0-8306-3903-9*) McGraw-Hill Prof.

New Stereo Soundbook. 2nd rev. ed. F. Alton Everest & Ron Streicher. (Illus.). 272p. 1998. text 54.50 (*0-9665162-0-6*) Audio Engineer.

New Stitches for Needlecraft. Edith John. (Illus.). 1990. 11.25 (*0-8446-5051-X*) Peter Smith.

New Stock Trend Detector. W. D. Gann. (Illus.). 191p. 1976. 49.00 (*0-939093-16-2*) Lambert Gann Pub.

***New Stoicism.** Lawrence C. Becker. 272p. 1999. pap. 16.95 (*0-691-00964-3*, Pub. by Princeton U Pr) Cal Prin Full Svc.

New Stone Technology, Design, & Construction for Exterior Wall Systems. Ed. by Barry Donaldson. LC 88-2358. (Special Technical Publication Ser.: No. 996). (Illus.). 196p. 1988. text 34.00 (*0-8031-1164-9*, STP996) ASTM.

New Store Workbook: MSA's Guide to Remodeling, Expanding & Opening the Museum Store. Museum Store Association, Inc. Staff. (Illus.). 107p. (Orig.). 1994. student ed., spiral bd. 69.95 (*0-9616104-3-3*) Museum Store.

New Stores in the U. S. A. Ed. by LArchivolto Editors. (Illus.). 240p. 1999. 79.95 (*88-7685-105-4*, Pub. by LArchivolto) Bks Nippan.

New Stories by Southern Women. Ed. by Mary E. Gibson. LC 89-30840. 301p. 1989. pap. 16.95 (*0-87249-634-1*) U of SC Pr.

New Stories from the South: The Year's Best, 1987. Ed. by Shannon Ravenel. 248p. 1987. pap. 10.95 (*0-912697-73-3*) Algonquin Bks.

New Stories from the South: The Year's Best, 1991. Intro. by Shannon Ravenel. 256p. 1991. pap. 9.95 (*0-945575-82-3*) Algonquin Bks.

New Stories from the South: The Year's Best, 1992. Intro. by Shannon Ravenel. 368p. 1992. pap. 10.95 (*1-56512-011-6*) Algonquin Bks.

New Stories from the South: The Year's Best, 1993. Ed. by Shannon Ravenel. 374p. 1993. pap. 11.95 (*1-56512-053-1*) Algonquin Bks.

New Stories from the South: The Year's Best, 1994. Shannon Ravenel. 368p. 1994. pap. 10.95 (*1-56512-088-4*) Algonquin Bks.

New Stories from the South: The Year's Best, 1995. Ed. by Shannon Ravenel. (New Stories from the South Ser.). 280p. 1995. pap. 10.95 (*1-56512-123-6*, 72123) Algonquin Bks.

New Stories from the South: The Year's Best, 1996. Ed. & Intro. by Shannon Ravenel. (New Stories from the South Ser.). 286p. 1996. pap. 10.95 (*1-56512-155-4*) Algonquin Bks.

New Stories from the South: The Year's Best, 1997. Ed. by Shannon Ravenel. 324p. 1997. pap. 12.95 (*1-56512-175-9*, 72175) Algonquin Bks.

New Stories from the South: The Year's Best 1998. Shannon Ravenel. (New Stories from the South Ser.). 324p. 1998. pap. 12.95 (*1-56512-219-4*) Algonquin Bks.

An Asterisk (*) at the beginning of an entry indicates that the title is appearing for the first time.

***New Stories from the South: The Year's Best 1999.** Ed. by Shannon Ravenel. 312p. 1999. pap. 14.95 (*1-56512-247-X*) Algonquin Bks.

***New Stories from the South: The Year's Best, 2000.** Ed. by Shannon Ravenel. 320p. 2000. pap. 14.95 (*1-56512-295-X*) Algonquin Bks.

New Story: Comments on the Origin, Identification & Transaurian of Values. Thomas Berry. (Teilhard Studies: No. 1). 1978. 3.50 (*0-89012-012-9*) Am Teilhard.

***New Story Collection.** Sam Shepard. 2001. 24.00 (*0-375-40505-4*, Evrymans Lib Childs) Knopf.

New Story, New God. Dennis Pakula. 251p. 1998. pap. 11.95 (*1-891929-05-4*) Four Seasons.

New Story of O. (New Tempo Ser.). 200p. 1993. mass mkt. 7.95 (*0-929654-98-6*) Blue Moon Bks.

New Story Writers. Ed. by John Metcalf. 256p. 1992. pap. 18.95 (*1-55082-038-9*, Pub. by Quarry Pr) LPC InBook.

***New Strangers in Paradise: The Immigrant Experience & Contemporary American Fiction.** Gilbert H. Muller. LC 99-24008. 288p. 1999. 29.95 (*0-8131-2134-5*) U Pr of Ky.

New Strategic Perspectives on Social Policy. John E. Tropman & Roger M. Lind. (Policy Studies). 1981. text 120.00 (*0-08-025554-X*, Pergamon Pr); pap. text 35.00 (*0-08-025553-1*, Pergamon Pr) Elsevier.

New Strategic Selling: The Unique Sales System Proven Successful by the World's Best Companies, Revised & Updated for the 21st Century. rev. ed. Stephen E. Heiman. LC 97-29935. 433p. 1998. mass mkt. 14.99 (*0-446-67346-3*, Pub. by Warner Bks) Little.

New Strategies for America's Watersheds. National Research Council Staff. LC 98-58156. 328p. (C). 1999. text 49.00 (*0-309-06417-1*) Natl Acad Pr.

New Strategies for Free Children: A Leader's Manual of the Child Assault Prevention Projects. Sally Cooper. Ed. by Jan Britton. LC 91-62365. (Illus.). 220p. 1991. 21.25 (*1-880326-49-3*) Natl Assault.

New Strategies for Improving Rural Family Life. Philip H. Coombs. 72p. 1981. 3.00 (*0-318-16926-6*) ICED Pubns.

New Strategies for Innovations in Medical Information Systems. Mary Poulin. 50p. 1984. 7.50 (*0-318-19205-5*, R-61) Inst Future.

New Strategies for Marketing Information Technology. Ed. by C. Field. (Illus.). 384p. 1995. mass mkt. 75.00 (*0-412-61520-7*) Chapman & Hall.

New Strategies for New Challenges: Corporate Innovation in the United States & Japan. National Research Council Staff. 54p. 1999. pap. 18.00 (*0-309-05848-1*) Natl Acad Pr.

New Strategies for Public Pay: Rethinking Government Compensation Programs. Howard W. Risher & Charles H. Fay. LC 96-53433. (Jossey-Bass Public Administration Ser.). 1997. 34.95 (*0-7879-0826-6*) Jossey-Bass.

New Strategies for Regional Cooperation: A Model for the Tri-State New York-New Jersey-Connecticut Area. Edward N. Costikyan & Maxwell Lehman. LC 73-9388. (Special Studies in U. S. Economic, Social & Political Issues). 1973. 32.50 (*0-275-28777-7*) Irvington.

New Strategies for Treating Children's Articulation & Phonological Disorders. Ken Bleile. 1998. 110.00 incl. VHS (*1-58041-017-0*, 0112092) Am Speech Lang Hearing.

New Strategies in Clinical Nutrition. Ed. by P. Furst. (Clinical Nutrition Ser.: Vol. 33). (Illus.). 88p. 1993. text 35.00 (*3-88603-462-3*, Pub. by W Zuckschwerdt) Scholium Intl.

New Strategies in Contests for Corporate Control 1999. Dennis J. Block. LC 99-177620. (Corporate & Practice Course Handbook Ser.). 696 p. 1999. 99.00 (*0-87224-558-6*) PLI.

New Strategies in Fungal Disease. Ed. by John E. Bennett et al. (Frontiers of Infectious Diseases Ser.). (Illus.). 312p. (Orig.). 1992. pap. text 66.95 (*0-443-04684-0*) Church.

New Strategies in Higher Education Marketing. Ed. by Thomas J. Hayes. LC 91-25330. (Journal of Marketing for Higher Education). (Illus.). 193p. 1991. lib. bdg. 49.95 (*1-56024-198-5*) Haworth Pr.

New Strategies in Locust Control. Ed. by S. Krall et al. LC 97-14016. write for info. (*3-7643-5442-9*) Birkhauser.

New Strategies in Locust Control. S. Krall et al. LC 97-14016. 1997. write for info. (*0-8176-5442-9*) Birkhauser.

New Strategies in Social Research: An Introduction & Guide. Derek Layder. LC 92-30551. 1992. pap. 26.95 (*0-7456-0881-7*) Blackwell Pubs.

New Strategists: Creating Leaders at All Levels. Stephen J. Wall & Shannon R. Wall. (Illus.). 272p. 1995. 24.50 (*0-02-874058-0*) Free Pr.

New Strategy of Style. 2nd ed. Winston Weathers & Otis Winchester. 192p. (C). 1978. 53.75 (*0-07-068692-0*) McGraw.

New Strategy Through Space. Neville Brown. 352p. 1990. text 52.50 (*0-7185-1279-0*, Pub. by Leicester U Pr) Cassell & Continuum.

New Stretching Book. Maxine Tobias. 1992. write for info. (*0-679-40908-4*) McKay.

New Strong's Concise Concordance of the Bible. LC 96-19866. 768p. 1996. pap. 14.99 (*0-7852-1166-7*) Nelson.

New Strong's Exhaustive Concordance. Thomas Nelson Publishers Staff. 1997. 15.97 (*0-7852-0931-X*) Nelson.

New Strong's Exhaustive Concordance of the Bible: With Main Concordance, Appendix to the Main Concordance, Hebrew & Aramaic Dictionary of the Old Testament, Greek Dictionary of the New Testament see Supervalue Reference Promotional Superset

New Strong's Exhaustive Concordance of the Bible With Main Concordance, Appendix to the Main Concordance, Topical Index, Greek & Hebrew Dictionaries. James Strong. LC 98-138045. 1990. 34.99 (*0-8407-6750-1*) Nelson.

New Strong's Guide to Bible Words. James Strong. LC 96-36197. 292p. 1997. 14.99 (*0-7852-1197-7*) Nelson.

New Strong's Guide to Bible Words. Thomas Nelson Publishers Staff. 1997. 9.97 (*0-7852-0959-X*) Nelson.

New Structure for National Security Policy Planning: Revisiting the National Security Act of 1947. Stephen A. Cambone. LC 98-37026. (Significant Issue Ser.). 272p. 1998. pap. text 23.95 (*0-89206-345-9*) CSIS.

New Structure of School Improvement: Inquiring Schools & Achieving Students Bruce R. Joyce et al. LC 98-55535. 9p. 1999. 29.95 (*0-335-20294-2*) OpUniv Pr.

New Structures in Jazz & Improvised Music: From the 1960s into the 1980s. Roger T. Dean. 176p. 1991. pap. 41.95 (*0-335-09897-5*) OpUniv Pr.

New Structures of Campus Power. John D. Millett. LC 77-82911. (Jossey-Bass Higher Education Ser.). 316p. reprint ed. pap. 98.00 (*0-608-17772-5*, 20565700072) Bks Demand.

New Struggle for Democracy in Africa. John A. Wiseman. 208p. 1996. 72.95 (*1-85972-332-2*, Pub. by Avebry) Ashgate Pub Co.

***New Student Handbook 1998-1999.** 240p. (C). 1998. pap. 7.00 (*0-536-01101-X*) Pearson Custom.

***New Student Handbook 1999-2000.** 2nd ed. 208p. (C). 1999. pap. text 9.00 (*0-536-02329-8*) Pearson Custom.

New Student Seminar. 3rd ed. Zadra. 168p. (C). 1998. pap. text 13.00 (*0-536-01320-9*) Pearson Custom.

***New Students Guide Research Unthinkable.** 2nd ed. Ed. by Bensel-Meyers. 168p. 1998. pap. text 12.70 (*0-536-01816-2*) P-H.

New Students in Karate: The First Three Months. rev. ed. Merlin T. Taylor, Jr. (Illus.). 118p. (Orig.). 1995. pap. 9.95 (*0-911921-21-4*) Palmerston & Reed.

New Studies in Bonhoeffer's Society. Ed. by William J. Peck. LC 87-7944. (Toronto Studies in Theology: Vol. 30). 284p. 1987. lib. bdg. 89.95 (*0-88946-775-7*) E Mellen.

New Studies in Deontic Logic: Norms, Actions & the Foundations of Ethics. Ed. by Risto Hilpinen. 265p. 1981. lib. bdg. 104.50 (*90-277-1278-6*, D Reidel) Kluwer Academic.

New Studies in Engine Oil Rheology & Tribology. 1996. 55.00 (*1-56091-825-X*, SP-1182) Soc Auto Engineers.

New Studies in Greek Poetry. Heather White. (London Studies in Classical Philology: Vol. 22). 146p. 1989. pap. 34.00 (*90-5063-036-7*, Pub. by Gieben) J Benjamins Pubng Co.

New Studies in Latin Linguistics: Proceedings from the 4th International Colloquium on Latin Linguistics, Cambridge, April 1987. Ed. by Robert Coleman. LC 91-8624. (Studies in Language Companion: Vol. 21). x, 480p. 1991. 148.00 (*90-272-3024-2*) J Benjamins Pubng Co.

New Studies in Mystical Religion. Rufus M. Jones. 1973. 250.00 (*0-87968-102-0*) Gordon Pr.

New Studies in Philosophy, Politics, Economics & the History of Ideas. Friedrich A. Hayek. LC 77-88475. viii, 314p. (C). 1985. reprint ed. pap. text 12.50 (*0-226-32070-7*) U Ch Pr.

New Studies in Post-Cold War Security. K. R. Dark. LC 96-16535. 296p. 1996. text 82.95 (*1-85521-728-7*, Pub. by Dartmuth Pub) Ashgate Pub Co.

New Studies in Richard Wagner's "The Ring of the Nibelung" Ed. by Herbert W. Richardson. LC 91-38295. (Studies in the History & Interpretation of Music: Vol. 20). 200p. 1992. lib. bdg. 79.95 (*0-88946-445-6*) E Mellen.

New Studies in Russian Language & Literature. Ed. by Anna L. Crone & Catherine V. Chvany. (Illus.). 302p. 1987. 22.95 (*0-89357-168-7*) Slavica.

New Studies in the Philosophy of John Dewey. Ed. by Steven M. Cahn. LC 76-62914. 223p. reprint ed. pap. 69.20 (*0-7837-0374-0*, 204069400018) Bks Demand.

New Studies in the Politics & Culture of U. S. Communism. Ed. by Michael E. Brown et al. 384p. (C). 1993. text 38.00 (*0-85345-851-0*, Pub. by Monthly Rev); pap. text 18.00 (*0-85345-852-9*, Pub. by Monthly Rev) NYU Pr.

New Studies of Tropical American Birds. Alexander F. Skutch. (Publications of the Nuttall Ornithological Club: No. 19). (Illus.). 281p. 1981. 29.50 (*1-877973-29-7*) Nuttall Ornith.

New Studies on the Black Sea Littoral. Ed. by Gocha R. Tsetskhladze. (Colloquia Pontica Ser.: Vol. 1). (Illus.). 160p. 1995. pap. 32.50 (*1-900188-01-5*, Pub. by Oxbow Bks) David Brown.

New Study Guide to Steinbeck's Major Works with Critical Explications. Ed. by Tetsumaro Hayashi. LC 92-37198. 312p. 1993. 45.00 (*0-8108-2611-9*) Scarecrow.

New Study of the Sonnets of Shakespeare. Parke Godwin. LC 78-168172. reprint ed. 41.50 (*0-404-02848-9*) AMS Pr.

New-Style Tai Chi Ch'uan The Official Chinese System. Wei Yue Sun. LC 99-21090. 1999. pap. text 13.95 (*0-8069-9703-6*) Sterling.

New Subediting: Apple-Mac, QuarkXpress & After. 3rd ed. F. W. Hodgson. LC 99-166803. (Media Manuals Ser.). 248p. 1998. 32.95 (*0-240-51534-X*, Focal) Buttrwrth-Heinemann.

New Subjectivism: Art in the 1980s. Donald Kuspit. LC 88-12224. (Studies in the Fine Arts: No. 28). 602p. reprint ed. pap. 186.70 (*0-8357-1888-3*, 207073000004) Bks Demand.

New Subjectivism: Art in the 1980s. Donald Kuspit. (Illus.). 602p. 1993. reprint ed. pap. 17.95 (*0-306-80538-3*) Da Capo.

New Success: Redefining, Creating & Surviving Your Own Success. Pamela Murray. 200p. 1993. pap. 12.95 (*0-9638021-0-0*) Many Waters.

***New Success Rules for Women: 10 Surefire Strategies for Reaching Your Career Goals.** Susan L. Abrams. LC 00-27647. 288p. 2000. 24.95 (*0-7615-2348-0*) Prima Pub.

New Successful Coin Hunting. rev. ed. Charles L. Garrett. LC 88-93045. (Illus.). 259p. 1997. pap. 9.95 (*0-915920-67-0*) Ram Pub.

New Succulent Spiny Euphorbias from East Africa. S. Carter. (Illus.). vi, 118p. 1982. pap. 20.00 (*1-878762-72-9*, Pub. by Royal Botnic Grdns) Balogh.

New Sufferings of Young W. Ulrich Plenzdorf. Tr. by Kenneth P. Wilcox. 84p. 1996. reprint ed. pap. text 7.50 (*0-88133-891-5*) Waveland Pr.

New Sufferings of Young W. And Other Stories from the German Democratic Republic. G. Kunert et al. LC 96-53312. (German Library). 348p. 1997. 39.50 (*0-8264-0953-9*) Continuum.

New Sufferings of Young W. And Other Stories from the German Democratic Republic. U. Plenzdorf et al. Ed. by Therese Hornigk & Alexander Stephan. LC 96-53312. (The German Library). 348p. 1997. pap. 19.95 (*0-8264-0952-0*) Continuum.

New Suit for Santa. Kath Mellentin & Tim Wood. (Illus.). 12p. (J). 1997. 6.95 (*0-7641-5059-6*) Barron.

New Summit Hiker & Ski Touring Guide: Fifty Historic Hiking & Ski Trails. 2nd ed. Mary E. Gilliland. LC 83-71361. (Illus.). 120p. 1997. spiral bd. 14.95 (*0-9603624-2-8*) Alpenrose Pr.

New Sun. Hilda Charlton. Ed. by Golden Quest Staff. (Golden Quest Ser.: Vol. 4). (Illus.). 160p. (Orig.). 1989. pap. text 8.95 (*0-927383-01-2*) Golden Quest.

New Sun: The Solar Results from Skylab. 1994. lib. bdg. 250.75 (*0-8490-6409-0*) Gordon Pr.

***New Suns Will Arise: From the Journals of Henry David Thoreau.** Ed. by Frank Crocitto. 80p. (YA). (gr. 7 up). 2000. 24.99 (*0-7868-0539-0*, Pub. by Hyprn Child) Time Warner.

New Super Antioxidant Plus. Richard A. Passwater. 46p. 1992. pap. 3.95 (*0-87983-589-3*, 35893K, Keats Publng) NTC Contemp Pub Co.

New Superconducting Electronics: Proceedings of the NATO Advanced Study Institute, Waterville Valley, New Hampshire, U. S. A. August 9-20, 1992. Ed. by Harold Weinstock & Richard W. Ralston. LC 93-31752. (NATO ASI Series E, Applied Sciences). 462p. (C). 1993. text 267.50 (*0-7923-2515-X*) Kluwer Academic.

New Superconductors. F. J. Owens & C. P. Poole. LC 96-43014. (Selected Topics in Superconductivity Ser.). (Illus.). 215p. (C). 1996. text 47.00 (*0-306-45453-X*, Kluwer Plenum) Kluwer Academic.

New Superconductors: From Granular to High TC. 300p. 1997. text 33.00 (*981-02-3089-3*) World Scientific Pub.

New Superfamily & Three New Families of Tetraodontiform Fishes from the Upper Cretaceous: The Earliest & Most Morphologically Primitive Plectognaths. James C. Tyler & Lorenzo Sorbini. LC 95-46251. (Smithsonian Contributions to Paleobiology Ser.: Vol. 82). 65p. 1996. reprint ed. pap. 30.00 (*0-608-02428-7*, 206307100004) Bks Demand.

New Superfund Program: Redefining the Federal-State Partnership. Christine O'Donnell. Ed. by Karen Glass. 32p. (Orig.). 1988. pap. text 7.50 (*1-55877-009-7*) Natl Governor.

New Supernutrition. Richard A. Passwater. 337p. 1991. mass mkt. 6.99 (*0-671-70071-5*) PB.

New Supervisor. 3rd ed. Martin M. Broadwell. 1984. pap. text 18.95 (*0-201-10353-2*) Addison-Wesley.

New Supervisor: A Guide for the Newly Promoted. 3rd rev. ed. Elwood N. Chapman. Ed. by Michael G. Crisp. LC 91-77082. (Fifty-Minute Ser.). Orig. Title: Fifty-Minute Supervisor. (Illus.). 68p. 1992. pap. 10.95 (*1-56052-120-1*) Crisp Pubns.

New Supervisor: BUS 101. California College for Health Sciences Staff. 148p. (C). 1992. ring bd. write for info. (*0-933915-36-5*) CA College Health Sci.

New Supervisor: How to Thrive in Your First Year As a Manager. 5th ed. Martin M. Broadwell. LC 98-14806. 304p. 1998. pap. 15.00 (*0-201-33992-7*) Addison-Wesley.

New Supervisor: Skills for Success. Bruce B. Tepper. LC 93-22351. (Business Skills Express Ser.). 128p. (Orig.). 1993. pap. 10.95 (*1-55623-762-6*, Irwn Prfssnl) McGraw-Hill Prof.

New Supervisor's EEO Handbook. 1992. pap. 9.95 (*0-7816-0073-1*) Exec Ent Pubns.

New Supervisor's EEO Handbook: A Guide to Federal Antidiscrimination Laws & Regulations. 5th ed. James H. Coil. 64p. 1994. pap. 32.95 (*0-471-11282-8*) Wiley.

New Supervisor's Survival Manual. William A. Salmon. LC 98-8085. 224p. 1998. pap. 27.95 (*0-8144-7027-0*) AMACOM.

New Surfactants for New Applications. 378p. 1993. 2475.00 (*0-89336-954-3*, C-145) BCC.

New Surrealism. Akhter Ahsen. 542p. 1992. pap. 25.00 (*0-913412-52-X*) Brandon Hse.

New Survey Methods in Transport: 2nd International Conference, Australia, 1983. Ed. by E. S. Amp et al. 387p. 1985. lib. bdg. 99.50 (*90-6764-051-4*, Pub. by VSP) Coronet Bks.

New Survival of the RV Snowbird. rev. ed. Joe Peterson & Kay Peterson. 256p. 1995. 10.95 (*0-910449-08-2*) RoVers Pubns.

New Sweatshops. Ross. (Illus.). (C). text. write for info. (*0-472-10941-3*) U of Mich Pr.

New Sweden in America. Ed. by Carol E. Hoffecker et al. LC 94-36142. 1995. write for info. (*0-87413-520-6*) U Delaware Pr.

New Sweden on the Delaware, 1638-1655. C. A. Weslager. (Illus.). 256p. (Orig.). 1988. pap. 9.95 (*0-912608-65-X*) Mid Atlantic.

New Swedish Plays. Ed. & Tr. by Gunilla Anderman. Tr. by Duncan Foster et al. 212p. 1993. pap. 25.00 (*1-870041-19-4*, Pub. by Forest Bks) Dufour.

New Swedish Style: A Practical Decorating Guide. Sasha Waddell. LC 96-67703. (Illus.). 96p. 1996. 24.95 (*0-8478-1976-0*, Pub. by Rizzoli Intl) St Martin.

New Sweet Style: A Novel. Vassily Aksyonov. LC 99-13313. 496p. 1999. 29.95 (*0-679-44401-7*) Random.

New Switzerland: Problems & Policies. Ed. by Rolf Kieser & Kurt R. Spillmann. LC 96-3011. (Illus.). 425p. 1997. 39.50 (*0-930664-16-7*) SPOSS.

***New Symmetries & Integrable Models.** Ed. by Andrzej Frydryszak et al. 240p. 2000. 86.00 (*981-02-4270-0*) World Scientific Pub.

New Symmetry Principles in Quantum Field Theory. J. Frolich et al. LC 92-18441. (NATO ASI Ser.: Vol. 295). (Illus.). 538p. (C). 1992. text 145.00 (*0-306-44240-X*, Kluwer Plenum) Kluwer Academic.

New Syntax of the Verb in New Testament Greek: An Aspectual Approach. K. L. McKay. LC 92-44671. (Studies in Biblical Greek: Vol. 5). 203p. (Orig.). (C). 1994. pap. text 29.95 (*0-8204-2123-5*) P Lang Pubng.

New Syntheses with Carbon Monoxide. Ed. by Jurgen Falbe. (Reactivity & Structure Ser.: Vol. 11). (Illus.). 450p. 1980. 228.95 (*0-387-09674-4*) Spr-Verlag.

New Synthetic Test Circuit for Ultra-High-Voltage Circuit Breakers. Baoliang Sheng. (Illus.). viii, 164p. (Orig.). 1995. pap. 59.50 (*90-407-1210-7*, Pub. by Delft U Pr) Coronet Bks.

***New System for the Formal Analysis of Kinship.** Sydney H. Gould & David B. Kronenfeld. LC 99-88552. 472p. 2000. 57.50 (*0-7618-1622-4*) U Pr of Amer.

***New System of Domestic Cookery by a Lady: Mrs. Maria Eliza Rundell's Original 1806 Classic - Fort Niagara Edition.** Maria E. Rundell. Ed. by R. Arthur Bowler. (Illus.). 320p. 1998. reprint ed. 14.95 (*0-941967-20-4*) Old Fort Niagara Assn.

New System of Education. B. Everard Blanchard. LC 74-23970. 1975. 19.95 (*0-88280-012-4*) ETC Pubns.

New System of National Accounts. Ed. by John W. Kendrick. (Recent Economic Thought Ser.). 480p. (C). 1996. lib. bdg. 230.00 (*0-7923-9602-2*) Kluwer Academic.

New Systematics. Ed. by Julian S. Huxley. LC 40-35139. 583p. 1940. reprint ed. 49.00 (*0-403-01786-6*) Scholarly.

New Systemic Ideas from the Italian Mental Health Movement. Laura Fruggeri et al. 112p. 1992. pap. text 22.00 (*1-85575-016-3*, Pub. by H Karnac Bks Ltd) Other Pr LLC.

New Table of Reciprocals of Factorials & Some Derived Numbers. Horace S. Uhler. (Connecticut Academy of Arts & Sciences Ser., Trans.: Vol. 32). 1937. pap. 49.50 (*0-685-22916-5*) Elliots Bks.

New Tactics for Real Estate Syndication under the 1984 Tax Act. Law & Business Inc. Staff & Michael I. Sanders. (Illus.). write for info. (*0-318-59551-6*) Harcourt.

New Tagalog English Dictionary Including Everyday Tagalog. Colton Bk Staff. 1994. pap. 5.50 (*971-686-041-2*) Colton Bk.

New Talent Design 1999. 4th ed. Ed. by B. Martin Pedersen. (Illus.). 256p. 1999. text 60.00 (*1-888001-60-7*, Pub. by Graphis US) Watsn-Guptill.

New Tales for Old: Folktales as Literary Fictions for Young Adults. Gail De Vos & Anna E. Altmann. LC 99-33150. 250p. 1999. pap. 35.00 (*1-56308-447-3*) Teacher Ideas Pr.

New Tales of Mystery & Crime from Latin America. Amelia S. Simpson. LC 90-56416. 160p. 1992. 32.50 (*0-8386-3453-2*) Fairleigh Dickinson.

New Tales of Old Rome. Rodolfo Lanciani. LC 67-29707. (Illus.). 1972. reprint ed. 22.95 (*0-405-08727-6*, Pub. by Blom Pubns) Ayer.

New Tales of Robin's Wood. unabridged ed. Marion Ford Park. 20p. 1995. spiral bd. 5.00 (*1-929326-44-0*) Hal Bar Pubg.

New Tales of the Arabian Nights: The Last Voyage of Sindbad. 2nd ed. Jan Strnad. (Illus.). 96p. 1995. pap. 21.95 (*1-884924-01-8*) Fantagor Pr.

New Talkamatics: Easy Way to Verbal Power & Persuasion. Cathy Handley. 1977. 4.95 (*0-13-616102-2*, Parker Publishing Co) P-H.

New Talkpower: A "Pain Clinic" for Public Speaking. Natalie H. Rogers. LC 98-28266. (Illus.). 300p. 1998. 24.95 (*1-892123-03-7*) Capital VA.

***New Talkpower: The Mind-Body Way to Speak Like a Pro.** Natalie H. Rogers. 2000. pap. 15.95 (*1-892123-24-X*) Capital VA.

New Talmudic Readings. Emmanuel Levinas. LC 99-6128. 136p. 1999. 24.00 (*0-8207-0297-8*) Duquesne.

New Targets in Cancer Chemotherapy. David J. Kerr. 236p. 1994. lib. bdg. 189.00 (*0-8493-4905-2*, RC268) CRC Pr.

New Targets in Inflammation: Inhibitors of COX-2 or Adhesion Molecules. Ed. by N. Bazan. 160p. (C). 1996. lib. bdg. 74.00 (*0-614-24339-4*) Kluwer Academic.

New Tarot. Rachel Pollack. (Illus.). 176p. 1990. 22.50 (*0-87951-395-0*, Pub. by Overlook Pr) Penguin Putnam.

New Tarot: Modern Variations of Ancient Images. Rachel Pollack. (Illus.). 176p. 1992. pap. 14.95 (*0-87951-475-2*, Pub. by Overlook Pr) Penguin Putnam.

***New Taste of Chocolate: A Guide to Fine Chocolate with Recipes.** Maricel E. Presilla. (Illus.). 160p. 2000. 17.95 (*1-58008-143-6*) Ten Speed Pr.

***New Tastes from Texas.** Stephan Pyles. LC 99-23443. 1999. pap. 21.95 (*0-609-80497-9*) Crown Pub Group.

New Tastes of Iowa. Peg Hein. Ed. by Mary Ullrich. (Illus.). 124p. (Orig.). 1993. pap. 8.50 (*0-9613881-2-9*) Hein & Assocs.

N

New Tastes of Texas. Peg Hein. Ed. by Mary Ullrich. (Illus.). 180p. 1995. pap. 12.95 (*0-9613881-3-7*) Hein & Assocs.

New Tattoo. Victoria Lautman. LC 94-5033. (Illus.). 128p. 1994. 35.00 (*1-55859-785-9*) Abbeville Pr.

New Tattoo. Victoria Lautman. (Illus.). 128p. 1996. pap., bds. 24.95 (*0-7892-0233-6*) Abbeville Pr.

New Tax Developments Doctors Version, 1990. (C). 1990. pap. 5.95 (*0-13-620758-8*) P-H.

New Tax Developments Over 55, 1990 (C). 1990. pap. 6.85 (*0-13-620741-3*) P-H.

New Tax Guide for Performers, Writers, Directors, Designers & Other Show Biz Folk: 1999 Edition. rev. ed. R. Brendon Hanlon. LC 99-187201. (Illus.). 139p. 1999. pap. 12.95 (*0-87910-276-4*) Limelight Edns.

New Tax Rule for Employee Reimbursements, 1989. Nicholas Economides. (C). 1989. pap. 4.95 (*0-13-612011-3*) P-H.

New Tax Structure for the United States. Donald H. Skadden. LC 77-29249. (Key Issues Lecture Ser.). 1978. write for info. (*0-672-97222-0*); pap. write for info. (*0-672-97223-9*) Macmillan.

New Tax Superstar: S Corporation. Irving L. Blackman & Gregory G. Andresen. (Special Report Ser.: No. 17). 61p. 1991. pap. 29.00 (*0-916181-16-2*) Blackman Kallick Bartelstein.

***New Tea Lover's Treasury: The Classic True Story of Tea.** (Illus.). 210p. 1999. 24.95 (*0-9701283-0-4*) P T A Pubng.

New Teacher: An Introduction to Teaching in Comprehensive Education. Nigel Tubbs. LC 96-222632. (Quality in Secondary Schools & Colleges Ser.). 176p. 1996. pap. text 24.95 (*1-85346-424-4*, Pub. by David Fulton) Taylor & Francis.

New Teacher, New Student. Connie Jensen. (Illus.). 128p. 1997. pap. 4.95 (*1-880505-51-7*, CLC0203) Pieces of Lrning.

New Teacher Orientation: A Practical Guide for School Administration. 1995. 92.00 (*0-8342-0458-4*) Aspen Pub.

New Teachers. Don M. Flournoy et al. LC 77-184957. (Jossey-Bass Higher Education Ser.). 224p. reprint ed. 69.50 (*0-8357-9339-7*, 201381700087) Bks Demand.

***New Teachers for a New Century, the Future of Early Childhood Professional Preparation.** Diane Horm-Wingerd. 99p. 2000. per. 22.00 (*0-16-050296-9*) USGPO.

New Teachers Helping New Teachers: Preservice Peer Coaching. Elizabeth A. McAllister & Gloria A. Neubert. LC 94-49407. 132p. (Orig.). 1995. pap. 19.95 (*1-883790-14-X*, 100-1272, EDINFO Pr) Grayson Bernard Pubs.

New Teacher's Survival Guide: Everything They Forget to Tell You During Credentialing. Mark N. Remy. LC 97-92217. (Illus.). 134p. 1997. pap. 15.95 (*0-9659349-1-8*, 001) Siena Pub.

New Teaching Elementary Science: Who's Afraid of Spiders? 2nd rev. ed. Selma Wasserman & J. W. Ivany. LC 95-41119. 336p. (C). 1996. pap. text 22.95 (*0-8077-3512-4*) Tchrs Coll.

New Teaching, New Learning: Current Issues in Higher Education, 1971. Ed. by G. Kerry Smith. LC 72-173856. (Jossey-Bass Higher Education Ser.). 284p. reprint ed. 88.10 (*0-8357-9340-0*, 201390100087) Bks Demand.

***New Teaching Safer Sex.** Peggy Brick. 129p. 1998. 25.00 (*0-9609366-1-0*) Plan Parenthood.

New Teachings for an Awakening Humanity. Ed. by Virginia Essene. 208p. (Orig.). 1987. pap. 8.95 (*0-937147-00-1*) SEE Pub Co.

New Teachings for an Awakening Humanity. Ed. by Virginia Essene. (SPA.). 217p. (Orig.). 1989. pap. 9.95 (*0-937147-04-4*) SEE Pub Co.

New Teachings for an Awakening Humanity, 1994-1995 Update. Ed. by Virginia Essene. 264p. 1995. pap. 9.95 (*0-937147-09-5*) SEE Pub Co.

New Technical Trader: Boost Your Profit by Plugging into the Latest Indicators. Tushar S. Chande & Stanley Kroll. (Finance Editions Ser.). 224p. 1994. 64.95 (*0-471-59780-5*) Wiley.

New Technique for Simulating Composite Material: Final Report, September 1991. John L. Volakis. LC QC0670.. (University of Michigan Report Ser.: No. 025921-23-T). 80p. reprint ed. pap. 30.00 (*0-7837-1948-5*, 204216300001) Bks Demand.

New Techniques & Applications in Lipid Analysis. Richard E. McDonald & Magdi M. Mossoba. LC 97-3204. 1997. 105.00 (*0-935315-80-2*) Am Oil Chemists.

New Techniques & Approaches for Wood Carving. D. V. Semenick. (Illus.). 168p. (Orig.). 1988. pap. 14.95 (*0-9692582-0-8*) Gordon Soules Bk.

New Techniques & Instrumentation in Ultrasonography. Ed. by P. N. Wells & Marvin C. Ziskin. LC 80-18689. (Clinics in Diagnostic Ultrasound Ser.: No. 5). (Illus.). 255p. reprint ed. pap. 79.10 (*0-7837-2575-2*, 204273400006) Bks Demand.

New Techniques & Technologies for Statistics II. LC 97-70213. 350p. (gr. 12). 1997. 102.00 (*90-5199-326-9*) IOS Press.

New Techniques for Aligning & Maintaining Large Ring Gears. Mike Antosiewicz. (Technical Papers: Vol. P159.04A). (Illus.). 11p. 1981. pap. text 30.00 (*1-55589-207-8*) AGMA.

New Techniques for Characterizing Corrosion & Stress Corrosion. Ed. by R. H. Jones & D. R. Baer. (Illus.). 331p. 1995. 20.00 (*0-87339-325-2*, 3252) Minerals Metals.

New Techniques for Efficient Teaching. Paul W. Nesbit. (Illus.). 1947. 1.75 (*0-911746-03-X*); pap. 1.00 (*0-911746-05-6*) Nesbit.

New Techniques for Future Accelerators. Ed. by M. Puglisi et al. LC 87-20248. (Ettore Majorana International Science Series, Life Sciences: Vol. 29). (Illus.). 292p. 1987. 85.00 (*0-306-42608-0*, Plenum Trade) Perseus Pubng.

New Techniques for Future Accelerators Vol. 3: High-Intensity Storage Rings: Status & Prospects for Superconducting Magnets. Ed. by G. Torelli. (Ettore Majorana International Science Ser., Life Sciences: Vol. 53). (Illus.). 242p. (C). 1990. 107.00 (*0-306-43703-1*, Kluwer Plenum) Kluwer Academic.

New Techniques for Future Accelerators II: RF & Microwave Systems. Ed. by M. Puglisi et al. (Ettore Majorana International Science Series, Life Sciences: Vol. 36). (Illus.). 322p. 1989. 95.00 (*0-306-43090-8*, Plenum Trade) Perseus Pubng.

New Techniques for Modelling the Management of Stormwater Quality Impacts. Ed. by William James. 560p. 1992. lib. bdg. 99.95 (*0-87371-898-4*, L898) Lewis Pubs.

New Techniques for the Study of Electrodes & Their Reaction. Ed. by R. G. Comton & A. Hammett. (Comprehensive Chemical Kinetics Ser.: 29). xivi,504p. 1989. 411.50 (*0-444-42999-9*) Elsevier.

New Techniques for Welding & Extending Sprinkler Pipes. Ernest W. Pyle. 1976. 2.50 (*0-686-17608-1*, TR 76-2) Society Fire Protect.

***New Techniques for Winning Jury Trials.** (C). 2000. 120.00 (*0-8087-4683-9*) Pearson Custom.

New Techniques in Acquisitions & Takeovers. Kenneth J. Bialkin, Jr. et al. vi, 528p. write for info. (*0-318-58372-0*) Harcourt.

New Techniques in Aqua Therapy. Kiss Agnes. LC 98-46877. (Illus.). 330p. 1999. 19.95 (*1-58141-006-9*) Rivercross Pub.

New Techniques in Biophysics & Cell Biology, Vol. 1. Ed. by B. J. Smith & Roger H. Pain. LC 72-8611. 259p. 1974. reprint ed. pap. 80.30 (*0-608-14370-7*, 201615600098) Bks Demand.

New Techniques in Biophysics & Cell Biology, 1975, Vol. 2. Ed. by B. J. Smith & Roger H. Pain. LC 72-8611. 407p. 1975. reprint ed. pap. 126.20 (*0-7837-8634-4*, 201615600002) Bks Demand.

New Techniques in Biophysics & Cell Biology, 1976, Vol. 3. fac. ed. Ed. by B. J. Smith & Roger H. Pain. LC 72-8611. 253p. 1976. pap. 78.50 (*0-7837-8635-2*, 201615600003) Bks Demand.

New Techniques in Food & Beverage Microbiology. Ed. by R. G. Kroll et al. LC 93-15223. 1993. 60.00 (*0-632-03755-5*) Blackwell Sci.

New Techniques in Hob Sharping. F. Stelzer. (Technical Papers: Vol. P129.29). (Illus.). 10p. 1982. pap. text 30.00 (*1-55589-543-3*) AGMA.

New Techniques in Labor Dispute Resolution: A Report of the 23rd Conference of the Association of Labor Mediation Agencies. Howard J. Anderson. LC 76-13538. 259p. reprint ed. pap. 80.30 (*0-608-12743-4*, 202434200036) Bks Demand.

New Techniques in Reconstructive Urology. Jack W. McAninch. (Illus.). 160p. 1996. write for info. (*0-89640-281-9*) Igaku-Shoin.

New Techniques in SI & Diesel Engine Modeling. 120p. 1998. pap. 59.00 (*0-7680-0203-6*, SP-1366) Soc Auto Engineers.

New Techniques in Space Astronomy: Proceedings of the I. A. U. Symposium, No. 41, Muenchen, Germany, Aug. 10-14, 1970. International Astronomical Union Staff. Ed. by F. Labuhn & R. Luest. LC 75-15658. (I.A.U. Symposia Ser.). 418p. 1971. text 121.50 (*90-277-0202-0*) Kluwer Academic.

New Techniques in the Analysis of Foods. Michael Tunick et al. LC 98-48207. (C). 1999. text. write for info. (*0-306-46035-1*, Kluwer Plenum) Kluwer Academic.

New Techniques of Inner Healing. D. Scott Rogo. 248p. (Orig.). 1994. pap. 12.95 (*1-56924-930-X*) Marlowe & Co.

New Techniques of Optical Microscopy & Microspectroscopy. Ed. by Richard J. Cherry. 1991. 105.00 (*0-8493-7117-1*, QH) CRC Pr.

New Techniques of Osteosynthesis of the Hand. F. Schuind. (Reconstruction Surgery & Traumatology Ser.: Vol. 21). (Illus.). x, 156p. 1990. 137.50 (*3-8055-5194-0*) S Karger.

New Techniques That Catch More Bluegill. Steve L. Wunderle. (Illus.). 90p. 1983. pap. 6.95 (*0-9611162-1-8*) Wunderle Outdoor.

New Techniques That Catch More Crappie. Steve L. Wunderle. (Illus.). 64p. (Orig.). 1983. pap. text 6.95 (*0-9611162-0-X*) Wunderle Outdoor.

***New Technological & Design Developments in Deep Foundations: Proceedings of Sessions of Geo-Denver 2000, August 5-8, 2000, Denver, Colorado.** Geo-Denver 2000 Staff et al. LC 00-40139. (Geotechnical Special Publication Ser.). 2000. pap. write for info. (*0-7844-0511-5*) Am Soc Civil Eng.

New Technologies: A Challenge to Privacy Protection? Council of Europe Staff. 1989. 15.00 (*92-871-1617-2*, Pub. by Council of Europe) Manhattan Pub Co.

New Technologies: New Architecture. William Zuk & Thomas Zuk. (Illus.). 176p. (Orig.). 1994. pap. write for info. (*0-9640572-0-4*) W Zuk.

New Technologies: Their Impact on Employment & the Working Environment. International Labour Office Staff. 174p. 1984. pap. 10.00 (*0-86346-044-5*, Tycooly Pub) Weidner & Sons.

New Technologies & Art Education: Implications for Theory, Research, & Practice. Ed. by Diane Gregory. 189p. (C). 1997. pap. text 22.00 (*0-937652-74-1*, 218) Natl Art Ed.

New Technologies & Concepts for Reducing Drug Toxicities. Harry Salem & Steven I. Baskin. 176p. 1992. lib. bdg. 95.00 (*0-8493-8896-1*, RA1238) CRC Pr.

New Technologies & Corporation Aviation: 25th Annual Meeting of Corporate Aviation Safety Seminar, March 23-25, 1980 St. Louis, Missouri. Corporate Aviation Safety Seminar Staff. LC TL0545.F55. 174p. reprint ed. pap. 54.00 (*0-608-13064-8*, 201463500096) Bks Demand.

***New Technologies & Law of the Marine Environment (Nouvelles Technologies et Droit de l'Environnement Marin)** Ed. by Jean-Pierre Beurier et al. (International Environmental Law & Policy Ser.: Vol. 55). 304p. 2000. text 135.00 (*90-411-9756-7*) Kluwer Law Intl.

New Technologies & New Skills: Two Year Colleges at the Vanguard of Modernization. Stuart A. Rosenfeld. 159p. (Orig.). (C). 1995. 20.00 (*0-9636927-2-0*) Reg Tech Strat.

New Technologies & Services: Impacts on Cities & Jobs. Thierry J. Noyelle. (Urban Studies: No. 5). 55p. (Orig.). 1986. pap. text 6.00 (*0-913749-03-6*) U MD Urban Stud.

New Technologies & Technological Capability-Building at the Enterprise Level: Some Policy Implications. LC 96-226292. (Science & Technology Issues Ser.). 52p. pap. 10.00 (*92-1-112392-5*) UN.

New Technologies & the Employment of Disabled Persons. Ed. by H. Allan Hunt & Monroe Berkowitz. v, 162p. (Orig.). 1992. pap. 18.00 (*92-2-107757-8*) Intl Labour Office.

New Technologies & the Future of Food & Nutrition. Ed. by Gerald E. Gaull & Ray A. Goldberg. LC 91-18915. 192p. 1991. 90.00 (*0-471-55408-1*) Wiley.

New Technologies, Defense Policy & Arms Control. Kosta Tsipis. 144p. 1989. text 24.95 (*0-88730-382-X*, HarpBusn) HarpInfo.

New Technologies for Education: A Beginner's Guide. 3rd ed. Ann E. Barron & Gary W. Orwig. LC 96-39108. 265p. 1997. pap. 40.00 (*1-56308-477-5*) Libs Unl.

New Technologies for Exploration & Exploitation for Oil & Gas Resources, 2 vols., Set. Commission of the European Communities. 338p. 1988. lib. bdg. 475.50 (*1-85333-226-7*) G & T Inc.

New Technologies for Gas Energy Supply & Efficient Use, 1983 Update. American Gas Association. Policy Evaluation & Anal. (Illus.). 43p. write for info. (*0-318-57841-7*) Am Gas Assn.

New Technologies for Healthy Foods & Nutraceuticals. Ed. by Manssur Yalpani. (Frontiers in Foods & Food Ingredients Ser.: Vol. 2). 344p. 1997. pap. 125.00 (*1-882360-11-7*) ATL Pr Sci.

New Technologies for Healthy Foods & Nutraceuticals. Ed. by Manssur Yalpani. LC 96-36413. (Frontiers in Foods & Food Ingredients Ser.: Vol. 2). (Illus.). 344p. (C). 1997. 225.00 (*1-882360-10-9*) ATL Pr Sci.

New Technologies for Liver Resections. Ed. by R. Dionigi & Juan Madariaga. LC 97-6443. (Medical Intelligence Unit Ser.). (Illus.). xiv, 268p. 1997. 98.00 (*3-8055-6564-X*) S Karger.

New Technologies for Low Emissions Vehicle Testing: SAE International Congress & Exposition 1994, 16 papers. (Special Publications). 112p. 1994. pap. 49.00 (*1-56091-466-1*, SP-1014) Soc Auto Engineers.

New Technologies for Rainfed Rice-Based Farming Systems in the Philippines & Sri Lanka. Ed. by Bibliotech Anutech Pty., Ltd. Staff. 1988. pap. 36.00 (*0-949511-63-3*, Pub. by ACIAR) St Mut.

New Technologies for Supercolliders. Ed. by L. Cifarelli & T. Ypsilantis. (Ettore Majorana International Science Ser., Life Sciences: Vol. 57). (Illus.). 408p. (C). 1992. text 155.00 (*0-306-44058-X*, Kluwer Plenum) Kluwer Academic.

New Technologies for the Exploration & Exploitation of Oil & Gas Resources, 2 vols., Vol. 1. E. Millich et al. (C). 1900. lib. bdg. 574.00 (*1-85333-058-2*) Kluwer Academic.

New Technologies for the Exploration & Exploitation of Oil & Gas Resources, 2 vols., Vol. 2. E. Millich et al. (C). 1900. lib. bdg. 108.00 (*1-85333-059-0*) Kluwer Academic.

New Technologies in Clinical Laboratory Science. Ed. by K. Shinton. 1985. text 147.50 (*0-85200-927-5*) Kluwer Academic.

New Technologies in Electron Microscopy & Microdiffraction Tutorial, Austin, 1987. (American Crystallographic Association Lecture Notes Ser.: No. 7). 1991. pap. 15.00 (*0-685-51612-1*) Polycrystal Bk Serv.

New Technologies in Exploration Geophysics. H. Roice Nelson. LC 82-21120. 293p. 1983. reprint ed. pap. 90.90 (*0-608-01577-6*, 206199700001) Bks Demand.

New Technologies in Hospital Information Systems. Ed. by J. Dudeck et al. LC 97-75049. (Studies in Health Technology & Informatics: Vol. 45). 250p. Date not set. 86.00 (*90-5199-363-3*, 363-3) IOS Press.

New Technologies in Language Learning & Teaching. 1997. 18.00 (*92-871-3254-2*, Pub. by Council of Europe) Manhattan Pub Co.

New Technologies in Reproductive Medicine, Neonatology & Gynecology: The Proceedings of the 1st International Symposium, Folgaria, Italy. Ermelando V. Cosmi. LC 99-21828. (Illus.). 368p. 1999. 88.00 (*1-85070-065-6*) Prthnon Pub.

New Technologies in Retailing: Card Readers, Scanners, & Monitors. McGowan. 162p. 1998. 3150.00 (*1-56965-092-6*, G-226) BCC.

***New Technologies in the Fight Against Transboundary Animal Diseases.** FAO Staff. (Animal Production & Health Papers: No. 145). 130p. 2000. pap. 16.00 (*92-5-104358-2*, F43582, Pub. by FAO) Bernan Associates.

New Technologies in the Humanities. Christine Mullings et al. 1996. 75.00 (*1-85739-113-6*) Bowker-Saur.

New Technologies in Urban Drainage: UDT 91. Ed. by C. Maksimovic. (Illus.). 540p. (C). (gr. 13). 1991. text 200.00 (*1-85166-650-8*) Elsevier Applied Sci.

New Technologies of Birth & Death: Medical, Legal & Moral Dimensions. Ed. by Donald G. McCarthy. LC 80-83425. xvi, 196p. (Orig.). 1980. pap. 8.95 (*0-935372-07-5*) NCBC.

New Technology: The Bargaining Issues. Ed. by Jonathan Winterton & Ruth Winterton. (C). 1985. 40.00 (*0-900572-64-7*) St Mut.

New Technology: The Bargaining Issues. Jonathan Winterton & Ruth Winterton. (C). 1988. text 35.00 (*0-7855-3174-2*, Pub. by Univ Nottingham) St Mut.

New Technology & Employment in Insurance, Banking & Building Societies. A. Raijan. (C). 1984. 275.00 (*0-7855-4070-9*, Pub. by Witherby & Co) St Mut.

New Technology & Human Error. fac. ed. Ed. by Jens Rasmussen et al. LC 86-5607. (New Technologies & Work Ser.). 370p. 1987. reprint ed. pap. 114.70 (*0-7837-8271-3*, 204905200009) Bks Demand.

New Technology & Industrial Relations in Fleet Street. Roderick Martin. 1981. 55.00 (*0-19-827243-X*) OUP.

New Technology & Insurance. S. Curran. (C). 1980. 85.00 (*0-7855-4069-5*, Pub. by Witherby & Co) St Mut.

New Technology & Insurance. Susan Curran. 1981. 60.00 (*0-7855-7333-X*, Pub. by Fourmat Pub) St Mut.

New Technology & Manufacturing Management: Strategic Choices for Flexible Production Systems. fac. ed. Ed. by Malcolm Warner et al. LC 89-70549. (New Technologies & Work Ser.). 287p. pap. 89.00 (*0-7837-7371-4*, 204718100005) Bks Demand.

New Technology & Practical Police Work: The Social Context of Technical Innovation. Stephen Ackroyd et al. 100p. 1992. 113.00 (*0-335-09459-7*); pap. 41.95 (*0-335-09458-9*) OpUniv Pr.

New Technology & Public Relations: A Guide for Public Relations & Public Affairs Practitioners. Ed. by Kalman B. Druck. LC 87-105313. 188p. reprint ed. pap. 58.30 (*0-7837-0081-4*, 204033900016) Bks Demand.

New Technology & Rural Development see Technology & the Rural Community: The Social Impact

New Technology & the Process of Labour Regulation. Eric Batstone et al. 272p. 1987. 65.00 (*0-19-827274-X*) OUP.

New Technology & the Workers' Response: Microelectronics, Labour & Society. Ed. by Amiya K. Bagchi. LC 94-19449. 348p. 1995. 39.95 (*0-8039-9198-3*) Sage.

New Technology As Organizational Innovation: The Development & Diffusion of Microelectronics. Ed. by Johannes M. Pennings & Arend Buitendam. LC 86-32110. 328p. 1987. text 32.00 (*0-88730-186-X*, HarpBusn) HarpInfo.

New Technology at Work. Arthur Francis. 224p. 1987. 55.00 (*0-19-878016-8*) OUP.

***New Technology-Based Firms at the Turn of the Century.** W. E. During et al. LC 00-25523. 2000. write for info. (*0-08-043791-5*, Pergamon Pr) Elsevier.

***New Technology-Based Firms in the 1990's.** Raymond P. Oakey et al. 320p. 1999. 90.00 (*0-08-042761-8*, Pergamon Pr) Elsevier.

New Technology-Based Firms in the 1990s. Ed. by Raymond P. Oakey. LC 95-113964. 256p. 1994. 75.00 (*1-85396-274-0*, Pub. by P Chapman) Taylor & Francis.

New Technology-Based Firms in the 1990s, Vol. II. Raymond P. Oakey. 208p. 1996. pap. 85.00 (*1-85396-343-7*, Pub. by P Chapman) Taylor & Francis.

New Technology-Based Firms in the 1990s, Vol. III. Ed. by Ray Oakey & Syeda-Masooda Mukhtar. 240p. 1997. pap. 89.00 (*1-85396-369-0*, Pub. by P Chapman) Taylor & Francis.

New Technology-Based Firms in the 1990s, Vol. IV. Ray Oakley. 1998. 79.95 (*1-85396-386-0*, Pub. by P Chapman) P H Brookes.

***New Technology Batteries Guide.** William J. Ingram. (Illus.). 52p. (C). 2000. pap. text 20.00 (*0-7881-8806-2*) DIANE Pub.

New Technology Demonstration: A Unit Report from the Energy Task Force of the Urban Consortium. 80p. 1981. 10.00 (*0-318-17346-8*, DG81-306) Pub Tech Inc.

New Technology Developments Impacting Broadcasting Businesses, Markets, & Operations. 110p. (Orig.). 1990. pap. 40.00 (*0-89324-084-2*) Natl Assn Broadcasters.

New Technology for Geosciences see Proceedings of the 30th International Geological Congress

New Technology in Hydrometry: Developments in the Acquisition & Management of Streamflow Data. fac. ed. Ed. by Reginald W. Herschy. LC 85-24515. (Illus.). 254p. 1986. reprint ed. pap. 78.80 (*0-7837-8008-7*, 204776400008) Bks Demand.

New Technology in Language Learning: Proceedings of the 1989 Man & the Media Symposium. Ed. by Graham Davies & Michael Hussey. LC 92-27589. (Illus.). 127p. 1992. 32.00 (*3-631-44890-2*) P Lang Pubng.

New Technology in Medical Plastics. Ed. by M. Weiselberg & R. H. Bauman. 177p. 1990. reprint ed. pap. 42.00 (*0-938648-20-9*) T-C Pr CA.

New Technology in Medical Plastics: Proceedings West Coast Medical Plastics Conference, Grand Hotel, Anaheim, California, March 21-22 ,1984. Society of Plastics Engineers Staff. LC TA0455.. 174p. reprint ed. pap. 54.00 (*0-608-14554-8*, 202472300038) Bks Demand.

New Technology in Nuclear Power Plant Instrumentation & Control: Proceedings of the Symposium, Hyatt Regency Crystal City Hotel, Washington, D. C., November 28-30, 1984. Instrument Society of America Staff. LC 85-218690. (Illus.). 409p. reprint ed. pap. 126.80 (*0-608-15522-5*, 202974800064) Bks Demand.

New Technology in Sociology: Practical Applications in Research & Work. Ed. by Grant Blank et al. 170p. 1989. pap. 21.95 (*0-88738-769-1*) Transaction Pubs.

An Asterisk (*) at the beginning of an entry indicates that the title is appearing for the first time.

New Technology in the Office: Planning for People. Tora K. Bikson. (Studies in Productivity: Highlights of the Literature Ser.: Vol. 40). 1985. 55.00 (0-08-029514-2) Work in Amer.

New Technology in Water Services: Proceedings of a Symposium Organized by the Institution of Civil Engineers. 260p. 1985. 42.00 (0-7277-0239-4, Pub. by T Telford) RCH.

New Technology of Financial Management. Dimitris N. Chorafas. LC 92-1023. (Finance Editions Ser.). 304p. 1992. 55.00 (0-471-57402-3) Wiley.

New Technology of Pest Control. Ed. by Carl B. Huffaker. LC 79-4369. (Environmental Science & Technology Ser.). (Illus.). 516p. reprint ed. pap. 160.00 (0-8357-6235-1, 205680600089) Bks Demand.

New Technology Policy & Social Innovations in the Firm. Ed. by Jorge Niosi. LC 94-15090. 1995. 60.00 (1-85567-259-6) St Martin.

New Technology to Reduce Fire Losses & Costs. Ed. by S. J. Grayson & D. A. Smith. (C). 1986. 350.00 (0-7855-4068-7, Pub. by Witherby & Co) St Mut.

***New Teen Book: An A-Z Guide for Parents of 9 to 16 Year Olds.** Wade Horn & Carol Keough. LC 98-68019. 160p. 1999. pap. 16.95 (0-696-20933-0) Meredith Bks.

New Teen Titans. Marv Wolfman. 224p. 1989. pap. 2.95 (0-8125-0354-6, Pub. by Tor Bks) St Martin.

New Teen Titans Archives, Vol. 1. Marv Wolfman. (Illus.). 240p. 1999. 49.95 (1-56389-485-8, Pub. by DC Comics) Time Warner.

New Teenage Body Book. rev. ed. Kathy McCoy & Charles Wibbelsman. (Illus.). 288p. (YA). (gr. 9-12). 1992. pap. 15.95 (0-399-51725-1, Body Pr-Perigee) Berkley Pub.

New Telecommunications: A Political Economy of Network Evolution. Robin E. Mansell. (C). 1994. text 65.00 (0-8039-8535-5); pap. text 24.95 (0-8039-8536-3) Sage.

New Telecommunications Environment: Opportunities for Electric Cooperatives. Keller et al. LC 96-35724. 1996. write for info. (0-917599-19-5) Natl Rural.

New Telecommunications Industry: Meeting the Competition. rev. ed. Leonard S. Hyman et al. 500p. 1997. pap. 89.00 (0-910325-66-9) Public Util.

New Telecommunications Landscape. Law & Business Inc. Staff et al. iv, 199p. write for info. (0-318-58373-9) Harcourt.

New Television Showstoppers. rev. ed. Ed. by Carol Cuellar. 256p. (Orig.). (YA). 1996. pap. text 18.95 (1-57623-519-X, MF9637) Wrner Bros.

New Temperance: The American Obsession with Sin & Vice. David Wagner. LC 96-51514. (C). 1997. pap. text 25.00 (0-8133-2569-2, Pub. by Westview) HarpC.

New Temple for Corinth: Rhetorical & Archaeological Approaches to Pauline Imagery. John R. Lanci. LC 96-33594. (Studies in Biblical Literature: Vol. 1). 155p. (C). 1997. text 39.95 (0-8204-3676-3) P Lang Pubng.

New Temple for Hathor at Memphis Vol. 1: Egyptology Today. Abdulla. 1978. pap. 32.50 (0-85668-089-3, Pub. by Aris & Phillips) David Brown.

New Tenant see Three Plays

New Tendencies in the Hungarian Economy. Geza Kilenyi & V. Lamm. (Studies on Hungarian State & Law: Vol. 2). 179p. (C). 1990. pap. 72.00 (963-05-5760-6, Pub. by Akade Kiado) St Mut.

New Term at Lechlade College. L. Brown. mass mkt. 6.95 (0-7472-5409-5, Pub. by Headline Bk Pub) Trafalgar.

New Ternary Alloy Systems for Infrared Detectors. Antoni Rogalski. LC 94-10019. 1994. 91.00 (0-8194-1583-9, PM14/HC); pap. 76.00 (0-8194-1582-0) SPIE.

New Terracotta Gardener: Creative Ideas from Leading Gardeners. Jim Keeling. (Illus.). 176p. 1997. pap. 19.95 (1-57076-066-7, Trafalgar Sq Pub) Trafalgar.

New Terrier Handbook. Kerry V. Kern. 1988. pap. 9.95 (0-8120-3951-3) Barron.

New Territories: The Computer Visions of Jurgen Ziewe. Text by Nigel Suckling. LC 97-9781. (Illus.). 128p. (Orig.). 1997. pap. 24.95 (0-87951-811-1, Pub. by Overlook Pr) Penguin Putnam.

New Territory: Contemporary Indiana Fiction. Ed. by Michael Wilkerson & Deborah Galyan. LC 90-30118. 176p. 1990. 23.95 (0-253-36544-9); pap. 5.95 (0-253-20595-6, MB-595) Ind U Pr.

***New Terror: Facing the Threat of Biological & Chemical Weapons.** Ed. by Sidney D. Drell et al. LC 99-41989. (Publication Series: Archival Documentaries: Vol. 462). 500p. 1999. pap. 24.00 (0-8179-9702-4) Hoover Inst Pr.

New Terrorism: Fanaticism & the Arms of Mass Destruction. Walter Laquer. LC HV6431.L35 1999. 320p. 1999. 30.00 (0-19-511816-2) OUP.

New Tertiary Mathematics. C. A. Plumpton & P. S. Macilwaine. 1250p. 1981. text 590.00 (0-08-021646-3) Franklin.

New Tesla Electromagnetics. (Nikola Tesla Ser.). 1991. lib. bdg. 250.00 (0-8490-4322-0) Gordon Pr.

New Tesla Electromagnetics. 1987. 11.50 (0-914119-19-2) Tesla Bk Co.

***New Testament.** 1999. 34.99 (0-521-51302-2) Cambridge U Pr.

New Testament. (Praying with...Ser.). 1988. 5.95 (0-687-86037-7) Abingdon.

New Testament. Bellerophon Books Staff. (J). (gr. 1-9). 1992. pap. 4.95 (0-88388-004-0) Bellerophon Bks.

***New Testament.** Broadman & Holman Publishing Staff. LC 99-54017. (Shepherd's Notes Bible Summary Ser.). 1999. pap. 5.95 (0-8054-9378-6) Broadman.

***New Testament, 1vol.** Davidson Press Staff. 2000. pap. text 30.00 (1-891833-13-8) Davidson Pr.

New Testament. Frank Schaffer Publications Staff. 1997. pap. text 5.95 (0-7647-0098-7) Schaffer Pubns.

New Testament. Frank Schaffer Publications Staff. 1997. pap. text 9.95 (0-7647-0248-3) Schaffer Pubns.

New Testament. Richmond Lattimore. 608p. 1997. pap. text 16.00 (0-86547-524-5) N Point Pr.

New Testament. Alfred Martin. (Survey of the Scriptures Study Guides Ser.). 1995. pap. 8.99 (1-56570-000-7) Meridian MI.

New Testament. William Tyndale. Ed. by David Daniell. LC 88-37936. 429p. (C). 1989. 40.00 (0-300-04419-4) Yale U Pr.

***New Testament.** Warner Press Staff. (Illus.). (J). 1999. pap. 3.95 (0-87162-862-7) Warner Pr.

New Testament. 4th ed. Duling. (C). 1999. text. write for info. (0-15-507856-9) Harcourt Coll Pubs.

New Testament see Zondervan NIV Bible Commentary

New Testament: A Course on Jesus & His Disciples: Keystone Edition. Norman F. Josaitis & Michael J. Lanning. (Faith & Witness Program Ser.). (Illus.). 192p. (J). (gr. 7-9). 1999. pap. text 11.40 (0-8215-5601-0) Sadlier.

New Testament: A Critical Introduction. Edwin D. Freed. 449p. (C). 1985. pap. write for info. (0-534-05388-2) Wadsworth Pub.

New Testament: A Critical Introduction. 2nd ed. Edwin D. Freed. 462p. (C). 1990. 46.50 (0-534-13872-1) Wadsworth Pub.

New Testament: A Critical Introduction. 3rd ed. Edwin D. Freed. LC 99-56609. (Religion Ser.). 478p. 2000. pap. 45.95 (0-534-52139-8) Wadsworth Pub.

New Testament: A Guide to Its Writings. Gunther Bornkamm. LC 73-79009. 174p. (Orig.). reprint ed. pap. 54.00 (0-608-15538-1, 202977100064) Bks Demand.

New Testament: A Historical Introduction to the Early Christian Writings. 2nd ed. Bart D. Ehrman. LC 99-22360. (Illus.). 508p. (C). 1999. pap. 36.95 (0-19-512639-4) OUP.

New Testament: A Manual for College Students. Wayne W. Mahan. 111p. (Orig.). 1997. pap. text 11.95 (0-87563-722-1) Stipes.

New Testament: A Modern Introduction. Vanvoorst. (Religion). 2001. pap. 34.00 (0-534-54180-1) Wadsworth Pub.

New Testament: A Pictorial Archive from Nineteenth-Century Sources. Ed. by Don Rice. (Pictorial Archive Ser.). (Illus.). 192p. (Orig.). 1986. pap. 9.95 (0-486-25073-3) Dover.

New Testament: A Rendering. Jon Madsen. pap. 29.50 (0-86315-184-1, 1869, Pub. by Floris Bks) Anthroposophic.

New Testament: A Student's Introduction. 3rd ed. Stephen L. Harris. LC 97-51733. 440p. 1999. pap. text 36.95 (0-7674-0014-3) Mayfield Pub.

New Testament: A Study Aid. Tessa Krailing. (Barron's Book Notes Ser.). (Orig.). 1986. pap. text 2.50 (0-8120-3530-5) Barron.

New Testament: A Thematic Introduction. J. Christiaan Beker. LC 93-32244. 152p. 1994. pap. 15.00 (0-8006-2775-X, 1-2775) Augsburg Fortress.

New Testament: A Timeless Book for All People. Selvidge. LC 98-19234. 492p. 1998. pap. text 37.33 (0-13-269580-4) St Martin.

New Testament: A Translation by William Barclay. William Barclay. (William Barclay Library). 598p. 1999. pap. 18.95 (0-664-22174-2) Westminster John Knox.

New Testament: An Introduction. Paul N. Tarazi. LC 98-40713. 1998. write for info. (0-88141-188-4) St Vladimirs.

New Testament: An Introduction to Its History & Literature. J. Gresham Machem. 1976. pap. 15.99 (0-85151-449-9) Banner of Truth.

New Testament: Classic Premier Edition. Premier League Staff. (Believer's Lifesystem Ser.). 1996. pap. 8.99 (0-8024-2766-9) Moody.

New Testament: Devotions for Litle Boys & Girls. Joan C. Webb. LC 91-3770. (Devotions for Little Boys & Girls). (Illus.). 112p. (J). 1992. pap. 6.99 (0-87403-682-8, 02822) Standard Pub.

New Testament: Expanded Translation. Kenneth S. Wuest. 1994. pap. text 20.00 (0-8028-0882-4) Eerdmans.

New Testament: Its Background & Message. Thomas D. Lea. LC 93-46945. 640p. 1995. pap. 34.99 (0-8054-1078-3, 4210-78) Broadman.

New Testament: Its Background, Growth & Content. enl. ed. Bruce M. Metzger. 310p. 1983. 21.95 (0-687-27914-3) Abingdon.

New Testament: King James Version. Ed. by Everyman's Library Staff. LC 99-214312. 1999. 22.00 (0-375-40550-X) Everymns Lib.

New Testament: King James Version. Tr. by Richmond Lattimore. 592p. 1996. 35.00 (0-86547-499-0) N Point Pr.

New Testament: KJV Bible Bed Books for Seniors. large type unabridged ed. Ed. by A. L. Wilson. 400p. 1999. pap. write for info. (1-892113-01-5) Lightside.

New Testament: Little Angel. Date not set. 1.95 (0-88271-208-X, 1808) Regina Pr.

New Testament: Proclamation & Parenesis, Myth & History. 3rd ed. Dennis C. Duling & Norman Perrin. Ed. by Robert L. Ferm. LC 93-79968. 512p. (C). 1994. pap. text 47.50 (0-15-500378-X, Pub. by Harcourt Coll Pubs) Harcourt.

New Testament: Sinaitic Version. Dalmer R. Ford. 1993. pap. 24.95 (0-533-10622-2) Vantage.

***New Testament Bk. 1: The Hinge of History.** David Pawson & Andy Peck. (Unlocking the Bible Ser.). 2000. pap. 13.00 (0-551-03187-5, Pub. by M Pickering) Trafalgar.

***New Testament Bk. 2: The Thirteenth Apostle.** David Pawson & Andy Peck. (Unlocking the Bible Ser.). 2000. pap. 13.00 (0-551-03190-5, Pub. by M Pickering) Trafalgar.

New Testament - A Translation by William Barclay. 1988. 65.00 (0-85305-289-1); pap. 55.00 (0-85305-288-3) St Mut.

New Testament - An Orthodox Perspective Vol. 1: Scripture, Tradition, Hermeneutics. Theodore G. Stylianopoulos. LC 96-40125. 271p. (Orig.). (C). 1997. pap. 16.95 (1-885652-13-5, Pub. by Holy Cross Orthodox) BookWorld.

New Testament--International Standard Version: Preview Release Edition. Tr. by Learn Foundation Translation Committee. LC 98-84061. 624p. 1998. pap. 15.95 (1-891833-02-2) Davidson Pr.

***New Testament Activity Bible.** Chariot Victor Publishing Staff. 2000. pap. text 12.99 (0-7814-3318-5) Chariot Victor.

New Testament Activity Book. Linda Giampa. (Illus.). 32p. (Orig.). (J). (gr. k-3). 1992. pap. 3.99 (0-570-04725-0) Concordia.

***New Testament among the Writings of Antiquity.** Detlev Dormeyer. (Biblical Seminar Ser.: No. 55). 328p. 1998. pap. 28.50 (1-85075-860-3, Pub. by Sheffield Acad) CUP Services.

New Testament, An Introduction, Parish. Gloria Hutchinson. (Faith & Witness Program Ser.). (Illus.). 208p. (YA). (gr. 7-8). pap. 15.00 (0-8215-5661-4) Sadlier.

New Testament, An Introduction, Parish Edition. Norman F. Josaitis & Michael J. Lanning. (Faith & Witness Program Ser.). (Illus.). 128p. (YA). (gr. 7-8). 7.50 (0-8215-5651-7) Sadlier.

New Testament & Criticism see Critica Del Nuevo Testamento

New Testament & Early Christianity. Joseph B. Tyson. 480p. (C). 1984. text 54.00 (0-02-421890-1, Macmillan Coll) P-H.

New Testament & Gnosis. Ed. by A. H. Logan & A. J. Wedderburn. 272p. 1983. 47.95 (0-567-09344-1, Pub. by T & T Clark) Bks Intl VA.

New Testament & Hellenistic Judaism. Ed. by Peder Borgen & Soren Giversen. 300p. (Orig.). (C). 1995. 39.00 (87-7288-458-4, Pub. by Aarhus Univ Pr) David Brown.

New Testament & Hellenistic Judaism. Ed. by Peder Borgen & Soren Giversen. LC 96-52508. 294p. (Orig.). 1997. pap. 24.95 (1-56563-261-3) Hendrickson MA.

New Testament & Homosexuality. Robin Scroggs. LC 82-48588. 160p. 1984. pap. 16.00 (0-8006-1854-8, 1-1854, Fortress Pr) Augsburg Fortress.

***New Testament & Mission: Historical & Hermeneutical Perspectives.** Johannes Nissen. 199p. 1999. pap. 35.95 (3-631-34500-3) P Lang Pubng.

***New Testament & Mission: Historical & Hermeneutical Perspectives.** Johannes Nissen. LC 99-48713. 199p. (C). 1999. pap. 35.95 (0-8204-4309-3) P Lang Pubng.

New Testament & Mythology & Other Basic Writings. Rudolf Bultmann. Ed. & Tr. by Schubert M. Ogden. LC 84-47921. 192p. 1984. pap. 14.00 (0-8006-2442-4, 1-2442, Fortress Pr) Augsburg Fortress.

New Testament & Other Early Christian Writings: A Reader. Bart D. Ehrman. LC 96-43600. 416p. 1997. pap. 25.95 (0-19-511192-3) OUP.

New Testament & Psalms: An Inclusive Version. Victor Gold. 512p. 1996. text 12.95 (0-19-528460-7) OUP.

New Testament & Psalms, Authorized Version. 1995. 36.00 (0-19-120923-6) OUP.

New Testament & Rabbinic Judaism. David Daube. 496p. 1994. pap. 24.95 (1-56563-141-2) Hendrickson MA.

New Testament & Rabbinic Judaism. David Daube. LC 73-2191. (Jewish People; History, Religion, Literature Ser.). 1979. reprint ed. 42.95 (0-405-05257-X) Ayer.

New Testament & Structuralism: A Collection of Essays. Ed. & Tr. by Alfred M. Johnson, Jr. LC 76-25447. (Pittsburgh Theological Monographs: No. 11). 1976. pap. text 11.50 (0-915138-13-1) Pickwick.

New Testament & the Christian Church. R. Edward Mangrum. LC 98-90075. 1998. pap. 14.95 (0-533-12701-7) Vantage.

New Testament & the Latter-Day Saints. Sperry Symposium '87 Staff. pap. 7.95 (1-55517-013-7) CFI Dist.

***New Testament & the Law: A New Testament Study on the Validity of Jewish Law.** Michael Marks. 128p. 1999. pap. 10.00 (0-939513-36-6) Joy Pub SJC.

New Testament & the People of God Vol. 1: Christian Origins & the Question of God. N. T. Wright. LC 92-19348. 510p. 1992. 35.00 (0-8006-2681-8, 1-2681) Augsburg Fortress.

New Testament Apocrypha Vol. 1: Gospels & Related Writings. rev. ed. Ed. by Wilhelm Schneemelcher. Tr. by R. M. Wilson. 1990. text 44.95 (0-664-21878-4) Westminster John Knox.

New Testament Apocrypha Vol. 2: Writings Relating to the Apostles; Apocalypses & Related Topics. rev. ed. Wilhelm Schneemelcher. Ed. by R. M. Wilson. 896p. 1993. text 54.95 (0-664-21879-2) Westminster John Knox.

New Testament Apostles Testify of Christ: A Guide to Acts Through Revelation. D. Kelly Ogden & Andrew C. Skinner. LC 98-35953. 1998. 19.95 (1-57345-304-8) Deseret Bk.

New Testament Archaeology. Dan P. Cole. Ed. by Hershel Shanks. 48p. (Orig.). 1986. pap. text 159.50 (1-880317-38-9, 5091) Biblical Arch Soc.

New Testament As Canon: A Reader in Canonical Criticism. Robert W. Wall & Eugene E. Lemcio. (Journal for the Study of the New Testament, Supplement Ser.: No. 76). 376p. (C). 1992. 90.75 (1-85075-374-1, Pub. by Sheffield Acad) CUP Services.

New Testament As Canon: An Introduction. Brevard S. Childs. LC 94-9101. 608p. (C). 1992. reprint ed. pap. 25.00 (1-56338-089-7) TPI PA.

New Testament As Personal Reading. Ed. by Ronan Drury. 158p. 1983. pap. 7.95 (0-87243-122-3) Templegate.

New Testament as True Fiction: Literature, Literary Criticism, Aesthetics. Douglas A. Templeton. (Playing the Texts Ser.: Vol. 3). 392p. 1999. 95.00 (1-85075-945-6, Pub. by Sheffield Acad); pap. 33.00 (1-85075-950-2, Pub. by Sheffield Acad) CUP Services.

New Testament At-a-Glance. J. G. Horton. (Bible At-a-Glance Study & Teaching Tools Ser.). (Illus.). 1992. pap. 4.95 (1-880426-00-5) Bible At A Glance.

New Testament Background: Selected Documents:Revised & Expanded Edition. expanded rev. ed. C. K. Barrett. LC 95-16264. 400p. 1995. pap. 18.00 (0-06-060881-1, Pub. by Harper SF) HarpC.

New Testament Backgrounds: A Sheffield Reader. Ed. by Craig A. Evans & Stanley E. Porter. (Biblical Seminar Ser.: No. 43). 335p. 1997. pap. 19.95 (1-85075-796-8, Pub. by Sheffield Acad) CUP Services.

New Testament Believers & the Law. Paul O'Higgins & Nuala O'Higgins. pap. 3.95 (0-944795-04-8) Recon Outreach.

New Testament Bible Adventure Kit: Bible Storyboard Adventures for Kids. Dawn Reagan. Ed. by Toon Takes. (Illus.). 16p. (ps-5). 1999. pap. 29.95 (1-929456-01-8) Myrtle Seal Pubg.

New Testament Bible Origami. Florence Temko. (My Favorite Origami Ser.). (Orig.). 1994. pap. 5.95 (0-89346-801-0) Heian Intl.

New Testament Bible Stories. (Magic Pad Ser.). (J). 1993. pap. 1.75 (1-895877-10-5) Novar Cottage.

New Testament Canon: Its Making & Meaning. Harry Y. Gamble. LC 85-4509. (Guides to Biblical Scholarship Ser.). 96p. 1985. pap. 12.00 (0-8006-0470-9, 1-470, Fortress Pr) Augsburg Fortress.

New Testament Characters. Carolyn Nystrom. (LifeGuide Bible Studies). 64p. (Orig.). 1993. pap., wbk. ed. 4.99 (0-8308-1069-2, 1069) InterVarsity.

New Testament Christology: A Critical Assessment & Annotated Bibliography, 12. Compiled by Arland J. Hultgren. LC 88-24645. (Bibliographies & Indexes in Religious Studies: No. 12). 500p. 1988. lib. bdg. 105.00 (0-313-25188-6, HNT/, Greenwood Pr) Greenwood.

New Testament Christology: The Christology in the Story. Frank J. Matera. LC 98-42257. 304p. 1999. pap. 26.00 (0-664-25694-5) Westminster John Knox.

New Testament Chronology. Kenneth F. Doig. LC 91-45430. 464p. 1992. pap. text 89.95 (0-7734-9920-2) E Mellen.

New Testament Church. Bernard Rossier. 104p. (Orig.). 1990. pap. 8.00 (0-930401-31-X) Artex Pub.

New Testament Church & Its Ministries. Bill Scheidler. (Illus.). 118p. (C). 1980. pap. 12.99 (0-914936-43-3) City Bible Pub.

New Testament Church & Its Symbols. Fred Pruitt. 131p. 3.00 (0-686-29157-3) Faith Pub Hse.

New Testament Church Finance. Bruce H. Hanson. LC 97-93186. iv, 84p. (Orig.). 1997. pap. 8.95 (0-9657099-0-6) Hanson Minist.

New Testament Church Organization. Donald L. Norbie. 1977. pap. 6.00 (0-937396-28-1) Walterick Pubs.

New Testament Church Principles. Arthur G. Clarke. 1996. pap. 6.99 (0-946351-11-2, Pub. by John Ritchie) Loizeaux.

New Testament Commentaries of H. P. Blavatsky. Compiled by H. J. Spierenburg. LC 87-61398. 350p. 1987. pap. 15.00 (0-913004-51-0) Point Loma Pub.

New Testament (Confraternity Edition) 691p. 1997. vinyl bd. 9.95 (0-933932-77-4) Scepter Pubs.

New Testament Deacon. Alexander Strauch. 191p. pap., teacher ed. 9.99 (0-89900-437-7); pap., student ed. 5.99 (0-89900-438-5) College Pr Pub.

New Testament Deacon: The Church's Minister of Mercy. Alexander Strauch. LC 92-29609. 192p. (Orig.). 1992. pap. text 9.99 (0-936083-07-7) Lewis-Roth.

New Testament Deacon: The Church's Minister of Mercy: A Study Guide. Alexander Strauch. 96p. 1994. pap., student ed. 6.99 (0-936083-10-7) Lewis-Roth.

New Testament Dictionary of Sins. Kingdom Quotes Staff. pap. write for info. (0-930179-37-4) Johns Enter.

New Testament Digest. John D. Hawkes. 160p. 1968. pap. 3.95 (0-89036-014-6) Liahona Pub Trust.

New Testament Documents: Are They Reliable? Ed. by F. F. Bruce. (Orig.). 1960. pap. 8.00 (0-8028-1025-X) Eerdmans.

New Testament Documents: Are They Reliable? F. F. Bruce. 120p. (Orig.). 1967. pap. 5.99 (0-87784-691-X, 691) InterVarsity.

New Testament Environment. Edward Lohse. Tr. by John E. Steely from GER. LC 75-43618. 320p. 1976. pap. 14.95 (0-687-27944-5) Abingdon.

New Testament Epistles. Drane. (Orig.). 1999. text. write for info. (0-312-22514-8) St Martin.

***New Testament Epistles: Early Christian Wisdom.** Ed. by John Drane. LC 99-15307. 382p. 1999. pap. 13.95 (0-312-22103-7) St Martin.

New Testament Epistles Study Guide, Bk. 1. Constance. 86p. 1988. pap., student ed. 12.99 (1-889015-50-4) Explrs Bible.

New Testament Epistles Study Guide, Bk. 2. Constance. 95p. 1988. pap., student ed. 12.99 (1-889015-51-2) Explrs Bible.

New Testament Epistles Study Guide, Bk. 3. Constance. 130p. 1988. pap., student ed. 12.99 (1-889015-52-0) Explrs Bible.

New Testament Era: The World of the Bible from 500 B. C. to A.D. 100. Bo I. Reicke. LC 68-15864. 352p. 1974. pap. 20.00 (0-8006-1080-6, 1-1080, Fortress Pr) Augsburg Fortress.

New Testament Eschatology: Historical & Cultural Background. George W. Buchanan. LC 93-28572. (Biblical Press Ser.: Vol. 15). 316p. 1993. text 99.95 (0-7734-2378-8, Mellen Biblical Pr) E Mellen.

New Testament Essays. Gary Meadors. 1991. 17.50 (0-88469-231-0) BMH Bks.

N

An Asterisk (*) at the beginning of an entry indicates that the title is appearing for the first time.

New Testament Ethics: An Introduction. fac. ed. Dale Goldsmith. LC 88-2863. 191p. 1988. pap. 59.30 (*0-7837-7339-0*, 204729200007) Bks Demand.

New Testament Ethics: The Legacies of Jesus & Paul. Frank J. Matera. LC 96-16563. 352p. 1996. 34.95 (*0-664-22069-X*) Westminster John Knox.

New Testament Exegesis see Exegesis Del Nuevo Testamento

New Testament Exegesis: A Handbook for Students & Pastors. rev. ed. Gordon D. Fee. LC 82-24829. 176p. 1993. pap. 16.95 (*0-664-25442-X*) Westminster John Knox.

New Testament Explorer, 1. Mark Bailey. LC 99-39608. 1999. 34.99 (*0-8499-1448-5*) Word Pub.

New Testament Explorer: Supersaver ed., 1. Mark Bailey. 1999. 29.97 (*0-8499-1600-3*) Word Pub.

New Testament Exposition: From Text to Sermon. Walter L. Liefeld. 176p. (C). 1984. 15.95 (*0-310-45910-9*, 12607) Zondervan.

New Testament, 1 & 2 Corinthians. Lloyd J. Ogilvie & Kenneth L. Chafin. (Communicator's Commentary Ser.: Vol. 7). 298p. 1985. 22.99 (*0-8499-0347-5*) Word Pub.

New Testament for Latter-Day Saint Families. Ed. by Thomas Valletta. LC 98-73233. 1998. 39.95 (*1-57008-530-7*) Bookcraft Inc.

New Testament for Spiritual Reading, 25 vols. Ed. by J. L. McKenzie. Incl. Pt. 1. Revelation of St. John. pap. 4.95 Pt. 2. Revelation of St. John. pap. 4.95 Vol. 1, Pt. 1. Gospel According to St. Matthew. pap. 4.95 Vol. 2, Pt. 1. Gospel According to St. Matthew. pap. 4.95 Vol. 3, Pt. 1. Gospel According to St. Mark. pap. 4.95 Vol. 4, Pt. 2. Gospel According to St. Mark. pap. 4.95 (*0-8245-0337-6*); Vol. 5, Pt. 1. Gospel According to St. Luke. pap. 4.95 Vol. 6, Pt. 2. Gospel According to St. Luke. pap. 4.95 Vol. 7, Pt. 1. Gospel According to St. John. pap. 4.95 Vol. 8, Pt. 2. Gospel According to St. John. 4.95 (*0-8164-1079-8*); Vol. 9, Pt. 3. Gospel According to St. John. pap. 4.95 Vol. 10. Acts of the Apostles, Pt. 1. pap. Vol. 11. Acts of the Apostles, Pt. 2. pap. 4.95 Vol. 12. Epistle to the Romans. pap. 4.95 Vol. 13. First Epistle to the Corinthians. pap. 4.95 Vol. 14. Second Epistle to the Corinthians. pap. 4.95 (*0-8245-0347-3*); Vol. 14. Second Epistle to the Corinthians. (*0-8245-0123-3*); Vol. 15. Epistle to the Galatians. pap. 4.95 Vol. 16. Epistle to the Ephesians. pap. 4.95 Vol. 17. Epistle to the Philippians, Epistle to the Colossians. pap. 4.95 (*0-8164-1088-7*); Vol. 18. First Epistle to the Thessalonians. Second Epistle to the Thessalonians. pap. 4.95 Vol. 19. First Epistle to Timothy. Second Epistle to Timothy. pap. 4.95 Vol. 20. Epistle to Titus. Epistle to Philemon. pap. 4.95 (*0-8245-0354-6*); Vol. 20. Epistle to Titus. Epistle to Philemon. (*0-8245-0129-2*); Vol. 21. Epistle to the Hebrews, Epistle to James. pap. 4.95 Vol. 22. First Epistle to Peter. Second Epistle to Peter. pap. 4.95 Vol. 23. Epistle to Jude, Three Epistles of John. pap. 4.95 123.75 (*0-8245-0135-7*) Crossroad NY.

New Testament for Today: Bible Stories with Modern Parallels. W. Jeffrey Marsh & Ron R. Munns. 1995. 10.95 (*0-88494-965-6*) Bookcraft Inc.

New Testament for Winning Souls. 68p. 1995. pap. 19.99 (*0-8499-5147-X*) Word Pub.

New Testament for Winning Souls with Helps: King James Version. LC 95-18137. 1995. 19.99 (*0-8499-5145-3*) Word Pub.

***New Testament Foundations Vol. 1: A Guide for Christian Students.** Ralph P. Martin. 326p. 1999. pap. 26.00 (*1-57910-310-3*) Wipf & Stock.

***New Testament Foundations Vol. 2: A Guide for Christian Students.** Ralph P. Martin. 470p. 1999. pap. 36.00 (*1-57910-312-X*) Wipf & Stock.

New Testament Foundations for Christian Ethics. Willi Marxsen. Tr. by O. C. Dean.Tr. of Christliche und Christliche Ethik im Neuen Testament. 320p. 1998. pap. 29.95 (*0-567-29223-1*, Pub. by T & T Clark) Bks Intl VA.

New Testament Fun Activities - First & Second Grade. Cindy Jackson. (Illus.). 16p. (J). (gr. 1-2). 1998. wbk. ed. 3.95 (*1-878669-80-X*, CRE 3544) Crea Tea Assocs.

New Testament Fun Activities - Pre-School & Kindergarten. Cindy Jackson. (Illus.). 16p. (J). (ps-k). 1998. 3.95 (*1-878669-79-6*, CRE 3543) Crea Tea Assocs.

New Testament Fun Activities - Third & Fourth Grade. Cindy Jackson. (Illus.). 16p. (J). (gr. 3-4). 1998. wbk. ed. 3.95 (*1-878669-81-8*, CRE 3545) Crea Tea Assocs.

New Testament Fundamentals. rev. ed. Stevan L. Davies. LC 93-48825. (Illus.). 256p. 1994. pap. 17.95 (*0-944344-41-0*) Polebridge Pr.

New Testament Greek. Gerald L. Stevens. 298p. (C). 1994. pap. text, student ed., wbk. ed. 28.50 (*0-8191-9599-5*); lib. bdg. write for info. (*0-8191-9600-2*) U Pr of Amer.

New Testament Greek. 2nd ed. Gerald L. Stevens. 304p. (C). 1997. pap. text, wbk. ed. 19.95 (*0-7618-0891-4*) U Pr of Amer.

New Testament Greek. 2nd ed. Gerald L. Stevens. LC 97-34018. (ENG.). 524p. (C). 1997. text 29.00 (*0-7618-0892-2*) U Pr of Amer.

New Testament Greek: A Beginning & Intermediate Grammar. James A. Hewett. LC 89-11123. 234p. 1986. 19.95 (*0-913573-32-9*) Hendrickson MA.

New Testament Greek: An Introductory Grammar. 2nd ed. Watson E. Mills. LC 85-11540. 1989. lib. bdg. 79.95 (*0-88946-201-1*) E Mellen.

New Testament Greek: Key to Exercises. James A. Hewett. 26p. 1987. pap. text 1.95 (*0-913573-83-3*) Hendrickson MA.

New Testament Greek Beginnings. Thompson. (C). 1980. pap. text, student ed. 25.60 (*0-02-420650-4*, Macmillan Coll) P-H.

***New Testament Greek for Beginners.** J. Gresham Machen. 300p. 1998. pap. 25.00 (*1-57910-180-1*) Wipf & Stock.

***New Testament Greek for Beginners.** rev. ed. J. Gresham Machen. Ed. by John W. Robbins. 287p. (C). 2000. 16.95 (*0-940931-77-X*); pap. 10.95 (*0-940931-55-9*) Trinity Found.

***New Testament Greek for Beginners.** 2nd abr. ed. J. Gresham Machen. LC 99-21889. 416p. 2000. 19.99 (*0-8010-2211-8*) Baker Bks.

New Testament Greek for Preachers & Teachers: Five Areas of Application. Neal Windham. 264p. (Orig.). (C). 1991. pap. text 24.50 (*0-8191-8326-1*) U Pr of Amer.

New Testament Greek Grammar. Charles A. Schism. 159p. 1994. student ed. 15.95 (*0-9641158-4-0*) Redemp Fellowship.

New Testament Greek Manuscripts: John. Reuben J. Swanson. (Manuals Ser.: No. 11). 321p. 1995. pap. 35.00 (*1-85075-775-5*, Pub. by Sheffield Acad) CUP Services.

New Testament Greek Manuscripts: Luke. Reuben J. Swanson. (Manuals Ser.: No. 10). 448p. 1995. pap. 40.00 (*1-85075-774-7*, Pub. by Sheffield Acad) CUP Services.

New Testament Greek Manuscripts: Mark. Reuben J. Swanson. (Manuals Ser.: No. 9). 299p. 1995. pap. 28.50 (*1-85075-773-9*, Pub. by Sheffield Acad) CUP Services.

New Testament Greek Manuscripts: Matthew. Ed. by Reuben J. Swanson. (Manuals Ser.: No. 8). 332p. 1995. pap. 35.00 (*1-85075-772-0*, Pub. by Sheffield Acad) CUP Services.

***New Testament Greek Manuscripts: The Acts of the Apostles.** Ed. by Reuben J. Swanson. 513p. 1998. pap. 43.95 (*0-86585-055-0*) Wm Carey Intl.

New Testament Greek I Study Sheets. Jeffrey L. Chadwick. 65p. 1998. pap. text 14.95 (*0-9646272-2-1*); ring bd., wbk. ed. 14.95 (*0-9646272-1-3*) Alpine Pub OR.

New Testament Greek Primer. S. M. Baugh. 248p. 1995. pap. text 29.99 (*0-87552-099-5*) P & R Pubng.

New Testament Greek Primer. Alfred Marshall. 176p. (C). 1986. 46.95 (*0-310-20540-9*, 6246) Zondervan.

New Testament Greek Workbook: An Inductive Study of the Complete Text of the Gospel of John. James A. Walther. LC 80-23762. (Illus.). 280p. 1981. pap. text 30.00 (*0-226-87239-4*) U Ch Pr.

***New Testament Guide to the Holy Land.** 2nd ed. John J. Kilgallen. LC 97-47704. (Illus.). 220p. 1998. pap. 14.95 (*0-8294-1041-4*) Loyola Pr.

***New Testament Hidden Pictures: Bible Story Puzzle.** (Illus.). (J). 1998. pap. 5.95 (*0-7647-0436-2*) Schaffer Pubns.

New Testament History. F. F. Bruce. LC 78-144253. 480p. 1983. pap. 16.95 (*0-385-02533-5*, Anchor NY) Doubleday.

New Testament History. Richard L. Niswonger. 368p. 1988. 19.95 (*0-310-31200-0*, 18436) Zondervan.

New Testament History. Richard L. Niswonger. (History - New Testament Studies). 336p. 1992. pap. 19.99 (*0-310-31201-9*) Zondervan.

New Testament History - Acts. 11th ed. Gareth Reese. (Bible Study Textbook Ser.). (Illus.). 1056p. 1976. 24.99 (*0-89900-055-X*) College Pr Pub.

New Testament Image of the Ministry. W. T. Purkiser. 148p. 1969. pap. 9.99 (*0-8341-0509-8*) Beacon Hill.

New Testament in Fiction & Film: On Reversing the Hermeneutical Flow. Larry J. Kreitzer. (Biblical Seminar Ser.: Vol. 17). 180p. 1993. pap. 23.75 (*1-85075-364-4*, Pub. by Sheffield Acad) CUP Services.

New Testament in Greek: The Gospel According to St. Luke, Vol. 3, Pt. 1. American & British Committee for the International. (New Testament in Greek Ser.). 314p. 1984. text 160.00 (*0-19-826167-5*) OUP.

New Testament in Greek: The Gospel According to St. Luke, Vol. 3, Pt. 2. 266p. 1987. 145.00 (*0-19-826171-3*) OUP.

New Testament in Its Literary Environment. David E. Aune. LC 86-18949. (Library of Early Christianity: Vol. 8). 262p. 1985. pap. 24.95 (*0-664-25018-1*) Westminster John Knox.

New Testament in Its Social Environment. John E. Stambaugh & David L. Balch. LC 85-15516. (Library of Early Christianity: Vol. 2). (Illus.). 208p. (C). 1986. reprint ed. pap. 24.95 (*0-664-25012-2*) Westminster John Knox.

New Testament in Modern English. J. B. Phillips. 1995. 14.98 (*0-88486-127-9*) Galahad Bks.

New Testament in Modern English. rev. ed. John B. Phillips. 576p. 1972. 14.95 (*0-02-596970-6*) Macmillan.

New Testament in Modern Speech. Richard F. Weymouth. 624p. 1996. 10.95 (*1-57562-025-1*) K Copeland Pubns.

New Testament in Modern Speech. Tr. by R. F. Weymouth. LC 78-9536. 752p. 1994. reprint ed. pap. 24.99 (*0-8254-3986-8*) Kregel.

New Testament in Pictures for Little Eyes see Nuevo Testamento en Cuadros para Ninos

New Testament in Survey. Paul Southern. 1958. pap. 4.35 (*0-89137-550-3*) Quality Pubns.

New Testament in the Original Greek: According to the Byzantine-Majority Textform. Ed. by William G. Pierpont. LC 91-60094. (ENG & GEC.). 576p. 1991. pap. 24.95 (*0-9626544-3-4*) Original Word.

New Testament in the Original Greek: According to the Byzantine-Majority Textform. deluxe limited ed. Ed. by William G. Pierpont. LC 91-60094. (ENG & GEC.). 576p. 1991. 74.95 (*0-9626544-2-6*) Original Word.

New Testament Index. Ed. by R. G. Bratcher. vii, 37p. 1963. pap. 4.99 (*0-8267-0003-9*, 102670) Untd Bible Soc.

New Testament Interpretation. 1997. pap. 7.99 (*0-85364-424-1*, Pub. by Paternoster Pub) McClelland & Stewart.

New Testament Interpretation. 5th rev. ed. Ed. by I. Howard Marshall. (Biblical & Theological Classics Library: Vol. 16). 406p. 1997. reprint ed. pap. 9.99 (*0-85364-841-7*, Pub. by Paternoster Pub) OM Literature.

New Testament Interpretation: Essays on Principles & Methods. fac. ed. Ed. by I. Howard Marshall. LC 77-9619. 406p. 1977. reprint ed. pap. 125.90 (*0-7837-7962-3*, 204771800008) Bks Demand.

New Testament Interpretation & Methods: A Sheffield Book. Ed. by Craig A. Evans & Stanley E. Porter. (Biblical Seminar Ser.: No. 45). 321p. 1997. pap. 19.95 (*1-85075-794-1*, Pub. by Sheffield Acad) CUP Services.

New Testament Interpretation Through Rhetorical Criticism. George A. Kennedy. LC 83-23577. (Studies in Religion). x, 171p. 1984. pap. 12.95 (*0-8078-4120-X*) U of NC Pr.

New Testament Introduction. Stanley E. Porter & Lee M. McDonald. LC 95-25608. (IBR Bibliographies Ser.: Vol. 12). 240p. 1996. pap. 14.99 (*0-8010-2060-3*) Baker Bks.

New Testament Introduction. rev. ed. Donald Guthrie. LC 90-30404. 1054p. 1990. 39.99 (*0-8308-1402-7*, 1402) InterVarsity.

New Testament Journal. Helen Hemmer. (Faith & Witness Program Ser.). (Illus.). 64p. (YA). (gr. 7-8). 4.50 (*0-8215-5631-2*) Sadlier.

New Testament Living. Norman B. Harrison. 1972. pap. 2.00 (*0-911802-30-4*) Free Church Pubns.

New Testament Logia on Divorce. V. Norskov Olsen. vi, 161p. 1994. pap. 36.50 (*3-16-131441-7*, Pub. by JCB Mohr) Coronet Bks.

***New Testament Mazes: Bible Story Puzzle.** (Illus.). (J). 1998. pap. 5.95 (*0-7647-0432-X*) Schaffer Pubns.

New Testament Me, 5. (Following God Ser.). 1999. pap. 16.99 (*0-89957-304-5*) AMG Pubs.

New Testament Notes. Charles H. Patterson. (Cliffs Notes Ser.). 104p. 1965. pap. 4.95 (*0-8220-0880-7*, Cliff) IDG Bks.

New Testament of the Inclusive Language Bible. LC 94-71047. 260p. 1994. 19.95 (*0-940121-22-0*, H213, Cross Roads Bks) Cross Cultural Pubns.
This inclusive language version of the New Testament gives due reverence to the Word of God & faithfulness to its original meaning. The translation seeks to address men & women as equals. The change in language & gender does not alter God's message as conveyed in the Bible, but recognizes that a change in our culture & society point up the need for the language of the Bible to reflect that change. Those who translated previous versions found it necessary to use the language of their time which often emerged from a male-dominated society.
Publisher Paid Annotation.

New Testament Picture Bible. Iva Hoth. (Illus.). 1998. pap. text 9.99 (*0-7814-3056-9*) Chariot Victor.

New Testament Postcards: Swindoll Bible Study Guides. rev. ed. Charles R. Swindoll. 1996. pap. text 5.99 (*0-8499-8737-7*) Word Pub.

New Testament Priests of the Gospel. Witness Lee. 145p. 1989. per. 6.75 (*0-87083-471-1*, 13-010-001) Living Stream Ministry.

***New Testament Profiles, 3 vols.** Incl. John: Evangelist & Interpreter. rev. ed. Stephen Smalley. LC 98-20199. 287p. 1998. pap. 19.99 (*0-8308-1514-7*, 1514); Luke: Historian & Theologian. I. Howard Marshall. LC 98-23480. 252p. 1998. reprint ed. pap. 19.99 (*0-8308-1513-9*, 1513); Matthew: Evangelist & Teacher. R. T. France. LC 98-20153. 345p. 1998. reprint ed. pap. 22.99 (*0-8308-1511-2*, 1511); 1999. Set pap. 62.97 (*0-8308-1541-4*) InterVarsity.

New Testament Prophet. large type ed. Ted J. Hanson. 96p. (Orig.). Date not set. pap. 6.00 (*0-9653393-0-0*) Hse of Bread.

New Testament Quotations from the Old. William Wright. pap. 1.49 (*0-87377-120-6*) GAM Pubns.

New Testament, Recovery Version see Nuevo Testamento, Version Recobro, Black

New Testament, Recovery Version see Nuevo Testamento, Version Recobro, Maroon

New Testament Recovery Version. Living Street Ministry Staff. 450p. 1985. 7.50 (*0-87083-697-8*, 01-001-901) Living Stream Ministry.

New Testament Recovery Version. Living Street Ministry Staff. 450p. 1993. per. 5.00 (*0-87083-698-6*, 01-002-001) Living Stream Ministry.

New Testament, Recovery Version (Economy Black, 6 3/4 see Nuevo Testamento, Version Recobro, Edicion Economica en Rustica (Black)

New Testament, Recovery Version (Economy Burgundy, 6 3/4 see Nuevo Testamento, Version Recobro, Edicion Economica en Rustica (Maroon)

New Testament Revelations of Jesus of Nazareth. James E. Padgett & Daniel G. Samuels. 555p. 1995. pap. 20.00 (*1-887621-04-0*) Found Ch Divine Truth.

New Testament Scholarship: Paraphrases on the Letters to Timothy, Titus & Philemon, the Letters of Peter & Jude, the Letter of James, the Letters of John, & the Letter to the Hebrews. Desiderius Erasmus. Tr. & Anno. by John J. Bateman. (Collected Works of Erasmus: No. 44). 352p. 1993. text 120.00 (*0-8020-0541-1*) U of Toronto Pr.

New Testament, School Annotated Guide: A Course on Jesus Christ & His Disciples. Gloria Hutchinson. (The Faith & Witness Program). (Illus.). 272p. (YA). (gr. 7-8). pap. 21.90 (*0-8215-5611-8*) Sadlier.

New Testament Scriptures. Michael Castoro, Sr. 1998. 3.99 (*0-9660781-6-0*) St Michael Archangel Soc.

New Testament Service. Witness Lee. 158p. 1986. per. 7.00 (*0-87083-229-8*, 13-011-001) Living Stream Ministry.

New Testament Set. 50.00 (*0-687-09611-1*) Abingdon.

New Testament Spirituality. Michael Green & Paul Stephens. 224p. 1996. pap. 11.99 (*0-86347-113-7*, Pub. by Eagle Bks) Shaw Pubs.

***New Testament Stories from the Back Side.** Elaine Ward. LC 99-59768. 144p. 2000. pap. 11.00 (*0-687-07306-5*) Abingdon.

New Testament Story. 3rd ed. Barr. (Religion Ser.). 2001. pap. 50.00 (*0-534-54163-1*) Wadsworth Pub.

New Testament Story: An Introduction. David L. Barr. 379p. (C). 1987. pap. 42.95 (*0-534-07284-4*) Wadsworth Pub.

New Testament Story: An Introduction. 2nd ed. David L. Barr. LC 94-27204. 574p. 1994. pap. 67.95 (*0-534-16380-7*) Wadsworth Pub.

New Testament Studies. Rudolf Frieling. pap. 29.50 (*0-86315-185-X*, 1868, Pub. by Floris Bks) Anthroposophic.

New Testament Survey see Nuestro Nuevo Testamento

New Testament Survey see Apercu du Nouveau Testament

***New Testament Survey.** Walter M. Dunnett. (Discovery Ser.). Orig. Title: Broadening Your Biblical Horizons - New Testament Survey. (Illus.). 110p. 1999. pap. text. write for info. (*1-891110-02-0*, ATTS Pubns) Africa Theolog Trng.

New Testament Survey. Robert G. Gromacki. LC 74-83793. 434p. (gr. 13). 1974. 27.99 (*0-8010-3677-1*) Baker Bks.

New Testament Survey. Ken Malmin & Kevin Conner. 35p. 1975. pap. 5.99 (*0-914936-22-0*) City Bible Pub.

New Testament Survey. Russell K. Tardo. 111p. 1992. 10.00 (*1-881210-04-9*) Faithful Wrd.

New Testament Survey. rev. ed. Merrill C. Tenney. 473p. 1985. 27.00 (*0-8028-3611-9*) Eerdmans.

New Testament Survey, Pt. 2. Charles Porter. (TEE Ser.). 216p. 1981. 6.95 (*1-879892-17-0*) Editorial Bautista.

New Testament Survey, Vol. 1. Charles Porter. (TEE Ser.). 223p. 1981. 6.95 (*1-879892-15-4*) Editorial Bautista.

New Testament Survey: Broadening Your Biblical Horizons. LC 63-7410. 90p. 1983. teacher ed., ring bd. 24.95 (*0-910566-19-4*) Evang Trg Assn.

New Testament Survey: Broadening Your Biblical Horizons. Walter M. Dunnett. LC 63-7410. 96p. 1963. pap. text 9.95 (*0-910566-03-8*) Evang Trg Assn.

New Testament Teaching on Tongues. Merrill F. Unger. LC 70-165057. 184p. 1971. pap. 9.99 (*0-8254-3900-0*) Kregel.

New Testament Text & Language: A Sheffield Reader. Ed. by Craig A. Evans & Stanley E. Porter. (Biblical Seminar Ser.: No. 44). 311p. 1997. pap. 19.95 (*1-85075-795-X*, Pub. by Sheffield Acad) CUP Services.

New Testament Textual Criticism: A Concise Guide. David A. Black. (Illus.). 80p. (C). 1994. pap. 9.99 (*0-8010-1074-8*) Baker Bks.

New Testament Textual Criticism: Its Significance for Exegesis. Ed. by Eldon J. Epp & Fee D. Gordon. (Illus.). 1982. 120.00 (*0-19-826175-6*) OUP.

***New Testament, the Christian & the State.** Archie Penner. (Mennonite Reprint Series: 3). 128p. (YA). 2000. pap. text 6.95 (*1-883453-07-0*) Deutsche Buchhandlung.

New Testament Theology. Donald Guthrie. LC 81-47066. 1064p. 1981. 39.99 (*0-87784-965-X*, 965) InterVarsity.

New Testament Theology. Joachim Jeremias. LC 70-143936. 352p. 1977. 45.00 (*0-684-15157-X*, Scribners Ref) Mac Lib Ref.

New Testament Theology. Leon Morris. 448p. 1986. 20.95 (*0-310-45570-7*, 12391) Zondervan.

New Testament Theology. Leon Morris. 368p. 1990. pap. 19.99 (*0-310-45571-5*) Zondervan.

New Testament Theology. G. B. Caird. Ed. by L. D. Hurst. 518p. 1995. reprint ed. pap. text 26.00 (*0-19-826388-0*) OUP.

***New Testament Today.** Ed. by Mark A. Powell. LC 98-42329. 168p. 1999. pap. 18.00 (*0-664-25824-7*) Westminster John Knox.

New Testament Traditions & Apocryphal Narratives. Francois Bovon. (Princeton Theological Monographs: No. 36). 253p. (Orig.). 1995. pap. 25.00 (*1-55635-024-4*) Pickwick.

New Testament Verses One. Phil Huneke. (W Cross RDS Ser.). 38p. 1993. pap. 2.95 (*1-884488-25-0*) Bonjour Tigre.

***New Testament with Psalms & Proverbs, 1vol.** Davidson Press Staff. 2000. 60.00 (*1-891833-12-X*) Davidson Pr.

New Testament with the Joseph Smith Translation. rev. ed. Steven J. Hite & Julie M. Hite. 375p. 1994. pap. 19.95 (*0-9642325-1-0*) Veritas Grp.

New Testament Women, Vol. 13. Ed. by Dennis E. Smith & Michael E. Williams. 208p. 1999. 18.00 (*0-687-08272-2*) Abingdon.

New Testament Word Book: A Glossary. Eric Partridge. LC 70-117907. (Select Bibliographies Reprint Ser.). 1977. reprint ed. 21.95 (*0-8369-5359-2*) Ayer.

New Testament Word Search Puzzles. Gertrude Knabbe. 72p. (Orig.). (YA). (gr. 3 up). 1995. pap. 1.99 (*0-87813-561-8*) Christian Light.

New Testament Words. William Barclay. LC 73-12737. (William Barclay Library). 96p. 2000. pap. 17.95 (*0-664-24761-X*, Pub. by Westminster John Knox) Presbyterian Pub.

New Testament World: Insights from Cultural Anthropology. rev. ed. Bruce J. Malina. 224p. 1993. pap. 19.95 (*0-664-25456-X*) Westminster John Knox.

New Testament Writings: History, Literature, Interpretation. James M. Efird. LC 79-87750. 1982. pap. 17.95 (*0-8042-0246-X*) Westminster John Knox.

***New Testment Tyndale's Version in English with Numerous Readings Comparisons of Texts.** Francis Fry. 1999. pap. 25.00 (*1-57074-380-0*) Greyden Pr.

New Testment Walk with Oswald Chambers. Oswald Chambers. LC 97-37467. 208p. 1998. 14.99 (*0-8007-1753-8*) Revell.

New Texas Cuisine. Stephan Pyles & John Harisson. LC 92-31496. 448p. 1993. 38.95 (*0-385-42336-5*) Doubleday.

New Texas Wild Game Cookbook. rev. ed. Judith Morehead & Richard Morehead. (Illus.). 104p. 1985. pap. 13.95 (*0-89015-526-7*) Sunbelt Media.

New Textiles: Trends & Traditions. Chloe Colchester. LC 96-61511. (Illus.). 192p. (Orig.). 1997. pap. 24.95 (*0-500-27737-0*, Pub. by Thames Hudson) Norton.

New Theatre & Cinema of Soviet Russia. Huntly Carter. LC 74-124001. (Literature of Cinema, Ser. 1). 1970. reprint ed. 19.95 (*0-405-01607-7*) Ayer.

***New Theatre Quarterly, Vol. 62.** Ed. by Clive Barker & Simon Trussler. (Illus.). 96p. 2000. pap. write for info. (*0-521-78902-8*) Cambridge U Pr.

***New Theatre Quarterly, Vol. 63.** Ed. by Clive Barker & Simon Trussler. (Illus.). 96p. 2000. pap. write for info. (*0-521-78903-6*) Cambridge U Pr.

New Theatre Vistas: Modern Movements in International Theatre. Judy L. Oliva. Ed. by Kimball King. LC 95-30422. (Studies in Modern Drama: Vol. 7). 234p. 1995. text 46.00 (*0-8153-1670-4*, H1840) Garland.

New Themes for the Protestant Clergy. Stephen Colwell. LC 71-83417. (Religion in America, Ser. 1). 1975. reprint ed. 35.95 (*0-405-00243-2*) Ayer.

New Themes in Christian Philosophy. Ed. by Ralph McInerny. LC 68-20439. 1968. 40.95 (*0-8290-1654-6*); pap. text 9.50 (*0-8290-1606-6*) Irvington.

New Themes in Palliative Care. David Clark et al. LC 97-12123. 336p. 1997. pap. 37.95 (*0-335-19605-5*) OpUniv Pr.

New Themes in Palliative Care. Clark et al. LC 97-12123. 306p. 1997. 105.00 (*0-335-19606-3*) OpUniv Pr.

New Theogony: Mythology for the Real World. Maria M. Colavito. LC 91-22107. 163p. (C). 1992. text 19.50 (*0-7914-1067-6*) State U NY Pr.

New Theoretical Concepts for Understanding Organic Reactions. Ed. by J. Bertran & Imre G. Csizmadia. (C). 1989. text 202.50 (*0-7923-0151-X*) Kluwer Academic.

New Theories in Physics: Proceedings of the XI International Symposium on Elementary Particle Physics. Ed. by Z. Ajduk et al. 584p. 1989. text 125.00 (*9971-5-0691-2*) World Scientific Pub.

New Theories of Discourse: Laclau, Mouffe & Zizek. Jacob Torfing. LC 98-28667. 320p. 1999. write for info. (*0-631-19557-2*); pap. write for info. (*0-631-19558-0*) Blackwell Pubs.

New Theories on the Ancient Maya. Ed. by Elin C. Danien & Robert J. Sharer. (University Museum Monographs: University Museum Symposium Ser.: Nos. 77 & III). (Illus.). xvi, 224p. (C). 1992. text 50.00 (*0-924171-13-8*) U Museum Pubns.

New Theory for the Design of Helical Gears for Surface Fatigue Using Hertzian Point Contact Stresses. C. Bagci. (Nineteen Eighty-Seven Fall Technical Meeting Ser.: Vol. 87FTM1). (Illus.). 11p. 1985. pap. text 30.00 (*1-55589-477-1*) AGMA.

New Theory of Arthritis Based on the Edgar Cayce Readings. Carol Baraff. 43p. 1981. 2.00 (*1-882545-01-X*) Herit Pubns.

New Theory of Reference: Kripke, Marcus, & Its Origins. Paul Humphreys & James H. Fetzer. LC 97-47064. (Synthese Library). 1998. lib. bdg. write for info. (*0-7923-4898-2*) Kluwer Academic.

New Theory of the Earth: Its Original, to the Consummation of All Things Wherein the Creation of the World in Six Days. William Whiston. Ed. by Claude C. Albritton, Jr. LC 77-6545. (History of Geology Ser.). 1978. lib. bdg. 41.95 (*0-405-10463-4*) Ayer.

New Theory of Time. L. Nathan Oaklander & Quentin Smith. LC 93-47500. 400p. 1994. 45.00 (*0-300-05796-2*) Yale U Pr.

New Theory of Urban Design. Christopher Alexander et al. (Illus.). 272p. 1987. 45.00 (*0-19-503753-7*) OUP.

New Theory of Value: The Canadian Economics of H. A. Innis. Robin Neill. LC 77-185867. (Canadian University Paperbooks Ser.: No. 120). 167p. reprint ed. pap. 51.80 (*0-8357-4162-1*, 203693600007) Bks Demand.

New Theosophy (1929) Ernest Wood. 90p. 1998. reprint ed. pap. 14.95 (*0-7661-0331-5*) Kessinger Pub.

New Therapeutic Agents in Thrombosis & Thrombolysis. Ed. by Loscalzo & Arthur A. Sasahara. LC 97-12542. (Illus.). 700p. 1997. text 195.00 (*0-8247-9866-X*) Dekker.

New Therapeutic Indications of Antidepressants: Workshop, Bruges, March 1996. Ed. by Julien Mendlewicz et al. LC 97-4322. (International Academy for Biomedical & Drug Research Ser.: Vol. 12, 1997). (Illus.). vi, 138p. 1997. 139.25 (*3-8055-6436-8*) S Karger.

New Therapeutic Strategies in Hypertension. Ed. by Norman M. Kaplan et al. LC 86-43104. (Perspectives in Hypertension Ser.: Vol. 3). 333p. 1989. reprint ed. pap. 103.30 (*0-608-00319-0*, 206103600007) Bks Demand.

New Therapeutic Strategies in Nephrology: Proceedings of the 3rd International Meeting on Current Therapy in Nephrology. Ed. by Vittorio E. Andreucci & Antonio D. Canton. (Developments in Nephrology Ser.). 576p. 1991. text 197.00 (*0-7923-1199-X*) Kluwer Academic.

New Therapeutic Uses of Calcium Channel Blockers. Ed. by H. Glossmann. (Journal of Neural Transmission: Suppl. 31). (Illus.). 65p. 1990. 52.95 (*0-387-82200-3*) Spr-Verlag.

New Therapeutic Visions. Ed. by Arnold Goldberg. (Progress in Self Psychology Ser.: Vol. 8). 288p. 1992. text 45.00 (*0-88163-150-7*) Analytic Pr.

New Therapeutics & Diagnostics for Women's Disorders, No. C-177. 1994. 2450.00 (*1-56965-013-6*) BCC.

New Therapies for Neonatal Respiratory Failure: A Physiological Approach. Ed. by Bruce R. Boynton et al. (Illus.). 377p. (C). 1994. text 130.00 (*0-521-43161-1*) Cambridge U Pr.

New Thermoset Developments for Wire & Cable Insulation: Regional Technical Conference, Society of Plastics Engineers, June 19-20, 1979. Society of Plastics Engineers Staff. LC TK3331.N4. 148p. reprint ed. pap. 45.90 (*0-608-30754-8*, 201138600080) Bks Demand.

***New "Thin" You: The Simple Safe Secret to Lose Weight Once & Forever Naturally.** A. Tony Martin. LC 99-75513. 180p. 1999. reprint ed. pap. 9.95 (*1-884820-56-5*) SAFE GOODS.

New Thing Breathing. Gavin Bantock. Date not set. 14.95 (*0-900977-03-5*, Pub. by Anvil Press) Dufour.

***New Thing Breathing: Recent Work by Tony Cragg.** Lewis Biggs. (Illus.). 156p. 2000. pap. 40.00 (*1-85437-324-2*) U of Wash Pr.

New Think. Edward De Bono. 224p. 1985. mass mkt. 4.95 (*0-380-01426-2*, Avon Bks) Morrow Avon.

New Thinking about Quality Control. rev. ed. LC 95-60042. 112p. 1995. pap. text 29.95 (*0-942004-63-9*) Throwkoff Pr.

New Thinking & American Defense Technology. 2nd ed. Carnegie Commission on Science, Technology, & Gove & William J. Perry. 48p. 1993. pap. write for info. (*1-881054-12-8*) Carnegie Comm Sci.

New Thinking & Developments in International Politics: Opportunities & Dangers, Vol. III. Ed. by Neal Riemer & Kenneth Thompson. (Miller Center Series on a World in Change). 206p. (C). 1991. pap. text 23.50 (*0-8191-8309-1*); lib. bdg. 46.00 (*0-8191-8308-3*) U Pr of Amer.

New Thinking for a New Millennium. Ed. by Richard A. Slaughter. LC 95-31961. (Illus.). 256p. (C). 1996. pap. 25.99 (*0-415-12943-5*) Routledge.

New Thinking for a New Millennium. William J. Williams. LC 99-70437. (Illus.). 112p. 1999. pap. 11.95 (*1-57197-173-4*) Pentland Pr.

***New Thinking for the New Millennium.** Edward De Bono. 2000. 22.95 (*1-893224-05-8*) New Millenn Enter.

New Thinking in Design: Conversations on Theory & Practice. C. Thomas Mitchell. (Illus.). 192p. 1996. pap. 62.95 (*0-442-01733-2*, VNR) Wiley.

New Thinking in Design: Conversations on Theory & Practices. C. Thomas Mitchell. (Architecture Ser.). 208p. 1996. 69.95 (*0-471-28604-4*, VNR) Wiley.

New Thinking in International Relations Theory. Ed. by Michael W. Doyle & G. John Ikenberry. LC 97-15796. 304p. (C). 1997. pap. 28.00 (*0-8133-9966-1*, Pub. by Westview) HarpC.

New Thinking in Organizational Behaviour: From Social Engineering to Reflective Action. Haridimos Tsoukas. LC 94-204039. (Management Readers Ser.). (Illus.). 268p. reprint ed. pap. 83.10 (*0-608-06256-1*, 206658500008) Bks Demand.

***New Thinking in Technical Analysis: Trading Models from the Masters.** Rick Bensignor. (Professional Library). 2000. 55.00 (*1-57660-049-1*) Bloomberg NJ.

New Thinking in TEFL. Ed. by Tim Caudery. (The Dolphin Ser.: No. 21). 192p. (C). 1992. pap. 19.95 (*87-7288-371-5*, Pub. by Aarhus Univ Pr) David Brown.

New Thinking on Financing & Regulating Long-Term Care. Wendy Fox-Grage. 1998. 20.00 incl. audio (*1-55516-821-3*) Natl Conf State Legis.

New Thinking on Higher Education: Creating a Context for Change. Joel W. Meyerson. (Forum Ser.: Vol. 1). 208p. 1998. 34.95 (*1-882982-23-1*) Anker Pub.

New Third World. 2nd ed. Ed. by Alfonso Gonzalez & Jim Norwine. LC 98-2634. 336p. (C). 1998. 79.00 (*0-8133-2250-2*, Pub. by Westview); pap. 29.00 (*0-8133-2251-0*, Pub. by Westview) HarpC.

New Thought: A Practical American Spirituality. C. Alan Anderson & Deborah G. Whitehouse. LC 94-47380. 160p. 1995. 19.95 (*0-8245-1480-7*) Crossroad NY.

New Thought Christian. William A. Warch. LC 77-90509. 100p. 1987. reprint ed. pap. 7.95 (*0-87516-591-5*) DeVorss.

New Thought Essays. Charles B. Patterson. 103p. 1997. pap. 9.00 (*0-89540-271-8*, SB-271) Sun Pub.

New Thought for a New Millennium: Twelve Powers for the 21st Century. Ed. by Michael A. Maday. LC 97-26296. 235p. 1998. 19.95 (*0-87159-205-3*, 001) Unity Bks.

New Thought Healing Made Plain. Kate A. Boehme. 142p. 1997. pap. 12.00 (*0-89540-272-6*, SB-272) Sun Pub.

***New Threat: Honest Rustlers.** Virgil R. Cooper. 218p. 2000. 4.99 (*0-9668804-2-0*) A-bar-V.

New Threat of Drug Resistant Microbes. 3rd rev. ed. Sharon Krystofiak. Ed. by Barbara Halliburton. 172p. 1996. pap. 24.95 (*1-57801-002-0*) Western Schls.

New Three Minute Meditator see Three Minute Meditator: 30 Simple Ways to Unwind Your Mind While Enhancing Your Emotional Intelligence

New Three Year Garden Journal: With Regional Planning Guides. rev. ed. Louise Carter & JoAnne Lawson. LC 98-20536. (Illus.). 114p. 1999. 29.95 (*1-55591-392-X*) Fulcrum Pub.

New Thresholds of Faith see Nuevos Umbrales de Fe

New Thresholds of Faith. 2nd ed. Kenneth E. Hagin. 1972. pap. 5.95 (*0-89276-070-2*) Faith Lib Pubns.

New Tides in the Pacific: Pacific Basin Cooperation & the Big Four (Japan, PRC, U. S. A, U. S. S. R., 188. Ed. by Roy Kim & Hilary Conroy. LC 87-8406. (Contributions in Political Science Ser.: No. 188). 229p. 1987. 59.95 (*0-313-25625-X*, KNE/) Greenwood.

New Tigers & Old Elephants: The Development Game in the 1990s & Beyond. Scott B. MacDonald & Jane E. Hughes. LC 99-53931. 364p. 1999. pap. 29.95 (*0-7658-0633-9*) Transaction Pubs.

New Tigers & Old Elephants: The Development Game in the 1990s & Beyond. Scott B. MacDonald et al. LC 95-18142. 1995. 44.95 (*1-56000-204-2*) Transaction Pubs.

New Time. Leslie Scalapino. LC 98-47528. (Wesleyan Poetry Ser.). 100p. 1999. pap. 11.95 (*0-8195-6356-0*, Wesleyan Univ Pr); text 25.00 (*0-8195-6355-2*, Wesleyan Univ Pr) U Pr of New Eng.

New Time & Place: Preparing Yourself to Receive God's Best. Jack W. Hayford. LC 97-3905. 160p. 1997. 12.99 (*1-57673-028-X*, Multnomah Bks) Multnomah Pubs.

New Time for Mexico. Carlos Fuentes. Tr. by Marina G. Castanede. LC 96-10540. 215p. 1996. 22.00 (*0-374-22170-7*) FS&G.

New Time for Mexico. Carlos Fuentes. Tr. by Marina G. Gutman. LC 97-8427. 216p. 1997. pap. 13.95 (*0-520-21183-9*, Pub. by U CA Pr) Cal Prin Full Svc.

New Time Management Methods for You & Your Staff. 2nd ed. R. Alec Mackenzie. 250p. 1990. ring bd. 91.50 (*0-85013-168-5*) Dartnell Corp.

New Time Manager. Angela V. Woodhull. LC 96-30372. 250p. 1997. 51.95 (*0-566-07835-X*, Pub. by Gower) Ashgate Pub Co.

New Times & Old Enemies: Essays on Cultural Studies & America. John Clarke. LC 91-40869. 224p. (C). 1992. text 55.00 (*0-04-445474-0*) Routledge.

New Times Best of Phoenix Restaurant Guide, 1995. rev. ed. Howard Seftel. 192p. 1994. pap. 7.95 (*0-9639272-1-3*) New Times AZ.

New Times Nature Diary. Derwent May. (Illus.). 127p. 1995. 18.95 (*0-86051-850-7*, Robson-Parkwest) Parkwest Pubns.

New Times Nature Diary. Derwent May. LC 94-77100. (Illus.). 128p. 1996. pap. 9.95 (*0-86051-946-5*, Robson-Parkwest) Parkwest Pubns.

New Times, New Competencies, New Professional. 108p. 1997. pap. 20.00 (*1-57744-057-9*) Nat Acad Public Admin.

New Times to Invest? The Rediscovery of Smaller Enterprises in Theory & Practice see neue Grunderzeit?: Die Wiederentdeckung kleiner Unternehmen in Theorie und Praxis

New Timon: A Romance of London. Edward Bulwer Lytton & Algernon Charles Swinburne. Ed. by Ira B. Nadel et al. 320p. 1986. lib. bdg. 20.00 (*0-8240-8619-8*) Garland.

New Titles Library, 6 bks. & 6 cass., Set. 39.95 incl. audio (*0-86545-170-2*) Spizzirri.

***New to Kew?** Jane Cox. 1999. pap. 12.95 (*1-873162-40-5*) PRO Pubns.

New to North America: Writing by Immigrants, Their Children & Grandchildren. Ed. by Abby Bogomolny. LC 97-24186. 400p. 1997. pap. 24.95 (*0-9650665-9-2*) Burning Bush CA.

New to the U. K. A Guide to Your Life & Rights in the U. K. Genevieve Muinzer. 224p. 1987. 35.00 (*0-7102-0852-9*, 08529, Routledge Thoemms) Routledge.

New Toes for Tia. Larry Dinkins. 1987. pap. 2.95 (*9971-972-59-X*) OMF Bks.

New Tolerance see Nueva Tolerancia

New Tolerance. Josh McDowell & Bob Hostetler. LC 98-27048. 1998. pap. 9.99 (*0-8423-7088-9*) Tyndale Hse.

New Tolkien Companion. 2nd rev. ed. J. E. Tyler. LC 79-323111. (Picador Ser.). xiii, 651 p. 1979. write for info. (*0-330-25801-X*, Pub. by Pan) Trafalgar.

New Tonality. Ed. by Paul Moravec. (Contemporary Music Review Ser.). 126p. 1992. pap. text 15.00 (*3-7186-5187-4*, Harwood Acad Pubs) Gordon & Breach.

New Tongue & Quill: Your Practical (And Humorous) Guide to Better Communication. Hank Staley. 256p. 1990. pap. 17.00 (*0-08-035975-2*) Brasseys.

New Tools & Techniques for Product & Process Integration: 1996 International Congress & Exposition. LC 96-207932. (Special Publications). 254p. 1996. pap. 94.00 (*1-56091-776-8*, SP-1146) Soc Auto Engineers.

New Tools for Agriculture & Forestry: Statistics Proc of the Oporto Workshop. Eurostat Staff. 148p. 1997. pap. 30.00 (*92-827-9455-5*, CA-01-96-026ENC, Pub. by Comm Europ Commun) Bernan Associates.

New Tools for Balancing Theater Combat & Support. David B. Kassing et al. 61p. (Orig.). 1996. pap. text 6.00 (*0-8330-2429-9*, DB-150-A) Rand Corp.

***New Tools for Failure & Risk Analysis: Anticipatory Failure Determination (AFD) & the Theory of Scenario Structuring.** Stan Kaplan et al. (Illus.). 86p. 1999. 35.00 (*1-928747-05-1*) Ideation Intl.

New Tools for New Times: The Impact of Electronic Commerce on Information Technology. Ed. & Intro. by Layna Fischer. (Electronic Commerce Ser.: Bk. 3). (Illus.). 350p. (Orig.). 1996. pap. 29.95 (*0-9640233-3-4*) Future Strat.

New Tools for New Times - The Workflow Paradigm: The Impact of Information Technology on Business Process Reengineering. 2nd ed. Ed. by Layna Fischer. LC 94-72343. (Illus.). 432p. 1995. pap. 34.95 (*0-9640233-2-6*) Future Strat.

New Tools for Preservation: Assessing Long-Term Environmental Effects on Library & Archive Collections. James M. Reilly et al. LC 96-126478. 35p. 1995. pap. 10.00 (*1-887334-46-7*) Coun Lib & Info.

New Tools for Social Scientists: Advances & Applications in Research Methods. Ed. by William D. Berry & Michael S. Lewis-Beck. LC 85-19653. (Illus.). 288p. 1986. reprint ed. pap. 89.30 (*0-608-01186-X*, 205948400001) Bks Demand.

New Tools in Turbulence Modelling: Course Held in Les Houches, 21-31 May 1996. Ed. by O. Metais & J. H. Ferziger. (Illus.). xvii, 298p. 1997. pap. 84.95 (*3-540-63090-2*) Spr-Verlag.

New Tools of Technology: A User Friendly Guide to the Latest Technology. Dan Burrus & Patti Thomsen. 187p. (Orig.). 1991. pap. 19.95 (*1-880136-50-3*) Intl Mgmt Pubns.

New Top of the Country Charts: 41 Smash Country Hits from 1989-1990. (Piano-Vocal-Guitar Ser.). 208p. 1991. per. 14.95 (*0-7935-0405-8*, 00490578) H Leonard.

New Topiary: Imaginative Techniques from Longwood Gardens. Patricia R. Hammer. (Illus.). 264p. 1991. 39.50 (*1-870673-21-2*, Pub. by Garden Art Pr) Antique Collect.

New Topics in Learning Automata Theory & Applications. N. Baba. (Lecture Notes in Control & Information Sciences: Vol. 71). 150p. 1985. pap. 22.00 (*0-387-15613-5*) Spr-Verlag.

New Topographical Dictionary of Ancient Rome. L. Richardson, Jr. (Illus.). 480p. 1992. text 65.00 (*0-8018-4300-6*) Johns Hopkins.

New Toughness Training for Sports. James E. Loehr. (Illus.). 224p. 1995. pap. 12.95 (*0-452-26998-9*, Plume) Dutton Plume.

New Town. Leslie Higgs. 240p. 1982. 40.00 (*0-85335-215-1*, Pub. by Stuart Titles Ltd) St Mut.

New Towns: An Emphasis on the American Enterprise, No. 982. James A. Clapp. 1976. 10.00 (*0-686-20387-9*, Sage Prdcls Pr) Sage.

New Towns for Colonial Brazil: Spatial & Social Planning of the 18th Century. Roberta M. Delson. Ed. by David J. Robinson. LC 79-9347. (Dellplain Latin American Studies: No. 2). 228p. 1979. reprint ed. pap. 70.70 (*0-8357-0439-4*, 202259600028) Bks Demand.

New Towns in East & South-East Asia. Ed. by David R. Phillips & Anthony G. Yeh. (Illus.). 268p. 1987. 36.00 (*0-19-584087-9*) OUP.

New Towns in Israel. Alexander Berler. 384p. 1970. boxed set 39.95 (*0-87855-174-3*) Transaction Pubs.

New Towns in the New World: Images of Nineteenth Century Urban Frontiers. David Hamer. (Illus.). 320p. 1990. text 46.00 (*0-231-06620-1*) Col U Pr.

New Towns Planning & Development: A World-Wide Bibliography. Gideon Golany. LC 72-93819. (Urban Land Institute, ULI Research Reports: No. 20). 256p. reprint ed. pap. 79.40 (*0-608-11922-9*, 202323700032) Bks Demand.

New Tracks for Thomas. W. Audry. LC 93-85588. (Pictureback Shapes Ser.). (Illus.). 24p. (J). (ps-2). 1994. pap. 3.25 (*0-679-85699-4*, Pub. by Random Bks Yng Read) Random.

New Trade Agenda. Geza Feketekuty. (Occasional Paper Ser.: No. 40). 30p. 1992. pap. text 10.00 (*1-56708-087-1*) Grp of Thirty.

New Trading Dimensions: How to Profit from Chaos in Stocks, Bonds & Commodities. Bill Williams. LC 98-3765. (Trading Advantage Ser.). 288p. 1998. 59.95 (*0-471-29541-8*) Wiley.

New Traditional Garden: A Practical Guide to Creating & Restoring Authentic American Gardens for Homes of All Ages. Michael Weishan. LC 98-46043. 400p. 1999. 35.00 (*0-345-42041-1*) Ballantine Pub Grp.

New Traditions from Nigeria: Seven Artists of the Nsukka Group. Simon Ottenberg. LC 97-7666. 1997. text 49.95 (*1-56098-800-2*) Smithsonian.

New Traditions in Business: Spirit & Leadership in the 21st Century. Ed. by John Renesch. LC 92-52970. (Illus.). 270p. 1992. pap. 17.95 (*1-881052-03-6*) Berrett-Koehler.

New Traditions in Business: Spirit & Leadership in the 21st Century. Ed. by John Renesch. 256p. 1991. 24.75 (*0-9630390-0-8*) New Leaders.

New Tragedy & Comedy in France, 1945-1970. Peter Norrish. LC 87-11571. 192p. (C). 1988. text 50.00 (*0-389-20746-2*, N8305) B&N Imports.

New Trails: Twenty-Three Original Stories of the West from Western Writers of America. large type ed. Ed. by John Jakes & Martin H. Greenberg. LC 95-2633. 478p. 1995. lib. bdg. 23.95 (*0-7838-1248-5*, G K Hall Lrg Type) Mac Lib Ref.

New Trails in Mexico. Carl Lumholtz. LC 90-30449. (Southwest Center Ser.). 411p. 1990. reprint ed. pap. 20.95 (*0-8165-1175-6*) U of Ariz Pr.

New Trainer's Self-Study Workshop. Kervin. 1999. 99.95 (*0-07-134482-9*) McGraw.

New Training Strategies for a High Performance Metalworking Industry. Robert Howard. 42p. 1991. pap. 20.00 (*1-887410-61-9*) Jobs for Future.

***New Transatlantic Agenda.** LC 98-211743. iii, 90p. 1998. write for info. (*0-16-057294-0*) USGPO.

New Transatlantic Agenda & the Future. Kluwer Law International Staff. LC 98-31550. 1998. text 83.00 (*90-411-9676-5*) Kluwer Law Intl.

New Transatlantic Economy. Ed. by Matthew B. Canzoneri et al. LC 97-108427. 348p. (C). 1996. text 59.95 (*0-521-56205-8*) Cambridge U Pr.

New Transatlantic Partnership: Report by the Trans-Europe Policy Studies Association. Geoffrey Denton. 77p. 1999. pap. 20.00 (*0-901573-87-6*, Kogan Pg Educ) Stylus Pub VA.

New Translations. Ed. by Doris Meyer & Margarite Fernandez-Olmos. (Contemporary Women Authors of Latin America Ser.: Vol. II). 331p. 1984. pap. 12.50 (*0-930888-21-9*) Brooklyn Coll Pr.

New Transparent Decorations. D. M. Campana. 9.95 (*0-939608-27-8*) Campana Art.

New Travels in North America, 1770-1772. Jean-Bernard Bossu. Ed. by Samuel D. Dickinson. LC 82-81335. 163p. 1982. 17.50 (*0-917898-07-9*) NSU Pr LA.

New Travels in the United States: Performed in 1788. Jean P. Brissot De Warville. LC 74-11214. (On America Ser.: Vol. 1). 483p. 1970. reprint ed. lib. bdg. 57.50 (*0-678-04028-1*) Kelley.

N

New Travels Through North America. Abbe Robin. Ed. by Peter Decker. Tr. by Philip Freneau. LC 73-77110. (Eyewitness Accounts of the American Revolution Ser.). 1969. reprint ed. 16.95 (*0-405-01176-8*) Ayer.

New Treasures: A Perspective of New Testament Teachings Through Hebraic Eyes. rev. ed. E. William Bean. 208p. (Orig.). 1999. pap. 13.95 (*0-9623950-2-1*) Cornerstn Pub.

New Treasury of Cat Stories. Roger Caras. 512p. 1997. 27.00 (*0-88486-172-4*, Bristol Park Bks) Arrowood Pr.

New Treasury of Christmas Recipes. (Favorite All Time Recipes Ser.). (Illus.). 96p. 1993. spiral bd. 3.50 (*1-56173-610-4*, 2019102) Pubns Intl Ltd.

New Treasury of Great Racing Stories. Ed. by John Welcome. 236p. 1992. 19.95 (*0-393-03102-0*) Norton.

New Treasury of Poetry. Illus. by John Lawrence. LC 89-49089. 256p. 1990. 27.50 (*1-55670-145-4*) Stewart Tabori & Chang.

New Treasury of Scripture Knowledge. rev. ed. Ed. by Jerome H. Smith. 1664p. 1992. 39.99 (*0-8407-7694-2*) Nelson.

New Treasury of War Poetry: Poems of the Second World War. Ed. by George H. Clark. 1977. 18.95 (*0-8369-6009-2*) Ayer.

New Treatise on Accompaniment: With the Harpsichord, the Organ, & with Other Instruments. De Saint Lambert. Ed. & Tr. by John S. Powell from FRE. LC 90-33591. (Publications of the Early Music Institute). 176p. 1991. pap. 15.95 (*0-253-34561-8*) Ind U Pr.

New Treatise on Accompaniment: With the Harpsichord, the Organ & with Other Instruments. Michael D. Saint-Lambert. Ed. & Tr. by John S. Powell. LC 90-33591. (Publications of the Early Music Institute Ser.). (Illus.). 172p. Date not set. reprint ed. pap. 53.40 (*0-608-20565-6*, 205447900002) Bks Demand.

New Treatment of Alcohol & Substance Abuse in Akhter Absen's Eidetic Image Therapy. Toni Nixon. 308p. 1997. pap. 25.00 (*0-913412-39-2*) Brandon Hse.

New Treatment of Disease: Abridged Therapeutics Founded upon Histology & Cellular Pathology. abr. ed. W. H. Schuessler. 1996. reprint ed. spiral bd. 19.50 (*0-7873-0743-2*) Hlth Research.

New Treatment of Diseases: Therapeutics Founded upon Histology & Cellular Pathology. W. H. Schussler. 1991. lib. bdg. 79.95 (*0-8490-4106-6*) Gordon Pr.

New Treatments for Chemical Addictions. Ed. by Elinore F. McCance-Katz & Thomas R. Kosten. (Review of Psychiatry Ser.). 211p. 1998. pap. text 31.00 (*0-88048-838-7*, 8838) Am Psychiatric.

New Treatments for Opiate Dependence. Ed. by Susan M. Stine & Thomas R. Kosten. LC 97-3244. (Substance Abuse Ser.). 286p. 1997. lib. bdg. 38.00 (*1-57230-190-2*) Guilford Pubns.

N

*__New Treatments in Neurology AA Summary.__ Neil Scolding. (Illus.). 224p. 2000. pap. 45.00 (*0-7506-3918-0*) Buttrwrth-Heinemann.

New Tree Biology; A New Tree Biology Dictionary, 2 vols., Set. 2nd ed. Alex L. Shigo. (Dr. Shigo's Tree Ser.). (Illus.). 132p. 1986. reprint ed. 65.00 (*0-943563-12-7*) Shigo & Trees Assocs.

New Tree Health. Alex L. Shigo. (Illus.). 1989. reprint ed. pap. text 3.00 (*0-943563-02-X*) Shigo & Trees Assocs.

New Trek Programme Guide. Paul Cornell et al. 1995. mass mkt. 5.95 (*0-86369-922-7*, Pub. by Virgin Bks) London Brdge.

New Trend in Indian Irrigation: Commercialisation of Ground Water. Niranjan Pant. (C). 1992. 14.50 (*81-7024-467-6*, Pub. by Ashish Pub Hse) S Asia.

New Trends & Advanced Techniques in Clinical Neurophysiology. P. M. Rossini & Francois Mauguiere. (Supplement to EEG Ser.: Vol. 41). 382p. 1991. 270.50 (*0-444-81352-7*) Elsevier.

New Trends & Developments in African Religions, 186. Ed. by Peter B. Clarke. LC 97-32006. (Contributions in Afro-American & African Studies: Vol. 186). 328p. 1998. 59.95 (*0-313-30128-X*, Greenwood Pr) Greenwood.

New Trends & Developments in Carotid Artery Disease. Ed. by Alain Branchereau & Michael Jacobs. LC 98-6275. (Illus.). 284p. 1998. 110.00 (*0-87993-403-4*) Futura Pub.

New Trends & Developments in Papermaking. Ed. by Kelly Ferguson. (Illus.). 210p. 1994. pap. 54.00 (*0-87930-302-6*) Miller Freeman.

New Trends & Developments in the World of Islam. Peter B. Clarke. LC 97-182446. x, 400 p. 1997. 60.36 (*1-898942-17-X*, Pub. by Luzac Oriental) Weatherhill.

New Trends & Generations in African Literature No. 20: African Literature Today. Ed. by Eldred D. Jones & Marjorie Jones. 192p. 1996. 49.95 (*0-86543-506-5*); pap. 16.95 (*0-86543-507-3*) Africa World.

New Trends & Issues in Teaching Japanese Language & Culture. Ed. by Haruko M. Cook et al. (Technical Report Ser.: Vol. 15). 184p. 1998. pap. text 20.00 (*0-8248-2067-3*) Sec Lang Tching.

New Trends & Shifts in the Asia Pacific Travel Market: Proceedings from the Fifth Asia Business Forum Held July 3, 1995. 85p. 1995. pap. 40.00 (*981-00-6951-0*) Pac Asia Trvl.

New Trends for Hamiltonian Systems & Celestial Mechanics. LC 96-205725. 408p. 1996. lib. bdg. 62.00 (*981-02-2645-4*) World Scientific Pub.

New Trends in Aging Research. Ed. by Giancarlo Pepeu et al. (FIDIA Research Ser.: Vol. 15). viii, 237p. 1989. 79.00 (*0-387-96911-X*) Spr-Verlag.

New Trends in Allergy. Ed. by G. Burg & Johannes Ring. (Illus.). 350p. 1981. 79.95 (*0-387-10346-5*) Spr-Verlag.

New Trends in Allergy, No. III. Ed. by B. Przybilla & Johannes Ring. (Illus.). 568p. 1991. 249.00 (*0-387-52993-4*) Spr-Verlag.

New Trends in Allergy IV, Together with Environmental Allergy & Allergotoxicology III: Joint International Symposium, Hamburg, April 29-May 1, 1995. Johannes Ring et al. LC 96-42937. (Illus.). 280p. 1996. 199.00 (*3-540-61120-7*) Spr-Verlag.

New Trends in Animation & Visualization. Ed. by Nadia M. Thalmann & Daniel Thalmann. LC 91-19182. (Illus.). 287p. reprint ed. pap. 89.00 (*0-608-20235-5*, 207149400012) Bks Demand.

New Trends in Antivirals: Highlighting Antisense Oligonucleotides. BCC Staff. 156p. 1990. 2450.00 (*0-89336-619-6*, C109) BCC.

New Trends in Astronomy Teaching. Ed. by L. Gouguenheim et al. LC 98-7171. (Illus.). 400p. (C). 1998. 69.95 (*0-521-62373-1*) Cambridge U Pr.

New Trends in Basement Membrane Research: Tenth Workshop Conference Hoechst, Eibsee, May 11-14, 1981. fac. ed. Ed. by Klaus Kuehn et al. LC 81-48593. (Illus.). 309p. pap. 95.80 (*0-7837-7196-7*, 204710300005) Bks Demand.

New Trends in Basic Lymphology. 1980. 63.50 (*0-8176-0115-5*) Birkhauser.

New Trends in Biological Chemistry. Ed. by T. Ozawa. (Illus.). 440p. 1991. 149.95 (*0-387-53935-2*) Spr-Verlag.

New Trends in Canadian Federalism. Ed. by Francois Rocher & Miriam Smith. 380p. 1995. pap. 29.95 (*1-55111-019-9*) Broadview Pr.

New Trends in Cerebral Hemodynamics & Neurosonology: Proceedings of the 10th International Symposium on Cerebral Hemodynamics, Munich, Germany, 29 August-1 September, 1996. Jurgen Klingelhofer et al. LC 97-41501. 845p. 1997. 287.50 (*0-444-82631-9*) Elsevier.

New Trends in Clinical Pharmacology. D. Bartko et al. (Current Problems in Neurology Ser.: Vol. 7). 320p. 1988. 74.95 (*0-86196-146-3*, Pub. by J Libbey Med) Bks Intl VA.

New Trends in Coal Preparation Technologies & Equipment. Ed. by Wieslaw Blaschke. (Recent Advances in Coal Processing Ser). 1016p. 1995. text 198.00 (*2-88449-139-2*) Gordon & Breach.

New Trends in Coal Science. Ed. by Yuda Yurum. (C). 1988. text 266.50 (*90-277-2790-2*) Kluwer Academic.

New Trends in Colloid Science: Progress in Colloid & Polymer Science, Vol. 73. Ed. by H. Hoffmann. 196p. 1987. 94.00 (*0-387-91308-4*) Spr-Verlag.

New Trends in Conceptual Representation: Challenges to Piaget's Theory. Ellin K. Scholnick. (Jean Piaget Symposia Ser.). 304p. (C). 1983. text 59.95 (*0-89859-260-7*) L Erlbaum Assocs.

New Trends in Design of Control Systems. M. Huba & J. Mikles. LC 95-144357. (IFAC Postprint Volume Ser.). 446p. 1995. 87.75 (*0-08-042367-1*, Pergamon Pr) Elsevier.

New Trends in Diagnosis & Management of Stroke. Ed. by Klaus Poeck et al. (Illus.). 169p. 1988. pap. 33.10 (*0-387-18369-8*) Spr-Verlag.

New Trends in Discrete & Computational Geometry. Ed. by Janos Pach. LC 92-23684. (Algorithms & Combinatorics Ser.: Vol. 10). 1993. 89.00 (*0-387-55713-X*) Spr-Verlag.

*__New Trends in Distribution Logistics.__ Ed. by M. Grazia Speranza & Paul Stahly. LC 99-49218. (Lecture Notes in Economics & Mathematical Systems Ser.: Vol. 480). (Illus.). x, 319p. 2000. pap. 73.00 (*3-540-66617-6*) Spr-Verlag.

New Trends in Dynamic Games & Appications, Vol. 3. Ed. by Geert J. Olsder. LC 95-33319. (Annals of the International Society of Dynamic Games Ser.). 482p. 1995. 104.00 (*0-8176-3812-1*) Birkhauser.

New Trends in Employment Practices: An International Survey, 34. Walter Galenson. LC 90-45325. (Contributions in Labor Studies: No. 34). 168p. 1990. 57.95 (*0-313-27629-3*, GNT, Greenwood Pr) Greenwood.

New Trends in Farm Machinery Development & Agriculture. 1996. 61.00 (*1-56091-846-2*, SP-1194) Soc Auto Engineers.

New Trends in Formal Languages: Control, Cooperation, & Combinatorics, Vol. 121. Ed. by Gheorghe Paun et al. LC 97-12652. (Lecture Notes in Computer Science Ser.: No. 1218). ix, 465p. 1997. pap. 73.00 (*3-540-62844-4*) Spr-Verlag.

New Trends in Fuzzy Logic: Proceedings of the WILK, '95 Italian Workshop on Fuzzy Logic, 21-22 September 1995, Naples, Italy. Andrea Bonarini. LC 96-22862. 400p. 1996. write for info. (*981-02-2794-9*) World Scientific Pub.

New Trends in Fuzzy Logic II: Proceedings of the WILF '97 - Italian Workshop on Fuzzy Logic, 1997 Bari, Italy, 19-20 March, 1997. Ed. by Marcello Castellano et al. 300p. 1998. 78.00 (*981-02-3309-4*) World Scientific Pub.

New Trends in Fuzzy Systems: Proceedings of the International Joint Workshop on Current Issues on Fuzzy Technologies & Methods & Environments for Planning & Programming CIFT/MEPP '96 Aversa, Italy 10 October, 1996 Napoli, Italy 11 October, 1996. Ed. by Dario Mancini et al. 300p. 1997. 78.00 (*981-02-3245-4*) World Scientific Pub.

New Trends in Ganglioside Research: Neurochemical & Neuroregenerative Aspects. Ed. by Robert W. Ledeen et al. (FIDIA Research Ser.: Vol. 14). xiv, 660p. 1988. 189.00 (*0-387-96797-4*) Spr-Verlag.

New Trends in Gastric Cancer. Ed. by P. I. Reed et al. (Developments in Oncology Ser.). (C). 1990. text 123.00 (*0-7923-8917-4*) Kluwer Academic.

New Trends in Geometric Function Theory & Applications: Proceedings of the International Conference. A. Gnanam & R. Parvatham. 196p. 1991. text 74.00 (*981-02-0482-5*) World Scientific Pub.

New Trends in Graphemics & Orthography: Kolloquium Siegen 22-24 August, 1985. Ed. by Gerhard Augst. xii, 464p. 1986. 119.25 (*3-11-010804-6*) De Gruyter.

New Trends in Haemostasis: Coagulation Proteins, Endothelium, & Tissue Factors. Ed. by F. Gotthard Schettler et al. (Sitzungsberichte der Heidelberger Akademie der Wissenschaften Ser., Mathematisch-Naturwissenschaftliche Klasse, Jahrgang 1991: Suppl. 3). (Illus.). 280p. 1990. pap. 44.00 (*0-387-53275-7*) Spr-Verlag.

New Trends in Heart Transplantation. Ed. by M. Havel. (Bibliotheca Cardiologica Ser.: No. 43). viii, 168p. 1989. 127.00 (*3-8055-4792-7*) S Karger.

New Trends in Hepatology, Vol. 15. Ed. by Paolo Gentilini. 352p. (C). 1996. text 129.00 (*0-7923-8703-1*) Kluwer Academic.

New Trends in Hepatology, 1996: Proceedings of the Falk Symposium No. 92, St. Petersburg. Ed. by W. Gerok et al. (Falk Symposium Ser.: No. 92). 256p. 1997. text 120.50 (*0-7923-8723-6*) Kluwer Academic.

New Trends in HERA Physics: Proceedings of the Ringberg Workshop Ringberg Castle, Tegernsee, Germany 25-30 May, 1997. Ed. by Bernd Kniehl. LC 98-227418. 350p. 1998. 86.00 (*981-02-3398-1*) World Scientific Pub.

*__New Trends in Hera Physics, 1999: Proceedings of the Ringberg Workshop Held at Tegernsee, Germany, 30 May-4 June, 1999.__ G. Grindhammer et al. LC 00-26908. (Lecture Notes in Physics Ser.). xvi, 460p. 2000. 98.00 (*3-540-67156-0*) Spr-Verlag.

New Trends in Indian Art & Archaeology, 2 vols. B. U. Nayak & N. C. Ghosh. 571p. 1991. pap. 183.50 (*81-85689-12-1*, Pub. by Aditya Prakashan) S Asia.

New Trends in Indian Art & Archaeology: S. R. Rao's 70th Birthday Felicitation Volume, Vol. I. B. U. Nayak. (C). 1992. write for info. (*81-85689-13-X*, Pub. by Aditya Prakashan) S Asia.

New Trends in Indian Art & Archaeology: S. R. Rao's 70th Birthday Felicitation Volume, Vol. II. B. U. Nayak. (C). 1992. write for info. (*81-85689-14-8*, Pub. by Aditya Prakashan) S Asia.

New Trends in Instrumentation for Hypersonic Research. Ed. by A. Boutier. LC 92-33756. (NATO Advanced Study Institutes Series E, Applied Sciences: Vol. 224). (C). 1993. text 340.50 (*0-7923-2024-7*) Kluwer Academic.

New Trends in Ion Beam Processing of Materials & Beam Induced Nanometric Phenomena: Proceedings of Symposium I & Symposium K of the 1996 E-MRS Spring Conference, Strasbourg, France, June 4-7, 1996. F. Priolo et al. 640p. 1997. 373.00 (*0-444-20506-3*) Elsevier.

New Trends in Kramers' Reaction Rate Theory. Ed. by Peter Talkner. LC 94-20434. (Understanding Chemical Reactivity Ser.: Vol. 11). 256p. (C). 1995. text 144.00 (*0-7923-2940-6*) Kluwer Academic.

New Trends in Lipid & Lipoprotein Analyses. Ed. by E. G. Perkins & J. L. Sebedio. 384p. 1995. 90.00 (*0-935315-59-4*) Am Oil Chemists.

New Trends in Logistics in Europe. ECMT Staff. LC 99-204591. (ECMT Round Table Ser.: No. 104). 178p. 1997. pap. 42.00 (*92-821-1224-1*, 75-97-05-1, Pub. by Org for Econ) OECD.

New Trends in Magnetism. Ed. by Mauricio D. Coutinho-Filho & Sergio M. Rezende. 336p. (C). 1990. text 151.00 (*981-02-0013-7*) World Scientific Pub.

New Trends in Magnetism, Magnetic Materials & Their Applications. J. L. Moran-Lopez & J. M. Sanchez. LC 94-39745. (Illus.). 486p. (C). 1994. text 135.00 (*0-306-44829-7*, Kluwer Plenum) Kluwer Academic.

New Trends in Management of Cerebro-Vascular Malformation: Proceedings of the International Conference, Verona, Italy, June 8-12, 1992. Ed. by A. Pasqualin & R. Da Pian. LC 94-7680. 1994. 280.00 (*0-387-82528-2*) Spr-Verlag.

New Trends in Management of Cerebro-Vascular Malformation: Proceedings of the International Conference, Verona, Italy, June 8-12, 1992. Ed. by A. Pasqualin & R. DaPian. LC 94-7680. 1994. write for info. (*3-211-82528-2*) Spr-Verlag.

New Trends in Materials Chemistry. C. R. Catlow. LC 97-29915. (NATO ASI, Series C, Mathematical & Physical Sciences). 1997. text 264.50 (*0-7923-4714-5*) Kluwer Academic.

New Trends in Materials Processing: Papers Presented at a Seminar of the American Society for Metals, October 19-20, 1974. American Society for Metals Staff. LC 75-42155. (Illus.). 371p. reprint ed. pap. 115.10 (*0-608-11708-0*, 201947600013) Bks Demand.

New Trends in Mathematical Programming: Homage to Steven Vajda. S. Vajda et al. LC 98-13123. (Applied Optimization Ser.). 1998. 140.00 (*0-7923-5036-7*) Kluwer Academic.

New Trends in Medical Technologies & Hospital Management: French Experiences. Asian Productivity Organization Staff. 126p. 1991. pap. text 15.00 (*92-833-2099-9*, 320999) Productivity Inc.

New Trends in Microlocal Analysis, Vol. VIII. Ed. by J. M. Bony & M. Morimoto. (Illus.). 244p. 1997. 74.95 (*4-431-70192-3*) Spr-Verlag.

New Trends in Natural Product Chemistry. Attaur Rahman & M. Iqbal Choudhary. 288p. 1998. text 44.00 (*90-5702-287-7*, Harwood Acad Pubs) Gordon & Breach.

New Trends in Neural Computation: Proceedings of the International Workshop on Artificial Neural Networks IWANN '93, Sitges, Spain, June 9 - 11, 1993. Ed. by A. Prieto et al. (Lecture Notes in Computer Science Ser.: Vol. 686). xvi, 746p. 1993. 108.95 (*0-387-56798-4*) Spr-Verlag.

New Trends in Neutrino Physics: Proceedings of the Ringberg Euroconference. Bernd A. Kniehl. 350p. 1999. 78.00 (*981-02-3783-9*); pap. 38.00 (*981-02-3784-7*) World Scientific Pub.

New Trends in Nonlinear Dynamics & Pattern-Forming Phenomena: The Geometry of Nonequilibrium. Ed. by P. Coullet & P. Huerre. (NATO ASI Ser.: Vol. 231). (Illus.). 368p. (C). 1990. text 144.00 (*0-306-43692-2*, Kluwer Plenum) Kluwer Academic.

New Trends in Nuclear Collective Dynamics: Proceedings of the Nuclear Physics Part of the Fifth Nishinomiya-Yukawa Memorial Symposium Nishinomiya, Japan, October 25-26, 1990. Ed. by Y. Abe et al. (Proceedings in Physics Ser.: Vol. 58). (Illus.). viii, 297p. 1992. 86.95 (*0-387-53606-X*) Spr-Verlag.

New Trends in Nuclear Neurology & Psychiatry. Costa. 192p. 42.00 (*0-86196-401-2*, Pub. by J Libbey Med) Bks Intl VA.

New Trends in Optical Soliton Transmission Systems: Proceedings of the Symposium Held in Kyoto, Japan, 18-21 November, 1997. Akira Hasegawa. LC 98-8192. (Solid-State Science & Technology Library). 1998. 219.00 (*0-7923-5147-9*) Kluwer Academic.

New Trends in Osteoarthritis. Ed. by E. C. Huskisson & G. Katona. (Rheumatology Ser.: Vol. 7). (Illus.). vi, 198p. 1982. 69.75 (*3-8055-3487-6*) S Karger.

New Trends in Particle Theory: Proceedings of the 9th Johns Hopkins Workshop on Current Problems in Particle Theory, Firenze, Italy, June 5-7, 1985. Ed. by L. Lusanna. 184p. 1985. 46.00 (*9971-5-0044-2*) World Scientific Pub.

New Trends in Patient Education: A Trans-Cultural & Inter-Disease Approach: Proceedings of the Patient Education 2000 Congress, Geneva, 1-4 June 1994. Ed. by Jean-Philippe Assal et al. (International Congress Ser.: Vol. 1076). 400p. 1995. 212.50 (*0-444-82234-8*) Elsevier.

New Trends in Pattern Formation in Active Nonlinear Media. V. P. Villar et al. LC 96-145810. (World Scientific Series on Nonlinear Science). 324p. 1996. text 106.00 (*981-02-2179-7*) World Scientific Pub.

New Trends in Pharmacokinetics. Ed. by A. Rescigno & A. K. Thakur. (NATO ASI Ser.: Vol. 221). (Illus.). 456p. (C). 1992. text 168.00 (*0-306-44089-X*, Kluwer Plenum) Kluwer Academic.

New Trends in Physics. L. Vicek. 90p. 1996. 80.00 (*1-898326-42-8*) CISP.

New Trends in Physics & Physical Chemistry of Polymers. Ed. by L. H. Lee. LC 89-22965. (Illus.). 672p. 1989. 155.00 (*0-306-43383-4*, Plenum Trade) Perseus Pubng.

New Trends in Plant Physiology. K. K. Dhir et al. Ed. by I. S. Dua & K. S. Chark. (Illus.). 300p. 1991. 69.00 (*1-55528-217-2*, Pub. by Today Tomorrow) Scholarly Pubns.

New Trends in Probability & Statistics, Vol. 1. Ed. by V. V. Sazonov. 718p. 1991. 225.00 (*90-6764-133-2*) Coronet Bks.

New Trends in Probability & Statistics Vol. 3: Multivariate Statistics & Matrices in Statistics; Proceedings of the 5th Tartu Conference, Estonia, May 1994. Ed. by E. M. Tiit et al. 342p. 1995. 195.00 (*90-6764-195-2*, Pub. by VSP) Coronet Bks.

New Trends in Quantum Field Theory: Proceedings of the Second Bulgarian Workshop. Ed. by A. Ganchev et al. (Illus.). 368p. 1997. 89.95 (*954-580-022-4*, Pub. by Heron Pr) Intl Scholars.

*__New Trends In Quantum Structures.__ Anatolij Dvureicenskij & Sylvia Pulmannova. LC 00-42414. (Mathematics & Its Applications Ser.). 2000. write for info. (*0-7923-6471-6*) Kluwer Academic.

New Trends in Radiopharmaceutical Synthesis, Quality Assurance & Regulatory Control. Ed. by A. M. Emran. (Illus.). 536p. (C). 1991. text 174.00 (*0-306-44035-0*, Kluwer Plenum) Kluwer Academic.

New Trends in Referred Pain & Hyperalgesia. Ed. by L. Vecchiet et al. LC 93-10736. (Pain Research & Clinical Management Ser.). 468p. 1993. 282.75 (*0-444-89631-7*) Elsevier.

New Trends in Reproductive Medicine. Ed. by K. H. Broer & I. Turanli. LC 95-44731. 448p. 1996. 139.00 (*3-540-58981-3*) Spr-Verlag.

New Trends in Research & Utilization of Solar Energy Through Biological Systems. Ed. by R. Bachofen & H. Mislin. (Experientia Supplementa Ser.: Vol. 43). 156p. 1982. 46.50 (*0-8176-1335-8*) Birkhauser.

New Trends in School Finance. 12p. 1992. 4.00 (*0-317-05349-3*) NASBE.

New Trends in Stochastic Analysis. 423p. 1997. lib. bdg. 61.00 (*981-02-2867-8*) World Scientific Pub.

New Trends in Strong Coupling Gauge Theories. Ed. by T. Muta et al. 364p. (C). 1989. text 115.00 (*9971-5-0846-X*) World Scientific Pub.

New Trends in Suicide Prevention. Julien Mendlewicz. Ed. by J. Wilmotte. (Bibliotheca Psychiatrica Ser.: No. 162). (Illus.). vi, 106p. 1982. pap. 41.75 (*3-8055-3430-2*) S Karger.

*__New Trends in Synthetic Medicinal Chemistry.__ Ed. by Fulvio Gualtieri. 370p. 2000. 155.00 (*3-527-29799-5*) Wiley.

New Trends in System Reliability Evaluation. Ed. by Krishna B. Misra. LC 93-38228. (Fundamental Studies in Engineering: Vol. 16). 732p. 1993. 289.00 (*0-444-81660-7*) Elsevier.

New Trends in Systems Theory. G. Conte et al. (Progress in Systems & Control Theory Ser.: Vol. 7). xvii, 722p. 1991. 181.00 (*0-8176-3548-3*) Birkhauser.

New Trends in the Description of the General Mechanism & Regulation of Enzymes: Symposium on Enzyme Action, 9-12 July 1978, Debrecen, Hungary. S. Damjanovich et al. (Symposia Biologica Hungarica Ser.: No. 21). 312p. (C). 1978. 75.00 (*963-05-1881-3*, Pub. by Akade Kiado) St Mut.

An Asterisk (*) at the beginning of an entry indicates that the title is appearing for the first time.

New Trends in the Design of Control Systems 1997: A Proceedings Volume from the Second IFAC Workshop, Smolenice, Slovak Republic, 7-10 September 1997. S. Koz Ak & M. Huba. Ed. by International Federation of Automatic Control, Tri et al. LC 98-14486. 1998. write for info. (*0-08-042935-1*) Elsevier.

New Trends in the Diagnosis & Therapy of Alzheimer's Disease. Ed. by K. A. Jellinger et al. 146p. 1996. 83.00 (*3-211-82620-3*) Spr-Verlag.

New Trends in the Diagnosis & Therapy of Non-Alzheimer's Dementia. Ed. by K. A. Jellinger & M. Windisch. (Journal of Neural Transmission Ser.: Vol. 47). 290p. 1996. pap. 131.00 (*3-211-82823-0*) Spr-Verlag.

New Trends in the Therapy of Liver Disease: Proceedings of the International Symposium on Tirrenia, June, 1974. Ed. by A. Bertelli. 300p. 1975. 54.50 (*3-8055-2118-9*) S Karger.

New Trends in Theoretical & Experimental Nuclear Physics: Predeal International Summer School. A. A. Raduta et al. 600p. 1992. text 106.00 (*981-02-0906-1*) World Scientific Pub.

New Trends in Tractor & Farm Machinery. LC 97-67966. 81p. 1997. pap. 44.00 (*0-7680-0056-4*) Soc Auto Engineers.

New Trends in Ulcer Disease. F. Di Mario et al. 314p. 1988. text 40.00 (*1-57235-018-0*) Piccin Nuova.

New Trends in Ulcer Disease. F. Di Mario et al. (Advances in Gastroenterology Ser.: Vol. 2). (Illus.). 314p. 1988. text 44.00 (*88-299-0633-6*, Pub. by Piccin Nuova) Gordon & Breach.

New Trends in Urinary Tract Infections. Ed. by H. C. Neu & J. D. Williams. (Illus.). x, 358p. 1988. 214.00 (*3-8055-4637-8*) S Karger.

New Trends in Youth Organizations: A Comparative Survey. UNESCO Staff. (Education Studies & Documents: No. 35). 1974. reprint ed. pap. 25.00 (*0-8115-1359-9*) Periodicals Srv.

New Tribalism. rev. ed. Intro. by Donald E. Hardy. (Tattootime Ser.). (Illus.). 64p. (Orig.). 1988. pap. text 10.00 (*0-945367-02-3*) Hardy Marks Pubns.

New Tribalisms: The Resurgence of Race & Ethnicity. Michael W. Hughey. LC 97-39574. (Main Trends of the Modern World Ser.). 320p. 1998. text 55.00 (*0-8147-3540-1*); pap. text 18.50 (*0-8147-3541-X*) NYU Pr.

New Tricks. Vivienne Joseph. LC 93-9286. (Illus.). (J). 1994. write for info. (*0-383-03704-2*) SRA McGraw.

New Tricks I Can Do! Robert Lopshire. LC 95-36104. (Illus.). (J). 1996. lib. bdg. 11.99 (*0-679-97715-5*) Beginner.

New Tricks I Can Do! Robert Lopshire. (Illus.). (J). (ps-2). 1996. 7.99 (*0-679-87715-0*, Pub. by Random Bks Yng Read) Random.

New Tripoli. Ethel Braun. 400p. 1990. 125.00 (*1-85077-147-2*, Pub. by Darf Pubs Ltd) St Mut.

New Trition: How to Achieve Optimum Health. George E. Meinig. (Illus.). 326p. (Orig.). 1988. pap. write for info. (*0-945196-08-3*) Bion Pub.

New Trucks: Prices & Reviews Includes: Vans, Pickups & Sport Utilities, Winter 1999. St. Martin's Press Staff. (Edmund's New Trucks: Prices & Reviews Ser.). 576p. 1999. pap. text 8.99 (*0-87759-644-1*) Edmund Pubns.

New Trucks: Vans, Pickups & Sport Utilities. Consumer Information Express Staff. (Edmunds New Trucks Ser.). 1998. pap. text 8.99 (*0-87759-630-1*) Edmund Pubns.

New Trucks for Greater Productivity & Less Road Wear: An Evaluation of the Turner Proposal. (Special Reports: No. 227). 234p. 1990. 21.00 (*0-309-04963-6*) Transport Res Bd.

New Trucks Prices & Reviews: American & Import. Edmunds Publications Staff. 1998. pap. text 8.99 (*0-87759-626-3*) Edmund Pubns.

***New Trucks Prices & Reviews: Includes: Vans, Pickups & Sport Utilities.** Edmunds Publications Staff. (Prices & Reviews Ser.). 592p. 1999. pap. 8.99 (*0-87759-635-2*) Edmund Pubns.

***New Trucks Prices & Reviews: Includes: Vans, Pickups & Sport Utilities, 2000.** Edmunds Staff. (Edmund's New Trucks: Prices & Reviews Ser.). 1999. pap. 8.99 (*0-87759-651-4*) Edmund Pubns.

New Truth about Learning Disabilities. Susan Du Plessis. Ed. by Robert J. Heller. (Illus.). 160p. (Orig.). 1997. pap. 12.95 (*0-9657005-1-8*) Bobrich Pub.

New Tug-of-War: Congress, the Executive Branch, & National Security. Jeremy D. Rosner. LC 95-17583. 117p. 1995. pap. 10.95 (*0-87003-062-0*) Carnegie Endow.

New Turing Omnibus: Sixty-Six Excursions in Computer Science. A. K. Dewdney. LC 93-17330. 458p. (C). 1993. pap. text 24.95 (*0-7167-8271-5*) W H Freeman.

New Turnaround. Leonard Bertain. 196p. 1993. 30.00 (*0-88427-096-3*) North River.

New Twilight Zone. Ed. by Martin H. Greenberg. 296p. 1996. 7.98 (*1-56731-083-4*, MJF Bks) Fine Comms.

New Twilight Zone: Original Stories. Ed. by Martin H. Greenberg. 304p. (Orig.). 1991. pap. 10.00 (*0-380-75926-8*, Avon Bks) Morrow Avon.

New Twist: Developing Arithmetic Skills Through Problem Solving. Jean J. Pedersen. 1979. text 16.00 (*0-201-05712-3*) Addison-Wesley.

New Twist on Tatting. Co-Edition Staff. 1999. write for info. (*0-8069-8145-8*) Sterling.

New Twist on Tatting: More Than One Hundred Glorious Designs. Catherine Austin. (Illus.). 144p. 1994. pap. 14.95 (*0-8069-0290-6*, Chapelle) Sterling.

New Twist on Triangles. Mary Sue Suit. LC 98-49820. (Illus.). 96p. 1999. 25.95 (*1-56477-247-0*, B372) Martingale & Co.

New Types of Cardiovascular Diseases: Topics in Clinical Cardiology. Ed. by J. Willis Hurst. LC 93-11899. (Illus.). 312p. 1994. 69.50 (*0-89640-245-2*) Igaku-Shoin.

New Types of Metal Powders: Proceedings of a Symposium, Cleveland, Ohio, October 24, 1963. Ed. by Henry H. Hausner. LC 64-18802. (Metallurgical Society Conference Ser.: Vol. 23). 177p. reprint ed. pap. 54.90 (*0-608-11215-1*, 200151100079) Bks Demand.

***New Types of Persistent Halogenated Compounds.** Ed. by J. Paasivirta. (Handbook of Environmental Chemistry Ser.: Vol. 3, Pt. K). (Illus.). 336p. 2000. 175.00 (*3-540-65838-6*) Spr-Verlag.

New Typographic Logo. Gerry Rosentsweig. LC 96-76801. (Illus.). 176p. 1996. 37.50 (*0-942604-55-5*) Madison Square.

New Typographics, Vol. 2. Pie Books Editorial Staff. 59.95 (*4-89444-056-3*, Pub. by Pie Bks) Bks Nippan.

New Typography. Jan Tschichold. (Weimar & Now: German Cultural Criticism Ser.: Vol. 8). 270p. 1995. 50.00 (*0-520-07146-8*, Pub. by U CA Pr) Cal Prin Full Svc.

New Typography: A Handbook for Modern Designers. Jan Tschichold. 280p. 1998. pap. 24.95 (*0-520-07147-6*, Pub. by U CA Pr) Cal Prin Full Svc.

New Tyrolean Architecture. Liesbeth Waechter-Bohm. 1998. pap. 55.00 (*3-211-83128-2*) Spr-Verlag.

New U. K. Securities Legislation & the E. C. 1992 Program. J. H. Dalhuisen. (Verhandelingen der Koninklijke Nederlandse Akademie van Wetenschappen, Afd. Letterkunde, Nieuwe Reeks Ser.: No. 142). viii, 158p. 1989. pap. text 47.00 (*0-444-85709-5*) Elsevier.

New U. S. Farm Policy for Changing World Food Needs. Committee for Economic Development. LC 74-84123. 1974. pap. 2.00 (*0-87186-056-2*) Comm Econ Dev.

New U. S. Strategic Debate. Ronald D. Asmus. 120p. 1994. pap. 15.00 (*0-8330-1537-0*, MR-240-1-A) Rand Corp.

New Ulm, Minnesota: J. H. Strasser's 1892 History of a German-American Settlement. Ed. by Don H. Tolzmann & Frederic R. Steinhauser. LC 97-216911. (Illus.). 80p. 1997. pap. 9.00 (*1-880788-09-8*) NCSA Lit.

New Ultra Cool Parents Guide to All of New York: Excursions & Activities in & Around Our City That Your Children Will Love & You Won't Think Are Too Bad Either. 2nd rev. ed. Alfred Gingold & Helen Rogan. LC 98-30503. Orig. Title: The Cool Parents Guide to All of New York. 144p. 1996. pap. 14.95 (*1-885492-76-6*) City & Co.

New Unblocked Manager: A Practical Guide to Self-Development. rev. ed. Dave Francis & Mike Woodcock. LC 95-40203. 200p. 1996. 61.95 (*0-566-07639-X*, Pub. by Gower); pap. 29.95 (*0-566-07705-1*, Pub. by Gower) Ashgate Pub Co.

New Understanding of Parent Involvement: Family - Work - School, Conference Proceedings. Ed. by Peter J. Cookson, Jr. et al. 91p. (Orig.). (C). 1997. pap. text 30.00 (*0-7881-4569-X*) DIANE Pub.

New Unemployed: Joblessness & Poverty in the Market Economy. Ed. by Frank Gaffikin & Mike Morrissey. 256p. (C). 1992. text 59.95 (*1-85649-067-X*, Pub. by Zed Books); text 22.50 (*1-85649-068-8*, Pub. by Zed Books) St Martin.

New Unger's Bible Dictionary. Cyril J. Barber et al. Ed. by R. K. Harrison. (Illus.). 1416p. 39.99 (*0-8024-9037-9*, 228) Moody.

New Unger's Bible Handbook see Nuevo Manual Biblico de Unger

New Unger's Bible Handbook. rev. ed. Merrill F. Unger. (Illus.). 34.99 (*0-8024-9049-2*, 229) Moody.

New Unger's Bible Handbook: Student Edition. Merrill Unger. 352p. 1998. student ed. 14.99 (*0-8024-6332-0*) Moody.

New Unified Performance Graphs & Comparisons for Streamlined Human Powered Vehicles. Douglas J. Malewicki. 20p. 1983. 3.50 (*0-912468-29-7*) CA Rocketry.

New Unionism: Employee Involvement in the Changing Corporation. Charles C. Heckscher. (ILR Press Book). 360p. 1996. pap. text 17.95 (*0-8014-8357-3*) Cornell U Pr.

New Unionism in the New Society: Public Sector Unions in the Redistributive State. Leo Troy. LC 94-2667. 236p. 1994. 46.00 (*0-913969-69-9*) Univ Pub Assocs.

New United States Immigration Law: How to Avoid Getting into Trouble with U. S. I. N. S. Paul Kimani. Ed. by Jane Kimani. 170p. (Orig.). 1997. pap. 14.95 (*0-9657641-0-9*) Wambui Pub.

New Universal Garzanti Encyclopedia (La Nuova Enciclopedia Universale Garzanti) Garzanti. (ITA.). 1525p. 1982. pap. 49.95 (*0-8288-1986-6*, M14444) Fr & Eur.

***New Universe.** Robert Houston. LC 99-36492. 1999. pap. 28.00 (*1-57733-057-9*) B Dolphin Pub.

New Universities & Regional Context: Papers from an International Seminar. Ed. by Urban Dahllof & Staffan Selander. 291p. (Orig.). 1994. pap. 62.50 (*91-554-3337-5*) Coronet Bks.

New Universities Overseas. Alexander M. Carr-Saunders. LC 77-7518. (Illus.). 1977. reprint ed. lib. bdg. 69.50 (*0-8371-9665-5*, CSNU, Greenwood Pr) Greenwood.

New Untouchables: How America Sanctions Police Violence. John Desantis. LC 94-18643. 288p. 1994. 22.95 (*1-879360-31-4*) Noble Pr.

***New Upholstery: Step-by-Step Solutions for Creating Fresh & Modern Furnishings.** Diane Wallis. LC 98-3897. (Illus.). 176p. 1998. 17.98 (*0-7651-0834-8*) Smithmark.

New Uprooted: Single Mothers in Urban Life. Elizabeth A. Mulroy. LC 95-2084. 206p. 1995. 59.95 (*0-86569-038-3*, Auburn Hse); pap. 18.95 (*0-86569-039-1*, Auburn Hse) Greenwood.

New Urban America: Growth & Politics in Sunbelt Cities. rev. ed. Carl Abbott. LC 86-40490. (Illus.). 350p. 1987. reprint ed. pap. 108.50 (*0-7837-9018-X*, 204977000003) Bks Demand.

New Urban Environments: British Architecture & Its European Context. Ed. by Peter Murray & MaryAnne Stevens. LC 98-181768. (Illus.). 192p. 1998. 65.00 (*3-7913-1937-X*) te Neues.

New Urban Frontier: Gentrification & the Revanchist City. Neil Smith. (Illus.). 288p. (C). 1996. 85.00 (*0-415-13254-1*); pap. 24.99 (*0-415-13255-X*) Routledge.

New Urban Frontier: Urbanization & City Building in Australasia & the American West. Lionel Frost. 1991. pap. 24.95 (*0-86840-268-0*, Pub. by New South Wales Univ Pr) Intl Spec Bk.

New Urban Housing: Fresh Thinking from the Pittsburgh Design Competition. Community Design Center of Pittsburgh, Inc. Staff. (Illus.). 72p. 1994. pap. 21.95 (*0-9641302-0-3*) Comm Design.

New Urban Infrastructure: Cities & Telecommunications. Ed. by Jurgen Schmandt et al. LC 89-72101. 344p. 1990. 65.00 (*0-275-93591-4*, C3591, Praeger Pubs) Greenwood.

New Urban Landscape. Ed. by Richard Martin. LC 89-63218. (Illus.). 132p. 1990. pap. 29.95 (*0-9624916-0-8*) Drenttel Doyle.

***New Urban Leadership.** Joyce A. Ladner. 2000. 22.95 (*0-8157-5108-7*) Brookings.

New Urban Paradigm: Critical Perspectives on the City. Joe R. Feagin. LC 97-26345. 356p. 1997. pap. 24.95 (*0-8476-8499-7*); text 63.00 (*0-8476-8498-9*) Rowman.

New Urban Reality. Ed. by Paul E. Peterson. LC 84-45848. 301p. 1985. 36.95 (*0-8157-7018-9*); pap. 16.95 (*0-8157-7017-0*) Brookings.

New Urban Sociology. Mark Gottdiener. LC 93-23576. (C). 1993. text 53.25 (*0-07-023912-6*) McGraw.

New Urban Studies Literature: A Review with Special Reference to Australia. M. Huxley & J. B. McLoughlin. 86p. 1985. pap. 22.00 (*0-08-033668-X*, K120, Pub. by PPL) Elsevier.

New Urbanism: Hope or Hype for American Communities? William Fulton. 32p. 1996. pap. 14.00 (*1-55844-129-8*) Lincoln Inst Land.

New Urbanism: Toward an Architecture of Community. P. Katz. LC 92-47474. (Illus.). 288p. 1992. 49.95 (*0-07-033889-2*) McGraw.

***New Urbanisms: Mostar, Bosnia & Herzegovina** Richard Plunz. LC 98-73349. (MSAUD New Urbanisms Ser.). 83p. 1998. write for info. (*1-883584-13-2*) CUGSA.

New, Used & Improved: Art in 80's. Peter Frank & Michael McKenzie. LC 86-32273. (Illus.). 160p. 1987. 39.95 (*0-89659-650-8*) Abbeville Pr.

New User's Guide to the Sun Workstation. Michael Russo. 203p. 1990. 53.95 (*0-387-97249-8*) Spr-Verlag.

New Uses for New Phylogenies. Ed. by Paul H. Harvey et al. (Illus.). 368p. 1996. 70.00 (*0-19-854985-7*); pap. text 35.00 (*0-19-854984-9*) OUP.

New Uses for Obsolete Buildings. Urban Land Institute Staff et al. LC 96-61393. 178p. 1996. pap. 64.95 (*0-87420-802-5*, N03) Urban Land.

New Uses of Sulfur: A Symposium Sponsored by the Division of Industrial & Engineering Chemistry at the 167th Meeting of the American Chemical Society, Los Angeles, CA, April 2-3, 1974. Ed. by James R. West. LC 75-14440. (Advances in Chemistry Ser.: No. 140). (Illus.). 246p. 1975. reprint ed. pap. 76.30 (*0-608-06739-3*, 206693600009) Bks Demand.

New Uses of Sulfur II. Ed. by Douglas J. Bourne. LC 78-1004. (Advances in Chemistry Ser.: No. 165). 1978. 32.95 (*0-8412-0391-1*) Am Chemical.

New Uses of Sulfur II: A Symposium. Douglas J. Bourne. LC 78-1004. (Advances in Chemistry Ser.: No. 165). (Illus.). 293p. 1978. reprint ed. pap. 90.90 (*0-608-04357-5*, 206513800001) Bks Demand.

New Uses of Systems Theory in Archaeology. Ed. by E. Gary Stickel & Thomas C. Blackburn. LC 82-13811. (Anthropological Papers: No. 24). (Illus.). 104p. 1982. pap. 9.95 (*0-87919-096-5*) Ballena Pr.

New Utah's Heritage. rev. ed. S. George Ellsworth. LC 84-14043. (Illus.). 392p. 1992. text 21.95 (*0-87905-475-1*) Gibbs Smith Pub.

New Utopians: A Study of System Design & Social Change. enl. ed. Robert Boguslaw. LC 80-18602. 1981. pap. text 17.95 (*0-8290-0115-8*) Irvington.

New Vaccine Development - Establishing Priorities Vol. 2: Diseases of Importance in Developing Countries. Institute of Medicine Staff. 432p. 1986. pap. text 43.50 (*0-309-03679-8*) Natl Acad Pr.

New Vaccine for Child Safety. Murl Harmon. LC 76-8726. (Illus.). 1976. pap. 7.50 (*0-917066-00-6*) Safety Now.

New Vade Mecum: Or a Pocket Companion for Lawyers, Deputy Sheriffs & Constables; Suggesting Many Grievous Abuses & Alarming Evils, Which Attend the Present Mode of Administering the Laws of New Hampshire: Together with the Most Obvious Means of Redressing & Removing Them. Publicola Staff. LC 94-26147. xv, 155p. 1995. reprint ed. 42.50 (*0-8377-2551-8*, Rothman) W S Hein.

New Valaam at Monks' Lagoon: On St. Herman's Spruce Island. St. Herman of Alaska Brotherhood Staff. LC 97-61962. (American Paradise Ser.: Vol. IV). (Illus.). 176p. 1997. pap. 10.00 (*1-887904-01-8*) St Herman Pr.

***New Vampire Miyu: The Shinma Menace.** Toshihiro Kirano. Ed. by Stephen R. Bennett. Tr. by Kuni Kimura from JPN. (Illus.). 224p. 1999. pap. 17.95 (*1-929090-08-0*, GNM01) Studio Ironcat.

***New Vampire Miyu Vol. 2: The Western Shinma Strike Back.** Toshihiro Hirano. Ed. by Stephen R. Bennett. Tr. by Sachiko Uchida from JPN. (Illus.). 196p. 2000. 17.95 (*1-929090-04-8*, GNM02) Studio Ironcat.

New Varieties to Know & Grow, 1998 Edition. Sara Rowekamp. (Illus.). 96p. 1998. pap. write for info. (*0-9662978-0-6*) Oak Leaf Pubns.

New Variorum Edition of Shakespeare. William Shakespeare. (BCL1-PR English Literature Ser.). 1992. reprint ed. lib. bdg. 75.00 (*0-7812-7268-8*) Rprt Serv.

New Variorum Edition of Shakespeare, 27 vols., Set. William Shakespeare. Incl. As You Like It. 500p. 1999. reprint ed. lib. bdg. 98.00 (*1-58201-289-X*); King Lear. 500p. 1999. reprint ed. lib. bdg. 98.00 (*1-58201-286-5*); Life & Death of King John. 500p. 1999. reprint ed. lib. bdg. 98.00 (*1-58201-300-4*); Life & Death of King Richard II. 500p. 1999. reprint ed. lib. bdg. 98.00 (*1-58201-308-X*); Life & Death of King Richard II. 500p. 1999. reprint ed. lib. bdg. 98.00 (*1-58201-306-3*); Love's Labour's Lost. 500p. 1999. reprint ed. lib. bdg. 98.00 (*1-58201-295-4*); Macbeth. 500p. 1999. reprint ed. lib. bdg. 98.00 (*1-58201-283-0*); Merchant of Venice. 500p. 1999. reprint ed. lib. bdg. 98.00 (*1-58201-288-1*); Midsommer Nights Dreame. 500p. 1999. reprint ed. lib. bdg. 98.00 (*1-58201-291-1*); Much Ado about Nothing. 500p. 1999. reprint ed. lib. bdg. 98.00 (*1-58201-293-8*); Othello. 500p. 1999. reprint ed. lib. bdg. 98.00 (*1-58201-287-3*); Romeo & Juliet. 500p. 1999. reprint ed. lib. bdg. 98.00 (*1-58201-282-2*); Sonnets. 500p. 1999. reprint ed. lib. bdg. 98.00 (*1-58201-305-5*); Tempest. 1999. reprint ed. 98.00 (*1-58201-290-3*); Tragedie of Anthonie & Cleopatra. 500p. 1999. reprint ed. lib. bdg. 98.00 (*1-58201-296-2*); Tragedie of Coriolanus. 500p. 1999. reprint ed. lib. bdg. 98.00 (*1-58201-301-2*); Tragedie of Cymbeline. 500p. 1999. reprint ed. lib. bdg. 98.00 (*1-58201-299-7*); Tragedie of Julius Caesar. 500p. 1999. reprint ed. lib. bdg. 98.00 (*1-58201-298-9*); Tragedy of Richard the Third with the Landing of Earle Richmond & the Battell at Bosworth Field. 500p. 1999. reprint ed. lib. bdg. 98.00 (*1-58201-297-0*); Troilus & Cressida. 500p. 1999. reprint ed. lib. bdg. 98.00 (*1-58201-307-1*); Twelfth Night: or What You Will. 500p. 1999. reprint ed. lib. bdg. 98.00 (*1-58201-294-6*); Winter's Tale. 500p. 1999. reprint ed. lib. bdg. 98.00 (*1-58201-292-X*); Pt. 1. Hamlet. 500p. 1999. reprint ed. lib. bdg. 98.00 (*1-58201-284-9*); Pt. 1. Henry IV. 500p. 1999. reprint ed. lib. bdg. 98.00 (*1-58201-302-0*); Pt. 2. Hamlet. 500p. 1999. reprint ed. lib. bdg. 98.00 (*1-58201-285-7*); Pt. 2. Henry IV. 500p. 1999. reprint ed. lib. bdg. 98.00 (*1-58201-303-9*); Pt. 3. Henry IV. 500p. 1999. reprint ed. lib. bdg. 98.00 (*1-58201-304-7*); 1999. reprint ed. Set lib. bdg. 2646.00 (*1-58201-281-4*) Classic Bks.

New Variorum Edition of Shakespeare, Vol. 21, Pt. 1. Henry the Fourth & William Shakespeare. LC PR2753.. 566p. reprint ed. pap. 175.50 (*0-608-14334-0*, 205197600023) Bks Demand.

N

New Vegetables on Your Barbecue. Black. 1995. pap. 6.95 (*0-572-01623-9*, Pub. by Foulsham UK) Assoc Pubs Grp.

New Vegetarian: The Ultimate Guide to Gourmet Cooking & Healthy Living. Colin Spencer. (Illus.). 256p. 1986. pap. 19.95 (*1-55013-379-9*) Firefly Bks Ltd.

New Vegetarian Baby. Christine H. Beard & Sharon Yntema. LC 99-47876. (Orig.). 1999. pap. 15.95 (*0-935526-63-3*) McBooks Pr.

New Vegetarian Cookbook. Gary Null. 250p. 1980. pap. 13.95 (*0-02-010040-X*) Macmillan.

New Vegetarian Cookbook. Gary Null. 1987. pap. 15.95 (*0-02-590890-1*) Macmillan.

New Vegetarian Cookbook. Gary Null. 1998. pap. text 9.99 (*1-57866-014-9*) Promntory Pr.

New Vegetarian Cookbook. Heather Thomas. 144p. 1998. pap. 14.99 (*1-57145-652-X*, Laurel Glen Pub) Advantage Pubs.

New Vegetarian Cuisine: Two Hundred & Fifty Satisfying Recipes for Superior Health. Linda Rosensweig. Ed. by Prevention Magazine Food Editors. LC 93-17792. 376p. 1993. 26.95 (*0-87596-168-1*) Rodale Pr Inc.

New Vegetarian Cuisine: Two Hundred & Fifty Satisfying Recipes for Superior Health. Linda Rosensweig. LC 93-17792. (Illus.). 376p. 1996. pap. 14.95 (*0-87596-314-5*) Rodale Pr Inc.

New Vegetarian Epicure: Plain & Fancy Menus for Family & Friends. Anna Thomas. (Illus.). 448p. 1996. pap. 19.00 (*0-679-76588-3*) Knopf.

New Vegetarian Gourmet. Byron Ayanoglu. (Illus.). 192p. (Orig.). 1996. pap. 17.95 (*1-896503-26-8*, Pub. by R Rose Inc) Firefly Bks Ltd.

New Vegetarian Gourmet Recipes. Jean Conil. 96p. (Orig.). 1995. pap. 6.95 (*0-572-01852-5*, Pub. by Foulsham UK) Assoc Pubs Grp.

New Vegetarian Tofu Recipes. Christopher Conil. 128p. 1995. pap. 5.95 (*0-572-01727-8*, Pub. by Foulsham UK) Assoc Pubs Grp.

New Vegetarians. Rynn Berry. (Illus.). 192p. 1989. pap. 10.95 (*0-9626169-0-7*) Pythago Bks.

New Vegetative Approaches to Soil & Moisture Conservation. Montague Yudelman et al. LC 90-40382. (Illus.). 56p. 1990. reprint ed. pap. 30.00 (*0-608-04187-4*, 206492200011) Bks Demand.

New Vehicle Comparison & Pricing Guide: A VMR Standard Auto Guide. (VMR Standard Auto Guides Ser.). 1998. pap. 6.99 (*1-883899-28-1*) VMR Intl.

***New Vehicle Comparison & Pricing Guide: Covers All 1998 Cars & Trucks.** V. M. R. International, Inc. Staff. 1998. pap. text 6.99 (*1-883899-27-3*) VMR Intl.

New Venture. Reginald Wallis. 32p. (J). (gr. 3-7). 1935. pap. 0.85 (*0-87213-914-X*) Loizeaux.

***New Venture Adventure: Succeed with Professional Business Planning.** Ueli Looser & Bruna Schlapfer. 240p. 2001. 29.95 (*1-58799-003-2*) Texere.

New Venture Creation: Entrepreneurship for the 21st Century. 4th rev. ed. Jeffry A. Timmons. (C). 1995. text 57.25 (*0-256-19348-7*, Irwn McGrw-H) McGraw-H Hghr Educ.

New Venture Creation: Entrepreneurship for the 21st Century. 5th ed. Jeffry A. Timmons. LC 98-43156. 1998. write for info. (*0-256-19756-3*) Irwinton.
New Venture Experience. Karl H. Vesper. (Illus.). 800p. (C). 1993. text 54.95 (*1-884021-00-X*) Vector Bks.
New Venture Experience. rev. ed. Karl H. Vesper. (Illus.). 811p. (C). 1995. text 64.95 (*1-884021-25-5*) Vector Bks.
New Venture Financial Planning Kit: A Planning Tool for Entrepreneurs & Their Advisors. T. Jefferson Straus. 25p. 1996. ring bd. 4.95 (*0-9651660-1-5*) Profit Mgnt.
New Venture Formations in United States Manufacturing: The Role of Industry Environments. Thomas J. Dean. LC 95-38868. (Studies in Entrepreneurship). (Illus.). 216p. 1995. text 20.00 (*0-8153-2128-7*) Garland.
New Venture Handbook: Everything You Need to Know to Start & Run Your Own Business. Ronald E. Merrill & Henry D. Sedgwick. LC 86-47818. 366p. reprint ed. pap. 113.50 (*0-7837-4237-1*, 204392600012) Bks Demand.
New Venture Mechanics. Karl H. Vesper. 400p. 1992. pap. text 54.00 (*0-13-620790-1*) P-H.
New Venture Strategies. Karl H. Vesper. 1980. 22.95 (*0-13-615948-6*) P-H.
New Venture Strategies. rev. ed. Karl H. Vesper. 530p. 1989. pap. text 47.00 (*0-13-615907-9*) P-H.
New Venture Strategy: Timing, Enviromental Uncertainty & Performance. Dean A. Shepherd & Mark Shanley. LC 98-25305. (Entrepreneurship & the Management of Growing Enterprises Ser.). 112p. 1998. 54.95 (*0-7619-1353-X*); pap. 25.95 (*0-7619-1354-8*) Sage.
New Venturers. John W. Wilson. LC 85-755. 1985. 17.95 (*0-201-09681-1*) Addison-Wesley.
New Versions of Victims: Feminists Struggle with the Concept. Sharon Lamb. LC 99-17521. 1999. pap. text 18.50 (*0-8147-5153-9*) NYU Pr.
New Versions of Victims: Feminists Struggle with the Concept. Ed. by Sharon Lamb. LC 99-17521. 192p. 1999. text 55.00 (*0-8147-5152-0*) NYU Pr.
New Vice Presidency for a New Century. Richard D. MacCann. LC 91-76548. (Illus.). vi, 90p. (Orig.). 1991. pap. write for info. (*0-934570-01-9*) Image & Idea.
New Vico Studies, No. 2. Ed. by Giorgio Tagliacozzo & Donald Phillip Verene. 178p. 1985. pap. 15.00 (*0-391-03675-0*) Humanities.
New Vico Studies, Vol. 1. Ed. by Giorgio Tagliacozzo & Donald Phillip Verene. 138p. 1983. pap. 12.50 (*0-391-03674-2*) Humanities.
New Vico Studies, Vol. 15. Ed. by Donald Phillip Verene. 128p. 1997. pap. 42.95 (*0-391-04073-1*) Humanities.
New Vico Studies, 1989, Vol. 7. Ed. by Giorgio Tagliacozzo & Donald Phillip Verene. 232p. 1990. pap. 39.95 (*0-391-03680-7*) Humanities.
New Vico Studies, 1986, Vol. 4. Ed. by Giorgio Tagliacozzo & Donald Phillip Verene. 224p. 1988. pap. 25.00 (*0-391-03677-7*) Humanities.
New Vico Studies, 1990, Vol. 8. Ed. by Giorgio Tagliacozzo & Donald Phillip Verene. 212p. 1991. pap. 39.95 (*0-391-03697-1*) Humanities.
New Vico Studies, 1995, Vol. 3. Giorgio Tagliacozzo. (C). 1996. pap. 39.95 (*0-391-03903-2*) Humanities.
New Vico Studies, 1991, Vol. 9. Ed. by Giorgio Tagliacozzo & Donald Phillip Verene. 200p. (C). 1992. pap. 39.95 (*0-391-03746-3*) Humanities.
New Vico Studies, 1996, Vol. 14. Giorgio Tagliacozzo. (C). 1997. pap. 39.95 (*0-391-03972-5*) Humanities.
New Vico Studies, 1992, Vol. 10. Ed. by Giorgio Tagliacozzo & Donald Phillip Verene. 192p. (C). 1993. pap. 39.95 (*0-391-03778-1*) Humanities.
New Vico Studies, 1992, Vol. 11. Ed. by Giorgio Tagliacozzo & Donald Phillip Verene. 192p. 1993. pap. 39.95 (*0-391-03833-8*) Humanities.
New Victorians: A Young Woman's Challenge to the Old Feminist Order. Rene Denfeld. 352p. 1995. 21.95 (*0-446-51752-6*) Warner Bks.
New Video Encyclopedia. Larry Langman & Joseph Molinari. LC 90-3605. (Illus.). 328p. 1990. text 15.00 (*0-8240-8244-3*, H1221) Garland.
***New Videomaker Handbook.** Ed. by Videomaker Magazine Editors. (Illus.). 352p. 2001. pap. 24.95 (*0-240-80435-X*, Focal) Buttrwrth-Heinemann.
New View Almanac: The First All-Visual Resource of Vital Facts & Statistics: The Only Almanac You Will Ever Need for the Millennium. rev. ed. Jenny Tesar. Ed. by Bruce Glassman. (Illus.). 608p. (J). (gr. 5 up). 1999. lib. bdg. 34.95 (*1-56711-150-5*) Blackbirch.
New View from the Castle: The Smithsonian's Museum & Garden Complex on the National Mall. Edwards Park & Jean Paul Carlhian. LC 87-42555. (Illus.). 160p. (C). 1987. pap. 15.95 (*0-87474-749-X*) Smithsonian.
New View of a Woman's Body. Federation of Feminist Women's Health Centers Staf. (Illus.). 176p. 1991. reprint ed. pap. 19.95 (*0-9629945-0-2*) Feminist Hlth.
New View of Chaucer. George G. Williams. LC 64-8173. 217p. reprint ed. pap. 67.30 (*0-608-15050-9*, 202621800048) Bks Demand.
New View of Comparative Economy. Kennett. (C). 1999. text 65.50 (*0-03-018959-4*) Harcourt Coll Pubs.
New View of Economic Growth. Maurice F. Scott. (Illus.). 642p. 1991. reprint ed. pap. text 45.00 (*0-19-828742-9*) OUP.
New View of Insanity: The Duality of the Mind Proved by the Structure, Functions, & Diseases of the Brain, & by the Phenomena of Mental Derangement. Arthur L. Wigan. LC 78-72829. (Brainedness, Handedness, & Mental Abilities Ser.). reprint ed. 37.50 (*0-404-60897-3*) AMS Pr.
***New View of Self: How Genes & Neurotrasnmitters Shape Your Mind, Your Personality, & Your Mental Health.** Larry J. Siever & William Frucht. 257p. 1999. reprint ed. text 25.00 (*0-7881-6483-X*) DIANE Pub.
New View of Society, 1816. Robert Owen. Ed. & Intro. by Jeffrey Stern. (Classics in Education Ser.). 184p. 1996. reprint ed. 75.00 (*1-85506-300-X*) Bks Intl VA.
New View of Society. Robert Owen. LC 70-134407. reprint ed. 36.00 (*0-404-08453-2*) AMS Pr.
New View of Society. Robert Owen. LC 91-31814. 194p. 1991. reprint ed. 48.00 (*1-85477-077-2*) Continuum.
New View of the World: A Handbook to World Map: Peters Projection. Ward L. Kaiser. 44p. (Orig.). 1987. pap. 7.00 (*0-377-00175-9*) Friendship Pr.
New View of Two Carmona Ivories. Vivian A. Hibbs. (Illus.). 62p. 1979. reprint ed. 3.00 (*0-87535-139-5*) Hispanic Soc.
New View of You. LaSalle R. Vaughn. 72p. 1997. pap. 10.00 (*1-886065-07-1*) N Life Christian.
New View World War II. Gerhard Weinberg. (Illus.). 0.00 (*0-691-03194-0*) Princeton U Pr.
New Viewpoints in American History. Arthur Meier Schlesinger, Jr. (BCL1 - U. S. History Ser.). 299p. 1991. reprint ed. lib. bdg. 79.00 (*0-7812-6025-6*) Rprt Serv.
New Viewpoints in American History. Arthur Meier Schlesinger, Sr. LC 76-49146. 299p. 1977. reprint ed. lib. bdg. 65.00 (*0-8371-9314-1*, SCNV, Greenwood Pr) Greenwood.
New Views of Borderlands History. Ed. by Robert H. Jackson. LC 98-24572. (Illus.). 224p. 1998. pap. 19.95 (*0-8263-1938-6*); lib. bdg. 40.00 (*0-8263-1937-8*) U of NM Pr.
New Views of Christianity, Society, & the Church: The Works of Orestes Augustus Brownson. Orestes A. Brownson. 1989. reprint ed. lib. bdg. 79.00 (*0-7812-2105-6*) Rprt Serv.
New Views of Co-Operation. Ed. by Stephen Yeo. (History Workshop Ser.). 272p. 1989. 57.50 (*0-415-02523-0*) Routledge.
New Views of Mormon History: A Collection of Essays in Honor of Leonard J. Arrington. Ed. by Davis Bitton & Maureen U. Beecher. LC 87-18787. 500p. reprint ed. pap. 155.00 (*0-7837-6871-0*, 204670100003) Bks Demand.
***New Views of the Constitution.** John Taylor. 2000. 35.00 (*0-89526-217-7*) Regnery Pub.
New Views of the Nature of Man. Ed. by John R. Platt. LC 65-24980. 1994. lib. bdg. 10.00 (*0-226-67080-5*) U Ch Pr.
New Views of the Nature of Man. Ed. by John R. Platt. LC 65-24980. (C). 1993. reprint ed. pap. text 1.95 (*0-226-67081-3*, P389) U Ch Pr.
New Views of the Origin of the Tribes & Nations of America. Benjamin S. Barton. (LC History-America-E). 133p. 1999. reprint ed. lib. bdg. 69.00 (*0-7812-4306-8*) Rprt Serv.
New Views on an Old Planet: A History of Global Change. Tjeerd H. Van Andel. (Illus.). 457p. (C). 1994. text 69.95 (*0-521-44243-5*) Cambridge U Pr.
New Views on an Old Planet: A History of Global Change. Tjeerd H. Van Andel. (Illus.). 457p. (C). 1994. pap. text 29.95 (*0-521-44755-0*) Cambridge U Pr.
New Views on Chaucer: Essays in Generative Criticism. Ed. by William C. Johnson, Jr. & Loren C. Gruber. 1973. pap. 2.50 (*0-9502699-6-4*) Soc New Lang Study.
New Villagers: Urban Pressure on Rural Areas in Worchester. Ed. by Elizabeth Radford. (Illus.). 76p. 1970. 25.00 (*0-7146-1585-4*, Pub. by F Cass Pubs) Intl Spec Bk.
New Villages: Case Studies Christiania, Copenhagen. Carl Bray. (C). 1981. 29.00 (*0-7855-3864-X*, Pub. by Oxford Polytechnic) St Mut.
New Villages: Case Studies New Ash Green, Kent. Carl Bray. (C). 1981. 29.00 (*0-7855-3866-6*, Pub. by Oxford Polytechnic) St Mut.
New Villages: Case Studies South Woodham Ferrers, Essex. Carl Bray. (C). 1981. 35.00 (*0-7855-3865-8*, Pub. by Oxford Polytechnic) St Mut.
New Villeneuve: The Life of Jacques Villeneuve. Timothy Collings. LC 97-10909. (Illus.). 200p. 1997. 24.95 (*0-7603-0411-4*) MBI Pubg.
***New Virgin Book of Baby Names.** Emily Wood. 320p. 2000. mass mkt. 7.95 (*0-7535-0406-5*) Virgin Pubng.
New Virginia One-Day Trip Book. Jane Ockershausen. LC 96-26634. 352p. 1996. 14.95 (*1-889324-00-0*, EPM) Howell Pr VA.
New Virginia Review, Vol. 4. Ed. by Dave Smith. 300p. 1986. pap. 13.50 (*0-317-62283-8*) New VA.
New Virginia Review Anthology, Vol. 5. Ed. by David Bradley. 300p. (Orig.). 1987. pap. 13.50 (*0-939233-01-0*) New VA.
New Virginia Review Anthology 4. Ed. by Dave Smith. 300p. 1986. 13.50 (*0-939233-00-2*) New VA.
New Virginia Review Anthology 3. Ed. by Virginius Dabney et al. (Illus.). 304p. (Orig.). 1984. 13.50 (*0-318-01379-7*) New VA.
New Virginia Review Anthology 2. Ed. by Walton Beacham et al. LC 79-644281. (Illus.). 336p. 1981. 13.50 (*0-318-20431-2*) New VA.
***New Virtual Money: Law & Practice.** Olivier Hance et al. LC 99-41162. 500p. 1999. 135.00 (*90-411-9442-8*) Kluwer Law Intl.
New Vision: Photography Between the World Wars, Ford Motor Company Collection at the Metropolitan Museum of Art. Maria Morris Hambourg & Christopher Phillips. (Illus.). 328p. 1989. pap. 45.00 (*0-87099-550-2*, 0-8109-6428-7) Metro Mus Art.
New Vision for Human Resources. Jac Fitz-Enz & Jack J. Phillips. Ed. by Bill Christopher. LC 98-73101. (Management Library: Vol. 19). 96p. 1998. pap. 12.95 (*1-56052-488-X*) Crisp Pubns.
New Vision for Staff Development. Dennis Sparks & Stephanie Hirsh. LC 97-21007. 108p. (Orig.). 1997. pap. 17.95 (*0-87120-283-2*, 197018) ASCD.
New Vision in Poetry. Sirley J. Russell. 45p. 1995. pap. write for info. (*0-9643885-1-0*) Personal Profiles.
New Vision of an Old Cluster: Untangling Coma Berenices Marseille, France, 17-20 June, 1997. Ed. by A. Mazure et al. 250p. 1998. 78.00 (*981-02-3322-1*) World Scientific Pub.
New Vision of Board Leadership: Governing the Community College. John Carver & Miriam Mayhew. 175p. 1994. 35.00 (*1-886237-01-8*) Assn Commun Coll.
New Vision of Israel: The Teachings of Jesus in National Context. Scot McKnight. LC 98-43795. (Studying the Historical Jesus Ser.). 352p. 1999. pap. 21.00 (*0-8028-4212-7*) Eerdmans.
New Vision of Reality. Bede Griffiths. 304p. 1990. pap. 14.95 (*0-87243-180-0*) Templegate.
New Vision of Religious Education: Theory, History, Practice, & Spirituality for DREs, Catechists, & Teachers. Kevin Treston. LC 92-63178. 120p. (Orig.). 1993. pap. 12.95 (*0-89622-558-5*) Twenty-Third.
New Visionaries: Art from Mt. Shasta. Ed. & Compiled by Walter Von Finck. LC 89-85586. (Illus.). 126p. (Orig.). 1989. pap. 29.50 (*0-9623960-8-7*) Lapis Dragon.
New Visions: Tools for Change in Museums. 60p. 1995. ring bd. 60.00 (*0-931201-23-3*) Am Assn Mus.
New Visions for Canadian Business: Strategies for Competing in the Global Economy. Alan M. Rugman & Joseph R. D'Cruz. (Illus.). 48p. (Orig.). (C). 1993. pap. text 25.00 (*1-56806-691-0*) DIANE Pub.
New Visions for Metropolitan America. Anthony Downs. LC 93-47483. (Integrating National Economies: Promise & Pitfalls Ser.). 272p. (Orig.). (C). 1995. 38.95 (*0-8157-1926-4*); pap. 16.95 (*0-8157-1925-6*) Brookings.
New Visions for the Americas: Religious Engagement & Social Transformation. Ed. by David Batstone. LC 93-28257. 280p. 1993. 18.00 (*0-8006-2690-7*) Augsburg Fortress.
New Visions for the Developmental Assessment of Infants & Young Children. Ed. by Samuel J. Meisels & Emily Fenichel. 408p. (Orig.). 1996. pap. 35.00 (*0-943657-35-0*) ZERO TO THREE.
New Visions for the Long Pastorate. Roy M. Oswald et al. LC 83-73205. 111p. (Orig.). 1983. pap. 10.95 (*1-56699-010-6*, AL73) Alban Inst.
New Visions in Asian American Studies: Diversity, Community, Power. Ed. by Franklin Ng et al. LC 93-36427. (Association for Asian American Studies). 296p. (C). 1994. pap. text 30.00 (*0-87422-102-1*) Wash St U Pr.
***New Visions in Celtic Art: The Modern Tradition.** David James. LC 99-208988. 1999. 27.95 (*0-7137-2736-5*) Blandford Pr.
New Visions in Drawing & Painting. Robert Henkes. 80p. 1984. 8.95 (*0-89697-151-1*) Intl Univ Pr.
New Visions, New Perspectives: Voices of Contemporary Australian Women Artists. Anna Voigt. LC 96-205370. (Illus.). 312p. 1996. text 39.00 (*976-8097-92-2*, ECU50, Harwood Acad Pubs) Gordon & Breach.
New Visions of Collaborative Writing. Ed. by Janis Forman. LC 91-29274. 200p. (C). 1991. pap. text 27.50 (*0-86709-295-5*, 0295, Pub. by Boynton Cook Pubs) Heinemann.
New Visions of Isaiah. Ed. by Roy F. Melugin & Marvin A. Sweeney. (JSOT Supplement Ser.: No. 214). 344p. 1996. 90.75 (*1-85075-584-1*, Pub. by Sheffield Acad) CUP Services.
New Vistas, Bk. 1. 2nd ed. H. Douglas Brown. LC 98-14842. 144p. (C). 1998. pap. text 14.60 (*0-13-908195-X*) P-H.
New Vistas, Bk. 4. 2nd ed. Brown. 1998. pap., wbk. ed. 10.27 (*0-13-908328-6*) P-H.
New Vistas: Contemporary American Landscapes. Janice C. Oresman. (Illus.). 55p. (Orig.). 1984. pap. 4.75 (*0-943651-20-4*) Hudson Riv.
New Vistas, Getting Started. H. Douglas Brown. LC 97-44199. 128p. (C). 1998. pap. text 14.00 (*0-13-908351-0*) P-H.
***New Vistas in Aquatic Microbial Ecology: A Tribute to Jurgen Overbeck on Occasion of His 75th Birthday.** Ed. by Karl-Paul Witzel & Tom Berman. (Advances in Limnology Ser.: No. 54). (Illus.). vi, 386p. 1999. pap. 99.00 (*3-510-47056-7*, Pub. by E Schweizerbartsche) Balogh.
New Vistas in Depression. Ed. by S. Z. Langer et al. (Illus.). 339p. 1982. 81.00 (*0-08-027388-2*, Pergamon Pr) Elsevier.
New Vistas in Electro-Nuclear Physics. Ed. by E. L. Tomusiak et al. (NATO ASI Series B, Physics: Vol. 142). 500p. 1986. 125.00 (*0-306-42388-X*, Plenum Trade) Perseus Pubng.
New Vistas in Grammar: Invariance & Variation: Proceedings of the Second International Roman Jakobson Conference, New York University, Nov. 5-8, 1985. Ed. by Linda R. Waugh & Stephen Rudy. LC 91-27655. (Current Issues in Linguistic Theory Ser.: Vol. 49). x, 540p. 1991. 97.00 (*90-272-3543-0*); pap. 34.95 (*90-272-3585-6*) J Benjamins Pubng Co.
New Vistas in Nuclear Dynamics. Ed. by P. J. Brussard & J. H. Koch. (NATO ASI Series B, Physics: Vol. 139). 410p. 1986. 105.00 (*0-306-42371-5*, Plenum Trade) Perseus Pubng.
New Vistas in Parkinson's Disease. Ed. by T. Caraceni et al. (Journal of Neural Transmission: Suppl. 22). (Illus.). 280p. 1986. pap. 68.00 (*0-387-81929-0*) Spr-Verlag.
New Vistas in Physics with High-Energy Pion Beams: Preconference Workshop. J. B. McClelland & B. F. Gibson. 180p. 1993. text 95.00 (*981-02-1275-5*) World Scientific Pub.
New Vistas in Psychology: An Anthroposophical Contribution. Stewart C. Easton. 146p. 1986. pap. 10.95 (*0-85440-454-6*, Pub. by R Steiner Pr) Anthroposophic.
New Vistas in Transatlantic Science & Technology Cooperation. National Research Council Staff. Ed. by Charles W. Wessner. 178p. 1999. pap. 38.00 (*0-309-06197-0*) Natl Acad Pr.
New Vistas Student 2nd ed. Brown. 1999. pap. text 10.95 (*0-13-908237-9*) S&S Trade.
New Vistas Student, 4. 2nd ed. Brown. 1998. pap. 15.33 (*0-13-908310-3*) S&S Trade.
New Vitality in General Education. Task Group on General Education Staff. 61p. (Orig.). (C). 1988. pap. text 10.00 (*0-911696-41-5*) Assn Am Coll.
New Vocabularies in Film Semiotics: Structuralism, Poststructuralism & Beyond. Robert Stam et al. (Sightlines Ser.). 256p. (C). (gr. 13). 1992. pap. 22.99 (*0-415-06595-X*, A7041) Routledge.
New Vocabulary for Governing in the 1990s: A Lexicon for Governors' Policy Advisors. Thomas W. Bonnett. LC 94-43274. 60p. (Orig.). 1995. pap. 8.95 (*0-934842-14-0*) CSPA.
New Vocabulary of Medical Terms (Uj Magyar Orvosi Szotar) J. Brencsan. 544p. 1993. 45.00 (*963-05-6497-1*, Pub. by Akade Kiado) St Mut.
New Vocal Repertory, Vol. 2. Jane Manning. (Illus.). 336p. 1999. text 55.00 (*0-19-879018-X*); pap. text 19.95 (*0-19-879019-8*) OUP.
New Vocal Repertory: An Introduction. Jane Manning. LC 93-30975. (Illus.). 290p. 1994. pap. text 27.95 (*0-19-816413-0*) OUP.
New Voice for a New People: Midwestern Poetry, 1800-1910. Ed. by Bernard F. Engel & Patricia W. Julius. 148p. 1985. pap. text 18.00 (*0-8191-4452-5*); lib. bdg. 43.50 (*0-8191-4451-7*) U Pr of Amer.
New Voice of Old - Five Centuries of Puerto Rican History. Ursula Acosta. (Illus.). 176p. (Orig.). 1987. pap. 9.95 (*0-317-61628-5*) Perm Pr.
New Voice Pedagogy. Marilee David. LC 94-30743. 220p. 1995. 47.50 (*0-8108-2943-6*) Scarecrow.
***New Voices.** Donna Jo Napoli. (Angelwings Ser.: Vol. 12). (Illus.). 80p. (J). (gr. 2-5). 2000. pap. 3.99 (*0-689-83573-6*) Aladdin.
***New Voices.** 5th ed. Pamela Bourgeois. 122p. (C). 1999. per. 19.95 (*0-7872-6424-5*, 41642401) Kendall-Hunt.
New Voices: Contemporary Soviet. Koulaef. (C). 1966. pap. 26.50 (*0-15-504472-9*, Pub. by Harcourt Coll Pubs) Harcourt.
New Voices: Contemporary Soviet Short Stories. Ed. by Kenneth E. Harper et al. (RUS.). 191p. (C). 1966. pap. text 22.00 (*0-15-565727-5*) Harcourt Coll Pubs.
New Voices: Essays from Colorado State University. Ed. by David Milofsky. 165p. (Orig.). (C). 1995. pap. text 10.00 (*1-885635-01-X*) CO St U Ctr Literary.
New Voices: Poetry & Fiction from Colorado State University. Ed. by David Milofsky. 300p. (C). 1994. pap. text 10.00 (*1-885635-00-1*) CO St U Ctr Literary.
New Voices: Self-Advocacy by Persons with Disabilities. Ed. by Gunnar Dybwad & Hank Bersani. 274p. (C). 1996. pap. text 29.95 (*1-57129-004-4*) Brookline Bks.
New Voices: Student Political Activism in the '80s & '90s. Tony Vellela. LC 88-4454. 275p. 1988. 35.00 (*0-89608-342-X*); pap. 12.00 (*0-89608-341-1*) South End Pr.
New Voices Vol. 1: Immigrant Students in U. S. Public Schools. 2nd ed. Joan M. First et al. (Illus.). 176p. 1991. reprint ed. pap. 14.95 (*1-880002-01-9*) Natl Coal Advocates.
New Voices from the Longhouse: An Anthology of Modern Iroquois Literature. Ed. by Joseph Bruchac. 1988. 12.95 (*0-912678-68-2*, Greenfld Rev Pr) Greenfld Rev Lit.
New Voices from West Africa. Ed. by Henry Corder. 1979. 11.00 (*0-686-33149-4*) Arden Assocs.
***New Voices in Irish Criticism.** P. J. Matthews. 272p. 2000. pap. 19.95 (*1-85182-545-2*, Pub. by Four Cts Pr) Intl Spec Bk.
***New Voices in Irish Criticism.** Ed. by P. J. Matthews. 272p. 2000. 35.00 (*1-85182-544-4*, Pub. by Four Cts Pr) Intl Spec Bk.
New Voices in Latin American Literature. Gabriel J. Cairo et al. Ed. & Intro. by Pedro R. Monge-Rafuls. LC 93-85756. (Literature/Conversation Ser.: Vol. III). (ENG & SPA.). 260p. 1993. pap. 17.00 (*0-9625127-0-2*) Ollantay Pr.
New Voices in Native American Literary Criticism. Ed. by Arnold Krupat. LC 92-18673. (Series in Native American Literatures). 704p. 1993. pap. text 34.95 (*1-56098-226-8*) Smithsonian.
New Voices in the Field: The Work Lives of First-Year Assistant Principals. Gary N. Hartzell et al. LC 95-792. 200p. 1995. 55.95 (*0-8039-6190-1*); pap. 24.95 (*0-8039-6191-X*) Corwin Pr.
New Voices in the Nation: Women & the Greek Resistance, 1941-1964. Janet Hart. (Wilder House Ser.). (Illus.). 368p. 1996. text 42.50 (*0-8014-3044-5*); pap. text 17.95 (*0-8014-8219-4*) Cornell U Pr.
New Voices of the Southwest. Hilton R. Greer. 1993. reprint ed. lib. bdg. 75.00 (*0-7812-5932-0*) Rprt Serv.
New Voices 1 from Aunt Lute. DeeAnne Davis et al. LC 95-13818. 152p. (Orig.). 1995. pap. 10.95 (*1-879960-38-9*); lib. bdg. 20.95 (*1-879960-39-7*) Aunt Lute Bks.
New Volunteerism: A Community Connection. Barbara Feinstein & Catherine Cavanaugh. LC 76-7838. 208p. 1978. pap. 13.95 (*0-87073-781-3*) Schenkman Bks Inc.
New Voter's Guide to Practical Politics. League of Women Voters of Cleveland Educational Fu. 61p. (YA). (gr. 7-12). 1982. reprint ed. pap. 2.00 (*1-880746-02-6*) LOWV Cleve Educ.
New Voyage Round the World, by a Course Never Sailed Before. Daniel Defoe. LC 74-13444. (Illus.). reprint ed. write for info. (*0-404-07924-5*) AMS Pr.

N

An Asterisk (*) at the beginning of an entry indicates that the title is appearing for the first time.

New Voyage to Carolina. John Lawson. Ed. by Hugh T. Lefler. LC 67-23498. liv, 305p. 1984. pap. 19.95 (*0-8078-4126-9*) U of NC Pr.

New Voyage to Guinea. William Smith, Jr. 282p. 1967. reprint ed. 39.50 (*0-7146-1018-6*, Pub. by F Cass Pubs) Intl Spec Bk.

New VW Beetle. Matt DeLorenzo. LC 98-30034. 1998. pap. 13.95 (*0-7603-0644-3*) MBI Pubg.

New W. E. T. Workout: Water Exercise Techniques for Strengthening, Toning, & Lifetime Fitness. Jane Katz. LC 95-48450. 224p. 1996. 26.95 (*0-8160-3268-8*) Facts on File.

New W. E. T. Workout: Water Exercise Techniques for Strengthening, Toning, & Lifetime Fitness. Jane Katz. LC 95-48450. (Illus.). 224p. 1996. pap. text 14.95 (*0-8160-3342-0*) Facts on File.

New Walker's Logbook. Mark Fenton. 144p. 1995. pap. 12.95 (*0-9630398-3-0*) Walking.

New Wall Street. Rudolph L. Weissman. LC 75-2684. (Wall Street & the Security Market Ser.). 1975. reprint ed. 28.95 (*0-405-07245-7*) Ayer.

New Wallpaper: Creative Ideas for Decorating Walls, Ceilings & Home Accessories. Liz R. Manning. (Illus.). 160p. 1999. pap. 24.99 (*1-56496-544-9*) Rockport Vitae Pub.

New War. Ed. by Harlequin Books Staff. (Executioner Ser.: Vol. 39). 1989. per. 2.25 (*0-373-15128-4*) Harlequin Bks.

New Washington One-Day Trip Book: One Hundred One Offbeat Excursions in & Around the Nation's Capital. 4th ed. Jane Ockershausen. LC 91-46710. 271p. 1992. pap. 9.95 (*0-939009-59-5*, EPM) Howell Pr VA.

New Water. James Forte. 55p. (Orig.). 1995. pap. 16.00 (*1-889560-10-3*) Wildflower Pub.

New Water. Roy Jacobsen. Tr. by William H. Halverson from NOR. LC 96-71723. 192p. 1997. pap. 18.00 (*0-9645238-1-7*) Peer Gynt.

New Waterfront: A Worldwide Urban Success Story. Ann Breen & Dick Rigby. (Illus.). 224p. 1996. 69.95 (*0-07-007454-2*) McGraw.

New Wave. Acarya T. Avadhuta & Jayanta Kumar. 150p. (Orig.). (C). 1985. pap. text 3.95 (*0-317-93884-3*) Proutist Universal.

New Wave & Human Rights of Constitutional Law Against the Dark Age in America: God's Truth Against the Secular Machine. John-Claude Redfern. LC 87-60754. 82p. (Orig.). (C). 1988. pap. 19.95 (*0-9618238-0-1*) SBCAP.

New Wave in Fashion: Three Japanese Designers. Jean C. Hildreth. (Illus.). 44p. (Orig.). 1983. pap. 12.50 (*0-910407-01-0*) Phoenix Art.

New Wave in Information Technology. Dimitris Chorafas & Heinrich Steimann. (Illus.). 416p. 1996. pap. 37.95 (*0-304-33608-4*) Continuum.

New Wave in Information Technology. N.Dimitris Chorafas & Heinrich Steimann. (Illus.). 416p. 1996. text 90.00 (*0-304-33607-6*) Continuum.

New Wave Media. Wayne F. Kelly & Richard G. Frohnen. 448p. (C). 1996. per. write for info. (*0-697-21946-1*) Brown & Benchmark.

New Wave Millenium, Rural Economies, & Human Rights. John-Claude Redfern. (New Wave Ser.). (Illus.). 93p. 1999. per. 19.95 (*0-9618238-3-6*) SBCAP.

New Wave of the Future: The Sequel. John-Claude Redfern. LC 95-92767. 151p. (Orig.). 1996. spiral bd. 19.95 (*0-9618238-2-8*) SBCAP.

New Wave Pharmaceutical Selling. Vincent F. Peters. Ed. by Carolyn R. Peters. (Illus.). ii, 50p. (Orig.). 1996. pap. 29.95 (*0-9656231-0-6*) Black Dog Pub.

New Wavenumber Calibration Tables from Heterodyne Frequency Measurements. Arthur G. Maki & Joseph S. Wells. (Illus.). 62p. (Orig.). (C). 1992. pap. text 30.00 (*1-56806-136-6*) DIANE Pub.

New Way: A Study in the Rise & Establishment of a Gnostic Society, Vols. 1 & 2. Patrizia Norelli-Bachelet. (Illus.). 601p. (Orig.). 1981. pap. text 36.00 (*0-945747-06-3*) Aeon Bks.

New Way Around an Old World. Francis E. Clark. LC 70-115519. (Russia Observed, Series I). 1970. reprint ed. 23.95 (*0-405-03014-2*) Ayer.

New Way of Eating: The Proper Foods, Combinations, & Recipes to Start You on the Road to Good Health. Marilyn Diamond. 176p. (Orig.). 1987. mass mkt. 8.99 (*0-446-38404-6*, Pub. by Warner Bks) Little.

New Way of Eating from the Fit for Life Kitchen. Marilyn Diamond. 176p. 1993. mass mkt. 5.99 (*0-446-36488-6*, Pub. by Warner Bks) Little.

New Way of Life: A Discipleship Manual for New Christians. Robert L. Brandt. Ed. by Clancy P. Hayes. LC 95-76164. 96p. 1995. pap. text 9.95 (*0-88243-204-4*) Gospel Pub.

New Way of Life: A Discipleship Manual for New Christians. Robert L. Brandt. Ed. by Clancy P. Hayes. LC 95-79773. (Spiritual Discovery Ser.). 96p. (YA). (gr. 9 up). 1995. pap. text, student ed. 4.95 (*0-88243-104-8*) Gospel Pub.

New Way of Living. Larry Kreider. (Biblical Foundation Ser.: Vol. 2). (Illus.). 48p. 1997. pap. 2.95 (*1-886973-01-6*) Dove Chr Fel.

New Way of Manufacturing Bevel & Hypoid Gears in a Continuous Process. Hermann J. Stadtfeld. (Technical Papers: Vol. 96FTM2). (Illus.). 11p. 1996. pap. text 30.00 (*1-55589-669-3*) AGMA.

New Way of the Cross. Renzo Agasso. (Illus.). 1996. pap. 45.00 (*0-85439-487-7*, Pub. by St Paul Pubns) St Mut.

New Way Things Work. David Macaulay. LC 98-14224. (Illus.). 400p. 1998. 35.00 (*0-395-93847-3*) HM.

New Way to Carry out the Increase & Spread of the Church see Nueva Manera de Llevar a Cabo el Aumento y la Extension de la Iglesia

New Way to Fight Child Poverty & Welfare Dependence: The Child Support Assurance System (CSAS) 32p. (Orig.). 1992. pap. text 6.00 (*0-926582-05-4*) NCCP.

New Way to Fly: An Alternative Way to Achieve Freedom from Alcohol & Drugs. Ken Mills. LC 87-60845. 184p. (Orig.). 1987. pap. text 6.95 (*0-942267-00-1*) Profile Press.

New Way to Grow Edible Mushrooms: White Pleurotus. G. M. Ola'h. (Illus.). xii, 92p. 1981. pap. text 15.00 (*2-7637-6963-2*) Lubrecht & Cramer.

***New Way to Learn Astrology: Presenting the Noel Tyl Method.** Basil Fearrington. LC 99-33969. (Illus.). 264p. 1999. pap. 14.95 (*1-56718-739-0*) Llewellyn Pubns.

New Way to Live. Neta Jackson. LC 82-83392. 104p. 1983. pap. 5.99 (*0-8361-3323-4*) Herald Pr.

New Way to Pay Old Debt, a Comedie. Philip Massinger. LC 76-25773. (English Experience Ser.: No. 262). 92p. 1970. reprint ed. 20.00 (*90-221-0262-9*) Walter J Johnson.

New Way to Pay Old Debts. Philip Massinger. (New Mermaids Ser.). (C). 1984. pap. text 9.75 (*0-393-90009-6*) Norton.

New Way to Take Charge of Your Medical Treatment: A Patient's Guide. Barbara Hardt & Katharine R. Halkin. 144p. (Orig.). 1994. pap. 10.95 (*1-56833-034-0*) Madison Bks UPA.

New Ways: Tiltrotor Aircraft & Magnetically Levitated Vehicles. (Illus.). 107p. (Orig.). (C). 1992. pap. text 40.00 (*0-941375-82-X*) DIANE Pub.

New Ways & Means: Reform & Change in a Congressional Committee. Randall Strahan. LC 89-22660. 236p. 1990. reprint ed. pap. 73.20 (*0-608-00201-1*, 206098400006) Bks Demand.

New Ways for Old Jugs: Tradition & Innovation at the Jugtown Pottery. Ed. by Douglas DeNatale et al. LC 94-11701. 1994. pap. write for info. (*0-938983-11-3*) McKissick.

New Ways in Content-Based Instruction. Ed. by Donna M. Brinton & Peter Master. LC 96-61208. 312p. 1997. pap. 25.95 (*0-939791-67-2*) Tchrs Eng Spkrs.

***New Ways in English for Specific Purposes.** Peter A. Master & Donna Brinton. LC 98-60381. (New Ways in Tesol Ser.: 2). 337 p. 1998. 29.95 (*0-939791-49-8*) Tchrs Eng Spkrs.

New Ways in Germanistik. Ed. by Richard Sheppard. LC 89-35881. 336p. 1990. 19.50 (*0-85496-288-3*) Berg Pubs.

New Ways in Psychoanalysis. Karen Horney. 320p. pap. 15.95 (*0-393-31230-5*) Norton.

New Ways in Psychoanalysis. Karen Horney. 1964. pap. 4.95 (*0-393-00132-6*) Norton.

***New Ways in Statistical Methodology: From Significance Tests to Bayesian Inference.** Henry Rouanet et al. LC 98-42942. (European University Studies: Series 6, Vol. 618). xviii, 276p. 1998. 44.95 (*3-906760-68-5*, Pub. by P Lang) P Lang Pubng.

New Ways in Teacher Education. Ed. by Donald Freeman & Steve Cornwell. LC 93-60126. 223p. 1993. pap. 22.95 (*0-939791-46-3*) Tchrs Eng Spkrs.

New Ways in Teaching Adults. Ed. by Marilyn Lewis. LC 96-61905. 266p. 1997. pap. 24.95 (*0-939791-68-4*) Tchrs Eng Spkrs.

New Ways in Teaching Culture. Ed. by Alvino Fantini. 236p. 1997. pap. 24.95 (*0-939791-70-6*) Tchrs Eng Spkrs.

***New Ways in Teaching English at the Secondary Level.** Ed. by Deborah J. Short. LC 98-61415. (New Ways in TESOL II). (Illus.). 326p. 1999. pap. 29.95 (*0-939791-77-3*) Tchrs Eng Spkrs.

New Ways in Teaching Grammar. Ed. by Martha C. Pennington. 205p. 1995. pap. 22.95 (*0-939791-56-0*) Tchrs Eng Spkrs.

New Ways in Teaching Listening. Ed. by David Nunan & Linsday Miller. 290p. 1995. pap. 24.95 (*0-939791-58-7*) Tchrs Eng Spkrs.

New Ways in Teaching Reading. Ed. by Richard R. Day. LC 93-60127. 300p. 1993. pap. 22.95 (*0-939791-45-5*) Tchrs Eng Spkrs.

New Ways in Teaching Speaking. Ed. by Kathleen Bailey & Lance Savage. 365p. 1994. pap. 22.95 (*0-939791-54-4*) Tchrs Eng Spkrs.

New Ways in Teaching Vocabulary. Ed. by Paul Nation. 218p. 1994. pap. 22.95 (*0-939791-51-X*) Tchrs Eng Spkrs.

New Ways in Teaching Writing. Ed. by Ronald V. White. 271p. 1995. pap. 25.95 (*0-939791-57-9*) Tchrs Eng Spkrs.

New Ways in Teaching Young Children. Ed. by Linda Schinke-Llano & Rebecca Rauff. LC 95-62078. (New Ways in TESOL: Innovative Classroom Techniques Ser.). (Illus.). 179p. 1996. pap. 25.95 (*0-939791-63-3*) Tchrs Eng Spkrs.

***New Ways in Using Authentic Materials in the Classroom.** Ed. by Ruth E. Larimer & Leigh Schleicher. LC 98-61418. (New Ways in Tesol Ser.: Vol. II). 233p. 1999. pap. 29.95 (*0-939791-80-3*) Tchrs Eng Spkrs.

***New Ways in Using Communicative Games in Language Teaching.** Nikhat Shameem & Makhan Tickoo. (New Ways in Tesol Ser.: Vol. II). 214p. 1999. pap. text 29.95 (*0-939791-78-1*) Tchrs Eng Spkrs.

New Ways of Classroom Assessment. Ed. by J. D. Brown. LC 97-61577. 397p. 1998. pap. 27.95 (*0-939791-72-2*) Tchrs Eng Spkrs.

New Ways of Knowing: The Sciences, Society & Reconstructive Knowledge. Ed. by Marcus G. Raskin et al. 352p. 1987. pap. 26.50 (*0-8476-7463-0*) Rowman.

New Ways of Learning the Library - & Beyond. Ed. by Linda Shirato. (Library Orientation Ser.: No. 27). 1997. pap. 40.00 (*0-87650-347-4*) Pierian.

New Ways of Looking at Old Texts: Papers of the Renaissance English Text Society, 1985-1991. Ed. by W. Speed Hill. LC 93-936. (Renaissance English Text Society Series, Medieval & Renaissance Texts & Studies: Vol. 107). 320p. 1993. 25.00 (*0-86698-153-5*, MR107) MRTS.

New Ways of Looking at Old Texts Vol. II: Papers of the Renaissance English Text Society, 1992-1996. Ed. by W. Speed Hill. LC 98-19258. (Medieval & Renaissance Texts & Studies: Vol. 188). (Illus.). 192p. 1998. 25.00 (*0-86698-230-2*, MR188) MRTS.

***New Ways of Loving: How Authenticity Transforms Relationships.** 4th rev. ed. James Leonard Park. 264p. 2000. pap. 45.00 (*0-89231-520-2*) Existential Bks.

New Ways of Making Babies: The Case of Egg Donation. Ed. by Cynthia B. Cohen. LC 95-51471. (Medical Ethics Ser.). (Illus.). 352p. (C). 1996. 39.95 (*0-253-33058-0*) Ind U Pr.

New Ways of Managing Conflict. Rensis Likert & Jane G. Likert. LC 75-23216. (Illus.). 383p. reprint ed. pap. 118.80 (*0-8357-3611-3*, AU0039600004) Bks Demand.

New Ways of Managing Infrastructure Provision. OECD Staff. 200p. (Orig.). 1994. pap. 23.00 (*92-64-14306-8*) OECD.

New Ways of Ontology. Nicolai Hartmann. Tr. by Reinhard C. Kuhn from GER. LC 75-1112. 145p. 1975. reprint ed. lib. bdg. 49.50 (*0-8371-7989-0*, HANW, Greenwood Pr) Greenwood.

New Ways of Paying for College. Ed. by Arthur M. Hauptman & Robert H. Hoff. LC 90-20222. (American Council on Education/Macmillan Series on Higher Education). 240p. reprint ed. pap. 74.40 (*0-608-20852-3*, 207195100003) Bks Demand.

New Ways of Produce Textiles. P. W. Harrison. 274p. 1972. 70.00 (*0-7855-7207-4*) St Mut.

New Ways of Training for School Leadership: A Special Issue of Peabody Journal of Education, Vol. 72, No. 2. Ed. by Naftaly S. Glasman. 184p. 1997. pap. 20.00 (*0-8058-9858-1*) L Erlbaum Assocs.

New Ways of Using Computers in Language Teaching. Ed. by Tim Boswood. 309p. 1997. pap. 27.95 (*0-939791-69-2*) Tchrs Eng Spkrs.

New Ways of Using Drama & Literature in Language Teaching. Ed. by Valerie Whiteson. LC 96-61035. 155p. 1996. pap. 21.95 (*0-939791-66-8*) Tchrs Eng Spkrs.

New Ways of Working with Local Laws to Prevent Crime. Lauren Brosler. Ed. by Judy Kirby. (Special Focus Ser.). 80p. (Orig.). 1996. pap. 14.95 (*0-934513-10-4*, LAW1) Natl Crime DC.

New Ways of Writing. Susan Miller & Kyle Knowles. 199p. (C). 1996. spiral bd. 24.80 (*0-13-531260-4*) P-H.

New Ways of Writing: A Hanbook for Writing with Computers. 1996. write for info. (*0-13-849290-5*) P-H.

New Ways of Writing Trade. Susan Miller & Kyle Knowles. 1996. spiral bd. 19.20 (*0-13-652215-7*) P-H.

New Ways to Assess the Performance of School Principals: A Special Issue of the Peabody Journal of Education, Vol. 68, No. 2, 1996. Ed. by Glasman & Heck. 1996. reprint ed. pap. 20.00 (*0-8058-9902-2*) L Erlbaum Assocs.

New Ways to Assess the Performance of School Principals Pt. I: A Special Issue of the Peabody Journal of Education, Vol. 68, No. 1, 1996. Ed. by Glasman & Heck. 1996. reprint ed. pap. 20.00 (*0-8058-9903-0*) L Erlbaum Assocs.

New Ways to Care for Older People: Building Systems Based on Evidence in Managed Care. Ed. by Evan Calkins et al. LC 98-38606. (Illus.). 280p. 1998. 42.95 (*0-8261-1220-X*) Springer Pub.

New Ways to Learn a Foreign Language. Robert A. Hall, Jr. LC 73-15154. viii, 180p. (C). 1980. reprint ed. pap. 10.00 (*0-87950-293-2*) Spoken Lang Serv.

New Ways to Save Energy. Ed. by Albert S. Strub & H. Ehringer. 1238p. 1980. text 211.50 (*90-277-1078-3*) Kluwer Academic.

New Ways to Teach Using Cable Television: A Step-by-Step Guide. Randi Stone. LC 96-51273. 104p. 1997. 39.95 (*0-8039-6562-1*); pap. 16.95 (*0-8039-6563-X*) Corwin Pr.

New Ways to Tell the Old, Old Story. H. M. S. Richards, Jr. Ed. by Tim Crosby. 64p. 1991. pap. 1.49 (*0-8163-1074-2*) Pacific Pr Pub Assn.

New Ways to Tell the Old, Old Story: Choosing & Using Bible Stories with Children & Youths. Delia T. Halverson. 80p. (J). 1992. pap. 11.95 (*0-687-27946-1*) Abingdon.

New Ways to Use Test Meters: A Modern Guide to Electronic Servicing. Robert G. Middleton. 256p. 1986. 22.95 (*0-13-616169-3*, Busn) P-H.

New Ways with Polymer Clay: The Next Generation of Projects & Techniques. Kris Richards. LC 96-42125. (Illus.). 112p. 1997. pap. 19.95 (*0-8019-8869-1*) Krause Pubns.

New Ways with Vegetables. (Recipes of the World Ser.). (Illus.). 1998. write for info. (*1-886614-91-1*) Intl Masters Pub.

New Ways with Vegetables. (Mini Cook Bks.). 148p. pap. 1.95 (*3-8290-0378-1*, 770116) Konemann.

New Wealth of Nations. John Raven. 372p. 1995. pap. 20.00 (*0-89824-232-0*, 2320) Trillium Pr.

New Wealth of Nations. Guy Sorman. (Publication Ser.: No. 391). 232p. (C). 1990. pap. text 5.60 (*0-8179-8912-9*, P391) Hoover Inst Pr.

New Wealth of Nations. Guy Sorman. Tr. by Asha Puri from FRE. (Publication Ser.: No. 391). 232p. (C). 1990. text 20.00 (*0-8179-8911-0*, P391) Hoover Inst Pr.

New Wealth Private Fortunes. 1997. 155.00 (*1-56995-050-4*) Taft Group.

New Wealth Private Fortunes, 1995. 1995. 155.00 (*1-56995-048-2*) Taft Group.

New Wealth Private Fortunes, 1996. 1996. 155.00 (*1-56995-049-0*) Taft Group.

New Wealth Private Fortunes, 1994. 94th ed. Catherine M. Ehr. 1993. 155.00 (*1-56995-047-4*, 600518) Taft Group.

New Weapons & NATO: Solutions or Irritants?, 66. Robert Kromer. LC 87-8649. (Contributions in Military Studies Ser.: No. 66). 191p. 1987. 49.95 (*0-313-25588-1*, KNW/, Greenwood Pr) Greenwood.

New Weapons, Old Politics: America's Military Procurement Muddle. Thomas L. McNaugher. 252p. 1989. 36.95 (*0-8157-5626-7*); pap. 15.95 (*0-8157-5625-9*) Brookings.

New Webster Spelling Dictionary. Donald O. Borlander. 1990. mass mkt. 5.99 (*0-425-12474-6*) Berkley Pub.

New Webster's Crossword Dictionary. Lawrence Lexicon. pap. 5.99 (*0-425-13096-7*) Berkley Pub.

New Webster's Crossword Dictionary. Lexicon Publications Staff. 1991. mass mkt. 5.99 (*0-425-12882-2*) Berkley Pub.

New Webster's Crossword Puzzle Dictionary. Ed. by I. Vidyadhar & K. Lee. 256p. (Orig.). 1991. pap. 5.95 (*0-938261-07-X*) PSI & Assocs.

New Webster's Desk Reference. Donald O. Bolander et al. 1991. mass mkt. 5.99 (*0-425-12884-9*) Berkley Pub.

New Webster's Dictionary. Neufeldt. 1992. 4.50 (*0-446-77618-1*) Warner Bks.

New Webster's Dictionary. Ed. by R. F. Patterson. 256p. (Orig.). 1993. pap. 5.95 (*0-938261-80-0*) PSI & Assocs.

New Webster's Dictionary. Ed. by R. F. Patterson. 256p. (Orig.). 1994. pap. write for info. (*1-884907-02-4*) Paradise Pr FL.

New Webster's Dictionary. Sears. 1984. mass mkt. 3.50 (*0-446-31324-6*, Pub. by Warner Bks) Little.

New Webster's Dictionary - Roget's Thesaurus. Ed. by R. F. Patterson. 512p. 1994. pap. write for info. (*1-884907-00-8*) Paradise Pr FL.

New Webster's Dictionary & New Roget's Thesaurus. Ed. by R. F. Patterson. 512p. (Orig.). 1990. pap. 12.95 (*0-938261-39-8*) PSI & Assocs.

New Webster's Expanded Dictionary. Ed. by R. F. Patterson. 384p. (Orig.). 1988. pap. 6.95 (*0-938261-79-7*) PSI & Assocs.

New Webster's Expanded Dictionary. R. F. Patterson. 384p. (Orig.). 1994. pap. write for info. (*1-884907-01-6*) Paradise Pr FL.

New Webster's French-English Dictionary. (ENG & FRE.). 256p. 1994. pap. write for info. (*1-884907-07-5*) Paradise Pr FL.

New Webster's Giant Print Dictionary. Ed. by R. F. Patterson. 288p. (Orig.). 1990. pap. 5.95 (*0-938261-81-9*) PSI & Assocs.

New Webster's Grammar Guide. Madeline Semmelmeyer & Donald O. Bolander. 247p. 1991. mass mkt. 5.99 (*0-425-12557-2*) Berkley Pub.

New Webster's International Encyclopedia: The New Illustrated Home Reference Guide, 2 vols. rev. ed. Ed. by Michael D. Harkavy. (Illus.). 1312p. 1998. reprint ed. 129.95 (*1-888777-83-4*) Trident Pr Intl.

New Webster's International Padded Encyclopedia: The New Illustrated Home Reference Guide. rev. ed. Ed. by Michael D. Harkavy. (Illus.). 1312p. 1998. reprint ed. 99.95 (*1-888777-76-1*) Trident Pr Intl.

New Webster's Large Print Dictionary. large type ed. Ed. by R. F. Patterson. 256p. 1994. pap. 5.95 (*1-884907-03-2*) Paradise Pr FL.

New Webster's Pocket Dicionary. 192p. 1994. pap. write for info. (*1-884907-10-5*) Paradise Pr FL.

New Webster's Pocket Pal Dictionary. Ed. by R. F. Patterson. 192p. (Orig.). 1989. pap. 3.95 (*0-938261-20-7*) PSI & Assocs.

New Webster's Spanish-English Dictionary. (ENG & SPA.). 256p. 1994. pap. write for info. (*1-884907-06-7*) Paradise Pr FL.

New Webster's Spanish-English, English-Spanish Dictionary. (ENG & SPA.). 256p. (Orig.). 1989. pap. 5.95 (*0-938261-09-6*) PSI & Assocs.

New Webster's Universal Dictionary. Dalton Edition Staff. 1997. write for info. (*0-517-18554-7*) Random Hse Value.

New Wedding Cake Designs. 1999. 19.95 (*1-85391-631-5*, Pub. by Merehurst Ltd) Tuttle Pubng.

***New Wedding Cake Designs.** Linda Pawsey. 2000. pap. 34.95 (*1-85391-884-9*, Pub. by Merehurst Ltd) Tuttle Pubng.

New Well Pregnancy Book: Fully Revised & Updated. rev. ed. Mike Samuels & Nancy H. Samuels. 496p. 1996. per. 20.00 (*0-684-81057-3*) S&S Trade Pap.

New Well-Tempered Sentence: A Punctuation Handbook for the Innocent, the Eager, & the Doomed. enl. rev. ed. Karen E. Gordon. LC 93-18454. (Illus.). 148p. 1993. reprint ed. 14.95 (*0-395-62883-0*, Pub. by Ticknor & Fields) HM.

New Wellness Encyclopedia. Ed. by University of California, Berkeley, Wellness Lette. 540p. 1995. pap. 25.00 (*0-395-73345-6*) HM.

New Welsh Dictionary. 1997. pap. 29.95 (*0-8464-4904-8*) Beekman Pubs.

New West. Kevin Siembieda & Chris Kornmann. Ed. by Alex Marciniszyn & James Osten. (Rifts Worldbook Ser.: Vol. 14). (Illus.). 192p. (Orig.). (YA). (gr. 8 up). 1997. pap. 20.95 (*1-57457-001-3*, 826) Palladium Bks.

New West Highland White Terrier. Gentry. 1996. per. 25.00 (*0-87605-363-0*) Howell Bks.

New West Highland White Terrier. Daphne S. Gentry. LC 98-12606. 256p. 1998. 27.95 (*0-87605-356-8*) Howell Bks.

New West of Edward Abbey. Ann Ronald. LC 87-32074. 271p. 1988. pap. 84.10 (*0-608-01265-3*, 206201400001) Bks Demand.

***New West of Edward Abbey.** 2nd ed. Ann Ronald. 300p. 2000. pap. 18.95 (*0-87417-357-4*) U of Nev Pr.

N

New West Virginia One-Day Trip Book: More Than 200 Affordable Adventures in the Mountain State. Colleen Anderson. LC 98-22753. 1998. pap. 12.95 (*1-889324-13-2*, EPM) Howell Pr VA.

New Western Frontier: An Illustrated History of Greater Las Vegas. Gary Elliott. LC 97-78262. (Illus.). 1999. 39.95 (*1-886483-17-5*) Heritge Media.

New Western History. Ed. by Forrest G. Robinson. LC 98-19251. 220p. 1998. 40.00 (*0-8165-1915-3*) U of Ariz Pr.

New Western History: An Assessment. Ed. by Forrest G. Robinson. LC 98-19251. 220p. 1998. pap. 17.95 (*0-8165-1916-1*) U of Ariz Pr.

New Westers: The West in Contemporary American Culture. Michael L. Johnson. LC 96-426. (Illus.). 424p. 1996. 29.95 (*0-7006-0763-3*) U Pr of KS.

New Westminster Dictionary of Liturgy & Worship. Ed. by J. G. Davies. LC 86-9219. (Illus.). 560p. 1986. 39.95 (*0-664-21270-0*) Westminster John Knox.

New Wheels Without Getting the Shaft. Stephen Ruback. vii, 71p. 1998. pap. 19.95 (*0-9651551-4-5*) Dynamic Pubng.

New Whole Foods Encyclopedia: A Comprehensive Resource for Healthy Eating. Rebecca Wood. LC 98-47431. (Illus.). 426p. 1999. pap. 18.95 (*0-14-025032-8*) Viking Penguin.

New Whole Heart Book. 2nd ed. James J. Nora. (Illus.). 350p. 1989. reprint ed. 18.95 (*0-922811-02-4*); reprint ed. pap. 10.95 (*0-922811-03-2*) Mid-List.

***New Why Teams Don't Work: What Went Wrong & How to Make It Right.** rev. ed. Harvey Robbins & Michael Finley. 270p. 2000. pap. 17.95 (*1-57675-110-4*, Pub. by Berrett-Koehler) Publishers Group.

***New Wicker/Whicker Family.** Richard Fenton Wicker, Jr. 2000. pap. 99.00 (*0-7404-0046-0*) Higginson Bk Co.

***New Wicker/Whicker Family.** rev. ed. Ed. by Richard Fenton Wicker, Jr. 839p. 2000. reprint ed. 109.00 (*0-7404-0045-2*) Higginson Bk Co.

New Wigmore. 5th ed. David P. Leonard. LC 95-77279. 986p. 1995. 155.00 (*0-316-26232-3*) Little.

New Wilderness Letter, No. 11: The Book Spiritual Instrument see Book, Spiritual Instrument

New Wilson's Old Testament Word Studies. rev. ed. William Wilson. LC 86-7210. 584p. 1987. lib. bdg. 34.99 (*0-8254-4030-0*, Kregel Class) Kregel.

N

New Wind: Changing Identities in South Asia. Ed. by Kenneth David. (World Anthropology Ser.). xvi, 537p. 1977. 61.55 (*90-279-7959-6*) Mouton.

New Window (La Ventana Nueva), Vol. 1. Laurence A. Frame. LC 95-190033. (Native American - Mission Ser.). (ENG & SPA., Illus.). 30p. (J). (gr. 2-8). 1994. pap. 10.00 (*1-884480-54-3*) Spts Curriculum.

New Windows on the Universe: XIth European Meeting of the International Astronomical Union, 2 vols., Set. Ed. by M. Vazquez & F. Sanchez. 1063p. (C). 1991. text 145.00 (*0-521-40177-1*) Cambridge U Pr.

New Wine: A Commentary on Religion & the Bible. S. Mallard. LC 94-72833. 232p. 1995. pap. 24.95 (*0-9643891-9-3*) AMI Bk Bldrs.

New Wine: Christian Witness of the Family. Carlo M. Martini. Tr. by Mary J. Berger from ITA. 319p. (Orig.). 1994. pap. 11.95 (*0-8198-5131-0*) Pauline Bks.

***New Wine: In Search of Jesus in History & Myth.** Victoria H. Doren. LC 99-184198. 128p. 1999. pap. 12.50 (*0-9668518-0-3*) Polarity Pr.

New Wine: Spiritual Roots/12 Step Miracle. B. Mel. 1991. pap. 12.95 (*0-89486-772-5*) Hazelden.

New Wine: The Cultural Shaping of Japanese Christianity. David Reid. LC 91-7732. (Nanzan Studies in Asian Religions: Vol. 2). (Illus.). 250p. (C). 1991. pap. text 20.00 (*0-89581-932-5*) Asian Humanities.

New Wine: The Story of Women Transforming Leadership & Power in the Episcopal Church. Pamela W. Darling. LC 94-10734. 258p. 1994. pap. 16.95 (*1-56101-094-4*) Cowley Pubns.

New Wine & Old Bottles: International Politics & Ethical Discourse. Jean B. Elshtain. LC 97-49698. (Notre Dame Studies on International Peace). 99p. 1998. pap. 14.95 (*0-268-01483-3*) U of Notre Dame Pr.

New Wine Companion. 2nd ed. David Burroughs. 244p. 1993. pap. 34.95 (*0-7506-1274-6*) Buttrwrth-Heinemann.

New Wine Companion. 2nd ed. David Burroughs & Norman Bezzant. LC 94-27192. 256p. reprint ed. pap. 79.40 (*0-608-09704-7*, 206987000007) Bks Demand.

***New Wine in Old Bottles: Poems from Hollywood.** Mark Dunster. 11p. 1999. pap. 5.00 (*0-89642-980-6*) Linden Pubs.

New Wine in Old Wineskins: Evangelicals & Liberals in a Small-Town Church. R. Stephen Warner. 367p. 1988. pap. 17.95 (*0-520-07204-9*, Pub. by U CA Pr) Cal Prin Full Svc.

New Wine into Fresh Wineskins: Contextualizing the Early Christian Confessions. Richard N. Longenecker. LC 99-46070. 220p. 1999. pap. 14.95 (*1-56563-098-X*) Hendrickson MA.

New Wine Is Better. Robert Thom. 240p. 1974. mass mkt. 5.99 (*0-88368-036-X*) Whitaker Hse.

New Wine or Old Deception. 2nd rev. ed. Roger Oakland. 117p. 1995. reprint ed. pap. 4.99 (*0-936728-62-0*) Word for Today.

New Wines of Spain. Tony Lord. (Illus.). 160p. 24.95 (*0-932664-59-8*, 6517) Wine Appreciation.

***New Wineskins: Faithful Mission in the 21st Century.** Ed. by Rena M. Yocom. (Illus.). 145p. 1999. pap. 6.95 (*1-890569-13-5*, 2809) Gnl Brd Glbl Minis.

New Winter Soldiers: GI & Veteran Dissent During the Vietnam Era. Richard Moser. (Sights on the Sixties Ser.). (Illus.). 300p. (C). 1996. text 50.00 (*0-8135-2241-2*) Rutgers U Pr.

New Wisconsin Photography. Tom Bamberger. (Illus.). 27p. 1994. pap. 5.00 (*0-944110-49-5*) Milwauk Art Mus.

***New Wisdom of Business.** Richard Haasnoot. LC 99-88244. 204p. 2000. pap. 17.95 (*0-7931-3761-6*) Dearborn.

New Witness for Christ: Chiastic Structures in the Book of Mormon. H. Clay Gorton. 480p. 1997. 27.98 (*0-88290-600-3*, 1078) Horizon Utah.

***New Wittgenstein.** Ed. by Alice Marguerite Crary & Rupert J. Read. LC 99-48803. 416p. (C). 2000. pap. write for info. (*0-415-17319-1*) Routledge.

***New Wittgenstein.** Ed. by Alice Marguerite Crary & Rupert J. Read. LC 99-48803. 416p. (C). 2000. text 90.00 (*0-415-17318-3*) Routledge.

New Wok Cooking: Easy, Healthy, One-Pot Meals. Rosa Ross. LC 99-49909. (Illus.). 224p. 2000. 25.00 (*0-609-60418-X*) C Potter.

New Wolff Olins Guide to Identity: How to Create & Sustain Change Through Managing Identity. Wally Olins. 110p. 1996. pap. 33.95 (*0-566-07737-X*, Pub. by Gower) Ashgate Pub Co.

New Wolves. Rick Bass. LC 98-36557. 128p. 1998. 18.95 (*1-55821-697-9*) Lyons Pr.

New Wolves. Rick Bass. LC 98-36557. 1998. lib. bdg. 18.95 (*1-55821-773-8*) Lyons Pr.

New Woman see Mujer Nueva: Cinderella Twin

New Woman. Qasim Amin. Tr. by Samiha S. Peterson. 128p. 1996. 25.00 (*977-424-366-8*, Pub. by Am Univ Cairo Pr) Col U Pr.

New Woman. Ledger. LC 96-29804. 272p. 1997. pap. 27.95 (*0-7190-4093-0*) St Martin.

New Woman. large type ed. Janine Boissard. 304p. 1984. 27.99 (*0-7089-1154-4*) Ulverscroft.

New Woman: A Tribute to Mercedes Sosa. Nestor R. Lacoren. Ed. by Latin Culture Productions Staff. LC 90-61383. (ENG & SPA., Illus.). 150p. (Orig.). 1990. pap. 14.95 (*0-9627004-0-1*) Latin Cul Prod.

New Woman: Women's Voices, 1880-1918. Ed. by Juliet Gardiner. 310p. 1994. pap. 15.95 (*1-85585-159-8*) Trafalgar.

New Woman & Other Emancipated Woman Plays. Ed. by Jean Chothia. LC 97-31284. (Oxford World's Classics Ser.). 352p. 2001. pap. 12.95 (*0-19-282427-9*) OUP.

New Woman & the Old Academe: Sexism & Higher Education. Jonah R. Churgin. LC 77-91470. 1979. 15.00 (*0-87212-076-7*) Libra.

New Woman & the Victorian Novel. Gail Cunningham. LC 78-6179. 172p. 1978. text 44.00 (*0-06-491347-3*, N6417) B&N Imports.

New Woman & the Victorian Novel Gail Cunningham. LC 79-301111. viii, 172 p. 1978. write for info. (*0-333-21617-2*) Trans-Atl Phila.

***New Woman Fiction: Women Writing First-Wave Feminism.** Ann Heilmann. LC 00-42059. 2000. (*0-312-23627-1*) St Martin.

New Woman in Alabama: Social Reforms & Suffrage, 1890-1920. Mary M. Thomas. LC 91-13069. 280p. (C). 1992. text 34.95 (*0-8173-0564-5*) U of Ala Pr.

***New Woman in Fiction & in Fact: Fin de Si Ecle Feminisms.** Angelique Richardson et al. LC 00-27246. 2000. write for info. (*0-312-23490-2*) St Martin.

New Woman in Indian-English Women Writers since the 1970's. Vijayalakshmi Seshadri. LC 95-906273. (C). 1995. 11.00 (*81-7018-825-3*, Pub. by BR Pub) S Asia.

New Woman Manager: Fifty Fast & Savvy Solutions for Executive Excellence. rev. ed. Sharon Willen. LC 92-40066. 300p. 1993. reprint ed. pap. 14.95 (*0-944031-11-0*) Aslan Pub.

New Woman, New Church, New Priestly Ministry: Proceedings of the Second Conference on the Ordination of Roman Catholic Women. Intro. by Maureen Dwyer. LC 89-183386. (Illus.). 178p. (Orig.). (C). 1980. pap. 5.00 (*0-9623386-0-5*) Women's Ord Conf.

New Woman, New Earth: Sexist Ideologies & Human Liberation. Rosemary Radford Ruether. LC 95-16969. 256p. (C). 1995. pap. 14.00 (*0-8070-6503-X*) Beacon Pr.

New Woman Plays. Linda Fitzsimmons. 189p. (C). 1991. pap. 17.95 (*0-413-64200-3*, A0501, Methuen Drama) Methn.

New Woman Revised: Painting & Gender Politics on Fourteenth Street. Ellen W. Todd. 450p. 1993. 55.00 (*0-520-07471-8*, Pub. by U CA Pr) Cal Prin Full Svc.

New Woman's Broken Heart: Short Stories. Andrea Dworkin. LC 79-55919. 56p. (Orig.). 1980. pap. 4.00 (*0-9603628-0-0*) Frog in Well.

New Woman's Diary: A Journal for Women in Search of Themselves. Judith Finlayson. LC 93-20019. 1994. 16.00 (*0-517-59248-7*, Crown) Crown Pub Group.

***New Wombs: Electronic Bodies & Architectural Disorder.** Maria Luisa Palumbo. (Illus.). 96p. 2000. pap. 12.50 (*3-7643-6294-4*, Pub. by Birkhauser) Princeton Arch.

New Women for God: Canadian Presbyterian Women & India Missions, 1876-1914. Ruth C. Brouwer. (Social History of Canada Ser.). 376p. 1990. text 50.00 (*0-8020-2718-0*); pap. text 19.95 (*0-8020-6750-6*) U of Toronto Pr.

New Women, New Novels: Feminism & Early Modernism. Ann Ardis. LC 90-35039. 225p. (Orig.). (C). 1990. text 40.00 (*0-8135-1581-5*); pap. text 15.00 (*0-8135-1582-3*) Rutgers U Pr.

New Women of Lusaka. Ilsa M. Glazer. Ed. by Robert B. Edgerton & L. L. Langness. LC 78-51540. (Illus.). 209p. (C). 1979. pap. text 18.95 (*0-87484-428-2*, 428) Mayfield Pub.

New Women of Wonder. Ed. by Pamela Sargent. LC 77-76577. 1978. pap. 3.95 (*0-394-72438-0*) Random.

New Women Poets. Intro. by Carol Rumens. 176p. (Orig.). 1990. pap. 17.95 (*1-85224-145-4*, Pub. by Bloodaxe Bks) Dufour.

New Women's Dress for Success. John T. Molloy. 272p. (Orig.). 1996. mass mkt. 13.99 (*0-446-67223-8*, Pub. by Warner Bks) Little.

New Women's Writing from Israel. Ed. by Risa Domb. LC 96-21338. (Illus.). 235p. 1996. 42.50 (*0-85303-307-2*, Pub. by M Vallentine & Co); pap. 19.50 (*0-85303-308-0*, Pub. by M Vallentine & Co) Intl Spec Bk.

New Wonder, a Woman Never Vext: An Old-Spelling, Critical Edition. William D. Rowley. Ed. by George Cheatham. LC 92-27581. (Renaissance & Baroque Studies & Texts: Vol. 6). XII, 264p. (C). 1993. text 49.95 (*0-8204-1916-8*) P Lang Pubng.

New Wood Architecture. Naomi Stungo. (Illus.). 240p. 1998. 59.95 (*3-927258-88-1*) Gingko Press.

New Wood Architecture in Scandinavia. Christoph Affentranger. (Illus.). 240p. 1997. 75.00 (*3-7643-5458-5*, Pub. by Birkhauser) Princeton Arch.

New Wood Finishing Book. Michael Dresdner. LC 99-13395. 1999. pap. 19.95 (*1-56158-299-9*) Taunton.

New Woodburner's Handbook: A Guide to Safe, Healthy & Efficient Woodburning. Stephen Bushway. Ed. by Mary Twitchell. LC 91-51125. (Illus.). 168p. 1992. pap. 12.95 (*0-88266-788-2*, Garden Way Pub) Storey Bks.

New Woodstock & Vicinity, Past & Present. Anzolette D. Ellsworth & Mary E. Richmond. (Illus.). 141p. 1997. reprint ed. pap. 19.00 (*0-8328-6184-7*); reprint ed. lib. bdg. 29.00 (*0-8328-6183-9*) Higginson Bk Co.

New Word. Charles H. Grandgent. LC 75-121471. (Essay Index Reprint Ser.). 1977. 19.95 (*0-8369-1707-3*) Ayer.

***New Word Presents Sister Chula: Women from Around the Way.** Garrett R. Fortner. 146p. 2000. 25.00 (*0-9652010-2-3*) Boss Publns.

New Word Puzzles. Gerald L. Kaufman. 1957. pap. 3.50 (*0-486-20344-1*) Dover.

New Words. Dan E. Slocum. (Illus.). 33p. 1996. pap. 12.00 (*0-9654245-0-2*) Child Hospital.

New Words Vol. I: A Collection of 15 Bicinia Hungarica Composed by Zoltan Kodaly with New English Lyrics by Peter S. Thompson. Faith Knowles et al. (Orig.). 1997. pap. 11.95 (*0-935432-11-6*) Kodaly Ctr Am.

New Words for Selected Bacinia: A Collection of 30 Bicinia Hungarica Composed by Zoltan Kodaly with New English Lyrics by Peter S. Thompson. Faith Knowles et al. 64p. 1998. pap. 14.95 (*0-935432-12-4*) Kodaly Ctr Am.

New Words-Meanings Dictionary. N. Z. Kotelova. (RUS.). 806p. 1984. 49.95 (*0-8288-2004-X*, F84380) Fr & Eur.

New Words, Old Songs: Understanding the Lives of Ancient Peoples in Southwest Florida Through Archaeology. Charles E. Blanchard. LC 94-46955. (Illus.). 136p. (Orig.). 1995. 24.95 (*1-881448-02-9*) IAPS Bks.

New Words, Old Songs: Understanding the Lives of Ancient Peoples in Southwest Florida Through Archaeology. Charles E. Blanchard. LC 94-46955. (Illus.). 136p. (Orig.). 1995. pap. 14.95 (*1-881448-03-7*) IAPS Bks.

New Work: From the Institute of American Indian Arts. Ed. by Henry Eteitly & Irvin Morris. (IAIA Anthology Ser.: No. 1). 56p. 1989. pap. 6.00 (*1-881396-00-2*) IOA Indian Arts.

New Work by Award Winners II. 176p. 1987. pap. 6.00 (*0-685-19184-2*) Crosscurrents Anthologies.

New Work Culture: HRD Strategies for Transformational Management. Philip R. Harris. 1998. pap. text 44.95 (*0-87425-420-5*) HRD Press.

New Work Order. James Gee & Glynda Hull. 240p. (C). 1996. pap. text 25.00 (*0-8133-3261-3*, Pub. by Westview) HarpC.

New Work Order: Behind the Language of the New Capitalism. James P. Gee et al. LC 96-218230. 208p. 1996. pap. 24.95 (*1-86448-052-1*, Pub. by Allen & Unwin Pty) Paul & Co Pubs.

New Work Schedules for a Changing Society: Complete Study. Jerome M. Rosow & Robert Zager. 128p. 1981. pap. 12.00 (*0-89361-025-9*) Work in Amer.

New Work Schedules for a Changing Society: Executive Summary. Jerome M. Rosow & Robert Zager. 55p. 1981. pap. 5.50 (*0-89361-026-7*) Work in Amer.

New Workbook of Basic Writing Skills. 4th ed. Cora L. Robey et al. 240p. (C). 1996. teacher ed. 19.50 (*0-15-503706-4*, Pub. by Harcourt Coll Pubs) Harcourt.

New Working Class. Ed. by Serge Mallet. Tr. by Andree Shepherd from FRE. 210p. 1975. 25.00 (*0-85124-131-X*, Pub. by Spksman) Coronet Bks.

New Working Fluids for Gas-Fired Cycle Heat Pumps. Allied Chemical Corporation Staff & M. J. Mastroianni. 104p. 1975. pap. 4.50 (*0-318-12658-3*, M50077) Am Gas Assn.

***New Working Woman's Guide to Retirement Planning: Saving & Investing Now for a Secure Future.** 2nd ed. Martha Priddy Patterson. LC 99-36954. 1999. pap. text 19.95 (*0-8122-1703-9*) U of Pa Pr.

New Worklife Expectancy Tables: For Persons with & Without Disability by Gender & Level of Educational Attainment. rev. ed. Anthony M. Gamboa, Jr. LC 95-60103. 51p. 1995. pap. 59.95 (*1-886870-00-4*) Vocat Econ.

New Worklife Expectancy Tables, 1998. 4th rev. ed. A. M. Gamboa, Jr. 58p. 1998. pap. 59.95 (*1-886870-02-0*) Vocat Econ.

New Workplace: Transforming the Character & Culture of Our Organizations. Ed. by Systems Thinker Staff. LC 98-14807. (Illus.). 128p. 1998. pap. 24.95 (*1-883823-25-0*, OL009) Pegasus Comm.

New Workplace & Trade Unionism. Ed. by Chris Smith et al. LC 95-8637. (Critical Perspectives on Work & Organization Ser.). 240p. (C). 1995. pap. 18.99 (*0-415-11677-5*) Thomson Learn.

New Workplace & Trade Unionism. Ed. by Chris Smith et al. LC 95-8637. (Critical Perspectives on Work & Organization Ser.). 240p. (C). (gr. 13). 1995. pap. 47.00 (*0-415-11676-7*) Thomson Learn.

New Workplaces for New Workstyles. Marilyn Zelinsky. LC 97-30216. (Illus.). 288p. 1998. 69.95 (*0-07-063324-X*) McGraw.

New Works: An Anthology of Ten Contemporary Poets. Ed. by Kirk Robertson. LC 81-65314. (Windriver Ser.). (Illus.). (Orig.). (C). 1981. pap. 5.95 (*0-916918-13-0*) Duck Down.

New Works: Visiting Hours; House;The Prairie Church of Buster Galloway;Wetland Roy; Murray McRae et al. LC 88-107476. 548p. (Orig.). 1997. pap. 18.95 (*0-88754-451-7*) Theatre Comm.

New Works Fellowships: Northern Telecom. Donald Kuspit et al. Ed. by Nancy H. Margolis. LC 94-67898. (Illus.). (Orig.). 1994. pap. 5.00 (*1-885449-00-3*) City Gallery Cntmprry Art.

New Works for Readers' Theatre. Ed. & Compiled by Steven Porter. 112p. 1994. pap. 10.00 (*81-87848-91-X*) Phantom Pubns.

New Works for Readers' Theatre. Compiled by Steven Porter. LC 93-47112. 112p. 1994. pap. 10.00 (*0-88734-644-8*) Players Pr.

New Workspace, New Culture: Office Design As a Catalyst for Change. Gavin Turner & Jeremy Myerson. LC 97-9613. (Design Council Ser.). 135p. 1998. 61.95 (*0-566-08028-1*, Pub. by Gower) Ashgate Pub Co.

New World. Winston L. S. Churchill. 1994. lib. bdg. 29.95 (*1-56849-505-6*) Buccaneer Bks.

New World. Gillian Cross. (J). 1996. 10.00 (*0-606-11679-6*, Pub. by Turtleback) Demco.

New World. Suzanne Gardinier. 160p. (C). 1994. pap. 15.95 (*0-8229-5516-4*); text 29.95 (*0-8229-3771-9*) U of Pittsburgh Pr.

New World. Frederick Turner. LC 84-24788. (Illus.). 200p. 1985. pap. 12.95 (*0-691-01420-5*, Pub. by Princeton U Pr); text 35.00 (*0-691-06641-8*, Pub. by Princeton U Pr) Cal Prin Full Svc.

***New World, Pt.. 1.** F. A. Hayek. Ed. by Stephen Kresge. LC HB171.H426 1989 vol.. (Good Money Ser.). (Illus.). 288p. 1999. 45.00 (*0-226-32095-2*) U Ch Pr.

New World: A History of the United States Atomic Energy Commission, 1939-1946, Vol. I. Richard G. Hewlett & Oscar E. Anderson, Jr. 781p. 1990. pap. 40.00 (*0-520-07186-7*, Pub. by U CA Pr) Cal Prin Full Svc.

***New World: A Novel.** Amit Chaudhuri. 224p. 2000. 23.00 (*0-375-41093-7*) Knopf.

New World: An Epic of Colonial America from the Founding of Jamestown to the Fall of Quebec. Arthur Quinn. 544p. 1995. pap. 15.95 (*0-425-14956-0*) Berkley Pub.

***New World: History of Immigration to the United States.** Duncan Clarke et al. 2000. 24.98 (*1-57145-280-X*, Thunder Bay) Advantage Pubs.

New World: Neo-Classical Drawings from the Collection of Lodewijk Houthakker, Amsterdam. Roland D. Kollewijn. Ed. by M. Kirby Talley, Jr. (Illus.). 93p. 1986. pap. 12.50 (*0-317-47574-6*) Ober Coll Allen.

New World: Stories. Russell Banks. LC 78-10646. (Illinois Short Fiction Ser.). 144p. 1996. 11.95 (*0-252-00722-0*) U of Ill Pr.

New World A-Coming: Inside Black America. Roi Ottley. LC 68-29014. (American Negro: His History & Literature, Series 1). 1969. reprint ed. 17.95 (*0-405-01833-9*) Ayer.

New World Agaoninae (Pollinators of Figs) J. T. Wiebes. LC 96-150207. 60p. pap. 22.00 (*0-444-85798-2*) Elsevier.

New World & the New World Order: Domestic Instability in the Americas & the End of the Cold War. K. R. Dark & A. L. Harris. (Illus.). 184p. 1996. text 59.95 (*0-312-16212-X*) St Martin.

New World Architecture. Sheldon W. Cheney. LC 72-100513. (BCL Ser.: No. II). (Illus.). reprint ed. 55.00 (*0-404-01487-9*) AMS Pr.

New World Architecture. 2nd ed. Matthew Graham. LC 84-81137. 52p. (Orig.). 1985. 12.95 (*0-913123-07-2*); pap. 6.95 (*0-913123-05-6*) Galileo.

New World Avenue & Vicinity. Tadeusz Konwicki. Tr. by Walter Arndt. 212p. 1991. 24.95 (*0-374-22182-0*) FS&G.

New World Babel: Languages & Nations in Early America. Edward G. Gray. LC 98-35157. xiv, 185p. 1999. 35.00 (*0-691-01705-0*, Pub. by Princeton U Pr) Cal Prin Full Svc.

New World Balance & Peace in the Middle East - Reality or Mirage? A Colloquium. Ed. by Seymour M. Finger. 308p. 1975. 15.00 (*0-317-18477-6*) Fairleigh Dickinson.

New World Balance & Peace Mid. 1974. 15.00 (*0-8386-1675-5*) Fairleigh Dickinson.

New World Blackbirds: The Icterids. Alvaro Jaramillo & Peter Burke. LC 98-34714. 431 p. 1999. 49.50 (*0-691-00680-6*, Pub. by Princeton U Pr) Cal Prin Full Svc.

New World Border: Prophecies, Poems, & Loqueras for the End of the Century. Guillermo Gomez-Pena. (Illus.). 216p. (Orig.). 1996. pap. 16.95 (*0-87286-313-1*) City Lights.

New World Chinese Cooking. Bill Jones & Stephen Wong. (Illus.). 192p. 1998. pap. 17.95 (*1-896503-70-5*, Pub. by R Rose Inc) Firefly Bks Ltd.

New World Chronicles, 2 vols. rev. ed. Peter Martyr. Incl. Vol. 1. New World Chronicles. rev. ed. Tr. by Francis McNutt from LAT. (Illus.). 1996. (*1-887954-08-2*); Vol. 2. New World Chronicles. rev. ed. Tr. by Francis A. McNutt from LAT. (Illus.). 1996. (*1-887954-09-0*); 19.95 (*1-887954-07-4*) Athena FL.

New World Chronicles see New World Chronicles

New-World Collection of Polyphony for Holy Week & the Salve Service: Guatemala City, Cathedral Library, Music. Ed. & Intro. by Robert J. Snow. (Monuments of Renaissance Music Ser.: Vol. 9). 496p. 1996. lib. bdg. 185.00 (*0-226-76744-2*) U Ch Pr.

An Asterisk (*) at the beginning of an entry indicates that the title is appearing for the first time.

*New World Coming: American Security in the 21st Century, Phase 1, Major Themes & Implications. 12p. 1999. pap. 3.50 (0-16-059056-6); pap. 3.50 (0-16-059171-6) USGPO.

*New World Coming: American Security in the 21st Century, Phase 1, Supporting Research & Analysis. 159p. 1999. per. 15.00 (0-16-059057-4) USGPO.

*New World Coming: American Security In The 21st Century, Phase 1, Supporting Research & Analysis. 159p. 1999. per. 15.00 (0-16-059172-4) USGPO.

New World Dictionary Concordance to the New American Bible. 1984. pap. 7.99 (0-529-04540-0, 2416) World Publng.

New World Disorder: How the Power Elite Manipulates History. Roy J. Giampaoli. (Illus.). 614p. 1998. pap. 25.00 (0-9664373-0-6) R J Giampoli.

New World Disorder: The Leninist Extinction. Kenneth Jowitt. LC 91-28260. 345p. (C). 1992. 45.00 (0-520-07762-8, Pub. by U CA Pr) Cal Prin Full Svc.

New World Disorder: The Lenninist Extinction. Kenneth Jowitt. 1993. pap. 16.95 (0-520-08272-9, Pub. by U CA Pr) Cal Prin Full Svc.

New World Dutch Barn: A Study of Its Characteristics, Its Structural System, & Its Probable Erectional Procedures. John Fitchen. LC 68-20485. (Illus.). 204p. reprint ed. pap. 63.30 (0-8357-4212-1, 2036989000003) Bks Demand.

New World Dutch Studies: Dutch Arts & Culture in Colonial America, 1609-1776. Ed. by Roderic H. Blackburn & Nancy A. Kelley. (Illus.). 219p. (Orig.). 1987. pap. 21.95 (0-939072-10-6) Albany Hist & Art.

New World Economics. 5th ed. McKenzie & Gordon Staff. (C). 1994. pap. text 22.50 (0-07-045667-4) McGraw.

New World Economies: The Growth of the Thirteen Colonies & Early Canada. Marc Egnal. 256p. 1998. text 49.95 (0-19-511482-5) OUP.

New World Encounters. Ed. by Stephen Greenblatt. LC 92-19328. (Representation Bks.: No. 6). (C). 1993. 50.00 (0-520-08020-3, Pub. by U CA Pr); pap. 17.95 (0-520-08021-1, Pub. by U CA Pr) Cal Prin Full Svc.

New World Figurine Project, Vol. 1. Ed. by Terry Stocker. (Illus.). 170p. (C). 1991. 23.00 (0-934893-09-8) Res Press UT.

New World Fiscal Order. Ed. by C. Eugene Steuerle & Masahiro Kawai. 250p. 1996. pap. text 24.00 (0-87766-641-5); lib. bdg. 60.50 (0-87766-640-7) Urban Inst.

New World Folk Art: Old World Survivals & Cross-Cultural Inspirations, 1492-1992. Ed. by John Hunter & Gene Kangas. (Illus.). 88p. (Orig.). 1992. pap. 15.00 (0-9634556-0-5) CSU OH.

New World Guide to Beer. rev. ed. Michael Jackson. (Illus.). 256p. 1997. 24.95 (0-7624-0091-9) Running Pr.

New World Haggadah (El Hagada de Neuvo Mundo) Ed. by Harry A. Ezratty. (ENG, HEB & SPA.). 100p. 1996. per. 9.95 (0-942929-10-1) Omni Arts.

New World Hasidim: Ethnographic Studies of Hasidic Jews in America. Ed. by Janet S. Belcove-Shalin. LC 94-300. (SUNY Series in Anthropology & Judaic Studies). 285p. (C). 1995. text 57.50 (0-7914-2245-3); pap. text 18.95 (0-7914-2246-1) State U NY Pr.

*New World Hegemony in the Malay World. Geoffrey C. Gunn. LC 99-59269. 2000. pap. write for info. (0-86543-816-1) Africa World.

*New World Hegemony in the Malay World. Geoffrey C. Gunn. 2000. 79.95 (1-56902-134-1); pap. 21.95 (1-56902-135-X) Red Sea Pr.

New World Immigrants: A Consolidation of Ship Passenger Lists & Associated Data from Periodical Literature, 2 vols. Michael H. Tepper. LC 79-84392. 1170p. 1988. 60.00 (0-8063-0854-0) Genealog Pub.

New World in a Small Place: Church & Religion in the Diocese of Rieti, 1188-1378. Robert Brentano. LC 92-35862. 1994. 48.00 (0-520-08076-9, Pub. by U CA Pr) Cal Prin Full Svc.

New World in Our Hearts: The Faces of Spanish Anarchism. Ed. by Albert Meltzer. 1979. pap. 4.50 (0-932366-00-7) Black Thorn Bks.

New World in the Making. Danilo Dolci. Tr. by R. Munroe from ITA. LC 75-3990. 327p. 1976. reprint ed. lib. bdg. 69.50 (0-8371-7419-8, DONW, Greenwood Pr) Greenwood.

New World Information & Communication Order: A Selective Bibliography. 152p. 15.00 (92-1-000035-8, E/F.84.I.15) UN.

New World Jerusalem: The Swedenborgian Experience in Community Construction, 65. Mary A. Meyers. LC 82-11997. (Contributions in American Studies: No. 65). (Illus.). 217p. 1983. 55.00 (0-313-23602-X, MNJ/, Greenwood Pr) Greenwood.

New World Jewry, 1493-1825: Requiem for the Forgotten. Seymour B. Liebman. 25.00 (0-87068-277-6) Ktav.

New World Journeys: Contemporary Italian Writers & the Experience of America, 33. Ed. by Angela M. Jeannet & Louise K. Barnett. LC 77-14144. (Contributions in American Studies: No. 33). 249p. 1977. 55.00 (0-8371-9758-9, BAI/, Greenwood Pr) Greenwood.

New World Maths, Bk. 1. Fox. Date not set. pap. text. write for info. (0-582-76550-1, Pub. by Addison-Wesley) Longman.

New World Maths, Bk. 2. Fox. Date not set. pap. text. write for info. (0-582-76553-6, Pub. by Addison-Wesley) Longman.

New World Maths, Bk. 3. Fox. Date not set. pap. text. write for info. (0-582-76582-X, Pub. by Addison-Wesley) Longman.

New World Media Textbook. Adams. (Mass Communication Ser.). 1919. pap. 35.00 (0-534-57285-5) Wadsworth Pub.

New World Merchants of Rouen, 1559-1630. Gayle K. Brunelle. (Sixteenth Century Essays & Studies: Vol. 16). (Illus.). 190p. 1991. 40.00 (0-940474-17-4, SCJP) Truman St Univ.

New World Mine Proposed Buyout: Hearing Before the Subcommittee on Energy & Mineral Resources of the Committee on Resources, House of Representatives, 105th Congress, 1st Session, May 20, 1997, Washington, D. C., 1997. USGPO Staff. LC 98-110641. iii, 59 p. 1997. pap. write for info. (0-16-055796-8) USGPO.

New World Myth: Postmodernism & Postcolonialism in Canadian Fiction. Marie Vautier. 368p. 1998. text 60.00 (0-7735-1669-7, Pub. by McG-Queens Univ Pr) CUP Services.

New World Myth: Postmodernism & Postcolonialism in Canadian Fiction. Marie Vautier. 376p. 1998. pap. 24.95 (0-7735-1748-0) McG-Queens Univ Pr.

New World, New Roles: A Documentary History of Women in Pre-Industrial America, 65. Sylvia R. Frey & Marian J. Morton. LC 85-27159. (Contributions in Women's Studies: No.65). (Illus.). 255p. 1986. 59.95 (0-313-24896-6, FNVX, Greenwood Pr) Greenwood.

New World, New Rules: The Changing Role of the American Corporation. Marina V. Whitman. LC 98-45835. 272p. 1999. 29.95 (0-87584-858-3) Harvard Busn.

New World, 1939 Through 1946 see History of the U. S. Atomic Energy Commission: AEC Technical Information Center

New World Noodles. Stephen Wong & Bill Jones. (Illus.). 192p. 1997. pap. 17.95 (1-896503-01-2, Pub. by R Rose Inc) Firefly Bks Ltd.

New World of Business: Ethics & Free Enterprise in the Global 1990s. Robert C. Solomon. 360p. (Orig.). (C). 1994. text 54.00 (0-8476-7890-3); pap. text 18.95 (0-8226-3030-3) Rowman.

New World of Eating. Paula Duvall. (Illus.). 470p. 1994. 19.95 (0-9645980-0-0) P Duvall Nutrit.

New World of Educational Thought. Ed. by Frank A. Stone. 280p. 1974. 34.50 (0-8422-5067-0); pap. text 12.95 (0-8422-0282-X) Irvington.

New World of English Words: or A General Dictionary. Edward Phillips. (Anglistica & Americana Ser.: No. 48). 358p. 1969. reprint ed. 76.70 (0-685-66500-3, 05102596) G Olms Pubs.

New World of English Words: or A Gereral Dictionary Containing the Interpretation of Such Hard Words As Are Derived from Other Languages. Edward Phillips. (Anglistica & Americana Ser.: No. 48). 358p. 1969. reprint ed. lib. bdg. 132.50 (3-487-02596-5) G Olms Pubs.

*New World of Faith. Avery Dulles. LC 00-130460. 176p. 2000. pap. 14.95 (0-87973-692-5) Our Sunday Visitor.

New World of James Fenimore Cooper. Wayne Franklin. LC 81-16121. 1982. pap. text 17.00 (0-226-26080-1) U Ch Pr.

New World of James Fenimore Cooper. Wayne Franklin. LC 81-16121. 285p. reprint ed. pap. 88.40 (0-608-09299-1, 205417300004) Bks Demand.

*New World of Knowledge: Canadian Universities & Globalization. Sheryl L. Bond. 1999. pap. 19.95 (0-88936-893-7) IDRC Bks.

New World of Microenterprise Finance: Building Healthy Financial Institutions for the Poor. Ed. by Maria Otero & Elisabeth H. Rhyne. LC 93-47513. (Library of Management for Development). (Illus.). 318p. 1994. 37.00 (1-56549-031-2); pap. 26.95 (1-56549-030-4) Kumarian Pr.

New World of Mr. Tompkins: George Gamow's Classic Mr. Tompkins in Paperback Fully Revised & Updated by Russell Stannard. George Gamow. LC 98-50379. (Illus.). 256p. 1999. 24.95 (0-521-63009-6) Cambridge U Pr.

New World of Politics: An Introduction to Political Science. 4th ed. Neal Riemer & Douglas Simon. (Illus.). 488p. (C). 1997. pap. text 41.75 (0-939693-41-0) Collegiate Pr.

New World of Quantum Chemistry: Proceedings of the International Congress of Quantum Chemistry, 2nd, New Orleans, April, 1976. International Congress of Quantum Chemistry Staff. Ed. by Bernard Pullman & Robert G. Parr. 1976. text 126.50 (90-277-0762-6) Kluwer Academic.

New World of Russian Small Arms & Ammo. Charlie Cutshaw. LC 99-190375. (Illus.). 160p. 1998. 39.95 (0-87364-993-1) Paladin Pr.

New World of Science. Ed. by Robert M. Yerkes. LC 68-58818. (Essay Index Reprint Ser.). 1977. 30.95 (0-8369-1166-0) Ayer.

New World of the Gothic Fox: Culture & Economy in English & Spanish America. Claudio Veliz. LC 93-23709. 1994. 45.00 (0-520-08316-4, Pub. by U CA Pr) Cal Prin Full Svc.

New World of Travel. Arthur Frommer. 1995. pap. 16.95 (0-671-52015-6, P-H Travel) Prntice Hall Bks.

New World of Wine. Max Allen et al. (Illus.). 160p. 1998. 29.95 (1-85732-520-6, Pub. by Mitchell Beazley) Antique Collect.

New World of Wonders: European Images of the Americas, 1492-1700. Ed. by Rachel Doggett et al. LC 92-28277. (Illus.). 1992. pap. 12.95 (0-9629254-2-X) Folger.

New World of Words: Redefining Early American Literature. William C. Spengemann. LC 93-21015. 288p. 1994. 32.50 (0-300-05794-6) Yale U Pr.

New World Order. John Bennett. LC 91-90037. 88p. 1991. pap. 10.95 (0-912292-94-6) Smith.

*New World Order. James A. Clayton. 269p. 1999. pap. 19.95 (0-9670687-0-3) Betoi Pubg.

New World Order. Ed. by Ashtar Commance. (Illus.). 160p. (Orig.). 1990. 15.00 (0-938294-11-3) Inner Light.

New World Order. Ralph Epperson. 390p. 1990. pap. 16.95 (0-9614135-1-4) Publius Pr.

New World Order. Ilija Poplasen. 301p. 1983. 20.00 (0-935352-12-0) MIR PA.

New World Order. Ilija Poplasen. (Illus.). 301p. 1984. 20.00 (0-935352-17-1) MIR PA.

New World Order. Pat Robertson. 1992. mass mkt. 5.99 (0-8499-3394-3) Word Pub.

New World Order. Ed. by Sundeep Waslekar. xiv, 214p. 1991. 27.50 (81-220-0241-2) Advent Bks Div.

New World Order. 4th ed. Maulana M. Ali. 86p. (Orig.). 1989. pap. 4.95 (0-913221-33-3) Ahmadiyya Anjuman.

New World Order. 4th ed. Muhammad A. Maulana. 86p. 1989. pap. 4.95 (0-913321-33-8) Ahmadiyya Anjuman.

*New World Order: An Economic Global Regime. Carlo James. 122p. (C). 1999. pap. 19.95 (1-58112-076-1) Dissertation.

*New World Order: Contrasting Theories. Birthe Hansen & Bertel Heurlin. LC 00-26985. 2000. write for info. (0-312-23469-4) St Martin.

New World-Order: Essays. Ed. by Francis S. Marvin. LC 67-30221. (Essay Index Reprint Ser.). 1977. 19.95 (0-8369-0683-7) Ayer.

New World Order? Global Transformations in the Late Twentieth Century. Ed. by Jozsef Borocz & David A. Smith. LC 94-47418. 272p. 1995. pap. 21.95 (0-275-95122-7, Praeger Pubs) Greenwood.

New World Order? Global Transformations in the Late Twentieth Century, 164. Ed. by Jozsef Borocz & David A. Smith. LC 94-47418. (Contributions in Economics & Economic History Ser.: No. 164). 272p. 1995. 65.00 (0-313-29573-5, Greenwood Pr) Greenwood.

New World Order: Grassroots Movements for Global Change. Paul Ekins. 256p. (C). 1992. pap. 24.99 (0-415-07115-1, A6537) Routledge.

*New World Order: Internationalism, Regionalism & the Multinational Corporations. Ed. by K. Fatemi. (Series in International Business & Economics). 312p. 2000. 75.00 (0-08-043628-5, Pergamon Pr) Elsevier.

New World Order: Manuscript Edition. Harold Pinter. 1992. pap. 2.50 (0-8222-1449-0) Dramatists Play.

*New World Order: Now il the Dawning of the New Age. Dennis L. Cuddy. 2000. pap. 12.95 (1-57558-059-4) Hearthstone OK.

New World Order? Socialist Register, 1992. Ed. by Ralph Miliband & Leo Panitch. 360p. (C). 1992. pap. text 18.00 (0-85345-855-3, Pub. by Monthly Rev) NYU Pr.

New World Order: Sovereignty, Human Rights & the Self-Determination of Peoples. Ed. by M. N. Sellers. (Baltimore Studies in Nationalism & Internationalism). 340p. 1996. 55.00 (1-85973-059-0, Pub. by Berg Pubs); pap. 19.50 (1-85973-064-7, Pub. by Berg Pubs) NYU Pr.

New World Order: The Ancient Plan of Secret Societies. William Still. LC 90-80397. 208p. (Orig.). 1990. pap. 10.99 (0-910311-64-1) Huntington Hse.

New World Order: The Reconstruction of the Middle East. Ed. by Haifaa A. Jawad. LC 94-9889. 1994. text 65.00 (0-312-12201-2) St Martin.

New World Order: Tribalism, Nationalism, & Religious Fundamentalism. Richard Hobbs. 218p. 1995. spiral bd. 19.95 (0-9647788-1-5) ColDoc Pubng.

New World Order: What's Behind the Headlines. Russell Burrill. (Illus.). 192p. (Orig.). 1992. pap. 1.95 (1-882704-00-2) Seminars Unltd.

New World Order - Can It Bring Security to the World's People? Essays on Restructuring the United Nations. Ed. by Walter Hoffmann et al. 122p. 1991. pap. 5.00 (1-880533-02-2) Wrld Federal.

New World Order & Other Secret Combinations. Greg West. pap. 11.95 (1-55517-400-0) CFI Dist.

New World Order & the Security Council: Testing the Legality of Its Acts. Mohammed Bedjaoui. LC 93-41072. 1993. write for info. (0-7923-2562-1) Kluwer Academic.

New World Order & The Third World. Ed. by Dave Broad & Lori Foster. LC 91-72978. 160p. 1991. pap. 19.99 (1-895431-16-6, Pub. by Black Rose) Consort Bk Sales.

New World Order & the Third World. Ed. by Dave Broad & Lori Foster. LC 91-72978. 160p. 1991. 48.99 (1-895431-17-4, Pub. by Black Rose) Consort Bk Sales.

New World Order in Historical Perspective. Ed. by David M. Kirkham. LC 93-77746. 216p. 1993. pap. 19.50 (1-881019-06-3) High Plns WY.

New World Order in International Finance. Geoffrey R. Underhill. LC 96-21863. (International Political Economy Ser.). 331p. 1997. text 49.95 (0-312-16335-5) St Martin.

New World Order Through Cooperative Democracy. James P. Warbasse. 1972. 59.95 (0-8490-0725-9) Gordon Pr.

New World Ordered & Delivered: A Collection of Poetry. David J. Knowles. LC 98-157976. 19p. 1997. pap. 22.95 (0-9648480-1-5) Stndpt Pubng.

New World Orders. Blouet. 1997. pap. text 29.00 (0-02-311081-3) P-H.

New World Orders: Casta Painting & Colonial Latin America. Ilona Katzew et al. (ENG & SPA., Illus.). 144p. 1996. pap. 25.00 (1-879128-14-4) Americas Soc.

New World Order's Defining Crises: The Clash of Promise & Essence. C. G. Jacobsen. LC 96-18841. (Illus.). 124p. 1996. text 72.95 (1-85521-883-6, Pub. by Dartmth Pub) Ashgate Pub Co.

New World Paleoethnobotany: Collected Papers in Honor of Leonard W. Blake. Ed. by Eric E. Voigt & Deborah M. Pearsall. (Missouri Archaeologist Ser.: Vol. 47). (Illus.). 255p. (Orig.). (C). 1989. pap. 12.00 (0-943414-69-5) MO Arch Soc.

New World Parrots in Crisis: Solutions from Conservation Biology. Ed. by Steven R. Beissinger & Noel F. Snyder. LC 91-52867. (Illus.). 256p. (C). 1991. pap. text 17.95 (1-56098-136-9) Smithsonian.

New World Plants & Their Uses: A Guide to Selected Literature & Genetic Resources 1980-1993. Joanne Meil. (Illus.). 39p. (Orig.). (C). 1995. pap. text 20.00 (0-7881-1613-4) DIANE Pub.

New World Politics: Power, Ethnicity & Democracy. 1993. pap. 19.95 (0-614-04160-0) Acad Poli Sci.

New World Primates: Adaptive Radiation & the Evolution of Social Behavior, Languages & Intelligence. Martin Moynihan. LC 75-3467. (Illus.). 273p. 1976. reprint ed. pap. 84.70 (0-608-06642-7, 206683900009) Bks Demand.

New World Primates: Ecology, Evolution, & Behavior. Ed. by Warren G. Kinzey. LC 96-38566. (Evolutionary Foundations of Human Behavior Ser.). (Illus.). 453p. 1997. pap. text 32.95 (0-202-01186-0); lib. bdg. 64.95 (0-202-01185-2) Aldine de Gruyter.

New World Regionalism. David M. Jordan. (Theory - Culture Ser.). (Illus.). 176p. (C). 1994. text 45.00 (0-8020-0568-3); pap. text 17.95 (0-8020-6989-4) U of Toronto Pr.

New World Religion. Gary Kah. 1998. pap. 12.99 (0-921714-52-1, Pub. by Fon3tier Res) Spring Arbor Dist.

New World Religion. Gary Kah. 1999. pap. 12.99 (0-921714-50-5) Fon3tier Res.

New World Religion. Gary Kah. Ed. by Rick Blanchette. 300p. 1999. pap. 12.99 (0-9670098-0-4) Hope Intl.

New World Screwworm Eradication Programme: North Africa, 1988-92. FAO Staff. 1992p. 1992. pap. 47.00 (92-5-103200-9, F32009, Pub. by FAO) Bernan Associates.

New World Shipwrecks, 1492-1825: A Comprehensive Guide. Robert Marx & Jenifer Marx. LC 94-65593. (Illus.). 400p. 1994. 16.95 (0-915920-84-0) Ram Pub.

New World Soundings: Culture & Ideology in the Americas. Richard M. Morse. LC 89-1730. (Johns Hopkins Studies in Atlantic History & Culture). 312p. reprint ed. pap. 96.80 (0-608-08795-5, 206943400004) Bks Demand.

New World Spanish-English, English-Spanish Dictionary. rev. ed. Andrew Morehead & Salvatore Ramondino. 1296p. 1996. pap. 29.95 incl. disk (0-525-94205-X) Viking Penguin.

New World Strategy: A Military Policy for America's Future. Harry G. Summers, Jr. LC 95-32868. 269p. 1995. pap. 11.00 (0-684-81208-8, Touchstone) S&S Trade Pap.

N

New World Symphonies: How American Culture Changed European Music. Jack Sullivan. LC 98-3641. (Illus.). 266p. 1999. 30.00 (0-300-07231-7) Yale U Pr.

New World Thesaurus. Charleton Grant Liard. 1986. mass mkt. 9.95 (0-446-38412-7, Pub. by Warner Bks) Little.

*New World Trade Organization Agreements: Globalizing Law Through Services & Intellectual Property. Christopher Arup. (Cambridge Studies in Law & Society). 336p. 2000. 54.95 (0-521-77355-5) Cambridge U Pr.

New World Trading System: Readings. OECD Staff. 240p. (Orig.). 1994. pap. 29.00 (92-64-14245-2) OECD.

New World Vistas: Air & Space Power for the 21st Century (Summary) Gene H. McCall & John A. Corder. (Illus.). 90p. (Orig.). (C). 1996. pap. text 35.00 (0-7881-3385-3) DIANE Pub.

New World Vultures with Old World Affinities. P. V. Rich. (Contributions to Vertebrate Evolution Ser.: Vol. 5). (Illus.). 1979. pap. 34.00 (3-8055-0280-X) S Karger.

New World Wide Stamp Kit. rev. ed. Ed. by Glenn Hinceman & George A. Tlamsa. (Illus.). 400p. 1994. reprint ed. boxed set 65.00 (0-912236-29-9, Minkus Pubns) Novus Debut.

*New World Wines: The Complete Guide. Julie Arkell. (Illus.). 224p. 2000. 39.95 (0-304-35160-1, Pub. by Cassell) Sterling.

*New World Won. Barrington King. LC 99-17836. 1999. 24.95 (0-7862-1886-X) Thorndike Pr.

New Worldly Order: John Paul II & Human Freedom - A Centesimus Annus Reader. Ed. by George Weigel. 196p. (Orig.). (C). 1992. 29.95 (0-89633-170-9); pap. 14.95 (0-89633-171-7) Ethics & Public Policy.

New Worlds. (English for Academic Purposes Ser.). 288p. (J). 1996. mass mkt. 27.95 (0-8384-1670-5) Heinle & Heinle.

*New Worlds. Bart Farkas. (Official Strategies & Secrets Ser.). 240p. 1999. pap. 19.99 (0-7821-2673-1) Sybex.

New Worlds. annot. ed. (English for Academic Purposes Ser.). (J). 1990. teacher ed. 27.95 (0-8384-1702-7) Heinle & Heinle.

New Worlds, Vol. 1. Ed. by David Garnett. (New Anthology Ser.). (Orig.). 1997. pap. 12.99 (1-56504-190-9, 12190, Borealis) White Wolf.

New Worlds: A Course in Guided Composition, with Readings & Conversation, 3 vols. Florence Baskoff. (C). 1992. 25.16 (0-395-52632-9) HM.

New Worlds: A Course in Guided Composition, with Readings & Conversation, 3 vols. 3rd ed. Florence Baskoff. (C). 1992. text 23.96 (0-395-43196-4) HM.

*New Worlds: An Introduction to College Reading. Joe Cortina & Janet Elder. LC 99-43522. 2000. write for info. (0-07-366029-9) McGrw-H Hghr Educ.

New Worlds, Ancient Texts: The Power of Tradition & the Shock of Discovery. Anthony Grafton. 282p. 1995. pap. 16.95 (0-674-61876-9, GRANEX) Belknap Pr.

New Worlds, Ancient Texts: The Power of Tradition & the Shock of Discovery. Anthony Grafton et al. LC 92-10692. (Illus.). 320p. (C). 1992. text 29.95 (0-674-61875-0) HUP.

New Worlds for All: Indians, Europeans, & the Remaking of Early America. Colin G. Calloway. LC 96-20625. (Illus.). 216p. 1997. 24.95 (0-8018-5448-2) Johns Hopkins.

N

New Worlds for All: Indians, Europeans, & the Remaking of Early America. Colin G. Calloway. LC 96-20625. (The American Moment Ser.). (Illus.). 256p. 1998. reprint ed. pap. text 14.95 (*0-8018-5959-X*) Johns Hopkins.

New Worlds for Old. unabridged ed. H. G. Wells. (Classic Reprint Ser.). 333p. 1997. reprint ed. 35.00 (*0-936128-59-3*) De Young Pr.

New Worlds for Old: Reports from the New World & Their Effect on the Development of Social Thought in Europe, 1500-1800. William Brandon. LC 85-25818. 226p. 1986. pap. text 14.95 (*0-8214-0819-4*) Ohio U Pr.

New Worlds Four. Ed. by David Garnett. (Illus.). 224p. 1994. pap. 13.95 (*0-575-05147-7*, Pub. by V Gollancz) Trafalgar.

New Worlds from the Lowlands: Fantasy & Science Fiction of Dutch & Flemish Writers. Compiled by Manuel Van Loggem. 256p. 1982. 20.00 (*0-89304-053-3*, CCC150); pap. 12.00 (*0-89304-054-1*) Cross-Cultrl NY.

New Worlds in Astroparticle Physics: Proceedings of the International Workshop Faro, Portugal 8-10 September, 1996. Ed. by A. M. Mourao et al. LC 98-215439. 430p. 1998. 94.00 (*981-02-3389-2*) World Scientific Pub.

***New Worlds in Astroparticle Physics: Proceedings of the Second International Workshop.** Ed. by Ana M. Mourao et al. 500p. 1999. 108.00 (*981-02-4087-2*) World Scientific Pub.

New Worlds in Information & Documentation: Proceedings of the Forty-Sixth Conference & Congress Held in Madrid, Spain, 22-29 October, 1992. Ed. by Jose R. Alvarez-Ossorio & Ben G. Goedegebuure. LC 94-10009. 506p. 1994. 126.75 (*0-444-81891-X*) Elsevier.

***New Worlds in Old Books.** Leona Rostenberg. 1999. 29.95 (*1-58574-001-2*) Lyons Pr.

New Worlds in Old Books. Leona Rostenberg & Madeleine B. Stern. LC 98-56395. (Illus.). 210p. 1999. 29.95 (*1-884718-89-2*, No. 53940RB) Oak Knoll.

New Worlds, New Animals: From Menagerie to Zoological Park in the Nineteenth Century. Ed. by R. J. Hoage & William A. Deiss. LC 95-33006. (Illus.). 224p. (C). 1996. pap. 15.95 (*0-8018-5373-7*); text 34.95 (*0-8018-5110-6*) Johns Hopkins.

***New Worlds, New Civilizations.** Michael Friedman. 288p. 1999. 35.00 (*0-671-88103-5*, Star Trek) PB.

New Worlds, New Geographies. John R. Short. LC 97-29244. (Space, Place, & Society Ser.). 1998. 29.95 (*0-8156-0527-7*) Syracuse U Pr.

***New Worlds, New Geographies.** John R. Short. 244p. 2000. pap. 22.95 (*0-8156-2838-2*) Syracuse U Pr.

New Worlds, New Technologies, New Issues. Ed. by Stephen H. Cutcliffe et al. LC 91-58102. (Research in Technology Studies: Vol. 6). 240p. 1992. 36.50 (*0-934223-24-6*) Lehigh Univ Pr.

New Worlds of Dvorak. Michael B. Beckerman. (Illus.). 200p. 1999. 27.95 (*0-393-04706-7*) Norton.

New Worlds of Edgard Varese: Papers & Discussion from a Varese Symposium at the City University of New York. Ed. by Sherman Van Solkema. LC 79-50357. (I.S.A.M. Monographs: No. 11). 90p. 1979. pap. 10.00 (*0-914678-11-6*) Inst Am Music.

New Worlds of Literature: Writings from America's Many Cultures. Ed. by Jerome Beaty & J. Paul Hunter. LC 93-9921. (C). 1994. pap. text. write for info. (*0-393-96355-1*) Norton.

New Worlds of Literature: Writings from America's Many Cultures. 2nd ed. Ed. by Jerome Beaty & J. Paul Hunter. (C). 1994. pap. text 44.50 (*0-393-96354-3*) Norton.

New Worlds of Women: Sapphic Science Fiction Erotica. 2nd expanded rev. ed. Ed. by Cecilia Tan. LC 97-169959. 1996. pap. 10.95 (*1-885865-15-5*) Circlet Pr.

***New Worlds to Seek: Pioneer Heinrich Lienhard in Switzerland & America, 1824-1846.** Heinrich Lienhard et al. Ed. by John Cushman Abbott. Tr. by Raymond Jhurgen Spahn. LC 99-21412. 352p. 2000. 39.95 (*0-8093-2233-1*) S Ill U Pr.

New Worship: Straight Talk on Music & the Church. Barry Liesch. LC 95-2576. (Illus.). 272p. (Orig.). 1995. pap. 15.99 (*0-8010-9001-6*) Baker Bks.

New Wrinkles. Roger Lewin. LC 96-85400. (Illus.). 64p. (Orig.). 1996. pap. 9.95 (*1-886094-42-X*) Chicago Spectrum.

New Writers. R. M. Frew & R. Siegfried. LC 97-178739. 225p. 1997. spiral bd. 24.95 (*0-917962-58-3*) T H Peek.

New Writer's Activity Book, Bk. 1. Fry. 1996. pap. 23.30 (*0-8092-0887-3*) NTC Contemp Pub Co.

New Writer's Activity Book, Bk. 2. Fry. 1996. pap. 23.30 (*0-8092-0888-1*) NTC Contemp Pub Co.

New Writer's Activity Book, Bk. 3. Fry. 1996. pap. 23.30 (*0-8092-0890-3*) NTC Contemp Pub Co.

New Writer's Activity Book, Bk. 4. Fry. 1996. pap. 23.30 (*0-8092-0891-1*) NTC Contemp Pub Co.

New Writer's Activity Book, Bk. 5. Fry. 1996. pap. 23.30 (*0-8092-0893-8*) NTC Contemp Pub Co.

New Writers for the Eighties. Ed. by Joe D. Bellamy. LC 81-71004. (Fiction International Ser.: No. 13). 282p. (Orig.). 1981. pap. 10.00 (*0-931362-06-7*) Fiction Intl.

New Writing: Spring, 1938. Ed. by John Lehmann. LC 72-178450. (Short Story Index Reprint Ser.). 1977. reprint ed. 19.95 (*0-8369-4051-2*) Ayer.

New Writing Environment: Writers at Work in a World of Technology. Ed. by M. Sharples & T. Van Der Geest. LC 96-4805. 278p. 1996. pap. 69.95 (*3-540-76011-3*) Spr-Verlag.

New Writing from Drost, Hewett, Hilburger, Hopkins, Lulat, McGoldrick: Poetry & Prose. J. Drost et al. LC 92-8884. 309p. (Orig.). 1992. pap. 18.99 (*0-944265-09-X*) Librosmondiale.

New Writing from Mexico. Intro. by Reginald Gibbons. (Illus.). 448p. 1992. 27.00 (*0-916384-12-8*, TriQuart); pap. 15.00 (*0-916384-13-6*, TriQuart) Northwestern U Pr.

New Writing from Southern Africa: Authors Who Have Become Prominent Since 1980. Ed. by Emmanuel Ngara. LC 95-39814. 320p. 1996. pap. 24.95 (*0-435-08971-4*, 08971) Heinemann.

New Writing from the Philippines: A Critique & Anthology. Leonard Casper. LC 66-18506. 429p. reprint ed. pap. 133.00 (*0-608-15205-6*, 202739700055) Bks Demand.

New Writing in Japan. Ed. by Yukio Mishima, pseud & Geoffrey Bownas. 256p. 1998. reprint ed. pap. text 25.00 (*1-873410-79-4*, Pub. by Curzon Pr Ltd) UH Pr.

New Writings by Swinburne: or Miscellanea Nova et Curiosa: Being a Medley of Poems, Critical Essays, Hoaxes & Burlesques. Algernon Charles Swinburne. LC 64-8669. 279p. reprint ed. pap. 86.50 (*0-608-18340-7*, 203301700082) Bks Demand.

New X Window System: An Internet Architecture for Clustered. Charles F. Bowman. LC 99-57912. 153p. (C). 2000. pap. text 32.95 (*0-201-18463-X*) Addison-Wesley.

New Xenophobia in Europe. Ed. by Bernd Baumgartl & Adrian Favell. 416p. (C). 1995. lib. bdg. 91.00 (*90-411-0865-3*) Kluwer Academic.

New Xhosa Phrase Book. H. Tsolwana. 120p. 1999. pap. 10.00 (*0-627-02006-2*, Pub. by J L Van Schaik) BHB Intl.

New Yalta, Commemorating the 50th Anniversary of the Declaration of Human Rights in RBEC Region. 190p. 45.00 (*92-1-126108-2*) UN.

New Yankee Workshop. Norm Abram. (Illus.). 196p. 1989. 29.95 (*0-316-00453-7*); pap. 21.95 (*0-316-00454-5*) Little.

New Yankee Workshop Kids' Stuff. Norm Abram. LC 97-17889. (Illus.). 208p. 1998. pap. 19.95 (*0-316-00492-8*) Little.

New Yankee Workshop Outdoor Projects. Norm Abram & Roland Walker. LC 93-42574. 204p. 1994. pap. 22.00 (*0-316-00486-3*) Little.

New Yawk Tawk: A Dictionary of New York City Expressions. Robert Hendrickson. LC 97-51156. 1998. pap. 14.95 (*0-8160-3869-4*, Checkmark) Facts on File.

New Yawk Tawk: A Dictionary of New York Expressions. Hendrickson. LC 97-51156. (Dictionary of American Regional Expressions Ser.). 256p. 1998. 24.95 (*0-8160-2114-7*) Facts on File.

New Year. Lass Small. (Desire Ser.). 1994. per. 2.99 (*0-373-05830-6*, 5-05830-0) Silhouette.

New Year. Michele Spirn. LC 98-12118. (World Celebrations & Ceremonies Ser.). (Illus.). 24p. (J). (gr. 3-5). 1998. lib. bdg. 15.95 (*1-56711-249-8*) Blackbirch.

New Year Ceremony at Basak (South Laos) Charles Archimault. Tr. by Simone B. Boas from FRE. 137p. 1988. reprint ed. pap. 20.00 (*0-923135-03-0*) Dalley Bk Service.

New Year... New Family. Grace Green. (Romance Ser.: Bk. 3586). 185p. 2000. per. 3.50 (*0-373-03586-1*, 1-03586-4) Harlequin Bks.

New Year, New Love. Cameron Dokey et al. 176p. (Orig.). (YA). 1996. mass mkt. 3.99 (*0-380-78663-X*, Avon Bks) Morrow Avon.

New Yearbook of Jazz. Leonard Feather. (Roots of Jazz Ser.). 188p. 1985. reprint ed. lib. bdg. 29.50 (*0-306-76288-9*) Da Capo.

New Year's. Nancy Reese. Ed. by Alton Jordan. (Holiday Set). (Illus.). (J). (gr. k-3). 1984. 7.95 (*0-89868-026-3*, Read Res); pap. 3.95 (*0-89868-059-X*, Read Res) ARO Pub.

***New Year's Babies.** Eugenia Riley et al. 400p. 1999. mass mkt. 5.99 (*0-505-52345-0*, Love Spell) Dorchester Pub Co.

New Year's Conviction. Cassie Miles. 1997. per. 3.75 (*0-373-22402-8*, 1-22402-1) Silhouette.

New Year's Daddy. Lisa Jackson. 1996. per. 3.75 (*0-373-24004-X*, 1-24004-3) Silhouette.

***New Year's Day.** David F. Marx. (Illus.). (J). 2000. write for info. (*0-516-22205-8*) Childrens.

***New Year's Day.** David F. Marx. (Rookie Read-About Holidays Ser.). (Illus.). 32p. (J). (gr. 1-2). 2000. pap. 5.95 (*0-516-27156-3*) Childrens.

***New Year's Day.** Dana Meachen Rau. LC 99-86740. (Illus.). (J). 2000. 22.00 (*0-516-21516-7*) Childrens.

***New Years' Day.** Dana Meachen Rau. (True Bks.). (Illus.). 48p. (J). (gr. 3-5). 2000. pap. 6.95 (*0-516-27062-1*) Childrens.

New Year's Day Killings of the Nuns in Nicaragua: A Report on an Investigation. Americas Watch Staff. 40p. 1990. 5.00 (*0-929692-92-6*, Am Watch) Hum Rts Watch.

New Year's Eve. Gwynne Garfinkle. 72p. (Orig.). (C). 1989. pap. write for info. (*0-9623512-0-2*) Typical Girls.

New Year's Eve. Lisa Grunwald. LC 98-15406. 384p. 1998. mass mkt. 13.99 (*0-446-67403-6*, Pub. by Warner Bks) Little.

New Year's Eve. Beth Henderson. (Special Edition Ser.). 1995. per. 3.50 (*0-373-09935-5*, 1-09935-7) Silhouette.

New Year's Eve. large type ed. Lisa Grunwald. (Niagara Large Print Ser.). 1997. 29.50 (*0-7089-5876-1*) Ulverscroft.

New Year's Eve Compendium: Toasts, Tips, Trivia & Tidbits for Bringing in the New Year. Todd Lyon. 1998. pap. write for info. (*0-609-80341-7*) C Potter.

New Year's Eve Compendium: Toasts, Tips, Trivia & Tidbits for Bringing in the New Year. Todd Lyon. LC 98-16943. (Illus.). 112p. 1998. 12.00 (*0-609-60374-4*) C Potter.

New Year's Eve Flood on Oahu, Hawaii: December 31, 1987-January 1, 1988. National Research Council, Committee on Vision Sta. (Natural Disaster Studies: Vol. 1). 88p. 1990. pap. text 19.00 (*0-309-04433-2*) Natl Acad Pr.

New Year's Eve in Whiting, Indiana. James Hazard. LC 85-62417. 80p. (Orig.). 1985. pap. 6.50 (*0-935399-00-3*) Main St Pub.

New Year's Eve Murder. Lee Harris. (Christine Bennett Mystery Ser.). 1997. mass mkt. 5.99 (*0-449-15018-6*, GM) Fawcett.

New Year's Eve, 1929. James T. Farrell. LC 67-30058. 144p. 1960. pap. 10.00 (*0-912292-02-4*) Smith.

New Year's Eve, 1929. James T. Farrell. LC 67-30058. 144p. 1967. 15.00 (*0-912292-84-9*) Smith.

New Year's Evil. Carolyn Keene. Ed. by Anne Greenberg. (Nancy Drew & Hardy Boys Super Mystery Ser.: No. 11). 224p. (YA). (gr. 6 up). 1991. mass mkt. 3.99 (*0-671-67467-6*, Archway) PB.

New Year's Evil. Carolyn Keene. (Nancy Drew & Hardy Boys Super Mystery Ser.: No. 11). (YA). (gr. 6 up). 1991. 9.09 (*0-606-00644-3*, Pub. by Turtleback) Demco.

New Year's Knight. Lyn Ellis. 1997. per. 3.50 (*0-373-25718-X*, 1-25718-7) Silhouette.

New Year's Party. R. L. Stine, pseud. (Fear Street Super Chiller Ser.: No. 9). (J). (gr. 7 up). 1995. mass mkt. 3.99 (*0-671-89425-0*, Archway) PB.

New Year's Party. R. L. Stine, pseud. (Fear Street Super Chiller Ser.: No. 9). (YA). (gr. 7 up). 1995. 9.09 (*0-606-08515-7*, Pub. by Turtleback) Demco.

New Year's Poetry Party at the Imperial Court: Two Decades in Postwar Years, 1960-1979. Marie Philomene. (Illus.). 250p. 1983. 39.95 (*4-590-00653-7*, Pub. by Hokuseido Pr) Book East.

New Year's Resolution. Elley Crain. (Intimate Moments Ser.). 1993. per. 3.50 (*0-373-07533-2*, 5-07533-8) Silhouette.

New Year's Resolution: Baby. Margot Dalton & Anne Stuart. 1997. per. 5.99 (*0-373-83320-2*, 1-83320-1) Silhouette.

New Year's Resolution: Family. Barbara Bretton & Anne McAllister. (Harlequin Promotion Ser.). 1998. per. 5.99 (*0-373-83332-6*, 1-883332-6) Harlequin Bks.

New Year's Resolution: Husband. Rebecca Brandewyne & Anne Stuart. LC 96-3538. 377p. 1996. per. 4.99 (*0-373-83312-1*, 1-83312-8) Harlequin Bks.

***New Year's Resolutions Diet, Exercise, & Weight Loss Log Book: A Useful One-Year Self-Help Record to Accomplish Your Health & Fitness Goals.** Masquerade Masters Staff. (Illus.). 190p. 1998. vinyl bd. 12.00 (*1-886197-29-6*) Joy Books.

New Year's Resolutions Diet, Exercise & Weight Loss Log Book: A Useful One-Year Self-Help Record to Accomplish Your Health & Fitness Goals. deluxe ed. Masquerade Masters. (Illus.). 190p. 1997. vinyl bd. 24.50 (*1-886197-11-3*) Joy Books.

New Year's Revolution! Diana G. Gallagher. (Secret World of Alex Mack Ser.: No. 22). (J). (gr. 3-6). 1997. pap. 3.99 (*0-671-01555-9*) PB.

***New Year's to Kwanzaa: Original Stories of Celebration.** Kendall Haven. 288p. (J). (gr. 3-8). 1999. pap. 16.95 (*1-55591-962-6*) Fulcrum Pub.

New Year's Wife. Linda Varner. 1997. per. 3.25 (*0-373-19200-2*, 1-19200-4) Silhouette.

New Yoga for People over 50: A Comprehensive Guide for Midlife & Older Beginners. Suza Francina. LC 97-20984. (Illus.). 230p. 1997. pap. 11.95 (*1-55874-453-3*) Health Comm.

New York see From Sea to Shining Sea

New York see World Cities

New York see One Nation Series

New York see Celebrate the States - Group 1

***New York.** 208p. 2000. spiral bd. 16.95 (*1-56251-330-3*, Pub. by AAA) S&S Trade.

New York. 1997. pap. 6.95 (*1-872876-39-0*, 311698Q) Assoc Pubs Grp.

New York. 64p. pap. text 9.95 (*88-8029-128-9*, Pub. by Bonechi) Eiron.

New York. (Ultimate Sticker Books Ser.). (J). 1998. pap. 6.95 (*0-7894-3468-7*) DK Pub Inc.

New York. (Nelles Guides Ser.). (Illus.). 256p. pap. 14.95 (*3-88618-903-1*, Pub. by Nelles Verlag) Seven Hills Bk.

New York. (Prestel Postcard Bks.). (Illus.). 18p. 1994. 8.95 (*3-7913-1377-0*, Pub. by Prestel) te Neues.

New York. (Baedeker's Ser.). (Illus.). 1991. pap. 17.00 (*0-13-094780-6*, P-H Travel) Prntice Hall Bks.

New York. (Windsor Destination Guides Ser.). (Illus.). 64p. 1992. pap. 16.95 (*1-874111-04-9*) Seven Hills Bk.

New York. Eleanor Berman. LC 92-53471. (Eyewitness Travel Guides Ser.). (Illus.). 432p. 1993. pap. 24.95 (*1-56458-184-5*) DK Pub Inc.

***New York.** Mary Bowman-Kruhm. (Illus.). 64p. (gr. 1-5). 2000. pap. 5.95 (*1-892920-49-2*) G H B Pubs.

New York. Capstone Press Geography Department Staff. (One Nation Ser.). (Illus.). 48p. (J). (gr. 3-7). 1996. lib. bdg. 19.00 (*0-516-20107-7*) Childrens.

***New York.** Dorling Kindersley Publishing Inc., Staff. LC 99-53294. (Kids' Travel Guides Ser.). (Illus.). 64p. (J). 2000. pap. 7.95 (*0-7894-5248-0*, D K Ink) DK Pub Inc.

New York. Mark Dunster. LC 74-229035. 1973. 4.00 (*0-89642-029-9*) Linden Pubs.

New York. William Eisner. (Illus.). 140p. 1986. pap. 13.95 (*0-87816-020-5*) Kitchen Sink.

New York. John Escott. (Illus.). 24p. 1996. pap. text 6.95 (*0-19-422800-2*) OUP.

New York. Dennis B. Fradin. (Illus.). 64p. (J). (gr. 3-5). 1994. pap. 7.95 (*0-516-43832-8*) Childrens.

New York. Amy Gelman. Ed. by Lerner Geography Department Staff. (Hello U. S. A. Ser.). (Illus.). 72p. (J). (gr. 3-6). 1992. lib. bdg. 19.95 (*0-8225-2720-0*, Lerner Publctns) Lerner Pub.

New York. Amy Gelman. (Illus.). 72p. 1995. pap. text 5.95 (*0-8225-9702-0*) Lerner Pub.

New York. Michael Gottlieb. 1993. pap. 10.00 (*0-935724-52-4*) Figures.

New York. Ann Heinrichs & R. Conrad Stein. LC 98-27784. (America the Beautiful Ser.). 144p. (YA). (gr. 5-8). 1999. write for info. (*0-516-20691-5*) Childrens.

New York. Horwitz. 1999. pap. write for info. (*0-312-09352-7*) St Martin.

New York. Insight Guides Staff. (Insight Guides). 1998. pap. text 7.95 (*0-88729-550-9*) Langenscheidt.

***New York.** James Kavanagh. (Pocket Traveller City Ser.). (Illus.). 2000. 5.95 (*1-58355-020-8*, Pub. by Waterford WA) Falcon Pub Inc.

New York. Knopf Guides Staff. (Knopf Guide Ser.). 446p. 1994. pap. 25.00 (*0-679-75065-7*) Knopf.

New York. Edward Irving Koch. LC 99-54412. (Illus.). 1999. write for info. (*1-881096-76-9*) Towery Pub.

New York. Sabina Lietzmann. LC 81-7564. (Illus.). 80p. 1999. pap. 19.95 (*0-86565-023-3*) Vendome.

New York. National Geographic Society Staff. LC 99-11701. (National Geographic Traveler Ser.). 272p. 1999. per. 22.95 (*0-7922-7430-X*, Pub. by Natl Geog) S&S Trade.

New York. NTC Publishing Group Staff. (Passport Essential Guide Ser.). 128p. 1998. pap. 8.95 (*0-8442-0124-3*, Passprt Bks) NTC Contemp Pub Co.

New York. Ramker. (Discover America Ser.). 1979. 6.99 (*0-8442-7469-0*) NTC Contemp Pub Co.

New York. Tamas Revesz. 14.95 (*0-393-05023-8*) Norton.

New York. Esther Selsdon. (Great Cities Ser.). (Illus.). 96p. 1999. 20.00 (*1-85995-520-7*) Parkstone Pr.

***New York.** Antony Shugaar. (Illus.). 2000. 9.99 (*0-7858-1239-3*) Bk Sales Inc.

New York. Susanna Sirefman. (Architecture Guides Ser.). (Illus.). 320p. 1998. pap. 5.95 (*3-89508-641-X*, 520205) Konemann.

New York Smith. 272p. text 74.00 (*0-471-98829-4*) Wiley.

New York. Gail Stewart. (Great Cities of the U. S. A. Ser.). (Illus.). 48p. (YA). (gr. 5 up). 1989. lib. bdg. 23.93 (*0-86592-541-0*) Rourke Enter.

***New York.** Lynn M. Stone. (American Wildlife Ser.). (Illus.). 32p. (J). (gr. 2-7). 2001. lib. bdg. 22.60 (*1-58340-011-7*) Smart Apple.

New York. Kathleen Thompson. LC 95-9608. (Portrait of America Library). (Illus.). 48p. (J). (gr. 3-6). 1996. lib. bdg. 22.83 (*0-8114-7377-5*) Raintree Steck-V.

New York. Kathleen Thompson. LC 95-9608. (Portrait of America Library). (Illus.). 48p. (J). (gr. 4-8). 1996. pap. 5.95 (*0-8114-7458-5*) Raintree Steck-V.

New York. Santi Visalli. (Illus.). 208p. 1995. pap. 25.00 (*0-7893-0003-6*, Pub. by Universe) St Martin.

New York. Anne Welsbacher. LC 97-34110. (United States Ser.). (Illus.). 32p. (J). 1998. lib. bdg. 19.93 (*1-56239-891-1*, Checkerboard Library) ABDO Pub Co.

New York. rev. ed. Compiled by Nelles Verlag. (Nelles Guides Ser.). (Illus.). 256p. 1993. pap. 14.95 (*3-88618-390-4*, Pub. by Nelles Verlag) Seven Hills Bk.

***New York.** rev. ed. Virgin Publishing Staff. (City Guides Ser.). (Illus.). 2000. pap. 17.95 (*0-7627-0780-1*) Globe Pequot.

New York. 2nd ed. Thomas Cook. (Passport's Illustrated Travel Guides Ser.). (Illus.). 192p. 1998. pap. 14.95 (*0-8442-4846-0*, 48460, Passprt Bks) NTC Contemp Pub Co.

New York. 2nd ed. Deborah Williams. (Country Roads of... Ser.). 176p. 1999. pap. 12.95 (*0-8442-4308-6*, 43086, Cntry Rds Pr) NTC Contemp Pub Co.

New York. 2nd rev. ed. Carol Von Pressentin Wright. LC 90-21262. (Illus.). 761p. 1991. pap. 25.00 (*0-393-30486-8*) Norton.

***New York.** 8th ed. Penguin Books Staff. (Time Out Travel Guides Ser.). (Illus.). 2000. pap. 14.95 (*0-14-028943-7*) Penguin Putnam.

***New York.** 15th ed. Petersons. (Peterson's Colleges in New York Ser.). 139-357p. 1999. pap. 17.95 (*0-7689-0253-3*) Petersons.

New York: A City Guide. Federal Writers' Project Staff. LC 39-27593. (American Guidebook Ser.). (Illus.). 708p. 1939. reprint ed. 89.00 (*0-403-02921-X*) Somerset Pub.

New York: A Geography. Richard T. Lewis. 1996. text 35.00 (*0-86531-227-3*) Westview.

New York: A Geography. Richard T. Lewis. (C). 1996. pap. text 20.00 (*0-86531-485-3*) Westview.

New York: A Guide to Information & Reference Sources, 1979-1986. Manuel D. Lopez. LC 87-16531. 384p. 1987. 39.50 (*0-8108-2018-8*) Scarecrow.

New York: A Guide to the Empire State. Federal Writers' Project Staff & Writers Program-WPA Staff. (American Guide Ser.). 1989. reprint ed. lib. bdg. 99.00 (*0-7812-1031-3*, 1031) Rprt Serv.

New York: A Guide to the Metropolis. 2nd ed. G. E. Wolfe. (Illus.). 559p. 1994. pap. 25.00 (*0-07-071397-9*) McGraw.

New York: A Literary Companion. Ed. by William Cole. 1992. 13.95 (*0-916366-59-6*, Pub. by Pushcart Pr) Norton.

***New York: Amerique du Nord.** 11th ed. (FRE.). 1998. pap. text 18.00 (*2-06-054811-X*) Michelin.

New York: An Illustrated History. Ric Burns & James Sanders. Ed. by Lisa Ades. LC 99-23569. (Illus.). 480p. 1999. 60.00 (*0-679-45482-9*) Knopf.

New York: An Illustrated History of the People. Allon Schoener. LC 98-10533. (Illus.). 416p. 1998. 59.95 (*0-393-04581-1*) Norton.

New York: City of Islands. Jake Rajs. LC 98-30246. 272p. 1998. 60.00 (*1-58093-009-3*, Pub. by Monacelli Pr) Penguin Putnam.

New York: Cobb's America Guyed Books. Irvin S. Cobb. (Collected Works of Irvin S. Cobb). 61p. 1998. reprint ed. lib. bdg. 88.00 (*1-58201-601-1*) Classic Bks.

New York: Das Insider-Lexikon. M. Gisela. (GER.). 29.95 (*0-7859-8336-8*, 3406340148) Fr & Eur.

New York: Deluxe Gift Edition. DK Publishing Staff. (Eyewitness Travel Guides Ser.). 432p. 1999. pap. 40.00 (*0-7894-4976-5*, D K Ink) DK Pub Inc.

New York: Drive by Shootings. David Bradford & Gerhard Waldherr. (Illus.). 440p. 1999. pap. 19.95 (*3-8290-2891-1*, 810155) Konemann.

New York: Exploring Wild & Scenic Places. 2nd ed. Deborah Williams. LC 98-46867. (Natural Wonders of... Ser.). (Illus.). 192p. (Orig.). 1994. reprint ed. pap. 14.95 (*1-56626-028-0*, 60280, Cntry Rds Pr) NTC Contemp Pub Co.

New York: Index of Awards on Claims of the Soldiers of the War of 1812. New York Adjutant-General's Office Staff. LC 74-75352. 579p. 1994. reprint ed. pap. 42.50 (*0-8063-0258-5*) Clearfield Co.

New York: Its Land & Its People. James Killoran et al. (Illus.). 433p. (J). (gr. 4 up). 1997. 21.95 (*1-882422-26-0*) Jarrett Pub.

New York: Its Upper Ten & Lower Million. George Lippard. LC 70-104514. 1989. reprint ed. pap. text 19.95 (*0-8290-1855-7*) Irvington.

New York: Manhattan. 2nd ed. Vanessa Letts. (Cadogan Guide Ser.). (Illus.). 224p. 1997. pap. text 14.95 (*1-86011-072-X*, Pub. by Cadgn Bks) Globe Pequot.

New York: Masterpieces of Architecture. Andras Kaldor. (Illus.). 96p. 1999. 19.95 (*1-85149-308-5*) Antique Collect.

New York: Metropolis of the American Dream. Martin Mayer & Deborah G. Faria. LC 95-38123. (Urban Tapestry Ser.). (Illus.). 384p. 1995. 39.50 (*1-881096-22-X*) Towery Pub.

*__New York: Not Only Buildings.__ Italo Rota. (Illus.). 400p. 2000. pap. 22.50 (*3-8238-5475-5*) te Neues.

New York: Off the Beaten Path: A Guide to Unique Places. 5th ed. William G. Scheller & Kay Scheller. LC 98-41609. (Illus.). 290p. 1999. pap. text 10.95 (*0-7627-0433-0*) Globe Pequot.

New York: Songs of the City. Nancy J. Groce. LC 99-11122. (Illus.). 192p. 1999. text 35.00 (*0-8230-8349-7*) Watsn-Guptill.

New York: State & City. David M. Ellis. LC 78-15759. (Illus.). 267p. 1979. text 39.95 (*0-8014-1180-7*) Cornell U Pr.

*__New York: The Best Cross-Country Ski & Snowshoe Trails.__ Ron Farra & Johanna Farra. (Winter Trails Ser.). (Illus.). 2000. pap. 14.95 (*0-7627-0557-4*) Globe Pequot.

New York: The Canal State. Francis P. Kimball. 105p. 1993. reprint ed. lib. bdg. 69.00 (*0-7812-5216-4*) Rprt Serv.

New York: The City in More Than 500 Memorable Quotations. Vladimir F. Wertsman. LC 99-23473. Orig. Title: New York, the City in More Than 500 Memorable Quotations: From More Than 500 Authors (American & Foreign) & More Than 500 Reference Sources. 208p. 1999. reprint ed. pap. 14.95 (*1-57886-005-9*, Pub. by Scarecrow Trade) Natl Bk Netwk.

New York: The Planting & the Growth of the Empire State, 2 vols. Ellis H. Roberts. LC 72-3763. (American Commonwealths Ser.: Nos. 8-9). reprint ed. 76.50 (*0-404-57221-9*) AMS Pr.

New York: The Planting & the Growth of the Empire State, 2 vols., Set. Ellis H. Roberts. 1993. reprint ed. lib. bdg. 99.00 (*0-7812-5197-4*) Rprt Serv.

New York: The Politics of Urban Regional Development. Michael N. Danielson & Jameson W. Doig. LC 81-7480. (Lane Studies in Regional Government: No. 4). 352p. 1982. 55.00 (*0-520-04371-5*, Pub. by U CA Pr); pap. 16.95 (*0-520-04551-3*, Pub. by U CA Pr) Cal Prin Full Svc.

New York: The Spirit of America, State by State. Nina Sonenberg. Ed. by Diana Landau. LC 98-14183. (Art of the State Ser.). (Illus.). 120p. 1998. 12.95 (*0-8109-5557-1*, Pub. by Abrams) Time Warner.

New York: The State & Its Educational System. Harold L. Hodgkinson. 12p. 1987. 7.00 (*0-937846-86-4*) Inst Educ Lead.

New York: The Thirties. Samuel Fuller. 1997. pap. 12.95 (*0-614-27471-0*) DAP Assocs.

New York: The Travel Notebook. Pascale Loiseau. 104p. 1997. 14.95 (*2-911141-00-8*, Pub. by Les Edtns Pascale) Assoc Pubs Grp.

*__New York: The Ultimate Photographic Journey.__ Mark Crosby. (Illus.). 2000. 29.95 (*0-7893-0504-6*) Universe.

New York: Trends & Traditions. Roberto Schezen & Chessy Rayner. LC 97-28070. 1997. 65.00 (*1-885254-74-1*, Pub. by Monacelli Pr) Penguin Putnam.

New York - A Feast of Memories: A Re-Sampling of Times Past. David D. Carroll. LC 92-61110. (Illus.). 96p. 1994. 14.95 (*1-881554-01-5*) Skyward Pub.

New York - Collected Works of Federal Writers Project, 2 vols., Set. Federal Writers' Project Staff. 1991. reprint ed. lib. bdg. 148.00 (*0-7812-5688-7*) Rprt Serv.

New York Abolitionists: A Case Study of Political Radicalism, 11. Gerald Sorin. LC 73-105981. 172p. 1970. 52.95 (*0-8371-3308-4*, SNY/, Greenwood Pr) Greenwood.

*__New York Abstract Expressionists: Artists Choice by Artists.__ Marika Herskovic. (Illus.). 496p. 2000. 95.00 (*0-9677994-0-6*) NY Schl Pr.

New York Academy of Medicine, 1947-1997: Enhancing the Health of the Public. Marvin Lieberman & Leon J. Warshaw. LC 97-29698. 428p. 1998. 69.50 (*0-89464-984-1*) Krieger.

New York Actions & Remedies, Vol. 5, Family Law, Wills & Trusts see New York Actions & Remedies, Vols. 1-5

New York Actions & Remedies Vols. 1-5, 5 vols., Set. Ed. by Mark Rhodes. Incl. Set. New York Actions & Remedies Vols. 3 & 4: Corporate & Commercial Law., 2 vols. 1300p. 1991. ring bd. 170.00 (*0-88063-445-6*, MICHIE); Vol. 5. New York Actions & Remedies Vol. 5: Family Law, Wills & Trusts. 500p. 1991. ring bd. 85.00 (*1-56257-165-6*, MICHIE); Vols. 1 & 2. New York Actions & Remedies Vols. 1 & 2: Tort Law. 1000p. 1991. ring bd. 170.00 (*1-56257-164-8*, MICHIE); 1991. Set ring bd. 400.00 (*1-56257-661-5*, MICHIE) LEXIS Pub.

New York Actions & Remedies, Vols. 1 & 2, Tort Law see New York Actions & Remedies, Vols. 1-5

New York Actions & Remedies, Vols. 3 & 4, Corporate & Commercial Law see New York Actions & Remedies, Vols. 1-5

New York Administration, 1998 Supplement. Margaret V. Turano & C. Raymond Radigan. 200p. 1998. write for info. (*0-327-00828-8*, 6890511) LEXIS Pub.

New York Agent: Get the Agent You Need & the Career You Want. 4th ed. Ed. by Kristi Nolte. 300p. 1995. 17.95 (*1-878355-03-1*) Sweden Pr.

New York Agent Book. 5th ed. K. Callan. 1998. pap. text 17.95 (*1-878355-07-4*) Sweden Pr.

*__New York Agent Book: Get the Agent You Need for the Career You Want.__ 6th ed. K. Callan. Ed. by Kristi Nolte. 290p. 2000. pap. 18.95 (*1-878355-13-9*, Pub. by Sweden Pr) SCB Distributors.

New York Alcoholic Beverage Control Law. Ed. by Gould Staff. 168p. 1991. pap. 6.00 (*0-87526-377-1*) Gould.

New York & Its Emblems. Emily McAuliffe. LC 97-40685. (States & Their Emblems Ser.). (J). 1998. lib. bdg. write for info. (*1-56065-767-7*, Hilltop Bks) Capstone Pr.

New York & Its Western Hemispheric Neighbors. Linda Biemer. (Illus.). 208p. 1989. 21.00 (*0-87905-326-7*) Gibbs Smith Pub.

*__New York & New England: Woodall's 2000 Regional Camping Guide.__ Woodall's Publishing Staff. 372p. 1999. pap. text 6.99 (*0-7627-0585-X*) Globe Pequot.

*__New York & New England Camping Guide 2001.__ Woodalls Publishing Staff. (Regional Camping Guides Ser.). (Illus.). 2000. pap. 6.99 (*0-7627-0860-3*) Globe Pequot.

*__New York & New Jersey Area Contingency Plan.__ 950p. 1999. ring bd. 65.00 (*0-16-059082-5*) USGPO.

New York & New Jersey Parks Guide. Barbara Sinotte. (State & National Parks Ser.). (Illus.). 203p. (Orig.). 1996. pap. 14.95 (*1-55650-737-2*) Hunter NJ.

New York & Other State Greats (Biographies) Carole Marsh. (Carole Marsh New York Bks.). (Illus.). (J). 1994. pap. 19.95 (*1-55609-919-3*); lib. bdg. 29.95 (*1-55609-918-5*); disk 29.95 (*1-55609-920-7*) Gallopade Intl.

New York & Pennsylvania & New Jersey. Randall S. Peffer et al. LC 97-22435. (Driving Guides to America Ser.). 1997. write for info. (*0-7922-3431-6*) Natl Geog.

New York & the China Trade. David S. Howard. 144p. 1984. pap. 18.95 (*0-914366-22-X*) Columbia Pub.

New York & the New Europe: A Guide to Business Opportunities. (Illus.). 157p. (Orig.). (C). 1994. pap. text 40.00 (*0-7881-0229-X*) DIANE Pub.

New York Appellate Practice, 2 vols. Thomas R. Newman. 1985. ring bd. 365.00 (*0-8205-1519-1*) Bender.

New York Area Golf Guide, 1992: A Guide to Facilities Open to the Public. Briarcliff Press Staff. 1992. pap. 12.95 (*0-9631658-0-1*) Briarcliff NY.

New York Art from Warhol to Now. Matthew Collings. 1998. pap. text 29.95 (*1-901785-03-3*) Twenty-One.

New York As an Eighteenth Century Municipality, 2 pts., Set. George W. Edwards & Arthur E. Peterson. LC 68-56681. (Columbia University. Studies in the Social Sciences: Nos. 177-178). reprint ed. 67.50 (*0-404-51697-1*) AMS Pr.

New York As Washington Knew It after the Revolution. W. L. Andrews. 1973. 59.95 (*0-8490-0726-7*) Gordon Pr.

New York at Gettysburg, 3 vols., Set. William F. Fox. 1462p. 1994. reprint ed. lib. bdg. 139.00 (*0-8328-3804-7*) Higginson Bk Co.

New York at Its Best. Robert S. Kane. (Illus.). 416p. 1995. pap. 12.95 (*0-8442-9583-3*, Passprt Bks) NTC Contemp Pub Co.

New York at Mid-Century: The Impellitteri Years, 147. Salvatore J. Lagumina. LC 92-8844. 272p. 1992. 55.00 (*0-313-27205-0*, LBC, Greenwood Pr) Greenwood.

*__New York at Night.__ 2nd ed. M. K. Publishing Group Staff. (Illus.). 2000. pap. 11.95 (*0-9666057-2-1*) Nightlife Inc.

*__New York @ Night: A Personal Guide to New York's Nightlife.__ C. Dagan McCann. (Illus.). 2000. pap. 11.95 (*0-9660570-5-8*) Preserv Pubns.

New York Athlete: Sports, Fitness & Fun in the Big Apple. Jane Goldman et al. 1983. pap. 8.95 (*0-686-45252-6*) S&S Trade.

New York Atlas. Stephan Van Dam. (City Atlas Ser.). 1998. pap. 10.95 (*0-931141-90-7*) VanDam Inc.

*__New York Atlas.__ 5th ed. DeLorme Mapping Co. Staff. (Illus.). 2000. pap. 19.95 (*0-89933-275-7*) DeLorme Map.

New York Attorney's-Secretary's Handbook. 3rd ed. (Illus.). 475p. 1993. ring bd. 65.00 (*1-881131-01-7*) Plymouth Pub.

New York Automotive Directory. Ed. by T. L. Spelman. 1985. 24.95 (*1-55527-023-9*) Auto Contact Inc.

New York Bandits, Bushwackers, Outlaws, Crooks, Devils, Ghosts, Desperadoes & Other Assorted & Sundry Characters! Carole Marsh. (Carole Marsh New York Bks.). (Illus.). (J). 1994. pap. 19.95 (*0-7933-0816-X*); lib. bdg. 29.95 (*0-7933-0817-8*); disk 29.95 (*0-7933-0818-6*) Gallopade Intl.

New York Banking Law. annuals Gould Editorial Staff. 950p. (C). ring bd. 59.00 (*0-87526-235-X*) Gould.

New York Bartender's Guide. Black Dog & Leventhal Publis. Staff. (Illus.). 256p. 9.98 (*1-884822-13-4*) Blck Dog & Leventhal.

New York Basic Competency Tests (BCT-NY) Jack Rudman. (Admission Test Ser.: Vol. 55). 43.95 (*0-8373-5155-3*) Nat Learn.

New York Basic Competency Tests (BCT-NY) Jack Rudman. (Admission Test Ser.: ATS-55). 1994. pap. 23.95 (*0-8373-5055-7*) Nat Learn.

New York Beautiful. Wallace Nutting. 305p. 1993. reprint ed. lib. bdg. 89.00 (*0-7812-5131-1*) Rprt Serv.

New York Before Chinatown: Orientalism & the Shaping of American Culture, 1776-1882. John J. Weitchen. LC 99-10665. 400p. 1999. 42.50 (*0-8018-6006-7*) Johns Hopkins.

New York Bicycle Touring Guide: Includes Route EM, Route HC, Route PC & Route ST. William N. Hoffman. 1983. pap. 2.95 (*0-9612050-1-6*); pap. 2.95 (*0-9612050-2-4*); pap. 2.50 (*0-9612050-3-2*); pap. 3.50 (*0-9612050-4-0*) Spring Garden Pubns.

New York Bicycle Touring Guide: Includes Route EM, Route HC, Route PC & Route ST, 4 bks., Set. William N. Hoffman. 1983. pap. 9.95 (*0-9612050-0-8*) Spring Garden Pubns.

New York Biking Guide. Barbara McCaig. Ed. by Gretchen Vanderboom. 100p. (Orig.). 1989. pap. text 5.95 (*0-935201-83-1*) Affordable Adven.

New York "BIO" Bingo! 24 Must Know State People for Kids to Learn about While Having Fun! Carole Marsh. (Bingo! Ser.). (Illus.). (J). (gr. 2-8). 1998. pap. 14.95 (*0-7933-8618-7*) Gallopade Intl.

New York Birds. James Kavanagh. (Pocket Naturalist Ser.). (Illus.). 1997. 5.95 (*1-889903-39-6*, Pub. by Waterford WA) Falcon Pub Inc.

New York Bond Market, 1920-1930. Charles C. Abbott. LC 75-2618. (Wall Street & the Security Market Ser.). 1975. reprint ed. 26.95 (*0-405-06945-6*) Ayer.

New York Book of Coffee & Cake see Big Cup: A Guide to New York's Coffee Culture

New York Book of Tea: Where to Take Tea & Buy Tea & Teaware. 2nd rev. ed. Bo Niles & Veronica McNiff. LC 97-8247. (Illus.). 128p. 1997. 18.00 (*1-885492-37-5*) City & Co.

New York Bookstore Book: A Surprising Guide to Our State's Bookstores & Their Specialties for Students, Teachers, Writers & Publishers. Carole Marsh. (Carole Marsh New York Bks.). (Illus.). 1994. pap. 19.95 (*0-7933-2952-3*); lib. bdg. 29.95 (*0-7933-2951-5*); disk 29.95 (*0-7933-2953-1*) Gallopade Intl.

New York Botanical Garden Illustrated Encyclopedia of Horticulture, 10 vols. T. H. Everett. 1980. 107.00 (*0-318-52572-0*) Garland.

New York Botanical Garden Illustrated Encyclopedia of Horticulture, 10 vols., Set. T. H. Everett. 1980. lib. bdg. 1070.00 (*0-8153-0256-8*) Garland.

New York, Brooklyn Census Index, 1870. Ronald V. Jackson. 1991. 320.00 (*0-685-52205-9*, Accel Indexing) Genealogical Srvcs.

*__New York Business Directory, 2000 Edition.__ rev. ed. American Business Directories Staff. 6160p. 1999. boxed set 520.00 incl. cd-rom (*0-7687-0167-8*) Am Busn Direct.

New York Business Directory 1998. American Business Directories Staff. Incl. New York Metro Business Directory, 1998. rev. ed. 3648p. 1997. boxed set 595.00 (*1-56105-957-9*); Upstate New York Business Directory, 1998. rev. ed. 2384p. 1997. boxed set 465.00 (*1-56105-958-7*); 795.00 (*1-56105-956-0*) Am Busn Direct.

*__New York Business Law.__ Helewitz. (C). 2002. pap. 18.75 (*0-7668-2320-2*) Delmar.

New York by Gas-Light & Other Urban Sketches. George G. Foster. LC 90-35290. (Illus.). 251p. 1990. 40.00 (*0-520-06721-5*, Pub. by U CA Pr) Cal Prin Full Svc.

New York by Gas-Light & Other Urban Sketches. George G. Foster. LC 90-35290. (Illus.). 251p. 1991. pap. 15.95 (*0-520-06722-3*, Pub. by U CA Pr) Cal Prin Full Svc.

New York by the Numbers: State & City in Perpetual Crisis. LC 96-37327. 656p. 1997. write for info. (*0-7618-0622-9*) U Pr of Amer.

New York by the Numbers: State & City in Perpetual Crisis. Raymond J. Keating. 656p. 1997. pap. 14.95 (*1-56833-087-1*) U Pr of Amer.

New York Cab Driver & His Fare. Charles Vidich. 196p. 1976. pap. text 21.95 (*0-87073-926-3*) Transaction Pubs.

*__New York Calendar of Wills: On File & Recorded in the Office of the Clerk of the Court of Appeals, of the County Clerk at Albany, & of the Secretary of State, 1626 - 1836.__ Berthold Fernow. 657p. 1999. pap. 47.50 (*0-8063-0110-4*, Pub. by Clearfield Co) ACCESS Pubs Network.

New York Canudo on Criminal Law. annuals John Copertino. 1000p. ring bd. 44.95 (*0-87526-201-5*) Gould.

New York Canudo on Evidence Laws. annuals Gary Shaw. 490p. ring bd. 39.95 (*0-87526-175-2*) Gould.

New York Cases in Business Law. Morris. (LA - Business Law Ser.). 1993. pap. 21.50 (*0-314-00494-7*) West Pub.

New York Census Index, 1890 Union Vets. (Illus.). lib. bdg. write for info. (*0-89593-442-6*, Accel Indexing) Genealogical Srvcs.

New York Central: Lightning Stripes. David R. Sweetland. (Illus.). 128p. 1990. 45.00 (*0-9619058-6-7*) Morning NJ.

New York Central: Steam-Locomotives & Trains from 1933 to 1943. 2nd rev. ed. Robert K. Durham. LC 94-69691. (Steam of the Thirties Ser.). (Illus.). 64p. 2000. pap. 21.00 (*0-9644480-0-9*) Durham Publng.

New York Central & the Trains of the Future. Geofrey J. Doughty. (Illus.). 112p. 1997. 25.95 (*1-883089-27-1*) TLC VA.

New York Central Color Photography of Ed Nowak, Bk. I. Ed Nowak & Robert J. Yanosey. LC 91-67986. (Illus.). 128p. 1992. 45.00 (*1-878887-09-2*) Morning NJ.

New York Central Color Photography of Ed Nowak, Bk. II. Ed Nowak & Robert J. Yanosey. LC 91-67986. (Illus.). 128p. 1992. 49.95 (*1-878887-17-3*) Morning NJ.

New York Central Color Photography of Ed Nowak, Bk. 3. Ed Nowak & Robert J. Yanosey. LC 91-67986. (Illus.). 128p. 1993. 49.95 (*1-878887-24-6*) Morning NJ.

New York Central Lightning Stripes, Vol. 2. David R. Sweetland. (Illus.). 128p. 1993. 49.95 (*1-878887-16-5*) Morning NJ.

New York, Central Park: New York City, First Annual Report. LC 71-143064. 1982. 15.95 (*0-8434-0446-9*, Pub. by McGrath NH) Ayer.

New York Central Railroad. Brian Solomon & Mike Schafer. LC 99-31914. (Illus.). 128p. 1999. pap. 21.95 (*0-7603-0613-3*, Pub. by MBI Pubg) Motorbooks Intl.

*__New York Central Stations & Terminals.__ Geoffrey H. Doughty. (Illus.). 160p. 2000. 28.95 (*1-883089-47-6*, 130061AE, Pub. by TLC VA) Motorbooks Intl.

New York Central Steam in Color. David R. Sweetland. (Illus.). 128p. 1994. 49.95 (*1-878887-31-9*) Morning NJ.

New York Central System: Great Steel Fleet 1948-1968. rev. ed. Geoffrey H. Doughty. (Illus.). 160p. 1999. 28.95 (*1-883089-46-8*, Pub. by TLC VA) Motorbooks Intl.

New York Central System Diesel Locomotives. William Edson. (Illus.). 212p. 1996. 42.95 (*1-883089-16-6*) TLC VA.

New York Central Trackside with Eugene Van Dusen. Bill Marvel. LC 97-72732. (Illus.). 128p. 1997. 49.95 (*1-878887-81-5*) Morning NJ.

New York Central's Early Power, 1831-1916. Alvin F. Staufer et al. LC 67-18364. (Illus.). 352p. 1967. 50.00 (*0-944513-01-8*) Staufer Bks.

New York Central's Great Steel Fleet, 1948-1967. Geoffrey H. Doughty. (Illus.). 120p. 1996. 22.95 (*1-883089-18-2*) TLC VA.

New York Central's Lightweight Passenger Cars, Trains & Travel. J. Geoffrey Doughty. (Illus.). 160p. 1996. 28.95 (*1-883089-25-5*) TLC VA.

New York Central's Mercury. Richard Cook, Sr. 60p. 1996. pap. 14.95 (*0-9622003-4-4*) TLC VA.

New York, Chicago, Los Angeles: America's Global Cities. Janet L. Abu-Lughod. LC 99-20783. (Illus.). 580p. 1999. 39.95 (*0-8166-3335-5*, Pub. by U of Minn Pr) Chicago Distribution Ctr.

New York, Chicago, Los Angeles: America's Global Cities Janet L. Abu-Lughod. LC 99-20783. 1999. write for info. (*0-8166-3336-3*) U of Minn Pr.

New York Chocolate Lover's Guide: The Best Candy, Cakes, & Chocolate Treats in Town. Patricia MacKenzie & William Gillen. LC 97-152384. 144p. 1996. 16.00 (*1-885492-36-7*) City & Co.

New York Christmas. Photos by Mark Crosby. (Illus.). 96p. 1999. 20.00 (*0-7893-0370-1*, Pub. by Universe) St Martin.

New York City see Cities of the World

New York City. Barbara Johnston Adams. LC 88-20245. (Downtown America Ser.). (Illus.). 60p. (J). (gr. 3 up). 1988. lib. bdg. 13.95 (*0-87518-384-0*) Silver Burdett Pr.

New York City. Griffin Trade Paperbacks Publishing Staff. (Illus.). 368p. 1999. pap. 16.99 (*0-312-24477-0*, St Martin Griffin) St Martin.

New York City. Deborah Kent. (Cities of the World Ser.). 64p. (J). 1997. pap. 9.95 (*0-516-26072-3*) Childrens.

New York City. H. C. Landphair. LC 96-43088. (Illus.). 128p. 1997. 14.99 (*0-517-18330-7*) Random Hse Value.

New York City. David F. Marx. LC 98-37342. (Rookie Read-About Geography Ser.). (Illus.). 32p. (J). (gr. 1-2). 1999. 19.00 (*0-516-21552-3*) Childrens.

*__New York City.__ David F. Marx. (Rookie Read-About Geography Ser.). (J). 2000. pap. text 5.95 (*0-516-26558-X*) Childrens.

New York City. St. Martin's Press Staff. (Marcellino's Restaurant Report Ser.). 1997. pap. 9.99 (*0-312-16921-3*) St Martin.

New York City. Nancy Ann VanWei. (Travels with Max Ser.). (Illus.). 47p. (J). (gr. 1-7). 1997. pap. 5.95 (*1-888575-02-6*) Maxs Pubns.

*__New York City.__ rev. ed. Let's Go Staff. (Let's Go 2001 Ser.). (Illus.). 368p. 2000. pap. 16.99 (*0-312-24684-6*, St Martin Griffin) St Martin.

*__New York City.__ 2nd ed. Ed. by Fodors Travel Publications, Inc. Staff. 2000. pap. 13.50 (*0-679-00384-3*) Fodors Travel.

*__New York City.__ 2nd ed. Ed. by Fodors Travel Publications, Inc. Staff. (Fodor's Citypack Ser.). 528p. 2000. pap. 19.00 (*0-679-00408-4*) Fodors Travel.

New York City. 2nd ed. Insight Guides Staff. (Insight Guides). 1998. pap. text 21.95 (*0-88729-726-9*) Langenscheidt.

*__New York City.__ 2nd ed. New Holland Publishing Staff. 2001. pap. 14.95 (*1-85974-480-X*) New5 Holland.

*__New York City.__ 2nd ed. New Holland Staff. (Globetrotter Travel Guides Ser.). (Illus.). 2001. pap. 10.95 (*1-85974-478-8*) New5 Holland.

*__New York City.__ 2nd ed. David Ellis. 2000. reprint ed. pap. 16.99 (*1-86450-180-4*) Lonely Planet.

New York City. 3rd ed. (Insight Guides Ser.). (Illus.). 1999. pap. 21.95 (*0-88729-158-9*) Langenscheidt.

*__New York City.__ 3rd ed. Ed. by Fodors Travel Publications, Inc. Staff. 96p. 2000. pap. 12.00 (*0-679-00483-1*) Fodors Travel.

New York City. 4th ed. Insight Guides Staff. (Insight Guides). 1998. pap. text 12.95 (*0-88729-921-0*) Langenschiedt.

New York City: A Basic Guide to Services & Community Resources. Ed. by Patricia A. Friedland et al. 1997. pap. 15.00 (*0-88156-203-3*) Comm Serv Soc NY.

New York City: A Photographic Celebration. Courage Books Staff. LC 97-66816. (Illus.). 128p. 13.98 (*0-7624-0284-9*, Courage) Running Pr.

New York City: A Pictorial Guide. K. J. Dumond & Ann Merlin. Ed. by Anne Du Bois. 64p. 1992. pap. 8.95 (*1-56540-033-X*) Impact Photograph.

New York City: Downtown America. Barbara Johnston Adams. (Illus.). 64p. (J). (gr. 4-7). 1996. pap. text 7.95 (*0-382-24794-9*) Silver Burdett Pr.

New York City: English Edition - Country, City & Region. (Green Guides). pap. 14.95 (*0-686-56392-1*) Fr & Eur.

*__New York City: Insiders' Guide for Cosmopolitan Travelers.__ 2nd ed. Dan Levine. (Avant-Guide Bks.). (Illus.). 2000. pap. 19.95 (*1-891603-08-6*) Empire Pr.

New York City: Our Community. 2nd ed. Linda Biemer. (Illus.). 100p. (J). (gr. 4). 1994. 9.30 (*0-87905-139-6*) Gibbs Smith Pub.

New York City: The Five Boroughs. Carol M. Highsmith & Ted Landphai. LC 97-16565. (Pictorial Souvenir Ser.). (Illus.). 64p. 1997. 7.99 (*0-517-20147-X*) Random Hse Value.

New York City: Ulysses Travel Guide. Francois Remillard. Ed. by Ulysses Travel Guide Staff. (Ulysses Travel Guide Ser.). (Illus.). 432p. 1998. pap. 14.95 (*2-89464-088-9*) Ulysses Travel.

New York City: Views of Lower Manhattan. (Album Ser.: No. 2). 1976. pap. 7.95 (*0-87130-052-4*) Eakins.

New York City: 1999 Edition. Zagat Publishers Staff. 1999. 19.95 (*1-57006-167-X*) Zagat.

New York City Almanac: The Ultimate Fact Book for the Five Boroughs. Edward Forlie. LC 94-20045. (Illus.). 352p. 1994. 14.95 (*0-8065-1574-0*, Citadel Pr) Carol Pub Group.

New York City & Vicinity: The Best 200 Restaurants. Ed. by Tom Demaree. (Menu Ser.). (Illus.). 448p. (Orig.). 1993. pap. 12.95 (*0-9628274-4-4*) D Thomas Pub.

New York City at the Turn of Century. Ed. by Elizabeth Beirne. (Illus.). 160p. (Orig.). 1996. pap. write for info. (*0-9652331-0-3*) Hist NYCP.

New York City Ballet. Anatole Chujoy. (Series in Dance). (Illus.). xxviii, 382p. 1981. reprint ed. lib. bdg. 39.50 (*0-306-76035-5*) Da Capo.

New York City Ballet Workout: Fifty Stretches & Exercises Anyone Can Do for a Strong, Graceful & Sculpted Body. Peter Martins & New York City Ballet. LC 96-36245. 1997. 40.00 (*0-688-14843-3*, Wm Morrow) Morrow Avon.

New York City Ballet Workout: Fifty Stretches And Exercises Anyone Can Do For A Strong, Graceful, And SculptedBody. Peter Martins. 352p. 1997. pap. 22.00 (*0-688-15202-3*, Wm Morrow) Morrow Avon.

New York City Ballet's the Sleeping Beauty. Brooke Allen. (J). 1993. write for info. (*0-316-03459-2*) Little.

New York City Baseball: The Last Golden Age, 1947-1957. Harvey Frommer. (Illus.). 234p. 1992. pap. 9.95 (*0-15-665500-4*, Harvest Bks) Harcourt.

*__New York City Birds.__ James Kavanagh. (Pocket Naturalist Ser.). (Illus.). 1999. 5.90 (*1-58355-012-7*, Pub. by Waterford WA) Falcon Pub Inc.

New York City Building Code. annuals Gould Editorial Staff. 750p. ring bd. 49.95 (*0-87526-128-0*) Gould.

New York City Buildings see Edificios de Nueva York

New York City Buildings. Ann Mace. (Books for Young Learners). (Illus.). 12p. (J). (gr. k-2). 1997. pap. text 5.00 (*1-57274-077-9*, A2475) R Owen Pubs.

New York City Cab Driver's Joke Book. Jim Pietsch. 1986. mass mkt. 5.99 (*0-446-34487-7*, Pub. by Warner Bks) Little.

New York City Cab Driver's Joke Book, Vol. 2. Jim Pietsch. 288p. 1998. mass mkt. 5.99 (*0-446-60487-9*, Pub. by Warner Bks) Little.

New York City Cab Driver's Joke Book, Vol. 2. Jim Pietsch. 1998. mass mkt. 35.94 (*0-446-16570-0*) Warner Bks.

New York City Community Health Atlas. Compiled by Division of Research, Analysis, & Planning Staff. LC 85-675630. 1985. 40.00 (*0-934459-15-0*) United Hosp Fund.

New York City Community Health Atlas, 1988. Melvin I. Krasner. LC 85-645644. 216p. 1988. 40.00 (*0-934459-51-7*) United Hosp Fund.

New York City Community Health Atlas, 1994. Melvin I. Krasner. LC 94-6675. 192p. 1994. 50.00 (*1-881277-00-3*) United Hosp Fund.

New York City Contest Problem Book. Saul Book Staff. 1997. pap. text 19.95 (*0-86651-307-8*) Seymour Pubns.

New York City Court Records, 1797-1801: Genealogical Data from the Court of General Sessions. Kenneth Scott. LC 88-1634. (Special Publication: No. 56). 200p. 1988. lib. bdg. 24.95 (*0-915156-56-3*) Natl Genealogical.

New York City Court Records, 1684-1760: Genealogical Data from the Court of Quarter Sessions. Kenneth Scott. (Special Publication - National Genealogical Society Ser.: No. 50). 161p. 1982. lib. bdg. 22.75 (*0-915156-44-X*) Natl Genealogical.

New York City Criminal Court: The Case for Abolition. Harry I. Subin. Ed. by Graham Hughes. (Occasional Papers: Vol. XII). 22p. (Orig.). (C). 1992. pap. text 10.00 (*1-878429-62-0*) NYU Ctr for Rsch in Crime Justice.

New York City Culture Catalog: A Guide to New York City's Museums, Concert Halls, Theaters, Zoos, Botanical Gardens, Historic Houses & Libraries. Alliance for the Arts Staff et al. LC 93-34782. (Illus.). 224p. 1994. pap. 12.95 (*0-8109-2578-8*, Pub. by Abrams) Time Warner.

New York City Draft Riots: Their Significance for American Society & Politics in the Age of the Civil War. Iver Bernstein. (Illus.). 384p. 1991. reprint ed. pap. text 24.95 (*0-19-507130-1*) OUP.

New York City During the American Revolution. H. B. Dawson. 1972. 59.95 (*0-8490-0727-5*) Gordon Pr.

New York City 1870 Census Index, 3 vols. Raeone Christensen Steuart & Precision Indexing Staff. LC 98-168949. xix, 2179p. 1997. write for info. (*1-877677-13-2*) Herit Quest.

*__New York City Entertainment, 2000.__ (Illus.). 806p. 1999. pap. 25.00 (*1-880248-50-6*, 0034) Enter Pubns.

New York City Federal Census, 1850 (Excludes New York County), 2 vols., Set. Ronald V. Jackson. LC 77-86120. (Illus.). lib. bdg. 350.00 (*0-89593-101-X*, Accel Indexing) Genealogical Srvcs.

New York City Federal Census, 1830. Ronald V. Jackson. LC 77-86117. (Illus.). lib. bdg. 151.00 (*0-89593-099-4*, Accel Indexing) Genealogical Srvcs.

New York City Federal Census Index, 1800. Ronald V. Jackson. LC 77-86124. (Illus.). lib. bdg. 68.00 (*0-89593-096-X*, Accel Indexing) Genealogical Srvcs.

New York City Federal Census Index, 1820. Ronald V. Jackson. LC 77-86116. (Illus.). 1975. lib. bdg. 98.00 (*0-89593-098-6*, Accel Indexing) Genealogical Srvcs.

New York City Federal Census Index, 1840. Ronald V. Jackson. LC 77-86118. (Illus.). lib. bdg. 187.00 (*0-89593-100-1*, Accel Indexing) Genealogical Srvcs.

New York City Federal Census Index, 1850 (New York County) Ronald V. Jackson & Gary R. Teeples. LC 77-86121. (Illus.). 1978. lib. bdg. 125.00 (*0-89593-102-8*, Accel Indexing) Genealogical Srvcs.

New York City Federal Index, 1810. Ronald V. Jackson. LC 77-86125. (Illus.). lib. bdg. 68.00 (*0-89593-097-8*, Accel Indexing) Genealogical Srvcs.

*__New York City Financial District.__ Randall Gabrielan. LC 00-100871. (Postcard History Ser.). (Illus.). 128p. 2000. pap. 18.99 (*0-7385-0068-2*) Arcadia Publng.

New York City Fire Law Handbook. annuals Gould Editorial Staff. 310p. ring bd. 19.95 (*0-87526-335-6*) Gould.

New York City Fire Patrol: An Illustrated History. Arthur C. Smith. Ed. & Intro. by Charles J. Adams, III. (Illus.). 81p. (Orig.). 1997. pap. 12.95 (*1-880683-10-5*) Exeter Hse.

New York City Fiscal Crisis. U. S. House of Representatives Committee on Bankin. LC 77-74954. (American Federalism-the Urban Dimension Ser.). (Illus.). 1978. reprint ed. lib. bdg. 29.95 (*0-405-10498-7*) Ayer.

New York City Flash Maps. 1990. pap. 4.95 (*0-528-92966-6*) Rand McNally.

*__New York City for Dummies.__ Bruce Murphy. (For Dummies Ser.). 352p. 2000. pap. 15.99 (*0-7645-6160-X*) IDG Bks.

New York City from a Cab Driver's View. Da Silva. 1994. 5.50 (*0-9644600-1-7*) NY Publ.

New York City Get-a-Grip Gripe Book: Raising Hell & Getting Satisfaction with the 51 Most Maddening Hassles, Vol. 1. Raymond Alvin. (Illus.). 256p. (Orig.). 1995. pap. 10.95 (*0-9644961-2-7*) Streetbeat.

New York City Ghost Stories. Charles J. Adams, III. (Illus.). 185p. (Orig.). 1996. pap., per. 10.95 (*1-880683-09-1*) Exeter Hse.

*__New York City Green Guide.__ Michelin Staff. 1999. pap. 18.00 (*2-06-155113-0*) Michelin.

New York City Green Guide. 11th ed. Michelin Staff. 1997. pap. 19.95 (*0-7859-9128-X*) Fr & Eur.

New York City Green Guide: Amerique du Nord/North America. (JPN.). 1992. per. 36.00 (*4-408-01313-7*, 9593) Michelin.

New York City Green Guide French Edition. Michelin Staff. (FRE.). 1997. pap. 19.95 (*0-7859-7215-3*, 2067005480) Fr & Eur.

New York City Health Facts: A Profile from the National Health Interview Survey. United Hospital Fund Staff. 56p. 1989. 20.00 (*0-934459-54-1*) United Hosp Fund.

New York City Health Trends, 1979-1989. 56p. 1993. pap. 20.00 (*0-934459-99-1*) United Hosp Fund.

New York City Housing Maintenance Code. annuals Gould Editorial Staff. 540p. (C). ring bd. 19.95 (*0-87526-278-3*) Gould.

New York City Law Digest. annuals 340p. ring bd. 15.95 (*0-87526-302-X*) Gould.

New York City Man. Elaine Louie. 240p. (Orig.). 1989. mass mkt. 8.95 (*0-446-38708-8*, Pub. by Warner Bks) Little.

New York City Methodist Marriages, 1785-1893, 2 vols., Set. William S. Fisher. 1994. 89.50 (*0-89725-181-4*, 1526) Picton Pr.

New York City Model Agency Directory, Vol. 9. Peter Glenn Staff. 1998. pap. 13.95 (*0-87314-131-8*) Peter Glenn.

*__New York City Model Agency Directory, Vol. 10.__ Ed. by Tricia Blount. 80p. 2000. pap. 13.95 (*0-87314-132-6*, Pub. by Peter Glenn) SCB Distributors.

*__New York City Motorists' Parking Survival Guide: A Primer on How to Avoid & Deal with Parking Tickets Effectively.__ Louis A. Camporeale. LC 98-91641. (Motorist Educational Bks.). (Illus.). 147p. 1998. pap. 11.95 (*0-9664678-0-9*) Park Pal Co.

New York City Museum Guide. Ed. by Candace Ward. (Illus.). 144p. 1995. pap. text 3.95 (*0-486-28639-8*) Dover.

*__New York City Museum Guide.__ 2nd rev. ed. Candace Ward. (Illus.). (J). 2000. pap. 4.95 (*0-486-41000-5*) Dover.

New York City Neighborhoods: The Eighteenth Century. Nan A. Rothschild. 264p. 1990. text 65.00 (*0-12-598725-0*) Acad Pr.

New York City, NY. (Streetfinder Ser.). (Illus.). 1995. pap. 11.95 (*0-528-91349-2*) Rand McNally.

New York City One Hundred Years Ago: Central Park. Compiled by Skip Whitson. (Historical Ser.). (Illus.). (Orig.). 1976. pap. 3.50 (*0-89540-019-7*, SB-019) Sun Pub.

New York City Police Corruption Investigation Commissions, 1894-1994, 6 vols. Ed. by Gabriel J. Chin. LC 97-70840. 1997. 325.00 (*1-57588-211-6*, 310740) W S Hein.

*__New York City Police Department's "Stop & Frisk" Practices: A Report to the People of the State of New York from the Office of the Attorney General.__ Eliot Spitzer. (Illus.). 400p. (C). 2000. pap. text 40.00 (*0-7881-8753-8*) DIANE Pub.

New York City Records, 1760-1797: Genealogical Data from the Court of Quarter Sessions. Kenneth Scott. LC 83-13397. (Special Publication - National Genealogical Society Ser.: No. 52). 250p. 1983. lib. bdg. 22.75 (*0-915156-52-0*) Natl Genealogical.

New York City Reservoirs in the Catskill Mountains. 1985. pap. 3.00 (*0-939166-07-0*) Outdoor Pubns.

New York City Restaurant. Zagat Publishers Staff. (Zagat Survey: New York City Restaurants Ser.). 254p. 1998. pap. 11.95 (*1-57006-149-1*) Zagat.

*__New York City Restaurants.__ Andre Gayot. (Gayot Restaurants Ser.: Vol. 3). (Illus.). 352p. 2000. pap. 14.00 (*1-881066-70-3*, Pub. by Gault Millau) Publishers Group.

New York City Specialized Science High School Admissions Test. 4th ed. Stephen Krane. LC 97-70054. (Illus.). 192p. 1997. pap. 15.95 (*0-02-861695-2*, Arc) IDG Bks.

New York City Star Walks: A Guide to the Exclusive Haunts, Habitats, & Havens of the Big Apple's Happening Celebs. Larry Horwitz. (Illus.). 176p. (Orig.). 1993. pap. 12.95 (*0-312-09885-5*) St Martin.

New York City Street Games: The Greatest Games Ever Played on Concrete. Ray Vignola & Dennis Vignola. LC 93-79775. (Illus.). 64p. (Orig.). 1993. pap. 14.95 (*0-944661-22-X*) MIG Comns.

New York City Subway Guide. Oscar Israelowitz. LC 88-83966. (Illus.). 259p. 1989. 6.95 (*0-9611036-7-1*) Israelowitz Pub.

New York City Tattoo: The Oral History of an Urban Art. Michael McCabe. (Illus.). 1997. pap. 25.00 (*0-614-28151-2*) Dist Art Pubs.

New York City Tattoo: The Oral History of an Urban Art. Michael McCabe. 1997. pap. text 25.00 (*0-945367-20-1*) Hardy Marks Pubns.

New York City Tax Handbook, 1998. rev. ed. Robert D. Plattner & Mark S. Klein. 212p. 1997. pap. text 45.00 (*0-7811-0186-7*) Res Inst Am.

New York City Tax Handbook, 1999. rev. ed. Robert D. Plattner & Mark S. Klein. 234p. 1998. pap. text 35.75 (*0-7811-0198-0*) Res Inst Am.

New York City Taxi-Limousine Drivers Guide. 136p. 1994. 8.95 (*0-88097-620-9*, 976209) Am Map.

New York City Traffic Rules. annuals Gould Editorial Staff. 145p. ring bd. 6.95 (*0-87526-329-1*) Gould.

New York City Travel Guide. Globe Pequot Press Staff. (Illus.). 128p. 1997. pap. text 16.25 (*1-85368-709-X*, Pub. by New5 Holland) Globe Pequot.

New York City 2000. Fodors Travel Publications, Inc. Staff. 1999. pap. 15.50 (*0-679-00321-5*) Fodors Travel.

New York City 2000. Fodors Travel Publications, Inc. Staff. (Guides Ser.). (Illus.). 1999. pap. 9.00 (*0-679-00350-9*) Fodors Travel.

*__New York City 2001.__ Fodor's Staff. 2000. pap. 15.50 (*0-679-00549-8*) Fodors Travel.

*__New York City 2000-2001.__ 2nd ed. Francois Remillard. (Illus.). 2000. pap. 14.95 (*2-89464-236-9*, Pub. by Ulysses Travel) Globe Pequot.

New York City Water Supply Studies - Watershed Restoration, Management: American Water Resources Association, Symposium Proceedings. American Water Resources Association Staff. Ed. by Jeffrey J. McDonnell et al. LC 96-85384. (American Water Resources Association Technical Publication Ser.: No. TPS-96-2). (Illus.). 192p. 1996. reprint ed. pap. 59.60 (*0-608-04278-1*, 206503100012) Bks Demand.

New York City with Kids. 5th ed. Holly Hughes. 1996. 15.95 (*0-02-860893-3*) Macmillan.

New York City Woman. Elaine Louie. 240p. (Orig.). 1989. mass mkt. 8.95 (*0-446-38706-1*, Pub. by Warner Bks) Little.

New York City, Yesterday & Today: Thirty Timeless Walking Adventures. Judith H. Browning. Ed. by Midge Bacon. LC 90-81118. (Illus.). 414p. (Orig.). 1990. pap. 21.95 (*0-9626067-0-7*) Corsair Pubns.

*__New York City 2001.__ Fodors Travel Publications, Inc. Staff. (Pocket Guides Ser.). 2000. pap. 10.00 (*0-679-00572-2*, Pub. by Fodors Travel) Random House.

New York City's African Slaveowners: A Social & Material Culture History. Sherrill D. Wilson. LC 94-2813. (Studies in African American History & Culture). 136p. 1994. text 42.00 (*0-8153-1536-8*) Garland.

New York City's Buried Past: A Guide to Excavated New York City's Revolutionary War Artifacts 1776-1783. 2nd ed. Robert Apuzzo. (Illus.). 164p. (Orig.). 1992. pap. 24.95 (*0-9629913-0-9*) R & L Pub.

New York City's Hospital Occupancy Crisis: Caring for a Changing Patient Population. Bigel Institute for Health Policy Staff & United Hospital Fund Staff. 36p. 1988. 25.00 (*0-934459-50-9*) United Hosp Fund.

New York City's Labor Market, 1994-1997: Profiles & Perspectives. Mark Levitan. 124p. 1998. 15.00 (*0-88156-253-X*) Comm Serv Soc NY.

*__New York Civil Practice.__ Jeffrey A. Helenitz. 224p. (C). 2000. pap. text 29.95 (*0-929563-58-1*) Pearson Pubns.

New York Civil Practice: CPLR, 14 vols. Jack B. Weinstein & Harold L. Korn. 1963. ring bd. write for info. (*0-8205-1805-0*) Bender.

New York Civil Practice: EPTL, 7 vols. Patrick J. Rohan. 1969. ring bd. 1260.00 (*0-8205-1806-9*) Bender.

New York Civil Practice: Family Court Proceedings, 4 vols. James Zett & Michael E. Edmonds. 1972. ring bd. 970.00 (*0-8205-1814-X*) Bender.

New York Civil Practice: Matrimonial Actions, 4 vols., Vols. 11-11c. James Zett & Michael E. Edmonds. 1971. ring bd. 950.00 (*0-8205-1809-3*) Bender.

New York Civil Practice: SCPA, 6 vols. Joseph A. Cox et al. 1970. ring bd. 1380.00 (*0-8205-1808-5*) Bender.

New York Civil Practice, 1995. (Litigation & Administrative Practice Course Handbook, 1983-84 Ser.). 193p. 1995. pap. 12.00 (*0-6851-56914-4*, H4-5230) PLI.

New York Civil Practice Rules & Law Handbook. annuals Gould Editorial Staff. 1030p. (C). pap. 21.95 (*0-87526-390-9*) Gould.

New York Civil Service Law. annuals Ed. by Gould Editorial Staff. 220p. (C). ring bd. 9.95 (*0-87526-363-1*) Gould.

New York Classic Christmas Trivia: Stories, Recipes, Activities, Legends, Lore & More! Carole Marsh. (Carole Marsh New York Bks.). (Illus.). (J). 1994. lib. bdg. 29.95 (*0-7933-0820-8*); disk 29.95 (*0-7933-0821-6*) Gallopade Intl.

New York Classic Christmas Trivia: Stories, Recipes, Activities, Legends, Lore & More! Carole Marsh. (Carole Marsh New York Bks.). (Illus.). (J). 1997. pap. 19.95 (*0-7933-0819-4*) Gallopade Intl.

New York Coastales. Carole Marsh. (Carole Marsh New York Bks.). (J). 1994. lib. bdg. 29.95 (*0-7933-7297-6*) Gallopade Intl.

New York Coastales. Carole Marsh. (Carole Marsh New York Bks.). (Illus.). (J). 1994. pap. 19.95 (*1-55609-913-4*); lib. bdg. 29.95 (*1-55609-912-6*); disk 29.95 (*1-55609-914-2*) Gallopade Intl.

New York Code of Professional Responsibility: Opinions, Commentary & Caselaw, 2 vols. Ed. by Mary C. Daly. LC 97-37283. 1997. ring bd. 300.00 (*0-379-20677-3*) Oceana.

New York Collections. Joseph Rubin. LC 80-81138. (Practice Systems Library Manual). ring bd. 120.00 (*0-317-00518-9*) West Group.

New York Collections. Joseph Rubin. LC 80-81138. (Practice Systems Library Manual). 1993. suppl. ed. 75.00 (*0-317-04327-7*) West Group.

New York Collects: Drawings & Watercolors, 1900-1950. Emily Braun & Pierpont Morgan Library Staff. LC 99-21145. 1999. 45.00 (*0-87598-128-3*) Pierpont Morgan.

New York Colony. Dennis B. Fradin. LC 87-35803. (Thirteen Colonies Ser.). (Illus.). 160p. (J). (gr. 4 up). 1988. lib. bdg. 30.00 (*0-516-00389-5*) Childrens.

New York Coloring Book. Annie Campbell. (Illus.). 32p. (Orig.). 1996. pap. 6.95 (*0-935526-26-9*); pap. 6.95 (*0-935526-27-7*); pap. 6.95 (*0-935526-28-5*); pap. 6.95 (*0-935526-29-3*) McBooks Pr.

New York Commercial Law, Goldbook. write for info. (*0-8205-1751-8*) Bender.

New York Commercial Law, Goldbook. 1973. pap. write for info. (*0-8205-3495-1*) Bender.

New York Condominium & Cooperative Law. Vincent M. Di Lorenzo. LC 84-82172. 1991. suppl. ed. 55.00 (*0-317-03257-7*) West Group.

New York Condominium & Cooperative Law. 2nd ed. Vincent M. Di Lorenzo. LC 84-82172. 1984. 135.00 (*0-318-04263-0*) West Group.

New York Conference, 1958 see Research Opportunities in Renaissance Drama: The Reports of the Modern Language Association Conferences

New York Confidential. Camille Lubro & Stephanie Chayet. 168p. 45.00 (*2-84323-173-6*, Pub. by Assouline) Rizzoli Intl.

New York Connection. (Passport to America Ser.). 1987. 6.99 (*0-8325-0425-4*) NTC Contemp Pub Co.

New York Considered & Improved, from the Original Mss. in the British Museum. John Miller. Ed. & Intro. by Victor H. Paltsits. (Illus.). 135p. 1997. reprint ed. pap. 18.50 (*0-8328-6092-1*); reprint ed. lib. bdg. 28.50 (*0-8328-6091-3*) Higginson Bk Co.

New York Consolidated Law Service Advance Legislative Service, 1999, No. 3. Lexis Law Publishing Staff. 100p. 1999. 77.50 (*0-327-08709-9*, 40983-12) LEXIS Pub.

New York Consolidated Law Service ALS No. 6: September 1998. 600p. 1998. pap. write for info. (*0-327-06315-7*, 4098611) LEXIS Pub.

New York Consolidated Law Service ALS No. 7: October 1998. 600p. 1998. pap. write for info. (*0-327-06320-3*, 4098711) LEXIS Pub.

New York Consolidated Law Service ALS No. 8: November 1998. 600p. 1998. pap. write for info. (*0-327-06333-5*, 4098811) LEXIS Pub.

New York Consolidated Law Service ALS No. 9: December 1998. 600p. 1998. pap. write for info. (*0-327-06336-X*, 4098911) LEXIS Pub.

New York Consolidated Law Service ALS, May 1999, No. 2. 1999. pap. write for info. (*0-327-08392-1*, 40982-12) LEXIS Pub.

New York Consolidated Law Service CLS Quarterly Update, April 1999. 300p. 1999. pap. write for info. (*0-327-08415-4*, 57256-12) LEXIS Pub.

New York Consolidated Laws (NYCU), 9 vols., Set. annuals Gould Editorial Staff. 1300p. 1999. pap. 179.00 (*0-87526-344-5*) Gould.

New York Consolidated Laws Service, 135+ Vols. 2070.00 (*0-327-10666-2*) LEXIS Pub.

New York Consolidated Laws Service, 124 vols. 1992. suppl. ed. 2070.00 (*0-318-57151-X*) West Group.

*__New York Consolidated Laws Service ALS, 1999.__ 715p. 1999. pap. write for info. (*0-327-08391-3*) LEXIS Pub.

*__New York Consolidated Laws Service ALS 1999: July 1999, No. 4.__ 600p. 1999. Price not set. (*0-327-09109-6*, 4098412) LEXIS Pub.

*__New York Consolidated Laws Service ALS 1999 Vol. 7: October 1999.__ 365p. 1999. pap. write for info. (*0-327-09876-7*, 4098712) LEXIS Pub.

*__New York Consolidated Laws Service ALS 1999 Number 5: August 1999.__ 370p. 1999. Price not set. (*0-327-09176-2*, 4098512) LEXIS Pub.

An Asterisk (*) at the beginning of an entry indicates that the title is appearing for the first time.

***New York Consolidated Laws Service ALS 1999 (September 1999), Vol. 6.** 1185p. 1999. pap. write for info. (0-327-09238-6, 4098612) LEXIS Pub.

***New York Consolidated Laws Service (CLS) Quarterly Update Service, July 1999.** 1660p. 1999. Price not set. (0-327-09093-6, 5725712) LEXIS Pub.

New York Consolidated Laws Service, 1998: Stat & Later Case Service Quarterly Update Pamphlets. 3000p. 1998. pap. write for info. (0-327-06319-X, 5725711) LEXIS Pub.

New York Consolidated Laws Service 1998 Supplement Research Guide Volume. 450p. 1999. write for info. (0-327-07437-X, 5740012) LEXIS Pub.

New York Consolidated Laws Service 1998 Session Laws, Vol. 1. 2200p. 1999. write for info. (0-327-07577-5, 4095611) LEXIS Pub.

New York Consolidated Laws Service 1998 Session Laws, Vol. 2. 2200p. 1999. write for info. (0-327-07578-3, 4095711) LEXIS Pub.

***New York Consolidated Laws Service (NY CLS) Quarterly Update Service, October 1999.** 2160p. 1999. pap. write for info. (0-327-09839-2, 5725812) LEXIS Pub.

***New York Consolidated Laws Service (NY CLS) 2000 General Indexes, 4 vols.** Ed. by LEXIS Law Publishing Editors. 4423p. 2000. write for info. (0-327-11216-6, 4094613) LEXIS Pub.

New York Consumer Law Training Manual. 246p. 1988. 28.00 (0-317-03753-6, 44,165) NCLS Inc.

New York Contemporary Art Galleries: The Complete Annual Guide. Ed. & Intro. by Renee Phillips. 254p. 1995. pap. 16.95 (0-9646358-2-8) Manhattan Arts Intl.

New York Contemporary Art Galleries: The Complete Annual Guide. 3rd rev. ed. Renee Phillips. 264p. 1998. mass mkt. 18.95 (0-9646358-4-4) Manhattan Arts Intl.

New York Contemporary Art Galleries: The Complete Annual Guide, Vol. 2. 2nd rev. ed. Ed. by Renee Phillips. 252p. 1997. pap. 18.95 (0-9646358-3-6) Manhattan Arts Intl.

New York Contemporary Art Galleries: The Complete Annual Guide 2000 Edition. 4th rev. ed. Renee Phillips. 264p. 2000. pap. 18.95 (0-9646358-9-5) Manhattan Arts Intl.

New York Cookbook. Molly O'Neill. LC 92-50280. (Illus.). 512p. 1992. pap. 17.95 (0-89480-698-X, 1698) Workman Pub.

New York Cooking. B. Carlson. (Illus.). 160p. 1997. spiral bd. 5.95 (1-57166-079-8) Hearts N Tummies.

New York Cops Talk Back: A Study of a Beleaguered Minority. Nicholas Alex. LC 76-1852. 235p. reprint ed. pap. 72.90 (0-8357-9942-5, 201646000004) Bks Demand.

New York Corporation Law Handbook. annuals 1340p. (C). ring bd. 24.95 (0-87526-330-5) Gould.

New York Corporation Law, Whitebook. 1968. pap. write for info. (0-8205-3499-4) Bender.

New York Corporations: Legal Aspects of Organization & Operation. John R. Alexander. (Corporate Practice Ser.: No. 2-3). 1999. 95.00 (1-55871-403-0) BNA.

New York Correction Law Handbook. annuals Gould Editorial Staff. 480p. ring bd. 12.95 (0-87526-403-4) Gould.

New York Court Forms. annuals Eugene W. Salisbury. 410p. ring bd. 39.95 (0-87526-250-3) Gould.

New York Court of Appeals Case Name Citations: All Inclusive Subscriptions. text 320.00 (0-7698-1987-7) Shepards.

New York Court of Appeals on Criminal Law. William C. Donnino. LC 85-50869. 1985. 105.00 (0-318-18300-5) West Group.

New York Court of Appeals on Criminal Law. William C. Donnino. LC 85-50869. 1993. suppl. ed. 52.50 (0-317-03275-5) West Group.

New York Court of Appeals on Criminal Law. 2nd ed. William C. Donnino. LC 97-29386. 1997. write for info. (0-8366-1150-0) West Group.

New York Court Records, 1801-1804: Genealogical Data from the Court of General Sessions. Kenneth Scott. LC 88-2070. (Special Publication: No. 57). 148p. 1988. lib. bdg. 24.95 (0-915156-82-2) Natl Genealogical.

New York Courtroom Evidence. 2nd ed. John E. Durst, Jr. & Abraham Fuchsberg. 400p. 1993. spiral bd. 120.00 (0-250-40706-X, MICHIE) LEXIS Pub.

***New York Courtroom Evidence: 1999 Edition.** Abraham Fuchsberg & John E. Durst, Jr. 400p. 1999. 125.00 (0-327-04988-X, 8218111) LEXIS Pub.

New York Courts. Jeffrey A. Helewitz. 72p. (C). 1999. pap. 15.50 (0-929563-50-6) Pearson Pubns.

New York Courts Manual of Procedure. annuals Eugene W. Salisbury. 310p. ring bd. 34.95 (0-87526-180-9) Gould.

New York CPLR. text 31.00 (0-8205-4189-3) Bender.

New York CPLR, Redbook. 1963. write for info. (0-8205-3046-8) Bender.

***New York Crime in Perspective 2000.** Ed. by Kathleen O'Leary Morgan & Scott E. Morgan. 22p. 2000. spiral bd. 19.00 (0-7401-0331-8) Morgan Quitno Corp.

New York Crime Perspective, 1998. Ed. by Kathleen O'Leary Morgan & Scott E. Morgan. 20p. 1998. pap. 19.00 (1-56692-931-8) Morgan Quitno Corp.

New York Crime Perspectives, 1999. Kathleen O'Leary Morgan. 22p. 1999. spiral bd. 19.00 (0-7401-0131-5) Morgan Quitno Corp.

New York Criminal & Traffic Law Manual, 1998. 1271p. 1998. write for info. (0-327-05392-5, 30700-10) LEXIS Pub.

New York Criminal Law. text 35.00 (0-8205-4228-8) Bender.

New York Criminal Law. Richard A. Greenberg et al. LC 96-60313. (New York Practice Ser.). xxxix, 1090p. 1996. 105.00 (0-314-09441-5) West Pub.

New York Criminal Law Designed for Criminal Justice (Paralegal Students) 3rd ed. Sam Maislin. 240p. 1990. per. 39.95 (0-8403-6105-X) Kendall-Hunt.

New York Criminal Law Handbook. annuals Gould Editorial Staff. 1470p. (C). ring bd. 24.95 (0-87526-309-7) Gould.

New York Criminal Practice, 11 vols. Marvin Waxner & James Zett. 1974. ring bd. 1950.00 (0-8205-1463-2) Bender.

New York Criminal Practice Handbook. Intro. by Robert W. Vinal. LC 90-53691. 920p. 1991. text 95.00 (0-942954-36-X) NYS Bar.

New York Criminal Practice Handbook, 1994 Supplement. New York State Bar Association Staff. Ed. by Lawrence N. Gray. 229p. 1994. pap. text 40.00 (0-942954-72-6) NYS Bar.

New York Criminal Procedure Law. annuals Gould Editorial Staff. 520p. pap. 6.95 (0-87526-262-7); ring bd. 6.95 (0-87526-138-8) Gould.

New York Criminal Procedure Law: Questions & Answers. annuals Gould Editorial Staff. 300p. ring bd. 12.95 (0-87526-314-3) Gould.

New York "Crinkum-Crankum" A Funny Word Book about Our State. Carole Marsh. (Carole Marsh New York Bks.). (Illus.). (J). 1994. pap. 19.95 (0-7933-4905-2); lib. bdg. 29.95 (0-7933-4904-4); disk 29.95 (0-7933-4906-0) Gallopade Intl.

New York Cruciform Lectionary. Jeffrey C. Anderson. (Illus.). 192p. 1992. 47.50 (0-271-00743-5) Pa St U Pr.

New York Dada, 1915-23. Francis M. Naumann. LC 93-34280. (Illus.). 256p. 1994. 60.00 (0-8109-3676-3, Pub. by Abrams) Time Warner.

New York Dance. large type ed. Donald E. Westlake. 524p. 1981. 27.99 (0-7089-0605-2) Ulverscroft.

New York Dance Schools - Studios Guide. 6th ed. Eri Misaki. Ed. by Elizabeth Belton. (ENG & JPN., Illus.). 84p. 1998. pap. 15.00 (1-888275-03-0) Dance Project.

***New York Dance School/Studio Guide.** 7th rev. ed. Eri Misaki. Ed. by Julia Kocich. (Illus.). 80p. 1999. pap. 12.00 (1-888275-04-9) Dance Project.

New York Dead. Stuart Woods. 352p. 1992. mass mkt. 6.99 (0-06-109080-8, Harp PBks) HarpC.

***New York Department of Education Reports, Vol. 38.** 950p. 1999. write for info. (0-327-09402-8, 5622111) LEXIS Pub.

New York Detail: A Treasury of Ornamental Splendor. Yumiko Kobayashi & Ryo Watanabe. (Illus.). 132p. 1995. pap. 22.95 (0-8118-1056-9) Chronicle Bks.

New York Detective. William Marshall. 288p. 1990. mass mkt. 4.95 (0-445-40921-5, Pub. by Warner Bks) Little.

New York Diaries. Daniel Drennan. LC 98-19282. 234p. 1998. pap. 11.95 (0-345-41643-0) Ballantine Pub Grp.

New York Diary. Julie Doucet. 1999. pap. text 13.95 (1-896597-24-6) LPC InBook.

New York Diary of Lieutenant Jabez Fitch of the 17th Connecticut Regiment from August 22, 1776 to December 15, 1777. Ed. by William H. Sabine. LC 78-140881. (Eyewitness Accounts of the American Revolution Ser.). (Illus.). 1971. reprint ed. 19.95 (0-405-01218-7) Ayer.

New York Dingbats! A Fun Book of Games, Stories, Activities & More about Our State That's All in Code! for You to Decipher, Bk. 1. Carole Marsh. (Carole Marsh New York Bks.). (Illus.). (J). (gr. 3-12). 1994. pap. 19.95 (0-7933-3870-0); lib. bdg. 29.95 (0-7933-3869-7); disk 29.95 (0-7933-3871-9) Gallopade Intl.

New York Directory for 1786. Sachs, H. J., & Company Staff. 127p. 1998. reprint ed. pap. 11.00 (0-7884-0810-0, S013) Heritage Bk.

New York Directory for 1786. Noah Webster. 215p. 1994. reprint ed. lib. bdg. 27.50 (0-8328-3801-2) Higginson Bk Co.

New York Divorce Book: Do It Yourself Step-by-Step Manual Complete with Forms. Bernard Clyne. 256p. 1994. pap. 29.95 (0-918825-25-3) Moyer Bell.

New York Dogs. Andrea Mohin & Jack Robertiello. LC 96-35980. (Illus.). 1997. 14.95 (0-8118-1658-3) Chronicle Bks.

New York Dolls: Too Much. Nina Antonia. (Illus.). 208p. 1998. pap. text 17.95 (0-7119-6777-6) Music Sales.

New York Domestic Relations Reporter. Willard H. DaSilva. text 260.00 (0-8205-2083-7) Bender.

New York Driving While Intoxicated. Edward L. Fiandach. LC 92-81960. 1992. 120.00 (0-317-05367-1) West Group.

New York Driving While Intoxicated. Edward L. Fiandach. Ed. by John Gebauer. LC 96-76214. 900p. 1996. text. write for info. (0-7620-0049-X) West Group.

New York E. P. T. L. & S. C. P. A. annuals rev. ed. Gould Editorial Staff. 790p. (C). pap. text 21.95 (0-87526-342-9) Gould.

New York Early Census, Vol. 1. Ronald V. Jackson. (Illus.). 1978. lib. bdg. 30.00 (0-89593-585-6, Accel Indexing) Genealogical Srvcs.

New York Eats (More) The Food Shopper's Guide to the Freshest Ingredients, the Best Take-out & Baked Goods, & the Most Unusual Marketplaces in All of New York. Ed Levine. LC 97-11456. 1997. pap. 18.95 (0-312-15605-7) St Martin.

New York Edge 1998 Savvy Shoppers' Survey: Everything from Pearls to Plumbers, Rated for Quality, Style, Service & Value. 2nd unabridged ed. Susan B. Dollinger & Jane R. Lockshin. 500p. 1997. pap. 14.95 (1-889782-51-3) Custom Databanks.

New York Edge 1997 Savvy Shoppers' Survey: Everything from Pearls to Plumbers, Rated for Quality, Style, Service & Value, Vol. 1. Susan B. Dollinger & Jane R. Lockshin. 478p. (Orig.). 1996. pap. 14.95 (1-889782-50-5) Custom Databanks.

New York Edge Savvy Shopper's Survey: Everything from Pearls to Plumbers Rated for Quality, Style, Service & Value. Susan B. Dollinger & Jane R. Lockshiv. (Illus.). 418p. 1998. pap. 14.95 (1-889782-52-1) Custom Databanks.

New York Education Department Reports, April 1999. 100p. 1999. pap. write for info. (0-327-08420-0, 56216-13) LEXIS Pub.

New York Education Department Reports, August, 1998. 120p. 1998. pap. write for info. (0-327-06458-7, 5620813) LEXIS Pub.

***New York Education Department Reports, August 1999.** 100p. 1999. ring bd. write for info. (0-327-09214-9, 5620814) LEXIS Pub.

***New York Education Department Reports, December 1998.** 120p. 1998. ring bd. write for info. (0-327-06812-4, 5621213) LEXIS Pub.

New York Education Department Reports, December, 1998. 120p. 1999. ring bd. write for info. (0-327-07818-9, 5621313) LEXIS Pub.

***New York Education Department Reports, December 1999.** 175p. 1999. ring bd. write for info. (0-327-09218-1, 5621214) LEXIS Pub.

New York Education Department Reports, February 1999. 100p. 1999. ring bd. write for info. (0-327-08412-X, 56214-13) LEXIS Pub.

New York Education Department Reports, July 1998. 50p. 1998. pap. write for info. (0-327-06309-2, 5620713) LEXIS Pub.

***New York Education Department Reports, July 1999.** 100p. 1999. ring bd. write for info. (0-327-09213-0, 5620714) LEXIS Pub.

***New York Education Department Reports, June 1999.** 250p. 1999. Price not set. (0-327-09099-5, 5621813) LEXIS Pub.

New York Education Department Reports, March 1999. 150p. 1999. pap. write for info. (0-327-08417-0, 56215-13) LEXIS Pub.

New York Education Department Reports, November 1998. 120p. 1998. ring bd. write for info. (0-327-06809-4, 5621113) LEXIS Pub.

***New York Education Department Reports, November 1999.** 150p. 1999. ring bd. write for info. (0-327-09217-3, 5621114) LEXIS Pub.

New York Education Department Reports, October 1998. 120p. 1998. ring bd. write for info. (0-327-06807-8, 5621013) LEXIS Pub.

New York Education Department Reports, September, 1998. 120p. 1998. pap. write for info. (0-327-06501-X, 5620913) LEXIS Pub.

***New York Education Department Reports, September 1999.** 120p. 1999. ring bd. write for info. (0-327-09215-7, 562914) LEXIS Pub.

New York Education Laws: 1999-2000 Edition. 759p. pap. 40.00 (0-327-11364-2) LEXIS Pub.

New York 1880: Architecture & Urbanism in the Gilded Age. Robert A. M. Stern et al. LC 99-17892. (Illus.). 1164p. 1999. 85.00 (1-58093-027-1, Pub. by Monacelli Pr) Penguin Putnam.

New York, 1870: Long Island Federal Census Index (Dutchess, Queens, Richmond, & Suffolk Counties) 1990. 190.00 (0-89593-586-4, Accel Indexing) Genealogical Srvcs.

New York Elder Law Handbook. expanded ed. Institute on Law & Rights of Older Adults, Brookda. Ed. by Annette L. Kasle. 752p. 1995. ring bd. 95.00 (0-614-17126-1, F3-1202) PLI.

New York Election Laws. Lewis Abrahams. lxi, 588p. 1950. suppl. ed. 40.00 (0-89941-598-9, 501850) W S Hein.

***New York Employer's Guide: A Handbook of Employment Laws & Regulations.** 8th rev. ed. Summers Press, Inc. Staff. 550p. 1999. ring bd. 92.50 (1-56759-039-X) Summers Pr.

New York Employment Discrimination Handbook. text 69.00 (0-8205-4178-8) Bender.

New York Employment Discrimination Handbook. Proskauer et al. LC 92-41658. 1993. write for info. (0-8205-2788-2) Bender.

New York Employment Law, 4 vols., Set. Jonathan L. Salds. 1992. 400.00 (0-8205-1796-8) Bender.

New York End-of-Life Issues: Health Care Proxies, Living Wills, & Do-Not-Resuscitate Orders. James R. Sahlem & Mary E. Roche. 1996. write for info. (1-57588-340-6, 308630) W S Hein.

New York Environment Book. Eric Goldstein & Mark Izeman. LC 90-4024. (Illus.). 263p. 1990. pap. 19.95 (1-55963-018-3); text 32.50 (1-55963-019-1) Island Pr.

New York Environmental Conservation Law. annuals rev. ed. Ed. by Gould Editorial Staff. 1360p. (C). 1991. ring bd. 14.95 (0-87526-255-4) Gould.

New York Environmental Law. Ed. by Nicholas A. Robinson. LC 92-53528. 1000p. 1992. 110.00 (0-942954-48-3) NYS Bar.

New York Environmental Law Handbook. 5th ed. Nixon, Hargrave, Devons & Doyle Staff. LC 98-120602. 317p. 1999. pap. text 95.00 (0-86587-653-3) Gov Insts.

New York Estate Administration. Margaret V. Turano & C. Raymond Radigan. (Hornbook Ser.). 676p. Date not set. text 38.50 (0-314-98675-8, 68900, MICHIE) LEXIS Pub.

New York Estate Administration: 1991 Pocket Parts. Margaret V. Turano. (Hornbook Ser.). 125p. (C). 1991. pap. text 15.00 (0-314-92782-4) West Pub.

***New York Estate Administration: 1999 Edition.** C. Raymond Radigan & Margaret Valentine Turano. 900p. 1999. write for info. (0-327-04987-1, 6890011) LEXIS Pub.

New York Estate Administration, 1998 Supplement. C. Raymond Radigan & Margaret V. Turano. 200p. 1998. write for info. (0-327-00855-5, 6890511) LEXIS Pub.

New York Estates, Powers & Trusts Law. annuals Gould Editorial Staff. 220p. ring bd. 9.95 (0-87526-140-X) Gould.

New York Estates Practice Guide, 3 vols. 4th ed. John W. Tarbox. LC 84-81334. 1993. suppl. ed. 68.50 (0-317-03258-5) West Group.

New York Estates Practice Guide, 3 vols., Set. 4th ed. John W. Tarbox. LC 84-81334. 1984. 300.00 (0-318-04270-3) West Group.

New York Estate's Surrogate's Court Procedure Act. Ed. by New York State Staff & Matthew Bender Publishers Staff. 1997. write for info. (0-8205-3496-X) Bender.

New York Evidence Courtroom Manual. pap. 60.00 (1-58360-152-X) Anderson Pub Co.

New York Evidence-Proof of Cases, 2 vols. 2nd ed. Gabriel V. Mottla. LC 66-275456. 1658p. 190.00 (0-317-00483-2) West Group.

New York Evidence-Proof of Cases, 2 vols. 2nd ed. Gabriel V. Mottla. LC 66-275456. 1658p. 1993. suppl. ed. 89.50 (0-317-03184-8) West Group.

New York Evidentiary Foundations. 2nd ed. Randolph N. Jonakait et al. LC 98-85217. 368p. 1998. text 85.00 (0-327-00135-6, 63570-11) LEXIS Pub.

New York Evidentiary Foundations: 1993 Edition. Randolph N. Jonakait et al. 343p. 1993. text 85.00 (1-55834-058-0, 63570-10, MICHIE) LEXIS Pub.

New York Evidentiary Foundations, 1999 Supplement. 2nd ed. Randolph N. Jonakait et al. 22p. 1999. write for info. (0-327-01271-4, 6357114) LEXIS Pub.

New York Express. Deborah Wicentowski. (Illus.). 127p. (J). (gr. 3-5). 1988. pap. 8.95 (0-935063-47-1) CIS Comm.

New York Extra, 1693-1939, Vol. 1. Eric Caren. 1999. 24.99 (0-7858-1138-9) Bk Sales Inc.

New York, Eyewitness Travel Guide (French Edition) 1993. pap. 59.95 (0-7859-9026-7) Fr & Eur.

New York, Eyewitness Travel Guide (German Edition) 1993. pap. 69.56 (0-7859-9027-5) Fr & Eur.

New York, Eyewitness Travel Guide (Italian Edition) 1994. pap. 59.95 (0-7859-9028-3) Fr & Eur.

New York, Eyewitness Travel Guide (Spanish Edition) 2nd ed. Maria A. Sanchez. 432p. 1995. pap. 59.95 (0-7859-9025-9) Fr & Eur.

New York Facts & Factivities. Carole Marsh. (Carole Marsh State Bks.). (Illus.). (J). (gr. 4-7). 1996. pap., teacher ed. 19.95 (0-7933-7911-3, C Marsh) Gallopade Intl.

New York Facts & Symbols. Emily McAuliffe. (States & Their Symbols Ser.). 24p. (J). 1998. lib. bdg. 14.00 (0-531-11552-6) Watts.

New York Family Law. text 35.00 (0-8205-4198-2) Bender.

New York Family Law. Schechter. LC 97-141233. (Paralegal). 500p. (C). 1997. mass mkt. 49.95 (0-314-20622-1) West Pub.

New York Family Law Handbook. annuals Gould Editorial Staff. 1120p. 1989. pap. 21.95 (0-87526-374-7) Gould.

New York Family Law (Yellowbook) 1971. pap. write for info. (0-8205-2682-7) Bender.

New York Fashion: The Evolution of American Style. Caroline R. Milbank. (Illus.). 304p. 1996. pap. text 29.95 (0-8109-2647-4, Pub. by Abrams) Time Warner.

New York Federal Census Index, 1860 North. (Illus.). 1988. lib. bdg. 340.00 (0-89593-438-8, Accel Indexing) Genealogical Srvcs.

New York Federal Census Index, 1860 NY City (New York County) (Illus.). lib. bdg. 375.00 (0-89593-439-6, Accel Indexing) Genealogical Srvcs.

New York Federal Census Index, 1860 Buffalo (Erie County) (Illus.). 1987. lib. bdg. 255.00 (0-89593-437-X, Accel Indexing) Genealogical Srvcs.

New York Federal Census Index, 1860 Brooklyn (Kings & Queens Counties) (Illus.). 1988. lib. bdg. 375.00 (0-89593-436-1, Accel Indexing) Genealogical Srvcs.

New York Federal Census Index, 1860 South (Excludes Kings, New York & Queens Counties), 2 vols., Set. (Illus.). 1988. lib. bdg. 375.00 (0-89593-440-X, Accel Indexing) Genealogical Srvcs.

New York Federal Census Index, 1790. Ronald V. Jackson. (Illus.). 1978. lib. bdg. 63.00 (0-89593-752-2, Accel Indexing) Genealogical Srvcs.

New York Festival, Vol. 6. New York Festivals Staff. 1998. 59.95 (0-688-16043-3, Wm Morrow) Morrow Avon.

New York Festival Fun for Kids! Carole Marsh. (Carole Marsh New York Bks.). (Illus.). (J). (gr. 3-12). 1994. pap. 19.95 (0-7933-4023-3); lib. bdg. 29.95 (0-7933-4022-5) Gallopade Intl.

New York Festival Fun for Kids! Carole Marsh. (Carole Marsh New York Bks.). (Illus.). (YA). (gr. 3-12). 1994. disk 29.95 (0-7933-4024-1) Gallopade Intl.

New York Festivals. Sponsored Publications Staff. 1993. 55.00 (0-688-13179-4, Wm Morrow) Morrow Avon.

New York Festivals. 3rd ed. New York Festivals Staff. 1995. 59.95 (0-688-14258-3, Wm Morrow) Morrow Avon.

***New York Festivals: International Advertising Awards 8.** New York Festivals Staff & Gerald M. Goldberg. (Illus.). 392p. 2000. 69.95 (0-9655403-4-0, Pub. by NY Festivals) Watsn-Guptill.

New York Festivals Annual of Advertising. 5th ed. Gerald M. Goldberg. (Illus.). 384p. 1997. 69.95 (0-9655403-1-6) NY Festivals.

New York Festivals Annual of Advertising, Vol. 6. Gerald M. Goldberg. (Illus.). 370p. 1997. 69.95 (0-9655403-2-4) NY Festivals.

New York Festivals Annual of Advertising, Vol. 7. Ed. by Gerald M. Goldberg. (Illus.). 396p. 1998. text 69.95 (0-9655403-3-2, Pub. by NY Festivals) Watsn-Guptill.

New York Fictions: Modernity, Postmodernism, the New Modern. Peter Brooker. Ed. by Stan Smith. LC 95-24903. (Studies in Twentieth Century Literature Ser.). 256p. (C). 1996. pap. text 30.94 (0-582-09954-4, Pub. by Addison-Wesley) Longman.

N

New York Fictions: Modernity, Postmodernism, the New Modern. Peter Brooker. Ed. by Stan Smith. LC 95-24903. (Studies in Twentieth Century Literature). 256p. (C). 1996. 90.00 (*0-582-09955-2*) Longman.

New York Field Codes, 1850-1865, 5 vols. New York State Staff. Incl. Vol. I. Code of Civil Procedure of the State of New York, 1850. LC 97-42137. 1998. reprint ed. Not sold separately (*1-886363-34-X*); Vol. II. Code of Criminal Procedure of the State of New York, 1850. LC 97-42136. 1998. reprint ed. Not sold separately (*1-886363-35-8*); Vol. III. Civil Code of the State of New York, 1865. LC 97-42138. 1998. reprint ed. Not sold separately (*1-886363-38-2*); Vol. IV. Penal Code of the State of New York, 1865. LC 97-42135. 1998. reprint ed. Not sold separately (*1-886363-36-6*); Vol. V. Political Code of the State of New York, 1860. LC 97-38750. 1998. reprint ed. Not sold separately (*1-886363-37-4*); LC 97-38809. 1997. reprint ed. 495.00 (*1-886363-40-4*) Lawbk Exchange.

New York Film & Video Guide: Feature Film Edition. 96p. 1996. pap. 8.50 (*1-886494-02-9*) NY Film & Video.

New York Film & Video Guide: Feature Film Edition - 1998. Ed. by Michael Gordon. 112p. 1998. pap. 14.95 (*1-886494-04-5*) NY Film & Video.

New York Film & Video Guide: TV Commercial. Michael Gordon. 96p. (Orig.). 1997. pap. 14.95 (*1-886494-03-7*) NY Film & Video.

New York Film Festival Programs, 1963-1975. Nicolbas de Lafora & Lawrence Kinnaird. 1977. 65.95 (*0-405-07619-3*, 11479) Ayer.

New York Finance. Robert M. Simmons. 400p. (Orig.). 1995. 24.99 (*0-9642137-0-2*) Investar.

New York Fine Arts Resources. Renee Phillips. 264p. 1999. pap. 18.95 (*0-9646358-0-1*) Manhattan Arts Intl.

New York Fire District Officer's Guide. Raymond S. DiRaddo & Jerome M. Komfeld. 1998. write for info. (*1-58012-034-2*) James Pub Santa Ana.

***New York Fly Fishing Guide.** Robert W. Streeter. (Illus.). 112p. 2000. pap. 19.95 (*1-57188-157-3*, NYFG) F Amato Pubns.

New York for Less. (For Less Compact Guides Ser.). 1999. pap. 9.95 (*1-901811-80-8*) IPG Chicago.

New York for Less. Christina Prostano. (Illus.). 288p. 1997. pap. 19.95 (*0-9525437-8-8*, Pub. by Metropolis International) IPG Chicago.

New York for Less Compact Guide: 2nd Ed. 2nd ed. Christina Prostano. 1999. pap. text 19.95 (*1-901811-31-X*) Metropolis International.

New York for New Yorkers: A Historical Treasury & Guide to the Buildings & Monuments of Manhattan. Liza M. Greene. (Illus.). 128p. 1995. 17.95 (*0-393-03883-1*) Norton.

New York for the Independent Traveler: Fun Self-Guided Tours with Special Maps, Step-by-Step Itineraries & Floor Plans. 3rd rev. ed. Ruth Humleker. LC 96-50110. (Illus.). 228p. 1997. pap. 14.95 (*0-943400-93-7*) Marlor Pr.

New York Forms - Legal & Business, 12 vols. LC 75-134916. 1993. suppl. ed. 1365.00 (*0-318-57153-6*) West Group.

***New York Founding Hospital: An Index to the Federal, State & Local Census Records, 1870-1925.** Carolee Inskeep. 339p. 1999. pap. 27.50 (*0-8063-4590-X*) Clearfield Co.

***New York Friars Club.** Barry Dougherty. 2000. 21.95 (*0-87131-918-7*) M Evans.

New York from on High: A Guide to the View from the Empire State Building. Tauranac, Ltd. Staff. LC 98-211263. (Illus.). 48p. 1997. write for info. (*1-878892-09-6*) Tauranac Ltd.

New York from the Air. Yann Arthus-Bertrand. LC 98-26701. (Illus.). 160p. 1998. 45.00 (*0-8109-3692-5*, Pub. by Abrams) Time Warner.

New York Fun-ics: Yuze Can Tawk Like the Big Apple. Michael L. Ellis, III. LC 88-50184. (Illus.). (Orig.). 1993. pap. text 3.50 (*0-929178-21-1*) Valley Forge Pub.

New York Gardener's Guide: The What, Where, When, How & Why of Gardening in New York. Ralph Snodsmith. (Illus.). 424p. 2000. pap. 19.95 (*1-888608-45-5*) Cool Springs Pr.

New York Genealogical Research. George K. Schweitzer. 254p. 1995. pap. 15.00 (*0-913857-11-4*) Genealog Sources.

New York "GEO" Bingo! 38 Must Know State Geography Facts for Kids to Learn While Having Fun! Carole Marsh. (Bingo! Ser.). (Illus.). (J). (gr. 2-8). 1998. pap. 14.95 (*0-7933-8619-5*) Gallopade Intl.

New York Giants. Bob Italia. LC 95-883. (Inside the NFL Ser.). (Illus.). 32p. (J). (gr. 3-8). 1996. lib. bdg. 15.98 (*1-56239-457-6*) ABDO Pub Co.

New York Giants. New York Giants. Ed. by CWC Sports Inc. (NFL Team Yearbooks Ser.). (J). (gr. 1-12). 1998. pap. 9.99 (*1-891613-09-X*) Everett Sports.

New York Giants. rev. ed. John Steinbreder. LC 99-36495. 1999. pap. write for info. (*0-87833-159-X*) Taylor Pub.

***New York Giants.** 3rd rev. ed. Julie Nelson. (Pro Football Today Ser.). (Illus.). 32p. (YA). (gr. 3-12). 2000. lib. bdg. 22.60 (*1-58341-052-X*, Creat Educ) Creative Co.

***New York Giants: Seventy-Five Years.** Jerry Izenberg. LC 99-2852. (Illus.). 188p. 1999. 195.00 (*1-887656-13-8*) Tehabi Bks.

***New York Giants: Seventy-Five Years.** anniversary ed. Jerry Izenberg. LC 99-28527. (Illus.). 180p. 1999. 39.95 (*0-7370-0066-X*); pap. 24.95 (*0-7370-0067-8*) T-L Custom Pub.

***New York Giants: Seventy-Five Years.** deluxe ed. Jerry Izenberg. LC 99-2852. (Illus.). 188p. 1999. 50.00 (*1-887656-18-9*) Tehabi Bks.

***New York Giants: 75 Years of Football Memories.** New York Daily News Editors. 200p. 1999. 24.95 (*1-58261-134-3*, Pub. by Sprts Pubng) Partners-West.

New York Giants Baseball Club: The Growth of a Team & a Sport, 1870 to 1900. James D. Hardy, Jr. LC 96-23281. (Illus.). 251p. 1996. lib. bdg. 28.50 (*0-7864-0231-8*) McFarland & Co.

New York Girls. Richard Kern. (Photo & Sexy Bks.). (Illus.). 208p. 1997. 29.99 (*3-8228-8180-5*) Taschen Amer.

New York Girls. Taschen, Benedikt Staff. 1996. pap. 3.99 (*3-8228-8164-3*) Taschen Amer.

New York Girls Postcardbook. Taschen, Benedikt Staff. 1997. pap. 5.99 (*3-8228-8088-4*) Taschen Amer.

New York Gitlitz on Divorces & Annulments. James P. Gitlitz. 730p. ring bd. 44.95 (*0-87526-258-9*) Gould.

***New York Glory: Religions in the City.** Ed. by Tony Carnes & Anna Karpathakis. 2000. text 60.00 (*0-8147-1600-8*); pap. text 19.50 (*0-8147-1601-6*) NYU Pr.

New York Government! The Cornerstone of Everyday Life in Our State! Carole Marsh. (Carole Marsh New York Bks.). (Illus.). (J). (gr. 3-12). 1996. pap. 19.95 (*0-7933-6278-4*); lib. bdg. 29.95 (*0-7933-6277-6*); disk 29.95 (*0-7933-6279-2*) Gallopade Intl.

New York Government's Performance Standards, 1990. Ed. by Greg Michels. (Governments Performance Standards Ser.). (Illus.). 150p. 1990. text 125.00 (*1-55507-495-2*) Municipal Analysis.

***New York Graphic.** Adam L. Baker. LC 99-88713. 308p. 2000. pap. 13.00 (*0-385-49843-8*, Anchor NY) Doubleday.

New York Guide. 5th ed. Penguin Books Staff. (Time Out Ser.). 352p. 1998. pap. 14.95 (*0-14-026441-8*, Penguin Bks) Viking Penguin.

***New York Guide.** 7th ed. Penguin Staff. (Time Out Guide Ser.). (Illus.). 352p. 1999. pap. 14.95 (*0-14-027452-9*, Penguin Bks) Viking Penguin.

New York Guide to Peace & Quiet. pap. 4.95 (*0-685-39067-5*) Pimog Pr.

***New York Guide to Tax, Estate & Financial Planning for the Elderly.** David Goldfarb. LC 98-46495. 1998. 130.00 (*0-8205-4066-8*) Bender.

New York Handbook of Intellectual Property. H. Hansen. 1991. Price not set. (*0-8205-2787-4*) Bender.

New York Harbor Book. Francis J. Duffy & William H. Miller. (Illus.). xvi, 208p. 1986. 22.50 (*0-931474-33-7*); pap. 17.95 (*0-931474-34-5*) TBW Bks.

New York Harbor to Chesapeake Bay (Regional) (N. O. A. A. Tide & Tidal Current Tables, 1999 Ser.). 1998. 17.95 (*1-57785-064-5*, 81599NYC) ProStar Pubns.

***New York Health Care in Perspective 2000.** Ed. by Kathleen O'Leary Morgan & Scott E. Morgan. 21p. 2000. spiral bd. 19.00 (*0-7401-0231-1*) Morgan Quitno Corp.

New York Health Care Perspective, 1998. Ed. by Kathleen O'Leary Morgan & Scott E. Morgan. 20p. 1998. pap. 19.00 (*1-56692-831-1*) Morgan Quitno Corp.

New York Health Care Perspective, 1999. Kathleen O'Leary Morgan. 21p. 1999. spiral bd. 19.00 (*0-7401-0081-5*) Morgan Quitno Corp.

New York, Hello! Vincent Katz & Rudy Burckhardt. (Offset Offshoot Ser.: No. 9). 1990. 8.00 (*0-941240-12-6*) Ommation Pr.

***New York, Here We Come.** Melanie Stewart. 128p. 1999. mass mkt. 3.99 (*0-307-23450-9*) Gldn Bks Pub Co.

New York "HISTO" Bingo! 42 Must Know State History Facts for Kids to Learn While Having Fun! Carole Marsh. (Bingo! Ser.). (Illus.). (J). (gr. 2-8). 1998. pap. 14.95 (*0-7933-8620-9*) Gallopade Intl.

New York Historical & Biographical Index, Vol. 1. Ronald V. Jackson. LC 78-53710. (Illus.). 1984. lib. bdg. 30.00 (*0-89593-193-1*, Accel Indexing) Genealogical Srvcs.

New York Historical Manuscripts: Dutch Kingston Papers, 2 vols. Peter R. Christoph. Ed. by Kenneth Scott & Kenn Stryker-Rodda. Tr. by Dingman Versteeg. LC 75-5971. (Illus.). xxii, 849p. 1999. pap. 60.00 (*0-8063-0720-X*) Clearfield Co.

New York History! Surprising Secrets about Our State's Founding Mothers, Fathers & Kids! Carole Marsh. (Carole Marsh New York Bks.). (Illus.). (J). (gr. 3-12). 1996. pap. 19.95 (*0-7933-6125-7*); lib. bdg. 29.95 (*0-7933-6124-9*); disk 29.95 (*0-7933-6126-5*) Gallopade Intl.

***New York Holiday & Millennium Guide: Where to Eat, Drink, Shop & Celebrate.** Charles Suisman & Carol Molesworth. (Illus.). 144p. 1999. pap. 12.00 (*1-885492-87-1*) City & Co.

New York Hospital: A History of the Psychiatric Service, 1771-1936. William L. Russell. LC 73-2414. (Mental Illness & Social Policy; the American Experience Ser.). 1973. reprint ed. 40.95 (*0-405-05224-3*) Ayer.

New York Hot Air Balloon Mystery. Carole Marsh. (Carole Marsh New York Bks.). (Illus.). (J). (gr. 2-9). 1994. 29.95 (*0-7933-2606-0*); pap. 19.95 (*0-7933-2607-9*); disk 29.95 (*0-7933-2608-7*) Gallopade Intl.

New York Hot & Hip. David Andrusia. LC 97-32298. (Illus.). 144p. 1998. 9.95 (*0-87131-849-0*) M Evans.

New York Hot Zones! Viruses, Diseases, & Epidemics in Our State's History. Carole Marsh. (Hot Zones! Ser.). (Illus.). (J). (gr. 3-12). 1998. pap. 19.95 (*0-7933-8925-9*); lib. bdg. 29.95 (*0-7933-8924-0*) Gallopade Intl.

New York Hotel Industry: A Labor Relations Study. Morris A. Horowitz. LC 60-7992. (Wertheim Publications in Industrial Relations). (Illus.). 285p. 1960. 18.50 (*0-674-61900-5*) HUP.

New York in Aerial Views: Eighty-Six Photographs. William Fried & Edward B. Watson. (Illus.). 176p. (Orig.). 1981. pap. 12.95 (*0-486-24018-5*) Dover.

New York in American History. Cappell & Howard. 64p. 1987. student ed. 4.50 (*0-910307-14-8*) Comp Pr.

New York in Fiction. A. B. Maurice. 1972. 59.95 (*0-8490-0728-3*) Gordon Pr.

New York in Perspective, 1998. Ed. by Kathleen O'Leary Morgan & Scott E. Morgan. 24p. 1998. pap. 19.00 (*1-56692-881-8*) Morgan Quitno Corp.

New York in Perspective, 1999. Ed. by Kathleen O'Leary Morgan. 26p. 1999. spiral bd. 19.00 (*1-56692-981-4*) Morgan Quitno Corp.

***New York in Perspective 2000.** Ed. by Kathleen O'Leary Morgan & Scott E. Morgan. 26p. 2000. spiral bd. 19.00 (*0-7401-0281-8*) Morgan Quitno Corp.

New York in the Age of the Constitution, 1775-1800. Ed. by Paul A. Gilje & William Pencak. LC 91-55094. 208p. 1992. 38.50 (*0-8386-3455-9*) Fairleigh Dickinson.

New York in the American Revolution. W. C. Abbott. LC 72-7428. (American History & Americana Ser.: No. 47). 1973. reprint ed. lib. bdg. 75.00 (*0-8383-1668-9*) M S G Haskell Hse.

New York in the Confederation. Thomas C. Cochran. LC 72-77054. (Reprints of Economic Classics Ser.). (Illus.). ix, 220p. 1972. reprint ed. 35.00 (*0-678-00911-2*) Kelley.

New York in the Critical Period, 1783-1789. Ernest W. Spaulding. 334p. 1993. reprint ed. lib. bdg. 89.00 (*0-7812-5199-0*) Rprt Serv.

New York in the Fifties. Dan Wakefield. LC 98-50902. 1999. pap. 14.95 (*0-312-19935-X*) St Martin.

New York in the Forties. Andreas Feininger. LC 77-8734. (New York City Ser.). (Illus.). 181p. 1978. pap. 12.95 (*0-486-23585-8*) Dover.

New York in the Forties. Andreas Feininger. (GER., Illus.). 96p. (C). 1995. 41.00 (*3-8170-2512-2*, Pub. by Knstvrlag Weingrtn) Intl Bk Import.

New York in the Nineteenth Century: Engravings from Harper's Weekly & Other Contemporary Sources. John Grafton. LC 77-73339. (Illus.). 256p. 1977. pap. 12.95 (*0-486-23516-5*) Dover.

New York in the Revolution: As Colony & State, 2 vols. in 1. James A. Roberts & Frederick G. Mather. (Illus.). 900p. 1996. reprint ed. 60.00 (*0-8063-1489-3*) Genealog Pub.

New York in the Revolution As Colony & State: These Records Were Discovered, Arranged & Classified 1895, 1896-1897 & 1898. Ed. by James A. Roberts. 534p. 1993. reprint ed. lib. bdg. 53.50 (*1-56012-127-0*, 124) Kinship Rhinebeck.

New York in the Sixties. Klaus Lehnartz. LC 78-53190. (Illus.). 144p. 1978. pap. 9.95 (*0-486-23674-9*) Dover.

New York in the Thirties. Berenice Abbott. LC 73-77375. Orig. Title: Changing New York. (Illus.). 97p. 1973. reprint ed. 11.95 (*0-486-22967-X*) Dover.

New York in Your Pocket Guide. Michelin Staff. (In Your Pocket Guides Ser.). 1996. per. 9.95 (*2-06-650401-7*, 6504) Michelin.

New York Indian Dictionary for Kids! Carole Marsh. (Carole Marsh State Bks.). (J). (gr. 2-9). 1996. 29.95 (*0-7933-7740-4*, C Marsh); pap. 19.95 (*0-7933-7741-2*, C Marsh) Gallopade Intl.

New York Institute of Finance Guide to Investing. New York Institute of Finance Staff. LC 87-11323. (Illus.). 320p. (C). 1987. pap. 15.95 (*0-13-620436-8*) NY Inst Finance.

New York Institute of Finance Guide to Investing. 2nd ed. New York Institute of Finance Staff. 320p. (C). 1992. pap. text 19.95 (*0-13-617598-8*) P-H.

***New York Institute of Finance Guide to Investing.** 3rd ed. Michael Steinberg. 2000. pap. 20.00 (*0-7352-0117-X*) PH Pr.

New York Institute of Finance Guide to Mutual Funds, 1999. Kirk Kazanjian. LC 98-38867. 464p. 1999. pap. text 20.00 (*0-7352-0074-2*) PH Pr.

***New York Institute of Finance Guide to Mutual Funds 2000.** Kirk Kazanjian. 352p. 1999. pap. 20.00 (*0-7352-0130-7*) PH Pr.

New York Insurance Law, 4 vols. W. B. Dunham. 1991. 530.00 (*0-8205-1484-5*) Bender.

New York Insurance Laws, 1986. 770p. 1986. pap. 24.50 (*0-317-52119-5*) West Pub.

New York Intellect: A History of Intellectual Life in New York City from 1750 to the Beginnings of Our Own Time. Thomas Bender. 448p. 1988. reprint ed. pap. 19.95 (*0-8018-3639-5*) Johns Hopkins.

New York Intellectuals: From Vanguard to Institution. Hugh Wilford. LC 95-4043. 320p. 1995. text 79.95 (*0-7190-3988-6*, Pub. by Manchester Univ Pr) St Martin.

New York Intellectuals: The Rise & Decline of the Anti-Stalinist Left from the 1930s to the 1980s. Alan M. Wald. LC 86-24922. (Illus.). xvi, 440p. (C). 1987. text 39.95 (*0-8078-1716-3*) U of NC Pr.

New York Interiors. Beate Wedekind. LC 99-461711. (Jumbo Ser.). (Illus.). 300p. 1997. 39.99 (*3-8228-8182-1*) Taschen Amer.

New York Interiors at the Turn of the Century. Joseph Byron. (Illus.). 176p. (Orig.). 1976. pap. 14.95 (*0-486-23359-6*) Dover.

New York International Chess: Tournament, 1984. Jeffrey Naier. 1985. 17.50 (*0-911971-11-4*) Effect Pub.

***New York Investment & Business Guide: Business, Investment, Export-Import Opportunities, 50 vols., Vol. 32.** Global Investment Center, USA Staff. (U. S. Regional Investment & Business Library-99: Vol. 32). (Illus.). 350p. (Orig.). 1999. pap. 59.95 (*0-7397-1131-8*) Intl Business Pubns.

New York Irish. Ed. by Ronald H. Bayor & Timothy J. Meagher. LC 95-20319. (Illus.). 720p. 1996. 50.00 (*0-8018-5199-8*) Johns Hopkins.

New York Irish. Ed. by Ronald H. Bayor & Timothy J. Meagher. LC 95-20319. 758p. 1997. reprint ed. pap. text 25.95 (*0-8018-5764-3*) Johns Hopkins.

New York Irish: Their View of American Foreign Policy, 1914-1921. John P. Buckley. LC 76-6327. (Irish Americans Ser.). 1976. 34.95 (*0-405-09324-1*) Ayer.

New York Is a Rubber's Paradise: A Guide to New York's City's Cemeteries in the Five Boroughs. 2nd rev. ed. Roberta Halporn. LC 97-68304. (Illus.). 76p. (Orig.). 1998. pap. 12.95 (*0-930194-54-3*) Ctr Thanatology.

New York Islanders see NHL Today

New York Islanders. Jim Stevens. LC 98-21713. (Inside the NHL Ser.). (J). 1999. 16.48 (*1-57765-049-2*) ABDO Pub Co.

New York Jeopardy! Answers & Questions about Our State! Carole Marsh. (Carole Marsh New York Bks.). (Illus.). (J). (gr. 3-12). 1994. pap. 19.95 (*0-7933-4176-0*); lib. bdg. 29.95 (*0-7933-4175-2*); disk 29.95 (*0-7933-4177-9*) Gallopade Intl.

New York Jets. Bob Italia. LC 95-34979. (Inside the NFL Ser.). (Illus.). 32p. (J). (gr. 3-8). 1996. lib. bdg. 15.98 (*1-56239-550-5*) ABDO Pub Co.

New York Jets. New York Jets. Ed. by CWC Sports Inc. (NFL Team Yearbooks Ser.). (J). (gr. 1-12). 1998. pap. 9.99 (*1-891613-17-0*) Everett Sports.

***New York Jets.** 3rd rev. ed. Julie Nelson. LC 99-15747. (Pro Football Today Ser.). (Illus.). 32p. (YA). 2000. lib. bdg. 22.60 (*1-58341-053-8*, Creat Educ) Creative Co.

***New York Jets Family Cookbook.** Glenn Foley WINGS Foundation Staff. 288p. 1999. 21.95 (*0-9675962-0-3*, Pub. by G Foley WINGS) Wimmer Bks.

New York Jew. Alfred Kazin. LC 96-25816. (New York Classics Ser.). 307p. 1996. reprint ed. pap. 17.95 (*0-8156-0413-0*, KANYP) Syracuse U Pr.

***New York Jews & the Great Depression: Uncertain Promise.** Beth S. Wenger. LC 99-37948. 288p. 1999. pap. text 19.95 (*0-8156-0617-6*) Syracuse U Pr.

New York Jews & the Great Depression: Uncertain Promise. Beth S. Wenger. LC 96-17786. (Illus.). 288p. 1996. 30.00 (*0-300-06265-6*) Yale U Pr.

***New York JobBank, 2000 (Metro)** Adams Media Corporation Staff. 640p. 1999. pap. 16.95 (*1-58062-230-5*) Adams Media.

***New York JobBank, 2001 (Metro)** (JobBank Ser.). 656p. 2000. pap. 16.95 (*1-58062-382-4*) Adams Media.

New York "Jography" A Fun Run Thru Our State! Carole Marsh. (Carole Marsh New York Bks.). (Illus.). (J). 1994. pap. 19.95 (*1-55609-898-7*); lib. bdg. 29.95 (*1-55609-897-9*); disk 29.95 (*1-55609-899-5*) Gallopade Intl.

New York Judge Reviews, Vol. 1. Benedene Cannata. Ed. by Cynthia Millican-Glenn. 540p. 1997. pap. 125.00 (*1-58012-004-0*) James Pub Santa Ana.

***New York Judge Reviews & Court Directory: 2000 Edition.** Francis K. Kenna & Linda Z. Sideri. 2000. pap. write for info. (*1-58012-057-1*) James Pub Santa Ana.

New York Jurisprudence, 133 vols., Set. 2nd ed. LC 79-90263. 1993. suppl. ed. 8645.00 incl. cd-rom (*0-318-57150-1*) West Group.

New York Juvenile Delinquency Practice. Stephen J. Bogacz. LC 98-87339. 1122p. 1998. 99.00 (*0-327-00341-3*, 6012010) LEXIS Pub.

New York Kid's Cookbook: Recipes, How-To, History, Lore & More! Carole Marsh. (Carole Marsh New York Bks.). (Illus.). (J). 1994. pap. 19.95 (*0-7933-0828-3*); lib. bdg. 29.95 (*0-7933-0829-1*); disk 29.95 (*0-7933-0830-5*) Gallopade Intl.

New York Knicks see Pro Basketball Today

New York Knicks. Paul Joseph. LC 96-39607. (Inside the NBA Ser.). (Illus.). 32p. (J). (gr. 3-8). 1997. lib. bdg. 16.95 (*1-56239-767-2*) ABDO Pub Co.

New York Knicks: The Official 50th Anniversary Celebration. George Kalinsky. (Illus.). 247p. 1997. pap. text 22.95 (*0-02-861991-9*, Pub. by Macmillan) S&S Trade.

***New York Knicks Basketball Team.** Randy Schultz. LC 99-53164. (Great Sports Teams Ser.). (Illus.). 48p. (YA). (gr. 4-10). 2000. lib. bdg. 18.95 (*0-7660-1281-6*) Enslow Pubs.

New York Labor Pool: Alucinaciones de un Immigrante. Jorge Cevallos. (SPA., Illus.). 174p. 1997. pap. 19.95 (*0-9654237-2-7*) Town Compass.

New York Landlord & Tenant: Including Summary Proceedings. 4th ed. Joseph Rasch. LC 98-22395. 1998. write for info. (*0-8366-1250-7*) West Group.

New York Landlord & Tenant: Rent Control & Rent Stabilization. 2nd ed. Joseph Rasch. LC 87-80713. 1987. 95.00 (*0-317-01506-0*) West Group.

New York Landlord & Tenant: Rent Control & Rent Stabilization. 2nd ed. Joseph Rasch. LC 87-80713. 1993. suppl. ed. 52.50 (*0-317-03311-5*) West Group.

New York Landlord & Tenant Handbook. annuals Jeffrey Gallett. Ed. by Gould Staff. 370p. ring bd. 39.95 (*0-87526-311-9*) Gould.

New York Landlord & Tenant, Summary Proceedings, 3 vols. 3rd ed. Joseph Rasch. LC 71-154362. 1988. 285.00 (*0-317-03188-0*) West Group.

New York Landlord & Tenant, Summary Proceedings, 3 vols. 3rd ed. Joseph Rasch. LC 71-154362. 1993. suppl. ed. 60.00 (*0-317-03189-9*) West Group.

New York Landlord-Tenant Law (Tanbook) annuals 1990. write for info. (*0-8205-2785-8*) Bender.

New York Landlord's Law Book. Mary Ann Hallenborg. LC 99-28062. 496p. 1999. pap. 39.95 (*0-87337-539-4*) Nolo.com.

New York Landmarks: A Collection of Architecture & Historical Details. Charles J. Ziga. 64p. 1993. 9.95 (*0-9636673-0-0*) DoveTail Bks.

New York Law Addendum - Life & Health Insurance. rev. ed. Steven C. Kleinman. 96p. 1999. pap. text 12.95 (*1-884803-04-0*) Werbel Pub.

New York Law & Practice of Real Property, 3 vols. 2nd ed. Joseph Rasch. LC 62-4443. 285.00 (*0-317-00514-6*) West Group.

New York Law & Practice of Real Property, 3 vols. 2nd ed. Joseph Rasch. LC 62-4443. 1993. suppl. ed. 50.00 (*0-317-05565-8*) West Group.

N

An Asterisk (*) at the beginning of an entry indicates that the title is appearing for the first time.

New York Law Digest. annuals Gould Editorial Staff. 850p. ring bd. 14.95 (0-87526-252-X) Gould.

New York Law of Product Liability. Paul D. Rheingold. 250p. 1990. ring bd. 65.00 (0-929179-49-8) Juris Pubng.

New York Law of Wills, Descent & Distribution. George F. Keenan. LC 58-10383. xii, 538p. 1958. 35.00 (0-89941-604-7, 501980) W S Hein.

New York Law School Human Rights Annual, 1983-1994/95, 13 vols., Set. 1983. 487.50 (0-8377-9068-9, Rothman) W S Hein.

New York Law School Journal of International & Comparative Law, 1979-1994/95, 17 vols., Set. 1979. 675.00 (0-8377-9119-7, Rothman) W S Hein.

New York Lawyer's Deskbook. New York State Bar Association Staff. LC 89-64413. 1172p. 1990. ring bd. 115.00 (0-942954-33-5) NYS Bar.

New York Lawyer's Formbook. New York State Bar Association Staff. LC 90-50851. 1364p. 1991. ring bd. 115.00 (0-942954-35-1) NYS Bar.

New York Legal Assistant Handbook. Patricia Derby et al. 772p. 1996. ring bd. 89.98 (0-938065-96-3) James Pub Santa Ana.

New York Legal Forms & Procedures Handbook. Gould Editorial Staff. 660p. 1989. ring bd. 49.95 (0-87526-362-3) Gould.

New York Legal Research Guide. Ellen M. Gibson. LC 88-80721. xi, 404p. 1988. lib. bdg. 38.50 (0-89941-622-5, 305440) W S Hein.

New York Legal Research Guide. 2nd ed. Ellen M. Gibson. LC 98-20121. xviii,486,x,236p. 1998. 68.00 (1-57588-220-5, 311220) W S Hein.

New York Liberty: Teamwork. Thomas S. Owens & Diana S. Helmer. LC 98-16487. (Women's Professional Basketball Ser.). 24p. (J). 1999. 18.60 (0-8239-5239-8, PowerKids) Rosen Group.

New York Library Book: A Surprising Guide to the Unusual Special Collections in Libraries Across Our State for Students, Teachers, Writers & Publishers - Includes Reproducible Mailing Labels Plus Activities for Young People! Carole Marsh. (Carole Marsh New York Bks.). (Illus.). 1994. pap. 19.95 (0-7933-3102-1); lib. bdg. 29.95 (0-7933-3101-3); disk 29.95 (0-7933-3103-X) Gallopade Intl.

New York Life at the Turn of the Century in Photographs. Joseph Byron. (New York City Ser.). (Illus.). 144p. 1985. pap. 12.95 (0-486-24863-1) Dover.

New York Limited Liability Companies & Partnerships: A Guide to Law & Practice. Karon S. Walker. LC 95-8483. 700p. (C). 1995. text. write for info. (0-314-05987-3) West Pub.

New York Limited Liability Company Forms & Practice Manual, 2 vols. 3rd ed. Howard N. Lefkowitz. LC 97-51696. 790p. 1998. ring bd. 239.90 (1-57400-035-7) Data Trace Pubng.

New York Literary Lights: William Corbett. William Corbett. LC 97-80077. 338p. 1998. pap. 16.95 (1-55597-272-1) Graywolf.

New York Litigation Checklists, 2 vols., Set. Lawyers Cooperative Publishing Staff. LC 92-73799. 1992. ring bd. 150.00 (0-317-05372-8) West Group.

New York Living. Lisa Lovatt-Smith. LC 99-62116. (Illus.). 216p. 1999. 35.00 (0-8230-3182-9) Watsn-Guptill.

New York Living Rooms. Dominique Nabokov. LC 98-16619. (Illus.). 1998. text 29.95 (0-87951-875-8, Pub. by Overlook Pr) Penguin Putnam.

New York Loyalists. Philip Ranlet. LC 85-29601. 317p. reprint ed. pap. 98.30 (0-608-08627-4, 206915000003) Bks Demand.

***New York Magazine: Crosswords.** Maura Jacobson. 1999. pap. 9.95 (0-8129-3212-9) Random.

***New York Manhattan Changing Times.** Andreas Weber. (Illus.). 148p. 2000. 85.00 (3-8238-5474-7) te Neues.

New York Manufacturers Register. 2nd rev. ed. Ed. by Frank Lambing. 1999. 145.00 (1-58202-060-4) Manufacturers.

New York Mapguide: The Esssential Guide to Manhattan. Michael Middleditch. 64p. 1998. pap. 8.95 (0-14-026562-7) Viking Penguin.

***New York Marble Cemetary Interments, 1830-1937: With Additional Biographical Information.** Anne W. Brown. (Illus.). 238p. 1999. lib. bdg. 37.95 (1-56012-157-2, 161) Kinship Rhinebeck.

New York Marriages Previous to 1784. New York Colony Committee. LC 67-30757. 618p. 1999. reprint ed. pap. 45.00 (0-8063-0259-3) Clearfield Co.

New York Math! How It All Adds up in Our State. Carole Marsh. (Carole Marsh New York Bks.). (Illus.). (YA). (gr. 3-12). 1996. pap. 19.95 (0-7933-6584-8); lib. bdg. 29.95 (0-7933-6583-X) Gallopade Intl.

New York Matrimonial Practice. Willard H. DaSilva. LC 79-91156. (Practice Systems Library Manual). ring bd. 125.00 (0-317-00469-7) West Group.

New York Matrimonial Practice. Willard H. DaSilva. LC 79-91156. (Practice Systems Library Manual). 1993. suppl. ed. 60.00 (0-317-03180-5) West Group.

New York Media Book: A Surprising Guide to the Amazing Print, Broadcast & Online Media of Our State for Students, Teachers, Writers & Publishers - Includes Reproducible Mailing Labels Plus Activities for Young People! Carole Marsh. (Carole Marsh New York Bks.). (Illus.). 1994. pap. 19.95 (0-7933-3258-3); lib. bdg. 29.95 (0-7933-3257-5); disk 29.95 (0-7933-3259-1) Gallopade Intl.

New York Metro - Northern New Jersey Pocket Guide. Warren M. Silverman. 188p. 1995. pap. 13.95 (0-939430-18-5) Scanner Master.

New York Metro Business Directory, 1998 see New York Business Directory 1998

***New York Metro Business Directory, 2000 Edition.** rev. ed. American Business Directories Staff. 3680p. 1999. boxed set 415.00 incl. cd-rom (0-7687-0168-6) Am Busn Direct.

New York Metro Directory, 1996-97. Patrick Dalton. 1998. pap. 135.00 (1-882893-17-4) Dalton.

New York Metro/Northern New Jersey Guide: The Tri-State's Complete Resource of Public Safety Operations & Two-Way Radio Communications. 6th ed. Warren M. Silverman. (Illus.). 660p. 1997. pap. 38.95 (0-939430-36-3) Scanner Master.

New York Mets. George Salinsky. (Illus.). 240p. 1996. 19.95 (0-02-861248-5) Macmillan USA.

New York Mets. Chris W. Sehnert. LC 96-8144. (America's Game Ser.). (Illus.). 32p. (J). (gr. 3-8). 1997. lib. bdg. 16.48 (1-56239-665-X) ABDO Pub Co.

New York Mets: A Photographic History. George Kalinsky. (Illus.). 240p. 1994. 40.00 (0-02-860000-2) Macmillan.

New York Mets: A Photographic History. George Kalinsky. (Illus.). 240p. 1996. pap. text 19.95 (0-02-860858-5) Macmillan.

***New York Mets Encyclopedia.** Peter C. Bjarkman. (Illus.). 250p. 2001. 34.95 (1-58261-035-5) Sports Pub.

New York Missal: A Paleographic & Phonetic Analysis. Andrew R. Corin. (UCLA Slavic Studies: Vol. 21). 272p. 1991. 29.95 (0-89357-224-1) Slavica.

New York Modern: The Arts & the City. William B. Scott & Peter M. Rutkoff. LC 98-41864. (Illus.). 448p. 1999. 39.95 (0-8018-5998-0) Johns Hopkins.

New York Money Market, 4 vols. Ed. by Benjamin H. Beckhart. LC 79-155152. reprint ed. 210.00 (0-404-04550-2) AMS Pr.

New York Money Market & the Finance of Trade, 1900-1913. Charles A. Goodhart. LC 69-12723. (Economic Studies: No. 132). 247p. 1969. 15.00 (0-674-61950-1) HUP.

New York Mosaic: Do I Wake or Sleep; The Christmas Tree; Many Mansions. Isabel Bolton. LC 97-18480. 401p. 1997. 35.00 (1-883642-28-0) Steerforth Pr.

New York Mosaic: Do I Wake or Sleep; The Christmas Tree; Many Mansions. Isabel Bolton. LC 97-18480. (Illus.). 401p. 1998. reprint ed. pap. 18.00 (1-883642-89-2) Steerforth Pr.

***New York Motor Vehicle Accidents.** Gary B. Pillersdorf et al. 1999. write for info. (1-58012-050-4) James Pub Santa Ana.

New York Multiple Dwelling Law. annuals Gould Editorial Staff. 300p. ring bd. 16.95 (0-87526-285-6) Gould.

New York Municipal Formbook. Herbert A. Kline. Ed. by Nancy E. Kline. 700p. 1994. ring bd. 102.60 (0-614-26700-5, 4160); ring bd. 156.60 incl. disk (0-614-26701-3, 4160) NYS Bar.

New York Murder Mystery: The True Story Behind the Crime Crash of the 1990s. Andrew Karmen. 320p. 2000. 27.95 (0-8147-4717-5) NYU Pr.

New York Musical World 1852-1860, 4 vols. Ed. by H. Robert Cohen. (Repertoire International de la Presse Musicale Ser.). 1993. lib. bdg. 570.00 (0-8357-2255-4) UMI.

***New York Musicals of Comden & Green.** Betty Comden & Adolph Green. (Illus.). 328p. 1998. pap. 19.95 (1-55783-360-5) Applause Theatre Bk Pubs.

New York Musicals of Comden & Green: On the Town, Wonderful Town & Bells Are Ringing. Betty Comden & Adolph Green. (Illus.). 328p. 1996. 35.00 (1-55783-242-0) Applause Theatre Bk Pubs.

New York Mystery Van Takes Off! Handicapped New York Kids Sneak Off on a Big Adventure. Carole Marsh. (Carole Marsh New York Bks.). (Illus.). (J). (gr. 3-12). 1994. pap. 19.95 (0-7933-5058-1); disk 29.95 (0-7933-5059-X) Gallopade Intl.

New York Mystery Van Takes Off! Handicapped New York Kids Sneak Off on a Big Adventure, Bk. 1. Carole Marsh. (Carole Marsh New York Bks.). (Illus.). (J). (gr. 3-12). 1994. 29.95 (0-7933-5057-3) Gallopade Intl.

New York Natural History Survey: Zoology of New York, 5 vols., Set. James E. DeKay. 1993. reprint ed. lib. bdg. 375.00 (0-7812-5142-7) Rprt Serv.

New York Naturally, 1989: A Resource Directory for Natural Living in the Tri-State Area. Jerome Rubin. 168p. (Orig.). 1988. pap. write for info. (0-318-65041-X) City Spirit Pubns.

New York Naturally, 1990: A Resource Directory for Natural Living in the Tri-State Area, Including New Jersey & Connecticut. Ed. by Jerome Rubin & Stephen Donaldson. (Orig.). 1990. pap. 4.95 (0-9622953-1-0) City Spirit Pubns.

New York Navigation Law. annuals Gould Editorial Staff. 170p. ring bd. 7.00 (0-87526-234-1) Gould.

New York Negligence Reporter. Ed. by David A. Slavin. text 270.00 (0-8205-2081-0) Bender.

New York Neighborhood Cookbook. Denton S. Harewood. LC 95-79905. (Illus.). 100p. (Orig.). 1996. pap. 24.95 (0-934789-01-0) Hands-On Pub Co.

New York Neighborhoods: A Food Lovers Walking, Eating & Shopping Guide to Ethnic Enclaves in New York's Five Boroughs. Eleanor Berman. LC 99-22940. (Illus.). 256p. 1999. pap. 14.95 (0-7627-0442-X) Globe Pequot.

New York, New York. Kander & Ebb. 1994. pap. text 14.95 (0-7935-3647-2, 00673251) H Leonard.

New York, New York. Peter Kuper. (Illus.). 80p. (Orig.). 1988. pap. 9.95 (0-930193-54-7) Fantagraph Bks.

New York, New York! Ann M. Martin. (Baby-Sitters Club Super Special Ser.: No. 6). 256p. (J). (gr. 3-7). 1991. pap. 4.50 (0-590-43576-0) Scholastic Inc.

New York, New York! Ann M. Martin. (Baby-Sitters Club Super Special Ser.: No. 6). (J). 1991. 9.60 (0-606-04991-6, Pub. by Turtleback) Demco.

New York, New York. Layle Silbert. 104p. (Orig.). 1996. pap. 10.00 (1-879934-39-6) St Andrews Pr.

New York, New York: Apartments. Elizabeth B. Hawes. 1995. pap. 16.95 (0-8050-3258-4) H Holt & Co.

New York, New York: Conquistare Manhattan. Judith Krantz. 1987. pap. 12.95 (84-01-50726-X) Plaza.

New York, New York: Selections from the Columbia News Service. 1981. write for info. (0-318-50860-5) Ayer.

New York, New York: Selections from the Columbia News Service, Columbia University Graduate School of Journalism. Ed. by Donald H. Johnston. pap. 6.95 (0-405-14213-7) Ayer.

New York, New York: The Prints & Drawings of Martin Lewis & Armin Landeck. Robert Henning, Jr. LC 84-51865. (Illus.). (Orig.). 1984. pap. 5.50 (0-89951-054-X) Santa Barb Mus Art.

New York, New York Address Book. Metropolitan Museum of Art Staff. (Illus.). 124p. 1998. 18.95 (0-8212-2489-1, Pub. by Bulfinch Pr) Little.

New York, New York Postcard Book. Metropolitan Museum of Art Staff. (Illus.). 30p. 1998. pap. 9.95 (0-8212-2488-3, Pub. by Bulfinch Pr) Little.

New York-Newark Air Freight System. Arthur J. Stevenson. LC 82-16011. (University of Chicago, Department of Geography, Research Paper Ser.: Nos. 199-200). 459p. 1982. reprint ed. pap. 142.30 (0-608-02264-0, 206290500004) Bks Demand.

***New York Nightlife 2000** Zagat Publishers Staff. 2000. pap. text 10.95 (1-57006-217-X) Zagat.

New York Nightmare! Erica Pass. (Secret World of Alex Mack Ser.: No. 31). (J). (gr. 3-6). 1998. pap. 3.99 (0-671-01957-0) PB.

New York 1985, The Manhattan Chess Club International. Tim Taylor. 105p. (Orig.). 1987. pap. 6.00 (0-931462-62-2) Chess Ent.

New York 1900: Metropolitan Architecture & Urbanism 1890-1915. Robert A. Stern et al. LC 83-42995. (Illus.). 440p. 1995. pap. 49.50 (0-8478-1934-5, Pub. by Rizzoli Intl) St Martin.

New York 1970 Census Index: Heads of Families. pap. 30.00 (1-877677-47-7) Herit Quest.

New York, 1960: Architecture & Urbanism Between the Second World War & the Bicentennial. Robert A. Stern et al. (Illus.). 1376p. 49.95 (1-885254-85-7, Pub. by Monacelli Pr) Penguin Putnam.

New York, 1960: Architecture & Urbanism Between the Second World War & the Bicentennial. Robert A. Stern et al. LC 94-76581. (Illus.). 1376p. (C). 1995. 125.00 (1-885254-02-4, Pub. by Monacelli Pr) Penguin Putnam.

New York, 1930s. Samuel Fuller. (Pocket Archives Ser.). 1997. pap. text 12.95 (2-85025-534-3) Hazan.

New York, 1930: Architecture Between the Two World Wars. Robert A. Stern et al. LC 86-17662. (Illus.). 848p. 1994. pap. 49.50 (0-8478-1838-1, Pub. by Rizzoli Intl) St Martin.

New York, 1932: The Wonder City. W. Parker Chase & Paul Goldberger. (Illus.). 304p. 1983. 18.95 (0-9608788-3-1) NY Bound.

New York Noir: Crime Photos from the Daily News Archive. William Hannigan. (Illus.). 160p. 1999. 29.95 (0-8478-2172-2, Pub. by Rizzoli Intl) St Martin.

New York Nonprofit Law & Practice: With a Tax Analysis. Victoria B. Bjorklund et al. LC 97-71606. 795p. 1997. text 100.00 (1-55834-494-2, 62546-10, MICHIE) LEXIS Pub.

New York Nonprofit Law & Practice: With Tax Analysis: 1998 Supplement. LC 97-71606. 100p. 1998. suppl. ed. write for info. (0-327-00252-2, 62547-10) LEXIS Pub.

New York Not-for-Profit Organization Manual. rev. ed. Ed. by Council of New York Law Associates Staff & Community Law Offices Staff. 190p. 1985. reprint ed. pap. 25.00 (0-686-37424-X) Coun NY Law.

New York Notary Law Primer. 3rd ed. National Notary Association Editors. LC 87-61369. 124p. 1997. pap. 16.00 (0-933134-88-6) Natl Notary.

New York Notes. Stephen Ratcliffe. 32p. (Orig.). 1983. pap. text 3.50 (0-939180-22-7) Tombouctou.

New York Novels. Edith Wharton. LC 98-5465. 958p. 1998. 27.95 (0-679-60302-6) Modern Lib NY.

New York Objections. Helen E. Freedman. 1998. spiral bd. 89.98 (1-58012-023-7) James Pub Santa Ana.

New York on Fire. Hilton Obenzinger. LC 89-10224. (Illus.). 144p. (Orig.). 1989. 24.95 (0-941104-40-0); pap. 12.95 (0-941104-39-7) Real Comet.

New York on One Thousand Dollars a Day (Before Lunch) Ferne Kadish & Shelley Clark. 416p. 1990. 29.95 (0-8442-9539-6, Passprt Bks) NTC Contemp Pub Co.

New York on One Thousand Dollars a Day (Before Lunch) Ferne Kadish & Shelley Clark. 416p. 1994. pap. 14.95 (0-8442-9543-4, Passprt Bks) NTC Contemp Pub Co.

New York on the Rise. Janet Parks. (Illus.). 80p. 1999. 24.95 (0-85331-763-1) Antique Collect.

New York, Ontario & West Railway & the Industry of Central New York State: Milk Cans, Mixed Trains & Motor Cars. Robert E. Mohowski. LC 95-17349. (Illus.). x, 350p. 1996. 62.50 (0-9620844-6-8) Garrigues Hse.

New York Ontario & Western in Color. Paul Lubliner. LC 96-78483. (Illus.). 128p. 1997. 49.95 (1-878887-73-4) Morning NJ.

New York, Ontario & Western in the Diesel Age. Robert Mohowski. (Illus.). 96p. (Orig.). 1994. pap. 29.95 (0-944119-15-8) Andover Junction.

New York Outline Map Pad. 1990. pap. write for info. (0-89359-072-X) Afton Pub.

New York Paintings Postcards. Hayward Cirker. 1996. pap. text 4.95 (0-486-29058-1) Dover.

New York Panorama: A Comprehensive View of the Metropolis Presented in a Series of Articles. Federal Writers' Project Staff. LC 76-145121. (American Guidebook Ser.). 1981. reprint ed. lib. bdg. 89.00 (0-403-02152-9) Somerset Pub.

New York Parks Guide. Chris Boyce. Ed. by Barbara McCaig. 150p. (Orig.). 1988. pap. text 5.95 (0-935201-39-4) Affordable Adven.

New York Part-Ease. Patricia S. Lefkowitz & Joy S. Zimmer. 1982. pap. 7.95 (0-9607664-0-5) Part-Ease.

New York Party Directory. 2nd ed. Ed. by Lauren Mihaly. (Illus.). 72p. 1986. 9.95 (0-933255-00-4) NY Party Pub Ass.

New York Passengership Lists, 1820-1824. Ronald V. Jackson. (Illus.). lib. bdg. 45.00 (0-89593-548-1, Accel Indexing) Genealogical Srvcs.

New York Pattern Jury Instructions - Civil: Committee on Pattern Jury Instructions of the Association of Supreme Court Justices, 2 vols. LC 74-15279. 1779p. 200.00 (0-317-00462-X) West Group.

New York Pattern Jury Instructions - Civil: Committee on Pattern Jury Instructions of the Association of Supreme Court Justices, 2 vols. LC 74-15279. 1779p. 1992. suppl. ed. 70.00 (0-317-04325-0) West Group.

New York Penal Law. annuals Gould Editorial Staff. 420p. ring bd. 6.95 (0-87526-145-0) Gould.

New York Penal Law: Annual Edition. annuals Gould Editorial Staff. 6.00 (0-87526-287-2) Gould.

New York Penal Law: Questions & Answers. annuals Gould Editorial Staff. 170p. (C). 1985. ring bd. 12.95 (0-87526-313-5) Gould.

New York Penal Law & Criminal Procedure Law. Gould Editorial Staff. 970p. ring bd. 9.95 (0-87526-326-7) Gould.

New York Philharmonic Guide to the Symphony. Edward Downes. LC 76-13813. 1976. 65.00 (0-8027-0540-5) Walker & Co.

***New York Pocket Guide.** Berlitz Editors. (Pocket Guides Ser.). (Illus.). 144p. 2000. pap. 8.95 (2-8315-7170-7) Berlitz.

New York Political Almanac: The Constitutional Officers, the Senate, the Assembly, & the U. S. Congressional Delegation, 1995 Edition. rev. ed. Ed. by Chris Lakis. 355p. 1995. 19.95 (0-926766-14-7) Ctr Leader Stu.

New York Politics & Government: Competition & Compassion. Sarah F. Liebschutz. LC 97-26898. (Politics & Governments of the American States Ser.). (Illus.). xxv, 235p. 1998. text 50.00 (0-8032-2925-9); pap. text 22.00 (0-8032-7971-X) U of Nebr Pr.

New York Pop-Up Book: New York City: Historic New York, Celebrating the Century. New York City 100 Staff. Ed. by Marie Salerno & Arthur Gelb. (Illus.). 8p. 1999. 39.95 (0-7893-0374-4, Pub. by Universe) St Martin.

New York Postal History: The Post Offices & First Postmasters from 1775-1980. Chester M. Smith, Jr. & John L. Kay. 556p. 1982. 40.00 (0-933580-05-3) Am Philatelic Society.

New York Power of Attorney Handbook. William P. Coyle & Edward A. Haman. LC 97-40127. (Legal Survival Guides Ser.). 144p. 1997. pap. 12.95 (1-57071-188-7) Sourcebks.

New York Practical Tips for Law Enforcement. Barry Kamins. 25p. 1994. pap. 5.95 (0-87526-423-9) Gould.

New York Practice. 2nd ed. David D. Siegel. 1068p. 1991. pap. 42.00 (0-314-82881-8) West Pub.

New York Practice: 1998-1999 Supplement. 2nd ed. David A. Siegel. (Hornbook Ser.). 100p. 1998. pap. 12.00 (0-314-23263-X) West Pub.

New York Practice Vol. 5: Evidence in New York State & Federal Courts. Robert A. Barker & Vincent C. Alexander. LC 95-62237. xxxv, 1050p. 1996. 99.00 (0-314-08636-6) West Pub.

New York Practice Vols. 2, 3 & 4: Commercial Litigation in New York State Courts. Robert L. Haig. 1995. text. write for info. (0-614-08298-6) West Pub.

New York Practice, Cases & Other Materials. 4th ed. Herbert Peterfreund & Joseph M. McLaughlin. (University Casebook Ser.). 1583p. 1991. reprint ed. text 38.50 (0-88277-434-4) Foundation Pr.

New York Practice Guide: Business & Commercial, 4 vols. E. M. Lach. (New York Practice Guides Ser.). 1987. ring bd. 510.00 (0-8205-1517-5) Bender.

New York Practice Guide: Domestic Relations, 3 vols. (New York Practice Guides Ser.: No. 518). 1988. 530.00 (0-8205-1518-3) Bender.

New York Practice Guide: Negligence, 4 vols. Henry Miller et al. 1989. ring bd. 540.00 (0-8205-1521-3) Bender.

New York Practice Guide: Probate & Estate Administration, 2 vols. Joseph T. Arenson et al. 1985. ring bd. 385.00 (0-8205-1522-1) Bender.

New York Practice Guide: Real Estate, 5 vols. Eugene J. Morris et al. 1986. ring bd. 760.00 (0-8205-1523-X) Bender.

New York Practice, 1995 Pocket Part. 2nd ed. David D. Siegel. (Practitioner Treatise Ser.). 116p. (C). 1995. pap. text. write for info. (0-314-06872-4) West Pub.

New York Practice, 1997-98 Supplement. David D. Siegel. (Hornbook Ser.). 96p. (C). 1997. pap. text. write for info. (0-314-22790-3) West Pub.

New York Practice, 1996 Pocket Part. 2nd ed. David D. Siegel. (Practitioner Treatise Ser.). 1996. write for info. (0-314-20129-7) West Pub.

New York Practice, 1996-97 Supplement. 2nd ed. David D. Siegel. (Hornbook Ser.). 100p. 1996. pap. text. write for info. (0-314-20407-5) West Pub.

New York Pretrial Criminal Procedure. Lawrence K. Marks. LC 96-60314. (New York Practice Ser.). xxviii, 831p. 1996. pap. 105.00 incl. disk (0-314-09764-3) West Pub.

New York Printmakers: A Dozen Directions, Essay. Mia Feroleto. Ed. by Nancy Liddle. (Illus.). 16p. 1985. pap. 2.00 (0-910763-01-1) U Albany Art Mus.

New York Probate, 3 vols., Set. Edward S. Schlesinger & Michael M. Mariani. LC 86-82156. (New York Practice Systems Library). 1986. ring bd. 321.00 (0-318-21802-X) West Group.

N

An Asterisk (*) at the beginning of an entry indicates that the title is appearing for the first time.

New York Production Manual, 1981: The Producer's Masterguide for Motion Picture, Television, Commercials & Videotape Industries. 2nd ed. Ed. by Shmuel Bension. 1100p. 1981. pap. 58.00 (0-935744-01-0) Prod Mstrguide.

New York Production Manual, 1979-80: The Producer's Masterguide for Motion Picture, Television, Commercials & Videotape Industries. Shmuel Bension. LC 79-644582. 600p. 1979. pap. 35.00 (0-935744-00-2) Prod Mstrguide.

New York Prudent Investor Act, Proposed Revised Uniform Principal & Income Act, & Marital Deduction Planning. 450p. 1995. pap. 30.00 (0-614-26735-8, 1441); pap. 175.00 incl. VHS (0-614-26736-6, 34411) NYS Bar.

New York Public Library. 960p. 1998. 34.95 (0-02-862835-7) Macmillan.

New York Public Library: A History of Its Founding & Early Years. Phyllis Dain. LC 70-163359. (Illus.). 466p. (Orig.). 1972. 35.00 (0-87104-131-6) NY Pub Lib.

***New York Public Library: A Universe.** Phyllis Dain. (Illus.). 144p. 2000. pap. write for info. (1-85759-234-4, Pub. by Scala Books) Antique Collect.

New York Public Library African American Desk Reference. New York Public Library Staff. 624p. 1999. 34.95 (0-471-23924-0) Wiley.

New York Public Library Amazing African American History: A Book of Answers for Kids. Diane Patrick. LC 97-16938. (NYPL Answer Books for Kids). 176p. (J). 1997. pap. 12.95 (0-471-19217-1) Wiley.

New York Public Library Amazing Hispanic American History: A Book of Answers for Kids. George Ochoa. LC 98-23797. (New York Public Library Answer Books for Kids Ser.). (Illus.). 192p. (YA). (gr. 6). 1998. pap. 12.95 (0-471-19204-X) Wiley.

New York Public Library Amazing Mythology: A Book of Answers for Kids. New York Public Library Staff et al. LC 99-32203. 192p. (YA). (gr. 5-9). 2000. pap. text 12.95 (0-471-33205-4) Wiley.

New York Public Library Amazing Native American History: American History: A Book of Answers for Kids. New York Public Library Staff & Liz Sonneborne. LC 99-22916. 170p. (YA). (gr. 5-9). 1999. pap. 12.95 (0-471-33204-6) Wiley.

New York Public Library Amazing Space: A Book of Answers for Kids. Ann-Jeanette Campbell. LC 96-29785. 192p. (J). 1997. pap. 12.95 (0-471-14498-3) Wiley.

New York Public Library Amazing Women in American History: A Book of Answers for Kids. Sue Heinemann. LC 97-18465. (New York Public Library Kids Books of Answers). (Illus.). 192p. (J). (gr. 5-9). 1998. pap. 12.95 (0-471-19216-3) Wiley.

New York Public Library American History Desk Reference. Macmillan Publishing Company Staff. Ed. by Marian Faux. LC 96-16054. (Illus.). 640p. 1997. 39.95 (0-02-861322-8) Macmillan.

New York Public Library American History Desk Reference. Stonesong Press Staff. 1997. 39.95 (0-614-28228-4) Macmillan USA.

New York Public Library Book of Answers: Movies & TV. Melinda Corey & George Ochoa. 256p. (Orig.). (J). (gr. 5-9). 1992. pap. 10.00 (0-671-77538-3, Fireside) S&S Trade Pap.

New York Public Library Book of Chronologies. Bruce Wetterau. 640p. 1994. pap. 16.00 (0-671-89265-7) Macmillan.

New York Public Library Book of Popular Americana. Tad Tuleja. LC 93-45362. 451p. 1994. 27.50 (0-671-89987-2) Macmillan.

New York Public Library Book of Twentieth-Century American Quotations. Stephen Donadio et al. 640p. 1992. 24.45 (0-446-51639-2, Pub. by Warner Bks) Little.

***New York Public Library Business Desk Reference.** New York Public Library Staff. 512p. 1999. pap. 19.95 (0-471-32835-9) Wiley.

New York Public Library Business Desk Reference: Essential Information for Every Office at Your Fingertips. New York Public Library Staff. LC 97-7408. 512p. 1997. 29.95 (0-471-14442-8) Wiley.

New York Public Library Desk Reference. 2nd ed. New York Public Library Staff. LC 93-18299. (Illus.). 944p. 1993. 40.00 (0-671-85014-8) Macmillan.

New York Public Library Desk Reference. 3rd ed. Paul Fargis. LC 98-25132. 960p. 1998. 34.95 (0-02-862169-7) Macmillan.

New York Public Library Desk Reference to the Performing Arts. New York Public Library Staff. 1996. 16.95 (0-02-861447-X) Macmillan.

New York Public Library Incredible Earth: A Book of Answers for Kids. New York Public Library Staff et al. LC 96-22112. (Illus.). 192p. 1996. pap. 12.95 (0-471-14497-5) Wiley.

New York Public Library Kid's Guide to Research. Deborah Heiligman. LC 97-28939. (Illus.). 134p. (YA). (gr. 4-9). 1998. 14.95 (0-590-30715-0, Pub. by Scholastic Inc) Penguin Putnam.

New York Public Library Manuscripts, Pt. 1. Ed. by Elise B. Jorgens. (English Song 1600-1675 Ser.). 312p. 1987. text 25.00 (0-8240-8239-7) Garland.

New York Public Library Manuscripts Pt. II: Drexel Ms. 4257 (John Gamble, "His Booke, Amen 1659") Ed. by Elise B. Jorgens. (English Song 1600-1675 Ser.). 480p. 1987. text 30.00 (0-8240-8240-0) Garland.

New York Public Library Performing Arts Desk Reference. New York Public Library Staff. (Illus.). 432p. 1994. 35.00 (0-671-79912-6) Macmillan.

New York Public Library Science Desk Reference. Patricia L. Barnes-Svarney. (Illus.). 758p. 1995. 39.95 (0-02-860403-2) Macmillan.

New York Public Library Student's Desk Reference. New York Public Library Staff. LC 93-22842. (Illus.). 528p. 1995. 14.95 (0-02-860418-0) Macmillan.

New York Public Library Writer's Guide to Style & Usage. Ed. by Andrea Sutcliffe. LC 93-33255. (Illus.). 848p. 1994. 40.00 (0-06-270064-2, Harper Ref) HarpC.

New York Public Library's Books of the Century. Ed. by Elizabeth Diefendorf. (Illus.). 240p. (C). 1996. 19.95 (0-19-510897-3) OUP.

New York Public Library's Books of the Century. Ed. by Elizabeth Diefendorf. (Illus.). 240p. 1997. reprint ed. pap. 8.95 (0-19-511790-5) OUP.

New York Public Records Guide. Fred D. Knapp. 240p. 1994. pap. 49.95 (0-9629879-7-2) REYN.

New York Pursuits: Manhattan's Guide to Adult Education Courses, Winter-Spring '96. Daryl G. Stern. 160p. 1995. pap. 7.95 (0-9648644-8-7) Persnl Pursuits.

New York Pursuits: The Tri-State Guide to Adult Education Courses, 1996-1997. Daryl G. Stern. 1996. pap. 7.95 (0-9648644-1-X) Persnl Pursuits.

New York Quik-Finder. Rand McNally Staff. 1991. pap. 4.95 (0-88433-005-2) Geographia.

New York Quiz Bowl Crash Course! Carole Marsh. (Carole Marsh New York Bks.). (Illus.). (J). 1994. pap. 19.95 (1-55609-916-9); lib. bdg. 29.95 (1-55609-915-0); disk 29.95 (1-55609-917-7) Gallopade Intl.

New York Railways: The Green Line. (Illus.). 64p. (Orig.). 1994. pap. 19.95 (0-934088-30-6, 7615) NJ Intl Inc.

New York Rangers see NHL Today

New York Rangers. Morgan Hughes. LC 98-12304. (Inside the NHL Ser.). (J). 1999. 14.95 (1-57765-050-6) ABDO Pub Co.

New York Rangers: Broadway's Longest Running Hit. John Krieser & Lou Friedman. (Illus.). 360p. 1996. 39.95 (1-57167-041-6) Sports Pub.

***New York Rangers: Millennium Memories.** New York Daily News Editors. (Illus.). 128p. 2000. 19.95 (1-58261-147-5, Pub. by Sports Pub) Partners Pubs Grp.

***New York Rangers: Seventy-Five Years.** limited ed. John Halligan. LC 00-41779. (Illus.). 2000. write for info. (1-887656-35-9) Tehabi Bks.

New York Rangers: Stanley Cup Champions, 1939-1940, Vol. 7. Hockey Information Service Staff. 1997. pap. text. write for info. (1-894014-06-5) Hockey Info.

New York Rangers Guide, 1993-94 ed. Simon & Schuster Staff. 1993. pap. text 8.00 (0-671-89022-0) S&S Trade.

New York Rangers Hockey Team. Michael J. Sullivan. LC 97-21310. (Great Sports Teams Ser.). (Illus.). 48p. (J). (gr. 4-10). 1998. lib. bdg. 18.95 (0-7660-1023-6) Enslow Pubs.

New York Real Estate. 2nd ed. Charles J. Jacobus & Melissa Martin. LC 96-6717. 700p. (C). 1997. 50.00 (0-13-226796-9) P-H.

New York Real Estate Exam Review. Ed. by Real Estate Educ. Co. Staff. 142p. 1998. pap. text 19.95 (0-7931-2678-9, 1510-3901, Real Estate Ed) Dearborn.

***New York Real Estate Exam Review.** 2nd ed. Real Estate Educ. Co. Staff. 2000. 21.95 (0-7931-3724-1) Dearborn.

New York Real Estate for Brokers. 2nd ed. Spada. LC 99-15639. 390p. 1999. pap. 34.67 (0-13-010580-5) S&S Trade.

***New York Real Estate for Brokers Blando.** 2nd ed. (C). 1999. 31.20 (0-13-018370-9) P-H.

***New York Real Estate for Salespersons: Special Edition.** 2nd ed. Marcia Darvin Spada. 436p. 1999. pap. 21.80 (0-13-014562-9, Prentice Hall) P-H.

New York Real Estate Salespersons. 2nd ed. Spada. LC 99-11345. 436p. 1999. pap. 32.00 (0-13-010591-0) S&S Trade.

New York Real Property Forms, 9 vols. Bergman & Roth. 1948. ring bd. 1220.00 (0-8205-1140-4) Bender.

New York Real Property Law Handbook. annuals Gould Editorial Staff. 1000p. (C). pap. 24.95 (0-87526-340-2) Gould.

New York Real Property Service. LC 87-81741. 1987. 1500.00 (0-317-03790-0) West Group.

New York Real Property Service. 1994. suppl. ed. 345.00 (0-318-67057-7) West Group.

New York Red Pages: A Radical Tourist Guide. Gene Glickman & Toby Glickman. LC 84-2157. 156p. 1984. 55.00 (0-275-91173-X, C1173, Praeger Pubs) Greenwood.

New York Regents Exam. Kaplan Staff. 240p. 1997. 14.95 (0-684-84538-5) S&S Trade.

New York Regents Exam: Biology. Kaplan Staff. 256p. 1997. 14.95 (0-684-84540-7) S&S Trade.

New York Regents Exam: English. Kaplan Staff. 224p. 1998. pap. 14.95 (0-684-84543-1) S&S Trade.

New York Regents Exam: Math 1. Kaplan Staff. 176p. 1997. 14.95 (0-684-84536-9) S&S Trade.

New York Regents Exam: Math 2. Kaplan Staff. 160p. 1997. 14.95 (0-684-84537-7) S&S Trade.

New York Regents Exam: U. S. History/Government. Kaplan Staff. 240p. 1997. 14.95 (0-684-84542-3) S&S Trade.

New York Regents Exam Global Studies. Kaplan Staff. 272p. 1997. 14.95 (0-684-84539-3) S&S Trade.

New York Residency Audit Handbook. Paul R. Comeau & Mark S. Klein. 1993. pap. 39.95 (0-9639171-0-2) Guaranty NY.

New York Residency Audit Handbook, 1995-1996. 2nd ed. Paul R. Comeau & Mark S. Klein. 200p. 1995. 59.95 (0-9639171-2-9) Guaranty NY.

New York Residency Audit Handbook, 1995-1996. 2nd ed. Paul R. Comeau & Mark S. Klein. 200p. 1996. pap. 19.95 (0-9639171-1-0) Guaranty NY.

New York Retirement & Relocation Guide. large type ed. (Retirement & Relocation Guides Ser.). (Illus.). 350p. Date not set. pap. 24.95 (1-56559-134-8) HGI-Over Fifty.

New York Review. (Illus.). 1970. 63.95 (0-405-18317-8) Ayer.

New York Review, 1905-1908. Michael J. De Vito. LC 77-75637. (Monographs: No. 34). (Illus.). 1977. 13.95 (0-930060-14-8) US Cath Hist.

New York Review of Books, 1963-1973, 10 vols. LC 71-88614. 1969. reprint ed. 955.00 (0-405-00090-1) Ayer.

New York Revisited. Henry James. LC 93-43414. 1994. 14.95 (1-879957-14-0, Franklin Sq Pr) Harpers Mag Found.

New York Road Atlas. Susan Farewell et al. (State Road Atlases Ser.). 64p. 1990. pap. 4.95 (0-13-616194-4, H M Gousha) Prntice Hall Bks.

New York Road Atlas. H. M. Gousha. 1995. 7.95 (0-671-53598-6) S&S Trade.

New York Road Runners Club Complete Book of Running. 3rd rev. ed. New York Road Runner 's Club Staff. LC 97-23114. 704p. 1997. pap. 18.00 (0-679-78010-6) Random Ref & Info.

New York Rollercoasters! Carole Marsh. (Carole Marsh New York Bks.). (Illus.). (J). (gr. 3-12). 1994. pap. 19.95 (0-7933-5321-1); lib. bdg. 29.95 (0-7933-5320-3) Gallopade Intl.

New York Rollercoasters! Carole Marsh. (Carole Marsh New York Bks.). (Illus.). (YA). (gr. 3-12). 1994. disk 29.95 (0-7933-5322-X) Gallopade Intl.

New York Running Guide. Bob McCullough & Miles Jaffe. LC 98-6094. (City Running Guide Ser.). (Illus.). 168p. 1998. pap. 16.95 (0-88011-765-6, PMCC0765) Human Kinetics.

***New York Sawed in Half: An Urban Historical.** Joel Rose. (Illus.). 2001. 19.95 (1-58234-098-6) Bloomsbury Pubg.

New York Scene, 1996-97. Gerard Raymond. (Illus.). 256p. 1996. pap. 10.95 (0-85449-228-3, Pub. by Gay Mens Pr) LPC InBook.

New York School. Ed. by Larry Gagosian. 20p. 1998. 20.00 (1-880154-21-8) Gagosian Gallery.

New York School: A Cultural Reckoning. Dore Ashton. LC 92-11669. 1973. reprint ed. pap. 18.95 (0-520-08106-4, Pub. by U CA Pr) Cal Prin Full Svc.

New York School: A Cultural Reckoning. Dore Ashton. LC 92-11669. 1992. reprint ed. 45.00 (0-520-08107-2, Pub. by U CA Pr) Cal Prin Full Svc.

New York School Poets As Playwrights: O'Hara, Ashberry, Koch, Schuyler & the Visual Arts. Philip Auslander. (Literature & the Visual Arts Ser.: Vol. 3). 187p. (C). 1989. text 37.50 (0-8204-1094-2) P Lang Pubng.

New York School Trivia: An Amazing & Fascinating Look at Our State's Teachers, Schools & Students! Carole Marsh. (Carole Marsh New York Bks.). (Illus.). (J). 1994. pap. 19.95 (0-7933-0825-9); lib. bdg. 29.95 (0-7933-0826-7); disk 29.95 (0-7933-0827-5) Gallopade Intl.

New York Search & Seizure. rev. ed. Barry Kamins. 850p. (C). 1996. ring bd. 44.95 (0-87526-383-6) Gould.

New York Search & Seizure for Law Enforcement Officers. Barry Kamins. 95p. 1996. pap. 9.95 (0-87526-430-1) Gould.

New York Secrets. Gerald Grey. 1998. mass mkt. 6.95 (1-56333-675-8) Masquerade.

New York Securities Law: Practice & Policy. Ed. by Raymond W. Merritt & Clifford R. Ennico. 244p. 1990. pap. 32.00 (0-614-26659-9, 4165) NYS Bar.

New York Security Officer Training Manual. Thomas Lenahan & Thomas Blanchfield. 120p. pap. 12.95 (0-87526-425-5) Gould.

New York Self Help. Citizens Committee for New York City. 1978. pap. 4.95 (0-9601496-1-9) Citizens Comm NY.

New York Sex: Stories. Ed. by Jane DeLynn. LC 98-34182. 204p. 1998. pap. 12.00 (1-891305-03-4) Painted Leaf.

New York Silly Basketball Sportsmysteries, Vol. 1. Carole Marsh. (Carole Marsh New York Bks.). (Illus.). (J). 1994. pap. 19.95 (0-7933-0822-4); lib. bdg. 29.95 (0-7933-0823-2); disk 29.95 (0-7933-0824-0) Gallopade Intl.

New York Silly Basketball Sportsmysteries, Vol. 2. Carole Marsh. (Carole Marsh New York Bks.). (Illus.). (J). 1970. lib. bdg. 29.95 (0-7933-1824-6) Gallopade Intl.

New York Silly Basketball Sportsmysteries, Vol. 2. Carole Marsh. (Carole Marsh New York Bks.). (Illus.). (J). 1994. pap. 19.95 (0-7933-1825-4); disk 29.95 (0-7933-1826-2) Gallopade Intl.

New York Silly Football Sportsmysteries, Vol. 1. Carole Marsh. (Carole Marsh New York Bks.). (Illus.). (J). 1994. pap. 19.95 (1-55609-907-X); lib. bdg. 29.95 (1-55609-906-1); disk 29.95 (1-55609-908-8) Gallopade Intl.

New York Silly Football Sportsmysteries, Vol. 2. Carole Marsh. (Carole Marsh New York Bks.). (Illus.). (J). 1994. pap. 19.95 (1-55609-910-X); lib. bdg. 29.95 (1-55609-909-6); disk 29.95 (1-55609-911-8) Gallopade Intl.

New York Silly Trivia! Carole Marsh. (Carole Marsh New York Bks.). (Illus.). (J). 1994. pap. 19.95 (1-55609-103-6); lib. bdg. 29.95 (1-55609-895-2); disk 29.95 (1-55609-896-0) Gallopade Intl.

New York Small Claims Guide. Herbert A. Kline. 40p. 1994. pap. 5.95 (0-87526-327-5) Gould.

New York Smells. Caroline McKeldin. 1995. mass mkt. 9.99 (0-312-95632-0) St Martin.

New York Society on Parade. Ralph Pulitzer. LC 75-1866. (Leisure Class in America Ser.). (Illus.). 1975. reprint ed. 15.95 (0-405-06932-4) Ayer.

***New York Soldiers in the Civil War Vol. 1: A-K - A Roster of Military Officers & Soldiers Who Served in NY Regiments in the Civil War.** Richard A. Wilt. LC 99-219953. 408p. 1999. pap. 58.00 (0-7884-1141-1, W336) Heritage Bk.

***New York Soldiers in the Civil War Vol. 2: L-Z.** Richard A. Wilt. LC 99-219953. 393p. 1999. pap. 57.00 (0-7884-1209-4, W354) Heritage Bk.

New York Spanish American War Vets Index, 1898. Ronald V. Jackson. 1992. 250.00 (0-89593-863-4, Accel Indexing) Genealogical Srvcs.

New York Spelling Bee! Score Big by Correctly Spelling Our State's Unique Names. Carole Marsh. (Carole Marsh New York Bks.). (Illus.). (YA). (gr. 3-12). 1996. pap. 19.95 (0-7933-6737-9); lib. bdg. 29.95 (0-7933-6736-0) Gallopade Intl.

New York Standard Civil Practice Service Desk Book, Vol. 1. rev. ed. LC 93-79603. 1991. 99.00 (0-317-04266-1) West Group.

***New York Standard Civil Practice Service Desk Book: 2000 Supplement.** Compiled by Publisher's Editorial Staff. 2000. pap. write for info. (0-327-10181-4, 6891111) LEXIS Pub.

New York Standard Civil Practice Service Desk Book, 1999 Edition. 2800p. 1998. pap. write for info. (0-327-06697-0, 6891012) LEXIS Pub.

***New York Standard Civil Practice Service Desk Book 99 Supplement.** 97p. 1999. Price not set. (0-327-08865-6, 6891110) LEXIS Pub.

New York State. 3rd ed. Insight Guides Staff. (Insight Guides). 1998. pap. text 22.95 (0-88729-727-7) Langenscheidt.

New York State: A Guide to the Empire State. Federal Writers' Project Staff. (American Guidebook Ser.). 782p. 1940. reprint ed. 95.00 (0-403-02151-0) Somerset Pub.

New York State: Gateway to America. David M. Ellis. 1988. 19.95 (0-89781-426-6) Am Historical Pr.

New York State: Gateway to America. David M. Ellis. (Illus.). 400p. (YA). (gr. 7 up). 1988. 19.95 (0-89781-246-8) Am Historical Pr.

New York State & Federal Criminal Practice & Procedure. Andrew M. Cohen. LC 96-14376. 1996. write for info. (1-57588-079-2, 310460) W S Hein.

New York State Astronomy. Ed. by A. G. Davis Philip. 184p. 1992. 32.00 (0-933485-16-6) L Davis Pr.

New York State Bar Association: Section on Antitrust Law, Antitrust Law Symposium, 1949-1971, Set. 1949. 295.00 (0-685-42628-9) W S Hein.

New York State Bar Examination (NYBE) Jack Rudman. (Admission Test Ser.: ATS-25). 1994. pap. 49.95 (0-8373-5025-5) Nat Learn.

New York State Canals: A Short History. F. Daniel Larkin. LC 97-40532. (Illus.). 104p. 1998. pap. 12.00 (0-935796-90-8) Purple Mnt Pr.

New York State Cemeteries Name/Location Inventory, 1995-1997. Association of Municipal Historian of NY State Staff. LC 99-199258. 1248p. 1999. pap. 83.50 (0-7884-1084-9, A534) Heritage.

***New York State Census for the Town of Guilford, Chenango County, New York, 1865.** Compiled & Transcribed by Shirley B. Goerlich. LC 99-70212. 150p. 1999. pap. text 25.00 (1-887530-35-5) RSG Pub.

***New York State Census for the Town of Guilford, Chenango County, New York, 1875.** Compiled & Transcribed by Shirley B. Goerlich. LC 99-63674. 140p. 1999. pap. text. write for info. (1-887530-37-1) RSG Pub.

***New York State Census for the Town of Guilford, Chenango County, New York, 1905.** Compiled & Transcribed by Shirley B. Goerlich. LC 99-63675. 124p. 1999. pap. text 25.00 (1-887530-38-X) RSG Pub.

***New York State Census for the Town of Unadilla, Otsego County, New York, 1875.** Compiled & Transcribed by Shirley B. Goerlich. LC 99-63673. 139p. 1999. pap. text 25.00 (1-887530-36-3) RSG Pub.

New York State Census for the Year 1845 of Masonville, Delaware County. Compiled & Transcribed by Shirley B. Goerlich. LC 98-68621. 72p. 1999. pap. 25.00 (1-887530-27-4) RSG Pub.

New York State Census for the Year 1850 of Sidney, Delaware County, New York. Compiled & Transcribed by Shirley B. Goerlich. LC 98-68768. 106p. 1999. pap. text 25.00 (1-887530-28-2) RSG Pub.

New York State Census Index, 1815 (St. Lawrence) (Illus.). lib. bdg. 25.00 (0-89593-443-4, Accel Indexing) Genealogical Srvcs.

New York State Census, Town of Guilford, Chenango County, 1855. Compiled & Transcribed by Shirley B. Goerlich. LC 99-70213. 136p. 1999. pap. 25.00 (1-887530-30-4) RSG Pub.

New York State Census, Town of Unadilla, Otsego County, New York, 1855. Compiled & Transcribed by Shirley B. Goerlich. LC 98-68767. 106p. 1999. pap. 25.00 (1-887530-29-0) RSG Pub.

***New York State Census, Town of Unadilla, Otsego County, New York, 1865.** Compiled & Transcribed by Shirley B. Goerlich. LC 99-70211. 106p. 1999. pap. 25.00 (1-887530-34-7) RSG Pub.

***New York State Census, Town of Unadilla, Otsego County, 1892: With an Added Map of Residences of Wells Bridge.** Compiled & Transcribed by Shirley B. Goerlich. LC 99-90802. 160p. 1999. pap. 25.00 (1-887530-39-8) RSG Pub.

New York State Constitution: A Reference Guide, 3. Peter J. Galie. LC 90-36627. (Reference Guides to the State Constitutions of the United States Ser.: No. 3). 372p. 1990. lib. bdg. 79.50 (0-313-26156-3, GNY, Greenwood Pr) Greenwood.

New York State Constitution: Sources of Legislative Intent. Robert A. Carter. ix, 204p. 1988. reprint ed. 40.00 (0-8377-0459-6, Rothman) W S Hein.

***New York State Corporation Tax Law & Regulations: 2000 Edition.** CCH Tax Law Editors. 544p. 2000. pap. 99.00 (0-8080-0456-5) CCH INC.

An Asterisk (*) at the beginning of an entry indicates that the title is appearing for the first time.

***New York State Credit Directory, 2000 Edition.** rev. ed. American Business Directories Staff. 1664p. 1999. boxed set 195.00 incl. cd-rom (*0-7687-0314-X*) Am Busn Direct.

New York State Directory: 1999/2000 Edition. Ed. by E. T. Walsh. 698p. 1999. pap. 129.00 (*1-879346-37-0*) Walkers Research.

New York State Directory: 2000-2001 Edition. Ed. by E. T. Walsh. 698p. 2000. pap. 129.00 (*1-879346-40-0*) Walkers Research.

***New York State Directory: 2001-2002 Edition.** Ed. by E. T. Walsh. 704p. 2001. pap. 129.00 (*1-879346-43-5*) Walkers Research.

New York State Directory, 1998-1999. Ed. by E. T. Walsh. 624p. 1998. pap. 129.00 (*1-879346-34-6*) Walkers Research.

New York State Documents: An Introductory Manual. Dorothy Butch. 138p. 1987. 10.00 (*0-318-22980-3*) NYS Library.

New York State Drunk Driving Penalties & Sanctions Handbook. Stuart Meyer. LC 97-72029. 99p. 1997. text 49.95 (*0-8318-0770-9*) Am Law Inst.

New York State Education Department Reports, Vol. 37. 825p. 1998. write for info. (*0-327-06015-8*, 56222-10) LEXIS Pub.

New York State Education Department Reports, Vol. 37 SB. 825p. 1998. pap. 91.75 (*0-327-06016-6*, 56221-10) LEXIS Pub.

New York State Education Department Reports, Judicial Decisions of the Commissioner of Education. Judicial Decisions of the Commissioner of Education. 89.25 (*0-327-12358-3*) LEXIS Pub.

New York State Employment Laws & Regulations: How to Comply. Ed. by Keith A. Reed et al. 140p. 1995. pap. 75.00 (*0-923606-01-7*) Amer CC Pubs.

New York State Environmental Externalities Cost Study: Report & Computer Model, 2 vols. Empire State Electric Energy Research Corporation. (Illus.). 1996. pap. text 200.00 incl. disk (*0-379-21359-1*) Oceana.

New York State Foundations. 5th ed. Foundation Center Staff. LC 97-183431. 1095p. 1997. 180.00 (*0-87954-717-0*) Foundation Ctr.

***New York State Foundations.** 6th ed. 1095p. 1999. 180.00 (*0-87954-891-6*) Foundation Ctr.

New York State Grants Guide 1999-2000. 1120p. 1999. pap. 199.00 (*0-9658306-6-7*) Grantseeker.

New York State, History of Smithboro, along the Susquehanna River in Tioga County, 1787-1997. Roberta L. Bostwick. LC 98-111366. (Illus.). xviii, 524p. (Orig.). 1997. 37.95 (*0-9661819-1-3*); ring bd. 27.95 (*0-9661819-0-5*) Oakwood Est.

***New York State in the 21st Century.** Ed. by Thomas A. Hirschl & Tim B. Heaton. LC 98-44671. 304p. 1999. 75.00 (*0-275-96339-X*, Praeger Pubs) Greenwood.

New York State in the Year 2000. Ed. by Jeryl L. Mumpower & Warren F. Ilchman. LC 87-6486. 572p. (C). 1988. text 34.50 (*0-88706-602-X*) State U NY Pr.

New York State Law Including Law Provisions Imposing Admissions & Sales Tax December 1998. Ed. by CCH Tax Law Editors. (Orig.). pap. 65.00 (*0-8080-0143-4*) CCH INC.

New York State Low-Level Radioactive Waste Transportation Report. 15p. (Orig.). (C). 1993. pap. text 25.00 (*1-56806-761-5*) DIANE Pub.

New York State Map Skills Resource Guide. Bernard Whitman. (Illus.). 85p. (Orig.). (J). (gr. 4-7). 1984. teacher ed. 18.00 (*0-918433-00-2*) In Educ.

New York State Municipal Profiles, 1996, 2 vols. 3rd rev. ed. Ed. by Louise L. Hornor. 1718p. (Orig.). 1996. pap. 99.95 (*0-931845-50-5*) Info Pubns.

New York State of Crime. Michael Jahn et al. 1999. per. 6.99 (*0-373-26317-1*, Wrldwide Lib) Harlequin Bks.

New York State Office of Mental Health Psychotherapeutic Drug Manual. 3rd rev. ed. Ed. by Julie M. Zito. (Series in General & Clinical Psychiatry). 334p. 1994. 75.00 (*0-471-30530-8*) Wiley.

New York State Parks. State Council of Parks Staff. 88p. 1993. reprint ed. lib. bdg. 69.00 (*0-7812-5264-4*) Rprt Serv.

New York State Parks: A Complete Outdoor Recreation Guide. Bill Bailey. 400p. 1997. pap. 15.95 (*1-881139-18-2*) Glovebox Guidebks.

***New York State Personal Income Tax Law & Regulations: 2000 Edition.** CCH Tax Law Editors. 624p. 2000. pap. 99.00 (*0-8080-0457-3*) CCH INC.

New York State Regents Biology Laboratory Manual. Marianna L. Reep & Richard M. Plass. (Illus.). 138p. (YA). (gr. 8-11). 1989. 5.95 (*0-685-29317-3*) Amer Scholastic.

New York State Regents Exam: Chemistry. Kaplan Staff. 192p. 1997. 14.95 (*0-684-84541-5*) S&S Trade.

New York State Reports Official Edition (including Court of Appeals, Appellate Division & Miscellaneous Courts), 396 vols., Set. write for info. (*0-318-68089-0*) West Group.

New York State Road Atlas. Hagstrom Map Company Staff. LC 93-675673. 1992. write for info. (*0-88097-051-0*) Hagstrom Map.

***New York State Sales & Use Tax Law & Regulations: 2000 Edition.** CCH Tax Law Editors. 1120p. 2000. pap. 95.00 (*0-8080-0454-9*) CCH INC.

New York State Security Guard Handbook: Version 1.0. Security Press, Inc. Staff. (Security Guard Solution Ser.: Vol. 7). 218p. 1994. ring bd. 29.95 (*1-892594-14-5*) Security Pr Inc.

New York State Society of Certified Public Accountants: Foundation for a Profession. Ed. by Julia Grant. LC 95-32129. (New Works in Accounting History). 320p. 1995. text 68.00 (*0-8153-2238-0*) Garland.

New York State Tax Handbook, 1998. rev. ed. Robert D. Plattner & Mark S. Klein. 336p. 1997. pap. text 45.00 (*0-7811-0185-9*) Res Inst Am.

New York State Tax Handbook, 1999. rev. ed. Robert D. Plattner & Mark S. Klein. Ed. by Richard E. Jenis. 386p. 1998. pap. text 35.75 (*0-7811-0197-2*) Res Inst Am.

New York State Tax Law. CCH Editorial Staff. 1150p. 1998. pap. 37.95 (*0-8080-0251-1*) CCH INC.

***New York State Tax Law: 2000 Edition.** CCH Tax Law Editors. 1248p. 2000. pap. 80.00 (*0-8080-0455-7*) CCH INC.

***New York State Teacher Certification Exam.** Norman Levy & Joan U. Levy. (Illus.). 256p. 1999. pap. text 19.95 (*0-02-863534-5*) S&S Trade.

New York State Trivia. Michael Mendrick. LC 97-34333. 192p. 1997. pap. 6.95 (*1-55853-534-9*) Rutledge Hill Pr.

New York State Union Catalog of Film & Video, 2 vols. Ed. by Mary Keelan. LC 85-25977. (Illus.). 974p. (Orig.). 1985. pap. write for info. (*0-936213-83-3*) Mid-Hudson Lib.

New York State, Yesterday & Today. Mary A. Wheeler. 432p. 1993. reprint ed. lib. bdg. 99.00 (*0-7812-5205-9*) Rprt Serv.

New York Statements: Ten Artists - Nancy Brett, Katie Degroot, Joan Duff-Bohrer, Cynthia Lin, Carol Luce, David Miller, Michael Phelan, Jason Stewart, Richard Tsao, & Michael Volonakis. Ken Johnson. Ed. by Michael Goodman. LC 95-77113. (Illus.). 23p. (Orig.). 1995. pap. 10.00 (*1-883967-03-1*) Art in General.

New York Stock Exchange. Francis L. Eames. LC 68-28628. 139p. 1968. reprint ed. lib. bdg. 38.50 (*0-8371-0066-6*, EANY, Greenwood Pr) Greenwood.

New York Stock Exchange: A Guide to Information Sources. Lucy Heckman. LC 92-118. (Research & Information Guides in Business, Industry & Economic Institutions Ser.: Vol. 6). 368p. 1992. text 20.00 (*0-8240-3328-0*, SS#759) Garland.

***New York Stock Exchange: Another Century.** 2nd rev. ed. James E. Buck. LC 98-49162. (Illus.). 264p. 1998. write for info. (*0-944641-34-2*) Greenwich Pub Group.

New York Stock Exchange: The First 200 Years. Ed. by James E. Buck. LC 92-10465. (Illus.). 264p. 1992. write for info. (*0-944641-02-4*) Greenwich Pub Group.

New York Stock Exchange, Inc. 728p. 1996. pap. 27.00 (*0-614-26802-8*, 04761101) CCH INC.

***New York Stock Exchange, Inc. Constitution & Rules.** 760p. 1999. pap. text 36.50 (*0-8080-0420-4*) CCH INC.

New York Stock Market: An Original Anthology. Ed. by Vincent P. Carosso. LC 75-2656. (Wall Street & the Security Market Ser.). 1975. 52.95 (*0-405-06981-2*) Ayer.

New York StreetSmart City Edition. Stephan Van Dam. (StreetSmarts Ser.). 1998. pap. 4.95 (*0-931141-49-4*) VanDam Inc.

New York StreetSmart Metro Edition. Stephan Van Dam. (StreetSmarts Ser.). 1998. pap. 5.95 (*0-931141-74-5*) VanDam Inc.

***New York Student Supplement for Litigation.** Joseph Napoli. LC 99-52329. 1999. pap. text 21.95 (*0-7355-1285-X*) Panel Pubs.

***New York Style.** PBC International Staff. (Illus.). 2000. 42.50 (*0-86636-789-6*) Universe.

New York Styles - Spring & Summer 1917 Catalog, No. 67 see Women's & Children's Fashions of 1917: The Complete Perry, Dame & Co., Catalog

New York Subway: Its Construction & Equipment. 2nd ed. Interborough Rapid Transit Co. Staff. LC 90-85874. (Illus.). 150p. 1991. reprint ed. 50.00 (*0-8232-1319-6*) Fordham.

New York Subway Cars. James C. Greller. LC 94-60874. (Illus.). 250p. 1994. pap. 50.00 (*0-9645765-0-3*) Xplorer Pr.

New York Subway Finder: Manhattan. rev. ed. Barry Krusch & Margaret Chesser. 32p. 1989. pap. 2.95 (*0-9620981-1-6*) Stanhope Pr.

New York Subway System. Tim McNeese. LC 96-48700. (Building History Ser.). (Illus.). (J). (gr. 4-12). 1997. lib. bdg. 22.45 (*1-56006-427-7*) Lucent Bks.

***New York Suite.** Ken Hatfield. 24p. 1999. pap. 15.00 (*1-929807-02-3*, KHSG102) Arthur Circle.

New York Supression Manual. L. R. Katz. 1991. 145.00 (*0-8205-1652-X*) Bender.

New York Surrogate's Court Procedure Act (S.C.P.A.) annuals Gould Editorial Staff. 570p. ring bd. 10.95 (*0-87526-129-9*) Gould.

New York Survival. Betty L. Hall & Ralph Roberts. 160p. (Orig.). (gr. 10-12). 1979. pap. text 5.84 (*0-936159-04-9*) Westwood Pr.

New York Survival Guide. Curt Northrup. LC 93-71212. (City Survival Guides Ser.). 170p. (Orig.). (C). 1993. pap. 7.95 (*0-9634720-1-1*) Arkobaleno.

New York Tax Cases, 48 vols., Set. Paul R. Comeau & Arthur R. Rosen. 1988. ring bd. 3995.00 (*0-89941-640-3*, 305590) W S Hein.

New York Tax Handbook. Seymour F. Bernstein. 480p. 1988. 19.50 (*0-13-620469-4*) P-H.

New York Tax Handbook. Seymour F. Bernstein. 400p. 1988. 18.95 (*0-13-620485-6*, Busn) P-H.

New York Tax Handbook, 1984. Seymour F. Bernstein. 436p. 1984. 11.00 (*0-686-89040-X*, 62061-7) P-H.

New York Tax Handbook, 1985. Seymour F. Bernstein. write for info. (*0-318-58208-2*) P-H.

New York Tax Handbook, 1992. 500p. 1992. 27.50 (*0-7811-0008-9*, Maxwell Macmillan) Macmillan.

New York, the City in More Than 500 Memorable Quotations: From More Than 500 Authors (American & Foreign) & More Than 500 Reference Sources. Selected by Vladimir Wertsman. LC 95-38622. 192p. 1997. 35.00 (*0-8108-3088-4*) Scarecrow.

New York, the City in More Than 500 Memorable Quotations: From More Than 500 Authors (American & Foreign) & More Than 500 Reference Sources see New York: The City in More Than 500 Memorable Quotations

New York Theatre Experience Book of the Year 1998. Martin Denton. ii, 322p. 1999. pap. 29.50 (*0-9670234-0-8*) NY Theatre Exp.

New York Theatre Sourcebook. Chuck Lawliss. 1990. pap. 12.95 (*0-671-69970-9*) S&S Trade.

New York Theatrical Sourcebook. Association of Theatrical Artists & Craftspeople S. Ed. by Leslie E. Rollins. (Illus.). 550p. 1994. pap. 24.00 (*0-9642679-7-7*) Sourcebk Pr.

***New York Then & Now.** Alan Hall. LC 99-86164. (Then & Now Ser.). (Illus.). 144p. 2000. 17.98 (*1-57145-190-0*, Thunder Bay) Advantage Pubs.

New York Then & Now: 83 Manhattan Sites Photographed in the Past & Present. Edward B. Watson. (Illus.). 192p. (Orig.). 1976. pap. 12.95 (*0-486-23361-8*) Dover.

***New York Time Guide to Economics.** Murphy & Cheryl D. Jennings. LC 00-21220. 100p. 2000. pap. text 20.95 (*0-324-04159-4*) Sth-Wstrn College.

New York Timeline: A Chronology of New York History, Mystery, Trivia, Legend, Lore & More. Carole Marsh. (Carole Marsh New York Bks.). (Illus.). (J). (gr. 3-12). 1994. pap. 19.95 (*0-7933-5972-4*); lib. bdg. 29.95 (*0-7933-5971-6*); disk 29.95 (*0-7933-5973-2*) Gallopade Intl.

New York Times. 464p. 1999. 29.99 (*1-57866-066-1*) Galahad Bks.

New York Times Acrostic Crossword Puzzles, Vol. 7. Tom Middleton. 1997. pap. 10.00 (*0-8129-2704-4*, Times Bks) Crown Pub Group.

New York Times Acrostic Crosswords, Vol. 6. Thomas H. Middleton. 80p. 1995. pap. 8.50 (*0-8129-2620-X*, Times Bks) Crown Pub Group.

New York Times Acrostics, Vol. 5. 5th ed. Thomas H. Middleton. 1995. pap. 10.00 (*0-8129-2537-8*, Times Bks) Crown Pub Group.

New York Times Acrostics Omnibus. Thomas H. Middleton. 1999. pap. 11.50 (*0-8129-3178-5*, Times Bks) Crown Pub Group.

***New York Times Advertising: Spring 1999.** (C). 1998. write for info. (*0-13-082953-6*) P-H.

***New York Times Almanac 2000.** Ed. by John W. Wright. (Illus.). 1008p. 1999. pap. 10.95 (*0-14-051457-0*, Penguin Bks) Viking Penguin.

***New York Times Almanac 2001.** John W. Wright. 2000. pap. 10.95 (*0-14-051487-2*) Penguin Putnam.

New York Times American Studies Program, 3 pts. Allen Associates Staff. 64p. 1981. pap. text. write for info. (*0-912853-07-7*); write for info. (*0-912853-09-3*); write for info. (*0-912853-08-5*) NY Times.

New York Times Annual Review, 1980. Ed. by Arleen Keylin et al. (Illus.). 256p. 1980. lib. bdg. 18.95 (*0-405-13288-3*) Ayer.

New York Times at the Movies. Arleen Keylin & Christine Bent. 1979. 11.95 (*0-405-12415-5*) Ayer.

New York Times Atlas of the World. abr. ed. Time-Life Books Staff. LC 93-3189. 1993. pap. 22.50 (*0-8129-2266-2*, Times Bks) Crown Pub Group.

New York Times Atlas of the World: Family Edition. LC 92-53666. 1992. 37.50 (*0-8129-2075-9*, Times Bks) Crown Pub Group.

New York Times Beginner Crossword Dictionary. Stanley Newman. 512p. 1999. 23.00 (*0-8129-3043-6*, Times Bks) Crown Pub Group.

New York Times Best Crosswords, Vol. 2. New York Times Staff. Ed. by Eugene T. Maleska. 64p. 1996. pap. 8.50 (*0-8129-2707-9*, Times Bks) Crown Pub Group.

New York Times Best Diagramless Crosswords, Vol. 1. Stanley Newman. Vol. 1. 64p. 1995. pap. 8.50 (*0-8129-2608-0*, Times Bks) Crown Pub Group.

New York Times Book of Great Chess Victories & Defeats. Robert Byrne. (Illus.). 1990. pap. 8.95 (*0-8129-1844-4*, Times Bks) Crown Pub Group.

New York Times Book of Health. Jane E. Brody. 464p. 1998. pap. 15.00 (*0-8129-3012-6*, Times Bks) Crown Pub Group.

New York Times Book of Science Questions & Answers: Answers by Leading Scientists to the Most Commonly Asked Science Questions. C. Claiborne Ray. LC 96-36828. 240p. 1997. pap. 12.95 (*0-385-48660-X*) Doubleday.

New York Times Book of the Civil War. Ed. by Arleen Keylin & Douglas J. Bowen. LC 80-7799. (Illus.). 1980. lib. bdg. 18.95 (*0-405-13396-0*) Ayer.

New York Times Book of Wine. Terry Robards. 480p. 1977. pap. 8.95 (*0-380-01720-2*, Avon Bks) Morrow Avon.

***New York Times Book of Women's Health: The Latest on Feeling Fit, Eating Right & Healthy Living.** Jane E. Brody & Reporters of the New York Times Staff. Ed. by Denise Grady. (Illus.). 356p. 2000. 29.95 (*0-86730-806-0*) Lebhar Friedman.

New York Times Book of World War I. Christine Bent. 1980. 18.95 (*0-405-13465-7*) Ayer.

New York Times Book Review, 1896-1981, 141 vols. LC 68-57778. 9781.00 (*0-685-32624-1*, Times Bks) Crown Pub Group.

New York Times Book Review Index, 5 vols. 1973. 600.00 (*0-405-12494-5*) Ayer.

New York Times Book Review, July-December 1979. 1979. reprint ed. 75.00 (*0-686-64655-X*, Times Bks) Crown Pub Group.

New York Times Bread & Soup Cookbook. Yvonne Y. Tarr. LC 72-83084. 1972. write for info. (*0-8129-0291-2*, Times Bks) Crown Pub Group.

New York Times Bread & Soup Cookbook. Yvonne Y. Tarr. LC 72-83084. 1983. pap. 8.95 (*0-8129-6247-8*, Times Bks) Crown Pub Group.

***New York Times Business Communication: Spring 1999.** (C). 1998. write for info. (*0-13-082955-2*) P-H.

***NYT Business Financing: 25 Keys to Raising Money.** Dick Cardozo & Dileep Rao. LC 99-27690. 104p. 1999. pap. 12.95 (*0-86730-770-6*) Lebhar Friedman.

New York Times Century of Business. Floyd Norris & Christine Bockelmann. (Illus.). 336p. 1999. 29.95 (*0-07-135589-8*) McGraw.

New York Times Co. vs. U. S. Pentagon Papers Litigation, 2 vols. Ed. by James C. Goodale. LC 72-173288. 1971. 90.95 (*0-405-00100-2*) Ayer.

New York Times Complete Manual of Home Repair. Bernard Gladstone. 1979. pap. write for info. (*0-8129-6307-5*, Times Bks) Crown Pub Group.

New York Times Cookbook. Craig Claiborne. Incl. New York Times Menu Cookbook. 1975. (Illus.). 1975. 30.50 (*0-06-010775-8*) HarperTrade.

New York Times Cookbook. rev. ed. Craig Claiborne. LC 89-45640. 800p. 1990. 32.50 (*0-06-016010-1*) HarperTrade.

New York Times Cookbook: The Classic Gourmet Cookbook for the Home Kitchen with Hundreds of New Recipes. rev. ed. Craig Claiborne. 1990. reprint ed. 25.00 (*0-317-99579-0*) HarperTrade.

New York Times Crossword Companion. 1995. pap. 29.95 (*1-57495-013-4*) Herbko Intl.

New York Times Crossword Companion, Vol. 1. 1994. pap. 25.00 (*1-57495-000-2*) Herbko Intl.

New York Times Crossword Companion, Vol. 2. 1994. pap. 12.00 (*1-57495-001-0*) Herbko Intl.

New York Times Crossword Companion, Vol. 3. 1994. pap. 12.00 (*1-57495-002-9*) Herbko Intl.

New York Times Crossword Companion, Vol. 4. 1994. pap. 12.00 (*1-57495-003-7*) Herbko Intl.

New York Times Crossword Companion, Vol. 5. 1994. pap. 12.00 (*1-57495-004-5*) Herbko Intl.

New York Times Crossword Companion, Vol. 6. 1995. pap. 12.00 (*1-57495-005-3*) Herbko Intl.

New York Times Crossword Companion, Vol. 7. 1995. pap. 12.00 (*1-57495-006-1*) Herbko Intl.

New York Times Crossword Companion, Vol. 8. 1995. pap. 12.00 (*1-57495-007-X*) Herbko Intl.

New York Times Crossword Companion, Vol. 9. 1995. pap. 12.00 (*1-57495-008-8*) Herbko Intl.

New York Times Crossword Companion, Vol. 10. 1995. pap. 12.00 (*1-57495-009-6*) Herbko Intl.

New York Times Crossword Companion, Vol. 11. 1995. pap. 12.00 (*1-57495-010-X*) Herbko Intl.

New York Times Crossword Companion, Vol. 12. 1995. pap. 12.00 (*1-57495-011-8*) Herbko Intl.

New York Times Crossword Companion, Vol. 13. 1995. pap. 12.00 (*1-57495-012-6*) Herbko Intl.

New York Times Crossword Dictionary. 3rd ed. Tom Pulliam. 656p. 1997. pap. 18.00 (*0-8129-2823-7*, Times Bks) Crown Pub Group.

New York Times Crossword Puzzle. 1993. write for info. (*0-394-14869-X*, Times Bks) Crown Pub Group.

NY Times Crossword Puzzle Dictionary. 3rd ed. Tom Pulliam & Claire Grundman. LC 84-40108. 1457p. 1999. pap. 7.99 (*0-8129-3122-X*, Times Bks) Crown Pub Group.

New York Times Crossword Puzzle Dictionary. 2nd ed. Tom Pulliam & Clare Grundman. 624p. 1989. pap. 15.99 (*0-446-38265-5*) Warner Bks.

New York Times Crossword Puzzle Dictionary. 3rd rev. ed. Tom Pulliam & Clare Grundman. LC 95-11416. 640p. 1995. 27.50 (*0-8129-2606-4*, Times Bks) Crown Pub Group.

New York Times Crossword Puzzle Omnibus, Vol. 1. Ed. by Will Weng. 1977. pap. 8.95 (*0-8129-0733-7*, Times Bks) Crown Pub Group.

New York Times Crossword Puzzle Omnibus, Vol. 6. 6th ed. Will Weng. Vol. 6. 1992. pap. 11.00 (*0-8129-2124-0*, Times Bks) Crown Pub Group.

New York Times Crossword Puzzle Omnibus, Vol. 7. Will Weng. 1995. pap. 11.00 (*0-8129-2541-6*, Times Bks) Crown Pub Group.

New York Times Crossword Puzzle Omnibus, Vol. 8. New York Times Staff. 128p. 1996. pap. 11.00 (*0-8129-2759-1*, Times Bks) Crown Pub Group.

New York Times Crossword Puzzle Omnibus, Vol. 9. Eugene Maleska. 1997. pap. 11.00 (*0-8129-2951-9*, Times Bks) Crown Pub Group.

New York Times Crossword Puzzles. 1976. mass mkt. 5.95 (*0-446-87128-1*, Pub. by Warner Bks) Little.

New York Times Crossword Puzzles. 1977. mass mkt. 6.95 (*0-446-87710-7*, Pub. by Warner Bks) Little.

New York Times Crossword Puzzles, 10. 10th ed. Will Weng. 1999. pap. 9.00 (*0-8129-3104-1*, Times Bks) Crown Pub Group.

New York Times Crossword Puzzles, Vol. 34. Ed. by Eugene T. Maleska. 1993. write for info. (*0-8129-2264-6*) Random.

New York Times Crossword Puzzles, Vol. 37. Ed. by Eugene T. Maleska. 1994. pap. 8.50 (*0-8129-2358-8*) Random.

New York Times Crossword Puzzles Omnibus, Vol. 1. Will Weng. Vol. 1. 1983. pap. 11.00 (*0-8129-1094-X*, Times Bks) Crown Pub Group.

New York Times Crossword Puzzles Omnibus, Vol. 2. Will Weng. Vol. 2. 1982. pap. 11.00 (*0-8129-1018-4*, Times Bks) Crown Pub Group.

New York Times Crossword Puzzles Omnibus, Vol. 3. Ed. by Will Weng. Vol. 3. 224p. 1983. pap. 11.00 (*0-8129-1066-4*, Times Bks) Crown Pub Group.

New York Times Crossword Puzzles Omnibus, Vol. 4. Ed. by Will Weng. Vol. 4. 224p. 1984. pap. 11.00 (*0-8129-1117-2*, Times Bks) Crown Pub Group.

New York Times Cryptic Handbook. E. Cox & H. Ravthon. 224p. 1996. pap. 14.00 (*0-8129-2621-8*) Random.

N

***New York Times Daily Crossword Puzzles, Vol. 24.** Eugene Maleska. 2000. pap. 9.95 (*0-8129-3288-9*) Random.

New York Times Daily Crossword. Eugene Maleska. 1998. pap. 9.00 (*0-8129-3073-8*, Times Bks) Crown Pub Group.

New York Times Daily Crossword. Will Weng. 1999. pap. 9.50 (*0-8129-3133-5*, Times Bks) Crown Pub Group.

New York Times Daily Crossword, Vol. 6. Will Weng. 1998. pap. 9.00 (*0-8129-3074-6*, Times Bks) Crown Pub Group.

New York Times Daily Crossword, Vol. 11. Will Weng. 1999. pap. 9.50 (*0-8129-3131-9*, Times Bks) Crown Pub Group.

New York Times Daily Crossword, Vol. 12. Will Weng. 1999. pap. 9.50 (*0-8129-3132-7*, Times Bks) Crown Pub Group.

New York Times Daily Crossword, Vol. 49. Will Shortz. 1998. pap. 9.00 (*0-8129-3026-6*, Times Bks) Crown Pub Group.

***New York Times Daily Crossword Puzzle, Vol. 23.** Will Weng. 2000. pap. 9.95 (*0-8129-3234-X*, Times Bks) Crown Pub Group.

***New York Times Daily Crossword Puzzles.** Will Weng. 1999. pap. 9.95 (*0-8129-3226-9*, Times Bks) Crown Pub Group.

NY Times Daily Crossword Puzzles, 6. Will Weng. Vol. 6. 64p. 1998. pap. 9.00 (*0-8129-3079-7*, Times Bks) Crown Pub Group.

NY Times Daily Crossword Puzzles, 7. Will Weng. Vol. 7. 64p. 1998. pap. 9.00 (*0-8129-3077-0*, Times Bks) Crown Pub Group.

NY Times Daily Crossword Puzzles, 8. Will Weng. 1998. pap. 9.00 (*0-8129-3075-4*, Times Bks) Crown Pub Group.

New York Times Daily Crossword Puzzles, Vol. 1. Ed. by Will Weng. 1977. pap. 8.50 (*0-8129-0669-1*, Times Bks) Crown Pub Group.

New York Times Daily Crossword Puzzles, Vol. 3. Will Weng. 1998. pap. 9.00 (*0-8129-3044-4*, Times Bks) Crown Pub Group.

New York Times Daily Crossword Puzzles, Vol. 4. 40th ed. Will Shortz. Vol. 4. 1995. pap. 9.00 (*0-8129-2538-6*, Times Bks) Crown Pub Group.

***New York Times Daily Crossword Puzzles, Vol. 14.** Will Weng. Vol. 14. 64p. 1999. pap. 9.50 (*0-8129-3182-3*, Times Bks) Crown Pub Group.

New York Times Daily Crossword Puzzles, Vol. 15. Will Weng. 64p. 1984. spiral bd. 5.95 (*0-317-05200-4*, Times Bks) Crown Pub Group.

***New York Times Daily Crossword Puzzles, Vol. 15.** Will Weng. Vol. 15. 64p. 1999. pap. 9.50 (*0-8129-3181-5*, Times Bks) Crown Pub Group.

***New York Times Daily Crossword Puzzles, Vol. 17.** Will Weng. Vol. 17. 64p. 1999. pap. 9.50 (*0-8129-3184-X*, Times Bks) Crown Pub Group.

***New York Times Daily Crossword Puzzles, Vol. 18.** Will Weng. 1999. pap. 9.95 (*0-8129-3227-7*, Times Bks) Crown Pub Group.

New York Times Daily Crossword Puzzles, Vol. 22. Ed. by Will Weng. 64p. 1988. pap. 8.00 (*0-8129-1682-4*, Times Bks) Crown Pub Group.

***New York Times Daily Crossword Puzzles, Vol. 27.** Eugene T. Maleska. 64p. 2000. pap. 9.95 (*0-8129-3363-X*, Times Bks) Crown Pub Group.

New York Times Daily Crossword Puzzles, Vol. 27. 27th ed. Eugene T. Maleska. 1990. pap. 7.50 (*0-8129-1879-7*, Times Bks) Crown Pub Group.

***New York Times Daily Crossword Puzzles, Vol. 28.** Ed. by Eugene T. Maleska & Stanley Newman. 64p. 2000. pap. 9.95 (*0-8129-3361-3*, Times Bks) Crown Pub Group.

New York Times Daily Crossword Puzzles, Vol. 28. 28th ed. Eugene T. Maleska. Vol. 28. 1991. pap. 7.00 (*0-8129-1899-1*, Times Bks) Crown Pub Group.

New York Times Daily Crossword Puzzles, Vol. 29. 29th ed. Ed. by Eugene T. Maleska. 64p. 1991. pap. 7.00 (*0-8129-1937-8*, Times Bks) Crown Pub Group.

***New York Times Daily Crossword Puzzles, Vol. 30.** Eugene T. Maleska. 2000. pap. 9.95 (*0-8129-3380-X*, Times Bks) Crown Pub Group.

***New York Times Daily Crossword Puzzles, Vol. 31.** Eugene T. Maleska. 2000. pap. 9.95 (*0-8129-3383-4*, Times Bks) Crown Pub Group.

New York Times Daily Crossword Puzzles, Vol. 31. 31st ed. Eugene T. Maleska. 1992. pap. 8.00 (*0-8129-2043-0*, Times Bks) Crown Pub Group.

***New York Times Daily Crossword Puzzles, Vol. 32.** Eugene T. Maleska. 2000. pap. 9.95 (*0-8129-3385-0*, Times Bks) Crown Pub Group.

***New York Times Daily Crossword Puzzles, Vol. 33.** Eugene T. Maleska. 2000. pap. 9.95 (*0-8129-3388-5*, Times Bks) Crown Pub Group.

New York Times Daily Crossword Puzzles, Vol. 33. 33rd ed. Eugene T. Maleska. Vol. 33. 1993. pap. 8.50 (*0-8129-2183-6*, Times Bks) Crown Pub Group.

New York Times Daily Crossword Puzzles, Vol. 34. 34th ed. Eugene T. Maleska. Vol. 34. 1993. pap. 8.00 (*0-8129-2209-3*, Times Bks) Crown Pub Group.

New York Times Daily Crossword Puzzles, Vol. 38. Ed. by Eugene T. Maleska. Vol. 38. 64p. 1994. pap. 9.00 (*0-8129-2450-9*, Times Bks) Crown Pub Group.

New York Times Daily Crossword Puzzles, Vol. 39. Eugene T. Maleska. Vol. 39. 1995. pap. 9.95 (*0-8129-2481-9*, Times Bks) Crown Pub Group.

New York Times Daily Crossword Puzzles, Vol. 41. Will Shortz. Vol. 41. 64p. 1995. pap. 8.50 (*0-8129-2617-X*, Times Bks) Crown Pub Group.

New York Times Daily Crossword Puzzles, Vol. 42. 42nd ed. Ed. by Will Shortz. 80p. 1996. pap. 9.00 (*0-8129-2706-0*, Times Bks) Crown Pub Group.

New York Times Daily Crossword Puzzles, Vol. 43. New York Times Staff. 80p. 1996. pap. 9.00 (*0-8129-2760-5*, Times Bks) Crown Pub Group.

New York Times Daily Crossword Puzzles, Vol. 44. Will Shortz. Vol. 44. 1996. pap. 9.00 (*0-8129-2801-6*, Times Bks) Crown Pub Group.

New York Times Daily Crossword Puzzles, Vol. 45. Will Shortz. 1996. pap. 9.00 (*0-8129-2893-8*, Times Bks) Crown Pub Group.

New York Times Daily Crossword Puzzles, Vol. 47. 47th ed. Will Shortz. 1998. pap. 9.00 (*0-8129-2942-X*, Times Bks) Crown Pub Group.

New York Times Daily Crossword Puzzles, Vol. 50. 50th ed. Will Shortz. 1992. pap. 13.50 (*0-8129-3060-6*, Times Bks) Crown Pub Group.

NY Times Daily Crossword Puzzles, Vol. 51. Will Shortz. 1999. pap. 9.50 (*0-8129-3125-4*, Times Bks) Crown Pub Group.

***New York Times Daily Crossword Puzzles, Vol. 52.** Will Shortz. Vol. 52. 80p. 1999. pap. 9.50 (*0-8129-3164-5*, Times Bks) Crown Pub Group.

***New York Times Daily Crossword Puzzles, Vol. 55.** Will Shortz. 64p. 2000. pap. 9.95 (*0-8129-3365-6*, Times Bks) Crown Pub Group.

New York Times Daily Crossword Puzzles Friday, Skill Level 5, Vol. 1. Eugene T. Maleska. 1997. mass mkt. 2.99 (*0-8041-1583-4*) Ivy Books.

New York Times Daily Crossword Puzzles (Monday), Vol. I. Eugene T. Maleska. Vol. I. 1997. mass mkt. 2.99 (*0-8041-1579-6*) Ivy Books.

New York Times Daily Crossword Puzzles Saturday, Skill Level 6, Vol. 1. Eugene T. Maleska. 1997. mass mkt. 2.99 (*0-8041-1584-2*) Ivy Books.

New York Times Daily Crossword Puzzles (Thursday), Vol. 2. Eugene T. Maleska. 1997. mass mkt. 2.99 (*0-8041-1582-6*) Ivy Books.

New York Times Daily Crossword Puzzles (Tuesday), Vol. I. Eugene T. Maleska. 1997. mass mkt. 2.99 (*0-8041-1580-X*) Ivy Books.

New York Times Daily Crossword Puzzles, Vol. 35, Vol. 26. Eugene T. Maleska. 1990. pap. 6.95 (*0-8129-1860-6*) Random.

New York Times Daily Crossword Puzzles, Vol. 35, Vol. 30. Ed. by Eugene T. Maleska. 1992. pap. 7.50 (*0-8129-1997-1*) Random.

New York Times Daily Crossword Puzzles, Vol. 35, Vol. 35. Eugene T. Maleska. Vol. 35. 1993. pap. 8.50 (*0-8129-2270-0*, Times Bks) Crown Pub Group.

New York Times Daily Crossword Puzzles, Vol. 35, Vol. 35. Ed. by Eugene T. Maleska. 1994. pap. 8.50 (*0-8129-2340-5*) Random.

New York Times Daily Crossword Puzzles (Wednesday), Vol. I. Eugene T. Maleska. 1997. mass mkt. 2.99 (*0-8041-1581-8*) Ivy Books.

New York Times Daily Crosswords, Vol. 46. 46th ed. Will Shortz. Vol. 46. 80p. 1997. pap. 9.00 (*0-8129-2915-2*, Times Bks) Crown Pub Group.

New York Times Daily Crosswords, Vol. 48. 48th ed. Will Shortz. 1998. pap. 9.00 (*0-8129-2968-3*, Times Bks) Crown Pub Group.

New York Times Dictionary of Misunderstood, Misused & Mispronounced Words. Laurence Urdang. LC 98-51456. 384p. 1999. 10.98 (*1-57912-060-1*) Blck Dog & Leventhal.

New York Times Encyclopedia of Film, 13 vols., Set. Ed. by Gene Brown. 1992. 495.00 (*0-8153-0349-1*) Garland.

New York Times Encyclopedia of Film, Vol. 1: 1896-1928. 1988. text 38.00 (*0-8240-6765-7*) Garland.

New York Times Encyclopedia of Film, Vol. 2: 1929-1936. 1987. text 38.00 (*0-8240-6766-5*) Garland.

New York Times Encyclopedia of Film, Vol. 4: 1941-1946. 1987. text 38.00 (*0-8240-6768-1*) Garland.

New York Times Encyclopedia of Film, Vol. 5: 1947-1951. 1987. text 38.00 (*0-8240-6769-X*) Garland.

New York Times Encyclopedia of Film, Vol. 6: 1952-1957. 1987. text 38.00 (*0-8240-6770-3*) Garland.

New York Times Encyclopedia of Film, Vol. 7: 1958-1963. 1987. text 38.00 (*0-8240-6771-1*) Garland.

New York Times Encyclopedia of Film, Vol. 8: 1964-1968. 1987. text 38.00 (*0-8240-6772-X*) Garland.

New York Times Encyclopedia of Film, Vol. 9: 1969-1971. 1987. text 38.00 (*0-8240-6773-8*) Garland.

New York Times Encyclopedia of Film, Vol. 10: 1972-1974. 1987. text 38.00 (*0-8240-6774-6*) Garland.

New York Times Encyclopedia of Film, Vol. 11: 1975-1976. 1987. text 38.00 (*0-8240-6775-4*) Garland.

New York Times Encyclopedia of Film, Vol. 12: 1977-1979. 1987. text 38.00 (*0-8240-6776-2*) Garland.

New York Times Encyclopedia of Film, Vol. 13: Index. 1987. text 38.00 (*0-8240-6777-0*) Garland.

New York Times Film Reviews, Vol. 10: 1975-1976. Random House Staff. 1988. text 180.00 (*0-8240-7584-6*) Garland.

New York Times Film Reviews, Vol. 11: 1977-1978. Random House Staff. 1988. text 180.00 (*0-8240-7585-4*) Garland.

New York Times Film Reviews, Vol. 12: 1979-1980. Random House Staff. 1988. text 180.00 (*0-8240-7586-2*) Garland.

New York Times Film Reviews, Vol. 13: 1981-1982. Random House Staff. 350p. 1989. text 180.00 (*0-8240-7587-0*) Garland.

New York Times Film Reviews, Vol. 14: 1983-1984. Random House Staff. 1988. text 180.00 (*0-8240-7588-9*) Garland.

New York Times Film Reviews, 1993-1994, 17 vols. 1992. 165.00 (*0-318-69658-4*); 275.00 (*0-8150-7580-4*) Garland.

New York Times Film Reviews, 1995-1996. (New York Times Film Reviews Ser.: Vol. 20). 500p. 1998. 165.00 (*0-8153-3052-9*) Garland.

New York Times Film Reviews, 1993-1994, 19. 520p. 1992. 165.00 (*0-8153-0350-5*) Garland.

New York Times Film Reviews, 1993-1994, Vol. 1. LC 70-112777. 528p. 1996. reprint ed. text 180.00 (*0-8240-7593-5*) Garland.

New York Times Film Reviews, 1913-1974, 11 vols. (Illus.). 840.00 (*0-405-02191-7*, Times Bks) Crown Pub Group.

New York Times Film Reviews, 1913-1931, No. 1. New York Times Staff & Random House Staff. 787p. 1990. text 165.00 (*0-8240-7575-7*) Garland.

New York Times Film Reviews 1959-1968, Vol. 5. LC 70-112777. (New York Times Film Reviews Ser.). 720p. 1990. reprint ed. text 180.00 (*0-8240-7579-X*) Garland.

New York Times Giant Sunday Crossword, Vol. 4. New York Times Information Bank. 1994. mass mkt. write for info. (*0-394-59843-1*) Random.

NYT Going Global: 25 Keys to International Operations. Jeffrey H. Bergstrand. Ed. by Tom Redburn. LC 99-27693. 104p. 1999. pap. 12.95 (*0-86730-779-X*) Lebhar Friedman.

***New York Times Guide to Business Communication Today.** Murphy. LC 99-52892. 1999. pap. text 20.95 (*0-324-04161-6*) Sth-Wstrn College.

***New York Times Guide to Business Law.** Murphy. 2000. pap. text 20.95 (*0-324-04160-8*) Sth-Wstrn College.

***New York Times Guide to Finance.** Murphy. 2000. pap. text 20.95 (*0-324-04158-6*) Sth-Wstrn College.

***New York Times Guide to Hotels in New York City, 2000.** Charles Suisman. 400p. 1999. pap. 14.95 (*0-9668659-3-6*, Pub. by NY Times) Publishers Group.

***New York Times Guide to Management.** Jamie Murphy & Daniel J. Montgomery. LC 00-21221. 112p. 2000. pap. text 20.95 (*0-324-04157-8*) Sth-Wstrn College.

***New York Times Guide to Marketing.** Murphy. LC 99-49442. 1999. pap. text 20.95 (*0-324-04182-9*) Sth-Wstrn College.

***New York Times Guide to New York City 2001.** New York Times Staff. (Illus.). 300p. 2000. pap. 16.95 (*0-9668659-8-7*, Pub. by NY Times) Publishers Group.

New York Times Guide to Restaurants in New York City. Bryan Miller. LC 86-5896. 448p. 1987. pap. 12.95 (*0-8129-1313-2*, Times Bks) Crown Pub Group.

New York Times Guide to Restaurants in New York City. Bryan Miller. 1992. pap. 15.00 (*0-8129-2089-9*, Times Bks) Crown Pub Group.

New York Times Guide to Restaurants in New York City. rev. ed. Bryan Miller. (Illus.). 448p. 1988. pap. 12.95 (*0-8129-1735-9*, Times Bks) Crown Pub Group.

New York Times Guide to Restaurants in New York City, 1993-1994. Bryan Miller. 1992. 15.00 (*0-8129-1859-2*, Times Bks) Crown Pub Group.

New York Times Guide to Restaurants in New York City, 2000. Ruth Reichl et al. 400p. 1999. pap. 14.95 (*0-9668659-2-8*, Pub. by NY Times) Publishers Group.

***New York Times Guide to Restaurants in New York City 2001.** 2nd ed. William Grimes et al. (Illus.). 450p. 2000. pap. 14.95 (*0-9668659-9-5*, Pub. by NY Times) Publishers Group.

***New York Times Guide to the Best Children's Videos.** Kids First Staff. 478p. 1999. per. 16.00 (*0-671-03669-6*, PB Trade Paper) PB.

New York Times Guide to the Best 1,000 Movies Ever Made. Vincent Canby et al. LC 98-45289. (Illus.). 1024p. 1999. pap. 25.00 (*0-8129-3001-0*, Times Bks) Crown Pub Group.

New York Times Home Repair Almanac: A Season-by-Season Guide for Maintaining Your Home. Edward R. Lipinski. LC 99-10048. (Illus.). 308p. 1999. pap. 19.95 (*0-86730-759-5*, Pub. by Lebhar Friedman) Natl Bk Netwk.

New York Times Large Print Crossword Puzzle Omnibus, Vol. 1. large type ed. Ed. by Eugene T. Maleska. 1994. pap. 13.00 (*0-679-75144-0*) Random Hse Lrg Prnt.

New York Times Large Print Crossword Puzzles, Vol. 7. large type ed. Ed. by Eugene T. Maleska. 1992. pap. 10.00 (*0-679-74118-6*) Random Hse Lrg Prnt.

New York Times Large-Type Crossword Puzzles, Vol. 1. large type ed. Ed. by Will Weng. 96p. (Orig.). 1983. pap. 10.00 (*0-8129-1044-3*, Times Bks) Crown Pub Group.

New York Times Large-Type Crossword Puzzles, Vol. 2. Ed. by Will Weng. Vol. 2. 64p. (Orig.). 1984. pap. 10.00 (*0-8129-1105-9*, Times Bks) Crown Pub Group.

New York Times Large-Type Crosswords, Vol. 3. Ed. by Will Weng. 96p. 1986. pap. 10.00 (*0-8129-1598-4*, Times Bks) Crown Pub Group.

NYT Leadership & Vision: 25 Keys to Motivation. Raymond Aldag & Buck Joseph. LC 99-27688. 104p. 1999. pap. 12.95 (*0-86730-780-3*) Lebhar Friedman.

NYT Managing Investment: 25 Keys to Profitable Capital Investment. Robert Taggart. LC 99-27694. 104p. 1999. pap. 12.95 (*0-86730-778-1*) Lebhar Friedman.

New York Times Manual of Style: The Official Style Guide Used by the Writers & Editors of the New York Times. rev. expanded ed. Allan M. Siegal & William G. Connolly. LC 99-10630. 480p. 1999. 30.00 (*0-8129-6388-1*, Times Bks) Crown Pub Group.

New York Times Menu Cookbook see New York Times Cookbook

New York Times Natural Foods Dieting Book. Yvonne Y. Tarr. LC 75-190484. 1972. write for info. (*0-8129-0277-7*, Times Bks) Crown Pub Group.

New York Times New England Heritage Cookbook. Jean Hewitt. 350p. 1991. 7.98 (*0-89009-444-6*) Bk Sales Inc.

New York Times New Natural Foods Cookbook. rev. ed. Jean Hewitt. 438p. 1983. pap. 10.00 (*0-380-62687-X*, Avon Bks) Morrow Avon.

New York Times 1999 Almanac. Ed. by John W. Wright. 982p. 1998. pap. 10.95 (*0-14-051411-2*) Viking Penguin.

NY Times Omnibus, 2. large type ed. Ed. by Eugene T. Maleska. 1998. pap. 13.00 (*0-8129-3069-X*, Times Bks) Crown Pub Group.

New York Times on Film. Vernon Young. 1980. 1.00 (*0-394-59564-5*) Random.

***New York Times on the Sopranos.** New York Times Staff. 176p. 2000. per. 9.95 (*0-7434-0021-6*, Pub. by ibooks) S&S Trade.

***NYT Organizing a Company: 25 Keys to Choosing a Business Structure.** S. Jay Skylar & Joseph N. Bongiovanni. Ed. by Tom Redburn. LC 99-27691. 104p. 1999. pap. 12.95 (*0-86730-772-2*) Lebhar Friedman.

New York Times Parent's Guide to the Best Books for Children. Eden R. Lipson. (Illus.). 448p. 1988. 22.50 (*0-8129-1649-2*, Times Bks); pap. 12.95 (*0-8129-1688-3*, Times Bks) Crown Pub Group.

New York Times Parent's Guide to the Best Books for Children. Eden R. Lipson. (Illus.). 1991. 15.00 (*0-8129-1943-2*, Times Bks) Crown Pub Group.

New York Times Parent's Guide to the Best Books for Children. rev. ed. Eden R. Lipson. LC 91-2675. (Illus.). 464p. 1991. pap. 17.00 (*0-8129-1889-4*, Times Bks) Crown Pub Group.

New York Times Parent's Guide to the Best Books for Children. 3rd ed. Eden Ross Lipson. (Illus.). 560p. 2000. pap. 18.00 (*0-8129-3018-5*, Three Riv Pr) Crown Pub Group.

New York Times Passover Cookbook: More Than 175 Holiday Recipes from Top Chefs & Writers. New York Times Staff. Ed. by Linda Armster. LC 98-41282. (Illus.). 320p. 1999. 25.00 (*0-688-15590-1*, Wm Morrow) Morrow Avon.

New York Times Pocket MBA Series. 1999. pap. 115.40 (*0-86730-785-4*) Lebhar Friedman.

***New York Times Pocket MBA Series.** New York Times Staff. 1999. pap. 155.40 (*0-86730-810-9*) Lebhar Friedman.

New York Times Puzzle Dictionary. 3rd ed. Tom Pulliam. 1995. 27.50 (*0-8129-2373-1*) Random.

New York Times Quiz Book, Vol. 1. Raymond Hamel. LC 99-20688. Vol. 1. 256p. 1999. pap. 12.50 (*0-8129-3057-6*, Times Bks) Crown Pub Group.

New York Times Reader Philosphy. New York Times Staff. 1999. pap. 16.00 (*0-13-977497-1*) P-H.

New York Times Reading Experience. Kitty Bateman et al. 40p. 1979. pap. text. write for info. (*0-912853-02-6*) NY Times.

New York Times Report from Red China. Tillman Durdin et al. 1976. pap. 1.95 (*0-380-01363-0*, Avon Bks) Morrow Avon.

New York Times Season-by-Season Guide to Home Maintenance. John Warde. 1992. 25.00 (*0-685-54872-4*, Times Bks) Crown Pub Group.

New York Times Season by Season Home Maintenance. 4th ed. John Warde. 1994. pap. write for info. (*0-394-27118-1*) Random.

New York Times Sixty-Minute Gourmet. Pierre Franey. LC 79-51427. 1979. 19.95 (*0-8129-0834-1*, Times Bks) Crown Pub Group.

New York Times Skillbuilder Crosswords: Three Star Strategiest Level, Vol. 4. 4th ed. New York Times Staff. 1995. pap. 8.50 (*0-8129-2557-2*, Times Bks) Crown Pub Group.

New York Times Skillbuilder Crosswords: Three,Star Strategist Level, Vol. 3. 3rd ed. New York Times Staff. 1995. pap. 8.50 (*0-8129-2310-3*, Times Bks) Crown Pub Group.

New York Times Skillbuilder Crosswords Vol. 5: Three-Star Strategist Puzzles. Stanley Newman. 64p. 1995. pap. 8.50 (*0-8129-2611-0*, Times Bks) Crown Pub Group.

New York Times Skillbuilder Omnibus. 1998. pap. 12.50 (*0-8129-2970-5*, Times Bks) Crown Pub Group.

New York Times Sports Hall of Fame. New York Times Staff. 1980. 14.95 (*0-405-13942-X*) Ayer.

***New York Times Sunday Crossword, 25.** Will Shortz. 1999. pap. 14.00 (*0-8129-3208-0*) Random.

New York Times Sunday Crossword, Vol. 8. Will Weng. 1998. pap. 9.00 (*0-8129-3076-2*, Times Bks) Crown Pub Group.

New York Times Sunday Crossword Omnibus, Vol. 2. Will Weng. Vol. 2. 1989. pap. 11.00 (*0-8129-1791-X*, Times Bks) Crown Pub Group.

New York Times Sunday Crossword Puzzle, Vol. 1. Will Weng. 1977. pap. 9.00 (*0-8129-0670-5*, Times Bks) Crown Pub Group.

New York Times Sunday Crossword Puzzle Omnibus, Vol. 1. Will Weng. (Orig.). 1984. pap. 11.50 (*0-8129-1139-3*, Times Bks) Crown Pub Group.

New York Times Sunday Crossword Puzzles, 5. 10th ed. Eugene Maleska. Vol. 10. 64p. 1999. pap. 9.00 (*0-8129-3105-X*, Times Bks) Crown Pub Group.

NY Times Sunday Crossword Puzzles, 7. Will Weng. 1998. pap. 9.00 (*0-8129-3078-9*, Times Bks) Crown Pub Group.

NY Times Sunday Crossword Puzzles, 9. Eugene Maleska. Vol. 9. 64p. 1998. pap. 9.00 (*0-8129-3087-8*, Times Bks) Crown Pub Group.

New York Times Sunday Crossword Puzzles, Vol. II. Ed. by Eugene T. Maleska. Vol. II. 1985. pap. 9.00 (*0-8129-1115-6*, Times Bks) Crown Pub Group.

New York Times Sunday Crossword Puzzles, Vol. 2. Will Weng. 1998. pap. 9.00 (*0-8129-3051-7*, Times Bks) Crown Pub Group.

New York Times Sunday Crossword Puzzles, Vol. 10. Ed. by Eugene T. Maleska. Vol. 10. 64p. 1984. pap., spiral bd. 9.00 (*0-8129-1083-4*, Times Bks) Crown Pub Group.

New York Times Sunday Crossword Puzzles, Vol. 12. Ed. by Eugene T. Maleska. Vol. 12. 64p. 1985. pap. 9.00 (*0-8129-1166-0*, Times Bks) Crown Pub Group.

New York Times Sunday Crossword Puzzles, Vol. 13. Ed. by Eugene T. Maleska. Vol. 13. 64p. 1986. pap. 9.00 (*0-8129-1191-1*, Times Bks) Crown Pub Group.

N

New York Times Sunday Crossword Puzzles, Vol. 14. Ed. by Eugene T. Maleska. 64p. 1988. pap. 9.00 (*0-8129-1681-6*, Times Bks) Crown Pub Group.

New York Times Sunday Crossword Puzzles, Vol. 15. Eugene T. Maleska. 1989. pap. 9.00 (*0-8129-1781-2*, Times Bks) Crown Pub Group.

New York Times Sunday Crossword Puzzles, Vol. 16. Eugene T. Maleska. 1990. pap. 9.00 (*0-8129-1839-8*, Times Bks) Crown Pub Group.

New York Times Sunday Crossword Puzzles, Vol. 17. Eugene T. Maleska. 1990. pap. 9.00 (*0-8129-1878-9*, Times Bks) Crown Pub Group.

New York Times Sunday Crossword Puzzles, Vol. 18. Eugene T. Maleska. 1994. pap. 9.95 (*0-8129-2268-9*, Times Bks) Crown Pub Group.

New York Times Sunday Crossword Puzzles, Vol. 19. Eugene T. Maleska. Vol. 19. 1992. pap. 9.00 (*0-8129-2083-X*, Times Bks) Crown Pub Group.

New York Times Sunday Crossword Puzzles, Vol. 20. Ed. by Eugene T. Maleska. Vol. 20. 64p. 1995. pap. 9.00 (*0-8129-2451-7*, Times Bks) Crown Pub Group.

New York Times Sunday Crossword Puzzles, Vol. 21. Eugene T. Maleska. Vol. 21. 64p. 1995. pap. 9.00 (*0-8129-2615-3*, Times Bks) Crown Pub Group.

New York Times Sunday Crossword Puzzles, Vol. 22. 22nd ed. Eugene T. Maleska. Vol. 22. 64p. 1996. pap. 9.00 (*0-8129-2803-2*, Times Bks) Crown Pub Group.

New York Times Sunday Crossword Puzzles, Vol. 23. 23rd ed. Eugene T. Maleska. 1997. pap. 9.00 (*0-8129-2939-X*, Times Bks) Crown Pub Group.

New York Times Sunday Crossword Puzzles, Vol. 24. 24th ed. Will Shortz. 1998. pap. 9.00 (*0-8129-3061-4*, Times Bks) Crown Pub Group.

New York Times Sunday Crosswords Omnibus, Vol. 4. Eugene T. Maleska. 1995. pap. 11.00 (*0-8129-2480-0*, Times Bks) Crown Pub Group.

New York Times Sunday Omnibus, Vol. 3. 3rd ed. Ed. by Eugene T. Maleska. Vol. 3. 240p. 1991. pap. 11.00 (*0-8129-1936-X*, Times Bks) Crown Pub Group.

*__NYT the Board of Directors: 25 Keys to Corporate Governace.__ Marianne Jennings. LC 99-27692. 104p. 1999. pap. 12.95 (*0-86730-781-1*) Lebhar Friedman.

New York Times Theater Reviews, Vol. 20: 1977-1978. Random House Staff. 1988. text 80.00 (*0-8240-7568-4*) Garland.

New York Times Theater Reviews, Vol. 22: 1981-1982. Random House Staff. 1988. text 80.00 (*0-8240-7570-6*) Garland.

New York Times Theater Reviews, Vol. 24: 1985-1986. Random House Staff. 550p. 1989. text 80.00 (*0-8240-7572-2*) Garland.

New York Times Theater Reviews, Vol. 25: 1987-1988. Random House Staff. 500p. 1990. text 80.00 (*0-8240-7573-0*) Garland.

New York Times Theater Reviews, 1995-1996. (New York Times Theater Review Ser.: Vol. 29). 456p. 1998. 180.00 (*0-8153-0645-8*) Garland.

New York Times Theater Reviews, 1870-1990, 26 vols. 1992. 165.00 (*0-318-69659-2*); 350.00 (*0-318-69660-6*) Garland.

New York Times Theater Reviews, 1870-1990, 26 vols., Set. 1992. 3555.00 (*0-8153-0351-3*) Garland.

New York Times Theatre Review, Vol. 1: 1870-1885. Random House Staff. 550p. 1990. text 80.00 (*0-8240-7549-8*) Garland.

New York Times Theatre Review, Vol. 2: 1886-1895. Random House Staff. 1988. text 80.00 (*0-8240-7550-1*) Garland.

New York Times Theatre Reviews, Vol. 3: 1896-1903. Random House Staff. 550p. 1990. text 80.00 (*0-8240-7551-X*) Garland.

New York Times Theatre Reviews, Vol. 4: 1904-1911. Random House Staff. 1988. text 80.00 (*0-8240-7552-8*) Garland.

New York Times Theatre Reviews, Vol. 5: 1912-1919. Random House Staff. 1988. text 80.00 (*0-8240-7553-6*) Garland.

New York Times Theatre Reviews, Vol. 6: Index 1870-1919. Random House Staff. 550p. 1991. text 195.00 (*0-8240-7554-4*) Garland.

New York Times Theatre Reviews, Vol. 15: Index 1920-1970. Random House Staff. 550p. 1990. text 195.00 (*0-8240-7563-3*) Garland.

New York Times Theatre Reviews, 1870-1919, 6 vols., Set. 1976. 975.00 (*0-405-06664-3*, Times Bks) Crown Pub Group.

New York Times Theatre Reviews, 1991-92. Random House Staff. (New York Times Theater Reviews Ser.: Vol. 27). 1994. text 180.00 (*0-8153-0643-1*) Garland.

New York Times Theatre Reviews, 1920-1980, 15 vols., Set. (Illus.). 1580.00 (*0-405-00696-9*, Times Bks) Crown Pub Group.

New York Times Theatre Reviews, 1993-1994, Vol. 28. New York Times Staff. 568p. 1996. text 180.00 (*0-8153-0644-X*) Garland.

New York Times Toughest Crossword Puzzles, Vol. 7. 7th ed. Will Shortz. 1998. pap. 10.00 (*0-8129-3070-3*, Times Bks) Crown Pub Group.

*__New York Times Toughest Crossword Puzzle Megaomnibus.__ Eugene T. Maleska. 336p. (Orig.). 1999. pap. 13.50 (*0-8129-3166-1*, Times Bks) Crown Pub Group.

New York Times Toughest Crossword Puzzles, Vol. 1. Eugene T. Maleska. 1988. pap. 9.00 (*0-8129-1694-8*, Times Bks) Crown Pub Group.

New York Times Toughest Crossword Puzzles, Vol. 2. Eugene T. Maleska. 1989. pap. 9.00 (*0-8129-1828-2*, Times Bks) Crown Pub Group.

New York Times Toughest Crossword Puzzles, Vol. 3. Eugene T. Maleska. Vol. 3. 1991. pap. 10.00 (*0-8129-1912-2*, Times Bks) Crown Pub Group.

New York Times Toughest Crossword Puzzles, Vol. 4. 4th ed. Eugene T. Maleska. Vol. 4. 1993. pap. 9.00 (*0-8129-2178-X*, Times Bks) Crown Pub Group.

New York Times Toughest Crossword Puzzles, Vol. 5. Eugene T. Maleska. Vol. 5. 64p. 1995. pap. 9.00 (*0-8129-2618-8*, Times Bks) Crown Pub Group.

New York Times Toughest Crossword Puzzles, Vol. 6. 6th ed. Eugene Maleska. 1998. pap. 10.00 (*0-8129-2805-9*, Times Bks) Crown Pub Group.

New York Times Update, 1979, Set 1. New York Times Staff. (Great Contemporary Issues Ser.). 1979. 38.95 (*0-405-18421-2*, 1772) Ayer.

New York Times Update, 1979, Vol. 2. New York Times Staff. (Great Contemporary Issues Ser.). 38.95 (*0-405-18422-0*, 1773) Ayer.

New York Times vs. Sullivan: Affirming Freedom of the Press. Harvey Fireside. LC 98-36959. (Landmark Supreme Court Cases Ser.). 128p. (YA). (gr. 6 up). 1999. lib. bdg. 20.95 (*0-7660-1085-6*) Enslow Pubs.

New York Times vs. United States: National Security & Censorship. D. J. Herda. LC 93-32156. (Landmark Supreme Court Cases Ser.). (Illus.). 104p. (YA). (gr. 6 up). 1994. lib. bdg. 20.95 (*0-89490-490-6*) Enslow Pubs.

*__New York Times Weekends: Great Getaways for All Four Seasons.__ 2nd ed. 418p. 1999. pap. 15.95 (*0-02-863151-X*, Pub. by Macmillan) S&S Trade.

New York to Nome. Rick Steber. 1989. pap. 7.95 (*0-318-42733-8*) PB.

New York to Nome. Rick Steber. (Illus.). 168p. 1996. reprint ed. pap. 11.95 (*0-945134-44-4*) Bonanza Pub.

New York to Oberplan. James N. Hardin. 172p. 1946. 29.95 (*0-89839-044-3*) Battery Pr.

New York Tombs, Its Secrets & Its Mysteries. Charles Sutton. Ed. by James B. Mix & Samuel A. Mackeever. LC 76-172588. (Criminology, Law Enforcement, & Social Problems Ser.: No. 178). (Illus.). 1973. reprint ed. 32.00 (*0-87585-178-9*) Patterson Smith.

New York Town Law. annuals Gould Editorial Staff. 495p. ring bd. 17.95 (*0-87526-303-8*) Gould.

New York Transit Memories. Harold Smith. 1997. pap. 16.95 (*0-915276-56-9*) Quadrant Pr.

New York Trial Guide, 5 vols., Set. Seymour H. Moskowitz et al. 1990. 475.00 (*0-8205-1599-X*, 599) Bender.

New York Trilogy: City of Glass; Ghosts; The Locked Room. Paul Auster. LC 89-70997. (Illus.). 448p. 1990. pap. 20.99 (*0-14-013155-8*, Penguin Bks) Viking Penguin.

New York Trilogy: City of Glass; Ghosts; The Locked Room. rev. ed. Paul Auster. (New American Fiction Ser.: No. 4-6). 472p. 1995. 21.95 (*1-55713-166-X*) Sun & Moon CA.

New York Trilogy: New York Underground; Trapped; Love & Sex. Paul Hallasy. 147p. (Orig.). 1990. pap. 7.95 (*0-9627135-0-3*) P Hallasy.

New York Triumvirate: A Study of the Legal & Political Careers of William Livingston, John Morin Scott, & William Smith Jr. Dorothy R. Dillon. LC 68-58567. (Columbia University. Studies in the Social Sciences: No. 548). reprint ed. 20.00 (*0-404-51548-7*) AMS Pr.

New York 2000! Coming Soon to a Calendar Near You - The 21st Century! - Complete Set of AL 2000 Items. Carole Marsh. (Two Thousand! Ser.). (Illus.). (J). (gr. 3-12). 1998. pap. 75.00 (*0-7933-9373-6*); lib. bdg. 85.00 (*0-7933-9374-4*) Gallopade Intl.

New York 2000! Coming Soon to a Calendar near You-The 21st Century! Carole Marsh. (Two Thousand! Ser.). (Illus.). (J). (gr. 3-12). 1998. pap. 19.95 (*0-7933-8772-8*); lib. bdg. 29.95 (*0-7933-8771-X*) Gallopade Intl.

New York UFO's & Extraterrestrials! A Look at the Sightings & Science in Our State. Carole Marsh. (Carole Marsh New York Bks.). (Illus.). (J). (gr. 3-12). 1997. pap. 19.95 (*0-7933-6431-0*); lib. bdg. 29.95 (*0-7933-6430-2*) Gallopade Intl.

New York Underground. Ed. by Colgan Bryan. 112p. (Orig.). 1997. pap. text 19.95 (*1-57623-926-8*) Wrner Bros.

New York Understanding the Penal Law. Richard C. Moriarty. 190p. 1994. ring bd. 25.95 (*0-87526-416-6*) Gould.

New York Unfolds. Stephan Van Dam. (World Unfolds Ser.). 1998. pap. 6.95 (*0-931141-00-1*) VanDam Inc.

New York Uniform Commercial Code, 4 vols., Set. Lawyers Cooperative Publishing Staff. LC 92-74149. 1993. ring bd. 375.00 (*0-317-05379-5*) West Group.

New York University & the City: An Illustrated History, 1831-1996. Thomas J. Frusciano & Marilyn H. Pettit. LC 97-9655. 1997. 35.00 (*0-8135-2347-8*) Rutgers U Pr.

New York University Annual Conference on Tax Planning for 501 (c) (3) Organizations. write for info. (*0-8205-1480-2*) Bender.

New York University Annual Conference on Tax Planning for 501(c)(3) Organizations. text 100.00 (*0-8205-4229-6*) Bender.

New York University Annual Institute on Federal Taxation. annuals Melvin Cornfield. (New York University School of Continuing Education Ser.). 1986. ring bd. write for info. (*0-8205-1500-0*) Bender.

New York University Institute of Philosophy Symposia. Ed. by Sidney Hook. Incl. Religious Experience & Truth: A Symposium. 333p. 1961. pap. 12.50 (*0-8147-3393-X*); pap. write for info. (*0-318-54711-2*) NYU Pr.

New York University Institute on Federal Taxation. 57th ed. text 445.00 (*0-8205-4602-X*) Bender.

New York University Institute on State & Local Taxation, 1998. Contrib. by Paul H. Frankel & Peter L. Faber. LC 99-160651. 1998. 99.00 (*0-8205-3941-4*) Bender.

New York University Journal of International Law & Politics, 1968-1994/95, 24 vols. 1968. mic. film 295.00 (*0-318-57449-7*) W S Hein.

New York University Journal of International Law & Politics, 1968-1994/95, 29 vols., Set. 1995. 1315.00 (*0-8377-9120-0*, Rothman) W S Hein.

New York University Law Review, 1924-1996, 72 vols., Set. 1924. 3900.00 (*0-8377-9123-5*, Rothman) W S Hein.

New York University Medical Center Family Guide to Staying Healthy in a Risky Environment. Ed. by Arthur C. Upton & Eden Graber. LC 93-2634. (Illus.). 960p. 1993. 32.50 (*0-671-76815-8*) S&S Trade.

New York University Review of Law & Social Change, 1971-1994/95, 22 vols., Set. 1971. 932.50 (*0-8377-9124-3*, Rothman) W S Hein.

New York University's Stern School of Business: A Centennial Retrospective. Abraham L. Gitlow. LC 94-49200. 307p. (C). 1995. text 42.50 (*0-8147-3077-9*) NYU Pr.

New York Vehicle & Traffic Law. James M. Rose. LC 92-70344. 1984. 120.00 (*0-318-01917-5*) West Group.

New York Vehicle & Traffic Law. James M. Rose. LC 84-80365. 1993. suppl. ed. 45.00 (*0-317-03245-3*) West Group.

New York Vehicle & Traffic Law. annuals rev. ed. Gould Editorial Staff. 720p. (C). pap. 9.95 (*0-87526-373-9*) Gould.

New York Vehicle & Traffic Law: Annual Edition. annuals Gould Editorial Staff. 6.00 (*0-87526-288-0*) Gould.

New York Vehicle & Traffic Law Flip Code. Ed. by Gould Editorial Staff. 32p. 1988. student ed. 8.95 (*0-87526-333-X*) Gould.

New York Venture Capital Directory. Mervin Evans. 250p. 1995. 49.99 incl. 3.5 hd (*0-914396-40-4*) Comm People Pr.

New York Vertical. Photos by Horst Hamann. (Illus.). 168p. 1998. 98.00 (*3-8238-2119-9*); 29.95 (*3-8238-0370-0*) te Neues.

*__New York Vertical.__ Horst Hamann. (Illus.). 168p. 2000. 19.95 (*3-8238-5473-9*) te Neues.

New York Village Law. annuals Gould Editorial Staff. 250p. ring bd. 15.95 (*0-87526-308-9*) Gould.

*__New York Virgin Guide.__ Virgin City Guides Staff. (Illus.). 176p. 1999. pap. 16.95 (*0-7627-0563-9*) Globe Pequot.

New York Vision: Interpretations of New York City in the American Novel. Robert A. Gates. LC 87-5054. 170p. (C). 1987. pap. text 19.50 (*0-8191-6270-1*); lib. bdg. 42.00 (*0-8191-6269-8*) U Pr of Amer.

New York Walk Book. 5th ed. 1984. 12.95 (*0-385-15583-2*) Doubleday.

New York Walk Book. 6th ed. New York-New Jersey Trail Conference Staff. LC 97-35069. 1998. 19.95 (*1-880775-11-5*) NY-NJ Trail Confer.

New York Waterfront. Kevin Bone. LC 96-53253. 280p. 1997. pap. 35.00 (*1-885254-54-7*, Pub. by Monacelli Pr) Penguin Putnam.

New York Wedding Planner. Tiger Oak Editors. (Regional Wedding Planners Ser.). (Illus.). 124p. 2000. pap. 14.95 (*1-928728-03-0*, Pub. by Tiger Oak) Natl Bk Netwk.

*__New York Weekly Museum: An Annotated Index of the Literary Prose, 1800-1811.__ Edward William Pitcher. LC 99-55511. (Studies in British & American Magazines : Vol. 4). (Illus.). 496p. 2000. text 109.95 (*0-7734-7840-X*) E Mellen.

New York West Federal Census Index 1860 West (Excludes Erie County) Ed. by Ronald Vern Jackson. LC 99-198171. (Illus.). 1988. lib. bdg. 375.00 (*0-89593-441-8*, Accel Indexing) Genealogical Srvcs.

New York Wildlife Viewing Guide. Frank Knight. LC 97-44030. (Illus.). 96p. 1998. pap. 8.95 (*1-56044-513-0*) Falcon Pub Inc.

New York Wills. Lawrence P. Keller. LC 87-82545. 1992. suppl. ed. 52.50 (*0-317-03320-4*) West Group.

New York Wills. 2nd ed. Lawrence P. Keller. LC 93-80273. 1987. 200.00 (*0-318-33010-5*) West Group.

New York Wills & Trust, 2 vols. 3rd ed. Fingar et al. 1328p. Date not set. text 277.50 (*0-07-172147-9*, 68919, MICHIE) LEXIS Pub.

New York Wills & Trust: 1999 Cumulative Supplement with Disk, 2 vols. 3rd ed. William P. LaPiana et al. 300p. 1999. 37.00 incl. disk (*0-327-01277-3*, 6892713); ring bd. 74.00 (*0-327-01154-8*, 6892312) LEXIS Pub.

New York Workers' Compensation Law Handbook. annuals Ed. by Gould Staff. 770p. (C). ring bd. 39.95 (*0-87526-380-1*) Gould.

New York Workers' Compensation Law Reporter, Vol. 1. Ed. by LRP Publications Staff. 1987. text 605.00 (*0-934753-22-9*) LRP Pubns.

New York World's Fair, 1939-1940 in 155 Photographs. Richard Wurts. LC 77-70029. (Illus.). 170p. 1978. pap. 9.95 (*0-486-23494-0*) Dover.

New York Yacht Club, 1844-1994. Melissa Harrington. Ed. by Ceila D. Robbins. (Illus.). 176p. 1994. write for info. (*0-944641-07-5*) Greenwich Pub Group.

New York Yankee Encyclopedia: The Complete Record of Yankee Baseball. Harvey Frommer. LC 97-7455. (Illus.). 432p. 1997. 39.95 (*0-02-861511-5*) Macmillan.

New York Yankee Openers: An Opening Day History of Baseball's Most Famous Team. Lyle Spatz. LC 97-16785. (Illus.). 494p. 1997. pap. 32.50 (*0-7864-0368-3*) McFarland & Co.

New York Yankees. Jay David, pseud. LC 97-1326. 1997. pap. 9.95 (*0-688-15505-7*, Wm Morrow) Morrow Avon.

New York Yankees. Paul Joseph. LC 96-23089. (America's Game Ser.). (Illus.). 32p. (J). (gr. 3-8). 1997. lib. bdg. 16.48 (*1-56239-673-0*) ABDO Pub Co.

New York Yankees: Informal History. Frank Graham. 1976. 25.95 (*0-8488-1592-0*) Amereon Ltd.

New York Yankees Baseball Team. David Pietrusza. LC 97-19611. (Great Sports Teams Ser.). (Illus.). 48p. (J). (gr. 4-10). 1998. lib. bdg. 18.95 (*0-7660-1018-X*) Enslow Pubs.

New York Yankees Collectibles: An Exhaustive Guide to Memorabilia from America's Favorite Team. Beckett Publications Editors. LC 99-236284. 1999. pap. text 24.95 (*1-887432-65-5*) Beckett Pubns.

New York Yankees: Seasons of Glory: A Salute to the 50 Greatest Seasons by Individual Yankee Players. William Hageman & Warren Wilbert. LC 99-10732. 360p. 1998. 29.95 (*0-8246-0416-4*) Jonathan David.

New York Yanquis. Bill Granger. LC 94-39262. 288p. 1995. 21.45 (*1-55970-289-3*, Pub. by Arcade Pub Inc) Time Warner.

*__New York Years: Stories.__ Felice Picano. LC 99-89539. 232p. 2000. pap. 12.95 (*1-55583-522-8*, Pub. by Alyson Pubns) Consort Bk Sales.

New York Zoning Law & Practice, 2 vols. 3rd ed. Robert M. Anderson. LC 84-81189. 1984. 220.00 (*0-318-03855-2*) West Group.

New York Zoning Law & Practice, 2 vols. 3rd ed. Robert M. Anderson. LC 84-81189. 1993. suppl. ed. 60.00 (*0-317-03252-6*) West Group.

*__New Yorker: Book of Political Cartoons.__ Robert Mankoff. (Illus.). 128p. 2000. 21.95 (*1-57660-080-7*) Bloomberg NJ.

New Yorker Book of All-New Cat Cartoons. New Yorker Editors. (Illus.). 112p. 1997. 20.00 (*0-375-40108-3*) Knopf.

New Yorker Book of Business Cartoons from the New Yorker. Ed. by Robert Mankoff. (Illus.). pap. 12.00 (*1-57660-042-4*, Pub. by Bloomberg NJ) Norton.

New Yorker Book of Business Cartoons from the New Yorker. Ed. by Robert Mankoff. LC 98-33461. (Illus.). 128p. 1998. 21.95 (*1-57660-056-4*, Pub. by Bloomberg NJ) Norton.

New Yorker Book of Cat Cartoons. New Yorker Magazine Editors. (Illus.). 1990. 20.00 (*0-394-58795-2*) Knopf.

New Yorker Book of Cat Cartoons. New Yorker Magazine Editors. LC 90-53070. (Illus.). 112p. 1992. pap. 10.00 (*0-679-74276-X*) Knopf.

New Yorker Book of Doctor Cartoons: Mini-Edition. New Yorker Magazine Editors. (Illus.). 96p. 1996. pap. 10.00 (*0-679-76573-5*) Knopf.

New Yorker Book of Doctor Cartoons & Psychiatrist Cartoons. New Yorker Magazine Editors. (Illus.). 96p. 1993. 22.00 (*0-679-43069-5*) Knopf.

New Yorker Book of Dog Cartoons. New Yorker Magazine Editors. LC 95-21555. (Illus.). 112p. 1995. pap. 10.00 (*0-679-76542-5*) Knopf.

New Yorker Book of Dog Cartoons. New Yorker Staff & Carolyn B. Mitchell. LC 92-70913. (Illus.). 1992. 20.00 (*0-679-41680-3*) Knopf.

New Yorker Book of Lawyer Cartoons. New Yorker Magazine Editors. (Illus.). 96p. 1993. 22.00 (*0-679-43068-7*) Knopf.

New Yorker Book of Lawyer Cartoons: Mini-Edition. New Yorker Magazine Editors. (Illus.). 96p. 1996. pap. 10.00 (*0-679-76574-3*) Knopf.

*__New Yorker Book of Literary Cartoons.__ Ed. by Bob Mankoff. 112p. 2000. 19.95 (*0-671-03557-6*) PB.

New Yorker Book of Literary Cartoons. Ed. by New Yorker Staff. 1999. pap. write for info. (*0-671-03558-4*) S&S Trade.

*__New Yorker Book of Money Cartoons.__ Ed. by Robert Mankoff. LC 99-36941. (Illus.). 128p. 1999. text 21.95 (*1-57660-033-5*, Pub. by Bloomberg NJ) Norton.

*__New Yorker Book of Technology Cartoons.__ Robert Mankoff. LC 00-30390. (Illus.). 2000. 24.95 (*1-57660-075-0*, Pub. by Bloomberg NJ) Norton.

New Yorker Book of True Love Cartoons. New Yorker Staff. LC NC1428.N47 1999. 112p. 1999. 20.00 (*0-375-40313-2*) Random.

New Yorker Book of War Pieces. New Yorker Magazine Editors. LC 75-167394. (Essay Index Reprint Ser.). 1977. reprint ed. 31.95 (*0-8369-2470-3*) Ayer.

New Yorker Desk Diary, 1996. New Yorker Magazine Editors. 1995. 25.95 (*0-00-221154-8*); 28.95 (*0-00-221155-6*) Harper SF.

New Yorker Desk Diary 2000. (Illus.). 205p. 1999. 27.95 (*1-57499-112-4*) Per Annum.

*__New Yorker Desk Diary 2001.__ 205p. 2000. 27.95 (*1-57499-096-9*) Per Annum.

*__New Yorker Profiles, 1925-1992.__ Gail Shivel. 210p. 2000. 47.50 (*0-7618-1714-X*) U Pr of Amer.

*__New Yorker 75th Anniversary Cartoon Collection.__ rev. ed. Ed. & Frwd. by Bob Mankoff. (Illus.). 304p. 1999. 40.00 (*0-671-03555-X*, PB Hardcover) PB.

New Yorker Unlimited: The Memoirs of Edward Larocque Tinker. Edward L. Tinker. (Illus.). 1970. 17.50 (*0-87959-066-1*) U of Tex H Ransom Ctr.

New Yorkers. Ed. by Tricia Hedge. (Illus.). 48p. 1991. pap. text 5.95 (*0-19-422679-4*) OUP.

New Yorker's 75th Anniversary Cartoon Collection. Ed. by New Yorker Magazine Editors. 1999. pap. write for info. (*0-671-03556-8*) S&S Trade.

New York/New Jersey/Pennsylvania Green Guide: North America. Michelin Staff. 1998. per. 20.00 (*2-06-154901-2*, 1549) Michelin.

New York's Architectural Holdouts. unabridged ed. Andrew Alpern & Seymour Durst. LC 96-45227. (Illus.). 172p. 1997. reprint ed. pap. text 12.95 (*0-486-29425-0*) Dover.

New York's Detailed Census of 1855 Greene County, Extracted & Systematized. Fred Q. Bowman. Ed. by Arthur C. Kelly. LC F127.G7B69 1986. 277p. 1988. lib. bdg. 21.95 (*1-56012-090-8*, 90) Kinship Rhinebeck.

New York's Fabulous Luxury Apartments: With Original Floor Plans from the Dakota, River House, Olympic Tower & Other Great Buildings. Andrew Alpern. (Illus.). 176p. 1987. reprint ed. pap. 10.95 (*0-486-25318-X*) Dover.

New York's 50 Best Art in Public Places. David Masello. LC 99-35693. (Illus.). 128p. 1999. pap. 12.00 (*1-885492-80-4*) City & Co.

N

New York's 50 Best Bookstores for Book Lovers. Eve Claxton. LC 99-52459. (Illus.). 128p. 2000. pap. 12.00 (*1-885492-84-7*) City & Co.

***New York's 50 Best Fun-Filled Family Getaways.** Heidi Arthur & Jane Pollock. (Illus.). 128p. 2000. pap. 12.00 (*1-885492-92-8*) City & Co.

***New York's 50 Best Museums for Cool Parents & Their Kids.** Alfred Gingold & Helen Rogan. LC 99-52058. (Illus.). 128p. 1999. pap. 14.00 (*1-885492-83-9*) City & Co.

New York's 50 Best Places to Discover & Enjoy in Central Park. Karen Putnam & Marianne Cramer. LC 99-20604. 144p. 1998. pap. 12.00 (*1-885492-64-2*) City & Co.

New York's 50 Best Places to Eat Southern. Bruce Lane & Scott Wyatt. LC 98-2928. 128p. 1998. pap. 12.00 (*1-885492-57-X*) City & Co.

***New York's 50 Best Places to Find Spiritual Renewal: A Peace & Quiet Book.** Beth Donnelly & Andrea Martin. 128p. 2000. pap. 14.00 (*1-929439-00-8*) City & Co.

New York's 50 Best Places to Find Peace & Quiet. 2nd ed. Allan Ishac. LC 97-43420. 128p. 1998. pap. 12.00 (*1-885492-52-9*) City & Co.

New York's 50 Best Places to Go Birding in & Around the Big Apple. John Thaxton. LC 98-36761. 160p. 1998. pap. 15.00 (*1-885492-66-9*) City & Co.

New York's 50 Best Places to Have a Kid's Party. Katherine Goldman. LC 99-20182. (Illus.). 112p. 1999. pap. 12.00 (*1-885492-78-2*) City & Co.

New York's 50 Best Places to Have Brunch. Ann Volkwein & Jason Nixon. LC 99-35442. (Illus.). 128p. 1999. pap. 12.00 (*1-885492-69-3*) City & Co.

New York's 50 Best Places to Take Children. Allan Ishac. LC 97-10911. 128p. (Orig.). 1997. pap. 12.00 (*1-885492-30-8*) City & Co.

New York's 50 Best Skyscrapers. E. Nash. LC 97-29334. 128p. 1997. pap. text 12.00 (*1-885492-47-2*) City & Co.

New York's Finger Lakes, Pioneer Families Especially Tompkins County: A Genealogical Notebook. Helen F. Lewis. LC 91-196260. 403p. 1991. lib. bdg. 69.95 (*1-56012-111-4*, 105) Kinship Rhinebeck.

New York's Firearms & Weapons Laws: Gun Control in New York. unabridged ed. Lee O. Thomas & Jeffrey Chamberlain. 330p. 2000. ring bd. 31.95 (*1-889031-04-6*) Looseleaf Law.

New York's First Theatrical Center: The Rialto at Union Square. John W. Frick. Ed. by Oscar G. Brockett. LC 84-16255. (Theater & Dramatic Studies: No. 26). 221p. reprint ed. 68.60 (*0-8357-1612-0*, 207054600001) Bks Demand.

New York's Forts in the Revolution. Robert B. Roberts. LC 77-74395. 500p. 1979. 38.50 (*0-8386-2063-9*) Fairleigh Dickinson.

New York's Great Industries. Ed. by Richard Edwards. LC 73-2504. (Big Business; Economic Power in a Free Society Ser.). 1980. reprint ed. 34.95 (*0-405-05086-0*) Ayer.

New York's Health Care System: Making the Transition to Managed Care & Competition. Ed. by Martin A. Strosberg. LC 97-77569. (Dialogues on Public Policy Ser.). 1997. pap. 25.95 (*0-9658339-3-3*) Educ Intl Pr.

New York's Jewish Jews: The Orthodox Community in the Interwar Years. Jenna W. Joselit. LC 89-45197. (Modern Jewish Experience Ser.). (Illus.). 208p. 1990. 29.95 (*0-253-33151-X*) Ind U Pr.

New York's (Most Devasting!) Disasters & (Most Calamitous!) Catastrophies! Carole Marsh. (Carole Marsh New York Bks.). (Illus.). (J). 1994. pap. 19.95 (*0-7933-0813-5*); lib. bdg. 29.95 (*0-7933-0814-3*); disk 29.95 (*0-7933-0815-1*) Gallopade Intl.

New York's New & Avant-Garde Art Galleries. Barbara Stone. (Illus.). 128p. 1999. pap. 14.00 (*1-885492-82-0*) City & Co.

New York's 100 Best Little Places to Shop. Eve Clayton. LC 98-35314. (Illus.). 160p. (Orig.). 1998. pap. 14.00 (*1-885492-70-7*) City & Co.

New York's 100 Best Party Places. Hilarie Sheets. LC 99-52394. (Illus.). 128p. 2000. pap. 14.00 (*1-885492-85-5*) City & Co.

New York's Part in History. Sherman Williams. 390p. 1993. reprint ed. lib. bdg. 89.00 (*0-7812-5206-7*) Rprt Serv.

New York's Role As a Center for Health Care: An Analysis of Nonresident Patients Served by New York City Hospitals. Steven Finkler et al. (Papers: No. 4). 40p. 1986. 5.00 (*0-934459-29-0*) United Hosp Fund.

***New York's 75 Best Hot Nightspots.** Angela Tribelli. (Illus.). 128p. 1999. pap. 12.00 (*1-885492-86-3*) City & Co.

New York's 60 Best Wonderful Little Hotels. Allen Sperry. LC 99-38166. Orig. Title: New York's 50 Best Wonderful Little Hotels. (Illus.). 160p. 1999. pap. 15.00 (*1-885492-81-2*) City & Co.

New York's Strongest. Peter Lauria. 181p. 1992. pap. 3.50 (*0-9635713-0-3*) Longshot Prod.

New York's Unsolved Mysteries (& Their "Solutions") Includes Scientific Information & Other Activities for Students. Carole Marsh. (Carole Marsh New York Bks.). (Illus.). (J). (gr. 3-12). 1994. pap. 19.95 (*0-7933-5819-1*); lib. bdg. 29.95 (*0-7933-5818-3*); disk 29.95 (*0-7933-5820-5*) Gallopade Intl.

New York's 50 Best Wonderful Little Hotels see New York's 60 Best Wonderful Little Hotels

New You. Kathleen Leverich. LC 97-32322. 128p. (YA). (gr. 5-9). 1998. 15.00 (*0-688-16076-X*, Grenwillow Bks) HarpC Child Bks.

***New You.** Kathleen Leverich. (Illus.). 112p. (J). (gr. 4-7). 2000. pap. 4.50 (*0-439-10801-2*) Scholastic Inc.

***New Young American Poets: An Anthology.** Ed. by Kevin Prufer. LC 99-37043. 264p. 2000. pap. 16.95 (*0-8093-2309-5*) S Ill U Pr.

New Young Messiah. 120p. 1994. per. 16.95 (*0-7935-3980-3*, 00310006) H Leonard.

New Young Oxford Book of Ghost Stories. Ed. by Dennis Pepper. (Illus.). 224p. (YA). (gr. 8 up). 1999. 22.95 (*0-19-278154-5*) OUP.

***New Young Oxford Book of Ghost Stories, 2 vols., Vol. 2.** Ed. by Dennis Pepper. (Illus.). 224p. (YA). 2000. pap. 12.95 (*0-19-278178-2*) OUP.

New Younger Irish Poets. Gerald Dawe. 176p. 1991. pap. 14.95 (*0-85640-460-8*) Dufour.

New Youth Challenge: A Model for Working with Older Children in School-Age Child Care. Steve Musson & Maurice Gibbons. LC 88-62241. (Illus.). 107p. (Orig.). (C). 1988. pap. text, teacher ed. 12.95 (*0-917505-02-6*) School Age.

New Youth Pastor's Handbook: Guidelines for the 1990's & Beyond. rev. ed. E. S. Caldwell. Ed. by Alan H. Peterson. 200p. 1992. pap. text 34.95 (*1-877858-08-0*, TNYPH2) Amer Focus Pub.

New Zealand see Festivals of the World

New Zealand see Cultures of the World - Group 16

New Zealand. (Landmark Visitors Guide Ser.). (Illus.). 320p. 1999. pap. 18.95 (*1-901522-36-9*) Hunter NJ.

***New Zealand.** Allan Edie. (AAA Essential Guides Ser.). (Illus.). 2000. pap. 8.95 (*0-658-01148-0*, Passprt Bks) NTC Contemp Pub Co.

New Zealand. Griffin Trade Paperbacks Staff. 416p. 1999. pap. 18.99 (*0-312-24478-9*, St Martins Paperbacks) St Martin.

New Zealand. Ray Grover. (World Bibliographical Ser.: No. 18). 254p. 1981. lib. bdg. 50.00 (*0-903450-31-3*) ABC-CLIO.

New Zealand. Insight Guides Staff. (Insight Guides). 1998. pap. text 12.95 (*0-88729-922-9*) Langenscheidt.

New Zealand. Patrick J. Kennedy. LC 81-8086. (World Education Ser.). (Illus.). 96p. (Orig.). 1981. pap. text 12.00 (*0-910054-61-4*) Am Assn Coll Registrars.

***New Zealand.** Christina J. Moose. LC 00-29071. (Dropping in on Ser.). (Illus.). 2000. write for info. (*1-55916-283-X*) Rourke Bk Co.

New Zealand. NTC Publishing Group Staff. (Passport Essential Guide Ser.). (Illus.). 128p. 1998. pap. 8.95 (*0-8442-0129-4*, 01294, Passprt Bks) NTC Contemp Pub Co.

New Zealand. Compiled by Brad Patterson & Kathryn Patterson. (World Bibliographic Ser.: Vol. 18). 416p. 1998. lib. bdg. 98.00 (*1-85109-279-X*) ABC-CLIO.

New Zealand. Ravenstein Verlag Staff. 1993. 11.95 (*3-87660-862-7*) Ravenstein Vrlg.

New Zealand. Pat Ryan. LC 98-11692. (Illus.). 32p. (J). 1999. lib. bdg. 22.79 (*1-56766-577-2*) Childs World.

New Zealand. Contrib. by Fay Smith. 304p. 1999. pap. 16.95 (*1-86315-114-1*) Pelican.

New Zealand. Survival Books Staff. (Living & Working Guides). 448p. 1998. pap. 21.95 (*1-901130-05-3*, Pub. by Survival Books) Seven Hills Bk.

***New Zealand.** Ed. by Thomas Cook Publishing Staff. (Must-See Guides Ser.). (Illus.). 2000. pap. 14.95 (*1-84157-045-1*) Thomas Cook Pub.

New Zealand. Ngaio Marsh. 1976. reprint ed. lib. bdg. 24.95 (*0-88411-489-9*) Amereon Ltd.

New Zealand see Enchantment of the World Series

***New Zealand.** rev. ed. Let's Go Staff. (Let's Go 2001 Ser.). (Illus.). 416p. 2000. pap. 18.99 (*0-312-24685-4*, St Martin Griffin) St Martin.

New Zealand. 2nd ed. Elizabeth Booz. LC 90-63333. (Asian Guides Ser.). (Illus.). 232p. 1993. reprint ed. pap. 12.95 (*0-8442-9724-0*, Passprt Bks) NTC Contemp Pub Co.

New Zealand. 3rd ed. Elisabeth B. Booz. LC 98-32374. (Odyssey Passport Ser.). (Illus.). 301p. 1999. pap. 19.95 (*962-217-533-3*) Norton.

New Zealand. 3rd rev. ed. Nick Hanna. (Passport's Illustrated Travel Guides). (Illus.). 192p. 1999. pap. 14.95 (*0-8442-1179-6*, 11796, Passprt Bks) NTC Contemp Pub Co.

New Zealand. 3rd rev. ed. Nelles Verlag Staff. (Nelles Guides Ser.). (Illus.). 256p. 1999. pap. 15.95 (*3-88618-905-8*) Hunter NJ.

***New Zealand.** 6th ed. Fodors Travel Publications, Inc. Staff. 2000. pap. 16.00 (*0-679-00666-4*, Pub. by Fodors Travel) Random House.

New Zealand. 6th ed. Insight Guides Staff. (Insight Guides). 1998. pap. text 22.95 (*0-88729-481-2*) Langenscheidt.

New Zealand. 9th ed. Nancy Keller et al. (Lonely Planet Travel Guides Ser.). (Illus.). 689p. 1998. pap. 19.95 (*0-86442-565-1*) Lonely Planet.

New Zealand, 32. Harold G. Miller. LC 82-24157. (British Empire History Ser.). 155p. 1983. reprint ed. lib. bdg. 55.00 (*0-313-22997-X*, MINZ, Greenwood Pr) Greenwood.

New Zealand: A Complete Guide. Passport Books Staff. 1991. pap. 12.95 (*0-8442-9722-4*, Passprt Bks) NTC Contemp Pub Co.

***New Zealand: A Country Study Guide.** Global Investment & Business Center, Inc. Staff. (World Country Study Guides Library: Vol. 124). (Illus.). 350p. 2000. pap. 59.00 (*0-7397-2422-3*) Intl Business Pubns.

***New Zealand: Aotearoa.** Peter Hooper. (Illus.). 146p. 2000. 49.95 (*0-908598-50-5*, Pub. by New Holland) BHB Intl.

New Zealand: Chapters by W. T. G. Airey (And Others) W. T. Airey et al. LC 81-23727. (United Nations Ser.). (Illus.). 329p. 1982. reprint ed. lib. bdg. 69.50 (*0-313-23410-8*, BENZ, Greenwood Pr) Greenwood.

New Zealand: Land of the Long White Cloud. Valerie Keyworth. LC 89-11716. (Discovering Our Heritage Ser.). (Illus.). 128p. (YA). (gr. 5 up). 1990. lib. bdg. 14.95 (*0-87518-414-6*, Dillon Silver Burdett) Silver Burdett Pr.

New Zealand: Land of the Long White Cloud. 2nd ed. Valerie Keyworth. LC 97-19365. (Discovering Our Heritage Ser.). (J). 1998. 23.00 (*0-382-39815-7*, Dillon Silver Burdett) Silver Burdett Pr.

***New Zealand: Mountains to the Sea.** Warren Jacobs. (Illus.). 173p. 2000. 49.95 (*0-908598-59-9*, Pub. by New Holland) BHB Intl.

New Zealand: Nelle's Guide. rev. ed. Compiled by Nelles Verlag. (Nelles Guides Ser.). (GER., Illus.). 256p. 1995. pap. 14.95 (*3-88618-044-1*, Pub. by JARR UK) Seven Hills Bk.

New Zealand: Picturesque Land. 3rd ed. Elizabeth Booz. (Illus.). 232p. 1996. pap. 15.95 (*0-8442-9886-7*, Passprt Bks) NTC Contemp Pub Co.

New Zealand: The Rough Guide. Laura Harper et al. LC 98-165657. (Illus.). 704p. 1998. pap. 19.95 (*1-85828-233-0*) Viking Penguin.

***New Zealand: The Rough Guide.** 2nd ed. Rough Guides Staff. 2000. pap. 19.95 (*1-85828-555-0*, Rough Guides) Viking Penguin.

New Zealand - A Country Study Guide: Basic Information for Research & Pleasure. Global Investment Center, USA Staff. (World Country Study Guide Library: Vol. 124). (Illus.). 350p. 1999. pap. 59.00 (*0-7397-1521-6*) Intl Business Pubns.

New Zealand - North Island. (Illus.). 350p. 1996. pap. 10.95 (*1-86958-179-2*) Hunter NJ.

New Zealand Administrative Reports. John Cottle & Judith Fairley. ring bd. 351.00 (*0-614-05552-0*, NZ, MICHIE) LEXIS Pub.

New Zealand Adopts Proportional Representation: Accident? Design? Evolution? Keith Jackson & Alan McRobie. LC 98-24974. 382p. 1998. text 68.95 (*1-84014-472-6*, JF1075.N45J33, Pub. by Ashgate Pub) Ashgate Pub Co.

New Zealand & Japan, 1945-1952: The Occupation & the Peace Treaty. Ann Trotter. LC 90-656. 240p. (C). 1990. text 49.95 (*0-485-11398-8*, Pub. by Athlone Pr) Humanities.

New Zealand & the Korean War: Combat Operations, Vol. II. Ian McGibbon. (Illus.). 592p. 1997. 85.00 (*0-19-558343-4*) OUP.

New Zealand & the Pacific. Roderic Alley. (Replica Edition Ser.). (Illus.). 300p. (C). 1983. pap. text 1.75 (*0-86531-929-4*, Pub. by Westview) HarpC.

New Zealand at Cost. Fay Smith. (At Cost Travel Guide Ser.). (Illus.). 352p. 1996. pap. 16.95 (*1-86315-054-4*) Pelican.

New Zealand at the Polls: The General Election of 1978. Ed. by Howard R. Penniman. LC 80-16464. (AEI Studies: No. 273). (Illus.). 312p. reprint ed. pap. 96.80 (*0-8357-4514-7*, 203737200008) Bks Demand.

New Zealand Banking Law. Alan Tyree. 1987. pap. 108.00 (*0-409-70223-4*, NZ, MICHIE) LEXIS Pub.

***New Zealand Bed & Breakfast Book.** 10th ed. J. J. Thomas. (Illus.). 768p. 1999. pap. 17.95 (*1-56554-648-2*) Pelican.

***New Zealand Bed & Breakfast Book.** 11th ed. J. & J. Thomas Staff. (Illus.). 784p. 2000. pap. text 18.95 (*1-56554-743-8*) Pelican.

New Zealand Beeches. John Wardle. 1984. 25.00 (*0-477-05753-5*, Pub. by Manaaki Whenua) Balogh.

New Zealand Blouse. Martha C. Pullen. LC 99-70132. (Illus.). 72p. 1999. 19.95 (*1-878048-20-1*) M Pullen.

***New Zealand Books in Print: 2000.** 28th ed. Bowker Staff. 2000. 60.00 (*1-86452-036-1*) D W Thorpe.

***New Zealand Books in Print, 1999.** 27th ed. 800p. 1999. 60.00 (*1-86452-028-0*) D W Thorpe.

***New Zealand Business Intelligence Report, 190 vols.** Global Investment & Business Center, Inc. Staff. (World Business Intelligence Library: Vol. 124). (Illus.). 350p. 2000. pap. 99.95 (*0-7397-2622-6*) Intl Business Pubns.

***New Zealand Business Law Handbook, 190 vols.** Global Investment & Business Center, Inc. Staff. (Global Business Law Handbooks Library: Vol. 124). (Illus.). 350p. 2000. pap. 99.95 (*0-7397-2022-8*) Intl Business Pubns.

***New Zealand Business Opportunity Yearbook.** Global Investment & Business Center, Inc. Staff. (Global Business Opportunity Yearbooks Library: Vol. 124). (Illus.). 2000. pap. 99.95 (*0-7397-2222-0*) Intl Business Pubns.

***New Zealand Business Opportunity Yearbook: Export-Import, Investment & Business Opportunities.** International Business Publications, U. S. A. Staff & Global Investment Center, U. S. A. Staff. (Global Business Opportunity Yearbooks Library: Vol. 124). (Illus.). 350p. 1999. pap. 99.95 (*0-7397-1322-1*) Intl Business Pubns.

New Zealand by Bike. 2nd ed. Bruce Ringer. (Illus.). 240p. 1994. pap. 16.95 (*0-89886-409-7*) Mountaineers.

***New Zealand by Motorcycle.** Gregory W. Frazier. (Illus.). 150p. 2000. pap. 24.95 (*0-935151-22-2*) Arrowstar Pub.

New Zealand by Motorhome. David Shore & Patty Campbell. (Illus.). 208p. 1989. pap. 13.95 (*0-938297-04-X*) Shore Campbell.

New Zealand Company Law Casebook. Catherine Watson. 189p. 1984. pap. 36.00 (*0-409-70177-7*, NZ, MICHIE) LEXIS Pub.

New Zealand Conservation Estate & International Visitors New Zealand Tourism Board Staff. LC 94-179551. vi, 44 p. 1993. pap. write for info. (*0-478-02150-X*, Pub. by Manaaki Whenua) Balogh.

New Zealand Conveyancing & Property Reports, Vol. 1. P. G. Haig. 575p. boxed set 81.00 (*0-409-70141-6*, NZ, MICHIE) LEXIS Pub.

New Zealand Conveyancing & Property Reports, Vol. 2. P. G. Haig. 651p. boxed set 221.00 (*0-409-70154-8*, NZ, MICHIE) LEXIS Pub.

***New Zealand Country Review 2000.** Robert C. Kelly et al. (Illus.). 60p. 1999. pap. 39.95 (*1-58310-548-4*) CountryWatch.

New Zealand Curriculum Framework. Ed. by Ministry of Education of New Zealand Staff. 28p. (Orig.). (C). 1994. pap. text 14.95 (*1-878450-96-4*, 511, Pub. by Lrning Media) R Owen Pubs.

New Zealand Domestic Travel Study, 1986-1987, 18 vols. LC 88-178052. (Domestic Research Ser.). 1987. write for info. (*0-478-02042-2*, Pub. by Manaaki Whenua) Balogh.

New Zealand, 1898-99 Great Barrier Island Pigeon Post Stamps. J. Reg Walker et al. (Illus.). 110p. 1969. pap. 12.50 (*0-912574-22-4*) Collectors.

***New Zealand English.** Ed. by Allan Bell & Koenraad Kuiper. LC 99-42693. (Varieties of English Around the World General Ser.: Vol. 25). 368p. 2000. 75.00 (*1-55619-723-3*) J Benjamins Pubng Co.

New Zealand English Grammar - Fact or Fiction? A Corpus-Based Study in Morphosyntactic Variation. Marianne Hundt. LC 98-23346. (Varieties of English Around the World General Ser.: No. 23). xvi, 212p. 1998. 59.00 (*1-55619-721-7*) J Benjamins Pubng Co.

New Zealand European Connection. Martin O'Connor. 172p. (C). 1988. 65.00 (*1-86934-018-3*, Pub. by Grantham Hse) St Mut.

New Zealand Experiment. 2nd ed. Jane Kelsey. LC 97-198500. 416p. 1997. pap. 29.95 (*1-86940-179-4*, Pub. by Auckland Univ) Paul & Co Pubs.

New Zealand Family Law Reports. Christine O'Brien & N. Karunaharan. ring bd. write for info. (*0-409-79037-0*, NZ, MICHIE) LEXIS Pub.

New Zealand Film, 1912-1995. Helen Martin & Sam Edwards. (Illus.). 222p. 1998. pap. 29.95 (*0-19-558336-1*) OUP.

New Zealand Foreign Affairs Handbook. 2nd ed. Steve Hoadley. (Illus.). 192p. (C). 1993. pap. text 29.95 (*0-19-558248-9*) OUP.

***New Zealand Foreign Policy & Government Guide.** Contrib. by Global Investment & Business Center, Inc. Staff. (World Foreign Policy & Government Library: Vol. 119). (Illus.). 350p. 1999. pap. 99.00 (*0-7397-3617-5*) Intl Business Pubns.

***New Zealand Foreign Policy & Government Guide.** Global Investment & Business Center, Inc. Staff. (World Foreign Policy & Government Library: Vol. 119). (Illus.). 350p. 2000. 99.95 (*0-7397-3822-4*) Intl Business Pubns.

New Zealand Forms & Precedents, 5 vols., Set. Justice Barker. ring bd. write for info. (*0-409-70208-0*, NZ, MICHIE) LEXIS Pub.

New Zealand Framework for Cultural Statistics, 1995. New Zealand Dept. of Scientific & Industrial Research. LC 96-131419.Tr. of Te Anga Tatauranga Tikanga-ea-iwi O Aotearoa, 1995.. vi, 115p. 1995. write for info. (*0-478-04422-4*) Manaaki Whenua.

New Zealand Fungi: An Illustrated Guide. Greta Stevenson. (Illus.). 128p. 1994. pap. 19.95 (*0-908812-29-9*, Pub. by Canterbury Univ) Accents Pubns.

***New Zealand Government & Business Contacts Handbook: Strategic Government & Business contacts for Conducting Successful Business, Export-Import & Investment Activity.** International Business Publications, USA Staff & Global Investment Center, USA Staff. (World Export-Import & Business Library: 107). (Illus.). 250p. 2000. pap. 99.95 (*0-7397-6096-3*) Intl Business Pubns.

New Zealand Guide to Miniature Roses. Margaret Hayward. 144p. (C). 1988. 75.00 (*1-86934-014-0*, Pub. by Grantham Hse) St Mut.

New Zealand Health Policy: A Comparative Study. Robert H. Blank. (Readings in New Zealand Politics Ser.). (Illus.). 160p. 1994. pap. text 39.95 (*0-19-558319-1*) OUP.

***New Zealand Immigration Guide.** Adam Starchild. 1999. pap. text 14.95 (*1-893626-03-2*) Breakout Prods Inc.

New Zealand in Pictures. Lerner Publications, Department of Geography Staff. (Visual Geography Ser.). (Illus.). 64p. (YA). (gr. 5 up). 1990. lib. bdg. 19.95 (*0-8225-1862-7*, Lerner Publctns) Lerner Pub.

New Zealand Inheritance. large type ed. Essie Summers. (Romance Ser.). 384p. 1993. 11.50 (*0-7089-2921-4*) Ulverscroft.

New Zealand Intellectual Property. Andrew Brown. 744p. 1989. boxed set 192.00 (*0-409-78736-1*, NZ, MICHIE) LEXIS Pub.

New Zealand International Visitor Arrival Forecasts, 1989 to 1993. LC 89-143674. (NZTP Economic Research Ser.). 138p. 1988. write for info. (*0-478-02088-0*, Pub. by Manaaki Whenua) Balogh.

New Zealand International Visitor Arrival Forecasts, 1991 to 1995, 2000 (December Year) Final Report Joanna Savage. LC 92-214198. (NZTP Economic Research Ser.). 138p. 1991. pap. write for info. (*0-478-02136-4*, Pub. by Manaaki Whenua) Balogh.

New Zealand International Visitors Product Survey, April 1985-March 1986: Regional Report. LC 88-135157. (International Visitors Research Ser.). vi, 213 p. 1987. write for info. (*0-477-02468-8*, Pub. by Horticult & Food Res) St Mut.

New Zealand International Visitors Survey, 1986-87: Demographic Report Andrew Barnard. LC 88-209795. (NZTP International Visitors Research Ser.). 171 p. 1988. write for info. (*0-478-02079-1*, Pub. by Manaaki Whenua) Balogh.

***New Zealand Investment & Business Guide.** Global Investment & Business Center, Inc. Staff. (Global Investment & Business Guide Library: Vol. 124). (Illus.). 2000. pap. 99.95 (*0-7397-1822-3*) Intl Business Pubns.

***New Zealand Investment & Business Guide: Export-Import, Investment & Business Opportunities.** International Business Publications, USA Staff & Global Investment Center, USA Staff. (World Investment & Business Guide Library-99: Vol. 124). (Illus.). 350p. 1999. pap. 99.95 (*0-7397-0319-6*) Intl Business Pubns.

N

An Asterisk (*) at the beginning of an entry indicates that the title is appearing for the first time.

New Zealand Jewish Community. Stephen Levine. LC 98-52719. 384p. 1999. 65.00 (*0-7391-0003-3*) Lxngtn Bks.

New Zealand Journal, 1842-1844. Ed. by Robert W. Kenny. 1956. 10.00 (*0-87577-012-6*, Peabody Museum) Peabody Essex Mus.

New Zealand Law Dictionary. 3rd rev. ed. G. W. Hinde. 417p. 1986. pap. 72.00 (*0-409-78762-0*, NZ, MICHIE) LEXIS Pub.

New Zealand Law Dictionary. 4th ed. P. Spiller. 341p. 1995. pap. write for info. (*0-409-78829-5*, MICHIE) LEXIS Pub.

New Zealand Liberals: The Years of Power, 1891-1912. David Hamer. (Illus.). 432p. 1988. 45.00 (*1-86940-014-3*) OUP.

New Zealand Literature Today. Ed. by R. K. Dhawan & Walter Tonett. 192p. (C). 1992. 30.00 (*81-85218-69-2*, Pub. by Prestige) Advent Bks Div.

New Zealand Lizards: An Annotated Bibliography. B. Thomas & T. Whitaker. 1989. 20.00 (*0-477-02550-1*, Pub. by Manaaki Whenua) Balogh.

***New Zealand Love Stories.** 352p. 2000. 45.00 (*0-19-558399-X*) OUP.

New Zealand Macroeconomy: A Briefing on the Reforms. Paul Dalziel. LC 96-225149. (Illus.). 142p. 1996. pap. text 28.00 (*0-19-558330-2*) OUP.

New Zealand Macroeconomy: A Briefing on the Reforms. 3rd ed. Dalziel Paul. LC 99-462631. (Illus.). 150p. 1999. pap. text 24.95 (*0-19-558402-3*) OUP.

New Zealand, 1984-1991: Economic Reforms, 1984-1991. Alan Bollard. LC 92-8467. 52p. 1992. pap. 9.95 (*1-55815-214-8*) ICS Pr.

New Zealand, 1901-1929: The Penny 'Universal' & Penny 'Dominion' Issues. Mark A. Juvisich. (Illus.). ix, 129p. 1995. text 225.00 (*1-887657-00-2*) Edenbridge Grp.

New Zealand Official Yearbook, 1987-88. 92nd ed. 760p. 1987. pap. write for info. (*0-8002-4198-3*) Taylor & Francis.

***New Zealand Pocket Guide.** Berlitz Publishing Staff. (Berlitz Pocket Guide Ser.). (Illus.). 144p. 1999. pap. 8.95 (*2-8315-7224-X*) Berlitz.

New Zealand Pohutukawa. Geoff Conly & Maurice Conly. 88p. (C). 1988. 59.00 (*1-86934-016-7*, Pub. by Grantham Hse) St Mut.

New Zealand Politics in Transition, Vol. 1. Ed. by Raymond Miller. LC 97-223557. (Illus.). 464p. 1997. pap. text 65.00 (*0-19-558339-6*) OUP.

New Zealand Politics Source Book. Ed. by Paul Harris et al. 447p. (Orig.). 1992. pap. 39.95 (*0-86469-173-4*) Intl Spec Bk.

New Zealand Prayer Book -Rev ed. He Karakia Mihinare O Aotearoa. rev. ed. Church of the Province of New Zealand Staff. LC 97-3716. (ENG & MAO.). 992p. 1997. 28.00 (*0-06-060199-X*, Pub. by Harper SF) HarpC.

New Zealand Protected Natural Areas: A Scientific Focus. Ed. by G. C. Kelly & G. N. Park. 1987. 18.70 (*0-477-06794-8*, Pub. by Manaaki Whenua) Balogh.

New Zealand School Publications Branch. UNESCO Staff. (Education Studies & Documents: No. 25). 1974. reprint ed. 25.00 (*0-8115-1349-1*) Periodicals Srv.

New Zealand, 1769-1840: Early Years of Western Contact. Harrison M. Wright. LC 59-12979. (Historical Monographs: No. 42). 235p. 1959. 20.00 (*0-674-62000-3*) HUP.

New Zealand Shake-Up, Vol. 6. Stacy T. Morgan. LC 97-4706. (Ruby Slippers School Ser.). 8p. (J). (gr. 2-5). 1997. pap. 3.99 (*1-55661-605-8*) Bethany Hse.

New Zealand Short Story Collection. Ed. by Marion McLeod & Bill Manhire. LC 98-146593. 1997. pap. 19.95 (*0-7022-3030-8*, Pub. by Univ Queensland Pr) Intl Spec Bk.

New Zealand Soil Classification. A. E. Hewitt. 1993. 35.00 (*0-478-04508-5*, Pub. by Manaaki Whenua) Balogh.

New Zealand Soil Classification. 2nd ed. A. E. Hewitt. LC 98-212778. (Landcare Research Science Ser.: No. 1). 133p. 1998. pap. 35.00 (*0-478-09317-9*) Balogh.

New Zealand Stories. Katherine Mansfield. Ed. by Vincent O'Sullivan. 302p. 1998. text 35.00 (*0-19-558364-7*) OUP.

***New Zealand Tax Guide.** Global Investment & Business Center, Inc. Staff. (World Tax Guide Library: Vol. 7). (Illus.). 350p. 1999. pap. 99.00 (*0-7397-0181-9*) Intl Business Pubns.

***New Zealand 2001.** Thomas Cook Publishing Staff. (Independent Traveller's Guide Ser.). (Illus.). 2000. pap. 19.95 (*0-7627-0769-0*) Globe Pequot.

New Zealand Wars, 2 vols. James Cowan. LC 76-100514. (BCL Ser. II). reprint ed. 64.00 (*0-404-00600-0*) AMS Pr.

New Zealand Ways of Speaking English. Ed. by Allan Bell & Janet Holmes. (Multilingual Matters Ser.: No. 65). 300p. 1990. 99.00 (*1-85359-083-5*, Pub. by Multilingual Matters); pap. 44.95 (*1-85359-082-7*, Pub. by Multilingual Matters) Taylor & Francis.

New Zealand Women Artists: A Survey of 150 Years. Anne Kirker. (Illus.). 256p. 1993. text 46.00 (*976-8097-30-2*) Gordon & Breach.

New Zealand's Alpine Plants Inside & Out. Bill Malcolm & Nancy Malcolm. (Illus.). 136p. 1996. pap. 14.95 (*0-908802-04-8*, Pub. by C Potton Pubng) Timber.

New Zealand's Economic Native Plants. R. C. Cooper & R. C. Cambie. (Illus.). 248p. 1992. text 55.00 (*0-19-558229-2*) OUP.

New Zealand's Remarkable Reforms: Fifth IEA Annual Hayek Memorial Lecture. Donald T. Brash. (Occasional Paper Ser.: No. 100). 56p. 1996. pap. 13.95 (*0-255-36400-8*, Pub. by Inst Economic Affairs) Coronet Bks.

New Zealand's Secret Heroes: Don Stott & the "Z" Special Unit. Gabrielle McDonald. LC 93-120100. xvi, 168 p. 1991. write for info. (*0-7900-0216-7*) Reed Pubng.

New Zealand's Top Trout Fishing Waters. John Kent et al. (Fly Fishing International Ser.). (Illus.). 192p. 1999. pap. 24.95 (*0-8117-2862-5*) Stackpole.

New Zionism & the Foreign Policy System of Israel. Ofira Seliktar. LC 85-26103. (Middle East Research Institute Special Studies). 320p. 1986. text 36.95 (*0-8093-1287-5*) S Ill U Pr.

New Zones: East-West Europe & North-South America. Ed. by Richard L. Bolin. 84p. 1992. pap. 40.00 (*0-945951-07-8*) Flagstaff Inst.

New Zucchini Cookbook: And Other Squash. Nancy C. Ralston & Marynor Jordan. LC 89-46018. (Illus.). 176p. 1990. pap. 12.95 (*0-88266-589-8*, Garden Way Pub) Storey Bks.

New Zucchini Cookbook: And Other Squash. Nancy C. Ralston & Marynor Jordan. LC 89-46018. (Illus.). 176p. 1990. 16.95 (*0-88266-590-1*, Garden Way Pub) Storey Bks.

***New 35mm Photographers Handbook, Vol. 1.** 3rd ed. Julian Calder. 1999. pap. 19.95 (*0-609-80422-7*) Crown Pub Group.

***Newamerica.** Michael A. Smith. 384p. 2000. mass mkt. 6.99 (*0-8125-6669-6*, Pub. by Forge NYC) St Martin.

Newar Nepali Angrejee Shabdakosh. I. N. Shresthacharya. 1997. pap. 27.00 (*0-7855-7467-0*, Pub. by Ratna Pustak Bhandar) St Mut.

Newari Root Verbs. Iswaranand Shresthacharya. 175p. (C). 1882. 120.00 (*0-89771-110-6*, Pub. by Ratna Pustak Bhandar) St Mut.

Newari Root Verbs. Iswaranand Shresthacharya. 1981. 75.00 (*0-7855-0283-1*, Pub. by Ratna Pustak Bhandar) St Mut.

Newari Root Verbs. Iswaranand Shresthacharya. 1982. 60.00 (*0-7855-0319-6*, Pub. by Ratna Pustak Bhandar) St Mut.

Newark. Jean-Rae Turner & Richard T. Koles. LC 97-205640. (Images of America Ser.). 1997. pap. 16.99 (*0-7524-0547-0*) Arcadia Publng.

Newark Collection of American Art Pottery. Ulysses G. Dietz. Ed. by Mary S. Sweeney. LC 84-4818. (Illus.). 128p. (Orig.). 1984. pap. 19.95 (*0-932828-19-1*) Newark Mus.

Newark Experiment: A New Direction for Urban Health Care. John Kolesar. 1975. 3.00 (*0-943136-14-8*) Ctr Analysis Public Issues.

Newark Museum Cookbook. Ed. by Mary S. Sweeney & Theron L. Marsh. (Illus.). 176p. (Orig.). 1983. spiral bd. 10.95 (*0-932828-18-3*) Newark Mus.

Newark Museum Tibetan Buddhist Altar. Valrae Reynolds. Ed. by Lori VanDecker & Mary S. Price. (Illus.). 32p. (Orig.). 1991. pap. 8.00 (*0-932828-25-6*) Newark Mus.

Newark Museum Tibetan Collection: Sculpture & Painting, Vol. III. 2nd rev. ed. Valrae Reynolds et al. (Illus.). 208p. 1987. pap. 20.00 (*0-932828-15-9*) Newark Mus.

Newark, the Nation's Unhealthiest City, 1832-1895. Stuart Galishoff. 263p. (C). 1988. text 45.00 (*0-8135-1281-6*) Rutgers U Pr.

Newark's Little Italy: The Vanished First Ward. Michael Immerso. LC 97-5674. (Illus.). 172p. (C). 1997. 32.95 (*0-8135-2417-2*) Rutgers U Pr.

Newark's Little Italy: The Vanished First Ward. Michael Immerso. (Illus.). 172p. 1999. pap. 23.00 (*0-8135-2757-0*) Rutgers U Pr.

Newark's Riverside Heritage: Millgate, a Guided Walk. David Marcombe. LC 98-138962. (Illus.). 52p. 1997. pap. 5.95 (*1-85041-086-0*, Pub. by U of Nottingham) Intl Spec Bk.

Newaygo White Pine Heritage: A Pictorial History of the Lumbering Era along the Muskegon River in Newaygo County, 1837-1899. Robert I. Thompson. (Illus.). 91p. 1995. reprint ed. pap. 18.00 (*0-8328-5043-8*); reprint ed. lib. bdg. 25.00 (*0-8328-5042-X*) Higginson Bk Co.

Newbaker: A Genealogical Record of the Descendants of Andrew Newbaker of Hardwick Township, Warren County, N.J., with History & Biographical Sketches. A. J. Fretz. (Illus.). 42p. 1992. reprint ed. lib. bdg. write for info. (*0-8328-6572-9*) Higginson Bk Co.

Newberg on Class Actions: 1996 Supplement. 3rd ed. Alba Conte. Ed. by Russ Davis. 600p. 1996. pap. text. write for info. (*0-7620-0094-5*) West Group.

Newberry & Caldecott Awards: A Guide to the Medal & Honor Books, 1998 Edition. American Library Association Staff. LC 93-648805. (Newbery & Caldecott Awards Ser.). 160p. 1999. pap. text 17.00 (*0-8389-3495-1*) ALA.

***Newberry Awards.** Aladdin Paperbacks Publishing Staff. 1998. pap. 143.10 (*0-689-00462-1*) Aladdin.

***Newberry County, South Carolina Deed Abstracts: Deed Books C, D-2 & D 1794-1800 (1765-1800), Vol. II.** Brent H. Holcomb. 215p. 2000. 30.00 (*0-913363-39-1*) SCMAR.

Newberry County South Carolina Deed Abstracts Vol. 1: Deed Books A-B 1785-1794 (1751-1794) Brent H. Holcomb. LC 98-75025. 200p. 1999. 30.00 (*0-913363-33-2*) SCMAR.

Newberry Crater: A Ten-Thousand-Year Record of Human Occupation & Environmental Change. Thomas J. Connolly. LC 99-27479. (Anthropological Papers: No. 121). (Illus.). 287p. 1999. pap. 34.50 (*0-87480-574-0*) U of Utah Pr.

Newberry National Volcanic Monument: An Oregon Documentary. expanded ed. Stuart G. Garrett & Bert Webber. LC 91-13081. (Illus.). 128p. 1997. pap. 12.95 (*0-936738-61-8*) Webb Research.

Newberry Reference Bible. 1994. lthr. 59.99 (*0-946351-39-2*) Loizeaux.

Newberry Reference Bible. Ed. by Thomas Newberry. LC 73-189203. 1112p. 1992. lib. bdg. 49.99 (*0-8254-3315-0*, Kregel Class); boxed set, bond lthr. 84.99 (*0-8254-3298-7*, Kregel Class); boxed set, bond lthr. 79.99 (*0-8254-3299-5*, Kregel Class) Kregel.

Newberry Zoo. Martin H. Greenberg. (J). 1996. 24.95 (*0-385-30993-7*) BDD Bks Young Read.

Newbery & Caldecott Awards. Association for Library Service Staff. 160p. 1998. pap. text 16.00 (*0-8389-3484-6*) ALA.

Newbery & Caldecott Awards: A Guide to the Medal & Honor Books. Association for Library Service to Children Staff. LC 91-9909. (Illus.). 143p. 1991. reprint ed. pap. 44.40 (*0-7837-5966-5*, 204576700007) Bks Demand.

Newbery & Caldecott Awards: A Guide to the Medal & Honor Books 1995 Edition. Association for Library Service to Children Staff. LC Z 1037.A2N47. 157p. 1995. reprint ed. pap. 48.70 (*0-608-02967-X*, 206343200006) Bks Demand.

Newbery & Caldecott Awards: A Guide to the Medal & Honor Books 1998. Library Service to Children Staff. 1998. pap. 16.00 (*0-8389-3473-0*) ALA.

Newbery & Caldecott Awards, 1994: A Guide to the Medal & Honor Books. Association for Library Service to Children Staff. LC Z 1037.A2N47. 151p. 1994. reprint ed. pap. 46.90 (*0-7837-9675-7*, 206040300005) Bks Demand.

Newbery & Caldecott Books in the Classroom. Claudette H. Comfort. 160p. (J). (gr. 1-4). 1991. pap. text 12.95 (*0-86530-178-6*, IP 194-0) Incentive Pubns.

Newbery & Caldecott Medal & Honor Books in Other Media. Paulette B. Sharkey. Ed. by Jim Roginski. 157p. 1992. 39.95 (*1-55570-119-1*) Neal-Schuman.

Newbery & Caldecott Medal Books, 1966-1975. Ed. by Lee Kingman. LC 75-20167. (Illus.). 321p. 1975. 22.95 (*0-87675-003-X*) Horn Bk.

Newbery & Caldecott Medal Books, 1976-1985. Ed. by Lee Kingman. LC 86-15223. (Illus.). 321p. 1986. 24.95 (*0-87675-004-8*) Horn Bk.

Newbery & Caldecott Medalists & Honor Book Winners: Bibliographies & Resource Materials Through 1991. 2nd ed. Muriel Brown & Rita S. Foudray. Ed. by Jim Roginski. 530p. 1992. 65.00 (*1-55570-118-3*) Neal-Schuman.

***Newbery & Caldecott Trivia & More for Every Day of the Year.** Claudette Hegel. 200p. 2000. 26.00 (*1-56308-830-4*) Libs Unl.

Newbery Authors of the Eastern Seaboard: Integrating Social Studies & Literature Grades 5-8. Joanne Kelly. (Illus.). ix, 159p. 1994. pap. text 20.00 (*1-56308-122-9*) Teacher Ideas Pr.

Newbery Award Library II: And Now Miguel - Bridge to Terabithia - Sarah, Plain & Tall - The Wheel on the School, 4 bks., Set. Joseph Krumgold et al. (Trophy Bk.). (Illus.). (J). (gr. 4-6). 1988. pap. 19.80 (*0-06-440277-0*, HarpTrophy) HarpC Child Bks.

Newbery Award Library I: It's Like This Cat - Julie of the Wolves - Onion John - Sounder, 4 bks., Set. Emily C. Neville. (J). (gr. 4-6). 1985. pap. 19.80 (*0-06-440162-6*) HarpC Child Bks.

Newbery Award Reader. Ed. by Charles Waugh & Martin H. Greenberg. 252p. (YA). (gr. 7 up). 1984. 14.95 (*0-15-257034-9*, Harcourt Child Bks) Harcourt.

Newbery Award Treasures, 5 vols., Set. (J). (gr. 4-7). 1990. pap., boxed set 16.25 (*0-440-36002-1*) Dell.

Newbery Awards, 5 vols., Set. Scott O'Dell et al. (J). (gr. 4-7). 1990. pap., boxed set 16.75 (*0-440-45963-X*) Dell.

Newbery Awards Collection, 5 bks. Elizabeth George Speare. Incl. Witch of Blackbird Pond. (J). (gr. k-9). 1987. Set pap. 12.40 (*0-685-19117-6*) Dell.

Newbery Books. 2nd ed. Virginia T. Mealy. (Illus.). 128p. 1991. pap. 12.95 (*1-879287-02-1*, BL012) Pieces of Lrning.

***Newbery Books a World of Award-winners Carton Pack.** Alladin Paperbacks Staff. 1999. per. 215.28 (*0-689-00889-9*) Aladdin.

Newbery Christmas. Martin H. Greenberg. Ed. by Charles G. Waugh. 208p. (J). (gr. 4-7). 1991. 19.95 (*0-385-30485-4*) Delacorte.

***Newbery Companion: Booktalk & Related Materials for Newbery Medal & Honor Books.** John T. Gillespie. 460p. 2001. 56.00 (*1-56308-813-4*) Libs Unl.

Newbery Companion: Booktalk & Related Materials for Newbery Medal & Honor Books. John T. Gillespie & Corinne J. Naden. LC 96-23699. 450p. 1996. lib. bdg. 48.00 (*1-56308-356-6*) Libs Unl.

Newbery Halloween: Thirteen Scary Stories by Newbery Award-Winning Authors. Ed. by Charles G. Waugh. LC 92-43877. 208p. (J). 1993. 16.95 (*0-385-31028-5*) Doubleday.

Newbery Library Award, Set. Incl. Johnny Tremain: Illustrated American Classics. Esther Forbes. Twenty-One Balloons. William Pene du Bois. 1983. Witch of Blackbird Pond. Elizabeth George Speare. 1983. (J). (gr. 5 up). 1983. Set pap., boxed set 12.30 (*0-440-46256-8*) Dell.

Newbery Library III: Walk Two Moons, Catherine, Called Birdy, Indian Captive, 4 vols., Set. Lois Lenski & Karen Cushman. (J). 1996. pap., boxed set 14.85 (*0-06-449627-9*, HarpTrophy) HarpC Child Bks.

Newbery Medal. Virginia Hamilton et al. (J). 1997. pap. text 13.50 (*0-689-81766-5*) Aladdin.

Newbery Medal Books, 1922-1955. Ed. by Bertha M. Miller & Elinor W. Field. LC 55-13968. (Illus.). 458p. 1955. 22.95 (*0-87675-396-9*) Horn Bk.

Newbery Medal Collection, 5 vols., No. 3. (J). (gr. 4 up). 1988. boxed set 16.25 (*0-440-36003-X*) Dell.

Newbery on the Net: Reading & Internet Activities. Ru Story-Huffman. LC 98-39811. 100p. 1999. pap. 16.95 (*1-57950-021-8*, PC8-37693, Alleyside) Highsmith Pr.

Newbery 1 Teacher's Guide. (Thematic Library). 56p. 1996. pap. text, teacher ed. 29.95 (*1-58303-019-0*) Pthways Pubng.

Newbery 2 Teacher's Guide. (Thematic Library). 56p. 1996. pap. text 29.95 (*1-58303-020-4*) Pthways Pubng.

Newbery Zoo: A Dozen Animal Stories by Newbery Award-Winning Authors. Martin H. Greenberg. LC 94-32712. 192p. (J). (gr. 4-7). 1995. 16.95 (*0-385-32263-1*) Delacorte.

Newbie's Guide to the Microsoft Network. Michael Lehman. (Newbie's Guide Ser.). (Illus.). 240p. (Orig.). 1995. pap. 24.95 (*0-9637025-8-0*) Albion Bks.

***Newbies' Money Guide: For Rookies & Late Starters; Simple Steps to Wealth & Security.** Coleen Moore. 309p. 2000. pap. 14.95 (*0-9676954-1-4*, Pub. by Pnt of View) ACCESS Pubs Network.

Newbold Astbury & Its History. J. E. Cartlidge. 256p. (C). 1982. text 39.00 (*0-947818-00-6*, Pub. by Old Vicarage) St Mut.

Newborn see Recien Nacido!

Newborn. Kathy Henderson. Ed. by Phyllis Fogelman & Toby Sherry. LC 98-33674. (Illus.). 32p. (J). (ps-3). 1999. 15.99 (*0-8037-2434-9*, Dial Yng Read) Peng Put Young Read.

Newborn. Photos by Howard Schatz. LC 95-23313. (Illus.). 80p. 1996. 14.95 (*0-8118-1195-6*) Chronicle Bks.

Newborn: Alive in Christ, the Savior. Jack W. Hayford. (Orig.). 1984. pap. 3.95 (*0-916847-00-4*) Living Way.

Newborn Attention: Biological Constraints & Influence of Experience. Ed. by Michael J. Weiss & Philip R. Zelazo. 552p. 1991. text 125.00 (*0-89391-525-4*) Ablx Pub.

Newborn Baby. 5th ed. V. C. Harrison et al. (Illus.). 464p. (C). 1994. reprint ed. pap. text 54.00 (*0-7021-1848-6*, Pub. by Juta & Co) Intl Spec Bk.

Newborn Behavioral Organization Nursing Research & Implications. Ed. by Beverly S. Raff & Gene C. Anderson. LC 79-2597. (Alan R. Liss Ser.: Vol. 15, No. 7). 1979. 29.00 (*0-685-03294-9*) March of Dimes.

Newborn Care Video Step-by-Step: A Parents' Complete Medical Guide to Safe & Happy Beginnings with Your New Baby. Jenet Langjahr & Anita Sebree. 32p. 19.95 incl. VHS (*0-8431-2288-9*) U Studios Home Vid.

Newborn Child. 6th ed. David G. Vulliamy & Peter G. Johnston. LC 87-10324. (Illus.). 273p. 1987. pap. text 30.00 (*0-443-03668-3*) Church.

Newborn Child. 8th ed. Peter G. B. Johnston & David G. Vulliamy. LC 97-15115. 1998. pap. 32.95 (*0-443-05510-6*) Church.

Newborn Death: For Parents Experiencing the Death of an Infant. Joy Johnson et al. (SPA.). 1997. 3.50 (*1-56123-113-4*) Centering Corp.

***Newborn Expectations: My First Journal.** Terry Lee Bilsky. (Illus.). 128p. 2000. pap. 10.95 (*0-7407-0988-7*) Andrews & McMeel.

Newborn Feeding & Care Kit for Cleft Lip and/or Palate Infants. Renee L. Howard. (Illus.). 24p. (Orig.). (C). pap. 5.00 (*0-935801-00-6*) Howard & Assocs.

Newborn in the Intensive Care Unit: A Neuropsychoanalytic Prevention Model. Romana Negri. 288p. 1994. pap. text 32.00 (*1-85575-073-2*, Pub. by H Karnac Bks Ltd) Other Pr LLC.

Newborn in the Intensive Care Unit: A Neuropsychoanalytic Prevention Model. Romana Negri. 285p. 1994. pap. text 34.95 (*0-614-07215-8*, Pub. by H Karnac Bks Ltd) Brunner-Mazel.

Newborn Intensive Care: What Every Parent Needs to Know. Ed. by Jeanette G. Zaichkin. LC 96-21773. (Illus.). 463p. (Orig.). 1996. pap. 24.95 (*0-9622975-8-5*) NICU Ink.

***Newborn Intensive Care: What Every Parent Needs to Know.** 2nd ed. Ed. by Jeanette Goodnow Zaichkin. (Illus.). xii, 460p. 2001. pap. 24.95 (*1-887571-05-1*) NICU Ink.

Newborn Intensive Care: What Every Parent Needs to Know see Cuidado Intensiveo Neonatal: Lo Que Todo Padre Necesita Saber

Newborn Joy. Linda Sunshine. (Illus.). 96p. 1994. 15.00 (*0-8362-8052-0*) Andrews & McMeel.

Newborn King. Cindy Holtrop. (Scripture Alive Ser.). 22p. 1998. pap. 14.95 (*1-56212-371-8*, 2290-0030) CRC Pubns.

Newborn Medicine & Society: European Background & American Practice (1750-1975) Murdina M. Desmond. LC 97-43737. 1998. 26.95 (*1-57168-219-8*, Eakin Pr) Sunbelt Media.

Newborn Might & Strength Everlasting: A Christmas Offering. Rudolf Steiner. Ed. by Gilbert Church. (Illus.). 19p. (Orig.). 1977. pap. 3.95 (*0-88010-100-8*) Anthroposophic.

Newborn Mother. Andrea B. Eagan. LC 87-333. 224p. 1995. pap. 7.95 (*0-8050-0250-2*, Owl) H Holt & Co.

Newborns at Risk: Medical Care & Psychoeducational Intervention. 2nd ed. Gail L. Ensher & David A. Clark. 400p. 1994. 56.00 (*0-8342-0555-6*) Aspen Pub.

Newboy: The Autobiography of Herbert Hill Peyton. Herbert H. Peyton. LC 97-91993. (Illus.). 240p. 1997. 18.95 (*0-9658277-0-4*) Gate Petrol.

Newbridge Early Skills Library, 12 vols., Set. (Illus.). 1995. pap. write for info. (*1-56784-526-6*) Newbridge Educ.

Newburger's Manual of Cosmetic Analysis. 2nd ed. Ed. by Alan J. Senzel. 150p. 1977. pap. 39.00 (*0-935584-09-9*) AOAC Intl.

Newburgh Baseball Club: Rules of 1858. 1960. pap. 5.00 (*0-87556-224-8*) Saifer.

Newbury: A Photographic Records, 1850-1935. Sue Hopson. 104p. 1987. pap. 30.00 (*0-905392-25-6*) St Mut.

Newbury: History & Guide. Susan Tolman. (Illus.). 128p. 1994. pap. 13.95 (*0-7509-0318-X*, Pub. by Sutton Pub Ltd) Intl Pubs Mktg.

N

Newbury Childhood. Joan Booker. 128p. 1987. pap. 30.00 (*0-9506044-3-7*) St Mut.

Newbury House Basic English Dictionary. Philip M. Rideout. LC 98-152110. 550p. (J). 1998. mass mkt. 19.95 (*0-8384-6015-1*) Heinle & Heinle.

Newbury House Dictionary. 3rd ed. Ed. by Heinle Publishers Inc. (C). 1999. 25.95 (*0-8384-0259-3*) Heinle & Heinle.

Newbury House Dictionary: ELS Edition. Philip M. Rideout. (Miscellaneous/Catalogs Ser.). (J). 1996. pap. 13.95 (*0-8384-7069-6*) Wadsworth Pub.

Newbury House Dictionary of American English. Philip M. Rideout. (College ESL Ser.). (J). 1995. pap. 17.95 (*0-8384-5532-8*) Heinle & Heinle.

Newbury House Dictionary of American English. 2nd ed. Philip M. Rideout. LC 98-167539. 1024p. (J). 1998. pap. 19.95 (*0-8384-7812-3*) Heinle & Heinle.

Newbury House Dictionary of American English: An Essential Reference for Learners of American English & Culture. Philip M. Rideout. (College ESL Ser.). Date not set. pap. 18.95 (*0-614-10351-7*) Heinle & Heinle.

Newbury House Dictionary of American English: An Essential Reference for Learners of American English & Culture. Philip M. Rideout. (College ESL Ser.). 1031p. (J). 1996. mass mkt. 28.95 (*0-8384-5613-8*) Heinle & Heinle.

Newbury House Guide to Writing. M. E. Sokolik. (College ESL Ser.). 400p. (J). 1995. mass mkt. 32.95 (*0-8384-4681-7*) Heinle & Heinle.

Newbury House TOEFL. Daniel B. Kennedy. (YA). 1989. pap., teacher ed. 20.00 (*0-8384-2675-1*) Heinle & Heinle.

Newbury House TOEFL: Prep. for TWE. Daniel B. Kennedy & Hamp-Lyons. (J). 1989. mass mkt. 21.95 (*0-8384-3903-9*) Heinle & Heinle.

Newburyport. L. Sullivan. (Images of America Ser.). 1997. pap. 16.99 (*0-7524-0879-8*) Arcadia Publng.

***Newburyport: Stories from the Waterside.** Liza Nelson. (Town Memoirs Ser.). (Illus.). 144p. 2000. pap. 14.95 (*1-889833-12-6*, Commonwealth Eds) Memoirs Unltd.

Newburyport, MA. Historical Briefs, Inc. Staff. Ed. by Thomas Antonucci & Michael Antonucci. 176p. 1992. pap. 19.95 (*0-89677-029-X*) Hist Briefs.

Newcastle, a Duke Without Money: Thomas Pelham-Holles, 1693-1768. Ray A. Kelch. LC 73-83064. 232p. reprint ed. pap. 72.00 (*0-608-18295-8*, 203154500075) Bks Demand.

Newcastle Disease. Ed. by David J. Alexander. (Developments in Veterinary Virology Ser.). (C). 1988. text 240.00 (*0-89838-392-7*) Kluwer Academic.

Newcastle Disease & Its Control in Southeast Asia: Proceedings of a UNESCO-Sponsored Training Course & Workshop on Viral Vaccines in Poultry. Ed. by K. F. Shortridge. LC 83-159845. 117p. reprint ed. pap. 36.30 (*0-8357-6667-5*, 203533500094) Bks Demand.

Newcastle Disease in Village Chickens: Control with Thermostable Oral Vaccines. P.H. Spradbrow. 189p. 1992. pap. 126.00 (*1-86320-062-2*, Pub. by ACIAR) St Mut.

Newcastle Disease, Laboratory Diagnosis & Vaccine Evaluation. K. F. Shortridge et al. LC SF0995.6.N4S. (Illus.). 61p. reprint ed. pap. 30.00 (*0-8357-6668-3*, 203533600094) Bks Demand.

Newcastle Disease Virus: An Evolving Pathogen, Proceedings of an International Symposium. Ed. by Robert P. Hanson. LC 64-25078. 394p. 1964. reprint ed. pap. 122.20 (*0-608-01877-5*, 206252900003) Bks Demand.

Newcastle Earthquake Study. Intro. by M. A. Sargent. (Illus.). 155p. (Orig.). 1990. pap. 96.00 (*0-85825-516-2*, Pub. by Inst Engrs Aust-EA Bks) Accents Pubns.

Newcastle Guide to Healing with Crystals: Balancing the Human Energy Field for Physical & Spiritual Well-Being. Pamela L. Chase & Jonathan Pawlik. 171p. 1988. pap. 10.95 (*0-87877-134-4*) Newcastle Pub.

Newcastle Guide to Healing with Gemstones. Pamela L. Chase & Jonathan Pawlik. (Illus.). 260p. (Orig.). 1989. pap. 12.95 (*0-87877-140-9*) Newcastle Pub.

Newcastle upon Tyne. J. J. Anderson. (Records of Early English Drama Ser.). (Illus.). 264p. 1982. text 60.00 (*0-8020-5610-5*) U of Toronto Pr.

Newcastle's New York: Anglo-American Politics, 1732-1753. Stanley N. Katz. LC 68-14261. 299p. 1968. reprint ed. pap. 92.70 (*0-7837-2285-0*, 205737300004) Bks Demand.

Newcat: Parsing Natural Language Using Left-Associative Grammar. R. Hausser. (Lecture Notes in Computer Science Ser.: Vol. 231). ii, 540p. 1986. 53.00 (*0-387-16781-1*) Spr-Verlag.

Newcomb Pottery: An Enterprise for Southern Women, 1895-1904. Jessie Poesch et al. LC 83-51776. (Illus.). 208p. 1984. pap. 24.95 (*0-916838-99-4*) Schiffer.

Newcomb's Wildflower Guide: An Ingenious New Key System for Quick, Positive Field Identification of Wildflowers, Flowering Shrubs & Vines. Lawrence Newcomb. (Illus.). 490p. 1989. pap. 19.00 (*0-316-60442-9*) Little.

***Newcomer.** Margot Dalton. (Superromance Ser.: Vol. 940). 2000. mass mkt. 4.50 (*0-373-70940-4*, 1-70940-1) Harlequin Bks.

Newcomer. Janet Thomas. 33p. (J). (gr. k-3). 1987. pap. 6.00 (*0-87602-268-9*) Anchorage.

Newcomer & the Bible. A. Lacoque & F. R. Vasquez. 24p. 1971. 3.00 (*0-913256-46-3*) CMS.

***Newcomer in New Albany.** Phil Hardwick. (Mississippi Mysteries Ser.: Vol. 4). 112p. 1999. pap. 9.95 (*1-893062-06-6*) Quail Ridge.

Newcomer Phonics. Addison-Wesley Publishing Staff. 96p. 1999. pap. text 14.60 (*0-201-43703-1*, Prentice Hall) P-H.

Newcomer Programs: Innovative Efforts to Meet the Educational Challenges of Immigrant Students. Hedy N. Chang. 59p. 1990. pap. 15.00 (*1-887039-04-X*) Calif Tomorrow.

Newcomers. Myron Ladue. 389p. (Orig.). 1989. pap. 15.00 (*0-9623443-0-3*) M Ladue.

Newcomers: Negroes & Puerto Ricans in a Changing Metropolis. Oscar Handlin. LC 59-14737. (New York Metropolitan Region Study). 184p. 1959. 16.95 (*0-674-62101-8*) HUP.

Newcomers Among Us: The Alien Nation Companion. Edward Gross et al. (Illus.). 112p. (Orig.). 1991. pap. 12.95 (*0-685-50338-0*) Retro Vision.

Newcomer's Guide to Hawaii. David Paxman. (Illus.). 144p. 1993. pap. 8.95 (*0-935180-32-X*) Mutual Pub HI.

Newcomer's Guide to Home Gardening in North & Central Florida. Karl M. Touraine. 126p. 1993. 9.95 (*0-9632916-0-2*) F R Pubns FL.

Newcomers Guide to Living in the U. S. A. Leon J. Snaid. 115p. 1988. 89.95 (*0-685-44525-9*) Intl Busn Seminars.

Newcomer's Guide to North Carolina: Everything You Need to Know to Be a Tar Heel. 2nd rev. ed. Bill Lee. (Illus.). 286p. 1999. pap. 15.95 (*1-878086-73-1*, Pub. by Down Home NC) Blair.

***Newcomer's Guide to the Afterlife: On the Other Side Known Commonly As "The Little Book"** Daniel Quinn & Tom Whalen. (Illus.). 160p. 1998. pap. 13.95 (*0-553-37979-8*) Bantam.

Newcomer's Guide to the Bible: Themes & Timelines. Michael C. Armour. LC 99-30558. 300p. 1999. pap. 17.99 (*0-89900-859-3*) College Pr Pub.

Newcomer's Handbook for Boston. 2nd ed. Marietta Hitzemann & Ed Golden. LC 99-158612. 218p. 1998. 14.95 (*0-912301-40-6*) First Bks.

***Newcomer's Handbook for Chicago.** 3rd ed. Ed. by Mark Wukas & Thor Ringler. LC 98-168264. (Newcomer's Handbook Ser.). 192p. 1998. 14.95 (*0-912301-39-2*) First Bks.

***Newcomer's Handbook for Los Angeles: Third Edition.** 3rd ed. 296p. 2000. pap. 17.95 (*0-912301-43-0*) First Bks.

Newcomer's Handbook for Los Angeles, 2nd Edition. 2nd ed. First Books Inc. Staff. (Newcomer's Handbook Ser.). (Illus.). 144p. 1996. 13.95 (*0-912301-30-9*) First Bks.

Newcomer's Handbook for Minneapolis St. Paul. First Books Inc. Staff. LC 97-197550. (Newcomer's Handbook Ser.). (Illus.). 196p. 1997. 14.95 (*0-912301-33-3*) First Bks.

Newcomer's Handbook for New York City. 17th rev. ed. First Books Inc. Staff. (Newcomer's Handbook Ser.). (Illus.). 312p. (Orig.). 1998. 17.95 (*0-912301-37-6*) First Bks.

***Newcomer's Handbook for New York City.** 18th ed. (Newcomer's Handbook Ser.). (Illus.). 416p. 1999. pap. 18.95 (*0-912301-42-2*) First Bks.

Newcomer's Handbook for San Francisco. Michael Bower. (Newcomer's Handbook Ser.). (Illus.). 168p. 1997. 13.95 (*0-912301-34-1*) First Bks.

Newcomer's Handbook for Seattle. Amy Bellamy. LC 99-234184. 248p. 1998. pap. 14.95 (*0-912301-35-X*) First Bks.

Newcomer's Handbook for Washington, DC. 2nd ed. First Books Editors. LC 98-115451. (Newcomer's Handbook Ser.). (Illus.). 160p. 1997. 13.95 (*0-912301-36-8*) First Bks.

Newcomers in the Workplace: Immigrants & the Restructuring of the U. S. Economy. Ed. by Louise Lamphere et al. LC 93-15205. (Labor & Social Change Ser.). 320p. (C). 1994. pap. 22.95 (*1-56639-131-8*); text 69.95 (*1-56639-124-5*) Temple U Pr.

Newcomers to America: Stories of Today's Young Immigrants. Judith E. Greenberg. LC 95-40519. (In Their Own Words Ser.). (Illus.). 144p. (YA). (gr. 7-11). 1996. lib. bdg. 24.00 (*0-531-11256-X*) Watts.

Newcomers to the United States: Children & Families. Ed. by Mary Frank. 89p. 1991. pap. 19.95 (*1-56024-120-9*) Haworth Pr.

Newcomes. William Makepeace Thackeray. 416p. 1994. 8.50 (*0-460-87495-0*, Everyman's Classic Lib) Tuttle Pubng.

Newcomes. William Makepeace Thackeray. Ed. by Peter L. Shillinsburg. LC 96-4229. 1104p. (C). 1996. text 90.00 (*0-472-10675-9*, 10675) U of Mich Pr.

Newcomes see Complete Works of William Makepeace Thackeray

Newdick's Season of Frost: An Interrupted Biography of Robert Frost. Ed. by William A. Sutton & Robert S. Newdick. LC 75-22009. 1976. text 29.50 (*0-87395-316-9*) State U NY Pr.

Newe Booke, Containing the Arte of Ryding. Thomas Blundeville. LC 75-25640. (English Experience Ser.: No. 118). (Illus.). 232p. 1969. reprint ed. 55.00 (*90-221-0118-5*) Walter J Johnson.

Newe Iewell of Health. Conrad Gesner. LC 73-171759. (English Experience Ser.: No. 381). 540p. 1971. reprint ed. 75.00 (*90-221-0381-1*) Walter J Johnson.

Newe Natekwinappeh: Shoshoni Stories & Dictionary. Wick R. Miller. (Utah Anthropological Papers: No. 94). reprint ed. 24.00 (*0-404-60694-6*) AMS Pr.

Newe Natekwinappeh: Shoshoni Stories & Dictionary. Wick R. Miller. LC 72-612763. (Anthropological Papers: No. 94). 180p. reprint ed. pap. 55.80 (*0-7837-2606-6*, 204277000006) Bks Demand.

Newell D. Goff: The Life of a Young Entrepreneur at the Turn of the Twentieth Century. Mary E. Robinson. LC 92-27885. (Illus.). 1992. 9.95 (*0-914659-57-X*) Phoenix Pub.

Newell. Descendants of Thomas Newell (1730-1803) Rachel S. Tefft. 68p. 1997. pap. 14.00 (*0-8328-9479-6*); lib. bdg. 24.00 (*0-8328-9478-8*) Higginson Bk Co.

Newell Lectureships, Vol. 2. Date not set. pap. write for info. (*0-87162-640-3*) Warner Pr.

Newell Lectureships, Vol. 3. John N. Oswalt & William L. Lane. Ed. by Timothy Dwyer. 1996. 19.95 (*0-87162-678-0*) Warner Pr.

Newell Lectureships Vol. 4: Essays on Romans - Implications of a Contextual Approach to Paul's Letter. Robert Jewett. Ed. by Timothy Dwyer. 1996. 19.95 (*0-87162-693-4*) Warner Pr.

Newell Lectureships 1, Vol. 1. Ed. by Timothy Dwyer. 1992. 16.95 (*0-87162-638-1*, D3075) Warner Pr.

***Newer Deal: Social Work & Religion in Partnership.** Ram A. Cnaan et al. LC 99-30601. 316p. 1999. 49.50 (*0-231-11624-1*); pap. 26.50 (*0-231-11625-X*) Col U Pr.

Newer Dimensions of Patient Care, 3 pts. Esther L. Brown. Incl. Pt. 1. Use of the Physical & Social Environment of the General Hospital for Therapeutic Purposes. 160p. 1961. pap. 16.50 (*0-87154-183-1*); Pt. 2. Improving Staff Motivation & Competence in the General Hospital. 194p. 1962. pap. 19.95 (*0-87154-184-X*); Pt. 3. Patients As People. 164p. 1965. pap. 14.95 (*0-87154-185-8*); 160p. pap. write for info. (*0-318-55563-8*) Russell Sage.

Newer Dimensions of Patient Care, 3 vols., Set. Esther L. Brown. Incl. Pt. 1. Use of the Physical & Social Environment of the General Hospital for Therapeutic Purposes. 160p. 1961. pap. 16.50 (*0-87154-183-1*); Pt. 2. Improving Staff Motivation & Competence in the General Hospital. 194p. 1962. pap. 19.95 (*0-87154-184-X*); Pt. 3. Patients As People. 164p. 1965. pap. 14.95 (*0-87154-185-8*); 160p. write for info. (*0-87154-182-3*) Russell Sage.

Newer Ideals of Peace. Jane Addams. LC 71-137523. (Peace Movement in America Ser.). xviii, 243p. 1972. reprint ed. lib. bdg. 34.95 (*0-89198-050-4*) Ozer.

***Newer Insights into Marketing: Cross-Cultural & Cross-National Perspectives.** Ed. by Camille P. Schuster & Phil Harris. LC 99-27560. (Journal of Euromarketing Ser.: Vol. 7, No. 2). 94p. (C). 1999. 24.95 (*0-7890-0752-5*) Haworth Pr.

Newer Islamic Movements in Western Europe. Lars Pedersen. LC 98-74759. (Research in Migration & Ethnic Relations Ser.). 296p. 1999. text 69.95 (*1-84014-388-6*) Ashgate Pub Co.

Newer Spiritualism. Frank Podmore. LC 75-7392. (Perspectives in Psychical Research Ser.). 1975. reprint ed. 26.95 (*0-405-07041-1*) Ayer.

Newer Tests & Procedures in Pediatric Gastroenterology. Ed. by G. Dinari et al. (Frontiers of Gastrointestinal Research Ser.: Vol. 15). (Illus.). vii, 332p. 1989. 258.50 (*3-8055-4646-7*) S Karger.

Newer Tests & Procedures in Pediatric Gastroenterology: Function & Laboratory Tests; Nutrition, 2. Ed. by G. Dinari et al. (Frontiers of Gastrointestinal Research Ser.: Vol. 16). (Illus.). viii, 296p. 1989. 233.25 (*3-8055-4900-8*) S Karger.

Newer Trace Elements in Nutrition. Ed. by Walter Mertz & W. E. Cornatzer. LC 70-157834. (Illus.). 451p. reprint ed. pap. 139.90 (*0-608-30254-6*, 205501500007) Bks Demand.

Newer World: Kit Carson, John C. Fremont & the Claiming of the American West. David Roberts. LC 99-41816. 320p. 2000. pap. text 25.00 (*0-684-83482-0*) S&S Trade.

Newer World: The Progressive Republican Vision of America. Ed. by James Leach & William P. McKenzie. LC 88-21529. 172p. 1988. 16.95 (*0-8191-6827-0*) Madison Bks UPA.

Newes from America. John G. Underhill. LC 79-25747. (English Experience Ser.: No. 348). 44p. 1971. reprint ed. 40.00 (*90-221-0348-X*) Walter J Johnson.

Newes from Italy of a Second Moses: or The Life of Galeacius Carracciolus the Noble Marquese of Vico. Niccolo Balbani. Tr. by W. Crashaw. LC 79-84085. (English Experience Ser.: No. 905). 92p. 1979. reprint ed. lib. bdg. 15.00 (*90-221-0905-4*) Walter J Johnson.

Newes from Virginia, the Lost Flocke Triumphant. Barnaby Rich. LC 70-25514. (English Experience Ser.: No. 269). 16p. 1970. reprint ed. 15.00 (*90-221-0269-6*) Walter J Johnson.

Newes Itinerarium Italiae. Joseph Furttenbach. (Illus.). xxiv, 295p. 1971. reprint ed. write for info. (*0-318-71597-X*) G Olms Pubs.

Newes of the Complement of the Art of Navigation & of the Mightie Empire of Cataia. Anthony Linton. LC 72-215. (English Experience Ser.: No. 204). 1969. reprint ed. 30.00 (*90-221-0204-1*) Walter J Johnson.

Newes Out of the Coast of Spaine. Henry Haslop. LC 78-38200. (English Experience Ser.: No. 466). 16p. 1972. reprint ed. 15.00 (*90-221-0466-4*) Walter J Johnson.

Newest Americans: Report of the American Jewish Committee's Task Force on the Acculturation of Immigrants to American Life. Gary E. Rubin. LC 87-70998. 36p. 1987. pap. 5.00 (*0-87495-089-9*) Am Jewish Comm.

Newest & Coolest Dinosaurs. Phillip Currie & Colleayan Martin. LC 96-910710. (Illus.). 32p. (J). (gr. 4-8). 1998. text 18.95 (*1-895910-41-2*) Grasshopper Bks.

Newest Discipline: Managing Legally Driven Issues: Providing Public Affairs Advice in the Lawyer-Dominated Problem Environment. James E. Lukaszewski. 14p. 1996. pap. 20.00 (*1-883291-18-6*) Lukaszewski.

Newest Discoveries in Nutrition. Raymond W. Bernard. 1996. spiral bd. 10.00 (*0-7873-1012-3*) Hlth Research.

Newest England: A County Without Strikes. Henry D. Lloyd. (Notable American Authors Ser.). 1999. reprint ed. lib. bdg. 125.00 (*0-7812-3803-X*) Rprt Serv.

Newest Explosions of Terrorism: Latest Sites of Terrorism in the 1990's & Beyond. 3rd rev. ed. Beau Grosscup. LC 97-76208. (Illus.). 405p. 1998. pap. 19.95 (*0-88282-163-6*) New Horizon NJ.

Newest Logo from California. Gerry Rosentswieg. 1998. pap. text 35.00 (*0-8230-6601-0*) Watsn-Guptill.

Newest Logo from California, Vol. 3. 3rd ed. Supon Phornirunlit. (Illus.). 2192p. 1997. 37.50 (*0-942604-58-X*) Madison Square.

Newest Peruvian Poetry in Translation. Ed. by Luis A. Ramos-Garcia & Edgar O'Hara. 1979. 4.95 (*0-934840-00-8*) Studia Hispanica.

Newest Weapons - Oldest Psychology: The Dialectics of American Nuclear Strategy. Ron Hirschbein. LC 89-2811. (Conflict & Consciousness: Studies in War, Peace & Social Thought: Vol. 1). 278p. (C). 1989. text 31.95 (*0-8204-1074-8*) P Lang Pubng.

Newey: The Official Referees' Courts - Practice & Procedure. Judge Newey. 68p. 1988. pap. 38.00 (*0-406-11340-8*, U.K., MICHIE) LEXIS Pub.

Newf. Marie Killilea. LC 91-31157. (Illus.). 32p. (J). (ps up). 1992. 14.95 (*0-399-21875-0*, Philomel) Peng Put Young Read.

Newf. Marie Killilea. (J). 1996. 11.15 (*0-606-11680-X*, Pub. by Turtleback) Demco.

Newfane, 1774-1874: Centennial Proceedings & Other Historical Facts & Incidents, Relating to Newfane, the County Seat of Windham County. Ed. by J. J. Green et al. (Illus.). 256p. 1995. reprint ed. lib. bdg. 35.00 (*0-8328-4724-0*) Higginson Bk Co.

(Newfane) 1774-1874: Centennial Proceedings & Other Historical Facts & Incidents Relating to Newfane, the County Seat of Windham Co. (Illus.). 255p. 1997. reprint ed. lib. bdg. 34.00 (*0-8328-6504-4*) Higginson Bk Co.

Newfangled: A Novel. Debra Monroe. LC 97-36281. 320p. 1998. 21.50 (*0-684-81905-8*) S&S Trade.

***Newfangled: A Novel.** Debra Monroe. 304p. 2000. per. 12.00 (*0-684-85197-0*) S&S Trade.

Newfangled Fairy Tales. Ed. by Bruce Lanskey. (J). 1998. 3.95 (*0-88166-299-2*) Meadowbrook.

Newfangled Fairy Tales. Ed. by Bruce Lansky. (Illus.). 120p. (J). (gr. 3-7). 1998. lib. bdg. 3.95 (*0-671-57704-2*) S&S Childrens.

Newfangled Fairy Tales Bk. 2. Bruce Lansky. 120p. (J). (gr. 2-8). 1998. 3.95 (*0-689-82211-1*, Pub. by Meadowbrook) S&S Trade.

Newfangled Fairy Tales book 3. (J). (gr. 4-6). 2000. pap. 3.95 (*0-689-83290-7*) S&S Childrens.

Newfound. rev. ed. Jim W. Miller. LC 96-77903. 214p. (J). 1996. reprint ed. pap. 13.50 (*0-917788-59-1*) Gnomon Pr.

***Newfoundland.** (Canada in the Twenty First Century Ser.). (Illus.). (J). 2000. 18.95 (*0-7910-6065-9*) Chelsea Hse.

Newfoundland. Harry Beckett. LC 97-2211. (Journey Across Canada Ser.). 24p. (J). (gr. 3-5). 1997. lib. bdg. 18.60 (*1-55916-197-3*) Rourke Bk Co.

Newfoundland. Emmy Bruno. Ed. by Luana Luther & Ellen Young. Tr. by Louis Palmisano from ITA. LC 97-65308. (Pure Breds Ser.). (Illus.). 168p. 1997. 34.95 (*0-944875-47-5*) Doral Pub.

Newfoundland: A Personal Voyage of Discovery. Farley Mowat. 448p. 1990. pap. 7.99 (*0-7704-2419-8*) Bantam.

Newfoundland: Companion Dog - Water Dog. Joan C. Bendure. (Illus.). 256p. 1994. 25.95 (*0-87605-242-1*) Howell Bks.

Newfoundland: Economic, Diplomatic & Strategic Studies. Ed. by Robert A. Mackay. LC 76-46180. reprint ed. 49.50 (*0-404-15366-6*) AMS Pr.

Newfoundland: Learning about Dogs. Charlotte Wilcox. LC 98-37632. (Illus.). 48p. 21.26 (*0-7368-0160-X*, Capstone Bks) Capstone Pr.

Newfoundland Air Mails. Cyril H. C. Harmer. 181p. 1985. 18.00 (*0-939429-12-8*) Am Air Mail.

***Newfoundland & Labrador.** Lawrence Jackson. (Hello Canada Ser.). 1999. pap. 7.95 (*1-55041-261-2*) Fitzhenry & W Ltd.

Newfoundland & Labrador. Lawrence Jackson. LC 94-28964. (Hello Canada Ser.). (Illus.). 76p. (J). 1995. lib. bdg. 19.95 (*0-8225-2757-X*, Lerner Publctns) Lerner Pub.

Newfoundland & Labrador Prehistory. James A. Tuck. (Canadian Prehistory Ser.). (Illus.). 136p. 1976. pap. 16.95 (*0-660-00096-7*, Pub. by CN Mus Civilization) U of Wash Pr.

Newfoundland Birds: Exploitation, Study, Conservation. William A. Montevecchi & Leslie M. Tuck. (Publications of the Nuttall Ornithological Club: No. 21). (Illus.). 273p. 1987. 10.50 (*1-877973-31-9*) Nuttall Ornith.

***Newfoundland Discovered English Attempts at Colonial.** Cell. 1998. 52.95 (*0-904180-13-1*) Ashgate Pub Co.

Newfoundland Fireside Stories. Jack Fitzgerald. 148p. 1990. reprint ed. pap. 7.95 (*0-920021-78-6*) Creative Bk Pub.

Newfoundland from Fishery to Colony. Ed. & Comment by David B. Quinn. xxvi, 454p. 1979. 65.95 (*0-405-10763-3*) Arno Press.

Newfoundland in the Nineteenth & Twentieth Centuries: Essays in Interpretation. Ed. by James Hiller & Peter Neary. LC 80-506730. 297p. reprint ed. pap. 92.10 (*0-608-16860-2*, 205613400050) Bks Demand.

Newfoundland in the North Atlantic World, 1929-1949. Peter Neary. (Illus.). 488p. (C). 1988. text 65.00 (*0-7735-0668-3*, Pub. by McG-Queens Univ Pr) CUP Services.

Newfoundland in the North Atlantic World, 1929-1949. Peter Neary. 400p. 1996. pap. text 24.95 (*0-7735-1518-6*, F1123, Pub. by McG-Queens Univ Pr) CUP Services.

Newfoundland Law Reports Vols. 1-15: Decisions of the Supreme Court, 1817-1946, Set. 1980. 750.00 (*1-57588-341-4*, 302570) W S Hein.

Newfoundland National Convention, 1946-1948: Debates, Reports & Papers, 2 vols., Set. Ed. by James K. Hiller & Michael F. Harrington. (Illus.). 2064p. 1995. 260.00 (*0-7735-1257-8*, Pub. by McG-Queens Univ Pr) CUP Services.

An Asterisk (*) at the beginning of an entry indicates that the title is appearing for the first time.

Newfoundland Pony. Andrew F. Fraser. 224p. 1992. reprint ed. pap. 11.95 (*1-895387-14-0*) Creative Bk Pub.

Newfoundland Pony Tales. Andrew F. Fraser. 110p. 1996. pap. 6.95 (*1-895387-67-1*) Creative Bk Pub.

Newfoundland Recipes: Recipes From The Kitchens Of Newfoundland. Carol Over. 56p. 1979. reprint ed. pap. 3.15 (*0-920021-69-7*) Creative Bk Pub.

Newfoundland Souvenir. John Devisser. 240p. 1997. pap. text 15.95 (*1-55046-203-2*, Pub. by Boston Mills) Genl Dist Srvs.

Newfoundlands: AKC Rank #50. Kiny Drury & Bill Linn. (Illus.). 1997. pap. 9.95 (*0-7938-2318-8*, KW-174S) TFH Pubns.

Newfoundlands: Everything about Purchase, Care, Nutrition, Diseases, Breeding, Behavior, & Training. Joanna Kosloff. (Complete Pet Owner's Manual Ser.). (Illus.). 1996. pap. 6.95 (*0-8120-9489-1*) Barron.

Newfoundlands Today. Peter Newman & Delphine Richards. LC 97-34518. 176p. 1997. 29.95 (*0-87605-246-4*) Howell Bks.

Newgames: Strategic Competition in the PC Revolution. John Steffens. LC 93-43104. 522p. 1994. text 48.25 (*0-08-040791-9*, Pergamon Pr) Elsevier.

NewGAP. John McLeod & Rita McLeod. 40p. (Orig.). 1990. pap. text 24.00 (*0-87879-892-7*); 22.00 (*0-87879-893-5*); 6.00 (*0-87879-894-3*) Acad Therapy.

NewGAP, Set. John McLeod & Rita McLeod. 40p. (Orig.). 1990. teacher ed. 55.00 (*0-685-46301-X*) Acad Therapy.

Newgate Novel, 1830-1847: Bulwer, Ainsworth, Dickens & Thackeray. William Makepeace Thackeray. LC 62-14875. (Illus.). 288p. reprint ed. pap. 89.30 (*0-7837-3669-X*, 204354300009) Bks Demand.

Newgate of Connecticut: Its Origin & Early History. Richard H. Phelps. LC 96-69650. 128p. 1996. 12.95 (*0-89725-271-3*, 1765) Picton Pr.

Newgrange: Archaeology, Art & Legend. Michael J. O'Kelly. LC 81-86413. (New Aspects of Antiquity Ser.). (Illus.). 240p. 1995. pap. 22.50 (*0-500-27371-5*, Pub. by Thames Hudson) Norton.

Newhall & Williams College: Selected Papers of a History Teacher at New England College, 1917-1973. Russell H. Bostert. XIII, 403p. 1989. text 25.00 (*0-8204-0542-6*) P Lang Pubng.

Newhall Incident: America's Worst Uniformed Cop Massacre. John Anderson & Marsh Cassady. (Illus.). 212p. 1999. 24.95 (*1-884956-09-2*) Quill Driver.

Newhall Incident: America's Worst Uniformed Cop Massacre. John P. Anderson & Marsh Cassady. LC 98-40994. (Illus.). 1998. pap. 14.95 (*1-884956-01-7*) Quill Driver.

Newhaven on Forth: Port of Grace. T. McGowran. (Illus.). 248p. (C). 1996. pap. 30.00 (*0-85976-130-4*, Pub. by J Donald) St Mut.

Newhouse Empire. Carol Felsenthal. 528p. 1999. text 29.95 (*0-670-85674-6*, Viking) Viking Penguin.

Newington, New Hampshire: A Heritage of Independence since 1630. John F. Rowe. LC 87-2235. (Illus.). 336p. 1987. 18.00 (*0-914659-25-1*) Phoenix Pub.

Newington, New Hampshire Families in the Eighteenth Century. Henry W. Hardon. 222p. (Orig.). 1992. pap. 20.00 (*1-55613-540-8*) Heritage Bk.

***Newjack: Guarding Sing Sing.** Ted Conover. LC 99-87895. 352p. 2000. 24.95 (*0-375-50177-0*) Random.

Newk Phillips Papers. Gary P. Walton. 240p. (Orig.). 1996. pap. 14.95 (*1-881168-17-4*) Red Dancefir.

Newlands Reclamation Project Water Rights: A Personal Property Issue. Ernest C. Schank. 17p. 1994. 10.00 (*1-886306-10-9*) Nevada Policy.

***Newletters in Print.** 12th ed. Gale Group Staff. 1242p. 1999. 265.00 (*0-7876-2294-X*) Gale.

Newllano: History of the Llano Movement. James N. Davison. 98p. 1994. pap. 7.95 (*0-9646846-5-9*) Dogwood TX.

Newly Acquired Wealth. 96th ed. Edwards. LC 98-184284. 1996. pap. text 35.00 (*0-15-601841-1*) Harcourt.

Newly Born Woman. Helene Cixous & Catherine Clement. Tr. by Betsy Wing from FRE. LC 85-30898. (Theory & History of Literature Ser.: Vol. 24).Tr. of La/Jeune Nee. 186p. (Orig.). 1986. pap. 13.95 (*0-8166-1466-0*); text 42.95 (*0-8166-1465-2*) U of Minn Pr.

Newly Divorced Book of Protocol: How to Be Civil When You Hate Their Guts. Gloria Lintermans. LC 94-44570. 272p. 1995. 17.95 (*1-56980-037-5*) Barricade Bks.

Newly Floated Public Companies. Grinyer Vaughan & Birley Vaughan. 1980. boxed set 30.00 (*0-7855-7124-8*) St Mut.

Newly Independent States (NIS) Industrial Directories Vol. 1: 500 Largest Companies. Russian Information & Business Center, Inc. Staff. 200p. 1997. pap. 99.00 (*1-57751-202-2*) Intl Business Pubns.

Newly Independent States (NIS) Industrial Directories Vol. 2: 1000 Largest Companies. Russian Information & Business Center, Inc. Staff. 1997. pap. 99.00 (*1-57751-203-0*) Intl Business Pubns.

Newly Independent States (NIS) Industrial Directories Vol. 3: Automobile Industry. Russian Information & Business Center, Inc. Staff. 200p. 1997. pap. 99.00 (*1-57751-204-9*) Intl Business Pubns.

Newly Independent States (NIS) Industrial Directories Vol. 4: Building Materials Industry. Russian Information & Business Center, Inc. Staff. 200p. 1997. pap. 99.00 (*1-57751-205-7*) Intl Business Pubns.

Newly Independent States (NIS) Industrial Directories Vol. 5: Chemical, Pharmaceutical & Microbiology Industry. Russian Information & Business Center, Inc. Staff. 200p. 1997. pap. 99.00 (*1-57751-206-5*) Intl Business Pubns.

Newly Independent States (NIS) Industrial Directories Vol. 6: Clothing Industry. Russian Information & Business Center, Inc. Staff. 200p. 1997. pap. 99.00 (*1-57751-207-3*) Intl Business Pubns.

Newly Independent States (NIS) Industrial Directories Vol. 7: Coal Mining & Peat Industry. Russian Information & Business Center, Inc. Staff. 200p. 1997. pap. 99.00 (*1-57751-208-1*) Intl Business Pubns.

Newly Independent States (NIS) Industrial Directories Vol. 8: Consumer Goods, Household & Cultural Foods. Russian Information & Business Center, Inc. Staff. 200p. 1997. pap. 99.00 (*1-57751-209-X*) Intl Business Pubns.

Newly Independent States (NIS) Industrial Directories Vol. 9: Electrical Engineering. Russian Information & Business Center, Inc. Staff. 200p. 1997. pap. 99.00 (*1-57751-210-3*) Intl Business Pubns.

Newly Independent States (NIS) Industrial Directories Vol. 10: Fishing & Fish Processing. Russian Information & Business Center, Inc. Staff. 200p. 1997. pap. 99.00 (*1-57751-211-1*) Intl Business Pubns.

Newly Independent States (NIS) Industrial Directories Vol. 11: Food & Food Processing Industry. Russian Information & Business Center, Inc. Staff. 200p. 1997. pap. 99.00 (*1-57751-212-X*) Intl Business Pubns.

Newly Independent States (NIS) Industrial Directories Vol. 12: Footwear & Tanning Industry. Russian Information & Business Center, Inc. Staff. 200p. 1997. pap. 99.00 (*1-57751-213-8*) Intl Business Pubns.

Newly Independent States (NIS) Industrial Directories Vol. 13: Forestry & Timber Processing. Russian Information & Business Center, Inc. Staff. 200p. 1997. pap. 99.00 (*1-57751-214-6*) Intl Business Pubns.

Newly Independent States (NIS) Industrial Directories Vol. 14: High-Tech Products, PC, Research & Design. Russian Information & Business Center, Inc. Staff. 1997. pap. 99.00 (*1-57751-215-4*) Intl Business Pubns.

Newly Independent States (NIS) Industrial Directories Vol. 15: Machine-Building Industry. Russian Information & Business Center, Inc. Staff. 200p. 1997. pap. 99.00 (*1-57751-201-4*) Intl Business Pubns.

Newly Independent States (NIS) Industrial Directories Vol. 16: Medical Equipment Industry. Russian Information & Business Center, Inc. Staff. 200p. 1997. pap. 99.00 (*1-57751-216-2*) Intl Business Pubns.

Newly Independent States (NIS) Industrial Directories Vol. 17: Metal-Working Industry. Russian Information & Business Center, Inc. Staff. 200p. 1997. pap. 99.00 (*1-57751-200-6*) Intl Business Pubns.

Newly Independent States (NIS) Industrial Directories Vol. 18: Metallurgy. Russian Information & Business Center, Inc. Staff. 200p. 1997. pap. 99.00 (*1-57751-217-0*) Intl Business Pubns.

Newly Independent States (NIS) Industrial Directories Vol. 19: Mining (Building Materials) Russian Information & Business Center, Inc. Staff. 200p. 1997. pap. 99.00 (*1-57751-218-9*) Intl Business Pubns.

Newly Independent States (NIS) Industrial Directories Vol. 20: Oil & Gas Industry. Russian Information & Business Center, Inc. Staff. 200p. 1997. pap. 99.00 (*1-57751-219-7*) Intl Business Pubns.

Newly Independent States (NIS) Industrial Directories Vol. 21: Oil Refining & Gas Processing. Russian Information & Business Center, Inc. Staff. 200p. 1997. pap. 99.00 (*1-57751-220-0*) Intl Business Pubns.

Newly Independent States (NIS) Industrial Directories Vol. 22: Gold Mining & Mining. Russian Information & Business Center, Inc. Staff. 200p. 1997. pap. 99.00 (*1-57751-221-9*) Intl Business Pubns.

Newly Independent States (NIS) Industrial Directories Vol. 23: Power Industry. Russian Information & Business Center, Inc. Staff. 200p. 1997. pap. 99.00 (*1-57751-222-7*) Intl Business Pubns.

Newly Independent States (NIS) Industrial Directories Vol. 24: Publishing & Printing. Russian Information & Business Center, Inc. Staff. 200p. 1997. pap. 99.00 (*1-57751-223-5*) Intl Business Pubns.

Newly Independent States (NIS) Industrial Directories Vol. 25: Pulp & Paper Industry. Russian Information & Business Center, Inc. Staff. 200p. 1997. pap. 99.00 (*1-57751-224-3*) Intl Business Pubns.

Newly Independent States (NIS) Industrial Directories Vol. 26: Radio-Electronic Industry. Russian Information & Business Center, Inc. Staff. 200p. 1997. pap. 99.00 (*1-57751-225-1*) Intl Business Pubns.

Newly Independent States (NIS) Industrial Directories Vol. 27: Rubber & Plastic Industry. Russian Information & Business Center, Inc. Staff. 200p. 1997. pap. 99.00 (*1-57751-226-X*) Intl Business Pubns.

Newly Independent States (NIS) Industrial Directories Vol. 28: Scrap & Waste Processing. Russian Information & Business Center, Inc. Staff. 200p. 1997. pap. 99.00 (*1-57751-227-8*) Intl Business Pubns.

Newly Independent States (NIS) Industrial Directories Vol. 29: Textile Industry. Russian Information & Business Center, Inc. Staff. 200p. 1997. pap. 99.00 (*1-57751-228-6*) Intl Business Pubns.

Newly Independent States (NIS) Industrial Directories Vol. 30: Tobacco Industry. Russian Information & Business Center, Inc. Staff. 200p. 1997. pap. 99.00 (*1-57751-229-4*) Intl Business Pubns.

Newly Independent States (NIS) Industrial Directories Vol. 31: Transport & Civil Engineering. Russian Information & Business Center, Inc. Staff. 200p. 1997. pap. 99.00 (*1-57751-230-8*) Intl Business Pubns.

Newly Independent States of Eurasia: Handbook of Former Soviet Republics. 2nd ed. Stephen K. Batalden & Sandra L. Batalden. LC 97-3893. (Illus.). 248p. (J). (gr. 7). 1997. pap. 39.50 (*0-89774-940-5*) Oryx Pr.

Newly Industrialized Countries & the Information Technology Revolution: The Brazillian Experience. Arlindo Villaschi. 224p. 1994. 66.95 (*1-85628-699-1*, Pub. by Avebry) Ashgate Pub Co.

Newly Industrializing Asia in Transition: Policy Reform & American Response. Tun-jen Cheng & Stephan Haggard. LC 87-80821. (Policy Papers in International Affairs: No. 31). (Illus.). x, 106p. (C). 1987. pap. text 8.50 (*0-87725-531-8*) U of Cal IAS.

Newly Industrializing Countries in the World Economy. Neil McMullen. (British-North American Committee Ser.). 1982. 7.00 (*0-685-06045-4*) Natl Planning.

Newly Industrializing Countries in the World Economy: Challenges for U. S. Policy. Ed. by Randall B. Purcell. LC 89-30730. 250p. 1989. lib. bdg. 37.00 (*1-55587-154-2*) L Rienner.

Newly Industrializing Countries of Asia. 2nd ed. Gerald Tan. LC 95-948158. 400p. 1995. pap. 28.00 (*981-210-075-X*, Pub. by Times Academic) Intl Spec Bk.

Newly Industrializing Economies of East Asia. Anis Chowdhury & Iyanatul Islam. LC 93-16568. (Illus.). 304p. (C). 1993. pap. 29.99 (*0-415-09749-5*, B2338) Routledge.

Newly Made Mason: What He & Every Mason Should Know about Masonry. 6th ed. Ed. by H. L. Haywood. (Illus.). 256p. 1993. reprint ed. text 15.95 (*0-88053-030-8*, M-80) Macoy Pub.

Newlywed: A Survival Guide to the First Years of Marriage. Pamela A. Piljac. LC 85-21288. (Illus.). 256p. (Orig.). 1985. pap. 8.95 (*0-913339-02-4*) Bryce-Waterton Pubns.

Newlywed Bath Book: A Soak for Two Souls. Elizabeth O'Dowd & Cynthia Good. (Illus.). 10p. 1998. pap. 9.95 (*1-56352-459-7*) Longstreet.

Newlywed Book. William Coleman. LC 85-1345. 144p. (Orig.). 1985. pap. 6.99 (*0-87123-799-7*) Bethany Hse.

***Newlywed Cookbook.** Robin Vitetta-Miller. LC 99-16755. (Illus.). 240p. 1999. pap. 14.95 (*1-57071-458-4*) Sourcebks.

Newlywed Game (In Name Only) Bonnie K. Winn. LC 96-2467. (American Romance Ser.). 248p. 1996. mass mkt. 3.75 (*0-373-16624-9*, 1-16624-8) Harlequin Bks.

***Newlywed Games.** Mary Davis. LC 99-89172. 384p. 2000. mass mkt. 6.99 (*1-57673-268-1*, Pub. by Multnomah Pubs) GL Services.

***Newlyweds: Forty-eight Inspirational Stories of the Britnell Family from Writings in the Family Tree.** Charlie Britnell. LC 98-211039. (Illus.). 1998. write for info. (*0-89315-402-4*) Lambert Bk.

Newlyweds: The Crucial First Years of Marriage. 3rd ed. Basil J. Sherlock & Ingrid K. S. Moller. 144p. 1992. per. 21.95 (*0-8403-6753-8*) Kendall-Hunt.

Newlyweds' Guide to Sex on the First Night. Richard Smith. LC 84-40318. (Illus.). 144p. 1984. pap. 4.95 (*0-89480-773-0*, 773) Workman Pub.

Newlyweds' Predictionary: A Safe-Deposit Box of Hopes, Plans, Promises, & Expectations for Your First Ten Years. Text by Erika Wood. 1998. 19.95 (*0-8362-5260-8*) Andrews & McMeel.

Newman. Barnett Newman. (Illus.). 336p. 1999. 65.00 (*3-7757-0795-6*, Pub. by Gerd Hatje) Dist Art Pubs.

Newman: A Bibliography of Secondary Studies. John R. Griffin. LC 80-68760. 150p. (Orig.). 1980. pap. text 12.00 (*0-931888-04-2*) Christendom Pr.

Newman: From Oxford to the People. Ed. by Paul Vaiss. 306p. 1997. pap. 24.95 (*0-85244-269-6*, 954, Pub. by Gra1cewing) Morehouse Pub.

Newman: Paul Newman - A Celebration. Eric Lax. (Illus.). 1999. pap. 24.95 (*1-85793-955-7*, Pub. by Pavilion Bks Ltd) Trafalgar.

Newman: Towards the Second Spring. Michael Ffinch. 230p. 1996. pap. 19.95 (*0-00-599301-6*, Pub. by T & T Clark) Bks Intl VA.

Newman: Towards the Second Spring. Michael Finch. LC 91-76069. 232p. (Orig.). 1992. reprint ed. pap. 14.95 (*0-89870-388-3*) Ignatius Pr.

Newman after a Hundred Years. Ed. by Ian Ker & Alan G. Hill. 488p. (C). 1990. 95.00 (*0-19-812891-6*) OUP.

***Newman American Historical.** Holly Newman. 2000. text 22.95 (*0-312-86869-3*) St Martin.

Newman & Conversion. Ed. by Ian Ker. LC 98-153006. (C). 1997. pap. text 18.00 (*0-268-01482-5*) U of Notre Dame Pr.

Newman & Gadamer: Toward a Hermeneutics of Religious Knowledge. Thomas K. Carr. LC 96-28988. (AAR Reflection & Theory in the Study of Religion Ser.). 214p. 1996. 34.95 (*0-7885-0303-0*, 01 10 10) OUP.

Newman & Heresy: The Anglican Years. Stephen B. Thomas. 349p. (C). 1991. text 75.00 (*0-521-39208-X*) Cambridge U Pr.

Newman & the Fullness of Christianity. Ian Ker. 160p. 1993. pap. text 27.95 (*0-567-29225-8*, Pub. by T & T Clark) Bks Intl VA.

Newman Assignment. Kurt Haberl. (Illus.). 12p. (Orig.). 1996. teacher ed., spiral bd. 5.00 (*0-943864-82-8*) Davenport.

Newman Assignment. Kurt Haberl. LC 95-83550. (Illus.). 321p. (Orig.). (YA). (gr. 9-12). 1996. pap. text 10.95 (*0-943864-78-X*) Davenport.

Newman Brothers: An Essay in Comparative Intellectual Biography. William Robbins. LC 66-4976. (Illus.). 214p. 1966. 26.50 (*0-674-62200-6*) HUP.

Newman Compendium for Sundays & Feasts. Ed. by James Tolhurst. 270p. 1995. pap. 15.95 (*0-85244-292-0*, 953, Pub. by Gra1cewing) Morehouse Pub.

Newman for Everyone: 101 Questions Answered Imaginatively by Newman. John Henry Newman. Ed. by Jules M. Brady. LC 96-1267. 170p. (Orig.). 1996. pap. 5.95 (*0-8189-0736-3*) Alba.

Newman on Being a Christian. Ian Ker. 1997. pap. 25.95 (*0-00-599319-9*, Pub. by T & T Clark) Bks Intl VA.

Newman on Being a Christian. Ian Ker. LC 89-40752. 200p. (C). 1990. text 29.00 (*0-268-01468-X*) U of Notre Dame Pr.

Newman on Being a Christian. Ian Ker. LC 89-40752. (C). 1992. pap. text 14.00 (*0-268-01474-4*) U of Notre Dame Pr.

Newman Report: Interim Report, Eighth Coast Guard District Offshore Operations Liaison Staff, 1 June 1973. C. T. Newman. 109p. (Orig.). 1985. pap. text 50.85 (*0-934114-67-6*, BK-515) Marine Educ.

Newman the Theologian: A Reader. Ed. by Ian Ker. LC 90-70863. 288p. (C). 1990. pap. text 11.50 (*0-268-01469-8*) U of Notre Dame Pr.

Newmann: The Pioneer Mentalist. James B. Alfredson. (Illus.). 78p. 1989. 22.50 (*0-916638-42-1*, D M Magic Bks) Meyerbooks.

Newman's Birds of Southern Africa. Kenneth Newman. LC 96-144471. (Illus.). 1998. 19.95 (*1-86812-623-4*) Menasha Ridge.

Newman's Birds of Southern Africa: The Green Edition. Kenneth Newman. (Illus.). 461p. (Orig.). (C). 1996. pap. 39.95 (*0-8130-1427-1*) U Press Fla.

***Newman's Birds Of Southern Africa: 7th Ed., 1.** 7th ed. Kenneth Newman. (Illus.). 510p. 1999. pap. 19.95 (*1-86812-757-5*) Southern Appeal.

***Newman's Challenge.** Stanley L. Jaki. LC 99-46845. 331p. 2000. pap. 20.00 (*0-8028-4395-6*) Eerdmans.

Newman's Conveyancing Practice & Procedure. Vera D. Gittins & Phyllis E. Newman. 128p. 1985. 85.00 (*0-906840-91-0*, Pub. by Fourmat Pub) St Mut.

Newman's Conveyancing Practice & Procedure. Phyllis E. Newman & Sue Craven. 214p. (C). 1991. 110.00 (*1-85190-108-6*, Pub. by Tolley Pubng) St Mut.

Newman's Mariology. Michael Perrott. 104p. 1997. pap. 15.95 (*1-901157-45-8*) St Austin.

Newmans of Hollywood. Burlingame. 2000. 32.50 (*0-02-864770-X*) S&S Trade.

Newman's Own Cookbook. Paul Newman & A. E. Hotchner. LC 98-35430. (Illus.). 224p. 1998. 24.50 (*0-684-84832-5*) Simon & Schuster.

Newmark's U. K. Asset Management Yearbook, 1997/98. Wade Newmark. 192p. 1997. boxed set 185.00 (*1-85573-325-0*, Pub. by Woodhead Pubng) Am Educ Systs.

Newnes Audio & Hi-Fi Engineer's Pocket Book. 2nd rev. ed. Vivian Capel. (Illus.). 216p. 1995. text 29.95 (*0-7506-2001-3*) Buttrwrth-Heinemann.

Newnes Building Services (Mechanical) Pocket Book. Peter Jones & John Knight. LC 95-21923. 272p. 1995. 29.95 (*0-7506-2148-6*) Buttrwrth-Heinemann.

Newnes Circuit Ideas Pocket Book. Electronics World & Wireless World Magazine Editor. (Illus.). 312p. 1995. 29.95 (*0-7506-2336-5*, Pub. by Newtech) Buttrwrth-Heinemann.

Newnes Computer Engineer's Pocket Book. Michael H. Tooley. 1988. 22.00 (*0-434-91967-5*) CRC Pr.

Newnes Computer Engineer's Pocket Book. 2nd ed. Michael H. Tooley. 1990. 22.00 (*0-434-91969-1*) CRC Pr.

Newnes Computer Engineer's Pocket Book. 4th ed. Michael H. Tooley. 272p. 1999. text 28.95 (*0-7506-2095-1*) Buttrwrth-Heinemann.

Newnes Control Engineering Pocket Book. W. Bolton. (Illus.). 304p. 1998. text 29.95 (*0-7506-3928-8*, Newnes) Buttrwrth-Heinemann.

Newnes Data Communications Pocket Book. 3rd ed. Michael H. Tooley. LC 96-42136. (Illus.). 256p. 1999. text 28.95 (*0-7506-2884-7*) Buttrwrth-Heinemann.

Newnes Dictionary of Electronics. 4th ed. G. W. Dummer et al. LC 99-461824. 400p. 1999. 36.95 (*0-7506-4331-5*) Buttrwrth-Heinemann.

Newnes Digital IC Pocket Book. Ray M. Marston. (Illus.). 256p. 1999. text 29.95 (*0-7506-3018-3*) Buttrwrth-Heinemann.

Newnes 8086 Family Pocket Book: Up to & Including 80486. Ian Sinclair. LC 91-137669. 348p. 1990. pap. 107.90 (*0-608-04992-1*, 206561000004) Bks Demand.

***Newnes Electrical Engineer's Handbook.** D. F. Warne. 448p. 2000. 56.95 (*0-7506-4879-1*, Newnes) Buttrwrth-Heinemann.

Newnes Electrical Engineer's Pocket Book. 23rd ed. Ed. by D. F. Warne. (Illus.). 333p. 2000. text 24.95 (*0-7506-3515-0*, Newnes) Buttrwrth-Heinemann.

***Newnes Electrical Pocket Book.** Martin Heathcote & E. A. Reeves. 608p. 2000. 29.95 (*0-7506-4758-2*, Newnes) Buttrwrth-Heinemann.

Newnes Electrical Pocket Book. E. A. Reeves. 1988. 21.00 (*0-434-91716-8*) CRC Pr.

Newnes Electrical Pocket Book. 22nd ed. Ed. by E. A. Reeves. LC 95-20183. (Illus.). 544p. 1995. pap. text 29.95 (*0-7506-2566-X*) Buttrwrth-Heinemann.

Newnes Electronic Components Pocket Book. M. Tooley. (Illus.). 208p. 1999. 24.95 (*0-7506-2700-X*) Buttrwrth-Heinemann.

Newnes Electronics Engineer's Pocket Book. 2nd ed. Keith Brindley & Joseph Carr. (Illus.). 368p. 2000. 28.95 (*0-7506-3972-5*, Newnes) Buttrwrth-Heinemann.

Newnes Electronics Pocket Book. E. A. Parr. 1988. 22.00 (*0-434-91519-X*) CRC Pr.

Newnes Engineering & Physical Science Pocket Book. 2nd ed. J. O. Bird. LC 96-17119. (Illus.). 624p. 1996. 32.95 (*0-7506-2897-9*, Pub. by Newtech) Buttrwrth-Heinemann.

***Newnes Engineering Materials Pocket Book.** Bolton. 2000. 28.95 (*0-7506-4974-7*, Newnes) Buttrwrth-Heinemann.

***Newnes Engineering Mathematics Pocket Book.** Bird. 384p. 2001. 32.95 (*0-7506-4992-5*, Newnes) Buttrwrth-Heinemann.

***Newnes Engineering Science Pocket Book.** Bird. 512p. 2001. 32.95 (*0-7506-4991-7*, Newnes) Buttrwrth-Heinemann.

Newnes File Formats Pocket Book. Stephen Morris. 352p. 2000. text 22.95 (*0-7506-3423-5*) Buttrwrth-Heinemann.

N

*Newnes Guide to Audio & Hi-Fi: A Conprehensive Introduction to Audio & Hi-Fi Systems. Nick Beer. 384p. 1999. pap. text 28.95 (0-7506-4418-4, Newnes) Buttrwrth-Heinemann.
*Newnes Guide to Digital Television. Richard Brice. 258p. 2000. 49.95 (0-7506-4586-5, Newnes) Buttrwrth-Heinemann.
Newnes Instrumentation & Measurement Pocket Book. William Bolton. 240p. 1991. text 32.95 (0-7506-0039-X) Buttrwrth-Heinemann.
Newnes Instrumentation & Measurement Pocket Book. 2nd ed. William Bolton. LC 96-47098. (Illus.). 320p. 1996. 29.95 (0-7506-2885-5) Buttrwrth-Heinemann.
Newnes Mathematics Pocket Book for Engineers. J. O. Bird. (Illus.). 352p. 1988. 26.95 (0-7506-0264-3) Buttrwrth-Heinemann.
Newnes Mathematics Pocket Book for Engineers. J. O. Bird. 1988. 21.00 (0-434-90129-6) CRC Pr.
Newnes Mathematics Pocket Book for Engineers. 2nd ed. J. O. Bird. LC 97-27319. (Pocket Book Ser.). 384p. 1999. text 28.95 (0-7506-3004-3, Newnes) Buttrwrth-Heinemann.
Newnes Mechanical Engineers Pocket Book. 2nd ed. Roger Timings. LC 97-27318. (Illus.). 650p. 1998. text 34.95 (0-7506-3262-3) Buttrwrth-Heinemann.
Newnes Microprocessor Pocket Book. Steve Money. 1990. 22.00 (0-8493-7146-5) CRC Pr.
Newnes Microprocessor Pocket Book. Steve A. Money. LC 89-45982. (Illus.). 260p. 1989. pap. 80.60 (0-608-04989-1, 206560700004) Bks Demand.
Newnes Passive & Discrete Circuits Pocket Book. R. M. Marston. (Illus.). 400p. Date not set. 29.95 (0-7506-4192-4) Buttrwrth-Heinemann.
Newnes PC Networking Pocket Book. Steve Heath. (Illus.). 300p. 1998. text 28.95 (0-7506-3449-9, Newnes) Buttrwrth-Heinemann.
Newnes PC Troubleshooting Pocket Book. 2nd ed. Michael Tooley. (Illus.). 320p. 1998. text 28.95 (0-7506-3901-6, Newnes) Buttrwrth-Heinemann.
Newnes Physical Science Pocket Book for Engineers. 4201st ed. J. O. Bird & P. Chivers. 1988. 22.00 (0-408-01343-5) CRC Pr.
Newnes Radio Amateur & Listener's Pocket Book. Steve Money. 1988. 27.00 (0-434-91259-X) CRC Pr.
Newnes Radio & Electronic Engineer's Pocket Book. Keith Brindley. 1988. 27.00 (0-434-90179-2) CRC Pr.
*Newnes Radio & RF Engineers Pocket Book. John Davies & Joseph Carr. 608p. 2000. 29.95 (0-7506-4600-4, Newnes) Buttrwrth-Heinemann.
Newnes Radio Engineer's Pocket Book. John Davies. (Illus.). 280p. 1995. text 29.95 (0-7506-1738-1) Buttrwrth-Heinemann.
Newnes Service Engineer's Pocket Book. Geoffrey E. Lewis & Ian R. Sinclair. LC 97-27320. 272p. 1998. text 29.95 (0-7506-3789-7, Newnes) Buttrwrth-Heinemann.
Newnes 68000 Family Pocket Book. Michael H. Tooley. LC 92-160615. (Illus.). 263p. 1992. pap. 81.60 (0-608-04987-5, 206560500004) Bks Demand.
Newnes Telecommunications Pocket Book. E. A. Edis & J. E. Varrall. LC 92-14810. (Illus.). 352p. 1992. text 34.95 (0-7506-0307-0) Buttrwrth-Heinemann.
Newnes Television & Video Engineer's Pocket Book. Trundle. 1988. 27.00 (0-434-90197-0) CRC Pr.
Newnes Television & Video Engineer's Pocket Book. 3rd ed. Eugene Trundle. (Illus.). 503p. 1999. 29.95 (0-7506-4194-0, Newnes) Buttrwrth-Heinemann.
Newnes UNIX Pocket Book. 2nd rev. ed. Steve Heath. 450p. 1994. 29.95 (0-7506-2073-0) Buttrwrth-Heinemann.
Newnes Unix Pocket Book. 3rd ed. Steve Heath. LC 99-180913. 340p. 1999. text 28.95 (0-7506-4108-8, Newnes) Buttrwrth-Heinemann.
Newnes Windows 95 Pocket Book. Ian R. Sinclair. LC 96-113828. 400p. 1995. text 29.95 (0-7506-2227-X, Digital DEC) Buttrwrth-Heinemann.
Newnes Windows NT Version 4 Pocket Book. 2nd ed. Steve Heath. LC 96-37276. 300p. 1997. text 28.95 (0-7506-3422-7) Buttrwrth-Heinemann.
*Newnes Windows Programming Pocket Book. Conor Sexton. (Illus.). 300p. 1999. 24.95 (0-7506-1853-1, Digital DEC) Buttrwrth-Heinemann.
*Newnes Workshop Engineer's Pocket Book. Roger Timings. 224p. 2000. 29.95 (0-7506-4719-1, Newnes) Buttrwrth-Heinemann.
Newnes Z80 Pocket Book. Chris Roberts. LC 92-225477. 191p. 1992. pap. 59.30 (0-608-04988-3, 206560600004) Bks Demand.
Newness of Life. Richard Howard. 48p. 1984. pap. 1.99 (0-8341-0925-5) Nazarene.
Newness of the Unchanging. Kenneth G. Mills. pap. 10.95 incl. audio (0-919842-02-X, KGOM5) Sun-Scape Ent.
Newpapers. Bill Balcziak. (Communication Today & Tomorrow Ser.). (Illus.). 48p. (J). (gr. 4-8). 1989. lib. bdg. 25.27 (0-86592-069-9) Rourke Enter.
Newport. Rob Lewis. (Images of America Ser.). 128p. 1996. pap. 16.99 (0-7524-0405-9) Arcadia Publng.
*Newport. Barbara Malloy. (Images of America Ser.). 128p. 1999. pap. 18.99 (0-7385-0298-7) Arcadia Publng.
Newport: A Short History. C. P. Jefferys. 96p. 1992. pap. 9.95 (0-9633200-0-9); spiral bd. 100.00 (0-9633200-1-7) Newport Hist Soc.
Newport: Our Social Capital. May K. Van Rensselaer. LC 75-910. (Leisure Class in America Ser.). (Illus.). 1975. reprint ed. 36.95 (0-405-06936-7) Ayer.
Newport & Narragansett Bay Book: A Complete Guide with Block Island. 2nd rev. ed. Pamela Petro. LC 97-32467. (Great Destinations Ser.). (Illus.). 320p. 1998. pap. 17.95 (0-936399-93-7) Berkshire Hse.
Newport Beach, California: Celebrating 90 Years. Steven Simon, Jr. (Illus.). 112p. 1996. 34.95 (0-9652771-0-0) Simon Fine Art.
Newport Biennial. 3rd ed. Marilu Knode et al. LC 91-15760. (Illus.). 80p. 1991. pap. 14.95 (0-917493-19-2) Orange Cnty Mus.
Newport Cookbook. rev. ed. Ceil Dyer. (Illus.). 256p. reprint ed. pap. 5.95 (0-940078-08-2) Foremost Pubs.
Newport Cooks & Collects. Preservation Society of Newport County Staff. LC 95-72320. (Illus.). 176p. 1996. 16.95 (0-9646888-1-6) Preserv Soc Newport.
Newport Houses. Richard Carbotti. (Birds Pack Ser.). 8p. (J). (gr. k-2). 1993. pap. write for info. (1-882563-01-8) Lamont Bks.
Newport Houses. Illus. by Roberto Schezen. LC 88-43445. 228p. 1989. reprint ed. 65.00 (0-8478-0912-9, Pub. by Rizzoli Intl) St Martin.
Newport, Illustrated: A Series of Pen & Pencil Sketches by the Editor of "The Newport Mercury" (Illus.). 110p. 1997. reprint ed. pap. 16.00 (0-8328-6480-3); reprint ed. lib. bdg. 24.00 (0-8328-6479-X) Higginson Bk Co.
Newport in the Rockies: The Life & Good Times of Colorado Springs Revised for the 1990's. rev. ed. Marshall Sprague. LC 80-52995. 400p. 1987. pap. 14.95 (0-8040-0899-X) Swallow.
Newport Mansions: The Gilded Age. Thomas Gannon. Ed. by James B. Patrick. (Illus.). 88p. 1982. 20.00 (0-940078-01-5) Foremost Pubs.
*Newportraits. Eileen Warburton & Newport Art Museum Staff. LC 99-44802. (Illus.). 344p. 2000. 50.00 (1-58465-018-4) U Pr of New Eng.
News. Peggy Burns. (Stepping Through History Ser.). (Illus.). 32p. (J). 1995. lib. bdg. 5.00 (1-56847-342-7) Raintree Steck-V.
*News: A Reader. Ed. by Howard Tumber. LC 99-15284. (Oxford Media Readers Ser.). 432p. 2000. pap. text 24.95 (0-19-874231-2) OUP.
News: Reporting & Writing. 2nd ed. (C). 2000. text 45.33 (0-205-29576-2, Longwood Div) Allyn.
News: Reporting & Writing for Print, Broadcast, & Public Relations. John H. Vivian & Alfred Lorenz. LC 95-14806. 608p. 1995. pap. text 58.00 (0-205-13975-2) Allyn.
News: The Politics of Illusion. 3rd ed. W. Lance Bennett. LC 95-3575. (700 (College) Ser.). 256p. (C). 1995. pap. 45.00 (0-8013-1167-5, 79661) Longman.
*News: The Politics of Illusion. 4th ed. W. Lance Bennett. 304p. 2000. pap. 39.00 (0-8013-1921-8) Longman.
News - the Evolution of Journalism in Canada. Andrew M. Osler. pap. text. write for info. (0-7730-5193-7) Addison-Wes.
News about Dinosaurs. 1995. pap. 10.00 (0-15-305211-2) Harcourt Schl Pubs.
News about Dinosaurs. HarBrace Staff. 1995. pap. text 13.10 (0-15-305583-9) Harcourt.
News about Dinosaurs. Houghton Mifflin Company Staff. (Literature Experience 1993 Ser.). (J). (gr. 4). 1992. pap. 10.24 (0-395-61800-2) HM.
News about Dinosaurs. Lauber. (J). 1998. pap. 6.95 (0-87628-976-6) Ctr Appl Res.
News about Dinosaurs. Patricia Lauber. LC 88-24140. (Illus.). 48p. (J). (gr. 1-5). 1989. lib. bdg. 17.00 (0-02-754520-2, Bradbury S&S) S&S Childrens.
News about Dinosaurs. Patricia Lauber. LC 94-2373. 1994. 12.15 (0-606-06620-9, Pub. by Turtleback) Demco.
News Aesthetic. Ed. by Lawrence Mirsky & Silvana Tropea. LC 97-215283. (Illus.). 64p. (Orig.). 1995. pap. 19.95 (1-56898-051-5) Princeton Arch.
News Agencies Pool of Non-Aligned Countries. 303p. 1983. 19.95 (0-940500-76-0, Pub. by Indian Inst Comm) Asia Bk Corp.
News Agencies Pool of Non-Aligned Countries: A Perspectve. Indian Institute of Mass Communication Staff. 303p. 1983. 24.95 (0-318-37279-7) Asia Bk Corp.
News Agencies, Their Structure & Operation. UNESCO Staff. LC 76-88957. 208p. 1970. reprint ed. lib. bdg. 65.00 (0-8371-2501-4, UNNA, Greenwood Pr) Greenwood.
News Analysis: Case Studies of International & National News in the Press. Teun A. Van Dijk. (Communication Series Jennings Bryant). 348p. (C). 1987. text 69.95 (0-8058-0064-6) L Erlbaum Assocs.
News & Dissent: The Press & the Politics of Peace in Canada. Robert A. Hackett. Ed. by Brenda Dervin. (Communication & Information Science Ser.). 336p. 1991. 73.25 (0-89391-769-9); pap. 39.50 (0-89391-815-6) Ablx Pub.
News & Information in a Digital World: And That Is the Way It Will Be. Christopher Harper. 1999. pap. 18.95 (0-8147-3608-4) NYU Pr.
*News & Journalism in the U. K. A Textbook. 3rd ed. Brian McNair. LC 98-47256. 240p. 1999. pap. write for info. (0-415-19924-7) Routledge.
*News & Journalism in the U. K. A Textbook. 3rd ed. Brian McNair. LC 98-47256. 1999. write for info. (0-415-19923-9) Routledge.
News & Newsmaking: Essays. Contrib. by Stephen Hess. 148p. (C). 1996. 24.95 (0-8157-3634-7) Brookings.
News & Numbers: A Guide to Reporting Statistical Claims & Controversies in Health & Other Fields. Victor Cohn. 190p. (C). 1988. pap. text 16.95 (0-8138-1437-5) Iowa St U Pr.
News & Observer's Raleigh: A Living History of North Carolina's Capital. Ed. by David Perkins. LC 93-72410. (Illus.). 202p. (Orig.). 1994. 22.95 (0-89587-121-1) Blair.
News & Politics in the Age of Revolution: Jean Luzac's "Gazette de Leyde" Jeremy D. Popkin. LC 89-31379. (Illus.). 304p. 1989. text 45.00 (0-8014-2301-5) Cornell U Pr.
News & Power. Rodney Tiffen. 228p. (C). 1990. pap. 21.95 (0-04-372043-9) Routledge.
*News & Smoke: Selected Poems. Sharon Thesen. 160p. 2000. pap. 12.95 (0-88922-417-X, Pub. by Talonbks) Genl Dist Srvs.
News & Society in the Greek Polis. Sian Lewis. (Studies in the History of Greece & Rome). 224p. (C). 1996. 55.00 (0-8078-2309-0); pap. 19.95 (0-8078-4621-X) U of NC Pr.
*News & the Culture of Lying. 1998. per. 22.95 (0-684-86364-2) Free Pr.
News & the Culture of Lying: How Journalism Really Works. Paul Weaver. 250p. 1994. 22.95 (0-02-934021-7) Free Pr.
News & the Human Interest Story. Helen M. Hughes. LC 80-19176. (Social Science Classics Ser.). 313p. (C). 1980. text 39.95 (0-87855-326-6); pap. text 24.95 (0-87855-729-6) Transaction Pubs.
News & Weather: Seven Canadian Poets. Ed. by August Kleinzahler. 92p. 1982. pap. 9.95 (0-919626-17-3, Pub. by Brick Bks) Genl Dist Srvs.
News As Hegemonic Reality: American Political Culture & the Framing of New Accounts. Allan Rachlin. LC 88-12009. 168p. 1988. 52.95 (0-275-92534-X, C2534, Praeger Pubs) Greenwood.
News at the Hearth: A Drama of Reading in Nineteenth-Century America. Thomas C. Leonard. 1993. pap. 7.00 (0-944026-42-7) Am Antiquarian.
News Behind Newspapers: A Study of the Indian Press. Phani B. Chakraborty & Brojen Bhattacharya. (C). 1989. 17.50 (81-85195-16-1, Pub. by Minerva) S Asia.
News Book. J. Gosling et al. (Sun Technical Reference Library). (Illus.). ix, 235p. 1990. 64.95 (0-387-96915-2) Spr-Verlag.
News Cameras in the Courtroom: A Free Press-Fair Trial Debate. Susanna Barber. Ed. by Melvin J. Voigt. LC 86-10858. (Communication & Information Science Ser.). 176p. 1987. text 73.25 (0-89391-349-9) Ablx Pub.
*News Corporation, Technology & the Workplace: Global Strategies, Local Change. Timothy Majoribanks. (Illus.). 240p. (C). 2000. 54.95 (0-521-77280-X); pap. 19.95 (0-521-77535-3) Cambridge U Pr.
News Coverage of Violence Against Women: Engendering Blame. Marian Meyers. LC 96-25357. 148p. 1996. 38.95 (0-8039-5635-5); pap. 18.95 (0-8039-5636-3) Sage.
News Crew: Story Rhyme Coloring Book. Alfreda Doyle. (Illus.). 24p. (J). (gr. 3-8). 1998. pap. 8.95 (1-56820-326-8) Story Time.
*News, Crime & Culture Maggie Wykes. LC 99-37924. 2000. write for info. (0-7453-1331-0) Pluto GBR.
*News, Crime & Culture. Maggie Wykes. LC 00-9908. 2001. pap. write for info. (0-7453-1326-4, Pub. by Pluto GBR) Stylus Pub VA.
News Culture Stuart Allan. LC 99-19412. (Issues in Cultural & Media Studies). 1999. 24.95 (0-335-19915-1) OpUniv Pr.
*News Culture. Stuart Allan. 176p. 1999. pap. text 24.95 (0-335-19956-9) OpUniv Pr.
News Effects in a High Frequency Model of the Sterling-Dollar Exchange Rate. C. A. Goodhart et al. LC HG3823.. (Bank of England. Discussion Papers. Technical Ser.: No. 41). 14p. reprint ed. pap. 30.00 (0-7837-5377-2, 204514100005) Bks Demand.
*News for a Change: An Advocate's Guide to Working with the Media. Lawrence M. Wallack. LC 99-6310. 1999. write for info. (0-7619-1924-4) Sage.
*News for a Change: An Advocate's Guide to Working with the Media. Ed. by Lawrence Wallak. LC 99-6310. 152p. 1999. 59.95 (0-7619-1923-6) Sage.
News for All: America's Coming-of-Age with the Press. Thomas C. Leonard. (Illus.). 304p. 1995. text 30.00 (0-19-506454-2) OUP.
News for Babylon: The Chatto Book of Westindian-British Poetry. Ed. by James Berry. 1998. pap. 22.95 (1-85224-379-1, Pub. by Bloodaxe Bks) Dufour.
News for Everyman: Radio & Foreign Affairs in Thirties America. David H. Culbert. LC 75-23862. 238p. 1976. 62.95 (0-8371-8260-3, CRC/, Greenwood Pr) Greenwood.
News for Now Book 1. Karen L. Blanchard & Christine B. Root. 19.95 (0-534-83556-2, Pub. by Heinle & Heinle) Thomson Learn.
News for Now Book 2. Karen L. Blanchard & Christine B. Root. 19.95 (0-534-83548-1, Pub. by Heinle & Heinle) Thomson Learn.
News for Now Student Book 3. Karen L. Blanchard & Christine B. Root. 19.95 (0-534-83557-0, Pub. by Heinle & Heinle) Thomson Learn.
News Formula. Mitchell & West. pap. text, wbk. ed. write for info. (0-312-10242-9) St Martin.
News 4 You. Jacquie Clark. 400p. (J). (ps-6). 1996. spiral bd. 32.00 (1-884135-29-3) Mayer-Johnson.
News from Abroad & the Foreign Policy Public. Donald R. Shanor et al. LC 80-68024. (Headline Ser.: No. 250). (Illus.). 64p. (Orig.). 1980. pap. 5.95 (0-87124-063-7) Foreign Policy.
News from Brownsville: Helen Chapman's Letters from the Texas Military Frontier, 1848-1852. Ed. by Caleb Coker. (Barker Texas History Center Ser.: No. 2). (Illus.). 452p. 1992. 29.95 (0-87611-115-0) Tex St Hist Assn.
News from Brownsville: Helen Chapman's Letters from the Texas Military Frontier, 1848-1852. limited ed. Ed. by Caleb Coker. (Illus.). 452p. 1992. boxed set 85.00 (0-87611-114-2) Tex St Hist Assn.
News from down to the Cafe: New Poems. David Lee. LC 99-6576. 145p. 1999. pap. 14.00 (1-55659-132-2, Pub. by Copper Canyon) SPD-Small Pr Dist.
News from End of Earth: A Portrait of Chile. Hickman. LC 98-6194. 256p. 1998. text 35.00 (0-312-21567-3) St Martin.
News from Fort God. William L. Sutherland. LC 93-2231. (First Novel Ser.). 224p. 1993. pap. 12.00 (0-922811-17-2) Mid-List.
News from Marion: Marion County, OH, 1844-1861. Sharon Moore. 211p. (Orig.). 1995. pap. 63.50 (0-7884-0343-5) Heritage Bk.
News from Nowhere. William Morris. Ed. by Krishan Kumar. (Cambridge Texts in the History of Political Thought Ser.). 263p. (C). 1995. text 59.95 (0-521-42007-5); pap. text 19.95 (0-521-42233-7) Cambridge U Pr.
News from Nowhere. William Morris. Ed. by James Redmond. (English Texts Ser.). 1972. pap. 10.95 (0-7100-6756-9, Routledge Thoemms) Routledge.
News from Nowhere. Ed. by James Redmond. (Routledge English Texts Ser.). 236p. (C). 1972. pap. 20.99 (0-415-07581-5) Routledge.
*News from Nowhere: Television & the News. Edward J. Epstein. LC 99-88936. 352p. 2000. pap. 16.95 (1-56663-300-1, Pub. by I R Dee) Natl Bk Netwk.
News from Nowhere, A Dream of John Ball, A King's Lesson see Collected Works of William Morris
News from Nowhere & Other Writings. William Morris. Ed. & Intro. by Clive Wilmer. 480p. 1994. pap. 12.95 (0-14-043330-9, Penguin Classics) Viking Penguin.
News from Russia see International Press Institute Surveys
News from Somewhere: Connecting Health & Freedom at the Workplace, 151. Gary A. Lewis. LC 85-27269. (Contributions in Political Science Ser.: No. 151). (Illus.). 226p. 1986. 55.00 (0-313-24869-9, LNF/, Greenwood Pr) Greenwood.
*News from Tartary. Peter Fleming. LC 99-27722. 384p. 1999. pap. 16.95 (0-8101-6071-4, Marlboro) Northwestern U Pr.
News from the Edge: Insanity, Illinois, No. 2. Mark Sumner. 1998. mass mkt. 5.99 (0-441-00511-X) Ace Bks.
News from the Fringe: True Stories of Weird People & Weirder Times. Ed. by John J. Kohut & Roland Sweet. (Illus.). 204p. 1998. pap. text 8.00 (0-7881-5448-6) DIANE Pub.
*News from the Front: War Correspondents on the Western Front, 1914-1918. Martin Farrar. 1999. pap. text 21.95 (0-7509-2326-1) Sutton Pub Ltd.
News From the Hidden Forest. (J). 2001. 16.00 (0-689-82582-X) Atheneum Yung Read.
News from the Land of Freedom: German Immigrants Write Home. Ed. by Walter D. Kamphoefner et al. Tr. by Susan C. Vogel from GER. LC 91-10835. (Documents in American Social History Ser.). (Illus.). 656p. 1993. pap. text 18.95 (0-8014-8120-1) Cornell U Pr.
News from the Middle East see International Press Institute Surveys
News from the Past-Mistakes Hermitage. Lee Bassett. (Illus.). 24p. 1983. 5.00 (0-911287-01-9) Blue Begonia.
News from the South: Poems. 2nd ed. Stephen Mooney. LC 66-14773. 78p. reprint ed. pap. 30.00 (0-608-14399-5, 202178100023) Bks Demand.
News from the Spirit World: A Checklist of American Spiritualist Periodicals, 1847-1900. Ann Braude. (Illus.). 63p. 1990. reprint ed. pap. 7.50 (0-944026-21-4) Am Antiquarian.
*News from the Volcano: Stories. Gladys Swan. 200p. 2000. pap. 17.95 (0-8262-1296-4) U of Mo Pr.
News from the White House: The Presidential-Press Relationship in the Progressive Era. George Juergens. LC 81-7634. (C). 1995. 33.95 (0-226-41472-8) U Ch Pr.
News from the White House: The Presidential-Press Relationship in the Progressive Era. George Juergens. LC 81-7634. (Illus.). 360p. reprint ed. pap. 111.60 (0-608-09416-1, 205421600004) Bks Demand.
News from Thrush Green. Miss Read. LC 92-40907. lib. bdg. 21.95 (0-8488-1455-X) Amereon Ltd.
News from Thrush Green. large type ed. Miss Read. 1993. 22.00 (0-8161-5504-6, G K Hall Lrg Type) Mac Lib Ref.
News from Thrush Green. large type ed. Miss Read. LC 92-40907. (General Ser.). (Illus.). 325p. 1993. lib. bdg. 21.95 (0-8161-5503-8, G K Hall Lrg Type) Mac Lib Ref.
News from Thrush Green. Miss Read. LC 92-40907. (Illus.). 240p. 1990. reprint ed. pap. 20.00 (0-89733-334-9, G K Hall Lrg Type) Mac Lib Ref.
News from True Cultivators, Vol. I. Heng Sure & Heng Chau. 130p. 1983. pap. 6.00 (0-88139-508-0) Buddhist Text.
News from True Cultivators, Vol. II. Heng Sure & Heng Ch'au. 122p. (Orig.). 1983. pap. 6.00 (0-88139-024-0) Buddhist Text.
News from Where I Live: Poems by Martin Lammon. Martin Lammon. LC 97-39769. 1998. 20.00 (1-55728-507-1); pap. 12.00 (1-55728-508-X) U of Ark Pr.
News, Gender, & Power. Cynthia Carter et al. LC 98-12179. (Illus.). 296p. (C). 1998. 75.00 (0-415-17015-X) Routledge.
News, Gender, & Power. Cynthia Carter et al. LC 98-12179. (Illus.). 296p. (C). 1998. pap. 24.99 (0-415-17016-8) Routledge.
News' History of Passaic, from the Earliest Settlement to the Present Day, Embracing a Descriptive History of Its Municipal, Religious, Social & Commerical Institutions, with Biographical Sketches. Ed. by William J. Pape & William W. Scott. (Illus.). 320p. 1996. reprint ed. lib. bdg. 39.00 (0-8328-5068-3) Higginson Bk Co.
*News Hounds Catch a Wave: A Geography Adventure. Amy Axelrod. LC 99-47056. (Illus.). (J). 2001. write for info. (0-689-82410-6) S&S Childrens.

N

An Asterisk (*) at the beginning of an entry indicates that the title is appearing for the first time.

***News Hounds in the Great Balloon Race: A Geography Adventure.** Amy Axelrod. LC 98-47638. (Illus.). 40p. (J). (gr. 1-4). 2000. pap. 13.00 (*0-689-82409-2*) S&S Childrens.

News in A New Century: Reporting in An Age of Converging Media. Jerry Lanson & Barbara Croll Fought. LC 98-25449. 339 p. 1999. write for info. (*0-7619-8506-9*) Sage.

News in the Mail: The Press, Post Office, & Public Information, 1700-1860s, 138. Richard B. Kielbowicz. LC 89-11859. (Contributions in American History Ser.: No. 138). 221p. 1989. 52.95 (*0-313-26638-7*, KNM/, Greenwood Pr) Greenwood.

***News Information: Online, CD-ROM & Internet Resources.** Nigel Spencer. (Key Resource Ser.). 72p. 1998. pap. 55.00 (*0-7123-0833-4*) L Erlbaum Assocs.

News Interviews: A Pragmalinguistic Analysis. Andreas H. Jucker. LC 86-26371. (Pragmatics & Beyond Ser.: Vol. VII:4). ix, 195p. 1986. pap. 44.00 (*1-55619-003-4*) J Benjamins Pubng Co.

News is Not a Verb. Pete Hamill. LC 98-5896. (YA). (gr. 6-12). 1998. pap. 8.95 (*0-345-42528-6*) Ballantine Pub Grp.

News Manipulators: Why You Can't Trust the News. Reed Irvine et al. write for info. (*0-9625053-1-5*) Bk Distributors.

News Media & Foreign Relations: A Multifaceted Perspective. Ed. by Abbas Malek. (Communication, Culture & Information Studies Ser.). 268p. 1996. pap. 39.50 (*1-56750-273-3*); text 78.50 (*1-56750-272-5*) Ablx Pub.

News Media & Public Policy: An Annotated Bibliography, Vol. 2. Joseph P. McKerns & L. E. Atwood. LC 83-49290. (Public Affairs & Administration Ser.: Vol. 11). 192p. 1985. text 15.00 (*0-8240-9004-7*) Garland.

News Media As a Necessary Supplement to the Text in Education. 3rd rev. ed. Marion C. Ullrich. (Illus.). 6p. (Orig.). (YA). (gr. 7-12). 1981. write for info. (*0-318-69523-5*) M C Ullrich Pub.

News Media, Civil War, & Humanitarian Action: A Handbook for Practitioners. Larry Minear et al. LC 96-17327. 123p. 1996. lib. bdg. 25.00 (*1-55587-662-5*) L Rienner.

News Media, Civil War & Humanitarian Action: A Handbook for Practitioners. Larry Minear et al. LC 96-17327. 123p. 1996. pap. text 12.50 (*1-55587-676-5*) L Rienner.

News Media Guide to Firearms. (Illus.). 38p. (Orig.). (C). 1994. pap. text 20.00 (*0-7881-0396-2*) DIANE Pub.

News Media Law in New Zealand. 3rd ed. J. F. Burrows. 476p. 1991. pap. 49.95 (*0-19-558208-X*, 12309) OUP.

News Media Librarianship: A Management Handbook. Ed. by Barbara P. Semonche. LC 92-43158. (Library Management Collection). 680p. 1993. lib. bdg. 85.00 (*0-313-27946-2*, SKQ, Greenwood Pr) Greenwood.

News, Newspapers & Society in Early Modern Britain. Ed. by Joad Raymond. LC 98-45230. (Prose Studies). 158p. 1999. pap. 24.50 (*0-7146-8003-6*, Pub. by F Cass Pubs) Intl Spec Bk.

***News, Newspapers & Society in Early Modern Britain.** Ed. by Joad Raymond. LC 98-45230. (Prose Studies). 158p. 1999. 52.50 (*0-7146-4944-9*, Pub. by F Cass Pubs) Intl Spec Bk.

News of a Kidnapping. Gabriel Garcia Marquez. Tr. by Edith Grossman from SPA. LC 97-5445. 1997. 25.00 (*0-375-40051-6*) Pantheon.

News of a Kidnapping. Gabriel Garcia Marquez. Tr. by Edith Grossman. LC 97-5445. (Penguin Great Books of the 20th Century Ser.). 291p. 1998. pap. 13.95 (*0-14-026944-4*) Viking Penguin.

News of Crime: Courts & Press in Conflict, 1. Edward J. Gerald. LC 83-10732. (Contributions to the Study of Mass Media & Communications Ser.: No. 1). 227p. 1983. 59.95 (*0-313-23876-6*, GNC/, Greenwood Pr) Greenwood.

News of Home. Debra K. Dean. LC 98-72186. (New Poets of America Ser.: No. 19). 96p. 1998. pap. 12.50 (*1-880238-66-7*) BOA Edns.

News of the Arab's Horse-Breeding & of the Arabian Horses. Karl W. Ammon. Tr. by Helen Staubli. 400p. 1992. reprint ed. write for info. (*0-318-71574-0*) G Olms Pubs.

News of the Day . . . Yesterday. Ed. by Donald E. Loker. (Illus.). 94p. (Orig.). 1971. pap. 3.00 (*0-685-29126-X*) Niagara Cnty Hist Soc.

News of the Islands & the Mainland Newly Discovered in India by the Captain of His Imperial Majesty's Fleet. Andrea Calvo. Ed. by Edward F. Tuttle. (Illus.). 1985. pap. 10.00 (*0-911437-29-0*) Labyrinthos.

News of the Plains & Rockies, 1803-1865: Original Narratives of Overland Travel & Adventure Selected from the Wagner-Camp & Becker Bibliography of Western Americana, 8 vols., Set. annot. ed. Anno. & Compiled by David A. White. Date not set. 400.00 (*0-87062-231-5*) A H Clark.

News of the Plains & Rockies, 1803-1865 Vol. 1: Early Explorers, Fur Hunters. annot. ed. Anno. & Compiled by David A. White. (Illus.). 300p. 1996. 50.00 (*0-87062-251-X*) A H Clark.

News of the Plains & Rockies, 1803-1865 Vol. 2: Original Narratives of Overland Travel & Adventure - Santa Fe Traders & Travelers, Settlers. Ed. by David A. White. (Illus.). 300p. 1996. 50.00 (*0-87062-252-8*) A H Clark.

News of the Plains & Rockies, 1803-1865 Vol. 3: Missionaries & Mormons, Indian Agents & Captives. Ed. by David A. White. (Illus.). 450p. Date not set. 50.00 (*0-87062-253-6*) A H Clark.

News of the Plains & Rockies, 1803-1865 Vol. 4: Warriors, Scientists & Artists. Ed. by David A. White. (Illus.). 450p. 1997. 50.00 (*0-87062-254-4*) A H Clark.

News of the Plains & Rockies, 1803-1865 Vol. 5: Later Explorers, 1847-1865. Ed. by David A. White. (Illus.). 536p. 1999. 50.00 (*0-87062-255-2*) A H Clark.

News of the Spirit: Stories. Lee Smith. LC 98-96296. 1998. pap. 11.00 (*0-449-00226-8*) Fawcett.

News of the Spirit: Stories. Lee Smith. LC 97-11660. 320p. 1997. 23.95 (*0-399-14281-9*, G P Putnam) Peng Put Young Read.

***News of the Stoopids: (NotS)** Gremlin. (Illus.). xiv, 242p. 2000. pap. 14.95 (*0-9669059-9-7*) Rain Ridge Pubns.

News of the Universe: Poems of Twofold Consciousness. Intro. & Selected by Robert Bly. LC 79-12812. 320p. 1995. pap. 12.00 (*0-87156-368-1*, Pub. by Sierra) Random.

News of the World. Peter Fallon. LC 98-153648. 138 p. 1998. write for info. (*1-85235-214-0*) Dufour.

News of the World. Peter Fallon. LC 93-60785. 79p. 1993. 13.95 (*0-916390-57-8*); pap. 8.95 (*0-916390-56-X*) Wake Forest.

News of the World: Last Poems. Maurice Lindsay. 1990. pap. 21.00 (*1-898218-32-3*) St Mut.

News of the World: World Cultures Look at Television News. Klaus Jensen. LC 97-47559. (Research in Cultural & Media Studies). (Illus.). 248p. (C). 1998. 75.00 (*0-415-16107-X*) Routledge.

***News of the World Football Annual 1999-2000.** Eric Brown. 1999. pap. 10.95 (*0-00-218883-X*, Pub. by HarpC) Trafalgar.

News on a Knife Edge. Richard Bourne. LC 96-196350. 1997. 26.00 (*1-86020-524-0*, Pub. by U of Luton Pr) Bks Intl VA.

News on Aliens. Stephen Measday. LC 97-188212. 163p. (YA). 1997. pap. 12.95 (*0-7022-2887-7*, Pub. by Univ Queensland Pr) Intl Spec Bk.

News on Skis. Peter Ganick. 1992. pap. 8.00 (*0-939691-06-X*) Avenue B.

News over the Wires: The Telegraph & the Flow of Public Information in America 1844-1897. Menahem Blondheim. LC 93-28731. (Studies in Business History: No. 42). 216p. 1994. text 39.95 (*0-674-62212-X*) HUP.

News: Politics Illusion. 2nd ed. W. Lance Bennett. 216p. (C). 1989. pap. text 28.50 (*0-582-28664-6*, 71680) Addison-Wesley.

News Radio. (Stereo Boom Box Ser.: Vol. 1). 157p. (J). (gr. 1-6). 1994. ring bd. 159.95 incl. audio, VHS, sl. (*1-57405-048-6*) CharismaLife Pub.

***News Releases: Working with the Media & Getting the Media to Work for You.** Kate Becker-Burridge. Ed. by Sally Steis & Drew Steis. (Art Calendar Guide Ser.). (Illus.). 48p. 1999. pap. 9.95 (*0-945388-28-4*) Art Calendar.

***News Releases & Book Publicity: From Pre-Publication Galleys Through a Continuing Review Program.** 5th ed. Dan Poynter. (Book Publishing Consultation with Dan Poynter Ser.). (Illus.). 35p. 2000. pap. 19.95 (*1-56860-054-2*) Para Pub.

News Reporters & News Sources: Accomplices in Shaping & Misshaping the News. 2nd rev. ed. Herbert Strentz. 190p. (C). 1989. pap. text 21.95 (*0-8138-1887-7*) Iowa St U Pr.

News Reporting: Science, Medicine, & High Technology. Warren Burkett. LC 85-23102. 170p. 1986. reprint ed. pap. 52.70 (*0-608-00080-9*, 206084300006) Bks Demand.

News Reporting & Writing. Brian S. Brooks. LC 80-50144. 542 p. 1980. write for info. (*0-312-57202-6*) St Martin.

News Reporting & Writing Melvin Mencher. LC 77-81895. 437 p. 1977. write for info. (*0-697-04308-8*, WCB McGr Hill) McGrw-H Hghr Educ.

News Reporting & Writing. Contrib. by Missouri Group Staff. 1995. pap. text 48.00 (*0-312-14502-0*) McGraw.

News Reporting & Writing. 4th ed. Brian S. Brooks et al. LC 90-71645. 192p. (C). 1992. pap. text, teacher ed. 0.84 (*0-312-06246-X*) St Martin.

News Reporting & Writing. 5th ed. Missouri Group Staff. 1995. pap. text, teacher ed. 10.00 (*0-312-13800-8*) St Martin.

News Reporting & Writing. 5th ed. Missouri Group Staff. 160p. 1996. pap. text, wbk. ed. 24.95 (*0-312-11716-7*) St Martin.

News Reporting & Writing. 6th ed. Missouri Group Staff. LC 98-84337. 1999. pap. 55.95 (*0-312-18019-5*); pap. text, wbk. ed. 24.95 (*0-312-18018-7*) St Martin.

News Reporting & Writing. 6th ed. Missouri Group Staff. 2000. pap. text, teacher ed. 10.00 (*0-312-18020-9*) St Martin.

News Reporting & Writing. 7th ed. Mencher. 1997. 16.25 (*0-697-28902-8*, WCB McGr Hill) McGrw-H Hghr Educ.

News Reporting & Writing. 7th ed. Melvin Mencher. LC 95-83695. 736p. (C). 1996. text 46.75 (*0-697-28901-X*) Brown & Benchmark.

News Reporting & Writing. 7th ed. Melvin Mencher. 288p. (C). 1997. text, wbk. ed. 22.50 (*0-697-28903-6*) Brown & Benchmark.

News Reporting & Writing. 7th ed. Melvin Mencher. 736p. (C). 1997. per. write for info. (*0-07-114585-0*) McGraw.

News Reporting & Writing. 8th ed. Mencher. LC 99-25513. 1999. 38.50 (*0-07-230011-6*); pap. 25.31 (*0-07-230012-4*) McGraw.

News Revolution: Political & Economic Decisions about Global Information. Mark D. Alleyne. 252p. 1996. pap. 19.95 (*0-312-16498-X*); text 45.00 (*0-312-15894-7*) St Martin.

News Revolution in England: Cultural Dynamics of Daily Information. C. John Sommerville. 208p. 1996. text 45.00 (*0-19-510667-9*) OUP.

News Shapers: The Sources Who Explain the News. Lawrence C. Soley. LC 91-33606. 192p. 1992. 52.95 (*0-275-94033-0*, C4033, Praeger Pubs) Greenwood.

News, Surprise, & Nostalgia. Tracy L. Adler et al. (Illus.). 24p. 1995. pap. text. write for info. (*1-885998-06-6*) Hunter College.

News that Matters: Television & American Opinion. Shanto Iyengar & Donald R. Kinder. LC 86-30845. (American Politics & Political Economy Ser.). (Illus.). 200p. 1987. 19.95 (*0-226-38856-5*) U Ch Pr.

News that Matters: Television & American Opinion. Shanto Iyengar & Donald R. Kinder. LC 86-30845. (American Politics & Political Economy Ser.). (Illus.). 200p. 1989. pap. text 11.95 (*0-226-38857-3*) U Ch Pr.

News They Didn't Use. Stephen Measday. (YA). 1995. pap. 12.95 (*0-7022-2711-0*, Pub. by Univ Queensland Pr) Intl Spec Bk.

NEWS 3X/400 Technical Reference Series. LC 96-10149. 1996. pap. write for info. (*1-882419-11-1*) News Four-Hund.

NEWS 3X/400's Power Tools for the AS/400, Vol. II. Ed. by Dan Riehl & Frederick Dick. 702p. 1995. pap. 129.00 incl. disk (*1-882419-08-1*) News Four-Hund.

News under Russia's Old Regime: The Development of a Mass-Circulation Press. Louise McReynolds. LC 91-13671. 327p. 1991. reprint ed. pap. 101.40 (*0-608-04577-2*, 206534600003) Bks Demand.

News Values: Ideas for an Information Age. Jack Fuller. LC 95-33951. (Illus.). xiv, 252p. 1996. 22.95 (*0-226-26879-9*) U Ch Pr.

News Values: Ideas for an Information Age. Jack Fuller. xiv, 252p. 1997. pap. 12.95 (*0-226-26880-2*) U Ch Pr.

News Verdicts, the Debates, & Presidential Campaigns. James B. Lemert et al. LC 91-8749. 312p. 1991. 62.95 (*0-275-93758-5*, C3758, Praeger Pubs) Greenwood.

News Views. Flatt & Rankin-Eagles. 1990. pap. text. write for info. (*0-582-86908-0*, Pub. by Addison-Wesley) Longman.

News Writing, 5 vols. Hough. (C). 1995. pap., teacher ed. 11.96 (*0-395-70879-6*) HM.

News Writing. Rich. (Mass Communication). 1995. pap., teacher ed. 54.25 (*0-534-19073-1*) Wadsworth Pub.

News Writing, 5 vols. 5th ed. George A. Hough. LC 94-76509. (C). 1994. pap. text 47.56 (*0-395-70877-X*) HM.

News Writing: Student Telecourse. Rich & Berkow. (Mass Communication Ser.). 1995. pap., student ed. 17.50 (*0-534-19079-0*) Wadsworth Pub.

News Writing & Reporting for Today's Media. 4th ed. Bruce D. Itule & Dauglas A. Anderson. LC 96-11924. (C). 1996. text 48.00 (*0-07-032874-9*) McGraw.

News Writing & Reporting for Today's Media. 4th ed. Bruce D. Itule & Douglas A. Anderson. (C). 1996. pap., wbk. ed. 29.38 (*0-07-032876-5*) McGraw.

***News Writing & Reporting for Today's Media.** 5th ed. Bruce D. Itule. LC 99-18951. 1999. 55.60 (*0-07-365498-1*) McGraw-Hill Pubng.

***News Writing & Reporting for Today's Media.** 5th ed. Bruce D. Itule & Douglas Anderson. 232p. (C). 1999. pap. 28.13 (*0-07-230007-8*) McGrw-H Hghr Educ.

News Writing Student Telecourse. 2nd ed. Rich. (Mass Communication Ser.). 1996. pap. 21.00 (*0-534-52254-8*) Wadsworth Pub.

Newscomer's Handbook for Atlanta. First Books Inc. Staff. (Newcomer's Handbook Ser.). (Illus.). 160p. 1996. 13.95 (*0-912301-31-7*) First Bks.

Newscraft. 2nd ed. (C). 1988. write for info. (*0-8087-7331-3*) Pearson Custom.

Newsday's Guide to Long Island Wines. Peter M. Gianotti. (Illus.). 204p. 1998. pap. 12.95 (*1-885134-15-0*) Newsday.

***Newsday's Year 2000 Business Almanac.** Newsday Staff. 1999. pap. 19.95 (*1-885134-22-3*) Newsday.

Newsgathering & the Law. C. Thomas Dienes et al. LC 97-70137. 1005p. 1997. text 105.00 (*1-55834-462-4*, 65190, MICHIE) LEXIS Pub.

***Newsgathering & the Law.** 2nd ed. C. Thomas Dienes et al. 1280p. 1999. 105.00 (*0-327-04972-3*, 6519011) LEXIS Pub.

***Newsgathering on the Net: An Internet Guide for Australian Journalists.** Stephen C. Quinn. 250p. 1999. pap. 29.95 (*0-7329-5599-8*, Pub. by Macmill Educ) Paul & Co Pubs.

Newsies. Adapted by Jonathan Fast. LC 91-73973. (Junior Novelization Ser.). (Illus.). 136p. (J). (gr. 2-6). 1992. pap. 3.50 (*1-56282-115-6*, Pub. by Disney Pr) Time Warner.

Newsletter, Vols. 1-3. Mongolia Society Staff. 1964. pap. 5.00 (*0-910980-01-2*) Mongolia.

Newsletter Design: A Step-by-Step Guide to Creative Publications. Edward A. Hamilton. 192p. 1995. 29.95 (*0-442-01668-9*, VNR) Wiley.

Newsletter Design: A Step-by-Step Guide to Creative Publications. Edward A. Hamilton. (Design & Graphic Design Ser.). 192p. 1995. pap. 34.95 (*0-471-28592-7*) Wiley.

Newsletter Editor's Desk Book. 2nd rev. ed. Marvin Arth & Helen Ashmore. LC 80-83042. (Illus.). 168p. 1980. pap. 9.95 (*0-938270-00-1*) Parkway Pr Ltd.

Newsletter Editor's Desk Book. 3rd ed. Marvin Arth & Helen Ashmore. LC 81-83398. 188p. 1984. pap. 11.50 (*0-938270-03-6*) Parkway Pr Ltd.

Newsletter Editor's Handbook: A Quick-Start Guide to Writing, Interviewing & Copyright Law. 5th rev. ed. Elaine Floyd et al. (Illus.). 268p. 1997. pap. 24.99 (*0-9630222-6-1*) EFG Inc MO.

Newsletter Needs, No. 1457. (Illus.). 48p. 1989. reprint ed. 5.95 (*1-878259-12-1*) Neibauer Pr.

Newsletter Principles, Pitfalls & Pizzazz! Carolynn M. Andrews. (Illus.). 42p. 1996. reprint ed. pap. text 7.00 (*0-9653191-0-5*) Designer Bytes.

Newsletter Publishing with PageMaker: Macintosh & IBM Editions. Frederic E. Davis et al. 350p. 1988. pap. 25.00 (*1-55623-064-8*, Irwn Prfssnl) McGraw-Hill Prof.

Newsletter Sourcebook. 2nd ed. Mark Beach & Elaine Floyd. LC 97-42969. (Illus.). 144p. 1998. pap. 27.99 (*0-89879-869-8*, Wrtrs Digest Bks) F & W Pubns Inc.

Newsletter Yearbook Directory. 450p. 1995. 145.00 (*0-685-55412-0*) B Klein Pubns.

Newsletters. Pbc International Staff. 1997. pap. 24.95 (*0-688-15885-4*, Wm Morrow) Morrow Avon.

Newsletters: Informing Your Public: Everything You Need to Know to Produce an Eye-Catching, Professional Newsletter see Communications Series

Newsletters: The Art & Design of Small Publications. Steven Heller. LC 95-12990. (Illus.). 160p. 1996. 35.00 (*0-86636-338-6*) PBC Intl Inc.

Newsletters for the 90s. Sheryl Roush. 1992. write for info. (*1-880878-02-X*) Creative Comns.

***Newsletters from the Archpresbyterate of George Birkhead.** Ed. by M. C. Questier. (Camden Fifth Ser.: No. 12). 321p. (C). 2000. 64.95 (*0-521-65260-X*) Cambridge U Pr.

***Newsletters in Print.** 13th ed. 1250p. 2000. 275.00 (*0-7876-2295-8*, UXL) Gale.

Newsletters Simplified: Valuable Material to Print in Your Newsletter Plus Helpful Newsletter Tips. Marge Knoth. (Illus.). 300p. (Orig.). 1993. per. 21.99 (*0-927935-06-6*) Valley Pr IN.

Newsletters with Impact. Lea Leever Oldham. 72p. 1998. pap. text 7.95 (*0-942923-09-X*) NETWIC.

Newsmakers, 1985: Cumulation. 85th ed. Ed. by Ann Evory & Peter M. Gareffa. 1986. 89.00 (*0-8103-2201-3*) Gale.

Newsmakers, 1989 Subscription. 89th ed. Ed. by Peter M. Gareffa. 1989. 129.00 (*0-8103-2208-0*) Gale.

Newsmakers, 1987: Cumulation. 87th ed. Ed. by Peter M. Gareffa. 440p. 1988. 89.00 (*0-8103-2203-X*) Gale.

Newsmakers, 1986: Cumulation. 86th ed. Ed. by Peter M. Gareffa. 1987. 89.00 (*0-8103-2202-1*) Gale.

Newsmakers, 1995 Subscription. 95th ed. 1995. 129.00 (*0-8103-5741-0*, 00002487) Gale.

Newsmakers, 1994 Subscription. 94th ed. Louise Mooney. 1994. 129.00 (*0-8103-8560-0*, 001820) Gale.

Newsmakers, 1991. 91st ed. Peter M. Gareffa. 1991. 129.00 (*0-8103-5452-7*) Gale.

Newsmakers, 1997 Subscription. 97th ed. 1997. 129.00 (*0-7876-0103-9*, 00108812) Gale.

Newsmakers, 1996 Subscription. 96th ed. L. Collins. 1996. 129.00 (*0-8103-9320-4*) Gale.

Newsmakers, 1990 Subscription. 90th ed. Ed. by Peter M. Gareffa. 1990. 129.00 (*0-8103-2209-9*) Gale.

Newsmakers, 1992 Subscription. 92nd ed. 1992. 129.00 (*0-8103-2245-5*) Gale.

***Newsmakers 2000.** 2000. 135.00 (*0-7876-3066-7*) Gale.

***Newsmakers 99.** Pollack. 1999. 135.00 (*0-7876-2108-0*) Gale.

Newsmaking. Bernard Roshco. LC 75-5076. x, 160p. 1979. pap. text 3.95 (*0-226-72815-3*) U Ch Pr.

Newsmaking. Bernard Roshco. LC 75-5076. x, 160p. 1995. lib. bdg. 14.50 (*0-226-72814-5*) U Ch Pr.

Newsmen Speak: Journalists on Their Craft. Ed. by Edmond E. Coblentz. LC 68-14900. (Essay Index Reprint Ser.). 1977. 19.95 (*0-8369-0318-8*) Ayer.

Newsmen's Holiday. LC 73-84330. (Essay Index Reprint Ser. Harvard Univ. Neiman Essays, First Ser.). 1977. reprint ed. 20.95 (*0-8369-1100-8*) Ayer.

Newsom Papers. Caroline L. Riley. 150p. 1988. 35.00 (*0-9621609-0-3*) C L Riley.

Newspaper: A Reference Book for Teachers & Librarians. Edward F. DeRoche. LC 91-633. 170p. 1991. lib. bdg. 35.00 (*0-87436-584-8*) ABC-CLIO.

Newspaper: A Subscription for Success. rev. ed. Lisa C. O'Connor. Ed. by Cindy Drolet & C. Gilles-Brown. (Language for Living Ser.). 143p. 1992. spiral bd. 37.00 (*0-9609464-8-9*, 8004) Imaginart Intl.

Newspaper: An Alternative Textbook. J. Rodney Short & Beverly Dickerson. LC 79-54759. 1980. pap. 9.99 (*0-8224-4661-8*) Fearon Teacher Aids.

***Newspaper: Everything You Need to Know to Make It in the Newspaper Business.** Leonard Mogel. (Illus.). 264p. (C). 2000. pap. 40.00 (*0-88362-235-1*) GATFPress.

***Newspaper Abstracts Hardin County, Kentucky, 1829-1893.** Compiled by Carolyn Wimp. 374p. 1999. pap. 31.00 (*1-889221-44-9*) Ancestral Trails.

Newspaper Accounts of B. F. Wright, Esq., & Others of Louisa County, Iowa. Robert L. Johnson. LC 67-31310. (Illus.). 209p. reprint ed. pap. 64.80 (*0-8357-3614-8*, AU0039900004) Bks Demand.

Newspaper Advertising Handbook. Don Watkins. LC 80-10996. (Illus.). 112p. 1980. pap. 8.95 (*0-936294-00-0*) Dynamo Inc.

Newspaper Advertising Sales: The Complete Guide to Job Finding, Facts, & Forecasts. Harry Chin. Ed. by Laura Utterback. LC 93-87294. 240p. 1994. pap. 19.95 (*0-9637975-0-6*) Newspaper Res.

Newspaper & Newsmagazine Evaluation: Score Book & Judge's Review. 1997. 3.50 (*0-318-19225-X*) Quill & Scroll.

Newspaper & Public Affairs Frederick J. Fletcher & David V. Bell. LC 82-135440. (Research Publications). ix, 123p. 1981. 5.95 (*0-660-11062-8*, Pub. by Can7 Govern Pub) Intl Spec Bk.

Newspaper & the Law. Walter A. Steigleman. LC 74-141419. 427p. 1971. reprint ed. lib. bdg. 79.50 (*0-8371-3059-X*, STNE, Greenwood Pr) Greenwood.

Newspaper Anti-Coloring Book. Susan Striker. (Illus.). 64p. (J). (gr. 2 up). 1995. pap. 6.95 (*0-8050-1599-X*, Owl) H Holt & Co.

Newspaper As a Necessary Supplement to the Text in Education. 3rd rev. ed. Marion C. Ullrich. (Illus.). 35p. (Orig.). 1981. reprint ed. write for info. (*0-9617091-1-1*) M C Ullrich Pub.

Newspaper As a Teaching Tool. Eileen E. Sargent. 192p. 9.95 (*0-318-13724-0*) Communacad.

N

An Asterisk (*) at the beginning of an entry indicates that the title is appearing for the first time.

Newspaper Chinese ABC: An Introductory Reader. Li Zhenjie & Wang Shixun. (C & T Asian Language Ser.). 189p. (Orig.). (C). 1988. reprint ed. pap. text 9.95 (0-88727-059-X) Cheng & Tsui.

Newspaper Correspondent's Manual. Donald K. Ross. LC PN4781.R67. 40p. reprint ed. pap. 30.00 (0-608-12670-5, 202511000042) Bks Demand.

Newspaper Credibility: Two Hundred Six Practical Approaches to Heighten Reader Trust. Compiled by ASNE's Credibility Committee Staff. 63p. 1988. 2.25 (0-317-01534-6) Nwspaper Assn Amer.

Newspaper Credit & Collection Management. Technical Publications Committee Staff. (Illus.). 100p. (Orig.). 1989. pap. 49.95 (1-877888-09-5) Intl Newspaper.

Newspaper Crusaders. Silas Bent. LC 77-90609. (Essay Index Reprint Ser.). 1977. 21.95 (0-8369-1245-4) Ayer.

Newspaper Days. Theodore Dreiser. Ed. by T. D. Nostwich. LC 91-30225. (Dreiser Edition Ser.). 840p. (C). 1991. text 54.95 (0-8122-3095-7) U of Pa Pr.

*Newspaper Days: An Autobiography. Theodore Dreiser. Ed. by T. D. Nostwich. 750p. 2000. 30.00 (1-57423-139-1); pap. 18.00 (1-57423-138-3) Black Sparrow.

Newspaper Days, 1899-1906. H. L. Mencken. LC 95-52240. (Maryland Paperback Bookshelf Ser.). 336p. 1996. reprint ed. pap. 15.95 (0-8018-5340-0) Johns Hopkins.

Newspaper Designer's Handbook. 4th ed. Tim Harrower. LC 97-11842. 1997. 28.25 (0-697-32720-5, WCB McGr Hill) McGrw-H Hghr Educ.

Newspaper Educational Uses: Possibilities & Workpages. Frieda Carrol Staff. (Illus.). 60p. 1997. ring bd. 39.95 (1-890928-29-1) Frieda Carrol.

Newspaper Extracts from the Martin County Sentinel, Fairmont, Minnesota, 1 January, 1879-27 September, 1889. Mary L. Hackett-Magnuson. LC 97-34359. 1997. pap. 15.00 (0-915709-38-4) Pk Geneal Bk.

Newspaper Feature Writing. 2nd rev. ed. Len Granato. 85p. (C). 1995. pap. 65.00 (0-7300-1424-X, Pub. by Deakin Univ) St Mut.

Newspaper Financial Management: An Introduction. Jay Matthews & Chester Rozak. 72p. (Orig.). 1988. pap. 49.95 (1-877888-05-2) Intl Newspaper.

Newspaper Fun. Bobbye S. Goldstein & Gabriel F. Goldstein. 1992. pap. 11.99 (0-86653-967-0) Fearon Teacher Aids.

Newspaper Genealogical Column Directory. 6th rev. ed. Anita C. Milner. x, 110p. (Orig.). 1996. pap. 14.00 (0-7884-0507-1, M347) Heritage Bk.

Newspaper German. Colin Good. 200p. 1995. 20.00 (0-7083-1261-6, Pub. by Univ Wales Pr) Paul & Co Pubs.

Newspaper Gleanings of Andrew County (MO) & Surrounding Area. Compiled by Dorothy J. McMackin. LC 86-82190. 584p. 1986. 15.00 (0-939810-05-0) Jordan Valley.

Newspaper Holdings of the California State Library. Compiled by Marianne Leach. 396p. 1986. pap. 40.00 (0-929722-09-4) CA State Library Fndtn.

Newspaper in Art. Garry Apgar et al. LC 97-181483. (Illus.). 232p. 1996. 75.00 (0-923910-05-0) NMV.

Newspaper Indexes, Vol. 1. Anita C. Milner. LC 77-7130. 210p. 1977. 26.50 (0-8108-1066-2) Scarecrow.

Newspaper Indexes, Vol. II. Anita C. Milner. LC 77-7130. 203p. 1979. 28.00 (0-8108-1244-4) Scarecrow.

Newspaper Indexes, Vol. III. Anita C. Milner. LC 77-7130. 192p. 1982. 28.00 (0-8108-1493-5) Scarecrow.

Newspaper Indian: Native American Identity in the Press, 1820-90. John M. Coward. LC 98-19663. (History of Communication Ser.). 264p. 1998. text 39.95 (0-252-02432-X) U of Ill Pr.

Newspaper Indian: Native American Identity in the Press, 1820-90. John M. Coward. LC 98-19663. (The History of Communication Ser.). 264p. 1999. pap. 18.95 (0-252-06738-X) U of Ill Pr.

Newspaper, Its Making & Its Meaning. New York Times Staff. LC 80-2891. (BCL Ser.: Vols. I & II). reprint ed. 26.00 (0-404-18069-8) AMS Pr.

Newspaper Kids. Juanita Phillips. (Illus.). (J). 1998. pap. 5.95 (0-207-19160-3) HarpC.

*Newspaper Kids #4. Juanita Phillips. 1999. pap. 5.95 (0-207-19052-6) Collins Angus & Robertson Pubs.

Newspaper Kurdish. Ed. by Jamal Abdulla & Ernest N. McCarus. (Kurdish Readers Ser.: Vol. 1). vii, 115p. 1967. 14.00 (0-916798-61-5) UM Dept NES.

Newspaper Language. Nicholas Bagnall. 280p. 1993. pap. 39.95 (0-7506-0399-2) Buttrwrth-Heinemann.

Newspaper Layout & Design. Daryl R. Moen. (Illus.). 274p. (C). 1989. wbk. ed. 21.95 (0-8138-1228-3) Iowa St U Pr.

Newspaper Layout & Design: A Team Approach. 3rd ed. Daryl R. Moen. LC 94-15567. (Illus.). 248p. 1995. pap. text 34.95 (0-8138-1225-9) Iowa St U Pr.

*Newspaper Layout & Design: A Team Approach. 4th rev. ed. Daryl R. Moen. 280p. 2000. pap. 39.95 (0-8138-0729-8) Iowa St U Pr.

Newspaper Libel: A Handbook for the Press. Samuel Merrill. (Handbook for the Press Ser.). 304p. 1995. reprint ed. 45.00 (0-8377-2476-7, Rothman) W S Hein.

Newspaper Libraries: A Bibliography, 1933-1985. Celia J. Wall. LC 86-14604. 134p. 1986. reprint ed. pap. 41.60 (0-608-00761-7, 206155900010) Bks Demand.

Newspaper Libraries in the U. S. & Canada: An SLA Directory. Ed. by Elizabeth L. Anderson. LC 80-25188. 331p. reprint ed. pap. 102.70 (0-7837-6301-8, 204601600010) Bks Demand.

Newspaper Markets for Travel Writers. Shelly Steig. LC 99-72764. 128p. 1999. pap. 17.95 (0-9639260-8-X) Aletheia.

Newspaper Organization & Management. 5th ed. Herbert L. Williams. LC 78-15799. (Illus.). 509p. 1978. reprint ed. pap. 157.80 (0-608-00131-7, 206091200006) Bks Demand.

Newspaper Power: The New National Press in Britain. Jeremy Tunstall. 456p. (C). 1996. 65.00 (0-19-871132-8) OUP.

Newspaper Power: The New National Press in Britain. Jeremy Tunstall. (Illus.). 452p. (C). 1996. pap. text 26.00 (0-19-871133-6) OUP.

Newspaper Preservation & Access: Proceedings of the Symposium Held in London, August 12-15, 1987, Vol. I. Ed. by Willem R. Koops. (IFLA Publications: Vol. 45). 231p. 1988. lib. bdg. 37.50 (3-598-21775-7) K G Saur Verlag.

Newspaper Preservation & Access: Proceedings of the Symposium Held in London, August 12-15, 1987, Vol. II. Ed. by Willem R. Koops. (IFLA Publications: Vol. 46). 449p. 1988. lib. bdg. 37.50 (3-598-21776-5) K G Saur Verlag.

Newspaper Press Directory, 1999, 2 vols., Set. 1992. 950.00 (0-7855-7126-4) St Mut.

Newspaper Press in Kentucky. Herndon J. Evans. LC 76-24340. (Kentucky Bicentennial Bookshelf Ser.). 133p. reprint ed. pap. 41.30 (0-7837-5802-2, 204546800006) Bks Demand.

Newspaper Press in the French Revolution. Hugh Gough. LC 88-70716. 264p. (C). 1988. pap. text 35.95 (0-925065-01-3) Lyceum IL.

Newspaper Press of Charleston, S. C. William L. King. LC 72-125701. (American Journalists Ser.). 1978. reprint ed. 20.95 (0-405-01680-8) Ayer.

Newspaper Readings: The U. S. A. in the People's Daily. Chih-p'ing Chou & Xuedong Wang. 255p. 1993. pap. text 24.50 (0-691-00070-0, Pub. by Princeton U Pr) Cal Prin Full Svc.

Newspaper Records Management. rev. ed. George K. Dahl. 64p. 1988. pap. 49.95 (1-877888-04-4) Intl Newspaper.

Newspaper Recycling Workbook Based on the Story Newspaper Recycling Association. A. Doyle. (Illus.). 20p. 1999. pap., wbk. ed. 15.95 (1-56820-390-X) Story Time.

Newspaper Reporters. Marzella Brown. Ed. by Sharon Coan. (Illus.). 48p. (J). (gr. 3-6). 1990. student ed. 7.95 (1-55734-137-0) Tchr Create Mat.

Newspaper Scavenger Hunts. Tom Burt. Ed. by Rita Seho. 144p. 1998. pap., teacher ed. 14.95 (1-57690-353-2, TCM2353) Tchr Create Mat.

Newspaper Spanish. Charles Kelley et al. LC 95-228005. 178p. 1995. pap. 20.00 (0-7083-1277-2, Pub. by Univ Wales Pr) Paul & Co Pubs.

Newspaper Stories & Other Poems. Patricia Dienstfrey. 36p. (Orig.). 1979. pap. 9.95 (0-917658-11-6) BPW & P.

Newspaper Survival Book: An Editor's Guide to Marketing Research. Philip Meyer et al. LC 84-48042. (Illus.). 183p. reprint ed. pap. 56.80 (0-608-09350-5, 205409600002) Bks Demand.

Newspaper Theatre. Alice Morin. (J). (gr. 1-8). 1989. pap. 8.99 (0-8224-6349-0) Fearon Teacher Aids.

Newspaper Use & Community Ties: Towards a Dynamic Theory. Keith R. Stamm. Ed. by Melvin J. Voigt. LC 85-7330. (Communication & Information Science Ser.). 216p. 1985. text 73.25 (0-89391-136-4) Ablx Pub.

Newspaper Writings, 4-vols. Ed. by Ann P. Robson & John M. Robson. (Collected Works of John Stuart Mill: Vols. 22-25). (Illus.). 1986. text 195.00 (0-8020-2602-8) U of Toronto Pr.

Newspaperman, News & Society. Warren Breed. Ed. by Harriet Zuckerman & Robert K. Merton. LC 79-8979. (Dissertations on Sociology Ser.). 1980. lib. bdg. 44.95 (0-405-12955-6) Ayer.

Newspaperman's Guide to the Law. 5th ed. William Lane et al. 352p. 1990. pap. 86.00 (0-409-05769-X, SA, MICHIE); boxed set 126.00 (0-409-05770-3, SA, MICHIE) LEXIS Pub.

Newspaperman's President: Harry S. Truman. Herbert L. Williams. LC 84-1115. 255p. 1984. text 34.95 (0-8304-1064-3) Burnham Inc.

Newspapers. Sharon Coan. (Illus.). 15p. 1993. pap., teacher ed. 7.95 (1-55734-138-9) Tchr Create Mat.

Newspapers. Peter Grundy. Ed. by Alan Maley. (Illus.). 142p. 1993. pap. text 13.95 (0-19-437192-1) OUP.

Newspapers: A Reference Guide. Richard A. Schwarlose. LC 87-246. 454p. 1987. lib. bdg. 99.50 (0-313-23613-5, SNW/, Greenwood Pr) Greenwood.

Newspapers, A Lost Cause? Strategic Management of Newspaper Firms in the United States & the Netherlands. Patrick Hendriks. LC 99-10320. 1999. write for info. (0-7923-5608-X) Kluwer Academic.

Newspapers & Nationalism. Marie L. Legg. LC 99-191735. 240p. 1999. boxed set 49.50 (1-85182-341-7, Pub. by Four Cts Pr) Intl Spec Bk.

*Newspapers & New Media: The Digital Awakening of the Newspaper Industry. Steve Outing. LC 99-68450. (Illus.). 72p. (C). 2000. pap. text 25.00 (0-88362-302-1) GATFPress.

Newspapers & Periodicals of Jordan: In the Press Archive of the Moshe Dayan Center. Compiled by Haim Gal. LC 96-969680. 47 p. 1996. write for info. (965-224-022-2) Moshe Dayan Ctr.

Newspapers Career Directory. 4th ed. Bradley J. Morgan. Ed. by Diane Dupuis. (Career Advisor Ser.). 1993. 17.95 (0-8103-9438-3, 089142) Visible Ink Pr.

Newspapers Handbook. 2nd ed. Richard Keeble. LC 97-34625. (Media Practice Ser.). 336p. (C). 1998. 85.00 (0-415-18409-6) Routledge.

Newspapers Handbook. 2nd ed. Richard Keeble. LC 97-34625. (Media Practice Ser.). 416p. (C). 1998. pap. write for info. (0-415-15827-3) Routledge.

*Newspapers in the E-Age: Re-Engineering for Electronic Commerce. Matt Adams. (Gastric Stimulation for Wannabe Dinosaurs Ser.: Vol. 2). 180p. 1999. pap. 19.95 (0-9665796-6-6) Insiders Guide.

Newspapers in the E-Age Vol. 1: Re-Engineering for Electronic Commerce. Matt Adams. LC 99-64868. (Gastric Stimulation for Wannabe Dinosaurs Ser.). 240p. 1999. pap. 16.95 (0-9665796-5-8) Insiders Guide.

Newspapers in the Library: New Approaches to Management & Reference Work. Ed. by Lois N. Upham. LC 87-29866. (Serials Librarian Supplement Ser.: No. 4). (Illus.). 160p. 1988. text 39.95 (0-86656-688-0) Haworth Pr.

Newspapers in the State Historical Society of Wisconsin: A Bibliography with Holdings, 2 vols. Intro. by James P. Danky & Maureen E. Hady. Incl. Vol. I. Newspapers in the State Historical Society of Wisconsin: A Bibliography with Holdings. LC 92-60505. xiv, 256p. 1994. lib. bdg. (0-88354-700-7); Vol. II. Newspapers in the State Historical Society of Wisconsin: A Bibliography with Holdings. LC 92-60505. viii, 488p. 1994. lib. bdg. Not sold separately (0-88354-701-5); Set lib. bdg. 110.00 N Ross.

Newspapers in the State Historical Society of Wisconsin: A Bibliography with Holdings see Newspapers in the State Historical Society of Wisconsin: A Bibliography with Holdings

Newspapers of Maryland's Eastern Shore. Dickson J. Preston. LC 85-40533. (Illus.). 290p. 1986. reprint ed. pap. 89.90 (0-7837-9082-1, 204983200003) Bks Demand.

Newspapers of Nevada: A History & Bibliography, 1854-1979. Richard E. Lingenfelter & Karen R. Gash. LC 83-16790. (Illus.). 368p. 1984. 50.00 (0-87417-075-3) U of Nev Pr.

Newspapers of Record in a Digital Age: From Hot Type to Hot Link. Shannon E. Martin & Kathleen A. Hansen. LC 97-47232. (Praeger Series in Political Communication). 176p. 1998. 55.00 (0-275-95960-0, Praeger Pubs) Greenwood.

Newspapers on the Minnesota Frontier, 1849-1860. George S. Hage. LC 67-63489. (Publications of the Minnesota Historical Society). (Illus.). 191p. 1967. reprint ed. pap. 59.30 (0-608-06673-7, 206687000009) Bks Demand.

*Newspapers, Politics & English Society, 1695-1855. Hannah Barker. LC 99-35486. (Themes in British Social History Ser.). 248p. 1999. pap. 29.06 (0-582-31217-5) Longman.

*Newspapers, Politics & English Society, 1695-1855. Hannah Barker. LC 99-35486. (Themes in British Social History Ser.). 256p. (C). 1999. 79.95 (0-582-31216-7) Longman.

Newspapers, Politics, & Public Opinion in Late Eighteenth-Century England. Hannah Barker. (Oxford Historical Monographs). (Illus.). 216p. 1998. text 65.00 (0-19-820741-7) OUP.

Newspeak: A Dictionary of Jargon. Jonathan Green. 263p. 1984. 25.00 (0-7100-9685-2, Routledge Thoemms) Routledge.

Newspeak: A Dictionary of Jargon. Jonathon Green. 263p. 1985. 12.95 (0-685-42925-3); pap. 12.95 (0-7102-0673-9) Routledge.

Newspring in Hong Kong: A Strategic Entry Report, 1998. Compiled by Icon Group International Staff. (Country Industry Report). (Illus.). 128p. 1999. ring bd. 1280.00 incl. audio compact disk (0-7418-0521-9) Icon Grp.

Newsprint: Canadian Supply & American Demand. Thomas R. Roach. LC 94-6940. (Issues Ser.). viii, 56p. 1994. pap. 6.95 (0-89030-050-X) Forest Hist Soc.

Newsprint Forum, 1993: Marriott Marquis, Atlanta, Georgia, April 21-23. Technical Association of the Pulp & Paper Industry. LC TS1124.. (TAPPI Course Notes Ser.). 292p. 1993. reprint ed. pap. 90.60 (0-608-00263-1, 204538600005) Bks Demand.

*Newsprint in Hong Kong: A Strategic Entry Report, 1998. Compiled by Icon Group International Staff. (Illus.). 117p. 1999. ring bd. 1170.00 incl. audio compact disk (0-7418-1534-6) Icon Grp.

Newsprint Mask: The Tradition of the Fictional Journalist. Ed. by Welford D. Taylor. LC 90-40072. (Illus.). 268p. 1991. reprint ed. pap. 83.10 (0-608-06864-0, 206707000009) Bks Demand.

Newsreel: Documentary Filmaking on the American Left. Bill Nichols. Ed. by Garth S. Jowett. LC 79-6681. (Dissertations on Film Ser.). 313p. 1980. 23.95 (0-405-12914-9) Ayer.

Newsreels in Film Archives: A Survey Based on the FIAF Newsreel Symposium. Ed. by Roger Smither & Wolfgang Klaue. LC 95-52394. (Illus.). 256p. 1996. 38.50 (0-8386-3696-9) Fairleigh Dickinson.

Newsroom Brain: A Working Guide to Journalism Decisions. Ed. by Stacy Lynch & Michael P. Smith. 62p. 1998. pap. 35.00 (0-9656018-2-X) NMC.

Newsroom Guide to Abortion & Family Planning. David Anderson. 102p. (Orig.). 1993. pap. 8.95 (1-883068-00-2) Comm Consort.

Newsroom Guide to Civil Rights. David Anderson. 146p. (Orig.). 1994. pap. 8.95 (1-883068-01-0) Comm Consort.

Newsroom Guide to Polls & Surveys. G. Cleveland Wilhoit & David H. Weaver. LC 89-36942. (Illus.). 82p. 1990. 20.95 (0-253-36543-0) Ind U Pr.

Newsroom Guide to Polls & Surveys. G. C. Wilhoit. LC 89-36942. (Illus.). 82p. Date not set. reprint ed. pap. 30.00 (0-608-20734-9, 205449000002) Bks Demand.

Newsroom Management: A Guide to Theory & Practice. Robert H. Giles. LC 87-71124. (Illus.). 739p. 1987. 67.50 (0-89730-181-1); student ed. 34.95 (0-89730-189-7) R J Berg.

Newsroom Management: A Guide to Theory & Practice. Robert H. Giles. (Illus.). 739p. (C). 1991. reprint ed. lib. bdg. 19.95 (1-962109-40-2) Media Mgt Bks.

Newsroom Management: A Guide to Theory & Practice. 3rd ed. Robert H. Giles. 742p. (C). 1995. reprint ed. 39.95 (0-9621094-0-1) Media Mgt Bks.

Newsroom Management Handbook. LC 85-70343. 107p. 1985. ring bd. 15.00 (0-943086-04-3) Am Soc News.

Newsroom Management Handbook. American Society of Newspaper Editors. 1985. 15.00 (0-318-33451-8) Am Soc News.

Newsschool: Using the Newspaper to Teach Math, Science & Health. Marilyn Olson. 1997. pap. text 11.85 (0-86651-261-6) Seymour Pubns.

Newsschool: Using the Newspaper to Teach Social Studies. Marilyn Olson. 1997. pap. text 11.85 (0-86651-262-4) Seymour Pubns.

Newstart Lifestyle Cookbook: More Than 260 Heart-Healthy Recipes Whole Plant Foods. Weimar Institute Staff. LC 98-134405. (Illus.). 224p. 1997. 19.99 (0-7852-7140-6) Nelson.

Newstrom Organizational Behavior. 9th ed. Chown. 1992. teacher ed. 51.56 (0-07-015621-2) McGraw.

*Newsweek Business School Admissions Adviser. rev. ed. Kaplan Staff. 320p. 1998. pap. 20.00 (0-684-84976-3) Kaplan.

Newsweek Business School Admissions Advisor: Expert Advice to Help You Get Into the School of Yo. Kaplan Educational Center, Ltd. Staff. LC 98-646671. (Illus.). 288p. 1999. pap. 20.00 (0-684-85957-2) S&S Trade.

Newsweek College Catalog. Kaplan. 1400p. 1998. pap. 25.00 (0-684-85247-0) S&S Trade.

*Newsweek College Catalog 2000. Kaplan Educational Center Staff. (College Catalog Ser.). (Illus.). 100p. 1999. pap. text 25.00 (0-684-85953-X) Free Pr.

Newsweek Graduate School Admissions Advisor: Expert Advice to Help You Get Into the School of Yo. Kaplan Educational Center, Ltd. Staff. LC 99-111871. (Illus.). 288p. 1999. pap. 20.00 (0-684-85955-6) S&S Trade.

*Newsweek Interactive Guide Workbook. Shirley R. Wachtel. (C). 1999. pap. text, wbk. ed. 8.25 (0-321-05528-4) Addison-Wesley.

Newsweek Law School Admissions Advisor: Expert Advice to Help You Get Into the School of Your Ch. Kaplan Educational Center, Ltd. Staff. LC 98-660820. (Illus.). 304p. 1999. pap. 20.00 (0-684-85958-0) S&S Trade.

Newsweek Medical School Admissions Advisor: Expert Advice to Help You Get Into the School of You. Kaplan Educational Center, Ltd. Staff. LC 98-660821. (Illus.). 272p. 1999. pap. 20.00 (0-684-85956-4) S&S Trade.

Newsweek Score Kaplan Guide to Educational Software & Web Sites, 1998. Kaplan Staff. 360p. 1997. 18.00 (0-684-84533-4) S&S Trade.

Newsworkers: Toward a History of the Rank & File. Ed. by Hanno Hardt & Bonnie Brennen. 256p. 1995. text 49.95 (0-8166-2706-1); pap. text 19.95 (0-8166-2707-X) U of Minn Pr.

Newsworthy: The Lives of Media Women. Susan Crean. 350p. 1985. mass mkt. 5.95 (0-88780-150-1, Pub. by Formac Publ Co) Formac Dist Ltd.

Newsworthy: The Lives of Media Women. Susan Crean. (Illus.). 350p. 1985. 24.95 (0-7737-0081-1) Genl Dist Srvs.

Newswriter's Handbook: An Introduction to Journalism. M. L. Stein. LC 97-43709. 1998. pap. text 29.95 (0-8138-2719-1) Iowa St U Pr.

Newswriter's Handbook: An Introduction to Journalism. M. L. Stein & Susan F. Paterno. 1998. pap., teacher ed. 9.95 (0-8138-2720-5) Iowa St U Pr.

Newswriting. Gerald Stone. (C). 1997. pap. 52.00 (0-06-046457-7, Perennial) HarperTrade.

Newswriting. 2nd ed. Ken Metzler. (Illus.). 208p. (C). 1987. pap. text 38.20 (0-13-611641-8) P-H.

Newswriting & Reporting for Today's Media. Bruce D. Itule & Douglas Anderson. 612p. (C). 1987. student ed. 12.95 (0-685-13257-9) McGraw.

Newswriting & Reporting Public Affairs. 2nd ed. Chilton R. Bush. LC 71-127596. x, 576p. 1970. write for info. (0-8019-6002-9) NP-Chilton.

Newswriting Guide: A Handbook for Student Reporters. 2nd rev. ed. Rachel Bard. LC 79-55986. 96p. 1988. reprint ed. pap. 10.95 (0-9603666-4-4) Blue Zoo.

Newswriting Guide: A Handbook for Student Reporters. 3rd ed. Rachel Bard. LC 79-55986. write for info. (0-929838-09-2) Blue Zoo.

Newswriting in Transition. Ray Laakaniemi. (Mass Communication Ser.). 1995. pap. text 34.95 (0-8304-1347-2) Thomson Learn.

Newszak & News Media. Bob Franklin. LC 97-20880. 320p. 1997. pap. text 21.00 (0-340-61416-1, Pub. by E A) OUP.

Newt. Ron Dakron. 205p. 1992. pap. 10.95 (0-930773-19-5) Black Heron Pr.

Newt. Matt Novak. LC 95-13286. (I Can Read Bks.). (Illus.). 48p. (J). (gr. 1-3). 1996. lib. bdg. 15.89 (0-06-024502-6) HarpC Child Bks.

Newt. Matt Novak. (I Can Read Bks.). (Illus.). 48p. (J). (gr. 1-3). 1997. pap. 3.95 (0-06-444236-5, HarpTrophy) HarpC Child Bks.

Newt. Matt Novak. (I Can Read Bks.). (J). (gr. 1-3). 1997. 8.95 (0-606-11681-8, Pub. by Turtleback) Demco.

Newt: A Study Guide. Duncan Searl. Ed. by J. Friedland & R. Kessler. (Novel-Ties Ser.). (J). (gr. k-2). 1998. pap. text, student ed. 15.95 (0-7675-0312-0) Lrn Links.

Newt Gingrich: Capitol Crimes & Misdemeanors. John K. Wilson. 300p. 1996. 24.95 (1-56751-097-3) Common Courage.

Newtisms: Newt Gingrich on the Issues--From A to Z. Geoff Rodkey. 1995. mass mkt. 5.00 (0-671-53533-1) PB.

Newton. Wayne McCabe & Kate Gordon. LC 98-87868. (Images of America Ser.). (Illus.). 128p. 1998. pap. 16.99 (0-7524-1239-6) Arcadia Publng.

*Newton. Newton Historical Society Staff. (Images of America Ser.). (Illus.). 128p. 1999. pap. 18.99 (0-7524-1319-8) Arcadia Publng.

N

*Newton. Taschen America Staff. 2000. pap. text 4.99 (3-8228-6087-5) Taschen Amer.

*Newton: An Iowa Story. Will Stuart. LC 99-91565. 1999. 25.00 (0-7388-0874-1); pap. 18.00 (0-7388-0875-X) Xlibris Corp.

Newton: Texts, Backgrounds, Commentaries. Ed. by Richard S. Westfall. LC 92-21165. (Critical Editions Ser.). 436p. (C). 1995. pap. text 12.50 (0-393-95902-3) Norton.

Newton: The Father of Modern Astronomy. Jean-Pierre Maury. Tr. by I. Mark Paris. (Discoveries Ser.). (Illus.). 144p. 1992. pap. 12.95 (0-8109-2835-3, Pub. by Abrams) Time Warner.

Newton: The Law & Regulation of Derivatives. Alan Newton. 266p. 1996. write for info. (0-406-04965-3, NLRD, MICHIE) LEXIS Pub.

Newton among Poets: Shelley's Use of Science in Prometheus Unbound. Carl A. Grabo. LC 68-19138. 1968. reprint ed. lib. bdg. 55.50 (0-8154-0085-3) Cooper Sq.

Newton among Poets: Shelley's Use of Science in Prometheus Unbound. Carl H. Grabo. LC 68-24046. 220p. 1968. reprint ed. 50.00 (0-87752-044-5) Gordian.

Newton among Poets: Shelley's Use of Science in Prometheus Unbound. Carl H. Grabo. (BCL1-PR English Literature Ser.). 208p. 1992. reprint ed. lib. bdg. 79.00 (0-7812-7652-7) Rprt Serv.

Newton & Gravity. Paul Strathern. LC 97-52135. (Big Idea Ser.). (Illus.). 112p. 1998. pap. 9.95 (0-385-49241-3, Anchor NY) Doubleday.

Newton & Howe, Hale & Carter: The Ancestors & Descendants of James Newton & Esther Hale of Hubbardston & Greenfield, Massachusetts. Franklin H. White. LC 89-50894. (Illus.). 180p. 1989. 35.00 (0-9623187-0-1) WHE OH.

*Newton & Religion: Context, Nature, & Influence. James E. Force & Richard H. Popkin. LC 99-15083. (International Archives of the History of Ideas Ser.). 1999. write for info. (0-7923-5744-2) Kluwer Academic.

Newton & Russia: The Early Influence, 1698-1796. Valentin Boss. LC 73-188352. (Russian Research Center Studies: No. 69). 367p. reprint ed. pap. 113.80 (0-7837-2225-7, 205731500004) Bks Demand.

Newton & the Culture of Newtonianism. Betty Jo Dobbs et al. LC 98-52947. 1998. write for info. (1-57392-545-4) Prometheus Bks.

Newton & the Culture of Newtonianism. Margaret C. Jacob & Betty J. T. Dobbs. LC 94-18946. (Control of Nature Ser.). 152p. (C). 1995. pap. 12.50 (0-391-03877-X) Humanities.

Newton & the Culture of Newtonianism. Jo Teeter. LC 98-52947. 1998. write for info. (1-57392-547-0) Prometheus Bks.

Newton & the Scientific Revolution. Richard S. Westfall. (Illus.). 87p. 1987. pap. 5.00 (1-879598-09-4) IN Univ Lilly Library.

Newton at the Bat: The Science in Sports. Ed. by Eric W. Schrier & William F. Allman. LC 84-1299. (Illus.). 192p. reprint ed. pap. 59.60 (0-7837-6744-7, 204637200011) Bks Demand.

Newton Boys: Portrait of an Outlaw Gang. Willis Newton & Joe Newton. LC 93-43267. (Illus.). 332p. 1994. pap. 16.95 (1-880510-16-2) State House Pr.

Newton Boys: Portrait of an Outlaw Gang. limited ed. Willis Newton & Joe Newton. LC 93-43267. (Illus.). 332p. 1994. 60.00 (1-880510-17-0) State House Pr.

Newton-Cauchy Framework: A Unified Approach to Unconstrained Nonlinear Minimization. John L. Nazareth. LC 93-49417. (Lecture Notes in Computer Science Ser.: Vol. 769). xii, 101p. 1994. 29.95 (0-387-57671-1) Spr-Verlag.

Newton Co., Ms. Census, 1840. Compiled by Berniece D. Coyle. 19p. 1989. pap. text 10.00 (1-882111-85-0) Coyle Data Co.

Newton County: Collection of Historical Facts & Personal Recollections Concerning Newton Co., from 1853 to 1911. John Ade. (Illus.). 314p. 1997. reprint ed. lib. bdg. 37.50 (0-8328-6661-X) Higginson Bk Co.

Newton County, MO to 1990. Donna J. Whitchurch. (Illus.). 147p. 1992. 30.00 (0-88107-202-8) Curtis Media.

Newton Demands the Muse: Newton's "Opticks" & the Eighteenth Century Poets, 2. Marjorie H. Nicholson. LC 78-13146. 178p. 1979. reprint ed. lib. bdg. 35.00 (0-313-21044-6, NIND, Greenwood Pr) Greenwood.

Newton Forster or the Merchant Service. Frederick Marryat. LC 98-14726. 1998. pap. 13.95 (0-935526-44-7) McBooks Pr.

Newton Handbook. Derek Gjertsen. 576p. 1987. 59.95 (0-7102-0279-2, 02792, Routledge Thoemms) Routledge.

Newton, His Friends & His Foes. A. Rupert Hall. (Collected Studies: Vol. CS390). 344p. 1993. 115.95 (0-86078-347-2, Pub. by Variorum) Ashgate Pub Co.

Newton in 90 Minutes. John Gribbin & Mary Gribbin. (Scientists in 90 Minutes Ser.). 80p. 1997. pap. 7.95 (0-09-477040-9, Pub. by Constable & Co) Trafalgar.

Newton Letter. John Banville. 96p. 1987. pap. 10.95 (1-56792-096-9) Godine.

Newton Letter. John Banville. 1991. pap. 8.99 (0-446-39283-9) Warner Bks.

Newton, Massachusetts, 1679-1779: A Biographical Directory. Priscilla Ritter & Thelma Fleishman. 152p. 1982. pap. 11.95 (0-88082-001-2) New Eng Hist.

Newton Messagepad Version of Practical Guide to the Care of the Medical Patient. 3rd ed. Fred F. Ferri. 2p. (C). 1996. write for info. (0-8151-3168-2) Mosby Inc.

Newton Polyhedra Without Coordinates - Newton Polyhedra of Ideals. Boris Youssin. LC 90-595. (Memoirs Ser.: No. 87/433). 99p. 1990. pap. 20.00 (0-8218-2495-3, MEMO/87/433) Am Math.

Newton Programmer's Guide. Apple Computer, Inc. Staff. 944p. 1996. pap. text 50.95 (0-201-47947-8) Addison-Wesley.

Newton, Rev. Roger Newton, Deceased 1683, & One Line of His Descendants, & Abner Newton, 1764-1852, His Ancestors & Descendants. Caroline G. Newton. (Illus.). 280p. 1995. reprint ed. pap. 44.00 (0-8328-4560-4); reprint ed. lib. bdg. 54.00 (0-8328-4559-0) Higginson Bk Co.

Newton Rules Biology: A Physical Approach to Biological Problems. C. J. Pennycuick. (Illus.). 128p. 1992. pap. text 25.00 (0-19-854021-3) OUP.

Newton to Aristotle: Towards a Theory of Models for Living Systems. John L. Casti & Anders Karlqvist. (Mathematical Modeling Ser.: No. 4). 296p. 1989. 73.00 (0-8176-3435-5) Birkhauser.

Newton to Einstein: The Trail of Light: An Excursion to the Wave-Particle Duality & the Special Theory of Relativity. Ralph Baierlein. (Illus.). 345p. (C). 1992. text 42.95 (0-521-41171-8) Cambridge U Pr.

Newton 2.0 User Interface Guidelines. Apple Computer, Inc. Staff. LC 96-20168. 320p. (C). 1996. pap. text 29.95 (0-201-48838-8) Addison-Wesley.

Newtonian Casino. Blass. 1990. text. write for info. (0-582-05752-3, Pub. by Addison-Wesley) Longman.

Newtonian Dynamics. Baierlein. 1983. student ed. 20.62 (0-07-003017-0) McGraw.

Newtonian Dynamics. Ralph Baierlein. (Illus.). 336p. (C). 1983. 88.44 (0-07-003016-2) McGraw.

Newtonian Electrodynamics. 304p. 1996. lib. bdg. 25.00 (981-02-2681-0) World Scientific Pub.

Newtonian Electrodynamics. Peter Graneau & Neal Graneau. 350p. 1996. text 61.00 (981-02-2284-X) World Scientific Pub.

Newtonian Mechanics. Anthony P. French. (M.I.T. Introductory Physics Ser.). (Illus.). (C). 1971. pap. text 34.25 (0-393-09970-9) Norton.

Newtonians & the English Revolution, 1689-1720. M. C. Jacob. (Classics in the History & Philosophy of Science Ser.: Vol. 7). iv, 288p. 1990. pap. text 55.00 (2-88124-400-9) Gordon & Breach.

Newtonians & the English Revolution, 1689-1720. Margaret C. Jacob. LC 75-36995. reprint ed. pap. 74.90 (0-608-17742-3, 2032049) Bks Demand.

Newton's Cannon. J. Gregory Keyes. LC 98-10473. (Age of Unreason Ser.: 1). 480p. 1998. pap. 14.00 (0-345-40605-2) Ballantine Pub Grp.

Newton's Cannon. J. Gregory Keyes. 1999. mass mkt. 6.99 (0-345-43378-5, Del Rey) Ballantine Pub Grp.

Newton's Clock: Chaos in the Solar System. Ivars Peterson. LC 93-7176. (Illus.). 317p. 1995. pap. text 15.95 (0-7167-2724-2) W H Freeman.

Newton's Dream. Ed. by Marcia S. Stayer. 144p. (C). 1988. text 65.00 (0-7735-0689-6, Pub. by McG-Queens Univ Pr) CUP Services.

*Newton's Gift: How Sir Isaac Newton Unlocked the System of the World. David Berlinski. 2000. 24.00 (0-684-84392-7) Free Pr.

Newton's Law: The Brave New World of Apple's Personal Digital Assistant. Mitch Ratcliffe. 480p. 1993. pap. 24.00 (0-679-74647-1) Random.

Newton's Laws of Motion. School Mathematics Project Staff. (School Mathematics Project 16-19 Ser.). (Illus.). 125p. 1993. pap. text 13.95 (0-521-40878-4) Cambridge U Pr.

Newton's Laws of Motion. School Mathematics Project Staff. (Mathematics Series: Ages 16-19). (Illus.). 125p. (C). 1993. pap. text 11.95 (0-521-38845-7) Cambridge U Pr.

Newton's Method & Dynamical Systems. Ed. by Heinz-Otto Peitgen. (C). 1989. text 160.00 (0-7923-0113-7) Kluwer Academic.

Newton's Optical Writings: A Guided Study. Dennis L. Sepper. LC 93-26703. (Masterworks of Discovery: Guided Studies of Great Texts in Science Ser.). 250p. (C). 1994. text 42.00 (0-8135-2037-1); pap. text 19.00 (0-8135-2038-X) Rutgers U Pr.

Newton's Philosophy of Nature: Selected Writings. Sir Isaac Newton. 1970. pap. 16.95 (0-02-849700-7) Free Pr.

Newton's Physics & the Conceptual Structure of the Scientific Revolution. Zev Bechler. 624p. (C). 1991. lib. bdg. 292.50 (0-7923-1054-3, Pub. by Kluwer Academic) Kluwer Academic.

Newton's Principia: The Central Argument. Dana Densmore. Tr. & Illus. by William H. Donahue. 473p. 1995. pap. 26.95 (1-888009-00-4) Grn Lion Pr.

Newton's Principia for the Common Reader. S. Chandrasekhar. (Illus.). 616p. 1995. text 145.00 (0-19-851744-0) OUP.

Newton's Scientific & Philosophical Legacy. Ed. by P. B. Scheurer & G. Debrock. (C). 1988. lib. bdg. 201.00 (90-247-3723-0) Kluwer Academic.

Newton's Second Law. Sam Forman. 1995. 3.50 (0-87129-569-5, N39) Dramatic Pub.

Newton's Sleep: The Two Cultures & the Two Kingdoms. Raymond Tallis. LC 95-18080. 180p. 1995. text 59.95 (0-312-12865-7) St Martin.

Newton's Telecom Dictionary. 11th ed. Harry Newton. 1996. pap. 27.95 (0-936648-87-2) Telecom Bks.

Newton's Telecom Dictionary. 14th ed. Harry Newton. 1998. pap. text 29.95 (1-57820-023-7) Telecom Bks.

*Newton's Telecom Dictionary: The Official Dictionary of Telecommunications & the Internet. 16th ed. Harry Newton & Ray Horak. (Illus.). 1008p. 2000. pap. 32.95 (1-57820-053-9, Pub. by Miller Freeman) Publishers Group.

*Newton's Tyranny: The Suppressed Scientific Discoveries of Steven Gray & John Flamsteed. David Clark & Stephen P. H. Clark. 2000. 23.95 (0-7167-4215-2) W H Freeman.

Newtopia: How to Build a Bright New Utopia. D. K. Paul. LC 96-119926. 120p. (Orig.). (YA). 1995. pap. 9.95 (0-9642761-0-0) PakDonald Pubng.

Newtown. Daniel Cruson. (Images of America Ser.). (Illus.). 128p. 1998. pap. 16.99 (0-7524-0948-4) Arcadia Publng.

Newtown, Connecticut: Directions & Images. League of Women Voters of Newtown Staff. Ed. by Carol Telfair & Carolyn Greene. (Illus.). 1989. text 30.00 (0-9623444-0-0) LWV Newtown.

Newtown, Connecticut's, History & Historian. Ed. by Jane E. Johnson. (Illus.). 457p. 1992. reprint ed. lib. bdg. 49.00 (0-8328-2892-0) Higginson Bk Co.

Newtown's Slaves: A Case Study in Early Connecticut Rural Black History. Daniel Cruson. (Illus.). 92p. 1995. pap. 10.00 (1-888006-01-3) Newtown Hist Soc.

Newts. Jordan Patterson. (Illus.). 68p. 1995. pap. text 9.95 (0-7938-0274-1, RE131) TFH Pubns.

Newts: Their Care in Captivity. Jordan Patterson. (Basic Domestic Reptile & Amphibian Library). (Illus.). 64p. (YA). (gr. 3 up). 1999. lib. bdg. 17.95 (0-7910-5131-5) Chelsea Hse.

Newts & Salamanders. Frank Indiviglio. LC 97-1166. (More Complete Pet Owner's Manual Ser.). (Illus.). 96p. 1997. pap. text 6.95 (0-8120-9779-3) Barron.

Newts & Salamanders of Europe. Ed. by Richard A. Griffiths. (Poyser Natural History Ser.). (Illus.). 224p. 1996. text 39.95 (0-12-303955-X) Acad Pr.

Newts of the British Isles. P. J. Wisniewski. (Natural History Ser.: No. 47). (Illus.). 24p. 1989. pap. 5.25 (0-7478-0029-4, Pub. by Shire Pubns) Parkwest Pubns.

*NewYork Times Daily Crossword Puzzles, Vol. 16. Will Weng. Vol. 16. 64p. 1999. pap. 9.50 (0-8129-3183-1, Times Bks) Crown Pub Group.

NewYorkwalks: The Ninety-Second Street Y. Ed. by Batia Plotch. (Walks Ser.). (Illus.). 272p. 1995. pap. 12.95 (0-8050-1660-0, Owl) H Holt & Co.

NEXAFS Spectroscopy. Joachim Stohr. LC 96-15834. (Series in Surface Sciences: Vol. 25). 1996. write for info. (3-540-54422-4) Spr-Verlag.

NEXAFS Spectroscopy: And the Structure of Adsorbed Molecules. Joachim Stohr. (Springer Series in Surface Sciences: Vol. 25). (Illus.). 403p. 1996. 59.95 (0-387-54422-4) Spr-Verlag.

Nexis (R) Product Guide, 4 vols. Ed. by Bob Bernard. 1992. write for info. (0-318-72162-7); write for info. (0-318-72163-5); write for info. (0-318-72164-3); write for info. (0-318-72165-1) LEXIS-NEXIS.

Nexis (R) Product Guide, 4 vols., Set. Ed. by Bob Bernard. 1992. 65.00 (0-926578-09-X) LEXIS-NEXIS.

Nexrad User's Guide 1.1. ACCU-Weather, Inc. Staff. 64p. 1995. pap. text, ring bd. 5.00 (0-7872-1098-6) Kendall-Hunt.

Next: A Poetic Odyssey. Lee Frank. LC 97-91189. 326p. 1998. pap. 12.95 (0-533-12581-2) Vantage.

Next! An Actor's Guide to Auditioning. Ellie Kanner & Paul G. Bens, Jr. LC 96-46181. 168p. (Orig.). 1997. pap. 19.95 (0-943728-71-1) Lone Eagle Pub.

Next! Auditioning for the Musical Theatre. Steven M. Alper. LC 95-19090. 105p. 1995. pap. 12.95 (0-435-08686-3, 08686) Heinemann.

Next: New Poems. Lucille Clifton. (American Poets Continuum Ser.: No. 15). 85p. 1987. pap. 10.00 (0-918526-61-2) BOA Edns.

Next: The Coming Era in Medicine, Vol. 1. Holcomb B. Noble. 1988. pap. 9.95 (0-316-61134-4, Little Brwn Med Div) Lppncott W & W.

Next: The Coming Era in Science. Ed. by Holcomb B. Noble. 192p. 1988. pap. 9.95 (0-316-61133-6) Little.

*Next: The New Generation in Graphic Design. Jesse Marinoff Reyes. LC 00-29201. (Illus.). 160p. 2000. write for info. (0-89134-999-5) North Lght.

Next: Trends for the Near-Future. Marian Salzman & Ira Matathia. LC 99-11457. 432p. 1999. text 26.95 (0-87951-943-6, Pub. by Overlook Pr) Penguin Putnam.

*Next: Trends for the Near Future. Marian Salzman & Ira Matathia. 2000. pap. 16.95 (1-58567-083-9, Pub. by Overlook Pr) Penguin Putnam.

Next: Young American Writers on the New Generation. Eric Liu. LC 93-38794. 1994. pap. 12.95 (0-393-31191-0) Norton.

Next American Metropolis: Ecology, Community & the American Dream. Peter Calthorpe. LC 93-10170. (Illus.). 160p. (Orig.). 1993. pap. 24.95 (1-878271-68-7) Princeton Arch.

Next American Nation: The New Nationalism & the Fourth American Revolution. Michael Lind. 350p. 1995. 25.00 (0-02-919103-3) Free Pr.

Next American Nation: The New Nationalism & the Fourth American Revolution. Michael Lind. LC 96-2144. 448p. 1996. per. 15.00 (0-684-82503-1) Free Pr.

Next American Spirituality: Finding God in the Twenty-first Century. George H. Gallup, Jr. LC 99-88255. 225p. 2000. 19.99 (0-7814-3316-9) Chariot Victor.

Next Arab Decade: Alternative Futures. Hisham Sharabi. LC 87-6550. 1988. write for info. (0-932568-14-9) GU Ctr CAS.

Next Archaeology Workbook. Nicholas David & Jonathan Driver. LC 89-40406. (Illus.). 118p. (C). 1989. pap. text 19.95 (0-8122-1293-2) U of Pa Pr.

Next Balcony Down. Veronique Borg. (Child's World Library). (Illus.). 32p. (J). (gr. k-5). 1992. lib. bdg. 18.50 (0-89565-757-0) Childs World.

Next Bend in the River. C. J. Stevens. LC 89-51183. 177p. (Orig.). 1989. text 18.00 (0-9623934-0-1); pap. text 8.95 (0-9623934-1-X) J Wade.

*Next Best Thing: Helping Sexually Active Teens Avoid Pregnancy. John Hutchins. (Illus.). 25p. 2000. pap. 5.00 (1-58671-027-3) Natl Cpgn Teen Preg.

Next Best Thing to Paradise. Mary Jane Edwards. LC 98-88474. 325p. 1998. pap. 15.00 (0-7388-0164-X) Xlibris Corp.

Next Best Thing to Paradise. Mary Jane Edwards. LC 98-88474. 325p. 1999. 25.00 (0-7388-0163-1) Xlibris Corp.

Next Bible. 2nd ed. Clapp. 1991. pap. 29.95 (0-13-617200-8) P-H.

Next Book. (C). 1990. text. write for info. (0-201-50970-9) Addison-Wesley.

*Next Book of the Lockes: Descendants of William Locke of Woburn, Massachusetts. Jerry Harrison. 619p. 2000. pap. write for info. (0-7884-1457-7, 1457) Heritage Bk.

Next Bottom Line: Making Sustainable Development Tangible. Matthew Arnold & Robert Day. LC 98-88622. (Illus.). 64p. 1998. pap. 20.00 (1-56973-283-3) World Resources Inst.

Next by Default Too. Peter Ganick. 32p. 1997. pap. 7.00 (0-935350-97-7) Luna Bisonte.

*Next Canada: In Search of Our Future Nation. Myrna Kostash. (Illus.). 350p. 2000. 28.95 (0-7710-4561-1) McClland & Stewart.

Next Canadian Century. David Crane. 224p. 1992. 26.95 (0-7737-2569-5) Genl Dist Srvs.

*Next Century: Why Canada Wins. Nuala Beck. LC 99-182175. 2000. pap. 18.00 (0-00-638527-3) HarpC.

Next Chance to Last. Louisa Dixon. LC 98-217129. 345p. 1998. 24.95 (1-885478-39-9, Pub. by Genesis Press) BookWorld.

Next Chapter after the Last. A. W. Tozer. LC 87-70164. 111p. (Orig.). 1988. pap. 9.99 (0-87509-391-4, PSPUM 35) Chr Pubns.

*Next Church. Now: Creating New Faith Communities. Craig Kennet Miller. LC 99-68755. 192p. 2000. pap. text 21.95 (0-88177-293-3, DR293) Discipleship Res.

Next Cold War? American Alternatives for the Twenty-First Century. Jim Hanson. LC 95-40581. 208p. 1996. 57.95 (0-275-95473-0, Praeger Pubs) Greenwood.

Next Common Sense: Mastering Corporate Complexity Through Coherence. Michael Lissack & Johan Roos. LC 98-32271. 256p. 1999. 25.00 (1-85788-240-7) Nicholas Brealey.

*Next Common Sense: Mastering Corporate Complexity Through Coherence. Michael Lissack & Johan Roos. (Illus.). 256p. 2000. pap. 16.00 (1-85788-235-0, Pub. by Nicholas Brealey) Natl Bk Netwk.

Next Critical Step. Bernard Theroux. LC 95-190156. 80p. 1995. pap. 8.95 (0-9645910-0-6) Morning Light Pubns.

*Next Dance. Franklin S. Yudkin. LC 98-88758. 192p. 1999. pap. 11.95 (1-56315-201-0) SterlingHse.

*Next Deal: The Choice Revolution & the New Responsibility. Andrei Cherny. 224p. 2000. 24.00 (0-465-00971-9, Pub. by Basic) HarpC.

Next Development Tools. Next Computer Inc. Staff. 1991. pap. text 26.95 (0-201-58132-9) Addison-Wesley.

Next Dimension Is Love. Dorothy Roeder. 148p. (Orig.). 1993. pap. 11.95 (0-929385-50-0) Light Tech Pubng.

Next Dominant Species. Milo Lawrence. LC 93-74163. 403p. 1994. 19.95 (0-9639372-5-1) Altos Pubng.

Next Door. Kurt Vonnegut, Jr. 1994. 3.50 (0-87129-433-8, N23) Dramatic Pub.

Next-Door Neighbors. Sarah Ellis. LC 89-37923. 160p. (J). (gr. 4-7). 1990. 16.00 (0-689-50495-0) McElderry Bks.

Next Door to Power. G. Wayne Dailey. Date not set. 24.95 (0-8488-2088-6); pap. 14.95 (0-8488-2089-4) Amereon Ltd.

Next Door to Power: Human Interest Stories about 45 Vice Presidents. G. Wayne Dailey. (Illus.). 268p. (Orig.). 1997. pap. 11.95 (0-9653544-0-7) G W Dailey.

Next Door Witch. Mary Stanton. (Magical Mystery Ser.). 160p. (J). (gr. 3-7). 1997. mass mkt. 3.99 (0-425-15905-1) Berkley Pub.

Next Efficiency Revolution: Creating a Sustainable Materials Economy. John E. Young & Aaron Sachs. LC 94-61212. 54p. (Orig.). 1994. pap. 5.00 (1-878071-22-X) Worldwatch Inst.

Next Environmental Battleground: Indoor Air. Dwight Lee. 1992. pap. 10.00 (0-943802-78-4, 174) Natl Ctr Pol.

Next Erase. Patrick Zale. LC 91-91287. 58p. (Orig.). 1992. pap. 7.50 (0-9631141-3-1) PAZ Pubns.

*Next Exit: U. S. A. Interstate Exit Directory. 9th ed. (Illus.). 542p. 2000. pap. 18.95 (0-9630103-8-7) Next Exit.

Next Exit: U. S. A. Interstate Highway Exit Guide. 7th ed. (Illus.). vii, 520p. 1998. pap. 17.95 (0-9630103-6-0) Next Exit.

Next Exit: U. S. A. Interstate Highway Guide. 8th ed. vii, 534p. 1999. pap. 18.95 (0-9630103-7-9) Next Exit.

Next Exit: USA Interstate Highway Guide. LC 92-141884. 375p. 1991. write for info. (0-9630103-0-1) Next Exit.

Next Fifty Years: Health, Physical Education, Recreation, Dance. Ed. by Larry L. Neal. 179p. 1971. pap. 10.00 (0-943272-08-4) Inst Recreation Res.

Next Fifty Years: The United Nations & the United States. Tom Barry & Erik Leaver. LC 96-14989. 202p. (Orig.). 1996. pap. 11.95 (0-911213-61-9) Interhemisp Res Ctr.

Next Fine Day. 2nd ed. Elizabeth Yates. (Pennant Ser.). (Illus.). 150p. (J). 1994. pap. 6.49 (0-89084-735-5, 078220) Bob Jones Univ.

Next Four Years: A Vision of Victory. Howard Phillips. 190p. 1992. pap. 10.00 (0-9633469-3-8) Policy Analysis.

Next Four Years: The U. S. & the World Economy. William D. Eberle et al. 20p. (Orig.). 1984. pap. text 13.00 (0-8191-5874-7) U Pr of Amer.

Next Generation. James Preller. 32p. (gr. 2-4). 1998. pap. text 7.99 (0-590-37240-8) Scholastic Inc.

Next Generation: Dialogues Between Leaders & Students. Ronald M. Peters, Jr. LC 92-54133. 320p. 1992. pap. 9.95 (0-8061-2430-X) U of Okla Pr.

N

An Asterisk (*) at the beginning of an entry indicates that the title is appearing for the first time.

Next Generation: Jewish Children & Adolescents. Ariela Keysar et al. LC 00-24953. (C). 2000. text 47.50 (0-7914-4543-7) State U NY Pr.

Next Generation: Jewish Children & Adolescents. Ariela Keysar et al. LC 00-24953. (Illus.). 192p. (C). 2000. pap. text 15.95 (0-7914-4544-5) State U NY Pr.

Next Generation: Preparing Graduate Student for the Professional Responsibilities of College Teachers. Jim Slevin. 32p. 1993. pap. 5.00 (0-685-62734-9) Assn Am Coll.

Next-Generation Attack Fighter: Affordability & Mission Needs. Donald Stevens et al. LC 97-8161. (Illus.). 71p. 1997. pap. 15.00 (0-8330-2497-3, MR-719) Rand Corp.

Next Generation Attack Fighter: Design Tradeoffs & Notional System Concepts. Rand Corp. Staff & Daniel P. Raymer. LC 96-23122. 1996. pap. text 13.00 (0-8330-2406-X, MR-595-AF) Rand Corp.

Next Generation Blessing see Break the Generation Curse

Next Generation CASE Tools. Ed. by Kalle Lytinen & Veli-Pekka Tahvanainen. LC 91-59042. (Studies in Computer & Communications Systems: Vol. 3). 240p. (gr. 12). 1992. pap. 70.00 (90-5199-076-6, Pub. by IOS Pr) IOS Press.

Next Generation Computing: Distributed Objects for Business. Ed. by Peter Fingar et al. (SIGS Reference Library: No. 4). 307p. 1996. pap. 49.95 (0-13-261892-3) Cambridge U Pr.

Next Generation Environmental Models & Computational Methods. Ed. by George Delic & Mary F. Wheeler. LC 96-71103. (Proceedings in Applied Mathematics Ser.: No. 87). (Illus.). xii, 375p. 1997. pap. 69.50 (0-89871-378-1, PR87) Soc Indus-Appl Math.

Next Generation Information System Technology: Proceedings of First International East-West Database Workshop, Kiev, U. S. S. R., October 9-12, 1990. Ed. by J. William Schmidt & A. A. Stogny. (Lecture Notes in Computer Science Ser.). ix, 450p. 1991. 47.95 (0-387-54141-1) Spr-Verlag.

***Next Generation Information Technologies & Systems: 4th International Workshop, NGITS'99, Zikhron-Yaakov, Israel, July 5-7, 1999, Proceedings.** Ed. by Ron Y. Pinter et al. LC 99-33674. (Lecture Notes in Computer Science Ser.: Vol. 1649). ix, 327p. 1999. pap. 56.00 (3-540-66225-1) Spr-Verlag.

N

Next Generation Infrared Space Observatory. Ed. by S. J. Burnell et al. LC 92-32222. 1992. text 171.00 (0-7923-1983-4) Kluwer Academic.

Next Generation Internet: Hearing Before the Committee on Science, U.S. House of Representatives, One Hundred Fifth Congress, First Session, September 10, 1997. United States Government. LC 98-142379. iii, 120 p. 1997. write for info. (0-16-056105-1) USGPO.

***Next Generation Manufacturing: Methods & Techniques.** James A. Jordan et al. LC 99-53198. (National Association of Manufacturers Ser.). 464p. 2000. text 55.00 (0-471-36006-6) Wiley.

***Next Generation Modems: A Professional Guide to DSLs & Cable Modems.** Gilbert Held. LC 99-58050. 384p. 2000. pap. 49.99 (0-471-35981-5) Wiley.

***Next Generation Nucleon Decay & Neutrino Detector, NNN99.** Ed. by Milind V. Diwan & Chang Kee Jung. (AIP Conference Proceedings Ser.: Vol. 533). (Illus.). ix, 248p. 2000. 115.00 (1-56396-956-4) Am Inst Physics.

Next-Generation Nursing Information Systems: Essential Characteristics for Professional Practice. Rita Zielstorff et al. (Illus.). 59p. (C). 1993. pap. text 14.95 (1-55810-083-0, NP-83) Am Nurses Pub.

Next Generation of Information Systems: From Data to Knowledge - A Selection of Papers Presented at Two IJCAI-91 Workshops, Sydney, Australia, August 26, 1991. Ed. by Joerg H. Siekmann et al. LC 92-21889. (Lecture Notes in Artificial Intelligence Ser.: Vol. 611). viii, 310p. 1992. write for info. (3-540-55616-8); 52.00 (0-387-55616-8) Spr-Verlag.

Next Generation of Nuclear Power Plants: A Status Report Topical Meeting, San Francisco, CA, Nov. 11-14, 1991. 211p. 1991. 45.00 (0-89448-166-5, 700167) Am Nuclear Soc.

***Next Generation Phone Systems: How to Choose & Implement PBX Alternatives.** David Krupinski et al. 250p. 2000. pap. 34.95 (1-57820-038-5, Pub. by Miller Freeman) Publishers Group.

Next Generation TCAD: Models & Methods. Enrico Sangiorgi et al. 1999. 400.00 (0-7803-5305-6) IEEE Standards.

Next Generation Websites. Vanessa Donnelly. (C). 2000. text. write for info. (0-201-67468-8) Addison-Wesley.

Next Giant Leap for Mankind. Theodore Coates. 125p. 1995. 27.95 (0-9648675-6-7) EMC Pubng.

Next Great Thing: The Sun, the Stirling Engine, & the Drive to Change the World. Mark L. Shelton. LC 93-34409. 1994. 25.00 (0-393-03619-7) Norton.

Next Greatest Thing: Fifty Years of Rural Electrification. Ed. by Richard A. Pence & Patrick Dahl. (Illus.). 256p. 1984. 29.85 (0-917599-00-4) Natl Rural.

Next in Line: The American Vice Presidency. Barbara S. Feinberg. LC 96-11617. (Democracy in Action Ser.). 160p. (J). 1996. lib. bdg. 24.00 (0-531-11283-7) Watts.

Next Karate Kid. B. B. Hiller. 176p. (YA). 1994. pap. 3.50 (0-590-48444-3) Scholastic Inc.

Next Karate Kid. B. B. Hiller. 120p. (J). (gr. 4-7). 1994. pap. 3.50 (0-590-48445-1) Scholastic Inc.

Next Learning System: And Why Home-Schoolers Are Trailblazers. Roland Meighan. 1997. pap. 13.95 (1-900219-04-2, Pub. by Educ Heretics) Intl Spec Bk.

Next Level. James Wood. 1998. write for info. (0-201-36093-4) Addison-Wesley.

***Next Level: Essential Strategies for Achieving Breakthrough Growth.** James B. Wood & Larry Rothstein. (Illus.). 224p. 1999. pap. text 16.00 (0-7382-0159-6, Pub. by Perseus Pubng) HarpC.

Next Level Leader's Guide: 4 Complete Youth Meetings That Guide Student Disciples through the Ne. Youth Specialties Staff. LC 98-55380. 1999. pap. text 8.99 (0-310-22986-3) Zondervan.

Next Level Spiritual Challenge Journal. Youth Specialties Staff & Mike Yaconelli. 1999. pap. 6.99 (0-310-22985-5) Zondervan.

Next Life: A Guide to Living Conditions on the Next Plane. C. C. Zain. (Brotherhood of Light Home Study Ser.: Course 20). 239p. 1995. pap. 16.95 (0-87887-392-9) Church of Light.

Next Man in Texas: Boots & Booties. Kristine Rolofson. 1997. per. 3.50 (0-373-25725-2, 1-25725-2) Harlequin Bks.

Next Marketing Handbook for Independent Schools. Rick Cowen. 1991. 27.00 (0-934338-75-2) NAIS.

Next Mediterranean Enlargement of the European Community: Turkey, Cyprus & Malta? John Redmond. 165p. 1993. 72.95 (1-85521-281-1, Pub. by Dartmth Pub) Ashgate Pub Co.

Next Millennium: Cities for People in a Globalizing World. (Roundtable Ser.: No. 1). 64p. pap. 10.00 (92-1-126057-4) UN.

Next Million Years. Charles G. Darwin. LC 73-5264. 210p. 1973. reprint ed. lib. bdg. 35.00 (0-8371-6876-7, DANM, Greenwood Pr) Greenwood.

Next Move of God. Fuchsia Pickett. pap. 9.99 (0-88419-384-5) Creation House.

Next New Madrid Earthquake: A Survival Guide for the Midwest. William Atkinson. LC 86-31637. (Shawnee Bks.). (Illus.). 192p. 1989. pap. 14.95 (0-8093-1320-0) S Ill U Pr.

Next New World. Bob Shacochis. 240p. 1990. pap. 10.95 (0-14-012105-6, Penguin Bks) Viking Penguin.

Next Newspapers: Future of Newspapers Report. 70p. 1988. 8.00 (0-318-41379-5) Nwspaper Assn Amer.

Next Nuclear Gamble: Transportation & Storage of Nuclear Waste. Marvin Resnikoff. 378p. 1985. 39.95 (0-88738-095-6) Transaction Pubs.

Next of Kin. Joanna Trollope. 1997. pap. 10.00 (0-552-99700-5) Bantam.

Next of Kin. Paul Wagner & Terrill Wagner. (Illus.). 242p. 1985. 19.95 (0-87770-363-9) Ye Galleon.

Next of Kin. Marianne L. Zeitlin. LC 91-65950. 188p. 1991. pap. 9.95 (0-939010-15-1) Zephyr Pr.

Next of Kin. large type ed. Stan Barstow. (General Ser.). 448p. 1993. 11.50 (0-7089-2907-9) Ulverscroft.

Next of Kin. large type ed. George Goodchild. (Linford Mystery Library). 464p. 1995. pap. 16.99 (0-7089-7729-4, Linford) Ulverscroft.

Next of Kin: Fossils in the Great Halls of the American Museum of Natural History. Lowell Dingus. LC 95-48881. (Illus.). 160p. 1996. 40.00 (0-8478-1929-9, Pub. by Rizzoli Intl) St Martin.

Next of Kin: Looking at the Great Apes. unabridged ed. Ron Platt et al. (Illus.). 48p. (Orig.). 1995. pap. 12.00 (0-938437-50-X) MIT List Visual Arts.

Next of Kin: My Conversations with Chimpanzees. Roger Fouts. 432p. 1998. pap. 14.00 (0-380-72822-2, Avon Bks) Morrow Avon.

***Next of Kin: What Chimpanzees Have Taught Me about Who We Are.** Roger Fouts & Stephen Tukel Mills. (Illus.). 420p. 2000. reprint ed. text 25.00 (0-7881-6927-0) DIANE Pub.

Next of (Non) Kin: The Importance of Primary Relationships for Adults' Well Being. Pearl A. Dykstra. viii, 248p. 1990. 40.75 (90-265-1104-3) Swets.

Next Operating System Software. NeXT Computer Inc. Staff. 1991. pap. text 24.95 (0-201-58131-0) Addison-Wesley.

Next Parish Over: A Collection of Irish American Writing. Ed. & Intro. by Patricia Monaghan. LC 93-83973. (Many Minnesotas Project Ser.). 367p. (Orig.). 1993. pap. 17.95 (0-89823-150-7) New Rivers Pr.

***Next Passage.** K. A. Applegate. (Animorphs: No. 2). (Illus.). 128p. (J). (gr. 3-7). 2000. mass mkt. 4.99 (0-439-14263-6) Scholastic Inc.

***Next Passage.** K. A. Applegate. (Illus.). (J). 2000. 10.34 (0-606-18506-2) Turtleback.

Next Phase in Foreign Policy. Ed. by Henry Owen. LC 73-1077. 357p. reprint ed. pap. 110.70 (0-608-12460-5, 202539700043) Bks Demand.

Next Place. Warren Hanson. LC 99-13135. (Illus.). 36p. (gr. k-4). 1997. 15.95 (0-931674-32-8) Waldman Hse Pr.

***Next, Please!** Christopher Inns. LC 00-36457. (Illus.). (J). 2001. write for info. (1-58246-038-8) Tricycle Pr.

***Next Pope, The - Revised & Updated: A Behind-the-Scenes Look at How the Successor to John Paul II Will be Elected & Where He Will Lead The Church.** Peter Hebblethwaite. LC 99-58506. (Illus.). 208p. 2000. pap. 13.00 (0-06-063777-3) Harper SF.

Next Power Frontier! Marla M. Branson. 337p. (Orig.). 1996. per. 19.95 (0-9651317-0-X) Unvrsal Spirit.

Next Presidency - Leadership. Robert M. Rueth. LC 97-67141. 176p. 1998. 18.95 (1-57197-072-X) Pentland Pr.

Next President. Joseph Flynn. LC 99-59476. 384p. 2000. 23.95 (0-553-10533-7, Spectra) Bantam.

***Next Religious Establishment: National Identity & Political Theology in Post-Protestant America.** Eldon J. Eisenach. LC 99-56786. (American Intellectual Culture Ser.). 192p. 2000. 65.00 (0-8476-9618-9); pap. 22.95 (0-8476-9619-7) Rowman.

***Next Revolution.** Charles C. Jung. 2000. 22.95 (0-533-13394-7) Vantage.

***Next Santini Bride.** Maureen Child. (Desire Ser.: Vol. 1317). 2000. mass mkt. 3.99 (0-373-76317-4, 1-76317-6) Harlequin Bks.

Next Season: A Novel. Michael Blakemore. 364p. 1995. pap. 12.95 (1-55783-223-4) Applause Theatre Bk Pubs.

Next Services. Michalea Moore. LC 80-5677. (Lucky Heart Bk.). (Illus.). 27p. 1980. reprint ed. pap. 30.00 (0-7837-9152-6, 204985200003) Bks Demand.

Next Seven Great Events of the Future: And What They Mean to You. Randal Ross. LC 97-65690. 1997. pap. text 9.99 (0-88419-457-4) Creation House.

Next Seventy Years: Population, Food & Resources. Gilland. vii, 134p. 1979. text 49.00 (0-85626-176-9) Gordon & Breach.

Next Software Guide. Clapp. 1991. pap. 29.95 (0-13-617218-0) P-H.

Next Spring an Oriole. Laurie Diamond. Ed. by Joyce Friedland & Rikki Kessler. (Novel-Ties Ser.). (J). (gr. 1-3). 1991. pap. text, student ed. 15.95 (0-88122-565-7) Lrn Links.

Next Spring an Oriole. Gloria Whelan. LC 87-4910. (Stepping Stone Bks). (Illus.). 64p. (J). (ps-3). 1987. pap. 3.99 (0-394-89125-2, Pub. by Random Bks Yng Read) Random.

Next Spring an Oriole. Gloria Whelan. LC 87-4910. (Stepping Stone Bks). (Illus.). 64p. (J). (ps-3). 1987. lib. bdg. 6.99 (0-394-99125-7, Pub. by Random Bks Yng Read) Random.

Next Spring an Oriole. Gloria Whelan. (Stepping Stone Bks.). (J). 1987. 9.19 (0-606-03037-9, Pub. by Turtleback) Demco.

Next Stage Guitar Book: Learn How to Play Scale Patterns & Tabs Easily & Quickly! Chris Lopez. 1999. spiral bd. 18.95 (0-9667719-2-3) C Winkle Prods.

Next Station Will Be . . . Ed. by Wilson E. Jones. LC 94-74870. (Next Station Will Be...Ser.: Vol. 1 3). 62p. (Orig.). (YA). 1995. pap. 20.00 (0-941652-13-0) NJ Midland Railroad.

Next Station Will Be . . ., Vol. 11. Ed. by Wilson E. Jones. LC 85-62575. (Illus.). 88p. (Orig.). 1990. pap. 26.00 (0-941652-10-6) NJ Midland Railroad.

Next Station Will Be . . ., Vol. 12. Ed. by Wilson E. Jones. LC 82-62628. (Illus.). 52p. (Orig.). 1993. pap. 16.00 (0-941652-12-2) NJ Midland Railroad.

***Next Station Will Be... An Album of Photographs of Railroad Depots in 1910.** 2nd rev. ed. Ed. by Curt Carlough et al. LC 99-67001. (Illus.). 64p. 1999. pap. 17.95 (0-941652-15-7) NJ Midland Railroad.

Next Step Babywise II: Parenting Your Pretoddler. Gary Ezzo & Robert Buckham. LC 94-220126. 134p. (Orig.). pap. text 6.95 (1-883035-98-8) Grow Families.

Next Step. Jack T. Chick. (Illus.). 64p. 1978. pap. 3.50 (0-937958-04-2) Chick Pubns.

Next Step, Pt. II. John-Paul Morgaite. (Basic Christian Training Ser.). 64p. 1993. pap. 2.50 (1-880322-03-X) Champions Christ.

Next Step: A Daily Walk in Recovery. F. Alvin Dungan. Ed. by Christy McBride. LC 93-9834. 220p. (Orig.). 1993. pap. 11.95 (1-880292-10-6) LangMarc.

Next Step: A Guide to Balanced Recovery. Todd Weber. LC 91-32096. 160p. pap. 8.95 (0-934125-25-2) Hazelden.

Next Step: A Life Skills Workbook for Adult Survivors of Emotional Abuse. Jill Raiguel. 288p. (Orig.). 1991. pap. 12.95 (0-944256-08-2) ACCESS Pubs Network.

Next Step: A National Conference Focusing on Issues Related to Substance Abuse in Deaf & Hard of Hearing Population. (Illus.). iv, 209p. 1993. pap. 20.00 (1-893891-13-5) Gallaudet U Contin Ed.

Next Step: Distributing Independent Films & Videos. 2nd rev. ed. Ed. by Morrie Warshawski. LC 96-172288. (Illus.). 184p. (Orig.). 1995. pap. 24.95 (0-9622448-1-3) FIVF.

Next Step: Etiology & Treatment of Addiction. Joseph Rosenfeld. LC 95-16788. 1995. 15.95 (0-938475-06-1) Lighthouse Inst.

Next Step: Fifty More Things You Can Do to Save the Earth. Earth Works Group Staff. 120p. 1990. pap. text 5.95 (0-8362-2302-0) Andrews & McMeel.

Next Step: Integrating the Software Life Cycle with SAS(R) Programming. Paul Gill. 384p. (C). 1997. pap. 39.95 (1-58025-030-0, BR55697) SAS Publ.

Next Step: Poems by the Women of the Mini Twelve Step House, Inc. Poetry Workshop with Merilene M. Murphy. 52p. 1994. pap. write for info. (0-9644606-0-2) Telepoetics.

Next Step: The Real World: Aggressive Tactics to Get Your Professional Life off to a Fast Start. Jack O'Brien. LC 99-37352. 243p. (C). 1999. pap. 14.95 (0-938721-65-8, Pub. by Kiplinger Bks) Natl Bk Netwk.

Next Step: 50 More Things You Can Do to Save the Earth. Works Group Earth. 1991. 11.05 (0-606-04853-7, Pub. by Turtleback) Demco.

Next Step . . . Re-Unification with the Presence of God Within Our Hearts. 2nd ed. Patricia D. Cota-Robles. Ed. by Picas & Points. (Illus.). 369p. 1989. 17.00 (0-9615287-1-0) New Age Study Human.

Next Step Forward: Music Therapy with the Terminally Ill. Ed. by Jenny A. Martin. 95p. 1989. spiral bd. 17.95 (0-930194-46-2) Ctr Thanatology.

Next Step in Community Ministry: Hands-On Leadership. Carl S. Dudley. LC 95-83892. xviii, 138 p. 1996. pap. 15.75 (1-56699-168-4, AL172) Alban Inst.

Next Step in Database Marketing: Consumer Guided Marketing. Dick Shaver. LC 95-51506. 482p. 1996. 39.95 (0-471-13359-0) Wiley.

Next Step in Religion: An Essay Toward the Coming Renaissance. Roy W. Sellars. LC 75-3360. reprint ed. 34.50 (0-404-59358-5) AMS Pr.

Next Step in the Dance. Tim Gautreaux. LC 97-33374. 352p. 1998. text 23.00 (0-312-18143-4) St Martin.

Next Step in the Dance. Tim Gautreaux. LC 98-51203. 352p. 1999. pap. 13.00 (0-312-19936-8) St Martin.

Next Step Leader's Guide. Don Dinkmeyer, Sr. et al. (Next Step Ser.). 1987. pap. text 42.95 (0-913476-67-6, 4801) Am Guidance.

Next Step on the Ladder: Assessment & Management of the Multi-Handicapped Child. G. B. Simon. 144p. 1985. pap. 65.00 (0-906054-26-5) St Mut.

Next Steps Report, 1997. (Command Papers). 122p. 1998. pap. 100.00 (0-10-138892-6, HM88926, Pub. by Statnry Office) Bernan Associates.

Next Step to Greater Energy: A Unique Perspective on Bioenergy, Addictions & Transformation. 2nd rev. ed. Jack Tips. LC 90-84755. (Illus.). 209p. 1990. pap. text 15.95 (0-929167-04-X) Apple-a-Day.

Next Step Toward Welfare Reform: A Manual for Enacting Tax Credits for Charitable Contributions. David G. Tuerck. 39p. 1998. pap. text. write for info. (1-886320-04-7) BHIFPPR.

Next Step with Spirit. Charles Sommer. LC 95-70038. 185p. (Orig.). 1995. pap. 12.95 (0-87516-684-9) DeVorss.

Next Step Workbook: Exercises in Gratitude, Forgiveness, & Action. Todd Weber. 112p. (Orig.). pap., wbk. ed. 7.95 (0-934125-26-0) Hazelden.

Next Steps: Improving Management in Government. Ed. by Barry O'Toole & A. Grant Jordan. 224p. 1995. 77.95 (1-85521-491-1) Ashgate Pub Co.

Next Steps: Research & Practice to Advance Indian Education. Ed. by Karen G. Swisher & John W. Tippeconnic, III. LC 98-50364. 400p. 1999. pap. 28.00 (1-880785-21-8) ERIC-CRESS.

Next Steps for a New Administration. Ed. by Marcus G. Raskin. 48p. 1976. pap. 21.95 (0-87855-657-5) Transaction Pubs.

Next Steps for New Christians see Proximos Pasos para Nuevos Creyentes

Next Steps for Summitry: Report of the Twentieth Century Fund International Conference on Economic Summitry. 61p. (Orig.). (C). 1984. pap. text 7.50 (0-87078-155-3) Century Foundation.

Next Steps in Arms Control & Non-Proliferation: Final Report of the U. S.-Japan Study Group on Arms Control & Non-Proliferation After the Cold War. U. S. - Japan Study Group on Arms Control & Non-Pr. Ed. by William Clark & Ryukichi Imai. LC 96-53440. 1996. 14.95 (0-87003-105-8) Carnegie Endow.

Next Steps in Central America. Ed. by Bruce L. Smith. 187p. 1991. pap. 9.95 (0-8157-5063-3) Brookings.

Next Steps in Cross Stitch. Angela Beazley. 1999. 16.95 (1-85391-529-7) Merehurst Ltd.

Next Steps in Global Education: A Handbook for Curriculum Development. William Kniep. 220p. (C). 1987. ring bd. 30.00 (0-944675-01-8) Amer Forum.

Next Steps in Public-Private Partnerships. Madeleine B. Hemmings. 20p. 1984. 3.00 (0-318-22161-6, OC103) Ctr Educ Trng Employ.

Next Steps on the Creation of an Accidental Nuclear War Prevention Center. Ed. by John W. Lewis & Coit D. Blacker. (Special Report of the Center for International Security & Arms Control, Stanford University Ser.). 45p. (Orig.). 1983. pap. 8.00 (0-935371-07-9) CFISAC.

Next Stop: Nowhere. Sheila S. Klass. LC 94-20235. (Illus.). 176p. (YA). (gr. 7-9). 1995. 14.95 (0-590-46686-0) Scholastic Inc.

Next Stop: Troubletown. Lloyd Dangle. (Illus.). 120p. (Orig.). 1996. pap. 10.95 (0-916397-44-0) Manic D Pr.

Next Stop, Freedom: The Story of a Slave Girl. Dorothy Hoobler & Thomas Hoobler. (Her Story Ser.). (Illus.). 64p. (J). (gr. 4-6). 1991. pap. 3.95 (0-382-24347-1); lib. bdg. 9.95 (0-382-24145-2) Silver Burdett Pr.

Next Stop Grand Central. Maira Kalman. LC 98-25135. (Illus.). 32p. (YA). (ps-5). 1999. lib. bdg. 15.99 (0-399-22926-4) Putnam Pub Group.

Next Stop, New York City! The Polk Street Kids on Tour. Patricia Reilly Giff. (Polk Street Special Ser.). 1997. 9.09 (0-606-11682-6, Pub. by Turtleback) Demco.

Next Stop, New York City! The Polk Street Kids on Tour. Patricia Reilly Giff. (Polk Street Special Ser.: No. 9). (Illus.). 128p. 1997. pap. 3.99 (0-440-41362-1) Dell.

Next Stop, the White House! Judy Delton. LC 95-11602. (Lottery Luck Ser.: No. 6). (Illus.). 96p. (J). (gr. 2-5). 1995. pap. 3.95 (0-7868-1023-8, Pub. by Hyprn Ppbks) Little.

Next Stop Westchester! People & the Railroad. John R. Stilgoe et al. LC 96-33980. (Illus.). 28p. 1996. pap. 7.00 (0-943651-26-3) Hudson Riv.

Next Teller: A Book of Canadian Storytelling. Ed. by Dan Yashinsky. LC 94-154439. (Illus.). 256p. (YA). (gr. 7 up). 1994. pap. 12.95 (0-921556-46-2, Pub. by Gynergy-Ragweed) U of Toronto Pr.

Next Texas Energy Boom: Power Choices for the 21st Century. Michael Brower et al. (Illus.). 71p. 1997. reprint ed. pap. text 30.00 (0-7881-4579-7) DIANE Pub.

Next Threat: Western Perceptions of Islam. Hippler. LC 94-43473. (Transnational Institute Ser.).Tr. of Feindbild Islam. (ARA & ENG.). 168p. (C). 59.00 (0-7453-0954-2, Pub. by Pluto GBR); pap. 16.95 (0-7453-0953-4) Pluto GBR.

Next Three Futures: Paradigms of Things to Come. W. Warren Wagar. LC 91-8277. (Contributions in Sociology Ser.: No. 48). 192p. 1991. pap. 17.95 (0-275-94049-7, B4049, Praeger Pubs) Greenwood.

Next Three Futures: Paradigms of Things to Come, 98. W. Warren Wagar. LC 91-9251. (Contributions in Sociology Ser.: No. 48). 176p. 1991. 49.95 (0-313-26528-3, WNX/, Greenwood Pr) Greenwood.

Next Thursday. Dick Beyer. LC 96-90440. 306p. 1996. pap. 3.95 (0-9635404-7-5) TwoForYou Bks.

***Next Time.** Karen Stokes. LC 99-91854. 264p. 2000. 25.00 (0-7388-1326-5); pap. 18.00 (0-7388-1327-3) Xlibris Corp.

Next Time see Works of Henry James Jr.: Collected Works

Next Time - Hash! Abby Westenberg. 64p. pap. 9.95 (0-9630779-1-0) PPC Bks.

Next-Time Forever. Sherryl Woods. (Desire Ser.: No. 601). 1990. per. 2.50 (0-373-05601-X) Silhouette.

Next Time I Fall in Love. Chap Clark. 1992. 29.99 incl. VHS (*0-310-54518-8*) Zondervan.

Next Time I Fall in Love Journal. 1991. pap. 6.95 (*0-310-58051-X*) Zondervan.

Next Time I'll Sing to You. James Saunders. 1966. pap. 5.25 (*0-8222-0814-8*) Dramatists Play.

Next Time Round in Provence: The Vaucluse & the Bouchers-du-Rhone. Ian Norrie. LC 97-125767. (Illus.). 224p. (Orig.). 1996. pap. text 14.95 (*1-85410-239-7*, Pub. by Aurum Pr) London Brdge.

Next Time Round in the Dordogne. Ian Norrie. (Illus.). 208p. (Orig.). 1997. pap. text 14.95 (*1-85410-394-6*, Pub. by Aurum Pr) London Brdge.

Next Time Round in Tuscany. Ian Norrie. 1998. pap. 17.95 (*1-85410-541-8*, Pub. by Aurum Pr) London Brdge.

Next Time Say Where You're Going. Carole M. Longmeyer. (Lost Colony Collection). (Illus.). (Orig.). (J). (gr. 4-9). 1994. pap. 19.95 (*0-935326-42-1*) Gallopade Intl.

***Next Time She'll Be Dead.** Ann Jones. LC 99-45252. 2000. pap. 15.00 (*0-8070-6789-X*) Beacon Pr.

Next Time, She'll Be Dead: Battering & How to Stop It. Ann Jones. 1994. pap. 15.00 (*0-8070-6771-7*) Beacon Pr.

Next Time We Strike: Labor in Utah's Coal Fields, 1900-1933. Allen K. Powell. (Illus.). 292p. 1985. pap. text 24.95 (*0-87421-161-1*) Utah St U Pr.

Next-to-Final Solution: A Belgian Detention Camp for Hitler Refugees. Joseph Fabry. LC 90-23285. 146p. (C). 1992. text 42.95 (*0-8204-1527-8*) P Lang Pubng.

Next to Mother's Milk ... An Engelhard Lecture on the Book, Presented at the Library of Congress on Tuesday, April 8, 1986. Contrib. by Lawrence C. Powell. LC 87-4160. 25p. 1989. reprint ed. 3.95 (*0-8444-0551-5*) Lib Congress.

Next to Shakespeare. Aline M. Taylor. LC 50-10282. reprint ed. 32.50 (*0-404-06351-9*) AMS Pr.

Next to the Last Word: Stopping the Cycle of Competition in Human Relationships. Dwight L. Barr. LC 98-83084. 208p. 2000. pap. 13.95 (*0-88739-241-5*) Creat Arts Bk.

Next to You: (Movie Tie-In for How I Created My Perfect Prom Date) Todd Strasser. LC 96-10569. (Illus.). 208p. (YA). (gr. 5-9). 1999. mass mkt. 4.99 (*0-689-83115-3*) Aladdin.

***Next 25 Years of ERISA: The Future of Private Retirement Plans: An EBRI-ERF Policy Forum.** Dallas L. Salisbury & Employee Benefit Research Institute, Washington, D. LC 00-29409. 2000. write for info. (*0-86643-095-4*) Empl Benefit Res Inst.

Next Twenty-Five Years of Public Choice. Ed. by Charles K. Rowley et al. LC 93-21577. (DIVS-Diverse Ser.). 232p. (C). 1993. lib. bdg. 145.50 (*0-7923-2450-1*) Kluwer Academic.

***Next Twenty Years of Your Life: A Personal Guide into the Year 2017.** R. Worzel. LC 99-231841. 1998. pap. 19.95 (*0-7737-5996-4*) Stoddart Publ.

Next Twenty Years of Your Life: A Personal Guide into Your Life. Richard Worzel. 304p. 1998. 21.95 (*0-7737-3013-3*) Stoddart Publ.

Next Valley Over: An Angler's Progress. Charles Gaines. LC 99-49508. 256p. 2000. 23.00 (*0-609-60539-9*, Crown) Crown Pub Group.

Next Voice You Hear: Sermons We Preach Together. David Steele. LC 99-11360. 128p. 1999. pap. 10.95 (*0-664-50040-4*) Geneva Press.

Next War. Caspar W. Weinberger & Peter Schweizer. 320p. 1996. 27.50 (*0-89526-447-1*) Regnery Pub.

Next Wave. Ed. by Mark Pirie. LC 98-228811. 280p. 1998. pap. 24.95 (*1-877133-44-2*, Pub. by Univ Otago Pr) Intl Spec Bk.

Next Wave: The World of Surfing. Ed. by Nick Carroll. (Illus.). 240p. 1991. 29.98 (*1-55859-162-1*) Abbeville Pr.

Next Week East Lynne: Domestic Drama in Performance, 1820-1874. Gilbert B. Cross. LC 74-25573. (Illus.). 281p. 1976. 38.50 (*0-8387-1646-6*) Bucknell U Pr.

Next Week, Swan Lake: Reflections on Dance & Dances. Ed. by Selma J. Cohen. LC 82-2614. (Illus.). 207p. 1982. pap. 17.95 (*0-8195-6110-X*, Wesleyan Univ Pr) U Pr of New Eng.

***Next Week Will Be Better: A Cat Wilde Mystery.** Jean Ruryk. 1999. per. 4.99 (*0-373-26333-3*) Harlequin Bks.

Next Week Will Be Better: A Cat Wilde Mystery. Jean Ruryk. LC 97-37119. 256p. 1998. text 21.95 (*0-312-18144-2*) St Martin.

Next West: Public Lands, Community & Economy in the American West. Ed. by John A. Baden & Donald Snow. LC 96-52664. 272p. 1997. pap. 22.95 (*1-55963-460-X*, Shearwater Bks); text 45.00 (*1-55963-459-6*, Shearwater Bks) Island Pr.

Next World. Gratton E. Coffman. 222p. 1996. pap. 8.95 (*0-9655206-1-7*) Caster Ent.

Next World War: Computers Are the Weapons & the Front Line Is Everywhere. James Adams. LC 98-21135. 288p. 1998. 25.00 (*0-684-83452-9*) S&S Trade.

Next-Year Country: A Study of Rural Social Organization in Alberta. Jean Burnet. LC HN0110.H3B8. (Social Credit in Alberta: Its Background & Development Ser.: No. 3). 204p. reprint ed. pap. 63.30 (*0-8357-8248-4*, 203407200088) Bks Demand.

Next Year I'll Be Special. Patricia Reilly Giff. LC 92-20749. (J). 1996. 10.19 (*0-606-09680-9*, Pub. by Turtleback) Demco.

Next Year I'll Be Special. Patricia G. Reilly. (Illus.). 32p. (J). (gr. k-3). 1996. pap. 4.99 (*0-440-41031-2*) Dell.

Next Year in Cuba: A Cuban Emigre's Coming of Age in America. Mem. of Gustavo P. Firmat. LC 94-42347. 320p. 1995. 22.95 (*0-385-47296-X*, Anchor NY) Doubleday.

Next Year in Jerusalem. Howard Schwartz. 1999. pap. 6.99 (*0-14-037559-7*) Viking Penguin.

Next Year in Jerusalem: 3000 Years of Jewish Stories. Howard Schwartz. 1998. 12.19 (*0-606-13659-2*, Pub. by Turtleback) Demco.

Next Year in Salem: A Chronicle of the Home Front During W. W. II 1940-1945. William A. Cormier. LC 96-92726. (Illus.). xii, 206p. 1996. 28.50 (*0-9655477-0-1*) New Perth.

Next Year Jeruslaum, Vol. 2. Avital Scharansky. 1999. pap. write for info. (*0-394-75281-3*) Vin Bks.

NextPresident.com. William T. Powers. 450p. 1999. 24.95 (*0-9672701-0-3*) Coyote Pubng.

NeXTstep Applications Programming. S. Garfinkle. (Illus.). 672p. 1993. text 49.95 (*0-387-97884-4*) Spr-Verlag.

NeXTstep Database Kit Concepts. Next Computer Inc. Staff. LC 93-46024. (Nextstep Developer's Library). 208p. (C). 1994. pap. text 24.95 (*0-201-40741-8*) Addison-Wesley.

NeXTstep Development Tools: Release 3. Next Computer Inc. Staff. 480p. (C). 1992. pap. text 30.95 (*0-201-63249-7*) Addison-Wesley.

NeXtstep General Reference: Release 3. Next Computer Inc. Staff. 1992. pap. 49.95 (*0-201-63248-9*) Addison-Wesley.

NeXTstep User Interface Guidelines: Release 3. Next Computer Inc. Staff. 208p. (C). 1992. pap. text 24.95 (*0-201-63250-0*) Addison-Wesley.

Nexus see Rosy Crucifixion

Nexus: A Book about Youth Work. Mark Krueger. (Studies in Youth Work). 96p. 1995. pap. text 10.95 (*0-9646955-0-2*) Univ Wisconsin.

Nexus: Live Action Roleplaying. Rick Dutton & Walter O. Freitao. Ed. by Les Brooks. (Play This Bk.: Vol. 1). (Illus.). 136p. (Orig.). 1994. pap. 19.95 (*1-56882-030-5*, 6500) Chaosium.

Nexus: The Rosy Crucifixion III, Vol. III. Henry Miller. LC 87-16. 320p. 1987. pap. 12.95 (*0-8021-5178-7*, Grove) Grove-Atltic.

Nexus Collection, Vol. 1. Mike Baron & Steve Rude. Ed. by Anina Bennett. (Nexus Ser.). (Illus.). 144p. 1993. pap. 14.95 (*1-878574-54-X*) Dark Horse Comics.

Nexus Collection, Vol. 2. Mike Baron & Steve Rude. (Nexus Ser.). (Illus.). 144p. 1993. pap. 15.95 (*1-878574-80-9*) Dark Horse Comics.

Nexus DNA: Artography. Steve Stone. (Illus.). 1998. pap. 20.00 (*1-892519-01-1*) Archangel Ent.

Nexus-Lex: A Multimedia Chinese-English Lexicon of Characters. Scott A. Hart. Ed. by Ramon F. Reiser. (CHI., Illus.). 27p. 1995. pap., student ed. 249.00 incl. cd-rom (*1-887866-51-5*) Nexus Lab.

***Nexus Sisterhood of the Institute.** Rey Maria Del. 2000. mass mkt. 6.95 (*0-352-33456-8*) London Bridges.

Neyman. C. Reid. (Illus.). 308p. 1997. pap. 34.95 (*0-387-98357-0*) Spr-Verlag.

Neysa Grassi: Recent Paintings. Text by Sid Sachs. (Illus.). 27p. 1996. pap. 20.00 (*1-879173-30-1*) Locks Gallery.

***Neysa Grassi with Essay by Barry Schwabsky.** LC 99-65346. (Illus.). 34p. 1999. pap. 20.00 (*1-879173-42-5*) Locks Gallery.

Nez-Bits. Paul W. Nesbit. (Illus.). 1946. pap. 0.75 (*0-911746-04-8*) Nesbit.

Nez Perce see Nez Perce

***Nez Perce.** Richard Gaines. LC 99-59864. (Native Americans Ser.). 2000. lib. bdg. 21.35 (*1-57765-375-0*) ABDO Pub Co.

Nez Perce. Kathi Howes. (Native American People Ser.). (Illus.). 32p. (J). (gr. 5-8). 1990. lib. bdg. 11.95 (*0-685-36389-9*) Rourke Corp.

Nez Perce. Kathi Howes. (Native American People Ser.: Set II). (Illus.). 32p. (J). (gr. 4-8). 1994. lib. bdg. 22.60 (*0-86625-379-3*) Rourke Pubns.

Nez Perce. Kathi Howes. (Pueblos Americanos Nativos Ser.).Tr. of Nez Perce. (SPA.). 32p. (J). (gr. 5-8). 1990. lib. bdg. 21.27 (*0-86625-452-8*) Rourke Pubns.

Nez Perce. Alice Osinski. LC 88-11822. (New True Books Ser.). (Illus.). 48p. (J). (gr. 2-4). 1988. pap. 5.50 (*0-516-41154-3*); lib. bdg. 21.00 (*0-516-01154-5*) Childrens.

Nez Perce. Virginia Driving Hawk Sneve. LC 93-38598. (Illus.). 32p. (J). (gr. 4-6). 1994. lib. bdg. 16.95 (*0-8234-1090-0*) Holiday.

Nez Perce Buffalo Horse. William E. Sanderson. LC 77-137771. (Illus.). 169p. reprint ed. pap. 52.40 (*0-8357-4119-2*, 203694900005) Bks Demand.

Nez Perce Country: A Guide to Nez Perce National Historical Park. 224p. 1984. pap. 103.00 (*0-16-003458-2*) USGPO.

Nez Perce Coyote Tales: The Myth Cycle. Deward E. Walker, Jr. & Daniel N. Matthews. LC 97-40106. 256p. (Orig.). 1998. pap. 13.95 (*0-8061-3032-6*) U of Okla Pr.

Nez Perce Dictionary. Haruo Aoki. LC 93-11792. (Publications in Linguistics: Vol. 122). 1993. 155.00 (*0-520-09763-7*, Pub. by U CA Pr) Cal Prin Full Svc.

Nez Perce Indians see Junior Library of American Indians

Nez Perce Indians & the Opening of the Northwest. Alvin M. Josephy. LC 96-54278. (Illus.). 736p. 1997. pap. 18.00 (*0-395-85011-8*) HM.

Nez Perce Indians & the Opening of the Northwest. abr. ed. Alvin M. Josephy, Jr. LC 79-14847. (Illus.). xvi, 667p. 1979. pap. 16.95 (*0-8032-7551-X*, Bison Books) U of Nebr Pr.

Nez Perce Joseph. Oliver O. Howard. LC 70-39379. (Law, Politics & History Ser.). (Illus.). 274p. 1972. reprint ed. lib. bdg. 32.50 (*0-306-70461-7*) Da Capo.

Nez Perce National Forest Story. rev. ed. Edward E. Laven. Ed. by Shirley T. Moore & Mary Zabinski. (Illus.). 57p. 1991. pap. 4.95 (*0-914019-30-9*) NW Interpretive.

***Nez Perce Summer, 1877: The U. S. Army & the Nee-Me-Poo Crisis.** Jerome A. Greene. LC 00-32924. 2000. write for info. (*0-917298-68-3*) MT Hist Soc.

Nez Perce Texts. Archie Phinney. LC 73-82344. (Columbia University. Contributions to Anthropology Ser.: Vol. 25). reprint ed. 49.50 (*0-404-50575-9*) AMS Pr.

***Nez Perce Tribe.** Allison Lassieur. LC 99-53167. (Native Peoples Ser.). 24p. (J). (ps-3). 2000. lib. bdg. 15.93 (*0-7368-0500-1*) Capstone Pr.

Nez Perce Women in Transition, 1877-1990. Caroline James. (Illus.). 1996. 49.95 (*0-89301-188-6*) U of Idaho Pr.

Nez Perces: Tribesmen of the Columbia Plateau. Francis Haines. LC 55-9626. (Civilization of the American Indian Ser.: No. 42). (Illus.). 1955. pap. 17.95 (*0-8061-0982-3*) U of Okla Pr.

Nez-Perces First Book for Children & New Beginners. Henry H. Spalding. Ed. by Tom Trusky. 6p. 1994. reprint ed. 5.00 (*0-932129-21-8*) Heming W Studies.

Nez Perces since Lewis & Clark. Kate McBeth. (Idaho Yesterdays Ser.). (Illus.). 288p. (C). 1993. reprint ed. pap. 15.95 (*0-89301-160-6*) U of Idaho Pr.

Nezahualcoyotl: Vida y Obra (Life & Work) Jose L. Martinez. (SPA.). 335p. 1992. reprint ed. 16.99 (*968-16-0509-8*, Pub. by Fondo) Continental Bk.

Nezdeshnie Vechera: Stikhi Nineteen Fourteen to Nineteen Twenty. Mikhail A. Kuzmin. LC 79-66376. (RUS.). pap. 5.95 (*0-89830-010-X*) Russica Pubs.

Nezumi Choja see Old Man & the Mice

Nezumi No Yomeiri see Mouse's Wedding

NFA 20th-Anniversary Anthology of American Flute Music. Ed. by John Solum. 236p. 1993. text 75.00 (*0-19-385875-4*) OUP.

NFAIS Yearbook of the Information Industry, 1992. Arthur W. Elias. 122p. 1992. 40.00 (*0-938734-64-4*) Info Today Inc.

NFAIS Yearbook of the Information Industry, 1993. Arthur W. Elias. 130p. 1993. 40.00 (*0-938734-74-1*) Info Today Inc.

NFE-TV: Television for Nonformal Education. Jonathan F. Gunter. 286p. (Orig.). (C). 1975. spiral bd. 6.00 (*0-932288-33-2*) Ctr Intl Ed U of MA.

***NFL ABC Book.** Kindersley Dorling. 36p. (ps-k). 2000. 6.95 (*0-7894-6374-1*) DK Pub Inc.

NFL Adventures. James Buckley. 1996. mass mkt. 3.99 (*0-590-16211-X*) Scholastic Inc.

***NFL, Big & Small.** DK Publishing Staff. LC 99-24167. (NFL Board Bks.). 22p. (J). (gr. k-2). 1999. 6.95 (*0-7894-4720-7*) DK Pub Inc.

NFL Blitz: Prima's Official Strategy Guide. (Games Ser.). 96p. 1998. per. 12.99 (*0-7615-1867-3*) Prima Pub.

NFL Blitz Official Strategy Guide. Bradygames Staff. LC 98-73166. 1998. pap. 11.99 (*1-56686-814-9*) Brady Pub.

***NFL Blitz 2000: Official Strategy Guide.** BradyGames Staff. 1999. pap. 12.99 (*1-56686-912-9*) Brady Pub.

***NFL Blitz 2000: Prima's Official Strategy Guide.** Prima Development Staff. 1999. pap. 12.99 (*0-7615-2325-1*, Prima Games) Prima Pub.

***NFL Century: The Complete Story of the National Football League, 1920-2000.** Will McDonough. LC 99-23696. (Illus.). 320p. 1999. 19.98 (*0-7651-1062-8*) Smithmark.

***NFL Colors.** DK Publishing Staff. (NFL Board Bks.). (Illus.). 22p. (J). (ps-k). 2000. 6.95 (*0-7894-5538-2*, D K Ink) DK Pub Inc.

NFL Magic: Bloopers, Pranks, Upsets, & Touchdowns. Jim Buckley. LC 97-80387. (NFL/ABC Monday Night Football Club Ser.: No. 5). (Illus.). 96p. (J). (gr. 3-7). 1998. pap. 3.95 (*0-7868-1271-0*, Pub. by Hyprn Ppbks) Little.

NFL Mixed Display. DK Publishing Staff. 1999. 166.80 (*0-7894-4962-5*) DK Pub Inc.

***NFL 1999 Championship Spec Mkt.** NFL Staff. 2000. pap. 15.00 (*0-06-107593-0*) HarpC.

***NFL Rising Stars: The 10 Best Young Players in the NFL.** Richard Deitsch & Alan Schwarz. Ed. by Sherie Holder. 32p. (J). (gr. 3-8). 2000. pap. 3.99 (*1-930623-03-8*) SI For Kids.

***NFL Rules!** Jim Buckley. 96p. (J). 1999. pap. 3.95 (*0-7868-1412-8*, Pub. by Disney Pr) Little.

***NFL 1-2-3.** LC 99-24168. (NFL Board Bks.). 22p. (J). (gr. k-2). 1999. 6.95 (*0-7894-4721-5*) DK Pub Inc.

NFLC Guide for Basic Chinese Language Programs. Cornelius C. Kubler et al. LC 97-26834. (Pathways to Advanced Skills Ser.: Vol. 3). 1997. 26.95 (*0-87415-315-8*, PA03) Foreign Lang.

NFL/Monday Night Football. Gordon Korman. (J). 1997. pap. write for info. (*0-614-29241-7*) Hyprn Child.

***NFL's Greatest: Pro Football's Best Players, Teams, & Games.** Kindersley Dorling. 2000. 30.00 (*0-7894-5955-8*) DK Pub Inc.

***NFL's Greatest Upsets.** James Buckley. LC 00-24795. (Illus.). (gr. 4-7). 2000. pap. 3.95 (*0-7894-6756-9*) DK Pub Inc.

***NFL's Greatest Upsets.** James Buckley. LC 00-24795. (gr. 4-7). 2000. 12.95 (*0-7894-6379-2*) DK Pub Inc.

NFNA Flight Nursing Review Manual. Ed. by Angela Golden et al. 128p. Date not set. pap. text 33.00 (*0-935890-21-1*) Emerg Nurses IL.

NFO: A Farm Belt Rebel. Don Muhm. LC 98-89806. (Illus.). 400p. 2000. pap. 16.95 (*1-883477-30-1*); lib. bdg. 24.95 (*1-883477-29-8*) Lone Oak MN.

NFPA Annotated OSHA Regulations see NFPA Guide to OSHA Fire Protection Regulations

***NFPA Electrical Inspection Manual: With Checklists.** Jeffrey S. Sargent & Noel Williams. LC 99-75181. (Illus.). 350p. 1999. pap. 65.00 (*0-87765-447-6*, 99NECCL) Natl Fire Prot.

***NFPA Fire Prevention Code Handbook.** Carl E. Peterson et al. LC 98-65473. x, 614 p. 1998. write for info. (*0-87765-414-X*) Natl Fire Prot.

NFPA Guide to OSHA Fire Protection Regulations, 5 vols. 2nd rev. ed. Incl. Nos. 10-22. OSHA-NFPA Standards. Nos. 24-28. OSHA-NFPA Standards. Nos. 59-80. OSHA-NFPA Standards. Nos. 86a-664. OSHA-NFPA Standards. Vol. 1. NFPA Annotated OSHA Regulations. rev. ed. 15.00 55.00 (*0-685-44150-4*) Natl Fire Prot.

***NFT: Not for Tourists, Guide to Manhattan 2000.** Happy Mazza Media LLC Staff. (Illus.). 1999. pap. 19.95 (*0-9672303-0-6*) Happy Mazza.

NG Protocols. Robert Hinden. (C). 1998. text. write for info. (*0-201-63486-4*) Addison-Wesley.

NGA Garden Library, Set. National Gardening Association Staff. Incl. Beans. 36p. 1980. pap. 3.50 (*0-915873-08-7*, 1-1010C); Cauliflower, Broccoli, & Cabbage. 36p. 1980. pap. 3.50 (*0-915873-14-1*, 1-1010H); Corn. 36p. pap. 3.50 (*0-915873-16-8*, 1-1010J); Cucumbers, Melons & Squash. 36p. 1980. pap. 3.50 (*0-915873-12-5*, 1-1010F); Eggplant, Okra & Peppers. 36p. 1980. pap. 3.50 (*0-915873-15-X*, 1-1010I); Lettuce & Greens. 36p. pap. 3.50 (*0-915873-11-7*, 1-1010E); Onions. 36p. 1980. pap. 3.50 (*0-915873-07-9*, 1-1010A); Peas & Peanuts. 36p. 1980. pap. 3.50 (*0-915873-17-6*, 1-1010K); Potatoes. pap. 3.50 (*0-915873-13-3*, 1-1010G); Root Crops. 36p. 1980. pap. 3.50 (*0-915873-10-9*, 1-1010D); Tomatoes. 36p. 1980. pap. 2.50 (*0-915873-09-5*, 1-1010B); 32p. Set pap. 29.50 (*0-915873-18-4*, 1-1009C) Natl Gardening Assn.

Nga Iwi o Tainui: The Traditional History of the Tainui People - Nga Koorero Tuku Iho a Nga Tuupuna. Pe Te H. Jones & Bruce Biggs. (ENG & MAO., Illus.). 416p. 1995. 39.95 (*1-86940-119-0*, Pub. by Auckland Univ) Paul & Co Pubs.

Nga Morehu: The Survivors. Judith Binney & Gillian Chaplin. 144p. 1987. pap. 34.50 (*0-19-558135-0*) OUP.

Nga Morehu/The Survivors: The Life Story of Eight Maori Women. Judith Binney. 228p. 1996. pap. 39.95 (*1-86940-147-6*, Pub. by Auckland Univ) Paul & Co Pubs.

Nga Tangata Taumata Rau, 1901-1920, Vol. 3. (MAO.). 336p. 1997. 57.50 (*1-86940-201-4*, Pub. by Auckland Univ) Paul & Co Pubs.

Ngaio: Tied up in Tinsel. 288p. 1999. mass mkt. 5.99 (*0-312-97195-8*) St Martin.

Ngaio Marsh, 5 vols. Incl. Vol. 1. Black As He's Painted. 1982. Vol. 2. Enter a Murderer. Ngaio Marsh. 1982. pap. Vol. 3. Killer Dolphin. 1982. pap. Vol. 4. Last Ditch. 1982. Vol. 5. Overture to Death. 1982. pap. 1982. Set boxed set 12.50 (*0-515-06816-0*, Jove) Berkley Pub.

N

Ngaio Marsh. Kathryne S. McDorman. (Twayne's English Authors Ser.: No. 481). 190p. (C). 1991. 22.95 (*0-8057-6999-4*, Twyne) Mac Lib Ref.

Ngaio Marsh: A Life. Margaret Lewis. 1995. 20.00 (*1-883402-86-7*) S&S Trade.

Ngaio Marsh: A Life. Margaret Lewis. 275p. 1998. reprint ed. 24.95 (*1-890208-05-1*) Poisoned Pen.

Ngaio Marsh: A Life. 2nd large type ed. Margaret Lewis. 448p. 1993. 24.95 (*1-85089-327-6*, Pub. by ISIS Lrg Prnt) Transaction Pubs.

Ngaio Marsh: The Woman & Her Work. Ed. by B. J. Rahn. LC 95-5785. (Illus.). 274p. 1995. 34.50 (*0-8108-3023-X*) Scarecrow.

***Ngalangangpum Jarrakpu Purrurn: Mother & Child.** Women of Warmun Community. (Illus.). 128p. 1999. pap. 19.95 (*1-875641-50-5*, Pub. by Magabala Bks) Intl Spec Bk.

Ngambika: Studies of Women in African Literature. Ed. by Carole B. Davies & Anne A. Graves. LC 85-71385. 298p. (C). 1986. 59.95 (*0-86543-017-9*); pap. 18.95 (*0-86543-018-7*) Africa World.

Nganasan: The Material Culture of the Tavgi Samoyeds. A. A. Popov. Tr. by Elaine K. Ristenen. LC 66-63668. (Uralic & Altaic Ser.: Vol. 56). (Orig.). 1966. pap. text. write for info. (*0-87750-020-7*) Curzon Pr Ltd.

Ngando, Victoire de l'Amour, Le Mystere de l'Enfant Disparu. Paul Lomami-Tshibamba et al. (B. E. Ser.: No. 28). (FRE.). 1962. 35.00 (*0-8115-2979-7*) Periodicals Srv.

Ngandong Fossil Hominids: A Comparative Study of a Far Eastern Homo Erectus Group. A. P. Santa Luca. LC 80-52035. (Publications in Anthropology: No. 78). 1980. pap. 13.50 (*0-913516-11-2*) Yale U Anthro.

Ngarrindjeri Wurruwarrin: A World That Is, Was & Will Be. Diane Bell. LC 98-213203. 1999. pap. 27.95 (*1-875559-71-X*, Pub. by SpiniFex Pr) LPC InBook.

Ngatik Massacre: History & Identity on a Micronesian Atoll. Lin Poyer. LC 92-37911. (Series in Ethnographic Inquiry). (Illus.). 312p. (C). 1993. pap. text 17.95 (*1-56098-262-4*) Smithsonian.

***Ngay Janijirr Ngank - This Is My Word.** Ed. by Mackie Williams & Pat Torres. (Illus.). 1999. pap. 16.95 (*1-875641-47-5*, Pub. by Magabala Bks) Intl Spec Bk.

NGC 2000.0: The Complete New General Catalogue & Index Catalogues of Nebulae & Star Clusters by J. L. E. Dreyer. Ed. by Roger W. Sinnott. LC 88-29962. (Illus.). 304p. (Orig.). 1988. pap. 19.95 (*0-933346-51-4*) Sky Pub.

NGCSA: A Retrospective. Azim L. Mayadas. 14p. 1985. 15.00 (*0-318-21719-8*) NGCSA.

Ngea Mahi Auraki Summary of Mainstreaming. LC 96-137298. 13 p. 1994. write for info. (*0-478-04341-4*) Manaaki Whenua.

Ngea Tikanga Pono Weahanga Hauora Health Sector Ethics : Mechanisms for Meaori into Ethical Review : A Discussion Document. LC 96-137338. 107 p. 1994. write for info. (*0-478-04338-4*) Manaaki Whenua.

Ngea Waka O Neherea: The First Voyaging Canoe Jeff Evans. LC 97-221524. 223p. 1997. write for info. (*0-7900-0557-3*) Reed Pubng.

Ngealao te Oranga Hinengaro Meaori (Trends in Meaori Mental Health, 1984-1993) LC 98-148235. 50p. 1996. write for info. (*0-478-09116-8*) Manaaki Whenua.

NGF's Golf Course Directory. National Golf Foundation Staff. 1147p. 1999. 199.00 (*1-57701-105-8*) Natl Golf.

An Asterisk (*) at the beginning of an entry indicates that the title is appearing for the first time.

NGF's Golf Course Directory & Range Directory: Combo Pack, 2 vols. (Illus.). 1321p. 1999. pap. 250.00 (*1-57701-164-3*, 99GR045) Natl Golf.

***Nghi Quan Viet Quanh.** Hoang Hon.Tr. of Wandering Thinking, Wandering Writing. (VIE., Illus.). 610p. 2000. pap. 20.00 (*1-889880-07-8*) Nguoi Dan.

Nghi Thuc Tung Niem: Roan Bang Qnoc Van. 2nd ed. Thich Nhat Hahn. (VIE.). 449p. 1994. reprint ed. pap. 15.00 (*1-891667-29-7*) La Boi Soc.

Nghin Trung Xa Cach see Ocean Apart: Vietnamese Contemporary Art from the United States & Vietnam

NGNA Care Curriculum for Gerontological Nurses & Associates. National Gerontologic Nurses Association Staff. (Illus.). 768p. (C). (gr. 13). 1995. pap. text 46.95 (*0-8151-6424-6*, 24848) Mosby Inc.

NGNA Core Curriculum for Gerontological Advance Practice Nurses. Ann S. Luggen et al. LC 98-9043. 717p. 1998. 99.95 (*0-7619-1300-9*); pap. 55.00 (*0-7619-1301-7*) Sage.

***NGO Development Initiative & Public Policy.** Shivani Dharmarajan. LC 98-908067. 1998. 36.00 (*81-7391-265-3*, Pub. by Kaniska Pubs Dist) S Asia.

NGO Directory. 400p. 1994. write for info. (*92-806-3064-4*) U N I C E.

Ngola: The Weapon As Authority, Identity, or Ritual Object in Sub-Saharan Africa. Norman Hurst. (Illus.). 44p. (Orig.). 1994. 25.00 (*0-9628074-6-X*) Hurst Gal.

Ngoma: Discourses of Healing in Central & Southern Africa. John M. Janzen. (Comparative Studies of Health Systems & Medical Care: Vol. 34). (C). 1992. 50.00 (*0-520-07265-0*, Pub. by U CA Pr) Cal Prin Full Svc.

Ngondro: The Four Foundational Practices of Tibetan Buddhism. Ole Nydahl. (Illus.). 96p. (Orig.). 1990. pap. 9.95 (*0-931892-23-6*) B Dolphin Pub.

Ngondro Commentary: Instructions for the Concise Preliminary Practices of the New Treasure of Dudjom. Jane Tromge. LC 95-18666. (Illus.). 160p. 1995. pap., student ed. write for info. (*1-881847-06-3*, Pub. by Padma Pub CA) Bookpeople.

Ngoni. Nwankwo T. Nwaezeigwe. LC 96-22945. (Heritage Library of African Peoples: Set 3). (Illus.). 64p. (YA). (gr. 7-12). 1996. lib. bdg. 16.95 (*0-8239-2006-2*, D2006-2) Rosen Group.

Ngoni of Nyasaland. Margaret Read. LC 57-994. 220p. reprint ed. pap. 68.20 (*0-8357-3223-1*, 205711700010) Bks Demand.

N

***NGOS & Civil Society: Democracy by Proxy?** Ann C. Hudock. 140p. 1999. 59.95 (*0-7456-1648-8*, Pub. by Polity Pr); pap. text 24.95 (*0-7456-1649-6*, Pub. by Polity Pr) Blackwell Pubs.

NGOs & Environmental Policies: Asia & Africa. Ed. by David Potter. LC 95-26760. 352p. (Orig.). (C). 1996. pap. 22.50 (*0-7146-4215-0*, Pub. by F Cass Pubs) Intl Spec Bk.

NGOs & Grassroots in Development Work in South India: Elizabeth Moen Mathiot. Elizabeth M. Mathiot. Ed. by Sue M. Charlton & Jana Everett. LC 97-37089. 152p. (C). 1997. text 36.00 (*0-7618-0931-7*) U Pr of Amer.

***NGO's & Socio-Economic Development Opportunities.** Ed. by Kamta Prasad. 2000. 38.00 (*81-7629-258-3*, Pub. by Deep & Deep Pubns) S Asia.

NGOs in Indonesia: Issues of Hegemony & Social Change. Mansour Fakih. (Occasional Paper Ser.). 16p. 1991. 3.00 (*0-932288-84-7*) Ctr Intl Ed U of MA.

NGOs in Latin America: Issues & Characteristics of NGOs Involved in Development. Eloy Anello. (Occasional Paper Ser.). 31p. 1991. 3.00 (*0-932288-85-5*) Ctr Intl Ed U of MA.

NGOs in the Sahel: Issues in Cooperation for Natural Resources Management. Jonathan Otto. (Occasional Paper Ser.). 1991. 3.00 (*0-932288-86-3*) Ctr Intl Ed U of MA.

NGOs, States & Donors: Too Close for Comfort? David Hulme & Michael Edwards. LC 96-27848. (International Political Economy Ser.). 320p. 1997. text 59.95 (*0-312-16190-5*) St Martin.

NGOs, States & Donors: Too Close for Comfort? Ed. by David Hulme & Michael Edwards. LC 96-27848. (International Political Economy Ser.). 320p. 1997. pap. 18.95 (*0-312-16191-3*) St Martin.

NGOs, the United Nations, & Global Governance. Ed. by Thomas G. Weiss & Leon Gordenker. 250p. 1996. pap. text 19.95 (*1-55587-626-9*, 87-626-9) L Rienner.

NGOs, the United Nations & Global Governance. Ed. by Thomas G. Weiss & Leon Gordenker. 250p. (Orig.). 1996. lib. bdg. 45.00 (*1-55587-613-7*, 87-613-7) L Rienner.

Nguchiro Na Panyae. Godfrey Nyotumba. LC 95-981889. 1995. pap. text 4.95 (*9966-884-51-3*) Nocturnal Sun.

Ngugi Wa Thiong'o. Ed. by Charles Cantalupo. 390p. 1995. pap. 19.95 (*0-86543-445-X*) Africa World.

***Ngugi Wa Thiong'o.** Patrick Williams. 1999. text 59.95 (*0-7190-4730-7*, Pub. by Manchester Univ Pr) St Martin.

Ngugi Wa Thiong'o. Patrick Williams. 1999. pap. text 19.95 (*0-7190-4731-5*, Pub. by Manchester Univ Pr) St Martin.

Ngugi Wa Thiong'o: A Bibliography of Primary & Secondary Sources, 1957-1987. Carol Sicherman. (Bibliographical Research in African Written Literature Ser.: Vol. 1). 270p. 1990. 70.00 (*0-905450-71-X*, Pub. by H Zell Pubs) Seven Hills Bk.

Ngugi Wa Thiong'o: An Exploration of His Writings. David Cook & Michael Okenimkpe. LC 97-219198. 283p. 1997. pap. write for info. (*0-435-07430-X*) Heinemann.

Ngugi Wa Thiong'o: Text & Contexts. Ed. by Charles Cantalupo. LC 95-21818. 390p. 1995. 69.95 (*0-86543-444-1*) Africa World.

***Ngugi waThiong'o.** Simon Gikandi. LC PR9381.9.N45Z67 2000. (Cambridge Studies in African & Caribbean Literature: No. 8). 368p. (C). 2000. 64.95 (*0-521-48006-X*) Cambridge U Pr.

Ngugi's Novels & African History. James Ogude. LC 99-23065. 1999. write for info. (*0-7453-1436-8*) LPC InBook.

Ngugi's Novels & African History: Narrating the Nation. James Ogude. 1999. pap. 19.95 (*0-7453-1431-7*, Pub. by Pluto GBR) Stylus Pub VA.

Nguoi Viet Dau Tu Luat Thue Vu 1986 Cua Hoa Ky (The Vietnamese & the Tax Reform Act of 1986) Ngoc N. Nam. 135p. (Orig.). 1987. pap. 8.00 (*0-9614634-1-4*) N N Nguyen.

Nguoi Viet Dau Tu (The Vietnamese Investor) Ngoc N. Nam. 267p. (Orig.). 1985. pap. 15.00 (*0-9614634-0-6*) N N Nguyen.

Nguyen Cochinchina: Southern Vietnam in the Seventeenth & Eighteenth Centuries. Li Tana. (Studies on Southeast Asia: Vol. 23). 194p. 1998. pap. 16.00 (*0-87727-722-2*) Cornell SE Asia.

Nguzo Saba & Festival of First Fruits. James W. Johnson. LC 97-111499. 1997. pap. 9.95 (*0-936073-20-9*) Gumbs & Thomas.

NGV (Natural Gas Vehicle) Activity Book. Steve McCrea. (Illus.). 20p. (J). 1995. pap. text 4.00 (*1-57074-246-4*) Greyden Pr.

Ngwa History: A Study of Social & Economic Changes in Igbo Mini-States in Time Perspective. 2nd ed. John N. Oriji. LC 98-141338. XII, 195p. 1998. pap. 24.95 (*0-8204-4042-6*) P Lang Pubng.

NH Color Guide to Freight & Passenger Equipment. David R. Sweetland. (Illus.). 1995. 49.95 (*1-878887-47-5*) Morning NJ.

NHA Examination Review Manual. Robert W. Haacker. (C). 1998. 55.00 (*0-929442-30-X*, 2200PP) Prof Prnting & Pub.

NHA Practice Examination A. Robert Haacker. 1998. 10.00 (*0-929442-44-X*, 2209PP) Prof Prnting & Pub.

NHA Practice Examination B. Robert Haacker. 1998. 10.00 (*0-929442-42-3*, 2202PP) Prof Prnting & Pub.

NHA Practice Examination C. Robert Haacker. 1998. 10.00 (*0-929442-46-6*, 2213PP) Prof Prnting & Pub.

NHA Practice Examination D. Robert Haacker. 1998. 10.00 (*0-929442-45-8*, 2212PP) Prof Prnting & Pub.

NHA Practice Examination E. rev. ed. Robert Haacker. 1999. 10.00 (*0-929442-47-4*, 2219PP) Prof Prnting & Pub.

NHA Practice Examination F. Robert Haacker. 1998. 13.50 (*0-929442-43-1*, 2204PP) Prof Prnting & Pub.

Nhat Tung Thien Mon Nam 2000. Thich Nhat Hahn. (VIE.). 228p. 1997. 25.00 (*1-891667-48-3*) La Boi Soc.

NHE ESL System 1 Texas. 2nd ed. Michael Walker, Jr. 1984. 401.02 (*0-201-20046-5*) Addison-Wesley.

NHE ESL System 2 Texas. 2nd ed. Michael Walker, Jr. 1984. 401.02 (*0-201-20048-1*) Addison-Wesley.

NHE ESL System 3 Texas. 2nd ed. Michael Walker, Jr. 1984. 401.02 (*0-201-20050-3*) Addison-Wesley.

NHE Lifeskills Workbook I. Judy Defilippo. 1981. pap. text 8.48 (*0-201-05048-X*) Addison-Wesley.

NHE Lifeskills Workbook II. Judy Defilippo. 1982. pap. text 9.75 (*0-201-05049-8*) Addison-Wesley.

NHK's Let's Learn Japanese: A Practical Conversation Guide, Bk. II. NHK Overseas Broadcasting Department Staff & Nobuko Mizutani. Ed. by Jun Maeda. (Illus.). 176p. 1993. pap. 15.00 (*4-7700-1784-7*); audio 40.00 (*4-7700-1785-5*) Kodansha.

NHK's Let's Learn Japanese: A Practical Conversation Guide, Bk. III. NHK Overseas Broadcasting Department Staff & Nobuko Mizutani. Ed. by Jun Maeda. (Illus.). 176p. 1994. pap. 15.00 (*4-7700-1786-3*) Kodansha.

NHK's Let's Learn Japanese: A Practical Conversation Guide, Bk. IV. NHK Overseas Broadcasting Department Staff & Nobuko Mizutani. Ed. by Jun Maeda. (Illus.). 176p. 1994. audio 40.00 (*4-7700-1789-8*) Kodansha.

NHL Coaches: The Best Coaching Legends from Lester Patrick to Pat Burns. Stanley I. Fischler. (Illus.). 224p. (Orig.). 1994. pap. 14.95 (*1-895629-41-1*) Warwick Publ.

NHL Goalies: Legends of the Toughest Job in Professional Sports. Stanley I. Fischler. (Illus.). 224p. (Orig.). 1994. pap. 14.95 (*1-895629-40-3*) Warwick Publ.

NHL Hockey: An Official Fan's Guide. John MacKinnon. 128p. 1998. 23.95 (*1-892049-04-X*) Triumph Bks.

***NHL Hockey: An Official Fans' Guide.** John MacKinnon & John McDermott. (Illus.). 128p. 2000. 19.95 (*1-84222-101-9*) Carlton Bks Ltd.

NHL Hockey: The Official Fans' Guide: The NHL's Complete Authorized Guide. 2nd rev. ed. John MacKinnon. LC 98-1528. (Illus.). 128p. 1997. 19.95 (*1-57243-215-2*) Triumph Bks.

***NHL Hockey: An Offical Fans' Guide: The NHL's Complete Authorized Guide.** 4th ed. John MacKinnon. 1999. pap. 23.95 (*1-57243-338-8*) Triumph Bks.

NHL Official Guide & Record Book: 1999-2000 Edition. Dan Diamond. 544p. 1999. 21.95 (*1-892129-11-6*) Total Sprts.

***NHL Official Guide & Record Book, 2001: New & Revised for the 2000-01 Season.** Illus. by Dan Diamond. 608p. 2000. pap. 23.95 (*1-892129-46-9*) Total Sprts.

NHL Official Guide & Record Book, 1998-1999. NHL Staff. 1998. pap. text 19.95 (*1-892049-02-3*) Benchmark Press.

***NHL Quick Series Guide to Hockey Rules.** Seven Hills Publishing Staff. (Quick Series Guide). 1998. pap. text 5.95 (*2-922164-11-X*) Luxart.

***Nhl Quick Series Guide to The Coolest Game on Earth.** Seven Hills Publishing Staff. 1998. pap. text 5.95 (*2-922164-12-8*) Luxart.

NHL Today, 26 bks. Incl. Anaheim Mighty Ducks. Jeff Babineau. LC 94-46768. (Illus.). 32p. (YA). (gr. 3 up). 1995. lib. bdg. 21.30 (*0-88682-746-9*, Creat Educ); Boston Bruins. Vartan Kupelian. LC 93-48437. (Illus.). 32p. (YA). (gr. 3 up). 1996. lib. bdg. 21.30 (*0-88682-669-1*, Creat Educ); Buffalo Sabres. John Gilbert. LC 93-47952. (Illus.). 32p. (YA). (gr. 3 up). 1996. lib. bdg. 21.30 (*0-88682-670-5*, Creat Educ); Calgary Flames. Terry Jones. LC 93-48431. (Illus.). 32p. (YA). (gr. 3 up). 1996. lib. bdg. 21.30 (*0-88682-671-3*, Creat Educ); Colorado Avalanche. Gary Olson. LC 93-48453. (Illus.). 32p. (YA). (gr. 3 up). 1996. lib. bdg. 21.30 (*0-88682-685-3*, Creat Educ); Dallas Stars. John Gilbert. LC 93-48448. (Illus.). 32p. (YA). (gr. 3 up). 1996. lib. bdg. 21.30 (*0-88682-743-4*, Creat Educ); Detroit Red Wings. Vartan Kupelian. LC 93-47951. (Illus.). 32p. (YA). (gr. 3 up). 1996. lib. bdg. 21.30 (*0-88682-674-8*, Creat Educ); Edmonton Oilers. Terry Jones. LC 93-47950. (Illus.). 32p. (YA). (gr. 3 up). 1996. lib. bdg. 21.30 (*0-88682-675-6*, Creat Educ); Florida Panthers. Jeff Babineau. LC 94-46767. (Illus.). 32p. (YA). (gr. 3 up). 1996. lib. bdg. 21.30 (*0-88682-738-8*, Creat Educ); Hartford Whalers. Gary Olson. LC 93-48433. (Illus.). 32p. (YA). (gr. 3 up). 1996. lib. bdg. 21.30 (*0-88682-676-4*, Creat Educ); Los Angeles Kings. Joan St. Peter. LC 93-48432. (Illus.). 32p. (YA). (gr. 3 up). 1996. lib. bdg. 21.30 (*0-88682-677-2*, Creat Educ); Montreal Canadiens. Chrys Goyens. LC 94-1362. (Illus.). 32p. (YA). (gr. 3 up). 1996. lib. bdg. 21.30 (*0-88682-678-0*, Creat Educ); New Jersey Devils. Alex Yannis. LC 93-48436. (Illus.). 32p. (YA). (gr. 3 up). 1996. lib. bdg. 21.30 (*0-88682-679-9*, Creat Educ); New York Islanders. Mark Everson. LC 93-48435. (Illus.). 32p. (YA). (gr. 3 up). 1996. lib. bdg. 21.30 (*0-88682-680-2*, Creat Educ); New York Rangers. Mark Everson. LC 93-48434. (Illus.). 32p. (YA). (gr. 3 up). 1996. lib. bdg. 21.30 (*0-88682-681-0*, Creat Educ); Ottawa Senators. Roy MacGregor. LC 93-48454. (Illus.). 32p. (YA). (gr. 3 up). 1996. lib. bdg. 21.30 (*0-88682-682-9*, Creat Educ); Philadelphia Flyers. John Gilbert. LC 93-48455. (Illus.). 32p. (YA). (gr. 3 up). 1996. lib. bdg. 21.30 (*0-88682-683-7*, Creat Educ); Pittsburgh Penguins. John Gilbert. LC 93-48449. (Illus.). 32p. (YA). (gr. 3 up). 1996. lib. bdg. 21.30 (*0-88682-684-5*, Creat Educ); St. Louis Blues. Bruce Brothers. LC 93-48456. (Illus.). 32p. (YA). (gr. 3 up). 1996. lib. bdg. 21.30 (*0-88682-686-1*, Creat Educ); Tampa Bay Lightning. Jeff Babineau. LC 94-4305. (Illus.). 32p. (YA). (gr. 3 up). 1996. lib. bdg. 21.30 (*0-88682-688-8*, Creat Educ); Toronto Maple Leafs. Chrys Goyens. LC 94-1361. (Illus.). 32p. (YA). (gr. 3 up). 1996. lib. bdg. 21.30 (*0-88682-689-6*, Creat Educ); Washington Capitals. David Smale. LC 94-4304. (Illus.). 32p. (YA). (gr. 3 up). 1996. lib. bdg. 21.30 (*0-88682-691-8*, Creat Educ); Winnipeg Jets. Jess Myers. LC 93-48451. (Illus.). 32p. (YA). (gr. 3 up). 1996. lib. bdg. 21.30 (*0-88682-692-6*, Creat Educ); 1996. 553.80 (*0-88682-668-3*, Creat Educ) Creative Co.

NHL Today's Stars - Tomorrow's Legends. James Duplacey. 112p. 14.99 (*1-57215-237-0*, JG2370) World Pubns.

***NHL 2K: Prima's Official Strategy Guide.** Keith M. Kolmos. LC 99-69303. (Official Strategy Guides Ser.). (Illus.). 104p. (YA). 2000. pap. 14.99 (*0-7615-2732-X*) Prima Pub.

***NHL 2000: Official Strategy Guide.** Prima Development Staff. 1999. pap. 12.99 (*0-7615-2294-8*) Prima Pub.

NHS & Ideological Conflict. Paul Higgs. 233p. 1993. 66.95 (*1-85628-346-1*, Pub. by Avebury Technical) Ashgate Pub Co.

NHS Complaints: Litigation & Professional Discipline. Vivienne Harpwood. 250p. 1996. pap. write for info. (*1-85941-012-X*, Pub. by Cavendish Pubng) Gaunt.

NHS Data Book. John Fry et al. 1984. text 90.50 (*0-85200-735-3*) Kluwer Academic.

NHS Wales: Putting Patients First, Command Paper 3841. LC 98-147247. (Command Papers (All) Ser.: 81011068). 1998. 25.00 (*0-10-138412-2*, HM84122, Pub. by Statnry Office) Bernan Associates.

Nhung Giot Khong: Tuyen Tap Nhac Lang Mai. Ed. by Anh Viet. (VIE.). 220p. 1997. pap. 27.00 (*1-891667-49-1*) La Boi Soc.

Nhung Nam Thang Khong The Nao Quen see Unforgettable Months & Years

Ni Ange, Ni Bete. Andre Maurois. (FRE.). 1927. 10.95 (*0-8288-9883-9*, F114080) Fr & Eur.

Ni Caida, Ni Cambios. Eduardo De Acha. LC 93-72350. (Coleccion Cuba y sus Jueces). (SPA.). 85p. (Orig.). 1993. pap. 9.95 (*0-89729-702-4*) Ediciones.

***Ni Era Vaca, Ni Era Caballo...** Miguel Angel Jusayu. (Illus.). 48p. (J). 1999. pap. 7.95 (*980-257-212-8*, Pub. by Ediciones Ekare) Kane-Miller Bk.

Ni Hao I: Traditional Character Edition. Shumang & Paul Fredlein. 1996. pap. text 19.95 (*0-646-25096-5*); pap. text, wbk. ed. 12.95 (*0-646-25097-3*) Cheng & Tsui.

Ni-Kso-Ko-Wa: Blackfoot Spirituality, Traditions, Values & Beliefs. Long Standing Bear Chief. 1995. 9.95 (*0-614-06313-2*) Spirit Talk Pr.

Ni Macho . . . Ni Raton . . . Sino Verdadero Varon! Victor Ricardo. (SPA.). 36p. (Orig.). 1996. pap. 1.15 (*1-885630-39-5*) HLM Producciones.

Ni Nickel Pt. 3: Organonickel Compounds: Mononuclear Compounds. 8th ed. (Gmelin Ser.). (Illus.). xii, 406p. 1996. suppl. ed. 1689.00 (*3-540-93732-3*) Spr-Verlag.

Ni Organonickel Compounds: Mononuclear Compounds - Ni Bonded by One Carbon Atom. 8th ed. Gmelin Institute For Inorganic Chemistry for the M. (Gmelin Handbook of Inorganic & Organometallic Chemistry Ser.). (Illus.). xi, 381p. 1993. 1570.00 (*0-387-93681-5*) Spr-Verlag.

Ni Tan Solo Una Hora. Larry Lea.Tr. of Could You Not Tarry One Hour. (SPA.). 176p. (Orig.). 1992. pap. 7.99 (*0-88113-053-2*) Caribe Betania.

Ni Tiempo para Pedir Auxilio. Fausto Canel. LC 90-84964. (Coleccion Caniqui). (SPA.). 202p. (Orig.). 1991. pap. 18.00 (*0-89729-587-0*) Ediciones.

***Ni una Bomba Mas: Vieques vs. U. S. Navy.** Lisa Mullenneaux. LC 00-190931. (Illus.). 164p. 2000. pap. 12.00 (*0-615-11307-9*) Penington Pr.

***Ni Vue, Ni Connue.** Mary Higgins Clark. 1999. pap. 12.95 (*2-253-17056-9*) Midwest European Pubns.

***Niagara.** Tanya Lloyd. Ed. by Whitecap Books Staff. (Illus.). 96p. 2000. 14.95 (*1-55285-019-6*) Carlton Bks Ltd.

Niagara. Richard Watson. LC 93-16592. 192p. 1993. 19.95 (*1-56689-006-3*) Coffee Hse.

Niagara: A History of the Falls. Pierre Berton. (Illus.). 480p. 1998. pap. text 7.00 (*0-7881-5350-1*) DIANE Pub.

Niagara: A History of the Falls. Pierre Berton. Ed. by Philip Turner. (Illus.). 480p. 1997. 27.00 (*1-56836-154-8*) Kodansha.

Niagara: A History of the Falls. Pierre Berton. 1993. pap. 8.99 (*0-7710-1217-9*) McCland & Stewart.

Niagara: A History of the Falls. Pierre Berton. LC 96-44821. 371p. 1998. pap. 14.95 (*0-14-027016-7*) Viking Penguin.

Niagara & Southwestern Ontario. Ed. by Paul Knowles. (Illus.). 207p. 1998. pap. 16.95 (*0-88780-426-8*, Pub. by J Lorimer) Formac Dist Ltd.

Niagara Attracting the World. Philip Nyhuis et al. LC 97-16127. 288p. 1997. 45.00 (*1-885352-58-1*); pap. write for info. (*1-885352-59-X*) Community Comm.

Niagara County, One of the Most Wonderful Regions in the World: A Concise Record of Her Progress & People, 1821-1921, 2 vols. Edward T. Williams. (Illus.). 850p. 1997. reprint ed. lib. bdg. 95.00 (*0-8328-6185-5*) Higginson Bk Co.

***Niagara 1814: America Invades Canada.** Richard V. Barbuto. 2000. 39.95 (*0-7006-1052-9*) U Pr of KS.

Niagara Escarpment: A Portfolio. Pat Keough & Rosemarie Keough. (Illus.). 204p. 1990. 24.99 (*0-7737-2414-1*) Genl Dist Srvs.

Niagara Escarpment: From Tobermory to Niagara Falls. William Gillard & Thomas Tooke. LC 73-84434. (Illus.). 147p. reprint ed. pap. 45.60 (*0-8357-8249-2*, 203398500088) Bks Demand.

Niagara Falls. Jim Daniels. 39p. 1994. pap. 7.00 (*0-938566-63-6*) Adastra Pr.

***Niagara Falls.** Sarah De Capua. LC 99-42013. (Rookie Read-About Geography Ser.). (J). 2001. write for info. (*0-516-22016-0*) Childrens.

Niagara Falls. Daniel Martin Dumych. (Images of America Ser.). 128p. 1996. pap. 16.99 (*0-7524-0432-6*) Arcadia Publng.

Niagara Falls, Vol. II. Daniel Martin Dumych. (Images of America Ser.). (Illus.). 128p. 1998. pap. 16.99 (*0-7524-1201-9*) Arcadia Publng.

Niagara Falls: A Picture Book. Pierre Berton. (Illus.). 160p. 1993. 29.95 (*0-7710-0218-1*) McCland & Stewart.

Niagara Falls: A Selected Topical History of the City's Formative Years. expanded rev. ed. Hamilton B. Mizer. 210p. 1991. 12.95 (*0-614-13514-1*) Niagara Cnty Hist Soc.

Niagara Falls: Nature's Wonder. Leonard Everett Fisher. (Illus.). 64p. (J). (gr. 4-6). 1996. 16.95 (*0-8234-1240-7*) Holiday.

Niagara Falls Mystery. Created by Gertrude Chandler Warner. LC 97-6155. (Boxcar Children Ser.: No. 8). (J). (gr. 2-5). 1997. pap. 3.95 (*0-8075-5603-3*); lib. bdg. 13.95 (*0-8075-5602-5*) A Whitman.

Niagara Falls Mystery. Created by Gertrude Chandler Warner. LC 97-6155. (Boxcar Children Ser.: No. 8). (J). (gr. 2-5). 1997. 9.05 (*0-606-11163-8*, Pub. by Turtleback) Demco.

Niagara Falls Picture Book. Kathleen Berton. 1994. 19.95 (*0-7710-1214-4*) McCland & Stewart.

Niagara Falls Q & A: Answers to the Most Common Questions about Niagara Falls. 6th ed. Paul Gromosiak & Brian Meyer. (Illus.). 52p. 1991. reprint ed. pap. 3.95 (*0-9620314-8-8*) WNY Wares.

Niagara Flavours Guidebook & Cookbook. Brenda Matthews. (Illus.). 128p. 1999. pap. 16.95 (*1-55028-606-4*, Pub. by J Lorimer) Formac Dist Ltd.

Niagara Mist. Donald Verger. (Moving Pictures Ser.). (Illus.). 64p. 1998. pap. 4.95 (*1-887716-07-6*) Designs Disc.

***Niagara River.** Melissa Whitcraft. LC 00-39928. (Library). 2001. write for info. (*0-531-11903-3*) Watts.

Niagara's Gold. Jeff Maynard. LC 96-150087. 1996. pap. text 16.95 (*0-86417-766-6*, Pub. by Kangaroo Pr) Seven Hills Bk.

NIAM Information Analysis Method: Theory & Practice. J. J. Wintraecken. 484p. 1990. text 388.50 (*0-7923-0263-X*) Kluwer Academic.

***Niara.** Elizabeth Griffin Gore. Ed. by Marietta Brown. 227p. (YA). (gr. 8 up). 2000. pap. write for info. (*0-9701447-0-9*) Gore Pubns.

Nia's in Love. Runett N. Ebo. (Illus.). 28p. (Orig.). 1992. pap. 8.00 (*1-883753-03-1*) Jwand Ent.

Nibbana - The Ultimate Truth of Buddhism. Chinda Chandrkaew. 254p. 1982. 12.95 (*0-318-36661-4*) Asia Bk Corp.

Nibbana As Living Experience. Lily De Silva. 56p. 1996. 3.75 (*955-24-0128-3*, Pub. by Buddhist Pub Soc) Vipassana Res Pubns.

Nibble Nibble: Poems for Children. Margaret W. Brown. LC 84-43128. (Illus.). 64p. (J). (ps-3). 1998. 15.95 (*0-06-027997-4*) HarpC Child Bks.

Nibble, Nibble, Jenny Archer. Ellen Conford. LC 92-34306. (Illus.). 61p. (J). (gr. k-3). 1993. 14.95 (*0-316-15371-0*) Little.

***Nibble, Nibble, Jerry Archer.** Ellen Conford. 64p. (J). (gr. 3-7). 1999. pap. 4.50 (*0-316-15206-4*) Little.

Nibble Nibble Mousekin: A Tale of Hansel & Gretel. Joan W. Anglund. LC 62-14422. (Illus.). 32p. (J). (gr. k-3). 1962. 10.95 (*0-15-257400-X*, Harcourt Child Bks) Harcourt.

An Asterisk (*) at the beginning of an entry indicates that the title is appearing for the first time.

Nibble Nibble Mousekin: A Tale of Hansel & Gretel. Joan W. Anglund. LC 62-14422. (Illus.). 32p. (J). (gr. k-3). 1977. pap. 4.95 (*0-15-665588-8*, Voyager Bks) Harcourt.

Nibble Theory & the Kernel of Power. Kaleel Jamison. LC 83-63112. 74p. (Orig.). 1984. pap. 6.95 (*0-8091-2621-4*) Paulist Pr.

Nibbled to Death by Ducks. Robert Campbell. Ed. by Jane Chelius. 288p. 1990. reprint ed. mass mkt. 4.99 (*0-671-67583-4*) PB.

Nibbler's Diet: Ultimate Solution to America's Weight & Cholesterol Problems. Sita R. Kaura & Diane Collins. (Illus.). 250p. 1996. 21.95 (*0-9650621-0-4*) Manisha Pr.

***Nibbles: Poems from Hollywood.** Mark Dunster. 11p. 1999. pap. 5.00 (*0-89642-918-0*) Linden Pubs.

Nibbles: Schoolbound. Doug Macaraeg. (Illus.). 22p. (J). (gr. k-3). 1997. pap. 6.95 (*0-9666833-0-7*) Coconut Works.

***Nibbles O'Hare.** Illus. by Betty Paraskevas & Michael Paraskevas. LC 99-31242. (J). 2001. 16.00 (*0-689-82865-9*) S&S Childrens.

Nibbles the Rabbit Has a Good Habit. Kathy Craner. (Illus.). (Orig.). (J). (ps-2). 1998. pap. 12.95 (*0-7880-1404-8*, Fairway Pr) CSS OH.

Nibbly Mouse. David Drew. LC 92-21397. (Voyages Ser.). (Illus.). (J). 1993. 4.25 (*0-383-03587-2*) SRA McGraw.

Nibelunge Not in Auswahl: Mit Kurzem Woerterbuch. 11th ed. Ed. by Karl Langosch. (Sammlung Goeschen Ser.: No. 1). (C). 1966. 6.00 (*3-11-002722-4*) De Gruyter.

Nibelunge Noth und die Klage: Nach den Aeltesten Ueberlieferungen mit Bezeichnung des Unechten und mit den Abweichungen der gemeinen Lesart. 6th ed. Ed. by Karl Lachmann. (C). 1960. 18.55 (*3-11-000177-2*); pap. 20.75 (*3-11-000178-0*) De Gruyter.

Nibelungen Prosody. Ray M. Wakefield. (De Proprietatibus Litterarum Ser.: No. 112). 1976. pap. 30.80 (*90-279-3066-X*) Mouton.

***Nibelungen Tradition: An Encyclopedia.** Ed. by Werner Wunderlich et al. 700p. 1999. 100.00 (*0-8153-1785-9*) Garland.

Nibelungenlied. Tr. by A. T. Hatto. (Classics Ser.). 416p. 1965. pap. 12.95 (*0-14-044137-9*, Penguin Classics) Viking Penguin.

Nibelungenlied. Tr. by Robert Lichtenstein from GER. LC 91-44798. (Studies in German Language & Literature: Vol. 9). 260p. 1992. lib. bdg. 89.95 (*0-7734-9470-7*) E Mellen.

Nibelungenlied: An Interpretative Commentary. D. G. Mowatt & Hugh Secker. LC 68-83851. 152p. reprint ed. pap. 47.20 (*0-8357-4145-1*, 203691800006) Bks Demand.

Nibelungenlied: Eine Einfuehrung. Joachim Heinzle. 128p. 1994. pap. 11.75 (*3-596-11843-3*, Pub. by Fischer Tasch) Intl Bk Import.

Nibelungenlied Vol. 1: Mittelhochdeutscher Text mit Uebertragung. 23rd ed. Ed. by Helmut Brackert. (GEH & GER.). 304p. 1998. pap. 15.25 (*3-596-26038-8*, Pub. by Fischer Tasch) Intl Bk Import.

Nibelungenlied Vol. 2: Mittelhochdeutscher Text mit Uebertragung. 21st ed. Ed. by Helmut Brackert. (GEH & GER.). 310p. 1997. pap. 15.25 (*3-596-26039-6*, Pub. by Fischer Tasch) Intl Bk Import.

***Nibelungenlied in der wissenschaftlichen Literatur zwischen 1945 und 1985: Ein Beitrag zur Geschichte der Nibelungenforschung.** Sabine B. Sattel. 2000. 68.95 (*3-631-35513-0*) P Lang Pubng.

Nibelungenlied Today. Werner A. Mueller. LC 70-181961. (North Carolina. University. Studies in the Germanic Languages & Literatures: No. 34). reprint ed. 27.00 (*0-404-50934-7*) AMS Pr.

Niblack Family: Chronicles & Genealogy. Ellen N. Frew. 200p. 1997. 35.00 (*1-57860-000-6*) Guild Pr IN.

Nibsy's Christmas. Jacob A. Riis. LC 71-90590. (Short Story Index Reprint Ser.). 1977. 15.95 (*0-8369-3073-8*) Ayer.

Nicander: Poems. Ed. by A. Gow & A. Scholfield. (BCP Classic Greek Texts Ser.). (GEC.). 256p. 1997. pap. 33.95 (*1-85399-528-2*, Pub. by Brist Class Pr) Focus Pub-R Pullins.

Nicandri Colophonii Carminum. Nicandrus. Ed. by Albertus Bernabe. write for info. (*0-318-70986-4*) G Olms Pubs.

Nicandrus: Nicandri Colophonii Carminum Index et Concordantia. Ed. by Albertus Bernabe. write for info. (*0-318-71954-1*) G Olms Pubs.

Nicandrus - Nicandri Theriacorum et Alexipharmacorum Concordantia. Manolis Papathomopoulos. 431p. 1996. write for info. (*3-487-10206-4*) G Olms Pubs.

Nicaragua see American Nations Past & Present

Nicaragua see Statements of the Laws of the OAS Member States in Matters Affecting Business

Nicaragua see Cultures of the World - Group 9

***Nicaragua.** Bernan Press Staff & World Trade Organization Staff. (Trade Policy Review Ser.). 2000. 50.00 (*0-89059-201-2*) Bernan Pr.

Nicaragua. Nicolas Caillens. (Illus.). 46p. 1994. 40.00 (*1-880515-52-0*) Schl Mus Fine.

Nicaragua. William F. Gentile. (Illus.). 1989. pap. 19.95 (*0-393-30603-8*) Norton.

Nicaragua. Smith. (C). 66.50 (*0-7453-0480-X*, Pub. by Pluto GBR); pap. 19.95 (*0-7453-0475-3*, Pub. by Pluto GBR) Stylus Pub VA.

Nicaragua. U. S. Government Staff. (Country Studies). 1995. 18.00 (*0-614-30806-2*, UNICAR) Claitors.

Nicaragua. Ed. by Ralph L. Woodward, Jr. (World Bibliographical Ser.: No. 44). 254p. 1994. lib. bdg. 73.00 (*0-903450-79-8*) ABC-CLIO.

***Nicaragua.** 2nd ed. Carol Wood. (Ulysses Travel Guide Ser.). 1999. pap. 17.95 (*2-89464-148-6*) Ulysses Travel.

Nicaragua. 2nd rev. ed. Ed. by Ralph L. Woodward. (World Bibliographical Ser.: Vol. 44). 322p. 1983. lib. bdg. 73.00 (*1-85109-189-0*) ABC-CLIO.

Nicaragua: A Country Guide. 2nd ed. Kent Norsworthy & Tom Barry. 226p. 1990. pap. 9.95 (*0-911213-29-5*) Interhemisp Res Ctr.

***Nicaragua: A Country Study.** 3rd ed. Ed. by Tim L. Merrill. (Illus.). 300p. 1999. reprint ed. text 50.00 (*0-7881-8115-7*) DIANE Pub.

***Nicaragua: A Country Study Guide.** Global Investment & Business Center, Inc. Staff. (World Country Study Guides Library: Vol. 125). (Illus.). 350p. 2000. pap. 59.00 (*0-7397-2423-1*) Intl Business Pubns.

Nicaragua: A Decade of Revolution. Anthony Jenkins. 1991. 39.95 (*0-393-02965-4*) Norton.

Nicaragua: An Introduction to the Sandinista Revolution. 2nd ed. Arnold Weissberg. 45p. 1987. reprint ed. pap. 3.50 (*0-87348-442-8*) Pathfinder NY.

Nicaragua: Dynamics of an Unfinished Revolution. Alan Benjamin. 186p. (Orig.). 1989. write for info. (*0-929405-02-1*); pap. 7.95 (*0-929405-03-X*) Walnut Pub.

Nicaragua: Major World Nations. John Griffiths. LC 98-6399. (Major World Nations Ser.). (Illus.). 144p. (YA). (gr. 5 up). 1999. lib. bdg. 19.95 (*0-7910-4976-0*) Chelsea Hse.

Nicaragua: Politics, Economics & Society. David Close. 220p. 1988. text 49.00 (*0-86187-434-X*, Pub. by P P Pubs); text 17.50 (*0-86187-435-8*, Pub. by P P Pubs) Cassell & Continuum.

Nicaragua: Portrait of a Tragedy. William J. Murray. 128p. 1987. pap. 6.95 (*0-940917-03-3*) MFM Publish.

Nicaragua: Reconciliation Awaiting Recovery. 37p. 1991. 6.00 (*0-929513-18-5*) WOLA.

Nicaragua: Revolution & Democracy. Jose L. Coraggio. 160p. (C). 1986. pap. text 13.95 (*0-04-497019-6*) Routledge.

Nicaragua: Struggling with Change. Faith Adams. LC 86-11608. (Discovering Our Heritage Ser.). (Illus.). 152p. (YA). (gr. 5 up). 1987. lib. bdg. 14.95 (*0-87518-340-9*, Dillon Silver Burdett) Silver Burdett Pr.

Nicaragua: The Chamorro Years. David Close. LC 98-27844. 244p. 1998. lib. bdg. 52.00 (*1-55587-643-9*) L Rienner.

Nicaragua: The First Five Years. Ed. by Thomas W. Walker. LC 85-3467. 572p. 1985. 79.50 (*0-275-90177-7*, C0177, Praeger Pubs); pap. 29.95 (*0-275-91660-X*, B1660, Praeger Pubs) Greenwood.

Nicaragua: The First War We Can Drive To. Georgie A. Geyer. 300p. 1990. 24.95 (*0-88738-219-3*) Transaction Pubs.

Nicaragua: The Human Rights Record, 1986-1986. Amnesty International Staff. (SPA.). 67p. (Orig.). 1989. pap. 6.00 (*0-939994-50-X*, Pub. by Amnesty Intl Pubns) Science Pubs.

Nicaragua: The Human Tragedy of War, April-June, 1986. Washington Office on Latin America Staff. 53p. (Orig.). 1987. pap. 4.00 (*0-929513-00-2*) WOLA.

Nicaragua: The Making of U. S. Policy, 1978-1990, Guide & Index, 2 vols., Set. National Security Archive Staff & Chadwyck-Healey Staff. Ed. by Deter Kornbluh. (Making of U. S. Policy Ser.). (Illus.). 1991. write for info. (*0-89887-088-7*) Chadwyck-Healey.

Nicaragua: The People Speak. Alvin Levie. LC 85-13485. (Illus.). 221p. 1985. pap. 12.95 (*0-89789-084-1*, Bergin & Garvey) Greenwood.

Nicaragua: The People Speak. Alvin Levie. (Illus.). 221p. 1985. 34.94 (*0-89789-083-3*, Bergin & Garvey) Greenwood.

Nicaragua: The Price of Intervention, Reagan's Wars Against the Sandinistas. Peter Kornbluh. LC 87-21387. 287p. (Orig.). 1987. pap. 8.95 (*0-89758-040-0*) Inst Policy Stud.

Nicaragua: The Sandinista People's Revolution. Tomas Borge et al. LC 85-61096. (Illus.). 412p. (C). 1985. pap. 21.95 (*0-87348-653-6*); lib. bdg. 60.00 (*0-87348-652-8*) Pathfinder NY.

Nicaragua: The Threat of a Good Example? Dianna Melrose. 80p. (C). 1985. pap. text 30.00 (*0-85598-070-2*, Pub. by Oxfam Pubns) St Mut.

Nicaragua: Violations of the Laws of War by Both Sides, February-December 1985. Mary Dutcher. 44p. (Orig.). (C). 1986. pap. text 6.50 (*0-9613249-3-7*) WOLA.

Nicaragua: War of the Filibusters . . . Daniel B. Lucas. 2194p. 1986. reprint ed. 25.00 (*0-913129-10-0*) La Tienda.

Nicaragua - A Country Study Guide: Basic Information for Research & Pleasure. Global Investment Center, USA Staff. (World Country Study Guide Library: Vol. 125). (Illus.). 350p. 1999. pap. 59.00 (*0-7397-1522-4*) Intl Business Pubns.

***Nicaragua Business Intelligence Report, 190 vols.** Global Investment & Business Center, Inc. Staff. (World Business Intelligence Library: Vol. 125). (Illus.). 350p. 2000. pap. 99.95 (*0-7397-2623-4*) Intl Business Pubns.

***Nicaragua Business Law Handbook.** Global Investment & Business Center, Inc. Staff. (Global Business Law Handbooks Library: Vol. 125). (Illus.). 2000. pap. 99.95 (*0-7397-2023-6*) Intl Business Pubns.

Nicaragua Business Law Handbook-98. Russian Information & Business Center, Inc. Staff. (World Business Law Library-98). (Illus.). 350p. 1998. pap. 99.00 (*1-57751-842-X*) Intl Business Pubns.

***Nicaragua Business Opportunity Yearbook.** Global Investment & Business Center, Inc. Staff. (Global Business Opportunity Yearbooks Library: Vol. 125). (Illus.). 2000. pap. 99.95 (*0-7397-2223-9*) Intl Business Pubns.

***Nicaragua Business Opportunity Yearbook: Export-Import, Investment & Business Opportunities.** International Business Publications, U. S. A. Staff & Global Investment Center, U. S. A. Staff. (Global Business Opportunity Yearbooks Library: Vol. 125). (Illus.). 350p. 1999. pap. 99.95 (*0-7397-1323-X*) Intl Business Pubns.

***Nicaragua Country Review 2000.** Robert C. Kelly et al. (Illus.). 60p. 1999. pap. 39.95 (*1-58310-549-2*) CountryWatch.

Nicaragua Country Studies: Area Handbook. 3rd ed. Helen C. Metz & Tim L. Merrill. LC 94-43019. (Area Handbook DA Pam Ser.). 1994. write for info. (*0-8444-0831-X*) Lib Congress.

Nicaragua: Cronica de Una Sangre Inocente la Guerra Sucia De "Los Paladines de la Libertad" see Blood of the Innocent: Victims of the Contras' War in Nicaragua

Nicaragua Divided: La Prensa & the Chamorro Legacy. Patricia T. Edmisten. 128p. 1990. 39.95 (*0-8130-0972-3*) U Press Fla.

Nicaragua for Beginners. Ruis. (Illus.). 160p. 1984. pap. 7.95 (*0-86316-067-0*) Writers & Readers.

***Nicaragua Foreign Policy & Government Guide.** Contrib. by Global Investment & Business Center, Inc. Staff. (World Foreign Policy & Government Library: Vol. 120). (Illus.). 350p. 1999. pap. 99.00 (*0-7397-3618-3*) Intl Business Pubns.

***Nicaragua Foreign Policy & Government Guide.** Global Investment & Business Center, Inc. Staff. (World Foreign Policy & Government Library: Vol. 120). (Illus.). 350p. 2000. 99.95 (*0-7397-3823-2*) Intl Business Pubns.

Nicaragua Guide: Spectacular & Unspoiled. Paul Glassman. (Illus.). 288p. (Orig.). 1995. pap. 16.95 (*0-930016-22-X*) Pass Pr Trvl Line.

Nicaragua in Focus: A Guide to the People, Politics & Culture. Hazel Plunkett. LC 99-19668. 1999. pap. 12.95 (*1-56656-286-4*) Interlink Pub.

Nicaragua in Pictures. Nathan A. Haverstock. (Visual Geography Ser.). (Illus.). 64p. (YA). (gr. 5 up). 1993. lib. bdg. 19.95 (*0-8225-1817-1*, Lerner Publctns) Lerner Pub.

Nicaragua in Reconstruction & at War: The People Speak. Ed. by Marc Zimmerman. LC 85-61046. (Studies in Marxism: Vol. 17). (Illus.). 314p. 1985. 19.95 (*0-930656-41-5*); pap. 8.95 (*0-930656-42-3*) MEP Pubns.

Nicaragua in Revolution. Ed. by Thomas W. Walker. LC 81-17746. 410p. 1981. 65.00 (*0-275-90737-6*, C0737, Praeger Pubs); pap. 15.95 (*0-275-91766-5*, B1766, Praeger Pubs) Greenwood.

Nicaragua in Revolution: The Poets Speak. Ed. by Bridget Aldaraca et al. LC 80-16304. (Studies in Marxism: Vol. 5). 301p. 1980. 18.95 (*0-930656-10-5*); pap. 8.95 (*0-930656-09-1*) MEP Pubns.

***Nicaragua Investment & Business Guide.** Global Investment & Business Center, Inc. Staff. (Global Investment & Business Guide Library: Vol. 125). (Illus.). 2000. pap. 99.95 (*0-7397-1823-1*) Intl Business Pubns.

Nicaragua Investment & Business Guide: Economy, Export-Import, Business & Investment Climate, Business Contacts. Contrib. by Russian Information & Business Center, Inc. Staff. (Russia, NIS & Emerging Markets Investment & Business Library-98). (Illus.). 350p. 1998. pap. 99.00 (*1-57751-899-3*) Intl Business Pubns.

***Nicaragua Investment & Business Guide: Export-Import, Investment & Business Opportunities.** International Business Publications, USA Staff & Global Investment Center, USA Staff. (World Investment & Business Guide Library-99: Vol. 125). (Illus.). 350p. 1999. pap. 99.95 (*0-7397-0320-X*) Intl Business Pubns.

Nicaragua, Its People, Scenery, Monuments, Resources, Condition & Proposed Canal. Ephraim G. Squier. LC 73-176006. (Illus.). reprint ed. 79.50 (*0-404-06220-2*) AMS Pr.

Nicaragua Route. LC 73-180827. (University of Utah Publications in the American West: Vol. 8). 187p. reprint ed. pap. 58.00 (*0-608-16286-8*, 202717000054) Bks Demand.

Nicaragua Water Fire. Gioconda Belli. (C). 1990. pap. 40.00 (*0-906887-37-2*, Pub. by Greville Pr) St Mut.

Nicaragua Without Illusions: Regime Transition & Structural Adjustment in the 1990s. Ed. by Thomas W. Walker. LC 96-45590. (Latin American Silhouettes Ser.). 352p. 1997. pap. 21.95 (*0-8420-2579-0*) Scholarly Res Inc.

Nicaragua Without Illusions: Regime Transition & Structural Adjustment in the 1990s. Ed. by Thomas W. Walker. LC 96-45590. (Latin American Silhouettes Ser.). 352p. 1997. text 55.00 (*0-8420-2578-2*) Scholarly Res Inc.

Nicaraguan Church & the Revolution. Joseph E. Mulligan. LC 90-63486. 320p. (Orig.). (C). 1991. pap. 17.95 (*1-55612-411-2*, LL1411) Sheed & Ward WI.

Nicaraguan Constitution of 1987: English Translation & Commentary. Ed. by Kenneth J. Mijeski. LC 90-47132. (Monographs in International Studies, Latin America Ser.: No. 17). 355p. (Orig.). (C). 1991. pap. 25.00 (*0-89680-165-9*) Ohio U Pr.

Nicaraguan Family. Michael Malone. LC 97-13827. (Journey Between Two Worlds Ser.). 1998. lib. bdg. write for info. (*0-8225-9779-9*) Lerner Pub.

Nicaraguan Family. Michael Malone. LC 97-13827. (Journey Between Two Worlds Ser.). (J). 1998. lib. bdg. 22.60 (*0-8225-3412-6*) Lerner Pub.

Nicaraguan National Bibliography, 1800-1978, 3 vols. 1986. 450.00 (*0-914369-01-6*) Latin Am Biblio.

Nicaraguan National Bibliography, 1800-1978, 3 vols., I. 1986. write for info. (*0-914369-02-4*) Latin Am Biblio.

Nicaraguan National Bibliography, 1800-1978, 3 vols., II. 1986. write for info. (*0-914369-03-2*) Latin Am Biblio.

Nicaraguan National Bibliography, 1800-1978, 3 vols., III. 1986. write for info. (*0-914369-04-0*) Latin Am Biblio.

Nicaraguan Peasant Poetry from Solentiname. Tr. & Intro. by David Gullette. (ENG & SPA.). 209p. (Orig.). (C). 1988. pap. 11.95 (*0-931122-48-1*) West End.

Nicaraguan Revolution. Ed. by Gary E. McCuen. (Ideas in Conflict Ser.). (Illus.). 184p. (YA). (gr. 7-12). 1986. lib. bdg. 15.95 (*0-86596-058-5*) G E M.

Nicaraguan Revolution in Health: From Somoza to the Sandinistas. John M. Donahue. LC 85-31562. 188p. 1986. 55.00 (*0-89789-101-5*, Bergin & Garvey); pap. 17.95 (*0-89789-170-8*, Bergin & Garvey) Greenwood.

Nicaragua's Continuing Revolution, 1977-1990: A Chronology. David A. Ridenour & David Almasi. LC 90-61757. pap. 20.00 (*0-930095-12-X*) Signal Bks.

Nicaragua's Continuing Struggle: In Search of Democracy. Arturo J. Cruz. Ed. by James Finn. LC 87-28072. (Focus on Issues Ser.: No. 4). 1988. 12.95 (*0-932088-20-1*); pap. 5.95 (*0-932088-19-8*) Freedom Hse.

Nicaragua's Mosquito Shore: The Years of British & American Presence. Craig L. Dozier. LC 84-237. (Illus.). 280p. 1985. pap. 86.80 (*0-7837-8371-X*, 205918100009) Bks Demand.

Nicaragua's Other Revolution: Religious Faith & Political Struggle. Michael Dodson & Laura N. O'Shaughnessy. LC 89-35448. xii, 280p. (C). 1990. pap. 18.95 (*0-8078-4266-4*) U of NC Pr.

Nicaragua's Slow March to Communism. Joshua Muravchik. 1986. 3.00 (*0-317-90495-7*) Cuban Amer Natl Fndtn.

Niccola Sacco & Bartolomeo Vanzetti: The Letters of Sacco & Vanzetti. Ed. by Marion D. Frankfurter et al. LC 96-29901. lxi, 414p. 1997. pap. 13.95 (*0-14-118026-9*) Penguin Putnam.

Niccolo & Nicolette. Allan Cullen. (J). (gr. 1-9). 1957. 6.00 (*0-87602-162-3*) Anchorage.

Niccolo Machiavelli: An Annotated Bibliography of Modern Criticism & Scholarship, 13. Compiled by Silvia R. Fiore. LC 89-25602. (Bibliographies & Indexes in Law & Political Science Ser.: No. 13). 824p. 1990. lib. bdg. 145.00 (*0-313-25238-6*, RFM/, Greenwood Pr) Greenwood.

Niccolo Machiavelli's The Prince: New Interdisciplinary Essays. Ed. by Martin Coyle. LC 95-910. (Texts in Culture Ser.). 224p. 1995. text 69.95 (*0-7190-4195-3*, Pub. by Manchester Univ Pr); text 26.95 (*0-7190-4196-1*, Pub. by Manchester Univ Pr) St Martin.

Niccolo Manucci: A Venetian's Odyssey in Mogul India. John H. Waller. 277p. 1984. 11.95 (*0-89697-142-2*) Intl Univ Pr.

Niccolo Rising: The First Book of the House of Niccolo. Dorothy Dunnett. LC 86-45306. (House of Niccolo Series: Vol. I). 470p. 1999. pap. 15.00 (*0-375-70477-9*) Vin Bks.

Niccolo Rising: The First Book of the House of Niccolo. Dorothy Dunnett. 1992. reprint ed. lib. bdg. 33.95 (*0-89966-963-8*) Buccaneer Bks.

***Niccolo's Smile: A Biography of Machiavelli.** Maurizio Viroli. Tr. by Antony Shugaar from ITA. LC 00-29380. (Illus.). 288p. 2000. 25.00 (*0-374-22187-1*) FS&G.

Nice. Jen Sacks. LC 98-19407. 208p. 1998. text 21.95 (*0-312-19306-8*) St Martin.

Nice. Jen Sacks. 256p. 1999. mass mkt. 5.99 (*0-312-96925-2*, St Martins Paperbacks) St Martin.

Nice & Easy French Grammar. C. Beswick. (FRE., Illus.). 136p. 1995. pap. 4.95 (*0-8442-9497-7*, 94977, Natl Textbk Co) NTC Contemp Pub Co.

Nice & Easy German Grammar. Isabel Willshaw. (GER., Illus.). 176p. 1995. pap. 4.95 (*0-8442-9498-5*, 94985, Natl Textbk Co) NTC Contemp Pub Co.

Nice & Easy Spanish Grammar. Sandra Truscott. LC 98-8724. (SPA., Illus.). 128p. 1994. pap. 4.95 (*0-8442-9496-9*, 94969, Natl Textbk Co) NTC Contemp Pub Co.

Nice & the Good. Iris Murdoch. 1978. pap. 13.95 (*0-14-003034-4*, Penguin Bks) Viking Penguin.

Nice & the Nasty. Mark O'Donnell. 1987. pap. 5.25 (*0-8222-0815-6*) Dramatists Play.

***Nice Bloke.** Catherine Cookson. 2000. pap. 10.95 (*0-552-14086-4*, Pub. by Transworld Publishers Ltd) Trafalgar.

Nice Boy. George Veltri. 186p. (Orig.). 1995. pap. 9.95 (*0-87286-302-6*) City Lights.

Nice City Plan. (Grafocarte Maps Ser.). 1995. 8.95 (*2-7416-0029-5*, 80029) Michelin.

Nice Couples Do: How to Turn Your Secret Dreams into Sensational Sex. Joan E. Lloyd. 1991. mass mkt. 13.99 (*0-446-39258-8*, Pub. by Warner Bks) Little.

Nice Day for a Funeral. large type ed. Hartley Howard. (Linford Mystery Large Print Ser.). 368p. 1998. pap. 17.99 (*0-7089-5211-9*, Linford) Ulverscroft.

Nice Day in the City. David B. Simpson. LC 83-49478. (Illus.). 48p. (J). (gr. 1-4). 1984. 12.95 (*0-06-025641-9*) HarpC Child Bks.

Nice Day in the Park. Ev Miller. 1984. pap. 1.75 (*0-912963-03-4*) Eldridge Pub.

Nice Deity. Martha Baird. LC 55-11012. 1955. 8.95 (*0-910492-04-2*) Definition.

Nice Derangement of Epitaphs. Ellis Peters. 208p. 1992. mass mkt. 5.99 (*0-446-40069-6*, Pub. by Warner Bks) Little.

Nice Derangement of Epitaphs. large type ed. Ellis Peters. 1993. 18.95 (*0-7505-0311-4*, Pub. by Mgna Lrg Print) Ulverscroft.

Nice Fish: New & Selected Prose Poems. Louis Jenkins. 70p. (Orig.). (YA). (gr. 10 up). 1995. pap. text 10.00 (*0-930100-61-1*) Holy Cow.

Nice Flyers. Ed. by Meg Bowman. (Illus.). 155p. 1996. spiral bd. 8.95 (*0-940483-14-9*) Hot Flash Pr.

Nice Girl Like You. Alexandra Sellers. 1996. per. 3.50 (*0-373-52033-6*, 1-52033-7) Silhouette.

N

Nice Girl Like You. Norma Johnston. LC 99-60483. (Keeping Days Ser.). 222p. (YA). 1999. reprint ed. pap. 16.00 (*1-892323-32-X*, Pierce Harris Pr) Vivisphere.

***Nice Girls & Rude Girls; Women Workers in World War I.** Deborah Thom. 2000. pap. 22.50 (*1-86064-477-5*, Pub. by I B T) St Martin.

***Nice Girl's Book of Naughty Spells: Get Rich, Get Lucky, Get Even.** Deborah Gray. (Illus.). 128p. 1999. pap. 11.95 (*1-885203-88-8*) Jrny Editions.

Nice Girls Don't Drink: Stories of Recovery. Sarah Hafner. LC 91-18924. 264p. 1992. 24.95 (*0-89789-246-1*, H246, Bergin & Garvey); pap. 12.95 (*0-89789-247-X*, Bergin & Garvey) Greenwood.

Nice Girls Don't Finish Last: 2-Act Comedy Drama. Lewis F. Spitzer. (Illus.). 64p. (YA). (gr. 7-12). 1983. pap. 4.00 (*0-88680-138-9*) I E Clark.

Nice Girls Don't Wear Cha Cha Heels: Camp Lines from Classic Films. Ed. by Leigh W. Rutledge. LC 99-36926. 196p. 1999. pap. 10.95 (*1-55583-440-X*, Pub. by Alyson Pubns) Consort Bk Sales.

Nice Girls Finish Last. Sparkle Hayter. 1997. pap. 5.99 (*0-14-024516-2*) Viking Penguin.

Nice Girl's Guide to Sensational Sex. Nancy Kalish. 224p. 1994. mass mkt. 5.99 (*0-380-77229-9*, Avon Bks) Morrow Avon.

Nice Guys Don't Get Laid. rev. ed. Marcus P. Meleton, Jr. LC 93-83581. 112p. 1993. pap. 7.95 (*0-9635826-0-7*) Sharkbait Pr.

Nice Guys Finish First. Jay Hall & Susan M. Donnell. 1988. 19.95 (*0-945804-47-4*) Woodstead Pr.

Nice Guys Finish First: The Autobiography of Monte Irvin. Monte Irvin & James A. Riley. (Illus.). 256p. 1996. 22.00 (*0-7867-0254-0*) Carroll & Graf.

Nice Guys Finish Last. Gary Jonas. 11p. 1998. pap. 3.00 (*1-893816-01-X*) Ozark Tri.

Nice Guys Finish Last: Management Myths & Reality. Lawrence L. Steinmetz. (Illus.). 247p. 1992. 24.95 (*0-8159-6316-5*) Horizon Pubns.

Nice Jewish Girls: Growing up in America. Ed. by Marlene A. Marks. 352p. 1996. pap. 12.95 (*0-452-27397-8*, Plume) Dutton Plume.

Nice Job! The Guide to Cool, Odd, Risky & Gruesome Ways to Make a Living. Jamie H. Rosen & John Westerdahl. LC 98-56096. 224p. 1999. pap. 14.95 (*1-58008-033-2*) Ten Speed Pr.

Nice Knight for Murder. large type ed. Philip Daniels. (Linford Mystery Library). 240p. 1988. pap. 16.99 (*0-7089-6625-X*, Linford) Ulverscroft.

Nice Little Mystery. large type ed. Eileen Dewhurst. (Mystery Ser.). 416p. 1992. 27.99 (*0-7089-2601-0*) Ulverscroft.

Nice Little Stories Jam-Packed with Depraved Sex & Violence. Michael Hemmingson. 76p. 1995. pap. 5.00 (*1-886988-00-5*) Jasmine Sail.

Nice Murder for Mom. James Yaffe. 1990. mass mkt. 3.50 (*0-373-26044-X*) Harlequin Bks.

Nice New Neighbors. Franz Brandenberg. (Illus.). 32p. (J). (ps-2). 1990. pap. 2.75 (*0-590-44117-5*) Scholastic Inc.

Nice Nurse Nevin. large type ed. Jan Tempest. (Linford Romance Library). 368p. 1989. pap. 11.95 (*0-7089-6661-6*, Linford) Ulverscroft.

Nice People. Clare Curzon. LC 95-1717. 1995. 20.95 (*0-312-13132-1*) St Martin.

Nice People. large type ed. Clare Curzon. 336p. 1995. pap. 20.95 (*0-7862-0361-7*) Thorndike Pr.

Nice People: A Collection of Dutch Short Stories. Gerrit Bussink. (Prose Ser.: No. 23). 195p. 1993. pap. 12.00 (*0-920717-89-6*) Guernica Editions.

Nice People Dancing to Good Country Music. Lee Blessing. 1983. pap. 5.25 (*0-8222-0816-4*) Dramatists Play.

Nice Place to Live: Creating Communities, Fighting Sprawl. 28p. pap. text. write for info. (*0-7872-6483-0*) Kendall-Hunt.

Nice Shot! see Homeplay: Joyful Learning for Children & Adults, Series I

Nice Shot, Snoopy! Charles M. Schulz. (Way of the Fussbudget Is Not Easy Ser.: Vol. 3). (Illus.). 128p. 1988. mass mkt. 3.99 (*0-449-21404-4*, Crest) Fawcett.

Nice Shot, Snoopy! Charles M. Schulz. (J). 1984. 9.09 (*0-606-03872-8*, Pub. by Turtleback) Demco.

Nice Storm for a New Birth. Skie Bender. 80p. 1992. pap. 7.95 (*1-881168-05-0*) Red Danceflr.

Nice Things about Growing Older. William W. Meyer. 68p. (Orig.). 1990. pap. 7.75 (*1-877871-11-7*, 3530) Ed Ministries.

***Nice Timing: Gourmet Meals in Minutes.** Pamela Steel. (Illus.). 208p. 2000. pap. 24.95 (*0-13-018185-4*) P-H.

Nice to See You. Ed. by Anne Waldman. LC 90-2696. (Illus.). 256p. (Orig.). 1991. 24.95 (*0-918273-11-0*) Coffee Hse.

Nice to See You: Homage to Ted Berrigan. Ed. by Anne Waldman. LC 90-2696. (Illus.). 256p. (Orig.). 1991. pap. 14.95 (*0-918273-13-7*) Coffee Hse.

Nice Tries. Ed. by Stuart Barnes & Mike Seabrook. 192p. 1996. pap. 13.95 (*0-575-60044-6*, Pub. by V Gollancz) Trafalgar.

***Nice Try: A Murray Whelan Mystery.** Shane Maloney. LC 99-59581. 272p. 2000. 23.95 (*1-55970-513-2*, Pub. by Arcade Pub Inc) Time Warner.

Nice Try, Tooth Fairy. Mary V. Olson. LC 98-22749. Orig. Title: Dear Tooth Fairy. (Illus.). 32p. (J). (ps-3). 2000. per. 15.00 (*0-689-82422-X*) S&S Bks Yung.

Nice Tuesday: A Memoir. Pat Jordan. LC 98-48779. 352p. 1999. text 23.00 (*1-58238-028-7*, Whitman Coin) St Martin.

***Nice Tuesday: A Memoir.** Pat Jordan. 352p. 2000. pap. 13.95 (*0-312-26362-7*, St Martin Griffin) St Martin.

Nice Wanton. LC 71-133717. (Tudor Facsimile Texts. Old English Plays Ser.: No. 28). reprint ed. 49.50 (*0-404-53328-0*) AMS Pr.

Nice Weekend for a Murder. Max Allan Collins. 208p. 1994. mass mkt. 3.99 (*0-8125-0138-1*, Pub. by Tor Bks) St Martin.

Nice When They Are Young: Contemporary Christianity in Families & Schools. Mairi Levitt. 181p. 1996. text 63.95 (*1-85972-388-8*, Pub. by Avebry) Ashgate Pub Co.

Nice Work. David Lodge. 288p. 1990. pap. 12.95 (*0-14-013396-8*, Penguin Bks) Viking Penguin.

***Nice Work: The Continuing Scandal of Canada's Senate.** Claire Hoy. 320p. 2000. 32.50 (*0-7710-4212-4*) McCland & Stewart.

Nice Work If You Can Get It: My Life in Rhythm & Rhyme. Michael Feinstein. LC 95-2165. (Illus.). 416p. (J). 1995. 24.45 (*0-7868-6093-6*, Pub. by Hyperion) Time Warner.

Nice Work If You Can Get It: My Life in Rhythm & Rhyme. Michael Feinstein. (Illus.). 416p. (J). 1996. pap. 14.45 (*0-7868-8220-4*, Pub. by Hyperion) Time Warner.

Nice Work If You Can Get It - Local Attorney's Fees. 50p. 1971. 9.00 (*0-943136-15-6*) Ctr Analysis Public Issues.

Nicel Legal Life Skills. 1998. mass mkt. 17.00 (*0-314-05445-6*) West Pub.

Nicel Violence Problem. 1995. mass mkt. 4.50 (*0-314-05381-6*) West Pub.

Nicelies at Home. Sandra J. Ross. LC 93-70084. (Nicelies Ser.). (Illus.). 76p. (Orig.). (J). (ps-1). 1993. pap. 5.95 (*1-881235-01-7*) Creat Opport.

Nicelies Go to School. Sandra J. Ross. LC 93-74878. (Nicelies Ser.). (Illus.). 74p. (J). (ps-1). 1994. pap. 5.95 (*1-881235-02-5*) Creat Opport.

Nicelies Series, 4 vols. Sandra J. Ross. (Illus.). (J). (ps-1). 1994. pap. 19.95 (*1-881235-04-1*) Creat Opport.

NICEM Thesaurus. National Information Center for Educational Media. LC 98-72499. 300p. 1998. pap. 59.95 (*0-89320-200-2*) Natl Info Ctr NM.

Nicene & Post-Nicene Fathers Series 2, Vol. 1: Eusebius. Ed. by Philip Schaff & Henry Wace. (Early Church Fathers Ser.). 1952. 30.00 (*0-8028-8115-7*) Eerdmans.

Nicene & Post-Nicene Fathers Series 2, Vol. 2: Socrates Scholasticus. Ed. by Philip Schaff & Henry Wace. (Early Church Fathers Ser.). 1952. 30.00 (*0-8028-8116-5*) Eerdmans.

Nicene & Post-Nicene Fathers Series 2, Vol. 3: Theodoret, Vol. 3. Ed. by Philip Schaff & Henry Wace. (The Early Church Fathers Ser.). 1953. 30.00 (*0-8028-8117-3*) Eerdmans.

Nicene & Post-Nicene Fathers Series 2, Vol. 4: Athanasius. Ed. by Philip Schaff & Henry Wace. (Early Church Fathers Ser.). 1953. 30.00 (*0-8028-8118-1*) Eerdmans.

Nicene & Post-Nicene Fathers Series 2, Vol. 5: Gregory of Nyssa. Ed. by Philip Schaff & Henry Wace. (Early Church Fathers Ser.). 1954. 30.00 (*0-8028-8119-X*) Eerdmans.

Nicene & Post-Nicene Fathers Series 2, Vol. 6: St. Jerome. Ed. by Philip Schaff & Henry Wace. (Early Church Fathers Ser.). 1954. 30.00 (*0-8028-8120-3*) Eerdmans.

Nicene & Post-Nicene Fathers Series 2, Vol. 7: St. Cyril. Ed. by Philip Schaff & Henry Wace. (Early Church Fathers Ser.). 1955. 30.00 (*0-8028-8121-1*) Eerdmans.

Nicene & Post-Nicene Fathers Series 2, Vol. 8: St. Basil. Ed. by Philip Schaff & Henry Wace. (Early Church Fathers Ser.). 1955. 30.00 (*0-8028-8122-X*) Eerdmans.

Nicene & Post-Nicene Fathers Series 2, Vol. 9: St. Hilary of Poitiers. Ed. by Philip Schaff & Henry Wace. (Early Church Fathers Ser.). 1955. 30.00 (*0-8028-8123-8*) Eerdmans.

Nicene & Post-Nicene Fathers Series 2, Vol. 10: St. Ambrose. Ed. by Philip Schaff & Henry Wace. (Early Church Fathers Ser.). 1955. 30.00 (*0-8028-8124-6*) Eerdmans.

Nicene & Post-Nicene Fathers Series 2, Vol. 11: Sulpitius Severus. Ed. by Philip Schaff & Henry Wace. (Early Church Fathers Ser.). 1955. 30.00 (*0-8028-8125-4*) Eerdmans.

Nicene & Post-Nicene Fathers Series 2, Vol. 12: Leo the Great. Ed. by Philip Schaff & Henry Wace. (Early Church Fathers Ser.). 1956. 30.00 (*0-8028-8126-2*) Eerdmans.

Nicene & Post-Nicene Fathers Series 2, Vol. 13: Gregory the Great. Ed. by Philip Schaff & Henry Wace. (Early Church Fathers Ser.). 1956. 30.00 (*0-8028-8127-0*) Eerdmans.

Nicene & Post-Nicene Fathers Series 2, Vol. 14: Seven Ecumenical Councils. Ed. by Philip Schaff & Henry Wace. (Early Church Fathers Ser.). 1956. 30.00 (*0-8028-8128-9*) Eerdmans.

Nicene & Post-Nicene Fathers, Series 1--St. Augustine Vol. 1: Prolegomena. Ed. by Philip Schaff. LC 96-211918. (Early Church Fathers Ser.). 1956. 30.00 (*0-8028-8098-3*) Eerdmans.

Nicene & Post-Nicene Fathers, Series 1 -- St. Augustine Vol. 2: City of God. Ed. by Philip Schaff. (Early Church Fathers Ser.). 1956. 30.00 (*0-8028-8099-1*) Eerdmans.

Nicene & Post-Nicene Fathers, Series 1--St. Augustine Vol. 3: Doctrinal-Moral Treatises. Ed. by Philip Schaff. (Early Church Fathers Ser.). 1956. 30.00 (*0-8028-8100-9*) Eerdmans.

Nicene & Post-Nicene Fathers, Series 1--St. Augustine Vol. 4: Anti-Manicheean & Anti-Donatist. Ed. by Philip Schaff. (Early Church Fathers Ser.). 1956. 30.00 (*0-8028-8101-7*) Eerdmans.

Nicene & Post-Nicene Fathers, Series 1 -- St. Augustine Vol. 5: Anti-Pelagian. Ed. by Philip Schaff. (Early Church Fathers Ser.). 1956. 30.00 (*0-8028-8102-5*) Eerdmans.

Nicene & Post-Nicene Fathers, Series 1--St. Augustine Vol. 6: Sermon on the Mount, Etc. Ed. by Philip Schaff. (Early Church Fathers Ser.). 1956. 30.00 (*0-8028-8103-3*) Eerdmans.

Nicene & Post-Nicene Fathers, Series 1--St. Augustine Vol. 7: Homilies. Ed. by Philip Schaff. (Early Church Fathers Ser.). 1956. 30.00 (*0-8028-8104-1*) Eerdmans.

Nicene & Post-Nicene Fathers, Series 1-St. Augustine Vol. 8: Exposition on Psalms. Ed. by Philip Schaff. (Early Church Fathers Ser.). 1956. 30.00 (*0-8028-8105-X*) Eerdmans.

Nicene & Post-Nicene Fathers, Series 1--St. Chrysostom Vol. 13: Homilies on the Epistles. Ed. by Philip Schaff. (Early Church Fathers Ser.). 1956. 30.00 (*0-8028-8111-4*) Eerdmans.

Nicene & Post-Nicene Fathers, Series 1--St. Crysistom Vol. 12: Homilies on Corinthians. Ed. by Philip Schaff. (Early Church Fathers Ser.). 1956. 30.00 (*0-8028-8110-6*) Eerdmans.

Nicene & Post-Nicene Fathers, Series 1--St. Crysostom Vol. 1: Prolegomena. Ed. by Philip Schaff. (Early Church Fathers Ser.). 1956. 30.00 (*0-8028-8107-6*) Eerdmans.

Nicene & Post-Nicene Fathers, Series 1--St. Crysostom Vol. 10: Homilies on Matthew. Ed. by Philip Schaff. 1956. 30.00 (*0-8028-8108-4*) Eerdmans.

Nicene & Post-Nicene Fathers, Series 1--St. Crysostom Vol. 11: Homilies on Acts, Romans. Ed. by Philip Schaff. (Early Church Fathers Ser.). 1956. 30.00 (*0-8028-8109-2*) Eerdmans.

Nicene & Post-Nicene Fathers, Series 1--St. Crysostom Vol. 14: Homilies on John, Hebrews. Ed. by Philip Schaff. (Early Church Fathers Ser.). 1956. 30.00 (*0-8028-8112-2*) Eerdmans.

Nicene Creed for Today. Gregory Simpson. LC 99-41516. 112p. 1999. pap. 8.95 (*1-55725-236-X*, 930-023, Pub. by Paraclete MA) BookWorld.

Nicene Creed, Illumined by Modern Thought. Geddes MacGregor. LC 80-19348. 163p. reprint ed. pap. 50.60 (*0-608-11916-4*, 202322000032) Bks Demand.

Nicephore Gregoras: Calcul de l'Eclipse de Soleil du 16 Juillet, 1330. Joseph Mogenet et al. (Corpus des Astronomes Byzantins Ser.: Vol. I). (FRE.). 222p. (C). 1983. pap. 54.00 (*90-70265-34-6*, Pub. by Gieben) J Benjamins Pubng Co.

Nicephori Archiepiscopi Constantinopolitani Opuscula Historica. Nicephorus. Ed. by Carl G. De Boor. LC 75-7311. (Roman History Ser.). (GRE.). 1975. reprint ed. 28.95 (*0-405-07193-0*) Ayer.

Nicephori Basilacae. Ed. by Garzya. (GRE.). 1984. 47.50 (*3-322-00164-4*, T1551, Pub. by B G Teubner) U of Mich Pr.

Nicest Guy in America. Angela Benson. 352p. 1997. mass mkt. 4.99 (*0-7860-0443-6*, Pinncle Kensgtn) Kensgtn Pub Corp.

Nicest Guy in America. large type ed. Angela Benson. LC 98-3737. 1998. 23.95 (*0-7862-1461-9*) Thorndike Pr.

Nicest Thing That Happened to Me Today Was... Joel Ehrendreich. 112p. (Orig.). 1994. pap. 9.50 (*0-9640540-0-0*) Nicest Thing.

Niceta of Remesiana: Sulpicius Severus, Vincent of Lerins, Prosper of Aquitaine: Grace & Free Will. Nicetas. Tr. by Gerald G. Walsh et al. LC 50-5703. (Fathers of the Church Ser.: Vol. 7). 449p. 1970. reprint ed. pap. 139.20 (*0-7837-9204-2*, 204995400004) Bks Demand.

Nicetae Choniatae Historiae, 2 vols. Ed. by Ioannes Van Dieten. (Corpus Fontium Historiae Byzantinae Ser.: Berolinensis Vol. XI). (C). 1975. 638.50 (*3-11-004528-1*) De Gruyter.

Nicetas Eugenianus: De Drospillae et Chariclis Amoribus Libros IX. Ed. by Fabricus Conca. (London Studies in Classical Philology: Vol. 24). (GRE & LAT.). 295p. 1991. 94.00 (*90-70265-95-8*, Pub. by Gieben) J Benjamins Pubng Co.

Nich Nur Fur Johnny see Not for Johnny Only: Recollections by My American Son

***Niche E-Tailing Report: Quantitative Data, Case Studies, Analyses.** unabridged ed. Harry Wolhandler. Ed. by Margaret Gurney. (Illus.). 171p. 1999. 2895.00 (*1-58637-006-5*) ActivMedia.

Niche Market Report: Discovering, Understanding & Selling to the Niche Consumer of the 21st Century. Walt F. Goodridge. (Illus.). 175p. 1999. pap. 39.95 (*0-9629202-8-2*) Co Called W.

Niche Marketing for Radio. Godfrey W. Herweg & Ashley P. Herweg. LC 97-16724. 288p. 1997. pap. text 37.95 (*0-240-80202-0*, Focal) Buttrwrth-Heinemann.

Niche Marketing for Writers, Speakers, & Entrepreneurs: How to Make Yourself Indispensable, Slightly Immortal, & Lifelong Rich in 18 Months! Gordon Burgett. 192p. (Orig.). 1993. pap. 14.95 (*0-910167-22-2*) Comm Unltd CA.

***Niche Narrows: New & Selected Poems.** Samuel Menashe. 2000. 37.95 (*1-58498-013-3*); pap. 16.95 (*1-58498-012-5*) Talisman Hse.

Niche of Lights. Tr. by David Buchman. LC 98-25466. (slamic Translations Ser.). 300p. 1998. 24.95 (*0-8425-2353-7*, Pub. by Brigham) U Ch Pr.

Niche Selling: How to Find Your Customer in a Crowded Market. William T. Brooks. 225p. 1991. text 30.00 (*1-55623-499-6*, Irwn Prfssnl) McGraw-Hill Prof.

Niche Series. Beth Linn. (Illus.). 48p. 1991. pap. 16.95 (*0-89822-066-1*) Visual Studies.

Niche Strategies for Downtown Revitalization. N. David Milder. LC 97-65110. 140p. 1997. pap. 69.95 (*0-915910-40-3*) Downtown Res.

Niche Threat: Deterring the Use of Chemical & Biological Weapons. Ed. by Stuart E. Johnson. 125p. (C). 1998. pap. text 30.00 (*0-7881-4858-3*) DIANE Pub.

Niche Threat: Deterring the Use of Chemical & Biological Weapons. Stuart E. Johnson. 135p. 1997. per. 5.50 (*0-16-054403-3*) USGPO.

Nichecraft: The Art of Being Special. 2nd rev. ed. Lynda C. Falkenstein. (Illus.). 272p. 1993. pap. 17.95 (*0-9625747-9-1*) Niche OR.

***Nichecraft: Using Your Specialness to Focus Your Business, Corner Your Market & Make Customers Seek You Out.** 2nd ed. Lynda Falkenstein. 320p. 2000. pap. 24.95 (*0-9625747-2-4*) Niche OR.

Nichecraft - The Art of Being Special: How to Make Niches That Work in Business, Profession, & Career. Lynda C. Falkenstein. 200p. (Orig.). 1990. pap. 14.95 (*0-9625747-0-8*) Niche OR.

Nichemanship: How to Carve Your Niche in Life & Business. 2nd rev. ed. Larry Perry & Ernie Arthur. 150p. 1996. 14.95 (*0-942442-06-7*) Perry Publns.

Niches in the World of Textiles: Papers Presented at the Textile Institute's 1996 World Conference Tampere, Finland. 1998. 395.00 (*1-870812-97-2*, Pub. by Textile Inst) St Mut.

***Nichiren: Leader of Buddhist Reformation in Japan.** J. A. Christensen. LC 99-88875. 2000. pap. write for info. (*0-87573-086-8*) Jain Pub Co.

Nichiren: Selected Writings. Laurel R. Rodd. LC 79-17054. (Asian Studies at Hawaii: No. 26). 201p. reprint ed. pap. 62.40 (*0-608-13710-3*, 202044400018) Bks Demand.

Nichiren's Senji-Sho: An Essay on the Selection of the Proper Time. Kenneth Dollarhide. LC 82-21687. (Studies in Asian Thought & Religion: Vol. 1). 184p. 1983. lib. bdg. 79.95 (*0-88946-051-5*) E Mellen.

Nichol Pocket Bible Encyclopedia. C. R. Nichol. 1984. pap. 2.50 (*0-915547-55-4*) Abilene Christ U.

Nicholas. J. O. Schrag. (Illus.). 35p. (Orig.). (J). (gr. k-3). 1991. pap. 7.95 (*0-945530-05-6*) Wordsworth KS.

Nicholas: The Boy Who Became Santa. CCC of America Staff. (Illus.). 35p. (J). (ps-4). 1989. 14.99 incl. VHS (*1-56814-003-7*) CCC of America.

Nicholas: The Boy Who Became Santa. CCC of America Staff. (Illus.). 35p. (J). (ps-6). 1989. pap. text 1.49 (*0-685-62400-5*) CCC of America.

Nicholas Africano: Paintings, 1976-1983. Mitchell D. Kahan. (Illus.). 20p. (Orig.). 1983. 3.00 (*0-88259-097-9*) NCMA.

***Nicholas & Alexandra.** Abrams Staff. (YA). 1998. pap. 9.41 (*0-8109-2768-3*, Pub. by Abrams) Time Warner.

Nicholas & Alexandra. Robert K. Massie. 624p. 1985. mass mkt. 7.99 (*0-440-36358-6*, LE) Dell.

Nicholas & Alexandra: The Last Family of Tsarist Russia. George Vilinbakhov et al. LC 98-27383. (Illus.). 400p. 1998. 75.00 (*0-8109-3687-9*, Pub. by Abrams) Time Warner.

***Nicholas & Alexandra: The Story of the Love That Ended an Empire.** Robert K. Massie. (Illus.). 624p. 2000. pap. 18.00 (*0-345-43831-0*) Ballantine Pub Grp.

***Nicholas & Alexandra Paper Dolls.** Tom Tierney. (Illus.). 1998. pap. 4.95 (*0-486-40372-6*) Dover.

***Nicholas & the Elves.** Terry Corbett. (Illus.). 20p. (Orig.). (J). 1999. pap. 5.99 (*1-929731-03-5*) Rowfant.

Nicholas at the Library. Hazel J. Hutchins. (Illus.). 32p. (J). (ps-2). 1990. pap. 5.95 (*1-55037-132-0*, Pub. by Annick); text 16.95 (*1-55037-134-7*, Pub. by Annick) Firefly Bks Ltd.

Nicholas Bentley Stoningpot III. Ann McGovern. LC 91-77614. (Illus.). 32p. (J). (ps-3). 1992. lib. bdg. 14.95 (*1-56397-104-6*) Boyds Mills Pr.

Nicholas Bentley Stoningpot III. Ann McGovern. 1997. 11.19 (*0-606-12782-8*, Pub. by Turtleback) Demco.

Nicholas Berdyaev. G. Seaver. 1973. 59.95 (*0-8490-0730-5*) Gordon Pr.

Nicholas Biddle in Greece: The Journals & Letters of 1806. Ed. by R. A. McNeal. LC 92-35459. (Illus.). 240p. 1993. 40.00 (*0-271-00914-4*) Pa St U Pr.

Nicholas Biddle, Nationalist & Public Banker, 1786-1844. Thomas P. Govan. LC 59-12286. (Midway Reprint Ser.). 441p. reprint ed. pap. 136.80 (*0-608-16150-0*, 202404200035) Bks Demand.

Nicholas Blood, Candidate. Arthur Henry. LC 71-38654. (Black Heritage Library Collection). 1977. reprint ed. 18.95 (*0-8369-9012-9*) Ayer.

***Nicholas Claus Hollyberry: A Christmas Story.** large type ed. Sandy Cook. (Illus.). 59p. 1999. pap. 24.99 (*0-9674142-0-2*, 001) Roseheart Pubng.

Nicholas County Kentucky, 1850 Census: 1850 Census. Rowena Lawson. iv, 92p. (Orig.). 1983. pap. 12.50 (*0-917890-34-5*) Heritage Bk.

***Nicholas County, KY Execution Bk. A: 1801-1878 (Sheriff's Orders)** Carrie Eldridge. (Illus.). 51p. 1999. pap. 15.00 (*1-928979-30-0*) C Eldridge.

***Nicholas County, KY Stray Bk. 1: 1805-1811.** Carrie Eldridge. (Illus.). 66p. 1999. pap. 15.00 (*1-928979-31-9*) C Eldridge.

***Nicholas County, KY Stray Bk. 2: 1813-1820.** Carrie Eldridge. (Illus.). 62p. 1999. pap. 15.00 (*1-928979-32-7*) C Eldridge.

***Nicholas County, KY Stray Bk. 3: 1820-1870.** Carrie Eldridge. (Illus.). 77p. 1999. pap. 15.00 (*1-928979-33-5*) C Eldridge.

Nicholas Crabbe: or The One & the Many, a Romance. Frederick C. Rolfe & Cecil Woolf. LC 77-11680. 1977. reprint ed. lib. bdg. 65.00 (*0-8371-9816-X*, RONC, Greenwood Pr) Greenwood.

Nicholas Cricket. Joyce Maxner. LC 88-33076. (Illus.). 32p. (J). (gr. k-3). 1989. 14.00 (*0-06-024216-7*); lib. bdg. 13.89 (*0-06-024222-1*) HarpC Child Bks.

Nicholas Cricket. Joyce Maxner. LC 88-33076. (Trophy Picture Bk.). (Illus.). 28p. (J). (gr. k-3). 1991. pap. 4.95 (*0-06-443275-0*, HarpTrophy) HarpC Child Bks.

***Nicholas Effect: A Boy's Gift to the World.** Reg Green. Ed. by Linda Lamb. LC 99-22558. (Illus.). 246p. 1999. 24.95 (*1-56592-597-1*) OReilly & Assocs.

***Nicholas Effect: A Boy's Gift to the World.** Reg Green. (Illus.). 247p. 2000. pap. 12.95 (*1-56592-860-1*) OReilly & Assocs.

***Nicholas F. Forell.** Joseph P. Nicoletti & Nicholas F. Forell. LC 99-54561. (EERI Oral History Ser.). 1999. write for info. (*0-943198-98-4*) Earthquake Eng.

An Asterisk (*) at the beginning of an entry indicates that the title is appearing for the first time.

Nicholas Ferrar of Little Gidding. A. L. Maycock. LC 80-16684. 334p. reprint ed. pap. 103.60 (0-8357-9131-9, 201934500011) Bks Demand.

Nicholas Gengenbach's Musica Nova: Newe Singekunst, Commentary, Critical Edition & Translation. (Theorists in Translation Ser.: No. 14). (ENG, GER & LAT.). vi, 294p. 1996. lib. bdg. 52.00 (0-931902-44-4) Inst Mediaeval Mus.

Nicholas Gouin Dufief of Philadelphia: Franco-American Bookseller, 1776-1834. Madeleine B. Stern. (Philobiblon Series in Philadelphia Booklore: No. 1). (Illus.). 75p. 1988. 37.50 (0-9620773-0-5) Philobiblon Club.

Nicholas Grimshaw & Partners. Ed. by D. McCorquodale & Monica Pidgeon. (Illus.). 24p. 1997. pap. 39.95 incl. cd-rom (1-901033-00-7, Pub. by Art Bks Intl) Partners Pubs Grp.

Nicholas Hawksmoor & the Replanning of Oxford. Roger White. (Illus.). 90p. 1998. pap. 15.95 (1-85444-094-2, 0942) OUP.

Nicholas Hilliard (1546/7-1618) The Arte of Limning. Ed. by R. K. Thornton & T. G. Cain. pap. write for info. (0-85635-971-8, Pub. by Carcanet Pr) Paul & Co Pubs.

Nicholas Homoky LC 98-192466. 48 p. 1997. write for info. (1-899296-03-4) Am Acad Hospice.

Nicholas Horsfield: Walker Art Gallery Liverpool 18 July-28 September 1997. Nicolas Horsfield & Walker Art Gallery Staff. LC 98-165906. 111p. 1997. write for info. (0-906367-86-7) Natl Mus & Galls.

Nicholas Hutchins of Lynn & Groton, Massachusetts & His Descendants with a Genealogy of Allied Families. Marvin C. Hutchins. LC 88-70559. (Illus.). xviii, 398p. 1989. 14.50 (0-936124-13-X) C Boyer.

Nicholas I, Patriarch of Constantinople: Miscellaneous Writings. Ed. by L. G. Westerink. LC 80-70736. (Dumbarton Oaks Texts: Vol. 6). 160p. 1983. 28.00 (0-88402-089-4) Dumbarton Oaks.

Nicholas II. Dominic C. Lieven. 304p. 1996. pap. 16.95 (0-312-14379-6) St Martin.

Nicholas II: Last of the Tsars. Marc Ferro. Tr. by Brian Pearce. (Illus.). 336p. 1995. reprint ed. pap. 17.95 (0-19-509382-8) OUP.

Nicholas Kaldor: The Economics & Politics of Capitalism As a Dynamic System. Ferdinando Targetti. (Illus.). 416p. 1992. text 65.00 (0-19-828348-2) OUP.

Nicholas Kaldor & the Real World. Marjorie S. Turner. LC 93-21759. 254p. (gr. 13). 1993. text 79.95 (1-56324-147-1) M E Sharpe.

Nicholas Lanier: Master of the Kings of Musick. Michael I. Wilson. (Illus.). 320p. 1994. 83.95 (0-85967-999-3, Pub. by Scolar Pr) Ashgate Pub Co.

Nicholas Love at Waseda: Proceedings of the International Conference, 20-22 July, 1995. Ed. by Shoichi Oguro et al. LC 97-1851. (Illus.). 305p. 1997. 75.00 (0-85991-500-X, DS Brewer) Boydell & Brewer.

Nicholas Love's: Mirror of the Blessed Life of Jesus Christ, a Critical Edition. Ed. by Michael Sargent. LC 92-30252. (Medieval Texts Ser.: Vol. 18). (Illus.). 496p. 1992. text 80.00 (0-8240-5896-8, H1233) Garland.

Nicholas Minorita: Chronica (The Early 13th Century Poverty Controversey) Gedeon Gal & David Flood. (History Ser.: No. 12). 1996. pap. 85.00 (1-57659-118-2) Franciscan Inst.

Nicholas Nickleby. Charles Dickens. LC 93-1856. 1993. 20.00 (0-679-42307-9) Everymns Lib.

Nicholas Nickleby. Charles Dickens. 926p. 1998. pap. 6.95 (0-19-283623-4) OUP.

Nicholas Nickleby. Charles Dickens. 992p. 1998. mass mkt. 5.99 (0-8125-6584-3, Pub. by Tor Bks) St Martin.

Nicholas Nickleby. Charles Dickens. 864p. 1999. pap. 7.95 (0-14-043512-3, Penguin Classics) Viking Penguin.

Nicholas Nickleby. Charles Dickens. (Classics Library). (YA). (gr. 7 up). Date not set. pap. 3.95 (1-85326-264-1, 2641WW, Pub. by Wrdsworth Edits) NTC Contemp Pub Co.

Nicholas Nickleby. Intro. by David Parker. 416p. 1994. 5.95 (0-460-87480-2, Everyman's Classic Lib) Tuttle Pubng.

Nicholas Nickleby. Charles Dickens. 1990. reprint ed. lib. bdg. 49.95 (0-89966-681-7) Buccaneer Bks.

Nicholas Nickleby: Playscript. Guy Williams. LC 91-51102. 1992. pap. 6.00 (0-88734-515-8) Players Pr.

Nicholas Nickleby - Full. Charles Dickens. 1981. 5.50 (0-87129-416-8, N27) Dramatic Pub.

Nicholas Nickleby, 1-Act. Tim Kelley. 27p. (YA). (gr. 10 up). 1981. pap. 3.95 (0-87129-901-1, N29) Dramatic Pub.

Nicholas Nixon: Pictures of People. Peter Galassi & Nicholas Nixon. (Illus.). 128p. 1990. pap. 22.50 (0-8109-6057-5, Pub. by Abrams) Time Warner.

Nicholas Nixon: Pictures of People. Peter Galassi & Nicholas Nixon. (Illus.). 1988. 45.00 (0-87070-437-0, 0-8109-6056-7); pap. 22.50 (0-87070-438-9, 0-8109-6057-5, Pub. by Mus of Modern Art) Abrams.

Nicholas of Autrecourt: His Correspondence with Master Giles & Bernhard of Arezzo: a Critical Edition from the Two Persian Manuscripts. Tr. & Intro. by L. M. De Rijk. LC 93-48276. (Studien und Texte zur Geistesgeschichte des Mittelalters Ser.: No. 42). ix, 241p. 1994. 113.50 (90-04-09988-3) Brill Academic Pubs.

Nicholas of Cusa: In Search of God & Wisdom. Ed. by Gerald Christianson & Thomas M. Izbicki. LC 90-22415. (Studies in the History of Christian Thought: No. 45). xvi, 298p. 1990. 105.50 (90-04-09362-1) Brill Academic Pubs.

Nicholas of Cusa: Metaphysical Speculations. Nicholas of Cusa. Tr. & Pref. by Jasper Hopkins. LC 97-72945. xii, 333p. (C). 1998. text 25.00 (0-938060-47-3) Banning Pr.

Nicholas of Cusa: Selected Spiritual Writings. Tr. & Intro. by H. Lawrence Bond. LC 96-44466. (Classics of Western Spirituality Ser.: No. 89). 384p. (Orig.). 1997. 34.95 (0-8091-0482-2); pap. 24.95 (0-8091-3698-8) Paulist Pr.

Nicholas of Cusa: The Catholic Concordance. Paul E. Sigmund. (Cambridge Texts in the History of Political Thought Ser.). 377p. (C). 1996. pap. text 24.95 (0-521-56773-4) Cambridge U Pr.

***Nicholas of Cusa Vol. 2: Metaphysical Speculations.** Jasper Hopkins. LC 97-72945. x, 437p. (C). 2000. text 30.00 (0-938060-48-1) Banning Pr.

Nicholas of Cusa & the Renaissance. F. Edward Cranz. Ed. by Thomas M. Izbicki & Gerald Christianson. (Variorum Collected Studies Ser.: Vol. CS654). 280p. 1999. text 97.95 (0-86078-801-6, Pub. by Ashgate Pub) Ashgate Pub Co.

Nicholas of Cusa on God As Not-Other: A Translation & an Appraisal of De Li Non Aliud. 3rd rev. ed. Jasper Hopkins. xii, 212p. (C). 1987. text 20.00 (0-938060-38-4) Banning Pr.

Nicholas of Cusa on Interreligious Harmony: Text, Concordance & Translation of De Pace Fidei. Ed. by James E. Biechler & H. Lawrence Bond. LC 90-25778. (Texts & Studies in Religion: Vol. 55). 254p. 1991. lib. bdg. 89.95 (0-88946-736-6) E Mellen.

Nicholas of Cusa on Learned Ignorance: A Translation & an Appraisal of De Docta Ignorantia. 2nd ed. Jasper Hopkins. LC 80-82907. ix, 205p. (C). 1985. text 23.00 (0-938060-30-9); pap. text 10.00 (0-938060-27-9) Banning Pr.

Nicholas of Cusa on Wisdom & Knowledge. Jasper Hopkins. xii, 543p. (C). 1996. text 35.00 (0-938060-46-5) Banning Pr.

Nicholas of Cusa's De Pace Fidei & Cribratio Alkorani: Translation & Analysis. rev. ed. Jasper Hopkins. LC 89-85812. viii, 252p. (C). 1990. text 30.00 (0-938060-41-4) Banning Pr.

Nicholas of Cusa's Debate with John Wenck: A Translation & an Appraisal of De Ignota Litteratura & Apologia Doctae Ignorantiae. 3rd rev. ed. Jasper Hopkins. LC 80-82908. viii, 119p. (C). 1988. text 23.00 (0-938060-40-6) Banning Pr.

Nicholas of Cusa's Dialectical Mysticism: Text, Translation, & Interpretive Study of De Visione Dei. 2nd ed. Jasper Hopkins. ix, 397p. 1998. pap. text 10.00 (0-938060-45-7) Banning Pr.

Nicholas of Cusa's Dialectical Mysticism: Text, Translation, & Interpretive Study of De Visione Dei. 2nd rev. ed. Jasper Hopkins. LC 84-71736. ix, 397p. (C). 1988. text 25.00 (0-938060-39-2) Banning Pr.

Nicholas of Cusa's Metaphysic of Contraction. Jasper Hopkins. LC 82-71704. ix, 197p. (C). 1983. text 23.00 (0-938060-25-2) Banning Pr.

***Nicholas Of Lyra: The Senses of Scripture.** Philip D.W. Krey & Lesley Smith. (Studies in the History of Christian Thought: Vol. 90). (Illus.). 360p. 1999. text 84.00 (90-04-11295-2) Brill Academic Pubs.

Nicholas of Lyra's Apocalypse Commentary. Nicholas & Consortium for the Teaching of the Middle Ages Sta. Tr. by Philip D. Krey from LAT. LC 96-52918. (Commentary Ser.). 1997. pap. 10.00 (1-879288-78-8) Medieval Inst.

***Nicholas Pipe.** Robert D. San Souci. (Picture Puffin Ser.). (Illus.). 32p. (J). (gr. k-4). 2000. pap. 6.99 (0-14-056520-5, PuffinBks) Peng Put Young Read.

Nicholas Poussin. Janina Michalkow. (GER.). 164p. 1980. 99.00 (0-7855-1600-X, Pub. by Collets) St Mut.

Nicholas Poussin: Friendship & the Love of Painting. Elizabeth Cropper & Charles Dempsey. LC 95-5243. 336p. 1996. text 95.00 (0-691-04449-X, Pub. by Princeton U Pr) Cal Prin Full Svc.

Nicholas Roerich. 2nd ed. G. Paelian. LC 74-11757. 1996. pap. 12.00 (0-911794-34-4) Saraydarian Inst.

Nicholas Roerich: A Short Biography. Roerich, Nicholas, Museum Staff. 1.50 (0-686-79662-4) Agni Yoga Soc.

Nicholas Roerich: The Life & Art of a Russian Master. Jacqueline Decter. (Illus.). 224p. 1989. 39.95 (0-89281-156-0, Park St Pr) Inner Tradit.

Nicholas Rowe & Christian Tragedy. John D. Canfield. LC 76-39917. (Illus.). 224p. reprint ed. pap. 69.50 (0-7837-4945-7, 204461100004) Bks Demand.

Nicholas Rubakin: A Life for Books. Alfred E. Senn. (Russian Biography Ser.: No. 1). (Illus.). 1977. 16.00 (0-89250-125-1) Orient Res Partners.

Nicholas I: Emperor & Autocrat of All the Russias. W. Bruce Lincoln. 424p. 1989. reprint ed. pap. text 16.00 (0-87580-548-5) N Ill U Pr.

Nicholas I & Official Nationality in Russia, 1825-1855. Nicholas V. Riasanovsky. LC 59-11316. (Russian & East European Studies). 308p. reprint ed. pap. 95.50 (0-7837-4750-0, 204449700003) Bks Demand.

Nicholas, The Pumpkins & the Squirrel. Ann C. VanderMaten. (Illus.). 32p. (J). (gr. k-3). 1994. pap. text 6.95 (0-9643247-0-9) AtwoZ Pubng.

Nicholas II. Helene Carrere D'Encausse. Tr. by George Holoch from FRE. LC 99-48898. 336p. 2000. 39.95 (0-8419-1397-8) Holmes & Meier.

Nicholas II: The Life & Reign of Russia's Last Monarch. Robert D. Warth. LC 97-5862. 360p. 1997. 65.00 (0-275-95832-9, Praeger Pubs) Greenwood.

Nicholas Vasilieff: A Retrospective Exhibition. Stephanie Terenzio et al. 144p. 1978. write for info. (0-918386-21-7) W Benton Mus.

Nicholas White Family, 1643-1900. T. J. Lothrop. (Illus.). 493p. 1989. reprint ed. pap. 74.00 (0-8328-1253-6); reprint ed. lib. bdg. 82.00 (0-8328-1252-8) Higginson Bk Co.

Nicholas Wiseman & the Transformation of English Catholicism. Richard J. Schiefen. LC 84-7763. (Illus.). 416p. 1984. 32.50 (0-915762-15-3) Patmos Pr.

Nichole Digs a Hole. Barbara Gregorich. (Start to Read! Ser.). (Illus.). 32p. (J). (ps-3). 1993. 3.99 (0-88743-420-7, 06072) Sch Zone Pub Co.

Nicholi. Cooper Edens. LC 94-34340. (Illus.). (J). 1996. 15.00 (0-671-50545-9) S&S Bks Yung.

Nicholi. Cooper Edens. LC 94-34340. (Illus.). 40p. (J). (ps-2). 1997. mass mkt. 16.00 (0-689-80495-4) S&S Childrens.

Nicholl's Concise Guide to the Navigation Examinations, Vol. 2. 12th ed. Edward Coolen. (Illus.). 492p. 1995. 125.00 (0-85174-635-7) Sheridan.

Nicholls of Nesbit Street. large type ed. Mary L. Temple. 240p. 1994. 27.99 (0-7089-3140-5) Ulverscroft.

Nicholl's Seamanship & Nautical Knowledge. 27th ed. Ed. by A. N. Cockroft. 383p. 1997. text 75.00 (0-85174-654-3) Sheridan.

Nicholls's Concise Guide to the Navigation Examinations, Vol. 1. 10th rev. ed. Rev. by E. J. Coolen. (Illus.). 1012p. 1987. reprint ed. text 155.00 (0-85174-539-3, Pub. by Brown Son & Ferguson) Sheridan.

Nicholls's Seamanship & Nautical Knowledge. rev. ed. Rev. by A. N. Cockroft. (C). 1987. 150.00 (0-85174-462-1) St Mut.

Nichols Cyclopedia of Legal Forms, 1925-1990, 31 vols. Ed. by Publisher's Editorial Staff. LC 73-165177. 1320.00 (0-685-09239-9) West Group.

Nichols Debtor-Creditor Practice Forms, 3 vols. CBC Editorial Staff. (Commercial Law Ser.). 1993. 320.00 (0-685-68856-9) West Group.

Nichols Debtor-Creditor Practice Forms, 3 vols. John Tingley. 1993. 350.00 (0-318-70282-7) West Group.

Nichols File of "The Gentleman's Magazine" Attributions of Authorship & Other Documentation in Editorial Papers at the Folger Library. James M. Kuist. LC 80-52296. 347p. 1982. reprint ed. pap. 107.60 (0-608-01959-3, 206261400003) Bks Demand.

Nichols Monthly: A Magazine of Social Science & Progressive Literature, Set, Vols. 1-3. (Free Love in America Ser.). reprint ed. 84.50 (0-404-60976-7) AMS Pr.

Nichols on Eminent Domain, 18 vols. Julius Sackman. 1956. ring bd. 2620.00 (0-8205-1460-8) Bender.

Nichols Plays 1. Peter Nichols. (Methuen World Dramatists Ser.). 376p. (C). 1991. pap. 17.95 (0-413-64870-2, A0560) Heinemann.

Nichols Plays 2. Peter Nichols. (Methuen World Dramatists Ser.). 498p. (C). 1992. pap. 13.95 (0-413-65070-7, A0561) Heinemann.

Nicholson Children's London. Guides Nicholson. 1996. pap. text 11.95 (0-7028-2943-9) Hammond World.

Nicholson London Guide: The Most Comprehensive Guide to London. Guides Nicholson. 1997. pap. text 12.95 (0-7028-2743-6) Hammond World.

Nicholson's Small Press Tirade. Jeff Nicholson. (Illus.). 104p. (Orig.). 1994. pap. 7.95 (1-885047-01-0) Bad Habit.

Nichomachean Ethics. Aristotle. (Classics of World Literature Ser.). 1997. pap. 5.95 (1-85326-461-X, 461XWW, Pub. by Wrdsworth Edits) NTC Contemp Pub Co.

Nichomachean Ethics. Tr. by J. E. Welldon. LC 86-64008. (Great Books in Philosophy). 354p. 1987. pap. 8.95 (0-87975-378-1) Prometheus Bks.

Nicht - Assyrer Neuassyrischer Darstellungen. Markus Wafler. (Alter Orient und Altes Testament Ser.: Vol. 26). (GER.). 344p. 1975. text 59.50 (3-7887-0468-3) NeukirchenerV.

Nicht (Aus, in, Uber, Von) Osterreich: Zur Osterreichischen Literatur, Zu Celan, Bachmann, Bernhard und Anderen 2., Unverand. Auflage. 2nd ed. Tamas Lichtmann. (GER.). 319p. 1996. 57.95 (3-631-30811-6) P Lang Pubng.

Nicht-Euklidische Geometrie. Felix Klein. LC 59-10281. 14.95 (0-8284-0129-2) Chelsea Pub.

Nicht Mehr Bretonisch? Sprachkonflikt in der Landlichen Bretagne. Eva Vetter. (Sprache Im Kontext Ser.: Bd. 2). (Illus.). 196p. 1997. 42.95 (3-631-30484-6) P Lang Pubng.

Nicht O' the Blunt Claymore: A Jacobean Farce Alan Richardson. LC 75-325713. (Scottish Plays Ser.). 95p. 1975. write for info. (0-85174-220-3) Brown Son & Ferguson.

Nicht-Seminomatoese Hodentumoren. Ed. by H. J. Illiger et al. (Beitraege Zur Onkologie, Contributions to Oncology Ser.: Vol. 8). (Illus.). x, 298p. 1982. pap. 43.50 (3-8055-3065-X) S Karger.

Nicht Umsonst und Nicht aus Liebe. Brunhilde Wagner. (Hildesheimer Schriftenreihe Zur Sozialpadagogik und Sozialarbeit Ser.: Vol. 3). (GER.). iv, 204p. 1993. write for info. (3-487-09724-9) G Olms Pubs.

Nicht Wie Die Schafe Zur Schlachbank see Against All Hope: Resistance in the Nazi Concentration Camps, 1938-1945

Nicht wie die Schafe zur Schlachtbank: Widerstand in den nationalsozialistischen Konzentrationslagern. Hermann Langbein. (GER.). 1997. pap. 18.00 (3-596-23486-7, Pub. by Fischer Tasch) Intl Bk Import.

***Nichteheliche Lebensgemeinschaften Als Problem Fur das Staatliche und Kirchliche Recht.** Gerhard Hoppler. (Illus.). 402p. 1999. 56.95 (3-631-34250-0) P Lang Pubng.

Nichtov M'Aleph V'ad Tav: Spirit Duplicating Writing Primer. Avivia Langsam. (Illus.). 1997. pap., teacher ed. 18.00 (0-915152-03-7, A041) Langsam Publishing Co.

Nichtpriesterliche Josephsgeschichte (Gen 37-50) Hans-Christoph Schmitt. (C). 1979. 82.35 (3-11-007834-1) De Gruyter.

Nichu: A Japanese School. John Singleton. Ed. by Louise S. Spindler & George D. Spindler. (Case Studies in Education & Culture). 144p. 1982. reprint ed. pap. text 16.95 (0-8290-0322-3) Irvington.

***Nici de Nuevo.** Charles W. Colson. (SPA.). 1999. pap. 7.99 (0-7899-0778-X) Spanish Hse Distributors.

***Nick.** Genell Dellin. (Renegades Ser.: Vol. 2). 384p. 2000. mass mkt. 5.99 (0-380-80353-4, Avon Bks) Morrow Avon.

Nick. Alma J. Yates. LC 95-36488. (Orig.). (YA). (gr. 7 up). 1995. pap. 9.95 (1-57345-062-6) Deseret Bk.

Nick Adams Stories. Ernest Hemingway. 1976. 22.95 (0-8488-0524-0) Amereon Ltd.

Nick Adams Stories. Ernest Hemingway. 268p. 1981. pap. 10.95 (0-684-16940-1, Scribners Ref) Mac Lib Ref.

Nick Adams Stories. Ernest Hemingway. (Hudson River Editions Ver.). 268p. 1987. 40.00 (0-02-550780-X, Scribners Ref) Mac Lib Ref.

***Nick & Pete Stories.** Toulla Palazetti. Ed. by Noreen Wise. (Book-a-Day Collection). (Illus.). 48p. (J). (ps up). 2000. pap. 6.95 (1-58584-417-9) Huckleberry CT.

Nick & Peter: The Fire Island Murder. James Robiscoe. 186p. (Orig.). 1995. pap. 10.95 (0-9642911-1-8) Tanner Long.

Cal 98: Nick at Nite Classic TV: 365 More Classic TV Tidbits. 1997. 9.95 (0-684-82493-0, S&S Edns) Simon & Schuster.

Nick Bollettieri's Mental Efficiency Program for Playing Great Tennis. Nick Bollettieri & Charles A. Maher. (Illus.). 248p. 1996. pap. 12.95 (0-8092-3282-0, 328200, Contemporary Bks) NTC Contemp Pub Co.

Nick Cave: The Birthday Party & Other Epic Adventures. Robert Brokenmouth. (Illus.). 96p. (Orig.). 1996. pap. 17.95 (0-7119-5601-4, OP47826) Omnibus NY.

Nick Cerio's Kenpo, the Master's Text. Nick Cerlo. Ed. by Elena Y. Harootunian & Nicci Cataldo. (Illus.). viii, 192p. (Orig.). 1997. pap. 34.95 (0-9660178-0-3) N Cerios Kenpo.

***Nick Chase's Great Escape.** Christopher Orcutt. LC 99-91079. 1999. 25.00 (0-7388-0602-1); pap. 18.00 (0-7388-0603-X) Xlibris Corp.

Nick Drake: The Biography. Patrick Humphries. 224p. 1998. 24.95 (1-58234-006-4) Bloomsbury Pubg.

Nick Drake: The Biography. Patrick Humphries. 1999. pap. 14.95 (1-58234-035-8) Bloomsbury Pubg.

Nick Drives the Car. Date not set. pap. write for info. (1-58453-040-5) Pioneer MA.

***Nick Engler's Woodworking Wisdom.** Rick Engler. LC 99-39197. 392p. 1999. 29.95 (0-7621-0178-4, Pub. by RD Assn) Penguin Putnam.

N

Nick Faldo: In Search of Perfection. Nick Faldo. (Illus.). 160p. 1997. pap. 24.95 (0-297-83606-4, Pub. by Weidenfeld & Nicolson) Trafalgar.

***Nick Fury, Agent of S. H. I. E. L. D.** Jim Steranko. (Marvels Finest Ser.). (Illus.). 248p. 2000. pap. 17.95 (0-7851-0747-9, Pub. by Marvel Entrprs) LPC Group.

***Nick Fury, Agent of Shield: Empyre.** Will Murray. 1999. mass mkt. 6.50 (0-425-16816-6) Berkley Pub.

Nick Hardeman: A Civil War Novel with an Appendix of Selected Short Stories. Benjamin M. Hord. Ed. by Lewright B. Sikes. 384p. (C). 1993. pap. text 39.50 (0-8191-9245-7); lib. bdg. 64.50 (0-8191-9244-9) U Pr of Amer.

Nick Harvey's Practical Reloading Manual. Nick Harvey. 244p. 1994. pap. write for info. (0-9643068-0-8) Trigger Pr.

Nick Joins In. Joe Lasker. Ed. by Kathleen Tucker. LC 79-29637. (Albert Whitman Concept Bks.: Level 1). (Illus.). 32p. (J). (gr. 1-3). 1980. lib. bdg. 14.95 (0-8075-5612-2) A Whitman.

***Nick Malgieri's Perfect Pastry: Create Fantastic Desserts by Mastering the Basic Techniques.** Nick Malgieri. 352p. 1998. pap. text 19.95 (0-02-862335-5, Pub. by Macmillan) S&S Trade.

Nick Nairn's Island Harvest. Nick Nairn. 1999. pap. text 26.95 (1-884656-10-2) W One Hund Seventy Five.

Nick Nolte: Caught in the Act. Mel Weiser. LC 99-18046. (Illus.). 208p. 1999. 27.95 (1-879094-59-2) Momentum Bks.

Nick of the Woods. Robert M. Bird. Ed. by Curtis Dahl. (Masterworks of Literature Ser.). 1967. pap. 15.95 (0-8084-0235-8) NCUP.

Nick of the Woods. Robert M. Bird. (Works of Robert Montgomery Bird). 1989. reprint ed. lib. bdg. 79.00 (0-7812-1992-2) Rprt Serv.

Nick of Time. Casey Claybourne. (Time Passages Romance Ser.). 304p. 1997. mass mkt. 5.99 (0-515-12189-4, Jove) Berkley Pub.

Nick of Time. Janelle Denison. 1999. mass mkt. 4.50 (0-373-82597-8, 1-82597-5) Harlequin Bks.

Nick of Time. George A. Effinger. Ed. by Arthur B. Cover. Date not set. pap. write for info. (1-893475-22-0) Alexander Pubg.

Nick Ribbeck of Ribbeck of Havelland. Theodor Fontane. Tr. by Anthea Bell from GER. LC 90-7164. (Illus.). 32p. (J). (gr. k up). 1991. pap. 14.95 (0-88708-149-5, Picture Book Studio) S&S Childrens.

***Nick Sharratt.** Nick Sharratt. 2000. 13.95 (0-7641-7429-0) Barron.

Nick Stellino's Family Kitchen. Nick Stellino. LC 99-15967. (Illus.). 304p. 1999. 27.95 (0-399-14533-8, G P Putnam) Peng Put Young Read.

Nick Stellino's Glorious Italian Cooking: Romantic Meals, Menus & Music from "Cucina Amore" Nick Stellino. 256p. 1996. 24.95 (0-399-14171-5, G P Putnam) Peng Put Young Read.

Nick Stellino's Mediterranean Flavors. Nick Stellino. LC 96-52935. (Illus.). 256p. 1997. 25.95 (0-399-14266-5, G P Putnam) Peng Put Young Read.

***Nick Stellino's Passione: Pizza, Pasta & Panini.** Nick Stellino. 304p. 2000. 27.95 (0-399-14657-1) Putnam Pub Group.

***Nick Tosches Reader.** Nick Tosches. 624p. 2000. pap. text 18.95 (0-306-80969-9) Da Capo.

Nickalsain: The Life & Times of John Nicholson, Brigadier-General in the Army of the Honourable East India Company, 1822-1857. R. H. Haigh & P. W. Turner. 371p. 1980. pap. text 46.00 (*0-89126-092-7*) MA-AH Pub.

Nickel. (Metals & Minerals Ser.). 1993. lib. bdg. 262.95 (*0-8490-9003-2*) Gordon Pr.

Nickel. (Environmental Health Criteria Ser.: No. 108). (ENG, FRE & SPA.). 383p. 1991. pap. text 60.00 (*92-4-157108-X*, 1160108) World Health.

Nickel & a Dream. Ines Dotson. LC 97-92541. 54p. 1997. pap. write for info. (*0-9660537-0-2*) Dotson Pubns.

Nickel & Chromium Plating. 3rd ed. J. K. Dennis & T. E. Such. 464p. 1993. 170.00 (*1-85573-081-2*, 6337, Pub. by Woodhead Pubng) Am Educ Systs.

***Nickel & Dime.** Gary Soto. LC 99-6778. 195p. 2000. 29.95 (*0-8263-2185-2*); pap. 16.95 (*0-8263-2186-0*) U of NM Pr.

Nickel & Dime Decade: American Popular Culture During the 1930s. Gary D. Best. LC 93-2855. 184p. 1993. 49.95 (*0-275-94395-X*, C4395, Praeger Pubs) Greenwood.

Nickel & Human Health: Current Perspectives. Ed. by Evert Nieboer & Jerome O. Nriagu. LC 91-31093. (Advances in Environmental Science & Technology Ser.). 704p. 1992. 235.00 (*0-471-50076-3*) Wiley.

Nickel & the Skin. Ed. by Howard I. Maibach. 232p. 1989. boxed set 166.95 (*0-8493-6976-2*, RL803) CRC Pr.

Nickel Buys a Rhyme. Alan Benjamin. LC 92-6475. (Illus.). 40p. (J). (ps up). 1993. 15.00 (*0-688-06698-4*, Wm Morrow) Morrow Avon.

Nickel Chimera. Steven D. Lakey. LC 80-65824. (Illus.). 60p. (C). 1980. 4.95 (*0-936748-00-1*); pap. 2.95 (*0-936748-01-X*) Fade In.

Nickel Dreams. Tanya Tucker. 1998. mass mkt. 188.73 (*0-7868-9485-7*) Hyperion.

Nickel Dreams: My Life. Tanya Tucker & Patsi B. Cox. (Illus.). 384p. 1997. 23.45 (*0-7868-6305-6*, Pub. by Disney Pr) Time Warner.

Nickel Dreams: My Life. large type ed. Tanya Tucker & Patsi B. Cox. LC 97-21415. (Americana Series). 682p. 1997. 25.95 (*0-7862-1182-2*) Thorndike Pr.

Nickel Dreams: My Life. Tanya Tucker. (Illus.). 1996p. 1998. reprint ed. mass mkt. 6.99 (*0-7868-8936-5*, Pub. by Hyperion) Time Warner.

***Nickel Eclipse Iroquois Moon.** Eric Gansworth. 176p. 2000. pap. 19.95 (*0-87013-564-3*) Mich St U Pr.

Nickel Hydroxide Electrodes: Proceedings of the Symposium. Symposium on Nickel Hydroxide Electrodes (1989: Ho. Ed. by Dennis A. Corrigan & Albert H. Zimmerman. LC 90-81016. (Electrochemical Society Proceedings Ser.: Vol. 90-4). 448p. reprint ed. pap. 138.90 (*0-7837-5647-X*, 205249900005) Bks Demand.

Nickel in the Environment, Pt. 1. Ed. by Jerome O. Nriagu. LC 80-16600. (Environmental Science & Technology Ser.). 848p. 1980. 140.00 (*0-471-05885-8*) Krieger.

Nickel Miseries. Ivan Gold. Ed. by Jane Rosenman. 224p. 1992. pap. 10.00 (*0-671-75605-2*, WSP) PB.

Nickel, Nickel Carbonyl & Some Nickel Compounds Health & Safety Guide. (Health & Safety Guides Ser.: No. 62). 46p. 1991. pap. text 5.00 (*92-4-151062-5*, 1860062) World Health.

Nickel-Organische Verbibdunger Register - Organical Compounds Index for Pts. 1 & 2 of the Gmelin Handbuch, Vol. 18. Planck, Max, Society for the Advancement of Scienc. 129p. 1975. 130.00 (*0-387-93296-8*) Spr-Verlag.

Nickel Plate Color Photography of Willis McCaleb Vol. 1: Buffalo-Bellevue. Bruce Dicken & James Semon. LC 95-79970. (Illus.). 128p. 1995. 49.95 (*1-878887-52-1*) Morning NJ.

Nickel Plate Color Photography of Willis McCaleb Vol. 2: Bellevue-Chicago-Wheeling District. Bruce Dicken & Jim Semon. (Illus.). 1996. 49.95 (*1-878887-66-1*) Morning NJ.

Nickel Plate Road Diesel Locomotives. Kevin Holland. (Illus.). 112p. 1998. 26.95 (*1-883089-35-2*) TLC VA.

Nickel Plate Road Publicity Photos, 1943-1952, Vol. 2. John B. Corns. (Illus.). 126p. 1998. 25.95 (*1-883089-22-0*) TLC VA.

Nickel Plate Story. John A. Rehor. (Illus.). 484p. 1966. 74.95 (*0-89024-012-4*) Kalmbach.

Nickel-Plated Beauty. Patricia Beatty. 1993. 10.05 (*0-606-05508-8*, Pub. by Turtleback) Demco.

Nickel Rate Color Photography Vol. 3: The Railfan Perspective. Fred D. Cheney. LC 95-79970. (Illus.). 127p. 1997. 49.95 (*1-878887-71-8*) Morning NJ.

Nickel That Laughed & Other Stories. Muriel Taylor. (Illus.). 56p. (Orig.). 1974. pap. 3.50 (*1-880960-07-9*) Script Memory Fl.

Nickel Toxicology. Ed. by Stanley S. Brown & F. William Sunderman, Jr. 1981. text 104.00 (*0-12-137680-X*) Acad Pr.

Nickel Was for the Movies - Film in the Novel: Pirandello to Pulg. Gavriel Moses. LC 93-16283. 1994. 48.00 (*0-520-07943-4*, Pub. by U CA Pr) Cal Prin Full Svc.

Nickelodeon: The Mystery Files of Shelby Woo. (J). 1997. write for info. (*0-614-29163-1*, Minstrel Bks) PB.

Nickelodeon Hands-Free Guide, No. 3. Johnston. (J). 1999. 12.95 (*0-689-80819-4*) S&S Childrens.

Nickelodeon Hands-Free Guide, No. 4. Johnston. (J). 1999. 12.95 (*0-689-80820-8*) S&S Childrens.

Nickelodeon Theatres & Their Music. Q. David Bowers. LC 86-5594. (Illus.). 212p. 1986. 24.95 (*0-911572-49-X*, Vestal Pr); pap. 14.95 (*0-911572-50-3*, Vestal Pr) Madison Bks UPA.

Nickelodeon's the Big Help Book: 365 Ways You Can Make a Difference by Volunteering. Alan Goodman. LC 95-203901. (Illus.). (J). (gr. 3-6). 1994. pap. 3.99 (*0-671-51927-1*, Minstrel Bks) PB.

Nickels & Pennies see Math Set A

Nickel's Worth of Skim Milk: A Boy's View of the Great Depression. Robert J. Hastings. (Shawnee Bks.). 168p. 1986. pap. 9.95 (*0-8093-1305-7*) S Ill U Pr.

Nickerson Family Vol. IV: The Descendants of William Nickerson. Pauline W. Derick. Ed. by Elbert O. Derick. LC 97-68761. (Illus.). 768p. 1997. 50.00 (*0-9659269-1-5*) Nickerson Fam.

Nickerson Family Vols. 1-3: The Descendants of William Nickerson. 2nd rev. ed. Pauline W. Derick et al. Ed. by Elbert O. Derick. LC 97-68760. (Illus.). 500p. 1997. 50.00 (*0-9659269-0-7*) Nickerson Fam.

Nickerson's Four-Star Management Workshop. Patricia Nickerson. 384p. 1988. 39.95 (*0-685-37794-6*) P-H.

Nicketty-Nacketty, Noo-Noo-Noo. Joy Cowley. LC 98-17759. (J). (ps-2). 1999. pap. 4.95 (*1-57255-558-0*) Mondo Pubng.

Nickie's Ghost. Lynn Lockhart. (American Romance Ser.). 1994. per. 3.50 (*0-373-16527-7*, 1-16527-3) Harlequin Bks.

Nicklaus. Mark Shaw. LC 97-501. (Illus.). 400p. 1997. 24.95 (*0-87833-961-2*) Taylor Pub.

Nicknames: Past & Present. Christine Rose. 29p. 1991. pap. 4.50 (*0-929626-04-4*) Rose Family Assn.

Nicknames: Past & Present. 2nd enl. rev. ed. LC 95-92110. viii, 42p. 1995. pap. write for info. (*0-929626-08-7*) Rose Family Assn.

Nicknames & Sobriquets of U. S. Cities, States, & Counties. 3rd ed. Joseph N. Kane & Gerard L. Alexander. LC 79-20193. 445p. 1979. 42.00 (*0-8108-1255-X*) Scarecrow.

Nicknight: The Photographs of Nick Knight. Photos by Nick Knight. (Illus.). 162p. 1997. 125.00 (*3-8238-2123-7*) te Neues.

Nickommoh: A Thanksgiving Celebration. Jackie F. Koller. LC 97-37087. (Illus.). 32p. (J). (gr. k-3). 1999. 17.00 (*0-689-81094-6*) Atheneum Yung Read.

***Nick's a Chick.** (Jersey Ser.: No. 3). (Illus.). 128p. (J). (gr. 3-7). 2000. pap. 4.99 (*0-7868-4423-X*) Disney Pr.

Nick's Child. Tina Vasilos. (Intrigue Ser.). 1998. per. 3.99 (*0-373-22463-X*, 1-22463-3) Harlequin Bks.

Nick's Kind of Woman. Margot Early. 1997. per. 3.99 (*0-373-70724-X*, 1-70724-9) Silhouette.

Nick's Long-Awaited Honeymoon. Sandra Steffen. 1998. per. 3.50 (*0-373-19290-8*, 1-19290-5) Silhouette.

Nick's Mission. Claire H. Blatchford. LC 95-856. (J). 1995. lib. bdg. 19.95 (*0-8225-0740-4*, Lerner Publctns) Lerner Pub.

Nicks, 1998: The Annual Guide to Sire & Broodmare Sire Crosses. Ed. by Raymond S. Paulick & Dan Liebman. 500p. 1998. pap. 44.95 (*1-58150-005-X*) Blood-Horse.

***Nick's Secret.** Claire H. Blatchford. LC 00-8274. (Mysteries Ser.). (Illus.). 180p. (J). (gr. 4-7). 2000. 19.93 (*0-8225-0743-9*, Carolrhoda) Lerner Pub.

***Nick's Trip.** George P. Pelecanos. 1999. pap. 12.00 (*1-85242-714-0*, Pub. by Serpents Tail) Consort Bk Sales.

Nicky: Divorce Through the Eyes of a Child. Karen J. Todd. (Illus.). 60p. 1998. pap. 6.95 (*0-9649210-1-4*) Motivo Pubng.

Nicky & the Big, Bad Wolves. Valeri Gorbachev. LC 97-36314. (Illus.). 32p. (J). (ps-2). 1998. 15.95 (*1-55858-917-1*, Pub. by North-South Bks NYC); lib. bdg. 15.88 (*1-55858-918-X*, Pub. by North-South Bks NYC) Chronicle Bks.

***Nicky & the Big, Bad Wolves.** Valeri Gorbachev. (Illus.). 32p. (ps-2). 2000. pap. 6.95 (*0-7358-1334-5*) North-South Bks NYC.

***Nicky & the Fantastic Birthday Gift.** Valeri Gorbachev. LC 00-35126. (Illus.). 32p. (ps-2). 2000. 15.95 (*0-7358-1378-7*) North-South Bks NYC.

***Nicky & the Fantastic Birthday Gift.** Valeri Gorbachev. LC 00-35126. (Illus.). 32p. (J). (ps-2). 2000. write for info. (*0-7358-1379-5*) North-South Bks NYC.

***Nicky & the Twins' Lost Rabbit.** Tony Bradman. (Illus.). (J). 1998. pap. 9.95 (*0-00-664511-9*, Pub. by HarpC) Trafalgar.

Nicky at the Magic House. Lieve Baeten. (Illus.). 32p. (J). (ps-2). 1993. pap. 6.95 (*1-55037-271-8*, Pub. by Annick); lib. bdg. 14.95 (*1-55037-273-4*, Pub. by Annick) Firefly Bks Ltd.

Nicky D. A Narrative Portrait of Nicholas Detommaso. Warren Lehrer. LC 95-5814. (Portrait Ser.). (Illus.). 268p. (Orig.). 1995. pap. 12.95 (*0-941920-37-2*) Bay Pr.

Nicky Epstein's Knitted Embellishments: 350 Ways to Enhance Your Knitting. Nicky Epstein. LC 98-32299. 272 p. 1999. pap. 31.95 (*1-883010-39-X*) Interweave.

***Nicky Epstein's Knitting for Your Home.** Nicky Epstein. LC 99-89552. (Illus.). 160p. 2000. pap. 24.95 (*1-56158-294-8*) Taunton.

Nicky, 1-2-3. Cathryn Falwell. 28p. (J). (ps up). 1998. bds. 4.95 (*0-395-92952-0*, Clarion Bks) HM.

Nicky, 1-2-3. Harriet Ziefert. (Illus.). 20p. (J). (ps). 1995. pap. 5.99 (*0-14-050767-1*, PuffinBks) Peng Put Young Read.

Nicky the Nature Detective. Ulf Svedberg. Tr. by Ingrid Selberg. LC 87-28355. (Illus.). 52p. (J). (gr. 5 up). 1988. 12.95 (*91-29-58786-7*, Pub. by R & S Bks) FS&G.

Nicky Upstairs & Down Level 1, Blue, Level. Harriet Ziefert & Richard Brown. (Easy-to-Read Bks.). (Illus.). (J). (ps-2). 1994. pap. 3.99 (*0-14-036852-3*, PuffinBks) Peng Put Young Read.

Nicky Visits the Airport. Harriet Ziefert. 1997. pap. 5.99 (*0-14-055948-5*) Viking Penguin.

Nicky's Birthday. Lieve Baeten. (Illus.). 32p. (J). (ps-2). 1993. pap. 9.95 (*1-55037-464-8*, Pub. by Annick); text 16.95 (*1-55037-465-6*, Pub. by Annick) Firefly Bks Ltd.

Niclous Garber Family Record. 310p. 1999. 56.50 (*0-8328-9875-9*); pap. 46.50 (*0-8328-9876-7*) Higginson Bk Co.

Nico. Richard Witts. 1994. pap. text 9.95 (*0-86369-655-4*, Pub. by Virgin Bks) London Brdge.

Nico: Recipes & Recollections from One of Our Most Brilliant & Controversial Chefs. Nico Ladenis. (Illus.). 240p. 1997. pap. 37.50 (*0-333-71102-5*, Pub. by Macmillan) Trans-Atl Phila.

Nico: The End. James Young. (Illus.). 216p. 1993. 21.95 (*0-87951-504-X*, Pub. by Overlook Pr) Penguin Putnam.

Nico: The End. James Young. (Illus.). 207p. 1994. pap. 11.95 (*0-87951-545-7*, Pub. by Overlook Pr) Penguin Putnam.

Nico: The Life & Lies of an Icon. Richard Witts. (Illus.). 1995. pap. 9.95 (*0-86368-655-9*, Pub. by Virgin Bks) London Brdge.

Nico le Petit Garcon Change en Chien. Andre Maurois. 9.95 (*0-686-55495-7*) Fr & Eur.

Nico the Unicorn. Frank Sacks. (J). (gr. 3-7). pap. 3.99 (*0-614-19256-0*) Tor Bks.

Nico the Unicorn. Frank Sacks. 1996. pap. text 3.99 (*0-8125-5171-0*, Pub. by Tor Bks) St Martin.

***Nico y los Lobos Feroces.** Valeri Gorbachev. Tr. by Ariel Almohar. (SPA., Illus.). 32p. (gr. k-3). 2000. pap. 6.95 (*0-7358-1336-1*) North-South Bks NYC.

***Nico y los Lobos Feroces.** Valeri Gorbachev. Tr. by Ariel Almohar. (SPA., Illus.). 32p. (ps-3). 2000. 15.95 (*0-7358-1335-3*) North-South Bks NYC.

Nicobar Islands & Their People. Edward H. Man. LC 77-86996. (Royal Anthropological Institute of Great Britain & Ireland. Publication Ser.). reprint ed. 55.00 (*0-404-16767-5*) AMS Pr.

Nicobarase Vocabulary. E.H. Man. 1858. 19.95 (*0-7859-9825-X*) Fr & Eur.

Nicobarese. Anstice Justin. (C). 1991. 10.50 (*81-7046-082-4*, Pub. by Seagull Bks) S Asia.

Nicobarese of Great Nicobar: An Ethnography. Anshu P. Nandan. 1993. 14.00 (*81-212-0403-8*, Pub. by Gian Publng Hse) S Asia.

Nicobobinus. large type ed. Terry Jones. (Lythway Ser.). 224p. (J). (gr. 3-7). 1991. 17.95 (*0-7451-1319-2*, G K Hall Lrg Type) Mac Lib Ref.

Nicodemos of the Holy Mountain: A Handbook of Spiritual Counsel. Tr. by Peter A. Chamberas. (Classics of Western Spirituality Ser.). 1989. pap. 12.95 (*0-8091-3038-6*) Paulist Pr.

Nicola Pio As a Collector of Drawings. Per Bjurstrom. (Illus.). 291p. 1995. 67.50 (*91-7042-151-X*, Pub. by P Astroms) Coronet Bks.

Nicola Pisano's Arca di San Domenico & Its Legacy. Anita F. Moskowitz. LC 92-35734. (College Art Association Monographs on the Fine Arts: Vol. L). (Illus.). 160p. (C). 1994. 65.00 (*0-271-00946-2*) Pa St U Pr.

Nicolae: The Rise of Antichrist. Tim F. LaHaye & Jerry B. Jenkins. LC 97-20356. (Left Behind Ser.: Bk. 3). 432p. 1997. 16.95 (*0-8423-2914-5*) Tyndale Hse.

Nicolae: The Rise of Antichrist. Tim F. LaHaye & Jerry B. Jenkins. (Left Behind Ser.: Bk. 3). 415p. 1998. pap. 13.99 (*0-8423-2924-2*, 910666Q) Tyndale Hse.

***Nicolae: The Rise of Antichrist.** large type ed. Tim F. LaHaye & Jerry B. Jenkins. LC 99-87744. (Left Behind Ser.: Bk. 3). 2000. write for info. (*0-7862-2469-X*) Thorndike Pr.

***Nicolae Bretan, His Life & His Music.** Hartmut Gagelmann. LC 00-37314. (Lives in Music Ser.). (Illus.). (J). 2000. pap. write for info. (*1-57647-021-0*) Pendragon NY.

Nicolae High: The Young Trib Force Goes Back to School, Vol. 5. Jerry B. Jenkins & Tim LaHaye. (Left Behind: Bk. 5). (YA). (gr. 5 up). 1999. pap. text 5.99 (*0-8423-4325-3*) Tyndale Hse.

Nicolai Case: A Biography. Wolf W. Zuelzer. LC 82-1990. (Illus.). 473p. reprint ed. pap. 146.70 (*0-608-16054-7*, 203318400084) Bks Demand.

Nicolai Fechin: Across Two Continents. Photos by Dan Morse. LC 78-58003. (Illus.). 84p. 1997. pap. 25.00 (*0-935037-87-X*) G Peters Gallery.

Nicolai Gedda: My Life & Art. Nicolai Gedda. Tr. by Tom Geddes. LC 98-42923. (Opera Biography Ser.: Vol. 12). (Illus.). 270p. 1999. 24.95 (*1-57467-048-4*, Amadeus Pr) Timber.

Nicolai Hartmann's New Ontology. William H. Werkmeister. 288p. 1990. 49.95 (*0-8130-1008-X*) U Press Fla.

Nicolai Kantchev - Medusa: Selected Poems. Nicolai Kantchev. Tr. by Kessler & Shurbanov. (QRL Poetry Bks.: Vol. XXVI). 1986. 20.00 (*0-614-06418-X*) Quarterly Rev.

Nicolaitanism, the Rise & Growth of the Clergy. F. W. Grant. Ed. by R. P. Daniel. pap. 3.95 (*0-88172-139-5*) Believers Bkshelf.

***Nicolas.** Tim F. LaHaye. (Left Behind Ser.: Vol. 3). (SPA.). 2000. pap. 9.99 (*0-7899-0457-8*) Editorial Unilit.

Nicolas: Complete Chansons Published by Le Roy Ballard. LC 91-750087. (Sixteenth-Century Chanson Ser.: Vol. 20). 242p. 1991. text 30.00 (*0-8240-3119-9*) Garland.

Nicolas Cage: Hollywood's Wild Talent. Brian Robb. 144p. 1998. pap. text 16.95 (*0-85965-264-5*, Pub. by Plexus) Publishers Group.

***Nicolas Cage: The Biography.** Ian Markham-Smith & Liz Hodgson. 2000. 26.00 (*1-85782-396-6*, Pub. by Blake Publng) Seven Hills Bk.

Nicolas Cotheret's Annals of Citeaux, Outlined from the Original French. Louis J. Lekai. (Cistercian Studies: 57). 1983. pap. 13.95 (*0-87907-857-X*) Cistercian Pubns.

***Nicolas de Clamanges: Spirituality, Personal Reform & Pastoral Renewal on the Eve of the Reformations.** Christopher M. Bellitto. LC 00-30311. 2001. write for info. (*0-8132-0996-X*) Cath U Pr.

Nicolas Fatio de Duillier & the Prophets of Paris. Ed. by Charles Domson & I. Bernard Cohen. LC 80-2086. (Development of Science Ser.). (Illus.). 1981. lib. bdg. 18.95 (*0-405-13852-0*) Ayer.

Nicolas Flamel: His Exposition of the Hieroglypical Figures (1624) Ed. by Laurinda Dixon. LC 94-8101. (Illus.). 208p. 1994. text 37.00 (*0-8240-5838-0*, H979) Garland.

Nicola's Floating Home. Bobbie Kalman. (Crabapple Ser.). (Illus.). 32p. (J). (ps-3). 1995. pap. 5.95 (*0-86505-726-5*); lib. bdg. 19.96 (*0-86505-626-9*) Crabtree Pub Co.

Nicola's Floating Home. Bobbie Kalman. LC 95-35940. (Crabapples Ser.). (J). 1995. 11.15 (*0-606-09681-7*, Pub. by Turtleback) Demco.

Nicolas Gueudeville & His Work 1652-1725. A. Rosenberg. 1982. lib. bdg. 177.50 (*90-247-2533-X*) Kluwer Academic.

Nicolas Guillen: Popular Poet of the Caribbean. Ian I. Smart. 208p. 1990. text 29.95 (*0-8262-0756-1*) U of Mo Pr.

Nicolas Guillen's New Love Poems. Nicholas Guillen. Ed. & Tr. by Keith Ellis from SPA. (Romance Ser.). (Illus.). 136p. 1994. text 40.00 (*0-8020-0427-X*) U of Toronto Pr.

Nicolas Legat: Heritage of a Ballet Master. Andre Eglevsky & John Gregory. (Illus.). 124p. 1978. 39.95 (*0-903102-43-9*, Pub. by Dance Bks) Princeton Bk Co.

Nicolas Medtner: His Life & Music. Barrie Martyn. (Illus.). 288p. 1995. 86.95 (*0-85967-959-4*) Ashgate Pub Co.

Nicolas Millot, Merchandy, Nicolas de Marle, Thomas Champion (Mithou), Pierre Moulu, Jean Mouton, Pagnier, Hilaire Penet, Claude Petit Jehan. Ed. by Jane A. Bernstein. LC 90-755315. (Sixteenth Century Chanson Ser.: Vol. 19). 280p. 1991. 90.00 (*0-8240-3118-0*) Garland.

Nicolas Nickleby & Livres de Noel. Charles Dickens. (FRE.). 1966. 99.50 (*0-8288-3433-4*, F77430) Fr & Eur.

Nicolas of Cusa on Christ & the Church: Essays in Memory of Chandler McCuskey Brooks. American Cusanus Society Staff. Ed. by Gerald Christianson & Thomas M. Izicki. LC 96-5099. (Studies in the History of Christian Thought, 0081-8607: No. 71). xviii, 362p. 1996. 139.00 (*90-04-10519-0*) Brill Academic Pubs.

Nicolas Pashkevich. Nicolas Pashkevich. LC 94-77354. (Illus.). 168p. 1996. 35.00 (*0-9617756-8-8*) Galerija.

Nicolas Poussin. Alain Merot. (Illus.). 336p. 1990. 125.00 (*1-55859-120-6*) Abbeville Pr.

Nicolas Poussin: Dialectics of Painting. Oskar Batschmann. 228p. 1997. 50.00 (*0-948462-10-8*, Pub. by Reaktion Bks) Consort Bk Sales.

Nicolas Poussin: Dialectics of Painting. Oskar Batschmann. (Illus.). 174p. 1999. pap. 29.95 (*0-948462-43-4*, Pub. by Reaktion Bks) Consort Bk Sales.

***Nicolas Poussin: Friendship & the Love of Painting.** Elizabeth Cropper. 2000. pap. text 35.00 (*0-691-05067-8*, Pub. by Princeton U Pr) Cal Prin Full Svc.

Nicolas Poussin, 1594-1665. Richard Verdi et al. LC 95-219504. (Illus.). 336p. 1995. 70.00 (*0-302-00647-8*) Sothebys Pubns.

Nicolas Poussin, 1594-1665: Catalogue Raissone des Dessins. Pierre Rosenberg & Louis-Antoine Prat. (FRE., Illus.). 1218p. 1994. 800.00 (*88-355-0258-6*, Pub. by Art Bks Intl) Partners Pubs Grp.

Nicolas Poussin's Landscape Allegories. Sheila McTighe. (Illus.). 226p. (C). 1996. text 74.95 (*0-521-48214-3*) Cambridge U Pr.

Nicolas Roeg Film by Film. Scott Salwolke. LC 92-56690. (Illus.). 232p. 1993. lib. bdg. 42.50 (*0-89950-881-2*) McFarland & Co.

Nicolas Tarkhoff: A Retrospective Exhibition. Annabel Armstrong. (Illus.). 64p. 1989. pap. 20.00 (*0-8150-0014-6*) Wittenborn Art.

Nicola's Winter. large type ed. Mary Mackie. (Linford Romance Library). 336p. 1996. pap. 16.99 (*0-7089-7967-X*, Linford) Ulverscroft.

Nicolaus Copernicus, 1473-1543, 500th Anniversary Celebration. Smithsonian Institution Staff. 0.25 (*0-940962-14-4*) Polish Inst Art & Sci.

Nicolaus Damascenus de Plantis: Five Translations. Nicolaus of Damascus. Ed. by H. J. Drossaart Lulofs & E. L. Poortman. (Verhandelingen der Koninklijke Nederlandse Akademie van Wetenschappen, Afd. Letterkunde, Nieuwe Reeks Ser.: No. 139). 732p. 103.25 (*0-444-85703-6*) Elsevier.

Nicolaus of Autrecourt. Julius R. Weinberg. LC 76-91776. 242p. 1969. reprint ed. lib. bdg. 59.50 (*0-8371-2529-4*, WENA, Greenwood Pr) Greenwood.

Nicole. Jack Weyland. LC 93-27308. 196p. (YA). (gr. 8-12). 1993. 11.95 (*0-87579-787-3*) Deseret Bk.

Nicole & the Ice Cream Bear! Connie M. Hardan. (Nicole Adventure Ser.: Vol. 3). (Illus.). 30p. (Orig.). (J). (gr. 1 up). 1996. pap. 7.99 (*1-889039-01-2*) Hrtline Publng.

Nicole Bobek. Veda B. Jones. LC 98-21902. (Female Figure Skating Legends Ser.). (Illus.). 64p. (YA). (gr. 3 up). 1999. lib. bdg. 16.95 (*0-7910-5029-7*) Chelsea Hse.

Nicole Digs a Hole. Barbara Gregorich. Ed. by Joan Hoffman. (Start to Read! Ser.). (Illus.). 16p. (J). (gr. k-2). 1991. pap. 2.29 (*0-88743-026-0*, 06026) Sch Zone Pub Co.

Nicole Oresme: Highlights from His French Commentary on Aristotle's Politics. Tr. by Albert D. Menut. 237p. 1979. 25.00 (*0-87291-132-2*) Coronado Pr.

Nicole Oresme & the Kinematics of Circular Motion: Tractatus de Commensurabilitate Vel Incommensurabilitate Motuum Celi. Nicole Oresme. Ed. & Tr. by Edward Grant. LC 79-133238. (Publications in Medieval Science). (Illus.). 438p. reprint ed. pap. 135.80 (*0-608-20431-5*, 207168400002) Bks Demand.

Nicole Oresme & the Marvels. Nicole Oresme. Ed. by Bert Hansen. pap. text 59.43 (*0-88844-068-5*) Brill Academic Pubs.

Nicole Oresme & the Medieval Geometry of Qualities & Motions: A Treatise on the Uniformity & Difformity of Intensities Known As Tractatus de

An Asterisk (*) at the beginning of an entry indicates that the title is appearing for the first time.

Configurationibus Qualitatum et Motuum. Nicole Oresme. Ed. by Marshall Clagett. LC 68-14031. (University of Wisconsin Publications in Medieval Science). (Illus.). 736p. reprint ed. pap. 200.00 (*0-7837-5901-0*, 204569200007) Bks Demand.

Nicole Routhier's Fruit Cookbook. Nicole Routhier. (Illus.). 480p. 1996. 25.95 (*0-7611-0506-9*, 10506); pap. 15.95 (*1-56305-565-1*, 3565) Workman Pub.

Nicole's Boat. Allen Morgan. (Annick Toddler Ser.). (Illus.). 24p. (J). (ps-1). 1986. 12.95 (*0-920303-60-9*, Pub. by Annick); pap. 4.95 (*0-920303-61-7*, Pub. by Annick) Firefly Bks Ltd.

***Nicole's Boat.** rev. ed. Allen Morgan. 24p. (J). (ps-k). 2000. per. 5.95 (*1-55037-630-6*, Pub. by Annick Pr) Firefly Bks Ltd.

***Nicole's Boat.** rev. ed. Allen Morgan & Jirina Marton. (Illus.). 24p. (J). (ps-k). 2000. lib. bdg. 15.95 (*1-55037-631-4*, Pub. by Annick Pr) Firefly Bks Ltd.

Nicole's Orphan Calf. Connie M. Hardan. (Nicole Adventure Ser.: Vol. 3+). (Illus.). 36p. (Orig.). (J). (gr. 2 up). 1996. pap. 7.99 (*1-889039-00-4*) Hrtline Publng.

Nicole's Revenge. Lisette Allen. (Black Lace Ser.). 1995. mass mkt. 5.95 (*0-352-32984-X*, Pub. by Virgin Bks) London Brdge.

Nicole's Story: A Book about a Girl with Juvenile Rheumatoid Arthritis. Virginia T. Aldape. LC 95-35622. (Illus.). (J). 1996. lib. bdg. 19.95 (*0-8225-2578-X*, Lerner Publctns) Lerner Pub.

Nicolo d'Alessandro: Italian Art. Nicolo D'Alessandro. 95p. 1985. 25.00 (*0-89304-570-5*, CCC181); pap. 10.00 (*0-89304-595-0*) Cross-Cultrl NY.

Nicolo G - And the Days of November. Frank Menchaca. LC 90-84969. 56p. (Orig.). 1990. pap. 4.95 (*0-9628159-0-X*) Front Rm.

Nicolo Paganini. McGee. 49.95 (*1-85928-400-0*) Ashgate Pub Co.

Nicolo Paganini. Jacques G. Prod'Homme. LC 74-24195. reprint ed. 29.50 (*0-404-13096-8*) AMS Pr.

Nicolo Paganini: His Life & Work. Stephen S. Stratton. 205p. 1990. reprint ed. lib. bdg. 69.00 (*0-7812-9102-X*) Rprt Serv.

Nicolo-Peccavi: ou L'Affaire Dreyfus a Carpentras. Armand Lunel. (FRE.). 1976. pap. 10.95 (*0-7859-4064-2*) Fr & Eur.

Nicomachean Ethics. Aristotle. Tr. by D. P. Chase. LC 97-39242. (Thrift Editions Ser.). 256p. 1998. pap. 2.00 (*0-486-40096-4*) Dover.

Nicomachean Ethics. Aristotle. Tr. by H. Rackham. (Loeb Classical Library: No. 73). 684p. 1926. 18.95 (*0-674-99081-1*) HUP.

Nicomachean Ethics. Aristotle. Tr. & Intro. by David Ross. (Oxford World's Classics Ser.). 320p. 1998. pap. 8.95 (*0-19-283407-X*) OUP.

Nicomachean Ethics. Aristotle. Ed. & Comment by Gottfried Ramsauer. LC 86-29529. 1987p. 1987. reprint ed. 80.00 (*0-8240-6901-3*) Garland.

Nicomachean Ethics. 2nd ed. Aristotle. Ed. by Hippocrates G. Apostle. LC 84-60009. (Apostle Translations of Aristotle's Works: Vol. 6). 372p. 1984. reprint ed. pap. 19.00 (*0-911589-03-1*) Peripatetic.

Nicomachean Ethics. 2nd ed. Aristotle. Ed. by Hippocrates G. Apostle. LC 84-60009. (Apostle Translations of Aristotle's Works: Vol. 6). 372p. 1991. reprint ed. 40.00 (*0-911589-02-3*) Peripatetic.

***Nicomachean Ethics.** 2nd rev. ed. Aristotle. Tr. by Terence Irwin from GRE. LC 99-26709. 480p. (C). 2000. pap. 9.95 (*0-87220-464-2*); lib. bdg. 34.95 (*0-87220-465-0*) Hackett Pub.

Nicomachean Ethics, Bks. 8-11. Aristotle. Tr. & Comment by Michael Pakaluk. LC 98-37479. (Clarendon Aristotle Ser.). 254p. 1999. text 65.00 (*0-19-875103-6*, Clarendon Pr); pap. text 19.95 (*0-19-875104-4*, Clarendon Pr) OUP.

Nicomachean Ethics, Vol. 6. Aristotle. Tr. by L. H. Greenwood. LC 72-9290. (Philosophy of Plato & Aristotle Ser.). (ENG & GRE.). 1977. reprint ed. 18.95 (*0-405-04842-4*) Ayer.

Nicomachean Ethics: Aristotle. Aristotle. Ed. by Martin Ostwald. 352p. (C). 1962. pap. text 10.00 (*0-02-389530-6*, Pub. by P-H) S&S Trade.

Nicomede. Pierre Corneille. (FRE.). 202p. 1977. pap. 8.95 (*0-7859-0924-9*, F36134) Fr & Eur.

Nicopolis Ad Istrum: The Finds. A. G. Poulter et al. LC 97-47439. (Reports of the Research Committee of the Society of Antiquaries of London). (Illus.). 384p. 1999. 145.00 (*0-7185-0168-3*) Bks Intl VA.

Nicopolis 1396, Vol. 64. David Nicolle. 1999. pap. text 17.95 (*1-85532-918-2*) Greenhill Bks.

Nicotina & Caffeina. Adnan Sarhan. 64p. 1988. pap. 5.00 (*1-884328-04-0*) Sufi Fnd Amer.

Nicotine. Judy Monroe. LC 94-47280. (Drug Library Ser.). (Illus.). 128p. (YA). (gr. 6 up). 1995. lib. bdg. 20.95 (*0-89490-505-8*) Enslow Pubs.

Nicotine: An Old-Fashioned Addiction. Jack E. Henningfield. (Encyclopedia of Psychoactive Drugs Ser.: No. 1). (Illus.). 124p. (YA). (gr. 7 up). 1985. lib. bdg. 19.95 (*0-87754-751-3*) Chelsea Hse.

Nicotine Addiction. John Hicks. 128p. (YA). (gr. 7 up). 1999. 21.40 (*0-7613-0322-7*, Copper Beech Bks) Millbrook Pr.

Nicotine Addiction: Principles & Management. Ed. by C. Tracy Orleans & John Slade. LC 92-29443. (Illus.). 456p. 1993. text 69.50 (*0-19-506441-0*) OUP.

***Nicotine Addiction among Adolescents.** Eric F. Wagner. LC 00-38851. 2000. write for info. (*0-7890-1171-9*) Haworth Pr.

Nicotine & Caffeine, 8 vols. Richard S. Lee & Mary Price Lee. LC 94-2279. (Drug Abuse Prevention Library). (Illus.). 64p. (YA). (gr. 7-12). 1998. lib. bdg. 17.95 (*0-8239-2745-8*) Rosen Group.

Nicotine & Cigarettes. Ed. by Steven L. Jaffe. LC 99-28647. (Illus.). 80p. (J). (gr. 4-8). 1999. lib. bdg. 19.95 (*0-7910-5175-7*) Chelsea Hse.

Nicotine, Caffeine & Social Drinking: Behaviour & Brain Function. Ed. by Jan Snel & Monicque Lorist. 488p. 1997. text 44.00 (*90-5702-218-4*, Harwood Acad Pubs) Gordon & Breach.

***Nicotine Doohickeys: The Fairly Intelligent Person's Guide to Smoking & Quitting.** Bill Howard. (Illus.). 127p. 1999. pap. 9.75 (*0-9686164-0-2*, Pub. by W Howard) Genl Dist Srvs.

Nicotine Fit: A Nightmare. D. V. Thomas. Ed. by F. L. Miller. 65p. (Orig.). 1988. pap. 9.95 (*0-929623-00-2*) Paranoid Pr.

***Nicotine in Cigarettes & Smokeless Tobacco Products Is a Drug & These Products Are Nicotine Delivery Devices & under the Federal Food, Drug & Cosmetic Act - Appendices.** Ed. by Barry Leonard. 313p. (C). 1999. reprint ed. pap. text 60.00 (*0-7881-8222-6*) DIANE Pub.

Nicotine in Cigarettes & Smokeless Tobacco Products is a Drug & These Products Are Nicotine Delivery Devices Under the Federal Food, Drug & Cosmetic Act: Appendices. 313p. 1995. per. 24.00 (*0-16-061413-9*) USGPO.

***Nicotine in Psychiatry: Psychopathology & Emerging Therapeutics.** Melissa Piasecki. LC 99-40827. (Clinical Practice Ser.). 2000. 40.00 (*0-88048-797-6*) Am Psychiatric.

Nicotine Jukebox. Marc C. Jachsina. 32p. 1998. pap. 7.00 (*1-881168-04-2*) Red Danceflr.

Nicotine Management: Air Cigarettes. Alice Morin. (Illus.). 66p. 1997. pap. 5.95 (*0-9658854-0-2*) Los Abuelos.

Nicotine Psychopharmacology: Molecular, Cellular, & Behavioural Aspects. S. Wonnacott et al. (Illus.). 448p. 1990. 80.00 (*0-19-261614-5*) OUP.

Nicotine Replacement: A Critical Evaluation. Ed. by Ovide F. Pomerleau & Cynthia S. Pomerleau. 325p. 1992. pap. 29.95 (*1-56024-250-7*) Haworth Pr.

Nicotine Safety & Toxicity. Ed. by Neal L. Benowitz. LC 97-46155. (Illus.). 224p. 1998. text 59.50 (*0-19-511496-5*) OUP.

Nicotine, Smoking, & the Low Tar Program. Ed. by Nicholas J. Wald & P. Froggatt. (Illus.). 256p. 1989. 75.00 (*0-19-261729-X*) OUP.

Nicotinic Acetylcholine Receptor. Ed. by A. Maelicke. (NATO ASI Series H: Vol. 3). xvi, 489p. 1986. 165.95 (*0-387-17168-1*) Spr-Verlag.

Nicotinic Acetylcholine Receptors. Francisco J. Barrantes. 208p. 1998. 159.00 (*1-57059-514-3*) Landes Bioscience.

Nicotinic Acetylcholine Receptors. Ed. by Francisco J. Barrantes & Bahia Blanca. (Biotechnology Intelligence Unit Ser.). 208p. 1998. 159.00 (*3-540-64258-7*) Spr-Verlag.

Nicotinoid Insecticides & the Nicotinic Acetylcholine Receptor. Izuru Yamamoto & John E. Casida. LC 99-20210. 300p. 1999. write for info. (*4-431-70213-X*) Spr-Verlag.

Nictitating Membrane. deluxe ed. David Benedetti. (Illus.). 64p. 1976. pap. 10.00 (*0-935724-54-0*) Figures.

Nidation: A Symposium Held in Honor of Professor M.C. Shelesnyak. M. C. Shelesnyak et al. LC 86-23862. 217p. 1986. write for info. (*0-89766-348-9*) NY Acad Sci.

Nidd Valley Light Railway. D. J. Croft. 80p. (C). 1985. 39.00 (*0-85361-337-0*) St Mut.

Niddah, 2 vols. (ENG & HEB.). 30.00 (*0-910218-87-0*) Bennet Pub.

Niddah, No. 1. Schottenstein. 47.99 (*0-89906-712-3*, TNI1) Mesorah Pubns.

Niddy Noddy the Noodlemaker. Virginia Maas. (Color-A-Story Ser.). (Illus.). 12p. (J). (ps-2). 1981. pap. 2.75 (*0-933992-15-7*) Coffee Break.

Nido de Amor (No Place for Love) Susanne McCarthy. (SPA.). 1996. per. 3.50 (*0-373-33381-1*, 1-33381-4) Harlequin Bks.

Nido de la Tortuga. Lola Schaefer. Tr. by Alberto Romo. (Books for Young Learners).Tr. of Turtle Nest. (SPA., Illus.). 16p. (J). (gr. k-2). 1998. pap. text 5.00 (*1-57274-205-4*, A2883) R Owen Pubs.

***Nidoran's New Friend.** Gregg Sacon. (Pokemon Junior Ser.: Vol. 7). (Illus.). (J). 2000. pap. 3.99 (*0-439-20096-2*) Scholastic Inc.

Nidos de Pajoros. Arthur Morton. Tr. by Angelita L. Aguilar. (SPA.). (J). (gr. k-3). 1994. 12.50 (*1-57842-025-3*) Delmas Creat.

Nid's Exciting Day. Mary Gurtler. 1989. pap. 2.95 (*9971-972-81-6*) OMF Bks.

Nie-Boska Komedia see Undivine Comedy

Nie Weiping on Go: The Art of Positional Judgment. Nie Weiping. Tr. by Sidney W. Yuan from CHI. LC 96-163995. (Illus.). 200p. 1995. pap. text 14.95 (*0-9641847-2-9*) Yutopian Ent.

Niebla. Miguel de Unamuno. (SPA.). pap. 13.95 (*84-376-0347-1*, Pub. by Ediciones Catedra) Continental Bk.

Niebla. Miguel de Unamuno. Ed. by German Gullon. (Nueva Austral Ser.: Vol. 115). (SPA.). pap. 14.95 (*84-239-1915-3*) Elliots Bks.

Niebla. Miguel de Unamuno. (SPA.). 1989. 9.95 (*0-8288-2577-7*) Fr & Eur.

Niebla. Miguel de Unamuno. (Clasicos Esenciales Ser.). (SPA.). (C). 1998. pap. 9.95 (*84-294-4628-1*) Santillana.

Niebla. 24th ed. Miguel de Unamuno. (SPA.). 264p. 1991. pap. write for info. (*0-7859-5141-5*) Fr & Eur.

***Niebla de Miguel de Unamuno A Favor de Cervantes, en Contra de los (Cervantofilos), Estudio de Narratologia Estilistica.** Benedicte Vauthier. (Illus.). 200p. 1999. 32.95 (*3-906762-10-6*, Pub. by P Lang) P Lang Pubng.

Niebuhr & His Age: Reinhold Niebuhr's Prophetic Role in the Twentieth Century. Charles C. Brown. LC 92-25356. 334p. 1992. 35.00 (*1-56338-042-0*) TPI PA.

***Niebuhr, Hromadka, Troeltsch & Barth: The Significance of Theology of History of Christian Social Ethics.** Kosuke Nishitani. LC 98-30468. (American University Studies, VII: Vol. 209). XVII, 400p. (C). 1999. text 64.00 (*0-8204-4188-0*) P Lang Pubng.

Niedecker & the Correspondence with Zukofsky, 1931-1970. Jenny Penberthy. LC 92-34643. (Illus.). 395p. (C). 1993. text 74.95 (*0-521-44369-5*) Cambridge U Pr.

Nieder-Sachsisches Koch-Buch. Mrcus Looft. (GER.). 557p. 1988. reprint ed. write for info. (*3-487-08218-7*) G Olms Pubs.

Niederdeutsch im Nationalsozialismus. Ed. by K. Dohnke et al. (GER.). 552p. 1994. write for info. (*3-487-09809-1*) G Olms Pubs.

Niedere Zahlentheorie, 2 Vols. in 1. Paul Bachmann. LC 66-20395. 902p. 1968. reprint ed. text 39.50 (*0-8284-0217-5*) Chelsea Pub.

***Niederlaendisches Buergerliches Gesetzbuch Buch 2: Juristische Personen.** 2nd ed. Ed. by Michael Lange et al. 460p. 1998. 108.00 (*90-411-0600-6*) Kluwer Law Intl.

Niederlage und Zukunft des Sozialismus see Downfall & Future of Socialism

Niederlandisch Am Niederrhein. Ed. by Helga Bister-Broosen et al. (Duisburger Arbeiten zur Sprach- und Kulturwissenschaft Ser.: Band 35). (GER., Illus.). 171p. 1998. pap. 37.95 (*3-631-32578-9*) P Lang Pubng.

Niederlandisch Ohne Muhe. Albert O. Cherel. 24.95 (*0-685-11422-8*); audio 125.00 (*0-685-01743-5*) Fr & Eur.

Niederlandisch ohne Muhe: Dutch for German Speakers. Assimil Staff. (DUT & GER.). 28.95 (*0-8288-4350-3*, M14896) Fr & Eur.

Niederlandisch ohne Muhe: Dutch for German Speakers, 3 cass., Set. Assimil Staff. (DUT & GER.). audio 125.00 (*0-685-53020-5*) Fr & Eur.

***Niederlandische Einflu & Bria; Auf Den Kirchenbau in Brandenburg und Anhalt Im 17. und 18. Jahrhundert.** Stephan Schonfeld. (Europaische Hochschulschriften Ser.: Vol. 28). 205p. 1999. 35.95 (*3-631-34961-0*) P Lang Pubng.

Niederlandisches Burgerliches Gesetzbuch, Buch 8 Verkehrsmittel und Beforderun, Vol. LETR 13. Nieper. 1997. 130.00 (*90-411-0388-0*) Kluwer Law Intl.

Niedermayr: Momentary Resorts. Walter Niedermayr. Ed. by AR/GE Kunst Bozen. (Illus.). 114p. 1999. 50.00 (*3-89322-962-0*) Edition Cantz.

Niederrheinische Musik-Zeitung, 3 vols. Ed. by H. Robert Cohen. (Repertoire International de la Presse Musicale Ser.). (GER.). 1990. 360.00 (*0-8357-0936-1*) Univ Microfilms.

Niederrheinisches Sagenbuch. Erich Bockemuhl. (GER.). 286p. 1997. reprint ed. write for info. (*3-487-05972-X*) G Olms Pubs.

Niedersachsische Schul- und Bildungsgeschichte im 19. und Fruhen 20. Jahrhundert. Hans-Joachim Schild. Ed. by Brigitte Schild. 1997. write for info. (*3-487-10273-0*) G Olms Pubs.

***Niehs Report on Health Effects from Exposure to Power-Line Frequency Electric & Magnetic Fields.** Ed. by Kenneth Olden. 67p. (C). 1999. pap. text 20.00 (*0-7881-8373-7*) DIANE Pub.

Niels Bohr: A Centenary Volume. Ed. by A. P. French & P. J. Kennedy. LC 85-8542. (Illus.). 440p. 1985. 39.95 (*0-674-62415-7*) HUP.

Niels Bohr: A Centenary Volume. Ed. by A. P. French & P. J. Kennedy. (Illus.). 440p. 1987. pap. 17.95 (*0-674-62416-5*) HUP.

Niels Bohr: Cientifico, Filosofo. Leopoldo Garcia-Colin. (Ciencia para Todos Ser.). (SPA.). pap. 6.99 (*968-16-2458-0*, Pub. by Fondo) Continental Bk.

Niels Bohr: Gentle Genius of Denmark. Ray Spangenburg & Diane K. Moser. LC 94-23815. (Makers of Modern Science Ser.). (Illus.). 128p. (YA). (gr. 7-12). 1995. 19.95 (*0-8160-2938-5*) Facts on File.

Niels Bohr: Physics & the World. Herman Feshbach et al. xx, 364p. 1988. text 87.00 (*3-7186-0484-1*); pap. text 43.00 (*3-7186-0494-9*) Gordon & Breach.

Niels Bohr & Contemporary Philosophy. Ed. by Jan Faye & Henry J. Folse, Jr. LC 93-24825. (Boston Studies in the Philosophy of Science: Vol 153). 406p. 1994. lib. bdg. 196.50 (*0-7923-2378-5*, Pub. by Kluwer Academic) Kluwer Academic.

Niels Bohr's Philosophy of Physics. D. R. Murdoch. (Illus.). 304p. 1989. pap. text 39.95 (*0-521-37927-X*) Cambridge U Pr.

Niels Bohr's Times: In Physics, Philosophy, & Polity. Abraham Pais. (Illus.). 582p. 1991. 35.00 (*0-19-852049-2*) OUP.

Niels Bohr's Times: In Physics, Philosophy, & Polity. Abraham Pais. (Illus.). 582p. 1994. reprint ed. pap. 19.95 (*0-19-852048-4*) OUP.

Niels Hendrik Abel, Mathematician Extraordinary. Oystein Ore. LC 73-14693. (Illus.). viii, 277p. 1974. reprint ed. text 19.95 (*0-8284-0274-4*) Chelsea Pub.

***Niels Henrik Abel & His Times: Called Too Soon by Flames Afar.** A. Stubhaug. Tr. by R. Daly. (Illus.). 550p. 2000. 44.95 (*3-540-66834-9*) Spr-Verlag.

Niels Lyhne. 2nd ed. Jens Peter Jacobsen. Tr. by Tiina Nunnally from DAN. LC 89-82139. (Fjord Modern Classics Ser.: No. 2). 217p. (Orig.). 1994. pap. 14.00 (*0-940242-65-6*) Fjord Pr.

Niels Stensen: Scientist & Saint. Erik K. Palsson. 75p. (Orig.). 1989. pap. 30.00 (*0-7855-6979-0*, Pub. by Veritas Pubns) St Mut.

Nielsen Theory & Dynamical Systems: AMS-IMS-SIAM Joint Summer Research Conference on Nielsen Theory & Dynamical Systems. Ed. by Christopher K. McCord. LC 93-26685. (Contemporary Mathematics Ser.: No. 152). 350p. 1993. pap. 52.00 (*0-8218-5181-0*, CONM/152) Am Math.

Nien Army & Their Guerrilla Warfare, 1851-1868. Ssu-yu Teng. LC 84-15874. 254p. 1984. reprint ed. lib. bdg. 65.00 (*0-313-24386-7*, TENI, Greenwood Pr) Greenwood.

Nieper Burgerliches, 8 vols., Set. 1997. lib. bdg. 555.00 (*90-411-0410-0*) Kluwer Law Intl.

Nieper Niederland Burgerliches. 1995. lib. bdg. 154.00 (*90-411-0131-4*) Kluwer Law Intl.

Nieto, Vol. 1. limited ed. Lauren Monsen. (Illus.). 80p. 1996. boxed set, lthr. 5000.00 (*0-9632328-2-7*) Marco Fine Arts.

Nietos de Felicidad Dolores. Cubena. LC 89-83579. (Coleccion Ebano y Canela). (SPA.). 233p. (Orig.). 1991. pap. 18.00 (*0-89729-528-5*) Ediciones.

Nietzche. 1997. write for info. (*0-8387-1069-7*) Bucknell U Pr.

Nietzche's French Legacy: A Genealogy of Poststructuralism. Alan D. Schrift. 250p. (C). 1995. pap. 20.99 (*0-415-91147-8*) Routledge.

***Nietzche's Postmoralism: Essays on Nietzche's Prelude to Philosophy's Future.** Richard Schacht. LC 99-56851. 2000. write for info. (*0-521-64085-7*) Cambridge U Pr.

Nietzsche. Gerald Abraham. LC 73-20387. (Nietzsche Ser.: No. 89). 1974. lib. bdg. 75.00 (*0-8383-1764-2*) M S G Haskell Hse.

Nietzsche. Ronald Hayman. LC 99-24217. (Great Philosophers Ser. : Vol. 5). 64p. 1999. pap. 6.00 (*0-415-92380-8*) Routledge.

Nietzsche. J. M. Kennedy. LC 73-21622. (Nietzsche Ser.: No. 89). 1974. lib. bdg. 75.00 (*0-8383-1791-X*) M S G Haskell Hse.

Nietzsche. Alfred Rosenberg. 1975. lib. bdg. 250.00 (*0-8490-0732-1*) Gordon Pr.

Nietzsche. Richard Schacht. (Arguments of the Philosophers Ser.). 560p. 1983. pap. 19.95 (*0-7102-0544-9*, Routledge Thoemms) Routledge.

***Nietzsche.** Michael Tanner. (Very Short Introductions Ser.). (Illus.). 112p. 2000. pap. 8.95 (*0-19-285414-3*) OUP.

***Nietzsche.** White. 592p. 2000. 165.00 (*0-7546-2069-7*) Ashgate Pub Co.

Nietzsche. Paul Carus. LC 72-2039. (Studies in German Literature: No. 13). 1972. reprint ed. lib. bdg. 75.00 (*0-8383-1464-3*) M S G Haskell Hse.

Nietzsche, 2 Vols, Set. 4th ed. Martin Heidegger. (GER.). 1982. 111.25 (*3-7885-0115-4*) Adlers Foreign Bks.

Nietzsche: A Critical Reader. Ed. by Peter R. Sedgwick. LC 94-40792. (Critical Readers Ser.). 300p. (C). 1995. pap. 28.95 (*0-631-19045-7*) Blackwell Pubs.

Nietzsche: A Frenzied Look. Robert J. Ackermann. LC 90-31323. 224p. 1990. 30.00 (*0-87023-722-5*) U of Mass Pr.

Nietzsche: A Frenzied Look. Robert J. Ackermann. LC 90-31323. 1993. pap. 16.95 (*0-87023-841-8*) U of Mass Pr.

Nietzsche: A Novel. David F. Krell. LC 96-12165. (SUNY Series in Contemporary Continental Philosophy). 364p. (C). 1996. text 57.50 (*0-7914-2999-7*); pap. text 18.95 (*0-7914-3000-6*) State U NY Pr.

Nietzsche: A Philosophical Biography. Gary Elsner. 206p. (Orig.). (C). 1992. pap. text 26.50 (*0-8191-8697-X*); lib. bdg. 49.50 (*0-8191-8696-1*) U Pr of Amer.

Nietzsche: A Re-Examination. Irving M. Zeitlin. 200p. 1994. pap. 26.95 (*0-7456-1291-1*) Blackwell Pubs.

Nietzsche: A Self-Portrait from His Letters. Friedrich Wilhelm Nietzsche. Ed. by Peter Fuss & Henry Shapiro. LC 73-134953. 208p. reprint ed. pap. 64.50 (*0-8357-9170-X*, 201465500093) Bks Demand.

Nietzsche: An Introduction to the Understanding of His Philosophical Activity. Karl Jaspers. Tr. by C. F. Wallraff & F. J. Schmitz from GER. LC 97-20966. 512p. 1997. reprint ed. pap. text 16.95 (*0-8018-5779-1*) Johns Hopkins.

Nietzsche: Critical Assessments. Daniel W. Conway. LC 97-29031. 1998. write for info. (*0-415-13562-1*) Routledge.

Nietzsche: Daybreak: Thoughts on the Prejudices of Morality. Friedrich Wilhelm Nietzsche. Ed. by Maudemarie Clark & Brian Leiter. (Cambridge Texts in the History of Philosophy Ser.). 292p. (C). 1997. text 49.95 (*0-521-59050-7*); pap. text 16.95 (*0-521-59963-6*) Cambridge U Pr.

Nietzsche: Einfuehrung in das Verstaendnis Seines Philosophierens. 4th ed. Karl Jaspers. (GER.). (C). 1974. 44.65 (*3-11-004892-2*); pap. 40.00 (*3-11-008658-1*) De Gruyter.

Nietzsche: Great Philosophers. Richard Schacht. (Arguments of the Philosophers Ser.). 608p. (C). 1985. pap. 27.99 (*0-415-09071-7*) Routledge.

Nietzsche: Great Philosophers. Michael Tanner. 94p. 1995. pap. text 8.95 (*0-19-287680-5*) OUP.

Nietzsche: His Philosophy of Contradictions & the Contradictions of His Philosophy. Wolfgang Muller-Lauter. LC 98-25391. (International Nietzsche Studies). 296p. 1999. 39.95 (*0-252-02452-4*); pap. 21.95 (*0-252-06758-4*) U of Ill Pr.

Nietzsche: Life As Literature. Alexander Nehamas. LC 85-5589. 240p. 1985. 29.95 (*0-674-62435-1*) HUP.

Nietzsche: Life as Literature. Alexander Nehamas. LC 85-5589. 240p. 1985. pap. 17.95 (*0-674-62426-2*) HUP.

Nietzsche: Literature & Values. Ed. by Volker Durr et al. LC 87-40145. (Monatshefte Occasional Volumes Ser.: Vol. 6). 229p. 1988. reprint ed. pap. 71.00 (*0-608-07440-3*, 206766700009) Bks Demand.

Nietzsche: Man, Knowledge, & Will to Power. George J. Stack. LC 91-3486. 1994. text 35.00 (*0-89341-672-X*, Longwood Academic) Hollowbrook.

N

Nietzsche: Naturalism & Interpretation. Christopher Cox. LC 99-30107. 241p. 1999. text 45.00 (*0-520-21553-2*, Pub. by U CA Pr) Cal Prin Full Svc.

Nietzsche: Philosopher, Psychologist, Antichrist. 4th ed. Walter Kaufmann. 532p. 1975. pap. text 17.95 (*0-691-01983-5*, Pub. by Princeton U Pr) Cal Prin Full Svc.

Nietzsche: The Body & Culture: Philosophy As a Philological Genealogy. Eric Blondel. Tr. by Sean Hand from FRE. LC 89-51665. 296p. 1991. 47.50 (*0-8047-1551-3*); pap. 17.95 (*0-8047-1906-3*) Stanford U Pr.

Nietzsche: The Ethics of an Immoralist. Peter Berkowitz. LC 94-34119. 336p. 1995. text 41.00 (*0-674-62442-4*, BERNIE) HUP.

Nietzsche: The Ethics of an Immoralist. Peter Berkowitz. 336p. 1996. pap. 17.50 (*0-674-62443-2*) HUP.

Nietzsche: The Great Philosophers. Friedrich Wilhelm Nietzsche. Ed. by Richard Schacht. LC 92-38158. 330p. (Orig.). (C). 1993. pap. text 15.60 (*0-02-406681-8*, Macmillan Coll) P-H.

Nietzsche: The Man & His Philosophy. R. J. Hollingdale. LC 65-17723. 344p. reprint ed. pap. 106.70 (*0-608-11818-4*, 205097300076) Bks Demand.

Nietzsche: The Man & His Philosophy. rev. ed. R. J. Hollingdale. LC 98-33299. 300p. 1999. 27.95 (*0-521-64091-1*) Cambridge U Pr.

Nietzsche: The Mind's Greatest Storyteller. Anthony M. Mlikotin. (Series in Avant-Garde Thoughts & the Arts). 303p. 1991. pap. write for info. (*0-9629448-0-7*) New Dimens Pr.

Nietzsche: The Politics of Power. Ike Okonta. LC 91-31790. (American University Studies: Philosophy: Ser. V, Vol. 132). 192p. (C). 1992. text 38.95 (*0-8204-1727-0*) P Lang Pubng.

Nietzsche: Untimely Meditations. Friedrich Wilhelm Nietzsche. Ed. by Daniel Breazeale. Tr. by R. J. Hollingdale. LC 96-37028. (Cambridge Texts in the History of Philosophy Ser.). 328p. (C). 1997. text 49.95 (*0-521-58458-2*); pap. text 15.95 (*0-521-58584-8*) Cambridge U Pr.

Nietzsche: Volumes One & Two, 2 vols., Pt. 1, Vols. I & II. Martin Heidegger. Ed. by David F. Krell. LC 78-19509. Vol. 1. 608p. 1991. reprint ed. pap. 23.00 (*0-06-063841-9*, Pub. by Harper SF) HarpC.

Nietzsche: Volumes Three & Four, 2 vols., Pt. 2, Vols. III & IV. Martin Heidegger. Ed. by David F. Krell. LC 78-19509. Vol. 2. 608p. 1991. reprint ed. pap. 24.00 (*0-06-063794-3*, Pub. by Harper SF) HarpC.

Nietzsche - Briefweshsel, Kritische Gesamtausgabe: I, Abtielung, Vierter Band Nachbericht Zu Abteilung I: Briefe Von und An Friedrich Nietzsche Oktober 1849-April 1869. Ed. by Norbert Miller & Jorg Salaquarda. (GER.). viii, 960p. 1993. lib. bdg. 276.95 (*3-11-012277-4*) De Gruyter.

Nietzsche - Human, All Too Human: A Book for Free Spirits. Friedrich Wilhelm Nietzsche. Ed. by Richard Schacht. Tr. by R. J. Hollingdale. LC 96-10969. (Cambridge Texts in the History of Philosophy Ser.). 420p. (C). 1996. pap. text 16.95 (*0-521-56704-1*) Cambridge U Pr.

Nietzsche - Human, All Too Human: A Book for Free Spirits. Friedrich Wilhelm Nietzsche. Tr. by R. J. Hollingdale. LC 96-10969. (Cambridge Texts in the History of Philosophy Ser.). 429p. (C). 1996. text 54.95 (*0-521-56200-7*) Cambridge U Pr.

Nietzsche - Werke: Kritische Gesamtausgabe, Vol. 1, Sect. 7. Ed. by G. Colli & Mazzino Montinari. (C). 1976. 160.00 (*3-11-004979-1*) De Gruyter.

Nietzsche, Aesthetics & Modernity. Matthew Rampley. LC 99-19420. 336p. (C). 1999. 59.95 (*0-521-65155-7*) Cambridge U Pr.

***Nietzsche Against the Crucified.** Alistair Kee. 1998. pap. 26.00 (*0-334-02783-7*) TPI PA.

Nietzsche Als Herausforderung: Nietzsche-Interpretationen II. Wolfgang Muller-Lauter. 312p. 1998. 99.00 (*3-11-013452-7*) De Gruyter.

Nietzsche & "An Architecture of the Mind" Ed. by Alexandre Kostka & Irving Wohlfarth. LC 98-26304. (Issues & Debates Ser.). 378p. 1999. pap. 45.00 (*0-89236-485-8*, Pub. by J P Getty Trust) OUP.

Nietzsche & Art. A. Ludovici. LC 72-148824. (Studies in German Literature: No. 13). 1971. reprint ed. lib. bdg. 75.00 (*0-8383-1229-2*) M S G Haskell Hse.

Nietzsche & Asian Thought. Ed. by Graham Parkes. 266p. 1991. 32.50 (*0-226-64683-1*) U Ch Pr.

Nietzsche & Asian Thought. Graham Parkes. 254p. 1996. pap. text 14.95 (*0-226-64685-8*) U Ch Pr.

Nietzsche & Buddhism. Freny Mistry. (Monographien und Texte zur Nietzscge-Forschung Ser.: Vol. 6). 211p. 1981. 83.10 (*3-11-008305-1*) De Gruyter.

Nietzsche & Buddhism: A Study in Nihilism & Ironic Affinities. Robert G. Morrison. LC 96-53341. 260p. 1997. text 62.00 (*0-19-823556-9*) OUP.

Nietzsche & Buddhism: A Study in Nihilism & Ironic Affinities. Robert G. Morrison. 260p. 1999. pap. text 24.95 (*0-19-823865-7*) OUP.

Nietzsche & Christianity, Vol. 145. Ed. by Claude Geffre & Jean-Pierre Jossua. (Concilium Ser.). 128p. (Orig.). 1981. 6.95 (*0-8164-2312-1*) Harper SF.

Nietzsche & Depth Psychology. Ed. by Jacob Golomb et al. LC 98-26836. 364p. (C). 1999. pap. text 27.95 (*0-7914-4140-7*) State U NY Pr.

Nietzsche & Depth Psychology. Ed. by Jacob Golomb et al. LC 98-26836. 384p. (C). 1999. text 81.50 (*0-7914-4139-3*) State U NY Pr.

Nietzsche & Emerson: An Elective Affinity. George J. Stack. LC 92-27599. 392p. (C). 1992. text 39.95 (*0-8214-1037-7*) Ohio U Pr.

Nietzsche & Emerson: An Elective Affinity. George J. Stack. LC 92-27599. 392p. (C). 1994. reprint ed. pap. text 24.95 (*0-8214-1068-7*) Ohio U Pr.

Nietzsche & Jewish Culture. Ed. by Jacob J. Golomb. 296p. (C). 1997. 80.00 (*0-415-09512-3*); pap. 25.99 (*0-415-09513-1*) Routledge.

Nietzsche & Jung: Quest for Wholeness. Patricia E. Dixon. LC 89-13134. (Contemporary Existentialism Ser.). XVI, 459p. (C). 1999. text 68.00 (*0-8204-1161-2*) P Lang Pubng.

Nietzsche & Metaphor. Sarah Kofman. 210p. (C). 1993. 39.50 (*0-8047-1975-6*) Stanford U Pr.

Nietzsche & Metaphysics. Michel Haar. Ed. & Tr. by Michael Gendre. LC 95-12888. (SUNY Series in Contemporary Continental Philosophy). 214p. (C). 1996. pap. text 16.95 (*0-7914-2788-9*) State U NY Pr.

Nietzsche & Metaphysics. Michel Haar. Ed. & Tr. by Michael Gendre. LC 95-12888. (SUNY Series in Contemporary Continental Philosophy). 214p. (C). 1996. text 49.50 (*0-7914-2787-0*) State U NY Pr.

Nietzsche & Metaphysics. Peter Poellner. (Oxford Philosophical Monographs). 332p. 1995. text 60.00 (*0-19-823517-8*) OUP.

***Nietzsche & Metaphysics.** Peter Poellner. 336p. 2000. pap. 24.95 (*0-19-825063-0*) OUP.

Nietzsche & Modern Consciousness. Janko Lavrin. LC 72-2094. (Studies in German Literature: No. 13). 1972. reprint ed. lib. bdg. 75.00 (*0-8383-1481-3*) M S G Haskell Hse.

Nietzsche & Modern Times: A Study of Bacon, Descartes, Nietzsche. Laurence Lampert. 1995. pap. 19.00 (*0-300-06510-8*) Yale U Pr.

Nietzsche & Music. Georges Liebert. 1997. pap. text 17.50 (*0-226-48088-7*); lib. bdg. 44.00 (*0-226-48087-9*) U Ch Pr.

Nietzsche & Other Exponents of Individualism. Paul Carus. LC 14-1736. (Illus.). 171p. reprint ed. pap. 53.10 (*0-608-10197-4*, 200907700070) Bks Demand.

Nietzsche & Pascal on Christianity. Charles M. Natoli. LC 83-49020. (American University Studies: Philosophy: Ser. V, Vol. 3). 197p. (Orig.). (C). 1985. pap. text 24.25 (*0-8204-0071-8*) P Lang Pubng.

Nietzsche & Philosophy. Gilles Deleuze. Tr. by Hugh Tomlinson from FRE. LC 82-17676. (European Perspectives Ser.). 275p. 1985. pap. text 19.00 (*0-231-05669-9*) Col U Pr.

Nietzsche & Philosophy. Gilles Deleuze. Tr. by Hugh Tomlinson. LC 82-17676. (European Perspectives Ser.). 237p. reprint ed. pap. 73.50 (*0-7837-0428-3*, 204075100018) Bks Demand.

Nietzsche & Political Thought. Mark Warren. (German Social Thought Ser.). 336p. 1988. 39.50 (*0-262-23135-2*) MIT Pr.

Nietzsche & Political Thought. Mark Warren. (Studies in Contemporary German Social Thought). 320p. 1991. reprint ed. pap. text 14.95 (*0-262-73094-4*) MIT Pr.

Nietzsche & Psychoanalysis. Daniel Chapelle. LC 92-35535. 258p. (C). 1993. text 21.50 (*0-7914-1527-9*) State U NY Pr.

Nietzsche & Schiller: Untimely Aesthetics. Nicholas Martin. (Oxford Modern Languages & Literature Monographs). 230p. (C). 1996. text 57.00 (*0-19-815913-7*) OUP.

Nietzsche & Soviet Culture: Ally & Adversary. Ed. by Bernice G. Rosenthal. LC 93-29255. (Cambridge Studies in Russian Literature). (Illus.). 439p. (C). 1994. text 69.95 (*0-521-45281-3*) Cambridge U Pr.

***Nietzsche & the Divine.** Ed. by Jim Urpeth & John M. Lippitt. 216p. 2000. pap. 29.95 (*1-903083-12-5*, Pub. by Clinamen Pr) Paul & Co Pubs.

Nietzsche & the Feminine. Ed. & Intro. by Peter J. Burgard. LC 93-34551. (Feminist Issues Ser.). 384p. (C). 1994. pap. text 19.50 (*0-8139-1495-7*) U Pr of Va.

Nietzsche & the Jews: Exaltation & Denigration. Siegfried Mandel. LC 98-21368. 350p. 1998. 49.95 (*1-57392-223-4*) Prometheus Bks.

Nietzsche & the Modern Crisis of the Humanities. Peter Levine. LC 94-11021. 279p. (C). 1995. pap. text 18.95 (*0-7914-2328-X*) State U NY Pr.

Nietzsche & the Modern Crisis of the Humanities. Peter Levine. LC 94-11021. 279p. (C). 1995. text 57.50 (*0-7914-2327-1*) State U NY Pr.

Nietzsche & the Origin of Virtue. Lester H. Hunt. (Nietzsche Studies). 224p. (C). 1993. pap. 24.99 (*0-415-09580-8*, B0293) Routledge.

***Nietzsche & The Philosophy of The Future.** James I. Porter. 1999. pap. text 19.95 (*0-8047-3698-7*) Stanford U Pr.

Nietzsche & the Political. Daniel W. Conway. LC 96-7867. (Thinking the Political Ser.). 176p. (C). 1997. 70.00 (*0-415-10068-2*); pap. 20.99 (*0-415-10069-0*) Routledge.

Nietzsche & the Politics of Aristocratic Radicalism. Bruce Detwiler. LC 89-375. 252p. 1999. 29.95 (*0-226-14354-6*) U Ch Pr.

Nietzsche & the Problem of Sovereignty. Richard J. White. LC 96-25212. 224p. 1997. text 34.95 (*0-252-02300-5*); pap. text 15.95 (*0-252-06603-0*) U of Ill Pr.

Nietzsche & the Promise of Philosophy. Wayne Klein. LC 97-3885. (SUNY Series in Contemporary Continental Philosophy). 256p. (C). 1997. text 59.50 (*0-7914-3549-0*); pap. text 19.95 (*0-7914-3550-4*) State U NY Pr.

Nietzsche & the Question of Interpretation. Alan D. Schrift. 256p. (C). 1990. pap. 23.99 (*0-415-90312-2*, A4605) Routledge.

Nietzsche & the Vicious Circle. Pierre Klossowski. Tr. by Daniel W. Smith. LC 97-14379.Tr. of Nietzsche et le Cercle Vicieux. xx, 282p. 1997. pap. text 19.95 (*0-226-44387-6*); lib. bdg. 50.00 (*0-226-44386-8*) U Ch Pr.

Nietzsche & Wagner: A Lesson in Subjugation. Joachim Kohler. Tr. by Ronald Taylor from GER. LC 98-87833. (Illus.). 190p. 1998. 25.00 (*0-300-07640-1*) Yale U Pr.

Nietzsche As Affirmative Thinker. Ed. by Yirmiahu Yovel. 244p. 1986. text 129.50 (*90-247-3269-7*) Kluwer Academic.

Nietzsche As Anti-Socialist. William A. Preston. 1998. 60.00 (*0-391-04076-6*) Humanities.

Nietzsche As Cultural Physician. Daniel R. Ahern. LC 94-31510. 1995. 38.50 (*0-271-01425-3*) Pa St U Pr.

Nietzsche As Educator. Gary Lemco. LC 92-4107. 160p. 1992. lib. bdg. 69.95 (*0-7734-9962-8*) E Mellen.

Nietzsche As Philosopher. Arthur C. Danto. 250p. 1980. reprint ed. pap. text 19.50 (*0-231-05053-4*) Col U Pr.

Nietzsche As Postmodernist: Essays Pro & Contra. Ed. by Clayton Koelb. LC 89-27506. (SUNY Series in Contemporary Continental Philosophy). 350p. (C). 1990. text 21.50 (*0-7914-0341-6*) State U NY Pr.

Nietzsche-Briefwechsel: Briefe an Nietzsche, 1869-1872, Vol. 2, Section 2. Ed. by C. Colli & Mazzino Montinari. (C). 1977. 213.85 (*3-11-006635-1*) De Gruyter.

Nietzsche-Briefwechsel: Briefe April, 1869-1872, Vol. 2, Section 1. Ed. by G. Colli & Mazzino Montinari. (C). 1977. 113.85 (*3-11-006633-5*) De Gruyter.

Nietzsche, Briefwechsel, Kritische Gesamtausgabe: Section II. Incl. Vol. 3. Nietzsches Briefe, Mai 1872-Dezember 1874. 1978. 60.00 (*3-11-007194-0*); Vol. 4. Briefe an Nietzsche Mai 1872-Dezember 1874. 1978. 102.00 (*3-11-007196-7*); (C). 1978. write for info. (*0-318-51630-6*) De Gruyter.

Nietzsche Canon: A Publication History & Bibliography. William H. Schaberg. LC 95-16815. 192p. 1995. pap. text 14.95 (*0-226-73576-1*) U Ch Pr.

Nietzsche Canon: A Publication History & Bibliography. William H. Schaberg. LC 95-16815. 298p. 1996. 36.50 (*0-226-73575-3*) U Ch Pr.

Nietzsche Contra Democracy. Fredrick Appel. LC 98-27125. 160p. 1998. 29.95 (*0-8014-3424-6*) Cornell U Pr.

Nietzsche Contra Nietzsche: Creativity & the Anti-Romantic. Adrian Del Caro. LC 88-37659. 336p. 1989. text 47.50 (*0-8071-1493-6*) La State U Pr.

Nietzsche Contra Rousseau: A Study of Nietzsche's Moral & Political Thought. Keith Ansell-Pearson. 302p. (C). 1991. text 59.95 (*0-521-41173-4*) Cambridge U Pr.

Nietzsche Critical Assessments, 4 vols. Conway. Ed. by Daniel Conway. 1608p. (C). 1998. reprint ed. 660.00 (*0-415-13561-3*) Routledge.

Nietzsche. Die Dynamik der Willen Zur Macht und die Ewige Wiederkehr Vol. 2: Um ein Vorwort Erweiterte Auflage. Gunter Abel. 504p. 1998. 36.00 (*3-11-015191-X*) De Gruyter.

***Nietzsche, Epistemology & the Philosophy of Science: Nietzsche & the Sciences II.** Ed. by Babette E. Babich. LC 99-15081. (Boston Studies in the Philosophy of Science). 368p. 1999. 171.00 (*0-7923-5743-4*) Kluwer Academic.

Nietzsche et le Cercle Vicieux see Nietzsche & the Vicious Circle

Nietzsche, Feminism, & Political Theory. Ed. by Paul Patton. LC 92-33978. 272p. (C). 1993. pap. 24.99 (*0-415-08256-0*, B0699) Routledge.

Nietzsche for Beginners. Marc Sautet. (Documentary Comic Bks.). (Illus.). 192p. (Orig.). 1990. pap. 11.95 (*0-86316-118-9*) Writers & Readers.

Nietzsche, Genealogy, Morality: Essays on Nietzsche's Genealogy of Morals. Ed. by Richard Schacht. LC 93-12082. (Philosophical Traditions Ser.: Vol. 5). 1994. pap. 24.95 (*0-520-08318-0*, Pub. by U CA Pr) Cal Prin Full Svc.

Nietzsche, God, & the Jews: His Critique of Judeo-Christianity in Relation to the Nazi Myth. Weaver Santaniello. LC 93-46690. 232p. (C). 1994. pap. text 19.95 (*0-7914-2136-8*) State U NY Pr.

Nietzsche, God, & the Jews: His Critique of Judeo-Christianity in Relation to the Nazi Myth. Weaver Santaniello. LC 93-46690. 232p. (C). 1994. text 59.50 (*0-7914-2135-X*) State U NY Pr.

Nietzsche, Heidegger, & Bubber Vol. 2: Discovering the Mind. Walter Kaufmann. 453p. (C). 1991. pap. 24.95 (*0-88738-394-7*) Transaction Pubs.

Nietzsche, Heidegger & the Transition to Postmodernity. Gregory B. Smith. LC 95-14678. 376p. 1995. pap. text 16.00 (*0-226-76340-4*) U Ch Pr.

Nietzsche, Heidegger & the Transition to Postmodernity. Gregory B. Smith. LC 95-14678. 376p. 1999. lib. bdg. 42.00 (*0-226-76339-0*) U Ch Pr.

Nietzsche in American Literature & Thought. Ed. by Manfred Putz. LC 95-9731. (GERM Ser.). vi, 382p. (C). 1995. 75.00 (*1-57113-028-4*) Camden Hse.

Nietzsche in China. Lixin Shao. LC 98-26798. (Literature & the Sciences of Man Ser.: Vol. 11). XI, 146p. (C). 1999. text 40.95 (*0-8204-2853-1*) P Lang Pubng.

Nietzsche in China, 1904-1992: An Annotated Bibliography. Chiu-yee Cheung. (Faculty of Asian Studies Monographs: Vol. 19). 185p. 1997. pap. text 25.00 (*0-7315-1438-6*, Pub. by Aust Nat Univ) UH Pr.

Nietzsche in England, 1890-1914: The Growth of a Reputation. David S. Thatcher. LC 75-149322. 343p. reprint ed. pap. 106.40 (*0-608-10026-9*, 201443200093) Bks Demand.

Nietzsche in Italy. Ed. by Thomas J. Harrison. (Illus.). 340p. 1988. pap. 56.50 (*0-915838-99-0*) Anma Libri.

Nietzsche in 90 Minutes. Paul Strathern. LC 96-28105. (Philosophers in 90 Minutes Ser.). 96p. 1996. pap. 6.95 (*1-56663-121-1*, Pub. by I R Dee); lib. bdg. 14.95 (*1-56663-120-3*, Pub. by I R Dee) Natl Bk Netwk.

Nietzsche in Outline & Aphorism. Alfred R. Orage. 1974. 250.00 (*0-8490-0733-X*) Gordon Pr.

Nietzsche in Russia. Ed. by Bernice G. Rosenthal. LC 86-12290. (Illus.). 441p. 1986. reprint ed. pap. 136.80 (*0-608-07153-6*, 206737800009) Bks Demand.

Nietzsche in the Early Work of Thomas Mann. Roger A. Nicholls. LC 55-9553. (University of California Publications in Social Welfare: Vol. 45). 128p. reprint ed. pap. 39.70 (*0-608-14168-2*, 202125200021) Bks Demand.

Nietzsche in Turin: An Intimate Biography. Lesley Chamberlain. LC 98-51549. 272p. 1998. pap. 13.00 (*0-312-19938-4*) St Martin.

Nietzsche Legacy in Germany, 1890-1990. Steven E. Aschheim. (Weird & Horrible Library: No. 2). (Illus.). 337p. (C). 1992. pap. 18.95 (*0-520-08555-8*, Pub. by U CA Pr) Cal Prin Full Svc.

Nietzsche on Truth & Philosophy. Maudemarie Clark. (Modern European Philosophy Ser.). 312p. (C). 1991. text 64.95 (*0-521-34368-2*) Cambridge U Pr.

Nietzsche on Truth & Philosophy. Maudemarie Clark. (Modern European Philosophy Ser.). 312p. (C). 1991. pap. text 20.95 (*0-521-34850-1*) Cambridge U Pr.

Nietzsche, Philosophy & the Arts. Ed. by Salim Kemal et al. LC 97-18726. (Studies in Philosophy & the Arts). (Illus.). 370p. (C). 1998. text 69.95 (*0-521-59381-6*) Cambridge U Pr.

Nietzsche, Politics & Modernity: A Critique of Liberal Reason. David Owen. 192p. 1995. 69.95 (*0-8039-7766-2*); pap. 26.95 (*0-8039-7767-0*) Sage.

Nietzsche Reader. Friedrich Wilhelm Nietzsche. Ed. & Tr. by R. J. Hollingdale from GER. (Classics Ser.). 288p. (Orig.). 1978. pap. 12.95 (*0-14-044329-0*, Penguin Classics) Viking Penguin.

Nietzsche-Rezeption im Lichte des Faschismus: Thomas Mann und Menno ter Braak. Sung-Hyun Jang. (Germanistische Texte und Studien: Vol. 48). (GER.). viii, 222p. 1994. write for info. (*3-487-09943-8*) G Olms Pubs.

Nietzsche-Studien, Vol. 4. Friedrich Wilhelm Nietzsche. Ed. by Mazzino Montinari. (Internationales Jahrbuch fuer die Nietzsche-Forschung Ser.). (GER.). 1975. 142.35 (*3-11-005844-8*) De Gruyter.

Nietzsche-Studien, Vol. 6. Friedrich Wilhelm Nietzsche. (C). 1977. 113.85 (*3-11-007166-5*) De Gruyter.

Nietzsche-Studien, Vol. 7. Friedrich Wilhelm Nietzsche. (Internationales Jahrbuch fuer die Nietzsche-Forschung Ser.). (GER.). 1978. 126.95 (*3-11-007338-2*) De Gruyter.

Nietzsche-Studien, Vol. 8. Friedrich Wilhelm Nietzsche. (Internationales Jahrbuch fuer die Nietzsche-Forschung Ser.). (GER.). 1979. 150.00 (*3-11-007861-9*) De Gruyter.

Nietzsche-Studien, Vol. 9. Friedrich Wilhelm Nietzsche. Ed. by Ernst Behler et al. (Internationales Jahrbuch fuer die Nietzsche-Forschung Ser.). (GER.). 1980. 157.70 (*3-11-008241-1*) De Gruyter.

Nietzsche-Studien, Vol. 10-11. Friedrich Wilhelm Nietzsche. (Internationales Jahrbuch fuer die Nietzsche-Forchung Ser.). (GER.). 1982. 215.40 (*3-11-008638-7*) De Gruyter.

Nietzsche-Studien, Vol. 12. Friedrich Wilhelm Nietzsche. (Internationales Jahrbuch fuer die Nietzsche-Forschung Ser.). (GER.). 1982. 176.95 (*3-11-009507-6*) De Gruyter.

Nietzsche-Studien, Vol. 13. Friedrich Wilhelm Nietzsche. (Internationales Jahrbuch fuer die Nietzsche-Forschung Ser.). (GER.). 1984. 234.65 (*3-11-009648-X*) De Gruyter.

Nietzsche-Studien, Vol. 14. Friedrich Wilhelm Nietzsche. (Internationales Jahrbuch fuer die Nietzsche-Forchung Ser.). (GER.). 1985. 153.85 (*3-11-010207-2*) De Gruyter.

Nietzsche-Studien, Vol. 15. Friedrich Wilhelm Nietzsche. (Internationales Jahrbuch fuer die Nietzsche-Forschung Ser.). (GER.). 1986. 176.95 (*3-11-010540-3*) De Gruyter.

Nietzsche-Studien, Vol.5. Friedrich Wilhelm Nietzsche. (Internationales Jahrbuch fuer die Nietzsche-Forschung Ser.). (GER.). (C). 1976. 134.65 (*3-11-006656-4*) De Gruyter.

Nietzsche-Studien: Internationales Jahrbuch fuer die Nietzsche - Forschung, Vol. 2. Friedrich Wilhelm Nietzsche. Ed. by Mazzino Montinari et al. (Internationales Jahrbuch fuer die Nietzsche-Forschung Ser.). vi, 368p. (C). 1973. 112.35 (*3-11-004332-7*) De Gruyter.

Nietzsche-Studien: Internationales Jahrbuch fuer die Nietzsche-Forschung, Vol. 1. Friedrich Wilhelm Nietzsche. Ed. by Mazzino Montinari et al. 470p. (C). 1972. 142.35 (*3-11-002224-9*) De Gruyter.

Nietzsche-Studien: Internationales Jahrbuch fuer die Nietzsche-Forschung, Vol. 2. (GER.). 620p. (C). 1997. lib. bdg. 206.00 (*3-11-015725-X*) De Gruyter.

Nietzsche-Studien: Internationales Jahrbuch fuer die Nietzsche-Forschung, Vol. 3. Friedrich Wilhelm Nietzsche. Ed. by Mazzino Montinari et al. (GER.). (C). 1974. 73.10 (*3-11-004726-8*) De Gruyter.

Nietzsche-Studien Gesamtregister der Bande 1-20. Kurt Dite & Jorg Salaquarda. 504p. 1997. 124.00 (*3-11-013885-9*) De Gruyter.

Nietzsche und der Deutsche Geist, Vol. 1. Richard F. Krummel. (Monographien und Texte Zur Nietzsche-Forschung Ser.). 737p. 1998. 240.00 (*3-11-016074-9*) De Gruyter.

Nietzsche und der Deutsche Geist, Vol. 2. Richard F. Krummel. 688p. 1983. 253.85 (*3-11-008867-3*) De Gruyter.

Nietzsche und der Deutsche Geist, Vol. 2. Richard F. Krummel. (Monographien und Texte Zur Nietzsche-Forschung Ser.). 861p. 1998. 265.35 (*3-11-016075-7*) De Gruyter.

Nietzsche und der Deutsche Geist, Vol. 3. Richard F. Krummel. (Monographien und Texte Zur Nietzsche-Forschung Ser.). 931p. 1998. 285.35 (*3-11-015613-X*) De Gruyter.

Nietzsche und der Deutsche Geist: Ausbreitung und Wirkung des Nietzscheschen Werkes im Deutschen Sprachraum bis zum Todesjahr des Philosophen: ein Schrifttumsverzeichnis der Jahre 1867-1900, Vol. 1. Richard F. Krummel. LC 72-81559. (Monographien und Texte zur Nietzscge-Forschung Ser.: Vol. 3). (C). 1974. 150.00 (*3-11-004019-0*) De Gruyter.

N

An Asterisk (*) at the beginning of an entry indicates that the title is appearing for the first time.

Nietzsche und die Dialektik der Aufklaerung. Heinz Roettges. (Monographien und Texte zur Nietzscge-Forschung Ser.: Vol. 2). (C). 1972. 130.80 (*3-11-004018-2*) De Gruyter.

Nietzsche und die Metaphysik. Mihailo Djuric. (Monographien und Texte zur Nietzscge-Forschung Ser.: Band 16). (GER.). viii, 326p. 1985. 130.80 (*3-11-010169-6*) De Gruyter.

Nietzsche Und die Musik. Gunther Poltner & Helmuth Vetter. 140p. 1997. 32.95 (*3-631-49940-X*) P Lang Pubng.

Nietzsche und Emerson. Stanley Hubbard. LC 80-2538. reprint ed. 25.50 (*0-404-19264-5*) AMS Pr.

Nietzsche und Freud. Reinhard Gasser. (Monographien und Texte Zur Nietzsche-Forschung Ser.: Vol. 38). (GER.). 800p. (C). 1997. lib. bdg. 289.00 (*3-11-014960-5*) De Gruyter.

Nietzsche-Wagner Rift. Francis Neilson. 1979. lib. bdg. 150.00 (*0-685-96632-1*) Revisionist Pr.

Nietzsche Werke. Incl. Sect. 3, Vol. 3. Nachgelassene Fragmente, 1869-1872. 1978. 35.20 (*3-11-007469-9*); Vol. 4. Nachgelassene Fragmente, 1872-1873. 1978. 45.00 (*3-11-007471-0*); (C). 1978. write for info. (*0-318-51632-2*) De Gruyter.

Nietzsche Werke. Ed. by Friedrich Wilhelm Nietzsche. Incl. Sect 4, Vol. 1. Richard Wagner in Bayreuth: Unzeitgemaesse Betrachtungen, Nummer 4; Nachgelassene Fragmente, Anfang 1875 bis Fruehjahr, 1876. iv, 366p. 1967. 68.00 (*3-11-005170-2*); Sect. 4, Vol. 2. Menschliches, Allzumenschliches: Band 1; Nachgelassene Fragmente, 1876 bis Winter, 1877-78. Ed. by Giorgio Colli & Mazzino Montinari. (GER.). iv, 586p. 1967. 108.00 (*3-11-005171-0*); Sect 4, Vol. 3. Menschliches, Allzumenschliches: Band 2; Nachgelassene Fragmente, Fruehling, 1878 Bis November, 1879. Ed. by Giorgio Colli & Mazzino Montinari. (GER.). iv, 482p. 1967. 89.35 (*3-11-005172-9*); Sect 4, Vol. 4. Nachbericht Zur Vierten Abteilung: Richard Wagner in Bayreuth; Menschliches, Allzumenschliches, Baende 1 & 2, Nachgelassene Fragmente, 1875-79. Ed. by Giorgio Colli & Mazzino Montinari. (GER., Illus.). viii, 615p. 1969. 118.75 (*3-11-002553-1*); Sect. 6, Vol. 1. Also Sprach Zarathustra: Ein Buch fuer Alle und Keinen, 1883-85. Ed. by Giorgio Colli & Mazzino Montinari. (GER.). iv, 410p. 1968. 77.35 (*3-11-005174-5*); Sect. 6, Vol. 2. Jenseits von Gut und Boese - Zur Genealogie der Moral, 1886-1887. Ed. by Giorgio Colli & Mazzino Montinari. (GER.). iv, 436p. 1968. 80.00 (*3-11-005175-3*); Sect. 6, Vol. 3. Fall Wagner; Goetzen-Daemmerung; Nachgelassene Schriften, August, 1888 Bis Anfang Januar, 1889; der Antichrist; Ecce Homo; Dionysius-Dithyramben; Nietzsche Contra Wagner. Ed. by Giorgio Colli & Mazzino Montinari. (GER.). iv, 449p. 1969. 84.00 (*3-11-002554-X*); Sect. 8, Vol. 2. Nachgelassene Fragmente: Herbst, 1887 Bis Maerz, 1888. Ed. by Giorgio Colli & Mazzino Montinari. (GER.). xii, 477p. 1970. 82.70 (*3-11-006393-X*); (GER.). (C). write for info. (*0-318-51631-4*) De Gruyter.

Nietzsche Werke: Kritische Gesamtausgabe. Ed. by Wolfgang Mueller-Lauter & Karl Pestalozzi. (GER.). xvii, 1704p. (C). 1996. lib. bdg. 453.60 (*3-11-007774-4*) De Gruyter.

Nietzsche Werke: Kritische Gesamtausgabe: I.Abteilung, Bd. 1: Nachgelassene Aufzeichnungen Anfang 1852 - Sommer 1858. Friedrich Wilhelm Nietzsche. Ed. by Johann Figl. (GER.). xiv, 397p. (C). 1995. lib. bdg. 144.60 (*3-11-013007-6*) De Gruyter.

Nietzsche Werke: Kritische Gesamtausgabe: II. Abteilung: Philologica Band 5: Vorlesungsaufzeichnungen (WS 1874/75-WS1878/79) Ed. by Fritz Bornmann. (GER.). vi, 527p. (C). 1995. lib. bdg. 180.75 (*3-11-013913-8*) De Gruyter.

Nietzsche Werke: Kritische Gesamtausgabe Sect. 8, Vol. 3: Nachgelasssene Fragmente Anfang 1888-Anfang Januar 1889. Friedrich Wilhelm Nietzsche. Ed. by Giorgio Colli & Mazzino Montinari. LC 68-84293. 484p. (C). 1972. 104.65 (*3-11-004192-8*) De Gruyter.

Nietzsche Werke Abteilung II, Bd. 4: Kritische Gesamtausgabe: Vorlesungsaufzeichnungen (WS 1871-72 - WS 1874-75) Ed. by Fritz Bornmann. 643p. (C). 1995. lib. bdg. 207.70 (*3-11-013912-X*) De Gruyter.

Nietzsche Werke Sect. 5, Vol. 2: Kritische Gesamtausgabe: Idyllen aus Messina. Die Froehliche Wissenschaft. Nachgelassene Fragmente Fruehjahr 1881 bis Sommer 1882. Friedrich Wilhelm Nietzsche. (GER.). viii, 587p. (C). 1973. 127.70 (*3-11-004476-5*) De Gruyter.

Nietzsche Werke Sect. 7, Vol. 2: Kritische Gesamtausgabe: Nachgelassene Fragmente Fruehjahr bis Herbst 1884. Friedrich Wilhelm Nietzsche. iv, 324p. (C). 1973. 69.25 (*3-11-004797-7*) De Gruyter.

Nietzsche Werke Sect. 7, Vol. 3: Kritische Gesamtausgabe: Nachgelassene Fragmente Herbst 1884 bis Herbst 1885. Friedrich Wilhelm Nietzsche. iv, 476p. (C). 1974. 101.55 (*3-11-004983-X*) De Gruyter.

Nietzsche Werke, Kritische Gesamtausgabe Sect. 3, Vol. 1: Die Geburt der Tragoedie. Unzeitgemaesse Betrachtungen I-III (1872-1874) Friedrich Wilhelm Nietzsche. Ed. by Giorgio Colli & Mazzino Montinari. (GER.). iv, 427p. (C). 1972. 92.35 (*3-11-004294-0*) De Gruyter.

Nietzsche Werke, Kritische Gesamtausgabe Sect. 3, Vol. 2: Sect. 3, Vol. 2: Nachgelassene Schriften 1870-1873. Friedrich Wilhelm Nietzsche. Ed. by Giorgio Colli & Mazzino Montinari. (GER.). 400p. (C). 1973. 86.15 (*3-11-004312-2*) De Gruyter.

Nietzsche Werke, Kritische Gesamtausgabe Sect. 5, Vol. 1: Morgenroethe, Nachgelassene Fragmente Anfang 1880 bis Fruehjahr 1881. Friedrich Wilhelm Nietzsche. (GER.). (C). 1971. 150.80 (*3-11-001828-4*) De Gruyter.

Nietzsche Werke, Kritische Gesamtausgabe Sect. 8, Vol. 1: Nachgelassene Fragmente, Herbst 1885 bis Herbst 1887. Friedrich Wilhelm Nietzsche. Ed. by Giorgio Colli & Mazzino Montinari. (GER.). viii, 360p. (C). 1974. 73.85 (*3-11-004741-1*) De Gruyter.

Nietzsche Werke Two, Bd. 2-3: Kritische Gesamtausgabe, Bd. 2-3. Ed. by Wolfgang Mueller-Lauter & Karl Pestalozzi. (GER.). xii, 446p. (C). 1992. lib. bdg. 153.85 (*3-11-009922-5*); lib. bdg. 149.25 (*3-11-013915-4*) De Gruyter.

Nietzschean Defense of Democracy: An Experiment in Postmodern Politics. Lawrence J. Hatab. 340p. 1995. 39.95 (*0-8126-9295-0*); pap. 21.95 (*0-8126-9296-9*) Open Court.

Nietzschean Narratives. Gary Shapiro. LC 88-45451. (Studies in Phenomenology & Existential Philosophy). 192p. 1989. 17.95 (*0-253-34063-2*); pap. 6.95 (*0-253-20523-9*, MB-523) Ind U Pr.

Nietzsche's Aesthetic Turn: Reading Nietzsche After Heidegger, Deleuze, Derrida. James J. Winchester. LC 94-4928. (SUNY Series in Contemporary Continental Philosophy). 208p. (C). 1994. text 59.50 (*0-7914-2117-1*); pap. text 19.95 (*0-7914-2118-X*) State U NY Pr.

***Nietzsche's Affirmative Morality: A Revaluation Based in the Dionysian World-View.** Peter D. Murray. LC 99-32855. 320p. 1999. 155.00 (*3-11-016601-1*) De Gruyter.

Nietzsches Briefe, Mai 1872-Dezember 1874 see Nietzsche, Briefwechsel, Kritische Gesamtausgabe: Section II

Nietzsche's Case: Philosophy As - And Literature. Bernd Magnus et al. 350p. (C). 1992. pap. 23.99 (*0-415-90095-6*, A2728) Routledge.

Nietzsche's Conscience: Six Character Studies from the "Genealogy" Aaron Ridley. 208p. 1998. 39.95 (*0-8014-3557-9*); pap. 16.95 (*0-8014-8553-3*) Cornell U Pr.

Nietzsche's Corps/e: Aesthetics, Politics, Prophecy, or, The Spectacular Technoculture of Everyday Life. Geoff Waite. LC 95-42018. (Post-Contemporary Interventions Ser.). (Illus.). 576p. (C). 1996. text 54.95 (*0-8223-1709-5*) Duke.

Nietzsche's Corpse: Aesthetics, Politics, Prophecy, or, The Spectacular Technoculture of Everyday Life. Geoff Waite. LC 95-42018. (Post-Contemporary Interventions Ser.). (Illus.). 576p. 1996. pap. text 18.95 (*0-8223-1719-2*) Duke.

Nietzsche's Dangerous Game: Philosophy in the Twilight of the Idols. Daniel W. Conway. LC 96-46726. (Modern European Philosophy Ser.). 279p. 1997. text 57.95 (*0-521-57371-8*) Cambridge U Pr.

Nietzsche's Enticing Psychology of Power. Jacob J. Golomb. LC 87-35363. 350p. (C). 1989. text 32.95 (*0-8138-1122-8*) Iowa St U Pr.

Nietzsche's Ethics & His War on 'Morality' Simon May. LC 99-28678. 232p. 2000. 45.00 (*0-19-823846-0*) OUP.

Nietzsche's Existential Imperative. Bernd Magnus. LC 77-9864. (Studies in Phenomenology & Existential Philosophy). 254p. reprint ed. pap. 78.80 (*0-8357-6686-1*, 205686500094) Bks Demand.

Nietzsche's Futures. Lippitt. LC 98-21080. 1998. text 55.00 (*0-312-21559-2*) St Martin.

Nietzsche's Genealogy: Nihilism & the Will to Knowledge. Randall Havas. 272p. 1995. text 37.50 (*0-8014-2962-5*) Cornell U Pr.

***Nietzsche's Legacy for Education: Past & Present Values.** Paul Smeyers. Ed. by Michael Peters & James Marshall. LC 00-36056. (Critical Studies in Education & Culture Ser.). 272p. 2000. 60.00 (*0-89789-656-4*, H656, Bergin & Garvey) Greenwood.

Nietzsches Mensch und Nietzsches Gott: Das Spatwerk Als Philosophisch-Theologisches Programm. 2nd ed. Rainer Bucher. (Wurzburger Studien Zur Fundamentaltheologie Ser.: Bd. 1). (GER.). XIX, 434p. 1993. 59.80 (*3-631-46374-X*) P Lang Pubng.

***Nietzsche's Middle Period.** Ruth Abbey. LC 99-49373. 224p. 2000. text 45.00 (*0-19-513408-7*) OUP.

***Nietzsche's Mirror: The World as Will to Power.** Linda L. Williams. LC 00-38701. 2000. pap. write for info. (*0-8476-9795-9*) Rowman.

Nietzsche's Moral Philosophy. John A. Bernstein. LC 85-46001. 216p. 1987. 36.50 (*0-8386-3283-1*) Fairleigh Dickinson.

Nietzsche's New Seas: Explorations in Philosophy, Aesthetics, & Politics. Ed. by Michael A. Gillespie & Tracy B. Strong. 248p. 1991. pap. text 16.95 (*0-226-29379-3*) U Ch Pr.

Nietzsche's New Seas: Explorations in Philosophy, Aesthetics, & Politics. Tracy B. Strong. Ed. by Michael A. Gillespie. 248p. 1988. 27.50 (*0-226-29378-5*) U Ch Pr.

Nietzsche's Noontide Friend: The Self as Metaphoric Double. Sheridan Hough. LC 96-38366. (Literature & Philosophy Ser.). 1997. 35.00 (*0-271-01649-3*) Pa St U Pr.

***Nietzsche's Perspectivism** Steven D. Hales & Rex Welshon. LC 99-6699. (International Studies). 2000. 40.00 (*0-252-02535-0*) U of Ill Pr.

Nietzsche's Philosophical & Narrative Styles. John C. Pettey. LC 91-30171. (North American Studies in German Literature: Vol. 10). XV, 215p. (C). 1992. text 42.95 (*0-8204-1550-2*) P Lang Pubng.

Nietzsche's Philosophy of Art. Julian Young. 184p. (C). 1994. pap. text 17.95 (*0-521-45575-8*) Cambridge U Pr.

Nietzsche's Philosophy of Nature & Cosmology. Alistair Moles. (American University Studies: Philosophy: Ser. V, Vol. 80). XVII, 435p. (C). 1990. text 35.95 (*0-8204-0970-7*) P Lang Pubng.

Nietzsche's Philosophy of Science: Reflecting Science on the Ground of Art & Life. Babette E. Babich. LC 93-17271. (SUNY Series, The Margins of Literature). 350p. (C). 1994. text 64.50 (*0-7914-1865-0*); pap. text 21.95 (*0-7914-1866-9*) State U NY Pr.

Nietzsche's Philosophy of the Eternal Recurrence of the Same. Karl Lowith. Tr. by J. Harvey Lomax from GER. LC 96-19802. 1997. 40.00 (*0-520-06519-0*, Pub. by U CA Pr) Cal Prin Full Svc.

Nietzsche's Presence in Freud's Life & Thought: On the Origins of a Psychology of Dynamic Unconscious Mental Functioning. Ronald Lehrer. LC 94-571. 370p. (C). 1994. text 69.50 (*0-7914-2145-7*); pap. text 23.95 (*0-7914-2146-5*) State U NY Pr.

***Nietzsche's Prophecy: The Crisis in Meaning.** Harvey Sarles. 240p. 2001. 54.95 (*1-57392-872-0*) Prometheus Bks.

Nietzsche's Revaluation of Values: A Study in Strategies. E. E. Sleinis. LC 93-40385. (International Nietzsche Studies). 264p. 1994. text 37.50 (*0-252-02090-1*); pap. text 19.95 (*0-252-06383-X*) U of Ill Pr.

Nietzsche's St. Peter: Genesis & Cultivation of an Illusion. Frederick R. Love. (Monographien und Texte zur Nietzsche-Forschung Ser.: Vol. 5). xvi, 296p. (C). 1981. 80.00 (*3-11-007875-9*) De Gruyter.

Nietzsche's System. John Richardson. 328p. 1996. 42.00 (*0-19-509846-3*) OUP.

Nietzsche's Teaching: An Interpretation of "Thus Spake Zarathustra" Laurence Lampert. LC 86-9209. 400p. (C). 1989. reprint ed. pap. 19.00 (*0-300-04430-5*) Yale U Pr.

Nietzsches Theorie des Bewulbstein. Erwin Schlimgen. (Mongraphien und Texte zur Nietzsche-Forschung). 264p. 1998. 119.00 (*3-11-016066-8*) De Gruyter.

Nietzsche's Theory of Knowledge. Ruediger H. Grimm. (Monographien und Texte zur Nietzscge-Forschung Ser.: Vol. 4). 1977. 97.70 (*3-11-006568-1*) De Gruyter.

Nietzsche's Thought of Eternal Return. Joan Stambaugh. LC 75-171553. 157p. reprint ed. pap. 48.70 (*0-608-16131-4*, 201256400082) Bks Demand.

Nietzsche's Thought of Eternal Return. Joan Stambaugh. LC 88-187. (Current Continental Research Ser.: No. 807). 152p. (C). 1988. reprint ed. pap. text 18.25 (*0-8191-6911-0*) Taylor & Francis.

Nietzsches Totalismus: Philosophie der Natur Zwischen Verklarung und Verhangnis. Walter Gebhard. (GER.). 398p. 1983. 134.65 (*3-11-008958-0*) De Gruyter.

Nietzsche's Tragic Regime: Culture, Aesthetics, & Political Education. Thomas W. Heilke. LC 97-24737. 242p. 1997. lib. bdg. 32.00 (*0-87580-233-8*) N Ill U Pr.

Nietzsche's Voice. Henry Staten. LC 90-55131. 240p. 1993. text 42.50 (*0-8014-2500-X*); pap. text 16.95 (*0-8014-9739-6*) Cornell U Pr.

Nietzsches Werke: Historisch - Kritische Ausgabe (Macintosh) Friedrich Wilhelm Nietzsche. Ed. by Malcolm Brown. (Past Masters Ser.). (C). write for info. incl. cd-rom (*1-57085-079-8*) Intelex.

Nietzsche's Women: Beyond the Whip. Carol Diethe. LC 96-6241. (Monographien und Texte Zur Nietzsche-Forschung Ser.: No. 31). 1996. 88.90 (*3-11-014819-6*) De Gruyter.

Nietzsche's Women: Beyond the Whip. Carol Diethe. (Illus.). xiv, 177p. (C). 1996. pap. text 19.95 (*3-11-014820-X*) De Gruyter.

Nietzsche's Zarathustra. Kathleen M. Higgins. LC 86-30133. (C). 1987. 39.95 (*0-87722-482-X*) Temple U Pr.

Nietzsche's Zarathustra. Kathleen M. Higgins. 328p. 1989. pap. 19.95 (*0-87722-687-3*) Temple U Pr.

Nietzsche's Zarathustra: Notes of the Seminar Given in 1934-1939, 2 vols., Set. C. G. Jung. Ed. by James L. Jarrett. LC 87-32897. (Bollingen Ser.: No. XCIX). (Illus.). 1574p. 1988. text 225.00 (*0-691-09953-7*, Pub. by Princeton U Pr) Cal Prin Full Svc.

***Nieuport Aces of World War I.** Norman Franks. (Aircraft of the Aces Ser.: Vol. 33). (Illus.). 96p. 2000. 17.95 (*1-85532-961-1*, Pub. by Ospry) Motorbooks Intl.

Nieuwe Engels zonder Moeite: English for Dutch Speakers. Assimil Staff. (DUT & ENG.). 28.95 (*0-8288-4322-8*, M14922) Fr & Eur.

Nieve. Isidro Sanchez & Carme Peris. (World of Sports Ser.). (SPA., Illus.). 32p. (J). (ps-1). 1992. pap. 6.95 (*0-8120-4870-9*) Barron.

Nieve. Lisa Trumbauer. Ed. by Don Curry. Tr. by Leyla Torres from ENG. (Spanish Discovery Links Ser.). (SPA.). 8p. (J). (gr. k). 1997. pap. text 2.75 (*1-56784-972-5*) Newbridge Educ.

***Niezapomiane Jutro.** Gryzelda N. Lachocki. LC 99-28765.Tr. of Goodbye Tomorrow. (ENG & POL., Illus.). 144p. 1999. pap. 14.95 (*1-55618-180-9*) Brunswick Pub.

Niezapomniane Jutro see Goodbye Tomorrow

Nifty (And Thrifty) Science Activities. Dennis Stacy. (J). (gr. 2-6). 1988. pap. 7.99 (*0-8224-4777-0*) Fearon Teacher Aids.

Nifty 'Fifties' Fords: An Illustrated History of the Early Post-War Fords. Ray Miller & Glenn Embree. LC 73-93879. (Ford Road Ser.: Vol. 5). (Illus.). 320p. 1974. 44.95 (*0-913056-05-7*) Evergreen Pr.

Nifty Fifty: Five Hundred Thinking Challenges about 50 Familiar Things. Greta Rasmussen. LC 87-51619. (Illus.). 112p. 1988. pap. 11.95 (*0-936110-06-6*) Tin Man Pr.

Nifty Neckwear. Virginia Avery. Ed. by Barbara K. Kuhn & Sally Lanzarotti. LC 94-20797. (Illus.). 32p. 1995. pap. 11.95 (*0-914881-84-1*, 10105) C & T Pub.

***Nifty New Jersey Coloring Book.** Carole Marsh. (New Jersey Experience! Ser.). (Illus.). (J). (gr. k-5). 2000. pap. 3.95 (*0-7933-9473-2*) Gallopade Intl.

***Nifty North Carolina Coloring Book.** Carole Marsh. (North Carolina Experience! Ser.). (Illus.). (J). (gr. k-5). 2000. pap. 3.95 (*0-7933-9472-4*) Gallopade Intl.

Nifty Number Names: Integrated Activities for Numbers 1-20. Jill Gasquet. 1998. pap. 12.95 (*1-56822-671-3*) Instruct Fair.

Nifty, Thrifty, No-Sew Costumes & Props: Make Costumes for a Wide Variety of Characters, & Animals. Carol A. Bloom. LC 97-209832. (Illus.). 208p. 1997. pap. text 14.95 (*0-673-36372-4*, GoodYrBooks) Addson-Wesley Educ.

Nigamas: For the Age. Som P. Ranchan. 93p. 1989. text 15.95 (*81-220-0156-4*, Pub. by Konark Pubs Pvt Ltd) Advent Bks Div.

***Nigel Coates: Designing the City.** Jonathan Glancey. (Cutting Edge Ser.). (Illus.). 64p. 1999. 16.95 (*0-8230-1211-5*) Watsn-Guptill.

Nigel Foster's Guide to Surf Kayaking. Nigel Foster. LC 98-24363. (Illus.). 128p. 1998. pap. 16.95 (*0-7627-0218-4*) Globe Pequot.

Nigel Foster's Sea Kayaking. 2nd ed. Nigel Foster. LC 97-13211. 96 p. 1997. write for info. (*1-898660-42-5*) Fernhurst Bks.

Nigel Foster's Sea Kayaking: Secrets from the Pro. 2nd rev. ed. Nigel Foster. LC 97-13211. (Illus.). 96p. 1997. pap. 14.95 (*0-7627-0132-3*) Globe Pequot.

Nigel Mansell's Autobiography. Nigel Mansell. 1996. pap. 11.95 (*0-00-218703-5*, Pub. by HarpC) Trafalgar.

Nigel Short: Quest for the Crown. Cathy Forbes. 128p. 1993. 15.95 (*1-85744-048-X*) S&S Trade.

Nigel Short: World Chess Challenger. Raymond Keene. (Batsford Chess Library). 160p. 1993. pap. 16.95 (*0-8050-2634-7*, Owl) H Holt & Co.

Nigel Short's Best Games. Nigel Short. 64p. 1995. pap. 14.95 (*0-8050-3051-4*, Pub. by Batsford Chess) H Holt & Co.

***Niger.** Ann Heinrichs. LC 00-21243. (Enchantment of the World Ser.). (Illus.). (J). 2001. write for info. (*0-516-21633-3*) Childrens.

Niger. Lydia Salonga. (OIES Country Guide Ser.). (C). 1995. 22.00 (*0-929851-30-7*) Am Assn Coll Registrars.

Niger. Lynda F. Zamponi. LC 95-114746. (World Bibliographical Ser.). 277p. 1994. lib. bdg. 66.50 (*1-85109-204-8*) ABC-CLIO.

***Niger, 6 vols. , Set.** Rabah Seffal. LC 99-55064. (Cultures of the World Ser.: Vol. 20). 128p. (YA). (gr. 4-7). 2000. lib. bdg. 35.64 (*0-7614-0995-5*, Benchmark NY) Marshall Cavendish.

***Niger: A Country Study Guide.** Global Investment & Business Center, Inc. Staff. (World Country Study Guides Library: Vol. 126). (Illus.). 350p. 2000. pap. 59.00 (*0-7397-2424-X*) Intl Business Pubns.

Niger: Personal Rule & Survival in the Sahel. Robert B. Charlick. (Profiles - Nations of Contemporary Africa Ser.). 189p. 1991. pap. 58.50 (*0-89158-968-6*) Westview.

Niger: Profile of Agricultural Potential. L. Lamarque. 1993. pap. 25.00 (*0-85954-361-7*, Pub. by Nat Res Inst) St Mut.

Niger - A Country Study Guide: Basic Information for Research & Pleasure. Global Investment Center, USA Staff. (World Country Study Guide Library: Vol. 126). (Illus.). 350p. 1999. pap. 59.00 (*0-7397-1523-2*) Intl Business Pubns.

Niger & Its Neighbors: Environmental History & Hydrobiology, Human Use & Health Hazards of the Major West African Rivers. Ed. by A. T. Grove. 342p. (C). 1985. text 155.00 (*90-6191-512-0*, Pub. by A A Balkema) Ashgate Pub Co.

***Niger Business Intelligence Report, 190 vols.** Global Investment & Business Center, Inc. Staff. (World Business Intelligence Library: Vol. 126). (Illus.). 350p. 2000. pap. 99.95 (*0-7397-2624-2*) Intl Business Pubns.

***Niger Business Law Handbook.** Global Investment & Business Center, Inc. Staff. (Global Business Law Handbooks Library: Vol. 126). (Illus.). 2000. pap. 99.95 (*0-7397-2024-4*) Intl Business Pubns.

***Niger Business Opportunity Yearbook.** Global Investment & Business Center, Inc. Staff. (Global Business Opportunity Yearbooks Library: Vol. 126). (Illus.). 2000. pap. 99.95 (*0-7397-2224-7*) Intl Business Pubns.

***Niger Business Opportunity Yearbook: Export-Import, Investment & Business Opportunities.** International Business Publications, U. S. A. Staff & Global Investment Center, U. S. A. Staff. (Global Business Opportunity Yearbooks Library: Vol. 126). (Illus.). 350p. 1999. pap. 99.95 (*0-7397-1324-8*) Intl Business Pubns.

***Niger Country Review 2000.** Robert C. Kelly et al. (Illus.). 60p. 1999. pap. 39.95 (*1-58310-550-6*) CountryWatch.

Niger Delta Rivalry, 1884. Ikime. Date not set. pap. text. write for info. (*0-582-64638-3*, Pub. by Addison-Wesley) Longman.

Niger Flora. W. J. Hooker et al. (Illus.). 1966. reprint ed. 160.00 (*3-7682-0359-X*) Lubrecht & Cramer.

***Niger Foreign Policy & Government Guide.** Contrib. by Global Investment & Business Center, Inc. Staff. (World Foreign Policy & Government Library: Vol. 121). (Illus.). 350p. 1999. VHS 99.00 (*0-7397-3619-1*) Intl Business Pubns.

***Niger Foreign Policy & Government Guide.** Global Investment & Business Center, Inc. Staff. (World Foreign Policy & Government Library: Vol. 121). (Illus.). 350p. 2000. 99.95 (*0-7397-3824-0*) Intl Business Pubns.

Niger Household Energy Project: Promoting Rural Fuelwood Markets & Village Management of Natural Woodlands. Gerald Foley et al. (Technical Papers: No. 362). 128p. 1997. pap. 22.00 (*0-8213-3918-4*, 13918) World Bank.

Niger Ibos. G. T. Basden. (Illus.). 456p. 1966. reprint ed. 45.00 (*0-7146-1632-X*, Pub. by F Cass Pubs) Intl Spec Bk.

***Niger Investment & Business Guide.** Global Investment & Business Center, Inc. Staff. (Illus.). (Global Investment & Business Guide Library: Vol. 126). (Illus.). 2000. pap. 99.95 (*0-7397-1824-X*) Intl Business Pubns.

N

An Asterisk (*) at the beginning of an entry indicates that the title is appearing for the first time.

***Niger Investment & Business Guide: Export-Import, Investment & Business Opportunities.** International Business Publications, USA Staff & Global Investment Center, USA Staff. (World Investment & Business Guide Library-99: Vol. 126). (Illus.). 350p. 1999. pap. 99.95 (0-7397-0321-8) Intl Business Pubns.

Nigeria see MacDonald Countries

Nigeria see Enchantment of the World Series

Nigeria see Festivals of the World

Nigeria. (Case Studies in Population Policy). 38p. pap. 7.50 (92-1-151215-8, 90.XIII.28) UN.

Nigeria. Ed. by Robert A. Myers. (World Bibliographical Ser.: No. 100). (Illus.). 496p. 1989. lib. bdg. 80.00 (1-85109-083-5, Pub. by Clio Pr) ABC-CLIO.

Nigeria. Mary N. Oluonye. LC 97-16567. (Globe-Trotters Club Ser.). 1998. 22.60 (1-57505-113-3, Carolrhoda) Lerner Pub.

***Nigeria.** Revue Noire Magazine Editors. (Revue Noire Magazine Ser.: 30). (Illus.). 1999. pap. 22.00 (2-909571-41-6) Revue Noire.

Nigeria. Alasdair Tenquist. LC 95-42013. (Economically Developing Countries Ser.). (Illus.). (J). (gr. 4-7). 1996. lib. bdg. 24.26 (0-8172-4527-8) Raintree Steck-V.

Nigeria. Kristin Thoennes. LC 98-36964. (Countries of the World Ser.). (J). (gr. 3-4). 1999. 14.00 (0-7368-0154-5) Capstone Pr.

Nigeria. Kristin Thoennes. (Countries of the World Ser.). (Illus.). 24p. (J). (ps-3). 1999. 14.00 (0-516-21752-6) Childrens.

***Nigeria.** rev. ed. Ruby A. Bell-Gam & David Uru Iyam. (World Bibliographical Ser.: Vol. 100). 342p. 1999. 92.00 (1-85109-327-3) ABC-CLIO.

Nigeria see Cultures of the World - Group 6

Nigeria: A Country Study. Helen Chapin Metz. 428p. 1992. boxed set 28.00 (0-16-040401-0) USGPO.

***Nigeria: A Country Study Guide.** Global Investment & Business Center, Inc. Staff. (World Country Study Guides Library: Vol. 127). (Illus.). 350p. 2000. pap. 59.00 (0-7397-2425-8) Intl Business Pubns.

Nigeria: A Critique of British Colonial Administration. Walter R. Crocker. LC 76-160964. (Select Bibliographies Reprint Ser.). 1977. reprint ed. 28.95 (0-8369-5832-2) Ayer.

Nigeria: A Handy Guide to the Federal Republic. 1992. 15.00 (0-9632145-0-0) Chaneta Intl.

Nigeria: A Nation of Many Peoples. John Owhonda. LC 96-26165. (Discovering Our Heritage Ser.). 128p. (J). (gr. 4-8). 1997. lib. bdg. 14.95 (0-382-39454-2, Dillon Silver Burdett) Silver Burdett Pr.

Nigeria: Experience with Structural Adjustment. Gary G. Moser et al. LC 97-1966. (Occasional Papers). 1997. write for info. (1-55775-630-9) Intl Monetary.

Nigeria: Hundred Questions & Answers. Joseph Okpaku, Sr. 100p. 1992. 19.95 (0-89388-226-7); pap. 9.95 (0-89388-227-5) Okpaku Communications.

Nigeria: Its Peoples & Its Problems. 3rd ed. Edmund D. Morel. (Illus.). 264p. 1968. reprint ed. 45.00 (0-7146-1703-2, BHA-01703, Pub. by F Cass Pubs) Intl Spec Bk.

Nigeria: Its Petroleum Geology, Resources & Potential, Vol. 1. Ed. by Graham & Trotman, Ltd. Staff. 176p. 1982. lib. bdg. 135.50 (0-86010-264-5) G & T Inc.

Nigeria: Its Petroleum Geology, Resources & Potential, Vol. 2. Arthur Whiteman. 238p. 1982. lib. bdg. 135.50 (0-86010-265-3) G & T Inc.

Nigeria: Major World Nations. Nicholas Freville. LC 99-13782. (Major World Nations Ser.). (Illus.). 144p. (J). 1999. 19.95 (0-7910-5390-3) Chelsea Hse.

Nigeria: On the Eve of "Change", Transition to What? Karen Sorensen. Ed. by Human Rights Watch Staff. 62p. (Orig.). 1991. pap. 7.00 (1-56432-045-6) Hum Rts Watch.

Nigeria: One Land, Many Cultures see Exploring Cultures of the World - Group 1

Nigeria: Power & Democracy in Africa. Jean Herskovits. (Headline Ser.: No. 257). (Illus.). 72p. (gr. 11-12). 1982. pap. 5.95 (0-87124-073-4) Foreign Policy.

***Nigeria: Real Problems, Real Solutions.** Frwd. by Imeh Inyang. xxi, 120p. 2000. 13.00 (0-9677699-0-6) B N Umez.

Nigeria: Reorganization & Development since the Mid-Twentieth Century. Charles Jarmon. Ed. by K. Ishwaran. LC 87-20878. (Monographs & Theoretical Studies in Sociology & Anthropology in Honour of Nels Anderson: Vol. 23). x, 169p. (Orig.). 1988. pap. 56.00 (90-04-08340-5) Brill Academic Pubs.

Nigeria: The Illusions of Power. Timothy M. Shaw & Julius O. Ihonvbere. (Profiles - Nations of Contemporary Africa Ser.). 200p. 1988. text. write for info. (0-8133-0463-6) Westview.

Nigeria: The Political Economy of Oil. Sarah A. Khan. LC 95-114629. (Oxford Institute for Energy Studies). (Illus.). 248p. 1994. text 52.00 (0-19-730014-6) OUP.

Nigeria: The Politics of Adjustment & Democracy. Julius O. Ihonvbere. LC 92-36996. 256p. (C). 1993. text 44.95 (1-56000-093-7) Transaction Pubs.

Nigeria: The Price of Oil: Corporate Responsibility & Human Rights Violations. Human Rights Watch, Africa Staff. LC 99-60123. 224p. 1999. pap. 15.00 (1-56432-225-4) Hum Rts Watch.

Nigeria: The Prospects for Democracy. H. Oladipo Davies. (B. E. Ser.: No. 176). 1961. 30.00 (0-8115-3086-8) Periodicals Srv.

Nigeria: The Tribes, the Nation, or the Race; The Politics of Independence. Frederick A. Schwarz. LC 83-1528. (Illus.). 316p. (C). 1983. reprint ed. lib. bdg. 75.00 (0-313-23886-3, SCNI, Greenwood Pr) Greenwood.

Nigeria: World Development. Phiner Dike. (Illus.). 69p. (C). Date not set. pap. text 9.95 (0-9643652-0-0) Phiners Intl.

Nigeria - A Country Study Guide: Basic Information for Research & Pleasure. Global Investment Center, USA Staff. (World Country Study Guide Library: Vol. 127). (Illus.). 350p. 1999. pap. 59.00 (0-7397-1524-0) Intl Business Pubns.

Nigeria - Dilemma of Nationhood: An African Analysis of the Biafran Conflict. Ed. by Joseph Okpaku. LC 73-83162. 426p. 1974. reprint ed. pap. 15.95 (0-89388-088-4) Okpaku Communications.

Nigeria, Africa, & the United States: From Kennedy to Reagan. Robert B. Shepard. LC 90-44509. (Illus.). 208p. 1991. 26.95 (0-253-35209-6) Ind U Pr.

***Nigeria & Her Garbage Dumps: The Environmental Sensitive Nigeria.** Boniface Obiadi. Ed. by Gary Fowler. 69p. 1999. pap. 12.95 (0-9677864-2-8) Bons Diversified Invest.

Nigeria & Its British Invaders. J. U. Asiegbu. LC 83-62253. (Illus.). 409p. (C). 1984. 27.95 (0-88357-101-3); pap. 12.95 (0-685-08183-4) NOK Pubs.

Nigeria & Its Tin Fields. Albert F. Calvert. Ed. by Mira Wilkins. LC 76-29763. (European Business Ser.). (Illus.). 1977. reprint ed. lib. bdg. 35.95 (0-405-09778-6) Ayer.

Nigeria & the International Capitalist System. Toyin Falola & Julius O. Ihonvbere. LC 87-23183. (GSIS Monograph in World Affairs). 154p. 1987. lib. bdg. 22.00 (1-55587-087-2) L Rienner.

Nigeria & the Organisation of African Unity: In Search of an African Reality. Ed. by Joseph Okpaku, Sr. LC 91-67250. 446p. 1991. 50.00 (0-685-59746-6) Okpaku Communications.

Nigeria & the Politics of Survival As a Nation-State. E. Ike Udogu. LC 96-39800. (Studies in African Economic & Social Development: Vol. 8). 312p. 1996. text 99.95 (0-7734-8785-9) E Mellen.

Nigeria & the Struggle for the Liberation of Zimbabwe: A Study of Foreign Policy of an Emerging Nation. Olayiwola Abegunrin. LC 92-29433. 268p. 1992. text 89.95 (0-7734-9178-3) E Mellen.

Nigeria & the U. N. Mission to the Democratic Republic of the Congo: A Case Study of the Formative Stages of Nigeria's Foreign Policy. Festus U. Ohaegbulam. LC 82-11193. 198p. 1982. reprint ed. pap. 61.40 (0-608-04502-0, 206524700001) Bks Demand.

Nigeria, Around the World, Vol. 4. Betsy Franco. (Illus.). 48p. (J). (gr. 1-3). 1994. pap. text 7.95 (1-55799-269-X, EMC 278) Evan-Moor Edu Pubs.

Nigeria at the Crossroads. J. O. Irukwu. 324p. 1983. pap. 90.00 (0-900886-71-4, Pub. by Witherby & Co) St Mut.

Nigeria at the United Nation: Partnership for a Better World. Ed. by Joseph Okpaku, Sr. LC 91-67251. 742p. 60.00 (0-89388-211-9) Okpaku Communications.

Nigeria at the United Nations Security Council, 1994-1995. LC 98-60020. 1998. write for info. (1-889218-06-5); pap. write for info. (1-889218-07-3) Sungai Bks.

Nigeria-Australia Collaborative Agricultural Research. Saka Nuru & J. G. Ryan. 146p. 1985. pap. 60.00 (0-949511-07-2) St Mut.

***Nigeria Business Intelligence Report, 190 vols.** Global Investment & Business Center, Inc. Staff. (World Business Intelligence Library: Vol. 127). (Illus.). 350p. 2000. pap. 99.95 (0-7397-2625-0) Intl Business Pubns.

***Nigeria Business Law Handbook.** Global Investment & Business Center, Inc. Staff. (Global Business Law Handbooks Library: Vol. 127). (Illus.). 2000. pap. 99.95 (0-7397-2025-2) Intl Business Pubns.

***Nigeria Business Opportunity Yearbook.** Global Investment & Business Center, Inc. Staff. (Global Business Opportunity Yearbooks Library: Vol. 127). (Illus.). 2000. pap. 99.95 (0-7397-2225-5) Intl Business Pubns.

***Nigeria Business Opportunity Yearbook: Export-Import, Investment & Business Opportunities.** International Business Publications, U. S. A. Staff & Global Investment Center, U. S. A. Staff. (Global Business Opportunity Yearbooks Library: Vol. 127). (Illus.). 350p. 1999. pap. 99.95 (0-7397-1325-6) Intl Business Pubns.

Nigeria Census, 1931, 7 vols. in 6. LC 74-15073. reprint ed. 285.00 (0-404-12117-9) AMS Pr.

***Nigeria Country Review 2000.** Robert C. Kelly et al. (Illus.). 60p. 1999. pap. 39.95 (1-58310-551-4) CountryWatch.

Nigeria, Dilemma of Nationhood: An African Analysis of the Biafran Conflict, 12. Ed. by Joseph Okpaku. LC 78-111266. (Contributions in Afro-American & African Studies: No. 12). 426p. (C). 1970. 47.95 (0-8371-4668-2, OKN/, Greenwood Pr) Greenwood.

Nigeria Fertilizer Sector Present Situation & Future Prospects. A. O. Falusi & L. B. Williams. (Technical Bulletin Ser.: No. T-18). (Illus.). 96p. (Orig.). 1981. pap. 4.00 (0-88090-017-2) Intl Fertilizer.

***Nigeria Foreign Policy & Government Guide.** Contrib. by Global Investment & Business Center, Inc. Staff. (World Foreign Policy & Government Library: Vol. 122). (Illus.). 350p. 1999. pap. 99.00 (0-7397-3620-5) Intl Business Pubns.

***Nigeria Foreign Policy & Government Guide.** Global Investment & Business Center, Inc. Staff. (World Foreign Policy & Government Library: Vol. 122). (Illus.). 350p. 2000. 99.95 (0-7397-3825-9) Intl Business Pubns.

Nigeria in Maps. J. S. Oguntoyinbo et al. Ed. by K. M. Barbour et al. 160p. 1982. 49.50 (0-8419-0763-3) Holmes & Meier.

Nigeria in Pictures. Department of Geography, Lerner Publications. (Visual Geography Ser.). (Illus.). 64p. (YA). (gr. 5 up). 1988. lib. bdg. 19.95 (0-8225-1826-0, Lerner Publctns) Lerner Pub.

***Nigeria Investment & Business Guide.** Global Investment & Business Center, Inc. Staff. (Global Investment & Business Guide Library: Vol. 127). (Illus.). 2000. pap. 99.95 (0-7397-1825-8) Intl Business Pubns.

Nigeria Investment & Business Guide: Economy, Export-Import, Business & Investment Climate, Business Contacts. Contrib. by Russian Information & Business Center, Inc. Staff. (Russia, NIS & Emerging Markets Investment & Business Library-98). (Illus.). 350p. 1998. pap. 99.00 (1-57751-904-3) Intl Business Pubns.

***Nigeria Investment & Business Guide: Export-Import, Investment & Business Opportunities.** International Business Publications, USA Staff & Global Investment Center, USA Staff. (World Investment & Business Guide Library-99: Vol. 127). (Illus.). 350p. 1999. pap. 99.95 (0-7397-0322-6) Intl Business Pubns.

***Nigeria Past to the Present.** Oliver I. Anyabolu. 2000. pap. text. write for info. (0-9663234-1-6) Classic Publ.

Nigeria, Policy Responses to Shocks, 1970-1990. David Bevan et al. LC 92-22772. 48p. 1992. pap. 9.95 (1-55815-224-5) ICS Pr.

***Nigeria the Culture.** Anne Rosenberg. (Lands, Peoples & Cultures Ser.). (Illus.). 32p. (YA). (gr. 4-9). 2000. pap. 7.95 (0-86505-329-4); lib. bdg. 20.60 (0-86505-249-2) Crabtree Pub Co.

***Nigeria the Land.** Anne Rosenberg. (Lands, Peoples & Cultures Ser.). (Illus.). 32p. (YA). (gr. 4-9). 2000. pap. 7.95 (0-86505-327-8); lib. bdg. 20.60 (0-86505-247-6) Crabtree Pub Co.

***Nigeria the People.** Anne Rosenberg. (Lands, Peoples & Cultures Ser.). (Illus.). 32p. (YA). (gr. 4-9). 2000. pap. 7.95 (0-86505-328-6); lib. bdg. 20.60 (0-86505-248-4) Crabtree Pub Co.

Nigeria, Which Way Forward: Hearing Before the Subcommittee on Africa of the Committee on Foreign Affairs, House of Representatives, One Hundred Third Congress, First Session, August 4, 1993. United States Staff. LC 95-155953. iii, 123 p. 1994. write for info. (0-16-046207-X) USGPO.

Nigerian Annual of International Law. Ed. by T. O. Elias. 1979. pap. 49.50 (0-19-575455-7) OUP.

Nigerian Arabic-English Dictionary. A. S. Kaye. (Bibliotheca Afroasiatica Ser.: Vol. 3). viii, 90p. 1986. 40.00 (0-89003-190-8); pap. 30.00 (0-89003-191-6) Undena Pubns.

Nigerian Artists: A Who's Who & Bibliography. Ed. by Janet L. Stanley. LC 92-40052. (Illus.). 608p. 1993. 175.00 (0-905450-82-5, Pub. by H Zell Pubs) Seven Hills Bk.

Nigerian Banking System. Charles V. Brown. LC 66-19192. 212p. reprint ed. pap. 65.80 (0-608-13176-8, 201528900001) Bks Demand.

***Nigerian Chiefs: Traditional Power in Modern Politics, 1890-1990s.** Olufemi Vaughan. LC 99-88099. (Rochester Studies in African History & the Diaspora: No. 1092-5227). 302p. 2000. 79.00 (1-58046-040-2) Univ Rochester Pr.

Nigerian Civil War Literature: Seeking an "Imagined Community" Craig W. McLuckie. LC 90-6689. (Studies in African Literature: Vol. 3). 172p. 1990. lib. bdg. 79.95 (0-88946-727-7) E Mellen.

Nigerian Cooking: Epicurean Delight of the Rich & Famous - Stay Slim & Healthy Forever! 2nd ed. Phiner Dike. (Stay Slim Forever Ser.). (Illus.). 90p. 1996. reprint ed. pap. 14.95 (0-9643652-1-9) Phiners Intl.

Nigerian Economy: A Macroeconometric & Input-Output Model. Temitope W. Oshikoya. LC 89-16352. 203p. 1990. 57.95 (0-275-93417-9, C317, Greenwood Pr) Greenwood.

Nigerian Foreign Policy Towards Africa: Continuity & Change. Okon Akiba. LC 96-19565. (American University Studies X: Vol. 45). XIII, 230p. (C). 1998. pap. text 26.95 (0-8204-3371-3) P Lang Pubng.

Nigerian Historical Studies. E. A. Ayandele. 305p. 1979. 47.50 (0-7146-3113-2, Pub. by F Cass Pubs) Intl Spec Bk.

Nigerian Images. William B. Fagg. (Illus.). 194p. (C). 1990. 70.00 (0-85331-566-3, Pub. by Lund Humphries) Antique Collect.

***Nigerian Letter.** Thomas Hill. 299p. 2000. pap. 14.95 (1-928704-78-6, Fusion Pr) Authorlink.

Nigerian Military: A Sociological Analysis of Authority & Revolt, 1960-67. Robin Luckham. LC 73-152643. (African Studies: No. 4). 390p. reprint ed. pap. 111.20 (0-608-17521-8, 2030607) Bks Demand.

Nigerian Military & the State. Jim Peters. (Military & Security Studies). 224p. 1997. text 59.50 (1-85043-874-9) St Martin.

Nigerian Modernization. Ukandi G. Damachi. LC 75-183394. 160p. 1972. 24.95 (0-89388-030-2) Okpaku Communications.

Nigerian Musical Styles, Africa's Rhythm of Unity. Taiwo Ogunade. LC 92-90729. 78p. 1991. lib. bdg. 11.95 (1-881549-01-1) Oluweri Pubns.

Nigerian Oil Frauds: Special Report. International Maritime Organization Staff. (C). 1989. 120.00 (0-948691-97-2, Pub. by Witherby & Co) St Mut.

Nigerian Pidgin. Nicholas G. Faraclas. LC 95-24906. 320p. (C). 1996. 185.00 (0-415-02291-6) Routledge.

Nigerian Political Parties: Power in an Emergent African Nation. R. Sklar. LC 62-21107. 1983. reprint ed. pap. text 12.50 (0-88357-100-5) NOK Pubs.

Nigerian Political Scene. Archibald Callaway et al. Ed. by Robert O. Tilman & Taylor Cole. LC 62-18315. (Duke University Commonwealth-Studies Center Publication Ser.: No. 17). 352p. reprint ed. pap. 109.20 (0-608-13805-3, 201793900010) Bks Demand.

Nigerian Press, Hegemony, & the Social Construction of Legitimacy, 1960-1983. Adigun A. Agbaje. LC 92-19202. 352p. 1992. lib. bdg. 99.95 (0-7734-9555-X) E Mellen.

Nigerian Public Finance. Pius N. Okigbo. LC 65-15473. (Northwestern University African Studies Ser.: No. 15). 259p. reprint ed. pap. 80.30 (0-608-13053-2, 201485500096) Bks Demand.

Nigerian Scam Masters: An Expose of a Modern International Gang. Harold Baines. 171p. 2000. 34.00 (1-56072-282-7); pap. 23.95 (1-56072-267-3, Nova Kroshka Bks) Nova Sci Pubs.

Nigerian State: Political Economy, State Class & Political System in the Post-Colonial Era. William D. Graf. 281p. (C). 1989. text 40.00 (0-435-08028-8, 08028) Heinemann.

Nigerian State: Political Economy, State Class & Political System in the Post-Colonial Era. William D. Graf. 281p. (C). 1990. pap. text 26.50 (0-435-08029-6) Heinemann.

Nigerian Theatre in English. Chris Dunton. 1998. 100.00 (1-873836-71-6) Bowker-Saur.

***Nigerian Video Films.** 2nd rev. expanded ed. Ed. by Jonathan Haynes. (Research in International Studies: No. 73). (Illus.). 264p. 2000. pap. text 28.00 (0-89680-211-6, Ohio U Ctr Intl) Ohio U Pr.

Nigerian Women in Development: A Research Bibliography. Catherine M. Coles & Barbara Entwisle. 170p. 1986. pap. 25.00 (0-918456-58-4, Crossroads) African Studies Assn.

Nigeria's Financial System. Pius N. Okigbo. LC 82-158952. 300p. reprint ed. pap. 93.00 (0-8357-2969-9, 203923100011) Bks Demand.

Nigeria's Foreign Policy under Two Military Governments, 1966-1979: An Analysis of the Gowan & Muhammed - Obasanjo Regimes. Kenoye K. Eke. LC 89-13424. (African Studies: Vol. 16). (Illus.). 216p. 1990. lib. bdg. 89.95 (0-88946-171-6) E Mellen.

Nigeria's Leadership Role in Africa. Joseph Wayas. LC 80-452623. vii, 132 p. 1979. write for info. (0-333-27037-1) Macmillan.

Nigeria's Presidential Constitution: The Second Experiment in Constitutional Democracy. Benjamin O. Nwabueze. LC 84-19438. 502p. 1985. pap. 155.70 (0-608-05252-3, 206579000001) Bks Demand.

Nigeria's Third Republic. Ojo Bamidele. LC 98-28665. 1999. 75.00 (1-56072-580-X) Nova Sci Pubs.

Nigger. Dick Gregory & Robert Lipsyte. 209p. 1990. per. 5.99 (0-671-73560-8, WSP) PB.

Nigger. Edward Sheldon. Ed. by Walter J. Meserve & Mollie A. Meserve. (When Conscience Trod the Stage Ser.). 1998. pap., spiral bd. 4.95 (0-937657-45-X) Feedbk Theabks & Prospero.

Nigger. Dick Gregory. 1993. reprint ed. lib. bdg. 29.95 (1-56849-116-6) Buccaneer Bks.

Nigger Bible. Robert H. Decoy. 304p. 1998. mass mkt. 6.99 (0-87067-981-3) Holloway.

Nigger Factory. Gil Scott-Heron. 237p. 1996. reprint ed. pap. 12.95 (0-86241-527-6, Pub. by Payback Pr) AK Pr Dist.

***Nigger Heaven** Carl Van Vechten. LC 99-36777. 2000. pap. 15.95 (0-252-06860-2) U of Ill Pr.

Nigger Heaven. Carl Van Vechten. 1973. reprint ed. 20.50 (0-374-98069-1) FS&G.

Nigger of the Narcissus see Three Great Tales

Nigger of the Narcissus. Joseph Conrad. LC 99-35223. (Thrift Editions Ser.). 128p. 1999. pap. text 1.50 (0-486-40880-9) Dover.

Nigger of the Narcissus. Joseph Conrad. Ed. by Robert Kimbrough. (Critical Editions Ser.). (Illus.). (C). 1979. pap. text 12.50 (0-393-09019-1) Norton.

Nigger of the Narcissus. Joseph Conrad. Ed. & Intro. by Cedric P. Watts. 208p. 1989. pap. 12.95 (0-14-018094-X, Penguin Classics) Viking Penguin.

Nigger of the Narcissus. Joseph Conrad. 1976. 22.95 (0-8488-0969-6) Amereon Ltd.

Nigger of the Narcissus. Joseph Conrad. 1991. lib. bdg. 21.95 (0-89966-055-X) Buccaneer Bks.

Nigger of the 'Narcissus' Joseph Conrad. Ed. by Alan Simmons. (Everyman Paperback Classics). 480p. 1997. pap. 4.95 (0-460-87789-5, Everyman's Classic Lib) Tuttle Pubng.

Nigger of the 'Narcissus' A Tale of the Sea. Joseph Conrad. Ed. by Jacques Berthoud. (World's Classics Ser.). 244p. 1985. pap. 6.95 (0-19-281623-3) OUP.

***Nigger of the 'Narcissus' A Tale of the Sea.** Joseph Conrad. (Oxford World Classics Ser.). 232p. 1999. pap. 7.95 (0-19-283649-8) OUP.

Nigger, Please: Bold, Raw, Provocative Truth. Rosie Milligan. LC 97-104348. (Orig.). 1996. pap. 14.95 (1-881524-06-X) Milligan Bks.

Niggered Amen. Zu-Bolton Ahmos, II. 1975. 6.85 (0-941490-11-4) Solo Pr.

Niggers & Po' White Trash. Carl L. Shears. LC 79-167825. 72p. pap. 2.95 (0-912444-15-0) DARE Bks.

Niggers This Is Canada. rev. ed. Odimumba Kwamdela, pseud & J. Ashton Brathwaite. LC 82-82922. 80p. 1986. pap. text 8.00 (0-941266-02-8) Kibo Bks.

Niggun: Stories Behind the Chasidic Songs That Inspire Jews. Mordechai Staiman. LC 93-34028. 312p. 1994. 40.00 (1-56821-047-7) Aronson.

***Nighantu & the Nirukta: Oldest Indian Treatise on Etymology, Philolgy & Semantics.** Lakshman Sarup. 1998. 36.00 (81-208-1381-2) Motilal Bnarsidass.

Night. 32p. (YA). 1998. 9.95 (1-56137-804-6, NU8046); 11.95 (1-56137-805-4, NU8054SP) Novel Units.

Night. A. Alvarez. (Illus.). 224p. 1996. pap. 13.00 (0-393-31434-0, Norton Paperbks) Norton.

***Night.** Harold Bloom. (Modern Critical Interpretations Ser.). 2000. 36.95 (0-7910-5924-3) Chelsea Hse.

Night. Bruce Coville. LC 97-155113. (J). 1997. mass mkt. 3.99 (0-590-85295-7) Scholastic Inc.

An Asterisk (*) at the beginning of an entry indicates that the title is appearing for the first time.

Night. Ed. by Magnum Photos Agency Staff. (Terrail Photo Ser.). (Illus.). 64p. 1998. pap. text 11.95 (*2-87939-155-5*, Pub. by Pierre Terrail) Rizzoli Intl.

*__Night.__ Wendy Mass. LC 99-55870. (Literary Companion Ser.). 224p. 2000. pap. 13.96 (*0-7377-0369-5*) Greenhaven.

*__Night.__ Wendy Mass. LC 99-55870. (Literary Companion Ser.). 224p. (YA). 2000. 17.45 (*0-7377-0370-9*) Greenhaven.

Night. Elie Wiesel. 1982. mass mkt. 4.99 (*0-553-54083-1*) Bantam.

Night. Elie Wiesel. 128p. 1982. mass mkt. 5.50 (*0-553-27253-5*, Bantam Classics) Bantam.

Night. Elie Wiesel. 1987. 9.84 (*0-606-01692-9*, Pub. by Turtleback) Demco.

Night: A Holocaust Memoir. Jakob Littner & Kurt Grubler. 240p. 1999. 24.50 (*0-8264-1197-5*) Continuum.

Night: A Novel. Bilge Karasu. Tr. by Guneli Gun. LC 93-37912. 152p. (C). 1994. 19.95 (*0-8071-1849-4*) La State U Pr.

Night: A Study Guide. K. Fischer. Ed. by J. Friedland & R. Kessler. (Novel-Ties Ser.). (YA). (gr. 9-12). 1997. pap. text 15.95 (*0-7675-0168-3*) Lrn Links.

Night: A Unit Plan. Barbara M. Linde. 158p. 1998. teacher ed., ring bd. 26.95 (*1-58337-166-4*) Teachers Pet Pubns.

Night: Curriculum Unit. Center for Learning Network Staff & Elie Wiesel. (Novel Ser.). 101p. (YA). (gr. 9-12). 1992. spiral bd. 18.95 (*1-56077-225-5*) Ctr Learning.

Night: Reproducible Teaching Unit. James Scott. 50p. (YA). (gr. 7-12). 1999. teacher ed., ring bd. 29.50 (*1-58049-134-0*, TU94) Prestwick Hse.

Night Action. large type ed. Alan Evans. 1990. 27.99 (*0-7089-2301-1*) Ulverscroft.

Night After. 2nd ed. James Ralston. 100p. 1986. pap. text 6.00 (*0-945073-01-1*) Nightsun MD.

Night after Christmas. J. Thomas Moore. (J). (gr. k up). 1990. pap. 5.95 (*0-925928-07-0*) Tiny Thought.

Night after Christmas. James Stevenson. LC 81-1022. (Illus.). 32p. (J). (gr. k-3). 1981. 16.00 (*0-688-00547-0*, Grenwillow Bks) HarpC Child Bks.

Night after Christmas. James Stevenson. LC 92-43786. (Illus.). 32p. (J). (ps-3). 1993. pap. 4.95 (*0-688-04590-1*, Wm Morrow) Morrow Avon.

Night After Christmas. James Stevenson. 1993. 10.15 (*0-606-05954-7*, Pub. by Turtleback) Demco.

Night after Night. Neil Barlett. 80p. 1994. pap. 11.95 (*0-413-68500-4*, A0709, Methuen Drama) Methn.

Night after Night. Diana S. Cooper. LC 93-44947. (Illus.). 1994. 20.00 (*1-55963-306-9*) Island Pr.

Night, Again: Contemporary Fiction from Vietnam. Ed. by Linh Dinh. 176p. 1996. 25.00 (*1-888363-02-9*) Seven Stories.

Night, Again: Contemporary Fiction from Vietnam. Ed. by Linh Dinh. 176p. 1996. pap. 12.95 (*1-888363-07-X*) Seven Stories.

Night Air Dancing. George McCauley. 80p. (Orig.). 1990. pap. 8.95 (*0-9622889-1-8*) Something More.

*__Night Airwar: Personal Recollections of the Conflict over Europe, 1939-45.__ Theo Boiten. (Illus.). 192p. 2000. 44.95 (*1-86126-298-1*, 129770AE, Pub. by Crolwood) Motorbooks Intl.

Night Alone in the Camp. Helen Trowbridge. Ed. by JoAnne Cramberg. 48p. 1998. pap. 4.00 (*0-9657706-9-9*) Phos Pub.

Night & Day. Doris Johnson. 320p. 1997. mass mkt. 4.99 (*0-7860-0375-8*, Pinncle Kensgtn) Kensgtn Pub Corp.

Night & Day. John Leslie. 1996. pap. 5.99 (*0-671-86423-8*) PB.

Night & Day. Mira Markovic. LC 97-199993. 240p. 1997. 14.95 (*1-55082-168-7*, Pub. by Quarry Pr) LPC InBook.

Night & Day. Ian Murray-Clark. 1989. 4.95 (*0-945603-02-9*) Dinnerman Bks.

*__Night & Day.__ Ellen Weiss. (Bear in the Big Blue House Ser.). (Illus.). 10p. (J). (ps). 2000. bds. 7.99 (*1-57584-674-8*, Pub. by Rdrs Digest) S&S Trade.

Night & Day. Virginia Woolf. Ed. by Suzanne Raitt. (World's Classics Ser.). 582p. 1992. pap. write for info. (*0-19-281842-2*) OUP.

Night & Day. Virginia Woolf. Ed. & Intro. by Julia Briggs. LC 96-145376. (Illus.). 496p. 1996. pap. 13.95 (*0-14-018568-2*) Penguin Putnam.

*__Night & Day.__ Virginia Woolf. 2000. 37.95 (*0-7658-0782-3*) Transaction Pubs.

Night & Day. Virginia Woolf. LC 73-5730. 516p. 1973. reprint ed. pap. 12.95 (*0-15-665600-0*, HB263, Harvest Bks) Harcourt.

Night & Day, Bk. 1. Banks & Orlando. (C). 1993. pap. text 21.27 (*0-13-043696-8*) S&S Trade.

*__Night & Day: A Book of Eye-Catching Opposites.__ Herve Tullet. LC 98-35357. (Illus.). 144p. (J). (gr. k-3). 1999. 14.95 (*0-316-84244-3*) Little.

Night & Day: Reading for the Adult Learner of ESL - EFL, Bk. 2. Caroline Banks. 144p. 1993. pap. text 21.27 (*0-13-043704-2*) P-H.

*__Night & Day: The Double Lives of Artists in America.__ Gloria Klaiman. LC 00-26. 256p. 2000. 62.00 (*0-275-97029-9*, C7029) Greenwood.

Night & Day Book 3: Reading for the Adult Learner of ESL EFL, Bk. 3. Caroline Banks. 128p. 1993. pap. text 21.27 (*0-13-043712-3*) P-H.

Night & Her Stars. Richard Greenberg. LC 98-115332. 1997. pap. 5.25 (*0-8222-1500-4*) Dramatists Play.

Night & Hope. Arnost Lustig. Tr. by George Theiner from CZE. 219p. 1985. reprint ed. pap. 9.95 (*0-8101-0702-3*) Northwestern U Pr.

*__Night & Horses & the Desert: An Anthology of Classical Arabic Literature.__ Robert Irwin. 462p. 2000. 40.00 (*1-58567-064-2*, Pub. by Overlook Pr) Penguin Putnam.

*__Night & Light & the Half-Light.__ Henry G. Fischer. vi, 74p. 1998. pap. 6.00 (*0-936015-79-9*) Pocahontas Pr.

Night & Low-Light Photography: A Complete Guide. Bob Gibbons & Peter Wilson. (Illus.). 192p. 1993. pap. 19.95 (*0-304-34331-5*, Pub. by Cassell) Sterling.

*__Night & Morning (1845)__ Edward Bulwer Lytton. 254p. 1999. reprint ed. pap. 19.95 (*0-7661-0789-2*) Kessinger Pub.

Night & Shift Work - Biological & Social Aspects: Proceedings of the 5th International Symposium on Night & Shift Work-Scientific Committee on Shift Work of the Permanent Commission & International Association on Occupational Health (PCIAIH, Rouen, 12-16 May 1980. Ed. by Alain Reinberg et al. (Illus.). 509p. 1981. 100.00 (*0-08-025516-7*, Pergamon Pr) Elsevier.

Night & Sleep. Jalal al-Din Rumi Maulana. Tr. by Coleman Barks & Robert Bly from PER. (Illus.). 48p. (Orig.). 1980. pap. 6.00 (*0-938756-02-8*) Yellow Moon.

*__Night & the Candlemaker.__ Wolfgang Somary. (Illus.). 32p. (YA). (gr. 4 up). 2000. 16.99 (*1-84148-137-8*) Barefoot Bks NY.

Night & the Moon. Vincent DiPaolo. LC 82-13724. 1987. pap. 13.95 (*0-87949-214-7*) Ashley Bks.

Night Animals see Zoobooks

Night Animals. Iqbal Hussain. (Totally Amazing Ser.). 32p. 1999. pap. 5.99 (*0-307-20166-X*) Gldn Bks Pub Co.

Night Animals. Judy Nayer. (At Your Fingertips Ser.). (Illus.). 10p. (J). (ps-3). 1992. bds. 6.95 (*1-56293-223-3*, McClanahan Book) Learn Horizon.

Night Animals. John B. Wexo. (Zoobooks Ser.). 24p. (J). (gr. 1-7). 1993. 13.95 (*0-937934-99-2*) Wildlife Educ.

Night Animals. Wildlife Education, Ltd. Staff & John B. Wexo. (Zoobooks Ser.). (Illus.). 20p. (Orig.). (YA). (gr. 5 up). 1995. pap. 2.75 (*0-937934-26-7*) Wildlife Educ.

Night As Frontier: Colonizing the World after Dark. Murray Melbin. 1987. text 29.95 (*0-02-920940-4*) Free Pr.

Night at Acadie see Collected Works of Kate Chopin

Night at an Inn. unabridged ed. Lord Dunsany. Ed. by William-Alan Landes. LC 97-10228. 55p. (Orig.). 1997. pap. 5.00 (*0-88734-398-8*) Players Pr.

Night at the Ballet. (In Classical Mood Ser.: Vol. 25). (Illus.). 1998. write for info. incl. cd-rom (*1-886614-36-9*) Intl Masters Pub.

Night at the Fair. Donald Crews. LC 96-48780. (Illus.). 24p. (J). (ps-3). 1998. 15.00 (*0-688-11483-0*, Grenwillow Bks) HarpC Child Bks.

*__Night at the Fair.__ Donald Crews. LC 96-48780. (Illus.). 24p. (J). (ps-3). 1998. 14.93 (*0-688-11484-9*, Grenwillow Bks) HarpC Child Bks.

Night at the Hotel Pyramid. Lane Riosley. 57p. (Orig.). 1993. pap. 4.00 (*1-57514-115-9*, 1151) Encore Perform Pub.

Night at the Movies: or You Must Remember This. 2nd ed. Robert Coover. LC 92-14178. 197p. 1997. reprint ed. pap. 11.95 (*1-56478-160-7*) Dalkey Arch.

Night at the Museum. Milan Trenc. 1993. 11.15 (*0-606-13660-6*, Pub. by Turtleback) Demco.

Night at the Opera. (In Classical Mood Ser.: Vol. 35). (Illus.). 1998. write for info. incl. cd-rom (*1-886614-61-X*) Intl Masters Pub.

Night at the Opera. Denis Forman. LC 98-21454. 1998. 21.95 (*0-375-75176-9*) Modern Lib NY.

Night at the Opera. Denis Forman. LC 95-13398. 992p. 1995. 40.00 (*0-679-44553-6*) Random.

Night at the Opera. Ray Smith. 240p. 1992. pap. write for info. (*0-88984-137-3*) Porcup Quill.

Night at the Vulcan. Ngaio Marsh. 1998. mass mkt. 5.99 (*0-312-96668-7*) St Martin.

Night at the Vulcan. Ngaio Marsh. 1976. reprint ed. lib. bdg. 24.95 (*0-88411-490-2*) Amereon Ltd.

Night at the Y. Robert Garner McBrearty. LC 99-12912. 160p. 1999. pap. 12.00 (*1-880284-36-7*) J Daniel.

Night Autopsy Room: Seven Tales of Life, Death & Hope. Yoshio Sakabe. LC 94-71050. 350p. 1994. 39.95 (*0-940121-20-4*, H207, Cross Roads Bks) Cross Cultural Pubns.

In this intriguing book, the troubled characters in each tale take up important issues of wartime life in Japan. These include death, eschatology & the problems of lust, prejudice & discrimination. Above all, it tells of the horror & sorrows of war set against the fascinating backdrop of historical events & social conditions in Japan before, during & just after World War II. *Publisher Paid Annotation.*

---

*__Night Awakens: A Mystery Writers of America Anthology.__ Ed. by Mary Higgins Clark. 320p. 2000. reprint ed. per. 6.99 (*0-671-51918-2*, Pocket Star Bks) PB.

Night Ballon Fever Rising. Jim Dewitt. (Libraries-School Libraries). 64p. 1985. pap. 5.00 (*0-915199-10-6*) Pen-Dec.

Night Battle. William Logan. LC 99-19548. (Penguin Poets Ser.). 97p. 1999. pap. 15.95 (*0-14-058798-5*, Penguin Bks) Viking Penguin.

Night Battles: Witchcraft & Agrarian Cults in the Sixteenth & Seventeenth Centuries. Carlo Ginzburg. Tr. by John Tedeschi & Anne C. Tedeschi from ITA. 232p. 1992. reprint ed. pap. 15.95 (*0-8018-4386-3*) Johns Hopkins.

Night Beat: A Shadow History of Rock & Roll. Mikal Gilmore. 496p. 1999. pap. 15.95 (*0-385-48436-4*) Doubleday.

Night Bees. Anthony Holcroft. (Storybridge Ser.). (Illus.). 80p. (J). (gr. 2-7). 1995. pap. 9.95 (*0-7022-2669-6*, Pub. by Univ Queensland Pr) Intl Spec Bk.

Night Before: A Cookbook. Victoria Lewis. 1998. 16.00 (*0-207-18849-1*) HarpC.

Night Before Baby: Loving the Boss. Karen Rose Smith. 1999. per. 3.50 (*0-373-19348-3*, Harlequin) Harlequin Bks.

Night Before Cat-Mas. Virginia Unser. LC 99-162009. (Charming Petites Ser.). (Illus.). 64p. 1998. 4.95 (*0-88088-834-2*) Peter Pauper.

Night Before Christmas see Xmas Nutshell Library

Night Before Christmas see Santa's Take-Along Library: Five Favorite Read-to-Me Books

Night Before Christmas. (Little Golden Books Book 'n Tape Ser.). (Illus.). (J). (ps-2). 1995. 6.99 incl. audio (*0-307-14456-9*, 14456, Goldn Books) Gldn Bks Pub Co.

Night Before Christmas. (Illus.). 24p. (J). (gr. k-2). 1991. 3.95 (*1-56144-070-1*, Honey Bear Bks) Modern Pub NYC.

Night Before Christmas. (Christmas Titles Ser.: No. S808-20). (Illus.). (J). 1989. pap. 3.95 (*0-7214-5205-1*, Ladybrd) Penguin Putnam.

Night Before Christmas. (Illus.). 12p. (J). 1993. pap. 6.95 (*0-8167-3154-3*) Troll Communs.

Night Before Christmas. Illus. by Jan Brett. LC 98-4998. 32p. (J). 1998. 16.99 (*0-399-23190-0*, G P Putnam) Peng Put Young Read.

Night Before Christmas. Gabriele. (J). 1985. pap. 1.95 (*0-911211-77-2*) Penny Lane Pubns.

Night Before Christmas. Rick Geary. LC 96-155277. (Illus.). 32p. 1994. 9.95 (*1-56971-054-6*) Dark Horse Comics.

Night Before Christmas. Anita Lobel. 32p. 1988. mass mkt. 3.95 (*0-552-52384-4*) Bantam.

Night Before Christmas, 1 vol. Love Spell Staff. 400p. 1998. mass mkt. 5.99 (*0-505-52318-3*) Dorchester Pub Co.

Night Before Christmas. Kees Moerbeek. (Triangle Pop-up Ser.). 12p. (J). (ps up). 1992. pap. 10.99 (*0-8431-3445-3*, Price Stern) Peng Put Young Read.

Night Before Christmas. Moore. LC 98-15890. 32p. (J). 1999. 16.00 (*0-15-201713-5*, Harcourt Child Bks) Harcourt.

Night Before Christmas. Moore. LC 97-40335. (Illus.). 32p. (J). (ps-k). 1998. lib. bdg. 13.49 (*0-7868-2252-X*, Pub. by Hyperion) Time Warner.

Night Before Christmas. Clement Clarke Moore. (Children's Classics Ser.). (Illus.). 32p. (J). 1991. 6.95 (*0-8362-4917-8*) Andrews & McMeel.

Night Before Christmas. Clement Clarke Moore. (Illus.). 16p. 1992. 4.95 (*0-8362-3027-2*) Andrews & McMeel.

*__Night Before Christmas.__ Clement Clarke Moore. (Illus.). (J). 2000. pap. 1.00 (*0-486-41031-5*) Dover.

Night Before Christmas. Clement Clarke Moore. pap. 6.95 (*0-8378-8504-3*) Gibson.

Night Before Christmas. Clement Clarke Moore. (Super Shape Bks.). (Illus.). 24p. (J). (ps-k). 1991. 3.29 (*0-307-10038-3*, 10038) Gldn Bks Pub Co.

Night Before Christmas. Clement Clarke Moore. (Look-Look Bks.). (J). 1996. pap. text 3.29 (*0-307-13080-0*, 13080, Goldn Books) Gldn Bks Pub Co.

Night Before Christmas. Clement Clarke Moore. (Little Golden Storybks.). (J). 1997. 3.99 (*0-307-16178-1*, 16178, Goldn Books) Gldn Bks Pub Co.

Night Before Christmas. Clement Clarke Moore. (Illus.). 24p. (J). (ps-2). 1984. pap. 2.95 (*0-89542-498-3*, Ideals Child) Hambleton-Hill.

Night Before Christmas. Clement Clarke Moore. (Illus.). 16p. (J). (ps-1). 1994. pap. 7.95 (*1-57102-011-X*, Ideals Child) Hambleton-Hill.

Night Before Christmas. Clement Clarke Moore. LC 97-34352. (Illus.). 40p. (J). 1999. 16.95 (*0-06-026608-2*) HarpC.

Night Before Christmas. Clement Clarke Moore. LC 90-22388. (Merry Christmas Bk.). (Illus.). 24p. (J). (ps up). 1991. 2.95 (*0-694-00365-4*) HarpC Child Bks.

Night Before Christmas. Clement Clarke Moore. LC 97-34352. (Illus.). 40p. (J). (ps-3). 1999. lib. bdg. 16.89 (*0-06-028380-7*) HarpC Child Bks.

Night Before Christmas. Clement Clarke Moore. (Chubby Board Bks.). (Illus.). 16p. (J). (ps up). 1984. pap. 3.95 (*0-671-50952-7*) Litle Simon.

Night Before Christmas. Clement Clarke Moore. (Illus.). 32p. (J). (ps-1). 1986. pap. 5.95 (*0-671-62209-9*) Litle Simon.

Night Before Christmas. Clement Clarke Moore. LC 96-28153. (Illus.). 32p. (J). (gr. k-3). 1997. 13.95 (*0-316-57963-7*) Little.

Night Before Christmas. Clement Clarke Moore. LC 98-21623. (Illus.). 32p. (J). (gr. k-3). 1999. 14.95 (*0-316-85579-0*) Little.

Night Before Christmas. Clement Clarke Moore. LC 96-48760. (Illus.). 64p. (J). 1997. per. 18.00 (*0-689-81375-9*) McElderry Bks.

Night Before Christmas. Clement Clarke Moore. (Illus.). 10p. (J). (ps-7). 1989. pap. 3.95 (*0-922589-06-2*) More Than a Card.

Night Before Christmas. Clement Clarke Moore. LC 95-1775. (Illus.). 32p. (J). (ps-2). 1995. lib. bdg. 16.88 (*1-55858-466-8*, Pub. by North-South Bks NYC) Chronicle Bks.

Night Before Christmas. Clement Clarke Moore. LC 92-27138. (All Aboard Bks.). (Illus.). 32p. (J). (ps-3). 1993. pap. 2.95 (*0-448-40482-6*, G & D) Peng Put Young Read.

*__Night Before Christmas.__ Clement Clarke Moore. (Jellybean Bks.). (Illus.). 24p. (J). (ps-k). 1999. lib. bdg. 7.99 (*0-375-90147-7*, Pub. by Random Bks Yng Read) Random.

Night Before Christmas. Clement Clarke Moore. LC 98-67793. (Jellybean Bks.). (Illus.). 24p. (J). (ps-3). 1999. 1.99 (*0-375-80147-2*, Pub. by Random Bks Yng Read) Random.

Night Before Christmas. Clement Clarke Moore. (Illus.). 40p. (J). (ps up). 1996. 10.95 incl. audio (*0-689-80793-7*) S&S Bks Yung.

*__Night Before Christmas.__ Clement Clarke Moore. (Illus.). 60p. (J). (ps-1). 1999. pap. 12.98 (*1-58048-065-9*) Sandvik Pub.

Night Before Christmas. Clement Clarke Moore. 1987. pap. 1.75 (*0-8167-1223-9*) Troll Communs.

Night Before Christmas. Clement Clarke Moore. LC 87-15343. (Illus.). 48p. (J). (gr. k-3). 1988. lib. bdg. 19.95 (*0-8167-1209-3*) Troll Communs.

Night Before Christmas. Clement Clarke Moore. (Blue Ribbon Bks.). (J). 1985. 10.15 (*0-606-01915-4*, Pub. by Turtleback) Demco.

Night Before Christmas. Clement Clarke Moore. (Illus.). 32p. (J). (ps up). 1994. mass mkt. 16.00 (*0-02-767646-3*, Mac Bks Young Read) S&S Childrens.

*__Night Before Christmas.__ Clement Clarke Moore & Donald Mills. LC 00-20434. 2000. write for info. (*0-8249-4186-1*, Candy Cane Pr) Ideals.

Night Before Christmas. Clement Clarke Moore & Jenny Williams. (Glitter Glow Board Bks.). (Illus.). 12p. (J). (ps-2). 1997. 4.99 (*0-689-81692-8*) Simon & Schuster.

Night Before Christmas. Illus. by Stephanie Ryder. 32p. (J). (ps-2). 1995. 3.98 (*0-86112-892-3*) Brimax Bks.

*__Night Before Christmas.__ William Wegman. (Illus.). 32p. (J). 2000. 16.99 (*0-7868-0608-7*, Pub. by Hyprn Child) Time Warner.

Night Before Christmas. abr. ed. James Marshall. (Illus.). (J). (ps-3). 1992. 4.95 (*0-590-45977-5*, Blue Ribbon Bks) Scholastic Inc.

Night Before Christmas. abr. ed. Clement Clarke Moore. (Classic Christmas Sticker Storybook Ser.). (Illus.). 18p. (J). (ps-3). 1996. 3.50 (*0-689-80256-0*) Aladdin.

Night Before Christmas. abr. ed. Clement Clarke Moore. LC 95-20326. (Wee Books for Wee Folks). (Illus.). 64p. (ps-3). 1995. 6.95 (*1-55709-410-1*) Applewood.

Night Before Christmas. abr. ed. Clement Clarke Moore. LC 80-84842. (Illus.). 12p. (J). (ps-3). 1995. 12.95 (*0-8050-0900-0*, Bks Young Read) H Holt & Co.

Night Before Christmas. abr. ed. Clement Clarke Moore. (Illus.). 32p. (J). (ps-3). 1993. pap. 5.95 (*0-395-66508-6*, Clarion Bks) HM.

Night Before Christmas. abr. ed. Clement Clarke Moore. LC 98-16589. (Illus.). 24p. (J). (ps-2). 1998. 6.95 (*1-57102-135-3*, Ideals Child) Hambleton-Hill.

Night Before Christmas. abr. ed. Clement Clarke Moore. LC 80-11758. (Illus.). 32p. (J). (ps-3). 1980. pap. 6.95 (*0-8234-0417-X*); lib. bdg. 16.95 (*0-8234-0414-5*) Holiday.

Night Before Christmas. abr. ed. Clement Clarke Moore. LC 92-22712. (Illus.). 40p. (J). (ps-3). 1992. 14.95 (*0-88708-261-0*, Rabbit Ears) Litle Simon.

Night Before Christmas. abr. ed. Clement Clarke Moore. LC 95-1775. (Illus.). 32p. (J). (ps-3). 1995. 16.95 (*1-55858-465-X*, Pub. by North-South Bks NYC) Chronicle Bks.

Night Before Christmas. abr. ed. Clement Clarke Moore. LC 75-7511. (Illus.). 32p. (J). (ps-3). 1975. pap. 3.25 (*0-394-83019-9*, Pub. by Random Bks Yng Read) Random.

Night Before Christmas. abr. ed. Clement Clarke Moore. LC 88-35019. (Illus.). 40p. (J). (ps-3). 1990. 8.99 (*0-394-82698-1*, Pub. by Random Bks Yng Read) Random.

Night Before Christmas. abr. ed. Clement Clarke Moore. LC 88-35019. (Illus.). 32p. (J). (ps-3). 1989. pap. 3.25 (*0-671-68408-6*) S&S Trade.

Night Before Christmas. abr. ed. Clement Clarke Moore. LC 89-22386. (Illus.). 32p. (J). (ps-3). 1989. pap. 2.99 (*0-590-42758-X*) Scholastic Inc.

Night Before Christmas. abr. ed. Clement Clarke Moore. LC 87-15343. (Illus.). 48p. (J). (ps-3). 1989. pap. 5.95 (*0-8167-1210-7*) Troll Communs.

Night Before Christmas. abr. ed. Clement Clarke Moore. (Illus.). 32p. (J). (gr. 1-4). 1996. pap. 2.95 (*0-8167-4058-5*, Whistlstop) Troll Communs.

Night Before Christmas. abr. ed. Clement Clarke Moore. LC 87-15343. (Illus.). 48p. (J). (ps up). 1997. pap. 2.95 (*0-8167-1890-3*) Troll Communs.

Night Before Christmas. Clement Clarke Moore. LC 95-67986. (Illus.). 32p. (J). (ps-3). 1997. reprint ed. pap. 3.99 (*0-7636-0351-1*) Candlewick Pr.

Night Before Christmas. Clement Clarke Moore. (Illus.). 40p. 1971. reprint ed. pap. 2.95 (*0-486-22797-9*) Dover.

Night Before Christmas. Clement Clarke Moore. LC 98-66375. (Illus.). 26p. (J). 1998. reprint ed. 14.95 (*1-56352-533-X*) Longstreet.

Night Before Christmas. Clement Clarke Moore. LC 89-34789. (Illus.). 32p. (J). 1990. reprint ed. 14.95 (*0-88289-755-1*) Pelican.

Night Before Christmas. Jacquin Sanders. 1993. reprint ed. 35.95 (*1-56849-012-7*) Buccaneer Bks.

Night Before Christmas. rev. ed. Clement Clarke Moore. (Illus.). 24p. (J). (ps-1). 1995. 6.95 (*1-57102-082-9*, Ideals Child); pap. 2.49 (*1-57102-076-4*, Ideals Child) Hambleton-Hill.

Night Before Christmas. unabridged ed. Clement Clarke Moore. (Illus.). (J). (gr. k-3). 1984. 24.95 incl. audio (*0-941078-39-6*); pap. 15.95 incl. audio (*0-941078-37-X*) Live Oak Media.

Night Before Christmas, Mini Edition. Clement Clarke Moore. (Illus.). 32p. (J). 1996. 4.99 (*0-679-87930-7*) Knopf.

Night Before Christmas, 4 bks., Set. Clement Clarke Moore. LC 87-15343. (Illus.). (J). (gr. k-3). 1984. pap., teacher ed. 37.95 incl. audio (*0-941078-38-8*) Live Oak Media.

Night Before Christmas: A Classic Illustrated Edition. Clement Clarke Moore et al. LC 97-4101. (Illus.). (J). (ps up). 1998. 16.95 (*0-8118-1712-1*) Chronicle Bks.

N

N

***Night Before Christmas: A Collection of Festive Tales & Festive Traditions.** Yvonne Guilbert. LC 00-23261. (Illus.). 96p. (gr. 4-7). 2000. write for info. (*0-7894-6661-9*, Pub. by DK Pub Inc) Pub Resources Inc.

Night Before Christmas: A Reproduction of an Antique Christmas Classic. Clement Clarke Moore. LC 88-19600. (Illus.). 32p. (J). 1989. 17.95 (*0-399-21614-6*, Philomel) Peng Put Young Read.

***Night Before Christmas: A Trim-a-tree Story.** Clement Clarke Moore. 1999. 6.99 (*1-57866-076-9*) Galahad Bks.

***Night Before Christmas: A Victorian Vision of the Christmas Classic.** Clement Clarke Moore. (Illus.). 32p. (J). (ps-3). 2000. pap. 6.99 (*0-375-81047-1*) Random.

Night Before Christmas: Full-Color Sturdy Book. C. Moore. LC 98-20335. (Illus.). 12p. (J). 1998. pap. 1.00 (*0-486-40256-8*) Dover.

Night Before Christmas: Memories of an Old Time Country Christmas. large type ed. Alice Taylor. 21.95 (*1-85695-064-6*, Pub. by ISIS Lrg Prnt) Transaction Pubs.

Night Before Christmas: The Classic Edition. abr. ed. Clement Clarke Moore. LC 95-67238. (Children's Illustrated Classics Ser.). (Illus.). 48p. (J). (ps-3). 1995. 9.98 (*1-56138-476-3*, Courage) Running Pr.

Night Before Christmas: The Classic Poem. Clement Clarke Moore. LC 97-11482. (Illus.). 32p. (J). (gr. k-2). 1997. 11.95 (*0-8249-4084-9*, Candy Cane Pr); bds. 6.95 (*0-8249-4089-X*, Candy Cane Pr) Ideals.

Night Before Christmas: Told in Signed English. Clement Clarke Moore. (Awareness & Caring Ser.). (Illus.). 64p. (J). (gr. k-6). 1995. lib. bdg. 17.95 (*1-56674-109-2*) Forest Hse.

Night Before Christmas: Told in Signed English. Clement Clarke Moore. LC 94-11477. (Illus.). 64p. 1994. 14.95 (*1-56368-020-3*, Pub. by K Green Pubns) Gallaudet Univ Pr.

Night Before Christmas Board Book. abr. ed. Clement Clarke Moore. LC 91-46766. (Illus.). 26p. (J). (ps up). 1992. 6.95 (*0-694-00424-3*) HarpC Child Bks.

Night Before Christmas Coloring Book. Clement Clarke Moore. (J). 1986. pap. 2.95 (*0-671-62959-X*) Litle Simon.

Night Before Christmas Coloring Book. 80th ed. Nina Barbaresi. (Illus.). (J). 1990. pap. 1.00 (*0-486-25737-1*) Dover.

Night Before Christmas Coloring Book. 81st ed. John Obrien. (Illus.). (J). (gr. k-3). 1981. pap. 2.95 (*0-486-24169-6*) Dover.

Night Before Christmas Gift Set. Clement Clarke Moore. 1999. 17.98 (*0-7624-0644-5*) Running Pr.

Night Before Christmas Holiday Crafts & Activity Center. unabridged large type ed. Illus. by Melinda Bell. LC 96-79052. 32p. (J). (gr. k-5). 1996. 24.95 incl. cd-rom (*0-9654458-0-1*, Play Again Inter) Bell-Ford Ent.

Night Before Christmas in California. Catherine Smith. (Little Night Before Christmas Ser.). (Illus.). 60p. 1992. 5.95 (*0-87905-487-5*) Gibbs Smith Pub.

Night Before Christmas in Chicago. Catherine Smith. (Little Night Before Christmas Ser.). (Illus.). 60p. 1992. 5.95 (*0-87905-488-3*) Gibbs Smith Pub.

***Night Before Christmas in Colorado.** Sue Carabine. (Little Night Before Christmas Ser.: Vol. 18). (Illus.). 60p. 2000. 5.95 (*0-87905-997-4*) Gibbs Smith Pub.

Night Before Christmas in Florida. Sue Carabine. (Little Night Before Christmas Bks.: Vol. 15). (Illus.). 60p. 1999. 5.95 (*0-87905-928-1*) Gibbs Smith Pub.

Night Before Christmas in Hawaii. Clement Clarke Moore. (Illus.). 32p. (J). 1991. text 8.98 (*0-9627294-2-6*) Hawaiian Resources.

Night Before Christmas in New York City. Francis Morrone. LC 94-220441. (Illus.). 60p. 1994. 5.95 (*0-87905-615-0*) Gibbs Smith Pub.

***Night Before Christmas in Seattle.** Sue Carabine. (Little Night Before Christmas Bks.: Vol. 16). (Illus.). 60p. 1999. 5.95 (*0-87905-929-X*) Gibbs Smith Pub.

Night Before Christmas in Texas. Catherine Smith. (Little Night Before Christmas Ser.). (Illus.). 60p. 1992. 5.95 (*0-87905-485-9*) Gibbs Smith Pub.

***Night Before Christmas in Utah.** Sue Carabine. (Little Night Before Christmas Ser.: Vol. 17). (Illus.). 60p. 2000. 5.95 (*0-87905-981-8*) Gibbs Smith Pub.

***Night Before Christmas Mini Book.** Clement Clarke Moore. (Illus.). 32p. (J). 1999. 7.95 (*0-7358-1226-8*, Pub. by North-South Bks NYC) Chronicle Bks.

Night Before Christmas Sticker Storybook. Clement Clarke Moore & Anna Pomaska. (Illus.). 16p. (Orig.). (J). 1996. pap. text 1.00 (*0-486-29197-9*) Dover.

Night Before Dark. large type ed. Clodagh Chapman. 1989. 27.99 (*0-7089-2187-6*) Ulverscroft.

Night Before Dog-Mas. Claudine Gandolfi. LC 99-162019. (Charming Petites Ser.). (Illus.). 64p. 1998. 4.95 (*0-88088-835-0*) Peter Pauper.

Night Before Easter. 1996. 5.99 (*0-8341-9538-0*, ME-49) Lillenas.

Night Before Easter. Natasha Wing. LC 98-41054. (All Aboard Reading Ser.). (Illus.). 32p. (ps-3). 1999. pap. 3.49 (*0-448-41873-8*, G & D) Peng Put Young Read.

***Night Before Halloween.** Natasha Wing. LC 99-14898. 32p. (J). 1999. pap. text 2.99 (*0-448-41965-3*, G & D) Peng Put Young Read.

Night Before Jesus. Herbert F. Brokering. 36p. (J). (ps-4). 1983. 7.99 (*0-570-04084-1*, 56-1439) Concordia.

Night Before the Night Before Christmas! Richard Scarry. (Illus.). 48p. (J). (gr. k-3). 2000. 14.00 (*0-375-80202-9*, Pub. by Random Bks Yng Read) Random.

Night Bird Cantata. Donald Rawley. LC 97-44611. 256p. 1998. mass mkt. 23.00 (*0-380-97609-9*, Avon Bks) Morrow Avon.

Night Bird Cantata. Donald Rawley. 256p. 1999. reprint ed. pap. 12.00 (*0-380-79584-1*) Morrow Avon.

Night Birds. Alice K. Flanagan. LC 95-42386. (New True Books Ser.). (Illus.). 48p. (J). (gr. 1-4). 1996. lib. bdg. 21.00 (*0-516-01089-1*) Childrens.

Night Birds. Alice K. Flanagan. (New True Books Ser.). 48p. (J). (ps-3). 1996. pap. 5.50 (*0-516-20075-5*) Childrens.

Night Birds: Indian Prostitutes from Devadasis to Call Girls. K. Lakshmi Raghuramaiah. (C). 1991. text 19.50 (*81-7001-084-5*, Pub. by Chanakya) S Asia.

Night Bites: Vampire Stories by Women. Victoria A. Brownworth. LC 95-43877. 280p. (Orig.). 1996. pap. text 12.95 (*1-878067-71-0*) Seal Pr WA.

Night Blitz, 1940-41. John Ray. (Illus.). 224p. 1996. 24.95 (*1-85409-270-7*, Pub. by Arms & Armour) Sterling.

Night Blood. Eric Flanders. 384p. 1993. mass mkt. 4.50 (*0-8217-4063-6*, Zebra Kensgtn) Kensgtn Pub Corp.

Night Bloom. Mary Cappello. LC 98-19582. 280p. 1998. 24.00 (*0-8070-7216-8*) Beacon Pr.

Night Bloom: An Italian-American Life. Mary Cappello. LC 98-19582. 280p. 1999. pap. 16.00 (*0-8070-7217-6*) Beacon Pr.

Night Blooms: Reflections. Richard A. Bunch. Ed. by Edward Mycue. (Took Modern Essays in English Ser.: No. 1). (Illus.). 54p. (Orig.). 1992. pap. 5.00 (*1-879457-30-X*) Norton Coker Pr.

Night Boat. Robert R. McCammon. Ed. by Sally Peters. 1988. mass mkt. 5.99 (*0-671-73281-1*) PB.

Night Boat on the Potomac. Harry Jones & Timothy Jones. Ed. by Edwin L. Dunbaugh & John H. Shaum, Jr. (Illus.). 117p. 1996. reprint ed. 38.00 (*0-913423-08-4*) Steamship Hist Soc.

Night Boat to New England, 1815-1900, 128. Edwin L. Dunbaugh. LC 91-22368. (Contributions in Economics & Economic History Ser.: No. 116). (Illus.). 384p. 1992. 65.00 (*0-313-27733-8*, DNB, Greenwood Pr) Greenwood.

Night Boats. rev. ed. Edward Mycue. (Illus.). 64p. (Orig.). 1999. pap. 10.00 (*1-879457-38-5*) Norton Coker Pr.

Night Bombing with the Bedouins. Robert H. Reece. (Great War Ser.: No. 12). (Illus.). 120p. 1991. reprint ed. 29.95 (*0-89839-161-X*) Battery Pr.

Night Book: Exploring Nature after Dark with Activities, Experiments & Information. unabridged ed. Pamela Hickman. (Illus.). 48p. (J). (gr. 2-6). 1999. 16.99 (*1-55074-318-X*, Pub. by Kids Can Pr); pap. 9.99 (*1-55074-306-6*, Pub. by Kids Can Pr) Genl Dist Srvs.

***Night-Born.** Jack London. (Collected Works of Jack London). 290p. 1998. reprint ed. lib. bdg. 88.00 (*1-58201-730-1*) Classic Bks.

Night Brothers. Sidney Williams. 1989. mass mkt. 4.50 (*1-55817-290-4*, Pinncle Kensgtn) Kensgtn Pub Corp.

Night Buddies. Sands Hetherington. (Illus.). 64p. (J). (gr. k-6). 1999. pap. 8.00 (*0-8059-4754-X*) Dorrance.

***Night Bus.** Janice Law. LC 00-23938. 352p. 2000. 24.95 (*0-312-84882-X*, Pub. by Forge NYC) St Martin.

Night Bus. Janice Law. 19.95 (*0-312-87599-1*) St Martin.

Night Came to the Farms of the Great Plains. Raymond North. LC 91-71312. 286p. 1991. pap. 17.50 (*0-911311-29-7*) Acres USA.

***Night Cars.** Teddy Jam. (Illus.). (J). 2000. 16.95 (*0-88899-413-3*) Grndwd Bks.

Night Cats. Bird & Falk. (New Trend Fiction A Ser.). (J). 1993. pap. text. write for info. (*0-582-80033-1*, Pub. by Addison-Wesley) Longman.

Night Chant: A Navaho Ceremony. Washington Matthews. LC 74-7991. reprint ed. 94.50 (*0-404-11880-1*) AMS Pr.

Night Chant: A Navaho Ceremony. Washington Matthews. (Illus.). 376p. 1995. reprint ed. pap. 19.95 (*0-87480-491-4*); reprint ed. text 45.00 (*0-87480-490-6*) U of Utah Pr.

Night Child. large type ed. Alan Scholefield. 480p. 1994. 27.99 (*0-7089-3082-4*) Ulverscroft.

Night Chills. Dean Koontz. 384p. 1986. mass mkt. 7.99 (*0-425-09864-8*) Berkley Pub.

Night Chills. Dean Koontz. 1976. 12.09 (*0-606-03684-9*, Pub. by Turtleback) Demco.

Night Chills. large type ed. Dean Koontz. LC 97-41962. 1997. 25.95 (*1-57490-107-9*, Beeler LP Bks) T T Beeler.

Night Church. Whitley Strieber. 1990. pap. 3.95 (*0-380-70899-X*, Avon Bks) Morrow Avon.

Night City. Monica Wellington. LC 97-38874. (Illus.). 32p. (ps-4). 1998. 14.99 (*0-525-45948-0*) NAL.

Night City Sourcebook. Sam Shirley et al. Ed. by Colin Fisk et al. (Cyberpunk Ser.). (Illus.). 144p. (C). 1991. pap. text 18.00 (*0-937279-11-0*, CP3501) Talsorian.

Night City Stories. Scott Mackay. (Cyberpunk Ser.). 144p. 1992. pap. 15.00 (*1-887801-34-0*, Atlas Games) Trident MN.

***Night Club Era.** Stanley Walker. LC 99-28135. 327p. 1999. pap. 17.95 (*0-8018-6291-4*) Johns Hopkins.

Night Club Promotions Manual & Source List: How to Create Exciting, Profitable Event Calendars for Your Bar. 2nd ed. K. S. Jones. (Illus.). 144p. 1997. pap. 22.50 (*0-9648379-8-6*) Hughes Co.

Night Coach, Vol. 1. Marco Fraticelli. 48p. pap. 5.00 (*0-919349-27-7*) Guernica Editions.

Night Combat. 1996. lib. bdg. 250.95 (*0-8490-6019-2*) Gordon Pr.

Night Combat. Alfred Toppe. (Illus.). 49p. 1998. reprint ed. pap. text 20.00 (*0-7881-7080-5*) DIANE Pub.

***Night Comes On.** Steve Duffy. vi, 284p. 1998. 40.00 (*1-899562-44-3*) Ash-Tree.

Night Comes to the Cretaceous: Comets, Craters, Controversy & the Last Days of the Dinosaurs. James Lawrence Powell. LC 99-26503. 272p. 1999. pap. text 14.00 (*0-15-600703-7*, Harvest Bks) Harcourt.

Night Comes to the Cumberlands: Biography of a Depressed Area. Harry M. Caudill. 394p. 1964. pap. 15.95 (*0-316-13212-8*) Little.

Night Cometh: Two Wealthy Evangelicals Face the Nation. Rebecca J. Winter. LC 77-87594. 84p. 1977. pap. 3.95 (*0-87808-429-0*) William Carey Lib.

Night Conversations with None Other. Shreela Ray. (American Dust Ser.: No. 6). 85p. 1977. 6.95 (*0-913218-32-4*); pap. 2.95 (*0-913218-31-6*) Dustbooks.

Night Cooling Control Strategies - Final Report. A. Martin. 1996. pap. 80.00 (*0-86022-437-6*, Pub. by Build Servs Info Assn) St Mut.

Night Country. Loren S. Eiseley. LC 97-1507. (Illus.). xvii, 241p. 1997. pap. 14.95 (*0-8032-6735-5*, Bison Books) U of Nebr Pr.

***Night Crawlers.** Sherry Galloway. LC 00-39049. 205p. 2000. 18.95 (*1-58141-043-3*) Rivercross Pub.

Night Crawlers: After Hours at the ER. Andrew Malekoff. LC 97-32928. (Illus.). 56p. 1998. pap. 7.95 (*0-9646450-7-6*) DeeMar Commun.

Night Creature. Rodman Philbrick. (Werewolf Chronicles Ser.: No. 1). (J). (gr. 4-7). 1996. pap. 3.99 (*0-590-68950-9*) Scholastic Inc.

Night Creatures. Gallimard Jeunesse. LC 97-22765. (First Discovery Book). (Illus.). 24p. (J). (ps-2). 1998. 11.95 (*0-590-11765-3*) Scholastic Inc.

Night Creatures. Andrea Holden-Boone. (Eye to Eye Bks.). (Illus.). 32p. (J). (gr. 1-7). 1998. pap. 11.99 (*1-894042-17-4*) Somerville Hse.

Night Creatures. Andrea Holden-Boone. (Eye To Eye Ser.). (Illus.). 32p. (J). (gr. 1-7). 1998. pap. 11.99 (*1-58184-006-3*) Somerville Hse.

Night Creatures. Malcolm Penny. (Remarkable World Ser.). (Illus.). 48p. (J). (gr. 3-8). 1996. lib. bdg. 24.26 (*1-56847-371-0*) Raintree Steck-V.

Night Creatures. Joyce Pope. LC 91-45171. (Nature Club Ser.). (Illus.). 32p. (J). (gr. 3-6). 1997. pap. 4.95 (*0-8167-2784-8*) Troll Communs.

Night Creatures. Susanne Santoro Whayne. LC 91-24654. (Illus.). 48p. (J). (gr. 2-7). 1993. mass mkt. 15.00 (*0-671-73395-8*) S&S Bks Yung.

Night Crew. John Sandford, pseud. 1998. mass mkt. 7.50 (*0-425-16338-5*) Berkley Pub.

Night Crew. John Sandford, pseud. LC 97-1344. 368p. 1997. 23.95 (*0-399-14237-1*, G P Putnam) Peng Put Young Read.

Night Crew. large type ed. John Sandford, pseud. LC 97-34583. 1997. 25.95 (*1-56895-497-2*) Wheeler Pub.

Night Cries. John Cassidy. 1982. pap. 12.95 (*0-906427-45-2*, Pub. by Bloodaxe Bks) Dufour.

Night Cries. Barbara Steiner. 144p. (Orig.). (J). (gr. 4). 1993. pap. 3.50 (*0-380-76990-5*, Avon Bks) Morrow Avon.

Night Crossing. Karen Ackerman. (Illus.). 1995. pap. 4.50 (*0-679-87040-7*) Random.

Night Crossing. Karen Ackerman. (J). 1995. 9.70 (*0-606-07944-0*, Pub. by Turtleback) Demco.

Night Crossings. 2nd ed. Jon H. Gates. Ed. by Beverly Hanly. (Illus.). 129p. (C). 1990. reprint ed. pap. 8.95 (*1-878136-00-3*) Moonstone Pub.

Night Crossings. 3rd ed. J. Humboldt Gates. (Illus.). 129p. 1992. pap. 8.95 (*0-614-08082-7*) Moonstone Pub.

Night Cry. Phyllis Reynolds Naylor. LC 83-15569. 168p. (J). (gr. 5-9). 1984. 16.00 (*0-689-31017-X*) Atheneum Yung Read.

Night Cry. Phyllis Reynolds Naylor. 160p. (J). (gr. 4-7). 1993. pap. 3.99 (*0-440-40017-1*, YB BDD) BDD Bks Young Read.

Night Cry. Phyllis Reynolds Naylor. 1988. 9.09 (*0-606-12450-0*, Pub. by Turtleback) Demco.

Night Currents. Frances L. Steele. x, 320p. 1998. pap. 16.95 (*0-9662075-0-5*) Flemming Hse.

Night Daddy. Eileen Spinelli. LC PZ8.3.S759Ni 1999. (Illus.). 32p. (J). 2000. lib. bdg. 15.49 (*0-7868-2424-7*, Pub. by Hyperion) Time Warner.

Night Daddy. Eileen Spinelli. LC 98-52499. (Illus.). 32p. (J). (ps-2). 2000. 14.99 (*0-7868-0495-5*, Pub. by Hyperion) Time Warner.

Night Dance. Reynolds Price. 1991. pap. 5.25 (*0-8222-0819-9*) Dramatists Play.

Night, Dawn, Day. Elie Wiesel. Tr. by Stella Rodway from FRE. LC 85-71510. 320p. 1996. reprint ed. 30.00 (*0-87668-897-0*) Aronson.

Night Departure & No Place (Case Dismissed) Emmanuel Bove. Tr. by Carol Volk from FRE. LC 92-43032. 468p. 1995. 25.00 (*0-941423-91-3*); pap. 14.95 (*0-941423-98-0*) FWEW.

Night Depositories, UL 771. 8th ed. (C). 1998. pap. 95.00 (*1-55989-605-1*) Underwrtrs Labs.

Night Desk. George Ryga. 128p. reprint ed. pap. 6.95 (*0-88922-089-1*, Pub. by Talonbks) Genl Dist Srvs.

Night Dive. Dean Honma. 1985. pap. 3.50 (*0-932136-09-5*) Petronium HI.

Night Diver Manual. (Illus.). 68p. pap. text 12.95 (*1-878663-14-3*) PADI.

Night Diving: A Consumer's Guide to the Specialty of Night Diving. Ken Loyst et al. 1992. pap. 12.95 (*0-922769-33-8*) Watersport Pub.

Night Dog & Other Poems. Norman H. Russell. (Orig.). 1971. pap. 1.00 (*0-685-30029-3*) Cottonwood KS.

Night Dogs. Kent Anderson. 544p. 1999. reprint ed. mass mkt. 6.50 (*0-553-57877-4*) Bantam.

Night Drawings: Poems. Marjorie Stelmach. (Winner of the 1994 Marianne Moore Poetry Prize Ser.). 86p. (Orig.). 1995. pap. 9.95 (*1-884235-12-3*) Helicon Nine Eds.

Night Dreams. David Chereb. LC 86-90369. (Illus.). 65p. (Orig.). 1986. pap. 8.95 (*0-937001-05-8*) Merz Prod.

Night Drifter. Susan Carroll. LC PS3553.A7654N54 1999. 336p. 1999. 19.95 (*0-345-43312-2*) Ballantine Pub Grp.

***Night Drifter.** Susan Carroll. 2000. mass mkt. 6.99 (*0-449-00585-2*) Fawcett.

Night Driving. John Coy. LC 95-6063. (Illus.). 32p. (J). (ps-2). 1995. 14.95 (*0-8050-2931-1*, B Martin BYR) H Holt & Co.

Night Driving. John Coy. (Illus.). (J). 1996. 14.95 (*0-8050-4586-4*) H Holt & Co.

Night Duty: A Novel. Melitta Breznik. Tr. by Roslyn Theobold from GER. LC 99-12851. 131p. 1999. pap. 12.00 (*1-883642-85-X*) Steerforth Pr.

Night Errands: How Poets Use Dreams. Ed. by Roderick Townley. LC 98-19748. (Illus.). 184p. 1998. text 24.95 (*0-8229-4077-9*) U of Pittsburgh Pr.

***Night Errands: How Poets Use Dreams.** Roderick Townley. 2000. pap. text 14.95 (*0-8229-5730-2*) U of Pittsburgh Pr.

Night Eternal: The Lost Earth. James Axler. (Outlanders Ser.: No. 9). 1999. per. 5.99 (*0-373-63822-1*, 1-63822-0, Wrldwide Lib) Harlequin Bks.

Night Face & Other Stories. Poul Anderson. LC 77-28644. 221p. 1978. 25.00 (*0-89366-148-1*) Ultramarine Pub.

***Night Falls Fast: Understanding Suicide.** Kay Redfield Jamison. LC 99-311227. 320p. 1999. 26.00 (*0-375-40145-8*) Knopf.

***Night Falls Fast: Understanding Suicide.** Kay Redfield Jamison. 2000. pap. 14.00 (*0-375-70147-8*) Vin Bks.

Night Fantasies: Piano. 25.00 (*0-7935-5255-9*, 50482551) H Leonard.

Night Feet. Celia Watson. 88p. 1989. pap. 10.00 (*0-912292-82-2*) Smith.

Night Fell: Poems & Drawings. Rabindra Danks & P. Schneidre. (Illus.). 48p. (Orig.). 1975. pap. 2.95 (*0-915242-06-0*) Pygmalion Pr.

Night Fell at Harry's Farm. Carey E. Hedlund. LC 96-5414. (Illus.). 32p. (J). 1997. 15.00 (*0-688-14932-4*, Grenwillow Bks) HarpC Child Bks.

Night Ferry to Death. Patricia Moyes. LC 85-5567. 192p. 1995. pap. 5.95 (*0-8050-0116-6*, Owl) H Holt & Co.

Night Field. McKay. 1991. pap. 16.95 (*0-7710-5762-8*) McCland & Stewart.

Night Fighter's Handbook. Dennis J. Popp. (Illus.). 72p. 1986. pap. 18.00 (*0-87364-361-5*) Paladin Pr.

Night Fighters over Korea. G. G. O'Rourke & E. T. Wooldridge. LC 98-16424. 1998. 34.95 (*1-55750-653-1*) Naval Inst Pr.

Night Fire. large type ed. Catherine Coulter. LC 97-15890. (Wheeler Large Print Book Ser.). 1997. 23.95 (*1-56895-457-3*) Wheeler Pub.

Night Fire. Catherine Coulter. 400p. 1989. reprint ed. mass mkt. 6.99 (*0-380-75620-X*, Avon Bks) Morrow Avon.

Night Fire. Catherine Coulter. 392p. 1995. reprint ed. 18.00 (*0-7278-4787-2*) Severn Hse.

Night Fires. Linda Cook. (Zebra Bks.). 352p. 1998. mass mkt. 4.99 (*0-8217-6043-2*, Zebra Kensgtn) Kensgtn Pub Corp.

***Night Fires.** Justine Dare. 2000. mass mkt. 6.50 (*0-451-40938-8*, Onyx) NAL.

Night Fishing: A Woman's Dream Journal. Katherine M. Nelson. LC 96-40966. (Illus.). 160p. 1997. pap. 19.95 (*0-87905-790-4*) Gibbs Smith Pub.

Night-Fishing on Irish Buffalo Creek. Stephen Knauth. LC 82-37. 55p. 1982. pap. 5.00 (*0-87886-117-3*, Greenfld Rev Pr) Greenfld Rev Lit.

Night Flame. Catherine Hart. 480p. 1995. pap. text, mass mkt. 5.50 (*0-8439-3681-9*) Dorchester Pub Co.

***Night Flame.** Catherine Hart. 480p. 2000. mass mkt. 5.99 (*0-505-52386-8*, Love Spell) Dorchester Pub Co.

Night Flier. Elizabeth Ring. LC 93-40115. (Illus.). 32p. (J). (gr. k-3). 1994. lib. bdg. 21.90 (*1-56294-467-3*) Millbrook Pr.

Night Flight. Lita Hornick. 1982. pap. 5.00 (*0-936538-03-1*) Kulchur Foun.

Night Flight. Gloria Repp. (Light Line Ser.). 164p. (YA). 1991. pap. 6.49 (*0-89084-563-8*, 052191) Bob Jones Univ.

Night Flight. Joanne Ryder. (Illus.). 32p. (J). (ps-3). 1998. per. 5.99 (*0-689-82150-6*) S&S Childrens.

Night Flight. Antoine de Saint-Exupery. Tr. by Stuart Gilbert from FRE. LC 73-16016.Tr. of Vol De Nuit. 100p. 1974. reprint ed. pap. 7.00 (*0-15-665605-1*, Harvest Bks) Harcourt.

Night Flight Techniques & Procedures. 1995. lib. bdg. 256.00 (*0-8490-6623-9*) Gordon Pr.

Night Flower. Max Brand. (Library of Crime Classics). 311p. 1987. pap. 4.95 (*0-930330-48-X*) Intl Polygonics.

Night Flower. Shirl Henke. 352p. 1990. mass mkt. 4.95 (*0-446-34646-2*, Pub. by Warner Bks) Little.

Night Flyer: Tales from the Id. James S. Prine. 125p. (Orig.). Date not set. pap. 12.95 (*0-9653752-1-8*) J S Prine.

***Night Flyers.** Elizabeth McDavid Jones. LC 98-47806. (American Girl History Mysteries Ser.). 160p. (J). (gr. 5-9). 1999. 9.95 (*1-56247-815-X*) Pleasant Co.

Night Flyers. Elizabeth McDavid Jones. LC 98-47806. (American Girl History Mysteries Ser.). (Illus.). 145p. (J). (gr. 5-9). 1999. pap. 5.95 (*1-56247-759-5*) Pleasant Co.

Night Flying. Courtney Flatau. (Illus.). 224p. 1989. 24.95 (*0-8306-9456-0*); pap. 15.95 (*0-8306-2456-2*) McGraw-Hill Prof.

Night Flying. Richard F. Haines & Courtney Flatau. 312p. 1992. 29.95 (*0-8306-3780-X*, 4098); pap. 16.95 (*0-8306-3773-7*, 4098) McGraw-Hill Prof.

***Night Flying.** Rita Murphy. LC 00-20781. (Illus.). (J). 2000. 14.95 (*0-385-32748-X*) Delacorte.

Night Flying. Roger Nash. 83p. 1990. pap. 7.95 (*0-86492-116-0*, Pub. by Goose Ln Edits) Genl Dist Srvs.

Night Flying Avenger. Pete Grant. LC 89-64418. 320p. 1990. 19.95 (*0-938539-02-7*) Newmark Pub.

Night Flying Woman: An Ojibway Narrative. Ignatia Broker. LC 83-13360. (Illus.). xiv, 135p. (Orig.). 1983. pap. 9.50 (*0-87351-167-0*) Minn Hist.

***Night Freight.** Bill Pronzini. 368p. 2000. pap. 5.50 (*0-8439-4706-3*, Leisure Bks) Dorchester Pub Co.

Night Freight. Clyde Rice. LC 87-808. 144p. 1987. 17.95 (*0-932576-50-8*); pap. 7.95 (*0-932576-57-5*) Breitenbush Bks.

An Asterisk (*) at the beginning of an entry indicates that the title is appearing for the first time.

Night Frights: Thirteen Scary Stories. J. B. Stamper. (J). 1993. 8.15 (*0-606-02807-2*, Pub. by Turtleback) Demco.

Night Frights: Thirteen Scary Stories. Judith B. Stamper. 80p. (J). (gr. 4-6). 1993. pap. 2.95 (*0-590-46046-3*) Scholastic Inc.

Night Frost. R. D. Wingfield. 368p. 1995. mass mkt. 5.99 (*0-553-57167-2*) Bantam.

Night Frost. large type ed. Basil Copper. (Linford Mystery Library). 368p. 1996. pap. 16.99 (*0-7089-7868-1*, Linford) Ulverscroft.

Night Fun. Patricia M. Quinlan. (Illus.). 24p. (J). (ps-2). 1997. 16.95 (*1-55037-487-7*, Pub. by Annick) Firefly Bks Ltd.

Night G. A. A. Died. Jack Ricardo. (Stonewall Inn Mysteries Ser.). 208p. 1993. 8.95 (*0-312-09353-5*) St Martin.

Night Game. Greg Jenkins. LC 98-71499. 205p. 1999. pap. 13.95 (*0-88739-183-4*) Creat Arts Bk.

Night Game. Carol D. Luce. 1996. mass mkt. 4.99 (*0-8217-5287-1*, Zebra Kensgtn) Kensgtn Pub Corp.

Night Games. Jose Cabanis. Tr. by Peter Briscoe from FRE. LC 92-62605. (Illus.). 92p. (Orig.). 1993. pap. 12.95 (*0-9634898-0-1*) Palo Verde Pr.

Night Games. Robert Currie. 120p. 1983. pap. 5.95 (*0-919926-19-3*) Coteau.

Night Games. R. L. Stine, pseud. (Fear Street Ser.: No. 41). (YA). (gr. 7 up). 1996. per. 3.99 (*0-671-52958-7*) PB.

Night Games. R. L. Stine, pseud. (Fear Street Ser.: No. 41). (YA). (gr. 7 up). 1996. 9.09 (*0-606-10894-7*, Pub. by Turtleback) Demco.

Night Games: A Kate Henry Mystery. Alison Gordon. 1996. pap. 6.99 (*0-7710-3424-5*) McCland & Stewart.

Night Games: Secret Fantasies. Janice Kaiser. LC 95-4599. (Temptation Ser.). 216p. 1995. per. 2.99 (*0-373-25622-1*, 1-25622-1) Harlequin Bks.

***Night Garden: Poems from the World of Dreams.** Janet S. Wong. LC 98-46302. (Illus.). 32p. (J). (gr. 2-5). 2000. pap. 16.00 (*0-689-82617-6*) McElderry Bks.

***Night Gardener: A Search for Home.** Marjorie Sandor. LC 99-22601. 208p. 1999. 22.95 (*1-55821-931-5*) Lyons Pr.

Night Gardening. E. L. Swann. 215p. 1999. 16.95 (*0-7868-6498-2*, Pub. by Hyperion) Time Warner.

Night Gardening. E. L. Swann. 208p. 2000. mass mkt. 6.50 (*0-7868-8952-7*, Pub. by Hyperion) Time Warner.

***Night Gardening.** large type ed. E. L. Swann. (Core Ser.). 303p. 2000. write for info. (*0-7838-9036-2*, G K Hall Lrg Type) Mac Lib Ref.

Night Gliders. Joanne Ryder. (Illus.). 32p. (J). (ps-2). 1997. pap. 4.95 (*0-8167-3821-1*) Troll Communs.

Night Golf. William Miller. LC 98-47168. (Illus.). 32p. (J). (ps-3). 1999. 15.95 (*1-880000-79-2*, Pub. by Lee & Low Bks) Publishers Group.

Night Hank Williams Died. Larry L. King. LC 89-42894. (Southwest Life & Letters Ser.). (Illus.). 144p. 1989. pap. 9.95 (*0-87074-303-1*) SMU Press.

Night Hank Williams Died: A Play in Two Acts, with Incidental Music. Larry L. King. LC 89-42894. (Southwest Life & Letters Ser.). (Illus.). 144p. 1989. text 17.95 (*0-87074-292-2*) SMU Press.

Night Has a Naked Soul: Witchcraft & Sorcery among the Western Cherokee. Alan Kilpatrick. LC 97-12690. xviii, 160p. 1997. 29.95 (*0-8156-0471-8*); pap. 19.95 (*0-8156-0539-0*) Syracuse U Pr.

Night Has a Thousand Eyes: A Naked-Eye Guide to the Sky, Its Science, & Lore. Arthur Upgren. LC 98-13412. (Illus.). 314p. (C). 1998. 27.95 (*0-306-45790-3*, Plenum Trade) Perseus Pubng.

Night Has Ears: African Proverbs. Ashley Bryan. LC 98-48772. (Illus.). 32p. (J). (gr. 2-4). 1999. 16.00 (*0-689-82427-0*) Atheneum Yung Read.

Night Hawk. Wallace E. Burke. (Anasazi Ser.: Bk. II). (Illus.). 225p. (Orig.). (YA). 1994. pap. 10.95 (*0-9639014-1-9*) WEB Pubng.

Night He Was Betrayed: Bible Studies in Our Lord's Preparation for His Passion. Reginald E. White. LC 82-13783. 141p. reprint ed. pap. 43.80 (*0-608-14517-3*, 202534900043) Bks Demand.

***Night Heat.** Heather Graham Pozzessere. 2001. pap. 12.95 (*1-55166-787-8*, Mira Bks) Harlequin Bks.

Night Heat. Simona Taylor. 1999. mass mkt. 4.99 (*1-58314-026-3*) BET Bks.

Night Heat: Blaze. Lyn Ellis. (Temptation Ser.: No. 666). 1998. per. 3.50 (*0-373-25766-X*, 1-25766-6) Harlequin Bks.

Night Hit. Don Pendleton. (Executioner Ser.: No. 154). 1991. mass mkt. 3.50 (*0-373-61154-4*) Harlequin Bks.

***Night Hoops.** Carl Deuker. LC 99-47882. (Illus.). 256p. (YA). (gr. 7-12). 2000. 15.00 (*0-395-97936-6*) HM.

Night Horseman. large type ed. Max Brand. (Sagebrush Large Print Westerns Ser.). 300p. 1995. lib. bdg. 18.95 (*1-57490-007-2*) T T Beeler.

Night House, Bright House. Monica Wellington. LC 96-24550. (Illus.). 24p. (J). 1997. 11.99 (*0-525-45491-8*) Viking Penguin.

Night Hunter. Michael Reaves. 1997. mass mkt. 5.99 (*0-8125-1994-9*, Pub. by Tor Bks) St Martin.

Night Hurdling. James Dickey. 1983. 50.00 (*0-89723-038-8*) Bruccoli.

Night Hurdling. limited ed. James Dickey. 1983. 100.00 (*0-89723-040-X*) Bruccoli.

Night I Cry & Other Stories. Antonio R. Enriquez. (Illus.). 129p. (Orig.). (C). 1990. pap. 10.75 (*971-10-0343-0*, Pub. by New Day Pub) Cellar.

Night I Followed the Dog. Nina Laden. LC 93-31008. (Illus.). 40p. (J). (ps-5). 1994. 14.95 (*0-8118-0647-2*) Chronicle Bks.

Night in a Moorish Harem, No. 2. George Herbert & Gregory Baisden. (Illus.). 64p. 1997. pap. 10.95 (*1-56163-176-0*, Amerotica) NBM.

Night in a Moorish Harem, Vol. 1. George Herbert & Greg Baisden. LC 97-199802. (Illus.). 64p. 1996. pap. 11.95 (*1-56163-168-X*, Amerotica) NBM.

Night in Acadie. Kate Chopin. 1972. 69.95 (*0-8490-0734-8*) Gordon Pr.

Night in Alexandria: A Dramatic Poem in One Act. Ludwig Lewisohn. (Collected Works of Ludwig Lewisohn). 60p. 1998. reprint ed. lib. bdg. 98.00 (*1-58201-683-6*) Classic Bks.

Night in at the Opera. Lutton Staff. LC 95-182149. 1997. pap. 34.95 (*0-86196-466-7*, Pub. by J Libbey Med) Bks Intl VA.

Night in Bombay. Louis Bromfield. 1976. reprint ed. lib. bdg. 25.95 (*0-88411-503-8*) Amereon Ltd.

Night in Eden. Candice Proctor. 1997. mass mkt. 5.99 (*0-449-00125-3*, GM) Fawcett.

Night in Eden. Candice Proctor. 1997. mass mkt. 5.99 (*0-8041-1758-6*) Ivy Books.

Night in Gotham. Walter Hunt. 1989. pap. 7.00 (*0-912771-51-8*) Mayfair Games.

Night in Lisbon. Erich-Maria Remarque. LC 98-96092. 1998. pap. 13.95 (*0-449-91243-4*) Fawcett.

Night in November. Marie Jones. 48p. 1995. pap. 10.95 (*1-874597-24-3*) Dufour.

Night in November (An Afternoon in June) Marie Jones. (New Island Plays Ser.). 96p. (Orig.). 1996. pap. 12.95 (*1-85459-258-0*, Pub. by N Hern Bks) Theatre Comm.

Night in Question: Stories. Tobias Wolff. LC 96-17560. 206p. 1996. 25.00 (*0-679-40218-7*) Knopf.

Night in Question: Stories. Tobias Wolff. 1997. pap. 12.00 (*0-679-78155-2*) Vin Bks.

Night in Terror Tower. J. Miranda & P. Mercado. (Goosebumps Ser.). (Illus.). 144p. 1996. 6.98 incl. audio (*0-7643-0086-5*) Schiffer.

Night in Terror Tower. R. L. Stine, pseud. (Goosebumps Ser.: No. 27). 160p. (J). (gr. 3-7). 1995. pap. 3.99 (*0-590-48351-X*) Scholastic Inc.

Night in Terror Tower. R. L. Stine, pseud. (Goosebumps Ser.: No. 27). (J). 1995. 9.09 (*0-606-07945-9*, Pub. by Turtleback) Demco.

***Night in the Afternoon & Other Erotica.** Caroline Lamarche. Tr. by Howard Curtis from FRE. 96p. 2000. pap. 12.00 (*0-8021-3709-1*, Pub. by Grove-Atltic) Publishers Group.

Night in the Barn. Faye Gibbons. LC 94-43776. (Illus.). 32p. (J). (gr. 1-4). 1995. lib. bdg. 14.93 (*0-688-13327-4*, Wm Morrow) Morrow Avon.

Night in the Barn. Faye Gibbons. LC 94-43776. (Illus.). 32p. (J). (ps-3). 1995. 16.00 (*0-688-13326-6*, Wm Morrow) Morrow Avon.

***Night in the Barracks: Authentic Accounts of Sex in the Armed Forces.** Alex Buchman. 2000. 12.95 (*1-56023-988-3*); 39.95 (*1-56023-987-5*) Haworth Pr.

Night in the Catacombs: Fictional Portraits of Ireland's Literati. David M. Kiely. LC 95-169182. 208p. 1995. 31.95 (*1-874675-61-9*); pap. 16.95 (*1-874675-66-X*) Dufour.

Night in the Country. Cynthia Rylant. LC 85-70963. (Illus.). 32p. (J). (ps-1). 1986. lib. bdg. 14.95 (*0-02-777210-1*, Bradbury S&S) S&S Childrens.

Night in the Country. Cynthia Rylant. (J). 1991. 10.15 (*0-606-04760-3*, Pub. by Turtleback) Demco.

Night in the Country. Cynthia Rylant. LC 90-1043. (Illus.). 32p. (J). (ps-2). 1991. reprint ed. mass mkt. 4.95 (*0-689-71473-4*) Aladdin.

Night in the Dinosaur Graveyard: A Prehistoric Story with Ten Spooky Holograms. A. J. Wood. LC 95-148752. (Illus.). 24p. (J). (ps-3). 1994. 15.95 (*0-694-00641-6*, HarpFestival) HarpC Child Bks.

Night in the Lonesome October. Roger Zelazny. (Illus.). 288p. 1994. mass mkt. 4.99 (*0-380-77141-1*, Avon Bks) Morrow Avon.

Night in the Lonesome October. Roger Zelazny. LC 93-18414. (Illus.). vii, 280p. 2000. 18.00 (*0-380-97223-9*, Avon Bks) Morrow Avon.

Night in the Museum. Milan Trenc. (Illus.). 32p. (J). (ps-3). 1993. pap. 5.95 (*0-8120-1523-1*) Barron.

Night in the Tree House. Kris Jamsa. (Happy & Max Ser.). 64p. 1998. 18.95 incl. cd-rom (*1-884133-89-4*, Jamsa Press) Gulf Pub.

Night in Tunisia: Imaginings of Africa in Jazz. Norman C. Weinstein. LC 93-16888. 256p. 1993. reprint ed. pap. 13.95 (*0-87910-167-9*) Limelight Edns.

Night in Werewolf Woods. R. L. Stine, pseud. (Give Yourself Goosebumps Ser.: No. 5). (J). (gr. 3-7). 1996. pap. 3.99 (*0-590-67319-X*) Scholastic Inc.

Night in Werewolf Woods. R. L. Stine, pseud. (Give Yourself Goosebumps Ser.: No. 5). (J). 1996. 9.09 (*0-606-09682-5*, Pub. by Turtleback) Demco.

Night Inside. Nancy Baker. 1999. pap. write for info. (*0-451-18327-4*, Sig) NAL.

***Night Inspector.** Frederick Busch. 304p. 2000. pap. 14.00 (*0-449-00615-8*, Ballantine) Ballantine Pub Grp.

Night Inspector: A Novel. Frederick Busch. LC 99-11890. 288p. 1999. 23.00 (*0-609-60235-7*) Harmony Bks.

Night into Day. Thomas Feeny. LC 93-36175. 64p. 1993. pap. 14.95 (*0-7734-2797-X*, Mellen Poetry Pr) E Mellen.

Night Is a Jungle: A Collection of 14 Talks Delivered by Kirpal Singh. 409p. 1984. pap. 11.00 (*0-89142-017-7*) Ruhani Satsang.

Night Is Colder Than Autumn. Jerry D. Miley. (Original Poetry Ser.). 20p. 1991. 3.00 (*0-916397-18-1*) Manic D Pr.

Night Is Fallin' in My Heart. D. Linde. (Piano-Vocal-Guitar Ser.). 8p. 1994. pap. 3.95 (*0-7935-4285-5*, 00351047) H Leonard.

Night Is for Music. George Selcamm. 1964. 3.95 (*0-393-08525-2*) Norton.

Night Is Large, 1938-95. 3rd ed. Martin Gardner. 608p. 1997. pap. 17.95 (*0-312-16949-3*) St Martin.

Night Is Like an Animal. Candace Whitman. LC 94-44359. (Illus.). 32p. (J). (ps-3). 1995. 13.00 (*0-374-35521-5*) FS&G.

Night Is Like an Animal. Candace Whitman. 32p. (J). (ps-k). 1997. pap. text 4.95 (*0-374-45502-3*) FS&G.

Night Is Once Before. James Conroy. LC 97-14673. 48p. 1997. pap. 14.95 (*0-7734-2830-5*, Mellen Poetry Pr) E Mellen.

***Night Is the Time.** Elizabeth Bennett. 24p. (J). 1999. 1.99 (*0-679-89274-5*, Pub. by Random Bks Yng Read) Random.

***Night Is the Time.** Elizabeth Bennett. 2000. 7.99 (*0-375-90097-7*) Random Hse Chldrns.

***Night Is the Time.** Elizabeth Greenaway. (Jellybean Bks.). (Illus.). 24p. (J). (ps-k). 1999. 1.99 (*0-375-89274-5*, Pub. by Random Bks Yng Read); lib. bdg. 7.99 (*0-375-99274-X*, Pub. by Random Bks Yng Read) Random.

Night Is the Time. Elizabeth Greenaway. (J). 1999. lib. bdg. 7.99 (*0-679-99274-X*, Pub. by Random Bks Yng Read) Random.

Night Jasmine: Blossoms of the South. Erica Spindler. 1993. per. 3.50 (*0-373-09838-3*, 5-09838-9) Silhouette.

Night Jessie Sang at the Opry. John Killinger. 65p. (Orig.). (C). 1996. pap., teacher ed. 7.00 (*1-887730-04-4*) Angel Books.

***Night Jesus Christ Returned to Earth.** Tom Hudgens. 1999. pap. 9.95 (*0-937177-01-6*) B I L R Corp.

Night John. Gary Paulsen. (J). 1994. mass mkt. 4.99 (*0-440-82072-3*) BDD Bks Young Read.

Night Journey. Stephen King. (Green Mile Ser.: No. 5). 1996. mass mkt. 2.99 (*0-451-19056-4*, Sig) NAL.

Night Journey. Kathryn Lasky. (Novels Ser.). (Illus.). 152p. (J). (gr. 5-9). 1986. pap. 4.99 (*0-14-032048-2*, PuffinBks) Peng Put Young Read.

Night Journey. Kathryn Lasky. 1986. 10.09 (*0-606-00929-9*, Pub. by Turtleback) Demco.

***Night Journeys.** Avi. LC 93-50233. 160p. (J). (gr. 3-7). 2000. mass mkt. 4.99 (*0-380-73242-4*, Avon Bks) Morrow Avon.

Night Journeys. Avi. LC 93-50233. 1994. 10.05 (*0-606-06621-7*, Pub. by Turtleback) Demco.

Night Journeys. Avi. LC 93-50233. 160p. (J). (gr. 5 up). 1994. reprint ed. mass mkt. 4.95 (*0-688-13628-1*, Wm Morrow) Morrow Avon.

Night Journeys, Homework Set. unabridged ed. Avi. (YA). 1997. 40.20 incl. audio (*0-7887-1838-X*, 40618) Recorded Bks.

Night Judgement at Sinos. Jack Higgins. 1997. mass mkt. 6.99 (*0-425-16199-4*) Berkeley Pr.

Night Just Before the Forest; Struggle of the Dogs & the Black: A Book of Two Plays. Bernard Marie Koltes. Tr. by Timothy Johns & Matthew Ward from FRE. 248p. (Orig.). 1982. pap. text 8.95 (*0-913745-01-4*) Ubu Repertory.

***Night Kills.** Ed Gorman. LC 98-44602. 1999. 19.95 (*0-7862-1704-9*, Five Star MI) Mac Lib Ref.

Night Kills. Charlotte Hughes. 288p. 1998. mass mkt. 5.99 (*0-380-79220-6*, Avon Bks) Morrow Avon.

Night Kitchen (La Cocina de Noche) Maurice Sendak. (SPA., Illus.). (J). (gr. 1-6). 14.95 (*84-204-4570-3*) Santillana.

Night Kites. M. E. Kerr. LC 85-45386. (Trophy Keypoint Bk.). 224p. (YA). (gr. 7 up). 1987. mass mkt. 4.95 (*0-06-447035-0*, HarpTrophy) HarpC Child Bks.

Night Kites. M. E. Kerr. LC 85-45386. 1987. 9.60 (*0-606-03523-0*, Pub. by Turtleback) Demco.

Night, Knight, 4 vols. Harriet Ziefert. (J). 1997. 10.95 (*0-395-81560-6*) HM.

Night, Knight. Harriet Ziefert. LC 96-34989. (J). 1997. 10.95 (*0-395-85160-2*) HM.

Night-Knight. Harriet Ziefert. (Illus.). (J). (ps-1). 1997. 10.95 (*0-614-28828-2*) HM.

Night Lace. Emma F. Merritt. 320p. 1996. mass mkt. 5.50 (*0-8217-5251-0*, Zebra Kensgtn) Kensgtn Pub Corp.

Night Lake. limited large type ed. Jean Valentine. Ed. by John Wheatcroft. (Bucknell University Fine Editions: Series in Contemporary Poetry). (Illus.). 48p. 1992. 150.00 (*0-916375-15-3*) Press Alley.

***Night Lamp.** Vance. 1998. mass mkt. write for info. (*0-8125-5067-6*) Tor Bks.

Night Lamp. Jack Vance. 1998. pap. 14.95 (*0-312-86472-8*) St Martin.

Night Land. William H. Hodgson. 1976. lib. bdg. 12.95 (*0-89968-179-4*, Lghtyr Pr) Buccaneer Bks.

Night Landing: A Short History of West Coast Smuggling. David Heron. LC 98-50889. (Illus.). 134p. 1999. pap. 13.95 (*1-55571-449-8*, NVMPP, Hellgate Pr) PSI Resch.

Night Larry Kramer Kissed Me. David Drake. LC 93-21339. 112p. 1994. pap. 10.95 (*0-385-47204-8*, Anchor NY) Doubleday.

Night Launch. Jake Garn & Stephen P. Cohen. 1990. mass mkt. 4.95 (*0-445-21023-0*, Pub. by Warner Bks) Little.

Night Letter. Kerry Tomlinson. (Illus.). 36p. (Orig.). 1982. 7.00 (*0-930012-29-1*) J Mudfoot.

Night Letters: A Journey Through Switzerland & Italy. Robert Dessaix. LC 97-17701. 276p. 1997. text 22.95 (*0-312-16950-7*, Wyatt Bk) St Martin.

Night Letters: A Journey Through Switzerland & Italy. Robert Dessaix. LC 98-49197. 276p. 1999. pap. 13.00 (*0-312-19939-2*, Picador USA) St Martin.

Night Life. Jack Ellis. 352p. 1996. mass mkt. 4.99 (*0-8217-5404-1*, Zebra Kensgtn) Kensgtn Pub Corp.

Night Life. Sidney Kingsley. 1966. pap. 5.25 (*0-8222-0820-2*) Dramatists Play.

Night Life. William Matthews. Ed. by John Wheatcroft. (Bucknell University Fine Editions, a Series in Contemporary Poetry). (Illus.). 60p. 1997. 150.00 (*0-916375-28-5*) Press Alley.

Night Life. Paul Schmidt. LC 96-18390. 81p. (Orig.). 1996. pap. 10.00 (*0-9651558-0-3*) Painted Leaf.

Night Life: Nature from Dusk to Dawn. Kappel. LC 96-22318. 312p. 1996. pap. 17.95 (*0-8165-1702-9*) U of Ariz Pr.

Night Life of the Gods. Thorne Smith. 23.95 (*0-89190-117-5*) Amereon Ltd.

Night Light. (Illus.). (J). (ps-2). 1991. pap. 5.10 (*0-8136-5612-5*); lib. bdg. 7.95 (*0-8136-5112-3*) Modern Curr.

***Night Light.** James C. Dobson. 2000. 19.99 (*1-57673-674-1*, Multnomah Bks) Multnomah Pubs.

Night Light. Gina Erikson. (Get Ready...Get Set...Read! Ser.). (Illus.). 26p. (J). (gr. k-3). 1996. pap. 3.95 (*0-8120-9335-6*) Barron.

Night Light. Kelli C. Foster. LC 95-45820. (Get Ready - Get Set - Read! Ser.). 1996. 9.15 (*0-606-10269-8*, Pub. by Turtleback) Demco.

Night Light. Kelli C. Foster & Gina C. Erickson. (Get Ready...Get Set...Read! Ser.: Set 4). (Illus.). (J). 1996. lib. bdg. 11.95 (*1-56674-194-7*) Forest Hse.

Night Light: A Book of Nighttime Meditations. Amy Dean. (Illus.). 400p. pap. 10.00 (*0-89486-381-9*, 5030A) Hazelden.

Night Light: A Story for Children Afraid of the Dark. Jack Dutro. LC 91-19612. (Illus.). 32p. (J). (ps-2). 1991. 11.95 (*0-945354-37-1*) Am Psychol.

Night Light Tales. Andy Holmes. LC 96-206839. (Illus.). 256p. (J). (ps-3). 1996. 16.99 (*1-56476-575-X*, 6-3575, Victor Bks) Chariot Victor.

Night Lights. Mindy Aloff. Ed. by Vi Gale. LC 79-84510. (First Bk.). (Illus.). 1979. pap. 5.00 (*0-915986-14-0*) Prescott St Pr.

***Night Lights.** Steven Schnur. LC 99-22386. (Illus.). 32p. (YA). 2000. 16.00 (*0-374-35522-3*, Frances Foster) FS&G.

Night Lights. limited ed. Mindy Aloff. Ed. by Vi Gale. LC 79-84510. (First Bk.). (Illus.). 1979. 20.00 (*0-915986-13-2*) Prescott St Pr.

Night Lights: Nineteenth & Twentieth Century American Nocturne Paintings. Heather Hallenberg. (Illus.). 20p. (Orig.). 1985. pap. 5.00 (*0-915577-05-4*) Taft Museum.

Night Lights: 24 Poems to Sleep On. Denys Cazet. LC 96-42282. (Illus.). 32p. (J). (ps-1). 1997. 15.95 (*0-531-30010-2*); lib. bdg. 16.99 (*0-531-33010-9*) Orchard Bks Watts.

Night Lights & Pillow Fights: A Trip to Storyland. 2nd rev. ed. Guy Gilchrist. (Illus.). 48p. (J). (ps-6). 1997. reprint ed. 14.95 (*0-9660473-1-1*, 01) Gilchrist Publ.

***Night Lights & Pillow Fights Comics Featuring Mudpie.** Guy Gilchrist. LC 99-96575. (Illus.). 80p. 1999. pap. 4.95 (*0-9660473-6-2*) Gilchrist Publ.

***Night Lights & Pillow Fights Genius Club Bk. 1: Let's Draw Cartoons!** Guy Gilchrist. LC 99-96576. (Illus.). 80p. 1999. pap. 4.95 (*0-9660473-0-3*) Gilchrist Publ.

Night Lights & Pillow Fights II: The Box Set. unabridged ed. Guy Gilchrist. (Illus.). 144p. (J). (ps-6). 1997. 14.95 (*0-9660473-8-9*, 02) Gilchrist Publ.

Night-Limited Visibility Diving. Gary Clark. (Specialty Diver Ser.). 30p. 1990. teacher ed. 6.95 (*1-880229-01-3*); pap. text 10.95 (*0-943717-98-1*) Concept Sys.

Night Line. Ambrose Clancy & Peter M. Donahoe. (Illus.). 127p. 27.00 (*0-941533-45-X*, NAB) I R Dee.

Night Listener: A Novel. Armistead Maupin. LC 00-38907. 352p. 2000. 26.00 (*0-06-017143-X*, HarpCollins) HarperTrade.

Night Lives On. Walter Lord. 1976. 22.95 (*0-8488-0568-2*) Amereon Ltd.

***Night Lives On: Keating & Charles, Set.** Walter Lord. 1998. audio 18.00 (*0-694-52107-8*) HarperAudio.

***Night Lives On: The Untold Stories & Secrets Behind the Sinking of the "Unsinkable" Ship - Titanic!** large type ed. Walter Lord. 272p. 1999. 31.99 (*0-7089-9096-7*, Linford) Ulverscroft.

***Night Lives On: The Untold Stories & Secrets Behind the Sinking of the Unsinkable Ship-Titanic.** Walter Lord. 1998. mass mkt. 5.99 (*0-380-73203-3*, Avon Bks) Morrow Avon.

Night Lover. Elisabeth Stevens. LC 94-72882. (Illus.). 56p. (Orig.). 1995. pap. 11.50 (*0-913559-26-1*) Birch Brook Pr.

Night Magic. Charlotte Vale Allen. 1989. 18.95 (*0-689-11884-8*) Atheneum Yung Read.

Night Magic. Charlotte Vale Allen. 288p. 1989. 22.95 (*0-385-25212-9*) Doubleday.

Night Magic. Lynn Emery. (Arabesque Ser.). 320p. 1995. mass mkt. 4.99 (*0-7860-0179-8*, Pinncle Kensgtn) Kensgtn Pub Corp.

Night Magic. Karen Robards. 1987. mass mkt. 3.95 (*0-446-30058-6*, Pub. by Warner Bks) Little.

Night Magic. Karen Robards. 384p. 1988. mass mkt. 6.99 (*0-446-35391-4*, Pub. by Warner Bks) Little.

Night Magic. Thomas Tryon. 1995. 23.00 (*0-684-80393-3*) S&S Trade.

***Night Magic.** 2nd ed. Charlotte Vale Allen. 274p. 1998. reprint ed. pap. 20.00 (*0-9657437-3-X*) Isld Nation.

Night Mail: Selected Poems. Novica Tadic. Tr. & Intro. by Charles Simic. LC 92-80959. (Field Translation Ser.: No. 19). 119p. 1992. 24.95 (*0-932440-60-6*); pap. 14.95 (*0-932440-59-2*) Oberlin Coll Pr.

Night, Make My Day. 6p. 1995. pap. 3.95 (*0-7935-4238-3*) H Leonard.

Night Manager: A Novel. John Le Carre, pseud. 1994. mass mkt. 6.99 (*0-345-38576-4*) Ballantine Pub Grp.

Night Manager: A Novel. John Le Carre, pseud. 1997. pap. 12.00 (*0-345-41830-1*) Ballantine Pub Grp.

Night Manager: A Novel. John Le Carre, pseud. LC 92-55070. 1993. 24.00 (*0-679-42513-6*) Knopf.

Night Maneuver. Howard Korder. 1995. pap. 5.25 (*0-8222-1485-7*) Dramatists Play.

Night Mare. Piers Anthony. LC 82-90817. (Magic of Xanth Ser.). 320p. 1987. mass mkt. 6.99 (*0-345-35493-1*, Del Rey) Ballantine Pub Grp.

Night Mare. Piers Anthony. (Magic of Xanth Ser.). (J). 1982. 12.09 (*0-606-02597-9*, Pub. by Turtleback) Demco.

N

An Asterisk (*) at the beginning of an entry indicates that the title is appearing for the first time.

Night Mares, 1. Manda Scott. 320p. 1999. mass mkt. 5.50 (*0-553-57968-1*) Bantam.

Night Mares & Other Stories of Fantasy & Horror. Leoncio P. Deriada. 129p. (Orig.). (C). 1988. pap. 10.75 (*971-10-0367-8*, Pub. by New Day Pub) Cellar.

Night Market. Joshua Horwitz. LC 85-45401. (Trophy Nonfiction Bk.). (Illus.). 96p. (J). (gr. 2-6). 1986. pap. 6.95 (*0-06-446046-0*, HarpTrophy) HarpC Child Bks.

Night Market: Sexual Cultures & the Thai Economic Miracle. Ryan Bishop & Lillian S. Robinson. LC 97-29451. 288p. 1997. pap. 20.99 (*0-415-91429-9*) Routledge.

Night Market: Sexual Cultures & the Thai Economic Miracle. Ryan Bishop & Lillian S. Robinson. LC 97-29451. 288p. (C). 1997. 75.00 (*0-415-91428-0*) Routledge.

Night Mask. William W. Johnstone. 352p. 1994. mass mkt. 4.50 (*0-8217-4743-6*, Zebra Kensgtn) Kensgtn Pub Corp.

***Night Masks: Cleric Quintet, Book III.** R. A. Salvatore. (Cleric Quintet Ser.: Vol. 3). 320p. 2000. mass mkt. 7.99 (*0-7869-1606-0*) TSR Inc.

Night Mayor. Kim Newman. 202p. 1992. mass mkt. 3.95 (*0-88184-768-2*) Carroll & Graf.

***Night Mist.** 1999. per. 4.50 (*0-373-65112-0*) Harlequin Bks.

Night Mist. Helen R. Myers. (Shadows Ser.: No. 6). 1993. per. 3.50 (*0-373-27006-2*) Silhouette.

Night Monkeys. Dana Simson. (Legend Bks.). (Illus.). 32p. (J). 1996. 14.95 (*0-8362-1281-9*) Andrews & McMeel.

'Night, Mother. Marsha Norman. 1983. pap. 5.25 (*0-8222-0821-0*) Dramatists Play.

'Night, Mother. Marsha Norman. 92p. 1983. pap. 9.00 (*0-374-52138-7*) FS&G.

Night Movements. Mike Gunderloy. LC 88-45200. 140p. 1988. pap. 12.00 (*0-915179-79-2*, 70024) Loompanics.

***Night Moves.** Joe Jackson. LC 00-24292. (Illus.). 240p. 2000. pap. 14.95 (*0-312-19821-3*) St Martin.

Night Moves. Heather G. Pozzessere. 1996. per. 5.50 (*1-55166-160-8*, 1-66160-2, Mira Bks) Harlequin Bks.

Night Moves. Nora Roberts. (NR Flowers Ser.: No. 7). 1992. mass mkt. 3.59 (*0-373-51007-1*, 5-51007-8) Harlequin Bks.

Night Moves. large type ed. Alan Scholefield. 432p. 31.50 (*0-7089-3691-1*) Ulverscroft.

***Night Moves: Blaze.** Thea Devine. (Harlequin Temptation Ser.). 1999. mass mkt. 3.75 (*0-373-25860-7*, Harlequin) Harlequin Bks.

Night Moves Linda Howard Omnibus. Linda Howard. 1998. pap. 12.00 (*0-671-02747-6*) PB.

Night Music. Shelia B. Garner. 1992. mass mkt. 3.99 (*1-55817-567-9*, Pinncle Kensgtn) Kensgtn Pub Corp.

Night Music. Sara Mitchell. (Love Inspired Ser.). 1998. per. 4.50 (*0-373-87013-2*, 1-87013-8) Harlequin Bks.

Night Music: Poems by L. E. Sissman. L. E. Sissman. LC 98-50890. 160p. 1999. pap. 14.00 (*0-395-92570-3*) HM.

***Night Music: The Black Watch.** BJ James. 2000. per. 3.99 (*0-373-76286-0*) Silhouette.

Night, My Friend: Stories of Crime & Suspense by Edward D. Hoch. Edward D. Hoch. Ed. by Francis M. Nevins, Jr. LC 91-20984. 292p. (Orig.). 1992. pap. 21.95 (*0-8214-1011-3*) Ohio U Pr.

***Night My Mother Met Bruce Lee: Observations on Not Fitting In.** Paisley Rekdal. 224p. 2000. 22.00 (*0-375-40937-8*) Pantheon.

Night, Night! Mark Burgess. (Illus.). 12p. (J). (ps). 1996. bds. 2.99 (*0-689-80673-6*) Litle Simon.

***Night-Night, Baby: A Touch & Feel Book.** Grosset & Dunlap Staff. (Illus.). 12p. (J). (ps-k). 2000. pap. 6.99 (*0-448-42296-4*, Planet Dexter) Peng Put Young Read.

Night, Night Baby Mouseling. Cara. (Tiny Touch Bks.). (Illus.). 1994. 7.50 (*0-8378-7623-0*) Gibson.

***Night, Night Cuddly Bear.** Martin Waddell. LC 99-53125. (Illus.). 32p. (YA). (ps up). 2000. 14.99 (*0-7636-1195-6*) Candlewick Pr.

Night, Night, God Bless! Illus. by Jane Conteh-Morgan. (First Blessings Flap Bks.). 20p. (J). 1998. bds. 4.99 (*0-8054-1263-8*) Broadman.

Night, Night, God Bless! large type ed. Reader's Digest Editors. (First Blessings Flap Bks.: Vol. 1). (Illus.). 18p. (J). (gr. k-3). 1998. bds. 3.99 (*1-57584-079-0*, Pub. by Rdrs Digest) Random.

Night Night Knight. Harriet Ziefert. 1999. pap. 5.99 (*0-14-055734-2*) NAL.

Night, Night, Knight: Level Three, Blue. Michael Rosen. LC 98-88075. (Reading Together Ser.). (Illus.). 32p. (J). 1999. pap. write for info. (*0-7636-0856-4*) Candlewick Pr.

Night-Night, Roo. Mouseworks Staff. LC 99-162657. 18p. (J). 1998. 3.99 (*1-57082-984-5*, Pub. by Mouse Works) Time Warner.

Night-Night, Sleep Tight. Jerry Smath. LC 97-75337. (Illus.). 24p. (J). 1998. mass mkt. 5.99 (*0-448-41746-4*, G & D) Peng Put Young Read.

Night Noises. Mem Fox. LC 89-2162. (Illus.). 32p. (J). (ps-2). 1989. 15.00 (*0-15-200543-9*, Gulliver Bks) Harcourt.

Night Noises. Mem Fox. LC 89-216. (Illus.). 32p. (J). (ps-2). 1992. pap. 4.95 (*0-15-257421-2*, Gulliver Bks) Harcourt.

Night Noises. Mem Fox. 1989. 10.15 (*0-606-01020-3*, Pub. by Turtleback) Demco.

Night Notes. Maryam Riess. LC 96-222883. (Cliffs Notes Ser.). 72p. 1996. pap. text 4.95 (*0-8220-0893-9*, Cliff) IDG Bks.

Night Ocean. H. P. Lovecraft. (Illus.). (Orig.). 1986. pap. 2.50 (*0-940884-16-X*) Necronomicon.

Night of a Thousand Claws. R. L. Stine, pseud. (Give Yourself Goosebumps Ser.: No. 28). (J). 1998. pap. text 3.99 (*0-590-40034-7*, Little Apple) Scholastic Inc.

Night of a Thousand Claws. R. L. Stine, pseud. (Give Yourself Goosebumps Ser.: No. 28). (YA). 1998. 9.09 (*0-606-13661-4*, Pub. by Turtleback) Demco.

Night of a Thousand Stars. large type ed. Mona Newman. 320p. 1987. 27.99 (*0-7089-1628-7*) Ulverscroft.

Night of a Thousand Suicides: The Japanese Outbreak at Cowra. Teruhiko Asada. LC 75-597929. 125p. 1970. write for info. (*0-207-12052-8*) Consort Bk Sales.

Night of Affliction & Morning of Recovery. J. H. Magee. LC 77-89397. (Black Heritage Library Collection). 1977. 15.95 (*0-8369-8622-9*) Ayer.

Night of Amber: A Novel. Sylvie Germain. Tr. by Christine Donougher from FRE. LC 98-33650. (Verba Mundi Ser.). 336p. 1999. 22.95 (*1-56792-090-X*) Godine.

***Night of Anguish, Morning of Hope.** rev. ed. Jean Mize. (Illus.). xi, 200p. 2000. reprint ed. pap. 10.95 (*0-9678287-0-8*, 0001) Quest Pubng AR.

Night of Broken Souls. Thomas F. Monteleone. 448p. 1998. mass mkt. 6.50 (*0-446-60577-8*, Pub. by Warner Bks) Little.

Night of Error. Kay Thorpe. (Presents Ser.: No. 446). 1992. pap. 2.89 (*0-373-11446-X*, 1-11446-1) Harlequin Bks.

Night of Fear. Peg Kehret. 1996. 9.09 (*0-606-10895-5*, Pub. by Turtleback) Demco.

Night of Fear. Peg Kehret. (J). (gr. 3-6). 1996. reprint ed. per. 3.99 (*0-671-89217-7*) PB.

***Night of Fire.** Barbara Samuel. 384p. 2000. mass mkt. 5.99 (*0-06-101391-9*, Avon Bks) Morrow Avon.

Night of Fire: The Black Napoleon & the Battle for Haiti. Martin Ros. Tr. by Karen Ford from DUT. (Illus.). 256p. 1994. 27.50 (*0-9627613-8-9*); pap. 14.95 (*0-9627613-7-0*) Sarpedon.

Night of Fire: The Black Napoleon & the Battle for Haiti. Martin Ros. 256p. 1997. 68.00 (*1-873376-35-9*, Pub. by Spellmnt Pubs); 40.00 (*1-873376-36-7*, Pub. by Spellmnt Pubs) St Mut.

Night of Fires & Other Breton Studies. Anatole Le Braz. Tr. by Frances M. Gostling from FRE. LC 77-87696. (Illus.). reprint ed. 45.00 (*0-404-16492-7*) AMS Pr.

Night of Four Hundred. Elizabeth Peters. Date not set. mass mkt. write for info. (*0-380-73120-7*) Morrow Avon.

Night of Four Hundred Rabbits. Elizabeth Peters, pseud. 1989. mass mkt. 4.50 (*0-8125-0773-8*, Pub. by Tor Bks) St Martin.

Night of Four Hundred Rabbits. Elizabeth Peters, pseud. 1996. mass mkt. 5.99 (*0-8125-6360-3*, Pub. by Tor Bks) St Martin.

Night of Freedom. William W. Hebbard. LC 72-170696. (Black Heritage Library Collection). 1977. reprint ed. 13.95 (*0-8369-8886-8*) Ayer.

***Night of Frost.** R. D. Wingfield. 2000. pap. 10.95 (*0-552-14558-0*, Pub. by Transworld Publishers Ltd) Trafalgar.

Night of Ghosts & Hermits: Nocturnal Life on the Seashore. Mary Stolz. LC 84-15665. (Illus.). 48p. (J). (gr. 3-7). 1985. 12.95 (*0-15-257333-X*, Harcourt Child Bks) Harcourt.

Night of Glory. Scott Ciencin. (Eleven Ways Ser.: No. 3). 256p. 1998. mass mkt. 5.99 (*0-380-77983-8*, Eos) Morrow Avon.

Night of January 16th. Ayn Rand. 17.95 (*0-89190-772-6*) Amereon Ltd.

Night of January 16th. Ayn Rand. 1971. pap. 10.95 (*0-452-26486-3*, Plume) Dutton Plume.

Night of January 16th: A Play Book. Ayn Rand. 1979. pap. 10.00 (*0-679-39100-2*) McKay.

Night of January 16th: A Play Book. Ayn Rand. 1980. pap. 10.00 (*0-679-39051-0*) McKay.

Night of Las Posadas. Tomie De Paola. LC 98-36405. (Illus.). 32p. (J). (ps-3). 1999. 15.99 (*0-399-23400-4*, G P Putnam) Peng Put Young Read.

Night of Long Knives, June 29-30, 1934. Max Gallo. Tr. by Lily Emmet from FRE. LC 96-45123.Tr. of La Nuit des Longs Couteaux. (Illus.). 346p. 1997. reprint ed. pap. 14.95 (*0-306-80760-2*) Da Capo.

Night of Love. John M. Haffert. 162p. 1997. pap. text 7.00 (*1-890137-02-2*) One Hund-One Fnd.

Night of Love: Man of the Month. Diana Palmer. (Desire Ser.). 1993. mass mkt. 2.99 (*0-373-05799-7*, 5-05799-7) Silhouette.

***Night of Madness.** Lawrence Watt-Evans. 2000. text 24.95 (*0-312-87368-9*) St Martin.

Night of Many Dreams. Gail Tsukiyama. LC 97-40807. 288p. 1998. text 22.95 (*0-312-17194-3*) St Martin.

Night of Many Dreams. Gail Tsukiyama. LC 98-50903. 288p. 1999. pap. 12.95 (*0-312-19940-6*, Pub. by Tor Bks) St Martin.

Night of Many Dreams, Set. unabridged ed. Gail Tsukiyama. 1999. pap. 44.95 incl. audio (*0-7861-1335-9*, 2229) Blckstn Audio.

***Night of Many Dreams Newsleter Kit.** Tsukiyama. 1999. pap. write for info. (*0-312-20782-4*) St Martin.

Night of Morningstar. large type ed. Peter O'Donnell. 560p. 1996. 27.99 (*0-7089-3543-5*) Ulverscroft.

Night of Music. Marjorie Sandor. 1989. 17.95 (*0-88001-236-6*) HarpC.

***Night of No Return.** Eileen Wilks. (Intimate Moments Ser.: Vol. 1028). 2000. mass mkt. 4.50 (*0-373-27098-4*, 1-27098-2) Harlequin Bks.

Night of Pet Zombies. A. G. Cascone. 1997. pap. 3.50 (*0-8167-4397-5*) Troll Communs.

***Night of Pompon.** Sarah Jett. 160p. (J). 1999. per. 4.99 (*0-671-78633-4*, Archway) PB.

Night of Power. Gregory R. Gillespie. 216p. mass mkt. 4.99 (*1-896329-32-2*) Picasso Publ.

***Night of Questions: A Passover Haggadah.** Ed. by Joy Levitt & Michael Strassfeld. (Illus.). 160p. 2000. pap. 12.95 (*0-935457-49-6*, Pub. by Reconstructionist Pr) Fordham.

Night of Reunion. Michael Allegretto. 288p. 1991. mass mkt. 4.99 (*0-380-71442-6*, Avon Bks) Morrow Avon.

Night of Serious Drinkng. Rene Daumal. 1979. 8.95 (*0-394-50766-5*) Random.

Night of Shadows. large type ed. Edward Gorman. LC 95-16012. 261p. 1995. 19.95 (*0-7838-1370-8*, G K Hall Lrg Type) Mac Lib Ref.

Night of Shame. Miranda Lee. Vol. 1990. 1998. per. 3.75 (*0-373-11990-9*, 1-11990-8) Harlequin Bks.

Night of Shame. large type ed. Miranda Lee. (Harlequin Romance Ser.). 1997. 20.95 (*0-263-15168-9*) Mac Lib Ref.

***Night of Stone.** Catherine Merridale. 2001. 29.95 (*0-670-89474-5*, Viking) Viking Penguin.

Night of Terror. 1988. pap. 5.25 (*0-19-580748-0*) OUP.

Night of Terror & Tales. 2nd ed. Ed. by D. H. Howe. (Illus.). 110p. 1993. pap. text 5.95 (*0-19-585464-0*) OUP.

Night of Terror, Devastation, Suffering & Awful Woe: The Spokane Fire of 1889. Edward W. Nolan. 64p. 1989. pap. 10.95 (*0-910524-12-2*) Eastern Wash.

Night of the Aliens. Dayle C. Gaetz. (Out of This World Ser.). 72p. (J). (gr. 3-7). 1995. pap. 4.95 (*1-896184-08-1*) Roussan Pubs.

Night of the Assasin. Robert Vaughan. (Wild, Wild West Ser.: No. 3). 1998. pap. 5.99 (*0-425-16517-5*) Blvd Books.

Night of the Avenging Blowfish: A Novel of Covert Operations, Love & Luncheon Meat. John Welter. 304p. 1994. pap. 10.95 (*1-56512-050-7*) Algonquin Bks.

***Night of the Axe.** 2nd ed. William Mulvihill. 168p. 1999. reprint ed. pap. 9.00 (*1-891380-07-9*) Brickiln Pr.

Night of the Bear: A Mission of Mercy Through a Nightmare of Ice & Fire. William Smethurst & Julian Spilsbury. 512p. 1994. mass mkt. 13.95 (*0-7472-4239-9*, Pub. by Headline Bk Pub) Trafalgar.

Night of the Broken Glass. Peter Broner. 336p. 1997. pap. text 10.95 (*1-886449-43-0*) Barrytown Ltd.

Night of the Broken Glass. Peter Broner. 316p. 1991. pap. 10.95 (*0-88268-141-9*) Station Hill Pr.

Night of the Broken Glass. Peter Broner. 304p. 1991. 19.95 (*0-88268-132-X*) Station Hill Pr.

***Night of the Carnival.** Fletcher McGhee & Jared Wolf. 209p. 1999. pap. write for info. (*0-7541-1066-4*, Pub. by Minerva Pr) Unity Dist.

Night of the Chupacabras. Marie G. Lee. LC 98-7996. (Avon Camelot Bks.). 144p. (J). (gr. 3-7). 1998. 14.00 (*0-380-97706-0*, Avon Bks) Morrow Avon.

***Night of the Chupacabras.** Marie G. Lee. 128p. 1999. 3.99 (*0-380-79773-9*, Avon Bks) Morrow Avon.

Night of the Circus Monsters. Geoffrey Hayes. LC 94-43103. (Step into Reading Ser.: A Step 3 Book). (Illus.). 48p. (J). (gr. 2-3). 1996. pap. 3.99 (*0-679-87113-6*) McKay.

Night of the Circus Monsters. Geoffrey Hayes. LC 94-43103. (Step into Reading Ser.: A Step 3 Book). (J). (gr. 2-3). 1996. 9.19 (*0-606-09683-3*, Pub. by Turtleback) Demco.

Night of the Claw. Ramsey Campbell. 1992. mass mkt. 4.99 (*0-8125-1280-4*) Tor Bks.

***Night of the Comanche Moon.** T. T. Flynn. 240p. 2000. mass mkt. 4.50 (*0-8439-4689-X*, Leisure Bks) Dorchester Pub Co.

Night of the Comanche Moon. large type ed. T. T. Flynn. 299p. 1996. lib. bdg. 16.95 (*0-7862-0716-7*) Thorndike Pr.

Night of the Comanche Moon: A Western Story. large type ed. T. T. Flynn, LC 95-9437. (Five-Star Western Ser.). 200p. 1995. 16.95 (*0-7862-0508-3*) Thorndike Pr.

Night of the Cooters: More Neat Stories. Howard Waldrop. (Illus.). xiii, 231 p. 1991. 25.00 (*0-942681-05-3*) Ursus Imprints.

Night of the Cotillion. large type ed. Janet Dailey. LC 77-376591. 188p. (J). 1976. write for info. (*0-263-09032-9*, Pub. by Mills & Boon) Chivers N Amer.

Night of the Crash-Test Dummies. Gary Larson. (Illus.). 104p. 1988. pap. 7.95 (*0-8362-2049-8*) Andrews & McMeel.

Night of the Cruel Moon: Cherokee Removal & the Trail of Tears. Stan Hoig. LC 95-22039. (Illus.). 144p. (J). (gr. 7-12). 1996. text 19.95 (*0-8160-3307-2*) Facts on File.

Night of the Cruel Moon: Cherokee Removal & the Trail of Tears. Stanley Hoig. (Library of American Indian History). (Illus.). 144p. 1996. pap. 9.95 (*0-8160-3491-5*) Facts on File.

Night of the Death Train. Robert Vaughan. (Wild, Wild West Ser.). 1998. mass mkt. 5.99 (*0-425-16449-7*) Blvd Books.

Night of the Dinosaurs. Joan Stimson. (Scary Stories Ser.: No. S903-1). (J). 1990. pap. 3.95 (*0-7214-5265-5*, Ladybrd) Penguin Putnam.

Night of the Dolphins. Gavan Daws. (C). 1982. 45.00 (*0-86828-156-5*, Pub. by Deakin Univ) St Mut.

Night of the Dragon's Blood. William Pridgen. LC 96-78145. 192p. 1997. 17.95 (*0-9636512-6-9*) Hodge & Braddock.

Night of the Dunce. Frank Gagliano. 1967. pap. 5.25 (*0-8222-0822-9*) Dramatists Play.

Night of the Eye. Mary Kirchoff. (DragonLance Defenders of Magic Ser.). 320p. (Orig.). 1994. pap. 5.99 (*1-56076-840-1*, Pub. by TSR Inc) Random.

Night of the Fair. large type ed. Jay Baker. (Linford Mystery Library). 560p. 1997. pap. 16.99 (*0-7089-5020-5*, Linford) Ulverscroft.

Night of the Falling Stars. Terry Baltz & Wayne Baltz. LC 95-70986. 181p. (Orig.). (YA). (gr. 5 up). 1995. pap. 6.50 (*1-884610-51-X*) Prairie Divide.

Night of the Fireflies. Beverly Lewis. LC 95-43838. (Summerhill Secrets Ser.: Vol. 4). 144p. (Orig.). (J). (gr. 6-9). 1995. pap. 5.99 (*1-55661-479-9*) Bethany Hse.

Night of the Five Aunties. Mesa Somer. (Illus.). 32p. (J). (ps-4). 1996. lib. bdg. 14.95 (*0-8075-5631-9*) A Whitman.

Night of the Fox. Jack Higgins. 1987. mass mkt. 5.95 (*0-671-64058-5*, Pocket Books) PB.

Night of the Fox. Jack Higgins. 352p. 1991. pap. 5.95 (*0-671-72820-2*) PB.

Night of the Full Moon. Gloria Whelan. LC 93-6706. (Illus.). 64p. (J). (gr. 2-4). 1993. lib. bdg. 15.99 (*0-679-94464-8*, Pub. by Knopf Bks Yng Read) Random.

Night of the Full Moon. Gloria Whelan. LC 95-5386. (Illus.). 64p. (J). (gr. 2-4). 1996. pap. 3.99 (*0-679-87276-0*) Random.

Night of the Full Moon. Gloria Whelan. LC 95-5386. (J). 1996. 9.19 (*0-606-09684-1*, Pub. by Turtleback) Demco.

Night of the Full Moon & Other Stories. Kartar S. Duggal. (C). 1992. text 8.00 (*81-7201-228-4*, Pub. by National Sahitya Akademi) S Asia.

Night of the Gargoyle. Lloyd Alan. (House of Horrors). (J). 1995. 9.05 (*0-606-08455-X*, Pub. by Turtleback) Demco.

Night of the Gargoyles. Eve Bunting. LC 93-8160. (Illus.). 32p. (J). (gr. 3 up). 1994. 14.95 (*0-395-66553-1*, Clarion Bks) HM.

Night of the Gargoyles. Eve Bunting. (Illus.). 32p. (J). (gr. k-3). 1999. pap. 7.95 (*0-395-96887-9*, Clarion Bks) HM.

Night of the Goat Children. J. Patrick Lewis. Ed. by Michele Foley. LC 95-45186. (Illus.). 32p. (J). (ps-3). 1999. 15.99 (*0-8037-1870-5*, Dial Yng Read) Peng Put Young Read.

Night of the Green Dragon. Dorothy Dixon. (Illus.). 32p. 1996. pap. text 4.95 (*0-19-421947-X*) OUP.

Night of the Grizzlies. Jack Olsen. LC 96-3072. 224p. 1996. reprint ed. pap. 14.95 (*0-943972-48-5*) Homestead WY.

Night of the Hawk. Dale Brown. 576p. 1993. mass mkt. 7.99 (*0-425-13661-2*) Berkley Pub.

Night of the Hawk. large type ed. Dale Brown. LC 92-33396. 906p. 1994. reprint ed. lib. bdg. 22.95 (*1-56054-586-0*) Thorndike Pr.

Night of the Hippoflytamus. Rhyk Gilbar. (Illus.). (J). 1997. 14.95 (*1-888588-13-6*); pap. 6.95 (*1-888588-14-4*) Positive Press.

Night of the Hippoflytamus. Rhyk Gilbar. (Illus.). 32p. (J). (gr. k-6). 1997. pap. 6.95 (*0-614-17775-8*); lib. bdg. 14.95 (*0-614-17774-X*) Positive Press.

Night of the Hunter. Jennifer Greene. (Men at Work Ser.: Vol. 12). 1998. mass mkt. 4.50 (*0-373-81024-5*, 1-81024-1) Harlequin Bks.

Night of the Hunter. Davis Grubb. (Film Ink Ser.). 1999. pap. 13.00 (*1-85375-320-3*, Pub. by Prion) Trafalgar.

Night of the Hunter. Davis Grubb. 1993. reprint ed. lib. bdg. 18.95 (*0-89968-431-9*, Lghtyr Pr) Buccaneer Bks.

***Night of the Hunter.** unabridged large type ed. Davis Grubb. 2000. 24.95 (*0-7531-6124-9*, 161249, Pub. by ISIS Lrg Prnt) ISIS Pub.

Night of the Ice Storm. David Stout. 368p. 1992. mass mkt. 4.99 (*0-446-40110-2*, Pub. by Warner Bks) Little.

Night of the Iguana see Best American Plays: Fifth Series, 1958-1963

Night of the Iguana. Tennessee Williams. 1963. pap. 5.25 (*0-8222-0823-7*) Dramatists Play.

Night of the Iquana see Three by Tennessee Williams

Night of the Jaguar. Laura Pendleton & Don Pendleton. (Stony Man Ser.: No. 31). 1997. per. 5.50 (*0-373-61915-4*, 1-61915-4, Wrldwide Lib) Harlequin Bks.

Night of the Jaguar. large type ed. Merline Lovelace. (Silhouette Ser.). 1998. 20.95 (*0-373-59862-9*, Harlequin) Harlequin Bks.

Night of the Jaguar: IM Extra, Code Name - Danger. Merline Lovelace. (Intimate Moments Ser.). 1995. per. 3.75 (*0-373-07637-1*, 1-07637-1) Silhouette.

Night of the Kachina. Nichole Salas. (Bestsellers I Ser.). (J). 1977. 16.60 (*0-606-02422-0*, Pub. by Turtleback) Demco.

Night of the Letter. Dorothy Eden. 1996. 19.50 (*0-7451-8694-7*, Black Dagger) Chivers N Amer.

***Night of the Letter.** large type ed. Dorothy Eden. LC 99-38780. 294p. 1999. 23.95 (*0-7862-2150-X*) Thorndike Pr.

Night of the Litani. Andrea Brunais. 254p. 1996. pap. 18.50 (*0-931541-55-7*) Mancorp Pub.

Night of the Living Bar-B-Q. Charles Podrebarac. Ed. by Jake Morrissey. (Illus.). 160p. 1997. pap. 9.95 (*0-9604884-3-X*) Kansas City Star.

Night of the Living Cavemen. Eric Weiner. (Ghostwriter Ser.). 1995. 8.60 (*0-606-07574-7*, Pub. by Turtleback) Demco.

Night of the Living Clay. Betsy Haynes. (Bone Chillers Ser.: No. 12). (J). (gr. 4-8). 1996. 9.09 (*0-606-10144-6*, Pub. by Turtleback) Demco.

Night of the Living Dad. Rick Kirkman & Jerry Scott. LC 95-80754. (Baby Blues Scrapbook Ser.: No. 6). (Illus.). 128p. (Orig.). 1996. pap. 9.95 (*0-8362-1310-6*) Andrews & McMeel.

Night of the Living Dummy see Noche del Muneco Viviente

Night of the Living Dummy. R. L. Stine, pseud. (Goosebumps Ser.: No. 7). 160p. (J). (gr. 3-7). 1993. pap. 3.99 (*0-590-46617-8*) Scholastic Inc.

Night of the Living Dummy. R. L. Stine, pseud. (Goosebumps Ser.: No. 7). 1993. 9.09 (*0-606-05509-6*, Pub. by Turtleback) Demco.

Night of the Living Dummy see Goosebumps

Night of the Living Dummy III. R. L. Stine, pseud. LC 00-5342. (Goosebumps Ser.: No. 40). (J). (gr. 3-7). 1996. pap. 3.99 (*0-590-56877-9*) Scholastic Inc.

Night of the Living Dummy III. R. L. Stine, pseud. (Goosebumps Ser.: No. 40). (J). 1995. 9.09 (*0-606-07946-7*, Pub. by Turtleback) Demco.

Night of the Living Dummy III. R. L. Stine, pseud. (Goosebumps Ser.: No. 40). 1996. 9.09 (*0-606-08832-6*, Pub. by Turtleback) Demco.

An Asterisk (*) at the beginning of an entry indicates that the title is appearing for the first time.

Night of the Living Dummy II. Adapted by Carol Ellis. (Goosebumps Presents Ser.: No. 5). 1996. 9.19 (0-606-10200-0, Pub. by Turtleback) Demco.

Sound & Music. Adapted by Carol Ellis. LC 49-119020. (Let's Explore Science Ser.: No. 5). (Illus.). 64p. (J). (gr. 2-5). 1996. text 3.99 (0-590-74590-5) Scholastic Inc.

Night of the Living Dummy II. R. L. Stine, pseud. LC 00-3754. (Goosebumps Ser.: No. 31). 160p. (YA). (gr. 3-7). 1995. pap. 3.99 (0-590-48349-8) Scholastic Inc.

Night of the Living Gerbil. Elizabeth Levy. 96p. 14.95 (0-06-028588-5) HarpC.

Night of the Living Gerbil. Elizabeth Levy. 96p. (J). (gr. 2-5). 14.89 (0-06-028589-3) HarpC.

Night of the Living Mad Libs: World's Greatest Word Game. Roger Price & Leonard Stern. LC 96-153860. (Mad Libs Ser.). (Illus.). 48p. (J). (gr. 3 up). 1994. pap. 3.99 (0-8431-3735-5, Price Stern) Peng Put Young Read.

Night of the Living Rerun. Arthur Byron Cover. (Buffy the Vampire Slayer Ser.: No. 4). 178p. (YA). (gr. 7-12). 1998. pap. 4.50 (0-671-01715-2) PB.

Night of the Living Tiki. P. J. Neri. (Hawaii Chillers Ser.: Vol. 4). 128p. (J). (gr. 3-6). 1998. pap. 4.95 (1-57306-043-7) Bess Pr.

Night of the Living Yogurt. William DeAndrea. (Orig.). (J). 1996. 9.09 (0-606-09685-X, Pub. by Turtleback) Demco.

Night of the Living Yogurt. William L. DeAndrea & Matthew DeAndrea. 112p. (Orig.). (J). (gr. 3-7). 1996. pap. 3.99 (0-380-78358-4, Avon Bks) Morrow Avon.

Night of the Luminarias. Pat Carr. 120p. (Orig.). (C). 1986. write for info. (0-941720-30-6); pap. 5.95 (0-941720-29-2) Slough Pr TX.

Night of the Magician. Stephanie James, pseud. 1999. mass mkt. 4.50 (0-373-80682-5, 1-80682-7) Harlequin Bks.

***Night of the Magician.** Stephanie James, pseud. 2000. mass mkt. 4.50 (0-373-80694-9, 1-80694-2, Harlequin) Harlequin Bks.

Night of the Milky Way Railway. Miyazawa Kenji. Ed. & Tr. by Sarah M. Strong from JPN. LC 91-6608. (Illus.). 192p. (YA). (gr. 7 up). 1991. 44.95 (0-87332-820-5) M E Sharpe.

Night of the Mist. Eugene Heimler. LC 77-28508. 191p. 1978. reprint ed. lib. bdg. 35.00 (0-313-20229-X, HENM, Greenwood Pr) Greenwood.

Night of the Mist. 2nd ed. Eugene Heimler. 192p. 1997. reprint ed. 12.95 (965-229-165-X) Gefen Bks.

Night of the Moon Children. rev. ed. Regina C. Rapier. 1995. reprint ed. 20.00 (0-614-06251-9) R C Rapier.

Night of the Nile. Lynn Leslie. (Intrigue Ser.). 1994. per. 2.99 (0-373-22287-4, 1-22287-6) Harlequin Bks.

Night of the Ninjas. Mary Pope Osborne. LC 94-29142. (Magic Tree House Ser.: No. 5). (Illus.). (J). (gr. k-3). 1995. pap. 3.99 (0-679-86371-0) Random.

Night of the Ninjas. Mary Pope Osborne. LC 94-29142. (Magic Tree House Ser.: No. 5). (Illus.). (J). (gr. k-3). 1995. lib. bdg. 11.99 (0-679-96371-5) Random.

Night of the Ninjas. Mary Pope Osborne. (Magic Tree House Ser.: No. 5). (Illus.). (J). (gr. k-3). 1995. 9.19 (0-606-07947-5, Pub. by Turtleback) Demco.

***Night of the November Moon.** Ann C. Ulrich. LC 99-63384. 208p. 1999. pap. 11.95 (0-944851-17-7) Earth Star.

Night of the Old South Ball: And Other Essays & Fables. Edwin M. Yoder, Jr. 248p. 1984. 17.95 (0-916242-53-6) Yoknapatawpha.

Night of the Paper Bag Monsters. Helen Craig. LC 92-44610. (Illus.). 32p. (J). (ps up). 1994. reprint ed. pap. 4.95 (1-56402-120-3) Candlewick Pr.

Night of the Phantom. large type ed. Anne Stuart. 340p. 1992. reprint ed. lib. bdg. 19.95 (1-56054-293-4) Thorndike Pr.

Night of the Poor. Frederic Prokosch. LC 71-178789. 359p. 1972. reprint ed. lib. bdg. 52.50 (0-8371-6288-2, PRNP, Greenwood Pr) Greenwood.

Night of the Potato. David Oates. (Chapbook Ser.: No. 3). 56p. 1994. pap. 5.00 (1-885912-00-5) Sows Ear Pr.

Night of the Pterodactyls. Julian Wiles. 1965p. (YA). (gr. 7 up). 1988. pap. 5.50 (0-87129-911-9, N32) Dramatic Pub.

Night of the Red Moon. Angi Ma Wong. LC 94-68680. (Illus.). 96p. (J). (gr. 4 up). 1994. text 16.00 (0-9635906-1-8) Pacific Herit.

Night of the Running Man. Lee Wells. 448p. 1987. mass mkt. 3.95 (0-373-62112-4) Harlequin Bks.

Night of the Scorpion. large type ed. John Winton. 448p. 1996. 27.99 (0-7089-3474-9) Ulverscroft.

Night of the Sea Turtle. Lynn M. Stone. (Animal Odysseys Ser.). 48p. (J). (gr. 3-8). 1991. lib. bdg. 16.95 (0-86593-102-X) Rourke Corp.

Night of the Shark. Bruce Cordell. Ed. by John Rateliff. 1997. 9.95 (0-7869-0718-5, Pub. by TSR Inc) Random.

Night of the Shepherds: A Christmas Experience. Juliana Quaglini. Tr. by Anne J. Flanagan from ITA. LC 93-25027. (Illus.). 31p. (Orig.). (J). (gr. 4 up). 1993. pap. 3.95 (0-8198-5128-0) Pauline Bks.

***Night of the Shifter's Moon.** Mary Stanton. (Unicorns of Balinor Ser.: Vol. 7). (Illus.). 144p. (J). (gr. 3-7). 2000. mass mkt. 4.50 (0-439-16786-8) Scholastic Inc.

Night of the Silent Drums. John L. Anderson. (Illus.). 449p. 1992. reprint ed. 29.95 (0-926330-05-5); reprint ed. pap. 19.95 (0-926330-06-3) Mapes Monde.

Night of the Silver Stars: The Battle of Lang Vei. William R. Phillips. LC 97-29824. (Special Warfare Ser.). (Illus.). 208p. 1997. 29.95 (1-55750-691-4) Naval Inst Pr.

Night of the Stars. Douglas Gutierrez. Tr. by Carmen D. Dearden from SPA. Orig. Title: La Noche de las Estrellas. (Illus.). 24p. (J). (ps-1). 1988. 9.95 (0-916291-17-0) Kane-Miller Bk.

Night of the Stars. Douglas Gutierrez. Tr. by Carmen D. Dearden from SPA. Orig. Title: La Noche de las Estrellas. (Illus.). 24p. (J). (ps-2). 1997. reprint ed. pap. 5.95 (0-916291-74-X, Cranky Nell Bks) Kane-Miller Bk.

Night of the Storm. L. Townsend. 1996. text 35.00 (0-340-64720-5, Pub. by Hodder & Stought Ltd) Trafalgar.

Night of the Storm. L. Townsend. 1996. mass mkt. 13.95 (0-340-64721-3, Pub. by Hodder & Stought Ltd) Trafalgar.

Night of the Storm. Lindsay Townsend. LC 98-8440. 608 p. 1998. write for info. (0-7540-1204-2) Chivers N Amer.

Night of the Storm. large type ed. Lindsay Townsend. LC 98-8440. 1998. 30.00 (0-7862-1534-8) Thorndike Pr.

Night of the Tribades. Per Olov Enquist. Tr. by Ross Shideler. 1978. pap. 5.25 (0-8222-0824-5) Dramatists Play.

Night of the Twister. Ivy Ruckman. 1986. 10.05 (0-606-02536-7, Pub. by Turtleback) Demco.

Night of the Twisters. Ivy Ruckman. LC 83-46168. 160p. (J). (gr. 3-6). 1984. lib. bdg. 15.89 (0-690-04409-7) HarpC Child Bks.

***Night of the Twisters.** Anne Troy. 32p. 1999. 9.95 (1-56137-654-X) Novel Units.

Night of the Twisters. Ivy Ruckman. LC 83-46168. (Trophy Bk.). 160p. (J). (gr. 4-7). 1986. reprint ed. pap. 4.95 (0-06-440176-6, HarpTrophy) HarpC Child Bks.

Night of the Vampire. Christopher Pike, pseud. (Spooksville Ser.). (J). (gr. 4-6). 1997. per. 3.99 (0-671-00267-8) PB.

Night of the Vampire. Christopher Pike, pseud. (Spooksville Ser.). (J). (gr. 4-6). 1997. 9.09 (0-606-13036-5, Pub. by Turtleback) Demco.

Night of the Vanishing Lights. Lee Roddy. LC 94-15779. (Ladd Family Adventure Ser.: No. 10). (J). (gr. 3-7). 1994. pap. 5.99 (1-56179-256-X) Focus Family.

Night of the Walking Dead. William W. Connors. (Advanced Dungeons & Dragons, Second Edition; Al-Qadim Ser.). 1992. 10.95 (1-56076-351-5) TSR Inc.

Night of the Walking Dead, Prt. 1. Erica Farber. (Mercer Mayer's Critters of the Night Ser.). (J). 1997. 10.19 (0-606-13001-2, Pub. by Turtleback) Demco.

Night of the Walking Dead, Prt. 2. Erica Farber. (Mercer Mayer's Critters of the Night Ser.). (J). 1997. 10.19 (0-606-13002-0, Pub. by Turtleback) Demco.

Night of the Weeping Women. Lawrence Naumoff. LC 97-20028. 256p. 1997. pap. 11.00 (0-15-600364-3) Harcourt.

Night of the Werecat. R. L. Stine, pseud. (Ghosts of Fear Street Ser.: No. 12). (J). (gr. 4-7). 1996. per. 3.99 (0-671-00184-1) PB.

Night of the Werecat. R. L. Stine, pseud. (Ghosts of Fear Street Ser.: No. 12). (J). (gr. 4-7). 1996. 9.09 (0-606-10814-9, Pub. by Turtleback) Demco.

Night of the Werepoodle. Constance Hiser. LC 93-25732. (Illus.). 128p. (J). (gr. 4-6). 1994. 14.95 (0-8234-1116-8) Holiday.

Night of the Werewolf. Franklin W. Dixon. Ed. by Ann Greenberg. (Hardy Boys Mystery Stories Ser.: No. 59). 192p. (J). (gr. 3-6). 1990. pap. 3.99 (0-671-70993-3, Minstrel Bks) PB.

Night of the Werewolf. Edward Packard. (Choose Your Own Nightmare Ser.: No. 1). (J). (gr. 4-8). 1995. 8.70 (0-606-07365-5, Pub. by Turtleback) Demco.

Night of the Werewolf. gif. ed. Franklin W. Dixon. (Hardy Boys Mystery Stories Ser.:). (J). (gr. 3-6). 1984. pap., boxed set 8.85 (0-685-09390-5) PB.

Night of the Werewolf see Choose Your Own Nightmare Series

Night of the White Stag. Mary C. Helldorfer. LC 96-11771. (Illus.). 32p. (J). (gr. 2-4). 1999. 16.95 (0-385-32261-5, DD Bks Yng Read) BDD Bks Young Read.

Night of the Willow. large type ed. Maureen Peters. (Dales Large Print Ser.). (Illus.). 294p. 1996. pap. 18.99 (1-85389-647-0) Ulverscroft.

Night of the Wolf. Alice Borchardt. LC 99-31102. 464p. 1999. 24.50 (0-345-42362-3) Ballantine Pub Grp.

***Night of the Wolf.** Alice Borchardt. 480p. 2000. mass mkt. 6.99 (0-345-42363-1) Ballantine Pub Grp.

***Night of Three Ghosts.** (Adventures of Wishbone Ser.: Vol. 25). (Illus.). 144p. (J). (gr. 3-7). 2000. mass mkt. 3.99 (1-57064-391-1, Big Red) Lyrick Pub.

***Night of Tragedy, Dawning of Light: The Wedgwood Baptist Shootings.** Dan R. Crawford et al. LC 00-26551. 180p. 2000. 14.99 (0-87788-585-0, H Shaw Pubs) Waterbrook Pr.

Night of Weeping: When God's Children Suffer. Horatius Bonar. 1999. pap. text 7.99 (1-85792-441-X) Christian Focus.

Night of Wenceslas. Lionel Davidson. 1996. mass mkt. 6.99 (0-312-95876-5) St Martin.

Night of Wishes. Michael Ende. (Sunburst Ser.). (Illus.). 228p. (YA). (gr. 4-7). 1995. pap. 6.95 (0-374-45503-1) FS&G.

Night of Wishes: Or the Satanarchaeolidealcohellish Notion Potion. Michael Ende. (J). 1992. 12.30 (0-606-07948-3) Turtleback.

Night of Wonder: Service-Story for Christmas Eve. Nathan Aaseng & Michael L. Sherer. 1985. 3.50 (0-89536-762-9, 5869) CSS OH.

***Night on Avalanche Hill.** Michael Hulit & Kathleen Comstock. LC 99-80015. 128p. (J). (gr. 3-6). 2000. pap. write for info. (1-57197-210-2, Pub. by Pentland Pr) Assoc Pubs Grp.

Night on Bald Mountain. Patrick White. 98p. (Orig.). 1996. pap. 14.95 (0-86819-469-7, Pub. by Currency Pr) Accents Pubns.

Night on Fire. Diana Deverell. LC 99-14874. 304p. 1999. 23.00 (0-380-97611-0, Avon Bks) Morrow Avon.

Night on 'Gator Creek. Winnie Stewart. (Sundown Fiction Collection). 60p. (J). (gr. 3). 1993. pap. 3.95 (0-88336-215-5) New Readers.

Night on Hibernia. John Ennis. 62p. 1976. pap. 11.95 (0-902996-46-0) Dufour.

Night on Lone Wolf Mountain & Other Short Stories. Jack Weyland. LC 95-26314. vii, 210p. (YA). (gr. 8-12). 1996. 14.95 (1-57345-113-4) Deseret Bk.

Night on Needlepoint. Max C. Gougutly. 21p. (Orig.). 1994. pap. 2.50 (1-57514-224-4, 3021) Encore Perform Pub.

Night on Neighborhood Street. Eloise Greenfield. (J). 1996. 11.19 (0-606-08833-4, Pub. by Turtleback) Demco.

***Night on the Flint River.** Roberta C. Bondi. LC 99-19063. 1999. 17.00 (0-687-02455-2) Abingdon.

Night on the Ground, a Day in the Open: A Mountain Vagabond Hard at Work. Doug Robinson. LC 96-887. (Illus.). 320p. 1996. pap. 19.00 (1-879415-14-3) Mtn n Air Bks.

Night on the Tiles. Bruce Ingman. LC 98-36467. (Illus.). 32p. (J). (ps-3). 1999. 15.00 (0-395-93655-1) HM.

Night Ones. Patricia Grossman. (Illus.). 1997. pap. 5.00 (0-15-201503-5) Harcourt.

Night Open. Rolf Jacobsen. Tr. by Olav Grinde. 221p. 1993. pap. 15.00 (1-877727-33-4) White Pine.

Night Out. John Watson. LC 98-30014. 1998. pap. 6.00 (0-88734-792-4) Players Pr.

Night Out: A Comedy. Frank Vickery. LC 86-233843. ii, 33p. 1986. write for info. (0-573-12011-0) French.

Night Out: Poems about Hotels, Motels, Restaurants & Bars. Ed. by Kurt Brown & Laure-Anne Bosselaar. LC 96-47358. 384p. 1997. pap. 14.95 (1-57131-405-9) Milkweed Ed.

Night Out with the Girls: Women Having a Good Time. Gilda O'Neill. 212p. 1997. pap. 15.95 (0-7043-4353-3, Pub. by Womens Press) Trafalgar.

Night Outside. Patricia Wrightson. LC 85-7529. (Illus.). 64p. (J). (gr. 4-7). 1985. lib. bdg. 13.95 (0-689-50363-6) McElderry Bks.

Night over Day over Night. Watkins. 1992. pap. write for info. (0-09-965870-4, Pub. by Random) Random House.

Night over Day over Night. Paul Watkins. 304p. 1990. pap. 7.95 (0-380-70737-3, Avon Bks) Morrow Avon.

Night over Day over Night. Paul Watkins. LC 97-5814. 304p. 1997. pap. 13.00 (0-312-15608-1) St Martin.

Night over Day over Night. Paul Watkins. 1997. pap. 13.00 (0-614-27292-0, Picador USA) St Martin.

Night over the Solomons. Louis L'Amour. 192p. 1986. mass mkt. 4.50 (0-553-26602-0) Bantam.

Night over Vienna. Lili Korber. Tr. by Viktoria Hertling & Kay M. Stone from GER. (Studies in Austrian Literature, Culture, & Thought. Translation Ser.). 147p. (Orig.). 1989. pap. 14.95 (0-929497-12-0) Ariadne CA.

Night over Water. Ken Follett. 1992. pap. 5.99 (0-451-17410-0, Sig) NAL.

Night over Water. Ken Follett. 526p. 1992. mass mkt. 7.99 (0-451-17313-9, Sig) NAL.

Night Owl & the Rooster: A Haitian Legend. Ed. & Illus. by Charles Reasoner. LC 95-9983. 32p. (J). (gr. 2-6). 1995. pap., teacher ed. 4.95 (0-8167-3750-9) Troll Communs.

Night Owl & the Rooster: A Haitian Legend. Ed. & Illus. by Charles Reasoner. LC 95-9983. (Legends of the World Ser.). 32p. (J). (gr. 2-6). 1997. lib. bdg. 18.60 (0-8167-3749-5) Troll Communs.

Night Owl & the Rooster: A Haitian Legend. Charles Reasoner. (Legends of the World Ser.). (J). 1995. 9.15 (0-606-07949-1, Pub. by Turtleback) Demco.

Night Owls. Sharon P. Denslow. LC 89-33937. (Illus.). 32p. (J). (ps-2). 1990. lib. bdg. 13.95 (0-02-728681-9, Bradbury S&S) S&S Childrens.

Night Parade. Edward Hirsch. 1989. pap. 17.00 (0-679-72299-8) Knopf.

Night Parents. Michael S. Allen. (Cleveland Poets Ser.: No. 42). 28p. (Orig.). 1988. pap. 4.00 (0-914946-64-1) Cleveland St Univ Poetry Ctr.

Night Passage. Norman A. Fox. 176p. 1988. pap. 2.75 (0-380-70295-9, Avon Bks) Morrow Avon.

Night Passage. Carol D. Luce. 432p. 1995. mass mkt. 4.99 (0-8217-4966-8, Pinncle Kensgtn) Kensgtn Pub Corp.

Night Passage. large type ed. Robert B. Parker. LC 97-47199. (Compass Press Large Print Book Ser.). 1998. 26.95 (1-56895-530-8) Wheeler Pub.

Night Passage. Robert B. Parker. 336p. 1998. reprint ed. mass mkt. 6.99 (0-515-12349-8, Jove) Berkley Pub.

Night Path. Laurie Kutchins. LC 97-72085. (American Poets Continuum Ser.: Vol. 43). 96p. 1997. 20.00 (1-880238-48-9); pap. 12.50 (1-880238-49-7) BOA Edns.

Night Patrol & Other Stories. Mikhail Kuraev. Tr. by Margareta O. Thompson from RUS. LC 93-30236. 296p. 1994. text 49.95 (0-8223-1402-9) Duke.

Night Patrol & Other Stories. Mikhail Kuraev. Tr. by Margareta O. Thompson from RUS. LC 93-30236. 296p. 1994. pap. 16.95 (0-8223-1415-0) Duke.

Night People. Jack Finney. 1994. lib. bdg. 24.95 (1-56849-414-9) Buccaneer Bks.

Night People. Barry Gifford. LC 92-13449. 208p. 1993. pap. 11.00 (0-8021-3369-X, Grove) Grove-Atltic.

Night People: The Jazz Life of Dicky Wells. rev. ed. Rev. by Dicky Wells. LC 90-24916. (Illus.). 240p. (C). 1991. pap. 15.95 (1-56098-067-2) Smithsonian.

Night Perimeter: New & Selected Poems, 1958-1990. Carroll Arnet. 1991. pap. 9.95 (0-912678-81-X) Greenfld Rev Lit.

Night Physics. M. Travis Lane. LC 94-194883. 86p. 1994. pap. 11.95 (0-919626-70-X, Pub. by Brick Bks) Genl Dist Srvs.

Night-Pieces: Eighteen Tales. Thomas Burke. LC 78-150539. (Short Story Index Reprint Ser.). 1977. reprint ed. 20.95 (0-8369-3836-4) Ayer.

Night Plague. Graham Masterton. 1991. mass mkt. 4.50 (0-8125-2204-4) Tor Bks.

Night Porch. Jean Valentine. 20p. 1995. pap. 5.00 (1-885141-05-X) Harlequin Ink.

Night Prayer: From the Liturgy of the Hours. rev. ed. 80p. 1997. pap. text 4.95 (1-57455-148-5) US Catholic.

Night Prayers: A Vampire Novel. P. D. Cacek. LC 98-70434. 240p. 1998. pap. 15.95 (1-891946-01-3) Design Image.

Night Prayers: Full Score for String Quartet. G. Kancheli. 1994. pap. 9.50 (0-7935-3538-7, 50482203) H Leonard.

***Night Prayers: Qiyam & Tarawih.** 2nd unabridged ed. Muhummad Al-Jibaly. 198p. 1999. pap. 9.00 (1-891229-22-2) Al-Kitaab & As-Sunnah.

Night Prayers & Other Poems. Melech Ravitch. Tr. by Seymour Mayne & Rivka Augenfeld. 24p. pap. 5.00 (0-88962-563-8) Mosaic.

Night Preacher. Louise A. Vernon. LC 73-94378. (Illus.). 134p. (J). (gr. 3-8). 1969. pap. 6.99 (0-8361-1774-3) Herald Pr.

Night Prey. Carol D. Luce. 1992. mass mkt. 4.99 (0-8217-3661-2, Zebra Kensgtn) Kensgtn Pub Corp.

Night Prey. John Sandford, pseud. 400p. 1995. mass mkt. 7.50 (0-425-14641-3) Berkley Pub.

Night Prince. Muriel Jensen. (American Romance Ser.). 1994. per. 3.50 (0-373-16522-6, 1-16522-4) Harlequin Bks.

Night Probe! Clive Cussler. 352p. 1984. mass mkt. 7.99 (0-553-27740-5) Bantam.

Night Prowlers. Arthur Morton. (Illus.). (J). (gr. k-3). 1992. 12.50 (1-57842-057-1) Delmas Creat.

Night Prowlers. Arthur Morton. Tr. by Suon Thach. (CAM.). (J). (gr. k-3). 1994. 12.50 (1-57842-060-1) Delmas Creat.

Night Rabbits. Lee Posey. LC 98-34021. (Illus.). 32p. (J). (ps-3). 1999. 15.95 (1-56145-164-9, 51649) Peachtree Pubs.

***Night Rabbits.** Monica Wellington. 1999. pap. 13.40 (0-613-15036-8) Econo-Clad Bks.

Night Raiders: Israel's Naval Commandos at War. Samuel M. Katz. 1997. per. 6.50 (0-671-00234-1) PB.

Night Raiders along the Cape - Cape Cod, 1779. John Waters. LC 96-758. (Mysteries in Time Ser.). (Illus.). 80p. (J). (gr. 4-6). 1997. lib. bdg. 14.95 (1-881889-85-8) Silver Moon.

Night Rain. Thomas Wiloch. (Illus.). 55p. (Orig.). 1991. pap. 3.00 (0-926935-55-0) Runaway Spoon.

***Night Rainbow.** Barbara Juster Esbensen. LC 99-30880. (Illus.). 32p. (J). (gr. k-4). 2000. 16.95 (0-531-30244-X) Orchard Bks Watts.

***Night Rainbow.** Barbara Juster Esbensen. LC 99-30880. (Illus.). 32p. (J). (gr. k-4). 2000. lib. bdg. 17.99 (0-531-33244-6) Orchard Bks Watts.

Night Rape. Deborah Gulliver. Ed. by Barry Lane. (Opening Doors Ser.: No. 1). (Illus.). 32p. (Orig.). 1989. pap. 4.00 (1-877829-01-3) Homegrown Bks.

***Night Raven.** Elaine Barbieri. 400p. 2000. mass mkt. 5.99 (0-8439-4723-3, Leisure Bks) Dorchester Pub Co.

Night Relics. James P. Blaylock. LC 93-14261. 320p. 1994. pap. 18.95 (0-441-00022-3) Ace Bks.

Night Remembers. Kathleen Eagle. LC 96-46832. 384p. 1998. mass mkt. 5.99 (0-380-78491-2, Avon Bks) Morrow Avon.

Night Reversing. Morgan Yasbineck. 1996. pap. 12.95 (1-86368-166-3, Pub. by Fremantle Arts) Intl Spec Bk.

Night Rhythms. Elda Minger. 1997. per. 3.50 (0-373-25749-X, 1-25749-2) Harlequin Bks.

Night Ribbons. Cynthia Gallaher. 64p. (Orig.). 1989. pap. 6.95 (0-9623803-0-X) Polar Bear Pr.

Night Ride. Mary Morgan. LC 95-45779. (Illus.). (J). 1999. 16.00 (0-689-80545-4) Atheneum Yung Read.

Night Ride. Mary Morgan. (J). 1997. 14.95 (0-02-767460-6) S&S Bks Yung.

Night Ride Home. Vicki Covington. LC 92-15907. 1992. 20.00 (0-671-74345-7) S&S Trade.

Night Ride Home. Barbara Esstman. LC 97-9305. 352p. 1997. 22.00 (0-15-100288-6) Harcourt.

Night Ride Home. large type ed. Vicki Covington. (Americana Series). 385p. 1993. reprint ed. lib. bdg. 19.95 (1-56054-672-7) Thorndike Pr.

Night Ride Home: A Novel. Barbara Esstman. LC 98-24571. 336p. 1998. pap. 13.00 (0-06-097754-X, Perennial) HarperTrade.

***Night Ride to Nanna's.** Jenny Koralek. LC 99-58229. 32p. (YA). (ps up). 2000. 15.99 (0-7636-1192-1) Candlewick Pr.

Night Rider. Doyle Trent. 1992. mass mkt. 3.50 (0-8217-3695-7, Zebra Kensgtn) Kensgtn Pub Corp.

Night Rider. Robert Penn Warren. LC 92-82382. (Southern Classics Ser.). 480p. 1992. reprint ed. pap. 14.95 (1-879941-14-7) J S Sanders.

Night Riders. large type ed. Todhunter Ballard. LC 98-15051. (Sagebrush Large Print Westerns Ser.). 1998. 18.95 (1-57490-125-7) T T Beeler.

Night Riders. large type ed. Jeff Kincaid. (Linford Western Library Ser.). 272p. 1997. pap. 16.99 (0-7089-5133-3, Linford) Ulverscroft.

Night Riders: Defending Community in the Black Patch, 1890-1915. Christopher Waldrep. LC 93-10077. 278p. (C). 1993. text 49.95 (0-8223-1359-6); pap. text 18.95 (0-8223-1393-6) Duke.

Night Riders of Harper's Ferry. Kathleen Ernst. LC 96-2524. (WM Kids Ser.: No. 2). (Illus.). 139p. (Orig.). (YA). (gr. 5 up). 1996. pap. 7.95 (1-57249-013-6, WM Kids) White Mane Pub.

Night Riley Chase Fell in the Icy Housatonic River. Bernard A. Drew. 48p. 1994. pap. 6.50 (0-941583-22-8) Attic Rev Pr.

Night Roamers & Other Stories. Knut Hamsun. Tr. by Tiina Nunnally from NOR. LC 92-3337. (European Short Stories Ser.: No. 3). 156p. (Orig.). 1992. 21.95 (0-940242-24-9) Fjord Pr.

Night Room. E.M. Goldman. LC 94-30727. (J). 1997. 10.09 (0-606-11683-4, Pub. by Turtleback) Demco.

Night Ructions. Dara O. Conaola. Tr. by Gabriel Rosenstock from IRI. (Illus.). 58p. (Orig.). 1990. pap. 9.95 (0-948259-93-0, Pub. by Forest Bks) Dufour.

***Night Ructions: Selected Short Stories.** Dara O Conaola. 58p. 2000. pap. 7.95 (1-900693-15-1, Pub. by Clo Iar-Chonnachta) Dufour.

An Asterisk (*) at the beginning of an entry indicates that the title is appearing for the first time.

Night Sale. Richard Broderick. LC 82-61652. (Minnesota Voices Project Ser.: No. 8). (Illus.). 135p. 1982. pap. 0.75 (*0-89823-040-3*) New Rivers Pr.

Night Santa Got Stuck. (Illus.). 13p. (J). (gr. k-3). 1996. pap. 2.95 (*0-8167-2193-9*) Troll Communs.

Night Scary Beasties Popped out of My Melon. Daniel Kamish & David Kamish. LC 97-31367. 40p. (J). (gr. k-3). 1998. 14.00 (*0-679-89039-4*, Pub. by Random Bks Yng Read) Random.

Night Scary Beasties Popped Out of My Melon. Daniel Kamish & David Kamish. LC 97-31367. (J). 1998. lib. bdg. 15.99 (*0-679-99039-9*, Pub. by Random Bks Yng Read) Random.

Night Scene: The Garden. Meena Alexander. 32p. 1992. pap. 3.00 (*0-87376-074-3*) Red Dust.

Night Scented Air. large type ed. D. Y. Cameron. 1990. pap. 16.99 (*0-7089-6915-1*, Linford) Ulverscroft.

Night-Scented Stock in Bloom? Martha Robertson. (C). 1989. pap. text 49.00 (*1-85821-035-6*, Pub. by Pentland Pr) St Mut.

Night Scents. Carla Neggers. 1997. per. 5.99 (*0-671-56769-1*) PB.

Night School. Caroline Cooney. LC 95-235817. 176p. (YA). (gr. 7-9). 1995. pap. 3.50 (*0-590-47878-8*) Scholastic Inc.

Night School. Caroline B. Cooney. 1995. 8.60 (*0-606-07950-5*, Pub. by Turtleback) Demco.

***Night School.** Loris Lesynski. (Illus.). 32p. 2000. 15.95 (*1-55037-585-7*, Pub. by Annick Pr); pap. 5.95 (*1-55037-584-9*, Pub. by Annick Pr) Firefly Bks Ltd.

Night Screams. Alan S. Kessler. 49p. (Orig.). 1986. pap. 3.95 (*0-9616206-0-9*) Blk Pumpkin Pr.

Night Screams. Daniel Ransom. 176p. (Orig.). (J). 1996. pap. 3.99 (*0-380-72561-4*, Avon Bks) Morrow Avon.

Night Screams: Twenty-Two New Stories of Horror. Ed. by Ed Gorman & Martin H. Greenberg. 352p. 1996. pap., mass mkt. 6.99 (*0-451-45512-6*, ROC) NAL.

Night, Sea & Stars. Heather Graham. LC 96-42510. (Star-Romance Ser.). 320p. 1997. 23.95 (*0-7862-0906-2*) Five Star.

Night, Sea & Stars. Heather Graham. 352p. 1996. mass mkt. 5.99 (*0-8217-5325-8*, Zebra Kensgtn) Kensgtn Pub Corp.

***Night Sea & Stars.** Heather Graham. 2000. mass mkt. 6.99 (*0-8217-6983-9*, Knsington) Kensgtn Pub Corp.

Night, Sea & Stars. large type ed. Heather Graham. LC 96-3208. 1996. pap. 22.95 (*1-56895-374-7*, Compass) Wheeler Pub.

***Night-Sea Journey.** Michael Alpert. 381p. 2000. pap. 14.95 (*0-913006-72-6*) Puckerbrush.

Night Sea Journey. Rahul Ranchan. vii, 46p. 1989. text 12.50 (*81-220-0157-2*, Pub. by Konark Pubs Pvt Ltd) Advent Bks Div.

Night Sea Sky. Laurie S. Robertson. Ed. by Kathleen Iddings. (Illus.). 29p. (Orig.). 1988. pap. text 6.00 (*0-931721-09-1*) La Jolla Poets.

Night Search. large type ed. Kate Chamberlin. LC 96-39005. (Turtle Bks.). (Illus.). 32p. (J). (gr. k-3). 1997. pap. 8.95 (*0-944727-31-X*); lib. bdg. 14.95 (*0-944727-32-8*) Jason & Nordic Pubs.

Night Search, Print & Braille Ed. braille large type ed. Kate Chamberlin. (Turtle Bks.). (Illus.). 32p. (J). (gr. k-3). 1997. lib. bdg. 24.95 (*0-944727-33-6*) Jason & Nordic Pubs.

Night Season. Paul Bowdring. LC 98-152315. 256p. 1997. pap. 12.95 (*1-895387-89-2*) Creative Bk Pub.

Night Seasons. Horton Foote. 1996. pap. 5.25 (*0-8222-1482-2*) Dramatists Play.

Night Secrets. Thomas H. Cook. 1991. mass mkt. 5.99 (*0-446-36177-1*, Pub. by Warner Bks) Little.

***Night Secrets.** Doris Johnson. 1999. mass mkt. 5.99 (*1-58314-091-3*) BET Bks.

Night Secrets. Doris Johnson. (Arabesque Ser.). 288p. 1998. mass mkt. 4.99 (*0-7860-0475-4*, Pinncle Kensgtn) Kensgtn Pub Corp.

***Night Secrets.** Kat Martin. 368p. 1999. mass mkt. 6.99 (*0-312-97002-1*) St Martin.

***Night Shade: Gothic Tales by Women.** Ed. by Victoria A. Brownworth & Judith M. Redding. LC 99-13306. 288p. 1999. pap. 14.95 (*1-58005-024-7*) Seal Pr WA.

Night Shadow. Catherine Coulter. 400p. 1989. mass mkt. 6.99 (*0-380-75621-8*, Avon Bks) Morrow Avon.

Night Shadow. large type ed. Catherine Coulter. LC 97-34584. (Large Print Bks.). 1997. 24.95 (*1-56895-499-9*) Wheeler Pub.

Night Shadow. large type ed. Nora Roberts. 329p. 1991. reprint ed. lib. bdg. 19.95 (*1-56054-175-X*) Thorndike Pr.

Night Shadows. Ron Ely. 1996. per. 5.50 (*0-373-26218-3*, 1-26218-7, Wrldwide Lib) Harlequin Bks.

Night Shadows. Ron Ely. LC 93-30415. 1994. 20.00 (*0-671-87280-X*) S&S Trade.

Night Shadows. Shirley K. Gilfert. Ed. by Linda J. Dageforde. LC 97-68325. (Illus.). 200p. (Orig.). 1997. pap. 10.95 (*1-886225-25-7*, 500) Dageforde Pub.

***Night She Died.** Dorothy Simpson. (Missing Mysteries Ser.: Vol. 4). 206p. 1998. reprint ed. pap. 8.95 (*1-890208-06-X*) Poisoned Pen.

***Night Shield.** Nora Roberts. (Intimate Moments Ser.: Vol. 1027). 2000. mass mkt. 4.50 (*0-373-27097-6*, 1-27097-4) Silhouette.

Night Shift. Maria Gitin. LC 77-21969. (Orig.). 1978. pap. 9.95 (*0-912652-37-3*) Blue Wind.

Night Shift. Carl Hanni. 76p. (Orig.). 1996. pap. 7.95 (*1-882550-22-6*) Quiet Lion Pr.

Night Shift. Stephen King. LC 77-75146. 368p. 1993. 30.00 (*0-385-12991-2*) Doubleday.

Night Shift. Stephen King. 352p. 1979. mass mkt. 7.99 (*0-451-17011-3*, Sig) NAL.

Night Shift. Stephen King. 1979. 12.09 (*0-606-02411-5*, Pub. by Turtleback) Demco.

Night Shift. large type ed. Stephen King. LC 93-38623. 541p. 1994. lib. bdg. 23.95 (*0-8161-5687-5*, G K Hall Lrg Type) Mac Lib Ref.

Night Shift: New Poems. Valerie Sinason. 109p. 1995. pap. 12.50 (*1-85575-113-5*, Pub. by H Karnac Bks Ltd) Other Pr LLC.

Night Shift in a Pickle Factory. Steve Turner. (Little Bks.). 61p. 1980. pap. 2.25 (*0-917300-13-0*) Singlejack Bks.

Night Shots. Alex Larg. (Pro-Lighting Ser.). (Illus.). 160p. 1997. pap. 35.00 (*2-88046-324-6*, Rotovision) Watsn-Guptill.

***Night Show.** R. Laymon. 1998. mass mkt. 13.95 (*0-7472-4782-X*, Pub. by Headline Bk Pub) Trafalgar.

Night-Side: Chronic Fatigue Syndrome & the Illness Experience. Floyd Skloot. LC 96-8218. 224p. (Orig.). 1996. pap. 12.00 (*1-885266-31-6*) Story Line.

Night Side of Dickens: Cannibalism, Passion, Necessity. Harry Stone. LC 92-26043. (Victorian Life & Literature Ser.). (Illus.). 726p. 1994. text 75.00 (*0-8142-0547-X*) Ohio St U Pr.

Night-Side of Nature. Catherine Crowe. 1988. pap. 14.95 (*0-85030-519-5*, Pub. by Aqrn Pr) HarpC.

Night Siege: The Hudson Valley UFO Sightings. 2nd expanded rev. ed. J. Allen Hyneck et al. LC 98-10769. (Illus.). 288p. 1999. pap. 9.95 (*1-56718-362-X*) Llewellyn Pubns.

Night Signals. 1989. 6.00 (*0-87259-428-9*) Am Radio.

Night Sins. Tami Hoag. LC 94-23910. 576p. 1995. mass mkt. 7.50 (*0-553-56451-X*, Fanfare) Bantam.

Night Skies. Diane Webber & Linda Hall. LC 91-91632. (Illus.). 61p. 1991. pap. 4.95 (*1-55105-007-2*) Lone Pine.

Night Sky. DK Publishing Staff. LC 93-644. (Eyewitness Explorers Ser.). 64p. (J). (gr. k-3). 1997. pap. 5.95 (*0-7894-2214-X*) DK Pub Inc.

Night Sky. Harper Collins Staff. 1985. pap. 8.00 (*0-00-458817-7*) Collins.

Night Sky. N. Henbest. (Spotter's Guides Ser.). (Illus.). 64p. (YA). (gr. 4-7). 1993. pap. 4.95 (*0-86020-284-4*) EDC.

Night Sky. Nigel Henbest. (Spotter's Guide Ser.). (Illus.). 64p. (YA). (gr. 8-12). 1992. lib. bdg. 12.95 (*0-88110-987-8*, Usborne) EDC.

Night Sky. James Kavanagh. (Pocket Naturalist Ser.). (Illus.). 1997. 5.95 (*1-889903-06-X*, Pub. by Waterford WA) Falcon Pub Inc.

***Night Sky.** Gary Mechler. LC 98-51876. (National Audubon Society First Field Guides Ser.). (Illus.). 160p. (YA). (gr. 3-7). 1999. 17.95 (*0-590-64085-2*, Pub. by Scholastic Inc); vinyl bd. 11.95 (*0-590-64086-0*, Pub. by Scholastic Inc) Penguin Putnam.

Night Sky. Mary Morris. LC 97-799. 288p. 1997. pap. 13.00 (*0-312-15609-X*) St Martin.

***Night Sky.** Scholastic, Inc. Staff. (Super Science Readers Ser.). (Illus.). 16p. 2000. pap. text 10.95 (*0-439-18618-8*) Scholastic Inc.

Night Sky. Donald M. Silver. (One Small Square Ser.). (Illus.). 48p. (J). (gr. 1-4). 1998. pap. 7.95 (*0-07-058045-6*) McGraw.

***Night Sky: An Explore Your World Handbook.** Contrib. by Robert Burnham. LC 99-35934. (Illus.). 192p. 1999. pap. 13.95 (*1-56331-801-6*) Discovery.

Night Sky: An Interactive Journey Throughout the Night Sky. Carole Stott. (DK Action Packs Ser.). (Illus.). 16p. (J). (gr. 3-7). 1994. boxed set 19.95 (*1-56458-685-5*) DK Pub Inc.

Night Sky: An Observer's Guide. George R. Kepple. 1998. pap. 34.95 (*0-943396-59-X*) Willmann-Bell.

***Night Sky: An Observer's Guide.** George R. Kepple. 1998. 34.95 (*0-943396-58-1*) Willmann-Bell.

Night Sky: The Science & Anthropology of the Stars & Planets. 2nd ed. Richard Grossinger. LC 88-13974. 512p. 1992. reprint ed. pap. 12.95 (*1-55643-142-2*) North Atlantic.

Night Sky Book. Jamie Jobb. (Brown Paper School Bks.). 127p. (YA). (gr. 5 up). 1977. pap. 12.95 (*0-316-46552-6*) Little.

Night Sky Book: An Everyday Guide to Every Night. Jamie Jobb. (Brown Paper School Bks.). (J). 1977. 18.05 (*0-606-04020-X*, Pub. by Turtleback) Demco.

***Night Sky Book: An Everyday Guide to Every Night.** Jamie Jobb. (Illus.). 127p. (YA). (gr. 7-10). 1999. reprint ed. pap. text 10.00 (*0-7881-6695-6*) DIANE Pub.

Night Sky Guide. Sky & Telescope Magazine. 19.95 (*1-893770-01-X*) S Lewers.

Night Sky Mine. Melissa Scott. 384p. 1997. pap. 14.95 (*0-312-86156-7*) St Martin.

***Night Sky, Morning Star.** Evelina Zuni Lucero. LC 00-8119. (First Book Awards Ser.). 235p. 2000. pap. 16.95 (*0-8165-2055-0*) U of Ariz Pr.

Night Sky of the Southwest. Dan Heim. (Easy Field Guide Ser.). (Illus.). 32p. (J). 1997. pap. 1.50 (*0-935810-62-5*) R H Pub.

Night Slayer. John Ilich. 200p. 1983. pap. 5.95 (*0-935650-04-0*) Bengal Pr.

Night Smoke. Nora Roberts. 1994. per. 3.50 (*0-373-07595-2*, 1-07595-1) Harlequin Bks.

Night Smoke, Vol. 595. Nora Roberts. (Intimate Moments Ser.). 1998. 21.95 (*0-373-59929-3*) Silhouette.

Night Song. Beverly Jenkins. 384p. (Orig.). 1994. mass mkt. 5.99 (*0-380-77658-8*, Avon Bks) Morrow Avon.

Night Song. Andres Rodriquez. 78p. (Orig.). 1994. pap. 7.95 (*1-882688-05-8*) Tia Chucha Pr.

Night Song of the Personal Shadow: Selected Poems. Gyorgy Petri. Tr. by C. Wilmer & G. Gomori from HUN. 80p. (Orig.). 1991. pap. 14.95 (*1-85224-107-1*, Pub. by Bloodaxe Bks) Dufour.

Night Songs. Anne Miranda. LC 92-251. (Illus.). 32p. (J). (ps-1). 1993. lib. bdg. 13.95 (*0-02-767250-6*, Bradbury S&S) S&S Childrens.

Night Sounds see Sonidos de la Noche (Night Sounds)

Night Sounds. Lois G. Grambling. LC 95-71536. (Illus.). 40p. (J). (ps-6). 1996. 12.95 (*1-877810-77-0*, NSH); pap. 6.95 (*1-877810-83-5*, NSP) Rayve Prodns.

Night Sounds. Warner Lee. Ed. by Eric Tobias. 288p. (Orig.). 1992. mass mkt. 4.99 (*0-671-70426-5*) PB.

Night Speaks. Steven Forrest. 192p. (Orig.). 1992. pap. 12.95 (*0-935127-25-9*) ACS Pubns.

Night Spell. David Yanoff. LC 89-388. 1991. pap. 13.95 (*0-87949-293-7*) Ashley Bks.

Night Squawker. Dahlia Kosinski. (Bone Chillers Ser.). 1997. 9.09 (*0-606-11154-9*, Pub. by Turtleback) Demco.

Night Squawker, The (BC 19) Betsy Haynes. (Bone Chillers Ser.). 128p. (J). (gr. 4-8). 1997. mass mkt. 3.99 (*0-06-106451-3*) HarperTrade.

Night Stalker. Philip Carlo. LC 97-208386. 576p. 1997. mass mkt. 5.99 (*0-7860-0379-0*, Pinncle Kensgtn) Kensgtn Pub Corp.

***Night Stalker.** Philip Carlo. 2000. mass mkt. 6.50 (*0-7860-1362-1*, Pinncle Kensgtn) Kensgtn Pub Corp.

Night Stalker. Carol D. Luce. 1990. mass mkt. 4.99 (*0-8217-4245-0*, Zebra Kensgtn) Kensgtn Pub Corp.

Night Stalker. large type ed. Tex Larrigan. (Linford Western Large Print Ser.). 224p. 1998. pap. 17.99 (*0-7089-5277-1*, Linford) Ulverscroft.

Night Stalker: The Life & Crimes of Richard Ramirez. Philip Carlo. 1996. 16.95 incl. audio (*1-882071-83-2*, 634043) B&B Audio.

Night Stalker: The True Story of America's Most Feared Serial Killer. Phillip Carlo. LC 96-75279. 432p. 1996. pap. 22.95 (*1-57566-030-X*) Kensgtn Pub Corp.

Night Stalking: A Twentieth Century Anniversary Kolchak Companion. Mark Dawidziak. (Illus.). 160p. (Orig.). 1991. pap. 14.95 (*0-685-50339-9*) Retro Vision.

Night Stick. Lewis Valentine. (American Autobiography Ser.). 320p. 1995. reprint ed. lib. bdg. 89.00 (*0-7812-8655-7*) Rprt Serv.

Night Stick Justice. Henry Hardee. 45p. 1991. pap. 10.00 (*1-884978-16-9*) Black Boys Dream.

Night Stone. Rick Hautala. 624p. 1986. mass mkt. 3.95 (*0-8217-1843-6*, Zebra Kensgtn) Kensgtn Pub Corp.

Night Storm. Catherine Coulter. 400p. 1990. mass mkt. 6.99 (*0-380-75623-4*, Avon Bks) Morrow Avon.

Night Storm. large type ed. Catherine Coulter. LC 98-6712. 1998. 25.95 (*1-56895-558-8*, Wheeler) Wheeler Pub.

Night Story. Nancy Willard. LC 85-17677. (Illus.). 32p. (J). (ps-2). 1986. 13.95 (*0-15-257348-8*, Harcourt Child Bks) Harcourt.

Night Story. Nancy Willard. LC 85-17677. (Illus.). 32p. (J). (ps-2). 1994. pap. 4.95 (*0-15-200075-5*, Harcourt Child Bks) Harcourt.

Night Strike. Gregory G. Vanhee. 384p. (Orig.). 1990. pap. 3.95 (*0-380-75868-7*, Avon Bks) Morrow Avon.

Night Striker. Amii Lorin, pseud. 288p. 1991. reprint ed. pap. text, mass mkt. 3.99 (*0-8439-3187-6*) Dorchester Pub Co.

Night Studies: A Novelistic Investigation of Race Relations in America. Cyrus Colter. LC 97-16024. 1997. pap. text 19.95 (*0-8101-5065-4*, TriQuart) Northwestern U Pr.

Night Studio: A Memoir of Philip Guston. Musa Mayer. LC 96-43818. (Illus.). 320p. 1997. pap. 17.95 (*0-306-80767-X*) Da Capo.

Night Summons. Anita Gentry. (WWL Mystery Ser.). 1998. per. 4.99 (*0-373-26276-0*, 1-26276-5, Wrldwide Lib) Harlequin Bks.

Night Sun: An Initiation Trilogy, 3 vols., Set. Thomas R. Crowe. LC 93-92604. 250p. (Orig.). 1993. boxed set 24.95 (*1-883197-00-7*) New Native Pr.

Night Sun, Our Wounds, Prometheus in Evin, Poems, & Leave to Remain. Iraj J. Ataie & Rob Ritchie. (Methuen New Theatrescripts Ser.). 179p. (Orig.). (C). 1989. pap. write for info. (*0-413-62250-9*, A0395, Methuen Drama) Methn.

Night Surfing. Fiona Capp. 213p. (Orig.). 1997. pap. 12.95 (*1-86373-913-0*, Pub. by Allen & Unwin Pty) IPG Chicago.

***Night Swimmer - A Man in London: A Collection of 19 Short Stories.** Lowell B. Komie. 1999. pap. 14.95 (*0-9641957-2-0*) Swordfish-Chicago.

Night Swimmers. Betsy C. Byars. (J). 1980. 9.09 (*0-606-03873-6*, Pub. by Turtleback) Demco.

Night Swimmers. Betsy C. Byars. (Illus.). 144p. (J). (gr. 5-9). 1983. pap. 4.50 (*0-440-45857-9*, YB BDD) BDD Bks Young Read.

Night Swimming. Pete Fromm. LC 99-22213. 192p. 1999. text 23.00 (*0-312-20936-3*, Picador USA) St Martin.

***Night Swimming: Stories.** Pete Fromm. 192p. 2000. pap. 12.00 (*0-312-26363-5*, Picador USA) St Martin.

Night Symbols: 11,000 Dreams Interpreted. R. M. Soccolich. Ed. by Sam Chekwas. 344p. 1998. pap. 12.95 (*1-885778-36-8*) Seaburn.

***Night Tales: Night Shift; Night Shadow; Nightshade; Night Smoke, 4 bks. in 1.** Nora Roberts. (Silhouette Promo Ser.). 768p. 2000. pap. 14.95 (*0-373-48410-0*, 1-48410-4) Harlequin Bks.

Night Tales from Long Ago. Michael J. Katz. LC 92-40322. 568p. 1993. 50.00 (*0-87668-590-4*) Aronson.

Night Tales Remembered: Fables from the Shammas. Michael J. Katz. LC 90-167. 568p. 1990. 50.00 (*0-87668-816-4*) Aronson.

Night Talk. Elizabeth Cox. LC 97-71190. 267p. 1997. 23.95 (*1-55597-267-5*) Graywolf.

Night Talk. Elizabeth Cox. LC 98-36888. 272p. 1998. pap. 13.95 (*0-312-19516-8*) St Martin.

Night Talk & Other Poems. Richard Pevear. LC 77-2533. (Princeton Series of Contemporary Poets). 73p. reprint ed. pap. 30.00 (*0-8357-2778-5*, 203990400014) Bks Demand.

Night Terrors. Nicole Davidson. 192p. (Orig.). (YA). 1994. mass mkt. 3.99 (*0-380-72243-7*, Avon Bks) Morrow Avon.

Night Terrors. Lois Duncan. (J). 1997. per. 3.99 (*0-689-80724-4*) S&S Childrens.

Night Terrors. Jim Murphy. LC 92-27102. 192p. (J). (gr. 7-9). 1993. 13.95 (*0-590-45341-6*) Scholastic Inc.

Night Terrors. Jim Murphy. 192p. (YA). (gr. 7-9). 1994. pap. 3.50 (*0-590-45342-4*) Scholastic Inc.

Night Terrors. Jim Murphy. 1993. 8.60 (*0-606-07058-3*, Pub. by Turtleback) Demco.

Night Terrors: Stories of Shadow & Substance. Ed. by Lois Duncan. LC 95-44901. 176p. (YA). (gr. 7 up). 1996. per. 16.00 (*0-689-80346-X*) S&S Bks Yung.

Night Terrors: Stories of Shadow & Substance. Lois Duncan. 1997. 9.09 (*0-606-13662-2*, Pub. by Turtleback) Demco.

Night the Angels Sang. (Little Treasures Ser.). (Illus.). 88p. 1994. 4.99 (*1-57051-023-7*) Brownlow Pub Co.

Night the Angels Sang: Luke 2: 8-20. Concordia Staff. 24p. (J). (ps-3). 1973. pap. 1.99 (*0-570-06095-8*, 59-1213) Concordia.

Night the Animals Talked. Patricia B. Rumble. 36p. (YA). 1992. pap. 3.00 (*1-57514-179-5*, 1105) Encore Perform Pub.

Night the Baby-Sitter Didn't Come. Beverly Keller. 144p. (J). (gr. 4-7). 1994. pap. 3.25 (*0-590-43726-7*) Scholastic Inc.

Night the Bear Ate Goombaw. Patrick F. McManus. 88p. 1995. 19.95 (*0-8050-1033-5*); pap. 7.95 (*0-8050-1340-7*, Owl) H Holt & Co.

Night the Bear Ate Goombaw. large type ed. Patrick F. McManus. (General Ser.). 253p. 1990. lib. bdg. 18.95 (*0-8161-4889-9*, G K Hall Lrg Type) Mac Lib Ref.

***Night the Bells Rang.** Natalie Kinsey-Warnock. (Illus.). 80p. (gr. 2-5). 2000. pap. 3.99 (*0-14-130986-5*, PuffinBks) Peng Put Young Read.

Night the Dog Smiled. John Newlove. 80p. (C). 1986. 18.00 (*0-920763-33-2*, Pub. by ECW); pap. 9.00 (*0-920763-31-6*, Pub. by ECW) Genl Dist Srvs.

***Night the Fitz Went Down.** Hugh E. Bishop. LC 00-30459. 2000. pap. write for info. (*0-942235-37-1*) LSPC Inc.

Night the Grandfathers Danced. Linda T. Raczek. (Illus.). 32p. (J). (gr. k-3). 1998. pap. 7.95 (*0-87358-720-0*, Rising Moon Bks) Northland AZ.

Night the Heads Came. Puffin Books Staff. (Illus.). 160p. (J). 1998. pap. 4.99 (*0-14-038441-3*, PuffinBks) Peng Put Young Read.

Night the Heads Came. William Sleator. LC 95-32321. 160p. (J). (gr. 5 up). 1996. 16.99 (*0-525-45463-2*, Dutton Child) Peng Put Young Read.

Night the Heads Came. William Sleator. 1998. 10.09 (*0-606-13663-0*, Pub. by Turtleback) Demco.

Night the Lights Went Out see All Day & Night Set

Night the Mice Danced the Quadrille: Five Years in the Backwoods, 1875-1879. Thomas Osborne. LC 95-190486. (Illus.). 192p. 1995. pap. 15.95 (*1-55046-135-4*, Pub. by Boston Mills) Genl Dist Srvs.

Night the Moon Blew Kisses. Lynn Manuel. LC 95-24391. (Illus.). 32p. (J). (ps-3). 1996. 14.95 (*0-395-73979-9*) HM.

***Night the Moon Fell.** Pat Mora. (Illus.). 32p. (ps-k). 2000. 16.95 (*0-88899-398-6*) Grndwd Bks.

Night the Moon Fell. Jane Norman & Frank Beazley. 24p. (J). (ps-3). 1993. pap. write for info. (*1-883585-06-6*) Pixanne Ent.

***Night the Moon Slept.** Susan K. Baggette. LC 99-76580. (Illus.). 32p. (J). (ps-3). 2000. 16.95 (*0-9660172-8-5*, Pub. by Brookfield Read) Book Wholesalers.

Night the New Jesus Fell to Earth & Other Stories from Cliffside, North Carolina. Ron Rash. LC 94-18350. 1994. pap. 14.95 (*0-930769-11-2*) Bench Pr SC.

Night the Stars Danced for Joy A Story for Christmas. Bob Hartman. (ps-3). 1999. 5.99 (*0-7459-4086-2*) Lion USA.

Night the War Was Lost. Charles L. Dufour. LC 93-47281. (Illus.). iv, 443p. (C). 1994. pap. 14.95 (*0-8032-6599-9*, Bison Books) U of Nebr Pr.

Night the Water Came. Clive King. LC 81-43318. 160p. (J). (gr. 5-7). 1982. lib. bdg. 9.89 (*0-690-04163-2*) HarpC Child Bks.

Night the White Deer Died. Gary Paulsen. 112p. (YA). 1991. mass mkt. 3.99 (*0-440-21092-5*, YB BDD) BDD Bks Young Read.

Night the Whole Class Slept Over. Stella Peusner. Ed. by Patricia McDonald. 176p. (J). (gr. 3-6). 1992. reprint ed. pap. 3.50 (*0-671-78157-X*, Minstrel Bks) PB.

Night There Was Thunder & Stuff. Cynthia. (Illus.). 32p. (J). Date not set. pap. 4.95 (*1-895562-67-8*, Pub. by Wood Lake Bks) Logos Prods.

Night They Burned the Mountain. Tom Dooley. 1993. reprint ed. lib. bdg. 21.95 (*1-56849-119-0*) Buccaneer Bks.

Night They Raided Minsky's. Rowland Barber. 23.95 (*0-88411-097-4*) Amereon Ltd.

Night They Stole the Stanley Cup see Screech Owls Series Boxed Set: Mystery at Lake Placid; The Night They Stole the Stanley Cup; The Screech Owls' Northern Adventure

Night Thief. Valerie Allen. LC 89-28459. (Illus.). 32p. (J). (ps-3). 1990. 14.95 (*0-88289-774-8*) Pelican.

Night Things. Michael Talbot. 256p. (Orig.). 1989. pap. 3.95 (*0-380-70897-3*, Avon Bks) Morrow Avon.

Night Thoreau Spent in Jail. Jerome Lawrence. 1982. 11.09 (*0-606-12451-9*, Pub. by Turtleback) Demco.

Night Thoreau Spent in Jail. Jerome Lawrence & Robert E. Lee. 128p. (YA). (gr. 8-12). 1982. mass mkt. 5.99 (*0-553-27838-X*) Bantam.

Night Thoreau Spent in Jail: Curriculum Unit. Center for Learning Network Staff et al. (Novel Ser.). 72p. (YA). (gr. 9-12). 1990. spiral bd. 18.95 (*1-56077-371-5*) Ctr Learning.

N

An Asterisk (*) at the beginning of an entry indicates that the title is appearing for the first time.

Night Thoughts: Reflections of a Sex Therapist. rev. ed. Avodah K. Offit. LC 94-45758. 256p. 1995. pap. 25.00 (*1-56821-458-8*) Aronson.

Night Thoughts & Terminal: Two Short Plays. Corinne Jacker. 1977. pap. 5.25 (*0-8222-0825-3*) Dramatists Play.

Night Thoughts of a Classical Physicist. Russell K. McCormmach. LC 81-6674. (Illus.). 29.95p. 1982. 31.00 (*0-674-62460-2*) HUP.

Night Thoughts of a Classical Physicist. Russell K. McCormmach. (Illus.). 232p. 1991. pap. text 14.50 (*0-674-62461-0*, MCCNIX) HUP.

Night Thoughts: or The Complaint & the Consolation. William Blake. Ed. by Robert Essick & Jenijoy LaBelle. LC 96-12356. Orig. Title: The Complaint, & The Consolation. (Illus.). 128p. 1996. reprint ed. pap. text 8.95 (*0-486-29214-2*) Dover.

Night-Threads: The Calling of the Three. Ru Emerson. 1990. pap. 4.50 (*0-441-58085-8*) Ace Bks.

Night Threads: The Craft of Light. Ru Emerson. 288p. (Orig.). 1993. mass mkt. 4.99 (*0-441-58088-2*) Ace Bks.

Night Threads No. 2: Two in Hiding. Ru Emerson. 1991. mass mkt. 4.99 (*0-441-58086-6*) Ace Bks.

Night Threads No. 3: One Land, One Duke. Ru Emerson. 1992. mass mkt. 4.99 (*0-441-58087-4*) Ace Bks.

Night Threads No. 6: The Science of Power. Ru Emerson. (Orig.). 1995. pap. text 5.99 (*0-441-00286-2*) Ace Bks.

***Night Thunder.** Ruby J. Jensen. 2000. mass mkt. 5.99 (*0-7860-1238-2*, Pinncle Kensgtn) Kensgtn Pub Corp.

Night Thunder. Ruby-Jean Jensen. 1995. pap. 4.50 (*0-8217-5005-4*) NAL.

Night Thunder & the Queen of the Wild Horses. Lynn W. Reiser. LC 93-25734. (Illus.). 32p. (J). (ps-3). 1995. 15.00 (*0-688-11791-0*, Grenwillow Bks) HarpC Child Bks.

Night Thunder's Bride. Karen Kay. 384p. 1999. mass mkt. 5.99 (*0-380-80339-9*, Avon Bks) Morrow Avon.

Night Time. Eileen Pettigrew. (Illus.). 24p. (J). (ps-1). 1992. pap. 4.95 (*1-55037-242-4*, Pub. by Annick); lib. bdg. 14.95 (*1-55037-235-1*, Pub. by Annick) Firefly Bks Ltd.

Night Time Animals. Rayston Angela Kindersley. LC 92-12294. (Eye Openers Ser.). (Illus.). 24p. (J). (ps-k). 1992. pap. 7.95 (*0-689-71646-X*) Aladdin.

Night Time Mystery. Mouse Works Staff. (Illus.). 10p. (J). (ps-k). 1994. bds. write for info. (*1-57082-968-3*) Mouse Works.

Night-Time Numbers: A Scary Counting Book. Susan L. Roth. 32p. (J). (ps-1). 1999. 15.95 (*1-84148-001-0*) Barefoot Bks NY.

Night Time Twinkles. Nadine B. Lammers. 20p. (J). (gr. k-5). 1994. pap. 4.95 (*0-9642971-0-8*) N B Lammers.

Night to Day. David S. Tanner. 22p. 1993. pap. 2.45 (*0-9639385-0-9*) D H C.

Night to Remember. Ellen Conford et al. 160p. (Orig.). (YA). (gr. 7 up). 1995. mass mkt. 3.99 (*0-380-78038-0*, Avon Bks) Morrow Avon.

Night to Remember. Walter Lord. 1987. 23.95 (*0-8488-0065-6*) Amereon Ltd.

Night to Remember. Walter Lord. 224p. 1997. mass mkt. 6.50 (*0-553-27827-4*) Bantam.

Night to Remember. Walter Lord. (Henry Holt Classics Library). 224p. 1995. 30.00 (*0-8050-1733-X*) H Holt & Co.

Night to Remember. Walter Lord. 1991. 11.09 (*0-606-01137-4*, Pub. by Turtleback) Demco.

Night to Remember. Niqui Stanhope. (Arabesque Ser.). 256p. 1998. mass mkt. 4.99 (*0-7860-0477-0*, Pinncle Kensgtn) Kensgtn Pub Corp.

Night to Remember. Gina F. Wilkins. 1997. per. 3.50 (*0-373-25720-1*, 1-25720-3) Silhouette.

Night to Remember. Kate William. (Sweet Valley High Magna Edition Ser.). (YA). (gr. 7 up). 1993. 10.09 (*0-606-05640-8*, Pub. by Turtleback) Demco.

Night to Remember. large type ed. Walter Lord. 1976. 12.00 (*0-85456-444-6*) Ulverscroft.

Night to Remember. large type ed. Walter Lord. (Niagara Large Print Ser.). 240p. 1997. 29.50 (*0-7089-5874-5*) Ulverscroft.

Night to Remember. Walter Lord. 300p. 1991. reprint ed. 25.95 (*0-89966-794-5*) Buccaneer Bks.

Night to Remember & Streams to the river, River to the Sea: Curriculum Unit. Center for Learning Network Staff et al. (Novel Ser.). 91p. (YA). (gr. 4-12). 1995. spiral bd. 18.95 (*1-56077-318-9*) Ctr Learning.

Night Tokyo Burned. Hoito Edoin. 1989. mass mkt. 4.95 (*0-312-91385-0*) St Martin.

Night Touch. Stephen Gresham. 1988. mass mkt. 3.95 (*0-8217-2552-1*, Zebra Kensgtn) Kensgtn Pub Corp.

Night Train. Martin Amis. LC 97-28163. 175p. 1998. 20.00 (*0-609-60128-8*) Harmony Bks.

Night Train. Martin Amis. 175p. 1999. pap. 11.00 (*0-375-70114-1*) Vintage Am.

***Night Train.** Judith Clarke. LC 99-27966. 176p. (J). 2000. 16.95 (*0-8050-6151-7*) H Holt & Co.

Night Train. Friederike Mayrocker. Tr. & Afterword by Beth Bjorklund. (Studies in Austrian Literature, Culture, & Thought. Translation Ser.). 126p. 1992. 17.00 (*0-929497-53-8*) Ariadne CA.

Night Train. W. Loran Smith. LC 96-69876. 80p. 1997. 24.00 (*1-887628-00-2*); pap. 12.00 (*1-887628-01-0*) Plinth Bks.

Night Train. Caroline Stutson. LC 98-44865. 1999. write for info. (*0-7894-2518-1*) DK Pub Inc.

Night Train. large type ed. Martin Amis. LC 98-7829. 1998. 25.95 (*1-56895-570-7*, Compass) Wheeler Pub.

***Night Train: Little Lionel Book about Opposites.** Catherine Lukas. (Night Train : No. 4). (Illus.). 48p. (J). (gr. k-3). 2000. bds. 4.99 (*0-689-83366-0*) Litle Simon.

Night Train & Other Stories. Sathya Saran. (C). 1996. pap. 18.00 (*81-241-0389-5*, Pub. by Har-Anand Pubns) S Asia.

Night Train & the Golden Bird. Peter Meinke. LC 76-43966. (Pitt Poetry Ser.). 79p. reprint ed. pap. 30.00 (*0-608-16768-1*, 202631600049) Bks Demand.

Night Train at Wiscasset Station. Lew Dietz. LC 97-36446. (Illus.). 192p. 1998. reprint ed. pap. 21.95 (*0-89272-430-7*) Down East.

Night Train Blues. Edward Hower. LC 95-19559. 208p. 1996. 22.00 (*1-877946-71-0*) Permanent Pr.

Night Train Through the Brenner. Harry Clifton. LC 94-151864. 70p. 1994. pap. 12.95 (*1-85235-122-5*) Dufour.

Night Train to Memphis. Elizabeth Peters, pseud. 368p. 1995. mass mkt. 6.99 (*0-446-60248-5*, Pub. by Warner Bks) Little.

Night Train to Memphis. unabridged ed. Elizabeth Peters, pseud. (Vicky Bliss Mysteries Ser.). 1997. 28.95 incl. audio (*1-885608-26-8*) Airplay.

Night Train to Nykobing. Kristjana Gunnars. LC 99-211238. 128p. 1998. pap. 14.95 (*0-88995-187-X*, Pub. by Red Deer) Genl Dist Srvs.

Night Train to Turkistan: Modern Adventures along China's Ancient Silk Road. Stuart Stevens. LC 87-30019. (Travel Ser.). 256p. 1988. pap. 12.00 (*0-87113-190-0*, Atlntc Mnthly) Grove-Atltic.

Night Trains. Peter H. Fine. 1976. 21.95 (*0-8488-0864-9*) Amereon Ltd.

Night Trains: The Pullman System in the Golden Years of American Rail Travel. Peter T. Maiken. LC 92-12586. (Illus.). 416p. 1992. pap. 24.95 (*0-8018-4503-3*) Johns Hopkins.

Night Trains: The Pullman System in the Golden Years of American Rail Travel. Peter T. Maiken. (Illus.). 416p. (C). 1989. boxed set 49.95 (*0-9621480-0-8*) Lakme Pr.

Night Tree. Eve Bunting. LC 90-36178. (Illus.). 32p. (J). (ps-3). 1991. 13.95 (*0-15-257425-5*, Harcourt Child Bks) Harcourt.

Night Tree. Eve Bunting. LC 90-36178. (Illus.). 32p. (C). (ps-3). 1994. pap. 6.00 (*0-15-200121-2*) Harcourt.

Night Tree. Eve Bunting. 1994. 11.45 (*0-606-12452-7*) Turtleback.

Night Tribes. Christopher Golden & Tom Sniegoski. (Illus.). 48p. 1999. pap. 4.95 (*1-56389-553-6*, Pub. by DC Comics) Diamond Comic Distributors Inc.

Night Trilogy: Night; Dawn; The Accident. Elie Wiesel. 318p. 1987. pap. 11.00 (*0-374-52140-9*) FS&G.

Night Two Thousand Men Came to Dinner: And Other Appetizing Anecdotes. Douglas G. Meldrum. (Illus.). 160p. 1994. 16.95 (*0-02-583960-8*, Scribners Ref) Mac Lib Ref.

Night unto Night. Philip Wylie. 1994. lib. bdg. 21.95 (*1-56849-442-4*) Buccaneer Bks.

Night unto Night: The Night Scenes in the Bible. Christian Chen. (Illus.). 118p. 1997. pap. 12.00 (*0-9661121-0-5*) Liv Word.

Night Vision. Laura Adams. LC 97-10007. 256p. (Orig.). 1997. pap. 11.95 (*1-56280-182-1*) Naiad Pr.

Night Vision. Neal Bowers. LC 92-6036. 1993. pap. 8.00 (*0-933532-94-6*) BkMk.

Night Vision. King. 1989. mass mkt. write for info. (*0-8125-2071-8*) Tor Bks.

Night Vision. Paul Levine. 448p. 1992. mass mkt. 5.99 (*0-553-29762-7*) Bantam.

***Night Vision: A First to Third World Vampyre Opera.** Fred Ho & Ruth Margraff. 90p. 2000. pap. 20.00 (*1-57027-103-8*) Autonomedia.

Night Vision: Basic, Clinical & Applied Aspects. Ed. by R. F. Hess et al. (Illus.). 562p. (C). 1990. text 145.00 (*0-521-32736-9*) Cambridge U Pr.

Night-Vision: Illuminating War & Class on the Neo-Colonial Terrain. Butch Lee & Red Rover. 188p. (Orig.). 1993. pap. 14.95 (*1-883780-00-4*) Vagabond NY.

Night Vision: Praying Through Change. Anita M. Constance. LC 98-5152. 96p. 1998. pap. 11.95 (*0-8091-3783-6*) Paulist Pr.

Night Visions: Searching the Shadows of Advent & Christmas. Jan Richardson. LC 97-45177. 144p. (Orig.). 1998. 18.95 (*0-8298-1255-5*) Pilgrim OH.

Skin Trade: Night Visions V. Stephen King-Hall. 1990. mass mkt. 5.99 (*0-425-12003-1*) Berkley Pub.

***Night Visit.** large type ed. Priscilla Masters. LC 99-22225. 1999. pap. 19.95 (*0-7838-8653-5*, G K Hall & Co) Mac Lib Ref.

Night Visitor. B. Traven. reprint ed. lib. bdg. 22.95 (*0-89190-160-4*, Rivercity Pr) Amereon Ltd.

Night Visitor: A Shaman Mystery. James D. Doss. LC 99-25049. 400p. 1999. 23.00 (*0-380-97721-4*, Avon Bks) Morrow Avon.

***Night Visitor: A Shaman Mystery.** James D. Doss. 384p. 2000. mass mkt. 5.99 (*0-380-80393-3*, Avon Bks) Morrow Avon.

Night Visitor & Other Stories. Arnold Bennett. LC 74-17062. (Collected Works of Arnold Bennett: Vol, 59). 1977. reprint ed. 31.95 (*0-518-19140-0*) Ayer.

Night Visitor & Other Stories. B. Traven. LC 93-11240. 252p. 1993. reprint ed. pap. 14.95 (*1-56663-039-8*, Pub. by I R Dee) Natl Bk Netwk.

Night Visitors. Ed Young. LC 94-33355. (Illus.). 32p. (J). (ps-3). 1995. 15.95 (*0-399-22731-8*, Philomel) Peng Put Young Read.

Night Visits. Ron Butlin. 128p. 1990. pap. text 21.00 (*1-84017-000-X*) St Mut.

Night Visits to a Wolf's Howl. George Roberts. 1979. 12.50 (*0-933114-03-6*); pap. 3.50 (*0-933114-02-8*) Oyster Pr.

Night Voices. Compiled by Thomas L. Crain. (Illus.). 164p. 1991. pap. text 12.95 (*0-9627099-0-5*) Zephyr Pub Corp.

***Night Voices.** June Hubbard. 1998. pap. 13.95 (*1-892419-00-9*) Chameleon Publ.

Night Voyage. Eric Sellin. 1964. pap. 10.00 (*0-685-62612-1*) Atlantis Edns.

Night Voyager: A Reading of Celine. Philip H. Solomon. LC 88-62811. (ENG & FRE.). 238p. 1988. lib. bdg. 27.95 (*0-917786-66-1*) Summa Pubns.

Night Voyagers. unabridged ed. Donn Kushner. LC 96-136653. 242p. (YA). (gr. 7 up). 1997. 16.95 (*1-895555-69-8*) STDK.

Night Walk see Caminando por la Noche

Night Walk. Michael Kenna. LC 88-81567. (Untitled Ser.: No. 47). (Illus.). 60p. 1988. pap. 17.95 (*0-933286-51-1*) Frnds Photography.

Night Walk. Ann Kenny. (Books for Young Learners). (Illus.). 12p. (J). (gr. k-2). 1996. pap. text 5.00 (*1-57274-021-3*, A2478) R Owen Pubs.

Night Walk. Eddie Williams. 54p. (Orig.). 1993. pap. text 5.00 (*1-880994-05-4*) Mt Olive Coll Pr.

Night Walk: Selected Poems. Roo Borson. 92p. (C). 1994. pap. (*0-19-541082-3*) OUP.

Night Walker. Diane Hoh. (Nightmare Hall Ser.: No. 9). (YA). 1994. pap. 3.50 (*0-590-47688-2*) Scholastic Inc.

Night Walker. Sylvie Sommerfield. 400p. 1998. mass mkt. 5.99 (*0-8439-4359-9*, Leisure Bks) Dorchester Pub Co.

Night Walker. large type ed. Jean Hager. 335p. 1991. reprint ed. lib. bdg. 18.95 (*1-56054-114-8*) Thorndike Pr.

Night Walker. Jean Hager. 1991. reprint ed. mass mkt. 3.99 (*0-373-26085-7*) Harlequin Bks.

***Night Warriors: Darkstalkers' Revenge.** Run Ishida. (Night Warriors Ser.). (Illus.). 168p. 2000. pap. text 15.95 (*1-56931-428-4*, Pub. by Viz Commns Inc) Publishers Group.

Night Watch. Lucille Fletcher. 1972. pap. 5.25 (*0-8222-0826-1*) Dramatists Play.

***Night Watch.** Peter Scupham. 76p. 2000. pap. 18.95 (*0-85646-319-1*, Pub. by Anvil Press) Dufour.

Night Watch. Frida A. Sigurdardottir & Katjana Edwardsen. 168p. 1995. pap. 16.95 (*1-899197-20-6*) Dufour.

Night Watch. Sean Stewart. LC 96-6546. 384p. 1997. 21.95 (*0-441-00445-8*) Ace Bks.

Night Watch. Sean Stewart. 384p. 1997. 21.95 (*0-441-00448-2*) Ace Bks.

Night Watch. Sean Stewart. 338p. 1998. reprint ed. mass mkt. 6.50 (*0-441-00554-3*) Ace Bks.

Night Watch: Lovers & Legends. Carla Neggers. (Temptation Ser.). 1993. per. 2.99 (*0-373-25561-6*, 1-25561-1) Harlequin Bks.

Night Watch on the Chesapeake. Peter Meinke. LC 86-25040. (Poetry Ser.). 96p. 1987. pap. 10.95 (*0-8229-5390-0*) U of Pittsburgh Pr.

Night Watches. Gary Metras. 48p. 1981. pap. 10.00 (*0-938566-06-7*) Adastra Pr.

Night Watches. deluxe limited ed. Gary Metras. 48p. 1981. 25.00 (*0-938566-08-3*) Adastra Pr.

Night Watches: Inventions on the Life of Maria Mitchell. Carole S. Oles. LC 85-70621. 72p. 1985. 6.95 (*0-914086-56-1*); pap. 9.95 (*0-914086-57-X*) Alice James Bks.

Night Watchman. James Bernhard. 180p. 1997. pap. write for info. (*1-891239-00-7*) Primeval Pr.

Night We Buried Road Dog. Jack Cady. 204p. 1998. 27.00 (*1-892058-00-6*) Dreamhaven.

Night We Get Rich. large type ed. William Newton. 1990. pap. 16.99 (*0-7089-7000-1*, Linford) Ulverscroft.

Night We Stood up for Our Rights. Morty Sklar. LC 77-8539. 53p. (Orig.). 1977. pap. 8.00 (*0-915124-11-4*) Coffee Hse.

Night When Dreams Come True. Dale Terry. Ed. by J. Richards. LC 96-86394. 66p. (Orig.). 1996. pap. 7.95 (*1-887303-14-6*) Blu Lantern Pub.

***Night When Moon Follows.** Cheryl Boyce Taylor. 96p. 2000. pap. 12.00 (*0-9654738-4-8*) Lng Shot Prods.

Night Whisper. Patricia Wallace. 368p. 1987. mass mkt. 4.50 (*0-8217-2901-2*, Zebra Kensgtn) Kensgtn Pub Corp.

Night Whispers. Lynn Erickson. 1997. pap. 5.99 (*1-55166-178-0*, 1-66178-4, Mira Bks) Harlequin Bks.

Night Whispers. Leslie Kelly. (Temptation Ser.). 1999. per. 3.75 (*0-373-25847-X*, 1-25847-4) Harlequin Bks.

Night Whispers. Judith McNaught. LC 99-228998. 400p. 1998. 24.00 (*0-671-00085-3*) S&S Trade.

Night Whispers. Judith McNaught. 1998. mass mkt. write for info. (*0-671-02834-0*) S&S Trade.

***Night Whispers.** Judith McNaught. 451p. 1999. per. 7.99 (*0-671-52574-3*) S&S Trade.

***Night Whispers.** Judith McNaught. LC 99-19122. 1999. write for info. (*1-56895-647-9*) Wheeler Pub.

***Night Whispers, 1 vol.** Karen W. Sandler. 1999. mass mkt. 5.99 (*0-515-12584-9*, Jove) Berkley Pub.

***Night Whispers.** large type ed. Judith McNaught. 2000. pap. 11.95 (*1-56895-968-0*) Wheeler Pub.

Night Whispers: A Novel of Evil. Emmett Clifford. LC 98-6928. 448p. 1998. 22.95 (*1-888952-81-4*) Cumberland Hse.

Night Wind. Aimee Thurlo. (Intrigue Ser.: No. 175). 1991. pap. 2.79 (*0-373-22175-4*, 1-22175-3) Harlequin Bks.

***Night Wind Howls: The Complete Supernatural Stories.** Frederick Cowles. Ed. by Hugh Lamb. xx, 400p. 1999. 50.00 (*1-899562-66-4*) Ash-Tree.

***Night Winds.** Gwyneth Atlee. 2000. mass mkt. 5.99 (*0-8217-6642-2*, Zebra Kensgtn) Kensgtn Pub Corp.

Night Wind's Woman. Shirl Henke. 448p. (Orig.). 1999. mass mkt. 5.99 (*0-8439-4507-9*) Dorchester Pub Co.

***Night Wind's Woman.** Sheri Whitefeather. (Desire Ser.: Bk. 1332). 2000. mass mkt. 3.99 (*0-373-76332-8*, 1-76332-5) Silhouette.

Night Witches: The Amazing Story of Russia's Women Pilots in WWII. 3rd ed. Bruce Myles. (Illus.). 272p. 1997. reprint ed. pap. 13.00 (*0-89733-288-1*) Academy Chi Pubs.

Night with the Hants & Other Alabama Folk Experiences. Ed. by Ray B. Browne. LC 76-43449. 1976. 17.95 (*0-87972-075-1*); pap. 11.95 (*0-87972-167-7*) Bowling Green Univ Popular Press.

***Night Without Armor.** unabridged ed. Jewel. 1998. audio 12.00 (*0-694-52043-8*) HarperAudio.

Night Without Armor: Poems. Jewel Kilcher. LC 98-21593. 160p. 1998. 18.00 (*0-06-019198-8*) HarpC.

Night Without Armor: Poems. Jewel Kilcher. 160p. 1999. pap. 11.00 (*0-06-107362-8*) HarpC.

Night Without Armor Pt. 2: The Revenge. Beau Sia. (Illus.). 128p. (C). 1998. pap. 10.00 (*0-9662042-9-8*) Mouth Almighty.

***Night Without Armor Cd.** unabridged ed. Jewel Kilcher. 1998. audio 15.00 (*0-694-52046-2*) HarperAudio.

***Night Without Darkness** Illus. by Timothy M. Robinson & James A. Madsen. LC 99-33984. 1999. write for info. (*1-57345-504-0*) Deseret Bk.

Night Without End. Alistair MacLean. LC 60-6893. (J). 1960. 6.95 (*0-385-00546-6*) Doubleday.

Night Without End. Alistair MacLean. reprint ed. lib. bdg. 21.95 (*0-89190-174-4*, Rivercity Pr) Amereon Ltd.

***Night Without End: (A Memory Away...)** Susan Kearney. (Intrigue Ser.: No. 552). 2000. per. 4.25 (*0-373-22552-0*, 1-22552-3, Harlequin) Harlequin Bks.

Night Without Stars. James Howe. (Illus.). 192p. (J). (gr. 3-7). 1996. per. 4.50 (*0-689-80832-1*) Aladdin.

Night Without Stars. James Howe. LC 82-16278. 192p. (J). (gr. 4-7). 1983. 16.00 (*0-689-30957-0*) Atheneum Yung Read.

Night Without Stars. James Howe. 192p. (YA). (gr. 7 up). 1985. pap. 2.95 (*0-380-69877-3*, Avon Bks) Morrow Avon.

Night Without Stars. James Howe. 192p. (YA). 1993. pap. 3.50 (*0-380-71867-7*, Avon Bks) Morrow Avon.

Night Without Stars. James Howe. LC 82-16278. (J). 1996. 9.60 (*0-606-09686-8*, Pub. by Turtleback) Demco.

Night Woman. Nancy Price. 352p. 1993. mass mkt. 5.99 (*0-671-74994-3*, Pocket Star Bks) PB.

Night Woman. large type ed. Nancy Price. LC 92-33705. 550p. 1993. reprint ed. lib. bdg. 18.95 (*1-56054-583-6*) Thorndike Pr.

Night Words. Justine Wittich. LC 96-95287. 192p. 1997. 18.95 (*0-8034-9187-5*, Avalon Bks) Bouregy.

Night Work. Dennis Foley. pap. write for info. (*0-449-90894-1*) Fawcett.

***Night Work.** Laurie R. King. 2000. mass mkt. 6.50 (*0-553-57825-1*) Bantam.

***Night Work: A Kate Martinelli Mystery.** Laurie R. King. LC 99-57060. 339p. 2000. 23.95 (*0-553-10713-5*) Bantam.

Night Work: A Novel of Vietnam. Dennis Foley. (Orig.). 1995. mass mkt. 5.99 (*0-8041-0724-6*) Ivy Books.

***Night Worker.** Kate Banks. LC 99-27595. 2000. text 16.00 (*0-374-35520-7*) St Martin.

Night World & the Word Night. Franz Wright. LC 92-71506. (Poetry Ser.). 63p. 1993. pap. 11.95 (*0-88748-155-8*) Carnegie-Mellon.

Night Wrestling: Struggling for Answers & Finding God. Leslie Williams. LC 96-48118. 224p. 1997. 15.99 (*0-8499-1327-6*) Word Pub.

Night Wrighters' Chapbook. Roy Andresen et al. 103p. 1999. mass mkt. 8.00 (*0-9657568-4-X*) J B Strout.

***Night You Were Born.** Wendy McCormick. (Illus.). 32p. (J). (ps-2). 2000. 15.95 (*1-56145-225-4*) Peachtree Pubs.

Nightbane. Kevin Siembieda & C. J. Carella. Ed. by Alex Marciniszyn et al. (Nightbane Ser.). (Illus.). 200p. (Orig.). 1995. pap. 20.95 (*0-916211-86-X*, 730) Palladium Bks.

Nightbird. Edward Dee. LC 99-14591. 304p. 1999. 23.95 (*0-446-52039-X*, Pub. by Warner Bks) Little.

***Nightbird.** Edward Dee. 338p. 2000. mass mkt. 6.99 (*0-446-60913-7*) Warner Bks.

Nightbirds on Nantucket. Joan Aiken. 248p. (YA). (gr. 5). 1999. pap. 5.95 (*0-395-97185-3*) HM.

Nightblind. Helene Davis. Ed. by Peter Kaplan. 1976. 3.00 (*0-915176-17-3*) Pourboire.

Nightblood. T. Chris Martindale. 336p. (Orig.). 1990. mass mkt. 4.95 (*0-446-35530-5*) Warner Bks.

Nightbrood First Contact: Silent Death Races Book. K. Barrett. (Silent Death - The Next Millennium Ser.). (Illus.). 60p. 1996. pap. 16.00 (*1-55806-264-5*, 7213) Iron Crown Ent Inc.

Nightcharmer & Other Tales of Claude Seignolle. Claude Seignolle. Tr. by Eric H. Deudon. LC 83-45104. (Illus.). 120p. 1983. 10.95 (*0-89096-169-7*) Tex A&M Univ Pr.

***Nightchild: A Clans Novel.** J. A. Cummings. (Vampire Clans Ser.). 328p. 1999. pap. 15.95 (*0-9670668-0-8*) Kresnak Pr.

Nightclub Cantata. Elizabeth Swados. 1979. spiral bd. 8.95 (*0-8222-0827-X*) Dramatists Play.

***Nightclub/Bar Daily Logbook - Management.** Bob Johnson. (Illus.). 120p. 1999. pap. 29.95 (*1-928605-01-X*) BMS Pubg Co.

Nightcomers. S. Price. 1997. mass mkt. 11.95 (*0-340-65605-0*, Pub. by Hodder & Stought Ltd) Trafalgar.

Nightcrawler Manual: A Complete Guide to the Collecting & Storing of the Nightcrawler. Ray Edwards. (Illus.). 1981. pap. 10.00 (*0-914116-20-7*) Shields.

Nightcrawlers, Bait & Beer to Go. Hal Shymkus. LC 90-50960. (Illus.). 170p. (Orig.). 1991. pap. 10.95 (*0-923568-19-0*) Wilderness Adventure Bks.

Nightdances. James Skofield. LC 80-8943. (Illus.). 32p. (J). (ps-3). 1981. 12.95 (*0-06-025741-5*) HarpC Child Bks.

Nightdreams & Daymares: Introspection from the Inner City. Ivan Miller. Ed. by Shia Barnett. 1999. pap. 12.00 (*0-9655430-2-1*) Blckberry Bks.

Nightfall. Isaac Asimov & Robert Silverberg. 1991. mass mkt. 5.50 (*0-553-18042-8*) Bantam.

Nightfall. Isaac Asimov & Robert Silverberg. 352p. 1991. mass mkt. 6.99 (*0-553-29099-1*, Spectra) Bantam.

Nightfall. Loure Bussey-Jackson. 304p. 1996. mass mkt. 4.99 (*0-7860-0332-4*, Pinncle Kensgtn) Kensgtn Pub Corp.

Nightfall. Katharine Marlowe, pseud. 352p. 1994. mass mkt. 4.99 (*0-8125-2415-2*, Pub. by Tor Bks) St Martin.

Nightfall. large type ed. Anne Stuart. LC 96-29609. 1996. lib. bdg. 23.95 (*1-57490-077-3*, Beeler LP Bks) T T Beeler.

***Nightfall.** Katharine Marlowe, pseud. 234p. 1999. reprint ed. pap. 20.00 (*1-892738-28-7*) Isld Nation.

Nightfall & Other Stories. Daniel Corkery. 204p. 1988. pap. 12.95 (*0-85640-414-4*, Pub. by Blackstaff Pr) Dufour.

***Nightfall at Algemron.** 1999. pap. 5.99 (*0-7869-1419-X*) TSR Inc.

***Nightfall at Algemron.** Diane Duane E. (Harbinger Trilogy Ser.: Vol. 3). (Illus.). 352p. 2000. mass mkt. 5.99 (*0-7869-1563-3*) TSR Inc.

Nightfall, Country Lake. David Cunningham. LC 94-26352. (Illus.). (J). (gr. 1-4). 1995. lib. bdg. 15.95 (*0-8075-5624-6*) A Whitman.

Nightfall of Diamonds. Ed. by Melissa Mitchell. 1997. 69.95 (*1-57553-351-0*) Nat Lib Poetry.

Nightfather. Carl Friedman. Tr. by Arnold J. Pomerans & Erica Pomerans from DUT. 144p. 1994. 18.50 (*0-89255-193-3*) Persea Bks.

Nightfather. Carl Friedman. Tr. by Arnold J. Pomerans & Erica Pomerans from DUT. 144p. 1995. pap. 7.95 (*0-89255-210-7*) Persea Bks.

Nightfeathers: Black Goose Rhymes. Sundaira Morninghouse. LC 89-63264. (Illus.). 32p. (J). (gr. 1-4). 1989. 9.95 (*0-940880-27-X*); pap. text 4.95 (*0-940880-28-8*) Open Hand.

Nightfighter Ace. Tony Spooner. (Illus.). 192p. 1997. 33.95 (*0-7509-1621-4*, Pub. by Sutton Pub Ltd) Intl Pubs Mktg.

Nightfighters Over the Reich. LC 96-39871. (Luftwaffe at War Ser.). (Illus.). 72p. 1997. 12.95 (*1-85367-271-8*) Stackpole.

Nightfire. large type ed. Barbara McCauley. (Silhouette Romance Ser.). 1995. 18.95 (*0-373-59632-4*) Thorndike Pr.

***Nightfire: Lord of the Seas Trilogy.** (Executioner Ser.: Bk. 259). 2000. per. 4.50 (*0-373-64259-8*, 1-64259-4, Wrldwide Lib) Harlequin Bks.

***Nightfisherman: Selected Letters.** W. S. Graham. 400p. 2000. pap. 24.95 (*1-85754-445-5*, Pub. by Carcanet Pr) Paul & Co Pubs.

Nightflower. large type ed. Mary Mackie. 1990. pap. 16.99 (*0-7089-6883-X*, Linford) Ulverscroft.

Nightflyers. George R. R. Martin. 304p. 1987. reprint ed. pap. 3.50 (*0-8125-4564-8*, Pub. by Tor Bks) St Martin.

Nightgown Countdown. Frank B. Edwards. (New Reader Ser.). (J). (gr. k-1). text 14.95 (*1-894323-05-X*, Pub. by Pokeweed Pr) Genl Dist Srvs.

Nightgown Countdown. Frank B. Edwards. (New Reader Ser.). (Illus.). (J). (gr. k-1). pap. 4.95 (*1-894323-04-1*, Pub. by Pokeweed Pr) Genl Dist Srvs.

Nighthawk. Kristen Kyle. 368p. 1997. mass mkt. 5.50 (*0-505-52184-9*) Dorchester Pub Co.

Nighthawk. Rachel Lee. (Conard County Ser.). 1997. per. 3.99 (*0-373-07781-5*, 1-07781-7) Silhouette.

Nighthawk. Artemis OakGrove. 1998. mass mkt. 6.95 (*1-56333-634-0*, Rosebud) Masquerade.

Nighthawk. large type ed. Charles Burnham. (Linford Western Library). 256p. 1997. pap. 16.99 (*0-7089-5002-7*, Linford) Ulverscroft.

***Nighthawk.** large type ed. Rachel Lee. (Silhouette Romance Ser.). 1999. 21.95 (*0-373-59650-2*) Harlequin Bks.

Nighthawks: Insider's Guide to the Heraldry & Insignia of the Lockheed F-117A Stealth Fighter. Patrick A. Blazek. LC 98-86279. (Illus.). 80p. (Orig.). 1999. pap. 24.95 (*0-7643-0681-2*) Schiffer.

Nighthouse Anthology. (International Anthology Ser.). 120p. (J). (gr. 7-9). 1981. pap. 12.50 (*0-939622-24-6*) Four Zoas Night Ltd.

Nightime Prayers. Date not set. 3.95 (*0-88271-536-4*, 10337) Regina Pr.

Nightingale see Naktergalen

Nightingale see Nattergalen

Nightingale. Hans Christian Andersen.Tr. of Nattergalen. (Illus.). 32p. (J). (ps-3). 1992. 6.95 (*0-8362-4927-5*) Andrews & McMeel.

Nightingale. Hans Christian Andersen. LC 85-2765.Tr. of Nattergalen. (Illus.). 32p. (J). (ps-3). 1988. pap. 3.95 (*0-15-257428-X*, Voyager Bks) Harcourt.

Nightingale. Hans Christian Andersen. Tr. by Eva Le Gallienne. LC 64-18574.Tr. of Nattergalen. (Illus.). 48p. (J). (gr. 3 up). 1965. 13.95 (*0-06-023780-5*) HarpC Child Bks.

***Nightingale.** Hans Christian Andersen. Tr. by Anthea Bell from DAN. LC 98-45563.Tr. of Nattergalen. (Illus.). 32p. (J). (gr. k-3). 1999. pap. 6.95 (*0-7358-1120-2*, Pub. by North-South Bks NYC) Chronicle Bks.

***Nightingale.** Hans Christian Andersen. Tr. by Anthea Bell from DAN. LC 98-45563.Tr. of Nattergalen. (Illus.). 32p. (J). (gr. k-3). 1999. 15.95 (*0-7358-1118-0*, Pub. by North-South Bks NYC) Chronicle Bks.

Nightingale (A Participation Play) John Urquhart et al. (J). (gr. k up). 1983. pap. 6.00 (*0-87602-245-X*) Anchorage.

Nightingale by Hans Christian Andersen. Diane Stanley. 1924. write for info. (*0-688-17135-4*, Wm Morrow) Morrow Avon.

Nightingale By Hans Christian Andersen. Diane Stanley. 1924. lib. bdg. write for info. (*0-688-17136-2*, Wm Morrow) Morrow Avon.

Nightingale, Fantasia for Four Viols (Two Trebles, Tenor, Bass) Rosemary Thorndycraft. 21p. 1991. pap. text 10.00 (*1-56571-034-7*) PRB Prods.

Nightingale Gallery: Being the First of the Sorrowful Mysteries of Brother Athelstan. Paul Harding. 256p. 1993. mass mkt. 4.99 (*0-380-71751-4*, Avon Bks) Morrow Avon.

Nightingale Legacy. Catherine Coulter. 464p. 1995. mass mkt. 6.99 (*0-515-11624-6*, Jove) Berkley Pub.

***Nightingale (Musical)** William Electric Black et al. 44p. 1999. pap. 5.50 (*0-87129-880-5*, N04) Dramatic Pub.

***Nightingale Sang in Fernhurst Road.** C. Matthew. 1998. text 29.95 (*0-7195-5899-9*, Pub. by John Murray) Trafalgar.

Nightingale Sings. Bingham. LC 96-209224. 1997. mass mkt. 8.99 (*0-553-40895-X*) Bantam.

***Nightingale Sings.** Bingham. 2000. 29.95 (*0-385-40610-X*, Pub. by Transworld Publishers Ltd) Trafalgar.

Nightingale Summer. large type ed. Betty O'Rourke. (Ulverscroft Large Print Ser.). 400p. 1997. 27.99 (*0-7089-3794-2*) Ulverscroft.

Nightingale Will Sing. large type ed. Sheila Belshaw. (Linford Romance Library). 272p. 1995. pap. 16.99 (*0-7089-7773-1*, Linford) Ulverscroft.

Nightingale's Burden: Women Poets & American Culture Before 1900. Cheryl Walker. LC 81-48514. 207p. reprint ed. pap. 64.20 (*0-8357-3951-1*, 205704600004) Bks Demand.

Nightingale's Lament: Selections from the Poems & Fables of Parvin Etesami (1907-41) Heshmat Moayyad et al. LC 84-60071. (Iran-e NO Literary Collection Ser.). 289p. 1985. pap. 11.95 (*0-939214-20-2*) Mazda Pubs.

Nightingale's Song. Jo-Ann Power. 1997. per. 5.99 (*0-671-52997-8*, Pocket Books) PB.

Nightingale's Song. Robert Timberg. LC 95-3446. 582p. 1995. 27.50 (*0-684-80301-1*) S&S Trade.

Nightingale's Song. Robert Timberg. LC 95-3446. (Illus.). 544p. 1996. per. 14.00 (*0-684-82673-9*) S&S Trade.

Nightingales under the Snow. Annemarie Schimmel. LC 96-37540. 106p. 1995. pap. 0.95 (*0-933546-54-8*) KNP.

Nightingales under the Snow: Poems. Annemarie Schimmel. 110p. 1996. pap. 8.95 (*0-614-21652-4*, 1393) Kazi Pubns.

Nightjar. Peter Tate. (Natural History Ser.: No. 48). (Illus.). 24p. 1989. pap. 5.25 (*0-7478-0030-8*, Pub. by Shire Pubns) Parkwest Pubns.

Nightjars. Marjory Wentworth. 32p. (Orig.). 1995. pap. 7.00 (*0-9655612-0-8*) Laurel Pub SC.

Nightjars: A Guide to the Nightjars, Nighthawks & Their Relatives. Nigel Cleere. LC 98-60961. (Illus.). 256p. 1998. 40.00 (*0-300-07457-3*) Yale U Pr.

NightJohn. Gary Paulsen. (J). 1994. mass mkt. 4.99 (*0-440-91014-5*) BDD Bks Young Read.

NightJohn. Gary Paulsen. 112p. (YA). (gr. 6 up). 1995. mass mkt. 4.50 (*0-440-21936-1*) Dell.

NightJohn. Gary Paulsen. LC 92-1222. 96p. (YA). (gr. 6 up). 1993. 15.95 (*0-385-30838-8*) Doubleday.

Nightjohn. Gary Paulsen. 1995. 9.60 (*0-606-07951-3*, Pub. by Turtleback) Demco.

Nightkill. F. Paul Wilson & Steve Lyon. LC 97-16824. 304p. 1997. text 23.95 (*0-312-85910-4*) St Martin.

Nightkill. F. Paul Wilson & Steve Lyon. 1999. mass mkt. 6.99 (*0-8125-6536-3*, Pub. by Tor Bks) St Martin.

Nightlands. C. J. Carella & Kevin Siembieda. Ed. by Alex Marciniszyn et al. (Nightbane Worldbook Ser.: Vol. 2). (Illus.). 144p. (Orig.). (YA). (gr. 8 up). 1996. pap. 16.95 (*0-916211-97-5*, 732) Palladium Bks.

Nightlands: Nordic Building. Christian Norberg-Schulz. Tr. by Thomas McQuillan. (Illus.). 240p. 1996. 40.00 (*0-262-14057-8*) MIT Pr.

Nightlands: Nordic Building. Christian Norberg-Schulz. (Illus.). 240p. 1997. reprint ed. pap. text 18.50 (*0-262-64036-8*) MIT Pr.

***Nightlife.** Jack Ellis. 2000. mass mkt. 5.99 (*0-7860-1259-5*, Pinnacle Kensgtn) Kensgtn Pub Corp.

Nightlife of the Gods. Thorne Smith. LC 99-36286. 2000. pap. 12.95 (*0-375-75306-0*) Modern Lib NY.

Nightlights. Debby Boone. LC 97-12443. (Illus.). 40p. (Orig.). (J). 1997. 14.99 (*1-56507-734-2*) Harvest Hse.

Nightlights, UL 1786. 2nd ed. (C). 1995. pap. text 330.00 (*1-55989-856-9*) Underwrtrs Labs.

Nightline. Ted Koppel. 1997. pap. 16.00 (*0-8129-2927-6*, Times Bks) Crown Pub Group.

Nightlines. Neil Jordan. 192p. 1995. 21.00 (*0-679-44438-6*) Random.

Nightly Horrors: Crisis Coverage in Television Network News. Dan Nimmo & James E. Combs. LC 84-10464. 232p. 1985. pap. 17.95 (*0-87049-625-5*) U of Tenn Pr.

Nightman. Whitley Strieber. 1999. pap. 21.00 (*0-525-93620-3*) NAL.

Nightmare. Bonnie Bryant. (Saddle Club Super Edition Ser.: No. 6). 208p. (Orig.). (J). (gr. 4-7). 1997. pap. 4.99 (*0-553-48428-1*) BDD Bks Young Read.

Nightmare. Marjorie Dorner. 384p. 1988. mass mkt. 3.95 (*0-446-35016-8*, Pub. by Warner Bks) Little.

Nightmare. LeRoma Greth. 1961. pap. 3.50 (*0-87129-084-7*, N13) Dramatic Pub.

Nightmare. David Pelham. 1999. pap. 19.95 (*0-670-82402-X*) Viking Penguin.

Nightmare. Willo D. Roberts. LC 89-7038. 192p. (J). (gr. 5-9). 1989. 16.00 (*0-689-31551-1*) Atheneum Yung Read.

Nightmare. Willo Davis Roberts. 1992. 9.60 (*0-606-00881-0*, Pub. by Turtleback) Demco.

Nightmare: Psychological & Biological Foundations. Ed. by Henry Kellerman. LC 86-13675. 320p. 1987. text 69.50 (*0-231-05892-6*) Col U Pr.

***Nightmare: The Underside of the Nixon Years.** 3rd ed. J. Anthony Lukas. LC 75-30667. 626p. 1999. reprint ed. pap. 24.95 (*0-8214-1287-6*) Ohio U Pr.

Nightmare Abbey, Crotchet Castle. Thomas Love Peacock. Ed. by Raymond Wright. 284p. 1982. pap. 13.95 (*0-14-043045-8*, Penguin Classics) Viking Penguin.

Nightmare Abbey, 1818. Thomas Love Peacock. LC 93-3948. (Revolution & Romanticism Ser.). 236p. 1992. 48.00 (*1-85477-123-X*) Continuum.

Nightmare Abroad: Stories of Americans Imprisoned in Foreign Lands. Peter Laufer. LC 92-15811. (Illus.). 208p. 1993. 20.00 (*1-56279-028-5*) Mercury Hse Inc.

Nightmare & Dawn. Mark Aldanov. Tr. by Joel Carmichael. LC 73-21489. 343p. 1974. reprint ed. lib. bdg. 65.00 (*0-8371-6406-0*, ALND, Greenwood Pr) Greenwood.

Nightmare & Network. K. Srinivasa Sastry. LC 96-60335. 120p. (Orig.). 1996. pap. 10.00 (*0-938999-08-7*) Yuganta Pr.

Nightmare Asylum. Dark Horse Comics Staff. (Aliens Ser.). (Illus.). 1997. pap. text 16.95 (*1-56971-217-4*) Dark Horse Comics.

Nightmare at Mystery Mansion. Phil Roxbee-Cox. (Spinechillers Ser.). (Illus.). 48p. (J). (gr. 4-7). 1996. pap. 5.95 (*0-7460-2089-9*, Usborne) EDC.

Nightmare at Mystery Mansion. Phil Roxbee-Cox. (Spinechillers Ser.). (Illus.). 48p. (J). (gr. 4 up). 1996. lib. bdg. 13.95 (*0-88110-824-3*, Usborne) EDC.

Nightmare Before Christmas. Tim Burton. LC 92-54867. (Illus.). 40p. (J). 1993. 15.95 (*1-56282-411-2*, Pub. by Hyprn Child) Little.

Nightmare Before Christmas. Tim Burton. LC 92-54867. (Illus.). 40p. (J). 1994. pap. 6.70 (*0-7868-1014-9*, Pub. by Hyprn Ppbks) Little.

Nightmare Before Christmas: The Film, the Art, the Vision. Frank Thompson. (Illus.). 192p. (J). 1994. pap. 15.45 (*0-7868-8066-X*, Pub. by Hyperion) Time Warner.

Nightmare Begins. Jerry Ahern. (Survivalist Ser.: No. 2). (Orig.). 1981. mass mkt. 2.50 (*0-89083-810-0*, Zebra Kensgtn) Kensgtn Pub Corp.

Nightmare Begins Responsibility. fac. ed. Michael S. Harper. LC 74-10974. 104p. 1974. reprint ed. pap. 32.30 (*0-7837-8068-0*, 204782100008) Bks Demand.

Nightmare Begins Responsibility, Poems. Michael S. Harper. LC 74-10974. 106p. 1975. text 14.95 (*0-252-00466-3*) U of Ill Pr.

***Nightmare Chronicles.** Douglas Clegg. 368p. 1999. mass mkt. 5.50 (*0-8439-4580-X*, Pub. by Dorchester Pub Co) CMG.

Nightmare Considered: Critical Essays on Nuclear War Literature. Ed. by Nancy Anisfield. LC 91-72619. 282p. (C). 1991. 35.95 (*0-87972-529-X*); pap. 18.95 (*0-87972-530-3*) Bowling Green Univ Popular Press.

Nightmare Creatures: The Official Strategy Guide. Odom. LC 97-69339. (Secrets of the Game Ser.). 128p. 1997. per. 12.99 (*0-7615-1256-X*) Prima Pub.

Nightmare Creatures 64: Prima's Official Strategy Guide. Prima Publishing Staff. LC 98-73121. (Secrets of the Game Ser.). 96p. 1998. per. 12.99 (*0-7615-1795-2*) Prima Pub.

***Nightmare Creatures II Vol. 1: Official Strategy Guide.** BradyGames Staff. LC 99-73428. (Illus.). 112p. 2000. pap. 12.99 (*1-56686-915-3*) Brady Pub.

Nightmare Dream. 352p. 1991. pap. 4.95 (*0-87431-303-1*, 20603) West End Games.

Nightmare Factory. Thomas Ligotti. 576p. 1996. pap. 12.95 (*0-7867-0302-4*) Carroll & Graf.

Nightmare Farm. Jack Mann. 1975. 6.50 (*0-685-54480-X*) Bookfinger.

Nightmare for Dr. Morelle. Ernest Dudley. 1998. 19.50 (*0-7540-8506-6*, Black Dagger) Chivers N Amer.

Nightmare Has Triplets: Smirt, Smith & Smire. James Branch Cabell. LC 70-156179. 311p. 1972. reprint ed. lib. bdg. 52.50 (*0-8371-6122-3*, CANT, Greenwood Pr) Greenwood.

Nightmare Help: A Guide for Adults & Children. Ann S. Wiseman. (Dream Exploration Ser.). (Illus.). 137p. (Orig.). (J). (gr. 1-12). 1986. pap. text 9.00 (*0-937369-00-4*) Ansayre Pr.

***Nightmare Hour: Time for Terror.** R. L. Stine, pseud. LC 99-63663. (Illus.). 160p. (J). (gr. 3 up). 1999. 9.95 (*0-06-028688-1*) HarpC Child Bks.

***Nightmare Hour: Time for Terror.** R. L. Stine, pseud. LC 99-63663. (Illus.). 160p. (J). (gr. 5 up). 2000. mass mkt. 4.99 (*0-06-440842-6*) HarpC Child Bks.

Nightmare House. large type ed. Rae Foley. LC 97-16228. 258p. 1997. lib. bdg. 21.95 (*0-7838-8227-0*, G K Hall Lrg Type) Mac Lib Ref.

Nightmare in Broken Bow. large type ed. Wayne D. Overholser. LC 98-10488. 238p. 1998. pap. 18.95 (*0-7838-8456-7*, G K Hall & Co) Mac Lib Ref.

Nightmare in Broken Bow large type ed. Wayne D. Overholser. LC 98-10488. (A Large Print Western Ser.). 194p. 1998. write for info. (*0-7540-3292-2*) Chivers N Amer.

Nightmare in Broken Bow - Day of Judgment. Wayne D. Overholser. 384p. 1996. pap. text, mass mkt. 4.99 (*0-8439-3910-9*) Dorchester Pub Co.

Nightmare in Dallas: The "Babushka Lady" Beverly Oliver. LC 94-66617. 304p. 1994. 19.95 (*0-914984-60-8*) Starburst.

Nightmare in Death Valley. Created by Francine Pascal. (Sweet Valley High Ser.: No. 116). 208p. (YA). (gr. 7-12). 1995. mass mkt. 3.99 (*0-553-56634-2*) Bantam.

Nightmare in Death Valley. Kate William. (Sweet Valley High Ser.: No. 116). (YA). (gr. 7 up). 1995. 9.09 (*0-606-08221-2*, Pub. by Turtleback) Demco.

Nightmare in Heaven. Cherie Bennett. (Teen Angels Ser.: No. 5). (YA). 1996. mass mkt. 3.99 (*0-380-78578-1*, Avon Bks) Morrow Avon.

Nightmare in History: The Holocaust 1933-1945. Miriam Chaikin. (Illus.). 160p. 1992. pap. 10.00 (*0-395-61580-1*, Clarion Bks) HM.

Nightmare in History: The Holocaust, 1933-1945. Miriam Chaikin. 1987. 15.10 (*0-606-01476-4*, Pub. by Turtleback) Demco.

Nightmare in Nagano see Screech Owls Series Boxed Set: The Quebec City Crisis; The Screech Owls' Home Loss; Nightmare in Nagano

Nightmare in New Orleans. Carolyn Keene. (Nancy Drew & Hardy Boys Super Mystery Ser.: No. 30). (YA). (gr. 6 up). 1997. pap. 3.99 (*0-671-53749-0*, Archway) PB.

Nightmare in New Orleans. Carolyn Keene. (Nancy Drew & Hardy Boys Super Mystery Ser.: No. 30). (YA). (gr. 6 up). 1997. 9.09 (*0-606-11667-2*, Pub. by Turtleback) Demco.

Nightmare in New York. Don Pendleton. (Executioner Ser.: No. 7). 1988. mass mkt. 3.50 (*1-55817-066-9*, Pinncle Kensgtn) Kensgtn Pub Corp.

Nightmare in Pink. John D. MacDonald. 1996. mass mkt. 5.99 (*0-449-22414-7*) Fawcett.

Nightmare in Red: The McCarthy Era in Perspective. Richard M. Fried. 256p. 1991. reprint ed. pap. text 10.95 (*0-19-504361-8*) OUP.

Nightmare in the Greenhouse: The True Story of a Woman's Fight for Survival. Neva Kent. vi, 118p. (Orig.). 1995. pap. 9.95 (*0-9650712-1-9*) Teller Press.

Nightmare in 3-D. R. L. Stine, pseud. (Ghosts of Fear Street Ser.: No. 4). (J). (gr. 4-7). 1996. pap. 3.99 (*0-671-52944-7*, Pocket Books) PB.

Nightmare in 3-D. R. L. Stine, pseud. (Ghosts of Fear Street Ser.: No. 4). (J). (gr. 4-9). 1996. 9.09 (*0-606-08524-6*, Pub. by Turtleback) Demco.

Nightmare in 3-D see Pesadilla en 3 Dimensiones

Nightmare Lands. TSR Inc. Staff. (Advanced Dungeons & Dragons, 2nd Edition: Ravenloft Campaign World Ser.). 1995. 20.00 (*0-7869-0174-8*, Pub. by TSR Inc) Random.

Nightmare Machine. John Whitman. LC 49-253820. (Star Wars: No. 4). 144p. (J). (gr. 3-7). 1997. pap. 4.99 (*0-553-48453-2*, Skylark BDD) BDD Bks Young Read.

Nightmare Machine. John Whitman. (Star Wars: No. 4). (J). (gr. 4-8). 1997. 10.09 (*0-606-11891-8*, Pub. by Turtleback) Demco.

Nightmare Machine see Galaxy of Fear Boxed Set

Nightmare Man. large type ed. Michael Fisher. (Niagara Large Print Ser.). 443p. 1996. 29.50 (*0-7089-5854-0*) Ulverscroft.

Nightmare Mountain. Peg Kehret. Ed. by Patricia MacDonald. 176p. (J). 1991. mass mkt. 3.99 (*0-671-72864-4*, Minstrel Bks) PB.

Nightmare Mountain. Peg Kehret. 176p. (J). 1991. per. 2.95 (*0-671-77965-6*) PB.

Nightmare Mountain Reissue Edition, Vol. 1. Peg Kehert. (J). 1999. pap. 4.99 (*0-14-130645-9*, PuffinBks) Peng Put Young Read.

Nightmare Never Ends: The Official History of Freddy Krueger & the Nightmare on Elm Street Films. James Spencer. (Illus.). 224p. 1992. pap. 17.95 (*0-8065-1368-3*, Citadel Pr) Carol Pub Group.

Nightmare of Ecstasy: The Life & Art of Edward D. Wood. 2nd ed. Rudolph Grey. (Illus.). 232p. 1994. pap. 14.95 (*0-922915-24-5*) Feral Hse.

Nightmare of Falling Teeth. Mari Alschuler. 20p. 1998. pap. 7.95 (*0-944754-54-6*) Pudding Hse Pubns.

Nightmare of God. Daniel Berrigan. LC 81-51877. (Sunburst Originals Ser.: No. 9). (Illus.). 144p. (Orig.). 1983. pap. 6.00 (*0-934648-08-5*) Sunburst Pr.

Nightmare of History: The Fictions of Virginia Woolf & D. H. Lawrence. Helen Wussow. LC 98-16573. 208p. 1998. 36.00 (*0-934223-46-7*) Lehigh Univ Pr.

Nightmare of Mouse. Lynn Strongin. LC 77-75173. 82p. 1977. per. 3.75 (*0-934332-06-1*) LEpervier Pr.

Nightmare or Reality, Guatemala in the 1980's. Angela Delli Sante. 1996. pap. text 35.00 (*90-5538-010-5*, Pub. by Bonechi) Eiron.

Nightmare of Success: The Fallacy of the Super-Success Dream. William J. Ruzicka. LC 73-90028. 155p. 1973. 6.95 (*0-914372-01-7*) Peninsula Pubns.

Nightmare of the Apocalypse: The Rabbi Conspiracy. Philip Moore. LC 97-91511. (Illus.). 365p. (Orig.). 1997. pap. 15.00 (*1-57915-998-2*) Rams Head Pr.

Nightmare on Elm Street V: The Dream Child. Jack Barstow. Ed. by New Line Cinema Staff. LC 92-499. 1992. lib. bdg. 13.95 (*1-56239-160-7*) ABDO Pub Co.

Nightmare on Main Street: Angels, Sadomasochism, & the Culture of Gothic. Mark Edmundson. LC 97-20270. 224p. 1997. 22.95 (*0-674-87484-6*) HUP.

Nightmare on Main Street: Angels, Sadomasochism & the Culture of Gothic. Mark Edmundson. 208p. 1999. pap. 14.00 (*0-674-62463-7*) HUP.

Nightmare on Planet X. A. G. Cascone. (Deadtime Stories Ser.: No. 11). (J). (gr. 3-7). 1997. pap. 3.50 (*0-8167-4292-8*) Troll Communs.

Nightmare on the Nile. large type ed. Charles Leader. (Linford Mystery Large Print Ser.). 384p. 1998. pap. 17.99 (*0-7089-5296-8*, Linford) Ulverscroft.

Nightmare on University Way: The Rise of the Post-Sixties Aliens. Fred K. Ginther. (Illus.). 192p. 1997. pap. 14.95 (*0-9651590-2-7*) Infnty Pub.

Nightmare Overhanging Darkly: Essays on Black Culture & Resistance. rev. ed. Acklyn Lynch. 276p. 1993. reprint ed. pap. 14.95 (*0-88378-142-5*) Third World.

Nightmare Passage. James Axler. (Deathlands Ser.: No. 40). 1998. per. 5.50 (*0-373-62540-5*, 1-62540-9, Wrldwide Lib) Harlequin Bks.

Nightmare Realm Baba Yaga. Curtis Smith. (Advanced Dungeons & Dragons Adventure Gamebks.: No. 8). 1986. pap. 2.95 (*0-685-14569-7*) Random.

***Nightmare Room, No. 5.** R. L. Stine, pseud. (J). 2001. pap. write for info. (*0-06-440903-1*, HarpTrophy) HarpC Child Bks.

***Nightmare Room, No. 6.** R. L. Stine, pseud. 2001. pap. write for info. (*0-06-440904-X*, HarpTrophy) HarpC Child Bks.

***Nightmare Room, No. 7.** R. L. Stine, pseud. 2001. pap. write for info. (*0-06-440905-8*, HarpTrophy) HarpC Child Bks.

***Nightmare Room, No. 8.** R. L. Stine, pseud. 2001. pap. write for info. (*0-06-440906-6*, HarpTrophy) HarpC Child Bks.

Nightmare Room, No. 9. R. L. Stine, pseud. Date not set. pap. write for info. (*0-06-440907-4*, HarpTrophy) HarpC Child Bks.

An Asterisk (*) at the beginning of an entry indicates that the title is appearing for the first time.

Nightmare Room, No. 10. R. L. Stine, pseud. Date not set. pap. write for info. (*0-06-440908-2*, HarpTrophy) HarpC Child Bks.

Nightmare Room, No. 11. R. L. Stine, pseud. (J). Date not set. pap. write for info. (*0-06-440909-0*, HarpTrophy) HarpC Child Bks.

Nightmare Room, No. 12. R. L. Stine, pseud. (J). Date not set. pap. write for info. (*0-06-440910-4*, HarpTrophy) HarpC Child Bks.

***Nightmare Room: Don't Forget Me!, No. 1.** R. L. Stine, pseud. LC 00-101108. (Nightmare Room Ser.: No. 1). 160p. (J). (gr. 4-7). 2000. mass mkt. 3.99 (*0-06-440899-X*) HarpC Child Bks.

***Nightmare Room: Liar Liar, No. 4.** R. L. Stine, pseud. (Nightmare Room Ser.: No. 4). 160p. (J). (gr. 5 up). 2000. mass mkt. 3.99 (*0-06-440902-3*) HarpC Child Bks.

***Nightmare Room: Locker 13, No. 2.** R. L. Stine, pseud. LC 00-190244. (Nightmare Room Ser.: No. 2). 144p. (J). (gr. 4-7). 2000. mass mkt. 3.99 (*0-06-440900-7*, HarpTrophy) HarpC Child Bks.

***Nightmare Room: My Name Is Evil, No. 3.** R. L. Stine, pseud. LC 00-190245. (Nightmare Room Ser.: No. 3). 160p. (J). (gr. 4-7). 2000. mass mkt. 3.99 (*0-06-440901-5*, HarpTrophy) HarpC Child Bks.

Nightmare Snow. Judith A. Green. (Adult Learner Ser.). (Illus.). 220p. 1985. pap. text 8.98 (*0-89061-283-8*, Jamestwn Pub) NTC Contemp Pub Co.

Nightmare Tales. Helena P. Blavatsky. 139p. 1971. reprint ed. spiral bd. 14.00 (*0-7873-1219-3*) Hlth Research.

Nightmare Tales. Helena P. Blavatsky. 135p. 1992. reprint ed. pap. 12.95 (*1-56459-251-0*) Kessinger Pub.

Nightmare Time: A Pierre Chambrun Mystery Novel. large type ed. Hugh Pentecost. (Linford Mystery Library). 304p. 1988. pap. 16.99 (*0-7089-6563-6*, Linford) Ulverscroft.

Nightmare Town. Dashiell Hammett. Ed. by Kirby McCauley et al. LC 99-37237. 432p. 1999. 25.00 (*0-375-40111-3*) Knopf.

Nightmare Trail. large type ed. E. B. Majors. LC 98-41737. 1998. 21.95 (*0-7838-0387-7*, G K Hall Lrg Type) Mac Lib Ref.

Nightmare Works: Tibor Hajas. Laszlo Beke et al. (Illus.). 82p. (Orig.). 1990. 10.00 (*0-935519-11-4*) Anderson Gal.

***Nightmares: Dreams from the Dark.** Alex Lukeman. LC 00-37134. 224p. 2000. 19.95 (*0-87131-917-9*) M Evans.

Nightmares: Terrifying Tales from Beyond the Grave. J. H. Brennan. 144p. 1996. pap. 8.95 (*1-85371-632-4*, Pub. by Poolbeg Pr) Dufour.

***Nightmares: The Sleepwalker; The Secret Bedroom; Bad Dreams.** R. L. Stine, pseud. (Fear Street Collector's Edition Ser.: No. 2). (YA). (gr. 7 up). 1998. per. 6.99 (*0-671-02298-9*, Archway) PB.

Nightmares Lf. Jack Prelutsky. LC 76-4820. (Illus.). 40p. (J). (gr. 4-7). 1976. 14.89 (*0-688-84053-1*, Grenwillow Bks) HarpC Child Bks.

Nightmares & Dreamscapes. Stephen King. 1994. pap. 6.99 (*0-451-18302-9*, Sig) NAL.

Nightmares & Dreamscapes. Stephen King. LC 92-46881. 1993. 13.09 (*0-606-06623-3*, Pub. by Turtleback) Demco.

Nightmares & Dreamscapes. large type ed. Stephen King. LC 93-35475. (General Ser.). (Illus.). 1071p. 1994. lib. bdg. 28.95 (*0-8161-5881-9*, G K Hall Lrg Type) Mac Lib Ref.

Nightmares & Dreamscapes. large type ed. Stephen King. LC 93-35475. (General Ser.). (Illus.). 1071p. 1994. pap. 20.95 (*0-8161-5882-7*, G K Hall Lrg Type) Mac Lib Ref.

Nightmares & Dreamscapes. Stephen King. LC 92-46881. 692p. 1994. reprint ed. mass mkt. 7.99 (*0-451-18023-2*, Sig) NAL.

Nightmares & Hobbyhorses: Swift, Sterne, & Augustan Ideas of Madness. Michael V. DePorte. LC 73-78048. (Illus.). 176p. reprint ed. pap. 54.60 (*0-7837-6679-3*, 204629500011) Bks Demand.

Nightmares & Human Conflict. John Mack. 288p. 1989. text 64.50 (*0-231-07102-7*); pap. text 22.50 (*0-231-07103-5*) Col U Pr.

***Nightmares Desire Kept for Me.** Alex S. Defazio. (Illus.). 100p. (C). 1999. pap. 17.99 (*0-9676282-1-0*) Elixir Prods.

Nightmare's Disciple. Joseph S. Pulver, Sr. (Call of Cthulhu Fiction Ser.). 396p. 1999. pap. 14.95 (*1-56882-118-2*, Chaosium Fiction) Chaosium.

Nightmare's Dozen: Stories from the Dark. Michael Stearns. 256p. (YA). 1999. mass mkt. 4.99 (*0-440-22746-1*) Bantam.

Nightmare's Dozen: Stories from the Dark. Ed. by Michael Stearns. LC 96-3382. (Illus.). 240p. (J). 1996. 17.00 (*0-15-201247-8*) Harcourt.

Nightmares in Paradise. Robyn Sheahan. (YA). 1995. 11.95 (*0-7022-2705-6*, Pub. by Univ Queensland Pr) Intl Spec Bk.

Nightmares in the Mist. Leslie McGuire. LC 92-46876. (Illus.). 40p. (J). (gr. k-4). 1994. 14.95 (*1-56844-003-0*) Enchante Pub.

Nightmares in the Mist. 2nd rev. ed. Leslie McGuire. Ed. by Gudrun Hoy & Bobi Martin. (Emotional Literacy Ser.). (Illus.). 40p. (J). (gr. k-5). 1996. 14.95 (*1-56844-103-7*) Enchante Pub.

Nightmares in the Sky: Gargoyles & Grotesques. Stephen King. 1999. pap. write for info. (*0-14-026565-1*) Viking Penguin.

Nightmares of a Journalist. Newton S. Lee. (Orig.). 1991. pap. 4.79 (*0-9627016-1-0*) VTLS.

***Nightmares of Mine: RPG Sourcebook.** Kenneth Hite. (Illus.). 176p. (YA). (gr. 7 up). 1999. pap. 14.00 (*1-55806-367-6*, 5704) Iron Crown Ent Inc.

Nightmarks. Carlos Reyes. LC 88-26747. 1990. 15.95 (*0-89924-060-7*); pap. 8.00 (*0-89924-059-3*) Lynx Hse.

Nightmists of Mansfield. Raymond E. Ward. LC 98-83101. 365p. 1999. 25.00 (*0-7388-0329-4*); pap. 15.00 (*0-7388-0330-8*) Xlibris Corp.

Nightmonsters. Sharon Shebar. Ed. by Dan Wasserman. (Ten Word Book Ser.). (Illus.). (J). (gr. k-1). 1979. 9.95 (*0-89868-068-9*); pap. 3.95 (*0-89868-079-4*) ARO Pub.

Nightmonsters: Big Big Book. Sharon Shebar. Ed. by Dan Wasserman. (Ten Word Book Ser.). (Illus.). (J). (gr. k-1). 1979. 22.00 (*0-614-24514-1*) ARO Pub.

***Nightmusic.** Wignall. 2001. write for info. (*0-15-100580-X*) Harcourt.

Nightpool. Houghton Mifflin Company Staff. (Literature Experience 1991 Ser.). (J). (gr. 8). 1990. pap. 11.04 (*0-395-55187-0*) HM.

Nightpool. Houghton Mifflin Company Staff. (Literature Experience 1993 Ser.). (J). 1992. pap. 11.04 (*0-395-61879-7*) HM.

Nightprowlers. Jerry Emory. LC 93-27547. (Gulliver Green Book Ser.). (Illus.). 48p. (J). (gr. 3-7). 1994. pap. 14.95 (*0-15-200694-X*, Gulliver Bks) Harcourt.

Nightreaver. Michael D. Weaver. 192p. 1988. pap. 2.95 (*0-380-75197-6*, Avon Bks) Morrow Avon.

Nightrider: A Play Based on a Legend from Oregon's Mt. Hood. Michael P. Jones. (Illus.). 84p. 1984. text 14.00 (*0-89904-091-8*); pap. text 9.00 (*0-89904-090-X*) Crumb Elbow Pub.

Nightrider: A Working Copy of a Play. Michael P. Jones. Tr. by Ole E. Petterson. (Illus.). 54p. 1984. pap. 5.50 (*0-89904-088-8*); text 10.00 (*0-89904-089-6*) Crumb Elbow Pub.

Nightriders. Jim Walker. (Wells Fargo Trail Ser.: Bk. 2). 272p. 1994. pap. 8.99 (*1-55661-429-2*) Bethany Hse.

Nightriders. large type ed. Jim Walker. LC 97-259. (Christian Fiction Ser.). 448p. 1997. 22.95 (*0-7862-1066-4*) Thorndike Pr.

Nightriders: Inside Story of the West & Kimbrell Clan. Richard Briley, 3rd. 102p. 1992. reprint ed. pap. 10.00 (*0-9646846-3-2*) Dogwood TX.

Nightrider's Moon. Lauran Paine. 160p. 1988. 16.95 (*0-8027-4083-9*) Walker & Co.

Nightriffer. Stanley Nelson. (Illus.). 108p. 1988. pap. 5.95 (*0-913559-02-4*) Birch Brook Pr.

Nightriffer. deluxe ed. Stanley Nelson. (Illus.). 108p. 1988. pap. 30.00 (*0-913559-01-6*) Birch Brook Pr.

Nightrose. Dorothy Garlock. 384p. 1990. mass mkt. 5.50 (*0-446-35607-7*, Pub. by Warner Bks) Little.

Nightrose. large type ed. Dorothy Garlock. LC 97-1516. 1997. 26.95 (*0-7838-8098-7*, G K Hall Lrg Type) Mac Lib Ref.

Nightrunners. Joe R. Lansdale. 248p. 1995. mass mkt. 4.95 (*0-7867-0289-3*) Carroll & Graf.

Nights. Alfred De Musset.Tr. of Nuit. 48p. 1999. pap. 12.95 (*1-892355-02-7*) Fifth Season.

Nights. H. D., pseud. LC 85-28472. 192p. 1986. 19.95 (*0-8112-0979-2*, Pub. by New Directions) Norton.

Nights. Edna O'Brien. 1987. pap. 12.00 (*0-374-52051-8*) FS&G.

Nights: The Official Strategy Guide. PCS Staff. LC 96-69704. 96p. 1996. pap., per. 14.99 (*0-7615-0866-X*) Prima Pub.

Nights & Days on the Gypsy Trail: Through Andalusia & Other Mediterranean Shores. Irving H. Brown. LC 75-3452. (Illus.). reprint ed. 49.50 (*0-404-16885-X*) AMS Pr.

Nights As Day, Days As Night. Michel Leiris. Tr. by Richard Sieburth from FRE. LC 87-83301.Tr. of Nuit sans Nuit. 198p. 1988. pap. 13.00 (*0-941419-07-X*, Eridanos Library) Marsilio Pubs.

Nights at the Circus. Angela Carter. (Fiction Ser.). 304p. 1986. pap. 12.95 (*0-14-007703-0*, Penguin Bks) Viking Penguin.

Nights Below Station Street. David Adams Richards. 1994. pap. 12.95 (*0-7710-7465-4*) McCland & Stewart.

Nights Below Station Street. David Adams Richards. 224p. 1997. reprint ed. pap. 11.95 (*0-7710-7467-0*) McCland & Stewart.

Night's Black Agent. Fritz Leiber. 1976. reprint ed. lib. bdg. 21.95 (*0-88411-932-7*) Amereon Ltd.

Night's Black Agent. Fritz Leiber. 1990. reprint ed. 27.95 (*0-89968-538-2*) Buccaneer Bks.

Night's Black Agents. Fritz Leiber. LC 76-363952. x, 237p. (J). 1975. write for info. (*0-85978-013-9*) C W Daniel.

Night's Black Agents. large type ed. David Armstrong. (Linford Mystery Library). 352p. 1998. pap. 17.99 (*0-7089-5214-3*, Linford) Ulverscroft.

***Night's Dream, 5 vols.** Steck-Vaughn Company Staff. (Illus.). (J). 2000. pap. 26.95 (*0-8114-6969-7*) Raintree Steck-V.

Nights in Aruba. Andrew Holleran. LC 84-4885. 244p. 1984. pap. 10.95 (*0-452-26395-6*, Plume) Dutton Plume.

Nights in the Big City: Paris, Berlin, London, 1840-1930. Joachim Schlor. LC 99-490307. (Topographics Ser.). (Illus.). 304p. 1998. pap. 26.00 (*1-86189-015-X*, Pub. by Reaktion Bks) Consort Bk Sales.

Nights in the Gardens of Brooklyn. Harvey Swados. LC 71-128751. (Short Story Index Reprint Ser.). 1977. 19.95 (*0-8369-3642-6*) Ayer.

Nights in Vienna. (In Classical Mood Ser.: Vol. 4). (Illus.). 1997. write for info. incl. cd-rom (*1-886614-26-1*) Intl Masters Pub.

Nights in White Satin: A Laura Principal Novel. Michelle Spring. LC 98-55777. 288p. 1999. 23.00 (*0-345-42493-X*) Ballantine Pub Grp.

***Nights in White Satin: A Laura Principal Novel.** Michelle Spring. 2000. mass mkt. 6.50 (*0-345-42494-8*) Fawcett.

Night's Journey. Bahman Sholevar. 1988. write for info. (*0-911323-12-0*) Concourse Pr.

Night's Journey & the Coming of the Messiah. Bahman Sholevar. LC 84-70283. (Literature-Fiction Ser.). 230p. 1984. 18.00 (*0-911323-06-6*) Concourse Pr.

Night's Journey & the Coming of the Messiah. Bahman Sholevar. 1988. write for info. (*0-911323-13-9*) Concourse Pr.

***Night's Lies.** Gesualdo Bufalino. Tr. by Patrick Creagh. 160p. 2000. pap. text 13.00 (*1-86046-110-7*) Harvill Press.

Nights of Fire, Nights of Rain. Amy Uyematsu. LC 97-40146. 112p. 1998. pap. text 12.00 (*1-885266-52-9*) Story Line.

Nights of Ice. Spike Walker. LC 97-6207. 208p. 1997. text 20.95 (*0-312-15611-1*) St Martin.

Nights of Ice. Spike Walker. LC 99-10810. 224p. 1999. pap. 12.95 (*0-312-19993-7*) St Martin.

Nights of Labor: The Workers' Dream in Nineteenth-Century France. Jacques Ranciere. Tr. by John Drury from FRE. 448p. (C). 1989. 49.95 (*0-87722-625-3*) Temple U Pr.

Nights of Labor: The Worker's Dream in Nineteenth-Century France. Jacques Ranciere. Tr. by John Drury. 448p. 1991. pap. 22.95 (*0-87722-833-7*) Temple U Pr.

Nights of 1990. Richard McCann. (Illus.). 22p. 1994. pap. 6.00 (*1-879294-08-7*) Warm Spring Pr.

Nights of Summer, Nights of Autumn. Paula I. Robbins. (Illus.). 195p. (C). 1992. pap. 12.95 (*0-9632975-0-3*) Sampo Pub.

Nights of Summer, Nights of Autumn: Self-Care for Bodyworkers. Paula I. Robbins. (Illus.). 195p. (Orig.). (C). 1992. spiral bd. 12.95 (*0-9632875-0-8*) Sampo Pub.

Nights of the Pufflings. Bruce Mcmillan. (Illus.). 32p. (J). 1997. pap. 4.95 (*0-395-85693-0*) HM.

Nights of the Pufflings. Bruce McMillan. LC 94-14808. (Illus.). 32p. (J). (gr. k-5). 1995. 16.00 (*0-395-70810-9*) HM.

Nights of the Pufflings. Bruce McMillan. 1997. 10.15 (*0-606-11684-2*, Pub. by Turtleback) Demco.

***Nights of the Round Table.** Margery Lawrence. Ed. by Richard Dalby. xx, 220p. 1998. 39.50 (*1-899562-63-X*) Ash-Tree.

Nights on the Heights. Giuseppe Bonaviri. Tr. by Giovanni R. Bussino from ITA. LC 90-40033. XIV, 204p. (C). 1991. text 42.95 (*0-8204-1355-0*) P Lang Pubng.

Night's Soft Folds: Reflections...Life & Poetry of Josephine Van Gasse Basiliko. J. J. Van Gasse. LC 97-68595. 80p. (Orig.). 1997. pap. 10.95 (*1-882792-46-7*) Proctor Pubns.

Nights That Make the Night: Selected Poems of Vicent Andres Estelles. Vicent A. Estelles. Tr. & Intro. by David H. Rosenthal. LC 91-42692. 96p. (Orig.). 1992. pap. 9.95 (*0-89255-172-0*) Persea Bks.

Nights to Imagine: Magical Places to Stay in America. Peter Guttman. 80p. 1996. 17.00 (*0-679-03341-6*) Fodors Travel.

Nights under a Tin Roof. James A. Autry. 1983. 15.95 (*0-916242-26-9*) Yoknapatawpha.

Nightscape. Stephen R. George. 352p. 1992. mass mkt. 4.50 (*0-8217-3849-6*, Zebra Kensgtn) Kensgtn Pub Corp.

Nightseasons. Peter Cooley. LC 82-74302. 1983. 20.95 (*0-915604-82-5*); pap. 11.95 (*0-915604-83-3*) Carnegie-Mellon.

Nightseer. Laurell K. Hamilton. 304p. 1992. mass mkt. 5.99 (*0-451-45143-0*, ROC) NAL.

Nightshade. Laurell K. Hamilton. Ed. by Dave Stern. (Star Trek: The Next Generation Ser.: No. 24). 288p. 1992. mass mkt. 5.50 (*0-671-79566-X*) PB.

***Nightshade.** John Saul. LC 00-25918. 336p. 2000. 25.95 (*0-345-43329-7*) Ballantine Pub Grp.

***Nightshade.** John Saul. LC 00-39680. 2000. pap. write for info. (*0-7838-9070-2*, G K Hall & Co) Mac Lib Ref.

Nightshade. Rachel Weininger. LC 88-63135. (Illus.). 64p. (Orig.). (J). (gr. 4-6). 1989. pap. 5.95 (*0-931093-11-2*) Red Hen Pr.

Nightshade. Karen Williams. 256p. (Orig.). 1995. pap. 11.99 (*1-883061-08-3*) Rising AZ.

Nightshade: American Hero, Night Tales. Nora Roberts. (Intimate Moments Ser.). 1993. mass mkt. 3.50 (*0-373-07529-4*, 5-07529-6) Silhouette.

Nightshade Nightstand Reader. Ed. by Roy Zarucchi & Carolyn Page. (Illus.). 276p. (Orig.). 1995. pap. 13.95 (*1-879205-63-7*) Nightshade Pr.

***Nightshades.** Greg Chupita. 1999. pap. write for info. (*1-58235-355-7*) Watermrk Pr.

Nightshift. Pete McKenna. 128p. 1996. pap. 12.95 (*1-898927-40-5*, Pub. by S T Pubng) AK Pr Dist.

Nightshift Workers. George Charlton. LC 88-51785. 64p. (Orig.). 1989. pap. 11.95 (*1-85224-070-9*, Pub. by Bloodaxe Bks) Dufour.

Nightside the Long Sun. Gene Wolfe. 352p. 1993. mass mkt. 4.99 (*0-8125-1625-7*, Pub. by Tor Bks) St Martin.

Nightson, Vol. 15. Ed. by Douglas DeMars. 60p. (Orig.). 1995. 6.50 (*1-878306-07-3*) Nightsun Frostburg.

Nightsong. Margaret E. Kelchner. 168p. 1995. pap. 9.99 (*0-8341-1529-8*) Beacon Hill.

Nightsong: Performance, Power & Practice in South Africa. Veit Erlmann. LC 94-24977. 462p. 1996. pap. text 24.95 (*0-226-21721-3*); lib. bdg. 75.00 (*0-226-21720-5*) U Ch Pr.

Nightsong: The Video. Veit Erlmann. 1996. lib. bdg. 50.00 (*0-226-21719-1*) U Ch Pr.

Nightsounds. Pamela R. Young. LC 99-64384. 300p. 1997. 25.00 (*0-7388-0446-0*); pap. 18.00 (*0-7388-0447-9*) Xlibris Corp.

Nightspawn. John Banville. 200p. 1993. pap. 16.95 (*1-85235-126-8*) Dufour.

Nightstalker Companion: A 25th Anniversary Tribute. Mark Dawidziak. LC 97-67156. (Illus.). 208p. 1997. pap. 17.95 (*0-938817-44-2*) Pomegranate Pr.

Nightstar. Fern Michaels. 1998. per. 5.50 (*1-55166-458-5*, 1-66458-0, Mira Bks) Harlequin Bks.

Nightstar. Fern Michaels. (Best of the Best Ser.). 1993. per. 4.50 (*0-373-48274-4*, 5-48274-0) Silhouette.

Nightstar, 1973-1978. Mari Evans. (Special Publications). (Illus.). 78p. 1981. pap. 4.95 (*0-934934-07-X*) CAAS Pubns.

Nightsun. Ed. by Douglas DeMars. 60p. (Orig.). 1993. pap. 5.00 (*1-878306-05-7*) Nightsun Frostburg.

Nightsun. Ed. by Douglas DeMars & Barbara Wilson. 52p. (Orig.). 1991. pap. text 5.00 (*1-878306-02-2*) Nightsun Frostburg.

Nightsun. Ed. by Wilson DeMars. LC 89-63279. 50p. (Orig.). 1989. pap. 5.00 (*1-878306-00-6*) Nightsun Frostburg.

Nightsun, No. 17. Ed. by Barbara Hurd. 56p. 1997. pap. 5.00 (*1-878306-09-X*) Nightsun Frostburg.

Nightsun, No. 18. Ed. by Barbara Hurd. 56p. 1998. pap. 5.00 (*1-878306-10-3*) Nightsun Frostburg.

***Nightsun, No. 19.** Barbara Hurd. 56p. 1999. pap. 5.00 (*1-878306-11-1*) Nightsun Frostburg.

Nightsun, Vol. 16. Ed. by Douglas DeMars. 64p. (Orig.). (C). 1996. pap. 6.50 (*1-878306-08-1*) Nightsun Frostburg.

Nightswimmer. Joseph Olshan. 320p. 1996. reprint ed. mass mkt. 6.99 (*0-425-15190-5*) Berkley Pub.

Nightswimming: Stephen Barker. Photos by Stephen Barker. (Illus.). 96p. 1999. 60.00 (*0-944092-54-3*) Twin Palms Pub.

Nightswimming: Stephen Barker. limited ed. Photos by Stephen Barker. (Illus.). 96p. 1999. 400.00 (*0-944092-55-1*) Twin Palms Pub.

Nightsword: A Starshield Novel. Margaret Weis & Tracy Hickman. 1999. mass mkt. 6.99 (*0-345-42462-X*, Del Rey) Ballantine Pub Grp.

Nightsword: A Starshield Novel, Vol. 2. Margaret Weis & Tracy Hickman. LC 98-5897. 384p. 1998. 24.95 (*0-345-39762-2*, Del Rey) Ballantine Pub Grp.

Nighttime at the Zoo. Dale Smith. LC 96-94349. (Grandad, Tell Us a Story Ser.). (Illus.). 32p. (J). (ps-1). 1997. 14.95 (*1-886864-10-1*) Goldn Anchor Pr.

Nighttime Guardian. Aaron Werner. 237p. 1994. text 15.95 (*1-885006-14-4*); pap. text 12.95 (*1-885006-15-2*) Three Beacons.

Nighttime in the Desert Vol. 1: And Other Desert Songs, Vol. 1. Patty Horn. (Illus.). (Orig.). (J). (gr. k-5). 1995. pap. text 7.95 (*0-9644105-4-0*) Two Geckos Mus.

Nighttime in the Desert & Other Desert Songs, Vol. 1. unabridged ed. Patty Horn. (Illus.). (J). (gr. k-5). 1995. pap. 15.95 incl. audio (*0-9644105-5-9*) Two Geckos Mus.

***Nighttime Is Just Daytime with Your Eyes Closed.** Mark Lowry. LC 99-40180. (The Adventures of Piper the Hyper Mouse Ser.). (Illus.). 32p. (gr. k-4). 1999. 14.99 (*1-58229-076-8*) Howard Pub LA.

***Nighttime Nonsense: A Picture-It Storybook - A Reader Illustrated Storybook.** Julia Kalin. (Illus.). 12p. (J). (ps-6). 1999. pap. 12.95 (*0-9672430-7-6*) Stay Play.

Nighttime Parenting. William M. Sears. 1993. pap. 10.00 (*0-452-27196-7*, Plume) Dutton Plume.

***Nighttime Parenting: How to Get Your Baby & Child to Sleep.** William Sears. 1999. pap. 12.95 (*0-452-28148-2*, Plume) Dutton Plume.

Nighttime Parenting: How to Get Your Baby & Child to Sleep. 2nd rev. ed. William Sears. LC 99-63632. (Growing Family Ser.). (Illus.). 1999. pap. 9.95 (*0-912500-53-0*) La Leche.

Nighttime Quests of Irwin Botski. Mary Rutkovsky-Ruskin. 18p. (Orig.). 1994. pap. text 8.95 (*1-885902-02-6*) Printable Arts.

Nightwalk & Other Poems. Constance Hunting. LC 79-57074. 47p. 1979. pap. 8.95 (*0-89101-041-6*) U Maine Pr.

***Nightwalker.** Stephanie James, pseud. 2000. mass mkt. 4.50 (*0-373-80695-7*, 1-80695-9, Harlequin) Harlequin Bks.

Nightwalker - The Villee Affair: Three Assignments for the Millenniums End Contemporary Roleplaying Game System. Charles Ryan. (Illus.). 88p. (Orig.). 1991. pap. text 11.95 (*0-9628748-1-7*) Chameleon Eclectic.

Nightwalker & the Buffalo. Althea Bass. (Indian Culture Ser.). 32p. (J). (gr. 5-9). 1972. pap. 4.95 (*0-89992-032-2*) Coun India Ed.

Nightwalkers. Judy K. Morris. LC 96-16241. (Illus.). 144p. (J). (gr. 3-7). 1996. 14.95 (*0-06-027200-7*) HarpC Child Bks.

Nightwalkers: Gothic Horror Movies; The Modern Era. Bruce L. Wright. LC 95-4858. (Illus.). 176p. 1995. pap. 17.95 (*0-87833-879-9*) Taylor Pub.

Nightwalking: Voices from Kent State. Sandra Perlman. 80p. (Orig.). 1995. pap. 10.00 (*1-885663-01-3*) Franklin Mills.

Nightwatch. Richard P. Henrick. LC 99-20897. 336p. 1999. 23.00 (*0-380-97423-1*, Avon Bks) Morrow Avon.

Nightwatch. large type ed. Frank Palmer. 1997. pap. 21.95 (*0-7838-2041-0*) Thorndike Pr.

Nightwatch: A Novel. John Leax. 144p. 1990. pap. 6.99 (*0-310-21861-6*) Zondervan.

Nightwatch: A Practical Guide to Viewing the Universe. 3rd rev. expanded ed. Terence Dickinson. (Illus.). 176p. 1998. 45.00 (*1-55209-300-X*); pap. 29.95 (*1-55209-302-6*) Firefly Bks Ltd.

Nightwatch: An Equinox Guide to Viewing the Universe. rev. ed. Terence Dickinson. (Illus.). 159p. 1999. reprint ed. pap. text 22.00 (*0-7881-6407-4*) DIANE Pub.

Nightwatch: New & Selected Poems 1968-1996. Dennis Lee. 208p. 1996. pap. 15.99 (*0-7710-5215-4*) McCland & Stewart.

Nightwatch: Nightlife in the Tropical Rain Forest. Peter Riley & Sherry Gerstein. LC 98-65524. (Windows on Science Ser.). (Illus.). 16p. (J). (gr. 3-7). 1999. 12.99 (*1-57584-251-3*, Pub. by Rdrs Digest) Random.

Nightwatch: The Making of a Movement in the Peruvian Andes. Orin Starn. LC 98-41295. (Latin America Otherwise Ser.). 1999. 49.95 (*0-8223-2301-X*); pap. 17.95 (*0-8223-2321-4*) Duke.

N

Nightwatch over Nature: People, Natures & Politics. Alexander Cockburn. 2000. 24.00 (*0-8133-3054-8*) Westview.

Nightwatcher. Charles Wilson. 288p. 1997. reprint ed. mass mkt. 4.99 (*0-8439-4275-4*, Leisure Bks) Dorchester Pub Co.

Nightway. Janet Dailey. 1993. per. 6.99 (*0-671-87509-4*) PB.

Nightway: A History & a History of Documentation of a Navajo Ceremonial. James C. Faris. LC 90-30005. (Illus.). 288p. 1994. pap. 18.95 (*0-8263-1564-X*) U of NM Pr.

Nightwing. Ed. by Fotonovel Publications Staff. (Illus.). (Orig.). 1979. pap. 2.75 (*0-686-52702-X*) Fotonovel.

Nightwing. Lynn Michaels. LC 95-13947. (Temptation Ser.). 218p. 1995. per. 3.25 (*0-373-25642-6*, 1-25642-9) Harlequin Bks.

Nightwing. Martin Cruz Smith. 224p. 1991. mass mkt. 5.99 (*0-345-37059-7*) Ballantine Pub Grp.

***Nightwing.** Martin Cruz Smith. 2000. mass mkt. 6.99 (*0-345-91705-7*) Ballantine Pub Grp.

Nightwing: A Knight in Bludhaven. Schuck Dixon. (Illus.). 192p. 1998. pap. text 14.95 (*1-56389-425-4*, Pub. by DC Comics) Time Warner.

***Nightwing: Love & Bullets.** Chuck Dixon. (Illus.). 144p. 2000. pap. 17.95 (*1-56389-613-3*, Pub. by DC Comics) Time Warner.

Nightwing: Rough Justice. Chuck Dixon. (Illus.). 224p. 1999. text 17.95 (*1-56389-523-4*, Pub. by DC Comics) Time Warner.

Nightwing: Ties that Bind. Dennis O'Neil & Alan Grant. Ed. by Greg Land & Dick Giordano. LC 98-100054. (Illus.). 144p. 1997. pap. text 12.95 (*1-56389-328-2*, Pub. by DC Comics) Time Warner.

***Nightwood.** Djuna Barnes. LC 99-56308. 224p. 2000. 18.95 (*0-679-64024-X*) Modern Lib NY.

Nightwood. Djuna Barnes. LC 49-1384. 1961. pap. 9.95 (*0-8112-0005-1*, NDP98, Pub. by New Directions) Norton.

Nightwood. Robert Muller. 32p. 1991. 17.00 (*0-385-25305-2*) Doubleday.

Nightwood. Robin Muller. 32p. 1995. mass mkt. 9.95 (*0-385-25544-6*) Doubleday.

Nightwood: The Original Version & Related Drafts. Djuna Barnes. Ed. by Cheryl J. Plumb. LC 94-36949. 319p. 1995. 23.95 (*1-56478-080-5*) Dalkey Arch.

Nightwords: 50 Poems. Samuel Hazo. 95p. 1987. pap. 12.95 (*0-935296-74-3*, Pub. by Sheep Meadow) U Pr of New Eng.

Nightwork. Joseph Hansen. LC 83-12846. (Dave Brandsetter Mystery Ser.). 88p. 1995. pap. 5.95 (*0-8050-1055-6*, Owl) H Holt & Co.

***Nightwork.** Christine Schutt. LC 00-20978. 129p. 2000. reprint ed. pap. 10.95 (*1-56478-239-5*, Pub. by Dalkey Arch) Chicago Distribution Ctr.

Nightwork: Sexuality, Pleasure & Corporate Masculinity in a Tokyo Hostess Club. Anne Allison. LC 93-34877. 228p. 1994. pap. text 15.00 (*0-226-01487-8*) U Ch Pr.

Nightwork: Sexuality, Pleasure & Corporate Masculinity in a Tokyo Hostess Club. Anne Allison. LC 93-34877. 228p. 1996. lib. bdg. 37.00 (*0-226-01485-1*) U Ch Pr.

Nightworks. Prod. by Zobeida Perez. 20p. (Orig.). 1993. pap. 5.50 (*0-89898-652-4*, F3313P9X) Wrner Bros.

***Nightworks: Poems, 1962-2000.** Marvin Bell. 360p. 2000. 28.00 (*1-55659-147-0*) Copper Canyon.

Nightworld. F. Paul Wilson. 400p. 1993. mass mkt. 6.99 (*0-515-11159-7*, Jove) Berkley Pub.

Nighty-Night. Dawn Apperley. LC 98-66851. (Illus.). 8p. (J). (ps). 1999. 5.95 (*0-316-60427-5*) Little.

Nighty-Night. Wendy Lewison. (Poke & Look Bks.). (Illus.). 16p. (J). (ps-1). 1992. spiral bd., bds. 9.95 (*0-448-40391-9*, G & D) Peng Put Young Read.

Nighty-Night, Teddy Beddy Bear. Illus. by Tina Marksbury. (Cuddle Cloth Bks.). 12p. (J). (ps). 1986. 4.99 (*0-394-88244-X*, Pub. by Random Bks Yng Read) Random.

Nighty-Nightmare. James Howe. LC 86-22334. (Bunnicula Ser.). (Illus.). 128p. (J). (gr. 3-5). 1987. 15.00 (*0-689-31207-5*) Atheneum Yung Read.

Nighty-Nightmare. James Howe. (Bunnicula Ser.). 128p. (J). (gr. 3-7). 1997. per. 4.50 (*0-689-81724-X*) S&S Childrens.

Nighty-Nightmare. James Howe. (Bunnicula Ser.). (J). (gr. 3-5). 1997. 9.85 (*0-606-12453-5*) Turtleback.

Nighty-Nightmare. James Howe. (Bunnicula Ser.). (Illus.). 128p. (J). (gr. 3-5). 1988. reprint ed. pap. 3.99 (*0-380-70490-0*, Avon Bks) Morrow Avon.

Niginik Katittigaangapta. large type ed. Margaret Nickerson.Tr. of Gathering Food. (ESK., Illus.). 8p. (J). (gr. k-3). 1999. pap. text 14.50 (*1-58084-133-3*) Lower Kuskokwim.

Nigredo. Norman Weinstein. LC 82-748. 96p. 1982. pap. 5.50 (*0-930794-68-0*) Station Hill Pr.

NIH Readings on the Protection of Human Subjects in Behavioral & Social Science Research. Ed. by Joan E. Sieber. LC 84-7563. 203p. 1984. lib. bdg. 55.00 (*0-313-27071-6*, U7071, Greenwood Pr) Greenwood.

***Nih Telephone & Service Directory, November 1999.** 556p. 2000. spiral bd. 52.00 (*0-16-050245-4*) USGPO.

Nihancan's Feast of Beaver: Animal Tales of the North American Indians. Edward Lavitt & Robert McDowell. (Illus.). 120p. 1990. pap. 12.95 (*0-89013-211-9*) Museum NM Pr.

Nihil Obstat: Religion, Politics & Social Change in East-Central Europe & Russia. Sabrina P. Ramet. LC 97-23350. ix, 425p. 1998. text 69.95 (*0-8223-2056-8*); pap. text 23.95 (*0-8223-2070-3*) Duke.

Nihil Obstat in Story Telling. S. A. Bonebakker. (Mededelingen der Koninklijke Nederlandse Akademie van Wetenschappen, Afd. Letterkunde Ser.: No. 55(8)). 1992. pap. 15.00 (*0-444-85756-7*) Elsevier.

Nihilesthete. Richard Kalish. LC 86-62449. 160p. 1987. 22.00 (*0-932966-77-2*) Permanent Pr.

Nihilism: A Philosophical Essay. Stanley Rosen. LC 70-81428. 261p. reprint ed. pap. 81.00 (*0-8357-8250-6*, 203387700087) Bks Demand.

***Nihilism: A Philosophical Essay.** unabridged ed. Stanley Rosen. LC 99-48134. 272p. 2000. reprint ed. pap. 25.00 (*1-890318-45-0*, Pub. by St Augustines Pr) Chicago Distribution Ctr.

Nihilism: Its Origin & Nature with a Christian Answer. Helmut Thielicke. Tr. by John W. Doberstein from GER. LC 81-7186.Tr. of Der/Nihilismus. 190p. 1981. reprint ed. lib. bdg. 55.00 (*0-313-23143-5*, THIN, Greenwood Pr) Greenwood.

Nihilism: The Root of the Revolution of the Modern Age. Eugene Rose. 104p. 1994. pap. 5.95 (*0-938635-15-8*) St Herman Pr.

Nihilism Before Nietzsche. Michael A. Gillespie. 336p. 1994. 27.50 (*0-226-29347-5*) U Ch Pr.

Nihilism Before Nietzsche. Michael A. Gillespie. xxiv, 312p. 1996. pap. text 15.95 (*0-226-29348-3*) U Ch Pr.

Nihilism Incorporated: European Civilization & Environmental Destruction. Arran Gare. 190p. 1994. pap. 24.95 (*0-646-14871-0*, Pub. by White Horse Pr) Paul & Co Pubs.

***Nihilism Now.** Keith Ansell-Pearson. LC 99-88249. 2000. text 59.95 (*0-312-23209-8*) St Martin.

Nihilist Princess. Louise M. Gagneur. 256p. 1999. pap. 12.00 (*1-886625-05-0*) III Pub.

Nihilistic Egoist. Paterson. 336p. 1993. 63.95 (*0-7512-0258-4*) Ashgate Pub Co.

Nihmmachi: A Story of San Francisco's Japantown. Suzie K. Diazaki. (Illus.). 135p. (Orig.). 1985. pap. text 25.00 (*0-9615546-0-6*) SKO Studios.

Nihon no Seiji see Political Dynamics of Japan

Nihon to Koza: Lectures on Japanese Swords, 10 vols. Tr. by Harry A. Watson from JPN. (Nihon to Koza Ser.). (Illus.). 500p. Date not set. write for info. (*1-888612-10-X*) Afu Res Enter.

Nihon to Koza: Shinshinto, 1772-1925. 2nd ed. Ed. & Tr. by Harry A. Watson. (Nihon to Koza Ser.: Vol. IV). (JPN., Illus.). 500p. 1993. 150.00 (*1-888612-00-2*) Afu Res Enter.

Nihon to Koza Pt. 1: Kodogu. 2nd ed. Ed. by Harry A. Watson. (Nihon to Koza Ser.: Vol. VI). (Illus.). Date not set. lib. bdg. 150.00 (*1-888612-02-9*) Afu Res Enter.

Nihon to Koza Pt. 1: Koto. rev. ed. Ed. by Harry A. Watson. (Nihon to Koza Ser.: Vol. II). (Illus.). 1996. lib. bdg. 150.00 (*1-888612-03-7*) Afu Res Enter.

Nihon to Koza Pt. 2: Koto. Ed. by Harry A. Watson. (Nihon to Koza Ser.: Vol. III). (Illus.). 1996. 150.00 (*1-888612-05-3*) Afu Res Enter.

Nihon to Koza Pt. 3: Koto. 2nd ed. Ed. by Harry A. Watson. (Nihon to Koza Ser.: Vol. IX). (Illus.). 500p. 1996. lib. bdg. 150.00 (*1-888612-04-5*) Afu Res Enter.

Nihon to Koza Vol. IV: Shinto, 1596-1771. 2nd ed. Ed. by Harry A. Watson. (Nihon to Koza Ser.: Vol. IV). (Illus.). 420p. 1993. 150.00 (*1-888612-01-0*) Afu Res Enter.

Nihonga: Transcending the Past: Japanese-Style Painting, 1868-1968. Ellen P. Conant. Tr. by J. Thomas Rimer & Stephen D. Owyoung. (Illus.). 352p. 1996. 80.00 (*0-8348-0363-1*) Weatherhill.

Nihonga, Transcending the Past: Japanese-Style Painting, 1868-1968. Ellen P. Conant et al. Ed. by Reiko Tomii & Mary A. Steiner. (Illus.). 352p. 1995. pap. text 40.00 (*0-89178-044-0*) St Louis Art Mus.

Nihongi: Chronicles of Japan from the Earliest Times to A.D. 697. Tr. by William G. Aston. LC 70-152110. (Illus.). 852p. 1971. pap. 19.95 (*0-8048-0984-4*) Tuttle Pubng.

Nihongo: In Defence of Japanese. Roy A. Miller. LC 85-23007. 260p. (C). 1986. text 45.00 (*0-485-11251-5*, Pub. by Athlone Pr) Humanities.

Nihongo: Introductory Japanese, Vol. 1. Yutaka Sato & Margaret Y. Yamashita. 248p. 1992. 24.95 (*0-935848-94-0*); pap. 19.95 (*1-880188-19-8*) Bess Pr.

Nihongo: Introductory Japanese, Vol. 1. Yutaka Sato & Margaret Y. Yamashita. 248p. 1992. pap., teacher ed. 24.95 (*0-935848-98-3*) Bess Pr.

Nihongo Vol. 1: Introductory Japanese. Yutaka Sato & Margaret Y. Yamashita. 248p. 1992. pap., student ed. 12.95 (*0-935848-99-1*) Bess Pr.

Nihongo Vol. 2: Introductory Japanese, Vol. 2. Yutaka Sato & Margaret Y. Yamashita. (Illus.). 192p. 1993. pap. text 19.95 (*1-880188-73-2*) Bess Pr.

Nihongo Vol. 2: Introductory Japanese, Vol. 2. Yutaka Sato & Margaret Y. Yamashita. (Illus.). 192p. 1994. text 24.95 (*1-880188-81-3*) Bess Pr.

Nihongo Vol. 2: Introductory Japanese, Vol. 2. Yutaka Sato & Margaret Y. Yamashita. (Illus.). 128p. 1995. pap. text, wbk. ed. 12.95 (*1-880188-75-9*) Bess Pr.

Nihongo Vol. 2: Introductory Japanese, Vol. 2. 2nd ed. Yutaka Sato & Margaret Y. Yamashita. (Illus.). 192p. 1994. pap. text, teacher ed. 24.95 (*1-880188-76-7*) Bess Pr.

Nihongo Daisuki! Japanese Language Activities for Children. Susan H. Hirate & Noriko Kawaura. LC 89-81822. (ENG & JPN., Illus.). 208p. (J). (gr. k-6). 1990. pap., teacher ed. 14.95 (*0-935848-82-7*) Bess Pr.

Nihongo Pera Pera: A User's Guide to Japanese Onomatopoeia. Susan Millington. 152p. 1993. pap. 9.95 (*0-8048-1890-8*) Tuttle Pubng.

Niigugis Maqaxtazaqangis: Atkan Historical Traditions. 2nd ed. Ed. & Tr. by Knut Bergslad. 114p. 1979. pap. 4.00 (*0-933769-16-4*) Alaska Native.

Ni'ihau: The Last Hawaiian Island. Ruth M. Tabrah. 243p. 1987. pap. 12.95 (*0-916630-59-5*) Pr Pacifica.

Niihau: The Traditions of a Hawaiian Island. Rerioterai Tava & Moses K. Keale, Sr. 160p. 1989. pap. 16.95 (*0-935180-80-X*) Mutual Pub HI.

Niihau Incident. Allan Beekman. LC 82-83137. (Illus.). 128p. 1982. pap. 6.95 (*0-9609132-0-3*) Heritage Pac.

Ni'ihau Shell Leis. Linda P. Moriarty. LC 86-50306. (Illus.). 104p. 1986. 39.95 (*0-8248-0998-X*, Kolowalu Bk) UH Pr.

Niiwam & Taaw. Sembene Ousmane. Tr. by Catherine Glenn-Lauga. (African Writers Ser.). 110p. (C). 1992. pap. 8.95 (*0-435-90671-2*, 90671) Heinemann.

Niiwan. Taaw, Nouvelles. Ousmane Sembene. (FRE.). 1987. pap. 14.95 (*0-7859-3301-8*, 2708704869) Fr & Eur.

Nijhoff, Van Ostaijen, "De Stijl" Bulhof. 1976. pap. text 82.00 (*90-247-1857-0*) Kluwer Academic.

Nijinsky. Lesley I. Sampson. 320p. 1990. 64.00 (*0-85131-411-2*, Pub. by J A Allen) St Mut.

Nijinsky - Death of a Faun. David Ponwall. (Oberon Bks.). 72p. 1997. pap. 12.95 (*1-84002-000-8*) Theatre Comm.

Nijinsky Dancing! From the Golden Age of the Ballets Russe. Anne Holliday. (Illus.). 22p. (Orig.). 1996. pap. 10.00 (*1-877809-58-6*) Park Pl Pubns.

Nijinsky, Pavlova, Duncan: Three Lives in Dance. Ed. by Paul Magriel. (Series in Dance). 1977. reprint ed. lib. bdg. 35.00 (*0-306-70845-0*) Da Capo.

Nijinsky, Pavlova, Duncan: Three Lives in Dance. Ed. by Paul Magriel. (Series in Dance). (Illus.). 288p. 1977. reprint ed. pap. 14.95 (*0-306-80035-7*) Da Capo.

Nijinsky's Crime Against Grace: Rite of Spring. Hodson. (Dance & Music Ser.: Vol. 8). 1996. 64.00 (*0-945193-43-2*) Pendragon NY.

Nijinsky's Faune Restored, Vol. 3. Ann H. Guest. (Language of Dance Ser.). xiv, 204p. 1991. text 22.00 (*2-88124-819-5*) Gordon & Breach.

Nijole's House. Hannah Weiner. 32p. (Orig.). 1981. pap. 5.50 (*0-937013-02-1*) Potes Poets.

NIK: Now I Know. Aidan Chambers. LC 87-30836. (Charlotte Zolotow Bk.). 288p. (YA). (gr. 7 up). 1988. 13.95 (*0-06-021208-X*) HarpC Child Bks.

Nika Hazelton Way with Vegetables. Nika Hazelton. 370p. 1995. 9.98 (*0-7858-0396-3*) Bk Sales Inc.

Nika Hazelton's the Regional Italian Kitchen. Nika Hazelton. 370p. 1995. 9.98 (*0-7858-0459-5*) Bk Sales Inc.

Nike: A Romance. Nicholas Flokos. LC 98-11869. 192p. 1998. 20.00 (*0-395-88396-2*) HM.

***Nike: A Romance.** Nicholas Flokos. 176p. 2000. pap. 10.00 (*0-618-00207-3*) HM.

Nike: Nike. William Gould. (VGM's Business Portraits Ser.). (Illus.). 48p. (YA). 1998. 14.95 (*0-8442-4706-5*, VGM Career) NTC Contemp Pub Co.

Nike Culture: The Sign of the Swoosh. Robert Goldman. LC 98-61739. (Core Culture Icons Ser.). 194 p. 1998. 74.50 (*0-7619-6148-8*) Sage.

Nike, Inc. The WetFeet.com Insider Guide. 4th ed. WetFeet.com Staff. (Insider Guides Ser.). 35p. 1999. spiral bd. 25.00 (*1-58207-053-9*) WetFeet.

***Nike Is a Goddess: The History of Women in Sports.** Lissa Smith. LC 98-27049. 352p. 1998. 25.00 (*0-87113-726-7*, Atlntc Mnthly) Grove-Atltic.

***Nike Is a Goddess: The History of Women in Sports.** Ed. by Lissa Smith. 352p. 1999. pap. 14.00 (*0-87113-761-5*, Atlntc Mnthly) Grove-Atltic.

Nikephoros 8, 1995. (GER.). 1996. 98.00 (*3-615-00183-4*, Pub. by Weidmann) Lubrecht & Cramer.

Nikephoros 5, 1992. (GER.). 128.00 (*3-615-00097-8*, Pub. by Weidmann) Lubrecht & Cramer.

Nikephoros, Patriarch of Constantinople, Short History. Tr. & Comment by Cyril A. Mango. LC 89-17058. (Dumbarton Oaks Texts: Vol. 10). (Illus.). 264p. 1990. 30.00 (*0-88402-184-X*, MANI, Dumbarton Rsch Lib) Dumbarton Oaks.

Nikephoros 7, 1994. (GER.). 98.00 (*3-615-00174-5*, Pub. by Weidmann) Lubrecht & Cramer.

Nikephoros 6, 1993. (GER.). 128.00 (*3-615-00137-0*, Pub. by Weidmann) Lubrecht & Cramer.

Nikephoros, Zeitschrift fur Sport und Kultur im Altertum. Wolfgang Decker et al. (GER., Illus.). 288p. 1996. 98.00 (*3-615-00191-5*) G Olms Pubs.

Niketas Choniates: Erlaeuterungen zu den Reden und Briefen Nebst Einer Biographie. Jan-Louis Van Dieten. (Supplementa Byzantina Ser.: Vol. 2). (C). 1971. 108.50 (*3-11-002290-7*) De Gruyter.

Niki de Saint Phalle: Insider-Outsider--World Inspired Art. Ed. by Martha W. Longenecker. (Illus.). 120p. 1998. 35.00 (*0-914155-10-5*) Mingei Intl Mus.

Niki de Saint Phalle: The Tarot Garden. Pierre Restany et al. LC 99-178176. (Illus.). 120p. 1998. pap. 25.00 (*88-8158-167-1*, Pub. by Charta) Dist Art Pubs.

Niki de Saint Phalle Traces, 1930-1949: Autobiography. Niki De Saint Phalle. (Illus.). 220p. 1999. 24.95 (*2-940033-43-9*, Pub. by Acatos Edit) Antique Collect.

***Nikita Khrushchev.** William Taubman & Nikita Khruschchev. Tr. by David Gehrenbeck. (Illus.). 464p. 2000. 45.00 (*0-300-07635-5*) Yale U Pr.

Nikita Khrushchev & the Creation of a Superpower, 2 vols. Sergei N. Khrushchev. Tr. by Shirley Benson from RUS. LC 98-54931. 848p. 2000. 59.95 (*0-271-01927-1*) Pa St U Pr.

Nikita's Shadows. rev. ed. Soma Vira. LC 96-71651. (Planet Keepers Ser.: Vol. 3). 223p. 1997. pap. 12.95 (*0-9646057-3-2*) Space Link Bks.

Nikkei Donburi: A Japanese American Cultural Survival Guide. Chris Aihara. LC 98-7207. (Illus.). (J). 1999. pap. 18.95 (*1-879965-18-6*) Polychrome Pub.

Nikkei Legacy: The Story of Japanese Canadians from Settlement to Today. Toyo Takata. (Illus.). 192p. 1993. 21.95 (*0-919601-94-4*, Pub. by NC Ltd) U of Toronto Pr.

Nikkei Microdevices: 1998 Flat Panel Display Yearbook. Ed. by Jack Bernstein. (Illus.). 218p. 1998. 495.00 (*1-884730-13-2*, Interlingua) JB & Me.

Nikkei Microdevices 1999 Flat Panel Display Yearbook. Ed. by Jack Bernstein. (Illus.). 220p. 1999. 995.00 (*1-884730-16-7*, Interlingua) JB & Me.

Nikkei Placement Guide International, 1994-1995. Ed. by Jennifer Kos. pap. 10.00 (*0-9642587-8-1*) Disco Intl.

***Nikken Sekkel: Building Future Japan, 1900-2000.** Botond Bognar. (Illus.). 352p. 2000. text 65.00 (*0-8478-2246-X*) Rizzoli Intl.

***Nikki.** Gustav BenJava. LC 00-190327. 318p. 2000. 25.00 (*0-7388-1723-6*); pap. 18.00 (*0-7388-1724-4*) Xlibris Corp.

Nikki & David Goldbeck's American Wholefoods Cuisine: Over 1300 Meatless Wholesome Recipes from Short Order to Gourmet. Nikki Goldbeck & David Goldbeck. 590p. 1984. pap. 16.95 (*0-452-26280-1*, Plume) Dutton Plume.

***Nikki & the Rocking Horse.** Alan Brown. (Illus.). (J). (ps-3). 1999. pap. 9.95 (*0-00-664517-8*, Pub. by HarpC) Trafalgar.

Nikki Giovanni. Virginia C. Fowler. LC 92-16731. (United States Authors Ser.: No. 613). 150p. 1992. 28.95 (*0-8057-3983-1*, Twyne) Mac Lib Ref.

***Nikki Giovanni: Poet of the People.** Judith Pinkerton Josephson. LC 99-50864. (African-American Biographies Ser.). (Illus.). 128p. (YA). (gr. 6 up). 2000. lib. bdg. 20.95 (*0-7660-1238-7*) Enslow Pubs.

***Nikki Giovanni in the Classroom: The Same ol Danger but a Brand New Pleasure.** Carol Jago. LC 99-36770. 90p. 1999. pap. 12.95 (*0-8141-5212-0*, 52120) NCTE.

Nikki Haskell's Star Diet: Look & Feel Like a Star. Balanced Products, Inc. Staff & Nikki Haskell. 256p. 1998. 20.00 (*1-57566-283-3*, Knsington) Kensgtn Pub Corp.

Nikki, Rooster & Chick-a-Biddy. Naomi Russell. (Illus.). 100p. (J). 1998. 15.00 (*0-89904-761-0*); pap. 10.00 (*0-89904-762-9*) Crumb Elbow Pub.

Nikki's Adventures. Carol L. Ballard & Bryan L. Ballard. (Illus.). 40p. (J). (gr. k-6). 1999. pap. 18.00 (*0-8059-4675-6*) Dorrance.

Niklas Vogt, 1756-1836: A Personality of the Late German Enlightenment & Early Romantic Movement. Steven A. Stargardter. LC 91-12412. (Modern European History Outstanding Studies & Dissertations). 176p. 1991. text 15.00 (*0-8240-2539-3*) Garland.

Nikola Tesla: A Bibliography. Nikola Tesla. 1991. lib. bdg. 99.95 (*0-8490-4107-4*) Gordon Pr.

Nikola Tesla: A Spark of Genius. Carol Dommermuth-Costa. LC 93-43123. (Lerner Biography Ser.). (Illus.). 144p. (J). (gr. 5 up). 1994. lib. bdg. 23.95 (*0-8225-4920-4*, Lerner Publctns) Lerner Pub.

Nikola Tesla: Colorado Springs Notes, 1899-1900. Nikola Tesla. (Nikola Tesla Ser.). 1986. lib. bdg. 250.00 (*0-8490-3837-5*) Gordon Pr.

Nikola Tesla: Colorado Springs Notes (1899-1900) unabridged ed. Ed. & Compiled by Nikola Tesla Museum Staff. 437p. 1978. reprint ed. 40.00 (*0-945001-69-X*) GSG & Assocs.

Nikola Tesla: Complete Patents. unabridged ed. Compiled by John T. Ratzlaff. 500p. 1983. reprint ed. 40.00 (*0-945001-70-3*) GSG & Assocs.

Nikola Tesla: Free Energy & the White Dove. Commander X. 148p. 1990. 15.00 (*0-938294-82-2*) Inner Light.

Nikola Tesla: Incredible Scientist & Prodigal Genius the Life of Nikola Tesla. Morrison Colladay & John J. O'Neill. 76p. 1996. reprint ed. pap. 12.95 (*1-56459-738-5*) Kessinger Pub.

Nikola Tesla: Lectures, Patents, Articles, 2 vols. Nikola Tesla. 1000+p. 1992. 65.00 (*0-685-52649-6*) Tesla Bk Co.

Nikola Tesla: The Lost Inventions. Nikola Tesla. 1991. lib. bdg. 250.00 (*0-8490-4808-7*) Gordon Pr.

***Nikola Tesla: The Man Who Harnessed Niagara Falls.** Marc Seifer. (Illus.). 2000. pap. 12.95 (*1-56649-169-X*) Welcome Rain.

Nikola Tesla - Colorado Springs Correspondence: Material Related to the Early History of Radio in the United States. annot. ed. Nikola Tesla. Ed. by Gary L. Peterson. (Illus.). spiral bd. write for info. (*0-9636012-3-7*) Twty Frst Cent.

Nikola Tesla - Guided Weapons & Computer Technology. Nikola Tesla. Ed. by Leland I. Anderson et al. LC 98-22686. (Tesla Presents Ser.: Pt. 3). (Illus.). xv, 241p. 1998. 31.95 (*0-9636012-5-3*); pap. 18.95 (*0-9636012-9-6*) Twty Frst Cent.

Nikola Tesla - Lecture Before the New York Academy of Sciences, April 6, 1897: The Streams of Lenard & Roentgen: a Novel Apparatus for Their Production. Nikola Tesla. Ed. by L. I. Anderson. LC 94-61004. (Tesla Presents Ser.: Part 2). (Illus.). xix, 123p. 1994. pap. 12.95 (*0-9636012-7-X*) Twty Frst Cent.

Nikola Tesla, Dreamer: His Three-Day Trip to Europe & His Scheme to Split the Earth. Allan L. Benson. 29p. 1996. reprint ed. spiral bd. 8.00 (*0-7873-0093-4*) Hlth Research.

Nikola Tesla, 1856-1943: Lectures, Patents, Articles, 2 vols., Set. Ed. by Nikola Tesla Museum Staff. 1996. reprint ed. 89.50 (*0-7873-0634-7*) Hlth Research.

Nikola Tesla on His Work with Alternating Currents: Their Application to Wireless Telegraphy, Telephony & Transmission of Power. Nikola Tesla. Ed. by Leland I. Anderson. (Tesla Presents Ser.: Pt. 1). (Illus.). xvi, 237p. 1992. spiral bd. 26.95 (*0-9636012-4-5*) Twty Frst Cent.

Nikola Tesla Research. Nikola Tesla et al. (Nikola Tesla Ser.). 1991. lib. bdg. 75.00 (*0-8490-4279-8*) Gordon Pr.

Nikola Tesla Research. Ed. by Health Research Staff. 50p. 1996. reprint ed. spiral bd. 12.00 (*0-7873-0404-2*) Hlth Research.

Nikola Tesla Returns: 20th Anniversary Edition. 20th ed. Robert R. Leichtman. 96p. 1998. pap. text 7.95 (*0-89804-840-0*) Ariel GA.

Nikola Tesla's Earthquake Machine: With Tesla's Original Patents Plus New Blueprints to Build Your Own Working Model. Dale Pond & Walter Baumgartner. LC 95-76243. (Illus.). 176p. (Orig.). 1995. pap. 16.95 (*1-57282-008-X*, D2008X) Message NM.

An Asterisk (*) at the beginning of an entry indicates that the title is appearing for the first time.

Nikola Tesla's Teleforce & Telegeodynamics Proposals. Nikola Tesla. Ed. by Leland I. Anderson. LC 99-49562. (Tesla Presents Ser.: Pt. 4). (Illus.). 119p. 1998. pap. 24.95 (*0-9636012-8-8*) Twty Frst Cent.

***Nikola the Outlaw.** Ivan Olbracht. 2001. pap. 18.95 (*0-8101-1827-0*) Northwestern U Pr.

Nikolai Bukharin & the Transition from Capitalism to Socialism. Michael Haynes. LC 85-2582. 144p. 1985. 29.50 (*0-8419-1026-X*) Holmes & Meier.

Nikolai Gogol. Vladimir Nabokov. LC 44-8135. 1961. pap. 9.95 (*0-8112-0120-1*, NDP78, Pub. by New Directions) Norton.

Nikolai Gogol: The Overcoat, 2 cassettes, Set. 72p. (YA). 1993. pap. 39.50 incl. audio (*1-57970-012-8*, SRU120) Audio-Forum.

Nikolai Gogol & the Baroque Cultural Heritage. Gavriel Shapiro. 276p. (C). 1993. 45.00 (*0-271-00861-X*) Pa St U Pr.

Nikolai Gogol's Quest for Beauty: An Exploration into His Works. Jesse Zeldin. LC 78-2693. x, 246p. 1978. 25.00 (*0-7006-0173-2*) U Pr of KS.

Nikolai Gumilev, 1886-1986: Papers from the Gumilev Centenary Symposium Held at Ross Priory, University of Strathclyde, 1986. Ed. by Sheelagh D. Graham. (Illus.). 332p. 1987. pap. 16.00 (*0-933884-60-5*) Berkeley Slavic.

Nikolai Ivanovich Bukharin: A Centenary Appraisal. Nicholas N. Kozlov & Eric D. Weitz. LC 89-22828. 192p. 1990. 57.95 (*0-275-93261-3*, C3261, Greenwood Pr) Greenwood.

Nikolai Leskov: The Man & His Art. Hugh McLean. 796p. 1977. 50.00 (*0-674-62471-8*) HUP.

Nikolai Strakhov. Linda Gerstein. LC 79-139720. (Russian Research Center Studies: No. 65). 247p. 1971. 29.00 (*0-674-62475-0*) HUP.

***Nikolai Zabolotsky: Enigma & Cultural Paradigm.** Sarah Pratt. 368p. 1999. 69.95 (*0-8101-1421-6*) Northwestern U Pr.

Nikolai Zabolotsky: Play for Mortal Stakes. Darra Goldstein. LC 92-46108. (Studies in Russian Literature). (Illus.). 322p. (C). 1994. text 74.95 (*0-521-41896-8*) Cambridge U Pr.

Nikolaus Grass: Alm und Wein. Louis Carlen & Hans C. Faussner. (GER.). x, 436p. 1990. 128.00 (*3-615-00036-6*, Pub. by Weidmann) Lubrecht & Cramer.

Nikolaus Grass: Ausgewahlte Aufsatze zum 80. Geburtstag. Louis Carlen & Hans C. Faussner. (GER.). xix, 545p. 1993. 148.00 (*3-615-00095-1*, Pub. by Weidmann) Lubrecht & Cramer.

Nikolaus Lenau. Hugo Schmidt. LC 68-17227. (Twayne's World Authors Ser.). 1971. lib. bdg. 20.95 (*0-8057-2520-2*) Irvington.

Nikolaus Pevsner. Charles Rennie Mackintosh. 1998. pap. text 7.99 (*88-86502-89-3*, Pub. by Canal & Stamperia) Antique Collect.

Nikolaus von Amsdorf, 1483-1565: Popular Polemics in the Preservation of Luther's Legacy. Robert Kolb. 296p. 1978. text 77.50 (*90-6004-354-5*, Pub. by B De Graaf) Coronet Bks.

***Nikon Camera Repair Handbook.** Thomas Tomosy. (Illus.). 144p. 2000. pap. 39.95 (*1-58428-041-7*, Pub. by Amherst Media) IPG Chicago.

Nikon Classic Cameras, Vol. 1. Paul Comon. (Magic Lantern Guides). (Illus.). 176p. (Orig.). (C). 1998. pap. 19.95 (*1-883403-31-6*, H 191, Silver Pixel Pr) Saunders Photo.

Nikon Classic Cameras, Vol. 2. B. Moose Peterson. (Magic Lantern Guides). (Illus.). 176p. (Orig.). (C). 1998. pap. 19.95 (*1-883403-38-3*, H 192, Silver Pixel Pr) Saunders Photo.

***Nikon F100.** Artur Landt. LC 99-39067. (Magic Lantern Guides Ser.). 176p. 1999. pap. 19.95 (*1-883403-61-8*, Silver Pixel Pr) Saunders Photo.

Nikon F50-N50. Hove Foto Books Staff. (Illus.). 220p. 1996. pap. text 19.95 (*1-874031-50-9*, Pub. by Hove Foto) Watsn-Guptill.

Nikon F5. Gunter Richter. LC 97-178221. (Magic Lantern Guides Ser.). (Illus.). 176p. (Orig.). (C). 1998. pap. 19.95 (*1-883403-24-3*, H 131, Silver Pixel Pr) Saunders Photo.

Nikon F4-F3. B. Moose Peterson. LC 95-128067. (Magic Lantern Guides Ser.). (Illus.). 176p. (Orig.). (C). 1998. pap. 19.95 (*1-883403-12-X*, H 130, Silver Pixel Pr) Saunders Photo.

Nikon Field Guide: A Photographer's Portable Reference. Thom Hogan. LC 97-51846. (Illus.). 288p. 1998. pap. 19.95 (*1-883403-44-8*, H 606, Silver Pixel Pr) Saunders Photo.

Nikon Field Guide: A Photographer's Portable Reference. 2nd ed. Thom Hogan. LC 99-36397. (Illus.). 288p. 1999. pap. 19.95 (*1-883403-58-8*, Pub. by Saunders Photo) Sterling.

Nikon Flash Systems SB24-25-26. Hove Foto Books Staff. (Illus.). 220p. 1996. pap. text 19.95 (*1-874031-26-6*, Pub. by Hove Foto) Watsn-Guptill.

Nikon F90-N90. Hove Foto Books Staff. LC 70-1017. (Illus.). 220p. 1993. pap. text 19.95 (*1-874031-01-0*, Pub. by Hove Foto) Watsn-Guptill.

Nikon F70-N70 John Clements. Hove Foto Books Staff. (Illus.). 220p. 1996. pap. text 19.95 (*1-874031-70-3*, Pub. by Hove Foto) Watsn-Guptill.

Nikon F601 AF & M-N6006-N6000-N5005. (User's Guides Bks.). (Illus.). 220p. text 19.95 (*0-906447-71-2*, Pub. by Hove Foto) Watsn-Guptill.

Nikon Lenses. B. Moose Peterson. LC 94-182693. (Magic Lantern Guides Ser.). (Illus.). 176p. (Orig.). (C). 1998. pap. 19.95 (*1-883403-07-3*, H 138, Silver Pixel Pr) Saunders Photo.

***Nikon Lenses.** 2nd ed. B. Peterson. LC 99-38318. (Magic Lantern Guides Ser.). 176p. 2000. pap. 19.95 (*1-883403-63-4*, Silver Pixel Pr) Saunders Photo.

Nikon Modern Classics F2, EL, FM FE2, FT2, FA. (Modern Classics Ser.). (Illus.). 196p. text 19.95 (*0-906447-75-5*, Pub. by Hove Foto) Watsn-Guptill.

Nikon N90s/F90x. 2nd ed. Michael Huber & B. Moose Peterson. Tr. by Hayley Ohlig from GER. LC 98-134660. (Magic Lantern Guides Ser.). (Illus.). 192p. 1998. pap. 19.95 (*1-883403-45-6*, H 133, Silver Pixel Pr) Saunders Photo.

Nikon N50-F50. Peter K. Burian & Gunter Richter. Tr. by Hayley Ohlig from GER. LC 95-128048. (Magic Lantern Guides Ser.). (Illus.). 176p. (Orig.). (C). 1998. pap. 19.95 (*1-883403-13-8*, H 134, Silver Pixel Pr) Saunders Photo.

Nikon N4004s-N4004. Hove Foto Books Staff. LC 70-3009. (Illus.). 220p. 1993. text 19.95 (*0-86343-300-6*, Pub. by Hove Foto) Watsn-Guptill.

Nikon N70-F70. Gunter Richter & Peter K. Burian. Tr. by Hayley Ohlig from GER. (Magic Lantern Guides Ser.). (Illus.). 176p. (Orig.). (C). 1998. pap. 19.95 (*1-883403-19-7*, H 141, Silver Pixel Pr) Saunders Photo.

Nikon N6006-N8008s-N6000. Paul Comon. LC 95-128074. (Magic Lantern Guides Ser.). (Illus.). 176p. (Orig.). (C). 1998. pap. 19.95 (*1-883403-11-1*, H 139, Silver Pixel Pr) Saunders Photo.

Nikon N60. Artur Landt. LC 99-10123. (Magic Lantern Guides Ser.). (Illus.). 176p. 1999. pap. 19.95 (*1-883403-56-1*, Pub. by Saunders Photo) Sterling.

Nikon Pro-Guide: Nikkor AF Lenses & Their Uses. John Clements. 208p. 1997. pap. text 29.95 (*1-874031-37-1*, Pub. by Hove Foto) Watsn-Guptill.

Nikon SB-28 Flash System. Michale Huber. LC 98-36469. (Magic Lantern Guides Ser.). 1999. pap. write for info. (*1-883403-52-9*, Silver Pixel Pr) Saunders Photo.

Nikon SB-26 Flash System. B. Moose Peterson & Michael Huber. Tr. by Phyllis M. Riefler-Bonham from GER. (Magic Lantern Guides Ser.). (Illus.). 176p. (C). 1998. pap. 19.95 (*1-883403-29-4*, H 140, Silver Pixel Pr) Saunders Photo.

Nikon System Handbook. Moose Peterson. 164p. 1991. pap. 19.95 (*0-929667-03-4*, 10252) Images NY.

Nikon System Handbook. 5th rev. ed. B. Moose Peterson & Heather Angel. LC 98-28426. (Illus.). 184 p. 1998. pap. 24.95 (*1-883403-50-2*, H 609, Silver Pixel Pr) Saunders Photo.

***Nikon System Handbook.** 6th ed. B. Peterson. LC 99-26695. 176p. 2000. pap. 24.95 (*1-883403-64-2*, Silver Pixel Pr) Saunders Photo.

Nikonian Chronicle, Vol. III. Ed. & Tr. by Serge A. Zenkovsky. 305p. 1986. 35.00 (*0-940670-02-X*) Darwin Pr.

Nikonian Chronicle, Vol. IV. Ed. & Tr. by Serge A. Zenkovsky from RUS. Tr. by Betty J. Zenkovsky from RUS. LC 84-210330. 256p. 1988. 35.00 (*0-940670-03-8*) Darwin Pr.

Nikonian Chronicle, Vol. V. Ed. & Tr. by Serge A. Zenkovsky from RUS. Tr. by Betty J. Zenkovsky from RUS. LC 88-80729. 325p. 1989. 35.00 (*0-940670-04-6*) Darwin Pr.

***Nikopol Trilogy.** deluxe ed. Enki Bilal. (Illus.). 176p. 1999. 39.95 (*0-9672401-2-3*) Humanoids.

Nikos Kazantzakis Novelist. Peter Bien. (Studies in Modern Greek). 115p. (Orig.). (C). 1989. pap. text 16.00 (*0-89241-484-7*); lib. bdg. 25.00 (*0-89241-483-9*) Caratzas.

Nikos the Fisherman. Fiona French. (Illus.). 32p. (J). Date not set. write for info. (*0-19-279971-1*) OUP.

Nil Sorsky: The Complete Writings. Ed. & Tr. by George A. Maloney from RUS. (Classics of Western Spirituality Ser.). 192p. 2000. 24.95 (*0-8091-0497-0*); pap. 18.95 (*0-8091-3810-7*) Paulist Pr.

Nil und Euthenia. Gertrud Platz-Horster. (Winckelmannsprogramm der Archaologischen Gesellschaft zu Berlin Ser.: No. 133). (GER.). 47p. (C). 1992. pap. text 29.25 (*3-11-013779-8*) De Gruyter.

Nilda. 2nd ed. Nicholasa Mohr. LC 87-70274. 292p. (YA). (ps up). 1986. pap. 11.95 (*0-934770-61-1*) Arte Publico.

Nile see Great Rivers

Nile. Cari Meister. LC 98-29324. (Rivers & Lakes Ser.). (J). 2002. lib. bdg. 19.92 (*1-57765-098-0*) ABDO Pub Co.

Nile. Illus. by Claire Mumford. (Butterfly Bks.). 32p. (J). (gr. 3-5). 1983. 9.95 (*0-86685-447-9*) Intl Bk Ctr.

***Nile.** Kazuyoshi Nomachi. LC 98-46908. 1998. 34.95 (*962-217-543-0*, Pub. by China Guides) Norton.

Nile. 2nd ed. Insight Guides Staff. (Insight Guides). 1998. pap. text 23.95 (*0-88729-729-3*) Langenscheidt.

***Nile: Histories, Cultures, Myths.** Ed. by Haggai Erlich & Israel Gershoni. LC 99-21066. 308p. 1999. lib. bdg. 55.00 (*1-55587-672-2*) L Rienner.

Nile: Notes for Travelers in Egypt (1901) E. A. Wallis Budge. 700p. 1998. reprint ed. pap. 49.95 (*0-7661-0360-9*) Kessinger Pub.

Nile: Sharing a Scarce Resource: An Historical & Technical Review of Water Management & of Economic & Legal Issues. Ed. by P. P. Howell & J. A. Allan. (Illus.). 426p. (C). 1994. text 85.00 (*0-521-45040-3*) Cambridge U Pr.

***Nile: The Longest River.** Aileen Weintraub. LC 00-23908. (Illus.). 2000. write for info. (*0-8239-5638-5*) Rosen Group.

Nile & Egyptian Civilization. Alexandre Moret. (African Studies). reprint ed. 50.00 (*0-938818-99-6*) ECA Assoc.

Nile & Its Environment. Ed. by Mohamed Kassas & I. Ghabbour. 136p. 1980. pap. 24.00 (*0-08-026081-0*, Pergamon Pr) Elsevier.

Nile Basin. 2nd ed. Richard F. Burton. LC 65-23403. (Middle East in the 20th Century Ser.). 1967. reprint ed. 25.00 (*0-306-70926-0*) Da Capo.

Nile Empire Sourcebook. (Torg Ser.). 128p. 18.00 (*0-87431-305-8*, 20506) West End Games.

Nile Journeys. Charles Derowitsch. LC 97-75987. (Illus.). 160p. 1998. 19.95 (*1-57197-106-8*) Pentland Pr.

Nile Mosaic of Palestrina: Early Evidence of Egyptian Religion in Italy. Paul G. Meyboom. 424p. 1994. text 152.00 (*90-04-10137-3*) Brill Academic Pubs.

Nile Nightmare: A Novel of Suspense. Will H. Ryan. 288p. (Orig.). 1993. pap. 12.95 (*1-56474-049-8*) Fithian Pr.

Nile Notes of a Howadji. Harriot Curtis. (Works of Harriot Curtis). 1990. reprint ed. lib. bdg. 79.00 (*0-685-44776-6*) Rprt Serv.

Nile Quest. Harry Johnston. 1971. 39.00 (*0-403-00378-4*) Scholarly.

Nile Quest. Harry Johnston. 2003. pap. 19.00 (*0-685-47614-6*) Scholarly.

Nile Quest. Harry Johnston. 1988. reprint ed. lib. bdg. 49.00 (*0-7812-0926-9*) Rprt Serv.

Nile River. Allan Fowler. LC 98-43962. (Rookie Read-About Geography Ser.). 32p. (J). (gr. 1-2). 1999. 19.00 (*0-516-21559-0*) Childrens.

***Nile River.** Allan Fowler. (Rookie Read-About Geography Ser.). (J). 2000. pap. text 5.95 (*0-516-26559-8*) Childrens.

Nile Valley Contributions to Civilization. Anthony T. Browder et al. (Illus.). 64p. 1994. pap., student ed. 10.00 (*0-924944-05-6*) Inst Karmic.

Nile Valley Contributions to Civilization: Exploding the Myths, Vol. 1. Anthony T. Browder. LC 92-73935. (Illus.). 296p. 1992. 39.95 (*0-924944-04-8*); pap. 16.95 (*0-924944-03-X*) Inst Karmic.

Niles Likes to Smile: Big Book. large type ed. Cass Hollander & Patrick Girouard. (Little Books & Big Bks.). (Illus.). 8p. (J). (gr. k-2). 1997. pap. text 19.47 (*0-8215-0932-2*) Sadlier.

Niles-Merton Songs: Opus 171 & 172. John J. Niles & Thomas Merton. (Illus.). 95p. 1981. spiral bd. 15.95 (*0-916656-16-0*, MF755) Mark Foster Mus.

Niles, Songs of John Jacob: Low Voice & Piano. J. Niles. 1993. per. 12.95 (*0-7935-2334-6*) H Leonard.

Nili Ancyrani. Ed. by Conca. (GRE.). 1983. 29.95 (*3-322-00150-4*, T1907, Pub. by B G Teubner) U of Mich Pr.

Nili Spies. Anita Engle. 1997. 47.50 (*0-7146-4803-5*, Pub. by F Cass Pubs) Intl Spec Bk.

Nili Spies. 2nd ed. Anita Engle. 256p. 1997. pap. 19.50 (*0-7146-4293-2*, Pub. by F Cass Pubs) Intl Spec Bk.

Nilla's Big Adventure. Sue Barbetta. (Illus.). 32p. (J). (gr. k-3). 1998. pap. 4.95 (*1-892774-00-3*) Bullfrog Pubg.

Nilo & the Tortoise. Ted Lewin. LC 98-27489. (J). 1999. write for info. (*0-590-73912-3*) Scholastic Inc.

Nilo & the Tortoise. Ted Lewin. LC 98-27489. 40p. (J). (gr. k-3). 1999. 16.95 (*0-590-96004-0*) Scholastic Inc.

Nilo-Saharan Proceedings. Ed. by M. C. Bender & T. C. Schadeberg. x, 349p. 1981. pap. 83.10 (*90-70176-26-2*) Mouton.

Nilopolitics: A Hydrological Regime, 1870-1990. Mohamed-Hate El-Atawy. 62p. 1997. pap. 10.00 (*977-424-407-9*, Pub. by Am Univ Cairo Pr) Col U Pr.

Nilos Law of Sea Yearbook, 1994. 1996. 565.00 (*90-411-0173-X*) Kluwer Law Intl.

Nilotic World: The Atuot-speaking Peoples of the Southern Sudan, 1. John W. Burton. LC 86-31790. (Contributions to the Study of Anthropology Ser.: No. 1). 188p. 1987. 49.95 (*0-313-25501-6*, BND/, Greenwood Pr) Greenwood.

Nilpferd In der Vorstellungswelt der Alten Agypter. Almuth Behrmann. 203p. 1996. 42.95 (*3-631-48964-1*) P Lang Pubng.

Nilpotence & Periodicity in Stable Homotopy Theory. Douglas C. Ravenel. LC 92-26785. (Annals of Mathematics Studies: No. 128). 209p. (C). 1993. text 79.50 (*0-691-08792-X*, Pub. by Princeton U Pr); pap. text 29.95 (*0-691-02572-X*, Pub. by Princeton U Pr) Cal Prin Full Svc.

Nilpotent Groups & Their Automorphisms. Evgenii I. Khukhro. LC 93-16401. (Expositions in Mathematics Ser.: No. 8). xiv, 252p. (C). 1993. lib. bdg. 99.95 (*3-11-013672-4*) De Gruyter.

Nilpotent Lie Algebras. Michel Goze & Yusupdjan Khakimdjanov. LC 95-48426. (Mathematics & Its Applications Ser.: Vol. 361). 352p. (C). 1996. text 180.50 (*0-7923-3932-0*) Kluwer Academic.

Nilpotent Orbits: Primitive Ideals & Characteristic Classes. Jean-Luc Brylinski & R. D. MacPherson. (Progress in Mathematics Ser.: No. 78). 144p. 1989. 45.00 (*0-8176-3473-8*) Birkhauser.

Nilpotent Orbits in Semisimple Lie Algebras. David H. Collingwood & William M. McGovern. LC 92-30461. 192p. (gr. 13). 1993. ring bd. 94.95 (*0-534-18834-6*, Chap & Hall CRC) CRC Pr.

Nils Alwall Festschrift. Ed. by C. M. Kjellstrand. (Journal: Nephrology: Vol. 39, No. 2). (Illus.). 88p. 1984. pap. 48.00 (*3-8055-4001-9*) S Karger.

Nils Discovers America Adventures: Adventures with Erik. Julie McDonald. 96p. (J). (gr. 2-6). 1990. pap. 8.95 (*0-941016-74-9*) Penfield.

Nilsson: The Autobiography of Birgit Nilsson. unabridged ed. Birgit Nilsson. (Great Voices Ser.). 500p. 1997. 42.00 (*1-880909-57-X*) Baskerville.

Nilsson Electric Circuits Translation: Translation. 4th ed. James W. Nilsson. (C). 1995. pap. text. write for info. (*0-201-42044-9*) Addison-Wesley.

Niltown Neighbors in "Don't Tell Stephen" Anthony D. Luck. (J). (gr. k). 1996. pap. 6.95 (*0-533-11969-3*) Vantage.

Nim: A Chimpanzee Who Learned Sign Language. Herbert S. Terrace. LC 85-26928. (Animal Intelligence Ser.). (Illus.). 303p. 1987. pap. text 20.00 (*0-231-06341-5*) Col U Pr.

Nim & the War Effort. Milly Lee. (Illus.). 40p. (J). (gr. 1 up). 1997. 16.00 (*0-374-35523-1*) FS&G.

Nimai Coloring Book. large type ed. Bonnie McElroy. (Illus.). 32p. (J). 1992. pap. 4.95 (*0-945475-30-6*, 1204, Pub. by Mandala Pub Grp) Words Distrib.

Nimbe on Growing Golden. Katina Kefalus. (Illus.). 14p. 1999. pap. 4.95 (*1-929172-03-6*) Emerald Prodns.

Nimbe on Growing Up. Katina Kefalus. (Illus.). 14p. 1999. pap. 4.95 (*1-929172-05-2*) Emerald Prodns.

Nimbe on Life & Death. Katina Kefalus. (Illus.). 14p. 1999. pap. 4.95 (*1-929172-06-0*) Emerald Prodns.

Nimbe's Family. Katina Kefalus. (Illus.). 14p. 1999. pap. 4.95 (*1-929172-02-8*) Emerald Prodns.

Nimbe's Journey. Katina Kefalus. (Illus.). 14p. 1999. pap. 4.95 (*1-929172-01-X*) Emerald Prodns.

Nimbe's Key. Katina Kefalus. (Illus.). 14p. 1999. pap. 4.95 (*1-929172-04-4*) Emerald Prodns.

***Nimble Believing: Dickinson & the Unknown.** James McIntosh. LC 99-54534. 208p. (C). 2000. text 42.50 (*0-472-11080-2*, 11080) U of Mich Pr.

Nimble Documentation: The Practical Guide to World Class Organizations. Adrienne Escoe. LC 97-15785. (Illus.). 247p. 1997. 47.00 (*0-87389-423-5*, H0961) ASQ Qual Pr.

Nimble Reader: Literary Theory & Children's Literature. Roderick McGillis. LC 95-36099. 1996. 30.00 (*0-8057-9033-0*, Hall Reference) Macmillan.

Nimble with Numbers. Laura Childs. 160p. (ps-3). 1999. pap. text 15.95 (*1-57232-983-1*) Seymour Pubns.

Nimble with Numbers. Leigh Childs. 160p. (J). 1997. pap. text 14.95 (*1-57232-439-2*) Seymour Pubns.

Nimble with Numbers. Leigh Childs. 1998. pap. text 14.95 (*1-57232-986-6*) Seymour Pubns.

Nimble with Numbers. Leigh Childs. 160p. 1999. pap. text 15.95 (*1-57232-985-8*) Seymour Pubns.

Nimble with Numbers. Leigh Childs. 1999. pap. text 15.95 (*1-57232-984-X*) Seymour Pubns.

Nimble with Numbers. Leigh Childs & Laura Choate. Ed. by Patricia Brill et al. (Practice Bookshelf Ser.). (Illus.). 162p. (J). (gr. 3-4). 1997. pap. text 14.95 (*1-57232-842-8*, 21850) Seymour Pubns.

Nimbus. Alexander Jablokov. 2000. 22.00 (*0-380-97228-X*, Avon Bks) Morrow Avon.

Nimbus Story: Technology Serving the Arts. John Griffiths. 288p. 1995. 50.00 (*0-233-98888-2*, Pub. by Andre Deutsch) Trafalgar.

Nimby. Jasper Tomkins. 1987. pap. 6.95 (*0-310-57091-3*, 16109P) Zondervan.

NIMBY Case Studies: Overcoming Exclusion in Rural Communities. Housing Assistance Council Staff. 135p. 1994. 7.00 (*1-58064-057-5*) Housing Assist.

Nimby Politics in Japan: Energy Sitting & the Management of Environmental Conflict. S. Hayden Lesbirel. LC 98-38148. (Illus.). 187p. 1999. 33.95 (*0-8014-3537-4*) Cornell U Pr.

NIMBYs & LULUs: Not-in-My-Backyard & Locally-Unwanted-Land-Uses. Jan Horah & Heather Scott. 23p. 1993. pap. 10.00 (*0-86602-302-X*, Sage Prdcls Pr) Sage.

Nimes at War: Religion, Politics, & Public Opinion in the Gard, 1938-1944. Robert Zaretsky. 328p. (C). 1995. 60.00 (*0-271-01326-5*); pap. 15.95 (*0-271-01327-3*) Pa St U Pr.

Nimes City Plan. (Grafocarte Maps Ser.). 1994. 8.95 (*2-7416-0030-9*, 80030) Michelin.

Nimes Pont du Gard. Casa Bonechi. 32p. pap. text 8.95 (*88-7009-397-2*, Pub. by Bonechi) Eiron.

Nimieri & the Revolution of Dismay. Mansour Khalid. 300p. 1985. 39.50 (*0-7103-0111-1*) Routledge.

***Nimisha's Ship.** Anne McCaffrey. LC 98-45500. 388p. 1999. 25.00 (*0-345-38825-9*, Del Rey) Ballantine Pub Grp.

***Nimisha's Ship.** Anne McCaffrey. 2000. mass mkt. 6.99 (*0-345-43425-0*, Del Rey) Ballantine Pub Grp.

Nimitz. E. B. Potter. LC 76-1056. (Illus.). 507p. 1976. 36.95 (*0-87021-492-6*) Naval Inst Pr.

Nimitz: Reflections on Pearl Harbor. 1985. pap. 2.00 (*0-934841-04-7*) Adm Nimitz Foun.

Nimitz: Steamboat Hotel. Herman Toepperwein. (Illus.). 12p. (Orig.). 1987. pap. 2.00 (*0-934841-09-8*) Adm Nimitz Foun.

Nimitz: The Man & His Wars. Randall Brink. LC 95-50254. 368p. 1999. pap. 24.95 (*1-55611-478-8*) D I Fine.

Nimitz - The Story of Pearl Harbor from the Japanese Perspective (English-Japanese) Nobuo Fukuchi. 1986. 2.00 (*0-934841-08-X*) Adm Nimitz Foun.

Nimitz Class. Patrick Robinson. 2000. mass mkt. 6.99 (*0-06-109594-X*, Harp PBks) HarpC.

***Nimitz Class: Export Edition.** Patrick Robinson. 528p. 1998. mass mkt. 6.99 (*0-06-109684-9*) HarpC.

Nimitz Class: Sanders,&Jay O. abr. ed. Patrick Robinson. 1997. audio 18.00 (*0-694-51799-2*, CPN 2641) HarperAudio.

Nimmer on Copyright, 6 vols. Melville B. Nimmer. 1978. ring bd. 1160.00 (*0-8205-1465-9*) Bender.

Nimodipine: Pharmacological & Clinical Results in Cerebral Ischemia. Ed. by A. Scriabine et al. (Illus.). xiv, 277p. 1991. 86.95 (*0-387-53405-9*) Spr-Verlag.

Nimrod Hunt see Mind Pool

Nimrud Wine Lists see Cuneiform Texts from Nimrud

***Nim's Island.** Wendy Orr. 2001. mass mkt. 16.99 (*0-375-91123-5*, Pub. by Random Bks Yng Read); mass mkt. 14.95 (*0-375-81123-0*, Pub. by Random Bks Yng Read) Random.

Nimslo 3D Book see Reel 3-D Enterprises' Guide to the Nimslo 3D Camera

Nimue & Other Poems. Terri Hardin. 50p. (Orig.). 1983. pap. 4.00 (*0-941062-10-4*) Begos & Rosenberg.

Nimue & Other Poems. limited ed. Terri Hardin. 50p. (Orig.). 1983. pap. 30.00 (*0-941062-11-2*) Begos & Rosenberg.

Nimzo-Indian Capablanca Variation (E32-E39) S. L. Edritrice. (Illus.). (Orig.). 1995. pap. 20.95 (*88-86127-43-X*) Thinkers Pr.

N

Nimzo Indian 4. Qc2. Max Dlugy. 230p. (Orig.). 1990. pap. 14.95 (*0-945470-07-X*) Chess Ent.

***Nimzo-Larsen Attack.** Tim Wall. 2000. pap. 19.95 (*1-85744-286-5*, Pub. by Everyman Chess) Globe Pequot.

***Nin.** Cass Dalglish. 352p. 2000. pap. 12.00 (*1-883523-39-7*, Pub. by Spinsters Ink) Words Distrib.

***Nina: Urban Fairy Tales: Paperdoll.** Sarah C. Bell. 24p. 1999. pap. 5.00 (*1-887997-15-6*, Pub. by Baksun Bks) SPD-Small Pr Dist.

Nina Balatka: The Story of a Maiden of Prague, 2 vols. Anthony Trollope. Ed. by N. John Hall. LC 80-1885. (Selected Works of Anthony Trollope). 1981. reprint ed. 55.95 (*0-405-14148-3*) Ayer.

Nina Balatka: (trollope 1996) Skilton. 1996. 37.00 (*1-870587-47-2*) Ashgate Pub Co.

Nina Bonita. Ana M. Machado. (SPA., Illus.). 24p. (J). (ps-3). pap. 6.95 (*980-257-165-2*, Pub. by Ediciones Ekare) Kane-Miller Bk.

Nina Bonita. Ana M. Machado. Tr. by Elena Iribarren from POR. LC 95-81577. (Illus.). 24p. (J). (ps-3). 1996. 9.95 (*0-916291-63-4*) Kane-Miller Bk.

***Nina Campbell's Decorating Secrets: 100 Ways to Achieve a Professional Look.** Nina Campbell. (Illus.). 176p. 2000. 40.00 (*0-609-60675-1*) C Potter.

Nina de Nueva York. Jose M. Oveido. (SPA.). pap. 7.99 (*968-16-3247-8*, Pub. by Fondo) Continental Bk.

***Nina Glaser-Recomposed.** Nina Glaser. (Illus.). 96p. 1998. pap. 35.00 (*1-890377-02-3*) Pohlmann Pr.

Nina Hartley's Scandal. unabridged ed. Ed. by Nina Hartley & Edi Birsan. (Illus.). 54p. 1999. 13.69 (*0-9669776-0-2*) Mdnght Games.

***Nina Hartley's Sex Tips for Straight Men.** Nina Hartley. (Illus.). 200p. 2000. pap. 14.95 (*1-57344-102-3*, Pub. by Cleis Pr) Publishers Group.

Nina in the Wilderness. Sarah Aldridge. LC 97-93762. 288p. 1997. 18.00 (*0-9646648-4-4*); pap. 11.95 (*0-9646648-3-6*) A&M Bks.

Nina Invisible (The Invisible Girl) J. L. Garcia Sanchez. (SPA.). (J). (gr. k-3). 1994. pap. 8.95 (*0-88272-041-4*) Santillana.

Nina Invisible (The Invisible Girl) J. L. Sanchez & M. A. Pacheco. (Derechos del Nino Ser.). (SPA., Illus.). 42p. (J). (gr. k-2). 1988. write for info. (*84-372-1829-2*) Santillana.

***Nina, Nina & the Copycat Ballerina.** Jane O'Connor. LC 99-48179. (All Aboard Reading Ser.). (Illus.). 32p. (J). 2000. 13.89 (*0-448-42152-6*, G & D); pap. 3.99 (*0-448-42151-8*, G & D) Peng Put Young Read.

Nina, Nina Ballerina. Jane O'Connor. LC 92-24465. (All Aboard Reading Ser.: Level 1). (Illus.). 32p. (J). (ps-1). 1993. pap. 3.99 (*0-448-40511-3*, G & D) Peng Put Young Read.

Nina, Nina Star Ballerina. Jane O'Connor. LC 96-30741. (All Aboard Reading Ser.). (Illus.). 32p. (J). (ps-1). 1997. lib. bdg. 13.89 (*0-448-41611-5*, G & D) Peng Put Young Read.

Nina, Nina Star Ballerina. Jane O'Connor. LC 96-30741. (All Aboard Reading Ser.: Level 1). (Illus.). 32p. (J). (ps-1). 1997. pap. 3.99 (*0-448-41492-9*, G & D) Peng Put Young Read.

Nina Que Amaba Los Caballos Salvajes. Paul Goble. 1998. 11.19 (*0-606-13556-1*, Pub. by Turtleback) Demco.

Nina Que Aprendia los Nombres y Otros Cuentos. Carlos Murciano. (Punto Infantil Ser.). (SPA.). (J). 1989. 10.70 (*0-606-05403-0*, Pub. by Turtleback) Demco.

***Nina Shapes Up.** Katherine Applegate. (Making Out Ser.: No. 10). 192p. (YA). (gr. 7-12). 1999. mass mkt. 3.99 (*0-380-80743-2*, Avon Bks) Morrow Avon.

Nina sin Nombre. Garcia. 1995. pap. 8.95 (*1-56014-208-1*) Santillana.

Nina the Gobbledegoat. Penny Ives. (Illus.). 32p. (J). pap. 7.95 (*0-14-038702-1*, Pub. by Pnguin Bks Ltd) Trafalgar.

***Nina Won't Tell.** Katherine Applegate. (Making Out Ser.: No. 3). 224p. (YA). (gr. 7-12). 1998. reprint ed. mass mkt. 3.99 (*0-380-80213-9*, Avon Bks) Morrow Avon.

Nina's Adventures. Nina Paley. (Illus.). 96p. 1993. pap. 7.95 (*0-9637283-1-8*) Pentshack Pr.

***Nina's Book of Little Things.** Keith Haring. (Illus.). 70p. 2000. 19.95 (*3-7913-2453-5*) Prestel.

Nina's Book of Little Things. Keith Haring et al. (Illus.). 70p. (J). (gr. 1-6). 1997. 19.95 (*3-7913-1380-0*, Pub. by Prestel) te Neues.

Ninas Madres - Madres Adolescentes. A. Martin. (Serie Actualidades - Actualities Ser.).Tr. of Child Mothers - Teen Mothers. (SPA.). 2.29 (*1-56063-660-2*, 496253) Editorial Unilit.

Nina's Magic. Lisa K. Butenhoff. Ed. by Nancy R. Thatch. LC 92-18293. (Books for Students by Students). (Illus.). 26p. (J). (gr. 3-4). 1992. lib. bdg. 15.95 (*0-933849-40-0*) Landmark Edns.

Nina's North Shore Guide: Big Lake, Big Woods, Big Fun. 2nd ed. Nina A. Simonowicz. LC 99-12102. (Illus.). 349p. 1999. pap. 14.95 (*0-8166-3326-6*) U of Minn Pr.

Nina's People. Mark Blaylock. Ed. by Karen Fischbach. 216p. 1998. spiral bd. 13.50 (*0-9654440-4-X*) Ironwood Pr AZ.

Nina's Treasures. large type ed. Stefan Czernecki & Timothy Rhodes. (Illus.). 40p. (J). (gr. k-4). 1994. pap. write for info. (*1-895340-02-0*) Hyperion Pr.

***Nina's Waltz.** Corinne Demas. LC 99-54152. (Illus.). 32p. (J). (gr. k-4). 2000. 16.95 (*0-531-30281-4*); 17.99 (*0-531-33281-0*) Orchard Bks Watts.

Nina's War. Clyde Briggs. LC 95-76887. 224p. 1996. text 12.95 (*1-885487-13-4*) Brownell & Carroll.

Nindo Ryu Gendai Ninjutsu: Introduction to Theories & Applications in the Modern Art of Perseverance. Carlos Febres. (Illus.). 90p. Date not set. pap. 13.95 (*0-7392-0143-3*, P03078) Morris Pubng.

***Nine.** Theodore Enslin. LC 00-28765. 2000. pap. write for info. (*1-881471-49-7*) S Duyvil.

Nine. Ed. by Milton Okun. pap. 17.95 (*0-89524-820-4*) Cherry Lane.

9: Knight of Shadows. Roger Zelazny. 256p. 1990. mass mkt. 5.99 (*0-380-75501-7*, Avon Bks) Morrow Avon.

9: The Official Strategy Guide. Kip Ward. LC 96-70602. 144p. 1996. per. 19.99 (*0-7615-0951-8*) Prima Pub.

Nine African-American Inventors. rev. ed. Robert C. Hayden. (Achievers: African Americans in Science & Technology Ser.). (Illus.). 171p. (J). (gr. 5-8). 1995. reprint ed. lib. bdg. 19.90 (*0-8050-2133-7*) TFC Bks NY.

***Nine American Jewish Thinkers.** Milton R. Konvitz. 132p. 2000. 29.95 (*0-7658-0028-4*) Transaction Pubs.

Nine & a Half Weeks. Elizabeth McNeill. 128p. 1993. reprint ed. lib. bdg. 27.95 (*1-56849-171-9*) Buccaneer Bks.

***Nine & Counting: American Politics as Seen by the Most Influential Women Who Make & Shape It.** Barbara Boxer & Women of the Senate Members. 288p. 2000. 25.00 (*0-06-019767-6*) HarpC.

Nine & Death Makes Ten. Carter Dickson, pseud. LC 87-82442. 175p. 1987. reprint ed. pap. 5.95 (*0-930330-69-2*) Intl Polygonics.

Nine Annual Reports on the Noxious, Beneficial & Other Insects of the State of Missouri, 1869-1877: With a General Index & Supplement, 10 vols. Charles V. Riley. Ed. by Keir B. Sterling. LC 77-81105. (Biologists & Their World Ser.). 1979. reprint ed. lib. bdg. 145.95 (*0-405-10745-5*) Ayer.

Nine Answers. limited ed. George Bernard Shaw. (Bucknell University, Limited Editions, Ellen Clarke Bertrand Library). (Illus.). 48p. 1988. reprint ed. 125.00 (*0-916375-08-0*) Press Alley.

Nine Armenians. Leslie Ayvasian. 1998. pap. 5.25 (*0-8222-1602-7*) Dramatists Play.

Nine Artists - Nine Visions, 1991. Rachel R. Lafo & Nicholas Capasso. 1991. bds. 6.00 (*0-945506-07-4*) DeCordova Mus.

9 Artists/9 Visions: 1996. Rachel R. Lafo & Nick Capasso. LC 96-84236. (Illus.). 13p. (Orig.). Date not set. pap. write for info. (*0-945506-19-8*) DeCordova Mus.

Nine at Carnival. Errol Lloyd. LC 78-4776. (Illus.). (J). (ps-2). 1979. 11.95 (*0-690-03891-7*) HarpC Child Bks.

9 Attitudes That Keep a Christian Going & Growing. Stuart Briscoe. 144p. 1995. pap. 8.99 (*0-87788-581-8*, H Shaw Pubs) Waterbrook Pr.

Nine Ayres for Two Bass Viols. 2nd rev. ed. Simon Ives. Ed. by Gordon Sandford. (Viol Consort Ser.: No. 11). i, 22p. 1994. pap. text 14.00 (*1-56571-124-6*) PRB Prods.

Nine Basic Exercises for Alto Recorder. Hans U. Staeps. Ed. by Gerald Burakoff. 1970. 5.00 (*0-913334-07-3*, CM1004) Consort Music.

***Nine Battles to Stanley.** Van der Bijk Nick. 1999. 36.95 (*0-85052-619-1*) Pen & Sword.

Nine Bells at the Breaker: An Immigrant's Story. Geraldine Glodek. LC 98-73047. viii, 248p. 1998. 24.00 (*0-9665943-0-4*); pap. 15.00 (*0-9665943-1-2*) Barn Peg Pr.

Nine Below Zero. Kevin Canty. LC 98-41402. 384p. 1999. 23.95 (*0-385-49160-3*, N A Talese) Doubleday.

***Nine Below Zero.** Kevin Canty. (Contemporaries Ser.). 384p. 2000. pap. 13.00 (*0-375-70799-9*) Vin Bks.

IX Bericht Ueber die Ausgrabungen in Olympia: Herbst, 1962 Bis Fruehjahr, 1966. Ed. by Deutschen Archaeologischen Institut Staff. (Bericht Ueber die Ausgrabungen in Olympia Ser.: No. 9). (GER.). vii, 229p. (C). 1995. lib. bdg. 176.95 (*3-11-014243-0*) De Gruyter.

Nine Bible Principles for Judging Prophecy. John Hagee & Rick Randall. 31p. (Orig.). 1991. pap., per. 3.00 (*1-56908-002-X*) Global Evang.

Nine Biggest Pitfalls of Home Construction: Avoiding Them Can Save You Money. Jeff Howe. 70p. (Orig.). 1997. pap. 29.95 (*1-57502-493-4*, P01462) Morris Pubng.

Nine Billion Names of God: The Best Short Stories of Arthur C. Clarke. Arthur C. Clarke. Date not set. lib. bdg. 23.95 (*0-8488-2181-5*) Amereon Ltd.

Nine Black Women: Anthology of Nineteenth Century Writers from the United States, Canada, Bermuda & the Caribbean. Moira Ferguson. LC 97-26460. 320p. (C). 1997. 75.00 (*0-415-91904-5*); pap. 19.99 (*0-415-91905-3*) Routledge.

Nine Boats & Nine Kids: A True Chronicle. Jeanne S. Merkel. LC 84-19422. (Illus.). 162p. (Orig.). 1984. 14.95 (*0-931447-01-1*); pap. 9.95 (*0-931447-00-3*) Ledge Bks.

Nine Bottles: An Adventure in Chemical Identification. Jay Young et al. 8p. (C). 1995. pap. text 1.50 (*0-87540-503-7*, REAC 503-7) Chem Educ Res.

Nine Bright Shiners. large type ed. Anthea Fraser. 1990. 25.99 (*0-7089-2173-6*) Ulverscroft.

Nine by Nine. Photos by David Bailey et al. (Illus.). 96p. 1984. pap. 12.95 (*0-912810-47-5*) Lustrum Pr.

9 by 13 Pan Cookbook. Barbara Karoff. (Illus.). 160p. 1991. pap. 8.95 (*1-55867-031-9*, Nitty Gritty Ckbks) Bristol Pub Ent CA.

***9x12 Sketchbook.** 160p. 2000. 16.95 (*1-55156-179-4*); spiral bd. 16.95 (*1-55156-178-6*) Paperblank.

9 Candles. Maria Testa. (Illus.). (J). 1996. lib. bdg. 19.93 (*0-87614-940-9*, Carolrhoda) Lerner Pub.

Nine Canvases. Herman M. Ward. LC 86-71030. 196p. (Orig.). 1987. pap. 10.00 (*0-9610346-6-1*) Belle Mead Pr.

Nine Carnival Plays. Hans Sachs. Tr. by Randall W. Listerman. 95p. 1985. pap. 8.95 (*0-919473-68-7*, PDH56, Pub. by Dovehouse) Sterling.

***Nine Centuries of Etruscan Civilization: A Cultural History.** Sybille Haynes. LC 00-25732. (Illus.). 490p. 2000. 55.00 (*0-89236-575-7*, J P Getty Museum) J P Getty Trust.

Nine Challenges for Parents: Leading Your Child into Responsible Adulthood. Lucy Hulme & William Hulme. 128p. 1993. pap. 12.99 (*0-8066-2657-7*, 9-2657) Augsburg Fortress.

9 Chances to Feel Good About Yourself. Judy A. Laslie. 128p. 1997. reprint ed. pap. 14.95 (*0-9650218-3-1*) Radnor Hse.

Nine Changed Lives. Cynthia S. Baker. 1991. pap. 5.50 (*1-55673-282-1*, 9115) CSS OH.

***Nine Chapters on the Mathematical Art: Companion & Commentary.** Ed. by Shen Kangshen et al. LC 99-37443. 616p. 2000. write for info. (*0-19-853936-3*) OUP.

Nine Character Traits Separating the Men from the Boys: Encouragement for Men Trying to Grow Up. Nate Adams. LC 94-8449. 256p. 1994. pap. 9.99 (*1-55661-458-6*) Bethany Hse.

Nine Coaches Waiting. Mary Stewart. 1988. mass mkt. 5.99 (*0-449-21572-5*, Crest) Fawcett.

***Nine Commandments: Uncovering a Hidden Pattern of Crime & Punishment in the Hebrew Bible.** David Noel Freedman et al. LC 00-29492. 2000. 24.95 (*0-385-49986-8*) Doubleday.

Nine Commandments of Golf . . . According to the Pro Upstairs. Mark Oman. LC 88-81603. (Illus.). 112p. (Orig.). 1988. pap. 8.95 (*0-917346-07-6*) Golfaholics Anon.

Nine Commentaries on Frank Lloyd Wright. Edgar J. Kaufmann, Jr. (Illus.). 156p. 1990. 32.50 (*0-262-11144-6*) MIT Pr.

9 Creativity-Required Businesses You Can Start from Home: And How to Make Them Profitable Careers. Bill Watson. LC 99-94895. (Illus.). 256p. 2000. pap. 23.95 (*0-9670751-6-5*) Creatv Books.

Nine-Day Inner Cleansing & Blood Wash for Renewed Youthfulness & Health. I. E. Gaumont. 228p. (C). 1979. text 25.95 (*0-13-622506-3*) P-H.

Nine Dayak Nights. William R. Geddes. (Illus.). 148p. 1985. reprint ed. pap. 15.95 (*0-19-582621-3*) OUP.

Nine Days in Union: The Search for Alex & Michael Smith. Gary Henderson. (Illus.). 160p. (Orig.). 1995. pap. text 12.95 (*1-885354-00-2*) Honoribus Pr.

Nine Days Queen. Mary Luke. 448p. 1994. reprint ed. lib. bdg. 49.95 (*1-56849-526-9*) Buccaneer Bks.

Nine Days to Christmas. Marie H. Ets & Aurora Labastida. (Illus.). 48p. (J). (ps-3). 1991. pap. 4.99 (*0-14-054442-9*, PuffinBks) Peng Put Young Read.

Nine Days to Christmas: A Story of Mexico. Marie H. Ets. (Picture Puffin Ser.). (Illus.). (J). 1991. 10.19 (*0-606-00655-9*, Pub. by Turtleback) Demco.

Nine Days to Istanbul. Jeanne Frankel de Corrales. 128p. 1994. pap. 7.95 (*1-85168-037-3*, Pub. by Oneworld Pubns) Penguin Putnam.

Nine Days to Kill. large type ed. Julie Ellis. LC 96-53539. 228p. 1997. pap. 21.95 (*0-7838-8078-2*, G K Hall Lrg Type) Mac Lib Ref.

Nine Decades: The Northern California Craft Movement 1907-Present. Ted Cohen et al. 32p. (Orig.). 1993. pap. write for info. (*1-877742-03-1*) SF Craft & Folk.

Nine Decades of Scholarship. Ed. by Richard Newman. 83p. 1986. pap. 3.00 (*0-87104-288-6*) NY Pub Lib.

Nine-Dollar Daddy: Texas Grooms Wanted! Day Leclaire. (Romance Ser.: No. 3543). 1999. per. 3.50 (*0-373-03543-8*, 1-03543-5) Harlequin Bks.

Nine-Dollar Daddy: Texas Grooms Wanted! large type ed. Day Leclaire. (Larger Print Ser.: No. 389). 1999. mass mkt. 3.50 (*0-373-15789-4*, 1-15789-0) Harlequin Bks.

***Nine-Dollar Daddy: Texas Grooms Wanted!** large type ed. Day Leclaire. 288p. 1999. 25.99 (*0-263-16139-0*, Pub. by Mills & Boon) Ulverscroft.

Nine Dragons. large type ed. Justin Scott. (Adventure Suspense Ser.). 656p. 1992. 27.99 (*0-7089-8635-8*) Ulverscroft.

Nine Ducks Nine. Sarah Hayes. LC 95-38453. (Illus.). 32p. (J). 1996. 5.99 (*1-56402-830-5*) Candlewick Pr.

***Nine Ducks Nine.** Sarah Hayes. (Illus.). 32p. (J). (ps-2). 2000. pap. 19.99 (*0-7636-1284-7*, Pub. by Candlewick Pr) Penguin Putnam.

***Nine Easy Hymn Preludes, Bk. 3.** Edward H. Meyer. 36p. 1998. pap. 13.50 (*0-8100-0957-9*) Northwest Pub.

911-912 Porsche. Brett Johnson. (Authenticity Ser.). (Illus.). 112p. (Orig.). 1988. pap. 19.95 (*0-929758-00-5*) Beeman Jorgensen.

Nine Essays. Arthur Platt. LC 68-16969. (Essay Index Reprint Ser.). 1977. reprint ed. 19.95 (*0-8369-0793-0*) Ayer.

Nine Essays on Concrete Poems. Wally Depew. (Illus.). 68p. (Orig.). 1974. pap. 5.95 (*0-914974-00-9*) Holmgangers.

Nine Essays on Homer. Ed. by Miriam Carlisle & Olga Levaniouk. LC 99-11159. (Greek Studies). 272p. 1999. pap. 21.95 (*0-8476-9424-0*) Rowman.

***Nine Essays on Homer.** Ed. by Miriam Carlisle & Olga Levaniouk. LC 99-11159. (Greek Studies). 10p. 1999. 57.50 (*0-8476-9423-2*) Rowman.

***9 Essential Laws for Becoming Influential.** Tony Zeiss. Ed. by Tom A. Rutherford & Todd Rutherford. 112p. 2000. pap. 9.95 (*1-929496-01-X*) Triumphant Pubs.

Nine Etched from Life. Emil Ludwig. LC 70-90658. (Essay Index Reprint Ser.). 1977. 26.95 (*0-8369-1225-X*) Ayer.

Nine Faces of Christ see Nueve Caras de Cristo: La Busqueda del Verdadero Iniciado

Nine Faces of Christ: A Narrative of Nine Great Mystic Initiations of Joseph, Bar, Joseph in the Eternal Religion. Eugene E. Whitworth. 381p. 1993. reprint ed. 24.95 (*0-87516-666-0*); reprint ed. pap. 19.95 (*0-87516-665-2*) DeVorss.

Nine Faces of Christ - Quest of the True Initiate see Die Neun Gesichter Christi: Die Suche des Wahren Eingeweihten

Nine Faces of God. Peter Hannon. 308p. (Orig.). 1992. pap. 14.95 (*1-85607-059-X*, Pub. by Columba Press) Whitecap Bks.

Nine Fairy Tales & One More Thrown in for Good Measure. Karel Capek & Dagmar Herrmann. LC 96-24156. (European Classics Ser.). 253p. (J). 1996. pap. 15.95 (*0-8101-1464-X*) Northwestern U Pr.

Nine Fantasies for the Japanese Consort (Three to Six Viols) David Loeb. (Contemporary Consort Ser.: No. 13). ii, 45p. 1991. 12.00 (*1-56571-015-0*) PRB Prods.

Nine Fantasies That Will Ruin Your Life & the Eight Realities That Will Save You. abr. ed. Joy Browne. LC 98-36245. 272p. 1998. 23.00 incl. audio (*0-609-60354-X*, Three Riv Pr) Crown Pub Group.

***Nine Fantasies That Will Ruin Your Life & the Eight Realities That Will Save You, Vol. 1.** Joy Browne. 1999. pap. 13.00 (*0-609-80473-1*) Crown.

Nine Fast Profit Angles 90. Ph. 1990. pap. text 6.85 (*0-13-621137-2*) P-H.

Nine Florida Stories: A Florida Sand Dollar Book. Marjory S. Douglas. Ed. by Kevin M. McCarthy. 216p. 1990. 22.95 (*0-8130-0988-X*); pap. 17.95 (*0-8130-0994-4*) U Press Fla.

Nine for California. Sonia Levitin. LC 96-1958. (Illus.). 32p. (J). (gr. k-4). 1996. 15.95 (*0-531-09527-4*) Orchard Bks Watts.

***Nine for California.** Sonia Levitin. 40p. 2000. pap. 6.95 (*0-531-07176-6*) Orchard Bks Watts.

***914 Porsche: A Restorer's Guide to Authenticity.** Johnson. (Illus.). 112p. (Orig.). 2000. pap. 19.95 (*0-929758-21-8*, Pub. by Beeman Jorgensen) Motorbooks Intl.

914 Porsche: A Restorer's Guide to Authenticity. Brett Johnson. (Authenticity Ser.). (Illus.). 110p. (Orig.). 1989. pap. 19.95 (*0-929758-01-3*) Beeman Jorgensen.

Nine Freedoms. George King. LC 78-262002. (Illus.). 200p. 1963. 24.95 (*0-937249-04-1*) Aetherius Soc.

9 Fun to Learn Books. 1991. pap. text 9.00 (*0-486-26584-6*) Dover.

Nine Gates: Entering the Mind of Poetry. Jane Hirshfield. LC 97-2793. 240p. 1997. 22.00 (*0-06-017456-0*) HarpC.

Nine Gates: Entering the Mind of Poetry. Jane Hirshfield. LC 97-2793. 240p. 1998. pap. 13.00 (*0-06-092948-0*, Perennial) HarperTrade.

Nine Gates to the Chasidic Mysteries. Jiri Langer. Tr. by Stephen Jolly. LC 92-28679. 312p. 1993. 40.00 (*0-87668-249-2*) Aronson.

Nine Girls. Wilfrid H. Pettitt. 101p. (YA). (gr. 10 up). 1942. pap. 5.50 (*0-87129-923-2*, N14) Dramatic Pub.

Nine Great English Poets: Poemsby Shakespeare, Keats, Blake, Coleridge, Wordsworth, Mrs. Browning, Fitzgerald, Tennyson, & Kipling, 6 vols., Set. Dover Staff. 704p. 1992. pap., boxed set 9.00 (*0-486-27633-3*) Dover.

Nine Guardians. Rosario Castellanos. Tr. by Irene Nicholson from SPA. 272p. 1992. pap. 14.95 (*0-930523-90-3*) Readers Intl.

Nine-Headed Dragon River: Zen Journals, 1969-1985. Peter Matthiessen. 1998. pap. 17.00 (*1-57062-367-8*, Pub. by Shambhala Pubns) Random.

9 Highland Road. Michael Winerip. 1999. pap. 25.00 (*0-670-84037-8*) Viking Penguin.

9 Highland Road. Michael Winerip. 1995. pap. 15.00 (*0-679-76160-8*) Vin Bks.

Nine Humorous Tales. Anton Chekhov. LC 76-106262. (Short Story Index Reprint Ser.). 1918. 7.50 (*0-8369-3299-4*) Ayer.

900 Bible Questions Answered. William L. Pettingill. LC 90-20615. Orig. Title: Bible Questions Answered - Enlarged Edition. 416p. 1991. reprint ed. pap. 19.99 (*0-8254-3541-2*) Kregel.

Nine Hundred Days: The Siege of Leningrad. Harrison Salisbury. (Quality Paperbacks Ser.). (Illus.). 456p. 1985. reprint ed. pap. 16.95 (*0-306-80253-8*) Da Capo.

***985 - The Discovery of America.** Brian Cherry. 160p. 1999. pap. 14.95 (*1-928547-01-X*, QuickWorks) Q W Inc.

Nine Hundred Fifty-Nine Study Plan. 1976. 8.50 (*0-918403-02-2*) Agape Ministries.

900 Gold: Marketing Secrets for Success in the 900 Business. Richard Wills. Ed. by Maureen Twyman. LC 95-71788. (Illus.). 142p. (Orig.). 1995. pap. 19.95 (*0-9622822-8-6*) Dragon Marina.

900 Know-How: How to Succeed with Your Own 900-Number Business. 3rd ed. Robert Mastin. LC 95-83157. 350p. 1996. pap. 19.95 (*0-9632790-3-3*) Aegis Pub Grp.

Nine Hundred Miles on the Butterfield Trail. A. C. Greene. LC 94-20107. (Illus.). 293p. 1994. 24.95 (*0-929398-73-4*) UNTX Pr.

999: New Stories of Horror & Suspense. Ed. by Al Sarrantonio. LC 99-20895. 688p. 1999. 27.50 (*0-380-97740-0*, Avon Bks) Morrow Avon.

999 Lies for Every Occasion. Jo Donnelly. LC 95-19917. 240p. 1995. pap. 8.95 (*0-8065-1672-0*, Citadel Pr) Carol Pub Group.

999 Nonquantitative Problems for FE Examination Review. Kenton Whitehead. LC 97-12586. 180p. (Orig.). 1997. pap. 28.95 (*1-888577-11-8*, FESP) Prof Pubns CA.

999 Questions. John Colombo. 1989. mass mkt. 14.95 (*0-385-25207-2*) Doubleday.

999 Tips, Trends & Guidelines for Successful Direct Mail & Telephone Fundraising. Mal Warwick. (Illus.). 320p. 1993. reprint ed. pap. 34.95 (*0-9624891-2-3*) Strathmoor Pr.

Nine Hundred One Best Jokes There Ever Was. J. R. Miller. LC 91-24866. (Illus.). 192p. (Orig.). 1991. pap. 6.95 (*1-55853-122-X*) Rutledge Hill Pr.

Nine Hundred Shows a Year. Stuart B. Palonsky. 288p. (C). 1985. pap. 32.19 (*0-07-554645-0*) McGraw.

N

An Asterisk (*) at the beginning of an entry indicates that the title is appearing for the first time.

910's Guide to the Beatles' Outtakes. Doug Sulpy. LC 95-69773. 240p. 1995. pap. 29.95 (*0-9643869-1-7*) The NineTen.

930 Matchbook Advertising Cuts of the Twenties & Thirties. Ed. by Trina Robbins. LC 96-40194. (Clip-Art Ser.). 80p. 1997. pap. 8.95 (*0-486-29564-8*) Dover.

Nine Hundred Twenty-Four Elementary Problems & Answers in Solar System Astronomy. James A. Van Allen. LC 93-24605. (Illus.). 259p. 1993. pap. 12.95 (*0-87745-434-5*); text 29.95 (*0-87745-433-7*) U of Iowa Pr.

920 O'Farrell Street: A Jewish Girlhood in Old San Francisco. Harriet L. Levy. 216p. 1996. pap. 12.95 (*0-930588-91-6*) Heyday Bks.

9226 Kercheval: The Storefront that Did Not Burn, New Edition. Nancy Milio. (Illus.). 224p. (C). pap. text 16.95 (*0-472-08695-2*, 08695) U of Mich Pr.

Nine Hundred Words of Wisdom: The Real Truth about 900. Sean Naughton. Ed. by Barbara DeMarco. (Orig.). 1993. student ed. 99.00 (*0-9638246-1-9*); pap. 198.00 (*0-9638246-0-0*); audio 98.00 (*0-9638246-2-7*) Future Freedom.

900 Years: The Restorations of Westminster Abbey. Thomas H. Cocke. (Illus.). 160p. 1995. text 45.00 (*1-872501-77-X*, Pub. by Harvey Miller) Gordon & Breach.

Nine in One. Houghton Mifflin Company Staff. (Literature Experience 1993 Ser.). (J). 1992. pap. 9.48 (*0-395-61789-8*) HM.

Nine-in-One, Grr! Grr! Illus. by Nancy Hom. LC 89-9891. 32p. (YA). (ps-5). 1989. 14.95 (*0-89239-048-4*) Childrens Book Pr.

Nine-in-One, Grr! Grr! Illus. by Nancy Hom. 32p. (YA). (ps-3). 1993. pap. 7.95 (*0-89239-110-3*) Childrens Book Pr.

Nine-In-One, Grr! Grr! A Folktale From The Hmong People Of Laos. Blia. 1989. 12.15 (*0-606-05510-X*, Pub. by Turtleback) Demco.

Nine Inch Nails: Tear-Out Photo Book. (Illus.). 22p. (Orig.). 1993. pap. 11.95 (*1-870049-44-6*, OB 11007) Oliver Bks.

Nine Inch Will Please a Lady. Compiled by Richard Styff. (Illus.). 128p. 1994. pap. 9.95 (*0-89804-999-7*, Kudzu Hse) Ariel GA.

Nine Indian Women Poets: An Anthology. Ed. by Eunice De Souza. LC 98-902943. 106p. 1998. text 12.95 (*0-19-564077-2*) OUP.

Nine Innings: The Anatomy of a Baseball Game. Daniel Okrent. 288p. 1994. pap. 12.00 (*0-395-71040-5*) HM.

9 Innings with Cal Ripken Jr. By the People Who Know Him Best. Alex Rodriquez. (Illus.). 1998. 19.95 (*1-887432-46-9*) Beckett Pubns.

9 Insights of the Wealthy Soul. Michael R. Norwood. 1999. pap. write for info. (*0-911649-02-6*) Global Pub GA.

***Nine Jazz Duets for Guitar & Bass.** Ken Hatfield. 58p. 1998. pap. 22.50 (*1-929807-00-7*, KHJGB100) Arthur Circle.

9 Kantaten fur 4 Singstimmen & Instrumente, Pt. 1. Dieterich Buxtehude. Ed. by Dietrich Kilian. (Dietrich Buxtehudes Werke Ser.: Vol. 8). (Illus.). 1978. reprint ed. pap. 85.00 (*0-89371-018-0*) Broude Intl Edns.

Nine Keys to a High Income Retirement 1989. (C). 1989. pap. text 6.85 (*0-13-624065-8*, Macmillan Coll) P-H.

Nine Keys to Effective Small Group Leadership: How Lay Leaders Can Establish Dynamic & Healthy Cells, Classes or Teams. Carl F. George. 232p. pap. 12.97 incl. audio (*1-883906-13-X*) Kingdom Prods.

***Nine Keys to Happiness: Collected Speeches & Writings of Dr. John S. Madara, M. D.** John S. Madara. LC 99-91727. 2000. 25.00 (*0-7388-1202-1*); pap. 18.00 (*0-7388-1203-X*) Xlibris Corp.

Nine Keys to Successful Volunteer Programs. Kathleen B. Fletcher. LC 87-10174. 87p. (Orig.). 1994. 21.95 (*0-914756-28-1*, 600010) Taft Group.

9 Kirchenkantaten & Arien fur zwei Soprane & Bass mit Continuo & Instrumenten see Dietrich Buxtehudes Werke

Nine Language Universal Dictionary: How to Write It & Say It in Arabic, English, French, German, Italian, Japanese, Portuguese, Russian, Spanish. rev. ed. Jean M. De Lafayette. Ed. by ACUPAE Group Staff & NASCU Staff. (Illus.). 186p. (Orig.). 1991. pap. 30.00 (*0-939877-28-7*) ACUPAE.

Nine Levels: The Path of Welsh Witchcraft. Rhuddlwm Gawr. LC 85-73757. (Illus.). 192p. (Orig.). 1989. 14.95 (*0-931760-41-0*, CP 10119); pap. 12.95 (*0-931760-19-4*) Camelot GA.

Nine Levels Down. William R. Dantz. 320p. 1999. mass mkt. 6.99 (*0-8125-2416-0*, Pub. by Forge NYC) St Martin.

9 Lives. Messerschmi. LC 99-45726. 2000. 59.00 (*0-8133-6666-6*) Westview.

9 Lives. Messerschmid. LC 99-45726. 2000. 20.00 (*0-8133-6667-4*) Westview.

Nine Lives: A Cat Photo Memory Album. 1997. 15.99 (*1-57977-200-5*) Havoc Pub.

Nine Lives: A Journal for My Cat. Louise Reinoehl Max. 80p. 1999. 12.95 (*0-87905-889-7*) Gibbs Smith Pub.

***Nine Lives: An Oral History.** Aaron Elson. (Illus.). 192p. 2000. per. 13.95 (*0-9640611-5-5*) Chi Chi Pr.

Nine Lives: Ethnic Conflict in the Polish-ukrainian Borderlands. Waledman Lotnik. 1999. pap. text 14.95 (*1-897959-40-0*) Serif.

Nine Lives: The Reincarnation Story. rev. ed. Joseph A. Myers & Jean M. Myers. 220p. 1994. pap. 14.95 (*0-913911-08-9*) Akashic Pr.

Nine Lives of Big Meg O'Shannessy. John Millett. 64p. (Orig.). 1989. pap. 9.95 (*0-934257-30-2*) Story Line.

Nine Lives of Catseye Gomez. Simon Hawke. (Orig.). 1992. mass mkt. 4.99 (*0-446-36241-7*, Pub. by Warner Bks) Little.

Nine Lives of Frank & Natalie. 2nd rev. ed. Katherine H. Brooks. LC 98-84839. 52p. (Orig.). 1998. pap. 5.00 (*1-886467-33-1*) WJM Press.

Nine Lives to Live: A Classic Felix Celebration. Otto Messmer. 144p. 1996. 39.95 (*1-56097-308-0*, Pub. by Fantagraph Bks) Seven Hills Bk.

Nine Lives to Murder. Marian Babson. 1995. mass mkt. 4.99 (*0-312-95580-4*) St Martin.

Nine Madrigals to Five Voices from Musica Transalpina, 1588 see Old English Edition

***Nine Magic Wishes.** Shirley Jackson. 2000. text. write for info. (*0-374-35525-8*) FS&G.

Nine Man-Eaters & One Rogue. Kenneth Anderson. 264p. 1997. 21.95 (*1-887269-11-8*) J Culler & Sons.

***Nine Man Tree.** Robert Newton Peck. 192p. (gr. 5-9). 2000. pap. 4.99 (*0-375-80250-9*) Random.

Nine Man Tree. Robert Newton Peck. LC 97-43624. 170p. (YA). (gr. 5-8). 1998. 17.00 (*0-679-89257-5*, Pub. by Random Bks Yng Read); lib. bdg. 18.99 (*0-679-99257-X*, Pub. by Random Bks Yng Read) Random.

9 Marks of a Healthy Church. Mark Dever. 29p. 1997. pap. 4.00 (*0-9654955-4-X*) Founders Pr.

***Nine Marks of a Healthy Church.** rev. expanded ed. Mark Dever. LC 00-9045. 304p. 2000. pap. 15.99 (*1-58134-163-6*) Crossway Bks.

Nine Martinis. Lita Hornick. 1987. 10.00 (*0-936538-12-0*); pap. 5.00 (*0-936538-13-9*) Kulchur Foun.

Nine Meditations on Christmas Hymns: For Organ. Ed. by Dale Tucker. 32p. (Orig.). (C). 1997. pap. text 7.95 (*0-7692-0179-2*, GB9706) Wrner Bros.

Nine Men: A Political History of the Supreme Court from 1790 to 1955. Fred Rodell. xii, 338p. 1988. reprint ed. 45.00 (*0-8377-2541-0*, Rothman) W S Hein.

Nine Men Chase a Hen. Barbara Gregorich. Ed. by Joan Hoffman. (Start to Read! Ser.). (Illus.). 16p. (J). (gr. k-2). 1984. pap. 2.29 (*0-88743-009-0*, 06009) Sch Zone Pub Co.

Nine Men Chase a Hen. Barbara Gregorich. Ed. by Joan Hoffman. (Start to Read! Ser.). (Illus.). 32p. (J). (ps-3). 1993. pap. 3.99 (*0-88743-407-X*, 06059) Sch Zone Pub Co.

Nine Men in Gray. Charles L. Dufour. LC 93-9529. (Illus.). xix, 372p. (C). 1993. reprint ed. pap. 16.00 (*0-8032-6596-4*, Bison Books) U of Nebr Pr.

9MM Parabellum: The History & Development of the World's 9MM Pistols & Ammunition. Klaus-Peter Konig & Martin Hugo. Tr. by Tim Russell from GER. LC 91-66337. (Illus.). 304p. 1992. 39.95 (*0-88740-342-5*) Schiffer.

Nine-Month Bride: Virgin Brides. Judy Christenberry. (Silhouette Romance Ser.: No. 1324). 1998. per. 3.50 (*0-373-19324-6*, 1-19324-2) Harlequin Bks.

Nine-Month Marriage: Conveniently Yours. Christine Rimmer. (Special Edition Ser.: No. 1148). 1998. per. 3.99 (*0-373-24148-8*, 1-24148-8) Silhouette.

Nine Months: 36 Hours. Beverly Barton. (Thirty-Six Hours Ser.: Vol. 10). 1998. per. 4.50 (*0-373-65015-9*, 1-65015-9) Harlequin Bks.

Nine Months & a Day: A Pregnancy, Labor & Delivery Companion. Linda H. Holt & Adrienne B. Lieberman. LC 99-25178. (Illus.). 160p. 2000. pap. 7.95 (*1-55832-150-0*) Harvard Common Pr.

Nine Months & Counting... Baby in the Middle & The Forever Night, 2 vols. in 1. Marie Ferrarella & Myrna Temte. (By Request 2's Ser.). 512p. 2000. mass mkt. 4.99 (*0-373-21709-9*, 1-21709-0) Harlequin Bks.

***Nine Months & Counting: Bible Promises & Bright Ideas for Pregnancy & After.** Alice Z. Chapin. LC 99-26601. 1999. pap. text 8.99 (*0-8423-7363-2*) Tyndale Hse.

Nine Months Is a Year at Baboquivari School. fac. ed. Eulalia Bourne. LC 68-57760. (Southwest Chronicle Ser.). (Illus.). 282p. 1969. reprint ed. pap. 87.50 (*0-7837-8020-6*, 204777600008) Bks Demand.

Nine Months to Gettysburg: Stannard's Vermonters & the Repulse of Pickett's Charge. Howard Coffin. LC 97-20031. (Illus.). 340p. 1997. 29.95 (*0-88150-400-9*, Pub. by Countryman) Norton.

Nine Most Troublesome Teenage Problems & How to Solve Them. Lawrence Bauman & Robert Riche. 186p. 1986. 15.95 (*0-8184-0392-6*) Carol Pub Group.

Nine Muses: A Mythological Path to Creativity. Angeles Arrien. (Illus.). 160p. 1999. 23.95 (*0-87477-999-5*, Tarcher Putnam) Putnam Pub Group.

Nine Myths of Aging: Maximizing the Quality of Later Life, Vol. 1. Douglas H. Powell. LC 97-51718. 250p. 1998. pap. text 23.95 (*0-7167-3104-5*) W H Freeman.

Nine Myths That Damage a Child's Confidence: What Parents Think, What Children Say, What Professionals Observe. Pat Holt. LC 99-24186. 109p. 1999. pap. 8.99 (*0-87788-591-5*, H Shaw Pubs) Waterbrook Pr.

Nine Nations of North America. Joel Garreau. 448p. 1992. pap. 12.50 (*0-380-57885-9*, Avon Bks) Morrow Avon.

Nine Natural Laws of Leadership. Warren Blank. LC 95-33153. 288p. 1995. 27.95 (*0-8144-0309-3*) AMACOM.

Nine Naughty Kittens. Linda Jennings. (Illus.). 20p. (J). (gr. k-1). 1999. 14.95 (*1-888444-62-2*, Pub. by Little Tiger) Futech Educ Prods.

Proceedings of the International Symposium on Earth Tides, 9, New York City, August 17-22, 1981. Ed. by J. T. Kuo. (Illus.). xxiv, 747p. 1983. lib. bdg. 53.00 (*3-510-65113-8*, Pub. by E Schweizerbartsche) Balogh.

***Nine Nights on the Windy Tree: A Bertha Brannon Mystery.** Martha Miller. 224p. 2000. pap. 10.95 (*1-892281-11-2*, Pub. by New Victoria Pubs) LPC InBook.

Nine-Note Recorder Method: Easy Duets for Beginners. Penny Gardner. 92p. 1998. pap. text 9.95 (*1-57636-057-1*) SunRise Pbl.

Nine, Novena, Vol. 104. Osman Lins. Tr. by Adria Frizzi from POR. LC 95-35738. (Sun & Moon Classics Ser.: No. 104). 250p. (Orig.). 1995. pap. 12.95 (*1-55713-229-1*) Sun & Moon CA.

***Nine Numbers of the Cosmos.** Michael Rowan-Robinson. LC 99-42817. (Illus.). 192p. 1999. 24.95 (*0-19-850444-6*) OUP.

Nine O'Clock in the Morning: An Episcopal Priest Discovers the Holy Spirit. Dennis Bennett. LC 72-85205. 209p. 1984. pap. 8.99 (*0-88270-629-2*) Bridge-Logos.

Nine O'Clock Lullaby. Marilyn Singer. LC 90-32116. (Illus.). 32p. (J). (ps-3). 1993. pap. 5.95 (*0-06-443319-6*, HarpTrophy) HarpC Child Bks.

Nine O'Clock Lullaby. Marilyn Singer. LC 90-32116. 1991. 10.15 (*0-606-10270-1*, Pub. by Turtleback) Demco.

Nine O'Clock Tide. Mignon G. Eberhart. reprint ed. lib. bdg. 19.95 (*0-88411-770-7*) Amereon Ltd.

Nine Old Men. Drew Pearson & Robert S. Allen. LC 73-21727. (American Constitutional & Legal History Ser). 325p. 1974. reprint ed. lib. bdg. 45.00 (*0-306-70609-1*) Da Capo.

911. Don Goldman. 265p. mass mkt. 4.99 (*1-55197-104-6*) Picasso Publ.

911: Calling for Help in a Violent World. abr. ed. Bonny M. Wynia. (Life Wise Ser.). 34p. 1995. pap., teacher ed. 7.95 (*1-56212-120-0*, 1210-4008) CRC Pubns.

911: Emergency Communication Manual. 3rd ed. PPI (Pivetta) Staff. LC 97-212828. 512p. 1997. per. 54.50 (*0-7872-4445-7*) Kendall-Hunt.

911: The School Administrator's Guide to Crisis Management. Keen J. Babbage. LC 96-60906. 180p. 1996. pap. text 29.95 (*1-56676-454-8*) Scarecrow.

***9-1-1 Beauty Secrets: An Emergency Guide to Looking Great at Every Age, Size & Budget.** Diane Irons. LC 99-37644. 336p. 1999. pap. 14.95 (*1-57071-446-0*) Sourcebks.

***9-1-1 Dispatching: A Best Practices Review.** Jody Hauer. (Illus.). 118p. (C). 1999. reprint ed. pap. text 25.00 (*0-7881-8125-4*) DIANE Pub.

911 Handbook: Biblical Solutions to Everyday Problems. Kent Crockett. LC 97-23128. 232p. 1997. 16.95 (*1-56563-295-8*) Hendrickson MA.

9-1-1 Liability: A Call for Answers. Charles C. Ormsby, Jr. & Philip M. Salafia, Jr. LC 97-75907. (Illus.). 208p. 1998. 69.95 (*0-9661395-0-X*) PowerPhone.

911 Management. Joseph Bannon. 1999. pap. 29.95 (*1-57167-132-3*) Sagamore Pub.

911 Operator. (Career Examination Ser.: C-3594). 1994. pap. 23.95 (*0-8373-3594-9*) Nat Learn.

911 until Help Arrives. Ethan P. Allen. 304p. (C). 1994. pap. text, spiral bd., vinyl bd. 25.95 (*0-8403-9204-4*) Kendall-Hunt.

***911 Urgent Dating Solutions.** Gail Burgess. 210p. 1999. pap. 14.98 (*0-9668986-0-5*) Any Key Pr.

***9-1-1's: Help Haiku.** Evie Ivy & Tom Oleszczuk. (Illus.). 40p. 1999. pap. 4.00 (*1-893043-04-5*) Petit Pois.

Nine Papers from the International Congress of Mathematicians, 1986. I. Bashmakova. LC 90-22430. (Translations Ser.: Series 2, Vol. 147). 100p. 1990. 56.00 (*0-8218-3133-X*, TRANS2/147) Am Math.

Nine Papers in Analysis. M. S. Brodsky et al. LC 51-5559. (Translations Ser.: Series 2, Vol. 103). 203p. 1974. 55.00 (*0-8218-3053-8*, TRANS2/103) Am Math.

Nine Papers on Analysis. V. M. Adamjan et al. LC 78-5442. (Translations Ser.: Series 2, Vol. 111). 219p. 1978. 57.00 (*0-8218-3061-9*, TRANS2/111) Am Math.

Nine Papers on Analysis. N. I. Aheizer et al. LC 51-5559. (Translations Ser.: Series 2, Vol. 22). 370p. 1962. 42.00 (*0-8218-1722-1*, TRANS2/22) Am Math.

Nine Papers on Analysis. M. S. Budjanu et al. LC 77-11203. (Translations Ser.: Series 2, Vol. 110). 188p. 1977. 62.00 (*0-8218-3060-0*, TRANS2/110) Am Math.

Nine Papers on Foundations, Algebra, Topology, Functions of a Complex Variable. V. S. Carin et al. (Translations Ser.: Series 2, Vol. 15). 349p. 1960. 41.00 (*0-8218-1715-9*, TRANS2/15) Am Math.

Nine Papers on Foundations, Measure Theory, & Analysis. S. Fomin et al. (Translations Ser.: Series 2, Vol. 57). 307p. 1966. 51.00 (*0-8218-1757-4*, TRANS2/57) Am Math.

Nine Papers on Functional Analysis. Ju. M. Berezanskii et al. (Translations Ser.: Series 2, Vol. 93). 253p. 1970. 44.00 (*0-8218-1793-0*, TRANS2/93) Am Math.

Nine Papers on Functional Analysis & Numerical Analysis. Oleg V. Besov et al. (Translations Ser.: Series 2, Vol. 40). 290p. 1964. 36.00 (*0-8218-1740-X*, TRANS2/40) Am Math.

Nine Papers on Functional Analysis & Partial Differential Equations. Ju. A. Dubinskii et al. (Translations Ser.: Series 2, Vol. 67). 288p. 1968. 50.00 (*0-8218-1767-1*, TRANS2/67) Am Math.

Nine Papers on Hilbert's Sixteenth Problem. D. A. Gudkov & G. A. Utkin. LC 78-10201. (American Mathematical Society Translations Ser. 2: Vol. 112). 172p. 1978. text 59.00 (*0-8218-3062-7*, TRANS2/112) Am Math.

Nine Papers on Logic & Group Theory. S. D. Berman et al. LC 51-5559. (Translations Ser.: Series 2, Vol. 64). 256p. 1967. 47.00 (*0-8218-1764-7*, TRANS2/64) Am Math.

Nine Papers on Logic & Quantum Electrodynamics. V. K. Detlovs et al. LC 51-5559. (Translations Ser.: Series 2, Vol. 23). 335p. 1963. 38.00 (*0-8218-1723-X*, TRANS2/23) Am Math.

Nine Papers on Number Theory & Operator Theory. M. S. Brodskii et al. LC 51-5559. (Translations Ser.: Series 2, Vol. 13). 346p. 1960. reprint ed. pap. 62.00 (*0-8218-1713-2*, TRANS2/13) Am Math.

Nine Papers on Partial Differential Equations & Functional Analysis. Mikhail S. Brodskii et al. LC 51-5559. (American Mathematical Society Ser.: Series 2, 65). 300p. 1987. pap. 93.00 (*0-608-05171-3*, 205259200001) Bks Demand.

Nine Papers on Topology, Lie Groups, & Differential Equations. A. D. Aleksandrov et al. LC 51-5559. (Translations Ser.: Series 2, Vol. 21). 416p. 1962. 45.00 (*0-8218-1721-3*, TRANS2/21) Am Math.

Nine Parts of Desire: The Hidden World of Islamic Women. Geraldine Brooks. 272p. 1995. reprint ed. pap. 14.00 (*0-385-47577-2*) Doubleday.

Nine Patch Design Variations. Betty Boyink. 72p. (Orig.). 1991. pap. 14.50 (*0-925623-04-0*) B Boyink.

Nine Patch Wonders. Blanche Young & Helen Prost. 60p. 1991. pap. text 15.95 (*0-9633917-0-4*) First Star AZ.

Nine Pathological Mechanisms. Katherine E. Anderson. 30p. (Orig.). 1996. pap., spiral bd. 4.95 (*1-57876-901-9*) Triple U Enterprises.

Nine Pieces for Theater. B. Z. Niditch. Ed. by Joyce Carbone. 40p. (Orig.). 1995. pap. 4.95 (*1-878116-42-8*) JVC Bks.

Nine Plays by Black Women. Margaret B. Wilkerson. 1986. 12.09 (*0-606-00274-X*, Pub. by Turtleback) Demco.

Nine Plays of the Modern Theater: Waiting for Godot; The Visit; Tango; The Caucasian Chalk Circle; The Balcony; Rhinoceros; American Buffalo; The Birthday Party; Rosencrantz & Guildenstein are Dead. Ed. by Harold Clurman. LC 79-52121. 912p. 1981. pap. 21.00 (*0-8021-5032-2*, Grove) Grove-Atltic.

Nine + One: Ten Young Dutch Architectural Offices. Ed. by Michael Speaks & Christophe Grafe. LC 98-118169. (Illus.). 128p. 1998. pap. 36.00 (*90-5662-068-1*, 810762, Pub. by NAi Uitgevers) Dist Art Pubs.

Nine Portraits of Jesus: Discovering Jesus Through the Enneagram. Robert J. Nogosek. 1987. pap. 14.95 (*0-87193-260-1*) Dimension Bks.

Nine Princes in Amber. large type ed. Roger Zelazny. LC 97-48919. 254p. 1998. 22.95 (*0-7838-8425-7*, G K Hall & Co) Mac Lib Ref.

Nine Princes in Amber. Roger Zelazny. 176p. (YA). (gr. 9 up). 1977. reprint ed. mass mkt. 5.99 (*0-380-01430-0*, Avon Bks) Morrow Avon.

***Nine Public Lectures on Important Subjects in Religion.** Nicholaus Ludwig Count von Zinzendorf. Ed. by George W. Forell. 170p. 1998. pap. 17.00 (*1-57910-152-6*) Wipf & Stock.

9 Puzzling Mysteries. Andrew Gutelle. (Lunch Box Library). (Illus.). 208p. (J). (gr. 3-5). 1997. pap. 6.95 (*0-7611-0729-0*, 10729) Workman Pub.

Nine Questions People Ask about Judaism. Dennis Prager & Joseph Telushkin. 224p. 1986. pap. 11.00 (*0-671-62261-7*, Touchstone) S&S Trade Pap.

Nine Quills & a Red Pencil. Joseph Friedman et al. Tr. by Gladys Heitin. LC 89-11040. (ENG & YID., Illus.). 210p. (Orig.). 1989. pap. 11.95 (*0-9623737-0-2*) Jewish Cmnty Hse Elderly.

9 Scorpions. Paul Levine. LC 98-15064. 448p. 1999. 23.00 (*0-671-01939-2*, Pocket Books) PB.

9 Scorpions. Paul Levine. 1999. reprint ed. per. 7.50 (*0-671-01940-6*, Pocket Books) PB.

Nine Scorpions in a Bottle: Great Judges & Cases of the Supreme Court. Max Lerner. Ed. by Richard Cummings, Jr. LC 93-24463. 352p. 1995. pap. 13.45 (*1-55970-291-5*, Pub. by Arcade Pub Inc) Time Warner.

Nine Scorpions in a Bottle: Great Judges, & Cases of the Supreme Court. Max Lerner. LC 93-24463. 544p. 1994. 27.45 (*1-55970-168-4*, Pub. by Arcade Pub Inc) Time Warner.

Nine Secrets of Perfect Horsemanship. Don Blazer. Ed. by Meribah Small. LC 97-91294. 149p. 1998. pap. 19.95 (*0-9660127-1-2*) Success is Easy.

9 Secrets of Spiritually Successful People. Marilyn Hickey. 1999. pap. 7.95 (*1-56441-037-4*) M Hickey Min.

9 Secrets of Women Who Get Even. Kate White. 1999. pap. 12.00 (*0-609-80434-0*) Random Hse Value.

Nine Ships: A Book of Tales. Tony Cohan. (Illus.). 1975. 12.00 (*0-918226-02-3*); pap. 9.95 (*0-918226-00-7*) Acrobat.

Nine Short Plays: For Classroom Cooperative Learning Presentations. rev. ed. James Scott. 72p. (YA). (gr. 7-12). 1995. pap., wbk. ed. 4.50 (*1-58049-101-4*, CO01A) Prestwick Hse.

Nine Sisters Dancing. Ed Moses. 248p. (Orig.). 1996. pap. 12.95 (*1-56474-162-1*) Fithian Pr.

Nine Skies: Poems. A. V. Christie. LC 96-45773. (National Poetry Ser.). 72p. 1997. 11.95 (*0-252-06644-8*) U of Ill Pr.

Nine Sonnets. C. H. Sisson. (C). 1990. 35.00 (*0-906887-51-8*, Pub. by Greville Pr) St Mut.

Nine Soviet Portraits. Raymond A. Bauer & Edward Wasiolek. LC 79-4609. (Illus.). 190p. 1979. reprint ed. lib. bdg. 55.00 (*0-313-20929-4*, BANS, Greenwood Pr) Greenwood.

Nine Specimens of English Dialects: Edited from Various Sources. Ed. by Walter W. Skeat. (English Dialect Society Publications: No. 76). 1974. reprint ed. pap. 30.00 (*0-8115-0494-8*) Periodicals Srv.

***Nine Spiritual Gifts.** Ronald C. Dubrul. (Ministering the Gifts Ser.: No. II). ii, 118p. 1998. pap. 9.95 (*1-929138-13-X*, MINGI2) Christ Fellow Min.

Nine Spoons: A Chanukah Story. Marci Stillerman. Ed. by D. L. Rosenfeld. LC 97-74049. (Illus.). 32p. (J). (gr. k-2). 1998. 11.95 (*0-922613-84-2*) Hachai Pubng.

Nine Stages of Spiritual Apprenticeship: Understanding the Student-Teacher Relationship. Greg Bogart. 250p. (Orig.). 1997. pap. 17.95 (*0-9639068-5-2*) Dawn Mtn Pr.

***Nine Star Ki.** Robert Sachs. 352p. 1999. pap. 12.95 (*1-86204-485-6*, Pub. by Element MA) Penguin Putnam.

Nine Star Ki: Introducing Oriental Astrology. Michio Kushi & Edward Esko. 128p. 1991. pap. 12.95 (*0-9628528-0-5*) One Peaceful World.

N

***Nine Star Ki: Your Astrological Companion to Feng Shui.** Robert Sachs. 1999. pap. text 77.70 (*1-86204-652-2*, Pub. by Element MA) Penguin Putnam.

Nine Steps from Ignition to Extinguishment. 2nd ed. Rexford Wilson. 50p. 1994. pap. 19.95 (*1-885231-00-8*) Firecom Inst.

***Nine Steps to Becoming a Better Lector.** Nick Wagner. LC 00-20961. 96p. 2000. pap. 10.95 (*0-89390-503-8*) Resource Pubns.

9 Steps to Financial Freedom. Suze Orman. LC 97-143886. 278p. 1997. 23.00 (*0-517-70791-8*, Crown) Crown Pub Group.

9 Steps to Financial Freedom. Suze Orman. LC 98-3320. 288p. 2000. pap. 13.95 (*0-609-80186-4*) Crown Pub Group.

***9 Steps to Financial Freedom.** large type ed. Suze Orman. LC 99-23036. 1999. pap. 29.95 (*0-7838-8637-3*, G K Hall Lrg Type) Mac Lib Ref.

***9 Steps to Your New Home: A Home Building Guide.** Stephanie G. Davis. (Illus.). viii, 73p. 2000. pap. 6.95 (*0-615-11247-1*) S G Davis.

Nine Stories. J. D. Salinger. LC 52-12626. 302p. (gr. 8). 1953. 24.95 (*0-316-76956-8*) Little.

***Nine Stories.** J. D. Salinger. 320p. 2001. pap. 13.95 (*0-316-76772-7*, Back Bay) Little.

Nine Stories. J. D. Salinger. 1991. 10.09 (*0-606-04992-4*, Pub. by Turtleback) Demco.

Nine Stories. J. D. Salinger. 198p. 1991. reprint ed. mass mkt. 5.99 (*0-316-76950-9*) Little.

Nine Strikes of Death. Camella B. Schreyer. LC 88-7829. 1990. pap. 13.95 (*0-87949-281-3*) Ashley Bks.

Nine Stupid Things People Do to Mess up Their Resume: And 16 Ways to Avoid the Traps. Angela K. Durden. 80p. Date not set. pap. 11.95 (*0-9701356-0-2*) Writer Hire.

Nine Symphonies of Beethoven. 2nd rev. ed. Anthony Hopkins. LC 96-24730. 296p. 1996. 61.95 (*1-85928-246-6*, Pub. by Scolar Pr) Ashgate Pub Co.

Nine Tailors. Dorothy L. Sayers. 320p. Date not set. 24.95 (*0-8488-2388-5*) Amereon Ltd.

Nine Tailors. Dorothy L. Sayers. LC 34-6048. (Modern Classic Ser.). 420p. 1966. pap. 10.00 (*0-15-665899-2*, Harvest Bks) Harcourt.

Nine Tailors. Dorothy L. Sayers. LC 34-6048. (Modern Classic Ser.). 331p. 1989. 15.95 (*0-15-165897-8*) Harcourt.

Nine Tales. Forrest A. Abell. LC 96-71909. 112p. (Orig.). 1997. pap. 11.95 (*1-56167-344-7*) Am Literary Pr.

Nine Tales. Hugh De Selincourt. LC 79-103506. (Short Story Index Reprint Ser.). 1977. 21.95 (*0-8369-3248-X*) Ayer.

Nine Talmudic Readings by Emmanuel Levinas. Emmanuel Levinas. Tr. by Annette Aronwicz. LC 89-46329. 240p. 1990. 31.95 (*0-253-33379-2*) Ind U Pr.

Nine Talmudic Readings by Emmanuel Levinas. Emmanuel Levinas. Tr. by Annette Aronwicz. LC 89-46329. 240p. 1994. pap. 14.95 (*0-253-20876-9*) Ind U Pr.

Nine-Tenths. James Oppenheim. LC 68-57543. (Muckrakers Ser.). 1979. reprint ed. lib. bdg. 29.00 (*0-8398-1453-4*) Irvington.

Nine-Tenths Unseen: A Novel. Kenneth J. Harvey. 210p. pap. 19.95 (*1-895897-65-3*) Somerville Hse.

Nine Thousand Miles to Adventure: The Story of an American Boy in the Philippines. John P. Santacroce. LC 98-93986. 191 p. 1998. write for info. (*0-9668760-0-8*) Four Oaks Pubg.

9009. James M. Hopper & Fred R. Bechdolt. LC 68-57532. (Muckrakers Ser.). reprint ed. lib. bdg. 37.50 (*0-8398-0790-2*) Irvington.

Nine Times Nine. Anthony Boucher. 254p. 1986. pap. 4.95 (*0-930330-37-4*) Intl Polygonics.

***Nine-to-Five Affair.** large type ed. Jessica Steele. 1999. 21.95 (*0-263-16210-9*, Pub. by Mills & Boon) Ulverscroft.

Nine to Five & Spiritually Alive. Sheila Jones. 194p. 1997. pap. 11.99 (*1-57782-035-5*) Discipleshp.

9 to 5 Beats Ten to Life: How to (Re)Enter Society. Mike Davis. LC 96-152602. 125p. 1996. 12.00 (*1-56991-041-3*) Am Correctional.

Nine-to-Five Bride. Robin Wells. (Romance Ser.). 1998. per. 3.50 (*0-373-19311-4*, 1-19311-9) Silhouette.

***9 to 5 Guide to Combating Sexual Harassment: Candid Advice from 9 to 5, the National Association of Working Women.** Ellen Bravo & Ellen Cassedy. 208p. 1999. pap. 15.00 (*0-9673398-0-4*) Nine Five Wrk.

9 to 5 Guide to Combating Sexual Harassment: Candid Advice from 9 to 5, the National Association of Working Women. Ellen Bravo & Ellen Cassedy. LC 92-9793. 160p. 1992. pap. 12.95 (*0-471-57576-3*) Wiley.

Nine to Five Mindpoems, Vol. 1. Robert Clymire. (Perfect Gift Ser.). 85p. (Orig.). 1990. pap. 9.95 (*0-9621806-0-2*) Northstar VA.

Nine to Five Series, Set. Marilyn Cunningham & Margaret M. Scariano. (Illus.). (J). (gr. 3-9). 1985. pap. 17.00 (*0-87879-502-2*) High Noon Bks.

Nine to Five Wife see Esposa de Nueve a Cinco

Nine-Ton Cat: And Other True Tales of An Art Museum. Peggy Thomson et al. LC 96-18809. (Illus.). 96p. (J). 1997. 21.95 (*0-395-82655-1*); pap. 14.95 (*0-395-82683-7*) HM.

Nine Troubled Years. Samuel Templewood. LC 75-36363. (Illus.). 448p. 1976. reprint ed. lib. bdg. 75.00 (*0-8371-8633-1*, TENT, Greenwood Pr) Greenwood.

Nine True Dolphin Stories. Margaret Davidson & Roger Wilson.Tr. of Neuf Histoires Vraies de Dauphins. (FRE.). (J). mass mkt. 4.99 (*0-590-71188-1*) Scholastic Inc.

***Nine Truths about Weight Loss.** Daniel Kirschenbaum. 2001. pap. 12.00 (*0-8050-6394-3*) St Martin.

***9 Truths about Weight Loss: The No-Tricks, No-Nonsense Plan for Life-Long Weight Control.** Daniel Kirschenbaum. LC 99-49927. 288p. 2000. text 23.00 (*0-8050-6393-5*) H Holt & Co.

Nine-Twenty O'Farrell Street. Harriet L. Levy. LC 74-29501. (Modern Jewish Experience Ser.). (Illus.). 1975. reprint ed. 25.95 (*0-405-06728-3*) Ayer.

9 Types of Lovers: Why We Love the People We Do & How They Drive Us Crazy. Daphne R. Kingma. LC 99-24077. 240p. 1999. pap. 14.95 (*1-57324-160-1*) Conari Press.

Nine Ulster Lives. Ed. by G. O'Brien & P. Roebuck. 178p. 1992. pap. 16.95 (*0-901905-51-8*, Pub. by Ulster Hist Fnd) Irish Bks Media.

***Nine Visits to the Mythworld: Ghandl of the Qayahl Llaanas.** Tr. by Robert Bringhurst. 224p. 2000. 29.95 (*0-8032-1316-6*) U of Nebr Pr.

Nine Waxed Faces. Francis Beeding. 1994. lib. bdg. 21.95 (*1-56849-472-6*) Buccaneer Bks.

9 Ways of Working: How to Use the Enneagram to Discover Your Natural Strengths & Work More Effectively. Michael J. Goldberg. LC 98-52204. 1999. 13.95 (*1-56924-688-2*) Marlowe & Co.

9 Ways to Avoid Estate Taxes. Denis Clifford & Mary Randolph. LC 98-36075. (Quick & Legal Ser.). 200p. 1999. pap. 24.95 (*0-87337-466-5*) Nolo com.

***Nine Ways to Body Wisdom: Blending Natural Therapies to Nourish Body, Emotions & Soul.** Jennifer Harper. 2000. pap. 16.95 (*0-7225-4016-7*) Thorsons PA.

Nine Ways to Buy a House. Ralph E. Lee. 100p. (Orig.). 1981. pap. 6.95 (*0-9606268-0-8*) ProPress Pub.

Nine Women. Galina O. Sokolnikova. Tr. by H. C. Stevens. LC 71-93375. (Essay Index Reprint Ser.). 1977. 21.95 (*0-8369-1314-0*) Ayer.

Nine Women. Shirley A. Grau. (Southern Writers Ser.). 208p. 1987. reprint ed. mass mkt. 6.95 (*0-380-70107-3*, Avon Bks) Morrow Avon.

Nine Women: Drawn from the Epoch of the French Revolution. Galina O. Sokolnikova. Tr. by H. C. Stevens from RUS. (Essay Index Reprint Ser.). 287p. 1982. reprint ed. lib. bdg. 21.00 (*0-8290-0802-0*) Irvington.

Nine Wonderful Months: B'Sha'ah Tovah: The Complete Clinical & Halachic Guide to Pregnancy & Childbirth. Baruch Finkelstein & Michal Finkelstein. LC 93-9493. 1993. 26.95 (*0-87306-629-4*) Feldheim.

Nine Wrong Answers. John Dickson Carr. 168p. 1995. mass mkt. 3.95 (*0-7867-0174-9*) Carroll & Graf.

Nine Years Between Two Poems. Pit M. Pinegar. 1996. pap. 5.00 (*0-916897-23-0*) Andrew Mtn Pr.

Nine Years in the Saddle. James V. Lee. LC 98-161436. (Illus.). 138p. 1998. pap. 14.95 (*0-9663870-0-7*) Salado Pr.

***Nine Young Men from Kentucky.** 2nd ed. George H. Yater & Carolyn S. Denton. (We Proceeded on Supplementary Publication Ser.: Vol. 11). 24p. 2000. reprint ed. pap. 8.00 (*0-9678887-2-7*) L & C Trail.

90210 Guide Annex '94. Venice L. Holmes, Jr. 60p. (Orig.). 1994. pap. text 3.95 (*0-9638305-0-3*) New King Pub.

90210 Guide Annex '95. Venice L. Holmes, Jr. 60p. (Orig.). 1995. 3.95 (*0-9638305-1-1*) New King Pub.

Ninemile Wolves. Rick Bass. 170p. 1993. pap. 10.00 (*0-345-38251-X*) Ballantine Pub Grp.

Ninepenny Flute: Twenty-One Tales. Alfred E. Coppard. LC 71-106277. (Short Story Index Reprint Ser.). 1977. 20.95 (*0-8369-3314-1*) Ayer.

Nines see Ennead III.6: On the Impassivity of the Bodiless

19. (Detect-a-Word Ser.). (J). 1997. pap. write for info. (*1-56144-789-7*, Honey Bear Bks) Modern Pub NYC.

***1970s.** Mark Ray Schmidt. LC 99-47627. (America's Decades Ser.). 360p. (YA). 2000. lib. bdg. 22.45 (*0-7377-0308-3*) Greenhaven.

***1970s.** Mark Ray Schmidt. LC 99-47627. (America's Decades Ser.). 360p. (YA). 2000. pap. 17.96 (*0-7377-0307-5*) Greenhaven.

19 Articles You Can Use: To Acquire More Planned Gifts. G. Roger Schoenhals. 60p. (Orig.). 1995. pap. 49.00 (*0-9645517-0-5*) Planned Giving.

Nineteen Beautiful Years. Frances E. Willard. (Notable American Authors Ser.). 1999. reprint ed. lib. bdg. 125.00 (*0-7812-9975-6*) Rprt Serv.

Nineteen Day Feast Compilation. 1989. pap. 4.25 (*0-909991-48-0*) Bahai.

Nineteen Days: The Final Campaign Across Northwest Italy. 15th ed. (Combat Arms Ser.). 256p. 1987. 29.95 (*0-89839-105-9*) Battery Pr.

Nineteen Dollars & Eighty-Four Cents. William Wegman. (Illus.). 22p. 1984. pap. 15.00 (*0-939784-10-6*) CEPA Gall.

1918. Horton Foote. 1987. pap. 5.25 (*0-8222-0828-8*) Dramatists Play.

1918: The Unexpected Victory. J. H. Johnson. LC 98-111567. (Illus.). 208p. 1998. 27.95 (*1-85409-346-0*, Pub. by Arms & Armour) Sterling.

***1918 the Unexpected Victory.** J. H. Johnson. (Military Classics). (Illus.). 2000. pap. 9.95 (*0-304-35331-0*) Continuum.

1980s. Jane Duden & Gail B. Stewart. LC 90-46827. (Timelines Ser.). (Illus.). 48p. (J). (gr. 6). 1991. lib. bdg. 11.95 (*0-89686-599-1*, Crstwood Hse) Silver Burdett Pr.

***1980s.** Flametree. (Collins Gem Ser.). (Illus.). 256p. 2000. pap. 7.95 (*0-00-472312-0*, Pub. by HarpC) Trafalgar.

1980s. Stuart A. Kallen. LC 98-28564. (Cultural History of the United States Through the Decades Ser.). (Illus.). (YA). (gr. 4-12). 1998. lib. bdg. 23.70 (*1-56006-558-3*) Lucent Bks.

1980s. John Peacock. LC 98-60250. (Fashion Sourcebks.). (Illus.). 64p. 1998. pap. 10.95 (*0-500-28076-2*, Pub. by Thames Hudson) Norton.

***1980s.** James D. Torr. LC 99-55864. (America's Decades Ser.). 360p. (YA). 2000. pap. 17.96 (*0-7377-0309-1*); lib. bdg. 22.45 (*0-7377-0310-5*) Greenhaven.

1980s. Clint Twist. LC 92-40348. (Take Ten Years Ser.). (Illus.). 48p. (J). (gr. 3-7). 1993. lib. bdg. 5.00 (*0-8114-3081-2*) Raintree Steck-V.

***1980s from Ronald Reagan to MTV.** Stephen C. Feinstein. LC 99-39594. (Decades of the 20th Century Ser.). (Illus.). 64p. (YA). (gr. 5 up). 2000. lib. bdg. 17.95 (*0-7660-1424-X*) Enslow Pubs.

1980s, Payoff Decade for Advanced Materials: 25th National SAMPE Symposium & Exhibition, Town & Country Hotel, San Diego, California, May 6-8, 1980. National SAMPE Symposium & Exhibition Staff. LC 80-133416. (Science of Advanced Materials & Process Enginnering Ser.: No. 25). 790p. reprint ed. pap. 200.00 (*0-7837-1278-2*, 204141900020) Bks Demand.

1980's Pop. Bob Brunning. LC 99-27664. (Sound Trackers Ser.). 32p. (YA). 1999. 15.95 (*0-87226-579-X*, 6579XB, P Bedrick Books) NTC Contemp Pub Co.

1980's the United States in Crisis: United States in Crisis. Eli Raitport. Ed. by F. R. Duplantier. (United States in Crises Ser.). (Illus.). 214p. (Orig.). (C). 1989. reprint ed. pap. 19.50 (*0-944182-01-1*) Raitport Co.

1980 see Ferrous Division Conference.

1980 see Studies in Bibliography: Papers of the Bibliographical Society of the University of Virginia

1988. Andrew McGahan. LC 96-44519. 314p. 1996. 22.95 (*0-312-15043-1*) St Martin.

1988. Andrew McGahan. 320p. 1998. pap. 12.95 (*0-312-18032-X*, 837237) St Martin.

1988 see Studies in Bibliography: Papers of the Bibliographical Society of the University of Virginia

1988: A Novel of Politics. Richard D. Lamm & Arnold Grossman. 1986. pap. 3.95 (*0-685-43593-8*) St Martin.

1988: An Artist's Diary. Tod Thilleman. (Poetry New York Pamphlet Ser.: Vol. 7). 20p. 1999. pap. 5.00 (*0-923389-24-5*) Meet Eyes Bind.

1988 ACL Proceedings. pap. 60.00 (*1-55860-971-7*) Morgan Kaufmann.

1988 & All That: New Views of Australia's Past. Ed. by George Shore. 140p. (Orig.). (C). 1989. pap. text 29.95 (*0-7022-2168-6*, Pub. by Univ Queensland Pr) Intl Spec Bk.

1988 Applied Natural Language Processing Proceedings. pap. 60.00 (*1-55860-988-1*) Morgan Kaufmann.

1988 Candidate Profiles: A Look at the Leading Presidential Contenders. Ed. by James Skillen. 96p. 1988. pap. 2.95 (*0-310-20862-9*, 6328P) Zondervan.

1988 Connecticut Models Summer School: Proceedings. Ed. by David S. Touretzky et al. 550p. 1998. pap. text 29.95 (*1-55860-035-3*) Morgan Kaufmann.

1988 Defense Budget. Joshua M. Epstein. LC 87-7116. (Studies in Defense Policy). 57p. 1987. pap. 8.95 (*0-8157-2459-4*) Brookings.

1988 Election in South Dakota. Alan L. Clem. 1989. pap. 1.00 (*1-55614-131-9*) U of SD Gov Res Bur.

1988 Gold Book of Photography Prices. Thomas I. Perrett. 300p. (Orig.). 1988. pap. text 29.95 (*0-915827-07-7*) Photo Res Inst Carson Endowment.

1988 Graphics Interface Proceedings. pap. 40.00 (*1-55860-999-7*) Morgan Kaufmann.

1988 Media Guide: A Critical Review of the Print Media. Ed. by Jude Wanniski. 400p. 1988. 17.95 (*0-317-90505-8*) Polyconomics.

1988 Music & Video Yearbook. Joel Whitburn. 192p. 1989. pap. 14.95 (*0-89820-072-5*) Record Research.

1988 National Maternal & Infant Health Survey: Methods & Response Characteristics. Maureen Sanderson et al. LC 97-52830. (Vital & Health Statistics Ser.: Series 3, No. 125). 1998. write for info. (*0-8406-0540-4*) Natl Ctr Health Stats.

1988 Presidential Election in the South: Continuity Amidst Change in Southern Party Politics. Laurence W. Moreland et al. LC 90-23761. 320p. 1991. 65.00 (*0-275-93145-5*, C3145, Praeger Pubs) Greenwood.

1988-89 Who's Who among Play-by-Mail Gamers. 2nd rev. ed. Ed. by Kieron B. Mitchell. 125p. 1989. per. 9.95 (*0-9620846-1-1*) K & C Enterp.

1980 Election in South Dakota: End of an Era. Alan L. Clem. 1981. 1.00 (*1-55614-069-X*) U of SD Gov Res Bur.

1980 Eruptions of Mount St. Helens, Washington: Early Results of Studies of Volcanic Events in 1980, Geophysical Monitoring of Activity, & Studies of Volcanic Deposits, Effects, & Potential Hazards. Ed. by Peter W. Lipman & Donal R. Mullineaux. LC 81-600142. (Illus.). 872p. 1997. 35.00 (*0-295-97623-3*) U of Wash Pr.

1985 see Studies in Bibliography: Papers of the Bibliographical Society of the University of Virginia

1985 ACL Proceedings. pap. 60.00 (*1-55860-974-1*) Morgan Kaufmann.

1985, an Escape from Orwell's 1984: A Conservative Path to Freedom. Rhodes Boyson. LC 76-363799. ix, 146 p. 1975. write for info. (*0-902782-20-7*) Churchill Pr.

1985 Defense Budget. William W. Kaufmann. LC 84-71380. (Studies in Defense Policy). 54p. 1984. pap. 8.95 (*0-8157-4875-2*) Brookings.

1985-86 Hormel Meat-Packers Strike in Austin, Minnesota. Fred Halstead. 44p. 1986. pap. 5.00 (*0-87348-489-4*) Pathfinder NY.

1985 European ACL Proceedings. pap. 60.00 (*1-55860-983-0*) Morgan Kaufmann.

1985 Excavations at the Hodges Site, Pima County, Arizona. Ed. by Robert W. Layhe. (Archaeological Ser.: No. 170). (Illus.). 436p. 1986. pap. 19.95 (*1-889747-42-4*) Ariz St Mus.

1985 Federal Tax Course. Prentice-Hall Staff. 1984. write for info. (*0-318-58023-3*) P-H.

1985 Music Yearbook. Joel Whitburn. 240p. 1986. pap. 14.95 (*0-89820-057-1*) Record Research.

1985 Proceedings of the National Association of Insurance Commissioners, Vol. II. National Association of Insurance Commissioners St. Ed. by Karen P. Miller. 772p. 1985. 175.00 (*0-89382-165-9*) Nat Assn Insurance.

1985 Supplement to Agricultural Law. Julian C. Juergensmeyer & James B. Wadley. 1985. 46.00 (*0-316-47613-7*, Aspen Law & Bus) Aspen Pub.

1985 Supplement to Federal Litigation Practice Manual. 68p. 1985. pap. 6.00 (*0-317-02661-5*, 40,000B) NCLS Inc.

1985 Symposium Proceedings: Test Ranges & Facilities: The Next Ten Years. 1986. 30.00 (*0-317-01268-1*) Int Test Eval.

1985-1992 Master Cumulation, Vols. 1-6. 92nd ed. Ed. by Neil E. Walker & Beverly Baer. 8500p. 1993. 1360.00 (*0-8103-9626-2*) Gale.

***1984.** (YA). 1999. 9.95 (*1-56137-413-X*) Novel Units.

Nineteen Eighty-Four. Harold Bloom. (Bloom's Notes Ser.). 1998. pap. 4.95 (*0-7910-4140-9*) Chelsea Hse.

***1984.** Ed. by Cliffs Notes Staff. (Cliffs Notes Ser.). 80p. 2000. pap. 4.99 (*0-7645-8585-1*) IDG Bks.

***1984.** Kathleen Millin & Mary Dennis. 36p. (YA). 1999. 11.95 (*1-56137-414-8*) Novel Units.

1984. George Orwell. 1991. pap. text. write for info. (*0-582-06018-4*, Pub. by Addison-Wesley) Longman.

1984. George Orwell. 1998. pap. 5.95 (*0-451-52493-4*) Addson-Wesley Educ.

1984. George Orwell. 1963. 5.60 (*0-87129-542-3*, N15) Dramatic Pub.

***1984.** George Orwell. 1999. pap. 13.35 (*0-88103-036-8*) Econo-Clad Bks.

1984. George Orwell. LC 92-52906. 384p. 1992. 17.00 (*0-679-41739-7*) Everymns Lib.

1984. George Orwell. LC 83-18442. 320p. 1983. 12.95 (*0-15-166038-7*) Harcourt.

1984. George Orwell. write for info. (*0-614-22114-5*, Sig Classics) NAL.

1984. George Orwell. 294p. 1989. pap. 12.95 (*0-452-26293-3*) NAL.

1984. George Orwell. (Signet Classics). 1949. 11.05 (*0-606-00199-9*, Pub. by Turtleback) Demco.

1984. Liz Winner. (Novel-Ties Ser.). (YA). (gr. 9-12). 1983. pap. text, student ed. 15.95 (*0-88122-027-2*) Lrn Links.

1984. George Orwell. 1982. reprint ed. 29.95 (*0-89966-368-0*) Buccaneer Bks.

1984 see Studies in Bibliography: Papers of the Bibliographical Society of the University of Virginia

1984: A Preview. Ed. by Sean H. Elwood. (Illus.). 168p. (Orig.). 1983. pap. 10.00 (*0-914661-00-0*) Feldman Fine Arts.

1984: Past, Present & Future. Patrick Reilly. (Masterwork Studies). 160p. 1989. 25.95 (*0-8057-8065-3*, Twyne); pap. 13.95 (*0-8057-8110-2*, Twyne) Mac Lib Ref.

1984: Reproducible Teaching Unit. rev. ed. James Scott. 48p. (YA). (gr. 7-12). 1996. teacher ed., ring bd. 29.50 (*1-58049-070-0*, TU68/U) Prestwick Hse.

***1984: Selected Letters.** Samuel R. Delany. 384p. 2000. pap. 17.95 (*0-9665998-1-0*) Voyant Pubg.

1984: The Facsimile of the extant manuscript. fac. ed. George Orwell. LC 81-3848. 416p. 1984. 75.00 (*0-15-166034-4*) Harcourt.

1984: The Fascimile of the Extant Manuscript. deluxe limited ed. George Orwell. Ed. by Peter Davison. 406p. 1984. boxed set 525.00 (*0-87730-015-1*); lthr. 275.00 (*0-87730-012-7*) M & S Pr.

1984: The Ultimate Van Halen Trivia Book. Lucas Aykroyd. 155p. 1997. spiral bd. 18.00 (*1-55212-089-9*, No. 97-0007) Trafford Pub.

1984 & After. Dimitrios I. Roussopoulos. Ed. by Marsha Hewitt. 234p. 1984. 43.99 (*0-920057-28-4*, Pub. by Black Rose); pap. 14.95 (*0-920057-29-2*, Pub. by Black Rose) Consort Bk Sales.

1984 Budget. Ed. by Joseph A. Pechman. 248p. 1983. 34.95 (*0-8157-6994-6*); pap. 14.95 (*0-8157-6993-8*) Brookings.

1984 by George Orwell: Curriculum Unit. Center for Learning Network Staff. (Novel - Drama Ser.). 89p. 1996. teacher ed., spiral bd. 18.95 (*1-56077-323-5*) Ctr Learning.

1984 Election in Historical Perspective. William E. Leuchtenburg. LC 86-72071. (Charles Edmondson Historical Lectures). 43p. (Orig.). 1986. pap. 5.95 (*0-918954-45-2*) Baylor Univ Pr.

1984 Election in South Dakota. Alan L. Clem. 1985. 1.00 (*1-55614-070-3*) U of SD Gov Res Bur.

1984 Hazardous Waste Amendments & Superfund Developments. 35.00 (*0-317-29652-3*, #CO3395) Harcourt.

1984 in 1984: Orwell As Prophecy. Robert L. Fishman et al. Ed. by Richard Waldron. (Illus.). 76p. (Orig.). 1986. pap. 5.00 (*0-938766-03-1*) NJ State Mus.

1984 Music Yearbook. Joel Whitburn. 264p. 1985. pap. 14.95 (*0-89820-055-5*) Record Research.

1984 Notes. Gilbert Borman & Frank H. Thompson, Jr. (Cliffs Notes Ser.). 56p. 1967. pap. 4.95 (*0-8220-0899-8*, Cliff) IDG Bks.

1984 Presidential Election in the South: Patterns of Southern Party Politics. Ed. by Robert P. Steed et al. LC 85-12246. 348p. 1985. 59.95 (*0-275-90043-6*, C0043, Praeger Pubs) Greenwood.

1984 Proceedings - 1st National Conference & Workshop, Tailoring Environmental Standards to Control Contract Requirements. LC 62-38584. 200p. 1984. pap. text 75.00 (*0-915414-79-1*) IEST.

1984 Show. Ed. by Sean Elwood. (Illus.). 160p. 1984. pap. 10.95 (*0-930794-99-0*) Station Hill Pr.

1984 Symposium Proceedings: Impact of High Technology on Test & Evaluation. 1984. 25.00 (*0-317-01201-0*) Int Test Eval.

1984 World Review: The Ten Years since the World Food Conference - Urbanization, Agriculture & Food Systems see State of Food & Agriculture

1984 World's Fair: The Official Guidebook. Ed. by Linda Delery. (Illus.). 160p. 1984. pap. 6.25 (*0-685-08335-7*) Picayune Pr.

1980 Grain Embargo Negotiations: The United States, Argentina, & the Soviet Union. Aldo C. Vacs. (Pew Case Studies in International Affairs). 50p. (C). 1992. pap. text 3.50 (*1-56927-118-6*) Geo U Inst Dplmcy.

1989 see Studies in Bibliography: Papers of the Bibliographical Society of the University of Virginia

1989: The Year the World Changed. Jeffrey B. Symynkywicz. LC 95-14703. (YA). (gr. 6 up). 1995. pap. 7.95 (*0-382-39191-8*, Dillon Silver Burdett); lib. bdg. 14.95 (*0-87518-631-9*, Dillon Silver Burdett) Silver Burdett Pr.

1989 ACL Proceedings. pap. 60.00 (*1-55860-970-9*) Morgan Kaufmann.

1989 Conference Issue. J. Miles. 74p. 1990. text 76.00 (*3-7186-5103-3*, Harwood Acad Pubs) Gordon & Breach.

1989 European ACL Proceedings. pap. 60.00 (*1-55860-981-4*) Morgan Kaufmann.

1989 Fall Consumer Catalog. Osborne. 1989. write for info. (*0-07-881569-X*) McGraw.

1989 Fall International Catalog. Osborne. 1989. write for info. (*0-07-881571-1*) McGraw.

1989 Forensic Services Directory. 1300p. 1989. 87.50 (*0-9602962-5-5*) Natl Forensic.

1989 Gold Book of Photography Prices. Thomas I. Perrett. 300p. 1989. spiral bd. 39.95 (*0-915827-09-3*) Photo Res Inst Carson Endowment.

1989 Graphics Interface Proceedings. pap. 40.00 (*1-55860-998-9*) Morgan Kaufmann.

1989 Indian National Elections: A Retrospective Analysis. Leon J. Weil & Lewis R. McFarlane. ii, 40p. 1990. pap. 6.00 (*1-879720-72-8*) Intl Fndt Elect.

1989 Media Guide. Jude Wannisky. 1989. write for info. (*0-318-64949-8*) Polyconomics.

1989 Mediaguide: A Critical Review of the Print Media. Jude Wanniski. 1989. 34.95 (*0-938081-03-9*); pap. 19.95 (*0-938081-02-0*) Polyconomics.

1989 Music & Video Yearbook. Joel Whitburn. 216p. 1990. pap. 29.95 (*0-89820-075-X*) Record Research.

1989 Paraguayan Elections: A Foundation for Democratic Change. National Democratic Institute for International Af. 68p. 1989. pap. 6.00 (*1-880134-02-0*) Natl Demo Inst.

1989 Revision of the U. S. Standard Certificates & Reports: PHS 91-1465. (Vital & Health Statistics Ser.: Series 4, No. 28). 34p. 1991. 3.25 (*0-685-61571-5*, 017-022-01134-4) Natl Ctr Health Stats.

1989-2000 Greater Atlanta Newcomer's Guide, Vol. 10. 10th rev. ed. Missy Hardee. (Illus.). 192p. 1999. 5.95 (*1-886760-03-9*) Atl Chamber Publ.

1989 Vacuum Metallurgy Conference Proceedings. 146p. 1989. 40.00 (*0-932897-45-2*) Iron & Steel.

1981 see Studies in Bibliography: Papers of the Bibliographical Society of the University of Virginia

1980 Proceedings of the Annual Technical Meeting of the Institute of Environmental Sciences: Life Cycle Problems & Environmental Technology, Philadelphia, PA, April, 1980. Institute of Environmental Sciences & Technology Staff. LC 62-38584. (Illus.). 456p. 1980. pap. 75.00 (*0-915414-20-1*) IEST.

1987 see Studies in Bibliography: Papers of the Bibliographical Society of the University of Virginia

1987 ACL Proceedings. pap. 60.00 (*1-55860-972-5*) Morgan Kaufmann.

1987 Annual Precision Engineering Conference - Abstracts & Agenda. 68p. 1987. pap. write for info. (*1-887706-01-1*) Am Soc Prec Engr.

1987 Corporation & Partnership, Statutes, Rules, & Forms. Conrad et al. 1987. pap. text 15.25 (*0-88277-597-9*) Foundation Pr.

1987 Defense Budget. Joshua M. Epstein. LC 85-48175. (Studies in Defense Policy). 61p. 1986. pap. 8.95 (*0-8157-2457-8*) Brookings.

1987 Directory of Literary Magazines. rev. ed. 94p. (Orig.). 1987. pap. 6.95 (*0-317-61506-8*) Coord Coun Lit Mags.

1987 European ACL Proceedings. pap. 60.00 (*1-55860-982-2*) Morgan Kaufmann.

1987 Music & Video Yearbook. Joel Whitburn. 240p. 1988. pap. 14.95 (*0-89820-065-2*) Record Research.

1987 Ohio Selection: Graphics. Dominique H. Vasseur. 36p. 1987. pap. text 6.00 (*0-937809-01-2*) Dayton Art.

1987 Supplement to the Design Guide to the 1985 Uniform Building Code. Alfred Goldberg. (Illus.). 70p. (Orig.). 1987. pap. 6.00 (*0-9614808-3-1*) GRDA Pubns.

1987 Survey of Income & Expenditure of Urban Households of China. China Statistical Information & Consultancy Servic. 176p. 1991. pap. text 32.95 (*0-86638-125-2*) EW Ctr HI.

1986 see Animal Health Yearbook

1986 see Studies in Bibliography: Papers of the Bibliographical Society of the University of Virginia

1986 ACL Proceedings. pap. 60.00 (*1-55860-973-3*) Morgan Kaufmann.

1986 All States Guide to Garnishment Law & Procedures. U. S. Army Judge Advocate General's School Staff. 123p. 1986. 10.00 (*0-685-23173-9*, 42,107) NCLS Inc.

1986 Defense Budget. William W. Kaufmann. LC 84-45858. (Studies in Defense Policy). 59p. 1985. pap. 8.95 (*0-8157-4877-9*) Brookings.

1986 Directory of Literary Magazines. rev. ed. 94p. (Orig.). 1986. pap. 5.95 (*0-942332-08-3*) Coord Coun Lit Mags.

1986 Election in South Dakota. Alan L. Clem. 1987. pap. 1.00 (*1-55614-127-0*) U of SD Gov Res Bur.

1986 MediaGuide. Jude Wanniski. 102p. (Orig.). 1986. pap. 14.95 (*0-938081-00-4*) Polyconomics.

1986 Music Yearbook. Joel Whitburn. 216p. 1987. pap. 14.95 (*0-89820-063-6*) Record Research.

1986 Supplement to the Design Guide to the Nineteen Eighty-Five Uniform Building Code. Alfred Goldberg. (Illus.). (Orig.). 1986. pap. 6.00 (*0-9614808-2-3*) GRDA Pubns.

1986 Symposium Proceedings: Challenges of Space Testing. 1986. 30.00 (*0-318-21790-2*) Int Test Eval.

1983 see World Statistics in Brief: United Nations Statistical Pocketbook

1983 see FAO Trade Yearbook

1983 ACL Proceedings. pap. 60.00 (*1-55860-976-8*) Morgan Kaufmann.

1983 Annual Report of the Former Secretaries of State, 1983: The Need to Develop Bipartisanship & Continuity in U. S. Foreign Policy. Alexander Haig et al. Ed. by Julia A. White. LC 85-50887. (Papers on International Issues). 30p. (Orig.). (C). 1985. pap. text 5.00 (*0-935082-06-9*) Southern Ctr Intl Stud.

1983 Applied Natural Language Processing Proceedings. pap. 60.00 (*1-55860-989-X*) Morgan Kaufmann.

Nineteen Eighty-Three Budget. Ed. by Joseph A. Pechman. 268p. 1982. 34.95 (*0-8157-6992-X*); pap. 14.95 (*0-8157-6991-1*) Brookings.

1983 European ACL Proceedings. pap. 60.00 (*1-55860-984-9*) Morgan Kaufmann.

1983 Symposium Proceedings. 1983. 25.00 (*0-318-22042-3*) Int Test Eval.

1983 Travis Papers in the Integration of Psychology & Theology. Ed. by Christopher H. Rosik & H. Newton Malony. 1986. pap. 10.00 (*0-9609928-5-5*) Integ Pr.

1983 View of Non-Conventional Energy Sources. Ed. by G. Furlan et al. 700p. 1985. 121.00 (*9971-966-36-0*) World Scientific Pub.

1983 Music Yearbook. Joel Whitburn. 276p. 1984. pap. 14.95 (*0-89820-052-0*) Record Research.

1980-1989. Robert Dunbar. (Yearbooks in Science Ser.). (Illus.). 80p. (J). (gr. 5-8). 1995. lib. bdg. 20.40 (*0-8050-3438-2*) TFC Bks NY.

1980-1981 see Selected Articles

1982 see Winter Simulation Conference Proceedings

1982 see Studies in Bibliography: Papers of the Bibliographical Society of the University of Virginia

1982-1983 see Selected Articles

1982 ACL Proceedings. pap. 60.00 (*1-55860-977-6*) Morgan Kaufmann.

1982 Annual Report on Mining Activities. Bureau of Deep Mine Safety & Mining & Reclamation. Ed. by Nichols Patsie & Gloria Keffer. 485p. (C). 1982. 8.05 (*0-8182-0028-6*) Commonweal PA.

1982 Carnegie International. Gene Baro. (Illus.). 128p. 1982. pap. text 7.95 (*0-88039-004-2*) Mus Art Carnegie.

1982 Cuban Joint Venture Law: Context, Assessment, & Prospects. Jorge F. Perez-Lopez. 93p. (C). 1985. pap. text 14.95 (*1-56000-662-5*, CP307) Transaction Pubs.

1982 Election in South Dakota. Alan L. Clem. 1983. 1.00 (*1-55614-071-1*) U of SD Gov Res Bur.

1982 Mexican Debt Negotiations. Roger S. Leeds & Gale Thompson. (Pew Case Studies in International Affairs). 50p. (C). 1993. pap. text 3.50 (*1-56927-201-8*) Geo U Inst Dplmcy.

1982 Proceedings Seminar on Designing Electronic Equipment for Random Vibration Environments: Los Angeles, CA. 98p. 50.00 (*0-915414-68-6*) IEST.

1982 Register. Michael Laurence et al. (Illus.). 124p. 1983. 30.00 (*0-9610384-0-3*) US Pict Res.

1982 Supplement to Estate Planning. 4th ed. A. James Casner. 1982. pap., student ed. 16.00 (*0-316-13171-7*, Aspen Law & Bus) Aspen Pub.

1982 Supplement to Federal Income Taxation of Corporate Transactions. William D. Andrews. (C). 1982. pap. 12.00 (*0-316-04224-2*) Little.

1982-1984 Excavations at Las Colinas - The Mound 8 Precinct. Contrib. by Gregory et al. (Archaeological Ser.: Vol. 162, No. 3). (Illus.). 78p. 1988. 5.00 (*1-889747-58-0*) Ariz St Mus.

1982-1984 Excavations at Las Colinas Research Design. Contrib. by David A. Gregory et al. (Archaeological Ser.: Vol. 162, No. 1). (Illus.). 54p. 1985. 5.00 (*1-889747-57-2*) Ariz St Mus.

1980 U. S. Census Population & Housing Characteristics, 5 vols. Thomas R. Gay. Incl. Bk. 1. State, SMSA, ADI, City, County Data & Indices. James D. Shaffer. 1983. Bk. 2. Place Data & Indices. James D. Shaffer. 1983. Bk. 3. Census Tract Data (Alaska-Iowa) James D. Shaffer. 1983. Bk. 4. Census Tract Data (Kansas-North Dakota) James D. Shaffer. 1983. Bk. 5. Census Tract Data (Ohio-Wyoming) Ed. by James D. Shaffer. 1983. 1000p. 1983. Set pap. 395.00 (*0-686-46735-3*) Natl Decision.

1911 Revolution in China. Ed. by Shinkichi Eto & Harold Z. Shiffrin. 316p. 1985. 37.50 (*0-86008-349-7*, Pub. by U of Tokyo) Col U Pr.

1915. Roger McDonald. (Paperbacks Ser.). 434p. (YA). (gr. 10 up). 1989. reprint ed. pap. 16.95 (*0-7022-2134-1*, Pub. by Univ Queensland Pr) Intl Spec Bk.

1915, the Cultural Moment: The New Politics, the New Woman, the New Psychology, the New Art, & the New Theater in America. Ed. by Adele Heller & Lois Rudnick. LC 91-6634. (Illus.). 400p. (C). 1991. pap. 19.95 (*0-8135-1721-4*); text 60.00 (*0-8135-1720-6*) Rutgers U Pr.

History of the Reorganized Church of Jesus Christ of Latter Day Saints Vol. 7: 1915-1925, Vol. 7. F. Henry Edwards. 1973. 31.50 (*0-8309-0075-6*) Herald Pub Hse.

1950s. Jane Duden. LC 89-34400. (Timelines Ser.). (Illus.). 48p. (J). (gr. 6). 1989. lib. bdg. 11.95 (*0-89686-476-6*, Crstwood Hse) Silver Burdett Pr.

***1950's.** Flametree Staff. (Collins Gem Ser.). (Illus.). 256p. 2000. pap. 7.95 (*0-00-472309-0*, Pub. by HarpC) Trafalgar.

***1950s.** Stuart A. Kallen. LC 99-47628. (America's Decades Ser.). 360p. (YA). 2000. lib. bdg. 22.45 (*0-7377-0304-0*) Greenhaven.

***1950s.** Stuart A. Kallen. LC 99-47628. (America's Decades Ser.). 360p. (YA). 2000. pap. 17.96 (*0-7377-0303-2*) Greenhaven.

***1950s.** Stuart A. Kallen. LC 98-26669. (Cultural History of the United States Through the Decades Ser.). (Illus.). (YA). (gr. 4 up). 1998. lib. bdg. 23.70 (*1-56006-555-9*) Lucent Bks.

1950s. John Peacock. LC 96-61232. (Fashion Sourcebooks Ser.). (Illus.). 64p. (Orig.). 1997. pap. 10.95 (*0-500-27931-4*, Pub. by Thames Hudson) Norton.

1950s. Ed. by Nick Yapp. (Decades of the 20th Century Ser.). (Illus.). 400p. 1998. pap. 9.95 (*3-8290-0522-9*, 810151) Konemann.

***1950s from the Korean War to Elvis.** Stephen Feinstein. (Decades of the 20th Century Ser.). (Illus.). 64p. (YA). (gr. 5 up). 2000. lib. bdg. 17.95 (*0-7660-1427-4*) Enslow Pubs.

1950s Scrapbook. Robert Opie. 1998. 24.95 (*1-872727-63-8*, Pub. by New Cavendish) Pincushion Pr.

1953: Chronicle of a Birth Foretold. France Daigle. Tr. by Robert Majzels from FRE. LC 98-104627. (ENG & FRE.). 176p. 1999. pap. 13.95 (*0-88784-604-1*) Genl Dist Srvs.

***1950, Crossroads of American Religious Life.** Robert S. Ellwood. LC 99-56256. (Illus.). 192p. 2000. pap. 18.95 (*0-664-25813-1*, Pub. by Westminster John Knox) Presbyterian Pub.

1958 see Studies in Bibliography: Papers of the Bibliographical Society of the University of Virginia

1950-51 see Studies in Bibliography: Papers of the Bibliographical Society of the University of Virginia

1955 see Studies in Bibliography: Papers of the Bibliographical Society of the University of Virginia

1955-1959 see Cumulative Index of Hospital Literature: 1950-1954

1955-1966 Definitive Rock 'n Roll Collection: Alto Saxophone. 96p. 1991. pap. 9.95 (*0-7935-1302-2*, 00847209) H Leonard.

1955-1966 Definitive Rock 'n Roll Collection: Clarinet. 96p. 1991. pap. 9.95 (*0-7935-1301-4*, 00847208) H Leonard.

1955-1966 Definitive Rock 'n Roll Collection: Flute. 96p. 1991. pap. 9.95 (*0-7935-1300-6*, 00847207) H Leonard.

1955-1966 Definitive Rock 'n Roll Collection: Trombone. 96p. 1991. pap. 9.95 (*0-7935-1304-9*, 00847211) H Leonard.

1955-1966 Definitive Rock 'n Roll Collection: Trumpet. 96p. 1991. pap. 9.95 (*0-7935-1303-0*, 00847210) H Leonard.

1954, Vol. 3. 12.00 Destiny.

1954 Infinite Way Letters. Joel S. Goldsmith. LC 96-26081. xi, 115p. 1996. 15.95 (*1-889051-03-9*, I Lvl) Acrpls Bks CO.

1959 see Studies in Bibliography: Papers of the Bibliographical Society of the University of Virginia

1959-1960 see Indice Cultural

1950-1959 see Times in Review: New York Times Decade Books

1950-1951 see Yearbook of the United Nations, 1946-1977

1951-52 see Studies in Bibliography: Papers of the Bibliographical Society of the University of Virginia

1957-1975 Microfiche see Yearbook of National Accounts Statistics

1957 Code Article 27 see Michie's Annotated Code of Maryland, 1998 Supplement

1957 Code Articles 1-26A see Michie's Annotated Code of Maryland, 1998 Supplement

1957 Code Articles 27A-41 see Michie's Annotated Code of Maryland, 1998 Supplement

1957 Excavations at Beth-Zur. Paul W. Lapp. (Annuals of the American Schools of Oriental Research Ser.: Vol. 38). 87p. 1968. text 39.50 (*0-89757-038-3*, Pub. by Sheffield Acad) CUP Services.

1957-1958 see Indice Cultural

1956-1965 see Librairie Francaise, Tables Decennales

1956 & All That: The Making of Modern British Drama. Dan Rebellato. LC 98-29159. 1999. 65.00 (*0-415-18938-1*); pap. 21.99 (*0-415-18939-X*) Routledge.

1956 Counter-Revolution in Hungary: Words & Weapons. rev. ed. Janos Berecz. Tr. by Istvan Butykai from HUN. 223p. (C). 1986. 45.00 (*963-05-4370-2*, Pub. by Akade Kiado) St Mut.

1956 Presidential Campaign. Charles A. Thomson & Frances M. Shattuck. LC 74-11990. 382p. 1974. reprint ed. lib. bdg. 69.50 (*0-8371-7707-3*, THPC, Greenwood Pr) Greenwood.

***1956 War: Collusion & Rivalry in the Middle East.** Ed. by David Tal. (Cummings Center Ser.: Vol. 11). 304p. 2000. pap. text 18.50 (*0-7146-4394-7*) F Cass Pubs.

1953-54 see Studies in Bibliography: Papers of the Bibliographical Society of the University of Virginia

1953 Humes Herald. Jerry Osborne. (Illus.). 112p. 1988. 19.95 (*0-932117-09-0*) Osborne Enterps.

1950-1959. Mona Kerby. (Yearbooks in Science Ser.). (Illus.). 80p. (J). (gr. 5-8). 1995. lib. bdg. 20.40 (*0-8050-3435-8*) TFC Bks NY.

1952-53 see Studies in Bibliography: Papers of the Bibliographical Society of the University of Virginia

***1940's.** Center for Gifted Education Staff. 364p. 1998. boxed set 65.95 (*0-7872-5343-X*, 41534301) Kendall-Hunt.

1940s. Jane Duden. LC 89-34401. (Timelines Ser.). (Illus.). 48p. (J). (gr. 6). 1989. lib. bdg. 11.95 (*0-89686-475-8*, Crstwood Hse) Silver Burdett Pr.

***1940s.** Louise Gerdes. LC 99-56323. (America's Decades Ser.). 360p. (YA). 2000. lib. bdg. 22.45 (*0-7377-0302-4*) Greenhaven.

***1940s.** Louise Gerdes. LC 99-56323. (America's Decades Ser.). (Illus.). 360p. (YA). 2000. pap. 17.96 (*0-7377-0301-6*) Greenhaven.

1940s. John Peacock. LC 97-61657. (Fashion Sourcebooks Ser.). (Illus.). 64p. 1998. pap. 10.95 (*0-500-28041-X*, Pub. by Thames Hudson) Norton.

1940s. Michael V. Uschan. (Cultural History of the United States Through the Decades Ser.). (Illus.). 128p. 1998. lib. bdg. 18.96 (*1-56510-554-0*) Lucent Bks.

1940s. Michael V. Uschan. LC 98-21005. (Cultural History of the United States Through the Decades Ser.). (Illus.). (YA). (gr. 4-12). 1998. lib. bdg. 23.70 (*1-56006-554-0*) Lucent Bks.

1940s. Ed. by Nick Yapp. (Decades of the 20th Century Ser.). (Illus.). 400p. 1998. pap. 9.95 (*3-8290-0521-0*, 810150) Konemann.

***1940s from World War II to Jackie Robinson.** Stephen Feinstein. LC 99-50710. (Decades of the 20th Century Ser.). (Illus.). 64p. (YA). (gr. 5 up). 2000. lib. bdg. 17.95 (*0-7660-1428-2*) Enslow Pubs.

1940: Myth & Reality. Clive Ponting. 272p. 1991. text 24.95 (*0-929587-68-5*) I R Dee.

1940: Myth & Reality. Clive Ponting. LC 93-11244. 276p. 1993. reprint ed. pap. 14.95 (*1-56663-036-3*, Elephant Paperbacks) I R Dee.

1940 Destroyer Deal with Great Britain. Ole R. Holsti. (Pew Case Studies in International Affairs). 50p. (C). 1993. pap. text 3.50 (*1-56927-457-6*) Geo U Inst Dplmcy.

1948 & After: Israel & the Palestinians. Benny Morris. (Illus.). 304p. 1991. 75.00 (*0-19-828784-4*) OUP.

1948-49 see Studies in Bibliography: Papers of the Bibliographical Society of the University of Virginia

1948, Italy. limited ed. Donald Windham. (Illus.). 132p. 1998. 75.00 (*0-917366-11-5*) S Campbell.

1948-1956 see Indice Cultural

1948 Zanzibar General Strike. Anthony Clayton. (Research Report Ser.: No. 32). 66p. 1976. write for info. (*91-7106-094-4*, Pub. by Nordic Africa) Transaction Pubs.

1945. Newt Gingrich. 1996. per. 6.99 (*0-671-87739-9*) PB.

1945. Newt Gingrich & William R. Forstchen. 382p. 1995. 24.00 (*0-671-87676-7*) Baen Bks.

1945. Newt Gingrich & William R. Forstchen. 400p. 1996. mass mkt. 6.99 (*0-614-20498-4*) Baen Bks.

1944: The Allies Triumph. John Westwoo. 1994. 15.98 (*1-55521-955-1*) Bk Sales Inc.

1949. David French. (NFS Canada Ser.). 176p. 1989. pap. 13.95 (*0-88922-266-5*, Pub. by Talonbks) Genl Dist Srvs.

1949: The First Israelis. Tom Segev. Tr. by Arlen N. Weinstein. (Illus.). 384p. 1998. pap. 15.95 (*0-317-43428-4*, Owl) H Holt & Co.

1949: The First Israelis. Tom Segev. Tr. by Arlen N. Weinstein. LC 97-42451. (Illus.). 384p. 1998. pap. 15.95 (*0-8050-5896-6*) St Martin.

1949-50 see Studies in Bibliography: Papers of the Bibliographical Society of the University of Virginia

1940-1949 see Times in Review: New York Times Decade Books

1947: When All Hell Broke Loose. Barber. 31.95 (*0-8488-1564-5*) Amereon Ltd.

1947: When All Hell Broke Loose in Baseball. Red Barber. (Quality Paperbacks Ser.). 380p. 1984. pap. 14.95 (*0-306-80212-0*) Da Capo.

1946. Matthew Graham. 55p. (Orig.). 1991. pap. text 9.95 (*0-913123-34-X*) Galileo.

1946-1955 see Librairie Francaise, Tables Decennales

1945 Year of Liberation. Ed. by Kevin Mahoney. 1995. pap. 19.95 (*0-89604-700-8*, Holocaust Library) US Holocaust.

1943: The Victory. J. Grigg. 1985. pap. 3.50 (*0-8217-1596-8*) Kensgtn Pub Corp.

1943: The Victory That Never Was. John Grigg. 1982. mass mkt. 2.95 (*0-89083-971-9*, Zebra Kensgtn) Kensgtn Pub Corp.

1940-1945 Remembered: Translated from My Diary & Retold. Nelleke Nix. (Illus.). 40p. 1992. 300.00 (*1-881067-01-7*); teacher ed. 60.00 (*1-881067-04-1*); pap. 200.00 (*1-881067-00-9*); lib. bdg. 200.00 (*1-881067-03-3*); 280.00 (*1-881067-02-5*) N Nelleke Studio.

1942: Issue in Doubt. Wayman C. Mullins. LC 94-5234. 320p. 1994. 29.95 (*0-89015-968-8*) Sunbelt Media.

1940s: A Decade of Change: A Language Arts Unit for High-ability Learners. Center for Gifted Education Staff. 332p. (C). per. 28.95 (*0-7872-5344-8*) Kendall-Hunt.

1914. Gerald Gliddon. (VCs of the First World War Ser.). (Illus.). 224p. (Orig.). 1997. pap. 22.95 (*0-7509-1444-0*, Pub. by Sutton Pub Ltd) Intl Pubs Mktg.

1914-1916 see Diario de Sidney Sonnino

***1914-1918: Voices & Images of the Great War.** Lyn MacDonald. (Illus.). 346p. 2000. pap. 27.50 (*0-14-014674-1*, Pub. by Pnguin Bks Ltd) Trafalgar.

1914-1939: German Reflections of the Two World Wars. Ed. by Reinhold Grimm & Jost Hermand. LC 91-33074. (Monatshefte Occasional Ser.: Vol. 12). (Illus.). 196p. (C). 1992. lib. bdg. 25.00 (*0-299-97074-4*) U of Wis Pr.

***1944-45 British Soldier: Headress, Uniforms & Equipment, 2.** Jean Bouchery. 1998. 34.95 (*2-908182-74-2*, 182742) Histoire.

19 Further Articles You Can Use (to Inspire Planned Gifts), Bk. 4. G. Roger Schoenhals. 60p. 1998. pap. 59.00 (*0-9645517-7-2*) Planned Giving.

19 Gifts of the Spirit. Leslie B. Flynn. LC 74-91027. 204p. 1974. pap. 7.99 (*0-88207-701-5*, Victor Bks) Chariot Victor.

19 Gifts of the Spirit. rev. ed. Leslie Flynn. LC 94-8320. 208p. 1994. reprint ed. pap. 9.99 (*1-56476-337-4*, 6-3337, Victor Bks) Chariot Victor.

N

***1900.** Ed. by Mike R. Jay & Michael Neve. (Illus.). 384p. 2000. pap. 14.95 (*0-14-118083-8*, Penguin Bks) Viking Penguin.

***1900: Art at the Crossroads.** Robert Rosenblum et al. LC 99-69361. (Illus.). 448p. 2000. 75.00 (*0-8109-4303-4*, Pub. by Abrams) Time Warner.

***Nineteen Hundred: The Magic Year.** Nola L. McDonald. (Illus.). 64p. 1999. pap. 9.95 (*1-928547-03-6*, QuickWorks) Q W Inc.

1900 - Musik Zur Jahrhundertwende. Ed. by Werner Keil. (Hildesheimer Musikwissenschaftliche Arbeiten Ser.: Vol. 1). (GER.). 210p. 1995. write for info. (*3-487-10006-1*) G Olms Pubs.

1900-1919. Tom McGowen. (Yearbooks in Science Ser.). (Illus.). 80p. (J). (gr. 5-8). 1995. lib. bdg. 20.40 (*0-8050-3431-5*) TFC Bks NY.

1900-1970 see History of Medicine in South Carolina

1900-1920 Sevier County Census. Bruce D. Price. 80p. 1999. pap. 26.00 (*1-56664-155-1*) WorldComm.

Wearable Art Accessories & Jewelry, 1900-2000. Leslie Pina & Shirley Friedland. (Illus.). 184p. 1999. 39.95 (*0-7643-0971-4*) Schiffer.

1907-Bibliography of Statistical Literature, 3 vols. Maurice G. Kendall. 1981. 27.95 (*0-405-13882-2*) Arno Press.

***1902 Edition of the Sears, Roebuck Catalogue.** Sears, Roebuck & Company Staff. LC 00-39359. (Illus.). 704p. 2000. pap. 14.99 (*0-517-16288-1*) Bell T.

1900 ASME COGEN-TURBO: International Symposium on Gas Turbines in Cogeneration, Repowering, & Peak-Load Power Generation, 4th, Held in New Orleans, Louisiana, August 27-29, 1990. Ed. by I. S. Ondryas & T. H. Fransson. LC 90-195623. (IGTI Ser.: Vol. 5). 264p. 1990. reprint ed. pap. 81.90 (*0-7837-1448-3*, 205242300017) Bks Demand.

1900 Census of Carter County, Tennessee. Ed. by Connie J. Latner. vi, 304p. 1997. pap. 38.50 (*0-9659386-0-3*) C L Latner.

***1900 Census, Turtle Mountain Chippewa, Rolette County, N. D.** Gail Morin. 88p. 2000. 12.95 (*1-58211-215-0*) Quintin Pub RI.

1908 Olympic Games: Results for All Competitors in All Events, with Commentary. Bill Mallon & Ian Buchanan. LC 99-57985. (Illus.). 516p. 2000. lib. bdg. 49.50 (*0-7864-0598-8*) McFarland & Co.

***1988 Uprising in Burma.** U. Maung Maung. (Monograph Series, Yale Southeast Asia Studies: Vol. 49). 306p. 1999. pap. 22.00 (*0-938692-72-0*); lib. bdg. 35.00 (*0-938692-71-2*) Yale U SE Asia.

1915: The Death of Innocence. Lyn MacDonald. LC 94-25654. 1995. write for info. (*0-8050-3499-4*) H Holt & Co.

1950s Plastics Design: Everyday Elegance. 2nd rev. ed. Holly Wahlberg. LC 98-89660. (Illus.). 112p. (Orig.). 1999. pap. 19.95 (*0-7643-0783-5*) Schiffer.

1905 & All That: Essays on Rugby Football, Sport & Welsh Society. Gareth Williams. 245p. 1998. pap. 26.95 (*0-8464-4721-5*) Beekman Pubs.

1905 & All That: Essays on Rugby Football, Sport & Welsh Society. Gareth Williams. 245p. (C). 1991. pap. 35.00 (*0-86383-758-1*, Pub. by Gomer Pr) St Mut.

1905-Folk Dances of European Countries. Anne S. Duggan et al. (Anne Schley Duggan, 1905 Folk Dance Library). (Illus.). 160p. 1980. 23.95 (*0-8369-9285-7*) Bks for Libraries.

1905-Folk Dances of Scandinavia. Anne S. Duggan et al. (Anne Schley Duggan, 1905 Folk Dance Library). (Illus.). 118p. 1980. 23.95 (*0-8369-9284-9*) Bks for Libraries.

1905-Folk Dances of the United States & Mexico. Anne S. Duggan et al. (Anne Schley Duggan, 1905 Folk Dance Library). (Illus.). 159p. 1980. 23.95 (*0-8369-9287-3*) Bks for Libraries.

1905 Folk Dances of the British Isles. Anne S. Duggan et al. (Anne Schley Duggan, 1905 Folk Dance Library). 120p. 1980. 23.95 (*0-8369-9286-5*) Bks for Libraries.

1905 in St. Petersburg: Labor, Society, & Revolution. Gerald D. Surh. LC 88-38696. 480p. 1989. 52.50 (*0-8047-1499-1*) Stanford U Pr.

1905-The Teaching of Folk Dance. Anne S. Duggan et al. (Anne Schley Duggan, 1905 Folk Dance Library). (Illus.). 116p. 1980. 23.95 (*0-8369-9283-0*) Bks for Libraries.

***1905-1906 Unger Bros. Supplemental Catalogue.** Ulysses G. Dietz. Ed. by Benjamin A. Randolph. (Historical Catalogue Ser.: Vol. 9). (Illus.). 64p. 1999. pap. 29.95 (*0-9656139-5-X*) Eden Sterling.

1905-1907 Breasted Expeditions to Egypt & the Sudan: A Photographic Study, 2 vols., Vol. 1. Oriental Institute Staff. LC 76-22621. (Illus.). 21p. 1976. lib. bdg. 15.00 incl. fiche (*0-226-69471-2*) U Ch Pr.

1905-1907 Breasted Expeditions to Egypt & the Sudan: A Photographic Study, 2 vols., Vol. 2. Oriental Institute Staff. LC 76-22621. (Illus.). 24p. 1976. lib. bdg. 15.00 incl. fiche (*0-226-69472-0*) U Ch Pr.

1905 U. S. Navy Dive Manual. Ed. by Joe Strykowski. LC 99-162311. (Illus.). 64p. 1997. reprint ed. pap. 10.00 (*1-879488-22-1*) Sundiver.

1904 Olympic Games: Complete Results for All Competitors in All Events, with Commentary. Bill Mallon. LC 98-30989. 287p. 1999. lib. bdg. 39.50 (*0-7864-0550-3*) McFarland & Co.

Nineteen Hundred Luger-U. S. Test Trials. 2nd rev. ed. Michael Reese, II. Ed. by Pioneer Press Staff. LC 71-117532. (Illus.). 1976. pap. 7.00 (*0-913150-35-5*) Pioneer Pr.

1900-1920: Linen & Lace see 20th-Century Fashion

1900-20: The Birth of Modernism see 20th Century Design

***1998 Resin & Blending Seminar Proceedings.** Ed. by John Bradfield. 176p. 1999. pap. 45.00 (*1-892529-05-X*, 7266) Forest Prod.

***1998-1999 Administrative Compensation Survey.** 125p. 1999. 155.00 (*1-878240-70-6*) Coll & U Personnel.

***1998-1999 National Faculty Salary Survey by Discipline & Rankin Private Four-Year Colleges & Universities.** 48p. 1999. 52.50 (*1-878240-73-0*) Coll & U Personnel.

1995 Directory of Licensed Administrators & Child Care Institutions. 76p. (Orig.). 1995. pap. write for info. (*1-878353-39-X*) Silent Partners.

Nineteen Hundred Ninety-Nine Facts about Blacks. Raymond M. Corbin. 1995. pap. 14.95 (*0-931761-53-0*) Beckham Pubns.

***1999 General Election Opinion Poll: How Voters Assess Politics, Parties & Politicians.** S. Sharma & P. K. Sen. 1999. pap. 25.00 (*0-7855-7585-5*) St Mut.

***1999 Information Systems & eBusiness Spending: Volume 1, Budget & Technology Trends Analysis: Volume 2 Budget & Technology Trends Planner, 2 vols.** Ed. by Catherine Huneke. 400p. 1999. ring bd. 2000.00 (*0-945052-37-5*) Computer Econ.

***1999-2000 Management Company Compensation Report.** 160p. 2000. pap. 495.00 (*1-893772-06-3*) J R Zabka.

***1999-2000 Administrative Compensation Survey.** 120p. 2000. 310.00 (*1-878240-78-1*) Coll & U Personnel.

***1999-2000 Mid-Level Administrative - Professional Salary Survey.** 2000. 190.00 (*1-878240-79-X*) Coll & U Personnel.

***1999-2000 National Faculty Salary Survey by Discipline & Rank in Private Four-Year Colleges & Universities.** (Illus.). 60p. 2000. 105.00 (*1-878240-80-3*) Coll & U Personnel.

***1999-2000 National Faculty Salary Survey by Discipline & Rank in Public Four-Year Colleges & Universities.** (Illus.). 88p. 2000. 105.00 (*1-878240-81-1*) Coll & U Personnel.

1999-2000 Guide to Museum Studies & Training in the United States. 4th ed. Tom Ritzenthaler. Ed. by Roxana Adams. 190p. 1999. pap. 21.50 (*0-931201-59-4*, 830) Am Assn Mus.

***1999-2000 AAHSA Assissted Living Salary & Benefit Report, Vol. 2.** 236p. 2000. pap. 250.00 (*1-893772-05-5*) J R Zabka.

***1999-2000 Nursing Department Compensation Report, Vol. 8.** 200p. 1999. pap. 195.00 (*1-893772-02-0*) J R Zabka.

***1999-2000 Wisconsin School Directory.** 600p. 1999. 18.00 (*1-57337-077-0*) WI Dept Pub Instruct.

1991 Lectures in Complex Systems. Lynn Nadel. (C). 1992. 54.00 (*0-201-57834-4*) Addison-Wesley.

1996 IEEE Intelligent Vehicles Symposium. IEEE (Industrial Electronics Society). Ed. by IEEE (Institute of Electrical & Electronics Engine. LC 96-77960. 420p. 1996. pap. write for info. (*0-7803-3652-6*, 96TH8230); mic. film. write for info. (*0-7803-3653-4*, 96TH8230) Inst Electrical.

1990 Summary of Coal Resources in Colorado. Carol M. Tremain et al. (Special Publications: No. 36). (Illus.). 33p. (Orig.). 1991. pap. 3.00 (*1-884216-48-X*) Colo Geol Survey.

1900 Olympic Games. Bill Mallon. LC 97-36094. 351p. 1997. lib. bdg. 39.50 (*0-7864-0378-0*) McFarland & Co.

1901 Eaton's Catalogue. T. Eaton Company Staff. 1999. pap. 16.95 (*0-7737-5923-9*) Genl Dist Srvs.

1901-1908, 7 vols. in 1. William Butler Yeats. Ed. by Samhain. 324p. 1970. reprint ed. 45.00 (*0-7146-2101-3*, Pub. by F Cass Pubs) Intl Spec Bk.

***1900 Scrip Vol. 1: Abbott Through Bone.** Gail Morin. 300p. 2000. pap. 30.00 (*1-58211-045-X*) Quintin Pub RI.

***1900 Scrip Vol. 2: Bone Through Cardinal.** Gail Morin. 300p. 1998. pap. 30.00 (*1-58211-121-9*) Quintin Pub RI.

1907 Mace Toy Catalogue. Flora G. Jacobs. (Illus.). 126p. 1977. reprint ed. pap. 6.00 (*0-686-35939-9*) Wash Dolls Hse.

1906 Bing Toy Catalogue: Including 1907 Supplement. Ed. by Allen Levy. (Illus.). 500p. 1992. 55.00 (*0-904568-52-0*) Pincushion Pr.

1906 Olympic Games: Complete Results for All Competitors in All Events, with Commentary. Bill Mallon. LC 98-46197. 250p. 1999. lib. bdg. 39.50 (*0-7864-0551-1*) McFarland & Co.

***1900s.** Myra Immell. LC 99-56322. (America's Decades Ser.). 360p. (YA). 2000. pap. 17.96 (*0-7377-0293-1*); lib. bdg. 22.45 (*0-7377-0294-X*) Greenhaven.

1900s. Gail B. Stewart. LC 89-9936. (Timelines Ser.). (Illus.). 48p. (J). (gr. 6). 1989. lib. bdg. 11.95 (*0-89686-471-5*, Crstwood Hse) Silver Burdett Pr.

1900's. Adam Woog. LC 98-27964. (Cultural History of the United States Through the Decades Ser.). (Illus.). (YA). (gr. 4-12). 1998. lib. bdg. 23.70 (*1-56006-550-8*) Lucent Bks.

Nineteen Impressions. John D. Beresford. LC 71-103492. (Short Story Index Reprint Ser.). 1977. 19.95 (*0-8369-3234-X*) Ayer.

Nineteen Letters. Samson R. Hirsch. LC 94-40778.Tr. of Neunzehn Briefe uber Judenthum. 1994. 25.95 (*0-87306-696-0*) Feldheim.

Nineteen Letters of Ben Uziel. Samson R. Hirsch. Tr. by Karen Paritzky from GER. LC 69-131727. 15.95 (*0-87306-045-8*) Feldheim.

Nineteen Letters of Ben Uziel: A Spiritual Presentation of the Principles of Judaism. Somson R. Hirsch. Tr. by Bernard Drachman. (ENG & GER.). 500p. 27.50 (*0-87559-076-4*) Shalom.

Nineteen Masks for the Naked Poet. Nancy Willard. LC 83-22734. (Illus.). 32p. 1984. 9.95 (*0-15-166039-5*) Harcourt.

19 Minute: Bible Study, Pt. 1. Tim H. Gumm. 1998. 37.99 (*0-8100-0803-3*, 22N0879) Northwest Pub.

19 More Articles You Can Use: To Inspire Planned Gifts. G. Roger Schoenhals. LC 97-132104. 60p. (Orig.). 1998. pap. 59.00 (*0-9645517-2-1*) Planned Giving.

Nineteen Negro Men: Personality & Manpower Retraining. Aaron L. Rutledge & Gertrude Z. Gass. LC 67-13277. (Jossey-Bass Social & Behavioral Science Ser.). 228p. reprint ed. 70.70 (*0-8357-9341-9*, 201383100088) Bks Demand.

1995-96 State Issues Report. 132p. 1996. pap. 20.00 (*0-614-30581-0*, IS-96-5) Ed Comm States.

1919. John Dos Passos. 27.95 (*0-88411-345-0*) Amereon Ltd.

***1919, Vol. 2.** John Dos Passos. (U. S. A. Trilogy Ser.: Vol. 2). 464p. 2000. pap. 13.00 (*0-618-05682-3*) HM.

1998 Asia Pacific Software Engineering Conference: Proceedings, December 2-4, 1998, Taipei, Taiwan. Asia-Pacific Software Engineering Conference Staff et al. LC 98-87889. xiv, 387 p. 1998. write for info. (*0-8186-9186-7*) IEEE Comp Soc.

1919-1930: The Year Our World Began. William K. Klingaman. 1987. 27.95 (*0-317-59967-4*) St Martin.

1919-1933 see Trade Unionism in Germany from Bismarck to Hitler, 1869-1933

1919 Report: The Final & Interim Reports of the Adult Education Committee of the Ministry of Reconstruction, 1918-1919. H. C. Wiltshire et al. 562p. (C). 1980. text 60.00 (*0-7855-3195-5*, Pub. by Univ Nottingham) St Mut.

1919-1930 Merger Movement in American Industry. Carl Eis. LC 77-14773. (Dissertations in American Economic History Ser.). 1978. 21.95 (*0-405-11032-4*) Ayer.

1919-1920 Breasted Expedition to the Near East. Oriental Institute Staff. LC 77-2731. 36p. 1978. lib. bdg. 20.50 incl. fiche (*0-226-69473-9*) U Ch Pr.

***1990s.** Stuart A. Kallen. LC 99-49999. (America's Decades Ser.). 360p. (YA). 2000. lib. bdg. 22.45 (*0-7377-0312-1*) Greenhaven.

***1990s.** Stuart A. Kallen. LC 99-49999. (America's Decades Ser.). 360p. (YA). 2000. pap. 17.96 (*0-7377-0311-3*) Greenhaven.

1990s. Stuart A. Kallen. LC 98-30359. (Cultural History of the United States Through the Decades Ser.). (Illus.). (YA). (gr. 4-12). 1998. lib. bdg. 23.70 (*1-56006-559-1*) Lucent Bks.

1990s Art from Cuba: A National Residency & Exhibition Program. Contrib. by Lupe Alvarez & Ernesto Pujol. (Illus.). 55p. 1997. pap. 10.00 (*1-883967-07-4*) Art in General.

1990's Handbook: Modern Background for Cthulhu. rev. ed. Gregory Rucka. Ed. by Janice Sellers. (Call of Cthulhu Roleplaying Game Ser.). (Illus.). 80p. (Orig.). 1995. pap. 12.95 (*1-56882-048-8*, 2355) Chaosium.

1990s Slump: Causes & Cures. Ed. by Mario Baldassarri et al. 400p. 1996. text 85.00 (*0-312-16012-7*) St Martin.

Nineteen Ninety. Michael Klein. (Provincetown Poets Ser.: No. 2). 64p. 1993. 35.00 (*0-944854-09-5*); pap. 10.00 (*0-944854-08-7*) Provincetown Arts.

1990: Challenge in the 90's/Foreign Language Program. Aausc. (Teaching Methods Ser.). (C). 1991. mass mkt. 11.95 (*0-8384-2548-8*) Heinle & Heinle.

1998 Washoe County School Bond: Is Accountability Still the Issue: Washoe County School Bond. George Kucera & Ted Harris. Date not set. lib. bdg. 10.00 (*1-886306-28-1*) Nevada Policy.

***1999 Trading the Four Year Presidental Election Cycle: The Preelection Years.** Frank A. Taucher. 222p. 1998. pap. 98.00 (*1-879591-59-6*) Mkt Movements.

1990 ACL Proceedings. pap. write for info. (*1-55860-969-5*) Morgan Kaufmann.

1990 & Beyond. Herma Silverstein. (Yearbooks in Science Ser.). (Illus.). 80p. (J). (gr. 5-8). 1995. lib. bdg. 20.40 (*0-8050-3439-0*) TFC Bks NY.

***1990 Coach of the Year Clinics Football Manual.** Ed. by Earl Browning. (Illus.). 256p. 2000. pap. 22.95 (*1-57167-402-0*) Coaches Choice.

1990 College Relations & Recruitment Survey. College Placement Council Staff. LC 91-131725. 127p. 1990. write for info. (*0-913936-25-1*) Coll Placement.

1990 Defense Budget. William W. Kaufmann & Lawrence J. Korb. 91p. 1989. pap. 8.95 (*0-8157-4951-1*) Brookings.

1990 Directory of the Transportation Research Board. 316p. 1990. 30.00 (*0-309-05011-1*) Transport Res Bd.

1998 Money Adviser. 225p. (gr. 7). 1999. 24.95 (*1-883013-35-6*) Time-Life.

1998: The Year of Destiny, 2 bks., Bk. 1. Raymond Ouellette. LC 77-89344. (Illus.). 1978. 9.95 (*0-936450-27-4*) Aero Pr.

1998: The Year of Destiny, 2 bks., Bk. 2. Raymond Ouellette. LC 77-89344. (Illus.). 1978. 8.95 (*0-936450-29-0*) Aero Pr.

1998: The Year of Destiny, 2 bks., Set. Raymond Ouellette. LC 77-89344. (Illus.). 1978. write for info. (*0-936450-28-2*) Aero Pr.

1998: The Year of the Beast. Chris Cawood. Ed. by Gaynell Seale. LC 96-94050. 312p. (Orig.). 1996. pap. 12.95 (*0-9642231-9-8*) Magnolia Hill.

1998-1999 Northwest Senior Housing Book. 6th rev. ed. Terry Fahey. Ed. by Lori Fahey. (Senior Housing Ser.). (Illus.). 380p. 1998. pap. 65.00 (*1-893583-00-7*) Research West.

1998-1999 Yearbook: Church & School Directory of Heritage Netherlands Reformed Congregations. Intro. by Joel R. Beeke. 91p. 1998. pap. 4.00 (*1-892777-03-7*) Reform Heritage Bks.

1998-99 AAHSA Continuing Care Retirement Community Salary & Benefits Report. 281p. 1998. pap. 250.00 (*0-939326-38-8*) Hosp & Hlthcare.

1998-99 AAHSA Nursing Home Salary & Benefits Report. 370p. 1998. pap. 250.00 (*0-939326-39-6*) Hosp & Hlthcare.

1998-99 Directory of Corporate Counsel. Aspen Law & Business Editorial Staff. boxed set 799.00 incl. cd-rom (*1-56706-658-5*, 66585) Panel Pubs.

1998-99 Home Care Salary & Benefits Report. 424p. 1998. pap. 250.00 (*0-939326-40-X*) Hosp & Hlthcare.

1998-99 Hospital Salary & Benefits Report. 336p. 1998. pap. 295.00 (*0-939326-42-6*) Hosp & Hlthcare.

1998-99 Hospice Salary & Benefits Report. 260p. 1998. pap. 195.00 (*0-939326-41-8*) Hosp & Hlthcare.

1998/99 Houston/Texas Oil Directory. 28th ed. Ed. by James W. Self. 970p. 1998. pap. 65.00 (*1-889879-10-X*) Atlantic Commun.

1998-99 Matching Gift Details. 43rd ed. 224p. (Orig.). 1998. pap. 130.00 (*0-89964-335-3*, 21898) Coun Adv & Supp Ed.

1998/99 North American Biotechnology Directory. 7th ed. Ed. by James W. Self. 525p. (Orig.). 1998. pap. 105.00 (*1-889879-09-6*) Atlantic Commun.

1998/99 North American Biotechnology Directory, Vol. 6. 6th rev. ed. Ed. by James W. Self. 500p. (Orig.). 1997. pap. 105.00 (*1-889879-05-3*) Atlantic Commun.

1998-99 Nursing Department Report. 1998. pap. 195.00 (*0-939326-44-2*) Hosp & Hlthcare.

1998-99 Public Human Services Directory, Vol. 59. 580p. 1998. pap. 90.00 (*0-910106-29-0*) Am Human Servs.

1998 Arden Shakespeare Library Edition Collection. William Shakespeare. 349.00 (*0-17-443624-6*) Spring Jrnl.

***1998-99 AAHSA Assisted Living Salary & Benefits Reports.** 200p. 1999. pap. 250.00 (*0-939326-43-4*) Hosp & Hlthcare.

***1998-99 Management Company Compensation Report, Vol. 15.** 180p. 1999. pap. 495.00 (*0-939326-45-0*) Hosp & Hlthcare.

1998 AABGA/AZH Salary Survey. rev. ed. AABGA Staff & AZH Staff. Orig. Title: AABGA Salary Survey. 41p. 1998. 50.00 (*0-934843-09-0*) Am Assn Botanical Gdns.

1998 AACE International Transactions. Ed. by Marvin Gelhausen. (Illus.). 312p. 1998. pap. 84.95 (*1-885517-11-4*) AACE Intl.

***1998 Academic Library Trends & Statistics: Associate of Arts Colleges.** 150p. (C). 1999. pap. 75.00 (*0-8389-8069-4*) Assn Coll & Res Libs.

***1998 Academic Library Trends & Statistics: Doctoral-Granting/Master's/Baccalaureate Institutions.** 322p. (C). 1999. pap. 135.00 (*0-8389-8070-8*) Assn Coll & Res Libs.

1998 AIDS & STDS, 9. Parsons. 46p. 1998. pap. text, student ed. 3.00 (*0-536-01166-4*) Pearson Custom.

1998 Alabama Manufacturers Register. 9th rev. ed. Ed. by Louise M. West & Frank Lambing. 1998. 79.00 (*1-58202-014-0*) Manufacturers.

1998 Alaska Manufacturers Directory. 3rd rev. ed. Ed. by Louise M. West & Frank Lambing. 1998. 45.00 (*1-58202-033-7*) Manufacturers.

1998 American Control Conference, 6 vols. IEEE, Control Systems Society Staff & Institute of Electrical & Electronics Engineers, I. LC 99-215063. 4100p. 1998. lib. bdg., boxed set. write for info. (*0-7803-4531-2*, 98CH36207) Inst Electrical.

1998 Animation Industry Directory. 2nd ed. 1998. pap. 75.00 (*1-891010-01-8*) Animation Mag.

1998 Annual Reliability & Maintainability Symposium. IEEE (Reliability Society) Staff. Ed. by IEEE (Institute of Electrical & Electronics Engine. 464p. 1997. pap. text. write for info. (*0-7803-4362-X*, 98CH36161); lib. bdg. write for info. (*0-7803-4363-8*, 98CH36161) Inst Electrical.

1998 Annual Meeting of the North American Fuzzy Information Processing Society. IEEE, Neural Networks Council, Systems, Man & Cybe. Ed. by Institute of Electrical & Electronics Engineers, I. LC 97-81139. 540p. 1998. pap. 150.00 (*0-7803-4453-7*, 98TH8353); fiche. write for info. (*0-7803-4454-5*) Inst Electrical.

1998 Annual Pulp & Paper Industry Technical Conference. IEEE (Industry Applications Society) Staff & IEEE (Institute of Electrical & Electronics Engine. LC 74-136000. 250p. 1998. pap. 122.00 (*0-7803-4785-4*, 98CH36219); lib. bdg. write for info. (*0-7803-4786-2*) Inst Electrical.

***1998 Annual Report of the Scientific Registry & the OPTN.** Ed. by UNOS Staff. (Illus.). 494p. 1999. pap. 10.00 (*1-886651-35-3*) United Network.

1998 Annual Review of Development Effectiveness. Robert Buckley. (Operations Evaluation Department Ser.). 80p. 1999. pap. 22.00 (*0-8213-4474-9*, 14474) World Bank.

1998 Annual Survey of Letter of Credit Law & Practice. Ed. by James E. Byrne. 677p. 1998. 175.00 (*1-888870-16-8*) Inst Intl Bnking.

1998 Annual Survey Report. Susan L. MacLean. 1999. 500.00 (*0-935890-33-5*) Emerg Nurses IL.

1998 Annual Treasure Coast Magazine Vol. 9: The Best of South Florida from North Palm Beach to Vero Beach. (Illus.). 128p. 1998. pap. 7.95 (*1-883117-08-9*) Mohr Graphics.

1998 APA Membership Register. American Psychological Association Staff. 1998. 35.00 (*1-55798-502-2*) Am Psychol.

1998 APICS Remanufacturing Symposium Proceedings, May 18-19, 1998, San Diego, California: New Oportunities in Remanufacturing, Strategies & Tactics for Improving Your Business. Remanufacturing Symposium et al. LC 98-170466. 1998. write for info. (*1-55822-141-7*) Am Prod & Inventory.

1998 Arkansas Manufacturers Register. 3rd rev. ed. Ed. by Louise M. West & Frank Lambing. 1997. 61.00 (*1-58202-021-3*) Manufacturers.

1998 Asia & South Pacific Design Automation Conference. IEEE, Circuits & Systems Society Staff. Ed. by Institute of Electrical & Electronics Engineers, I. LC 97-80907. 700p. 1998. pap. write for info. (*0-7803-4425-1*, 98EX121) Inst Electrical.

N

1998 ASME - IEEE Joint Railroad Conference. IEEE, Vehicular Technology Society Staff. Ed. by Institute of Electrical & Electronics Engineers, I. LC 90-644036. 300p. 1998. pap. text 128.00 (*0-7803-4852-4*, 98CH44036); lib. bdg. write for info. (*0-7803-4853-2*, 98CH36223) Inst Electrical.

1998 ASPE Survey of Compensation & Benefits. unabridged ed. (Illus.). 380p. 1999. pap. 9.95 (*1-891255-05-3*) Am Soc Plumb Eng.

1998 ASSE Professional Development Conference Proceedings. (Illus.). 688p. 1998. pap. text 99.95 (*1-885581-17-3*, 4367) ASSE.

1998 ASTD Training & Performance Yearbook. James Cortada & John Woods. 544p. 1997. 79.95 (*0-07-071855-5*) McGraw.

1998 Asteroid Ephemeris - Zodiacal Order. annuals Compiled by Marianne Alexander. 300p. (Orig.). 1997. pap. write for info. (*1-888760-07-9*) Pandora Pubng.

1998 Asteroid Ephemeris - Alphabetical Order. annuals Compiled by Marianne Alexander. 300p. 1997. pap. 25.00 (*1-888760-06-0*) Pandora Pubng.

1998 Audio Blue Book. rev. ed. 1997. lib. bdg. 200.00 (*0-932089-86-0*) Orion Res.

1998 Austin Wedding Directory. Ed. by Gina Brown & Jean Brown. (Illus.). 116p. 1998. pap. 12.95 (*0-9635013-2-1*) JP Ink.

***1998 Australasian Computer Human Interaction Conference, Ozchi '98: Proceedings, November 30 December 4, 1998, Adelaide, South Australia.** Australasian Computer Human Interaction Conference Staff et al. LC 98-88396. xii, 350 p. 1998. write for info. (*0-8186-9207-3*) IEEE Comp Soc.

1998 Baseball Insight Annual. Phil Erwin. 212p. 1998. spiral bd. 29.95 (*0-9663525-0-5*) Parrish Pubns.

1998 Behavioral Outcomer & Guideliner Sourcebook: A Practical Guide to Measuring, Managing & Standardizing Mental Health & Substance Abuse Treatment. Ed. by Kenneth M. Coughlin. 672p. 1997. pap. 295.00 (*1-57987-030-9*) Faulkner & Gray.

1998 Biennial Exhibition Catalog. Robert F. Schroeder. 1998. pap. 10.00 (*0-917185-09-9*) Fort Wayne.

1998 Big Bad Baseball Annual: The Book Baseball Deserves. Don Malcolm et al. (Illus.). 428p. 1998. pap. 19.95 (*1-57028-201-3*, Mstrs Pr) NTC Contemp Pub Co.

1998 BioSupplyNet Source Book. (Illus.). 1998. pap. 24.95 (*1-890574-03-1*) BioSupplyNet.

1998 Book of Lists. 192p. 1997. pap. 30.00 (*0-9650400-4-6*) Houston Busin Jrnl.

1998 Book of Lists. 1998. pap. 34.50 (*0-932439-12-8*) Denver Busn Media.

1998 Year Book of Oncology. 2nd ed. Robert F. Ozols. (Illus.). 408p. (C). (gr. 13). 1998. text 86.00 (*0-8151-9710-1*, 24997) Mosby Inc.

1998 Year Book of Psychiatry & Applied Mental Health. Talbott. (Illus.). 528p. 1998. text 73.00 (*0-8151-9733-0*, 25020) Mosby Inc.

***1998 Business Work-Life Study: A Sourcebook.** Ellen Galinsky & James T. Bond. 84p. 1998. pap. 59.00 (*1-888324-26-0*) Families & Work.

1998 Calendar of Louisiana Festivals & Events. Julie Posner. (Illus.). 28p. (Orig.). 1997. pap. 11.95 (*0-9654906-4-5*) Huli Pub.

1998 Calendar of Musical Personalities. Ed. by Tony Esposito. 32p. 1997. pap. 7.95 (*0-7692-1653-6*, BMP1998) Wrner Bros.

1998 California - Nevada Senior Housing Book. 2nd rev. ed. Terry Fahey. Ed. by Lori Fahey. (Senior Housing Ser.). (Illus.). 380p. 1998. pap. 65.00 (*1-893583-01-5*) Research West.

1998 Camera Blue Book. rev. ed. 1997. lib. bdg. 200.00 (*0-932089-42-9*) Orion Res.

1998 Car Stereo Blue Book. 1997. lib. bdg. 200.00 (*0-932089-90-9*) Orion Res.

1998 Cars. Ed. by Consumer Guide Editors. 448p. 1998. mass mkt. 6.99 (*0-451-19436-5*, Sig) NAL.

1998 Cases & Documentary Supplement for Use with Basic Corporation Law, Materials-Cases-Test. Detlev F. Vogts. (University Casebook Ser.). 200p. 1998. pap. text 9.50 (*1-56662-662-5*) Foundation Pr.

1998 Cases & Statutory Supplement to Products Liability & Safety, Cases & Materials. 3rd ed. David G. Owen & Mary J. Davis. (University Casebks.). 600p. 1998. pap. text 16.95 (*1-56662-678-1*) Foundation Pr.

1998 CCH Federal Taxation Comprehensive Topics. Ephraim P. Smith. (CCH Federal Taxation Ser.). 1314p. 1997. text. write for info. (*0-8080-0137-X*) CCH INC.

1998 CCH Federal Taxation Basic Principles. Ephraim P. Smith. (CCH Federal Taxation Ser.). 846p. 1997. text. write for info. (*0-8080-0138-8*) CCH INC.

1998 Center Watch Industry Directory: A Comprehensive Resource for the Clinical Trials Industry. Ed. by Robert Whitaker. (Illus.). vi, 425p. 1998. pap. 395.00 (*1-892369-00-1*) C W Pubns.

1998 CFO's Guide to Credit Union Investments: Including Detailed Information on Corporate Credit Unions. 4th ed. Ed. by Callahan & Associates, Inc. Staff. Orig. Title: Corporate Sourcebook. (Illus.). 188p. 1998. pap. 95.00 (*1-889265-11-X*) Callahan & Assocs.

1998 Civil Procedure Supplement for Use with All Pleading & Procedure Casebooks. John J. Cound et al. (American Casebook Ser.). 500p. 1998. pap. 20.50 (*0-314-23248-6*) West Pub.

1998 CLC Integrative Medicine: A Balanced Account of the Data. rev. ed. Steven Wirth & May Farkas. Ed. by Sandra Wirth & Larry Reed. (Illus.). 80p. 1998. pap. text 7.95 (*0-9661161-3-5*, 161-35) Creat Logic.

1998 Clinician's Therapeutic Quickie. Afshine A. Emrani. 1998. pap. 9.95 (*0-9654687-3-9*) Emrani Publns.

1998 Comparative Performance Data Sourcebook. Ed. by Gwen Segre. 496p. 1997. pap. 245.00 (*1-57987-033-3*) Faulkner & Gray.

1998 Competition Act Explained. David Pickersgill. LC 99-210002. (Point of Law Ser.). 1999. 50.00 (*0-11-702683-2*, Pub. by Statnry Office) Balogh.

1998 Compleat Jazz Calendar. Vince Danca. (Illus.). 28p. 1997. pap. 9.95 (*0-9602390-2-2*) V Danca.

1998 Computer Monitor Troubleshooting Tips. Robert Yount. (Illus.). 272p. 1998. pap. 49.95 (*0-7906-1160-0*) Prompt Publns.

1998 Computers in Cardiology Conference. IEEE Engineering in Medicine & Biology Society Sta. Ed. by IEEE (Institute of Electrical & Electronics Engine. LC 80-641097. 850p. 1998. pap. 182.00 (*0-7803-5200-9*, 98CH36292) Inst Electrical.

1998 Conference on Lasers & Electro-Optics. IEEE (Lasers & Electro-Optics Society) Staff. Ed. by IEEE (Institute of Electrical & Electronics Engine. 500p. 1997. lib. bdg. write for info. (*0-7803-4417-0*, 98CH36178) Inst Electrical.

1998 Conference on Precision Electromagnetic Measurements Digest. IEEE Staff. LC 98-86197. 720p. 1998. pap. text 168.00 (*0-7803-5018-9*, 98CH36254); lib. bdg. 168.00 (*0-7803-5019-7*, 98CH36254) IEEE Standards.

1998 Conference on High-Temperature Electronic Materials, Devices & Sensors Proceedings. IEEE, Electron Devices Society & Instrumentation &. Ed. by Institute of Electrical & Electronics Engineers, I. LC 97-81042. 500p. 1998. pap. write for info. (*0-7803-4437-5*, 98EX132) Inst Electrical.

1998 Conference on Lasers & Electro-Optics Europe. IEEE (Lasers & Electro-Optics Society) Staff. LC 97-80073. 360p. 1998. pap. 128.00 (*0-7803-4233-X*, 98TH8326) Inst Electrical.

1998 Conference on Optoelectronic & Microelectronic Materials & Devices: Proceedings. IEEE (Electron Devices Society) Staff & IEEE (Lasers & Electro-Optics Society) Staff. Ed. by IEEE (Institute of Electrical & Electronics Engine. 500p. 1998. pap. text 146.00 (*0-7803-4513-4*, 98EX140) Inst Electrical.

1998 Connecticut State Register & Manual. annuals Secretary of the State's Office Editors. (Connecticut State Register & Manual Ser.). 900p. 1998. 19.00 (*1-888951-04-4*); pap. 10.00 (*1-888951-05-2*) CT Secy Sts Ofc.

1998 Copier Blue Book. 1997. lib. bdg. 200.00 (*0-932089-91-7*) Orion Res.

1998 Corporate Homes for Wildlife. 10th anniversary ed. Jana Goldman. (Illus.). 112p. 1997. pap. 10.95 (*1-889685-00-3*) Wildlife Habitat.

***1998 Corporation & Partnership Tax Return Guide.** rev. ed. Research Inst. of America Staff. 140p. 1999. pap. text 15.75 (*0-7811-0214-6*) Res Inst Am.

1998 CPA's Guide to the Internet. John Graves & Kim H. Torrence. (AICPA Technology Ser.). 500p. 1998. pap. 49.95 (*0-9654000-9-3*) Kent Info Srvcs.

1998 CPI (Consumer Price Index) Ed. by Deborah P. Klein. (Illus.). 83p. (C). 1997. pap. text 30.00 (*0-7881-4497-9*) DIANE Pub.

1998 Credit Union Directory: The First Guide to All Credit Unions. 13th rev. ed. Ed. by Callahan & Associates, Inc. Staff. (Illus.). 578p. 1997. pap. 135.00 (*1-889265-06-3*) Callahan & Assocs.

1998 Credit Union Yearbook, 5 vols. 11th ed. Ed. by Callahan & Associates, Inc. Staff. (Illus.). 316p. 1998. pap. 555.00 (*1-889265-02-0*) Callahan & Assocs.

1998 Crime & Disorder Act Explained. Richard Powers. LC 99-209992. (Point of Law Ser.). 1999. 50.00 (*0-11-702685-9*, Pub. by Statnry Office) Balogh.

1998 Cumulative Supplement Connecticut Evidence. Benedict M. Holden & John J. Daly. 1006p. 1998. pap. 78.00 (*1-878698-50-8*) Atlantic Law.

1998 Cumulative Supplement to Connecticut Law of Torts. Douglas B. Wright et al. 146p. 1988. pap. 55.00 (*1-878698-47-8*) Atlantic Law.

1998 Cumulative Supplement, Waters & Water Rights Vol. 1: 1991 Edition. Ed. by Robert E. Beck. 1998. write for info. (*0-327-00777-X*, 52691-16) LEXIS Pub.

1998 Cumulative Supplement, Waters & Water Rights Vol. 2: 1991 Edition. Ed. by Robert E. Beck. 1998. write for info. (*0-327-00778-8*, 526592-16) LEXIS Pub.

1998 Cumulative Supplement, Waters & Water Rights Vol. 3: 1991 Edition. Ed. by Robert E. Beck. 1998. write for info. (*0-327-00779-6*, 52693-16) LEXIS Pub.

1998 Cumulative Supplement, Waters & Water Rights Vol. 4: 1991 Edition. Ed. by Robert E. Beck. 1998. write for info. (*0-327-00780-X*, 52694-16) LEXIS Pub.

1998 Cumulative Supplement, Waters & Water Rights Vol. 6: 1991 Edition. Ed. by Robert E. Beck. 1998. write for info. (*0-327-00781-8*, 52696-16) LEXIS Pub.

1998 Cumulative Supplement, Waters & Water Rights Vol. 7: 1991 Edition. Ed. by Robert E. Beck. 1998. write for info. (*0-327-00782-6*, 52697-16) LEXIS Pub.

1998 Dale Earnhardt Signature Series Calendar. (Illus.). 24p. 1997. pap. 14.95 (*1-890929-03-4*) Comp Motorsport.

1998 Dale Jarrett Signature Series Calendar. (Illus.). 24p. 1997. pap. 14.95 (*1-890929-07-7*) Comp Motorsport.

1998 DeCordova Annual Exhibition, 13 June-September 7: Bethany Bristow, Tom Chapin, Stephanie Chubbuck, Vico Fabbris, Ben Freeman, Thomas Halloran, John Hughes, Abelardo Morell, Irene Valincius, Lucy White. Rachel Rosenfield Lafo & DeCordova Museum & Sculpture Park Staff. LC 98-71568. 24p. 1998. write for info. (*0-945506-26-0*) DeCordova Mus.

1998 Defense Credit Union Council Directory. 2nd rev. ed. Ed. by Callahan & Associates, Inc. Staff. (Illus.). 178p. 1998. pap. 95.00 (*1-889265-08-X*) Callahan & Assocs.

1998 Design Automation Conference. IEEE, Circuits & Systems Society Staff. Ed. by Institute of Electrical & Electronics Engineers, I. LC 85-644924. 840p. 1998. lib. bdg. write for info. (*0-7803-4409-X*, 98CH36175) Inst Electrical.

***1998 Development Report Card for the States: Economic Benchmarks for State & Corporate Decision-Makers.** Corporation for Enterprise Development Staff. 111p. 1998. pap. 75.00 (*1-883187-20-6*) Corp Ent Dev.

1998 Directory of Major Mailers & What They Mail: The Most Powerful Database on Direct Mail Ever Created. Ed. by Paul Bobnak. 1312p. 1998. pap. 395.00 (*1-888576-37-5*) North Am Pub Co.

1998 Directory of Religious Media, Vol. 20. Ed. by Karen M. Hawkins. (Illus.). 384p. (Orig.). 1997. pap. 79.95 (*1-880040-07-7*) Natl Relig Broad.

1998 Directory of Tennessee Manufacturers. Ed. by Mary K. Weber. 724p. 1998. pap. 92.00 (*0-925773-43-3*) M Lee Smith.

1998 Directory to Medical Product Manufacturing Consultants. 164p. 1998. pap. 10.00 (*1-884551-04-1*) Canon Comns.

1998 Ed Database Summary. Susan L. MacLean. 1999. 30.00 (*0-935890-32-7*) Emerg Nurses IL.

1998 Edition Introducing the Family Limited Partnership: How to Save Mega Bucks in Taxes & Maintain Control of Your Assets. 2nd ed. Charles S. Stoll & Ronald C. White. (Illus.). 250p. 1998. pap. 24.95 (*0-9654605-1-7*) Fortune Pr Pubs.

1998 8th International Conference on Harmonics & Power Quality. IEEE, Power Engineering Society Staff. Ed. by Institute of Electrical & Electronics Engineers, I. 1000p. 1998. pap. text. write for info. (*0-7803-5105-3*, 98EX227) Inst Electrical.

***1998 Election Update.** 2nd ed. Simon & Schuster Staff. 28p. (C). 1999. write for info. (*0-13-012966-6*) S&S Trade.

***1998 Electric Furnace Conference & Process Technology Conference Proceedings, Vol. 56.** Iron & Steel Society Staff. LC 46-22879. (Illus.). 728p. 1998. pap. 110.00 (*1-886362-29-7*) Iron & Steel.

1998 Electro. IEEE Staff. LC 98-85330. 350p. 1998. pap. text 132.00 (*0-7803-4940-7*); lib. bdg. write for info. (*0-7803-4941-5*) Inst Electrical.

1998 11th Annual IEEE International ASIC Conference & Exhibit. IEEE (Rochester Section) Staff. 400p. 1998. pap. 138.00 (*0-7803-4980-6*, 98TH8372) IEEE Standards.

1998 EMC, Wireless, Computer & Electronics Desk Reference Encyclopedia. Donald R. White. (Illus.). 400p. 1998. text 45.00 (*0-944916-96-1*) emf-emi Control.

1998 EnviroSafety Directory. 5th ed. Ed. by James W. Self. 600p. 1998. pap. 65.00 (*1-889879-12-6*) Atlantic Commun.

1998 ESPN/Information Please Sports Almanac. INSO Corporation Staff. (Illus.). 950p. (J). 1997. pap. 11.95 (*0-7868-8296-4*) Hyperion.

1998 Ethanol Vehicle Challenge. (Special Publications). 140p. 1999. pap. 40.00 (*0-7680-0385-7*, SP-1453) Soc Auto Engineers.

1998 Eurail & Train Travel Guide to Europe. 3rd ed. 696p. 1998. pap. 15.00 (*0-395-88161-7*) HM.

1998 Eurail & Train Travel Guide to the World. 28th ed. 998p. 1998. pap. 19.00 (*0-395-88160-9*) HM.

1998 European Accounting Guide. 2nd ed. Ed. by David Alexander. 1998. pap. text 119.00 (*0-15-606261-5*) Harcourt Coll Pubs.

1998 European Quantum Electronics Conference. IEEE (Lasers & Electro-Optics Society) Staff. LC 97-80072. 250p. 1998. pap. write for info. (*0-7803-4231-3*, 98TH8325) Inst Electrical.

***1998 FAA Environmental Conference: "Environmental Risk: Working with Uncertainty"** 109p. 1998. ring bd. 10.00 (*1-56986-217-6*, ENV-98-109) Federal Bar.

***1998 Fall Simulation Interoperability Workshop: Workshop Papers.** (Simulation Interoperability Workshop Ser.). (Illus.). 1300p. 1998. 75.00 (*1-930638-05-1*) S I S O.

***1998 Fars Network Version.** Fasb. 1999. 36.95 (*0-471-32825-1*) Wiley.

1998 Federal Staff Directory, Fall: White House, Departments, Agencies, Biographies, 3 vols. 28th ed. 1648p. 1998. pap. 89.00 (*0-87289-145-3*) C Q Staff.

1998 Federal Tax Withholding Tables with Highlights, Effective January 1, 1998. CCH Editors. LC 99-202854. 40p. 1998. pap. 17.50 (*0-8080-0209-0*) CCH INC.

1998 Fedex Championship Series Media Guide. Cartstaff. Ed. by Steve Bronder et al. (Illus.). 368p. (Orig.). 1998. pap. 14.95 (*0-9647598-2-9*) Chmpship Auto.

1998 Fee & Billing Survey of A/E/P & Environmental Consulting Firms. Zweig White & Association Staff. 206p. 1998. pap. text 250.00 (*1-885002-48-3*) Zweig White.

1998 Fee Schedule & Payment Policies for Physicians' Medicare Services. CCH Editors. (Health Law Professional Ser.). 300p. 1997. pap. 45.00 (*0-8080-0200-7*) CCH INC.

***1998 Fiduciary Tax Return Guide.** rev. ed. Research Inst. of America Staff. 160p. 1999. pap. text 15.75 (*0-7811-0215-4*) Res Inst Am.

1998 15th Annual IEEE/AESS Dayton Chapter Symposium Sensing the World. IEEE (Dayton Section) Staff. Ed. by IEEE Staff. LC 98-85215. 100p. 1998. pap. 108.00 (*0-7803-4922-9*, 98EX178) IEEE Standards.

1998 5th IEEE International Conference on Electronics, Circuits & Systems. IEEE Staff. LC 98-86105. 1600p. 1998. pap. 254.00 (*0-7803-5008-1*, 98EX196) IEEE Standards.

1998 5th International Conference on Solid-State & Integrated Circuit Technology. IEEE (Electron Devices Society & Beijing Section). LC 97-80249. 1100p. 1998. pap. write for info. (*0-7803-4306-9*, 97EX105) Inst Electrical.

1998 5th IEEE International Workshop on Cellular Neural Networks & Their Applications Proceedings. IEEE (Region 8, Circuits & Systems Society) Staff. Ed. by IEEE (Institute of Electrical & Electronics Engine. 500p. 1998. pap. 146.00 (*0-7803-4867-2*, 98TH8359) Inst Electrical.

1998 5th International Workshop on Advanced Motion Control. IEEE, Industrial Electronics Society Staff. Ed. by Institute of Electrical & Electronics Engineers, I. LC 97-81372. 700p. 1998. pap. 166.00 (*0-7803-4484-7*, 98TH8354) Inst Electrical.

1998 Film Writers Guide. 7th ed. Ed. & Compiled by Susan Avallone. 675p. 1998. pap. 70.00 (*0-943728-98-3*) Lone Eagle Pub.

1998 Finance & Accounting Survey of Architecture, Engineering & Planning Firms. Zweig White & Association Staff. 210p. 1998. pap. text 250.00 (*1-885002-49-1*) Zweig White.

1998 1st International Conference on Integrated Circuit Yield. IEEE (Electron Devices Society) Staff. Ed. by IEEE (Institute of Electrical & Electronics Engine. 100p. 1998. pap. 104.00 (*0-7803-4387-5*, 98EX118) Inst Electrical.

1998 Florida Almanac. 14th ed. Del Marth & Marty Marth. (Illus.). 536p. (Orig.). 1997. pap. 14.50 (*1-885034-09-1*) Suwannee River.

1998 Florida Manufacturers Register. 13th rev. ed. Ed. by Louise M. West & Frank Lambing. 1998. 149.00 (*1-58202-011-6*) Manufacturers.

1998 Foreign Policy Overview & the President's Fiscal Year 1999 Budget Request: Hearing Before the Committee on Foreign Relations, United States Senate, 105th Congress, Second Session, February 10, 1998. LC 98-165805. (S. Hrg. Ser.). iii, 71p. 1998. write for info. (*0-16-056496-4*) USGPO.

1998 48th Electronic Components & Technology Conference. IEEE, Components, Packaging & Manufacturing Techno. Ed. by Institute of Electrical & Electronics Engineers, I. LC 78-647174. 1300p. 1998. pap. text 226.00 (*0-7803-4526-6*, 98CH36206); lib. bdg. write for info. (*0-7803-4527-4*, 98CH36206) Inst Electrical.

1998 Fourth International Conference on Signal Processing Proceedings. IEEE (Beijing Section) Staff. Ed. by IEEE (Institute of Electrical & Electronics Engine. LC 97-80337. 1600p. 1998. pap. 254.00 (*0-7803-4325-5*, 98TH8344) Inst Electrical.

1998 4th International Symposium on Advanced Packaging Materials. IEEE (Components, Packaging & Manufacturing Techno. Ed. by IEEE (Institute of Electrical & Electronics Engine. 180p. 1998. pap. 128.00 (*0-7803-4795-1*, 98EX153); mic. film 128.00 (*0-7803-4796-X*, 98EX153) Inst Electrical.

1998 4th International Conference on Actual Problems of Electronic Instrument Engineering Proceedings. IEEE (Electron Devices Society) Staff. Ed. by IEEE Staff. LC 98-85265. 500p. 1998. pap. 146.00 (*0-7803-4938-5*, 98EX179) IEEE Standards.

1998 4th International High Temperature Electronics Conference. IEEE, Electron Devices Society & Components, Packa. Ed. by Institute of Electrical & Electronics Engineers, I. LC 98-84231. 450p. 1998. pap. 142.00 (*0-7803-4540-1*, 98EX145) Inst Electrical.

1998 Fourth International High Temperature Electronics Conference: Hitec, Albuquerque, New Mexico, U.S.A, June 14-18, 1998. Conference International High Temperature Electronics et al. LC 98-84231. vii, 332 p. 1998. write for info. (*0-7803-4541-X*) IEEE Standards.

1998 IEEE Frequency Control Symposium. IEEE (Ultrasonics, Ferroelectrics & Frequency Cont. Ed. by IEEE (Institute of Electrical & Electronics Engine. LC 87-654207. 1000p. 1998. lib. bdg. write for info. (*0-7803-4374-3*, 98CH36165) Inst Electrical.

1998 Freshman Achievement Award. 76th ed. Lide. ring bd. write for info. (*0-8493-0594-2*) CRC Pr.

1998 Frontiers in Education. IEEE (Power Electronics Society) Staff. Ed. by IEEE (Institute of Electrical & Electronics Engine. 1300p. 1998. pap. text 226.00 (*0-7803-4762-5*); lib. bdg. write for info. (*0-7803-4763-3*) Inst Electrical.

***1998 Fuel Cell Seminar Abstracts.** Contrib. by Fuel Cell Seminar Organizing Committee Staff. (Fuel Cell Information Ser.: Vol. XX). (Illus.). 785p. 1998. lib. bdg. 345.00 (*0-89934-358-9*, BT992) Bus Tech Bks.

1998 Fun Book. Newsday Staff. (Illus.). 176p. 1998. pap. 4.95 (*1-885134-17-7*) Newsday.

1998 Future Car Challenge. (Special Publications). 130p. 1999. pap. 40.00 (*0-7680-0384-9*, SP-1452) Soc Auto Engineers.

1998 GaAs IC Symposium. IEEE, Electron Devices Society & Microwave Theory. Ed. by Institute of Electrical & Electronics Engineers, I. 350p. 1998. pap. text 132.00 (*0-7803-5049-9*) Inst Electrical.

***1998 Global Telecoms Tax Profiles: A Resource for Business, Tax, & Market Strategies.** Coopers & Lybrand Staff. 446p. 1998. pap. 175.00 (*0-471-31841-8*) Wiley.

1998 Gold Book Annual. Frank Veneroso. Ed. by James U. Blanchard, III & Brien F. Lundin. (Illus.). 230p. 1998. pap. 295.00 (*0-9629019-3-8*) Jeffrsn Finan.

1998 Gold Book of Photography Prices. Thomas I. Perrett. 328p. 1998. pap. 49.95 (*0-915827-20-4*) Photo Res Inst Carson Endowment.

1998 Good Curry. P. Chapman. mass mkt. 13.95 (*0-340-68032-6*, Pub. by Hodder & Stought Ltd) Trafalgar.

N

An Asterisk (*) at the beginning of an entry indicates that the title is appearing for the first time.

*1998 **Governor's Race: An Inside Look at the Candidates & Their Campaign by the People Who Managed Them.** Ed. by Gerald C. Lubenow. LC 99-38459. 310p. 1999. pap. 21.95 (*0-87772-390-7*) UCB IGS.

*1998 **Graphics Interface Proceedings.** Kellogg S. Booth & Alain Fournier. Ed. by Wayne Davis. 246p. 1998. pap. 50.00 (*2-558-60550-X*) Morgan Kaufmann.

1998 Guide to Healthcare Resources on the Internet. Ed. by John W. Hoben. 638p. 1997. pap. 245.00 (*1-57987-034-1*) Faulkner & Gray.

1998 Guide to Intranets in Healthcare: A Comprehensive Guide to New Developments in Networks, Extranets & Electronic Commerce. Jeffery Muscarella. Ed. by Luci Koizumi. (Illus.). 1997. pap. 245.00 (*1-57987-032-5*) Faulkner & Gray.

1998 Guidebook to Massachusetts Taxes. CCH Editorial Staff. 1998. pap. 37.95 (*0-8080-0231-7*) CCH INC.

1998 Guidebook to New Jersey Taxes. CCH Editorial Staff. 1998. pap. 37.95 (*0-8080-0230-9*) CCH INC.

1998 Guidebook to Pennsylvania Taxes. rev. ed. Ed. by CCH Editorial Staff. 320p. 1998. pap. 37.95 (*0-8080-0219-8*) CCH INC.

1998 Guidebook to New York Taxes. CCH Editorial Staff. 1998. pap. 37.95 (*0-8080-0232-5*) CCH INC.

1998 Guidebook to California Taxes. 49th ed. CCH Tax Law Editors. 648p. 1998. pap. 37.50 (*0-8080-0207-4*) CCH INC.

1998 Guidelines for Treatment of Sexually Transmitted Diseases. Centers for Disease Control & Prevention Staff & U. S. Department of Health & Human Services Editor. (C). 1998. pap. 7.95 (*1-883205-45-X*) Intl Med Pub.

1998 Guitars & Musical Instruments Blue Book. rev. ed. 1997. lib. bdg. 200.00 (*0-932089-87-9*) Orion Res.

1998 Gulf Coast Oil Directory. 46th ed. Ed. by James W. Self. 989p. 1997. pap. 69.00 (*1-889879-08-8*) Atlantic Commun.

1998 Gulf Coast Oil Directory, Vol. 46. 46th rev. ed. Ed. by James W. Self. 950p. 1998. pap. 69.00 (*1-889879-01-0*) Atlantic Commun.

N

1998 Gun Blue Book. 1997. lib. bdg. 200.00 incl. audio compact disk (*0-932089-92-5*) Orion Res.

1998 Harp Almanac: International Resource Guide for All Harps. Ed. by Fred Schlomka. (Illus.). 113p. 1998. pap. 25.00 (*0-9662113-0-8*) Maxemilian Prods.

1998 Hawaii Manufacturers Directory. 3rd rev. ed. Ed. by Louise M. West & Frank Lambing. 1998. 49.00 (*1-58202-034-5*) Manufacturers.

1998 Health Care Almanac & Yearbook: The Single Volume Desk Reference for Facts, Figures & Resources. Ed. by Luci Koizumi & Daniel Moskowitz. (Illus.). 576p. 1997. pap. 195.00 (*1-57987-043-0*) Faulkner & Gray.

*1998 **Health Care & Culture: April 29-30, 1998 at Lakeview Resort & Conference Center, Morgantown, West Virginia : Proceedings of the Fourth International & Interdisciplinary Health Research Symposium.** International and Interdisciplinary Health Research Symposium et al. LC 98-60785. 1998. write for info. (*0-930284-72-0*) Morgantown Print & Bind.

1998 Health Network & Alliance Sourcebook. Ed. by Daniel Moskowitz. (Illus.). 642p. 1997. pap. 250.00 (*1-57987-042-2*) Faulkner & Gray.

1998 Healthcare Guide to the Internet, Vol. 1. Ed. by Jennifer Wayne-Doppke. (Illus.). 64p. 1998. pap. 68.00 (*0-9645360-5-6*) Cor Hlthcare.

1998 Holdings Statements for Bibliographic Items, Z39.71-1999. National Information Standards Organization Staff. LC 99-10693. 50p. 1999. 55.00 (*1-880124-39-4*) NISO.

1998 Home Equity Lending Directory. Ed. by Paul Muolo. 1997. write for info. (*1-57987-039-2*) Faulkner & Gray.

*1998 **House Staff Employment Study.** Bradley S. Keare. (Illus.). 107p. 1998. pap. text 15.00 (*1-930473-04-4*) Congressional Mgmt Fdnt.

1998 Human Rights Act Explained. David Leckie. LC 99-210009. (Point of Law Ser.). 1999. 50.00 (*0-11-702684-0*, Pub. by Statnry Office) Balogh.

*1998 **ICD-9-CM Code Book, Vols. 1-3.** St. Anthony's Staff. (Medical Assisting Ser.). (C). 1998. pap. (*0-7668-1060-7*) Delmar.

1998 IEEE Aerospace Conference. IEEE, Aerospace & Electronic Systems Society Staff. Ed. by Institute of Electrical & Electronics Engineers, I. 4000p. 1998. pap. write for info. (*0-7803-4311-5*, 98TH8339) Inst Electrical.

1998 IEEE Annual Textile, Fiber & Film Industry Technical Conference. IEEE (Industry Applications Society) Staff. Ed. by IEEE (Institute of Electrical & Electronics Engine. LC 90-657367. 90p. 1998. lib. bdg. 106.00 (*0-7803-4963-6*) Inst Electrical.

1998 IEEE Annual Textile, Fiber & Film Industry Technical Conference. IEEE (Industry Applications Society) Staff. Ed. by IEEE (Institute of Electrical & Electronics Engine. LC 90-657367. 90p. 1998. pap. text 106.00 (*0-7803-4962-8*, 98CH36246) Inst Electrical.

1998 IEEE Antennas & Propagation Society International Symposium. IEEE (Antennas & Propagation Society) Staff. Ed. by IEEE (Institute of Electrical & Electronics Engine. LC 90-640397. 2700p. 1998. pap. text. write for info. (*0-7803-4478-2*, 98CH36194); lib. bdg. write for info. (*0-7803-4479-0*, 98CH36194) Inst Electrical.

1998 IEEE Applied Power Electronics Conference. IEEE (Power Electronics Society & Industry Applica. Ed. by IEEE (Institute of Electrical & Electronics Engine. LC 90-643607. 1120p. 1998. pap. text. write for info. (*0-7803-4340-9*, 98CH36154); lib. bdg. write for info. (*0-7803-4341-7*, 98CH36154) Inst Electrical.

1998 IEEE-APS Conference on Antennas & Propagation for Wireless Communications. IEEE, Antennas & Propagation Society & Boston Sect. Ed. by Institute of Electrical & Electronics Engineers, I. LC 98-85596. 400p. 1998. pap. 138.00 (*0-7803-4955-5*, 98EX184) Inst Electrical.

1998 IEEE Asia-Pacific Conference on Circuits & Systems Proceedings. IEEE, Circuits & Systems Society Staff. Ed. by Institute of Electrical & Electronics engineers, Inc.,Staff. LC 98-87938. 850p. 1998. pap. text. write for info. (*0-7803-5146-0*, 98EX242) Inst Electrical.

1998 IEEE ATM Workshop. IEEE Staff. 550p. 1998. pap. 152.00 (*0-7803-4874-5*, 98EX164) Inst Electrical.

1998 IEEE Autotestcon. IEEE (Aerospace & Electronics Systems Society) Sta & IEEE (Instrumentation & Measurement Society) Staff. Ed. by IEEE (Institute of Electrical & Electronics Engine. 750p. 1998. pap. text 172.00 (*0-7803-4420-0*, 98CH36179); lib. bdg. write for info. (*0-7803-4421-9*, 98CH36179) Inst Electrical.

1998 IEEE Bipolar/BICMOS Circuits & Technology Meeting Proceedings. IEEE (Electron Devices Society) Staff. Ed. by IEEE (Institute of Electrical & Electronics Engine. 250p. 1998. pap. text 122.00 (*0-7803-4497-9*, 98CH36198); lib. bdg. write for info. (*0-7803-4498-7*, 98CH36198) IEEE Standards.

1998 IEEE Cement Industry Technical Conference. IEEE, Industry Applications Society Staff. Ed. by Institute of Electrical & Electronics Engineers, I. 550p. 1998. pap. text. write for info. (*0-7803-3941-X*, 98CH36070); lib. bdg. write for info. (*0-7803-3942-8*, 98CH36070) IEEE Standards.

1998 IEEE Conference on Control Applications. IEEE (Control Systems Society) Staff. Ed. by IEEE (Institute of Electrical & Electronics Engine. 1500p. 1998. pap. text. write for info. (*0-7803-4104-X*, 98CH36104); lib. bdg. write for info. (*0-7803-4105-8*, 98CB36104) Inst Electrical.

*1998 **IEEE Conference on Information Visualization: An International Conference on Computer Visualization & Graphics : Proceedings, July 29-31, 1998, London, England.** IEEE Conference on Information Staff et al. LC 98-218170. xi, 352 p. 1998. write for info. (*0-8186-8509-3*) IEEE Comp Soc.

1998 IEEE Conference on Electrical Insulation & Dielectric Phenomena. IEEE, Dielectrics & Electrical Insulation Society. Ed. by Institute of Electrical & Electronics Engineers, I. LC 79-649806. 900p. 1998. pap. text 186.00 (*0-7803-5035-9*, 98CH36257); lib. bdg. 186.00 (*0-7803-5036-7*, 98CH36257) IEEE Standards.

1998 IEEE Custom Integrated Circuits Conference. IEEE (Electron Devices Society) Staff. LC 85-653738. 660p. 1998. pap. text. write for info. (*0-7803-4292-5*, 98CH36143); lib. bdg. write for info. (*0-7803-4293-3*, 98CH36143) Inst Electrical.

1998 IEEE Electrical Performance of Electronic Packaging. IEEE, Microwave Theory & Techniques Society & Comp & IEEE, Components, Packaging & Manufacturing Techno. Ed. by Institute of Electrical & Electronics Engineers, I. LC 98-85598. 270p. 1998. pap. 124.00 (*0-7803-4965-2*, 98TH8370) Inst Electrical.

1998 IEEE 11th Annual International Workshop on Micro Electro Mechanical Systems. IEEE (Robotics & Automation Society) Staff. Ed. by IEEE (Institute of Electrical & Electronics Engine. LC 98-179821. 750p. 1998. pap. text. write for info. (*0-7803-4412-X*, 98CH36176); lib. bdg. write for info. (*0-7803-4413-8*, 98CH36176) Inst Electrical.

1998 IEEE 11th International Vacuum Microelectronics Conference. IEEE (Electron Devices Society) Staff. Ed. by IEEE (Institute of Electrical & Electronics Engine. 358p. 1998. pap. 134.00 (*0-7803-5096-0*, 98TH8382) IEEE Standards.

1998 IEEE Engineering in Medicine & Biology 20th Annual Conference. IEEE (Engineering in Medicine & Biology Society) S. Ed. by Institute of Electrical & Electronics Engineers, I. LC 99-214652. 3200p. 1998. pap. text. write for info. (*0-7803-5164-9*, 98CH36286) Inst Electrical.

1998 IEEE Fifth International Symposium on Spread Spectrum Techniques & Applications: Proceedings, September 2-4, 1998, Sun City, South Africa: Technical Program, Proceedings, 3 vols. IEEE International Symposium on Spread Spectrum Techniques & Applications Staff & Institute of Electrical & Electronics Engineers Staff. LC 97-80169. 1011 p. 1998. pap. write for info. (*0-7803-4282-8*) IEEE Standards.

1998 IEEE 48th Vehicular Technology Conference. IEEE (Vehicular Technology Society) Staff. Ed. by IEEE (Institute of Electrical & Electronics Engine. 1150p. 1998. lib. bdg. write for info. (*0-7803-4321-2*, 98CH36151) Inst Electrical.

1998 IEEE 45th Petroleum & Chemical Industry Conference. IEEE (Industry Applications Society) Staff. Ed. by IEEE (Institute of Electrical & Electronics Engine. LC 73-641120. 350p. 1998. pap. text 132.00 (*0-7803-4897-4*, 98CH36234); lib. bdg. 132.00 (*0-7803-4898-2*, 98CH36234) Inst Electrical.

1998 IEEE 14th Annual Semiconductor Thermal Measurement & Management Symposium. IEEE (Components, Packaging & Manufacturing Techno. Ed. by IEEE (Institute of Electrical & Electronics Engine. 200p. 1998. pap. text. write for info. (*0-7803-4486-3*, 98CH36195); lib. bdg. write for info. (*0-7803-4487-1*, 98CH36195) Inst Electrical.

1998 IEEE 4th Workshop Interactive Voice Technology for Telecommunications Applications. IEEE Staff. LC 98-86195. 230p. 1998. pap. 120.00 (*0-7803-5028-6*, 98TH8376) IEEE Standards.

1998 IEEE Holm Conference on Electrical Contacts. IEEE (Components, Packaging & Manufacturing Techno. Ed. by IEEE Staff. 400p. 1998. lib. bdg. 138.00 (*0-7803-4925-3*) Inst Electrical.

1998 IEEE Hong Kong Electron Devices Meeting. IEEE (Electron Devices Hong Kong Chapter) Staff. Ed. by IEEE Staff. LC 98-85263. 180p. 1998. pap. 116.00 (*0-7803-4932-6*, 98TH8368) IEEE Standards.

1998 IEEE Industrial & Commercial Power Systems Technical Conference. IEEE, Industry Applications Society Staff. Ed. by Institute of Electrical & Electronics Engineers, I. LC 88-641172. 260p. 1998. pap. text 118.00 (*0-7803-4509-6*, 98CH36202); lib. bdg. 118.00 (*0-7803-4510-X*, 98CH36202) Inst Electrical.

1998 IEEE Industry Applications Society Conference. IEEE Staff. 2800p. 1998. lib. bdg. write for info. (*0-7803-4944-X*) Inst Electrical.

1998 IEEE Industry Applications Society Conference. IEEE Staff. 2800p. 1998. pap. text 372.00 (*0-7803-4943-1*) Inst Electrical.

1998 IEEE Infocom. IEEE, Computer Society, Communications Society Sta. Ed. by Institute of Electrical & Electronics Engineers, I. 1600p. 1998. lib. bdg. write for info. (*0-7803-4384-0*, 98CH36169) Inst Electrical.

1998 IEEE Information Technology Conference. IEEE Staff. 200p. 1998. pap. text 118.00 (*0-7803-9914-5*, 98EX228) Inst Electrical.

1998 IEEE Instrumentation & Measurement Technology Conference. IEEE, Instrumentation & Measurement Society Staff. Ed. by Institute of Electrical & Electronics Engineers, I. 1400p. 1998. pap. text 234.00 (*0-7803-4797-8*, 98CH36222); lib. bdg. write for info. (*0-7803-4798-6*, 98CH36222) Inst Electrical.

1998 IEEE Intelligent Network Workshop. IEEE (Communications Society & France Communicatio. Ed. by IEEE Staff. LC 98-85024. 250p. 1998. pap. 122.00 (*0-7803-4905-9*, 98TH8364) Inst Electrical.

1998 IEEE International Conference on Communications. IEEE (Communications Society) Staff & IEEE (Institute of Electrical & Electronics Engine. LC 81-649547. 1726p. 1998. pap. text 266.00 (*0-7803-4788-9*, 98CH36220); lib. bdg. write for info. (*0-7803-4789-7*, 98CH36220) Inst Electrical.

1998 IEEE International Symposium on Electrical Insulation. IEEE (Dielectrics & Electrical Insulation Society). Ed. by IEEE Staff. 960p. 1998. lib. bdg. write for info. (*0-7803-4928-8*) Inst Electrical.

1998 IEEE International Symposium on Electrical Insulation. IEEE (Dielectrics & Electrical Insulation Society). Ed. by IEEE Staff. 960p. 1998. pap. text 192.00 (*0-7803-4927-X*) Inst Electrical.

1998 IEEE International Reliability Physics Symposium. IEEE (Electron Devices Society & Reliability Socie. Ed. by IEEE (Institute of Electrical & Electronics Engine. LC 82-640313. 400p. 1998. pap. text. write for info. (*0-7803-4400-6*, 98CH36173); lib. bdg. write for info. (*0-7803-4401-4*, 98CH36173) Inst Electrical.

1998 IEEE International Interconnect Technology Conference Technical Digest. IEEE (Electron Devices Society) Staff. Ed. by IEEE (Institute of Electrical & Electronics Engine. LC 97-80205. 200p. 1998. pap. write for info. (*0-7803-4285-2*, 98EX102) Inst Electrical.

1998 IEEE International Integrated Reliability Workshop Final Report. IEEE (Electron Devices Society) Staff & IEEE (Reliability Society) Staff. Ed. by IEEE (Institute of Electrical & Electronics Engine. LC 98-84868. 176p. 1999. pap. 116.00 (*0-7803-4881-8*, 98TH8363) Inst Electrical.

1998 IEEE International Symposium on Industrial Electronics. IEEE (Industrial Electronics Society) Staff. Ed. by IEEE (Institute of Electrical & Electronics Engine. LC 98-84437. 1000p. 1998. pap. 196.00 (*0-7803-4756-0*, 98TH8357) Inst Electrical.

1998 IEEE International Test Conference. IEEE (Institute of Electrical & Electronics Engine. LC 99-208103. 1100p. 1998. pap. 206.00 (*0-7803-5092-8*, 98CH36270) IEEE Standards.

1998 IEEE International Conference on Evolutionary Computation. IEEE (Neural Network Council, Alaska Section) Staf. Ed. by IEEE (Institute of Electrical & Electronics Engine. LC 98-84865. 600p. 1998. pap. 156.00 (*0-7803-4869-9*, 98TH8360) Inst Electrical.

1998 IEEE International Conference on Plasma Science. IEEE (Nuclear & Plasma Science Society) Staff & IEEE (Institute of Electrical & Electronics Engine. LC 81-644315. 300p. 1998. pap. text 128.00 (*0-7803-4792-7*, 98CH36221); lib. bdg. write for info. (*0-7803-4793-5*, 98CH36221) Inst Electrical.

1998 IEEE International Conference on Robotics & Automation. IEEE (Robotics & Automation Society) Staff. LC 90-640158. 3500p. 1998. pap. text. write for info. (*0-7803-4300-X*, 98CH36146); lib. bdg. write for info. (*0-7803-4301-8*, 98CH36146) Inst Electrical.

1998 IEEE International Conference on Acoustics, Speech, & Signal Processing Proceedings. IEEE (Signal Processing Society) Staff. Ed. by IEEE (Institute of Electrical & Electronics Engine. 3,520p. 1999. pap. 442.00 (*0-7803-5041-3*, 99CH36258) IEEE Standards.

1998 IEEE International Solid-State Circuits Conference. IEEE (Solid-State Circuits Council) Staff. LC 81-644810. 512p. 1998. pap. text. write for info. (*0-7803-4344-1*, 98CH36156); lib. bdg. write for info. (*0-7803-4345-X*, 98CH36156) Inst Electrical.

1998 IEEE International Conference on Systems, Man & Cybernetics. IEEE (Systems, Man & Cybernetics Society) Staff & IEEE (Institute of Electrical & Electronics Engine. 3900p. 1998. pap. text 478.00 (*0-7803-4778-1*, 98CH36218); lib. bdg. write for info. (*0-7803-4779-X*, 98CH36218) Inst Electrical.

1998 IEEE International Symposium on Circuits & Systems. IEEE, Circuits & Systems Society Staff. Ed. by Institute of Electrical & Electronics Engineers, I. LC 80-646530. 3700p. 1997. pap. text. write for info. (*0-7803-4455-3*, 98CH36187); lib. bdg. write for info. (*0-7803-4456-1*, 98CH36187); fiche. write for info. (*0-7803-4457-X*) Inst Electrical.

1998 IEEE International Non-Voltile Memory Technology Conference. IEEE, Components, Packaging & Manufacturing Techno. Ed. by Institute of Electrical & Electronics Engineers, I. LC 98-84111. 180p. 1998. pap. 116.00 (*0-7803-4518-5*, 98EX141) Inst Electrical.

1998 IEEE International Performance, Computing & Communications Conference. IEEE, Computer Society & Communications Society St. Ed. by Institute of Electrical & Electronics Engineers, I. 700p. 1998. pap. text 166.00 (*0-7803-4468-5*, 98CH36191); lib. bdg. 166.00 (*0-7803-4469-3*, 98CH36191) Inst Electrical.

1998 IEEE International Conference on Consumer Electronics. IEEE, Consumer Electronics Society Staff. Ed. by Institute of Electrical & Electronics Engineers, I. LC 84-643147. 480p. 1998. pap. text. write for info. (*0-7803-4357-3*, 98CH36160); lib. bdg. write for info. (*0-7803-4358-1*, 98CH36160) Inst Electrical.

1998 IEEE International Symposium on Electromagnetic Compatibility. IEEE, Electromagnetic Compatibility Staff. Ed. by Institute of Electrical & Electronics Engineers, I. LC 83-645449. 1200p. 1998. pap. text 216.00 (*0-7803-5015-4*, 98CH36253); lib. bdg. 216.00 (*0-7803-5016-2*, 98CH36253) IEEE Standards.

1998 IEEE International Conference on Microelectronic Test Structures. IEEE, Electron Devices Society Staff. Ed. by Institute of Electrical & Electronics Engineers, I. LC 97-80476. 250p. 1998. pap. text. write for info. (*0-7803-4348-4*, 98CH36157); lib. bdg. write for info. (*0-7803-4349-2*, 98CH36157) Inst Electrical.

1998 IEEE International SOI Conference. IEEE, Electron-Devices Society Staff. Ed. by Institute of Electrical & Electronics Engineers, I. 186p. 1998. pap. text 116.00 (*0-7803-4500-2*, 98CH36199); lib. bdg. 116.00 (*0-7803-4501-0*, 98CH36199); fiche 116.00 (*0-7803-4502-9*, 98CH36199) Inst Electrical.

1998 IEEE International Information Theory Workshop. IEEE, Information Theory Society Staff. Ed. by Institute of Electrical & Electronics Engineers, I. LC 97-80963. 150p. 1998. pap. write for info. (*0-7803-4408-1*, 98EX131); fiche. write for info. (*0-7803-4411-1*, 98EX131) Inst Electrical.

1998 IEEE International Symposium on Information Theory. IEEE, Information Theory Society Staff. Ed. by Institute of Electrical & Electronics Engineers, I. LC 72-179437. 526p. 1998. pap. text. write for info. (*0-7803-5000-6*, 98CH36252); lib. bdg. write for info. (*0-7803-5001-4*, 98CH36252) Inst Electrical.

1998 IEEE International Conference on Semiconductor Electronics. IEEE, Malaysia Section Staff. Ed. by Institute of Electrical & Electronics Engineers, I. LC 98-85600. 400p. 1998. pap. 138.00 (*0-7803-4971-7*, 98EX187) Inst Electrical.

1998 IEEE International Conference on Neural Networks. IEEE, Neural Networks Council, Alaska Section Staf. Ed. by Institute of Electrical & Electronics Engineers, I. 3000p. 1998. pap. text. write for info. (*0-7803-4859-1*, 98CH36227); lib. bdg. write for info. (*0-7803-4860-5*, 98CH36227) Inst Electrical.

1998 IEEE International Conference on Fuzzy Systems. IEEE, Neural Networks Council, Alaska Section Staf. Ed. by Institute of Electrical & Electronics Engineers, I. 2000p. 1998. pap. text. write for info. (*0-7803-4863-X*, 98CH36228); lib. bdg. write for info. (*0-7803-4864-8*, 98CH36228) Inst Electrical.

1998 IEEE International Professional Communication Conference. IEEE, Professional Communication Society Staff. Ed. by Institute of Electrical & Electronics Engineers, I. LC 98-84968. 400p. 1998. pap. text 138.00 (*0-7803-4890-7*, 98CH36232); lib. bdg. 138.00 (*0-7803-4891-5*, 98CH36232) Inst Electrical.

1998 IEEE International Conference on Acoustics, Speech & Signal Processing. IEEE, Signal Processing Society Staff. Ed. by Institute of Electrical & Electronics Engineers, I. LC 97-80964. 4100p. 1998. pap. text. write for info. (*0-7803-4428-6*, 98CH36181); lib. bdg. write for info. (*0-7803-4429-4*, 98CH36181); fiche. write for info. (*0-7803-4430-8*, 98CH36181) Inst Electrical.

1998 IEEE International Power Electronics Congress. IEEE Staff. LC 98-86102. 350p. 1998. pap. 132.00 (*0-7803-5006-5*, 98TH8375) IEEE Standards.

1998 IEEE International Workshop on Integrated Power Packaging. IEEE Staff. LC 98-86190. 400p. 1998. pap. 138.00 (*0-7803-5033-2*, 98EX203) IEEE Standards.

1998 IEEE International Engineering Management Conference. IEEE Staff (Engineering Mgmt. Society, Region 9, P & IEEE Staff (Inst. of Electrical & Electronics Engi. LC 98-86887. 700p. 1998. pap. text 166.00 (*0-7803-5082-0*, 98CH36266) IEEE Standards.

1998 IEEE International Symposium on Electronics & the Environment. IEEE, Technical Activities Board Staff. Ed. by Institute of Electrical & Electronics Engineers, I. 326p. 1998. pap. text. write for info. (*0-7803-4295-X*, 98CH36145); lib. bdg. write for info. (*0-7803-4296-8*, 98CH36145); fiche. write for info. (*0-7803-4297-6*, 98CH36145) Inst Electrical.

1998 IEEE Leos Summer Topical Meetings. IEEE, Lasers & Electro-Optics Society Staff. Ed. by Institute of Electrical & Electronics Engineers, I. LC 98-234090. 300p. 1998. pap. text. write for info. (*0-7803-4953-9*, 98TH8369) Inst Electrical.

1998 IEEE MTT-S International Microwave Symposium Digest. IEEE (Microwave Theory & Techniques Society, Elect. Ed. by IEEE (Institute of Electrical & Electronics Engine. LC 77-645125. 2000p. 1998. pap. text. write for info. (*0-7803-4471-5*, 98CH36192); lib. bdg. write for info. (*0-7803-4472-3*, 98CH36192) Inst Electrical.

1998 IEEE National Aerospace & Electronics Conference - NAECON. IEEE, Aerospace & Electronic Systems Society Staff. Ed. by Institute of Electrical & Electronics Engineers, I. LC 79-640977. 1000p. 1998. pap. text. write for info. (*0-7803-4449-9*, 98CH36185); lib. bdg. write for info. (*0-7803-4450-2*, 98CH36185) Inst Electrical.

1998 IEEE Network Operations & Management Symposium. IEEE, Communications Society Staff. Ed. by Institute of Electrical & Electronics Engineers, I. LC 97-80477. 850p. 1998. pap. text 182.00 (*0-7803-4351-4*, 98CH36158); lib. bdg. write for info. (*0-7803-4352-2*, 98CH36158) Inst Electrical.

1998 IEEE 9th Workshop on Local & Metropolitan Area Networks. IEEE, Communications Society Staff. Ed. by Institute of Electrical & Electronics engineers, Inc.,Staff. LC 98-87489. 360p. 1998. pap. text. write for info. (*0-7803-5116-9*, 98EX229) Inst Electrical.

1998 IEEE Nonlinear Optics: Materials, Fundamentals & Applications. IEEE, Lasers & Electro-Optics Society Staff. Ed. by Institute of Electrical & Electronics Engineers, I. LC 98-85597. 476p. 1998. pap. text 144.00 (*0-7803-4950-4*, 98CH36244) Inst Electrical.

1998 IEEE Nonlinear Optics: Materials, Fundamentals & Applications. IEEE, Lasers & Electro-Optics Society Staff. Ed. by Institute of Electrical & Electronics Engineers, I. LC 98-85597. 476p. 1998. lib. bdg. 144.00 (*0-7803-4951-2*, 98CH36244) Inst Electrical.

1998 IEEE Open Architectures & Network Programming. IEEE (Communications Society) Staff & IEEE (Institute of Electrical & Electronics Engine. LC 98-84565. 260p. 1998. pap. 124.00 (*0-7803-4783-8*, 98EX152) Inst Electrical.

1998 IEEE Open Architectures & Network Programming: Openarch'98: 3-4 April 1998, San Francisco, Ca, USA. Aurel A. Lazar & IEEE Staff. LC 98-84565. v, 145p. 1998. pap. write for info. (*0-7803-4784-6*) IEEE Standards.

1998 IEEE Position Location & Navigation Symposium. IEEE (Aerospace & Electronic Systems Society) Staf. Ed. by IEEE (Institute of Electrical & Electronics Engine. LC 97-80352. 850p. 1998. pap. text. write for info. (*0-7803-4330-1*, 98CH36153); lib. bdg. write for info. (*0-7803-4331-X*, 98CB36153) Inst Electrical.

1998 IEEE Power Electronics Specialists Conference. IEEE (Power Electronics Society) Staff. Ed. by IEEE (Institute of Electrical & Electronics Engine. LC 80-646675. 2000p. 1998. pap. text. write for info. (*0-7803-4489-8*, 98CH36196); lib. bdg. write for info. (*0-7803-4490-1*, 98CH36196) Inst Electrical.

1998 IEEE Radar Conference. IEEE, Aerospace & Electronic Systems Society Staff. Ed. by Institute of Electrical & Electronics Engineers, I. LC 99-192675. 500p. 1998. pap. text 146.00 (*0-7803-4492-8*, 98CH36197); lib. bdg. write for info. (*0-7803-4493-6*, 98CH36197) Inst Electrical.

1998 IEEE Radiation Effects Data Workshop. IEEE, Nuclear & Plasma Sciences Society Staff. Ed. by Institute of Electrical & Electronics Engineers, I. LC 98-87423. 190p. 1998. pap. text. write for info. (*0-7803-5109-6*, 98TH8385) Inst Electrical.

1998 IEEE Radio Frequency Integrated Circuit Symposium. IEEE, Microwave Theory & Techniques Society & Comp. Ed. by Institute of Electrical & Electronics Engineers, I. 300p. 1998. pap. text 128.00 (*0-7803-4439-1*, 98CH36182); lib. bdg. 128.00 (*0-7803-4440-5*, 98CH36182) Inst Electrical.

1998 IEEE Rural Electric Power Conference. IEEE, Industry Applications Society Staff. Ed. by Institute of Electrical & Electronics Engineers, I. LC 83-641006. 200p. 1998. pap. text. write for info. (*0-7803-4459-6*, 98CH36188); lib. bdg. write for info. (*0-7803-4460-X*, 98CH36188); fiche. write for info. (*0-7803-4461-8*, 98CH36188) Inst Electrical.

1998 IEEE 2nd Workshop on Multimedia Signal Processing. IEEE, Signal Processing Society Staff. Ed. by Institute of Electrical & Electronics Engineers, I. LC 98-85150. 750p. 1999. pap. write for info. (*0-7803-4919-9*, 98EX175) Inst Electrical.

1998 IEEE 6th International Conference on Terahertz Electronics. IEEE (Microwavey Theory & Techniques Society) Staf. Ed. by IEEE Staff. LC 98-85025. 300p. 1998. pap. 128.00 (*0-7803-4903-2*, 98EX171) Inst Electrical.

1998 IEEE South African Symposium on Communications & Signal Processing. IEEE, South African Section Staff. Ed. by Institute of Electrical & Electronics Engineers, I. LC 98-86398. 180p. 1998. pap. 116.00 (*0-7803-5054-5*, 98EX214) Inst Electrical.

1998 IEEE Southeastcon. IEEE (Region 3, Orlando Section) Staff. Ed. by IEEE (Institute of Electrical & Electronics Engine. LC 84-643372. 500p. 1998. pap. text 146.00 (*0-7803-4391-3*, 98CH36170); lib. bdg. write for info. (*0-7803-4392-1*, 98CH36170) Inst Electrical.

1998 IEEE Southwest Symposium on Image Analysis & Interpretation. IEEE, Tucson Section Staff. Ed. by Institute of Electrical & Electronics Engineers, I. LC 98-157777. 286p. 1998. pap. 126.00 (*0-7803-4876-1*, 98EX165) Inst Electrical.

1998 IEEE-SP International Symposium on Time-Frequency & Time-Scale Analysis. IEEE Staff. LC 98-86762. 700p. 1998. pap. 166.00 (*0-7803-5073-1*, 98TH8380) IEEE Standards.

1998 IEEE Symposium on Autonomous Underwater Vehicle Technology. IEEE (Oceanic Engineering Society) Staff. Ed. by IEEE Institute of Electrical & Electronics Engineers, Inc. Staff. 300p. 1998. pap. 128.00 (*0-7803-5190-8*, 98CH36290) Inst Electrical.

1998 IEEE Symposium on Advances in Digital Filtering & Signal Processing. IEEE, Victoria Section Staff. Ed. by Institute of Electrical & Electronics Engineers, I. LC 98-85595. 200p. 1998. pap. 118.00 (*0-7803-4957-1*, 98EX185) Inst Electrical.

1998 IEEE TENCON. IEEE (Delhi Section, Region 10) Staff. Ed. by IEEE (Institute of Electrical & Electronics Engine. 500p. 1999. pap. text 147.00 (*0-7803-4886-9*, 98CH36229); lib. bdg. 146.00 (*0-7803-4887-7*, 98CH36229) Inst Electrical.

1998 IEEE 3rd International Conference on Multimedia Engineering & Education. IEEE, Hong Kong Section, Computer Society Hong Kon. Ed. by Institute of Electrical & Electronics Engineers, I. 66p. 1998. pap. text. write for info. (*0-7803-5111-8*, 98TH8386) Inst Electrical.

1998 IEEE 24th Annual Conference of the IEEE Industrial Electronics Society Proceedings. IEEE, Industrial Electronics Society Staff. Ed. by Institute of Electrical & Electronics Engineers, I. LC 98-84110. 1500p. 1998. pap. text 244.00 (*0-7803-4503-7*, 98CH36200) Inst Electrical.

1998 IEEE 24th Annual Conference of the IEEE Industrial Electronics Society Proceedings. IEEE, Industrial Electronics Society Staff. Ed. by Institute of Electrical & Electronics Engineers, I. LC 98-84110. 1500p. 1998. lib. bdg. write for info. (*0-7803-4504-5*, 98CH36200) Inst Electrical.

1998 IEEE Workshop on Visual Surveillance: Bombay, India, January 2, 1998: Proceedings. IEEE Workshop on Visual Surveillance et al. LC 97-80959. 94 p. 1998. write for info. (*0-8186-8320-1*) IEEE Comp Soc.

***1998 IEEE Workshop on Application-Specific Software Engineering & Technology: Proceedings Asset-98: March 26-28, 1998, Clarion Hotel & University of Texas at Dallas, Richardson, Texas.** IEEE Workshop on Application Specific Software Engineering & Technology Staff et al. LC 98-86107. 1998. write for info. (*0-8186-8584-0*) IEEE Comp Soc.

1998 IEEE Workshop on Computers in Power Electronics. IEEE (Power Electronics Society) Staff. Ed. by IEEE (Institute of Electrical & Electronics Engine. 250p. 1998. pap. 122.00 (*0-7803-4856-7*, 98TH8358); mic. film 122.00 (*0-7803-4857-5*, 98TH8358) Inst Electrical.

1998 IEEE Workshop on Signal Processing Systems Design & Implementation. IEEE (Signal Processing Society & Circuits & Syste. Ed. by IEEE (Institute of Electrical & Electronics Engine. 600p. 1998. pap. 110.00 (*0-7803-4997-0*, 98TH8374) IEEE Standards.

1998 IEEE 16th International Semiconductor Laser Conference. IEEE Staff. LC 99-159845. 230p. 1998. pap. text 116.00 (*0-7803-4223-2*); lib. bdg. write for info. (*0-7803-4224-0*) Inst Electrical.

1998 IEEE 2nd International Conference Biomedical Engineering Days. IEEE Staff. LC 97-80100. 500p. 1998. pap. write for info. (*0-7803-4242-9*) Inst Electrical.

1998 IEEE 5th International Symposium on Spread Spectrum Techniques & Applications. IEEE (Communications Society, Region 8) Staff. LC 97-80169. 1200p. 1998. pap. write for info. (*0-7803-4281-X*, 98TH8333) Inst Electrical.

1998 IEEE 6th International Conference on Conduction & Breakdown in Solid Dielectrics. IEEE Staff. LC 97-80099. 700p. 1998. pap. text. write for info. (*0-7803-4237-2*); lib. bdg. write for info. (*0-7803-4238-0*) Inst Electrical.

1998 IEEE/AIAA 17th Digital Avionics Systems Conference. IEEE Staff (Aerospace & Electronic Systems Society & IEEE Staff (Institute of Electrical & Electronics. LC 98-86916. 350p. 1998. pap. text 132.00 (*0-7803-5086-3*, 98CH36267) IEEE Standards.

***1998 IEEE/IEOS Summer Topical Meetings: Digest, 20-24 July, 1998, Monterey Palza Hotel, Monterey, Ca.** Institute of Electrical & Electronics Engineers Staff & Lasers & Electro-Optics Society (Institute of Electrical & Electronics Engineers) Staff. LC 98-234090. 1998. pap. write for info. incl. fiche (*0-7803-4954-7*) Inst Electrical.

1998 IEEE/RSJ International Conference on Intelligent Robots & Systems: Proceedings Innovatiions in Theory, Practice & Applications October 13-17, 1998, Victoria Conference Centre, Victoria, B. C. Canada, 3 vol. IEEE/RSJ International Conference on Intelligent Robots and Systems Staff & IEEE (Industrial Electronics Society, Tokyo Sectio. LC 97-81244. 1998. pap. write for info. (*0-7803-4467-7*) IEEE Standards.

1998 IEEE/Semi Advanced Semiconductor Manufacturing Conference & Workshop. IEEE, Electron Devices Society & Components, Packa. Ed. by Institute of Electrical & Electronics Engineers, I. 500p. 1998. pap. text. write for info. (*0-7803-4380-8*, 98CH36168); lib. bdg. write for info. (*0-7803-4381-6*, 98CH36168) Inst Electrical.

1998 IFIP/IEEE International Workshop on Distributed Systems, Operations & Management. IEEE (Communications Society) Staff. Ed. by IEEE (Institute of Electrical & Electronics Engine. LC 98-86654. 300p. 1998. pap. 128.00 (*0-7803-5065-0*, 98EX218) Inst Electrical.

1998 Illinois Agricultural Pest Management Handbook. (Illus.). 382p. 1997. pap. 20.00 (*1-883097-18-5*) U Ill Ofc Agricult.

1998 Illinois Manufactures Directory. 15th rev. ed. Ed. by Louise M. West & Frank Lambing. 1998. 169.00 (*1-58202-007-8*) Manufacturers.

1998 Illinois Services Directory. 15th rev. ed. Ed. by Louise M. West & Frank Lambing. 1997. 179.00 (*1-58202-025-6*) Manufacturers.

1998 Index of Economic Freedom. 4th ed. Bryon T. Johnson et al. (Index of Economic Freedom Ser.: Vol. IV). 408p. 1997. pap. 19.95 (*0-89195-244-6*) Heritage Found.

1998 Indiana Manufacturers Directory. 17th rev. ed. Ed. by Louise M. West & Frank Lambing. 1998. 109.00 (*1-58202-015-9*) Manufacturers.

***1998 Individual Tax Return Guide.** rev. ed. Research Inst. of America Staff. 160p. 1999. pap. text 15.75 (*0-7811-0213-8*) Res Inst Am.

1998 Information Systems Spending: Technology Trends Planner: Budget Trends Analysis: Technology Trends Planner Update, Vols. 1-3. Ed. by Edward Pasahow. 550p. 1998. ring bd. 1995.00 (*0-945052-34-0*) Computer Econ.

1998 Information Technology Survey of Architecture, Engineering, Planning & Environmental Consulting Firms. 2nd ed. Dana Weinstein. 294p. 1998. pap. text 250.00 (*1-885002-61-0*) Zweig White.

1998 International Conference on Microwave & Millimeter Wave Technology. IEEE (Beijing Section) Staff. LC 97-80251. 650p. 1998. pap. write for info. (*0-7803-4308-5*, 98EX106) Inst Electrical.

1998 International Conference on Indium Phosphide & Related Materials. IEEE (Lasers & Electro Optics Society & Electron D. Ed. by IEEE (Institute of Electrical & Electronics Engine. 800p. 1998. pap. text. write for info. (*0-7803-4220-8*, 98CH36129); lib. bdg. write for info. (*0-7803-4221-6*, 98CH36129) Inst Electrical.

1998 International Symposium on Technology & Society on Technology & Society. IEEE (Social Implications of Technology Society) S. LC 97-80379. 650p. 1998. pap. text. write for info. (*0-7803-4327-1*, 98CH36152); lib. bdg. write for info. (*0-7803-4328-X*, 98CH36152) Inst Electrical.

1998 International Conference on Multichip Modules & High Density Packaging. IEEE (Components, Packaging, Manufacturing Technol. Ed. by IEEE (Institute of Electrical & Electronics Engine. LC 98-84630. 450p. 1998. pap. 142.00 (*0-7803-4850-8*, 98EX154); mic. film 142.00 (*0-7803-4851-6*, 98EX154) Inst Electrical.

1998 International Conference on Ion Implantation Technology. IEEE (Electron Devices Society) Staff. Ed. by IEEE (Institute of Electrical & Electronics Engine. LC 98-84232. 700p. 1998. pap. write for info. (*0-7803-4538-X*, 98EX144) Inst Electrical.

1998 International Conference on Advanced Semiconductor Devices & Microsystems. IEEE (Electron Devices Society) Staff. Ed. by IEEE Staff. LC 98-85040. 350p. 1998. pap. 92.00 (*0-7803-4909-1*, 98EX172) Inst Electrical.

1998 International Conference on Information Technology Applications in Biomedicine. IEEE (Engineering in Medicine & Biology Society) S. LC 98-179886. 166p. 1998. pap. 114.00 (*0-7803-4973-3*, 98EX188) IEEE Standards.

1998 International Conference on Power System Technology Proceedings. IEEE (Power Electronics Society) Staff. Ed. by IEEE (Institute of Electrical & Electronics Engine. LC 98-84360. 800p. 1998. pap. 176.00 (*0-7803-4754-4*, 98EX151) Inst Electrical.

1998 International Conference on Power Electronics, Drives & Energy Systems for Industrial Growth. IEEE (Power Electronics Society) Staff & IEEE (Industry Applications Society) Staff. Ed. by IEEE (Institute of Electrical & Electronics Engine. 1200p. 1999. pap. 216.00 (*0-7803-4879-6*, 98TH8362) Inst Electrical.

1998 International Conference on Intelligent Robots & Systems Proceedings. IEEE (Reliability Society & Industrial Electronics. LC 97-81244. 1900p. 1998. pap. text 284.00 (*0-7803-4465-0*, 98CH36190); lib. bdg. write for info. (*0-7803-4466-9*, 98CH36190) Inst Electrical.

1998 International Conference on Mathematical Methods in Electromagnetic Theory. IEEE, Antennas & Propagation Society Staff et al. Ed. by Institute of Electrical & Electronics Engineers, I. LC 97-80498. 935p. 1998. write for info. (*0-7803-4361-1*, 98EX114); pap. write for info. (*0-7803-4360-3*, 98EX114) Inst Electrical.

1998 International Conference on Microelectronics. IEEE, Electron Devices Society Staff. Ed. by Institute of Electrical & Electronics Engineers, I. LC 98-85599. 100p. 1999. pap. 108.00 (*0-7803-4969-5*, 98EX186) Inst Electrical.

1998 International Conference on Energy Management & Power Delivery. IEEE, Singapore Chapter Staff. Ed. by Institute of Electrical & Electronics Engineers, I. LC 97-81439. 750p. 1998. pap. 172.00 (*0-7803-4495-2*, 98EX137) Inst Electrical.

1998 International Conference of Application of Concurrency to System Design: March 23-26, 1998, Fukushima, Japan / IEEE Computer Society. LC 97-77796. xii, 295 p. 1998. write for info. (*0-8186-8350-3*) IEEE Comp Soc.

1998 International Electron Devices Meeting. IEEE (Electron Devices Society) Staff. Ed. by IEEE (Institute of Electrical & Electronics Engine. 980p. 1998. lib. bdg. write for info. (*0-7803-4775-7*) Inst Electrical.

1998 International Electron Devices Meeting. IEEE (Electron Devices Society) Staff. Ed. by IEEE (Institute of Electrical & Electronics Engine. 980p. 1999. pap. text 194.00 (*0-7803-4774-9*) Inst Electrical.

1998 International Fiber Optics Yellow Pages. Date not set. pap. 89.95 (*1-56851-162-0*) Info Gatekeepers.

1998 International Geoscience & Remote Sensing Symposium. IEEE (Geoscience & Remote Sensing Society) Staff. Ed. by IEEE (Institute of Electrical & Electronics Engine. LC 97-80873. 2950p. 1998. pap. text 386.00 (*0-7803-4403-0*, 98CH36174); lib. bdg. write for info. (*0-7803-4404-9*, 98CH361745) Inst Electrical.

1998 International ISDN Yellow Pages. Date not set. pap. 69.95 (*1-56851-158-2*) Info Gatekeepers.

1998 International Quantum Electronics Conference. IEEE (Lasers & Electro-Optics Society). Ed. by IEEE Staff. 1998. lib. bdg. 128.00 (*0-7803-4914-8*, 98CH36236) IEEE Standards.

1998 International Semiconductor Conference. IEEE (Electron Devices Society) Staff. Ed. by IEEE (Institute of Electrical & Electronics Engine. LC 97-81049. 650p. 1998. pap. 162.00 (*0-7803-4432-4*, 98TH8351) Inst Electrical.

1998 International Symposium on Power Semiconductor Devices & IC's. IEEE (Electron Devices Society) Staff. Ed. by IEEE (Institute of Electrical & Electronics Engine. 500p. 1998. lib. bdg. 146.00 (*0-7803-4752-8*, 98CH36212) Inst Electrical.

1998 International Symposium on Micro Mechatronics & Human Science. IEEE (Robotics & Automation Society) Staff. Ed. by IEEE Institute of Electrical & Electronics Engineers, Inc. Staff. LC 98-87750. 250p. 1998. pap. text. write for info. (*0-7803-5130-4*, 98TH8388) Inst Electrical.

1998 International Symposium on Signals, Systems, & Electronics. IEEE, Communications Society, Microwave Theory & T. Ed. by Institute of Electrical & Electronics Engineers, I. LC 98-84972. 600p. 1998. pap. 156.00 (*0-7803-4900-8*, 98EX167) Inst Electrical.

1998 International Symposium on Discharges & Electrical Insulation in Vacuum Proceedings. IEEE, Dielectrics & Electrical Insulation Society. 1100p. 1998. pap. text. write for info. (*0-7803-3953-3*, 98CH36073); lib. bdg. write for info. (*0-7803-3954-1*, 98CH36073) Inst Electrical.

1998 International Symposium on Applications of Ferroelectrics. IEEE, Ultrasonics, Ferroelectrics & Frequency Cont. Ed. by Institute of Electrical & Electronics Engineers, I. 1000p. 1999. pap. 196.00 (*0-7803-4959-8*, 98CH36245); lib. bdg. 196.00 (*0-7803-4960-1*, 98CH36245) Inst Electrical.

1998 International Topical Meeting on Microwave Photonics Technical Digest. IEEE (Lasers & Electro-Optics Society & Electron D. Ed. by IEEE Staff. LC 98-85266. 300p. 1998. pap. 128.00 (*0-7803-4936-9*, 98EX181) IEEE Standards.

***1998 International Workshop on Innovative Architecture (IWIA '98)** LC 99-60129. 136p. 1999. pap. 150.00 (*0-7695-0125-7*) IEEE Comp Soc.

1998 International Zurich Seminar on Broadband Communications. IEEE (Communications Society) Staff. Ed. by IEEE (Institute of Electrical & Electronics Engine. LC 97-70755. 400p. 1998. pap. write for info. (*0-7803-3893-6*, 98TH8277); fiche. write for info. (*0-7803-3894-4*, 98TM8277) Inst Electrical.

1998 Internet Directory of the Banking Industry, Vol. 1. Bobby Fisher. (Illus.). viii, 232p. 1997. spiral bd. 69.00 (*0-9661549-9-1*) Compet Res.

1998 Intersociety Conference on Thermal & Thermomechanical Phenomena in Electronic Systems. IEEE (Components, Packaging & Manufacturing Techno. Ed. by IEEE (Institute of Electrical & Electronics Engine. 500p. 1998. pap. text. write for info. (*0-7803-4475-8*, 98CH36208); lib. bdg. write for info. (*0-7803-4476-6*, 98CH36208) Inst Electrical.

1998 Invertebrates in Captivity Conference Proceedings. annuals 6th ed. (Illus.). 200p. 1998. pap. text 20.00 (*0-9626629-1-7*) Sonoran Arthropod.

1998 Investment Allocation Percentages for New York State & New York City. CCH Tax Law Editors. 680p. 1999. pap. text 32.95 (*0-8080-0356-9*) CCH INC.

1998 Iowa Manufacturers Register. 16th rev. ed. Ed. by Louise M. West & Frank Lambing. 1998. 76.00 (*1-58202-010-8*) Manufacturers.

1998 ISIC - CIRA - ISAS. IEEE, Control Systems Society Staff. Ed. by Institute of Electrical & Electronics Engineers, I. LC 97-80924. 1500p. 1998. pap. 244.00 (*0-7803-4423-5*, 98EX124) Inst Electrical.

1998 Kansas Manufacturers Directory. 3rd rev. ed. Ed. by Louise M. West & Frank Lambing. 1998. 69.00 (*1-58202-013-2*) Manufacturers.

1998 Karting Industry Buyer's Guide. 4th rev. ed. Robert Cycon & Darrell Sitarz. (Illus.). 106p. 1998. pap. 5.95 (*0-9661467-0-0*) Kart Mktg Grp.

1998 Kentucky Manufacturers Register. 14th rev. ed. Ed. by Louise M. West & Frank Lambing. 1997. 76.00 (*1-58202-022-1*) Manufacturers.

1998 League of Utah Writers Anthology. Ed. by Carole O. Cole. 100p. 1999. pap. 15.00 (*0-945767-04-8*) Write Place.

1998 Legal Guide Update. William S. Greene et al. Ed. by Barry Umansky. 397p. 1998. pap. 99.95 (*0-89324-321-3*, 3837) Natl Assn Broadcasters.

1998 Leos Annual Meeting. IEEE Staff. LC 98-36243. 1000p. 1998. pap. text 196.00 (*0-7803-4947-4*); lib. bdg. write for info. (*0-7803-4948-2*) Inst Electrical.

1998 Louisiana Manufacturers Register. 8th rev. ed. Ed. by Louise M. West & Frank Lambing. 1998. 69.00 (*1-58202-035-3*) Manufacturers.

1998 Management Compensation Survey of A/E/P & Environmental Consulting Firms. 184p. 1998. pap. 250.00 (*1-885002-65-3*) Zweig White.

1998 Management Stock Incentive Plan. 98th ed. Ed. by Harcourt Brace Staff. (C). 1998. 595.00 (*0-15-606282-8*) Harcourt.

1998 Marketing Survey of A/E/P & Environmental Consulting Firms. 5th ed. Zweig White & Associates Staff. 362p. 1998. pap. 250.00 (*1-885002-63-7*) Zweig White.

1998 Maryland/D. C. Manufacturers Directory. 6th rev. ed. Ed. by Louise M. West & Frank Lambing. 4p. 1998. 72.00 (*1-58202-028-0*) Manufacturers.

1998 McGraw-Hill Team & Organization Development Sourcebook. Ed. by Mel Silberman. 304p. 1997. pap. 34.95 (*0-07-058002-2*) McGraw.

1998 McGraw-Hill Team & Organization Development Sourcebook. Mel Silberman. 304p. 1997. pap. 79.95 (*0-07-058001-4*) McGraw.

1998 McGraw-Hill Training & Performance Sourcebook. Ed. by Mel Silberman. 304p. 1997. pap. 79.95 (*0-07-058003-0*) McGraw.

1998 Medicaid Managed Care Sourcebook. Ed. by Kenneth M. Coughlin & Lois Wingerson. 558p. 1997. pap. 245.00 (*1-57987-041-4*) Faulkner & Gray.

1998 Medicaid Managed Behavioral Care Sourcebook. Ed. by Ken Coughlin. (Illus.). 495p. 1997. pap. text 195.00 (*1-57987-008-2*) Faulkner & Gray.

1998 Medical & Health Care Market Research Handbook. Terri C. Walker & Richard K. Miller. 350p. 1997. 985.00 (*1-881503-80-1*) R K Miller Assocs.

1998 Medicare Explained. CCH Editorial Staff Publication. (Health Law Professional Ser.). 200p. 1998. pap. 25.00 (*0-8080-0215-5*) CCH INC.

1998 Medicare & Medicaid Benefits. rev. ed. Ed. by CCH Editorial Staff Publication. (Health Law Professional Ser.). 340p. 1998. pap. text 10.00 (*0-8080-0214-7*) CCH INC.

1998 Membership Directory. rev. ed. 200p. 1998. write for info. (*1-888340-10-X*) Psychedelic Lit.

1998 Mercer Guide to Social Security & Medicare. 26th ed. Dale Detlefs & Robert J. Myers. (Illus.). 200p. 1997. pap. 9.95 (*1-880754-98-3*) W M Mercer.

1998 Metroplex Wedding Directory. Ed. by Gina Brown & Jean Brown. (Illus.). 118p. 1998. pap. 12.95 (*0-9635013-1-3*) JP Ink.

1998 Michael Cooper's Buyer's Guide to New Zealand Wines. Michael Cooper. LC 98-202319. 314p. 1997. write for info. (*1-86958-570-4*) Moa Beckett.

1998 Milcom. IEEE (Communications Society) Staff. Ed. by IEEE (Institute of Electrical & Electronics Engine. LC 98-84051. 1200p. 1998. pap. text 216.00 (*0-7803-4506-1*); lib. bdg. write for info. (*0-7803-4507-X*) Inst Electrical.

1998 Minnesota Golfing Insider. Ed. by Randy A. Salas. (Illus.). 96p. 1998. pap. 5.95 (*0-9647179-6-4*) Star MN.

1998 Minnesota Manufacturers Register. 15th rev. ed. Ed. by Louise M. West & Frank Lambing. 1997. 106.00 (*1-58202-024-8*) Manufacturers.

1998 Mississippi Manufacturers Register. 4th rev. ed. Ed. by Louise M. West & Frank Lambing. 1998. 66.00 (*1-58202-004-3*) Manufacturers.

1998 Missouri Manufacturers Register. 11th rev. ed. Ed. by Louise M. West & Frank Lambing. 1998. 99.00 (*1-58202-017-5*) Manufacturers.

1998 Models with the Language of RVing, an Extensive Glossary of Words & Terms. 3rd ed. 352p. 1998. per. 48.00 (*1-890049-05-0*) R V Consumer Grp.

1998 Moravian Daily Texts. large type ed. 454p. 1997. per. 8.00 (*1-878422-33-2*) Moravian Ch in Amer.

1998 Motorsports Conference Proceedings: Engines & Drivetrains, No. 2. 1998. pap. 79.00 (*0-7680-0319-9*, P-340/2) Soc Auto Engineers.

1998 Motorsports Engineering Conference Proceedings, 2 vols. 1998. pap. 150.00 (*0-7680-0320-2*, P-340) Soc Auto Engineers.

1998 Motorsports Engineering Conference Proceedings: Vehicle Design & Safety Issues, No. 1. 1998. pap. 109.00 (*0-7680-0318-0*, P-340/1) Soc Auto Engineers.

1998 Multimedia Modeling: Mmm '98 : October 12-15, 1998, Lausanne, Switzerland : Proceedings. Nadia Magnenat-Thalmann et al. LC 98-86890. x, 231 p. 1998. write for info. (*0-8186-8911-0*) IEEE Comp Soc.

1998 Multimedia World Journal. (Illus.). 133p. 1998. pap. 100.00 (*0-89324-306-X*, 3866) Natl Assn Broadcasters.

1998 Music Yearbook. Joel Whitburn. 264p. 1999. pap., suppl. ed. 34.95 (*0-89820-131-4*) Record Research.

1998 National Hispanic Media Directory Pt. 1: U. S. Media Companies. Kirk Whisler & Octavio Nuiry. (Marketing Guidepost Ser.). 321p. 1998. pap. 95.00 (*1-889379-08-5*) WPR Pubng.

1998 National Roundtable on Family Group Decision Making: Summary of Proceedings. Illus. by American Humane Association Staff. 90p. 1999. pap. 25.00 (*0-930915-27-5*) Am Humane Assn.

1998 Nebraska Manufacturers Register. 6th rev. ed. Ed. by Louise M. West & Frank Lambing. 1998. 65.00 (*1-58202-032-9*) Manufacturers.

1998 Neural Networks for Signal Processing IX. IEEE, Signal Processing Society Staff. Ed. by Institute of Electrical & Electronics Engineers, I. 620p. 1998. pap. 112.00 (*0-7803-5060-X*, 98TH8378) Inst Electrical.

1998 New Jersey Manufacturers Register. Ed. by Louise M. West & Frank Lambing. 1998. 105.00 (*1-58202-003-5*) Manufacturers.

1998 New Mexico Manufacturers Register. 2nd rev. ed. Ed. by Louise M. West & Frank Lambing. 1998. 62.00 (*1-58202-012-4*) Manufacturers.

1998 New Orleans Triennial. William A. Fagaly & Charlotta Kotik. (Illus.). 60p. 1998. 14.95 (*0-89494-068-6*) New Orleans Mus Art.

1998 New York City Apartment Management Checklist. 14th rev. ed. Ed. by Susan R. Lipp et al. (Illus.). 355p. 1997. pap. 72.50 (*0-913828-00-9*) Brownstone NYC.

1998-1999 Liturgy & Appointment Calendar. (Illus.). 1998. pap. 15.00 (*1-56854-231-3*, APPCA9) Liturgy Tr Pubns.

1998-1999 National Directory of Law Schools. 672p. 1998. pap. 80.00 (*1-55733-013-1*) NALP.

***1998-1999 National Faculty Salary Survey by Discipline & Rank in Public Four-Year Colleges & Universities.** 74p. 1999. 52.50 (*1-878240-72-2*) Coll & U Personnel.

1998-1999 Supertrader's Book of Linear Time Cycles. Frank A. Taucher. 452p. 1998. pap. 98.00 (*1-879591-53-7*) Mkt Movements.

1998-1999 Scholarship Book. 6th ed. Cassidy. (C). 1998. pap. 24.95 (*0-13-095093-9*, Macmillan Coll) P-H.

1998-1999 Pocket Book of Pediatric Antimicrobial Therapy. 13th ed. John D. Nelson. 116p. 1997. pap. 14.95 (*0-683-30484-4*) Lppncott W & W.

1998 9th International Symposium on Personal, Indoor & Mobile Radio Communications. IEEE (Communications Society, Boston Section) Staf. Ed. by IEEE (Institute of Electrical & Electronics Engine. LC 98-84864. 400p. 1998. pap. 138.00 (*0-7803-4872-9*, 98TH8361) Inst Electrical.

***1998-99 Directory of Packaging Consultants.** IOPP Packaging Consultants Council Staff. (Illus.). 58p. 1998. pap. 25.00 (*1-930268-02-5*, CC98) Packaging Prof.

1998-99 Freelance Editorial Association Yellow Pages & Code of Fair Practice. rev. ed. Yellow Pages Committee. 107p. 1998. pap. 47.50 (*0-9628636-8-8*) Free Edit Assn.

***1998-99 Annual Supplement to the Piano Book.** Larry Fine. 101p. 1998. pap. 14.95 (*0-9617512-9-0*, 9-0) Brookside Pr MA.

1998-99 Directory of Community Services: First Call for Help. 15th ed. United Way of Minneapolis Area Staff. Ed. by Lael J. Tryon. 769p. 1998. pap. 20.00 (*1-887418-04-0*) United Way MN.

1998-99 State DOT Market for A/E/P & Environmental Consulting Firms. 2nd ed. Zweig White & Associates Staff. 410p. 1998. pap. 395.00 (*1-885002-60-2*) Zweig White.

1998-99 V.I.P. Address Book. Ed. by James M. Wiggins. 1998. lib. bdg. 94.95 (*0-938731-13-0*) Assoc Media Cos.

1998/99 Zagat Paris Restaurant Survey. Zagat Publishers Staff. 1998. pap. text 11.95 (*1-57006-134-3*) Zagat.

1998 9th Asia-Pacific Conference on Nondestructive Testing in Conjunction with ASNT's 1998 Spring Conference & 7th Annual Research Symposium Short Papers. (Illus.). 384p. (C). 1998. per. 31.00 (*1-57117-026-X*, 1361) Am Soc Nondestructive.

1998 9th IEEE Signal Processing on Statistical Signal & Array Processing. IEEE Staff. LC 98-86103. 500p. 1998. pap. write for info. (*0-7803-5010-3*, 98EX197) IEEE Standards.

1998 9th Mediterranean Electrotechnical Conference. IEEE (Region 8) Staff. Ed. by IEEE (Institute of Electrical & Electronics Engine. LC 97-70759. 1000p. 1998. pap. text. write for info. (*0-7803-3879-0*, 98CH36056); lib. bdg. write for info. (*0-7803-3880-4*, 98CH36056) Inst Electrical.

1998 North Carolina Advance Legislative Service Series, 3 vols. 1998. pap. 27.50 (*0-327-05170-1*, 46570-15) LEXIS Pub.

1998 North Carolina Advance Legislative Service, No. 1. 27p. 1998. pap. write for info. (*0-327-05169-8*, 46571-15) LEXIS Pub.

1998 North Carolina Data Guide to Child Well-Being. Madhuri Bhat & Jonathan P. Sher. 156p. 1998. pap. 15.00 (*0-9665180-0-4*) NC Child.

1998 North Carolina Manufacturers Register. 5th rev. ed. Ed. by Louise M. West & Frank Lambing. 1998. 106.00 (*1-58202-009-4*) Manufacturers.

1998 Northcon. IEEE Staff. LC 98-86795. 200p. 1998. pap. 118.00 (*0-7803-5075-8*, 98CH36264) IEEE Standards.

1998 Northern Front Range R & D: Manufacturers Directory. annuals Ed. by Chris Wood. 96p. 1998. pap. 30.00 (*1-891973-00-2*) Boulder Busn.

1998 Northern Plains States Senior Housing Book. 2nd rev. ed. Terry Fahey. Ed. by Lori Fahey. (Senior Housing Ser.). (Illus.). 380p. 1998. pap. 65.00 (*1-893583-09-0*) Research West.

1998 Nuclear Science Symposium. IEEE Staff. 1000p. 1999. pap. text 196.00 (*0-7803-5021-9*, 98CH36255); lib. bdg. 196.00 (*0-7803-5022-7*, 98CH36255) IEEE Standards.

1998 Nunavut Handbook. Marion Soubliere. 366p. 1997. pap. 21.56 (*1-55036-574-6*) NIDL.

1998 Nursing Licensure Guidelines: State Information Manual for Nursing in U. S. Doctor's Licensure Group, Inc. Staff. 290p. 1998. 65.00 (*1-887617-57-4*) St Bart Pr Ltd.

1998 Oceans. IEEE, Oceanic Engineering Society Staff. Ed. by Institute of Electrical & Electronics Engineers, I. LC 98-86363. 2300p. 1998. pap. text 322.00 (*0-7803-5045-6*, 98CH36259) Inst Electrical.

1998 Official ACC Basketball Handbook. abr. ed. Atlantic Coast Conference Staff & Atlantic Coast Conference Schools' (Clemson, Duke, Florida State, VA, Wake Forest, GA Tech, Maryland, NC, NC State) Staff. (Illus.). 176p. 1998. pap. 6.95 (*0-9642611-5-4*) BellSouth Advert.

1998 Official Guide Book to Sarasota, Bradenton & Venice, FL: Steve Rabow's Guide Book. 7th rev. ed. Steve Rabow. (Illus.). 360p. 1997. pap. 12.95 (*0-9639551-4-4*) Primitive Pr.

1998 Official Jr. Sport Source Club Guide. rev. ed. Ed. by Charlie Kadupski. (J). (gr. 2-12). Date not set. pap. 12.95 (*0-9631148-4-0*) Spt Source TX.

1998 Official P. G. A. Golf Directory of the South Central Section, Vol. 3. Ed. by Roger Runge. (Illus.). 144p. 1997. pap. 8.95 (*0-9662780-0-3*) Resource Design.

1998 Official Travel Industry Directory: The Sourcebook for Travel Professionals. 528p. 1998. spiral bd. 31.95 (*0-9644529-3-6*) Universal Media.

1998 Ohio Manufacturers Directory. 16th rev. ed. Ed. by Louise M. West & Frank Lambing. 1997. 154.00 (*1-58202-019-1*) Manufacturers.

1998 Oklahoma Manufacturers Register. 7th rev. ed. Ed. by Louise M. West & Frank Lambing. 1997. 73.00 (*1-58202-020-5*) Manufacturers.

1998 Optical Fiber Communication Conference. IEEE (Lasers & Electro Optics Society & Electron D. Ed. by IEEE (Institute of Electrical & Electronics Engine. 376p. 1998. lib. bdg. write for info. (*0-7803-4415-4*, 98CH36177) Inst Electrical.

1998 OR Product Directory. Ed. by Deb Reno. 458p. 1998. pap. 25.00 (*1-888460-01-6*) Assn Oper Rm Nurses.

1998 PA Abstract. PASDC Staff. Ed. by Jennifer Shultz. (Illus.). 310p. 1998. pap. 50.00 (*1-58036-059-9*) Penn State Data Ctr.

1998 Pacific Northwest Festivals Directory & Resource Guide. Ed. by Theano Petersen. 232p. 1997. pap. 14.50 (*0-9631954-6-8*) NW Folklife.

***1998 Pan-Pacific & International Printing & Graphic Arts Conference.** (Conference Preprints Ser.). 220p. 1998. 51.00 (*1-896742-39-4*) Pulp & Paper.

1998 Passport to the Web, to Accompany Strategic Management & Business Policy. 6th ed. Thomas Wheelen. (C). 1998. ring bd. write for info. (*0-201-32268-4*) Addison-Wesley.

1998 Petro Process Directory. 9th ed. Ed. by James W. Self. 650p. 1998. pap. 65.00 (*1-889879-11-8*) Atlantic Commun.

1998 Phoenix Triennial. David S. Rubin. LC 98-33837. (Illus.). 88p. 1998. pap. write for info. (*0-910407-35-5*) Phoenix Art.

1998 Physician. 368p. 1998. pap. 250.00 (*0-939326-37-X*) Hosp & Hlthcare.

1998 Plumber's Business Planner. R. Dodge Woodson. (Illus.). 480p. 1997. 39.95 (*0-07-071834-2*) McGraw-Hill Prof.

1998 Pocket Book of Infectious Disease Therapy. 9th ed. John G. Bartlett. LC 98-194526. 357p. 1998. pap. 14.95 (*0-683-30632-4*) Lppncott W & W.

1998 Pocket ImmunoFacts. Facts & Comparisons Staff. Ed. by John D. Grabenstein & Laurie A. Grabenstein. 1998. pap. text 34.95 (*1-57439-035-X*) Facts & Comparisons.

1998 Portland Museum of Art Biennial. (Illus.). 64p. 1998. pap. 10.00 (*0-916857-16-6*) Port Mus Art.

1998 Power Tool Blue Book. rev. ed. 1998. lib. bdg. 200.00 (*0-932089-55-0*) Orion Res.

1998 Prayer Journal. Ed. by Leo Zanchettin. (Illus.). 208p. 1997. spiral bd. 12.95 (*0-932085-11-3*) Word Among Us.

1998 Presidential Mid-Election Cycle. Frank A. Taucher. 222p. 1997. pap. 98.00 (*1-879591-54-5*) Mkt Movements.

1998 Principal's Survey of A/E/P & Environmental Consulting Firms. 7th ed. Ed. by Dana Weinstein. 242p. 1998. pap. text 250.00 (*1-885002-43-2*) Zweig White.

1998 Professional Sound Blue Book. 1997. lib. bdg. 200.00 (*0-932089-88-7*) Orion Res.

1998 Summer Programs Guide. Maureen Ramagnoli. 106p. 1998. ring bd. 6.98 (*1-891486-02-0*) Romagnoli.

1998 Project Management Survey of Architecture, Engineering, Planning & Environmental Consulting Firms. 3rd ed. Zweig White & Associates Staff. 1998. pap. text 250.00 (*1-885002-55-6*) Zweig White.

1998 Random Lengths Buyers' & Sellers' Guide: A Directory of the Forest Products Industry. Ed. by Jon P. Anderson. 1044p. 1998. 185.00 (*1-884311-03-2*) Random Lgths Pubns.

1998 Random Lengths Yearbook: Forest Product Market, Prices & Statistics. 250p. 1999. pap. 38.95 (*1-884311-07-5*) Random Lgths Pubns.

1998 Real Estate Market Research Handbook. Terri C. Walker et al. 300p. 1997. 275.00 (*1-881503-81-X*) R K Miller Assocs.

1998 Reference Guide to the Occupational Therapy Code of Ethics. rev. ed. AOTA Staff. 58p. 1999. pap. 20.00 (*1-56900-113-8*, 1139) Am Occup Therapy.

1998 Registered Company Directory, North America. 2500p. 278.95 (*0-07-047219-X*) McGraw-Hill Prof.

***1998 Rehabilitation Services Administration Consumer Satisfaction Survey.** M. Davis. 102p. 1998. pap. write for info. (*1-888557-91-5*) No Ariz Univ.

***1998 Rehabilitation Services Administration Consumer Satisfaction Survey.** M. Davis & F. J. Meaney. 1998. write for info. (*1-888557-90-7*) No Ariz Univ.

***1998 Rehabilitation Services Administration Needs Assessment of Arizonans with Disabilities.** R. Vanderbilt. 71p. 1998. write for info. (*1-888557-89-3*) No Ariz Univ.

1998 Residency Directory, Vol. 2. rev. ed. Accreditation Services Division Staff. 176p. 1997. pap. text 19.00 (*1-879907-74-7*, P509) Am Soc Hlth-Syst.

1998 Residency Directory, Vols. 1 & 2. rev. ed. Accreditation Services Division Staff. 324p. 1997. pap. text 31.00 (*1-879907-73-9*, P508) Am Soc Hlth-Syst.

1998 Rhode Island Manufacturers Register. 2nd rev. ed. Ed. by Louise M. West & Frank Lambing. 1998. 56.00 (*1-58202-036-1*) Manufacturers.

1998 RI Acts & Resolves, Vol. 3. 2000p. Date not set. write for info. (*0-327-07621-6*, 4778011) LEXIS Pub.

1998 RI Public Laws, Vol. 1. 2000p. Date not set. write for info. (*0-327-07622-4*, 4777811) LEXIS Pub.

1998 RI Public Laws, Vol. 2. 2000p. Date not set. write for info. (*0-327-07623-2*, 4777911) LEXIS Pub.

1998 Ringside Wrestling: '99 Photo Album #2. (Illus.). 1998. pap. 3.99 (*0-934551-47-2*) Starlog Grp Inc.

1998 Risk Management for Health Care Provider Groups. Ed. by Lois Wingerson. 496p. 1997. pap. 235.00 (*1-57987-006-6*) Faulkner & Gray.

1998 Roster of Tennessee Architects, Engineers, Landscape Architects, & Registered Interior Designers: 1998 Edition. 315p. 1998. pap. write for info. (*0-327-06316-5*, 3322610) LEXIS Pub.

1998 Satellite Office Survey of A/E/P & Environmental Consulting Firms. 6th ed. Zweig White & Associates Staff. 224p. 1998. pap. text 250.00 (*1-885002-62-9*) Zweig White.

1998 SBT/IEEE International Telecommunications Symposium. IEEE Staff. LC 98-86192. 800p. 1998. pap. 176.00 (*0-7803-5030-8*, 98EX202) IEEE Standards.

***1998 Season Replay Yearbook.** (Illus.). 104p. 1999. pap. 34.95 (*0-9700351-0-1*) Replay Pubng.

1998 2nd Electronic Packaging Technology Conference. IEEE, Singapore Chapter Staff. Ed. by Institute of Electrical & Electronics Engineers Staff. LC 98-87866. 240p. 1999. pap. text 122.00 (*0-7803-5141-X*, 98EX235) Inst Electrical.

1998 2nd IEEE Caracas Conference on Devices, Circuits & Systems Proceedings. IEEE, Venezuela Section & Electron Devices Society. Ed. by Institute of Electrical & Electronics Engineers, I. LC 97-81048. 500p. 1998. pap. 146.00 (*0-7803-4434-0*, 98TH8350) Inst Electrical.

***1998 2nd IEMT/IMC Symposium: April 15-17, 1998, Sonic City-Omiya, Tokyo, Japan.** IEMT\IMC Symposium Staff et al. LC 98-191569. xvii, 391 p. 1998. write for info. (*0-7803-5091-X*) IEEE Comp Soc.

1998 2nd International Conference on Bioelectromagnetism. IEEE (Engineering in Medicine & Biology Society) S. Ed. by IEEE (Institute of Electrical & Electronics Engine. LC 97-70762. 450p. 1998. pap. write for info. (*0-7803-3867-7*, 98TH8269) Inst Electrical.

1998 2nd International Enterprise Distributed Object Computing Workshop Proceedings. IEEE, Communications Society Staff. Ed. by \Institute of Electrical & Electronics Engineers, Inc., Staff. LC 98-88034. 400p. 1998. pap. text. write for info. (*0-7803-5158-4*, 98EX244) Inst Electrical.

1998 Second International Conference on Knowledge-Based Intelligent Engineering Systems Proceedings. IEEE, South Australia Section Staff. Ed. by Institute of Electrical & Electronics Engineers, I. LC 97-80276. 800p. 1998. pap. write for info. (*0-7803-4316-6*, 97EX111); fiche. write for info. (*0-7803-4317-4*, 97EX111) Inst Electrical.

1998 Security Transactions: Taxation of Your Stock & Bond Transactions. Ed. by Denise Davidson et al. 56p. 1998. pap. text 9.95 (*0-8080-0316-X*) CCH INC.

1998 Selected Standards on Professional Responsibility Including California Rules. Thomas D. Morgan & Ronald D. Rotunda. 648p. 1997. pap. write for info. (*1-56662-515-7*) Foundation Pr.

1998 Semiconductor & Insulating Materials Conference. IEEE, Electron Devices Society Staff. Ed. by Institute of Electrical & Electronics Engineers, I. LC 97-80479. 600p. 1998. pap. text. write for info. (*0-7803-4354-9*, 98CH36159); lib. bdg. write for info. (*0-7803-4355-7*, 98CH36159) Inst Electrical.

1998 17th International Conference on Thermoelectrics. IEEE (Components, Packaging & Manufacturing Techno. Ed. by IEEE Staff. LC 98-85026. 450p. 1998. pap. 142.00 (*0-7803-4907-5*, 98TH8365) Inst Electrical.

1998 7th IEEE International Conference on Universal Personal Communications. IEEE, Communications Society Staff. 1,300p. 1998. pap. 226.00 (*0-7803-5106-1*, 98TH8384) Inst Electrical.

1998 Sixth International Workshop on Computational Electronics. IEEE (Electron Devices Society) Staff. Ed. by IEEE (Institute of Electrical & Electronics Engine. LC 97-80530. 300p. 1998. pap. write for info. (*0-7803-4369-7*, 98EX116) Inst Electrical.

1998 6th International Workshop on Quality of Service. IEEE, Communications Society Staff. Ed. by Institute of Electrical & Electronics Engineers, I. LC 97-81374. 324p. 1998. pap. 92.00 (*0-7803-4482-0*, 98EX136) Inst Electrical.

1998 Social Security Explained. rev. ed. CCH Editorial Staff Publication. 320p. 1998. pap. 30.00 (*0-8080-0216-3*) CCH INC.

1998 Social Security Benefits: Including Medicare. rev. ed. CCH Editoral Staff Publication. 56p. 1998. pap. 10.00 (*0-8080-0217-1*) CCH INC.

1998 Source Book on Collective Bargaining: Wages, Benefits, & Other Contract Issues. Ed. by Joyce T. Bagot. 1998. 75.00 (*1-55871-366-2*, XCMP 45) BNA PLUS.

1998 South Carolina Manufacturers Register. 4th rev. ed. Ed. by Louise M. West & Frank Lambing. 1997. 67.00 (*1-58202-018-3*) Manufacturers.

1998 South Dakota Manufacturers Register. 2nd rev. ed. Ed. by Louise M. West & Frank Lambing. 1998. 55.00 (*1-58202-006-X*) Manufacturers.

1998 Southern N. H. Children's Directory. 356p. 1998. 9.98 (*1-891486-00-4*) Romagnoli.

1998 Southwest Senior Housing Book. 2nd rev. ed. Terry Fahey. Ed. by Lori Fahey. (Senior Housing Ser.). (Illus.). 38p. 1998. pap. 65.00 (*1-893583-03-1*) Research West.

1998 Sport Summit Sports Business Directory. rev. ed. Ed. by Michael Patino. 1152p. (Orig.). 1998. pap. 189.00 (*0-9644259-3-9*) E J Krause.

***1998 Spring Simulation Interoperability Workshop: Workshop Papers.** (Simulation Interoperability Workshop Ser.). (Illus.). 1300p. 1998. 75.00 (*1-930638-04-3*) S I S O.

1998 State by State Guide to Human Resources Law. annuals Ronald M. Green et al. Ed. by John F. Buckley, IV. 904p. pap., suppl. ed. 168.00 (*1-56706-790-5*, S91) Panel Pubs.

1998 State Medical Licensure Guidelines: Information Manual for Physicians in the U. S. Worldwide Medical Services Staff. 136p. 1998. 89.00 (*1-887617-59-0*) St Bart Pr Ltd.

1998 State of the Future: Issues & Opportunities. Ed. by Jerome C. Glenn & Theodore J. Gordon. (Illus.). 304p. 1998. pap. 38.50 (*0-9657362-1-0*, 0-9657362) Am Coun Unit Nat.

1998 State Tax Handbook. CCH Tax Law Editors. Ed. by Victor Sotelo & Brian Plunkett. 388p. 1998. pap. 39.95 (*0-8080-0211-2*) CCH INC.

1998 Statute, Rule & Case Supplement for Use with Cases & Materials on Admiralty. Jo Desha Lucas. (University Casebook Ser.). 300p. 1998. pap. text. write for info. (*1-56662-690-0*) Foundation Pr.

An Asterisk (*) at the beginning of an entry indicates that the title is appearing for the first time.

1998 Stock Trader's Almanac. 31st ed. (Illus.). 1997. spiral bd. 34.00 (*1-889223-98-0*) Hirsch Orgn.

***1998 Summer Computer Simulation Conference.** Ed. by Mohammad S. Obaidat. 696p. 1998. 90.00 (*1-56555-149-4*) Soc Computer Sim.

1998 Summer Library Program Manual - "Make Waves: Read" Jane A. Roeber. (Illus.). 200p. (Orig.). 1997. pap. text 18.00 (*1-57337-045-2*) WI Dept Pub Instruct.

1998 Super Register. Ed. by Allan Simpson et al. 664p. 1998. pap. text 17.95 (*0-945164-03-3*) Baseball Amer.

1998 Supercross: Collectors Edition, 1. Brent Madaraza. 136 p. 1998. 19.95 (*0-9683708-0-2*) Aspire Ent.

1998 Supertrader's Almanac: Second Half Edition. Frank A. Taucher. 400p. 1998. pap. 69.00 (*1-879591-55-3*) Mkt Movements.

1998 Supplement to American Criminal Procedure Cases & Commentary. 5th ed. Stephen A. Saltzburg & Daniel J. Capra. (American Casebook Ser.). 185p. 1998. pap. 16.00 (*0-314-23254-0*) West Pub.

1998 Supplement to Cases & Materials on Legislation Policy. William Eskridge et al. (American Casebks.). 100p. 1998. pap. 20.00 (*0-314-23317-2*) West Pub.

1998 Supplement to Cases & Materials on Conflict of Laws. Peter Hay et al. (University Casebook Ser.). 41p. 1998. pap. text. write for info. (*1-56662-639-0*) Foundation Pr.

1998 Supplement to Cases & Materials on Pleadings & Procedure, State & Federal. Geoffrey C. Hazard et al. (University Casebook Ser.). 125p. 1998. pap. text. write for info. (*1-56662-696-X*) Foundation Pr.

1998 Supplement to Cases & Materials on Criminal Justice Administration. 4th ed. Frank W. Miller et al. (University Casebook Ser.). 236p. 1998. pap. text, suppl. ed. 10.50 (*1-56662-677-3*) Foundation Pr.

1998 Supplement to Cases & Materials on Mass Media Law. 5th ed. Marc A. Franklin & David A. Anderson. (University Casebook Ser.). 197p. 1998. pap. text 9.95 (*1-56662-695-1*) Foundation Pr.

1998 Supplement to Cases & Materials on Corporations. 7th unabridged ed. Melvin A. Eisenberg. (University Casebook Ser.). 250p. 1998. pap. text. write for info. (*1-56662-502-5*) Foundation Pr.

1998 Supplement to Cases & Materials on Evidence. 8th ed. Roger C. Park & Jon R. Waltz. (University Casebook Ser.). 119p. (C). 1998. pap. text 7.95 (*1-56662-670-6*) Foundation Pr.

1998 Supplement to Cases & Materials on Federal Courts. 9th ed. Charles A. Wright & John B. Oakley. (University Casebook Ser.). 150p. (C). 1998. pap. text. write for info. (*1-56662-671-4*) Foundation Pr.

1998 Supplement to Cases & Materials on Constitutional Law: Themes for the Constitution's Third Century. 2nd ed. Daniel A. Farber et al. (American Casebook Ser.). 78p. 1998. pap. text, suppl. ed. 8.00 (*0-314-23250-8*) West Pub.

1998 Supplement to Civil Rights Actions: Section 1983 & Related Statutes. 2nd ed. Peter W. Low & John C. Jeffries. (University Casebook Ser.). 160p. 1998. pap. text, suppl. ed. write for info. (*1-56662-654-4*) Foundation Pr.

1998 Supplement to Connecticut Jury Instructions (Civil) 4th ed. Douglass B. Wright & William L. Ankerman. 203p. 1998. pap. 54.00 (*1-878698-46-X*) Atlantic Law.

1998 Supplement to Constitutional Law - The American Constitution - Constitutional Rights & Liberties, Cases, Comments, Questions. Yale Kamisar et al. 100p. 1998. pap. text 9.36 (*0-314-23321-0*) West Pub.

1998 Supplement to Constitutional Law, Civil Liberty & Individual Rights. 4th ed. William Cohen & David J. Danelski. (Pamphlet Ser.). 75p. 1998. pap. text, suppl. ed. 6.50 (*1-56662-664-1*) Foundation Pr.

1998 Supplement to Constitutional Law, Cases & Materials. 10th ed. William Cohen & Jonathan D. Varat. (University Casebook Ser.). 229p. 1998. pap. text, suppl. ed. 9.95 (*1-56662-663-3*) Foundation Pr.

1998 Supplement to Criminal Procedure: An Analysis on Cases & Concepts. 3rd ed. Charles Whittereal & Christopher Slobogin. (University Textbook Ser.). 86p. 1998. pap. text, suppl. ed. 6.95 (*1-56662-697-8*) Foundation Pr.

1998 Supplement to Federal Income Taxation of Corporations. Paul R. McDaniel et al. 86p. 1998. pap. text. write for info. (*1-56662-666-8*) Foundation Pr.

1998 Supplement to Federal Income Taxation of Business Organizations. 2nd ed. Paul R. McDaniel et al. (University Casebook Ser.). 134p. (C). 1998. pap. text. write for info. (*1-56662-668-4*) Foundation Pr.

1998 Supplement to Federal Income Taxation & Partnerships & S Corporations. 2nd ed. Paul R. McDaniel et al. (University Casebook Ser.). 82p. 1998. pap. text. write for info. (*1-56662-669-2*) Foundation Pr.

1998 Supplement to Federal Courts & the Law of Federal-State Relations. 4th ed. Peter W. Low & John C. Jeffries, Jr. (University Casebook Ser.). 50p. 1998. pap. text, suppl. ed. 4.95 (*1-56662-721-4*) Foundation Pr.

1998 Supplement to Federal Income Tax: A Casebook on the Basics. Philip H. Wile. (American Casebook Ser.). 40p. (C). 1998. pap. text. write for info. (*0-314-23334-2*) West Pub.

1998 Supplement to Federal Courts: Cases & Comments on Judicial Federation & Judicial Power. Louise Weinberg. 350p. 1998. pap. 20.50 (*0-314-23256-7*) West Pub.

1998 Supplement to Intellectual Property Cases & materials on Trademark, Copyright & Patent Law. Rochelle Druyfuss & Roberta Keavall. (University Casebks.). 50p. 1998. pap. text 5.50 (*1-56662-684-6*) Foundation Pr.

1998 Supplement to Local Government Law. 2nd ed. Gerald E. Frug. (American Casebook Ser.). 125p. 1998. 12.50 (*0-314-23309-1*) West Pub.

1998 Supplement to Modern Constitutional Law Cases & Notes. 5th ed. Ronald D. Rotunda. (American Casebks.). 192p. 1998. pap. text 13.25 (*0-314-23253-2*) West Pub.

1998 Supplement to Modern Criminal Procedure, Basic Criminal Procedure & Advanced Criminal Procedure. 8th ed. Yale Kamisar et al. (American Casebook Ser.). 300p. 1998. pap. text 19.25 (*0-314-23252-4*) West Pub.

1998 Supplement to Securities Regulation, Cases & Materials. Richard W. Jennings et al. (University Casebook Ser.). 512p. 1998. pap. text 28.95 (*1-56662-672-2*) Foundation Pr.

1998 Supplement to Sexuality Gender, & the Law. William N. Esteridge, Jr. & Nan S. Hunter. (University Casebook Ser.). 250p. 1998. pap. text, suppl. ed. 9.50 (*1-56662-705-2*) Foundation Pr.

1998 Supplement to the Federal Courts & the Federal System. 4th ed. Richard H. Fallon et al. (University Casebook Ser.). 120p. 1998. pap. text, suppl. ed. 9.95 (*1-56662-685-4*) Foundation Pr.

1998 Survey of Corporate University Future Directions. unabridged ed. Jeanne Meister. Ed. by Adam Eisenstat & Stephanie Roberts. (Illus.). 100p. 1998. pap. 895.00 (*0-9656453-1-2*) Corp Univ Xchange.

***1998 Symposium on the Performance Evaluation of Computer & Telecommunication Systems.** Ed. by Mohammad S. Obaidat. 352p. 1998. 50.00 (*1-56555-150-8*) Soc Computer Sim.

1998 Symposium on VLSI Technology. IEEE (Electron Devices Society) Staff. Ed. by IEEE (Institute of Electrical & Electronics Engine. 226p. 1998. pap. text 120.00 (*0-7803-4770-6*); lib. bdg. write for info. (*0-7803-4771-4*) Inst Electrical.

1998 Taste of Home Annual Recipes. Reiman Publications Staff. Ed. by Julie Schnittke. 324p. 1997. 24.95 (*0-89821-216-2*, 24510) Reiman Pubns.

1998 Tax Legislation Law, Explanation & Analysis: IRS Restructuring & Reform. CCH Staff. 816 p. 1998. pap. text 34.95 (*0-8080-0281-3*) CCH INC.

1998 Tax Return Practice Problems for Corporation, S Corporations, & Partnerships. Dalton. 1999. pap. 21.95 (*0-87393-883-6*) Dame Pubns.

1998 Tax Year in Review. CCH Editors. 260p. 1999. pap. text 42.95 (*0-8080-0339-9*) CCH INC.

1998 Tennessee Manufacturers Register. 2nd rev. ed. Ed. by Louise M. West & Frank Lambing. 1997. 74.00 (*1-58202-023-X*) Manufacturers.

1998 10th IEEE International Conference on Tools with AI. IEEE (Computer Society) Staff. Ed. by IEEE(Institute of Electrical & Electronics Engineers, Inc.) Staff. 500p. 1998. pap. 146.00 (*0-7803-5214-9*, 98CH36294) Inst Electrical.

1998 Texas Manufacturers Register. 14th rev. ed. Ed. by Louise M. West & Frank Lambing. 1998. 154.00 (*1-58202-037-X*) Manufacturers.

1998 Texas Senior Housing Book. 2nd rev. ed. Terry Fahey. Ed. by Lori Fahey. (Senior Housing Ser.). (Illus.). 380p. 1998. pap. 65.00 (*1-893583-07-4*) Research West.

1998 3rd International Workshop on Statistical Metrology. IEEE (Electron Devices Society) Staff. LC 97-80378. 130p. 1998. pap. write for info. (*0-7803-4338-7*, 98EX113) Inst Electrical.

1998 3rd Annual Symposium on Plasma Process-Induced Damage. annuals Ed. by Moritaka Nakamura et al. LC 98-65928. (Illus.). 1998. pap. 65.00 (*0-9651577-2-5*) Nrthrn CA Chapter.

1998 3rd International Conference on Adhesives Joining & Coating Technology in Electronic Manufacturing Proceedings. IEEE (Components, Packaging & Manufacturing Techno. Ed. by IEEE Staff. LC 98-85262. 450p. 1998. pap. 142.00 (*0-7803-4934-2*, 98EX180) IEEE Standards.

1998 13th Annual Battery Conference on Applications & Advances. IEEE (Aerospace & Electronic Systems Society) Staff. Ed. by IEEE (Institute of Electrical & Electronics Engine. 360p. 1998. pap. write for info. (*0-7803-4098-1*, 98TH8299) Inst Electrical.

1998 30th Southeastern Symposium on System Theory. IEEE, Computer Society, Circuits, & Systems Societ. Ed. by Institute of Electrical & Electronics Engineers, I. 600p. 1998. pap. 156.00 (*0-7803-4547-9*, 98EX148) Inst Electrical.

1998 32nd Annual International Carnahan Conference on Security Technology. IEEE, Aerospace & Electronics Systems Staff. Ed. by Institute of Electrical & Electronics Engineers, I. LC 79-644630. 250p. 1998. pap. text. write for info. (*0-7803-4535-5*, 98CH36209); lib. bdg. write for info. (*0-7803-4536-3*, 98CH36209) IEEE Standards.

1998 32nd Asilomar Conference on Signals, Systems & Computers. IEEE, Signal Processing Society Staff. Ed. by Institute of Electical & Electronics Engineers, Inc., Staff. 1800p. 1999. pap. text. write for info. (*0-7803-5148-7*, 98CH36284) Inst Electrical.

1998 37th IEEE Conference on Decision & Control. IEEE (Control Systems Society) Staff. Ed. by IEEE (Institute of Electrical & Electronics Engine. LC 79-640961. 5000p. 1998. pap. text. write for info. (*0-7803-4394-8*, 98CH36171); lib. bdg. write for info. (*0-7803-4395-6*, 98CH36171) Inst Electrical.

1998 37th Sice Annual Conference. IEEE, Industrial Electronics Society, Robotics & A. Ed. by Institute of Electrical & Electronics Engineers, I. 376p. 1998. pap. 134.00 (*0-7803-5052-9*, 98TH8377) Inst Electrical.

1998-2000 Graduate Faculty & Programs in Political Science. 16th rev. ed. Ed. by Elizabeth Weaver Engel & Catherine E. Rudder. 356p. (C). 1995. pap. 60.00 (*1-878147-43-9*) Am Political.

1998-1999 Illinois Commercial Landscape & Turfgrass Pest Management Handbook. 152p. 1998. pap. 10.00 (*1-883097-19-3*) U Ill Ofc Agricult.

***1998-1999 Mid-Level Administrative - Professional Salary Survey.** 118p. 1999. 95.00 (*1-878240-71-4*) Coll & U Personnel.

1998-1999 Medical Student's Guide to Successful Residency Matching. Lee T. Miller & Leigh G. Donowitz. 102p. 1998. pap. 14.95 (*0-683-30613-8*) Lppncott W & W.

1998-99 Guide to Superfund Sites. Ed. by Ron DiGregorio. 864p. 1998. pap. 495.00 incl. cd-rom (*0-935453-87-3*) Pasha Pubns.

1998-99 Model & Talent Bible: The Ultimate Modeling Research Guide. Sarah Giovinetti. 340p. 1998. pap. 24.95 (*1-57502-681-3*, PO1924) Morris Pubng.

1998-99 School Technology Funding Directory. Ed. by Rebecca Flowers. 200p. 1998. pap. 145.00 (*1-890773-03-4*) IAQ Pubns.

1998-2000 Comprehensive Accreditation Manual for Health Care Networks. rev. ed. Joint Commission on Accreditation of Healthcare Organizations. (Illus.). 490p. 1997. pap. 195.00 (*0-86688-582-X*, CHCN-98) Joint Comm Hlthcare.

1998-2000 Standards for Health Care Networks. rev. ed. Joint Commission on Accreditation of Healthcare Organizations. 1997. pap. 70.00 (*0-86688-583-8*, HCN-98) Joint Comm Hlthcare.

1998 Topical Meeting on Silicon Monolithic Integrated Circuits in RF Systems. IEEE, Microwave, Theory & Techniques Society Staff. Ed. by IEEE Institute of Electrical & Electronics Engineers, Inc. Staff. LC 98-83181. 236p. 1998. pap. write for info. (*0-7803-5288-2*, 98EX271) Inst Electrical.

1998 Tour de France: Conquests & Crises. VeloNews Editors et al. (Illus.). 240p. (Orig.). 1998. pap. 19.95 (*1-884737-65-X*) VeloPress.

***1998 Trade Policy Agenda & 1997 Annual Report of the President of the U. S. on the Trade Agreement Program.** Charlene Barshefsky. 273p. 1999. pap. text 35.00 (*0-7881-8133-5*) DIANE Pub.

1998 Training Annual. Pfeiffer Staff. 320p. 1997. pap. 44.95 (*0-7879-1104-6*, Pfffr & Co) Jossey-Bass.

1998 Training Annual, 1. Pfeiffer Staff. 320p. 1997. 94.95 (*0-7879-1103-8*, Pfffr & Co) Jossey-Bass.

1998 Transmission & Driveline Systems Symposium: New Developments & Advanced Concepts in Systems & Components. 287p. 1998. 99.00 (*0-7680-0144-7*) Soc Auto Engineers.

1998 20th International Telecommunications Energy Conference (INTELEC) IEEE, Power Electronics Society Staff. Ed. by Institute of Electrical & Electronics Engineers, I. LC 88-656128. 850p. 1998. pap. text 182.00 (*0-7803-5069-3*, 98CH36263) Inst Electrical.

1998 24th Annual Northeast Bioengineering Conference. IEEE, Engineering in Medicine & Biology Society St. Ed. by Institute of Electrical & Electronics Engineers, I. LC 88-646567. 120p. 1998. lib. bdg. write for info. (*0-7803-4545-2*, 98CH36210) Inst Electrical.

1998 22nd IEEE/CPMT International Electronics Manufacturing Technology Symposium. IEEE (Components, Packaging & Manufacturing Techno. Ed. by IEEE (Institute of Electrical & Electronics Engine. LC 98-84340. 240p. 1998. pap. text 122.00 (*0-7803-4520-7*, 98CH36204); lib. bdg. write for info. (*0-7803-4521-5*, 98CH36204) Inst Electrical.

1998 Twenty-Third International Power Modulator Symposium. IEEE Staff. 400p. 1998. pap. text. write for info. (*0-7803-4244-5*); lib. bdg. write for info. (*0-7803-4245-3*) Inst Electrical.

1998 23rd IEEE - CPMT International Electronics Manufacturing Technology Symposium. IEEE, Components, Packaging & Manufacturing Techno. Ed. by Institute of Electrical & Electronics Engineers, I. 500p. 1998. pap. text 146.00 (*0-7803-4523-1*, 98CH36205); lib. bdg. 146.00 (*0-7803-4524-X*, 98CH36205) Inst Electrical.

1998 U. S. Hispanic Market Study. Strategy Research Corp. Staff. (Orig.). 1997. pap. write for info. (*1-888520-07-8*) Strategy Research.

1998 U. S. Master GAAP Guide. Bill D. Jarnagin. 1200p. 1998. pap. 59.95 (*0-8080-0220-1*) CCH INC.

1998 U. S. Master Pension Guide. Nicholas Kaster et al. 900p. 1998. pap. text 49.00 (*0-8080-0160-4*) CCH INC.

1998 U. S. Master Employee Benefits Guide. 3rd ed. Linda Panszczyk. 655p. 1997. pap. 59.00 (*0-8080-0151-5*) CCH INC.

1998 U. S. Master Accounting Guide. John Wisdom. Ed. by Lawrence Norris. 1400p. 1998. pap. text 47.95 (*0-8080-0266-X*) CCH INC.

1998 U. S. Master Depreciation Guide. Ed. by CCH Editorial Staff. 1998. pap. text 37.95 (*0-8080-0253-8*) CCH INC.

1998 U. S. Master Tax Guide. CCH Editorial Staff. 688p. Date not set. pap. 37.95 (*0-8080-0162-0*) CCH INC.

1998 U. S. Master Tax Guide. 98th ed. CCH Editors. 684p. 1997. text 54.95 (*0-8080-0173-6*) CCH INC.

1998 U. S./BNA Postage Stamp Catalog. rev. ed. (Illus.). 512p. 1997. pap. 9.95 (*0-937458-62-7*) Harris & Co.

1998 Underwater Technology Conference Proceedings. IEEE, Oceanic Engineering Society Staff. LC 97-80153. 300p. 1998. pap. 144.00 (*0-7803-4273-9*, 98EX101) Inst Electrical.

1998 Update for Law of Public Communication. 4th ed. Kent Middleton. (C). 1998. pap. text. write for info. (*0-8013-2042-9*) Addison-Wesley.

1998 URSI International Symposium on Signals, Systems & Electronics: Conference Proceedings, 29 September-2 October, 1998, Palazzo Dei Congressi, Pisa, Italy. URSI International Symposium on Signals Systems Staff & International Union of Radio Science Staff. LC 98-84972. xii, 494 p. 1998. write for info. (*0-7803-4901-6*) Inst Electrical.

1998 Used Cars Book. Consumer Guide Editors. 160p. 1998. mass mkt. 9.99 (*0-451-19438-1*, Sig) NAL.

1998 Variable Valve Actuation & Power Boost. 169p. 1998. 59.00 (*0-7680-0166-8*) Soc Auto Engineers.

1998 Video & T. V. Blue Book. 1997. lib. bdg. 200.00 (*0-932089-89-5*) Orion Res.

1998 Virginia Manufacturers Directory. 6th rev. ed. Ed. by Louise M. West & Frank Lambing. 1998. 79.00 (*1-58202-008-6*) Manufacturers.

1998 Vital Statistics: Clinton, Franklin & Essex County, New York. Compiled by Clyde M. Rabideau. LC 99-60840. iv, 503p. 1999. write for info. (*0-9662895-3-6*) C M Rabideau.

1998 Volume 11.2: Articles & Book Reviews. 22.95 (*0-567-08622-4*) T&T Clark Pubs.

1998 Washington State Yearbook: A Guide to Government in the Evergreen State. Ed. by Richard Yates & Charity Yates. 296p. (Orig.). 1996. pap. 21.95 (*0-911927-29-8*) Public Sector.

1998 Washoe County School Bond: Is Accountability Still the Issue. George Kucera & Ted Harris. (Illus.). 18p. 1998. lib. bdg. 10.00 (*1-886306-00-1*) Nevada Policy.

1998 Water Terminals Register, Vol. 1. Ed. by James W. Self. 504p. 1998. pap. 330.00 (*1-889879-07-X*) Atlantic Commun.

1998 Wescon Conference. IEEE, Los Angeles Council, San Francisco Bay Counc. Ed. by Institute of Electrical & Electronics Engineers, I. 300p. 1998. pap. text 128.00 (*0-7803-5078-2*, 98CH36265) Inst Electrical.

1998 West Virginia Manufacturers Register. 11th rev. ed. Ed. by Louise M. West & Frank Lambing. 1998. 56.00 (*1-58202-016-7*) Manufacturers.

1998 Wildflower Diary. Philippa Nikulinsky. 1997. pap. 19.95 (*1-86368-194-9*, Pub. by Fremantle Arts) Intl Spec Bk.

1998 Wisconsin Manufacturers Register. 15th rev. ed. Ed. by Louise M. West & Frank Lambing. 1997. 109.00 (*1-58202-031-0*) Manufacturers.

1998 Workshop on High Performance Electron Devices for Microwave & Optoelectronic Applications. IEEE (Electron Devices Society & Lasers & Electro-. Ed. by IEEE (Institute of Electrical & Electronics Engine. LC 97-80346. 200p. 1998. pap. 118.00 (*0-7803-4333-6*, 98TH8345) Inst Electrical.

1998 Workshop on Power Electronics in Transportation. IEEE (Power Electronics Society & Southeastern Mic. Ed. by IEEE (Institute of Electrical & Electronics Engine. LC 97-80778. 220p. 1998. pap. 120.00 (*0-7803-4398-0*, 98TH8349) Inst Electrical.

1998 Year Book Neonatal & Perinatal Medicine. 2nd ed. Avary A. Fanaroff. (Illus.). 480p. (C). (gr. 13). 1998. text 80.00 (*0-8151-9644-X*, 24981) Mosby Inc.

1998 Year Book Neurology & Neurosurgery. Walter G. Bradley. (Illus.). 440p. (C). (gr. 13). 1998. text 78.00 (*0-8151-9648-2*, 24985) Mosby Inc.

1998 Year Book Obstetrics & Gynecology. 2nd ed. Daniel R. Mishell. (Illus.). 600p. (C). (gr. 13). 1998. text 79.00 (*0-8151-9704-7*, 24991) Mosby Inc.

1998 Year Book of Medicine. Cline. (Illus.). 752p. (C). (gr. 13). 1998. text 75.00 (*0-8151-3156-9*, 26975) Mosby Inc.

1998 Year Book of Anesthesia & Pain Management. 2nd ed. John H. Tinker. (Illus.). 504p. (C). (gr. 13). 1998. text 79.00 (*0-8151-8781-5*, 24436) Mosby Inc.

1998 Year Book of Cardiology. 2nd ed. Robert C. Schlant. (Illus.). 576p. (C). (gr. 13). 1998. text 79.00 (*0-8151-7539-6*, 24312) Mosby Inc.

1998 Year Book of Chiropractic. Lawrence Phillips. (Illus.). 448p. (C). (gr. 13). 1997. text 73.00 (*0-8151-6737-7*, 21967) Mosby Inc.

1998 Year Book of Critical Care Medicine. Parrillo. (Illus.). 432p. (C). (gr. 13). 1998. text 78.00 (*0-8151-9605-9*, 24944) Mosby Inc.

1998 Year Book of Dentistry. Meskin. (Illus.). 528p. (C). (gr. 13). 1998. text 73.00 (*0-8151-7084-X*, 27509) Mosby Inc.

1998 Year Book of Dermatologic Surgery. Hubert T. Greenway. (Illus.). 368p. (C). (gr. 13). 1998. text 88.00 (*0-8151-9608-3*, 24947) Mosby Inc.

1998 Year Book of Dermatology. Sober. (Illus.). 512p. (C). (gr. 13). 1998. text 81.00 (*0-8151-9613-X*, 24950) Mosby Inc.

1998 Year Book Of Diagnostic Radiology. Anne G. Osborn. (Illus.). 640p. (C). (gr. 13). 1998. text 79.00 (*0-8151-9616-4*, 24953) Mosby Inc.

1998 Year Book of Digestive Diseases. Norton J. Greenberger. (Illus.). 264p. (C). (gr. 13). 1998. text 77.95 (*0-8151-9619-9*, 24956) Mosby Inc.

1998 Year Book of Drug Therapy. Louis Lasagna. (Illus.). 408p. (C). (gr. 13). 1998. text 79.95 (*0-8151-5296-5*, 24747) Mosby Inc.

1998 Year Book of Emergency Medicine. 2nd ed. David K. Wagner. (Illus.). 456p. (C). (gr. 13). 1998. text 83.00 (*0-8151-9623-7*, 24960) Mosby Inc.

1998 Year Book of Endocrinology. 2nd ed. John D. Bagdade. (Illus.). 432p. (C). (gr. 13). 1998. text 79.00 (*0-8151-9626-1*, 24963) Mosby Inc.

1998 Year Book of Geriatrics & Gerontology. Burton. (Illus.). 424p. (C). (gr. 13). 1998. text 69.95 (*0-8151-9631-8*, 24968) Mosby Inc.

1998 Year Book of Hand Surgery. Peter C. Amadio. (Illus.). 464p. (C). (gr. 13). 1998. text 80.00 (*0-8151-0163-5*, 25764) Mosby Inc.

1998 Year Book of Infectious Diseases. Gerald T. Keusch. (Illus.). 400p. (C). (gr. 13). 1998. text 80.00 (*0-8151-9387-4*, 24592) Mosby Inc.

1998 Year Book of Nuclear Medicine. Ed. by Alexander Gottschalk. (Illus.). 504p. (C). (gr. 13). 1998. text 86.00 (*0-8151-3821-0*, 25463) Mosby Inc.

1998 Year Book of Occupational & Environmental Health. 2nd ed. Edward A. Emmett. (Illus.). 360p. (C). (gr. 13). 1998. text 74.95 (*0-8151-9707-1*, 24994) Mosby Inc.

N

1998 Year Book of Ophthalmology. 2nd ed. Wilson. (Illus.). 408p. (C). (gr. 13). 1998. text 82.00 (*0-8151-9713-6*, 25000) Mosby Inc.

1998 Year Book of Orthopaedics. 2nd ed. Clement B. Sledge. (Illus.). 488p. (C). (gr. 13). 1998. text 83.00 (*0-8151-9716-0*, 25003) Mosby Inc.

1998 Year Book of Pathology & Laboratory Medicine. 2nd ed. Steve Raab. (Illus.). 568p. (C). (gr. 13). 1998. text 83.00 (*0-8151-9722-5*, 25009) Mosby Inc.

1998 Year Book of Pediatrics. 2nd ed. James A. Stockman. (Illus.). 680p. (C). (gr. 13). 1998. text 67.95 (*0-8151-9725-X*, 25012) Mosby Inc.

1998 Year Book of Plastic & Reconstructive Surgery. 2nd ed. Ronald D. Miller. (Illus.). 352p. (C). (gr. 13). 1998. text 82.00 (*0-8151-9728-4*, 25015) Mosby Inc.

1998 Year Book of Pulmonary Disease. 2nd ed. Jett James Jett. (Illus.). 472p. (C). (gr. 13). 1998. text 79.00 (*0-8151-9736-5*, 25023) Mosby Inc.

1998 Year Book of Sports Medicine. 2nd ed. Roy J. Shephard. (Illus.). 472p. (C). (gr. 13). 1998. text 74.95 (*0-8151-9740-3*, 25027) Mosby Inc.

1998 Year Book of Surgery. 2nd ed. Edward M. Copeland. (Illus.). 576p. (C). (gr. 13). 1998. text 74.00 (*0-8151-9743-8*, 25030) Mosby Inc.

1998 Year Book of Urology. 2nd ed. Andriole. (Illus.). 384p. (C). (gr. 13). 1998. text 82.00 (*0-8151-2548-8*, 24061) Mosby Inc.

1998 Year Book of Vascular Surgery. Porter. (Illus.). 544p. (C). (gr. 13). 1998. text 86.00 (*0-8151-9800-0*, 25037) Mosby Inc.

1998 Year Book of Podiatry. 2nd ed. Ed. by Stephen J. Kominsky. 348p. (C). (gr. 13). 1998. text 69.95 (*0-8151-9731-4*) Mosby Inc.

1998 Year-Round Fun Places for Families. Maureen Romagnoli. 1998. ring bd. 8.98 (*1-891486-03-9*) Romagnoli.

1998 Yearbook Supplement to McGraw-Hill's National Electrical Code Handbook. Joseph F. McPartland & Brian J. McPartland. (Illus.). 176p. 1998. 29.95 (*0-07-046604-1*) McGraw-Hill Prof.

1998 Yearbook: Scientific Contributions of William L. Johnston, DO, FAAO. Ed. by Myron C. Beal. (Illus.). 370p. 1998. pap. 50.00 (*0-940668-09-2*) Am Acad Osteopathy.

***1998 Yearbook of Labour Statistics.** Bulletin of Labour Statistics Staff. (FRE, SPA & ENG., Illus.). 1339p. 1999. 239.50 (*92-2-007357-9*, Pub. by Statnry Office) Balogh.

1998 Zagat St. Louis Restaurant Survey. Zagat Publishers Staff. 1998. pap. text 9.95 (*1-57006-130-0*) Zagat.

1998 1st IEEE International Conference on ATM, ICATM '98, June 22-24, 1998, Colmar, France. IEEE Conference on ATM Staff & IEEE Staff. LC 98-85755. x, 535 p. 1998. pap. write for info. (*0-7803-4983-0*) IEEE Standards.

1998/99 EnviroSafety Directory, Vol. 4. 4th rev. ed. Ed. by James W. Self. 525p. 1998. pap. 65.00 (*1-889879-00-2*) Atlantic Commun.

1998/99 PetroProcess Directory, Vol. 9. 9th rev. ed. Ed. by James W. Self. 650p. 1997. pap. 65.00 (*1-889879-03-7*) Atlantic Commun.

1998 Symposium on VLSI Circuits. IEEE (Solid-State Circuits Society) Staff & IEEE (Institute of Electrical & Electronics Engine. LC 98-84564. 200p. 1998. pap. text 118.00 (*0-7803-4766-8*, 98CH36215); lib. bdg. write for info. (*0-7803-4767-6*, 98CH36215) Inst Electrical.

1990 Election in South Dakota. Alan L. Clem. 1991. pap. 1.00 (*1-55614-133-5*) U of SD Gov Res Bur.

Nineteen Ninety Elections in Nicaragua & Their Aftermath. Ed. by Vanessa Castro & Gary Prevost. 1992. pap. 24.50 (*0-8476-7766-4*) Rowman.

Nineteen Ninety Elections in Nicaragua & Their Aftermath. Ed. by Vanessa Castro & Gary Prevost. 240p. (C). 1992. text 60.00 (*0-8476-7761-3*) Rowman.

1990 European Oil & Gas Management Directory. Ed. by Editions Technip Staff. 688p. (C). 1990. 685.00 (*1-872549-00-4*, Pub. by Edits Technip) Enfield Pubs NH.

1995 AEE Energy & Environmental Industry Survey. Ruth M. Bennett. LC 95-60080. 128p. 1995. pap. 200.00 (*0-88173-220-6*) Fairmont Pr.

1995 IEEE - CPMT 17th International Electronic Manufacturing Technology Symposium. IEEE (Components, Packaging & Manufacturing Techno. Ed. by IEEE (Institute of Electrical & Electronics Engine. LC 95-80331. 400p. 1995. pap. text 110.00 (*0-7803-2996-1*, 95CH35864); lib. bdg. 110.00 (*0-7803-2997-X*, 95CB35864); fiche 110.00 (*0-7803-2998-8*, 95CM35864) Inst Electrical.

1995 IEEE IECON - 21st International Conference on Industrial Electronics, Control & Instrumentation. IEEE (Industrial Electronics Society) Staff. Ed. by IEEE (Institute of Electrical & Electronics Engine. LC 95-80333. 2100p. 1995. pap. text 244.00 (*0-7803-3026-9*, 95CH35868); lib. bdg. 244.00 (*0-7803-3027-7*, 95CB35868); fiche 244.00 (*0-7803-3028-5*, 95CM35868) Inst Electrical.

1995 IEEE Electrical Performance of Electronic Packaging. IEEE (Microwave Theory & Techniques Society, Elect. Ed. by IEEE (Institute of Electrical & Electronics Engine. LC 95-80323. 270p. 1995. pap. 100.00 (*0-7803-3034-X*, 95TH8137) Inst Electrical.

1995 IEEE International Conference on Fuzzy Systems. IEEE (Neural Networks Council) Staff. Ed. by IEEE (Institute of Electrical & Electronics Engine. LC 94-73559. 2500p. 1995. pap. text. write for info. (*0-7803-2461-7*, 95CH35741); lib. bdg. write for info. (*0-7803-2462-5*, 95CH35741); mic. film. write for info. (*0-7803-2463-3*, 95CH35741) Inst Electrical.

1995 Black Mail Order Directory: Specializing in Black Ethnic Gifts, Crafts, Collectibles & Memorabilia. 4th ed. 64p. 1994. pap. 9.95 (*1-885716-01-X*) JAK Prods.

1995-1997 Directory of Fine Art & Artists in South Eastern Connecticut. (Orig.). 1995. pap. text 7.95 (*0-9646958-0-4*) Griffis Art Ctr.

1995 AACE International Transactions. Ed. by Sara Pritchard. (Illus.). 450p. (Orig.). 1995. pap. text 19.95 (*1-885517-01-7*) AACE Intl.

1995 AAFCO Official Publication. rev. ed. Ed. by Paul M. Bachman. 357p. 1995. 25.00 (*1-878341-06-5*) AAFCO.

1995 ACL Proceedings. pap. 63.00 (*1-55860-384-0*) Morgan Kaufmann.

1995 Advances in Bioengineering, Vol. 31. Ed. by M. L. Hull. (1995 ASME International Mechanical Engineering Congress & Exposition Ser.: BED-Vol. 31). 412p. 1995. 100.00 (*0-7918-1722-9*, H01004) ASME.

1995 Advances in Thermal Spray Science & Technology: Proceedings of the 8th National Thermal Spray Conference. Ed. by C. C. Berndt & S. Sampath. LC 95-211747. 774p. 1995. 108.00 (*0-87170-541-9*, 6537) ASM.

1995 AIAA-IEEE 14th Digital Avionics Systems Conference Proceedings. IEEE, Aerospace & Electronics Systems Society Staf. Ed. by Institute of Electrical & Electronics Engineers, I. LC 95-80703. 350p. 1995. pap. text 116.00 (*0-7803-3050-1*, 95CH35873); lib. bdg. 116.00 (*0-7803-3051-X*, 95CB35873); fiche 116.00 (*0-7803-3052-8*, 95CM35873) Inst Electrical.

1995 Almanac of Hospital Financial & Operating Indicators. William O. Cleverley. 516p. 1995. pap. 350.00 (*1-882733-04-5*) Ctr Hlthcare IPS.

1995 Almanac of Hospital Financial & Operating Indicators. 2nd ed. Timothy Carse & Jeffrey Slater. 1996. text 350.00 (*0-07-413128-1*, Irwn McGrw-H) McGrw-H Hghr Educ.

1995 American Control Conference. IEEE, Control Systems Society Staff. Ed. by IEEE Staff. LC 94-73164. 3700p. 1995. pap. text. write for info. (*0-7803-2445-5*, 95CH35736); lib. bdg. write for info. (*0-7803-2446-3*, 95CH35736); mic. film. write for info. (*0-7803-2447-1*, 95CH35736) Inst Electrical.

1995 & 1996 Report. Ed. by Marie R. Spiller. (Illus.). 64p. 1997. pap. write for info. (*0-933642-26-1*) Intl Ctr Photo.

1995-96 Directory of Key Health Legislators & Legislative Staff. NCSL Health Services Program Staff. 1995. 20.00 (*1-55516-608-3*, 6653) Natl Conf State Legis.

1995 Annual Reliability & Maintainability Symposium. IEEE (Reliability Society) Staff. 652p. 1995. pap. text 100.00 (*0-7803-2470-6*); lib. bdg. 100.00 (*0-7803-2471-4*, 95CB35743); fiche 100.00 (*0-7803-2472-2*, 95CM35743) Inst Electrical.

1995 Annual Index to Motion Picture Credits: Annual Index. Ed. by Byerly Woodward. 375p. 1996. 30.00 (*0-942102-24-X*) Acad Motion Pic.

1995 Annual Survey of Letter of Credit Law & Practice: Survey Handbook. Ed. by James E. Byrne et al. vi, 686p. 1995. pap. 99.00 (*1-888870-03-6*) Inst Intl Bnking.

1995 Annual Technical Session Proceedings. Ed. by James M. Ricles. 240p. (Orig.). 1995. pap. 40.00 (*1-879749-60-2*) Structural Stability.

1995 Federal Antitrust Guidelines for the Licensing of Intellectual Property: Commentary & Text. LC 96-78649. 124p. 1996. pap. 45.00 (*1-57073-350-3*, 503-0291, ABA Antitrust) Amer Bar Assn.

1995 ASME/JSME Fluids Engineering Conference Series, 23 bks., Set. 1995. 560.00 (*0-614-16700-0*, H95781) ASME.

1995 IEEE Autotestcon - Systems Readiness Technology Conference. IEEE, Aerospace & Electronics Systems Society Staf. Ed. by Institute of Electrical & Electronics Engineers, I. LC 95-76244. 750p. 1995. pap. text 138.00 (*0-7803-2621-0*, 95CH35786); lib. bdg. 138.00 (*0-7803-2622-9*, 95CB35786); fiche 138.00 (*0-7803-2623-7*, 95CM35786) Inst Electrical.

1995 Bankruptcy Yearbook & Almanac. 5th ed. Ed. by Christopher M. McHugh. 622p. 1995. pap. 175.00 (*0-9628991-4-3*) New Gen Research.

1995 Bar Activities Inventory. 400p. 1995. pap. 74.95 (*0-89707-661-3*, 171-0066, ABA Bar Servs) Amer Bar Assn.

1995 Bedside Astrologer. Francesca Stuart. LC 93-91010. 240p. (Orig.). 1994. mass mkt. 4.99 (*0-380-77571-9*, Avon Bks) Morrow Avon.

1995 Big Bad Baseball Annual. Brock Henke. 1995. pap. 19.95 (*0-9625846-6-5*) Mad Aztec Pr.

1995 Bioreclamation Symposium Set, 11 bks. 1995. 349.50 (*1-57477-001-2*) Battelle.

1995 Brookman: Price Guide for United States Stamps & Postal Collectibles. David S. MacDonald. 1995. pap. text 14.95 (*0-936937-38-6*) Brookman Stamp.

1995 Accessible Building Product Guide. John P. Salmen & Julee Quarve-Peterson. 335p. 1995. pap. 110.00 (*0-471-10947-9*) Wiley.

1995 Canadian Conference on Electrical & Computer Engineering Conference Proceedings. IEEE (Region Seven) Staff. Ed. by IEEE (Institute of Electrical & Electronics Engine. 1880p. 1995. pap. 216.00 (*0-7803-2766-7*, 95TH8103); fiche 216.00 (*0-7803-2767-5*, 95TM8103) Inst Electrical.

1995 Carburizing & Nitriding with Atmospheres Conference Proceedings. LC 95-81230. 394p. 1995. 98.00 (*0-87170-561-3*, 6464) ASM.

1995 Case Supplement to Legal Regulation of the Competitive Process. Edmund W. Kitch & Harvey S. Perlman. (University Casebook Ser.). 408p. 1995. pap. text 13.50 (*1-56662-295-6*) Foundation Pr.

1995 Challenge Report: Meeting the Challenge: The First Status Report on the Pro Bono Activities of America's Major Law Firms. Esther F. Lardent. 40p. (Orig.). 1997. pap. write for info. (*0-9659548-0-3*) Pro Bono Inst.

1995 China Medical Market Report Vol. 1: An Indepth Market Study on China's Pharmaceutical, Biotechnology & Medical Device Markets. Deborah Miller & Shannon Shi. 100p. (Orig.). 1995. pap. 79.95 (*0-9657889-0-3*) Golden Tri Org.

1995 Coach of the Year Clinics Football Manual. Ed. by Earl Browning. (Illus.). 256p. 1999. pap. 22.95 (*1-57167-406-3*) Coaches Choice.

1995 Comics Scene Presents: Batman. 1995. pap. 5.99 (*0-934551-01-4*) Starlog Grp Inc.

1995 Competitiveness Index. (Illus.). vi, 51p. (Orig.). 1995. pap. 15.00 (*1-889866-15-6*) Coun on Competitiveness.

1995 Complete Guide to Federal & State Benefits for Veterans, their Families & Survivors. Robert L. Berko. LC 94-31413. 240p. pap. 34.72 (*0-934873-16-X*) Consumer Ed Res.

1995 Computers in Cardiology. IEEE (Engineering in Medicine & Biology Society) S. Ed. by IEEE (Institute of Electrical & Electronics Engine. LC 80-641097. 900p. 1995. pap. text 150.00 (*0-7803-3053-6*, 95CH35874); lib. bdg. 150.00 (*0-7803-3054-4*, 95CB35874); fiche 150.00 (*0-7803-3055-2*, 95CM35874) Inst Electrical.

1995 Conference on Computational Intelligence for Financial Engineering. IEEE (Technical Activities Board) Staff. Ed. by IEEE Staff. LC 95-79210. 208p. 1995. pap. text 104.00 (*0-7803-2145-6*, 95TH8013) Inst Electrical.

1995 Conference on Computational Intelligence for Financial Engineering. IEEE (Technical Activities Board) Staff. Ed. by IEEE Staff. LC 95-79210. 1995. fiche 104.00 (*0-7803-2146-4*, 95TM8013) Inst Electrical.

1995 Conference on Lasers & Electro-Optics. LC 95-68677. (Nineteen Ninety-Five Technical Digest Ser.: Vol. 15). 600p. 1995. pap. 92.00 (*1-55752-400-9*, 95CH35800) Optical Soc.

1995 Corporation & Partnership Tax Return Guide. rev. ed. RIA In-House Professional Staff. 142p. 1996. pap. text 11.50 (*0-7811-0131-X*) Res Inst Am.

1995 Crimson Review: The Photographic Review of Indiana Athletics. Ed. & Photos by Garrett Ewald. (Illus.). 232p. 1995. lib. bdg. write for info. (*0-9647981-1-5*) Caravelle Communs.

1995 Crimson Review: The Photographic Review of Indiana Athletics. Ed. & Photos by Garrtt Ewald. (Illus.). 232p. 1995. 56.95 (*0-9647981-0-7*); pap. 34.95 (*0-9647981-2-3*) Caravelle Communs.

1995 CUES Staffing Manual for Credit Unions. 2nd rev. ed. Gary Morehead et al. 102p. 1995. pap. 99.00 (*1-889394-34-3*) Credit Union Execs.

1995 Cumulative Supplement to Connecticut Land Use Regulation. 2nd ed. Terry J. Tondro. 246p. 1995. pap. 55.00 (*1-878698-28-1*) Atlantic Law.

1995 Deposit Accounts Regulation Manual. rev. ed. Kenneth F. Hall. 700p. 1995. 99.00 (*0-8366-0032-0*) West Group.

1995 Deskbook Supplement. Western Attorneys General Conference Staff. 1995. pap. 9.95 (*0-87081-405-2*) Univ Pr Colo.

1995 Development Report Card for the States, Economic Benchmarks for State & Corporate Decisionmakers. 202p. 1995. 35.00 (*1-883187-05-2*) Corp Ent Dev.

1995 Digest of the LEOS Summer Topical Meetings. IEEE (Lasers & Electro-Optics Society) Staff. LC 94-73348. 360p. 1995. pap. 100.00 (*0-7803-2448-X*, 95TH8031); fiche 100.00 (*0-7803-2449-8*, 95TM8031) Inst Electrical.

1995 Digests of Intermag '95. IEEE, Magnetics Society Staff. Ed. by Institute of Electrical & Electronics Engineers, I. LC 72-649866. 1995. pap. text. write for info. (*0-7803-2605-9*); lib. bdg. write for info. (*0-7803-2606-7*); fiche. write for info. (*0-7803-2607-5*, 95CH35782) Inst Electrical.

1995 Directory of Convenience Stores: The Book of C-Store Market Facts. rev. ed. Ed. by Adrienne Toth et al. (Illus.). 648p. 1995. pap. 225.00 (*0-911790-30-6*) Trade Dimensns.

1995 Directory of Mass Merchandisers. rev. ed. Ed. by Adrienne Toth et al. (Illus.). 1994. pap. 199.00 (*0-911790-27-6*) Trade Dimensns.

1995 Directory of Members: American Statistical Association, Bernoulli Society, International Biometric Society: Eastern & Western North American Regions, Institute of Mathematical Statistics, & Statistical Society of Canada. (Orig.). 1995. pap. text 125.00 (*1-883276-02-0*) Amer Statist.

1995 Directory of Solid Workers. 414p. 1995. pap. write for info. (*1-878353-38-1*) Silent Partners.

1995 Directory of State Toxic Contacts. Chuck Costanza et al. 74p. 1995. 10.00 (*0-614-10574-9*, 6466) Natl Conf State Legis.

***1995 Domestic Engine Control Manual.** Keith Kraehmer. (Illus.). 737p. 1998. 120.00 (*1-887023-15-1*) Target Trning.

1995 Dung Annual: The Year of the Newet. Christopher L. Clutter & Legro Bennett. 90p. 1995. mass mkt. 13.30 (*0-9644321-1-0*) Camel Dung Writ.

1995 Eighteenth Convention of Electrical & Electronics Engineers in Israel. IEEE, Israel Section Staff. Ed. by IEEE Staff. 500p. 1995. pap. write for info. (*0-7803-2498-6*, 95TH8044); fiche. write for info. (*0-7803-2499-4*, 95TH8044) Inst Electrical.

1995 18th IEEE/CPMT International Electronic Manufacturing Technology. IEEE Components, Packaging, & Manufacturing Techno. LC 96-226643. 502p. 1996. pap. 122.00 (*0-7803-3622-4*) Inst Electrical.

1995 Electronic Market Data Book. annuals 250p. 1995. pap. text 150.00 (*0-7908-0056-X*) Elec Ind Assn.

1995 Eleventh Annual IEEE Semiconductor Thermal Measurement & Management Symposium. IEEE (Components, Packaging & Manufacturing Techno. Ed. by IEEE (Institute of Electrical & Electronics Engine. 200p. 1995. pap. text. write for info. (*0-7803-2434-X*, 95CH35733); fiche. write for info. (*0-7803-2436-6*, 95CM35733) Inst Electrical.

1995 Eleventh Annual IEEE Semiconductor Thermal Measurement & Management Symposium. IEEE, Components, Packaging & Mfg. Technol Soc. St. Ed. by IEEE Staff. 200p. 1995. lib. bdg. write for info. (*0-7803-2435-8*) Inst Electrical.

1995 Enlargement of the European Union. Ed. by John Redmond. LC 96-29590. 208p. 1997. 72.95 (*1-85521-823-2*, Pub. by Dartmth Pub) Ashgate Pub Co.

1995 National Equestrian Yellow Pages. 437p. 1995. pap. 12.00 (*1-56803-009-6*) G D Hall Co.

1995 ESD Tutorial: 95 TUT. (Illus.). 500p. 1995. pap. 75.00 (*1-878303-45-7*, 95TUT) EOS ESD.

***1995 European Community Convention on Insolvency Proceedings: An Insider's View.** Miguel Virgos. (Forum Internationale Ser.: Vol. 25). 66p. 1998. pap. 30.00 (*90-411-1017-8*) Kluwer Law Intl.

1995 Fall Frontlist Catalog. (Miscellaneous/Catalogs Ser.). 1995. pap. write for info. (*0-442-02192-5*, VNR) Wiley.

1995 Fiduciary Tax Return Guide. rev. ed. RIA In-House Professional Staff. 142p. 1996. pap. text 11.50 (*0-7811-0132-8*) Res Inst Am.

1995 5th International Symposium on the Physical & Failure Analysis of Integrated Circuits Conference Proceedings. IEEE (Electron Devices Society) Staff. LC 95-78165. 300p. 1995. pap. 102.00 (*0-7803-2797-7*, 95TH8113); fiche 102.00 (*0-7803-2798-5*, 95TM8113) Inst Electrical.

1995 53rd Annual Device Research Conference Digest. IEEE (Electron Devices Society) Staff. Ed. by IEEE (Institute of Electrical & Electronics Engine. 150p. 1995. pap. 92.00 (*0-7803-2788-8*, 95TH8109); fiche 92.00 (*0-7803-2789-6*, 95TM8109) Inst Electrical.

1995 First IEEE International Caracas Conference on Devices, Circuits & Systems. IEEE, Venezuela Section Staff. Ed. by Institute of Electrical & Electronics Engineers, I. LC 95-76339. 1200p. 1995. pap. 174.00 (*0-7803-2672-5*, 95TH8074); fiche 174.00 (*0-7803-2673-3*, 95TM8074) Inst Electrical.

1995 First Regional Conference of the IEEE Engineering in Medicine & Biology Society Proceedings. IEEE (Engineering in Medicine & Biology Society) S. Ed. by IEEE (Institute of Electrical & Electronics Engine. 450p. 1995. pap. write for info. (*0-7803-2711-X*, 95TH8089); mic. film. write for info. (*0-7803-2712-8*, 95TH8089) Inst Electrical.

1995 Florida Statistical Abstract. 29th ed. Ed. by Carol L. McLarty et al. 760p. 1995. 44.95 (*0-8130-1375-5*); pap. 29.95 (*0-8130-1376-3*) U Press Fla.

1995 14th Annual International Phoenix Conference on Computers & Communications. IEEE (Communication Society) Staff. LC 87-654239. 600p. 1995. lib. bdg. write for info. (*0-7803-2493-5*, 95CB35751) Inst Electrical.

1995 14th Annual International Phoenix Conference on Computers & Communications. IEEE (Communications Society) Staff. Ed. by IEEE (Institute of Electrical & Electronics Engine. LC 87-654239. 600p. 1995. pap. text. write for info. (*0-7803-2492-7*, 95CH35751); mic. film. write for info. (*0-7803-2494-3*, 95CM35751) Inst Electrical.

1995 Fourteenth Southern Biomedical Engineering Conference. IEEE, Engineering in Medicine & Biology Society St. Ed. by IEEE Staff. LC 94-77907. 350p. 1995. pap. write for info. (*0-7803-2083-2*, 95TH0703-9); fiche. write for info. (*0-7803-2084-0*, 95TH0703-9) Inst Electrical.

1995 Fourth IEEE International Conference on Universal Personal Communications Records. IEEE (Communications Society) Staff. Ed. by IEEE (Institute of Electrical & Electronics Engine. LC 95-79208. 1000p. 1996. pap. 158.00 (*0-7803-2955-4*, 95TH8128); fiche 158.00 (*0-7803-2956-2*, 95TM8128) Inst Electrical.

1995 Fourth International Conference on Solid-State & Integrated Circuit Technology Proceedings. IEEE, Electron Devices Society & Solid-State Circu. Ed. by Institute of Electrical & Electronics Engineers, I. LC 95-80704. 832p. 1995. pap. 158.00 (*0-7803-3062-5*, 95TH8143); fiche 158.00 (*0-7803-3063-3*, 95TM8143) Inst Electrical.

1995 Religious Funding Resource Guide. Ed. by Eileen Paul & Andrea Flores. 500p. 1995. 75.00 (*1-883542-04-9*) ResourceWomen.

1995 Genealogy Annual: A Bibliography of Published Sources. Ed. by Thomas J. Kemp. (Genealogy Annual Ser.). 397p. 1997. 95.00 (*0-8420-2661-4*) Scholarly Res Inc.

1995 Gold Book of Photography Prices. Thomas I. Perrett. (Illus.). 328p. 1995. pap. 39.95 (*0-915827-18-2*) Photo Res Inst Carson Endowment.

1995 Greater Puget Sound Bravo Bridal Resource Guide. 1994. 9.95 (*1-898471-04-5*) Bravo Pubns.

1995 Guide to Coal Contracts. Ed. by Anne Phelan. 690p. (Orig.). 1995. pap. 270.00 (*0-935453-76-8*) Pasha Pubns.

Guide to Federal Funding for Governments & Nonprofits, 2 vols., Set. Ed. by Charles J. Edwards et al. 1995. 339.00 (*0-933544-71-5*) Gov Info Srvs.

1995 Guide to the U. S. Membrane Industry. Crull. 175p. 1995. 1650.00 (*1-56965-319-4*, DMD95) BCC.

1995 Harvard Business School Core Collection: An Author, Title, & Subject Guide. Harvard Business School Press Staff. 1995. pap. text 65.00 (*0-07-103625-3*) McGraw.

1995 Helicopter Annual. Helicopter Assn. International Staff. 352p. 1995. per. write for info. (*0-614-04281-X*) Helicopter Assn Intl.

1995 Help Desk Salary Survey. Ed. by Patrice Rhoades-Baum et al. (Illus.). 52p. (Orig.). pap. write for info. (*1-57125-024-7*) Help Desk Inst.

1995 HEV Challenge: 1996 International Congress & Exposition. LC 96-207881. (Special Publications). 35p. 1996. pap. 59.00 (*1-56091-800-4*, SP-1170) Soc Auto Engineers.

1995 Hong Kong Electron Devices Meeting Proceedings. IEEE (Electron Devices Society) Staff. LC 96-231762. 80p. 1995. pap. 86.00 (*0-7803-2919-8*, 95TH8119); fiche 86.00 (*0-7803-2920-1*, 95TM8119) Inst Electrical.

1995 IEEE Compass. IEEE (Aerospace & Electronic Systems Society) Staf. Ed. by IEEE (Institute of Electrical & Electronics Engine. LC 95-76679. 150p. 1995. pap. text. write for info. (*0-7803-2680-6*, 95CH35802); lib. bdg. write for info. (*0-7803-2681-4*, 95CB35802); mic. film. write for info. (*0-7803-2682-2*, 95CM35802) Inst Electrical.

1995 IEEE - Semi Advanced Semiconductor Manufacturing Conference & Workshop. IEEE (Electron Devices Society & Components, Hybri. Ed. by IEEE (Institute of Electrical & Electronics Engine. 404p. 1995. pap. text 106.00 (*0-7803-2713-6*, 95CH35811); lib. bdg. 106.00 (*0-7803-2714-4*, 95CB35811); fiche 106.00 (*0-7803-2715-2*, 95CM35811) Inst Electrical.

1995 IEEE Annual Textile, Fiber & Film Industry Technical Conference. IEEE (Industry Applications Society) Staff. Ed. by IEEE (Institute of Electrical & Electronics Engine. 80p. 1995. pap. text. write for info. (*0-7803-2689-X*, 95CH35806); lib. bdg. write for info. (*0-7803-2690-3*, 95CH35806); mic. film. write for info. (*0-7803-2691-1*) Inst Electrical.

1995 IEEE Bipolar-BiCMOS Circuits & Technology Meeting Proceedings. IEEE (Electron Devices Society) Staff. LC 95-77998. 218p. 1995. pap. text 98.00 (*0-7803-2778-0*, 95CH35831); lib. bdg. 98.00 (*0-7803-2779-9*, 95CB35831); fiche 98.00 (*0-7803-2780-2*, 95CM35831) Inst Electrical.

1995 IEEE Cement Industry Technical Conference XXXVII. IEEE, Industry Applications Society Staff. Ed. by IEEE Staff. 500p. 1995. pap. text. write for info. (*0-7803-2456-0*, 95CH35740); lib. bdg. write for info. (*0-7803-2457-9*, 95CH35740); fiche. write for info. (*0-7803-2458-7*, 95CM35740) Inst Electrical.

1995 IEEE Conference on Control Applications. IEEE (Control Systems Society) Staff. Ed. by IEEE (Institute of Electrical & Electronics Engine. LC 95-75510. 1200p. 1995. pap. text 162.00 (*0-7803-2550-8*, 95CH35764); lib. bdg. 162.00 (*0-7803-2551-6*, 95CB35764); fiche 162.00 (*0-7803-2552-4*, 95CM35764) Inst Electrical.

1995 IEEE Cornell Conference on Advanced Concepts in High-Speed Semiconductor Devices & Circuits. IEEE, Electron Devices Society Staff. Ed. by IEEE Staff. 592p. 1995. pap. text 114.00 (*0-7803-2442-0*, 95CH35735); lib. bdg. 114.00 (*0-7803-2443-9*, 95CB35735); fiche 114.00 (*0-7803-2444-7*, 95CM35735) Inst Electrical.

1995 IEEE Engineering in Medicine & Biology 17th Annual Conference: Basic & Applied Biomedical Engineering - Building Block for Health Care. IEEE (Engineering in Medicine & Biology Society) S. Ed. by IEEE (Institute of Electrical & Electronics Engine. LC 94-73760. 2000p. 1995. pap. text 222.00 (*0-7803-2475-7*, 95CH35746); lib. bdg. 222.00 (*0-7803-2476-5*, 95CB35746); fiche 222.00 (*0-7803-2477-3*, 95CM35746); cd-rom 222.00 (*0-7803-2478-1*, 95CH35746) Inst Electrical.

1995 IEEE Globecom. IEEE (Communication Society) Staff. Ed. by IEEE (Institute of Electrical & Electronics Engine. LC 87-640337. 2600p. 1995. lib. bdg. 276.00 (*0-7803-2510-9*, 95CB35756) Inst Electrical.

1995 IEEE Globecom. IEEE (Communications Society) Staff. Ed. by IEEE (Institute of Electrical & Electronics Engine. LC 87-640337. 2600p. 1995. pap. text 276.00 (*0-7803-2509-5*, 95CH35756); mic. film 276.00 (*0-7803-2511-7*, 95CM35756) Inst Electrical.

1995 IEEE Instrumentation & Measurement Technology Conference. IEEE, Instrumentation & Measurement Society Staff. Ed. by IEEE, Institute of Electrical & Electronics Engine. LC 95-79751. 750p. 1995. pap. text. write for info. (*0-7803-2615-6*, 95CH35783); lib. bdg. write for info. (*0-7803-2616-4*, 95CH35783); fiche. write for info. (*0-7803-2617-2*, 95CH35783) Inst Electrical.

1995 IEEE Intelligent Vehicles Symposium. IEEE (Industrial Electronics Society) Staff. Ed. by IEEE (Institute of Electrical & Electronics Engine. LC 95-79386. 600p. 1995. pap. 126.00 (*0-7803-2983-X*, 95TH8132); mic. film 126.00 (*0-7803-2984-8*, 95TM8132) Inst Electrical.

1995 IEEE Internationl Conference on Communications. IEEE (Communications Society) Staff. Ed. by IEEE (Institute of Electrical & Electronics Engine. LC 81-649547. 2086p. 1995. pap. text 232.00 (*0-7803-2486-2*, 95CH35749) Inst Electrical.

1995 IEEE International Conference on Communications. IEEE (Communications Society) Staff. Ed. by IEEE (Institute of Electrical & Electronics Engine. LC 81-649547. 2086p. 1995. lib. bdg. 232.00 (*0-7803-2487-0*, 95CB35749); mic. film 232.00 (*0-7803-2488-9*, 95CM35749) Inst Electrical.

1995 IEEE International Test Conference Proceedings. IEEE (Computer Society) Staff. Ed. by IEEE (Institute of Electrical & Electronics Engine. LC 95-79385. 1024p. 1995. pap. text 166.00 (*0-7803-2991-0*, 95CH35858); lib. bdg. 166.00 (*0-7803-2992-9*, 95CB35858); fiche 166.00 (*0-7803-2993-7*, 95CM35858) Inst Electrical.

1995 IEEE International Symposium on Electromagnetic Compatibility. IEEE (Electromagnetic Comopatibility Society) Staf. Ed. by IEEE (Institute of Electrical & Electronics Engine. LC 83-645449. 680p. 1995. pap. text 126.00 (*0-7803-2573-7*, 95CN35772); lib. bdg. 126.00 (*0-7803-2574-5*, 95CB35772); fiche 126.00 (*0-7803-2575-3*, 95CM35772) Inst Electrical.

1995 IEEE International SOI Conference Proceedings. IEEE (Electron Devicers Society) Staff. Ed. by IEEE (Institute of Electrical & Electronics Engine. LC 95-75507. 236p. 1995. pap. text 92.00 (*0-7803-2547-8*, 95CH35763); lib. bdg. 92.00 (*0-7803-2548-6*, 95CB35763); fiche 92.00 (*0-7803-2549-4*, 95CM35763) Inst Electrical.

1995 IEEE International Symposium on Semiconductor Manufacturing. IEEE (Electron Devices Society & Components, Hybri. Ed. by IEEE (Institute of Electrical & Electronics Engine. LC 95-78629. 350p. 1995. pap. text 106.00 (*0-7803-2928-7*, 95CH35841); lib. bdg. 106.00 (*0-7803-2929-5*, 95CB35841); fiche 106.00 (*0-7803-2930-9*, 95CM35841) Inst Electrical.

1995 IEEE International Engineering Management Conference Proceedings. IEEE (Engineering Management Society) Staff. Ed. by IEEE (Institute of Electrical & Electronics Engine. 438p. 1995. pap. text 110.00 (*0-7803-2799-3*, 95CH35837); lib. bdg. 110.00 (*0-7803-2900-7*, 95CB35837); fiche 110.00 (*0-7803-2901-5*, 95CM35837) Inst Electrical.

1995 IEEE International Symposium on Industrial Electronics. IEEE (Industrial Electronics Society) Staff. Ed. by IEEE (Institute of Electrical & Electronics Engine. LC 95-76682. 1200p. 1995. pap. write for info. (*0-7803-2683-0*, 95TH8081); mic. film. write for info. (*0-7803-2684-9*, 95TH8081) Inst Electrical.

1995 IEEE International Workshop on Robot & Human Communication Proceedings. IEEE (Industrial Electronics Society) Staff. Ed. by IEEE (Institute of Electrical & Electronics Engine. 400p. 1995. pap. 110.00 (*0-7803-2904-X*, 95TH8115); fiche 110.00 (*0-7803-2905-8*, 95TM8115) Inst Electrical.

1995 IEEE International Professional Communication Conference IPCC 95 Proceedings. IEEE (Professional Communication Society) Staff. Ed. by IEEE (Institute of Electrical & Electronics Engine. LC 95-179311. 264p. 1995. pap. text 118.00 (*0-7803-2957-0*, 95CH35848); lib. bdg. 118.00 (*0-7803-2958-9*, 95CB35848); mic. film 118.00 (*0-7803-2959-7*, 95CM35848) Inst Electrical.

1995 IEEE International Conference on Image Processing. IEEE (Signal Processing Society) Staff. Ed. by IEEE (Institute of Electrical & Electronics Engine. LC 95-77540. 2500p. 1995. pap. text 300.00 (*0-7803-2733-0*, 95CH35819); lib. bdg. 300.00 (*0-7803-3122-2*, 95CH35819); fiche 300.00 (*0-7803-2735-7*, 95CM35819); cd-rom 300.00 (*0-7803-2749-7*, 95CH35819) Inst Electrical.

1995 IEEE International Solid State Circuits Conference Digest of Technical Papers. IEEE (Solid State Circuits Council) Staff. Ed. by IEEE (Institute of Electrical & Electronics Engine. LC 81-644810. 400p. 1995. pap. text. write for info. (*0-7803-2495-1*, 95CH35753); lib. bdg. write for info. (*0-7803-2496-X*, 95CH35753) Inst Electrical.

1995 IEEE International Symposium on Low Power Electronics - Digest of Technical Papers. IEEE (Solid-State Circuits Council) Staff. Ed. by IEEE (Institute of Electrical & Electronics Engine. LC 95-80264. 125p. 1995. pap. 90.00 (*0-7803-3036-6*, 95TH8138); fiche 90.00 (*0-7803-3037-4*, 95TM8138) Inst Electrical.

1995 IEEE International Conference on Systems, Man & Cybernetics. IEEE (Systems, Man & Cybernetics Society) Staff. Ed. by IEEE (Institute of Electrical & Electronics Engine. LC 95-75508. 5028p. 1995. pap. text 452.00 (*0-7803-2559-1*, 95CH35767); lib. bdg. 452.00 (*0-7803-2560-5*, 95CB35767); fiche 452.00 (*0-7803-2561-3*, 95CM35767) Inst Electrical.

1995 IEEE International Symposium on Power Semiconductor Devices & ICs. IEEE, Electron Devices Society Staff. Ed. by Institute of Electrical & Electronics Engineers, I. LC 95-76245. 350p. 1995. pap. text. write for info. (*0-7803-2618-0*, 95CH35785); lib. bdg. write for info. (*0-7803-2619-9*, 95CH35785); mic. film. write for info. (*0-7803-2620-2*, 95CH35785) Inst Electrical.

1995 IEEE International Workshop on Factory Communication Systems - WFCS '95. IEEE, Industrial Electronics Society Staff. Ed. by Institute of Electrical & Electronics Engineers, I. LC 95-80705. 250p. 1995. pap. 98.00 (*0-7803-3059-5*, 95TH8141); fiche 98.00 (*0-7803-3060-9*, 95TM8141) Inst Electrical.

1995 IEEE International Conference on Evolutionary Computation. IEEE, Neural Networks Council Staff. Ed. by Institute of Electrical & Electronics Engineers, I. LC 95-77674. 1500p. 1995. pap. 198.00 (*0-7803-2759-4*, 95TH8099); fiche 198.00 (*0-7803-2760-8*, 95TM8099) Inst Electrical.

1995 IEEE International Symposium on Electronics & the Environment. IEEE, Technical Activities Board Staff. Ed. by IEEE Staff. LC 94-79212. 336p. 1995. pap. text 96.00 (*0-7803-2137-5*, 95CH35718); lib. bdg. 96.00 (*0-7803-2138-3*, 95CB35718); fiche 96.00 (*0-7803-2139-1*, 95CM35718) Inst Electrical.

1995 IEEE LEOS Annual Meeting. IEEE (Lasers & Electro-Optics Society) Staff. LC 94-73347. 856p. 1995. pap. text 136.00 (*0-7803-2450-1*, 95CH35739); lib. bdg. 136.00 (*0-7803-2451-X*, 95CB35739); fiche 136.00 (*0-7803-2452-8*, 95CM35739) Inst Electrical.

1995 IEEE Micro Electro Mechanical Systems. IEEE (Robotics & Automation) Staff. Ed. by IEEE (Institute of Electrical & Electronics Engine. 450p. 1995. pap. text. write for info. (*0-7803-2503-6*, 95CH35754); lib. bdg. write for info. (*0-7803-2504-4*, 95CH35754) Inst Electrical.

1995 IEEE MTT-S International Microwave Symposium Digest. IEEE, Microwave Theory & Techniques Society & Comp. Ed. by Institute of Electrical & Electronics Engineers, I. LC 77-645125. 1995. pap. text. write for info. (*0-7803-2581-8*, 95CH35774); lib. bdg. write for info. (*0-7803-2582-6*, 95CH35774) Inst Electrical.

1995 IEEE National Telesystems Conference: The Microwave Systems Conference. IEEE (Aerospace & Electronic Systems Society) Staf & IEEE (Microwave Theory & Techniques Society, Elect. Ed. by Institute of Electrical & Electronics Engineers, I. LC 95-76065. 1995. pap. text. write for info. (*0-7803-2593-1*, 95CH35778); lib. bdg. write for info. (*0-7803-2594-X*, 95CB35778); fiche. write for info. (*0-7803-2595-8*, 95CM35778) Inst Electrical.

1995 IEEE Nuclear Science Symposium. IEEE (Nuclear & Plasma Sciences Society) Staff. Ed. by IEEE (Institute of Electrical & Electronics Engine. LC 96-75063. 1500p. 1996. pap. text 248.00 (*0-7803-3180-X*, 95CH35898); lib. bdg. 248.00 (*0-7803-3181-8*, 95CB35898); fiche 248.00 (*0-7803-3182-6*, 95CM35898) Inst Electrical.

1995 IEEE Pacific Rim Conference on Communications, Computers & Signal Processing. IEEE (Region Seven) Staff. Ed. by IEEE Staff. LC 90-655140. 400p. 1995. pap. text. write for info. (*0-7803-2553-2*, 95CH35765); lib. bdg. write for info. (*0-7803-2554-0*, 95Ch35765); mic. film. write for info. (*0-7803-2555-9*, 95CH35765) Inst Electrical.

1995 IEEE Radiation Effects Data Workshop. IEEE (Nuclear & Plasma Sciences Society Staff. Ed. by IEEE (Institute of Electrical & Electronics Engine. LC 95-81501. 180p. 1996. fiche 94.00 (*0-7803-3101-X*, 95TM8149) Inst Electrical.

1995 IEEE Radiation Effects Data Workshop. IEEE (Nuclear & Plasma Sciences Society) Staff. Ed. by IEEE (Institute of Electrical & Electronics Engine. LC 95-81501. 114p. 1995. pap. 94.00 (*0-7803-3100-1*, 95TH8149) Inst Electrical.

1995 IEEE Singapore International Conference on Networks/International Conference on Information Engineering. IEEE, Singapore Section Staff. Ed. by Institute of Electrical & Electronics Engineers, I. LC 95-75915. 1000p. 1995. pap. 158.00 (*0-7803-2579-6*, 95TH8061); fiche 158.00 (*0-7803-2580-X*, 95TM8061) Inst Electrical.

1995 IEEE Symposium on Emerging Technologies & Factory Automation. IEEE (Industrial Electronics Society) Staff. Ed. by IEEE Staff. LC 95-75166. 1966p. 1995. pap. 250.00 (*0-7803-2535-4*, 95TH8056); fiche 250.00 (*0-7803-2536-2*, 95TM8056) Inst Electrical.

1995 IEEE Tencon - IEEE Region Ten International Conference on Microelectronics & VLSI. IEEE, Region Ten Staff. Ed. by Institute of Electrical & Electronics Engineers, I. LC 95-76247. 516p. 1996. pap. text 126.00 (*0-7803-2624-5*, 95CB35787); lib. bdg. 126.00 (*0-7803-2625-3*, 95CB35787); fiche 126.00 (*0-7803-2626-1*, 95CM35787) Inst Electrical.

1995 IEEE Ultrasonics Symposium Proceedings. IEEE, Ultrasonics, Ferroelectrics & Frequency Cont. 2000p. 1996. pap. text 236.00 (*0-7803-2940-6*, 95CH35844); lib. bdg. 236.00 (*0-7803-2941-4*, 95CB35844); fiche 236.00 (*0-7803-2942-2*, 95CM35844) Inst Electrical.

1995 IEEE Wescanex: Communications, Power & Computing. IEEE, Region 7 Staff. Ed. by IEEE Staff. 1995. pap. text. write for info. (*0-7803-2725-X*); lib. bdg. write for info. (*0-7803-2726-8*, 95CH35816); mic. film. write for info. (*0-7803-2727-6*); cd-rom. write for info. (*0-7803-2741-1*) Inst Electrical.

1995 IEEE Workshop on Applications of Signal Processing to Audio & Acoustics. IEEE (Signal Processing Society) Staff. Ed. by IEEE (Institute of Electrical & Electronics Engine. 250p. 1995. pap. 98.00 (*0-7803-3064-1*, 95TH8144); fiche 98.00 (*0-7803-3065-X*, 95TM8144) Inst Electrical.

1995 IEEE 45th Vehicular Technology Conference. IEEE Staff. LC 83-645418. 800p. 1995. pap. text 156.00 (*0-7803-2742-X*, 95CH35821); lib. bdg. 156.00 (*0-7803-2743-8*, 95CB35821); fiche 156.00 (*0-7803-2744-6*, 95CM35821) Inst Electrical.

1995 Individual Tax Return Guide. rev. ed. RIA In-House Professional Staff. 160p. 1996. pap. text 11.50 (*0-7811-0130-1*) Res Inst Am.

1995 Information Systems Spending: An Analysis of Trends & Strategies. Ed. by Anne Zalatan. 340p. 1995. ring bd. 895.00 (*0-945052-27-8*) Computer Econ.

1995 Interdisciplinary Conference On: Knowledge Tools for a Sustainable Civilization. IEEE (Social Implications of Technology) Staff. Ed. by IEEE (Institute of Electrical & Electronics Engine. LC 97-124337. 400p. 1996. pap. 120.00 (*0-7803-3365-9*, 95TH8194); fiche 120.00 (*0-7803-3366-7*, 96TM8194) Inst Electrical.

1995 IEEE International Conference on Neural Networks Proceedings. IEEE (Neural Networks Council) Staff. Ed. by IEEE (Institute of Electrical & Electronics Engine. LC 95-77907. 2500p. 1995. pap. text 374.00 (*0-7803-2768-3*, 95CH35828); lib. bdg. 374.00 (*0-7803-2769-1*, 95CB35828); fiche 374.00 (*0-7803-2770-5*, 95CM35828) Inst Electrical.

1995 International Conference on Bond Graph Modeling & Simulation. Ed. by Cellier & Granda. 310p. 1995. 100.00 (*1-56555-037-4*, SS-27-1) Soc Computer Sim.

1995 International Conference on Advanced Technologies - at '95. IEEE (Electron Devices Society) Staff. Ed. by IEEE (Institute of Electrical & Electronics Engine. LC 95-78786. 50p. 1995. pap. 84.00 (*0-7803-2943-0*, 95TH8124); fiche 84.00 (*0-7803-2944-9*, 95TM8124) Inst Electrical.

1995 International Conference on Energy Management & Power Delivery. IEEE (Singapore Power Chapter) Staff. Ed. by IEEE (Institute of Electrical & Electronics Engine. LC 95-79383. 1080p. 1995. pap. 164.00 (*0-7803-2981-3*, 95TH8130); fiche 164.00 (*0-7803-2982-1*, 95TM8130) Inst Electrical.

1995 International Conference on Power Electronics & Drive Systems. IEEE (Singapore Section, Power Electronics Society. Ed. by IEEE (Institute of Electrical & Electronics Engine. LC 94-79802. 1000p. 1994. fiche. write for info. (*0-7803-2424-2*, 95TH8025) Inst Electrical.

1995 International Conference on Electromagnetic Interference & Compatibility (INCEMIC) IEEE, Madras Section Staff. 508p. 1995. pap. 110.00 (*0-7803-3229-6*, 95TH8121); fiche 110.00 (*0-7803-2939-2*, 95TM8121) Inst Electrical.

1995 International Conference on Power Electronics & Drive Systems. IEEE Singapore Sect. Power Electronics Society Sta. Ed. by IEEE Staff. LC 94-79802. 1000p. 1994. pap. write for info. (*0-7803-2423-4*) Inst Electrical.

1995 International Electron Devices Meeting. IEEE (Electron Devices Society) Staff. Ed. by IEEE (Institute of Electrical & Electronics Engine. LC 81-642284. 980p. 1995. pap. text 156.00 (*0-7803-2700-4*, 95CH35810); lib. bdg. 156.00 (*0-7803-2701-2*, 95CB35810); mic. film 156.00 (*0-7803-2702-0*, 95CM35810) Inst Electrical.

1995 International Electronics Packaging Conference Proceedings, Vol. 15. (Illus.). 825p. (Orig.). pap. 115.00 (*1-880433-17-6*) Intl Elect Pack.

1995 International Fiber Optics Yellow Pages. annuals rev. ed. 300p. 1996. pap. 89.95 (*1-56851-006-3*) Info Gatekeepers.

1995 International Geoscience & Remote Sensing Symposium Proceedings. IEEE, Geoscience & Remote Sensing Society Staff. Ed. by Institute of Electrical & Electronics Engineers, I. LC 95-75916. 2500p. 1995. pap. text 276.00 (*0-7803-2567-2*, 95CH35770); lib. bdg. 276.00 (*0-7803-2568-0*, 95CB35770); fiche 276.00 (*0-7803-2569-9*, 95CM35770) Inst Electrical.

1995 International Integrated Reliability Workshop - Final Report. IEEE Staff. LC 95-77004. 200p. 1996. pap. 96.00 (*0-7803-2705-5*, 95TH8086); fiche 96.00 (*0-7803-2706-3*, 95TM8086) Inst Electrical.

1995 International ISDN Yellow Pages. annuals rev. ed. 200p. 1996. pap. 49.95 (*1-56851-005-5*) Info Gatekeepers.

1995 International ISDN Yellow Pages. annuals 6th ed. 1995. 69.95 (*0-614-18410-X*, 126YP2) Info Gatekeepers.

1995 International Jt Power Generation Conference, 4 bks., Set. 1996. write for info. (*0-614-16701-9*) ASME.

1995 ASME International Mechanical Engineering Congress & Exposition Vol. 34: Heat Pump & Refrigeration Systems Design, Analysis & Applications - 1995. Ed. by D. L. O'Neal et al. 240p. 88.00 (*0-614-97062-8*, H01001) ASME.

1995 International Mechanical Engineering Congress & Exposition - Proceedings of the ASME Heat Transfer Division, Vol. 1. Ed. by R. J. Cochran et al. 488p. 110.00 (*0-614-97063-6*, H1032A) ASME.

1995 International Mechanical Engineering Congress & Exposition - Proceedings of the ASME Heat Transfer Division, Vol. 2. Ed. by A. Atreya et al. 592p. 150.00 (*0-614-97064-4*, H1032B) ASME.

1995 International Microelectronics Conference (ICVM) IEEE, Electron Devices Society Staff. Ed. by IEEE Staff. LC 94-79211. 200p. 1995. pap. 88.00 (*0-7803-2143-X*, 95TH8012); fiche 88.00 (*0-7803-2144-8*, 95TM8012) Inst Electrical.

1995 International Power Electronics Congress - CIEP. IEEE (Power Electronics Society) Staff. Ed. by IEEE (Institute of Electrical & Electronics Engine. LC 96-226207. 180p. 1995. pap. 94.00 (*0-7803-3071-4*, 95TH8145); mic. film 94.00 (*0-7803-3072-2*, 95TM8145) Inst Electrical.

1995 International Semiconductor Conference. IEEE, Electron Devices Society Staff. Ed. by Institute of Electrical & Electronics Engineers, I. LC 95-76251. 642p. 1995. pap. 126.00 (*0-7803-2647-4*, 95TH8071); fiche 126.00 (*0-7803-2648-2*, 95TM8071) Inst Electrical.

1995 International Symposium on VLSI Technology, Systems & Applications Proceedings of Technical Papers. IEEE (Computer Society, Electron Devices Society). Ed. by IEEE (Institute of Electrical & Electronics Engine. 380p. 1995. pap. write for info. (*0-7803-2773-X*, 95TH8104); mic. film. write for info. (*0-7803-2774-8*, 95TM8104) Inst Electrical.

1995 International Symposium on Electrical Insulating Materials. IEEE (Dielectrics & Electrical Insulation Society). Ed. by IEEE Staff. 600p. 1995. pap. 118.00 (*0-7803-2464-1*, 95TH8036); pap. 118.00 (*4-88686-047-8*, 95TH8036); fiche 118.00 (*0-7803-2465-X*, 95TM8036) Inst Electrical.

1995 International Symposium on Signals, Systems & Electronics. IEEE, Microwave Theory & Techniques Society & Comp. Ed. by IEEE Staff. LC 94-74516. 612p. 1995. pap. 136.00 (*0-7803-2516-8*, 95TH8047) Inst Electrical.

1995 International Travel Health Guide. Stuart R. Rose. 1994. pap. text 17.95 (*0-923947-06-X*) Travel Med.

1995 ISHM Industry Guide. 1995. pap. write for info. (*0-930815-43-2*) Intl Soc Hybrid.

Numerical Methods in Structural Mechanics, Vol. 2. Ed. by J. W. Ju. LC 95-77177. (1995 Joint ASME Applied Mechanics & Materials Summer Meeting Ser.: Vol. 204). 248p. 1995. 108.00 (*0-7918-1319-3*, H00951) ASME.

Recent Advances in Composite Materials Vol. 56: Recent Advances in Composite Materials. Ed. by S. R. White et al. LC 95-77176. (1995 Joint ASME Applied Mechanics & Materials Summer Meeting Ser.: Vol. 56). 260p. 1995. 108.00 (*0-7918-1314-2*, H00946) ASME.

N

Plastic & & Fracture Instabilities in Materils Vol. 200-57: Plastic & & Fracture Instabilities in Materials. Ed. by Nasr Ghoniem. LC 95-77291. (1995 Joint ASME Applied Mechanics & Materials Summer Meeting Ser.: Vol. 200). 236p. 1995. 108.00 (*0-7918-1315-0*, H00947) ASME.

Current Research in the Thermo-Mechanics of Polymers in the Rubbery-Glassy Range - 1995 Vol. 203: Current Research in the Thermo-Mechanics of Polymers in the Rubbery-Glassy Range - 1995. Ed. by Mehrdad Negahban. LC 95-77199. (1995 Joint ASME Applied Mechanics & Materials Summer Meeting Ser.: Vol. 203). 184p. 1995. 100.00 (*0-7918-1318-5*, H00950) ASME.

1995 Kentucky Media Guide. Bluegrass Chapter, Society of Professional Journal. 94p. 11.50 (*1-883589-22-3*) Clark Pub KY.

1995 Laser Video Disc Companion. Douglas R. Pratt. Ed. by Lee Royle & Peter Hajduk. 972p. (Orig.). 1995. pap. 39.95 (*0-918432-90-1*) Baseline Bks.

1995 Latin American Market Planning Handbook. Strategy Research Corporation Staff. 138p. (C). 1995. pap. write for info. (*1-888520-02-7*) Strategy Research.

1995 Legislative Council Elections in Hong Kong. Tr. by Kuan Hsin-Chi et al. 437p. 1997. pap. text 36.00 (*962-441-532-3*, Pub. by Chinese Univ of Hong Kong) St Mut.

1995 Local Telecommunications Competition. 1995. 2995.00 (*0-614-26468-5*) Info Gatekeepers.

1995 Machine Learning Proceedings. pap. 69.95 (*1-55860-377-8*) Morgan Kaufmann.

1995 Managers, Vol. 1. Frankel. 1995. 48.50 (*0-316-29125-0*) Little.

1995 Managers, Vol. 2. Frankel. 1995. 48.50 (*0-316-29128-5*) Little.

1995 Managers, Vol. 3. Frankel. 1995. 48.50 (*0-316-29132-3*) Little.

1995 Managers, Vol. 4. Frankel. 1995. 48.50 (*0-316-29135-8*) Little.

1995 Market Scope. 1995. 299.00 (*0-614-03640-2*) Trade Dimensns.

1995 Market Scope: The Desktop Guide to Supermarket Share & Category Sales. Bruce Levene. Ed. by Adrienne Toth et al. (Illus.). 940p. 1995. pap. 299.00 (*0-911790-28-4*) Trade Dimensns.

1995 Market Share Reports for Top 100 Life & Fraternal: Insurance Groups & Companies by State. 185p. 1996. pap. 150.00 (*0-89382-422-4*, MSR-LB) Nat Assn Insurance.

1995 Market Share Reports for Property/Casualty Groups & Companies: Top 10 by Line by State - Top 100 by Line Countrywide. 2nd rev. ed. 418p. (C). 1996. pap. 150.00 (*0-89382-421-6*, MSR-PB) Nat Assn Insurance.

1995 Marketing Guidebook. Ed. by Adrienne Toth et al. 1994. 320.00 (*0-911790-26-8*) Trade Dimensns.

1995 Mercer Guide to Social Security & Medicare Special Edition. 23rd rev. ed. Robert J. Myers et al. (Illus.). 184p. 1995. pap. 7.95 (*1-880754-95-9*) W M Mercer.

1995 Mobil Highway Atlas. H. M. Gousha. 1994. 4.95 (*0-671-89130-8*) S&S Trade.

1995 Mobil Pocket Atlas. H. M. Gousha. 1994. 4.95 (*0-671-89131-6*) S&S Trade.

1995 Music Yearbook. Joel Whitburn. 240p. 1996. pap. 22.95 (*0-7935-6676-2*, 00330233) H Leonard.

1995 Music Yearbook. Joel Whitburn. 256p. 1996. pap. 34.95 (*0-89820-116-0*, 00330233) Record Research.

1995 National Directory of Fire Chiefs & Emergency Departments, Vol. IV. Ed. by Span Publishing, Inc., Staff. Tr. by Laura J. Gross. 1132p. 1995. 49.00 (*1-880245-08-6*) SPAN Pub.

1995 National Directory of Law Enforcement Administrators, Correctional Institutions & Related Agencies, Vol. XXXI. 743p. 1995. 75.00 (*1-880245-10-8*) SPAN Pub.

1995 Neural Networks for Signal Processing, No. 5. IEEE (Signal Processing Society) Staff. Ed. by IEEE (Institute of Electrical & Electronics Engine. LC 95-77353. 650p. 1995. pap. write for info. (*0-7803-2739-X*, 95TH8094); mic. film. write for info. (*0-7803-2740-3*, 95TH8094) Inst Electrical.

1995-96 HomeTech Housebuilders Cost Estimator. Ed. by Henry Reynolds. (Illus.). (Orig.). 1995. pap. 69.50 (*1-882379-17-9*) HomeTech Info Systs.

1995-1996 Help Desk Buyers Guide. Ed. by Patrice Rhoades-Baum et al. (Illus.). 128p. (Orig.). pap. write for info. (*1-57125-052-2*) Help Desk Inst.

1995-1996 Irvine Spectrum Business Directory. rev. ed. Ed. by Bruce Clumpher. 184p. 1995. pap. text 39.95 (*0-9639578-1-3*) Coris Quill.

1995-96 Greeting Card Industry Directory: A Comprehensive Guide to the Products & Services of the Greeting Card Industry. 8th ed. Marianne McDermott. Ed. by Mila Albertson. 276p. (Orig.). 1995. pap. 75.00 (*0-938369-25-3*) Greeting Card Assn.

1995-96 Guide to Small Group Resources. Judy Hamlin. 400p. 1995. pap. 16.99 (*1-56476-496-6*, 6-3496, Victor Bks) Chariot Victor.

1995-96 Price Reference Handbook. 2nd ed. Kevin Timothy. Ed. by Joanne Collison. 96p. (Orig.). pap. 7.95 (*88-379-6075-1*) What It Is.

1995 Oceans. IEEE (Oceanic Engineering Society) Staff. Ed. by IEEE (Institute of Electrical & Electronics Engine. 2100p. 1995. lib. bdg. 310.00 (*0-7803-3042-0*, 95CB35870); fiche 310.00 (*0-7803-3043-9*, 95CM35870) Inst Electrical.

1995 Office Computing Bible: Using Personal Computers at Work. Nancy E. Dunn. (Illus.). 575p. 1999. reprint ed. pap. text 15.00 (*0-7881-6502-X*) DIANE Pub.

1995 Offshore Mechanics & Arctic Engineering Conference Vol. 1, Pt. A: Offshore Technology Symposium. Ed. by S. K. Chakrabarti et al. LC 82-70515. (OMAE 1995 Ser.). 524p. 1995. 170.00 (*0-7918-1306-1*, H00938) ASME.

1995 Offshore Mechanics & Arctic Engineering Conference Vol. 1, Pt. B: Offshore Technology Symposium. Ed. by S. K. Chakrabarti et al. 540p. 1995. 170.00 (*0-7918-1307-X*, H93839) ASME.

1995 Online/Internet Industry Review. (Report Ser.: No. DDI95). 305p. 1996. 1500.00 (*1-56965-412-3*) BCC.

1995 Pacific Rim Computer Law Conference. Ed. by Computer Law Association Staff. 500p. 1995. 80.00 (*1-885169-01-9*) Computer Law.

1995 Pacific Rim Transtech Conference. IEEE (Vehicular Technology Society) Staff. Ed. by IEEE (Institute of Electrical & Electronics Engine. LC 95-76064. 304p. 1995. pap. 104.00 (*0-7803-2610-5*, 95TH8064); fiche 104.00 (*0-7803-2611-3*, 95TM8064) Inst Electrical.

1995 Physician Salary Survey Report. annuals 19th ed. 1995. pap. 250.00 (*0-939326-88-4*) Hosp & Hlthcare.

1995 Pocket Book of Infectious Disease Therapy. 6th ed. John G. Bartlett. 282p. 1995. pap. 13.95 (*0-683-00445-X*) Lppncott W & W.

1995 Portland-Vancouver-Salem Bravo Bridal Resource Guide. 1994. 9.95 (*1-898471-05-3*) Bravo Pubns.

1995 Price Guide Annual. Jon R. Warren. 288p. 1994. write for info. (*0-9647033-0-0*) Wizard Pr NY.

1995 Proceedings of the 41st Annual Technical Meeting of the Institute of Environmental Sciences & Technology, Product Reliability - Design, Test & Evaluation: Developing Future Leaders of Technology. IEST Staff. 325p. 1995. pap. 115.00 (*1-877862-43-6*) IEST.

1995 Proceedings of the 34th SICE Annual Conference. IEEE (Industrial Electronics Society, Tokyo Sectio. Ed. by IEEE (Institute of Electrical & Electronics Engine. 450p. 1995. pap. write for info. (*0-7803-2781-0*, 95TH8107) Inst Electrical.

1995 Proceedings 45th Electronic Components & Technology Conference. IEEE Staff. LC 78-647174. 1995. pap. text. write for info. (*0-7803-2736-5*); lib. bdg. write for info. (*0-7803-2737-3*, 95CH35820); mic. film. write for info. (*0-7803-2738-1*) Inst Electrical.

1995 Program Directory: Educational Opportunities & Resources Pertaining to Hungary. rev. ed. Hungarian American Coalition Staff. 60p. 1995. write for info. (*0-9640129-0-1*) Hungarian Amer.

1995 Quantum Electronics & Laser Science (QELS) LC 95-68679. (Nineteen Ninety-Five Technical Digest Ser.: Vol. 16). 350p. 1995. pap. 92.00 (*1-55752-402-5*, 95CH35799) Optical Soc.

1995 Quantum Electronics & Laser Science Conference. IEEE, Lasers & Electro-Optics Society Staff. Ed. by Institute of Electrical & Electronics Engineers, I. 325p. 1995. lib. bdg. write for info. (*0-7803-2661-X*, 95CB35799); fiche. write for info. (*0-7803-2662-8*, 95CM35799) Inst Electrical.

1995 Quick Look Drug Book. Leonard L. Lance et al. 729p. 1995. pap. 34.00 (*0-683-07046-0*) Lppncott W & W.

1995 IEEE Radiation Effects Data Workshop (NSREC '95) I. E. E. E. Nuclear & Plasma Sciences Society Staf. Ed. by I. E. E. E. Institute of Electrical & Electronics. LC 95-81040. 600p. 1996. pap. write for info. (*0-7803-3093-5*, 95TH8149); fiche. write for info. (*0-7803-3094-3*, 95TM8149) Inst Electrical.

1995 Raoul Wallenberg Lecture: Daniel Libeskind: Traces of the Unborn. Daniel Libeskind & Annette W. LeCuyer. (Illus.). 50p. (Orig.). (C). 1995. pap. text 11.50 (*0-9614792-1-3*) U Mich Arch.

1995 Redstone Diary. Ed. by Stephen Frears. (Illus.). 1994. spiral bd. 18.99 (*1-85242-335-8*) Serpents Tail.

1995 Retail Tenant Directory. rev. ed. Ed. by Adrienne Toth et al. 1995. pap. 325.00 (*0-911790-29-2*) Trade Dimensns.

1995 RNNS-IEEE Symposium on Neuroinformatics & Neurocomputers. IEEE, Neural Networks Council Staff. Ed. by IEEE Staff. LC 94-74518. 508p. 1995. pap. 132.00 (*0-7803-2512-5*, 95TH8045); fiche 132.00 (*0-7803-2513-3*, 95TM8045) Inst Electrical.

1995 Mobil Road Atlas Trip Planning Guide. H. M. Gousha. 1994. 7.95 (*0-671-89132-4*) S&S Trade.

1995 Salaries & Benefits of Transportation Engineers in North America. ITE Survey Staff. (Illus.). 19p. 1995. pap. text 35.00 (*0-935403-15-9*, PP-050) Inst Trans Eng.

1995 SBMO - IEEE MTT-S International Microwave & Optoelectronics Conference. IEEE (Microwave Theory & Techniques Society, Elect. Ed. by IEEE (Institute of Electrical & Electronics Engine. LC 95-76610. 996p. 1995. pap. 158.00 (*0-7803-2674-1*, 95TH8080); fiche 158.00 (*0-7803-2675-X*, 95TM8080) Inst Electrical.

1995 Second International Workshop on Community Networking. IEEE (Communications Society) Staff. Ed. by IEEE (Institute of Electrical & Electronics Engine. LC 97-119321. 340p. 1995. pap. write for info. (*0-7803-2756-X*, 95TH8097); mic. film. write for info. (*0-7803-2757-8*, 95TM8097) Inst Electrical.

1995 Sidereal Astrological Almanac. P. Krishna Warriar et al. 118p. (Orig.). Date not set. pap. text 14.00 (*0-9618070-8-3*) Personal Insight.

1995 Sixth IEEE International Symposium on Personal, Indoor, & Mobile Radio Communications. IEEE (Communications Society) Staff. Ed. by IEEE (Institute of Electrical & Electronics Engine. LC 96-164608. 1478p. 1995. pap. 198.00 (*0-7803-3002-1*, 95TH8135); fiche 198.00 (*0-7803-3003-X*, 95TM8135) Inst Electrical.

1995 6th International Symposium on Micro Machine & Human Science Proceedings. IEEE (Robotics & Automation Society, Industrial El. Ed. by IEEE (Institute of Electrical & Electronics Engine. LC 95-76605. 300p. 1995. pap. 98.00 (*0-7803-2676-8*, 95TH8079); fiche 98.00 (*0-7803-2677-6*, 95TM8079) Inst Electrical.

1995 State Expenditure Report. annuals National Association of State Budget Officers Staff. (Illus.). 133p. 1996. pap. 35.00 (*1-887253-04-1*) NASBD.

1995 State Labor Laws. SHRM Government Affairs Department Staff. 51p. Date not set. pap. 25.00 (*0-939900-71-8*) Soc Human Resc Mgmt.

1995 State Legislation on Native American Issues. Compiled by Kimberly A. Morin. 35p. 1994. pap. 15.00 (*1-55516-923-6*, 9374) Natl Conf State Legis.

1995 State Legislative Summary: Children, Youth & Family. 1996. 25.00 (*1-55516-607-5*, 6135) Natl Conf State Legis.

1995 State Legislative Priorities: An Opinion Survey of Leading Lawmakers. NCSL Staff. 45p. 1995. 30.00 (*1-55516-925-2*, 9368) Natl Conf State Legis.

1995 Summer School in High Energy Physics & Cosmology 1995. 400p. 1997. lib. bdg. 60.00 (*981-02-2698-5*) World Scientific Pub.

1995 Supplement to UCC One to Five. Crandall. 1995. 150.00 (*0-316-16029-6*, Aspen Law & Bus) Aspen Pub.

1995 Supplement to Fundamentals of Modern Real Property Law, Suppl. 1. 3rd ed. Roberta R. Kwall. (University Casebook Ser.). 100p. 1995. pap. text 6.50 (*1-56662-307-3*) Foundation Pr.

1995 Supplement to Federal Income Taxation, Cases & Materials, Suppl. 1. 3rd ed. Paul R. McDaniel et al. (University Casebook Ser.). 31p. 1995. pap. text 4.95 (*1-56662-274-3*) Foundation Pr.

1995 Supplement to Securities Regulation, Cases & Materials, Suppl. 3. 7th ed. Joel Seligman. (University Casebook Ser.). 405p. 1996. pap. text 12.95 (*1-56662-285-9*) Foundation Pr.

1995 Supplement to Federal Income Taxation of Partnerships & S Corporations, Suppl. 5. Paul R. McDaniel et al. (University Casebook Ser.). 100p. 1995. pap. text 6.50 (*1-56662-267-0*) Foundation Pr.

1995 Supplement to Federal Income Taxation of Business Organizations, Suppl. 5. Paul R. McDaniel et al. (University Casebook Ser.). 169p. 1995. pap. text 9.50 (*1-56662-266-2*) Foundation Pr.

1995 Supplement to Bankruptcy. Lynn M. LoPucki. 1995. suppl. ed. 75.00 (*0-316-53101-4*, Aspen Law & Bus) Aspen Pub.

1995 Supplement to Cases & Comments on Criminal Procedure. James B. Haddad et al. (University Casebook Ser.). 216p. 1995. pap. text 9.50 (*1-56662-296-4*) Foundation Pr.

1995 Supplement to Cases & Materials on Fundamentals of Corporate Taxation. 3rd ed. Daniel J. Lathrope et al. (University Casebook Ser.). 59p. 1995. pap. text 4.95 (*1-56662-298-0*) Foundation Pr.

1995 Supplement to Cases & Materials on Criminal Justice Administration. 4th ed. Frank W. Miller et al. (University Casebook Ser.). 142p. 1995. pap. text 8.50 (*1-56662-301-4*) Foundation Pr.

1995 Supplement to Cases & Materials on Pleading & Procedure - State & Federal. 7th ed. Geoffrey C. Hazard, Jr. et al. (University Casebook Ser.). 70p. 1995. pap. text 5.50 (*1-56662-319-7*) Foundation Pr.

1995 Supplement to Cases & Materials on Employment Law, Suppl. 1. 3rd ed. Lance M. Liebman & Mark A. Rothstein. (University Casebook Ser.). 50p. 1995. pap. text 3.95 (*1-56662-309-X*) Foundation Pr.

1995 Supplement to Cases & Materials on Federal Courts, Suppl. 1. 9th ed. Charles A. Wright & John B. Oakley. (University Casebook Ser.). 59p. 1995. pap. text 5.50 (*1-56662-278-6*) Foundation Pr.

1995 Supplement to Civil Rights Actions: Section 1983 & Related Statutes. 2nd ed. Peter W. Low & John C. Jeffries, Jr. (University Casebook Ser.). 59p. 1995. pap. text 4.95 (*1-56662-299-9*) Foundation Pr.

1995 Supplement to Connecticut Law of Uninsured & Underinsured Motorist Coverage. Jon Berk & Michael C. Jaindell. 146p. 1995. pap. 56.00 (*1-878698-32-X*) Atlantic Law.

1995 Supplement to Connecticut Law of Torts. Douglass B. Wright et al. 128p. Date not set. pap. 55.00 (*1-878698-30-3*) Atlantic Law.

1995 Supplement to Constitutional Law, Civil LIberty, & Individual Rights. 3rd ed. William Cohen & David J. Danelski. 70p. 1995. pap. text 5.50 (*1-56662-325-1*) Foundation Pr.

1995 Supplement to Constitutional Law, Cases & Materials. 9th ed. Jonathan D. Varat & William Cohen. (University Casebook Ser.). 349p. 1995. pap. text 10.95 (*1-56662-288-3*) Foundation Pr.

1995 Supplement to Criminal Procedure, an Analysis of Cases & Concepts. Charles H. Whitebread & Christopher Slobogin. (University Textbook Ser.). 46p. 1995. pap. text 3.50 (*1-56662-303-0*) Foundation Pr.

1995 Supplement to Criminal Process, Cases, Comment, Questions. 5th ed. Lloyd L. Weinreb. (University Casebook Ser.). 88p. 1995. pap. text 4.95 (*1-56662-305-7*) Foundation Pr.

1995 Supplement to Estate Planning. John R. Price. 1995. suppl. ed. 82.50 (*0-316-71864-5*, Aspen Law & Bus) Aspen Pub.

1995 Supplement to Federal Courts & the Law of Federal-State Relations. 3rd ed. Peter W. Low & John C. Jeffries, Jr. (University Casebook Ser.). 93p. 1995. pap. text 5.95 (*1-56662-300-6*) Foundation Pr.

1995 Supplement to Motion. Herr. 1995. suppl. ed. 65.00 (*0-316-35744-8*, Aspen Law & Bus) Aspen Pub.

1995 Supplement to the Evolving Constitution. Jethro K. Lieberman. 55p. 1995. 14.95 (*0-614-13519-2*) Dialogue.

1995 Supplement to Women & the Law. Gerald E. Frug. (University Casebook Ser.). 148p. 1995. pap. text 7.50 (*1-56662-291-3*) Foundation Pr.

1995 Symposium on VLSI Circuits. IEEE (Solid State Circuits Council) Staff. Ed. by IEEE (Institute of Electrical & Electronics Engine. 140p. 1995. pap. text. write for info. (*0-7803-2599-0*, 95CH35780); lib. bdg. write for info. (*0-7803-2600-8*, 95CH35780); mic. film. write for info. (*0-7803-2601-6*, 95CH35780) Inst Electrical.

1995 Symposium on VLSI Technology. IEEE, Solid State Circuits Council Staff. Ed. by Institute of Electrical & Electronics Engineers, I. LC 90-655131. 1995. pap. text. write for info. (*0-7803-2602-4*); lib. bdg. write for info. (*0-7803-2603-2*, 95CH35781); fiche. write for info. (*0-7803-2604-0*) Inst Electrical.

1995 Tenth Annual Battery Conference on Applications & Advances. IEEE, Aerospace & Electronics Systems Society Staf. Ed. by IEEE Staff. 324p. 1995. pap. 88.00 (*0-7803-2459-5*, 95TH8035) Inst Electrical.

1995 10th International Pulsed Power Conference. IEEE (Nuclear & Plasma Sciences Society) Staff. LC 95-78039. 1750p. 1996. pap. text 218.00 (*0-7803-2790-X*, 95CH35833); lib. bdg. 218.00 (*0-7803-2791-8*, 95CB35833); mic. film 218.00 (*0-7803-2792-6*, 95CM35833) Inst Electrical.

1995 The Lab Manual Source Book. (Illus.). xviii, 168p. 1995. pap. 49.95 (*1-890574-00-7*) BioSupplyNet.

1995 Thirty-Second Design Automation Conference. IEEE (Circuits & Systems Society) Staff. Ed. by IEEE (Institute of Electrical & Electronics Engine. LC 85-644924. 800p. 1995. lib. bdg. write for info. (*0-7803-2716-0*, 95CB35812); mic. film. write for info. (*0-7803-2717-9*, 95CM35812) Inst Electrical.

1995 Timeline of Events: Central & Eastern Europe. Ed. by Anne D. Baylon & Ania Garlitski. (Timeline of Events Ser.). 62p. (Orig.). (C). Date not set. pap. 15.00 (*0-9631515-8-4*) Strategic Decisions.

1995-1996 AAO Yearbook: Osteopathic Vision. Ed. by Myron C. Beal. (Illus.). 205p. (Orig.). (C). 1996. pap. 40.00 (*0-940668-04-1*) Am Acad Osteopathy.

1995-96 Directory of Greeting Card Sales Representatives. 3rd ed. Marianne McDermott. Ed. by Mila Albertson. 124p. 1995. pap. 95.00 (*0-938369-24-5*) Greeting Card Assn.

1995-96 Home Care Salary & Benefits Report. annuals 5th ed. (Orig.). 1995. pap. 250.00 (*0-939326-91-4*) Hosp & Hlthcare.

1995-96 Hospice Salary & Benefits Report. annuals 4th ed. (Orig.). 1995. pap. 195.00 (*0-939326-92-2*) Hosp & Hlthcare.

1995-96 Hospital Salary & Benefits Report. annuals 25th ed. 304p. (Orig.). 1995. pap. 250.00 (*0-939326-90-6*) Hosp & Hlthcare.

1995-96 Management Company Report. 13th ed. 1995. pap. 495.00 (*0-939326-94-9*) Hosp & Hlthcare.

1995-96 Nursing Department Report. annuals 4th ed. 1995. pap. 195.00 (*0-939326-93-0*) Hosp & Hlthcare.

1995-96 Nursing Home Salary & Benefits Report. annuals 17th ed. 1995. pap. 250.00 (*0-939326-89-2*) Hosp & Hlthcare.

1995-96 PIA National Sales Compensation Survey. 195.00 (*0-614-25525-2*, 00HR4451) Print Indus Am.

1995-96 World Wide Guide to Gay Nude Resorts Beaches & Recreation. Alex Summers. (Illus.). 80p. (Orig.). 1995. pap. 14.95 (*1-887895-00-0*) Serengeti Pubng.

1995 Top 25 Lists. 1995. 28.00 (*0-932439-09-8*) Denver Busn Media.

1995 Trial Ethics. Underwood. 1995. 100.00 (*0-316-88826-5*, Aspen Law & Bus) Aspen Pub.

1995 20th International Conference on Microelectronics Proceedings. IEEE (Electron Devices Society) Staff. LC 95-77995. 1000p. 1995. pap. 158.00 (*0-7803-2786-1*, 95TH8108); fiche 158.00 (*0-7803-2787-X*, 95TM8108) Inst Electrical.

1995 U. S. Pharmacopeia & the National Formulary: USP 23-NF18. LC 83-64008. 2391p. 1994. 450.00 (*0-913595-76-4*) US Pharmacopeia.

1995 USENIX Technical Conference Proceedings, New Orleans: New Orleans, LA. 326p. (Orig.). 1995. pap. text 39.00 (*1-880446-67-7*) USENIX Assn.

1995 Vehicle Navigation & Information Systems Conference Proceedings. IEEE (Vehicular Technology Society) Staff. Ed. by IEEE (Institute of Electrical & Electronics Engine. LC 95-76029. 796p. 1995. pap. text 142.00 (*0-7803-2587-7*, 95CH35776); lib. bdg. 142.00 (*0-7803-2588-5*, 95CB35776); fiche 142.00 (*0-7803-2589-3*, 95CM35776) Inst Electrical.

1995 VLSI Signal Processing, VIII. IEEE (Signal Processing Society) Staff. Ed. by IEEE (Institute of Electrical & Electronics Engine. LC 95-76062. 660p. 1995. pap. 92.00 (*0-7803-2612-1*, 95TH8067); fiche 92.00 (*0-7803-2613-X*, 95TM8067) Inst Electrical.

1995 Washington Software Association & Industry Directory: Now Includes the Digital Media Alliance. rev. ed. 250p. 1995. 75.00 (*1-887925-00-7*) WA Software.

1995 Water Technology Review. (Report Ser.: No. DWA95). 302p. 1996. 1500.00 (*1-56965-410-7*) BCC.

1995 Workshop on High Performance Electron Devices for Microwave & Optoelectronic Applications - EDMO. IEEE (Electron Devices) Staff. Ed. by IEEE Staff. LC 95-75171. 120p. 1995. pap. 96.00 (*0-7803-2537-0*, 95TH8057); mic. film 96.00 (*0-7803-2538-9*, 95TM8057) Inst Electrical.

1995 Worldwide Electric Vehicle Directory. 7th ed. Philip Terpstra. (Illus.). 79p. pap. 20.00 (*1-883063-05-1*) Spirit Pub HI.

1995 Year in Review - U. S. Seafood Trade Report. Ed. by James L. Anderson & Barbara S. Gardiner. (Illus.). xii, 390p. 1996. pap. 19.95 (*0-9673524-0-1*) J L Anderson Assoc.

An Asterisk (*) at the beginning of an entry indicates that the title is appearing for the first time.

1995 2nd International Workshop on Active Matrix Liquid Crystal Displays. IEEE (Electron Devices Society) Staff. Ed. by IEEE (Institute of Electrical & Electronics Engine. LC 96-225450. 150p. 1995. pap. 92.00 (*0-7803-3056-0*, 95TH8139); fiche 92.00 (*0-7803-3057-9*, 95TM8139) Inst Electrical.

1995 22nd International Symposium on Compound Semiconductors. IEEE, Lasers & Electro-Optics Society & Electron D & Institute of Electrical & Electronics Engineers, I. 1000p. 1996. pap. 158.00 (*0-7803-2703-9*, 95TH8085); fiche 158.00 (*0-7803-2704-7*, 95TM8085) Inst Electrical.

1995 Conference on Lasers & Electro-Optics. IEEE, Lasers & Electro-Optics Society Staff. Ed. by Institute of Electrical & Electronics Engineers, I. 450p. 1995. lib. bdg. write for info. (*0-7803-2659-8*, 95CB35800); fiche. write for info. (*0-7803-2660-1*, 95CM35800) Inst Electrical.

1990 Forensic Services Directory. 1200p. 1990. 89.50 (*0-9602962-9-8*) Natl Forensic.

1994? Harold Camping. (POR.). 595p. 1994. pap. 14.95 (*1-885000-01-4*) Omega Pr Fmly Stat.

1994? Harold Camping. (ARA.). 605p. 1994. pap. 14.95 (*1-885000-02-2*) Omega Pr Fmly Stat.

1994. Harold Camping. Tr. by Anaceli G. Campins. (SPA.). 588p. (Orig.). (C). 1994. pap. 14.95 (*1-885000-00-6*) Omega Pr Fmly Stat.

1994: Faces in a Crowd. Aausc. (Teaching Methods Ser.). (C). 1995. mass mkt. 25.95 (*0-8384-6367-3*) Heinle & Heinle.

1994-1995 Internet Access Providers Marketplace Analysis. Joel Maloff. (Illus.). 159p. 1995. pap. text 200.00 (*1-57074-258-8*) Greyden Pr.

1994-95 Kentucky Writers' Resource Directory: August 1994. Ed. by Marguerite Floyd. 24p. (Orig.). 1994. pap. 8.00 (*0-9628089-3-8*) Lexington Pr.

1994-95 Home Care Salary & Benefits Report. annuals 4th ed. 440p. 1994. pap. 250.00 (*0-939326-84-1*) Hosp & Hlthcare.

1994-95 Hospice Salary & Benefits Report. 250p. 1994. pap. 195.00 (*0-939326-85-X*) Hosp & Hlthcare.

1994-95 Hospital Salary & Benefits Report. annuals 24th ed. 281p. 1994. pap. 250.00 (*0-939326-83-3*) Hosp & Hlthcare.

1994 a Year in Review for the Pacific Northwest Research Station (Long Version) Cynthia Miner et al. (Illus.). 84p. 1997. reprint ed. pap. 9.40 (*0-89904-908-7*, Ecosytems Resrch) Crumb Elbow Pub.

1994 ACL Proceedings. pap. 60.00 (*1-55860-365-4*) Morgan Kaufmann.

1994 Almanac of Hospital Financial & Operating Indicators. William O. Cleverley. 516p. 1994. pap. 350.00 (*1-882733-02-9*) Ctr Hlthcare IPS.

1994 Annual Convention (Reno, Nevada) Vol. 1: ASPRS Proceedings. ACSM Staff & ASPRS Staff. 762p. 1994. pap. 30.00 (*0-614-06102-4*, T727) Am Congrs Survey.

1994 Annual Convention (Reno, Nevada) Vol. 2: ACSM Proceedings. ACSM Staff & ASPRS Staff. 353p. 1994. pap. 30.00 (*0-614-06101-6*, T728) Am Congrs Survey.

1994 Annual Survey of Letter of Credit Law & Practice: Survey Handbook. Ed. by James E. Byrne et al. xv, 549p. 1994. pap. 99.00 (*1-888870-02-8*) Inst Intl Bnking.

1994 Anti-Crime Law: A Local Officials Guide. National League Cl Staff. 32p. 1994. pap. 10.00 (*1-886152-02-0*, 6016) Natl League Cities.

1994 Applied Natural Language Processing Proceedings. pap. 60.00 (*1-55860-986-5*) Morgan Kaufmann.

1994 Arms Deliveries: A Register of Deliveries from Public Sources. John Sislin & Siemon T. Wezeman. 80p. 1995. 25.00 (*1-885350-01-5*) Ctr Nonproliferation.

1994 IEEE Asia-Pacific Conference on Circuits & Systems. Institute of Electrical & Electronics Engineers, I. LC 94-73058. 800p. 1994. pap., per. write for info. (*0-7803-2440-4*); fiche. write for info. (*0-7803-2441-2*, 94TM8029) Inst Electrical.

1994 Asia Pacific Conference on Insurance Taxation. 1994. ring bd. write for info. (*1-56423-038-4*) Ntl Ctr Tax Ed.

1994 Beacon Awards. Contrib. by Patrick Whitney. (Illus.). 36p. 1995. pap. 10.00 (*0-941447-04-9*) Amer Ctr Design.

1994 Book of Lists. 1995. 24.95 (*0-932439-04-7*) Denver Busn Media.

1996 Book of Lists by Houston Business Journal. 168p. 1995. pap. 24.95 (*0-9650400-0-3*) Houston Busin Jrnl.

***1994 Coach of the Year Clinics Football Manual.** Ed. by Earl Browning. (Illus.). 256p. 1999. pap. 22.95 (*1-57167-405-5*) Coaches Choice.

1994 Compensation Report: The Executive Compensation Survey for Small to Medium-Sized Businesses. Howard B. Goldsmith. 395.00 (*1-56706-012-9*) Panel Pubs.

1994 Cumulative Supplement Connecticut Evidence. Benedict M. Holden & John J. Daly. 710p. 1994. pap. 70.00 (*1-878698-25-7*) Atlantic Law.

1994 Dallas, Fort Worth Medical Directory. rev. ed. American Medical Sales School, Inc. Staff. Ed. & Intro. by Diane Huggins. (Illus.). 737p. 1994. 42.50 (*1-882328-02-7*) Am Med Sales.

1994 Directory of Simulation Software. Ed. by Rodriguez. 56p. 1994. pap. 40.00 (*1-56555-064-1*, DSS-94) Soc Computer Sim.

1994 Domestic Engine Control Manual. Keith Kraehmer. (Illus.). 723p. 1997. 120.00 (*1-887023-14-3*) Target Trning.

1994 Dung Annual: Collector's Issue. Christopher L. Clutter et al. (Illus.). 62p. 1994. mass mkt. 13.30 (*0-9644321-0-2*, CDWC) Camel Dung Writ.

1994 Elections to the European Parliament. Ed. by Juliet Lodge. LC 95-31171. 242p. 1996. 99.00 (*1-85567-280-4*) Bks Intl VA.

1994 Essentials with CPE. 94th ed. William A. Duncan Ph.D. (C). 1994. pap. text 59.00 (*0-15-602249-4*) Harcourt Coll Pubs.

1994 Evaluation Results: A World Bank Operations & Evaluation Study. 152p. 1996. pap. 22.00 (*0-8213-3607-X*, 13607) World Bank.

1994 Extended Abstracts: Fall - Miami Beach, Florida. (Proceedings Ser.: Vol. 94-2). 1134p. 1994. 72.00 (*1-56677-083-1*) Electrochem Soc.

1994 Extended Abstracts: Spring - San Francisco, California. (Proceedings Ser.: Vol. 94-1). 1846p. 1994. 72.00 (*1-56677-081-5*) Electrochem Soc.

1994 First International Conference on Software Testing, Reliability & Quality Assurance Conference Proceedings. IEEE, Dehli Section, Computer Society Dehli Chapte. Ed. by Institute of Electrical & Electronics Engineers, I. LC 97-153151. 162p. 1995. pap. text 92.00 (*0-7803-2608-3*, 94TH8063); fiche. write for info. (*0-7803-2609-1*) Inst Electrical.

1994 Help Desk & Customer Support Practices Report. Ed. by Patrick Bultema et al. (Illus.). 58p. (Orig.). pap. write for info. (*1-57125-012-3*) Help Desk Inst.

1994 High School Transcript Study Tabulations: Comparative Data on Credits Earned & Demographics for 1994, 1990, 1987 & 1982 High School Graduates Stanley Legum et al. LC 97-188204. (E. D. Tabs Ser.). 1997. write for info. (*0-16-049176-2*) USGPO.

1994 IEEE Fourth Workshop on Computers in Power Electronics. IEEE, Power Electronics Society Staff. Ed. by IEEE Staff. LC 94-77989. 350p. 1994. pap. write for info. (*0-7803-2091-3*, 94TH0705-4); fiche. write for info. (*0-7803-2092-1*, 94TH0705-4) Inst Electrical.

1994 IEEE Bipolar-BiCMOS Circuits & Technology Meeting. IEEE, Electron Devices Society Staff. Ed. by IEEE Staff. LC 94-78759. 272p. 1994. pap. text. write for info. (*0-7803-2117-0*); lib. bdg. write for info. (*0-7803-2118-9*); fiche. write for info. (*0-7803-2119-7*, 94CH35709) Inst Electrical.

1994 IEEE-IMS Workshop on Information Theory & Statistics. IEEE (Information Theory Society) Staff. Ed. by IEEE (Institute of Electrical & Electronics Engine. 108p. 1995. pap. write for info. (*0-7803-2761-6*, 94TH8100); mic. film. write for info. (*0-7803-2762-4*, 94TH8100) Inst Electrical.

1994 IEEE Intelligent Vehicles Symposium. IEEE, Industrial Electronics Society Staff. Ed. by IEEE Staff. 500p. 1994. pap. write for info. (*0-7803-2135-9*); fiche. write for info. (*0-7803-2136-7*, 94th8011) Inst Electrical.

1994 IEEE International Conference on Personal Wireless Communications. IEEE (Bangalore Section, India Council) Staff. LC 94-76625. 250p. 1994. fiche. write for info. (*0-7803-1997-4*, 94TM0666-8) Inst Electrical.

1994 IEEE International Conference on Systems, Man & Cybernetics. IEEE, Systems, Man & Cybernetics Society Staff. LC 94-79102. 2900p. 1994. pap. text. write for info. (*0-7803-2129-4*, 94CH35715); lib. bdg. write for info. (*0-7803-2130-8*, 94CH35715); mic. film. write for info. (*0-7803-2131-6*, 94CH35715) Inst Electrical.

1994 International Seminar on Stained Glass: Proceedings. Ed. by Virginia C. Raguin. (Illus.). 240p. 1994. 25.00 (*0-614-14262-8*) Census Stained.

1994 International Conference on Object Oriented Information Systems, 19-21 December 1994, London : OOIS '94. Yanqing Sun. Ed. by D. Patel. LC 94-42658. 1995. 69.00 (*3-540-19927-6*) Spr-Verlag.

1994 International Electronics Packaging Conference: Proceedings. (Conference Proceedings Ser.: No. 14). (Illus.). 975p. (Orig.). 1994. pap. text 115.00 (*1-880433-16-8*) Intl Elect Pack.

1994 International GIS Sourcebook. 1994. 186.61 (*0-582-25687-9*) Addison-Wesley.

1994 Internet White Pages. Godin, Seth, Productions Staff. LC 94-75233. 812p. 1993. pap. 29.95 (*1-56884-300-3*) IDG Bks.

1994 Kentucky Media Guide. Bluegrass Chapter, Society of Professional Journal. 94p. 1994. 10.00 (*1-883589-18-5*) Clark Pub KY.

1994 Market Share Reports: For Top 100 Life & Fraternal Insurance Groups & Companies by State. annuals 186p. (Orig.). (C). 1995. per. 125.00 (*0-89382-338-4*) Nat Assn Insurance.

1994 Market Share Reports for P-C Groups & Companies: Top 10 by Line by State Top 100 by Line Countrywide. annuals 418p. (Orig.). (C). 1995. per. 125.00 (*0-89382-356-2*) Nat Assn Insurance.

1994 Motorsports Engineering Conference & Exposition Meeting Proceedings. 1994. pap. 149.00 (*1-56091-576-5*, P287SET) Soc Auto Engineers.

1994 Motorsports Engineering Conference & Exposition Meeting Proceedings Vol. I: Vehicle Design Issues. 1994. pap. 99.00 (*1-56091-570-6*, P287) Soc Auto Engineers.

1994 Motorsports Engineering Conference & Exposition Meeting Proceedings Vol. II: Engines & Drivetrains. LC 94-68064. 1994. pap. 86.00 (*1-56091-571-4*, P288) Soc Auto Engineers.

1994 Music Yearbook. Joel Whitburn. 240p. 1995. pap. 29.95 (*0-89820-110-1*) Record Research.

1994 National Survey of Freshman Seminar Programs: Continuing Innovations in the Collegiate Curriculum. Betsy O. Barefoot & Paul P. Fidler. (Freshman Year Experience Monograph: No. 20). 92p. (Orig.). 1996. pap. 35.00 (*1-889271-17-9*) Nat Res Ctr.

1994 National Directory of Fire Chiefs & Emergency Departments, Vol. 3. Ed. by Steve Cywinski. 950p. 1994. 41.00 (*1-880245-06-X*) SPAN Pub.

1994-1995 Help Desk Buyer's Guide: A Comprehensive Directory of Help Desk Products & Services. Ed. by Patrick Bultema et al. (Illus.). 106p. (Orig.). pap. write for info. (*1-57125-011-5*) Help Desk Inst.

1994-1995 Guide to Theater Missile Defense. Jeff W. Schomisch. (Illus.). 278p. 1994. pap. 293.00 (*0-935453-73-3*) Pasha Pubns.

1994-95 International Registry of Certified Corporate Wildlife Habitats. Christel M. Cothran. 120p. 1994. write for info. (*0-9646852-5-6*) Wildlife Habitat.

1994 NTSC Proceedings: Thermal Spray Industrial Applications. 804p. 1994. 98.00 (*0-87170-509-5*, 6416) ASM.

1994 Physician Salary Survey Report. annuals 18th ed. 247p. 1994. pap. 250.00 (*0-939326-81-7*) Hosp & Hlthcare.

1994 Pro & College Football Almanac. Ed. by Sports Illustrated Editors. 1994. pap. 1.05 (*0-316-80864-4*) Little.

1994 Proceedings of the Fortieth Holm Conference on Electrical Contacts. IEEE (Components, Packages & Manufacturing Technol. Ed. by IEEE Staff. LC 86-645722. 325p. 1994. pap. text. write for info. (*0-7803-2132-4*, 94CH35716); lib. bdg. write for info. (*0-7803-2133-2*, 94CB35716); fiche. write for info. (*0-7803-2134-0*, 94CM35716) Inst Electrical.

1994 Second Australian & New Zealand Conference on Intelligent Information Systems. IEEE (Queensland Chapter) Staff. Ed. by IEEE Staff. 500p. 1994. pap. write for info. (*0-7803-2404-8*, 94TH8019); mic. film. write for info. (*0-7803-2405-6*, 94TH8019) Inst Electrical.

1994 Sidereal Astrological Almanac. P. Krishna Warriar et al. 118p. (Orig.). Date not set. pap. text 14.00 (*0-9618070-7-5*) Personal Insight.

1994 Significant Developments. 1994. ring bd. write for info. (*1-56423-036-8*) Ntl Ctr Tax Ed.

1994 Special Sessions on Crime. Adelia Yee. 5p. 1995. 15.00 (*1-55516-391-2*, 7302-2013) Natl Conf State Legis.

1994 State Expenditure Report. National Association of State Budget Officers Staff. (Illus.). 127p. (Orig.). 1995. pap. text 35.00 (*1-887253-01-7*) NASBD.

1994 State Legislation on Native American Issues. Kimberly A. Morin. 35p. 1994. 10.00 (*1-55516-924-4*, 9369) Natl Conf State Legis.

1994 Summary of Children Youth & Family Legislation. NCSL Children Families Program Staff. 200p. 1994. 20.00 (*1-55516-649-0*, 6131) Natl Conf State Legis.

1994 Summer School in High Energy Physics & Cosmology: ICTP, Trieste, Italy, 13 June-29 June, 1994. E. Gava. Ed. by A. Masiero et al. (ICTP Series in Theoretical Physics: Vol. 11). 750p. 1995. text 146.00 (*981-02-2291-2*) World Scientific Pub.

1994 Supplement to Constitutional Law, Twelfth Edition & Individual Rights in Constitutional Law, Fifth Edition. Gerald Gunther. (University Casebook Ser.). 337p. 1994. 11.95 (*1-56662-222-0*) Foundation Pr.

1994 Supplement to the Evolving Constitution. Jethro K. Lieberman. 85p. (Orig.). 1994. pap. 16.95 (*0-9630136-1-0*) Dialogue.

1994 Tax Savings Book: Checkers, Simon & Rosner Certified Public Accountants. Checkers. 1994. pap. 6.95 (*1-878667-04-1*) H & S Media.

1994 Third International Workshop on Integrated Nonlinear Microwave & Millimeterwave Circuits Digest. IEEE, Microwave Theory & Techniques Chapter, Anten. Ed. by IEEE Staff. 300p. 1994. pap. write for info. (*0-7803-2409-9*, 94TH8020); mic. film. write for info. (*0-7803-2410-2*, 94TH8020) Inst Electrical.

1994 3rd Quarter Seminar Papers: A Collection of Available Papers from Jakarta. 227p. 1995. pap. 55.00 (*0-614-31031-8*) Pac Telecom.

1994 Third Topical Meeting on Electrical Performance of Electronic Packaging. IEEE (Microwave Theory & Techniques Society, Elect. Ed. by IEEE Staff. LC 95-134049. 200p. 1994. pap. 84.00 (*0-7803-2411-0*, 94TH8022); fiche 84.00 (*0-7803-2412-9*, 94TM8022) Inst Electrical.

1994-95 Annual Review of Corporate Reporting Practices. 75p. (Orig.). 1995. pap. text 30.00 (*1-879087-56-1*) RFICFA.

1994-95 Nursing Department Report. annuals 3rd ed. 152p. (Orig.). 1994. pap. 195.00 (*0-939326-86-8*) Hosp & Hlthcare.

1994-95 Nursing Home Salary & Benefits Report. annuals 16th ed. 1994. pap. 250.00 (*0-939326-82-5*) Hosp & Hlthcare.

1994-95 State Issues Report. 69p. 1995. pap. 12.50 (*0-614-30582-9*, IS-95-1) Ed Comm States.

1994-95 State-by-State Report. 86p. 1995. pap. 12.50 (*0-614-30583-7*, IS-95-2) Ed Comm States.

1994-96/97 Supplement (with Additions & Corrections) to You Really Got Me: An Illustrated World Discography . . . Compiled by Doug Hinman. LC 94-216558. (Kinks Ser.: Pt. 1). 64p. 1997. pap., suppl. ed. 7.00 (*0-9641005-2-5*) Rock n Roll Res.

1994 U. S. Hispanic Market. Strategy Research Corporation Staff. 306p. 1994. pap. write for info. (*1-888520-01-9*) Strategy Research.

1994 United Nations Convention on the Law of the Sea: Basic Documents. The Nineteen Ninety-Four United Nations. LC 94-39925. (Law Specials Ser.: Vol. 8). 1995. pap. text 51.50 (*0-7923-3271-7*, Pub. by M Nijhoff) Kluwer Academic.

1994 USAN (U. S. Adopted Names) & the USP Dictionary of Drug Names. 901p. 1993. pap. 105.00 (*0-913595-73-X*, 932041) US Pharmacopeia.

1994 USP DI: Advice for the Patient Drug Information in Lay Language, Vol. II. 1700p. 1994. 52.00 (*0-913595-78-0*, 920246) US Pharmacopeia.

1994 USP DI: Approved Drug Products & Legal Requirements, Vol. III. 1200p. 1994. 95.00 (*0-913595-79-9*, 920348) US Pharmacopeia.

1994 USP DI: Drug Information for the Health Care Professional, Vol. I. 3000p. 1994. 105.00 (*0-913595-77-2*, 920144) US Pharmacopeia.

1994 Video Supplement. Donnell Media Center Staff. 342p. 1994. pap. 20.00 (*0-87104-745-4*, Branch Libraries) NY Pub Lib.

1994 Video Yearbook. Joel Whitburn. 112p. 1995. pap. 19.95 (*0-89820-111-X*) Record Research.

1994 Violent Crime Control & Law Enforcement Act Today. Marcus Nieto. 42p. 1995. pap. write for info. (*1-58703-034-9*, CRB-95-001) CA St Libry.

1994 VLSI Signal Processing VII. IEEE (Signal Processing Society) Staff. Ed. by IEEE Staff. 550p. 1994. pap. write for info. (*0-7803-2123-5*); fiche. write for info. (*0-7803-2124-3*, 94TH8008) Inst Electrical.

1994 World Lottery Almanac. Terri LaFleur. 388p. 1994. pap. text 149.00 (*1-883567-64-5*) TLF Pubns.

1994 International Year of the Family: Building the Smallest Democracy at the Heart of Society. 3p. 1994. mass mkt. 3.00 (*92-1-100510-8*, E.93.I.12) UN.

1994/95 Tennessee Statistical Abstract. Betty B. Vickers & Vickie C. Cunningham. (Orig.). 1994. pap. text 36.00 (*0-940191-18-0*) Univ TN Ctr Bus Econ.

1990 General Elections in Guatemala. National Democratic Institute for International Af. 114p. 1991. pap. 10.95 (*1-880134-11-X*) Natl Demo Inst.

1990 General Elections in Haiti. National Democratic Institute for International Af. 123p. (Orig.). 1991. pap. 10.95 (*1-880134-08-X*) Natl Demo Inst.

1990 Geographic Codes Book, Pennsylvania. PASDC Staff. (Pennsylvania State Data Center Ser.). 72p. 1994. pap. 20.00 (*1-885925-00-X*) Penn State Data Ctr.

1990 Guide to Expert & Consultants Fees. 50p. 1990. spiral bd. 29.95 (*0-9602962-8-X*) Natl Forensic.

Abstracts: 1990 International Conference on Titanium Products & Applications. (Illus.). 36p. (Orig.). text 30.00 (*0-935297-13-8*, 9602) Intl Titanium.

1990 International Supplement. (C). 1990. text. write for info. (*0-201-51486-9*) Addison-Wesley.

1990 Marketer's Handbook Vol. II: Pennsylvania Zip Code Data. Glenn Bobb. 183p. 1995. pap. 45.00 (*1-885925-06-9*) Penn State Data Ctr.

1990 Music & Video Yearbook. Joel Whitburn. 216p. 1991. pap. 29.95 (*0-89820-078-4*) Record Research.

1999. Herbert L. Akin. LC 81-80962. (Illus.). 260p. 1981. 4.95 (*0-938736-03-5*) Life Enrich.

1999. Stanley C. Baldwin. LC 94-16540. 220p. (Orig.). 1994. pap. 9.99 (*0-8308-1363-2*, 1363) InterVarsity.

1999. Stanley C. Baldwin. LC 98-53616. (Orig.). 1999. pap. 23.95 (*0-7862-1807-X*) Thorndike Pr.

1999. Ed. by Clifford Kachline. (Illus.). 88p. 1985. pap. 6.00 Soc Am Baseball Res.

1999: Apocalypse Maybe. D. H. Robinson. LC 97-74722. 256p. 1997. pap. 12.95 (*0-9658820-0-4*) Kalos Pr.

1999: The Crash of America. Carroll Melton. 300p. 1997. 22.95 (*0-943015-30-8*) Power Press.

1999: The Global Challenges We Face in the Next Decade. Richard M. Nixon. 1988. 100.00 (*0-671-65992-8*) S&S Trade.

Censored, 1999: The News That Didn't Make the News. Peter Phillips & Project Censored Staff. (Illus.). 100p. 1999. pap. 18.95 (*1-888363-79-7*, Pub. by Seven Stories) Publishers Group.

1999: The World of Tomorrow. Ed. by Edward Cornish. 160p. 1978. pap. 15.95 (*0-930242-04-1*) Transaction Pubs.

1999 - King of Terror. Gerry Nelson. 200p. (Orig.). 1996. pap. 4.95 (*0-614-14396-9*) New Comet.

1999-2000 Directory of Kentucky Grantmakers: Grant & Scholarship Information. Ed. by Susan O. Wilson. 350p. 1998. pap. 69.95 (*1-886445-10-9*) Indiana Donors.

1999-2000 Directory of Indiana Grantmakers: Grant & Scholarship Information. expanded ed. Ed. by Susan O. Wilson. 400p. 1999. pap. 65.00 (*1-886445-11-7*) Indiana Donors.

1999-2000 Global Telecommunications. 2nd ed. P. W. Coopers. (C). 2000. pap. text 150.00 (*0-471-32854-5*) Wiley.

1999-2000 Guide to Manufacturers' Reps. Ed. by Abby Communications Staff. 176p. 1999. pap. 36.00 (*1-893677-04-4*) Abby Communs.

1999-2000 Irvine Spectrum Business Directory. Ed. by Bruce Clumpner. (Illus.). 160p. Date not set. 39.95 (*0-9639578-5-6*) Coris Quill.

1999-2000 National Directory of Law Schools. 720p. 1999. pap. 60.00 (*1-55733-017-4*) NALP.

1999-2000 Official Catholic College & University Guidebook. (Illus.). 152p. (C). 1999. pap. 8.95 (*1-893728-00-5*) NCCAA.

1999-2001 Worldwide IT Spending Forecast. Ed. by Michael Erbschloe. 150p. 1999. write for info. (*0-945052-36-7*) Computer Econ.

1999/2000 Public Human Services Directory. Ed. by Amy Plotnick. 600p. 1999. pap. 90.00i (*0-910106-30-4*) Am Human Servs.

1999-2000 Zagat Vancouver Restaurant Survey. Zagat Publishers Staff. 1999. pap. 9.95 (*1-57006-186-6*) Zagat.

1999-2000 Zagat Las Vegas Restaurant Survey. Zagat Publishers Staff. 1999. pap. 9.95 (*1-57006-158-0*) Zagat.

1999-2000 Zagat Paris Restaurant Survey. Zagat Publishers Staff. 1999. pap. 11.95 (*1-57006-183-1*) Zagat.

***1999-2000 Zagat Kansas City Restaurant Survey.** Zagat Publishers Staff. 1999. pap. 9.95 (*1-57006-182-3*) Zagat.

1999 AACE International Transactions. Ed. by Marvin Gelhausen. (Illus.). 400p. 1999. pap. 89.95 (*1-885517-16-5*) AACE Intl.

1999 Academy Awards Handbook. John Harkness. 352p. 1999. mass mkt. 5.99 (*0-7860-0637-4*) Kensgtn Pub Corp.

N

***1999 Accounting Department Management & Administration Report Yearbook.** Tim Harris. (Illus.). 200p. 1999. pap. 199.00 (*1-58673-007-X*) IOMA.

***1999 Additions & Revisions to the Official Methods & Recommended Practices of the AOCS.** 5th ed. 1999. ring bd. 100.00 (*1-893997-09-X*) Am Oil Chemists.

1999 Africon. IEEE (Region 8) Staff. LC 99-61203. 1150p. 1999. pap. write for info. (*0-7803-5546-6*, 99CH36342) Inst Electrical.

1999 Alabama Advance Legislative Service Pamphlet, No. 1. 200p. 1999. pap. write for info. (*0-327-08660-2*, 40176-13) LEXIS Pub.

***1999 Alabama Advance Legislative Service Pamphlet, No. 2.** 400p. 1999. Price not set. (*0-327-09050-2*, 4017713) LEXIS Pub.

***1999 Alabama Advance Legislative Service Pamphlet, No. 3.** 600p. 1999. Price not set. (*0-327-09051-0*, 4017813) LEXIS Pub.

***1999 Alliance for Children & Families Directory of Member Organizations.** Alliance Staff. 1999. pap. 365.00 (*0-87304-317-0*) Manticore Pubs.

***1999 American Drug Index.** rev. ed. Facts & Comparisons Staff. Ed. by Norman Billups. 992p. 1998. text 54.95 (*1-57439-041-4*) Facts & Comparisons.

***1999 American Drug Index: Bundled.** Facts & Comparisons Staff. 992p. 1999. 85.00 incl. cd-rom (*1-57439-043-0*) Facts & Comparisons.

1999 American Guide to U. S. Coins. French. (Illus.). 192p. 1998. per. 6.99 (*0-684-85363-9*) S&S Trade.

1999 Zagat America's Best Meal Deals. 1999. pap. 12.95 (*1-57006-172-6*) Zagat.

1999 Zagat America's Top Restaurants. Zagat Publishers Staff. pap. 12.95 (*1-57006-151-3*) Zagat.

1999 Anderson Guide to Enjoying Greenwich, CT. Carolyn Anderson. LC 98-88785. (Illus.). 200p. 1998. pap. 12.95 (*0-9661072-3-3*) Avocet Pr.

1999 Annual, 2 vols. Ed. by Elaine Biech. 320p. 1998. pap. 79.95 (*0-7879-4452-1*) Jossey-Bass.

1999 Annual Vol. 1: Training. Ed. by Elaine Biech. 320p. 1998. pap. 44.95 (*0-7879-4541-2*) Jossey-Bass.

1999 Annual Vol. 2: Consulting. Ed. by Elaine Biech. 320p. 1998. pap. 44.95 (*0-7879-4542-0*) Jossey-Bass.

1999 Annual Book of ASTM Standards: Electrical Insulation (II): D 2518-Latest. 670p. 1999. 91.00 (*0-8031-2682-4*, S100299) ASTM.

1999 Annual Book of ASTM Standards: Electronics (II) 816p. 1999. 114.00 (*0-8031-2685-9*, S100599) ASTM.

1999 Annual Book of ASTM Standards Vol. 00.01: Subject Index; Alphanumeric List. 1350p. 1999. 71.00 (*0-8031-2711-1*, S000199) ASTM.

1999 Annual Book of ASTM Standards Vol. 01.01: Steel - Piping, Tubing, Fittings. 790p. 1999. 116.00 (*0-8031-2626-3*, S010199) ASTM.

1999 Annual Book of ASTM Standards Vol. 01.02: Ferrous Castings; Ferroalloys. 1999. 102.00 (*0-8031-2627-1*, S010299) ASTM.

1999 Annual Book of ASTM Standards Vol. 01.03: Steel - Plate, Sheet, Strip, Wire; Stainless Steel Bar. 636p. 1999. 88.00 (*0-8031-2628-X*, S010399) ASTM.

1999 Annual Book of ASTM Standards Vol. 01.04: Steel - Structural, Reinforcing, Pressure Vessel, Railway. 680p. 1999. 98.00 (*0-8031-2629-8*, S010499) ASTM.

1999 Annual Book of ASTM Standards Vol. 01.06: Coated Steel Products. 628p. 1999. 85.00 (*0-8031-2631-X*, S010699) ASTM.

1999 Annual Book of ASTM Standards Vol. 01.07: Ships & Marine Technology. 1358p. 1999. 153.00 (*0-8031-2632-8*, S010799) ASTM.

1999 Annual Book of ASTM Standards Vol. 02.01: Copper & Copper Alloys. 922p. 1999. 129.00 (*0-8031-2634-4*, S020199) ASTM.

1999 Annual Book of ASTM Standards Vol. 02.02: Aluminum & Magnesium Alloys. 788p. 1999. 110.00 (*0-8031-2635-2*, S020299) ASTM.

1999 Annual Book of ASTM Standards Vol. 02.03: Electrical Conductors. 470p. 1999. 77.00 (*0-8031-2636-0*, S020399) ASTM.

1999 Annual Book of ASTM Standards Vol. 02.04: Nonferrous Metals - Nickel, Cobalt, Lead, Tin, Zinc, Cadmium, Precious Reactive, Refractory Metals & Alloys; Materials for Thermostats, Electrical Heating & Resistance, Contacts, & Connectors. 1098p. 1999. 112.00 (*0-8031-2637-9*, S020499) ASTM.

1999 Annual Book of ASTM Standards Vol. 02.05: Metallic & Inorganic Coatings; Metal Powders, Sintered P/M Structural Parts. 836p. 1999. 110.00 (*0-8031-2638-7*, S020599) ASTM.

1999 Annual Book of ASTM Standards Vol. 03.01: Metals - Mechanical Testing; Elevated & Low-Temperature Tests; Metallography. 1188p. 1999. 142.00 (*0-8031-2640-9*, S030199) ASTM.

1999 Annual Book of ASTM Standards Vol. 03.02: Wear & Erosion; Metal Corrosion. 708p. 1999. 85.00 (*0-8031-2641-7*, S030299) ASTM.

1999 Annual Book of ASTM Standards Vol. 03.03: Nondestructive Testing. 1074p. 1999. 123.00 (*0-8031-2642-5*, S030399) ASTM.

1999 Annual Book of ASTM Standards Vol. 03.04: Magnetic Properties. 336p. 1999. 82.00 (*0-8031-2643-3*, S030499) ASTM.

1999 Annual Book of ASTM Standards Vol. 03.05: Analytical Chemistry for Metals, Ores, & Related Materials (I): C 571 to E 354. 564p. 1999. 83.00 (*0-8031-2644-1*, S030599) ASTM.

1999 Annual Book of ASTM Standards Vol. 03.06: Analytical Chemistry for Metals, Ores, & Related Materials (II): E356 to Latest; Molecular Spectroscopy; Surface Analysis. 1056p. 1999. 129.00 (*0-8031-2645-X*, S030699) ASTM.

1999 Annual Book of ASTM Standards Vol. 04.01: Cement; Lime; Gypsum. 600p. 1999. 83.00 (*0-8031-2647-6*, S040199) ASTM.

1999 Annual Book of ASTM Standards Vol. 04.02: Concrete & Aggregates. 700p. 1999. 112.00 (*0-8031-2648-4*, S040299) ASTM.

1999 Annual Book of ASTM Standards Vol. 04.03: Road & Paving Materials; Vehicle - Pavement Systems. 900p. 1999. 116.00 (*0-8031-2649-2*, S040399) ASTM.

1999 Annual Book of ASTM Standards Vol. 04.04: Roofing, Waterproofing, & Bituminous Materials. 420p. 1999. 65.00 (*0-8031-2650-6*, S040499) ASTM.

1999 Annual Book of ASTM Standards Vol. 04.05: Chemical - Resistant Nonmetallic Materials; Vitrified Clay Pipe, Concrete, Fiber-Cement Products; Mortars & Grouts; Masonry. 1148p. 1999. 138.00 (*0-8031-2651-4*, S040599) ASTM.

1999 Annual Book of ASTM Standards Vol. 04.06: Thermal Insulation; Environmental Acoustics. 1088p. 1999. 138.00 (*0-8031-2652-2*, S040699) ASTM.

1999 Annual Book of ASTM Standards Vol. 04.07: Building Seals & Sealants; Fire Standards; Dimension Stone. 946p. 1999. 106.00 (*0-8031-2653-0*, S040799) ASTM.

1999 Annual Book of ASTM Standards Vol. 04.08: Soil & Rock (I): D 420-D 4914. 990p. 1999. 120.00 (*0-8031-2654-9*, S040899) ASTM.

1999 Annual Book of ASTM Standards Vol. 04.09: Soil & Rock (II): D 4943-Latest; Geosynthetics. 1380p. 1999. 120.00 (*0-8031-2655-7*, S040999) ASTM.

1999 Annual Book of ASTM Standards Vol. 04.10: Wood. 666p. 1999. 98.00 (*0-8031-2656-5*, S041099) ASTM.

1999 Annual Book of ASTM Standards Vol. 04.11: Building Constructions. 1252p. 1999. 138.00 (*0-8031-2657-3*, S041199) ASTM.

1999 Annual Book of ASTM Standards Vol. 05.01: Petroleum Products & Lubricants (I): D 56-D 2596. 1009p. 1999. 150.00 (*0-8031-2659-X*, S050199) ASTM.

1999 Annual Book of ASTM Standards Vol. 05.02: Petroleum Products & Lubricants (II): D 2597-D 4927. 1251p. 1999. 152.00 (*0-8031-2660-3*, S050299) ASTM.

1999 Annual Book of ASTM Standards Vol. 05.03: Petroleum Products & Lubricants (III): D 4928-Latest. 1600p. 1999. 165.00 (*0-8031-2661-1*, S050399) ASTM.

1999 Annual Book of ASTM Standards Vol. 05.04: Test Methods for Rating Motor, Diesel, & Aviation Fuels; Catalysts. 382p. 1999. 76.00 (*0-8031-2662-X*, S050499) ASTM.

1999 Annual Book of ASTM Standards Vol. 05.05: Gaseous Fuels; Coal & Coke. 534p. 1999. 79.00 (*0-8031-2663-8*, S050599) ASTM.

1999 Annual Book of ASTM Standards Vol. 06.01: Paint - Tests for Chemical, Physical, & Optical Properties; Appearance. 1134p. 1999. 144.00 (*0-8031-2665-4*, S060199) ASTM.

1999 Annual Book of ASTM Standards Vol. 06.02: Paint - Products & Applications; Protective Coatings; Pipeline Coatings. 900p. 1999. 109.00 (*0-8031-2666-2*, S060299) ASTM.

1999 Annual Book of ASTM Standards Vol. 06.03: Paint - Pigments, Drying Oils, Polymers, Resins, Naval Stores, Cellulosic Esters, & Ink Vehicles. 858p. 1999. 109.00 (*0-8031-2667-0*, S060399) ASTM.

1999 Annual Book of ASTM Standards Vol. 06.04: Paint - Solvents; Aromatic Hydrocarbons. 664p. 1999. 90.00 (*0-8031-2668-9*, S060499) ASTM.

1999 Annual Book of ASTM Standards Vol. 07.01: Textiles (I): D 76-D 3218. 934p. 1999. 125.00 (*0-8031-2670-0*, S070199) ASTM.

1999 Annual Book of ASTM Standards Vol. 07.02: Textiles (II): D 3333-Latest. 1192p. 1999. 141.00 (*0-8031-2671-9*, S070299) ASTM.

1999 Annual Book of ASTM Standards Vol. 08.01: Plastics (I): D 256-D 2343. 656p. 1999. 101.00 (*0-8031-2673-5*, S080199) ASTM.

1999 Annual Book of ASTM Standards Vol. 08.02: Plastics (II): D 2383-D 4322. 804p. 1999. 107.00 (*0-8031-2674-3*, S080299) ASTM.

1999 Annual Book of ASTM Standards Vol. 08.03: Plastics (III): D 4329-Latest. 1006p. 1999. 116.00 (*0-8031-2675-1*, S080399) ASTM.

1999 Annual Book of ASTM Standards Vol. 08.04: Plastic Pipe & Building Products. 1330p. 1999. 153.00 (*0-8031-2676-X*, S080499) ASTM.

1999 Annual Book of ASTM Standards Vol. 09.01: Rubber, Natural & Synthetic - General Test Methods; Carbon Black. 1070p. 1999. 129.00 (*0-8031-2678-6*, S090198) ASTM.

1999 Annual Book of ASTM Standards Vol. 09.02: Rubber Products, Industrial - Specifications & Related Test Methods; Gaskets; Tires. 502p. 1999. 93.00 (*0-8031-2679-4*, S090299) ASTM.

1999 Annual Book of ASTM Standards Vol. 10.01: Electrical Insulation (I): D 69-D 2484. 620p. 1999. 89.00 (*0-8031-2681-6*, S100199) ASTM.

1999 Annual Book of ASTM Standards Vol. 10.03: Electrical Insulating Liquids & Gases; Electrical Protective Equipment. 492p. 1999. 68.00 (*0-8031-2683-2*, S100399) ASTM.

1999 Annual Book of ASTM Standards Vol. 10.04: Electronics (I) 536p. 1999. 87.00 (*0-8031-2684-0*, S100499) ASTM.

1999 Annual Book of ASTM Standards Vol. 11.01: Water (I) 938p. 1999. 120.00 (*0-8031-2687-5*, S110199) ASTM.

1999 Annual Book of ASTM Standards Vol. 11.02: Water (II) 1086p. 1999. 144.00 (*0-8031-2688-3*, S110299) ASTM.

1999 Annual Book of ASTM Standards Vol. 11.03: Atmospheric Analysis; Occupational Health & Safety; Protective Clothing. 1106p. 1999. 127.00 (*0-8031-2689-1*, S110399) ASTM.

1999 Annual Book of ASTM Standards Vol. 11.04: Environmental Assessment; Hazardous Substances & Oil Spill Responses; Waste Management; Environmental Risk Management. 1386p. 1999. 138.00 (*0-8031-2690-5*, S110499) ASTM.

1999 Annual Book of ASTM Standards Vol. 11.05: Biological Effects & Environmental Fate; Biotechnology; Pesticides. 1608p. 1999. 164.00 (*0-8031-2691-3*, S110599) ASTM.

1999 Annual Book of ASTM Standards Vol. 12.01: Nuclear Energy (I) 1040p. 1999. 133.00 (*0-8031-2693-X*, S120199) ASTM.

1999 Annual Book of ASTM Standards Vol. 12.02: Nuclean (II), Solar, & Geothermal Energy. 1094p. 1999. 133.00 (*0-8031-2694-8*, S120299) ASTM.

1999 Annual Book of ASTM Standards Vol. 13.01: Medical Devices; Emergency Medical Services. 1362p. 1999. 142.00 (*0-8031-2695-6*, S130199) ASTM.

1999 Annual Book of ASTM Standards Vol. 14.01: Healthcare Informatics; Computerized Systems & Chemical & Material Information. 1034p. 1999. 102.00 (*0-8031-2697-2*, S140199) ASTM.

1999 Annual Book of ASTM Standards Vol. 14.02: General Test Methods; Chromatography; Forensic Sciences; Terminology; Conformity Assessment; Statistical Methods. 814p. 1999. 88.00 (*0-8031-2698-0*, S140299) ASTM.

1999 Annual Book of ASTM Standards Vol. 14.03: Temperature Measurement. 644p. 1999. 73.00 (*0-8031-2699-9*, S140399) ASTM.

1999 Annual Book of ASTM Standards Vol. 14.04: Laboratory Apparatus; Degradation of Materials; Filtration; SI; Oxygen Fire Safety. 795p. 1999. 87.00 (*0-8031-2700-6*, S140499) ASTM.

1999 Annual Book of ASTM Standards Vol. 15.01: Refractories; Carbon & Graphite Products; Activated Carbon; Advanced Ceramics. 894p. 1999. 89.00 (*0-8031-2702-2*, S150199) ASTM.

1999 Annual Book of ASTM Standards Vol. 15.02: Glass; Ceramic Whitewares. 536p. 1999. 73.00 (*0-8031-2703-0*, S150299) ASTM.

1999 Annual Book of ASTM Standards Vol. 15.03: Space Simulation; Aerospace & Aircraft; High Modulus Fibers & Composites. 946p. 1999. 114.00 (*0-8031-2704-9*, S150399) ASTM.

1999 Annual Book of ASTM Standards Vol. 15.04: Soaps & Other Detergents; Polishes; Leather; Resilient Floor Coverings. 788p. 1999. 98.00 (*0-8031-2705-7*, S150499) ASTM.

1999 Annual Book of ASTM Standards Vol. 15.05: Engine Coolants; Halogenated Organic Solvents & Fire Extinguishing Agents; Industrial Chemicals. 702p. 1999. 89.00 (*0-8031-2706-5*, S150599) ASTM.

1999 Annual Book of ASTM Standards Vol. 15.06: Adhesives. 562p. 1999. 77.00 (*0-8031-2707-3*, S150699) ASTM.

1999 Annual Book of ASTM Standards Vol. 15.07: End Use Products. 1656p. 1999. 156.00 (*0-8031-2708-1*, S150799) ASTM.

1999 Annual Book of ASTM Standards Vol. 15.08: Fasteners. 454p. 1999. 78.00 (*0-8031-2709-X*, S150899) ASTM.

1999 Annual Book of ASTM Standards Vol. 15.09: Paper; Packaging; Flexible Barrier Materials; Business Imaging Products. 1422p. 1999. 186.00 (*0-8031-2710-3*, S150999) ASTM.

1999 Annual Directory of Western Bed & Breakfasts. Tracey Menges. 1998. pap. 12.95 (*1-55853-681-7*) Rutledge Hill Pr.

1999 Annual Directory of Midwestern Bed & Breakfasts. Tracey Menges. 1998. pap. 9.95 (*1-55853-682-5*) Rutledge Hill Pr.

1999 Annual Directory of Southern Bed & Breakfasts. Tracey Menges. 1998. pap. 9.95 (*1-55853-683-3*) Rutledge Hill Pr.

1999 Annual Directory of Mid-Atlantic Bed & Breakfasts. Tracey Menges. 1998. pap. 9.95 (*1-55853-684-1*) Rutledge Hill Pr.

1999 Annual Directory of New England Bed & Breakfasts. Tracey Menges. 1998. pap. 9.95 (*1-55853-685-X*) Rutledge Hill Pr.

1999 Annual Meeting of the North American Fuzzy Information Processing Society. IEEE (Neural Networks Council) Staff. Ed. by IEEE(Institute of Electrical & Electronics Engineers, Inc.) Staff. LC 98-89050. 500p. 1999. pap. 146.00 (*0-7803-5211-4*, 99TH8397) Inst Electrical.

1999 Annual Pulp & Paper Industry Technical Conference. IEEE (Industry Applications Society & Seattle Section) Staff. LC 74-136000. 300p. (Orig.). 1999. pap. write for info. (*0-7803-5526-1*, 99CH36338) Inst Electrical.

1999 Annual Reliability & Maintainability Symposium. IEEE (Reliability Society) Staff. Ed. by IEEE (Institute of Electrical & Electronics Engine. LC 78-132873. 464p. 1999. pap. text 144.00 (*0-7803-5143-6*, 99CH36283) Inst Electrical.

***1999 Annual Report: Institute for Business & Home Safety.** (Illus.). 38p. 2000. pap. write for info. (*1-885312-23-7*) Inst for Busn.

1999 Annual Report Conference on Electrical Insulation & Dielectric Phenomena. IEEE (Dielectrics & Electrical Insulation Society) Staff. Ed. by IEEE Staff. LC 79-649806. 900p. 1999. pap. write for info. (*0-7803-5414-1*, 99CH36319) Inst Electrical.

***1999 Annual Report of the Scientific Registry & the OPTN.** Ed. by Carol Smith et al. (Illus.). 492p. 2000. pap. 15.00 (*1-886651-37-X*) United Network.

***1999 Annual Review of Development Effectiveness.** Nagy K. Hanna. 112p. 2000. 22.00 (*0-8213-4706-3*, 14706) World Bank.

***1999 Annual Survey of Letter of Credit Law Practice, 4 vols.** Ed. by James E. Byrne. vi, 486p. 1999. 99.00 (*1-888870-19-2*) Inst Intl Bnking.

***1999 Annual Treasure Coast Magazine Vol. 10: The Best of South Florida from North Palm Beach to Vero Beach.** (Illus.). 112p. 1999. pap. 7.95 (*1-883117-09-7*, Pub. by Mohr Graphics) Southern Bk Service.

***1999 APA Membership Register.** 980p. 1999. 37.50 (*1-55798-577-4*) Am Psychol.

1999 Archaeological Bulletin. 8th ed. AIA Staff. 160p. 1998. per. 12.00 (*0-7872-5693-5*, 41569301) Kendall-Hunt.

1999 Arizona High Tech Directory. 12th ed. Ed. by Jean Wendelboe. 1998. pap. 65.00 (*1-885797-18-4*, KE001) Keiland.

1999 Asia & South Pacific Design Automation Conference. IEEE Staff. LC 98-86104. 400p. 1999. pap. 138.00 (*0-7803-5012-X*, 99EX198) IEEE Standards.

1999 Asia-Pacific Conference on ASICs. IEEE (Seoul Section) Staff. Ed. by IEEE (Institute of Electrical & Electronics Engineers, Inc.) Staff. LC 99-63832. 450p. 1999. pap. write for info. (*0-7803-5705-1*, 99EX360) Inst Electrical.

***1999 Asia Pacific Microwave Conference.** IEEE Singapore Section Staff. LC 99-64621. 1200p. 1999. pap. write for info. (*0-7803-5761-2*, 99TH8473) IEEE Standards.

***1999 Assessment of the Office of Naval Research's Air & Surface Weapons Technology Program.** National Research Council Staff. 46p. 1999. pap. 12.00 (*0-309-06632-8*) Natl Acad Pr.

1999 ASTD Training & Performance Yearbook. James W. Cortada & John A. Woods. (ASQ Ser.). (Illus.). 528p. 1999. 128.95 (*0-07-024818-4*) McGraw-Hill Prof.

1999 Auction Prices Realized. 18th ed. Ed. by Bob Wilhite. LC 83-642434. (Illus.). 464p. 1999. per. 65.00 (*0-87341-784-4*) Krause Pubns.

1999 Audio Blue Book. rev. ed. 1998. lib. bdg. 200.00 (*0-932089-93-3*) Orion Res.

1999 Bahamas & Caribbean Pilot's Guide. 20th rev. ed. John Obradovich & Betty Obradovich. (Illus.). 450p. 1998. 44.95 (*0-9660854-1-8*) Pilot Pub.

1999 Bank Tax Guide. rev. ed. Ronald W. Blasi. Ed. by Kris Bond. 850p. 1999. pap. 175.00 (*0-8080-0340-2*) CCH INC.

1999 Bankruptcy Yearbook & Almanac. Ed. by Christopher M. McHugh. 472p. 1999. pap. 195.00 (*0-9628991-8-6*) New Gen Research.

1999 Behavioral Outcomes & Guidelines Sourcebook. Ed. by Kenneth M. Coughlin. 736p. 1998. pap. 295.00 (*1-57987-091-0*) Faulkner & Gray.

1999 Biennial. Bruce Guenther. LC 99-10034. (Illus.). 45p. 1999. pap. 14.95 (*0-917493-29-X*) Orange Cnty Mus.

1999 Big Bad Baseball Annual: The Book Baseball Deserves. Don Malcolm et al. (Illus.). 428p. 1999. pap. 19.95 (*0-8092-2655-3*) NTC Contemp Pub Co.

1999 Big Movie & TV Songs. Warner Brothers Publications Staff. 14.95 (*0-7692-9118-X*) Warner Bros.

***1999 Billiards Yearbook, Vol. 1, No. 1.** annuals Carl Hungness et al. (Illus.). 448p. 2000. pap. text 39.95 (*0-915088-84-3*) C Hungness.

***1999 Billiards Yearbook, Vol. 1, No. 1** annuals Carl Hungness et al. (Illus.). 448p. 2000. text 59.95 (*0-915088-85-1*) C Hungness.

1999 BioSupplyNet Source Book. (Illus.). 412p. 1999. pap. 24.95 (*1-890574-04-X*) BioSupplyNet.

1999 Bipolar/BICMOS Circuits & Technology Meeting Proceedings. IEEE (Electron Devices Society) Staff. Ed. by IEEE (Institute of Electrical & Electronics Engineers, Inc.) Staff. 182p. 1999. pap. write for info. (*0-7803-5712-4*, 99CH37024) Inst Electrical.

***1999 Blue Chip: Association Executive Compensation & Benefits Study.** (Illus.). xxii, 112p. 1999. pap. 195.00 (*0-88034-161-0*) Am Soc Assn Execs.

***1999 Board Member Manual.** Ed. by John Gillis. 80p. 1999. pap. 47.00 (*0-8342-1379-6*) Aspen Pub.

1999 Year Book of Endocrinology. 3rd ed. (Illus.). 460p. 1999. text 82.00 (*0-8151-9627-X*, 24964) Mosby Inc.

1999 Boston Datebook. 1998. 9.95 (*1-892528-03-7*) Datebook Pub.

1999 Budget & Planning Workbook. 10th ed. Ed. by Callahan & Associates, Inc. Staff. (Illus.). 71p. 1998. pap. 210.00 (*1-889265-10-1*) Callahan & Assocs.

1999 California - Nevada Senior Housing Book. 3rd rev. ed. Terry Fahey. Ed. by Lori Fahey. (Senior Housing Ser.). (Illus.). 380p. 1999. pap. 65.00 (*1-893583-05-8*) Research West.

1999 California Public Employees' Retirement Law. 647p. 1999. pap. write for info. (*0-327-07636-4*, 2130512) LEXIS Pub.

1999 Camera Blue Book. rev. ed. 1998. lib. bdg. 200.00 (*0-932089-95-X*) Orion Res.

1999 Camp Staff Salary Study. 160p. 1999. pap. 59.95 (*0-87603-164-5*) Am Camping.

1999 Canadian Conference on Electrical & Computer Engineering. IEEE, Region 7 Staff. Ed. by Institute of Electrical & Electronics Engineers, Inc. Staff. 1800p. 1999. pap. write for info. (*0-7803-5579-2*, 99TH8411) IEEE Standards.

***1999 Canadian Encyclopedia World Edition.** Ed. by McClelland & Stewart Staff. (Illus.). 1999. pap. text 19.99 (*0-7710-2041-4*) McCland & Stewart.

1999 Car Stereo Blue Book. rev. ed. 1998. lib. bdg. 200.00 (*0-932089-97-6*) Orion Res.

1999 Career Guide: Marketing. 96p. 1999. pap. 22.95 (*1-57851-187-9*) Harvard Busn.

1999 CCH Federal Taxation Study Manual. rev. ed. Edward C. Foth. 550p. (C). 1999. pap., student ed. 31.00 (*0-8080-0268-6*) CCH INC.

1999 CCH Federal Taxation: Basic Principles. Ephraim P. Smith et al. (Illus.). 880p. (C). 1998. text 67.00 (*0-8080-0243-0*, O-5375-100) CCH INC.

An Asterisk (*) at the beginning of an entry indicates that the title is appearing for the first time.

1999 CCH Federal Taxation: Comprehensive Topics. Ephraim P. Smith et al. (Illus.). 1360p. (C). 1998. text 82.00 (*0-8080-0244-9*, 0-5376-100) CCH INC.

1999 Charlotte Datebook. 1998. 9.95 (*1-892528-04-5*) Datebook Pub.

1999 Chicago Datebook. 1998. 9.95 (*1-892528-05-3*) Datebook Pub.

1999 CLC Integrative Medicine: A Balanced Account of the Data. Steven Wirth & Sandra Wirth. Ed. by Mary Farkas & Larry Reed. (Illus.). 88p. 1998. 7.95 (*0-9661161-1-9*, 161-1-9, Boitumelo Pub) Creat Logic.

1999 Cleveland Datebook. 1998. 9.95 (*1-892528-06-1*) Datebook Pub.

1999 Coach of the Year Clinics Football Manual. Ed. by Earl Browning. (Illus.). 256p. 1999. pap. 22.95 (*1-57167-401-2*) Coaches Choice.

1999 Coding Workbook: Physician's Office. 6th ed. Covell. (C). 1999. pap., wbk. ed. 25.95 (*0-7668-0853-X*) Thomson Learn.

***1999 Collection: Prepared for Sudbury Schools & Planning Groups.** 260p. 1999. pap. 25.00 (*1-888947-21-7*) Sudbury Valley.

1999 Comparative Performance Data Sourcebook. Ed. by Eric Levy. 496p. 1998. pap. 265.00 (*1-57987-082-1*) Faulkner & Gray.

1999 Compensation Handbook for Church Staff. James F. Cobble, Jr. & Richard R. Hammar. 152p. 1998. pap. 19.95 (*1-880562-32-4*) Christ Minist.

***1999 Comprehensive Accreditation Manual for Home Care.** rev. ed. Joint Commission on Accreditation of Healthcare Organizations. (Illus.). 530p. 1998. 195.00 (*0-86688-595-1*, CAHC-99) Joint Comm Hlthcare.

1999 Comprehensive Catalogue of United States Stamp Booklets: Postage & Airmail Booklets. Robert Furman. LC 98-87626. (Illus.). 192p. 1999. per. 17.95 (*0-87341-685-6*) Krause Pubns.

1999 Comprehensive Guide to Electronic Medical Records. Margret Amatayakul et al. 549p. 1999. pap. write for info. (*1-57987-108-9*) Faulkner & Gray.

1999 Computers in Cardiology. IEEE (Engineering in Medicine & Biology) Staff. Ed. by IEEE (Institute of Electrical & Electronics Engineers, Inc.) Staff. LC 80-641097. 850p. 1999. pap. write for info. (*0-7803-5614-4*, 99CH37004) Inst Electrical.

***1999 Congressional Staff Directory - Fall: Members Committees Staff Biographies.** 56th ed. Congressional Quarterly Staff. 1999. pap. 207.00 (*0-87289-160-7*) C Q Staff.

1999 Connecticut Manufacturers Register. 2nd rev. ed. Ed. by Louise M. West & Frank Lambing. 1998. 68.00 (*1-58202-005-1*) Manufacturers.

1999 Conservation Directory. 44th ed. National Wildlife Federation Staff. Ed. by Rue E. Gordon. 544p. 1999. pap. 61.00 (*1-55821-920-X*) Lyons Pr.

1999 Consultants Directory: A Comprehensive Directory to Medical Device Industry Consultants. Susan Wallace. 164p. 1999. pap. 10.00 (*1-884551-05-X*) Canon Comns.

***1999 Contractor's Business Management Report Yearbook.** Susan Sandler. Ed. by David Solomon. (Illus.). 200p. 1999. pap. 199.00 (*1-58673-012-6*) IOMA.

1999 Copies Blue Book. rev. ed. 1998. lib. bdg. 200.00 (*0-932089-98-4*) Orion Res.

***1999 Cowboy Artists of America: Thirty-Fourth Annual Exhibition Catalog.** Cowboy Artists of America Staff. (Illus.). 1999. pap. write for info. (*1-890752-06-1*) Cowboy Art Am.

***1999 CPT.** American Medical Association Staff. (Medical Assisting Ser.). (C). 1999. pap. (*0-89970-941-9*) Delmar.

1999 Credit Union Quarterly Reports. 8th rev. ed. 1999. pap. 300.00 (*1-889265-15-2*) Callahan & Assocs.

1999 Credit Union Financial Yearbook. 12th rev. ed. (Illus.). 1999. pap. 500.00 (*1-889265-12-8*) Callahan & Assocs.

1999 Credit Union Financial Yearbook $250 Million: Credit Unions over $250 Million. 12th rev. ed. (Illus.). 360p. 1999. pap. 195.00 (*1-889265-24-1*) Callahan & Assocs.

1999 Credit Union Financial Yearbook $100 Million: Credit Unions $100-$250 Million. 12th rev. ed. (Illus.). 568p. 1999. pap. 195.00 (*1-889265-17-9*) Callahan & Assocs.

1999 Credit Union Financial Yearbook $50 Million: Credit Unions $50-$100 Million. 12th rev. ed. (Illus.). 780p. 1999. pap. 195.00 (*1-889265-25-X*) Callahan & Assocs.

1999 Credit Union Technology Survey: Including Detailed Information on the Data Processors. 9th rev. ed. (Illus.). 250p. 1999. pap. 495.00 (*1-889265-14-4*) Callahan & Assocs.

1999 Credit Union Directory: The First Guide to All Credit Unions. 14th rev. ed. Ed. by Callahan & Associates, Inc. Staff. (Illus.). 578p. 1998. pap. 135.00 (*1-889265-07-1*) Callahan & Assocs.

1999 Credit Union 1st Quarter Report: Credit Unions over $100 Million. 8th rev. ed. 150p. 1999. pap. 95.00 (*1-889265-19-5*) Callahan & Assocs.

1999 Credit Union 1st Quarter Report: Credit Unions $50-$100 Million. 8th rev. ed. (Illus.). 150p. 1999. pap. 95.00 (*1-889265-18-7*) Callahan & Assocs.

1999 Credit Union 2nd Quarter Report: Credit Unions over $100 Million. 8th rev. ed. (Illus.). 150p. 1999. pap. 95.00 (*1-889265-21-7*) Callahan & Assocs.

1999 Credit Union 2nd Quarter Report: Credit Unions $50-$100 Million. 8th rev. ed. (Illus.). 150p. 1999. pap. 95.00 (*1-889265-20-9*) Callahan & Assocs.

1999 Credit Union 3rd Quarter Report: Credit Unions over $100 Million. (Illus.). 150p. 1999. pap. 95.00 (*1-889265-23-3*) Callahan & Assocs.

1999 Credit Union 3rd Quarter Report: Credit Unions $50-$100 Million. 8th rev. ed. (Illus.). 150p. 1999. pap. 95.00 (*1-889265-22-5*) Callahan & Assocs.

1999 Cruise Line Employment Manual. Jim Ross. 1999. pap. 19.99 (*0-9670568-0-2*) Cruise Ross.

***1999 Cumulative Supplement Connecticut Evidence.** Benedict M. Holden & John Daly. 1107p. 1999. pap. 78.00 (*1-878698-56-7*) Atlantic Law.

1999 Cumulative Supplement to Connecticut Law of Torts. 3rd ed. Douglass B. Wright et al. 157p. 1999. pap. 57.00 (*1-878698-54-0*) Atlantic Law.

***1999 Current Text Vol. 1: General Standards.** Financial Accounting Standards Board Staff. 1999. pap. 51.95 (*0-471-35519-4*) Wiley.

***1999 Current Text Vol. 2: Industry Standards.** Fasb. 1999. pap. 51.95 (*0-471-35520-8*) Wiley.

1999 Dallas Datebook. 1998. 9.95 (*1-892528-07-X*) Datebook Pub.

1999 Delaware Manufacturers Register. 3rd rev. ed. Ed. by Louise M. West & Frank Lambing. 1998. 47.00 (*1-58202-030-2*) Manufacturers.

1999 Denver Datebook. 1998. 9.95 (*1-892528-08-8*) Datebook Pub.

***1999 Design Firm Management & Administration Report Yearbook.** Stephen Kliment. Ed. by David Solomon. (Illus.). 200p. 1999. pap. 199.00 (*1-58673-011-8*) IOMA.

***1999 Design/Build Survey.** 3rd ed. Zweig White & Associates Staff. 154p. 1999. pap. text 275.00 (*1-885002-94-7*) Zweig White.

1999 Detroit Datebook. 1998. 9.95 (*1-892528-09-6*) Datebook Pub.

1999 Digest of the LEOS Summer Topical Meetings. IEEE (Lasers & Electro-Optics Society) Staff. Ed. by IEEE (Institute of Electrical & Electronics Engineers, Inc.) Staff. 276p. 1999. pap. write for info. (*0-7803-5633-0*, 99TH8455) IEEE Standards.

1999 Directory of Alternative Investment Programs. Steven P. Galante. 552p. 1999. pap. 495.00 (*0-9652137-7-3*) Asset Alternatives.

***1999 Directory of Health Care Management Companies.** 2nd rev. ed. Ed. by Susan Namovicz-Peat & James P. Swann. 564p. 1999. pap. 294.00 (*0-929156-68-4*) Atlantic Info Services Inc.

1999 Disease Management Sourcebook. Ed. by Lois Wingerson. 570p. 1998. pap. 250.00 (*1-57987-085-6*) Faulkner & Gray.

***1999 Drug Facts & Comparisons.** Facts & Comparisons Staff. 4048p. 1998. text 140.00 (*1-57439-038-4*) Facts & Comparisons.

***1999 Drug Interaction Facts.** rev. ed. Facts & Comparisons Staff. Ed. by David S. Tatro. 1264p. 1998. pap. 64.95 (*1-57439-039-2*) Facts & Comparisons.

1999 Educational Opportunity Guide: A Directory of Programs for the Gifted. rev. ed. Ed. by Daniel Trollinger. 322p. 1999. pap. 15.00 (*0-9639756-5-X*) Duke U TIP.

***1999 18th IEEE/NPS Symposium on Fusion Engineering.** IEEE (Nuclear & Plasma Sciences) Staff. Ed. by IEEE (Institute of Electrical & Electronics Engineers, Inc.) Staff. LC 85-653749. 750p. 2000. pap. write for info. (*0-7803-5829-5*, 00CH37050) Inst Electrical.

1999 18th International Conference on Thermoelectrics. IEEE, Components, Packaging & Manufacturing Techno. 650p. (Orig.). 1999. pap. write for info. (*0-7803-5451-6*, 99TH8407) Inst Electrical.

***1999 Electrical Insulation Conference & Electrical Manufacturing & Coil Winding Conference.** IEEE (Dielectrics & Electrical Insulation Society) Staff. Ed. by IEEE (Institute of Electrical & Electronics Engineers, Inc.) Staff. 700p. 1999. pap. write for info. (*0-7803-5757-4*, 99CH37035) Inst Electrical.

1999 EMC, Telecom & Computer Encyclopedia, Vol. 3. 3rd rev. ed. Don White. Orig. Title: EMC Digest. (Illus.). 736p. 1999. text 95.00 (*0-932263-36-4*) emf-emi Control.

***1999 Employment Relations Act Explanied.** Richard Hemmings. (Point of Law Ser.). vi, 243p. 2000. 50.00 (*0-11-702395-7*, Pub. by Statnry Office) Balogh.

1999 Employment Acts, Explained. Richard Hemmings. (Point of Law Ser.). 300p. 1999. pap. 50.00 (*0-11-702346-9*, Pub. by Statnry Office) Balogh.

***1999 Employment Law Update, 1.** Henry H. Perritt Jr. 544p. 1999. pap. text 150.00 (*0-7355-0348-6*) Panel Pubs.

***1999 Energy Market Research Report.** Euromoney Staff. 1999. pap. text 982.00 (*1-86186-093-5*, Pub. by Euromoney) Am Educ Systs.

1999 Environmental Assessment: Rising to the Challenge of a New Century. Ed. by Daniel P. Bourque et al. (Illus.). 114p. 1999. pap. 9.00 (*0-9667828-1-X*) VHA Inc.

***1999 Ethanol Vehicle Challenge.** (Special Publications). 126p. 2000. 35.00 (*0-7680-0570-1*, SP-1520) Soc Auto Engineers.

1999 Europe TravelBook: Travel with Someone You Trust, 1999 ed. 640p. 1999. pap. 14.95 (*1-56251-270-6*) AAA.

1999 Exploring America's National Parks. Ed. by Rand McNally Staff. LC 98-226172. 1998. pap. 4.95 (*0-528-84052-5*) Rand McNally.

1999 Facts about Blacks: A Sourcebook of African-American Accomplishment. rev. ed. Raymond M. Corbin. 263p. 1995. pap. 10.95 (*0-931761-06-9*) Beckham Pubns.

***1999 Fall Simulation Interoperability Workshop: Workshop Papers.** (Simulation Interoperability Workshop Ser.). 1200p. 1999. 75.00 (*1-930638-07-8*) S I S O.

1999 Fast-Growth Firm Survey of A-E-P & Environmental Consulting Firms. 298p. 1999. pap. 275.00 (*1-885002-67-X*) Zweig White.

***1999 FDA Directory Issue 2: July - December 1999.** 7th ed. Food & Drug Law Institute Staff. 225p. 1999. pap. 99.00 (*1-885259-59-X*) Food & Drug Law.

***1999 Federal Bar Association Annual Convention Program Materials.** 420p. 1999. spiral bd. 90.00 (*1-56986-144-7*, FBA-99-420) Federal Bar.

***1999 Federal Staff Directory - Fall: White House Departments Agencies Biographies.** 31st ed. Congressional Quarterly Staff. 1999. pap. 207.00 (*0-87289-159-3*) C Q Staff.

***1999 Federal Tax Forms for Individuals & Businesses: Including Sample Filled-In Tax Returns.** CCH Editors. 1568p. 2000. pap. text 99.00 (*0-8080-0465-4*) CCH INC.

1999 Federal Witholding Tables with Highlights, Effective January 1, 1999. CCH Editorial Staff. (Payroll Professional Management Ser.). 40p. 1998. pap. 17.50 (*0-8080-0300-3*) CCH INC.

***1999 Fee & Billing Survey of A/E/P & Environmental Consulting Firms.** 2nd ed. 210p. 1999. pap. text 275.00 (*1-885002-81-5*) Zweig White.

1999 Fee Schedule & Payment Policies for Physician's Medicare Services. rev. ed. CCH Editorial Staff. 300p. 1998. pap. 45.00 (*0-8080-0303-8*) CCH INC.

***1999 Fiduciary Tax Return Guide.** Ed. by Robert Rywick et al. 160p. 2000. pap. 16.50 (*0-7811-0237-5*) Res Inst Am.

1999 Fifth European Conference on Radiation & Its Effects on Components & Systems Proceedings. IEEE (Nuclear & Plasma Sciences Society) Staff. Ed. by IEEE (Institute of Electrical & Electronics Engineers, Inc.) Staff. LC 99-64034. 600p. 2000. pap. write for info. (*0-7803-5726-4*, 99TH8471) IEEE Standards.

1999 5th Seminar on Neural Network Applications in Electrical Engineering. IEEE (Yugoslavia Section) Staff. LC 99-60930. 350p. 1999. pap. write for info. (*0-7803-5512-1*, 99EX287) Inst Electrical.

***1999 Finance & Accounting Survey of Architecture, Engineering & Planning Firms.** 3rd ed. 232p. 1999. pap. text 275.00 (*1-885002-82-3*) Zweig White.

1999 Finance Career Guide. Ed. by Anthony L. Tillman. (Harvard Business School Career Guides). 176p. 1998. pap. text 24.95 (*0-87584-875-3*) Harvard Busn.

***1999 Financial Performance Survey of Environmental Consulting Firms.** 7th ed. 264p. 1999. pap. text 275.00 (*1-885002-83-1*) Zweig White.

***1999 1st IEEE/RPS Conference on Internet Technology & Services.** IEEE, Communications Society & Region 8 Staff. Ed. by Institute of Electrical & Electronics Engineers, Inc. Staff. LC 99-69253. 160p. 1999. pap. write for info. (*0-7803-5985-2*, 99EX391) Inst Electrical.

***1999 First State Insurance Tax Institute.** 1999. ring bd. write for info. (*1-56423-083-X*) Ntl Ctr Tax Ed.

1999 1st Workshop on Robot Motion & Control. IEEE (Industrial Electronics Society) Staff. Ed. by IEEE (Institute of Electrical & Electronics Engineers, Inc.) Staff. LC 99-62862. 280p. 1999. pap. write for info. (*0-7803-5655-1*, 99EX353) IEEE Standards.

1999 Florida Almanac. 15th ed. Del Marth & Marty Marth. 336p. 1998. pap. 14.50 (*1-885034-11-3*) Suwannee River.

1999 Fort Worth Datebook. 1998. 9.95 (*1-892528-10-X*) Datebook Pub.

1999 42nd Midwest Symposium on Circuits & Systems. IEEE (Circuits & Systems Society) Staff. LC 79-645128. 1100p. 1999. pap. write for info. (*0-7803-5491-5*, 99CH36356) Inst Electrical.

1999 14th Annual Applied Power Electronics Conference. IEEE, Power electronics Society & Industrial Electronics Society Staff. Ed. by Institute of Electrical & electronics Engineers, I. LC 90-643607. 1200p. 1999. pap. text. write for info. (*0-7803-5160-6*, 99CH36285) Inst Electrical.

1999 14th Annual Battery Conference on Applications & Advances. IEEE (Aerospace & Electronics Systems Society) Sta. Ed. by IEEE (Institute of Electrical & Electronics Engine. 450p. 1999. pap. 142.00 (*0-7803-4967-9*, 99TH8371) Inst Electrical.

1999 4th High Frequency Postgraduate Student Colloquium. IEEE (Microwave Theory & Techniques Society) Staff. Ed. by IEEE (Institute of Electrical & Electronics Engineers, Inc.) Staff. LC 99-61881. 180p. 1999. pap. write for info. (*0-7803-5577-6*, 99TH8409) IEEE Standards.

1999 4th International Symposium on Plasma Process-Induced Damage. Ed. by Thuy Dao et al. (Illus.). 250p. 1999. pap. write for info. (*0-9651577-3-3*) Nrthrn CA Chapter.

1999 4th International Workshop on Statistical Metrology. IEEE, Electron-Devices Society Staff. LC 98-88036. 100p. 1999. pap. text. write for info. (*0-7803-5154-1*, 99TH8391) Inst Electrical.

***1999 4th International Conference on Telecommunications in Modern Satellite, Cable & Broadcasting Services - Telsiks.** IEEE Staff. 700p. 1999. pap. write for info. (*0-7803-5768-X*) IEEE Standards.

1999 Frontiers in Education. IEEE (Education Society & Computer Society) Staff. Ed. by IEEE (Institute of Electrical & Electronics Engineers, Inc.) Staff. LC 79-640910. 1200p. 1999. pap. write for info. (*0-7803-5643-8*, 99CH37011) IEEE Standards.

1999 Full Size U. S. Road Atlas. American Map Publishing Staff. 1998. pap. 10.95 (*0-8416-2386-4*) Am Map.

***1999 Future Car Challenge.** (Special Publications). 126p. 2000. 35.00 (*0-7680-0571-X*, SP-1521) Soc Auto Engineers.

1999 GAAP from EITF Guide. 99th ed. Weiss. (C). 1998. pap. text 69.00 (*0-15-606308-5*, Pub. by Harcourt Coll Pubs) Harcourt.

1999 GAAP Guide. 98th ed. Williams. (C). 1998. pap. text 69.00 (*0-15-606311-5*, Pub. by Harcourt Coll Pubs) Harcourt.

1999 GAAS Guide. 99th ed. Bailey. (C). 1998. pap. text 69.00 (*0-15-606314-X*, Pub. by Harcourt Coll Pubs) Harcourt.

1999 Garden Conservancy Open Days Directory, 5th ed. Garden Conserv Staff. 480p. 1999. pap. 12.95 (*1-893424-00-6*) Garden Conserv.

1999 Georgia Manufacturers Register. 11th rev. ed. Ed. by Louise M. West & Frank Lambing. 1998. 103.00 (*1-58202-026-4*) Manufacturers.

1999 Graduate Programs in Physics, Astronomy, & Related Fields. Ed. by American Institute of Physics Staff. 962p. 1998. pap. 50.00 (*1-56396-822-3*) Am Inst Physics.

***1999 Guide to Entrepreneurial Venture Financing - South & Middle Atlantic.** Capital Growth, Inc. Staff. 120p. 1999. pap. 95.00 (*1-929744-09-9*) Penn Chamber of Bus.

1999 Guide to Healthy Restaurant Eating: What to Eat in America's Most Popular Family & Chain Restaurants. Hope Warshaw. LC 98-35395. 192p. 1998. pap. 13.95 (*1-58040-004-3*, 00043Q, Pub. by Am Diabetes) NTC Contemp Pub Co.

1999 Guide to Intranets in Health Care. Ed. by Jeffrey W. Muscarella & Luci Koizumi. (Illus.). 352p. 1998. pap. 275.00 (*1-57987-106-2*) Faulkner & Gray.

***1999 Guide to Sales & Use Taxes.** annuals rev. ed. Research Inst. of America Staff. 992p. 1999. pap. text 59.95 (*0-7811-0206-5*) Res Inst Am.

1999 Guidebook to California Taxes. 50th ed. CCH Tax Law Editors. (Illus.). 672p. 1999. text 41.95 (*0-8080-0286-4*) CCH INC.

1999 Guidelines for Infectious Diseases in Primary Care. Sherwood L. Gorbach et al. 345p. 1998. pap. 24.95 (*0-683-18343-5*) Lppncott W & W.

1999 Guitar & Musical Instrument Blue Book. rev. ed. 1998. lib. bdg. 200.00 (*0-932089-94-1*) Orion Res.

1999 Gulf Coast Oil Directory. 47th ed. Ed. by James W. Self. 1000p. 1998. pap. 69.00 (*1-889879-13-4*) Atlantic Commun.

1999 Gun Blue Book. rev. ed. 1998. lib. bdg. 200.00 (*0-932089-99-2*) Orion Res.

1999 Guns Illustrated: The Journal for Gun Buffs. 31st ed. Ed. by Harold A. Murtz. LC 69-11342. (Illus.). 352p. 1998. pap. 22.95 (*0-87349-204-8*, GI99) Krause Pubns.

***1999 Hart Gulf States Petroleum Directory.** 9th rev. ed. Ed. by Annemarie E. Alano. (Illus.). 746p. 1999. per. 129.00 (*1-58271-012-0*) Phillips Business.

***1999 Hart Midcontinent Petroleum Directory.** 14th ed. Contrib. by Richard G. Ghiselin. (Illus.). 439p. 1999. per. 129.00 (*1-58271-017-1*) Phillips Business.

***1999 Hart Rocky Mountain Petroleum Directory.** 45th rev. ed. Contrib. by Richard G. Ghiselin. (Illus.). 474p. 1999. per. 129.00 (*1-58271-013-9*) Phillips Business.

1999 Harvard Business School Core Collection. Ed. by Baker Library Staff. 464p. 1999. pap. 65.00 (*0-87584-888-5*) Harvard Busn.

***1999 HCPCS.** Ed. by American Medical Association Staff. 1998. pap. 44.00 (*0-89970-950-8*) Aspen Pub.

1999 HCPCS: Level II Codes. 240p. 1999. pap. 65.00 (*1-58383-010-3*, HCPCS9) Robert D Keene.

***1999 National Health Directory.** Ed. by Aspen Health & Administration Development Group. 400p. 1999. pap. 99.00 (*0-8342-1721-X*) Aspen Pub.

1999 Health Care Market for A/E/P & Environmental Consulting Firms. Zweig White & Associates Staff. (Illus.). 188p. 1999. pap. text 395.00 (*1-885002-73-4*) Zweig White.

1999 Health Network & Alliance Sourcebook: Purchasing & Selling Strategies for Payers & Providers, Including Blue Book Network, Coalition & Alliance Directories. Ed. by Daniel B. Moskowitz. (Illus.). 544p. 1998. pap. 265.00 (*1-57987-099-6*) Faulkner & Gray.

***1999 High Performance Electron Devices for Microwave & Optoelectronic Applications.** IEEE (UKRI/MTT Chapter) Staff. Ed. by Institute of Electrical & Electronics Engineers, Inc. Staff. LC 99-60116. 200p. 1999. pap. write for info. (*0-7803-5298-X*, 99TH8401) IEEE Standards.

1999 High-Profit Firm Survey of A-E-P & Environmental Consulting Films. Zweig White & Associates Staff. 216p. 1999. pap. 275.00 (*1-885002-68-8*) Zweig White.

1999 Hispanic Scholarship Directory: Over 1,000 Ways to Finance Your Education. 2nd rev. ed. Ed. by Andres Tobar & Kirk Whisler. (Stepping Stones to Success Ser.). 224p. 1998. pap. 19.95 (*1-889379-11-5*) WPR Pubng.

***1999 Hospital Accreditation Standards.** Joint Commission on Accreditation of Healthcare Organizations. 320p. 1998. pap. 95.00 (*0-86688-625-7*, HS-99) Joint Comm Hlthcare.

1999 Houston Datebook. 1998. 9.95 (*1-892528-11-8*) Datebook Pub.

***1999 Human Resource Department Management Report Yearbook.** Susan Patterson. (Illus.). 200p. 1999. pap. 199.00 (*1-58673-003-7*) IOMA.

1999 Human Resource Management: Issues & Trends. Bureau of Business Practice Staff. LC 99-183961. 1998. write for info. (*0-87622-782-5*) Aspen Pub.

***1999 HVAC Systems & Equipment.** Ed. by Robert Parsons. 1999. 134.00 (*1-883413-71-0*) Am Heat Ref & Air Eng.

***1999 Idea Regulations: A Practical Analysis.** Council of School Attorneys Members. 90p. 1999. pap. 25.00 (*0-88364-225-5*, 06-170, Pub. by Natl Sch Boards) PMDS-AACRAO.

***1999 IECON.** IEE Industrial Electronics Society Staff. LC 99-64256. 1600p. 1999. pap. write for info. (*0-7803-5735-3*, 99CH37029) IEEE Standards.

An Asterisk (*) at the beginning of an entry indicates that the title is appearing for the first time.

***1999 IEEE Aerospace Conference.** IEEE (Aerospace & Electronic Systems Society) Staff. Ed. by IEEE (Institute of Electrical & Electronics Engineers, Inc.) Staff. 2800p. 1999. pap. write for info. (*0-7803-5425-7*, 99TH8403) Inst Electrical.

1999 IEEE Annual Textile, Fiber & Film Industry Technical Conference. IEEE (Industry Applications Society) Staff. Ed. by IEEE (Institute of Electrical & Electronics Engineers, Inc.) Staff. LC 90-657367. 90p. 1999. pap. write for info. (*0-7803-5621-7*, 99CH37006) IEEE Standards.

1999 IEEE Antennas & Propagation Society International Symposium. IEEE (Antennas & Propagation Society) Staff. Ed. by IEEE (Institute of Electrical & Electronics Engineers, Inc.) Staff. LC 99-640397. 2984p. 1999. pap. write for info. (*0-7803-5639-X*, 99CH37010) Inst Electrical.

1999 IEEE-ASME International Conference on Advanced Intelligent Mechatronics. IEEE, Industrial Electronics Society & Robotics &. Ed. by Institute of Electrical & Electronics Engineers, I. LC 98-86331. 1200p. 1999. pap. 216.00 (*0-7803-5038-3*, 99EX213) Inst Electrical.

1999 IEEE Autotestcon. IEEE (Aerospace & Electronic System SOC, Instrumentation & Measurement SOC, Central Texas Section). Ed. by IEEE(Institute of Electrical & Electronics Engineers, Inc.) Staff. 860p. 1999. pap. write for info. (*0-7803-5432-X*, 99CH36323) Inst Electrical.

1999 IEEE Cement Industry Technical Conference. IEEE (Industry Applications Society) Staff. 426p. 1999. pap. write for info. (*0-7803-5523-7*, 99CH36335) Inst Electrical.

1999 IEEE Communications Theory Mini-Conference. IEEE (Communications Society) Staff. Ed. by IEEE (Institute of Electrical & Electronics Engineers, Inc.) Staff. LC 99-62836. 186p. 1999. pap. write for info. (*0-7803-5653-5*, 99EX352) IEEE Standards.

1999 IEEE Conference on Real-Time Computer Applications in Nuclear Particle & Plasma Physics. IEEE (Nuclear & Plasma Sciences Society) Staff. LC 99-61389. 800p. 1999. pap. write for info. (*0-7803-5463-X*, 99EX295) Inst Electrical.

1999 IEEE Custom Integrated Circuits Conference. IEEE (Solid-State Circuits Society) Staff. Ed. by IEEE (Institute of Electrical & Electronics Engineers, Inc.) Staff. LC 85-653738. 660p. 1999. pap. write for info. (*0-7803-5443-5*, 99CH36327) IEEE Standards.

1999 IEEE Electrical Performance of Electronic Packaging. IEEE (Microwave Theory & Techniques Society & Components, Packaging & Mfg. Technology Society) Staff. Ed. by IEEE (Institute of Electrical & Electronics Engineers, Inc.) Staff. LC 99-62322. 300p. 1999. pap. write for info. (*0-7803-5597-0*, 99TH8412) IEEE Standards.

1999 IEEE Emerging Technologies Symposium on Wireless Communications & Systems. IEEE, Dallas Section Staff. Ed. by Institute of Electrical & Electronics Engineers, Inc. Staff. LC 99-61656. 130p. 1999. pap. write for info. (*0-7803-5554-7*, 99EX297) IEEE Standards.

***1999 IEEE 15th Annual Semiconductor Thermal Measurement & Management Symposium.** IEEE (Components, Packaging & Manufacturing Techno. Ed. by IEEE (Institute of Electrical & Electronics Engine. 200p. 1999. pap. write for info. (*0-7803-5264-5*, 99CH36306) Inst Electrical.

1999 IEEE 50th Vehicular Technology Conference. IEEE (Vehicular Technology Society, Houston Section, Galveston Bay Section) Staff. Ed. by IEEE(Institute of Electrical & Electronics Engineers, Inc.) Staff. 2000p. 1999. pap. write for info. (*0-7803-5435-4*, 99CH36324) IEEE Standards.

1999 IEEE 57th Annual Device Research Conference. IEEE (Electron Devices Society) Staff. Ed. by IEEE(Institute of Electrical & Electronics Engineers, Inc.) Staff. LC 98-88247. 120p. 1999. pap. text 110.00 (*0-7803-5170-3*, 99TH8393) Inst Electrical.

1999 IEEE 49th Electronic Components & Technology Conference. IEEE (Components, Packaging & Manufacturing Techno. Ed. by Institute of Electrical & Electronics Engineers, I. LC 78-647174. 1400p. 1999. pap. write for info. (*0-7803-5231-9*, 99CH36299) Inst Electrical.

1999 IEEE 49th Vehicular Technology Conference Proceedings. IEEE, Vehicular Technology Society Staff. Ed. by Institute of Electrical & Electronics Engineers, Inc. Staff. 2700p. 1999. pap. write for info. (*0-7803-5565-2*, 99CH36363) IEEE Standards.

1999 IEEE GAAs IC Symposium. IEEE (Electron Devices Society & Microwave Theory & Techniques Society) Staff. Ed. by IEEE(Institute of Electrical & Electronics Engineers, Inc.) Staff. 318p. 1999. pap. write for info. (*0-7803-5585-7*, 99CH36369) Inst Electrical.

***1999 IEEE Global Telecommunications Conference - Globecom.** IEEE, Communications Society Staff. Ed. by Institute of Electrical & Electronics Engineers, Inc. Staff. LC 87-640337. 2700p. 2000. pap. write for info. (*0-7803-5796-5*, 99CH37042) Inst Electrical.

1999 IEEE Hong Kong Electron Devices Meeting. IEEE (Electron Devices Society) Staff. Ed. by IEEE (Institute of Electrical & Electronics Engineers, Inc.) Staff. LC 99-62712. 150p. 1999. pap. write for info. (*0-7803-5648-9*, 99TH8458) IEEE Standards.

1999 IEEE Industrial & Commercial Power Systems Technical Conference. IEEE (Industry Applications Society) Staff. Ed. by IEEE (Institute of Electrical & Electronics Engineers, Inc.) Staff. LC 88-641172. 180p. 1999. pap. write for info. (*0-7803-5593-8*, 99CH36371) IEEE Standards.

1999 IEEE Industry Applications Conference. IEEE (Industry Applications Society) Staff. Ed. by IEEE (Institute of Electrical & Electronics Engineers, Inc.) Staff. 2400p. 1999. pap. write for info. (*0-7803-5589-X*, 99CH36370) IEEE Standards.

1999 IEEE Infocom. IEEE Computer & Communication Society Staff. Ed. by IEEE Staff. 1680p. 1999. pap. write for info. (*0-7803-5417-6*, 99CH36320) Inst Electrical.

1999 IEEE Information Theory & Communications Workshop. Ed. by IEEE (Institute of Electrical & Electronics Engine & IEEE (Information Theory Society) Staff. LC 98-89843. 200p. 1999. pap. write for info. (*0-7803-5268-8*, 99EX253) Inst Electrical.

1999 IEEE Instrumentation & Measurement Technology Conferencer. IEEE Staff. 1700p. 1999. pap. write for info. (*0-7803-5276-9*, 99CH36309) Inst Electrical.

1999 IEEE Intelligent Transportation Systems Conference. IEEE (TAB Intelligent Transportation Systems Commi. LC 98-85686. 500p. 2000. pap. 146.00 (*0-7803-4975-X*, 98EX189) IEEE Standards.

1999 IEEE Intermag. IEEE, Magnetics Scoiety Staff. Ed. by Institute of Electrical & Electronics Engineers, Inc. Staff. LC 72-649866. 1900p. 1999. pap. write for info. (*0-7803-5555-5*, 99CH36359) IEEE Standards.

1999 IEEE International Symposium on Circuits & Systems. IEEE (Circuits & Sysyems Society) Staff. LC 80-646530. 3600p. 1999. pap. write for info. (*0-7803-5471-0*, 99CH36349) Inst Electrical.

1999 IEEE International Symposium on Electronics & the Environment. IEEE (Computer Society) Staff. 342p. 1999. pap. write for info. (*0-7803-5495-8*, 99CH36357) Inst Electrical.

1999 IEEE International Conference on Control Applications. IEEE (Control Society) Staff. Ed. by IEEE (Institute of Electrical & Electronics Engineers, Inc.) Staff. 1894p. 1999. pap. write for info. (*0-7803-5446-X*, 99CH36328) Inst Electrical.

1999 IEEE International Integrated Reliability Workshop Final Report. IEEE (Electron Devices Society & Reliability Society) Staff. Ed. by IEEE (Institute of Electrical & Electronics Engineers, Inc.) Staff. LC 99-62857. 200p. 2000. pap. write for info. (*0-7803-5649-7*, 99TH8460) IEEE Standards.

1999 IEEE International SOI Conference. IEEE (Electron Devices Society) Staff. 176p. 1999. pap. write for info. (*0-7803-5456-7*, 99CH36345) Inst Electrical.

1999 IEEE International Geoscience & Remote Sensing Symposium. IEEE (Geoscience & Remote Sensing Society) Staff. Ed. by IEEE(Institute of Electrical & Electronics Engineers, Inc.) Staff. LC 98-89048. 3000p. 1999. pap. 392.00 (*0-7803-5207-6*, 99CH36293) Inst Electrical.

1999 IEEE International Conference on Evolutionary Computation. IEEE (Neural Networks Council) Staff. LC 99-61143. 2100p. 1999. pap. write for info. (*0-7803-5536-9*) Inst Electrical.

1999 IEEE International Conference on Neural Networks. IEEE (Neural Networks Council) Staff. 5000p. 1999. pap. write for info. (*0-7803-5529-6*, 99CH36339) Inst Electrical.

1999 IEEE International Conference on Personal Wireless Communications. IEEE (Region 10, Communications Society) Staff. Ed. by IEEE Staff. LC 98-85084. 500p. 1999. pap. 146.00 (*0-7803-4912-1*, 99TH8366) Inst Electrical.

1999 IEEE International Conference on Robotics & Automation. IEEE (Robotics & Automation Society) Staff. Ed. by IEEE(Institute of Electrical & Electronics Engineers, Inc.) Staff. LC 90-640158. 3700p. 1999. pap. text. write for info. (*0-7803-5180-0*, 99CH36288) Inst Electrical.

1999 IEEE International Symposium on Assembly & Task Planning. IEEE (Robotics & Automation) Staff. Ed. by IEEE (Institute of Electrical & Electronics Engineers, Inc.) Staff. LC 99-63665. 500p. Date not set. pap. write for info. (*0-7803-5704-3*, 99TH8470) IEEE Standards.

1999 IEEE International Workshop on Multimedia Signal Processing. IEEE (Signal Processing Society) Staff. Ed. by IEEE (Institute of Electrical & Electronics Engineers, Inc.) Staff. LC 99-62563. 716p. 1999. pap. write for info. (*0-7803-5610-1*, 99TH8451) IEEE Standards.

1999 IEEE International Symposium on Technology & Society. IEEE (Social Implications of Technology) Staff. Ed. by IEEE (Institute of Electrical & Electronics Engineers, Inc.) Staff. LC 99-62551. 300p. 1999. pap. write for info. (*0-7803-5617-9*, 99CH37005) IEEE Standards.

1999 IEEE International ASIC Conference & Exhibit. IEEE (Solid State Circuits Society & Rochester Section) Staff. Ed. by IEEE (Institute of Electrical & Electronics Engineers, Inc.) Staff. 400p. 1999. pap. write for info. (*0-7803-5632-2*, 99TH8454) IEEE Standards.

1999 IEEE International Solid-State Circuits Conference. IEEE (Solid-State Circuits Society) Staff. Ed. by IEEE (Institute of Electrical & Electronics Engine. LC 81-644810. 512p. 1999. pap. text. write for info. (*0-7803-5126-6*, 99CH36278) Inst Electrical.

1999 IEEE International Frequency Control Symposium. IEEE (Ultrasonics, Ferroelectrics & Frequency Control Society Staff. Ed. by IEEE (Ultrasonics, Ferroelectrics & Frequency Control Society Staff). LC 87-654207. 1400p. 2000. pap. write for info. (*0-7803-5400-1*, 99CH36313) Inst Electrical.

1999 IEEE International Performance Computing & Communications Conference. IEEE, Communications Society Staff. Ed. by IEEE (Institute of Electrical & Electronics Engine. 466p. 1999. pap. write for info. (*0-7803-5258-0*) Inst Electrical.

1999 IEEE International Symposium on Electromagnetic Compatibility. IEEE, Electromagnetic Compatibility Society Staff. Ed. by Institute of Electrical & Electronics Engineers, I. LC 83-645449. 700p. 1998. pap. text 136.00 (*0-7803-5057-X*, 99CH36261) Inst Electrical.

1999 IEEE International Reliability Physics Symposium. IEEE Electron Devices Society & Reliability Society Staff. Ed. by IEEE(Institute of Electrical & Electronics Engineers, Inc.) Staff. LC 82-640313. 420p. 1999. pap. write for info. (*0-7803-5220-3*) Inst Electrical.

1999 IEEE International Vehicle Electronics Conference. IEEE, Industrial Electronics Society Staff. Ed. by IEEE Staff (Institute of Electrical & Electronics. LC 99-60117. 1100p. 1999. pap. write for info. (*0-7803-5296-3*, 99EX275) Inst Electrical.

1999 IEEE International Conference on Plasma Science. IEEE Nuclear & Plasma Sciences Society Staff. Ed. by IEEE Institute of Electrical & Electronics Engineers, Inc. Staff. LC 81-644315. 320p. 1999. pap. write for info. (*0-7803-5224-6*, 99CH36297) Inst Electrical.

***1999 IEEE International Professional Communication Conference.** IEEE Professional Communication Society Staff. LC 99-64043. 476p. 1999. pap. write for info. (*0-7803-5709-4*, 99CH37023) IEEE Standards.

***1999 IEEE International Symposium on Computational Intelligence in Robotics & Automation.** IEEE Robotics & Automation Society Staff. Ed. by IEEE Institute of Electrical & Electronics Engineers, Inc. Staff. 400p. 1999. pap. write for info. (*0-7803-5806-6*, 99EX375) IEEE Standards.

1999 IEEE International Conference on Microelectronic Test Structures Proceedings. IEEE Staff. LC 98-89942. 270p. 1999. pap. write for info. (*0-7803-5270-X*, 99CH36307) Inst Electrical.

1999 IEEE International Conference on Communications. IEEE Staff. LC 81-649547. 1920p. 1999. pap. write for info. (*0-7803-5284-X*, 99CH36311) Inst Electrical.

***1999 IEEE International Conference on Systems, Man & Cybernetics.** IEEE Systems, Man & Cybernetics Society Staff. 6500p. 1999. pap. write for info. (*0-7803-5731-0*, 99CH37028) IEEE Standards.

1999 IEEE LEOS Annual Meeting Conference Proceedings. IEEE (Lasers & Electro-Optics Society) Staff. Ed. by IEEE (Institute of Electrical & Electronics Engineers, Inc.) Staff. 950p. 1999. pap. write for info. (*0-7803-5634-9*, 99CH37009) IEEE Standards.

1999 IEEE Midnight-Sun Workshop on Soft Computing Methods in Industrial Applications. IEEE Staff. LC 98-83007. 316p. 1999. pap. write for info. (*0-7803-5280-7*, 99EX269) Inst Electrical.

1999 IEEE MTT-S International Topical Symposium on Technologies for Wireless Applications. IEEE (Microwave Theory & Techniques Society) Staff. Ed. by \Institute of Electrical & Electronics Engineers, Inc., Staff. LC 98-88037. 206p. 1999. pap. text. write for info. (*0-7803-5152-5*, 99TH8390) Inst Electrical.

1999 IEEE MTT-S International Microwave Symposium. IEEE (Microwave Theory & Techniques Society) Staff. Ed. by IEEE (Institute of Electrical & Electronics Engineers, Inc.) Staff. LC 77-645125. 2200p. 2000. pap. write for info. (*0-7803-5687-X*, 00CH37017) IEEE Standards.

1999 IEEE Nuclear Science Symposium. IEEE (Nuclear & Plasma Sciences Society) Staff. Ed. by IEEE (Institute of Electrical & Electronics Engineers, Inc.) Staff. 1960p. 1999. pap. write for info. (*0-7803-5696-9*, 99CH37019) IEEE Standards.

1999 IEEE Pacific Rim Conference on Communications, Computers & Signal Processing. IEEE (Region 7, Victoria Section) Staff. Ed. by IEEE (Institute of Electrical & Electronics Engineers, Inc.) Staff. LC 90-655140. 638p. 1999. pap. write for info. (*0-7803-5582-2*, 99CH36368) Inst Electrical.

1999 IEEE Petroleum & Chemical Industry Technical Conference. IEEE (Industry Applications Society) Staff. Ed. by IEEE (Institute of Electrical & Electronics Engineers, Inc.) Staff. LC 73-641120. 350p. 1999. pap. write for info. (*0-7803-5601-2*, 99CH37000) IEEE Standards.

1999 IEEE Power Engineering Society Summer Meeting. IEEE (Power Engineering Society) Staff. Ed. by IEEE (Institute of Electrical & Electronics Engineers, Inc.) Staff. LC 99-61883. 1100p. 1999. pap. write for info. (*0-7803-5569-5*, 99CH36364) IEEE Standards.

1999 IEEE Power Engineering Society Winter Meeting. IEEE, Power Engineering Society Staff. Ed. by Institute of Electrical & Electronics Engineers, I. LC 98-84970. 1400p. 1999. lib. bdg. 234.00 (*0-7803-4894-X*, 99CH36233) Inst Electrical.

1999 IEEE Power Engineering Society Winter Meeting. IEEE, Power Engineering Society Staff. Ed. by Institute of Electrical & Electronics Engineers, I. LC 98-84970. 1400p. 1999. pap. text 234.00 (*0-7803-4893-1*, 99CH36233) Inst Electrical.

1999 IEEE Radar Conference. IEEE (Aerospace & Electronic Systems Society) Staf. 300p. 1998. lib. bdg. 128.00 (*0-7803-4978-4*, 00CH36249) IEEE Standards.

1999 IEEE Radar Conference. IEEE (Aerospace & Electronic Systems Society) Staff. 300p. 1999. pap. text 128.00 (*0-7803-4977-6*, 99CH36249) IEEE Standards.

1999 IEEE Radio & Wireless Conference. IEEE (Microwave Theory & Techniques Society, Denver Section, Pikes Peak Section) Staff. LC 99-61247. 360p. 1999. pap. write for info. (*0-7803-5454-0*, 99EX292) Inst Electrical.

1999 IEEE Radio Frequency Integrated Circuits Symposium. IEEE (Microwave Theory & Techniques Society & Components, Packaging & Mfg. Technology Society) Staff. Ed. by IEEE (Institute of Electrical & Electronics Engineers, Inc.) Staff. 300p. 1999. pap. write for info. (*0-7803-5604-7*, 99CH37001) IEEE Standards.

***1999 IEEE 2nd Conference on Open Architectures & Network Programming.** IEEE (Communications Society) Staff. Ed. by IEEE (Institute of Electrical & Electronics Engine. LC 98-89714. 200p. 1999. pap. write for info. (*0-7803-5261-0*, 99EX252) Inst Electrical.

1999 IEEE 6th International Conference on Electronics, Circuits & Systems. IEEE (Circuits & Systems Society) Staff. Ed. by IEEE (Institute of Electrical & Electronics Engineers, Inc.) Staff. LC 99-63293. 2000p. 1999. pap. write for info. (*0-7803-5682-9*, 99EX357) IEEE Standards.

1999 IEEE South Africa Symposium on Communications & Signal Processing. IEEE (South Africa Section) Staff. Ed. by IEEE (Institute of Electrical & Electronics Engineers, Inc.) Staff. LC 99-62321. 180p. 1999. pap. write for info. (*0-7803-5598-9*, 99TH8413) IEEE Standards.

1999 IEEE Southeastcon. Dee Siegferth. Ed. by Institute of Electrical & Electronics Engineers, I. LC 84-643372. 400p. 1999. pap. 138.00 (*0-7803-5237-8*, 99CH36300) Inst Electrical.

***1999 IEEE Tencon.** IEEE Seoul Section Staff. LC 99-64255. 1850p. 1999. pap. write for info. (*0-7803-5739-6*, 99CH37030) IEEE Standards.

1999 IEEE 13th International Conference on Dielectric Liquids. IEEE (Dielectrics & Electrical Insulation Society) & IEEE (Institute of Electrical & Electronics Engine. LC 98-84562. 650p. 1999. pap. text 162.00 (*0-7803-4759-5*, 99CH36213); lib. bdg. write for info. (*0-7803-4760-9*, 99CH36213) Inst Electrical.

1999 IEEE 25th Annual Northeast Bioengineering Conf. IEEE, Engineering in Medicine & Biology Society Staff. LC 88-646567. 144p. 1999. pap. write for info. (*0-7803-5486-9*, 99CH36355) Inst Electrical.

1999 IEEE Ultrasonics Symposium Proceedings. IEEE (Ultrasonics, Ferroelectrics & Frequency Control Society) Staff. Ed. by IEEE (Institute of Electrical & Electronics Engineers, Inc.) Staff. LC 73-641406. 1900p. 2000. pap. write for info. (*0-7803-5722-1*, 99CH37027) IEEE Standards.

***1999 IEEE Visualization Conference.** IEEE (Computer Society) Staff. Ed. by IEEE (Institute of Electrical & Electronics Engineers, Inc.) Staff. 576p. 1999. pap. write for info. (*0-7803-5897-X*, 99CH37067) IEEE Standards.

***1999 IEEE Wireless Communications & Networking Conference.** IEEE Communications Society Staff. 1580p. 1999. pap. write for info. (*0-7803-5668-3*, 99TH8466) Inst Electrical.

1999 IEEE Workshop on Signal Processing Systems Design & Implementation. IEEE (Signal Processing Society & Circuits & Syste. Ed. by IEEE (Institute of Electrical & Electronics Engineers, Inc.) Staff. 600p. 1999. pap. write for info. (*0-7803-5650-0*, 99TH8461) IEEE Standards.

1999 IEEE Workshop on Speech Coding. IEEE (Signal Processing Society) Staff. Ed. by IEEE (Institute of Electrical & Electronics Engineers, Inc.) Staff. LC 99-62834. 200p. 1999. pap. write for info. (*0-7803-5651-9*, 99EX351) IEEE Standards.

1999 IEEE Workshop on Applications of Signal Processing to Audio & Acoustics. IEEE (Signal Processing Society) Staff. Ed. by IEEE (Institute of Electrical & Electronics Engineers, Inc.) Staff. LC 99-62555. 250p. 1999. pap. write for info. (*0-7803-5612-8*, 99TH8452) Inst Electrical.

***1999 IEEE Workshop on Knowledge & Data Exchange, KDEX'99.** 80p. 1999. 100.00 (*0-7695-0453-1*) IEEE Comp Soc.

***1999 IEEE/ACM International Conference on Computer-Aided Design.** IEEE (Computer Society & Circuits & Systems Society) Staff. Ed. by IEEE (Institute of Electrical & Electronics Engineers, Inc.) Staff. 800p. 1999. pap. write for info. (*0-7803-5832-5*, 99CH37051) IEEE Standards.

***1999 IEEE/AIAA 18th Digital Avionics Systems Conference.** IEEE Aerospace & Electrical Systems Society, St Louis Section Staff. LC 99-64624. 2400p. 1999. pap. write for info. (*0-7803-5749-3*, 99CH37033) IEEE Standards.

1999 IEEE/ASME Joint Railroad Conference. IEEE (Vehicular Technology Society) Staff. LC 90-644036. 24p. 1999. pap. write for info. (*0-7803-5533-4*, 99CH36340) Inst Electrical.

1999 IEEE/RSJ International Conference no Intelligent Robots & Systems Proceedings. IEEE (Industrial Electronics, Robotics & Automation Society) Staff. LC 98-88538. 2100p. 1999. pap. 304.00 (*0-7803-5184-3*, 99CH36289) Inst Electrical.

1999 IEEE/Semi Advanced Semiconductor Manufacturing Conference & Workshop. IEEE, Electron Devices Society & Components, Packa. Ed. by IEEE Institute of Electrical & Electronics Engineers, Inc. Staff. LC 82-640313. 500p. 1999. pap. write for info. (*0-7803-5217-3*, 99CH36296) Inst Electrical.

1999 Import Performance Directory, Vol. 1. Peter Macaj. 250p. 1999. pap. 9.95 (*0-9668418-0-8*) A Marketing.

1999 Index of Economic Freedom. Bryan T. Johnson. 1998. pap. 24.95 (*0-89195-245-4*) Heritage Found.

1999 Indiana Media Directory: The Most Up-to-Date, Detailed Listing of All Indiana Media. Ed. by Lori Brackemyre. (Illus.). 232p. 1998. pap. 49.50 (*0-944369-19-7*) Brackemyre Pub.

1999 Indianapolis Datebook. 1998. 9.95 (*1-892528-12-6*) Datebook Pub.

***1999 Indy Review: Complete Coverage of the 1998 Indy Racing League Season, Vol. 9.** Motorbooks Staff. (Illus.). 160p. 1999. 24.95 (*0-7603-0774-1*, 129030AP, Pub. by MBI Pubg) Motorbooks Intl.

1999 Information, Decision & Control. IEEE South Australian Section Staff. LC 98-89631. 600p. 1999. pap. write for info. (*0-7803-5256-4*, 99EX251) Inst Electrical.

An Asterisk (*) at the beginning of an entry indicates that the title is appearing for the first time.

1999 Information Technology Survey of A-E-P & Environmental Consulting Firm. 3rd ed. Zweig White & Associates Staff. 288p. 1994. pap. text 275.00 (*1-885002-77-7*) Zweig White.

1999 IEEE Power Electronics Specialists Conference. IEEE (Power Electronics Society) Staff. 1300p. 1999. pap. write for info. (*0-7803-5421-4*) IEEE Standards.

1999 Intelec. IEEE (Power Electronics Society) Staff. Ed. by IEEE (Institute of Electrical & Electronics Engineers, Inc.) Staff. LC 88-656128. 700p. 1999. pap. write for info. (*0-7803-5624-1*, 99CH37007) IEEE Standards.

***1998 Interconnect Directory: Service, Installation & Maintenance.** rev. ed. Ron Brandow. 133p. 1998. pap. 79.00 (*0-9659931-1-6*) Am Teleprocessing.

1999 Intenational Electron Devices Meeting Technical Digest. IEEE (Electron Devices Society) Staff. Ed. by IEEE Staff. LC 81-642284. 1000p. 1999. pap. write for info. (*0-7803-5410-9*, 99CH36318) Inst Electrical.

1999 International Conference on Transparent Optical Networks. IEEE (Lasers & Electro-Optics Society) Staff. Ed. by IEEE (Institute of Electrical & Electronics Engineers, Inc.) Staff. LC 99-62616. 300p. 1999. pap. write for info. (*0-7803-5637-3*, 99EX350) IEEE Standards.

1999 International Symposium on VLSI Technology Systems & Applications. IEEE (Taipei Section/Electron Devices) Staff. Ed. by IEEE (Institute of Electrical & Electronics Engineers, Inc.) Staff. 400p. 1999. pap. write for info. (*0-7803-5620-9*, 99TH8453) IEEE Standards.

***1999 International Ash Utilization Symposium Proceedings.** International Ash Utilization Symposium Staff. (International Ash Utilization Symposia Ser.: No. 3). 850p. (C). 1999. 120.00 (*0-9674971-0-8*) Univ of Ken.

***1999 International Conference on Web-Based Modeling & Simulation.** Ed. by Agostino G. Bruzzone et al. (Simulation Ser.: Vol. 31, No. 3). 256p. 1999. 100.00 (*1-56555-156-7*) Soc Computer Sim.

***1999 International Conference on Industrial Lasers.** Ed. by Fu X. Gan et al. 636p. 1999. pap. text 111.00 (*0-8194-3456-6*) SPIE.

1999 International Conference on Image Processing. IEEE (Signal Processing Society) Staff. 2700p. 1999. pap. write for info. (*0-7803-5467-2*, 99CH36348) Inst Electrical.

***1999 International Conference on Computational Electromagnetics & Applications Proceedings.** IEEE Beijing Section & Atennas & Propagation Society Staff. Ed. by IEEE Institute of Electrical & Electronics Engineers, Inc. Staff. 700p. 1999. pap. write for info. (*0-7803-5802-3*, 99EX374) IEEE Standards.

1999 International Conference on Consumer Electronics. IEEE Staff. LC 84-643147. 500p. 1999. pap. text. write for info. (*0-7803-5123-1*) Inst Electrical.

1999 International Conference on Indium Phosphide & Related Materials Conference Proceedings. IEEE, Swiss Section Staff. Ed. by Institute of Electrical & Electronics Engineers, Inc. Staff. 800p. 1999. pap. write for info. (*0-7803-5562-8*, 99CH36362) IEEE Standards.

***1999 International Conference on Mission Earth.** Ed. by Achim Sydow & Jin-Yi Yu. 122p. 1999. pap. 60.00 (*1-56555-162-1*) Soc Computer Sim.

***1999 International Conference on Bond Graph Modeling & Simulation: ICBGM '99.** Ed. by Jose J. Granda & Francois E. Cellier. (Simulation Ser.: Vol. 31, No. 1). 394p. 1999. 100.00 (*1-56555-155-9*) Soc Computer Sim.

1999 International Congress on Instrumentation in Aerospace Simulation Facilities. IEEE (Aerospace & Electronic Systems Society) Staff. Ed. by IEEE (Institute of Electrical & Electronics Engineers, Inc.) Staff. LC 81-644323. 500p. 1999. pap. write for info. (*0-7803-5715-9*, 99CH37025) IEEE Standards.

1999 International Electric Power Encyclopedia. 416p. 150.00 (*0-87814-757-8*) PennWell Bks.

1999 International Fiber Optics Yellow Pages. Date not set. pap. 89.95 (*1-56851-161-2*) Info Gatekeepers.

1999 IEEE International Fuzzy Systems Conference. IEEE (Neural Networks Council Staff). Ed. by IEEE (Institute of Electrical & Electronics Engine. 2200p. 1999. pap. write for info. (*0-7803-5406-0*, No. 99CH36315) IEEE Standards.

1999 International Interconnect Technology Conference. IEEE (Electron Devices Society) Staff. Ed. by IEEE(Institute of Electrical & Electronics Engineers, Inc.) Staff. LC 98-88249. 250p. 1999. pap. text 122.00 (*0-7803-5174-6*, 99EX247) Inst Electrical.

1999 International ISDN Yellow Pages. Date not set. pap. 69.95 (*1-56851-157-4*) Info Gatekeepers.

***1999 International Karting Industry Buyer's Guide, Vol. 5.** 5th rev. ed. Ed. by Darrell Sitarz & Robert Cycon. (Illus.). 114p. 1999. pap. 6.95 (*0-9661467-2-7*) Kart Mktg Grp.

1999 International Semiconductor Conference. IEEE, Electron Devices Society Staff & Institute of Electrical & Electronics Engineers Staff. LC 98-87865. 650p. 1999. pap. text 162.00 (*0-7803-5139-8*, 99TH8389) Inst Electrical.

***1999 International Symposium on Micro Mechatronics & Human Science.** IEEE, Industrial Electronics Society & Robotics & Automation Society Staff. Ed. by Institute of Electrical & Electronics Engineers, Inc. Staff. LC 99-65524. 260p. 1999. pap. write for info. (*0-7803-5790-6*, 99TH8478) IEEE Standards.

1999 International Tax Havens. Spitz. (C). 1998. text 149.00 (*0-15-606293-3*, Pub. by Harcourt Coll Pubs) Harcourt.

***1999 International Test Conference.** IEEE Computer Society, Philadelphia Section Staff. 1200p. 1999. pap. write for info. (*0-7803-5753-1*, 99CH37034) IEEE Standards.

1999 International Topical Meeting on Microwave Photonics. IEEE, Microwave Theory & Techniques Society & Lasers & Electro Optics Society Staff. Ed. by Institute of Electrical & Electronics Engineers, Inc. Staff. LC 99-61747. 250p. 1999. pap. write for info. (*0-7803-5558-X*, 99EX301) IEEE Standards.

***1999 International Workshop on Robot & Human Communication.** IEEE (Industrial Electronics Society) Staff. Ed. by IEEE (Institute of Electrical & Electronics Engineers, Inc.) Staff. LC 99-66631. 450p. 1999. pap. write for info. (*0-7803-5841-4*, 99TH8483) IEEE Standards.

***1999 Internet Workshop.** IEEE (Communications Society) Staff. Ed. by IEEE (Institute of Electrical & Electronics Engineers, Inc.) Staff. LC 99-59259. 312p. 1999. pap. write for info. (*0-7803-5925-9*, 99EX385) IEEE Standards.

1999 Investment Allocation Percentages. rev. ed. Ed. by CCH Editorial Staff. pap. text 35.00 (*0-8080-0488-3*) CCH INC.

***1999 Judicial Staff Directory - Summer: Members Committees Staff Biographies.** 14th ed. Congressional Quarterly Staff. 1999. pap. 207.00 (*0-87289-167-4*) C Q Staff.

1999 Kansas City Datebook. 1998. 9.95 (*1-892528-13-4*) Datebook Pub.

1999 Krause-Minkus Standard Catalog of U. S. Stamps. 2nd ed. Ed. by Fred Baumann & George Cuhaj. LC 98-84632. (Illus.). 602p. 1999. pap. 19.95 (*0-87341-682-1*, SCM02) Krause Pubns.

***1999 Laguna Beach Slam Team.** Buzzy Enniss et al. 36p. 1999. pap. 4.95 (*1-929250-08-8*) FarStarFire Pr.

***1999 Latino Film Festival Yearbook.** Jim Sullivan. (Illus.). 132p. 1999. pap. 19.95 (*1-889379-14-X*) WPR Pubng.

***1999 Law Office Management & Admisitration Report Yearbook.** Lisa Isom-Rodiguez. Ed. by Jan Christian Bernabe. (Illus.). 200p. 1999. pap. 199.00 (*1-58673-009-6*) IOMA.

***1999 Licensing Update.** Gregory J. Battersby & Charles W. Grimes. LC 99-26304. 1999. write for info. (*0-7355-0552-7*) Panel Pubs.

1999 London Restaurants. annuals Zagat Publishers Staff. Ed. by Sholto Douglas-Home & Susan Kessler. (Zagat Survey Ser.). 236p. 1998. pap. 11.95 (*1-57006-143-2*) Zagat.

1999 Los Angeles Datebook. 1998. 9.95 (*1-892528-14-2*) Datebook Pub.

1999 Management Consulting Career Guide. Ed. by Neil Hunn. (Harvard Business School Career Guides). 208p. 1998. pap. text 24.95 (*0-87584-876-1*) Harvard Busn.

***1999 Managing Accounts Payable Yearbook.** Mary L. Schaeffer. (Illus.). 200p. 1999. pap. 199.00 (*1-58673-006-1*) IOMA.

***1999 Managing Benefits Plans Yearbook.** Susan Patterson. Ed. by Jan Chrisctian Berabe. (Illus.). 200p. 1999. pap. 199.00 (*1-58673-013-4*) IOMA.

***1999 Managing Credit, Receivables & Collections Yearbook.** Mary L. Schaeffer. Ed. by Janice Prescott. (Illus.). 200p. 1999. pap. 199.00 (*1-58673-005-3*) IOMA.

***1999 Managing HR Information Systems Yearbook.** Ed. by Andy Dzamba & Janice Prescott. (Illus.). 200p. 1999. pap. 199.00 (*1-58673-008-8*) IOMA.

***1999 Marketing & Public Policy Conference, Vol. 9.** Ed. by Gregory T. Gundlach et al. 97p. 1999. 45.00 (*0-87757-277-1*) Am Mktg.

***1999 Marketing Survey of A/E/P & Environmental Consulting Firms.** 6th ed. 348p. 1999. pap. 275.00 (*1-885002-98-X*) Zweig White.

1999 Medicaid Managed Behavioral Care Sourcebook: Strategies & Opportunities for Providers & Purchasers. Ed. by Ken Coughlin. LC 99-192066. (Illus.). 560p. 1998. pap. 225.00 (*1-57987-047-3*) Faulkner & Gray.

1999 Medicaid Managed Care Sourcebook. Ed. by Kenneth M. Coughlin. 560p. 1998. pap. 265.00 (*1-57987-105-4*) Faulkner & Gray.

1999 Medical Outcomes & Guidelines Sourcebook: A Progress Report & Resource Guide on Medical Outcomes Research & Practice Guidelines: Developments Data, & Implementation. Laura Newman. (Illus.). 1998. pap. 295.00 (*1-57987-084-8*) Faulkner & Gray.

1999 Medical Quality Management Sourcebook: A Comprehensive Guide to Measuring Quality & Applying the Results. rev. ed. Ed. by Ken Coughlin. 608p. 1998. pap. 250.00 (*1-57987-087-2*) Faulkner & Gray.

1999 Medicare & Medicaid Benefits. rev. ed. CCH Editorial Staff. 48p. 1999. pap. 10.00 (*0-8080-0308-9*) CCH INC.

1999 Medicare Explained. CCH Editorial Staff. 224p. 1999. pap. 25.00 (*0-8080-0307-0*) CCH INC.

1999 Medicare Managed Care Sourcebook. Ed. by Melissa Glim. 546p. 1998. pap. 275.00 (*1-57987-104-6*) Faulkner & Gray.

1999 Membership Directory. 1999. pap. write for info. (*1-58534-026-X*) Points of Light.

1999 Membership Directory. rev. ed. 215p. 1999. 10.00 (*1-888340-19-3*) AAPM.

1999 Miami Datebook. 1998. 9.95 (*1-892528-15-0*) Datebook Pub.

1999 Miami/South Florida Restaurant Survey. Zagat Publishers Staff. Date not set. pap. 9.95 (*1-57006-144-0*) Zagat.

1999 Michigan Child Support Formula Manual. John F. Wagner, Jr. 100p. 1999. pap. write for info. (*0-327-07800-6*, 5704112) LEXIS Pub.

1999 Midwest Senior Housing Book. 3rd rev. ed. Terry Fahey. Ed. by Lori Fahey. (Senior Housing Ser.). (Illus.). 380p. 1999. pap. 65.00 (*1-893583-02-3*) Research West.

1999 MILCOM. IEEE (Communications Society) Staff. LC 99-61144. 1584p. 1999. pap. write for info. (*0-7803-5538-5*, 99CH36341) Inst Electrical.

1999 Milwaukee Datebook. 1998. 9.95 (*1-892528-16-9*) Datebook Pub.

1999 Zagat Minneapolis Restaurant Survey. 1999. pap. 9.95 (*1-57006-166-1*) Zagat.

1999 Minneapolis/St. Paul Datebook. 1998. 9.95 (*1-892528-17-7*) Datebook Pub.

1999 MTT-S International Microwave Symposium. IEEE (Microwave Theory & Techniques Society, Elect. Ed. by IEEE (Institute of Electrical & Electronics Engine. LC 77-645125. 2400p. 1999. pap. text 332.00 (*0-7803-5135-5*, 99CH36282) Inst Electrical.

1999 Multi-Diet: Taming the Beast. Anderson A. Anonymous. LC 98-87950. (Illus.). vii, 417p. 1999. pap. 23.95 (*0-9667945-6-7*, TMD21999) Hamilton Wolcott.

***1999 Multi-Office Firm Survey of A/E/P & Environmental Consulting Firms.** 2nd ed. 225p. 1999. pap. 275.00 (*1-885002-97-1*) Zweig White.

1999 Municipal Water & Wastewater Market for A/E/P & Environmental Consulting Firms. Zweig White & Associates Staff. 416p. 1999. pap. text 395.00 (*1-885002-74-2*) Zweig White.

***1999 Music Yearbook.** Joel Whitburn. 250p. 2000. pap. 39.95 (*0-89820-138-1*) Record Research.

1999 NAGWS Volleyball Rules. Ed. by Ann L. Sruechte. (Illus.). 254p. 1999. pap. text 9.95 (*0-88314-811-0*) NAGWS.

1999 National CUSO Directory: Your Guide to the Nation's Credit Union Service Organization. 2nd rev. ed. 225p. 1999. pap. 125.00 (*1-889265-13-6*) Callahan & Assocs.

***1999 National Hispanic Media Directory Pt. 1: U. S. Media Companies.** Ed. by Kirk Whisler & Octavio Nuiry. 336p. 1999. pap. 95.00 (*1-889379-17-4*) WPR Pubng.

1999 National Hispanic Media Directory Pt. 3: Latin American Media. Octavio Nuiry. Ed. by Kirk Whisler. (Marketing Guidepost Ser.). 220p. 1998. pap. 95.00 (*1-889379-10-7*) WPR Pubng.

1999 National Roundtable on Family Group Decision Making & International Conference: Summary of Proceedings. Ed. by American Humane Association Staff. (Illus.). 2000. pap. 25.00 (*0-930915-31-3*) Am Humane Assn.

1999 NBA Analyst: A Revolutionary Method for Evaluating NBA Players & Teams. David Claerbaut. LC 98-38723. 192p. 1998. pap. 16.95 (*0-87833-210-3*) Taylor Pub.

***1999 NCSL Workshop & Symposium Proceedings: Metrology - At the Threshold of the Century Are We Ready?** Ed. by National Conference Standards Laboratories Staff. (Illus.). 1097p. 1999. text 50.00 (*1-58464-029-4*) Natl Conf Stds Labs.

1999 New Orleans Datebook. 1998. 9.95 (*1-892528-18-5*) Datebook Pub.

1999 New York Datebook. 1998. 9.95 (*1-892528-19-3*) Datebook Pub.

1999 New York Manufacturers Register. rev. ed. Ed. by Louise M. West & Frank Lambing. 1998. 145.00 (*1-58202-002-7*) Manufacturers.

1999 New York State Corporation Tax Law & Regulations. rev. ed. Ed. by CCH Editorial Staff. 600p. 1999. pap. text 99.00 (*0-8080-0313-5*) CCH INC.

1999 New York State Sales & Use Tax Law & Regulations. rev. ed. CCH Editorial Staff. 1400p. 1999. pap. text 89.00 (*0-8080-0314-3*) CCH INC.

1999 New York State Tax Law. rev. ed. CCH Editorial Staff. 700p. 1999. pap. text 79.00 (*0-8080-0315-1*) CCH INC.

***1999 North American Brewers Resource Directory: Your Yellow Pages to the Craftbrewing Industry.** 15th ed. Compiled by Institute for Brewing Studies Staff. 170p. 1999. pap. 100.00 (*0-937381-71-3*) Brewers Pubns.

1999 North Dakota Manufacturers Register. 3rd rev. ed. Ed. by Louise M. West & Frank Lambing. 1998. 54.00 (*1-58202-027-2*) Manufacturers.

1999 Northern Plains States Senior Housing Book. 3rd rev. ed. Terry Fahey. Ed. by Lori Fahey. (Senior Housing Ser.). (Illus.). 380p. 1999. pap. 65.00 (*1-893583-08-2*) Research West.

1999 Oceans. IEEE (Oceanic Engineering Society) Staff. Ed. by IEEE (Institute of Electrical & Electronics Engineers, Inc.) Staff. LC 99-62617. 1500p. 1999. pap. write for info. (*0-7803-5628-4*, 99CH37008) IEEE Standards.

1999 Official Museum Directory. National Register Publishing Co. Staff. 1998. 286.25 (*0-87217-908-7*) Natl Register.

1999 Official PGA Golf Directory of the South Central Section. Mark Frace. Ed. by Roger Runge. (Illus.). 112p. 1998. pap. 8.95 (*0-9662780-1-1*, Pub. by Resource Design) Herveys Bklink.

1999 Official Travel Industry Directory: The Sourcebook for Travel Professionals. 528p. 1999. 31.95 (*0-9644529-4-4*) Advanstar Commns.

***1999 Offshore Insurance Operations Conference.** Ed. by Dennis Kabelis. 1999. ring bd. write for info. (*1-56423-082-1*) Ntl Ctr Tax Ed.

1999 Oklahoma City Datebook. 919th ed. 1998. 9.95 (*1-892528-20-7*) Datebook Pub.

***1999 Oncology Nursing Drug Handbook - Hoechst.** 3rd ed. Gail Wilkes et al. (Illus.). (C). 1998. pap. text 50.00 (*0-7637-0987-5*) JB Pubns.

1999 Oncology Nursing Drug Handbook. 3rd ed. Gail M. Wilkes et al. LC 98-42615. (Jones & Bartlett Oncology Ser.). 734p. 1999. 50.00 (*0-7637-0865-8*) Jones & Bartlett.

***1999 Ophthalmic Drug Facts.** rev. ed. Facts & Comparisons Staff. Ed. by Jimmy Bartlett. 416p. 1998. pap. 54.95 (*1-57439-040-6*) Facts & Comparisons.

***1999 Original Pronouncements, 2 vols., Vols. 1-2.** 1999. pap. 102.95 (*0-471-37285-4*) Wiley.

***1999 Original Pronouncements Vol. 1: FASB Statements.** Financial Accounting Standards Board Staff. 1500p. 1999. pap. 51.95 (*0-471-35521-6*) Wiley.

1999 Particle Accelerator Conference. IEEE (Nuclear & Plasma Sciences Society) Staff. Ed. by IEEE (Institute of Electrical & Electronics Engineers, Inc.) Staff. LC 88-647453. 4000p. 1999. pap. write for info. (*0-7803-5573-3*, 99CH36366) IEEE Standards.

1999 Patient Resources on the Internet. Ed. by Eric Levy. 512p. 1998. pap. 195.00 (*1-57987-044-9*) Faulkner & Gray.

***1999 Payroll Managers Report Yearbook.** Donis W. Ford. (Illus.). 2000p. 1999. pap. 199.00 (*1-58673-000-2*) IOMA.

***1999 Pennsylvania County Data Book: Bucks.** Jennifer Shultz. Ed. by Diane Shoop. (Illus.). 139p. 1999. pap. 45.00 (*1-58036-072-6*) Penn State Data Ctr.

***1999 Pennsylvania County Data Book: Lebanon.** Jennifer Shultz. Ed. by Diane Shoop. (Illus.). 117p. 1999. pap. 35.00 (*1-58036-100-5*) Penn State Data Ctr.

***1999 Pennsylvania Abstract.** PASDC Staff. Ed. by Jennifer Shultz. (Illus.). 303p. 1999. pap. 50.00 (*1-58036-134-X*) Penn State Data Ctr.

***1999 Pennsylvania County Data Book: Adams.** Jennifer Shultz. Ed. by Diane Shoop. (Illus.). 116p. 1999. pap. 35.00 (*1-58036-064-5*) Penn State Data Ctr.

***1999 Pennsylvania County Data Book: Allegheny.** Jennifer Shultz. Ed. by Diane Shoop. (Illus.). 196p. 1999. pap. 45.00 (*1-58036-065-3*) Penn State Data Ctr.

***1999 Pennsylvania County Data Book: Armstrong.** Jennifer Shultz. Ed. by Diane Shoop. (Illus.). 118p. 1999. pap. 40.00 (*1-58036-066-1*) Penn State Data Ctr.

***1999 Pennsylvania County Data Book: Beaver.** Jennifer Shultz. Ed. by Diane Shoop. (Illus.). 132p. 1999. pap. 45.00 (*1-58036-067-X*) Penn State Data Ctr.

***1999 Pennsylvania County Data Book: Bedfurd.** Jennifer Shultz. Ed. by Diane Shoop. (Illus.). 114p. 1999. pap. 40.00 (*1-58036-068-8*) Penn State Data Ctr.

***1999 Pennsylvania County Data Book: Blair.** Jennifer Shultz. Ed. by Diane Shoop. (Illus.). 114p. 1999. pap. 35.00 (*1-58036-070-X*) Penn State Data Ctr.

***1999 Pennsylvania County Data Book: Bradford.** Jennifer Shultz. Ed. by Diane Shoop. (Illus.). 121p. 1999. pap. 40.00 (*1-58036-071-8*) Penn State Data Ctr.

***1999 Pennsylvania County Data Book: Butler.** Jennifer Shultz. Ed. by Diane Shoop. (Illus.). 133p. 1999. pap. 45.00 (*1-58036-073-4*) Penn State Data Ctr.

***1999 Pennsylvania County Data Book: Cambria.** Jennifer Shultz. Ed. by Diane Shoop. (Illus.). 137p. 1999. pap. 45.00 (*1-58036-074-2*) Penn State Data Ctr.

***1999 Pennsylvania County Data Book: Cameron.** Jennifer Shultz. Ed. by Diane Shoop. (Illus.), 94p. 1999. pap. 30.00 (*1-58036-075-0*) Penn State Data Ctr.

***1999 Pennsylvania County Data Book: Carbow.** Jennifer Shultz. Ed. by Diane Shoop. (Illus.). 101p. 1999. pap. 30.00 (*1-58036-076-9*) Penn State Data Ctr.

***1999 Pennsylvania County Data Book: Centre.** Jennifer Shultz. Ed. by Diane Shoop. (Illus.). 118p. 1999. pap. 35.00 (*1-58036-077-7*) Penn State Data Ctr.

***1999 Pennsylvania County Data Book: Chester.** Jennifer Shultz. Ed. by Diane Shoop. (Illus.). 153p. 1999. pap. 45.00 (*1-58036-078-5*) Penn State Data Ctr.

***1999 Pennsylvania County Data Book: Clarion.** Jennifer Shultz. Ed. by Diane Shoop. (Illus.). 113p. 1999. pap. 40.00 (*1-58036-079-3*) Penn State Data Ctr.

***1999 Pennsylvania County Data Book: Clearfield.** Jennifer Shultz. Ed. by Diane Shoop. (Illus.). 118p. 1999. pap. 40.00 (*1-58036-080-7*) Penn State Data Ctr.

***1999 Pennsylvania County Data Book: Clinton.** Jennifer Shultz. Ed. by Diane Shoop. (Illus.). 111p. 1999. pap. 35.00 (*1-58036-081-5*) Penn State Data Ctr.

***1999 Pennsylvania County Data Book: Columbia.** Jennifer Shultz. Ed. by Diane Shoop. (Illus.). 115p. 1999. pap. 35.00 (*1-58036-082-3*) Penn State Data Ctr.

***1999 Pennsylvania County Data Book: Crawford.** Jennifer Shultz. Ed. by Diane Shoop. (Illus.). 118p. 1999. pap. 45.00 (*1-58036-083-1*) Penn State Data Ctr.

***1999 Pennsylvania County Data Book: Cumberland.** Jennifer Shultz. Ed. by Diane Shoop. (Illus.). 122p. 1999. pap. 35.00 (*1-58036-084-X*) Penn State Data Ctr.

***1999 Pennsylvania County Data Book: Dauphin.** Jennifer Shultz. Ed. by Diane Shoop. (Illus.). 124p. 1999. pap. 40.00 (*1-58036-085-8*) Penn State Data Ctr.

***1999 Pennsylvania County Data Book: Delaware.** Jennifer Shultz. Ed. by Diane Shoop. (Illus.). 128p. 1999. pap. 40.00 (*1-58036-086-6*) Penn State Data Ctr.

***1999 Pennsylvania County Data Book: Elk.** Jennifer Shultz. Ed. by Diane Shoop. (Illus.). 100p. 1999. pap. 30.00 (*1-58036-087-4*) Penn State Data Ctr.

***1999 Pennsylvania County Data Book: Erie.** Jennifer Shultz. Ed. by Diane Shoop. (Illus.). 131p. 1999. pap. 40.00 (*1-58036-088-2*) Penn State Data Ctr.

***1999 Pennsylvania County Data Book: Fayette.** Jennifer Shultz. Ed. by Diane Shoop. (Illus.). 119p. 1999. pap. 40.00 (*1-58036-089-0*) Penn State Data Ctr.

***1999 Pennsylvania County Data Book: Forest.** Jennifer Shultz. Ed. by Diane Shoop. (Illus.). 96p. 1999. pap. 30.00 (*1-58036-090-4*) Penn State Data Ctr.

***1999 Pennsylvania County Data Book: Franklin.** Jennifer Shultz. Ed. by Diane Shoop. (Illus.). 106p. 1999. pap. 30.00 (*1-58036-091-2*) Penn State Data Ctr.

***1999 Pennsylvania County Data Book: Futon.** Jennifer Shultz. Ed. by Diane Shoop. (Illus.). 98p. 1999. pap. 30.00 (*1-58036-092-0*) Penn State Data Ctr.

***1999 Pennsylvania County Data Book: Greene.** Jennifer Shultz. Ed. by Diane Shoop. (Illus.). 108p. 1999. pap. 35.00 (*1-58036-093-9*) Penn State Data Ctr.

***1999 Pennsylvania County Data Book: Huntington.** Jennifer Shultz. Ed. by Diane Shoop. (Illus.). 114p. 1999. pap. 40.00 (*1-58036-094-7*) Penn State Data Ctr.

N

An Asterisk (*) at the beginning of an entry indicates that the title is appearing for the first time.

***1999 Pennsylvania County Data Book: Indiana.** Jennifer Shultz. Ed. by Diane Shoop. (Illus.). 119p. 1999. pap. 40.00 (*1-58036-095-5*) Penn State Data Ctr.

***1999 Pennsylvania County Data Book: Jefferson.** Jennifer Shultz. Ed. by Diane Shoop. (Illus.). 117p. 1999. pap. 35.00 (*1-58036-130-7*) Penn State Data Ctr.

***1999 Pennsylvania County Data Book: Juniata.** Jennifer Shultz. Ed. by Diane Shoop. (Illus.). 100p. 1999. pap. 30.00 (*1-58036-096-3*) Penn State Data Ctr.

***1999 Pennsylvania County Data Book: Lackawanna.** Jennifer Shultz. Ed. by Diane Shoop. (Illus.). 125p. 1999. pap. 40.00 (*1-58036-097-1*) Penn State Data Ctr.

***1999 Pennsylvania County Data Book: Lancaster.** Jennifer Shultz. Ed. by Diane Shoop. (Illus.). 146p. 1999. pap. 45.00 (*1-58036-098-X*) Penn State Data Ctr.

***1999 Pennsylvania County Data Book: Lawrence.** Jennifer Shultz. Ed. by Diane Shoop. (Illus.). 115p. 1999. pap. 35.00 (*1-58036-099-8*) Penn State Data Ctr.

***1999 Pennsylvania County Data Book: Lehigh.** Jennifer Shultz. Ed. by Diane Shoop. (Illus.). 120p. 1999. pap. 35.00 (*1-58036-101-3*) Penn State Data Ctr.

***1999 Pennsylvania County Data Book: Luzerne.** Jennifer Shultz. Ed. by Diane Shoop. (Illus.). 152p. 1999. pap. 45.00 (*1-58036-102-1*) Penn State Data Ctr.

***1999 Pennsylvania County Data Book: Lycoming.** Amy Jonas. Ed. by Diane Shoop. (Illus.). 131p. 1999. pap. 45.00 (*1-58036-103-X*) Penn State Data Ctr.

***1999 Pennsylvania County Data Book: McKean.** Jennifer Shultz. Ed. by Diane Shoop. (Illus.). 113p. 1999. pap. 30.00 (*1-58036-104-8*) Penn State Data Ctr.

***1999 Pennsylvania County Data Book: Mercer.** Jennifer Shultz. Ed. by Diane Shoop. (Illus.). 123p. 1999. pap. 40.00 (*1-58036-105-6*) Penn State Data Ctr.

***1999 Pennsylvania County Data Book: Mifflin.** Jennifer Shultz. Ed. by Diane Shoop. (Illus.). 102p. 1999. pap. 30.00 (*1-58036-106-4*) Penn State Data Ctr.

***1999 Pennsylvania County Data Book: Monroe.** Jennifer Shultz. Ed. by Diane Shoop. (Illus.). 106p. 1999. pap. 30.00 (*1-58036-107-2*) Penn State Data Ctr.

***1999 Pennsylvania County Data Book: Montgomery.** Jennifer Shultz. Ed. by Diane Shoop. (Illus.). 150p. 1999. pap. 45.00 (*1-58036-108-0*) Penn State Data Ctr.

***1999 Pennsylvania County Data Book: Montour.** Jennifer Shultz. Ed. by Diane Shoop. (Illus.). 99p. 1999. pap. 30.00 (*1-58036-109-9*) Penn State Data Ctr.

***1999 Pennsylvania County Data Book: Northampton.** Jennifer Shultz. Ed. by Diane Shoop. (Illus.). 122p. 1999. pap. 40.00 (*1-58036-110-2*) Penn State Data Ctr.

***1999 Pennsylvania County Data Book: Northumberland.** Jennifer Shultz. Ed. by Diane Shoop. (Illus.). 121p. 1999. pap. 40.00 (*1-58036-111-0*) Penn State Data Ctr.

***1999 Pennsylvania County Data Book: Perry.** Jennifer Shultz. Ed. by Diane Shoop. (Illus.). 113p. 1999. pap. 35.00 (*1-58036-112-9*) Penn State Data Ctr.

***1999 Pennsylvania County Data Book: Philadelphia.** Jennifer Shultz. Ed. by Diane Shoop. (Illus.). 123p. 1999. pap. 30.00 (*1-58036-113-7*) Penn State Data Ctr.

***1999 Pennsylvania County Data Book: Pike.** Jennifer Shultz. Ed. by Diane Shoop. (Illus.). 98p. 1999. pap. 30.00 (*1-58036-114-5*) Penn State Data Ctr.

***1999 Pennsylvania County Data Book: Potter.** Jennifer Shultz. Ed. by Diane Shoop. (Illus.). 108p. 1999. pap. 35.00 (*1-58036-115-3*) Penn State Data Ctr.

***1999 Pennsylvania County Data Book: Schuylkill.** Jennifer Shultz. Ed. by Diane Shoop. (Illus.). 139p. 1999. pap. 45.00 (*1-58036-116-1*) Penn State Data Ctr.

***1999 Pennsylvania County Data Book: Snyder.** Jennifer Shultz. Ed. by Diane Shoop. (Illus.). 110p. 1999. pap. 30.00 (*1-58036-117-X*) Penn State Data Ctr.

***1999 Pennsylvania County Data Book: Somerset.** Jennifer Shultz. Ed. by Diane Shoop. (Illus.). 118p. 1999. pap. 45.00 (*1-58036-118-8*) Penn State Data Ctr.

***1999 Pennsylvania County Data Book: Sullivan.** Jennifer Shultz. Ed. by Diane Shoop. (Illus.). 96p. 1999. pap. 30.00 (*1-58036-119-6*) Penn State Data Ctr.

***1999 Pennsylvania County Data Book: Susquehanna.** Jennifer Shultz. Ed. by Diane Shoop. (Illus.). 115p. 1999. pap. 40.00 (*1-58036-120-X*) Penn State Data Ctr.

***1999 Pennsylvania County Data Book: Tioga.** Jennifer Shultz. Ed. by Diane Shoop. (Illus.). 114p. 1999. pap. 40.00 (*1-58036-121-8*) Penn State Data Ctr.

***1999 Pennsylvania County Data Book: Union.** Jennifer Shultz. Ed. by Diane Shoop. (Illus.). 100p. 1999. pap. 30.00 (*1-58036-122-6*) Penn State Data Ctr.

***1999 Pennsylvania County Data Book: Venango.** Jennifer Shultz. Ed. by Diane Shoop. (Illus.). 115p. 1999. pap. 35.00 (*1-58036-123-4*) Penn State Data Ctr.

***1999 Pennsylvania County Data Book: Warren.** Jennifer Shultz. Ed. by Diane Shoop. (Illus.). 109p. 1999. pap. 35.00 (*1-58036-124-2*) Penn State Data Ctr.

***1999 Pennsylvania County Data Book: Washington.** Jennifer Shultz. Ed. by Diane Shoop. (Illus.). 139p. 1999. pap. 45.00 (*1-58036-125-0*) Penn State Data Ctr.

***1999 Pennsylvania County Data Book: Wayne.** Jennifer Shultz. Ed. by Diane Shoop. (Illus.). 110p. 1999. pap. 35.00 (*1-58036-126-9*) Penn State Data Ctr.

***1999 Pennsylvania County Data Book: Westmoreland.** Jennifer Shultz. Ed. by Diane Shoop. (Illus.). 145p. 1999. pap. 45.00 (*1-58036-127-7*) Penn State Data Ctr.

***1999 Pennsylvania County Data Book: Wyoming.** Jennifer Shultz. Ed. by Diane Shoop. (Illus.). 101p. 1999. pap. 35.00 (*1-58036-128-5*) Penn State Data Ctr.

***1999 Pennsylvania County Data Book: York.** Jennifer Shultz. Ed. by Diane Shoop. (Illus.). 149p. 1999. pap. 45.00 (*1-58036-129-3*) Penn State Data Ctr.

***1999 Pennsylvania County Data Book No. 6: Berks.** Jennifer Shultz. Ed. by Diane Shoop. (Illus.). 149p. 1999. pap. 45.00 (*1-58036-069-6*) Penn State Data Ctr.

1999 Pennsylvania Manufacturers Register. 13th rev. ed. Ed. by Louise M. West & Frank Lambing. 1998. 154.00 (*1-58202-029-9*) Manufacturers.

***1999 Petro Process Directory.** 10th rev. ed. Ed. by James W. Self. 424p. 1999. pap. 65.00 (*1-889879-14-2*) Atlantic Commun.

1999 Philadelphia Datebook. 1998. 9.95 (*1-892528-21-5*) Datebook Pub.

1999 Phoenix Datebook. 1998. 9.95 (*1-892528-22-3*) Datebook Pub.

***1999 Physician ICD-9-CM, Compact Edition: International Classification of Diseases.** 9th rev. ed. Medicode, Inc. Staff. (Illus.). vi, 1478p. (C). 1999. pap. write for info. (*1-56337-284-3*) Thomson Learn.

1999 Physician ICD-9-CM: International Classification of Diseases, Clinical Modification. 9th ed. Medicode Staff. iii, 774p. (C). 1998. pap. write for info. (*1-56337-285-1*) Thomson Learn.

***1999 Physician Salary Survey Report, Vol. 23.** 390p. 1999. pap. 250.00 (*0-939326-46-9*) Hosp & Hlthcare.

***1999 PIA Ratios: All Printers by Product Specialty.** PIA Staff. (PIA Ratios Ser.: Vol. 3). (Illus.). 80p. (C). 1999. pap. text 199.00 (*0-88362-269-6*, 00FM99003) GATFPress.

***1999 PIA Ratios: All Printers by Sales Volume & Geographic Areas.** PIA Staff. (PIA Ratios Ser.: Vol. 2). (Illus.). 80p. (Orig.). (C). 1999. pap. text 199.00 (*0-88362-268-8*, 00FM99002) GATFPress.

***1999 PIA Ratios: Binders' Ratios.** PIA Staff. (PIA Ratios Ser.: Vol. 11). (Illus.). 80p. (C). 1999. pap. text 199.00 (*0-88362-277-7*, 00FM99011) GATFPress.

***1999 PIA Ratios: Book Manufacturer's Ratios.** PIA Staff. (PIA Ratios Ser.: Vol. 8). (Illus.). 80p. (C). 1999. pap. text 199.00 (*0-88362-274-2*, 00FM99008) GATFPress.

***1999 PIA Ratios: Business Forms Ratios.** PIA Staff. (PIA Ratios Ser.: Vol. 14). (Illus.). 80p. (C). 1999. pap. text 199.00 (*0-88362-280-7*, 00FM99014) GATFPress.

***1999 PIA Ratios: Combination Offset-Sheetfed/Web.** PIA Staff. (PIA Ratios Ser.: Vol. 7). (Illus.). 80p. (C). 1999. pap. text 199.00 (*0-88362-273-4*, 00FM99007) GATFPress.

***1999 PIA Ratios: Commercial & Advertising Printers.** PIA Staff. (PIA Ratios Ser.: Vol. 17). (Illus.). 80p. (C). 1999. pap. text 199.00 (*0-88362-283-1*, 00FM99017) GATFPress.

***1999 PIA Ratios: Digital Printers' Ratios.** PIA Staff. (PIA Ratios Ser.: Vol. 16). (Illus.). 80p. (C). 1999. pap. text 199.00 (*0-88362-282-3*, 00FM99016) GATFPress.

***1999 PIA Ratios: Label Printers' Ratios.** PIA Staff. (PIA Ratios Ser.: Vol. 15). (Illus.). 80p. (C). 1999. pap. text 199.00 (*0-88362-281-5*, 00FM99015) GATFPress.

***1999 PIA Ratios: Managament Guide to PIA Ratios.** PIA Staff. (PIA Ratios Ser.: Vol. 1). (Illus.). 80p. (C). 1999. pap. text 199.00 (*0-88362-267-X*, 00FM990001) GATFPress.

***1999 PIA Ratios: Prepress Specialists' Ratios.** PIA Staff. (PIA Ratios Ser.: Vol. 10). (Illus.). 80p. (C). 1999. pap. text 199.00 (*0-88362-276-9*, 00FM99010) GATFPress.

***1999 PIA Ratios: Printers with Sales over $10,000,000.** PIA Staff. (PIA Ratios Ser.: Vol. 9). (Illus.). 80p. (C). 1999. pap. text 199.00 (*0-88362-275-0*, 00FM99009) GATFPress.

***1999 PIA Ratios: Printers with Sales under $1,500,000.** PIA Staff. (PIA Ratios Ser.: Vol. 12). (Illus.). 80p. (C). 1999. pap. text 199.00 (*0-88362-278-5*, 00FM99012) GATFPress.

***1999 PIA Ratios: Quick Printers' Ratios.** PIA Staff. (PIA Ratios Ser.: Vol. 13). (Illus.). 80p. (C). 1999. pap. text 199.00 (*0-88362-279-3*, 00FM99013) GATFPress.

***1999 PIA Ratios: Sheetfed Printers by Size & Geographic Area.** PIA Staff. (PIA Ratios Ser.: Vol. 4). (Illus.). 80p. (C). 1999. pap. text 199.00 (*0-88362-270-X*, 00FM99004) GATFPress.

***1999 PIA Ratios: Web Offset Printers, Heatset.** PIA Staff. (PIA Ratios Ser.: Vol. 5). (Illus.). 80p. (C). 1999. pap. text 199.00 (*0-88362-271-8*, 00FM99005) GATFPress.

***1999 PIA Ratios: Web Offset Printers, Non-Heatset, Vol. 6.** PIA Staff. (PIA Ratios Ser.: Vol. 6). (Illus.). 80p. (C). 1999. pap. text 199.00 (*0-88362-272-6*, 00FM99006) GATFPress.

1999 Pilot Resource Guide. 4th ed. Ed. by Becky Dean & Montina L. Waymire. 64p. 1999. pap. 24.95 (*1-891726-23-4*, AIR Inc) Aviation Info.

1999 Pilot's Guide to Flying in the Guard & Reserve. Robert U. Black. Ed. by Montina L. Waymire & Dave Mattice. 368p. 1999. pap. 40.95 (*1-891726-22-6*, AIR Inc) Aviation Info.

1999 Pittsburgh Datebook. 1998. 9.95 (*1-892528-23-1*) Datebook Pub.

1999 Pocket Book of Antimicrobial Therapy & Prevention. 2nd ed. Sherwood L. Gorbach et al. 360p. 24.95 (*0-683-18379-6*) Lppncott W & W.

1999 Pocketax for Returns of 1998 Income. rev. ed. Ed. by CCH Editorial Staff. 85p. 1998. pap. text 7.50 (*0-8080-0319-4*) CCH INC.

1999 Policies, Procedures & Benefits Survey of A-E-P & Environmental Consulting Firms. 5th ed. Zweig White & Associates Staff. 312p. 1999. pap. text 275.00 (*1-885002-75-0*) Zweig White.

1999 Political Risk Yearbook, 8 vols. Incl. Vol. I. North & Central America. 675p. Date not set. 275.00 (*1-85271-394-1*); Vol. II. Middle East & North Africa. 730p. Date not set. 275.00 (*1-85271-395-X*); Vol. III. South America. 550p. Date not set. 275.00 (*1-85271-396-8*); Vol. IV. Sub-Saharan Africa. 700p. Date not set. 275.00 (*1-85271-397-6*); Vol. V. Asia & the Pacific. 850p. Date not set. 275.00 (*1-85271-376-3*); Vol. VI. West Europe. 1125p. Date not set. 275.00 (*1-85271-390-9*); Vol. VII. East Europe. Ed. by PRS Group Staff. 1999. pap. 275.00 (*1-85271-391-7*); Date not set. cd-rom 1200.00 (*1-85271-313-5*); 1200.00 (*1-85271-339-9*) PRS Grp.

1999 Portland Datebook. 1998. 9.95 (*1-892528-24-X*) Datebook Pub.

1999 Portrait World Atlas. 1998. 39.95 (*0-528-83995-0*) Rand McNally.

1999 Post Acute Outcomes Sourcebook: A Guide to Methods, Measures, & Strategies in Post-Acute Care. Ed. by Lois Wingerson. (Illus.). 496p. 1998. pap. 245.00 (*1-57987-049-X*) Faulkner & Gray.

1999 Power Tool Blue Book. rev. ed. 1999. lib. bdg. 200.00 (*0-932089-83-6*) Orion Res.

1999 Family Practice Sourcebook: Current Literature & Medical Evidence in Patient Care. Marshall. LC 98-15925. (Illus.). 405p. (C). (gr. 13). 1998. pap. text 49.95 (*0-8151-2785-5*, 31801) Mosby Inc.

***1999 PricewaterhouseCoopers Survey of U. S. Petroleum Accounting Practices.** Ed. by Teddy L. Coe et al. 261p. 1999. mass mkt. 125.00 (*0-926969-05-6*) UNTIPA.

1999 Principal's Survey of A/E/P & Environmental Consulting Firms. 8th ed. Zweig White & Associates Staff. 246p. 1999. pap. text 275.00 (*1-885002-76-9*) Zweig White.

***1999 Pro Football Ultimate Statistics.** Scott L. Perry. 152p. 1999. pap. 19.95 (*0-9674386-0-8*) Perry Rating.

***1999 Procedural Coding Crosswalk.** Medicode, Inc. Staff. ii, 329p. (C). 1999. pap. write for info. (*1-56337-288-6*) Thomson Learn.

***1999 Proceedings Ironmaking Conference, Vol. 58.** Iron & Steel Society Staff. LC 77-61344. (Illus.). 781p. 1999. pap. 110.00 (*1-886362-32-7*) Iron & Steel.

***1999 Proceedings of the 45th Annual Technical Meeting of the Institute of Environmental Sciences & Technology: Today's Training for Tomorrow's World, Ontario, CA, April, 1999.** Institute of Environmental Sciences & Technology Staff. LC 62-38584. 1999. pap. text 195.00 (*1-877862-66-5*) IEST.

1999 Professional Sound Blue Book. rev. ed. 1998. lib. bdg. 200.00 (*1-892761-00-9*) Orion Res.

***1999 Project Management Survey of A-E-P & Environmental Consulting Firms.** 4th ed. 228p. 1999. pap. text 275.00 (*1-885002-95-5*) Zweig White.

***1999 PUR Analysis of the NAtion's Largest Investor-Owned Electric & Gas Utilities.** Ed. by Bruce Kinsey & Joan M. Anderson. 475p. 1999. 998.00 incl. cd-rom (*0-910325-77-4*) Public Util.

1999 Random Lengths Buyers' & Sellers' Guide: A Directory of the Forest Products Industry. Ed. by Jon P. Anderson. 1102p. 1999. 195.00 (*1-884311-06-7*) Random Lgths Pubns.

***1999 Random Lengths Yearbook: Forest Product Market, Prices & Statistics.** 248p. 2000. pap. 42.95 (*1-884311-09-1*) Random Lgths Pubns.

1999 RBRVS. 100p. 1999. pap. 65.00 (*1-58383-043-X*) Robert D Keene.

1999 RBRVS: Resource Based Relative Value Scale. 250p. 1999. pap. 65.00 (*1-58383-008-1*, RBRVS9) Robert D Keene.

***1999 Report on Salary Surveys Yearbook.** Laime Vaitkus. (Illus.). 200p. 1999. pap. 199.00 (*1-58673-001-0*) IOMA.

1999 Residency Directory, 2 vols. rev. ed. Contrib. by Accreditation Services Division Staff. 448p. 1998. pap. text 31.00 (*1-879907-83-6*) Am Soc Hlth-Syst.

1999 Residency Directory, Vol. 2. rev. ed. Contrib. by Accreditation Services Division Staff. 256p. 1998. pap. text 31.00 (*1-879907-84-4*) Am Soc Hlth-Syst.

1999 River of Words: The Natural World As Views by Young People. Robert Hass. (Poetry from the Annual River of Words Contest Ser.). (Illus.). 48p. 1999. per. 5.00 (*0-9662771-3-9*) Intl Riv Ntwrk.

***1999 Robert H. Ebert Memorial Lecture: Understanding Health Behavior & Speaking Out on the Uninsured: Two Leadership Opportunities.** Steven A. Schroeder. 28p. 1999. pap. write for info. (*1-887748-33-4*) Milbank Memorial.

***1999 Rugby World Cup Essential Stats & Facts.** Steve Pearce. (Illus.). 160p. 1999. pap. 15.95 (*0-7522-1740-2*, Pub. by Boxtree) Trans-Atl Phila.

1999 S-Corporation Tax Guide. 99th ed. Jamison. (C). 1998. pap. text 129.00 (*0-15-606628-9*, Pub. by Harcourt Coll Pubs) Harcourt.

***1999 Salary Study.** Patrick Curtis & Anna Laitin. 1999. pap. 26.95 (*0-87868-782-3*) Child Welfare.

1999 San Antonio Datebook. 1998. 9.95 (*1-892528-25-8*) Datebook Pub.

1999 San Diego Datebook. 1998. 9.95 (*1-892528-26-6*) Datebook Pub.

1999 San Francisco Datebook. 1998. 9.95 (*1-892528-27-4*) Datebook Pub.

***1999 SBMO/IEEE-International Microwave & Optoelectronics Conference.** IEEE (Microwave Theory & Techniques Society) Staff. Ed. by IEEE (Institute of Electrical & Electronics Engineers, Inc.) Staff. 700p. 1999. pap. write for info. (*0-7803-5807-4*, 99TH8481) IEEE Standards.

1999 School Law in Review. NSBA Council of School Attorneys Members. 160p. 1999. pap. 35.00 (*0-88364-223-9*, 06-168) Natl Sch Boards.

***1999 Season Replay Yearbook.** (Illus.). 112p. 2000. pap. 39.95 (*0-9700351-2-8*) Replay Pubng.

1999 Seattle Datebook. 1998. 9.95 (*1-892528-28-2*) Datebook Pub.

1999 2nd IEEE Signal Processing Workshop on Signal Processing Advances in Wireless Communications. IEEE (Signal Processing Society) Staff. Ed. by IEEE (Institute of Electrical & Electronics Engineers, Inc.) Staff. LC 99-62323. 426p. 1999. pap. write for info. (*0-7803-5599-7*, 99EX304) IEEE Standards.

1999 2nd International Conference on ATM. IEEE (French Communications Chapter - French Computer Chapter) Staff. Ed. by IEEE(Institute of Electrical & Electronics Engineers, Inc.) Staff. LC 99-60529. 550p. 1999. pap. write for info. (*0-7803-5428-1*, 99EX284) IEEE Standards.

1999 2nd International Conference on Intelligent Processing & Manufacturing of Material. IEEE (Systems, Man & Cybernetics Society) Staff. LC 99-61516. 1494p. 1999. pap. write for info. (*0-7803-5489-3*, 99EX296) Inst Electrical.

1999 2nd International Conference on Information Application in Biomedicine. IEEE, Engineering in Medicine & Biology Society Staff. Ed. by IEEE (Institute of Electrical & Electronics Engineers, Inc.) Staff. LC 99-62713. 30p. 1999. pap. write for info. (*0-7803-5647-0*, 99TH8457) IEEE Standards.

***1999 Senate Staff Employment Study.** Sheree L. Beverly. (Illus.). 126p. 1999. pap. text 15.00 (*1-930473-00-1*) Congressional Mgmt Fdnt.

***1999 SERVSIG Services Research Conference: Jazzing into the New Millennium.** Ed. by Raymond P. Fisk & Liam Glynn. 185p. 1999. pap. 45.00 (*0-87757-279-8*) Am Mktg.

1999 7th International Symposium on the Physical Failure Analysis of Integrated Circuits. IEEE (Electron Devices Society) Staff. LC 98-88539. 300p. 1999. pap. 128.00 (*0-7803-5187-8*, 99TH8394) Inst Electrical.

1999 Sixteenth International Conference on Insurance Taxation. Ed. by Dennis Kabelis. 1999. ring bd. write for info. (*1-56423-084-8*) Ntl Ctr Tax Ed.

***1999 6th International Workshop on Multimedia Communications.** IEEE (Communications Society) Staff. Ed. by IEEE (Institute of Electrical & Electronics Engineers, Inc.) Staff. LC 99-67926. 400p. 1999. pap. write for info. (*0-7803-5904-6*, 99EX284) IEEE Standards.

***1999 6th International Conference on Neural Information Processing.** IEEE (Western Australia Section) Staff. Ed. by IEEE (Institute of Electrical & Electronics Engineers, Inc.) Staff. LC 99-67211. 650p. 1999. pap. write for info. (*0-7803-5871-6*, 99EX378) Inst Electrical.

***1999 6th International Conference on VLSI & CAD.** IEEE Staff. LC 99-64042. 500p. 1999. pap. write for info. (*0-7803-5727-2*, 99EX361) IEEE Standards.

***1999 6th Working Conference on Current Measurement.** IEEE (Oceanic Engineering Society) Staff. Ed. by IEEE (Institute of Electrical & Electronics Engineers, Inc.) Staff. LC 99-60894. 300p. 1999. pap. write for info. (*0-7803-5505-9*, 99CH36331) Inst Electrical.

1999 Social Security Benefits Including Medicare. rev. ed. CCH Editorial Staff. 64p. 1999. pap. 10.00 (*0-8080-0309-7*) CCH INC.

***1999 Social Security Explained.** rev. ed. 340p. 1999. pap. 30.00 (*0-8080-0304-6*) CCH INC.

1999 Software Developer's Guide. Whil Hentzen. Ed. by Jeffrey A. Donnici. 400p. 1999. pap. 49.95 (*0-9655093-2-X*) Hentzenwerke.

***1999 Source Book on Collective Bargaining: Wages, Benefits & Other Contract Issues.** Ed. by Joyce T. Bagot. 1999. ring bd. 80.00 (*1-55871-397-2*) BNA PLUS.

***1999 Southern Living Annual Recipes.** 1999. 34.95 (*0-8487-1904-2*) Oxmoor Hse.

1999 Southern New Hampshire Children's Directory. 366p. 1998. 14.98 (*1-891486-05-5*) Romagnoli.

1999 Southwest Senior Housing Book. 3rd rev. ed. Terry Fahey. Ed. by Lori Fahey. (Senior Housing Ser.). (Illus.). 380p. 1999. pap. 65.00 (*1-893583-04-X*) Research West.

1999 Southwest Symposium on Mixed-Signal Design. IEEE, Tucson Section Staff. LC 99-60929. 252p. 1999. pap. write for info. (*0-7803-5510-5*, 99EX286) Inst Electrical.

1999 Latino Speakers Directory. Kirk Whisler & Carlos Conejo. (Stepping Stones to Success Ser.). (Illus.). 194p. 1998. pap. 29.95 (*1-889379-13-1*) WPR Pubng.

***1999 Sport Summit Sports Business Directory.** rev. ed. Ed. by Michael Patino. 1096p. 1999. pap. 189.00 (*0-9644259-4-7*) E J Krause.

1999 Sports Collectors Almanac. 2nd ed. Editors of Sports Collectors Digest. (Illus.). 304p. 1999. per. 21.95 (*0-87341-744-5*) Krause Pubns.

***1999 Spring Simulation Interoperability Workshop: Workshop Papers.** (Simulation Interoperability Workshop Ser.). (Illus.). 1300p. 1999. 75.00 (*1-930638-06-X*) S I S O.

1999 St. Louis Datebook. 1998. 9.95 (*1-892528-29-0*) Datebook Pub.

1999 Starcycles Astrological Planning Book. 5th ed. Georgia Stathis. (Illus.). 80p. 1998. pap. 14.95 (*1-881229-18-1*) Starcycles.

***1999 State of the Future: Challenges We Face at the Millennium.** Jerome C. Glenn & Theodore J. Gordon. (Illus.). 348p. 1999. pap. 48.50 (*0-9657362-3-7*) Am Coun Unit Nat.

***1999 State Quarter Collector.** Krause Publications Staff. (Illus.). 64p. 2000. 9.95 (*0-87341-983-9*) Krause Pubns.

***1999 Statement of Financial Accounting Concepts.** Financial Accounting Standards Board Staff. 800p. 1999. pap. 30.95 (*0-471-35518-6*) Wiley.

1999 Strategic Systems Planning & Management, 1999. Bennet P. Lientz. 350p. 1999. pap. text 65.00 (*0-15-606075-2*) Harcourt.

***1999 Summer Computer Simulation Conference.** Ed. by Mohammad S. Obaidat et al. 658p. 1999. 180.00 (*1-56555-173-7*) Soc Computer Sim.

***1999 Supertrader's Almanac: Second Half Edition.** Frank A. Taucher. 400p. 1999. pap. 144.00 (*1-879591-58-8*) Mkt Movements.

***1999 Supertrader's Book of Linear Time Cycles.** Frank A. Taucher. 476p. 1999. pap. 144.00 (*1-879591-57-X*) Mkt Movements.

1995 Supplement to Cases & Materials on Conflict of Laws, Suppl. 4. 9th ed. Peter Hay et al. (University Casebook Ser.). 58p. 1995. pap. text 4.95 (*1-56662-271-9*) Foundation Pr.

An Asterisk (*) at the beginning of an entry indicates that the title is appearing for the first time.

***1999 Supplement to Connecticut Jury Instruction (Civil)** 4th ed. Douglas B. Wright & William L. Ankerman. 242p. 1999. pap. 59.00 (*1-878698-55-9*) Atlantic Law.

***1999 Supplement to the American Indian Law Deskbook.** 2nd ed. 80p. 1999. pap. 19.95 (*0-87081-535-0*) Univ Pr Colo.

***1999 Symposium of Higher Education (10th Annual Conference)** 240p. 1999. 45.00 (*0-87757-280-1*) Am Mktg.

***1999 Symposium on the Performance Evaluation of Computer & Telecommunication Systems.** Ed. by Mohammad S. Obaidat & Marco Ajmone Marsan. 414p. 1999. pap. 100.00 (*1-56555-174-5*) Soc Computer Sim.

1999 Taste of Home Annual Recipes. Ed. by Julie Schnittka. 324p. 1998. 24.95 (*0-89821-239-1*) Reiman Pubns.

***1999 Tax Year in Review.** CCH Tax Law Editors. 268p. 2000. pap. text 42.00 (*0-8080-0471-9*) CCH INC.

1999 Team & Organization Development Sourcebook. Mel Silberman. (ASQ Ser.). (Illus.). 350p. 1998. pap. 57.95 (*0-07-058096-0*); ring bd. 114.95 (*0-07-913778-4*) McGraw-Hill Prof.

***1999 Telecommunications Information Networking Architecture Conference Proceedings.** IEEE (Communication Society) Staff. Ed. by IEEE (Institute of Electrical & Electronics Engineers, Inc.) Staff. LC 99-65351. 400p. 1999. pap. write for info. (*0-7803-5785-X*, 99EX368) Inst Electrical.

1999 Telemedicine Sourcebook. Ed. by Eric Levy & Kenneth Coughlin. 512p. 1998. pap. 275.00 (*1-57987-046-5*) Faulkner & Gray.

1999 Television Writers Guide. 5th ed. Ed. by Lynne Naylor. 608p. 1999. pap. 55.00 (*0-943728-86-X*) Lone Eagle Pub.

1999 10th International Symposium on Electrets Proceedings. IEEE Staff. LC 98-86196. 750p. 1999. lib. bdg. 172.00 (*0-7803-5026-X*, 98CH36256) IEEE Standards.

1999 10th International Symposium on Electrets Proceedings. IEEE Staff. LC 98-86196. 750p. 1999. pap. text 172.00 (*0-7803-5025-1*, 98CH36256) Inst Electrical.

1999 Texas Senior Housing Book. 3rd rev. ed. Terry Fahey. Ed. by Lori Fahey. (Senior Housing Ser.). (Illus.). 380p. 1999. pap. 65.00 (*1-893583-06-6*) Research West.

***1999 3rd European Conference on High Temperature Electronics - HITEN '99.** IEEE, Electron Devices Society Staff. Ed. by Institute of Electrical & Electronics Engineers, Inc. Staff. LC 99-65668. 120p. 1999. pap. write for info. (*0-7803-5795-7*, 99EX372) IEEE Standards.

1999 3rd International Workshop on Design of Mixed-Mode Integrated Circuits & Applications. IEEE (Circuits & Systems Society, Cas Puebla Chapter) Staff. Ed. by IEEE (Institute of Electrical & Electronics Engineers, Inc.) Staff. LC 99-62172. 220p. 1999. pap. write for info. (*0-7803-5588-1*, 99EX303) IEEE Standards.

***1999 3rd International Enterprise Distributed Object Computing Conference.** IEEE (Communications Society & Computer Society) S. Ed. by IEEE (Institute of Electrical & Electronics Engineers, Inc.) Staff. LC 99-65352. 400p. 1999. pap. write for info. (*0-7803-5784-1*, 99EX366) Inst Electrical.

1999 3rd International Symposium Application of Conversion Research Results for International Cooperation. IEEE (Electron Devices Society) Staff. Ed. by IEEE Institute of Electrical & Electronics Engineers, Inc. Staff. LC 98-88248. 200p. 1999. pap. text 118.00 (*0-7803-5172-X*, 99EX246) Inst Electrical.

1999 3rd International Conference on Knowledge Based Intelligent Electronics Systems. IEEE (South Australia Section) Staff. Ed. by IEEE (Institute of Electrical & Electronics Engineers, Inc.) Staff. LC 99-61882. 400p. 1999. pap. write for info. (*0-7803-5578-4*, 99TH8410) IEEE Standards.

***1999 3rd Russian-Korean International Symposium on Science & Technology.** IEEE Electron Devices Society Staff. 800p. 1999. pap. write for info. (*0-7803-5729-9*, 99EX362) IEEE Standards.

1999 13th Biennial Univrsity/Gonernment/Industry Microelectronics Symposium. IEEE (Electron Devices Society) Staff. Ed. by Institute of Electrical & Electronics Engineers, I. 200p. 1999. pap. 118.00 (*0-7803-5240-8*, 99CH36301) Inst Electrical.

1999 How to Investigate by Computer. rev. ed. Ralph D. Thomas. 1999. spiral bd. 45.00 (*1-891247-27-1*) Thomas Investigative.

***1999-2000 Accredited Institutions of Post-Secondary Education.** 24th ed. Ed. by American Council on Education Staff. (Ace-Oryx Series on Higher Education). 736p. 2000. pap. 59.95 (*1-57356-282-3*) Oryx Pr.

1999-2000 Airline Fleet & Sim Directory. Kit Darby & Dan Gradwohl. Ed. by Montina L. Waymire & Becky Dean. 64p. 1999. pap. 29.95 (*1-891726-25-0*, AIR Inc) Aviation Info.

***1999-2000 Comprehensive Accreditation Manual for Behavioral Health Care.** rev. ed. Joint Commission on Accreditation of Healthcare Organizations. (Illus.). 520p. 1998. 225.00 (*0-86688-593-5*, CBHC-99) Joint Comm Hlthcare.

1999-2000 Finance Calendar of Duties for City & County Officials. Pref. by Gregory S. Allison. 1999. pap. 6.00 (*1-56011-357-X*) Institute Government.

***1999-2000 Hockey Annual: The Indispensible Guide to the Complete NHL Season.** Murray Townsend. (Illus.). 256p. 1999. pap. 17.95 (*1-894020-61-8*) Warwick Pub.

***1999-2000 PATA Chapter Directory.** 99p. 1999. pap. 50.00 (*1-882866-39-8*) Pac Asia Trvl.

***1999-2000 Standards for Behavioral Health Care.** Joint Commission on Accreditation of Healthcare Organizations. 305p. 1998. pap. 70.00 (*0-86688-594-3*, BHCS-99) Joint Comm Hlthcare.

***1999-2000 Standards for Home Care.** Joint Commission on Accreditation of Healthcare Organizations. 222p. 1998. pap. 70.00 (*0-86688-596-X*, HCS-99) Joint Comm Hlthcare.

***1999-2000 Annual Supplement to the Piano Book.** Larry Fine. 138p. 1999. pap. 14.95 (*1-929145-00-4*) Brookside Pr MA.

1999-2000 V. I. P. Address Book. Ed. by James M. Wiggins. 1999. lib. bdg. 94.95 (*0-938731-14-9*) Assoc Media Cos.

1999 Toy Shop Annual. Ed. by Editors of Toy Shop Magazine. (Illus.). 88p. 1999. per. 9.95 (*0-87341-785-2*) Krause Pubns.

1999 Trailer Life Campgrounds, RV Parks, & Services Directory. (Illus.). 1800p. 1998. mass mkt. 19.95 (*0-934798-58-3*, Trailer Life Bks) TL Enterprises.

1999 Training & Performance Sourcebook. Ed. by Mel Silberman. (ASQ Ser.). (Illus.). 350p. 1998. pap. 57.95 (*0-07-058095-2*); ring bd. 114.95 (*0-07-913777-6*) McGraw-Hill Prof.

1999 Transmission & Distribution Conference. IEEE (Power Engineering Society) Staff. LC 99-61042. 1000p. 1999. pap. write for info. (*0-7803-5515-6*, 99CH36333) Inst Electrical.

1999 Transmission & Driveline Systems Symposium. (Special Publications). 420p. 1999. pap. 109.00 (*0-7680-0372-5*, SP-1440) Soc Auto Engineers.

1999 Truckers Atlas. American Map Publishing Staff. 1998. pap. 19.95 (*0-8416-9228-9*) Am Map.

1999 12th IEEE International Micro Electro Mechanical Systems Conference. IEEE (Robotics & Automation Society) Staff. 600p. 1999. pap. 166.00 (*0-7803-5194-0*, 99CH36291) Inst Electrical.

1999 12th IEEE International Pulsed Power Conference. IEEE, Nuclear & Plasma Sciences Society Staff. Ed. by Institute of Electrical & Electronics Engineers, Inc. Staff. LC 99-61748. 1500p. 2000. pap. write for info. (*0-7803-5498-2*, 99CH36358) IEEE Standards.

1999 21st International Conference on Power Industry Computer Applications. IEEE (Power Engineering Society) Staff. 450p. 1999. pap. write for info. (*0-7803-5478-8*, 99CH36351) Inst Electrical.

1999 24th IEEE International Electronics Manufacturing Tech Symposium. IEEE, Components, Packaging & Manufacturing Techno. Ed. by IEEE Staff. 800p. 1999. pap. write for info. (*0-7803-5502-4*, 99CH36330) IEEE Standards.

1999 22nd International Conference on Microelectronics. IEEE Staff. LC 98-89413. 850p. 1999. pap. write for info. (*0-7803-5235-1*, 99EX250) Inst Electrical.

***1999-2000 Houston - Texas Oil Directory.** 29th rev. ed. Ed. by James W. Staff. 1134p. 1999. pap. 69.00 (*1-889879-16-9*) Atlantic Commun.

***1999-2000 AAHSA Nursing Home Salary & Benefits Report.** 370p. 1999. pap. 250.00 (*0-939326-49-3*) Hosp & Hlthcare.

***1999-2000 AAHSA Continuing Care Retirement Community Salary & Benefits Report, Vol. 2.** 300p. 1999. pap. 250.00 (*0-939326-48-5*) Hosp & Hlthcare.

***1999-2000 Colorado International Trade Directory.** Ed. by James F. Reis. 164p. 1999. pap. 50.00 (*0-9643267-3-6*) Wrld Trade Ctr.

***1999-2000 Home Care Salary & Benefits Report, Vol. 9.** 420p. 1999. pap. 250.00 (*1-893772-01-2*) Hosp & Hlthcare.

***1999-2000 Hospice Salary & Benefits Report.** 260p. 1999. pap. 195.00 (*1-893772-03-9*) Hosp & Hlthcare.

***1999-2000 Hospital Salary & Benefit Report, Vol. 29.** 320p. 1999. pap. 295.00 (*1-893772-00-4*) Hosp & Hlthcare.

1999-2000 Medical Student's Guide to Successful Residency Matching. Lee T. Miller & Leigh G. Donowitz. 112p. pap. text 14.95 (*0-7817-2163-6*) Lppncott W & W.

***1999-2000 PATA Membership Directory.** PATA Staff. 251p. 1999. pap. 250.00 (*1-882866-21-5*, D-002-99) Pac Asia Trvl.

***1999-2000 North American Biotechnology Directory.** 8th rev. ed. Ed. by James W. Self. 624p. 1999. pap. 105.00 (*1-889879-15-0*) Atlantic Commun.

1999 U. S. Master Depreciation Guide. rev. ed. CCH Editors. 560p. Date not set. pap. text 41.95 (*0-8080-0349-6*) CCH INC.

1999 U. S. Master Employee Benefits Guide. Linda Paszczyk. 700p. 1998. pap. 49.00 (*0-8080-0301-1*) CCH INC.

***1999 U. S. Master Payroll Guide.** Barbara Moore. 400p. 1999. pap. 75.00 (*0-8080-0305-4*) CCH INC.

1999 U. S. Master Pension Guide. Nicholas Kaster et al. 950p. 1999. pap. 49.00 (*0-8080-0302-X*) CCH INC.

1999 U. S. Master Tax Guide. CCH Editorial Staff. 720p. 1998. text 59.95 (*0-8080-0293-7*); pap. text 42.95 (*0-8080-0294-5*) CCH INC.

1999 U. S. Master Tax Guide CCH Federal Tax Service Edition. CCH Editorial Staff. 720p. 1998. pap. text 42.95 (*0-8080-0311-9*) CCH INC.

1999 U. S. Road Atlas. American Map Publishing Staff. 1998. pap. 7.95 (*0-8416-9227-0*) Am Map.

1999 U. S./BNA Postage Stamp Catalog. rev. ed. (Illus.). 304p. 1998. pap. 12.95 (*0-937458-63-5*) Harris & Co.

***1999 Update & Review: Bankruptcy Litigation & Bankruptcy Law.** Ed. by Norton Institute on Bankruptcy Law Staff. 550p. 1999. ring bd. 250.00 (*1-887617-69-8*) St Bart Pr Ltd.

***1999 Used Car Book.** Consumer Guide Editors. (Consumer Guide Used Car Book). 192p. 1999. mass mkt. 9.99 (*0-451-19916-2*) NAL.

1999 Valuation Survey of A-E-P & Environmental Consulting Firms. 9th ed. Zweig White & Associates Staff. 496p. 1999. pap. text 275.00 (*1-885002-72-6*) Zweig White.

***1999 Vehicle Thermal Management Systems Conference Proceedings.** 864p. 1999. 561.00 incl. cd-rom (*1-86058-218-4*, Pub. by Prof Eng Pubng) Soc Auto Engineers.

1999 Veterinary Drug Guide. Delmar Publishing Staff. (C). 1999. mass mkt. 22.50 (*0-7668-0754-1*) Delmar.

1999 Video & Television Blue Book. rev. ed. 1998. lib. bdg. 200.00 (*0-932089-96-8*) Orion Res.

1999 Volunteer Center Resource Directory. 70p. 1999. pap. write for info. (*1-58534-025-1*) Points of Light.

***1999 Wage & Benefit Survey.** Ed. by K. Kaufmann. (Wage & Benefit Survey Ser.). 235p. 1999. ring bd. 450.00 (*1-891872-00-1*) Mgmt Ctr.

1999 Wall Street in Advance: A Full Year's Schedule of Market Moving Events for Strategic Investors. Sandi Lynne. (Illus.). 32p. 1998. mass mkt. 21.95 (*0-9664730-0-0*) S Lynne.

1999 Washington D. C. Datebook. 1998. 9.95 (*1-892528-30-4*) Datebook Pub.

1999 Wellness & Prevention Sourcebook. Ed. by Eric Levy. 496p. 1998. pap. 235.00 (*1-57987-081-3*) Faulkner & Gray.

***1999 Wiley Expert Witness Update, 1.** 392p. 1998. pap. text 160.00 (*0-7355-0289-7*) Panel Pubs.

***1999 Wiley Medical Malpractice Update, 1.** Melvin A. Shiffman MD. 440p. 1998. pap. 155.00 (*0-7355-0183-1*) Panel Pubs.

1999 Wine Watch Guide. Ed. by Don Moyer. 128p. 1998. pap. 9.95 (*0-9667459-0-6*, WWG1999) AMS Press.

***1999 Winter Simulation Conference.** IEEE Computer Society & Systems, Man & Cybernetics. Ed. by IEEE (Institute of Electrical & Electronics Engineers, Inc.) Staff. LC 87-654182. 1600p. 1999. pap. write for info. (*0-7803-5780-9*, 99CH37038) Inst Electrical.

1999 Workers Comp Managed Care Sourcebook. Ed. by Mary G. Stefanchik. (Illus.). 512p. 1998. pap. 245.00 (*1-57987-075-9*) Faulkner & Gray.

***1999 World Book Year Book.** (Illus.). 528p. 1999. 29.00 (*0-7166-0499-X*) World Bk.

1999 Year Book Allergy & Clinical Immunology. 1999. 79.00 (*0-8151-9600-8*, 24939) Mosby Inc.

1999 Year Book Neurology & Neurosurgery. 2nd ed. Bradley. (Illus.). 448p. 1999. text 81.00 (*0-8151-9649-0*, 24986) Mosby Inc.

1999 Year Book Obstetrics & Gynecology. (Illus.). 608p. 1999. text 82.00 (*0-8151-9705-5*, 24992) Mosby Inc.

1999 Year Book of Anesthesia & Pain Management. Date not set. 75.95 (*0-8151-9601-6*) Mosby Inc.

***1999 Year Book of Anesthesiology & Pain Management.** John H. Tinker et al. 1999. write for info. (*0-323-00645-0*) Mosby Inc.

1999 Year Book of Cardiology. Schlant. (Illus.). 475p. 1999. text 82.00 (*0-8151-9602-4*, 24941) Mosby Inc.

1999 Year Book of Chiropractic. Lawrence. (Illus.). 416p. 1998. text 78.00 (*0-8151-9603-2*, 24942) Mosby Inc.

1999 Year Book of Critical Care Medicine. (Illus.). 350p. 1999. text 81.00 (*0-8151-9606-7*, 24945) Mosby Inc.

1999 Year Book of Dentistry. (Illus.). 520p. 1999. text 74.95 (*0-8151-7085-8*, 27510) Mosby Inc.

1999 Year Book of Dermatologic Surgery. 350p. 1999. text 84.95 (*0-8151-9610-5*) Mosby Inc.

1999 Year Book of Dermatology. Sober. 500p. 1999. text 84.00 (*0-8151-9614-8*, 24951) Mosby Inc.

1999 Year Book of Diagnostic Radiology. 1999. 83.00 (*0-8151-9617-2*, 24954) Mosby Inc.

1999 Year Book of Drug Therapy. 1999. 79.95 (*0-8151-9621-0*) Mosby Inc.

1999 Year Book of Emergency Medicine. 3rd ed. (Illus.). 408p. 1999. text 85.00 (*0-8151-9624-5*, 24961) Mosby Inc.

1999 Year Book of Family Practice. 3rd ed. (Illus.). 488p. 1999. text 69.00 (*0-8151-9630-X*, 24967) Mosby Inc.

1999 Year Book of Gastroenterology. (Illus.). 315p. 1999. text 79.00 (*0-8151-9620-2*, 24957) Mosby Inc.

1999 Year Book of Geriatrics & Gerontology. Date not set. 69.95 (*0-8151-9632-6*) Mosby Inc.

1999 Year Book of Hand Surgery. (Illus.). 360p. 1999. text 83.00 (*0-8151-0164-3*, 25765) Mosby Inc.

1999 Year Book of Hematology. 3rd ed. Spivak. 594p. (C). (gr. 13). 1998. text 82.95 (*0-8151-9635-0*) Mosby Inc.

1999 Year Book of Medicine. (Illus.). 670p. 1999. text 78.00 (*0-8151-2902-5*, 31813) Mosby Inc.

1999 Year Book of Neonatal & Perinatal Medicine. 3rd ed. (Illus.). 400p. 1999. text 83.00 (*0-8151-9645-8*, 24982) Mosby Inc.

1999 Year Book of Nephrology, Hypertension & Mineral Metabolism. 2nd ed. (Illus.). 283p. 1999. text 86.00 (*0-8151-9647-4*, 24984) Mosby Inc.

1999 Year Book Of Nuclear Medicine. (Illus.). 448p. 1999. text 88.00 (*0-8151-3822-9*, 25464) Mosby Inc.

1999 Year Book of Oncology. 3rd ed. Simone. (Illus.). 500p. 1999. text 86.00 (*0-8151-9711-X*, 24998) Mosby Inc.

1999 Year Book of Ophthalmology. 3rd ed. (Illus.). 500p. 1999. text 84.00 (*0-8151-9714-4*, 25001) Mosby Inc.

1999 Year Book of Orthopaedics. 3rd ed. Sledge. (Illus.). 450p. 1999. text 86.00 (*0-8151-9717-9*, 25004) Mosby Inc.

1999 Year Book of Pathology. 3rd ed. (Illus.). 536p. 1999. text, lab manual ed. 85.00 (*0-8151-9723-3*, 25010) Mosby Inc.

1999 Year Book of Pediatrics. 3rd ed. (Illus.). 632p. 1999. text 71.00 (*0-8151-9726-8*, 25013) Mosby Inc.

1999 Year Book of Plastic & Reconstructive Surgery. 3rd ed. 400p. 1999. text 85.00 (*0-8151-9729-2*, 25016) Mosby Inc.

1999 Year Book of Podiatry. Date not set. 73.00 (*0-8151-9732-2*) Mosby Inc.

1999 Year Book of Psychiatry. 2nd ed. (Illus.). 456p. 1999. text 76.00 (*0-8151-9734-9*, 25021) Mosby Inc.

1999 Year Book of Pulmonary Disease. 3rd ed. (Illus.). 539p. 1999. text 79.00 (*0-8151-9737-3*, 25024) Mosby Inc.

1999 Year Book of Rheumatology, Arthritis & Musculoskeletal Disease. (Illus.). 376p. 1999. text 86.00 (*0-8151-9738-1*, 25025) Mosby Inc.

1999 Year Book of Sports Medicine. 3rd ed. (Illus.). 450p. 1999. text 77.95 (*0-8151-9741-1*, 25028) Mosby Inc.

1999 Year Book of Surgery. 3rd ed. (Illus.). 552p. 1999. text 76.95 (*0-8151-9744-6*, 25031) Mosby Inc.

1999 Year Book of Thoracic & Cardiac Surgery. 1999. 79.95 (*0-8151-9745-4*, 25032) Mosby Inc.

1999 Year Book of Urology. 3rd ed. (Illus.). 550p. 1999. text 84.00 (*0-8151-2549-6*, 24062) Mosby Inc.

1999 Year Book of Vascular Surgery. 2nd ed. (Illus.). 560p. 1999. text 87.95 (*0-8151-9801-9*, 25038) Mosby Inc.

***1999 Yearbook of Labour Statistics.** (ENG, FRE & SPA.). xvi, 1353p. 1999. 182.00 (*92-2-011329-5*, Pub. by Intl Labour Off) Balogh.

1999 Zagat Connecticut/ Southern New York State Restaurant Survey. Zagat Publishers Staff. 1998. pap. text 9.95 (*1-57006-135-1*) Zagat.

1999 Zagat Dallas Restaurant Survey. Zagat Publishers Staff. 1999. pap. 9.95 (*1-57006-162-9*) Zagat.

1999 Zagat Hawaii Restaurant Survey. Zagat Publishers Staff. 1999. pap. 9.95 (*1-57006-163-7*) Zagat.

1999 Zagat Houston Restaurant Survey. Zagat Publishers Staff. 1999. pap. 9.95 (*1-57006-164-5*) Zagat.

1999 Zagat Long Island Restaurant Survey. Zagat Publishers Staff. 1998. pap. text 9.95 (*1-57006-136-X*) Zagat.

1999 Zagat Los Angeles/ Southern California Restaurant Survey. Zagat Publishers Staff. Ed. by Merrill Shindler & Karen Berk. 268p. pap. 10.95 (*1-57006-148-3*) Zagat.

1999 Zagat Los Angeles Marketplace Survey. Zagat Publishers Staff. 1999. pap. 10.95 (*1-57006-139-4*) Zagat.

1999 Zagat New Jersey Restaurant Survey. Zagat Publishers Staff. 1998. pap. text 9.95 (*1-57006-137-8*) Zagat.

1999 Zagat New Orleans Restaurant Survey, 1. Zagat Publishers Staff. 1999. pap. 9.95 (*1-57006-155-6*) Zagat.

1999 Zagat New York City Marketplace. Zagat Publishers Staff. 1999. pap. 10.95 (*1-57006-145-9*) Zagat.

1999 Zagat Ohio Restaurant Survey, 1. Zagat Publishers Staff. 1999. pap. 9.95 (*1-57006-156-4*) Zagat.

1999 Zagat Orlando/Central Florida Restaurant Survey. Zagat Publishers Staff. 1999. pap. 9.95 (*1-57006-146-7*) Zagat.

1999 Zagat Philadelphia Restaurant Survey. Zagat Publishers Staff. 1998. pap. text 10.95 (*1-57006-133-5*) Zagat.

1999 Zagat Rocky Mountain Restaurant Survey. Zagat Publishers Staff. 1999. pap. 9.95 (*1-57006-152-1*) Zagat.

1999 Zagat San Diego Restaurant Survey. Zagat Publishers Staff. 1999. pap. 9.95 (*1-57006-138-6*) Zagat.

1999 Zagat Seattle/Portland Restaurant Survey. Zagat Publishers Staff. 1999. pap. 9.95 (*1-57006-154-8*) Zagat.

1999 Zagat Southwest Arizona/ New MexicoRestaurant Survey. Zagat Publishers Staff. 1999. pap. 9.95 (*1-57006-153-X*) Zagat.

1999 Zagat Toronto Restaurant Survey: Toronto Restaurant Survey. Zagat Publishers Staff. 1999. pap. 9.95 (*1-57006-116-5*) Zagat.

1999 Zagat Washington D. C. / Baltimore Restaurant Survey. Zagat Publishers Staff. 1998. pap. 10.95 (*1-57006-141-6*) Zagat.

1999 Zip/Area Code Directory: The Quick, Easy Way to Locate Area Codes for All U. S. Postal Zip Codes... Without Operator Assistance. rev. ed. Pilot Books Staff. (Where to Find What You Want to Know Ser.). 80p. 1999. pap. 9.95 (*0-87576-254-9*) Pilot Bks.

***1999/2000 Legislative Directory.** rev. ed. Pennsylvania Chamber of Business & Industry Educational Foundation Staff. 96p. 1999. pap. 15.00 (*1-929744-06-4*) Penn Chamber of Bus.

1990-91 Gulf War: Crisis, Conflict, Aftermath: An Annotated Bibliography. Andrew Orgill. LC 94-28447. 224p. 1995. 110.00 (*0-7201-2174-4*) Continuum.

1991: Assessing Foreign Language Proficiency. Aausc. (Teaching Methods Ser.). (C). 1991. mass mkt. 11.95 (*0-8384-3915-2*) Heinle & Heinle.

1991 ACL Proceedings. pap. 60.00 (*1-55860-968-7*) Morgan Kaufmann.

1991 Businessowners Policy. Ed. by Laura Biddle-Bruckman. 76p. 1996. 19.95 (*1-56461-170-1*) Rough Notes.

1991 Care Guide: Comprehensive Automotive & Light Truck Service Specifications. Gousha. 1991. pap. 55.95 (*0-13-117540-8*) P-H.

***1991 Coach of the Year Clinics Football Manual.** Ed. by Earl Browning. (Illus.). 256p. 2000. pap. 22.95 (*1-57167-403-9*) Coaches Choice.

1991 Deprivation Index: A Review of Approaches & a Matrix of Results. 173p. 1995. pap. 45.00 (*0-11-753049-2*, HM30492, Pub. by Statnry Office) Bernan Associates.

1991 European ACL Proceedings. pap. 60.00 (*1-55860-980-6*) Morgan Kaufmann.

1991 Graphics Interface Proceedings. pap. 40.00 (*1-55860-996-2*) Morgan Kaufmann.

1991 INFE Software-Hardware Resource Database. rev. ed. Ed. by INFE Information Systems Committee Staff. 65p. (C). 1991. pap. 35.00 (*1-877888-15-X*) Intl Newspaper.

1991 International Directory of Noise & Vibration Manufacturers & Suppliers. Ed. by S. Barrett. 92p. 1991. pap. 54.00 (*1-85617-071-3*, Pub. by Elsvr Adv Tech) Elsevier.

N

An Asterisk (*) at the beginning of an entry indicates that the title is appearing for the first time.

1991 Music & Video Yearbook. Joel Whitburn. 288p. 1992. pap. 29.95 (*0-89820-081-4*) Record Research.

1991 Proceedings of the 37th Annual Technical Meeting of the Institute of Environmental Sciences, San Diego, CA, "Technical Solutions Through Technical Cooperation" 891p. 1991. pap. 125.00 (*1-877862-10-X*) IEST.

1991 Reforms in Massachusetts: An Assessment of Impact. John A. Gardner et al. LC 96-15348. 194p. (Orig.). 1996. pap. 50.00 (*0-935149-57-0*, WC-96-3) Workers Comp Res Inst.

1991 Road Atlas. Rand McNally Staff. (Illus.). pap. 190.80 (*0-528-80502-9*) Rand McNally.

1991 San Diego Home Buyer's-Seller's Guide. David Horsting. 1991. student ed. 9.95 (*0-9629862-0-8*) Am RE Analytical.

1991 Supplement to the 1985 Edition of Federal Fisheries Management: A Guidebook to the Magnuson Fishery Conservation & Management Act. Ed. by William Kabeiseman. 49p. (C). 1992. pap. text 4.50 (*0-945216-03-3*) U OR Ocean & Law Ctr.

1991/1994 Cross-Reference Directory to the U.B.C. & U.M.C. 55p. 1994. pap. text 11.25 (*1-884590-58-6*, 095S94) Intl Conf Bldg Off.

1991-1992 National Directory of Law Enforcement Administrators, Vol. XXVII. National Police Chiefs & Sheriffs Information Bure. 552p. 1991. 49.00 (*1-880245-01-9*) SPAN Pub.

1991 Vacuum Metallurgy Conference: Select Proceedings. LC 86-81028. 220p. 1992. 90.00 (*0-932897-79-7*) Iron & Steel.

1991 Year Book Annual Supplement to Merit Students Encyclopedia. 1990. suppl. ed. 27.95 (*0-02-943753-9*) Mac Lib Ref.

1990 Proceedings of the 36th Annual Technical Meeting of the Institute of Environmental Sciences - New Orleans, LA, "A Glimpse into the 21st Century" 798p. 1990. pap. 125.00 (*1-877862-00-2*) IEST.

1990 Recommendations of the International Commission on Radiological Protection: User's Edition. ICRP Staff. (International Commission on Radiological Protection Ser.). 83p. 1992. pap. 53.25 (*0-08-041998-4*, Pergamon Pr) Elsevier.

Selected Papers of Norman Levin, 1997 see Selected Papers of Norman Levinson

1997 Metroplex Wedding Directory. Ed. by Gina Brown et al. (Illus.). 101p. 1996. pap. 12.95 (*0-9635013-0-5*) JP Ink.

*__Fisheries of the United States, 1997.__ Barbara K. O'Bannon. 174p. 1998. per. 16.00 (*0-16-060919-4*) USGPO.

1997 see Selected Papers of Norman Levinson

1997-1998 Compensation & Benefits Survey. Barbara Darraugh. (Illus.). viii, 78p. 1998. pap. 49.00 (*1-892725-14-2*, RP150) Building Serv.

1997-1998 Guide to Programs in Geography in the United States & Canada/AAG Handbook & Directory of Geographers. 30th rev. ed. Association of American Geographers Staff. Ed. by Linda S. Bradshaw. LC 85-641423. (Illus.). 824p. 1997. pap. 50.00 (*0-89291-242-1*) Assn Am Geographers.

1997-1998 Arizona Atlas & Data Book: An Economic & Demographic & Political View of the Grand Canyon State. Ed. by Richard Yates & Charity Yates. (Illus.). 64p. 1998. pap. 13.95 (*0-911927-28-X*) Public Sector.

1997-98 Compensation Report on Management Employees in Hospital, Nursing Home, & Home Care Management Companies. 200p. 1998. pap. 495.00 (*0-939326-36-1*) Hosp & Hlthcare.

1997-98 Directory of Corporate Counsel, 2 vols. Aspen Law & Business Editorial Staff. 2686p. boxed set 449.00 (*1-56706-657-7*) Panel Pubs.

1997-98 Greeting Care Industry Directory: A Comprehensive Guide to the Products & Services of the Greeting Card Industry. 9th ed. Ed. by Mila Albertson. 332p. 1997. pap. 95.00 (*0-938369-30-X*) Grtng Card Creat Netwk.

1997-98 National Faculty Salary Survey by Discipline & Rank in Private Four-Year Colleges & Universities. 1998. 65.00 (*1-878240-64-1*) Coll & U Personnel.

1997 - The Beginning of the End. Stephen Gyamfi. LC 97-90597. 1998. pap. 8.95 (*0-533-12436-0*) Vantage.

*__1997 Survey of Compensation Practices in Higher Education.__ (Illus.). 28p. 1999. 85.00 (*1-878240-77-3*) Coll & U Personnel.

1997 Ad Revenue for TV Household: A Market by Market Analysis. Theresa J. Ottina. 62p. 1997. pap. 225.00 (*0-89324-305-1*, 3853) Natl Assn Broadcasters.

1997 Advanced Workshop on Frontiers in Electronics. IEEE (Electron Devices Society & Lasers & Electro-. LC 97-72648. 150p. 1997. pap. 108.00 (*0-7803-4059-0*, 97TH8292) Inst Electrical.

1997 Advertising Market Research Handbook. Terri C. Walker & Richard K. Miller. 350p. 1997. 275.00 (*1-881503-75-5*) R K Miller Assocs.

1997 AEE Energy & Environment Industry Survey. Ruth Bennett. LC 97-188601. 424p. (C). 1997. pap. text 95.00 (*0-13-762155-8*) P-H.

1997 AIAA Membership Directory: Newly Updated Resource Guide. 430p. 1997. 79.99 (*1-56347-191-4*, 91-4(9991)) AIAA.

1997 AIAA/IEEE 16th Digital Avionics Systems Conference. IEEE, Aerospace & Electronic Systems Society Staff. LC 97-72969. 900p. 1997. pap. text 178.00 (*0-7803-4150-3*, 97CH36116); lib. bdg. write for info. (*0-7803-4151-1*, 97CH36116); fiche. write for info. (*0-7803-4152-X*) IEEE Standards.

1997 AIMAC Conference Proceedings: Association Internationale pour le Management des Arts et de la Culture (International Association for the Management of Ars & Culture) Ed. by Anne W. Smith. (ENG & FRE.). 700p. 1998. pap. 75.00 (*0-9664473-0-1*) Golden Gate Univ.

1997 Alternative Budget: The Canadian Centre for Policy Alternatives & Choices, a Coalition for Social Justice. Canadian Centre for Policy Alternatives Staff & Coalition for Social Justice Staff. (Illus.). 200p. 1997. pap. 19.95 (*1-55028-548-3*, Pub. by J Lorimer) Formac Dist Ltd.

1997 Amateur Radio Almanac. Ed. by Doug Grant. LC 93-74224. (Illus.). 620p. (Orig.). 1996. pap. 19.95 (*0-943016-16-9*) CQ Commns Inc.

1997 American Control Conference. IEEE (Neural Networks Council) Staff. Ed. by IEEE (Inst. of Electrical & Electronics Engrs.). 5000p. 1997. pap. text. write for info. (*0-7803-3832-4*, 97CH36041); lib. bdg. write for info. (*0-7803-3833-2*, 97CH36041) IEEE Standards.

1997 Americans with Disabilities Act Compliance Manual. David K. Fram. 1997. ring bd. 100.00 (*1-890487-03-1*) Ntl Employ Law.

1997 Analysis of Workers' Compensation Laws. U. S. Chamber of Commerce Staff. 64p. (Orig.). 1997. pap. 25.00 (*0-89834-086-1*) US Chamber DC.

1997 Animation Industry Directory. (Illus.). 190p. 1997. pap. 75.00 (*1-891010-00-X*) Animation Mag.

1997 Annual Book of ASTM Standards: Nuclear, Solar, & Geothermal Energy, Section 12, 2 vols. Incl. Vol. 12.02. Nuclear (II), Solar, & Geothermal Energy. 1048p. 1997. 124.00 (*0-8031-2451-1*, 01-120297-35); 223.00 (*0-8031-2449-X*, PCN01-120097-35) ASTM.

1997 Annual Conference Handouts, 5 vols. Incl. Track 1: Personal Growth & Leadership. 80p. 1997. pap. 12.00 (*0-939900-76-9*); Track 2: HRM: a Strategic & Future Focus. 100p. 1997. pap. 14.00 (*0-939900-77-7*); Industry Group & Professional Emphasis Group (PEG) Sessions. 42p. 1997. pap. 9.00 (*0-939900-80-7*); 33p. 1997. pap. 8.00 (*0-939900-79-3*); Track 3: HRM: an Operational Focus. 290p. 1997. pap. 34.00 (*0-939900-78-5*); 65.00 (*0-939900-75-0*) Soc Human Resc Mgmt.

1997 Annual Index to Motion Picture Credits. Ed. by Byerly Woodward. 350p. 1998. lib. bdg. 30.00 (*0-942102-28-2*) Acad Motion Pic.

1997 Annual Meeting of the North American Fuzzy Information Processing Society. IEEE (Neural Networks Council, Systems, Man & Cybe. LC 97-72650. 550p. 1997. pap. write for info. (*0-7803-4078-7*, 97TH8297) Inst Electrical.

1997 Annual Report of the Scientific Registry & the OPTN. UNOS Staff. (Illus.). 290p. 1998. pap. 15.00 (*1-886651-25-6*) United Network.

1997 Annual Report on Mining Activities in the Commonwealth of PA, DEP. DEP, Bureau of Mining & Reclamation Staff. 410p. 1998. 13.38 (*0-8182-0233-5*) Commonweal PA.

1997 Annual Review of Develpoment Effectiveness. Alison Evans & William G. Battaile, Jr. (Operations Evaluation Department Studies). 88p. 1998. pap. 22.00 (*0-8213-4210-X*, 14210) World Bank.

1997 Annual Statement Instructions - Title. 6th rev. ed. Ed. by Patti Carli. 316p. (C). 1997. ring bd. 125.00 (*0-89382-472-0*, ASI-TM) Nat Assn Insurance.

1997 Annual Statement Instructions - Limited Health Services Organizations (LHSO) 6th rev. ed. Ed. by Patti Carli. 108p. (C). 1997. ring bd. 75.00 (*0-89382-471-2*, ASI-SM) Nat Assn Insurance.

1997 Annual Statement Instructions - Hospital, Medical, Dental Service & Indemnity Corporation (HMDI) 6th rev. ed. Ed. by Patti Carli. 252p. (C). 1997. ring bd. 75.00 (*0-89382-469-0*, ASI-MM) Nat Assn Insurance.

1997 Annual Statement Instructions - Health Maintenance Organization. 7th rev. ed. Ed. by Patti Carli. 137p. (C). 1997. ring bd. 175.00 (*0-89382-468-2*, ASI-HM) Nat Assn Insurance.

1997 Annual Statement Instructions - Fraternal. 11th rev. ed. Ed. by Patti Carli. 418p. (C). 1997. ring bd. 175.00 (*0-89382-473-9*, ASI-FM) Nat Assn Insurance.

1997 Annual Statement Instructions - Life. 13th rev. ed. Ed. by Patti Carli. 488p. (C). 1997. ring bd. 175.00 (*0-89382-474-7*, ASI-LM) Nat Assn Insurance.

1997 Annual Statistical Report on Profit Production Sales & Marketing Trends in the Men's & Boys Tailored Clothing Industry. (Orig.). 1997. write for info. (*0-614-24018-2*) Clothing Mfrs.

1997 Annual Survey of Letter of Credit Law & Practice Survey Handbook. Ed. by James E. Byrne et al. 635p. 1997. 149.00 (*1-888870-15-X*) Inst Intl Bnking.

1997 Annual Survey Report. Susan L. MacLean. (Illus.). 1999. 500.00 (*0-935890-31-9*) Emerg Nurses IL.

1997 Annual Treasure Coast Magazine Vol. 8: The Best of South Florida from North Palm Beach to Vero Beach. (Illus.). 128p. 1997. 7.95 (*1-883117-07-0*) Mohr Graphics.

1997 Appellate Military Judges Conference. 89p. 1997. ring bd. 15.00 (*1-56986-152-8*, CRT-91-89) Federal Bar.

1997 Archaeological Fieldwork Opportunities Bulletin. AIA (Meister) Staff. 144p. 1997. pap. text 11.00 (*0-7872-3022-7*) Kendall-Hunt.

1997 Artists of the Mohawk Hudson Region Juried Exhibition: June 17 Through July 31, 1997, University Art Museum, University at Albany, State University of New York. Mohawk Hudson Region Juried Exhibition et al. LC 97-60955. (Illus.). 1997. write for info. (*0-910763-16-X*) U Albany Art Mus.

1997 Asia & South Pacific Design Automation Conference ASP DAC. IEEE (Circuits & Systems Society) Staff. Ed. by IEEE (Institute of Electrical & Electronics Engine. LC 96-78107. 1997. mic. film. write for info. (*0-7803-3663-1*, 97TM8231) Inst Electrical.

1997 Asia & South Pacific Design Automation Conference ASP DAC. IEEE (Circuits & Systems Society) Staff. Ed. by IEEE (Institute of Electrical & Electronics Engine. LC 96-78107. 724p. 1997. pap. 140.00 (*0-7803-3662-3*, 97TH8231) Inst Electrical.

1997 ASNT Fall Conference & Quality Testing Show Paper Summaries. ASNT Staff. (Illus.). 316p. (C). 1997. per. 31.00 (*1-57117-068-5*, 1360) Am Soc Nondestructive.

1997 ASNT Infrared Thermography Topic Conference Paper Summaries. ASNT Staff. (Illus.). 180p. (C). 1997. per. 19.00 (*1-57117-061-8*, 1359) Am Soc Nondestructive.

1997 ASNT Spring Conference & Sixth Annual Research Symposium Paper Summaries. ASNT Staff. (Illus.). 192p. (C). 1997. per. 31.00 (*1-57117-056-1*, 1356) Am Soc Nondestructive.

1997 ASNT Spring Conference/5th Annual Research Symposium Paper Summaries. ASNT Staff. (Illus.). 252p. 1996. per. 31.00 (*1-57117-017-0*, 1351) Am Soc Nondestructive.

1997 ASTM International Directory of Testing Laboratories. 384p. 1996. pap. 69.00 (*0-8031-1805-8*, LAB98) ASTM.

1997 AT&T National Toll-Free Business Buyer's Guide: Business Edition. Patricia G. Selden. 964p. 1996. pap. text 24.99 (*0-938963-39-2*) AT&T Natl.

1997 AT&T National Toll-Free Shoppers Guide: Consumer Edition. Patricia G. Selden. 383p. 1996. pap. text 14.99 (*0-938963-40-6*) AT&T Natl.

1997 Atlas TBA. (Illus.). 252p. 1997. pap. text. write for info. (*1-57932-002-3*) Chek-Chart.

Chek Chart Manual Transmission (Shop) & Transaxles. (Illus.). 240p. pap. write for info. (*1-57932-001-5*) Chek-Chart.

1997 Audio Blue Book. 1996. lib. bdg. 200.00 (*0-932089-72-0*) Orion Res.

1997 AVMA Convention Notes. 1997. pap. write for info. (*1-882691-11-3*) Am Veterinary Med Assn.

1997 Bankruptcy Yearbook & Almanac. Ed. by Christopher M. McHugh. 554p. 1997. pap. 195.00 (*0-9628991-6-X*) New Gen Research.

1997 Behavioral Outcomes & Guidelines Sourcebook. Ed. by Ken Coughlin. (Illus.). 575p. 1996. pap. text 295.00 (*1-881393-93-3*) Faulkner & Gray.

1997 Beijing Scene Guidebook, Vol. 1. Ed. by Scott Savitt. (Illus.). 567p. (Orig.). 1997. pap. 26.50 (*0-9656922-0-5*) Scene Pub.

1997 Biennial. Bruce Cuenther. Ed. by Terry A. Neff. (Illus.). 40p. 1997. pap. 14.95 (*0-917493-25-7*) Orange Cnty Mus.

1997 Biennial Exhibition: Whitney Museum of Art. Lisa Phillips & Louise Neri. (Illus.). 256p. 1997. pap. 39.95 (*0-8109-6825-8*) Whitney Mus.

1997 Bioremediation Symposium Proceedings Set, 5 vols. Bruce C. Alleman & Andrea Leeson. LC 97-7991. 1997. 349.50 (*1-57477-031-4*) Battelle.

1997 BioSupplyNet Source Book. (Illus.). 1997. pap. 24.95 (*1-890574-02-3*) BioSupplyNet.

1997 Book of Lists. 178p. 1996. pap. 30.00 (*0-9650400-1-1*) Houston Busin Jrnl.

1997 Book of Lists. Suzette Brewer. 1997. 32.50 (*0-932439-11-X*) Denver Busn Media.

1997 Book of Vascular Surgery. Ed. by John M. Porter. (Illus.). 560p. (C). (gr. 13). 1997. text 86.00 (*0-8151-6800-4*, 22715) Mosby Inc.

1997 Business & Teacher Directory. Ed. by Julie M. Vosberg. 1997. pap. write for info. (*0-943883-35-0*) Natl Soc of Tole.

1997 Camera Blue Book. rev. ed. 1996. lib. bdg. 200.00 (*0-932089-70-4*) Orion Res.

1997 Canadian Conference on Electrical & Computer Engineering. IEEE (Region 7) Staff. 1100p. 1997. pap. write for info. (*0-7803-3716-6*, 97TH8244); fiche. write for info. (*0-7803-3717-4*, 97TM8244) Inst Electrical.

1997 Canadian Ethical Money Guide: The Best RRSPs, Mutual Funds, & Stocks for Ethical Investors. rev. ed. Eugene Ellmen. 225p. 1997. pap. 19.95 (*1-55028-542-4*, Pub. by J Lorimer); bds. 34.95 (*1-55028-543-2*, Pub. by J Lorimer) Formac Dist Ltd.

1997 Future Car Challenge. 127p. 1998. 25.00 (*0-7680-0179-X*) Soc Auto Engineers.

1997 Car Stereo Blue Book. rev. ed. 1996. lib. bdg. 200.00 (*0-932089-69-0*) Orion Res.

1997 Caribbean Basic Commercial Profile, 2 vols. annuals Ed. by Sam Skogstad, 3rd. 1997. pap. 59.75 (*976-8088-11-7*) Carib Imprint.

1997 Caribbean Island Handbook. 8th rev. ed. Ed. by Sarah Cameron & Ben Box. (Footprint Handbks.). (Illus.). 1024p. 1996. 21.95 (*0-8442-4907-6*, Passprt Bks) NTC Contemp Pub Co.

1997 Casino & Gaming Market Research Handbook. Terri C. Walker & Richard K. Miller. 350p. 1997. 275.00 (*1-881503-70-4*) R K Miller Assocs.

1997 Circuits & Systems in the Information Age. IEEE (Circuits & Systems Society) Staff. Ed. by IEEE (Institute of Electrical & Electronics Engine. LC 96-79979. 1996. fiche. write for info. (*0-7803-3766-2*, 97TM8252) Inst Electrical.

1997 Circuits & Systems in the Information Age. IEEE (Circuits & Systems Society) Staff. Ed. by IEEE (Institute of Electrical & Electronics Engine. LC 96-79979. 450p. 1997. pap. write for info. (*0-7803-3765-4*, 97TH8252) Inst Electrical.

1997 CMMS Directory. 6th ed. Thomas Publishing Company Staff. Ed. by Adrian Salee. 700p. 1997. 95.00 incl. cd-rom (*1-882554-07-8*) Thomas Pub NY.

1997 CMS Country Music Radio Directory. rev. ed. Ed. by Robert Unmacht & Pat McCrummen. Date not set. pap. 65.00 (*0-9647930-3-2*) M St Corp.

*__1997 Coach of the Year Clinics Football Manual.__ Earl Browning. (Illus.). 264p. 1999. pap. 22.95 (*1-57167-376-8*) Coaches Choice.

1997 Comparative Performance Data Sourcebook. Ed. by John Reichard. (Illus.). 558p. 1996. pap. text 195.00 (*1-881393-84-4*) Faulkner & Gray.

1997 Comprehensive Guide to Idaho - Montana's Craft Fairs, Festivals & Bazaars. Susan K. Carter. (Illus.). 125p. 1996. spiral bd. 23.00 (*1-888651-04-0*) Carters Guides.

1997 Comprehensive Guide to Washington's Craft Fairs, Festivals & Bazaars. 3rd ed. Susan K. Carter. (Illus.). 232p. 1996. spiral bd. 23.00 (*1-888651-03-2*) Carters Guides.

1997 Comprehensive Guide to Oregon's Craft Fairs, Festivals & Bazaars. 5th ed. Susan K. Carter. LC 95-96235. (Illus.). 248p. 1996. spiral bd. 23.00 (*1-888651-02-4*) Carters Guides.

1997 Computers in Cardiology. IEEE, Engineering in Medicine & Biology Society St. Ed. by Institute of Electrical & Electronics Engineers, I. LC 80-641097. 776p. 1997. pap. text. write for info. (*0-7803-4445-6*, 97CH36184); lib. bdg. write for info. (*0-7803-4446-4*, 97CH36184) Inst Electrical.

1997 Conference on Lasers & Electro-Optics. (Nineteen Ninety-Seven Technical Digest Ser.: Vol. 11). 568p. 1997. pap. 92.00 (*1-55752-485-8*, CH36110) Optical Soc.

1997 Conference on Lasers & Electro-Optics. IEEE (Lasers & Electro-Optics Society) Staff. LC 97-65506. 484p. 1997. lib. bdg. write for info. (*0-7803-4125-2*, 97CH36110) Inst Electrical.

1997 Conference on Lasers & Electro-Optics/Pacific Rim. IEEE (Lasers & Electro-Optics Society) Staff. Ed. by IEEE (Institute of Electrical & Electronics Engine. LC 97-70754. 450p. 1997. pap. write for info. (*0-7803-3889-8*, 97TH8275); fiche. write for info. (*0-7803-3890-1*, 97TH8275) Inst Electrical.

1997 Conference on the High Energy Background Radiation in Space Proceedings. IEEE (Nuclear & Plasma Sciences Society) Staff. Ed. by IEEE (Institute of Electrical & Electronics Engine. LC 97-80345. 150p. 1997. pap. write for info. (*0-7803-4335-2*, 97TH8356) Inst Electrical.

1997 Connecticut State Register & Manual. annuals Secretary of State's Editorial Staff. 900p. 1997. 19.00 (*1-888951-02-8*); pap. 10.00 (*1-888951-03-6*) CT Secy Sts Ofc.

1997 Constraints Management Symposium Proceedings. LC 98-142036. 92p. 1997. write for info. (*1-55822-135-2*) Am Prod & Inventory.

1997 Coopers & Lybrand L. L. P. Survey of Accounting Practices in the U. S. Oil & Gas Industry. Ed. by Teddy L. Coe et al. LC 99-162739. 266p. (Orig.). 1997. pap. 125.00 (*0-926969-04-8*) UNTIPA.

1997 Copier Blue Book. rev. ed. 1996. lib. bdg. 200.00 (*0-932089-79-8*) Orion Res.

1997 Core Release Supplement 8: 76 Chemicals. Dauber Danner. 440p. 1998. ring bd. 160.00 (*1-56032-766-9*) Hemisp Pub.

1997 Corporate & Partnership Tax Return Guide. rev. ed. 144p. 1998. pap. text 15.00 (*0-7811-0172-7*) Res Inst Am.

1997 Courthouse Guide. Ed. by Debbie Shain. 96p. (Orig.). 1997. spiral bd. write for info. (*1-57786-050-0*) Legal Communs.

1997 Credit Reference Directory, 12 vols. American Business Directories Staff. Incl. Pacific Region. rev. ed. 3456p. 1997. 325.00 (*1-56105-910-2*); 1997. 1295.00 (*1-56105-906-4*) Am Busn Direct.

1997 Cumulative Supplement Connecticut Evidence. Benedict M. Holden & John J. Daly. 919p. 1997. pap. 75.00 (*1-878698-44-3*) Atlantic Law.

1997 Cumulative Supplement to Connecticut Law of Torts. 3rd ed. Douglass B. Wright et al. 133p. 1997. pap. 55.00 (*1-878698-42-7*) Atlantic Law.

1997 Dallas Business Journal Book of Lists. 1996. 30.00 (*1-885549-02-4*) Dallas Business Journal.

1997 Decorative Fabrics Cross-Reference Guide. Kimberly Causey. 194p. (Orig.). 1997. pap. 39.95 (*1-888229-02-0*) Home Decor.

1997 Defense Budget: Potential Reductions & Rescissions to DOD's Procurement & RDT&E Programs. Louis J. Rodrigues. (Illus.). 64p. (Orig.). (C). 1996. pap. text 25.00 (*0-7881-3579-1*) DIANE Pub.

1997 Design Automation Conference. IEEE, Circuits & Systems Society Staff. Ed. by Institute of Electrical & Electronics Engineers, I. LC 85-644924. 900p. 1997. lib. bdg. write for info. (*0-7803-4093-0*, 97CH36101) Inst Electrical.

1997 Developer's Guide. Whil Hentzen. 320p. (Orig.). 1996. pap. 40.00 (*0-9655093-1-1*) Hentzenwerke.

1997 Development Report Card for the States: Economic Benchmarks for State & Corporate Decision-Makers, 1997. 9th ed. Daphne Clones & Carl Rist. 114p. 1997. pap. 58.00 (*1-883187-17-6*) Corp Ent Dev.

1997 Digest of the LEOS Summer Topical Meetings. IEEE (Lasers & Electro-Optics Society) Staff. Ed. by IEEE (Institute of Electrical & Electronics Engine. LC 97-70760. 325p. 1997. pap. write for info. (*0-7803-3891-X*, 97TH8276); fiche. write for info. (*0-7803-3892-8*, 97TH8276) Inst Electrical.

1997 Digests of Intermag. IEEE, Magnetics Society Staff. Ed. by Institute of Electrical & Electronics Engineers, I. LC 72-649866. 750p. 1997. pap. text. write for info. (*0-7803-3862-6*, 97CH36050); lib. bdg. write for info. (*0-7803-3863-4*, 97CH36050) Inst Electrical.

1997 Directory of Community Blood Centers. 1997. pap. text 70.00 (*1-56395-089-8*) Am Assn Blood.

1997 Directory of Key Health Legislators & Legislative Staff. Compiled by NCSL Health Program Staff. 79p. 1997. 20.00 (*1-55516-651-2*, 6661) Natl Conf State Legis.

1997 Directory of Mass Merchandisers. Ed. by Lynda Beatty et al. 1996. pap. 220.00 (*0-911790-36-5*) Trade Dimensns.

1997 Directory of U. S. Biotechnology Centers. 12th ed. Institute for Biotechnology Information Staff. 90p. 1998. pap. text 75.00 (*1-886041-14-8*) Inst Biotech Info.

1997 Directory to Medical Product Manufacturing Consultants. 164p. (Orig.). 1997. pap. 10.00 (*1-884551-03-3*) Canon Comns.

***1997 Domestic Wiring Diagram.** Motor Information Staff. 1998. pap. 136.00 (*0-87851-983-1*, Hearst) Hearst Commns.

1997 National E-Mail Postal Directory. Ron Perkins. 176p. (Orig.). 1996. pap. 8.95 (*0-9627185-4-8*) Newport Media.

1997 East Africa Handbook. 3rd rev. ed. Ed. by Michael Hodd. (Footprint Handbks.). (Illus.). 832p. 1996. 24.95 (*0-8442-4911-4*, Passprt Bks) NTC Contemp Pub Co.

1997 Ed Database Summary. Susan L. MacLean. (Illus.). 1999. 30.00 (*0-935890-30-0*) Emerg Nurses IL.

1997 8th International Conference on Advanced Robotics. IEEE, Robotics & Automation Society Staff. Ed. by Institute of Electrical & Electronics Engineers, I. LC 97-80005. 1052p. 1997. pap. 178.00 (*0-7803-4160-0*, 97TH8308) Inst Electrical.

1997 Electrical Overstress/Electrostatic Discharge Symposium. IEEE (Electron Devices Society) Staff. Ed. by IEEE (Institute of Electrical & Electronics Engine. 400p. 1997. mic. film. write for info. (*0-7803-3764-6*, 97TM8251) Inst Electrical.

1997 Electrical Overstress/Electrostatic Discharge Symposium. IEEE (Electron Devices Society) Staff. Ed. by IEEE (Institute of Electrical & Electronics Engine. 400p. 1998. pap. write for info. (*0-614-24673-3*, 97TH8251) Inst Electrical.

1997 Electrical Electronics Insulation Conference & Electrical Manufacturing & Coil Winding Conference. IEEE (Dielectrics & Electrical Insulation Society). Ed. by IEEE (Inst. of Electrical & Electronics Engrs.). 700p. 1997. pap. text. write for info. (*0-7803-3959-2*, 97CH36075); lib. bdg. write for info. (*0-7803-3960-6*, 97CH36075) IEEE Standards.

1997 Electronics Industries Forum. IEEE Region 1 Staff. Ed. by IEEE Staff. LC 97-72972. 308p. 1997. pap. text 136.00 (*0-7803-3987-8*, 97CH36084); lib. bdg. write for info. (*0-7803-3988-6*, 97CH36084); fiche. write for info. (*0-7803-3989-4*, 97CH36084) Inst Electrical.

1997 11th IEEE International Pulsed Power Conference. IEEE (Nuclear & Plasma Science Society) Staff. Ed. by IEEE (Institute of Electrical & Electronics Engine. LC 97-80047. 2000p. 1998. pap. text. write for info. (*0-7803-4213-5*, 97CH36127); lib. bdg. write for info. (*0-7803-4214-3*, 97CH36127) Inst Electrical.

***1997 11th IEEE International Pulsed Power Conference.** IEEE (Nuclear & Plasma Science Society) Staff. Ed. by IEEE (Institute of Electrical & Electronics Engine. LC 97-80047. 1998. cd-rom. write for info. (*0-7803-4216-X*, 97CH36127) Inst Electrical.

1997 EMC Encyclopedia. Donald R. White. Orig. Title: EMC Digest. (Illus.). 400p. 1997. 35.00 (*0-932263-99-2*) emf-emi Control.

1997 Employment Law Briefing Manual. Nancy L. Abell et al. 300p. 1997. ring bd., wbk. ed. 150.00 (*1-890487-02-3*) Ntl Employ Law.

1997 Experience Exchange Report. (Illus.). 496p. 1997. pap. 275.00 (*0-614-31135-7*, 137-02E97) Build Own & Man.

1997 Fall Simulation Interoperability Workshop: Workshop Papers. (Simulation Interoperability Workshop Ser.). (Illus.). 1300p. 1997. 75.00 (*1-930638-03-5*) S I S O.

1997 Fashion & Fun Diary. Ed. by Shirley Kennedy. (Illus.). 205p. 1996. 34.95 (*0-9632385-4-X*) S Kennedy.

1997 Federal Tax Course. Lewis D. Solomon & Susan F. Posner. 1852p. ring bd. 136.00 (*1-56706-330-6*, 63306) Panel Pubs.

1997 Fiduciary Tax Return Guide. rev. ed. 160p. 1998. text 15.00 (*0-7811-0173-5*) Res Inst Am.

1997 Film Directors: A Complete Guide. 12th ed. Ed. by Michael Singer. 798p. 1997. pap. 75.00 (*0-943728-85-1*) Lone Eagle Pub.

1997 Finance & Accounting Survey of A/E/P Firms. 188p. 1997. pap. text 250.00 (*1-885002-29-7*) Zweig White.

1997 Financial Performance Survey of Environmental Consulting Firms. 5th ed. 256p. 1997. pap. text 250.00 (*1-885002-32-7*) Zweig White.

1997 1st Electronic Packaging Conference. IEEE, Components, Packaging & Manufacturing Techno. LC 97-73111. 240p. 1997. pap. 116.00 (*0-7803-4157-0*, 97TH8307); fiche. write for info. (*0-7803-4158-9*) IEEE Standards.

1997 1st IEEE Enterprise Networking Mini-Conference. IEEE (Communications Society) Staff. LC 98-104803. 228p. 1997. pap. 116.00 (*0-7803-4112-0*, 97TH8300) Inst Electrical.

1997 1st International Conference on Information Communications & Signal Processing Proceedings. IEEE (Singapore Section) Staff. Ed. by IEEE (Institute of Electrical & Electronics Engine. LC 96-78212. 1600p. 1997. pap. write for info. (*0-7803-3676-3*, 97TH8237); fiche. write for info. (*0-7803-3677-1*, 97TM8237) Inst Electrical.

1997 Fish & Game Code of California. unabridged ed. State Department of Fish and Game Staff. LC 99-162678. (Qwik-Code Ser.). 527p. 1997. write for info. (*0-915905-58-2*) Lawtech Pub.

1997 Florida Almanac. 13th ed. Del Marth & Marty Marth. (Illus.). 520p. (Orig.). 1996. pap. 14.50 (*1-885034-05-9*) Suwannee River.

1997 Florida Statistical Abstract. (Illus.). 800p. 1997. 39.95 (*0-930885-25-2*) Bur Econ & Bus Res.

1997 FM Subcarrier MKT Report. 2nd ed. 70p. 1997. pap. 55.00 (*0-89324-271-3*, 3847) Natl Assn Broadcasters.

1997 40th Midwest Symposium on Circuits & Systems. IEEE (Circuits & Systems Society) Staff. Ed. by IEEE (Institute of Electrical & Electronics Engine. LC 79-645128. 2000p. 1998. pap. text. write for info. (*0-7803-3694-1*, 97CH36010); lib. bdg. write for info. (*0-7803-3695-X*, 97CB36010); mic. film. write for info. (*0-7803-3697-6*, 97CM36010) Inst Electrical.

1997 44th Annual Petroleum & Chemical Industry Conference. IEEE (Industry Applications Society) Staff. Ed. by IEEE (Institute of Electrical & Electronics Engine. LC 73-641120. 300p. 1997. pap. text 122.00 (*0-7803-4217-8*, 97CH36128) Inst Electrical.

1997 44th Annual Petroleum & Chemical Industry Conference. IEEE (Industry Applications Society) Staff. Ed. by IEEE (Institute of Electrical & Electronics Engine. LC 73-641120. 300p. 1997. lib. bdg. write for info. (*0-7803-4218-6*, 97CH36128) Inst Electrical.

1997 47th Electronic Components & Technology Conference. IEEE, Components, Packaging & Manufacturing Techno. Ed. by Institute of Electrical & Electronics Engineers, I. LC 78-647174. 1300p. 1997. pap. text. write for info. (*0-7803-3857-X*, 97CH36048); lib. bdg. write for info. (*0-7803-3858-8*, 97CH36048) Inst Electrical.

1997 43rd Annual Technical Meeting Proceedings of the Institute of Environmental Sciences: Integrated Product Development, 2 vols., Set. 640p. 1997. pap. 185.00 (*1-877862-53-3*) IEST.

1997 43rd Annual Technical Meeting Proceedings of the Institute of Environmental Sciences & Technology Vol. 2: Integrated Product Development. 274p. 1997. pap. 145.00 (*1-877862-55-X*) IEST.

1997 Fourth European Conference on Radiation & Its Effects on Components & Systems. IEEE (Nuclear & Plasma Sciences Society) Staff. LC 97-72652. 1997. pap. write for info. (*0-7803-4071-X*, 97TH8294) Inst Electrical.

1997 4th International Workshop on Community Networking Proceedings. IEEE (Communications Society) Staff. Ed. by IEEE (Institute of Electrical & Electronics Engine. LC 97-80204. 150p. 1997. pap. write for info. (*0-7803-4290-9*, 97TH8337) Inst Electrical.

1997 Frontiers in Education Conference. IEEE, Education Society & Computer Society Staff. Ed. by Institute of Electrical & Electronics Engineers, I. LC 79-640910. 1100p. 1997. pap. text. write for info. (*0-7803-4086-8*, 97CH36099); lib. bdg. write for info. (*0-7803-4087-6*, 97CH36099) Inst Electrical.

1997 GaAs Reliability Workshop. Jedec JG 147 Committee. LC 98-193590. 116p. 1998. write for info. (*0-7908-0064-0*) Elec Ind Assn.

1997 Garden Planner Mid-Atlantic Edition. Ortho Books Staff. 1996. pap. text 10.95 (*0-89721-308-4*, Ortho Bks) Meredith Bks.

1997 Garden Planner Midwest Edition. Ortho Books Staff. 1996. pap. text 10.95 (*0-89721-309-2*, Ortho Bks) Meredith Bks.

1997 Garden Planner Northwest Edition. Ortho Books Staff. 1996. pap. text 10.95 (*0-89721-306-8*, Ortho Bks) Meredith Bks.

1997 Garden Planner Southwest Edition. Ortho Books Staff. 1996. pap. text 10.95 (*0-89721-307-6*, Ortho Bks) Meredith Bks.

1997 Garden Planner South Edition. Ortho Books Staff. 1996. pap. text 10.95 (*0-89721-311-4*, Ortho Bks) Meredith Bks.

1997 Genealogy Annual: A Bibliography of Published Sources. Thomas Kemp. 2p. 1999. 95.00 (*0-8420-2741-6*) Scholarly Res Inc.

1997 IEEE Globecom. IEEE (Communications Society) Staff. LC 87-640337. 2360p. 1997. pap. text 300.00 (*0-7803-4198-8*, 97CH36125); lib. bdg. write for info. (*0-7803-4199-6*, 97CB36125) Inst Electrical.

1997 Graphics Interface Proceedings. 250p. 1997. pap. write for info. (*1-55860-488-X*) Morgan Kaufmann.

1997 Guide to Behavioral Resources on the Internet: A Review of Mental Health & Substance Abuse Web Sites, Mailing Lists & Support Forms. Ed. by Kenneth M. Coughlin. (Illus.). 519p. (Orig.). 1997. pap. text 245.00 (*1-881393-99-2*) Faulkner & Gray.

1997 Guide to Coal Contracts. Ed. by Susannah J. Harris. 754p. 1997. pap. 295.00 (*0-935453-86-5*) Pasha Pubns.

1997 Viewers Guide to the PGA Tour. Whitney McClelland. (Illus.). 240p. 1996. pap. 24.95 (*0-9631259-5-8*) Golfguide.

1997 Guidelines for the Re-evaluation Counseling Communities. 42p. 1998. pap. 2.00 (*1-58429-027-7*) Rational Isl.

1997 Guitar & Musical Instrument Blue Book. rev. ed. 1996. lib. bdg. 200.00 (*0-932089-71-2*) Orion Res.

1997 Gun Blue Book. rev. ed. 1996. lib. bdg. 200.00 (*0-932089-75-5*) Orion Res.

1997 Health Care Almanac & Yearbook. Ed. by Luci S. Koizumi & Daniel B. Moskowitz. 480p. (Orig.). 1996. pap. text 195.00 (*1-881393-94-1*) Faulkner & Gray.

1997 Healthcare Alliance & Network Sourcebook. Ed. by John Reichard. 700p. 1996. pap. 265.00 (*1-881393-22-4*) Faulkner & Gray.

1997 Healthcare Guide to the Internet: An Annotated Listing of Internet Resources for the Healthcare Professional. 2nd ed. Jennifer Wayne-Doppke. (Illus.). 140p. (Orig.). 1997. pap. 68.00 (*0-9645360-4-8*) Cor Hlthcare.

1997 High Frequency Postgraduate Student Colloquium. IEEE (Electron Devices Soc.) Staff. Ed. by IEEE (Inst. of Electrical & Electronics Engrs.). LC 97-71451. 100p. 1997. pap. write for info. (*0-7803-3951-7*, 97TH8284) Inst Electrical.

1997 High Power Microwave Electronics Measurements, Identifications, Applications. IEEE (Russia/Joint Chapter Microwave Theory & Tech. 300p. 1997. pap. text. write for info. (*0-614-30242-0*, 97TH8290) IEEE Standards.

1997 Hong Kong Electron Devices Meeting. IEEE, Electron Devices Society Staff. Ed. by Institute of Electrical & Electronics Engineers, I. LC 96-80457. 240p. 1997. pap. write for info. (*0-7803-3802-2*, 97TH8260); fiche. write for info. (*0-7803-3803-0*, 97TH8260) Inst Electrical.

1997 I-95 Exit Information Guide. Tom Gilligan. 138p. 1997. pap. write for info. (*1-57502-734-8*, PO1358) Morris Pubng.

***1997 Idea Amendments: A Guide for Educators, Parents & Attorneys.** 2nd ed. Nancy L. Jones & Steven R. Aleman. LC 99-51931. 1999. write for info. (*1-57834-013-6*) LRP Pubns.

1997 Idea Amendment: A Guide for Educators, Parents, & Attorneys. Nancy L. Jones & Steven R. Aleman. LC 97-44782. 1997. 33.40 (*1-57834-005-5*) LRP Pubns.

1997 Idea Book. Commission on Reform Jewish Outreach. LC 98-142429. ix, 374p. 1997. write for info. (*0-8074-0644-9*) UAHC.

1997 IEEE International Workshop on (IDDQ '97) 100p. 1997. pap. 100.00 (*0-8186-8123-3*) IEEE Comp Soc.

1997 IEEE Annual Report Conference on Electrical Insulation & Dielectric Phenomena. IEEE, Dielectrics & Electrical Insulation Society. Ed. by Institute of Electrical & Electronics Engineers, I. LC 79-649806. 900p. 1997. pap. text. write for info. (*0-7803-3922-3*, 97CH36065); lib. bdg. write for info. (*0-7803-3923-1*, 97CH36065) IEEE Standards.

1997 IEEE Annual Report Conference on Electrical Insulation & Dielectric Phenomena. IEEE, Dielectrics & Electrical Insulation Society. Ed. by Institute of Electrical & Electronics Engineers, I. LC 79-649806. 900p. 1997. pap. text. write for info. (*0-7803-3851-0*, 97CH36046); lib. bdg. write for info. (*0-7803-3852-9*, 97CH36046) Inst Electrical.

1997 IEEE Annual Textile, Fiber & Film Industry Technical Conference. IEEE, Industry Applications Society Staff. Ed. by Institute of Electrical & Electronics Engineers, I. LC 90-657367. 100p. 1997. pap. text. write for info. (*0-7803-4090-6*, 97CH36100); lib. bdg. write for info. (*0-7803-4091-4*, 97CH36100) Inst Electrical.

1997 IEEE Antennas & Propagation Society Meeting. IEEE Antennas & Propagation Society Staff. Ed. by IEEE Staff. LC 90-640397. 2684p. 1997. pap. text 242.00 (*0-7803-4178-3*, 97CH36122); lib. bdg. write for info. (*0-7803-4179-1*, 97CH36122) Inst Electrical.

1997 IEEE-ASME Joint Railroad Conference. IEEE, Vehicular Technology Society Staff. Ed. by Institute of Electrical & Electronics Engineers, I. LC 90-644036. 160p. 1997. pap. text. write for info. (*0-7803-3854-5*, 97CH36047); lib. bdg. write for info. (*0-7803-3855-3*, 97CH36047) Inst Electrical.

1997 IEEE ATM Workshop. IEEE, Communications Society Staff. Ed. by Institute of Electrical & Electronics Engineers, I. LC 97-80022. 700p. 1997. pap. 160.00 (*0-7803-4196-1*, 97TH8316); fiche. write for info. (*0-7803-4197-X*, 97TH8316) Inst Electrical.

1997 IEEE Autotestcon. IEEE, Aerospace & Electronic Systems Society Staff. 700p. 1997. pap. text 160.00 (*0-7803-4162-7*, 97CH36120); lib. bdg. write for info. (*0-7803-4163-5*, 97CH36120); fiche. write for info. (*0-7803-4164-3*) Inst Electrical.

1997 IEEE Bipolar - Bicmos Circuits & Technology Meeting. IEEE, Electron Devices Society Staff. Ed. by Institute of Electrical & Electronics Engineers, I. 224p. 1997. pap. text. write for info. (*0-7803-3916-9*, 97CH36063); lib. bdg. write for info. (*0-7803-3917-7*, 97CH36063); fiche. write for info. (*0-7803-3918-5*, 97CH36063) IEEE Standards.

1997 IEEE Cement Industry Technical Conference Record XXXVIIII. IEEE (Industry Applications Soc.) Staff. Ed. by IEEE (Inst. of Electrical & Electronics Engrs.). 400p. 1997. pap. text. write for info. (*0-7803-3962-2*, 97CH36076); lib. bdg. write for info. (*0-7803-3963-0*, 97CH36076) IEEE Standards.

1997 IEEE Conference Communications, Power & Computing - Wescanex. IEEE (Region 7) Staff. LC 98-106927. 350p. 1997. pap. text. write for info. (*0-7803-4147-3*, 97CH36117); lib. bdg. write for info. (*0-7803-4148-1*, 97CH36117) Inst Electrical.

1997 IEEE Electrical Performance of Electronic Packaging. IEEE (Microwave Theory & Techniques Society, Elect. LC 97-80029. 276p. 1997. pap. 120.00 (*0-7803-4203-8*, 97TH8318) Inst Electrical.

1997 IEEE Engineering in Medicine & Biology Annual Conference. IEEE, Engineering in Medicine & Biology Society St. LC 99-226406. 2400p. 1997. pap. text 332.00 (*0-7803-4262-3*, 97CH36136); lib. bdg. write for info. (*0-7803-4263-1*, 97CH36136) Inst Electrical.

1997 IEEE 55th Annual Device Research Conference Digest. IEEE (Electron Devices Society) Staff. Ed. by IEEE (Institute of Electrical & Electronics Engine. LC 97-71261. 100p. 1997. pap. 102.00 (*0-7803-3911-8*, 97TH8279) Inst Electrical.

1997 IEEE 47th Vehicular Technology Conference. IEEE, Vehicular Technology Society Staff. 2000p. 1997. pap. text. write for info. (*0-7803-3659-3*, 97CH36003); lib. bdg. write for info. (*0-7803-3660-7*, 97CB36003); fiche 106.00 (*0-7803-3661-5*, 97CM36003) Inst Electrical.

1997 IEEE Gallium Aresenide Integrated Circuits Symposium. IEEE, Electron Devices Society & Microwave Theory. Ed. by Institute of Electrical & Electronics Engineers, I. 350p. 1997. pap. text. write for info. (*0-7803-4083-3*, 97CH36098); lib. bdg. write for info. (*0-7803-4084-1*, 97CH36098) Inst Electrical.

1997 IEEE Industrial & Commercial Power Systems Technical Conference. IEEE Industry Applications Society Staff. Ed. by IEEE Staff. 208p. 1997. pap. text. write for info. (*0-7803-3825-1*, 97CH36040); lib. bdg. write for info. (*0-7803-3826-X*, 97CH36040); fiche. write for info. (*0-7803-3827-8*, 97CH36040) Inst Electrical.

1997 IEEE Industry Applications Society Annual Meeting. IEEE (Industry Applications Society) Staff. 3000p. 1997. pap. text. write for info. (*0-7803-4067-1*, 97CH36096); lib. bdg. write for info. (*0-7803-4068-X*, 97CH36096) IEEE Standards.

1997 IEEE Intelligent Network Workshop. IEEE (Communications Society) Staff. LC 97-191771. 640p. 1997. pap. write for info. (*0-7803-4129-5*, 97TH8302) Inst Electrical.

1997 IEEE Intelligent Transportation Systems Conference. IEEE, Vehicular Technology Society Staff et al. LC 97-80147. 2000p. 1998. pap. write for info. (*0-7803-4269-0*, 97TH8331) Inst Electrical.

1997 IEEE International Symposium on Circuits & Systems. IEEE (Circuits & Systems Society) Staff. Ed. by IEEE (Institute of Electrical & Electronics Engine. LC 80-646530. 1997. fiche. write for info. (*0-7803-3585-6*, 97CM35987) Inst Electrical.

1997 IEEE International Symposium on Circuits & Systems. IEEE (Circuits & Systems Society) Staff. Ed. by IEEE (Institute of Electrical & Electronics Engine. LC 80-646530. 2400p. 1997. pap. text. write for info. (*0-7803-3583-X*, 97CH35987); lib. bdg. write for info. (*0-7803-3584-8*, 97CB35987) Inst Electrical.

1997 IEEE International Test Conference. IEEE (Computer-Society) Staff. Ed. by IEEE (Institute of Electrical & Electronics Engine. 1000p. 1997. pap. text 188.00 (*0-7803-4209-7*, 97CH36126); lib. bdg. write for info. (*0-7803-4210-0*, 97CB36126); mic. film. write for info. (*0-7803-4211-9*, 97CM36126); cd-rom. write for info. (*0-7803-4212-7*, 97CH36126) Inst Electrical.

1997 IEEE International Symposium on Consumer Electronics. IEEE (Consumer Electronics Society) Staff. Ed. by IEEE (Institute of Electrical & Electronics Engine. LC 97-80529. 350p. 1997. pap. write for info. (*0-7803-4371-9*, 97TH8348) Inst Electrical.

N

1997 IEEE International Symposium on Intelligent Control. IEEE (Control Systems Soc.) Staff. Ed. by IEEE (Inst. of Electrical & Electronics Engrs.). LC 90-655042. 470p. 1997. pap. text. write for info. (*0-7803-4116-3*, 97CH36107); lib. bdg. write for info. (*0-7803-4117-1*, 97CH36107) Inst Electrical.

1997 IEEE International Integrated Reliability Workshop Final Report. IEEE (Electron Devices Society & Reliability Socie. LC 97-80028. 176p. 1998. pap. 110.00 (*0-7803-4205-4*, 97TH8319) Inst Electrical.

1997 IEEE International Reliability Physics Symposium. IEEE (Electron Devices Society, Reliability Societ. Ed. by IEEE (Institute of Electrical & Electronics Engine. LC 82-640313. 540p. 1997. pap. text. write for info. (*0-7803-3575-9*, 97CH35983); fiche. write for info. (*0-7803-3577-5*, 97CM35983) Inst Electrical.

1997 IEEE International Reliability Physics Symposium. IEEE (Electron Devices Society, Reliability Societ. Ed. by IEEE (Institute of Electrical & Electronics Engine. LC 82-640313. 540p. 1997. lib. bdg. write for info. (*0-7803-3576-7*, 97CB35983) Inst Electrical.

1997 IEEE International Workshop on Robot & Human Communication. IEEE (Industrial Electronics Society) Staff. LC 97-72653. 500p. 1997. pap. write for info. (*0-7803-4076-0*, 97TH8296) Inst Electrical.

1997 IEEE International Workshop on Factory Communication Systems. IEEE (Industrial Electronics Society) Staff. LC 97-80019. 400p. 1997. pap. write for info. (*0-7803-4182-1*, 97TH8313) Inst Electrical.

1997 IEEE International Conference on Intelligent Processing Systems. IEEE (Industrial Electronics Society) Staff. Ed. by IEEE (Institute of Electrical & Electronics Engine. LC 97-80206. 2000p. 1997. pap. write for info. (*0-7803-4253-4*, 97TH8335) Inst Electrical.

1997 IEEE International Symposium on Information Theory. IEEE (Info. Theory Soc.) Staff. Ed. by IEEE (Inst. of Electrical & Electronics Engrs.). LC 72-179437. 580p. 1997. pap. text. write for info. (*0-7803-3956-8*, 97CH36074); lib. bdg. write for info. (*0-7803-3957-6*, 97CH36074) IEEE Standards.

1997 IEEE International Symposium on Compound Semiconductors. IEEE (Lasers & Electro-Optics Society) Staff & IEEE (Electron Devices Society) Staff. Ed. by IEEE (Institute of Electrical & Electronics Engine. LC 97-70758. 800p. 1997. pap. 118.00 (*0-7803-3883-9*, 97TH8272); fiche. write for info. (*0-7803-3884-7*, 97TH8272) Inst Electrical.

1997 IEEE International Conference on Evolutionary Computation. IEEE (Neural Networks Council) Staff. Ed. by IEEE (Inst. of Electrical & Electronics Engrs.). LC 97-71449. 826p. 1997. pap. write for info. (*0-7803-3949-5*, 97TH8283) Inst Electrical.

1997 IEEE International Electric Machines & Drives Conference. IEEE (Power Electronics Soc., Industrial Electroni. Ed. by IEEE (Inst. of Electrical & Electronics Engrs.). LC 97-71443. 738p. 1997. pap. 150.00 (*0-7803-3946-0*, 97TH8282) Inst Electrical.

1997 IEEE International Professional Communication Conference. IEEE (Professional Communication Society) Staff. LC 97-80020. 350p. 1997. pap. text 126.00 (*0-7803-4184-8*, 97CH36123); lib. bdg. write for info. (*0-7803-4185-6*, 97CH36123) Inst Electrical.

An Asterisk (*) at the beginning of an entry indicates that the title is appearing for the first time.

1997 IEEE International Conference on Personal Wireless Communications. IEEE (Region 10) Staff. Ed. by IEEE (Institute of Electrical & Electronics Engine. LC 97-80207. 600p. 1997. pap. write for info. (*0-7803-4298-4*, 97TH8338) Inst Electrical.

1997 IEEE International Conference on Robotics & Automation. IEEE (Robotics & Automation Society) Staff. LC 90-640158. 3800p. 1997. pap. text. write for info. (*0-7803-3612-7*, 97CH35992); lib. bdg. write for info. (*0-7803-3613-5*, 97CB35992); fiche. write for info. (*0-7803-3614-3*, 97CM35992) Inst Electrical.

1997 IEEE International Performance, Computing & Communications Conference. IEEE Communications Society Staff. Ed. by IEEE Staff. LC 97-152378. 530p. 1997. pap. text. write for info. (*0-7803-3873-1*, 97CH36051); lib. bdg. write for info. (*0-7803-3874-X*, 97CH36051) Inst Electrical.

1997 IEEE International Conference on Communications. IEEE, Communications Society Staff. Ed. by Institute of Electrical & Electronics Engineers, I. 2016p. 1997. pap. text. write for info. (*0-7803-3925-8*, 97CH36067); lib. bdg. write for info. (*0-7803-3926-6*, 97CH36067); fiche. write for info. (*0-7803-3927-4*, 97CH36067); cd-rom. write for info. (*0-7803-3928-2*, 97CH36067) IEEE Standards.

1997 IEEE International Conference on Innovative Systems in Silicon. IEEE, Components, Packaging & Manufacturing Techno & IEEE, Computer Society Staff. 400p. 1997. pap. text. write for info. (*0-7803-4275-5*, 97CH36140); lib. bdg. write for info. (*0-7803-4276-3*, 97CH36140) Inst Electrical.

1997 IEEE International Conference on Control Applications. IEEE Control System Society Staff. Ed. by IEEE Staff. 1200p. 1997. pap. text. write for info. (*0-7803-3876-6*, 97CH36055); lib. bdg. write for info. (*0-7803-3877-4*, 97CH36055) Inst Electrical.

1997 IEEE International Conference on Properties & Applications of Dielectric Materials Conference Record. IEEE, Dielectrics & Electrical Insulation Society. Ed. by Institute of Electrical & Electronics Engineers, I. LC 95-76252. 1000p. 1997. pap. text. write for info. (*0-7803-2651-2*, 97CH35794); lib. bdg. write for info. (*0-7803-2652-0*, 97CH35794); mic. film. write for info. (*0-7803-2653-9*, 97CM35794) Inst Electrical.

1997 IEEE International SOI Conference. IEEE, Electron Devices Society Staff. Ed. by Institute of Electrical & Electronics Engineers, I. 250p. 1997. pap. text. write for info. (*0-7803-3938-X*, 97CH36069); lib. bdg. write for info. (*0-7803-3939-8*, 97CH36069) IEEE Standards.

1997 IEEE International Symposium on Power Semiconductor & ICs. IEEE, Electron Devices Society Staff. 550p. 1997. pap. text. write for info. (*0-7803-3993-2*, 97CH36086); lib. bdg. write for info. (*0-7803-3994-0*, 97CH36086) Inst Electrical.

1997 IEEE International Geoscience & Remote Sensing Symposium. IEEE, Geoscience & Remote Sensing Society Staff. Ed. by Institute of Electrical & Electronics Engineers, I. LC 97-70575. 2000p. 1997. pap. text. write for info. (*0-7803-3836-7*, 97CH36042); lib. bdg. write for info. (*0-7803-3837-5*, 97CH36042) IEEE Standards.

1997 IEEE International Conference on Fuzzy Systems Proceedings. IEEE, Neural Networks Council Staff. Ed. by Institute of Electrical & Electronics Engineers, I. LC 96-80276. 1997. pap. text. write for info. (*0-7803-3796-4*, 97CH36032); lib. bdg. write for info. (*0-7803-3797-2*, 97CH36032); fiche. write for info. (*0-7803-3798-0*, 97CH36032) Inst Electrical.

1997 IEEE International Conference on Neural Networks. IEEE, Neural Networks Council Staff. Ed. by Institute of Electrical & Electronics Engineers, I. LC 97-72856. 2818p. 1997. pap. text 374.00 (*0-7803-4122-8*, 97CH36109); lib. bdg. write for info. (*0-7803-4123-6*, 97CH36109) Inst Electrical.

1997 IEEE International Symposium on Assembly & Task Planning. IEEE Robotics & Automation Society Staff. Ed. by IEEE Staff. LC 97-70262. 304p. 1997. pap. 132.00 (*0-7803-3820-0*, 97TH8264) Inst Electrical.

1997 IEEE International Conference on Systems, Man & Cybernetics. IEEE, Systems, Man & Cybernetics Society Staff. 3300p. 1997. pap. text. write for info. (*0-7803-4053-1*, 97CH36088); lib. bdg. write for info. (*0-7803-4054-X*, 97CH36088) Inst Electrical.

1997 IEEE International Symposium on Electronics & the Environment. IEEE, Technical Activities Board Staff. Ed. by Institute of Electrical & Electronics Engineers, I. LC 96-80471. 300p. 1997. pap. text. write for info. (*0-7803-3808-1*, 97CH36035); lib. bdg. write for info. (*0-7803-3809-X*, 97CH36035); fiche. write for info. (*0-7803-3810-3*, 97CH36035) Inst Electrical.

1997 IEEE International Conference on Intelligent Processing Systems: October 28-31, 1997, Central Garden Hotel, Beijing, China. IEEE International Conference on Intelligent Processing Systems & IEEE Industrial Electronics Society Staff. LC 97-80206. 1997. write for info. (*0-7803-4255-0*) Inst Electrical.

1997 IEEE International Workshop on Factory Communication Systems, WFCs '97: Proceedings. IEEE International Workshop on Factory Communication Systems Staff et al. LC 97-80019. xiv, 390 p. 1997. pap. write for info. (*0-7803-4183-X*) IEEE Standards.

1997 IEEE International Integrated Reliability Workshop Final Report: Stanford Sierra Camp, Lake Tahoe, California, October 13-16, 1997. IEEE Electron Devices Society Staff et al. LC 97-80028. v, 161 p. 1997. pap. write for info. (*0-7803-4206-2*) IEEE Standards.

1997 IEEE International Symposium on Computational Intelligence in Robotics & Automation, CIRA '97: "Towards New Computational Principles for Robotics & Automation": Proceedings, July 10-11, 1997, Monterey, California, USA. IEEE Staff et al. LC 97-80006. xiii, 420p. 1997. write for info. (*0-8186-8140-3*) IEEE Comp Soc.

1997 IEEE Leos Annual Meeting. IEEE (Lasers & Electro-Optics Society) Staff. 876p. 1997. pap. text. write for info. (*0-7803-3895-2*, 97CH36057); lib. bdg. write for info. (*0-7803-3896-0*, 97CH36057); fiche. write for info. (*0-7803-3897-9*, 97CH36057) Inst Electrical.

1997 IEEE MTT-S International Microwave Symposium Digest. IEEE, Microwave Theory & Techniques Society & Comp. Ed. by Institute of Electrical & Electronics Engineers, I. LC 77-645125. 2000p. 1997. pap. text. write for info. (*0-7803-3814-6*, 97CH36037); lib. bdg. write for info. (*0-7803-3815-4*, 97CH36037); fiche. write for info. (*0-7803-3816-2*, 97CH36037); cd-rom. write for info. (*0-7803-3817-0*, 97CH36037) Inst Electrical.

1997 IEEE MTT-S Symposium on Technologies for Wireless Applications Digest. IEEE (Microwave Theory & Techniques Society, Elect. Ed. by IEEE (Institute of Electrical & Electronics Engine. LC 96-75959. 250p. 1997. pap. 106.00 (*0-7803-3318-7*, 97TH8188); fiche 106.00 (*0-7803-3319-5*, 97TM8188) Inst Electrical.

1997 IEEE Pacific Rim Conference on Communications, Computers & Signal Processing. IEEE (Region 7, Victoria Sec.) Staff. Ed. by IEEE (Inst. of Electrical & Electronics Engrs.). LC 90-655140. 700p. 1997. pap. text. write for info. (*0-7803-3905-3*, 97CH36060); lib. bdg. write for info. (*0-7803-3906-1*, 97CH36060) Inst Electrical.

1997 IEEE Power Industry Computer Applications Conference. IEEE (Power Engineering Society) Staff. LC 84-645085. 500p. 1997. pap. text. write for info. (*0-7803-3713-1*, 97CH36013); lib. bdg. write for info. (*0-7803-3714-X*, 97CB36013); fiche. write for info. (*0-7803-3715-8*, 97CM36013) Inst Electrical.

1997 IEEE Power Electronics Specialists Conference. IEEE, Power Electronics Society Staff. Ed. by Institute of Electrical & Electronics Engineers, I. LC 80-646675. 1600p. 1997. pap. text. write for info. (*0-7803-3840-5*, 97CH36043); lib. bdg. write for info. (*0-7803-3841-3*, 97CH36043) Inst Electrical.

1997 IEEE Radiation Effects Data Workshop. IEEE (Nuclear & Plasma Sciences Society) Staff. LC 97-72647. 125p. 1997. pap. write for info. (*0-7803-4061-2*, 97TH8293) Inst Electrical.

1997 IEEE Radio Frequency Integrated Circuits Symposium. IEEE (Microwave Theory & Techniques Society, Elect. LC 97-72646. 266p. 1997. pap. text 118.00 (*0-7803-4063-9*, 97CH36095); lib. bdg. write for info. (*0-7803-4064-7*, 97CH36095) Inst Electrical.

1997 IEEE Rural Electric Power Conference. IEEE, Industry Applications Society Staff. Ed. by Institute of Electrical & Electronics Engineers, I. LC 83-641006. 190p. 1997. pap. text. write for info. (*0-7803-3973-8*, 97CH36079); lib. bdg. write for info. (*0-7803-3974-6*, 97CH36079) Inst Electrical.

1997 IEEE South African Symposium on Communications & Signal Processing. IEEE (South African Section) Staff. Ed. by IEEE (Institute of Electrical & Electronics Engine. LC 97-80017. 180p. 1997. pap. 110.00 (*0-7803-4173-2*, 97TH8312); mic. film. write for info. (*0-7803-4174-0*, 97TH8312) IEEE Standards.

1997 IEEE Symposium on Visual Languages. 450p. 1997. pap. 120.00 (*0-8186-8144-6*) IEEE Comp Soc.

1997 IEEE Tencon. IEEE, Region 10 Staff. Ed. by Institute of Electrical & Electronics Engineers, I. LC 97-80497. 800p. 1997. pap. text. write for info. (*0-7803-4365-4*, 97CH36162); lib. bdg. write for info. (*0-7803-4366-2*, 97CH36162); fiche. write for info. (*0-7803-4367-0*, 97CH36162) Inst Electrical.

1997 IEEE 23rd Annual Conference of the Industrial Electronics Society Proceedings. IEEE (Industrial Electronics Society) Staff. Ed. by IEEE (Institute of Electrical & Electronics Engine. LC 97-71262. 1500p. 1997. pap. text 234.00 (*0-7803-3932-0*, 97CH36066); lib. bdg. write for info. (*0-7803-3933-9*, 97CH36066) Inst Electrical.

1997 IEEE U. S. Membership Salary & Fringe Benefit Survey. 1997. 119.95 (*0-87942-311-0*, UH2966-0-0-10) Inst Electrical.

1997 IEEE Ultrasonics Symposium. IEEE (Ultrasonics, Ferroelectrics & Frequency Cont. LC 73-641406. 1900p. 1998. pap. text. write for info. (*0-7803-4153-8*, 97CH36118); lib. bdg. write for info. (*0-7803-4154-6*, 97CH36118) Inst Electrical.

1997 IEEE Workshop on Automatic Speech Recognition & Understanding. IEEE (Signal Processing Society) Staff. Ed. by IEEE Staff. LC 96-78539. 600p. 1997. pap. write for info. (*0-7803-3698-4*, 97TH8241); mic. film. write for info. (*0-7803-3699-2*, 97TM8241) Inst Electrical.

1997 IEEE Workshop on Applications of Signal Processing to Audio & Acoustics. IEEE (Signal Processing Society) Staff. Ed. by IEEE (Institute of Electrical & Electronics Engine. LC 97-71260. 150p. 1997. pap. write for info. (*0-7803-3908-8*, 97TH8278) Inst Electrical.

1997 IEEE Workshop on Speech Coding for Telecommunications. IEEE (Signal Processing Society) Staff. LC 97-72649. 116p. 1997. pap. 104.00 (*0-7803-4073-6*, 97TH8295) Inst Electrical.

1997 IEEE Workshop on Signal Processing Advances in Wireless Communications. IEEE (Signal Processing Society) Staff. 450p. 1997. pap. write for info. (*0-7803-3944-4*, 97TH8281) Inst Electrical.

1997 IEEE Workshop on Neural Networks for Signal Processing. IEEE Staff. 680p. 1997. pap. 122.00 (*0-7803-4256-9*) Inst Electrical.

1997 IEEE Workshop on Speech Coding for Telecommunications Proceedings: Back to Basics--Attacking Fundamental Problems in Speech Coding, Pocono Manor Inn, Pocono Manor, Pennsylvania, U. S. A., September 7-10, 1997. IEEE Workshop on Speech Coding for Telecommunications Staff & Institute of Electrical & Electronics Engineers Staff. LC 97-72649. viii, 116 p. 1997. pap. write for info. (*0-7803-4074-4*) Inst Electrical.

1997 IEEE Workshop on Signal Processing Systems (SIPS) Design & Implementation. IEEE, Signal Processing Society Staff. Ed. by Institute of Electrical & Electronics Engineers, I. LC 96-80477. 660p. 1997. pap. write for info. (*0-7803-3806-5*, 97TH8262); fiche. write for info. (*0-7803-3807-3*, 97TH8262) Inst Electrical.

1997 IEEE 12th Applied Power Electronics Conference. IEEE (Power Electronics Society, Industry Applicat. LC 90-643607. 1200p. 1997. pap. text. write for info. (*0-7803-3704-2*, 97CH36011); lib. bdg. write for info. (*0-7803-3705-0*, 97CB36011); fiche. write for info. (*0-7803-3706-9*, 97CM36011) Inst Electrical.

1997 IEEE 23rd Northeast Bioengineering Conference. IEEE, Engineering in Medicine & Biology Society St. Ed. by Institute of Electrical & Electronics Engineers, I. LC 88-646567. 250p. 1997. pap. text. write for info. (*0-7803-3848-0*, 97CH36045); lib. bdg. write for info. (*0-7803-3849-9*, 97CH36045) Inst Electrical.

1997 IEEE 26th Photovoltaic Specialists Conference. IEEE (Electron Devices Society) Staff. Ed. by IEEE (Institute of Electrical & Electronics Engine. LC 84-640812. 1700p. 1998. lib. bdg. write for info. (*0-7803-3767-0*, 97CB36026); mic. film. write for info. (*0-7803-3768-9*, 97CM36026) Inst Electrical.

1997 IEEE 36th Conference on Decision & Control. IEEE Control Systems Society Staff. Ed. by IEEE Staff. LC 79-640961. 4500p. 1998. pap. text 514.00 (*0-7803-4187-2*, 97CH36124); lib. bdg. write for info. (*0-7803-4188-0*, 97CH36124); fiche. write for info. (*0-7803-4189-9*, 97CH36124); cd-rom. write for info. (*0-7803-4190-2*, 97CH36124) Inst Electrical.

1997 IEEE 6th International Conference on Emerging Technologies & Factory Automation Proceedings. IEEE (Industrial Electronics Society) Staff. LC 97-80024. 660p. 1997. pap. 156.00 (*0-7803-4192-9*, 97TH8314) Inst Electrical.

1997 IEEE 6th Human Factors & Power Plants. IEEE (Power Engineering Society) Staff. Ed. by IEEE (Institute of Electrical & Electronics Engine. LC 96-79978. 1996. fiche. write for info. (*0-7803-3771-9*, 97CH36027) Inst Electrical.

1997 IEEE 6th Human Factors & Power Plants. IEEE (Power Engineering Society) Staff. Ed. by IEEE (Institute of Electrical & Electronics Engine. LC 96-79978. 606p. 1997. pap. text. write for info. (*0-7803-3769-7*, 97CH36027) Inst Electrical.

1997 IEEE 6th Human Factors & Power Plants. IEEE (Power Engineering Society) Staff. Ed. by IEEE Staff. LC 96-79978. 606p. 1997. lib. bdg. write for info. (*0-7803-3770-0*, 97CH36027) Inst Electrical.

1997 IEEE/ASME International Conference on Advanced Intelligent Mechatronics. IEEE (Industrial Electronics Society & Robotics &. LC 97-72651. 1000p. 1997. pap. 188.00 (*0-7803-4080-9*, 97TH8298) Inst Electrical.

1997 IEEE/Cornell Conference on Advanced Concepts in High Speed Semiconductor Devices & Circuits. IEEE (Electron Devices Soc.) Staff. Ed. by IEEE (Inst. of Electrical & Electronics Engrs.). 580p. 1997. pap. text. write for info. (*0-7803-3970-3*, 97CH36078); lib. bdg. write for info. (*0-7803-3971-1*, 97CB36078) Inst Electrical.

1997 IEEE/CPMT 21st International Electronics Manufacturing Technology Symposium. IEEE (Components, Packaging & Manufacturing Techno. Ed. by IEEE (Institute of Electrical & Electronics Engine. 400p. 1997. pap. text. write for info. (*0-7803-3929-0*, 97CH36068); lib. bdg. write for info. (*0-7803-3930-4*, 97CB36068) Inst Electrical.

1997 IEEE/IAFE Conference on Computational Intelligence for Financial Engineering. IEEE (Neural Networks Council) Staff. LC 97-191635. 310p. 1997. pap. write for info. (*0-7803-4133-3*, 97TH8304) Inst Electrical.

1997 IEEE/IEEJ Joint IAS Power Conversion Conference. IEEE Industry Applications Society Staff. Ed. by IEEE Staff. LC 97-70237. 1000p. 1997. pap. write for info. (*0-7803-3823-5*, 97TH8266) Inst Electrical.

1997 IEEE/Semi Advanced Semiconductor Manufacturing Conference & Workshop. IEEE, Electron Devices Society & Components, Packa. 480p. 1997. pap. text. write for info. (*0-7803-4050-7*, 97CH36089); lib. bdg. write for info. (*0-7803-4051-5*, 97CH36089) Inst Electrical.

1997 Illinois Agricultural Pest Management Handbook. 400p. 1997. pap. 17.00 (*1-883097-11-8*) U Ill Ofc Agricult.

1997 Illinois Commercial Landscape & Turf Pest Management Handbook. 150p. 1997. pap. 8.00 (*1-883097-13-4*) U Ill Ofc Agricult.

1997 India Handbook. 6th rev. ed. Ed. by Robert W. Bradnock. (Footprint Handbks.). (Illus.). 1440p. 1996. 29.95 (*0-8442-4908-4*, Passprt Bks) NTC Contemp Pub Co.

1997 Indian Medical Market Report Vol. 1: An Indepth Market Study on India's Pharmaceutical, Biotechnology & Medical Device Industries. Amiya Nayak et al. 167p. (Orig.). 1997. pap. 299.95 (*0-9657889-1-1*) Golden Tri Org.

1997 Individual Tax Return Guide. rev. ed. 154p. 1997. pap. text 15.00 (*0-7811-0171-9*) Res Inst Am.

1997 Information Systems Spending Vol. 1-3: Technology Trends Planner/Budget Trends Analysis/Technology Trends Planner Update, 3 vols. Ed. by Edward Pasahow. LC 98-171673. 450p. 1997. ring bd. 595.00 (*0-945052-32-4*) Computer Econ.

1997 International Symposium on Industrial Electronics. IEE (Industrial Electronics Society) Staff. Ed. by IEEE (Institute of Electrical & Electronics Engine. LC 97-71259. 1600p. 1997. pap. write for info. (*0-7803-3936-3*, 97TH8280) Inst Electrical.

1997 International Symposium on Electromagnetic Compatibility Proceedings. IEEE (Electromagnetic Compatibility Society) Staff. Ed. by IEEE (Institute of Electrical & Electronics Engine. LC 96-77611. 950p. 1997. pap. write for info. (*0-7803-3608-9*, 97TH8218); mic. film. write for info. (*0-7803-3609-7*, 97TM8218) Inst Electrical.

1997 IEEE International Symposium on Electromagnetic Compatibility. IEEE (Electromagnetic Compatibility Society) Staff. LC 83-645449. 500p. 1997. pap. text. write for info. (*0-7803-4140-6*, 97CH36113); lib. bdg. write for info. (*0-7803-4141-4*, 97CB36113) Inst Electrical.

1997 International Symposium on VLSI Technology, Systems & Applications. IEEE (Electron Devices Society & Computer Society). 350p. 1997. pap. write for info. (*0-7803-4131-7*, 97TH8303) Inst Electrical.

1997 International Electron Devices Meeting. IEEE (Electron Devices Society) Staff. Ed. by IEEE (Institute of Electrical & Electronics Engine. LC 81-642284. 980p. 1997. pap. text. write for info. (*0-7803-4100-7*, 97CH36103); lib. bdg. write for info. (*0-7803-4101-5*, 97CH36103) Inst Electrical.

1997 International Symposium on Micro Mechatronics & Human Science. IEEE (Robotics & Automation Society & Industrial E. Ed. by IEEE (Institute of Electrical & Electronics Engine. LC 97-80016. 250p. 1997. pap. 118.00 (*0-7803-4171-6*, 97TH8311); mic. film. write for info. (*0-7803-4172-4*, 97TH8311) IEEE Standards.

1997 International Symposium on Technology & Society. IEEE (Social Implications of Technology Society) S. LC 97-71959. 520p. 1997. pap. text. write for info. (*0-7803-3982-7*, 97CH36081); lib. bdg. write for info. (*0-7803-3983-5*, 97CH36081) IEEE Standards.

1997 International Conference on Virtual Systems & MultiMedia (VSMM '97) 200p. 1997. pap. 110.00 (*0-8186-8150-0*) IEEE Comp Soc.

***1997 International Conference on Bond Graph Modeling & Simulation (ICBGM '97) Held in Phoenix, Arizona - January, 1997.** Ed. by Jose J. Granda & Genevieve Dauphin-Tanguy. (Simulation Ser.: Vol. 29, No. 1). 347p. 1998. 100.00 (*1-56555-103-6*, SS-29-1) Soc Computer Sim.

1997 International Conference on Multichip Modules. IEEE, Components, Packaging & Manufacturing Techno. Ed. by Institute of Electrical & Electronics Engineers, I. LC 96-80271. 425p. 1997. pap. write for info. (*0-7803-3787-5*, 97TH8258); fiche. write for info. (*0-7803-3789-1*, 97TH8258) Inst Electrical.

1997 International Conference on Software Engineering (ICSE-19) IEEE Computer Society Staff. 600p. 1997. pap. text 80.00 (*0-8186-7816-X*) IEEE Comp Soc.

1997 International Conference on Information Technology Applications in Biomedicine Proceedings. IEEE, Engineering in Medicine & Biology Society St. Ed. by Institute of Electrical & Electronics Engineers, I. LC 97-80277. 80p. 1997. pap. write for info. (*0-7803-4318-2*, 97TH8342) Inst Electrical.

1997 International Fiber Optics Yellow Pages. Date not set. pap. 89.95 (*1-56851-163-9*) Info Gatekeepers.

1997 International ISDN Yellow Pages. Date not set. pap. 69.95 (*1-56851-159-0*) Info Gatekeepers.

1997 International Laser Safety Conference Proceedings, Vol. 3. Ed. by Jerome Dennis. (Illus.). 649p. 1997. pap. text 109.00 (*0-912035-13-7*, 215) Laser Inst.

1997 International Mechanical Engineering Congress & Exposition, Dallas, Texas, November 16-21, 1997: Adaptive Structures & Material Systems, 1997. Ed. by D. Brei & J. Sirkis. LC 97-76721. (AD Ser.: Vol. 54). 252p. 1997. 110.00 (*0-7918-1822-5*, H01103) ASME Pr.

1997 International Mechanical Engineering Congress & Exposition, Dallas, Texas, November 16-21, 1997: Analysis & Design Issues for Modern Aerospace Vehicles, 1997. Ed. by G. J. Simitses. (AD Ser.: Vol. 55). 508p. 1997. 170.00 (*0-7918-1835-7*, H01116) ASME Pr.

1997 International Mechanical Engineering Congress & Exposition: Proceedings of the ASME Advanced Energy Systems Division, Dallas, Texas, November 16-21, 1997. Ed. by M. L. Ramalingam et al. LC 97-77360. (AES Ser.: Vol. 37). 504p. 1997. 170.00 (*0-7918-1845-4*, H01126) ASME Pr.

1997 International Mechanical Engineering Congress & Exposition, Dallas, Texas, November 16-21, 1997: Thermal Hydraulics of Advanced Nuclear Reactors & Thermal Hydraulics of Advanced Steam Generation & Heat Exchangers. Ed. by Y. A. Hassan et al. LC 97-76709. (NE Ser.: Vol. 21). 136p. 1997. 80.00 (*0-7918-1832-2*, H01113) ASME Pr.

1997 International Mechanical Engineering Congress & Exposition, Dallas, Texas, November 16-21, 1997 Vol. 1: Fluid-Structure Interaction, Aeroelasticity, Flow-Induced Vibration & Noise. Ed. by M. P. Paidoussis et al. (AD Ser.: Vol. 53-1). 480p. 1997. 160.00 (*0-7918-1821-7*, H1102A) ASME Pr.

1997 International Plumbing Code. ICBO Staff et al. (Illus.). 127p. 1997. pap. 45.00 (*1-892395-05-3*, 112S97); ring bd. 51.75 (*1-892395-06-1*, 112L97) Intl Code Coun.

1997 International Plumbing Code. International Code Council Staff. 135p. 1997. ring bd. 51.75 (*1-884590-99-3*, 112L97) Intl Conf Bldg Off.

N

An Asterisk (*) at the beginning of an entry indicates that the title is appearing for the first time.

1997 Internatioanl Satellite Directory. 1997. 15.00 (*0-936361-22-0*) Design Pubs.

1997 International Semiconductor Conference. IEEE, Electron Devices Society Staff. Ed. by Institute of Electrical & Electronics Engineers, I. LC 96-80472. 700p. 1997. pap. write for info. (*0-7803-3804-9*, 97TH8261) Inst Electrical.

1997 International Semiconductor Conference. IEEE, Electron Devices Society Staff. Ed. by Institute of Electrical & Electronics Engineers, I. LC 96-80472. 700p. 1997. fiche. write for info. (*0-7803-3805-7*, 97TH8261) Inst Electrical.

1997 International Solid-State Sensor & Actuators Conference. IEEE, Electron Devices Society Staff. Ed. by Institute of Electrical & Electronics Engineers, I. LC 97-70574. 2000p. 1997. pap. write for info. (*0-7803-3829-4*, 97TH8267) IEEE Standards.

1997 International Symposium on Personal, Indoor & Mobile Radio Communications Proceedings. IEEE (Communications Society) Staff. Ed. by IEEE (Institute of Electrical & Electronics Engine. LC 97-70761. 1300p. 1997. pap. write for info. (*0-7803-3871-5*, 97TH8271); fiche. write for info. (*0-7803-3872-3*, 97TM8271) Inst Electrical.

1997 International Symposium on Polymeric Electronics Packaging. IEEE (Components, Packaging & Manufacturing Techno. Ed. by IEEE (Institute of Electrical & Electronics Engine. LC 97-70763. 200p. 1997. pap. write for info. (*0-7803-3865-0*, 97TH8268) Inst Electrical.

1997 International Symposium on Microelectronics, Vol. 3235. 714p. 1997. 116.00 (*0-930815-50-5*) SPIE.

1997 International Vacuum Microelectronics Conference. IEEE (Electron Devices Society) Staff. Ed. by IEEE (Institute of Electrical & Electronics Engine. 700p. 1997. pap. write for info. (*0-614-25850-2*, 97TH8257) IEEE Comp Soc.

1997 International Vacuum Microelectronics Conference. IEEE (Electron Devices Society) Staff. Ed. by IEEE (Institute of Electrical & Electronics Engine. 1997. fiche. write for info. (*0-7803-3786-7*, 97TH8257) Inst Electrical.

1997 International Who's Who of Institutions & Mutual Funds. Carson Publications Staff. 1997. ring bd. 500.00 (*0-9646311-4-8*) Carson Grp.

1997 Investment Allocation Percentages. CCH Editorial Staff. 600p. 1998. pap. 29.95 (*0-8080-0252-X*) CCH INC.

1997 Irwin Finance Cluster. Irwin Staff. 1996. text. write for info. (*0-256-26058-3*, Irwn McGrw-H) McGrw-H Hghr Educ.

1997 Its Technology Review: Southwestern United States. (Illus.). 1998. pap. text 65.00 (*0-935403-23-X*, PP-065) Inst Trans Eng.

1997 ITS Technology Review: 4th World Congress on ITS, Berlin, Germany. Gerald H. Blair et al. LC 99-173357. (Illus.). 47p. 1998. pap. text. write for info. (*0-935403-20-5*, PP-066) Inst Trans Eng.

1997 IUCN Red List of Threatened Plants. Contrib. by Kerry S. Walter & Harriet J. Gillett. LC 98-156526. 861p. 1998. pap. text 60.00 (*2-8317-0328-X*, Pub. by IUCN) Island Pr.

1997 Just-in-Time for Decision Science. Prentice Hall Staff. (C). 1997. write for info. (*0-13-259524-9*, Macmillan Coll) P-H.

1997 Latin American Market Planning Report. Strategy Research Corp. Staff. 1997. pap. 450.00 (*1-888520-06-X*) Strategy Research.

1997 Lawyer's Plum Book: Political Appointments for Attorneys in the Second Clinton Administration. Richard L. Hermann & Linda P. Sutherland. Ed. by Jeanette J. Sobajian & Glenda Dominguez. 146p. 1997. lib. bdg. 39.95 (*0-929728-31-9*) Federal Reports Inc.

1997 Legal Directory. 117th ed. 719p. 1997. pap. 34.95 (*1-57786-054-3*) Legal Communs.

1997 Life Safety Code Field Guide for Health Care Facilities. David M. Birk & James K. Lathrop. (Illus.). 176p. 1998. pap. text 145.00 (*1-57839-045-1*) Opus Communs.

1997 Life Safety Code Workbook & Study Guide. David M. Birk & James K. Lathrop. (Illus.). 416p. 1998. pap. text 495.00 (*1-57839-046-X*) Opus Communs.

1997 Managed Home Care Sourcebook. Ed. by David Bech. LC 98-233104. (Illus.). 575p. 1997. pap. text 195.00 (*1-881393-97-6*) Faulkner & Gray.

1997 Manufacturing Enterprise Applications, Vols. 1 & 2. Thomas Publishing Company Staff. Ed. by Alice Greene. (Illus.). 1800p. 1997. 125.00 incl. cd-rom (*1-882554-06-X*) Thomas Pub NY.

1997 Market Scope: The Desktop Guide to Supermarket Share & Category Sales. Ed. by Lynda Gutierrez et al. (Illus.). 980p. 1997. pap. 325.00 (*0-911790-61-6*) Trade Dimensns.

1997 Marketing Guidebook: The Book of Supermarket Distribution Facts. rev. ed. Ed. by Lynda Beatty et al. (Illus.). 949p. 1996. 325.00 (*0-911790-31-4*, Progress Grocer) Trade Dimensns.

1997 Martindale-Hubbell International Arbitration & Dispute Resolution Directory. Ed. by Martindale-Hubbell Staff. 1997. 170.00 (*1-85739-104-7*) Martindale-Hubbell.

1997 Medicaid Managed Care Sourcebook. Ed. by Lois Wingerson. 560p. (Orig.). 1996. pap. text. write for info. (*1-881393-95-X*) Faulkner & Gray.

1997 Medical Outcomes & Guidelines Sourcebook: A Progress Report & Resource Guide on Medical Outcomes Research & Practice Guidelines: Developments, Data, & Documentation. 800p. (Orig.). (C). 1996. pap. 295.00 (*1-881393-66-6*) Faulkner & Gray.

1997 Medical Quality Management Sourcebook. Ed. by Ken Coughlin & Maralee Youngs. 524p. 1996. 275.00 (*1-881393-85-2*) Faulkner & Gray.

1997 Medicare & Medicaid Legislation: Law & Explanation. CCH Editorial Staff. 900p. Date not set. pap. text 85.00 (*0-8080-0169-8*) CCH INC.

1997 Medicare Explained. rev. ed. Ed. by CCH Editorial Staff. 192p. 1997. pap. text 22.00 (*0-8080-0147-7*, 4750) CCH INC.

1997 Membership Directory of the American Crystallographic Association. 108p. (C). 1997. pap. text 10.00 (*0-937140-40-6*) Am Crystallographic.

1997 Mexico & Central America Handbook. 7th rev. ed. Ed. by Ben Box. (Footprint Handbks.). (Illus.). 928p. 1996. 21.95 (*0-8442-4906-8*, Passprt Bks) NTC Contemp Pub Co.

1997 Multistate Corporate Tax Guide, 2 vols. William A. Raabe & Karen J. Boucher. 1248p. pap. 238.00 (*1-56706-405-1*, S78) Panel Pubs.

*__1997 Municipal Elections in Bosnia & Herzegovina: An Analysis of the Observations.__ Hans Schmeets. 9p. 1998. 120.00 (*0-7923-5303-X*) Kluwer Academic.

1997 Music Yearbook. Joel Whitburn. 256p. 1998. pap. text 34.95 (*0-89820-125-X*) Record Research.

1997 NAB/BCFM Television Market Analysis. Theresa J. Ottina. 140p. 1997. pap. 475.00 (*0-89324-303-5*) Natl Assn Broadcasters.

1997 Nagano Symposium on Sports Sciences. Ed. by Hiroshi Nose et al. LC 98-71207. 646p. 1998. text 75.00 (*1-884125-71-9*) Cooper Pubng.

1997 National Directory of Fire Chiefs & Emergency Departments. 6th ed. Tr. by Laura J. Gross. 1080p. 1997. 70.00 (*1-880245-14-0*) SPAN Pub.

1997 National Directory of Law Enforcement Administrators, Correctional Institutions & Related Agencies, Vol. XXXIII. 750p. 1997. 85.00 (*1-880245-16-7*) SPAN Pub.

1997 National Hispanic Media Directory. 9th ed. Kirk Whisler & Octavio Nuiry. 320p. 1997. pap. 95.00 (*1-889379-06-9*) WPR Pubng.

1997 National Roundtables on Family Group Decision Making: Summary of Proceedings. Ed. by American Humane Association, Children's Division Staff. LC 99-183360. (Illus.). 1998. pap. text 25.00 (*0-930915-21-6*, CFGD02) Am Humane Assn.

1997 National Study of the Changing Workforce. James T. Bond et al. (National Study of the Changing Workforce Ser.: Vol. 2). 176p. 1998. pap. 49.00 (*1-888324-09-0*, W98-01) Families & Work.

1997 Natural Gas Yearbook. Ed. by Robert E. Willett. 361p. 1996. 175.00 (*0-471-17073-9*) Wiley.

1997 New Year's Floods in Western Nevada. J. G. Rigby et al. (Special Publications: No. 23). (Illus.). 112p. 1998. pap. 24.95 (*1-888035-03-X*) Nev Bureau Mines & Geol.

1997-1998 Day School Directory. 1997. pap. 13.00 (*0-914131-15-X*, C260) Torah Umesorah.

1997-1998 Absite Combat Manual. unabridged ed. Hratch L. Karamanoukian et al. Ed. by John Pryor. 295p. 1997. spiral bd. 59.00 (*0-9663292-0-1*) Magalhaes Sci Pr.

1997-1998 Medical Student's Guide to Successful Residency Matching. Lee T. Miller & Leigh G. Donowitz. 101p. 1997. pap. 14.95 (*0-683-30207-8*) Lppncott W & W.

1997-1998 Film Composers Guide. 4th ed. Ed. & Compiled by Vincent Jacquet-Francillon. 500p. 1997. pap. 55.00 (*0-943728-93-2*) Lone Eagle Pub.

1997-98 Hospital Salary & Benefits Report. 227p. 1997. pap. 295.00 (*0-939326-30-2*) Hosp & Hlthcare.

1997-98 Home Care Salary & Benefits Report. 420p. 1997. pap. 250.00 (*0-939326-32-9*) Hosp & Hlthcare.

1997-98 Hospice Salary & Benefits Report. 260p. 1997. pap. 195.00 (*0-939326-33-7*) Hosp & Hlthcare.

1997-98 Nursing Department Report. 168p. 1997. pap. 195.00 (*0-939326-35-3*) Hosp & Hlthcare.

1997-98 AAHSA Nursing Home Salary & Benefits Report. 280p. 1997. pap. 250.00 (*0-939326-34-5*) Hosp & Hlthcare.

1997-98 Nursing Home Salary & Benefits Report. 19th ed. 300p. 1997. pap. 250.00 (*0-939326-29-9*) Hosp & Hlthcare.

1997-98 Directory of Greeting Card Sales Representatives. 4th ed. Ed. by Mila Albertson. 286p. 1997. pap. 95.00 (*0-938369-31-8*) Greeting Card Assn.

1997-98 Workers' Compensation Managed Care Sourcebook. Ed. by Gwen C. Segre. LC 98-183719. (Illus.). 480p. 1997. pap. text 235.00 (*1-57987-005-8*) Faulkner & Gray.

1997-99 Handbook of Emergency Cardiovascular Care for Healthcare Providers. (Illus.). 58p. 1997. pap. 7.95 (*0-87493-629-2*) Am Heart.

1997 Nominations for the U. S. Court of Veterans Appeals, the U. S. Department of Veterans Affairs & the U. S. Department of Labor: Hearing Before the Committee on Veterans' Affairs, United States Senate, 105th Congress, First Session, October 30, 1997. LC 98-213756. (S. Hrg. Ser.). iii, 155p. 1998. write for info. (*0-16-057233-9*) USGPO.

1997 North American Who's Who of Institutions & Mutual Funds. Carson Publications Staff. 2000p. 1997. ring bd. 799.00 (*0-9646311-1-3*) Carson Grp.

1997 North Carolina's Literary Resource Guide. rev. ed. Linda Hobson et al. Ed. by Bobbie Collins-Perry. 52p. 1997. pap. 6.50 (*1-883314-07-0*) NC Writers Network.

1997 Northern Ontario Outdoor Guide Book. Shawn Perich & Gord Ellis. 160p. (Orig.). Date not set. pap. 8.95 (*0-9649257-3-7*) Outdoor News.

1997 Nursing Licensure Guidelines: Information Manual for Nurses in the United States of America. Jason F. Janoulis & Brenda H. Janoulis. 224p. 1997. pap. 89.00 (*1-887617-54-X*) St Bart Pr Ltd.

1997 Nursing Licensure Guidelines: State, Provincial, Territorial Information Manual for Nurses in the United States of America & Canada. Jason F. Janoulis & Brenda H. Janoulis. 1997. audio compact disk 150.00 (*1-887617-55-8*) St Bart Pr Ltd.

1997 Oceans. IEEE (Oceanic Engineering Society) Staff. LC 97-72643. 1000p. 1997. lib. bdg. write for info. (*0-7803-4109-0*, 97CH36105) Inst Electrical.

1997 Officer Compensation Report. Goldsmith. 208p. 1996. 425.00 (*1-56706-353-5*) Panel Pubs.

1997 Official Guide Book to Sarasota, Bradenton & Venice, FL. 5th rev. ed. Steve Rabow. (Illus.). 342p. 1997. pap. 12.95 (*0-9639551-3-6*, Rabow) Primitive Pr.

1997 Oncology Nursing Drug Handbook. 2nd ed. Gail M. Wilkes et al. LC 97-3045. (Nursing Ser.). 752p. 1997. pap. 42.50 (*0-7637-0369-9*) Jones & Bartlett.

1997 Optical Data Storage Topical Meeting. IEEE (Lasers & Electro-Optics Society) Staff. Ed. by IEEE (Institute of Electrical & Electronics Engine. LC 97-70757. 110p. 1997. pap. write for info. (*0-7803-3885-5*, 97TH8273) Inst Electrical.

1997 Optical Data Storage Topical Meeting. IEEE (Lasers & Electro-Optics Society) Staff. Ed. by IEEE (Inst. of Electrical & Electronics Engrs.). LC 97-70757. 110p. 1997. fiche. write for info. (*0-7803-3886-3*, 97TH8273) Inst Electrical.

1997 Optical Fiber Communication Conference. IEEE, Lasers & Electro Optics Society Staff. Ed. by Institute of Electrical & Electronics Engineers, I. 376p. 1997. lib. bdg. write for info. (*0-7803-3860-X*, 97CH36049) Inst Electrical.

1997 Pacific Rim Conference on Stellar Astrophysics. Ed. by Kwing L. Chan et al. LC 98-70636. (Conference Series Proceedings: Vol. 138). 426p. 1998. 52.00 (*1-886733-58-9*) Astron Soc Pacific.

1997 Pacific Workshop on Distributed Multimedia Systems. Ed. by Knowledge Systems Institute Staff. (Illus.). 1997. pap. 65.00 (*0-9641699-6-7*) Knowldge Systs.

1997 Parent's Guide to Cambridge Schools K-8. Nancy Walser. 144p. (Orig.). 1996. pap. 14.95 (*0-9655642-0-7*) Huron Village.

1997 Particle Accelerator Conference. IEEE (Nuclear & Plasma Sciences Society) Staff. Ed. by IEEE (Institute of Electrical & Electronics Engine. LC 88-647453. 3200p. 1997. pap. text 410.00 (*0-7803-4376-X*, 97CH36167); lib. bdg. write for info. (*0-7803-4377-8*, 97CH36167) Inst Electrical.

*__1997 PATA Annual Statistical Report.__ Ed. by John Koldowski. 133p. 1998. pap. 150.00 (*1-882866-12-6*) Pac Asia Trvl.

1997 PDR Supplements, 2 supplements. Incl. Suppl. B. Supplement B. 51st ed. 200p. (Orig.). 1997. pap. text, suppl. ed. Not sold separately (*1-56363-223-3*); 21.95 (*1-56363-221-7*) Med Econ.

1997 Pennsylvania State Rules. Ed. by Thomas Davies & Tammy Garzarelli. (Orig.). Date not set. per. 59.00 (*1-57786-044-6*) Legal Communs.

1997 Pennsylvania Tax Handbook. Ed. by Thomas Davies. 604p. (Orig.). 1996. per. write for info. (*1-57786-077-2*) Legal Communs.

1997 Physician Salary Survey Report. 21st ed. 392p. 1997. pap. 250.00 (*0-939326-28-0*) Hosp & Hlthcare.

1997 Physicians' GenRx. 7th rev. ed. Physicians Genrx Staff. LC 99-33332. (Illus.). 880p. (C). (gr. 13). 1999. text 64.95 (*0-8151-9017-4*, 31745) Mosby Inc.

1997 Pocket Book of Antimicrobial Therapy & Prevention. Sherwood L. Gorbach et al. 400p. 1997. write for info. (*0-683-18309-5*) Lppncott W & W.

1997 Annual Potato Statistical Yearbook. Ed. by Carol A. Reszegh. (Illus.). 72p. 1997. 25.00 (*0-318-19543-7*) Natl Potato Coun.

1997 Power Tool Blue Book. rev. ed. 1997. lib. bdg. 200.00 (*0-932089-19-4*) Orion Res.

1997 Prayer Journal. Ed. by Leo Zanchettin. 208p. 1996. 12.95 (*0-932085-10-5*) Word Among Us.

1997 Proceedings of 43rd Annual Technical Meeting of the Institute of Environmental Sciences & Technology Vol. 1: Integrated Product Development. 366p. 1997. pap. 145.00 (*1-877862-54-1*) IEST.

1997 Professional Sound Blue Book. rev. ed. 1996. lib. bdg. 200.00 (*0-932089-73-9*) Orion Res.

1997 Propane Vehicle Challenge. 130p. 1998. 25.00 (*0-7680-0180-3*) Soc Auto Engineers.

1997 Prune Book: Making the Right Appointments to Manage Washington's Toughest Jobs. John H. Trattner. LC 96-48055. 420p. 1997. text 34.95 (*1-56833-076-6*) Madison Bks UPA.

1997 Quantum Electronics & Laser Science Conference. IEEE (Lasers & Electro-Optics Society) Staff. 284p. 1997. lib. bdg. write for info. (*0-7803-4127-9*, 97CH36111) Inst Electrical.

1997 Random Lengths Yearbook: Forest Product Market, Prices & Statistics. 242p. 1998. pap. 37.95 (*1-884311-05-9*) Random Lgths Pubns.

1997 Quick Reference to Erisa Compliance. annuals Barry M. Newman & Virginia S. Peabody. 512p. 1997. pap. 125.00 (*1-56706-363-2*, 63632) Panel Pubs.

1997 Reliability & Maintainability Symposium. IEEE (Reliability Society) Staff. Ed. by IEEE Staff. LC 78-132873. 460p. 1996. pap. text. write for info. (*0-7803-3783-2*, 97CH36029); lib. bdg. write for info. (*0-7803-3784-0*, 97CH36029) Inst Electrical.

1997 Reliability & Maintainability Symposium. IEEE (Reliability Society) Staff. Ed. by IEEE (Institute of Electrical & Electronics Engine. LC 78-132873. 1996. fiche. write for info. (*0-7803-3785-9*, 97CH36029) Inst Electrical.

1997 Report of Center Specific Graft & Patient Survival Rates, 7 vols. UNOS Staff. Incl. CS Executive Summary. (Illus.). (Orig.). 1997. pap. 13.00 (*1-886651-16-7*); CS Kidney Volume., **2 bks.** (Illus.). (Orig.). 1997. pap. 20.00 (*1-886651-17-5*); CS Liver Volume. (Illus.). (Orig.). 1997. pap. 13.00 (*1-886651-18-3*); CS Pancreas Volume. (Illus.). (Orig.). 1997. pap. 13.00 (*1-886651-19-1*); CS Heart Volume. (Illus.). (Orig.). 1997. pap. 13.00 (*1-886651-20-5*); CS Lung Volume. (Illus.). (Orig.). 1997. pap. 13.00 (*1-886651-21-3*); CS Heart-Lung Volume. (Illus.). (Orig.). 1997. pap. 13.00 (*1-886651-22-1*); 40.00 (*1-886651-14-0*) United Network.

1997 Report of the Committee on Infectious Diseases. 24th ed. American Academy of Pediatrics Staff. 764p. 1997. pap. 84.95 (*0-910761-85-X*) Am Acad Pediat.

1997 Retail Tenant Directory. Ed. by Lynda Gutierrez et al. (Illus.). 1568p. 1997. pap. 325.00 (*0-911790-62-4*) Trade Dimensns.

1997 Revisions to Standard Specifications for Highway Bridges. (Bridges & Structures Ser.). (Illus.). 326p. 1997. pap. 42.00 (*1-56051-079-X*) AASHTO.

1997 RI Acts & Resolves, Vol. 3. 2000p. Date not set. write for info. (*0-327-07618-6*, 4778010) LEXIS Pub.

1997 RI Public Laws. 2000p. Date not set. write for info. (*0-327-07619-4*, 4777810) LEXIS Pub.

1997 RI Public Laws, Vol. 2. 2000p. Date not set. write for info. (*0-327-07620-8*, 4777910) LEXIS Pub.

1997 RMIS Buyer's Guide. David Tweedy. 192p. (Orig.). 1997. pap. text 125.00 (*0-923240-18-7*) Stndrd Publishing.

1997 Robert H. Ebert Memorial Lecture. Frwd. by Samuel L. Milbank & Daniel M. Fox. 32p. 1997. pap. write for info. (*1-887748-16-4*) Milbank Memorial.

1997 World Satellite Yearly Update. Frank Baylin. (Illus.). 160p. (Orig.). 1997. pap. 60.00 (*0-917893-30-1*) Baylin Pubns.

1997 SBMO/IEEE MTT-S International Microwave & Optoelectronics Conference. IEEE, Microwave Theory & Techniques Society & Comp. LC 97-80012. 880p. 1997. pap. 176.00 (*0-7803-4165-1*, 97TH8309); fiche. write for info. (*0-7803-4166-X*) IEEE Standards.

*__1997 Scientific Visualization Conference.__ 200p. 1999. 110.00 (*0-7695-0504-X*) IEEE Comp Soc.

1997 Seacoast Children's Directory. 100p. (Orig.). 1997. pap. 9.98 (*0-9645068-7-4*) Romagnoli.

1997 2nd IEEE-CAS Region 8 Workshop on Analog & Mixed IC Design Proceedings. IEEE Staff. LC 97-80101. 130p. 1997. pap. write for info. (*0-7803-4240-2*) Inst Electrical.

1997 2nd IEEE International Workshop on Broadband Switching Systems. IEEE, Communications Society Staff. Ed. by Institute of Electrical & Electronics Engineers, I. LC 97-81044. 180p. 1997. pap. 116.00 (*0-7803-4443-X*, 97TH8352) Inst Electrical.

1997 2nd International Symposium on Intelligent Data Analysis. IEEE (Institute of Electrical & Electronics Engine. LC 96-79036. 500p. 1997. pap. write for info. (*0-7803-3739-5*, 97TH8247) Inst Electrical.

1997 2nd International Workshop on Statistical Metrology. IEEE, Electron Devices Society Staff. Ed. by Institute of Electrical & Electronics Engineers, I. LC 96-79035. 100p. 1997. pap. write for info. (*0-7803-3737-9*, 97TH8246); fiche. write for info. (*0-7803-3738-7*, 97TM8246) Inst Electrical.

1997 2nd International Symposium on Plasma Process Induced Damage. IEEE Electron Devices Society Staff. Ed. by IEEE Staff. 250p. 1997. pap. write for info. (*0-614-26158-9*, 97TH8265); fiche. write for info. (*0-7803-3822-7*, 97TH8265) Inst Electrical.

1997 Security Industry Buyers Guide. 10th ed. Jennifer O. Newman. 1996. pap., per. 169.00 (*1-881537-41-2*) Phillips Business.

1997 Security Transactions: Taxation of Your Stock & Bond Transactions. Ed. by CCH Editors. 64p. 1997. pap. text 7.75 (*0-8080-0206-6*) CCH INC.

*__1997 Self-Study Manual: U. S. Edition 1999.__ rev. ed. Ed. by David Staat. 2100p. 1999. spiral bd. 150.00 (*1-880853-06-X*) Coun Accred Srvs Fam & Child.

1997 Senate Staff Employment: Salary, Tenure, Demographics, & Benefits. Thomas J. Klouda. (Illus.). 132p. (C). 1998. pap. text 30.00 (*0-7881-7477-0*) DIANE Pub.

1997 17th IEEE/NPSS Symposium on Fusion Engineering. IEEE (Nuclear Plasma Sciences Society) Staff. Ed. by IEEE (Institute of Electrical & Electronics Engine. LC 85-653749. 1600p. 1998. pap. text 244.00 (*0-7803-4226-7*, 97CH36131); lib. bdg. write for info. (*0-7803-4227-5*, 97CH36131) Inst Electrical.

1997 7th International Workshop on Network & Operating System Support for Digital Audio & Video Proceedings. IEEE, Communications Society Staff. Ed. by Institute of Electrical & Electronics Engineers, I. LC 96-80423. 200p. 1997. pap. write for info. (*0-7803-3799-9*, 97TH8259) Inst Electrical.

1997 Shanghai International Conference on Laser Medicine & Surgery, Vol. 3344. Ed. by Jing Zhu. 1998. 80.00 (*0-8194-2791-8*) SPIE.

1997 Shopping Center Directory's Top Contacts. annuals LC 88-62383. 1996. 305.00 (*1-886257-18-3*) Natl Res Bur.

1997 Shopping Center Directory & Top Contacts, 5 vols. 37th ed. National Research Bureau Staff. 5800p. (Orig.). 1996. pap. 765.00 (*1-886257-19-1*) Natl Res Bur.

1997 Shopping Center Directory: East. annuals LC 88-62383. 1996. 305.00 (*1-886257-14-0*) Natl Res Bur.

1997 Shopping Center Directory: Midwest. annuals LC 88-62383. 1996. 305.00 (*1-886257-15-9*) Natl Res Bur.

1997 Shopping Center Directory: South. annuals LC 88-62383. 1996. 305.00 (*1-886257-16-7*) Natl Res Bur.

1997 Shopping Center Directory: West. annuals LC 88-62383. 1996. 305.00 (*1-886257-17-5*) Natl Res Bur.

An Asterisk (*) at the beginning of an entry indicates that the title is appearing for the first time.

1997 16th International Conference on Thermoelectrics. IEEE (Components, Packaging & Manufacturing Techno. Ed. by IEEE (Institute of Electrical & Electronics Engine. 450p. 1997. pap. 136.00 (0-7803-4057-4, 97TH8291) Inst Electrical.

1997 6th IEEE International Conference on Universal Personal Communications. IEEE, Communications Society Staff. Ed. by Institute of Electrical & Electronics Engineers, I. 1020p. 1997. pap. write for info. (0-7803-3777-8, 97TH8255); fiche. write for info. (0-7803-3778-6, 97TH8255); cd-rom. write for info. (0-7803-3779-4, 97TH8255) Inst Electrical.

1997 6th International Symposium on the Physical & Failure Analysis of Integrated Circuits. IEEE, Reliability/Components, Packaging & Manufact & Institute of Electrical & Electronics Engineers, I. LC 97-7002. 240p. 1997. pap. write for info. (0-7803-3985-1, 97TH8289) Inst Electrical.

1997 South Africa Handbook. rev. ed. Ed. by Sebastian Ballard & Rupert Linton. (Footprint Handbks.). 600p. 1996. 21.95 (0-8442-4913-0, Passprt Bks) NTC Contemp Pub Co.

1997 South American Handbook. 73rd rev. ed. Ed. by Ben Box. (Footprint Handbks.). (Illus.). 1552p. 1996. 39.95 (0-8442-4904-1, Passprt Bks) NTC Contemp Pub Co.

1997 South Carolina Legislative Handbook, Vol. 3. (Illus.). 103p. 1997. 30.00 (1-886629-05-6) Hendricks & Co.

1997 Southern California Funding Directory. 3rd rev. ed. OCVN Board of Advisors Staff. 250p. (Orig.). 1996. pap. 29.95 (0-9655378-0-3) Orange Cnty Venture.

1997 Southern Living Annual Recipes. Southern Living Staff. (Illus.). 368p. 1997. 34.95 (0-8487-1618-3) Oxmoor Hse.

1997 Sports Business Market Research Handbook. Joshua R. Pursell & Richard K. Miller. 260p. 1997. pap. 275.00 (1-881503-72-0) R K Miller Assocs.

1997 Sports Summit Business Directory. Michael Patino. 1000p. 1997. pap. text 179.00 (0-9644259-2-0) E J Krause.

1997 Spring Simulation Interoperability Workshop: Workshop Papers. (Simulation Interoperability Workshop Ser.). (Illus.). 1997. 75.00 (1-930638-02-7) S I S O.

1997 State Health Care Expenditure Report. Frwd. by Daniel M. Fox et al. (Illus.). 192p. 1999. pap. write for info. (1-887748-25-3) Milbank Memorial.

1997 State Legislative Summary: Children, Youth & Family Issues. Prod. by NCSL Children & Families Program Staff. 163p. 1998. 25.00 (1-55516-755-1, 6139) Natl Conf State Legis.

1997 State Medical Licensure Guidelines: Information Manual for MD & DO Physicians in the United States of America. Jason F. Janoulis & Brenda H. Janoulis. 1997. pap. 125.00 incl. audio compact disk (1-887617-56-6) St Bart Pr Ltd.

1997 State of the Future: Implications for Actions Today. Jerome C. Glenn & Theodore J. Gordon. LC 97-196789. (Orig.). 1997. pap. 19.95 (0-9657362-0-2) Am Coun Unit Nat.

1997 State Postsecondary Education Structures Sourcebook. 274p. 1997. 25.00 (0-318-22549-2, PS-97-3) Ed Comm States.

1997 Stock Trader's Almanac. 30th ed. (Illus.). 192p. 1996. spiral bd. 29.75 (1-889223-97-2) Hirsch Orgn.

1997 Summer Library Program Manual - "Zap into the Past" Jane A. Roeber. (Illus.). 218p. (Orig.). 1997. pap. text 18.00 (1-57337-040-1) WI Dept Pub Instruct.

1997 Supertraders Almanac. Frank A. Taucher. (Orig.). 1997. pap., spiral bd. 69.00 (1-879591-24-3) Mkt Movements.

1997 Supplement to Cases & Materials on Mass Media Law. 5th ed. Marc A. Franklin & David A. Anderson. (University Casebook Ser.). 150p. 1997. pap. text. write for info. (1-56662-556-4) Foundation Pr.

1997 Supplement to Cases & Materials on Federal Courts. 9th ed. Charles A. Wright & John B. Oakley. (University Casebook Ser.). 124p. 1997. pap. text. write for info. (1-56662-517-3) Foundation Pr.

1997 Supplement to Cases & Materials on Conflict of Laws. 10th ed. Peter Hay et al. (University Casebook Ser.). 25p. 1997. pap. text. write for info. (1-56662-546-7) Foundation Pr.

1997 Supplement to Arrest, Search, & Investigation in North Carolina. Robert L. Farb. 144p. (Orig.). (C). 1997. pap. text 12.00 (1-56011-312-X, 93.06A) Institute Government.

1997 Supplement to Complex Litigation, Advanced Civil Procedures. 2nd ed. Richard L. Marcus & Edward F. Sherman. (American Casebook Ser.). 85p. 1997. pap. text. write for info. (0-314-22757-1) West Pub.

1997 Supplement to Connecticut Law of Uninsured & Underinsured Motorist Coverage. Jon Berk & Michael C. Jainchill. 304p. 1998. pap. 64.00 (1-878698-45-1) Atlantic Law.

1997 Supplement to Coping with Psychiatric & Psychological Testimony. Jay Ziskin. Ed. by John T. Dunn. 192p. 1997. pap. 75.00 (1-879689-08-1) Law & Psych.

1997 Supplement to Federal Courts, Cases & Comments on Judicial Federalism & Judicial Power. Louise Weinberg. (American Casebook Ser.). 340p. 1996. pap. text, suppl. ed. write for info. (0-314-20603-5) West Pub.

1997 Supplement to Federal Income Taxation Principles & Policies. 3rd ed. Michael J. Graetz & Deborah H. Schenk. (University Casebook Ser.). 42p. (C). 1997. pap. text, suppl. ed. write for info. (1-56662-425-8) Foundation Pr.

1997 Supplement to Federal Income Taxation, Cases & Materials. 3rd ed. Paul R. McDaniel et al. (University Casebook Ser.). 101p. 1997. pap. text. write for info. (1-56662-507-6) Foundation Pr.

1997 Survey of Corporate University Future Directions. unabridged ed. Jeanne C. Meister. Ed. by Stephanie Roberts. (Illus.). 100p. 1997. pap. 895.00 (0-9656453-0-4) Corp Univ Xchange.

1997 Survey of the Current Status of North Carolina Minority & Women-Owned Businesses. 1997. write for info. (0-9633115-3-0) NC Inst Min Econ Devel.

1997 Symposium of Parallel Rendering. LC 98-140557. 120p. 1997. pap. 30.00 (1-58113-010-4, 428977) Assn Compu Machinery.

1997 Symposium on Cannabinoids, Vol. 1. Ed. by Patricia Reggio. 1997. write for info. (0-9658053-0-1) Intl Cannabinoid.

1997 Symposium on VLSI Circuits. IEEE (Electron Devices Society & Solid State Circu. LC 98-143583. 170p. 1997. lib. bdg. write for info. (0-7803-4145-7, 97CH36115) Inst Electrical.

1997 Symposium on VLSI Technology. IEEE (Electron Devices Society & Solid-State Circu. LC 90-655131. 170p. 1997. lib. bdg. write for info. (0-7803-4143-0, 97CH36114) Inst Electrical.

1997 Taste of Home Annual Recipes. Taste of Home Staff. 1997. 24.95 (0-89821-176-X, 24161) Reiman Pubns.

1997 Tax Year in Review. CCH Incorporated Staff. LC 98-147328. 200 p. 1998. write for info. (0-8080-0237-6) CCH INC.

1997 Tax Legislation Law, Explanation & Analysis: Taxpayer Relief Act of 1997. CCN Editorial Staff. LC 97-211656. 1200p. 1997. pap. text 42.50 (0-8080-0152-3) CCH INC.

1997 Tax Return Practice Problem for Corporations, S Corporations, & Partnerships. Dalton. 1998. pap. 21.95 (0-87393-789-9) Dame Pubns.

1997 Tenth Annual IEEE International ASIC Conference & Exhibit. IEEE (Solid State Circuits Council, Rochester Sect. 392p. 1997. pap. write for info. (0-7803-4283-6, 97TH8334) Inst Electrical.

1997 Vehicle Thermal Management Systems Conference Proceedings. 1997. 500.00 (0-7680-0030-0, P-314) Soc Auto Engineers.

1997 3rd International Conference on Algorithms & Architectures for Parallel Processing. IEEE (Victorian Section) Staff. LC 97-80070. 750p. 1997. pap. 164.00 (0-7803-4229-1, 97TH8324) Inst Electrical.

1997 13th International Conference on Digital Signal Processing Proceedings. IEEE, Signal Processing Society Staff. Ed. by Institute of Electrical & Electronics Engineers, I. LC 97-72854. 900p. 1997. pap. 178.00 (0-7803-4137-6, 97TH8306) Inst Electrical.

1997 31st Annual International Carnahan Conference on Security Technology. IEEE, Aerospace & Electronic Systems Society Staff. Ed. by Institute of Electrical & Electronics Engineers, I. LC 79-644630. 250p. 1997. pap. text. write for info. (0-7803-3913-4, 97CH36062); lib. bdg. write for info. (0-7803-3914-2, 97CH36062) IEEE Standards.

1997-1998 Grant Guides. 1996. 75.00 (0-614-24173-1) Foundation Ctr.

1997-1998 National Directory of Law Schools. Orig. Title: Employer's Guide to Law Schools (Before 1992). 720p. (Orig.). 1997. pap. write for info. (1-55733-011-5) NALP.

1997-1998 National Directory of Legal Employers. 1997. pap. 39.95 (0-15-900248-6) Harcourt Legal.

1997-1999 National Juvenile Detention Directory. Ed. by American Correctional Association Staff. 258p. 1997. pap. 50.00 (1-56991-072-3, 628) Am Correctional.

1997-1998 Naree Source Book. 3rd ed. 200p. 1997. ring bd. 100.00 (0-614-14041-2) Natl Assn REE.

1997-1998 Irvine Spectrum Business Directory. 4th ed. Bruce Clumpner. 1997. pap. 39.95 (0-9639578-3-X, 97-001) Coris Quill.

1997-1998 Arizona Yearbook: A Guide to Government in the Grand Canyon State. Ed. by Richard Yates & Charity Yates. (Illus.). 184p. 1998. pap. 19.95 (0-911927-27-1) Public Sector.

1997-1998 Directory of Indiana Foundations Vol. 2: Grant & Scholarship Information. expanded ed. Ed. by Susan O. Wilson. (Directory of Indiana Foundations Ser.). 520p. (Orig.). 1997. pap. 45.00 (1-886445-08-7) Indiana Donors.

1997-98 Directory of Professional Personnel. 1997. 18.00 (0-614-13554-0) SHEEO.

1997-98 Graduate Programs of Physis, Astronomy & Related Fields. American Institute of Physics Staff. 1997. pap. 48.00 (1-56396-771-5) Am Inst Physics.

1997-98 Guide to Public Policy Experts. Thomas C. Atwood. 695p. 1995. pap. 16.95 (0-89195-068-0) Heritage Found.

1997/98 Houston Texas Oil Directory. 27th rev. ed. Ed. by James W. Self. 850p. 1997. pap. 65.00 (1-889879-06-1) Atlantic Commun.

1997-98 Indiana Media Directory: The Most Up-to-Date, Detailed Listing of All Indiana Media. (Illus.). 224p. 1997. pap. 47.00 (0-944369-18-9); pap. 47.00 (0-614-28397-3) Brackemyre Pub.

1997-98 Physician Practice Acquisition Resource Book. William O. Cleverley & Patrick J. Knott. 280p. 1997. pap. 295.00 (1-882733-09-6) Ctr Hlthcare IPS.

1997-98 Registry of Certified & Internationally Accredited Corporate Wildlife Programs. (Illus.). 144p. 1997. pap. 12.00 (1-889685-02-X) Wildlife Habitat.

1997 Topical Symposium on Millimeter Waves. IEEE (Microwave Theory & Techniques Society, Elect. Ed. by IEEE (Institute of Electrical & Electronics Engine. LC 97-70756. 200p. 1997. pap. write for info. (0-7803-3887-1, 97TH8274); fiche. write for info. (0-7803-3888-X, 97TH8274) Inst Electrical.

1997 Transactions of AACE International. Ed. by Sara Pritchard. (Illus.). 500p. (Orig.). 1997. pap. 47.95 (1-885517-06-8) AACE Intl.

1997 Transmission & Driveline Systems Symposium: Transmission Systems, Components, Gears & Friction & Fluid Materials. 1997. 86.00 (1-56091-953-1, SP-1241) Soc Auto Engineers.

1997 Travel & Tourism Market Research Handbook. Richard K. Miller. 400p. 1997. 275.00 (1-881503-79-8) R K Miller Assocs.

1997 TV Employee Compensation & Fringe Benefits Report. Theresa J. Ottina. 65p. 1997. pap. 225.00 (0-89324-302-7, 3857) Natl Assn Broadcasters.

1997 TV Financial Report. Theresa J. Ottina. 179p. 1997. pap. 375.00 (0-89324-301-9, 3851) Natl Assn Broadcasters.

1997 TV Regional Report. Theresa J. Ottina. (Illus.). 81p. 1997. pap. 225.00 (0-89324-309-4, 3856) Natl Assn Broadcasters.

1997 20th IEEE - CPMT International Electronic Manufacturing Technology Symposium Held Jointly with 1997 1st International Microelectronics Conference. IEEE, Components, Packaging & Manufacturing Techno. Ed. by Institute of Electrical & Electronics Engineers, I. 420p. 1997. lib. bdg. write for info. (0-7803-3901-0, 97CH36059); fiche. write for info. (0-7803-3902-9, 97CH36059) Inst Electrical.

1997 21st International Conference on Microelectronics Proceedings. IEEE (Electron Devices Society) Staff. Ed. by IEEE (Institute of Electrical & Electronics Engine. LC 96-78106. 800p. 1997. pap. write for info. (0-7803-3664-X, 97TH8232); mic. film. write for info. (0-7803-3665-8, 97TM8232) Inst Electrical.

1997 U. S. Market Forecasts: Economic & Demographic Profiles of 14,639 U. S. Markets. Ed. by Tom Dahlin. 500p. (Orig.). 1996. pap. write for info. (0-9646364-4-1) ASM Communs.

1997 U. S. Master Depreciation Guide. Ed. by CCH Editorial Staff. 560p. 1997. pap. text 32.95 (0-8080-0150-7) CCH INC.

1997 United Nations List of Protected Areas. World Conservation Monitoring Centre Staff & IUCN World Comission on Protected Areas. LC 98-173120. (SPA.). lix, 412p. 1998. write for info. (2-8317-0426-X, Pub. by IUCN) Island Pr.

1997 United States Biotechnology Regulations Handbook. Edward L. Korwek. LC 97-228902. 1997. 199.00 (1-885259-46-8) Food & Drug Law.

1997 Variable Valve Actuation & Power Boost. 1997. 56.00 (1-56091-970-1, SP-1258) Soc Auto Engineers.

1997 Video & Television Blue Book. rev. ed. 1996. lib. bdg. 200.00 (0-932089-74-7) Orion Res.

1997 Vital Statistics: Clinton, Franklin & Essex County, New York. LC 98-65601. 650p. 1998. 30.00 (0-9662895-1-X) C M Rabideau.

1997 Waste Treatment Technology Industry Review. Karen Lindsey. 286p. 1998. 1500.00 (1-56965-515-4) BCC.

1997 WebPointers Internet Guide: Invaluable Excursions Onto the World Wide Web. Kitty Williams & Robin Lind. (Illus.). viii, 268p. (Orig.). 1997. pap. 29.95 (0-9639531-2-5) Hope Springs.

1997 WESCON Conference. IEEE (Region 6) Staff. Ed. by IEEE (Institute of Electrical & Electronics Engine. 200p. 1997. pap. text. write for info. (0-7803-4303-4, 97CH36148); lib. bdg. write for info. (0-7803-4305-0, 97CH36148) Inst Electrical.

1997 Westmoreland County (PA) Court Rules. Ed. by Thomas Davies. 176p. 1997. per. 52.50 (1-57786-001-2) Legal Communs.

1997 Winter Simulation Conference Proceedings. IEEE Staff. 1500p. 1997. lib. bdg. write for info. (0-7803-4278-X) Inst Electrical.

1997 Wireless Communications Conference Proceedings. IEEE (Microwave Theory & Techniques Society, Elect. LC 97-80023. 268p. 1997. pap. 110.00 (0-7803-4194-5, 97TH8315) Inst Electrical.

1997 Workshop on High Performance Electron Devices for Microwave & Optoelectronic Applications - EDMO. IEEE, Electron Devices Society Staff. Ed. by Institute of Electrical & Electronics Engineers, I. LC 97-72855. 200p. 1997. pap. 112.00 (0-7803-4135-X, 97TH8305) Inst Electrical.

1997 Worldwide Guide to Gay Resorts Beaches & Recreation, No. III. Alex Summers. (Illus.). 92p. pap. text 14.95 (1-887895-11-6) Serengeti Pubng.

1997 Year Book of Sports Medicine. annuals Roy J. Shephard. (Illus.). 560p. (C). (gr. 13). 1998. text 74.95 (0-8151-9739-X, 25026) Mosby Inc.

1997 Year Book of Allergy & Clinical Immunology. 4th ed. Lanny J. Rosenwasser. (Illus.). 520p. (C). (gr. 13). 1997. text 74.95 (0-8151-7278-8, 23107) Mosby Inc.

1997 Year Book of Anesthesia & Pain Management. John H. Tinker. (Illus.). 568p. (C). (gr. 13). 1997. text 79.00 (0-8151-8780-7, 24435) Mosby Inc.

1997 Year Book of Dentistry. Lawrence Meskin. (Illus.). 552p. (C). (gr. 13). 1997. text 73.00 (0-8151-7083-1, 27508) Mosby Inc.

1997 Year Book of Dermatology. Arthur J. Sober. (Illus.). 696p. (C). (gr. 13). 1997. text 81.00 (0-8151-9611-3, 24949) Mosby Inc.

1997 Year Book of Digestive Diseases. Norton J. Greenberger. (Illus.). 544p. (C). (gr. 13). 1997. text 81.00 (0-8151-9618-0, 24955) Mosby Inc.

1997 Year Book of Drug Therapy. Louis Lasagna. (Illus.). 488p. (C). (gr. 13). 1997. text 79.95 (0-8151-5295-7, 24746) Mosby Inc.

1997 Year Book of Endocrinology. John D. Bagdade. (Illus.). 512p. (C). (gr. 13). 1997. text 79.00 (0-8151-9625-3, 24962) Mosby Inc.

1997 Year Book of Family Practice. Alfred O. Berg. (Illus.). 592p. (C). (gr. 13). 1997. text 66.95 (0-8151-9628-8, 24965) Mosby Inc.

1997 Year Book of Medicine. Ed. by Martin J. Cline et al. (Illus.). 1024p. (C). (gr. 13). 1997. text 75.00 (0-8151-3155-0, 26974) Mosby Inc.

1997 Year Book of Neurology & Neurosurgery. Walter G. Bradley. (Illus.). 608p. (C). (gr. 13). 1997. text 78.00 (0-8151-1209-2, 23003) Mosby Inc.

1997 Year Book of Obstetrics & Gynecology & Women's Health. Morrow et al. (Illus.). 728p. (C). (gr. 13). 1997. text 79.00 (0-8151-6019-4, 22714) Mosby Inc.

1997 Year Book of Occupational & Environmental Health. Edward A. Emmett. (Illus.). 392p. (C). (gr. 13). 1997. text 74.95 (0-8151-9706-3, 24993) Mosby Inc.

1997 Year Book of Ophthalmology. Wilson. (Illus.). 608p. (C). (gr. 13). 1997. text 82.00 (0-8151-9712-8, 24999) Mosby Inc.

1997 Year Book of Pathology & Laboratory Medicine. Ed. by Mark Stoler. (Illus.). 472p. (C). (gr. 13). 1997. text 83.00 (0-8151-9721-7, 25008) Mosby Inc.

1997 Year Book of Pediatrics. James A. Stockman. (Illus.). 744p. (C). (gr. 13). 1997. text 67.95 (0-8151-9724-1, 25011) Mosby Inc.

1997 Year Book of Plastic & Reconstructive Surgery. Ronald D. Miller. (Illus.). 480p. (C). (gr. 13). 1997. text 82.00 (0-8151-9727-6, 25014) Mosby Inc.

1997 Year Book of Podiatry. Ed. by Stephen J. Kominsky. (Illus.). 392p. (C). (gr. 13). 1997. text 73.00 (0-8151-9730-6, 25017) Mosby Inc.

1997 Year Book of Psychiatric & Applied Mental Health. John A. Talbott. (Illus.). 616p. (C). (gr. 13). 1997. text 73.00 (0-8151-8945-1, 24105) Mosby Inc.

1997 Year Book of Pulmonary Diseases. Petty. (Illus.). 560p. (C). (gr. 13). 1997. text 79.00 (0-8151-9735-7, 25022) Mosby Inc.

1997 Year Book of Rheumatology. 4th ed. Ed. by John S. Sergent. (Illus.). 480p. (C). (gr. 13). 1997. text 86.00 (0-8151-7863-8, 23010) Mosby Inc.

1997 Year Book of Surgery. Edward M. Copeland. (Illus.). 672p. (C). (gr. 13). 1997. text 74.00 (0-8151-9742-X, 25029) Mosby Inc.

1997 Year-End Tax Strategies. Ed. by Mildred Carter & Neil A. Ringquist. 48p. 1997. pap. text 12.95 (0-8080-0157-4) CCH INC.

***1997 Year in Review - U. S. Seafood Trade Report.** 3rd ed. Ed. by James L. Anderson & Barbara S. Gardiner. (Illus.). iv, 420p. 1998. pap. 39.95 (0-9673524-2-8) J L Anderson Assoc.

1997 Year-Round Fun Places for Families: New Hampshire & Massachusetts. 112p. (Orig.). 1997. pap., spiral bd. 9.98 (0-9645068-5-8) Romagnoli.

1997 1st International Conference Control of Oscillations & Chaos. IEEE (Circuits & Systems Society) Staff. Ed. by IEEE (Institute of Electrical & Electronics Engine. LC 97-80111. 500p. 1997. pap. write for info. (0-7803-4247-X, 97TH8329); fiche. write for info. (0-7803-4248-8, 97TM8329) Inst Electrical.

1997 12th Annual Conference on Computer Assurance. IEEE (Aerospace & Electronic Systems Society) Staf. LC 97-71843. 190p. 1997. pap. text. write for info. (0-7803-3979-7, 97CH36080); lib. bdg. write for info. (0-7803-3980-0, 97CH36080) IEEE Standards.

1997 14th Annual IEEE/AES Dayton Chapter Symposium "Synthetic Visualization: Systems & Applications" IEEE (Dayton Section) Staff. LC 97-71844. 68p. 1997. pap. 104.00 (0-7803-3965-7, 97TH8285) IEEE Standards.

1997 16th Southern Biomedical Engineering Conference. IEEE Engineering in Medicine & Biology Society Sta. Ed. by IEEE Staff. 600p. 1997. pap. write for info. (0-7803-3869-3, 97TH8270) Inst Electrical.

1997 17th International Congress on Instrumentation in Aerospace Simulation Facilities. IEEE Aerospace & Electronic Systems Society Staff. Ed. by IEEE Staff. LC 81-644323. 600p. 1997. pap. text 150.00 (0-7803-4167-8, 97CH36121); lib. bdg. write for info. (0-7803-4168-6, 97CH36121); fiche. write for info. (0-7803-4169-4, 97CH36121) Inst Electrical.

1997 20th Anniversary of Elvis. 1997. pap. 5.99 (0-934551-20-0) Starlog Grp Inc.

1997 9th International Conference on Indium Phosphide & Related Materials. IEEE, Lasers & Electro-Optics Society & Electron D. 800p. 1997. pap. text. write for info. (0-7803-3898-7, 97CH36058); lib. bdg. write for info. (0-7803-3899-5, 97CH36058) Inst Electrical.

1997/98 Consultants Directory: Aerospace, Automotive, ISO 9000Quality Systems/Mgt. 400p. 1997. 43.00 (0-7680-0061-0) Soc Auto Engineers.

1997 IEEE - RSJ International Conference on Intelligent Robots & Systems. IEEE, Industrial Electronics Society & Robotics &. Ed. by Institute of Electrical & Electronics Engineers, I. LC 97-72857. 2000p. 1997. pap. text 280.00 (0-7803-4119-8, 97CH36108); lib. bdg. write for info. (0-7803-4120-1, 97CH36108) Inst Electrical.

1997 International Symposium on Advanced Packaging Materials. IEEE, Components, Packaging & Manufacturing Techno. Ed. by Institute of Electrical & Electronics Engineers, I. LC 97-70176. 200p. 1997. pap. write for info. (0-7803-3818-9, 97TH8263) Inst Electrical.

1996 Mercer Guide to Social Security & Medicare. 24th ed. Dale Detlefs & Robert J. Myers. 200p. 1995. pap. 9.95 (1-880754-96-7) W M Mercer.

1996-1997 Financial & Operating Ratios Study. Barbara Darraugh. (Illus.). v, 60p. 1996. pap. 50.00 (1-892725-07-X, RP125) Building Serv.

Chicago Bulls: Authorized Pictorial. Roland Lazenby. LC 97-21212. (Illus.). 120p. 1997. 39.99 (1-56530-270-2); pap. 24.99 (1-56530-271-0) Summit TX.

1996-1997 ASTM Directory of Scientific & Technical Consultants & Expert Witnesses. 165p. 1996. pap. 40.00 (0-8031-1826-0) ASTM.

1996 AACE International Transactions. Ed. by Sara Pritchard. (Illus.). 500p. (Orig.). 1996. pap. text 47.95 (1-885517-04-1) AACE Intl.

An Asterisk (*) at the beginning of an entry indicates that the title is appearing for the first time.

1996 Addendum to the Teacher's Manual, Legal Ethics in the Practice of Law. Richard A. Zitrin & Carol M. Langford. (Michie Contemporary Legal Education Ser.). 30p. 1998. pap. text. write for info. (*0-327-00578-5*, 1347510) LEXIS Pub.

1996 AIAA/IEEE 15th Digital Avionics Systems Conference - 15th DASC. IEEE, Aerospace & Electronics Systems Society Staf. Ed. by IEEE, Institute of Electrical & Electronics Engine. LC 96-76777. 550p. 1996. pap. text. write for info. (*0-7803-3385-3*, 96CH35959); lib. bdg. write for info. (*0-7803-3386-1*, 96CH35959); fiche. write for info. (*0-7803-3387-X*, 96CH35959) Inst Electrical.

1996 Allied Health Graduate Program Directory in Exercise Science, Physical Therapy, Physician Assistant & Occupational Therapy. Victor L. Katch et al. 190p. (C). 1996. pap. text 17.95 (*0-9640591-1-8*) Fitness Tech.

1996 AMA Superbike Series Media Guide. American Motorcyclist Association Staff. Ed. by Larry Lawrence. (Illus.). 306p. (Orig.). 1996. pap. 18.95 (*0-9649722-1-2*) D Bull.

1996 American Payroll Association: Basic Guide to Payroll. Delores Risteau. 1995. 125.00 (*0-87622-678-0*) Aspen Pub.

1996 Annual Conference of the Society of Instrument & Control (SICE) IEEE Instrumentation & Measurement Society Staff. 458p. 1996. pap. 116.00 (*0-7803-3751-4*) Inst Electrical.

1996 Annual Reliability & Maintainability Symposium. IEEE (Reliability Society) Staff. Ed. by IEEE (Institute of Electrical & Electronics Engine. LC 78-132873. 500p. 1996. pap. text 118.00 (*0-7803-3112-5*, 96CH35885); lib. bdg. 118.00 (*0-7803-3113-3*, 96CB35885); fiche 118.00 (*0-7803-3114-1*, 96CM35885) Inst Electrical.

1996 Annual Statement Instructions - Title. Ed. by Todd Sells. 510p. (Orig.). (C). 1996. ring bd. 75.00 (*0-89382-404-6*, ASI-TM) Nat Assn Insurance.

1996 Annual Statement Instructions - Limited Health Service Organizations. 5th rev. ed. 62p. (Orig.). (C). 1996. ring bd. 75.00 (*0-89382-412-7*, ASI-SM) Nat Assn Insurance.

1996 Annual Statement Instructions - Hospital, Medical, Dental Service or Indemnity Corporations. 5th rev. ed. Ed. by Todd Sells. 206p. (Orig.). (C). 1996. ring bd. 75.00 (*0-89382-411-9*, ASI-MM) Nat Assn Insurance.

1996 Annual Statement Instructions - Health Maintenance Organizations. 7th rev. ed. Ed. by Todd Sells. 82p. (C). 1996. ring bd. 175.00 (*0-89382-408-9*, ASI-HM) Nat Assn Insurance.

1996 Annual Survey of Letter of Credit Law & Practice. James E. Byrne. 768p. 1996. 149.00 (*1-888870-11-7*) Inst Intl Bnking.

1996 Applied Electromagnetism. IEEE (Electron Devices) Staff. Ed. by IEEE (Institute of Electrical & Electronics Engine. 200p. 1996. fiche 102.00 (*0-7803-3333-0*, 96TH8191) Inst Electrical.

1996 APPMA National Pet Owners Survey. (Illus.). xii, 272p. (Orig.). 1996. pap. 150.00 (*0-9632552-0-7*) Am Pet Prods.

1996 ASEE Membership Handbook. ASEE Staff. 421p. 1996. spiral bd. 30.00 (*0-87823-153-6*, HANDBK 96) Am Soc Eng Ed.

1996 Asian Fuzzy Systems Symposium. IEEE (Neural Networks Council) Staff. LC 96-78417. 600p. 1996. pap. write for info. (*0-7803-3687-9*, 96TH8239); fiche. write for info. (*0-7803-3688-7*, 96TH8239) Inst Electrical.

1996 ASME Pressure Vessels & Piping Conference, Montreal, Quebec, Canada, July 21-26, 1996 Vol. 1: Pressure Vessel & Piping Codes & Standards. (PVP Ser.: Vol. 338). 296p. 1996. 110.00 (*0-7918-1785-7*, H01066) ASME Pr.

1996 ASME Pressure Vessels & Piping Conference, Montreal, Quebec, Canada, July 21-26, 1996 Vol. 2: Pressure Vessel & Piping Codes & Standards. (PVP Ser.: Vol. 339). 228p. 1996. 100.00 (*0-7918-1786-5*, H01067) ASME Pr.

1996 ASNT Fall Conference & Quality Testing Show Paper Summaries. ASNT Staff. (Illus.). 246p. (C). 1996. per. 31.00 (*1-57117-053-7*, 1355) Am Soc Nondestructive.

1996 Offshore Atlas of World Oil & Gas Theatres. (Illus.). 200p. 1995. 285.00 (*0-87814-457-9*) PennWell Bks.

1996 Australian-New Zealand Conference on Intelligent Information Systems Proceedings. IEEE (South Australia Section) Staff. Ed. by IEEE (Institute of Electrical & Electronics Engine. LC 96-78176. 350p. 1996. pap. write for info. (*0-7803-3667-4*, 96TH8234); fiche. write for info. (*0-7803-3668-2*, 96TH8234) Inst Electrical.

1996 Bankruptcy Yearbook & Almanac. 6th ed. Ed. by Christopher M. McHugh. 624p. 1996. pap. 195.00 (*0-9628991-5-1*) New Gen Research.

1996 BCC Plastics Fact Book. Howard Kibbel. 115p. 1995. 295.00 (*1-56965-348-8*, DPF96) BCC.

1996 Bibliography of Published Studies Using the Child Behavior Checklist & Related Materials. Denise Yignoe & Thomas M. Achenbach. 150p. (Orig.). 1996. pap. text 45.00 (*0-938565-41-9*) U of VT Psych.

1996 Biennial Conference of the North American Fuzzy Information Processing Society - NAFIPS. IEEE, Neural Networks Council & Systems, Man & Cyb. Ed. by IEEE, Institute of Electrical & Electronics Engine. LC 96-75373. 622p. 1996. pap. 142.00 (*0-7803-3225-3*, 96TH8171); fiche 142.00 (*0-7803-3226-1*, 96TH8171) Inst Electrical.

1996 Black Mail Order Directory: Specializing in Black Ethnic Products by Mail. 5th ed. (Orig.). 1995. 9.95 (*1-885716-02-8*) JAK Prods.

1996 Blue Book of Optometrists. 447p. 1995. pap. 95.00 incl. disk (*0-7506-9682-6*) Buttrwrth-Heinemann.

1996 Book of Lists. Suzette Brewer. 1996. 30.00 (*0-932439-10-1*) Denver Busn Media.

1996 Bosnia Herzegovina Elections: An Analysis of the Observations. LC 97-10300. 1997. lib. bdg. 107.00 (*0-7923-4505-3*) Kluwer Academic.

1996 Broadband Communications. IEEE (Communications Society) Staff. Ed. by IEEE (Institute of Electrical & Electronics Engine. LC 96-75515. 600p. 1996. pap. 126.00 (*0-7803-3234-2*, 96TH8176); fiche 126.00 (*0-7803-3235-0*, 96TM8176) Inst Electrical.

1996 Business Owner's Policy. Ed. by Laura Biddle-Bruckman. 72p. 1996. 19.95 (*1-56461-174-4*) Rough Notes.

1996 Cable Industry Directory. 3rd ed. Ed. by Jennifer O. Newman. 1996. pap., per. 229.00 (*1-881537-40-4*) Phillips Business.

1996 Canadian Conference on Electrical & Computer Engineering. IEEE (Region 7) Staff. 700p. 1996. pap. 134.00 (*0-7803-3143-5*, 96TH8157); fiche 134.00 (*0-7803-3144-3*, 96TH8157) Inst Electrical.

1996 Canadian Electronic Commerce Directory. Jennifer O. Newman. 1996. pap. 169.00 (*1-881537-49-8*) Phillips Business.

1996 Caribbean Basin Commercial Profile, 2 vols. annuals 59.75 (*976-8088-09-5*) Carib Imprint.

1996 CIE International Conference of Radar Proceedings. IEEE (Aerospace & Electronic Systems Society) Staf. Ed. by IEEE (Institute of Electrical & Electronics Engine. LC 95-78308. 860p. 1996. pap. write for info. (*0-7803-2914-7*, 96TH8117); fiche. write for info. (*0-7803-2915-5*, 96TM8117) Inst Electrical.

1996 Civil Procedure Supplement for Use with All Pleading & Procedure Casebooks. John J. Cound et al. (American Casebook Ser.). 478p. 1996. pap. text, suppl. ed. write for info. (*0-314-20239-0*) West Pub.

1996 Collection: Prepared for Sudbury-Model Schools & Planning Groups. 296p. (Orig.). 1996. pap. 25.00 (*1-888947-18-7*) Sudbury Valley.

1996 Comprehensive Guide to Oregon's Craft Fairs, Festivals & Bazaars. LC 95-96235. (Illus.). 262p. 1995. pap. 23.00 (*1-888651-00-8*) Carters Guides.

1996 Computers in Cardiology. IEEE (Engineering in Medicine & Biology Society) S. LC 80-641097. 850p. 1996. pap. text. write for info. (*0-7803-3710-7*, 96CH36012); lib. bdg. write for info. (*0-7803-3711-5*, 96CH36012); fiche. write for info. (*0-7803-3712-3*, 96CH36012) Inst Electrical.

1996 Conference on Lasers & Electro-Optics Europe. IEEE, Lasers & Electro-Optics Society Staff. Ed. by Institute of Electrical & Electronics Engineers, I. LC 95-82415. 350p. 1996. pap. 106.00 (*0-7803-3171-0*, 96TH8162); fiche 106.00 (*0-7803-3172-9*, 96TM8162) Inst Electrical.

1996 Conference on Lasers & Electro-Optics. IEEE (Lasers & Electro-Optics Society) Staff. Ed. by IEEE (Institute of Electrical & Electronics Engine. LC 95-72764. 560p. 1926. lib. bdg. write for info. (*0-7803-3183-4*, 96CB35899) Inst Electrical.

1996 Conference on Lasers & Electro-Optics. IEEE (Lasers & Electro-Optics Society) Staff. Ed. by IEEE (Institute of Electrical & Electronics Engine. LC 95-72764. 1996. fiche 126.00 (*0-7803-3184-2*, 96CM35899) Inst Electrical.

1996 Conference on Precision Electromagnetic Measurements Digest. IEEE, Instrumentation & Measurement Society Staff. Ed. by IEEE, Institute of Electrical & Electronics Engine. LC 96-76668. 700p. 1996. pap. text. write for info. (*0-7803-3376-4*, 96CH35956); lib. bdg. write for info. (*0-7803-3377-2*, 96CH35956) Inst Electrical.

1996 World Congress on Coastal & Marine Tourism-Abstracts: Experiences in Management & Development. 48p. 1996. pap. 12.00 (*1-881826-09-0*) OR Sea Grant.

1996 Congressional Report Card & Presidential Activity Report. Arpi Vartanian. (Illus.). 1996. pap. write for info. (*0-925428-09-4*) Armenian Assembly.

1996 Connecticut State Register & Manual. Secretary of the State's Office Editorial Staff. (Illus.). xiii, 900p. 1996. 19.00 (*1-888951-00-1*); pap. 10.00 (*1-888951-01-X*) Conn Secy.

1996 Consular Posts Handbook. Ed. by Seymour Rosenberg. 150p. 1996. 35.00 (*1-878677-96-9*, 52.60) Amer Immi Law Assn.

1996 Consumer RX Drug Price Guide Vol. 1: Spring Issues. (Consumer RX Drug Price Guide Ser.). 128p. (Orig.). 1996. pap. 19.95 (*0-9652203-0-3*) Greystone Pubng.

1996 Corporation & Partnership Tax Return Guide. rev. ed. 141p. 1997. pap. text 12.00 (*0-7811-0153-0*) Res Inst Am.

1996 CUES Compensation Manual. 15th rev. ed. Aon Consulting, Inc. Staff. 161p. 1996. pap. 119.00 (*1-889394-13-0*) Credit Union Execs.

1996 Cumulative Supplement Connecticut Evidence. Benedict M. Holden & John J. Daly. 854p. 1996. pap. 25.00 (*1-878698-36-2*) Atlantic Law.

1996 Cumulative Supplement to Connecticut Land Use Regulation. 2nd ed. Terry J. Tondro. 341p. 1996. pap. 60.00 (*1-878698-34-6*) Atlantic Law.

1996 Defense Budget: Potential Reductions, Rescissions, & Restrictions in RDT&E & Procurement. (Illus.). 105p. (Orig.). (C). 1996. pap. text 30.00 (*0-7881-2752-7*) DIANE Pub.

1996 Deposit Accounts Regulation Manual. rev. ed. Kenneth F. Hall. (Tax Law Ser.). 779p. 1996. pap. write for info. (*0-8366-0034-7*) West Group.

1996 Development Report Card for the States: Economic Benchmarks for State & Corporate Decision-Makers. 10th ed. Corporation for Enterprise Development Staff. 202p. (C). 1996. ring bd. 45.00 (*1-883187-09-5*) Corp Ent Dev.

1996 Digest of the LEOS Summer Topical Meetings. IEEE, Lasers & Electro-Optics Society Staff. Ed. by Institute of Electrical & Electronics Engineers, I. LC 95-82412. 360p. 1996. pap. 108.00 (*0-7803-3175-3*, 96TH8164); fiche 108.00 (*0-7803-3176-1*, 96TM8164) Inst Electrical.

1996 Digests of Intermag '96. IEEE, Magnetics Society Staff. Ed. by Institute of Electrical & Electronics Engineers, I. LC 72-649866. 710p. 1996. pap. text 136.00 (*0-7803-3240-7*, 96CH35912); lib. bdg. 136.00 (*0-7803-3241-5*, 96CB35912); fiche 136.00 (*0-7803-3242-3*, 96CM35912) Inst Electrical.

1996 Directory GIS Education. Morgan Group, Inc. Staff. LC 96-76028. 408p. 1996. pap. text 59.95 (*0-7872-2149-X*) Kendall-Hunt.

1996 Directory of Coaches & Accompanists. Ed. by Maryalice Foster. 104p. (Orig.). 1996. write for info. (*0-614-13038-7*) NY Opera Newsletter.

1996 Directory of Colorado Manufacturers. 30th rev. ed. Ed. by Ginny S. Hayden et al. 538p. (Orig.). 1996. pap. 80.00 (*0-89478-071-9*) U CO Busn Res Div.

1996 Directory of Convenience Stores: The Book of C-store Market Facts. Ed. by Vivian Jonokuchi et al. (Illus.). 639p. 1996. pap. 225.00 (*0-911790-35-7*) Trade Dimensns.

1996 Directory of Mass Merchandisers. Ed. by Adrienne Toth et al. (Illus.). 1995. pap. 220.00 (*0-911790-32-2*, Progress Grocer) Trade Dimensns.

1996 (E) (ISO/IEC) (ANSI/IEEE Std. 802.3, 1996 Edition), LAN/MAN CSMA/CD Access Method Standards Package: 8802-3: 1996. 905p. 1996. 200.00 (*1-55937-729-1*, SH94415-QOE) IEEE Standards.

1996 EDI Yellow Pages. 11th ed. Ed. by Jennifer O. Newman. 1996. pap., per. 199.00 (*1-881537-36-6*) Phillips Business.

1996 8th International Conference on Indium Phosphide & Related Materials. IEEE Staff. LC 96-75713. 400p. 1996. pap. 146.00 (*0-7803-3283-0*, 96CH35930); lib. bdg. 146.00 (*0-7803-3284-9*, 96CB35930); fiche 146.00 (*0-7803-3285-7*, 96CM35930) Inst Electrical.

1996 Election Results Directory. Legislative Management Staff. 1995. 35.00 (*1-55516-772-1*, 9371) Natl Conf State Legis.

1996 Eleventh Annual Battery Conference on Applications & Advances Proceedings. IEEE (Aerospace & Electronics Systems Society) Sta. Ed. by IEEE (Institute of Electrical & Electronics Engine. LC 95-79384. 1996. fiche 108.00 (*0-7803-2995-3*, 96TM8133) Inst Electrical.

1996 Eleventh Annual Battery Conference on Applications & Advances Proceedings. IEEE (Aerospace & Electronics Systems Society) Sta. Ed. by IEEE (Institute of Electrical & Electronics Engine. LC 95-79384. 358p. 1997. pap. 108.00 (*0-7803-2994-5*, 96TH8133) Inst Electrical.

1996 11th International Conference on Ion Implantation Technology. IEEE Staff. LC 96-75709. 1000p. 1996. pap. 158.00 (*0-7803-3289-X*); fiche 158.00 (*0-7803-3290-3*, 96TM8182) Inst Electrical.

1996 Emerging Technologies: Designing Low Power Digital Systems. IEEE, Circuits & Systems Society Staff. LC 96-76158. 526p. 1996. pap. 136.00 (*0-7803-3328-4*, 96TH8189); fiche 136.00 (*0-7803-3329-2*, 96TM8189) Inst Electrical.

AEE Energy & Environmental Industry Survey '96. Ruth Bennett & Fairmont Press Staff. 134p. (C). 1996. pap. text 95.00 (*0-13-264508-4*) P-H.

***1996 Eruptions in the Karynsky Volcanic Centre & Related Events.** L. Rykunov. 120p. 1998. pap. text 112.00 (*90-5699-197-3*, Harwood Acad Pubs) Gordon & Breach.

1996 ESD Tutorial. Contrib. by Electrostatic Discharge Association Staff. (Illus.). 539p. (Orig.). 1996. pap. 75.00 (*1-878303-66-X*, 96 TUT) EOS ESD.

1996 ESL/EFL Decision Guide. Heinle & Heinle Staff. (College ESL Ser.). (J). 1995. pap. write for info. (*0-8384-6742-3*) Heinle & Heinle.

***1996 European Community Law, Vol. VII, Bk. 1.** Ed. by Academy of European Law Staff. (Collected Courses of the Academy of European Law Ser.: Vol. 13).Tr. of Recueil des Cours de l'Academie de Droit Europeen. 416p. 1999. 129.00 (*90-411-1200-6*) Kluwer Law Intl.

1996 European Quantum Electronics Conference. IEEE, Lasers & Electro-Optics Society Staff. Ed. by Institute of Electrical & Electronics Engineers, I. LC 95-82410. 270p. 1996. pap. 100.00 (*0-7803-3169-9*, 96TH8161); fiche 100.00 (*0-7803-3170-2*, 96TM8161) Inst Electrical.

1996 Europese Ondernemingsgraad. E. Peeters. 1998. 56.95 (*90-6831-857-8*, Pub. by Peeters Pub) Bks Intl VA.

1996 Federal Tax Course. annuals Lewis D. Solomon & Susan F. Posner. 1544p. 1995. 136.00 (*1-56706-255-5*) Panel Pubs.

1996 Fiduciary Tax Return Guide. rev. ed. 142p. 1997. pap. text 12.00 (*0-7811-0154-9*) Res Inst Am.

1996 15th Southern Biomedical Engineering Conference. IEEE (Engineering in Medicine & Biology Society) S. Ed. by IEEE (Institute of Electrical & Electronics Engine. LC 96-212640. 350p. 1996. pap. 128.00 (*0-7803-3131-1*, 96TH8154); fiche 128.00 (*0-7803-3132-X*, 96TM8154) Inst Electrical.

1996 5th IEEE International Conference on Universal Personal Communications Record. IEEE Staff. LC 96-75876. 600p. 1996. pap. text 136.00 (*0-7803-3300-4*, 96TH8185); mic. film 136.00 (*0-7803-3301-2*, 96TM8185) Inst Electrical.

1996 First Australian Data Fusion Symposium Proceedings. IEEE South Australian Section Staff. Ed. by IEEE Staff. LC 96-77508. 248p. 1996. pap. 102.00 (*0-7803-3601-1*, 96TH8216); fiche. write for info. (*0-7803-3602-X*, 96TH8216) Inst Electrical.

1996 1st International Workshop on Wireless Image/Video Communications Proceedings. IEEE (Communications Society) Staff. 250p. 1996. pap. write for info. (*0-7803-3610-0*, 96TH8220); fiche. write for info. (*0-7803-3611-9*, 96TM8220) Inst Electrical.

1996 1st International Symposium on Plasma Process - Induced Damage. IEEE (Electron Devices Society) Staff. Ed. by IEEE (Institute of Electrical & Electronics Engine. 120p. 1996. fiche 88.00 (*0-7803-3061-7*, 95TM8142) Inst Electrical.

1996 First International Conference on Digital Power System Simulators. IEEE, Power Electronics Society Staff. Ed. by IEEE, Institute of Electrical & Electronics Engine. LC 96-176666. 402p. 1996. pap. write for info. (*0-7803-3227-X*, 96TH8172); fiche. write for info. (*0-7803-3228-8*, 96TH8172) Inst Electrical.

1996 Florida Almanac. 12th ed. Del Marth & Martha J. Marth. (Illus.). 520p. 1995. pap. 14.50 (*1-885034-03-2*) Suwannee River.

1996 Florida Lawyers Diary & Manual Including Bar Directory of Florida. rev. ed. Skinder-Strauss Staff. 1345p. 1995. 49.00 (*1-57741-010-6*) Skinder-Strauss.

1996 Florida Lawyers Diary & Manual Including Bar Directory of Florida. rev. ed. Skinder-Strauss Staff. 1996. cd-rom 49.00 (*1-57741-014-9*) Skinder-Strauss.

1996 Florida Statistical Abstract. 30th ed. Ed. by Susan S. Floyd & Gayle Thompson. (Illus.). 700p. 1996. 39.95 (*0-930885-10-4*); disk 75.00 (*0-930885-11-2*) Bur Econ & Bus Res.

1996 Food & Wine: An Entire Year's Recipes from America's Favorite Food Magazine. LC 96-37982. 1997. write for info. (*0-916103-34-X*) Am Express Food.

1996 42nd Annual Technical Meeting for the Institute of Environmental Sciences: Expanding Our Technical Excellence Through Education, 2 vols., Set. 914p. 1996. pap. 185.00 (*1-877862-50-9*) IEST.

1996 42nd Annual Technical Meeting for the Institute of Environmental Sciences & Technology: Expanding Our Technical Excellence Through Education - Contamination Control. 515p. 1996. pap. 145.00 (*1-877862-51-7*) IEST.

1996 42nd Annual Technical Meeting for the Institute of Environmental Sciences & Technology: Expanding Our Technical Excellence Through Education - Product Reliability - Design Test, & Evaluation. LC 96-205322. 399p. 1996. pap. 100.00 (*1-877862-52-5*) IEST.

1996 Fourth IEEE International Workshop on Cellular Neural Networks & Their Applications Proceedings. IEEE (Circuits & Systems Society) Staff. Ed. by IEEE (Institute of Electrical & Electronics Engine. LC 96-75666. 500p. 1996. pap. 118.00 (*0-7803-3261-X*, 96TH8180); fiche 118.00 (*0-7803-3262-8*, 96TM8180) Inst Electrical.

1996 4th International Conference on Millimeter Wave & Far Infrared Science & Technology Proceedings. IEEE (Beijing Section) Staff. Ed. by IEEE Staff. LC 97-124266. 350p. 1996. pap. write for info. (*0-7803-3619-4*, 96TH8221); fiche. write for info. (*0-7803-3620-8*, 96TM8221) Inst Electrical.

1996 4th International Workshop on Advanced Motion Control Proceedings. IEEE, Industrial Electronics Society Staff. Ed. by IEEE, Institute of Electrical & Electronics Engine. LC 96-75374. 822p. 1996. pap. 150.00 (*0-7803-3219-9*, 96TH8168); fiche 150.00 (*0-7803-3220-2*, 96TM8168) Inst Electrical.

1996 Future Car Challenge. 1997. 31.00 (*1-56091-946-9*, SP-1234) Soc Auto Engineers.

1996 FWCC Friends Directory of Meetings & Churches in the Section of the Americas & Resource Guide. Friends World Committee for Consultation Staff. 240p. 1995. pap. text 7.50 (*0-9649661-0-7*) Friends Wrld Cttee.

1996 GAAP Guide CPE, Module 1. 96th ed. Harcourt Brace Staff. 1995. 59.00 (*0-15-602166-8*); 59.00 (*0-15-602167-6*) Harcourt Legal.

1996 GAAP Guide CPE, Module 3. 96th ed. Harcourt Brace Staff. 1995. 59.00 (*0-15-602168-4*) Harcourt Legal.

1996 GAAP Guide CPE, Module 4. 96th ed. Harcourt Brace Staff. 1995. 59.00 (*0-15-602169-2*) Harcourt Legal.

1996 GAAS Guide CPE. 96th ed. Harcourt Brace Staff. 1995. 59.00 (*0-15-602152-8*) Harcourt Legal.

1996 GAAS Guide CPE, Module 2. 96th ed. Harcourt Brace Staff. 1995. 59.00 (*0-15-602153-6*) Harcourt Legal.

1996 GAAS Guide CPE, Module 3. 96th ed. Harcourt Brace Staff. 1995. 59.00 (*0-15-602154-4*) Harcourt Legal.

1996 Genealogy Annual: A Bibliography of Published Sources. Ed. by Thomas J. Kemp. (Genealogy Annual Ser.). 364p. 1997. 95.00 (*0-8420-2740-8*, SR Bks) Scholarly Res Inc.

1996 Gold Book of Photography Prices. Thomas I. Perrett. 328p. 1996. pap. 39.95 (*0-915827-19-0*) Photo Res Inst Carson Endowment.

1996 Government GAAP CPE, Module 2. 96th ed. Harcourt Brace Staff. 1995. 59.00 (*0-15-602148-X*) Harcourt Legal.

1996 Government GAAP Guide, Module 1. 96th ed. Harcourt Brace Staff. 1995. 59.00 (*0-15-602146-3*) Harcourt Legal.

1996 Guide to the Evaluation of Educational Experiences in the Armed Forces, 3 vols. American Council on Education Staff. Incl. Vol. 2: Navy. 624p. 1996. pap. 35.00 (*1-57356-056-1*); 1996. Set pap. 85.00 (*1-57356-054-5*) Oryx Pr.

1996 Healthcare Guide to the Internet. Ed. by Jennifer Wayne-Doppke.Tr. of Nineteen Ninety-Six Healthcare Guide to the Inter. (Illus.). 123p. (Orig.). 1996. pap. text 68.00 (*0-9645360-1-3*) Cor Hlthcare.

N

An Asterisk (*) at the beginning of an entry indicates that the title is appearing for the first time.

Nineteen Ninety-Six Healthcare Guide to the Inter see **1996 Healthcare Guide to the Internet**

1996 High Performance Electron Devices for Microwave & Optoelectronic Applications Workshop - EDMO. IEEE Staff. Ed. by Institute of Electrical & Electronics Engineers, I. LC 95-82086. 120p. 1996. pap. write for info. (*0-7803-3130-3*, 96TH8155); fiche. write for info. (*0-7803-3133-8*) Inst Electrical.

1996 National Home Based Business Directory. Ed. by Darleen J. Hoffman. (Illus.). 196p. 1996. otabind 24.95 (*0-9650208-0-0*) ProMark Pubg.

1996 HomeTech Remodeling & Renovation Cost Estimator, Field Manual. rev. ed. Ed. by Henry Reynolds. 278p. 1995. pap. 34.50 (*1-882379-18-7*) HomeTech Info Systs.

1996 HomeTech Remodeling & Renovation Cost Estimator, Manager's Manual. rev. ed. Ed. by Henry Reynolds. 278p. 1995. pap. 69.50 (*1-882379-19-5*) HomeTech Info Systs.

1996 House Elections: Reaffirming the Conservative Trend. David W. Brady et al. LC 97-9037. (Essays in Public Policy Ser.: No. 75). 1997. pap. 5.00 (*0-8179-5802-9*) Hoover Inst Pr.

***1996 House Staff Employment: Salary, Tenure, Demographics & Benefits.** Thomas J. Klouda. (Illus.). 116p. 1999. reprint ed. pap. text 30.00 (*0-7881-8001-0*) DIANE Pub.

1996 Houston Area Exhibition. Don Bacigalupi & Nancy Hixon. (Illus.). 36p. 1996. pap. 10.00 (*0-941193-11-X*) U Houst Sarah.

1996 Human Resource Administration Handbook. 96th ed. Osborne. 1995. 79.00 (*0-15-601922-1*); 79.00 (*0-15-601923-X*) Harcourt Legal.

1996 Human Service Yellow Pages of Massachusetts & Rhode Island. 530p. 1995. pap. 19.95 (*1-56803-010-X*) G D Hall Co.

1996 Human Service Yellow Pages of Connecticut. 219p. 1995. pap. 19.95 (*1-56803-011-8*) G D Hall Co.

1996 HVAC Systems & Equipment. rev. ed. Ed. by Robert Parsons. (ASHRAE Handbook Ser.). (Illus.). 1500p. 1996. 134.00 (*1-883413-35-4*); 134.00 (*1-883413-34-6*) Am Heat Ref & Air Eng.

1996 I. E. E. E. Hong Kong Device Meeting. I. E. E. E. (Electron Devices Society) Staff. Ed. by I. E. E. E. Institute of Electrical & Electronics. LC 95-81041. 100p. 1996. pap. 88.00 (*0-7803-3091-9*, 96TH8146); fiche 88.00 (*0-7803-3092-7*, 96TM0146) Inst Electrical.

1996 IEEE International Symposium on Circuits & Systems. I. E. E. E. Circuits & Systems Society Staff. Ed. by I. E. E. E. Institute of Electrical & Electronics. LC 80-646530. 2500p. 1996. lib. bdg. write for info. (*0-7803-3074-9*, 96CB35876); fiche. write for info. (*0-7803-3075-7*, 96CM35876) Inst Electrical.

1996 IEEE International Symposium on Circuits & Systems. IEEE Circuits & Systems Society Staff. Ed. by IEEE Institute of Electrical & Electronics Enginee. LC 80-646530. 2500p. 1996. pap. text. write for info. (*0-7803-3073-0*, 96CH35876) Inst Electrical.

1996 IECON 22nd International Conference on Industrial Electronics, Control & Instrumentation. IEEE (Industrial Electronics Society) Staff. LC 95-77996. 2400p. 1996. pap. text 268.00 (*0-7803-2775-6*, 96CH35830); lib. bdg. 268.00 (*0-7803-2776-4*, 96CB35830); mic. film 268.00 (*0-7803-2777-2*, 96CM35830) Inst Electrical.

1996 IEEE Aerospace Applications Conference. IEEE, Aerospace & Electronics Systems Staff. Ed. by Institute of Electrical & Electronics Engineers, I. LC 88-640065. 1800p. 1996. pap. text 238.00 (*0-7803-3196-6*, 96CH35904); lib. bdg. 238.00 (*0-7803-3197-4*, 96CB35904); fiche 238.00 (*0-7803-3198-2*, 96CM35904) Inst Electrical.

1996 IEEE Africon - 4th Africon Conference in Africa. IEEE (Region 8) Staff. Ed. by IEEE (Institute of Electrical & Electronics Engine. LC 95-80272. 800p. 1996. pap. text 142.00 (*0-7803-3019-6*, 95CH35866); lib. bdg. 142.00 (*0-7803-3020-X*, 95CB35866); fiche 142.00 (*0-7803-3021-8*, 95CM35866) Inst Electrical.

1996 IEEE Annual Textile, Fiber & Film Industry Technical Conference. IEEE (Industry Applications Society) Staff. Ed. by IEEE Staff. LC 90-657367. 96p. 1996. 94.00 (*0-7803-3299-7*, 96CM35933); pap. text 94.00 (*0-7803-3297-0*, 96CH35933); lib. bdg. 94.00 (*0-7803-3298-9*, 96CB35933) Inst Electrical.

1996 IEEE Asia Pacific Conference on Circuits & Systems Proceedings. IEEE (Circuits & Systems Society) Staff. Ed. by IEEE (Institute of Electrical & Electronics Engine. LC 96-78659. 680p. 1996. pap. write for info. (*0-7803-3702-6*, 96TH8243); fiche. write for info. (*0-7803-3703-4*, 96TM8243) Inst Electrical.

1996 IEEE Autotestcon. IEEE (Aerospace & Electrical Systems Society) Staff. Ed. by IEEE (Institute of Electrical & Electronics Engine. LC 97-188797. 700p. 1996. pap. text. write for info. (*0-7803-3379-9*, 96CH35955); lib. bdg. write for info. (*0-7803-3380-2*, 96CB35955); mic. film. write for info. (*0-7803-3381-0*, 96CM35933) Inst Electrical.

1996 IEEE Bipolar/Bicmos Circuits & Technology Meeting: Proceedings. IEEE (Electron Devices Society) Staff. 1996. pap. text. write for info. (*0-7803-3516-3*, 96CH35966); lib. bdg. write for info. (*0-7803-3517-1*, 96CH35966); fiche. write for info. (*0-7803-3518-X*, 96CH35966) Inst Electrical.

1996 IEEE Cement Industry Technical Conference. IEEE (Industry Applications Society) Staff. Ed. by IEEE Staff. 392p. 1996. pap. text 118.00 (*0-7803-3014-5*, 96CH35863); lib. bdg. 118.00 (*0-7803-3015-3*, 96CB35863); fiche 118.00 (*0-7803-3016-1*, 96CM35863) Inst Electrical.

1996 IEEE Compass. IEEE (Aerospace & Electronic Systems Society) Staf. Ed. by IEEE (Institute of Electrical & Electronics Engine. LC 96-179434. 272p. 1996. pap. text 112.00 (*0-7803-3390-X*, 96CH35960); lib. bdg. 112.00 (*0-7803-3391-8*, 96CB35960); fiche 112.00 (*0-7803-3392-6*, 96CM35960) Inst Electrical.

1996 IEEE Conference on Emerging Technologies & Factory Automation. IEEE (Industrial Electronics Society) Staff. LC 96-78418. 950p. 1996. pap. write for info. (*0-7803-3685-2*, 96TH8238); fiche. write for info. (*0-7803-3686-0*, 96TH8238) Inst Electrical.

1996 IEEE Conference on Electrical Insulation & Dielectric Phenomena. IEEE (Dielectrics & Electrical Insulation Society). Ed. by IEEE (Institute of Electrical & Electronics Engine. LC 79-649806. 880p. 1996. pap. text. write for info. (*0-7803-3580-5*, 96CH35985); lib. bdg. write for info. (*0-7803-3581-3*, 96CB35985); fiche. write for info. (*0-7803-3582-1*, 96CM35985) Inst Electrical.

1996 IEEE Digital Signal Processing Workshop Proceedings. IEEE (Signal Processing Society) Staff. Ed. by IEEE (Institute of Electrical & Electronics Engine. LC 96-217763. 550p. 1996. pap. write for info. (*0-7803-3629-1*, 96TH8225); mic. film. write for info. (*0-7803-3630-5*, 96TH8225) Inst Electrical.

1996 IEEE Electrical Performance of Electronic Packaging. IEEE (Microwave Theory & Techniques Society, Elect. Ed. by IEEE (Institute of Electrical & Electronics Engine. LC 96-77051. 250p. 1996. pap. text. write for info. (*0-7803-3514-7*, 96TH8203); mic. film. write for info. (*0-7803-3515-5*, 96TH8203) Inst Electrical.

1996 IEEE 54th Annual Device Research Conference. IEEE (Electronic Devices Society) Staff. LC 96-76294. 180p. 1996. pap. 100.00 (*0-7803-3358-6*, 96TH8193); fiche 100.00 (*0-7803-3359-4*) Inst Electrical.

1996 IEEE 46th Vehicular Technology Conference. IEEE, Vehicular Technology Society Staff. Ed. by Institute of Electrical & Electronics Engineers, I. LC 83-645418. 1000p. 1996. pap. text 246.00 (*0-7803-3157-5*, 96CH35894); lib. bdg. 246.00 (*0-7803-3158-3*, 96CB35894); fiche 246.00 (*0-7803-3159-1*, 96CM35894) Inst Electrical.

1996 IEEE Instrumentation & Measurement Technology Conference Proceedings. IEEE Instrumentation & Measurement Society Staff. Ed. by IEEE Staff. LC 96-76385. (Illus.). 1608p. 1996. pap. text 212.00 (*0-7803-3312-8*, 96CH35936); lib. bdg. 212.00 (*0-7803-3313-6*, 93CB35936); fiche 212.00 (*0-7803-3314-4*, 96CM35936) Inst Electrical.

1996 IEEE Intelligent Network Workshop. IEEE (Communication Society) Staff. Ed. by IEEE (Institute of Electrical & Electronics Engine. LC 96-75554. 500p. 1996. pap. 118.00 (*0-7803-3230-X*, 96TH8174); fiche 118.00 (*0-7803-3231-8*, 96TM8174) Inst Electrical.

1996 IEEE International Integrated Reliability Workshop Final Report. IEEE Electron Devices Society & Reliability Societ. Ed. by IEEE Staff. LC 96-77509. 175p. 1997. pap. write for info. (*0-7803-3598-8*, 96TH8215); fiche. write for info. (*0-7803-3599-6*, 96TM8215) Inst Electrical.

1996 IEEE International Symposium on Personal Indoor & Mobile Radio Communication. IEEE (Communication Society) Staff. LC 96-78419. 1000p. 1996. pap. write for info. (*0-7803-3692-5*, 96TH8240); fiche. write for info. (*0-7803-3693-3*, 96TM8240) Inst Electrical.

1996 IEEE International Conference on Control Applications. IEEE (Control Systems Society) Staff. Ed. by IEEE (Institute of Electrical & Electronics Engine. 1996. 206.00 incl. fiche (*0-7803-2977-5*, 94CH35854); pap. text 206.00 (*0-7803-2975-9*, 94CH35854); lib. bdg. 206.00 (*0-7803-2976-7*, 94CB35854) Inst Electrical.

1996 IEEE International Reliability Physics Proceedings. IEEE (Electron Devices Society) Staff. LC 82-640313. 404p. 1996. pap. text 120.00 (*0-7803-2753-5*, 96CH35825); lib. bdg. 120.00 (*0-7803-2754-3*, 96CB35825); fiche 120.00 (*0-7803-2755-1*, 96CM35825) Inst Electrical.

1996 IEEE International Conference on Semiconductor Electronics - Proceedings. IEEE, Electron Devices Society Staff. Ed. by IEEE, Institute of Electrical & Electronics Engine. LC 96-76775. 300p. 1996. pap. write for info. (*0-7803-3388-8*, 96TH8198); fiche. write for info. (*0-7803-3389-6*, 96TH8198) Inst Electrical.

1996 IEEE International Conference on Neural Networks. IEEE, Neural Networks Council Staff. Ed. by IEEE, Institute of Electrical & Electronics Engine. LC 96-75377. 3800p. 1996. pap. text. write for info. (*0-7803-3210-5*, 96CH35907); lib. bdg. write for info. (*0-7803-3211-3*, 96CH35907); fiche. write for info. (*0-7803-3212-1*, 96CH35907) Inst Electrical.

1996 IEEE International Conference on Microelectronic Test Structures. IEEE (Electron Devices Society) Staff. LC 95-77997. 338p. 1996. pap. text 106.00 (*0-7803-2783-7*, 96CH35832); lib. bdg. 106.00 (*0-7803-2784-5*, 95CB35832); mic. film 106.00 (*0-7803-2785-3*, 96CM35832) Inst Electrical.

1996 IEEE International Conference on Evolutionary Computation Proceedings. IEEE (Neural Networks Council) Staff. LC 95-78170. 1000p. 1996. pap. 158.00 (*0-7803-2902-3*, 96TH8114); mic. film 158.00 (*0-7803-2903-1*, 96TM8114) Inst Electrical.

1996 IEEE International Conference on Acoustics, Speech & Signal Processing, ICASSP-96. IEEE (Signal Processing Society) Staff. Ed. by IEEE (Institute of Electrical & Electronics Engine. LC 84-645139. 3800p. 1996. pap. text 378.00 (*0-7803-3192-3*, 96CH35903); lib. bdg. 378.00 (*0-7803-3193-1*, 96CB35903); fiche 378.00 (*0-7803-3194-X*, 96CM35903) Inst Electrical.

1996 IEEE International Conference on Image Processing Proceedings. IEEE (Signal Processing Society) Staff. Ed. by IEEE (Institute of Electrical & Electronics Engine. LC 96-75667. 3200p. 1996. pap. text 332.00 (*0-7803-3258-X*, 96CH35919); lib. bdg. 332.00 (*0-7803-3259-8*, 96CB35919); fiche 332.00 (*0-7803-3260-1*, 96CM35919) Inst Electrical.

1996 IEEE International Conference on Communications. IEEE, Communications Society Staff. Ed. by Institute of Electrical & Electronics Engineers, I. LC 81-649547. 2000p. 1996. pap. text 242.00 (*0-7803-3250-4*, 96CH35916); lib. bdg. 242.00 (*0-7803-3251-2*, 96CB35916); fiche 242.00 (*0-7803-3252-0*, 96CM35916) Inst Electrical.

1996 IEEE International Conference on Personal Wireless Communications. IEEE, Delhi Section, India Chapter Staff. Ed. by Institute of Electrical & Electronics Engineers, I. LC 95-82411. 250p. 1996. pap. 108.00 (*0-7803-3177-X*, 96TH8165); fiche 108.00 (*0-7803-3178-8*, 96TM8165) Inst Electrical.

1996 IEEE International Conference on Fuzzy Systems Proceedings. IEEE, Neural Networks Council Staff. 2650p. 1996. pap. text. write for info. (*0-7803-3645-3*, 96CH35998); lib. bdg. write for info. (*0-7803-3646-1*, 96CH35998); fiche. write for info. (*0-7803-3647-X*) Inst Electrical.

1996 IEEE International Conference on Acoustics, Speech & Signal Processing, ICASSP-96. IEEE, Signal Processing Society Staff. Ed. by Institute of Electrical & Electronic Engineers, In. LC 84-645139. 1996. cd-rom. write for info. (*0-7803-3195-8*) Inst Electrical.

1996 IEEE International Conference on Systems, Man & Cybernetics. IEEE Staff. 3000p. 1996. pap. text. write for info. (*0-7803-3280-6*); lib. bdg. write for info. (*0-7803-3281-4*); mic. film. write for info. (*0-7803-3282-2*) Inst Electrical.

1996 IEEE International Conference on Multi Media Engineering in Education Conference Proceedings. IEEE, Victorian Section Staff. Ed. by Institute of Electrical & Electronics Engineers, I. LC 95-82413. 800p. 1996. pap. 142.00 (*0-7803-3173-7*, 96TH8163); fiche 142.00 (*0-7803-3174-5*, 96TM8163) Inst Electrical.

1996 IEEE International Conference on Industrial Technology Proceedings. Industrial Electronics Society Staff. Ed. by Institute of Electrical & Electronics Engineers, I. LC 95-81731. 1000p. 1996. pap. write for info. (*0-7803-3104-4*, 96TH8151); fiche. write for info. (*0-7803-3105-2*, 96TH8151) Inst Electrical.

1996 IEEE International Engineering Management Conference. IEEE, Engineering Management Society Staff. Ed. by Institute of Electrical & Electronics Engineers, I. LC 96-77286. 700p. 1996. pap. text. write for info. (*0-7803-3552-X*, 96CH35979); lib. bdg. write for info. (*0-7803-3553-8*, 96CH35979); fiche. write for info. (*0-7803-3554-6*, 96CH35979) Inst Electrical.

1996 IEEE International Joint Symposia on Intelligence & Systems, Intelligence in Neural & Biological Systems (INBS); Intelligence in Automation & Robotics (IAR); & Image, Speech, & Natural Language Systems (ISNLS) LC 96-78147. 360p. 1996. pap. 80.00 (*0-8186-7728-7*, PR7728) IEEE Comp Soc.

1996 IEEE International Non-Volatile Memory Technology Conference. IEEE (Computer Society, Components, Packaging & Ma. Ed. by IEEE (Institute of Electrical & Electronics Engine. LC 96-215380. 180p. 1996. pap. write for info. (*0-7803-3510-4*, 96TH8200); fiche. write for info. (*0-7803-3511-2*, 96TM8200) Inst Electrical.

1996 IEEE International Professional Communication Conference. IEEE (Professional Communication Society) Staff. Ed. by IEEE (Institute of Electrical & Electronics Engine. 350p. 1996. pap. text. write for info. (*0-7803-3689-5*, 96CH36009); lib. bdg. write for info. (*0-7803-3690-9*, 96CH36009); fiche. write for info. (*0-7803-3691-7*, 96CH36009) Inst Electrical.

1996 IEEE International Symposium on Phased Array Systems & Technology. IEEE (Boston Section) Staff. LC 96-75516. 500p. 1996. pap. 118.00 (*0-7803-3232-6*, 96TH8175) Inst Electrical.

1996 IEEE International Symposium on Phased Array Systems & Technology. IEEE (Boston Section) Staff. Ed. by IEEE (Institute of Electrical & Electronics Engine. LC 96-75516. 500p. 1996. fiche 118.00 (*0-7803-3233-4*, 96TH8175) Inst Electrical.

1996 IEEE International Symposium on Computer-Aided Control System Design. IEEE (Control Systems Society) Staff. Ed. by IEEE (Institute of Electrical & Electronics Engine. LC 95-80332. 700p. 1996. pap. write for info. (*0-7803-3032-3*, 96TH8136); fiche. write for info. (*0-7803-3033-1*, 96TH8136) Inst Electrical.

1996 IEEE International Symposium on Electronics & the Environment. IEEE (Technical Activities Board) Staff. Ed. by IEEE (Institute of Electrical & Electronics Engine. LC 95-79200. 340p. 1996. pap. text 110.00 (*0-7803-2950-3*, 96CH35846); lib. bdg. 110.00 (*0-7803-2951-1*, 96CB35846); fiche 110.00 (*0-7803-2952-X*, 96CM35846) Inst Electrical.

1996 IEEE International Symposium on Applications of Ferroelectrics. IEEE (Ultrasonics, Ferroelectrics & Frequency Cont. LC 96-176293. 1000p. 1997. pap. text 170.00 (*0-7803-3355-1*, 96CH35948); lib. bdg. 170.00 (*0-7803-3356-X*, 96CB35948); fiche 170.00 (*0-7803-3357-8*, 96CM35948) Inst Electrical.

1996 IEEE International Symposium on Electromagnetic Compatibility. IEEE, Electromagnetic Compatibility Society Staff. Ed. by IEEE, Institute of Electrical & Electronics Engine. LC 83-645449. 700p. 1996. pap. text. write for info. (*0-7803-3207-5*, 96CH35906); lib. bdg. write for info. (*0-7803-3208-3*, 96CH35906); fiche. write for info. (*0-7803-3209-1*, 96CM35906) Inst Electrical.

1996 IEEE International Symposium on Power Semiconductor Devices & ICs. IEEE, Electron Devices Society Staff. LC 95-81730. 450p. 1996. pap. text 114.00 (*0-7803-3106-0*, 96CH35883); lib. bdg. 114.00 (*0-7803-3107-9*, 96CB35883) Inst Electrical.

1996 IEEE International Symposium on Industrial Electronics. IEEE, Industrial Electronics Society Staff. LC 96-76159. 1200p. 1996. pap. write for info. (*0-7803-3334-9*, 96TH8192); fiche. write for info. (*0-7803-3335-7*, 96TH8192) Inst Electrical.

1996 IEEE International Solid State Circuits Conference Digest of Technical Papers. IEEE, Solid-State Circuits Council Staff. LC 81-644810. 528p. 1996. pap. text 120.00 (*0-7803-3136-2*, 96CH35889); lib. bdg. 120.00 (*0-7803-3137-0*, 96CB35889) Inst Electrical.

1996 IEEE International SOI Conference Proceedings. IEEE Staff. 200p. 1996. pap. text. write for info. (*0-7803-3315-2*, 96CH35937); lib. bdg. write for info. (*0-7803-3316-0*, 96CH35937); mic. film. write for info. (*0-7803-3317-9*, 96CH35937) Inst Electrical.

1996 IEEE International Symposium On Electrical Insulation. IEEE Staff. 1000p. 1996. write for info. (*0-7803-3533-3*, 96CH35972); pap. text. write for info. (*0-7803-3531-7*); lib. bdg. write for info. (*0-7803-3532-5*) Inst Electrical.

1996 IEEE International Test Conference. IEEE Computer Society Staff. Ed. by IEEE Staff. LC 97-103140. 1100p. 1996. pap. text. write for info. (*0-7803-3540-6*, 96CH35976); lib. bdg. write for info. (*0-7803-3541-4*, 96CH35976); fiche. write for info. (*0-7803-3542-2*, 96CH35976) Inst Electrical.

1996 IEEE LEOS Annual Meeting. IEEE, Lasers & Electro-Optics Society Staff. Ed. by Institute of Electrical & Electronics Engineers, I. LC 95-82414. 830p. 1996. lib. bdg. write for info. (*0-7803-3161-3*, 96CH35895); fiche. write for info. (*0-7803-3162-1*) Inst Electrical.

1996 IEEE Micro Electro Mechanical Systems. IEEE (Robotics & Automation Society) Staff. Ed. by Institute of Electrical & Electronics Engineers, I. LC 97-131850. 400p. 1996. pap. text 116.00 (*0-7803-2985-6*, 96CH35856); lib. bdg. 116.00 (*0-7803-2986-4*, 96CB35856); fiche 116.00 (*0-7803-2987-2*, 96CM35856) Inst Electrical.

1996 IEEE MTT-S International Microwave Symposium Digest. IEEE, Microwave Theory & Techniques Society & Comp. Ed. by Institute of Electrical & Electronics Engineers, I. LC 77-645125. 2050p. 1996. pap. text 250.00 (*0-7803-3246-6*, 96CH35915); lib. bdg. 250.00 (*0-7803-3247-4*, 96CB35915); fiche 250.00 (*0-7803-3248-2*, 96CM35915); cd-rom. write for info. (*0-7803-3249-0*) Inst Electrical.

1996 IEEE Network Operations & Management Symposium. IEEE, Communications Society Staff. Ed. by IEEE Staff. LC 94-74519. 700p. 1996. pap. text. write for info. (*0-7803-2518-4*, 96CH35757); lib. bdg. write for info. (*0-7803-2519-2*, 96CB35757); fiche. write for info. (*0-7803-2520-6*, 96CM35757) Inst Electrical.

1996 IEEE Nuclear Science Symposium. IEEE, Nuclear & Plasma Sciences Society Staff. 2000p. 1997. pap. text. write for info. (*0-7803-3534-1*, 96CH35974); lib. bdg. write for info. (*0-7803-3535-X*, 96CB35974); fiche. write for info. (*0-7803-3536-8*, 96CM35974) Inst Electrical.

1996 IEEE Position, Location & Navigation Symposium - Plans '96. IEEE (Aerospace & Electronics Systems Society) Sta. LC 95-81044. 734p. 1996. pap. text 150.00 (*0-7803-3085-4*, 96CH35879); lib. bdg. 150.00 (*0-7803-3086-2*, 96CB35879); fiche 150.00 (*0-7803-3087-0*, 96CM35879) Inst Electrical.

1996 IEEE Radiation Effects Data Workshop. IEEE (Nuclear & Plasma Sciences Society) Staff. Ed. by IEEE (Institute of Electrical & Electronics Engine. LC 96-76986. 700p. 1996. pap. write for info. (*0-7803-3398-5*, 96TH8199); mic. film. write for info. (*0-7803-3399-3*, 96TH8199) Inst Electrical.

1996 IEEE Semiconducting & Insulating Materials Conference. IEEE (Electron Devices Society) Staff. Ed. by IEEE (Institute of Electrical & Electronics Engine. LC 96-75676. 500p. 1996. 84.00 (*0-7803-3096-X*, 96CH35881); pap. text 84.00 (*0-7803-3179-6*, 96CH35881); lib. bdg. 84.00 (*0-7803-3095-1*, 96CH35881) Inst Electrical.

1996 IEEE-SP International Symposium on Time-Frequency & Time-Scale Analysis. IEEE (Signal Processing Society) Staff. Ed. by IEEE (Institute of Electrical & Electronics Engine. LC 96-232814. 600p. 1996. pap. write for info. (*0-7803-3512-0*, 96TH8201); fiche. write for info. (*0-7803-3513-9*, 96TH8201) Inst Electrical.

1996 IEEE Symposium on Autonomous Underwater Vehicle Technology Proceedings. IEEE (Oceanic Engineering Society) Staff. Ed. by IEEE (Institute of Electrical & Electronics Engine. LC 96-75062. 496p. 1996. pap. text 118.00 (*0-7803-3185-0*, 96CH35900); lib. bdg. 118.00 (*0-7803-3186-9*, 96CB35900); fiche 118.00 (*0-7803-3187-7*, 96CM35900) Inst Electrical.

1996 IEEE Third Workshop on Interactive Voice Technology for Telecommunications Applications. IEEE (Communications Society) Staff. Ed. by IEEE (Institute of Electrical & Electronics Engine. LC 96-75519. 172p. 1996. pap. 92.00 (*0-7803-3238-5*, 96TH8178); fiche 92.00 (*0-7803-3239-3*, 96TM8178) Inst Electrical.

1996 IEEE Transmission & Distribution Conference. IEEE (Power Engineering Society) Staff. Ed. by IEEE (Institute of Electrical & Electronics Engine. LC 96-77049. 1000p. 1996. pap. text. write for info. (*0-7803-3522-8*, 96CH35968); lib. bdg. write for info. (*0-7803-3523-6*, 96CH35968); mic. film. write for info. (*0-7803-3524-4*, 96CH35968) Inst Electrical.

An Asterisk (*) at the beginning of an entry indicates that the title is appearing for the first time.

1996 IEEE 12th International Conference on Conduction & Breakdown in Dielectric Liquids. IEEE (Dielectrics & Electrical Insulation Society). Ed. by IEEE (Institute of Electrical & Electronics Engine. LC 96-77438. 500p. 1996. pap. text. write for info. (*0-7803-3560-0*, 96CH35981); lib. bdg. write for info. (*0-7803-3562-7*, 96CB35981); fiche. write for info. (*0-7803-3563-5*, 96CM35981) Inst Electrical.

1996 IEEE Ultrasonics Symposium Proceedings. IEEE (Ultrasonics, Ferroelectrics & Frequency Cont. LC 73-641406. 1900p. 1997. pap. text. write for info. (*0-7803-3615-1*, 96CH35993); lib. bdg. write for info. (*0-7803-3616-X*, 96CB35993); fiche. write for info. (*0-7803-3617-8*, 96CM35993); cd-rom. write for info. (*0-7803-3618-6*, 96CH35993) Inst Electrical.

1996 IEEE Workshop on Computers in Power Electronics. IEEE (Power Electronics Soc.) Staff. Ed. by IEEE (Inst. of Electrical & Electronics Engrs.). 190p. 1997. pap. write for info. (*0-7803-3977-0*, 96TH8288) Inst Electrical.

1996 IEEE Workshop on High-Assurance Software Engineering: HASE 96. LC 97-72097. 112p. 1997. pap. 115.00 (*0-8186-7629-9*) IEEE Comp Soc.

1996 IEEE Workshop on Neural Networks for Signal Processing. IEEE Signal Processing Society Staff. Ed. by IEEE Staff. 630p. 1996. pap. write for info. (*0-7803-3550-3*, 96TH8205); fiche. write for info. (*0-7803-3551-1*, 96TH8205) Inst Electrical.

1996 IEEE Workshop on Power Electronics in Transportation. IEEE Staff. LC 96-75710. 150p. 1996. write for info. (*0-7803-3293-8*, 96TH8184); pap. write for info. (*0-7803-3292-X*) Inst Electrical.

1996 IEEE 1st International Conference on Plasma Process-Induced Damage (P2IP) Ed. by Kin P. Chenng et al. 102.00 (*0-9651577-0-9*, 96TH8142) Nrthrn CA Chapter.

1996 IEEE 15th International Semiconductor Laser Conference. IEEE, Lasers & Electro-Optics Society Staff. Ed. by Institute of Electrical & Electronics Engineers, I. LC 95-82416. 1996. pap. text. write for info. (*0-7803-3163-X*) Inst Electrical.

1996 IEEE 15th International Semiconductor Laser Conference. IEEE, Lasers & Electro-Optics Society Staff. Ed. by Institute of Electrical & Electronics Engineers, I. LC 95-82416. 1996. lib. bdg. write for info. (*0-7803-3164-8*, 96CM35896); fiche. write for info. (*0-7803-3165-6*) Inst Electrical.

1996 IEEE 2nd International Conference on Algorithms & Architectures for Parallel Processing Proceedings. IEEE (Singapore Section, Singapore Computer Chapte. Ed. by IEEE (Institute of Electrical & Electronics Engine. LC 97-132314. 600p. 1996. pap. write for info. (*0-7803-3529-5*, 96TH8204); fiche. write for info. (*0-7803-3530-9*, 96TH8204) Inst Electrical.

1996 IEEE 4th International Symposium on Spread Spectrum Techniques & Applications. IEEE (Communications Society, Region 8) Staff. Ed. by IEEE (Institute of Electrical & Electronics Engine. LC 96-77389. 1700p. 1996. pap. write for info. (*0-7803-3567-8*, 96TH8210); fiche. write for info. (*0-7803-3568-6*, 96TM8210) Inst Electrical.

1996 IEEE 43rd Petroleum & Chemical Industry Conference. IEEE (Industry Applications Society) Staff. Ed. by IEEE (Institute of Electrical & Electronics Engine. LC 73-641120. 350p. 1996. pap. text. write for info. (*0-7803-3587-2*, 96CH35988); lib. bdg. write for info. (*0-7803-3588-0*, 96CH35988); fiche. write for info. (*0-7803-3589-9*, 96CH35988) Inst Electrical.

1996 IEEE 5th International Workshop on Robot & Human Communication. IEEE (Industrial Electronics Society) Staff. Ed. by IEEE (Institute of Electrical & Electronics Engine. LC 96-75514. 400p. 1996. pap. 110.00 (*0-7803-3253-9*, 96TH8179); fiche 110.00 (*0-7803-3254-7*, 96TH8179) Inst Electrical.

1996 IEEE 9th International Vacuum Microelectronics Conference Technical Digest. IEEE (Electron Devices Society) Staff. Ed. by IEEE (Institute of Electrical & Electronics Engine. 720p. 1996. pap. write for info. (*0-7803-3594-5*, 96TH8212); fiche. write for info. (*0-7803-3595-3*, 96TH8212) Inst Electrical.

1996 IEEE/IAFE Conference on Computational Intelligence for Financial Engineering. IEEE (Neural Networks Council) Staff. Ed. by IEEE (Institute of Electrical & Electronics Engine. LC 96-75520. 150p. 1996. pap. 108.00 (*0-7803-3236-9*, 96TH8177); fiche 108.00 (*0-7803-3237-7*, 96TM8177) Inst Electrical.

1996 IEEE/Semi Advanced Semiconductor Manufacturing Conference & Workshop. IEEE Staff. 426p. 1996. pap. text. write for info. (*0-7803-3371-3*, 96CH35953); lib. bdg. write for info. (*0-7803-3372-1*, 96CH35953); mic. film. write for info. (*0-7803-3373-X*, 96CH35953) Inst Electrical.

1996 Index for Advertising Law Anthology Series Vols. I-XVIII. Ed. by Allison P. Zabriskie. (National Law Anthology Ser.). 204p. (Orig.). (C). 1996. pap. 34.95 (*1-57024-030-2*) Intl Lib.

1996 Index for Banking Law Anthology Vols. I-X: 1983-1996. Ed. by Allison P. Zabriskie. (National Law Anthology Ser.). 115p. (Orig.). (C). 1996. pap. write for info. (*0-614-18612-9*) Intl Lib.

1996 Index for Public Utilities Law Anthology Ser., Set, Vols. I-XVIII (1974-1995) Ed. by Allison P. Zabriskie. 200p. (Orig.). 1996. pap. 34.95 (*1-57024-029-9*) Intl Lib.

1996 Index to the Directory of American Charities. Murray S. Weitzman et al. Tr. by Virginia A. Hodgkinson. 416p. (Orig.). 1996. pap. 8.95 (*0-9651579-0-3*) Philanthrc Res.

1996 Individual Tax Return Guide. rev. ed. 157p. 1997. pap. text 12.00 (*0-7811-0152-2*) Res Inst Am.

1996 IEEE Industrial & Commercial Power Systems Technical Conference. IEEE Industrial Applications Society Staff. Ed. by IEEE Staff. LC 88-641172. 250p. 1996. pap. text 98.00 (*0-7803-3263-6*, 96CH35920); lib. bdg. 98.00 (*0-7803-3264-4*, 96CB35920); fiche 98.00 (*0-7803-3265-2*, 96CM35920) Inst Electrical.

1996 Information Systems Spending Report. Ed. by Mark McManus. 200p. 1996. ring bd. 895.00 (*0-945052-31-6*) Computer Econ.

1996 Interactive Television Industry Directory. 2nd ed. 135p. 1995. pap. 65.00 (*0-614-25705-0*) Simba Info.

1996 International Conference on Simulation of Semiconductor Processes & Devices. IEEE (Electron Devices Society) Staff. 200p. 1996. pap. 96.00 (*0-7803-2745-4*, 96TH8095); fiche 96.00 (*0-7803-2746-2*, 96TM8095) Inst Electrical.

1996 International Conference on Power Electronics, Drives & Energy Systems for Industrial Growth. IEEE (Industry Applications Society) Staff. LC 95-78164. 1000p. 1996. pap. 158.00 (*0-7803-2795-0*, 96TH8111); mic. film 158.00 (*0-7803-2796-9*, 96TM8111) Inst Electrical.

1996 International Conference on Applications of Photonic Technology. IEEE (Region 7) Staff. Ed. by IEEE (Institute of Electrical & Electronics Engine. LC 95-82218. 600p. 1996. pap. 126.00 (*0-7803-3153-2*, 96TH8159); fiche 126.00 (*0-7803-3154-0*, 96TM8159) Inst Electrical.

1996 International Conference on Communication Technology Proceedings. IEEE, Communication Society Staff. Ed. by Institute of Electrical & Electronics Engineers, I. LC 95-78305. 2000p. 1996. pap. write for info. (*0-7803-2916-3*, 96TH8118) Inst Electrical.

1996 International Conference on Thermoelectrics. IEEE Components, Packaging & Manufacturing Technol. Ed. by IEEE Staff. LC 96-75531. 300p. 1996. pap. 102.00 (*0-7803-3221-0*, 96TH8169); fiche 102.00 (*0-7803-3222-9*, 96TM8169) Inst Electrical.

1996 International Conference on Intelligent Robots & Systems Proceedings. IEEE, Industrial Electronics & Robotics & Automati. Ed. by IEEE, Institute of Electrical & Electronics Engine. LC 96-75376. 2000p. 1996. pap. text. write for info. (*0-7803-3213-X*, 96CH35908); lib. bdg. write for info. (*0-7803-3214-8*, 96CH35908); fiche. write for info. (*0-7803-3215-6*, 96CM35908) Inst Electrical.

1996 International Conference on Spoken Language Processing Proceedings. IEEE, Signal Processing Society Staff. Ed. by Institute of Electrical & Electronics Engineers, I. 2600p. 1996. pap. write for info. (*0-7803-3555-4*, 96TH8206) Inst Electrical.

1996 International Conference on Spoken Language Processing Proceedings. IEEE, Signal Processing Society Staff. Ed. by Institute of Electrical & Electronics Engineers, I. 2600p. 1996. fiche. write for info. (*0-7803-3556-2*, 96TM8206) Inst Electrical.

1996 International Conference on Intelligent Systems Applications to Power Systems Proceedings. Power Engineering Society & Neural Networks Counci. Ed. by Institute of Electrical & Electronics Engineers, I. LC 95-81732. 500p. 1996. pap. 118.00 (*0-7803-3115-X*, 96TH8152) Inst Electrical.

1996 International Congress on Applied Lasers & Electro-Optics Proceedings. Ed. by Walter Duley & Kimihiro Shibata. (Illus.). 968p. 1997. pap. text 160.00 (*0-912035-54-4*, 581) Laser Inst.

1996 International Congress on Applied Lasers & Electro-Optics Proceedings: Lasers & Electro-Optics for Automotive Manufacturing. Ed. by Walter Duley & Kimihiro Shibata. (TCALEO 96 Ser.: Vol. 82). (Illus.). 173p. 1997. pap. text 60.00 (*0-912035-55-2*, 582) Laser Inst.

1996 International Design Resource Awards. Tom Johnson & Barbara Johnson. 60p. Date not set. 15.00 (*0-9644815-1-0*) Johnson Design.

1996 International Electron Devices Meeting. IEEE, Electron Devices Society Staff. Ed. by Institute of Electrical & Electronics Engineers, I. LC 81-642284. 980p. 1996. pap. text. write for info. (*0-7803-3393-4*, 96CH35961); lib. bdg. write for info. (*0-7803-3394-2*, 96CH35961); fiche. write for info. (*0-7803-3395-0*, 96CH35961); cd-rom. write for info. (*0-7803-3396-9*) Inst Electrical.

1996 International Fiber Optics Yellow Pages. Date not set. pap. 89.95 (*1-56851-164-7*) Info Gatekeepers.

1996 International Geoscience & Remote Sensing Symposium. IEEE, Geoscience & Remote Sensing Society Staff. Ed. by Institute of Electrical & Electronics Engineers, I. LC 95-80706. 2500p. 1996. pap. text 302.00 (*0-7803-3068-4*, 96CH35875); lib. bdg. 302.00 (*0-7803-3069-2*, 96CB35875); fiche 302.00 (*0-7803-3070-6*, 96CM35875) Inst Electrical.

1996 International Imaging Source Book. Ed. by Jennifer O. Newman. 1996. pap., per. 199.00 (*1-881537-44-7*) Phillips Business.

1996 International ISDN Yellow Pages. Date not set. pap. 69.95 (*1-56851-160-4*) Info Gatekeepers.

1996 International Mechanical Engineering Congress & Exposition, Atlanta, Georgia, November 17-22, 1996: Advanced Materials for Vibro-Acoustic Applications. (NCA Ser.: Vol. 23). 212p. 1996. 80.00 (*0-7918-1525-0*, G01020) ASME Pr.

1996 International Mechanical Engineering Congress & Exposition, Atlanta, Georgia, November 17-22, 1996: Thermal Science of Advanced Steam Generators - Heat Exchangers. (NE Ser.: Vol. 19). 64p. 1996. 56.00 (*0-7918-1544-7*, G01039) ASME Pr.

1996 International Satellite Directory. 1996. 15.00 (*0-936361-21-2*) Design Pubs.

1996 International Semiconductor Conference. IEEE, Electron Devices Society Staff. Ed. by IEEE, Institute of Electrical & Electronics Engine. LC 96-75375. 800p. 1996. pap. write for info. (*0-7803-3223-7*, 96TH8170); fiche. write for info. (*0-7803-3224-5*, 96TH8170) Inst Electrical.

1996 International Symposium on Circuits & Systems. 1996. pap. text 60.00 (*0-8186-7307-9*, PRO7307) IEEE Comp Soc.

1996 International Symposium on Technology & Society. IEEE (Social Implications of Technology Society) S. Ed. by IEEE (Institute of Electrical & Electronics Engine. LC 96-76267. 500p. 1996. pap. text 128.00 (*0-7803-3345-4*, 96CH35945); lib. bdg. 128.00 (*0-7803-3346-2*, 96CB35945); fiche 128.00 (*0-7803-3347-0*, 96CM35945) Inst Electrical.

1996 International Symposium on Low Power Electronics & Design. IEEE (Solid State Circuits Council & Circuits & Sy. Ed. by IEEE (Institute of Electrical & Electronics Engine. LC 96-77436. 420p. 1996. pap. 54.00 (*0-7803-3571-6*, 96TH8211); mic. film. write for info. (*0-7803-3572-4*, 96TH8211) Inst Electrical.

1996 International Symposium on Semiconductor Manufacturing. IEEE, Electron Devices Society, Components, Packag. 300p. 1996. lib. bdg. write for info. (*0-7803-3648-8*, 96CH35999); fiche. write for info. (*0-7803-3649-6*) Inst Electrical.

1996 International Symposium on Microelectronics, Vol. 2920. 610p. 1996. 94.00 (*0-930815-48-3*) SPIE.

1996 International Symposium/Workshop on Advanced Technologies: Neuro-Fuzzy Systems. IEEE, Electron Devices Society Staff. Ed. by Institute of Electrical & Electronics Engineers, I. LC 96-76486. 150p. 1996. pap. write for info. (*0-7803-3367-5*, 96TH8195); fiche. write for info. (*0-7803-3368-3*, 96TH8195) Inst Electrical.

1996 International Topical Meeting on Microwave Photonics (MWP) IEEE Microwave Theory & Techniques Society Staff. LC 98-149249. 200p. 1996. pap. 96.00 (*0-7803-3129-X*, TH8153) Inst Electrical.

1996 International Workshop on Human Factors in Offshore Operations Held December 16-18, 1996, New Orleans, Louisiana: Summary of Proceedings & Submitted Papers. unabridged ed. William Moore. Ed. by Robert G. Bea et al. (Illus.). 444p. 1998. pap. 50.00 (*0-943870-00-3*) Am Bur Shipping.

1996 International Who's Who of Institutions & Mutual Funds. Carson Publications Staff. Ed. by Ian Sax. 700p. 1996. ring bd. 400.00 (*0-9646311-2-1*) Carson Grp.

1996 Intersociety Conference on Thermal Phenomena in Electronic Systems Proceedings. IEEE Staff. 250p. 1996. pap. text. write for info. (*0-7803-3325-X*, 96CH35940); lib. bdg. write for info. (*0-7803-3326-8*, 96CH35940); mic. film. write for info. (*0-7803-3327-6*, 96CH35940) Inst Electrical.

1996 IPCC Guidelines for National Greenhouse Gas Inventories. rev. ed. 950p. 1997. pap. 187.00 (*92-64-15578-3*, Pub. by Org for Econ) OECD.

1996 IUCN List of Threatened Animals. Contrib. by Jonathan Baillie & Brian Groombridge. 368p. 1996. pap. text 40.00 (*2-8317-0335-2*, Pub. by IUCN) Island Pr.

1996 Latin American Market Planning Report. Strategy Research Corporation Staff. 293p. 1996. pap. 350.00 (*1-888520-04-3*) Strategy Research.

1996 Market Scope. Ed. by Adrienne Toth et al. (Illus.). 1996. pap. 325.00 (*0-911790-33-0*) Trade Dimensns.

1996 Market Share Reports for Property/Casualty Groups & Companies. annuals 3rd ed. Ed. by Natalia Webster. 472p. 1998. pap. 150.00 (*0-89382-495-X*, MSR-PB97) Nat Assn Insurance.

1996 Market Share Reports for Top 125 Life & Fraternal Insurance Groups & Companies by State. annuals 3rd ed. Ed. by Natalia Webster. 356p. (C). 1998. pap. 150.00 (*0-89382-494-1*, MSR-LB97) Nat Assn Insurance.

1996 Massachusetts Courts, Maps & Judges. rev. ed. Skinder-Strauss Staff. (Illus.). 160p. 1995. pap. 15.00 (*1-57741-002-5*) Skinder-Strauss.

1996 Massachusetts Courts, Maps & Judges; 1996 Massachusetts Lawyers Diary & Manual Including Bar Directory of Massachusetts, 2 bks., Set. rev. ed. Skinder-Strauss Staff. 1995. pap. 35.00 (*1-57741-004-1*) Skinder-Strauss.

1996 Massachusetts Courts, Maps & Judges: 1996 Massachusetts Lawyers Diary & Manual Including Bar Directory of Massachusetts, 2 bks. rev. ed. Skinder-Strauss Staff. 1995. pap. 35.00 (*1-57741-003-3*) Skinder-Strauss.

1996 Massachusetts Lawyers Diary & Manual Including Bar Directory of Massachusetts. rev. ed. Skinder-Strauss Staff. 1281p. 1995. pap. 35.00 (*1-57741-001-7*) Skinder-Strauss.

1996 Massachusetts Lawyers Diary & Manual Including Bar Directory of Massachusetts. rev. ed. Skinder-Strauss Staff. 1996. cd-rom 60.00 (*1-57741-015-7*) Skinder-Strauss.

1996 Mediterranean Electrotechnical Conference - Melecon. IEEE (Region 8) Staff. Ed. by Institute of Electrical & Electronics Engineers, I. LC 95-81728. 1500p. 1996. pap. text 198.00 (*0-7803-3109-5*, 96CH35884); lib. bdg. 198.00 (*0-7803-3110-9*, 96CB35884); fiche 198.00 (*0-7803-3111-7*, 96CM35884) Inst Electrical.

1996 Men. Sports Illustrated Staff. 1995. pap. 14.95 (*0-316-80869-5*) Little.

1996 MES Directory Vols. 1 & 2: Manufacturing Execution Systems. 2nd ed. Managing Automation Group Staff. Ed. by Alice H. Greene. (Illus.). 1500p. 1996. 125.00 incl. cd-rom (*1-882554-05-1*) Thomas Pub NY.

1996 Mid-Year Seminar Papers: A Collection of Available Papers from Singapore. 105p. 1996. pap. 20.00 (*0-614-31030-X*) Pac Telecom.

1996 Midsummer Classic. Gary Perkinson & Michael J. McCormick. (Illus.). 112p. 1996. 24.95 (*0-9638222-2-5*) Maj Leag Baseball.

1996 Motorsports Engineering Conference Proceedings, 2 vols. 1996. 125.00 (*1-56091-896-9*, P-304) Soc Auto Engineers.

1996 Motorsports Engineering Conference Proceedings Vol. I: Vehicle Design Issues. 1996. 93.00 (*1-56091-894-2*, P-304/1) Soc Auto Engineers.

1996 Motorsports Engineering Conference Proceedings Vol. II: Engines & Drivetrains. 1996. 61.00 (*1-56091-895-0*, P-304/2) Soc Auto Engineers.

1996 Multisensor Fusion & Integration for Intelligent Systems. IEEE (Industrial Electronics Society) Staff & IEEE (Robotics & Automation Society) Staff. Ed. by IEEE (Institute of Electrical & Electronics Engine. LC 96-78658. 900p. 1996. pap. write for info. (*0-7803-3700-X*, 96TH8242); fiche. write for info. (*0-7803-3701-8*, 96TH8242) Inst Electrical.

1996 Multistate Corporate Tax Guide Mid-Year Supplement. Raabe. 1996. 106.00 (*1-56706-311-X*) Panel Pubs.

1996 Music Yearbook. Joel Whitburn. 264p. 1997. pap. 34.95 (*0-89820-120-9*) Record Research.

1996 National Directory of Law Enforcement Administrators, Correctional Institutions & Related Agencies. 732p. 1996. 80.00 (*1-880245-13-2*) SPAN Pub.

1996 National Directory of Fire Chiefs & Emergency Departments, Vol. V. Tr. by Laura J. Gross. 1115p. 1996. 59.00 (*1-880245-11-6*) SPAN Pub.

1996 National Electrical Code Interpretive Diagrams. BNI Building News Staff. 270p. 1996. pap. text 34.95 (*1-55701-147-8*) BNI Pubns.

1996 National Emergency Department Annual Survey Report Summary. unabridged ed. Contrib. by Susan L. MacLean et al. 78p. 1997. pap. 30.00 (*0-935890-16-5*) Emerg Nurses IL.

1996 National Emergency Department Database Survey. unabridged ed. Contrib. by Susan L. MacLean et al. 311p. 1997. pap. 500.00 (*0-935890-17-3*) Emerg Nurses IL.

1996 National Radio Science Conference. IEEE (Electron Devices Society) Staff. Ed. by IEEE (Institute of Electrical & Electronics Engine. 700p. 1996. pap. 146.00 (*0-7803-3656-9*, 96TH8228); mic. film. write for info. (*0-7803-3635-6*, 96TM8228) Inst Electrical.

1996 National Trade Estimate Report on Foreign Trade Barriers. 267p. (Orig.). 1995. pap. text 50.00 (*0-7881-2904-X*) DIANE Pub.

1996 New Hampshire Law Directory & Daybook Including Bar Directory of New Hampshire. rev. ed. Skinder-Strauss Staff. 673p. 1995. 35.00 (*1-57741-009-2*) Skinder-Strauss.

1996 New York Lawyers Diary & Manual Including Bar Directory of the State of New York. rev. ed. Skinder-Strauss Staff. 1489p. 1995. 55.00 (*1-57741-008-4*); pap. 55.00 (*1-57741-007-6*) Skinder-Strauss.

1996 New York Lawyers Diary & Manual Including Bar Directory of the State of New York. rev. ed. Skinder-Strauss Staff. 1996. cd-rom 55.00 (*1-57741-013-0*) Skinder-Strauss.

1996-1997 World Trade Almanac: Economic, Marketing, Trade, Cultural, Legal, & Travel Surveys for the World's Top 100 Economies. Molly Thurmond et al. (Illus.). 842p. 1996. 87.00 (*1-885073-07-0*) Wrld Trade Pr.

1996 Nineteenth Convention of Electrical & Electronics Engineers in Israel. IEEE, Israel Section Staff. LC 96-76156. 600p. 1996. pap. write for info. (*0-7803-3330-6*, 96TH8190); fiche. write for info. (*0-7803-3331-4*, 96TH8190) Inst Electrical.

1996-97 Almanac of Hospital Financial & Operating Indicators. William O. Cleverley. (Illus.). 520p. 1996. pap. 350.00 (*1-882733-07-X*) Ctr Hlthcare IPS.

1996-97 Audiobook Reference Guide. 76p. (Orig.). 1996. pap. 20.00 (*0-9645649-1-2*) AudioFile.

1996-97 Hospice Salary & Benefits Report. 5th ed. 260p. 1996. pap. 195.00 (*0-939326-99-X*) Hosp & Hlthcare.

1996-97 Procedures Resource Book: A Guide to Inpatient Surgical Procedures. Susan E. White. (Illus.). 1996. pap. 295.00 (*1-882733-08-8*) Ctr Hlthcare IPS.

1996 9th International Symposium on Electrets. IEEE Staff. LC 95-77005. 1996. pap. text 158.00 (*0-7803-2695-4*, 96CH35808); lib. bdg. 158.00 (*0-7803-2696-2*, 96CB35808); mic. film 158.00 (*0-7803-2697-0*, 96CM35808) Inst Electrical.

1996 North American Emergency Response Guidebook. 354p. 1996. spiral bd. 8.75 (*1-877798-63-0*, 103ORS-6) J J Keller.

1996 North American Emergency Response Guidebook: A Guidebook for First Responders During the Initial Phase of a Hazardous Materials/Dangerous Goods Incident. 2nd ed. Ed. by Transport Canada-Transport Dangerous Goods Directo. 353p. 1996. pap. 12.95 (*0-660-16531-7*, Pub. by Canadian Govt Pub) Accents Pubns.

1996 Oceans. IEEE (Oceanic Engineering Society) Staff. Ed. by IEEE (Institute of Electrical & Electronics Engine. LC 96-77050. 2400p. 1996. lib. bdg. write for info. (*0-7803-3520-1*, 96CH35967); mic. film. write for info. (*0-7803-3521-X*, 96CH35967) Inst Electrical.

1996 Officer Compensation Report: The Executive Compensation Survey for Small to Medium-Sized Businesses. annuals Ed. by Mark Meltzer et al. 208p. 1995. pap. 395.00 (*1-56706-114-1*) Panel Pubs.

1996 Official Travel Industry Directory: The Sourcebook for Travel Professionals. 528p. 1996. spiral bd. write for info. (*0-9644529-1-X*) Universal Media.

1996 Olympic Games Cookbook: From Athens to Atlanta. Ed. by Bob Reardon et al. (Illus.). 24p. (Orig.). 1995. pap. 6.95 (*1-880970-19-8*) Aerial Photo.

1996 Olympic Arts Festival. Favorite Recipes Press Staff. LC 96-84330. 1996. pap. text 16.00 (*0-87197-446-0*) Favorite Recipes.

N

An Asterisk (*) at the beginning of an entry indicates that the title is appearing for the first time.

1996 Optical Fiber Communication Conference. IEEE (Lasers & Electro-Optics Society) Staff. Ed. by IEEE (Institute of Electrical & Electronics Engine. LC 95-72742. 328p. 1996. pap. 110.00 (*1-55752-422-X*, 96CH35901); lib. bdg. 110.00 (*0-7803-3188-5*, 96CB35901); fiche 110.00 (*0-7803-3189-3*, 96CM35901) Inst Electrical.

1996 PACE Conference & Workshop Proceedings. 40.00 (*0-87942-310-2*, UH29650010) Inst Electrical.

1996 PATA Annual Statistical Report. Ed. by Gil Lindberg. (Illus.). 133p. 1997. pap. 150.00 (*1-882866-11-8*) Pac Asia Trvl.

1996 Physician Salary Survey Report. 384p. (Orig.). 1996. pap. 250.00 (*0-939326-95-7*) Hosp & Hlthcare.

1996 Physicians Fee & Coding Guide. James R. Lyle & Hoyt W. Torras. 1996. pap. 109.95 (*1-879249-14-6*) HlthCare Consult.

1996 Pocket Book of Infectious Disease Therapy. Ed. by John G. Bartlett. (Illus.). 350p. 1997. pap. 14.95 (*0-683-18238-2*) Lppncott W & W.

1996 Portrait: Regional (Northwest) Economic Review & Outlook. 7th ed. (Illus.). 64p. (C). 1996. pap. text 35.00 (*0-7881-3093-5*) DIANE Pub.

1996 Presidential Campaign: A Communication Perspective. Ed. by Robert E. Denton, Jr. LC 97-33709. (Praeger Series in Political Communication). 320p. 1998. 65.00 (*0-275-95681-4*, Auburn Hse); pap. 24.95 (*0-275-96152-4*, Praeger Pubs) Greenwood.

1996 Presidential Elections in the Dominican Republic - El Consejo de Jefes de Gobierno Libremente Electos. LC 97-48931. (ENG & SPA.). 260p. (Orig.). 1998. pap. 10.95 (*1-880134-27-6*) Natl Demo Inst.

1996 Presidential Election in the South: Southern Party Systems in the 1990s. Ed. by Laurence W. Moreland & Robert P. Steed. LC 97-19236. 264p. 1997. 59.95 (*0-275-95951-1*, Praeger Pubs) Greenwood.

1996 Price Guide Annual. Jon R. Warren. 300p. 1995. write for info. (*0-9647033-1-9*) Wizard Pr NY.

1996 PIA Ratios, 16 vols., Set. Incl. Vol. I. Management Guide to PIA Ratios. 155.00 Vol. II. All Printers by Sales Volume & Geographic Areas. 155.00 Vol. III. All Printers by Product Specialty. 155.00 Vol. IV. Sheetfed Printers by Size & Geographic Area. 155.00 Vol. V. Web Offset Printers, Heatset. 155.00 Vol. VI. Wed Offset Printers, Non-Heatset. 155.00 Vol. VII. Combination Offset-Sheetfed Web. 155.00 Vol. VIII. Book Manufacturers' Ratios. 155.00 Vol. IX. Printers with Sales over $10,000,000. 155.00 Vol. X. Prepress Specialists' Ratios. 155.00 Vol. XI. Binders' Ratio. 155.00 Vol. XII. Printers with Sales under $1,500,000. 155.00 Vol. XIII. Quick Printers' Ratios. 155.00 Vol. XIV. Business Forms Ratios. 155.00 Vol. XV. Label Printers' Ratios. 1996. 155.00 Vol. XVI. Digital Printers' Ratios. 1996. 155.00 995.00 (*0-318-02606-6*) Print Indus Am.

1996 Private Sector State Labor Laws. Government Affairs Dept. Staff. 64p. Date not set. pap. 25.00 (*0-939900-56-4*) Soc Human Resc Mgmt.

1996 Proceedings Magnesium - A Material Advancing to the 21st Century. M. Avedesian et al. (Illus.). 1996. 80.00 (*0-910233-03-9*) Intl Magnesium.

1996 Proceedings 46th Electronic Components & Technology Conference. IEEE (Components, Packaging & Manufacturing Techno. Ed. by IEEE (Institute of Electrical & Electronics Engine. LC 78-647174. 1346p. 1996. pap. text 190.00 (*0-7803-3286-5*, 96CH35931); lib. bdg. 190.00 (*0-7803-3287-3*, 96CB35931); fiche 190.00 (*0-7803-3288-1*, 96CM35931) Inst Electrical.

1996 Propane Vehicle Challenge. 1997. 31.00 (*1-56091-969-8*, SP-1257) Soc Auto Engineers.

1996 Quantum Electronics & Laser Science Conference. IEEE (Lasers & Electro-Optics Society) Staff. Ed. by IEEE (Institute of Electrical & Electronics Engine. 284p. 1995. lib. bdg. write for info. (*0-7803-3190-7*, 96CH35902); fiche. write for info. (*0-7803-3191-5*, 96CH35902) Inst Electrical.

1996 Quick Reference to ERISA Compliance. annuals Alexander Consulting Group Staff. 512p. 1996. pap. 125.00 (*1-56706-306-3*) Panel Pubs.

1996 Regional Airline Directory. 5th ed. Jennifer O. Newman. 1996. pap., per. 247.00 (*1-881537-35-8*) Phillips Business.

1996 Religious Funding Resource Guide. Ed. by Eileen Paul & Jennifer E. Griffith. 500p. 1996. wbk. ed. 75.00 (*1-883542-05-7*) ResourceWomen.

1996 Remanufacturing Symposium Proceedings: Best in Class Basics. LC 97-147495. 87p. (Orig.). 1996. pap. 25.00 (*1-55822-152-2*) Am Prod & Inventory.

1996 Resident Year Book of Surgery. 5th ed. Edward Copeland. LC 98-4103. (Illus.). 528p. (C). (gr. 13). 1998. text 67.00 (*0-8151-2952-1*, 31833) Mosby Inc.

1996 Retail Tenant Directory. rev. ed. Ed. by Adrienne Toth et al. 1996. pap. 325.00 (*0-911790-34-9*) Trade Dimensns.

Road Altas 96. annuals Rand McNally Staff. (Illus.). 160p. pap. 13.95 (*0-528-81494-X*) Rand McNally.

1996 Rochester FORTH Conference: Open Systems, June 19-22, 1996, Ryerson Polytechnic University, Toronto, Ontario, Canada. Rochester FORTH Applications Conference et al. LC 97-191662. (Illus.). 1997. write for info. (*0-914593-16-1*) Inst Appl Forth.

1996 Rural Electric Power Conference. IEEE (Industry Applications Society) Staff. Ed. by IEEE (Institute of Electrical & Electronics Engine. LC 83-641006. 160p. 1996. pap. text 94.00 (*0-7803-3047-1*, 96CH35872); lib. bdg. 94.00 (*0-7803-3048-X*, 96CB35872); fiche 94.00 (*0-7803-3049-8*, 96CM35872) Inst Electrical.

1996 Russian Presidential Election. Jerry F. Hough et al. LC 97-60677. (Occasional Papers). 120p. 1996. pap. 12.95 (*0-8157-3751-3*) Brookings.

1996 Satellite Industry Directory: Formerly the World Satellite Directory. 18th ed. Ed. by Jennifer O. Newman. 1996. pap., per. 257.00 (*1-881537-37-4*) Phillips Business.

1996 2nd High Frequency Postgraduate Student Colloquium. IEEE (Electron Devices Society) Staff. Ed. by IEEE (Institute of Electrical & Electronics Engine. LC 95-82152. 120p. 1996. pap. 88.00 (*0-7803-3151-6*, 96TH8158); fiche 88.00 (*0-7803-3152-4*, 96TM8158) Inst Electrical.

1996 2nd International Conference on Asic Proceedings. IEEE (Circuits & Systems Society) Staff. Ed. by IEEE (Institute of Electrical & Electronics Engine. 600p. 1996. pap. write for info. (*7-5439-0940-5*, 96TH8140); fiche 126.00 (*0-7803-3058-7*, 96TM8140) Inst Electrical.

1996 Selected Standards on Professional Responsibility Including California Rules. Thomas D. Morgan. Ed. by Ronald D. Rotunda. 623p. 1995. 17.95 (*1-56662-336-7*) West Pub.

1996 7th Biennial IEEE Conference on Electromagnetic Field Computation. IEEE (Magnetics Society) Staff. Ed. by IEEE (Institute of Electrical & Electronics Engine. LC 95-82219. 1000p. 1996. pap. 158.00 (*0-7803-3155-9*, 96TH8160); fiche 158.00 (*0-7803-3156-7*, 96TH8160) Inst Electrical.

1996 7th International Symposium on Micro Machine & Human Science Proceedings. IEEE Reliability Society & Industrial Electronics. Ed. by IEEE Staff. LC 96-77510. 250p. 1996. pap. write for info. (*0-7803-3596-1*, 96TH8213); fiche. write for info. (*0-7803-3597-X*, 96TH8213) Inst Electrical.

1996 SHRM Innovative Benefits Survey. 32p. Date not set. pap. 30.00 (*0-939900-47-5*) Soc Human Resc Mgmt.

1996 SHRM Layoffs & Job Security Survey. Date not set. pap. 40.00 (*0-939900-49-1*) Soc Human Resc Mgmt.

1996 SHRM Workplace Violence Survey. Date not set. pap. 70.00 (*0-939900-48-3*) Soc Human Resc Mgmt.

1996 Solar Engineering. LC 96-217771. (ICONE 4 - Technical Papers). 544p. 1996. 130.00 (*0-7918-1765-2*, H01046) ASME.

1996 South Carolina Guide: Complete Media Information, Vol. 7. Ed. by Susan S. Hendricks. 124p. 1996. pap. text 40.00 (*1-886629-02-1*); disk 40.00 (*1-886629-03-X*) Hendricks & Co.

1996 Southwest Symposium on Image Analysis & Interpretation Proceedings. IEEE, Signal Processing Society Staff. Ed. by IEEE, Institute of Electrical & Electronics Engine. LC 96-75353. 300p. 1996. pap. 102.00 (*0-7803-3200-8*, 96TH8166); fiche 102.00 (*0-7803-3201-6*, 96TM8166) Inst Electrical.

1996 Starcycles Calendar Appointment Book. Georgia Stathis. Ed. & Illus. by Kathleen M. Savage. (Starcycles Appointment Bks.). 110p. (Orig.). 1995. pap. text 14.95 (*1-881229-15-7*) Starcycles.

1996 State by State Guide to Human Resources Law. annuals Ronald M. Green et al. Ed. by John F. Buckley, IV. 792p. 1996. pap. 164.00 (*1-56706-124-9*, S91) Panel Pubs.

1996 State Legislative Summary: Children, Youth & Family Issues. 1997. pap. 25.00 (*1-55516-605-9*, 6136) Natl Conf State Legis.

1996 Successful Strategies for Internet Marketing: An Executive Report. (Illus.). 100p. 1996. ring bd. 175.00 (*0-945052-28-6*) Computer Econ.

1996 Summary of Mineral Activity in Utah. Roger L. Bon et al. LC 97-199806. (Circular of the Utah Geological Survey Ser.: Vol. 98). (Illus.). 12p. 1997. pap. 3.40 (*1-55791-610-1*, C-98) Utah Geological Survey.

1996 Summer Library Program Manual - "Razzle Dazzle Read" Jane A. Roeber. 200p. (C). 1996. pap. text 18.00 (*1-57337-027-4*) WI Dept Pub Instruct.

1996 Supplement to Connecticut Jury Instructions (Civil) 4th ed. Douglass B. Wright & William L. Ankerman. 152p. 1996. pap. 50.00 (*1-878698-39-7*) Atlantic Law.

1996 Supplement to American Criminal Procedure, Cases & Commentary. 7th ed. Stephen A. Saltzburg & Daniel J. Capra. (American Casebook Ser.). 153p. (C). 1996. pap. text, suppl. ed. write for info. (*0-314-09928-X*) West Pub.

1996 Supplement to Cases & Materials on Constitutional Law, Themes for the Constitution's Third Century. Daniel A. Farber et al. (American Casebook Ser.). 250p. (C). 1996. pap. text, suppl. ed. write for info. (*0-314-09912-3*) West Pub.

1996 Supplement to Cases & Materials on Fundamentals of Corporate Taxation. 3rd ed. Stephen A. Lind et al. (University Casebook Ser.). 71p. 1996. pap. text, suppl. ed. write for info. (*1-56662-385-5*) Foundation Pr.

1996 Supplement to Cases & Materials on Corporate Finance. 4th ed. Victor Brudney & William W. Bratton. (University Casebook Ser.). 227p. 1996. pap. text, suppl. ed. write for info. (*1-56662-433-9*) Foundation Pr.

1996 Supplement to Cases & Materials on Fundamentals of Partnership Taxation. 4th ed. Stephen A. Lind et al. (University Casebook Ser.). 33p. 1996. pap. text. write for info. (*1-56662-410-X*) Foundation Pr.

1996 Supplement to Civil Rights Actions: Section 1983 & Related Statutes. 2nd ed. Peter W. Low & John C. Jeffries, Jr. (University Casebook Ser.). 90p. 1996. pap. text, suppl. ed. write for info. (*1-56662-386-3*) Foundation Pr.

1996 Supplement to Connecticut Law of Uninsured & Underinsured Motorist Coverage. Jon Berk & Michael C. Jainchill. 249p. 1996. pap. 62.00 (*1-878698-37-0*) Atlantic Law.

1996 Supplement to Connecticut Law of Torts. Douglass B. Wright et al. 126p. 1996. pap. 55.00 (*1-878698-35-4*) Atlantic Law.

1996 Supplement to Constitutional Law, Twelfth Edition & Individual Rights in Constitutional Law, Fifth Edition. Frederick F. Schauer. (University Casebook Ser.). 513p. 1996. pap. text, suppl. ed. write for info. (*1-56662-380-4*) Foundation Pr.

1996 Supplement to Constitutional Law, Civil Liberty & Individual Rights. 3rd ed. William Cohen. 179p. 1996. pap. text, suppl. ed. write for info. (*1-56662-372-3*) Foundation Pr.

1996 Supplement to Constitutional Law, the American Constitution, Constitutional Rights & Liberties, Cases, Comments, Questions. 8th ed. Yale Kamisar et al. (American Casebook Ser.). 100p. (C). 1996. pap. text, suppl. ed. write for info. (*0-314-09927-1*) West Pub.

1996 Supplement to Constitutional Law, Cases & Materials. 9th ed. Jonathan D. Varat & William Cohen. (University Casebook Ser.). 412p. 1996. pap. text, suppl. ed. write for info. (*1-56662-373-1*) Foundation Pr.

1996 Supplement to Criminal Procedure, an Analysis of Cases & Concepts. 3rd ed. Charles H. Whitebread & Christopher Slobogin. (University Textbook Ser.). 70p. 1996. pap. text, suppl. ed. write for info. (*1-56662-415-0*) Foundation Pr.

1996 Supplement to Criminal Process, Cases, Comment, Questions. 5th ed. Lloyd L. Weinreb. (University Casebook Ser.). 115p. 1996. pap. text, suppl. ed. write for info. (*1-56662-397-9*) Foundation Pr.

1996 Supplement to Federal Courts, Federalism & Separation of Powers, Cases & Materials. Donald L. Doernberg & C. Keith Wingate. (American Casebook Ser.). 166p. 1996. pap. text, suppl. ed. write for info. (*0-314-20054-1*) West Pub.

1996 Supplement to Federal Courts & the Law of Federal-State Relations. 3rd ed. Peter W. Low & John C. Jeffries, Jr. (University Casebook Ser.). 125p. 1996. pap. text, suppl. ed. write for info. (*1-56662-388-X*) Foundation Pr.

1996 Supplement to Local Government Law. 2nd ed. Gerald E. Frug. (American Casebook Ser.). 85p. 1996. pap. text, suppl. ed. write for info. (*0-314-20593-4*) West Pub.

1996 Supplement to Securities Regulation. 3rd ed. Larry D. Soderquist. (University Casebook Ser.). 99p. 1996. pap. text, suppl. ed. write for info. (*1-56662-395-2*) Foundation Pr.

1996 Supplement to the Environmental, Health & Safety Auditing Handbook. Lee Harrison. LC 96-47393. 121p. 1997. pap. 39.95 (*0-07-026921-1*) McGraw.

1996 Supplement to the Federal Courts & the Federal System. 4th ed. Richard H. Fallon, Jr. et al. (University Casebook Ser.). 80p. 1996. pap. text, suppl. ed. write for info. (*1-56662-408-8*) Foundation Pr.

1996 Supplement to the IPC & IPSDC. ICBO Staff et al. (Illus.). 17p. 1996. pap. text 50.00 (*1-892395-00-2*) Intl Code Coun.

1996 Supplement to the Wisconsin Directory of International Institutions. Karen L. Niesen & Christine Y. Onaga. 64p. 1996. pap. 12.95 (*0-299-15054-2*) U of Wis Pr.

1996 Supplement to the 1995 Editions of the Automotive, Burglary Protection, Mechanical Equipment, Gas & Oil Equipment, & Marine Products Directories. (C). 1996. pap. text 9.00 (*1-55989-970-0*) Underwrtrs Labs.

1996 Supplement to the 1996 Editions of the Building Materials Directory, Fire Protection Equipment Directory, Roofing Materials & Systems, & Fire Resistance Directory. (C). 1996. pap. text 15.50 (*1-55989-971-9*) Underwrtrs Labs.

1996 Supplement to the 1996 Editions of the Electrical Appliance & Utilization Equipment Directory, the Electrical Construction Materials Directory, & the Hazardous Locations Equipment Directory. (C). 1996. pap. text 15.00 (*1-55989-973-5*) Underwrtrs Labs.

1996 Survey Reports on Bank Retail Investment Services. American Brokerage Consultants Staff. (1996 Bank Representative Compensaion Survey Ser.: Vol. 2). Date not set. write for info. (*0-89982-021-2*) Am Bankers.

1996 Survey Reports on Bank Retail Investment Services. American Brokerage Consultants Staff. (1996 Banker's Report Card on Ihino-Party Marketing Companies Ser.: Vol. 3). Date not set. write for info. (*0-89982-022-0*) Am Bankers.

1996 Survey Reports on Bank Retail Investment Services. American Brokerage Consultants Staff. (1996 Bankers' Report Card on Mutual Fund Companies Ser.: Vol. 4). Date not set. write for info. (*0-89982-023-9*) Am Bankers.

1996 Survey Reports on Bank Retail Investment Services. American Brokerage Consultants Staff. (Nineteen Ninety-Six Bankers' Report Card on Proprietary Mutual Funds Ser.: Vol. 7). 1975. 17.50 (*0-89982-051-4*) Am Bankers.

1996 Survey Reports on Bank Retail Investment Services. American Brokerage Consultants Staff. (Nineteen Ninety-Six Bankers' Report Card on Variable Annuity Vendors Ser.: Vol. 6). 1976. 17.50 (*0-89982-050-6*) Am Bankers.

1996 Survey Reports on Bank Retail Investment Services. American Brokerage Consultants Staff. (Nineteen Ninety-Six Bankers' Report Card on Fixed Annuity Vendors Ser.: Vol. 5). 1978. 30.00 (*0-89982-024-7*) Am Bankers.

1996 Survey Reports on Bank Retail Investment Services. American Brokerage Consultants Staff. (1996 National Survey of Bank Retail Investment Services Ser.: Vol. 1). 1997. write for info. (*0-89982-020-4*) Am Bankers.

1996 Symposium on Smart Materials, Structures & MEMS Vol. 3321. Ed. by Vasu K. Aatre et al. LC 98-213336. 878p. 1998. 141.00 (*0-8194-2762-4*) SPIE.

1996 Symposium on VLSI Circuits. IEEE, Solid State Circuits Council Staff. LC 96-76157. 230p. 1996. pap. text 100.00 (*0-7803-3339-X*, 96CH35943); lib. bdg. 100.00 (*0-7803-3340-3*, 96CB35943); fiche 100.00 (*0-7803-3341-1*, 96CM35943) Inst Electrical.

1996 Symposium on VLSI Technology Digest of Technical Papers. IEEE (Electron Devices Society) Staff. Ed. by IEEE (Institute of Electrical & Electronics Engine. LC 90-655131. 264p. 1996. pap. text 102.00 (*0-7803-3342-X*, 96CH35944); lib. bdg. 102.00 (*0-7803-3344-6*, 96CB35944); fiche 102.00 (*0-7803-3343-8*, 96CM35944) Inst Electrical.

1996 Symposium on Volume Visualization. LC 97-104346. 1996. pap. text 30.00 (*0-89791-865-7*, 429965) Assn Compu Machinery.

1996 Tactical Communication Conference. IEEE (Fort Wayne Section) Staff. Ed. by IEEE (Institute of Electrical & Electronics Engine. LC 97-104412. 200p. 1996. pap. write for info. (*0-7803-3658-5*, 96TH8214); fiche. write for info. (*0-7803-3600-3*, 96TH8214) Inst Electrical.

1996 Tangshan, China Earthquake: Papers Presented at the Second U. S. National Conference on Earthquake Engineering & Not Included in the Proceedings. 109p. 1980. pap. 12.00 (*0-685-14407-0*) Earthquake Eng.

1996 Technical Digest of Solid State Sensor & Actuator Workshop, Vol. 1. Transducer Research Foundation Staff. Ed. by Roger T. Howe & David S. Eddy. (Technical Digest of Solid State Sensor & Actuator Workshop Ser.: No. 2). 275p. (Orig.). 1996. pap. 50.00 (*0-9640024-1-8*) Transducer Res.

1996 Telecom Act: An Antitrust Perspective : Hearing Before the Subcommittee on Antitrust, Business Rights, & Competition of the Committee on the Judiciary, United States Senate, One Hundred Fifth Congress, First Session ... September 17, 1997. USGPO Staff. LC 98-161357. iv, 130 p. 1998. write for info. (*0-16-056277-5*) USGPO.

1996 Telephone Industry Directory. 10th ed. Ed. by Jennifer O. Newman. 1996. pap., per. 249.00 (*1-881537-32-3*) Phillips Business.

1996 IEEE Tencon. IEEE (Region 10) Staff. LC 96-78415. 900p. 1996. pap. text. write for info. (*0-7803-3679-8*, 96CH36007); lib. bdg. write for info. (*0-7803-3680-1*, 96CH36007); fiche. write for info. (*0-7803-3681-X*, 96CH36007) Inst Electrical.

1996 The Lab Manual Source Book: The Comprehensive Product & Service Directory for Life Science Researchers. (Illus.). xx, 204p. 1996. pap. 24.95 (*1-890574-01-5*) BioSupplyNet.

1996 the Lawyer's Almanac. annuals 16th ed. Aspen Law & Business Editorial Staff. 1080p. 1996. 136.00 (*0-614-16676-4*) Panel Pubs.

1996 3rd IEEE International Workshop on Community Networking Proceedings. IEEE Staff. LC 96-75875. 146p. 1996. pap. 102.00 (*0-7803-3304-7*); fiche 102.00 (*0-7803-3305-5*) Inst Electrical.

1996 3rd International Conference on Signal Processing Proceedings. IEEE, Signal Processing Society Staff. Ed. by Institute of Electrical & Electronics Engineers, I. LC 95-78307. 1600p. 1996. pap. write for info. (*0-7803-2912-0*, 96TH8116); fiche. write for info. (*0-7803-2913-9*, 96TM8116) Inst Electrical.

1996 31st Intersociety Energy Conversion Engineering Conference. IEEE Electron Devices Society & Aerospace & Electr. Ed. by IEEE Staff. 2600p. 1996. pap. text 400.00 (*0-7803-3547-3*, 96CH35978); lib. bdg. write for info. (*0-7803-3548-1*, 96CH35978); fiche. write for info. (*0-7803-3549-X*, 96CH35978) Inst Electrical.

1996 39th Midwest Symposium on Circuits & Systems. IEEE (Circuits & Systems Society) Staff. Ed. by IEEE (Institute of Electrical & Electronics Engine. LC 79-645128. 1400p. 1996. pap. text. write for info. (*0-7803-3636-4*, 96CH35995); lib. bdg. write for info. (*0-7803-3637-2*, 96CB35995); mic. film. write for info. (*0-7803-3638-0*, 96CM35995) Inst Electrical.

1996 33rd Design Automation Conference. IEEE (Circuits & Systems Society) Staff. Ed. by IEEE (Institute of Electrical & Electronics Engine. LC 85-644924. 870p. 1996. pap. 152.00 (*0-7803-3364-0*, 96CH35932); lib. bdg. 152.00 (*0-7803-3294-6*, 96CB35932); fiche 152.00 (*0-7803-3295-4*, 96CM35932) Inst Electrical.

1996 Title Insurance. Burke. 1996. 75.00 (*0-316-11826-5*, Aspen Law & Bus) Aspen Pub.

1996-1997 Models. Date not set. per. 28.00 (*1-890049-01-8*) R V Consumer Grp.

1996-1997 Irvine Spectrum Business Directory. Ed. & Illus. by Bruce Clumpner. 128p. 1996. spiral bd. 39.95 (*0-9639578-2-1*) Coris Quill.

1996-1997 Medical Student's Guide to Successful Residency Matching. Lee T. Miller & Leigh G. Donowitz. 87p. (Orig.). 1996. pap. 14.95 (*0-683-18043-6*) Lppncott W & W.

1996/1997 Auctioneers Association of Arizona Directory. Ted W. Parod. 1996. pap. 9.95 (*0-9627432-1-6*) Echo Lake Pr.

1996/97 Book of Linear Time Cycles. Frank A. Taucher. 1996. spiral bd. 96.00 (*1-879591-22-7*) Mkt Movements.

1996-97 Compensation Report on Management Employees in Hospital, Nursing Home, & Home Care Management Companies. 13th ed. 200p. (Orig.). 1997. pap. 495.00 (*0-939326-87-6*) Hosp & Hlthcare.

1996-97 Eastern Region Directory of the INS Offices. Ed. by Neil Dornbaum & Jane Goldblum. 174p. 1996. 36.00 (*1-57370-008-8*, 53.26) Amer Immi Law Assn.

1996-97 Guide to Catholic Colleges & Universities: The National Catholic College Admission Association. rev. ed. Ed. by Elizabeth Hunt. (Illus.). 124p. (Orig.). (YA). (gr. 9-12). 1996. pap. 8.95 (*0-9645495-1-4*) R H Bailey.

1996-97 Home Care Salary & Benefits Report. 6th ed. 440p. 1996. pap. 250.00 (0-939326-98-1) Hosp & Hlthcare.

1996-97 Hospital Salary & Benefits Report. 300p. 1996. pap. 250.00 (0-939326-97-3) Hosp & Hlthcare.

1996/97 New York Attorney's/Secretary's Handbook. 4th ed. 675p. 65.00 (1-881131-03-3) Plymouth Pub.

1996-97 Nursing Home Salary & Benefits Report. 288p. (Orig.). 1996. pap. 250.00 (0-939326-96-5) Hosp & Hlthcare.

1996-97 Nursing Department Report. 5th ed. 152p. 1996. pap. 195.00 (0-939326-26-4) Hosp & Hlthcare.

1996/97 Pennsylvania Attorney's/Secretary's Handbook. 5th ed. 774p. 1996. 59.00 (1-881131-02-5) Plymouth Pub.

1996-97 Price Guide for Encyclopedia of Silhouette Collectibles on Glass. Shirley Mace. Ed. by Angela Ekvall. 12p. 1996. 5.00 (0-9633674-0-4) Shadow Enter.

1996-97 Supplement to Health Law, Cases, Materials, & Problems. Barry F. Furrow et al. (American Casebook Ser.). 350p. 1996. pap. text, suppl. ed. write for info. (0-314-20598-5) West Pub.

1996/97 Tennessee Statistical Abstract. Ed. by Betty Vickers & Vickie Cunningham. 1997. pap. text 40.00 (0-940191-22-9) Univ TN Ctr Bus Econ.

***1996 TOH Annual Recipes.** Ed. by Julie Schnittka. (Illus.). 310p. 1999. 29.99 (0-89821-265-0) Reiman Pubns.

1996 Trade Policy Agenda & 1995 Annual Report of the President of the U. S. on the Trade Agreements Program. Michael Kantor. (Illus.). 216p. (Orig.). 1996. pap. text 45.00 (0-7881-2630-X) DIANE Pub.

1996 Trademark Law Handbook, 2 vols. Ed. by Anthony L. Fletcher. Incl. Vol. I: U. S. 1996 Trademark Law Handbook. annuals Ed. by David J. Kera. 268p. 1996. pap. 75.00 Vol. II: International. 1996 Trademark Law Handbook. annuals Ed. by Theodore C. Max. 348p. 1996. pap. 60.00 115.00 (0-939190-19-2) Intl Trademark.

1996 Trademark Law Handbook see 1996 Trademark Law Handbook

1996 Treasure Coast Magazine: The Best of South Florida from North Palm Beach to Vero Beach. (Illus.). 112p. 1996. 5.95 (1-883117-06-2) Mohr Graphics.

1996 Twelfth Annual IEEE Semiconductor Thermal Measurement & Management Symposium. IEEE, Components, Hybrids & Manufacturing Technolo. 200p. 1996. pap. text. write for info. (0-7803-3139-7, 96CH35890); lib. bdg. write for info. (0-7803-3140-0, 96CH35890) Inst Electrical.

1996 Twenty-Fifth IEEE Photovoltaic Specialists Conference. IEEE, Electron Devices Society Staff. Ed. by Institute of Electrical & Electronics Engineers, I. LC 84-640812. 1996. pap. text. write for info. (0-7803-3166-4); lib. bdg. write for info. (0-7803-3167-2, 96CH35897); fiche. write for info. (0-7803-3168-0) Inst Electrical.

1996 Twenty-Second International Power Modulator Symposium Conference Record. IEEE (Electron Devices Society) Staff. Ed. by IEEE (Institute of Electrical & Electronics Engine. 1996. 110.00 incl. fiche (0-7803-3078-1, 96CM35877); pap. text 110.00 (0-7803-3076-5, 96CH35877); lib. bdg. 110.00 (0-7803-3077-3, 96CB35877) Inst Electrical.

1996 U. S. - BNA Postage Stamp Catalog. rev. ed. (Illus.). 464p. 1995. pap. 9.95 (0-937458-60-0) Harris & Co.

1996 U. S. Hispanic Market. Strategy Research Corporation Staff. 374p. 1995. pap. write for info. (1-888520-03-5) Strategy Research.

1996 United States Model Income Tax Convention: Analysis, Commentary & Comparison. Richard L. Doernberg & C. Van Raad. LC 97-5160. 1997. 85.00 (90-411-0998-6) Kluwer Law Intl.

1996 Update to Cataloging of Audiovisual Materials. 28p. 1996. pap. 6.00 (0-936996-73-0) Soldier Creek.

1996 Update to Cataloging Motion Pictures & Videorecordings. Nancy B. Olson. (Minnesota AACR Two Trainers Ser.). 24p. 1996. 4.00 (0-936996-71-4) Soldier Creek.

1996 Update to Cataloging Computer Files. Nancy B. Olson. (Minnesota AACR Two Trainers Ser.). 26p. 1996. 4.00 (0-936996-72-2) Soldier Creek.

1996 $upertraders Almanac, 2 vols., Set. Frank A. Taucher. 500p. (Orig.). 1996. pap., spiral bd. 110.00 (1-879591-20-0) Mkt Movements.

1996 Vedic Astrological Almanac. P. U. Warriar et al. 55p. (Orig.). 1995. pap. text 14.00 (0-9618070-9-1) Personal Insight.

1996 Viewers Guide to the PGA Tour. Whitney McClelland. (Illus.). 240p. 1995. pap. 24.95 (0-9631259-4-X) Golfguide.

1996 Virginia Lawyers Diary & Manual Including Bar Directory of Virginia. rev. ed. Skinder-Strauss Staff. 1039p. 1995. 45.00 (1-57741-011-4); pap. 20.00 (1-57741-012-2) Skinder-Strauss.

1996 VLSI Signal Processing. IEEE, Signal Processing Society Staff. Ed. by Institute of Electrical & Electronics Engineers, I. LC 95-82116. 1996. fiche. write for info. (0-7803-3135-4) Inst Electrical.

1996 VLSI Signal Processing, Vol. IX. IEEE, Signal Processing Society Staff. Ed. by Institute of Electrical & Electronics Engineers, I. LC 95-82116. 525p. 1996. pap. write for info. (0-7803-3134-6, 96TH8156) Inst Electrical.

1996 Waggish Chronicles: Proposterous Items of Curiosity. annuals Larry W. Smith. 50p. 1996. pap. 9.95 (1-57914-003-3) Campbell-Smith.

1996 Who's Who in Christian Hip-Hop Artist Directory. Lady J. Ed. by Fred D. Lynch et al. (Illus.). 74p. (Orig.). 1996. pap., spiral bd. 17.95 (1-889133-01-9) Rising Son Media.

1996 Who's Who in Electronic Commerce. 8th ed. Jennifer O. Newman. 1996. pap., per. 199.00 (1-881537-42-0) Phillips Business.

1996 Winter Simulation Conference Proceedings. IEEE, Computer Society, Systems, Man & Cybernetics. Ed. by Institute of Electrical & Electronics Engineers, I. LC 87-654182. 1600p. 1996. lib. bdg. write for info. (0-7803-3383-7, 96CB35957); fiche. write for info. (0-7803-3384-5, 9CB35957) Inst Electrical.

1996 Wireless Industry Directory. 7th ed. Ed. by Jennifer O. Newman. 1996. pap., per. 249.00 (1-881537-38-2) Phillips Business.

1996 Workshop on Cleanroom Software Engineering. 200p. 1996. pap. 40.00 (0-8186-7671-X, PR7671) IEEE Comp Soc.

1996 World Satellite Almanac: Incorporating the Satellite Systems Handbook. 8th ed. Ed. by Jennifer O. Newman. 1996. pap., per. 249.00 (1-881537-39-0) Phillips Business.

1996 XVIIth International Symposium on Discharges & Electrical Insulation in Vacuum. IEEE Dielectrics & Electrical Insulation Society S. Ed. by Institute of Electrical & Electronics Engineers, I. LC 95-78306. 1996. pap. text 134.00 (0-7803-2906-6, 96CH35839); lib. bdg. 134.00 (0-7803-2907-4, 96CB35839); fiche 134.00 (0-7803-2908-2, 96CM35839) Inst Electrical.

1996 Year in Review - U. S. Seafood Trade Report. 2nd ed. Ed. by James L. Anderson & Barbara S. Gardiner. (Illus.). v, 400p. 1997. pap. 29.95 (0-9673524-1-X) J L Anderson Assoc.

1996 New Zealand Petroleum Conference Proceedings: Confronting the Issues 1996, an International Perspective. New Zealand Petroleum Conference Staff & New Zealand Dept. of Scientific & Industrial Research. LC 98-210114. 1996. write for info. (0-478-00312-9) Manaaki Whenua.

1996 3rd IEEE International Conference on Electronics, Circuits & Systems. IEEE (Circuits & Systems Society) Staff. Ed. by IEEE (Institute of Electrical & Electronics Engine. LC 97-152822. 1400p. 1996. pap. write for info. (0-7803-3650-X, 96TH8229); mic. film. write for info. (0-7803-3651-8, 96TM8229) Inst Electrical.

1996 50-Day Spiritual Adventure: Grades 1-6 Leader's Guide. Scottie May et al. Ed. by Charlene Hiebert. (Illus.). 128p. (Orig.). 1995. pap., wbk. ed. 20.00 (1-879050-76-5) Chapel of Air.

1996 50-Day Spiritual Adventure: Grades 1-6 Leader's Guide & Sing-Along Tape. Paula Bussard et al. (Illus.). 128p. (Orig.). (J). (gr. k-2). 1995. pap. 30.00 incl. audio (1-879050-93-5) Chapel of Air.

1996/97 America's Best Meal Deals. Zagat Publishers Staff. 236p. 1996. pap. text 12.95 (1-57006-028-2) Zagat.

1996/97 World Satellite Yearly. Frank Baylin. (Illus.). 1996. 90.00 (0-917893-26-3) Baylin Pubns.

1990 Supplement to the German Commercial Code As Amended to Jan. 1, 1989. Tr. by Simon L. Goren. iii, 65p. 1992. pap. 18.50 (0-8377-0624-6, Rothman) W S Hein.

1993 Tax: Chapter One. Crimm. 1993. 20.00 (0-316-16113-6, Aspen Law & Bus) Aspen Pub.

1993: Dynamics of Language Learning. Aausc. (Teaching Methods Ser.). 1994. pap. 19.95 (0-8384-5456-9) Heinle & Heinle.

1993-94 Household Expenditure Survey, Australia. W. McLennan & Australian Bureau of Statistics Staff. LC 97-161157. 1996. write for info. (0-642-20707-0) Aust Inst Criminology.

1993 ACL Proceedings. pap. 60.00 (1-55860-966-0) Morgan Kaufmann.

1993 Almanac of Hospital Financial & Operating Indicators. William O. Cleverley. 520p. 1993. pap. 350.00 (1-882733-01-0) Ctr Hlthcare IPS.

1993 Annual Convention (New Orleans) Vol. 3: ASPRS. ACSM Staff & ASPRS Staff. 458p. 1993. 30.00 (0-614-06105-9, T724) Am Congrs Survey.

1993 Annual Survey of Letter of Credit Law & Practice: Survey Handbook. Ed. by James E. Byrne et al. 439p. 1993. pap. 99.00 (1-888870-01-X) Inst Intl Bnking.

1993 Baseball Sabermetric. Brock Hanke. 1993. pap. 15.95 (0-9625846-1-4) Mad Aztec Pr.

1993 Bioengineering Conference. Ed. by N. A. Langrana et al. LC 93-71951. (BED Ser.: Vol. 24). 677p. 1993. 70.00 (0-7918-0682-0) ASME.

1993 Case Supplement to Corporations. Cary & Eisenberg. 1988. write for info. (0-318-72442-1) Foundation Pr.

***1993 Coach of the Year Clinics Football Manual.** Ed. by Earl Browning. (Illus.). 280p. 1999. pap. 22.95 (1-57167-396-2) Coaches Choice.

1993 DARPA Message Understanding Proceedings. (C). 1993. pap. text 40.00 (1-55860-336-0) Morgan Kaufmann.

1993 Domestic Engine Control. Target Training Systems, Inc. Staff. (Illus.). 600p. 1995. 120.00 (1-887023-13-5) Target Trning.

1993 Elections in Senegal. National Democratic Institute for International Af. LC 94-38717. (ENG & FRE.). 250p. pap. 10.95 (1-880134-21-7) Natl Demo Inst.

1993 European ACL Proceedings. pap. 60.00 (1-55860-979-2) Morgan Kaufmann.

1993 Evaluation Results. 200p. 1995. pap. 22.00 (0-8213-3214-7, 13214) World Bank.

1993 Extended Abstracts: Fall - New Orleans, Louisiana. 963p. 1993. 72.00 (1-56677-032-7) Electrochem Soc.

1993 Extended Abstracts: Spring - Honolulu, Hawaii. 3018p. 1993. 84.00 (1-56677-031-9) Electrochem Soc.

1993 Graphics Interface Proceedings. pap. 40.00 (1-55860-994-6) Morgan Kaufmann.

1993 Hospice Personnel Compensation Study. National Hospice Organization Staff. 21p. 1993. 105.00 (0-931207-13-4) Natl Hospice.

1993 IEEE International Carnahan Conference on Security Technology. IEEE (Aerospace & Electronic Systems Society) Staf. LC 79-644630. 272p. 1993. lib. bdg. write for info. (0-7803-1480-8, 93CH3372-0) Inst Electrical.

IEEE International Carnahan Conference on Security Technology. IEEE (Aerospace & Electronic Systems Society) Staf. LC 79-644630. 272p. 1993. pap. text. write for info. (0-7803-1479-4, 93CH3372-0); fiche. write for info. (0-7803-1481-6, 93CM3372-0) Inst Electrical.

1993 International Emergency Management & Engineering Conference: Tenth Anniversary, Research & Applications. Ed. by James D. Sullivan. 275p. 1993. pap. 80.00 (1-56555-051-X, SMC-93-1) Soc Computer Sim.

1993 International Registry of Certified Corporate Wildlife Habitats. Christel M. Cothran. 102p. 1993. write for info. (0-9646852-4-8) Wildlife Habitat.

1993 Lectures & Memoirs, Vol. 84. British Academy Staff. (Proceedings of the British Academy Ser.: Vol. LXXXIV). (Illus.). 604p. 1995. text 95.00 (0-19-726149-3) OUP.

1993 Lectures in Complex Systems. Lynn Nadel & Daniel L. Stein. 639p. (C). 1995. 61.00 (0-201-48368-8) Addison-Wesley.

1993 Local Telecommunications Competition. 200p. 1993. 2995.00 (0-614-18352-9, IGIC-97) Info Gatekeepers.

1993 Machine Learning Proceedings. pap. 53.00 (1-55860-307-7) Morgan Kaufmann.

1993 Manual for Faith Development Research. 2nd rev. ed. Romney M. Moseley et al. Ed. by Karen B. De Nicola. 126p. (C). 1993. ring bd. 30.00 (0-9621113-2-5) Emory U Ctr Faith.

1993 Mariner's Book of Days: A Calendar & Compendium. Peter H. Spectre. 1992. pap. text 12.95 (0-07-060021-X) McGraw.

1993 Mid-Year Seminar Papers: A Collection of Available Papers from Taipei. 195p. 1993. pap. 45.00 (0-614-31032-6) Pac Telecom.

1993 Music Yearbook. Joel Whitburn. 240p. (Orig.). 1994. pap. 29.95 (0-89820-102-0, YB1993) Record Research.

1993 National Directory of Fire Chiefs & Emergency Departments, Vol. II. Span Publishing, Inc., Staff. Ed. by Steve Cywinski. 1993. 40.00 (1-880245-04-3) SPAN Pub.

1993-1994 North American Horsemen's Association Safety (Risk Reduction) Linda Liestman. (NAHA Risk Reduction Ser.). 96p. 1993. pap. text 30.00 (1-887811-06-0) N Amer Horsemens.

1993 Report on Unfair Trade Policies by Major Trading Partners. 185p. 1993. pap. 38.00 (4-8224-0618-0) Intl Pubns Serv.

1993 Statutory Supplement to Labor Law. Cox et al. 1993. pap. text 10.25 (1-56662-056-2) Foundation Pr.

1993 Supplement to Health Care Law & Policy. Havighurst. 1988. write for info. (0-318-72444-8) Foundation Pr.

1993 Symposium on VLSI Technology. IEEE (Electron Devices Society) Staff. Ed. by IEEE Staff. LC 90-655131. 130p. 1993. pap. text. write for info. (0-7803-1272-4); lib. bdg. write for info. (0-7803-1273-2, 93CH3303-5); fiche. write for info. (0-7803-1274-0) Inst Electrical.

1993 Tax: Chapter 2. Crimm. 1993. 30.00 (0-316-16116-0, Aspen Law & Bus) Aspen Pub.

1993 Tax Act, National Association of Manufacturers Edition: How the New Legislation Can Pay Off for You. Peter M. Berkery, Jr. 1993. text 10.95 (0-7863-0289-5, Irwn Prfssnl) McGraw-Hill Prof.

1993, the European Market: Myth or Reality? Ed. by Dennis Campbell & Charles Flint. LC 94-4588. 1994. 107.00 (90-6544-822-5) Kluwer Law Intl.

1993-1994 Debate on Health Care: Did the Polls Mislead the Policy Makers? Bowman. 50p. (Orig.). 1995. pap. 9.95 (0-8447-7031-0) Am Enterprise.

1993 Trail on the Curse of Ham. Wayne Perryman. 1995. pap. 6.99 (1-56229-423-7) Pneuma Life Pub.

1993 Video Yearbook. Joel Whitburn. 104p. (Orig.). 1994. pap. 19.95 (0-89820-103-9) Record Research.

1993 Viewer's Guide to Professional Golf. Whitney McClelland. 1992. pap. 24.95 (0-9631259-1-5) Golfguide.

Statistical Abstract of the United States, 1992, the National Data Book. 999p. 1992. pap. text 44.00 (0-16-060935-6) USGPO.

1992: Europe & North America - The Dialogue of the New Solidarities (Strasbourg, 19-20 June, 1992) 1993. 21.00 (92-871-2221-0, Pub. by Council of Europe) Manhattan Pub Co.

1992: The External Dimension. David Henderson. (Occasional Paper Ser.: No. 25). 23p. 1989. 10.00 (1-56708-024-3) Grp of Thirty.

1992: The Security Implications. K. G. Robertson. (C). 1990. 35.00 (0-907967-11-6, Pub. by Inst Euro Def & Strat) St Mut.

1992-93 Hospital Inpatient Charges - U. S. 1993. write for info. (1-880678-32-2) HCIA.

1992-93 Hospital Admission Rates - U. S. 1993. write for info. (1-880678-33-0) HCIA.

1992-93 LOS by Dx & Op - United States. 1992. write for info. (1-880678-15-2) HCIA.

1992-93 LOS by Dx & Op - North Carolina. 1992. write for info. (1-880678-16-0) HCIA.

1992-93 LOS by Dx & Op - Northeastern. 1992. write for info. (1-880678-17-9) HCIA.

1992-93 LOS by Dx & Op - Southern. 1992. write for info. (1-880678-18-7) HCIA.

1992-93 LOS by Dx & Op - Western. 1992. write for info. (1-880678-19-5) HCIA.

1992-93 LOS by Dx & Op - Pediatric. 1992. write for info. (1-880678-20-9) HCIA.

1992-93 LOS by Dx & Op - Geriatric. 1992. write for info. (1-880678-21-7) HCIA.

1992-93 LOS by DRG & Payment Source - United States. 1992. write for info. (1-880678-22-5) HCIA.

1992-93 Psychiatric LOS - United States. 1992. write for info. (1-880678-27-6) HCIA.

1992 ACL Proceedings. pap. 60.00 (1-55860-967-9) Morgan Kaufmann.

1992 & After. David S. Bell & John Gaffney. Ed. by Edgard Pisani. (Journal of Contemporary European Affairs Ser.: No. 1). 330p. 1989. pap. 25.20 (0-08-037391-7, Pergamon Pr) Elsevier.

1992 Applied Natural Language Processing Proceedings. pap. 60.00 (1-55860-987-3) Morgan Kaufmann.

1992 Baseball Sabermetric. Brock Hanke. 320p. 1992. text. write for info. (0-697-16612-0) Brown & Benchmark.

1992 Bold Shift Program: Survey Instruments. Jennifer Hawes-Dawson et al. LC 94-32573. 1994. pap. text 9.00 (0-8330-1591-5, MR-475-A) Rand Corp.

1992 Challenge from Europe: Development of the European Community's Internal Market. Michael Calingaert. 176p. 1990. pap. text 15.00 (0-89068-096-5, NPA 237) Natl Planning.

***1992 Coach of the Year Clinics Football Manual.** Ed. by Earl Browning. (Illus.). 256p. 2000. pap. 22.95 (1-57167-404-7) Coaches Choice.

1992 Columbus & Franklin County Cancer Incidence: Assessment & Mapping 5 Leading Cancer Sites. Columbus Health Department Staff. (Columbus Community Health Assessment Ser.: Vol. 8). (Illus.). iii, 93p. 1998. pap. write for info. (1-888492-54-6) Columbus Hlth.

Nineteen Ninety-Two Election. Gene Brown. LC 92-19963. (Headliners Ser.). (Illus.). 64p. (J). (gr. 5-8). 1992. pap. 6.95 (1-56294-806-7); lib. bdg. 23.40 (1-56294-080-5) Millbrook Pr.

1992 Federal Tax Course. Prentice-Hall Staff. (C). 1991. 129.00 (0-13-310418-4, Busn) P-H.

1992 Graphics Interface Proceedings. pap. 40.00 (1-55860-995-4) Morgan Kaufmann.

1992 Guide to Defense Cleanup. Ron DiGregorio. Ed. by Doug Rekenthaler, Jr. 245p. 1992. pap. 390.00 (0-935453-46-6) Pasha Pubns.

1992 Horizontal Merger Guidelines, with Commentary. LC 92-72646. 60p. 1992. pap. 20.00 (0-89707-764-4, 503-0223, ABA Antitrust) Amer Bar Assn.

1992 International Emergency Management & Engineering Conference: Managing Risk with Computer Simulation. Ed. by James D. Sullivan. 177p. 1992. pap. 50.00 (1-56555-005-6, SMC-92-1) Soc Computer Sim.

1992 International Energy Efficiency & DSM Conference. 839p. (Orig.). 1992. pap. text 115.00 (1-883128-00-5) SRC Intl.

1992 International Energy Efficiency & DSM Conference. 996p. (Orig.). 1993. pap. 150.00 (1-883128-01-3) SRC Intl.

1992 Lectures & Memoirs. British Academy. (Proceedings of the British Academy Ser.: Vol. 82). (Illus.). 532p. 1994. text 95.00 (0-19-726132-9) OUP.

1992 Letter of Credit Case Law Survey. Ed. by James E. Byrne et al. 439p. 1992. pap. 75.00 (1-888870-00-1) Inst Intl Bnking.

1992 Mid-Year Meeting Proceedings: Of the Seoul Meeting. 257p. 1992. pap. 45.00 (0-614-31034-2) Pac Telecom.

1992 Montgomery Biennial: In-Outsiders from the American South. Montgomery Museum of Fine Arts Staff. LC 92-25883. (Illus.). 68p. 1992. pap. 15.00 (0-89280-030-5) Montgomery Mus.

1992 Music & Video Yearbook. Joel Whitburn. 256p. 1993. pap. 29.95 (0-89820-096-2) Record Research.

1992 National Directory of Fire Chiefs, Rescue & Emergency Departments, Vol. I. Ed. by Steve Cywinski. 1992. 30.00 (1-880245-02-7) SPAN Pub.

1992-93 Dallas-Fort Worth Medical Director. Ed. by Diane E. Huggins. (Illus.). 826p. 1992. pap. 42.50 (1-882328-01-9) Am Med Sales.

1992 Presidential Campaign: A Communication Perspective. Ed. by Robert E. Denton. LC 93-50064. (Series in Political Communication). 288p. 1994. 75.00 (0-275-94559-6, Praeger Pubs); pap. 20.95 (0-275-94560-X, Praeger Pubs) Greenwood.

1992 Presidential Debates in Focus. Diana B. Carlin & Mitchell S. McKinney. LC 94-12350. (Political Communication Ser.). 296p. 1994. 65.00 (0-275-94846-3, Praeger Pubs) Greenwood.

1992 Presidential Election in the South. Ed. by Robert P. Steed et al. LC 93-11894. 240p. 1994. 62.95 (0-275-94534-0, Praeger Pubs) Greenwood.

1992 Project & the Future of Integration in Europe. Ed. by Dale L. Smith & James L. Ray. LC 92-13467. 252p. (C). (gr. 13). 1993. pap. text 36.95 (1-56324-255-9) M E Sharpe.

1992 Project & the Future of Integration in Europe. Ed. by Dale L. Smith & James Lee Ray. LC 92-13467. 252p. (C). 1992. text 70.95 (1-56324-022-X) M E Sharpe.

1992 State Expenditure Report. 110p. (Orig.). 1993. pap. 35.00 (1-55877-207-3) Natl Governor.

1992 State Legislative Summary: Children, Youth & Family Issues. 1992. 15.00 (1-55516-645-8) Natl Conf State Legis.

1992 3rd Quarter Seminar Proceedings: A Collection of Available Papers from Auckland. 309p. 1993. pap. 45.00 (0-614-31033-4) Pac Telecom.

1992-1993 National Directory of Law Enforcement Administrators, Vol. 28. 637p. 1992. 53.00 (1-880245-03-5) SPAN Pub.

1992-93 Home Care Salary & Benefits Report. 2nd ed. 1992. pap. 250.00 (0-939326-71-X) Hosp & Hlthcare.

N

An Asterisk (*) at the beginning of an entry indicates that the title is appearing for the first time.

1992 Year Book Annual Supplement to Merit Students Encyclopedia. 1992. suppl. ed. 45.00 (*0-02-943754-7*) Mac Lib Ref.

1990 Worlds Submarine Telephone Systems. 1990. 75.00 (*0-614-18426-6*) Info Gatekeepers.

1995 IEEE International Symposium on Circuits & Systems. IEEE (Circuits & Systems Society) Staff. Ed. by IEEE (Institute of Electrical & Electronics Engine. LC 80-646530. 5000p. 1995. pap. text. write for info. (*0-7803-2570-2*); lib. bdg. write for info. (*0-7803-2571-0*) Inst Electrical.

1996 Mergerstat Review. (Illus.). 250p. 1996. 249.00 (*1-888878-00-2*) Mergerstat Rev.

1998 IEEE Ultrasonics Symposium. IEEE, Ultrasonics, Ferroelectrics & Frequency Cont. Ed. by Institute of Electrical & Electronics Engineers, I. LC 73-641406. 1900p. 1999. pap. text. write for info. (*0-7803-4095-7*, 98CH36102); lib. bdg. write for info. (*0-7803-4096-5*, 98CH36102) Inst Electrical.

1998-1999 Guide to Cosmetology Licensing. Milady Inc. Staff & Donna Lewis. 192p. pap. 50.00 (*1-56253-446-7*, Pub. by Delmar) Thomson Learn.

***1998/99, the Penguin Good New Zealand Wine Guide.** 7th ed. Vic Williams. LC 98-174894. 1998. write for info. (*0-14-027789-7*) Penguin Books.

1995 Official Travel Industry Directory: The Sourcebook for Travel Professionals. 528p. 1995. spiral bd. 29.95 (*0-9644529-0-1*) Universal Media.

1999 Martindale-Hubbell Law Directory, 127 vols. 128th ed. Ed. by Martindale-Hubbell Staff. 1998. 695.00 (*1-56160-324-4*) Martindale-Hubbell.

1999 Money Adviser: Investing Moves for Today. Money Magazine Staff. 225p. 1999. write for info. (*1-883013-59-3*, People Bks) Tme Inc.

1999 the Professionals Guide to Purchase & Sale of a Business 2000. Tim Berry. 1999. pap. text 135.00 (*0-15-606831-1*) Harcourt.

1996 Yearbook Unequalled Coverage of the U. S. Carl Hungness. (Illus.). 160p. 1996. pap. 24.95 (*0-915088-77-0*) C Hungness.

1907 Census of Citizens of Miami, Oklahoma. Ed. by Hildred Hughes Ables. 51p. 1986. pap. 10.00 (*1-892744-06-6*, A-106) Maloy.

19 Other Articles You Can Use: To Inspire Planned Gifts. G. Roger Schoenhals. LC 97-132112. 60p. (Orig.). 1998. pap. 59.00 (*0-9645517-3-X*) Planned Giving.

Nineteen Out of Eighteen. Joel Lurie Grishaver. (Shema Is for Real Ser.). (Illus.). (Orig.). (J). (gr. 5-8). 1991. pap., student ed. 6.95 (*0-933873-63-8*) Torah Aura.

Nineteen Papers on Algebraic Semigroups. E. Shutov et al. LC 88-10352. (Translations Ser.: Series 2, Vol. 139). 210p. 1983. pap. text 84.00 (*0-8218-3115-1*, TRANS2/139) Am Math.

Nineteen Papers on Statistics & Probability. D. L. Berman et al. LC 61-9803. (Selected Translations on Mathematical Statistics & Probability Ser.: Vol. 5). 380p. 1965. 42.00 (*0-8218-1455-9*, STAPRO/5) Am Math.

Nineteen Papers on Statistics & Probability. A. A. Borovkov et al. LC 61-9803. (Selected Translations on Mathematical Statistics & Probability Ser.: Vol. 2). 251p. 1962. 34.00 (*0-8218-1452-4*, STAPRO/2) Am Math.

Nineteen Plus One, an Anthology of San Francisco Poetry. Ed. by A. D. Winans. LC 78-1139. 1978. 15.00 (*0-915016-17-6*) Second Coming.

19 Projects: Artists-in-Residence at the MIT List Visual Arts Center, Marina Abramovic & Ulay. Contrib. by Marie Cieri et al. LC 95-47172. 1996. pap. 25.00 (*0-938437-51-8*) MIT List Visual Arts.

19 Purchase Street. Gerald A. Browne. 480p. 1995. mass mkt. 6.50 (*0-446-36540-8*) Warner Bks.

1917: Red Banners, White Mantle. Warren H. Carroll. 168p. (Orig.). (C). 1981. pap. 6.95 (*0-931888-05-0*) Christendom Pr.

1970s. (Hutchinson Pocket Dictionaries Ser.). 192p. (C). Date not set. pap. write for info. (*1-85986-021-4*) OUP.

1970s. Jane Duden. LC 89-34630. (Timelines Ser.). (Illus.). 48p. (J). (gr. 6). 1989. lib. bdg. 11.95 (*0-89686-478-2*, Crstwood Hse) Silver Burdett Pr.

***1970s from Watergate to Disco.** Stephen C. Feinstein. LC 99-39425. (Decades of the 20th Century Ser.). (Illus.). 64p. (gr. 5 up). 2000. lib. bdg. 17.95 (*0-7660-1425-8*) Enslow Pubs.

***1970's.** Flametree Staff. (Collins Gem Ser.). (Illus.). 256p. 2000. pap. 7.95 (*0-00-472311-2*, Pub. by HarpC) Trafalgar.

1970s. John Peacock. LC 97-60236. (Fashion Sourcebooks Ser.). (Illus.). 64p. (Orig.). 1997. pap. 10.95 (*0-500-27972-1*, Pub. by Thames Hudson) Norton.

1970s. Gail Stewart. LC 98-24585. (Cultural History of the United States Through the Decades Ser.). (Illus.). (YA). (gr. 4-12). 1998. lib. bdg. 23.70 (*1-56006-557-5*) Lucent Bks.

1970s. Ed. by Nick Yapp. (Decades of the 20th Century Ser.). (Illus.). 400p. 1998. pap. 9.95 (*3-8290-0524-5*, 810153) Konemann.

1970s Pop. Bob Brunning. LC 98-45753. (Sound Trackers Ser.). 32p. (YA). (gr. 5-9). 1999. 15.95 (*0-87226-578-1*, 65781B, P Bedrick Books) NTC Contemp Pub Co.

1978 see Bulletin of Statistics on World Trade in Engineering Products: 1971-1980

1978 see Land Use & Environment Law Review, 1984

1978 see MLA International Bibliography of Books & Articles on the Modern Languages & Literatures

1978 see National Electrical Code

1978 see Socioeconomic Issues of Health

1978 see Statistics on Narcotic Drugs Furnished by Governments in Accordance with the International Treaties & Maximum Levels of Opium Stock

1978 see Statistics of World Trade in Steel, 1973-1981

1978 see United Nations Statistical Yearbook

1978 see WEP Research Working Papers

1978. 116p. 4.00 Soc Am Baseball Res.

1978 see Yearbook of Labor Statistics

1978 see Yearbook of the United Nations, 1978 & Beyond

1970-1971 see Liberian Studies Journal

1970-1973 see World Energy Supplies, 1964-1978

1971-1975 see World Energy Supplies, 1964-1978

1972-1976 see World Energy Supplies, 1964-1978

1970 Ballot Propositions in South Dakota. Thomas C. Geary & Frederick W. Zuercher. 1970. 1.00 (*1-55614-072-X*) U of SD Gov Res Bur.

1970 Census of Population: Characteristics of the Population, Part I, United States Summary, 2 vols., Set. U. S. Bureau of the Census Staff. LC 75-22864. (America in Two Centuries Ser.). (Illus.). 1977. reprint ed. 45.95 (*0-405-07747-5*) Ayer.

1970 Census of Population: Characteristics of the Population, Part I, United States Summary, 2 vols., Vol. 1. U. S. Bureau of the Census Staff. LC 75-22864. (America in Two Centuries Ser.). (Illus.). 1976. reprint ed. 27.95 (*0-405-07748-3*) Ayer.

1970 Census of Population: Characteristics of the Population, Part I, United States Summary, 2 vols., Vol. 2. U. S. Bureau of the Census Staff. LC 75-22864. (America in Two Centuries Ser.). (Illus.). 1976. reprint ed. 27.95 (*0-405-07749-1*) Ayer.

1978. 2nd ed. Ed. by Robert L. Davids. (Illus.). 116p. 1983. pap. 4.00 Soc Am Baseball Res.

1978: The Human Race Begins. Bert Hayes. (First Ser.). (Illus.). 64p. (Orig.). (J). 1989. pap. 4.95 (*0-318-41429-5*) M C Cook.

1978: When Baseball Was Still Baseball. Bert Sugar. LC 99-19917. 1999. 24.95 (*0-87833-230-8*) Taylor Pub.

1978 Data see Gas Facts

1978-1979 see Selected Articles

1975. 2nd ed. Ed. by Robert L. Davids. (Illus.). 112p. 1983. pap. 3.00 Soc Am Baseball Res.

1975-76 see Cahiers Elisabethains: Etudes sur la Pre-Renaissance et la Renaissance Anglaises

***Nineteen Seventy-Four.** David Peace. 2000. pap. 14.00 (*1-85242-634-9*) Serpents Tail.

***Nineteen Seventy Four.** David Peace. 320p. 2000. pap. 12.00 (*1-85242-741-8*) Serpents Tail.

1974: Les Mariages Mixtes see Ethnies: Proceedings

1974-1977 see WEP Research Working Papers

1974-1984 911, 912E & 930 Porsche. Mark Haab. (Authenticity Ser.). (Illus.). 112p. (Orig.). 1995. pap. 19.95 (*0-929758-02-1*) Beeman Jorgensen.

1974-1976 see Who Was Who in America, 1607-1996

1979. 160p. 1983. 5.00 Soc Am Baseball Res.

1979. 2nd ed. Ed. by Robert L. Davids. (Illus.). 1983. reprint ed. pap. 5.00 Soc Am Baseball Res.

1979 see Studies in Bibliography: Papers of the Bibliographical Society of the University of Virginia

1979-1983 Testing at Los Morteros (AZ AA-12-57 ASM) A Large Hohokam Village Site in the Tucson Basin, Vol. 177. Richard C. Lange & William L. Deaver. (Illus.). 352p. 1989. 16.95 (*1-889747-61-0*) Ariz St Mus.

1971: Anglo-French Conference on Race Relations in France & Great Britain, University of Sussex, Sept., 1968 see Ethnies: Proceedings

***1971 Honinbo Tournament.** Kaoru Iwamoto. 1999. pap. write for info. (*4-906574-07-6*) Kiseido Pubng Co.

1977 Data see Gas Facts

1977-1981 see Who Was Who in America, 1607-1996

1977-79 see Cahiers Elisabethains: Etudes sur la Pre-Renaissance et la Renaissance Anglaises

1976 Data see Gas Facts

Selected Poems II: Poems Selected & New, 1976-1986. Margaret Atwood. 160p. 1987. pap. 16.00 (*0-395-45406-9*) HM.

1976-1977 see Selected Articles

1973: Linguistique et Relations Interethiques see Ethnies: Proceedings

1973-1978 see World Energy Supplies, 1964-1978

1970-1979. Geraldine M. Gutfreund. (Yearbooks in Science Ser.). (Illus.). 80p. (J). (gr. 5-8). 1995. lib. bdg. 20.40 (*0-8050-3437-4*) TFC Bks NY.

1972, 3 vols., Tome 1: A-C. Cioranesco. (FRE.). 54.95 (*0-8288-9104-4*, F125000) Fr & Eur.

1972-1974 see Repertoire of the Practice of the Security Council

1972-1974 see Liberian Studies Journal

1972 Invasion of Military Region 1: Fall of Quang Tri & Defense of Hue. David K. Mann. 93p. 1993. reprint ed. pap. 11.50 (*0-923135-62-6*) Dalley Bk Service.

Nineteen Seventy-Two Simla Agreement: An Asymmetrical Negotiation. Imiaz H. Bokhari & Thomas P. Thornton. (Pew Case Studies in International Affairs). 51p. (Orig.). (C). 1988. pap. text 3.50 (*1-56927-420-7*) Geo U Inst Dplmcy.

1972-74 see Cahiers Elisabethains: Etudes sur la Pre-Renaissance et la Renaissance Anglaises

1972 Tutorial Proceedings of the Environmental Science-Challenge to EE Education in the Seventies! Institute of Environmental Sciences Staff. (Illus.). 1972. pap. 30.00 (*0-915414-46-5*) IEST.

1975-1997 Case Currents Index. Ed. by Wendy A. Larson. Tr. by Sarah Eveland. (Orig.). 1997. pap. 30.00 (*0-89964-327-2*, 22703) Coun Adv & Supp Ed.

1906 Souvenir of the City of Riverside by the Riverside Fire Department. Herman Charles. LC 87-61990. (Illus.). 128p. 1987. reprint ed. pap. 10.00 (*0-935661-16-6*) Riverside Mus Pr.

***1960's.** Flametree Staff. (Collins Gem Ser.). (Illus.). 256p. 2000. pap. 7.95 (*0-00-472310-4*, Pub. by HarpC) Trafalgar.

***1916: A Novel of the Irish Rebellion.** Morgan Llywelyn. LC 97-29838. 447p. 1998. text 24.95 (*0-312-86101-X*) St Martin.

1916: A Novel of the Irish Rebellion. Morgan Llywelyn. 544p. 1999. pap. 6.99 (*0-8125-7492-3*, Pub. by Tor Bks) St Martin.

***1916 Easter Rebellion Handbook.** Weekly Irish Times Staff. 1999. 39.95 (*1-57098-196-5*); pap. 19.95 (*1-57098-316-X*, R Rinehart Intl) Roberts Rinehart.

1916 Poets. Ed. by Desmond Ryan. LC 79-18768. 224p. 1980. reprint ed. lib. bdg. 59.50 (*0-313-22100-6*, RYNI, Greenwood Pr) Greenwood.

1916 Poets: Pearse, Plunkett, MacDonagh. Patrick Pearse et al. Ed. by Desmond Ryan. 179p. 1995. reprint ed. pap. 15.95 (*0-7171-2294-8*, Pub. by Gill & MacMill) Irish Bks Media.

***1916 Proclamation.** John O'Connor. (Illus.). 96p. 1999. pap. 10.95 (*0-937702-19-6*) Irish Bks Media.

1960s. 192p. (C). Date not set. pap. write for info. (*1-85986-020-6*) OUP.

1960s. Ariel Books Staff. LC 93-73362. (Illus.). 80p. 1994. 4.95 (*0-8362-3063-9*) Andrews & McMeel.

1960s. Jane Duden. LC 89-34399. (Timelines Ser.). (Illus.). 48p. (J). (gr. 6). 1989. lib. bdg. 11.95 (*0-89686-477-4*, Crstwood Hse) Silver Burdett Pr.

1960s. Ed. by William Dudley. LC 96-49282. (Opposing Viewpoints Ser.). (Illus.). (J). (gr. 5-12). 1996. pap. 16.20 (*1-56510-525-7*); lib. bdg. 26.20 (*1-56510-526-5*) Greenhaven.

***1960s.** William Dudley. LC 99-87776. (America's Decades Ser.). 360p. (YA). 2000. pap. 17.96 (*0-7377-0305-9*); lib. bdg. 22.45 (*0-7377-0306-7*) Greenhaven.

1960's. Gini Holland. LC 98-8826. (Cultural History of the U. S. Through the Decades Ser.). (Illus.). (YA). (gr. 4-12). 1998. lib. bdg. 23.70 (*1-56006-556-7*) Lucent Bks.

***1960s.** Jennnifer A. Hurley. LC 99-38546. (Opposing Viewpoints Digests Ser.). (Illus.). 144p. (YA). (gr. 6-10). 2000. pap. 14.95 (*0-7377-0210-9*); lib. bdg. 23.70 (*0-7377-0211-7*) Greenhaven.

1960s. John Peacock. LC 97-61658. (Fashion Sourcebooks Ser.). (Illus.). 64p. 1998. pap. 10.95 (*0-500-28040-1*, Pub. by Thames Hudson) Norton.

1960s. Ed. by Nick Yapp. (Decades of the 20th Century Ser.). (Illus.). 400p. 1998. pap. 9.95 (*3-8290-0523-7*, 810152) Konemann.

1960s: An Annotated Bibliography of Social & Political Movements in the United States, 24. Rebecca Jackson. LC 92-24261. (Bibliographies & Indexes in American History Ser.: No. 24). 256p. 1992. lib. bdg. 55.00 (*0-313-27255-7*, JSP, Greenwood Pr) Greenwood.

1960s: Words of a Decade. Ariel Books Staff. 374p. 1995. pap. 4.95 (*0-8362-0713-0*) Andrews & McMeel.

ABC-CLIO Companion to the 1960's Counterculture in America. Neil A. Hamilton. LC 97-36735. (Clio Companion Ser.). 386p. 1997. lib. bdg. 65.00 (*0-87436-858-8*) ABC-CLIO.

***1960s Cultural Revolution.** John C. McWilliams. LC 99-58963. (Greenwood Press Guides to Historic Events of the Twentieth Century Ser.). 2000. write for info. (*0-313-29913-7*, Greenwood Pr) Greenwood.

***1960s from the Vietnam War to Flower Power.** Stephen Feinstein. LC 99-39424. (Decades of the 20th Century Ser.). (Illus.). 64p. (YA). (gr. 5 up). 2000. lib. bdg. 17.95 (*0-7660-1426-6*) Enslow Pubs.

1960s Pop. Bob Brunning. LC 98-41697. (Sound Trackers Ser.). 32p. (YA). (gr. 5-9). 1999. 15.95 (*0-87226-576-5*, 65765B, P Bedrick Books) NTC Contemp Pub Co.

1960 see Studies in Bibliography: Papers of the Bibliographical Society of the University of Virginia

***1960: The Last Pure Season.** Kerry Keene. (Illus.). 200p. 2000. 22.95 (*1-58261-280-3*) Sprts Pubng.

1968-1969 see Liberian Studies Journal

1966-1968 see Repertoire of the Practice of the Security Council

1968. Tarig Ali. LC 98-5657. 224p. 1998. 27.00 (*0-684-85360-4*) S&S Trade.

1968. Michael Desmond & Christine Dixon. LC 95-61180. (Illus.). 112p. (Orig.). 1996. pap. 19.95 (*0-500-97433-0*, Pub. by Thames Hudson) Norton.

1968. Joe Haldeman. 1997. mass mkt. 5.99 (*0-614-27697-7*, Avon Bks) Morrow Avon.

1968 & Other Stories. Jim Martin. 60p. 1984. pap. 6.00 (*1-878124-00-5*) Flatland.

***1968.** rev. ed. Eugene J. McCarthy. LC 99-68858. 300p. 2000. pap. 24.95 (*1-883477-37-9*) Lone Oak MN.

1968: A History in Verse. Edward Sanders. LC 97-18698. 260p. 1997. pap. 14.00 (*1-57423-037-9*) Black Sparrow.

1968: The Election That Changed America. Lewis L. Gould. LC 92-35614. (American Ways Ser.). (Illus.). 192p. 1993. 18.95 (*1-56663-009-6*, Pub. by I R Dee); pap. text 9.95 (*1-56663-010-X*, Pub. by I R Dee) Natl Bk Netwk.

1968: The World Transformed. Ed. by Carole Fink et al. LC 98-23253. (Publications of the German Historical Insitute, Washington, D.C.). 350p. (C). 1998. 54.95 (*0-521-64141-1*); pap. 18.95 (*0-521-64637-5*) Cambridge U Pr.

***1968: Year of Media Decision.** Ed. by Robert Giles & Robert W. Snyder. LC 99-30870. 173p. 1999. pap. 24.95 (*0-7658-0621-5*) Transaction Pubs.

1968 - A Love Story. John E. Schwab. LC 94-65043. 210p. (Orig.). 1994. mass mkt. 4.50 (*0-945533-55-1*) April Day.

1968 Co. Joe Haldeman. 1997. mass mkt. 5.99 (*0-380-70803-5*, Avon Bks) Morrow Avon.

1968 Excavations at Mound 8 Las Colinas Ruins Group, Phoenix, Arizona. Ed. by Laurens C. Hammack & Alan P. Sullivan. (Archaeological Ser.: No. 154). (Illus.). 388p. 1981. pap. 19.95 (*1-889747-31-9*) Ariz St Mus.

1968 in America: Music, Politics, Chaos, Counterculture & the Shaping of a Generation. Charles Kaiser. 336p. 1997. pap. 13.00 (*0-8021-3530-7*, Grove) Grove-Atltic.

1968 Magnum Throughout the World. Eric J. Hobsbawm & Marc Weitzmann. (Illus.). 268p. 1998. 49.95 (*2-85025-588-2*) Hazan.

1968 Revolution in Iraq: Political Report of the 8th Congress of the Arab Ba'th Socialist Party. (Political Studies of the Middle East: No. 12). 176p. 1979. pap. write for info. (*0-903729-46-6*, Pub. by Ithaca Press); boxed set. write for info. (*0-903729-45-8*, Pub. by Ithaca Press) Evergreen Dist.

1965 see Studies in Bibliography: Papers of the Bibliographical Society of the University of Virginia

1964-1965 see Repertoire of the Practice of the Security Council

1964 Election: Has South Dakota Become a Two-Party State? Alan L. Clem. 1965. 1.00 (*1-55614-073-8*) U of SD Gov Res Bur.

1969 Supplement see Securities Regulation

1969-1971 see Repertoire of the Practice of the Security Council

1969-1972 see World Energy Supplies, 1964-1978

1969 Stingray Guidebook. Rick Bizzoco. LC 97-74519. 220p. 1995. pap. text 69.95 (*1-884562-01-9*) CA Trader.

1969-1973 see Who Was Who in America, 1607-1996

1960-1969 see Times in Review: New York Times Decade Books

1961 see Studies in Bibliography: Papers of the Bibliographical Society of the University of Virginia

1961-1962 see Indice Cultural

1960 Processors & Related Products. 3rd ed. Intel Corporation Staff. 1996. pap. text 23.95 (*0-07-032904-4*) McGraw.

1960 Processors & Related Products. Intel Corporation Staff. 1057p. 1996. pap. 23.95 (*1-55512-252-3*) McGraw.

1967, Many-Body Physics see Houches Lectures

1966 & All That. Dennis S. Lees & University of Nottingham Staff. LC 78-476829. (Inaugural Lecture Ser.). 14 p. 1970. write for info. (*0-900572-16-7*) Univ Nottingham.

***1966 Season Replay Yearbook.** (Illus.). 78p. 1999. pap. 32.95 (*0-9700351-1-X*) Replay Pubng.

1963 see Studies in Bibliography: Papers of the Bibliographical Society of the University of Virginia

1963 Five Hundred Days. John Lawton. (Illus.). 407p. 1993. text 45.00 (*0-340-50846-9*, Pub. by Headline Bk Pub) Trafalgar.

1963-1966 see Indice Cultural

1960-1969. Tom McGowen. (Yearbooks in Science Ser.). (Illus.). 80p. (J). (gr. 5-8). 1995. lib. bdg. 20.40 (*0-8050-3436-6*) TFC Bks NY.

1962 see Studies in Bibliography: Papers of the Bibliographical Society of the University of Virginia

1962 Supplement to Future Interests & Estate Planning. Leach & Logan. 1962. pap. text 6.25 (*0-88277-389-5*) Foundation Pr.

19 Stars: A Study in Military Character & Leadership. Edgar F. Puryear, Jr. LC 81-14365. 464p. 1997. reprint ed. pap. 17.95 (*0-89141-148-8*) Presidio Pr.

1910: The Emancipation of Dissonance. Thomas J. Harrison. LC 95-25990. (Illus.). 280p. (C). 1996. 35.00 (*0-520-20043-8*, Pub. by U CA Pr) Cal Prin Full Svc.

1910 Idaho Census Index. Upper Snake River Valley Family History Center Staff & David O. McKay Library Staff. LC 98-168401. 1998. write for info. (*1-877677-18-3*) Herit Quest.

1910 OSHA Guide. rev. ed. LC 89-80532. 1039p. 2000. ring bd. 199.00 (*0-934674-70-1*, 34-G) J J Keller.

1910 OSHA Guide: Workplace Safety, Regulations & Index. Keller, J. J., & Associates, Inc. Staff. LC 97-69939. 1200p. 1999. per. 199.00 (*1-57943-054-6*, 134-G) J J Keller.

1910-1929 - Building, Planning, & Urban Technology see Chicago

1910s. Gail B. Stewart. LC 89-9946. (Timelines Ser.). (Illus.). 48p. (J). (gr. 6). 1989. lib. bdg. 11.95 (*0-89686-472-3*, Crstwood Hse) Silver Burdett Pr.

1910s. Michael V. Uschan. LC 98-24574. (Cultural History of the United States Through the Decades Ser.). (Illus.). (YA). (gr. 4-12). 1998. lib. bdg. 23.70 (*1-56006-551-6*) Lucent Bks.

***1910s.** John F. Wukovits. LC 99-55859. (America's Decades Ser.). 360p. (YA). 2000. pap. 17.96 (*0-7377-0295-8*); lib. bdg. 22.45 (*0-7377-0296-6*) Greenhaven.

Nineteen Theses. 2000. text 27.50 (*0-312-20342-X*) St Martin.

Teddy Bears & Stuffed Animals: Hermann Teddy Originals 1913-1998. Milton R. Friedberg. (Illus.). 196p. 1999. pap. 39.95 (*0-7643-0933-1*) Schiffer.

1913-1968: Appendix Index. LC 70-112777. (New York Times Film Reviews Ser.). 750p. 1990. reprint ed. text 300.00 (*0-8240-7580-3*) Garland.

***1930s.** Louise I. Gerdes. LC 99-47626. (America's Decades Ser.). 2000. lib. bdg. 29.96 (*0-7377-0300-8*) Greenhaven.

***1930s.** Louise I. Gerdes. LC 99-47626. (America's Decades Ser.). 360p. (YA). 2000. pap. 17.96 (*0-7377-0299-0*) Greenhaven.

1930s. Ken Hills. LC 91-42164. (Take Ten Years Ser.). (Illus.). 48p. (J). (gr. 3-7). 1992. lib. bdg. 5.00 (*0-8114-3076-6*) Raintree Steck-V.

1930s. John Peacock. LC 97-60235. (Fashion Sourcebooks Ser.). (Illus.). 64p. (Orig.). 1997. pap. 10.95 (*0-500-27973-X*, Pub. by Thames Hudson) Norton.

1930's. Petra Press. LC 98-29895. (Cultural History of the United States Through the Decades Ser.). (Illus.). (YA). (gr. 4-12). 1998. lib. bdg. 23.70 (*1-56006-553-2*) Lucent Bks.

1930s. Gail B. Stewart. LC 89-34405. (Timelines Ser.). (Illus.). 48p. (J). (gr. 6). 1989. lib. bdg. 11.95 (*0-89686-474-X*, Crstwood Hse) Silver Burdett Pr.

An Asterisk (*) at the beginning of an entry indicates that the title is appearing for the first time.

1930s. Ed. by Nick Yapp. (Decades of the 20th Century Ser.). (Illus.). 400p. 1998. pap. 9.95 (*3-8290-0520-2*, 810149) Konemann.

***Nineteen Thirties Lighting: Deco & Traditional by Chase.** Donald Brian Johnson & Leslie Pina. (Illus.). 192p. 2000. 49.95 (*0-7643-1137-9*) Schiffer.

***1930s Scandinavia, 78.** Gennaro Postiglione. 1999. pap. text 35.00 (*88-85322-41-7*) Birkhauser.

1930s Scrapbook. Robert Opie. 1997. 24.95 (*1-872727-33-6*, Pub. by White Mouse) Abbeville Pr.

1938 . . . & the Consequences: Questions & Responses. Elfriede Schmidt. Tr. by Peter Lyth from GER. (Studies in Austrian Literature, Culture, & Thought. Translation Ser.). 382p. 1992. pap. 27.50 (*0-929497-34-1*) Ariadne CA.

1938 to the Present, Vol. 4. Facts on File Staff. (American Images on File Ser.). 1999. 125.00 (*0-8160-3968-2*) Facts on File.

1935: A Memoir. Sam Cornish. 181p. (C). 1990. 19.95 (*0-933277-03-2*); pap. 9.95 (*0-933277-04-0*) Ploughshares.

1930 Flying & Glider Manual. (Illus.). reprint ed. 6.95 (*0-614-13176-6*, 21-14168) EAA Aviation.

1934 Shortwave Radio Manual. Hugo Gernsback & Secor. 1987. pap. 15.95 (*0-917914-64-3*) Lindsay Pubns.

1939: Music & the World's Fair. Claudia Swan et al. (Illus.). 96p. 1998. 25.00 (*0-9648083-2-3*) Eos Music.

1939: The Alliance That Never Was & the Coming of World War II. Michael J. Carley. LC 99-24873. (Illus.). 352p. 1999. 28.95 (*1-56663-252-8*, Pub. by I R Dee) Natl Bk Netwk.

1939: The Last Season of Peace. large type ed. Angela Lambert. 387p. 1990. 10.97 (*0-685-56331-6*, Pub. by ISIS Lrg Prnt); 21.95 (*1-85089-370-5*, Pub. by ISIS Lrg Prnt) Transaction Pubs.

1939: The Lost World of the Fair. David Gelernter. 448p. 1996. pap. 13.50 (*0-380-72748-X*, Avon Bks) Morrow Avon.

1939: The Making of the Second World War. Sidney Aster. (Modern Revivals in History Ser.). 472p. (C). 1993. text 69.95 (*0-7512-0244-4*, Pub. by Gregg Revivals) Ashgate Pub Co.

1939-1970 see Modern Australia in Documents, 1901-1970

1939-1989: Fifty Years Progress in Allergy. A Tribute to Paul Kallos. Ed. by B. H. Waksman. (Chemical Immunology Ser.: Vol. 49). (Illus.). xii, 284p. 1990. 219.25 (*3-8055-5076-6*) S Karger.

1930-1939 see Times in Review: New York Times Decade Books

1931 Flying & Glider Manual. (Illus.). reprint ed. 6.95 (*0-614-13177-4*, 21-14169) EAA Aviation.

1931 Political Crisis. Reginald G. Bassett. 478p. 1986. 91.95 (*0-566-05138-9*, Pub. by Dartmth Pub) Ashgate Pub Co.

1937: Stalin's Year of Terror, Vol. 4. Vadim Z. Rogovin. Tr. by Frederick S. Choate from RUS. LC 97-50514. (Illus.). 550p. 1998. pap. 29.95 (*0-929087-77-1*) Mehring Bks.

1937 Newark Bears: A Baseball Legend. Ronald A. Mayer. (Illus.). 300p. (C). 1994. reprint ed. pap. 14.95 (*0-8135-2153-X*) Rutgers U Pr.

1937-1941. Harold S. Quigley. LC 73-3017. (Illus.). 369p. 1973. reprint ed. lib. bdg. 65.00 (*0-8371-6835-X*, QUFE, Greenwood Pr) Greenwood.

1936: McDermott & McGough. Claudia Gian Ferrari. 1996. pap. 19.95 (*88-8158-066-7*, Pub. by Charta) Dist Art Pubs.

1936: The Spanish Revolution. 1998. 25.00 (*1-873176-01-5*, AK Pr San Fran) AK Pr Dist.

1936-1970: Seven Quinquennial Consolidated Indexes to British Government Publications. 1952-1973. 1080p. 1974. pap. write for info. (*0-85964-006-X*) Chadwyck-Healey.

1933. Philip Metcalfe. LC 87-92040. 316p. 1988. 22.00 (*0-932966-87-X*) Permanent Pr.

1933: Characters in Crisis. Herbert Feis. (FDR & the Era of the New Deal Ser.). 1976. reprint ed. lib. bdg. 39.50 (*0-306-70807-8*) Da Capo.

1933: The Devil Comes to Henry County. limited ed. J. S. Roberts, pseud. Ed. by Robert Long. (Illus.). 571p. 1989. 29.95 (*0-938650-48-3*) Thinkers Pr.

1933 Cortes Elections. (Modern European History Ser.). 910710p. 1991. text. write for info. (*0-8153-0418-8*) Garland.

1933 Flying & Glider Manual. (Illus.). reprint ed. 6.95 (*0-614-13179-0*, 21-14171) EAA Aviation.

1933 Was a Bad Year. John Fante. LC 85-15626. 131p. 1995. reprint ed. 20.00 (*0-87685-656-3*); reprint ed. pap. 13.00 (*0-87685-655-5*) Black Sparrow.

1930-1970 - Building, Planning & Urban Technology see Chicago

1932 Campaign: An Analysis. Roy V. Peel & Thomas C. Donnelly. LC 73-454. (FDR & the Era of the New Deal Ser.). 252p. 1973. reprint ed. lib. bdg. 29.50 (*0-306-70567-2*) Da Capo.

1932 Flying & Glider Manual. (Illus.). reprint ed. 6.95 (*0-614-13178-2*, 21-14170) EAA Aviation.

1932-1938. LC 70-112777. (New York Times Film Reviews Ser.). 784p. 1990. reprint ed. text 180.00 (*0-8240-7576-5*) Garland.

***1932 Revolutionist: The Stage Play about Siamese Statesman Pridi Banomyong.** Kamron Gunatilaka. 2000. pap. 12.00 (*974-7449-19-6*, Pub. by CPNCOCAPB) Lantern Books.

1930's Something: A Nice Neighborhood with Tall Trees. Mary E. Ducklow. (Illus.). 145p. 1993. 29.95 (*0-929682-03-3*) Perin Pr.

Nineteen to the Dozen: Monologues & Bits & Bobs of Other Things. Sholem Aleichem. Ed. by Ken Frieden. Tr. by Ted Gorelick. LC 97-29985. (Judaic Traditions in Literature, Music, & Art Ser.). 177p. 1997. 24.95 (*0-8156-0477-7*) Syracuse U Pr.

***Nineteen to the Dozen: Monologues & Bits & Bobs of Other Things.** Sholem Aleichem. Ed. by Ken Frieden. Tr. by Ted Gorelick. 192p. 2000. pap. 17.95 (*0-8156-0634-6*) Syracuse U Pr.

1912 & 1915 Gustav Stickley Craftsman Furniture Catalogs. Gustav Stickley. (Furniture Ser.). (Illus.). 112p. 1991. reprint ed. pap. 9.95 (*0-486-26676-1*) Dover.

1912 Quaint Furniture Catalog. Ed. by Peter A. Copeland & Janet H. Copeland. (Illus.). 96p. (Orig.). 1993. pap. 23.50 (*0-9638771-0-0*) Parchment NJ.

1912 S. F. B. J. Catalog: Reproduction of Original Catalog. (Illus.). 72p. 1997. pap. 39.00 (*0-912823-69-0*, BT-166, Pub. by Gold Horse) Dollmasters.

1920's. Erica Hanson. LC 98-27965. (Cultural History of the United States Through the Decades Ser.). (Illus.). (YA). (gr. 4-12). 1998. lib. bdg. 23.70 (*1-56006-552-4*) Lucent Bks.

1920s. John Peacock. LC 96-61171. (Fashion Sourcebooks Ser.). (Illus.). 64p. (Orig.). 1997. pap. 10.95 (*0-500-27932-2*, Pub. by Thames Hudson) Norton.

1920s. Gail B. Stewart. (Timelines Ser.). (Illus.). 48p. (J). (gr. 6). 1989. lib. bdg. 11.95 (*0-89686-473-1*, Crstwood Hse) Silver Burdett Pr.

***1920s.** John F. Wukovitz. LC 99-87874. (America's Decades Ser.). 360p. (YA). 2000. pap. 17.96 (*0-7377-0297-4*) Greenhaven.

***1920s.** John F. Wukovitz. LC 99-87874. (America's Decades Ser.). 360p. (YA). 2000. lib. bdg. 22.45 (*0-7377-0298-2*) Greenhaven.

1920s. Ed. by Nick Yapp. (Decades of the 20th Century Ser.). (Illus.). 400p. 1998. pap. 9.95 (*3-8290-0519-9*, 810148) Konemann.

1920s & 1930s. 41.95 (*0-382-40680-X*) Cobblestone Pub Co.

1920s Fashion Design. Pepin Press Design Book Staff. (Illus.). 240p. 1998. pap. 29.95 (*0-89676-232-7*, Costume & Fashion Pr) QSMG Ltd.

1920s Fashions from B. Altman & Company. B. Altman & Co. Staff. Ed. by Blanche Cirker. (Illus.). 128p. 1999. pap. 12.95 (*0-486-40293-2*) Dover.

1920 see History of the Peace Conference of Paris

1920-1929. David E. Newton. (Yearbooks in Science Ser.). (Illus.). 80p. (J). (gr. 5-8). 1995. lib. bdg. 20.40 (*0-8050-3432-3*) TFC Bks NY.

1920 Census Index: Bucks County, PA. Thomas G. Myers. LC 93-91749. 190p. 1993. spiral bd. 13.00 (*0-9637799-0-7*) T G Myers.

1920 Diary. Isaac Babel. Ed. by Carol J. Avins. Tr. by H. T. Willetts from RUS. LC 94-24535. (Illus.). 192p. 1995. 27.50 (*0-300-05966-3*) Yale U Pr.

1920 Diary. Isaac Babel. Ed. & Intro. by Carol J. Avins. 192p. 1997. pap. 14.00 (*0-300-07054-3*) Yale U Pr.

1928 Campaign: An Analysis. Roy V. Peel & Thomas C. Donnelly. LC 73-19170. (Politics & People Ser.). (Illus.). 196p. 1974. reprint ed. 17.95 (*0-405-05892-6*) Ayer.

1928 Campaign: An Analysis. Roy V. Peel & Thomas C. Donnelly. LC 74-12758. (Illus.). 183p. 1975. reprint ed. lib. bdg. 45.00 (*0-8371-7749-9*, PENC, Greenwood Pr) Greenwood.

1924 see History of the Peace Conference of Paris

1924-1983: Commentary by a Social Servant. Ed. by National Institute for Social Work Staff. 1984. 35.00 (*0-7855-0829-5*, Pub. by Natl Inst Soc Work) St Mut.

1929 Again? rev. ed. Terry R. Rudd. (Illus.). 450p. (C). 1988. reprint ed. 27.50 (*0-9620011-0-4*) Bell Curve Rsch.

1929 Flying & Glider Manual. (Illus.). reprint ed. 6.95 (*0-614-13175-8*, 21-14167) EAA Aviation.

1920-1929 see Times in Review: New York Times Decade Books

1921 see History of the Peace Conference of Paris

1921 Tulsa Race Riot - "Angels of Mercy" Bob Hower. (Illus.). 238p. pap., per. 24.95 (*0-9665823-0-6*) Lucky Eight.

***1920 Population Census of Sabine County, Texas.** Robert Cecil McDaniel. 285p. 2000. pap. 20.00 (*1-887745-12-2*) Dogwood TX.

***1927: High Tide of the 1920s.** Gerald Leinwand. (Illus.). 368p. 2000. 32.00 (*1-56858-153-X*, Pub. by FWEW) Publishers Group.

***1927 Yankees.** Historical Briefs, Inc. Staff. Ed. by Thomas Antonucci & Michael Antonucci. 176p. 1999. pap. 19.95 (*0-89677-071-0*) Hist Briefs.

Nineteen Ways of Looking at Wang Wei: How a Chinese poem is translated. Eliot Weinberger & Octavio Paz. 64p. 1987. pap. 6.95 (*0-918825-14-8*) Moyer Bell.

***19 Years in a New Age Cult &Torn from the Arms of Satan.** Elizabeth Burchard & Judith Carlone. (Illus.). 330p. (C). 1999. pap. 14.95 (*1-881374-05-X*, Pub. by Ace Acad) Amazon Com.

Nineteenth- & Twentieth-Century Harpists: A Bio-Critical Sourcebook. Wenonah M. Govea. LC 95-1547. (Bio-Critical Sourcebooks on Music Performance Ser.). 368p. 1995. lib. bdg. 85.00 (*0-313-27866-0*, Greenwood Pr) Greenwood.

Nineteenth Amendment: Women's Right to Vote. Judy Monroe. LC 97-23363. (Constitution Ser.). (Illus.). 128p. (YA). (gr. 6 up). 1998. lib. bdg. 20.95 (*0-89490-922-3*) Enslow Pubs.

Nineteenth & Twentieth Centuries see Western Political Theory: From Its Origins to the Present

Nineteenth & Twentieth Century European Drawings. Ed. by Samuel H. Kress. (Illus.). 1966. 15.00 (*0-8079-0097-4*); pap. 7.95 (*0-8079-0098-2*) October.

Nineteenth & Twentieth Virginia Cavalry. Richard L. Armstrong. (Virginia Regimental Histories Ser.). (Illus.). 260p. 1994. 19.95 (*1-56190-061-3*) H E Howard.

Nineteenth Biennial Conference Proceedings. ICHCA Staff. 400p. (C). 1989. 510.00 (*0-7855-5090-9*, Pub. by ICHCA) St Mut.

***19th Century.** Ed. by Harold Bloom. 26p. (YA). 1998. 323.10 (*0-7910-4508-0*) Chelsea Hse.

19th Century. Sarah Halliwell. LC 97-29888. (Who & When Ser.). (J). 1998. lib. bdg. 28.55 (*0-8172-4728-9*) Raintree Steck-V.

***Nineteenth Century.** Colin Matthew. (Short History of the British Isle Ser.). 280p. 2000. pap. 19.95 (*0-19-873143-4*) OUP.

***19th Century.** Ed. by Salem Press Editors et al. (Dictionary of World Biography Ser.: Vol. 5 & 6). (Illus.). 2455p. 1999. lib. bdg. 195.00 (*0-89356-317-X*) Salem Pr.

Nineteenth Century, Pt. I. Ed. by M. G. Brock & M. C. Curthoys. (The History of the University of Oxford Ser.). (Illus.). 880p. 1998. text 145.00 (*0-19-951016-4*) OUP.

***Nineteenth Century: Europe 1789-1914.** Ed. by T. C. W. Blanning. (Short Oxford History of Europe Ser.). (Illus.). 260p. 2000. pap. 19.95 (*0-19-873135-3*); text 65.00 (*0-19-873136-1*) OUP.

***Nineteenth Century: The British Isles, 1815-1901.** Ed. by Colin Matthew. (Short Oxford History of the British Isles Ser.). (Illus.). 280p. 2000. text 65.00 (*0-19-873144-2*) OUP.

Nineteenth-Century Accounts of William Blake by Benjamin Heath Malkin, Henry Crabb Robinson, John Thomas Smith, Allan Cunningham, Frederick Tatham, & William Butler Yeats. Ed. by Joseph A. Wittreich, Jr. LC 78-133330. 300p. 1970. 50.00 (*0-8201-1085-X*) Schol Facsimiles.

***Nineteenth Century America.** (C). 1998. pap. text 53.33 (*0-201-57547-7*) Addison-Wesley.

Nineteenth-Century American Art. (Shorewood Art Programs for Education Ser.). 16p. 1975. teacher ed. 107.00 (*0-88185-059-4*); 143.00 (*0-685-07235-5*) Shorewood Fine Art.

Nineteenth Century American Art. Judith A. Barter & Frank A. Trapp. (Mead Art Museum Monographs: Vol. 5). (Illus.). 18p. 1985. pap. 3.00 (*0-914337-04-1*) Mead Art Mus.

***Nineteenth-Century American Art.** Barbara Groseclose. (Oxford History of Art Ser.). (Illus.). 256p. 2000. pap. 17.95 (*0-19-284225-0*) OUP.

Nineteenth Century American Carriages: Their Manufacture, Decoration & Use. Museums at Stony Brook Staff. LC 87-12282. (Illus.). 112p. (Orig.). 1987. pap. 15.00 (*0-943924-10-3*) Mus Stony Brook.

Nineteenth Century American Choral Music. David P. DeVenney. LC 87-80918. (Reference Books in Music: No. 8). xxi, 182p. (Orig.). 1987. pap. 19.95 (*0-914913-08-5*, Fallen Lef Pr) Scarecrow.

Nineteenth Century American Drama: A Finding Guide. Don L. Hixon & Don A. Hennessee. LC 77-12057. 581p. 1977. 40.00 (*0-8108-1083-2*) Scarecrow.

Nineteenth Century American Etchings in the Collection of the Parrish Art Museum. Maureen C. O'Brien & Patricia C. Mandel. LC 87-61051. 108p. 1987. pap. 15.00 (*0-943526-16-7*) Parrish Art.

***Nineteenth-Century American Fiction Writers.** Kent P. Ljungquist. LC 98-49304. (Dictionary of Literary Biography Ser.). 400p. 1999. text 155.00 (*0-7876-3096-9*) Gale.

Nineteenth-Century American Literature, 8 bks. (Modern Critical Interpretations Ser.). 1987. 269.60 (*0-7910-3575-1*) Chelsea Hse.

Nineteenth-Century American Painting: The Thyssen-Bornemisza Collection. Barbara Novak. (Illus.). 332p. 1991. 39.98 (*0-89660-026-2*, Artabras) Abbeville Pr.

Nineteenth Century American Plays. Myron Matlaw. 272p. Date not set. 22.95 (*0-8488-2367-2*) Amereon Ltd.

Nineteenth-Century American Plays. rev. ed. Ed. & Intro. by Myron Matlaw. Orig. Title: Black Crook & Other 19th Century American Plays. 262p. 1988. reprint ed. 24.95 (*1-55783-017-7*); reprint ed. pap. 14.95 (*1-55783-018-5*) Applause Theatre Bk Pubs.

Nineteenth-Century American Poetry. Ed. by William C. Spengemann & Jessica F. Roberts. LC 96-3466. 480p. 1996. pap. 14.95 (*0-14-043587-5*, Penguin Bks) Viking Penguin.

Nineteenth Century American Poetry: An Annotated Bibliography. Philip K. Jason. (Magill Bibliographies Ser.). 257p. 1989. 42.00 (*0-8108-2814-6*) Scarecrow.

Nineteenth-Century American Short Stories. Ed. by Christopher W. Bigsby. 336p. (Orig.). 1995. pap. 6.95 (*0-460-87552-3*, Everyman's Classic Lib) Tuttle Pubng.

Nineteenth-Century American Short Story. Ed. by A. Robert Lee. LC 85-15707. (Critical Studies). 224p. 1986. 56.50 (*0-389-20593-1*, N8151) B&N Imports.

19th Century American Western Writers, Vol. 186. LC 97-27436. (Dictionary of Literary Biography Ser.). 400p. 1997. text 155.00 (*0-7876-1682-6*, 111083) Gale.

Nineteenth-Century American Woman Theatre Managers, 143. Jane Kathleen Curry. LC 93-44333. (Contributions in Women's Studies). 168p. 1994. 55.00 (*0-313-29141-1*, Greenwood Pr) Greenwood.

Nineteenth Century American Women Poets: An Anthology. Ed. by Paula B. Bennett. LC 97-6863. (Blackwell Anthologies Ser.). 640p. 1997. 83.95 (*0-631-20398-2*); pap. 34.95 (*0-631-20399-0*) Blackwell Pubs.

Nineteenth-Century American Women Writers: A Bio-Bibliographical Critical Sourcebook. Ed. by Denise D. Knight. LC 96-35351. 552p. 1997. lib. bdg. 99.50 (*0-313-29713-4*, Greenwood Pr) Greenwood.

Nineteenth-Century American Women Writers: A Critical Reader. Karen L. Kilcup. LC 97-45807. 240p. 1998. pap. 29.95 (*0-631-20054-1*) Blackwell Pubs.

Nineteenth-Century American Women Writers: A Critical Reader. Karen L. Kilcup. LC 97-45807. 240p. 1998. 59.95 (*0-631-20053-3*) Blackwell Pubs.

Nineteenth-Century American Women Writers: An Anthology. Ed. by Karen L. Kilcup. LC 96-3113. (Anthologies Ser.). 660p. (C). 1996. pap. text 32.95 (*0-631-19986-1*) Blackwell Pubs.

Nineteenth-Century American Women Writers: An Anthology. Ed. by Karen L. Kilcup. LC 96-3113. (Anthologies Ser.). 601p. (C). 1997. text 77.95 (*0-631-19985-3*) Blackwell Pubs.

Nineteenth-Century American Writers, 11 bks. (Modern Critical Views Ser.). 1986. 334.45 (*0-7910-3584-0*) Chelsea Hse.

19th Century & Abolition. (Voices in African American History Ser.). (YA). 1994. pap. 6.35 (*0-8136-4968-4*); lib. bdg. 12.70 (*0-8136-4967-6*) Modern Curr.

Nineteenth-Century Anglican Theological Training: The Redbrick Challenge. David A. Dowland. LC 97-9923. (Oxford Theological Monographs). (Illus.). 250p. 1998. text 72.00 (*0-19-826929-3*) OUP.

Nineteenth Century Apprentices in New York City. Kenneth Scott. 474p. 1986. lib. bdg. 27.00 (*0-915156-55-5*) Natl Genealogical.

Nineteenth-Century Art. Robert Rosenblum & H. W. Janson. LC 83-3882. (Illus.). 528p. 1984. 65.00 (*0-8109-1362-3*, Pub. by Abrams) Time Warner.

Nineteenth Century Art: A Critical History. Stephen Eisenman. (C). 1994. pap. 34.95 (*0-500-27753-2*) Thames Hudson.

Nineteenth Century Art: A Critical History. Stephen F. Eisenman. LC 93-61271. (Illus.). 360p. 1994. 45.00 (*0-500-23675-5*, Pub. by Thames Hudson) Norton.

***Nineteenth Century Art: From Romanticism to Art Nouveau, The Walters Art Gallery, Baltimore.** William R. Johnston. Ed. by Deborah Horowitz. (Illus.). 160p. 2000. pap. 24.95 (*1-85759-226-3*, Pub. by Scala Books) Antique Collect.

Nineteenth Century Art (Abrams Book) Robert Rosenblum & H. W. Janson. (Illus.). 528p. (C). 1983. text 73.33 (*0-13-622621-3*) P-H.

Nineteenth-Century Attitudes: Men of Science. Sydney Ross. (C). 1991. text 122.00 (*0-7923-1308-9*) Kluwer Academic.

Nineteenth Century Australian Silver, 2 vols. J. B Hawkins. (Illus.). 720p. 1989. 250.00 (*1-85149-002-7*) Antique Collect.

Nineteenth Century Baseball: Year-by-Year Statistics for the Major League Team, 1871-1900. Marshall D. Wright. LC 96-19833. 350p. 1996. lib. bdg. 37.50 (*0-7864-0181-8*) McFarland & Co.

Nineteenth Century Bengal Society & the Christian Missionaries. Abhijit Dutta. (C). 1992. 23.00 (*81-85195-40-4*, Pub. by Minerva) S Asia.

Nineteenth Century Britain. A. Wood. 1984. pap. text. write for info. (*0-582-35311-4*, Pub. by Addison-Wesley) Longman.

Nineteenth-Century Britain: Integration & Diversity. Keith Robbins. (Ford Lectures 1986-1987). 212p. 1995. pap. text 21.00 (*0-19-820585-6*) OUP.

Nineteenth-Century British Literature, 9 bks. (Modern Critical Interpretations Ser.). 1987. 299.55 (*0-7910-3573-5*) Chelsea Hse.

***Nineteenth-Century British Music Studies, Vol. 1.** Ed. by Bennett Zon. LC 98-54371. (Music in Nineteenth-Century Britain Ser.). (Illus.). 272p. 1999. text 96.95 (*1-84014-259-6*) Ashgate Pub Co.

Nineteenth-Century British Novelists on the Novel. Ed. by George L. Barnett. LC 75-130791. (Goldentree Books in English Literature). (Orig.). (C). 1971. 42.00 (*0-89197-317-6*); pap. text 14.95 (*0-89197-318-4*) Irvington.

***Nineteenth-century British Women Writers: A Bio-bibliographical Critical Sourcebook.** Abigail Burnham Bloom. LC 99-43163. 472p. 2000. lib. bdg. 95.00 (*0-313-30439-4*) Greenwood.

Nineteenth Century British Working-Class Autobiographies: An Annotated Bibliography. Nan Hackett. LC 84-45278. (Studies in Social History: No. 5). 1985. 39.50 (*0-404-61605-4*) AMS Pr.

Nineteenth-Century British Writers - Novelists, 6 bks. (Modern Critical Views Ser.). 1987. 184.70 (*0-7910-3581-6*) Chelsea Hse.

Nineteenth-Century British Writers - Poets, 7 bks. (Modern Critical Views Ser.). 1987. 209.65 (*0-7910-3582-4*) Chelsea Hse.

Nineteenth Century Cairene Houses & Palaces. Nihal S. Tamraz. LC 98-961200. (Illus.). 176p. 1996. 29.00 (*977-424-378-1*, Pub. by Am Univ Cairo Pr) Col U Pr.

Nineteenth-Century Cape Breton: A Historical Geography. Stephen J. Hornsby. (Illus.). 304p. 1992. 34.95 (*0-7735-0889-9*, Pub. by McG-Queens Univ Pr) CUP Services.

Nineteenth Century Capital Accounting & Business Investment. Richard P. Brief. LC 75-18459. (History of Accounting Ser.). 1977. 18.95 (*0-405-07543-X*) Ayer.

19th Century Chamber Music. Stephen E. Hefling. LC 97-21884. 1997. 45.00 (*0-02-871034-7*) Macmillan.

Nineteenth Century Children's Fashions, Vol.9. Susan B. Sirkis. (Wish Booklets Ser.). 48p. 1972. pap. 5.95 (*0-913786-09-8*) Wish Bklets.

Nineteenth-Century Church & English Society. Frances Knight. (New Testament Theology Ser.). (Illus.). 256p. (C). 1999. pap. text 22.95 (*0-521-65711-3*) Cambridge U Pr.

Nineteenth-Century Cities: Essays in the New Urban History. Yale Conference on the Nineteenth-Century Industri. Ed. by Richard Sennett & Stephan A. Thernstrom. LC 73-89905. (Yale Studies of the City: No. 1). 444p. reprint ed. pap. 137.70 (*0-8357-8251-4*, 203390300087) Bks Demand.

Nineteenth Century Clothing see Historic Communities Series

Nineteenth-Century Costume & Fashion. unabridged ed. Herbert Norris & Oswald Curtis. LC 98-9926. (Illus.). 248p. 1998. pap. 12.95 (*0-486-40292-4*) Dover.

Nineteenth-Century Decoration: The Art of the Interior. Charlotte Gere. (Illus.). 384p. 1989. 95.00 (*0-8109-1382-8*, Pub. by Abrams) Time Warner.

N

Nineteenth Century Dutch Watercolors & Drawings from the Museum Boijmans Van Beuningen, Rotterdam. Museum Boijmans Van Beuningen Staff et al. LC 98-20287. 1998. 29.95 (0-88397-129-1) Art Srvc Intl.

19th Century Emigrants from Baden-Wurttemberg Vol. 1: The Enzkreis. Brigitte Burkett. LC 97-68243. 450p. 1997. 45.00 (0-89725-292-6, 1797) Picton Pr.

Nineteenth-Century Emigration from the Kreis Simmern (Hunsrueck), Rheinland-Pfalz, Germany, to Brazil, England, Russian Poland & the United States. Clifford N. Smith. (German-American Genealogical Research Monographs: No. 8). 80p. (Orig.). 1980. pap. 20.00 (0-915162-07-5) Westland Pubns.

Nineteenth-Century Emigration from the Siegkreis (Nordrhein-Westfalen, Germany) Mainly to the United States. Clifford N. Smith. (German-American Genealogical Research Monographs: No. 10). 1980. pap. 20.00 (0-915162-09-1) Westland Pubns.

Nineteenth-Century Emigration of "Old Lutherans" from Eastern Germany (Mainly Pomerania & Lower Silesia) to Australia, Canada, & the United States. Clifford N. Smith. (German-American Genealogical Research Monographs: No. 7). 1979. pap. 20.00 (0-915162-06-7) Westland Pubns.

Nineteenth-Century English. Richard Bailey. (Illus.). 384p. 1998. pap. text 19.95 (0-472-08540-9, 08540) U of Mich Pr.

Nineteenth Century English Prose: Early Essayists. Ed. by Frederick W. Roe. LC 73-152209. (Essay Index Reprint Ser.). 1977. reprint ed. 31.95 (0-8369-2331-6) Ayer.

Nineteenth-Century English Religious Traditions: Retrospect & Prospect, 44. D. G. Paz. LC 95-9665. (Contributions to the Study of Religion Ser.: 44). 248p. 1995. 59.95 (0-313-29476-3, Greenwood Pr) Greenwood.

Nineteenth Century English Verse Drama. Ed. by Gerald B. Kauvar & Gerald C. Sorensen. LC 79-146163. 355p. 1975. 45.00 (0-8386-7631-6) Fairleigh Dickinson.

Nineteenth Century Essays. Ed. by George Sampson. LC 75-152212. (Essay Index Reprint Ser.). 1977. reprint ed. 18.95 (0-8369-2255-7) Ayer.

Nineteenth-Century Etching Revival: Prints from the Collection of the Milton Public Library. Boyd G. Hill. (Illus.). 107p. (Orig.). 1990. pap. 20.00 (0-9624088-0-8) Trustees Milton.

Nineteenth-Century Europe: The Revolution of Life. Leo A. Loubere. LC 93-4487. 367p. (C). 1993. pap. text 54.00 (0-13-221086-X) P-H.

Nineteenth-Century European Art: A Topical Dictionary. Terry W. Strieter. LC 98-34720. 312p. 1999. lib. bdg. 89.50 (0-313-29898-X, Greenwood Pr) Greenwood.

19th Century European Furniture. Christopher Payne. (Illus.). 348p. 1986. 89.50 (1-85149-001-9) Antique Collect.

Nineteenth-Century European Piano Music. Ed. by John Gillespie. 343p. 1977. pap. 15.95 (0-486-23447-9) Dover.

Nineteenth Century Evangelical Theology. Fisher Humphreys. 416p. 1983. pap. 10.00 (0-8054-6579-0) Insight Pr.

Nineteenth Century Fiction, Vol. 1. Robert L. Wolff. LC 80-8511. 380p. 1981. text 20.00 (0-8240-9474-3) Garland.

Nineteenth Century Fiction: A Bibliographical Catalogue, 2 vols. Robert L. Wolff. (Illus.). 1700p. 1993. reprint ed. 175.00 (1-57898-034-8) Martino Pubng.

Nineteenth-Century Fiction: A Bibliographical Catalogue, Vol. 5. Robert L. Wolff. Ed. by Katherine Bruner. LC 80-8511. 240p. 1986. text 20.00 (0-8240-9337-2, H334) Garland.

Nineteenth Century Fiction: A Bibliographical Catalogue Based on the Collection Formed by Robert Lee Wolff, Vol. IV. Robert L. Wolff & Katherine Bruner. LC 80-8511. 352p. 1985. text 20.00 (0-8240-9336-4, H333) Garland.

XIX Century Fiction: A Bibliographical Record Based on His Own Collection, 2 vols. Michael Sadleir. (Illus.). 575p. 1992. reprint ed. 175.00 (1-57898-032-1) Martino Pubng.

***19th Century Fishing Lures: A Collector's Guide to U. S. Lures Manufactures Prior to 1901.** Arlan Carter. 304p. 2000. 29.95 (1-57432-165-X) Collector Bks.

Nineteenth Century Foreign Office of England. R. A. Jones. 240p. 1971. 22.95 (0-8464-0674-8) Beekman Pubs.

Nineteenth-Century French Caricatures & Comic Illustrations. Anne McCauley. (Illus.). 40p. 1986. pap. 6.00 (0-935213-02-3) J S Blanton Mus.

Nineteenth Century French Fiction Writers: Romanticism & Realism, 1800-1860. Ed. by Catharine S. Brosman. LC 92-17232. (Dictionary of Literary Biography Ser.: Vol. 119). 400p. 1992. text 155.00 (0-8103-7596-6) Gale.

Nineteenth-Century French Immigration into Louisiana, Vol. 1, 1820-1839. Carl A. Brasseaux. LC 90-81145. (Foreign French Ser.). 569p. 1990. 39.95 (0-940984-56-3) Univ LA Lafayette.

Nineteenth Century French Photography. Brooks Johnson. LC 83-70539. (Illus.). 40p. 1983. pap. 7.50 (0-940744-42-2) Chrysler Museum.

Nineteenth-Century French Poetry: Introductions to Close Reading. Ed. by Christopher Prendergast. 270p. 1990. pap. text 19.95 (0-521-34774-2) Cambridge U Pr.

***Nineteenth-Century French Short Stories: Contes et Nouvelles Franpcais du Xixe Siecle.** Stanley Appelbaum. LC 99-47448. 2000. pap. 9.95 (0-486-41126-5) Dover.

Nineteenth-Century French Song: Faur, Chausson, Duparc, & Debussy. Barbara Meister. LC 98-145953. 416p. 1998. 24.95 (0-253-21175-1) Ind U Pr.

Nineteenth-Century French Song: Faure, Chausson, Duparc & Debussy. Barbara Meister. LC 79-2171. 416p. 1980. 39.95 (0-253-34075-6) Ind U Pr.

***19th Century Friend: A Narrative in Verse.** Bruce Craig. 70p. 1999. pap. 10.00 (0-9665614-0-6) SkylondaWorks.

Nineteenth Century German, Austrian & Hungarian Drawings from Budapest. Terez Gerszi & Zsuzsa Gonda. LC 94-16212. 1994. pap. 29.95 (0-88397-111-9) Art Srvc Intl.

Nineteenth-Century German Lied. Lorraine Gorrell. LC 92-37138. (Illus.). 398p. 1993. 39.95 (0-931340-59-4, Amadeus Pr) Timber.

Nineteenth-Century German Plays: King Ottocar's Rise & Fall; The Talisman, & Agnes Bernauer. Johann N. Nestroy et al. Ed. by Egon Schwarz. LC 78-4300. (German Library: Vol. 31). 320p. 1990. 39.50 (0-8264-0331-X); pap. 19.95 (0-8264-0332-8) Continuum.

Nineteenth-Century German Writers to 1840. Ed. by James Hardin. LC 93-5366. (Dictionary of Literary Biography Ser.: Vol. 133). 400p. 1993. text 155.00 (0-8103-5392-X) Gale.

Nineteenth-Century History of English Studies. Alan Bacon. LC 98-8700. (Nineteenth Century Ser.). 330p. 1998. text 78.95 (1-84014-278-2, Pub. by Ashgate Pub) Ashgate Pub Co.

Nineteenth Century Home Architecture of Iowa City: A Silver Anniversary Edition. Margaret N. Keyes. LC 92-39535. (Bur Oak Bk.). (Illus.). 162p. (Orig.). 1993. pap. 14.95 (0-87745-343-8) U of Iowa Pr.

Nineteenth Century Houses in Lawrence, Kansas. rev. ed. Katie Armitage & John Lee. LC 90-70831. (Illus.). 71p. 1991. pap. 8.95 (0-913689-29-7) Spencer Muse Art.

Nineteenth Century Ireland: The Search for Stability. D. George Boyce. 256p. (C). 1990. text 69.00 (0-389-20934-1) B&N Imports.

Nineteenth Century Latin Americans in the United States: An Original Anthology. Ed. by Carlos E. Cortes. LC 79-6234. (Hispanics in the United States Ser.). 1981. lib. bdg. 31.95 (0-405-13182-8) Ayer.

Nineteenth-Century Legal Treatises: A Guide to the Microfiche Collection, Cume Unites 19-24. 328p. (C). 1991. text. write for info. (0-89235-132-2) Primary Srce Media.

Nineteenth-Century Legal Treatises: A Guide to the Microfiche Collections, Units 7-12. Ed. by Research Publications, Inc. Staff. 268p. 1987. lib. bdg. 250.00 (0-89235-123-3) Primary Srce Media.

Nineteenth-Century Legal Treatises: A Guide to the Microfilm Collections, Units 1-6. Ed. by Research Publications, Inc. Staff. 363p. 1987. lib. bdg. 250.00 (0-89235-118-7) Primary Srce Media.

Nineteenth Century Legal Treatises: Guide to the Microfiche Collection, Units 25-30. 442p. (C). 1990. text 275.00 (0-89235-138-1) Primary Srce Media.

Nineteenth-Century Legal Treatises: Guide to the Microfiche Collection, Units 31-36. 316p. (C). 1991. text 275.00 (0-89235-141-1) Primary Srce Media.

Nineteenth Century Legal Treatises: Guide to the Microfiche Collection, Units 37-42. 296p. 1993. 225.00 (0-89235-146-2) Primary Srce Media.

Nineteenth Century Legal Treatises: Guide to the Microfiche Collection, Vols. 13-18. (Units Ser.: Nos. 13-18). 304p. 1988. text 250.00 (0-89235-129-2) Primary Srce Media.

Nineteenth-Century Lighting. H. Parrott Bacot. LC 87-61704. (Illus.). 240p. 1987. 59.95 (0-88740-098-1) Schiffer.

Nineteenth-Century Lights: Historic Images of American Lighthouses. J. Candace Clifford & Mary Louise Clifford. LC 99-75177. (Illus.). 304p. Date not set. 34.95 (0-9636412-2-0); pap. 24.95 (0-9636412-3-9) Cypress Communs.

Nineteenth-Century Literary Criticism, Vol. 23. Ed. by Janet Mullane & Bob Wilson. 600p. 1989. text 150.00 (0-8103-5823-9) Gale.

Nineteenth-Century Literary Criticism, Vol. 24. Janet Mullane et al. 500p. 1989. text 150.00 (0-8103-5824-7) Gale.

Nineteenth-Century Literary Criticism, Vol. 25. Ed. by Janet Mullane & Bob Wilson. 500p. 1990. text 150.00 (0-8103-5825-5) Gale.

Nineteenth-Century Literary Criticism, Vol. 29. 500p. 1991. text 150.00 (0-8103-5829-8) Gale.

Nineteenth-Century Literary Criticism, Vol. 30. 500p. 1991. text 150.00 (0-8103-5830-1) Gale.

Nineteenth-Century Literary Criticism, Vol. 31. 500p. 1991. text 150.00 (0-8103-5831-X) Gale.

Nineteenth-Century Literary Criticism, Vol. 32. 500p. 1991. text 150.00 (0-8103-5832-8) Gale.

Nineteenth Century Literary Criticism, Vol. 33. Paula Kepos. 500p. 1992. text 150.00 (0-8103-5833-6) Gale.

Nineteenth Century Literary Criticism, Vol. 34. Paula Kepos. 500p. 1992. text 150.00 (0-8103-5834-4) Gale.

Nineteenth Century Literary Criticism, Vol. 35. Paula Kepos. 500p. 1992. text 150.00 (0-8103-5835-2) Gale.

Nineteenth Century Literary Criticism, Vol. 36. Paula Kepos. 500p. 1992. text 150.00 (0-8103-5836-0) Gale.

Nineteenth Century Literary Criticism, Vol. 37. Paula Kepos. 500p. 1992. text 150.00 (0-8103-7976-7) Gale.

Nineteenth Century Literary Criticism, Vol. 38. Ed. by Joann Cerrito. 507p. 1993. 150.00 (0-8103-9191-0, 100600) Gale.

Nineteenth Century Literary Criticism, Vol. 38. Paula Kepos. 500p. 1993. text 150.00 (0-8103-7977-5) Gale.

Nineteenth Century Literary Criticism, Vol. 39. Paula Kepos. 500p. 1993. text 150.00 (0-8103-7978-3) Gale.

Nineteenth Century Literary Criticism, Vol. 40. Paula Kepos. 500p. 1993. text 150.00 (0-8103-7979-1) Gale.

Nineteenth Century Literary Criticism, Vol. 41. Paula Kepos. 500p. 1993. text 150.00 (0-8103-8474-4) Gale.

Nineteenth Century Literary Criticism, Vol. 42. Paula Kepos. 1994. write for info. (0-8103-8475-2) Gale.

Nineteenth Century Literary Criticism, Vol. 43. Paula Kepos. 500p. 1994. text 150.00 (0-8103-8476-0) Gale.

Nineteenth Century Literary Criticism, Vol. 44. Paula Kepos. 500p. 1994. text 150.00 (0-8103-8477-9) Gale.

Nineteenth Century Literary Criticism, Vol. 53. Marie Lazzari. 500p. 1996. text 150.00 (0-8103-9299-2) Gale.

Nineteenth-Century Literary Criticism, Vol. 56. 400p. 1996. text 150.00 (0-8103-7005-0, 00108604) Gale.

Nineteenth-Century Literary Criticism, Vol. 57. 400p. 1996. text 150.00 (0-8103-7006-9, GML00597-002322) Gale.

Nineteenth-Century Literary Criticism, Vol. 58. 400p. 1997. text 150.00 (0-8103-7175-8, GML00597-002323) Gale.

Nineteenth-Century Literary Criticism, Vol. 59. Ed. by Denise Evans & Mary Onorato. (LCS Ser.). 400p. 1997. text 150.00 (0-8103-7106-5, GML00597-108705) Gale.

Nineteenth-Century Literary Criticism, Vol. 60. Ed. by Denise Evans & Mary Onorato. (LCS Ser.). 470p. 1997. text 150.00 (0-7876-1128-X, 00156232) Gale.

Nineteenth-Century Literary Criticism, Vol. 61. Ed. by Denise Evans & Mary Onorato. (LCS Ser.). 470p. 1997. 134.00 (0-7876-1127-1, 00156233) Gale.

Nineteenth-Century Literary Criticism, Vol. 62. Ed. by Denise Evans & Mary Onorato. (LCS Ser.). 470p. 1997. text 150.00 (0-7876-1243-X, 00156419) Gale.

Nineteenth-Century Literary Criticism, Vol. 63. 400p. 1997. text 150.00 (0-7876-1245-6, 00156420) Gale.

Nineteenth-Century Literary Criticism, Vol. 64. 400p. 1997. text 150.00 (0-7876-1247-2, 00156421) Gale.

Nineteenth Century Literary Criticism: Criticism of the Works of Novelists, Poets, Playwrights, Short Story Writers, Philosophers, & Other Creative Writers Who Died Between 1800 & 1899, from the First Published Critical Appraisals to Current Evaluations, Vol. 4. Ed. by Marie Lazzari. 450p. 1995. text 150.00 (0-8103-8940-1, 002314) Gale.

Nineteenth Century Literary Criticism: Criticism of the Works of Novelists, Poets, Playwrights, Short Story Writers, Philosophers, & Other Creative Writers Who Died Between 1800 & 1899, from the First Published Critical Appraisals to Current Evaluations, Vol. 5. Ed. by James E. Person. 450p. 1995. text 150.00 (0-8103-9295-X, 002315) Gale.

Nineteenth Century Literary Criticism: Excerpts from Criticism of the Works of Novelists, Poets, Playwrights, Short Story Writers, Philosophers & Other Creative Writers Who Died Between 1800 & 1899, from the First Published Critical Appraisals to Current Evaluations. Ed. by Joann Cerrito. (Nineteenth Century Literary Criticism Ser.: Vol. 46). 499p. 1994. text 140.00 (0-8103-8937-1) Gale.

Nineteenth Century Literary Criticism: Excerpts from Criticism of the Works of Novelists, Poets, Playwrights, Short Story Writers, Philosophers & Other Creative Writers Who Died Between 1800 & 1899, from the First Published Critical Appraisals to Current Evaluations. Ed. by Joann Cerrito & Marie Lazzari. (Nineteenth Century Literary Criticism Ser.: Vol. 46). 499p. 1994. text 140.00 (0-8103-9293-3) Gale.

Nineteenth Century Literary Criticism: Excerpts from Criticism of the Works of Novelists, Poets, Playwrights, Short Story Writers, Philosophers & Other Creative Writers Who Died Between 1800 & 1899, from the First Published Critical Appraisals to Current Evaluations, Vol. 45. Joann Cerrito. (Nineteenth Century Literary Criticism Ser.). 472p. 1994. text 150.00 (0-8103-8936-3) Gale.

Nineteenth Century Literary Criticism Vol. 47: Excerpts from Criticism of the Works of Novelists, Poets, Playwrights, Short Story Writers, Philosophers & Other Creative Writers Who Died Between 1800 & 1899, from the First Published Critical Appraisals to Current Evaluations. Ed. by Marie Lazzari. 460p. 1995. text 150.00 (0-8103-8938-X) Gale.

Nineteenth Century Literary Criticism Vol. 48: Excerpts from Criticism of the Works of Novelists, Poets, Playwrights, Short Story Writers, Philosophers & Other Creative Writers Who Died Between 1800 & 1899, from the First Published Critical Appraisals to Current Evaluations. Marie Lazzari. 460p. 1995. text 150.00 (0-8103-8939-8) Gale.

Nineteenth-Century Literary Criticism Vol. 60: Cumulative Index. 400p. 1997. text 150.00 (0-7876-1129-8, GML00597-110441) Gale.

Nineteenth Century Literary Criticism & Cumulative Index, Vol. 42. Ed. by Joann Cerrito. (Nineteenth Century Literary Criticism Ser.). 600p. 1994. text 150.00 (0-8103-9290-9) Gale.

***Nineteenth Century Literary Criticism & Cumulative Index, Vol. 63.** 400p. 1999. text 150.00 (0-7876-1246-4, 00156422) Gale.

Nineteenth-Century Literary Perspectives: Essays in Honor of Lionel Stevenson. Ed. by Benjamin F. Fisher et al. LC 73-84842. 318p. reprint ed. pap. 98.60 (0-608-11969-5, 202344300033) Bks Demand.

Nineteenth-Century Literary Realism: Through the Looking Glass. Katherine Kearns. 320p. (C). 1996. text 64.95 (0-521-49606-3) Cambridge U Pr.

Nineteenth Century Literature, Vol. 51. Marie Lazzari. 500p. 1995. text 150.00 (0-8103-9297-6) Gale.

Nineteenth Century Literature, Vol. 52. James E. Person. 500p. 1996. text 150.00 (0-8103-9298-4) Gale.

Nineteenth-Century Literature Criticism, Vol. 2. Laurie L. Harris. LC 81-6943. 648p. 1982. text 150.00 (0-8103-5802-6) Gale.

Nineteenth-Century Literature Criticism, Vol. 3. Ed. by Laurie L. Harris. 608p. 1983. text 150.00 (0-8103-5803-4) Gale.

Nineteenth-Century Literature Criticism, Vol. 4. Ed. by Laurie L. Harris & Sheila Fitzgerald. LC 81-6943. 648p. 1983. text 150.00 (0-8103-5804-2) Gale.

Nineteenth-Century Literature Criticism, Vol. 5. Ed. by Laurie L. Harris. LC 81-6943. 584p. 1984. text 150.00 (0-8103-5805-0) Gale.

Nineteenth-Century Literature Criticism, Vol. 6. Ed. by Laurie L. Harris & Sheila Fitzgerald. 612p. 1984. text 150.00 (0-8103-5806-9) Gale.

Nineteenth-Century Literature Criticism, Vol. 7. Ed. by Laurie L. Harris & Sheila Fitzgerald. LC 81-6943. 504p. 1984. text 150.00 (0-8103-5807-7) Gale.

Nineteenth-Century Literature Criticism, Vol. 8. Ed. by Laurie L. Harris. LC 81-6943. 552p. 1984. text 150.00 (0-8103-5808-5) Gale.

Nineteenth-Century Literature Criticism, Vol. 9. Ed. by Laurie L. Harris. LC 81-6943. 568p. 1985. text 150.00 (0-8103-5809-3) Gale.

Nineteenth-Century Literature Criticism, Vol. 10. Ed. by Laurie L. Harris & Sheila Fitzgerald. 572p. 1985. text 150.00 (0-8103-5810-7) Gale.

Nineteenth-Century Literature Criticism, Vol. 11. Ed. by Laurie Harris & Emily B. Tennyson. 600p. 1986. text 150.00 (0-8103-5811-5) Gale.

Nineteenth-Century Literature Criticism, Vol. 12. Ed. by Laurie L. Harris & Emily B. Tennyson. 600p. 1986. text 150.00 (0-8103-5812-3) Gale.

Nineteenth-Century Literature Criticism, Vol. 13. Ed. by Laurie L. Harris & Cherie D. Abbey. 600p. 1986. text 150.00 (0-8103-5813-1) Gale.

Nineteenth-Century Literature Criticism, Vol. 14. Ed. by Cherie D. Abbey. 600p. 1987. 150.00 (0-8103-5814-X) Gale.

Nineteenth-Century Literature Criticism, Vol. 15. Ed. by Cherie D. Abbey. 600p. 1987. text 150.00 (0-8103-5815-8) Gale.

Nineteenth-Century Literature Criticism, Vol. 16. Ed. by Cherie D. Abbey. 600p. 1987. text 150.00 (0-8103-5816-6) Gale.

Nineteenth-Century Literature Criticism, Vol. 17. Ed. by Cherie D. Abbey & Janet Mullane. LC 81-6943. 600p. 1988. 150.00 (0-8103-5817-4) Gale.

Nineteenth-Century Literature Criticism, Vol. 18. Ed. by Janet Mullane. 600p. 1988. 150.00 (0-8103-5818-2) Gale.

Nineteenth-Century Literature Criticism, Vol. 19. Ed. by Janet Mullane & Bob Wilson. 600p. 1988. 150.00 (0-8103-5819-0) Gale.

Nineteenth-Century Literature Criticism, Vol. 21. Ed. by Janet Mullane & Robert Wilson. 400p. 1989. text 150.00 (0-8103-5821-2) Gale.

Nineteenth-Century Literature Criticism, Vol. 22. Ed. by Janet Mullane & Bob Wilson. 400p. 1989. text 150.00 (0-8103-5822-0) Gale.

Nineteenth-Century Literature Criticism, Vol. 26. Ed. by Janet Mullane & Robert T. Wilson. LC 84-643008. (Illus.). 511p. 1990. text 150.00 (0-8103-5826-3) Gale.

Nineteenth-Century Literature Criticism, Vol. 27. Ed. by Janet Mullane & Laurie Sherman. LC 84-643008. (Illus.). 511p. 1990. text 150.00 (0-8103-5827-1) Gale.

Nineteenth-Century Literature Criticism, Vol. 28. Paula Kepos. 500p. 1990. text 150.00 (0-8103-5828-X, 001380-M99406) Gale.

Nineteenth-Century Literature Criticism, Vol. 54. James E. Person. 400p. 1996. text 150.00 (0-8103-6437-9) Gale.

Nineteenth-Century Literature Criticism, Vol. 55. James E. Person. 400p. 1996. text 150.00 (0-8103-5518-3) Gale.

Nineteenth Century Literature Criticism, Vol. 65. 480p. 1998. 140.00 (0-7876-1670-2, GML00198-111071) Visible Ink Pr.

***Nineteenth Century Literature Criticism, Vol. 66.** 400p. 1998. text 150.00 (0-7876-1905-1) Gale.

***Nineteenth Century Literature Criticism, Vol. 66.** Evans & Barterian. 500p. 1999. text 145.00 (0-7876-1671-0, GML00198-111072) Gale.

***Nineteenth Century Literature Criticism, Vol. 67.** 400p. 1998. text 150.00 (0-7876-1907-8) Gale.

***Nineteenth Century Literature Criticism, Vol. 68.** 400p. 1998. text 150.00 (0-7876-1908-6) Gale.

***Nineteenth Century Literature Criticism, Vol. 69.** 400p. 1998. text 150.00 (0-7876-1909-4) Gale.

***Nineteenth Century Literature Criticism, Vol. 70.** 400p. 1999. text 150.00 (0-7876-1910-8) Gale.

***Nineteenth Century Literature Criticism, Vol. 72.** 400p. 1999. text 150.00 (0-7876-2420-9) Gale.

***Nineteenth Century Literature Criticism, Vol. 73.** 400p. 1999. text 150.00 (0-7876-2875-1) Gale.

***Nineteenth-Century Literature Criticism, Vol. 74.** 480p. 1999. text 150.00 (0-7876-2876-X, GML00299-112436, Gale Res Intl) Gale.

***Nineteenth-Century Literature Criticism, Vol. 75.** Gale Group Staff. 500p. 1999. text 145.00 (0-7876-2877-8) Gale.

***Nineteenth-Century Literature Criticism, Vol. 76.** Gale Group Staff. 500p. 1999. text 145.00 (0-7876-2878-6) Gale.

Nineteenth Century Literature Criticism, Vol. 78. 500p. Date not set. text 145.00 (0-7876-1911-6) Gale.

Nineteenth Century Literature Criticism, Vol. 79. 500p. Date not set. text 145.00 (0-7876-3150-7) Gale.

Nineteenth Century Literature Criticism, Vol. 80. 500p. Date not set. text 145.00 (0-7876-3151-5) Gale.

***19th-Century Literature Criticism, Vol. 81.** 500p. 2000. text 150.00 (0-7876-3152-3, UXL) Gale.

***19th Century Literature Criticism, Vol. 82.** 500p. 2000. text 150.00 (0-7876-3258-9, UXL) Gale.

***19th-Century Literature Criticism, Vol. 83.** 500p. 2000. text 150.00 (0-7876-3259-7, UXL) Gale.

An Asterisk (*) at the beginning of an entry indicates that the title is appearing for the first time.

***19th Century Literature Criticism, Vol. 84.** 500p. 2000. text 150.00 (*0-7876-3260-0*, UXL) Gale.

***19th Century Literature Criticism, Vol. 85.** 500p. 2000. text 150.00 (*0-7876-3261-9*, UXL) Gale.

Nineteenth-Century Literature Criticism: Archives, Vol. 20. Ed. by Janet Mullane & Bob Wilson. 1988. 150.00 (*0-8103-5820-4*) Gale.

Nineteenth-Century Literature Criticism: Excerpts from Criticism of the Works of Nineteenth-Century Novelists, Poets, Playwrights, Short-Story Writers, & Other Creative Writers, Vol. 1. Laurie L. Harris. 588p. 1981. text 150.00 (*0-8103-5801-8*) Gale.

Nineteenth-Century Lives: Essays Presented to Jerome Hamilton Buckley. Ed. by Laurence S. Lockridge et al. LC 91-15552. (Illus.). 240p. (C). 1989. text 69.95 (*0-521-34181-7*) Cambridge U Pr.

***Nineteenth-Century Lumber Camp Cooking.** Maureen M. Fischer. (Exploring History Through Simple Recipes Ser.). 32p. (J). (gr. 2-7). 2000. lib. bdg. 22.60 (*0-7368-0604-0*, Blue Earth Bks) Capstone Pr.

19th Century Lustreware. Michael Gibson. LC 99-491028. (Illus.). 256p. 1999. 89.50 (*1-85149-306-9*) Antique Collect.

19th Century Macedonian Awakening: A Study of the Life & Works of Kiril Pejchinovich. Michael Seraphinoff. 184p. (C). 1995. lib. bdg. 34.50 (*0-7618-0012-3*) U Pr of Amer.

Nineteenth Century Markets. Phillips. 68.95 (*1-85928-058-7*) Ashgate Pub Co.

***Nineteenth-century Media & the Construction of Identities.** Laurel Brake. 2000. text 59.95 (*0-312-23215-2*) St Martin.

Nineteenth Century Medical Attitudes Toward Alcoholic Addiction: Six Studies, 1814 to 1867, an Original Anthology. Ed. by Gerald N. Grob. LC 80-1204. (Addiction in America Ser.). 1981. lib. bdg. 38.95 (*0-405-13562-9*) Ayer.

Nineteenth Century Memphis Families of Color, 1850-1900. Roberta Church & Ronald Walter. Ed. by Charles W. Crawford. (Illus.). 152p. 1987. pap. 8.95 (*0-937130-12-5*) Burkes Bk Store.

Nineteenth Century Miracles: or Spirits & Their Work in Every Country of the Earth. Emma H. Britten. LC 75-36831. (Occult Ser.). (Illus.). 1976. reprint ed. 47.95 (*0-405-07943-5*) Ayer.

Nineteenth-Century Mormon Architecture. Charles M. Hamilton. (Illus.). 352p. 1995. text 75.00 (*0-19-507505-6*) OUP.

Nineteenth-Century Music. Carl Dahlhaus. Tr. by J. Bradford Robinson. (Illus.). 427p. 1991. reprint ed. pap. 24.95 (*0-520-07644-3*, Pub. by U CA Pr) Cal Prin Full Svc.

Nineteenth-Century Music & the German Romantic Ideology. John J. Daverio. (Illus.). 274p. 1993. 45.00 (*0-02-870675-7*, Schirmer Books) Mac Lib Ref.

Nineteenth-Century Musical Chronicle: Events, 1800-1899, 21B. Compiled by Charles J. Hall. LC 89-17201. (Music Reference Collection: No. 21). 374p. 1989. lib. bdg. 55.00 (*0-313-26578-X*, HNM/, Greenwood Pr) Greenwood.

Nineteenth-Century New York in Rare Photographic Views. Frederick S. Lightfoot. (New York City Ser.). (Illus.). 96p. (Orig.). 1981. pap. 12.95 (*0-486-24137-8*) Dover.

19th Century Novelists: Critical Heritage, 7 vols., Set. Incl. Anthony Trollope. Ed. by Donald Smalley. 592p. (C). 1996. 160.00 (*0-415-13460-9*); Brontes. Ed. by Miriam Allott. 495p. (C). 1996. 140.00 (*0-415-13461-7*); Charles Dickens. Ed. by Philip Collins. 600p. (C). 1996. 160.00 (*0-415-13459-5*); George Eliot. 527p. (C). 1996. 160.00 (*0-415-13462-5*); William Thackeray. Ed. by Geoffrey Tillotson. 407p. (C). 1996. 140.00 (*0-415-13458-7*); Vol. 1. Jane Austen, 1811-1870. B. C. Southam. 286p. (C). 1996. 125.00 (*0-415-13456-0*); Vol. 2. Jane Austen, 1870-1940. B. C. Southam. 320p. (C). 1996. 125.00 (*0-415-13457-9*); 3227p. (C). 1996. Set text, boxed set 815.00 (*0-415-13455-2*) Routledge.

Nineteenth-Century Origins of Neuroscientific Concepts. Edwin Clarke & L. S. Jacyna. 593p. (C). 1998. pap. text 17.00 (*0-7881-5669-1*) DIANE Pub.

Nineteenth-Century Origins of Neuroscientific Concepts. Edwin Clarke & L. S. Jacyna. (C). 1992. pap. 19.95 (*0-520-07879-9*, Pub. by U CA Pr) Cal Prin Full Svc.

Nineteenth Century Painters of the Delaware Valley. Comment by Matthew Baigell. (Illus.). 60p. (Orig.). 1983. pap. 7.00 (*0-938766-01-5*) NJ State Mus.

Nineteenth-Century Painting: A Study in Conflict. John K. Rothenstein. LC 67-28739. (Essay Index Reprint Ser.). 1977. 18.95 (*0-8369-0838-4*) Ayer.

Nineteenth-Century Periodical Press in Britain: A Bibliography of Modern Studies, 1972-1987. Larry K. Uffelman et al. 132p. 1992. 19.95 (*0-9634626-0-1*) Vic Periodicals.

Nineteenth-Century Philosophy. Ed. by Patrick L. Gardiner. LC 69-10325. 1969. pap. 16.95 (*0-02-911220-6*) Free Pr.

Nineteenth Century Photographic Cases & Wall Frames. unabridged ed. Paul K. Berg. LC 95-94712. (Illus.). x, 418p. 1995. pap. 52.00 (*0-9659670-0-X*) P K Berg.

Nineteenth-Century Photographs at the University of New Mexico Art Museum. University of New Mexico Art Museum Staff. (Illus.). 191p. (Orig.). 1989. pap. 39.95 (*0-944282-09-1*) UNM Art Mus.

Nineteenth Century Piano Ballade: An Anthology. Edward MacDowell & Sigismond Thalberg. Ed. by James Parakilas. (Recent Researches in Music of the 19th & Early 20th Centuries Ser.: No. RRN9). (Illus.). 92, xxiip. 1990. pap. 40.00 (*0-89579-249-4*) A-R Eds.

Nineteenth Century Piano Music. Ed. by R. Larry Todd. 426p. 1994. 20.00 (*0-02-872555-7*, Schirmer Books) Mac Lib Ref.

Nineteenth Century Piano Music: Essays in Performance & Analysis. Ed. by David Witten & Michael Saffle. LC 96-34480. (Illus.). viii, 310p. 1997. text 59.00 (*0-8153-1502-3*) Garland.

Nineteenth-Century Pottery & Porcelain in Canada. 2nd rev. ed. Elizabeth Collard. (Illus.). 497p. 1984. 60.00 (*0-7735-0392-7*, Pub. by McG-Queens Univ Pr) CUP Services.

Nineteenth Century Questions. James F. Clarke. LC 71-37527. (Essay Index Reprint Ser.). 1977. reprint ed. 23.95 (*0-8369-2539-4*) Ayer.

Nineteenth Century Readers' Guide to Periodical Literature, 2 vols., Vol. 1. limited ed. 1516p. 1944. write for info. (*0-614-03204-0*) Wilson.

Nineteenth Century Readers' Guide to Periodical Literature, 2 Vols, Vol. 1 & 2. LC 44-5439. 1158p. 1944. 230.00 (*0-8242-0584-7*) Wilson.

Nineteenth Century Rhetoric: An Enumerative Bibliography. Forrest Houlette. LC 88-21765. 395p. 1989. text 20.00 (*0-8240-6645-6*, 787) Garland.

Nineteenth-Century Rhetoric in North America. Nan Johnson. LC 90-20983. 320p. (C). 1991. pap. 18.95 (*0-8093-1655-2*) S Ill U Pr.

Nineteenth-Century Rhetoric in North America. Nan Johnson. LC 90-20983. 320p. (C). 1991. 31.95 (*0-8093-1654-4*) S Ill U Pr.

Nineteenth-Century Russia: Opposition to Autocracy. Derek C. Offord. LC 98-55776. 160p. 1999. pap. 12.66 (*0-582-35767-5*) Addison-Wesley.

19th Century Russian Composers II: Borodin, Cul & Rimski-k. Kone Music Inc. Staff. (Illus.). 1999. pap. 7.95 (*963-9155-25-X*) Kone Music.

19th Century Russian Composers I: Borodin, Curl & Rimski-k. Kone Music Inc. Staff. (Illus.). 1999. pap. 7.95 (*963-9155-24-1*) Kone Music.

Nineteenth-Century Russian Literature in English: A Bibliography of Criticism & Translations. Compiled by Carl R. Proffer. (Illus.). 260p. 1990. 49.50 (*0-88233-943-5*) Ardis Pubs.

Nineteenth Century Scholasticism: The Search for a Unitary Method. 2nd ed. Gerald A. McCool. LC 89-85007. 301p. 1989. pap. 19.95 (*0-8232-1257-2*) Fordham.

***Nineteenth-Century Schoolgirl: The Diary of Caroline Cowles Richards, 1852-1854.** Kerry Graves. (Diaries, Letters & Memoirs Ser.). 32p. (J). (gr. 2-7). 1999. 21.00 (*0-516-21853-0*, Bridgestone Bks) Capstone Pr.

***19th Century Schoolgirl: The Diary of Caroline Cowles Richards, 1852-1855.** Ed. by Kerry Graves. (Diaries, Letters & Memoirs Ser.). (Illus.). 32p. (J). (gr. 2-7). 2000. lib. bdg. 22.60 (*0-7368-0342-4*, Blue Earth Bks) Capstone Pr.

***Nineteenth-Century Science.** Ed. by A. S. Weber. 420p. 2000. pap. 22.95 (*1-55111-165-9*) Broadview Pr.

Nineteenth-Century Scottish Rhetoric: The American Connection. Winifred B. Horner. LC 92-7435. 264p. (C). 1992. 31.95 (*0-8093-1470-3*) S Ill U Pr.

Nineteenth Century Sculpture. H. W. Janson. (Illus.). 288p. 1985. 65.00 (*0-8109-1369-0*, Pub. by Abrams) Time Warner.

Nineteenth Century Self-Help in Education - Mutual Improvement Societies. B. Graham. (C). 1983. 25.00 (*0-902031-91-0*, Pub. by Univ Nottingham) St Mut.

Nineteenth Century Self-Help in Education - Mutual Improvement Societies: A Case Study: The Carlisle Working Men's Reading Rooms. B. Graham. 72p. (C). 1983. text 60.00 (*0-7855-3184-X*, Pub. by Univ Nottingham) St Mut.

Nineteenth Century, 1798-1900, Vol. 4. Ed. by Brian Martin. LC 89-70174. (St. Martin's Anthologies of English Literature Ser.: Vol. No. 4.). 666p. 1990. text 20.00 (*0-312-04476-3*) St Martin.

Nineteenth-Century Shakespeare Burlesques, 5 vols., Set. Ed. by Stanley W. Wells. 1978. 150.00 (*0-89453-078-X*) Scholarly Res Inc.

Nineteenth-Century Spanish Story: Textual Strategies of a Genre in Transition. Lou Charnon-Deutsch. (Monografias A Ser.: No. 116). 176p. 1985. 58.00 (*0-7293-0213-X*, Pub. by Tamesis Bks Ltd) Boydell & Brewer.

Nineteenth Century Spanish Verse. Ed. by Jose Sanchez. LC 79-18739. (SPA.). 1979. reprint ed. pap. text 14.95 (*0-89197-538-1*) Irvington.

Nineteenth-Century Spectroscopy: Development of the Understanding of Spectra, 1802-1897. William McGucken. LC 74-94886. 249p. reprint ed. pap. 77.20 (*0-608-30476-X*, 201186800078) Bks Demand.

Nineteenth Century Stars. Ed. by Robert L. Tiemann & Mark Rucker. 144p. 1989. pap. 10.00 (*0-910137-35-8*) Soc Am Baseball Res.

Nineteenth Century Stories by Women: An Anthology. Ed. by G. Ennis Stephenson. 504p. (C). 1993. pap. 16.95 (*1-55111-000-8*) Broadview Pr.

Nineteenth Century Studies. Ed. by Herbert J. Davis et al. LC 69-10083. 1969. reprint ed. lib. bdg. 19.75 (*0-8371-0057-7*, DANC, Greenwood Pr) Greenwood.

Nineteenth Century Suspense: From Poe to Conan Doyle. Ed. by Clive Bloom et al. 192p. 1988. 24.95 (*0-317-66555-3*) St Martin.

Nineteenth-Century Theatrical Memoirs. Claudia D. Johnson & Vernon E. Johnson. LC 82-15576. 269p. 1982. lib. bdg. 59.95 (*0-313-23644-5*, JNT/, Greenwood Pr) Greenwood.

Nineteenth-Century Theories of Art. Ed. by Joshua C. Taylor. (California Studies in the History of Art: No. XXIV). (Illus.). 1987. pap. 19.95 (*0-520-04888-1*, Pub. by U CA Pr) Cal Prin Full Svc.

Nineteenth-Century Watercolors. Christopher Finch. (Illus.). 296p. 1991. 95.00 (*1-55859-019-6*) Abbeville Pr.

19th Century Whaling Tales: Stray Leaves from a Whaleman's Log; The Perils & Romance of Whaling. James T. Brown & Gustav Kobbe. Ed. by William R. Jones. 40p. 1996. pap. 3.95 (*0-89646-089-4*) Vistabooks.

***Nineteenth-Century Women at the Movies: Adapting Classic Women's Fiction to Film.** Ed. by Barbara Tepa Lupack. LC 99-38681. (Illus.). 331p. 1999. 59.95 (*0-87972-805-1*) Bowling Green Univ Popular Press.

***Nineteenth-Century Women at the Movies: Adapting Classic Women's Fiction to Film.** Ed. by Barbara Tepa Lupack. LC 99-38681. (Illus.). 331p. 1999. pap. 29.95 (*0-87972-806-X*) Bowling Green Univ Popular Press.

Nineteenth-Century Women Learn to Write. Ed. by Catherine Hobbs. 384p. (C). 1995. text 47.50 (*0-8139-1605-4*) U Pr of Va.

Nineteenth-Century Women Poets: An Oxford Anthology. Ed. by Isobel Armstrong et al. 872p. 1998. pap. text 19.95 (*0-19-818483-2*) OUP.

Nineteenth-Century Women Writers of the English-Speaking World, 69. Ed. by Rhoda B. Nathan. LC 85-27250. (Contributions in Women's Studies: No. 69). 299p. 1986. 57.95 (*0-313-25170-3*, NWW/, Greenwood Pr) Greenwood.

19th Century Wooden Boxes. Arene Burgess. LC 97-67261. (Schiffer Book for Collectors Ser.). (Illus.). 160p. 1997. pap. 29.95 (*0-7643-0319-8*) Schiffer.

Nineteenth Century Writings on Homosexuality: A Sourcebook. Chris White. LC 98-45703. 1999. 80.00 (*0-415-15305-0*); pap. 24.99 (*0-415-15306-9*) Routledge.

19th Hartford Institute on Insurance Taxation. Date not set. ring bd. write for info. (*1-56423-066-X*) Ntl Ctr Tax Ed.

Nineteenth Hole. Hal D. Stewart. LC 98-55470. 1999. pap. 5.00 (*0-88734-821-1*) Players Pr.

19th Hole: Stories & Yarns from the Fairways. B. Gallacher. (Illus.). 112p. 1998. pap. 15.95 (*0-233-99052-6*, Pub. by Andre Deutsch) Trafalgar.

19th Indiana Infantry at Gettysburg: Hoosiers' Courage. William Thomas Venner. LC 98-24758. 206p. 1998. pap. 16.95 (*1-57249-131-0*, Burd St Pr) White Mane Pub.

19th National Passive Solar Conference Proceedings. pap. 100.00 (*0-89553-209-3*) Am Solar Energy.

Nineteenth of April, 1775: Concord & Lexington. Harold Murdock. LC 68-58327. (Illus.). 1969. reprint ed. 15.00 (*0-87152-053-2*) Reprint.

XIX Olympiad: Mexico City, 1968, Sapporo, 1972. George G. Daniels. LC 96-28503. (Olympic Century Ser.: Vol. 17). (Illus.). 184p. 1996. write for info. (*1-888383-17-8*) Wld Sport Resch.

Nineteenth Precinct. Christopher Newman. 1992. mass mkt. 5.99 (*0-449-14732-0*, GM) Fawcett.

Nineteenth Session see Report of the Intergovernmental Group on Rice to the Committee on Commodity Problems

XIXe Siecle see Textes & Litterature

Nineteenth Street. rev. ed. Richard Marlitt. LC 78-73291. (Illus.). 218p. 1978. 19.95 (*0-87595-000-0*); pap. 12.95 (*0-87595-138-4*) Oregon Hist.

Nineteenth Symposium on Biotechnology for Fuels & Chemicals. Ed. by Mark Finkelstein & Brian H. Davison. (ABAB Symposium Ser.). 800p. 1998. 200.00 (*0-89603-651-0*) Humana.

Nineteenth Virginia Infantry. Ervin L. Jordan & Herbert A. Thomas, Jr. (Virginia Regimental Histories Ser.). (Illus.). 112p. 1987. 19.95 (*0-930919-42-4*) H E Howard.

XIXes Journees Nationales de Neonatologie, 1989. Ed. by J. P. Relier. (Progres en Neonatologie Ser.: Vol. 9). (Illus.). 268p. 1989. pap. 115.75 (*3-8055-5060-X*) S Karger.

19th Century Girls & Women see Historic Communities Series

1994 IEEE Nuclear Science Symposium. IEEE (Nuclear & Plasma Sciences Society) Staff. Ed. by IEEE (Institute of Electrical & Electronics Engine. 1900p. 1995. pap. text. write for info. (*0-7803-2544-3*); lib. bdg. write for info. (*0-7803-2545-1*); fiche. write for info. (*0-7803-2546-X*, 94CH35762) Inst Electrical.

9th Global Warming International Conference & Expo (GW9), June 8-11, 1998, Hong Kong, China: Abstracts. Sinyan Shen. (Global Warming International Center Ser.). (Illus.). 150p. 1998. pap. 85.00 (*1-884736-08-4*) Supcon Intl.

***Nineties.** Judith Condon. LC 99-37295. (Look at Life in Ser.). (Illus.). 48p. (J). (gr. 4-7). 2000. 25.69 (*0-7398-1342-0*) Raintree Steck-V.

***90s.** Dan Epstein. (Twentieth Century Pop Culture Ser.). (Illus.). (J). 2000. 17.95 (*0-7910-6089-6*) Chelsea Hse.

***Nineties.** Warner Brothers Staff. (80 Years of Popular Music Ser.). 1999. pap. 16.95 (*0-7692-7103-0*) Wrner Bros.

90's: A Look Back. Ed. by Tony Hendra & Peter Elbling. 208p. (Orig.). 1989. pap. 12.95 (*0-380-75866-0*, Avon Bks) Morrow Avon.

Nineties: Personal Recollections of the 20th Century. large type ed. Gloria Wood & Paul Thompson. 24.95 (*1-85695-086-7*, Pub. by ISIS Lrg Prnt) Transaction Pubs.

90s: The Digital Age see 20th Century Design

***Nineties: What the F**k Was That All About?** John Robb. (Illus.). 320p. 2000. pap. 15.00 (*0-09-187135-2*, Pub. by Ebury Pr) Trafalgar.

***'90s Chart Toppers.** 56p. 2000. otabind 16.95 (*1-57560-304-7*, Pub. by Cherry Lane) H Leonard.

Nineties Collection: New Scottish Tunes in the Traditional Style. Ed. by Ian Hardie. 152p. 1998. pap. 20.00 (*0-86241-599-3*) Interlink Pub.

Nineties Relationship with God the Creator. Lonna Traynor. 32p. 2000. pap. 8.00 (*0-8059-4711-6*) Dorrance.

90's Rock Music. 256p. (YA). 1996. pap. 16.95 (*1-57623-599-8*, MF9643) Wrner Bros.

Nineties Rock Sessions for Guitar. Ed. by Ed Lazano. 6p. 1998. pap. text 12.95 (*0-8256-1629-8*, AM945197) Music Sales.

Nineties Vegetarian. Ursula Ferrigno. 1994. 24.95 (*1-85391-309-X*) Merehurst Ltd.

Ninetieth Aero Squadron, American Expeditionary Forces. Leland Carver. (Great War Ser.: No. 4). (Illus.). 136p. 1990. reprint ed. 29.95 (*0-89839-146-6*) Battery Pr.

90th Division in World War I: The Texas-Oklahoma Draft Division in the Great War. Lonnie J. White. LC 96-145854. (Illus.). 266p. 1996. pap. 23.95 (*0-89745-191-0*) Sunflower U Pr.

Ninetieth U. S. Open. Gary Nuhn. Ed. by Bev Norwood. (Illus.). 64p. 1990. 15.00 (*1-878843-00-1*) Intl Merc OH.

***9TimeZones.com: An Email Screenplay Collaboration Between Hungary.** Alan C. Baird & Aniko J. Bartos. LC 99-91107. 349p. 1999. 25.00 (*0-7388-0612-9*); pap. 18.00 (*0-7388-0613-7*) Xlibris Corp.

Ninette de Valois: Idealist Without Illusions. Kathrine Sorley Walker & Ninette De Valois. 384p. pap. 24.95 (*1-85273-061-7*) Princeton Bk Co.

90 Basic Steps to Consider When Designing Your Home: Collection A139. Mike Tecton. (Illus.). 400p. 1998. reprint ed. pap. 35.00 (*0-922070-17-2*, A139) M Tecton Pub.

Ninety Best Day-Hikes: Southwest Oregon & Far Northern California. Art Bernstein. 192p. (Orig.). 1994. pap. text 12.95 (*0-9617525-7-2*) Cloudcap Bks.

90 Brain-Teasers for Trainers. Graham Roberts-Phelps & Anne McDougall. 362p. 1997. 72.95 (*0-566-07979-8*, Pub. by Gower) Ashgate Pub Co.

***90 Day Immune System Makeover.** Janet C. Maccaro. 2000. pap. 12.99 (*0-88419-692-5*) Creation House.

90-Day ISO 9000 Manual: Basics Manual & Implementation Guide. James R. Stewart et al. (Illus.). 184p. 1994. pap., lib. bdg., ring bd. 209.95 (*1-884015-11-5*) St Lucie Pr.

Ninety-Day Wife. Goldrick. 1997. per. 3.25 (*0-373-15710-X*) Harlequin Bks.

Ninety-Day Wife. Emma Goldrick. (Romance Ser.: No. 3464). 1997. per. 3.25 (*0-373-03464-4*, 1-03464-4) Harlequin Bks.

Ninety Days: Daily Reflections for Lent & Easter. Kay Murdy. LC 94-33529. 98p. (Orig.). 1995. pap. 8.95 (*0-89390-306-X*) Resource Pubns.

Ninety Days for Life: The Jailhouse Journal of Pro-Life Advocate, Fred Kerr. Fred W. Kerr. 200p. (Orig.). 1989. pap. 7.95 (*0-929292-07-3*) Hannibal Bks.

Ninety Days of Genevieve. Lucinda Carrington. (Black Lace Ser.). 288p. (Orig.). 1996. mass mkt. 5.95 (*0-352-33070-8*, Pub. by Virgin Bks) London Brdge.

***90 Days, One Day at a Time: A New Beginning for People in Recovery.** John Behnke. LC 99-29235. 160p. 1999. pap. 7.95 (*0-8091-3881-6*) Paulist Pr.

Ninety Days to Communication Excellence. Genie Z. Laborde. (Communication Ser.). 100p. 1985. 9.95 (*0-317-53169-7*) Syntony Inc Pub.

Ninety Days to Financial Fitness. Joan German & Donald R. German. 1986. pap. write for info. (*0-318-67221-9*) Macmillan.

Ninety Days to Fortune. Elizabeth M. Fowler. 1965. 10.95 (*0-8392-1137-6*) Astor-Honor.

***90 Days to Launch: Internet Projects on Time & on Budget.** Shayne Gilbert. 240p. 2000. 27.95 (*0-471-38826-2*) Wiley.

90 Days to Stress Free Living. C. Norman Shealy. LC 98-55289. 1999. pap. 14.95 (*1-86204-465-1*, Pub. by Element MA) Penguin Putnam.

90 Days to the Data Mart. Alan R. Simon. LC 97-52000. 352p. 1998. pap. 34.99 (*0-471-25194-1*) Wiley.

90 Days with Jesus: The Complete Life of Christ from the New Testament, New International Version: Arranged into 90 Daily Devotional Readings. Ed Stewart. LC 90-43076. 1991. 7.99 (*0-8307-1440-5*, Regal Bks) Gospel Lght.

90 Days with the Christian Classics. Augustine Stock. LC 99-15733. (One Minute Bible Ser.). 1999. 14.99 (*0-8054-9278-X*) Broadman.

Ninety Days' Worth of Europe. Edward E. Hale. (Notable American Authors Ser.). 1992. reprint ed. lib. bdg. 75.00 (*0-7812-2975-8*) Rprt Serv.

90 Degrees in the Shade. Clarence Cason. LC 83-1249. (Library of Alabama Classics). (Illus.). 216p. 1983. reprint ed. pap. 19.95 (*0-8173-0170-4*) U of Ala Pr.

98 Activities - Fast Fun for Tiny Hands: Creative Craft Ideas for Preschoolers. Joni Johnson. 40p. (J). (ps-2). 1999. pap. 3.95 (*1-880710-39-0*) Monterey Pacific.

'98 Champs: The Greatest Show: A Chronicle of the Yankees' Amazing Journey to the World Championship. Bob Klapisch et al. 250p. 1998. pap. 19.98 (*0-9654733-4-1*) Record Bks.

***Ninety-Eight Days: A Geographer's View of the Vicksburg Campaign.** Warren E. Grabau. LC 99-50509. (Illus.). 680p. 2000. 48.00 (*1-57233-068-6*, Pub. by U of Tenn Pr) U Ch Pr.

98 Degree: Backstage Pass, 1 vol. Nina Zier. LC 99-217186. (Illus.). 48p. (gr. 5-9). 1999. pap. text 5.99 (*0-439-08710-4*) Scholastic Inc.

98 (Degree Sign) The Unofficial Book. Angie Nichols. (Illus.). 64p. 1999. pap. 12.95 (*0-8230-8351-9*) Watsn-Guptill.

***98 Degrees.** Abr. by Andrews McMeel Publishing Staff. 1999. 4.95 (*0-7407-0418-4*) Andrews & McMeel.

98 Degrees: And Getting Hotter! 4th ed. Kristin Sparks. LC 99-205939. 176+8p. 1999. mass mkt. 4.99 (*0-312-97200-8*, St Martins Paperbacks) St Martin.

98 Degrees: The Official Book. K. M. Squires. 1999. per. 11.95 (*0-671-04169-X*) S&S Trade.

***98 Degrees: 98 Degrees & Rising.** 88p. 1999. otabind 16.95 (*0-634-00798-X*) H Leonard.

98 Degrees & Rising to the Top. Nancy Krulik. 1999. pap. 4.99 (*0-671-03676-9*, Archway) PB.

N

'98 Guide to Unique Meeting Facilities. 11th ed. Orig. Title: The Guide to Campus, Non-Profit & Retreat Meeting Facilities. 220p. 1997. 29.95 (*1-881761-13-4*) AMARC.

. . . 98, 99, 100! Ready, or Not. . . Here I Come! Teddy Slater. LC 98-7323. (Hello Reader! Ser.: Level 2). (Illus.). 32p. (J). (gr. k-2). 1999. pap. 3.99 (*0-590-12009-3*, Pub. by Scholastic Inc) Penguin Putnam.

Ninety-Eight Point Six. Ronald Sukenick. LC 74-24913. 188p. 1975. pap. 8.95 (*0-914590-09-X*) Fiction Coll.

'98 Reader: An Anthology of Song, Ballads, Prose & Poetry. Ed. by Padraic O'Farrell. LC 98-173366. 144p. 1998. pap. 11.95 (*1-901866-03-3*, Pub. by Lilliput Pr) Irish Bks Media.

98 Water Reuse Conference Proceedings: February 1-4, 1998, Lake Buena Vista, Florida. Water Reuse Conference Staff et al. LC 98-181212. 757 p. 1998. write for info. (*0-89867-950-8*) Am Water Wks Assn.

98 Ways to Cook Venison. (Illus.). 113p. 1997. pap. 10.95 (*0-9644922-3-7*) Newsday.

Ninety-Fifth Infantry Division History, 1918-1946. George M. Fuermann & F. Edward Cranz. (Divisional Ser.). (Illus.). 422p. 1988. reprint ed. 49.95 (*0-89839-114-8*) Battery Pr.

95th U. S. Open. Hubert Mizell. Ed. by Bev Norwood. (Illus.). 64p. 1995. 20.00 (*1-878843-13-3*) Intl Merc OH.

***Ninety-First Man.** Barbara V. Wilson. 136p. 2000. pap. write for info. (*0-7541-1014-1*, Pub. by Minerva Pr) Unity Dist.

Ninety-First Psalm Coloring Book. Susan Tate. (Petal Pals Ser.). (Illus.). 12p. (J). (gr. k-3). 1993. pap. 0.39 (*1-884395-05-8*) Clear Blue Sky.

Ninety-First U. S. Open. John Hopkins. Ed. by Bev Norwood. (Illus.). 64p. 1991. 15.00 (*1-878843-02-8*) Intl Merc OH.

95 Animals of the Bible. Nancy P. Johnson. LC 97-73934. (Illus.). 104p. (J). 1997. pap. 12.99 (*0-89051-190-X*) Master Bks.

Ninety-Five Classical Tunes. M. Frank. 1990. 9.95 (*0-685-32155-X*, O328) Hansen Ed Mus.

Ninety-Five Classical Tunes for the Flute. 1990. 7.95 (*0-685-32108-8*, 0353) Hansen Ed Mus.

95 Easy Piano Classics, No. 3. 192p. (Orig.). (YA). 1996. pap. 14.95 (*0-7692-0368-X*, PF0040) Wrner Bros.

Ninety-Five Essential Facts. Lee Eiferman. 16p. (Orig.). 1982. pap. 3.00 (*0-917061-14-4*) Top Stories.

Ninety-Five Forty-Seven Greely Street Vol. 1: Vignettes of My Childhood. Florence J. Goodman. (Illus.). 53p. (Orig.). 1988. pap. 13.00 (*0-917232-25-9*) Gee Tee Bee.

***Ninety-Five Languages & Seven Forms of Intelligence: Education in the Twenty-First Century.** D. Emily Hicks. LC 97-41077. (Counterpoints: Vol. 72). VIII, 187p. (C). 1999. pap. text 29.95 (*0-8204-3909-6*) P Lang Pubng.

95 Mind-Boggling Miniature Puzzles. David King. (Simon & Schuster Two Minute Crosswords Ser.: No. 4). 224p. 1996. pap. 5.95 (*0-684-81421-8*, Fireside) S&S Trade Pap.

95-96 Federal Audit Update Service. Broadus. 1995. 129.00 (*0-15-602139-0*) Harcourt Legal.

95-96 Federal Audit Update Service. 95th ed. Broadus. 1995. 79.00 (*0-15-601993-0*) Harcourt Legal.

95Talk 5Action. Mark Sonnenfeld. 20p. 1997. pap. 3.00 (*1-887379-15-0*) M Sonnenfeld.

95 Supplemental Life Insurance. Anderson. 1995. suppl. ed. 80.00 (*0-316-03975-6*) Aspen Pub.

Ninety-Five Theses. Morris L. Venden. 304p. 1987. pap. 11.99 (*0-8163-1081-5*) Pacific Pr Pub Assn.

95 Theses for the Church. Ben Johnson. 100p. 1995. pap. 8.95 (*1-885121-14-8*) CTS Press.

95 Traditional American Interior Doors & Interior Doorways: Collection A14. Mike Tecton. (Illus.). 64p. 1998. reprint ed. pap. 32.00 (*1-58203-003-0*, A14) M Tecton Pub.

95 Ways You Can Save Taxes in '95. (Illus.). 101p. (Orig.). 1995. pap. 9.95 (*0-9644913-0-3*) Loopholes Pr.

95 Years with John "Jack" Day: The Orphan Nobody Wanted. John Day. LC 97-73382. (Illus.). 266p. 1997. 24.95 (*1-878044-55-9*) Mayhaven Pub.

94 Jet & Propjet Corporate Directory. Peter T. Simmonds. 1994. pap. 19.95 (*0-941024-20-2*) Avcom Intl.

Ninety-Fourth U. S. Open. Hubert Mizell. Ed. by Bev Norwood. (Illus.). 64p. 1994. 20.00 (*1-878843-10-9*) Intl Merc OH.

90 French Styling Details: Collection A181. Mike Tecton. (Illus.). 64p. 1998. reprint ed. pap. 45.00 (*1-58203-082-0*, A181) M Tecton Pub.

Ninety Important Things You Must Know to Successfully Survive the 90s. Marshall B. Stearn. Ed. by Jon Campbell. 176p. (Orig.). 1992. pap. 7.95 (*0-9610480-5-0*) Park West.

Ninety Li a Day. David W. Swift. (Asian Folklore & Social Life Monographs: No. 69). 398p. 1975. 19.00 (*0-89986-064-8*) Oriental Bk Store.

Ninety Minute Hour: Combining Time-Saving Technology with New Age Psychology to Take You Beyond Time Management. Jay C. Levinson. 1990. 17.95 (*0-317-02816-2*, Dutt) Dutton Plume.

90-Minute Interview Prep Book: Get Yourself Ready for a Winning Interview - Fast! Peggy J. Schmidt. 160p. (Orig.). 1996. pap. 15.95 (*1-56079-634-0*) Petersons.

***99: My Life in Pictures, Vol. 1.** Wayne Gretzky & John Davidson. Ed. by Dan Diamond. (Illus.). 240p. 1999. 29.95 (*1-892129-19-1*) Total Sprts.

99: The New Meaning. Walter Abish. (Fiction Ser.). (Illus.). 112p. 1990. 20.00 (*0-930901-67-3*); pap. 8.00 (*0-930901-66-5*) Burning Deck.

99: The New Meaning. deluxe limited aut. ed. Walter Abish. (Fiction Ser.). (Illus.). 112p. 1990. 30.00 (*0-930901-68-1*) Burning Deck.

99 Answers to Questions about Angels, Demons & Spiritual Warfare. B. J. Oropeza. LC 97-14368. 216p. 1997. pap. 10.99 (*0-8308-1968-1*, 1968) InterVarsity.

Ninety-Nine Attributes of Allah: ASMAAA-UL-HUSNAA. Yasin T. Al-Jibouri. 177p. 1997. 20.00 (*1-879402-56-4*); pap. text 12.00 (*1-879402-55-6*) Tahrike Tarsile Quran.

Ninety-Nine Attributes of Allah: Read, Write & Color Names of Allah. Aunali Khalfan. LC 95-94057. 110p. (J). 1995. pap. 5.95 (*0-9645586-0-2*) A Khalfan.

Ninety-Nine Basic Points for Learners of British English. Wing-Fu Dai. (Orig.). 1995. pap. 9.95 (*0-533-11345-8*) Vantage.

Ninety-Nine Beautiful Names of God. Muhammad Al-Ghazali. Tr. by David B. Burrell. 205p. 1996. pap. 30.75 (*0-614-21186-7*, 895) Kazi Pubns.

Ninety-Nine Beautiful Names of God. Al-Ghazali. Tr. by David B. Burrell et al from ARA. (Al-Ghazali Ser.). 138p. 1995. reprint ed. 52.95 (*0-946621-30-6*, Pub. by Islamic Texts); reprint ed. pap. 21.95 (*0-946621-31-4*, Pub. by Islamic Texts) Intl Spec Bk.

***99 Beautiful Names of God: For All the People of the Book.** David Simmons Bentley. LC 99-42624. 112p. 1999. pap. 11.99 (*0-87808-299-9*) William Carey Lib.

99 Canadian Writers Before 1890. 400p. 1990. text 151.00 (*0-8103-4579-X*) Gale.

99 Casserole Dishes with 33 Colour Photographs. Mari Lajos & Karoly Henzo. (Illus.). 64p. 1999. 25.00 (*963-13-2774-4*, Pub. by Corvina Bks) St Mut.

Ninety-Nine Critical Shots in Pool. Ray Martin & Rosser Reeves. LC 75-36260. (Illus.). 256p. 1982. write for info. (*0-8129-0618-7*, Times Bks); pap. 12.00 (*0-8129-6313-X*, Times Bks) Crown Pub Group.

Ninety-Nine Critical Shots in Pool: Everything You Need to Know to Learn & Master the Game. Ray Martin. LC 75-36260. 240p. 1993. pap. 15.00 (*0-8129-2241-7*, Times Bks) Crown Pub Group.

Ninety-Nine Days & Get Up: A Pre- & Post-Release Survival Manual for Inmates & Their Loved Ones. 2nd ed. Ned Rollo. (Information Ser.). 29p. (Orig.). 1988. pap. 3.95 (*1-878436-04-X*) OPEN TX.

99 Dives from the San Juan Islands to Washington to the Gulf Islands & Vancouver Island in British Columbia. Betty Pratt-Johnson. 320p. 1997. pap. 28.95 (*1-895811-18-X*) Heritage Hse.

***99 Fear Street: House of Evil: The First Horror; The Second Horror; The First Horror.** 11th ed. R. L. Stine, pseud. (Fear Street Collector's Edition Ser.: No. 11). (YA). (gr. 7 up). 1998. mass mkt. 6.99 (*0-671-02307-1*, Archway) PB.

99 Film Scenes for Actors. Angela Nicholas. LC 99-230477. 480p. 1999. mass mkt. 5.99 (*0-380-79804-2*, Avon Bks) Morrow Avon.

99 Fun Things to Do in Columbia & Boone County. Pamela Watson. (Show Me Missouri Ser.). (Illus.). 168p. (Orig.). 1996. pap. 12.95 (*0-9646625-2-3*, MG3360) Pebble Pub.

Ninety-Nine Gnats, Nits, & Nibblers. May R. Berenbaum. LC 88-15420. (Illus.). 288p. 1989. 15.95 (*0-252-06027-X*) U of Ill Pr.

***99 Graphis Advertising.** Graphis Staff. 1999. 69.95 (*0-688-16487-0*, Wm Morrow) Morrow Avon.

'99 Guide to Unique Meeting Facilities. 11th ed. Orig. Title: The Guide to Campus, Non-Profit & Retreat Meeting Facilities. 240p. 1998. 29.95 (*1-881761-14-2*) AMARC.

Ninety-Nine Hundred Microprocessor: Architecture, Software, & Interface Techniques. Walter A. Triebel & Avtar Singh. (Illus.). 224p. (C). 1984. text 34.00 (*0-13-622853-4*); pap. text 16.95 (*0-13-622846-1*) P-H.

***99 Hungarian Dishes with 33 Colour Photographs.** Mari Lajos & Karoly Henzo. 64p. 1999. 25.00 (*963-13-4790-7*, Pub. by Corvina Bks) St Mut.

Ninety-Nine Iron. Wendell Givens. 128p. (Orig.). 1992. 18.99 (*1-878561-09-X*) Seacoast AL.

Ninety-Nine Iron: The Season Sewanee Won 5 Games in 6 Days. Wendell Givens. Ed. by Arthur B. Chitty & Elizabeth N. Chitty. (Illus.). 126p. 1992. 18.99 (*1-878050-50-8*) Univ South Pr.

99 Lives: Cats in History, Legend, & Literature. Howard Loxton. LC 98-16444. (Illus.). 144p. 1998. pap. 17.95 (*0-8118-2161-7*) Chronicle Bks.

99 Minutes to Your Ideal Job. William T. Mangum. 219p. 1995. pap. 12.95 (*0-471-11126-0*) Wiley.

Ninety-Nine More Maggots, Mites, & Munchers. May R. Berenbaum. LC 92-34639. (Illus.). 288p. 1993. 15.95 (*0-252-06322-8*); text 37.95 (*0-252-02016-2*) U of Ill Pr.

99 More Unuseless Japanese Inventions/101 Unuseless Japanese Inventions. Kenji Kawakami. 1997. pap. 189.25 (*0-393-31749-8*) Norton.

99 More Unuseless Japanese Inventions. Kenji Kawakami & Dan Papia. (Illus.). 164p. 1997. pap. 12.95 (*0-393-31743-9*) Norton.

***99 Most Common Grammar & Writing Errors . . . And How to Avoid Them.** Communication Briefings Editors. 48p. 1999. pap. 12.50 (*1-878604-33-3*) Briefings Pub Grp.

Ninety-Nine Names of Allah. M. I. Siddiqui. 1988. 8.50 (*1-56744-169-6*) Kazi Pubns.

99 Nursery Rhymes. Leonard C. Duncan. (Illus.). 110p. (J). 1995. spiral bd. 20.00 (*0-941414-15-9*) LCD.

***99 Officer Comp. Report.** Valusource Staff. 24p. 1999. 249.00 incl. disk (*0-471-17374-6*) Wiley.

99Fat-Free Italian Cooking: All Your Favorite Dishes with Less Than 1 Gram of Fat. Barry Bluestein & Kevin Morrissey. LC 98-41251. (Illus.). 288p. 1999. 27.50 (*0-385-48545-X*) Doubleday.

99 Percent Inspiration: Tips, Tales & Techniques for Liberating Your Business Creativity. Bryan W. Mattimore. LC 93-28469. 176p. 1993. pap. 17.95 (*0-8144-7788-7*) AMACOM.

Ninety-Nine Percent of Dance is Non-Movement: The 1999 Manual for Strategic Planners & Project Managers. unabridged ed. Illus. by Expert Software Staff. 62p. 1998. 35.00 (*0-9667543-0-1*) Schemata.

99 Poems in Translation. Ed. by Harold Pinter et al. 160p. 1997. reprint ed. pap. 11.00 (*0-8021-3489-0*, Grove) Grove-Atltic.

99 Poets/1999: An International Poetics Symposium: An International Poetics Symposium. Ed. by Charles Bernstein. Vol. 26, No. 1. 260p. 1999. pap. text 12.00 (*0-8223-6467-0*) Duke.

Ninety-Nine Programming Tips & Tricks for the IBM Personal Computer. Michael Fox. 128p. 1984. 8.95 (*0-86668-046-2*) ARCsoft.

99 Reasons Why No One Knows When Christ Will Return. B. J. Oropeza. LC 94-3576. 180p. (Orig.). 1994. pap. 10.99 (*0-8308-1636-4*, 1636, Saltshaker Bk) InterVarsity.

99 Salads with 33 Colour Photographs. 2nd ed. Mari Lajos & Karoly Henzo. (Illus.). 64p. 1999. 25.00 (*963-13-2664-0*, Pub. by Corvina Bks) St Mut.

Ninety-Nine Sermones Biblicos (Ninety-Nine Bible Messages) Ninety-Nine Bible Messages. Preston Taylor. Tr. by Arnoldo Canclini from ENG. (SPA.). 288p. (Orig.). 1993. pap. 9.99 (*0-311-43044-9*) Casa Bautista.

99 Surefire Ways to Stay Unemployed. Mike Davis. LC 98-5796. (Illus.). 144p. 1998. pap. 12.95 (*1-880090-53-8*) Galde Pr.

99 Teppiche - the Cremer Collection: Gabbeh, Baluchi & Tibetan Rugs. Volkma Gantzhorn. 1997. 95.00 (*3-925369-32-5*, Pub. by Arnoldsche Art Pubs) Antique Collect.

Ninety-Nine Tips & Tricks for the New Pocket Computers. Jim Cole. 128p. (Orig.). 1982. pap. 7.95 (*0-86668-019-5*) ARCsoft.

99 Uses for a Dead Cockroach. Michele Simos & Timothy O'Keefe. Ed. by Joyce S. LaFray Young. 1984. 3.95 (*0-942084-17-9*) SeaSide Pub.

Ninety-Nine Waves. Persis Gerdes. 303p. (Orig.). 2000. pap. 16.95 (*1-884097-18-9*) Depth Charge.

Ninety-Nine Ways to Be Happier Every Day. Terry Hampton & Ronnie Harper. LC 99-32346. (Illus.). 168p. 1999. pap. 9.95 (*1-56554-662-8*) Pelican.

***99 Ways to Beat the Casinos.** Walter Thomason. (Illus.). 2000. pap. 13.95 (*1-56625-144-3*) Bonus Books.

99 Ways to Get Kids to Love Reading. Mary Leonhardt. LC 96-51711. 1997. pap. 10.00 (*0-609-80113-9*) Crown Pub Group.

99 Ways to Get Kids to Love Writing: And 10 Easy Tips for Teaching Them Grammar. Mary Leonhardt. LC 98-21340. 128p. 1998. pap. 8.00 (*0-609-80320-4*) Crown Pub Group.

***99 Ways to get Your Kids to Do Their Homework: And Not Hate It.** Mary Leonhardt. LC 00-28660. (Illus.). 124p. 2000. pap. 10.00 (*0-609-80638-6*, EDU022000, Three Riv Pr) Crown Pub Group.

Ninety-Nine Ways to Start a Study Group & Keep It Growing. Lawrence O. Richards. 160p. (Orig.). 1987. pap. 6.95 (*0-310-31921-8*, 18145P) Zondervan.

Ninety-Nine Years of Navy: From Victoria to VJ Day Through Three Pairs of Eyes. Sam Morley. 1995. 19.95 (*1-899163-07-7*) Cimino Pub Grp.

Ninety-Nines Inc. International Women Pilots. Turner Publishing Company Staff. LC 95-60547. (Illus.). 368p. 1996. 54.95 (*1-56311-203-5*) Turner Pub KY.

99th Bomb Group. Turner Publishing Company Staff. (Illus.). 112p. Date not set. 52.50 (*1-56311-267-1*) Turner Pub KY.

99th U. S. Open Annual. Robert Sommers. Ed. by Bev Norwood. (Illus.). 72p. 1999. 20.00 (*1-878843-25-7*) Intl Merc OH.

91 Best Kept Tax Saving Secrets. (C). 1998. text 9.95 (*0-13-011300-X*) P-H.

91 Expressive Japanese Phrases. Mikio Kawarazaki. (JPN.). 275p. 1997. pap. 32.95 (*4-590-00983-8*, Pub. by Hokuseido Pr) Book East.

91 French Country, Normandy & Provincial Home Plans (Luxurious) Collection A68. Mike Tecton. (Illus.). 50p. 1993. 35.00 (*0-922070-52-0*, Collection A68) M Tecton Pub.

91Factor: Why Women Initiate 91of Divorce, End Most Relationships, & What Can Be Done about It. Ted Baiamonte. 251p. 1998. 21.95 (*0-9631799-2-6*) Am Polit Pr.

90 One-Story Luxury Homes: Collection A93. Mike Tecton. (Illus.). 34p. 1996. pap. 35.00 (*1-58203-057-X*, A93) M Tecton Pub.

90 Patterns for Dog Carvers. Tom James Wolfe. LC 96-13549. (Illus.). 64p. 1996. pap. 9.95 (*0-7643-0098-9*) Schiffer.

90of Helping Is Just Showing Up. James R. Kok. LC 96-8448. 121p. (Orig.). 1996. pap. 7.75 (*1-56212-168-5*) CRC Pubns.

90Off! How & Where to Get the Lowest Possible Price on Absolutely Anything. Laurence Leichman. 1995. pap. 14.95 (*0-9636867-5-5*) Leichman Assocs.

90Reading Goal: 90of Our Students Will Read at or above Grade Level by the End of Third Grade. Lynn Fielding et al. (Illus.). 144p. 1998. pap. 14.95 (*0-9666875-0-7*) New Foundation Pr.

Ninety Recipes from the Iona Community. Ed. by Wild Goose Publications Staff. (C). 1990. 30.00 (*0-947988-17-3*, Pub. by Wild Goose Pubns) St Mut.

92nd Bomb Group: Fame's Favored Few. Turner Publishing Company Staff. (Illus.). 176p. Date not set. 52.50 (*1-56311-241-8*) Turner Pub KY.

90 Second Lawyer: 100 Answers to Common Personal Questions. Robert Irwin & David Ganz. LC 95-54005. 320p. 1996. pap. 14.95 (*0-471-14724-9*) Wiley.

90 Second Lawyer's Guide to Buying Real Estate. Robert Irwin & Robert L. Ganz. LC 96-38521. 240p. 1997. pap. 18.95 (*0-471-16575-1*) Wiley.

Ninety-Second Tiger. Michael Gilbert. 193p. 1998. 19.50 (*0-7540-8520-1*, Black Dagger) Chivers N Amer.

Ninety Second U. S. Open. John Hopkins. Ed. by Bev Norwood. (Illus.). 64p. 1992. 20.00 (*1-878843-04-4*) Intl Merc OH.

***90 Seconds with God.** Roland G. Boyce. LC 00-102740. 203p. 2000. pap. 9.95 (*0-9678882-3-9*) MBrio Bks.

97 Auto Scopemeter. Delmar Staff. 126p. 1996. pap., student ed., wbk. ed. 15.75 (*0-8273-8289-8*) Delmar.

97 Savvy Secrets for Protecting Self & School: A Practical Guide for Today's Teachers & Administrators. Alice H. Sesno. LC 97-45461. 112p. 1998. 39.95 (*0-8039-6728-4*); pap. 16.95 (*0-8039-6729-2*) Corwin Pr.

97 Ways to Make a Baby Laugh. Jack Moore. 1997. pap. 83.40 (*0-7611-0860-2*) Workman Pub.

97 Ways to Make a Baby Laugh. Jack Moore. LC 97-6437. (Illus.). 112p. 1997. pap. text 6.95 (*0-7611-0736-3*, 10736) Workman Pub.

97 Ways to Protect What's Left of Your Privacy & Property Rights. 2nd ed. Ed. by Mark Nestmann. 35p. 1998. 25.00 (*1-891266-07-1*, Pub. by Asset Protection Intl) Pathway Bk Serv.

97th U. S. Open. Robert Sommers & Bev Norwood. (Illus.). 64p. 1997. 20.00 (*1-878843-19-2*) Intl Merc OH.

Ninety-Six: A Romance of Utopia. Frank Rosewater. LC 72-154460. (Utopian Literature Ser.). 1976. reprint ed. 23.95 (*0-405-03542-X*) Ayer.

Ninety-Six Billion Dollar Game - You Are Losing: How Personal Injury Litigation Has Become A Costly Game to You - How to Take Control & Save Money. Phillip J. Hermann. Ed. by Adnrew Hamilton. 264p. 1993. 24.95 (*0-9635375-1-2*) Legal Info Pubns.

96 Colonial Interior Doorways: Collection A31. Mike Tecton. (Illus.). 64p. 1998. reprint ed. pap. 32.00 (*1-58203-015-4*, A31) M Tecton Pub.

96 Great Interview Questions to Ask Before You Hire. Paul Falcone & Adrienne Hickey. 192p. (Orig.). 1996. pap. 17.95 (*0-8144-7909-X*) AMACOM.

96 Home Health, Vol. 1. Fay E. Rozovsky. 1996. 65.00 (*0-316-76103-6*, Little Brwn Med Div) Lppncott W & W.

'96 Jet & Propjet Corporate Directory. Peter T. Simmonds & David G. Richardson. 408p. (Orig.). 1996. pap. 21.95 (*0-941024-22-9*) Avcom Intl.

96-97 Photo Marketing Guidebook. Peter L. Gould & Shama T. Hekim. (Illus.). (Orig.). 1960. pap. 24.95 (*0-9648723-2-3*) Images Media.

96 Sonnets Facing Conviction. Leonard Cirino. 72p. 1999. pap. 10.00 (*1-891812-20-3*, 99-002) Cedar Hill Pubns.

Ninety-Six Tears. Michael Gottlieb. (Roof Bks.). 88p. 1983. pap. text 10.00 (*0-937804-07-X*) Segue NYC.

96 Tears (in My Jeans) R. M. Vaughan. 24p. 1997. pap. text 3.00 (*0-921411-65-0*) Genl Dist Srvs.

96 Theses: Interpreting the Doctrines of the 1st & 2nd Advents. Henry Evans. 218p. (Orig.). 1996. pap. write for info. (*1-57502-215-X*, D0859) Morris Pubng.

96 Traditional Exterior Details of Garden & Estates: Collection A111, Vol. 1. Mike Tecton. (Illus.). 1994. pap. 32.00 (*0-922070-07-5*, COLLECTION A111) M Tecton Pub.

96 Ways You Can Save Taxes in '96: Alabama Edition. Stanley C. Huner et al. 128p. (Orig.). Date not set. pap. 9.95 (*0-9644913-6-2*) Loopholes Pr.

96 Ways You Can Save Taxes in '96: California Edition. Gerry Herter et al. 128p. (Orig.). Date not set. pap. 9.95 (*1-888303-07-7*) Loopholes Pr.

96 Ways You Can Save Taxes in '96: Cincinnati, OH Edition. Tom Cooney & Crystal Faulkner. 128p. (Orig.). Date not set. pap. 9.95 (*1-888303-05-0*) Loopholes Pr.

96 Ways You Can Save Taxes in '96: Cleveland, Ohio Edition. Ed. by Lawrence D. Friedman et al. 128p. (Orig.). Date not set. pap. 9.95 (*0-9644913-1-1*) Loopholes Pr.

96 Ways You Can Save Taxes in '96: Florida Edition. Larry K. Hicks & McGee Lorren. Ed. by Ilona Borish & David A. Jacobi. 128p. (Orig.). Date not set. pap. 9.95 (*1-888303-02-6*) Loopholes Pr.

96 Ways You Can Save Taxes in '96: Grand Rapids, MI Edition. John G. Clark & Daniel L. Carter. 128p. (Orig.). Date not set. pap. 9.95 (*0-9644913-5-4*) Loopholes Pr.

96 Ways You Can Save Taxes in '96: Idaho Edition. Ruth Stevens & J. David Stoddard. 128p. (Orig.). Date not set. pap. 9.95 (*0-9644913-2-X*) Loopholes Pr.

96 Ways You Can Save Taxes in '96: Kansas City Edition. Joyce Morgan. Ed. by Steve Gershon & Scott Slabotsky. 128p. (Orig.). Date not set. pap. 9.95 (*1-888303-03-4*) Loopholes Pr.

96 Ways You Can Save Taxes in '96: Kentucky Edition. Robert R. Hill & Charles L. Stivers. 128p. (Orig.). Date not set. pap. 9.95 (*0-9644913-3-8*) Loopholes Pr.

96 Ways You Can Save Taxes in '96: Louisiana Edition. Boyle Henderson. 128p. (Orig.). Date not set. pap. 9.95 (*1-888303-08-5*) Loopholes Pr.

96 Ways You Can Save Taxes in '96: Minnesota Edition. Gerald M. Faletti & Michael J. Lethert. 128p. (Orig.). Date not set. pap. 9.95 (*1-888303-09-3*) Loopholes Pr.

96 Ways You Can Save Taxes in '96: Mississippi Edition. Thomas Wofford & Ronald Applewhite. 128p. (Orig.). Date not set. pap. 9.95 (*0-9644913-4-6*) Loopholes Pr.

96 Ways You Can Save Taxes in '96: Nevada Edition. Ed. by Gala Gorman & James Main. 128p. (Orig.). Date not set. pap. 9.95 (*0-9644913-8-9*) Loopholes Pr.

96 Ways You Can Save Taxes in '96: Oklahoma Edition. Robert L. Poplin & Thomas E. Ritchie. Ed. by William N. Magee. 128p. (Orig.). Date not set. pap. 90.95 (*0-9644913-7-0*) Loopholes Pr.

N

An Asterisk (*) at the beginning of an entry indicates that the title is appearing for the first time.

96 Ways You Can Save Taxes in '96: Pennsylvania Edition. Ronald Kramer et al. 128p. (Orig.). Date not set. pap. 9.95 (1-888303-06-9) Loopholes Pr.

96 Ways You Can Save Taxes in '96: Southeastern Michigan Edition. Howard Morof et al. 128p. (Orig.). Date not set. pap. 9.95 (1-888303-01-8) Loopholes Pr.

96 Ways You Can Save Taxes in '96: Washington Edition. Dennis Archer et al. 128p. (Orig.). Date not set. pap. 9.95 (1-888303-00-X) Loopholes Pr.

96 Ways You Can Save Taxes in '96: Wisconsin Edition. Mark McNally et al. 128p. (Orig.). Date not set. pap. 9.95 (0-9644913-9-7) Loopholes Pr.

*96th Illinois Volunteer Infantry of Jo Daviess & Lake Counties. unabridged ed. (Illus.). 331p. 1999. pap. 13.95 (0-9676889-0-6) P L Evans.

96th U. S. Open. Hubert Mizell. Ed. by Bev Norwood. (Illus.). 64p. 1996. 20.00 (1-878843-16-8) Intl Merc OH.

1960-1976 see National Party Platforms

90/10 Copper Nickel Alloy Piping for Offshore Applications: Tubes - Seamless & Welded. EEMUA Staff.Tr. of Ninety/Ten Copper Nickel Alloy Piping for Offshore. 1987. pap. 125.00 (0-85931-098-1, Pub. by EEMUA) St Mut.

Ninety-Third U. S. Open. Larry Dorman. Ed. by Bev Norwood. (Illus.). 64p. 1993. 20.00 (1-878843-08-7) Intl Merc OH.

Ninety Thousand Ninety-Nine: Environs of Infinity. George L. Lowe. LC 81-90003. 105p. (Orig.). 1981. pap. 4.95 (0-686-30362-8) G L Lowe.

90210 Guide Annex '96. Venice L. Holmes, Jr. 56p. (Orig.). 1996. pap. 3.95 (0-9638305-2-X) New King Pub.

Ninety-Three. Victor Hugo. 1976. 27.95 (0-8488-0820-7) Amereon Ltd.

Ninety-Three. Victor Hugo. 400p. 1998. pap. 11.95 (0-7867-0590-6) Carroll & Graf.

Ninety-Three. Victor Hugo. Tr. by Lowell Bair. 1998. reprint ed. pap. write for info. (1-56114-264-6) Second Renaissance.

Ninety-Three Health Benefits Planning Guide for Seniors. Phyllis Shelton. Ed. by Michael Goforth. 50p. (Orig.). 1993. pap. 10.00 (0-9633516-0-5) Shelton Mktg.

Ninety Times Guilty. Hickman Powell. LC 73-11909. (Metropolitan America Ser.). 356p. 1974. reprint ed. 23.95 (0-405-05411-4) Ayer.

90 Traditional Garage Plans One to Four Cars - Rooms Above: Collection A4. Mike Tecton. (Illus.). 1993. pap. 28.00 (0-922070-10-5, COLLECTION A4) M Tecton Pub.

Ninety Trillion Fausts. Jack L. Chalker. (Quintara Marathon Ser.: Bk. 3). 368p. 1992. mass mkt. 4.99 (0-441-58103-X) Ace Bks.

Ninety Trillion Fausts. Jack L. Chalker. 416p. 1999. per. 6.99 (0-671-57830-8) S&S Trade.

Ninety-Two & All That: Civil Liberties in the Balance. Michael Spencer. 128p. (C). 1990. pap. text 35.00 (0-900137-34-7, Pub. by NCCL) St Mut.

92 Days. Evelyn Waugh. 19.50 (0-7156-0960-2) G Duckworth.

Ninety-Two in the Shade. Thomas McGuane. LC 94-42801. 197p. 1995. pap. 12.00 (0-679-75289-7) Random.

*Ninety-two Poems & Hymns of Yehuda Halevi. Franz Rosenzweig. Ed. by Richard A. Cohen. Tr. by Thomas Kovach et al. LC 00-2655. 384p. (C). 2000. pap. text 25.95 (0-7914-4390-6) State U NY Pr.

*Ninety-two Poems & Hymns of Yehuda Halevi. Franz Rosenzweig. Ed. by Richard A. Cohen. Tr. by Thomas Kovach et al. LC 00-2655. 384p. (C). 2000. text 75.50 (0-7914-4389-2) State U NY Pr.

Ninety-Two Twenty-Six Kercheval: The Storefront That Did Not Burn. Nancy Milio. 224p. 1970. pap. text 17.95 (0-472-06180-1, 06180, Ann Arbor Bks) U of Mich Pr.

Ninety Years & Growing: Story of Lincoln National Corporation. Michael Hawfield. 1995. 19.95 (1-878208-68-3) Guild Pr IN.

Ninety Years in Aiken County (South Carolina) Gasper L. Toole, II. (Illus.). 404p. 1993. reprint ed. lib. bdg. 42.50 (0-8328-3545-5) Higginson Bk Co.

Ninety Years of Education in California, 1846-1936. William W. Ferrier. 1992. reprint ed. lib. bdg. 75.00 (0-7812-5032-3) Rprt Serv.

Ninety Years of Fashion. enl. rev. ed. Annalee Gold. (Illus.). 144p. 1990. 40.00 (0-87005-680-8) Fairchild.

90 Years of Ford. George H. Dammann. (Crestline Ser.). (Illus.). 608p. 1993. 44.95 (0-87938-682-7) MBI Pubg.

Ninety's Country Gold. 152p. 1993. per. 12.95 (0-7935-2106-8, 00311607) H Leonard.

90/10 Copper Nickel Alloy Piping for Offshore Applications: Fittings. EEMUA Staff. 1987. pap. 125.00 (0-85931-108-2, Pub. by EEMUA) St Mut.

Ninety/Ten Copper Nickel Alloy Piping for Offshore see 90/10 Copper Nickel Alloy Piping for Offshore Applications: Tubes - Seamless & Welded

90/10 Copper Nickel Piping for Offshore Applications: Flanges Composite & Solid. EEMUA Staff. 1987. pap. 125.00 (0-85931-103-1, Pub. by EEMUA) St Mut.

Ninez: Games, Stories & Verses of Spanish Childhood. Virginia Ebinger. Ed. by James C. Smith, Jr. LC 93-3215. (Illus.). 64p. (Orig.). 1993. pap. 8.95 (0-86534-175-3) Sunstone Pr.

Ninez de Jesucristo: Desde Su Nacimiento Hasta Sus 14 Anos. Josephine C. Trust. Orig. Title: Jesus Christ's Childhood. (SPA.). 44p. 1957. reprint ed. pap. 1.00 (1-892203-18-9, 17-S, Superet Pr) Mother Trust.

Ninfa: A Papal Retreat. Esme Howard & Lauro Marchetti. LC 99-30842. (Small Books of Great Gardens Ser.). 79p. 1999. text 18.95 (0-86565-205-8) Vendome.

Ninfa Gardens. Marella Agnelli. 1999. 55.00 (88-422-0797-7, Pub. by U Allemandi) Antique Collect.

Ningen No Ikigai see Meaningful Life

Ningen o Sodateru Kokoro see The Wholesome Family Life

Ningen Rashiku Ikiru see Richer Life

Ningun Beso Para Mama. Tomi Ungerer. 1998. pap. 11.00 (84-264-3590-4) Lectorum Pubns.

*Ningun Hombre para Ella (No Man for Her) The Seduction Game. Sara Craven. (Bianca Ser.: No. 187). 1999. per. 3.50 (0-373-33537-7, 1-33537-1) Harlequin Bks.

*Ningun Lugar Sagrado. Rosa R. Rey. (Biblioteca Breve Ser.). (SPA.). 1999. 14.95 (84-322-0762-4) E Seix Barral.

Ningyo: The Art of the Human Figurine - Traditional Japanese Display Dolls from the Ayervais Collection. Shigeki Kawakami. (Illus.). 95p. 1995. pap. 30.00 (0-913304-41-7) Japan Soc.

Ninib, the Determiner of Fates. Hugo Radau. (Publications of the Babylonian Section: Series D, Vol. V/2). (Illus.). x, 73p. 1910. pap. 10.00 (0-686-11919-3) U Museum Pubns.

Nini's Way, Bk. 1. Helen H. Kapelman. (Illus.). (J). (gr. k-2). 1988. 4.95 (0-9621807-0-X) H H Kapelman.

Ninja. Jerry Craven. LC 94-2528. (Illustrated History of Martial Arts Ser.). (Illus.). 32p. (J). (gr. 3-8). 1994. lib. bdg. 14.95 (0-86593-365-0) Rourke Corp.

Ninja. Eric Van Lustbader. 512p. 1985. mass mkt. 6.99 (0-449-20916-4, Crest) Fawcett.

Ninja. large type ed. Eric Van Lustbader. 800p. 1983. 27.99 (0-7089-8149-6, Charnwood) Ulverscroft.

Ninja: Secrets of Invisibility. Ashida Kim. (Illus.). 119p. 1984. pap. 7.95 (0-8065-0920-1, Citadel Pr) Carol Pub Group.

Ninja: The Official Strategy Guide. Kip Ward. LC 97-76271. (Illus.). 96p. 1998. pap. 12.99 (0-7615-1482-1) Prima Pub.

Ninja Vol. 1: Spirit of the Shadow Warrior. Stephen K. Hayes. Ed. by Bill Griffeth. LC 80-84678. (Japanese Arts Ser.). 1980. pap. 17.95 (0-89750-073-3, 411) Ohara Pubns.

Ninja Vol. 2: Warrior Ways of Enlightenment. Stephen K. Hayes. LC 81-83991. (Japanese Arts Ser.). (Illus.). 160p. (Orig.). 1981. pap. 17.95 (0-89750-077-6, 414) Ohara Pubns.

Ninja Vol. 3: Warrior Path of Togakure. Stephen K. Hayes. LC 83-61558. (Japanese Arts Ser.). (Illus.). (Orig.). 1983. pap. 19.95 (0-89750-090-3, 427) Ohara Pubns.

Ninja Vol. 4: Legacy of the Night Warrior. Stephen K. Hayes. Ed. by Mike Lee. LC 84-61831. (Japanese Arts Ser.). 192p. (Orig.). 1984. pap. 19.95 (0-89750-102-0, 437) Ohara Pubns.

Ninja Vol. 5: Lore of the Shinobi Warrior. Stephen K. Hayes. 1990. pap. 19.95 (0-89750-123-3, 463) Ohara Pubns.

Ninja & Their Secret Fighting Art. Stephen K. Hayes. LC 81-50105. (Illus.). 156p. 1981. 19.95 (0-8048-1374-4); pap. 10.95 (0-8048-1656-5) Tuttle Pubng.

Ninja Avenger. Jay Leibold. (Choose Your Own Adventure Ser.: No. 179). (Illus.). 112p. (J). (gr. 4-8). 1997. mass mkt. 3.50 (0-553-56750-0) BDD Bks Young Read.

Ninja Craft. Haha Lung. LC 97-72942. (Illus.). 144p. (Orig.). 1997. pap. 16.00 (0-939427-84-2) Alpha Pubns OH.

Ninja Cyborg. Jay Leibold. (Choose Your Own Adventure Ser.: No. 155). (J). (gr. 4-8). 1995. 8.60 (0-606-07952-1, Pub. by Turtleback) Demco.

*Ninja Justice: Six Tales of Murder & Revenge. Shotaro Ikenami. 2000. pap. 11.00 (4-7700-2537-8) Kodansha.

Ninja Mind Control. Ashida Kim. LC 98-232080. 158p. 1986. pap. 9.95 (0-8065-0997-X, Citadel Pr) Carol Pub Group.

Ninja Shuriken Manual. Takayuki Kubota. 64p. (Orig.). 1986. pap. 5.95 (0-934489-00-9, 560) I & I Sports.

Ninja, the Invisible Assassins. Andrew Adams. Ed. by Pat Alston. LC 75-130760. (Japanese Arts Ser.). (Illus.). 1970. 19.95 (0-89750-030-X, 302) Ohara Pubns.

Ninja Training Manual: Self-Defense & Fighting Secrets. Christopher Hunter. (Illus.). 188p. 1996. pap. 8.95 (0-8065-1781-6, Citadel Pr) Carol Pub Group.

Ninja Turtles: The Next Mutation. Catherine Clarke. (J). 1998. 3.99 (0-679-89301-6, Pub. by Random Bks Yng Read) Random.

Ninja Weapons: Chain & Shuriken. Charles V. Gruzanski. Orig. Title: Spike & Chain. (Illus.). 104p. 1991. pap. 9.95 (0-8048-1705-7) Tuttle Pubng.

Ninjak the Boss: Acclaim Adventure Zone. Evan Skolnick. (Acclaim Adventure Zone Ser.). 1997. pap. text 4.50 (1-57840-086-4, Pub. by Acclaim Bks) Penguin Putnam.

Ninjas & Superspies. rev. ed. Erick Wujcik. Ed. by Kevin Siembieda et al. (Illus.). 176p. (YA). (gr. 8 up). 1987. pap. 16.95 (0-916211-31-2, 525) Palladium Bks.

Ninja's Carnival. Espinet & Zaman. (Illus.). 24p. (J). (gr. k-5). 1994. per. write for info. (0-920813-63-1) Sister Vis Pr.

Ninjas Don't Bake Pumpkin Pies. Debbie Dadey & Marcia Thornton Jones. (Adventures of the Bailey School Kids Ser.: No. 38). (Illus.). 70p. (J). (gr. 2-5). 1999. pap. 3.99 (0-439-04398-0) Scholastic Inc.

Ninjas Kick Back. Todd Strasser. 208p. (J). (gr. 4-7). 1994. pap. 3.50 (0-590-48450-8) Scholastic Inc.

*Ninjitsu for Women: Ninja Secrets of Defensive Fighting. Ashida Kim. LC 99-16393. 1999. pap. text. write for info. (0-8065-2145-7) Carol Pub Group.

Ninjutsu. Stephen K. Hayes. (Illus.). 176p. (Orig.). 1984. pap. 16.95 (0-8092-5478-6, 547860, Contemporary Bks) NTC Contemp Pub Co.

Ninjutsu: The Art of Invisibility. 2nd ed. Donn F. Draeger. (Illus.). 128p. 1992. pap. 7.95 (0-8048-1597-6) Tuttle Pubng.

Ninjutsu History & Tradition. Masaaki Hatsumi. LC 81-70819. (Illus.). 205p. (Orig.). 1981. pap. 12.95 (0-86568-027-2, 105) Unique Pubns.

Ninnuock: The Algonkian People of New England. Steven F. Johnson. LC 93-34546. (Illus.). 282p. 1995. pap. 16.95 (0-9625144-2-X) Bliss Pub Co.

Nino. Clay Henry Will Fisher, pseud. 1994. lib. bdg. 17.50 (0-7451-4601-5, Gunsmoke) Chivers N Amer.

Nino. Anne D. Munson. 1999. pap. 7.95 (0-14-012977-4, Viking) Viking Penguin.

*Nino. Madeleine Nash. 2001. write for info. (0-446-52481-6) Warner Bks.

Nino: Children of the Streets, Mexico City. Elena Poniatowska. LC 98-51520. (Illus.). 168p. 1999. 45.00 (0-8156-0592-7) Syracuse U Pr.

Nino: How Fable & Fact Together Help Explain the Weather. Patricia Seibert. LC 99-13757. (Illus.). 32p. (J). (gr. 3-5). 1999. lib. bdg. 21.90 (0-7613-1273-0, Copper Beech Bks) Millbrook Pr.

Nino: Stories by Sharon Doubiago, No. 35. Sharon Doubiago. 152p. 1988. pap. 9.95 (0-918786-39-8) Lost Roads.

Nino: Stormy Weather for People & Wildlife. Caroline Arnold. LC 98-4826. 48p. (J). (gr. 3-6). 1998. 16.00 (0-395-77602-3, Clarion Bks) HM.

Nino! And La Nina. Sally Rose. LC 99-31149. (Weather Channel Ser.: No. 6). (Illus.). 63p. (J). (gr. 4-6). 1999. 3.99 (0-689-82015-1, Simon Spot) Litle Simon.

*Nino & La Nina: Weather in the Headlines. April Pulley Sayre. LC 00-25605. 2000. pap. write for info. (0-7613-1405-9) Millbrook Pr.

*Nino & the Southern Oscillation: Multiscale Variability & Global & Regional Impacts. Ed. by Henry F. Diaz & Vera Markgraf. (Illus.). 480p. (C). 2000. 90.00 (0-521-62138-0) Cambridge U Pr.

Nino Arribabajo see Upside down Boy: El Nino de Cabeza

Nino Campesino Deshabilitado: Una Guia Para Promotores de Salud, Trabajadores de Rehabilitation y Familias. David B. Werner. Ed. by Elizabeth De Avila & Martin Lamarque. LC 86-81738. (SPA., Illus.). 672p. (Orig.). 1990. pap. 22.00 (0-942364-07-4) Hesperian Found.

Nino Cocinero Latinoamericano. Coedicion Latinoamericana Staff. 36p. 1996. pap. 7.50 (968-494-063-7) Ediciones Huracan.

*Nino con los Panes y los Peces. Enid Blyton. (SPA.). 1999. pap. 4.99 (0-8254-1065-7, Edit Portavoz) Kregel.

Nino Cuervo (Crow Boy) Taro Yashima. Tr. by Maria Fiol. (Illus.). 40p. (J). (gr. 2-3). 1996. 14.95 (1-880507-21-8) Lectorum Pubns.

Nino de Belen.Tr. of Baby in Bethlehem. (SPA.). 12p. (J). 1994. write for info. (0-614-27086-3) Editorial Unilit.

Nino de Belen. Scripture Union Staff.Tr. of Baby in Bethlehem. (SPA.). (J). 1994. 9.99 (1-56063-698-X, 497713) Editorial Unilit.

Nino de Dos a Cinco Anos. Editorial America, S. A. Staff. Ed. by Maria E. Del Real. (SPA., Illus.). 264p. (Orig.). 1990. pap. write for info. (0-944499-69-4) Editorial Amer.

Nino de Guano. Lourdes G. Franca. LC 92-75211. (Coleccion Arte). (SPA., Illus.). 64p. (Orig.). 1993. pap. 19.00 (0-89729-666-4) Ediciones.

Nino de Seis a Trece Anos. Editorial America, S. A. Staff. Ed. by Maria E. Del Real. (SPA., Illus.). 304p. (Orig.). 1990. pap. write for info. (0-944499-88-0) Editorial Amer.

*Nino en el Templo. Enid Blyton. (SPA.). 1999. pap. 4.99 (0-8254-1066-5, Edit Portavoz) Kregel.

Nino Excepcional. Armando Rovira de Jesus. (SPA.). 342p. 1991. pap. write for info. (0-929441-16-8) Pubns Puertorriquenas.

Nino Fidencio: A Heart Thrown Open. Dore Gardner. 1992. 34.95 (0-89013-233-X) Museum NM Pr.

Nino Fidencio: A Heart Thrown Open. Dore Gardner. (Illus.). 112p. 1994. pap. 24.95 (0-89013-234-8) Museum NM Pr.

Nino Gigante (The Giant Child) J. L. Garcia Sanchez. (Derechos del Nino Ser.). (SPA., Illus.). 32p. (J). (gr. k-2). 1988. 9.95 (84-372-1346-0) Santillana.

Nino Gigante (The Giant Child) J. L. Garcia Sanchez. (SPA.). (J). (gr. 2-6). 1994. pap. 8.95 (1-56014-580-3) Santillana.

Nino Inocente de la Guardia. Lope de Vega. Ed. by Anthony J. Farrell. (Textos B Ser.: Vol. XXVII). (ENG & SPA.). 163p. 1985. 41.00 (0-7293-0215-6, Pub. by Tamesis Bks Ltd) Boydell & Brewer.

Nino Insoportable. Doris J. Rapp. Tr. by Lydia J. Zaragoza. Orig. Title: The Impossible Child. (SPA., Illus.). 170p. 1988. pap. 12.95 (1-880509-01-6); VHS 16.95 (1-880509-02-4) Practical Allergy.

*Nino Jesus. Enid Blyton. (SPA.). 1999. pap. 4.99 (0-8254-1067-3, Edit Portavoz) Kregel.

Nino Jesus: Little Baby Jesus. Patricia Shely. Tr. by Nola Granberry. (Libros Para Colorear Ser.). (SPA., Illus.). 16p. (J). (gr. 1-3). 1982. reprint ed. pap. 2.75 (0-311-38563-X) Casa Bautista.

Nino Jesus de Praga. Ludvik Nemec. (SPA.). 1987. pap. 2.95 (0-89942-439-2, 439/S) Catholic Bk Pub.

Nino Maicero: The Corn Boy. Patricia Van Rhijn. (SPA., Illus.). 35p. (J). (gr. k-4). 1990. 10.54 (968-494-042-4) Donars.

*Nino, 1997-1998: The Climate Event of the Century. Ed. by Stanley A. Changnon. LC 99-35619. (Illus.). 232p. 2000. pap. text 29.95 (0-19-513552-0) OUP.

*Nino, 1997-1998: The Climate Event of the Century. Ed. by Stanley A. Changnon. LC 99-35619. (Illus.). 232p. 2000. text 60.00 (0-19-513551-2) OUP.

Nino North: Nino Effects in the Eastern Subarctic Pacific Ocean. Ed. by Warren S. Wooster & David L. Fluharty. LC 85-15638. (Workshop Proceedings Ser.). (Illus.). viii, 312p. (Orig.). 1985. pap. text 10.00 (0-934539-01-4, WSG-WO 85-3) Wash Sea Grant.

Nino Que Buscaba a Ayer (The Boy Who Searched for Yesterday) Claribel Alegria. (Encuento/Literary Encounters Ser.). 1997. pap. text 10.95 (968-494-072-6) Donars.

Nino Que No Creia en la Primavera. Lucille Clifton. Tr. by Alma E. Ada.Tr. of Boy Who Didn't Believe in Spring. (SPA., Illus.). 32p. (J). (ps-3). 1996. pap. 4.99 (0-14-055892-6, PuffinBks) Peng Put Young Read.

Nino Que No Creia En La Primavera. Lucille Clifton. (SPA.). 1996. 10.19 (0-606-09235-8, Pub. by Turtleback) Demco.

Nino Que Pagaba El Pato. Sid Fleischman.Tr. of Whipping Boy. (SPA.). (J). 9.95 (84-204-4641-6) Santillana.

Nino Que Pagaba El Pato. Sid Fleischman.Tr. of Whipping Boy. 1996. 15.05 (0-606-10415-1, Pub. by Turtleback) Demco.

Nino Que Tenia Dos Ojos (The Boy Who Had Two Eyes) J. L. Garcia Sanchez. (SPA., Illus.). (J). (ps-3). 1994. pap. 8.95 (0-88272-136-4) Santillana.

Nino, Su Sufrimiento y la Pobreza. Elda Abrevaya. (SPA.). 160p. 1992. pap. write for info. (0-929441-37-0) Pubns Puertorriquenas.

Nino Survival Cookbook: Cooking Without Conveniences. Sue Oleson. (Illus.). xii, 89p. 2000. spiral bd. 17.95 (1-891829-00-9) Peaceful Angel.

Nino (The El Nino Effect) Climatico de la Naturaleza (A Climate Experiment of Nature) Wolf E. Arntz & Eberhard Fahrbach. (Ciencia para Todos Ser.). (SPA.). 312p. 1996. pap. 26.99 (968-16-5042-5, Pub. by Fondo) Continental Bk.

Nino, un Regalo (A Gift for Baby) Raye Morgan. (Deseo Ser.).Tr. of A Baby, a Gift. (SPA.). 1997. per. 3.50 (0-373-35212-3, 1-35212-9) Harlequin Bks.

Nino y el Rio (The Child & the River) Henri Bosco. Tr. by Jose L. Rivas. (SPA., Illus.). 120p. (J). (gr. 5-6). 1992. pap. 5.99 (968-16-4706-8, Pub. by Fondo) Continental Bk.

*Ninos. Miguel Delibes. 1999. pap. 9.95 (84-08-02902-9) Planeta Edit.

Ninos Alfabeticos. Lourdes Ayala & Margarita Isona-Rodriguez. LC 95-6187. (Illus.). 32p. (J). 1995. pap. 6.95 (0-88106-815-2) Charlesbridge Pub.

Ninos Como Yo. unabridged ed. Tr. by Rosealma Zubizarreta.Tr. of Children Just Like Me. (SPA., Illus.). 80p. (J). (gr. 2-6). 1995. 18.95 (0-9628720-2-4, MI72024) Mariuccia Iaconi Bk Imports.

Ninos con Problemas de Conducta y Aprendizaje: Temas Contemporaneos y Estrategias. Roberto Moran. 381p. 1984. pap. 12.50 (0-8477-2906-0) U of PR Pr.

Ninos de la Biblia. (SPA.). 9.00 (84-241-5410-X) E Torres & Sons.

Ninos de la Biblia. Jean-Francois Bourgeois. Ed. by Alberto Maecha. Orig. Title: Les Enfants de la Bible. (SPA., Illus.). 40p. (J). (gr. 3-5). 1984. pap. write for info. (0-942504-11-9) Overcomer Pr.

Ninos de la Biblia. Carine Mackenzie.Tr. of Children of the Bible. (SPA.). 48p. (J). 1993. 9.99 (1-56063-546-0, 498748) Editorial Unilit.

Ninos Desafiantes (Defiant Children) Materiales de Evaluacion y Folletos para los Padres (A Clinician's Manual for Assessment & Parent Training), Spanish Supplement. 2nd ed. Russell A. Barkley. LC 89-1862. (School Practitioner Ser.). (SPA.). 87p. 1997. pap. text 19.95 (1-57230-226-7, 0226) Guilford Pubns.

Ninos Desobedientes. Illus. by John I. Rojas.Tr. of Disobedient Children. (SPA.). 92p. (J). (gr. 4-6). 1994. 14.99 (958-07-0313-2, Pub. by Santillana) T R Bks.

Ninos Favoritos de la Biblia. Mig Holder. (SPA., Illus.). 20p. 1995. pap. 5.99 (0-8254-1318-4, Edit Portavoz) Kregel.

Ninos Inteligentes Con Problemas Escolares. Priscilla Vail. (SPA.). 310p. 1997. pap. text 22.98 (968-13-3007-2) Edit Diana.

Ninos International Family Cookbook. (Illus.). 268p. 1989. pap. 9.95 (0-935366-21-0) Los Ninos.

Ninos Mueren Tambien: Spanish-Children Die, Too. Joy Johnson. 1989. pap. 3.50 (1-56123-040-5) Centering Corp.

Ninos Tontos. Ana M. Matute. (SPA.). pap. 11.95 (84-233-0958-4, Pub. by Destino) Continental Bk.

Ninos y Ninas Que Exploran y Construyen: Curriculo para el Desarrollo Integral. Angeles Molina Iturrondo. (SPA.). 384p. 1994. pap. 19.95 (0-8477-0213-8) U of PR Pr.

Ninsori de Intuneric: Poeme. 2nd ed. Florentin Smarandache. Ed. by Xiquan Publishing House Staff. (RUM.). 120p. (Orig.). (C). 1991. reprint ed. pap. 12.99 (1-879585-05-7) Erhus Univ Pr.

Ninstints: Haida World Heritage Site. George F. MacDonald. (Illus.). 64p. 1986. pap. 15.95 (0-7748-0163-8) U of Wash Pr.

1956 see Studies in Bibliography: Papers of the Bibliographical Society of the University of Virginia

1998 Medical Practice Management Handbook. Reed Tinsley. 1997. pap. 99.00 (0-15-606088-4, Pub. by Harcourt Coll Pubs) Harcourt.

1998 Super Horoscopes: Pisces. Berkley Publishing Staff. (Berkley Super Horoscopes Ser.). 256p. 1997. pap. 6.99 (0-425-15897-7) Berkley Pub.

*1998 Topical Meeting On Silicon Monolithic integrated Circuits in Rf Systems: Digest of Papers: [17-18 September, 1998, Ann Arbor, Michigan, USA]. Sammy Kayali & IEEE, Microwave, Theory & Techniques Society Staff. LC 98-83181. viii, 219 p. 1998. pap. write for info. incl. fiche (0-7803-5289-0) IEEE Standards.

1998 Volume 11.1: Euthanasia. 22.95 (0-567-08621-6) T&T Clark Pubs.

1998 Year Book of Family Practice. Berg. (Illus.). 472p. 1998. text 66.95 (0-8151-9629-6, 24966) Mosby Inc.

***1999 Accounting Office Management & Administration Report Yearbook.** Susan Sandler. Ed. by David Solomon. (Illus.). 200p. 1999. pap. 199.00 (*1-58673-010-X*) IOMA.

1999 Pro Golf Scouting Report. John Gordon. (Illus.). 280p. 1999. pap. 16.95 (*1-894020-36-7*) Warwick Publ.

1999-2000 U. S. Airlines Salary Survey & Career Earnings Comparison. 3rd ed. Kit Darby & Dan Gradwohl. Ed. by Montina L. Waymire & Becky Dean. 144p. 1999. pap. 40.00 (*1-891726-27-7*, AIR Inc) Aviation Info.

1999 Yearbook of Otolaryngology-Head & Neck Surgery. 2nd ed. Paparella. (Illus.). 350p. 1999. text 79.00 (*0-8151-9719-5*, 25006) Mosby Inc.

1997 Civil Procedure Supplement for Use with All Pleading & Procedure Casebooks: 1997 Edition. annuals 11th ed. Jack Friedenthal. (American Casebook Ser.). 467p. (C). 1997. pap. text, suppl. ed. write for info. (*0-314-21180-2*) West Pub.

1997 Construction Manager. Andrew M. Civitello. 480p. 1996. text 39.95 (*0-07-011782-9*) McGraw.

1997 IEEE International Conference on Microelectronic Test Structures Proceedings. IEEE (Electron Devices Society) Staff. Ed. by IEEE (Institute of Electrical & Electronics Engine. LC 96-75517. 200p. 1997. fiche. write for info. (*0-7803-3245-8*, 97CM35914) Inst Electrical.

1997 IEEE International Conference on Microelectronic Test Structures Proceedings. IEEE (Electron Devices Society) Staff. Ed. by IEEE (Institute of Electrical & Electronics Engine. LC 96-75517. 200p. 1997. pap. text 96.00 (*0-7803-3243-1*, 97CH35914); lib. bdg. 96.00 (*0-7803-3244-X*, 97CB35914) Inst Electrical.

1996 New Jersey Lawyers Diary & Manual Including Bar Directory of New Jersey. rev. ed. Skinder-Strauss Staff. 1547p. 1995. 55.00 (*1-57741-005-X*) Skinder-Strauss.

1996 New Jersey Lawyers Diary & Manual Including Bar Directory of New Jersey. rev. ed. Skinder-Strauss Staff. 1996. cd-rom 55.00 (*1-57741-016-5*) Skinder-Strauss.

1992 Papua New Guinea Election: Change & Continuity in Electoral Politics. Yaw Saffu & Australian National University Press Staff. LC 98-144998. xii, 409 p. 1996. write for info. (*0-7315-2318-0*) Aust Nat Univ.

1998 Year Book of Nephrology, Hypertension & Mineral Metabolism. Steve Schwab. (Illus.). 312p. 1998. text 83.00 (*0-8151-9646-6*, 24983) Mosby Inc.

1998 Year Book of Otolaryngology - Head & Neck Surgery. Paparella. (Illus.). 368p. 1998. text 76.00 (*0-8151-9718-7*, 25005) Mosby Inc.

1968 - McCarthy - New Hampshire: I Hear American Singing. David C. Hoeh. Ed. by Ray Howe. (Illus.). 515p. (Orig.). 1995. pap. 22.50 (*1-883477-00-X*) Lone Oak MN.

Nineteen Thousand Three Hundred Six Large Boilers. Nceer. 1997. pap. text 12.00 (*0-13-910415-1*) P-H.

19th Century Thought in Bengal. Kalyan K. Sengupta & Tirthanath Bandyopadhyay. LC 98-915585. 226p. 1998. write for info. (*81-7023-798-X*) Allied Pubs.

Nintendo Book No. 4: Koopa Kapers, No. 4. Ed. by Ruth Ashby. 128p. (Orig.). (J). 1991. mass mkt. 3.50 (*0-671-74202-7*, Archway) PB.

***Nintendo Game Boy: Official Games Guide.** BradyGames Staff. 112p. 2000. pap. 12.99 (*1-56686-923-4*) Brady Pub.

***Nintendo Game Boy Official Games Guide.** Brady Games Staff. (Illus.). (J). 1999. pap. 7.99 (*1-56686-902-1*, BradyGAMES) Brady Pub.

Nintendo Games Secrets, Vol. 2. Rusel DeMaria & Zach Meston. (Secrets of the Games Ser.). (Illus.). 336p. 1991. pap. 11.95 (*1-55958-105-0*) Prima Pub.

Nintendo Games Secrets, Vol. 4. Rusel DeMaria & Zach Meston. (Secrets of the Games Ser.). (Illus.). 272p. 1992. pap. 9.99 (*1-55958-252-9*) Prima Pub.

Nintendo Secrets: The Power User's Guide. Rusel DeMaria. (Secrets of the Games Ser.). 368p. (Orig.). 1990. pap. 9.95 (*1-55958-062-3*) Prima Pub.

Nintendo 64 Game Secrets, Version 4, Vol. 4. Simon Hill et al. LC 96-70915. Vol. 4. (Illus.). 96p. 1998. per. 12.99 (*0-7615-1644-1*) Prima Pub.

***Nintendo 64 Game Secrets 1999.** Prima Staff. LC 99-209836. (Illus.). 144p. 1999. pap. 14.99 (*0-7615-2103-8*) Prima Pub.

Nintendo 64 Game Secrets Unauthorized, Vol. 3. Prima Publishing Staff. 144p. 1998. per. 12.99 (*0-7615-1464-3*) Prima Pub.

Nintendo 64 Player's Choice Pocket Power Guide. Ed. & Compiled by Nick Roberts. LC 98-65313. 96p. 1998. per. 7.99 (*0-7615-1565-8*) Prima Pub.

Nintendo 64 Pocket Power Guide, Vol. 3. LC 96-70916. Vol. 2. 96p. 1998. per. 7.99 (*0-7615-1465-1*) Prima Pub.

Nintendo 64 Pocket Power Guide: Unauthorized. Nick Roberts. LC 96-70916. 96p. 1997. pap. 7.99 (*0-7615-0971-2*) Prima Pub.

Nintendo 64 Pocket Power Guide Vol. 2: Unauthorized. Prima Publishing Staff. LC 96-70916. (Secrets of the Game Ser.). 96p. 1997. per. 7.99 (*0-7615-1121-0*) Prima Pub.

***Nintendo 64 Secret Codes, 3.** Bradygames. LC 99-72443. 1999. pap. text 7.99 (*1-56686-892-0*) Brady Pub.

Nintendo 64 Survival Guide. J. Douglas Arnold. 1997. pap. text 14.95 (*1-884364-45-4*) Sandwich Islands.

Nintendo 64 Survival Guide, Vol. 2. J. Douglas Arnold & Zach Meston. LC 98-60566. (Nintendo 64 Survival Guides). 1998. pap. 9.95 (*1-884364-34-9*) Sandwich Islands.

Nintendo 64 Unauthorized Game Secrets. PCS Staff. 128p. 1997. per. 12.99 (*0-7615-0970-4*) Prima Pub.

Nintendo 64 Unauthorized Game Secrets, Vol. 2. Prima Publishing Staff. 144p. 1997. per. 12.99 (*0-7615-1155-5*) Prima Pub.

Nintendo Super Hits, No. 138. 56p. 1992. pap. 7.95 (*0-7935-1498-3*, 00102238) H Leonard.

9th Aerospace Testing Seminar Proceedings, October, 1985. Compiled by Aerospace Corp. & IES Staffs. 300p. 1985. pap. 100.00 (*0-915414-87-2*) IEST.

Ninth Air Force Story. Kenn Rust. (Illus.). 72p. 1993. pap. text 15.95 (*0-911852-93-X*) Aviation Heritage.

Ninth Amendment: Preservation of the Constitutional Mind. Stephen K. Shaw. LC 90-35910. (Distinguished Studies in American Legal & Constitutional History: Vol. 24). 240p. 1990. reprint ed. text 10.00 (*0-8240-0030-7*) Garland.

Ninth Amendment & the Politics of Creative Jurisprudence: Disparaging the Fundamental Right of Popular Control. Marshall L. DeRosa. 148p. (C). 1996. text 39.95 (*1-56000-233-6*) Transaction Pubs.

Ninth Annual Coal Preparation, Utilization, & Environmental Control Contractors Conference: Proceedings. (Illus.). 663p. (Orig.). (C). 1994. pap. text 85.00 (*0-7881-0874-3*) DIANE Pub.

9th Annual Labor & Employment Law Institute: New Directions for Labor & Management in a Changing Economic Environment (University of Louisville School of Law, June 11-12, 1992) Ed. by William F. Dolson. LC 97-37614. ix, 275p. 1997. 72.50 (*0-8377-0564-9*, Rothman) W S Hein.

9th Australasia Conference on Insurance Taxation. 1998. ring bd. write for info. (*1-56423-076-7*) Ntl Ctr Tax Ed.

Ninth Avenue Truck Tailor & Occasional Timepiece Co. unabridged ed. Frank E. Cooke. 66p. (Orig.). (J). (gr. 6-10). 1998. pap. 24.95 (*0-940076-09-8*) Fiesta City.

Ninth Biennial Conference Proceedings. ICHCA Staff. 143p. (C). 1969. 50.00 (*0-7855-5083-6*, Pub. by ICHCA) St Mut.

Ninth Bridgewater Treatise Fragment. Charles Babbage. 270p. 1967. reprint ed. 22.50 (*0-7146-1106-9*, Pub. by F Cass Pubs) Intl Spec Bk.

Ninth Car. Anne R. Rooth & James P. White. 1978. 8.95 (*0-399-12284-2*) Putnam Pub Group.

Ninth Census of the United States: Agriculture. LC 72-89067. (Rural America Ser.). 1973. reprint ed. 37.00 (*0-8420-1491-8*) Scholarly Res Inc.

Ninth Circuit Criminal Law Reporter, 2 vols. Roger W. Haines, Jr. 1998. 250.00 (*0-938065-70-X*) James Pub Santa Ana.

Ninth Conference Proceedings. ICHCA Staff. 143p. (C). 1988. 75.00 (*0-7855-6141-2*, Pub. by ICHCA) St Mut.

Ninth Corps at Antietam. John W. Schildt. (Illus.). 203p. (Orig.). 1988. pap. write for info. (*0-318-68704-6*) Antietam.

Ninth Corps at Antietam. John W. Schildt. 203p. (Orig.). 25.00 (*1-56013-010-5*) Olde Soldier Bks.

Ninth Day. Dorothy Baker & Howard Baker. (Lost Play Ser.). 1967. pap. 1.25 (*0-912262-05-2*) Proscenium.

Ninth E. C. Photovoltaic Solar Energy Conference. Ed. by P. Helm et al. (C). 1989. text 492.00 (*0-7923-0497-7*) Kluwer Academic.

***9th Engineer Battalion, First Marine Division, in Vietnam: 35 Personal Accounts.** Jean Shellenbarger. LC 99-55654. (Illus.). 239p. 2000. boxed set 35.00 (*0-7864-0655-0*) McFarland & Co.

9th European Simulation Symposium. Ed. by Axel Lehmann & Winfried Hahn. 755p. 1997. 90.00 (*1-56555-125-7*) Soc Computer Sim.

***Ninth Federal Forecasters Conference, 1997, Papers & Proceedings.** Debra E. Gerald. 325p. 1998. pap. 20.00 (*0-16-049450-X*) USGPO.

Ninth Floor. Paula Kilpatrick & Cliff Dudley. LC 81-80942. 128p. 1981. pap. 4.95 (*0-89221-085-0*) New Leaf.

Ninth Garfield Treasury. Jim Davis. LC 97-93768. (Illus.). 128p. 1997. pap. 12.50 (*0-345-41670-8*) Ballantine Pub Grp.

Ninth General Programme of Work Covering the Period, 1996-2001. LC 95-126271. (Health for All Ser.: No. 11). (ARA, CHI, ENG, FRE & RUS.). iv, 61p. 1994. pap. text 10.00 (*92-4-180011-9*, 1130011) World Health.

Ninth Generation of One Hundred & One Aggie Jokes. Illus. by Bob Taylor. (One Hundred & One Aggie Jokes Ser.). 50p. (Orig.). 1981. 3.00 (*0-945430-09-4*) Gigem Pr.

Ninth Grade Math TAAS Instructional Packet. Patricia Enselek & Susan Griffin. (TAAS Instructional Packets (TIPs) Ser.). 73p. 1991. 19.95 (*1-883396-19-0*) Educ Etc.

Ninth Grade Reading TAAS Instructional Packet. Patricia Enselek & Susan Griffin. (TAAS Instructional Packets (TIPs) Ser.). 76p. 1991. 19.95 (*1-883396-17-4*) Educ Etc.

Ninth Grade Writing TAAS Instructional Packet. Patricia Enselek & Susan Griffin. (TAAS Instructional Packets (TIPs) Ser.). 73p. 1991. 19.95 (*1-883396-18-2*) Educ Etc.

Ninth Heaven to Ninth Hell: History of a Noble Chinese Experiment. Qin Huailu. Ed. by William Hinton. LC 95-15361. 672p. 1995. 24.95 (*1-56980-041-3*) Barricade Bks.

Ninth Hour. Gilbert Kilpack. (C). 1951. pap. 4.00 (*0-87574-063-4*) Pendle Hill.

Ninth IEEE International Symposium on Personal, Indoor & Mobile Radio Communications: Technical Program Proceedings, September 8-11, 1998, The Marriott Copely Place, Boston, Massachusetts, 3 vols. Institute of Electrical & Electronic Engineers Society Staff. LC 98-84864. 1574p. 1998. pap. write for info. (*0-7803-4873-7*) IEEE Standards.

Computer Applications in Industry & Engineering (CAINE-96), 9th International Conference, December 11-13, 1996, Orlando, Florida, U.S.A: CAINE-96, Dec. 11-13, 1996, Orlando, FL. Ed. by G. K. Lee. (C). 1996. write for info. (*1-880843-18-8*) Int Soc Comp App.

9th International Conference on Antennas & Propagation (ICAP 95), 2 vols., Set, IC407. 1000p. 1995. pap. 290.00 (*0-85296-637-7*) INSPEC Inc.

Ninth International Conference on Automated Deduction. Ed. by Ewing L. Lusk & R. Overbeek. (Lecture Notes in Computer Science Ser.: Vol. 310). 775p. 1988. 79.00 (*0-387-19343-X*) Spr-Verlag.

Parallel & Distributed Computing Systems (PDCS-96), 9th International Conference, September 25-27, 1996, Dijon, France: PDCS-96, Sept. 25-27, 1996, Dijon, FR., 2 vols. Ed. by K. Yetongnon & S. Hariri. (Illus.). 900p. (C). 1996. write for info. (*1-880843-17-X*) Int Soc Comp App.

9th International Conference on Road Transport Information & Control, No. IC454. Contrib. by IEEE Staff. LC 98-157278. (Conference Publications: No. 454). 271p. 1998. 114.00 (*0-85296-701-2*, IC454) INSPEC Inc.

9th International Conference on the Chemistry of the Organic Solid State, Set, Pts. 1 & 2. G. Di Silvestro. 642p. 1990. text 1917.00 (*2-88124-463-7*) Gordon & Breach.

Ninth International Congress on Advances in Non-Impact Printing Technologies: Japan Hardcopy '93: "Color Hardcopy Technology for the 21st Century" Final Program & Proceedings October 4-8, 1993, Pacifico Yokohama, Yokohama, Japan. International Congress on Advances in Non-Impact P. LC Z 0252.5.N46. 729p. 1993. reprint ed. pap. 200.00 (*0-608-02426-0*, 206306900004) Bks Demand.

9th International Congress on Marine Corrosion & Biofouling. Maureen E. Callow. 274p. 1997. pap. text 206.00 (*90-5702-110-2*, Harwood Acad Pubs) Gordon & Breach.

***9th International Congress on Rock Mechanics: Proceedings of the Comptes-Rendus, Berichte, Paris, France 1999, 3 vols.** Ed. by G. Vouille & P. Berest. (Illus.). 1481p. 1999. text 385.00 (*90-5809-069-8*) A A Balkema.

***9th International Meeting on Nuclear Reactro Thermal-Hydraulics (NURETH-9) San Francisco, California, October 3-8, 1999.** 1999. cd-rom 125.00 (*0-89448-650-0*, 700275) Am Nuclear Soc.

***9th International Symposium on Corrosion in the Pulp & Paper Industry.** (Conference Preprints Ser.). 270p. 1998. 78.20 (*1-896742-28-9*) Pulp & Paper.

9th International Symposium on Nondestructive Testing of Wood. 227p. 1994. 55.00 (*0-935018-66-2*, 7316) Forest Prod.

9th International Symposium on Wood & Pulping Chemistry: Oral Presentations. (Conference Preprints Ser.). 1997. 51.00 (*1-896742-14-9*) Pulp & Paper.

Ninth Justice: The Fight for Bork. Patrick B. McGuigan & Dawn M. Weyrich. LC 89-23661. 340p. (C). 1990. pap. 14.95 (*0-942522-15-X*) Free Congr Res.

Ninth Life. Lauren W. Douglas. LC 89-34012. 256p. 1990. pap. 9.95 (*0-941483-50-9*) Naiad Pr.

Ninth Life. Jack Mann. 1970. 6.50 (*0-685-26776-8*) Bookfinger.

Ninth Marine Defense & AAA Battalions. Francis E. Chadwick. LC 90-70003. (Illus.). 120p. 1990. 65.00 (*0-938021-85-0*) Turner Pub KY.

Ninth Marines: A History of the Ninth Marine Regiment in World War II; with Lists of the Officers & Men Who Served from Organization to Disbandment, 1942-1945. L. D. Burrus et al. 1985. reprint ed. 35.95 (*0-89201-116-5*) Zenger Pub.

Ninth Mental Measurements Yearbook. Ed. by James V. Mitchell, Jr. LC 39-3422. xxx, 2002p. 1985. 175.00 (*0-910674-29-9*) Buros Inst Mental.

Ninth National Space Symposium Proceedings Report. Beth A. Lipskin. 236p. 1993. text 50.00 (*0-9616962-7-3*) US Space Found.

Ninth Netsuke. large type ed. James Melville. 320p. 1986. 27.99 (*0-7089-1404-7*) Ulverscroft.

***Ninth of August: A Play - August Na** Manoranjan Das et al. LC 98-908050. xi, 59 p. 1998. write for info. (*81-260-0484-3*, Pub. by Rabindra Bhawn) S Asia.

IX Olympiad, Amsterdam, 1928 & Lake Placid, 1932. World Sport Research & Publications Staff. LC 99-13071. (Olympic Century Ser.: Vol. 9). (Illus.). 184p. 1999. 21.95 (*1-888383-09-7*, Wrld Spt) Wld Sport Resch.

Ninth PATA Adventure Travel & Ecotourism Conference: Proceedings of a Conference Held January 12-15, 1997. 115p. 1997. pap. 30.00 (*981-00-8954-6*) Pac Asia Trvl.

Ninth Pulsed Power Conference, 1993. IEEE Electron Devices Society & Nuclear & Plasma S. Ed. by IEEE Staff. LC 93-79733. 1360p. 1994. pap. text. write for info. (*0-7803-1415-8*, 93CH3350-6); lib. bdg. write for info. (*0-7803-1416-6*, 93CH3350-6); fiche. write for info. (*0-7803-1417-4*, 93CH3350-6) Inst Electrical.

9th Riddle of Time: Practical Time Travel. Steven Gibbs. (Illus.). 35p. 1997. 16.95 (*1-57179-053-5*) Intern Guild ASRS.

Ninth Session see Report of the FAO Conference

Ninth State: New Hampshire's Formative Years. Lynn W. Turner. LC 82-13386. 493p. reprint ed. pap. 152.90 (*0-7837-0309-0*, 204063100018) Bks Demand.

Ninth Statue. John C. Curbow. (Illus.). 80p. (Orig.). 1992. pap. 10.00 (*0-9632842-0-7*) Curbow Pubns.

Ninth Systems Administration Conference (LISA '95) Proceedings, Monterey, Ca. 1995. pap. text 38.00 (*1-880446-73-1*) USENIX Assn.

Ninth Tennessee Infantry: A Roster. James R. Fleming. LC 96-189. 168p. 1996. pap. 25.00 (*1-57249-026-8*) White Mane Pub.

Ninth Virginia Cavalry. Robert K. Krick. (Virginia Regimental Histories Ser.). (Illus.). 116p. 1982. 19.95 (*0-930919-01-7*) H E Howard.

Ninth Virginia Infantry. Benjamin H. Trask. (Virginia Regimental Histories Ser.). (Illus.). 106p. 1984. 19.95 (*0-930919-10-6*) H E Howard.

Ninth Wave. Iiya G. Ehrenburg. LC 74-10358. 895p. 1974. reprint ed. lib. bdg. 69.50 (*0-8371-7672-7*, EHNW, Greenwood Pr) Greenwood.

9th Workshop on Parallel & Distributed Simulation (PADS '95) Ed. by Jason Y. Lin & Mary L. Bailey. LC 95-76898. 212p. 1995. pap. 80.00 (*0-8186-7120-3*, PADS-95) Soc Computer Sim.

Nintotem: Indiana Stories. Joan Peternel. 1999. pap. 10.00 (*0-9646718-3-2*) Whelks Walk Pr.

90's Rock for Easy Guitar. 80p. 1996. pap. 12.95 (*0-7935-6673-8*) H Leonard.

Ninuch & Caguch. Theodore Barna & Dorothy Barna. LC 94-74842. (Illus.). 44p. (Orig.). 1994. pap. 6.00 (*1-878149-31-8*) Counterpoint Pub.

Niobe Poems. Kate Daniels. LC 88-4754. (Pitt Poetry Ser.). 79p. (Orig.). 1988. reprint ed. pap. 30.00 (*0-608-07694-5*, 206778400010) Bks Demand.

Niobium: Physico-Chemical Properties of Its Compounds & Alloys. (Atomic Energy Review Ser.: No. 2, Special Issue). 1968. pap. 25.00 (*92-0-149068-2*, IAER2, Pub. by IAEA) Bernan Associates.

Niobium: Proceedings of the International Symposium...Held in San Francisco, CA, November 8-11, 1981. Metallurgical Society of AIME Staff. LC 83-63096. (Technology of Metallurgy Ser.: No. 5). (Illus.). 1269p. reprint ed. pap. 200.00 (*0-8357-7507-0*, 203599900097) Bks Demand.

Nioka: Bride of Bigfoot. Paul Doyle. 476p. 1991. pap. 14.95 (*0-9630458-0-6*) Daily Plnt Pr.

Niort/Poitiers/Chateauroux Map. 1997. 6.95 (*2-06-700068-3*, 68) Michelin.

NIOSH Case Studies in Bioaerosols. Ed. by Shirley A. Ness. LC 96-182386. 316p. 1996. pap. text 39.00 (*0-86587-485-9*) Gov Insts.

NIOSH Case Studies in Ergonomics. Ed. by Shirley A. Ness. LC 96-183186. 321p. 1996. pap. text 39.00 (*0-86587-483-2*) Gov Insts.

NIOSH Case Studies in Indoor Air Quality. Ed. by Shirley A. Ness. LC 96-182385. 430p. 1996. pap. text 39.00 (*0-86587-482-4*) Gov Insts.

NIOSH Case Studies in Lead. Ed. by Shirley A. Ness. LC 96-183160. 308p. 1996. pap. text 39.00 (*0-86587-484-0*) Gov Insts.

NIOSH Case Studies in Personal Protective Equipment. Ed. by Shirley A. Ness. 309p. 1996. pap. text 39.00 (*0-86587-529-4*) Gov Insts.

NIOSH Guide to the Selection & use of Particulate Respirators Certified under 42 CFR 84. 22p. pap. text 30.00 (*0-7881-3922-3*) DIANE Pub.

NIOSH Manual of Analytical Methods, 2 vols. 382p. 1996. pap. text, suppl. ed. 55.00 (*1-57979-108-5*) DIANE Pub.

NIOSH Manual of Analytical Methods: Sampling & Analytical Methods, 4 vols. Ed. by Peter M. Eller & Mary E. Cassinelli. 1648p. 1994. pap. text 105.00 (*1-57979-102-6*) DIANE Pub.

NIOSH Manual of Analytical Methods: Sampling & Analytical Methods for Monitoring Occupational Exposures to Toxic Substances in Air & Biological Samples. Ed. by Peter M. Eller & Mary E. Cassinelli. (Illus.). 625p. (C). 1994. pap. text 95.00 (*0-7881-1500-6*) DIANE Pub.

NIOSH Manual of Analytical Methods, August 1994, , Vols. 1-3. 4th ed. Peter M. Eller. 1984. ring bd. 56.00 (*0-16-016953-4*) USGPO.

NIOSH Pocket Guide to Chemical Hazards. 400p. 1994. pap. text 50.00 (*1-57979-059-3*) DIANE Pub.

NIOSH Pocket Guide to Chemical Hazards. 251p. 1994. pap. 14.00 (*0-16-045338-0*, 017-033-00473-1) USGPO.

NIOSH Pocket Guide to Chemical Hazards. Contrib. by Health & Human Services Dept., Public Health Servi. 1997. ring bd. 18.00 (*0-16-054672-9*) USGPO.

NIOSH Pocket Guide to Chemical Hazards. Barry Leonard. (Illus.). 440p. 1998. pap. text 35.00 (*0-7881-4923-7*) DIANE Pub.

NIOSH Recommendations for Occupational Safety & Health: Compendium of Policy Documents & Statements. 208p. (Orig.). (C). 1994. pap. text 50.00 (*0-7881-0686-4*) DIANE Pub.

Nip & Tuck. Robert McConnell. (Illus.). 48p. 1990. 12.95 (*0-929141-01-6*) Napoleon Publ.

Nip & Tuck: Teacher's Resource Package, Grades 1-3. Robert McConnell. 1995. pap. text, teacher ed. 8.95 (*0-929141-46-6*) Napoleon Publ.

Nip in the Air. John Betjeman. 1976. pap. 2.50 (*0-393-04423-8*) Norton.

Nip the Buds, Shoot the Kids: A Novel. Kenzaburo Oe. Tr. by Paul S. Mackintosh & Maki Sugiyama from JPN. 189p. 1995. 22.95 (*0-7145-2997-4*) M Boyars Pubs.

Nip the Buds, Shoot the Kids: A Novel. Kenzaburo Oe. Tr. by Paul S. Mackintosh & Maki Sugiyama from JPN. 192p. 1996. reprint ed. pap. 11.00 (*0-8021-3463-7*, Grove) Grove-Atltic.

Nipper. Thomas A. Weston. 70p. (C). 1989. pap. text 39.00 (*1-872795-15-3*, Pub. by Pentland Pr) St Mut.

Nippon: A Chartered Survey of Japan, 1987-88. 32nd ed. 360p. 1987. 50.00 (*4-87549-307-X*) Taylor & Francis.

Nippon: A Chartered Survey of Japan, 1989-90. 34th ed. 360p. 1989. pap. 54.00 (*4-87549-309-6*) Taylor & Francis.

Nippon: Land of Beauty & Tradition. Philip Sandoz. (Illus.). 72p. 1996. pap. 17.95 (*0-8048-2067-8*) Tuttle Pubng.

Nippon - Eine Untergehende Sonne? Gero Jenner. 229p. 1997. 44.95 (*3-631-31748-4*) P Lang Pubng.

***Nippon Dolls & Playthings: Identification & Value Guide.** Linda Lau. (Illus.). 256p. 2000. 29.95 (*1-57432-201-X*) Collector Bks.

Nippon Kanryo Yo Doko e Yuku see Kanryo: Japan's Hidden Government

Nippon, 1995. 160p. 1995. pap. 22.00 (*4-8224-0705-5*, Pub. by JETRO) Taylor & Francis.

N

An Asterisk (*) at the beginning of an entry indicates that the title is appearing for the first time.

Nippon, 1994: Business Facts & Figures. 160p. 1994. pap. 18.00 (4-8224-0666-0) Intl Pubns Serv.

Nippon, 1996. (ENG & JPN.). 160p. 1996. 16.00 (4-8224-0751-9, Pub. by JETRO) Taylor & Francis.

Nippon, 1993: Business Facts & Figures. 160p. 1993. pap. 15.00 (4-8224-0615-6, Pub. by JETRO) Taylor & Francis.

Nippon Pop: Sounds from the Land of the Rising Sun. Steve McClure. (Illus.). 162p. 1998. pap. 26.95 (0-8048-2107-0) Tuttle Pubng.

Nippon Porcelain: Identification & Values. 5th ed. Joan Van Patten. LC NK4567.7.V36 1998. (Collector's Encyclopedia Ser.). 1998. 24.95 (1-57432-056-4, 5053) Collector Bks.

Nippon Rails. Mayfair Games Staff. 1992. 25.00 (0-923763-68-6) Mayfair Games.

Nippon Tech Sourcebook, Bk. 5. (Torg Ser.). 128p. 18.00 (0-87431-308-2, 20509) West End Games.

Nippon Very Sorry - Many Men Must Die. QLD Ex-POW Repatriation Committee. 123p. (C). 1990. 60.00 (0-86439-112-9, Pub. by Boolarong Pubns) St Mut.

Nippur Vol. 4: The Early Neo-Babylonian Governor's Archive from Nippur. S. W. Cole. LC 96-67507. (Publications: Vol. 114). (Illus.). xliv, 458p. 1996. text 65.00 (1-885923-03-1) Orient Inst.

Nippur at the Centennial: Papers Read at the 35th Rencontre Assyriologique Internationale, Philadelphia, 1988. Ed. by Maria D. Ellis. LC 92-37459. (Occasional Publications of the Samuel Noah Kramer Fund: No. 14). xix, 368p. 1992. 65.00 (0-924171-01-4) U Museum Pubns.

Nippur in Late Assyrian Times, c. 755-612 B. C. Steven W. Cole. (State Archives of Assyria Ser.: Vol. 4). x, 116p. (Orig.). 1996. pap. text 29.50 (951-45-7286-6, Pub. by Neo-Assyrian Text) Eisenbrauns.

Nippur Lament: Royal Rhetoric & Divine Legitimation in the Reign of Isme-Dagan of Isin (1953-1935 B.C.) Steve Tinney. LC 95-38176. (Occasional Publications of the Samuel Noah Kramer Fund: No. 16). (Illus.). xxii, 276p. 1996. 65.00 (0-924171-39-1) U Museum Pubns.

Nippur Neighborhoods. Elizabeth C. Stone. LC 86-63702. (Studies in Ancient Oriental Civilization: No. 44). (Illus.). xvii, 294p. 1987. pap. 45.00 (0-918986-50-8) Orient Inst.

Nippur 3: Kassite Buildings in Area WC-1. Richard L. Zettler. LC 92-82134. (Oriental Institute Publications: No. 111). (Illus.). xxxvii, 347p. 1993. lib. bdg. 60.00 (0-918986-91-5) Orient Inst.

Nippur II: The North Temple & Sounding E: Excavations of the Joint Expedition to Nippur of the American Schools of Oriental Research & the Oriental Institute of the University of Chicago. Donald E. McCown et al. LC 77-74719. (Oriental Institute Publications: No. 97). (Illus.). 1978. lib. bdg. 60.00 (0-918986-04-4) Orient Inst.

Nips Poems. John M. Bennett. (Illus.). 40p. (Orig.). 1980. pap. 3.00 (0-935350-00-4) Luna Bisonte.

Nips Poems. limited ed. John M. Bennett. (Illus.). 40p. (Orig.). 1980. pap. 6.00 (0-935350-83-7) Luna Bisonte.

Niquin el Cesante. Jose Sanchez-Boudy. LC 78-74694. (Coleccion Caniqui). (SPA., Illus.). 157p. (Orig.). 1980. pap. 9.95 (0-89729-218-9) Ediciones.

Niram: A Dusky Idyl. Laisdell Mitchell. LC 72-1513. (Black Heritage Library Collection). 1977. reprint ed. 17.95 (0-8369-9038-2) Ayer.

Nirex Collection: Nicaraguan Revolution Extracts. Intro. by Litext, Inc. Staff & Porfirio R. Solorzano. (Collection of Documents Ser.: Vols. 1-10). (Illus.). 9440p. (C). 1989. pap. 425.00 (0-685-27216-8) LITEXT Inc.

Nirex Collection: Nicaraguan Revolution Extracts, 10 vols. Compiled & Intro. by Porfirio R. Solorzano. (ENG & SPA., Illus.). 9440p. (C). 1994. text 775.00 (1-877970-01-8) LITEXT Inc.

Nirex Collection: Nicaraguan Revolution Extracts, 10 vols., Set. Ed. by Porfirio R. Solorzano. (ENG & SPA., Illus.). 9440p. (C). 1990. pap. 425.00 (1-877970-00-X) LITEXT Inc.

Nirmala. Premchand. Tr. by Alok Rai from HIN. LC 99-933485. 230p. 1999. text 17.95 (0-19-564580-4) OUP.

Nirmala. A. Premchand. Tr. by David Rubin. (C). 1988. 17.50 (81-7094-030-3, Pub. by Vision Books) Asia Bk Corp.

Nirodbaran's Correspondence with Sri Aurobindo, 2nd ed. Sri Aurobindo. Ed. by Nirodbaran. 1221p. 1995. pap. 39.50 (81-7058-020-X, Pub. by SAA) E-W Cultural Ctr.

***NIrV Kids' Books of Devotions: A 365-Day Adventure in God's Word.** Mark Littleton. LC 98-22806. 208p. (J). 1998. pap. 9.99 (0-310-22130-7) Zondervan.

NIrV Kids' Devotional Bible. rev. ed. 1650p. (J). (gr. 1-5). 1998. 24.99 (0-310-92657-2) Zondervan.

Nirv Young Discover. 19.99 (0-310-90867-1) HarpC.

***Nirvana.** Frank Lennon. (Poetry New York Pamphlet Ser.: No. 28). 30p. 1999. pap. 5.00 (0-923389-42-3) Meet Eyes Bind.

***Nirvana: A Day-by-Day Eyewitness Chronicle.** Carrie Borzillo. (Illus.). 2000. pap. 19.95 (1-56025-274-X, Thunders Mouth) Avalon NY.

Nirvana: A Story of Buddhist Psychology. Paul Carus. LC 98-904946. 93 p. 1997. 12.00 (81-206-1301-5, Pub. by Asian Educ Servs) S Asia.

Nirvana: Bleach Imp. Custom Print with Notes & Tablature. 64p. 1994. otabind 2.10 (0-7935-3726-6, 00694960) H Leonard.

***Nirvana: Bleach Imp. Custom Print with Notes & Tablature.** 104p. 1999. otabind 24.95 (0-7935-9572-X) H Leonard.

Nirvana: Bleach with Notes & Tablature. 64p. 1994. otabind 19.95 (0-7935-2682-5, 00694895) H Leonard.

Nirvana: Classic Rock Reads. Brad Morrell. (Classic Rock Read Ser.). (Illus.). 144p. pap. 16.95 (0-7119-5221-3, OP 47792) Omnibus NY.

***Nirvana: In Utero.** 144p. 1998. otabind 24.95 (0-7935-9246-1) H Leonard.

Nirvana: In Utero Imp. Custom Print with Notes & Tablature. 112p. 1994. otabind 2.64 (0-7935-3725-8, 00694961) H Leonard.

Nirvana: In Utero with Notes & Tablature. 112p. 1994. otabind 19.95 (0-7935-3141-1, 00694913) H Leonard.

Nirvana: Incesticide. 72p. 1995. otabind 19.95 (0-7935-2761-9, 00694901) H Leonard.

***Nirvana: Nevermind.** 120p. 1998. otabind 24.95 (0-7935-9244-5) H Leonard.

Nirvana: Nevermind. Susan Wilson. (Illus.). 80p. (Orig.). 1995. pap. 19.95 (1-873884-39-7, VX 03000, Pub. by UFO Books) Music Sales.

Nirvana: Nevermind with Notes & Tablature. 64p. 1993. otabind 19.95 (0-7935-2392-3, 00694883) H Leonard.

Nirvana: Revealed. Jeremy Dean. (Illus.). 128p. pap. 14.95 (0-7525-1860-7, Pub. by Parragon Pub) Music Sales.

Nirvana: The Bass Guitar Collection. 64p. 1997. otabind 17.95 (0-7935-4881-0, 00690066) H Leonard.

Nirvana: The Chosen Rejects. Thomas Kurt St. LC 99-15933. (Illus.). 272p. 2000. pap. 21.95 (0-312-20663-1) St Martin.

Nirvana: The Legacy. Mick Wall & Malcolm Dome. (Illus.). 96p. (Orig.). pap. 15.95 (0-7119-5220-5, OP47791, Pub. by Omnibus Press) Omnibus NY.

***Nirvana: The Muddy Banks of the Wishkah.** 72p. 1999. otabind 16.95 (0-7935-9340-9) H Leonard.

Nirvana: Unplugged in New York. 64p. 1995. otabind 19.95 (0-7935-4413-0, 00690026) H Leonard.

Nirvana, a Story of Buddhist Psychology. Paul Carus. LC 78-72395. (Illus.). reprint ed. 32.50 (0-404-15508-1); reprint ed. 32.50 (0-404-17254-7) AMS Pr.

Nirvana & Other Buddhist Felicities. Steven Collins. (Studies in Religious Traditions: Vol. 12). 708p. (C). 1998. text 85.00 (0-521-57054-9) Cambridge U Pr.

Nirvana & the Sound of Seattle. Brad Morrell. (Illus.). 96p. pap. 19.95 (0-7119-3492-4, OP 47326) Omnibus NY.

Nirvana Blues. John Nichols. 608p. 1983. mass mkt. 5.95 (0-345-30465-9) Ballantine Pub Grp.

Nirvana Blues. John Nichols. 1996. pap. 12.95 (0-345-41037-8) Ballantine Pub Grp.

Nirvana Blues. John Nichols. LC 99-39457. 540p. 2000. pap. 14.00 (0-8050-6340-4, Owl) H Holt & Co.

***Nirvana from the Muddy Banks of the Wishkah.** 128p. 1999. otabind 24.95 (0-7935-9559-2) H Leonard.

Nirvana in Tibetan Buddhism. E. Obermiller. Ed. by Harcharan S. Sobti. (C). 1987. 11.50 (81-85132-03-8) S Asia.

Nirvana-Tao: The Secret Meditation Techniques of the Taoist & Buddhist Masters. Daniel Odier. (Illus.). 208p. (Orig.). 1986. pap. 12.95 (0-89281-045-9) Inner Tradit.

Nirvana Tribute: The Life & Death of Kurt Cobain - The Full Story. Suzi Black. LC 95-188018. (Illus.). 48p. 1994. pap. 11.95 (0-7119-4244-7, OP 47696) Omnibus NY.

***NIS Automobile Industry.** Global Investment & Business Center, Inc. Staff. (NIS Industrial Directories Ser.: Vol. 3). (Illus.). 350p. 1999. pap. 99.00 (0-7397-0952-6) Intl Business Pubns.

***NIS Building Materials Industry.** Global Investment & Business Center, Inc. Staff. (NIS Industrial Directories Ser.: Vol. 4). (Illus.). 350p. 1999. pap. 99.00 (0-7397-0953-4) Intl Business Pubns.

***NIS Chemical, Pharmaceutical & Microbiology Industry.** Global Investment & Business Center, Inc. Staff. (NIS Industrial Directories Ser.: Vol. 5). (Illus.). 350p. 1999. pap. 99.00 (0-7397-0954-2) Intl Business Pubns.

***NIS Civil Engineering & Transport Industry.** Global Investment & Business Center, Inc. Staff. (NIS Industrial Directories Ser.: Vol. 31). (Illus.). 350p. 1999. pap. 99.00 (0-7397-0980-1) Intl Business Pubns.

***NIS Clothing Industry.** Global Investment & Business Center, Inc. Staff. (NIS Industrial Directories Ser.: Vol. 6). (Illus.). 350p. 1999. pap. 99.00 (0-7397-0955-0) Intl Business Pubns.

***NIS Coal Mining & Peat Industry.** Global Investment & Business Center, Inc. Staff. (NIS Industrial Directories Ser.: Vol. 7). (Illus.). 350p. 1999. pap. 99.00 (0-7397-0956-9) Intl Business Pubns.

***NIS Consumer Goods, Household & Cultural Goods Industry.** Global Investment & Business Center, Inc. Staff. (NIS Industrial Directories Ser.: Vol. 8). (Illus.). 350p. 1999. pap. 99.00 (0-7397-0957-7) Intl Business Pubns.

***NIS Electrical Engineering Industry.** Global Investment & Business Center, Inc. Staff. (NIS Industrial Directories Ser.: Vol. 9). (Illus.). 350p. 1999. pap. 99.00 (0-7397-0958-5) Intl Business Pubns.

***NIS Fishing & Fish Processing Industry.** Global Investment & Business Center, Inc. Staff. (NIS Industrial Directories Ser.: Vol. 10). (Illus.). 350p. 1999. pap. 99.00 (0-7397-0959-3) Intl Business Pubns.

***NIS 500 Largest Companies.** Global Investment & Business Center, Inc. Staff. (NIS Industrial Directories Ser.: Vol. 1). (Illus.). 350p. 1999. pap. 99.00 (0-7397-0950-X) Intl Business Pubns.

***NIS Food & Food Processing Industry.** Global Investment & Business Center, Inc. Staff. (NIS Industrial Directories Ser.: Vol. 11). (Illus.). 350p. 1999. pap. 99.00 (0-7397-0960-7) Intl Business Pubns.

***NIS Footwear & Tanning Industry.** Global Investment & Business Center, Inc. Staff. (NIS Industrial Directories Ser.: Vol. 12). (Illus.). 350p. 1999. pap. 99.00 (0-7397-0961-5) Intl Business Pubns.

***NIS Forestry & Timber Industry.** Global Investment & Business Center, Inc. Staff. (NIS Industrial Directories Ser.: Vol. 13). (Illus.). 350p. 1999. pap. 99.00 (0-7397-0962-3) Intl Business Pubns.

***NIS Gold Mining & Mining Industry.** Global Investment & Business Center, Inc. Staff. (NIS Industrial Directories Ser.: Vol. 22). (Illus.). 350p. 1999. pap. 99.00 (0-7397-0971-2) Intl Business Pubns.

***NIS High-Tech Products, PC, Research & Design Industry.** Global Investment & Business Center, Inc. Staff. (NIS Industrial Directories Ser.: Vol. 14). (Illus.). 350p. 1999. pap. 99.00 (0-7397-0963-1) Intl Business Pubns.

***NIS Machine Building Industry.** Global Investment & Business Center, Inc. Staff. (NIS Industrial Directories Ser.: Vol. 15). (Illus.). 350p. 1999. pap. 99.00 (0-7397-0964-X) Intl Business Pubns.

***NIS Medical Equipment Industry.** Global Investment & Business Center, Inc. Staff. (NIS Industrial Directories Ser.: Vol. 16). (Illus.). 350p. 1999. pap. 99.00 (0-7397-0965-8) Intl Business Pubns.

***NIS Metal-Working Industry.** Global Investment & Business Center, Inc. Staff. (NIS Industrial Directories Ser.: Vol. 17). (Illus.). 350p. 1999. pap. 99.00 (0-7397-0966-6) Intl Business Pubns.

***NIS Metallurgy Industry.** Global Investment & Business Center, Inc. Staff. (NIS Industrial Directories Ser.: Vol. 18). (Illus.). 350p. 1999. pap. 99.00 (0-7397-0967-4) Intl Business Pubns.

***NIS Mining (Building Materials) Industry.** Global Investment & Business Center, Inc. Staff. (NIS Industrial Directories Ser.: Vol. 19). (Illus.). 350p. 1999. pap. 99.00 (0-7397-0968-2) Intl Business Pubns.

***NIS Oil & Gas Industry.** Global Investment & Business Center, Inc. Staff. (NIS Industrial Directories Ser.: Vol. 20). (Illus.). 350p. 1999. pap. 99.00 (0-7397-0969-0) Intl Business Pubns.

***NIS Oil Refining & Gas Processing Industry.** Global Investment & Business Center, Inc. Staff. (NIS Industrial Directories Ser.: Vol. 21). (Illus.). 350p. 1999. pap. 99.00 (0-7397-0970-4) Intl Business Pubns.

***NIS 1000 Largest Companies.** Global Investment & Business Center, Inc. Staff. (NIS Industrial Directories Ser.: Vol. 2). (Illus.). 350p. 1999. pap. 99.00 (0-7397-0951-8) Intl Business Pubns.

***NIS Power Industry.** Global Investment & Business Center, Inc. Staff. (NIS Industrial Directories Ser.: Vol. 23). (Illus.). 350p. 1999. pap. 99.00 (0-7397-0972-0) Intl Business Pubns.

***NIS Publishing & Printing Industry.** Global Investment & Business Center, Inc. Staff. (NIS Industrial Directories Ser.: Vol. 24). (Illus.). 350p. 1999. pap. 99.00 (0-7397-0973-9) Intl Business Pubns.

***NIS Pulp & Paper Industry.** Global Investment & Business Center, Inc. Staff. (NIS Industrial Directories Ser.: Vol. 25). (Illus.). 350p. 1999. pap. 99.00 (0-7397-0974-7) Intl Business Pubns.

***NIS Radio-Electronic Industry.** Global Investment & Business Center, Inc. Staff. (NIS Industrial Directories Ser.: Vol. 26). (Illus.). 350p. 1999. pap. 99.00 (0-7397-0975-5) Intl Business Pubns.

***NIS Rubber & Plastic Industry.** Global Investment & Business Center, Inc. Staff. (NIS Industrial Directories Ser.: Vol. 27). (Illus.). 350p. 1999. pap. 99.00 (0-7397-0976-3) Intl Business Pubns.

***NIS Scrap & Waste Industry.** Global Investment & Business Center, Inc. Staff. (NIS Industrial Directories Ser.: Vol. 28). (Illus.). 350p. 1999. pap. 99.00 (0-7397-0977-1) Intl Business Pubns.

***NIS Textile Industry.** Global Investment & Business Center, Inc. Staff. (NIS Industrial Directories Ser.: Vol. 29). (Illus.). 350p. 1999. pap. 99.00 (0-7397-0978-X) Intl Business Pubns.

***NIS Tobacco Industry.** Global Investment & Business Center, Inc. Staff. (NIS Industrial Directories Ser.: Vol. 30). (Illus.). 350p. 1999. pap. 99.00 (0-7397-0979-8) Intl Business Pubns.

***Nisa: The Life & Words of a Kung Woman.** Marjorie Shostak. 288p. 2000. pap. 16.95 (0-674-00432-9) HUP.

Nisa, the Life & Words of a Kung Woman. Marjorie Shostak. LC 82-40050. (Illus.). 416p. (C). 1982. pap. 9.56 (0-394-71126-2) Knopf.

Nisbet's System of Heraldry, 2 vols. Aberdeen Rare Books Staff. (C). 1988. 500.00 (0-7855-3792-9, Pub. by Aberdeen Rare Bks) St Mut.

Nisei Daughter. Monica Sone. LC 79-4921. 238p. 1979. reprint ed. pap. 14.95 (0-295-95688-7) U of Wash Pr.

Nisei Soldier: Historical Essays on World War II. Edwin M. Nakasone. 96p. (C). 1997. pap. text 8.50 (0-9660111-3-9) J Press.

Nisei Soldier: Historical Essays on World War II & the Korean War. 2nd rev. ed. Edwin M. Nakasone. LC 98-75578. (Illus.). 206p. (Orig.). 1999. pap. 19.95 (0-9660111-5-5, Pub. by J Press) Baker & Taylor.

Nisei/Sansei: Shifting Japanese American Identities & Politics. Jere Takahashi. (Asian American History & Culture Ser.). 280p. 1998. pap. text 19.95 (1-56639-659-X) Temple U Pr.

Nishapur: Glass of the Early Islamic Period. Jens Kroger. LC 94-32633. 1995. 75.00 (0-87099-729-7) Metro Mus Art.

Nishapur: Metalwork from the Early Islamic Period. James W. Allen. (Illus.). 120p. 1981. 19.95 (0-87099-271-6, 0-8109-6464-3) Metro Mus Art.

Nishapur: Pottery of the Early Islamic Period. Charles K. Wilkinson. (Illus.). 420p. 1974. 45.00 (0-87099-076-4, 0-8109-6465-1) Metro Mus Art.

Nishapur: Some Early Islamic Buildings & Their Decoration. Charles K. Wilkinson. (Illus.). 328p. 1987. 75.00 (0-87099-402-6) Metro Mus Art.

Nishida Kitaro. Nishitani Keiji. Tr. by Yamamoto Seisaku & James W. Heisig from JPN. (Nanzan Studies in Religion & Culture: No. 15). 200p. 1991. 35.00 (0-520-07364-9, Pub. by U CA Pr) Cal Prin Full Svc.

Nishkamakarma. John G. Finch. LC 82-83498. (Orig.). (C). 1982. pap. 10.00 (0-9609928-0-4) Integ Pr.

Nishnabotna: Poems, Prose & Dramatic Scenes from the Natural & Oral History of Southwest Iowa. Michael Carey. (Illus.). 124p. 1995. pap. 12.95 (0-931209-62-5) Mid-Prairie Bks.

Nishnawbe: A Story of Indians in Michigan. 2nd ed. Lynne Deur. (Illus.). 54p. (J). (gr. 4-6). 1981. pap. 8.95 (0-938682-01-6) River Rd Pubns.

Nisho: A Potawatomi Fable. Jack Wooldridge. (Potawatomi Fables Ser.). (Illus.). 29p. (J). 1997. pap. 7.00 (1-887963-10-3) Pota Pr.

Nisin & Novel Lantibiotics: Proceedings of the 1st International Workshop on Lantibiotics, April 15-18, 1991, Physikzentrum Bad Honnef, F. R. G. Ed. by Gunther Jung & Hans-Georg Sahl. 508p. (C). 1991. text 303.00 (90-72199-11-1, Pub. by Escom Sci Pubs) Kluwer Academic.

Nisoldipine CC Investigators' Meeting, Wiesbaden, Germany, May 1996: Proceedings - Sessions I & II. Ed. by G. Heusch & J. L. Palma-Gamiz. (Journal Ser.: Vol. 88, Supplement 1, 1997). (Illus.). iv, 72p. 1996. pap. 33.25 (3-8055-6464-3) S Karger.

***Nisoldipine Coat-Core.** M. Rousseau. LC 99-33461. (Illus.). 100p. 1999. pap. 41.00 (3-540-66049-6) Spr-Verlag.

Nisqually Watershed: Glacier to Delta, a River's Legacy. deluxe ed. Photos by Mark R. Lembersky. LC 95-11067. (Illus.). 128p. 1995. pap. 19.95 (0-89886-453-4) Mountaineers.

Nissan: 240SX/Altima, 1993-98. Chilton Automotive Editorial Staff. (Total Car Care Ser.). 550p. (C). 1998. pap. 22.95 (0-8019-8970-1) Thomson Learn.

Nissan Bluebird Automotive Repair Manual. Tim Imhoff & John H. Haynes. LC 97-80267. (Haynes Auto Repair Manual Ser.). 1997. write for info. (1-56392-283-5) Haynes Manuals.

***Nissan Engine Control Systems.** Keith Kraehmer. (Illus.). 712p. 1998. 120.00 (1-887023-16-X) Target Trning.

Nissan Enigma: Flexibility at Work in a Local Economy. Philip Garrahan & Paul Stewart. 160p. 1992. pap. text 37.95 (0-7201-2155-8) Continuum.

Nissan-Infiniti Repair Manual, 1988-92. Chilton Automotive Editorial Staff. 256p. (C). 1992. pap. 19.95 (0-8019-8322-3) Thomson Learn.

Nissan Maxima: Automotive Repair Manual, 1985-91. rev. ed. Ken Freund & John H. Haynes. LC 91-75876. (Illus.). 304p. 1991. pap. 17.95 (1-56392-005-0) Haynes Manuals.

Nissan Maxima, 1985-92. (Illus.). 704p. (C). 1992. pap. 22.95 (0-8019-8261-8) Thomson Learn.

Nissan Maxima, 1985-92. Chilton Automotive Editorial Staff. 320p. 1992. pap. 16.95 (0-8019-8307-X) Nichols Pub.

Nissan-Maxima, 1993-98: Covers All U.S. & Canadian Models of Nissan Maxima. Chilton Automotive Editorial Staff. (Total Car Care Ser.). (C). 1999. pap. text 22.95 (0-8019-8961-2) Thomson Learn.

Nissan, 1973-1984: Datsun 200SX, 510, 610, 710, 810 & Maxima. Chilton Automotive Editorial Staff. (New Total Car Care Ser.). 512p. (C). 1997. pap. text 22.95 (0-8019-9070-X) Thomson Learn.

Nissan, 1973-1981: Datsun 210, 310, 1200 & F10. Chilton Automotive Editorial Staff. (New Total Car Care Ser.). 450p. (C). 1997. pap. text 22.95 (0-8019-9068-8) Thomson Learn.

Nissan on the Mojave Road. Dennis G. Casebier. LC 83-70971. (Illus.). 24p. 1983. 10.00 (0-914224-11-5) Tales Mojave Rd.

Nissan Patrol & Ford Maverick Automotive Repair Manual: 1988 Through 1997 Tim Imhoff & John H. Haynes. LC 97-80268. (Haynes Automotive Repair Manual Ser.). 1997. write for info. (1-56392-284-3) Haynes Manuals.

***Nissan Pick Up & Pathfinder 1980-96.** 2000. pap. 17.95 (1-56392-253-3, Pub. by Haynes Manuals) Motorbooks Intl.

Nissan Pick-Ups & Pathfinder, 1989-91. (Total Car Care Ser.). 672p. 1991. pap. 21.95 (0-8019-8145-X) Nichols Pub.

Nissan Pick-Ups & Pathfinder, 1989-91. (Total Car Care Ser.). 336p. (C). 1991. pap. 16.95 (0-8019-8146-8) Thomson Learn.

Nissan Pick-Ups & Pathfinder, 1989-1995. Chilton Automotive Editorial Staff. (Illus.). 688p. (C). 1995. pap. 22.95 (0-8019-8671-0) Thomson Learn.

Nissan Pulsar & Holden Astra Service & Repair Manual P. G. Strasman. LC 97-73897. (Haynes Automotive Repair Manual Ser.). 1997. write for info. (1-56392-270-3) Haynes Manuals.

Nissan Report: A Bold New Blueprint for Successful Innovation in American Business. Ed. by Steve Barnett. 224p. 1994. pap. 11.00 (0-380-72141-4, Avon Bks) Morrow Avon.

***Nissan Sentra 1982,94.** 2000. pap. 17.95 (1-56392-235-5, Pub. by Haynes Manuals) Motorbooks Intl.

Nissan Sentra, Pulsar, 1982-92. Chilton Automotive Editorial Staff. 416p. (C). 1992. pap. 16.95 (0-8019-8309-6) Thomson Learn.

Nissan Sentra, Pulsar, 1982-92: Total Car Care. (Illus.). 848p. 1992. pap. 21.95 (0-8019-8263-4) Nichols Pub.

Nissan Stanza, 200SX, 240SX, 1982-92. (Illus.). 960p. (C). 1992. pap. 22.95 (0-8019-8262-6) Thomson Learn.

Nissan Stanza, 200SX, 240SX, 1982-92. Chilton Automotive Editorial Staff. 424p. 1992. pap. 16.95 (0-8019-8308-8) Nichols Pub.

Nissan's Business Japanese, Set. Hajime Takamizawa. (JPN.). 300p. 1995. 59.95 incl. audio (0-8442-8419-X, 8419x, NTC Business Bks) NTC Contemp Pub Co.

Nissan's Business Japanese Plus, Set. Hajime Takamizawa. (JPN.). 300p. 1995. 59.95 incl. audio (0-8442-8422-X, 8422X, NTC Business Bks) NTC Contemp Pub Co.

N

Nissan's Business Japanese Plus: Intermediate. Hajime Takamizawa. (ENG & JPN.). 300p. (C). Date not set. pap. 29.95 (*0-8442-8423-8*, X8423-8) NTC Contemp Pub Co.

Nissa's Place. A. Lafaye. LC 99-12257. (Illus.). 224p. (J). 1999. per. 16.00 (*0-689-82610-9*) S&S Bks Yung.

Nisse Hos Fris Oren see Will Gets a Haircut

Nissequott. Margaret Dawe. LC 92-44444. 304p. 1994. pap. 10.95 (*0-8112-1260-2*, NDP775, Pub. by New Directions) Norton.

Nissim Ibn Shahin: The Arabic Original of Ibn Shahin's Book of Comfort. Ed. by Julian Obermann. LC 78-63561. (Yale Oriental Series: Researches: No. 17). reprint ed. 72.50 (*0-404-60287-8*) AMS Pr.

Nist Building & Fire Research Laboratory: Project Summaries, 1997. Noel J. Raufaste. 230p. 1998. per. 20.00 (*0-16-054773-3*) USGPO.

***NIST Calibration Service for Capacitance Standards at Low Frequencies.** Y. May Chang. 83p. 1998. pap. 7.00 (*0-16-060876-7*) USGPO.

***NIST Calibration Services for Gas Flow Meters: Piston Prover & Bell Prover Gas Flow Facilities.** John D. Wright, Jr. 47p. 1998. pap. 6.00 (*0-16-060879-1*) USGPO.

***Nist Calibration Services Users Guide, 1998.** J. L. Marshall. 231p. 1998. per. 19.00 (*0-16-054839-X*) USGPO.

Nist High-Accuracy Sampling Wattmeter. Gerard N. Stabakken. 57p. 1996. pap. 7.50 (*0-16-053342-2*) USGPO.

NIST Industrial Impacts: A Sampling of Successful Partnerships. 95p. pap. text. write for info. (*0-7881-8996-4*) DIANE Pub.

Nist International Activities. Peter L. M. Heydmann. 90p. 1997. pap. 7.50 (*0-16-054670-2*) USGPO.

***NIST International & Academic Activities for FY 1997/1998.** Marian F. McCurley. 86p. 1999. pap. 8.75 (*0-16-058873-1*) USGPO.

NIST Inventions. 152p. pap. text 40.00 (*0-7881-4557-6*) DIANE Pub.

NIST-JANAF Thermochemical Tables, 2 vols. 4th ed. M. W. Chase & National Institute of Standards & Technology Staff. LC 98-86732. (Journal of Physical & Chemical Reference Data Ser.). xi, 1951p. 1998. write for info. (*1-56396-820-7*) Am Inst Physics.

NIST JANAF Thermochemical Tables, 2 vols. 4th ed. Malcolm W. Chase, Jr. LC 98-86732. 1952p. 1998. 195.00 (*1-56396-831-2*) Am Inst Physics.

Nist Measurement Assurance Program for Resistance. Paul A. Boyton. 57p. 1998. pap. 5.25 (*0-16-054770-9*) USGPO.

***Nist Microwave Power Standards in Waveguide.** J. Wayde Allen. 50p. 1999. per. 4.50 (*0-16-056931-1*) USGPO.

***NIST Multifunction Calibration System.** Nile Oldham. 28p. 1998. pap. 3.00 (*0-16-060871-6*) USGPO.

Nist Serial Holdings 1999. Susan A. Sasnders. 264p. 1999. per. 21.00 (*0-16-056948-6*) USGPO.

***Nist Serial Holdings, Nineteen Ninety Eight.** Susan A. Sanders. 264p. 1998. per. 21.00 (*0-16-060880-5*) USGPO.

***NIST Serial Holdings, Two Thousand.** Susan A. Sanders. 264p. 2000. per. 24.00 (*0-16-059127-9*) USGPO.

Nist Standard Reference Materials Catalog, 1998-99. Nancy M. Trahey. 186p. 1998. per. 16.00 (*0-16-054862-4*) USGPO.

Nister's Work, 1907-1929: A Study of a Yiddish Symbolist. Delphine Bechtel. Ed. by Jean-Marie Valentin. (Contacts: Series Three, Etudes et Documents: Vol. 11). (Illus.). 306p. 1991. pap. 53.00 (*3-261-04239-7*) P Lang Pubng.

NIT, '90: Third International Conference on New Information Technology. Ed. by Ching-chih Chen. 354p. (Orig.). 1990. pap. text 59.50 (*0-931555-07-8*) MicroUse Info.

NITA Fire & Casualty Co. vs. Anthony Rubino, d. b. a. Rubino & Son. Anthony J. Bocchino & Louis M. Natali. 321p. 1982. pap. 22.95 (*1-55681-064-4*) Natl Inst Trial Ad.

Nita Hewitt Rutkosky's Advanced WordPerfect Desktop Publishing: Version 6.0 for DOS. Nita H. Rutkosky & Dineen K. Ebert. LC 94-43778. 1994. pap. text 32.95 (*1-56118-711-9*) Paradigm MN.

Nita Hewitt Rutkosky's WordPerfect 6.0 for Windows. Nita H. Rutkosky. LC 94-9731. 1994. pap. text 35.95 (*1-56118-685-6*) Paradigm MN.

Nita Hewitt Rutkosky's WordPerfect 6.0 for Windows. Nita H. Rutkosky. 1994. pap. text 19.00 (*1-56118-687-2*) Paradigm MN.

Nita Hewitt Rutkosky's WordPerfect Version 6.0 for DOS Essentials. Nita H. Rutkosky. LC 94-15026. 1994. pap. text 24.95 (*1-56118-737-2*) Paradigm MN.

NITA HEWITT RUTKOSKY'S WORDPERFECT 6.0 FOR DOS: Textbook with disk, 3.5. Nita Hewitt Rutkosky. text 43.95 (*1-56118-641-4*) EMC-Paradigm.

NITA HEWITT RUTKOSKY'S WORDPERFECT 6.0 FOR WINDOWS: Text with data disk, 3.5. Nita Hewitt Rutkosky. 752p. text 43.95 (*1-56118-688-0*) EMC-Paradigm.

Nite Lites: Three Bedtime Stories for Adults. John Siemens. (Illus.). 88p. 1996. pap. 7.95 (*1-55022-265-1*, Pub. by ECW) LPC InBook.

Nitidulidae (Coleoptera) of the Himalayas & Northern Indochina Pt. 1: Subfamily Epuraeinae. Alexander G. Kirejtshuk. Ed. by Ronald Fricke. (Theses Zoologicae Ser.: No. 28). (Illus.). 489p. (C). Date not set. lib. bdg. 120.00 (*3-87429-399-8*) Koeltz Sci Bks.

Nitnem: Spiritual Practices of Sikhism. Tr. by Swami Rama from PAN. LC 90-197892. 152p. 1989. pap. 12.95 (*0-89389-115-0*) Himalayan Inst.

Nitovikla Reconsidered. Gunnel Hult. (Museum of Mediterranean & Near Eastern Antiquities: Memoir 8). (Illus.). 176p. 1992. 78.00 (*91-7192-835-9*, Pub. by P Astroms) Coronet Bks.

Nitpicker's Guide for X-Philes. Phil Farrand. LC 97-14878. 400p. 1997. pap. 12.95 (*0-440-50808-8*, Delta Trade) Dell.

Nitrate: An Ailing Organism Calls for Healing. H. H. Koepf. (Bio-Dynamics Ser.: No. 73). 52p. 1977. pap. 3.25 (*0-938250-09-4*) Bio-Dynamic Farm.

Nitrate: Processes, Patterns, & Management. Ed. by T. P. Burt et al. LC 92-23877. 456p. 1993. 305.00 (*0-471-93476-3*) Wiley.

Nitrate Clippers. Basil Lubbock. (C). 1987. 125.00 (*0-85174-116-9*) St Mut.

Nitrate Clippers: History of Sailing Ships & Trade Along the West Coast of South America. Basil Lubbock. 1979. lib. bdg. 75.00 (*0-8490-2978-3*) Gordon Pr.

Nitrate Contamination: Exposure, Consequences & Control. Ed. by I. Bogardi & R. D. Kuzelka. (NATO ASI Series G: Ecological Sciences: Vol. 30). xii, 520p. 1991. 288.95 (*0-387-53088-6*) Spr-Verlag.

Nitrate Pollution & Politics: Great Britain, the Federal Republic of Germany & the Netherlands. Jobst Conrad. (Illus.). 88p. 1990. text 82.95 (*0-566-07147-9*, Pub. by Avebry) Ashgate Pub Co.

Nitrate Therapy & Nitrate Tolerance: Current Concepts & Controversies. Ed. by D. Rezakovic & J. S. Alpert. LC 92-49386. (Illus.). x, 548p. 1993. 252.25 (*3-8055-5669-1*) S Karger.

Nitrate Won't Wait: A History of Film Preservation in the United States. Anthony Slide. LC 91-50948. (Illus.). 240p. 1992. lib. bdg. 41.50 (*0-89950-694-1*) McFarland & Co.

Nitrates & Nitrites in Food & Water. Ed. by Michael Hill. 196p. 1991. text 179.95 (*0-7476-0067-8*) Technomic.

Nitrates & Nitrites in Foodstuffs. 1993. 15.00 (*92-871-2425-6*, Pub. by Council of Europe) Manhattan Pub Co.

Nitrates in Groundwater. Larry W. Canter. (Illus.). 320p. 1996. lib. bdg. 75.00 (*0-87371-569-1*, L569) Lewis Pubs.

Nitrates III - Cardiovascular Effects: Proceedings. Ed. by H. J. Engel & P. R. Lichtlen. (Illus.). 705p. 1981. 60.95 (*0-387-10761-4*) Spr-Verlag.

Nitrates Updated: Current Use in Angina, Ischemia, Infarction & Failure. Ed. by Udho Thadani. LC 95-14210. 236p. (C). 1997. text 174.00 (*0-7923-3466-3*) Kluwer Academic.

Nitrating Acetanilde or Methyl Benzoate: Electrophilic Aromatic Substitution. Carl T. Wigal. Ed. by J. Jeffers. (Modular Laboratory Program in Chemistry Ser.). 12p. (C). 1998. pap. text 1.75 (*0-87540-716-1*, REAC 716) Chem Educ Res.

Nitration: Methods & Mechanisms. George A. Olah & Ripudaman Malhotra. (Organic Nitro Chemistry Ser.). 330p. 1989. 120.00 (*0-471-18695-3*, Wiley-VCH) Wiley.

Nitration: Methods & Mechanisms. George A. Olah et al. LC 89-16582. (Organic Nitro Chemistry Ser.). 330p. 1989. 75.00 (*0-89573-144-4*, Wiley-VCH) Wiley.

Nitration: Recent Laboratory & Industrial Developments. Ed. by Lyle F. Albright et al. LC 96-11096. (ACS Symposium Ser.: No. 623). (Illus.). 296p. 1996. text 105.00 (*0-8412-3393-4*, Pub. by Am Chemical) OUP.

Nitric Acid & Fertilizer Nitrates. Cornelius Keleti. (Fertilizer Science & Technology Ser.: Vol. 4). (Illus.). 392p. (C). 1985. text 245.00 (*0-8247-7332-2*) Dekker.

Nitric Acid-Based Fertilizers & the Environment: Proceedings: International Workshop Nitric Acid-Based Fertilizers & the Environment (1993: Brussels, Belgium) R. G. Lee & International Workshop on Nitric Acid-Based Fertil. LC 94-23796. (Special Publications: No. SP-21). 443p. 1994. pap. 40.00 (*0-88090-108-X*) Intl Fertilizer.

***Nitric Oxide.** Ed. by B. Mayer et al. LC 99-87335. (Handbook of Experimental Pharmacology Ser.: 413). x, 630p. 2000. 399.00 (*3-540-66122-0*) Spr-Verlag.

***Nitric Oxide: Biology & Pathobiology.** Louis J. Ignarro. 2000. 149.95 (*0-12-370420-0*) Acad Pr.

Nitric Oxide: Brain & Immune System. Ed. by S. Moncada et al. (Proceedings Ser.: Vol. 5). 384p. (C). 1994. text 132.60 (*1-85578-046-1*, Pub. by Portland Pr Ltd) Ashgate Pub Co.

Nitric Oxide: Principles & Actions. Ed. by Jack Lancaster, Jr. (Illus.). 355p. 1996. text 79.95 (*0-12-435555-2*) Acad Pr.

Nitric Oxide: Roles in Neuronal Communication & Neurotoxicity. Ed. by Hiroshi Takagi et al. LC 94-15352. (Taniguchi Symposia on Brain Sciences Ser.: No. 17). 1994. 89.95 (*0-8493-7776-5*) CRC Pr.

Nitric Oxide Pt. A: Sources & Detection of NO; NO Synthase. Ed. by Lester Packer et al. LC 97-132273. (Methods in Enzymology Ser.: Vol. 268). (Illus.). 555p. 1996. text 95.00 (*0-12-182169-2*) Acad Pr.

Nitric Oxide Pt. B: Physiological & Pathological Processes. Ed. by Lester Packer et al. (Methods in Enzymology Ser.: Vol. 269). (Illus.). 528p. 1996. text 85.00 (*0-12-182170-6*) Acad Pr.

Nitric Oxide & Endothelin in the Pathogenesis of Glaucoma. Ivan O. Haefliger & J. Flammer. LC 97-34799. 280p. 1998. pap. text 65.00 (*0-7817-1600-4*) Lppncott W & W.

***Nitric Oxide & Free Radicals in Peripheral Neurotransmission.** Stanley Kaslner. LC 99-52761. (Nitrogen Oxides in Biology & Medicine Ser.). (Illus.). 360p. 2000. write for info. (*0-8176-4070-3*, Pub. by Birkhauser) Spr-Verlag.

***Nitric Oxide & Infection.** Ferric C. Fang. LC 99-30078. (C). 1999. text. write for info. (*0-306-46147-1*, Kluwer Plenum) Kluwer Academic.

Nitric Oxide & Radicals in the Pulmonary Vasculature. E. Kenneth Weir et al. LC 95-36634. (Illus.). 528p. 1996. 85.00 (*0-87993-631-2*) Futura Pub.

***Nitric Oxide & the Cardiovascular System.** Ed. by Joseph Loscalzo & Joseph A. Vita. (Contemporary Cardiology Ser.). 616p. 2000. 175.00 (*0-89603-620-0*) Humana.

Nitric Oxide & the Cell: Proliferation, Differentiation & Death. Ed. by S. Moncada et al. (Portland Press Proceedings Ser.: Vol. 13). 280p. 1998. 136.00 (*1-85578-120-4*, Pub. by Portland Pr Ltd) Ashgate Pub Co.

***Nitric Oxide & the Cell: Proliferation, Differentiation & Death: Proceedings of the Symposium Held in Calabria, Italy, in September 1996, under the Auspices of the British & Italian Pharmacological Societies.** Salvador Moncada et al. LC 98-44445. 1998. 99.50 (*0-691-00716-0*, Pub. by Princeton U Pr) Cal Prin Full Svc.

Nitric Oxide & the Kidney: Physiology & Pathophysiology. Michael S. Goligorsky & Steven S. Gross. LC 96-48721. 488p. 1997. 89.95 (*0-412-08061-3*) Kluwer Academic.

Nitric Oxide & the Lung. Ed. by Warren M. Zapol & Kenneth D. Bloch. LC 96-35124. (Lung Biology in Health & Disease Ser.: Vol. 98). (Illus.). 497p. 1996. text 185.00 (*0-8247-9725-6*) Dekker.

***Nitric Oxide & the Regulation of the Peripheral Circulation.** Ed. by Philip J. Kadowitz & D. B. McNamara. LC 99-27053. (Nitric Oxide in Biology & Medicine Ser.). (Illus.). 344p. 1999. 98.00 (*0-8176-4046-0*) Spr-Verlag.

Nitric Oxide, Cytochromes P450, & Sexual Steroid Hormones. Ed. by Jack R. Lancaster & J. F. Parkinson. LC 97-25453. (Ernst Schering Research Foundation Workshop Ser.: Vol. 21). (Illus.). 307p. write for info. (*3-540-63050-3*) Spr-Verlag.

Nitric Oxide in Bone & Joint Disease. Ed. by M. V. Hukkanen et al. LC 98-14672. (Postgraduate Medical Science Ser.: No. 7). (Illus.). 240p. (C). 1998. 69.95 (*0-521-59220-8*) Cambridge U Pr.

Nitric Oxide in Brain Development, Plasticity, & Disease. Ed. by R. Ranney Mize et al. LC 98-40803. (Progress in Brain Research Ser: Vol. 118). 302p. 1998. 210.00 (*0-444-82885-0*) Elsevier.

Nitric Oxide in Health & Disease. Jill Lincoln et al. (Biomedical Research Topics Ser.). (Illus.). 377p. (C). 1997. text 90.00 (*0-521-55038-6*); pap. text 39.95 (*0-521-55977-4*) Cambridge U Pr.

***Nitric Oxide in Pulmonary Processes: Role in Physiology & Pathophysiology of Lung Disease.** Ed. by M. G. Belvisi & J. A. Mitchell. LC 99-36128. (Respiratory Pharmacology & Pharmacotherapy Ser.). (Illus.). 330p. 1999. 119.00 (*3-7643-5718-5*, Pub. by Birkhauser) Spr-Verlag.

***Nitric Oxide in the Eye.** S. Kashii et al. LC 00-39483. 2000. write for info. (*4-431-70287-3*) Spr-Verlag.

Nitric Oxide in the Nervous System. Ed. by Steven R. Vincent. LC 96-7585. (Neuroscience Perspectives Ser.). (Illus.). 317p. 1995. text 74.00 (*0-12-721985-4*) Acad Pr.

Nitric Oxide in Transplant Rejection & Anti-Tumor Defense. Ed. by Stanislaw Lukiewicz & Jay L. Zweier. LC 98-45219. 376p. 1998. text 139.95 (*0-7923-8389-3*, QP535) Kluwer Academic.

Nitric Oxide Protocols. Ed. by M. A. Titheradge. (Methods in Molecular Biology Ser.: Vol. 100). (Illus.). 336p. 1997. spiral bd. 79.50 (*0-89603-537-9*) Humana.

Nitride Semiconductors Vol. 482: Materials Research Society Symposium Proceedings. Ed. by F. A. Ponce et al. LC 98-9636. 1224p. 1998. text 76.00 (*1-55899-387-8*) Materials Res.

***Nitride Semiconductors & Devices.** H. Morkoc. LC 99-14665. (Materials Science Ser.: Vol. 32). (Illus.). xxii, 475p. 1999. 116.00 (*3-540-64038-X*) Spr-Verlag.

***Nitrides & Oxynitrides: Proceedings of the Second International Symposium on Nitrides, Held in Limerick, Ireland, June 1998.** Ed. by S. Hampshire & M. J. Pomeroy. (Materials Science Forum Ser.: Vols. 325-326). 347p. 2000. text 156.00 (*0-87849-850-8*, Pub. by Trans T Pub) Enfield Pubs NH.

***Nitrides & Related Wide Band Gap Materials.** Ed. by A. Hangleiter et al. (European Materials Research Society Symposia Proceedings Ser.). 418p. 1999. 177.50 (*0-08-043615-3*) Elsevier.

Nitrification. Ed. by J. I. Prosser. (Society for General Microbiology Special Publications: Vol. 20). 228p. (C). 1987. 75.00 (*1-85221-013-3*); pap. text 44.00 (*1-85221-001-X*) OUP.

Nitrification Inhibition in the Treatment of Sewage. Richardson. 1989. 44.00 (*0-85186-596-8*) CRC Pr.

Nitrification Inhibitors: Potentials & Limitations. Ed. by J. J. Meisinger et al. (ASA Special Publications: No. 38). (Illus.). 129p. 1980. pap. 5.25 (*0-89118-063-X*) Am Soc Agron.

Nitrification Occurrence & Control in Chloraminated Water Systems. (Illus.). 156p. 1995. pap. 86.00 (*0-89867-801-3*, 90669) Am Water Wks Assn.

Nitrile Oxides, Nitrones & Nitronates in Organic Synthesis: Novel Strategies in Synthesis. Kurt B. Torssell. LC 87-23010. 330p. 1989. 80.00 (*0-89573-304-8*, Wiley-VCH) Wiley.

Nitrile Oxides, Nitrones & Nitronates in Organic Synthesis: Novel Strategies in Synthesis, 20. K. Torssell. (Organic Nitro Chemistry Ser.). 332p. 1988. 149.00 (*0-471-18687-2*, Wiley-VCH) Wiley.

Nitrite-Cured Meat: A Food Safety Issue in Perspective. Robert G. Cassens. 176p. 1990. 67.00 (*0-917678-27-3*) Food & Nut Pr.

Nitro Compounds: Recent Advances in Synthesis & Chemistry. Ed. by H. Feuer & A. T. Nielsen. (Organic Nitro Chemistry Ser.). 636p. 1990. 199.00 (*0-471-18714-3*, Wiley-VCH) Wiley.

Nitro Compounds: Recent Advances in Synthesis & Chemistry. Ed. by Henry Feuer & Arnold T. Nielsen. (Organic Nitro Chemistry Ser.). (Illus.). xvi, 636p. 1992. 150.00 (*0-89573-270-X*, Wiley-VCH) Wiley.

***Nitro Mania.** (World Championship Wrestling - New World Order Coloring & Activity Bks.). (Illus.). 32p. 1999. pap. write for info. (*0-7666-0424-1*, Honey Bear Bks) Modern Pub NYC.

Nitroarenes: Occurrence, Metabolism & Biological Impact. Ed. by P. C. Howard et al. LC 90-22875. (Environmental Science Research Ser.: Vol. 40). (Illus.). 342p. (C). 1990. text 132.00 (*0-306-43694-9*, Kluwer Plenum) Kluwer Academic.

Nitroazoles. Boyer. LC 86-15667. (Organic Nitro Chemistry Ser.). 368p. 1987. text 120.00 (*0-89573-148-7*, Wiley-VCH) Wiley.

Nitrocarbons. Arnold T. Nielsen. LC 94-41183. (Organic Nitro Chemistry Ser.). 1995. 115.00 (*1-56081-681-3*, Wiley-VCH) Wiley.

Nitrocarbons. Arnold T. Nielsen. Ed. by Henry Feuer. (Organic Nitro Chemistry Ser.). (Illus.). 190p. 1995. 150.00 (*0-471-18603-1*, Wiley-VCH) Wiley.

Nitrocelluloses: The Materials & Their Applications in Propellants, Explosives & Other Industries. Jean Quinchon & Jean Tranchant. (Physical Chemistry Ser.). 1989. text 84.95 (*0-470-21542-9*) P-H.

Nitrofurans: Chemistry, Metabolism, Mutagenesis, & Carcinogenesis. fac. ed. Ed. by George T. Bryan. LC 77-72824. (Carcinogenesis - A Comprehensive Survey Ser.: No. 4). 248p. pap. 76.90 (*0-7837-7171-1*, 204712600005) Bks Demand.

Nitrogen. (Metals & Minerals Ser.). 1993. lib. bdg. 250.95 (*0-8490-8991-3*) Gordon Pr.

Nitrogen. (Metals & Minerals Ser.). 1994. lib. bdg. 250.95 (*0-8490-5687-X*) Gordon Pr.

Nitrogen. Jean F. Blashfield. LC 98-4534. (Sparks of Life Ser.). (J). 1999. 27.12 (*0-8172-5039-5*) Raintree Steck-V.

Nitrogen. John Farndon. LC 97-37945. (Elements Ser.). 1999. lib. bdg. 22.79 (*0-7614-0877-0*, Benchmark NY) Marshall Cavendish.

Nitrogen & Air. Battino. (Solubility Data Ser.). 1982. 130.00 (*0-08-023961-7*, Pergamon Pr) Elsevier.

Nitrogen & Carbon Metabolism: Symposium on the Physiology & Bio-Chemistry of Plant Productivity. J. D. Bewley. (Development in Plant & Soil Sciences Ser.: No. 3). 1981. text 112.50 (*90-247-2472-4*) Kluwer Academic.

Nitrogen & Energy Nutrition of Ruminants. Raymond L. Shirley. (Animal Feeding & Nutrition Ser.). 1986. text 94.00 (*0-12-640260-4*) Acad Pr.

Nitrogen Assimilation of Plants. Ed. by E. J. Hewitt. 1979. text 283.00 (*0-12-346360-2*) Acad Pr.

Nitrogen-Centered Radicals, Aminoxyls & Related Radicals. H. Fischer. (Numerical Data & Functional Relationships in Science & Technology Ser.: Vol. 18). 624p. 1994. 2271.95 (*0-387-56056-4*) Spr-Verlag.

Nitrogen Compounds, Carboxylic Acids & Phosphorous Compounds see Comprehensive Organic Chemistry

Nitrogen-Containing Macromolecules in the Bio- & Geosphere, Vol. 707. Ed. by B. Artur Stankiewicz & Pim F. Van Bergen. LC 98-25956. (ACS Symposium Ser.: No. 707). (Illus.). 384p. 1999. text 130.00 (*0-8412-3582-1*) OUP.

Nitrogen Control. Ed. by O. K. Scheible & John L. Heidman. 322p. 1993. pap. 49.95 (*1-56676-135-2*) Technomic.

Nitrogen Control Manual for Water & Wastewater Management. 2nd ed. (Illus.). 311p. (C). 1996. reprint ed. pap. text 45.00 (*0-7881-3410-8*) DIANE Pub.

Nitrogen Cycling in Coastal Marine Environments: Scope 33. Ed. by T. Henry Blackburn & Jan Sorensen. LC 86-26803. (Scientific Committee on Problems of the Environment Ser.). 478p. 1988. 460.00 (*0-471-91404-5*) Wiley.

Nitrogen Cycling in Ecosystems of Latin America & the Caribbean. C. P. Robertson et al. 1982. text 211.50 (*90-247-2719-7*) Kluwer Academic.

Nitrogen Cycling in the North Atlantic Ocean & Its Watersheds. Ed. by Robert W. Howarth. LC 96-48824. 304p. 1996. text 81.00 (*0-7923-4281-X*) Kluwer Academic.

Nitrogen Economy in Tropical Soils: Proceedings of the International Symposium on Nitrogen Economy in Tropical Soils Held January 9-14, 1994 in Trinidad, W. I. Ed. by N. Ahmad. 444p. (C). 1996. text 294.00 (*0-7923-4094-9*) Kluwer Academic.

Nitrogen Economy of Flooded Rice Soils. Ed. by S. K. DeDatta & W. H. Patrick. (Developments in Plant & Soil Sciences Ser.). 1986. text 139.00 (*90-247-3361-8*) Kluwer Academic.

Nitrogen, Electrolytes Water & Metabolism. Ed. by Miloslav Rechcigl, Jr. (Comparative Animal Nutrition Ser.: Vol. 3). (Illus.). 1979. 113.25 (*3-8055-2829-9*) S Karger.

Nitrogen Fertilization in the Environment. Ed. by Peter E. Bacon. LC 94-42809. (Books in Soils, Plants & the Environment: Vol. 42). (Illus.). 624p. 1995. text 215.00 (*0-8247-8994-6*) Dekker.

Nitrogen Fixation. Ed. by M. Polsinelli et al. (Developments in Plant & Soil Sciences Ser.). 704p. (C). 1991. text 364.50 (*0-7923-1410-7*) Kluwer Academic.

Nitrogen Fixation. 3rd rev. ed. John Raymond Postgate. LC 98-15362. (Illus.). 100p. (C). 1998. 54.95 (*0-521-64047-4*); pap. 17.95 (*0-521-64853-X*) Cambridge U Pr.

***Nitrogen Fixation: From Molecules to Crop Productivity: Proceedings of the 12th International Congress on Nitrogen Fixation, Foz Do Iguawcu, Paranba, Brazil, September 12-27, 1999.** International Congress on Nitrogen Fixation Staff & Fbabio O. Pedrosa. LC 00-28156. 2000. write for info. (*0-7923-6233-0*) Kluwer Academic.

Nitrogen Fixation: Fundamentals & Applications: Proceedings of the 10th International Congress on Nitrogen Fixation, St. Petersburg, Russia, May 28-June 3, 1995. Ed. by Igor A. Tikhonovich et al. LC 95-31286. (Current Plant Science & Biotechnology in Agriculture Ser.). 1995. text 276.00 (*0-7923-3707-7*) Kluwer Academic.

Nitrogen Fixation Vol. 1: Proceedings of the First International Symposium, 1974, Pullman, WA. Ed. by William E. Newton & C. J. Nyman. LC TP0245.N8I61. (Illus.). 319p. reprint ed. pap. 98.90 (*0-608-18347-4*, 203302700001) Bks Demand.

Nitrogen Fixation & Its Research in China. Ed. by G. F. Hong. (Illus.). 628p. 1992. 272.95 (*0-387-54510-7*) Spr-Verlag.

Nitrogen Fixation & Nitrogen Cycle. Ed. by Hajime Takahashi. LC 77-359141. (JIBP Synthesis Ser.: No. 12). 169p. 1975. reprint ed. pap. 52.40 (*0-608-01557-1*, 206196800001) Bks Demand.

Nitrogen Fixation by Legumes in Mediterranean Agriculture. D. Beck & L. A. Materon. (Developments in Plants & Soil Sciences Ser.). (C). 1988. text 271.50 (*90-247-3624-2*) Kluwer Academic.

Nitrogen Fixation in Tropical Cropping Systems. K. Giller & K. Wilson. 320p. 1991. pap. 50.00 (*0-85198-842-3*) OUP.

***Nitrogen Fixation in Tropical Cropping Systems.** 2nd ed. K. Giller & K. Wilson. (CABI Publishing Ser.). (Illus.). 352p. 2000. text 90.00 (*0-85199-417-2*) OUP.

Nitrogen Fixation Research Progress. Ed. by William E. Newton et al. (Current Plant Science & Biotechnology in Agriculture Ser.). 1985. text 329.00 (*90-247-3255-7*) Kluwer Academic.

Nitrogen Fixation with Non-Legumes. Ed. by Kauser A. Malik et al. LC 97-43109. (Developments in Plant & Soil Sciences Ser.). 360p. 1998. lib. bdg. 169.00 (*0-7923-4873-7*) Kluwer Academic.

Nitrogen Fixation with Non-Legumes. Ed. by P. Uomala & Fredrick A. Skinner. (Developments in Plant & Soil Sciences Ser.). 1986. text 205.50 (*90-247-3283-2*) Kluwer Academic.

Nitrogen Fixation with Non-Legumes: The Sixth International Symposium on Nitrogen Fixation with Non-Legumes, Ismailia, Egypt, September 1993. Ed. by N. A. Hegazi et al. (World XEgypt Ser.). 620p. 1995. 150.00 (*977-424-355-2*, Pub. by Am Univ Cairo Pr) Col U Pr.

Nitrogen Fixing & Multipurpose Tree Species for Afforestation. Ed. by M. P. Singh. 275p. 1991. 65.00 (*1-55528-252-0*) Scholarly Pubns.

Nitrogen Fixing Organisms: Pure & Applied Aspects. Janet I. Sprent & Peter Sprent. (Illus.). 256p. (C). 1990. text 79.95 (*0-412-34680-X*, A4745) Chapman & Hall.

Nitrogen Fixation with Non-Legumes: Proceedings of the 4th International Symposium on Nitrogen Fixation with Non-Legumes, Rio de Janeiro, Brazil , August 23-28, 1987. Frederick A. Skinner et al. (Developments in Plant & Soil Sciences Ser.). (C). 1989. text 213.50 (*0-7923-0059-9*) Kluwer Academic.

Nitrogen Fluxes in Intensive Grassland Systems. Ed. by H. V. Van der Meer et al. (Developments in Plant & Soil Sciences Ser.). 1986. text 105.00 (*90-247-3309-X*) Kluwer Academic.

Nitrogen in Agricultural Soils. Ed. by F. J. Stevenson. (ASA Monograph Ser.: No. 22). 940p. (C). 1982. 30.00 (*0-89118-070-2*) Am Soc Agron.

Nitrogen in Crop Production. Ed. by R. D. Hauck. (Illus.). 804p. 1984. 48.00 (*0-89118-081-8*) Am Soc Agron.

Nitrogen in Organic Wastes Applied to Soils. Ed. by Jens A. Hansen. (ISWA Ser.). 381p. 1990. text 125.00 (*0-12-323440-9*) Acad Pr.

Nitrogen in Soils of China. Chao-Liang Chu et al. LC 96-49482. (Developments in Plant & Soil Sciences Ser.). 1997. text 234.00 (*0-7923-4372-7*) Kluwer Academic.

Nitrogen in Terrestrial Ecosystems: Questions of Productivity, Vegetational Changes & Ecosystem Stability. C. O. Tamm. Ed. by Hermann Remmert et al. (Ecological Studies: Vol. 81). (Illus.). 128p. 1991. 96.00 (*0-387-51807-X*) Spr-Verlag.

Nitrogen in the Marine Environment. Ed. by Edward J. Carpenter & Douglas G. Capone. LC 83-2829. 1983. text 142.00 (*0-12-160280-X*) Acad Pr.

Nitrogen in the Sea: Forms, Abundances & Rate Processes. Eitaro Wada & Hattori. 224p. 1990. lib. bdg. 210.00 (*0-8493-6273-3*, GC98) CRC Pr.

Nitrogen Industry, 2 vols., Set. G. D. Honti. 1413p. 1984. 300.00 (*963-05-0228-3*, Pub. by Akade Kiado) St Mut.

Nitrogen Industry, 2 vols., Set, Vols. 1 & 2. G. D. Honti. (C). 1976. 655.00 (*0-7855-4993-5*) St Mut.

Nitrogen Isotope Techniques. Ed. by Roger Knowles & T. Henry Blackburn. LC 92-13944. (Isotopic Techniques in Plant, Soil, & Aquatic Biology Ser.). (Illus.). 311p. 1992. text 79.00 (*0-12-416965-1*) Acad Pr.

Nitrogen Losses & Surface Run-Off from Landspreading of Manures: Proceedings of a Workshop in the EEC Programme of Co-Ordination & Research on Effluents from Livestock. J. C. Brogan. 487p. 1981. text 141.50 (*90-247-2471-6*) Kluwer Academic.

Nitrogen Management & Ground Water Protection. R. F. Follet. (Developments in Agricultural & Managed Forest Ecology Ser.: Vol. 21). (Illus.). xvi,396p. 1990. 170.00 (*0-444-87393-7*, DAF 21) Elsevier.

Nitrogen Management in Irrigated Agriculture. Roy S. Rauschkolb & Arthur G. Hornsby. (Illus.). 252p. 1994. text 65.00 (*0-19-507835-7*) OUP.

Nitrogen Metabolism & Excretion. Ed. by Patrick J. Walsh & Patricia Wright. LC 94-46469. (Evolutionary & Comparative Approaches Ser.). 352p. 1995. boxed set 179.95 (*0-8493-8411-7*, 8411) CRC Pr.

Nitrogen Metabolism in Plants. L. Beevers. 333p. (C). 1979. text 120.00 (*0-89771-548-9*, Pub. by Intl Bk Distr) St Mut.

Nitrogen Metabolism in Plants. Ed. by K. Mengel & D. J. Pilbeam. (Proceedings of the Phytochemical Society of Europe Ser.: No. 33). (Illus.). 304p. 1992. 95.00 (*0-19-857752-4*) OUP.

Nitrogen Metabolism in Plants. L. Beevers. 333p. 1979. reprint ed. 100.00 (*0-7855-6640-6*, Pub. by Intl Bk Distr) St Mut.

Nitrogen Nutrition & Plant Growth. Ed. by H. S. Srivastava & Rana P. Singh. (Illus.). 357p. 1999. 80.00 (*1-57808-032-0*) Science Pubs.

Nitrogen Nutrition of Cotton: Practical Issues. Ed. by W. N. Miley & D. M. Oosterhuis. 115p. 1990. 15.00 (*0-89118-105-9*) Am Soc Agron.

Nitrogen Oxides Control Technology Fact Book. Leslie L. Sloss et al. LC 92-3550. (Illus.). 635p. 1992. 129.00 (*0-8155-1294-5*) Noyes.

Nitrogen, Phosphorus & Sulphur Utilisation by Fungi. Ed. by L. Boddy et al. (British Mycological Society Symposium Ser.: No. 15). 316p. (C). 1989. text 110.00 (*0-521-37405-7*) Cambridge U Pr.

Nitrogen Source Control of Microbial Processes. Ed. by Sergio Sanchez-Esquivel. 224p. 1988. 123.00 (*0-8493-6223-7*, QR92, CRC Reprint) Franklin.

***Nitrogen, the Confer-N-S: First International Nitrogen Conference 1998: 23-27, March 1998 Noordwijkerhout, The Netherlands.** International Nitrogen Conference Staff. Ed. by Klass van der Hoek. LC 98-43518. 1999. write for info. (*0-08-043201-8*) Elsevier.

Nitrogen Turnover in the Soil-Crop System. Ed. by J. R. Groot et al. (Developments in Plant & Soil Sciences Ser.). (C). 1991. text 166.50 (*0-7923-1107-8*) Kluwer Academic.

Nitroglycerin 5. Ed. by Bodo E. Strauer. 125p. (C). 1987. pap. text 63.10 (*3-11-010879-8*) De Gruyter.

Nitroglycerin 7: Progress in Therapy. LC 91-28638. 103p. 1990. pap. 63.10 (*3-11-013396-2*) De Gruyter.

Nitroglycerin 6: Unstable Angina Pectoris & Extracardial Indications. Ed. by H. Roskamm. (Illus.). 165p. (C). 1990. pap. 60.00 (*3-11-012061-5*) De Gruyter.

Nitroglycerine & Nitroglycerine Explosives. Phokion Naoum. Tr. by E. M. Symmes. (World Wide Chemical Translation Ser.: No. 1). 512p. (C). 1928. reprint ed. 18.00 (*0-913022-46-2*) Angriff Pr.

Nitromethane from the People's Republic of China: An International Trade Investigation. (Illus.). 89p. (Orig.). (C). 1994. pap. text 25.00 (*0-7881-0776-3*) DIANE Pub.

Nitrones, Nitronates, & Nitroxides. Eli Breuer et al. Ed. by Saul Patai & Zvi Rappoport. LC 88-17388. (Chemistry of Functional Groups Ser.). (Illus.). 445p. reprint ed. pap. 138.00 (*0-608-20171-5*, 205280400012) Bks Demand.

Nitroquinolines. Ed. by Takashi Sugimura. LC 76-51087. (Carcinogenesis - A Comprehensive Survey Ser.: No. 6). (Illus.). 167p. 1981. reprint ed. pap. 51.80 (*0-608-00673-4*, 206126000007) Bks Demand.

Nitrosamines & Human Cancer. Ed. by Peter N. Magee. LC 82-12952. (Banbury Reports: Vol. 12). 599p. 1982. 67.00 (*0-87969-211-1*) Cold Spring Harbor.

Nitrosamines & Related N-Nitroso Compounds: Chemistry & Biochemistry. Ed. by Richard N. Loeppky & Christopher J. Michejda. LC 94-2014. (Symposium Ser.: Vol. 553). 381p. 1994. text 98.00 (*0-8412-2856-6*, Pub. by Am Chemical) OUP.

Nitroso Compounds: Biological Mechanism, Exposures & Cancer Etiology. O'Neill & Bartsch. (IARC Technical Report Ser.: No. 11). 149p. 1992. text 30.00 (*92-832-1425-0*) World Health.

Nitrous Oxide Injection Guide: How to Make Maximum Power with Nitrous Oxide Injection. Joe Pettitt. LC 99-218940. (Illus.). 128p. (Orig.). 1998. pap. 18.95 (*1-884089-22-4*, S-A Design) CarTech.

***Nitrox Mixing Handbook Vol. 1: U. S. Standard - Imperial.** A. E. Melton. (Illus.). 304p. (C). 1999. 50.00 (*0-915539-05-5*, M-6116) IANTD.

***Nitrox Mixing Handbook Vol. 2: Metric.** A. E. Melton. (Illus.). 192p. (C). 1999. 50.00 (*0-915539-06-3*, M-6117) IANTD.

Nitroxide Spin Labels: Reactions in Biology & Chemistry. Nickolai Kocherginsky & Harold M. Swartz. 288p. 1995. boxed set 179.95 (*0-8493-4204-X*, 4204) CRC Pr.

Nittany Lion: An Illustrated Tale. Jackie R. Esposito & Steven Herb. LC 97-1836. 1997. 28.50 (*0-271-01588-8*) Pa St U Pr.

Nitter Pitter. Stephen Cosgrove. (Serendipity Bks.). (Illus.). 32p. (J). (gr. 1-4). 1978. pap. 4.99 (*0-8431-0570-4*, Price Stern) Peng Put Young Read.

Nitty Gritty: A White Editor in Black Journalism. Ben Burns. LC 95-32890. 288p. 1996. 27.50 (*0-87805-812-5*) U Pr of Miss.

Nitty Gritty Bare Bones Method of Housekeeping. Toni Pighetti. (Illus.). 26p. (Orig.). 1985. pap. 6.95 (*0-913005-05-3*) TAM Assoc.

Nitty-Gritty Basketball Series, 9 bks. Sidney Goldstein. 1998. per. 97.05 (*1-884357-02-4*) Golden Aura.

Nitty-Gritty Basketball Series, 9 bks., Set. Sidney Goldstein. (Illus.). 323p. 1995. per. 93.55 (*1-884357-01-6*) Golden Aura.

Nitty-Gritty for Ministers' Wives. Bonnie J. Markham. LC 88-11750. (Illus.). 208p. (Orig.). 1988. pap. 7.99 (*0-932581-34-X*) Word Aflame.

***Nitty-Gritty Grammar: A Not-So-Serious Guide to Clear Communication.** Edith Fine & Judith Josephson. LC 97-44240. (Illus.). 102p. 1998. pap. 8.95 (*0-89815-966-0*) Ten Speed Pr.

Nitty Gritty Grammar: Sentence Essentials for Writers. Robert A. Young & Ann O. Strauch. 288p. (C). 1994. pap. text 21.95 (*0-521-65784-9*) Cambridge U Pr.

Nitty Gritty Grammar: Sentence Essentials for Writers: Instructor's Manual. Robert A. Young & Ann O. Strauch. 44p. (C). 1994. pap., teacher ed. 6.00 (*0-521-65783-0*) Cambridge U Pr.

Nitty-Gritty on Long Distance Savings: Cut Through the Hype & End the Confusion! Wanda C. Swenson. LC 95-92109. 128p. (Orig.). 1995. pap. 19.95 (*0-9645676-0-1*) ProSysts Consult.

Nityananda: In Divine Presence. M. U. Hatengdi & Swami Chetanananda. LC 97-51368. (Illus.). xix, 148p. 1998. pap. 14.95 (*0-915801-76-0*) Rudra Pr.

Niuatoputapu: The Prehistory of a Polynesian Chiefdom. Patrick V. Kirch. (Illus.). 295p. 1989. pap. 25.00 (*0-295-96833-8*) U of Wash Pr.

***Niue: A Country Study Guide, 110 vols.** International Business Publications, USA Staff & Global Investment Center, USA Staff. (World Country Study Guides Library Ser.: Vol. 215). (Illus.). 350p. 2000. pap. 69.95 (*0-7397-1038-9*) Intl Business Pubns.

N'iukheivenskie Sonety, 1989-1998 (New Haven Sonnets, 1989-1998) (The New Haven Sonnets; in Russian) Maxin D. Shrayer. (RUS., Illus.). 50p. 1998. pap. 7.95 (*1-888244-01-1*) APKA Pubs.

NIV: The Making of a Contemporary Translation. Ed. by Kenneth Barker. 240p. 1986. pap. 9.95 (*0-310-24181-2*, 12080P) Zondervan.

NIV Application Commentary: Exodus. Peter Enns. 2000. 26.99 (*0-310-20607-3*) Zondervan.

***NIV Application Commentary: 2 Corinthians.** Scott J. Hafemann. 2000. 24.99 (*0-310-49420-6*) Zondervan.

NIV Atlas of the Bible. Carl G. Rasmussen. 256p. 1989. 49.99 (*0-310-25160-5*) Zondervan.

NIV Bible Compact Dictionary. J. D. Douglas & Tenney. 2000. 6.99 (*0-310-21496-3*) Zondervan.

NIV Bible Companion: A Basic Commentary on the Old & New Testaments. Alister E. McGrath. LC 96-51874. 400p. 1997. 24.99 (*0-310-20547-6*) Zondervan.

NIV Bible Crosswords. Rick Jansen. 144p. 1991. pap. 5.99 (*0-310-54681-8*) Zondervan.

***NIV Compact Bible Commentary.** John H. Sailhamer. (NIV Compact Ser.). 1999. pap. text 7.97 (*0-310-22868-9*) Zondervan.

***NIV Compact Concordance.** Zondervan Publishing Staff. 1999. pap. text 9.99 (*0-310-22872-7*) Zondervan.

NIV Compact Dictionary of the Bible. J. D. Douglas. 1999. pap. text 7.97 (*0-310-22873-5*) Zondervan.

NIV Compact Dictionary of the Bible. Jack D. Douglas & Merrill C. Tenney. 640p. 1989. 17.99 (*0-310-33180-3*, 6752) Zondervan.

NIV Compact Nave's Topical Bible. John R. Kohlenberger, 3rd. (NIV Compact Ser.). 1999. pap. text 7.97 (*0-310-22869-7*) Zondervan.

NIV Exhaustive Concordance. Edward W. Goodrick & John R. Kohlenberger, III. 1850p. 1990. 39.99 (*0-310-43690-7*) Zondervan.

NIV Handy Concordance: The Complete English Concordance to the New International Version. Edward W. Goodrick. 1982. pap. 6.95 (*0-310-43662-1*) Zondervan.

NIV Handy Concordance: The Complete English Concordance to the New International Version. Edward W. Goodrick & John R. Kohlenberger, III. 384p. 1988. pap. 9.99 (*0-310-43661-3*, 12097P) Zondervan.

NIV Harmony of the Gospels. Stanley N. Gundry. 352p. 1988. 23.00 (*0-06-063523-1*, Pub. by Harper SF) HarpC.

NIV Interlinear Hebrew-English Old Testament, Vol. 3. John R. Kohlenberger. (ENG & HEB.). 1980. 24.95 (*0-310-44200-1*) Zondervan.

NIV Matthew Commentary in One Volume. Matthew Henry. 2016p. 1992. 32.99 (*0-310-26040-X*) Zondervan.

NIV New Testament. (Believer's Life System Women's Edition Ser.). 1998. ring bd. 8.99 (*0-8024-6983-3*) Moody.

NIV Reconsidered: A Fresh Look at a Popular Translation. Earl Radmacher & Zane C. Hodges. 155p. (Orig.). 1991. pap. 8.95 (*0-9607576-9-4*) Redencion Viva.

NIV Standard Lesson Commentary, 1998-99. Ed. by J. Underwood. 448p. 1998. pap., text 13.99 incl. cd-rom (*0-7847-0844-4*, 11-11999) Standard Pub.

***Niv Study Bible.** Zondervan Publishing Staff. 2208p. 1999. 39.99 (*0-310-90991-0*) Zondervan.

NIV Teen Study Bible. Larry Richards & Sue Richards. LC 99-191932. (Illus.). 1664p. (YA). (gr. 7-10). 1998. 29.99 (*0-310-90096-4*) Zondervan.

NIV Teen Study Bible. Zondervan Publishing Staff. 1664p. 2000. pap. 24.99 (*0-310-90394-7*) Zondervan.

NIV 25th Anniversary Edition New Testament with Psalms & Proverbs: The NIV Celebrates Its 25th Anniversary with This Popularly Requested Edition. 672p. 1998. lthr. 19.99 (*0-310-90091-3*) Zondervan.

NIV Vest Pocket Companion for Christian Workers. rev. ed. R. A. Torrey. 96p. 1980. pap. 1.70 (*0-310-33331-8*, 12152P) Zondervan.

Niveaux de Survie see Tiers of Survival: Selected Poems

Nivel Inferior y Otros Cuentos. Raul T. Estrella. LC 96-86698. (Coleccion Caniqui). (SPA.). 169p. (Orig.). 1996. pap. 13.00 (*0-89729-816-0*) Ediciones.

Nivel Limiar (The Threshold Level for Portuguese) Council of Europe Staff. (POR.). 1988. 25.00 (*92-871-1554-0*, Pub. by Council of Europe) Manhattan Pub Co.

Nivel Soleira (The Threshold Level for Galacian) 1993. 25.00 (*92-871-2255-5*, Pub. by Council of Europe) Manhattan Pub Co.

Nivel Umbral (The Threshold Level for Spanish) Council of Europe Staff. (SPA.). 1980. 18.00 (*92-871-0746-7*, Pub. by Council of Europe) Manhattan Pub Co.

Niven: The Family of Niven, with Biographical Sketches & the Voyages, Letters & Diaries of Capt. John Niven. John Niven. 252p. 1992. reprint ed. pap. 37.00 (*0-8328-2395-3*); reprint ed. lib. bdg. 47.00 (*0-8328-2394-5*) Higginson Bk Co.

Niven's Laws. Larry Niven. 108p. 1984. 12.00 (*0-913896-24-1*) Owlswick Pr.

Nix. Mame Farrell. Date not set. write for info. (*0-374-32289-9*) FS&G.

Nixes, Numens, & Muses. Matthew J. Jewel & James J. Molchan. (Illus.). 96p. 1998. pap. 9.00 (*0-9664700-1-X*) Prosody Pr.

Nixon: A Life. Jonathan Aitken. (Illus.). 640p. 1996. pap. 17.95 (*0-89526-720-9*) Regnery Pub.

Nixon: An Oliver Stone Film. Ed. by Eric Hamburg. LC 95-31302. (Illus.). 592p. (Orig.). (J). 1995. pap. 14.45 (*0-7868-8157-7*, Pub. by Hyperion) Time Warner.

Nixon: The Education of a Politician, 1913-1962. Stephen E. Ambrose. 1988. pap. 18.00 (*0-671-65722-4*, Touchstone) S&S Trade Pap.

Nixon Administration & the Making of U. S. Nuclear Strategy. Terry Terriff. (Studies in Security Affairs). 256p. 1995. text 37.50 (*0-8014-3082-8*) Cornell U Pr.

Nixon Administration & Vietnam: A Case Study in Negotiation & War Termination. Gary Geipel. (Pew Case Studies in International Affairs). 81p. (C). 1994. pap. text 3.50 (*1-56927-337-5*) Geo U Inst Dplmcy.

Nixon & I. Karen Kovacik. LC 97-31169. (Wick Poetry Chapbook Ser.). 1998. 4.75 (*0-87338-592-6*) Kent St U Pr.

***Nixon & the Environment.** J. Brooks Flippen. LC 00-8607. 2000. 24.95 (*0-8263-1993-9*) U of NM Pr.

Nixon & the Foxes of Watergate. Aldebaran. 1968. pap. 2.95 (*0-918680-12-3*) Griffon House.

Nixon Bio, Vol. II. Morris. 1995. 26.95 (*0-8050-1365-2*) H Holt & Co.

Nixon, Ford, & Carter. Eileen Lucas. LC 95-43537. (Complete History of Our Presidents Ser.: Vol. 11). (J). 1996. write for info. (*0-86593-412-6*) Rourke Corp.

Nixon Man. Cahill. 240p. 1999. pap. 12.95 (*0-312-24488-6*) St Martin.

Nixon Man. Michael Cahill. LC 98-13706. 224p. 1998. text 22.95 (*0-312-18749-1*) St Martin.

Nixon Memo: Political Respectability, Russia & the Press. Marvin Kalb. 258p. 1994. 19.95 (*0-226-42299-2*) U Ch Pr.

Nixon on Stage & Screen: The Thirty-Seventh President As Depicted in Films, Television, Plays, & Opera. Thomas Monsell. LC 97-44651. 247p. 1998. lib. bdg. 42.50 (*0-7864-0163-X*) McFarland & Co.

Nixon Presidency: Power & Politics in Turbulent Times, 259. Michael A. Genovese. LC 90-2713. (Contributions in Political Science Ser.: No. 259). 280p. 1990. 59.95 (*0-313-25506-7*, GRN/, Greenwood Pr) Greenwood.

N

Nixon Presidency: Twenty-Two Intimate Perspectives of Richard Nixon. Ed. by Kenneth W. Thompson. (Portraits of American Presidents Ser.: Vol. VI). 432p. (Orig.). (C). 1987. pap. text 34.00 (*0-8191-6416-X*, Pub. by White Miller Center) U Pr of Amer.

Nixon Reconsidered. Joan Hoff. 496p. 1995. pap. 16.00 (*0-465-05105-7*, Pub. by Basic) HarpC.

Nixon Tapes: Submission of Recorded Presidential Conversations to the Committee on the Judiciary of the House of Representatives. Richard M. Nixon. 1308p. 1974. reprint ed. 45.00 (*1-57588-342-2*, 200830) W S Hein.

Nixon Years, 1969-1974: White House to Watergate. Fred J. Maroon. LC 99-35265. 192p. 1999. 29.95 (*0-7892-0610-2*) Abbeville Pr.

Nixoncarver. Mark Maxwell. LC 97-40068. 192p. 1998. text 19.95 (*0-312-18146-9*) St Martin.

NixonCarver: A Novel. Mark Maxwell. 1999. pap. 11.95 (*0-312-20664-X*, St Martin Griffin) St Martin.

Nixon's Economy: Booms, Busts, Dollars, & Votes. Allen J. Matusow. LC 97-49995. 288p. 1998. 35.00 (*0-7006-0888-5*) U Pr of KS.

Nixon's Enemies. Kenneth Franklin Kurz. 336p. 1999. pap. 17.95 (*0-7373-0254-2*, 02542W) NTC Contemp Pub Co.

Nixon's Horoscope. Lynne Palmer. 176p. 1975. 10.00 (*0-86690-140-X*, P1367-014) Am Fed Astrologers.

Nixon's Nixon. Russell Lees. LC 98-178110. 1996. pap. 5.25 (*0-8222-1556-X*) Dramatists Play.

Nixon's Piano: Presidents & the Politics of Race from Washington to Clinton. Kenneth O'Reilly. 512p. 1995. 27.00 (*0-02-923685-1*) Free Pr.

Nixon's Ten Commandments of Statecraft: His Guiding Principles of Leadership & Negotiation. James C. Humes. 192p. 1998. pap. 11.00 (*0-684-84816-3*, Touchstone) S&S Trade Pap.

Nixon's Ten Commandments of Statecraft: His Guiding Principles of Leadership & Negotiation. Richard M. Nixon. LC 97-17420. 1997. 19.50 (*0-684-83795-1*) S&S Trade.

Nixon's Vietnam War. Jeffrey Kimball. LC 98-19431. 528p. 1998. 39.95 (*0-7006-0924-5*) U Pr of KS.

Niyamsara (The Perfect Law) Kundakunda Acharya. Tr. & Intro. by Uggar Sain. LC 73-3844. (Sacred Books of the Jainas: No. 9). reprint ed. 32.50 (*0-404-57709-1*) AMS Pr.

Nizam Ad-Din Awliya: Morals for the Heart. Ed. & Tr. by Bruce B. Lawrence. (Classics of Western Spirituality Ser.). 1991. 26.95 (*0-8091-0451-2*); pap. 18.95 (*0-8091-3280-X*) Paulist Pr.

Nizam al Islam al 'Aqa'idi fi al 'Asr al Hadith: The Credal System of Islam in the Modern Age. Muhammad A. Mubarak. (Silsilat Rasa'il Islamiyat al Ma'rifah Ser.: No. 2). (ARA.). 44p. (Orig.). 1989. pap. 2.00 (*1-56564-161-2*) IIIT VA.

Nizam-British Relations, 1724-1857. Sarojini Regani. (C). 1989. 28.50 (*81-7022-195-1*, Pub. by Concept) S Asia.

Nizami: Khamsa Miniatures. Kerim Kerimov. (Illus.). 142p. (C). 1983. text 400.00 (*0-7855-5804-7*, Pub. by Collets) St Mut.

Nizami das Alexanderbuch Iskandarname: Aus Dem Persischen Ubersetzt. J. Christoph Burgel. (PER.). 678p. 1991. text 28.00 (*3-7175-1810-0*) Bibliotheca Persica.

***Nizan: La Conspiration.** John Flower. 1999. pap. 35.00 (*0-85261-657-0*, Pub. by U of Glasgow) St Mut.

Nizari Ismaili Tradition in the Indo-Pakistan Subcontinent. Azim Nanji. LC 78-12990. (Monographs in Islamic Religion & Theology). 232p. 1979. 35.00 (*0-88206-020-1*) Caravan Bks.

Nizatidin. 1989. 45.95 (*0-387-50738-8*) Spr-Verlag.

Nize Baby. Milton Gross. LC 83-46020. (Classics of Modern American Humor Ser.). reprint ed. 28.00 (*0-404-19932-1*) AMS Pr.

***Nizhniy Novgorod Oblast Regional Investment & Business Guide.** Global Investment & Business Center, Inc. Staff. (Russian Regional Investment & Business Guides Ser.: Vol. 51). (Illus.). 350p. 1999. pap. 99.00 (*0-7397-0851-1*) Intl Business Pubns.

***Nizhniy Novgorod Oblast Regional Investment & Business Guide.** Contrib. by Global Investment & Business Center, Inc. Staff. (Russian Regional Investment & Business Guides Ser.: Vol. 10). (Illus.). 350p. 2000. pap. 99.95 (*0-7397-2999-3*) Intl Business Pubns.

Nizhoni: The Higher Self in Education. Chris Griscom. 202p. 1989. pap. 10.00 (*0-9623696-0-8*) Light Inst Fndtn.

Nizniy Novgorod Oblast: Economy, Industry, Government, Business. 2nd rev. ed. Russian Information & Business Center, Inc. Staff. (Russian Regional Business Directories Ser.). (Illus.). 200p. 1997. pap. 99.00 (*1-57751-400-9*) Intl Business Pubns.

Njal's Saga. Magnus Magnusson. (Classics Ser.). 384p. (Orig.). 1960. pap. 19.99 (*0-14-044103-4*, Penguin Classics) Viking Penguin.

Njal's Saga. Ed. by Carl F. Bayerschmidt & Lee M. Hollander. LC 79-10657. (Illus.). 389p. 1980. reprint ed. lib. bdg. 79.50 (*0-313-20814-X*, NJSA, Greenwood Pr) Greenwood.

Njamba Nene & the Flying Bus. Ngugi wa Thiong'o. Tr. by Wangui wa Goro. LC 88-70433. (Young Reader's Ser.). (Illus.). 34p. (J). (gr. 2-7). 1995. 12.95 (*0-86543-079-9*); pap. 5.95 (*0-86543-080-2*) Africa World.

Njamba Nene's Pistol. Ngugi wa Thiong'o. Tr. by Wangui wa Goro. LC 88-70432. (Young Reader's Ser.). (Illus.). 32p. (J). (gr. 2-7). 1995. 12.95 (*0-86543-081-0*); pap. 5.95 (*0-86543-082-9*) Africa World.

Njtyasumangali: Devidasi Tradition in South India. Saskia C. Kersenboon. (C). 1998. reprint ed. pap. 17.50 (*81-208-1527-0*, Pub. by Motilal Bnarsidass) S Asia.

NK Cell Medicated Cytotoxicology: Receptors, Signaling & Mechanics. Eva Lotzova. 512p. 1992. lib. bdg. 239.00 (*0-8493-6267-9*, QR188) CRC Pr.

NK Cells: Adhesive Interactions, Microvasculature, Extracellular Matrices & Angiogenesis. Ronald H. Goldfarb. (Journal Ser.: Vol. 15, Nos. 2 & 3, 1996-97). (Illus.). 94p. 1997. pap. 40.00 (*3-8055-6394-9*) S Karger.

NK Cells & Natural Immunity. Ed. by B. Bonavida & S. Golup. (Journal Ser.: Vol. 14, 2, 1995). (Illus.). 60p. 1995. pap. 47.00 (*3-8055-6263-2*) S Karger.

NK Cells in the Liver. Ed. by Luc Bouwens. LC 95-1069. (Medical Intelligence Unit Ser.). 136p. 1995. text 79.00 (*1-57059-249-7*) Landes Bioscience.

NK Lawn & Garden Guides: Growing Herbs. Roberta Floden. 80p. (Orig.). 1994. pap. 7.95 (*0-380-77425-9*, Avon Bks) Morrow Avon.

NK Lawn & Garden Guides: Growing Perennials. Peggy Henry. 80p. (Orig.). 1994. pap. 7.95 (*0-380-77426-7*, Avon Bks) Morrow Avon.

NK Lawn & Garden Guides: Pruning Made Simple. Barbara Ferguson Stremple. 80p. 1994. pap. 7.95 (*0-380-77427-5*, Avon Bks) Morrow Avon.

Nkore-Kiga. Charles Taylor. LC 85-3813. (Descriptive Grammars Ser.). 254p. 1985. 72.50 (*0-7099-2482-8*, Pub. by C Helm) Routldge.

Nkrumah & Ghana: The Dilemma of a Post-Colonial Power. Kofi B. Hadjor. 142p. 1989. text 45.00 (*0-7103-0322-X*) Routledge.

***Nkrumah & the Chiefs: The Politics of Chieftaincy in Ghana, 1951-1960.** Richard Rathbone. LC 99-46031. (West African Ser.). 200p. 1999. text 44.95 (*0-8214-1305-8*); pap. text 19.95 (*0-8214-1306-6*) Ohio U Pr.

Nkrumah's Consciencism. Charles Boateng. 188p. (C). 1995. pap. text, per. 35.95 (*0-7872-1396-9*, 41139601) Kendall-Hunt.

Nkrumah's Ghana & East Africa: Pan-Africanism & African Interstate Relations. Opoku Agyeman. LC 91-55093. 240p. 1992. 38.50 (*0-8386-3456-7*) Fairleigh Dickinson.

NL: Contemporary Art from the Netherlands. Stedelijk Van Abbemuseum Eindhoven. LC N6948.N58 1998. (Illus.). 128p. 1999. pap. 30.00 (*90-70149-69-9*, 915015, Pub. by S V Abbemuseum) Dist Art Pubs.

NLADA-NCLC Advanced Consumer Training Materials. 424p. 1986. 28.00 (*0-685-23174-7*, 41,263) NCLS Inc.

NLADA Substantive Law Conference Youth Law Materials. 583p. 1988. 45.00 (*0-685-30181-8*, 43,725) NCLS Inc.

NLADA Substantive Law Training, 1987: 1987. 206p. 1987. 12.00 (*0-685-30201-6*, 39,964) NCLS Inc.

NLADA Training: Health Law Section. 213p. 1987. 22.00 (*0-685-30151-6*, 42,675) NCLS Inc.

NLC's City Fiscal Conditions & Outlook for Fiscal, 1985. 52p. 1984. 15.00 (*0-933729-03-0*) Natl League Cities.

NLGI Lubricating Grease Guide see Guia para Grasas Lubricantes

NLGI Lubricating Grease Guide. 4th rev. ed. Natl. Lubricating Grease Inst. Staff. Ed. by Mel Ehrlich. (Illus.). 148p. 1996. pap. 26.00 (*0-9613935-1-3*) Natl Lubrica Grease.

NLGI Steady Flow Charts for Grease. rev. ed. National Lubricating Grease Institute Staff. (Illus.). 16p. 1982. reprint ed. pap., student ed. 6.00 (*0-9613935-3-X*) Natl Lubrica Grease.

NLN Criteria for Appraisal of Baccalaureate Programs: A Critical Hermeneutic Analysis. Nancy Diekelmann et al. Ed. by Linda Moody & Moira Shannon. 80p. 1989. 17.95 (*0-88737-429-8*) Natl League Nurse.

NLN Guide to Undergraduate RN Education. 5th ed. D. Louden. 200p. 1997. 19.95 (*0-88737-737-8*, 19-7378, NLN Pr) Natl League Nurse.

***NLN Official Guide to Graduate Nursing Schools.** 1999. 26.95 (*0-7637-1060-1*) Jones & Bartlett.

***NLN Official Guide to Undergraduate & Graduate Nursing Schools.** 1999. 34.95 (*0-7637-1107-1*) Jones & Bartlett.

***NLN Official Guide to Undergraduate Nursing Schools.** 1999. 26.95 (*0-7637-1108-X*) Jones & Bartlett.

Nlp: The New Technology. Steve Andreas. 1996. pap. 14.00 (*0-688-14619-8*, Quil) HarperTrade.

NLP: The New Technology of Achievement, Set. Charles Faulkner. 1993. audio 16.00 (*0-671-79638-0*) S&S Audio.

NLP - Going Meta: Going Meta: Advanced Modeling Using Meta-Levels. L. Michael Hall. 250p. 1997. pap. 25.00 (*1-890001-16-3*) Empowerment Tech.

NLP - Neuro Linguistic Programming: The Art & Science of Getting What You Want. Harry Alder. 224p. 1997. pap. 14.95 (*0-7499-1489-0*, Pub. by Piatkus Bks) London Brdge.

***NLP & Relationships: Simple Strategies to Make Your Relationships Work.** Joseph O'Connor & Robin Prior. 2000. pap. 16.00 (*0-7225-3868-5*, Pub. by Thorsons PA) HarpC.

NLP at Work: Neuro Linguistic Programming: The Difference That Makes a Difference in Business. Sue Knight. LC 95-222691. (People Skills for Professionals). (Illus.). 230p. 1996. reprint ed. pap. 17.95 (*1-85788-070-6*) Nicholas Brealey.

NLP for Business Success. Andrew Bradbury. (Better Management Skills Ser.). 1997. pap. 12.95 (*0-7494-2151-7*) Kogan Page Ltd.

NLP for Lazy Learning: Superlearning Strategies for Business & Personal Development. Diana Beaver. 208p. 1998. pap. 14.95 (*1-86204-412-0*, Pub. by Element MA) Penguin Putnam.

NLP for Managers: How to Achieve Excellence at Work. Harry Alder. 240p. 1998. pap. text 14.95 (*0-7499-1643-5*, Pub. by Piatkus Bks) London Brdge.

NLP for Trainers: Communicating for Excellence. Harry Alder. LC 95-49799. (Training Ser.). 1996. pap. write for info. (*0-07-709134-5*) McGraw.

NLP Personal Profile Guidebook, Pt. I. Gregory Engel & Lowell J. Arthur. 180p. (C). 1999. pap., teacher ed. 39.95 (*1-884180-05-1*) LifeStar.

NLP Solutions: How to Model What Works in Business & Make It Work for You. Sue Knight. LC 98-51519. (People Skills for Professionals Ser.). (Illus.). 256p. 1999. pap. 17.95 (*1-85788-227-X*) Nicholas Brealey.

NLRB Advice Memorandum Reporter. LRP Publications Staff. text 510.00 (*0-934753-08-3*) LRP Pubns.

NLRB Advice Memorandum Reporter, Vol. 14. Ed. by LRP Publications Staff. 1987. text. write for info. (*0-934753-26-1*) LRP Pubns.

NLRB & Management Decision Making. Robert A. Swift. LC 74-80052. (Labor Relations & Public Policy Ser.: No. 9). 156p. reprint ed. pap. 48.40 (*0-8357-3151-0*, 203941400012) Bks Demand.

NLRB & Managerial Discretion: Plant Closings, Relocations, Subcontracting, & Automation. Philip A. Miscimarra. LC 83-81557. (Labor Relations & Public Policy Ser.: No. 24). (Illus.). 368p. (Orig.). 1983. pap. 25.00 (*0-89546-038-6*) U PA Ctr Hum Res.

NLRB & Secondary Boycotts. rev. ed. Ralph M. Dereshinsky et al. LC 81-52616. (Labor Relations & Public Policy Ser.: No. 4). 349p. 1981. pap. 22.00 (*0-89546-027-0*) U PA Ctr Hum Res.

NLRB & Secondary Boycotts: Supplement 1981-1998. Alan D. Berkowitz & Philip A. Miscimarra. (Labor Relations & Public Policy Ser.: Vol. 4). 200p. 1998. 25.00 (*1-891496-06-9*) J M Olin.

NLRB & the Appropriate Bargaining Unit. rev. ed. John E. Abodeely et al. LC 80-85252. (Labor Relations & Public Policy Ser.: No. 3). 359p. 1981. pap. 20.00 (*0-89546-028-9*) U PA Ctr Hum Res.

NLRB & the Appropriate Bargaining Unit. 3rd ed. Lawrence W. Marquess. (Labor Relations & Public Policy Ser.: Vol. 3). 150p. 1998. 35.00 (*1-891496-05-0*) J M Olin.

NLRB Casehandling Manual Pt. 2. 359p. 1997. ring bd. 26.00 (*0-16-061840-1*) USGPO.

NLRB Election Report. Government Printing Office Staff. 1983. pap. 31.00 (*0-16-011554-X*) USGPO.

NLRB Law & Practice, 3 vols., Vol. 3. 1991. 330.00 (*0-8205-1614-7*) Bender.

NLRB Regulation of Election Conduct: Labor Relations & Public Policy. rev. ed. Robert E. Williams. LC 85-80312. 350p. 1985. pap. 27.50 (*0-89546-054-8*) U PA Ctr Hum Res.

NLRB Regulation of Election Conduct, 1985-97 Supplement. rev. ed. J. Hamilton Stewart. (Labor Relations & Public Policy Ser.: Vol. LR8). 86p. 1998. 22.50 (*1-891496-03-4*) J M Olin.

NLRB Remedies for Unfair Labor Practices. rev. ed. Jonathan Kane et al. LC 85-81945. (Labor Relations & Public Policy Ser.: Vol. 12). 266p. 1986. pap. 27.50 (*0-89546-056-4*) U PA Ctr Hum Res.

NLRB Remedies for Unfair Labor Practices, 1986-97 Supplement. rev. ed. H. Lane Dennard, Jr. (Labor Relations & Public Policy Ser.: Vol. 12). 158p. 1998. pap. 22.50 (*1-891496-02-6*) J M Olin.

NLRB Representation & Decertification Elections Statistics. 1997. 35.00 (*0-685-45812-1*) BNA PLUS.

NLRB Representation Elections: Law, Practice & Procedure, 3 vols. 3rd ed. John D. Feerick et al. 1848p. 1988. ring bd. 95.00 (*0-13-104506-7*) Aspen Law.

***NLRB Style Manual: Guide for Legal Writing in Plain English.** 104p. 2000. ring bd. 20.00 (*0-16-050308-6*) USGPO.

Act 2. David Self & R. Speakman. 167p. 1988. pap. 11.95 (*0-09-136591-0*) Dufour.

NLW Riders Official Compuserve Yellow Pages. New Riders Development Group Staff. LC 94-37840. 800p. 1994. pap. 29.99 (*1-56205-396-5*) New Riders Pub.

NM Const. see New Mexico 1999 Cumulative Supplement

NMA Handbook for Managers. National Management Association Staff. 416p. 1987. 39.95 (*0-13-622903-4*) P-H.

NMA Hidden Heritage Address Book. (Illus.). 1990. pap. 2.00 (*0-939802-64-3*) High Mus Art.

NMDA Receptor. 2nd ed. Ed. by Graham L. Collingridge & Jeffrey C. Watkins. (Illus.). 522p. 1995. 115.00 (*0-19-262371-0*) OUP.

NMDA Receptor. 2nd ed. Ed. by Graham L. Collingridge & Jeffrey C. Watkins. (Illus.). 516p. 1995. pap. text 54.50 (*0-19-262502-0*) OUP.

NMDA Receptor Protocols. Min Li. LC 98-53445. (Methods in Molecular Biology Ser.: Vol. 128). (Illus.). 208p. 1999. 79.50 (*0-89603-713-4*) Humana.

NMDA Receptor Related Agents: Biochemistry, Pharmacology & Behavior. Ed. by T. Kameyama et al. LC 90-64353. (Illus.). 414p. 1991. text 95.00 (*0-916182-08-8*) NPP Bks.

NMR: A Primer for Medical Imaging. Gerald L. Wolfe & Carol Popp. 96p. 1983. 30.95 (*0-316-95099-8*, Little Brwn Med Div) Lppncott W & W.

NMR: Principles & Applications to Biomedical Research. Ed. by J. W. Pettegrew. (Illus.). 640p. 1989. 132.95 (*0-387-97094-0*) Spr-Verlag.

NMR - Basic Principles & Progress Vol. 22: Solid-State NMR; Inorganic Matter, Vol. 31; Vol II. Ed. by P. Diehl et al. 162p. 1994. 219.95 (*0-387-57190-6*) Spr-Verlag.

NMR - Basic Principles & Progress Vol. 22: Solid-State NMR; Methods, Vol. 30; Vol. I. Ed. by B. Blumich et al. 268p. 1994. 185.95 (*0-387-57189-2*) Spr-Verlag.

NMR - Basic Principles & Progress Vol. 23: Deuterium & Shift Calculation. Ed. by P. Diehl et al. (Illus.). x, 263p. 1991. 142.95 (*0-387-52949-7*) Spr-Verlag.

NMR - Basic Principles & Progress Vol. 24: High Pressure NMR. Ed. by P. Diehl et al. (Illus.). x, 265p. 1991. 150.95 (*0-387-52938-1*) Spr-Verlag.

NMR - Basic Principles & Progress Vol. 25: NMR at Very High Field. Ed. by P. Diehl et al. (Illus.). x, 168p. 1991. 111.95 (*0-387-52946-2*) Spr-Verlag.

NMR - Basic Principles & Progress Vol. 27: In Vivo Magnetic Resonance Spectroscopy II: Localization & Spectral Editing. Ed. by P. Diehl et al. (Illus.). 298p. 1992. 130.95 (*0-387-55022-4*) Spr-Verlag.

NMR - Basic Principles & Progress Vol. 28: In Vivo Magnetic Resonance Spectroscopy III: In-Vivo MR Spectroscopy: Potential & Limitations. Ed. by P. Diehl et al. (Illus.). 202p. 1992. 118.95 (*0-387-55029-1*) Spr-Verlag.

NMR - Basic Principles & Progress Vol. 29: Special Applications. Ed. by P. Diehl et al. (Illus.). 176p. 1993. 119.95 (*0-387-56438-1*) Spr-Verlag.

NMR - Tomography, Diffusometry, Relaxometry. R. Kimmich. LC 97-1009. (Illus.). 640p. 1997. 149.95 (*3-540-61822-8*) Spr-Verlag.

NMR Analyses of Molecular Conformations & Conformational Equilibria with the Lanthanide Probe Method, Vol. 14, No. 2. Clive Emsley & T. Miyazawa. (Illus.). 45p. 1981. pap. 28.00 (*0-08-027104-9*, Pergamon Pr) Elsevier.

NMR & Biochemistry: A Symposium Honoring Mildred Cohn. Ed. by P. Lu & Stanley J. Opella. LC 79-19485. (Illus.). 448p. reprint ed. pap. 138.90 (*0-7837-0618-9*, 204096300019) Bks Demand.

NMR & Chemistry. 4th rev. ed. Brian E. Mann & James W. Akitt. (Illus.). 288p. 2000. pap. (*0-7487-4344-8*) S Thornes Pubs.

NMR & Its Applications to Living Systems. 2nd ed. David G. Gadian. (Illus.). 294p. 1996. text 80.00 (*0-19-855281-5*); pap. text 45.00 (*0-19-855803-1*) OUP.

NMR & Macromolecules: Sequence, Dynamic, & Domain Structure. Ed. by James C. Randall. LC 84-366. (ACS Symposium Ser.: No. 247). 181p. 1984. lib. bdg. 43.95 (*0-8412-0829-8*) Am Chemical.

NMR & Macromolecules: Sequence, Dynamic, & Domain Structure. Ed. by James C. Randall, Jr. LC 84-366. (ACS Symposium Ser.: Vol. 247). 297p. 1984. reprint ed. pap. 92.10 (*0-608-03127-5*, 206358000007) Bks Demand.

NMR & Nucleic Acids. Ed. by Thomas L. James et al. (Methods in Enzymology Ser.: Vol. 261). (Illus.). 644p. 1995. text 80.00 (*0-12-182162-5*) Acad Pr.

NMR & X-Ray Crystallography: Interfaces & Challenges. Ed. by M. C. Etter. (Transactions of the American Crystallographic Association Ser.: Vol. 24). 172p. 1988. 40.00 (*0-685-30537-6*); pap. 25.00 (*0-937140-32-5*) Polycrystal Bk Serv.

NMR Applications in Biopolymers. Ed. by J. W. Finley et al. (Basic Life Sciences Ser.: Vol. 56). (Illus.). 526p. (C). 1990. text 179.00 (*0-306-43719-8*, Kluwer Plenum) Kluwer Academic.

NMR As a Structural Tool for Macromolecules: Current Status & Future Directions. Ed. by B. D. Rao & Marvin D. Kemple. LC 96-21442. (Illus.). 400p. (C). 1996. text 144.00 (*0-306-45313-4*, Kluwer Plenum) Kluwer Academic.

NMR Data Processing. Jeffrey C. Hoch & Alan S. Stern. LC 96-4981. 196p. 1996. 79.95 (*0-471-03900-4*) Wiley.

NMR Data Tables for Organic Compounds, Vol. 1. Frank A. Bovey. LC 67-20258. 619p. reprint ed. pap. 191.90 (*0-8357-9943-3*, 201647400004) Bks Demand.

NMR Diffusion Studies. Karger. text. write for info. (*0-471-49003-2*) Wiley.

NMR Imaging: A Comprehensive Bibliography. Jozef Jaklovsky. 190p. 1983. write for info. (*0-201-11608-1*) Addison-Wesley.

NMR Imaging Health & Safety: An Annotated Bibliography. Louis Slesin & Amy Rosenberg. 30p. (Orig.). 1986. 18.95 (*0-9610580-2-1*) Microwave.

***NMR Imaging of Materials.** Bernhard Blumich. LC 99-87343. (Illus.). 560p. 2000. text 120.00 (*0-19-850683-X*) OUP.

NMR in Biomedicine: The Physical Basis. Ed. by Eiichi Fukushima. (Key Papers in Physics). (Illus.). 170p. 1989. 59.95 (*0-88318-603-9*); pap. 39.95 (*0-88318-609-8*) Spr-Verlag.

NMR in Drug Design. Ed. by David J. Craik. LC 95-34213. (Analytical Biotechnology Ser.). 496p. 1995. boxed set 209.95 (*0-8493-7824-9*, 7824) CRC Pr.

NMR in Living Systems. Ed. by T. Axenrod & G. Ceccarelli. 1986. text 186.00 (*90-277-2174-2*) Kluwer Academic.

NMR in Medicine: The Instrumentation & Clinical Applications: Proceedings of the AAPM 1985 Summer School Held at the University of Portland, Portland, Oregon, August 4-9, 1985. Ed. by Stephen R. Thomas & Robert L. Dixon. (American Association of Physicists in Medicine Symposium Ser.: No. 14). 608p. 1986. 70.00 (*0-88318-497-4*, Pub. by Am Inst Physics) Med Physics Pub.

NMR in Medicine & Biology: Structure Determination, Tomography, In-Vivo Spectroscopy. K. H. Hausser & H. R. Kalbitzer. (Illus.). 240p. 1991. 91.95 (*0-387-53195-5*) Spr-Verlag.

***NMR in Microbiology: Theory & Applications.** Jean-Noel Barbotin & Jean-Charles Portais. 500p. 2000. 169.99 (*1-898486-21-2*, Pub. by Horizon Sci) Intl Spec Bk.

NMR in Physiology & Biomedicine. Ed. by Robert J. Gillies. (Illus.). 471p. 1994. text 104.00 (*0-12-283980-3*) Acad Pr.

NMR in Structural Biology: A Collection of Papers by Kurt Wuthrich. Kurt Wuthrich. 760p. 1995. 34.00 (*981-02-2384-6*) World Scientific Pub.

NMR in Structural Biology: A Collection of Papers by Kurt Wuthrich. Ed. by Kurt Wuthrich. 650p. 1995. 84.00 (*981-02-2242-4*) World Scientific Pub.

***NMR in Supramolecular Chemistry.** M. Pons. LC 99-12333. (NATO ASI Ser.). 1999. write for info. (*0-7923-5621-7*) Kluwer Academic.

NMR in the Life Sciences. Ed. by E. Morton Bradbury & Claudio Nicolini. LC 86-9404. (NATO ASI Series A, Life Sciences: Vol. 107). 246p. 1986. 65.00 (*0-306-42279-4*, Plenum Trade) Perseus Pubng.

NMR Methods for Elucidating Macromolecule-Ligand Interactions: An Approach to Drug Design. Ed. by Robert E. Handschumacher & Ian M. Armitage. 140p. 1990. 55.00 (*0-08-040674-2*, Pergamon Pr) Elsevier.

NMR of Biological Macromolecules. Chariklia I. Stassinopoulu. 1994. write for info. (*3-540-58269-X*) Spr-Verlag.

NMR of Biological Macromolecules, 87. Ed. by Chariklia I. Stassinopoulou. 358p. 1994. 192.95 (*0-387-58269-X*) Spr-Verlag.

NMR of Humic Substances & Coal: Techniques, Problems, & Solutions. Ed. by Robert L. Wershaw & Michael A. Mikita. (Illus.). 236p. 1989. lib. bdg. 68.00 (*0-87371-082-7*) Lewis Pubs.

NMR of Macromolecules: A Practical Approach. Ed. by Gordon C. Roberts. LC 93-17466. (Practical Approach Ser.: Vol. 134). (Illus.). 418p. 1993. pap. text 55.00 (*0-19-963224-3*) OUP.

NMR of Molecules Oriented in Electric Fields. C. W. Hilbers & C. MacLean. (NMR-Basic Principles & Progress Ser.: Vol. 7). (Illus.). 1972. 38.00 (*0-387-05687-4*) Spr-Verlag.

Nmr of Paramagnetic Molecules in Biological Systems: Physical Bioinorganic Chemistry Series. Ivano Bertini & Claudio Luchinat. (Physical Bioinorganic Ser.). (Illus.). 300p. (C). 1986. text 44.25 (*0-8053-0780-X*) Benjamin-Cummings.

NMR of Polymers. Frank A. Bovey & Peter Mirau. LC 96-28240. (Illus.). 459p. 1996. text 95.00 (*0-12-119765-4*) Acad Pr.

NMR of Proteins. Ed. by G. M. Clore & A. M. Gronenborn. LC 93-25445. (Topics in Molecular & Structural Biology Ser.). 1993. 110.00 (*0-8493-7771-4*) CRC Pr.

NMR of Proteins & Nucleic Acids. Kurt Wuthrich. LC 86-7834. (Baker Lectures). 320p. 1986. 94.95 (*0-471-82893-9*) Wiley.

NMR Shift Reagents. Thomas J. Wenzel. 296p. 1987. 168.00 (*0-8493-5298-3*, CRC Reprint) Franklin.

NMR Spectra of Plastics. A. Brandolini & D. D. Haney. (Illus.). 573p. 2000. text. write for info. (*0-8247-8970-9*) Dekker.

NMR Spectra of Simple Heterocycles. T. J. Batterham. LC 80-11724. 560p. 1982. reprint ed. lib. bdg. 69.50 (*0-89874-140-8*) Krieger.

NMR Spectroscopy: An Introduction. Harald Gunther. LC 78-31736. 450p. reprint ed. pap. 139.50 (*0-7837-0113-6*, 204039000016) Bks Demand.

NMR Spectroscopy: Basic Principles, Concepts & Applications in Chemistry. 2nd ed. Harald Gunther. LC 94-23084. Orig. Title: NMR Spektroskopie. 602p. 1995. 185.00 (*0-471-95199-4*) Wiley.

NMR Spectroscopy: Basic Principles, Concepts & Applications in Chemistry. 2nd ed. Harald Gunther. LC 94-23084. Orig. Title: NMR Spektroskopie. 602p. (J). 1995. pap. 69.95 (*0-471-95201-X*) Wiley.

***NMR-Spectroscopy: Data Acquisition.** Christian Schorn & Peter Bigler. 250p. 2000. 170.00 (*3-527-28827-9*) Wiley.

***NMR-Spectroscopy: Modern Spectral Analysis.** Ursula Weber & Herbert Thiele. 410p. 1998. 280.00 incl. cd-rom (*3-527-28828-7*) Wiley.

An Asterisk (*) at the beginning of an entry indicates that the title is appearing for the first time.

NMR Spectroscopy: New Methods & Applications. Ed. by George C. Levy. LC 82-11458. (ACS Symposium Ser.: Vol. 191). 398p. 1982. reprint ed. pap. 123.40 (*0-608-03116-X*, 206356900007) Bks Demand.

NMR Spectroscopy & Its Application to Biomedical Research. Sustana K. Sarkar. LC 96-45701. 406p. 1996. 250.00 (*0-444-89410-1*) Elsevier.

NMR Spectroscopy & Polymer Mic. A. E. Tonelli. (Methods in Stereochemical Analysis Ser.). 252p. 1989. 120.00 (*0-471-18748-8*, Wiley-VCH) Wiley.

NMR Spectroscopy & Stereoregularity of Polymers. K. Matsuzaki et al. (Illus.). xviii, 278p. 1996. 287.00 (*3-8055-6298-5*) S Karger.

***NMR Spectroscopy in Drug Development & Analysis.** Ulrike Holzgrabe et al. 299p. 1999. 95.00 (*3-527-30092-9*) Wiley.

NMR Spectroscopy in Psychiatric Brain Disorders. Ed. by Henry A. Nasrallah & Jay W. Pettegrew. LC 94-34269. (Progress in Psychiatry Ser.: No. 47). 272p. 1995. text 16.95 (*0-88048-483-7*, 8483) Am Psychiatric.

NMR Spectroscopy of Cells & Organisms, 2 vols., Set. Ed. by Raj K. Gupta. LC 87-835. 1987. 199.00 (*0-8493-4304-6*, QH585, CRC Reprint) Franklin.

NMR Spectroscopy of Cells & Organisms, Vol. 1. R. K. Gupta. LC 87-835. 1987. 105.00 (*0-8493-4305-4*, CRC Reprint) Franklin.

NMR Spectroscopy of Cells & Organisms, Vol. 2. R. K. Gupta. LC 87-835. 1987. 94.00 (*0-8493-4306-2*, QH585, CRC Reprint) Franklin.

NMR Spectroscopy of the Non-Metallic Elements. Stefan Berger et al. Tr. by Jack Becconsall. LC 96-15919. 1098p. 1997. 485.00 (*0-471-96763-7*) Wiley.

NMR Spectroscopy Techniques. 2nd ed. Martha D. Bruch. (Pratical Spectroscopy Ser.: Vol. 21). (Illus.). 632p. 1996. text 215.00 (*0-8247-9450-8*) Dekker.

NMR Spektroskopie see NMR Spectroscopy: Basic Principles, Concepts & Applications in Chemistry

NMR Techniques & Applications in Geochemistry & Soil Chemistry. M. A. Wilson & Institute Energy & Earth Resources Staff. LC 87-35940. 300p. 1987. 165.00 (*0-08-034852-1*, Pub. by Pergamon Repr) Franklin.

NMR Techniques in Catalysis. Ed. by Alexis T. Bell & Alexander Pines. LC 93-43400. (Chemical Industries Ser.: Vol. 55). (Illus.). 448p. 1994. text 199.00 (*0-8247-9173-8*) Dekker.

NMS Anatomy. 2nd ed. Ernest W. April. (National Medical Ser.). 610p. 1990. 26.00 (*0-683-06200-X*) Lppncott W & W.

NMS Genetics. J. Friedman et al. (National Medical Ser.). 250p. 1992. 26.00 (*0-683-06218-2*) Lppncott W & W.

NMS Immunology. 4th ed. Richard M. Hyde. 315p. 27.00 (*0-683-30662-6*) Lppncott W & W.

NMS Introduction to Clinical Medicine. Judy Lewis & Janice Williams. (National Medical Ser.). (Illus.). 260p. 1991. 24.00 (*0-683-06212-3*) Lppncott W & W.

NMS Medicine. 4th ed. Allen R. Myers. 775p. pap. text 30.00 (*0-7817-2144-X*) Lppncott W & W.

NMS Neuroanatomy. W. DeMyer. (National Medical Ser.). 380p. 1990. 26.00 (*0-683-06236-0*) Lppncott W & W.

NMS Pediatrics. 2nd ed. Paul H. Dworkin. (National Medical Ser.). 460p. 1991. 27.00 (*0-683-06246-8*) Lppncott W & W.

NMS Pediatrics. 4th ed. Paul H. Dworkin. 675p. 30.00 (*0-683-30637-5*) Lppncott W & W.

NMS Pharmacology. 3rd ed. L. Jacobs. (National Medical Ser.). 336p. 1991. 26.00 (*0-683-06250-6*) Lppncott W & W.

NMS Physiology. 4th ed. John Bullock et al. 575p. 27.00 (*0-683-30603-0*) Lppncott W & W.

NMS Psychiatry. 4th ed. James H. Scully. 320p. 30.00 (*0-683-30791-6*) Lppncott W & W.

Nms Surgery. 4th ed. Bruce E. Jarrell & R. Anthony Carabasi, III. 650p. 30.00 (*0-683-30615-4*) Lppncott W & W.

***NMSS Licensee Newsletter, Dec 1999- Jan 2000 No. 99-4.** 16p. 2000. pap. 2.00 (*0-16-059184-8*) USGPO.

***NMSS Licensee Newsletter, No. 97-4, December 1997-January 1998.** 11p. 1998. pap. 1.50 (*0-16-062997-7*) USGPO.

***NMSS Licensee Newsletter, No. 98-1, March-April 1998.** 8p. 1998. pap. 1.25 (*0-16-063002-9*) USGPO.

***NMSS Licensee Newsletter, No. 98-2, June-July 1998.** 6p. 1998. pap. 1.25 (*0-16-063004-5*) USGPO.

***NMSS Licensee Newsletter, No. 98-3, September to October 1998.** 9p. 1999. pap. 1.25 (*0-16-063013-4*) USGPO.

Nnamdi Azikiwe: The Vision of the New Africa. Chukwudi O. Maduno. (Ekumeku Universal Foundation Ser.). 72p. (Orig.). 1996. pap. text 10.00 (*0-9644596-4-7*) Ekumeku Commun.

NNS Red Book. Nieson N. Shak. Ed. by Saul Berman. 80p. (C). 1988. write for info. (*0-9619751-0-5*) NNS Pub Co.

***No.** Carl Djerassi. (Illus.). (J). 2000. pap. 14.00 (*0-14-029654-9*) Penguin Putnam.

No. large type ed. David Michaeli. 242p. 1998. mass mkt. 7.50 (*965-494-002-7*, Pub. by Astrolog Pub) Assoc Pubs Grp.

No: A Novel. Carl Djerassi. LC 98-6748. xii, 270p. 1998. 24.95 (*0-8203-2032-3*) U of Ga Pr.

N/O: Non Oz; Being Two Parts of the Alphabet. Ron Sulliman. LC 94-66953. 107p. (Orig.). 1994. pap. 10.95 (*0-937804-56-8*) Segue NYC.

No - It's Not the Devil: It's You. Jack Rowe. 80p. (Orig.). 1990. spiral bd. 3.00 (*0-9621384-1-X*) Rowe Evangelistic Minist.

No - Kyogen Masks & Performance. Hubert Nearman et al. (Mime Journal Ser.). (Illus.). 236p. (Orig.). 1984. pap. 12.00 (*0-9611066-6-2*) Mime Jour.

No, a Zamboni Is Not a Pasta: Guide for the Beginning Skater. large type ed. Joan M. Douglas. Ed. by John H. Hanst. (Illus.). 50p. 1997. pap. 9.95 (*0-9657186-0-3*) J M Douglas.

No Abandons Nunca (Don't Quit Ever) Anne McAllister. (SPA.). 1997. per. 3.50 (*0-373-35203-4*, 1-35203-8) Harlequin Bks.

No Abode: The Record of Ippen. Ippen. Ed. by Dennis Hirota. LC 97-25770. (Ryukoku-IBS Studies in Buddhist Thought & Tradition). (Illus.). 272p. 1997. text 32.00 (*0-8248-1978-0*); pap. text 17.95 (*0-8248-1997-7*) UH Pr.

No Acting Please. Eric Morris. 1995. pap. text 11.95 (*0-9629709-3-X*) Ermor Enter.

No Aging in India: Alzheimer's, Bad Families, & Other Modern Things. Lawrence Cohen. LC 97-38659. 400p. 1998. 45.00 (*0-520-08396-2*, Pub. by U CA Pr) Cal Prin Full Svc.

***No Aging in India: Alzheimer's, the Bad Family & Other Modern Things.** Lawrence Cohen. LC 97-38659. (Illus.). 400p. 2000. pap. 18.95 (*0-520-22462-0*) U CA Pr.

***No Aim, No Gain: Aimless Life or Life of Aim... Which Describes You?** Jeff Wickwire. 192p. 1999. pap. 10.99 (*1-890900-02-8*) Insight Intl.

***No Aloha: The Friendly Happy Music of the Past.** Deran Ludd. (Native Agents Ser.: No. 14). 197p. 1999. pap. 10.00 (*1-58435-008-3*, Pub. by Semiotexte); pap. 10.00 (*1-58435-000-8*, Native Agents) Semiotexte.

No Alternative. large type ed. Josie Metcalfe. 288p. 1995. 23.99 (*0-263-14330-9*, Pub. by Mills & Boon) Ulverscroft.

No Amateur Did This: What Is the Truth about the Oklahoma City Bombing? large type ed. Ken Armstrong. (Illus.). 192p. (Orig.). 1997. 19.95 (*0-9657155-0-7*) Blckeye Pr.

No Ameis al Mundo. T. S. Nee. Orig. Title: Love Not the World. (SPA.). 96p. 1992. mass mkt. 3.99 (*0-8254-1502-0*, Edit Portavoz) Kregel.

No Americans Wanted. Sam Mims. (J). 1969. 4.95 (*0-87511-085-1*) Claitors.

No Anchovies on the Moon: Three Score & Ten Washington Pictures & Poems. Paul Boswell. LC 93-44800. (Illus.). 192p. 1994. 29.95 (*0-929765-33-8*) Seven Locks Pr.

No & Bunraku: Two Forms of Japanese Theatre. Donald Keene. 200p. 1990. pap. text 19.00 (*0-231-07419-0*) Col U Pr.

No & Kyogen in the Contemporary World. Ed. by James R. Brandon. LC 96-43429. 1997. text 39.00 (*0-8248-1810-5*) UH Pr.

NO & Nervous System Plasticity: Journal. Ed. by Sean Murphy. (Journal Ser.: Vol. 19, No. 3, 1997). (Illus.). 74p. 1997. pap. 40.00 (*3-8055-6525-9*) S Karger.

No & Run: A Program to Teach Children How to React to Strangers. Ken Smith. (Illus.). 10p. (Orig.). (J). (ps-3). 1996. pap. 6.95 (*1-57543-010-X*) Mar Co Prods.

No & Yes. Mary Baker Eddy. pap. 5.00 (*0-87952-237-2*) Writings of Mary Baker.

No & Yes. Mary M. Eddy. (Notable American Authors Ser.). 1992. reprint ed. lib. bdg. 75.00 (*0-7812-2753-4*) Rprt Serv.

No & Yes: On the Genesis of Human Communication. Rene A. Spitz. LC 57-12046. 182p. 1966. 27.50 (*0-8236-3620-8*) Intl Univs Pr.

***No Angel.** Marian Malone. (Sapphire Ser.). 1999. pap. text 9.95 (*0-352-33462-2*) London Brdge.

No Angels: Women Who Commit Violence. Ed. by Alice Myers & Sarah Wight. (Illus.). 256p. 1995. pap. text 17.50 (*0-04-440957-5*) NYU Pr.

No Angel's Grace. Linda Winstead. 368p. (Orig.). 1997. mass mkt. 5.50 (*0-8439-4223-1*) Dorchester Pub Co.

No Answer. R. L. Stine, pseud. (Fear Street Seniors Ser.: No. 4). (YA). (gr. 7 up). 1998. mass mkt. 3.99 (*0-307-24708-2*, Goldn Books) Gldn Bks Pub Co.

No Apologies: Texas Radicals Celebrate the Sixties. Ed. by Daryl Janes. LC 92-18782. (Illus.). 304p. (C). 1992. 16.95 (*0-89015-870-3*) Sunbelt Media.

No Apologies: The Truth about Life, Love & Sex. Jim Ware. LC 99-12969. (Life on the Edge (Tyndale) Ser.). 231p. (YA). (gr. 9 up). 1999. mass mkt. 5.99 (*1-56179-654-9*) Focus Family.

No Apologies Pricing: How to Price Your Services & Products for Profit. Valarie Neiman & Elleen J. Glick. 52p. 1995. pap. 9.95 (*1-887780-00-9*) HomeBased Busn Assn.

No Apology Necessary: How Hidden Prophecies in the Old Testament Foretold the Tragedy of Slavery. Earl Carter. 1997. pap. 10.99 (*0-88419-455-8*) Creation House.

No Appointment Necessary: The Hospital Emergency Department in the Medical Services World. Julius A. Roth & Dorothy Douglas. 324p. 1983. pap. text 27.50 (*0-8290-1255-9*) Irvington.

No Appointment Needed. Bernhard Aaen. 128p. 1981. pap. 5.99 (*0-8280-0025-5*) Review & Herald.

No Arm in Left Field. Matt Christopher. (Illus.). 131p. (J). (gr. 4-6). 1987. pap. 3.95 (*0-316-13990-4*) Little.

No Arm in Left Field. Matt Christopher. (J). 1974. 9.05 (*0-606-03046-8*, Pub. by Turtleback) Demco.

No Assembly Required: The Pocket Book of Answers to Questions You Never Got Around to Asking. Dorothy Wilhelm. 48p. (Orig.). 1994. pap. 3.95 (*0-9642738-0-2*) Nautilus West.

No Asylum: State Psychiatric Repression in the Former U. S. S. R. Theresa C. Smith & Thomas A. Oleszczuk. LC 96-16533. 320p. (C). 1996. text 47.50 (*0-8147-8061-X*) NYU Pr.

No Author Better Served: The Correspondence of Samuel Beckett & Alan Schneider. Samuel Beckett et al. LC 98-5207. 512p. 1998. 35.00 (*0-674-62522-6*) HUP.

***No Author Better Served: The Correspondence of Samuel Beckett & Alan Schneider.** Ed. by Maurice Harmon. 512p. 2000. pap. 19.95 (*0-674-00385-3*) HUP.

***No Authority.** Alix Strauss. 145p. 1999. mass mkt. 4.99 (*0-312-97431-0*, St Martins Paperbacks) St Martin.

No B. S: Business Success. 2nd rev. ed. Dan Kennedy. 192p. 1998. pap. text 10.95 (*1-55180-143-4*) Self-Counsel Pr.

No B. S. Guide to Linux: Just What You Need to Know to Install, Optimize, & Use Linux. Bob Rankin. LC 97-6234. 256p. 1997. pap. text 34.95 incl. cd-rom (*1-886411-04-2*) No Starch Pr.

No B. S. Guide to Red Hat Linux 6: Just What You Need to Know to Install, Optimize & Use Red Hat Linux. Bob Rankin. LC 99-18467. 421p. 1999. pap. 34.95 incl. cd-rom (*1-886411-30-1*) No Starch Pr.

No B. S. Guide to Windows 95: Just What You Need to Know to Upgrade, Install, Optimize, & Use Windows 95. Scott Spanbauer. LC 96-3193. 190p. 1995. pap. text 19.00 (*1-886411-05-0*) No Starch Pr.

No B. S. Guide to Windows NT 4.0: Just What You Need to Know to Upgrade, Install, Optimize, & Use Windows NT 4.0. Jim Forkner. LC 97-5966. 223p. 1997. pap. text 21.00 (*1-886411-14-X*) No Starch Pr.

***No B. S. Sales Success.** 2nd ed. Dan S. Kennedy. 150p. 1999. pap. 9.95 (*1-55180-230-9*) Self-Counsel Pr.

No B. S. Time Management: The Ultimate No Holds Barred, Kick Butt, Take No Prisoners Entrepreneur's Guide to Time, Productivity, & Sanity. Dan Kennedy. 120p. (Orig.). 1996. pap. 8.95 (*1-55180-033-0*) Self-Counsel Pr.

No Babies Asleep. W. Nikola-Lisa. LC 93-20589. (Illus.). 32p. (J). (ps-1). 1995. 15.00 (*0-689-31841-3*) Atheneum Yung Read.

No Baby but Mine: Lovers under Cover. Carly Bishop. (Intrigue Ser.: No. 538). 1999. per. 3.99 (*0-373-22538-5*, 1-22538-2) Harlequin Bks.

***No Backward Step: A Guide to Grant's Campaign in Virginia.** Charles G. Siegel. 304p. 2000. pap. 24.95 (*1-57249-097-7*, Burd St Pr) White Mane Pub.

No Bad Dogs: Training Dogs the Woodhouse Way. Barbara Woodhouse. 128p. 1984. pap. 11.00 (*0-671-54185-4*, Fireside) S&S Trade Pap.

No Bad Mothers: Sex Control. Frank Kubic. LC 96-67688. 112p. 1996. 12.50 (*0-9636320-6-X*) Nuggets Wisdom.

No Badge, No Gun. Harold Adams. LC 98-26095. (Carl Wilcox Mystery Ser.). 208p. 1998. 22.95 (*0-8027-3321-2*) Walker & Co.

No Badge, No Gun. Harold Adams. (Carl Wilcox Mystery Ser.). 212p. 1999. pap. 7.95 (*0-8027-7575-6*) Walker & Co.

No Bail for Dalton. Miriam Borgenicht. LC 73-10705. (Black Bat Mystery Ser). 192p. 1974. 5.95 (*0-672-51881-3*, Bobbs) Macmillan.

No Bail for the Judge see Henry Cecil Reprint Series

No Bajes al Sotano. R. L. Stine, pseud. (Escalofrios Ser.: No. 2). Orig. Title: Stay out of the Basement. (SPA.). (J). (gr. 3-7). 1996. pap. text 3.99 (*0-590-50212-3*) Scholastic Inc.

No Bajes al Sotano. R. L. Stine, pseud. (Escalofrios Ser.: No. 2). Orig. Title: Stay out of the Basement. (J). 1995. 9.09 (*0-606-08582-3*, Pub. by Turtleback) Demco.

No-Bake Desserts. Jean Pare. 80p. 1998. pap. 7.99 (*1-896891-24-1*) Companys Coming.

No Band of Brothers: Problems of the Rebel High Command. Steven E. Woodworth. LC 99-35480. (Shades of Blue & Gray Ser.). 208p. 1999. 29.95 (*0-8262-1255-7*) U of Mo Pr.

No-Bark Dog. (Illus.). (J). (ps-2). 1991. pap. 5.10 (*0-8136-5542-0*, TK2347); lib. bdg. 7.95 (*0-8136-5042-9*) Modern Curr.

No Barking at the Table: More Recipes Your Dog Will Beg For. Wendy Van Rees. 1996. pap. 9.95 (*0-614-20780-0*) Macmillan.

No Bath but Plenty of Bubbles: Oral History of the Gay Liberation Front 1970-73. Lisa Power. LC 96-156570. (Lesbian & Gay Studies). 352p. 1997. 69.95 (*0-304-33195-3*); pap. 21.95 (*0-304-33205-4*) Continuum.

No Bath Tonight. Jane Yolen. LC 77-26605. (Illus.). (J). (gr. k-3). 1978. 12.95 (*0-690-03881-X*) HarpC Child Bks.

No Bath Tonight! Harriet Ziefert & Emily Bolam. LC 97-27432. (J). 1997. write for info. (*0-7894-2226-3*) DK Pub Inc.

***No Bed of Roses.** Franklin I. Badgley. 164p. 1999. pap. 10.00 (*1-57579-163-3*, Pub. by Pine Hill Pr) Penmarch Pub.

No Beggars Just Balloons: A Practical Approach to Self-Transformation. Ted L. Orcutt. 248p. 1989. 19.95 (*0-9623434-2-0*) Global Village.

***No Bell for Dak To.** Michael P. Umhofer. LC 99-50256. 338p. 1999. pap. 49.95 incl. VHS (*1-877633-49-6*) Luthers.

No Bended Knee: The Battle for Guadalcanal. Merrill B. Twining. Ed. by Neil Carey. LC 95-21897. (Illus.). 240p. 1997. pap. 14.95 (*0-89141-640-4*) Presidio Pr.

No Better Place: Than in the Center of His Presence. Robert P. Pangburn. 308p. 1993. pap. write for info. (*0-9638693-0-2*) Pearl Pubng.

No Better Place to Die: The Battle of Stones River. Peter Cozzens. LC 89-30577. (Illus.). 304p. 1990. 29.95 (*0-252-01652-1*) U of Ill Pr.

No Better Place to Die: The Battle of Stones River. Peter Cozzens. (Illus.). 304p. 1991. 15.95 (*0-252-06229-9*) U of Ill Pr.

No Better Way to Teach Writing! Ed. by Jan Turbill. 96p. (Orig.). (C). 1995. pap. text 16.50 (*0-909955-39-5*, 00568) Heinemann.

No Big Deal. Ellen Jaffe McClain. (J). 1997. 10.09 (*0-606-11685-0*, Pub. by Turtleback) Demco.

***No Big Deal.** Glenn Meganck. LC 99-36906. (Illus.). (J). 2000. pap. write for info. (*1-892339-05-6*) Bchfront Pubng.

No Birds Sing. Jo Bannister. (WWL Mystery Ser.). 1998. per. 4.99 (*0-373-26283-3*, 1-26283-1, Wrldwide Lib) Harlequin Bks.

No Birds Sing. Jo Bannister. 240p. 1996. text 21.95 (*0-312-14382-6*) St Martin.

No Birds Sing. large type ed. Jo Bannister. (Ulverscroft Large Print Ser.). 464p. 1997. 27.50 (*0-7089-3732-2*) Ulverscroft.

No Black Sparrows: A Vivid Portrait of Jamaica in the 1930s. Namba Roy. (Caribbean Writers Ser.). 224p. (Orig.). (C). 1989. pap. 7.95 (*0-435-98812-3*, 98812) Heinemann.

No Bland Facility: Selected Writings on Literature Religion & Censorship. Peter Connolly. 239p. 1991. 40.00 (*0-86140-315-0*, Pub. by Smyth) Dufour.

No Blood! David A. Reed. 144p. (Orig.). 1995. pap. 7.95 (*0-9637448-2-8*) Comments Friends.

No Blood Relative. Terry Carroll. LC 95-175238. 1997. pap. 15.95 (*1-55128-021-3*, Pub. by Mercury Bk) LPC InBook.

No Blood Spilled. Les Daniels. 1991. pap. 3.95 (*0-8125-0932-3*, Pub. by Tor Bks) St Martin.

***No Bloodless Myth: A Guide Through Balthasar's Dramatics.** Aidan Nichols. LC 99-51509. 1999. pap. 23.95 (*0-8132-0981-1*) Cath U Pr.

***No Bloodless Myth: A Guide Through Balthasar's Dramatics.** Aidan Nichols. LC 99-51509. 2000. 23.95 (*0-8132-0980-3*) Cath U Pr.

No Bluebonnets, No Yellow Roses: Texas Women in the Arts. Sylvia Moore. LC 87-63478. (Women/Art Ser.). (Illus.). 138p. (Orig.). 1989. pap. 10.95 (*0-9602476-8-8*) Midmarch Arts.

No Body. Nancy Pickard. 1987. per. 5.99 (*0-671-73429-6*) PB.

No-Body: A Novel in Parts. Richard Foreman. 1996. 23.95 (*0-87951-621-6*, Pub. by Overlook Pr) Penguin Putnam.

No Bones: A Key to Bugs & Slugs, Worms, & Ticks, Spiders & Centipedes, & Other Creepy Crawlies. Elizabeth Shepherd. LC 87-1549. (Illus.). 96p. (J). (gr. 2-5). 1988. 13.95 (*0-02-782880-8*, Mac Bks Young Read) S&S Childrens.

No Bones about Driftiss. Audrey Penn. LC 89-13326. (Illus.). viii, 146p. (J). (gr. 2-6). 1989. 14.95 (*0-939923-11-4*); pap. 7.95 (*0-939923-12-2*) M & W Pub Co.

No Bones about It. Eleanor T. Bland. (Dead Letter Mysteries Ser.). 1998. mass mkt. 5.99 (*0-312-96423-4*) St Martin.

No Bones! No Bones! Patrick G. Metoyer. LC 87-90350. (Illus.). 24p. (Orig.). (J). (gr. k-2). 1988. pap. 3.95 (*0-944523-03-X*) Western Slope Pubns.

No Borders. Marty LaVor. (Illus.). 1992. 35.00 (*0-9632680-0-7*) LaVor Grp.

No Borders: Poems. Joseph Bruchac. LC 99-10867. 96p. 1999. pap. 12.95 (*0-930100-84-0*, Pub. by Holy Cow) Consort Bk Sales.

No Both. Michael Gizzi. LC 97-38286. 120p. 1997. pap. 12.00 (*1-889097-16-0*) Hard Pr MA.

No Bottom: A Masey Baldridge/Luke Williamson Mystery. James D. Brewer. LC 93-23341. 256p. 1994. 19.95 (*0-8027-3178-3*) Walker & Co.

No Boundaries: An Anthology of Poetry from Woodbourne Correctional Facility. Ed. by Janine P. Vega. 1996. 8.00 (*0-937804-65-7*) Segue NYC.

No Boundaries: Moving Beyond Supply Chain Management. James A. Tompkins. (Illus.). iv, 200p. 2000. 24.95 (*0-9658659-2-4*) Tompkins Assocs.

No Boundary: Eastern & Western Approaches to Personal Growth. Ken Wilber. 1981. pap. 13.00 (*0-394-74881-6*, Pub. by Shambhala Pubns) Random.

No Boundary: Eastern & Western Approaches to Personal Growth. Ken Wilber. LC 81-40489. (New Science Library). (Illus.). 174p. 1981. pap. 13.00 (*0-87773-213-2*, Pub. by Shambhala Pubns) Random.

No Box Seats in the Kingdom: Sermons for the Sundays after Pentecost (Last Third): Gospel Texts. William G. Carter. LC 96-11805. (Orig.). 1996. pap. 10.50 (*0-7880-0805-6*) CSS OH.

No Boys see Wildfire Bestsellers

No Boys Allowed. Marilyn Kaye. (Camp Sunnyside Friends Ser.: No. 1). 128p. (Orig.). (J). (ps-8). 1989. pap. 2.95 (*0-380-75700-1*, Avon Bks) Morrow Avon.

No Boys Allowed. Marilyn Levinson. LC 93-22335. (Illus.). 128p. (J). (gr. 5-8). 1996. pap. 13.95 (*0-8167-3135-7*) BrdgeWater.

No Boys Allowed. Marilyn Levinson. LC 93-22335. (Illus.). 128p. (J). (gr. 5-8). 1994. pap. 2.95 (*0-8167-3136-5*, Rainbow NJ) Troll Communs.

No Boys Allowed. Marilyn Levinson. 1993. 8.05 (*0-606-07059-1*, Pub. by Turtleback) Demco.

No-Boys Club. Ho Che Anderson. 160p. (J). (gr. 4-7). 1998. pap. write for info. (*0-88899-321-8*, Pub. by Gro1undwood-Douglas); text 14.95 (*0-88899-322-6*, Pub. by Gro1undwood-Douglas) Publishers Group.

No Brainer Nutrition: High Energy, Flavor Filled Foods with No Cholesterol, Low Fat & No Salt! Marc Seidman. 192p. (Orig.). 1996. pap. 14.95 (*0-9652015-0-3*) Liv Health.

No Brakes! Bicycle Track Racing in the United States. Sandra Sutherland. (Illus.). 304p. 1996. pap. 29.95 (*0-9645243-0-9*) Iris Pr CA.

No Braver Man: The Story of Fritz Rohm, Buglar, 16th PA, Cavalry. Frederic W. Rohm. LC 97-40047. 180p. 1998. pap. 19.95 (*1-887901-18-3*) Sergeant Kirk.

No Bread for Mandela: The Prison Years of Nelson Mandela. Kathrada. 1997. 25.00 (*0-684-19671-9*) S&S Trade.

No Breakfast Plan & the Fasting Cure. 2nd ed. Edward H. Dewey. 207p. 1998. reprint ed. pap. 20.00 (*0-7873-0283-X*) Hlth Research.

***No Bride but His: Lovers Under Cover.** Carly Bishop. 2000. per. 4.25 (*0-373-22564-4*) Harlequin Bks.

No Bridges Blown. William B. Dreux. LC 72-165994. 336p. reprint ed. pap. 104.20 (*0-608-12682-9*, 202436900037) Bks Demand.

No Bright Shield. George McCauley. 80p. (Orig.). 1989. pap. text 8.95 (*0-9622889-0-X*) Something More.

N

No Bugles Tonight. Bruce Lancaster. 1999. lib. bdg. 26.95 (*1-56723-142-X*, 151) Yestermorrow.

No Bugs! Writing Error-Free Code in C & C++ David Thielen. LC 92-14802. 224p. (C). 1992. pap. text 24.95 (*0-201-60890-1*) Addison-Wesley.

No Bull: Object Technology for Executives. William S. Perlman. LC 99-18286. (Managing Object Technology Ser.: No. 18). (Illus.). 211p. (C). 1999. pap. 24.95 (*0-521-64548-4*) Cambridge U Pr.

No Bull: The Unauthorized Biography of Dennis Rodman. Dan Bickley. LC 97-17046. (Illus.). 288p. 1997. text 23.95 (*0-312-17119-6*) St Martin.

No Bull . . . Betsy. S. Dale Seawright. (Illus.). (Orig.). 1997. pap. 6.95 (*0-9652702-1-1*) S D Seawright.

No Bull Diet: A Lifetime Beyond Dieting. Howard A. Rose. 1992. pap. 10.00 (*0-9631828-0-3*) Hart Mktg.

*__No Bull Guide to Citizenship.__ Achal Mehra. 80p. 1999. pap. 8.95 (*1-893333-04-3*, Pub. by Noble Pubs) ACCESS Pubs Network.

*__No Bull Management.__ Herb Gabora. Ed. by Joe Johnson. 1999. pap. 11.95 (*0-9673891-0-0*, Pub. by H Gabora) Herveys Bklink.

No-Bullying Program Grades 4-5: Preventing Bully/Victim Violence at School. Ed. by James Bitney. 75p. 1996. pap., teacher ed. 54.95 (*1-56246-121-4*, 3079, HazeldenJohnson Inst) Hazelden.

No-Bullying Program Grades K-1: Preventing Bully/Victim Violence at School. Ed. by James Bitney. (Illus.). 75p. (Orig.). 1996. pap., teacher ed. 54.95 (*1-56246-119-2*, 3077, HazeldenJohnson Inst) Hazelden.

No-Bullying Program Grades 2-3: Preventing Bully/Victim Violence at School. Ed. by James Bitney. (Illus.). 75p. (Orig.). 1996. pap., teacher ed. 54.95 (*1-56246-120-6*, 3078, HazeldenJohnson Inst) Hazelden.

No-Bullying Program Grades 6-8: Preventing Bully/Victim Violence at School. Ed. by James Bitney. (Illus.). 125p. (Orig.). 1996. pap., teacher ed. 54.95 (*1-56246-122-2*, 3081, HazeldenJohnson Inst) Hazelden.

No Burden to Carry: Narratives of Black Working Women in Ontario 1920s to 1950s. Dionne Brand et al. 288p. pap. 15.95 (*0-88961-163-7*, Pub. by Womens Pr) LPC InBook.

No Business Being a Cop: A Norah Mulcahaney Mystery. large type ed. Lillian O'Donnell. LC 92-33704. 346p. 1993. reprint ed. lib. bdg. 17.95 (*1-56054-372-8*) Thorndike Pr.

No Business Like Show Business. Gail Herman. (Full House Stephanie Ser.). (J). (gr. 4-6). 1998. per. 3.99 (*0-671-01725-X*) PB.

No Butts about It: How to Want to Stop Smoking. 3rd ed. John R. Parker. (Illus.). 88p. (Orig.). 1989. pap. 6.95 (*0-912095-00-8*) Johmax Bks Inc.

No Candy, No Flowers. Carl Shapiro. 158p. (Orig.). 1984. pap. 10.00 (*0-914937-00-6*) Ind Pubns.

No Capital Crime. Ed Lipman. 1975. pap. 5.00 (*0-915016-04-4*) Second Coming.

No Car, No Radio, No Liquor. Little. LC 99-177999. (Illus.). 320p. 1998. pap. text 26.50 (*0-19-541150-1*) OUP.

No Casual Traveller: Hartley Grattan & Australia. Laurie Hergenhan. LC 95-194318. 336p. 1995. pap. 34.95 (*0-7022-2753-6*, Pub. by Univ Queensland Pr) Intl Spec Bk.

No Catnapping in the Kitchen. Wendy Boyd-Smith. (Illus.). 160p. 1996. 9.95 (*0-87605-695-8*) Howell Bks.

No Catnapping in the Kitchen: Kitty Cat Cuisine Recipes. Wendy Van Rees. 1996. pap. 9.95 (*0-614-20779-7*) Macmillan.

No Cats Have Been Maimed or Mutilated During the Making of This Book . . . But Some of Them Are Disappointed - Deeply Disappointed - In Me. Dean Bleheri. Ed. by Alan Graham. LC 96-60834. (Illus.). 84p. 1996. pap. 8.95 (*0-9644857-5-3*) Wrds & Pict Pr.

No Cause of Death. James Fontana. 320p. pap. 15.95 (*1-55128-018-3*, Pub. by Mercury Bk) LPC InBook.

No Certain Time. Eva Holmquist. LC 84-90368. 1984. 10.95 (*0-87212-182-8*) Libra.

No Chairs Make for Short Meetings: And Other Business Maxims from Dad. Richard Rybolt. 128p. 1994. 12.95 (*0-525-93873-7*) NAL.

No Chance Encounter. Kay Pollak. Tr. by Britt Gaut & Philip Gaut from SWE. (Guidebooks for Growth Together). (Illus.). 112p. (Orig.). 1996. pap. 10.95 (*1-899171-46-0*, Pub. by Findhorn Pr) Words Distrib.

No Change? No Chance! The Politics of Choosing Green. Jean Lambert. LC 96-166142. 128p. 1998. pap. 16.95 (*1-897766-23-8*, Pub. by Jon Carpenter) Paul & Co Pubs.

No Chariot Let Down: Charleston's Free People of Color on the Eve of the Civil War. Ed. by Michael P. Johnson & James L. Roark. LC 83-25897. (Illus.). 188p. reprint ed. pap. 58.30 (*0-7837-6861-3*, 204669000003) Bks Demand.

No Cheap Padding: Seventy-Five Years of the Indiana Magazine of History. Compiled by Lorna L. Sylvester. 558p. 1980. 13.50 (*1-885323-30-1*) IN Hist Bureau.

No Cheering in the Press Box. expanded rev. ed. Jerome Holtzman. 352p. 1995. 25.00 (*0-8050-3824-8*, Owl); pap. 14.95 (*0-8050-3823-X*, Owl) H Holt & Co.

No China Doll: Enemy-in-Waiting. Harrison-Simms Rheinhardt. (Illus.). 308p. (Orig.). 1990. 25.00 (*0-9626181-1-X*); lib. bdg. 14.95 (*0-9626181-0-1*) Simms Pub.

No Choice. Jean P. DeForrest. 264p. (C). 1991. 17.95 (*0-9619272-1-6*) Stonegate Rancho.

*__No Choice: Autobiography of an Arabian-American Lady.__ Fadwa Kassis Naser. LC 99-90816. 1999. 25.00 (*0-7388-0516-5*); pap. 18.00 (*0-7388-0517-3*) Xlibris Corp.

No Choice: Library Services for the Mentally Handicapped. Della Pearlman. LC 82-181478. 65p. reprint ed. pap. 30.00 (*0-7837-5320-9*, 204505900005) Bks Demand.

No Choice but Surrender. Meagan McKinney. 384p. 1998. pap. 5.99 (*0-8217-5859-4*, Zebra Kensgtn) Kensgtn Pub Corp.

No Choice but Surrender. large type ed. Meagan McKinney. LC 98-39413. (Large Print Book Ser.). 1998. pap. 23.95 (*1-56895-676-2*) Wheeler Pub.

No Choice but War: The United States Embargo Against Japan & the Eruption of War in the Pacific. Roland H. Worth, Jr. LC 95-8392. 248p. 1995. lib. bdg. 42.50 (*0-7864-0141-9*) McFarland & Co.

No Cholesterol Passover Recipes. rev. ed. Debra Wasserman. LC 94-61632. (Illus.). 96p. 1995. pap. 8.95 (*0-931411-14-9*) Vegetarian Resc.

No Clean Technology: An Assessment of Market & Technological Potential. PROFILE Staff. LC 96-118074. pap. 463.00 (*1-85617-237-6*) Elsevier.

No Clear & Present Danger: A Skeptical View of the U. S. Entry into World War II. Bruce M. Russett. 112p. (C). 1997. pap. 17.00 (*0-8133-3195-1*, Pub. by Westview) HarpC.

No Closets for Love. Charles D. Ellsworth. 28p. (Orig.). 1992. pap. write for info. (*0-318-72306-9*) JM Pubng.

No Clothes Today! Catarina Kruusval. LC 95-67922. (Illus.). 28p. (J). (ps-k). 6.95 (*91-29-63074-6*) FS&G.

No Code Technician Class Radio Amateur FCC Test Manual. Martin Schwartz. 1997. 12.95 (*0-912146-29-X*, 78-01) Ameco.

No Coffin for the Corpse. Clayton Rawson. LC 87-82444. 254p. 1987. reprint ed. pap. 4.95 (*0-930330-74-9*) Intl Polygonics.

No Colder Place. large type ed. S. J. Rozan. LC 97-39743. (CD Ser.). 473p. 1997. lib. bdg. 26.95 (*0-7862-1251-9*) Thorndike Pr.

No Colder Place, Vol. 1. S. J. Rozan. Vol. 1. 304p. 1998. pap. 5.99 (*0-312-96664-4*, Pub. by Tor Bks) St Martin.

No Color Is My Kind: The Life of Eldrewey Stearns & the Integration of Houston. Thomas R. Cole. LC 96-44105. (Illus.). 272p. 1997. 40.00 (*0-292-71197-2*); pap. 17.95 (*0-292-71198-0*) U of Tex Pr.

No Comebacks. Frederick Forsyth. 320p. 1983. mass mkt. 6.99 (*0-553-27673-5*) Bantam.

No Comfort in Victory: A Sheriff Harry Starbranch Mystery. Gregory Bean. 1996. mass mkt. 5.99 (*0-312-95877-3*) St Martin.

No Comment: An Executive's Guide to the News Media. Donald W. Blohowiak. LC 87-15831. 237p. 1987. 59.95 (*0-275-92820-9*, C2820, Praeger Pubs) Greenwood.

"No Comment" Can Be a Comment, or, How to Handle Reporters (gently!) A Lawyer's Guide to the Press. American Bar Association Staff. LC 95-126982. (Young Lawyers Desktop Reference Guide Ser.). v, 13 p. 1994. write for info. (*1-57073-085-7*) Amer Bar Assn.

No Commercial Potential: The Saga of Frank Zappa. 3rd rev. ed. David Walley. (Illus.). 240p. 1996. pap. 13.95 (*0-306-80710-6*) Da Capo.

*__No Commitment Required.__ Seressia Glass. 2000. pap. 8.95 (*1-58571-028-8*, 909-108, Pub. by Genesis Press) BookWorld.

*__No Common Place: The Holocaust Testimony of Alina Bacall-Zwirn.__ Alina Bacall-Zwirn & Jared Stark. LC 99-12593. (Illus.). 124p. 1999. text 30.00 (*0-8032-1296-8*) U of Nebr Pr.

*__No Common Place: The Holocaust Testimony of Alina Bacall-Zwirn.__ Alina Bacall-Zwirn & Jared Stark. LC 99-12593. (Illus.). 124p. 2000. pap. 15.00 (*0-8032-6178-0*, Bison Books) U of Nebr Pr.

No Common Power. 3rd ed. Robert J. Lieber. LC 94-7217. 386p. (C). 1997. pap. text 57.00 (*0-673-52390-X*) Addson-Wesley Educ.

*__No Common Power: Understanding International Relations.__ 4th ed. Robert J. Lieber. 416p. 2000. pap. 34.67 (*0-13-011504-5*, Prentice Hall) P-H.

No Compromise! Arnold Whitridge. LC 73-11626. 212p. 1974. reprint ed. lib. bdg. 59.50 (*0-8371-7077-X*, WHNC, Greenwood Pr) Greenwood.

*__No Compromise.__ rev. expanded ed. Melody Green Sievright. LC 99-44489. 400p. 2000. pap. 11.99 (*0-7369-0319-4*) Harvest Hse.

No Compromise: Convictions. Kevin Scoleri. (Inter Acta Ser.). (Illus.). 6p. (C). 1994. teacher ed., ring bd. 1.25 (*1-885702-98-1*, 741-048t, Inter Acta); student ed., ring bd. 3.25 (*1-885702-99-X*, 741-048s, Inter Acta) WSN Pr.

No Compromise: The Life Story of Keith Green. Melody Green. Ed. by David Hazard. 304p. (Orig.). (C). 1989. pap. 9.95 (*0-917143-01-9*) Sparrow TN.

No Compromise & The Fool: Two Life-Centered Plays That Relate Biblical Themes to Contemporary Life. J. Mulholland. 1991. pap. text 8.99 (*0-00-528675-1*) Lillenas.

No Compromise & The Fool: Two Life-Centered Plays That Relate Biblical Themes to Contemporary Life. James Mulholland. 78p. 1987. 8.99 (*0-8341-9243-8*, MP-638) Lillenas.

No Compromises: Encouragement for the Workplace. Rhonda Owen-Smith. LC 99-179222. 224p. 1998. lthr. 4.97 (*1-57748-182-8*) Barbour Pub.

No Condemnation. Octavius Winslow. 400p. 1991. pap. text 9.99 (*0-85151-592-4*) Banner of Truth.

No Condemnation: A New Theology of Assurance. Michael A. Eaton. LC 96-48381. 261p. (Orig.). 1997. pap. 16.99 (*0-8308-1888-X*, 1888) InterVarsity.

No Condemnation: Rethinking Guilt Motivation in Counseling, Preaching & Parenting. Bruce S. Narramore. 208p. 1984. pap. 16.99 (*0-310-30401-6*, 11244P) Zondervan.

*__No Condition Is Permanent.__ Christina Kessler. LC 99-27265. 192p. (YA). (gr. 5 up). 2000. 16.99 (*0-399-23486-1*, Philomel) Peng Put Young Read.

No Condition Is Permanent: The Social Dynamics of Agrarian Change in Sub-Saharan Africa. Sara Berry. LC 93-7102. (Illus.). 288p. (C). 1993. pap. 22.95 (*0-299-13934-4*) U of Wis Pr.

No Constitutional Right to Be Ladies: Women & the Obligations of Citizenship. Linda K. Kerber. LC 98-21393. (Illus.). 352p. 1998. 25.00 (*0-8090-7383-8*) Hill & Wang.

*__No Constitutional Right to Be Ladies: Women & the Obligations of Citizenship.__ Linda K. Kerber. (Illus.). 432p. 1999. pap. 14.00 (*0-8090-7384-6*) Hill & Wang.

No! Contemporary American Dada, Vols. 1 & 2. Ileana B. Leavens & Chris Bruce. Ed. by Joseph N. Newland. LC 85-81311. (Illus.). (Orig.). 1986. pap. 35.00 (*0-935558-17-9*) Henry Art.

No Contest. R. Nader & W. J. Smith. 464p. 1998. pap. 13.00 (*0-375-75258-7*) Random.

No Contest: How the Power Lawyers Are Perverting Justice in America. Ralph Nader & Wesley J. Smith. (Illus.). 336p. 1996. 25.95 (*0-679-42972-7*) Random.

No Contest: The Case Against Competition. rev. ed. Alfie Kohn. LC 92-26141. 328p. 1992. pap. 14.00 (*0-395-63125-4*) HM.

No Continuing City - Poems, 1963-1968. Michael Longley. LC 72-84906. 56p. 1969. 15.95 (*0-8023-1248-9*) Dufour.

No Control. Stephen Solomita. 416p. 1999. mass mkt. 5.99 (*0-553-57659-3*) Bantam.

No-Cook Cookbook: No Pots & Pans to Scrub! Jayne Benkendorf. LC 99-64270. 150p. 1999. pap. 14.95 (*0-9651990-3-7*) Ludwig Pub OK.

No Cook Recipe Substitution Book for Pasteries & Desserts, Bk. 1. Cookbook Consortium Staff. 1993. ring bd. 19.95 (*0-318-04314-9*) Prosperity & Profits.

No-Cooking Cookbook for Kids. Margie Poe. (Illus.). (J). (gr. k-6). 1985. pap. 4.95 (*0-936985-75-5*, 1096A) Kidsmart.

No Copycats Allowed! Bonnie Graves. LC 97-18048. (Hyperion Chapters Ser.). (Illus.). 64p. (J). (gr. 1-3). 1998. pap. 3.95 (*0-7868-1166-8*, Pub. by Hyprn Ppbks); lib. bdg. 14.49 (*0-7868-2235-X*, Pub. by Hyprn Ppbks) Little.

*__No Copycats Allowed!__ Bonnie Graves. 1998. 9.05 (*0-606-13664-9*, Pub. by Turtleback) Demco.

No Costumes or Masks. Grace B. Freeman. (Red Clay Reader Ser.: Vol. 10, No. 2). 48p. 1983. reprint ed. pap. 9.00 (*0-9607730-2-9*) Johns Pr.

No Country for a Gentleman: British Rule in Egypt, 1833-1907, 25. William M. Welch, Jr. LC 87-31795. (Contributions in Comparative Colonial Studies: No. 25). 176p. 1988. 52.95 (*0-313-26134-2*, WEY/, Greenwood Pr) Greenwood.

No Coward Soul. Vesta O. Robbins. LC 74-7399. 119p. reprint ed. pap. 36.90 (*0-608-16268-X*, 202666000051) Bks Demand.

No Coward Soul Is Mine: Emily Bronte Poems. Emily Jane Bronte. LC 92-62239. 160p. 1992. lib. bdg. 21.95 (*0-9634340-0-4*) Odessa.

No Credit Required: How to Buy a House When You Don't Qualify for a Mortgage. Ray Mungo & Robert H. Yamaguchi. 192p. (Orig.). 1993. mass mkt. 5.99 (*0-451-17564-6*, Sig) NAL.

No Crime Like the Present. Bill Gleason. 60p. 1982. pap. 5.25 (*0-87129-627-6*, N28) Dramatic Pub.

No Crooked Death: Coatesville, Pennsylvania, & the Lynching of Zachariah Walker. Dennis B. Downey & Ramond M. Hyser. (Blacks in the New World Ser.). (Illus.). 200p. 1991. 28.95 (*0-252-01739-0*) U of Ill Pr.

No Cross, No Crown. William Penn & Anna Brinton. 1944. pap. text 4.00 (*0-87574-030-8*) Pendle Hill.

No Cross, No Crown. William Penn. (C). 1989. reprint ed. pap. 32.00 (*0-900657-57-X*, Pub. by W Sessions) St Mut.

No Cross No Crown. William Penn. 1999. reprint ed. pap. 30.00 (*0-900657-58-8*, Pub. by W Sessions) St Mut.

*__No Cross on Earth, No Crown in Heaven: The History of the Sisters of the Holy Family.__ Mary Bernard Deggs. 2000. 39.95 (*0-253-33630-9*) Ind U Pr.

*__No Crystal Stair.__ Eva Rutland. 480p. 2000. per. 5.99 (*1-55166-519-0*, 1-66519-9, Mira Bks) Harlequin Bks.

No Crystal Stair: A Novel. Mairuth Sarsfield. LC 99-165766. 224p. 1997. 14.95 (*1-896867-02-2*) Moulin Publ.

No Crystal Stair: An African American Booklist. Compiled by Betsy Crenshaw. 40p. 1996. pap. 8.00 (*0-87104-736-5*) NY Pub Lib.

No Crystal Stair: Black Life & the Messenger, 1917-1928, 20. Theodore Kornweibel, Jr. LC 75-16967. (Contributions in Afro-American & African Studies: No. 20). 306p. 1976. 62.95 (*0-8371-8284-0*, KCS/, Greenwood Pr) Greenwood.

No Crystal Stair: Visions of Race & Gender in Black Women's Fiction. Gloria Wade-Gayles. LC 96-47198. 288p. 1997. pap. 18.95 (*0-8298-1151-6*) Pilgrim OH.

No Cuffs: Police Issues Teenagers Face. Darrell Mulroy & Dinah Tallent. 91p. (Orig.). (YA). (gr. 7-12). 1995. pap. 6.95 (*1-57515-087-5*) PPI Pubng.

No Culpe a Dios! Kenneth E. Hagin.Tr. of Don't Blame God!. (SPA.). 1983. pap. 1.00 (*0-89276-156-3*) Faith Lib Pubns.

No Cure. G. B. Williams. LC 98-91412. 1998. 19.95 (*0-533-12658-4*) Vantage.

No Cure for Cancer. Dennis Leary. LC 92-16820. 160p. 1992. pap. 8.95 (*0-385-42581-3*, Anchor NY) Doubleday.

No Cure for Love. Tara T. Quinn. (Superromance Ser.). 1994. per. 3.50 (*0-373-70624-3*, 1-70624-1) Harlequin Bks.

No Cure for Love. Peter Robinson. mass mkt. write for info. (*0-14-025187-1*) Penguin Putnam.

No Dancin' in Anson: An American Story of Race & Social Change. Ricardo Ainslie. LC 95-18805. 368p. 1995. 27.50 (*1-56821-585-1*) Aronson.

No Dancing in the Bathtub. Mercer Mayer. (Pictureback Ser.). (J). 1998. pap. 3.25 (*0-679-88708-3*, Pub. by Random Bks Yng Read) Random.

No Dangerous Rival. large type ed. I. M. Freeson. (Linford Romance Library). 1989. pap. 16.99 (*0-7089-6778-7*, Linford) Ulverscroft.

No Dark Eternal. Herman M. Ward. LC 84-72937. 65p. (Orig.). 1984. pap. 5.00 (*0-9610346-5-3*) Belle Mead Pr.

No Dark Place. Joan Wolf. LC 98-35763. 288p. 1999. 19.95 (*0-06-019238-0*) HarpC.

*__No Dark Place.__ Joan Wolf. 448p. 2000. mass mkt. 5.99 (*0-06-109745-4*) HarpC.

No Darker Heaven. large type ed. Stella Whitelaw. (Black Satin Romance Ser.). 336p. 1997. 27.99 (*1-86110-044-2*) Ulverscroft.

No Daughter of the South. Cynthia Webb. LC 96-44569. 200p. (Orig.). 1997. pap. 10.95 (*0-934678-82-0*) New Victoria Pubs.

*__No, David!__ David Shannon. (SPA., Illus.). (ps-3). 1999. 12.95 (*84-241-5885-7*) Everest SP.

No, David! David Shannon. LC 97-35125. (Illus.). 32p. (J). (ps-1). 1998. 14.95 (*0-590-93002-8*, Pub. by Scholastic Inc) Penguin Putnam.

No Day Repeats Itself. Alfred O. Christiansen. 108p. 1987. 12.95 (*0-9615098-4-8*) Prairie Imp.

No Day too Long - An Hydrographer's Tale. G. S. Ritchie. 247p. (C). 1989. text 50.00 (*1-872795-63-3*, Pub. by Pentland Pr) St Mut.

No Day Without a Line: From Notebooks by Yury Olesha. IUrii Karlovich Olesha. Tr. by Judson Rosengrant from RUS. LC 98-17688. (Studies in Russian Literature & Theory). 272p. 1998. pap. text 19.95 (*0-8101-1382-1*) Northwestern U Pr.

No Dead Ends. Maralene Wesner & Miles Wesner. 112p. (Orig.). 1988. pap. 7.95 (*0-936715-23-5*) Diversity Okla.

No Deadly Drug. Tom Ferguson & Joe Graedon. Ed. by Sally Peters. 320p. 1993. reprint ed. mass mkt. 5.50 (*0-671-74870-X*) PB.

No Deal in Diamonds. Peter Leslie. 224p. 1992. 19.00 (*0-7278-4371-0*) Severn Hse.

No Dear, Not Here: The Marbled Murrelets' Quest for a Nest in the Pacific Northwest. Jean D. Okimoto. (Illus.). 32p. (J). (ps-2). 1995. 14.95 (*1-57061-019-3*) Sasquatch Bks.

No Death: God's Other Door. Edgar Cayce et al. LC 98-37645. 195p. 1999. pap. 12.95 (*0-87604-417-8*, 531) ARE Pr.

No Decent Gentleman. Patricia Grasso. 1999. mass mkt. 5.99 (*0-440-22434-9*) Dell.

No Deed Greater Than a Word: A New Approach to Biblical Preaching. William H. Shepherd, Jr. LC 97-28495. 156p. 1997. pap. 14.75 (*0-7880-1180-4*) CSS OH.

No Defense. Rangeley Wallace. 1997. mass mkt. 5.99 (*0-312-96169-3*) St Martin.

*__No Defense.__ Kate Wilhelm. 2001. mass mkt. 5.99 (*1-55166-785-1*, Mira Bks) Harlequin Bks.

*__No Defense.__ Kate Wilhelm. LC 99-56355. 384p. 2000. text 24.95 (*0-312-20953-3*) St Martin.

No Dejes Tu Cerebro en la Puerta. Josh McDowell & Bob Hostetler.Tr. of Don't Check Your Brains at the Door. (SPA.). 208p. 1993. 9.99 (*0-88113-197-0*, B008-1970) Caribe Betania.

No Deposit No Return. Gloria Copeland. 15p. 1994. pap. 1.00 (*0-88114-969-1*) K Copeland Pubns.

No Deposit No Return. Louisa Payne. 254p. 1999. 15.95 (*0-7414-0186-X*) Buy Books.

*__No Deposit No Return.__ Amy Sandrin. 200p. 1999. pap. 6.99 (*1-893108-32-5*) Neighbrhd Pr Pubng.

No Depression: An Introduction to Alternative Country Music. Ed. by Grant Alden & Peter Blackstock. 256p. 1998. pap. 16.95 (*1-891847-00-7*, D010024, Pub. by Dowling Pr) Music Sales.

No Difference. Fritz Hamilton. (Backpocket Poets Ser.). 36p. (Orig.). 1987. pap. 2.50 (*0-916155-07-2*) Trout Creek.

No Difference in the Fare: Dietrich Bonhoeffer & the Problem of Racism. Josiah U. Young, III. LC 98-28330. 190p. 1998. pap. 22.00 (*0-8028-4465-0*) Eerdmans.

No Digas Adios. Marie Ferrarella. (SPA.). 1996. per. 3.50 (*0-373-35162-3*, 1-35162-6) Harlequin Bks.

No Dignity for Joshua: More Vital Insight into Deaf Children, Deaf Education & Deaf Culture. Tom Bertling. LC 96-78647. 112p. (Orig.). 1997. per. 21.95 (*0-9637813-6-7*) Kodiak Media.

*__No Dinner! The Story of the Old Woman & the Pumpkin.__ Jessica Souhami. (Illus.). 32p. (J). (ps-2). 2000. 15.95 (*0-7614-5059-9*, Cav Child Bks) Marshall Cavendish.

No Direction Home: The Life & Music of Bob Dylan. unabridged ed. Robert Shelton. LC 97-2563. (Illus.). 573p. 1997. pap. 17.95 (*0-306-80782-3*) Da Capo.

No Disabled Souls: How to Welcome People with Disabilities into Your Life & Your Church. James O. Pierson. Ed. by Theresa C. Hayes. LC 98-9994. (Illus.). 160p. 1998. pap. 9.99 (*0-7847-0768-5*, 11-03140) Standard Pub.

No Disintergrations. (Star Wars Ser.). 15.00 (*0-87431-296-5*, 40151) West End Games.

No Disrespect. Sister Souljah. 360p. 1996. pap. 13.00 (*0-679-76708-8*) Vin Bks.

No Distinction of Sex? Women in British Universities, 1870-1939. Dyhouse. LC 95-875. (Women's History Ser.). 1995. 75.00 (*1-85728-458-5*, Pub. by UCL Pr Ltd); pap. write for info. (*1-85728-459-3*, Pub. by UCL Pr Ltd) Taylor & Francis.

No Divided Allegiance: Essays in Brownson's Thought. Ed. by Leonard Gilhooley. LC 79-56139. (Rose Hill Bk.). 209p. reprint ed. pap. 64.80 (*0-7837-5600-3*, 204550600005) Bks Demand.

*__No Doctors, Please.__ large type ed. Lydia Balmain. 320p. 2000. pap. 20.99 (*1-85389-905-4*, Dales) Ulverscroft.

N

An Asterisk (*) at the beginning of an entry indicates that the title is appearing for the first time.

No Dogs Allowed see No Se Permiten Perros

No Dogs Allowed. Jane Cutler. 112p. (J). (gr. 4-7). 1992. 14.00 (*0-374-35526-6*) FS&G.

No Dogs Allowed. Jane Cutler. (Illus.). 112p. (J). (gr. 2-5). 1994. pap. 4.95 (*0-374-45508-2*, Sunburst Bks) FS&G.

No Dogs Allowed. Jane Cutler. LC 92-7206. (J). 1994. 9.05 (*0-606-09687-6*, Pub. by Turtleback) Demco.

No Dogs Allowed. Suzanne Hardin. (Books for Young Learners). (Illus.). 12p. (J). (gr. k-2). 1997. pap. text 5.00 (*1-57274-114-7*, A2480) R Owen Pubs.

No Dogs Allowed (or Junket) Aurand Harris. 43p. (J). 1959. 6.00 (*0-87602-164-X*) Anchorage.

No Dogs & Not Many Chinese. F. Wood. text 50.00 (*0-7195-5758-5*, Pub. by John Murray) Trafalgar.

No Dogs in China: A Report on China Today. William Kinmond. LC DS774.K56. 223p. reprint ed. pap. 69.20 (*0-608-11796-X*, 201427300095) Bks Demand.

No Dogs in Heaven. Scott Mason. (Cleveland Poets Ser.: No. 24). 28p. 1980. pap. 2.50 (*0-914946-21-8*) Cleveland St Univ Poetry Ctr.

No Double Standards in International Law: Linkage of NAFTA with Hemispheric System of Human Rights Enforcement Is Needed - Canada, Mexico & the United States Must Become Full Partners. Minnesota Advocates for Human Rights Staff. 22p. (Orig.). 1992. pap. 5.00 (*0-929293-15-0*) MN Advocates.

No Doubt. Laura Peyton Roberts. (Clearwater Crossing Ser.). 208p. (YA). (gr. 5-8). 1999. mass mkt. 3.99 (*0-553-49261-6*) BDD Bks Young Read.

No Doubt: African-American Art of the 90s. Maurice Berger. (Illus.). 28p. (Orig.). 1996. spiral bd. 12.00 (*1-888332-02-6*) Aldrich Mus.

No Doubt: The Story Of. Kalen Rogers. LC 97-162236. (Illus.). 48p. 1997. pap. 12.95 (*0-8256-1383-3*) Omnibus NY.

No Doubt: Tragic Kingdom. 104p. 1997. otabind 16.95 (*0-7935-8457-4*); otabind 22.95 (*0-7935-8459-0*) H Leonard.

No Doubt about It: The Case for Christianity. Winfried Corduan. LC 97-8569. 1997. 19.99 (*0-8054-1647-1*) Broadman.

***No Down! No New Loan! The Cal-Equity Pactrust** Bill J. Gatten. LC 99-202764. xv, 152p. 1998. write for info. (*0-9663302-1-8*) Cal-Equity.

***No Dragons for Tea: Fire Safety for Kids (And Dragons)** Jean Pensziwol. (Illus.). (J). 1999. pap. 5.95 (*1-55074-571-9*) Kids Can Pr.

No Dragons for Tea: Fire Safety for Kids (And Dragons) unabridged ed. Jean Pendziwol. (Illus.). 32p. (J). (ps-2). 1999. 14.95 (*1-55074-569-7*, Pub. by Kids Can Pr) Genl Dist Srvs.

No Dreams for Sale. D. Roger Martin. 1983. pap. 6.00 (*0-938566-15-6*) Adastra Pr.

No Drugs Allowed: An Elementary Drug Education Curriculum. Berneta K. Sherck. Ed. by Erla K. Williams. (Illus.). 120p. 1989. 75.00 (*0-935589-19-8*) Elite Pub IN.

No-Drugs Guide to Better Health. Eleanore B. Busch & Bernd W. Busch. 223p. 1983. 19.95 (*0-13-623090-3*, Parker Publishing Co); pap. 5.95 (*0-13-623082-2*, Parker Publishing Co) P-H.

No Dry Season: Raising High God's Standard of Living for this Final Generation. Rod Parsley. 1997. 10.99 (*0-88419-456-6*) Creation House.

No Dry Season: Raising High God's Standard of Living for This Final Generation. Rod Parsley. 1997. pap. 11.99 (*0-88419-464-7*) Creation House.

No Duermes, Osito? (Can't You Sleep Little Bear?) Martin Waddell. (SPA.). (J). 1996. 16.50 (*84-88342-04-7*) Lectorum Pubns.

No Duress. Miriam Borgenicht. (Worldwide Library Mysteries). 1992. per. 3.99 (*0-373-26105-5*, 1-26105-6) Harlequin Bks.

No Duty to Retreat: Violence & Values in American History & Society. Richard M. Brown. 280p. 1992. 25.00 (*0-19-504510-6*) OUP.

No Duty to Retreat: Violence & Values in American History & Society. Richard M. Brown. LC 93-32549. 268p. 1994. reprint ed. pap. 13.95 (*0-8061-2618-3*) U of Okla Pr.

No Earthly Sunne. Margaret Ball. 1994. per. 5.99 (*0-671-87633-3*) S&S Trade.

No East or West: Discovering the Gifts of Diversity. Ed. by Blair G. Meeks. (Liturgy Ser.). (Illus.). 80p. 1994. pap. 10.95 (*0-918208-67-X*) Liturgical Conf.

No Easy Answers. Donald R. Gallo. 336p. (YA). (gr. 7). 1999. pap. 5.50 (*0-440-41305-2*) BDD Bks Young Read.

No Easy Answers: A Teen Guide to Why Divorce Happens see Divorce Resource Series

No Easy Answers: Christians Debate Today's Issues. (Dialog Ser.). 120p. 1985. pap. 6.50 (*0-8341-1065-2*); pap., teacher ed. 5.50 (*0-8341-1064-4*) Beacon Hill.

No Easy Answers: Helping Children with Attention & Activity Level Differences. Jerry Aldridge et al. LC 97-51877. 80p. 1998. pap. text 15.00 (*0-87173-140-1*) ACEI.

No Easy Answers: Research Findings on Programs to Reduce Teen Pregnancy. Douglas Kirby. 91p. 1997. pap. 10.00 (*1-58671-000-1*) Natl Cpgn Teen Preg.

No Easy Answers: Short Stories about Teenagers Making Tough Choices. Ed. by Donald R. Gallo. LC 97-1841. 336p. (YA). (gr. 7 up). 1997. 16.95 (*0-385-32290-9*) Delacorte.

No Easy Answers: The Learning Disabled Child at Home & at School. rev. ed. Sally L. Smith. LC 94-36478. 416p. 1995. pap. 13.95 (*0-553-35450-7*) Bantam.

No Easy Choice: Political Participation in Developing Countries. Samuel P. Huntington & Joan M. Nelson. LC 75-31883. 214p. reprint ed. pap. 66.40 (*0-7837-2275-3*, 205736300004) Bks Demand.

No Easy Exit: Salida dificil. Gary Geddes. Tr. by Gonzalo Millan. 1989. pap. text 9.95 (*0-88982-096-1*, Pub. by Oolichan Bks) Genl Dist Srvs.

***No Easy Out.** Dean Hughes. (Scrappers Ser.: No. 6). 128p. (J). (gr. 3-7). 1999. per. 3.99 (*0-689-81939-0*, 076714003996) Aladdin.

No Easy Out. Dean Hughes. LC 98-51951. (Scrappers Ser.: No. 6). 112p. (J). (gr. 3-7). 1999. 14.00 (*0-689-81929-3*) S&S Childrens.

No Easy Road. large type ed. Kay Winchester. 336p. 1988. 27.99 (*0-7089-1810-7*) Ulverscroft.

No Easy Road: Inspirational Thoughts on Prayer. Dick Eastman. LC 70-155861. 132p. (gr. 10). 1973. mass mkt. 4.99 (*0-8010-3259-8*) Baker Bks.

No Easy Road: The Early Years of the Augustinians in the United States, 1796-1874. Arthur J. Ennis. LC 93-2972. 472p. (C). 1993. text 49.95 (*0-8204-2124-3*) P Lang Pubng.

No Easy Roses: A Look at the Lives of City Teenagers. Olive Pierce. (Illus.). 94p. 1986. pap. write for info. (*0-9617101-0-1*) Olive Pierce.

No Easy Victories: Black Americans & the Vote. Clarence Lusane. LC 96-21469. (African-American Experience Ser.). 160p. (YA). (gr. 9-12). 1996. lib. bdg. 24.00 (*0-531-11270-5*) Watts.

No Easy Walk: Newark, 1980-1993. Helen M. Stummer. LC 94-6476. (Visual Studies). (Illus.). 128p. (C). 1994. pap. 24.95 (*1-56639-243-8*); lib. bdg. 69.95 (*1-56639-242-X*) Temple U Pr.

No Easy Walk: The Dramatic Journey of African-Americans. Harry L. Williams, II. LC 98-31012. 168p. 1999. pap. 9.99 (*0-8308-1792-1*, 1792) InterVarsity.

No Easy Walk to Freedom. Nelson Mandela. pap. 8.95 (*0-7493-0504-5*, AO452) Heinemann.

No Easy Walk to Freedom. Nelson Mandela. (African Writers Ser.). (Illus.). 189p. (C). 1986. pap. 8.95 (*0-435-90782-4*, 90782) Heinemann.

No Easy Walk to Freedom: Reconstruction & the Ratification of the Fourteenth Amendment. James E. Bond. LC 96-42481. 312p. 1997. 65.00 (*0-275-95703-9*, Praeger Pubs) Greenwood.

No Easy Way Out. large type ed. Paula D. Riggs. (Silhouette Romance Ser.). 1995. 18.95 (*0-373-59640-5*) Mac Lib Ref.

No Echo in the Sky. Harald Penrose. LC 78-169433. (Literature & History of Aviation Ser.). 1979. reprint ed. 35.95 (*0-405-03776-7*) Ayer.

No Effect. Daniel Hayes. 224p. 1995. mass mkt. 3.99 (*0-380-72392-1*, Avon Bks) Morrow Avon.

No Effect. Daniel Hayes. 1995. 9.09 (*0-606-07954-8*, Pub. by Turtleback) Demco.

No Elephants for the Maharaja: Social & Political Change in Travancore 1921-1947. Louise Ouwerkerk. (C). 1994. text 27.50 (*81-7304-068-0*, Pub. by Manohar) S Asia.

No End in Sight: A Family Survives a Repressed Memory Blast. Anonymous. 1997. pap. text 12.95 (*0-9641357-7-9*) Storm Peak.

No End to Alliance: The United States & Western Europe: Past, Present, & Future: Nobel Symposium 105. Geir Lundestad. LC 98-23856. 268p. 1998. text 69.95 (*0-312-21761-7*) St Martin.

No End to Her: Soap Opera & the Female Subject. Martha Nochimson. 1993. 48.00 (*0-520-07763-6*, Pub. by U CA Pr); pap. 16.95 (*0-520-07771-7*, Pub. by U CA Pr) Cal Prin Full Svc.

No Enemies Within: A Creative Process for Discovering What's Right about What's Wrong. Dawna Markova. 340p. (Orig.). 1994. pap. 14.95 (*0-943233-64-X*) Conari Press.

No Enemy. Ford Madox Ford. LC 84-6090. 302p. 1984. reprint ed. pap. 8.50 (*0-88001-062-2*) HarpC.

No Entry. Edward A. Nagel. LC 94-37598. 184p. 1995. 20.00 (*1-56858-025-8*) FWEW.

***No Entry: Immigration Policy in Europe.** Hans Korno Rasmussen. LC 98-106367. 1999. 32.00 (*87-16-13358-7*) Mksgaard.

No Equal in the World: An Interpretation of the Academic Presidency. Joseph N. Crowley. LC 93-37567. 320p. (C). 1994. 29.95 (*0-87417-237-3*) U of Nev Pr.

No Equal Justice: Race & Class in the American Criminal Justice System. David Cole. (Illus.). 224p. 1999. 25.00 (*1-56584-473-4*, Pub. by New Press NY) Norton.

No Equal Justice: Race & Class in the American Criminal Justice System. David Cole. 224p. 2000. pap. text 14.95 (*1-56584-566-8*, Pub. by New Press NY) Norton.

***No Es Con Ejercito, Ni Con Fuerza.** Douglas Petersen. 1999. pap. 8.99 (*0-8297-0345-4*) Vida Pubs.

No es Facil Ser Hombre. Richards Hicks.Tr. of Uneasy Manhood. 1996. pap. text 10.99 (*0-88113-156-3*) Caribe Betania.

***No Es Ninguna.** Sergio Davila. (SPA.). 2000. pap. 6.99 (*0-8297-2885-6*) Vida Pubs.

No Es Tu Culpa, Koko Oso (It's Not Your Fault, Koko Bear) Vicki Lansky. (SPA., Illus.). 32p. (J). (ps-2). 1999. pap. 7.99 (*0-916773-45-0*) Book Peddlers.

No Escape. James D. Brewer. LC 98-2826. (Masey Baldridge - Luke Williamson Mystery Ser.). 264p. 1998. 22.95 (*0-8027-3318-2*) Walker & Co.

No Escape. Madge Harrah. 110p. (Orig.). (J). 1998. pap. 4.95 (*1-57502-775-5*, PO2137) Morris Pubng.

No Escape. Madge Harrah. 112p. (Orig.). (YA). 1993. pap. 3.50 (*0-380-76569-1*, Avon Bks) Morrow Avon.

No Escape! Created by Francine Pascal. (Sweet Valley Twins Ser.: No. 118). 144p. (J). (gr. 3-7). 1998. pap. 3.50 (*0-553-48602-0*) BDD Bks Young Read.

No Escape. Nancy Sanra. 1998. pap. text 11.99 (*1-883061-23-7*) Rising AZ.

No Escape: Prisons, Therapy & Politics. Blanche Hampton. LC 95-225584. (Frontlines Ser.). 64p. 1995. pap. 9.95 (*0-86840-350-4*, Pub. by New South Wales Univ Pr) Intl Spec Bk.

No Escape from Greatness. Clarence Rutherford. LC 89-85364. (Orig.). (C). 1989. pap. 12.95 (*0-9622704-1-5*) Xylo Prods.

No Escape from Love. E. Ray Nichols. LC 89-285. 1991. 14.95 (*0-87949-312-7*) Ashley Bks.

No Escape from Love. large type ed. Bennie C. Hall. 1995. 27.99 (*0-7089-3329-7*) Ulverscroft.

No Escape from Love. large type ed. Irene Lawrence. (Linford Romance Library). 1991. pap. 16.99 (*0-7089-7099-0*) Ulverscroft.

No Estamos Pidiendo el Cielo: Huelga Portuaria de 1938. Taller de Formacion Politica Staff. LC 88-80500. (Coleccion Semilla). (SPA.). 200p. 1988. pap. 7.50 (*0-940238-60-8*) Ediciones Huracan.

No Evil Angel. Elizabeth Ogilvie. reprint ed. lib. bdg. 23.95 (*0-88411-335-3*) Amereon Ltd.

No Evil Shall Befall Thee. Ken Stewart. 144p. 1991. pap. 7.99 (*0-89274-770-6*, HH-770) Harrison Hse.

No Evil Star: Selected Essays, Interviews, & Prose. Anne Sexton. Ed. by Steven E. Colburn. (Poets on Poetry Ser.). 224p. 1985. pap. 14.65 (*0-472-06366-9*, 06366) U of Mich Pr.

No Excuse: Key Principles for Balancing Life & Achieving Success. 3rd rev. ed. Jay Rifenbary. Ed. by Mike Markowski & Marjie Markowski. LC 94-77875. (Personal Development Ser.). (Illus.). 336p. 2000. pap. 16.95 (*0-938716-22-0*, Possible Pr) Markowski Intl.

No Excuse! The Workbook: Your Companion to the Book to Help You Live the "No Excuse!" Lifestyle. Jay Rifenbary. Ed. by Mike Markowski & Marjie Markowski. (Personal Development Ser.). (Illus.). 64p. 1996. per., wbk. ed. 9.95 (*0-938716-27-1*) Markowski Intl.

No Excuses: Antonio Sabato Jr. Workout for Life. Greg Frietas & Antonio Sabato, Jr. (Illus.). 144p. 1999. 45.00 (*0-7893-0354-X*, Pub. by Universe); pap. 29.95 (*0-7893-0352-3*, Pub. by Universe) St Martin.

No Excuses: Moses. Dee Dee Rush. (Inter Acta Ser.). (Illus.). 6p. (C). 1994. teacher ed., ring bd. 1.25 (*1-885702-23-X*, 741-019t, Inter Acta); student ed., ring bd. 3.25 (*1-885702-22-1*, 741-019s, Inter Acta) WSN Pr.

No Excuses Allowed: My Fifteen Years in the Navy. Art Wilson. Ed. by Irina Alexandrovna. (Illus.). 338p. (Orig.). 1991. pap. text 19.95 (*0-935733-01-9*) Dead Reckoning.

***No Excuses Risk Management.** Bernard P. Maloy & Charles R. Higgins. 150p. 2000. pap. text 25.00 (*1-884125-77-8*) Cooper Pubng.

No Exit. abr. ed. Jean-Paul Sartre. LC 68-2657. 1988. audio 22.00 (*0-694-50856-X*, SWC 327, Caedmon) HarperAudio.

No Exit. large type ed. Hardiman Scott. 464p. 1986. 27.99 (*0-7089-1548-5*) Ulverscroft.

No Exit & Three Other Plays. Jean-Paul Sartre. (Vintage International Ser.). 1989. pap. 12.00 (*0-679-72516-4*) Vin Bks.

***No Experience Necessary.** Kelly A. Fryer. LC 99-46723. 1999. 9.99 (*0-8066-4042-1*, Augsburg) Augsburg Fortress.

No Experience Necessary. Scott Nelson. LC 90-60085. 1990. pap. 12.95 (*0-916990-25-7*) META Pubns.

No Experience Necessary! A "Learn by Doing" Guide for Creating Children's Worship. Elaine C. Harpine. Ed. by Rhonda Wray. LC 92-30575. (Illus.). 368p. (Orig.). (ps-5). 1992. pap. 14.95 (*0-916260-78-X*, B107) Meriwether Pub.

No-Experience-Necessary Writer's Course: A Unique Stress Free Approach to Writing Fiction & Poetry for Anyone Who Has Ever Wanted to Write. Scott Edelstein. LC 86-43058. 299p. 1990. 19.95 (*0-8128-8512-0*, Scrbrough Hse); pap. 11.95 (*0-8128-3134-9*, Scrbrough Hse) Madison Bks UPA.

***No Eyes: Lester Young.** David Meltzer. LC 00-36101. (Illus.). 200p. 2000. pap. 30.00 (*1-57423-130-8*) Black Sparrow.

***No Eyes: Lester Young.** David Meltzer. LC 00-36101. (Illus.). 200p. 2000. pap. 16.00 (*1-57423-129-4*) Black Sparrow.

***No Eyes: Lester Young.** aut. ed. David Meltzer. (Illus.). 200p. 2000. 40.00 (*1-57423-131-6*) Black Sparrow.

No Fading Star. Celeste Raspanti. 1979. pap. 3.50 (*0-87129-250-5*, N24) Dramatic Pub.

No Fail Art Projects: Ninety-Nine Successful Lessons for the Primary Grades. Arliss Burchard. 230p. 1990. pap. 24.95 (*0-13-622481-4*) P-H.

No Fair! Caren Holtzman. LC 96-8032. (Hello Math Reader Ser.: Level 2). (Illus.). (J). 1997. 3.50 (*0-590-92230-0*) Scholastic Inc.

No Fair! Caren Holtzman. (Hello Math Reader Ser.). 1997. 8.70 (*0-606-11686-9*, Pub. by Turtleback) Demco.

No Fair. Donna Jo Napoli. LC 99-38627. (Aladdin Angelwings Ser.). (gr. 4-6). 2000. pap. 3.99 (*0-689-83206-0*) Aladdin.

***No Fair!** Donna Jo Napoli. (Illus.). (J). 2000. 9.34 (*0-606-17909-7*) Turtleback.

***No Fair! A Tale in Which Monty Learns Contentment.** Alan Kieda. LC 00-22233. (Stories to Grow By Ser.). (Illus.). (J). 2000. write for info. (*1-56822-596-2*, In Celeb) Instruct Fair.

No Fair Peeking. Sara Parke. LC 90-85436. (Minnie 'n Me Ser.). (Illus.). 32p. (J). (gr. k-3). 1991. 5.95 (*1-56282-037-0*) Disney Pr.

No Fairer Land: Studies in Southern Literature Before 1900. Ed. by J. Lasley Dameron & James W. Mathews. LC 85-51200. x, 245p. 1986. 45.00 (*0-87875-305-2*) Whitston Pub.

No Faith in the System. Sarah Clarke. LC 96-144511. 216p. 1997. pap. 18.95 (*1-85635-128-9*, Pub. by Mercier Pr) Irish Amer Bk.

No Faith of My Own & Graceful Reason: The Contribution of Reason to Theology. J. V. Langmead Casserley & C. Don Keyes. 408p. 1984. reprint ed. pap. text 29.00 (*0-8191-3793-6*) U Pr of Amer.

No Fall Too Far: The Gordon Weekley Story. Don Jeffries. 240p. 1995. pap. 11.95 (*0-87483-409-0*) August Hse.

No Faster Than a Walk: The Covered Bridges of New Brunswick. Stephen Gillis & John Gillis. LC 98-174280. (Illus.). 101p. 1998. pap. 17.95 (*0-86492-195-0*, Pub. by Goose Ln Edits) Genl Dist Srvs.

No Fat Chicks: How Big Business Profits by Making Women Hate Their Bodies--How to Fight Back. Terry Poulton. LC 97-19002. 256p. 1997. 21.95 (*1-55972-423-4*) Carol Pub Group.

No Fat Fudge: Forever Changing the Way America Makes Fudge. Norman Rose. LC 94-233795. 100p. (Orig.). 1994. 19.95 (*0-9631847-5-X*) N Rose Co.

No Fathers. Robert Endleman. LC 96-29824. 165p. (C). 1997. text 45.00 (*1-885809-08-5*); pap. text 25.00 (*1-885809-09-3*) Psyche Pr NY.

No-Fault & Uninsured Motorist, 4 vols. 1984. ring bd. 880.00 (*0-8205-1469-1*) Bender.

No-Fault Divorce in Pennsylvania: A Guide to the Law, with Forms for Filing Your Own Divorce. Howard Gibson. LC 93-86539. (Illus.). (Orig.). 1994. pap. 24.95 (*0-9638424-0-4*) PA Full Court.

No Fault Divorce in Pennsylvania: A How to Guide. Steven Howell. LC 95-83187. 82p. (Orig.). 1995. pap. 24.95 (*0-9650321-0-8*) Aubergine Mktg.

No-Fault Negotiating: A Practical Guide to the New Dealmaking Strategy That Lets Both Sides Win. Len Leritz. 1990. pap. 12.95 (*0-446-39104-2*) Warner Bks.

No Fault of Their Own: Unemployment & the Canadian Welfare State, 1914-1941. James Struthers. (State & Economic Life Ser.). 280p. 1983. pap. text 19.95 (*0-8020-6502-3*) U of Toronto Pr.

No-Fault Parenting. Helen Neville & Mona Halaby. LC 82-2525. 484p. 1984. reprint ed. pap. 150.10 (*0-608-02848-7*, 206391400007) Bks Demand.

No-Fault Politics: Modern Presidents, the Press, & Reformers. Eugene McCarthy. LC 97-37297. 320p. 1998. 25.00 (*0-8129-3016-9*, Times Bks) Crown Pub Group.

No Fear. Beckett Publications Editors. LC 99-192215. 1998. pap. 24.95 (*1-887432-53-1*) Beckett Pubns.

No Fear. Steve Devereux. 1999. 26.00 (*1-85782-355-9*, Pub. by Blake Publng) Seven Hills Bk.

No Fear. Dean Hughes. LC 99-19155. (Scrappers Ser.: No. 8). (Illus.). 96p. (J). (gr. 3-7). 1999. 14.00 (*0-689-81931-5*) Atheneum Yung Read.

No Fear. Dean Hughes. LC 99-19155. (Scrappers Ser.: No. 8). (Illus.). 96p. (J). (gr. 3-7). 1999. pap. 3.99 (*0-689-81941-2*) S&S Childrens.

No Fear. Ernie Irvan et al. 224p. 2000. mass mkt. 6.50 (*0-7868-8940-3*, Pub. by Hyperion) Time Warner.

***No Fear: A Police Officer's Perspective.** Robert R. Surgenor. LC 99-67602. 256p. 2000. write for info. (*1-57736-159-8*, Hillsboro Pr) Providence Hse.

No Fear: Don't Let Your Fears Stand in the Way of Your Dreams. Rick Bolton. 64p. 1995. 12.95 (*0-446-52026-8*, Pub. by Warner Bks) Little.

No Fear! The Calling of Angels. Larry Calvin. LC 95-68829. (Faith Focus Adult Studies). 1995. pap. 9.95 (*0-8344-0245-9*) Sweet Pub.

No Fear: The Hard Life & Fast Times of Nascar Driver Ernie Irvan. Ernie Irvan & Peter Golenbock. LC 98-35956. 304p. (J). 1999. 21.00 (*0-7868-6443-5*, Pub. by Hyperion) Time Warner.

No Fear Management: Rebuilding Trust, Performance & Commitment in the New American Workplace. Harry Chambers & Robert Craft. (Illus.). 1997. lib. bdg. 39.95 (*1-57444-119-1*) St Lucie Pr.

No Fear of Globalization: Welfare & Work for All. Oskar Lafontaine & Christa Muller. 2000. 27.00 (*1-85984-751-X*, Pub. by Verso) Norton.

No Fear of the Storm see No Temas a la Tormenta

No Fear of the Storm: Why Christians Will Escape All the Tribulation. Tim F. LaHaye. 256p. 1994. pap. 12.99 (*0-88070-788-7*) Multnomah Pubs.

No Fear or Favour see Henry Cecil Reprint Series

***No Feet in Concrete Volume 1: Leadership in an Entrepreneurial World.** John F. Boogaert. LC 00-103862. (Illus.). 128p. 2000. 21.95 (*0-9700981-5-4*) Panagraph Inc.

No Fighting, No Biting! Else H. Minarik. (I Can Read Bks.). (Illus.). 64p. (J). (gr. 1-3). 1958. 13.00 (*0-06-024290-6*) HarpC Child Bks.

No Fighting, No Biting! Else H. Minarik. LC 58-5293. (I Can Read Bks.). (Illus.). 64p. (J). (ps-3). 1958. lib. bdg. 15.89 (*0-06-024291-4*) HarpC Child Bks.

No Fighting, No Biting! Else H. Minarik. (I Can Read Bks.). (Illus.). 64p. (J). (gr. 1-3). 1978. pap. 3.95 (*0-06-444015-X*, HarpTrophy) HarpC Child Bks.

No Fighting, No Biting! Else H. Minarik. (I Can Read Bks.). (J). (gr. 1-3). 1978. 8.95 (*0-606-12454-3*, Pub. by Turtleback) Demco.

***No Film in My Camera.** Bill Gibson. LC 00-30784. (Filmmakers Ser.). (Illus.). 2000. write for info. (*0-8108-3845-1*) Scarecrow.

No Film in the Camera. Nancy Lay. 64p. (Orig.). 1992. pap. 8.00 (*0-912449-21-7*) Floating Island.

No Fire, No Thunder: The Threat of Chemical & Biological Weapons. Sean Murphy et al. LC 84-20579. 160p. 1984. pap. 10.00 (*0-85345-662-3*, Pub. by Monthly Rev) NYU Pr.

N

No-First-Use. Ed. by Frank T. Blackaby et al. LC 84-2467. (Peace Studies). (Illus.). 156p. 1984. 45.00 (*0-85066-274-5*); pap. 21.00 (*0-85066-260-5*) Taylor & Francis.

No Fish & Our Lives. Cabot Martin. 224p. 1992. pap. 6.35 (*1-895387-12-4*) Creative Bk Pub.

No Five Fingers Are Alike: Cognitive Amplifiers in Social Context. Joseph C. Berland. LC 81-7154. (Illus.). 257p. 1982. 47.95 (*0-674-62540-4*) HUP.

*__No Fixed Abode.__ large type ed. Frances Ferguson. 384p. 1999. 31.99 (*0-7089-4100-1*, Linford) Ulverscroft.

No Fixed Abode: A History of Responses to the Roofless & the Rootless in Britain. Robert Humphreys. LC 99-26120. 1999. text 59.95 (*0-312-22563-6*) St Martin.

No Fixed Address: An Amorous Journey. Aritha Van Herk. (InPrints Ser.). 256p. 1998. reprint ed. pap. 14.95 (*0-88995-183-7*, Pub. by Red Deer) Genl Dist Srvs.

No Fixed Address: Life in the Foreign Service. Christine Hantel-Fraser. LC 93-93122. 400p. 1993. pap. 24.95 (*0-685-67319-7*); text 45.00 (*0-8020-2754-7*) U of Toronto Pr.

No Flight. unabridged ed. Norman E. Allison. 156p. 1998. pap. 13.95 (*1-892896-25-7*) Buy Books.

No Flowers for Their Graves: A Personal Glimpse into Death Row Life. Janalee Hoffman. 175p. (Orig.). 1992. pap. 10.00 (*0-939513-49-8*) Joy Pub SJC.

No Flowers on the Desert. Lawrence Wiener. LC 99-192775. 1999. pap. text 13.95 (*0-9683113-0-X*) PB Pubns.

No Flying in the Hall. Mercer Mayer. LC 96-45318. (J). 1997. pap. 3.25 (*0-679-87377-5*, Pub. by Random Bks Yng Read) Random.

No Flying in the House. Betty Brock. LC 79-104755. (Trophy Bk.). (Illus.). 144p. (J). (gr. 3-7). 1982. pap. 4.95 (*0-06-440130-8*, HarpTrophy) HarpC Child Bks.

No Flying in the House. Betty Brock. (Harper Trophy Book Ser.). 1982. 10.05 (*0-606-13665-7*, Pub. by Turtleback) Demco.

No Foal Yet. Jessie Haas. LC 94-6265. (Illus.). 24p. (J). (gr. 3 up). 1995. 16.00 (*0-688-12925-0*, Grenwillow Bks) HarpC Child Bks.

No Fold'em Hold'em: How to Win with the Little Cards & Send the Rocks to the Bar. D. R. Sherer. LC 96-71780. (Illus.). 112p. (Orig.). 1997. pap. 19.95 (*1-884466-24-9*) Poker Plus.

No Fool of Time. large type ed. Jean Graham. 320p. 1986. 27.99 (*0-7089-1459-4*) Ulverscroft.

*__No Foot, No Horse: Foot Balance, the Key to Soundness & Performance.__ Gail Williams & Martin Deacon. (Illus.). 144p. 1999. 42.95 (*1-872119-15-8*) Half Halt Pr.

No Foothold in the Swamp: A Story of One Man's Burnout in the Ministry. Charles Hollingsworth. 160p. 1988. 10.95 (*0-310-31770-3*, 18433) Zondervan.

No Footprints in the Bush. Arthur W. Upfield. 20.95 (*0-89190-560-X*) Amereon Ltd.

No Foreign Food: The American Diet in Time & Place. Richard Pillsbury. LC 97-47342. (Geographies of Imagination Ser.). 272p. (C). 1998. pap. text 23.00 (*0-8133-2739-3*, Pub. by Westview) HarpC.

No 4-Legged Meat Please: Origin of Diseases. large type ed. Andy Tsoi. (Illus.). Date not set. 19.95 (*0-9669256-1-0*) Gen Med Clinics.

No Free Ride. Kweisi Mfume. 1996. 24.00 (*0-614-95690-0*) Ballantine Pub Grp.

No Free Ride. Kweisi Mfume. LC 97-92949. 1997. pap. 12.00 (*0-345-41364-4*) Ballantine Pub Grp.

No Friend Like a Sister: A Celebration in Words & Memories. Barbara Alpert. LC 97-104871. 192p. 1996. pap. 11.00 (*0-425-15531-5*) Berkley Pub.

No Friendly Voice. Robert M. Hutchins. LC 69-13945. 196p. 1969. reprint ed. lib. bdg. 75.00 (*0-8371-0490-4*, HUNF, Greenwood Pr) Greenwood.

No Friends for Hannah. Hilda Stahl. LC 92-13272. (Best Friends Ser.: Vol. 8). 160p. (J). (gr. 4-7). 1992. pap. 4.99 (*0-89107-684-0*) Crossway Bks.

No-Frills Guide to Grammar & Syntax. Katzer & Livingston. LC 99-219043. 304p. (C). 1998. spiral bd. 19.95 (*0-7872-5239-5*) Kendall-Hunt.

No-Frills Statistics: A Guide for the First-Year Student, No. 380. Susan H. Gray. LC 83-11015. (Illus.). 188p. (C). 1984. pap. text 20.00 (*0-8226-0380-2*, A0380) Littlefield.

*__No Frogs for Dinner.__ Freida Wishinsky. (First Flight Ser.). (Illus.). 40p. (J). (gr. 1-3). 1999. lib. bdg. 9.95 (*1-55041-519-0*, Pub. by Fitzhenry & W Ltd) Genl Dist Srvs.

No Frogs for Dinner. Frieda Wishinsky. (First Flight Ser.). (Illus.). 40p. (J). (gr. 1-3). 1999. pap. 3.95 (*1-55041-521-2*, Pub. by Fitzhenry & W Ltd) Genl Dist Srvs.

No Frontiere: In a Place of Coincidence. Andrea Steinfl & Alexander Szadeczky. (Illus.). 112p. 2000. pap. 39.95 (*1-58423-014-2*) Gingko Press.

No Fui Yo. Alma F. Ada. (Cuentos para Todo el Ano Ser.). (SPA.). (J). (gr. k-12). pap. 7.95 (*1-56014-218-9*) Santillana.

No Fun on Sunday. Frederick Manfred, pseud. LC 89-40738. 296p. 1990. 24.95 (*0-8061-2273-0*) U of Okla Pr.

No Fun Without U. Jeremy Cooper. 50.00 (*1-899858-80-6*, Pub. by Ellipsis) Norton.

No-Fuss Diabetes Recipes for 1 or 2: 125 Healthy & Delicious Meals & Desserts. Jackie Boucher. 192p. 1999. pap. text 15.95 (*1-56561-178-0*) Wiley.

*__No Future Without Forgiveness.__ Desmond M. Tutu. LC 99-34451. 287p. (YA). (gr. 9-12). 1999. 23.95 (*0-385-49689-3*) Doubleday.

*__No Future Without Forgiveness.__ Desmond Tutu. 304p. 2000. reprint ed. pap. 14.95 (*0-385-49690-7*) Doubleday.

No Garden Gardener: The Essential Guide to Gardening in Small Spaces. Jane Courtier & Ruth Rogers Clausen. LC 98-30453. 1999. 29.95 (*0-7621-0127-X*, Pub. by RD Assn) Penguin Putnam.

No Gentle Love. 1986. mass mkt. 4.50 (*0-446-73370-9*, Pub. by Warner Bks) Little.

No Gentle Love. Rebecca Brandewyne. 592p. 1987. mass mkt. 6.50 (*0-446-34689-6*, Pub. by Warner Bks) Little.

No Gentle Love. Rebecca Brandewyne. 1994. reprint ed. lib. bdg. 22.00 (*0-7278-4686-8*) Severn Hse.

No Gentle Loving. large type ed. Sara Wood. (Magna Large Print Ser.). 285p. 1996. 27.99 (*0-7505-1013-7*, Pub. by Mgna Lrg Print) Ulverscroft.

No Gentle Seduction. Helen Bianchin. (Presents Ser.). 1993. pap. 2.89 (*0-373-11527-X*, 1-11527-8) Harlequin Bks.

No Gentle Seduction. large type ed. Helen Bianchin. 1992. reprint ed. lib. bdg. 18.95 (*0-263-12898-9*) Mac Lib Ref.

No Gentle Streets. Charles W. Sasser. LC 78-31638. 1984. 22.95 (*0-87949-166-3*) Ashley Bks.

No Gentleman. Andrea Young. 1997. mass mkt. 3.99 (*1-85487-929-4*) London Brdge.

No Germs Allowed! How to Avoid Infectious Diseases at Home & on the Road. Winkler G. Weinberg. LC 95-43235. (Illus.). 250p. (C). 1996. pap. 16.95 (*0-8135-2281-1*); text 49.00 (*0-8135-2280-3*) Rutgers U Pr.

No Gifts from Chance: A Biography of Edith Wharton. Shari Benstock & Barbara Grossman. LC 93-33704. (Illus.). 544p. 1994. 28.00 (*0-684-19276-4*, Scribners Ref) Mac Lib Ref.

*__No Girls Allowed!__ Steve Metzger. LC 99-10189. (Dinofours Ser.). (Illus.). (J). (ps-1). 2000. 20.01 (*0-439-06328-0*) Scholastic Inc.

No Girls Allowed. Created by Francine Pascal. (Sweet Valley Kids Ser.: No. 57). 96p. (J). (gr. 1-3). 1995. pap. 3.50 (*0-553-48208-4*) Bantam.

No Girls Allowed. Molly Mia Stewart. (Sweet Valley Kids Ser.: No. 57). (J). (gr. 1-3). 1995. 8.70 (*0-606-08231-X*, Pub. by Turtleback) Demco.

No Girls Allowed, Bk. 1. Jim O'Connor. LC 95-70654. (Illus.). (J). 1996. pap. 3.99 (*0-679-87858-0*) McKay.

*__No Girly-Girls Allowed!__ Jay Sinclair. (Jersey Ser.: No. 2). (Illus.). 128p. (J). 2000. pap. 4.99 (*0-7868-4422-1*, Pub. by Disney Pr) Time Warner.

No Glamour Grammar. Suzanna Mayer Watt. 399p. 1986. spiral bd. 41.95 (*1-55999-061-9*) LinguiSystems.

*__No Glamour Literature.__ Mary Conger. 195p. (YA). (gr. 5-13). 1999. spiral bd. 41.95 (*0-7606-0301-4*) LinguiSystems.

No Glamour Vocabulary. Diane M. Hyde. 278p. 1993. spiral bd. 41.95 (*1-55999-260-3*) LinguiSystems.

No Go: A Photographic Record of Free Derry. Barney McMonagle. Ed. by Adrein Kerr. LC 97-212807. (Illus.). 120p. 1997. pap. 21.95 (*0-946451-41-9*, Pub. by Guildhall Pr) Irish Bks Media.

No-Go King: Exodus 5-15: The Exodus. Mary M. Simon. LC 92-31888. (Hear Me Read Ser.: Level 2). (Illus.). 32p. (Orig.). (J). (gr. 1-3). 1993. pap. 3.99 (*0-570-04732-3*, 56-1689) Concordia.

No Go the Bogeyman: Scaring, Lulling & Making Mock. Marina Warner. LC 98-19243. (Illus.). 435p. 1999. 35.00 (*0-374-22301-7*) FS&G.

No God but God: Breaking with the Idols of Our Age. Ed. by Os Guinness & John Seel. 18.99 (*0-8024-6336-3*, 230) Moody.

*__No God but God: Egypt & the Triumph of Islam.__ Geneive Abdo. LC 99-58415. 240p. 2000. 25.00 (*0-19-512540-1*) OUP.

No God in Saguarro. large type ed. Lewis B. Patten. (Sagebrush Large Print Westerns Ser.). 176p. 1996. lib. bdg. 18.95 (*1-57490-022-6*) T T Beeler.

No God in the Holly. Lonnie D. Bailey. 1998. pap. write for info. (*1-57553-719-2*) Watermrk Pr.

No God Next Door. unabridged ed. Denis Fahey. 199p. 1935. reprint ed. pap. 13.00 (*0-945001-52-5*) GSG & Assocs.

No Gods & Precious Few Heroes: Scotland since 1914. Christopher T. Harvie. (New History of Scotland Ser.). 192p. 1993. pap. 20.00 (*0-7486-0387-5*, Pub. by Edinburgh U Pr) Col U Pr.

No Gods & Precious Few Heroes: Scotland, 1914-1980. Christopher T. Harvie. LC 81-175164. (New History of Scotland Ser.: No. 8). 192p. reprint ed. pap. 59.60 (*0-608-16597-2*, 202636500049) Bks Demand.

No Gods & Precious Few Heroes: Twentieth Century Scotland. 3rd ed. Christopher Harvie. (New History of Scotland Ser.). 1998. pap. 20.00 (*0-7486-0999-7*, Pub. by Edinburgh U Pr) Col U Pr.

No Gods No Masters, Bk. 1. Ed. by Daniel Guerin. 304p. (Orig.). 1997. pap. 16.95 (*1-873176-64-3*) AK Pr Dist.

No Gods No Masters, Bk. 2. Ed. by Daniel Guerin. 288p. (Orig.). 1997. pap. 16.95 (*1-873176-69-4*) AK Pr Dist.

No Going Back. large type ed. Stephanie Howard. (Magna Large Print Ser.). 252p. 1997. 27.99 (*0-7505-1133-8*) Ulverscroft.

No Golden Agers Here. Blaine Taylor. 101p. (Orig.). 1984. pap. 6.00 (*0-914527-33-9*) C-Four Res.

No Good Deed. Lynn S. Hightower. 400p. 1998. mass mkt. 6.50 (*0-440-22531-0*) Dell.

No Good Deed. Paul Nathan. LC 94-10137. 202p. 1995. 22.00 (*1-877946-56-7*) Permanent Pr.

*__No Good from a Corpse.__ Leigh Brackett. (Illus.). 576p. 1999. 35.00 (*0-939767-32-5*) D McMillan.

No Good in Art. Miriam Cohen. LC 79-16566. (Illus.). 32p. (J). (gr. k-3). 1980. 16.93 (*0-688-84234-8*, Grenwillow Bks) HarpC Child Bks.

No Good in Art. Miriam Cohen. (J). 1996. 10.19 (*0-606-09689-2*, Pub. by Turtleback) Demco.

No Goodbye. Marita Conlon-McKenna. 176p. 1997. pap. 6.95 (*0-86278-362-3*, Pub. by OBrien Pr) Irish Amer Bk.

No Goodbye. Stephen Philbrick. LC 81-615. 84p. (Orig.). 1981. pap. 6.00 (*0-912292-68-7*) Smith.

*__No Goodbyes: A Novel.__ Elaine Kagan. LC 99-44731. 288p. 2000. 24.00 (*0-688-15746-7*, Wm Morrow) Morrow Avon.

No Graven Image? Israelite Aniconism in Its Ancient Near Eastern Context. Tryggve N. Mettinger. (Coniectanea Biblica, Old Testament Ser.: No. 42). 252p. 1995. pap. 52.50 (*91-22-01664-3*) Coronet Bks.

No Graven Images: Studies in Art & the Hebrew Bible. Joseph Gutmann. (Library of Biblical Studies). 1970. 50.00 (*0-87068-063-3*) Ktav.

No Grazing for Sacred Cows: Tormenting Questions in a Bizarre World. Noel Francisco. LC 98-44909. 204p. 1999. pap. 17.50 (*0-7880-1329-7*) CSS OH.

*__No Great Mischief.__ Alistair MacLeod. LC 00-21801. (Illus.). 288p. 2000. 23.95 (*0-393-04970-1*) Norton.

No Great Mischief If You Fall: The Highland Experience. John Macleod. (Illus.). 240p. 1994. 34.95 (*1-85158-540-0*, Pub. by Mainstream Pubng) Trafalgar.

*__No Greater Gift.__ Geri Guillaume. 1999. mass mkt. 4.99 (*1-58314-040-9*) BET Bks.

No Greater Joy, Vol. 1. unabridged ed. Michael Pearl & Debi Pearl. (Illus.). 104p. 1997. pap. 4.00 (*1-892112-01-9*) Ch Cane Creek.

No Greater Joy: The Story of Ruth Woodworth, Missionary. rev. ed. Ruth A. Woodworth. LC 74-28952. (Illus.). 100p. (Orig.). 1996. pap. text 7.95 (*1-888796-11-1*) ABWE Pubng.

No Greater Love. Damien of Molokai & John Milsome. 112p. (C). 1989. 39.00 (*0-85439-308-0*, Pub. by St Paul Pubns) St Mut.

No Greater Love. Julie Ellis. 1991. mass mkt. 5.99 (*0-8217-3592-6*, Zebra Kensgtn) Kensgtn Pub Corp.

*__No Greater Love.__ Good News Publishing Company Staff. 2000. pap. 8.50 (*5-550-02137-4*) Nairi.

*__No Greater Love.__ William X. Kienzle. 2000. mass mkt. 6.99 (*0-345-42639-8*) Fawcett.

No Greater Love. Frwd. by Thomas Moore. LC 96-43158. 224p. 1997. 21.00 (*1-57731-006-3*) New Wrld Lib.

No Greater Love. Mother Teresa of Calcutta. 1997. 21.00 (*0-614-28615-8*) New World.

No Greater Love. Robbins Slocum. 1999. text. write for info. (*0-312-24553-X*); text 22.95 (*1-58238-056-2*, Whitman Coin) St Martin.

No Greater Love. Danielle Steel. 408p. 1991. 23.00 (*0-385-29909-5*) Delacorte.

No Greater Love. Danielle Steel. 400p. 1992. mass mkt. 6.99 (*0-440-21328-2*) Dell.

No Greater Love. Danielle Steel. 1991. 11.60 (*0-606-02811-0*, Pub. by Turtleback) Demco.

No Greater Love. large type ed. Mother Teresa of Calcutta et al. LC 97-43988. 240p. 1998. pap. 14.95 (*0-8027-2727-1*) Walker & Co.

No Greater Love. limited ed. Danielle Steel. 408p. 1991. 150.00 (*0-385-30510-9*) Delacorte.

*__No Greater Love: A Romance Blessed by God.__ Ed. by Cheryl Harris. 283p. 2000. pap. 5.99 (*0-9701168-0-2*) R E Horley.

*__No Greater Love: Bl. Gianna: Physician, Mother, Martyr.__ Ann M. Brown. (Illus.). 32p. 1999. pap. 3.00 (*1-892875-03-9*, 3007, Remnant Israel) New Hope Publicatns.

No Greater Love: The James Reeb Story. Duncan Howlett. 200p. 1993. pap. 12.00 (*1-55896-317-0*, 6108, Skinner Hse Bks) Unitarian Univ.

No Greater Privilege: The Making of a Physician. J. J. Kirschenfeld. 200p. 1992. 29.50 (*0-9622815-8-1*, Black Belt) Black Belt Communs.

No Greater Treasure. Ellen Kelley. 1998. mass mkt. 5.99 (*0-515-12408-7*, Jove) Berkley Pub.

No Greater Treasure: Stories of Extraordinary Women Drawn from the Talmud & Misdrash. Shoshana Lepon. 190p. 1990. 16.95 (*0-944070-62-0*) Targum Pr.

No Grown-Ups Allowed. Beverly Lewis. LC 95-23931. (Cul-de-Sac Kids Ser.: Vol. 4). (Illus.). 80p. (J). (gr. 2-5). 1995. pap. 3.99 (*1-55661-644-9*) Bethany Hse.

No Grown-Ups in Heaven: A T-A Primer for Christians. Art Greer. LC 74-33595. 1985. reprint ed. pap. 14.00 (*0-9624030-0-8*) Awareness Assocs.

No-Growth Society. Ed. by Mancur Olson, Jr. & Hans H. Landsberg. 259p. (C). 1974. 11.25 (*0-393-01111-9*) Norton.

No Guarantees. Robyn Donald. 1990. per. 2.50 (*0-373-11303-X*) Harlequin Bks.

No Guarantees. Cheryl Lanham. (Life at Sixteen Ser.). 208p. 1997. mass mkt. 4.50 (*0-425-15974-4*) Berkley Pub.

No Guarantees. large type ed. Chris Campbell. LC 93-42933. (J). 1994. lib. bdg. 15.95 (*0-7862-0146-0*) Thorndike Pr.

No Guarantees: A Young Woman's Fight to Overcome Drug & Alcohol Addiction. Chris Campbell. LC 92-25183. (Illus.). 192p. (YA). (gr. 6 up). 1993. lib. bdg. 19.00 (*0-02-716445-4*, Mac Bks Young Read) S&S Childrens.

No-Guilt Desserts. (Favorite All Time Recipes Ser.). (Illus.). 96p. 1993. spiral bd. 3.50 (*1-56173-574-4*, 2010500) Pubns Intl Ltd.

*__No Guns or Candy in This Line: Parenting with the Family Contract.__ 110p. 1999. spiral bd. write for info. (*0-9674873-0-7*) H Leftin.

No-H-In Snake: Music Theory for Children. Michiko Yurko. 282p. 1979. pap. text 20.95 (*0-88284-092-4*, 1472) Alfred Pub.

No Habra Mas Adioses (No More Good-Byes) Merline Lovelace. (SPA.). 1997. per. 3.50 (*0-373-35198-4*, 1-35198-0) Harlequin Bks.

No Habra Mas Penas ni Olvido see Funny, Dirty Little War

No Hair-Loss Hair Care Book: With Hair Replacement Solutions & Treatments. Emanuel Mamatas. 1988. pap. 14.95 (*0-13-623018-0*) P-H.

No Half-Way House: Selected Political Journalism, 1950-1977. Harri Webb. Ed. by Meic Stephens. LC 98-104800. 1997. pap. 14.95 (*0-86243-407-6*, Pub. by Y Lolfa) Intl Spec Bk.

No Handguns: The Postcard Activist. PGW Staff. 1991. pap. 4.95 (*1-879096-01-3*) Postcard Activist.

No Handle on the Cross: An Asian Meditation on the Crucified Mind. Kosuke Koyama. LC 76-23160. 128p. reprint ed. pap. 39.70 (*0-8357-4067-6*, 202512000042) Bks Demand.

No Hands: The Rise & Fall of the Schwinn Bicycle Company, An American Institution. Judith Crown & Glenn Coleman. (Illus.). 384p. 1995. 25.00 (*0-8050-3553-2*) H Holt & Co.

No Hang-Ups: Funny Answering Machine Messages. John Carfi & Cliff Carle. (Illus.). 132p. (Orig.). 1984. pap. 3.95 (*0-918259-00-2*) CCC Pubns.

No Hang-Ups III: Funny Answering Machine Messages. John Carfi & Cliff Carle. (Illus.). 96p. (Orig.). (YA). 1988. pap. 3.95 (*0-918259-12-6*) CCC Pubns.

No Hang-Ups II. Cliff Carle. (Illus.). 96p. (Orig.). 1986. pap. 3.95 (*0-918259-05-3*) CCC Pubns.

No Happy Ending. Paco Ignacio Talbo, II. Tr. by William I. Neuman. 192p. 1993. 17.95 (*0-89296-517-7*) Mysterious Pr.

No Happy Ending. Paco I. Taibo, II. Tr. by William I. Neuman. 192p. 1994. mass mkt. 5.50 (*0-446-40329-6*, Pub. by Warner Bks) Little.

No Harm. Wendy Hornsby. (Worldwide Ser.: No. 30). 1989. mass mkt. 3.50 (*0-373-26030-X*) Harlequin Bks.

No Harm: Ethical Principles for a Free Market. T. Patrick Burke. LC 93-12444. 1993. 24.95 (*1-55778-618-6*) Paragon Hse.

No Harm No Foul Referees. Wendell Trogdon. 1987. pap. 6.95 (*0-913617-06-7*) Highlander Pr.

No Harp Like My Own. large type ed. Marjorie Quarton. 1990. 27.99 (*0-7089-2177-9*) Ulverscroft.

No Hassles. Anne Waldman. (Illus.). pap. 3.50 (*0-686-09750-5*) Kulchur Foun.

*__No Haunui Laua 'O Hauiki.__ William H. Wilson. (HAW., Illus.). 17p. (J). (gr. 1-3). 1999. pap. 6.95 incl. audio (*1-58191-063-0*) Aha Punana Leo.

No Haven for the Oppressed: United States Policy Toward Jewish Refugees, 1938-1945. Saul S. Friedman. LC 72-2271. 316p. reprint ed. pap. 98.00 (*0-7837-3626-6*, 204349200009) Bks Demand.

No Hay Burlas Con el Amor. 7th ed. Pedro Calderon de la Barca. 232p. 1985. pap. 12.95 (*0-7859-5165-2*) Fr & Eur.

No Hay Fever & a Railway. Willa Walker. (Illus.). 186p. 1989. 24.95 (*0-86492-096-2*, Pub. by Goose Ln Edits) Genl Dist Srvs.

No Hay Ley en el Amor: Wife by Contract. Raye Morgan. (Silhouette Deseo Ser.: Vol. 236).Tr. of There Is No Law in Love. (SPA.). 1998. per. 3.50 (*0-373-35236-0*, 1-35236-8) Harlequin Bks.

No Hay Mal Que Dure 100 Anos Ni Mujer Que lo Resista. ROSAURA RODRIGUEZ. 1997. pap. text 11.98 (*970-05-0756-4*) Grijalbo Edit.

No Hay Olvido (The Wrong Kind of Wife) Roberta Leigh. (SPA.). 1996. per. 3.50 (*0-373-33382-X*, 1-33382-2) Harlequin Bks.

No Hay Otro Evangelio: No Other Gospel. Charles H. Spurgeon. (ENG & SPA.). 478p. 1997. pap. 9.99 (*0-85151-725-0*) Banner of Truth.

No Hero. John P. Marquand. reprint ed. lib. bdg. 23.95 (*0-88411-141-5*) Amereon Ltd.

No Heroes: Inside the FBI's Secret Counter-Terror Force. Danny O. Coulson. 2000. mass mkt. 7.99 (*0-671-02062-5*) S&S Trade.

No Heroes: Inside the FBI's Secret Counter-Terror Force. Danny O. Coulson & Elaine Shannon. LC 99-204502. 608p. 1999. 25.00 (*0-671-02061-7*, PB Hardcover) PB.

No Heroes, No Villains: New Perspectives on Kent State & Jackson State. Robert M. O'Neil et al. LC 72-6044. (Jossey-Bass Higher Education Ser.). 189p. reprint ed. pap. 58.60 (*0-608-15164-5*, 205216200045) Bks Demand.

No Heroes, No Villains: The Story of a Murder. Steven Phillips. 1978. pap. 11.00 (*0-394-72531-X*) Vin Bks.

No Heroics, Please. Raymond Carver. 1992. pap. write for info. (*0-679-74031-7*) McKay.

No Heroics, Please: Uncollected Writings. Raymond Carver. 1992. pap. 12.00 (*0-679-74007-4*) Vin Bks.

No Hiding Place. Tracey Herd. LC 97-163608. 62p. 1997. pap. 15.95 (*1-85224-381-3*, Pub. by Bloodaxe Bks) Dufour.

No Hiding Place. Warren Woessner. LC 79-67262. 1979. pap. 3.00 (*0-933180-06-3*) Spoon Riv Poetry.

No Hiding Place. large type ed. Rae Foley. LC 96-52700. 306p. 1997. write for info. (*0-7862-1014-1*) Thorndike Pr.

No Hiding Place: A Tamara Hayle Mystery. Valerie W. Wesley. LC 97-15676. 207p. 1997. 21.95 (*0-399-14318-1*, G P Putnam) Peng Put Young Read.

*__No Hiding Place: Child Sex Tourism & the Role of Extra-Territorial Legislation.__ Jeremy Seabrook. LC 00-32072. 2000. boxed set. write for info. (*1-85649-914-6*, Pub. by Zed Books) St Martin.

No Hiding Place: Essays on the New Nature & Poetry. John Barnie. 155p. 1997. pap. 18.95 (*0-7083-1342-6*, Pub. by Univ Wales Pr) Paul & Co Pubs.

*__No Hiding Place: Uncovering the Legacy of Charlotte-Area Writers.__ Ed. by Frye Gaillard et al. 300p. 1999. pap. 16.95 (*1-878086-69-3*, Pub. by Down Home NC) Blair.

No High Ground. Fletcher Knebel & Charles W. Bailey. LC 83-16384. 272p. 1983. reprint ed. lib. bdg. 65.00 (*0-313-24221-6*, KNHG, Greenwood Pr) Greenwood.

***No High Like the Most High: Divine Direction for Destiny.** Kent Mattox. 176p. 1999. pap. 9.99 (*1-884369-90-1*) McDougal Pubng.

No Higher Court: Contemporary Feminism & the Right to Abortion. Germain Kopaczynski. x, 247p. (C). 1995. text 29.95 (*0-940866-50-1*) U Scranton Pr.

***No Higher Honor: The U. S. S. Yorktown at the Battle of Midway.** Jeff Nesmith. LC 99-61750. (Illus.). 304p. 1999. 24.00 (*1-56352-552-6*) Longstreet.

***No Higher Law.** Philip Friedman. 1999. 34.65 (*1-55611-544-X*) D I Fine.

No Highway in the Sky. Nevil Shute. 24.95 (*0-88411-320-5*) Amereon Ltd.

No Hill Is Too High. Adrienne V. Sealy. (Illus.). (J). (gr. 2-5). 1978. lib. bdg. 4.95 (*0-9602670-0-X*) Assn Family Living.

No Hint of Scandal. large type ed. Sheila Bishop. (Large Print Ser.). 320p. 1997. 27.99 (*0-7089-3680-6*) Ulverscroft.

No-Hit Hall of Fame: No-Hitters of the Twentieth Century. Rich Coberly. LC 85-71539. 232p. (Orig.). 1985. pap. 13.95 (*0-934289-00-X*) R Coberly.

***No-Hitters: The 223 Games, 1893-1998.** Allen Lewis & Rich Westcott. LC 99-59282. (Illus.). 424p. 2000. lib. bdg. 45.00 (*0-7864-0722-0*) McFarland & Co.

No Holds Barred. Raving Beauties Editors. 128p. Date not set. pap. 8.95 (*0-7043-3963-3*, Pub. by Womens Press) Trafalgar.

No Holds Barred. Patricia Rosemoor. (Intrigue Ser.: No. 165). 1991. per. 2.75 (*0-373-22165-7*) Harlequin Bks.

No Holds Barred: My Life in Politics. John C. Crosbie. LC 98-107902. (Illus.). 384p. 1998. 27.95 (*0-7710-2427-4*) McCland & Stewart.

No Holds Barred: My Life in Politics. John C. Crosbie & Geoffrey Stevens. (Illus.). 512p. 1999. trans. 19.99 (*0-7710-2428-2*) McCland & Stewart.

No Holds Barred: The Final Congressional Testimony of Admiral Hyman Rickover. 103p. 1982. 1.50 (*0-936758-07-4*) Ctr Responsive Law.

No Holiness, No Heaven! Richard Alderson. 105p. (Orig.). 1986. pap. 6.50 (*0-85151-495-2*) Banner of Truth.

No Home to Return to but This. Geraldine Little. 40p. 1994. pap. 5.00 (*1-880286-19-X*) Singular Speech Pr.

No Homeless People Allowed: A Report on Anti-Homeless Laws, Litigation & Alternatives in 49 U. S. Cities. 136p. (Orig.). (C). 1994. pap. text 35.00 (*0-7881-1549-9*) DIANE Pub.

No Honeymoon for Death. Mary Krueger. 304p. 1996. mass mkt. 5.50 (*1-57566-110-1*, Knsington) Kensgtn Pub Corp.

***No Horn at Midnight.** Geoffrey Trease. 160p. (J). 2000. mass mkt. 5.99 (*0-330-34141-3*) Mcm Child Bks.

No Hot Water Tonight. 2nd ed. Jean W. Bodman & Michael Lanzano. (J). 1991. mass mkt. 18.95 (*0-8384-3231-X*) Heinle & Heinle.

No Howling in the House. Mercer Mayer & Erica Farber. (Step into Reading Ser.: A Step 2 Book). (Illus.). (J). (ps-3). 1996. lib. bdg. 11.99 (*0-679-97365-6*) McKay.

No Howling in the House. Mercer Mayer & Erica Farber. LC 95-13690. (Step into Reading Ser.: A Step 2 Book). 48p. (J). (gr. k-2). 1996. pap. 3.99 (*0-679-87365-1*) Random.

No Howling in the House. Mercer Mayer & Erica Farber. LC 95-13690. (Step into Reading Ser.: A Step 2 Book). (J). (gr. 1-3). 1996. 9.19 (*0-606-09690-6*, Pub. by Turtleback) Demco.

No Human Being Is Disposable: Social Cleansing, Human Rights & Sexual Orientation. Juan Pablo Ordonez. 78p. 1995. pap. 12.00 (*1-884955-01-0*) Intl Gay & Lesbian.

No Human Involved. Barbara Seranella. 304p. 1999. mass mkt. 6.99 (*0-06-101361-7*, Harp PBks) HarpC.

No Human Involved. Barbara Seranella. LC 97-6265. 256p. 1997. 22.95 (*0-312-15614-6*, Thomas Dunne) St Martin.

No Hunting. Sara H. Frommer. (Kaleidoscope Ser.: Set A). 1993. 2.95 (*0-88336-178-7*) New Readers.

***No Hurry to Get Home: The Captivating Memoir of the Unconventional Life & Far-Flung Adventures of a Veteran New York Writer.** Emily Hahn. 2000. 24.95 (*1-58005-045-X*) Seal Pr WA.

No Huyas de Mi: Maternity Bride. Maureen Child. (Deseo Ser.: No. 137).Tr. of Don't Run Away from Me. 1999. mass mkt. 3.50 (*0-373-35267-0*, 1-35267-3) Harlequin Bks.

No-Hysterectomy Option: Your Body--Your Choice. 2nd rev. ed. Herbert A. Goldfarb. LC 96-29848. 288p. 1997. pap. 15.95 (*0-471-16557-3*) Wiley.

No, I Tell a Lie, It Was the Tuesday . . . A Trudge Through His Life & Times. Alan Maclean. (Illus.). 182p. 1998. 35.00 (*1-85626-248-0*, Pub. by Cathie Kyle) Trafalgar.

No, I Won't Shut Up: Thirty Years of Telling It Like It Is. Barbara A. Reynolds. LC 98-67027. 332p. (C). 1998. pap. 17.95 (*0-9665073-0-4*) Reynolds News.

No Ifs, Ands or Butts. (Illus.). 32p. 1998. write for info. (*0-945100-48-5*) Parlay Intl.

No Ifs, Ands, or Butts: A Smoker's Guide to Kicking the Habit. Julie Waltz. LC 89-91978. (Illus.). 350p. 1989. pap., student ed. 15.95 (*0-931836-02-6*) Northwest Learn.

No Ifs, Ands, or Butts: Instruction Guide, Set. Julie Waltz. LC 89-91978. (Illus.). 288p. 1990. pap., suppl. ed. 39.95 (*0-931836-03-4*) Northwest Learn.

No Ifs, Ands, or Butts: The Smoker's Guide to Quitting. Harlan M. Krumholz & Robert H. Phillips. LC 92-29845. 192p. pap. 7.95 (*0-89529-534-2*, Avery) Penguin Putnam.

No Illusions, Some Hope & Fears: The Outlook Editorials of I. H. Burney. I. H. Burney. 564p. 1996. 35.00 (*0-19-577687-9*) OUP.

No, I'm Not Afraid. Irina Ratushinskaya. Tr. by David McDuff from RUS. 142p. 1987. reprint ed. 27.00 (*1-85224-057-1*, Pub. by Bloodaxe Bks) Dufour.

No, I'm Not Afraid. Irina Ratushinskaya. Tr. by David McDuff from RUS. 142p. 1992. reprint ed. pap. 16.95 (*0-906427-95-9*, Pub. by Bloodaxe Bks) Dufour.

No Immediate Danger? Prognosis for a Radioactive Earth. 2nd ed. Rosalie Bertell. LC 86-72223. 435p. 1986. pap. 11.95 (*0-913990-25-6*) Book Pub Co.

No Immediate Danger? Prognosis for a Radioactive Earth. 3rd ed. Rosalie Bertell. 400p. pap. write for info. (*0-88961-092-4*, Pub. by Womens Pr) LPC InBook.

No Immunity: A Kiernan O'Shaughnessy Mystery. Susan Dunlap. 1999. mass mkt. 5.99 (*0-440-22480-2*) Dell.

***No Immunity: A Kiernan O'Shaughnessy Mystery.** Susan Dunlap. LC 99-46184. 1999. pap. 22.95 (*1-56895-782-3*, Wheeler) Wheeler Pub.

No Importa de Espana y la Verdad en el Potro. Ed. by Julio R. Puertolas. (Textos B Ser.: No. 15). (SPA.). 205p. 1973. pap. 51.00 (*0-900411-57-0*, Pub. by Tamesis Bks Ltd) Boydell & Brewer.

No! In Thunder. Jake Hipple. LC 95-73120. 367p. 1995. 29.95 (*0-9646800-8-4*) On-Call Pub.

***No Intermissions: The Life of Agnes de Mille.** Carol Easton. 576p. 2000. pap. text 18.00 (*0-306-80975-3*) Da Capo.

***No Intermissions: The Life of Agnes de Mille.** Carol Easton. (Illus.). 548p. 2000. reprint ed. 30.00 (*0-7881-9377-5*) DIANE Pub.

No is a Complete Sentence: Learning the Sacredness of Personal Boundaries. Megan LeBoutillier. (Orig.). 1995. mass mkt. 5.99 (*0-345-37647-1*) Ballantine Pub Grp.

No Is a Love Word: How to Say "No" to Children of All Ages. Lonnie Carton. LC 91-77338. 250p. 1992. pap. 12.95 (*0-9627183-0-0*) Learn Ctr MA.

"No!" Is an Option: A Second Story in Recovery. Linda Macuga. 363p. 1999. pap. 12.95 (*1-891929-11-9*) Four Seasons.

No Island. Spencer Selby. 92p. 1995. 10.00 (*0-9628456-7-1*) Drogue Pr.

***No Island Is an Island: Four Glances at English Literature in a World Perspective.** Carlo Ginzburg. LC 00-35844. (Italian Academy Lectures). 2000. 19.95 (*0-231-11628-4*) Col U Pr.

No Island of Sanity: Paula Jones vs. Bill Clinton : The Supreme Court on Trial. Vincent Bugliosi. LC 97-50261. 147p. 1998. pap. 9.95 (*0-345-42487-5*) Ballantine Pub Grp.

No, It's Not Hot in Here: A Husband's Guide to Menopause. Dick Roth. 174p. 1999. 19.95 (*0-9655067-3-8*, Ant Hill Press) N Star Pubns.

No Jacket Required: Another Great Collection of Recipes from Incircle. Neiman Marcus InCirlce Staff. (Illus.). 292p. 1995. 25.00 (*0-15-100189-8*) Harcourt.

No Job? No Sweat! Make a Potful of Money at Home in Your Own Business. Michael Sharratt & Suzanne Sharratt. LC 83-90076. 160p. 1983. pap. 7.95 (*0-912295-00-7*) Sharratt & Co.

No-Job Dad. James H. Malone. LC 92-15873. (Illus.). 30p. (J). (gr. 1-2). 1992. pap. 13.95 (*1-878217-06-2*) Victory Press.

No Jumping on the Bed! Tedd Arnold. LC 86-13501. (Illus.). 32p. (J). (ps-2). 1987. 16.99 (*0-8037-0038-5*, Dial Yng Read) Peng Put Young Read.

No Jumping on the Bed! Tedd Arnold. LC 86-13501. (Illus.). 32p. (J). (ps-3). 1996. pap. 5.99 (*0-14-055839-X*, PuffinBks) Peng Put Young Read.

No Jumping on the Bed! Tedd Arnold. LC 86-13501. (J). 1996. 10.19 (*0-606-09691-4*, Pub. by Turtleback) Demco.

No Justice. Chris Raymondo. Ed. by Rodney Charles & Elizabeth Pasco. LC 96-69531. 500p. 1997. 23.95 (*1-887472-14-2*) Sunstar Pubng.

No Justice: A Masey Baldridge/Luke Williamson Mystery. James D. Brewer. LC 95-47226. 232p. 1996. 21.95 (*0-8027-3283-6*) Walker & Co.

No Justice for Millie: An HMO Tragedy. Fred Tenderella. LC 97-75005. 1998. pap. text 14.95 (*1-885221-73-8*) BookPartners.

No Justice, No Peace. Ed. by A. Gordon. (Orig.). 1997. pap. 11.95 (*0-932863-18-3*) Clarity Pr.

No Justice, No Peace: A Search for Truth. Arnold Staples. 240p. 1999. pap. 12.95 (*1-891231-16-2*) Word Assn.

No Justice, No Peace: From Emmett Till - Rodney King. Terry Morris. 128p. (Orig.). 1993. pap. 10.95 (*0-9635878-0-3*) Africentric.

No Justice, No Peace: The 1996 OPSEU Strike against the Harris Government in Ontario. David Rapaport. 60.00 (*0-7735-1858-4*); pap. 22.95 (*0-7735-1865-7*) McG-Queens Univ Pr.

No Ka Oi. Alluvial Staff. 1996. 39.95 (*0-9652009-0-6*) Alluvial Ent.

No Ka Oi. Alluvial Staff. 1996. 75.00 (*0-9652009-7-3*) Alluvial Ent.

No Kidding. Bruce Brooks. LC 88-22057. 224p. (YA). (gr. 7 up). 1989. 14.00 (*0-06-020722-1*) HarpC Child Bks.

No Kidding! A Primer for Teachers-Tutors New to Adult Education. Jane H. Combs. Ed. by Sandra Shaffer. 49p. (Orig.). 1990. pap. text, teacher ed. 5.56 (*0-9625440-0-0*) Longmuir Jones Pub.

No Kidding Around! America's Young Activists Are Changing Our World & You Can Too. Wendy S. Lesko. (Illus.). 250p. (Orig.). 1992. pap. 18.95 (*1-878346-10-5*) Info USA.

No Kidding, God. James C. Schaap. LC 89-48197. (Devotions for Today's Family Ser.). 153p. (Orig.). (J). 1990. pap. text 5.00 (*0-930265-86-6*) CRC Pubns.

No Kids or Dogs Allowed. Jane Gentry. (Special Edition Ser.). 1995. per. 3.75 (*0-373-09972-X*, 1-09972-0) Silhouette.

No King but Christ: Donald Cargill. Maurice Grant. 1988. pap. 13.99 (*0-85234-255-1*, Pub. by Evangelical Pr) P & R Pubng.

No King, No Popery: Anti-Catholicism in Revolutionary New England, 164. Francis D. Cogliano. LC 95-19322. (Contributions in American History Ser.: Vol. 164). 192p. 1996. 55.00 (*0-313-29729-0*, Greenwood Pr) Greenwood.

No Kiss for Mother. Tomi Ungerer. LC 97-44246. (Illus.). 40p. (J). (gr. 1-5). 1998. pap. text 5.95 (*1-57098-208-2*) Roberts Rinehart.

***No, Kitty! A Quick-Fix A-Z Problem Solver for Your Cat's Bad Behavior.** Steve Duno. 224p. 2000. pap. 5.99 (*0-312-97581-3*, St Martins Paperbacks) St Martin.

No Lace for Cricket: Sequel to Mountain Mama. Dora Axsom & Erra Pelham. 216p. (Orig.). (YA). (gr. 10 up). 1991. pap. 5.50 (*0-9621669-2-8*) Lil Red Hen OK.

No Lace for Cricket: Sequel to Mountain Mama. 2nd ed. Dora Axsom & Erra Pelham. 207p. (Orig.). (YA). 1997. reprint ed. pap. 10.00 (*0-9621669-3-6*) Lil Red Hen OK.

***No Lady.** Saskia Hope. 2000. mass mkt. 6.95 (*0-352-32857-6*) BLA4.

No Language but a Cry. Richard A. Dambrosio. (Laurel-Leaf Library). (J). 1971. 11.09 (*0-606-04186-9*, Pub. by Turtleback) Demco.

No-Lathe Saxony-Style Spinning Wheel Construction Manual. Richard Schneider & Myrna Schneider. (Spinster-Helper Ser.). (Illus.). 54p. (Orig.). 1984. pap. 4.95 (*0-936984-05-8*) Schneider Pubs.

***No Latitude for Fools.** Hans Albert. LC 99-91656. 2000. 25.00 (*0-7388-1156-4*); pap. 18.00 (*0-7388-1157-2*) Xlibris Corp.

No Laughing Matter. Carolyn Keene. Ed. by Anne Greenberg. (Nancy Drew Files: No. 79). 160p. (YA). (gr. 6 up). 1993. mass mkt. 3.99 (*0-671-73083-5*, Archway) PB.

No Laughing Matter. Carolyn Keene. (Nancy Drew Files: No. 79). (YA). (gr. 6 up). 1993. 9.09 (*0-606-02798-X*, Pub. by Turtleback) Demco.

No Laughing Matter: The Life & Times of Flann O'Brien. Anthony Cronin. LC 97-40342. (Illus.). 272p. 1998. reprint ed. 29.95 (*0-88064-183-5*) Fromm Intl Pub.

No Laughing Matter, 1991. Autonomedia Collective Staff & Nina Felshin. (Illus.). 48p. 1991. 8.00 (*0-916365-33-6*) Ind Curators.

No Laurels for De Gaulle. Robert Mengin. Tr. by Jay Allen from FRE. LC 78-179734. (Biography Index Reprint Ser.). 1977. reprint ed. 24.95 (*0-8369-8102-2*) Ayer.

No Law Against Mercy: Jailed for Sheltering a Child from the State. Barbara L. Lapp & Rachel B. Lapp. LC 96-94579. (Illus.). 428p. 1997. 24.95 (*0-9653547-0-9*) Hand of Hope.

No Law & Order. large type ed. Ernest Haycox. 1977. 12.00 (*0-7089-0018-6*) Ulverscroft.

No Lease on Life: A Novel. Lynne Tillman. LC 97-9304. 179p. 1998. 21.00 (*0-15-100272-X*) Harcourt.

No Lease on Life: A Novel. Lynne Tillman. 192p. 1999. pap. 12.00 (*0-15-600860-2*, Harvest Bks) Harcourt.

No Left Turns, a Handbook for Conservatives: Based on the Writings of John M. Ashbrook. Compiled by Randy McNutt. LC 85-80376. (Illus.). 128p. 1986. pap. 15.00 (*0-940152-03-7*) Hamilton Hobby.

No Leftovers! Child Care Cookbook: Kid-Tested Recipes & Menus for Centers & Home-Based Programs. Jac L. Dunkle & Martha S. Edwards. LC 92-15973. (Illus.). 210p. (Orig.). 1992. pap. 14.95 (*0-934140-64-2*, 5211) Redleaf Pr.

No Legacy for Lindsay. large type ed. Essie Summers. (Romance Ser.). 352p. 1993. 27.99 (*0-7089-2976-1*) Ulverscroft.

No Less a Man: Masculist Art in a Feminist Age. Douglas Robinson. LC 93-72885. 308p. (C). 1994. 45.95 (*0-87972-637-7*); pap. 18.95 (*0-87972-638-5*) Bowling Green Univ Popular Press.

No Less a Woman: Femininity, Sexuality & Breast Cancer. 2nd ed. Deborah H. Kahane. LC 95-37552. (Illus.). 320p. 1995. pap. 14.95 (*0-89793-187-4*) Hunter Hse.

No Less Than a Lifetime. Christine Rimmer. (Special Edition Ser.: No. 1040). (Orig.). 1996. per. 3.99 (*0-373-24040-6*, 1-24040-7) Silhouette.

No Less Zeal: A Spiritual Guide for Catholic Lay People. Douglas J. Morin. LC 92-34242. 156p. (Orig.). 1993. pap. 7.95 (*0-8189-0631-6*) Alba.

No Lesser Plea. Robert K. Tanenbaum. 368p. 1988. reprint ed. mass mkt. 7.50 (*0-451-15496-7*, Sig) NAL.

No Letters from the Grave. large type ed. Basil Cooper. (Linford Mystery Library). 240p. 1998. pap. 17.99 (*0-7089-5223-2*, Linford) Ulverscroft.

No Liar Shall Be President. Byron Buckeridge. (Illus.). 70p. (Orig.). (C). 1989. write for info. (*0-318-65083-5*) B Buckeridge.

No Liberty for License: The Forgotten Logic of the First Amendment. David Lowenthal & Harvey C. Mansfield. LC 97-30379. 344p. 1997. 27.95 (*0-9653208-4-7*) Spence Pub.

No Lie Like Love: Stories. Paul Rawlins. LC 96-11960. 1996. 24.95 (*0-8203-1868-X*) U of Ga Pr.

No Life for a Lady. Agnes M. Cleaveland. LC 77-6825. (Illus.). xii, 356p. 1977. pap. 12.95 (*0-8032-5868-2*, Bison Books) U of Nebr Pr.

No Life Like It: Canada'S Military Wives. Deborah Harrison & Lucie Laliberte. LC 95-109555. 266p. pap. 19.95 (*1-55028-446-0*, Pub. by J Lorimer) Formac Dist Ltd.

No Life Like It: Military Wives in Canada. Deborah Harrison & Lucie Laliberte. LC 95-109555. 266p. 29.95 (*1-55028-447-9*, Pub. by J Lorimer) Formac Dist Ltd.

No Life of My Own: An Autobiography. Frank Chikane. LC 89-2906. 158p. reprint ed. pap. 49.00 (*0-7837-5504-X*, 204527400005) Bks Demand.

No Life Without Roots: Culture & Authentic Development. Thierry Verhelst. LC 89-39009. 272p. (C). 1990. text 49.95 (*0-86232-848-9*, Pub. by Zed Books) St Martin.

No Limit: The Rise & Fall of Bob Stupak & Las Vegas' Stratosphere Tower. John L. Smith. LC 96-79031. (Illus.). 320p. 1997. 21.95 (*0-929712-18-8*) Huntington Pr.

No Limits: Developing Scientific Literacy Using Science Fiction. Julie E. Czerneda. (Illus.). (YA). (gr. 7-10). 1999. pap., teacher ed. write for info. (*1-895579-94-5*) Trifolium Inc.

No Limits: Fighting Speeding Tickets. Norman Fulcher & Sheila Moak. LC 96-76386. (Illus.). 160p. (Orig.). 1996. pap. 19.95 (*0-9652690-0-0*) Mariah Publns.

No Limits but the Sky: Inspiration for Teachers, Counselors, & Kids. 120p. (YA). (gr. k-12). 1991. pap. text, teacher ed. 14.95 (*1-56499-000-1*, IP9000, Pub. by Innerchoice Pub) Jalmar Pr.

No Limits to Learning: Bridging the Human Gap: The Club of Rome Report. James W. Botkin et al. LC 79-40911. (Pergamon International Library Science Technology Engineering & Social Studies). 1979. 82.00 (*0-08-024705-9*, Pub. by Pergamon Repr) Franklin.

No Limits to Love. David Mercer. 69p. (C). 1988. pap. 8.95 (*0-413-48260-X*, A0191) Heinemann.

***No Limits Together - Vision 7007.** Joe Noland. Ed. by Deborah Flagg. 242p. 2000. text. write for info. (*0-9675393-1-5*); pap. text. write for info. (*0-9675393-0-7*) Duden.

No Lion at All. (Choices & Decisions Ser.). (J). 1990. 35.24 (*0-8123-6458-9*); pap. 5.28 (*0-8123-6459-7*); audio 7.92 (*0-8123-6461-9*) McDougal-Littell.

No Little Places: The Untapped Potential of the Small-Town Church. John Koessler & Ronald Klassen. LC 95-47525. 128p. 1996. pap. 10.99 (*0-8010-9014-8*) Baker Bks.

***No Llores por Nosotros, Puerto Rico.** Luis Rafael Sanchez. (Rama Ser.: Vol. 11). (SPA.). 245p. (C). 1998. pap. 18.00 (*0-910061-42-4*) Ediciones Norte.

No lo Olvide: Nuevas Tecnicas para Aumentar su Memoria Extraordinariamente see Aumente su Memoria Extraordinariamente

No-Load Stocks: How to Buy Your First Share & Every Share Directly from the Company-With No Broker's Fee. expanded rev. ed. Charles B. Carlson. LC 96-36839. (Illus.). 275p. 1996. pap. 16.95 (*0-07-011880-9*) McGraw.

***No Logo: Taking Aim at the Brand Bullies.** Naomi Klein. 224p. 2000. text 28.00 (*0-312-20343-8*, Picador USA) St Martin.

No Longer a Dilly Dally. Carl Sommer. LC 96-24351. (Another Sommer-Time Story Ser.). (Illus.). 48p. (J). (ps-4). 1997. 9.95 (*1-57537-001-8*); lib. bdg. 14.95 (*1-57537-053-0*) Advance Pub.

No Longer a Minority: Latinos & Social Policy in California. David E. Hayes-Bautista et al. LC 92-8303. 47p. 1992. pap. 8.50 (*0-89551-092-8*) UCLA Chicano Studies.

No Longer a Stranger. large type ed. Margaret O'Neill. 288p. 1995. 23.99 (*0-263-14332-5*, Pub. by Mills & Boon) Ulverscroft.

No Longer a Victim. Carol J. Cole. (Illus.). 196p. (Orig.). 1996. pap. 19.95 (*1-890961-02-7*) C Communs.

No Longer a Victim. Malcolm Smith. 1992. mass mkt. 4.99 (*1-880089-14-9*) Albury Pub.

No Longer a Victim. P. Burton Stokes & Lynn Lucas. 224p. (Orig.). 1988. pap. 10.99 (*0-914903-72-1*) Destiny Image.

No Longer Afraid. Sue S. Elkind. 64p. (Orig.). 1985. pap. 5.95 (*0-931642-16-7*) Lintel.

No Longer Alone. large type unabridged ed. O. O'Banion. 2000. write for info. (*0-9637174-0-5*) Two O Bks.

No Longer Alone: Mental Health & the Church. John Toews & Eleanor Loewen. LC 94-73616. 176p. (Orig.). 1995. pap. 11.99 (*0-8361-9010-6*) Herald Pr.

No Longer an American Lake? Alliance Problems in the South Pacific. Ed. by John Ravenhill. LC 89-7612. (Research Ser.: No. 73). (Illus.). 240p. 1989. pap. text 14.95 (*0-87725-173-8*) U of Cal IAS.

No Longer at Ease. Chinua Achebe. (C). 1961. 12.95 (*0-8392-1077-9*); pap. 7.95 (*0-8392-5008-8*) Astor-Honor.

No Longer at Ease. Chinua Achebe. LC 94-13428. 208p. 1994. pap. 7.95 (*0-385-47455-5*, Anchor NY) Doubleday.

No Longer Barred from Prison: Social Injustice in Canada. rev. ed. Claire Culhane. 216p. (C). 1991. write for info. (*0-921689-95-0*) Black Rose.

No Longer Deprived: The Use of Minority Cultures & Languages in the Education of Disadvantaged Children & Their Teachers. Ruth Fedder & Jacqueline Gabaldon. LC 78-76318. (Series in Guidance & Student Personnel Administration). 223p. reprint ed. pap. 69.20 (*0-608-14931-4*, 202601000048) Bks Demand.

No Longer Disabled: The Federal Courts & the Politics of Social Security Disability, 7. Susan G. Mezey. LC 87-31783. (Studies in Social Welfare Policies & Programs: No. 7). 208p. 1988. 55.00 (*0-313-25424-9*, MNL/, Greenwood Pr) Greenwood.

No Longer Enemies, Not Yet Friends: An American Soldier Returns to Vietnam. Frederick Downs, Jr. Ed. by Eric Tobias. 424p. 1993. reprint ed. mass mkt. 5.99 (*0-671-79513-9*) PB.

No Longer Enemies, Not Yet Friends: An American Soldier Returns to Vietnam. Frederick Downs. 352p. 1998. reprint ed. text 23.00 (*0-7881-5150-9*) DIANE Pub.

No Longer Exiles: The Religious New Right in American Politics. Ed. by Michael Cromartie. 164p. 1992. 18.95 (*0-89633-172-5*) Ethics & Public Policy.

N

No Longer Forgotten: The Remarkable Story of the Christian Women's Job Corps. Charlene Gray. Ed. by Trudy O. Johnson. LC 98-216471. 138p. 1998. pap. text 11.95 (1-56309-250-6, N984106) Womans Mission Union.

No Longer Human. Osamu Dazai. Tr. & Intro. by Donald Keene. LC 58-9509. 192p. 1973. pap. 10.95 (0-8112-0481-2, NDP357, Pub. by New Directions) Norton.

No Longer I: Being Transformed into the Image of Christ. Larry E. Hall. LC 98-71881. (Illus.). 208p. 1999. pap. 12.95 (0-89112-032-7) Abilene Christ U.

No Longer Invisible: Afro-Latin Americans Today. Ed. by Minority Rights Group Staff. 336p. pap. 21.95 (1-873194-85-4, Pub. by Minority Rts Pubns) Paul & Co Pubs.

No Longer Invisible: Afro-Latin Americans Today. Ed. by Minority Rights Group Staff. 336p. 1995. 34.95 (1-873194-80-3, Pub. by Minority Rts Pubns) Paul & Co Pubs.

No Longer Leading: A Scorecard on U. S. Economic Performance. Lucy Gorham. (Studies). 1990. 12.00 (0-944826-32-6) Economic Policy Inst.

No Longer Lonely. Ken Parker. 21p. 1982. 0.50 (0-89814-056-0) Grace Publns.

No Longer Patient: Feminist Ethics & Health Care. Susan Sherwin. 304p. 1992. pap. 22.95 (1-56639-061-3) Temple U Pr.

No Longer Silent: World-Wide Memories of the Children of World War II. Ed. by C. Leroy Anderson et al. LC 95-70124. (Illus.). 370p. (Orig.). 1995. pap. 22.95 (1-57510-003-7) Pictorial Hist.

No Longer Strangers: A Biography of H. Stover Kulp. Mary A. Kulp. LC 68-4439. 188p. reprint ed. pap. 58.30 (0-608-13563-1, 202241300026) Bks Demand.

No Longer Strangers: Selected Writings of Bishop K. H. Ting. K. H. Ting. Ed. & Intro. by Raymond L. Whitehead. LC 89-15989. (Illus.). 215p. 1989. reprint ed. pap. 66.70 (0-7837-9843-1, 206057200005) Bks Demand.

No Longer Two but One. Darrell Huffman. LC 97-213892. 112p. 1997. pap. 6.99 (0-89274-997-0) Harrison Hse.

No Longer Voiceless. Luis Leal. (Illus.). 195p. (Orig.). (C). 1995. pap. 22.00 (0-927065-16-9) Marin Chula Vista.

No Looking Back. Thrower. 1994. pap. 3.99 (0-946462-09-7, Pub. by Evangelical Pr) P & R Pubng.

No Lost Certainties to Be Recovered. Gregorio Kohon. 1999. pap. text. write for info. (1-85575-210-7) H Karnac Bks Ltd.

No Lotus Garden. Gren Wedderburn. 1987. 55.00 (0-946270-37-6, Pub. by Pentland Pr) St Mut.

No Love Lost. Margery Allingham. 176p. 1991. mass mkt. 3.95 (0-88184-723-2) Carroll & Graf.

No Love Lost. Margery Allingham. 176p. 1998. lib. bdg. 20.95 (1-56723-015-6) Yestermorrow.

No Love Lost. William Dean Howells. (Notable American Authors Ser.). 1992. reprint ed. lib. bdg. 75.00 (0-7812-3227-9) Rprt Serv.

No Lover Ever Dies. Morpheus. (Illus.). 80p. 1985. 11.99 (0-9604512-1-8) Mortal Pr.

No Luck! Josie Stewart & Lynn Salem. (Illus.). 12p. (J). (gr. k-1). 1996. pap. 3.75 (1-880612-07-0) Seedling Pubns.

No Lye: The African American Woman's Guide to Natural Hair Care. Tulani Kinard. LC 96-37420. 176p. 1997. pap. 11.95 (0-312-15180-2) St Martin.

No Magic Bullet: A Social History of Venereal Disease in the United States Since 1880. Allan M. Brandt. (Illus.). 290p. 1987. pap. text 14.95 (0-19-504237-9) OUP.

No Magic Wands. Beverly S. Nichols. LC 98-89887. 365p. 1999. 25.00 (0-7388-0321-9); pap. 15.00 (0-7388-0322-7) Xlibris Corp.

***No Ma'ikoha a Me Ka Wauke.** Kawika Napoleon & William H. Wilson. (HAW., Illus.). 29p. (J). (gr. 1-3). 1999. pap. 6.95 incl. audio (1-58191-062-2) Aha Punana Leo.

No Mail for Mitchell. Catherine Siracusa. LC 89-70010. (Step into Reading Ser.: A Step 1 Book). (Illus.). 32p. (J). (ps-1). 1990. pap. 3.99 (0-679-80476-5, Pub. by Random Bks Yng Read); lib. bdg. 11.99 (0-679-90476-X, Pub. by Random Bks Yng Read) Random.

No Mail for Mitchell. Catherine Siracusa. (Step into Reading Ser.: A Step 1 Book). (J). (ps-1). 1990. pap. 9.19 (0-606-12455-1, Pub. by Turtleback) Demco.

No Man Ever Spoke As This Man: The Great I Am's of Jesus. Anthony M. Coniaris. 1969. pap. 10.95 (0-937032-18-2) Light&Life Pub Co MN.

No Man in the House. Cecil Foster. 1993. pap. 11.50 (0-394-22344-6) Beginner.

No Man in the House. Cecil Foster. 288p. 1994. pap. 10.00 (0-345-38899-2) One Wrld.

No Man Is an Island. Thomas Merton. 256p. 1994. pap. 21.00 (0-86012-004-X, Pub. by Srch Pr) St Mut.

No Man Is an Island. James Minchin. 384p. 1987. text 37.95 (0-86861-906-X) Routledge.

No Man Is an Island. large type ed. Thomas Merton. 384p. 1986. pap. 15.95 (0-8027-2527-9) Walker & Co.

No Man Is an Island. Thomas Merton. LC 78-7108. 288p. 1978. reprint ed. pap. 9.00 (0-15-665962-X, Harvest Bks) Harcourt.

No Man Is Safe. Carol Gaye. (Lythway Adult Ser.). 304p. 1991. 20.50 (0-7451-1355-9, G K Hall Lrg Type) Mac Lib Ref.

No Man Knows My History. Fawn M. Brodie. LC 90-50139. 576p. 1995. pap. 17.00 (0-679-73054-0) Random.

No Man Knows My History: The Life of Joseph Smith. Fawn M. Brodie. (Illus.). 1971. 35.00 (0-394-46967-4) Knopf.

No Man Knows My Pastries: The Secret (Not Sacred) Recipes of Sister Enid Christensen. Roger B. Salazar & Michael G. Wightman. LC 92-16709. (Illus.). 128p. (Orig.). 1992. pap. 8.95 (1-56085-028-0) Signature Bks.

No Man Knows My Story: Emotional Abuse. Susan Clay. 195p. 1998. pap. 14.95 (0-9660284-9-X) Nelson Bk.

No Man's a Mountain. John E. Cramer. LC 96-76312. 276p. 1996. 19.95 (1-878044-48-6) Mayhaven Pub.

No Man's Fortune. Kristie Knight. 1993. mass mkt. 3.99 (0-373-28758-5, 1-28758-0) Harlequin Bks.

***No Man's Garden: Thoreau & a New Vision for Civilization & Nature.** Daniel B. Botkin. (Illus.). 288p. 2000. 24.95 (1-55963-465-0, Shearwater Bks) Island Pr.

No Man's Land. Susan C. Bartoletti. LC 98-24714. 176p. (J). (gr. 5-9). 1999. 15.95 (0-590-38371-X, Blue Sky Press) Scholastic Inc.

No Man's Land. Kathleen Gerson. 1994. pap. 14.00 (0-465-05120-0) Bantam.

No Man's Land. Sam Johnson. (Call of Cthulhu Roleplaying Ser.). 80p. 1998. pap. 14.95 (1-56882-142-5) Chaosium.

No Man's Land. Kevin Major. 272p. 1995. 22.95 (0-385-25503-9) Doubleday.

No Man's Land. Harold Pinter. LC 75-13555. 96p. 1975. pap. 9.95 (0-8021-5187-6, Grove) Grove-Atltic.

No Man's Land. George Pratt. Ed. by Greg Baisden. (Illus.). 112p. 1992. pap. 14.95 (1-879450-64-X) Kitchen Sink.

No Man's Land. Johnny Quarles. 368p. (Orig.). 1993. mass mkt. 4.99 (0-380-76814-3, Avon Bks) Morrow Avon.

No Man's Land. large type ed. Reginald Hill. 496p. 1986. 27.99 (0-7089-8338-3, Charnwood) Ulverscroft.

***No Man's Land.** 2nd rev. ed. (Illus.). 2000. reprint ed. pap. text. write for info. (0-9679400-8-7) SSDC.

No Man's Land: An Anthology of Modern Danish Women's Literature. Intro. by Annegret Heitmann. LC 87-63150. (Series B: No. 4). 211p. (Orig.). 1987. pap. 22.00 (1-870041-05-4, Pub. by Norvik Pr) Dufour.

No Man's Land: East German Drama after the Wall. Ed. by David W. Robinson. (Contemporary Theatre Review Ser.: Vol. 4, Pt. 2). 220p. 1996. pap. text 24.00 (3-7186-5786-4, ECU31, Harwood Acad Pubs) Gordon & Breach.

No Man's Land: The Place of the Woman Writer in the Twentieth Century. Sandra M. Gilbert & Susan Gubar. 1996. pap. 19.00 (0-300-06660-0) Yale U Pr.

No Man's Land Vol. 2: The Place of the Woman Writer in the Twentieth Century: Sexchanges. Sandra M. Gilbert & Susan Gubar. LC 87-10560. (Illus.). 472p. (C). 1991. reprint ed. pap. 22.00 (0-300-05025-9) Yale U Pr.

No Man's Land - The Place of the Woman Writer in the Twentieth Century Vol. 1: The War of the Words. Sandra M. Gilbert & Susan Gubar. 320p. (C). 1989. reprint ed. pap. 18.00 (0-300-04587-5) Yale U Pr.

No Man's Land - The Place of the Woman Writer in the Twentieth Century Vol. 3: Letters from the Front. Sandra M. Gilbert & Susan Gubar. LC 87-10560. (Illus.). 496p. 1994. 45.00 (0-300-05631-1) Yale U Pr.

No Man's Stage: A Semiotic Study of Jean Genet's Major Plays. Una Chaudhuri. Ed. by Oscar G. Brockett. LC 85-28886. (Theater & Dramatic Studies: No. 34). 162p. reprint ed. 50.30 (0-8357-1731-3, 207046800095) Bks Demand.

No Man's Street. Beverley Nichols. LC 74-170790. 192 p. (J). 1973. write for info. (0-491-01121-0) Virgin Bks.

No Mardi Gras for the Dead. D. J. Donaldson. (WWL Mystery Ser.). 1995. mass mkt. 3.99 (0-373-26163-2, 1-26163-5) Harlequin Bks.

No Margin for Error: America in the Eighties. Howard H. Baker, Jr. 1980. 10.95 (0-686-65902-3, Times Bks) Crown Pub Group.

***No Marks for Trying.** large type ed. Stella Allan. 384p. 1999. 31.99 (0-7089-4093-5, Linford) Ulverscroft.

***No Marriage of Convenience.** Elizabeth Boyle. 384p. 2000. mass mkt. 5.99 (0-380-81534-6) Morrow Avon.

No Mas! Guia Para la Mujer Golpeada. Myrna M. Zambrano. LC 94-14397. (New Leaf Ser.). (SPA.). 60p. 1994. pap. 5.95 (1-878067-50-8) Seal Pr WA.

No Mask Required. Mike Strickland. 103p. 1996. pap. 8.99 (1-873796-55-2) Review & Herald.

No Mate for the Magpie. Frances Molloy. 1986. pap. 8.95 (0-89255-105-4) Persea Bks.

No Matter Evil. D. S. Gregory. 1999. pap. write for info. (0-525-93830-3) NAL.

No Matter How Good the Light Is: Poems by a Painter. Edward Boccia. LC 97-50548. 77p. 1998. 22.00 (1-56809-044-7); pap. 14.50 (1-56809-045-5) Time Being Bks.

No Matter How Loud I Shout: A Year in the Life of Juvenile Court. Edward Humes. 400p. 1996. 23.50 (0-684-81194-4) S&S Trade.

No Matter How Loud I Shout: A Year in the Life of Juvenile Court. Edward Humes. 1997. pap. 14.00 (0-684-81195-2, Touchstone) S&S Trade Pap.

No Matter No Fact. Alain Bosquet. Tr. by Samuel Beckett et al from FRE. LC 87-7910. 128p. 1988. 21.95 (0-8112-1039-1, Pub. by New Directions); pap. 9.95 (0-8112-1040-5, NDP646, Pub. by New Directions) Norton.

***No Matter What.** Debi Gliori. (J). 1999. student ed. 16.00 (0-15-202459-X) Harcourt.

No Matter What. Debi Gliori. LC 98-47277. (Illus.). 32p. (J). (ps-1). 1999. 16.00 (0-15-202061-6, Harcourt Child Bks) Harcourt.

No Matter What. Mary Saracino. LC 93-26212. 320p. (Orig.). 1993. pap. 9.95 (0-933216-91-2) Spinsters Ink.

***No Matter What, No Matter Where: God's Presence on the Road Ahead.** Larry Libby & Steve Halliday. LC 99-88476. 128p. 2000. 11.95 (1-57856-314-3) Waterbrook Pr.

No Matter Where You Travel, You Still Be Black. Houston A. Baker, Jr. LC 78-61608. 58p. 1979. per. 5.00 (0-916418-18-9) Lotus.

No Mattrr What. Joe R. 42p. 1999. pap. 4.00 (1-891408-09-7, GBP-10) Green Bean.

No Me Arrestes. Eric H. Bryant. Tr. by Karen Gurney. (SPA., Illus.). 50p. (Orig.). 1996. pap. text 6.00 (0-9640336-1-5, NMA9601) Arrest Me Not Pub.

No Me Asusto a Mi. Janet L. Goss & Jerome C. Harste. (SPA., Illus.). 23p. (J). (ps-3). 1998. pap. 4.95 (1-57255-488-6) Mondo Pubng.

No Me Comprenden. Charles M. Schulz. (Peanuts Ser.). (SPA.). 64p. (J). 1971. 4.95 (0-8288-4511-5) Fr & Eur.

***No Me Digas Mentiras.** Judy Baer. (SPA.). (J). (gr. 4-7). 1999. mass mkt. 3.99 (0-7899-0644-9) Spanish Hse Distributors.

No Me Quiten a Babucha. Gilles Gauthier. (Primeros Lectores Ser.). (SPA., Illus.). 60p. (J). (gr. 5 up). 1994. pap. 5.95 (958-07-0073-7) Firefly Bks Ltd.

***No Mean City? The Image of Dublin in the Novels of Dermot Bolger, Roddy Doyle & Val Mulkerns.** McArthur. 2000. pap. 10.95 (0-552-07583-3, Pub. by Transworld Publishers Ltd) Trafalgar.

No Mean City? The Image of Dublin in the Novels of Dermot Bolger, Roddy Doyle & Val Mulkerns. Ulrike Paschel. LC 98-30126. (Aachen British & American Studies: Vol. 10). X, 170p. 1998. pap. text 37.95 (0-8204-3611-9) P Lang Pubng.

No Mean Feet. Liz LeBlanc. (Dialogues on Dance Ser.: No. 4). 13p. 1985. pap. 4.00 (0-941240-01-0) Ommation Pr.

"No" Means Find Another Way to Do It: And Other Mental Morsels. Kamau Ramsey. (Illus.). 296p. 1998. per. 12.95 (0-9668786-3-9) Quiet Warrior.

No Means No. Laurie John. (Sweet Valley University Ser.: No. 10). (YA). (gr. 7 up). 1995. 9.09 (0-606-08249-2, Pub. by Turtleback) Demco.

No Means No. Created by Francine Pascal. (Sweet Valley University Ser.: No. 10). 240p. (YA). (gr. 7 up). 1995. mass mkt. 4.50 (0-553-56655-5) Bantam.

No Measles, No Mumps for Me. Paul Showers. LC 79-7106. (Let's-Read-&-Find-Out Science Bks.). (Illus.). 40p. (J). (gr. k-3). 1980. lib. bdg. 12.89 (0-690-04018-0) HarpC Child Bks.

No Medals for Trying: A Week in the Life of a Pro Football Team. Jerry Izenberg. 256p. 1990. text 18.95 (0-02-558215-1) Macmillan.

No Men Are Strangers. Joseph North. LC 58-11504. 300p. 1976. pap. 2.25 (0-7178-0462-3) Intl Pubs Co.

"No Mentor but Myself" Jack London on Writing & Writers. 2nd ed. Ed. by Dale L. Walker. 224p. 1999. 49.50 (0-8047-3635-9); pap. 17.95 (0-8047-3636-7) Stanford U Pr.

No Mercy. D. Buckley. text 35.00 (0-340-68062-8, Pub. by Hodder & Stought Ltd); mass mkt. 15.95 (0-340-68065-2, Pub. by Hodder & Stought Ltd) Trafalgar.

***No Mercy.** Pat Califia. LC 00-23866. 260p. 2000. pap. 14.95 (1-55583-542-2, Pub. by Alyson Pubns) Consort Bk Sales.

No Mercy. Jack Curtis. 160p. 1995. 19.95 (0-8027-4151-7) Walker & Co.

No Mercy. Franklin W. Dixon. Ed. by Anne Greenberg. (Hardy Boys Casefiles Ser.: No. 65). 160p. (Orig.). (YA). (gr. 6 up). 1992. pap. 3.99 (0-671-73101-7, Archway) PB.

No Mercy. large type ed. Jane Brindle. (Dales Large Print Ser.). 1995. pap. 18.99 (1-85389-540-7, Dales) Ulverscroft.

No Mercy: A Journey to the Heart of the Congo. Redmond O'Hanlon. LC 96-36677. (Illus.). 462p. 1997. 29.95 (0-679-40655-7) Knopf.

No Mercy: A Journey to the Heart of the Congo. Redmond O'Hanlon. 480p. 1998. pap. 14.00 (0-679-73732-4) Vin Bks.

No Mercy: How Conservative Think Tanks & Foundations Changed America's Social Agenda. Jean Stefancic & Richard Delgado. LC 96-14145. 208p. (C). 1996. text 29.95 (1-56639-469-4) Temple U Pr.

No Mercy: The Host of America's Most Wanted Hunts the Worst Criminals of Our Time - In Shattering True Crime Cases. John Walsh & Philip Lerman. (Illus.). 302p. 1998. 24.00 (0-671-01993-7, PB Hardcover) PB.

No Mercy: The Host of America's Most Wanted Hunts the Worst Criminals of Our Time - In Shattering True Crime Cases. John Walsh & Philip Lerman. (Illus.). 427p. 1999. mass mkt. 7.50 (0-671-01994-5, Pocket Star Bks) PB.

***No Messages.** Robert Hahn. (Ernest Sandeen Prize in Poetry Ser.). 136p. 2000. 25.00 (0-268-03652-7); pap. 15.00 (0-268-03653-5) U of Notre Dame Pr.

No Middle Ground. Ed. by Kathleen M. Blee. LC 97-21111. 329p. 1998. text 55.00 (0-8147-1279-7); pap. text 19.00 (0-8147-1280-0) NYU Pr.

No Middle Ground: Thomas Ward Osborn's Letters from the Field (1862-1864) Thomas W. Osborn. Ed. by Herb S. Crumb & Katherine Dhalle. LC 93-8590. (Illus.). 199p. 1993. 22.95 (0-9622393-4-8) Edmonston Publ.

No Milk! Jennifer A. Ericsson. LC 92-21806. (Illus.). 32p. (J). (ps up). 1993. 15.93 (0-688-11307-9, Wm Morrow) Morrow Avon.

No Milk! Jennifer A. Ericsson. (Illus.). 32p. (J). 1998. mass mkt. 4.95 (0-688-15848-X, Wm Morrow) Morrow Avon.

No Milk! Jennifer A. Ericsson. 1998. 10.05 (0-606-13666-5, Pub. by Turtleback) Demco.

No Milk: A Revolutionary Solution to Back Pain & Headaches. Daniel A. Twogood. (Illus.). (Orig.). (C). 1992. pap. text. write for info. (0-9631125-0-3) Wilhelmina.

No Mind the Flowers of Eternity. Osho. Ed. by Deva Sarito & Anand Robin. LC 97-212702. (Zen Ser.). (Illus.). 276p. 1992. 21.95 (3-89338-060-4, Pub. by Rebel Hse) Oshos.

***No Miracles Here: Fighting Urban Decline in Japan & the United States.** Theodore J. Gilman. (C). 2000. pap. text 19.95 (0-7914-4792-8) State U NY Pr.

***No Miracles Here: Fighting Urban Decline in Japan & the United States.** Theodore J. Gilman. (C). 2001. text 59.50 (0-7914-4791-X) State U NY Pr.

No Mires Ahora . . . y Otros Cuentos. Ramon L. Acevedo. (Aqui y Ahora Ser.). 1997. pap. 6.95 (0-8477-0317-7) U of PR Pr.

No Mirrors in My Nana's House. Ysaye M. Barnwell & Synthia Saint James. LC 97-33356. (Illus.). 32p. (J). (ps-2). 1998. 18.00 (0-15-201825-5) Harcourt.

No-Miss Lessons for Preteen Kids: 22 Faith-Building Lessons to Keep Kids Coming Back. LC 96-35339. 1997. pap. 16.99 (0-7644-2015-1) Group Pub.

No Molasses in the Wheat Paste. rev. ed. Stanley A. Warshaw. 120p. (Orig.). 1977. 28.00 (0-685-07025-5) US School Prof.

No Moment Too Small: Rhythms of Silence, Prayer, & Holy Reading. Norvene Vest. LC 94-436. (Cistercian Studies Ser.: Vol. 153). 145p. 1994. pap. 10.95 (1-56101-092-8) Cowley Pubns.

No Money down Financing for Franchising. Roger C. Rule. LC 98-45404. 240p. 1999. pap. 19.95 (1-55571-462-5, NMDFP, Oasis Pr) PSI Resch.

No Money, No Honey: A Study of Street Traders & Prostitutes in Jakarta. Allison J. Murray. (Illus.). 190p. (C). 1991. 37.00 (0-19-588991-6) OUP.

No, Monkey! No! Fiona Conboy. LC 98-20026. (Illus.). 12p. (J). (ps-k). 1998. 8.95 (0-7613-0390-1, Copper Beech Bks) Millbrook Pr.

No Monkey Too Big. Carl Spacone. Ed. by John Hoffman. (Life Changing Bks.). (Illus.). 224p. (Orig.). (YA). (gr. 9 up). 1987. 8.95 (0-944712-00-2); pap. text 8.95 (0-318-23727-X) Spacone Pub.

No Monoply on Suffering: Blacks & Jews in Crown Heights & Elsewhere. Herbert D. Daughtry. LC 97-7987. 287p. 1997. 24.95 (0-86543-586-3) Africa World.

No Monsters: A Storybook for Kids. Carman Ministries Staff. LC 97-163194. 32p. (J). (ps-3). 1996. 7.99 (1-880089-35-1, Pub. by Albury Pub) Appalach Bk Dist.

No Moon. Nancy Eimers. LC 96-45290. 1997. pap. 14.95 (1-55753-099-8) Purdue U Pr.

No Moon: New Poems. Linda E. Opyr. 72p. 1998. pap. 12.00 (0-925062-16-2) Writers Ink Pr.

No Moon, No Milk! Chris Babcock. (Illus.). 32p. (J). (ps-3). 1995. pap. 6.99 (0-517-88540-9) Random Hse Value.

No Moon, No Milk! Chris Babcock. 1995. 12.19 (0-606-07955-6, Pub. by Turtleback) Demco.

No More. Marguerite Duras. Tr. & Afterword by Richard Howard. LC 97-46209. Orig. Title: C'Est Tout. 128p. 1998. pap. 17.00 (1-888363-65-7) Seven Stories.

No More Aching Back: Dr. Root's New, Fifteen-Minute-a-Day Program for a Healthy Back. Leon Root. 240p. 1991. mass mkt. 5.99 (0-451-17091-1, Sig) NAL.

No More Allergies: Identifying & Eliminating Allergies & Sensitivity Reactions to Everything in Your Environment. Gary Null. LC 92-50149. 1992. pap. 14.00 (0-679-74310-3) Villard Books.

No More Amoxicillin. Mary Ann Block. LC 99-188647. 144p. 1998. pap. 12.00 (1-57566-316-3, Knsington) Kensgtn Pub Corp.

***No More Antibiotics: Preventing & Treating Ear & Respiratory Infections the Natural Way.** Mary A. Block. 128p. 2000. mass mkt. 5.99 (1-57566-500-X) Kensgtn Pub Corp.

No More Bad Hair Days: A Woman's Journey Through Cancer, Chemotherapy & Coping. Susan S. Hyde. LC 97-192514. 112p. 1997. 9.95 (1-56352-412-0) Longstreet.

***No More Bad Shots.** Hank Haney. (Illus.). 2001. pap. 24.95 (1-892129-97-3) Total Sprts.

No More Bedtime Battles. Lee Canter & Marlene Canter. (Lee Canter Effective Parenting Bks.). (Illus.). 48p. (Orig.). 1996. pap. 5.95 (0-939007-78-9) Canter & Assocs.

No More Bedwetting: How to Help Your Child Stay Dry. Samuel J. Arnold. LC 97-21709. 192p. 1997. pap. 12.95 (0-471-14690-0) Wiley.

No More Black Days: Complete Freedom from Depression, Eating Disorders & Other Compulsive Behaviors. Lauri A. Mallord. 128p. (Orig.). 1992. pap. 5.95 (0-9630069-0-8, 1000) Whi Stone.

No More Blue Mondays: Four Keys to Finding Fulfillment at Work. Robin A. Sheerer. LC 98-31585. 272p. 1999. pap. 16.95 (0-89106-131-2, 7816, Pub. by Consulting Psychol) Natl Bk Netwk.

No More Bottom. Richard Moore. LC 90-28176. 80p. (Orig.). 1991. pap. 10.00 (0-914061-22-4) Orchises Pr.

No More Boys. Janet Quin-Harkin. (J). 1997. pap. 3.50 (0-8167-3675-8) Troll Communs.

***No More Broken Promises.** Angela Elwell Hunt. (Cassie Perkins Ser.: Vol. 1). 140p. (gr. 4-7). 2000. pap. 10.95 (0-595-09004-4) iUniversecom.

No More Buffalo. Bob Scriver. LC 82-15194. (Illus.). 152p. 1982. 45.00 (0-913504-75-0) Lowell Pr.

***No More Bullies!** Marcia Shoshana Nass. (Illus.). 92p. (J). (gr. k-7). 1998. pap. 17.95 (1-882732-75-8, 61530) Childswork.

No More Bummers! 121 Ways to Add Levity to Your Life. Elaine M. Lundberg. (Illus.). 192p. 1999. pap. 6.95 (0-9670956-0-3) Sockboy Pubns.

***No More "Business as Usual" Women of Color in Corporate America: Report of the National Women of Color Work-Life Survey.** Jennifer Tucker et al. 1999. pap. 20.00 (1-877966-61-4) Ctr Women Policy.

No More Butterflies: Overcoming Stagefright, Shyness, Interview Anxiety & Fear of Public Speaking. Peter Desberg. LC 95-72226. 176p. 1996. pap. 13.95 (1-57224-041-5) New Harbinger.

An Asterisk (*) at the beginning of an entry indicates that the title is appearing for the first time.

No More Cats. (Kaleidoscope Ser.: Set A). 1993. 2.95 (0-88336-171-X) New Readers.

No More Chernobyls. Brown. 1996. lib. bdg. 12.95 (0-8057-3880-0, Twyne) Mac Lib Ref.

*No **More Chores.** Illus. by J. J. Rudisill et al. (Wimzie's House Bks.). 24p. (J). 1999. pap. 3.99 (0-88724-542-0, CD-4848) Carson-Dellos.

No More Cold Calls: The Complete Guide to Generating & Closing All the Prospects You Need to Become a Multi-Millionaire by Selling Your Service. Jeffrey Lant. 1993. pap. 39.95 (0-940374-24-2) JLA Pubns.

No More Corncraiks: Lord Moray's Feuars in Edinburgh's New Town. Ann Mitchell. 160p. 1994. pap. 30.00 (1-84017-017-4) St Mut.

No More Crumbs. Rod Parsley. LC 97-36037. 1997. 14.99 (0-88419-521-X); pap. 11.99 (0-88419-510-4) Creation House.

No More Dead Dogs. Gordon Korman. LC 00-24313. 160p. (J). (gr. 4-7). 2000. lib. bdg. 16.49 (0-7868-2462-X, Pub. by Disney Pr) Little.

*No **More Dead Dogs.** Gordon Korman. (Illus.). 160p. (YA). (gr. 5-9). 2000. 15.99 (0-7868-0531-5, Pub. by Hyprn Child) Time Warner.

No More Detours. Silvia Martinoli. 102p. 1992. pap. 6.95 (0-9634014-7-5) S Martinoli.

*No **More Diapers.** Debbie A. Atwood. (Illus.). 10p. (J). (ps-k). 2000. 6.95 (0-9701013-1-7) Novel Approach.

No More Diapers. B. Terrill. (Sesame Street Pop-up Ser.). 1999. pap. 3.25 (0-375-80410-2) Random.

No More Diapers for Elvis! large type unabridged ed. Judith Cohen & Michael Cohen. (Potti Pets Ser.). (Illus.). 15p. (J). (ps). 1997. pap. 2.99 (0-9664396-0-0) PPP Enterp.

No More Diapers for Elvis! Incl. Chart. large type unabridged ed. Judith Cohen & Michael Cohen. (Potti Pets Ser.). (Illus.). 15p. (J). (ps). 1997. pap. write for info. incl. audio (0-9664396-1-9) PPP Enterp.

No More Dodos: How Zoos Help Endangered Wildlife. Nicholas Nirgiotis & Theodore Nirgiotis. LC 95-45972. (J). 1996. 23.95 (0-8225-2856-8, Lerner Publctns) Lerner Pub.

No More Dragons: Feminist Fables, Folktales & Fantasies. Ed. by Susan Sparrow. (Illus.). 160p. 1998. pap. 10.95 (1-55082-207-1, Pub. by Quarry Pr) LPC InBook.

No More Dying: The Conquest of Aging & the Extension of Human Life. Joel Kurtzman & Phillip Gordon. LC 75-32856. 1976. 19.95 (0-87477-055-6) ETC Pubns.

No More Dying Then. Ruth Rendell. 21.95 (0-89190-373-9) Amereon Ltd.

*No **More Dying Then.** Ruth Rendell. LC 98-52546. (Vintage Crime/Black Lizard Series). 203p. 1999. pap. text 11.00 (0-375-70489-2) Vin Bks.

*No **More Dying Then: An Inspector Wexford Mystery.** Ruth Rendell. 224p. 1999. pap. 11.00 (0-679-70489-2) Vin Bks.

No More Excuses: Be the Man God Made You to Be. Tony Evans. LC 96-4894. 288p. 1996. 19.99 (0-89107-896-7) Crossway Bks.

*No **More Excuses: Choose to Be Fit, Healthy, & Happy.** Tawni Gomes. 250p. 2000. 21.95 (1-879706-86-5, Pub. by Paper Chase) LPC InBook.

No More Excuses - A New Approach to Tackling Youth Crime in England & Wales: Command Paper 3809. (Command Papers (All) Ser.: No. 81011068). 1997. 16.00 (0-10-138092-5, HM80925, Pub. by Statnry Office) Bernan Associates.

No More Fear. 2nd ed. Stephen M. Thompson. 144p. 1994. per. 20.95 (0-8403-8201-4) Kendall-Hunt.

*No **More Fleas.** Ann Peutrell. 1999. 7.95 (0-7641-5213-0) Barron.

*No **More Foot Pain: How Can You Fix Your Feet & Knees.** Mary Bakalian. LC 00-90782. (Illus.). 104p. 2000. pap. 19.95 (0-9700183-0-4) Goodfoot.

*No **More Free Markets or Free Beer: The Progressive Era in Nebraska, 1900-1924.** Burton W. Folsom, Jr. LC 98-48919. 208p. 1998. 40.00 (0-7391-0014-9) Lxngtn Bks.

No More Frogs to Kiss. Joline Godfrey. LC 95-9266. (Illus.). 240p. 1995. pap. 12.50 (0-88730-659-4, HarpBusn) HarpInfo.

No More Frogs to Kiss: 99 Ways to Give Economic Power to Girls. Joline Godfrey. (Illus.). 215p. 1998. pap. text 12.00 (0-7881-5347-1) DIANE Pub.

No More Gas. Nordhoff & Hall. 1999. write for info. (0-316-88839-7) Little.

No More Headaches, No More Migraines: A Proven Approach to Preventing Headaches & Migraines. Zuzana Bic & Frances Bic. 134p. 1999. pap. 10.95 (0-89529-924-0, Avery) Penguin Putnam.

*No **More Heartburn.** Sherry A. Rogers. 2000. pap. 15.00 (1-57566-510-7) Kensgtn Pub Corp.

No More Heroes: Madness & Psychiatry in War. Richard A. Gabriel. 1988. pap. 7.95 (0-8090-1539-0) Hill & Wang.

No More Heroines? Russia, Women & the Market. Sue Bridger et al. LC 95-19881. (Women in Politics Ser.). 240p. (C). 1995. pap. 22.99 (0-415-12460-3) Routledge.

No More Heroines? Russia, Women & the Market. Sue Bridger et al. LC 95-19881. (Women in Politics Ser.). 240p. (C). (gr. 13). 1995. 90.00 (0-415-12459-X) Routledge.

No More Homework. Ted Kowalski. (C). 1994. pap. text. write for info. (0-8013-1347-3) Longman.

No More Homework! No More Tests! Kids' Favorite Funny School Poems. Bruce Lansky. LC 97-12729. (Illus.). 80p. (J). (gr. 3-7). 1997. lib. bdg. 8.00 (0-671-57702-6) Litle Simon.

No More Homework! No More Tests! Kids' Favorite Funny School Poems. Ed. by Bruce Lansky. LC 97-12729. (Illus.). (J). 1997. pap. 8.00 (0-88166-290-9) Meadowbrook.

No More Hot Flashes & Other Good News. Penny W. Budoff. 376p. 1989. mass mkt. 5.99 (0-446-35879-7, Pub. by Warner Bks) Little.

No More Hot Flashes...and Even More Good News. Penny W. Budoff. (Illus.). 650p. 1999. mass mkt. 7.50 (0-446-60780-0, Pub. by Warner Bks) Little.

No More Hotels in Paris: How to Find Alternative Accommodations. Cynthia Lynn. LC 98-65293. 140p. 1999. per. 14.95 (1-879899-08-6) Newjoy Pr.

No More Hotels in Rome Vol. 2: How to Find Alternative Accommodations. Cynthia Lynn. 210p. 2000. pap. 14.95 (1-879899-22-1) Newjoy Pr.

No More Hurt. Wendy Deaton & Kendall Johnson. 32p. (J). (gr. 4-6). 1991. pap., student ed. 9.95 (0-89793-083-5); 17.95 (0-89793-085-1) Hunter Hse.

No More Hysterectomies. Vickie G. Hufnagel & Susan K. Golant. 336p. 1989. pap. 13.95 (0-452-26255-0, Plume) Dutton Plume.

*No **More Job Interviews! Self-Employment Strategies for People with Disabilities.** Alice Weiss Doyel. LC 00-23414. 184p. 2000. pap. 29.95 (1-883302-36-6) Trning Res.

No More Kidney Stones. John S. Rodman et al. LC 95-52786. 240p. 1996. pap. 15.95 (0-471-12587-3) Wiley.

No More Kin: Exploring Race, Class, & Gender in Family Networks. Anne R. Roschelle. LC 97-4677. (Understanding Families Ser.: Vol. 8). 272p. 1997. 45.00 (0-7619-0158-2); pap. 21.95 (0-7619-0159-0) Sage.

No More Lack Attacks. Judi James. 7.95 (0-911604-18-9) Wehman.

No More Lies. Dick Gregory. 1993. reprint ed. 41.95 (1-56849-115-8) Buccaneer Bks.

No More Lies about Africa: Here's the Truth from an African. Musamaali Nangoli. LC 86-72151. 210p. (Orig.). (C). 1987. 16.95 (0-940385-01-5); pap. 9.95 (0-940385-03-1) Holly-Star Bks.

No More Litter: How to Train Your Cat to Use the Toilet. Donna McCracken. (Illus.). 64p. (Orig.). 1991. pap. 7.95 (0-9629301-0-5) Purr Pubns.

No More Mac & Cheese: A Bachelor's Guide to Cooking with Ease. William C. Marks. (Illus.). 56p. 1990. ring bd. write for info. (0-9628453-0-2) Marks Pub CA.

No More Magic. Avi. 1997. 10.09 (0-606-11687-7, Pub. by Turtleback) Demco.

No More Masks: An Anthology of Twentieth-Century American Women Poets. rev. ed. Ed. by Florence Howe. LC 92-54843. 560p. 1993. pap. 17.00 (0-06-096517-7, Perennial) HarperTrade.

No More Me & Other Poems. Alain Bosquet & Roger Little. LC 96-102164. 160p. 1995. pap. 15.95 (1-873790-80-5) Dufour.

No More Menopause: A Safe, Tested Way to Prevent the Symptoms of Menopause. Vicki Georges Hufnagel. 256p. 2000. 21.95 (1-55972-538-9) Carol Pub Group.

*No **More Mess.** Ann Braybrooks. (My Feelings Ser.: No. 3). (Illus.). 24p. (J). (ps-3). 1999. 3.29 (0-307-13328-1, 13328, Goldn Books) Gldn Bks Pub Co.

No More Mistakes. James R. Sherman. LC 87-62216. (Do It! Success Ser.). 72p. 1987. pap. 4.95 (0-935538-08-9) Pathway Bks.

No More Mister Nice Guy. Linda R. Wisdom. (Intimate Moments Ser.). 1996. per. 3.99 (0-373-07741-6, 1-07741-1) Silhouette.

*No **More Mr. Nice Guy: The Inside Story of the Original Alice Cooper Group.** Michael Bruce & Billy James. (Illus.). 2000. pap. 17.95 (0-946719-17-9, Pub. by SAF Pub) Interlink Pub.

*No **More Mr. Nice Guy: World's Top Entertainment Publicist Tells his Superstar Clients Exactly What He Thinks of Them.** Keith Altham. (Illus.). 308p. 2000. 14.95 (1-85782-373-7) Blake Publng.

No More Moanin. Ed. by Sue Thrasher & Leah Wise. (Southern Exposure Ser.). (Illus.). 225p. (Orig.). (C). 1974. pap. 3.50 (0-943810-02-7) Inst Southern Studies.

No More Monkeys: A Photographic Version of the Children's Finger Game. Marietta Lynch & Patricia Perry. (Orig.). (J). (ps-3). pap. 2.95 (0-9610962-0-9) M Lynch.

No More Monsters for Me! Peggy Parish. LC 81-47111. (I Can Read Bks.). (Illus.). 64p. (J). (gr. k-3). 1981. lib. bdg. 15.89 (0-06-024658-8) HarpC Child Bks.

No More Monsters for Me! Peggy Parish. (I Can Read Bks.). (Illus.). 64p. (J). (ps-1). 1981. 14.00 (0-06-024657-X) HarpC Child Bks.

No More Monsters for Me! Peggy Parish. LC 81-47111. (I Can Read Bks.). (Illus.). 64p. (J). (ps-3). 1987. pap. 3.95 (0-06-444109-1, HarpTrophy) HarpC Child Bks.

No More Monsters for Me! Peggy Parish. (I Can Read Bks.). (J). (ps-1). 1987. 8.95 (0-606-03049-2, Pub. by Turtleback) Demco.

No More Monsters for Me! abr. ed. Peggy Parish. LC 81-47111. (I Can Read Bks.). 64p. (J). (ps-3). 1991. audio 8.95 (1-55994-353-X, TBC 353X) HarperAudio.

No More Morning Sickness: A Survival Guide for Pregnant Women. Miriam Erick. 192p. (Orig.). 1993. pap. 12.95 (0-452-26983-0, Plume) Dutton Plume.

*No **More Mr. Fat Guy.** J. Slie Savill. 1998. pap. 15.95 (0-09-181672-6, Pub. by Random) Trafalgar.

No More Mr. Nice. Renee Roszel. (Temptation Ser.). 1993. mass mkt. 2.99 (0-373-25568-3, 1-25568-6) Harlequin Bks.

No More Mr. Nice Guy: A Life of Hardball. Dick Williams & Bill Plaschke. (Illus.). 352p. 1990. 19.95 (0-15-166728-4) Harcourt.

No More Myths. Stefanie Schwartz. 256p. 1996. per. 22.95 (0-87605-692-3) Howell Bks.

*No **More Myths.** Stefanie D. Schwartz. LC 00-20337. 2000. 8.99 (0-517-20959-4) Random Hse Value.

No More Nagging, Nit-Picking, & Nudging: A Guide to Motivating, Inspiring, & Influencing Kids Aged 10-18. Jim Wiltens. LC 91-72741. (Illus.). 192p. (Orig.). 1991. pap. 9.95 (0-938525-07-7) Deer Crossing.

*No **More Neck Pain! 9-Step Program for Your Neck, Shoulders & Head.** HEIKE HOFLER. 96p. 1999. pap. text 11.95 (0-8069-5937-1) Sterling.

*No **More Nice.** Amy MacDonald. LC 96-7661. (Illus.). 144p. (gr. 3-7). 1998. mass mkt. 3.99 (0-380-73055-3, Avon Bks) Morrow Avon.

No More Nice. Amy MacDonald. LC 96-7661. (Illus.). 128p. (J). (gr. 3-7). 1996. 14.95 (0-531-09542-8); lib. bdg. 15.99 (0-531-08892-8) Orchard Bks Watts.

No More Nice Girls: Countercultural Essays. Ellen Willis. LC 92-53868. 294p. 1992. pap. 22.95 (0-8195-6284-X, Wesleyan Univ Pr) U Pr of New Eng.

*No **More Parades.** Ford Madox Ford. LC 99-57294. 300p. 1999. 29.95 (1-56000-468-1) Transaction Pubs.

No More Partings: An Examination of Long-Term Foster Family Care. Edith Fein et al. 1990. pap. 9.95 (0-87868-352-6, 3968) Child Welfare.

No More Peanuts. Jo Morris. (C). 1988. 21.00 (0-946088-08-X, Pub. by NCCL) St Mut.

No More Peas, Please! Anne A. Roth. LC 96-32819. (Illus.). (J). 1997. write for info. (1-56763-241-6); pap. write for info. (1-56763-242-4) Ozark Pub.

*No **More Pity Parties: A Guide to Celebrating Your Way Through Life.** June D. Hall. LC 99-45952. 2000. 16.95 (0-9653846-4-0) McGregor Pub.

No More Plastic Jesus: Global Justice & Christian Lifestyle. Adam D. Finnerty. LC 76-13174. 237p. reprint ed. pap. 73.50 (0-7837-5503-1, 204527300005) Bks Demand.

No More Prisons: Urban Life, Homeschooling, Hip-Hop Leadership, The Cool Rich Kids Movement, Community Organizing & Why Philanthropy Is the Greatest Artform of the 21st Century. William Upski Wimsatt. 200p. 1999. pap. 22.00 incl. cd-rom (1-887128-43-3, Pub. by Soft Skull Pr) Consort Bk Sales.

*No **More Prisons: Urban Life, Homeschooling, Hip-Hop Leadership, The Cool Rich Kids Movement, Community Organizing & Why Philanthropy Is the Greatest Artform of the 21st Century.** William Upski Wimsatt. 165p. 2000. pap. 12.00 (1-887128-42-5, Pub. by Soft Skull Pr) SPD-Small Pr Dist.

No More Promises: Slices of Life. Mary C. Winey & William West. LC 89-30717. 220p. (Orig.). 1989. pap. 12.00 (0-317-93116-4); pap. 12.00 (0-9546659-0-2) Cole & Sherwood.

No More Ritalin. Mary A. Block. 144p. 1996. pap. 14.00 (1-57566-126-8, Knsington) Kensgtn Pub Corp.

No More Ritalin. May A. Block. 160p. 1997. pap. 5.99 (1-57566-239-6) Kensgtn Pub Corp.

No More Rules. Suzanne Taylor-Moore. 64p. 1982. pap. 4.95 (0-938758-15-2) MTM Pub Co.

No More Sad Stories Coming. Randy Wright. (J). (gr. 4-7). 1993. pap. 9.95 (0-933905-23-8) Claycomb Pr.

No More Saturday Nights. Norma Klein. (J). 1988. 10.09 (0-606-02121-3, Pub. by Turtleback) Demco.

*No **More School.** (J). 1998. pap. 7.50 (0-7459-3963-5, Pub. by Lion Pubng) Trafalgar.

No More Secondhand Art: Awakening the Artist Within. Peter London. LC 89-42618. 208p. (Orig.). 1989. pap. 14.95 (0-87773-482-8, Pub. by Shambhala Pubns) Random.

No More Secrets. Nina Weinstein. LC 90-20603. 160p. (Orig.). (YA). 1991. pap. 8.95 (1-878067-00-1) Seal Pr WA.

No More Secrets. Linda R. Wisdom. (Intimate Moments Ser.). 1995. per. 3.75 (0-373-07640-1, 1-07640-5) Harlequin Bks.

*No **More Secrets.** Linda R. Wisdom. 2000. mass mkt. 4.50 (0-373-82244-8, 1-82244-4) Harlequin Bks.

No More Secrets. large type ed. Catherine George. (Harlequin Romance Ser.). 1997. 20.95 (0-263-14967-6) Mac Lib Ref.

No More Secrets for Me. Oralee Wachter. (Illus.). 48p. (J). (gr. 1-4). 1984. pap. 8.95 (0-316-91491-6) Little.

No More Secrets for Me: Parent Guide. Oralee Wachter. (J). 1985. write for info. (0-316-91137-2) Little.

No More Separate Spheres. Ed. by Cathy N. Davidson. (Best from American Literature Ser.: Vol. 70, No. 3). 275p. 1998. pap. 12.00 (0-8223-6462-X) Duke.

No More Setasides: Women, Minorities, Business, & Politics. Dolores M. Reed. Ed. by Antoine Polgar. (Inaugural Ser.). (Illus.). 19p. pap. text 5.90 (0-318-20009-0) Inst Political Res.

No More Sheets: The Truth About Sex. Juanita Bynum. 1998. 19.99 (1-56229-148-3) Pneuma Life Pub.

No More Sheets: Wholeness Through Holiness. Juanita Bynum. 1999. 11.99 (1-56229-126-2) Pneuma Life Pub.

No More Sheets - Quote Book. Juanita Bynum. 1998. pap. 6.99 (1-56229-154-8) Pneuma Life Pub.

No More Sheets Devotional: My Accident. Juanita Bynum. 1998. pap. 11.99 (1-56229-149-1) Pneuma Life Pub.

No More Sibling Rivalry: Increasing Harmony by Helping Your Children Become Better Friends. John F. Taylor. LC 95-78001. (Family Power Ser.). (Illus.). 34p. 1992. 4.95 (1-884063-74-8) Mar Co Prods.

No More Silence: An Oral History of the Assassination of President Kennedy. Larry A. Sneed. (Illus.). 627p. 1998. 35.00 (0-9637629-6-6) Three Forks.

*No **More Silence: Testimony & Perspectives of a Holocaust Survivor.** Isadore Gold. 137p. 1999. 22.95 (0-88400-203-9, Shengold Bks) Schreiber Pub.

No More Sleepless Nights. 2nd rev. ed. Peter J. Hauri & Shirley Linde. LC 96-7758. (Illus.). 284p. 1996. pap. 15.95 (0-471-14904-7) Wiley.

No More Snoring: A Proven Program to Conquer Snoring & Sleep Apnea. Victor Hoffstein & Shirley Linde. LC 98-16096. 185p. 1998. pap. 12.95 (0-471-24375-2) Wiley.

No More Social Lynchings. Robert W. Ikard. LC 97-68416. (Illus.). 192p. 1997. 24.95 (1-57736-031-1, Hillsboro Pr) Providence Hse.

No More Someday. Sandy Michel. (Illus.). 1973. pap. 2.00 (0-917178-16-5) Lenape Pub.

No More Sour Grapes. Don Nori. 1999. pap. 12.99 (0-7684-2037-7) Destiny Image.

No More Storms a Comin' Dedicated to Mama. large type ed. Wales Goebel & Janie Buck. Ed. by Clif Cox et al. LC 96-83778. (Illus.). 171p. (Orig.). 1996. pap. 13.95 (0-934530-09-2) Buck Pub.

No More Strangers: One American & Two Russians in a Race Around the World. Steve A. Rahawi. LC 96-90370. (Illus.). vii, 275p. (Orig.). 1997. pap. 14.95 (0-9652565-2-9) World Novels.

*No **More Strangers Now.** DK Publishing Staff. LC 97-47293. (Illus.). 112p. (YA). (gr. 5-9). 2000. pap. text 11.95 (0-7894-2663-3, D K Ink) DK Pub Inc.

No More Strangers Now: Young Voices from a New South Africa. Timothy S. McKee. LC 97-47293. (YA). (gr. 5 up). 1998. 19.95 (0-7894-2524-6) DK Pub Inc.

No More Strangers, Please! Alma J. Yates. LC 93-43954. 258p. (Orig.). (YA). (gr. 7-12). 1994. pap. 6.95 (0-87579-828-4) Deseret Bk.

No More Such Days. large type ed. Emmeline Morrison. 368p. 1985. 27.99 (0-7089-1352-0) Ulverscroft.

No More Sugar: Autobiographical Fiction. Valerie Hannah. Ed. by George H. Herrick. (Orig.). 1987. pap. 6.95 (0-941281-50-7) V H Pub.

No More Tantrums. Diane Mason et al. LC 96-34768. 176p. 1997. pap. 12.95 (0-8092-3070-4, 307040, Contemporary Bks) NTC Contemp Pub Co.

No More Teachers, No More Books: The Commercialization of Canada's Schools. Heather-Jane Robertson. 304p. 1998. 24.95 (0-7710-7575-8) McCland & Stewart.

*No **More Teachers, No More Books: The Commercialization of Canada's Schools.** Heather-Jane Robertson. 360p. 1999. pap. 17.95 (0-7710-7576-6) McClelland & Stewart.

No More Teams. Michael Schrage. 272p. 1995. pap. 15.95 (0-385-47603-5) Doubleday.

No More Tears... Struggles for Land in Mpumalanga, South Africa. Ed. by Richard Levin & Daniel Weiner. LC 96-45355. 300p. 1996. 69.95 (0-86543-508-1); pap. 18.95 (0-86543-509-X) Africa World.

No More Test Anxiety: Effective Steps for Taking Tests & Achieving Better Grades. Ed Newman. LC 95-78584. (Illus.). 172p. (Orig.). (YA). (gr. 9 up). 1996. pap. 17.95 (0-9650930-0-X) Lrning Skills.

*No **More Tithing.** George W. Greene. vi, 93p. 2000. pap. 12.95 (0-9679689-0-9) Nehemiah NE.

No More Tomorrow. Albert Lyon. 232p. mass mkt. 4.99 (1-55197-158-5) Picasso Publ.

No More Tomorrows. Alice LaBianca. LC 90-61382. (Illus.). 426p. 1991. 24.95 (0-9626453-0-3) MCM Entertainment.

No More Tomorrows 'Til Forever: Family Survivors of Homicide Victims' Advocacy from a Christian Perspective. Delia K. Shore. (Illus.). 256p. 1998. 30.00 (0-944551-26-2) Sundance Pr TX.

No More Trumpets & Other Stories. George Milburn. LC 79-134968. (Short Story Index Reprint Ser.). 1977. 20.95 (0-8369-3699-X) Ayer.

No More Us & Them: 100 Ways to Bring Your Youth & Church Together. Group Publishing Staff. LC 99-21489. 110p. 2000. pap. 14.99 (0-7644-2092-5) Group Pub.

No More Vietnams. Richard M. Nixon. 240p. 1986. reprint ed. mass mkt. 4.99 (0-380-70119-7, Avon Bks) Morrow Avon.

No More Wacos: What's Wrong with Federal Law Enforcement & How to Fix It. David B. Kopel. LC 96-37639. (Illus.). 524p. 1997. 26.95 (1-57392-125-4) Prometheus Bks.

No More Walking on Eggshells: Living Successfully with Screw. Elizabeth B. Brown. LC 99-25171. 256p. 1999. pap. 11.99 (0-8007-5708-4) Revell.

No More Water in the Tub! Sequel To: No Jumping on the Bed! Tedd Arnold. (Picture Puffin Ser.). (J). (ps-3). 1998. pap. 5.99 (0-14-056430-6, PuffinBks) Peng Put Young Read.

No More Welfare. Jack Hughes. Ed. by Giulio Minchella. 352p. 1995. pap. 19.95 (0-9648396-2-8) New Amer Pub.

No More Whiskers in the Sink. Colleen Henry & Sue Zeno. LC 98-101667. (Illus.). 220p. 1997. 14.95 (0-9658752-0-2) Granville Moore.

No More Wishy-Washy Watercolor. Margaret M. Martin. LC 98-39799. (Illus.). 128p. 1999. 27.99 (0-89134-876-X, 31183, North Lght Bks) F & W Pubns Inc.

No More Worthy. William Chalmers. 176p. 1996. text 14.95 (0-88982-157-7, Pub. by Oolichan Bks) Genl Dist Srvs.

*No **Mother to Guide Her.** Anita Loos. (Humour Classics Ser.). (Illus.). 224p. 2000. 13.95 (1-85375-366-1, Pub. by Prion) Trafalgar.

*No **Mothers We! Italian Women & Their Revolt Against Maternity.** Alba Amoia. 200p. 2000. 52.00 (0-7618-1717-4); pap. 29.50 (0-7618-1718-2) U Pr of Amer.

No Mountain High Enough: Secrets of Successful African American Women. Dorothy Ehrhart-Morrison. LC 96-44167. 224p. (Orig.). 1997. pap. 14.95 (0-943233-98-4) Conari Press.

No Mountain Too High. Andrea Gabbard. LC 98-7824. 240p. 1998. pap. text 16.00 (1-58005-008-5) Seal Pr WA.

N

No Moving Parts. 3rd ed. Susan S. Deal. Ed. by Orvis C. Burmaster. LC 80-67909. (Ahsahta Press Modern & Contemporary Poets of the West Ser.). 60p. 1980. pap. 6.95 (*0-916272-15-X*) Ahsahta Pr.

No Mystery Cooking Guide. Joe Govea. 50p. 1992. pap. 6.95 (*0-9636368-0-4*) Govea Pub.

No-Nag, No-Guilt: Do-It-Your-Own-Way Guide to Quitting Smoking. Tom Ferguson. 1989. mass mkt. 5.99 (*0-345-35578-4*, Del Rey) Ballantine Pub Grp.

No Name. Wilkie Collins. Ed. & Intro. by Virginia Blain. (Oxford World's Classics Ser.). (Illus.). 780p. 1998. pap. 10.95 (*0-19-283388-X*) OUP.

No Name. Wilkie Collins. (Classics Ser.). 640p. 1995. pap. 12.95 (*0-14-043397-X*, Penguin Classics) Viking Penguin.

No Name see Works of Wilkie Collins

No Name, a Novel. Wilkie Collins. (BCL1-PR English Literature Ser.). 609p. 1992. reprint ed. lib. bdg. 109.00 (*0-7812-7503-2*) Rprt Serv.

No Name Gang: Larry & Stretch. large type ed. Marshall Grover. (Linford Western Library Ser.). 272p. 1997. pap. 16.99 (*0-7089-5088-4*, Linford) Ulverscroft.

No Name in the Street. James Baldwin. 208p. 1986. mass mkt. 6.99 (*0-440-36461-2*, LE) Dell.

No Name, Pt. 2: Incl. the Little Novels: Mr. Cosway & the Landlady; Miss Mina & the Groom see Works of Wilkie Collins

No Nap. Eve Bunting. LC 88-35256. (Illus.). 32p. (J). (ps-1). 1989. 15.95 (*0-89919-813-9*, Clarion Bks) HM.

No Nap. Eve Bunting. (Illus.). 32p. (J). (ps-1). 1996. pap. 5.95 (*0-395-77283-4*, Clarion Bks) HM.

No Nap. Eve Bunting. 1989. 11.15 (*0-606-08834-2*, Pub. by Turtleback) Demco.

No Nation Is an Island: Language, Culture, & National Identity in the Faroe Islands. Tom Nauerby. LC 97-111483. (North Atlantic Studies: Vol. 3). (Illus.). 237p. (C). 1996. 27.00 (*87-983424-5-2*, Pub. by Aarhus Univ Pr) David Brown.

No Nature: New & Selected Poems. Gary Snyder. 1993. pap. 15.00 (*0-679-74252-2*) Pantheon.

***No Naughty Cats: The First Guide to Intelligent Cat Training.** Debra Pirotin. 2000. 7.99 (*0-517-16200-8*) Random Hse Value.

N

No Need for Love. Sandra Marton. 1997. per. 3.50 (*0-373-11880-5*, 1-11880-1) Harlequin Bks.

No Need for Love. large type ed. Sandra Marton. (Harlequin Ser.). 1994. lib. bdg. 19.95 (*0-263-13715-5*) Thorndike Pr.

No Need for Tenchi! Hitoshi Okuda. (Illus.). 184p. 1997. pap. text 15.95 (*1-56931-180-3*, Viz Comics) Viz Commns Inc.

***No Need for Tenchi: Dream a Little Scheme.** Hitoshi Okuda. (No Need for Tenchi Ser.). (Illus.). 176p. 1999. pap. text 15.95 (*1-56931-429-2*, Pub. by Viz Commns Inc) Publishers Group.

No Need for Tenchi: Sword Play. Hitoshi Okuda. (Illus.). 176p. 1998. pap. text 15.95 (*1-56931-254-0*, Viz Comics) Viz Commns Inc.

***No Need for Tenchi! Unreal Genius.** Hitoshi Okuda. (Illus.). 176p. 1999. pap. text 15.95 (*1-56931-365-2*) Viz Commns Inc.

No Need for Tenchi: Samurai Space Opera. Hitoshi Okuda. 1998. pap. text 15.95 (*1-56931-339-3*) Viz Commns Inc.

No Need for Violence. large type ed. Julie Burrows. 288p. 1989. 27.99 (*0-7089-1990-1*) Ulverscroft.

No Need to Be Afraid... First Pelvic Exam: A Handbook for Young Women & Their Mothers. Ellen Curro. (Illus.). 80p. (YA). (gr. 9-12). 1991. pap. text 4.95 (*0-9629417-1-9*) Linking Ed Med.

No Need to Die. Eddie McGee. 1996. pap. 18.95 (*0-901764-41-8*, 93228) P H Crompton.

***No Need to Fear: Overcoming Panic Disorder.** Victoria M. St. Christopher & Koz St. Christopher. 48p. 2000. pap. 10.95 (*1-930693-50-8*) Creative Sol.

***No Need to Fear: Overcoming Panic Disorder.** Victoria M. St. Christopher et al. 48p. 2000. 36.00 incl. audio, VHS (*0-9677405-0-9*) Creative Sol.

***No Need to Knead: Handmade Italian Breads in 90 Minutes.** Suzanne Dunaway. LC 99-24912. (Illus.). 272p. 1999. text 24.95 (*0-7868-6427-3*, Pub. by Hyperion) Time Warner.

No Need to Panic. Donnie Cramer. (Illus.). 170p. (Orig.). 1995. pap. 9.95 (*0-938711-27-X*) Tecolote Pubns.

***No Need to Regret & Nineteen Other Twisted Tales.** Amy Kristoff. LC 00-190434. 335p. 2000. pap. 18.00 (*0-7388-1710-4*) Xlibris Corp.

***No Need to Regret & Nineteen Twisted Tales.** Amy Kristoff. LC 00-190434. 335p. 2000. 25.00 (*0-7388-1709-0*) Xlibris Corp.

No Negatives: A Positive Guide to Successful Leadership. J. Victor McGuire. Ed. by Jan Prado. 130p. (Orig.). (YA). (gr. 9-12). 1989. pap., student ed. 7.95 (*0-685-26846-2*) Spice Life CO.

No Neutral Ground. Joel Carlson. 4.95 (*0-7043-3158-6*, Pub. by Quartet) Charles River Bks.

No Neutral Ground? Abortion Politics in an Age of Absolutes. Karen O'Connor. (Dilemmas in American Politics Ser.). 224p. (C). 1996. pap. 19.00 (*0-8133-1946-3*, Pub. by Westview) HarpC.

No Neutral Ground: Standing by the Values We Prize in Higher Education. Richard B. Young. LC 96-35693. 240p. 1997. 31.95 (*0-7879-0800-2*) Jossey-Bass.

No New Baby: For Children Whose Mommy Miscarries a Baby. Marilyn Gryte. LC 98-46420. (Illus.). 24p. (J). (ps-4). 1988. pap. 4.95 (*1-56123-041-3*, NNBC) Centering Corp.

No New Baby: For Siblings Whose Brother or Sister Dies. Marilyn Gryte. (SPA.). 1988. 4.95 (*1-56123-114-2*) Centering Corp.

No New Jokes: A Novel. Steven Bloom. LC 96-28799. 187p. 1997. 23.00 (*0-393-04047-X*) Norton.

No New Land. M. G. Vassanji. 224p. 1995. pap. 12.95 (*0-7710-8720-9*) McCland & Stewart.

No New Land. M. G. Vassanji. 244p. 1997. reprint ed. pap. 14.99 (*0-7710-8722-5*) McClelland & Stewart.

No New Loan! The Cal-Equity Pactrust. Bill Gatten. 138p. 1998. pap. 16.95 (*0-9663302-0-X*) Cal-Equity.

***No New Pants!** Marcia Leonard. LC 98-52514. (Illus.). 32p. (J). 1999. 16.90 (*0-7613-2063-6*, Copper Beech Bks) Millbrook Pr.

No New Pants! Marcia Leonard. LC 98-52514. (Real Kids Readers Ser.). (Illus.). 32p. (J). (gr. k-1). 1999. pap. 3.99 (*0-7613-2088-1*, Copper Beech Bks) Millbrook Pr.

***No News at Throat Lake.** Lawrence Donegan. LC 99-89574. 250p. 2000. 23.95 (*0-671-78540-0*, PB Hardcover) PB.

***No News Is Bad News.** 2000. write for info. (*0-582-41833-X*) Pearson Educ.

No Next of Kin. Doris M. Disney. 1990. mass mkt. 3.50 (*0-8217-2969-1*, Zebra Kensgtn) Kensgtn Pub Corp.

No Night Is Too Long. Barbara Vine, pseud. 352p. 1996. mass mkt. 5.99 (*0-451-40634-6*, Onyx) NAL.

No Nine Neighborly Tetrahedra Exist. Joseph Zaks. LC 91-11255. (Memoirs of the American Mathematical Society Ser.: No. 447). 106p. 1991. pap. 21.00 (*0-8218-2517-8*, MEMO/91/447C) Am Math.

No-No & the Secret Touch: The Gentle Story of a Little Seal Who Learns to Stay Safe, Say "No" & Tell! unabridged ed. Sherri Patterson et al. (Illus.). 70p. (J). (gr. 1-6). pap. 14.95 incl. audio (*0-9632276-2-9*) Natl Self Esteem.

No, No, Annette. ETR Associates Staff. (Illus.). (YA). (gr. 5 up). 1993. 3.00 (*1-56071-311-9*) ETR Assocs.

No-No Boy. John Okada. LC 79-55834. 176p. 1980. reprint ed. pap. 14.95 (*0-295-95525-2*) U of Wash Pr.

No No, Jo! Kate McMullan. LC 96-34738. (Illus.). 20p. (J). (ps-k). 1998. 9.95 (*0-694-00904-0*) HarpC Child Bks.

No! No! No! Kathy Long. (Illus.). 144p. (Orig.). 1994. pap. 10.95 (*0-399-51845-2*, Perigee Bks) Berkley Pub.

No! No! No! Anne Rockwell. (Illus.). 32p. (J). (ps-1). 1995. mass mkt. 14.00 (*0-02-777782-0*, Mac Bks Young Read) S&S Childrens.

No, No, Titus! see No, Tito, No!

No, No, Titus! see Non, Titus, Non!

No, No, Titus! Claire Masurel. LC 96-44501. (Illus.). 32p. (J). (ps-1). 1997. lib. bdg. 15.88 (*1-55858-726-8*, Pub. by North-South Bks NYC) Chronicle Bks.

***No, No, Titus!** Claire Masurel. LC 96-44501. (Illus.). 32p. (J). (ps-1). 1999. pap. 6.95 (*0-7358-1201-2*, Pub. by North-South Bks NYC) Chronicle Bks.

No! No! Word Bird. Jane Belk Moncure. LC 80-29491. (Word House Words Ser.). (Illus.). 32p. (J). (ps-2). 1981. lib. bdg. 21.36 (*0-89565-161-0*) Childs World.

No-Nonsense Credit: An Insider's Guide to Borrowing Money & Managing Debt. Richard H. Jorgensen. (Illus.). 260p. 1990. 21.95 (*0-8306-3546-7*, 3546) McGraw-Hill Prof.

No-Nonsense Credit Manual: How to Repair Your Credit Profile, Manage Personal Debts & Get the Right Home Loan or Car Lease. Shaun Aghili. LC 97-46356. 160p. 1998. pap. 19.95 (*0-9661164-2-9*) ILS Pub.

No Nonsense Doing Business. Woronoff. 1997. text 21.95 (*0-333-58501-1*, Pub. by Macmillan) St Martin.

No-Nonsense Guide to Achieving ISO 9000 Registration. Robert J. Craig. 200p. 1994. 39.95 (*0-7918-0032-6*, 800326) ASME Pr.

***"No Nonsense" Guide to Doing Business in Japan.** 2nd ed. Jon Woronoff. LC 00-42210. 2000. write for info. (*0-333-80437-6*, Pub. by Macmillan) St Martin.

No Nonsense Guide to Teaching Art. Sara Beggs. (Illus.). 1991. pap. text 11.95 (*0-513-02051-9*) Denison.

No-Nonsense Landlord: Building Wealth with Rental Properties. Richard H. Jorgensen. (Illus.). 208p. 1990. pap. 14.95 (*0-685-46359-1*, Liberty Hse) TAB Bks.

No Nonsense Leadership. John W. Bizzack. 122p. 1993. 28.95 (*0-8062-3956-5*) Autumn Hse KY.

No-Nonsense Management: A General Manager's Primer. Richard S. Sloma. LC 77-80559. 1977. 22.95 (*0-02-929220-4*) Free Pr.

No-Nonsense Marketing: 101 Practical Ways to Win & Keep Customers. Victor H. Prushan. LC 96-42473. 282p. 1997. pap. 19.95 (*0-471-15707-4*) Wiley.

No Nonsense Money Guide, Vol. 1. Don F. Eves. 183p. (Orig.). 1992. pap. 19.95 (*0-9633492-0-1*) PRI Pub.

No-Nonsense Mountain Bike Trail Guide for Flagstaff & Sedona, AZ. (Illus.). 72p. (Orig.). 1997. pap. 6.95 (*1-889450-00-6*) Shook Bk.

***No-Nonsense Nanny: That Special Woman!** Penny Richards. (Special Edition Ser.: No. 1279). 1999. per. 4.25 (*0-373-24279-4*, 1-24279-1) Silhouette.

No-Nonsense Negotiations: A Practical, Easy Method for Getting What You Want. Jack Pachuta. 180p. 1999. pap. 12.95 (*1-888475-09-9*) Mangmt Stratgies.

No-Nonsense Nonsense: Between Mathematics & Logic II. J. Fang. 250p. 1996. pap. 19.50 (*0-912490-24-1*) PAIDEIA & PM.

No-Nonsense Parents' Guide: What You Can Do about Teens & Alcohol, Drugs, Sex, Eating Disorders & Depression. Sheila Fuller & Leigh Rudd. Ed. by Robert F. Fuller. (Illus.). 152p. 1992. pap. 7.95 (*0-9631049-0-X*) Parents Pipeline.

No-Nonsense Parents' Guide, Connecticut Edition see Parents' Pipeline Guide, Connecticut Edition: Plain Talk about Teens & Alcohol, Drugs, Sex, Eating Disorders & Depression

No-Nonsense Principal Handbook for Educators. Alice C. Blair. LC 82-50907. (Illus.). 112p. 1982. 14.50 (*0-941484-02-5*) Urban Res Pr.

No Noose Is Good Noose. Tony Medina. 180p. 1996. pap. 12.00 (*0-86316-109-X*) Writers & Readers.

***No North Sea, the Anglo-German Evangelical Network in the Middle of the 19th Century.** N. M. Railton. (Studies in Christian Mission). 1999. 100.00 (*90-04-11573-0*) Brill Academic Pubs.

No, Not Bloomsbury. Malcolm Bradbury. 384p. 1988. text 46.00 (*0-231-06726-7*) Col U Pr.

No! Not My Child. Peaches Smith. LC 96-33897. (Illus.). 17p. (J). 1996. 12.95 (*1-56763-180-0*); pap. 2.95 (*1-56763-181-9*) Ozark Pub.

No! Not on the Pews. large type ed. Annie Ruth. (Illus.). 20p. (J). (gr. k-3). 1999. 2.50 (*0-9656306-1-7*) A Ruth Creations.

No-Note Miracle Music: Mathematical Music. Peggy Beaman. (Illus.). 100p. 1993. pap. 24.95 (*1-929604-02-5*) Beamans No-Note.

No-Note Miracle Music Bk. 1: Gospel. unabridged ed. Peggy Beaman. (Illus.). 31p. 1987. pap. 10.00 (*1-929604-00-9*) Beamans No-Note.

No-Note Miracle Music Bk. 1: Traditional. Peggy Beaman. (Illus.). 29p. 1987. pap. 10.00 (*1-929604-01-7*) Beamans No-Note.

***No-Nothings & Their Baby.** Anne Mazer. (Illus.). 40p. (J). (ps-3). 2000. 15.95 (*0-590-68049-8*, Apple Classics) Scholastic Inc.

No Nukes: Everyone's Guide to Nuclear Power. Anna Gyorgy. (Illus.). 478p. write for info. (*0-919618-95-2*) Black Rose.

No Nukes: Everyone's Guide to Nuclear Power. Anna Gyorgy et al. (Illus.). 478p. pap. write for info. (*0-919618-94-4*) Black Rose.

No Nukes: Everyone's Guide to Nuclear Power. Anna Gyorgy et al. LC 78-71203. (Illus.). 478p. 1979. 40.00 (*0-89608-007-2*); pap. 10.00 (*0-89608-006-4*) South End Pr.

No Nuts for Me! Aaron Zevy. 1998. pap. text 5.95 (*0-9680678-0-8*) Tumbleweed Pr.

No Objections. Kate Denton. (Romance Ser.). 1993. per. 2.99 (*0-373-03281-1*, 1-03281-2) Harlequin Bks.

No Offense Intended. Barbara Seranella. LC 98-42409. 272p. 1999. 24.00 (*0-06-019212-7*) HarpC.

No Offense Intended. Barbara Seranella. 336p. 1999. mass mkt. 6.99 (*0-06-109724-1*) HarpC.

No Olives Tonight! Vol. 7: A Book about Helping Others. Linda Porter Carlyle. Ed. by Aileen A. Sox. (Child's Steps to Jesus Ser.). (Illus.). 24p. (J). 1993. 7.99 (*0-8163-1124-2*) Pacific Pr Pub Assn.

No One a Neutral: Political Hostage-Taking in the Modern World. Mayer Nudell & Norm Antokol. LC 90-60358. 256p. 1990. pap. 12.95 (*0-939427-78-8*, 09052); boxed set 19.95 (*0-939427-59-1*, 09051) Alpha Pubns OH.

No One but Us. Gregory Spatz. LC 95-18897. 224p. 1995. 17.95 (*1-56512-037-X*, 72037) Algonquin Bks.

No One Can Hear Us: Somali Refugees in Kenya. MN. Advocates for Human Rights Staff. 57p. (Orig.). 1992. pap. 5.00 (*0-614-16436-2*) MN Advocates.

No One Dies in Branson. Kathryn Buckstaff. 1995. mass mkt. 4.99 (*0-312-95425-5*, Pub. by Tor Bks) St Martin.

***No One Else Is Lawrence: A Dozen of D. H. Lawrence's Best Poems with Introduction & Commentary.** Doug Beardsley & Al Purdy. LC 99-216188. 80p. 1998. pap. 14.95 (*1-55017-194-1*) Harbour Pub Co.

No One Else Like Me. Margie Burton et al. Ed. by Susan Evento. (Early Connections Ser.). 16p. (gr. k-2). 1998. pap. 4.25 (*1-892393-69-7*) Benchmark Educ.

***No One Ever Walks Alone.** Mike Francen. Ed. by Rochelle O'Hay. (Illus.). 47p. (YA). (gr. 7). 1999. pap. 5.00 (*1-888079-26-6*, FWO Bks) Francen Wrld.

No One Hears but Him. Taylor Caldwell. 1976. 21.95 (*0-8488-0442-2*) Amereon Ltd.

No One Here Gets Out Alive. Jerry Hopkins & Daniel Sugerman. (Orig.). 1985. mass mkt. 6.99 (*0-446-34268-8*, Pub. by Warner Bks) Little.

No One Here Gets Out Alive. rev. ed. Jerry Hopkins & Danny Sugerman. (Illus.). 432p. (Orig.). 1995. mass mkt. 7.50 (*0-446-60228-0*, Pub. by Warner Bks) Little.

No One Is a Mystery: How to Use the Planets to Understand Anybody. Randall Curtis. LC 99-172726. (Illus.). 242p. 1998. mass mkt. 15.95 (*0-9644459-5-6*) Amrita Pubns.

No One Is Perfect: Just Be the Best That You Can Be see Tena, Joshua, & Friends

No One Is Unemployable: Creative Solutions for Overcoming Barriers to Employment. Debra L. Angel & Elisabeth E. Harney. Ed. by Patricia Harney & Danial Wooley. LC 94-12045. (Illus.). 273p. (Orig.). 1997. pap. 29.95 (*0-9657057-0-6*) WorkNet Training.

No One Knows Their Names: Screenwriters in Hollywood. Jorja Prover. LC 94-70377. 176p. (C). 1994. 37.95 (*0-87972-657-1*); pap. 17.95 (*0-87972-658-X*) Bowling Green Univ Popular Press.

No One Left Behind: The Report of the Twentieth Century Fund Task Force on Retraining America's Workforce. Twentieth Century Fund Staff & Carl E. Van Horn. LC 96-22571. 160p. 1996. 9.95 (*0-87078-390-4*) Century Foundation.

***No One Left to Lie To: The Politics of America's Worst Family.** Christopher Hitchens. 128p. 2000. pap. 10.00 (*1-85984-284-4*, Pub. by Verso) Norton.

No One Left to Lie To: The Triangulations of William Jefferson Clinton. Christopher Hitchens. 122p. 1999. 19.00 (*1-85984-736-6*, Pub. by Verso) Norton.

No One Like a Brother. Hap Gilliland. (Indian Culture Ser.). 32p. 1970. pap. 4.95 (*0-89992-003-9*) Coun India Ed.

***No One Likes Us, We Don't Care: The Myth & Reality of Millwall Fandom.** Garry Robson. (Illus.). 192p. 2000. 65.00 (*1-85973-367-0*, Pub. by Berg Pubs); pap. 19.50 (*1-85973-372-7*, Pub. by Berg Pubs) NYU Pr.

No One May Ever Have the Same Knowledge Again: Letters to Mt. Wilson Observatory, 1915. Ed. by Sarah Simons. (Illus.). 120p. (Orig.). 1993. pap. 9.95 (*0-9647215-0-3*) Mus Jurassic Technol.

No One Need Apply. Bowes. 1987. 27.95 (*0-07-103214-2*) McGraw.

No One Noticed the Cat. Anne McCaffrey. LC 96-22033. 128p. 1996. text 13.95 (*0-451-45578-9*, ROC) NAL.

No One Prepared Me for This. Kathleen V. Nielson. 130p. (Orig.). 1989. pap. 7.95 (*0-317-93837-1*) IHC Home Health.

No One Prepared Me for This. Kathleen V. Nielson. (Orig.). 1991. pap. 9.95 (*0-9622967-0-8*) IHC Home Health.

No One Rides for Free. Larry Beinhart. 240p. 1987. pap. 3.95 (*0-380-70283-5*, Avon Bks) Morrow Avon.

***No One Said a Word.** Paula Varsavsky. Tr. by Anne McLean from SPA. Orig. Title: Nadie Alzaba La Voz. 150p. 2000. 22.95 (*0-86538-099-6*, Pub. by Ontario Rev NJ) Norton.

No One Saw My Pain: Why Teens Kill Themselves. Andrew E. Slaby & Lili F. Garfinkel. 224p. 1996. pap. 13.00 (*0-393-31392-1*) Norton.

No One Sees the Stems. Ruth Yarrow. 24p. 1981. pap. 2.00 (*0-913719-53-6*, High Coo Pr) Brooks Books.

No One Should Have... (Illus.). (J). (ps-2). 1991. pap. 5.10 (*0-8136-5625-7*); lib. bdg. 7.95 (*0-8136-5125-5*) Modern Curr.

No One Stands Alone! In the Fire & Rescue Service. 2nd ed. Jerry E. Smith. 75p. 1993. pap. text, per. 12.95 (*0-9628471-2-7*) Inter Consult Systs.

No One to Play With. rev. ed. Betty B. Osman. 1996. pap. 15.00 (*0-87879-687-8*) Acad Therapy.

No One Told Me: An Honest Look at Ministry. Ed. by Jim Hightower. LC 96-37770. 96p. 1997. pap. 11.00 (*1-57312-153-3*) Smyth & Helwys.

No One Told Me I Could Cry: A Teen's Guide to Hope & Healing after Abortion. Connie Nykiel. LC 95-90855. (Illus.). 85p. (Orig.). (YA). (gr. 7 up). 1997. pap. 8.00 (*1-888231-03-3*) For Teen Moms.

No One Told the Aardvark. Deborah Eaton. 1997. 12.15 (*0-606-13667-3*, Pub. by Turtleback) Demco.

No One Told the Aardvark. Deborah Eaton & Susan Halter. LC 95-20078. (Illus.). (J). 1997. pap. 6.95 (*0-88106-871-3*) Charlesbridge Pub.

No One Took a Country from Me. Jacqueline Frank. LC 81-72095. 64p. 1982. pap. 3.95 (*0-914086-37-5*) Alice James Bks.

No One Walks on My Father's Moon. Chara M. Curtis. LC 95-62447. (Illus.). 32p. (J). (gr. 2 up). 1996. lib. bdg. 16.95 (*0-9649454-1-X*) Voyage Pubng.

No One Was Killed: Documentation & Meditation: Convention Week, Chicago - August, 1968. John Schultz. LC 70-90883. (Illus.). 310p. Date not set. reprint ed. 24.95 (*0-9667557-1-5*) J Schultz Assocs.

***No One Was Turned Away.** Sandra Opdycke. (Illus.). 240p. 2000. pap. 18.95 (*0-19-514059-1*) OUP.

No One Was Turned Away: The Role of Public Hospitals in New York City Since 1900. Sandra Opdycke. LC 98-3753. (Illus.). 264p. 1999. 29.95 (*0-19-511950-9*) OUP.

No One Will Be Immune: And Other Plays & Pieces. David Mamet. LC 95-118215. 1994. pap. 5.25 (*0-8222-1321-4*) Dramatists Play.

No One Will Ever Know. Carl Sommer. LC 96-24344. (Another Sommer-Time Story Ser.). (Illus.). 48p. (J). (ps). 1997. lib. bdg. 14.95 (*1-57537-052-2*) Advance Pub.

No One Will Ever Know. Carl Sommer. LC 96-24344. (Another Sommer-Time Story Ser.). (Illus.). 48p. (J). (ps-4). 1997. 9.95 (*1-57537-006-9*) Advance Pub.

No One Will Marry a Princess with a Tree Growing Out of Her Head: A Musical. Michael Brill. 67p. 1996. pap. 6.50 (*0-87602-348-0*) Anchorage.

No One Writes to the Colonel. Gabriel Garcia Marquez. Tr. by J. S. Bernstein from SPA. LC 68-15977. 176p. 1979. pap. 12.00 (*0-06-090700-2*, CN 700, Perennial) HarperTrade.

***No One You Know: A Collection of Cartoons.** Bruce Eric Kaplan. LC 99-18358. (Illus.). 192p. 1999. pap. 12.95 (*0-684-85919-X*) Simon & Schuster.

No-One's Listening: Mothers, Fathers & Child Sexual Abuse. Joy Trotter. LC 99-231546. 136p. 1999. pap. 25.00 (*1-86177-024-3*, Pub. by Whiting & Birch) Paul & Co Pubs.

***No One's Perfect.** Hirotada Ototake. LC 00-33074. 2000. 19.95 (*4-7700-2500-9*) Kodansha Intl.

No Opera at the Opr'y House: or Too Good to Be True. Tim Kelly. 62p. 1972. pap. 5.25 (*0-87129-159-2*, N19) Dramatic Pub.

No Orchids by Request. large type ed. Essie Summers. 352p. 1986. 15.95 (*0-7089-1475-6*) Ulverscroft.

No Orchids for a Nurse. large type ed. Marjorie Harte. 1990. 27.99 (*0-7089-2219-8*) Ulverscroft.

No Orchids for Andrea! Chrystine Brouillet. Tr. by Linda Gaboriau. (FRE., Illus.). 96p. (J). (gr. 3-7). 1998. pap. 6.95 (*0-921556-62-4*, Pub. by Gynergy-Ragweed) U of Toronto Pr.

No Ordinary Bag of Bones: A Gumpesque Drama by Jonathan Studebaker. Jonathan Studebaker. (Illus.). xii, 234p. 1998. 12.95 (*0-9625847-4-6*) Mango Pubns.

No Ordinary Childhood. Barbara Corbett. LC 94-152972. 169p. 1994. pap. 16.95 (*0-7022-2592-4*, Pub. by Univ Queensland Pr) Intl Spec Bk.

No Ordinary Clam Book: A Cook Book. May H. Davis. LC 83-62033. (Illus.). 103p. 1983. pap. 6.95 (*0-9616663-0-7*) Megan Pubns.

No Ordinary Dog. Mary S. Wilson. (Illus.). 80p. (Orig.). (J). (gr. 3-7). 1996. pap. 7.95 (*0-9650845-0-7*) Wilsons Bks & Gifts.

No Ordinary General: Lt. General Sir Henry Bunbury (1778-1860) Desmond Gregory. LC 98-28164. (Best Soldier Historian Ser.). (Illus.). 144p. 1999. 32.50 (*0-8386-3791-4*) Fairleigh Dickinson.

An Asterisk (*) at the beginning of an entry indicates that the title is appearing for the first time.

No Ordinary Genius: The Illustrated Richard Feynman. Richard Phillips Feynman. Ed. by Christopher Sykes. (Illus.). 272p. 1996. pap. 19.95 (*0-393-31393-X*, Norton Paperbks) Norton.

No Ordinary Joe: The Biography of Joe Paterno. Michael O'Brien. LC 98-19014. 1998. 24.95 (*1-55853-668-X*) Rutledge Hill Pr.

No Ordinary Journey: John Rae, Arctic Explorer 1813-1893. Ian Bunyan et al. (Illus.). 128p. 1993. 65.00 (*0-7735-1106-7*, Pub. by McG-Queens Univ Pr); pap. 24.95 (*0-7735-1107-5*, Pub. by McG-Queens Univ Pr) CUP Services.

No Ordinary Land: Encounters in a Changing Environment. Virginia Beahan & Laura McPhee. (Illus.). 112p. 1998. 53.00 (*0-89381-733-3*) Aperture.

***No Ordinary Life: Parenting the Sexually Abused Child & Adolescent.** Sandra Knauer. LC 99-48414. 188p. 2000. text 39.95 (*0-398-07026-1*) C C Thomas.

***No Ordinary Life: Parenting the Sexually Abused Child & Adolescent.** Sandy Knauer. LC 99-48414. 188p. 2000. pap. text 24.95 (*0-398-07027-X*) C C Thomas.

No Ordinary Lives: A History of Richmond County, North Carolina, 1750-1900. John Hutchinson. LC 98-11034. 1998. write for info. (*1-57864-025-3*) Donning Co.

No Ordinary Love. Monique Gilmore. 304p. 1994. mass mkt. 4.99 (*0-7860-0073-2*, Pinncle Kensgtn) Kensgtn Pub Corp.

No Ordinary Love. Karen Wyman. 204p. 1999. 19.95 (*1-58244-019-0*) Rutledge Bks.

No Ordinary Man. W. Fullerton. 1997. pap. 8.99 (*0-907927-91-2*) Emerald House Group Inc.

No Ordinary Man. Simmons. LC 98-41985. 1999. 30.00 (*0-7862-1688-3*) Thorndike Pr.

No Ordinary Man, Vol. 1. Suzanne Simmons. 1998. 5.99 (*0-312-96495-1*, Pub. by Tor Bks) St Martin.

No Ordinary Man: Judge Forbes & His Library. Allison M. Lockwood. (Illus.). 136p. (Orig.). 1994. pap. 12.95 (*0-9618052-4-2*) Daily Hampshire.

No Ordinary Man: William Francis Quinn, His Role in Hawaii's History. Mary C. Richards. (Illus.). xv, 354p. 1998. pap. 24.95 (*0-9648963-2-X*) Hawaii Educ Assn.

No Ordinary Man (Dangerous Men) Suzanne Brockmann. (Intrigue Ser.). 1996. per. 3.75 (*0-373-22365-X*, 1-22365-0) Harlequin Bks.

No Ordinary Moments: A Peaceful Warrior's Guide to Daily Life. Dan Millman. Ed. by Nancy Carleton. LC 92-9545. 324p. 1992. pap. 12.95 (*0-915811-40-5*) H J Kramer Inc.

No Ordinary Princess. Pamela Morsi. 400p. 1997. mass mkt. 5.99 (*0-380-78643-5*, Avon Bks) Morrow Avon.

No Ordinary Princess. large type ed. Pamela Morsi. LC 98-24001. (Large Print Bks.). 1998. 25.95 (*1-56895-519-7*) Wheeler Pub.

No Ordinary Time: Franklin & Eleanor Roosevelt--The Home Front in World War II. Doris Kearns Goodwin. (Illus.). 768p. 1994. 29.50 (*0-671-64240-5*) S&S Trade.

No Ordinary Time: Franklin & Eleanor Roosevelt--The Home Front in World War II. Doris Kearns Goodwin. (Illus.). 768p. 1995. per. 17.00 (*0-684-80448-4*) S&S Trade Pap.

No Ordinary Time: Franklin & Eleanor Roosevelt--The Home Front in World War II. Doris Kearns Goodwin. (Reading Group Guides Ser.). 1997. pap. 13.00 (*0-684-00448-8*, Touchstone) S&S Trade Pap.

No Ordinary University: The History of a City Set on a Hill. John C. Stevens. Ed. by Charles Marler. LC 98-74874. (Illus.). 564p. 1998. 34.95 (*0-89112-031-9*) Abilene Christ U.

No Ordinary Vitamin: Vitamin E & Health. Ed. by Laura Pawlak & Michelle Albers. 160p. 1999. pap. 15.00 (*1-889549-00-3*) Biomed Genl.

***No Os Entristezcais.** Kenneth Copeland. (SPA.). 32p. 1999. pap. write for info. (*1-58633-008-X*) Libros Intern.

No Other Blue: His First Collection of Poetry. Craig Charles. 64p. pap. 11.95 (*0-14-058797-7*, Pub. by Pnguin Bks Ltd) Trafalgar.

***No Other Book: Selected Essays.** Randall Jarrell. 400p. 2000. pap. 15.00 (*0-06-095638-0*, Perennial) HarperTrade.

No Other Book: Selected Essays. Ed. by Randall Jarrell & Brad Leithauser. LC 98-55353. 400p. 1999. 27.50 (*0-06-118012-2*) HarperTrade.

No Other Business Here: A Haiku Correspondence. Steve Sanfield & John Brandi. 96p. 1999. pap. 12.00 (*1-888809-17-5*, Pub. by La Alameda Pr) SPD-Small Pr Dist.

No Other Doctrine. Cornelius R. Stam. 149p. 1970. pap. 7.50 (*1-893874-21-4*) Berean Bibl Soc.

No Other Gods. 5th rev. ed. Stephen Bell. 26p. Date not set. pap. 3.95 (*1-891050-02-8*) Key Ministries.

No Other Gods: A Defense of Biblical Christianity. Phil Fernandes. 200p. 1998. pap. text 8.95 (*0-9656486-1-3*) Inst of Biblical.

No Other Gods: An Interpretation of the Biblical Myth for a Transbiblical Age. Phyllis B. Moore. (Chiron Monographs: Vol. 6). 208p. (Orig.). 1992. pap. 5.95 (*0-933029-46-2*) Chiron Pubns.

No Other Gods: Emergent Monotheism in Israel. Robert K. Gnuse. (JSOTS Ser.: Vol. 241). 392p. 1997. 85.00 (*1-85075-657-0*, Pub. by Sheffield Acad) CUP Services.

No Other Gods: On Science & American Social Thought. expanded rev. ed. Charles E. Rosenberg. LC 96-51657. 352p. 1997. text 48.50 (*0-8018-5608-6*); pap. text 16.95 (*0-8018-5598-5*) Johns Hopkins.

No Other Gods: On Science & American Social Thought. Charles E. Rosenberg. LC 75-36942. 288p. reprint ed. pap. 89.30 (*0-8357-7882-7*, 203630000002) Bks Demand.

No Other Gods: The Continuing Struggle Against Idolatry. Kenneth Seeskin. Ed. by David Behrman. (Illus.). 1995. 17.95 (*0-87441-583-7*) Behrman.

No Other Help I Know: Sermons on Prayer & Spirituality. Ed. by J. Alfred Smith, Sr. LC 96-35562. 96p. 1996. pap. 13.00 (*0-8170-1251-6*) Judson.

No Other Lamb. Contrib. by Tom Fettke. 1984. 5.99 (*0-685-68633-7*, ME-37) Lillenas.

No Other Law. Florence O'Donoghue. 368p. 1986. reprint ed. pap. 13.95 (*0-947962-12-3*, Pub. by Anvil Books Ltd) Irish Bks Media.

No Other Life. Brian Moore. LC 97-14797. 224p. 1997. pap. 11.95 (*0-452-27878-3*, Plume) Dutton Plume.

No Other Life. large type ed. Brian Moore. LC 93-33308. 277p. 1993. lib. bdg. 22.95 (*0-8161-5897-5*, G K Hall Lrg Type) Mac Lib Ref.

***No Other Love.** Candace Camp. 2001. mass mkt. 6.50 (*1-55166-788-6*, Mira Bks) Harlequin Bks.

No Other Love. Shannon Drake. 1997. mass mkt. 6.50 (*0-614-27702-7*, Avon Bks); mass mkt. 6.50 (*0-380-78137-9*, Avon Bks) Morrow Avon.

No Other Love. large type ed. Lynne Collins. 1991. 27.99 (*0-7089-2427-1*) Ulverscroft.

No Other Man. Shannon Drake. 400p. (Orig.). 1995. mass mkt. 5.99 (*0-380-77171-3*, Avon Bks) Morrow Avon.

No Other Name? A Critical Survey of Christian Attitudes Toward the World Religions. Paul F. Knitter. LC 84-16491. 304p. (Orig.). 1985. pap. 18.00 (*0-88344-347-3*) Orbis Bks.

No Other Path to Go. Radha Burnier. 1985. pap. 5.50 (*81-7059-276-3*, Quest) Theos Pub Hse.

No Other Road to Take: Memoir of Mrs. Nguyen Thi Dinh. Tr. by Mai Van Elliot from VIE. 1976. pap. 10.00 (*0-87727-102-X*, DP 102) Cornell SE Asia.

No Other Standard: Theonomy & Its Critics. Greg L. Bahnsen. LC 91-18274. 345p. 1991. 25.00 (*0-930464-55-9*); pap. 9.95 (*0-930464-56-7*) Inst Christian.

No Other Tribute: Erotic Tales of Women in Submission. 2nd ed. Ed. by Laura Antoniou. 1997. mass mkt. 7.95 (*1-56333-603-0*, Rhinoceros) Masquerade.

No Other Way. Ben DeWitt. 256p. 1999. pap. 10.00 (*0-9665387-0-6*) Oso Pr.

No Other Way. Lasalle R. Vaughn. 296p. 1993. pap. 9.99 (*1-56043-765-0*, Treasure Hse) Destiny Image.

No Other Way: Selected Prose. Charles North. LC 97-46108. 176p. 1998. 22.00 (*1-882413-53-9*); pap. 13.50 (*1-882413-52-0*) Hanging Loose.

No Other Way to Tell It: Dramadoc/Docudrama on Television. Paget. LC 98-164426. 256p. 1998. 69.95 (*0-7190-4532-0*, Pub. by Manchester Univ Pr); pap. 19.95 (*0-7190-4533-9*, Pub. by Manchester Univ Pr) St Martin.

No Other Woman. Shannon Drake. 377p. (Orig.). 1996. mass mkt. 6.50 (*0-380-78136-0*, Avon Bks) Morrow Avon.

No Other World. Robert E. McDonough. (Cleveland Poets Ser.: No. 44). 64p. (Orig.). 1988. pap. 6.00 (*0-914946-72-2*) Cleveland St Univ Poetry Ctr.

No Outcasts: The Public Witness of Edmond L. Browning XXIVth Presiding Bishop of the Episcopal Church. Edmond L. Browning. Ed. by Brian J. Grieves. 228p. (Orig.). 1997. pap. 8.95 (*0-88028-177-4*, 1405) Forward Movement.

No Pain Like This Body. Harold S. Ladoo. (Caribbean Writers Ser.). 141p. (C). 1987. pap. 8.95 (*0-435-98874-3*, 98874) Heinemann.

No Pain, No Gain: Taxes, Productivity, & Economic Gain. Louis A. Ferleger & Jay R. Mandle. LC 92-42839. (Orig.). 1992. pap. 9.95 (*0-87078-346-7*) Century Foundation.

***No Pain, No Gain: Training Journal.** Ed. by Robert Kennedy & Mandy Morgan. (Illus.). 212p. 1999. pap. 10.95 (*1-55210-015-4*, Pub. by MuscleMag Intl) BookWorld.

No Pain, No Strain. Arnold Roth. (Illus.). 1996. pap. 7.95 (*0-614-20785-1*, St Martin Griffin) St Martin.

No Parole Today. Laura Tohe. 47p. 1998. pap. 8.95 (*0-931122-93-7*, Pub. by West End) SPD-Small Pr Dist.

No Part of Marriage! large type ed. Georgia Craig. (Linford Romance Library). 304p. 1993. pap. 16.99 (*0-7089-7330-2*, Linford) Ulverscroft.

***No Particular Destination.** David Hilliard. 512p. 2000. pap. 24.95 (*0-9675612-0-5*) Circuit Ave.

No Particular Place to Go: The Making of a Free High School. Steve Bhaerman & Joel Denker. LC 81-18248. 263p. (Orig.). 1982. pap. 14.95 (*0-8093-1056-2*) S Ill U Pr.

No Particular Place to Go Cycle B: Sermons for the Sundays after Pentecost (Middle Third), First Lesson Texts. Timothy J. Smith. LC 96-4986. (First Lessons Ser.). 77p. (Orig.). 1996. pap. 8.50 (*0-7880-0781-5*) CSS OH.

No Pass No Play Texas' Darkest Day: H. Ross Perot Runs Amok. E. R. Simmons. 275p. 1993. write for info. (*0-9635282-0-3*) E R Simmons.

No Passenger on the River. Tran Van Dinh. LC 88-63579. 107p. (C). 1989. reprint ed. pap. 9.50 (*0-923707-01-8*) Pratt CO.

No Passion Spent: Essays, 1978-1995. George Steiner. LC 96-62289. 448p. (C). 1996. 35.00 (*0-300-06630-9*) Yale U Pr.

No Passion Spent: Essays, 1978-1995. George Steiner. 448p. 1998. pap. 16.00 (*0-300-07440-9*) Yale U Pr.

***No Past--No Present--No Future! An Austrian Jew in the French Resistance.** Dolly Steindling & Haim Avni. LC 99-53812. (Studies & Texts in Jewish History & Culture). 2000. write for info. (*1-883053-53-6*) Univ Pr MD.

No Past, No Present, No Future. Y. Maddy. 1997. pap. 13.95 (*0-435-90522-8*) Heinemann.

No Pat Answers. Eugenia Price. 144p. 1983. reprint ed. pap. 6.95 (*0-310-31331-7*, 16244P) Zondervan.

No Peace for Amelia. Siobhan Parkinson. 224p. (YA). 1997. pap. 7.95 (*0-86278-378-X*, Pub. by OBrien Pr) Irish Amer Bk.

No Peace for the Wicked. large type ed. Peter Chambers. (Linford Mystery Library). 384p. 1998. pap. 17.99 (*0-7089-5220-8*, Linford) Ulverscroft.

No Peace with Napoleon. Armand A. Caulaincourt. Ed. by Jean Hanoteau. Tr. by George Libaire. LC 74-29631. 286p. 1975. reprint ed. lib. bdg. 35.00 (*0-8371-7984-X*, CANP, Greenwood Pr) Greenwood.

No Peeping under the Curtain: Tips & Scripts for School Drama Productions. Dorothy G. Beck. LC 93-40075. (Illus.). 330p. 1994. 39.50 (*0-8108-2545-7*) Scarecrow.

No Perdamos Tambien el Sigl. Carlos Alberto Montaner. (SPA.). 1997. pap. text 17.95 (*84-01-01077-2*, Pub. by Plaza) Lectorum Pubns.

No Permanent City: Stories from Mennonite History & Life. Harry Loewen. LC 92-73439. 224p. (Orig.). 1993. pap. 12.99 (*0-8361-3612-8*) Herald Pr.

No Pets: Stories. Jim Ray Daniels. (Working Lives Ser.). 133p. 1999. pap. 10.95 (*0-933087-54-3*, Pub. by Bottom Dog Pr) SPD-Small Pr Dist.

***No Pets Allowed.** Morgan R. Persun. LC 98-18971. (Illus.). 30p. (J). (ps-4). 1998. pap. 5.49 (*1-57924-077-1*) Bob Jones Univ.

No Pets Allowed! And Other Animal Stories. Highlights for Children Staff. LC 91-77000. (Illus.). 96p. (J). (gr. 3-7). 1992. pap. 3.95 (*1-56397-102-X*) Boyds Mills Pr.

No Physical Evidence. Gus Lee. LC 98-15860. 400p. 1998. 24.95 (*0-449-91139-X*) Fawcett.

No Physical Evidence: A Courtroom Novel. Gus Lee. LC 99-94420. 372p. 2000. mass mkt. 6.99 (*0-8041-1779-9*) Ivy Books.

No Picnic on Mount Kenya. Felice Benuzzi. LC 98-70651. (Adventure Library: No. 16). (Illus.). 240p. 1998. reprint ed. lib. bdg. 32.50 (*1-885283-15-6*) Advent Library.

***No Picnic on Mount Kenya.** Felice Benuzzi. LC 98-50951 . (Illus.). 240p. 1998. reprint ed. pap. 14.95 (*1-55821-876-9*) Lyons Pr.

***No Pidas Sardinas Fuera De Temporada.** Andreu Martin. 1998. pap. text 11.95 (*84-204-4796-X*) Santillana.

No Pine Tree in This Forest Is Perfect. Ellen Goldsmith. Ed. by Margo Stever & Stephanie Strickland. LC 98-129820. (Illus.). 31p. 1997. pap. 8.00 (*0-9624178-7-4*) Slapering Hol.

No Pity: People with Disabilities Forging a New Civil Rights Movement. Joseph P. Shapiro. LC 94-238965. 384p. 1994. pap. 16.00 (*0-8129-2412-6*, Times Bks) Crown Pub Group.

No Place. Kay Haugaard. (Illus.). 140p. (J). (gr. 3-8). 1999. 15.95 (*1-57131-616-7*); pap. 6.95 (*1-57131-617-5*) Milkweed Ed.

No Place but Here: A Teacher's Vocation in a Rural Community. Garret Keizer. LC 96-21989. 184p. 1996. reprint ed. pap. 13.95 (*0-87451-790-7*) U Pr of New Eng.

No Place Called Home. Margaret Woodward. 1997. write for info. (*0-449-91073-3*) Fawcett.

No Place Called Home. Margaret Woodward. 1997. mass mkt. 5.99 (*0-449-15061-5*, GM) Fawcett.

No Place Else: Exploration in Utopian & Dystopian Fiction. Ed. by Eric S. Rabkin et al. LC 83-4265. (Alternatives Ser.). 288p. 1983. 21.95 (*0-8093-1113-5*) S Ill U Pr.

No Place Else to Go: Homeless Mothers & Their Children Living in an Urban Shelter. rev. ed. Sharon R. Liff. LC 95-53203. (Children of Poverty Ser.). (Illus.). 192p. 1996. text 55.00 (*0-8153-2436-7*) Garland.

No Place for a Lady. Joan Smith. 1994. mass mkt. 3.99 (*0-449-22219-5*, Crest) Fawcett.

No Place for a Lady. Vivian Vaughan. 1996. mass mkt. 4.99 (*0-8217-5334-7*, Zebra Kensgtn) Kensgtn Pub Corp.

No Place for a Lady. large type ed. Joan Smith. LC 97-3573. (Large Print Book Ser.). 1997. pap. 23.95 (*1-56895-424-7*) Wheeler Pub.

No Place for a Lady: The Story of Canadian Women Pilots, 1928-1992. Shirley Render. (Illus.). 389p. 1992. 39.95 (*0-9694264-2-9*) Peguis Pubs Ltd.

***No Place for a Nervous Lady.** Ed. by Lucy Frost. 1999. reprint ed. pap. 19.95 (*0-7022-2723-4*, Pub. by Univ Queensland Pr) Intl Spec Bk.

No Place for a Picnic. Justin R. Taylan. LC 94-60516. (Illus.). 208p. 1994. pap. 19.95 (*1-885240-42-2*) Wanpela Bks.

No Place for a Prophet. large type ed. C. Dexter Wise, 3rd. 187p. 1998. pap. 14.95 (*0-9621228-2-3*) Wise Works Inc.

No Place for a Woman: A Life of Senator Margaret Chase Smith. Janann Sherman. LC 99-12901. (Illus.). 298p. 2000. 35.00 (*0-8135-2722-8*) Rutgers U Pr.

No Place for a Woman: Misogyny in the Republican Party. Tanya Melich. 1996. 23.95 (*0-614-15509-6*) Bantam.

***No Place for Amateurs: How Political Consultants Are Reshaping American Democracy.** Dennis W. Johnson. 2001. 75.00 (*0-415-92125-2*); pap. 19.95 (*0-415-92836-2*) Routledge.

No Place for Borders: The HIV AIDS Epidemic & Development in Asia & the Pacific. Doug Porter & Godfrey J. Linge. LC 96-52306. 224p. 1997. text 49.95 (*0-312-17354-7*) St Martin.

No Place for Cal. Jane Morton. 112p. (Orig.). (J). 1989. pap. 2.75 (*0-380-75548-3*, Avon Bks) Morrow Avon.

No Place for Death. Sherry Lewis. 256p. 1996. mass mkt. 5.99 (*0-425-15383-5*, Prime Crime) Berkley Pub.

No Place for Defeat. Daughters of St. Paul Staff. (Encounter Ser.). 96p. (J). (gr. 3-9). 1987. 3.00 (*0-8198-0241-7*); pap. 2.00 (*0-8198-5100-0*) Pauline Bks.

No Place for Fear, Al Lacy & JoAnna Lacy. LC 97-32512. (Hannah of Fort Bridger Ser.: Vol. 3). 300p. 1998. pap. 10.99 (*1-57673-083-2*, Multnomah Fiction) Multnomah Pubs.

No Place for Kids. Alison Lohans. 98p. (J). (gr. 3-5). pap. 4.95 (*1-896184-50-2*) Roussan Pubs.

No Place for Little Boys: Civil War Letters of a Union Soldier. Ed. by Melissa MacCrae & Maureen Bradford. LC 97-94233. (Illus.). v, 119p. 1997. pap. 14.95 (*0-9659377-0-4*) Goddess ME.

No Place for Love. Susanne McCarthy. (Forbidden! Ser.). 1997. per. 3.50 (*0-373-11885-6*, 1-11885-0) Harlequin Bks.

No Place for Love. large type ed. Peggy O'More. (Linford Romance Library). 320p. 1993. pap. 16.99 (*0-7089-7410-4*, Linford) Ulverscroft.

No Place for Memories. Sherry Lewis. 1999. mass mkt. 5.99 (*0-425-16736-4*) Berkley Pub.

No Place for Secrets. Sherry Lewis. 256p. (Orig.). 1995. mass mkt. 4.99 (*0-425-14835-1*, Prime Crime) Berkley Pub.

No Place for Sin. Sherry Lewis. (Fred Vickery Novel Ser.). 1997. mass mkt. 5.99 (*0-425-16113-7*, Prime Crime) Berkley Pub.

No Place for Sovereignty: What's Wrong with Freewill Theism. R. K. Wright. LC 96-2810. 264p. (C). 1996. pap. 17.99 (*0-8308-1881-2*, 1881) InterVarsity.

No Place for Tears. Sherry Lewis. (Orig.). 1997. mass mkt. 5.99 (*0-425-15626-5*, Prime Crime) Berkley Pub.

***No Place for Tears.** large type ed. Phyllis Demaine. 288p. 2000. pap. 18.99 (*0-7089-5649-1*, Linford) Ulverscroft.

No Place for Truth: or What Ever Happened to Evangelical Theory. David Wells. 330p. 1993. pap. 18.00 (*0-8028-0747-X*) Eerdmans.

No Place Left Called Home. James A. Cogswell. LC 82-24215. (Illus.). 139p. 1983. reprint ed. pap. 43.10 (*0-608-01655-1*, 206230700002) Bks Demand.

***No Place Like: And Other Stories.** Robin Malan. LC 00-38950. 2000. pap. write for info. (*0-86543-862-5*) Africa World.

***No Place Like Home.** (Rugrats (tv) Ser.). (J). (ps-3). 2000. per. write for info. (*0-7434-0853-5*) PB.

***No Place Like Home.** Christopher Carrington. 1998. pap. 17.00 (*0-226-09486-3*) U Ch Pr.

No Place Like Home. Margaret Conrad et al. (Illus.). 306p. 1995. pap. 19.95 (*0-88780-066-1*, Pub. by Formac Publ Co) Formac Dist Ltd.

No Place (Like Home) Richard Flood et al. LC 97-664. (Illus.). 144p. (Orig.). 1997. pap. 29.95 (*0-935640-55-X*) Walker Art Ctr.

No Place Like Home. Valerie Tripp. (ESL Theme Links Ser.). (Illus.). (Orig.). 1993. 35.00 (*1-56334-294-4*); audio 10.50 (*1-56334-293-6*) Hampton-Brown.

No Place Like Home. Joyce E. Voelker. (Illus.). 48p. (Orig.). 1993. pap. 3.49 (*0-87227-179-X*, RBP5215) Reg Baptist.

No Place Like Home: As Nursing Homes Profit from Pain, Communities Fight to Reform Them. Ed. & Pref. by Eric R. Bates. (Southern Exposure Ser.). (Illus.). 64p. (Orig.). (C). 1992. pap. 5.00 (*0-943819-54-7*) Inst Southern Studies.

No Place Like Home: Big Book. Valerie Tripp. (Illus.). 24p. (Orig.). (J). (gr. 1-3). 1991. pap. text 29.95 (*1-56334-046-1*) Hampton-Brown.

No Place Like Home: Domesticity, Family Life & Lesbian & Gay Relationships. Christopher Carrington. LC 99-19780. (Worlds of Desire Ser.). 275p. 2000. 27.50 (*0-226-09485-5*) U Ch Pr.

No Place Like Home: Mozambican Refugees Begin Africa's Largest Repatriation. (Issue Papers). 1993. pap. 4.00 (*0-614-25343-8*) US Comm Refugees.

No Place Like Home: Small Book. Valerie Tripp. (ESL Theme Links Ser.). (Illus.). 24p. (Orig.). (J). (gr. 1-3). 1991. pap. text 6.00 (*1-56334-052-6*) Hampton-Brown.

No Place Like Home: Teacher's Guide. (ESL Theme Links Ser.). (Illus.). (Orig.). 1993. teacher ed. 15.00 (*1-56334-343-6*) Hampton-Brown.

No Place Like Home Theme Link, 7 bks., Set. Valerie Tripp. (ESL Theme Links Ser.). (Illus.). (Orig.). 1993. pap., teacher ed. 99.50 incl. audio (*1-56334-295-2*) Hampton-Brown.

No Place Like Home...School. Fugate. 1996. pap. text 6.95 (*1-889700-00-2*) Foun Biblic Res.

No Place Like Lowe's: 50 Years of Retailing for the American Home. Deni McIntyre. LC 96-69933. (Illus.). 160p. 1996. 40.00 (*0-9653801-0-6*) Lowes Cos.

No Place Like Utopia: Modern Architecture & the Company We Kept. Peter Blake. 352p. 1996. pap. 18.95 (*0-393-31503-7*) Norton.

No Place of Grace: Antimodernism & the Transformation of American Culture, 1880-1920. Jackson T. Lears. LC 93-39767. 400p. 1994. pap. text 16.95 (*0-226-46970-0*) U Ch Pr.

No Place of Her Own. Joseph S. Salzburg. 214p. 1971. 7.00 (*0-685-18737-3*) Sovereign MD.

No Place of Safety. Robert Barnard. LC 97-32909. 192p. 1998. 21.50 (*0-684-84503-2*) Scribner.

No Place of Safety. large type ed. Robert Barnard. LC 98-14590. (Basic Ser.). 1998. 26.95 (*0-7862-1452-X*) Thorndike Pr.

No Place to Be: Voices of Homeless Children. Judith Berck. (Illus.). 144p. (J). (gr. 5 up). 1992. 17.00 (*0-395-53350-3*) HM.

No Place to Be a Child: Growing up in a War Zone. James Garbarino et al. LC 98-20012. (Health & Psychology Ser.). 208p. (gr. 7). 1998. reprint ed. pap. 22.95 (*0-7879-4375-4*) Jossey-Bass.

No Place to Cry see Sin Tener a Quien Clamar

No Place to Cry: The Hurt & Healing of Sexual Abuse. Doris Van Stone & Erwin W. Lutzer. 119p. pap. 9.99 (*0-8024-2278-0*, 231) Moody.

***No Place to Fall.** Jonathan Brannen. LC 98-86473. 78p. 1999. pap. 10.00 (*0-9623806-4-4*) SINK Pr.

No Place to Go: The Civil Commitment of Minors. Gary B. Melton et al. LC 97-28085. (Children & the Law Ser.). vii, 228p. 1998. text 45.00 (*0-8032-3095-8*) U of Nebr Pr.

No Place to Hide. Gerry Carroll. LC 94-45923. 432p. 1995. 23.00 (*0-671-86510-2*, PB Hardcover) PB.

N

An Asterisk (*) at the beginning of an entry indicates that the title is appearing for the first time.

No Place to Hide. Kate William. (Sweet Valley High Super Thriller Ser.). (YA). (gr. 7 up). 1988. 8.60 (*0-606-04117-6*, Pub. by Turtleback) Demco.

No Place to Hide: A Novel of the Vietnam War. Gerald Carroll. 1997. per. 6.99 (*0-671-86511-0*) PB.

No Place to Hide: Crisis & Future of American Habitats, 50. Manuel Marti, Jr. LC 83-22762. (Contributions in Sociology Ser.: No. 50). (Illus.). 245p. 1984. 59.95 (*0-313-24271-2*, MNO/, Greenwood Pr) Greenwood.

No Place to Hide: Facing Shame So We Can Find Self-Respect. Michael P. Nichols. LC 95-33135. 366p. 1995. pap. 18.95 (*1-57392-016-9*) Prometheus Bks.

No Place to Hide: The South & Human Rights, 2 vols., Vol. 1 & 2. Ed. by Cal M. Logue. LC 84-1044. 766p. 1984. 40.00 (*0-86554-108-6*, MUP-H101) Mercer Univ Pr.

No Place to Hide, 1946-1984. rev. ed. David Bradley. LC 83-40013. (Illus.). 241p. 1983. reprint ed. pap. 14.95 (*0-87451-275-1*) U Pr of New Eng.

No Place to Live. large type ed. Edward S. Aarons. (Mystery Ser.). 1994. pap. 16.99 (*0-7089-7628-X*, Linford) Ulverscroft.

No Place to Rest: Forced Removals & the Law in South Africa. Christina Murray & Catherine O'Regan. (Contemporary South African Debates Ser.). (Illus.). 256p. 1990. pap. text 15.95 (*0-19-570580-7*, 5164) OUP.

***No Place to Run: The Canadian Corps & Gas Warfare in the First World War.** Tim Cook. (Illus.). 352p. 1999. text 85.00 (*0-7748-0739-3*) UBC Pr.

***No Place to Run: The Canadian Corps & Gas Warfare in the First World War.** Tim Cook. (Illus.). 352p. 2000. pap. 24.95 (*0-7748-0740-7*, Pub. by UBC Pr) U of Wash Pr.

No Place to Shop. Zy Weinberg. 36p. (Orig.). 1995. pap. 10.00 (*1-881360-01-6*) Public Voice.

No Place to Shop: Challenges & Opportunities Facing the Development of Supermarkets in Urban America. Zy Weinberg. (Illus.). 94p. (Orig.). 1996. pap. 20.00 (*1-881360-04-0*) Public Voice.

***No Place to Sit Down.** John O'Flaherty. 2001. pap. 16.95 (*1-57532-230-7*) Press-Tige Pub.

No Place to Stand? Abandoning Monetary Targets: An Evaluation. Thomas J. Courchene. LC 83-136524. 120p. 1983. reprint ed. pap. 37.20 (*0-608-01378-1*, 206212600002) Bks Demand.

No Place Too Far. Robyn Donald. (Presents Ser.: No. 434). 1992. pap. 2.79 (*0-373-11434-6*, 1-11434-7) Harlequin Bks.

No Place Too Far. large type ed. Robyn Donald. 1991. reprint ed. 18.95 (*0-263-12675-7*) Mac Lib Ref.

No Plays of Japan. Arthur Waley. LC 75-28969. (Illus.). 270p. 1976. pap. 14.95 (*0-8048-1198-9*) Tuttle Pubng.

No Plays of Japan: An Anthology. Arthur Waley. LC 97-46053. 288p. 1998. pap. 9.95 (*0-486-40156-1*) Dover.

No Pleasure in Death. large type ed. Pauline Bell. 369p. 1994. pap. 18.99 (*1-85389-498-2*, Dales) Ulverscroft.

No Pockets in a Shroud. Horace McCoy. (Midnight Classics Ser.). 160p. 1998. pap. 11.99 (*1-85242-434-6*) Serpents Tail.

No Pockets in a Shroud. 2nd ed. Maxine E. Thompson. LC 97-200232. 242p. 2000. pap. 13.95 (*0-9647576-1-3*) Black Butterfly Pr.

***No Popery.** Herbert J. Thurston. 336p. 2000. reprint ed. 22.95 (*0-912141-83-2*) Roman Cath Bks.

No Popery & Radicalism: Opposition to Roman Catholic Relief in Scotland, 1778-1782. Robert K. Donovan. (Modern European History Ser.). 384p. 1987. text 15.00 (*0-8240-7804-7*) Garland.

No Post-Easter Slump: Gospel Sermons for Sundays after Pentecost (First Third), Cycle A. Wayne H. Keller. LC 98-9385. 60p. 1998. pap. 6.95 (*0-7880-1253-3*) CSS OH.

***No-Post Easter Slump: Sermons for Sundays after Pentecost.** Wayne H. Keller. (Gospel Ser.). 1998. cd-rom 6.50 (*0-7880-1256-8*) CSS OH.

No Prayer for the Wicked Verses. Vince S. Knight. 16p. 1996. pap. 6.00 (*0-8059-3767-6*) Dorrance.

***No Pretty Pictures: A Child of War.** Anita Lobel. LC 97-48392. (Illus.). 208p. (YA). (gr. 5-9). 1998. 15.95 (*0-688-15935-4*, Grenwillow Bks) HarpC Child Bks.

***No Pretty Pictures: A Child of War.** Anita Lobel. LC 97-48392. (Illus.). 208p. (YA). (gr. 5-9). 2000. mass mkt. 4.99 (*0-380-73285-8*, Avon Bks) Morrow Avon.

No Priest but Love: Excerpts from the Diaries of Anne Lister, 1824- 1828. Ed. by Helena Whitbread. LC 92-29498. (Women's Classics Ser.). (C). 1993. text 45.00 (*0-8147-5076-1*); pap. text 17.50 (*0-8147-5077-X*) NYU Pr.

No, Prime Minister! Ralph Harris Against the Consensus: A Selection of the Shorter Writings of Ralph Harris on the Occasion of his 70th Birthday. Ralph Harris. (IEA Occasional Paper Ser.: No. 94). 112p. 1994. pap. 29.50 (*0-255-36341-9*, Pub. by Inst Economic Affairs) Coronet Bks.

No Privacy for Writing: Shipboard Diaries, 1852-1879. Andrew Hassam. LC 96-102273. 304p. 1996. 39.95 (*0-522-84468-5*, Pub. by Melbourne Univ Pr) Paul & Co Pubs.

No Private Heaven. Faith Baldwin. 1976. reprint ed. lib. bdg. 21.95 (*0-88411-622-0*) Amereon Ltd.

No Problem. Meg Brogan et al. 50p. 1996. pap. 3.50 (*0-87129-683-7*, N43) Dramatic Pub.

No Problem. Eileen Browne. LC 92-53134. (Illus.). 40p. (J). (ps up). 1993. 14.99 (*1-56402-200-5*) Candlewick Pr.

No Problem! Worldwide Travel Tips for Mature Adventures. Janice Kenyon. (Illus.). 176p. (Orig.). 1996. pap. 15.95 (*1-55143-080-0*) Orca Bk Pubs.

No Problem, We'll Fix It. Lyle Weis. 112p. (gr. 3-6). 1996. pap. 4.95 (*0-7736-7297-4*) General Publishing Co.

No Problem, We'll Fix It. Lyle Weis. 112p. (J). (gr. 3-6). 1991. pap. write for info. (*0-614-17728-6*) Stoddart Publ.

No Promise of Love. Lilian Peake. 1994. per. 2.99 (*0-373-11700-0*, 1-11700-1) Harlequin Bks.

No Promise of Love. large type unabridged ed. (Harlequin Ser.). 1994. lib. bdg. 19.95 (*0-263-13898-4*) Mac Lib Ref.

***No Promises in the Wind.** 1999. 9.95 (*1-56137-739-2*) Novel Units.

No Promises in the Wind. Irene Hunt. 223p. (YA). (gr. 7-12). 1981. mass mkt. 4.99 (*0-425-09969-5*) Berkley Pub.

No Promises in the Wind. Irene Hunt. 1986. 10.05 (*0-606-02210-4*, Pub. by Turtleback) Demco.

No Promises in the Wind: A Study Guide. Laura Huerta. Ed. by J. Friedland & R. Kessler. (Novel-Ties Ser.). (J). (gr. 6-8). 1988. pap. text, student ed. 15.95 (*0-88122-120-1*) Lrn Links.

No Provocation. Sophie Weston. (Romance Ser.). 1993. per. 2.89 (*0-373-03262-5*, 1-03262-2) Harlequin Bks.

***No Publishers Needed: An Insider's Guide to Creating a Bestseller.** Joel Hochman & Larry Leichman. LC 99-95112. (Illus.). 224p. 2000. pap. 16.95 (*0-9671636-0-9*) Floating Gallery.

No Puedo Mas y Otros Cuentos. Uva A. Clavijo. LC 88-81562. (Coleccion Caniqui). (SPA.). 98p. (Orig.). 1989. pap. 9.00 (*0-89729-495-5*) Ediciones.

***No Punia Me Ka Lua Ula.** William H. Wilson. (HAW., Illus.). 35p. (J). (gr. 1-3). 1999. pap. 6.95 incl. audio (*1-58191-061-4*) Aha Punana Leo.

No Puppy Food in the Garden Vol. 9: A Book about Trust. Linda Porter Carlyle. Ed. by Aileen Sox. (Child's Steps to Jesus Ser.). (Illus.). 24p. (J). 1994. 7.99 (*0-8163-1181-1*) Pacific Pr Pub Assn.

***No Quarter, 1 vol.** Jack Brennan. 1999. mass mkt. 5.99 (*0-425-17115-9*) Berkley Pub.

No Quarter Asked. Janet Dailey. 1991. mass mkt. 3.50 (*0-373-83233-8*) Harlequin Bks.

No Quarter Given. (Torg Ser.). 12.00 (*0-87431-350-3*, 20578) West End Games.

No Quarter Given. Lindsay McKenna. (Special Ser.: No. 667). 1991. per. 3.25 (*0-373-09667-4*) Silhouette.

No Question: Poems from Hollywood. Mark Dunster. 11p. 1999. pap. 5.00 (*0-89642-650-5*) Linden Pub.

No Question about It God is Building Acmes: Associated Christian Ministries & Educational Serv, 1. Oletha Daniels Brawley. 1998. pap. text 15.95 (*1-887918-15-9*) Brockton Pubng.

No Questions Asked. Ross Thomas. 192p. 1993. mass mkt. 4.99 (*0-446-40180-3*, Pub. by Warner Bks) Little.

No Quick Fix: A Problem-Based Unit. CGE (VanTassel-Baska) Staff. 184p. (C). 1996. per. 32.95 (*0-7872-2846-X*, 41284601) Kendall-Hunt.

No Quick Fix: Rethinking Literacy Programs in America's Elementary Schools. Ed. by Richard Allington & Sean Walmsley. (Language & Literacy Ser.). 288p. (C). 1995. text 44.00 (*0-8077-3389-X*); pap. text 20.95 (*0-8077-3388-1*) Tchrs Coll.

No Quick Fixes: Schools in Difficulty. Ed. by Louise Stoll & Kate Myers. LC 98-124878. 253p. 1997. 89.95 (*0-7507-0714-3*, Falmer Pr); pap. 29.95 (*0-7507-0674-0*, Falmer Pr) Taylor & Francis.

***No Quiero: La Historia De Jonas.** Marilyn Lashbrook. (Libros Yo Tambien! Ser.).Tr. of I Don't Want To. (SPA., Illus.). 32p. (J). (ps-2). 2000. 5.95 (*1-58170-041-5*) Rainbow Studies.

No Quiero Derretirme! Alma F. Ada. (Cuentos para Todo el Ano Ser.). (SPA.). (J). (gr. k-12). pap. 7.95 (*1-56014-229-4*) Santillana.

No Quittin' Sense. C. C. White & Ada M. Holland. (Illus.). 238p. (C). 1995. pap. text 14.95 (*0-292-75508-2*) U of Tex Pr.

No Race of Imitators: Lynn & Her People, an Anthology. Elizabeth H. Cushing. LC 92-73334. 225p. 1992. pap. 18.50 (*1-882162-01-3*) Lynn Hist Soc.

No Rain, No Gain: Growing Through Life's Storms. Susan Lenzkes. 128p. (Orig.). 1995. pap. 10.99 (*0-929239-93-8*) Discovery Hse Pubs.

No Rattling of Sabers: An Anthology of Israeli War Poetry. Tr. by Esther Raizen from ENG. LC 95-83542. (Modern Middle Eastern Literature in Translation Ser.). 200p. (Orig.). 1996. pap. 13.95 (*0-292-77071-5*) U of Tex Pr.

No Reason for Murder. large type ed. E. Radford & M. A. Radford. (Linford Mystery Library). 400p. 1995. pap. 16.99 (*0-7089-7715-4*, Linford) Ulverscroft.

No Reason on Earth. Katharine Haake. LC 86-2004. 200p. 1987. pap. 8.00 (*0-937872-33-4*) Dragon Gate.

No Reason to Die. Eric Hadar. 32p. 1983. pap. 5.00 (*0-942494-76-8*) Coleman Pub.

No Reck'ning Made. Joanne Greenberg. LC 93-10198. 384p. 1995. 23.00 (*0-8050-2579-0*); pap. 12.95 (*0-8050-3849-3*, Owl) H Holt & Co.

No Red Meat. Brenda J. Shriver & Ann Tinsley. LC 89-11632. (Illus.). 320p. (Orig.). 1989. pap. 16.95 (*1-55561-021-8*) Fisher Bks.

No Red Ribbons. John E. Quirk. 1965. 10.00 (*0-8159-6306-8*) Devin.

***No Redeeming Social Merit: A Silly Souffle of Prose, Poems & Punchlines.** 52p. 2000. pap. 10.00i (*0-9621112-5-2*) Hens Teeth.

No Regrets. Mabel Edmund. LC 93-110506. (Black Australian Writers Ser.). 101p. 1992. write for info. (*0-7022-2426-X*, Pub. by Univ Queensland Pr) Intl Spec Bk.

No Regrets. Mildred E. Riley. LC 98-208436. (Indigo Love Stories). 295p. 1998. 15.95 (*1-885478-33-X*, Pub. by Genesis Press) BookWorld.

No Regrets. Joann Ross. 1997. per. 5.99 (*1-55166-282-5*, 1-66282-4, Mira Bks) Harlequin Bks.

No Regrets. Pat Warren. 384p. 1997. mass mkt. 6.50 (*0-446-60387-2*, Pub. by Warner Bks); mass mkt. 175.50 (*0-446-16395-3*) Warner Bks.

No Regrets. large type ed. Fern Kupfer. (General Ser.). 378p. 1990. pap. 13.95 (*0-8161-4947-X*, G K Hall Lrg Type); lib. bdg. 19.95 (*0-8161-4946-1*, G K Hall Lrg Type) Mac Lib Ref.

***No Regrets.** unabridged ed. Mildred E. Riley. 304p. 1999. pap. 8.95 (*1-885478-64-X*) Genesis Press.

***No Regrets: Dr. Ben Reitman & the Women Who Loved Him.** Mecca Reitman Carpenter. LC 97-91152. (Illus.). 212p. 1999. pap. 19.95 (*0-9650584-0-9*) Southside Pr.

No Regrets: Fischer-Spassky. Yasser Seirawan et al. Ed. by Jonathan Berry. (Illus.). vii, 313p. (Orig.). 1992. 34.95 (*1-879479-08-7*); pap. 24.95 (*1-879479-09-5*) ICE WA.

No Regrets: How Home Schooling Earned Me a Master's Degree at Age 16. Alexandra Swann. 141p. (Orig.). 1989. pap. 16.95 (*0-9623611-0-0*) Cygnet Pr.

No Regrets: How I Found My Way Out of Mormonism. Judy Robertson. LC 97-218415. 224p. (Orig.). 1997. pap. 10.99 (*0-89367-222-X*) Light & Life Comm.

No Regrets: Minnesota Women & the Joan Growe Senatorial Campaign. Barbara Stuhler. LC 86-70977. (Orig.). 1986. pap. 7.95 (*0-9616791-0-7*) Braemar Pr.

No Regrets: The Life of Marietta Tree. Caroline Seebohm. LC 97-23370. (Illus.). 512p. 1997. 27.50 (*0-684-81008-5*) Simon & Schuster.

No-Regrets Remodeling: Creating a Comfortable, Healthy Home That Saves Energy. Ed. by Editors of Home Energy Magazine. LC 97-39669. (Illus.). 222p. 1997. pap. 19.95 (*0-9639444-2-8*) Home Energy.

No Relation to the Hotel. David Hilton. (Morning Chapbook Ser.). 20p. (Orig.). 1989. pap. 20.00 (*0-918273-63-3*) Coffee Hse.

No Religion Higher Than Truth: A History of the Theosophical Movement in Russia, 1875-1922. Maria Carlson. LC 92-19451. (Illus.). 304p. (C). 1993. text 49.50 (*0-691-05682-X*, Pub. by Princeton U Pr) Cal Prin Full Svc.

No Religion is an Island: The Nostra Aetate Dialogues. Ed. by Edward W. Bristow. LC 98-38054. xi, 184p. 1998. 35.00 (*0-8232-1824-4*); pap. 18.00 (*0-8232-1825-2*) Fordham.

No Remorse. Bob Stewart. 320p. 1996. mass mkt. 5.99 (*0-7860-0231-X*, Pinncle Kensgtn) Kensgtn Pub Corp.

No Remorse: A Masey Baldridge/Luke Williamson Mystery. James D. Brewer. LC 97-4095. 224p. 1997. 22.95 (*0-8027-3302-6*) Walker & Co.

***No Remorse: The Untold Story of a Parent Killer.** Lori Carangelo. 150p. 2000. pap. 12.95 (*0-942605-13-6*) Access Pr CA.

No Reprieve. large type ed. Susan Napier. 1991. reprint ed. lib. bdg. 18.95 (*0-263-12624-2*) Mac Lib Ref.

No Reproduction. Selma A. Genge. 325p. mass mkt. 5.99 (*1-896329-30-6*) Picasso Publ.

No Reservations Required: A Guide to Dining at Home. Illus. by Marilyn Downs. 256p. 1992. 16.00 (*0-9632850-0-9*) Assist Leag IA.

No Respect: Intellectuals & Popular Culture. Andrew Ross. 288p. 1989. 32.50 (*0-415-90036-0*, A1574) Routledge.

No Respect: Intellectuals & Popular Culture. Andrew Ross. 288p. 1989. pap. 20.99 (*0-415-90037-9*, A1578) Routledge.

***No Rest for the Dove.** Margaret Miles. 336p. 2000. mass mkt. 5.99 (*0-553-57864-2*) Bantam Dell.

No Return. Eugene Lachocki. LC 96-37246. (Illus.). 150p. (Orig.). 1997. pap. 12.50 (*1-877633-35-6*) Luthers.

***No Return Address: A Memoir of Displacement.** Anca Vlasopolos. LC 99-98189. (Illus.). 2000. 24.95 (*0-231-12130-X*) Col U Pr.

***No Rhyme or Meter.** Jadeed Aziz. 2000. write for info. (*1-58235-613-0*) Watermrk Pr.

No Right-of-Way: How Democracy Came to the Oil Patch. Peter Lewington. LC 90-20444. (Illus.). 290p. 1991. reprint ed. pap. 89.90 (*0-608-06875-6*, 206708300009) Bks Demand.

No Right Turn. Elise Title. 1993. per. 2.89 (*0-373-22209-2*, 1-22209-0) Harlequin Bks.

No Right Way. Tracy Orr. 1995. pap. 12.95 (*1-85727-087-8*) LPC InBook.

No Risk Real Estate, Vol. 1. Robert Allen. 39.95 (*0-911505-19-9*) Lifecraft.

No-Risk Society. Yair Aharoni. LC 81-6144. (Chatham House Series on Change in American Politics). 238p. (Orig.). reprint ed. pap. 73.80 (*0-8357-4825-1*, 203776200009) Bks Demand.

No Risks, No Prizes. Emma Darcy. (Presents Ser.). 1993. per. 2.99 (*0-373-11570-9*, 1-11570-8) Harlequin Bks.

No Rival Love. Dwight H. Small. 201p. (Orig.). 1984. pap. 4.95 (*0-87508-495-8*) Chr Lit.

No Road: Bitumen All the Way. Stephen Muecke. LC 97-158779. 249p. 1997. pap. 16.95 (*1-86368-181-7*, Pub. by Fremantle Arts) Intl Spec Bk.

No Road Maps. Margaret P. Allen. LC 93-70617. 1993. 11.95 (*0-8158-0493-8*) Chris Mass.

No Roof but Sky: Poetry of the American West. Jane C. Coleman. LC 90-84811. 74p. (Orig.). 1990. pap. 9.95 (*0-931271-13-4*) Hi Plains Pr.

No Room at the Inn. Linda R. Wisdom. (American Romance Ser.). 1993. per. 3.50 (*0-373-16515-3*, 1-16515-8) Harlequin Bks.

No Room at the Top: Underemployment & Alienation in the Corporation. Beverly Burris. LC 82-18073. 331p. 1983. 65.00 (*0-275-90954-9*, C0954, Praeger Pubs) Greenwood.

No Room for a Dog. Joan K. Nichols. 96p. (Orig.). (J). (gr. 2-4). 1995. pap. 3.50 (*0-380-77973-0*, Avon Bks) Morrow Avon.

No Room for Francie. Maryann MacDonald. LC 94-8596. (Lots of O'Leary's Ser.). (J). 1995. 9.15 (*0-606-09693-0*, Pub. by Turtleback) Demco.

No Room for Francie, No. 2. Maryann MacDonald. LC 94-8596. (Lots of O'Learys Ser.). (Illus.). 64p. (J). (gr. 2-4). 1995. 13.95 (*0-7868-0032-1*, Pub. by Hyprn Child) Little.

No Room for Grace: Pastoral Theology & Dehumanization in the Global Economy. Barbara Rumsheidt. LC 98-28236. 152p. 1998. pap. 18.00 (*0-8028-4547-9*) Eerdmans.

***No Room for Neighbors: A Tale in Which Two Strangers Become Friends.** Kathryn Wheeler. LC 00-22231. (Stories to Grow By Ser.). (Illus.). (J). 2000. write for info. (*1-56822-594-6*, In Celeb) Instruct Fair.

No Room in the Play. Al Attwell & Betty Attwell. 1986. pap. 3.50 (*0-687-28039-7*) Abingdon.

No Room in the Well. Cecil F. Beeler. (Northern Lights Young Novels Ser.). 176p. (J). (gr. 4-9). 1993. pap. 7.95 (*0-88995-099-7*, Pub. by Red Deer) Genl Dist Srvs.

***No Room of Their Own: Gender & Nation in Israeli Women's Fiction.** Yael S. Feldman. LC 99-31641. (Gender & Culture Ser.). 248p. 1999. 47.50 (*0-231-11146-0*); pap. 16.50 (*0-231-11147-9*) Col U Pr.

No Room Save in the Heart: Poetry & Prose on Reverence for Life - Animals, Nature & Humankind. Ann C. Free. LC 86-82187. (Illus.). 138p. (Orig.). 1987. pap. 10.95 (*0-9617225-0-9*) Flying Fox Pr.

No Rooms in Tara & Other Red Clay Stories. Fred Causey. LC 95-73044. 121p. (Orig.). 1996. pap. text 8.95 (*1-884778-13-5*) Old Mountain.

No Rooms of Their Own: Women Writers of Early California, 1849-1869. 2nd ed. Ed. by Ida R. Egli. 1997. pap. 14.95 (*1-890771-01-5*) Heyday Bks.

***No Roosters in This Blue City: Selected Poems.** Cal E. Rollins. LC 99-16675. 1999. 9.95 (*1-890688-24-X*) Kalimat.

No Rootless Flower: An Ecology of Creativity. Frank Barron. Ed. by Mark A. Runco. LC 95-13623. (Perspectives on Creativity Ser.). 416p. 1995. text 75.00 (*1-881303-02-0*); pap. text 26.50 (*1-881303-03-9*) Hampton Pr NJ.

No Roses for Harry see **Harry No Quiere Rosas!**

No Roses for Harry! Gene Zion. LC 58-7752. (Illus.). 32p. (J). (gr. k-3). 1958. 15.95 (*0-06-026890-5*) HarpC Child Bks.

No Roses for Harry. Gene Zion. LC 58-7752. (Trophy Picture Bk.). (Illus.). 32p. (J). (ps-3). 1976. pap. 6.95 (*0-06-443011-1*, HarpTrophy) HarpC Child Bks.

No Roses for Harry. Gene Zion. (J). 1958. 11.15 (*0-606-02796-3*, Pub. by Turtleback) Demco.

No Roses in June. large type ed. Essie Summers. (General Ser.). 400p. 1993. 27.99 (*0-7089-2832-3*) Ulverscroft.

No Royal Road: Luca Pacioli & His Times. R. Emmett Taylor. Ed. by Richard P. Brief. LC 80-1530. (Dimensions of Accounting Theory & Practice Ser.). 1980. reprint ed. lib. bdg. 35.95 (*0-405-13549-1*) Ayer.

No Royal Road to Reconciliation. Gene K. Hoffman. 1995. pap. 4.00 (*0-87574-321-8*) Pendle Hill.

No Rules. Created by Francine Pascal. (Sweet Valley University Ser.: No. 48). (YA). (gr. 7 up). 1999. mass mkt. 3.99 (*0-553-49268-3*) BDD Bks Young Read.

No Rules: 21 Giant Lies about Success & How to Make It Happen Now. Dan S. Kennedy. LC 98-11800. 1998. pap. 12.95 (*0-452-27694-2*, Plume) Dutton Plume.

No Sacrifice Too Great. Barbara Hibschman. (Junior Jaffray Collection: Bk. 7). (Illus.). (Orig.). (J). (gr. k-3). 1993. pap. 3.99 (*0-87509-515-1*) Chr Pubns.

No Sacrifice Too Great. Ruth P. Hutchins. LC 93-70742. (Jaffray Collection of Missionary Portraits: Bk. 7). (Illus.). 208p. 1993. pap. 9.99 (*0-87509-512-7*) Chr Pubns.

No Sacrifice Too Great: The Life of Lewis L. Strauss. Richard Pfau. LC 84-13153. (Illus.). 326p. reprint ed. pap. 101.10 (*0-7837-4368-8*, 204407800012) Bks Demand.

***No Sad Songs.** Christian Hawkes. 46p. 1999. 5.25 (*1-57688-019-2*, 80192) Branch & Vine.

No Safe Haven: Male Violence Against Women at Home, at Work, & in the Community. Mary P. Koss et al. LC 94-15637. 344p. 1994. text 34.95 (*1-55798-237-6*); pap. text 24.95 (*1-55798-244-9*) Am Psychol.

No Safe Haven: Stories of Women in Prison. Lori B. Girshick. LC 98-48852. (Gender, Crime & Law Ser.). 216p. 1999. text 45.00 (*1-55553-373-6*) NE U Pr.

***No Safe Haven: Stories of Women in Prison.** Lori B. Girshick. (Series on Gender, Crime & Law). 216p. 2000. pap. 17.95 (*1-55553-467-8*) NE U Pr.

No Safe Place. Barbara Bretton. (Mira Bks.). 251p. 1995. per. 4.99 (*1-55166-044-X*, 1-66044-8, Mira Bks) Harlequin Bks.

No Safe Place. Richard North Patterson. 1999. mass mkt. 7.99 (*0-345-38612-4*) Ballantine Pub Grp.

No Safe Place. Richard North Patterson. LC 98-14573. 495p. 1998. 25.95 (*0-679-45042-4*) Knopf.

No Safe Place. large type ed. Richard North Patterson. LC 97-51822. 512p. 1998. pap. 25.95 (*0-375-70296-2*) Random.

No Safe Place, Vol. 2. Richard North Patterson. 1999. mass mkt. 7.99 (*0-345-40477-7*) Ballantine Pub Grp.

***No Safe Place: A Husband's Sick Demands Were a Prelude to Murder.** Bill G. Cox. (Pinnacle True Crime Ser.). 2000. mass mkt. 6.50 (*0-7860-1037-1*, Pinncle Kensgtn) Kensgtn Pub Corp.

No Safe Place: The Legacy of Family Violence. Christina Crawford. LC 94-17737. 176p. 1994. 12.95 (*0-88268-184-2*) Station Hill Pr.

No Safe Place: The Legacy of Family Violence. Christina Crawford. 1994. 24.95 (*0-88268-190-7*) Station Hill Pr.

No Safe Place: Toxic Waste, Leukemia & Community Action. Phil Brown & Edwin J. Mikkelsen. 284p. 1997. pap. text 17.95 (*0-520-21248-7*, Pub. by U CA Pr) Cal Prin Full Svc.

An Asterisk (*) at the beginning of an entry indicates that the title is appearing for the first time.

No Safe Place: Violence Against Women. Ed. by Connie Guberman & Margie Wolfe. 160p. reprint ed. pap. 11.95 (*0-88961-098-3*, Pub. by Womens Pr) LPC InBook.

No Safety in Numbers: How the Computer Quantified Everything & Made People Risk-Aversive. Henry Perkinson. Ed. by Lance Strate. (Communication Ser.). 208p. (C). 1996. text 45.00 (*1-57273-062-5*); pap. text 21.95 (*1-57273-063-3*) Hampton Pr NJ.

No! Said Joe. John Prater. LC 91-71828. (J). 1996. 11.19 (*0-606-09694-9*, Pub. by Turtleback) Demco.

No! Said Joe. John Prater. (J). (ps-2). reprint ed. pap. 5.99 (*0-614-15565-7*) Candlewick Pr.

No! Said Joe. John Prater. LC 91-71828. (Illus.). 32p. (J). (ps-3). 1996. reprint ed. pap. 5.99 (*1-56402-847-X*) Candlewick Pr.

No Sale for Haloes. large type ed. Anthony Graham. (General Ser.). 320p. 1993. 27.99 (*0-7089-2806-4*) Ulverscroft.

No Salt Cooking. Story Time Staff. (Alfreda's Recipe Ser.: No. 3). (Illus.). 30p. (Orig.). (YA). (gr. 6 up). 1997. pap. 18.95 (*1-56820-220-2*) Story Time.

*No Salt, Lowest Sodium Cookbook: Delicious Recipes to Combat Congestive Heart Failure & Serious Hypertension.** Donald A. Gazzaniga. 384p. 2000. 27.95 (*0-312-25252-8*, Thomas Dunne) St Martin.

No Salt No Sugar No Fat Cookbook. rev. ed. Jacqueline Williams & Goldie Silverman. (Illus.). 176p. (Orig.). 1993. pap. 8.95 (*1-55867-085-8*, Nitty Gritty Ckbks) Bristol Pub Ent CA.

No Salvation Outside the Church? A Critical Inquiry. Molly T. Marshall. LC 93-10803. 280p. 1993. text 89.95 (*0-7734-2854-2*) E Mellen.

No Sanctuary. Jack Hild. 1986. pap. 2.75 (*0-373-61613-9*) Harlequin Bks.

No Sanctuary. large type ed. Ted Harriott. (Dales Large Print Ser.). 407p. 1997. pap. 18.99 (*1-85389-711-6*) Ulverscroft.

No Sanctuary: The True Story of a Rabbi's Deadly Affair. Michele Samit. LC 92-39498. 1993. 19.95 (*1-55972-182-0*, Birch Ln Pr) Carol Pub Group.

No Satisfaction & the Happy Time: Two Novels. Ed Marsicano. Ed. by Richard Milazzo & Patricia Collins. LC 93-85692. 229p. (Orig.). 1994. pap. 8.95 (*0-9631022-1-4*) Ridgefld Pr.

No-Scalpel Vasectomy: An Illustrated Guide for Surgeons. 2nd ed. Betty Gonzales. LC 96-36490. (Illus.). 59p. 1997. 20.00 (*0-9604536-6-0*) AVSC Int.

*No Scare Science Fair: An Extra Out of the Ordinary Guide to Doing a Science Fair Project.** large type ed. Priscilla Clendenin. LC 94-68976. Orig. Title: So You Have to Do a Science Fair Project.... (Illus.). 67p. (J). (gr. 1-8). 1998. pap. 15.95 (*0-9679713-0-6*) Ribbitt Prodns.

No School for Penelope Pig. Nicole Rubel. LC 97-200931. (Illus.). (J). 1997. pap. 3.50 (*0-8167-4300-2*) Troll Communs.

No Score. Lawrence Block. 1996. lib. bdg. 22.36 (*0-614-16124-X*) G & G Pubng.

No Se lo Digas a Nadie (Don't Say Anything) Jaime Bayly. 1997. pap. 12.95 (*84-322-1503-1*, Pub. by E Seix Barral) Continental Bk.

No Se Permiten Perros. Suzanne Hardin. Tr. by Alberto Romo. (Books for Young Learners).Tr. of No Dogs Allowed. (SPA., Illus.). 12p. (J). (gr. k-2). 1998. pap. text 5.00 (*1-57274-201-1*, A2886) R Owen Pubs.

No Se Puede Dar el Lujo de Tener un Pensamiento Negativo. John-Roger. 614p. 1995. pap. text 8.95 (*0-914829-92-0*) Mandeville LA.

No Sea Reganon. 2nd ed. Ruth Bowdoin. (Bowdoin Method I Ser.). Orig. Title: Instead of Nagging. (SPA., Illus.). 28p. (Orig.). 1991. reprint ed. pap. write for info. (*1-55997-064-2*) Websters Intl.

No Second Chance. Drumbeat Publishing Staff. Date not set. pap. text. write for info. (*0-582-78578-2*, Drumbeat) Longman.

No Second Chance! Disarming the Armed Assailant. Bradley J. Steiner. (Illus.). 176p. 1986. pap. 25.00 (*0-87364-341-0*) Paladin Pr.

No Second Place Winner. Bill Jordan. (Illus.). 114p. 1990. text 14.95 (*0-936279-09-5*) Police Bkshelf.

No Second Place Winner. 2nd ed. Bill Jordan. (SPA., Illus.). 128p. 1990. text 15.95 (*0-936279-10-9*) Police Bkshelf.

No Second Prize. Tom Vaughan. 176p. 1994. 23.95 (*0-233-98837-8*, Pub. by Andre Deutsch) Trafalgar.

No Secrets: Gold Quill Winners Tell All, 1986. International Association of Business Communicator. Ed. by Elizabeth Allan. 125p. (Orig.). 1986. pap. text 35.00 (*0-943372-05-4*) Intl Assn Busn Comm.

No Secrets: Gold Quill Winners Tell All, 1987. International Association of Business Communicato. 1987. pap. text 35.00 (*0-317-64301-0*) Intl Assn Busn Comm.

No Secrets to Success: A Realistic Guide to True Success in Personal & Professional Relationships. Michael V. Wilkins. LC 96-68952. 128p. (Orig.). 1996. pap. 14.95 (*1-57087-261-9*) Prof Pr NC.

No Self to Be Found: The Search for Personal Identity. James Giles. LC 96-49236. 174p. 1997. pap. 26.50 (*0-7618-0668-7*) U Pr of Amer.

No Sense in Mathematics. 2nd rev. ed. Donald P. Skow. 120p. 1987. pap. text 10.00 (*0-911171-02-9*) D & R Ent.

No Sense of Place: The Impact of Electronic Media on Social Behavior. Joshua Meyrowitz. 431p. 1986. pap. text 15.95 (*0-19-504231-X*) OUP.

No Separate Refuge: Culture, Class & Gender on an Anglo-Hispanic Frontier in the American Southwest, 1880-1940. Sarah Deutsch. 368p. (C). 1989. reprint ed. pap. text 23.95 (*0-19-506073-3*) OUP.

No-Sew Drapery. Claira Dobry. 78p. 1986. spiral bd. 19.95 (*0-9615218-9-9*) Dobry Enter.

No Sew Ethnic Wraps, Vol. IV, Bk. 16. Vicki Corona. (Celebrate the Cultures Ser.). (Illus.). 34p. 1989. pap. 14.95 (*1-58513-049-4*) Dance Fantasy.

No-Sew, Low-Sew Interior Decor: Instant Style Using Easy Techniques: Gluing, Stapling, Fusing, Draping, Gathering. Janis Bullis. 128p. 1996. pap. 19.95 (*0-8019-8747-4*) Krause Pubns.

No-Sew Patchwork. Pam Aulson. (Illus.). 1984. pap. 3.00 (*0-9601896-7-X*) Patch As Patch.

*No-Sew Soft Furnishings: Quick & Easy Techniques for Effective Home Furnishings.** Juliet Bawden. LC 99-190256. (Illus.). 128p. 1999. 24.95 (*0-7063-7770-2*, Pub. by WrLock) Sterling.

No-Sew Special Effects. Donna Albert. (Illus.). 128p. 1996. pap. 19.95 (*0-8019-8718-0*) Krause Pubns.

No-Sex Handbook. Pamela Pettler & Amy Heckerling. 1990. mass mkt. 6.95 (*0-446-39054-2*, Pub. by Warner Bks) Little.

No Shades of Gray: A Poetry Art Anthology by Laura. 2nd ed. Illus. by Jacqueline. 40p. 1995. reprint ed. pap. 19.99 (*0-9652362-0-X*) Poetry In Mot.

No Shame in Love. Helen W. Baker. 330p. 1998. pap. 7.98 (*1-57502-672-4*, PO1905) Morris Pubng.

No Shame in My Game: The Working Poor in the Inner City. Katherine S. Newman. LC 98-38244. 400p. 1999. 27.95 (*0-375-40254-3*) Knopf.

*No Shame in My Game: The Working Poor in the Inner City.** Katherine S. Newman. 416p. 2000. pap. 15.00 (*0-375-70379-9*) Vin Bks.

No Shining Armor: The Marines at War in Vietnam. Otto J. Lehrack. LC 91-39414. (Modern War Studies). (Illus.). 400p. 1992. 35.00 (*0-7006-0533-9*); pap. 15.95 (*0-7006-0534-7*) U Pr of KS.

No Shirt, No Shoes...No Problem! Jeff Foxworthy. 256p. (J). 1996. 19.95 (*0-7868-6234-3*, Pub. by Hyperion) Time Warner.

No Shirt, No Shoes...No Problem! Jeff Foxworthy. 384p. (J). 1997. mass mkt. 5.99 (*0-7868-8916-0*, Pub. by Hyperion) Time Warner.

No Shit! There I Was... A Collection of Wild Stories from Wild People, Vol. 1. Ed. by Michael Hodgson. (Illus.). 92p. (Orig.). 1994. pap. 11.95 (*0-934802-97-1*) Globe Pequot.

No Shit! There I Was . . . Again, Vol. 2. Ed. by Michael Hodgson. LC 95-24427. (Illus.). 192p. 1995. pap. 11.95 (*1-57034-031-5*) Globe Pequot.

No Shit! There I Was . . . At Last, Vol. 4. Ed. by Michael Hodgson. LC 97-26962. (No Shit! There I Was ...Ser.). 160p. 1997. pap. 14.95 (*1-57034-075-7*) Globe Pequot.

No Shit! There I Was . . . Gone Wild, Vol. 3. Ed. by Michael Hodgson. (Illus.). 192p. 1996. pap. 11.95 (*1-57034-041-2*) Globe Pequot.

No Shoes! Marie M. Clay. 24p. pap. write for info. (*0-325-00236-3*) Heinemann.

No Shoes, No Shirt, No Trial. Deidra Hair. Ed. by M. Lynne Smith & Laura Pulfer. 134p. 1992. text 20.00 (*0-9633515-0-8*) Symetry Pubns.

No Short Journeys: The Interplay of Cultures in the History & Literature of the Borderlands. Cecil Robinson. LC 91-28170. 148p. 1992. 39.95 (*0-8165-1270-1*) U of Ariz Pr.

No-Sided Professor & Other Tales of Fantasy, Humour, Mystery & Philosophy. Martin Gardner. LC 86-30487. 224p. 1987. 28.95 (*0-87975-390-0*) Prometheus Bks.

No Sidewalks Here: A Pictorial History of Hillsborough, California. Michael Svanevik & Shirley Burgett. LC 99-21199. (Illus.). 120p. 1999. 40.00 (*1-881529-36-3*) Custom & Limited.

No Sign. Sidney Lea. LC 86-19160. (Contemporary Poetry Ser.). 112p. 1987. 14.95 (*0-8203-0916-8*) U of Ga Pr.

No Sign of Murder. Alan Russell. 240p. 1993. mass mkt. 4.99 (*0-380-71656-9*, Avon Bks) Morrow Avon.

No Sign of Murder. Alan Russell. 192p. 1990. 17.95 (*0-8027-5767-7*) Walker & Co.

No Signature. William Bell. 176p. 1995. mass mkt. 4.99 (*0-7704-2706-5*) Bantam.

No Signature. William Bell. 176p. (YA). (gr. 6-10). 1992. text 14.00 (*0-385-25379-6*) Doubleday.

No Silence: A Library Life. William R. Eshelman. LC 96-53095. (Illus.). 328p. 1997. 59.00 (*0-8108-3241-0*) Scarecrow.

No Silent Nights. 2nd ed. O. G. B. Steele. 340p. 1998. reprint ed. pap. 15.00 (*0-9667703-0-7*) Calico Intl.

*No Simple Wilderness: An Elegy for Swift River.** Gail Thomas. 72p. 2000. 16.95 (*1-884540-55-4*); pap. 10.00 (*1-884540-54-6*) Haleys.

No Sin Too Great. Jasmine Cresswell. (Mira Bks.). 408p. 1996. per. 5.99 (*1-55166-147-0*, 1-66147-9, Mira Bks) Harlequin Bks.

*No Single Currency Regime Is Right for All Countries or at All Times.** Jeffrey A. Frankel. LC 99-52719. (Essays in International Finance Ser.: No. 215). 1999. 10.00 (*0-88165-122-2*) Princeton U Int Finan Econ.

No Sink? No Counters? No Problem! One Pot Meals to Get You Through Kitchen Remodeling. Judith E. Sulik. (Illus.). 64p. 1997. pap. 7.95 (*0-9657193-2-4*) Finely Finish.

No Slouch. Tom McDevitt. LC 78-70914. 1979. 8.95 (*0-933046-00-6*) Little Red Hen.

No Small Change: 100 Years of Sutton High Street. Frank Burgess. 1985. pap. 35.00 (*0-907335-09-8*, Pub. by Sutton Libs & Arts) St Mut.

*No Small Courage: A History of Women in the United States.** Nancy F. Cott. (Illus.). 768p. 2000. 35.00 (*0-19-513946-1*) OUP.

No Small Feat: Taking Time for Change. Pearl G. Solomon. LC 95-14404. (Illus.). 216p. 1995. 61.95 (*0-8039-6281-9*); pap. 27.95 (*0-8039-6282-7*) Corwin Pr.

No Small Part: A History of Regional Organizations in American Psychology. Ed. by James L. Pate et al. LC 93-37085. 227p. 1993. text 29.95 (*1-55798-215-5*) Am Psychol.

No Small Wonder: Stories of Hope from the Nativity, Vol. 1.3. Virginia Wiles. (Good Ground Ser.: No. 1, Pt. 3). 43p. 1998. pap. 5.95 (*0-87303-353-1*) Faith & Life.

No Smile Cookies Today. Kathy K. Tapp. (Illus.). iii, 15p. (J). (ps-6). 1998. pap. 3.50 (*1-892254-00-X*) Preg & Infant.

*No Smoke.** 2nd ed. Vincent Ferrini. 112p. 1999. pap. 14.95 (*1-892839-04-0*) Curious Traveller Pr.

No Smoking. Illus. by Toni Goffe. LC 92-10848. 32p. (J). 1992. 5.99 (*0-85953-368-9*); pap. 3.99 (*0-85953-369-7*) Childs Play.

No Smoking. Michael Twinn. (J). 1996. lib. bdg. 11.95 (*0-85953-848-6*) Childs Play.

No Smoking: The Ethical Issues. Robert E. Goodin. 176p. 1994. lib. bdg. 25.95 (*0-226-30300-4*) U Ch Pr.

No Smoking: The Ethical Issues. Robert E. Goodin. 172p. 1999. pap. text 12.00 (*0-226-30301-2*) U Ch Pr.

No Smoking Book: How to Quit Permanently. 2nd ed. Isabel Gilbert. (Illus.). 104p. (Orig.). 1986. reprint ed. pap. 8.95 (*0-930298-25-X*) Westwood Pub Co.

No Soap Radio. Peter Ganick. 264p. (Orig.). 1994. pap. 13.50 (*0-9628456-5-5*) Drogue Pr.

No Sorrow Like Our Sorrow: Northern Protestant Ministers & the Assassination of Lincoln. David B. Chesebrough. LC 93-31508. (Illus.). 224p. 1994. 24.00 (*0-87338-491-1*) Kent St U Pr.

No Spark of Malice: The Murder of Martin Begnaud. William Arceneaux. LC 99-15677. (Illus.). 360p. 1999. 34.95 (*0-8071-2447-8*) La State U Pr.

No Sparrow Shall Fall: Leaving the Convent after Forty-Five Years Under Vows. Mary K. O'Rourke. (Illus.). 192p. 1988. 17.95 (*0-941974-10-3*) Baranski Pub Co.

No Standing Armies: The Antiarmy Ideology in Seventeenth-Century England. Lois G. Schwoerer. LC 73-19337. (Illus.). 224p. 1974. reprint ed. pap. 69.50 (*0-608-07391-1*, 206761800009) Bks Demand.

No Stars to Guide. Adrian Seligman. 336p. (Orig.). 1997. pap. 22.95 (*0-7509-1637-0*, Pub. by Sutton Pub Ltd) Intl Pubs Mktg.

No State in Earth. Murray, Keith, Publishing Staff. (C). 1990. pap. 55.00 (*1-870978-26-9*) St Mut.

No State Shall Abridge: The Fourteenth Amendment & the Bill of Rights. Michael K. Curtis. LC 86-6309. xii, 276p. 1990. text 49.95 (*0-8223-0599-2*) Duke.

No State Shall Abridge: The Fourteenth Amendment & the Bill of Rights. Michael K. Curtis. LC 86-6309. xii, 276p. (C). 1990. reprint ed. pap. text 19.95 (*0-8223-1035-X*) Duke.

*No Static: A Guide to Creative Radio Programming.** Quincy McCoy. 273p. 1999. 39.95 (*0-87930-594-0*) Miller Freeman.

No Stone Unturned. large type ed. Patricia Robins. 280p. 1989. pap. 12.95 (*0-8161-4438-9*, G K Hall Lrg Type) Mac Lib Ref.

No Stone Unturned: Saving Outdoor Sculpture. David Ruell. 34p. 1994. pap. write for info. (*0-9643014-0-7*) NH Pres Alliance.

No Stone Unturned & Under Earth. Peters. 2000. 51.00 (*0-7167-3133-9*) W H Freeman.

No Stoppin' Sense. Rebera E. Foston. 96p. 1993. pap. text 16.00 (*0-9641709-1-4*) Foston Adolescent.

No Strange Fire. Ted Wojtasik. LC 96-1197. 400p. (Orig.). 1996. pap. 14.99 (*0-8361-9041-6*) Herald Pr.

No Stranger. Stella Cameron. 1993. per. 5.50 (*0-373-20091-9*, 1-20091-4) Harlequin Bks.

No Stranger to My Heart. Janet Hopkins. 2000. pap. 14.95 (*0-9670967-1-5*) Heartfelt Pr CO.

No Strangers Here: A Simplified Guide to Travel in Newfoundland. Arthur Sullivan. (Illus.). 128p. 1995. pap. 6.95 (*1-895387-54-X*) Creative Bk Pub.

No Strangers to God. Julie A. Gorman. (Groupbuilders Series for Adults). 144p. 1991. pap. 6.50 (*0-89693-018-1*, 6-1018, Victor Bks) Chariot Victor.

No Streets of Gold: A Social History of Ukrainians in Alberta. Helen Potrebenko. 312p. 1977. pap. 9.95 (*0-919888-69-0*, Pub. by New Star Bks) Genl Dist Srvs.

No Strength Without Union: An Illustrated History of Ohio Workers, 1803-1980. Raymond Boryczka & Lorin L. Cary. (Illus.). 328p. 19.95 (*0-318-00987-0*) Ohio Hist Soc.

*No-Stress Guide to the MCAS 8th Grade Tests.** Kaplan Staff. 112p. 2000. pap. 8.00 (*0-684-87088-6*) Free Pr.

No-Strike Agreements & Pendulum Arbitration. Giles Burrows. Ed. by IPM Information & Advisory Services Staff. 112p. (C). 1986. 38.00 (*0-85292-388-0*) St Mut.

No Strings see Sin Ataduras: The You-Can't-Make-Me Bride

No Strings. (Vocal Score Ser.). 192p. 1981. pap. 40.00 (*0-88188-038-8*, 00312281) H Leonard.

No Strings: Vocal Selections. (Illus.). 32p. 1981. pap. 8.95 (*0-88188-098-1*, 00312280) H Leonard.

*No Strings Attached.** Judy Gill. 400p. 2000. pap. 5.99 (*0-505-52366-3*, Love Spell) Dorchester Pub Co.

No Strings Attached. Maris Soule. (Romance Ser.). 1993. per. 2.75 (*0-373-08965-1*, 5-08965-1) Silhouette.

No Strings Attached: The Inside Story of Jim Henson's Creature Factory. Matt Bacon. LC 97-23622. 192p. 1997. 35.00 (*0-02-862008-9*) Macmillan.

*No Strings Attached: Untangling the Risks of Fundraising & Collaborations.** Melanie L. Herman & Dennis M. Kirschbaum. 95p. 1999. pap. 15.00 (*1-893210-04-9*) Nonprof Risk Mgmt Ctr.

No Strings Attached Grant Program. Marjorie Beggs. 36p. (Orig.). 1995. pap. 5.00 (*0-936434-86-4*, Pub. by Zellerbach Fam Fund) Intl Spec Bk.

No Substitute for Persevering. Reuben Welch. 1983. pap. 4.95 (*0-310-70311-5*) Zondervan.

No Substitute for Quality: The Many Worlds of Lawrence A. Fleischman. Barbara G. Fleischman. (Illus.). 104p. 1995. write for info. (*0-944641-08-3*) Greenwich Pub Group.

No Substitutions see Strange Matter

No Success Like Failure: The American Love of Self-Destruction, Self-Aggrandizement, & Breaking Even. Ivan Solotaroff. LC 94-2092. 233p. 1994. pap. 12.95 (*1-878818-31-7*, Pub. by Sheep Meadow); text 25.00 (*1-878818-32-5*, Pub. by Sheep Meadow) U Pr of New Eng.

No Such Country. Gary Crew. LC 93-17619. 192p. (J). (gr. 5-9). 1994. pap. 15.00 (*0-671-79760-3*) S&S Bks Yung.

No Such Thing. Jackie Koller. LC 96-83929. (Illus.). 32p. (J). (ps-3). 1997. 14.95 (*1-56397-490-8*) Boyds Mills Pr.

*No Such Thing as a Bad Day: A Memoir.** Hamilton Jordan. LC 99-68571. 224p. 2000. 22.00 (*1-56352-578-X*) Longstreet.

No Such Thing As a Bad Kid: Understanding & Responding to the Challenging Behavior of Troubled Children & Youth. Charles D. Appelstein. LC 97-74764. 304p. 1998. pap. 19.95 (*0-9659836-0-9*) Gifford Schl.

No Such Thing As Doomsday: How to Prepare for Y2K, Earth Changes, War & Other Threats. Philip L. Hoag. LC 96-90037. (Illus.). 326p. 1996. pap. 29.95 (*1-888865-01-6*) Yellowstone Riv.

*No Such Thing As Over the Hill.** James Kok. 96p. 2000. pap. 7.75 (*1-56212-545-1*, 151350) CRC Pubns.

No Such Thing As Strangers. David S. Bloch. (Illus.). 32p. 1993. pap. 5.95 (*1-882817-02-8*) J Bloch.

No Such Things, 001. Bill Peet. LC 82-23234. (Illus.). 32p. (J). (gr. k-3). 1983. 16.00 (*0-395-33888-3*) HM.

No Such Things, 001. Bill Peet. LC 82-23234. (Illus.). 32p. (J). (gr. k-3). 1985. pap. 7.95 (*0-395-39594-1*) HM.

No Such Things. Bill Peet. (J). 1983. 12.15 (*0-606-04490-6*, Pub. by Turtleback) Demco.

No Sugar: Low Fat Recipes. unabridged ed. Darryl J. Zion. Orig. Title: Busting Sugar. 114p. 1998. pap. 16.95 (*0-9662150-0-1*) C Z Pub.

No Sugar Added: or Redesigning Our Children's Future. Nicholas Krilanovich. (Illus.). 300p. (Orig.). 1982. 14.00 (*0-941098-00-1*) November Bks.

No Summers - No Holidays - No Weekends. unabridged ed. Mel C. Thompson. (Mel C. Thompson's Collected Works: Vol. 12). 112p. 1998. pap. 5.00 (*1-879665-24-7*) Cyborg Prods.

No Sun in My Palace. Jake L. Varela. LC 88-90863. 213p. (Orig.). 1988. pap. 9.95 (*0-9620680-0-4*) Opa Pubns.

*No Sunshine without Shadow.** Paula Lindsay. 392p. 2000. 18.99 (*0-7089-5698-X*) Ulverscroft.

No Surprises: Controlling Risks in Volunteer Programs. Charles Tremper & Gwynne Kostin. 60p. 1993. pap. 9.95 (*0-9637120-0-4*) Nonprof Risk Mgmt Ctr.

No Surprises: Two Decades of Clinton - Watching. Paul Greenberg. 324p. 1996. 23.95 (*1-57488-005-5*) Brasseys.

*No Surprises Project Management: A Proven Early Warning System for Staying on Track.** Timm J. Esque. LC 99-66687. (Illus.). 259p. 1999. 44.95 (*1-882939-05-0*); pap. 34.95 (*1-882939-04-2*) ACT Pub.

No Surrender. Joe Cardillo. LC 93-85853. (Orig.). (YA). 1993. pap. 11.95 (*0-9624082-1-2*) Stone Buzzard.

No Surrender. large type ed. Mary Lyons. 215p. 1992. 11.50 (*0-7505-0313-0*, Pub. by Mgna Lrg Print) Ulverscroft.

No Surrender: An Ulster Childhood, Vol. 1. 3rd ed. Robert Harbinson. 220p. 1993. reprint ed. pap. 11.95 (*0-85640-383-0*, Pub. by Blackstaff Pr) Dufour.

No Surrender: Expectantly Yours. Lindsay Longford. (Intimate Moments Ser.: No. 947). 1999. per. 4.25 (*0-373-07947-8*, 1-07947-4) Silhouette.

*No Surrender: My Thirty-Year War.** Hiroo Onoda. LC 99-23484. 1999. pap. 15.95 (*1-55750-663-9*) Naval Inst Pr.

No Surrender: Reflections of a Tory Warrior. Hugh Segal. 1998. pap. 14.50 (*0-00-638635-0*) HarpC.

No Surrender No Retreat. Gill. LC 99-89782. 1999. text. write for info. (*0-312-21757-9*) St Martin.

No Survivors. Will Henry, pseud. LC 95-39311. (Illus.). v, 345p. 1996. pap. 12.00 (*0-8032-7282-0*, Bison Books) U of Nebr Pr.

No Swank. Sherwood Anderson. LC 70-105302. (Illus.). 130p. 1970. reprint ed. 12.50 (*0-911858-06-7*) Appel.

No Sweat: Fashion, Free Trade & the Rights of Garment Workers. Andrew Ross. LC 97-31601. (C). 1997. 65.00 (*1-85984-866-4*, Pub. by Verso) Norton.

No Sweat: Fashion, Free Trade & the Rights of Workers. Andrew Ross. LC 97-31601. (Illus.). 313p. 1997. pap. 20.00 (*1-85984-172-4*, Pub. by Verso) Norton.

No Sweat! How to Use Your Learning Style to Be a Better Student. Cindy U. Tobias & Pat B. Guild. Ed. by Dorothy Craig. (Illus.). 52p. (YA). (gr. 8-12). 1986. student ed. 5.95 (*0-9621619-0-X*) P Guild Assocs.

No Sweeter Conflict. Megan Paul. (Scarlet Ser.). 1998. mass mkt. 3.99 (*1-85487-999-5*, Pub. by Scarlet Bks) London Brdge.

No Sweeter Wine. Anita Mills. 1999. mass mkt. 5.99 (*0-451-40770-9*, Topaz) NAL.

No Sweetness Here & Other Stories. Ama Ata Aidoo. LC 95-18346. 170p. 1998. reprint ed. pap. 10.95 (*1-55861-119-3*) Feminist Pr.

No Symbols Where None Intended: Samuel Beckett at the Harry Ransom Humanities Research Center. Carlton Lake. (Illus.). 185p. 1984. 20.00 (*0-87959-101-3*) U of Tex H Ransom Ctr.

No System. Vinca Petersen. 1999. pap. text 19.95 (*3-88243-645-X*) Steidl.

No-Talk Therapy for Children & Adolescents. Martha B. Straus. LC 98-44978. 242p. 1999. 27.00 (*0-393-70286-3*) Norton.

*No Taxation Through Litigation.** Peter J. Ferrara. 1999. pap. write for info. (*1-57655-181-4*) Independ Inst.

N

An Asterisk (*) at the beginning of an entry indicates that the title is appearing for the first time.

***No Taxation Through Litigation.** Peter J. Ferrara. 17p. 1999. lib. bdg. 10.00 (*1-886306-36-2*) Nevada Policy.

***No Te Ahogues En Un Vaso De Agua.** Richard Carlson. 1998. pap. 22.95 (*84-253-3199-4*) Distribks Inc.

No Te Dejare Hasta Que Seas Perfecto. Luis Palau.Tr. of Peter Promise. (SPA.). 1997. pap. 7.99 (*0-88113-453-8*) Caribe Betania.

***No Te Preocupes, Gana Dinero: Los Metodos Mas Practicos de Crear Abundancia y Alegria en su Vida.** Richard Carlson. (SPA.). 1998. pap. 22.95 (*84-253-3247-8*) Distribks Inc.

No Tears for Mao. Tr. by Peter Amann & Enne Amann. 279p. 1995. 22.95 (*0-89733-410-8*) Academy Chi Pubs.

***No Tears in Ireland: A Memoir.** Sylvia Couturie. 2001. 24.00 (*0-7432-0193-0*) Free Pr.

***No Tears to the Gallows: The Strange Case of Frank McCullough.** Mark David Johnson. (Illus.). 240p. 2000. 25.95 (*0-7710-4417-8*) McCland & Stewart.

No Telephone to Heaven. Cliff. 1995. pap. 8.95 (*0-07-546059-9*) McGraw.

No Telephone to Heaven. Michelle Cliff. 224p. 1996. pap. 12.95 (*0-452-27569-5*, Plume) Dutton Plume.

No Temas! 2nd rev. ed. Stephen Bell.Tr. of Fear Not!. (ENG & SPA.). 12p. 1995. pap. 3.50 (*1-891050-04-4*) Key Ministries.

No Temas a la Tormenta. Tim F. LaHaye.Tr. of No Fear of the Storm. (SPA.). 260p. 1992. pap. 7.99 (*1-56063-708-0*, 498554) Editorial Unilit.

No Testimony Without a Test. Arletha F. Boykin. 99p. 1997. pap. 12.99 (*0-9649172-1-1*) Always Finding.

***No Thank You, I'm 1662.** Jim Cotter & Stuart Yerrell. 1999. pap. 22.00 (*0-85305-458-4*, Pub. by Arthur James) St Mut.

No Thanks. E. E. Cummings. LC 78-3827. 96p. 1998. pap. 12.00 (*0-87140-172-X*) Norton.

No Thanks - I'll Sell It Myself. Kathy Overfelt & Tony Overfelt. 128p. 1991. pap. 3.95 (*0-380-76186-6*, Avon Bks) Morrow Avon.

No Thanks, I'm Just Looking: Professional Retail Sales Techniques for Turning Shoppers into Buyers. Friedman Group Staff. 228p. 1995. boxed set 24.95 (*0-8403-7962-5*) Kendall-Hunt.

No Thanks Said a Lobster: By Post & Other Maine Limericks. unabridged ed. Bill Webster. (Illus.). 64p. 1996. pap. 7.95 (*0-9651946-0-4*) More Better.

No Thanks Thanksgiving. Ilene Cooper. 1999. pap. 3.99 (*0-14-037087-0*) Viking Penguin.

No! The Positive Response to Alcohol. Jerry D. Hull. 104p. 1989. pap. 7.99 (*0-8341-1301-5*) Beacon Hill.

No Thief Gives Warning Signs: The Death of the Mid & Post Tribulation Rapture Theories. Jay S. Snell. (Illus.). 192p. (Orig.). 1995. pap. 10.00 (*1-877744-02-6*) J Snell Evangelistic.

No-Thing Is Left to Tell: Zen Chaos Theory in the Dramatic Art of Samuel Beckett. John L. Kundert-Gibbs. LC 98-25241. (Illus.). 240p. 1999. 41.50 (*0-8386-3762-0*) Fairleigh Dickinson.

No Thornless Roses. Gyeorgos C. Hatonn. (The Phoenix Journals). 223p. 1993. pap. 6.00 (*1-56935-010-8*) Phoenix Source.

No Through Road. large type ed. Anne Cassidy. (J). 1997. pap. 16.95 (*0-7540-6005-5*, Galaxy Child Lrg Print) Chivers N Amer.

No Through Road. large type ed. Theresa Charles. 448p. 1986. 27.99 (*0-7089-1539-6*) Ulverscroft.

No Ticket? No Problem: How to Sneak into Sporting Events & Concerts. Scott Kerman. LC 96-35680. (Illus.). 182p. 1996. pap. 8.99 (*1-56530-226-5*) Summit TX.

No Ties: (Kids & Kisses) Rosemary A. Gibson. (Larger Print Ser.). 1995. pap. 2.99 (*0-373-15590-5*, 1-15590-2) Harlequin Bks.

No-Till Question & Answer. 1995. 8.95 (*0-944079-18-0*) Lessiter Pubns.

No-Tillage Seeding: Science & Practice. C. J. Baker et al. LC 97-142324. (CAB International Publication Ser.). 272p. (C). 1996. text 95.00 (*0-85199-103-3*) OUP.

No Time for Fear. Diane Fessler. 255p. 1997. reprint ed. pap. 22.95 (*0-87013-440-X*) Mich St U Pr.

***No Time for Goodbyes: Coping with Sorrow, Anger & Injustice After a Tragic Death.** 5th ed. Janice Harris Lord. 1999. pap. 12.95 (*0-934793-68-9*) Pathfinder CA.

No Time for Heaven: A Full-Length Play for the Whole Family. E. P. Conkle. 76p. 1955. pap. 4.00 (*0-88680-140-0*) I E Clark.

No Time for Heaven: Director's Script. E. P. Conkle. 76p. 1955. pap. 15.00 (*0-88680-141-9*) I E Clark.

No Time for Heroes. Brian Freemantle. 1996. mass mkt. 6.99 (*0-312-95927-3*) St Martin.

No Time for Jello: One Family's Experiences with the Doman-Delacato Patterning Program. Berneen Bratt. 202p. 1989. pap. 17.95 (*0-914797-56-5*) Brookline Bks.

***No Time for Love.** 240p. 2000. pap. 13.95 (*1-57734-652-1*) Covenant Comms.

***No Time for Love.** Barbara Cartland. LC 99-30988. (Thorndike Large Print Candlelight Series). 1999. 19.95 (*0-7862-2029-5*) Thorndike Pr.

No Time for Me. Richard E. Petitti. (Illus.). 150p. 1984. pap. 20.00 (*0-938582-01-1*) Sensitive Man.

No Time for Me: Learning to Live with Busy Parents. John M. Barrett. LC 78-21257. (Illus.). 32p. (J). (ps-3). 1985. 16.95 (*0-87705-385-5*, Kluwer Acad Hman Sci) Kluwer Academic.

No Time for Miracles. Jack Veasey. LC 89-39402. 64p. (Orig.). 1989. pap. 6.95 (*0-9620251-1-9*) Yardbird Bks.

No Time for Mother's Day. Laurie Halse Anderson. LC 98-33757. (J). 1999. lib. bdg. 14.95 (*0-8075-4955-X*) A Whitman.

No Time for Neutrality: A Bible Study on Joshua. Donald K. Campbell. LC 94-2716. 264p. 1994. pap. 12.99 (*0-929239-84-9*) Discovery Hse Pubs.

***No Time for Patience: My Road from Kaunas to Jerusalem; a Memoir of a Holocaust Survivor.** Zev Birger. LC 99-30229. 150p. 1999. 18.95 (*1-55704-386-8*, Pub. by Newmarket) Norton.

***No Time for Pilots.** James Owen. LC 99-74222. 368p. 2000. 26.95 (*1-57197-186-6*) Pentland Pr.

No Time for Rabbits. Jane McFann. 176p. 1991. pap. 2.95 (*0-380-76085-1*, Avon Bks) Morrow Avon.

No Time for Romance: An Autobiographical Account of a Few Moments in British & Personal History Lucilla Andrews. LC 78-308938. 239 p. 1977. write for info. (*0-245-53087-8*) H Larousse Ltd.

No Time for Sanity. Evan Skolnick. (Tick Ser.). 1997. pap. text 9.95 (*1-57840-155-0*, Pub. by Acclaim Bks) Penguin Putnam.

No Time for Sergeants see Best American Plays: Fourth Series, 1952-1957

No Time for Sergeants. Mac Hyman. 1976. 21.95 (*0-8488-0170-9*) Amereon Ltd.

No Time for Sergeants. Mac Hyman & Ira Levin. 1958. pap. 5.25 (*0-8222-0829-6*) Dramatists Play.

No Time for Sergeants. Mac Hyman. 1993. reprint ed. lib. bdg. 17.95 (*1-56849-206-5*) Buccaneer Bks.

No Time for Sergeants: A Novel. Mac Hyman. LC 54-9435. (Voices of the South Ser.). 224p. (C). 1995. pap. 10.95 (*0-8071-2032-4*) La State U Pr.

***No Time for Sex: Wacky Scientists Con the Government.** Tom Kyle. LC 99-90842. 356p. 1999. 24.00 (*1-892298-17-1*) Abique.

No Time for Silence: Evangelical Women in Public Ministry Around the Turn of the Century. Janette Hassey. 176p. 1986. pap. 9.95 (*0-310-29451-7*, 12786P) Zondervan.

No Time for Slaves. R. E. McMaster, Jr. 300p. 1986. 14.95 (*0-9605316-8-8*) Reaper Pub.

No Time for Tears. Lora W. Hughes. LC 85-8644. (Illus.). viii, 305p. 1985. reprint ed. pap. 7.95 (*0-8032-7229-4*, Bison Books); reprint ed. text 40.00 (*0-8032-2336-6*) U of Nebr Pr.

No Time for Tears: Transforming Tragedy into Triumph. Dorris R. Wilcox. Ed. by Richard N. Cote. LC 99-68983. 180p. 2000. 24.95 (*1-929175-07-8*, Corinthian Bks) Cote Lit Grp.

No Time for Tie-Ups: A Complete Series of Maps to Guide You Out of & Around Any Traffic Jam on 31 Major Highways in the Tri-State Region. Compiled by Joshua B. Isaacson. (Illus.). 335p. (Orig.). 1992. pap. text 16.95 (*0-9633567-0-4*) Herruth Pub.

No Time for Youth: Growth & Constraint in College Students. Joseph Katz. LC 68-21317. (Jossey-Bass Higher Education Ser.). 486p. reprint ed. pap. 150.70 (*0-608-30924-9*, 202108500020) Bks Demand.

No Time Like the Past. Michael Fairlie. 246p. (C). 1989. text 69.00 (*1-872795-49-8*, Pub. by Pentland Pr) St Mut.

No Time on My Hands. Grace Snyder & Nellie S. Yost. LC 85-28959. (Illus.). 545p. 1986. reprint ed. pap. 16.95 (*0-8032-9164-7*, Bison Books) U of Nebr Pr.

No Time Out: The Life-Story of George & Dorothy Thomas. Betty M. Hockett. LC 91-72897. (Illus.). 80p. (J). (gr. 3-6). 1991. pap. 5.00 (*0-943701-19-8*) George Fox Pr.

No-Time-To-Cook Book: An Afternoon of Cooking... A Week of Meals. Janet Chadwick. LC 85-70194. (Illus.). 192p. 1986. pap. 14.95 (*0-88266-393-3*, Garden Way Pub) Storey Bks.

No-Time-To-Cook Book: An Afternoon of Cooking... A Week of Meals. Janet Chadwick. LC 85-70194. (Illus.). 192p. 1986. 14.95 (*0-88266-394-1*, Garden Way Pub) Storey Bks.

No-Time-to-Cook Cookbook: Fabulous Dishes for Today's Fast-Paced Lifestyle. Ed. by Marie Caratozzolo & Joanne Abrams. LC 98-36064. (Illus.). 240p. Date not set. 19.95 (*0-89529-859-7*, Avery) Penguin Putnam.

No Time to Cry. Lurlene McDaniel. 160p. (YA). (gr. 5). 1996. mass mkt. 4.99 (*0-553-57079-X*) Bantam.

No Time to Cry. Lurlene McDaniel. (J). 1996. 9.09 (*0-606-09697-3*, Pub. by Turtleback) Demco.

***No Time to Die.** Grace F. Edwards. 224p. 2000. mass mkt. 5.99 (*0-553-57956-8*) Bantam.

No Time To Die. Grace F. Edwards. LC 98-56014. 272p. 1999. 22.95 (*0-385-49247-2*) Doubleday.

No Time to Die. Liz Tilberis. LC 97-45811. (Illus.). 304p. 1998. 23.95 (*0-316-77674-2*) Little.

No Time to Die: Living with Ovarian Cancer. Liz Tilberis. LC 97-45811. (Illus.). 291p. 1999. pap. 14.00 (*0-380-73226-2*, Avon Bks) Morrow Avon.

No Time to Lose: A Post-War Romance. David Stringer. 203p. 1998. 42.50 (*1-85776-292-4*, Pub. by Book Guild Ltd) Trans-Atl Phila.

No Time to Lose: The Fast Moving World of Bill Ivy. Alan Peck. (Illus.). 184p. 1997. 29.95 (*1-899870-21-0*, Pub. by Motor Racing) Motorbooks Intl.

No Time to Play: Youthful Offenders in Adult Correctional Systems. Barry Glick et al. LC 98-9196. 181p. 1998. pap. 36.95 (*1-56991-071-5*) Am Correctional.

No Time to Read During Lunch: Try the Next Few Minutes. Joseph Spallone. (Illus.). 38p. (YA). (gr. 9-12). 1998. pap. 6.95 (*0-9660227-1-8*) CTM Pub.

***No Time to Say Goodbye: Surviving the Suicide of a Loved One.** Carla Fine. 272p. 1999. pap. 12.95 (*0-385-48551-4*, Anchor NY) Doubleday.

No Time to Sew. Sandra Betzina. (Illus.). 256p. 1996. text 29.95 (*0-87596-744-2*) St Martin.

***No Time to Sew Sewing Pattern.** Zana Sandra Bet. 2001. text. write for info. (*0-87596-786-8*) Rodale Pr Inc.

***No Time to Waste: On the Run to Be Ready to Meet Jesus.** George B. Prude. 85p. 1999. pap. 10.00 (*0-7392-0343-6*, PO3518) Morris Pubng.

No Time to Waste: Poverty & the Global Environment. Joan Davidson et al. (Illus.). 224p. (C). 1992. 39.95 (*0-85598-182-2*, Pub. by Oxfam Pub); pap. 15.95 (*0-85598-183-0*, Pub. by Oxfam Pub) Stylus Pub VA.

No Title. Jim Allen. Ed. by Jerry Robeson. (Illus.). 1998. pap. write for info. (*1-891879-01-4*) Shiloh Pub.

No Title. Paul Buck. 64p. (Orig.). 1991. pap. 8.00 (*0-937013-38-2*) Potes Poets.

No Title. Geri De Paoli & Nancy D. Resler. Ed. by John Natsoulas. (Illus.). 75p. (C). 1998. pap. text. write for info. (*1-881572-54-4*) J Natsoulas.

No Title. Ed. by Bertha Rogers & William Jolliff. (Poetry Chapbook Ser.: Vol. 2). 26p. (Orig.). 1998. mass mkt. 6.00 (*0-9646844-8-9*) Bright Hill.

***No, Tito, No!** Claire Masurel. Tr. by Diego Lasconi. LC 99-20064.Tr. of No, No, Titus!. (SPA., Illus.). 32p. (J). (ps-1). 1999. 15.95 (*0-7358-1208-X*, Pub. by North-South Bks NYC); pap. 6.95 (*0-7358-1209-8*, Pub. by North-South Bks NYC) Chronicle Bks.

No Toads Allowed! Anna M. McLemore. 80p. 1992. pap. 8.95 (*0-9630120-0-2*) Relational Pr.

No Toads in Heaven. James M. Mallon. (Gene Florian in the Caribbean Ser.). 262p. (Orig.). 1996. pap. 13.00 (*1-886163-05-7*) SoloZone.

No-Tofu Vegetarian Cookbook. Sharon S. Claessens. LC 96-52652. 272p. 1997. pap. 14.00 (*1-55788-269-X*, HP Books) Berkley Pub.

No Tomorrow. Isabel Hoch. 1997. pap. 14.95 (*1-875998-35-7*, Pub. by Central Queensland) Accents Pubns.

No Tomorrow: The Ethics of Pleasure in the French Enlightenment. Catherine Cusset. LC 98-55780. 224p. 1999. 35.00 (*0-8139-1860-X*) U Pr of Va.

No Tooth, No Quarter! Jon Buller & Susan Schade. LC 89-30250. (Step into Reading Ser.: A Step 3 Book). (Illus.). 48p. (J). (gr. 2-3). 1989. lib. bdg. 11.99 (*0-394-94956-0*, Pub. by Random Bks Yng Read) Random.

No Tooth, No Quarter! Jon Buller & Susan Schade. LC 89-30250. (Step into Reading Ser.: A Step 3 Book). (Illus.). 48p. (J). (ps-3). 1989. pap. 3.99 (*0-394-84956-6*, Pub. by Random Bks Yng Read) Random.

No Tooth, No Quarter! Jon Buller & Susan Schade. (Step into Reading Ser.: A Step 3 Book). (J). (gr. 2-3). 1989. 9.19 (*0-606-04284-9*, Pub. by Turtleback) Demco.

***No Toys on Sunday.** Nancy Alberts. LC 98-11434. (Illus.). 32p. (J). (ps-4). 1998. 16.95 (*0-8192-1740-9*) Morehouse Pub.

***No Trace of Christmas: Discovering Advent in the Old Testament.** Christoph Domen. Tr. by Linda M. Maloney. 104p. 2000. pap. 11.95 (*0-8146-2715-3*) Liturgical Pr.

No Trace of the Gardener: Poems of Yang Mu. Yang Mu et al. Tr. by Lawrence R. Smith & Michelle M. Yeh from CHI. LC 97-15641. 264p. 1997. 25.00 (*0-300-07070-5*) Yale U Pr.

No Transfer: An American Security Principle. John A. Logan. 1961. 79.50 (*0-685-69838-6*) Elliots Bks.

No Treason. Lysander Spooner. LC 73-2173. (Libertarian Broadsides Ser.: No. 5). (Illus.). 1990. reprint ed. pap. 3.50 (*0-87926-017-3*) R Myles.

No Tree for Christmas: The Story of Jesus' Birth. Marilyn Lashbrook. (Me Too Bks.). (Illus.). 30p. (J). 1996. 8.95 (*0-87973-866-9*) Our Sunday Visitor.

No Tree for Christmas: The Story of Jesus' Birth. Marilyn Lashbrook. (J). (ps-2). 1998. pap. 5.95 (*0-933657-71-4*) Rainbow Studies.

***No Tree for Christmas: The Story of Jesus' Birth.** Marilyn Lashbrook. (Libros Yo Tambien! Ser.). (SPA., Illus.). 32p. (J). (ps-2). 2000. 5.95 (*1-58170-042-3*) Rainbow Studies.

No Tree for Christmas: The Story of Jesus' Birth. Marilyn Lashbrook. LC 88-62025. (Me Too! Bks.). (Illus.). 32p. (J). (ps-k). 1989. 6.95 (*0-86606-434-6*, 3000834) Treasure Pub.

No Trenches in Town - Pour une Ville Sans Tranchee: Proceedings of the International Conference No-DIG 92 Paris, Paris La Villette, France 12-14 October 1992. Ed. by Jean-Pierre Henry & Michel Mermet. (Illus.). 450p. (C). 1993. text 149.00 (*90-5410-085-0*, Pub. by A A Balkema) Ashgate Pub Co.

No Trespassing. Val Tillery. 1991. pap. 9.00 (*0-932526-64-0*) Nexus Pr.

No Trespassing. Shannon Waverly. (Romance Ser.: No. 3150). 1991. per. 2.79 (*0-373-03150-5*) Harlequin Bks.

No Trespassing! Squatting, Rent Strikes & Land Struggles Worldwide. Anders Corr. LC 98-56182. 256p. 1999. 40.00 (*0-89608-596-1*, Pub. by South End Pr); pap. 17.00 (*0-89608-595-3*, Pub. by South End Pr) Consort Bk Sales.

No Trophy, No Sword: An American Volunteer in the Israeli Air Force During the 1948 War of Independence. Harold Livingston. LC 93-49571. (Illus.). 224p. 1994. 21.95 (*1-883695-03-1*) Edition Q.

No Truce With the Furies. R. S. Thomas. 92p. 1996. 35.00 (*1-85224-360-0*, Pub. by Bloodaxe Bks) Dufour.

No Truce with the Furies. R. S. Thomas. 92p. 1996. pap. 17.95 (*1-85224-361-9*, Pub. by Bloodaxe Bks) Dufour.

No Truer Love. Ginna Gray. 304p. 1996. mass mkt. 4.99 (*0-7860-0321-9*, Pinncle Kensgtn) Kensgtn Pub Corp.

No Trump Play. Raymond Brock. Ed. by Tony Sowter. LC 98-39175. (How to Play Bridge Ser.). (Illus.). 96p. 1998. pap. 8.95 (*0-8442-0078-6*, 00786, Natl Textbk Co) NTC Contemp Pub Co.

No Trumpets, No Drums: Red Cross Adventure. Mary F. Howard. LC 91-66937. 1992. 10.00 (*0-933598-38-6*) NC Wesleyan Pr.

No Truth Except in the Details: Essays in Honor of Martin J. Klein. Ed. by A. J. Kox & Daniel M. Siegel. LC 94-38026. (Boston Studies in the Philosophy of Science: Vol. 167). 384p. (C). 1995. lib. bdg. 166.00 (*0-7923-3195-8*) Kluwer Academic.

No Turn Unstoned: The Worst Ever Theatrical Reviews. Compiled by Diana Rigg. LC 91-11430. (Illus.). 192p. 1991. reprint ed. pap. 13.95 (*1-879505-03-7*) Silman James Pr.

No Turning Back see No Vuelvas Atras

No Turning Back. 1997. pap. 4.99 (*1-85078-250-4*, Pub. by Sheffield Acad) CUP Services.

No Turning Back. Judy Baer. (Cedar River Daydreams Ser.: No. 13). 144p. (Orig.). (YA). (gr. 7-10). 1991. mass mkt. 4.99 (*1-55661-216-8*) Bethany Hse.

***No Turning Back.** Estelle Freedman. 2002. text (*0-374-22293-2*) FS&G.

No Turning Back. Rosie Gillis. pap. 11.50 (*0-9640873-0-8*) R M Gillis.

No Turning Back. Ken Hawkins. 24p. (Orig.). 1994. pap. text 2.50 (*1-880573-14-8*) Bible Search Pubns.

No Turning Back. George Verwer. 138p. (C). 1983. reprint ed. pap. 6.99 (*1-884543-00-6*) O M Lit.

No Turning Back: A Hopi Indian Woman's Struggle to Live in Two Worlds. Polingaysi Qoyawayma, pseud. LC 64-7652. (Illus.). 187p. 1977. reprint ed. pap. 12.95 (*0-8263-0439-7*) U of NM Pr.

No Turning Back: A Journey Through Grief to Healing. Barbara Vaughn. 169p. (Orig.). 1996. pap. 10.95 (*1-888813-05-9*, 006) Brghtside.

No Turning Back: A Novel of South Africa. Beverley Naidoo. LC 96-28980. 208p. (J). (gr. 3-7). 1997. lib. bdg. 15.89 (*0-06-027506-5*, HarpTrophy) HarpC Child Bks.

No Turning Back: A Novel of South Africa. Beverley Naidoo. LC 96-28980. 208p. (J). (gr. 3-7). 1999. pap. 4.95 (*0-06-440749-7*, HarpTrophy) HarpC Child Bks.

No Turning Back: Dillon Confronts Death on a Magic Journey. Beth Peterson. LC 95-30857. 112p. (J). (gr. 5-9). 1996. 14.00 (*0-689-31914-2*) Atheneum Yung Read.

No Turning Back: On the Loose in China & Tibet. John W. Meyer. (Illus.). 328p. (Orig.). 1991. pap. 10.95 (*0-911627-13-8*) Neither-Nor Pr.

No Uncertain Future: A Study-Guide Commentary to Revelation. Larry Spargimino. LC 96-164005. 152p. (Orig.). 1994. pap. 10.95 (*1-879366-83-5*) Hearthstone OK.

No Uncertain Sound. Selected by H. E. Schmul. 98p. 1997. pap. 6.99 (*0-88019-362-X*) Schmul Pub Co.

No Union with Slaveholders, 1841-1849 see Letters of William Lloyd Garrison

No Use Dying over Spilled Milk: A Pennsylvania-Dutch Mystery with Recipes. Tamar Myers. 272p. 1997. mass mkt. 5.99 (*0-451-18854-3*, Sig) NAL.

No Vacancies in Hell. Daniel M. Epstein. 1973. 4.95 (*0-87140-574-1*, Pub. by Liveright) Norton.

No Vacancy! Apartment Manager's Guide to Full Occupancy. Gary R. Chatfield. xii, 50p. 1999. pap. 10.95 (*0-9672105-0-X*) WordsNumbers.

***No Vaseline on My Teeth: The Memoirs of Phyllis Mattingly.** Phyllis Mattingly. (Illus.). 1998. pap. 14.95 (*0-9669482-0-3*) Style Media.

No Verdict: New Zealand's Hung Jury Crisis. John Goulter. LC 98-151738. 220 p. 1997. write for info. (*1-86941-298-2*) Random.

No Victor, No Vanquished: The Arab-Israeli War, 1973. Edgar O'Ballance. LC 76-58756. 384p. 1997. pap. 16.95 (*0-89141-615-3*) Presidio Pr.

No Villain Need Be. Vardis Fisher. 387p. 1936. 150.00 (*0-614-22019-X*, Idaho Center for the Bk) Heming W Studies.

No Vipers in the Vatican. Joseph Dunn. LC 96-156022. 236p. (Orig.). 1996. pap. 15.95 (*1-85607-167-7*, Pub. by Columba Press) Whitecap Bks.

No Virtue: A Masey Baldridge/Luke Williamson Mystery. James D. Brewer. LC 94-40125. 232p. (YA). 1995. 20.95 (*0-8027-3259-3*) Walker & Co.

No Virtue in Accident: Behavior Analysis & Utopian Literature. Bobby Newman. 120p. 1996. pap. 19.95 (*0-9668528-0-X*) Dove & Orca.

No Visible Wounds: Identifying Nonphysical Abuse of Women by Their Men. Mary S. Miller. 320p. 1996. pap. 12.00 (*0-449-91079-2*) Fawcett.

***No Voice from the Hall.** large type unabridged ed. John Harris. 214p. 1999. 26.95 (*0-7531-5452-8*, 154528, Pub. by ISIS Lrg Prnt) ISIS Pub.

No Voice from the Hall: Early Memories of a Country House Snooper. John Harris. LC 99-214889. 1998. 29.95 (*0-7195-5567-1*) John Murray.

No Voice Is Ever Wholly Lost. Louise J. Kaplan. 288p. 1995. 24.00 (*0-671-79868-5*) S&S Trade.

No Voice Is Ever Wholly Lost. Louise J. Kaplan. 285p. 1999. reprint ed. pap. text 24.00 (*0-7881-6402-3*) DIANE Pub.

No Voice Is Ever Wholly Lost: An Exploration of Everlasting Attachment Between Parent & Child. Louise J. Kaplan. 288p. 1996. per. 14.00 (*0-684-81820-5*, Touchstone) S&S Trade Pap.

No Vuelvas Atras. G. Verwer.Tr. of No Turning Back. 5.99 (*0-7899-0590-6*, 498221) Editorial Unilit.

No Walls Between Us. Naomi Horton. (Family Continuity Program Ser.: No. 26). 1999. per. 4.50 (*0-373-82174-3*, 1-82174-3) Harlequin Bks.

No Walls of Stone: An Anthology of Literature by Deaf & Hard of Hearing Writers. Ed. by Jill Jepson. LC 92-31943. (Illus.). 240p. 1992. 24.95 (*1-56368-019-X*) Gallaudet Univ Pr.

No Water: A True, Gripping Story about Demons & Children. Mable Peterson. 96p. 1987. write for info. (*0-936369-08-6*) Son-Rise Pubns.

No Water in My Cup. Ratibor-Ray M. Jurjevich. LC 68-9415. 1968. 12.95 (*0-87212-010-4*) Libra.

No Water in My Cup: Experiences & a Controlled Study of Psychotherapy of Delinquent Girls. Ratibor-Ray M. Jurjevich. 194p. 1968. 8.95 (*0-930711-03-3*) Ichthys Bks.

An Asterisk (*) at the beginning of an entry indicates that the title is appearing for the first time.

No Water No Moon. 6th ed. Osho. (Illus.). 275p. 1977. reprint ed. 26.95 (*3-89338-135-X*, Pub. by Rebel Hse) Oshos.

No Water, No Moon: Talks on Zen Stories. Osho. 1994. pap. 13.95 (*1-85230-490-1*, Pub. by Element MA) Penguin Putnam.

No Way! Paul Fehlner. LC 94-32422. (My First Hello Reader Ser.). (Illus.). 32p. (J). (ps-3). 1996. pap. 3.95 (*0-590-48514-8*, Cartwheel) Scholastic Inc.

No Way: A Guide for the Spiritually "Advanced" Ram Tzu. LC 90-92091. (Illus.). 112p. (Orig.). 1990. pap. 13.00 (*0-929448-13-8*) Advaita Pr CA.

No Way: Essays on the Nature of the Impossible. Ed. by Philip J. Davis & David Park. LC 86-19728. (Trade Ser.). (Illus.). 325p. 1988. pap. text 14.95 (*0-7167-1966-5*) W H Freeman.

No Way Back. large type ed. Kenneth Royce. 528p. 1988. 27.99 (*0-7089-1778-X*) Ulverscroft.

No Way Home. large type ed. Patricia J. MacDonald. 1991. 27.99 (*0-7089-2484-0*) Ulverscroft.

No Way in Wapping. NCCL Staff. 1988. 21.00 (*0-946088-27-6*, Pub. by NCCL) St Mut.

No Way of Escape. large type ed. Ruth Pattison. (Dales Large Print Ser.). 184p. 1997. pap. 18.99 (*1-85389-762-0*, Dales) Ulverscroft.

No Way Out. Franklin W. Dixon. Ed. by Anne Greenberg. (Hardy Boys Casefiles Ser.: No. 75). 160p. (J). (gr. 7 up). 1993. pap. 3.99 (*0-671-73111-4*, Archway) PB.

No Way Out. Franklin W. Dixon. (Hardy Boys Casefiles Ser.: No. 75). (YA). (gr. 6 up). 1993. 9.09 (*0-606-05336-0*, Pub. by Turtleback) Demco.

No Way Out. Beverly Hastings. 192p. (Orig.). (J). 1994. mass mkt. 3.99 (*0-425-14399-6*) Berkley Pub.

No Way Out. Tina Vasilos. 1997. per. 3.75 (*0-373-22403-6*, 1-22403-9) Silhouette.

No Way Out. large type ed. Joanna Dessau. 1996. 27.99 (*0-7089-3458-7*) Ulverscroft.

No Way Out. Ivy Ruckman. LC 87-47817. (Trophy Keypoint Bk.). 224p. (YA). (gr. 7 up). 1989. reprint ed. mass mkt. 4.95 (*0-06-447003-2*, HarpTrophy) HarpC Child Bks.

No Way Out? Pastoral Care of the Divorced & Remarried. Bernard Haring. 90p. (C). 1990. 35.00 (*0-85439-317-X*, Pub. by St Paul Pubns) St Mut.

No Way Out: The Politics of Polish Jewry, 1935-1939. Emmanuel Melzer. LC 96-30841. (Monographs of the Hebrew Union College: Vol. 19). Orig. Title: Ma'avak Medini Be-Malkodet. (HEB.). 248p. (C). 1997. 39.95 (*0-87820-418-0*) Hebrew Union Coll Pr.

No Way Out but Through. Hortense Cupo. LC 93-29519. 150p. (J). 1994. pap. 4.95 (*0-8198-5130-2*) Pauline Bks.

No Way Out, No Way In: The Crisis of Internal Displacement in Burma. (Issue Papers). 76p. 2000. 5.00 (*0-936548-04-5*) US Comm Refugees.

No Way to Begin. large type ed. Michelle Reid. 285p. 1991. reprint ed. lib. bdg. 18.95 (*0-263-12697-8*) Mac Lib Ref.

No Way to Live: Poor Women Speak Out. 2nd rev. ed. Sheila Baxter. (Illus.). 234p. 1995. pap. 14.00 (*0-921586-43-4*, Pub. by New Star Bks) Genl Dist Srvs.

***No Way to Pick a President.** Jules Witcover. LC 99-34933. 352p. 1999. text 26.00 (*0-374-22303-3*) FS&G.

No Way to Treat a Lady. William Goldman. 1993. reprint ed. lib. bdg. 29.95 (*1-56849-091-7*) Buccaneer Bks.

No Way, Winky Blue! Pamela Jane. LC 95-53367. (J). (gr. 2-6). 1998. 3.95 (*1-57255-138-0*) Mondo Pubng.

No Weakness No War: Peace & Principle in America's Third Century. John K. Andrews, Jr. 120p. (Orig.). 1989. pap. 8.00 (*0-317-93469-4*) Independ Inst.

***No Weapons Formed Against Me.** Rebecca Nails-Pierce. 288p. 1999. pap. 12.95 (*0-9673149-4-1*) Treasured Spirit.

No Where Is Heaven: or, The Tragedy of Fighting & Dying to Make Our Chains More & More Comfortable Rather Than Removing Them. Afrikadzata Deku. LC 91-72665. (Afrikan-Centric Play Ser.). 90p. 2000. pap. write for info. (*1-56454-011-1*) Cont Afrikan.

No Wider Than the Heart. Betty Andrews. 1994. 5.50 (*0-87129-495-8*, N37) Dramatic Pub.

No Wife Required! Rebecca Winters. 1997. per. 3.25 (*0-373-03477-6*, 1-03477-6) Harlequin Bks.

No Wife Required. large type ed. Winters. 1997. per. 3.25 (*0-373-15723-1*, Harlequin) Harlequin Bks.

No Wild Dog Howled. Bruce Embree. 36p. (Orig.). 1988. pap. 45.00 (*0-931659-03-5*) Limberlost Pr.

No Wimps Allowed! Tales of Courage. Judy Katschke. LC 98-88402. 1999. pap. text 3.99 (*0-7868-4307-1*, Pub. by Hyperion) Time Warner.

No Win No Fee. Kerry Underwood. LC 98-221623. 188p. 1998. pap. 48.00 (*1-85811-132-3*, Pub. by CLT Prof) Gaunt.

No Wind of Blame. Georgette Heyer. reprint ed. lib. bdg. 24.95 (*0-89190-645-2*, Rivercity Pr) Amereon Ltd.

No Winner. large type ed. Daphne Clair. 288p. 1993. 27.99 (*0-7505-0443-9*, Pub. by Mgna Lrg Print) Ulverscroft.

No Winners. Roger Larson. 1979. pap. 3.95 (*0-9602468-0-0*) Ipse Dixit Pr.

No Wit, No Help Like a Woman's. Thomas Middleton. Ed. by Lowell E. Johnson. LC 74-33673. (Regents Renaissance Drama Ser.). 168p. 1976. reprint ed. pap. 52.10 (*0-608-02674-3*, 206332700004) Bks Demand.

No Witnesses. Ridley Pearson. 480p. 1996. mass mkt. 7.50 (*0-440-22142-0*) Dell.

No Witnesses. Ridley Pearson. 384p. 1994. 22.45 (*0-7868-6066-9*, Pub. by Hyperion) Time Warner.

No Witnesses. Nancy Sanra. 1995. pap. 9.99 (*1-883061-05-9*) Rising AZ.

No Wonder They Call Him Savior see Con Razon Lo Llamen el Salvador

No Wonder They Call Him the Savior: Chronicles of the Cross. Max Lucado. 216p. 1998. 19.99 (*1-57673-389-0*); pap. 12.99 (*1-57673-388-2*) Multnomah Pubs.

No Wonder They Call Him the Savoir. large type ed. Max Lucado. (Large Print Inspirational Ser.). 224p. 1987. pap. 12.95 (*0-8027-2579-1*) Walker & Co.

No Word for Time: The Way of the Algonquin People. Evan T. Pritchard. LC 97-7492. 114p. (Orig.). 1997. pap. 12.95 (*1-57178-042-4*) Coun Oak Bks.

No Word from Winifred. Amanda Cross. 272p. 1987. mass mkt. 5.99 (*0-345-33381-0*) Ballantine Pub Grp.

***No Word of Farewell: Selected Poems, 1970-2000.** R. S. Gwynn. 180p. 2000. pap. 16.95 (*1-885266-91-X*, Pub. by Story Line) Consort Bk Sales.

No Work, No Place to Garden: Development & Poverty in a West Indian Village. 215th ed. Stephen Koester. (Latin American Perspectives Ser.). 215p. (C). 1999. pap. text 27.00 (*0-8133-7598-3*) Westview.

No-Work Paperwork for Children's Ministry: Every Quick-Copy Form You Need to Complete Record-Keepiing in Record Time! Group Publishing Staff. 1996. pap. text 19.99 (*1-55945-621-3*) Group Pub.

No (World Version) Larry Price. 1990. pap. 7.00 (*84-87467-04-0*, Pub. by Zasterle Pr) SPD-Small Pr Dist.

No Wrinkles on the Soul: A Book of Readings for Older Adults. Richard L. Morgan. 1990. pap. 9.95 (*0-687-60809-0*) Abingdon.

No Wrinkles on the Soul: A Book of Readings for Older Adults. Richard L. Morgan. LC 89-51765. 1990. pap. text 10.00 (*0-8358-0610-3*) Upper Room Bks.

***No! You Suck!** Eric Vaughn. 2000. pap. 12.95 (*0-9701079-1-9*) Jet Pubng.

No, You Wore Red. Michael Wolfe. 80p. (Orig.). 1980. pap. 5.00 (*0-939180-14-6*) Tombouctou.

No, You'd Better Watch Out. Scott Adams. LC 97-225658. (Little Bks.). (Illus.). 80p. (J). 1997. 4.95 (*0-8362-3739-0*) Andrews & McMeel.

No Youth Worker Is an Island. Ridge Burns & Pam Campbell. 216p. (Orig.). 1992. pap. 10.99 (*0-89693-735-6*, 6-1735, Victor Bks) Chariot Victor.

***No Zombies Allowed.** Matt Novak. LC 00-37125. (Illus.). 2001. write for info. (*0-689-84130-2*) Atheneum Yung Read.

No. 1 see Poems of Faiz Ahmad Faiz: A Poet of the Third World

No. 10-Itchy? Don't Know What To Do? Starting a Kadima Chapter from Scratch see Kadima Advisor's Aid Series

No. 2 see Poems of N. M. Rashed: A Poet of the Third World (Oriental Literature in Translation 2)

Noa Noa: The Tahitian Journal of Paul Gauguin. Paul Gauguin. Tr. by O. F. Theis. LC 93-7166. (Illus.). 168p. 1994. 19.95 (*0-8118-0366-X*) Chronicle Bks.

Noa Noa: The Tahitian Journal of Paul Gauguin. Paul Gauguin. (Fine Art Ser.). (Illus.). 96p. 1985. reprint ed. pap. 3.95 (*0-486-24859-3*) Dover.

NOAA Diving Manual: Diving for Science & Technology. 3rd ed. (Illus.). 200p. 1993. pap. text 75.00 (*1-56806-231-1*) DIANE Pub.

NOAA Diving Manual: Diving for Science & Technology. 4th rev. ed. (Illus.). 550p. 1998. write for info. (*0-934213-58-5*, PB98-137078) Natl Tech Info.

NOAA Diving Manual: Scuba Diving for Science & Technology, 2 vols. 1997. lib. bdg. 605.95 (*0-8490-8124-6*) Gordon Pr.

***NOAA Strategic Plan: A Vision for 2005, Executive Summary, September 1998.** 22p. 1998. pap. 2.50 (*0-16-060918-6*) USGPO.

NOAA's Arctic Research Initiative: Proceedings of a Workshop. National Research Council Staff. LC 98-138586. 190p. (C). 1997. pap. text 34.00 (*0-309-05992-5*) Natl Acad Pr.

***Noah.** (Bible Stories for the Very Young Ser.). (J). 1998. 7.95 (*2-7289-0893-1*) CE75.

Noah. Berthe Amoss. (Illus.). 10p. (J). (ps-7). 1989. pap. 2.95 (*0-922589-10-0*) More Than a Card.

***Noah.** Chariot Victor Publishing Staff. (Shadowbox Bks.). (J). 2000. write for info. (*0-7814-3422-X*) Chariot Victor.

Noah. Louie J. Fant, Jr. (Illus.). 14p. (J). (gr. 3-4). 1973. pap. text 9.95 (*0-917002-70-9*) Joyce Media.

Noah. Patricia Lee Gauch. (Illus.). (J). (ps-3). 1999. pap. 5.99 (*0-698-11756-5*, PapStar) Peng Put Young Read.

Noah. Illus. by Jonathan Green. LC 92-44283. 32p. (J). (ps up). 1994. 14.95 (*0-399-22548-X*, Philomel) Peng Put Young Read.

Noah. Mary R. Hopkins. LC 98-20419. (Illus.). 1998. 10.99 (*1-58134-002-8*) Crossway Bks.

***Noah.** Susan Martins Miller. (Young Reader's Christian Library). (Illus.). 224p. (J). (gr. 3-7). 1999. pap. 1.39 (*1-57748-654-4*) Barbour Pub.

Noah. Arnold Perrin. 1993. pap. 4.00 (*0-939736-50-0*) Wings ME.

Noah. Phyllis Vos Wezeman & Anna L. Liechty. LC 96-53070. (A to Z Ser.). (Illus.). 80p. 1997. pap. 9.99 (*0-8254-3960-4*) Kregel.

Noah. Linda Winder. (My Own Doorknob Book Ser.). (J). 1993. bds. 5.99 (*0-7814-0122-4*, Chariot Bks) Chariot Victor.

Noah: His Life & Times. Samuel W. Jennings. 1996. pap. 11.99 (*0-946351-44-9*) Loizeaux.

Noah: The Promises of God are Everlasting. C. R. Gibson Company, Staff. 1997. 6.95 (*0-7852-1553-0*) Gibson.

Noah - In Sign Language. Ed. by Louie J. Fant, Jr. pap. 9.95 (*0-917002-10-5*) Joyce Media.

***Noah & God's Promise.** Laura Derico. (Illus.). 10p. (J). 2000. 9.99 (*0-7847-1059-7*, 03535) Standard Pub.

Noah & God's Promises: Genesis 6-8. Gloria A. Truitt. (Arch Bks.). 24p. (Orig.). (J). (gr. k-4). 1985. pap. 1.99 (*0-570-06193-8*, 59-1294) Concordia.

Noah & His Great Ark. John Simons & Kay Ward. (Bible Stories for Today Ser.). (Illus.). 16p. (Orig.). (J). (gr. 3-7). 1987. pap. text 2.50 (*0-937039-00-4*) Sun Pr FL.

Noah & the Animals. Nina Filipek. (Press Out & Play Bks.). (Illus.). 16p. (J). 1995. 2.95 (*0-689-80258-7*, Mac Bks Young Read) S&S Childrens.

Noah & the Animals. Allia Zobel-Nolan. (Illus.). 6p. (gr. k-3). 2000. 5.99 (*1-57584-406-0*) Rdrs Digest.

Noah & the Ark see Noe y el Arca (Historias Biblicas)

Noah & the Ark. LC 93-14131. (J). 1993. mass mkt. 4.99 (*0-8407-4910-4*) Nelson.

Noah & the Ark. (J). Date not set. 8.95 (*0-88271-533-X*, 10521) Regina Pr.

***Noah & the Ark.** Barber. 2000. 17.95 (*0-385-40566-9*, Pub. by Transworld Publishers Ltd) Trafalgar.

Noah & the Ark. D. Brumi. (J). 1996. bds. 3.95 (*0-88271-452-X*) Regina Pr.

Noah & the Ark. Melody Carlson. (Story Pockets Ser.). 1997. 4.99 (*1-57673-167-7*, Gold n Honey) Zondervan.

Noah & the Ark. Illus. by Kate Davies. (Bible Pop-Ins Ser.). 10p. (J). 1997. bds. 4.99 (*1-884628-31-1*, Flyng Frog) Allied Pub MD.

Noah & the Ark. Anne De Graaf. (Little Children's Bible Bks.). (Illus.). 38p. (J). 1998. 5.99 (*0-8054-1781-8*) Broadman.

Noah & the Ark. Tomie De Paola. (Illus.). 32p. (Orig.). (J). (ps-2). 1984. 12.95 (*0-86683-819-8*, AY8451) Harper SF.

Noah & the Ark. Illus. by Toni Goffe. 10p. (J). (ps). 1997. bds. 7.99 (*0-7847-0630-1*, 03800) Standard Pub.

Noah & the Ark. Paul Guernsey. (Greatest Stories Ever Told Ser.). (Illus.). 40p. (J). (gr. k up). 1993. 14.95 (*0-88708-292-0*, Rabbit Ears); audio 19.95 (*0-88708-293-9*, Rabbit Ears) Litle Simon.

Noah & the Ark. Paul Guernsey. LC 92-36281. (Illus.). 40p. (J). (ps up). 1996. 19.95 incl. audio (*0-689-80607-8*, Rabbit Ears) Litle Simon.

Noah & the Ark. James R. Leininger. (Beginners Bible Ser.). (Illus.). 1997. 2.99 (*0-310-97539-5*) Zondervan.

Noah & the Ark. Little Moorings Staff. LC 96-221710. 1996. 5.99 (*0-679-87748-7*) Random.

Noah & the Ark. Regina Press. 1999. 5.99 (*0-88271-681-6*) Regina Pr.

Noah & the Ark. Regina Press Staff. 1999. 6.95 (*0-88271-645-X*) Regina Pr.

Noah & the Ark: Sing, Color'n Say. Lenore Paxton & Phillip Siadi. (World of Language Bible Story Ser.). (Illus.). 32p. (J). (ps-4). 1994. reprint ed. pap. 7.95 incl. audio (*1-880449-11-0*) Wrldkids Pr.

Noah & the Ark & the Animals. Andrew Clements. (Illus.). 40p. (J). (ps-3). 1992. pap. 4.95 (*0-590-44457-3*, Blue Ribbon Bks) Scholastic Inc.

Noah & the Big Boat. Robin Currie. LC 94-73989. (Bible Buddies Ser.). (Illus.). 12p. (J). 1995. bds. 4.29 (*0-7814-0198-4*) Chariot Victor.

Noah & the Big Boat. Alice J. Davidson. LC 97-184124. (My Bible Friends Board Bks.). (Illus.). 12p. (J). 1997. 3.99 (*0-310-97322-8*) Zondervan.

Noah & the Big Boat. Brenda Ward. LC 98-34345. (Bible Babies Ser.). (Illus.). 16p. (J). 1998. 7.95 (*0-8054-1779-6*) Broadman.

Noah & the Flood. John Walton & Kim Walton. (Tiny Tots Tubby Book). (Illus.). 12p. (J). 1995. 6.29 (*0-7814-0201-8*) Chariot Victor.

Noah & the Great Ark. Bix L. Doughty. (J). (gr. k up). 1978. 7.00 (*0-87602-163-1*) Anchorage.

Noah & the Great Flood see Noe y el Gran Diluvio

Noah & the Great Flood. Mordicai Gerstein. LC 97-19259. (Illus.). 32p. (J). 1999. 16.00 (*0-689-81371-6*) S&S Childrens.

Noah & the Rainbow. Shoshana Lepon. LC 92-26431. (Illus.). (J). (gr. k-4). 1993. 12.95 (*1-880582-04-X*); pap. 9.95 (*1-880582-05-8*) Judaica Pr.

Noah & the Rainbow. large type ed. Mrs. Alistair MacLean, pseud. (Yesterday & Tomorrow Bible Cartoon Ser.). (Illus.). 75p. (YA). 1996. spiral bd. 10.00 (*0-940178-82-6*) Sitare.

Noah & the Space Ark. Laura Cecil. LC 97-12428. (Illus.). 32p. (J). (ps-3). 1998. lib. bdg. 19.85 (*1-57505-255-5*, Carolrhoda) Lerner Pub.

Noah Builds a Big Boat. V. Gilbert Beers. 1999. 3.99 (*0-7814-3334-7*) Chariot Victor.

Noah Conspiracy. Michael Shaara. 1994. mass mkt. 5.99 (*0-671-89866-3*) PB.

Noah John Rondeau: Adirondack Hermit. 5th ed. Maitland C. De Sormo. (Illus.). 204p. 1969. reprint ed. pap. 16.00 (*0-932052-74-6*) North Country.

Noah Looks At Vol. 2: The Flood. Susan Payson. (Illus.). 48p. (J). (gr. 2-5). 1999. pap. 12.95 (*1-929078-14-5*, NLSF2) Gods Kids.

Noah Looks at Creation, Vol. 1. Susan Payson. (Illus.). 40p. (J). (gr. 2-5). 1999. pap. 12.95 (*1-929078-13-7*, NLSC1) Gods Kids.

Noah Makes a Boat. Pippa Goodhart. LC 97-563. (Illus.). 32p. (J). (ps-3). 1997. bds. 15.00 (*0-395-86957-9*) HM.

***Noah! Noah!** Jennifer Stewart. (Illus.). (J). 2000. 14.99 (*0-7847-1213-1*) Standard Pub.

Noah, Noah, Build an Ark. John K. Seagrove. 300p. (Orig.). (YA). 1998. per. 15.00 (*0-9647633-2-X*) Kendall Pubng.

Noah Paradox: Time As Burden, Time As Blessing. Carol Ochs. LC 90-50969. (C). 1991. text 23.00 (*0-268-01470-1*) U of Notre Dame Pr.

Noah Plan: An Educational Program in the Principle Approach: A Self-Directed Seminar in the Principle Approach, Audio Tapes, Grade-Level Guidelines Kindergarten Through Eighth Grade. Rosalie Slater et al. (Illus.). 590p. 1997. ring bd. 125.00 (*0-912498-17-X*, PNB) F A C E.

Noah Plan: An Educational Program in the Principle Approach: A Self-Directed Seminar in the Principle Approach, Audio Tapes, Subject Guidelines for High School Ninth Through Twelfth Grade. Rosalie Slater et al. (Illus.). 334p. 1997. ring bd. 125.00 (*0-912498-22-6*, PNHS) F A C E.

Noah Plan English Language Curriculum Guide: The Principle Approach Kindergarten Through Twelfth Grade. Carole G. Adams. Ed. by Elizabeth L. Youmans. (Noah Plan Principle Approach Subject Curriculum Guides Ser.). (Illus.). 314p. 1998. pap. 40.00 (*0-912498-20-X*, EGC) F A C E.

Noah Plan History & Geography Curriculum Guide: The Principle Approach Kindergarten Through Twelfth Grade. Elizabeth L. Youmans. (Noah Plan Principle Approach Subject Curriculum Guides Ser.). (Illus.). 384p. 1998. pap. 40.00 (*0-912498-21-8*, HSTG) F A C E.

Noah Plan Literature Curriculum Guide: The Principle Approach Kindergarten Through Twelfth Grade. Rosalie J. Slater. Ed. by Carole G. Adams. (Noah Plan Principle Approach Subject Curriculum Guides Ser.). (Illus.). 384p. 1997. pap. 40.00 (*0-912498-19-6*, LIT) F A C E.

Noah Plan Reading Curriculum Guide: The Principle Approach Kindergarten Through Twelfth Grade. Martha B. Shirley. Ed. by Elizabeth Youmans. (Noah Plan Principle Approach Subject Curriculum Guides Ser.). (Illus.). 128p. 1997. pap. 25.00 (*0-912498-18-8*, RDG) F A C E.

Noah Project. Ralph L. Kliem & Irwin S. Ludin. 208p. 1994. pap. 26.95 (*0-566-07469-9*) Ashgate Pub Co.

Noah Project: The Secrets of Practical Project Management. Ralph L. Kliem & Irwin S. Ludin. 208p. 1993. 51.95 (*0-566-07439-7*, Pub. by Gower) Ashgate Pub Co.

Noah Smernoff: A Life in Medicine. Robert T. King. (Great Basin History of Medicine Ser.: No. 1). (Illus.). 144p. 1990. lib. bdg. 36.00 (*1-56475-001-9*); fiche. write for info. (*1-56475-352-2*) U NV Oral Hist.

Noah Webster. Horace E. Scudder. (Notable American Authors Ser.). 1999. reprint ed. lib. bdg. 125.00 (*0-7812-8887-8*) Rprt Serv.

Noah Webster: Letters on Yellow Fever Adressed to Dr. William Currie. Noah Webster & William Currie. 1979. 17.95 (*0-405-10629-7*) Ayer.

Noah Webster: Master of Words. David Collins. (Sower Ser.). (Illus.). 146p. (YA). (gr. 5-9). 1989. pap. 7.99 (*0-88062-158-3*) Mott Media.

***Noah Webster: The Life & Times of an American Patriot.** Harlow G. Unger. LC 98-15707. 400p. 1998. 30.00 (*0-471-18455-1*) Wiley.

***Noah Webster & the American Dictionary.** David Micklethwait. LC 99-39094. (Illus.). 358p. 2000. lib. bdg. 49.95 (*0-7864-0640-2*) McFarland & Co.

Noah Webster's American Spelling Book: With an Introductory Essay by Henry Steele Commager. fac. ed. Noah Webster. LC 62-21960. (Classics in Education Ser.: No. 17). 187p. 1962. reprint ed. pap. 58.00 (*0-7837-8206-3*, 204796400009) Bks Demand.

Noah Webster's Pronunciation & Modern New England Speech. K. E. Lindblad. (Essays & Studies on American Language & Literature: Vol. 11). (Orig.). 1954. pap. 25.00 (*0-8115-0191-4*) Periodicals Srv.

Noah Webster's Reading Handbook. Darrel A. Trulson. (Illus.). 140p. (J). (gr. 1-3). 1993. pap. text 7.00 (*1-930092-24-5*, CLP29515) Christian Liberty.

Noah's Aardvark. Mary Jane Auch. 32p. 1999. 9.95 (*0-307-10229-7*) Golden Bks Pub.

Noah's ABC. Shoo Rayner. (Illus.). 32p. (J). pap. 9.95 (*0-14-054360-0*, Pub. by Pnguin Bks Ltd) Trafalgar.

Noah's Amazing Ark. Jane Morton. (Illus.). 6p. (J). 1994. 5.99 (*1-56476-170-3*, 6-3170, Victor Bks) Chariot Victor.

Noah's Animals Two by Two: Bag of Noah's Animals. Chariot. 8p. (J). (ps). 1993. 8.99 (*0-7814-0124-0*) Chariot Victor.

Noah's Ark. (Now You Can Read Bible Stories Ser.). 24p. (J). 1994. 3.98 (*0-86112-782-X*) Brimax Bks.

Noah's Ark. 16p. Date not set. 2.50 (*1-871676-48-7*, Pub. by Christian Focus) Spring Arbor Dist.

Noah's Ark. (Kid's a-Peel Ser.). 1994. pap. text 3.00 (*1-896044-27-1*) Novar Cottage.

Noah's Ark. (Children's Bible Stories Ser.). (Illus.). 24p. (J). 1993. 4.98 (*1-56173-718-6*) Pubns Intl Ltd.

Noah's Ark. LC 94-214761. (J). 1994. write for info. (*0-7853-0561-0*) Pubns Intl Ltd.

Noah's Ark. (Very Easy Coloring Bks.). (Illus.). 16p. (J). (ps). 1995. pap. 1.49 (*0-7847-0373-6*, 22003) Standard Pub.

Noah's Ark. (Beginners Bible Play-A-Sound Bks.). (Illus.). 16p. (J). (ps-3). 1996. 10.99 (*0-7847-0466-X*, 03886) Standard Pub.

***Noah's Ark.** Georgie Adams. LC 99-19530. (Illus.). 24p. (J). (ps-2). 1999. 12.99 (*0-8054-2037-1*) Broadman.

Noah's Ark. Pam Adams. (Bath Bks.). 10p. (J). (gr. 3 up). 1981. 7.99 (*0-85953-267-4*) Childs Play.

***Noah's Ark.** Pam Adams. 12p. 1999. 8.99 (*0-85953-586-X*) Childs Play.

Noah's Ark. Heather Amery. (Bible Tales Ser.). (Illus.). 16p. (J). (ps-k). 1997. pap. 4.50 (*0-7460-2741-9*, Usborne) EDC.

Noah's Ark. Heather Amery. (Bible Tales Ser.). (Illus.). 16p. (J). (ps up). 1997. lib. bdg. 12.95 (*0-88110-886-3*, Usborne) EDC.

Noah's Ark. Ariel Books Staff. LC 96-85803. (Little Bks.). (Illus.). 80p. 4.95 (*0-8362-2648-8*, Arie Bks) Andrews & McMeel.

***Noah's Ark** Illus. by Mary Auld & Diana Mayo. LC 99-15335. (Bible Stories Ser.). 2000. 7.95 (*0-531-15394-0*) Watts.

Noah's Ark. Vincent Campbell. 184p. (Orig.). 1987. pap. 7.95 (*0-9617742-0-7*) Decision Syst.

Noah's Ark. Eli A. Cantillon. (Illus.). (J). 1997. 12.98 (*1-58048-017-9*) Sandvik Pub.

N

Noah's Ark. Illus. by Jane Conteh-Morgan. (Pudgy Pal Board Bks.). 18p. (J). (ps up). 1994. bds. 3.99 (*0-448-40185-1*, G & D) Peng Put Young Read.

Noah's Ark. Illus. & Retold by Lucy Cousins. LC 92-54589. 40p. (J). (ps up). 1993. 15.99 (*1-56402-213-7*) Candlewick Pr.

Noah's Ark. Retold by Lucy Cousins. LC 92-54589. (Illus.). 32p. (J). (ps-k). 1993. pap. 5.99 (*1-56402-515-2*) Candlewick Pr.

Noah's Ark. Lucy Cousins. LC 92-54589. (Illus.). 24p. (J). (ps-k). 1997. bds. 6.99 (*0-7636-0250-7*) Candlewick Pr.

Noah's Ark. Lucy Cousins. 1995. 11.19 (*0-606-07957-2*, Pub. by Turtleback) Demco.

***Noah's Ark.** Dalmatian Press Staff. (Illus.). (J). 2000. pap. text 4.97 (*1-888567-37-6*) Dalmatian Pr.

Noah's Ark. Patricia Daniels. LC 95-36897. (Family Time Bible Stories Ser.). (Illus.). 28p. (J). (ps-2). 1999. 4.95 (*0-7835-4626-2*) Time-Life.

Noah's Ark. DK Publishing Staff. (J). 1998. pap. text 5.95 (*0-7894-3469-5*) DK Pub Inc.

Noah's Ark. Eric Elfman. 1999. 20.00 (*0-7871-1951-2*) NewStar Media.

Noah's Ark. Frank Schaffer Publications Staff. 1997. pap. text 5.95 (*0-7647-0100-2*); pap. text 2.49 (*0-7647-0246-7*) Schaffer Pubns.

Noah's Ark. Frank Schaffer Publications Staff. 1997. pap. text 9.95 incl. audio (*0-7647-0228-9*) Schaffer Pubns.

Noah's Ark. Gertrud Fussenegger. LC 87-45153.Tr. of Die/Arche Noah. (Illus.). 32p. (J). (gr. k-3). 1987. 9.95 (*0-397-32241-0*); lib. bdg. 11.89 (*0-397-32242-9*) HarpC Child Bks.

Noah's Ark. Good Little Books for Good Little Children Staff. 12p. (J). (ps). 1986. 3.25 (*0-8378-5205-6*) Gibson.

***Noah's Ark.** John-Marc Grob. (Bible Kingdom Ser.). (Illus.). 2000. pap. 1.99 (*0-8054-3324-4*) Broadman.

Noah's Ark. Susan T. Hall. (Illus.). 12p. (J). (ps). 1990. pap. text 5.95 (*0-927106-03-5*) Prod Concept.

***Noah's Ark.** Havoc Publishing Staff. 1999. 18.00 (*1-57977-887-9*) Havoc Pub.

Noah's Ark. Linda Hayward. LC 86-17790. (Step into Reading Ser.: A Step 1 Book). (Illus.). 32p. (J). (ps-1). 1987. lib. bdg. 11.99 (*0-394-98716-0*, Pub. by Random Bks Yng Read) Random.

N

Noah's Ark. Linda Hayward. LC 86-17790. (Step into Reading Ser.: A Step 1 Book). (Illus.). 32p. (J). (ps-3). 1987. pap. 3.99 (*0-394-88716-6*, Pub. by Random Bks Yng Read) Random.

Noah's Ark. Linda Hayward. (Step into Reading Ser.: A Step 1 Book). (J). (ps-1). 1987. 9.19 (*0-606-12456-X*, Pub. by Turtleback) Demco.

***Noah's Ark.** Greg Holder. (Record Your Own Voice Ser.). (Illus.). 10p. 1999. bds. 12.99 (*0-7847-1112-7*, 03537) Standard Pub.

***Noah's Ark.** Greg Holder. (Felt Board Bks.). (Illus.). 10p. (ps). 1999. bds. 9.99 (*0-7847-1117-8*, 03526) Standard Pub.

Noah's Ark. Heinz Janisch. Tr. by Rosemary Lanning. LC 97-14952. (Illus.). 36p. (J). (gr. k-3). 1997. 16.95 (*1-55858-784-5*, Pub. by North-South Bks NYC) Chronicle Bks.

Noah's Ark. Annie Kubler. (Panorama Ser.). 44p. (J). 1985. 4.99 (*0-85953-255-0*) Childs Play.

Noah's Ark. Illus. by Julie Lacome. (Sticker Stories Ser.). 16p. (J). (ps-1). 1996. pap. text 4.99 (*0-448-41256-X*, G & D) Peng Put Young Read.

Noah's Ark. Ladybird Books Staff. (Bible Stories Ser.: No. S846-2). (Illus.). (J). (ps-2). pap. 3.95 (*0-7214-5065-2*, Ladybrd) Penguin Putnam.

Noah's Ark. Ed. by Sharon Lerner. LC 77-92377. (Pictureback Ser.). (Illus.). (J). (ps-2). 1978. pap. 3.25 (*0-394-83861-0*, Pub. by Random Bks Yng Read) Random.

Noah's Ark. Roberta Letwenko & Edward Letwenko. (Jeremy the Bible Bookworm Ser.). (Illus.). 32p. (J). 3.95 (*0-614-22060-2*) Regina Pr.

Noah's Ark. Peter Lippman. (Mini House Bks.). (Illus.). 20p. (J). (ps-1). 1994. bds. 9.95 (*1-56305-662-3*, 3662) Workman Pub.

Noah's Ark. Illus. by Gena Neilson. (J). (ps-1). 1986. spiral bd. 9.95 (*0-937763-01-2*) Lauri Inc.

Noah's Ark. Mary Packard. (Illus.). 24p. (J). (ps). 1997. pap. text 1.29 (*0-307-98783-3*, Goldn Books) Gldn Bks Pub Co.

Noah's Ark. Rien Poortvliet. (Illus.). 240p. 1992. 49.50 (*0-8109-1371-2*, Pub. by Abrams) Time Warner.

***Noah's Ark.** Kelly R. Pulley. LC 99-178960. (Beginner's Bible Ser.). 1998. write for info. (*0-7853-2676-6*) Pubns Intl Ltd.

Noah's Ark. Rand McNally Staff. (Story Scenes Ser.). (Illus.). 6p. 1997. 6.95 (*0-528-83841-5*) Rand McNally.

Noah's Ark. Ronne Randall. (Illus.). 32p. (J). 1996. pap. 3.99 (*1-884628-17-6*, Flyng Frog) Allied Pub MD.

Noah's Ark. Reader's Digest Editors. (Little Bible Playbks.: Vol. 1). (Illus.). 18p. (J). (gr. k-3). 1998. bds. 4.99 (*1-57584-260-2*, Pub. by Rdrs Digest) Random.

Noah's Ark. Regina Press Staff. 1999. 4.95 (*0-88271-671-9*); 5.95 (*0-88271-712-X*) Regina Pr.

Noah's Ark. Samuel Salerno. 33p. (Orig.). 1995. pap. 6.00 (*0-9638322-1-2*) S Salerno.

***Noah's Ark.** Illus. by Christopher Santoro. (Let's Go Lift & Peek Bks.). 7p. (J). (ps). 1999. 4.99 (*0-679-89481-0*, Pub. by Random Bks Yng Read) Random.

Noah's Ark. Illus. by Pat Schories. (Read Along with Me Bible Stories Ser.). 24p. (J). (ps-3). 1992. 4.95 (*1-56288-223-6*) Checkerboard.

Noah's Ark. Solomon M. Skolnick. LC 96-228302. (Charming Petites Ser.). (Illus.). 80p. 1996. 4.95 (*0-88088-802-4*) Peter Pauper.

Noah's Ark. Snapshot Staff. LC 97-204257. (My First Bible Board Bks.). 24p. (J). 1997. bds. 2.95 (*0-7894-2202-6*) DK Pub Inc.

Noah's Ark. Peter Spier. (Illus.). 48p. (J). (ps-1). 1992. pap. 7.99 (*0-440-40693-5*, YB BDD) BDD Bks Young Read.

Noah's Ark. Peter Spier. LC 76-43630. (Illus.). 48p. (J). (gr. k-3). 1977. 16.95 (*0-385-09473-6*) Doubleday.

Noah's Ark. Peter Spier. 1977. 12.19 (*0-606-00916-7*, Pub. by Turtleback) Demco.

***Noah's Ark.** Ed. by Jennifer Stewart. (Illus.). 24p. (J). (ps-2). 1999. pap. 2.99 (*0-7847-1096-1*, 2208) Standard Pub.

Noah's Ark. Melissa Tyrrell. LC 99-185686. (Hide-Away Bks.). (Illus.). 12p. (J). (ps). 1998. bds. 9.99 (*0-7847-0792-8*, 03764) Standard Pub.

Noah's Ark. Kaye Umansky. (Illus.). 48p. (J). (gr. 2-6). 1998. pap. 16.95 (*0-7136-4340-4*, Pub. by A & C Blk) Midpt Trade.

Noah's Ark. Illus. by Phil Wilson. (I-See-You Ser.). 8p. (J). 1996. 3.50 (*1-56293-827-4*, McClanahan Book) Learn Horizon.

Noah's Ark. Tim Wood & Jenny Wood. (Illus.). 10p. (J). (ps-2). 1998. 11.99 (*0-8054-1797-4*) Broadman.

Noah's Ark. R. Woodman. Date not set. pap. 1.75 (*0-906731-24-0*, Pub. by Christian Focus) Spring Arbor Dist.

***Noah's Ark.** Allia Zobel. (Mini Handle Bks.). (Illus.). 5p. (J). (ps). 2000. bds. 7.99 (*1-57584-670-5*, Pub. by Rdrs Digest) S&S Trade.

***Noah's Ark.** Allia Zobel-Nolan. (Baby's First Bible). 10p. (J). 2000. 7.99 (*0-7847-1210-7*) Standard Pub.

Noah's Ark. unabridged ed. Peter Spier. (Stories to Remember Ser.). (J). (gr. 1-5). 1993. pap. 8.98 incl. audio (*1-879496-04-6*) Lightyear Entrtnmnt.

Noah's Ark, Vol. 10012. Lou E. Smith. (Illus.). (J). (gr. 1-8). 1996. 8.00 (*1-888535-05-9*) Firefly Prods.

***Noah's Ark: A Journey into Multiliteracy.** David Schwarzer. 2001. pap. text. write for info. (*0-325-00279-7*) Heinemann.

Noah's Ark: A Little Bible Playbook about Trust. Sally L. Jones. (Chunky Board Books). (Illus.). 18p. (J). (ps-k). 1999. 4.99 (*0-7847-0928-9*, 03503) Standard Pub.

Noah's Ark: A Story Rhyme. Lamp Light Press Staff. (Illus.). 23p. (J). (ps-6). 1992. pap. text 8.95 (*0-917593-11-1*, Lamp Light Pr) Prosperity & Profits.

Noah's Ark: An Annotated Encyclopedia of Every Animal Species in the Hebrew Bible. annot. ed. Donald Schwartz. LC 99-28887. 1998. 40.00 (*0-7657-6110-6*) Aronson.

Noah's Ark: And Other Bible Stories. Retold by Selina Hastings. (Bible Stories Ser.). (Illus.). 64p. (J). (gr. 3-7). 1996. pap. 5.95 (*0-7894-1191-1*) DK Pub Inc.

Noah's Ark: My Coloring Book. Golden Books Staff. (Precious Moments Ser.). (J). 1997. pap. text 1.09 (*0-307-08747-6*, 08747, Goldn Books) Gldn Bks Pub Co.

Noah's Ark: Pencil Fun Book. C. Cook David. Date not set. pap. text 0.89 (*1-55513-159-X*) Chariot Victor.

Noah's Ark: Precious Moments. LC 98-30869. (Precious Moments for Children Ser.). (Illus.). 32p. (J). (ps-2). 1998. 9.99 (*0-8010-4411-1*) Baker Bks.

Noah's Ark: Rainbow of Promise. Heather Amery. (Usborne Kid Kits Ser.). (Illus.). (J). (ps up). 1997. 13.95 (*0-88110-952-5*, Usborne) EDC.

Noah's Ark: Tickle Giggle Book. Susan T. Hall. 12p. (J). (ps). 1990. bds. 7.49 (*1-55513-739-3*, Chariot Bks) Chariot Victor.

Noah's Ark: With Press-Out Ark & Animals Play Set. Dawn Apperley. 20p. (J). 1998. pap. 6.95 (*1-86233-021-2*) Sterling.

Noah's Ark Activity Book. (J). 1992. pap. 1.49 (*0-88271-229-2*) Regina Pr.

Noah's Ark Activity Book: Colors. Earl Snellenberger & Bonita Snellenberger. (Illus.). 16p. (J). 1997. pap. 3.50 (*0-89051-179-9*) Master Bks.

Noah's Ark Activity Kit, Incl. toy. (Illus.). 12p. (J). (ps-k). 1997. bds. 14.99 (*0-8499-1409-4*) Tommy Nelson.

***Noah's Ark Activity Set, 1.** PUBLISHING Concordia Publishing. LC 99-21183. 1999. 12.99 (*0-570-05567-9*) Concordia.

Noah's Ark Alphabet. Earl Snellenberger & Bonita Snellenberger. (Illus.). 16p. (J). 1997. pap. 3.50 (*0-89051-187-X*) Master Bks.

Noah's Ark & Other Bible Stories: Color Plus Fun. Golden Books Staff. 40p. 1999. pap. text 3.99 (*0-307-27606-6*, 27606) Gldn Bks Pub Co.

Noah's Ark & Other First Bible Stories. Victoria Parker. (Discovering the Bible Ser.). (Illus.). 64p. (J). 1999. 12.95 (*0-7548-0205-1*, Lorenz Bks) Anness Pub.

Noah's Ark & the Ararat Adventure. rev. ed. John D. Morris. LC 93-80508. (Illus.). 64p. (J). (gr. 3-5). 1994. boxed set 13.95 (*0-89051-166-7*) Master Bks.

Noah's Ark & the Great Flood. Gloria Clanin. (Illus.). 32p. (J). (gr. 1-5). 1996. pap. 6.95 (*0-89051-213-2*, NOAGFL) Master Bks.

Noah's Ark & the Ziusudra Epic: Sumerian Origins of the Flood Myth. Robert M. Best. LC 98-93918. 304p. 1999. text 38.00 (*0-9667840-1-4*) Enlil Pr.

***Noah's Ark Animals.** Jennifer Stewart. (Illus.). 16p. (J). (ps-k). 2000. pap. 1.69 (*0-7847-1192-5*) Standard Pub.

Noah's Ark Basic Skills. Earl Snellenberger & Bonita Snellenberger. (Illus.). 16p. (J). 1997. pap. 3.50 (*0-89051-186-1*) Master Bks.

Noah's Ark Book & 3-D Model. Eric Johns. (Illus.). 48p. (Orig.). (J). (gr. k-2). 1995. pap. 6.95 (*0-943706-50-5*) Pitspopany.

Noah's Ark Book of Hat Patterns. Anne Diebel & Patt Newbold. (Religious Ser.). (Illus.). 30p. 1997. pap. text 9.95 (*1-56422-992-0*) Start Reading.

Noah's Ark Coloring Book. Heirborne. 1997. pap. 2.25 (*1-57562-180-0*) K Copeland Pubns.

Noah's Ark Coloring Book. Rhoda F. Showalter et al. 1994. pap. 3.95 (*0-87813-557-X*) Christian Light.

Noah's Ark Dot-to-Dot: Activity Book. Barbara Allman. (J). 1997. pap. text 2.29 (*0-7647-0249-1*) Schaffer Pubns.

***Noah's Ark, Giant Ed.** Pam Adams. 1999. 19.99 (*0-85953-579-7*) Childs Play.

Noah's Ark Manuscript Handwriting Practice. Karen Gentry. (J). 1997. pap. text 2.29 (*0-7647-0085-5*) Schaffer Pubns.

Noah's Ark Modern Manuscript Handwriting Practice. Karen Gentry. (J). 1997. pap. text 2.29 (*0-7647-0086-3*) Schaffer Pubns.

Noah's Ark, Noah's Flood: Lots of Water, Lots of Mud. John Morris. LC 98-66306. (Illus.). 32p. (J). 1998. boxed set 11.99 (*0-89051-234-5*) Master Bks.

Noah's Ark Nonsense. Howard M. Teeple. LC 78-53529. (Truth in Religion Ser.: No. 1). 156p. 1978. 10.00 (*0-914384-01-5*) Relig & Ethics.

Noah's Ark Numbers. Earl Snellenberger & Bonita Snellenberger. (Illus.). 16p. (J). 1997. pap. 3.50 (*0-89051-180-2*) Master Bks.

Noah's Ark Opposites. Earl Snellenberger & Bonita Snellenberger. (Illus.). 16p. 1997. pap. 3.50 (*0-89051-181-0*) Master Bks.

***Noah's Ark Shaped.** Havoc Publishing Staff. 1999. 8.00 (*1-57977-687-6*) Havoc Pub.

Noah's Ark Shapes. Earl Snellenberger & Bonita Snellenberger. (Illus.). 16p. (J). 1997. pap. 3.50 (*0-89051-185-3*) Master Bks.

Noah's Ark Today: Saving Rare Form Animal Breeds from Extinction. Carolyn J. Christman. 78p. (J). (gr. k-6). 1996. pap. text 130.00 (*1-887316-01-9*) Am Livestock.

Noah's Art: The Best of Zoo & Aquarium Graphics. Ed. by Wei Yew. (Illus.). 240p. 1992. 60.00 (*0-9694432-6-9*, Pub. by Quon Edns) Bks Nippan.

Noah's Big Boat. Laura Kelly. (Illus.). (J). 1996. 7.99 (*0-679-87941-2*, Pub. by Random Bks Yng Read) Random.

Noah's Big Boat. Carolyn Larsen. (Wee Sing Bible Songs & Stories Ser.). (Illus.). 12p. (J). (ps-3). 1998. bds. 9.99 incl. audio (*0-8431-7967-8*, Price Stern) Peng Put Young Read.

Noah's Big Boat. Sin Wee. 1998. bds. 9.99 (*0-8423-8046-9*) Tyndale Hse.

Noah's Cargo: Some Curious Chapters of Natural History. George Jennison. LC 70-174390. (Illus.). 270p. 1972. reprint ed. 24.95 (*0-405-08670-9*, Pub. by Blom Pubns) Ayer.

Noah's Daughters. Joan McNerney. (Kestrel Ser.: No. 10). 24p. (Orig.). 1984. pap. 3.00 (*0-914974-42-4*) Holmgangers.

***Noah's Family & the Flood: A Romantic Novel Based on Research.** Marjorie Mary Gilfillan. LC 99-48538. (Illus.). 92p. 2000. pap. 4.95 (*0-930887-34-4*) Wenzel Pr.

Noah's Family Carousel. Yaacov Peterseil. (Illus.). (J). (ps). 1993. 12.95 (*0-943706-10-6*) Pitspopany.

Noah's Flood: The Genesis Story in Western Thought. Norman Cohn. LC 96-18500. (Illus.). 166p. 1996. 35.00 (*0-300-06823-9*) Yale U Pr.

***Noah's Flood: The Genesis Story in Western Thought.** Norman Cohn. (Illus.). 166p. 1999. pap. 16.00 (*0-300-07648-7*) Yale U Pr.

Noah's Flood: The New Scientific Discoveries about the Event That Changed History. Walter Pitman & William Ryan. LC 98-45384. (Illus.). 320p. 1999. 24.50 (*0-684-81052-2*) S&S Trade.

***Noah's Flood: The New Scientific Discoveries about the Event That Changed History.** William B. F. Ryan & Walter C. Pitman. LC 98-45384. 320p. 2000. per. 13.00 (*0-684-85920-3*, Touchstone) S&S Trade Pap.

Noah's Flood, Joshua's Long Day, & Lucifer's Fall: What Really Happened? Ralph E. Woodrow. (Illus.). 1984. pap. 7.00 (*0-916938-07-7*) R Woodrow.

***Noah's Garden.** Rosemarie E. Bishop. LC 00-190569. 229p. 2000. 25.00 (*0-7388-1838-0*); pap. 18.00 (*0-7388-1839-9*) Xlibris Corp.

Noah's Garden: Restoring the Ecology of Our Own Backyards. Sara Stein. (Illus.). 304p. 1995. pap. 13.00 (*0-395-70940-7*) HM.

Noah's Great Adventure. Rodney Brown. (Illus.). 20p. (J). 1993. 15.95 (*1-883909-00-7*) Wisdom Tree.

Noah's Irish Art. Sean Lysaght. (C). 1990. 30.00 (*0-948268-63-8*, Pub. by Dedalus); pap. 15.00 (*0-948268-62-X*, Pub. by Dedalus) St Mut.

Noah's Journey. unabridged ed. Joe Loesch. Ed. by Cheryl J. Hutchinson. (Bible Stories for Kids Ser.). (Illus.). 50p. (J). (gr. 1 up). 1995. pap. 14.95 incl. audio (*1-887729-06-2*); pap. 16.95 incl. audio compact disk (*1-887729-07-0*) Toy Box Prods.

***Noah's Noisy Ark: A Peek-a-Boo Lift-the-Flap Book.** Susan Hood. (Baby Blessings Ser.). (Illus.). 18p. (J). 2000. bds. 9.99 (*0-7847-1140-2*, 04320) Standard Pub.

Noah's Promise. C. R. Gibson Company Staff. 1997. 6.00 (*0-7852-2773-3*) Gibson.

Noah's Rainbow. Thomas J. Gardiner. 32p. (Orig.). (J). (gr. 3-8). 1993. 3.00 (*1-57514-254-6*, 1058) Encore Perform Pub.

Noah's Square Dance. Rick Walton. LC 92-10257. (Illus.). 32p. (J). (ps up). 1995. 16.00 (*0-688-11186-6*) Lothrop.

Noah's Trees. Bijou Le Tord. LC 98-53468. (Illus.). 40p. (J). (ps-1). 1999. 15.95 (*0-06-028235-5*); lib. bdg. 15.89 (*0-06-028527-3*) HarpC Child Bks.

***Noah's Trees.** Bijou Le Tord. LC 98-53468. 40p. (J). (ps-1). 1999. pap. 5.95 (*0-06-443540-7*) HarpC Child Bks.

Noah's Very Big Boat. Sue Isbell. (Great Big Bks.). 16p. (J). 1997. pap. text 14.95 (*0-687-00275-3*) Abingdon.

Noah's Wife. Marty R. Figley. LC 95-31044. (Illus.). 32p. (J). (ps-3). 1998. pap. 7.50 (*0-8028-5133-9*, Eerdmans Bks) Eerdmans.

Noah's Woman. Sylvie Sommerfield. 400p. (Orig.). 1997. mass mkt. 5.99 (*0-8439-4298-3*, Leisure Bks) Dorchester Pub Co.

***Noah's Zoo.** Karyn Henley. (Karyn Henley's Playsongs Bks.). (Illus.). (J). 2000. pap. 5.99 (*0-8423-3466-1*) Tyndale Hse.

Noah's 2-by-2 Adventure. Arch Books Staff. LC 97-228735. 1997. 1.99 (*0-570-07538-6*) Concordia.

Noam Chomsky. Michael C. Haley & Ronald F. Lunsford. LC 93-26570. (Twayne's United States Authors Ser.). 222p. 1993. 23.95 (*0-8057-4013-9*, Twyne) Mac Lib Ref.

Noam Chomsky: A Life of Dissent. Robert Franklin Barsky. LC 96-29013. (Illus.). 256p. 1998. pap. text 16.50 (*0-262-52255-1*) MIT Pr.

Noam Chomsky: A Life Of Dissent. Robert Franklin Barsky. LC P85.C47B37 1997. (Illus.). 250p. 1997. text 32.95 (*1-55022-282-1*, Pub. by ECW) Genl Dist Srvs.

Noam Chomsky: A Life of Dissent, 3 vols., 2. Robert Franklin Barsky & Richard Brauer. Ed. by Warren J. Wong et al. (Illus.). 400p. 1980. 80.00 (*0-262-02148-X*) MIT Pr.

Noam Chomsky: A Life of Dissent, Vol. 1. Robert Franklin Barsky. LC P85.C47B37 1997. 248p. 1997. 33.00 (*0-262-02418-7*) MIT Pr.

Noam Chomsky: A Personal Bibliography, 1951-1986. Ed. by Matsuji Tajima. LC 86-26829. (Library & Information Sources in Linguistics: No. 11). xi, 217p. 1986. 46.00 (*90-272-1000-4*) J Benjamins Pubng Co.

Noam Chomsky: Critical Assessments, 4 vols., Set. Ed. by Carlos Otero. (cr). (Illus.). 1600p. (C). 1994. 660.00 (*0-415-10692-3*) Routledge.

Noam Chomsky: Critical Assessments, 8 vols., Set. Ed. by Carlos Otero. (Illus.). 3408p. (C). 1994. 1195.00 (*0-415-10697-4*) Routledge.

Noam Chomsky: Critical Assessments, 4 vols., Set. Ed. by Carlos P. Otero. LC 92-47084. 1600p. (C). (gr. 13). 1994. 660.00 (*0-415-01005-5*, B2431) Routledge.

***Noam Chomsky: Ideas & Ideals.** Neil Smith. LC 98-48326. 288p. (C). 1999. 54.95 (*0-521-47517-1*) Cambridge U Pr.

Noam Chomsky Lectures. Daniel Brooks & Guillermo Verdecchia. 96p. 1991. pap. 10.95 (*0-88910-413-1*) Genl Dist Srvs.

***Noam Chomsky Lectures: A Play.** 2nd ed. Daniel Brooks & Guillermo Verdecchia. 92p. 1998. pap. 10.95 (*0-88922-405-6*) Talonbks.

Nobel Crimes. Marie Smith. 271p. Date not set. 22.95 (*0-8488-2393-1*) Amereon Ltd.

Nobel Crimes: Stories of Mystery & Detection by Winners of the Nobel Prize for Literature. Ed. by Marie Smith. 256p. 1992. pap. 11.95 (*0-88184-914-6*) Carroll & Graf.

Nobel Laureates. McCarty. 2000. 29.95 (*0-07-135614-2*) McGraw.

***Nobel Laureates 1801-2000.** Alan Symons. (Illus.). 2000. 34.95 (*0-9523751-3-3*) Polo Pubg.

Nobel Laureates in Chemistry, 1901-1992. Ed. by Laylin K. James. LC 93-17902. (History in Modern Chemical Sciences Ser.). 798p. 1993. 69.95 (*0-8412-2459-5*); pap. 34.95 (*0-8412-2690-3*) Am Chemical.

Nobel Laureates in Economic Sciences: A Biographical Dictionary. Ed. by Bernard S. Katz. LC 89-1062. 339p. 1989. text 25.00 (*0-8240-5742-2*, H850) Garland.

Nobel Laureates in Literature: A Biographical Dictionary. Ed. by Rado Pribic. LC 89-11803. 497p. 1990. text 25.00 (*0-8240-5741-4*, H849) Garland.

Nobel Lecture in Literature, 1993. Toni Morrison. LC 94-75096. 1994. 20.00 (*0-679-43437-2*) Knopf.

Nobel Lectures in Chemistry 1981-1990. Bo G. Malmstrom. 800p. 1993. text 122.00 (*981-02-0788-3*) World Scientific Pub.

Nobel Lectures in Chemistry 1981-1990. Bo G. Malmstrom. 800p. 1993. pap. text 61.00 (*981-02-0789-1*) World Scientific Pub.

Nobel Lectures in Chemistry, 1991-1995. Bo G. Malmstrom. LC 97-178966. 296p. 1997. pap. text 26.00 (*981-02-2680-2*) World Scientific Pub.

Nobel Lectures in Chemistry, 1991-1995. Bo G. Malmstrom. LC 97-178966. 1997. 54.00 (*981-02-2679-9*) World Scientific Pub.

Nobel Lectures in Chemistry 1971-1980. S. Forsen. 500p. 1994. text 86.00 (*981-02-0786-7*) World Scientific Pub.

Nobel Lectures in Chemistry 1971-1980. S. Forsen. 500p. 1994. pap. text 46.00 (*981-02-0787-5*) World Scientific Pub.

Nobel Lectures in Economic Sciences 1969-1980. A. Lindbeck. 500p. 1992. text 86.00 (*981-02-0833-2*); pap. text 46.00 (*981-02-0834-0*) World Scientific Pub.

Nobel Lectures in Economic Sciences 1991-1995 - The Sveriges Riksbank (Bank of Sweden) Prize in Economics. 220p. 1997. text 33.00 (*981-02-3059-1*) World Scientific Pub.

Nobel Lectures in Economic Sciences 1991-1995 - The Sveriges Riksbank (Bank of Sweden) Prize in Economics. Torsten Persson. 220p. 1997. pap. text 19.00 (*981-02-3060-5*) World Scientific Pub.

Nobel Lectures in Literature 1968-1980. S. Allen. 208p. 1994. text 40.00 (*981-02-1174-0*); pap. text 21.00 (*981-02-1175-9*) World Scientific Pub.

Nobel Lectures in Literature 1981-1990. S. Allen. 176p. 1994. text 40.00 (*981-02-1176-7*); pap. text 21.00 (*981-02-1177-5*) World Scientific Pub.

Nobel Lectures in Literature 1991-1995. 150p. 1997. pap. text 11.00 (*981-02-2721-3*); lib. bdg. 22.00 (*981-02-2720-5*) World Scientific Pub.

Nobel Lectures in Peace 1971-1980. Irwin Abrams. LC 97-159577. 184p. 1997. text 52.00 (*981-02-1178-3*); pap. text 21.00 (*981-02-1179-1*) World Scientific Pub.

Nobel Lectures in Peace 1981-1990. Irwin Abrams. 196p. 1997. text 52.00 (*981-02-1180-5*); pap. text 21.00 (*981-02-1181-3*) World Scientific Pub.

Nobel Lectures in Peace 1991-1995. 150p. 1997. pap. text 11.00 (*981-02-2723-X*); lib. bdg. 27.00 (*981-02-2722-1*) World Scientific Pub.

Nobel Lectures in Physics, 1901-1970, 4 vols. Incl. Vol. 1. 1901-1921. 1967. 92.50 (*0-444-40416-3*); write for info. (*0-318-51821-X*) Elsevier.

Nobel Lectures in Physics 1971-1980. Ed. by S. O. Lundqvist. 600p. (C). 1994. text 97.00 (*981-02-0726-3*) World Scientific Pub.

Nobel Lectures in Physics 1971-1980. Ed. by S. O. Lundqvist. 600p. (C). 1994. pap. text 48.00 (*981-02-0727-1*) World Scientific Pub.

Nobel Lectures in Physics 1981-1990. Ed. by Gosta Ekspong. 600p. (C). 1993. text 97.00 (*981-02-0728-X*); pap. text 48.00 (*981-02-0729-8*) World Scientific Pub.

Nobel Lectures in Physics, 1991-1995. Gosta Ekspong. LC 97-166091. 1997. 54.00 (*981-02-2677-2*); pap. text 26.00 (*981-02-2678-0*) World Scientific Pub.

Nobel Lectures in Physiology-Medicine, 1901-1970, 4 vols. Incl. Vol. 1. 1901-1921. 1967. 87.25 (*0-444-40419-8*); Vol. 2. 1922-1941. 1965. 87.25 (*0-444-40420-1*); Vol. 4. 1963-1970. 1973. 87.25 (*0-444-40994-7*); write for info. (*0-318-51822-8*) Elsevier.

Nobel Lectures in Physiology or Medicine 1971-1980. J. Lindsten. 690p. 1992. text 122.00 (*981-02-0790-5*); pap. text 61.00 (*981-02-0791-3*) World Scientific Pub.

Nobel Lectures in Physiology or Medicine 1981-1990. J. Lindsten. 640p. 1993. text 118.00 (*981-02-0792-1*); pap. text 55.00 (*981-02-0793-X*) World Scientific Pub.

Nobel Lectures in Physiology or Medicine, 1991-1995. 300p. 1997. text 33.00 (*981-02-3061-3*) World Scientific Pub.

Nobel Lectures in Physiology or Medicine, 1991-1995. Nils Ringertz. 300p. 1997. pap. text 19.00 (*981-02-3062-1*) World Scientific Pub.

Nobel Peace Prize & the Laureates: An Illustrated Biographical History, 1901-1987. Irwin Abrams. 1988. 45.00 (*0-8161-8609-X*, Hall Reference) Macmillan.

Nobel Peace Prize & the Laureatis. 2nd ed. Abrams. 1998. 60.00 (*0-02-896900-6*) Mac Lib Ref.

Nobel Peace Prize, 1989. Kathleen Cahill. (Monograph Ser.). 113p. (C). 1990. 25.00 (*0-8161-7253-6*, Hall Reference) Macmillan.

Nobel Population, 1901-1937: A Census of the Nominators & Nominees for the Prizes in Physics & Chemistry. Compiled by Elisabeth Crawford et al. LC 87-60004. (Berkeley Papers in History of Science: No. 11). 337p. 1987. pap. 20.00 (*0-918102-15-4*) U Cal Hist Sci Tech.

***Nobel Prize: A History of Genius, Controversy & Prestige.** Burton Feldman. (Illus.). 2000. 29.95 (*1-55970-537-X*, Pub. by Arcade Pub Inc) Time Warner.

Nobel Prize Annual, 1988. Donald D. Jackson et al. (Illus.). 128p. 1989. write for info. (*0-9615344-6-X*) Intl Merc OH.

Nobel Prize Annual, 1989. Donald D. Jackson et al. (Illus.). 128p. 1990. write for info. (*0-9615344-9-4*) Intl Merc OH.

Nobel Prize Annual, 1990. 120p. 1991. 25.00 (*0-8161-7376-1*, Hall Reference) Macmillan.

Nobel Prize Economics Lectures: A Cross-Section of Current Thinking. William J. Zahka. 180p. 1992. 77.95 (*1-85628-086-1*, Pub. by Avebry) Ashgate Pub Co.

Nobel Prize in Literature: A Study of the Criteria Behind the Choices. Kjell Espmark. 193p. 1991. 35.00 (*0-8161-1842-6*, Hall Reference) Macmillan.

Nobel Prize Lectures in Chemistry, 1901-1970, 4 vols. Incl. Vol. 2. 1922-1941. Nobel Foundation Staff. 1966. 82.00 (*0-444-40414-7*); Vol. 4. 1963-1970. 1973. 97.50 (*0-444-40987-4*); write for info. (*0-318-51820-1*) Elsevier.

Nobel Prize Winners see Women in Profile Series

Nobel Prize Winners. Ed. by Tyler Wasson. LC 87-16468. 1120p. 1987. 90.00 (*0-8242-0756-4*) Wilson.

Nobel Prize Winners: Biographical Sketches for Listening & Reading. Lisa F. DeWitt. (Illus.). 142p. 1991. pap. text 12.50 (*0-86647-047-6*) Pro Lingua.

Nobel Prize Winners: Biographical Sketches for Listening & Reading, 3 cass., Set. Lisa F. DeWitt. (Illus.). 142p. 1991. audio 27.00 (*0-86647-049-2*) Pro Lingua.

Nobel Prize Winners: Chemistry, 3 vols., Set. Ed. by Frank N. Magill. LC 90-8092. (Chemistry Ser.). (Illus.). 1306p. 1990. lib. bdg. 210.00 (*0-89356-561-X*) Salem Pr.

Nobel Prize Winners: Literature, 3 vols., Set. Frank N. Magill. (Literature Ser.). (Illus.). 1090p. 1988. lib. bdg. 210.00 (*0-89356-541-5*) Salem Pr.

Nobel Prize Winners: Physics, 3 vols., Set. Ed. by Frank N. Magill. LC 89-6409. (Illus.). 1427p. 1989. lib. bdg. 210.00 (*0-89356-557-1*) Salem Pr.

Nobel Prize Winners: Physiology or Medicine, 3 vols., Set. Ed. by Frank N. Magill. LC 91-12143. (Physiology or Medicine Ser.). (Illus.). 1659p. 1991. lib. bdg. 210.00 (*0-89356-571-7*) Salem Pr.

Nobel Prize Winners: Supplement, 1987-1991. Ed. by Paula McGuire. LC 92-12197. 143p. 35.00 (*0-8242-0834-X*) Wilson.

Nobel Prize Winners in Literature, 1901-1931. Annie R. Marble. LC 70-84324. (Essay Index Reprint Ser.). 1977. 30.95 (*0-8369-1185-7*) Ayer.

Nobel Prize Winners in Physics, 1901-1950. Niels H. Heathcote. LC 76-167354. (Essay Index Reprint Ser. Life of Science Library). 1977. reprint ed. 39.95 (*0-8369-2455-X*) Ayer.

Nobel Prize Winners, 1992-1996. Ed. by Clifford Thompson. LC 97-669. 1997. 35.00 (*0-8242-0906-0*) Wilson.

Nobel Prize Winning Investment Strategies. R. D. Rockefeller. 1992. pap. 12.95 (*0-9632572-1-8*) MDMI Int Pubns.

Nobel Prize Women in Science: Their Lives, Struggles & Momentous Discoveries. Sharon B. McGrayne. (Illus.). 368p. 1992. 26.95 (*1-55972-146-4*, Birch Ln Pr) Carol Pub Group.

Nobel Prize Women in Science: Their Lives, Struggles & Momentous Discoveries. rev. ed. Sharon B. McGrayne. LC 98-39490. (Illus.). xi, 451p. 1998. pap. 19.95 (*0-8065-2025-6*, Citadel Pr) Carol Pub Group.

***Nobel Prize Women in Science: Their Lives, Struggles & Momentous Discoveries.** 2nd rev. ed. Sharon B. McGrayne. (Illus.). xi, 451p. 1998. pap. 19.95 (*0-9702256-0-1*) Birch Tree.

Nobel Prizes, 1988: Presentations, Biographies & Lectures. (Illus.). 392p. 1989. 84.50 (*0-685-46229-3*) Coronet Bks.

Nobel Prizes, 1984: Presentations, Biographies & Lectures. (Illus.). 288p. 1985. lib. bdg. 55.00 (*91-85848-08-5*) Coronet Bks.

Nobel Prizes, 1989: Presentations, Biographies & Lectures. Ed. by Tore Frangsmyr. (Illus.). 289p. 1990. 90.00 (*91-85848-10-7*) Coronet Bks.

Nobel Prizes, 1986: Presentations, Biographies & Lectures. Ed. by Almqvist & Wiksell. (Illus.). 344p. 1987. 74.50 (*91-85848-11-5*) Coronet Bks.

Nobel Prizes, 1990: Presentations, Biographies & Lectures. Ed. by Tore Frangsmyr. (Illus.). 348p. 1991. 110.00 (*91-85848-16-6*) Coronet Bks.

Nobel Prizes, 1994: Presentations, Biographies & Lectures. Ed. by Tore Frangsmyr. (Illus.). 349p. 1995. 87.50 (*91-85848-24-7*) Coronet Bks.

Nobel Prizes, 1991: Presentations, Biographies & Lectures. Ed. by Tore Frangsmyr. (Illus.). 202p. 1992. 108.00 (*91-85848-19-0*) Coronet Bks.

Nobel Prizes, 1996. Anders Barany et al. (Illus.). 401p. 1997. 92.50 (*91-85848-26-3*, Pub. by Nobel Fnd) Coronet Bks.

Nobel Prizes, 1997. Ed. by Tore Frangsmyr. (Illus.). 502p. 1998. 89.50 (*91-85848-28-X*, Pub. by Almqvist Wiksell) Coronet Bks.

Nobel Santuary. Scott Morrison. 288p. 1990. 22.95 (*0-385-25249-8*) Doubleday.

Nobel Symposium, '91: Trapped Charged Particles & Related Fundamental Physics, Lysekil, Sweden 18 - 26 August 1994. Ed. by I. Bergstrom et al. 400p. 1996. text 98.00 (*981-02-2481-8*, Po-P2952) World Scientific Pub.

Nobel Symposium '67: Unification of Fundamental Interactions. Ed. by L. Brink et al. 212p. (C). 1989. text 86.00 (*9971-5-0942-3*); pap. text 33.00 (*9971-5-0943-1*) World Scientific Pub.

Nobel Symposium '73, Physics of Low-Dimensional Systems. Ed. by S. O. Lundqvist & N. R. Nilsson. 168p. (C). 1989. text 81.00 (*9971-5-0971-7*); pap. text 36.00 (*9971-5-0972-5*) World Scientific Pub.

Nobel Symposium, '79: The Birth & Early Evolution of Our Universe. B. Gustafsson et al. 450p. 1991. text 99.00 (*981-02-0357-8*); pap. text 40.00 (*981-02-0358-6*) World Scientific Pub.

***Nobel Writers on Writing.** Ed. by Ottar G. Draugsvold. 303p. 2000. lib. bdg. 45.00 (*0-7864-0629-1*) McFarland & Co.

Nobe's Kitchen: Poems. Quintin Prout. LC 98-23115. 64p. 1998. pap. 10.00 (*0-914278-75-4*) Copper Beech.

Nobi see Fires on the Plain

Nobiah's Well: A Modern African Folktale. Donna Guthrie. LC 93-586. (Illus.). 32p. (J). (ps-2). 1993. 14.95 (*0-8249-8622-9*, Ideals Child); lib. bdg. 15.00 (*0-8249-8631-8*, Ideals Child) Hambleton-Hill.

***Nobility.** Tim McGuire. 288p. 1999. mass mkt. 4.50 (*0-8439-4526-5*, Leisure Bks) Dorchester Pub Co.

Nobility & Analogous Traditional Elites in the Allocutions of Pius XII: A Theme Illuminating American Social History. Plinio Correa de Oliveira. LC 93-60895. (Illus.). 592p. 1993. 29.95 (*0-8191-9310-0*) U Pr of Amer.

***Nobility & Annihilation in Marguerite Porete's Mirror of Simple Souls.** Joanne Maguire Robinson. (C). 2001. pap. text. write for info. (*0-7914-4968-8*) State U NY Pr.

***Nobility & Annihilation in Marguerite Porete's Mirror of Simple Souls.** Joanne Maguire Robinson. (C). 2001. text. write for info. (*0-7914-4967-X*) State U NY Pr.

Nobility & Excellence of Women & the Defects & Vices of Men. Lucrezia Marinella. LC 99-39095. 208p. 2000. pap. text 18.00 (*0-226-50546-4*); lib. bdg. 45.00 (*0-226-50545-6*) U Ch Pr.

Nobility & Privilege in Late Imperial Russia. Seymour Becker. 273p. 1988. pap. 16.00 (*0-87580-539-6*) N Ill U Pr.

***Nobility, Land & Service in Medieval Hungary.** Martyn C. Rady. Ed. by London University College Staff. LC 00-41491. (Studies in Russia & East Europe). 2000. write for info. (*0-312-23582-8*) St Martin.

Nobility of Failure: Tragic Heroes in the History of Japan. Ivan Morris. (Noonday Ser.). 500p. 1988. pap. 17.00 (*0-374-52120-4*) FS&G.

Nobility of Holland: From Knights to Regents, 1500-1650. H. K. Van Nierop. Tr. by Maarten Ultee. (Cambridge Studies in Early Modern History). (Illus.). 270p. (C). 1993. text 69.95 (*0-521-39260-8*) Cambridge U Pr.

Nobility of the Desert: The Arab Horse of the Bedouins. F. B. Klynstra. Tr. by K. Schmitt & S. Eicher from GER. (Documenta Hippologica Ser.). (Illus.). 170p. 1990. lib. bdg. 55.00 (*3-487-08318-3*) G Olms Pubs.

Nobility of Toulouse in the Eighteenth Century. Robert Forster. LC 78-64233. (Johns Hopkins University. Studies in the Social Sciences. Thirtieth Ser. 1912: 1). reprint ed. 31.50 (*0-404-61338-1*) AMS Pr.

Noble - Dougherty: Descendants & Antecedents of Milton Bird & Leonora Dougherty Noble. M. Birdie Feiner. (Illus.). 398p. 1996. reprint ed. pap. 61.00 (*0-8328-5591-X*); reprint ed. lib. bdg. 71.00 (*0-8328-5590-1*) Higginson Bk Co.

Noble Abstractions: American Liberal Intellectuals & World War II. Frank A. Warren. LC 98-44839. 350p. 1999. text 40.00 (*0-8142-0814-2*) Ohio St U Pr.

Noble Achievements: Ohio Wesleyan from 1942-1992. Ed. by Bernard Murchland. (Illus.). 316p. 20.00 (*0-9630909-1-7*) OH Wesleyan U.

Noble & Dignified Stream: The Piscataqua River Region in the Colonial Revival, 1860-1930. Ed. by Kevin D. Murphy & Sarah L. Giffen. 272p. 1992. 50.00 (*0-9631955-0-6*) Old York Hist Soc.

Noble & Ivy. Carole Howey. 368p. (Orig.). 1996. mass mkt. 5.50 (*0-8439-4118-9*) Dorchester Pub Co.

Noble & Joyous Histories: English Romances, 1375-1650. Ed. by J. Pheifer & Ni Cuilleanain. 1993. 39.50 (*0-7165-2379-5*, Pub. by Irish Acad Pr) Intl Spec Bk.

Noble & Patriotic: The Beaumont Gift, 1828. Felicity Owen et al. (Illus.). 64p. 1988. pap. 14.95 (*0-295-96898-2*) U of Wash Pr.

Noble Arabian Horse see Arabiens edle Pferde

Noble Arabian Horse see Asil Araber IV: Arabiens edle Pferde

Noble Art of Politics: Political Cartoons, 1994-96. Martyn Turner. LC 96-219500. 114p. 1997. pap. 14.95 (*0-85640-583-3*, Pub. by Blackstaff Pr) Dufour.

Noble Art of Vending: An African Centered Guide to Vending Success. Gabriel Bandele. LC 92-97193. 100p. (Orig.). 1992. pap. 10.00 (*1-882706-01-3*) Bandele Pubns.

Noble Beginnings. large type ed. Christine M. Fraser. 424p. 1995. pap. 19.95 (*0-7862-0370-6*) Thorndike Pr.

Noble Bondsmen: Ministerial Marriages in the Archdiocese of Salzburg, 1100-1343. John B. Freed. (Illus.). 344p. 1995. text 52.50 (*0-8014-2975-7*) Cornell U Pr.

***Noble Breed.** Bill Cosgrove. LC 99-65960. 304p. 1999. 19.95 (*1-58244-063-8*) Rutledge Bks.

Noble Brutes: Camels on the American Frontier. Eva J. Boyd. LC 94-12228. 278p. 1994. pap. 12.95 (*1-55622-379-X*, Rep of TX Pr) Wordware Pub.

Noble but Plain: The Shaker Meetinghouse at Mount Lebanon. Jerry V. Grant. (Illus.). 20p. 1994. pap. text 4.95 (*0-937942-17-0*) Shaker Mus.

Noble Calling: Teacher Education at Lutheran Normal School & Augustana College, 1889-1989. Lynwood E. Oyos. LC 90-30516. 100p. (Orig.). 1990. pap. 2.00 (*0-931170-45-1*) Ctr Western Studies.

***Noble Cause.** Gerard J. De Groot. (Modern Wars in Perspective Ser.). 391p. (C). 1999. pap. 30.73 (*0-582-28717-0*) Longman.

***Noble Cause.** Gerard J. De Groot. (Modern Wars in Perspective Ser.). 400p. (C). 1999. 79.95 (*0-582-28718-9*) Longman.

Noble Collection: The Spencer Albums of Old Master Prints. Marjorie B. Cohn. (Illus.). 368p. 1992. pap. 19.95 (*0-916724-80-8*, 480-8) Harvard Art Mus.

Noble Crusade: The History of Eighth Army, 1941-1945. Richard Doherty. 1999. write for info. (*1-885119-63-1*) Sarpedon.

Noble Crusade: The History of Eighth Army 1941-1945. Richard Doherty. 352p. 1997. 100.00 (*1-86227-045-7*, Pub. by Spellmount Pubs) St Mut.

Noble Daughters: Unheralded Women in Western Christianity, 13th To 18th Centuries, 60. Marie A. Conn. LC 99-22142. 60. 144p. 2000. 49.95 (*0-313-30669-9*, Greenwood Pr) Greenwood.

Noble Death: Graeco-Roman Martyrology & Paul's Concept of Salvation. David Seeley. (JSNT Supplement Ser.: Vol. 28). 170p. 1990. 52.50 (*1-85075-185-4*, Pub. by Sheffield Acad) CUP Services.

Noble Deception. Sara Blayne. 1995. pap. 4.50 (*0-8217-5173-5*) NAL.

Noble Deeds. large type ed. Christine M. Fraser. (General Ser.). 375p. 1996. pap. 20.95 (*0-7862-0576-8*) Thorndike Pr.

Noble Deeds of American Women. Ed. by J. Clement. 480p. 1975. reprint ed. 31.95 (*0-87928-061-1*) Corner Hse.

Noble Deeds of American Women: With Biographical Sketches of Some of the More Prominent. Ed. by Jesse Clement. LC 74-3935. (Women in America Ser.). (Illus.). 482p. 1979. reprint ed. 42.95 (*0-405-06082-3*) Ayer.

***Noble Dreams, Wicked Pleasures: Orientalism in America, 1870-1930.** Ed. by Holly Edwards. LC 00-36685. (Illus.). 224p. 2000. pap. 29.95 (*0-691-05004-X*, Pub. by Princeton U Pr) Cal Prin Full Svc.

***Noble Dreams, Wicked Pleasures: Orientalism in America, 1870-1930.** Ed. by Holly Edwards. LC 00-36685. (Illus.). 224p. 2000. 60.00 (*0-691-05003-1*, Pub. by Princeton U Pr) Cal Prin Full Svc.

Noble Eightfold Path. Bhikkhu Bodhi. 144p. 1994. 6.00 (*955-24-0116-X*, Pub. by Buddhist Pub Soc) Vipassana Res Pubns.

Noble Eightfold Path. Manly P. Hall. 32p. 1995. pap. 4.95 (*0-89314-337-5*) Philos Res.

Noble Enemy. Charles Fox. 400p. 1982. mass mkt. 3.50 (*0-446-90672-7*, Pub. by Warner Bks) Little.

Noble Exercise: The Sporting Ideal in Eighteenth-Century British Art. Stephen Deuchar. LC 82-50676. (Illus.). 48p. (Orig.). 1982. pap. 5.75 (*0-930606-41-8*) Yale Ctr Brit Art.

Noble Experyence of the Vertuous Handy Warke of Surgeri. Von Braunschweig Hieronymus. LC 76-60044. (English Experience Ser.: No. 531). 156p. 1973. reprint ed. 30.00 (*90-221-0531-8*) Walter J Johnson.

Noble Families among the Sephardic Jews. I. DaCosta. 1976. lib. bdg. 134.95 (*0-8490-2349-1*) Gordon Pr.

Noble Gas & High Temperature Chemistry. (Structure & Bonding Ser.: Vol. 73). (Illus.). 264p. 1990. 118.95 (*0-387-52124-0*) Spr-Verlag.

Noble Gas Compounds. Ed. by Herbert H. Hyman. LC 63-20907. 1995. lib. bdg. 18.00 (*0-226-36540-9*) U Ch Pr.

Noble-Gas Compounds. Herbert H. Hyman. LC 63-20907. (Illus.). 418p. reprint ed. pap. 129.60 (*0-608-09409-9*, 205420900004) Bks Demand.

Noble Gases & Their Compounds. G. M. Moody & J. Thomas. LC 64-17965. 1964. 40.00 (*0-08-010843-1*, Pub. by Pergamon Repr) Franklin.

Noble Gyn of Comedy in the Middle English Cycle Plays. Virginia S. Carroll. (American University Studies: English Language & Literature: Ser. IV, Vol. 79). 248p. (C). 1989. text 34.95 (*0-8204-0714-3*) P Lang Pubng.

***Noble Heart.** Sara Blayne. (Regency Romance Ser.). 2000. mass mkt. 4.99 (*0-8217-6653-8*, Zebra Kensgtn) Kensgtn Pub Corp.

Noble Heritage: Five Centuries of Portraits from the Hosokawa Family. Jared Lubarsky. LC 92-12047. (Illus.). 112p. (Orig.). 1992. pap. 24.95 (*1-56098-209-8*) Smithsonian.

Noble Heritage: Jerusalem & Christianity - A Portrait. Alistair Duncan. 1974. 17.95 (*0-86685-011-2*) Intl Bk Ctr.

*** Noble Horse.** Angela S. Rixon. 96p. 2000. pap. 9.95 (*1-84215-330-7*) Anness Pub.

Noble House see James Clavell Library

Noble House. James Clavell. 1376p. 1984. mass mkt. 7.99 (*0-440-16484-2*) Dell.

Noble Jilt - Did He Steal It?, 2 vols. Anthony Trollope. Ed. by N. John Hall. LC 80-1906. (Selected Works of Anthony Trollope). 1981. reprint ed. lib. bdg. 33.95 (*0-405-14205-6*) Ayer.

Noble Landowners & Agriculture in Austria, 1815-1848: A Study in the Origins of the Peasant Emancipation of 1848. Jerome Blum. LC 78-64204. (Johns Hopkins University. Studies in Historical & Political Science: Extra Volumes; New Ser.: No. 2 1947). reprint ed. 42.50 (*0-404-61310-1*) AMS Pr.

Noble, le Serf et le Revizor. D. Beauvois. 356p. 1985. write for info. (*2-903928-31-2*) Gordon & Breach.

Noble, le Serf et le Revizor. 2nd ed. D. Beauvois. vi, 365p. 1991. pap. text 46.00 (*2-88124-075-5*) Gordon & Breach.

Noble Lies & Decent Drapery: Conservatism & the Law. Ireland. 62.95 (*1-85521-665-5*) Ashgate Pub Co.

Noble Lies, Slant Truths, Necessary Angels: Aspects of Fictionality in the Novels of Christoph Martin Wieland. Ellis Shookman. LC 96-30545. (Studies in the Germanic Languages & Literatures). 1997. 39.95 (*0-8078-8118-X*) U of NC Pr.

Noble Lies, Slant Truths, Necessary Angels: Aspects of Fictionality in the Novels of Christoph Martin Wieland. Ellis Shookman. LC 96-30545. (Studies in the Germanic Languages & Literatures). 256p. (C). (gr. 13). 1997. lib. bdg. 34.95 (*0-8078-8302-6*) U of NC Pr.

***Noble Madness.** Laura Casal. (Illus.). 76p. 1999. pap. 15.00 (*0-9668545-0-0*) PeecaPress.

Noble McCloud: A Novel. Harvey Havel. 400p. 1999. 19.95 (*0-9670081-5-8*) First Amndmnt.

Noble Merchant: Problems of Genre & Lineage in Hervis de Mes. Catherine M. Jones. LC 92-80590. (Studies in the Romance Languages & Literatures: No. 243). 170p. (C). 1992. pap. 27.50 (*0-8078-9245-9*) U of NC Pr.

Noble Metal Alloys: Phase Diagrams, Alloy Phase Stability, Thermodynamic Aspects, Properties & Special Features: Proceedings of the TMS Alloy Phase Committee, the TMS Thermodynamics Committee, & American Society for Metals Alloy Phase Diagram Data Committee, Held at the Metallurgical Society of AIME Annual Meeting, February 24-28, 1985. AIME, Metallurgical Society Staff. Ed. by T. B. Massalski et al. LC 85-29754. 370p. reprint ed. pap. 114.70 (*0-7837-2209-5*, 205245900004) Bks Demand.

Noble Metals & Biological Systems. Robert R. Brooks. 416p. 1992. lib. bdg. 179.00 (*0-8493-6164-8*, QP532) CRC Pr.

Noble Mistress. Janis Laden. 1987. mass mkt. 3.95 (*0-8217-2169-0*, Zebra Kensgtn) Kensgtn Pub Corp.

Noble Nephew. Martha Kirkland. 224p. 1998. pap. 4.99 (*0-8217-5956-6*) Kensgtn Pub Corp.

Noble Numbers, Subtle Words: The Art of Mathematics in the Science of Storytelling. Barbara M. Fisher. LC 96-47598. (Illus.). 168p. 1997. 31.50 (*0-8386-3740-X*) Fairleigh Dickinson.

Noble Outlaw. Braun. 1996. pap. write for info. (*0-312-95772-6*) St Martin.

Noble Outlaw. Matt Braun. 1996. mass mkt. 5.99 (*0-312-95941-9*) St Martin.

Noble Philosopher: Condorcet & the Enlightenment. Edward Goodell. LC 93-49525. 251p. (C). 1994. 34.95 (*0-87975-875-9*) Prometheus Bks.

Noble Piety & Reformed Monasticism. 166p. pap. 2.00 (*0-87907-864-2*) Cistercian Pubns.

Noble Power During the French Wars of Religion: The Guise Affinity & the Catholic Cause in Normandy. Stuart Carroll. LC 97-38680. (Cambridge Studies in Early Modern History). (Illus.). 224p. (C). 1998. text 59.95 (*0-521-62404-5*) Cambridge U Pr.

Noble Pursuit. Sara Blayne. 256p. 1997. mass mkt. 4.99 (*0-8217-5756-3*, Zebra Kensgtn) Kensgtn Pub Corp.

Noble Pursuit: The Sesquicentennial History of the New England Historic Genealogical Society. John A. Schutz. xxi, 281p. 1995. 25.00 (*0-88082-037-3*) New Eng Hist.

Noble Pursuits: Literature & the Hunt. Connie L. Scarborough & Dennis P. Seniff. (Homenajes Ser.: No. 8). 162p. 1992. 22.00 (*0-936388-55-2*) Juan de la Cuesta.

Noble Qur'an. Ed. by Muhammad M. Khan. 1100p. (Orig.). 1995. text 29.95 (*1-56744-499-7*) Kazi Pubns.

Noble Qur'an: Concise Version. Muhammad M. Khan. 1100p. 1995. 29.95 (*1-56744-518-7*) Kazi Pubns.

N

Noble Qur'an, Arabic-English: A Summarized Version of At-Tabari, Al-Qurtubi & Ibn Kathir with comments from Sahih Al-Bukhari, I. M. M. Khan. 1987. 29.95 (*0-933511-05-1*) Kazi Pubns.

Noble Qur'an, Arabic-English: A Summarized Version of At-Tabari, Al-Qurtubi & Ibn Kathir with comments from Sahih Al-Bukhari, II. M. M. Khan. 1992. 29.95 (*0-933511-06-X*) Kazi Pubns.

Noble Qur'an, Arabic-English: A Summarized Version of At-Tabari, Al-Qurtubi & Ibn Kathir with comments from Sahih Al-Bukhari, III. M. M. Khan. 1992. 29.95 (*0-933511-07-8*) Kazi Pubns.

Noble Qur'an, Arabic-English: A Summarized Version of At-Tabari, Al-Qurtubi & Ibn Kathir with comments from Sahih Al-Bukhari, IV. M. M. Khan. 1992. 29.95 (*0-933511-08-6*) Kazi Pubns.

Noble Red Man: Lakota Wisdomkeeper Mathew King. Ed. & Frwd. by Harvey Arden. 128p. 1994. 16.95 (*1-885223-01-3*) Beyond Words Pub.

***Noble Red Man: Lakota Wisdomkeeper Mathew King.** Mathew King. Ed. by Harvey Arden. (Illus.). 108p. 1999. text 17.00 (*0-7881-6001-X*) DIANE Pub.

Noble Resolve. Sara Blayne. 256p. 1998. pap. 4.99 (*0-8217-5912-4*) Kensgtn Pub Corp.

Noble Rogue. Nancy Lawrence. 224p. 1998. pap. 4.99 (*0-8217-5994-9*) Kensgtn Pub Corp.

Noble Savage: Allegory of Freedom. Stelio Cro. 184p. (C). 1990. text 29.95 (*0-88920-983-9*) W Laurier U Pr.

Noble Savage: Jean-Jacques Rousseau, 1754-1762. Maurice W. Cranston. (Illus.). 414p. 1991. 37.50 (*0-226-11863-0*) U Ch Pr.

Noble Savage: Satyrs & Satyr Families in Renaissance Art. Lynn F. Kaufmann. Ed. by Ann S. Harris. LC 83-24275. (Studies in Renaissance Art History: No. 2). 215p. reprint ed. pap. 66.70 (*0-8357-1482-9*, 207034700087) Bks Demand.

Noble Savage in the New World Garden: Notes Toward a Syntactics of Place. Gaile McGregor. LC 87-72549. 357p. (C). 1988. 34.95 (*0-87972-416-1*); pap. 17.95 (*0-87972-417-X*) Bowling Green Univ Popular Press.

Noble Savage: Jean-Jacques Rousseau, 1754-1762: Jean-Jacques Rousseau, 1754-1762. Maurice Cranston. LC 90-28111. (Illus.). 400p. 1999. pap. 20.00 (*0-226-11864-9*) U Ch Pr.

N

Noble Science: A Study & Transcription of Sloane Ms. 2530, Papers of the Masters of Defence of London, Temp. Henry VIII to 1590. Herbert Berry. LC 91-50103. (Illus.). 152p. 1991. 32.50 (*0-87413-441-2*) U Delaware Pr.

Noble Seed. large type ed. Christine M. Fraser. LC 97-23793. 1997. 21.95 (*0-7862-1204-7*) Thorndike Pr.

***Noble 76: National Organization Black Law Enforcement Executives Justice** LC 98-88561. 128 p. 1998. write for info. (*1-56311-465-8*) Turner Pub KY.

Noble Soldier. Thomas Dekker. LC 74-133655. (Tudor Facsimile Texts. Old English Plays Ser.: No. 140). reprint ed. 49.50 (*0-404-53440-6*) AMS Pr.

Noble Spirit. Alvin Morton. (Illus.). 272p. 1998. 43.00 (*0-8059-4463-X*) Dorrance.

Noble Tradition: American Painting from the National Arts Club. Carol Lowrey. (Illus.). 31p. (Orig.). 1995. pap. 14.00 (*1-880897-04-0*) Lyme Hist.

***Noble Tradition Revisited: Contemporary American Still Life.** Gerrit Henry et al. (Illus.). 36p. 1999. pap. 20.00 (*0-945936-25-7*) Spanierman Gallery.

Noble Traveller: The Life & Selected Writings of Oscar V. de Lubicz Milosz. Oscar V. De Lubicz Milosz. Tr. by David Gascoyne et al from FRE. LC 84-25029. (Illus.). 504p. (Orig.). 1985. 24.95 (*0-940262-15-0*, Lindisfarne); pap. 14.95 (*0-940262-16-9*, Lindisfarne) Anthroposophic.

Noble Women, Restless Men: The Rippley (Rieple, Ripley, Ripli, Rippli) Family in Wisconsin, North Dakota, Minnesota & Montana. LaVern J. Rippley. LC 96-68411. (Illus.). 300p. 1996. 35.00 (*0-9622931-6-4*) St Olaf German.

***Noble, Wretched, & Redeemable: Protestant Missionaries to the Indians in Canada & the United States, 1820-1900.** C. L. Higham. 2000. 39.95 (*0-8263-2165-8*) U of NM Pr.

***Noblemen & Kinsmen: History of a Sikh Family.** Preminder Singh Sandhawalia. (Illus.). 116p. 1999. 22.50 (*81-215-0914-9*, Pub. by M Manoharial) Coronet Bks.

Nobler in the Mind: The Stoic-Skeptic Dialectic in English Renaissance Tragedy. Geoffrey Aggeler. LC 98-14035. 200p. 1998. 36.50 (*0-87413-661-X*) U Delaware Pr.

Nobler Than the Angels, Lower Than a Worm: The Pietist View of the Individual in the Writings of Heinrich Muller & August Hermann Francke. Gary R. Sattler. 206p. (C). 1989. lib. bdg. 46.00 (*0-8191-7518-8*) U Pr of Amer.

Nobles. Richard G. Friend. (Illus.). 20p. 1995. pap. write for info. (*0-9649421-0-0*) R G Friend.

***Nobles & Nobility in Medieval Europe: Concepts, Origins, Transformations.** Ed. by Anne J. Duggan. LC 99-87553. (Illus.). 352p. 2000. 75.00 (*0-85115-769-6*) Boydell & Brewer.

Nobles in Nineteenth-Century France: The Practice of Inegalitarianism. David Higgs. LC 86-7393. (Johns Hopkins University Studies in Historical & Political Science: No. 1). 312p. 1987. reprint ed. pap. 96.80 (*0-608-04052-5*, 206478800011) Bks Demand.

Nobles, Knights, & Men-at-Arms in the Middle Ages. Maurice H. Keen. LC 95-49139. 1996. 60.00 (*1-85285-087-6*) Hambledon Press.

Nobles Memorias. 2nd ed. Manuel Sanguily. LC 80-67889. (SPA.). 246p. (Orig.). 1982. reprint ed. pap. 12.00 (*0-89729-262-6*) Ediciones.

***Noblesse Oblige.** Trisha David. (Azur Ser.: No. 805). (FRE.). 2000. mass mkt. 3.99 (*0-373-34805-3*, 1-34805-1, Harlequin French) Harlequin Bks.

Noblesse Oblige. Frank MacShane. 1999. text 19.95 (*0-670-81527-6*) Viking Penguin.

Noblesse Oblige. Cynthia Smith. 272p. (Orig.). 1996. mass mkt. 3.99 (*0-425-15549-8*, Prime Crime) Berkley Pub.

Noblesse Oblige. large type ed. Helen Argers. LC 94-45659. 424p. 1995. reprint ed. lib. bdg. 22.95 (*0-7838-1230-2*, G K Hall Lrg Type) Mac Lib Ref.

Noblesse Oblige: Charity & Cultural Philanthropy in Chicago. Kathleen D. McCarthy. LC 81-21849. (Illus.). 244p. reprint ed. pap. 75.70 (*0-608-09470-6*, 205427000005) Bks Demand.

Noblesse Oblige: Charity & Cultural Philanthropy in Chicago, 1849-1929. Kathleen D. McCarthy. LC 81-21849. (Illus.). 240p. (C). 1996. 24.00 (*0-226-55580-1*) U Ch Pr.

Noblesse Oblige: Essays in Honour of David Kessler Obe on His Ninetieth Birthday. David Kessler. Ed. by Alan D. Crown. LC 98-6080. (ENG & FRE.). 224p. 1998. 45.00 (*0-85303-356-0*, Pub. by F Cass Pubs) Intl Spec Bk.

Noblesse Oblige: Essays in Honour of David Kessler Obe on His Ninetieth Birthday. David Kessler & Alan D. Crown. LC 98-6080. (ENG & FRE.). 1998. pap. write for info. (*0-7146-4349-1*, Pub. by F Cass Pubs) Intl Spec Bk.

Noblesse Oblige: The Book of Houses. Bryant Durrell. (Changeling: The Dreaming Ser.). 1998. pap. text 18.00 (*1-56504-719-2*) White Wolf.

Noblesse Workshop on Non-Linear Model Based Image Analysis: Proceedings of NWBIA, 1-3 July 1998, Glasgow. Ed. by S. Marshall et al. LC 98-20454. (Illus.). xvi, 346p. 1998. pap. 99.00 (*3-540-76258-2*) Spr-Verlag.

Noblest Agitator: Daniel O'Connoll & the German Catholic Movement 1830-1850. Geraldine Grogan. 225p. 1989. pap. 45.00 (*1-85390-196-2*, Pub. by Veritas Pubns) St Mut.

Noblest Animate Motion: Speech, Physiology & Medicine in Pre-Cartesian Linguistic Thought. Jeffrey L. Wollock. LC 97-5838. (Studies in the History of the Language Sciences: Vol. 83). l, 461p. 1997. lib. bdg. 160.00 (*1-55619-620-2*) J Benjamins Pubng Co.

Noblest Love: The Sacramentality of Sex in Marriage. Clifford J. Stevens. (Schuyler Spiritual Ser.: Vol. 4). 84p. 1992. pap. text 3.70 (*1-56788-003-7*, 10-004) BMH Pubns.

Noblest Minds: Fame, Honor & the American Founding. Ed. by Peter McNamara. LC 99-18815. 288p. 1999. pap. 22.95 (*0-8476-8682-5*) Rowman.

Noblest Minds: Fame, Honor, & the American Founding. Ed. by Peter McNamara. LC 99-18815. 288p. 1999. 59.00 (*0-8476-8681-7*) Rowman.

Noblest Roman: Marcus Brutus & His Reputation. M. L. Clarke. LC 80-69178. (Aspects of Greek & Roman Life Ser.). 157p. 1981. text 37.50 (*0-8014-1393-1*) Cornell U Pr.

Noblest Triumph: Property & Prosperity Through the Ages. Tom Bethell. LC 98-6010. 378p. 1998. 29.95 (*0-312-21083-3*) St Martin.

Noblest Triumph: Property & Prosperity Through the Ages. Tom Bethell. 384p. 1999. pap. 16.95 (*0-312-22337-4*) St Martin.

Nobleza Del Andalucia. Gonzalo Argote De Molina. (Textos y Estudios Clasicos De las Literaturas Hispanicas Ser.). xx, 696p. 1975. reprint ed. 290.00 (*3-487-05607-0*) G Olms Pubs.

Nobodaddy. Archibald Macleish. LC 74-1356. (Studies in Poetry: No. 38). 1974. lib. bdg. 75.00 (*0-8383-2034-1*) M S G Haskell Hse.

Nobodaddy's Children. Arno B. Schmidt. Tr. by John E. Woods from GER. LC 95-16363. (Collected Early Fiction Ser.: Vol. 2). 237p. 1995. pap. 13.95 (*1-56478-090-2*) Dalkey Arch.

Nobodaddy's Children Vol. 2: Collected Early Fiction. Arno B. Schmidt. Tr. by John E. Woods from GER. LC 95-16363. 237p. 1995. 32.00 (*1-56478-083-X*) Dalkey Arch.

Nobody. Nikolai Bokov. Tr. by April Fitzlyon from RUS. 1979. pap. 11.95 (*0-7145-3551-6*) Riverrun NY.

Nobody & Somebody. LC 75-133718. (Tudor Facsimile Texts. Old English Plays Ser.: No. 113). reprint ed. 49.50 (*0-404-53413-9*) AMS Pr.

Nobody Asked Me. Steve Henry. (J). 14.95 (*0-688-17865-0*, Wm Morrow); lib. bdg. 14.89 (*0-688-17866-9*, Wm Morrow) Morrow Avon.

Nobody Better, Better Than Nobody. Ian Frazier. LC 97-15030. 181p. 1997. reprint ed. pap. 14.95 (*1-55821-598-0*) Lyons Pr.

Nobody Boy. Sharon D. Wyeth. LC 96-38207. 1997. pap. 3.99 (*0-679-85645-5*) Random.

Nobody Boy. Sharon D. Wyeth. LC 96-38207. (J). 1997. lib. bdg. 11.99 (*0-679-95645-X*) Random.

Nobody Can Imagine Our Longing: Addresses from the Association of Women of the Mediterranean Region, 1996 Conference. Ed. by Yana M. Bland. LC 96-72590. (Foundation Ser.). (Illus.). 136p. (Orig.). 1997. pap. 12.95 (*0-911051-93-7*) Plain View.

Nobody Can Kick You Unless You Bend Over: A Book about People, Problems, & Personal Pride. Fred Maes. (Illus.). (Orig.). 1997. pap. write for info. (*1-890462-01-2*) J Francisco.

Nobody Club. Madge Harrah. 176p. 1989. pap. 2.50 (*0-380-75631-5*, Avon Bks) Morrow Avon.

Nobody Dies in a Casino. Marlys Millhiser. LC 99-12859. 288p. 1999. text 22.95 (*0-312-20344-6*) St Martin.

Nobody Does It Better. Elizabeth Cage. (Spy Girls Ser.: No. 3). (YA). (gr. 7 up). 1999. mass mkt. 4.50 (*0-671-02288-1*, Minstrel Bks) PB.

Nobody Does It Better. Jan Freed. (Women Who Dare Ser.). 1997. per. 3.99 (*0-373-70741-X*, 1-70741-3) Harlequin Bks.

***Nobody Does It Better.** Julie Kenner. (Temptation Ser.: Vol. 772). 2000. mass mkt. 3.99 (*0-373-25872-0*) Harlequin Bks.

Nobody Drowns in Mineral Lake. Michael B. Druxman. LC 99-10203. 286p. 1999. pap. 12.95 (*1-889198-04-8*) Ctr Pr CA.

***Nobody Else Has to Know.** Ingrid Tomey. LC 98-43059. 240p. 1999. 15.95 (*0-385-32624-6*) Dela Pr.

***Nobody Else Has to Know.** Ingrid Tomey. 2000. mass mkt. 4.99 (*0-440-22782-8*, LE) Dell.

Nobody Fixes Real Carrot Sticks Anymore. Marianne M. Jennings. 144p. (Orig.). 1994. pap. 10.00 (*0-9643174-0-0*) Woodchip Pub.

***Nobody Gave Me Permission.** Ora Mobley Sweeting. LC 99-91570. 1999. 25.00 (*0-7388-0884-9*); pap. 18.00 (*0-7388-0885-7*) Xlibris Corp.

Nobody Gets off the Bus: Viet Nam Generation Big Book. Ed. by Kali Tal & Dan Duffy. (Illus.). 426p. (Orig.). (C). 1994. pap. text 30.00 (*0-9628524-8-1*) Burning Cities Pr.

Nobody Gets Rich Working for Somebody Else: An Entrepreneur's Guide. Roger Fritz. Ed. by Brenda Machosky. LC 92-54354. 280p. (Orig.). 1993. pap. 15.95 (*1-56052-165-1*) Crisp Pubns.

Nobody Home. Jennifer L. Paul. 1977. 7.95 (*0-393-08766-2*) Norton.

Nobody Hurt in Small Earthquake. large type ed. Michael Green. 344p. 1991. 21.95 (*1-85089-496-5*, Pub. by ISIS Lrg Prnt) Transaction Pubs.

Nobody Is Perfick, 001. Bernard Waber. 128p. (J). (ps-3). 1991. pap. 6.95 (*0-395-31669-3*) HM.

Nobody Is Perfick. Bernard Waber. 1971. 11.05 (*0-606-01436-5*, Pub. by Turtleback) Demco.

Nobody Knew but God: Miriam & Baby Moses. Marilyn Lashbrook. (Me Too! Bks.). (J). (gr. k-5). 1998. 5.95 (*0-933657-86-2*, 30001064) Rainbow Studies.

Nobody Knows but Me. Eve Bunting. (FastBack Romance Ser.). 1984. 11.27 (*0-606-00352-5*, Pub. by Turtleback) Demco.

Nobody Knows My Name: More Notes of a Native Son. James Baldwin. LC 92-50565. 192p. 1993. pap. 11.00 (*0-679-74473-8*) Vin Bks.

Nobody Knows the Calories I've Seen. Arthur Sturges. LC 92-13686. 156p. 1992. pap. 12.95 (*0-87131-699-4*) M Evans.

***Nobody Knows the Trouble I've Seen.** Velma Maia Thomas. 2001. 29.95 (*0-609-60719-7*, Pub. by Crown Pub Group) Random House.

Nobody Knows the Truffles I've Seen: A Memoir. George Lang. LC 97-42598. 416p. 1998. 28.95 (*0-679-45094-7*) McKay.

Nobody Knows What the Stork Will Bring. Charles Criswell. 1958. 11.95 (*0-8392-1076-0*) Astor-Honor.

Nobody Laughs, Nobody Cries. Charles Philbrick. LC 73-93613. (Illus.). 128p. 1976. 15.00 (*0-912292-33-4*) Smith.

***Nobody Left to Hate: Teaching Compassion after Columbine.** Elliot Aronson. 2000. 19.95 (*0-7167-4132-6*) W H Freeman.

Nobody Like Me. Stan Campbell. 96p. (YA). (gr. 7-9). 1986. teacher ed. 2.80 (*0-89693-188-9*, Victor Bks); pap., student ed. 0.60 (*0-89693-515-9*, Victor Bks) Chariot Victor.

Nobody Likes a Smartass: Expert Testimony by Psychologists. R. Buckhout. (Monographs: No. CR-44). 1976. 5.00 (*1-55524-045-3*) Ctr Respon Psych.

Nobody Likes Me! Raoul Krischanitz & Rosemary Lanning. LC 98-42106. (J). (ps-2). 1999. lib. bdg. 15.88 (*0-7358-1055-9*, Pub. by North-South Bks NYC) Chronicle Bks.

Nobody Likes Me! Raoul Krischanitz & Rosemary Lanning. LC 98-42106. (Illus.). 32p. (J). (ps-2). 1999. 15.95 (*0-7358-1054-0*, Pub. by North-South Bks NYC) Chronicle Bks.

Nobody Likes Me. Fay Weldon. (Illus.). 32p. (J). (ps-2). 1998. 19.95 (*0-370-32462-5*, Pub. by Bodley Head) Trafalgar.

"Nobody Likes Me" Helping Your Child Make Friends. Elaine K. McEwan. 96p. 1996. pap. 6.99 (*0-87788-590-7*, H Shaw Pubs) Waterbrook Pr.

Nobody Listens. (Illus.). (J). (ps-2). 1991. pap. 5.10 (*0-8136-5959-0*) Modern Curr.

Nobody Listens to Andrew. Elizabeth Guilfoile. (Illus.). (J). (ps-2). 1991. lib. bdg. 7.95 (*0-8136-5201-4*) Modern Curr.

Nobody Lives Forever. Edna R. Buchanan. 1992. mass mkt. 5.99 (*0-8217-3712-0*, Zebra Kensgtn) Kensgtn Pub Corp.

Nobody Lives Forever. Edna R. Buchanan. 400p. 1997. mass mkt. 5.99 (*1-57566-123-3*, Knsington) Kensgtn Pub Corp.

Nobody Lives Here Who Saw This Sky. Greg Kosmicki. 128p. 1998. pap. 12.00 (*1-892034-01-8*) Missing Spoke.

Nobody Lives in Apartment N-2. Anne Schraff. Ed. by Liz Parker. (Take Ten Bks.). (Illus.). 45p. (J). (gr. 6-12). 1992. pap. text 3.95 (*1-56254-057-2*) Saddleback Pubns.

***Nobody Lives in Apartment N-2.** rev. ed. Anne Schraff. (Take Ten Ser.). (Illus.). 49p. (YA). (gr. 4-12). 1999. pap. 3.95 (*1-58659-001-4*) Artesian.

Nobody Lives on Arthur Godfrey Boulevard. Gerald Costanzo. (American Poets Continuum Ser.: Vol. 24). 77p. 1992. 20.00 (*0-918526-92-2*); pap. 10.00 (*0-918526-93-0*) BOA Edns.

Nobody Loves a Drunken Indian. Clair Huffaker. 1993. reprint ed. lib. bdg. 29.95 (*1-56849-031-3*) Buccaneer Bks.

Nobody Loves an Albatross. Ronald Alexander. 1964. pap. 5.25 (*0-8222-0830-X*) Dramatists Play.

Nobody Loves Me. A. B. Publishing Staff. 1998. pap. text 6.95 (*1-881545-83-0*) Angelas Bkshelf.

Nobody Nothing Never. Juan J. Saer. (Masks Ser.). 224p. 1994. pap. 14.99 (*1-85242-273-4*) Serpents Tail.

Nobody Nowhere. Donna Williams. 224p. 1992. 24.50 (*0-385-25372-9*) Doubleday.

Nobody Nowhere. Donna Williams. 224p. 1993. mass mkt. 14.95 (*0-385-25425-3*) Doubleday.

Nobody Nowhere..Autistic. Donna Williams. 248p. 1994. pap. 12.50 (*0-380-72217-8*, Avon Bks) Morrow Avon.

Nobody Overeats. Susan Madden. LC 97-61705. 176p. 1997. pap. 12.95 (*1-890394-10-6*, Sage Creek) Rhodes & Easton.

Nobody Owns the Sky: The Story of "Brave Bessie" Coleman. Reeve Lindbergh. LC 96-6901. (Illus.). 32p. (J). (gr. 1-4). 1996. 15.99 (*1-56402-533-0*) Candlewick Pr.

***Nobody Owns the Sky: The Story of "Brave Bessie" Coleman.** Reeve Lindbergh. (J). 1998. 11.19 (*0-606-13668-1*, Pub. by Turtleback) Demco.

Nobody Owns the Sky: The Story of "Brave Bessie" Coleman. Reeve Lindbergh. LC 96-6901. (Illus.). 32p. (J). (gr. 1-4). 1998. reprint ed. pap. 5.99 (*0-7636-0361-9*) Candlewick Pr.

***Nobody Rides the Unicorn.** Adrian Mitchell. LC 99-27374. (Illus.). 32p. (J). (ps-3). 2000. 16.95 (*0-439-11204-4*, A A Levine) Scholastic Inc.

Nobody Roots for Goliath: A Bomber Hanson Mystery. David Champion. LC 96-3399. 319p. 1996. 22.95 (*1-888310-44-8*) A A Knoll Pubs.

Nobody Said It Would Be Easy. Marilyn Halvorson. 208p. (YA). (gr. 7-12). 1993. reprint ed. pap. write for info. (*0-614-17737-5*) Stoddart Publ.

Nobody Said It Would Be Easy. unabridged ed. Marilyn Halverson. 208p. (YA). (gr. 7-11). 1984. pap. 4.95 (*0-7736-7396-2*) STDK.

Nobody Said No: The Real Story about How the Mounties Always Get Their Man. Jeff Sallot. 207p. 1979. 0.99 (*0-88862-286-4*, Pub. by J Lorimer) Formac Dist Ltd.

Nobody Said Not to Go: The Life, Loves & Adventures of Emily Hahn. Ken Cuthbertson. (Illus.). 400p. 1999. pap. 16.00 (*0-571-19965-8*) Faber & Faber.

Nobody Said Not to Go: The Remarkable Life of Emily Hahn. Ken Cuthbertson. LC 97-43687. (Illus.). 386p. 1998. 29.95 (*0-571-19950-X*) Faber & Faber.

Nobody to Somebody in 63 Days or Less: The Ultimate How-to Guide to Business Networking & Word of Mouth Advertising. Joseph C. Ilvento & Arnold Sanow. LC 97-215719. 180p. 1996. 30.00 (*0-9654362-0-9*) Applied Bus Comm.

Nobody Told Me I'd Have to Sell: How to Sell Your Services & Skills, Even If You're Not in Sales. Dick Kendall. 224p. 1995. 18.95 (*1-55972-302-5*, Birch Ln Pr) Carol Pub Group.

Nobody Wants Annie. Linda J. Altman. (Sundown Fiction Collection). (Illus.). (J). (gr. 3). 1993. 3.95 (*0-88336-209-0*) New Readers.

Nobody Wants Annie: Reading Level 3. (Sundown Fiction Collection). 1993. audio 17.95 (*0-88336-256-2*) New Readers.

"Nobody Wants to Hear Our Truth" Homeless Women & Theories of the Welfare State, 153. Meredith L. Ralston. LC 95-19319. (Contributions in Women's Studies: Vol. 153). 224p. 1996. 57.95 (*0-313-29292-2*, Greenwood Pr) Greenwood.

Nobody's Angel. Thomas McGuane. (Vintage Contemporaries Ser.). 1986. pap. 14.00 (*0-394-74738-0*) Vin Bks.

***Nobody's Angel.** Patricia Rice. 2001. mass mkt. 6.99 (*0-449-00602-6*) Ballantine Pub Grp.

Nobody's Angel. Karen Robards. 416p. 1992. mass mkt. 5.99 (*0-440-20828-9*) Dell.

Nobody's Angel. large type ed. Karen Robards. 575p. 1992. reprint ed. lib. bdg. 20.95 (*1-56054-449-X*) Thorndike Pr.

Nobodys Angel: A Book of Satanic Abuse. Greg Reid. LC 97-93064. 96p. 1998. pap. 14.95 (*0-9657066-9-9*) Magic Press.

Nobody's Angels: Middle-Class Women & Domestic Ideology in Victorian Culture. Elizabeth Langland. LC 94-24393. (Reading Women Writing Ser.). 288p. 1995. text 42.50 (*0-8014-3045-3*); pap. text 16.95 (*0-8014-8220-8*) Cornell U Pr.

Nobody's Baby. Barbara Bretton. (Men Made in America Ser.). 1994. per. 3.59 (*0-373-45178-4*, 1-45178-0) Harlequin Bks.

Nobody's Baby. Elizabeth Smith. 1997. mass mkt. 3.99 (*1-85487-931-6*) London Brdge.

Nobody's Baby. Jane Toombs. 1997. per. 3.99 (*0-373-24081-3*, 1-24081-1) Silhouette.

Nobody's Baby but Mine. Susan Elizabeth Phillips. LC 96-96877. 376p. 1997. mass mkt. 6.99 (*0-380-78234-0*, Avon Bks) Morrow Avon.

Nobody's Baby but Mine. large type ed. Susan Elizabeth Phillips. LC 97-6785. (Core Ser.). 501p. 1997. lib. bdg. 27.95 (*0-7838-8197-5*, G K Hall Lrg Type) Mac Lib Ref.

Nobody's Best Friend: Loving & Learning with Adoptive Dogs, 1. Lorraine Houston. 1998. pap. text 12.95 (*0-9648913-6-0*) MCE.

Nobody's Boy. Hector H. Malot. 301p. 1991. reprint ed. lib. bdg. 35.95 (*0-89966-760-0*) Buccaneer Bks.

Nobody's Business. Alida Brill. 1991. pap. 9.57 (*0-201-56754-7*) Addison-Wesley.

Nobody's Business. Smith. 224p. (J). 14.95 (*0-06-028242-8*); lib. bdg. 14.89 (*0-06-028243-6*) HarpC.

Nobody's Business: The Paradoxes of Privacy. Alida Brill. 1990. 17.26 (*0-201-06745-5*) Addison-Wesley.

Nobody's Business: The Political Intruder's Guide to Everyone's State Legislature. Toby Moffett. LC 73-83355. (Illus.). 196p. 1973. 9.50 (*0-85699-080-9*); pap. 3.95 (*0-85699-081-7*) Chatham Pr.

*Nobody's Business but Your Own: A Business Start-Up Guide with Advice from Today's Most Successful Young Entrepreneurs. Carolyn M. Brown. LC 98-41065. (Illus.). 352p. (Orig.). 1999. pap. 14.95 (0-7868-8301-4, Pub. by Hyperion) Time Warner.

Nobody's Cat. Barbara M. Joosse. LC 91-37619. (Illus.). 32p. (J). (gr. k-3). 1992. lib. bdg. 14.89 (0-06-020835-X) HarpC Child Bks.

Nobody's Child. Janet Dawson. 1996. mass mkt. 5.99 (0-449-22356-6) Fawcett.

Nobody's Child. Ann Major. 1997. per. 3.50 (0-373-76105-8, 1-76105-5) Silhouette.

Nobody's Child. Pat Warren. (Special Edition Ser.). 1995. per. 3.75 (0-373-09974-6, 1-09974-6) Silhouette.

Nobody's Child. Marie Balter & Richard Katz. 1992. reprint ed. pap. 13.00 (0-201-60816-2) Addison-Wesley.

Nobody's Child: The Marie Balter Story. Marie Balter. 1991. 17.95 (0-201-57073-4) Addison-Wesley.

*Nobody's Child Anymore: Grieving, Caring & Comforting When Parents Die. Barbara Bartocci. LC 00-102081. 128p. 2000. pap. 11.95 (1-893732-21-5) SORIN BKS.

Nobody's Children: Abuse & Neglect, Foster Drift & the Adoption Alternative. Elizabeth Bartholet. LC 99-22976. 320p. 1999. 28.50 (0-8070-2318-3) Beacon Pr.

*Nobody's Children: Abuse & Neglect, Foster Drift & the Adoption Alternative. Elizabeth Bartholet. 2000. pap. 17.50 (0-8070-2319-1) Beacon Pr.

Nobody's Children: Orphans of the HIV Epidemic. Steven Dansky. LC 96-48940. 1995. 39.95 (1-56024-881-5) Haworth Pr.

Nobody's Children: Orphans of the HIV Epidemic. Steven F. Dansky. LC 96-48940. 178p. 1997. 54.95 (1-56023-855-0, Harrington Park); pap. 14.95 (1-56023-923-9, Harrington Park) Haworth Pr.

Nobody's Darling. Teresa Medeiros. 400p. 1998. mass mkt. 5.99 (0-553-57501-5) Bantam.

Nobody's Darling. large type ed. Josephine Cox. 640p. 32.99 (0-7089-8827-X) Ulverscroft.

Nobody's Darling. large type ed. Teresa Medeiros. LC 98-39411. (Large Print Bks.). 1998. pap. 22.95 (1-56895-675-4) Wheeler Pub.

Nobody's Daughter. Susan Beth Pfeffer. 160p. (J). (gr. 3-7). 1996. pap. 3.99 (0-440-41160-2) Dell.

Nobody's Daughter. Susan Beth Pfeffer. LC 94-19681. (J). 1996. 9.09 (0-606-09698-1, Pub. by Turtleback) Demco.

*Nobody's Daughter. Susan Beth Pfeffer. 154p. (J). (gr. 5-7). 1999. reprint ed. text 15.00 (0-7881-6627-1) DIANE Pub.

Nobody's Daughter: A Woman's Poetic Journal. Katie Reilly. Ed. by Barbara Wolf. LC 96-71980. 100p. 1997. 13.95 (0-9656367-0-4) Slow Please Pr.

Nobody's Dog. Charlotte Towner Graeber. LC 97-25632. (Illus.). 32p. (J). (gr. k-2). 1998. 12.95 (0-7868-0109-3, Pub. by Hyperion); lib. bdg. 13.49 (0-7868-2093-4, Pub. by Hyperion) Little.

Nobody's Dog, 4. Ellen Weiss. (J). 1996. 9.09 (0-606-08476-2, Pub. by Turtleback) Demco.

Nobody's Ever Cried for Me . . . Dave Roever & Karen C. Crump. 157p. 1992. pap. 15.00 (0-9648148-1-1) Roever Commun.

Nobody's Family Is Going to Change. Louise Fitzhugh. LC 74-19152. (Sunburst Ser.). (Illus.). 221p. (J). (gr. 4-7). 1986. pap. 4.95 (0-374-45523-6) FS&G.

Nobody's Fault. Doreen Gale. 1997. pap. 9.95 (1-57532-064-9) Press-Tige Pub.

Nobody's Fault. Slightly Off Center Writers Group Staff. (Orig.). 1995. pap. 8.95 (1-56721-114-3) Twnty-Fifth Cent Pr.

Nobody's Fault, Everybody's Responsibility: What Parents Can Do When a Child Is Using Alcohol & Other Drugs. Joseph A. Muldoon. 48p. (Orig.). 1989. pap. 3.95 (0-945485-09-3) Comm Intervention.

Nobody's Fool. Marten Claridge. 312p. 1991. 19.95 (0-8027-5793-6) Walker & Co.

Nobody's Fool. Martin Gottfried. (Illus.). 400p. 1994. 24.00 (0-671-86494-7) S&S Trade.

Nobody's Fool. Cynthia Harrod-Eagles. 160p. 1997. 22.00 (0-7278-4934-4) Severn Hse.

Nobody's Fool. Richard Russo. 1994. pap. 14.00 (0-679-75333-8) Knopf.

Nobody's Girl. Hector H. Malot. 301p. 1991. reprint ed. 31.95 (0-89966-759-7) Buccaneer Bks.

Nobody's Girl: A Novel. Antonya Nelson. LC 97-34839. 285p. 1998. 21.50 (0-684-83932-6) S&S Trade.

Nobody's Girl: A Novel. Antonya Nelson. 288p. 1999. pap. 12.00 (0-684-85207-1) S&S Trade.

Nobody's Hell. Douglas Goetsch. LC 98-47420. 74p. 1999. pap. 13.00 (1-882413-60-1) Hanging Loose.

Nobodys Hell. Douglas Goetsch. LC 98-47420. 1999. 21.00 (1-882413-61-X) Hanging Loose.

Nobody's Hero (Rebels & Rogues) Patricia Keelyn. (Temptation Ser.). 1996. per. 3.50 (0-373-25682-5, 1-25682-5) Harlequin Bks.

Nobody's Home: Dreams & Reality in a New Suburb. Lyn Richards. 336p. 1990. pap. 19.95 (0-19-554761-6) OUP.

Nobody's Home: Speech, Self & Place in American Fiction from Hawthorne to DeLillo. Arnold Weinstein. LC 92-22792. 368p. (C). 1993. pap. text 29.95 (0-19-508022-X) OUP.

Nobody's King. Steven H. West. LC 96-92263. (Illus.). x, 54p. (Orig.). (J). (gr. 3-5). 1996. pap. 5.95 (0-9652042-1-9) PgeWorthy Bks.

Nobody's Mother . . . Nobody's Wife: (When Women Feel Alone) Beryl Hammonds. (Illus.). 28p. (Orig.). 1994. pap. 6.95 (1-883244-01-3) Distinct Prod.

Nobody's Mother Is in Second Grade. Robin Pulver. LC 91-16395. (Illus.). 32p. (J). (gr. k-3). 1992. 15.99 (0-8037-1210-3, Dial Yng Read) Peng Put Young Read.

Nobody's Orphan. Anne M. Lindbergh. (J). (gr. 3-7). 1987. pap. 2.95 (0-380-70395-5, Avon Bks) Morrow Avon.

Nobody's Perfect. John Bowman. 150p. 1998. pap. 9.95 (0-9650797-3-2) J L Bowman.

*Nobody's Perfect. Amanda Christie. 1999. pap. 4.99 (0-375-80433-1) Random.

Nobody's Perfect. Patricia Haley-Brown. LC 98-92837. (Illus.). 324p. 1998. pap. 12.95 (0-9663174-1-6) Anointed Vision.

Nobody's Perfect. Curt Johnson. LC 73-87508. (Illus.). 236p. 1974. pap. 12.50 (0-914140-01-9) Carpenter Pr.

Nobody's Perfect. Hendrie Weisinger & Norman Lobsenz. 288p. 1988. mass mkt. 4.50 (0-446-35360-4, Pub. by Warner Bks) Little.

Nobody's Perfect. Donald E. Westlake. 240p. 1989. mass mkt. 5.50 (0-445-40715-8, Pub. by Warner Bks) Little.

Nobody's Perfect. Donald E. Westlake. 1994. pap. write for info. (0-446-40715-1, Mysterious Paperbk) Warner Bks.

Nobody's Perfect: Living & Growing with Children Who Have Special Needs. Nancy B. Miller. LC 93-2556. (Illus.). 272p. 1993. pap. 21.00 (1-55766-143-X) P H Brookes.

Nobody's Perfect, Cassie! Katy Hall. (Paxton Cheerleaders Ser.: No. 6). (J). (gr. 3-6). 1995. mass mkt. 3.99 (0-671-52052-0, Minstrel Bks) PB.

Nobody's Perfect, Not Even My Mother. Norma Simon. Ed. by Kathleen Tucker. LC 81-520. (Albert Whitman Concept Bks.). (Illus.). 32p. (J). (gr. k-3). 1981. lib. bdg. 13.95 (0-8075-5707-2) A Whitman.

Nobody's Princess. Jennifer Greene. 1997. per. 3.50 (0-373-76087-6, 1-76087-5) Silhouette.

*Nobody's Safe. Richard Steinberg. 496p. 2000. mass mkt. 6.50 (0-553-58188-0) Bantam.

Nobody's Safe. Richard Steinberg. LC 98-19495. 416p. 1999. 23.95 (0-385-49258-8) Doubleday.

Nobody's Son. Sean Stewart. 288p. 1995. mass mkt. 5.50 (0-441-00128-9) Ace Bks.

*Nobody's Son. Sean Stewart. LC 99-54324. (Illus.). 288p. (J). (gr. 7-12). 2000. pap. 6.00 (0-15-202259-7) Harcourt.

Nobody's Son: Notes from an American Life. Luis A. Urrea. LC 98-8924. (Camino Del Sol Ser.). 190p. 1998. 19.95 (0-8165-1865-3) U of Ariz Pr.

Nobody's Story: The Vanishing Acts of Women Writers in the Marketplace, 1670-1820. Catherine Gallagher. (New Historicism Ser.: Vol. 31). 339p. 1995. pap. 16.95 (0-520-20338-0, Pub. by U CA Pr) Cal Prin Full Svc.

*Nobody's There. Joan Lowery Nixon. LC 99-55106. (Illus.). 192p. (YA). (gr. 4-7). 2000. 15.95 (0-385-32567-3, Delacorte Pr Bks) BDD Bks Young Read.

Nobody's Warriors. I. C. Modrick. LC 96-69085. 167p. (Orig.). 1997. pap. 14.95 (1-57197-034-7) Pentland Pr.

*Nobrow: The Culture of Marketing, the Marketing of Culture. John Seabrook. LC 99-31126. 240p. 2000. 23.00 (0-375-40504-6) Knopf.

Nobuyoshi Araki. Toshiharu Ito. (Illus.). 96p. 1997. 29.95 (4-7713-2832-3) Dist Art Pubs.

*Nobuyoshi Araki: Araki in Wein, 2 Vols. Nobuyoshi Araki. 1999. 65.00 (4-7713-0316-9) Dist Art Pubs.

Nobuyoshi Araki: Shijyo - Tokyo, Marketplace of Emotions. Zdenek Felix. (Illus.). 136p. 1998. 45.00 (3-908161-21-5) Abbeville Pr.

*Nobuyoshi Araki: Taipei. Nobuyoshi Araki. 1999. 120.00 (4-7713-0324-X) Dist Art Pubs.

Noces Barbares. Yann Queffelec. (Folio Ser.: No. 1856). (FRE.). 308p. 1985. pap. 9.95 (2-07-037856-X) Schoenhof.

*Noces de Feu. Helen Bianchin. (Azur Ser.: No. 789). (FRE.). 1999. mass mkt. 3.99 (0-373-34789-8, 1-34789-7) Harlequin Bks.

Noces et l'Ete. Albert Camus. (FRE.). 1972. pap. 10.95 (0-8288-3667-1, F90682) Fr & Eur.

Noces in Full Score. Igor Stravinsky. 1998. 10.95 (0-486-29366-1, 281837Q) Dover.

Noces in Full Score. unabridged ed. Igor Stravinsky. (Illus.). 144p. 1998. pap. 12.95 (0-486-40413-7) Dover.

Noces Sevillannes. Rebecca Winters. (Horizon Ser.). (FRE.). 1997. pap. 3.50 (0-373-39435-7, 1-39435-2) Harlequin Bks.

Noces Suivi de l'Ete. Albert Camus. (FRE.). 1972. pap. 10.95 (0-7859-1686-5, 2070360164) Fr & Eur.

Noch Etwas Teifer Losen Sich die Menschen in Nichtigkeiten Auf: Figuren in Robert Musils Roman der Mann Ohne Eigenschaften. Jelka Schilt. (GER.). 1995. 44.95 (3-906755-30-4) P Lang Pubng.

Noche Blanca (White Night) Kathleen O'Brien. (SPA.). 1997. per. 3.50 (0-373-33423-0, 1-33423-4) Harlequin Bks.

Noche Callada (Poemas) Mercedes Castro. (SPA., Illus.). 79p. (Orig.). pap. 3.75 (0-9604748-0-3) Castro.

Noche de Bodas: Mistress & Mother. Lynne Graham. (Bianca Ser.: Vol. 116).Tr. of Wedding Night. (SPA.). 1998. per. 3.50 (0-373-33466-4, 1-33466-3) Harlequin Bks.

Noche de Humo. Eve Bunting. Tr. by Gloria De Aragon Andujar. LC 98-15863.Tr. of Smoky Night. (SPA., Illus.). 36p. (Orig.). (J). 1999. pap. 6.00 (0-15-201946-4) Harcourt.

Noche de las Estrellas see Night of the Stars

Noche de las Estrellas. (Illus.). (J). pap. 6.95 (980-257-041-9, Pub. by Ediciones Ekare) Kane-Miller Bk.

*Noche del Muneco Viviente II. R. L. Stine, pseud. (SPA., Illus.). (J). 1999. 10.00 (0-606-16955-5) Turtleback.

*Noche del Muneco Viviente II, Vol. 31. R. L. Stine, pseud. (Escalofrios Ser.: Vol. 31). (SPA.). (J). (gr. 3-7). 1999. pap. 3.99 (0-439-06627-1) Scholastic Inc.

Noche de Paz: La Navidad, 1. Mary Manz Simon. (Hear Me Read Ser.). 1999. pap. text 2.75 (0-570-09927-7) Concordia.

Noche de Primavera sin Sueno: Comedia Humoristica en Tres Actos. Enrique J. Poncela. Ed. by Francisco C. Lacosta. LC 67-25113. (SPA.). (YA). (gr. 9 up). 1967. pap. text 6.95 (0-89197-320-6) Irvington.

Noche del Muneco Viviente. R. L. Stine, pseud. (Escalofrios Ser.: No. 7).Tr. of Night of the Living Dummy. (SPA.). 144p. (J). (gr. 3-7). 1997. mass mkt. 3.99 (0-590-04141-X) Scholastic Inc.

Noche del Muneco Viviente. R. L. Stine, pseud. (Escalofrios Ser.: No. 7).Tr. of Night of the Living Dummy. 1997. 9.09 (0-606-11543-9, Pub. by Turtleback) Demco.

Noche del Te: El Gaban. Vicente Cabrera. LC 84-50238. (SPA.). 61p. 1984. pap. 10.00 (0-89295-035-8) Society Sp & Sp-Am.

Noche en Sus Brazos. Penny Jordan. (Bianca Ser.: No. 173).Tr. of One Night in His Arms. (SPA.). 1999. per. 3.50 (0-373-33523-7, 1-33523-1) Harlequin Bks.

*Noche Especial. Penny Jordan. (Bianca Ser.).Tr. of Special Night. (SPA.). 2000. mass mkt. 3.50 (0-373-33569-5, 1-33569-4) Harlequin Bks.

Noche, Fuente: Poesia. 2nd ed. Carlos M. Passalacqua. LC 79-23317. (Illus.). 98p. 1981. 6.00 (0-8477-3226-6) U of PR Pr.

*Noche Juntos. Diane Pershing. Vol. 224. (SPA.). 2000. per. 3.50 (0-373-35354-5) S&S Trade.

*Noche Mas Larga. Juan Jose Benitez. (SPA.). 1999. pap. 14.95 (84-08-02857-X) Planeta.

Noche Oscura del Nino Aviles. Edgardo R. Julia. 456p. 1991. pap. 16.95 (0-8477-3664-4) U of PR Pr.

*Noche Que Se Caybo la Luna. Pat Mora. (SPA., Illus.). 32p. (ps-k). 2000. 16.95 (0-88899-399-4) Grndwd Bks.

Noche Vigilada. Reinaldo B. Bretana. (SPA.). 208p. 1999. pap. 15.00 (0-927534-87-8) Biling Rev-Pr.

Noche y la Poesia Tienen Algo Que Decir. Andres C. Rios. (Aqui y Ahora Ser.). 48p. 1996. pap. 6.95 (0-8477-0265-0) U of PR Pr.

Nochebuena. Geraldine McCaughrean. (SPA.). 1997. pap. 13.95 (84-261-3012-7) Juventud Edit.

Nochebuena Vol. 2: Complete Plays 2. Manuel P. Garcia. (SPA.). 98p. 1998. 4.95 (1-885901-52-6, Liberts) Presbyters Peartree.

Nochebuena South of the Border. James Rice. Tr. by Ana Smith. LC 93-13002. (ENG & SPA., Illus.). 32p. (J). (gr. 4-7). 1993. reprint ed. 14.95 (0-88289-966-X) Pelican.

Noches de la Chambelona. Hector Santiago. (SPA.). 56p. 1993. pap. text 3.95 (1-885901-02-X) Presbyters Peartree.

*Noches de Las Mil y una Noches. Najib Mahfuz. (SPA.). 1998. pap. 6.95 (84-01-42746-0, Pub. by Plaza) Lectorum Pubns.

*Noches de Viena. (Musica Clasica Para Toda Ocasion Ser.: Vol. 5).Tr. of Vienna Nights. (SPA., Illus.). 30p. 2000. write for info. (1-892207-60-5) Intl Masters Pub.

Noches del Riel de Oro. Magali G. Ramis & Phyllis Chesler. LC 94-21995. 204p. 1996. pap. text. write for info. (1-56758-039-4) Edit Cultl.

Nociones de Literature Espanola (Historia y Analisis) Antonio Sobrino. LC 79-50629. (Coleccion Textos). 1979. pap. 10.00 (0-89729-221-9) Ediciones.

Nociones Esenciales Del Hebreo Biblico: Essentials of Biblical Hebrew. Kyle M. Yates & J. J. Owens. Tr. by S. Daniel Daglio. 308p. 1978. reprint ed. 14.50 (0-311-42056-7) Casa Bautista.

Noctet: Tales of Madonna-Moloch. Albert J. Manachino. (Illus.). 200p. (Orig.). 1997. pap. 14.95 (0-9634181-3-0) Argo Pr.

Noctilucent Clouds. M. Gadsden & W. Schroder. (Physics & Chemistry in Space Ser.: Vol. 18). (Illus.). 190p. 1989. 97.00 (0-387-50685-3) Spr-Verlag.

Noctuary. Thomas Ligotti. 208p. 1995. pap. 8.95 (0-7867-0235-4) Carroll & Graf.

Noctuidae, Introduction, Fasc. 124A. Ed. by J. B. Heppner. 2001. pap. 32.50 (0-945417-73-X) Sci Pubs.

Nocturn Matinal. deluxe limited ed. Joan Brossa. (Ediciones Especiales y de Bibliofilo Ser.). (CAT., Illus.). 1993. 4750.00 (84-343-0110-5) Elliots Bks.

*Nocturnal: Global Highflyers. Phil Beddard. 2000. pap. 27.50 (1-86154-169-4) Abrams.

Nocturnal: Worldravecreativewave. 184p. 1998. 45.00 (3-927258-91-1) Gingko Press.

Nocturnal Animals. Ruth Soffer. 1998. pap. 1.00 (0-486-40306-8) Dover.

Nocturnal Animals & Classroom Nights. Rhonda Vansant & Barbara Dondiego. LC 97-5406. (Illus.). 144p. (J). (ps-3). 1997. pap., teacher ed. 12.95 (0-07-017911-5) McGraw.

*Nocturnal Butterflies of the Russian Empire. Jose Manuel Prieto. 2000. 24.00 (0-8021-1665-5, Grove) Grove-Atltic.

Nocturnal Creatures Coloring Book. Ruth Soffer. (Illus.). 48p. (J). 1998. pap. 2.95 (0-486-40362-9) Dover.

Nocturnal Enuresis: The Child's Experience. Richard J. Butler. LC 94-32797. (Illus.). 192p. 1995. pap. text 39.00 (0-7506-2132-X) Buttrwrth-Heinemann.

Nocturnal Minstrel: or The Spirit of the Wood. Eleanor Sleath. LC 70-131342. (Gothic Novels Ser.). 1974. reprint ed. 51.95 (0-405-00821-X) Ayer.

Nocturnal Poetics: Structural & Comparative Studies of the Arabian Nights. Ferial J. Shazoul. LC 97-142334. 256p. 1996. 40.00 (977-424-363-3, Pub. by Am Univ Cairo Pr) Col U Pr.

Nocturnal Rhythms. Ken Stange. 96p. 1979. 5.95 (0-920806-03-1, Pub. by Penumbra Pr) U of Toronto Pr.

Nocturnal Rites. Sekou J. Karanja. 40p. 1991. pap. 6.95 (0-941749-21-5) Black Tie Pr.

Nocturnal Scriptures. Antwoine Patton. 70p. 1997. pap. write for info. (1-57502-526-4, P01558) Morris Pubng.

Nocturnal Visit: A Tale, 2 vols. Regina M. Roche. Ed. by Devendra P. Varma. LC 77-2045. (Gothic Novels III Ser.). 1977. reprint ed. lib. bdg. 91.95 (0-405-10143-0) Ayer.

Nocturnal Woman Margaret K. Biggs. LC 98-67339. 95 p. 1998. write for info. (0-9636529-5-8) Mulberry Riv.

Nocturnals: Black Planet. Dan Brereton. Ed. by Jamie S. Rich. (Illus.). 184p. 1998. pap. 19.95 (0-9667127-0-6) Oni Pr Inc.

Nocturnas. Shawn Ryan. Ed. by Eric Tobias. 448p. (Orig.). 1995. mass mkt. 5.50 (0-671-88270-8) PB.

Nocturne. Louise Cooper. (Indigo Ser.: No. 4). 1990. mass mkt. 4.95 (0-8125-0798-3, Pub. by Tor Bks) St Martin.

Nocturne. Ed McBain, pseud. (87th Precinct Ser.). 1998. mass mkt. 188.73 (0-446-16558-1) Warner Bks.

Nocturne. Joyce A. Rebaric. (Illus.). 130p. (Orig.). 1995. 17.00 (0-9635084-2-3) Nightshadow Prods.

Nocturne. Mark Whittington & Chantal Whittington. LC 98-89008. 292p. 1999. 25.00 (0-7388-0185-2); pap. 18.00 (0-7388-0186-0) Xlibris Corp.

Nocturne. Jane Yolen. LC 96-24864. (Illus.). 32p. (J). (ps-3). 1997. 15.00 (0-15-201458-6) Harcourt.

Nocturne. Ed McBain, pseud. LC 96-42030. 352p. 1998. reprint ed. mass mkt. 6.99 (0-446-60538-7, Pub. by Warner Bks) Little.

Nocturne for a Dangerous Man. Marc Matz. LC 99-22968. 448p. 1999. 25.95 (0-312-86935-5, Pub. by Tor Bks) St Martin.

*Nocturne for a Dangerous Man. Marc Matz. 2000. mass mkt. 6.99 (0-8125-7537-7, Pub. by Tor Bks) St Martin.

Nocturne Murder. Audrey Peterson. 256p. 1988. pap. 5.50 (0-671-66102-7) PB.

*Nocturne Strategy Guide. Gathering of Developers Staff. 1999. pap. 19.99 (1-892817-31-4) Gathering Developers.

Nocturnes. Frederic Chopin. Ed. by Ignacy J. Paderewski. 128p. 1999. pap. 11.95 (0-934009-13-9, 410-41329) Presser Co.

Nocturnes. Thomas Mann. LC 79-140336. (Short Story Index Reprint Ser.). 1977. 11.95 (0-8369-3728-7) Ayer.

Nocturnes. Joyce Odam. 48p. 1995. pap. 6.00 (0-9648232-1-7) Frith Pr.

Nocturnes. Leopold S. Senghor. Tr. by John Reed & Clive Wake. LC 75-162958. 96p. 1971. 15.95 (0-89388-014-0); pap. 9.95 (0-89388-015-9) Okpaku Communications.

Nocturnes & Barcarolles for Solo Piano. Gabriel Faure. 208p. 1994. pap. 11.95 (0-486-27955-3) Dover.

Nocturnes & Polonaises. Frederic Chopin. (Music Ser.). viii, 272p. 1985. reprint ed. pap. 10.95 (0-486-24564-0) Dover.

Nocturnes for the King of Naples. Edmund White. (Stonewall Inn Editions Ser.). 160p. 1988. pap. 7.95 (0-312-02263-8) St Martin.

Nocturno de Canas Bravas. Jose Corrales. (SPA.). 49p. 1994. pap. text 3.95 (1-885901-15-1) Presbyters Peartree.

Nod. Fanny Howe. (Sun & Moon Classics Ser.: No. 124). 218p. (Orig.). 1997. 18.95 (1-55713-307-7) Sun & Moon CA.

NOD Mice & Related Strains: Research Applications in Diabetes, AIDS, Cancer & Other Diseases. Edward Leiter & Mark Atkinson. LC 97-31480. (Molecular Biology Intelligence Unit Ser.). 182p. 1999. 99.00 (1-57059-466-X) Landes Bioscience.

Noda B'yehuda. R. Weingarten. Tr. by David Shulman. 144p. (C). 1991. 15.95 (1-56062-062-5); pap. 12.95 (1-56062-063-3) CIS Comm.

Nodal Analysis of Power Systems. P. Dimo. (Abacus Bks.). 290p. 1975. text 82.00 (0-85626-001-0) Gordon & Breach.

Nodaway County, Missouri: A Pictorial History, 1910-1994. Opal E. Eckert. LC 94-29264. (Illus.). 1994. write for info. (0-89865-910-8) Donning Co.

Noddy & the Great Cake Bake-Off. Enid Blyton. (Illus.). 32p. (J). (ps-k). 1999. pap. 3.99 (0-06-102016-8, HarpEntertain) Morrow Avon.

*Noddy Food. (Noddy Soft Beads Ser.). 10p. (J). (ps). 2001. write for info. (1-57584-721-3, Pub. by Rdrs Digest) S&S Trade.

*Noddy Gives a Birthday Party. Enid Blyton. (Lift-the-Flap Bk.: No. 1). 32p. (ps up). 2000. mass mkt. 4.50 (0-06-107366-0) HarpC Child Bks.

*Noddy Hardcover Storybook, No. 2. Enid Blyton. 2001. write for info. (0-06-107365-2, HarpEntertain) Morrow Avon.

*Noddy Makes a Friend. Enid Blyton. (Lift-the-Flap Bk.: No. 2). 32p. (ps up). 2000. mass mkt. 4.50 (0-06-107367-9) HarpC Child Bks.

Noddy Meets Santa. Enid Blyton. (Illus.). 32p. (ps-1). 1999. 13.95 (0-06-107363-6) HarpC.

*Noddy on the Farm. (Noddy Soft Tabs Ser.). (Illus.). 10p. (J). (ps). 2001. 6.99 (1-57584-718-3, Pub. by Rdrs Digest) S&S Trade.

*Noddy Vehicles. (Noddy Soft Beads Ser.). 10p. (J). (ps). 2001. write for info. (1-57584-720-5, Pub. by Rdrs Digest) S&S Trade.

*Noddy's Busy Counting Day. Bonnie Randall. (Cuddly Tale Ser.). (Illus.). 10p. (J). (ps-k). 2000. bds. 6.99 (1-57584-685-3, Pub. by Rdrs Digest) S&S Trade.

Noddy's Super Busy Day. Enid Blyton. 32p. 1999. pap. 3.99 (0-06-102015-X) HarpC.

*Noddy's Tricky Shoelace. (Lace Up I Can Do It Ser.). (Illus.). (J). (ps-k). 2000. bds. write for info. (1-57584-684-5, Pub. by Rdrs Digest) S&S Trade.

*Noddy's Wash Day Mix-Up. (Noddy Soft Tabs Ser.). (Illus.). 10p. (J). (ps). 2001. 6.99 (1-57584-719-1, Pub. by Rdrs Digest) S&S Trade.

Nodena: An Account of 90 Years of Archeological Investigation in Southeast Mississippi County, Arkansas. Mary Lucas Powell. Ed. by Dan F. Morse. (Illus.). 150p. 1989. pap. 10.00 (1-56349-057-9, RS30) AR Archaeol.

Nodes in Transit with Aspects. Clara Darr. 44p. 1993. 6.00 (0-86690-436-0) Am Fed Astrologers.

N

Nodular Iron Gears in Industry. B. Hopper. (Technical Papers: Vol. P249.07). (Illus.). 7p. 1959. pap. text 30.00 (*1-55589-349-X*) AGMA.

Noe. Jean Giono. (Folio Ser.: No. 365). (FRE.). 1973. pap. 9.95 (*2-07-036365-1*) Schoenhof.

Noe: Chroniques. Jean Giono. (FRE.). 384p. 1973. 10.95 (*0-7859-1151-0*, 2070363651) Fr & Eur.

Noe y el Arca (Historias Biblicas) A. M. De Graaf.Tr. of Noah & the Ark. (SPA.). (J). 3.49 (*0-7899-0524-8*, 496641) Editorial Unilit.

Noe y el Gran Barco. Alice J. Davidson. (SPA.). 1998. 3.99 (*0-8297-2487-7*) Vida Pubs.

Noe y el Gran Diluvio. Penny Frank & Tony Morris. (Serie Historias de la Biblia - Children's Bible Story Books Ser.).Tr. of Noah & the Great Flood. (SPA.). 24p. (J). 1986. 1.79 (*0-8423-6303-3*, 490303) Editorial Unilit.

Noedgelines. Chris Reising. (Illus.). (Orig.). 1986. pap. 7.00 (*0-937061-00-X*) Earhart Pr.

Noel. Deroussy DeSales. 1994. pap. 13.99 (*0-8442-1008-0*) NTC Contemp Pub Co.

Noel & His Friends. Carlyn Coffin. (Illus.). 130p. (J). (ps up). 1987. pap., bds. 10.95 (*0-931474-30-2*) TBW Bks.

Noel Aubert de Verse: A Study in the Concept of Toleration. Paul J. Mormon. LC 87-21643. (Texts & Studies in Religion: Vol. 32). 290p. 1986. lib. bdg. 89.95 (*0-88946-822-2*) E Mellen.

Noel Counihan: Artist & Revolutionary. Bernard Smith. (Illus.). 576p. 1994. text 65.00 (*0-19-553587-1*) OUP.

Noel Coward. Philip Hoare. (Illus.). 624p. 1996. 29.50 (*0-684-80937-0*) S&S Trade.

Noel Coward. Philip Hoare. LC 97-46481. 605p. 1998. pap. 18.00 (*0-226-34512-2*) U Ch Pr.

Noel Coward. Milton Levin. (English Authors Ser.: No. 73). 130p. 1989. 22.95 (*0-8057-6978-1*, TEAS 73, Twyne) Mac Lib Ref.

Noel Coward. 2nd large type ed. Clive Fisher. (Illus.). 415p. 1993. 25.95 (*1-85695-135-9*, Pub. by ISIS Lrg Prnt) Transaction Pubs.

Noel Coward: A Bio-Bibliography, 44. Stephen Cole. LC 93-28704. (Bio-Bibliographies in the Performing Arts Ser.: No. 44). 344p. 1993. lib. bdg. 69.50 (*0-313-28599-3*, Greenwood Pr) Greenwood.

***Noel Coward: A Life in Quotes.** Compiled by Barry Day. (Illus.). 116p. 2000. 19.95 (*1-900512-84-X*, Pub. by Metro Bks) Trafalgar.

***Noel Coward: Collected Revue Sketches & Parodies.** Noel Coward. Ed. by Barry Day. (Illus.). 282p. 2000. pap. text 14.95 (*0-413-73390-4*) Methn.

***Noel Coward: Collected Short Stories.** Noel Coward. 630p. 2000. pap. 17.95 (*0-413-59970-1*) Methn.

***Noel Coward: Collected Verse.** Noel Coward. Ed. by Martin Tickner & Graham Payn. 212p. 2000. pap. 14.95 (*0-413-55150-4*) Methn.

Noel Coward: The Complete Lyrics. Ed. & Anno. by Barry Day. LC 98-17414. (Illus.). 356p. 1998. 65.00 (*0-87951-896-0*, Pub. by Overlook Pr) Penguin Putnam.

Noel Coward & Radclyffe Hall: Kindred Spirits. Terry Castle. LC 96-22750. 1996. pap. write for info. (*0-231-10597-5*) Col U Pr.

Noel Coward & Radclyffe Hall: Kindred Spirits. Terry Castle. LC 96-22750. (Illus.). 160p. 1996. 21.00 (*0-231-10596-7*) Col U Pr.

***Noel Coward Autobiography.** Noel Coward. (Illus.). 514p. 2000. pap. text 16.95 (*0-413-73380-7*) Methn.

***Noel Coward Collected Plays: Blithe Spirit; Present Laughter; This Happy Breed, Vol. 4.** Noel Coward. 496p. 2000. pap. 14.95 (*0-413-46120-3*, Methuen Drama) Heinemann.

***Noel Coward Collected Plays: Design for Living; Cavalcade;Conversation Piece, Vol. 3.** Noel Coward. 432p. 2000. pap. text 16.95 (*0-413-46100-9*, Methuen Drama) Methn.

***Noel Coward Collected Plays: Hay Fever; The Vortex, Fallen Angels; Easy Virtue, Vol. 1.** Noel Coward. 384p. 2000. pap. 16.95 (*0-413-46060-6*) Methn.

***Noel Coward Collected Plays: Private Lives; Bitter Sweet; The Marquise; Post Mortem, Vol. 2.** Noel Coward. 384p. 2000. pap. 16.95 (*0-413-46080-0*) Methn.

***Noel Coward Collected Plays: Quadrille; "Peace in Our Time";, Vol. 7.** Noel Coward. (Methuen World Classics: The Noel Coward Collection Ser.). 416p. 2000. pap. 16.95 (*0-413-73400-5*) Methn.

***Noel Coward Collected Plays: Relative Values; Look After Lulu; Waiting in the Wings; Suite in Three Keys, Vol. 5.** Noel Coward. 560p. 2000. pap. text 16.95 (*0-413-51740-3*, Methuen Drama) Methn.

***Noel Coward Collected Plays: Semi Monde; Point Valaine; South Sea Bubble; Nude with Violin, Vol. 6.** Noel Coward. (Methuen World Classics: The Noel Coward Collection Ser.). 448p. 2000. pap. 16.95 (*0-413-73410-2*) Methn.

***Noel Coward Diaries.** Ed. by Graham Payn & Sheridan Morley. 2000. pap. 22.50 (*0-306-80960-5*, Pub. by Da Capo) HarpC.

Noel Coward Gala Vol. 2: His Words & Music. 200p. 1981. per. 15.95 (*0-88188-168-6*, 00312108) H Leonard.

Noel Coward Songbook. Ed. by Noel Coward. (Illus.). 304p. 1984. pap. 15.95 (*0-416-00961-1*, NO. 9205) Routledge.

***Noel de l'Espoir.** Tara Taylor Quinn. (Amours d'Aujourd'Hui Ser.: No. 349). (FRE.). 2000. mass mkt. 5.50 (*0-373-38349-5*, 1-38349-6, Harlequin French) Harlequin Bks.

Noel de Maigret. Georges Simenon. (FRE.). pap. 3.95 (*0-685-11424-4*) Fr & Eur.

***Noel en Alaska.** Kate Hoffmann. (Rouge Passion Ser.: No. 537). (FRE.). 2000. mass mkt. 3.99 (*0-373-37537-9*, 1-37537-7, Harlequin French) Harlequin Bks.

Noel en Blanc. Lynne Graham. (Azur Ser.: Bk. 734). 1999. mass mkt. 3.50 (*0-373-34734-0*, 1-34734-3) Harlequin Bks.

***Noel en Robe Blanche.** Carole Mortimer. (Azur Ser.: No. 807). (FRE.). 2000. mass mkt. 3.99 (*0-373-34807-X*, 1-34807-7, Harlequin French) Harlequin Bks.

Noel Levitz Student Athlete Retention Program. Edward C. Anderson et al. (C). 1995. write for info. (*1-887842-00-4*) USA Grp N-Levitz.

Noel Levitz Student Athlete Retention Program: Leader's Guide. Edward C. Anderson et al. 282p. (C). 1995. teacher ed., ring bd. write for info. (*1-887842-02-0*) USA Grp N-Levitz.

Noel Levitz Student Athlete Retention Program: Work-Text: Planning for Success in Athletics, Academics, & Careers. Edward C. Anderson et al. (C). 1995. pap., wbk. ed. write for info. (*1-887842-01-2*) USA Grp N-Levitz.

Noel-l'Invite d'un Jour. Truman Capote. (ENG & FRE.). 145p. 1991. pap. 14.95 (*0-7859-2180-X*, 2070384373) Fr & Eur.

Noel Magique. Margot Early. (Amours d'Aujourd'Hui Ser.: Bk. 312). 1999. mass mkt. 4.99 (*0-373-38312-6*, 1-38312-4) Harlequin Bks.

Noel, Noel. Ed. by W. Strickland. 1975. 4.00 (*0-913334-29-4*, CM1030) Consort Music.

Noel Perrin Sampler: Elegant Humor & Lighthearted Essays by the Author of First Person Ruran & a Reader's Delight. Noel Perrin. LC 90-50907. 160p. Date not set. reprint ed. pap. 49.60 (*0-608-20688-1*, 207179600002) Bks Demand.

Noel Purcell: A Biography. Philip B. Ryan. (Illus.). 203p. 1993. 35.00 (*1-85371-197-7*, Pub. by Poolbeg Pr) Dufour.

Noel Rockmore Vol. 1. Gail Feigenbaum. LC 98-67768. (Illus.). 40p. 1998. pap. 14.95 (*0-89494-070-8*) New Orleans Mus Art.

Noel Streatfield. Nancy Huse. LC 94-18997. (Twayne's English Authors Ser.: No. 510). 184p. 1994. 23.95 (*0-8057-4515-7*, Twyne) Mac Lib Ref.

Noel the Coward. Robert Kraus. (Illus.). 32p. (J). (ps-3). 1988. pap. 12.95 (*0-671-66845-5*) S&S Bks Yung.

Noel the First. Kate McMullan. LC 96-85606. (Michael di Capua Bks.). (Illus.). 32p. (J). (ps up). 1996. 14.95 (*0-06-205142-3*) HarpC Child Bks.

***Noel Wien: Alaska Pioneer Bush Pilot.** Ira Harkey. Ed. & Frwd. by Terrence Cole. LC 99-23720. (Classic Reprint Ser.: No. 7). Orig. Title: Pioneer Bush Pilot: The Story of Noel Wien. (Illus.). xxviii, 307p. 1999. pap. 24.95 (*1-889963-16-X*) U of Alaska Pr.

***Noela: Two Novellas.** Muriel Maddox. 288p. 2000. 22.95 (*0-86534-309-8*) Sunstone Pr.

Noela Hjorth: Journey of a Fire Goddess. N. Hjorth. (Illus.). 192p. 1990. 60.00 (*0-947131-30-2*) Gordon & Breach.

Noelle. Lacey Dancer. 1996. pap. 1.78 (*0-8217-5557-9*) Kensgtn Pub Corp.

Noelle. Diana Palmer. 1995. mass mkt. 5.99 (*0-8041-1281-9*) Ivy Books.

Noelle of the Nutcracker. Pamela Jane. (Illus.). 80p. (J). (gr. 2-5). 1997. pap. 3.99 (*0-440-41418-0*) BDD Bks Young Read.

Noelle of the Nutcracker, 001. Pamela Jane. (Illus.). 64p. (J). (gr. 2-5). 1986. 17.00 (*0-395-39969-6*) HM.

Noelle of the Nutcracker. Pamela Jane. 1997. 9.19 (*0-606-12783-6*, Pub. by Turtleback) Demco.

Noel's Almost-Perfect Just-about-Wonderful Christmas. Mary M. Simon. LC 94-27298. (Illus.). 32p. (J). (ps-3). 1994. 4.99 (*0-7852-8194-0*) Tommy Nelson.

***Noels for Flute & Piano.** Mizzy McCaskill & Dona Gilliam. 64p. 1998. pap. 10.95 (*0-7866-4506-7*, 98259) Mel Bay.

Noerr-Pennington Doctrine. LC 92-75960. 100p. 1993. pap. 30.00 (*0-89707-812-8*, 503-0228, ABA Antitrust) Amer Bar Assn.

Noeth Leith Parish Church. James S. Marshall. 160p. 1993. 40.00 (*0-86153-161-2*, Pub. by St Andrew); pap. 30.00 (*0-86153-160-4*, Pub. by St Andrew) St Mut.

Noether-Lefschetz Theory & the Picard Group of Projective Surfaces. A. Lopez. LC 90-19299. (Memoirs Ser.: No. 89/438). 100p. 1991. pap. 20.00 (*0-8218-2500-3*, MEMO/89/438) Am Math.

Noetherian Rings & Their Applications. L. Small. LC 87-14997. (Mathematical Surveys & Monographs: Vol. 24). 118p. 1987. text 47.00 (*0-8218-1525-3*, SURV/24) Am Math.

***Noetic Effects of Sin: An Historical & Contemporary Exploration of How Sin Affects Our Thinking.** Stephen K. Moroney. LC 99-48063. 176p. 1999. 55.00 (*0-7391-0018-1*) Lxngtn Bks.

Noetic Magic: And the Coming Transformation in Human Consciousness. Daniel L. Wick. LC 97-76534. (Illus.). 320p. 1997. pap. 15.95 (*0-9660714-0-9*) Mirandola Pub.

Noetic Psychology. (Institute of World Culture Ser.). 128p. 1984. pap. 12.75 (*0-685-11932-7*) Concord Grove.

Noetic Universe, Bk. 3. 2001. pap. write for info. (*0-9615847-4-2*) Marwolf Pub.

***Noetical Theory of Gabriel Vasquez, Jesuit Philosopher & Theologian (1549-1604) His View of the Objective Concept.** Michael J. Lapierre. LC 99-45518. (Studies in the History of Philosophy: Vol. 53). 132p. 1999. text 69.95 (*0-7734-7888-4*) E Mellen.

Noeud de Viperes. Francois Mauriac. (Coll. Diamant). 9.50 (*0-685-23904-7*); pap. 3.95 (*0-686-55471-X*) Fr & Eur.

Noeud de Viperes. Francois Mauriac. (FRE.). 1979. pap. 12.95 (*0-7859-3057-4*) Fr & Eur.

Nofrontiere: Operating System. (Illus.). 112p. 1997. pap. 39.95 (*3-927258-41-5*) Gingko Press.

Nofziger. Lyn Nofziger. LC 92-15908. 352p. 1992. 21.95 (*0-89526-513-3*) Regnery Pub.

***Nog.** Rudy Wurlitzer. 164p. 2000. reprint ed. pap. 11.99 (*1-56649-115-0*) Welcome Rain.

Nog Vele Jaren: Each Year of Life - Its Symbolism & Meaning. Hans Kortweg. LC 96-51697. (Illus.). 105p. pap. 14.00 (*1-56838-146-8*) Hazelden.

Noggin & Boggin in the Garden. 2nd ed. Olivier Dunrea. (Let Me Read Ser.). (Illus.). 16p. (J). (ps-1). 1995. pap. 2.95 (*0-673-36237-X*, GoodYrBooks) Addson-Wesley Educ.

Nogs: Poems from Hollywood. Mark Dunster. 18p. 1998. pap. 5.00 (*0-89642-412-X*) Linden Pubs.

***Noguchi.** Sam Hunter. (Illus.). 64p. 2000. 25.00 (*0-295-98017-6*) U of Wash Pr.

Noguchi & His Patrons. Isabel R. Plesset. LC 78-66819. 320p. 1970. 38.50 (*0-8386-2347-6*) Fairleigh Dickinson.

Noguchi East & West. Dore Ashton. LC 92-36450. (Illus.). (C). 1993. 19.95 (*0-520-08340-7*, Pub. by U CA Pr) Cal Prin Full Svc.

Noguchi the Samurai. unabridged ed. Burt Konzak. (Illus.). 32p. (J). (gr. 1 up). 1996. 16.95 (*1-895555-54-X*) STDK.

Noh Drama & the Tale of Genji: The Art of Allusion in Fifteen Classical Plays. Janet E. Goff. LC 90-8960. (Princeton Library of Asian Translations). (Illus.). 304p. 1991. reprint ed. pap. 94.30 (*0-608-02556-9*, 206320100004) Bks Demand.

***Noh Drama & the Tale of Gensi: The Art of Allusion in Fifteen Classical Plays.** Janet E. Goff. 296p. 2000. reprint ed. pap. 17.00 (*0-7881-9422-4*) DIANE Pub.

Noh' or Accomplishment: A Study of the Classical Stage of Japan. Ernest F. Fenollosa & Ezra Pound. LC 98-55492. 272p. 1999. 25.00 (*1-56554-440-4*) Pelican.

Noh, or Accomplishment, a Study of the Classical Stage of Japan see Classic Noh Theatre of Japan

Noh Othello in English & Japanese. Kuniyoshi Munakata. (Illus.). 228p. 1998. 87.95 (*4-585-10025-3*, Pub. by Hokuseido Pr) Book East.

Nohow On. Samuel Beckett. 128p. 1993. pap. 12.95 (*0-7145-4112-5*) Riverrun NY.

Nohow On: Company, Ill Seen, Ill Said, Worstward Ho. Samuel Beckett. LC 95-43710. 144p. 1995. pap. 11.00 (*0-8021-3426-2*, Grove) Grove-Atltic.

***Noi Functii in Teoria Numerelor.** Florentin Smarandache. (RUM., Illus.). 119p. (C). 2000. pap. 16.95 (*1-879585-77-4*, Pub. by American Res Pr) UMI.

Noi Voi Nguoi Xuat Gia Tre Tuoi. Thich Nhat Hahn. (VIE.). 70p. 1996. pap. 7.00 (*1-891667-37-8*) La Boi Soc.

Noi Voi Tuoi Hai Muoi. 12th ed. Thich Nhat Hahn. (VIE.). 116p. 1988. reprint ed. pap. 7.00 (*1-891667-07-6*) La Boi Soc.

Noir. K.W. Jeter. 496p. 1999. mass mkt. 6.99 (*0-553-57638-0*) Bantam.

Noir: The Black Book. Franca Sozzani. 1998. pap. text 40.00 (*2-84323-068-3*, Pub. by Assouline) Rizzoli Intl.

Noir de Boudoukou: Koulangos-Kyoulas-Abrons, Etc. Louis Tauxier. (B. E. Ser.: No. 147). (FRE.). 1921. 85.00 (*0-8115-3068-X*) Periodicals Srv.

Noir du Soudan: Pays Mossi et Gourounsi. Louis Tauxier. (B. E. Ser.: No. 146). (FRE.). 1912. 85.00 (*0-8115-3067-1*) Periodicals Srv.

***Noir Fiction.** Paul Duncan. 2000. pap. 5.95 (*1-903047-11-0*, Pub. by Pocket Essentials) Trafalgar.

Noir Style. Alain Silver & James Ursini. LC 99-33581. 256p. 1999. text 50.00 (*0-87951-722-0*, Pub. by Overlook Pr) Penguin Putnam.

Noire Comme le Cafe, Blanc Comme la Lune see You Be Me, I'll Be You

Noirotica. Ed. by Thomas Roche. (Orig.). 1996. mass mkt. 6.95 (*1-56333-390-2*, Rhinoceros) Masquerade.

***Noirotica: An Anthology of Erotic Crime stories.** Thomas Roche. 240p. 2000. reprint ed. pap. 15.00 (*1-892723-04-2*) Black Books.

***Noirotica: Stolen Kisses, 4, 3.** Thomas Roche. 240p. (Orig.). 2000. pap. 15.00 (*1-892723-03-4*) Black Books.

Noirotica 2. Ed. by Thomas S. Roche. (Orig.). 1997. mass mkt. 7.95 (*1-56333-584-0*, Rhinoceros) Masquerade.

***Noirotica 2, 4.** Thomas Roche. 240p. (Orig.). 2001. reprint ed. pap. 15.00 (*1-892723-05-0*) Black Books.

Nous les Jeunes, 1990. Created by Harcourt Brace Staff. (FRE.). 1990. pap. text, teacher ed. 15.00 (*0-15-381757-7*) Holt R&W.

Nous les Jeunes, 1990. 90th ed. Created by Harcourt Brace Staff. (FRE.). 1990. pap. text, teacher ed., wbk. ed. 16.75 (*0-15-381755-0*); pap. text, student ed. 14.80 (*0-15-381756-9*) Holt R&W.

Noise. Jacques Attali. Tr. by Brian Massumi. LC 84-28069. (Theory & History of Literature Ser.: Vol. 16). 180p. 1985. pap. 14.95 (*0-8166-1287-0*) U of Minn Pr.

Noise. Alex Jones. (Nick Hern Bks.). 96p. 1998. pap. 13.95 (*1-85459-353-6*) Theatre Comm.

Noise: A Guide to Information Required from Equipment Vendors. EEMUA Staff. 1985. pap. 125.00 (*0-85931-040-X*, Pub. by EEMUA) St Mut.

Noise: Its Measurement, Analysis, Rating & Control. John Anderson & Magda Bratos-Anderson. 494p. 1993. 96.95 (*0-291-39794-8*, Pub. by Avebury Technical) Ashgate Pub Co.

Noise: Proceedings. 158p. 1974. 21.00 (*0-911890-15-7*) Indus Health Inc.

Noise: Profiles of the Artists of Alternative Rock. Wayne Jancik & Steve Roeser. 1998. pap. 15.00 (*0-8362-5207-1*) Andrews & McMeel.

Noise Vol. 9: Pen & Ben. large type ed. Jill Storm. (Illus.). 24p. (J). (gr. 1-2). 1999. pap. 3.95 (*1-929078-08-0*, APB09) Gods Kids.

Noise Abatement at Gas Pipeline Installations: Noise Suppression at Pressure Regulating & Metering Stations, Vol. II. James M. Sharp et al. 200p. 1960. pap. 7.50 (*0-318-12659-1*, L00230) Am Gas Assn.

Noise Abatement at Gas Pipeline Installations: Physiological, Psychological & Legal Aspects of Noise, Vol. I. American Gas Association, Pipeline Research Commit et al. 58p. 1959. pap. 1.50 (*0-318-12660-5*, L00210) Am Gas Assn.

Noise Abatement at Gas Pipeline Installations: Blow-off Noise Suppression & Regulator Valve Noise Generation, Vol. III. Glenn Damewood et al. 121p. 1961. pap. 5.50 (*0-318-12661-3*, L00280) Am Gas Assn.

Noise Analysis in Nuclear Systems: Proceedings. Ed. by Robert E. Uhrig. (AEC Symposium Ser.). 518p. 1964. pap. 21.00 (*0-87079-292-X*, TID-7679); fiche 9.00 (*0-87079-293-8*, TID-7679) DOE.

Noise & Acoustic Fatigue in Aeronautics. Ed. by E. J. Richards & D. J. Mead. LC 68-55813. (Illus.). 524p. reprint ed. pap. 162.50 (*0-608-11673-4*, 201614900098) Bks Demand.

Noise & Adverse Effects on Health: Medical Subject Analysis with Reference Bibliography. American Health Research Institute Staff. LC 85-48089. 150p. 1987. 47.50 (*0-88164-450-1*); pap. 44.50 (*0-88164-451-X*) ABBE Pubs Assn.

Noise & Diffusion in Bistable Nonequilibrium Systems. Malachow et al. 168p. (C). 1985. 80.00 (*0-685-46638-8*, Pub. by Collets) St Mut.

Noise & Fluids Engineering. Ed. by Robert Hickling. LC 77-87328. 252p. reprint ed. pap. 78.20 (*0-608-11603-3*, 201055200068) Bks Demand.

Noise & Health. Ed. by Thomas H. Fay. (Illus.). 110p. 1991. text 35.00 (*0-924143-01-0*) NY Acad Med.

Noise & Hearing: A Bibliography. 1995. lib. bdg. 250.95 (*0-8490-7501-7*) Gordon Pr.

Noise & Hearing Conservation Manual. 4th ed. AIHA Noise Committee. 606p. 1986. 51.00 (*0-932627-21-8*) Am Indus Hygiene.

Noise & Human Efficiency. Michel Loeb. LC 85-16781. (Wiley Series on Studies in Human Performance). (Illus.). 283p. reprint ed. pap. 87.80 (*0-7837-4409-9*, 204415200012) Bks Demand.

Noise & Its Effect on Communication. 2nd ed. Nelson M. Blachman. LC 81-8140. 274p. (C). 1982. lib. bdg. 31.50 (*0-89874-256-0*) Krieger.

Noise & Noise Control, Vol. II. Ed. by Malcolm J. Crocker & F. M. Kessler. 312p. 1982. 175.00 (*0-8493-5094-8*, TD892, CRC Reprint) Franklin.

Noise & Noise Law: A Practical Approach. M. Adams & F. McManus. 1994. pap. text 82.95 (*0-471-93708-8*) Wiley.

Noise & Nonlinear Phenomena in Nuclear Systems. Ed. by J. L. Munoz-Cobo & F. C. Difilippo. (NATO ASI Series B, Physics: Vol. 192). (Illus.). 482p. 1989. 125.00 (*0-306-43102-5*, Plenum Trade) Perseus Pubng.

Noise & Other Interfering Signals. Ralph Morrison. LC 91-15226. 160p. 1991. 99.95 (*0-471-54288-1*) Wiley.

Noise & Smell. Sanduik Bokforlag. (Illus.). 1997. pap. 9.99 (*1-58048-006-3*) Sandvik Pub.

Noise & Society. fac. ed. Ed. by Dylan M. Jones et al. LC 83-16907. (Wiley Series on Studies in Occupational Stress). 331p. pap. 102.70 (*0-7837-7378-1*, 204718800005) Bks Demand.

***Noise & Vibration.** (Special Publications). 72p. 2000. 55.00 (*0-7680-0564-7*, SP-1514) Soc Auto Engineers.

Noise & Vibration Control. rev. ed. Ed. by Leo L. Beranek. LC 89-80604. (Illus.). 672p. 1989. reprint ed. 38.00 (*0-9622072-0-9*) INCE NY.

Noise & Vibration Control Engineering: Principles & Applications. Ed. by Leo L. Beranek & I. L. Ver. LC 92-11347. 816p. 1992. 190.00 (*0-471-61751-2*) Wiley.

***Noise & Vibration for Off-Highway Applications.** (Special Publications). 56p. 1999. 40.00 (*0-7680-0468-3*, SP-1473) Soc Auto Engineers.

Noise & Vibration Measurement: Proceedings of a Symposium Sponsored by the Environmental Engineering Division. Ed. by William A. Redl. 145p. 1985. 19.00 (*0-87262-445-5*) Am Soc Civil Eng.

Noise & Vibration of Electrical Machines. Ed. by P. L. Timar. (Studies in Electrical & Electronic Engineering: No. 34). 340p. 1989. 226.00 (*0-444-98896-3*) Elsevier.

Noise & Vibration Research. 123p. 1998. 75.00 (*0-7680-0183-8*) Soc Auto Engineers.

Noise & Your Health. Billy R. Boyd. 32p. 1996. pap. 3.50 (*0-9616792-6-3*) Taterhill.

Noise-Con, '88: Proceedings - National Conference on Noise Control Engineering, Purdue University, June 20-22, 1988. Ed. by Stuart Bolton. 1988. 60.00 (*0-931784-17-4*) Noise Control.

Noise-Con, '85: Proceedings - National Conference on Noise Control Engineering 1985. Ed. by Rajendra Singh. 1985. 48.00 (*0-931784-12-3*) Noise Control.

Noise-Con, '81: Proceedings - National Conference on Noise Control Engineering 1981. Ed. by Franklin D. Hart et al. 488p. 1981. 42.00 (*0-931784-04-2*) Noise Control.

Noise-Con, '87: Proceedings - National Conference on Noise Control Engineering, Penn State University. Ed. by Jiri Ticky & Sabih Hayck. xx, 780p. 1987. 60.00 (*0-931784-16-6*) Noise Control.

Noise-Con, '83: Proceedings - National Conference on Noise Control Engineering 1983. Ed. by Robert Lotz. 512p. 1983. 42.00 (*0-931784-08-5*) Noise Control.

Noise-Con, '90: National Conference on Noise Control Engineering 1990 Proceedings. Ed. by Ilene J. Busch-Vishniac. xviii, 494p. 1990. 60.00 (*0-931784-21-2*) Noise Control.

Noise-Con, '91 - Twenty Years of Progress & Future Trends: Proceedings of Noise-Con, '91. Ed. by Daniel A. Quinlan & Marehalli G. Prasad. (Noise-Con Ser.). xviii, 766p. 1991. pap. 75.00 (*0-931784-22-0*) Noise Control.

Noise-Con, '96, 2 vols. Boeing Commercial Airplane Group Staff & Institute of Noise Control Engineering Staff. 974p. write for info. (*0-931784-35-2*) Noise Control.

Noise Control. Christopher N. Penn. 1979. 110.00 (*0-7219-0830-6*, Pub. by Scientific) St Mut.

Noise Control: A Guide for Workers & Employers. 133p. 1984. 20.00 (*0-939874-59-8*) ASSE.

Noise Control: Measurement, Analysis, & Control of Sound & Vibration. Charles E. Wilson. LC 94-148. 586p. (C). 1994. reprint ed. lib. bdg. 74.50 (*0-89464-879-9*) Krieger.

An Asterisk (*) at the beginning of an entry indicates that the title is appearing for the first time.

Noise Control & Acoustics Division. (1995 ASME International Mechanical Engineering Congress & Exposition Ser.). 1995. 10.00 (*0-614-16713-2*, 95-WA/NCA-1) ASME.

Noise Control & Acoustics Division. Ed. by Mardi Hastings. LC 99-183118. 471p. 1998. pap. text 140.00 (*0-7918-1594-3*) ASME.

Noise Control & Acoustics Division: Proceedings, ASME International Mechanical Engineering Congress & Exposition, Dallas, TX, 1997. Ed. by Theodore M. Farabee et al. LC 97-77215. (NCA Ser.: Vol. 24). 389p. 1997. pap. 140.00 (*0-7918-1848-9*, TD892) ASME Pr.

***Noise Control & Acoustics Division, 1999.** Ed. by Sean F. Wu. (NCA Ser.: Vol. 26). 530p. 1999. 130.00 (*0-7918-1637-0*) ASME Pr.

Noise Control for Engineers. Harold W. Lord et al. LC 87-22611. 448p. (C). 1987. reprint ed. lib. bdg. 53.50 (*0-89464-255-3*) Krieger.

Noise Control for Industry: NOISE-CON '94. Ed. by Joseph M. Cuschieri et al. (NOISE-CON Ser.). xxvii, 1060p. pap. 95.00 (*0-614-25012-9*) Noise Control.

Noise Control in Aeroacoustics: NOISE-CON '93. Ed. by Harvey H. Hubbard. (NOISE-CON Ser.). xx, 652p. pap. 85.00 (*0-614-25013-7*) Noise Control.

Noise Control in Automobile Helical Gears. AGMA Technical Committee. (Technical Papers: Vol. 299.02). 1963. pap. text 30.00 (*1-55589-145-4*) AGMA.

Noise Control in Industry. 3rd ed. Sound Research Laboratories Limited Staff. (Illus.). 420p. (C). 1991. 95.00 (*0-419-17170-3*, E & FN Spon) Routledge.

Noise Control in Industry: A Practical Guide. Ed. by Nicholas P. Cheremisinoff. LC 96-12580. 190p. 1996. 89.00 (*0-8155-1399-2*) Noyes.

Noise Control in the Built Environment. John Roberts. 352p. 1989. text 86.95 (*0-566-09001-5*) Ashgate Pub Co.

Noise Control Management. Howard K. Pelton. (Industrial Health & Safety Ser.). 267p. 1992. 89.95 (*0-471-28433-5*, VNR) Wiley.

Noise Control Management. Howard K. Pelton. LC 92-18950. 288p. 1993. text 70.95 (*0-442-00763-9*, VNR) Wiley.

Noise Control of Hydraulic Machinery. Stan Skaistis. (Fluid Power & Control Ser.: Vol. 8). (Illus.). 336p. 1988. text 175.00 (*0-8247-7934-7*) Dekker.

***Noise Handbook.** Alberto Behar. LC 99-40683. 131p. 1999. pap. 43.95 (*1-56593-992-1*) Singular Publishing.

Noise Handbook. Ed. by W. Tempest. 1985. text 188.00 (*0-12-685460-2*) Acad Pr.

Noise in Circuits & Systems, Selected Papers On. Madhu S. Gupta. LC 87-32427. 110p. 1988. pap. 24.95 (*0-87942-239-4*, PP02303) Inst Electrical.

Noise in Digital Magnetic Recording. L. L. Nunnelley & T. C. Arnoldssen. 250p. 1994. text 74.00 (*981-02-0865-0*); pap. text 48.00 (*981-02-1025-6*) World Scientific Pub.

Noise in Digital Optical Transmission Systems. Gunnar Jacobsen. LC 94-11382. 387p. 1994. write for info. (*0-89006-695-7*) Artech Hse.

Noise in Dog Kennelling. G. Sales et al. 1996. pap. 40.00 (*0-900767-95-2*, Pub. by Univs Fed Animal Welfare) St Mut.

Noise in Electrical Measurements. Ed. by T. Kemeny & K. Havrilla. 223p. (C). 1987. pap. text 175.00 (*0-941743-36-5*) Nova Sci Pubs.

Noise in Electronic Devices & Systems. Michael J. Buckingham. (Electrical & Electronic Engineering Ser.). 372p. 1985. pap. text 54.95 (*0-470-20164-9*) P-H.

***Noise in Fluid Machinery: Proceedings Seminar on Noise in Fluid Machinery, London, UK, 1999.** (IMechE Seminar Publication Ser.). 79p. 1999. 99.00 (*1-86058-246-X*) Prof Eng Pubng.

Noise in Measurements. Albert Van der Ziel. LC 76-12108. 240p. reprint ed. pap. 74.40 (*0-608-16959-5*, 205629200056) Bks Demand.

Noise in Nonlinear Dynamical Systems Vol. 3: Experiments & Simulation. Ed. by Frank Moss & P. V. McClintock. (Illus.). 296p. (C). 1989. text 120.00 (*0-521-35265-7*) Cambridge U Pr.

Noise in Physical Systems. 700p. 1997. text 89.00 (*981-02-3141-5*) World Scientific Pub.

Noise in Physical Systems: Proceedings of the 9th International Conference. C. M. Van Vliet. 640p. (C). 1987. text 144.00 (*9971-5-0397-2*) World Scientific Pub.

Noise in Physical Systems & I - F Fluctuations. Ed. by Peter H. Handel & Alma L. Chung. (AIP Conference Proceedings Ser.: No. 285). (Illus.). 784p. 1994. text 185.00 (*1-56396-270-5*, AIP Pr) Spr-Verlag.

Noise in Physical Systems & 1-f Fluctuations: Proceedings of the International Conference, ICNF 1991, November 24-27, 1991, Kyoto, Japan. Ed. by T. Musha et al. LC 92-52686. 800p. (gr. 12). 1992. 170.00 (*90-5199-083-9*, Pub. by IOS Pr) IOS Press.

Noise in Physical Systems & 1/f Fluctuations: Proceedings of the 13th International Conference. V. Bareikis & R. Katilius. 768p. 1995. text 148.00 (*981-02-2278-5*) World Scientific Pub.

***Noise in Semiconductor Structures & Devices for Microwave Electronics.** Hans Ludwig Hartnagel et al. 346p. 2001. 89.95 (*0-471-38432-1*) Wiley.

***Noise in Spatially Extended Systems.** J. Garcia-Ojalvo & J. Sancho. Ed. by H. D. Abarbanel et al. LC 99-14734. (Institute for Nonlinear Science Ser.). (Illus.). 320p. 1999. 54.95 (*0-387-98855-6*) Spr-Verlag.

Noise in the Military Environment. R. F. Powell & M. R. Forrest. (Land Warfare: Brassey's New Battlefield Weapons & Technology Ser.: Vol. 3). 126p. 1988. 40.00 (*0-08-035830-6*, Pub. by Brasseys) Brasseys.

Noise in the Military Environment. 3rd ed. R. F. Powell & M. R. Forrest. (Battlefield Weapons Systems & Technology Ser.: Vol. 3). 126p. 1988. 25.00 (*0-08-035831-4*, Pub. by Brasseys) Brasseys.

Noise in the Night. Barbara Gregorich. Ed. by Joan Hoffman. (Start to Read! Ser.). (Illus.). 16p. (Orig.). (J). (gr. k-2). 1991. pap. 2.29 (*0-88743-027-9*, 06027) Sch Zone Pub Co.

Noise in the Night. Bruce Witty. (Start to Read! Ser.). (Illus.). 32p. (J). (ps-3). 1993. 3.99 (*0-88743-421-5*, 06072) Sch Zone Pub Co.

***Noise in the Woods.** Karyn Henley. (Tails Ser.). (Illus.). 28p. (J). (ps-5). 2000. 9.99 (*0-8054-2197-1*) Broadman.

Noise-Induced Transitions. W. Horsthemke & R. Lefever. (Synergetics Ser.: Vol. 15). (Illus.). 335p. 1983. 83.00 (*0-387-11359-2*) Spr-Verlag.

Noise Investigation Flow Charts. Myron L. Brewer. LC 73-85629. (Specialized Ser.). (Illus.). 36p. (Orig.). (C). 1987. pap. text 14.95 (*1-56016-020-9*) ABC TeleTraining.

Noise Levels on Board Ships. International Maritime Organization Staff. 1982. text 85.00 (*0-89771-998-0*, Pub. by Intl Maritime Org) St Mut.

Noise Made by Poems. 2nd ed. Peter Levi. 108p. 1984. 24.95 (*0-85646-132-6*, Pub. by Anvil Press); pap. 17.95 (*0-85646-133-4*, Pub. by Anvil Press) Dufour.

Noise of Change: Russian Literature & the Critics (1891-1917) Tr. & Intro. by Stanley Rabinowitz. 244p. (C). 1986. pap. 14.95 (*0-88233-526-X*) Ardis Pubs.

Noise of Culture: Literary Texts in a World of Information. William R. Paulson. LC 87-47822. 208p. 1988. text 37.50 (*0-8014-2102-0*) Cornell U Pr.

Noise of Reason: Scepticism & the Art of Rochester. Mark Notzon. Ed. by Don Y. Lee. LC 84-81310. 83p. (C). 1984. 36.50 (*0-939758-09-1*) Eastern Pr.

Noise of Reason: Scepticism & the Art of Rochester. rev. ed. Mark Notzon. Ed. by Don Y. Lee. LC 92-72327. 170p. (C). 1992. 39.50 (*0-939758-23-7*) Eastern Pr.

Noise of Threatening Drum: Dramatic Strategy & Political Ideology in Shakespeare & the English Chronicle Plays. Larry S. Champion. LC 89-40380. 176p. 1990. 32.50 (*0-87413-387-4*) U Delaware Pr.

Noise of War: Caesar, Pompey, Octavian & the Struggle for Rome. A. J. Langguth. 1994. 25.00 (*0-671-70829-5*) S&S Trade.

***Noise, Oscillators & Algebraic Randomness: From Noise in Communication Systems to Number Theory: Lectures of a School Held in Chapelle des Bois, France, April 5-10, 1999.** Michel Planat. LC 00-32966. (Lecture Notes in Physics). 2000. write for info. (*3-540-67572-8*) Spr-Verlag.

Noise Performance Factors in Communication Systems. William W. Mumford et al. LC 68-5234. (Illus.). 97p. reprint ed. pap. 30.10 (*0-608-10236-9*, 201007500068) Bks Demand.

Noise Pollution. Zachary Inseth. LC 97-34541. (Illus.). 32p. (J). 1998. lib. bdg. 22.79 (*1-56766-509-8*) Childs World.

Noise Pollution. Walker. text 84.00 (*0-471-98562-7*); pap. text 28.00 (*0-471-98563-5*) Wiley.

Noise Pollution: A Source Guide. 1991. lib. bdg. 69.95 (*0-8490-4858-3*) Gordon Pr.

Noise Pollution: Its Scientific & Legal Perspective. Scientific Publishers Staff. 118p. (C). 1988. 100.00 (*81-85312-00-1*, Pub. by Scientific) St Mut.

Noise Pollution & the Law. James L. Hildebrand. LC 73-132695. viii, 354p. 1970. reprint ed. lib. bdg. 42.00 (*0-930342-81-X*, 300580) W S Hein.

Noise Pollution to Perfumes see Encyclopedia of Chemical Technology

Noise Procedure Specifications. EEMUA Staff. 1988. pap. 125.00 (*0-85931-078-7*, Pub. by EEMUA) St Mut.

Noise Reduction. Leo L. Beranek. LC 91-61139. 776p. 1991. reprint ed. 34.95 (*0-932146-58-9*) Peninsula CA.

Noise Reduction. 2nd ed. Charles E. Durst. (ABC Pocket Guide for the Field Ser.). (Illus.). 40p. (C). 1985. pap. text 7.95 (*1-56016-025-X*) ABC TeleTraining.

Noise Reduction in a Plastic & Powder Metal Gear Set Through Control of Mean Involute Slopes. Robert E. Smith & Irving Laskin. (1992 Fall Technical Meeting Ser.: Vol. 92FTM12). (Illus.). 8p. 1992. pap. text 30.00 (*1-55589-592-1*) AGMA.

Noise Reduction Techniques in Electronic Systems. 2nd ed. Henry W. Ott. 448p. 1988. 94.95 (*0-471-85068-3*) Wiley.

Noise Reduction Through Generated Engagement Relief Modification. Werner Kiess & Stephen Price. (Technical Papers: Vol. 96FTM3). (Illus.). 9p. 1996. pap. text 30.00 (*1-55589-670-7*) AGMA.

Noise Research in Semiconductor Physics. N. B. Lukyanchikova. Ed. by B. K. Jones. 416p. 1997. text 98.00 (*90-5699-006-3*) Gordon & Breach.

Noise the Earth Makes. Michael Carey. (Iowa Poets Ser.: No. 1). (Illus.). 56p. (Orig.). 1985. 25.00 (*0-931757-19-3*); pap. 15.00 (*0-931757-20-7*) Pterodactyl Pr.

Noise Theory of Linear & Nonlinear Circuits. J. Engberg & T. Larsen. LC 94-39501. 308p. 1995. 195.00 (*0-471-94825-X*) Wiley.

***Noise, Water, Meat: A History of Sound in the Arts.** Douglas Kahn. LC 98-51886. (Illus.). 464p. 1999. 45.00 (*0-262-11243-4*) MIT Pr.

Noiseless Tenor: The Bicycle in Literature. Ed. by James E. Starrs. LC 81-67758. (Illus.). 544p. 1982. 25.00 (*0-8453-4736-5*, Cornwall Bks) Assoc Univ Prs.

Noises Animals Make. Date not set. 5.95 (*0-89868-313-0*); pap. 4.95 (*0-89868-373-4*); lib. bdg. 10.95 (*0-89868-312-2*) ARO Pub.

Noises from under the Rug: The Barry Louis Polisar Songbook. Barry Louis Polisar. (Illus.). 208p. (J). (gr. k-6). 1985. 18.95 (*0-9615696-0-3*) Rainbow Morn.

Noises in the Attic. (Illus.). 24p. (J). (gr. 1-3). 1997. 3.98 (*1-890095-04-4*) Nesak Intl.

Noises in the Blood: Orality, Gender, & the "Vulgar" Body of Jamaican Popular Culture. Carolyn Cooper. LC 94-37826. 240p. 1995. text 49.95 (*0-8223-1580-7*); pap. text 17.95 (*0-8223-1595-5*) Duke.

***Noises in the Henhouse.** Gussie K. Johnson. (Illus.). 548p. 2000. 20.00 (*1-887301-07-0*) Palmetto Bookworks.

***Noises in the Night: The Habits of Bats.** Deborah Kovacs. LC 99-87097. (Turnstone Rain Forest Pilot Bks.). (J). 2000. pap. 27.12 (*0-7398-2218-7*) Raintree Steck-V.

***Noises in the Night: The Habits of Bats.** Deborah Kovacs. (Turnstone Rain Forest Pilot Bks.). (Illus.). (J). 2000. pap. 7.95 (*0-7398-2227-6*) Raintree Steck-V.

Noisette l'Ecureuil. Beatrix Potter. (FRE., Illus.). 58p. (J). 1990. 9.95 (*0-7859-3629-7*, 2070560759) Fr & Eur.

Noisette l'Ecureuil. Beatrix Potter. (Gallimard Ser.). (FRE.). 58p. (J). 1990. 10.95 (*2-07-056075-9*) Schoenhof.

Noisy Baby. Susan Hood. (J). 1999. text 8.99 (*1-56799-893-3*) M Friedman Pub Grp Inc.

Noisy Baby: Baby Books. Illus. by Alison Ross. 8p. (J). (ps). 1992. text 3.50 (*0-7214-1496-6*, S9212-1, Ladybrd) Penguin Putnam.

Noisy Farm: A Picture Puzzle Board Book. Siobhan Dodds & Dawn Bentley. (Picture Puzzle Board Bks.). (Illus.). 12p. (J). 1999. 6.95 (*1-58117-031-9*, Pub. by Intervisual Bks) Andrews & McMeel.

***Noisy Farm Animals: Mix & Match.** Steve Lavis. (Illus.). 21p. (J). (gr. 13). 2000. 9.95 (*1-929927-08-8*) Ragged Bears NY.

***Noisy Farm Friends.** Illus. by Maureen Roffey. (Squeak & Rattle Ser.). (J). (ps). 2001. write for info. (*1-57584-724-8*, Pub. by Rdrs Digest) S&S Trade.

***Noisy Friends.** Sarah Weeks. (Fisher-Price Step-by-Step Ser.). (Illus.). 8p. (J). (ps). 2001. 5.99 (*1-57584-717-5*, Pub. by Rdrs Digest) S&S Trade.

Noisy Information & Computational Complexity. Leszek Plaskota. 319p. (C). 1996. text 64.95 (*0-521-55368-7*) Cambridge U Pr.

Noisy Neighbors: A Book about Animal Sounds. Marcia Leonard. LC 89-4959. (Illus.). 24p. (J). (gr. k-2). 1990. pap. 2.50 (*0-8167-1727-3*); lib. bdg. 14.50 (*0-8167-1726-5*) Troll Communs.

Noisy Night. Mouse Works Staff. LC 98-121356. 16p. (J). 1998. 3.98 (*1-57082-746-X*, Pub. by Mouse Works) Time Warner.

Noisy Nora see Julieta Estate Quieta - Noisy Nora

***Noisy Nora.** Rosemary Wells. (Pied Piper Bks.: Vol. 1). (Illus.). 32p. (J). (ps-2). 2000. pap. 5.99 (*0-14-056728-3*, PuffinBks) Peng Put Young Read.

***Noisy Nora.** Rosemary Wells. 1999. 15.99 (*0-670-88722-6*, Viking) Viking Penguin.

Noisy Poems. Jill Bennett. (Illus.). 32p. (J). (gr. k-3). 1989. pap. 7.95 (*0-19-278219-3*) OUP.

Noisy Poems. Jill Bennett. (J). 1987. 12.15 (*0-606-02125-6*, Pub. by Turtleback) Demco.

Noisy Science Book & Kit. Sterling Publishing Company, Inc. Staff. (Science Book & Kit Ser.). (J). 1997. 19.95 (*0-8069-0539-5*) Sterling.

Noisy Soil: Selected Poems from the Collected Works 1980-1998. Ed Noonan. 80p. (Orig.). 1999. pap. 12.00 (*0-9668216-0-2*) Bedrock Edns.

***Noisy Wild Animals: Mix & Match.** Steve Lavis. (Illus.). 21p. (J). (gr. 13). 2000. 9.95 (*1-929927-07-X*) Ragged Bears NY.

Noisytime for Zoo Animals. Caroline Arnold. LC 98-24376. (Illus.). 32p. (J). (gr. k-2). 1999. 21.27 (*1-57505-289-X*, Carolrhoda) Lerner Pub.

***Noisytime for Zoo Animals.** Caroline Arnold. LC 98-24376. (Zoo Animals Ser.). 32p. (J). (gr. k-2). 1999. 9.95 (*1-57505-392-6*, Carolrhoda) Lerner Pub.

Nojoque: A Question for a Continent. Hinton R. Helper. (Notable American Authors Ser.). 1992. reprint ed. lib. bdg. 75.00 (*0-7812-3076-4*) Rprt Serv.

Nola: A Memoir of Faith, Art & Madness. Robin Hemley. LC 98-84451. (Illus.). 364p. 1998. 24.95 (*1-55597-278-0*) Graywolf.

Nola Figen Perla Draws the Figure. Robert Perine. (Illus.). 64p. (Orig.). 1993. pap. 20.00 (*0-936725-08-7*) Artra Pub.

Nola 46. Lafayette Haymaker. LC 95-80166. (Illus.). 211p. (Orig.). 1995. pap. 14.00 (*0-9641632-2-5*) Mainesburg.

Nolan: Prisoner of the Inquisition. Morton L. Yanow. (Fiction Program Ser.). 340p. 1998. 29.95 (*0-8245-1747-4*, Crsrd); pap. 14.95 (*0-8245-1728-8*, Crsrd) Crossroad NY.

Nolan Family Tree. Hugh P. O'Kane & Monica O'Kane. (Illus.). 253p. 1983. 25.00 (*0-9609198-2-1*) Diction Bks.

Nolan-Miller Family History. Lewis Nolan. LC 97-73438. (Illus.). write for info. (*0-89308-701-7*) Southern Hist Pr.

Nolan Ryan. Keith E. Greenberg. LC 92-40311. (Winning Spirit Ser.). 48p. (J). (gr. 4-8). 1993. lib. bdg. 21.27 (*0-86592-002-8*) Rourke Enter.

Nolan Ryan. Lois P. Nicholson. LC 95-3099. (Baseball Legends Ser.). (Illus.). 64p. (YA). (gr. 3 up). 1995. lib. bdg. 15.95 (*0-7910-2174-2*) Chelsea Hse.

***Nolan Ryan: Fastball to Cooperstown.** Ken Anderson. LC 99-42362. 1999. pap. 5.95 (*1-57168-349-6*, Eakin Pr) Sunbelt Media.

***Nolan Ryan: Fastball to Cooperstown.** Ken Anderson. LC 99-42362. 1999. 16.95 (*1-57168-350-X*, Eakin Pr) Sunbelt Media.

Nolan Ryan: From Alvin to Cooperstown. Ed. by Sporting News Editors. (Illus.). 175p. 1999. 29.95 (*1-57167-258-3*) Sports Pub.

Nolan Ryan: Strikeout King. Howard Reiser. LC 92-35741. (Sports Stars Ser.). (Illus.). 48p. (J). (gr. 3-4). 1993. lib. bdg. 19.00 (*0-516-04365-X*) Childrens.

Nolan Ryan: The Authorized Pictorial History. D. Kent Pingel & Jennifer Briggs. LC 91-58019. (Illus.). 1991. write for info. (*0-9626219-8-6*) Summit TX.

Nolan Ryan: The Road to Cooperstown. Nolan Ryan et al. LC 99-49223. (Illus.). 112p. 1999. 26.95 (*1-886110-82-4*, Pub. by Addax Pubng) Midpt Trade.

Nolan Ryan: The Ryan Express. Ken Rappoport. LC 92-3244. (Taking Part Ser.). (Illus.). 64p. (J). (gr. 3 up). 1992. lib. bdg. 13.95 (*0-87518-524-X*, Dillon Silver Burdett) Silver Burdett Pr.

Nolan Ryan's Pitcher's Bible: The Ultimate Guide to Power, Precision, & Long-Term Performance. Nolan Ryan & Tom House. LC 90-39634. (Illus.). 176p. (Orig.). 1991. per. 12.00 (*0-671-70581-4*, Fireside) S&S Trade Pap.

Nolan's Dream, Vol. 1. large type ed. Janice R. Tingley. Ed. by Janice Gong. (Illus.). 64p. (J). (gr. k-6). 1997. 12.95 (*0-9660985-0-1*) J R Tingley.

***Nola's Daily Doses: Registration Preparation.** Nola Pursiful. 23p. 1999. student ed., ring bd. 10.00 (*1-884048-30-7*) Natl Assn Parliamentarians.

Noli Me Tangere. Jose Rizal. Ed. by Raul L. Locsin. Tr. by Ma. S. Lacson-Locsin from SPA. (SHAPS Library of Translations). 472p. 1997. text 47.00 (*0-8248-1916-0*); pap. text 27.95 (*0-8248-1917-9*) UH Pr.

***Nolichucky Jack.** John T. Faris. 288p. 1999. 19.95 (*1-57072-094-0*) Overmountain Pr.

Noli's Story. Peter Dickinson. LC 97-51182. 211p. (J). (gr. 4-8). 1998. pap. text 3.99 (*0-448-41710-3*, G & D) Peng Put Young Read.

Nolo Contendere. Judson Crews. LC 78-73263. 1978. 25.00 (*0-930324-08-0*); pap. 15.00 (*0-930324-09-9*) Wings Pr.

Nolo's California Quick Corp: Incorporate Your Business Without a Lawyer, 1. Anthony Mancuso. LC 99-12534. (Quick & Legal Ser.). (Illus.). 250p. 1999. pap. text 19.95 (*0-87337-477-0*) Nolo com.

Nolo's Everyday Law Book: Answers to Your Most Frequently Asked Questions. 2nd rev. ed. Ed. by Shae Irving. LC 98-10497. (Illus.). 300p. 1999. pap. 24.95 (*0-87337-426-6*) Nolo com.

***Nolo's Guide to Social Security Disability: Getting & Keeping Your Benefits.** David A. Morton. LC 99-57186. 2000. 29.95 (*0-87337-574-2*) Nolo com.

Nolo's Law Form Kit: Personal Bankruptcy. 2nd ed. Stephen R. Elias et al. 169p. 1999. pap. 14.95 (*0-87337-180-1*) Nolo com.

Nolo's Law Form Kit: Personal Bankruptcy. 2nd ed. Stephen Elias et al. (Illus.). 169p. 1999. pap. 16.95 (*0-87337-493-2*) Nolo com.

Nolo's Law Form Kit: Wills. Steve Elias & Denis Clifford. LC 98-150849. 100p. (Orig.). 1996. reprint ed. pap. 14.95 (*0-87337-181-X*) Nolo com.

Nolo's Partnership Maker. (Illus.). 224p. 1998. pap. 79.95 incl. cd-rom (*0-87337-165-8*) Nolo com.

***Nolo's Patents for Beginners.** David Pressman. LC 00-27404. (Quick & Legal Ser.). (Illus.). 200p. 2000. pap. 29.95 (*0-87337-575-0*) Nolo com.

Nolo's Pocket Guide to California Law, 1. 6th ed. Lisa Guerin. (Orig.). 1999. pap. text 15.95 (*0-87337-504-1*) Nolo com.

Nolo's Pocket Guide to Family Law. 4th ed. Robin Leonard & Stephen R. Elias. LC 95-26806. (Illus.). 208p. 1996. pap. text 14.95 (*0-87337-322-7*) Nolo com.

***Nolo's Quick LLC.** Anthony Mancuso. LC 00-20580. (Quick & Legal Ser.). (Illus.). 200p. 2000. pap. 29.95 (*0-87337-573-4*) Nolo com.

Nolo's Simple Will Book see Nolo's Will Book

Nolo's Will Book. 3rd rev. ed. Denis Clifford. LC 97-14103. Orig. Title: Nolo's Simple Will Book. (Illus.). 336p. (Orig.). 1997. pap. 34.95 incl. disk (*0-87337-373-1*) Nolo com.

NOLS Cookery. 4th ed. Ed. by Claudia Pearson. (Illus.). 160p. 1997. pap. 12.95 (*0-8117-2860-9*) Stackpole.

NOLS Cookery: Experience the Art of Outdoor Cooking. National Outdoor Leadership School Staff. LC 88-60635. 112p. 1991. pap. 8.95 (*0-8117-3083-2*) Stackpole.

NOLS Soft Paths. 2nd rev. ed. Bruce Hampton & David Cole. LC 95-7079. (Illus.). 240p. 1994. pap. 14.95 (*0-8117-3092-1*) Stackpole.

NOLS Wilderness First Aid. Tod Schimelpfenig & Linda Lindsey. LC 92-19090. (Illus.). 368p. (Orig.). 1992. pap. 14.95 (*0-8117-3084-0*) Stackpole.

***Nols Wilderness First Aid.** 3rd ed. Tod Schimelpfenig & Linda Lindsey. LC 00-36586. 2000. pap. 14.95 (*0-8117-2864-1*) Stackpole.

NOLS Wilderness Mountaineering. Phil Powers. LC 93-6856. (Illus.). 256p. 1993. pap. 14.95 (*0-8117-3086-7*) Stackpole.

***Nols Wilderness Mountaineering.** 2nd ed. Phil Powers & National Outdoor Leadership School U. S. Staff. LC 00-24094. (Illus.). 2000. pap. 14.95 (*0-8117-2861-7*) Stackpole.

Nom Adsorption onto Iron-Oxide-Coated Sand. (Illus.). 116p. 1993. pap. 64.75 (*0-89867-693-2*, 90632) Am Water Wks Assn.

Nom de Code: Casanova. Carroll Dawn. (Rouge Passion Ser.). (FRE.). 1997. pap. 3.50 (*0-373-37430-5*, 1-37430-5) Harlequin Bks.

NOM, '88: Proceedings of the Ninth Annual, May 10-12, 1988. 456p. 1988. pap. 40.00 (*0-938734-26-1*) Info Today Inc.

NOM, '90: National Online Meeting: Proceedings, 11th, May 1-3, 1990. Ed. by Martha E. Williams. 474p. 1990. pap. 50.00 (*0-938734-44-X*) Info Today Inc.

NOM, '91: National Online Meeting: Proceedings of the 12th National Online Meeting. Ed. by Martha E. Williams. 1991. pap. 55.00 (*0-938734-51-2*) Info Today Inc.

NOM, '92: National Online Meeting: Proceedings of the 13th National Online Meeting, May 5-7, 1992. Ed. by Martha E. Williams. 525p. 1992. pap. 55.00 (*0-938734-63-6*) Info Today Inc.

Nomad. David Alexander. 1992. per. 4.99 (*0-373-62115-9*, 1-62115-0) Harlequin Bks.

Nomad. Maryann Fitzgerald. 1999. pap. 10.95 (*0-14-017890-2*, Viking) Viking Penguin.

Nomad: A Year in the Life of a Qashqa'i Tribesman in Iran. Lois Beck. (Illus.). 482p. 1991. 65.00 (*0-520-07003-8*, Pub. by U CA Pr); pap. 22.50 (*0-520-07495-5*, Pub. by U CA Pr) Cal Prin Full Svc.

N

Nomad of the Time Streams Vol. 4: The Eternal Champion, 3 bks. in 1. Michael Moorcock. Vol. 4. (Illus.). 1997. pap. 14.99 (*1-56504-194-1*, 12520, Borealis) White Wolf.

Nomad Shelves. Mary Appelhof. (Illus.). 14p. (Orig.). 1977. pap. 3.50 (*0-942256-02-6*, Flower Pr) Flowerfield Ent.

Nomadic Alternative. Thomas J. Barfield. LC 92-15067. 224p. (C). 1993. pap. text 20.00 (*0-13-624982-5*) P-H.

Nomadic Alternative: Modes & Models of Interaction in the African-Asian Deserts & Steppes. Ed. by Wolfgang Weissleder. (World Anthropology Ser.). (Illus.). xviii, 424p. 1978. 52.35 (*90-279-7520-5*) Mouton.

Nomadic Architecture. Albert Locher. 1998. 65.00 (*3-907044-44-4*) Lars Muller.

***Nomadic Identities: The Performance of Citizenship.** May Joseph. (Public Worlds Ser.). 1999. write for info. (*0-8166-2636-7*) U of Minn Pr.

Nomadic Identities: The Performance of Citizenship, Vol. 5. May Joseph. LC 98-43818. 1999. pap. text 18.95 (*0-8166-2637-5*) U of Minn Pr.

***Nomadic Nature: A New Gate.** Johnny D. Cox. (Illus.). 90p. (YA). 2000. pap. 19.95 (*0-9679972-0-8*) Servano.

Nomadic, '96 - Conference Proceedings. Ed. by Leonard Kleinrock. (Illus.). 450p. 1996. ring bd. 395.00 (*0-614-28393-0*) Tech Trans Inst.

***Nomadic Soul.** Irina Muravyova. (Glas Ser.: Vol. 22). 240p. 2000. pap. 14.95 (*1-56663-276-5*, Pub. by I R Dee) Natl Bk Netwk.

Nomadic Subjects: Embodiment & Sexual Difference in Contemporary Feminist Theory. Rosi Braidotti. LC 93-40638. (Gender & Culture Ser.). 326p. 1994. 61.50 (*0-231-08234-7*); pap. 17.50 (*0-231-08235-5*) Col U Pr.

Nomadic Trajectory. Pasquale Verdicchio. 54p. 1990. pap. 5.00 (*0-920717-10-1*) Guernica Editions.

Nomadic Voices: Conrad & the Subject of Narrative. Bruce Henricksen. 216p. (C). 1992. text 34.95 (*0-252-01936-9*); pap. text 13.95 (*0-252-06253-1*) U of Ill Pr.

***Nomadic Voices of Exile: Feminine Identity in Francophone Literature of the Maghreb.** Valerie Orlando. LC 98-32063. 256p. 1999. 36.95 (*0-8214-1262-0*) Ohio U Pr.

***Nomadness Journals: Tales of the Behemoth Era.** 2nd ed. Steven K. Roberts. (NRL Adventure Tales Ser.: Vol. NRL-217). (Illus.). 144p. 1999. pap. 12.95 (*1-929470-03-7*) Nomadic Research.

Nomadology. Gilles Deleuze & Felix Guattari. 147p. Date not set. 7.00 (*0-936756-09-8*) Autonomedia.

Nomads. Peter Carmichael. (Illus.). 160p. 1993. 45.00 (*1-85585-061-3*) Trafalgar.

Nomads & Crusaders, A.D. 1000-1368. Archibald Ross Lewis. LC 87-45588. (Illus.). 224p. 1988. 26.95 (*0-253-34787-4*) Ind U Pr.

Nomads & Listeners. Joseph Chamberlin. Ed. by Samuel M. Waxman. LC 68-22905. (Essay Index Reprint Ser.). 1977. 19.95 (*0-8369-0287-4*) Ayer.

Nomads & Ottomans in Medieval Anatolia. Rudi P. Lindner. LC 82-6127. (Uralic & Altaic Ser.: Vol. 144). 167p. 1983. pap. 20.00 (*0-933070-12-8*) Res Inst Inner Asian Studies.

Nomads & Sedentary Societies in Medieval Eurasia. Peter B. Golden. LC 98-36367. (Essays on Global & Comparative History Ser.). 1998. pap. write for info. (*0-87229-108-1*) Am Hist Assn.

Nomads & the Outside World. 2nd ed. Anatoly M. Khazanov. Tr. by Julia Crookenden. LC 93-41133. 1994. reprint ed. 21.95 (*0-299-14284-1*) U of Wis Pr.

Nomads & the State in Africa: The Political Roots of Marginality. Victor Azarya. (African Studies Centre Leiden). 108p. 1996. pap. 43.95 (*1-85972-576-7*, Pub. by Avebry) Ashgate Pub Co.

Nomads et Sedentarisation a Borneo see Nomads of the Borneo Rainforest: The Economics, Politics, & Ideology of Settling Down

Nomads, Exiles, & Emigres: The Rebirth of the Latin American Narrative, 1960-80. Ronald Schwartz. LC 80-20669. 168p. 1980. 21.00 (*0-8108-1359-9*) Scarecrow.

Nomads in Archaeology. Roger Cribb. (New Studies in Archaeology). (Illus.). 267p. (C). 1991. text 74.95 (*0-521-32881-0*) Cambridge U Pr.

***Nomads in the Sedentary Word.** Ed. by Anatoly M. Khazanov & Andre Wink. 290p. 2000. pap. 29.95 (*0-7007-1370-0*, Pub. by Curzon Pr Ltd) Paul & Co Pubs.

***Nomads in the Sedentary World.** Ed. by Anatoly M. Khazanov & Andre Wink. 290p. 2000. 75.00 (*0-7007-1369-7*, Pub. by Curzon Pr Ltd) Paul & Co Pubs.

Nomads Indians Saints. Composed by Indigo Girls. 72p. 1996. per. 14.95 (*0-7935-6538-3*) H Leonard.

***Nomad's Journal: International - 30 Day.** Brian Leslie Lewis. 32p. 1999. pap. 9.95 (*1-928693-03-2*) Novice Nomad.

***Nomad's Journal - 72 Page: (Magehan's Version)** Brian Leslie Lewis. 72p. 1999. pap. 7.95 (*1-928693-06-7*) Novice Nomad.

Nomads of Gor. John Norman. 1997. mass mkt. 6.95 (*1-56333-527-1*, Masquerade SF) Masquerade.

Nomads of Luristan & Their Material Culture. Inge Demant Mortensen. LC 93-60435. (Carlsberg Nomad Ser.). (Illus.). 496p. 1993. 50.00 (*0-500-01572-4*, Pub. by Thames Hudson) Norton.

Nomads of Niger. Photos by Carol Beckwith. LC 93-14899. (Illus.). 224p. 1993. pap. 29.98 (*0-8109-8125-4*, Pub. by Abrams) Time Warner.

Nomads of Niger. Marion Van Offelen & Carol Beckwith. (Illus.). 224p. 1983. 60.00 (*0-8109-0734-8*) Abrams.

Nomads of South Persia: The Basseri Tribe of the Khamseh Confederacy. Fredrik Barth. (Illus.). 161p. (C). 1986. reprint ed. pap. text 11.50 (*0-88133-207-0*) Waveland Pr.

Nomads of South Siberia: The Pastoral Economies of Tuva. Sevian I. Vainshtein. Ed. by Caroline Humphrey. Tr. by Michael Colenso. LC 78-54728. (Cambridge Studies in Social Anthropology: No. 25). 299p. reprint ed. pap. 85.30 (*0-608-15616-7*, 2031739) Bks Demand.

Nomads of the Balkans. Alan J. Wace. 1973. reprint ed. 25.00 (*0-8196-0136-5*) Biblo.

Nomads of the Balkans: An Account of Life & Customs among the Vlachs of Northern Pindus. Alan J. Wace & M. S. Thompson. LC 70-37358. (Select Bibliographies Reprint Ser.). 1977. reprint ed. 31.95 (*0-8369-6705-4*) Ayer.

Nomads of the Borneo Rainforest: The Economics, Politics, & Ideology of Settling Down. Bernard Sellato. Tr. by Stephanie Morgan from FRE. LC 94-4291.Tr. of Nomads et Sedentarisation a Borneo. 1994. text 36.00 (*0-8248-1566-1*) UH Pr.

Nomads of the North. James O. Curwood. 1919. 69.00 (*0-403-00802-6*) Scholarly.

Nomads of the North. James O. Curwood. LC 98-85545. 260p. 1998. reprint ed. pap. 12.00 (*1-892323-08-7*) Vivisphere.

Nomads of the North: A Story of Romance & Adventure under the Open Stars. James O. Curwood. LC 78-127911. (BCL Ser. I). (Illus.). reprint ed. 37.50 (*0-404-01896-3*) AMS Pr.

Nomads of the Pamir Plateau, 2 vols. Esther Fihl. LC 99-70845. (Carlsberg Nomad Ser.). (Illus.). 700p. 1999. 85.00 (*0-500-01931-2*, Pub. by Thames Hudson) Norton.

Nomads of the Present. Melucci. 1992. pap. write for info. (*0-09-172872-X*, Pub. by Random) Random House.

Nomads of the Wind: A Natural History of Polynesia. Peter Crawford. (Illus.). 272p. 1994. 32.95 (*0-563-36707-5*, BBC-Parkwest) Parkwest Pubns.

Nomads of Western Tibet: The Survival of a Way of Life. Melvyn C. Goldstein & Cynthia M. Beall. LC 90-10892. (Illus.). 200p. 1990. 55.00 (*0-520-07210-3*, Pub. by U CA Pr); pap. 24.95 (*0-520-07211-1*, Pub. by U CA Pr) Cal Prin Full Svc.

***Nomad/Y: The Moon Base Project.** Noah Bond. LC 99-75830. 317p. 1999. pap. 16.95 (*0-9673551-0-9*, 01-NOMAD/Y) Mission Invest.

Nomai Dance Drama: A Surviving Spirit of Medieval Japan, 47. Susan M. Asai. LC 98-14243. (Contributions to the Study of Music & Dance Ser.: Vol. 47). 280p. 1999. 65.00 (*0-313-30698-2*, Greenwood Pr) Greenwood.

Noman. Gwendolyn MacEwen. 120p. 1985. pap. 4.95 (*0-7736-7086-6*) Genl Dist Srvs.

Nomar Garciaparra: High 5! Michael Shalin. Ed. by Rob Rains. (Super Star Ser.). 96p. (J). 1999. pap. 4.95 (*1-58261-053-3*) Sprts Pubng.

***Nomar Garciaparra: Non-Stop Shortstop.** Mark Stewart. LC 99-31131. (Baseball's New Wave Ser.). 5p. (J). 2000. pap. 6.95 (*0-7613-1335-4*) Millbrook Pr.

***Nomar Garciaparra: Non-Stop Shortstop.** Mark Stewart. LC 99-31131. (Baseball's New Wave Ser.). 48p. (J). (gr. 4). 2000. 19.90 (*0-7613-1520-9*) Millbrook Pr.

Nombre de Dios, Durango. Ed. by Robert H. Barlow & George T. Smisor. LC 76-44684. 136p. 1983. reprint ed. 32.50 (*0-404-15901-X*) AMS Pr.

Nombres. Jaime Carrero. (UPREX, Ficcion Ser.: No. 13). 167p. (C). 1972. pap. 1.50 (*0-8477-0013-5*) U of PR Pr.

Nombres. Ladybird Books Staff. (French Language Editions Ser.: No. 563F-2). (FRE., Illus.). (J). 1990. 3.50 (*0-7214-1427-3*, Ladybrd) Penguin Putnam.

Nombres. Phillipe Sollers. (FRE.). 1966. pap. 17.95 (*0-7859-1237-1*, 2020019434) Fr & Eur.

Nombres: Nombres de Pila en Nuevo Mexico. Francisco Sisneros & Joe H. Torres.Tr. of Spanish Given Names in New Mexico. (ENG & SPA.). 129p. (Orig.). 1982. pap. 6.95 (*0-938476-01-7*) Las Campanas.

Nombres Cientificos de los Parasitos y Su Significado. 2nd ed. Oscar J. Lombardero. (SPA.). 90p. 1978. 12.95 (*0-8288-5257-X*, S33068) Fr & Eur.

***Nombres de Cristo.** T. C. Horton & C. E. Hurlburt. (SPA.). 176p. 1999. pap. 5.99 (*0-8254-1333-8*, Edit Portavoz) Kregel.

Nombres de Dios. Nathan J. Stone.Tr. of Names of God. (SPA.). 160p. 1996. pap. 5.99 (*0-8254-1687-6*, Edit Portavoz) Kregel.

***Nombres de los Angeles.** C. Fred Dickason. (SPA.). 160p. 1999. pap. 5.99 (*0-8254-1165-3*, Edit Portavoz) Kregel.

Nombres Exoticos Para Bebe. Monica Stevenson. (SPA., Illus.). 112p. 1997. pap. text 7.98 (*968-403-538-1*) Selector.

Nombres para el Bebe. (SPA.). 221p. 1997. pap. text 16.98 (*968-13-1040-3*) Edit Diana.

Nombres Perfectos Para Bebe. Monica Stevenson. (SPA.). 1997. pap. text 8.98 (*968-403-407-5*) Diana-Etna Inc.

Nombril du Monde. Jean-Marie Poupart. (Novels in the Roman Jeunesse Ser.). (FRE.). 160p. (YA). (gr. 8 up). 1990. pap. 8.95 (*2-89021-143-6*, Pub. by La Courte Ech) Firefly Bks Ltd.

Nome, Alaska, Telephone Directory, 1905. Telephone & Telegraph Co. Staff. 28p. 1986. reprint ed. pap. 10.00 (*0-8466-0014-5*, S-14, Shorey Pubns) Shoreys Bkstore.

Nome, City of the Golden Beaches. Alaska Geographic Society Staff. LC 84-294. (Alaska Geographic Ser.: Vol. 11, no. 1). (Illus.). 184p. 1984. pap. 19.95 (*0-88240-201-3*) Alaska Geog Soc.

Nome Della Rosa. Umberto Eco. 1999. 17.95 (*88-452-1066-9*) Distribks Inc.

Nome Gold. Kenneth J. Kutz. (Illus.). 240p. (C). 1991. 32.50 (*0-9620411-1-4*) Gold Fever Pub.

Nome Hermopolite: Toponymes et Sites. Marie Drew-Bear. LC 78-13005. (American Studies in Papyrology: No. 21). (Illus.). 432p. reprint ed. pap. 134.00 (*0-7837-5494-9*, 204525900005) Bks Demand.

Nome King's Shadow in Oz. Gilbert M. Sprague. (Illus.). 120p. (J). (gr. 3 up). 1992. pap. 9.95 (*0-929605-18-7*) Books of Wonder.

***Nome Poems.** Ken Waldman. 2000. pap. 9.95 (*0-931122-98-8*) West End.

Nomen et Gens: Zur Historischen Aussagekraft Fruhmittelalterlicher Personennamen. Dieter Geuenich et al. 400p. 1997. 143.00 (*3-11-015809-4*) De Gruyter.

***Nomenclator Alliorum (Allium Names & Synonyms) A World Guide.** Mark Gregory et al. (Illus.). vi, 83p. 1998. pap. 42.00 (*1-900347-64-4*, Pub. by Royal Botnic Grdns) Balogh.

Nomenclator Botanics. E. T. Steudel. 1662p. (C). 1981. reprint ed. 1500.00 (*0-7855-3089-4*, Pub. by Intl Bk Distr) St Mut.

Nomenclator Botanicus, Vols. 1-2. E. T. Steudel. 1662p. (C). 1981. text 2500.00 (*0-89771-658-2*, Pub. by Intl Bk Distr) St Mut.

Nomenclator Hadriani Junii Medici Ad Scholarum Usum Accomodatus. Matthias Schenckius. (Documenta Linguistica, Reihe I: Worterbucher Des Vol. 15 & 16. Jahrhunderts Ser.). (GER.). xvi, 288p. 1982. reprint ed. write for info. (*3-487-06715-3*) G Olms Pubs.

Nomenclator Lationsaxonicus. Nathan Chytraeus. (Documenta Linguistica, Reihe I Ser.). xvi, 626p. 1974. reprint ed. 130.00 (*3-487-05277-6*) G Olms Pubs.

***Nomenclator of Mexican & Central American Rubiaceae.** David H. Lorence. 177p. 1999. pap. 20.00 (*0-915279-62-2*) Miss Botan.

Nomenclator Omnium Rerum. Hadrianus Junius. (Documenta Linguistica, Reihe I: Worterbucher Des Vol. 15 & 16. Jahrhunderts Ser.). (GER.). 570p. 1976. reprint ed. write for info. (*3-487-06105-8*) G Olms Pubs.

Nomenclator Philologorum. Friedrich A. Eckstein. viii, 656p. 1966. reprint ed. write for info. (*0-318-70741-1*); reprint ed. write for info. (*0-318-71900-2*) G Olms Pubs.

Nomenclatoris Hadriani Junii Medici Epitome. Adam Siber. (Documenta Linguistica, Reihe I Ser.). 238p. 1986. reprint ed. write for info. (*3-487-07776-0*) G Olms Pubs.

Nomenclatura Rerum Domesticarum. Sebaldus Heyden. (GER.). 144p. write for info. (*0-318-70472-2*) G Olms Pubs.

Nomenclatura Rerum Domesticarum. Sebald Heyden. (Documenta Linguistica Ser.: Reihe I). 144p. 1997. reprint ed. 72.00 (*3-487-10304-4*) G Olms Pubs.

Nomenclaturai Typification of Some Unicellular & Colonial Algae. Christiaan Van Den Hoek. (Illus.). 1963. pap. 10.00 (*3-7682-0211-9*) Lubrecht & Cramer.

Nomenclatural Guide to R. H. Beddome's Ferns of South India & Ferns of British India. Subhas Chandra & Surjit Kaur. x, 140p. 1987. 15.00 (*1-55528-076-5*, Pub. by Today Tomorrow) Scholarly Pubns.

Nomenclature Anatomique Illustree. Guntz. (FRE.). 512p. 1975. pap. 69.95 (*0-8288-5941-8*, M6307) Fr & Eur.

Nomenclature & Criteria for Diagnosis of Diseases of the Heart & Great Vessels. 9th ed. Criteria Committee of the New York Heart Associati. Ed. by Martin Dolgin et al. LC 93-43623. 352p. 1994. pap. text 34.95 (*0-316-60538-7*, Little Brwn Med Div) Lppncott W & W.

Nomenclature & Definitions for Use in NRSCL & Other NCCLS Documents: Proposed Guideline (1996) 2nd ed. Contrib. by Harry S. Hertz. 1996. 85.00 (*1-56238-185-7*, NRSCL8-P3) NCCLS.

Nomenclature & Systematic Description see Enzyklopaedie der Philosophischen Wissenschaften

Nomenclature & Systematic Description see Enzyklopaedie der Pilze

Nomenclature & Terminology for Extension Type Variable Area Meters, Rotameters: ISA Standard RP16.4. 1960. pap. 20.00 (*0-87664-343-8*, RP16.4) ISA.

Nomenclature des Appelations d'emploi dans L' Industrie Papetiere Quebecoise: Anglais-Francais. Normand Cote & J. Gaumond. (ENG & FRE.). 114p. 1977. pap. 9.95 (*0-7859-0652-5*, M9234) Fr & Eur.

Nomenclature for Flexible Couplings. AGMA Technical Committee. (AGMA Standard Ser.: Vol. 510.03). 12p. 1984. pap. text 38.00 (*1-55589-062-8*) AGMA.

Nomenclature for Hazard & Risk Assessment. 2nd ed. Ed. by David Jones. 43p. 1992. pap. 21.00 (*0-85295-297-X*, 9CH6, Pub. by IChemE) Gulf Pub.

Nomenclature for Instrument Tube Fittings: ISA Standard RP42.1. ISA Staff. 1991. pap. 25.00 (*1-55617-256-7*, RP42-1) ISA.

Nomenclature Hazards & Risks. ICHEM Engineers Staff. 1986. pap. 8.75 (*0-08-033935-2*, Pergamon Pr) Elsevier.

Nomenclature of Energy Fundamentals. 295p. 1996. 11.80 (*7-03-002243-2*, Pub. by Sci Pr) Lubrecht & Cramer.

Nomenclature of Inorganic Chemistry: Definitive Rules, 1970. 2nd ed. IUPAC Staff. 1971. 61.00 (*0-08-020834-7*, Pub. by Pergamon Repr) Franklin.

Nomenclature of Inorganic Chemistry, the Red Book, 2 pts. IUPAC Staff. 1971. pap. 74.00 (*0-08-021999-3*, Pub. by Pergamon Repr) Franklin.

Nomenclature of Organic Chemistry: Definitive Rules for Section A. Hydrocarbons, Section B., Fundamental Heterocyclic Systems. 2nd ed. International Union of Pure & Applied Chemistry. LC QD0291.I35. (Illus.). 92p. reprint ed. pap. 30.00 (*0-608-30015-2*, 202071400018) Bks Demand.

Nomenclature of Organic Chemistry: Definitive Rules for Section C. Characteristic Groups Containing Carbon, Hydrogen, Oxygen, Nitrogen, Halogen, Sulfur, Selenium, & or Tellurium. International Union of Pure & Applied Chemistry. LC QD0007.I55. 276p. reprint ed. pap. 85.60 (*0-608-30021-7*, 202071500018) Bks Demand.

Nomenclature of Organic Compounds. Raj K. Bansal. (Illus.). 1979. text. write for info. (*0-07-096370-3*) McGraw.

Nomenclature of Organic Compounds: Principles & Practice. Ed. by J. H. Fletcher et al. LC 73-92675. (Advances in Chemistry Ser.: No. 126). 337p. 1974. 54.95 (*0-8412-0191-9*); pap. 34.95 (*0-8412-0234-6*) Am Chemical.

Nomenclature of Organic Compounds: Principles & Practice. Ed. by John H. Fletcher et al. LC 73-92675. (Advances in Chemistry Ser.: No. 126). (Illus.). 352p. 1973. reprint ed. pap. 109.20 (*0-608-06811-X*, 206700800009) Bks Demand.

***Nomenclature of Organic Compounds: Principles & Practice.** 2nd ed. Robert B. Fox & Warren H. Powell. LC 99-43801. (An American Chemical Society Publication). 608p. 2001. text 215.00 (*0-8412-3648-8*, Pub. by Am Chemical) OUP.

***Nomenclature of Particle Dispersion Technology for Ceramic Systems.** Vincent A. Hackley. 24p. 2000. pap. 2.50 (*0-16-059095-7*) USGPO.

Nomenklatur, Taxonomie & Systematik der Gattung Isoetes Linnaeus in Geschichtlicher Entwicklung. H. P. Fuchs. (Illus.). 1962. pap. 30.00 (*3-7682-5403-8*) Lubrecht & Cramer.

Nomenklatura: The Soviet Rulin. Michael Voslensky. 1992. text 55.00 (*0-8133-1317-1*) Westview.

Nomes Basileus. Marcello Gigante. Ed. by Gregory Vlastos. LC 78-19351. (Morals & Law in Ancient Greece Ser.). 1979. reprint ed. lib. bdg. 25.95 (*0-405-11544-X*) Ayer.

Nomic Probability & the Foundations of Induction. John L. Pollock. 368p. 1990. text 75.00 (*0-19-506013-X*) OUP.

Nomie Book: Growing up from Shy. Sunnie Williams. (Illus.). 104p. (Orig.). (J). (gr. 3-6). 1981. pap. 5.25 (*0-9605444-0-2*) Waking Light Pr.

Nomifensine-Clinical & Experimental Investigation. Ed. by W. Poeldinger & K. Taeuber. (Journal: International Pharmacopsychiatry: Vol. 17, Suppl. 1, 1982). iv, 148p. 1982. pap. 41.75 (*3-8055-3585-6*) S Karger.

Nomina Anatomica Veterinaria & Nomina Histologica. 267p. 1983. 15.00 (*0-9600444-5-0*) Wld Assn Vet.

Nomina Simplicium Medicinarum ex Synonymariis Medii Aevi Collecta: Semantische Untersuchungen zum Fachwortschatz Hoch- & Spaetmittelalterlicher Drogenkunde. Willem F. Daems. LC 92-42058. (Studies in Ancient Medicine: Vol. 6). (GER.). 563p. 1993. 186.00 (*90-04-09672-8*) Brill Academic Pubs.

Nominal Anaphors. E. Peters. LC 97-227407. 1998. 28.95 (*90-6831-798-9*, Pub. by Peeters Pub) Bks Intl VA.

Nominal & Verbal Plurality in Chadic. Paul Newman. (Publications in African Languages & Linguistics: No. 12). 164p. 1990. pap. 60.00 (*90-6765-499-X*) Mouton.

Nominal & Verbal System of Fula. D. W. Arnott. LC 77-18225. 469p. reprint ed. pap. 145.40 (*0-8357-3967-8*, AU0040100005) Bks Demand.

Nominal Christian Handbook. C. Michael Cunningham. 1991. pap. 5.95 (*1-55673-306-2*, 9130) CSS OH.

Nominal Classification in Aboriginal Australia. Ed. by Mark Harvey & Nicholas Reid. LC 97-26693. (Studies in Language Companion Ser.: Vol. 37). x, 296p. 1997. lib. bdg. 89.00 (*1-55619-848-5*) J Benjamins Pubng Co.

Nominal Sentence in Sanskrit & Middle Indo-Aryan. Andries Breunis. LC 89-71270. (Orientalia Rheno-Traiectina Ser.: Vol. 35). vii, 229p. 1989. 63.50 (*90-04-09123-8*) Brill Academic Pubs.

Nominalism & Contemporary Nominalism. Mia Gosselin. 274p. (C). 1990. lib. bdg. 124.00 (*0-7923-0904-9*, Pub. by Kluwer Academic) Kluwer Academic.

Nominalism, Constructivism, & Relativism in the Work of Nelson Goodman see Philosophy of Nelson Goodman: Selected Essays

Nominalistic Systems. R. A. Eberle. LC 78-131265. (Synthese Library: No. 30). 226p. 1970. text 94.00 (*90-277-0161-X*, D Reidel) Kluwer Academic.

Nominalizations. Maria Koptjevskaja-Tamm. LC 92-7229. (Theoretical Linguistics Ser.). 352p. (C). (gr. 13). 1993. 100.00 (*0-415-06020-6*, A7878) Routledge.

Nominalsatze in Altbabylonischen Briefen und der Stativ. F. R. Kraus. (Mededelingen der Koninklijke Nederlandse Akademie van Wetenschappen, Afd. Letterkunde Ser.: No. 47(2)). 52p. 1984. pap. 28.25 (*0-444-85606-4*) Elsevier.

Nominalstil und Fachkommunikation: Analyse Komplexer Nominalphrasen in Deutsch- und Finnischsprachigen Philologischen Fachtexten. Marja Jarventausta & Hartmut Schroder. (Werkstattreihe Deutsch als Fremdsprache Ser.: Bd. 54). (GER., Illus.). IX, 281p. 1996. 54.95 (*3-631-30985-6*) P Lang Pubng.

Nominating a President: The Process & the Press. Los Angeles Times Editors. LC 80-13824. 168p. 1980. 38.50 (*0-275-90509-8*, C0509, Praeger Pubs); pap. 14.95 (*0-03-057858-2*, Praeger Pubs) Greenwood.

Nominating Committee: Laying a Foundation for Your Organization's Future, No. 54. Ellen C. Hirzy. 16p. 1994. 12.00 (*0-925299-37-5*) Natl Ctr Nonprofit.

Nominating National Leaders: A Cross-National Survey. James W. Davis. LC 97-52297. 232p. 1998. lib. bdg. 65.00 (*0-313-30147-6*, Greenwood Pr) Greenwood.

Nominating the President. Ed. by Emmett H. Buell, Jr. & Lee Sigelman. LC 90-43212. 320p. 1991. 42.95 (*0-87049-686-7*); pap. text 18.95 (*0-87049-687-5*) U of Tenn Pr.

Nominating the Presidents: An Evaluation of Voters & Primaries, 236. John G. Geer. LC 89-2130. (Contributions in Political Science Ser.: No. 236). (Illus.). 176p. 1989. 52.95 (*0-313-26182-2*, GSR/, Greenwood Pr) Greenwood.

Nomination: Hearing of the Committee on Labor & Human Resources, United States Senate & Congress, Second Session, on Jane E. Henney, of New Mexico, to Be Commissioner of Food & Drugs, Department of Health & Human Services, September 2, 1998. LC 98-214943. (S. Hrg. Ser.). iii, 69p. 1998. write for info. (*0-16-057551-6*) USGPO.

N

An Asterisk (*) at the beginning of an entry indicates that the title is appearing for the first time.

Nomination of Andrew J. Pincus to be General Counsel of the U.s. Department of Commerce: Hearing Before the Committee on Commerce, Science, & Transportation, United States Senate, One Hundred Fifth Congress, First Session, April 30, 1997. United States. LC 98-161393. iii, 13 p. 1997. write for info. (*0-16-056011-X*) USGPO.

Nomination of Anthony Lake to Be Director of Central Intelligence: Hearing Before the Select Committee on Intelligence, United States Senate, One Hundred Fifth Congress, First Session, on Nomination of Anthony Lake to Be Director of the Central Intelligence, March 11th, 12th, 13th, 1997. United States. LC 98-166269. 266 p. 1998. write for info. (*0-16-056408-5*) USGPO.

***Nomination of Bill Lann Lee of California, to Be Assistant Attorney General, U.S. Department of Justice: Hearing Before the Committee on the Judiciary, United States Senate, One Hundred Fifth Congress, First Session on the Nomination of Bill Lann Lee of California, to Be Assistant Attorney General, Department of Justice, October 22, 1997.** USGPO Staff. LC 98-207512. (S. Hrg. Ser.). iv, 173 p. 1998. write for info. (*0-16-057182-0*) USGPO.

Nomination of David J. Barram: Hearing Before the Committee on Governmental Affairs, United States Senate, 105th Congress, 1st Session, on Nomination of David J. Barram, to be Administrator of the General Services Administration, February 25, 1997. USGPO Staff. LC 98-107117. iii, 117p. 1997. write for info. (*0-16-055482-9*) USGPO.

Nomination of G. Edward Deseve & Deidre A. Lee: Hearing Before the Committee on Governmental Affairs, United States Senate, One Hundred Fifth Congress, Second Session, April 22, 1998 : Nomination of G. Edward Deseve, to Be Deputy Director for Management, Office of Management & Budget, & Deidre A. Lee, to Be Administrator, Office of Federal Procurement Policy, Office of Management & Budget. United States Staff. LC 98-208198. 112 p. 1998. write for info. (*0-16-057107-3*) USGPO.

***Nomination of George J. Tenet to Be Director of Central Intelligence: Hearing Before the Select Committee on Intelligence of the United States Senate, One Hundred Fifth Congress, First Session on the Nomination of George J. Tenet to Be Director of Central Intelligence, Tuesday, May 6, 1997.** United States Government. LC 98-144148. (S. Hrg. Ser.). iii, 113 p. 1998. write for info. (*0-16-056075-6*) USGPO.

Nomination of Hon. Rodney E. Slater to Be Secretary of Transportation: Hearing Before the Committee on Commerce, Science & Transportation, United States Senate, One Hundred Fifth Congress, First Session, January 29, 1997. United States Government. LC 98-158400. (S. Hrg. Ser.). iii, 159 p. 1997. write for info. (*0-16-056158-2*) USGPO.

Nomination of Janet Louise Yellen: Hearing Before the Committee on Banking, Housing & Urban Affairs, United States Senate, One Hundred Fifth Congress, First Session, on Nomination of Janet Louise Yellen, of California, to Be Chairman of the Council of Economic Advisors, February 5, 1997. United States Government. LC 98-114888. (S. Hrg. Ser.). iii, 45 p. 1997. write for info. (*0-16-055778-X*) USGPO.

Nomination of Judge Clarence Thomas & the Testimony of Anita Hill, 10 vols., Set. 1994. lib. bdg. 5559.95 (*0-8490-8507-1*) Gordon Pr.

Nomination of Kenneth M. Mead to Be Inspector General of the U. S. Department of Transportation: Hearing Before the Committee on Commerce, Science & Transportation, United States Senate, 105th Congress, First Session, April 9, 1997. LC 98-168059. (S. Hrg. Ser.). iii, 27 p. 1998. write for info. (*0-16-056481-6*) USGPO.

Nomination of Kenneth R. Wykle: Hearing Before the Committee on Environment & Public Works, United States Senate, One Hundred Fifth Congress, First Session, on the Nomination of Kenneth R. Winkle to Be Administrator, Federal Highway Administration, October 28, 1997. United States. LC 98-138705. 25 p. 1997. write for info. (*0-16-055936-7*) USGPO.

Nomination of Kerri-Ann Jones & Jerry M. Melillo to Be Associate Directors of the Office of Science & Technology Policy: Hearing Before the Committee on Commerce, Science & Transportation, United States Senate, 105th Congress, First Session, April 23, 1997. LC 98-175804. (S. Hrg. Ser.). iii, 27 p. 1998. write for info. (*0-16-056552-9*) USGPO.

Nomination of Kevin Gover: Hearing Before the Committee on Indian Affairs, United States Senate, One Hundred Fifth Congress, First Session, Kevin Gover to Be Assistant Secretary for Indian Affairs, October 30, 1997. United States Staff. LC 98-153911. 90 p. 1998. write for info. (*0-16-056091-8*) USGPO.

Nomination of Melvin Randolph Wright: Hearing Before the Committee on Governmental Affairs, United States Senate, One Hundred Fifth Congress, Second Session, April 1, 1998, Nomination of Melvin Randolph Wright to Be Associate Judge of the Superior Court of the District of Columbia. United States. LC 98-207575. 18 p. 1998. write for info. (*0-16-057334-3*) USGPO.

Nomination of Seth Waxman to Be Solicitor General: Hearing Before the Committee on the Judiciary, United States Senate, One Hundred Fifth Congress, First Session on the Nomination of Seth Waxman, of the District of Columbia, to Be Solicitor General of the United States, November 5, 1997. United States. LC 98-190339. iii, 112p. 1998. write for info. (*0-16-057053-0*) USGPO.

Nomination Politics: Party Activists & Presidential Choice. Alan I. Abramowitz & Walter J. Stone. LC 84-17891. 158p. 1984. 52.95 (*0-275-91110-1*, C1110, Praeger Pubs) Greenwood.

***Nominations Before the Senate Armed Services Committee, 1st Session, 105th Congress: Hearings Before the Committee on Armed Services, United States Senate, 105th Congress, 1st Session, on Nominations of William S. Cohen; Federico F. Peana; Keith R. Hall; Gen. Wesley K. Clark, USA; Lt. Gen. Anthony C. Zinni, USMC; Rudy F. De Leon; John J. Hamre; Gen. Henry H. Shelton.** USGPO Staff. LC 98-147330. iv, 769 p. 1998. write for info. (*0-16-056255-4*) USGPO.

Nominations for Elective Office in the United States. Frederick W. Dallinger. LC 73-19140. (Politics & People Ser.). 304p. 1974. reprint ed. 23.95 (*0-405-05865-9*) Ayer.

Nominations Hearing of V. Ann Jorgensen & Lowell Lee Junkins: Hearing Before the Committee on Agriculture, Nutrition & Forestry, United States Senate, One Hundred Fifth Congress, First Session, on the Nominations Hearing for V. Ann Jorgensen, to Be a Member of the Farm Credit Administration Board & Lowell Lee Junkins, to Be a Member of the Farm Mac Board, U.S. Department of Agriculture, April 10, 1997. USGPO Staff. LC 98-212703. (S. Hrg. Ser.). iii, 72 p. 1998. write for info. (*0-16-057282-7*) USGPO.

Nominations of Ernesta Ballard, Virginia Dale Cabaniss, & Susanne T. Marshall: Hearing Before the Committee on Governmental Affairs, United States Senate, One Hundred Fifth Congress, First Session, on Nominations of Ernesta Ballard, to Be Member, Postal Board of Governors, Virginia Dale Cabaniss, to Be Member Federal Labor Relations Authority, & Susanne T. Marshall, to Be Member Merit Systems Protection Board, November 4, 1997. United States. LC 98-160944. iii, 38p. 1998. write for info. (*0-16-056185-X*) USGPO.

Nominations of George A. Omas & Janice R. Lachance: Hearing Before the Committee on Governmental Affairs, United States Senate, One Hundred Fifth Congress, First Session, on Nomination of George A. Omas, to Be Commissioner, U.s. Postal Rate Commission, & Jance R. Lachance, to Be Deputy Director, Office of Personnel Management, July 28, 1997. United States. LC 98-138708. 51 p. 1997. write for info. (*0-16-055842-5*) USGPO.

Nominations of James A. Harmon & Jackie Marie Clegg: Hearing Before the Committee on Banking, Housing, & Urban Affairs, United States Senate, One Hundred Fifth Congress, First Session, on Nominations of James, of New York, to Be President & Chairman of the Export-import Bank, Jackie Marie Clegg, of Utah, to Be First Vice President & Vice Chair of the Export-import Bank, May 22, 1997. United States. LC 98-195356. iii, 49 p. 1997. write for info. (*0-16-057051-4*) USGPO.

Nominations of Joel I. Klein & Eric H. Holder, Jr. Hearings Before the Committee on the Judiciary, United States Senate, One Hundred Fifth Congress, First Session on the Nomination of Joel I. Klein, of the District of Columbia, to Be an Assistant Attorney General, Department of Justice & Eric H. Holder, Jr., of the District of Columbia, to Be Deputy Attorney General, Department of Justice, April 29 & June 13, 1997. USGPO Staff. LC 98-137749. (S. Hrg. Ser.). iv, 131 p. 1997. write for info. (*0-16-055836-0*) USGPO.

Nominations of Raymond C. Fisher to Be U.s. Associate Attorney General: Hearing Before the Committee on the Judiciary, United States Senate, one Hundred Fifth Congress, First Session on the Nomination of Raymond C. Fisher, of California, to Be An Associate Attorney General, U.s. Department of Justice, September 30, 1997. United States. LC 98-160483. iii, 82 p. 1998. write for info. (*0-16-056360-7*) USGPO.

Nominations of Richard J. Tarplin & Kevin L. Thurm: Hearing Before the Committee on Finance, United States Senate, One Hundred Fifth Congress, Second Session, on the Nominations of Richard J. Tarplin, to Be Assistant Secretary for Legislation, Department of Health & Human Services, & Kevin L. Thurm, to Be Deputy Secretary, Department of Health & Human Services. United States. LC 98-215189. 29 p. 1997. write for info. (*0-16-057484-6*) USGPO.

Nominations of Rita Hayes, Kenneth S. Apfel, Nancy-ann Min Deparle, Olivia A. Golden, David A. Lipton, Timothy F. Geithner, Gary Gensler, & Nancy Killefer: Hearing Before the Committee on Finance, United States Senate, One Hundred Fifth Congress, First Session, on the Nominations of Rita Hayes, to Be Deputy U.s. Trade Representative ... September 10, 1997. United States. LC 98-175795. 276 p. 1997. write for info. (*0-16-056572-3*) USGPO.

Nominations of Robert S. Warshaw, to Be Associate Director & Thomas J. Umberg to Be Deputy Director for Supply Reduction: Hearing Before the Committee on the Judiciary, 105th Congress, First Session ... Both of the Office of National Drug Control Policy, November 6, 1997. LC 98-212905. (S. Hrg. Ser.). iii, 142 p. 1998. write for info. (*0-16-057219-3*) USGPO.

***Nominations of Thelma J. Askey, Jennifer Anne Hillman, Stephen Koplan & Patrick A. Mulloy: Hearing Before the Committee on Finance, United States Senate, 105th Congress, 2nd Session, on the Nominations of Thelma J. Askey, Jennifer Anne Hillman, Stephen Koplan, to Be Members of the U. S. International Trade Commission; & Patrick A. Mulloy, to be an Assistant Secretary of Commerce, April 23, 1998.** USGPO Staff. LC 98-192824. iv, 128p. 1998. write for info. (*0-16-056596-0*) USGPO.

Nominationsforschung Im Deutschen. Ed. by Irmhild Barz & Marianne Schroder. (Illus.). 499p. 1997. 73.95 (*3-631-31366-7*) P Lang Pubng.

Nominative Case. Edward Mackin. 192p. 1991. 18.95 (*0-8027-5780-4*) Walker & Co.

Nominies. Ian Duhig. LC 99-171046. 64p. 1998. pap. 16.95 (*1-85224-457-7*, Pub. by Bloodaxe Bks) Dufour.

Nomisma. Ed. by Hans Von Fritze & Hugo Gaebler. iv, 492p. 1974. reprint ed. write for info. (*3-487-05385-3*) G Olms Pubs.

Nomlaki Ethnography. fac. ed. Walter Goldschmidt. Ed. by Beals et al. (University of California Publications in American Archaeology & Ethnology: No. 42:4). 140p. (C). 1951. reprint ed. pap. 15.63 (*1-55567-319-8*) Coyote Press.

Nomme Jeudi. G. K. Chesterton. (FRE.). 248p. 1979. pap. 10.95 (*0-7859-1790-X*, 2070366057) Fr & Eur.

Nommo (The Word) Zizwe Ngafua. (Illus.). 56p. (Orig.). 1978. pap. 4.00 (*0-917886-04-6*) Shamal Bks.

Nomo! Lawrence Rocca. 1996. pap. 14.95 (*1-56931-052-1*) Viz Commns Inc.

Nomo the Inside Story on Baseball's Hottest Sensation. Herb Fagen. (J). 1996. 11.09 (*0-606-09699-X*, Pub. by Turtleback) Demco.

Nomodeiktes: Greek Studies in Honor of Martin Oswald. Ed. by Ralph M. Rosen & Joseph Farrell. (Illus.). 752p. (C). 1994. text 67.00 (*0-472-10297-4*, 10297) U of Mich Pr.

Nomography. E. Otto & J. Smolska. LC 63-10028. (International Series of Monographs on Pure & Applied Mathematics: Vol. 42). 1963. 140.00 (*0-08-010164-X*, Pub. by Pergamon Repr) Franklin.

"Nomoi" of Theophrastus. rev. ed. Andrew Szegedy-Maszak. Ed. by W. R. Connor. LC 80-2670. (Monographs in Classical Studies). 1981. lib. bdg. 22.95 (*0-405-14053-3*) Ayer.

***Nomonhan.** John Colvin. 2000. pap. 25.00 (*0-7043-7112-X*, Pub. by Quartet) Interlink Pub.

Nomonhan: Japan Against Russia, 1939, 2 vols. Alvin D. Coox. LC 81-85447. (Illus.). 1296p. 1985. pap. 4.95 (*0-8047-1835-0*) Stanford U Pr.

Nomonhan: Japan Against Russia, 1939, 2 vols., Set. Alvin D. Coox. LC 81-85447. (Illus.). 1296p. 1985. 135.00 (*0-8047-1160-7*) Stanford U Pr.

Noms Indigenes Dans l'Asie-Mineure Greco-Romaine: Premiere Partie. Louis Robert. (Bibliotheque Archeologique Et Historique De L'Institut Francais D'Archeologie D'Istanbul Ser.: No. XIII). (FRE.). 659p. 1991. pap. 130.00 (*0-685-50578-2*, Pub. by AM Hakkert) BookLink Distributors.

Non - Solar Gamma Rays: Proceedings of the COSPAR 22nd Plenary Meeting, Bangalore, India, 1979. COSPAR, Twenty-Second Plenary Meeting Staff. Ed. by R. Cowsik & R. D. Wills. 254p. 1980. 61.00 (*0-08-024440-8*, Pergamon Pr) Elsevier.

Non- Western Architecture. Ronald Lewcock. write for info. (*0-393-73044-1*) Norton.

Non-Abelian Cohomology Theory & Applications to the Yang-Mills & Backlund Problems. S. I. Andersson. 280p. 1998. text 54.00 (*9971-5-0013-2*) World Scientific Pub.

Non-Abelian Harmonic Analysis: Applications of SL (2, R) Russel F. Howe & E. C. Tan. (Universitext Ser.). (Illus.). 272p. 1992. 49.95 (*0-387-97768-6*) Spr-Verlag.

Non-Abelian Homological Algebra & Its Applications. Hvedri Inassaridze. LC 97-26712. (Mathematics & Its Applications Ser.: No. 421). 265p. 1997. text 160.50 (*0-7923-4718-8*) Kluwer Academic.

Non-Abelian Minimal Closed Ideals of Transitive Lie Algebras. Jack F. Conn. LC 79-24096. (Mathematical Notes Ser.: No. 25). 227p. 1981. reprint ed. pap. 70.40 (*0-608-06615-X*, 206681200009) Bks Demand.

Non-Accelerator Particle Physics. H. V. Klapdor-Kleingrothaus & A. Staudt. Tr. by S. S. Wilson. LC 98-3478. (Illus.). 534p. 1995. 287.00 (*0-7503-0305-0*) IOP Pub.

Non-Accelerator Particle Physics. H. V. Klapdor-Kleingrothaus & A. Staudt. Tr. by S. S. Wilson. LC 98-3478. (Illus.). 534p. 1998. pap. 60.00 (*0-7503-0502-9*) IOP Pub.

Non-Adhesive Binding: Books Without Paste or Glue, Vol. 1. rev. expanded ed. Keith A. Smith. LC 98-91061. (Illus.). 352p. 1999. pap. 30.00 (*0-9637682-6-3*) K A Smith Bks.

Non-Aerospace Applications of Titanium & Alloys. Ed. by F. H. Froes et al. LC 97-75878. (Illus.). 362p. 1998. 132.00 (*0-87339-394-5*, 3945) Minerals Metals.

Non-Agricultural Employment in India: Trends & Prospects. Pravin Visaria & Rakesh Basant. LC 94-22748. 344p. 1995. text 29.95 (*0-8039-9191-6*) Sage.

Non-Agricultural Pesticide Users: Guide to Pollution Prevention. 58p. (Orig.). (C). 1994. pap. text 30.00 (*0-7881-0658-9*) DIANE Pub.

Non-Aligned Nations: Arms Race & Disarmaments. Attar Chand. 375p. 1983. 36.95 (*0-940500-11-6*) Asia Bk Corp.

Non-Aligned Nations: Challenges of the '80s. Attar Chand. 312p. 1983. 34.95 (*0-317-12336-X*, Pub. by Select Bk Serv) Asia Bk Corp.

Non-Aligned Storyteller. Thomas McCarthy. 64p. 1984. pap. 14.95 (*0-85646-123-7*, Pub. by Anvil Press) Dufour.

Non-Aligned, the U. N., & the Superpowers. Richard L. Jackson. LC 83-13836. 336p. 1987. pap. 14.95 (*0-275-92640-0*, B2640, Praeger Pubs) Greenwood.

Non-Alignment: Origins, Growth & Potential for World Peace. Rikhi Jaipal. 214p. 1983. 24.95 (*0-318-37247-9*) Asia Bk Corp.

Non-Alignment & Algerian Foreign Policy. Lassassi Assassi. 249p. 1988. text 77.95 (*0-566-05470-1*, Pub. by Dartmth Pub) Ashgate Pub Co.

Non-Analytical Methods for Motor Control. R. Tomovic et al. 250p. 1995. text 59.00 (*981-02-2090-1*) World Scientific Pub.

Non-Antagonistic Games. Yu B. Germeier. 1986. lib. bdg. 201.00 (*90-277-2023-1*) Kluwer Academic.

Non-Anticoagulant Actions of Glycosaminoglycans. Ed. by Job Harenberg et al. LC 96-10228. (Protein Binding Studies). (Illus.). 288p. (C). 1996. text 107.00 (*0-306-45299-5*, Kluwer Plenum) Kluwer Academic.

Non-Appearance Before the International Court of Justice: Functional & Comparative Analysis. Jerome B. Elkind. 1984. lib. bdg. 101.00 (*90-247-2921-1*) Kluwer Academic.

Non-Aqueous Phase Liquids (NAPLS) in Subsurface Environment: Assessment & Remediation: Proceedings of the Specialty Conference Held in Conjunction with the ASCE National Convention, Washington, D. C., November 12-13, 1996. Lakshmi N. Reddi et al. LC 96-44713. 864p. 1996. 84.00 (*0-7844-0203-5*) Am Soc Civil Eng.

***Non-aqueous Solvents.** John Chipperfield. LC QD544.5.C57 1999. (Illus.). 96p. 1999. pap. text 12.95 (*0-19-850259-1*) OUP.

Non-Archimedean Analysis. Reinhold Remmert et al. (Grundlehren der Mathematischen Wissenschaften Ser.: Vol. 261). 450p. 1984. 182.95 (*0-387-12546-9*) Spr-Verlag.

Non-Archimedean Analysis: Quantum Paradoxes, Dynamical Systems & Biological Models. Andrei Khrennikov. LC 97-31467. (Mathematics & Its Applications Ser.). 392p. 1997. text 197.50 (*0-7923-4800-1*) Kluwer Academic.

Non-Archimedean L-Functions: Of Siegel & Hilbert Modular Forms. A. A. Panchishkin et al. Ed. by A. Dold et al. (Lecture Notes in Mathematics Ser.: Vol. 1471). vii, 157p. 1991. 28.95 (*0-387-54137-3*) Spr-Verlag.

Non-Archimedean Utility. Skala. 1975. lib. bdg. 124.50 (*90-277-0352-3*) Kluwer Academic.

Non-Aristotelian Drama in Eighteenth Century Germany & its Modernity: J. M. R. Lenz. Helga S. Madland. (European University Studies: German Language & Literature: Ser. 1, Vol. 621). 308p. 1982. pap. 53.00 (*3-261-05079-9*) P Lang Pubng.

Non-Associative Algebra & Its Applications, 303. Ed. by Santos Gonzalez. LC 94-33302. (Mathematics & Its Applications Ser.). 428p. (C). 1994. text 251.00 (*0-7923-3117-6*) Kluwer Academic.

Non-Attic Greek Vase Inscriptions. Rudolf Wachter. (Illus.). 380p. 2000. text 105.00 (*0-19-814093-2*) OUP.

Non-Attorney Justice in the United States: An Empirical Study. Linda J. Silberman. 432p. 1979. 6.00 (*0-318-14441-7*) IJA NYU.

Non-Authentic Nature of Freud's Observations, 2 vols., Set, Vols. 1-2. Max Scharnberg. (Uppsala Studies in Education: Nos. 47-48). (Orig.). 1993. pap. 82.50 (*91-554-3122-4*) Coronet Bks.

Non-Automated Sphygmomanometers. 15p. 1994. pap. 73.00 (*1-57020-020-3*, SP9-209) Assn Adv Med Instrn.

Non-Bank Safe Deposit Boxes: An International Directory. rev. ed. Alpha Pyramis Research Division Staff. 215p. 1997. ring bd. 32.95 (*0-913597-08-2*) Prosperity & Profits.

Non-Bantu Languages of North-Eastern Africa: With a Supplement on the Non-Bantu Languages of Southern Africa. Archibald N. Tucker & M. A. Bryan. LC 57-1706. (Handbook of African Languages Ser.: Pt. 3). 262p. 1956. reprint ed. pap. 81.30 (*0-8357-3231-2*, 205712500010) Bks Demand.

Non-Biostratigraphical Methods of Dating & Correlation. Ed. by R. E. Dunay & E. Hailwood. (Geological Society Special Publication Ser.: No. 89). (Illus.). 272p. 1995. 100.00 (*1-897799-30-6*, 330, Pub. by Geol Soc Pub Hse) AAPG.

Non-Bourgeois Theology: An African Experience of Jesus. Joseph G. Donders. LC 84-16677. 224p. (Orig.). 1985. pap. 15.00 (*0-88344-352-X*) Orbis Bks.

Non-Cardiac Thoracic Interventions. LC 96-52547. (Radiologic Interventions Ser.). 1997. write for info. (*4-260-14288-7*) Igaku-Shoin.

Non-Cardiac Thoracic Interventions. Alan Matsumoto. LC 96-52547. (Radiologic Interventions Ser.). (Illus.). 384p. 1997. write for info. (*0-89640-288-6*) Igaku-Shoin.

Non-Cartographical Maritime Works Published by Mount & Page: A Preliminary Hand-List. Thomas Randolph Adams et al. LC 86-134845. (Occasional Papers of the Bibliographical Society). xiv, 54 p. 1985. write for info. (*0-948170-01-8*) CE38.

Non-Causal Theory of Justice in Rumi's Work. Abdul K. Soroush. 26p. 1992. 3.00 (*1-883058-31-7*, SAG&IP) Global Pubns.

Non-Chemist's Safety Primer: Guide for Engineers, Scientists, Technicians & Intelligent Laypersons. Kathryn Uhrich & Martin L. Kaplan. 1999. 49.95 (*1-56670-278-X*, L1278) Lewis Pubs.

Non-Chew Cookbook. Randy J. Wilson & Madeleine Osberger. 204p. 1998. spiral bd. 23.95 (*0-9616299-0-8*) Wilson Pub Inc.

Non-Christian Quakers: Their Faith & Message. Raquel Wood & Ranan Banerji. Ed. by Kenneth Ives. (Studies in Quakerism: No. 9). 59p. (Orig.). 1983. pap. 5.00 (*0-89670-012-7*) Progresiv Pub.

***Non-Christian's Response to Christianity: "And Ye Shall Know the Truth... "** Moses Farrar. 152p. 2000. pap. 15.00 (*0-9650247-1-7*) Monami Pubns.

Non-Chromotographic Continuous Separation Techniques. Valcarcel. 1991. 109.00 (*0-85186-986-6*) CRC Pr.

Non-Classical Elastic Solids. Michele Ciarletta & Dorin Iesan. LC 93-4718. (Pitman Research Notes in Mathematics Ser.). 1993. lib. bdg. write for info. (*0-582-22716-X*) Longman.

N

An Asterisk (*) at the beginning of an entry indicates that the title is appearing for the first time.

Non-Classical Equations of Mixed Type & Their Applications in Gas Dynamics. A. G. Kuzmin. LC 92-36582. ix, 288p. 1992. 156.00 *(0-8176-2573-9)* Birkhauser.

***Non-Classical Problems in the Theory of Elastic Stability.** Isaac Elishakoff et al. (Illus.). 384p. 2000. write for info. *(0-521-78210-4)* Cambridge U Pr.

Non-Classical Problems of the Theory & Behavior of Structures Exposed to Complex Environmental Conditions. Ed. by L. Librescu. LC 93-71578. (AMD Ser.: Vol. 164). 183p. 1993. pap. 50.00 *(0-7918-1143-3,* G00787) ASME.

***Non-co 2 Greenhouse Gases: Scietific Understanding.** J. Van Ham et al. 660p. 2000. 270.00 *(0-7923-6199-7)* Kluwer Academic.

Non-Coloring Book: A Drawing Book for Mind Stretching & Fantasy Building. Denys Cazet. 64p. 1973. pap. 5.95 *(0-88316-501-5)* Chandler & Sharp.

Non-Combat Roles for the U. S. Military in the Post Cold-War Era. Ed. by James R. Graham. 140p. 1993. pap. text 35.00 *(1-57979-148-4)* DIANE Pub.

Non-Combat Roles for the U. S. Military in the Post Cold-War Era. Ed. by James R. Graham. 133p. (C). 1993. pap. text 30.00 *(0-7881-0033-5)* DIANE Pub.

Non-Combatant Immunity As a Norm of International Humanitarian Law. Judith G. Gardam. LC 93-7129. 1993. lib. bdg. 86.00 *(0-7923-2245-2)* Kluwer Academic.

Non-Commissioned Baby: The Bachelor Battalion. Maureen Child. (Desire Ser.: No. 1174). 1998. per. 3.75 *(0-373-76174-0,* 1-76174-1) Harlequin Bks.

Non-Commissioned Officers & Men of the Royal Navy & Commonwealth & Colonial Revies Who Died in Service 1914-1919, Vol. 4. Ed. by Roberts Staff. (C). 1989. 125.00 *(0-7855-2660-9,* Pub. by Roberts) St Mut.

Non Commutative Geometry, 001. Do Ngoc Diep. 351p. 1999. per. 64.95 *(1-58488-019-8,* Chap & Hall CRC) CRC Pr.

Non-Commutative Harmonic Analysis & Lie Groups. Ed. by J. Carmona et al. (Lecture Notes in Mathematics Ser.: Vol. 1243). v, 309p. 1987. 47.95 *(0-387-17701-9)* Spr-Verlag.

Non-Commutative Harmonic Analysis & Lie Groups. Ed. by J. Carmona & M. Vergne. (Lecture Notes in Mathematics Ser.: Vol. 1020). 187p. 1983. 32.95 *(0-387-12717-8)* Spr-Verlag.

Non-Commutative Spectral Theory for Affine Function Spaces on Convex Sets. Erik M. Alfsen & Frederick W. Shultz. LC 76-18309. (Memoirs Ser.: No. 6/172). 120p. 1976. pap. 22.00 *(0-8218-1872-4,* MEMO/6/172) Am Math.

Non-Commutative Valuation Rings & Semi-Hereditary Orders. LC 97-16607. 1997. text 107.00 *(0-7923-4562-2)* Kluwer Academic.

Non-Competitive Games for People of All Ages. Susan Butler. LC 85-28644. 28p. (Orig.). 1986. pap. 9.99 *(0-87123-812-8)* Bethany Hse.

Non-Competitive Motor Activities: A Guide for Elementary Classroom Teachers. Robert Gamble & Julie Wilkins. (Illus.). 212p. (C). 1996. pap. text 19.95 *(0-89641-291-1)* American Pr.

Non-Compliance: Four Strategies That Work. Ennio Cipani. LC 93-26753. 1993. pap. text 11.40 *(0-86586-238-9,* P389) Coun Exc Child.

Non-Compliance in Winnicott's Words: A Companion to the Writings & Work of D. W. Winnicott. Alexander Newman. 500p. (C). 1995. text 75.00 *(0-8147-5786-3)* NYU Pr.

Non-Compliance in Winnicott's Words: A Companion to the Writings & Work of D. W. Winnicott. Ed. & Compiled by Alexander Newman. 500p. (C). 1995. pap. text 25.00 *(0-8147-5785-5)* NYU Pr.

Non-Confrontational Power Selling: The Most Effective & Useful Book on Selling Ever Printed. David Jacobson. LC 98-97015. 1999. pap. text 16.95 *(0-9668974-3-9)* Capital Results.

Non-Connoisseur's Menu Guide: For French, Italian, Latin American & Spanish Cuisines. David D'Aprix. LC 99-35433. 320p. 1999. pap. 10.95 *(0-609-80493-6)* Liv Lang.

Non-Contentious Costs. Alan A. Barrett. (Practice Notes Ser.). 88p. 1992. pap. write for info. *(0-85121-530-0,* Pub. by Cavendish Pubng) Gaunt.

Non-Conventional Construction of Concrete Dams & Rock Formations. Yu A. Landau & Yu B. Mgalobelov. (Illus.). 300p. 1997. 107.00 *(90-5410-252-7,* Pub. by A A Balkema) Ashgate Pub Co.

Non-Conventional Energy Sources: Proceedings of the First Latin American School & Third International Symposium, Bogota, Colombia, July 13-30, 1982. Ed. by G. Furlan et al. 702p. (C). 1984. 121.00 *(9971-966-78-6)* World Scientific Pub.

Non-Conventional Preference Relations in Decision Making. Ed. by Janusz Kacprzyk & M. Roubens. (Lecture Notes in Economics & Mathematical Systems Ser.: Vol. 301). vii, 155p. 1988. 32.00 *(0-387-18954-8)* Spr-Verlag.

Non Conventional View on Rock Mechanics & Fracture Mechanics. J. Gramberg. 280p. (C). 1989. text 136.00 *(90-6191-806-5,* Pub. by A A Balkema) Ashgate Pub Co.

Non-Conventional Water Resources Use in Developing Countries. (Natural Resources-Water Ser.: No. 22). 515p. 1987. pap. 50.00 *(92-1-104214-3,* E.87.II.A.20) UN.

Non-Conventional-Weapons Proliferation in the Middle East: Tackling the Spread of Nuclear, Chemical, & Biological Capabilities. Ed. by Efraim Karsh et al. LC 93-9469. (Illus.). 312p. 1993. text 68.00 *(0-19-827768-7,* Clarendon Pr) OUP.

Non-Cooperative Planning Theories. LC 94-22845. 1994. 69.95 *(3-540-58361-0)* Spr-Verlag.

Non-Cooperative Planning Theory. Peter Bogetoft. LC 94-22845. 1994. write for info. *(0-387-58361-0)* Spr-Verlag.

Non-Coronary Angioplasty & Interventional Radiological Treatment of Vascular Malformations. Laszlo Szlavy & Juan M. Taveras. (Illus.). 700p. 1994. text 179.00 *(0-683-08066-0)* Lppncott W & W.

Non-CO2 Greenhouse Gases - Why & How to Control? Proceedings of an International Symposium, Maastricht, The Netherlands, 13-15 December 1993. Anna-Teresa Tymieniecka. Ed. by J. Van Ham. LC 94-30337. 588p. (C). 1994. text 251.00 *(0-7923-3043-9)* Kluwer Academic.

Non-Credit Instruction: A Guide for Continuing & Adult Education Programs. Lea Leever Oldham. Ed. by Donald Greive. 34p. (Orig.). (C). 1995. pap. text 5.95 *(0-940017-20-2)* Info Tec OH.

Non-Cryogenic Gas Separations: Technologies & Markets. Craig Campbell & Anna Crull. LC 98-120615. (Report Ser.: No. C-128R). 171p. 1997. 2950.00 *(1-56965-387-9)* BCC.

Non-Crystalline Solids. 120.00 *(0-87849-505-3,* Pub. by Trans T Pub) Enfield Pubs NH.

Non-Custodial Sanctions: Alternative Models for Post-Communist Societies. Tiberio Dianu. LC 98-123981. 163p. 1998. 65.00 *(1-56072-509-5)* Nova Sci Pubs.

Non-Cycle Plays & Fragments. Ed. by Norman Davis. (SS 1 Ser.). 1970. 19.50 *(0-19-722401-6)* OUP.

Non-Dairy Whip Toppings (with or Without Soy Protein) - Bibliography & Sourcebook, 1944 to 1994: Detailed Information on 115 Published Documents (Extensively Annotated Bibliography), 21 Commerical Whip Topping Products, 48 Original Interviews (Many Full Text) & Overviews, 49 Unpublished Archival Documents. Compiled by William Shurtleff & Akiko Aoyagi. 135p. 1994. spiral bd. 49.00 *(0-933332-88-2)* Soyfoods Center.

Non-Debye Relaxation in Condensed Matter: Proceedings of a Discussion Meeting, Bangalore, India. T. V. Ramakrishnan & M. Rajalakshmi. 416p. (C). 1987. text 100.00 *(9971-5-0381-6)* World Scientific Pub.

Non-Declarative Sentences. Richard Zuber. (Pragmatics & Beyond Ser.: Vol. IV:2). ix, 123p. 1983. pap. 41.00 *(90-272-2529-X)* J Benjamins Pubng Co.

***Non-Democratic Regimes: Theory, Government & Politics.** Paul Brooker. LC 99-36064. (Comparative Government & Politics Ser.). 2000. pap. 21.95 *(0-312-22755-8);* text 59.95 *(0-312-22754-X)* St Martin.

Non-Designer's Design Book: Design & Typographic Principles for the Visual Novice. Robin Williams. 144p. (C). 1995. pap. text 14.95 *(1-56609-159-4,* Pub. by Peachpit Pr) Addison-Wesley.

***Non-Designer's Scan & Print Book.** Robin C. Williams & Sandy Cohen. LC 99-211201. 264p. (C). 1999. pap. text 24.99 *(0-201-35394-6,* Pub. by Peachpit Pr) Addison-Wesley.

Non-Designer's Type Book. Robin Williams. Ed. by Nancy Davis. LC 98-217131. 240p. (C). 1998. pap. text 24.99 *(0-201-35367-9,* Pub. by Peachpit Pr) Addison-Wesley.

***Non-Designer's Web Book.** 2nd ed. Robin Williams & John Tollett. 320p. 2000. pap. text 34.99 *(0-201-71038-2)* Peachpit Pr.

Non-Designer's Web Book: An Easy Guide to Creating, Designing & Posting Your Own Web Site. Robin Williams & John Tollett. LC 98-114044. (Illus.). 288p. (C). 1997. pap. 29.95 *(0-201-68859-X,* Pub. by Peachpit Pr) Addison-Wesley.

Non-Destructive Evaluation & Testing of Masonry Structures, Vol. 2. Bruce A. Suprenant & Michael P. Schuller. (Illus.). 184p. 1994. 89.95 *(0-924659-57-2,* 4530) Hanley.

Non Destructive Evaluation of Materials by Infrared Thermography. Xavier P. Maldague. LC 92-33616. 1993. 238.95 *(0-387-19769-9)* Spr-Verlag.

Non-Destructive Examination of Concrete Structures. Tomsett. 304p. 1999. pap. 66.00 *(0-419-15190-7)* Thomson Learn.

***Non-Destructive Techniques Applied to Landscape Archaeology.** Ed. by Marinella Pasquinucci & Frederic Trement. (Archaeology of the Mediterranean Landscape, Populus Monograph: Vol. 4). 250p. 2000. 81.95 *(1-900188-74-0,* Pub. by Oxbow Bks) David Brown.

Non-Destructive Testing. Ed. by G. Honeyman. 300p. 1989. 52.50 *(0-901462-67-5,* Pub. by Inst Materials) Ashgate Pub Co.

Non-Destructive Testing. 2nd ed. R. Halmshaw. (Illus.). 334p. 1991. pap. 51.95 *(0-340-54521-6,* A6363, Pub. by E A) Routldge.

Non-Destructive Testing: An Expanded Market. (Illus.). 163p. 1995. 2750.00 *(1-56965-221-X,* GB177) BCC.

Non-Destructive Testing: Proceedings of the First Joint Belgian-Hellenic Conference on Non-Destructive Testing, Patras, Greece, May 1995. Ed. by D.Van Hemelrijck & A. Anastassopoulos. (Illus.). 320p. (C). 1996. text 123.00 *(90-5410-595-X,* Pub. by A A Balkema) Ashgate Pub Co.

***Non-Destructive Testing Vol. 4: Acoustic Wave Propagation & Scattering.** Ed. by A. Guran et al. 400p. 2000. 86.00 *(981-02-4271-9)* World Scientific Pub.

Non-Destructive Testing for Aircraft. Douglas C. Latia. (Illus.). 1994. pap. text 26.95 *(0-89100-415-7,* JS312640) Jeppesen Sanderson.

Non-Destructive Testing in Building Services: A General Introduction. T. Finch. (C). 1985. pap. 25.00 *(0-86022-197-0,* Pub. by Build Servs Info Assn) St Mut.

Non-Destructive Testing in Nuclear Technology, Vol. 1. IAEA Staff. (Proceedings Ser.). (Illus.). 393p. 1965. 40.00 *(92-0-530065-9,* ISP105-1, Pub. by IAEA) Bernan Associates.

Non-Destructive Testing in Nuclear Technology, Vol. 2. IAEA Staff. (Proceedings Ser.). (Illus.). 446p. 1965. 45.00 *(92-0-530165-5,* ISP105-2, Pub. by IAEA) Bernan Associates.

Non-Destructive Testing in the Fitness-for-Purpose Assessment of Welded Constructions. (Illus.). 256p. 1985. pap. 120.00 *(0-85300-184-7,* Pub. by Woodhead Pubng) Am Educ Systs.

Non-Destructive Testing Standards: A Review - STP 624. Ed. by H. Berger. 338p. 1977. 33.75 *(0-8031-0196-1,* STP624) ASTM.

Non-Deterministic Concurrent Logic Programming in Pandora. Reem Bahgat. LC 92-33357. 220p. 1993. text 61.00 *(981-02-1251-8)* World Scientific Pub.

Non-Dictionary of Another Usage. Joyce B. Sousa et al. (Illus.). 20p. 1998. pap. 4.00 *(0-9665078-1-9)* SPS Assocs.

Non-Dimensional Characterization of Gear Geometry, Mesh Loss & Windage. J. Phillip Barnes. (Technical Papers: Vol. 97FTM11). (Illus.). 12p. 1997. pap. text 30.00 *(1-55589-705-3)* AGMA.

Non-Dinosaurian Lower Vertebrates Across the Cretaceous-Tertiary Boundary in Northeastern Montana. Laurie J. Bryant. 1990. pap. 20.00 *(0-520-09735-1,* Pub. by U CA Pr) Cal Prin Full Svc.

Non-Disabling Surgical Rehabilitation of the Forefoot. Milton D. Roven. LC 76-176177. (Illus.). 416p. 1976. 32.50 *(0-87527-123-5)* Green.

Non Disclosure. Campbell. 1993. 19.95 *(0-07-881940-7)* McGraw.

Non Disclosure. Murray. 1993. 27.95 *(0-07-881945-8)* McGraw.

Non Disclosure. Sheldon. 1993. 27.95 *(0-07-881946-6)* McGraw.

***Non-Discrimination Law: Comparative Perspectives.** T. Loenen & P. R. Rodrigues. LC 99-29148. 464p. 1999. 111.00 *(90-411-1063-1)* Kluwer Law Intl.

Non-Disseminated Breast Cancer: Controversial Issues in Management. G. H. Fletcher et al. LC 93-20548. (Medical Radiology, Diagnostic Imaging & Radiation Oncology Ser.). (Illus.). 178p. 1993. 155.00 *(0-387-54514-X)* Spr-Verlag.

***Non-Drug European Secret.** Michael Loes. 1999. pap. 5.95 *(1-893910-03-2)* Freedom Pr Inc.

Non-Dues Sources of Income for Bar Associations: Mini-MAP. 300p. 1996. pap. 29.95 *(1-57073-266-3,* 171-0072, ABA Bar Servs) Amer Bar Assn.

***Non-Epileptic Seizures.** 2nd ed. Ed. by John R. Gates & A. James Rowan. LC 99-55305. 323p. 1999. text 95.00 *(0-7506-7026-6)* Buttrwrth-Heinemann.

Non-Equilibrium & Disorder, Vol. 2. 2nd ed. William Jones & Norman H. March. 1985. pap. 16.95 *(0-486-65016-2)* Dover.

Non-Equilibrium Condensation in High-Speed Gas Flows. V. N. Gorbunov et al. 330p. 1989. text 555.00 *(2-88124-676-1)* Gordon & Breach.

Non-Equilibrium Entropy & Irreversibility. Goran Lindblad. 1983. text 139.00 *(90-277-1640-4)* Kluwer Academic.

Non-Equilibrium Phenomena in Supercooled Fliuds, Glasses & Amorphous Materials: Proceedings of the Workshop. LC 97-111855. 408p. 1996. lib. bdg. 60.00 *(981-02-2795-7)* World Scientific Pub.

Non-Equilibrium Processing of Materials. C. Suryanarayana. (Materials Ser.: Vol. 2). 446p. 1999. 144.00 *(0-08-042697-2)* Elsevier.

Non-Equilibrium Statistical Mechanics. E. S. Hernandez. 204p. (C). 1990. text 92.00 *(981-02-0106-0)* World Scientific Pub.

Non-Equilibrium Statistical Thermodynamics Applied to Fluid Dynamics & Laser Physics. Xavier De Hemptinne. 300p. 1992. text 59.00 *(981-02-0926-6)* World Scientific Pub.

Non-Equilibrium Thermodynamics. S. R. DeGroot & P. Mazur. 544p. 1984. reprint ed. pap. 13.95 *(0-486-64741-2)* Dover.

Non-Equilibrium Thermodynamics: Field Theory & Variational Principles. I. Gyarmati. Tr. by W. F. Heinz. (Engineering Science Library). (Illus.). 1970. 39.95 *(0-387-04886-3)* Spr-Verlag.

Non-Equilibrium Thermodynamics with Application to Solids: Dedicated to the Memory of Professor Theodor Lehmann. Ed. by W. Muschik. (CISM International Centre for Mechanical Sciences Ser.: No. 336). ix, 329p. 1994. 76.95 *(0-387-82453-7)* Spr-Verlag.

Non-Equilibrium Two-Phase Flows: Papers Presented at the Winter Annual Meeting of ASME, Houston, TX, November 30-December 5, 1975. Ed. by Richard T. Lahey & Graham B. Wallis. LC 75-25192. 67p. reprint ed. pap. 30.00 *(0-608-30626-6,* 201683000005) Bks Demand.

Non-Equivalence: A Key to Unity. unabridged ed. Benadetto A. Soldano. LC 98-182875. (Limits of the Present Foundations of Physics Ser.: Vol. I). (Illus.). 1997. pap. 39.00 *(0-9658606-0-4)* Grenridge Pr.

Non-Euclidean Adventures on the Lenart Sphere. Istvan Lenart. (Illus.). 244p. (YA). (gr. 6 up). 1995. pap. text 15.95 *(1-55953-103-7)* Key Curr Pr.

Non-Euclidean Geometry. Roberto Bonola. Ed. by H. S. Carslaw. 431p. (C). 1955. pap. 10.95 *(0-486-60027-0)* Dover.

Non-Euclidean Geometry. S. Kluczycki & S. Knapowski. LC 60-14187. (International Series of Monographs on Pure & Applied Mathematics: Vol. 16). 1961. 94.00 *(0-08-009443-0,* Pub. by Pergamon Repr) Franklin.

***Non-Euclidean Geometry in the Theory of Automorphic Functions.** Jacques Hadamard et al. LC 99-31709. (History Of Mathematics Ser.). 95p. 1999. pap. write for info. *(0-8218-2030-3)* Am Math.

Non-Euclidean Hyperbolic Plane. P. Kelly & G. Matthews. (Universitext Ser.). (Illus.). 350p. 1981. 69.95 *(0-387-90552-9)* Spr-Verlag.

Non-Euclidean Revolution. Richard Trudeau. 1995. 49.50 *(0-8176-3311-1)* Birkhauser.

Non-Euclideon Geometry. 6th ed. H. S. Coxeter. LC 98-85640. 320p. 1998. pap. text 30.95 *(0-88385-522-4)* Math Assn.

Non-Existence of God: Linguistic Paradox in Tillich's Thought. Robert R. Ross. LC 78-65486. (Toronto Studies in Theology: Vol. 1). xiv, 216p. 1978. lib. bdg. 89.95 *(0-88946-905-9)* E Mellen.

Non-Expected Utility & Risk Management. Ed. by Christian Gollier & Mark Machina. (Geneva Papers: Vol. 20, No. 1). 156p. (C). 1995. reprint ed. lib. bdg. 133.00 *(0-7923-9642-1)* Kluwer Academic.

***Non-Exponential Relaxation & Rate Behavior.** Ed. by A. M. Glazer. 289p. 1998. pap. text 1049.00 *(90-5699-175-2)* Gordon & Breach.

Non-Ferrous Materials, Vol. 6. 512p. 1992. 130.00 *(1-878954-25-3)* Metal Powder.

Non-Ferrous Metal Data, 1991. 150p. 1992. 350.00 *(0-910064-24-5)* Am Bur Metal.

Non-Ferrous Metal Works of the World. 4th ed. 647p. 1986. write for info. *(0-8002-4033-2)* Taylor & Francis.

Non-Ferrous Metal Works of the World. 5th ed. Ed. by Richard Serjeantson. 607p. 1989. 167.00 *(0-947671-22-6)* Metal Bulletin.

Non-Ferrous Metals - World Markets & Opportunities Vol. 1: 1997-2002 Analysis & Forecasts. Alan Berger. 100p. 1997. pap. text 2400.00 *(1-878218-84-0)* World Info Tech.

Non-Ferrous Metals - World Markets & Opportunities Vol. 2: 1997-2002 Analysis & Forecasts. Alan Berger. 61p. 1998. pap. text 3900.00 *(1-878218-92-1)* World Info Tech.

Non-Fiction: A Guide to Writing & Publishing. David S. Thomas. LC 79-481610. 192p. 1970. write for info. *(0-7153-4802-7,* Pub. by D & C Pub) Sterling.

Non-Fiction - Befo de War (Verse, with Armistead Churchill Gordon) Thomas N. Page. (Notable American Authors Ser.). 1999. reprint ed. lib. bdg. 125.00 *(0-7812-4705-5)* Rprt Serv.

Non-Fiction for the 1990's. Thomas Fensch. 248p. 1991. pap. 36.00 *(0-8058-0785-3)* L Erlbaum Assocs.

Non-Fiction Poems & by the Blood: A Chapbook Duet. Bob Rogers & Ralph Dunn. (Illus.). 40p. 1985. pap. 5.00 *(0-929170-07-5)* Paper Plant.

***Non-Fiction Writing Strategies: Using Science Big Books as Models.** Marcia S. Freeman. LC 00-24192. (Illus.). 112p. 2000. pap. 19.95 *(0-929895-37-1)* Maupin Hse.

Non-Fired Technique: How to Paint Bisque Dolls. Paulette Morrissey. (Illus.). 28p. 1997. spiral bd. 9.95 *(1-893502-06-6)* Morrissey Co.

Non-Fixed or Fixed Networks, Complements or Alternatives? Background Issues. unabridged ed. Yoshihiro Sato. (Illus.). 64p. (Orig.). 1996. pap. text. write for info. *(1-879716-33-X,* P-96-3) Ctr Info Policy.

Non-Fluent Aphasia in a Multilingual World. Lise Menn et al. LC 95-14639. (Studies in Speech Pathology & Clinical Linguistics: No. 5). xvii, 212p. 1995. 65.00 *(1-55619-391-2);* pap. 24.95 *(1-55619-392-0)* J Benjamins Pubng Co.

Non-Fluorinated Propellants & Solvents for Aerosols. Domingo Aviado et al. (Solvents in the Environment Ser.). 1977. 36.50 *(0-8493-5199-5,* RA1270, CRC Reprint) Franklin.

Non-Food Franchising in Saudi Arabia: A Strategic Entry Report, 1997. Compiled by Icon Group International Staff. (Illus.). 135p. 1999. ring bd. 1350.00 incl. audio compact disk *(0-7418-0848-X)* Icon Grp.

Non-Food Franchising in Thailand: A Strategic Entry Report, 1997. Compiled by Icon Group International Staff. (Illus.). 146p. 1999. ring bd. 1460.00 incl. audio compact disk *(0-7418-0849-8)* Icon Grp.

***Non-Food Retail Franchising in Canada: A Strategic Entry Report, 1996.** Compiled by Icon Group International Staff. (Illus.). 131p. 1999. ring bd. 1310.00 incl. audio compact disk *(0-7418-1242-8)* Icon Grp.

Non-Food Uses of Agricultural Raw Materials: Economics, Biotechnology & Politics. C. Spelman. (Illus.). 160p. 1994. text 65.00 *(0-85198-769-9)* OUP.

Non-Formal Education: An Annotated International Bibliography. Ed. by Rolland G. Paulston. LC 72-186197. (Special Studies in International Economics & Development). 1972. 42.50 *(0-275-28623-1)* Irvington.

Non-Formal Education & the NAEP. Ed. by A. B. Shah & Susheela Bhan. 1981. 24.95 *(0-19-561256-6)* OUP.

Non-Formal Educational Strategies Vol. 4: Tradition & Innovation: Non-Formal & Non-Governmental Approaches. Ed. by James Lynch et al. (International Debates Ser.). 352p. 1996. text 130.00 *(0-304-32894-4)* Continuum.

***Non-Functional Requirements in Software Engineering.** Lawrence Chung. LC 99-46023. (International Series in Software Engineering). 1999. write for info. *(0-7923-8666-3)* Kluwer Academic.

Non-Government Organizations & Political Participation in Indonesia. Philip J. Eldridge. (South-East Asian Social Science Monographs). (Illus.). 296p. 1996. text 55.00 *(967-65-3091-3)* OUP.

Non-Governmental Development Organizations of Developing Countries: And the South Smiles . . . Ed. by Sjef Theunis. 384p. (C). 1992. lib. bdg. 131.00 *(0-7923-1407-7)* Kluwer Academic.

Non-Governmental Organisations & the State in Africa: Rethinking Roles in Sustainable Agricultural Development. Ed. by Kate Wellard & James G. Copestake. LC 93-15540. (Non-Governmental Organizations Ser.). (Illus.). 352p. (C). 1993. pap. 27.99 *(0-415-08850-X,* B0838) Routledge.

Non-Governmental Organisations & the State in Asia: Rethinking Roles in Sustainable Agricultural Development. Ed. by John W. Farrington & David J.

N

An Asterisk (*) at the beginning of an entry indicates that the title is appearing for the first time.

Lewis. LC 92-45820. (Non-Governmental Organizations Ser.). (Illus.). 400p. (C). 1993. pap. 27.99 (*0-415-08848-8*, B0849) Routledge.

Non-Governmental Organisations & the State in Asia: Rethinking Roles in Sustainable Agricultural Development. Ed. by John W. Farrington & David J. Lewis. LC 92-45820. (Non-Governmental Organizations Ser.). (Illus.). 400p. (C). (gr. 13). 1993. text 85.00 (*0-415-08847-X*, B0845) Routledge.

Non-Governmental Organisations & the State in Latin America: Rethinking Roles in Sustainable Agricultural Development. Ed. by Anthony Bebbington & Graham Thiele. (Non-Governmental Organizations Ser.). (Illus.). 320p. (C). 1993. pap. 27.99 (*0-415-08846-1*, B0856) Routledge.

Non-Governmental Organizations & Health in Developing Countries. Andrew Green & Ann Matthias. LC 96-27850. (Illus.). 240p. 1997. text 59.95 (*0-312-16428-9*) St Martin.

Non-Governmental Organizations in Malawi: Their Contribution to Development & Democratization. Sabine Paul et al. 248p. 1997. pap. text 16.95 (*3-8258-3030-6*) Transaction Pubs.

Non-gravitational Perturbations & Satellite Geodesy. A. Milani et al. (Illus.). 136p. 1987. 92.00 (*0-85274-538-9*) IOP Pub.

Non-Heart-Beating Organ Transplantation: Medical & Ethical Issues in Procurement. Institute of Medicine Staff. LC 98-114047. 104p. (C). 1997. pap. text 22.00 (*0-309-06424-4*) Natl Acad Pr.

***Non-Heart-Beating Organ Transplantation: Practice & Protocols.** Institute of Medicine Staff. 174p. 2000. pap. 42.00 (*0-309-06641-7*) Natl Acad Pr.

Non-Heatset Web Offset Directory, 1995. 242p. 115.00 (*0-614-25588-0*, 00GM74031); 155.00 incl. disk (*0-614-25589-9*, 00GM74033) Print Indus Am.

Non-Hodgkin's Lymphomas. 2nd ed. Ed. by Ian T. Magrath. 1108p. 1997. text 225.00 (*0-340-55793-1*, Pub. by E A) OUP.

Non-Hodgkin's Lymphomas: Making Sense of Diagnosis, Treatment & Options. Lorraine Johnston. Ed. by Linda Lamb. LC 98-55468. (Illus.). 580p. 1999. pap. 24.95 (*1-56592-444-4*) OReilly & Assocs.

Non-Hodgkin's Lymphomas: New Techniques & Treatments. Ed. by J. J. Sotto et al. (Illus.). viii, 232p. 1985. 141.00 (*3-8055-4064-7*) S Karger.

Non Holonomic Dynamic Control of Robotic: Manipulators with Applications to Autonomous Probing. Ralph Goddard. Ed. by Laura Goddard. 750p. (Orig.). 1996. write for info. (*0-9654606-0-6*) L Goddard.

Non-Homogeneous Boundary Value Problems & Applications, Vol. 1. J. L. Lions & E. Magenes. Tr. by P. Kenneth. LC 71-151407. (Grundlehren der Mathematischen Wissenschaften Ser.: Vol. 181). 355p. 1972. 127.95 (*0-387-05363-8*) Spr-Verlag.

Non-Homogeneous Boundary Value Problems & Applications, Vol. 3. J. L. Lions & E. Magenes. Tr. by P. Kenneth from FRE. LC 71-151407. (Grundlehren der Mathematischen Wissenschaften Ser.: Vol. 183). 330p. 1973. 103.95 (*0-387-05832-X*) Spr-Verlag.

Non-Horizontal Mergers: Law & Policy. LC 88-70120. (Antitrust Law Section Monographs: No. 14). 91p. 1988. pap. 35.00 (*0-89707-346-0*, 503-0070) Amer Bar Assn.

Non-Human Primates As Models for Study of Human Reproduction: Proceedings of the International Primatological Society 7th Congress, Bangalore, January, 1979. International Primatological Society Staff. Ed. by T. C. Anand Kumar. (Illus.). 252p. 1980. pap. 77.50 (*3-8055-0540-X*) S Karger.

Non-Identifier-Based High-Gain Adaptive Control. Achim Ilchmann. LC 93-26519. (Lecture Notes in Control & Information Sciences: Vol. 189). 1993. 54.00 (*0-387-19845-8*) Spr-Verlag.

Non-Imperial Seals VIth to IXth Centuries see Byzantine Lead Seals

Non-Industrial Robotic Markets, No. 9. Richard K. Miller & Terri C. Walker. LC 88-80487. (Survey on Technology & Markets Ser.). 52p. 1989. pap. text 200.00 (*1-55865-008-3*) Future Tech Surveys.

Non Infectious Diseases, Vol. 1. Jokobiec. 1996. 39.00 (*0-316-45545-8*) Little.

***Non-Inflatable Monty Python TV Companion.** Jim Yoakum. (Illus.). 224p. 1999. pap. text 16.95 (*1-891847-05-8*, DO10064, Pub. by Dowling Pr) Music Sales.

Non-Intervention: The Law & Its Import in the Americas. Ann V. Thomas & A. J. Thomas. LC 56-8946. 492p. reprint ed. pap. 152.60 (*0-8357-8971-3*, 203342900086) Bks Demand.

Non-Intimidating Computer Book: The Absolute Bare Bones, Nuts & Bolts Couldn't Be Simpler, Guide to Understanding & Using Personal Computers. Keith R. Orsolini. (Illus.). 84p. (Orig.). (C). 1989. pap. text. write for info. (*0-318-65725-2*) KRO Enterprises.

Non-Intrusive Combustion Diagnostics: Third International Symposium on Special Topics in Chemical Propulsion. Ed. by Kenneth K. Kuo & Timothy P. Parr. LC 94-32048. 763p. 1994. 155.00 (*1-56700-020-7*) Begell Hse.

Non-Invasive Cardiac Diagnosis. Ed. by Edward K. Chung. LC 75-38915. (Illus.). 331p. reprint ed. pap. 102.70 (*0-608-17893-4*, 205667800080) Bks Demand.

Non-Invasive Cardiac Imaging. Gibson. 1990. text 105.00 (*0-443-04200-4*, W B Saunders Co) Harcrt Hlth Sci Grp.

Non Invasive Cardiovascular Monitoring. Bernard Hayes. Ed. by C. E. Hahn & A. P. Adams. (Illus.). 229p. 1997. pap. 43.00 (*0-7279-1038-8*, Pub. by BMJ Pub) Login Brothers Bk Co.

Non-Invasive Diagnostics of the Left Heart: Biochemical Disturbances. B. Y. Kantor et al. 214p. (C). 1998. lib. bdg. 125.00 (*1-56072-243-6*) Nova Sci Pubs.

Non-Invasive Imaging of Atherosclerosis. Ed. by Michele Mercuri et al. LC 97-37849. (Developments in Cardiovascular Medicine Ser.: No. 199). 245p. 1997. text 159.50 (*0-7923-8036-3*) Kluwer Academic.

Non-Invasive Measurements of Bone Mass & Their Clinical Application. Ed. by S. H. Cohn. 240p. 1981. 138.00 (*0-8493-5789-6*, RC930, CRC Reprint) Franklin.

Non-Invasive Mechanical Methods in Cardiology & Cardiovascular Dynamics: Proceedings of the World Congress, 4th, Amsterdam, April 14-16, 1975. World Congress on Ballistocardiography & Cardiovas. Ed. by W. J. Goedhard. (Bibliotheca Cardiologica Ser.: No. 35). 275p. 1976. 123.50 (*3-8055-2295-9*) S Karger.

Non-Invasive Monitoring of Multiphase Flows. J. Chaouki et al. LC 96-43594. 608p. 1996. 273.00 (*0-444-82521-5*) Elsevier.

Non-Invasive Respiratory Support. A. K. Simonds. (Illus.). 192p. 1995. pap. text 29.95 (*0-412-56840-3*, Pub. by E A) OUP.

Non-Invasive, Semi-Invasive Surgical Procedures, No. C-140. Business Communications Co., Inc. Staff. 189p. 1991. 2250.00 (*0-89336-831-8*) BCC.

Non-Invasive Techniques in Cardiology Journal: Cardiology, Vol. 71, No. 2-3, 1984. Ed. by J. S. Borer. (Illus.). 112p. 1984. pap. 69.75 (*3-8055-3886-3*) S Karger.

Non-Invasive Thermometry of the Human Body. Ed. by Michio Miyakawa & Jean-Charles Bolomey. 272p. 1995. boxed set 169.95 (*0-8493-4738-6*, 4738) CRC Pr.

Non-Ionizing Radiation Guide Series. AIHA Nonionizing Radiation Committee. (Guide Ser.). 12.00 (*0-685-43790-6*) Am Indus Hygiene.

Non-Ionizing Radiation Microwaves, Ultraviolet & Laser Radiation. Henry Gwyn Jeffreys Moseley. (Medical Physics Handbook Ser.: No. 18). (Illus.). 308p. 1988. 124.00 (*0-85274-166-9*) IOP Pub.

Non-Isotopic In Situ Hybridization: Applications to Clinical Diagnosis & Molecular Gene. Matteo Adinolfi & Angela F. Davies. (Medical Intelligence Unit Ser.). 114p. 1994. 99.00 (*1-879702-85-1*, LN0285) Landes Bioscience.

Non-Isotopic Methods in Molecular Biology: A Practical Approach. Ed. by E. Levy & C. S. Herrington. (Practical Approach Ser.: Vol. 153). (Illus.). 244p. 1995. text 110.00 (*0-19-963456-4*) OUP.

Non-Isotopic Methods in Molecular Biology: A Practical Approach, No. 153. Ed. by E. Levy & C. S. Herrington. (Practical Approach Ser.: Vol. 153). (Illus.). 244p. 1995. pap. text 55.00 (*0-19-963455-6*) OUP.

Non-Jewish Origins of European Jewry. (Judaica Ser.). 1992. lib. bdg. 79.95 (*0-8490-5320-X*) Gordon Pr.

Non-Jewish Origins of the Sephardic Jews. Paul Wexler. LC 95-22275. (SUNY Series in Anthropology & Judaic Studies). 321p. (C). 1996. text 74.50 (*0-7914-2795-1*); pap. text 24.95 (*0-7914-2796-X*) State U NY Pr.

Non-Judgemental Sacred Dance: Simple Ways to Pray Through Dance. Lu Bellamak. 1984. pap. 3.00 (*0-941500-14-4*) Sharing Co.

***Non-Judicial Dispute Settlement in International Financial Transactions.** Norbert Horn & Joseph Jude Norton. LC 00-30154. (Studies in Transnational Economic Law). 2000. write for info. (*90-411-9798-2*) Kluwer Law Intl.

Non-Jury Case Files on Trial Advocacy. James R. Devine. (American Casebook Ser.). 258p. (C). 1991. 22.50 (*0-314-87894-7*) West Pub.

Non-Lawyer Book to Form a Corporation in Cd. Juarez, Chihuahua. Daniel Martinez. 400p. (Orig.). 1994. pap. 49.99 (*0-9642059-2-0*) Infomex.

Non-Lawyer Book to Form a Corporation in Guadalajara, Jalisco. Daniel Martinez. 400p. (Orig.). 1994. pap. 49.99 (*0-9642059-5-5*) Infomex.

Non-Lawyer Book to Form a Corporation in Mexico City. Daniel Martinez. 400p. (Orig.). 1994. pap. 49.99 (*0-9642059-0-4*) Infomex.

Non-Lawyer Book to Form a Corporation in Monterrey, N. L. Daniel Martinez. 400p. (Orig.). 1994. pap. 49.99 (*0-9642059-4-7*) Infomex.

Non-Lawyer Book to Form a Corporation in Nuevo Laredo, Tamaulipas. Daniel Martinez. 400p. (Orig.). 1994. pap. 49.99 (*0-9642059-1-2*) Infomex.

Non-Lawyer Book to Form a Corporation in Puebla, Puebla. Daniel Martinez. (Orig.). 1994. pap. 49.99 (*0-9642059-8-X*) Infomex.

Non-Lawyer Book to Form a Corporation in Queretaro, Mexico. Daniel Martinez. 400p. (Orig.). 1994. pap. 49.99 (*0-9642059-7-1*) Infomex.

Non-Lawyer Book to Form a Corporation in San Luis Potosi. Daniel Martinez. 400p. (Orig.). 1994. pap. 49.99 (*0-9642059-6-3*) Infomex.

Non-Lawyer Book to Form a Corporation in Tijuana, B. C. Daniel Martinez. 400p. (Orig.). 1994. pap. 49.99 (*0-9642059-3-9*) Infomex.

Non-Lawyer Book to Form a Corporation in Veracruz, Jalapa. Daniel Martinez. 400p. (Orig.). 1994. pap. 49.99 (*0-9642059-9-8*) Infomex.

Non-Lethal Weapons: A Fatal Attraction? Military Strategies & Technologies for 21st Century Conflict. Nicholas Lewer & Steven Schofield. LC 96-34465. 192p. 1997. pap. 19.95 (*1-85649-486-1*, Pub. by Zed Books) St Martin.

Non-Lieux see Non-Places: Introduction to an Anthropology of Supermodernity

Non-Life Insurance Mathematics. Erwin Straub. (Illus.). 150p. 1988. 79.95 (*0-387-18787-1*) Spr-Verlag.

Non-Life Insurance Mathematics. Erwin Straub. LC 97-20923. 1997. write for info. (*3-540-18787-1*) Spr-Verlag.

Non Linear Analysis & Boundary Value Problems for Ordinary Differential Equations. Ed. by F. Zanolin. (CISM International Centre for Mechanical Sciences Ser.: No. 371). (Illus.). ix, 211p. 1996. pap. 57.00 (*3-211-82811-7*) Spr-Verlag.

Non Linear & Collective Phenomena in Quantum Physics. Ed. by J. L. Gervais & Maurice Jacob. 522p. 1983. text 98.00 (*9971-950-64-2*); pap. text 46.00 (*9971-950-65-0*) World Scientific Pub.

Non-linear Circuits: Qualitative Analysis of Non-linear, Non-reciprocal Circuits. Marc Fosseprez. LC 91-2673. 188p. 1992. 235.00 (*0-471-92659-0*) Wiley.

Non-Linear Differential Equations. rev. ed. G. Sansone & R. Conti. LC 63-10064. (International Series of Monographs on Pure & Applied Mathematics: Vol. 67). 1964. 243.00 (*0-08-010194-1*, Pub. by Pergamon Repr) Franklin.

Non-Linear Dynamic Problems for Composite Cylindrical Shells. A. Bogdanovich. Ed. & Tr. by Charles W. Bert. xii, 300p. 1993. mass mkt. 119.95 (*1-85166-653-2*) Elsevier.

Non-Linear Dynamics & Endogenous Cycles. Ed. by G. Abraham-Frois. LC 98-15193. (Lecture Notes in Economics & Mathematical Systems Ser.: Vol. 463). (Illus.). vi, 204p. 1998. pap. 61.00 (*3-540-64321-4*) Spr-Verlag.

Non-Linear Dynamics in Economic Theory. Ed. by Marc Jarsulic. (International Library of Critical Writings in Economics: Vol. 28). 616p. 1993. 255.00 (*1-85278-809-7*) E Elgar.

Non-Linear Dynamics in Geophysics. J. Dubois. LC 97-41824. 286p. 1998. 85.00 (*0-471-97853-1*) Wiley.

Non-Linear Elastic Deformations. R. W. Ogden. LC 83-26592. (Mathematics & Its Applications Ser.: 1-176). 532p. 1984. text 126.00 (*0-470-27508-1*) P-H.

Non-Linear Elastic Deformations. R. W. Ogden. LC 97-16162. (Illus.). 544p. 1997. reprint ed. pap. text 16.95 (*0-486-69648-0*) Dover.

Non-Linear Elasticity & Theoretical Mechanics: In Honour of A. E. Green. Ed. by P. M. Nagdi et al. (Illus.). 286p. 1994. text 85.00 (*0-19-853486-8*) OUP.

Non-Linear Estimation. G. J. Ross. Ed. by David R. Brillinger et al. (Series in Statistics). (Illus.). viii, 189p. 1990. 58.95 (*0-387-97278-1*) Spr-Verlag.

Non-Linear Field Theories of Mechanics. 2nd ed. Clifford A. Truesdell.Tr. of Die/Nicht-Linearen Feldtheorien der Mechanik. (Illus.). x, 591p. 1992. 91.00 (*0-387-55098-4*) Spr-Verlag.

Non-Linear Finite Element Analysis of Solids & Structures: Advanced Topics, Vol. 2, Advanced Topics. M. A. Crisfield. 508p. 1997. 160.00 (*0-471-95649-X*) Wiley.

Non-Linear Finite Elements Analysis of Solids & Structures: Essentials, Vol. 1, Essentials. M. A. Crisfield. 362p. 1996. pap. 49.95 (*0-471-97059-X*) Wiley.

Non-Linear Fracture: Recent Advances. Ed. by W. G. Knauss & A. J. Rosakis. (C). 1990. text 304.50 (*0-7923-0658-9*) Kluwer Academic.

Non-Linear Fracture & Damage Mechanics. Ed. by M. H. Aliabadi. (Advances in Fracture Mechanics Ser.: Vol. 4). 300p. 1998. 150.00 (*1-85312-508-3*, 5083, Pub. by WIT Pr) Computational Mech MA.

***Non Linear Guided Waves & Their Applications.** (Nineteen Ninety-Eight OSA Technical Digest Ser.: Vol. 5). 200p. (C). 1998. pap. 75.00 (*1-55752-538-2*) Optical Soc.

***Non-Linear Instabilities in Plasmas & Hydrodynamics.** S. S. Moiseev. LC 99-49916. (Plasma Physics Ser.). 176p. 1999. 80.00 (*0-7503-0483-9*) IOP Pub.

Non-Linear Modelling of High Frequency Financial Time-Series. Christian Dunis. LC 97-44713. (Series in Financial Economics & Quantitative Analysis). 320p. 1998. 133.95 (*0-471-97464-1*) Wiley.

Non Linear Oscillation. Nicholas Minorsky. LC 74-8918. 734p. 1974. reprint ed. 72.50 (*0-88275-186-7*) Krieger.

Non-Linear Parametric Optimization. Ed. by B. Bank et al. 224p. 1983. 66.50 (*0-8176-1375-7*) Birkhauser.

Non-Linear Partial Differential Operators & Quantization Procedures. Ed. by S. I. Andersson & H. D. Doebner. (Lecture Notes in Mathematics Ser.: Vol. 1037). 334p. 1983. 42.95 (*0-387-12710-0*) Spr-Verlag.

Non-Linear Phenomena in Materials Science. Ed. by G. Martin & L. P. Kubin. 512p. 1988. text 176.00 (*0-87849-565-7*, Pub. by Trans T Pub) Enfield Pubs NH.

Non Linear Phenomena in Materials Science II. Ed. by G. Martin & L. P. Kubin. 520p. 1992. text 183.00 (*0-87849-635-1*, Pub. by Trans T Pub) Enfield Pubs NH.

Non Linear Phenomena in Materials Science III: Instabilities & Patterning. Ed. by G. Ananthakrishna et al. (Solid State Phenomena Ser.: Vols. 42-43). (Illus.). 352p. (C). 1995. text 183.00 (*3-908450-09-8*, Pub. by Scitec Pubns) Enfield Pubs NH.

Non-Linear Problems in Mechanics of Continua: Proceedings of the First Symposium in Applied Mathematics of the American Mathematical Society. Symposium in Applied Mathematics, 1st, 1947, Brown. LC 50-1183. (Proceedings of Symposia in Applied Mathematics Ser.: No. 1). 227p. reprint ed. pap. 70.40 (*0-608-09196-0*, 205270000003) Bks Demand.

Non Linear Programming, 2 vols. Philip E. Gill. (C). 1998. write for info. (*0-201-52819-3*) Addison-Wesley.

***Non-Linear Singularities in Deformation & Flow: Proceedings: IUTAM Symposium on Non-Linear Singularities in Deformation & Flow (1997: Haifa, Israel)** Ed. by D. Durband & J. R. A. Pearson. LC 98-54487. 360p. 1999. 170.00 (*0-7923-5349-8*) Kluwer Academic.

***Non-Linear Static & Cyclic Analysis of Steel Frames with Semi-Rigid Connections.** Siu L. Chan & Pui T. Chui. LC 99-46371. 350p. 2000. 152.50 (*0-08-042998-X*) Elsevier.

Non-Linear Structural Equation Models: Simulation Studies of the Kenny-Judd Model. Fan Y. Jonsson. LC 97-200287. (Acta Universitatis Upsaliensis: No. 4). (Illus.). 160p. 1997. pap. 44.50 (*91-554-3937-3*, Pub. by Almqvist Wiksell) Coronet Bks.

Non-Linear Theory of Elasticity. A. I. Lurie. (Applied Mathematics & Mechanics Ser.: No. 36). 618p. 1990. 227.50 (*0-444-87439-9*, North Holland) Elsevier.

Non-Linear Theory of Thin Elastic Shells. K. Mushtari & K. Z. Galimov. LC 61-62238. 383p. reprint ed. pap. 118.80 (*0-608-31012-3*, 200233300012) Bks Demand.

Non-Linear Time-Dependent Deformation Behaviour of High Density Polyethylene. Junbiao Lai. vi, 159p. (Orig.). 1995. pap. 59.50 (*90-407-1136-4*, Pub. by Delft U Pr) Coronet Bks.

Non-Linear Time Series: A Dynamical System Approach. Howell Tong. (Non-Linear Time Ser.: No. 6). (Illus.). 580p. 1993. reprint ed. pap. text 65.00 (*0-19-852300-9*) OUP.

Non-Linear Variability in Geophysics: Scaling & Fractals. Ed. by D. Schertzer & S. Lovejoy. (C). 1991. lib. bdg. 151.00 (*0-7923-0985-5*) Kluwer Academic.

Non-Linear Waves in Dispersive Media. V. I. Karpman. Tr. by Ferdinand Cap. 1975. 95.00 (*0-08-017720-4*, Pub. by Pergamon Repr) Franklin.

Non-Linearity & Breakdown in Soft Condensed Matter: Proceedings of a Workshop Held at Calcutta, India, 1-9 December, 1993. Ed. by K. K. Bardhan et al. LC 94-40085. (Lecture Notes in Physics Ser.: Vol. 437). 1994. 79.95 (*3-540-58652-0*) Spr-Verlag.

Non-Literacy Papyri: Private Documents see Papyri

Non-Literary Papyri: Public Documents see Papyri

Non-Living Ocean Resources. Roger H. Charlier. 1979. reprint ed. pap. 7.00 (*0-686-27713-9*) Maple Mont.

Non-Local Universe: The New Physics & Matters of the Mind. Robert Nadeau & Menas Kafatos. LC 99-17062. (Illus.). 256p. 1999. 27.50 (*0-19-513256-4*) OUP.

Non-Lymphoid Leukemias in Children. Ed. by Carl Pochedly. 256p. 1985. 45.00 (*0-275-90009-6*, C0009, Praeger Pubs) Greenwood.

Non-majors Biology. 3rd ed. (C). 1997. write for info. (*0-8087-9932-0*) Pearson Custom.

Non-Mammalian Models for Research on Ageing. Ed. by F. A. Lints. (Interdisciplinary Topics in Gerontology Ser.: Vol. 21). (Illus.). viii, 288p. 1985. 172.25 (*3-8055-4019-1*) S Karger.

N

Non-Manipulative Selling. Tony Alessandra et al. 256p. 1992. pap. 13.00 (*0-671-76448-9*, Fireside) S&S Trade Pap.

Non-Market Components of National Income. Ismail A. Sirageldin. LC 78-627964. (Illus.). 139p. reprint ed. pap. 43.10 (*0-608-18011-4*, 202913300058) Bks Demand.

Non-Mathematical Approach to Basic MRI. Hans J. Smith & Frank Ranallo. LC 87-28170. (Illus.). 200p. (C). 1989. pap. text 23.95 (*0-944838-02-2*) Med Physics Pub.

Non-Mendelian Genetics in Humans: Medelian & Non-Mendelian. Harry Ostrer. LC 97-20620. (Oxford Monographs on Medical Genetics: No. 35). (Illus.). 216p. 1998. text 42.50 (*0-19-506877-0*) OUP.

Non-Metaliferous Strata Bound. Milka K. De Brodtkorb. 332p. (gr. 13). 1989. mass mkt. 97.95 (*0-442-20522-8*) Chapman & Hall.

Non-Metallic Elements in Liquid Metals. Mitsuo Shimoji & T. Itami. (Molten Salt Forum Ser.: No. 4). (Illus.). 264p. 1996. text 116.00 (*0-87849-711-0*, Pub. by Trans T Pub) Enfield Pubs NH.

***Non-Metallic Expansion Joint Hydrotesting & Vacuum Testing Standard FSA-NMEJ-701-98.** 7p. 2000. pap. write for info. (*1-892965-06-2*) Fluid Sealing Assn.

Non-Metallic FRP Reinforcement for Concrete Structures: Proceedings of the Second International Rilem Symposium. L. Taerwe. (Illus.). 736p. (C). 1995. 180.00 (*0-419-20540-3*, E & FN Spon) Routledge.

Non-Metallic Inclusions in Steel. 2nd ed. R. Kiessling & N. Lange. 444p. 1978. text 100.00 (*0-904357-18-X*, Pub. by Inst Materials) Ashgate Pub Co.

Non-Metallic Inclusions in Steel, Part V. R. Keissling. 196p. 1989. text 60.00 (*0-901462-44-6*, Pub. by Inst Materials) Ashgate Pub Co.

Non-Metallic Material, What Part Will It Play in the Future of the Gear Industry? T. C. Roantree. (AGMA Technical Paper: Vol. P72). (Illus.). 9p. 1928. pap. text 30.00 (*1-55589-319-8*) AGMA.

Non-Metallic Mineral Ores: Proceedings of the 27th International Geological Congress, Vol. 15. International Geological Congress Staff. 452p. 1984. lib. bdg. 107.00 (*90-6764-024-7*, Pub. by VSP) Coronet Bks.

Non-Metallic Ores, Silicate Industries & Solid Minerals Fuels, 8 vols., Vol. 2. Intro. by John J. McKetta, Jr. 828p. 1971. 68.50 (*0-06-491103-9*) B&N Imports.

Non Military Aspects of International Security: Peace & Conflict Issues. UNESCO Staff. LC 95-235199. 285p. 1995. pap. 30.00 (*92-3-103073-6*, U3073, Pub. by UNESCO) Bernan Associates.

***Non-military Security & Global Order: The Impact of Extremism Violence.** Peter Chalk. LC 00-21169. 272p. 2000. text 69.95 (*0-312-23167-9*) St Martin.

Non-Monotonic Extensions of Logic Programming: ICLP '94 Workshop, Santa Margherita Ligure, Italy, June 17, 1994, Selected Papers. Luis M. Pereira & Joerg H. Siekmann. LC 95-20072. (Lecture Notes in Computer Science Ser.: Vol. 927). 229p. 1995. 43.00 (*3-540-59467-1*) Spr-Verlag.

Non-Monotonic Extensions of Logic Programming: Second International Workshop NMELP '96, Bad Honnef, Germany September 5-6, 1996, Selected Papers, Vol. 121. Ed. by J. Dix et al. LC 97-12651. (Lecture Notes in Artificial Intelligence Ser.: No. 1216). xii, 224p. 1997. pap. 43.00 (*3-540-62843-6*) Spr-Verlag.

Non-Monotonic Reasoning. Johan De Kleer et al. (Lecture Notes in Computer Science Ser.: Vol. 346). xiv, 237p. 1988. 37.00 (*0-387-50701-9*) Spr-Verlag.

An Asterisk (*) at the beginning of an entry indicates that the title is appearing for the first time.

Non-Muslim among Muslim States: Israel. Shiv Lal. 152p. 1986. 135.00 (*0-7855-1838-X*, Pub. by Archives Pubs) St Mut.

Non Muslims in the Islamic Society. Yusuf Al-Qaradawl. Tr. by Khalil M. Hamad & Sayed M. Shah. LC 83-72763. 68p. (Orig.). 1985. reprint ed. pap. 3.75 (*0-89259-049-1*) Am Trust Pubns.

Non-Muslims under Shari'ah. A. R. Doi. 1981. 6.50 (*1-56744-170-X*) Kazi Pubns.

Non-Native Educators in English Language Teaching. Ed. by George Braine. LC 98-50643. 256p. 1999. 49.95 (*0-8058-3204-1*); pap. 24.50 (*0-8058-3205-X*) L Erlbaum Assocs.

Non-Negative Matrices & Markov Chains. E. Seneta. (Series in Statistics). 279p. 1981. 87.95 (*0-387-90598-7*) Spr-Verlag.

Non-Neoplastic Diseases of the Anorectum: Proceedings of the 64th Falk Symposium, Held in Titisee - Black Forest, Germany, October 11-13, 1991. Ed. by L. Demling & P. Fruhmorgen. LC 92-15602. 400p. (C). 1992. text 191.50 (*0-7923-8979-4*) Kluwer Academic.

Non-Neuronal Cells in Alzheimer's Disease. M. Nicolini & Paolo F. Zatta. 200p. 1995. text 61.00 (*981-02-2092-8*) World Scientific Pub.

Non-Neutral Plasma Physics. Ed. by C. W. Roberson & C. F. Driscoll. LC 88-72275. (AIP Conference Proceedings Ser.: No. 175). 311p. 1988. lib. bdg. 65.00 (*0-88318-375-7*) Am Inst Physics.

***Non-Neutral Plasma Physics III.** Ed. by John J. Bollinger et al. LC 99-68554. (AIP Conference Proceeding Ser.). (Illus.). 487p. 1999. 130.00 (*1-56396-913-0*) Am Inst Physics.

Non-Neutral Plasma Physics II: Proceedings: Non-Neutral Plasma Physics Conference (1994: Berkeley, CA) Ed. by Joel Fajans & Daniel H. Dubin. LC 95-79630. (AIP Conference Proceedings Ser.: No. 331). (Illus.). 294p. 1995. 120.00 (*1-56396-441-4*) Am Inst Physics.

Non-Newtonian Flow. Raj Chhabra & J. F. Richardson. LC 99-36996. (Illus.). 436p. 2000. text 66.95 (*0-7506-3770-6*) Buttrwrth-Heinemann.

Non-Newtonian Fluid Mechanics. G. Bohme. (North-Holland Series in Applied Mathematics & Mechanics: Vol. 31). xii, 352p. 1987. 162.60 (*0-444-70186-9*, North Holland) Elsevier.

Non-Newtonian Fluids. 2nd ed. Wilkinson. 1999. write for info. (*0-08-041863-5*, Pergamon Pr) Elsevier.

Non Nova, Sed Nove: Melanges de Civilisation Medievale dedies a Willem Noomen. Ed. by Martin Gosman & Jaap Van Os. (ENG, FRE & GER., Illus.). x, 298p. (Orig.). 1984. 48.00 (*90-6088-092-7*, Pub. by Boumas Boekhuis) Gen Publ ON.

Non-Nuclear Conflicts in the Nuclear Age. Ed. by Sam C. Sarkesian. LC 80-15281. 404p. 1980. 79.50 (*0-275-90544-6*, C0544, Praeger Pubs) Greenwood.

Non-Nuclear Defense of Cities: The High Frontier Space-Based Defense Against ICBM Attack. Daniel O. Graham. (Illus.). 160p. 1984. reprint ed. lib. bdg. 52.50 (*0-8191-4101-1*) U Pr of Amer.

Non-Nuclear Energy Programme (1990-94) Joule II Synthesis of Key Findings . . . EUR 17650. 1997. 25.00 (*92-828-0752-5*, CG-NA-17650-ENC, Pub. by Comm Europ Commun) Bernan Associates.

Non-Nuclear Hazardous Wastes: A Source Guide. 1991. lib. bdg. 76.00 (*0-8490-4873-7*) Gordon Pr.

Non-Nuclear Submarines - The World Market. Charles LeMesurier & Marc Arnold. (Special Reports). 1996. 695.00 (*0-7106-1502-7*) Janes Info Group.

Non-Nucleonic Degrees of Freedom Detected in the Nucleus: Osaka, Japan, 2-5 September, 1996. Ed. by T. Minamisono et al. 430p. 1997. 68.00 (*981-02-3184-9*) World Scientific Pub.

Non-Objective Art. (Illus.). 1991. text 44.00 (*1-56290-076-5*, 6007) Crystal.

Non-Occupational Exposure to Mineral Fibres. Ed. by J. Bignon et al. (IARC Scientific Publications: No. 90). (Illus.). 500p. 1989. pap. 115.00 (*92-832-1190-1*) OUP.

Non-Occupational Exposure to Mineral Fibres. International Agency for Research on Cancer Staff. Ed. by J. Bignon et al. LC 89-212402. (IARC Scientific Publications: No. 90). (Illus.). 552p. reprint ed. pap. 171.20 (*0-608-20035-2*, 207130700010) Bks Demand.

Non-Offensive Defence: A Strategic Contradiction? David Gates. (C). 1990. 40.00 (*0-907967-88-4*, Pub. by Inst Euro Def & Strat) St Mut.

Non-Official Art: Soviet Artists of the 1960s. Andrei Erofeev. (Illus.). 120p. 1995. text 26.00 (*976-8097-84-1*) Gordon & Breach.

Non-Official British in India to 1920. Raymond K. Renford. (Illus.). 400p. 1987. text 34.00 (*0-19-561388-0*) OUP.

Non-Operative Aspects of Pediatric Surgery. Richard Owings. LC 72-176176. 160p. 1973. 10.00 (*0-87527-118-9*) Green.

Non-Opioid Analgesics in the Treatment of Acute Pain: Johannesbergs Slott, Sweden, March 14th, 1996. Michael J. Parnham. LC 97-513. 1997. write for info. (*0-8176-5680-4*); write for info. (*3-7643-5680-4*) Birkhauser.

Non-Opioids in Pain Management: Vancouver, August 19, 1996. Michael J. Parnham. LC 97-10915. 1997. write for info. (*0-8176-5700-2*); write for info. (*3-7643-5700-2*) Birkhauser.

Non-Ordination of Women & the Politics of Power. Ed. by Elizabeth Schussler-Fiorenza & Hermann Haring. 150p. 1999. pap. 15.00 (*1-57075-227-3*) Orbis Bks.

Non Orthodox: The Orthodox Teaching on Christians Outside of the Church. Patrick Barnes. 151p. 1999. pap. 19.95 (*0-9649141-6-6*) Regina Orthodox.

Non Palpable Breast Lesions. Ed. by M. R. Christiaens & I. De Wever. (Surgical Oncology Ser.: No. 3). (Illus.). 126p. (Orig.). 1996. pap. 49.50 (*90-6186-734-7*, Pub. by Leuven Univ) Coronet Bks.

Non-Paper Sports Collectibles: An Illustrated Price Guide. Ted Hake & Roger Steckler. (Illus.). 192p. (Orig.). 1986. pap. 18.00 (*0-918708-08-7*) Hake.

***Non-Parametric Statistical Diagnosis: Problems & Methods.** B. E. Brodsky & B. S. Darkhovsky. LC 00-38933. (Mathematics & Its Applications Ser.). (Illus.). 2000. write for info. (*0-7923-6328-0*, Kluwer Plenum) Kluwer Academic.

Non-Parents & Schools: Creating a New Team see Communication Alert Series

Non-Passerine Pleistocene Avifauna of the Talara Tar Seeps, Northwestern Peru. Kenneth E. Campbell, Jr. (Illus.). 208p. pap. 20.57 (*0-88854-230-5*) Brill Academic Pubs.

***Non-Payment in the Electricity Sector in Eastern Europe & the Former Soviet Union.** LC 99-32182. (Technical Paper Ser.: No. 423). 132p. 1999. pap. 22.00 (*0-8213-4542-7*, 14542) World Bank.

Non PCB Mounted Thermal Management Component Markets. Market Intelligence Staff. 1993. 1750.00 (*1-56753-477-5*) Frost & Sullivan.

Non-Person Singular: Selected Poems of Yang Lian. Yang Lian. Tr. by Brian Holton & Mabel Lee. LC 95-233707. (WellSweep Chinese Poets Ser.: Vol. 6). 128p. (C). 1994. pap. 14.95 (*0-948454-15-6*) Cheng & Tsui.

Non-Perturbative Aspects of Quantum Field Theory: Proceedings of the XII International GIFT Seminar, Sant Feliu de Guixols, Spain, June 1-5, 1981. Ed. by J. Julve & M. Ramon-Medrano. 264p. 1982. 52.00 (*9971-950-34-0*); pap. 29.00 (*9971-950-35-9*) World Scientific Pub.

Non-Perturbative Field Theory & QCD: Proceedings of the 1982 December Workshop Trieste, Italy. Ed. by R. Iengo et al. 291p. 1983. 60.00 (*9971-950-84-7*); pap. 30.00 (*9971-950-85-5*) World Scientific Pub.

Non-Perturbative Methods: Proceedings of the Workshop at Montpellier, France, July 9-13, 1985. Ed. by S. Narison. 480p. 1986. text 137.00 (*9971-5-0012-4*) World Scientific Pub.

Non-Perturbative Methods in Quantum Field Theory: Proceedings of the Conference, Siofok, Hungary, September 1-7, 1986. Ed. by Z. Horvath. 428p. 1987. pap. 39.00 (*9971-5-0222-4*); text 131.00 (*9971-5-0221-6*) World Scientific Pub.

Non Perturbative Methods in Two Dimensional Quantum Field Theory. Elcio Abdalla et al. 700p. 1991. text 109.00 (*981-02-0462-0*); pap. text 61.00 (*981-02-0463-9*) World Scientific Pub.

Non-Perturbative Particle Theory & Experimental Tests: Proceedings of the Johns Hopkins Workshop on Current Problems in Particle Theory 20, Heidelberg, Germany, 27-29 June 1996. Ed. by M. Kins Jamin et al. LC 97-12538. 490p. 1997. 86.00 (*981-02-3162-8*) World Scientific Pub.

Non-Perturbative Quantum Field Theory: Mathematical Aspects & Applications. J. Frohlich. 856p. 1992. text 109.00 (*981-02-0432-9*); pap. text 61.00 (*981-02-0433-7*) World Scientific Pub.

Non-Pharmacologic Therapy of Hypertension. Ed. by M. Donald Blaufox & H. G. Langford. (Bibliotheca Cardiologica Ser.: No. 41). (Illus.). vi, 150p. 1987. 121.75 (*3-8055-4459-6*) S Karger.

Non-Physician Personnel in Expanded Primary Care Roles: An Annotated Bibliography, No. 1131. Lois S. Sigel. 1976. 5.00 (*0-686-20407-7*, Sage Prdcls Pr) Sage.

Non-Places: Introduction to an Anthropology of Supermodernity. Marc Auge. Tr. by John Howe. LC 94-46299.Tr. of Non-Lieux. (ENG & FRE.). 128p. (C). 1995. 55.00 (*1-85984-956-3*, C0517, Pub. by Verso); pap. 18.00 (*1-85984-051-5*, C0518, Pub. by Verso) Norton.

***Non-Plan: Essays on Freedom, Participation & Change in Modern Architecture & Urbanism.** Jonathan Hughes & Simon Sadler. 256p. 2000. pap. 49.95 (*0-7506-4083-9*, Architectural Pr) Buttrwrth-Heinemann.

Non-Point Source River Pollution: The Case of the River Meuse: Technical, Legal, Economic & Political Aspects. LC 96-48712. 1997. 160.00 (*90-411-0910-2*) Kluwer Law Intl.

Non-Point Sources of Water Pollution: Proceedings of Southeastern Regional Conference Conducted on May 1, 1975, Blacksburg, Va. Ed. by Peter M. Ashton & Richard C. Underwood. LC TD0423.N6. 318p. reprint ed. pap. 98.60 (*0-608-11571-1*, 200512800050) Bks Demand.

Non-Policy Debating. David M. Berube. 390p. (Orig.). (C). 1994. pap. text 34.50 (*0-8191-9348-8*) U Pr of Amer.

***Non Product Consolidation Operation: A Novel.** John Ropa. LC 00-190637. 187p. 2000. 25.00 (*0-7388-1880-1*); pap. 18.00 (*0-7388-1881-X*) Xlibris Corp.

***Non-Profit Corporations in Kentucky.** 3rd ed. Jesse T. Mountjoy et al. 188p. 1999. pap. 43.00 (*1-58757-023-8*, BM030) Univ of KY.

Non-Profit Corporations, Organizations, & Associations. 4th ed. Howard L. Oleck. 1251p. 1980. 59.95 (*0-685-03913-7*, Busn) P-H.

Non-profit Fundraiser's Handbook. Schaff. 1996. pap. 14.00 (*0-8050-4396-9*) St Martin.

Non-Profit Guide to the Internet. 2nd ed. Michael Johnston. LC 98-45980. 240p. 1999. pap. 29.95 (*0-471-32857-X*) Wiley.

Non-Profit Handbook, 1997-98: National Edition. Gary M. Grobman. 302p. (Orig.). 1997. pap. 29.95 (*0-9653653-7-9*) White Hat.

Non-Profit Hospitals: Their Structure, Human Resources, & Economic Importance. Thomas A. Barocci. LC 80-22075. 251p. 1980. 59.95 (*0-86569-054-5*, Auburn Hse) Greenwood.

Non-Profit Housing Development in Hawaii. Peter G. Panet. 167p. (Orig.). (C). 1995. pap. text 30.00 (*0-7881-2517-6*) DIANE Pub.

Non-Profit Internet Handbook. Gary M. Grobman & Gary B. Grant. LC 97-61931. (Illus.). 216p. 1998. pap. 29.95 (*0-9653653-6-0*) White Hat.

Non Profit Organizations: Cases & Materials. James J. Fishman & Stephen Schwarz. (University Casebook Ser.). 1034p. 1995. text 47.95 (*1-56662-280-8*) Foundation Pr.

Non-Profit Organizations Accounting & Reporting. 2nd ed. John Listro. LC 97-76347. 288p. (C). 1998. per. 39.95 (*0-7872-4766-9*, 41476601) Kendall-Hunt.

Non-Profit Organizations, 1990. Practising Law Institute Staff. (Tax Law & Estate Planning Ser.). 231p. 1990. 70.00 (*0-685-38047-5*) PLI.

Non-Profit Organizations with Communication Interests in the Pacific Hemisphere. 4th ed. 99p. (C). 1995. pap. text 25.00 (*0-7881-2344-0*) DIANE Pub.

Non-Profit Public Policy Research Organizations: A Sourcebook on Think Tanks in Government. Robert L. Hollings. LC 93-19101. (Organizations & Interest Groups Ser.: Vol. 7). 240p. 1993. text 15.00 (*0-8153-0766-7*, SS905) Garland.

Non-Profit Sector. Walter W. Powell. LC 86-15984. 464p. (C). 1989. reprint ed. pap. 30.00 (*0-300-04497-6*) Yale U Pr.

Non-Profit Sector in Hungary. Eva Kuti. (Johns Hopkins Non-Profit Sector Ser.: Vol. 4). (Illus.). 256p. 1996. text 69.95 (*0-7190-4905-9*, Pub. by Manchester Univ Pr); text 27.95 (*0-7190-4906-7*, Pub. by Manchester Univ Pr) St Martin.

Non-Profits & Education Job Finder. Daniel Lauber. LC 96-92661. (Illus.). 336p. 1997. 32.95 (*1-884587-09-7*); pap. 16.95 (*1-884587-06-2*) Planning Comns.

Non-Proliferation: The Why & the Wherefore. Stockholm International Peace Research Institute S & Jozef Goldblat. 400p. 1985. 90.00 (*0-85066-304-0*) Taylor & Francis.

Non-Proliferation & Confidence-Building Measures in Asia & the Pacific. (Disarmament Topical Papers: No. 10). 183p. pap. 13.50 (*92-1-142185-3*, E.93.IX.3) UN.

Non-Proliferation Incentives for Russia & Ukraine. John C. Baker. LC 98-101324. (Adelphi Papers: No. 309). (Illus.). 92p. (Orig.). 1997. pap. text 32.00 (*0-19-829371-2*) OUP.

Non-Proliferation of Nuclear Weapons. Georges Fischer. Tr. by David Willey. LC 72-189811. 270p. 1971. 22.95 (*0-8290-0190-5*) Irvington.

Non-Proliferation Regime & Pakistan: The Comprehensive Test Ban Treaty as a Case Study. Babar Sattar. 176p. 2000. text 19.95 (*0-19-577941-X*) OUP.

Non-Proliferation Treaty: How to Remove the Residual Threats. (UNIDIR Research Papers: No. 13). 36p. pap. 10.00 (*92-9045-069-X*, E.GV.92.0.25) UN.

Non-Prophet. Unisa Asokan. (Poetry Ser.). 1994. pap. 5.00 (*1-880855-03-8*) Fifth Planet.

Non-Radioactive Labeling: A Practical Introduction. Andrew Garman. LC 96-37104. (Biological Techniques Ser.). (Illus.). 160p. 1997. text 49.95 (*0-12-276045-X*) Morgan Kaufmann.

Non-Radioactive Labeling & Detection of Biomolecules. Ed. by C. Kessler. LC 92-23517. (Laboratory Ser.). (Illus.). 432p. 1992. 89.00 (*0-387-55482-3*) Spr-Verlag.

Non-Random Walk down Wall Street. Andrew W. Lo et al. LC 98-31390. (Illus.). 424p. 1999. text 45.00 (*0-691-05774-5*, Pub. by Princeton U Pr) Cal Prin Full Svc.

Non-Reality of Free Will. Richard Double. 272p. 1990. text 55.00 (*0-19-506497-6*) OUP.

Non-Refundable Groom. Patty Salier. 1998. per. 3.75 (*0-373-76149-X*, 1-76149-3) Silhouette.

Non-Regular Differential Equations & Calculations of Electromagnetic Fields. N. E. Tovmasyan. LC 98-10860. 250p. 1998. 44.00 (*981-02-3336-1*) World Scientific Pub.

Non-Regular Statistical Estimation. Kei Takeuchi & Masafumi Akahira. (Lecture Notes in Statistics Ser.: Vol. 107). 1995. 48.95 (*0-387-94578-4*) Spr-Verlag.

Non-Relativistic Quantum Mechanics. 2nd ed. Anton Z. Capri. LC 85-14933. (Lecture Notes & Supplements in Physics Ser.: No. 19). (Illus.). 653p. (C). 1985. 61.00 (*0-8053-1505-5*) Addison-Wesley.

Non-Religious Christianity. Gerald Coates. LC 99-163774. 1998. pap. 10.99 (*1-56043-694-8*, Revival Pr) Destiny Image.

Non-Renewable Resources: Extraction Programs & Markets. John M. Hartwick. Ed. by Jacques Lesourne & Hugo Sonnenschein. (Fundamentals of Pure & Applied Economics Ser.: Vol. 33). x, 156p. 1989. pap. text 83.00 (*3-7186-4896-2*) Gordon & Breach.

Non-Renunciation: Themes & Interpretations of Hindu Culture. Triloki N. Madan. 196p. 1988. text 22.50 (*0-19-562040-2*) OUP.

Non-Renunciation: Themes & Interpretations of Hindu Culture. Triloki N. Madan. 198p. 1996. pap. text 10.95 (*0-19-563809-3*) OUP.

Non-Reproductive Actions of Sex Steroids: Symposium No. 191. CIBA Foundation Symposium Staff. LC 95-6957. (Ciba Foundation Symposium Ser.: Vol. 191). 307p. 1995. 128.00 (*0-471-95513-2*) Wiley.

Non-Residents: Taxation & Investment in India. 2nd ed. P. Pikale. (C). 1989. 350.00 (*0-7855-4725-8*) St Mut.

Non-Resonant Feedback in Lasers see Progress in Quantum Electronics

Non-Retaliation in Early Jewish & New Testament Texts: Ethical Themes in Social Contexts. Gordon M. Zerbe. (JSP Supplement Ser.: No. 13). 307p. 1993. 85.00 (*1-85075-389-X*, Pub. by Sheffield Acad) CUP Services.

Non-Ricardian Political Economy: Five Neglected Contributions. Barry J. Gordon. (Kress Library of Business & Economics Publication: No. 22). vii, 51p. 1967. pap. 9.95 (*0-678-09914-6*) Kelley.

Non-Riemannian Geometry. Luther P. Eisenhart. LC 28-28413. (Colloquium Publications: Vol. 8). 184p. 1922. reprint ed. pap. 41.00 (*0-8218-1008-1*, COLL/8) Am Math.

Non Role of Religion in Peace or How to Convince a Woman to Kill Her Child or Have It Killed by Others. (Analysis Ser.: No. 6). 1982. pap. 10.00 (*0-686-42841-2*) Inst Analysis.

Non-Runner's Marathon Trainer. David A. Whitsett et al. LC 97-49288. (Illus.). 224p. 1998. pap. 12.95 (*1-57028-182-3*, 81823H, Mstrs Pr) NTC Contemp Pub Co.

Non-Scatological Set of Preliminary Remarks see Paperplay Mini-Books

***Non-School Hours, Mobilizing School & Community Resources: Hearing Before the Committee on Labor & Human Resources, United States Senate, 105th Congress, 2nd Session ... February 25, 1998.** USGPO Staff. LC 98-193161. (S. Hrg. Ser.). iii, 75 p. 1998. write for info. (*0-16-056576-6*) USGPO.

Non Sequitur Survival Guide for the Nineties. Wiley. (Illus.). 112p. 1995. pap. 9.95 (*0-8362-1785-3*) Andrews & McMeel.

***Non Sequitur's Beastly Things.** Wiley. 256p. 1999. pap. 14.95 (*0-7407-0016-2*) Andrews & McMeel.

Non-Silicates. Ed. by L. L. Chang et al. (Rock-Forming Minerals Ser.: No. 5B). (Illus.). 392p. 1997. 125.00 (*1-897799-90-X*, Pub. by Geol Soc Pub Hse) AAPG.

Non-Slavic Languages of the U. S. S. R. Papers from the 4th Conference. Ed. by Howard I. Aronson. (Illus.). 309p. (Orig.). 1994. pap. 24.95 (*0-89357-250-0*) Slavica.

***Non-Sleeping Universe** M. T. Lago & A. Blanchard. LC 99-37370. 1999. write for info. (*0-7923-5877-5*, Kluwer Plenum) Kluwer Academic.

Non-Smoking. abr. ed. Roger W. Breternitz. 1985. pap. 9.95 incl. audio (*1-893417-07-7*) Vector Studios.

***Non-Smooth Mechanics.** Michel Fremond. (Illus.). 2000. 69.95 (*3-540-66500-5*) Spr-Verlag.

Non-Solar X-Gamma-Ray Astronomy: Proceedings of the I.A.U. Symposium, No. 37, Rome, Italy, May 8-18, 1969. International Astronomical Union Staff. Ed. by L. Gratton. LC 73-83561. (I.A.U. Symposia Ser.). 425p. 1970. lib. bdg. 117.50 (*90-277-0160-1*) Kluwer Academic.

Non-Specific Aspects of Treatment. Ed. by Norman Sartorius & M. Shepherd. LC 88-13504. 160p. 1989. 39.00 (*0-920887-32-5*) Hogrefe & Huber Pubs.

Non-Specific Factors Influencing Host Resistance: A Reexamination. Ed. by W. Braun & J. Ungar. (Illus.). 1973. 116.75 (*3-8055-1598-7*) S Karger.

Non-Specific Mesenteric Lymphadenitis. V. Tuchel. 1972. 55.75 (*3-8055-1251-1*) S Karger.

Non-Spherical Principal Series Representations of a Semisimple Lie Group. Alfred Magnus. LC 79-10157. (Memoirs Ser.: No. 19/216). 52p. 1979. pap. 17.00 (*0-8218-2216-0*, MEMO/19/216) Am Math.

Non-Spherical Principal Series Representations of a Semisimple Lie Group. Alfred Magnus. LC 79-10157. (American Mathematical Society Ser.: No. 216). 58p. reprint ed. pap. 30.00 (*0-608-09215-0*, 205271900005) Bks Demand.

Non-Standard Analysis. rev. ed. Abraham Robinson. LC 95-43750. (Landmarks in Mathematics & Physics Ser.). 308p. (C). 1996. pap. text 19.95 (*0-691-04490-2*, Pub. by Princeton U Pr) Cal Prin Full Svc.

Non-Standard & Improperly Posed Problems. Karen A. Ames & Brian Straughan. LC 97-21742. (Mathematics in Science & Engineering Ser.). (Illus.). 200p. 1997. text 99.00 (*0-12-056745-8*) Morgan Kaufmann.

Non-Standard Collection Management. Michael Pearce. 250p. 1992. 78.95 (*1-85742-020-9*) Ashgate Pub Co.

Non-Standard Computation. T. Gram. LC 98-173288. 240p. 1998. pap. 94.00 (*3-527-29427-9*) Wiley.

Non-Standard Logics for Automated Reasoning. Ed. by Philippe Smets et al. 334p. 1988. text 73.00 (*0-12-649520-3*) Acad Pr.

Non-Standard Medical Electives in the U. S. A. & Canada, 1998-1999. Kenneth V. Iserson. LC 98-22346. 1998. pap. 31.95 (*1-883620-00-7*) Galen AZ.

Non-Standard Rank Tests. A. J. Janssen & D. M. Mason. (Lecture Notes in Statistics Ser.: Vol. 65). vi, 252p. 1990. 57.95 (*0-387-97484-9*) Spr-Verlag.

***Non-Standard Work & Industrial Relations.** Ed. by Roger Blanpain & M. Biagi. (Bulletin of Comparative Labour Relations Ser.: Vol. 35). 200p. 1999. pap. 72.00 (*90-411-1117-4*) Kluwer Law Intl.

***Non-State Actors & Authority in the Global System.** Richard A. Higgott et al. LC 99-34775. 320p. 1999. 100.00 (*0-415-22085-8*) Routledge.

Non-State Nations in International Politics: Comparative System Analyses. Ed. by Judy S. Bertelsen. LC 75-36404. 272p. 1976. 59.95 (*0-275-90244-7*, C0244, Praeger Pubs) Greenwood.

Non-Stationary Time Series Analysis & Cointegration. Ed. by Colin Hargreaves. (Advanced Texts in Econometrics Ser.). 326p. 1994. text 59.00 (*0-19-877391-9*); pap. text 36.00 (*0-19-877392-7*) OUP.

Non-Stereoidal. 1986. 71.00 (*0-8176-1750-7*) Birkhauser.

Non-Steroidal Regulations in Reproductive Biology & Medicine: Proceedings of a Satellite Symposium to the 8th International Congress of Pharmacology, Tokyo, 26-27 July 1981, Vol. 34. T. Fujii & C. P. Channing. (Illus.). 266p. 1982. 87.50 (*0-08-027976-7*, H130, Pergamon Pr) Elsevier.

Non-Stipendiary Ministry in the Church of England: A History of the Development of an Idea. Patrick H. Vaughan. LC 90-6547. 382p. 1990. lib. bdg. 99.95 (*0-7734-9936-9*) E Mellen.

An Asterisk (*) at the beginning of an entry indicates that the title is appearing for the first time.

Non-Stipitate Stereoid Fungi in the Northeastern United States & Adjacent Canada: Mycologia Memoir. George P. Chamuris. (Mycologia Memoir Ser.: No. 14). (Illus.). 247p. 1988. 58.00 (*3-443-76004-X*, Pub. by Gebruder Borntraeger) Balogh.

Non-Stock Production: The Shingo System for Continuous Improvement. Shigeo Shingo. LC 88-42626. (Illus.). 479p. 1988. 50.00 (*0-915299-30-5*) Productivity Inc.

Non-Stoichiometric Compounds. Ed. by J. Nowotny & W. Weppner. (C). 1989. text 287.50 (*0-7923-0225-7*) Kluwer Academic.

Non-Stop. Brian W. Aldiss. 268p. 1989. pap. 3.95 (*0-88184-492-6*) Carroll & Graf.

Non-Stop Discussion Workbook! Problems for Intermediate & Advanced Students of English. 2nd ed. George M. Rooks. 162p. (Orig.). (C). 1996. mass mkt. 15.00 (*0-8384-2938-6*, Newbury) Heinle & Heinle.

Non-Stop Flight: A Life of Artie Show. John White. (East Note - Hull Studies in Jazz). 230p. 1998. pap. 19.95 (*0-85958-666-9*, Pub. by Univ of Hull Pr) Paul & Co Pubs.

Non-Stop Stories. Judith W. Hollands et al. 45p. (J). (gr. 3-10). 1986. pap. 6.00 (*0-8290-1227-3*) Irvington.

Non-Store Retailing. Ed. by Peter Allen. 250p. 1989. pap. 1495.00 (*0-941285-50-2*) FIND-SVP.

Non-Subscription to Texas Workers Comp: Lawyer's Edition. James Martin. 110.00 (*0-685-52373-X*, B10) Sterling TX.

Non-Suicidal Society. Andrew Oldenquist. LC 85-45804. 276p. 1986. pap. 85.60 (*0-608-05038-5*, 205969900004) Bks Demand.

Non-Suicidal Society. Andrew G. Oldenquist. LC 85-45804. (Illus.). 280p. (C). 1986. 10.95 (*0-253-34107-8*) Ind U Pr.

Non-Surgical Relief for Chronic Pain: Reconstructive Therapy. 1996. lib. bdg. 251.75 (*0-8490-5883-X*) Gordon Pr.

Non-Sustainable Land Use Practices in Upland Areas & Their Relation to Coastal Livelihood Patterns: A Case Study from the Philippines. Random DuBois. LC 90-11221. (Geography Ser.). (Illus.). 145p. 1991. pap. 14.50 (*0-685-39264-3*) U Ch Pr.

Non-Target Effects of Live Vaccines. (Developments in Biological Standardization Ser.: Vol. 84). (Illus.). xiv, 294p. 1995. pap. 239.25 (*3-8055-6107-5*) S Karger.

Non-Tax Sources of Revenue for Public Libraries. Mary J. Lynch. 1988. 6.00 (*0-8389-7253-5*) ALA.

Non-Technical Obstacles to the Use of Solar Energy, Vol. 4. A Strub et al. (European Applied Research Reports Special Topics Ser.). xii, 454p. 1980. text 349.00 (*3-7186-0050-1*) Gordon & Breach.

Non-Technical Workbook for Public Safety. 2nd ed. PPI (Pivetta) Staff. 152p. 1997. spiral bd. 42.95 (*0-7872-4470-8*) Kendall-Hunt.

***Non-Tetrahedrally Bonded Binary Compounds II: Supplement to Vol. III/17g (Print Version) Revised & Updated Edition of Vol. III/17g (CD-ROM)** Ed. by O. Madelung et al. (Numerical Data & Functional Relationships in Science & Technology - New Ser.: Pt. D). 2000. 3883.00 incl. cd-rom (*3-540-64966-2*) Spr-Verlag.

***Non-Tetrahedrally Bonded Elements & Binary Compounds I.** Ed. by O. Madelung et al. 470p. 1999. 2943.00 (*3-540-64583-7*) Spr-Verlag.

***Non-Thermal Plasma for Exhaust Emission Control: Nox, HC, & Particulates.** (Special Publications). 126p. 1999. 68.00 (*0-7680-0490-X*, SP-1483) Soc Auto Engineers.

Non-Thermal Plasma Techniques for Pollution Control, 2 vols. Ed. by Bernie M. Penetrante & Shirley E. Schultheis. LC 93-21307. (NATO ASI Series G: Ecological Sciences: Vol. 34). (Illus.). lxxii, 790p. 1994. 437.95 (*0-387-57174-4*) Spr-Verlag.

Non-Thinking Self. W. Norman Cooper. 112p. 1980. 9.50 (*0-87516-414-5*); pap. 6.50 (*0-87516-403-X*) DeVorss.

Non-Timber Forest Products in Southern Ghana: A Summary Report. J. Falconer. 1992. pap. 35.00 (*0-902500-43-0*, Pub. by Nat Res Inst) St Mut.

Non-Timber Forest Products of East Kalimantan: Potentials for Sustainable Forest Use. J. L. Van Valkenburgh. LC 98-164260. (Tropenbos Ser.: Vol. 16). (Illus.). 198p. 1997. pap. 45.00 (*90-5113-030-9*, Pub. by Backhuys Pubs) Balogh.

Non-Timber Products from Tropical Forests: Evaluation of a Conservation & Development Strategy. Ed. by Daniel Nepstad & Stephen Schwartzman. LC 92-14911. (Advances in Economic Botany Ser.: Vol. 9). 176p. 1992. pap. text 18.95 (*0-89327-376-7*) NY Botanical.

Non-Timber Tree Products: A Partial Inventory of Products Available in the Mount Cameroon Area. V. Papadopulos & A. Gordon. 1977. pap. 60.00 (*0-85954-465-6*, Pub. by Nat Res Inst) St Mut.

Non, Titus, Non! Claire Masurel.Tr. of No, No, Titus!. (FRE., Illus.). (J). (ps-1). pap. 15.95 (*3-314-21050-7*, Pub. by North-South Bks NYC) Chronicle Bks.

Non-Toxic Farming Handbook. Philip A. Wheeler & Ronald B. Ward. LC 98-73502. 256p. 1998. pap. 25.00 (*0-911311-56-4*) Acres USA.

Non-Toxic Pest Control. write for info. (*0-937844-06-3*) Caverne Pub.

Non-Traditional Agriculture & Economic Development: The Brazilian Soybean Expansion, Nineteen Sixty-Four to Nineteen Eighty-Two. Anthony B. Soskin. LC 87-30872. 172p. 1988. 47.95 (*0-275-92803-9*, C2803, Praeger Pubs) Greenwood.

Non-Traditional & Traditionally Understudied Families: Parenting & Child Development. Ed. by Michael E. Lamb. LC 98-18422. 400p. 1998. write for info. (*0-8058-2747-1*); pap. write for info. (*0-8058-2748-X*) L Erlbaum Assocs.

Non Traditional Feed Sources for Use in Swine Production. P. A. Thacker & R. N. Kirkwood. 514p. 1992. lib. bdg. 79.95 (*0-409-90190-3*) Buttrwrth-Heinemann.

Non-Traditional Incentive Pay Programs. (PPF Survey Ser.: No. 148). 59p. 1991. 50.00 (*1-55871-219-4*) BNA.

Non-Traditional Job Creation & Entrepreneurship. Kenneth Poole. Ed. by Jenny Murphy. 28p. (Orig.). 1988. pap. 18.00 (*0-317-04855-4*) Natl Coun Econ Dev.

Non-Traditional Machining Handbook. Carl Sommer. LC 99-20676. 437p. 1999. text 49.95 (*1-57537-325-4*) Advance Pub.

Non-Traditional Machining Processes. American Society of Tool & Manufacturing Engineers. Ed. by R. K. Springborn. LC 67-17078. (American Society of Tool & Manufacturing Engineers Manufacturing Data Ser.). 190p. reprint ed. pap. 58.90 (*0-608-11724-2*, 205119800085) Bks Demand.

Non-Traditional Military Training for Canadian Peacekeepers. 2nd ed. Paul LaRose-Edwards et al. LC 98-179945. 125p. 1997. pap. 14.95 (*0-660-16881-2*, Pub. by Canadian Govt Pub) Accents Pubns.

Non-Trivial Trivia Book: The Ultimate Book of Knowledge. Nilanjan Sen. Ed. by Ilana Sparrow. LC 97-93662. (In Plain English Ser.). (Illus.). 150p. (Orig.). 1997. pap. 12.95 (*1-890838-02-0*) Indus Pub.

Non-Trycyclic & Non-Monamine Oxydase Inhibitors. Ed. by H. E. Lehmann. (Modern Problems of Pharmacopsychiatry Ser.: Vol. 18). (Illus.). viii, 212p. 1982. 100.00 (*3-8055-3428-0*) S Karger.

Non-U. S. Worldwide Telecommunications: Asia-Oceania, Vol. 4. Richard Bryant. LC 95-231952. (Illus.). 471p. 1994. 1500.00 (*1-56965-053-5*, HG-148D) BCC.

Non-U. S. Worldwide Telecommunications: Europe, Vol. 1. Richard Bryant. LC 95-231952. (Illus.). 410p. 1994. 1500.00 (*1-56965-055-1*, G-148A) BCC.

Non-U. S. Worldwide Telecommunications: Latin America, Vol. 3. Richard Bryant. LC 95-231952. (Illus.). 346p. 1993. 1500.00 (*1-56965-052-7*, G-148C) BCC.

Non-U. S. Worldwide Telecommunications Vol. 2: Africa-Middle East. Richard Bryant. LC 95-231952. (Illus.). 208p. 1994. 1500.00 (*1-56965-054-3*, G-148B) BCC.

Non-Ulcer Dyspepsia. F. Di Mario et al. (Advances in Gastroenterology Ser.: No. 3). 130p. 1991. text 32.00 (*1-57235-019-9*) Piccin Nuova.

Non-Ulcer Dyspepsia. F. Di Mario et al. (Advances in Gastroenterology Ser.: Vol. 3). (Illus.). 130p. 1991. text 36.00 (*88-299-0970-X*, Pub. by Piccin Nuova) Gordon & Breach.

Non-Uniform Random Variate Generation. L. Devroye. 865p. 1986. 107.95 (*0-387-96305-7*) Spr-Verlag.

Non-Utility Electrical Power Generation, No. E-067. 149p. 1993. 2450.00 (*1-56965-150-7*) BCC.

Non-Vanishing of L-Functions & Applications. Maruti R. Murty & V. Kumar Murty. LC 97-38038. (Progress in Mathematics Ser.: Vol. 157). (Illus.). x, 196p. 1997. text 47.00 (*3-7643-5801-7*) Birkhauser.

Non-Vanishing of L-Functions & Applications. Maruti R. Murty & Vijaya K. Murty. LC 97-38038. (Progress in Mathematics Ser.). (Illus.). x, 196p. 1997. pap. write for info. (*0-8176-5801-7*) Birkhauser.

Non-Vasoactive Renal Hormones. Ed. by G. M. Eisenbach & Jan Brod. (Contributions to Nephrology Ser.: Vol. 13). (Illus.). 1978. pap. 29375.00 (*3-8055-2895-7*) S Karger.

Non-Vegetarian Indian Cookery. Pritam Uberoi. 203p. (Orig.). 1983. pap. 12.95 (*0-940500-62-0*) Asia Bk Corp.

***Non-Verbal Behavior in Psychodynamic Psychotherapy & Psychoanalysis.** Frances La Barre. LC 00-38089. 2000. write for info. (*0-88163-316-X*) Analytic Pr.

Non-Verbal Intelligence Tests for Use in China. Herman C. Liu. LC 76-177001. (Columbia University. Teachers College. Contributions to Education Ser.: No. 126). reprint ed. 37.50 (*0-404-55126-2*) AMS Pr.

Non-Verbal Intimacy & Exchange: A Special Issue of Journal of Nonverbal Behavior. Ed. by Miles L. Patterson. (Illus.). 169p. (Orig.). 1983. pap. 14.95 (*0-89885-224-2*, Kluwer Acad Hman Sci) Kluwer Academic.

Non-Verbal Selling Power. Gerhard Gschwandtner. LC 85-6358. 201p. 1985. 19.95 (*0-317-38246-2*) P-H.

Non-Vicious Circle: Twenty Poems of Aime Cesaire. Tr. by Gregson Davis from FRE. LC 83-42791. (Illus.). 168p. 1984. 12.95 (*0-8047-1207-7*) Stanford U Pr.

Non-Violence Central to Christian Spirituality: Perspectives from Scripture to the Present. Joseph T. Culliton. LC 82-7964. (Toronto Studies in Theology: Vol. 8). 312p. (C). 1982. lib. bdg. 99.95 (*0-88946-964-4*) E Mellen.

Non-Violent Action: How it Works. George Lakey. LC 63-17661. (C). 1963. pap. 4.00 (*0-87574-129-0*) Pendle Hill.

Non-Violent Coercion: A Study in Methods of Social Pressure. Clarence M. Case. LC 78-137530. (Peace Movement in America Ser.). viii, 423p. 1972. reprint ed. lib. bdg. 49.95 (*0-89198-058-X*) Ozer.

Non-Violent Models in Violent Communities: A Crime Prevention Model for African-American Urban Neighborhoods. Joseph Jones. (Illus.). 252p. (C). 1997. 69.95 (*1-57292-042-4*); pap. 49.95 (*1-57292-041-6*) Austin & Winfield.

Non-Violent Revelation to John. Thomas R. Jones. LC 98-60518. 173p. 1998. pap. 20.00 (*0-9664703-0-3*) Tobacco River Pubs.

Non-Violent Stories & Poems for Children. Teresa Macaulay. LC 96-67651. (Illus.). 128p. (Orig.). (J). (ps-3). 1996. 16.95 (*1-56167-244-0*) Noble Hse MD.

Non-Viral Genetic Therapeutics: Advances, Challenges & Applications for Self-Assembling Systems. Ed. by Bari Walsh. (Biomedical Library). 1996. pap. 795.00 (*1-57936-019-X*) IBC USA.

Non-Volatile Memory Technology Review Meeting, 1993. IEEE (Components, Hybrids, & Manufacturing Technol. LC 93-77837. 240p. 1993. pap. text. write for info. (*0-7803-1290-2*, 93TH0547-0); fiche. write for info. (*0-7803-1291-0*, 93TM0547-0) Inst Electrical.

Non-Waste Technology & Production: Proceedings of an International Seminar Held in Paris, Nov.-Dec. 1976. United Nations. Economic Commission for Europe. 1978. pap. 310.00 (*0-08-022028-2*, Pub. by Pergamon Repr) Franklin.

Non-Well-Founded Sets. Peter Aczel. LC 87-17857. (CSLI Lecture Notes Ser.: No. 14). 147p. 1988. 34.95 (*0-937073-21-0*); pap. 17.95 (*0-937073-22-9*) CSLI.

***Non-Western & Absolute Instruments.** Robert Dearling. (Encyclopedia of Musical Instruments Ser.). (Illus.). 2000. 17.95 (*0-7910-6095-0*) Chelsea Hse.

***Non Western Art.** 2nd ed. MacKenzie. LC 99-86441. (Illus.). 256p. 2000. pap. 26.67 (*0-13-900036-4*) P-H.

Non-Western Art: A Brief Guide. Lynn Mackenzie. LC 94-44273. 176p. (C). 1995. pap. text 17.33 (*0-13-104894-5*) P-H.

***Non-Western Educational Traditions: Alternate Approaches to Educational Thought & Practice.** 2nd ed. Timothy G. Reagan. LC 99-54729. 2000. pap. write for info. (*0-8058-3450-8*) L Erlbaum Assocs.

Non-Western Films of John Ford. J. A. Place. (Illus.). 1979. pap. 9.95 (*0-8065-0779-9*, Citadel Pr) Carol Pub Group.

Non-Western Political Process. Lucian W. Pye. (Reprint Series in Social Sciences). (C). 1993. reprint ed. pap. text 5.00 (*0-8290-3099-9*, PS-351) Irvington.

***Non-Western Religions.** Daniel L. Hawley. 69p. 1998. teacher ed. 27.50 (*1-881678-57-1*) CSEE.

Non-Western Theories of Development: Regional Norms Versus Global Trends. Howard J. Wiarda. LC 97-74698. 1998. pap. text 33.00 (*0-15-505366-3*, Pub. by Harcourt Coll Pubs) Harcourt.

Non-Wood Goods & Services of the Forest: Report of ECE/FAO Team of Specialists Linda L. Langner & United Nations Staff. LC 98-200292. (Geneva Timber & Forest Study Papers). (ENG & RUS.). vi, 44p. 1998. pap. write for info. (*92-1-116691-8*) UN.

Non-Woven Bonded Fabrics. Ed. by J. Lunenschloss & W. Albrecht. Tr. by Janet Hock. LC 84-25175. (Applied Science & Industrial Technology Ser.). 549p. 1985. text 173.00 (*0-470-20150-9*) P-H.

Non-Woven Fabrics. M. S. Burnip & A. Newton. 105p. 1970. 95.00 (*0-7855-7208-2*) St Mut.

Non-Wovens. Ed. by Wira Staff. 1984. 50.00 (*0-7855-1009-5*) St Mut.

Nonacademic Writing: Social Theory & Technology. Ed. by Ann H. Duin & Craig J. Hansen. 344p. 1995. pap. 36.50 (*0-8058-1628-3*); text 89.95 (*0-8058-1627-5*) L Erlbaum Assocs.

Nonaccelerator Particle Physics: Proceedings of the International Conference. R. Cowsik. 600p. 1995. text 109.00 (*981-02-1811-7*) World Scientific Pub.

Nonadrenergic Innervation of Blood Vessels, 2 vols., Vol. I: Putative Neurotransmitters. G. Burnstock & S. G. Griffith. LC 87-24283. 176p. 1988. 95.00 (*0-8493-6681-X*, QP109, CRC Reprint) Franklin.

Nonadrenergic Innervation of Blood Vessels, 2 vols., Vol. II: Regional Innervation. G. Burnstock & S. G. Griffith. LC 87-24283. 256p. 1988. 140.00 (*0-8493-6682-8*, QP109, CRC Reprint) Franklin.

Nonaesthetic Issues in the Philosophy of Art: Art As a Social Realm. L. B. Cebik. LC 94-44818. 376p. 1995. text 99.95 (*0-7734-8999-1*) E Mellen.

Nonaligned Movement: India's Chairmanship. Kashi P. Misra. vii, 248p. (C). 1987. 26.00 (*81-7095-001-5*, Pub. by Lancer India) S Asia.

***Nonaqueous Electrochemistry.** Doron Orbakh. LC 99-35915. (Illus.). 608p. 1999. text 195.00 (*0-8247-7334-9*) Dekker.

Nonaqueous-Phase Liquids: Remediation of Chlorinated & Recalcitrant Compounds. Godage B. Wickramanayake & Robert E. Hinchee. LC 98-24756. 1998. 79.95 (*1-57477-057-8*) Battelle.

***Nonassociative Algebra & Its Applications: The 4th International Conference.** Roberto Costa. LC 00-26394. (Lecture Notes in Pure & Applied Mathematics Ser.). 2000. write for info. (*0-8247-0406-1*) Dekker.

Nonassociative Algebraic Models. Ed. by Santos Gonzalez & H. C. Myung. 250p. (C). 1992. text 175.00 (*1-56072-050-6*) Nova Sci Pubs.

Nonassociative Algebras & Related Topics, International Symposium, Hiroshima, Japan, 30 August-1 September 1990. Ed. by K. Yamaguti & N. Kawamoto. 400p. (C). 1991. text 85.00 (*981-02-0655-0*) World Scientific Pub.

Nonassociative Algebras in Physics. J. Lohmus et al. LC 94-42052. (Monographs in Mathematics). 280p. 1994. pap. text 75.00 (*0-911767-71-1*) Hadronic Pr Inc.

Nonastronimical Adaptive Optics. Compiled by Optical Society of America Staff. LC 97-68221. (Nineteen Ninety-Seven Technical Digest Ser.: Vol. 13). (Illus.). 69p. 1997. pap. 75.00 (*1-55752-507-2*) Optical Soc.

Nonathambia. Doru Chirodea. 26p. 1995. pap. 3.00 (*1-57141-014-7*) Runaway Spoon.

Nonbelief & Evil: Two Arguments for the Nonexistence of God. Theodore M. Drange. LC 98-24173. 340p. 1998. 39.95 (*1-57392-228-5*) Prometheus Bks.

Noncanonical Writings & New Testament Interpretation. Craig A. Evans. LC 92-31247. 282p. 1992. 19.95 (*0-943575-95-8*) Hendrickson MA.

Noncapitalist Development: Struggle to Nationalize the Guyanese Sugar Industry. Paulette Pierce. LC 84-17882. 220p. (C). 1984. 42.00 (*0-86598-118-3*) Rowman.

Noncash Remuneration for Agricultural Labor: Market Segment Understanding. (Illus.). 14p. 1995. pap. 11.00 (*1-57402-319-5*) Athena Info Mgt.

Noncatecholic Phenylethylamines Pt. 1: Phenylethylamine: Biological Mechanisms & Clinical Aspects. Ed. by Aron D. Mosnaim & Marion E. Wolf. LC 77-26130. (Modern Pharmacology-Toxicology Ser.: No. 12). (Illus.). 552p. 1978. reprint ed. pap. 171.20 (*0-608-01192-4*, 206076800001) Bks Demand.

Noncatecholic Phenylethylamines Pt. 2: Phenylethanolamine, Tyramines, & Octapamine. Ed. by Aron D. Mosnaim & Marion E. Wolf. LC 77-26130. (Modern Pharmacology-Toxicology Ser.: No. 12). (Illus.). 383p. 1980. reprint ed. pap. 118.80 (*0-608-00253-4*, 206076800002) Bks Demand.

Nonchemical Treatment Processes for Disinfestation of Insects & Fungi in Library Collections. Johanna G. Wellheiser. (IFLA Publications: Vol. 60). 118p. 1992. lib. bdg. 45.00 (*3-598-21788-9*) K G Saur Verlag.

Nonchurchgoer's Guide to the Bible. Michael Gantt. 184p. (Orig.). 1996. pap. 9.95 (*1-56148-213-7*) Good Bks PA.

Nonchurchgoer's Guide to the Bible: A User-Friendly, Nonsectarian Introduction to the All-Time Bestseller. Michael Gantt. LC 95-35006. 192p. 1995. 15.95 (*1-56148-181-5*) Good Bks PA.

Nonclassical & Inverse Problems for Pseudoparabolic Equations. A. Asanov & E. R. Atamanov. (Inverse & Ill-Posed Problems Ser.). (Illus.). 156p. 1997. 125.00 (*90-6764-235-5*, Pub. by VSP) Coronet Bks.

Nonclassical Effects in Quantum Optics. Ed. by Pierre Meystre. 464p. 1991. 89.95 (*0-88318-784-1*) Spr-Verlag.

Nonclassical Logics & Information Processing: International Workshop, Berlin, Germany, November 9-10, 1990 Proceedings. Ed. by D. Pearce et al. (Lecture Notes in Computer Science, Lecture Notes in Artificial Intelligence Ser.: Vol. 619). vii, 171p. 1992. 38.00 (*0-387-55745-8*) Spr-Verlag.

***Nonclassical Physics: Beyond Newtons View.** 128p. (C). 1998. text 24.00 (*0-201-35715-1*) Addison-Wesley.

Nonclassical Physics: Beyond Newton's View. Randy Harris. LC 98-7460. 545p. (C). 1998. 95.00 (*0-201-83436-7*) Addison-Wesley.

Nonclimbing Species of the Genus Psychotria (Rubiaceae) in New Guinea & the Bismarck Archipelago. S. H. Sohmer. (Bishop Museum Bulletin in Botany Ser.: Vol. 1). (Illus.). 339p. (C). 1988. pap. 35.00 (*0-930897-22-6*) Bishop Mus.

N

Noncoercive Variational Problems & Related Results. D. Goeleven. LC 96-35719. (Pitman Research Notes in Mathematics Ser.). 1997. pap. 49.95 (*0-582-30402-4*) Longman.

Noncommercial Foodservice Management: An Administrator's Handbook. John Cornyn et al. LC 94-17566. 305p. 1994. 64.95 incl. disk (*0-471-00880-X*) Wiley.

Noncommercial, Institution & Contract Foodservice Management. Mickey Warner. LC 93-38883. 289p. 1994. 59.95 (*0-471-59573-X*) Wiley.

Noncommercial, Institutional & Contract Foodservice Management. Mickey Warner. 320p. 1994. pap. text, teacher ed. write for info. (*0-471-10285-7*) Wiley.

Noncommutative Algebra. Benson Farb & R. Keith Dennis. LC 93-17487. (Graduate Texts in Mathematics Ser.: Vol. 144). (Illus.). 223p. 1993. 49.95 (*0-387-94057-X*) Spr-Verlag.

Noncommutative Algebraic Geometry & Representations of Quantized Algebras. Alexander L. Rosenberg. (Mathematics & Its Applications Ser.). 328p. (C). 1995. text 155.00 (*0-7923-3575-9*) Kluwer Academic.

Noncommutative Distributions: Unitary Representation of Gauge Groups & Algebras. S. Albeverio et al. LC 93-9942. (Pure & Applied Mathematics Ser.: Vol. 175). (Illus.). 208p. 1993. text 125.00 (*0-8247-9131-2*) Dekker.

Noncommutative Geometry. Ed. by Alain Connes. LC 94-26550. (Illus.). 661p. 1994. text 70.00 (*0-12-185860-X*) Acad Pr.

Noncommutative Harmonic Analysis. Michael E. Taylor. LC 86-10924. (Mathematical Surveys & Monographs: Vol. 22). 328p. 1986. reprint ed. pap. 34.00 (*0-8218-1523-7*, SURV/22) Am Math.

Noncommutative Microlocal Analysis, Pt. 1. Michael E. Taylor. LC 84-18500. (Memoirs of the American Mathematical Society Ser.: No. 52/313). 182p. 1990. pap. 25.00 (*0-8218-2314-0*, MEMO/52/313) Am Math.

***Noncommutative Noetherian Rings.** J. C. McConnell & James C. Robson. LC 00-34990. (Graduate Studies in Mathematics). (Illus.). 616p. 2001. reprint ed. 72.00 (*0-8218-2169-5*) Am Math.

Noncommutative Probability. I. Cuculescu & A. G. Oprea. LC 94-32310. (Mathematics & Its Applications Ser.: Vol. 305). 368p. (C). 1994. text 217.50 (*0-7923-3133-8*) Kluwer Academic.

Noncommutative Ring Theory: Proceedings of a Conference Held in Athens, Ohio, September 29-30, 1989. Ed. by Subodh K. Jain et al. (Lecture Notes in Mathematics Ser.: Vol. 1448). v, 166p. 1990. 35.95 (*0-387-53164-5*) Spr-Verlag.

Noncommutative Rings. I. N. Herstein. (Carus Mathematical Monograph: No. 15). 216p. 1996. text 34.00 (*0-88385-015-X*, CAM-15) Math Assn.

Noncommutative Rings. Ed. by S. Montgomery et al. (Mathematical Sciences Research Institute Publications: Vol. 24). 200p. 1991. 53.95 (*0-387-97704-X*) Spr-Verlag.

Noncompact Lie Groups & Some of Their Applications: Proceedings of the NATO Advanced Research Workshop on Noncompact Lie Groups & Their Physical Applications, San Antonio, Texas, January 4-8, 1993. Ed. by Elizabeth A. Tanner. (NATO ASI Series C, Mathematical & Physical Sciences). 512p. (C). 1994. text 251.00 (*0-7923-2787-X*) Kluwer Academic.

Noncondensed Aromatic Derivatives, Part II. V. St. Georgiev. (Survey of Drug Research in Immunologic Disease Ser.: Vol. 3). x, 582p. 1983. 426.75 (*3-8055-3687-9*) S Karger.

Noncondensed Aromatic Derivatives, Pt. I. V. St. Georgiev. (Survey of Drug Research in Immunologic Disease Ser.: Vol. 2). xii, 656p. 1983. 426.25 (*3-8055-3566-X*) S Karger.

Noncondensed Aromatic Derivatives, Pt. III. Vassil St. Georgiev. (Survey of Drug Research in Immunologic Disease Ser.: Vol. 4). x, 334p. 1984. 252.25 (*3-8055-3799-9*) S Karger.

Noncondensed Aromatic Derivatives, Pt. IV. V. St. Georgiev. (Survey of Drug Research in Immunologic Disease Ser.: Vol. 5). x, 606p. 1984. 426.25 (*3-8055-3856-1*) S Karger.

Noncondensed Aromatic Derivatives, Pt. IV. V. St. Georgiev. (Survey of Drug Research in Immunologic Disease Ser.: Vol. 7). xii, 792p. 1986. 687.00 (*3-8055-4031-0*) S Karger.

Noncondensed Aromatic Derivatives, Pt. V. V. St. Georgiev. (Survey of Drug Research in Immunologic Disease Ser.: Vol. 6). x, 586p. 1985. 426.25 (*3-8055-3962-2*) S Karger.

Noncondensed Aromatic Derivatives, Pt. VII. V. St. Georgiev. (Survey of Drug Research in Immunologic Disease Ser.: Vol. 8). xiv, 794p. 1987. 687.00 (*3-8055-4240-2*) S Karger.

Nonconformist Art: The Soviet Experience, 1956-1986. Ed. by Alla Rosenfeld & Norton Dodge. LC 95-60469. (Illus.). 360p. 1995. 60.00 (*0-500-23709-3*, Pub. by Thames Hudson) Norton.

Nonconformist's Memorial: Poems. Susan Howe. LC 92-38489. 192p. (Orig.). 1993. pap. 13.95 (*0-8112-1229-7*, NDP755, Pub. by New Directions) Norton.

Nonconformity: Writing on Writing. Nelson Algren. Ed. & Intro. by Daniel Simon. LC 94-35205. 144p. 1996. 16.00 (*1-888363-05-3*) Seven Stories.

Nonconformity: Writing on Writing. Nelson Algren. Ed. & Afterword by Daniel Simon. 144p. 1997. pap. 9.95 (*1-888363-62-2*) Seven Stories.

Nonconformity & Social & Economic Life, 1660-1800. Evelyn D. Bebb. LC 80-21180. 198p. 1980. reprint ed. lib. bdg. 35.00 (*0-87991-867-5*) Porcupine Pr.

Nonconformity in Tipton, Staffs. (C). 1987. 40.00 (*0-7855-2102-X*, Pub. by Birmingham Midland Soc) St Mut.

Nonconscious Movements: From Mystical Messages to Facilitated Communication. Herman H. Spitz. LC 96-33566. 211p. 1997. pap. 22.50 (*0-8058-2564-9*) L Erlbaum Assocs.

Nonconscious Movements: From Mystical Messages to Facilitated Communication. Herman H. Spitz. 216p. (C). 1997. 45.00 (*0-8058-2563-0*) L Erlbaum Assocs.

Noncontract Surety Bonds. Robert N. Fox et al. LC 92-75014. 264p. (C). 1992. pap. 41.00 (*0-89462-074-6*, 15302) IIA.

Nonconventional Concrete Technologies: Renewal of the Highway Infrastructure. National Research Council Staff. LC 97-170982. 124p. (C). 1997. pap. text 24.25 (*0-309-05687-X*) Natl Acad Pr.

Nonconventional Feedstuffs in the Nutrition of Farm Animals. Ed. by K. Boda. (Developments in Animal & Veterinary Science Ser.: No. 23). 260p. 1990. 154.50 (*0-444-98780-0*) Elsevier.

Nonconventional Yeasts in Biotechnology: A Handbook. Klaus Wolf. LC 96-4935. (Illus.). 560p. 1996. 99.50 (*3-540-59482-5*) Spr-Verlag.

Nonconvex Optimization in Mechanics: Algorithms, Heuristics & Engineering Applications by the F. E. M. E. S. Mistakidis & G. E. Stavroulakis. LC 97-39880. (Nonconvex Optimization & Its Applications Ser.). 285p. 1998. lib. bdg. write for info. (*0-7923-4812-5*) Kluwer Academic.

Noncovariant Gauges: Quantization of Yang-Mills. G. Leibbrandt. 220p. 1994. text 48.00 (*981-02-1384-0*) World Scientific Pub.

Noncovex Programming. F. Forgo. 187p. (C). 1988. 100.00 (*963-05-4453-9*, Pub. by Akade Kiado) St Mut.

Noncrystalline & Nanoscale Materials: Proceedings of the 5th International Workshop on Noncrystalline Solids Santiago de Compostela, Spain 2-5 July, 1997. Ed. by J. Rivas & M. A. Lopez-Quintela. 600p. 1998. 128.00 (*981-02-3282-9*) World Scientific Pub.

Noncrystalline Semiconductors, 3 vols., Set. Ed. by Michael Pollak. 1987. 369.00 (*0-8493-5994-5*, QC611, CRC Reprint) Franklin.

Noncrystalline Semiconductors, 3 vols., Vol. I. Ed. by Michael Pollak. 304p. 1987. write for info. (*0-318-62343-9*, CRC Reprint) Franklin.

Noncrystalline Semiconductors, Vol. 1. M. Pollack. LC 86-31045. 280p. 1987. reprint ed. 157.00 (*0-8493-5998-8*, CRC Reprint) Franklin.

Noncrystalline Semiconductors, 3 vols., Vol. II. Ed. by Michael Pollak. 192p. 1987. write for info. (*0-318-62344-7*, CRC Reprint) Franklin.

Noncrystalline Semiconductors, Vol. 2. M. Pollack. LC 86-31045. 176p. 1987. reprint ed. 104.00 (*0-8493-5999-6*, CRC Reprint) Franklin.

Noncrystalline Semiconductors, 3 vols., Vol. III. Ed. by Michael Pollak. 192p. 1987. write for info. (*0-318-62345-5*, CRC Reprint) Franklin.

Noncrystalline Semiconductors, Vol. 3. M. Pollack. LC 86-31045. 184p. 1987. reprint ed. 109.00 (*0-8493-6000-5*, CRC Reprint) Franklin.

***Nonculturable Organisms in the Environment.** Ed. by Rita Colwell & D. Jay Grimes. (Illus.). 360p. 2000. 89.95 (*1-55581-196-5*) ASM Pr.

Nondecision-Making & Community Power: Residential Development Control in Rural Areas. H. Buller & Keith Hoggart. (Progress in Planning Ser.: Vol. 25). (Illus.). 74p. 1986. pap. 22.00 (*0-08-034277-9*, Pub. by PPL) Elsevier.

Nondescription Drug. Consumer Guide Editors. 1997. mass mkt. 7.99 (*0-451-19063-7*, Sig) NAL.

Nondestructive & Automated Testing for Soil & Rock Properties. W. A. Marr & Charles Fairhurst. LC 99-23150. 1999. write for info. (*0-8031-2493-7*) ASTM.

Nondestructive & Ultrasonic Testing for Aircraft: Advisory Circular 43-3-7. FAA Staff. (Aviation Technician Ser.). (Illus.). 96p. (C). 1992. reprint ed. pap. 7.95 (*1-56027-106-X*, ASA-AC43-3-7) ASA Inc.

Nondestructive Biomarkers in Higher Vertebrates. M. Cristina Fossi. Ed. by Claudio Leonzio. LC 93-10836. 368p. 1993. lib. bdg. 110.00 (*0-87371-648-5*, L648) Lewis Pubs.

Nondestructive Characterization of Composite Media. Ronald A. Kline. LC 92-61121. 200p. 1992. pap. text 84.95 (*0-87762-925-0*) Technomic.

Nondestructive Characterization of Materials. Ed. by Anthony L. Bartos et al. (Materials Science Forum Ser.: Vols. 210-213). 924p. 1996. 333.00 (*0-87849-708-0*, Pub. by Trans T Pub) Enfield Pubs NH.

Nondestructive Characterization of Materials. Ed. by P. Holler et al. (Illus.). xviii, 892p. 1989. 214.95 (*0-387-51856-8*) Spr-Verlag.

Nondestructive Characterization of Materials II. Ed. by J. F. Bussiere et al. LC 87-16609. (Illus.). 804p. 1987. 145.00 (*0-306-42610-2*, Plenum Trade) Perseus Pubng.

Nondestructive Characterization of Materials in Aging Systems Vol. 503: Materials Research Society Symposium Proceedings. Ed. by R. L. Crane et al. LC 98-28359. 342p. 1998. text 71.00 (*1-55899-408-4*) Materials Res.

Nondestructive Characterization of Materials IV. C. O. Ruud et al. (Illus.). 528p. (C). 1992. 174.00 (*0-306-44047-4*, Plenum Trade) Perseus Pubng.

***Nondestructive Characterization of Materials IX, Vol. 497.** Ed. by Robert E. Green, Jr. (AIP Conference Proceeding Ser.: Vol. 497). (Illus.). 732p. 1999. 185.00 (*1-56396-911-4*) Am Inst Physics.

Nondestructive Characterization of Materials VI. R. E. Green, Jr. et al. (Illus.). 846p. (C). 1994. 175.00 (*0-306-44816-5*, Plenum Trade) Perseus Pubng.

Nondestructive Characterization of Materials VIII: Proceedings of the Eighth International Symposium Held in Boulder, Colorado, June 15-20, 1997. Ed. by Robert E. Green. LC 98-28222. (Illus.). 860p. (C). 1998. 175.00 (*0-306-45900-0*, Plenum Trade) Perseus Pubng.

Nondestructive Characterization of Reactor Pressure Vessel Steels: A Feasibility Study. Harry I. McHenry. 104p. 1998. per. 12.00 (*0-16-056741-6*) USGPO.

Nondestructive Deflection Testing & Backcalculation for Pavements: Proceedings of a Symposium, August 19-21, 1991, Nashville, Tennessee. LC 92-47094. write for info. (*0-309-05420-6*) Transport Res Bd.

Nondestructive Evaluation: A Tool in Design, Manufacturing & Service. Donald E. Bray & Roderick K. Stanley. (Mechanical Engineering Ser.). 672p. 1989. 15.95 (*0-07-007352-X*) McGraw.

Nondestructive Evaluation: A Tool in Design, Manufacturing & Service. rev. ed. Don E. Bray & Roderic K. Stanley. LC 96-35233. 608p. 1996. boxed set 99.95 (*0-8493-2655-9*, 2655) CRC Pr.

Nondestructive Evaluation: Application to Materials Processing: Proceedings of a Symposium - Sponsored by the Energy & Resources Activity of the ASM at the TMS Fall Meeting, Philadelphia, PA, October 3-4, 1983. Ed. by Otto Buck & Stanley M. Wolf. LC 84-71516. (Illus.). 223p. reprint ed. pap. 69.20 (*0-8357-4099-4*, 203686500005) Bks Demand.

Nondestructive Evaluation: Microstructural Characterization & Reliability Strategies: Proceedings of a Symposium Held at the TMS Fall Meeting, Pittsburgh, PA, October 5-9, 1980. Metallurgical Society of AIME Staff. Ed. by Otto Buck & Stanley M. Wolf. LC 81-82177. 413p. reprint ed. pap. 128.10 (*0-8357-2512-X*, 205239200013) Bks Demand.

Nondestructive Evaluation & Flaw Criticality for Composite Materials - STP 696. Ed. by R. B. Pipes. 364p. 1979. 34.50 (*0-8031-0527-4*, STP696) ASTM.

Nondestructive Evaluation & Material Properties III. Ed. by P. K. Law et al. LC 96-80437. (Illus.). 127p. 1997. 94.00 (*0-87339-343-0*, 3430) Minerals Metals.

Nondestructive Evaluation & Material Properties of Advanced Materials: Proceedings of a Symposium, Held During the 1991 TMS Annual Meeting, New Orleans, LA, February, 17-21, 1991. Minerals, Metals & Materials Society Staff. Ed. by P. K. Liaw et al. LC 91-51085. (Illus.). 117p. 1991. reprint ed. pap. 36.30 (*0-608-05695-2*, 206621000007) Bks Demand.

Nondestructive Evaluation Applied to Process Control of Composite Fabrication: Conference Proceedings. Ed. by Gary W. Carriveau & Dianne Chong. (Illus.). vi, 273p. (Orig.). 1994. pap. 50.00 (*1-890596-01-9*) TX Res Inst.

Nondestructive Evaluation for Aerospace Requirements: Proceedings of a Conference Held 26-27 August 1987, Huntsville, Alabama. Ed. by Gary L. Workman. (Nondestructive Testing Monographs & Tracts: Vol. 5). x, 160p. 1989. pap. text 106.00 (*2-88124-305-3*) Gordon & Breach.

Nondestructive Evaluation for Process Control in Manufacturing, Vol. 2948. Ed. by Richard H. Bossi & Tom Moran. 310p. 1996. 85.00 (*0-8194-2352-1*) SPIE.

Nondestructive Evaluation in the Nuclear Industry: An International Conference, 13-15 February, 1978, Salt Lake City, Utah, Proceedings. American Society for Metals Staff. Ed. by R. Natesh. LC 78-25552. (Materials-Metalworking Technology Ser.). (Illus.). 536p. reprint ed. pap. 166.20 (*0-608-10729-8*, 201948800013) Bks Demand.

Nondestructive Evaluation in the Nuclear Industry: Ninth International Conference Held April 25-28, 1988, Tokyo, Japan. Ed. by Kunihiro Lida et al. LC 88-71719. (Illus.). 699p. 1988. reprint ed. pap. 200.00 (*0-608-02646-8*, 206330500004) Bks Demand.

Nondestructive Evaluation in the Nuclear Industry: Proceedings of the Third International Conference. American Society for Metals Staff. LC 81-67225. (Materials-Metalworking Technology Ser.). 695p. reprint ed. 200.00 (*0-608-17149-2*, 202698600053) Bks Demand.

***Nondestructive Evaluation (NDE) & Materials Properties IV.** Ed. by P. K. Liaw et al. LC 98-68629. (Illus.). 20p. 1999. 100.00 (*0-87339-431-3*, 4313) Minerals Metals.

Nondestructive Evaluation (NDE) Capabilities Data Book. Ward D. Rummel & George A. Matzkanin. (Illus.). iii, 338p. 1996. 100.00 (*1-890596-03-5*) TX Res Inst.

Nondestructive Evaluation, 1993. Ed. by D. E. Bray. (PD Ser.: Vol. 54). 68p. 1993. 36.00 (*0-7918-0951-X*, H00783) ASME.

Nondestructive Evaluation of Aging Aircraft, Airports & Aerospace Hardware, Vol. 2945. Ed. by Raymond D. Rempt & Alfred L. Broz. 462p. 1996. 94.00 (*0-8194-2349-1*) SPIE.

Nondestructive Evaluation of Aging Aircraft, Airports & Aerospace Hardware II, Vol. 3397. Ed. by Glenn A. Geithman & Gary E. Georgeson. LC 98-184990. 296p. 1998. 80.00 (*0-8194-2846-9*) SPIE.

***Nondestructive Evaluation of Aging Aircraft, Airports & Aerospace Hardware III.** Ed. by Ajit K. Mal. LC 99-226052. 364p. 1999. pap. text 92.00 (*0-8194-3056-0*) SPIE.

***Nondestructive Evaluation of Aging Materials & Composites III.** Ed. by George Y. Baaklini et al. LC 99-229031. 416p. 1999. pap. text 92.00 (*0-8194-3055-2*) SPIE.

Nondestructive Evaluation of Bridges & Highways, Vol. 2946. Ed. by Steven B. Chase. 340p. 1996. 66.00 (*0-8194-2350-5*) SPIE.

***Nondestructive Evaluation of Bridges & Highways III: 3-5 March 1999, Newport Beach, California.** Steve Chase & Society of Photo-optical Instrumentation Engineers. LC 99-226076. (Illus.). 294p. 1999. 72.00 (*0-8194-3057-9*) SPIE.

Nondestructive Evaluation of Ceramics. Ed. by Christopher H. Schilling & Joseph N. Gray. (Ceramic Transactions Ser.: Vol. 89). (Illus.). 346p. 1998. 95.00 (*1-57498-037-8*, CT089) Am Ceramic.

Nondestructive Evaluation of Materials & Composites, Vol. 2944. Ed. by Steven R. Doctor et al. 344p. 1996. 85.00 (*0-8194-2348-3*) SPIE.

Nondestructive Evaluation of Materials & Composites II, Vol. 3396. Ed. by Steven R. Doctor et al. LC 98-184991. 300p. 1998. 80.00 (*0-8194-2845-0*) SPIE.

Nondestructive Evaluation of Utilities & Pipelines II, Vol. 3398. Ed. by Walter G. Reuter. LC 98-209972. 224p. 1998. 59.00 (*0-8194-2847-7*) SPIE.

***Nondestructive Evaluation of Utilities & Pipelines III.** Ed. by Walter G. Reuter. 106p. 1999. pap. text 50.00 (*0-8194-3058-7*) SPIE.

Nondestructive Evalution of Utilities & Pipelines, Vol. 2947. Ed. by Martin Prager & Richard M. Tilley. 310p. 1996. 76.00 (*0-8194-2351-3*) SPIE.

Nondestructive Examination (NDE) Techniques II, Course 32. Center for Occupational Research & Development Staff. (Nuclear Technology Ser.). pap. text 30.00 (*1-55502-121-2*) CORD Commns.

***Nondestructive Examination of Underwater Welded Structures: Revision of Document IIS/IIW - 1033-89 'Information on Practices for Underwater Nondestructive Testing'** Ed. by V. S. Davey et al. 76p. 1999. pap. 117.00 (*1-85573-427-3*) Am Educ Systs.

Nondestructive Inspection & Quality Control. American Society for Metals Staff. Ed. by Howard E. Boyer. LC 76-382089. (Illus.). 465p. reprint ed. pap. 144.20 (*0-7837-1857-8*, 204205800001) Bks Demand.

Nondestructive Inspection of Composite Materials. Contrib. by Harold Berger & Thomas Jones. (Illus.). 389p. 1995. ring bd. 149.95 (*1-56676-339-8*) Technomic.

Nondestructive Ion Beam Analysis of Surfaces. F. F. Komarov et al. xiv, 232p. 1990. text 299.00 (*2-88124-726-1*) Gordon & Breach.

***Nondestructive Methods for Materials Characterization Vol. 591: Materials Research Society Symposium Proceedings.** Ed. by G. Baaklini et al. LC 00-23037. 322p. 2000. text 90.00 (*1-55899-499-8*) Materials Res.

Nondestructive Monitoring of Materials Properties Vol. 142: Materials Research Society Symposium Proceedings. Ed. by J. Holbrook & J. Bussiere. 374p. 1989. text 17.50 (*1-55899-015-1*) Materials Res.

Nondestructive Rapid Identification of Metals & Alloys by Spot Test. American Society for Testing & Materials Staff & M. A. Wilson. LC 73-90275. 550. 60p. reprint ed. pap. 25.00 (*0-317-08730-4*, 2006068) Bks Demand.

Nondestructive Rapid Identification of Metals & Alloys by Spot Tests, STP 550. 56p. 1986. pap. 12.00 (*0-8031-0528-2*, STP550) ASTM.

Nondestructive Structural Evaluation of Pavements. LC 92-31824. (Transportation Research Record Ser.: No. 1355). 107p. 1992. 22.00 (*0-309-05219-X*) Transport Res Bd.

Nondestructive Testing. Louis Cartz. 225p. 1995. 118.00 (*0-87170-517-6*, 6390) ASM.

Nondestructive Testing. 2nd ed. Warren J. McGonnagle. (Illus.). xiv, 456p. 1971. text 252.00 (*0-677-00500-8*) Gordon & Breach.

Nondestructive Testing: An Expanding Market. 153p. 1997. 2950.00 (*1-56965-454-9*, GB-177R) BCC.

***Nondestructive Testing & Computer Simulations in Science & Engineering.** Ed. by Alexander I. Melker. 488p. 1999. pap. text 92.00 (*0-8194-3161-3*) SPIE.

Nondestructive Testing & Evaluation for Manufacturing & Construction. Ed. by Henrique L. Dos Reis. 550p. 1989. 198.00 (*0-89116-926-1*) Hemisp Pub.

Nondestructive Testing Eddy Current, 3 pts. James E. Cox. Ed. by George Pherigo. Incl. Classroom Training Handbook. (Illus.). 377p. (C). 1997. reprint ed. pap. text 17.50 (*1-886630-17-8*); Vol. I. Basic Principles. (Illus.). 377p. (C). 1997. reprint ed. pap. text 32.25 (*1-886630-07-0*); Vol. II. Applications Vol. II. rev. ed. (Illus.). (C). 1997. pap. text (*1-886630-19-4*); write for info. (*1-886630-21-6*) PH Diversified.

Nondestructive Testing Introduction. Robert W. Smilie. Ed. by George Pherigo. (Programmed Instruction Handbook Ser.). (Illus.). 378p. 1995. reprint ed. pap. text 32.00 (*1-886630-00-3*) PH Diversified.

Nondestructive Testing Liquid Penetrant. Robert W. Smilie. Ed. by George Pherigo. (Programmed Instruction Handbook Ser.). (Illus.). 376p. (C). 1997. reprint ed. pap. text 20.75 (*1-886630-01-1*) PH Diversified.

Nondestructive Testing Liquid Penetrant: Classroom Training Handbook. Robert W. Smilie. Ed. by George Pherigo. (Classroom Training Handbook Ser.). (Illus.). 176p. (C). 1998. reprint ed. pap. text 12.50 (*1-886630-14-3*) PH Diversified.

Nondestructive Testing Magnetic Particle. Robert W. Smilie. Ed. by George Pherigo. Incl. Classroom Training Handbook. (Illus.). 211p. (C). 1997. reprint ed. pap. text 12.50 (*1-886630-15-1*); Vol. I. Basic Principles. (Illus.). 496p. (C). 1997. reprint ed. pap. text 32.25 (*1-886630-02-X*); Vol. II. Applications Vol. II. rev. ed. (Illus.). (C). 1997. pap. text 32.25 (*1-886630-20-8*); write for info. (*1-886630-22-4*, 3 pts.) PH Diversified.

Nondestructive Testing Methods for Civil Infrastructure: A Collection of Expanded Papers on Nondestructure Testing from Structures Congress '93: Approved for the Publication by the Structural Division of the American Society of Civil Engineers. Ed. by Hota V. S. GangaRao. LC 95-36308. 136p. 1995. pap. 22.00 (*0-7844-0131-4*) Am Soc Civil Eng.

Nondestructive Testing of Concrete Elements & Structures. Ed. by Farhad Ansari & Stein Sture. 240p. 1992. pap. text 28.00 (*0-87262-887-6*) Am Soc Civil Eng.

Nondestructive Testing of High-Performance Ceramics: Conference Proceedings, August 25-27, 1987, Boston, MA. Joint Conference on Nondestructive Testing of High. LC 88-118459. (Illus.). 549p. reprint ed. pap. 170.20 (*0-7837-4341-6*, 204405100012) Bks Demand.

Nondestructive Testing of Large-Diameter Pipes for Oil & Gas Transmission Lines. F. J. Weisweiler & G. N. Senge. LC 87-1992. 260p. 1987. lib. bdg. 265.00 (*0-89573-567-9*, Wiley-VCH) Wiley.

Nondestructive Testing of Materials. Ed. by R. Collins et al. LC 95-7902. (Studies in Applied Electromagnetics & Mechanics: Vol. 8). 362p. (YA). (gr. 12). 1996. 121.00 (*90-5199-239-4*, 239-4) IOS Press.

***Nondestructive Testing of Pavements & Backcalculation of Moduli, Vol. 3.** Shiraz D. Tayabji & Erland O. Lukanen. LC 00-23295. (Illus.). 546p. 2000. text 95.00 (*0-8031-2858-4*, STP1375) ASTM.

Nondestructive Testing of Pavements & Backcalculation of Moduli STP 1026. Ed. by Albert J. Bush, III & Gilbert Baladi. LC 89-38726. (Special Technical Publication Ser.). (Illus.). 725p. 1989. text 99.00 (*0-8031-1260-2*, STP1026) ASTM.

Nondestructive Testing of Pavements & Backcalculations of Moduli (STP 1198), Vol. 2. ASTM Committee D-18 on Soil & Rock & Subcommittee D-4 on Road & Paving Materials. Ed. by Harold L. Von Quintus et al. LC 94-24308. 1994. write for info. (*0-8031-1865-1*, STP1198) ASTM.

Nondestructive Testing of Water Mains for Physical Integrity. (Illus.). 128p. 1992. pap. 35.00 (*0-89867-620-7*, 90601) Am Water Wks Assn.

Nondestructive Testing Radiography. Robert W. Smilie. Ed. by George Pherigo. (Classroom Training Handbook Ser.). (Illus.). 296p. (C). 1998. reprint ed. pap. text 18.50 (*1-886630-18-6*) PH Diversified.

Nondestructive Testing Radiography, 5 vols., Set. Robert W. Smilie. Ed. by George Pherigo. (Programmed Instruction Handbook Ser.). (Illus.). 1362p. (C). 1999. reprint ed. pap. text 92.50 (*1-886630-08-9*) PH Diversified.

Nondestructive Testing Radiography Vol. I: Origin & Nature of Radiography. Robert W. Smilie. Ed. by George Pherigo. (Programmed Instruction Handbook Ser.). (Illus.). 200p. (C). 1999. reprint ed. pap. text 18.50 (*1-886630-09-7*) PH Diversified.

Nondestructive Testing Radiography Vol. II: Radiation Safety. Robert W. Smilie. Ed. by George Pherigo. (Programmed Instruction Handbook Ser.). (Illus.). 306p. (C). 1999. reprint ed. pap. text 18.50 (*1-886630-10-0*) PH Diversified.

Nondestructive Testing Radiography Vol. III: Radiographic Equipment. Robert W. Smilie. Ed. by George Pherigo. (Programmed Instruction Handbook Ser.). (Illus.). 243p. (C). 1999. reprint ed. pap. text 18.50 (*1-886630-11-9*) PH Diversified.

Nondestructive Testing Radiography Vol. IV: Making Radiographs. Robert W. Smilie. Ed. by George Pherigo. (Programmed Instruction Handbook Ser.). (Illus.). 413p. (C). 1999. reprint ed. pap. text 18.50 (*1-886630-12-7*) PH Diversified.

Nondestructive Testing Radiography Vol. V: Film Handling & Processing. Robert W. Smilie. Ed. by George Pherigo. (Programmed Instruction Handbook Ser.). (Illus.). 200p. (C). 1999. reprint ed. pap. text 18.50 (*1-886630-13-5*) PH Diversified.

N

An Asterisk (*) at the beginning of an entry indicates that the title is appearing for the first time.

Nondestructive Testing Standards - Present & Future. Ed. by Harold Berger & Leonard Mordfin. LC 92-20433. (STP Ser.: Vol. 1151). (Illus.). 250p. 1992. text 77.00 (*0-8031-1487-7*, STP1151) ASTM.

Nondestructive Testing Techniques. Ed. by Donald E. Bray & Don McBride. LC 91-37970. (New Dimensions in Engineering Ser.). 800p. 1992. 200.00 (*0-471-52513-8*) Wiley.

Nondestructive Testing Ultrasonics. Robert W. Smilie. Ed. by George Pherigo. (Classroom Training Handbook Ser.). (Illus.). 265p. (C). 1997. reprint ed. pap. text 29.00 (*1-886630-16-X*) PH Diversified.

Nondestructive Testing Ultrasonics, 3 vols., Set. Robert W. Smilie. Ed. by George Pherigo. (Programmed Instruction Handbook Ser.). (Illus.). 1109p. (C). 1995. reprint ed. pap. text 86.75 (*1-886630-03-8*) PH Diversified.

Nondestructive Testing Ultrasonics Vol. I: Basic Principles. Robert W. Smilie. Ed. by George Pherigo. (Programmed Instruction Handbook Ser.). (Illus.). 404p. (C). 1995. reprint ed. pap. text 29.00 (*1-886630-04-6*) PH Diversified.

Nondestructive Testing Ultrasonics Vol. II: Equipment. Robert W. Smilie. Ed. by George Pherigo. (Programmed Instruction Handbook Ser.). (Illus.). 298p. (C). 1995. reprint ed. pap. text 29.00 (*1-886630-05-4*) PH Diversified.

Nondestructive Testing Ultrasonics Vol. III: Applications. Robert W. Smilie. Ed. by George Pherigo. (Programmed Instruction Handbook Ser.). (Illus.). 407p. (C). 1995. reprint ed. pap. text 29.00 (*1-886630-06-2*) PH Diversified.

Nondestructive Wafer Characterization for Compound Semiconductor Materials - State-of-the-Art Program on Compound Semiconductors XXII. V. Swaminathan et al. LC 95-60441. (Proceedings Ser.: Vol. 95-6). 378p. 1995. pap. 53.00 (*1-56677-100-5*) Electrochem Soc.

Nondeterminism in Algebraic Specification & Algebraic Programs. Heinrich Hussman. LC 93-9340. (Progress in Theoretical Computer Science Ser.). (Illus.). xii, 253p. 1993. 60.50 (*0-8176-3700-1*) Birkhauser.

Nondifferentiable & Two-Level Mathematical Programming. Kiyotaka Shimizu. LC 96-44000. 488p. (C). 1996. lib. bdg. 159.50 (*0-7923-9821-1*) Kluwer Academic.

Nondifferentiable Optimization. V. F. Dem'Yanov & L. V. Vasil'ev. (Translation Series in Mathematics & Engineering). xvii, 452p. 1985. 146.95 (*0-387-90951-6*) Spr-Verlag.

Nondifferentiable Optimization. V. F. Dem'yanov & L. V. Vasil'ev. Ed. by A. V. Balakrishnan. Tr. by Tetsushi Sasagawa. LC 85-18736. (Translations Series in Mathematics & Engineering). 472p. 1985. text 96.00 (*0-911575-09-X*) Optimization Soft.

Nondifferentiable Optimization & Polynomial Problems. Naum Z. Shor. LC 98-5088. (Nonconvex Optimization & Its Applications Ser.). 394p. 1998. 179.00 (*0-7923-4997-0*) Kluwer Academic.

Nondiscrimination in International Tax Law. Kees Van Raad. (Series on International Taxation: Vol. 6). 304p. 1986. 96.00 (*90-6544-266-9*) Kluwer Law Intl.

Nondiscrimination on the Basis of Disability by Public Accomodations & in Commercial Facilities, Final Rule. (Illus.). 145p. (Orig.). (C). 1993. pap. text 40.00 (*1-56806-923-5*) DIANE Pub.

Nondiscriminatory Multifactored Assessment: A Sourcebook. David W. Barnett. (Illus.). 214p. 1983. pap. 20.95 (*0-89885-082-7*, Kluwer Acad Hman Sci) Kluwer Academic.

Nondramatic Works of John Ford. Ed. by L. E. Stock et al. (Renaissance English Text Society Series, Medieval & Renaissance Texts & Studies: Vol. 85). 480p. 1991. 36.00 (*0-86698-097-0*, MR85) MRTS.

Nonduality: A Study in Comparative Philosophy. David Loy. LC 97-2516. 356p. (Orig.). (C). 1997. pap. 22.50 (*0-391-04020-0*) Humanities.

Nonduality: A Study in Comparative Philosophy. David Loy. LC 99-10394. (Orig.). 1999. 18.95 (*1-57392-359-1*, Humanity Bks) Prometheus Bks.

Nonducted Heat Recovery Ventilators UL 1815. 2nd ed. (C). 1995. pap. text 175.00 (*1-55989-095-9*) Underwrtrs Labs.

None but He. large type ed. Patricia Robins. (Dales Large Print Ser.). 1995. pap. 18.99 (*1-85389-461-3*, Dales) Ulverscroft.

None but Our Words: Critical Literacy in Classroom & Community. Chris Searle. LC 97-46655. 1998. pap. 26.95 (*0-335-20127-X*) OpUniv Pr.

None but Our Words: Critical Literacy in Classroom & Community. Chris Searle. LC 97-46655. 172p. 1998. 85.00 (*0-335-20128-8*) OpUniv Pr.

None but the Brave. Arthur Schnitzler. Tr. by Richard L. Simon. LC 76-175441. reprint ed. 37.50 (*0-404-05613-X*) AMS Pr.

None but the Braves: A Pitcher, a Team, a Champion. Tom Glavine. (Illus.). 240p. 1996. 25.00 (*0-06-018649-6*) HarpC.

None but the Dead & Dying. Ellen Behrens. LC 95-47880. 272p. 1996. 20.00 (*1-880909-41-3*) Baskerville.

***None but the Lonely Heart & Other Songs: For High Voices.** Peter I. Tchaikovsky. 2000. pap. 14.95 (*0-486-41093-5*) Dover.

None but the Sinners: Religious Categories in the Gospel of Luke. David A. Neale. (JSNTS Ser.: Vol. 58). 217p. (C). 1991. 60.00 (*1-85075-314-8*, Pub. by Sheffield Acad) CUP Services.

None Can Be Called Deformed. Vernon Mallinson. Ed. by William R. Phillips & Janet Rosenberg. LC 79-6917. (Physically Handicapped in Society Ser.). 1980. reprint ed. lib. bdg. 24.95 (*0-405-13124-0*) Ayer.

None Dare Call It Conspiracy. Gary Allen. 22.95 (*0-8488-1232-8*) Amereon Ltd.

None Dare Call It Conspiracy. Gary Allen. 142p. 1990. reprint ed. 27.95 (*0-89966-661-2*) Buccaneer Bks.

None Dare Call It Conspiracy. unabridged ed. Gary Allen. 141p. 1971. reprint ed. pap. 10.00 (*0-945001-29-0*) GSG & Assocs.

None Dare Call It Education: What's Happening to Our Schools & Our Children? John Stormer. 224p. 1998. 21.95 (*0-914053-12-4*) Liberty Bell Pr.

None Dare Call It Treason. John A. Stormer. 25.95 (*0-8488-1474-6*) Amereon Ltd.

None Dare Call It Treason. John A. Stormer. 251p. 1990. reprint ed. lib. bdg. 24.95 (*0-89966-725-2*) Buccaneer Bks.

None Dare Call It Treason - 25 Years Later. John A. Stormer. 640p. 1999. pap. 9.95 (*0-914053-10-8*) Liberty Bell Pr.

None Died in Vain: The Saga of the American Civil War. Robert Leckie. LC 89-45832. 704p. 1991. reprint ed. pap. 19.00 (*0-06-092116-1*, Perennial) HarperTrade.

None Had Lances: The Story of the 24th Lancers. Leonard Wills. 240p. (C). 1987. 105.00 (*0-9510718-0-7*, Pub. by Picton) St Mut.

***None of the Above.** Gerald Gardner. 72p. 2000. pap. 8.95 (*0-9676061-2-8*) Tallfellow.

None of the Above: Case for a New Party Animal. Mark R. Koski. LC 92-81224. 256p. 1992. pap. 13.95 (*0-9632635-0-1*) Hyperthyroid.

None of the Above: The Truth Behind the SATs. David Owen & Marilyn Doerr. LC 99-16334. 352p. 1999. 60.00 (*0-8476-9506-9*) Rowman.

None of the Above: The Truth Behind the SATs. rev. ed. David Owen & Marilyn Doerr. LC 99-16334. 352p. 1999. pap. 17.95 (*0-8476-9507-7*, Pub. by Rowman) Natl Bk Netwk.

None of the Above: Why Non-Voters Are America's Political Majority. Sy Leon. 191p. 1996. reprint ed. pap. 12.95 (*0-930073-17-7*) Fox & Wilkes.

None of These Diseases see Nenhuma Enfermidade

None of These Diseases: A Famous Doctor's Biblical Prescription for Healthier & Happier Living. 2nd ed. S. I. McMillen. LC 63-13359. (Illus.). 160p. (YA). (gr. 10). 1993. reprint ed. mass mkt. 5.99 (*0-8007-8030-2*, Spire) Revell.

None of These Diseases: The Bible's Health Secrets for the 21st Century. 3rd rev. ed. S. I. McMillen & David E. Stern. LC 99-59836. (Illus.). 288p. 2000. pap. 12.99 (*0-8007-5719-X*) Revell.

None of This Fun Is My Fault. Rick Detorie. (One Big Happy Ser.). (Illus.). 128p. (J). 1998. pap. 9.95 (*1-56163-217-1*) NBM.

None of This Is on the Map. Dan Murray. LC 98-138601. write for info. (*0-935252-51-7*) Street Pr.

None of This Will Kill Me. Jefferson Carter. 24p. (Orig.). 1987. pap. 5.00 (*0-934910-01-4*) Moon Pony.

None of Your Black Business. Dorothy Morris. LC 90-82800. 105p. (Orig.). (C). 1991. pap. 12.95 (*0-9627732-0-4*) Dell-Morse.

None of Your Business: World Data Flows, Electronic Commerce & the European Privacy Directive. Peter P. Swire & Robert E. Litan. LC 98-25515. 115p. 1998. pap. 12.95 (*0-8157-8239-X*); text 32.95 (*0-8157-8240-3*) Brookings.

None Shall Look Back. Caroline Gordon. LC 92-89827. (Southern Classics Ser.). 398p. 1992. reprint ed. pap. 14.95 (*1-879941-11-2*) J S Sanders.

***None So Blind.** Haldeman. 2000. 23.00 (*0-380-97267-0*) Morrow Avon.

None So Blind. Joe Haldeman. LC 95-4497. 304p. 1996. 22.00 (*0-688-14779-8*, Wm Morrow); 22.00 (*0-614-96770-8*, Avon Bks); 22.00 (*0-614-96940-9*, Avon Bks) Morrow Avon.

None So Blind. Joe Haldeman. 304p. 1997. mass mkt. 5.99 (*0-380-70802-7*, Avon Bks) Morrow Avon.

None So Blind. large type ed. Ivy Preston. (Linford Romance Library). 336p. 1989. pap. 16.99 (*0-7089-6706-X*, Linford) Ulverscroft.

None the Worse for a Hanging. large type ed. Jonathan Ross. (Cloak & Dagger Ser.). 320p. 1995. 21.95 (*0-7862-0567-9*) Thorndike Pr.

None to Accompany Me. Nadine Gordimer. LC 94-7553. 324p. 1994. 22.00 (*0-374-22297-5*) FS&G.

None To Accompany Me. Nadine Gordimer. 336p. 1995. pap. 13.95 (*0-14-025039-5*, Penguin Bks) Viking Penguin.

None Too Fragile: Pearl Jam & Eddie Vedder. Malcolm Butt. 1997. pap. text 16.95 (*0-85965-257-2*, Pub. by Plexus) Publishers Group.

Nonequalibrium Dynamic Processes at Colloidal Interfaces. Yitzhak Shnidman. (ACS Symposium Ser.). 140.00 (*0-8412-3620-8*, Pub. by Am Chemical) OUP.

Nonequilibrium. Mazenko. 300p. (C). 2000. write for info. (*0-471-32841-3*) Wiley.

Nonequilibrium Effects in Ion & Electron Transport. Ed. by J. W. Gallagher et al. LC 90-7893. (Illus.). 480p. 1990. 135.00 (*0-306-43713-9*, Plenum Trade) Perseus Pubng.

Nonequilibrium Electrons & Phonons in Superconductors. A. M. Gulian & G. F. Zharkov. LC 99-30046. (Selected Topics in Superconductivity Ser.). (Illus.). 350p. (C). 1999. text. write for info. (*0-306-46075-0*, Kluwer Plenum) Kluwer Academic.

Nonequilibrium Flows, Vol. 1. Ed. by Peter P. Wegener. LC 71-78829. (Illus.). 268p. reprint ed. pap. 83.10 (*0-608-30552-9*, 205507000001) Bks Demand.

Nonequilibrium Interfacial Transport Processes: Presented at the 18th National Heat Transfer Conference, San Diego, California, August 6-8, 1979. National Heat Transfer Conference Staff. Ed. by J. C. Chen & S. G. Bankoff. LC 79-53412. (Illus.). 95p. reprint ed. pap. 30.00 (*0-8357-2868-4*, 203910400011) Bks Demand.

Nonequilibrium Materials. Ed. by J. Lendvai. (Key Engineering Materials Ser.: Vol. 103). 260p. 1995. 100.00 (*0-87849-694-7*, Pub. by Trans T Pub) Enfield Pubs NH.

Nonequilibrium Phase Transitions in Lattice Models. Joaquin Marro & Ronald Dickman. LC 98-29461. (Collection Alea - Saclay). (Illus.). 300p. (C). 1998. 100.00 (*0-521-48062-0*) Cambridge U Pr.

Nonequilibrium Phase Transitions in Semiconductors. E. Scholl. (Synergetics Ser.: Vol. 35). (Illus.). 330p. 1987. 141.95 (*0-387-17582-2*) Spr-Verlag.

Nonequilibrium Phenomena in Polyatomic Gases Vol. 1: Dilute Gases. Frederick R. McCourt et al. (International Series of Monographs on Chemistry: No. 18). (Illus.). 596p. 1990. text 115.00 (*0-19-855631-4*) OUP.

Nonequilibrium Phenomena in Polyatomic Gases Vol. 2: Cross Sections, Scattering, & Rarefied Gases. Frederick R. McCourt et al. (International Series of Monographs on Chemistry: No. 19). (Illus.). 346p. 1991. text 80.00 (*0-19-855648-9*) OUP.

Nonequilibrium Problems in Many-Particle Systems. Ed. by Carlo Cercignani & Mario Pulvirenti. (Lecture Notes in Mathematics Ser.: Vol. 1551). (Illus.). 158p. 1993. pap. write for info. (*3-540-56945-6*) Spr-Verlag.

Nonequilibrium Problems in Many-Particle Systems: Lectures Given at the 3rd Session of the Centro Internazionale Metematico Estive held in Montecatini, Italy, June 1992. L. Arkeryd. LC 93-5230. (Lecture Notes in Mathematics Ser.: Vol. 1551). 1993. 37.95 (*0-387-56945-6*) Spr-Verlag.

Nonequilibrium Processes in Catalysis. Oleg V. Krylov & Boris R. Shub.Tr. of Neravnovesnye Protsessy v Katalize. 320p. 1993. lib. bdg. 115.00 (*0-8493-4478-6*, QD505) CRC Pr.

Nonequilibrium Processes in Partially Ionized Gases. Ed. by M. Capitelli & J. N. Bardsley. (NATO ASI Ser.: Vol. 220). (Illus.). 706p. (C). 1990. text 186.00 (*0-306-43586-1*, Kluwer Plenum) Kluwer Academic.

Nonequilibrium Processes in the Planetary & Cometary Atmospheres: Theory & Applications. Mikhail I. Marov. LC 97-26117. (Astrophysics & Space Science Library). 1997. text 146.00 (*0-7923-4686-6*) Kluwer Academic.

***Nonequilibrium Statistical Mechanics.** Robert Zwanzig. (Illus.). 224p. 2001. text 60.00 (*0-19-514018-4*) OUP.

Nonequilibrium Statistical Mechanics: Ensemble Method. B. C. Eu. LC 98-10598. (Fundamental Theories of Physics Ser.). 387p. 1998. 173.00 (*0-7923-4980-6*) Kluwer Academic.

Nonequilibrium Statistical Mechanics in One Dimension. Ed. by Vladimir Privman. LC 96-45965. (Illus.). 488p. (C). 1997. text 110.00 (*0-521-55974-X*) Cambridge U Pr.

Nonequilibrium Statistical Mechanics of Heterogeneous Fluid Systems. Andrei G. Bashkirov. LC 94-23470. 176p. 1995. boxed set 149.95 (*0-8493-2860-8*) CRC Pr.

Nonequilibrium Statistical Mechanics of Open & Closed Systems. K. Lindenberg & B. J. West. 448p. 1990. 89.95 (*0-471-18683-X*) Wiley.

Nonequilibrium Statistical Mechanics of Open & Closed Systems. Katja Lindenburg & Bruce J. West. (Illus.). xi, 448p. 1990. 55.00 (*0-89573-347-1*, Wiley-VCH) Wiley.

Nonequilibrium Statistical Thermodynamics. Bernard H. Lavenda. LC 84-26992. 213p. reprint ed. pap. 66.10 (*0-7837-4010-7*, 204384000011) Bks Demand.

Nonequilibrium Superconductivity. Ed. by Vitaly L. Ginzburg. (Proceedings of the Lebedev Physics Institute Ser.: Vol. 174). 289p. 1988. text 165.00 (*0-941743-09-8*) Nova Sci Pubs.

Nonequilibrium Systems in Natural Water Chemistry. American Chemical Society, Division of Water, Air,. LC 76-170252. (Advances in Chemistry Ser.: No. 106). (Illus.). 352p. 1971. reprint ed. pap. 109.20 (*0-608-03277-8*, 206379500007) Bks Demand.

Nonequilibrium Theory & Extremum Principles. Ed. by Stanislaw Sieniutycz & Peter Salamon. (Advances in Thermodynamics Ser.: Vol. 3). 557p. 1990. 79.00 (*0-8448-1667-1*, Pub. by Tay Francis Ltd) Taylor & Francis.

Nonequilibrium Thermodynamics in Biophysics. Aharon Katzir-Katchalsky & Peter F. Curran. LC 65-22045. (Harvard Books in Biophysics: No. 1). 260p. reprint ed. pap. 80.60 (*0-7837-2283-4*, 205737100004) Bks Demand.

***Nonesuch.** Georgette Heyer. 2000. per. 5.99 (*0-373-83444-6*) Harlequin Bks.

Nonesuch. Georgette Heyer. 1997. 23.95 (*1-56723-054-7*) Yestermorrow.

Nonesuch Creek: Selected Poems, 1969 to '79. Al Masarik. Ed. by Kirk Robertson. LC 80-65779. (Windriver Ser.). 112p. (Orig.). 1980. pap. 4.50 (*0-916918-12-2*) Duck Down.

Nonexistent Compounds: Compounds of Low Stability. W. E. Dasent. LC 65-27436. 191p. reprint ed. pap. 59.30 (*0-608-30362-3*, 205503500008) Bks Demand.

Nonexistent Knight & the Cloven Viscount. Italo Calvino. Ed. by J. Ferrone & H. Wolff. LC 76-39699. 264p. 1977. pap. 11.00 (*0-15-665975-1*, Harvest Bks) Harcourt.

Nonexistent Objects. Terence Parsons. LC 79-21682. 280p. 1980. 50.00 (*0-300-02404-5*) Yale U Pr.

Nonexistent Objects: Meinong & Contemporary Philosophy. Kenneth J. Perszyk. LC 93-11875. (Nijhoff International Philosophy Ser.). 324p. (C). 1993. lib. bdg. 174.50 (*0-7923-2461-7*, Pub. by Kluwer Academic) Kluwer Academic.

Nonextrapolative Methods in Business Forecasting: Scenarios, Vision, & Issues Management. Ed. by Jay S. Mendell & F. John Pessolano. LC 84-18093. (Illus.). 222p. 1985. 65.00 (*0-89930-066-9*, MHF/, Quorum Bks) Greenwood.

Nonfederal Housing Programs: How States & Localities Are Responding to Federal Cutbacks in Low-Income Housing Programs. 2nd ed. Michael A. Stegman & J. David Holden. LC 99-61432. 231p. 1987. pap. 44.95 (*0-87420-673-1*, N09) Urban Land.

Nonferrous-Electrical Conference, 1984. 30.00 (*0-318-04237-1*) Wire Assn Intl.

Nonferrous-Electrical Conference, 1983. Wire Association International Staff. 30.00 (*0-318-03215-5*, 7831) Wire Assn Intl.

Nonferrous-Electrical Conference, 1982. Wire Association International Staff. 30.00 (*0-318-03218-X*, 7822) Wire Assn Intl.

Nonferrous-Electrical Conference, 1980. Wire Association International Staff. 30.00 (*0-318-03225-2*, 7802) Wire Assn Intl.

Nonferrous-Electrical Conference, 1978. Wire Association International Staff. 30.00 (*0-318-03227-9*, 7781) Wire Assn Intl.

Nonferrous Extractive Metallurgy. C. B. Gill. LC 87-29393. 360p. (C). 1988. reprint ed. lib. bdg. 59.50 (*0-89464-264-2*) Krieger.

Nonferrous Metals: Industry Structure. (Illus.). 90p. (Orig.). (C). 1992. pap. text 40.00 (*1-56806-120-X*) DIANE Pub.

Nonferrous Wire Handbook, 2 vols. Wire Association International Staff. 40.00 (*0-685-09392-1*, 8521) Wire Assn Intl.

Nonferrous Wire Handbook, Vol. 1. Wire Association International Staff. 65.00 (*0-318-03176-0*, 8529) Wire Assn Intl.

Nonferrous Wire Handbook, 2 vols., Vol. 2. Wire Association International Staff. 40.00 (*0-685-09391-3*, 8520) Wire Assn Intl.

Nonferrous Wire Handbook: Principles & Practice, Vol. 3. Ed. by Horace Pops. (Illus.). 678p. (C). 1995. text 125.00 (*1-877836-20-6*) Wire Assn Intl.

Nonferrous Wire Handbook Vol. 1: Nonferrous Wire Rod. 2nd ed. Ed. by Laurence W. Collins et al. (Illus.). 417p. 1979. 50.00 (*0-685-26881-0*) Wire Assn Intl.

Nonferrous Wire Handbooks, 2 vols. 2nd ed. Ed. by Laurence W. Collins et al. (Illus.). 1981. 80.00 (*0-685-26882-9*) Wire Assn Intl.

Nonfiction see Young Adult Reading Activities Library

Nonfiction: A Critical Approach. Center for Learning Network Staff. 275p. spiral bd. 37.95 (*1-56077-396-0*) Ctr Learning.

***Nonfiction Book Proposal Anybody Can Write: A Contract & Advance Before You Write Your Book.** 2nd ed. Elizabeth Lyon. 2000. pap. 18.95 (*0-936085-45-2*) Blue Heron OR.

Nonfiction Book Proposals Anybody Can Write: How to Get a Contract & Advance Before You Write Your Book. Elizabeth C. Lyon. LC 96-167212. 240p. (Orig.). (C). 1995. pap. 17.95 (*0-936085-31-2*) Blue Heron OR.

Nonfiction Books for Children: Activities for Thinking, Learning, & Doing. Carol A. Doll. x, 117p. 1990. pap. text 19.50 (*0-87287-710-8*) Teacher Ideas Pr.

Nonfiction English 4 Syllabus. Ed. by Elizabeth Horton & Elisabeth Dousey. Orig. Title: English 4 Syllabus. 28p. (YA). (gr. 10-12). 1998. pap. text 4.95 (*1-57896-037-1*, 1911) Hewitt Res Fnd.

Nonfiction English 1 Syllabus. 2nd ed. Ed. by Elizabeth Horton & Elisabeth Doucey. Orig. Title: English Syllabus 1. (Illus.). 24p. (YA). (gr. 10-12). 1998. pap. text 4.95 (*1-57896-034-7*, 1908) Hewitt Res Fnd.

Nonfiction English 3 Syllabus. Ed. by Elizabeth Horton & Elisabeth Dousey. Orig. Title: English 3 Syllabus. 44p. (YA). (gr. 10-12). 1998. pap. text 4.95 (*1-57896-036-3*, 1910) Hewitt Res Fnd.

Nonfiction English 2 Syllabus. Ed. by Elizabeth Horton & Elisabeth Doucey. Orig. Title: English 2 Syllabus. 22p. (YA). (gr. 10-12). 1998. pap. text 4.95 (*1-57896-035-5*, 1909) Hewitt Res Fnd.

Nonfiction Film: A Critical History. rev. ed. Richard M. Barsam. LC 91-26985. (Illus.). 504p. 1992. text 72.50 (*0-253-31124-1*); pap. text 24.95 (*0-253-20706-1*, MB 706) Ind U Pr.

Nonfiction Matters: Reading, Writing, & Research in Grades 3-8. Stephanie Harvey. LC 97-36584. (Illus.). 248p. 1998. pap. text 19.50 (*1-57110-072-5*) Stenhse Pubs.

Nonfinancial Economics: The Case for Shorter Hours of Work. Eugene McCarthy & William McGaughey. LC 88-28833. 244p. 1989. 55.00 (*0-275-92514-5*, C2514, Praeger Pubs) Greenwood.

Nonformal Education & National Development: A Critical Assessment of Policy, Research, & Practice. Ed. by John C. Bock & George J. Papagiannis. LC 83-4031. (Praeger Studies in Comparative Education). 390p. 1983. 38.95 (*0-275-90949-2*, C0949, Praeger Pubs) Greenwood.

Nonformal Education & the Poor in Latin America & the Caribbean: Stability, Reform, or Revolution. Thomas J. LaBelle. LC 85-25783. 384p. 1986. 36.95 (*0-275-92078-X*, C2078, Praeger Pubs) Greenwood.

Nonformal Education As an Empowering Process. Suzanne Kindervatter. Ed. by Center for International Education Staff. 281p. 1979. spiral bd. 6.00 (*0-932288-54-5*) Ctr Intl Ed U of MA.

Nonformal Education for Women in Zimbabwe: Empowerment Strategies & Status Improvement. Christine Hausmann. (Erziehungskonzeptionen Und Praxis. Bd. : Vol. 751). xxii, 172p. 1998. pap. 37.95 (*3-631-33683-7*) P Lang Pubng.

Nonformal Education for Women in Zimbabwe Vol. 751: Empowerment Strategies & Status Improvement. Christine Hausmann. (European University Studies: No. 11). XXII, 172p. 1998. pap. text 37.95 (*0-8204-3616-X*) P Lang Pubng.

Nonformal Education in Ecuador. 232p. (Orig.). 1975. pap. 6.00 (*0-932288-31-6*) PERC.

N

An Asterisk (*) at the beginning of an entry indicates that the title is appearing for the first time.

Nonformal Education in Ghana. Ed. by David C. Kinsey & John W. Bing. 203p. (Orig.). (C). 1978. pap. 6.00 (*0-932288-52-9*) Ctr Intl Ed U of MA.

Nonformal Education in Latin America: An Annotated Bibliography. Susan L. Poston. LC 75-620142. (Reference Ser.: Vol. 8). 268p. 1976. 16.95 (*0-87903-108-5*) UCLA Lat Am Ctr.

Nonfoundationalism. John E. Thiel. LC 94-2159. 112p. 1994. pap. 14.00 (*0-8006-2692-3*, 1-2692, Fortress Pr) Augsburg Fortress.

Nonfuel Minerals: Foreign Dependence & National Security. Raymond F. Mikesell. LC 86-27247. (Illus.). 269p. reprint ed. pap. 83.40 (*0-7837-4719-5*, 205907100003) Bks Demand.

Nongenotoxic Carcinogenesis. Ed. by A. Cockburn & L. Smith. (Ernst Schering Research Foundation Workshop Ser.: Vol. 10). (Illus.). 252p. 1994. 69.95 (*0-387-58342-4*) Spr-Verlag.

Nongenotoxic Mechanisms in Carcinogenesis. Ed. by Bryon Butterworth & Thomas J. Slaga. (Banbury Reports: No. 25). 385p. 1987. text 70.00 (*0-87969-225-1*) Cold Spring Harbor.

Nongolfer's Cookbook. Elizabeth Klungness & James G. Klungness. (Illus.). 160p. 1982. pap. 5.95 (*0-910431-00-0*) Tower Ent.

Nongonococcal Urethritis & Other Selected Sexually Transmitted Diseases of Public Health Importance. (Technical Report Ser.: No. 660). 142p. 1981. pap. text 9.00 (*92-4-120660-8*) World Health.

Nongovernmental Organizations & Local Development, No. 40. Ed. by Michael M. Cernea. LC 88-27971. (Discussion Paper Ser.). 70p. 1988. pap. 22.00 (*0-8213-1148-4*, 20040) World Bank.

Nongovernmental Organizations & the Ideas of Human Rights. Lowell W. Livezey. (World Order Studies Program Occasional Paper: No. 15). 199p. (Orig.). 1988. pap. text 11.00 (*0-945101-00-7*) Princeton CIS.

Nongovernmental Organizations & the Ideas of Human Rights. Lowell W. Livezey. LC 87-34939. (World Order Studies Program Occasional Paper: No. 15). 201p. (Orig.). reprint ed. pap. 62.40 (*0-8357-8527-0*, 203482500091) Bks Demand.

Nongovernments: NGOs & the Political Development of the Third World. Julie Fisher. LC 97-14228. (Books on International Development). (Illus.). 256p. 1997. 45.00 (*1-56549-075-4*); pap. 24.95 (*1-56549-074-6*) Kumarian Pr.

N

Nongraded Elementary School. 2nd rev. ed. John I. Goodlad & Robert Anderson. 296p. 1987. reprint ed. pap. text 18.95 (*0-8077-2845-4*) Tchrs Coll.

Nongraded Primary: Making Schools Fit Children. American Association of School Administrators Staf. 28p. 1992. pap. 2.50 (*0-87652-184-7*, 21-00192) Am Assn Sch Admin.

Nongradedness: Helping It to Happen. Robert Anderson & Barbara N. Pavan. LC 92-62813. 250p. 1999. pap. text 24.95 (*0-87762-980-3*) Scarecrow.

Nongynecologic Cytologic Specimens: Collection & Cytopreparatory Techniques; Proposed Guideline (1997) 1997. 25.00 (*1-56238-338-8*, GP23-P) NCCLS.

***Nonholonomic Motion of Rigid Mechanical Systems from a DAE Viewpoint.** Patrick J. Rabier & Werner C. Rheinboldt. LC 99-53790. (Miscellaneous Titles in Applied Mathematics Ser.: No. 68). (Illus.). 140p. 2000. pap. 36.00 (*0-89871-446-X*, OT0068) Soc Indus-Appl Math.

Nonholonomic Motion Planning. Ed. by Zexiang Li & J. F. Canny. LC 92-27560. (Kluwer International Series in Engineering & Computer Science). 1992. text 187.00 (*0-7923-9275-2*) Kluwer Academic.

Nonhuman Environment in Normal Development & in Schizophrenia. Harold F. Searles. LC 60-9579. (Monograph Series on Schizophrenia: No. 5). 464p. 1960. 70.00 (*0-8236-3660-7*) Intl Univs Pr.

Nonhuman Primate Models for Human Diseases. Ed. by W. Richard Dukelow. LC 82-4519. 208p. 1983. 123.00 (*0-8493-6466-3*, RB125, CRC Reprint) Franklin.

Nonhuman Primates. Ed. by Phyllis Dolhinow & Augustin Fuentes. LC 98-45272. 1999. pap. text 32.95 (*1-55934-974-3*) Mayfield Pub.

Nonhuman Primates, 2 vols. Ed. by R. D. Hunt et al. Incl. Vol. I. LC 92-45285. (Illus.). 221p. 1993. 320.00 (*0-944398-15-4*); Vol. II. LC 92-45285. (Illus.). 264p. 1993. 320.00 (*0-944398-16-2*); (Monographs on Pathology of Laboratory Animals). 600.00 (*0-614-23193-0*, 398618) ILSI.

Nonhuman Primates, No. I. Ed. by Thomas C. Jones et al. LC 92-45285. (Monographs on Pathology of Laboratory Animals). 1995. 289.00 (*0-387-56465-9*) Spr-Verlag.

Nonhuman Primates & Human Diseases see Primatology: Proceedings of the International Congress of Primatology, 4th, Portland, 1972

Nonhuman Primates in Biomedical Research. William Montagna. LC 76-7881. (Wesley W. Spink Lectures on Comparative Medicine: No. 3). (Illus.). 161p. reprint ed. pap. 50.00 (*0-8357-8972-1*, 203327300085) Bks Demand.

Nonhuman Primates in Biomedical Research: Diseases. Ed. by B. Taylor Bennett et al. (Illus.). 512p. 1998. 132.00 (*0-12-088665-0*) Acad Pr.

Nonhuman Primates in Biomedical Research Vol. 1: Biology & Management. Ed. by B. Taylor Bennett et al. (Illus.). 428p. 1995. text 132.00 (*0-12-088661-8*) Acad Pr.

Nonhuman Primates in Perinatal Research. Ed. by Yves W. Brans & Thomas J. Kuehl. LC 87-29578. 500p. (C). 1988. text 85.00 (*0-471-84916-2*) Krieger.

Nonhydrocarbon Methods of Geophysical Formation Evaluation. James K. Hallenburg. LC 97-29081. 288p. 1997. lib. bdg. 59.95 (*1-56670-262-3*) Lewis Pubs.

Noni. Rita Elkins. (The Woodland Health Ser.). 1997. pap. text 3.95 (*1-885670-67-2*) Woodland UT.

Noni: Aspirin of the Ancients. 2nd large type ed. Diana Fairechild. (Illus.). 152p. 1998. pap. 9.95 (*0-9630198-6-4*, Pub. by Flyana) New Leaf Dist.

***Noni Phenomenon.** Neil Solomon. (Illus.). 1999. pap. 14.95 (*1-887938-87-7*) Snd Concepts.

Nonideal Plasma. E. V. Fortov & I. T. Iakubov. 360p. 1998. 68.00 (*981-02-3305-1*) World Scientific Pub.

Nonie of the Everglades, Vol. 1. Ann O'Connell Rust. Ed. by Allen F. Rust. LC 98-74242. 72p. (J). (gr. 4-7). 1998. pap. 7.95 (*1-883203-04-X*) Amaro Bks.

***Nonimaging Optics.** Ed. by Roland Winston. 1999. pap. text 72.00 (*0-8194-3267-9*) SPIE.

Nonimaging Optics: Maximum Efficiency Light Transfer IV. Ed. by Roland Winston. LC 98-122020. 25p. 1997. pap. 59.00 (*0-8194-2561-3*) SPIE.

Nonincendive Electrical Equipment for Use in Class I & II, Division 2 & Class III, Divisions I & 2 Hazardous: S12.12. ANSI/ISA Staff. 1994. pap. 55.00 (*1-55617-518-3*, S12.12) ISA.

Nonindigenous Fishes Introduced into Inland Waters of the United States. Ed. by P. L. Fuller et al. LC 98-88571. (Special Publication Ser.: Vol. 27). (Illus.). 624p. 1999. text 49.00 (*1-888569-14-X*, 510.27) Am Fisheries Soc.

***Nonindigenous Freshwater Organisms: Biology & Impact.** Renata Claudi. (Illus.). 500p. 1999. text 89.95 (*0-8493-4104-3*) CRC Pr.

Nonindigenous Freshwater Organisms: Vectors, Biology & Impacts. Ed. by Renata Claudi & Joseph H. Leach. LC 99-28607. 480p. 1999. boxed set 89.95 (*1-56670-449-9*) Lewis Pubs.

Nonindustrial Photoelectric Switches for Lighting Control, UL 773A. 4th ed. 1995. write for info. (*1-55989-886-0*) Underwrtrs Labs.

Nonindustrial Private Forests: A Review of Economic & Policy Studies: Symposium Proceedings, April 19-20, 1983. Ed. by Jack P. Royer & Christopher D. Risbrudt. LC SD0387.W6N66. (Illus.). 406p. reprint ed. pap. 125.90 (*0-8357-8252-2*, 203395800087) Bks Demand.

Nonindustrial Private Forests: Data & Information Needs: Conference Proceedings, April 17-18, 1980, Duke University, Durham, North Carolina. Ed. by Jack P. Royer & Frank J. Convery. LC SD0143.N65. (Illus.). 136p. reprint ed. pap. 42.20 (*0-7837-6037-X*, 204585000008) Bks Demand.

Noninfectious Diseases of Wildlife. 2nd ed. Ed. by Anne Fairbrother et al. LC 96-33967. (Illus.). 246p. 1996. text 52.95 (*0-8138-0451-5*) Iowa St U Pr.

Noninstitutional Senior Market for Healthcare Products & Services. 2nd ed. Ed. by Peter Allen. 250p. 1984. pap. 295.00 (*0-931634-46-6*) FIND-SVP.

Noninsulin-Dependent Diabetes: A Management Guide for Patients. (Illus.). 90p. (Orig.). (C). 1994. pap. text 20.00 (*0-7881-1033-0*) DIANE Pub.

Nonintegral Marine Fuel Tanks, UL 1102. 5th ed. (C). 1999. pap. text 230.00 (*1-55989-242-0*) Underwrtrs Labs.

Noninteracting Control with Stability for Nonlinear System. Stefano Battilotti. LC 94-11384. (Lecture Notes in Control & Information Sciences: Vol. 196). 1994. write for info. (*0-387-19891-1*) Spr-Verlag.

Noninvasive Access to Cardiovascular Dynamics: Experimental & Applied. Ed. by G. Juznic et al. (Bibliotheca Cardiologica Ser.: No. 37). (Illus.). 1979. pap. 122.75 (*3-8055-2970-8*) S Karger.

Noninvasive Approaches to Pain Management in the Terminally Ill. Ed. by Caryn S. Feldman. LC 92-1485. (Hospice Journal: Vol. 8, Nos. 1-2). (Illus.). 232p. 1992. pap. text 19.95 (*1-56024-301-5*) Haworth Pr.

Noninvasive Approaches to Pain Management in the Terminally Ill. Ed. by Caryn S. Feldman. LC 92-1485. (Hospice Journal: Vol. 8, Nos. 1-2). (Illus.). 232p. 1992. lib. bdg. 49.95 (*1-56024-300-7*) Haworth Pr.

Noninvasive Assessment of the Visual System. Ed. by Dean Yager. LC 96-72423. (Trends in Optics & Photonics Ser.: Vol. 11). (Illus.). 209p. 1997. pap. 55.00 (*1-55752-471-8*) Optical Soc.

Noninvasive Cardiac Assessment Technology. Ed. by Dhanjoo N. Ghista. (Advances in Cardiovascular Physics Ser.: Vol. 6). (Illus.). x, 190p. 1989. 165.25 (*3-8055-4839-7*) S Karger.

Noninvasive Cardiac Imaging. Ed. by Joel Morganroth et al. LC 82-11095. (Illus.). 458p. reprint ed. pap. 142.00 (*0-8357-7624-7*, 205694700096) Bks Demand.

Noninvasive Diagnosis of Kidney Disease. G. Lubec. (Continuing Education Ser.: Vol. 3). (Illus.). xii, 368p. 1983. 85.25 (*3-8055-3051-X*) S Karger.

Noninvasive Diagnosis of Peripheral Vascular Disease. Ed. by W. Robert Felix, Jr. LC 87-13004. (Illus.). 264p. 1988. reprint ed. pap. 81.90 (*0-608-05782-7*, 205974700007) Bks Demand.

Noninvasive Diagnosis of Vascular Disease. Ed. by Falls B. Hershey et al. LC 83-22310. (Illus.). 371p. 1984. text 52.50 (*0-941022-01-3*) Davies Pubng.

Noninvasive Diagnostic Techniques in Ophthalmology. Ed. by Barry R. Masters. (Illus.). 632p. 1990. 199.00 (*0-387-96992-6*) Spr-Verlag.

Noninvasive Electrocardiology. Moss. 1995. text 65.00 (*0-7020-1925-9*, W B Saunders Co) Harcrt Hlth Sci Grp.

Noninvasive Evaluation of Hemodynamcis in Congenital Heart Disease: Doppler Ultrasound Applications in the Adult & Pediatric Patient with Congenital Heart Disease. Ed. by James V. Chapman & George R. Sutherland. (Developments in Cardiovascular Medicine Ser.). (C). 1990. text 268.50 (*0-7923-0836-0*) Kluwer Academic.

Noninvasive Evaluation of Human Circulation: Clinical Clinicopharmacological & Data Processing Aspects. J. Simonyi & J. Fischer. 250p. (C). 1976. 45.00 (*963-05-0787-0*, Pub. by Akade Kiado) St Mut.

Noninvasive Imaging of Cardiac Metabolism. Ed. by Ernst E. Van der Wall. (Developments in Cardiovascular Medicine Ser.). 1987. text 272.50 (*0-89838-812-0*) Kluwer Academic.

Noninvasive Imaging of Congenital Heart Disease: Before & after Surgical Reconstruction. Alvin J. Chin. LC 93-39613. (Illus.). 400p. 1994. 128.00 (*0-87993-574-X*) Futura Pub.

Noninvasive Methods in Atherosclerosis Research. fac. ed. Ed. by Ruth J. Hegyeli. LC 82-40287. (Atherosclerosis Reviews Ser.: No. 10). (Illus.). 214p. pap. 66.40 (*0-7837-7504-0*, 204700200005) Bks Demand.

Noninvasive Respiratory Monitoring. Ed. by Michael L. Nochomovitz & Neil S. Cherniak. (Contemporary Issues in Pulmonary Disease Ser.: Vol. 3). (Illus.). 229p. 1986. text 42.00 (*0-443-08342-8*) Church.

Noninvasive Respiratory Monitoring. fac. ed. Ed. by Michael L. Nochomovitz & Neil S. Cherniack. LC 85-24275. (Contemporary Issues in Pulmonary Disease Ser.: No. 3). (Illus.). 239p. 1986. reprint ed. pap. 74.10 (*0-7837-7824-4*, 204758000008) Bks Demand.

Noninvasive Techniques for Assessment of Atherosclerosis in Peripheral, Carotid, & Coronary Arteries. fac. ed. Ed. by Thomas F. Budinger et al. LC 82-20437. (Illus.). 269p. pap. 83.40 (*0-7837-7207-6*, 204709200005) Bks Demand.

Noninvasive Techniques in Cardiology for the Nurse & Technician. Alberto Benchimol. LC 78-9047. (Illus.). 332p. reprint ed. pap. 103.00 (*0-608-30220-1*, 201584700097) Bks Demand.

Noninvasive Techniques in Cell Biology. Ed. by J. Kevin Foskett & Sergio Grinstein. LC 90-12359. (Modern Cell Biology Ser.: Vol. 9). 423p. 1990. 245.00 (*0-471-56809-0*) Wiley.

Noninvasive Vascular Diagnosis. Ed. by Ali F. AbuRahma & John J. Bergan. LC 98-50138. 1999. 265.00 (*1-85233-128-3*, Pub. by Spr-Verlag) Spr-Verlag.

Noninvasive Vascular Laboratory: Current Issues & Clinical Developments. Ed. by Marsha M. Neumyer & Arthur I. Auer. Date not set. text. write for info. (*0-941022-28-5*) Davies Pubng.

Nonionic Surfactants: Chemical Analysis. John Cross. (Surfactant Science Ser.: Vol. 19). (Illus.). 432p. 1986. text 215.00 (*0-8247-7626-7*) Dekker.

Nonionic Surfactants: Organic Chemistry. Ed. by Van Os. LC 97-43114. (Surfactant Science Ser.). (Illus.). 312p. 1997. text 145.00 (*0-8247-9997-6*) Dekker.

Nonionic Surfactants: Physical Chemistry. 2nd rev. ed. Martin J. Schick. (Surfactant Science Ser.: Vol. 23). (Illus.). 1158p. 1987. text 295.00 (*0-8247-7530-9*) Dekker.

Nonionic Surfactants: Polyoxyalkylerie Block Copolymers. Ed. by Vaughn M. Nace. (Surfactant Science Ser.: Vol. 60). (Illus.). 280p. 1996. text 150.00 (*0-8247-9700-0*) Dekker.

***Nonionic Surfactants in Western Europe, North America & Japan: Potential Applications & Markets 1998-2003-2008.** Willinger. LC 99-474318. 250p. 1999. pap. 4500.00 (*0-471-34909-7*) Wiley.

Nonionizing Electromagnetic Radiations & Ultrasound: Proceedings of the Twenty Second Annual Meeting of the National Council on Radiation Protection & Measurements. LC 88-9974. (Annual Meeting Proceedings Ser.: No. 8). 384p. (Orig.). 1988. pap. text 40.00 (*0-913392-95-2*) NCRP Pubns.

Nonionizing Radiation: A Case for Federal Standards? Jane Clemmensen. (Illus.). 1984. pap. 20.00 (*0-911302-51-4*) San Francisco Pr.

Nonionizing Radiation: Questions & Answers. M. G. Yost. (Illus.). 1988. pap. 10.00 (*0-911302-61-1*) San Francisco Pr.

Nonionizing Radiation Protection. 2nd ed. Ed. by Michael J. Seuss & D. A. Benwell-Morison. (WHO Regional Publications, European Ser.: No. 25). xiv, 346p. 1989. pap. text 34.40 (*92-890-1101-7*, 1310025) World Health.

Nonionizing Radiation Protection. 2nd ed. Suess & Benwell-Morison. (WHO Regional Publications, European Ser.: No. 25). 350p. 1989. text 43.00 (*92-890-1116-5*) World Health.

Nonisotopic Alternatives to Radioimmunoassay: Principles & Applications. Ed. by Lawrence A. Kaplan & Amadeo J. Pesce. LC 81-17310. (Clinical & Biochemical Analysis Ser.: No. 10). (Illus.). 356p. reprint ed. pap. 110.40 (*0-7837-4737-3*, 204454500004) Bks Demand.

Nonisotopic DNA Probe Techniques. Larry J. Kricka. (Illus.). 358p. 1992. pap. 53.00 (*0-12-426296-1*) Acad Pr.

Nonisotopic Immunoassay. T. T. Ngo. LC 87-36105. (Illus.). 512p. (C). 1988. text 125.00 (*0-306-42811-3*, Kluwer Plenum) Kluwer Academic.

Nonisotropic & Variable Outflows from Stars. Ed. by L. Drissen et al. (ASP Conference Series Proceedings: Vol. 22). 408p. 1992. 34.00 (*0-937707-41-4*) Astron Soc Pacific.

Nonisotropic Probing, Blotting, & Sequencing. 2nd ed. Ed. by Larry J. Kricka. (Illus.). 518p. 1995. 42.00 (*0-12-426292-9*); text 84.00 (*0-12-426291-0*) Acad Pr.

***Noniterative Coordination in Multilevel Systems** Todor Stoilov & Krassimira Stoilova. LC 99-37723. (Nonconvex Optimization & Its Applications Ser.). 1999. write for info. (*0-7923-5879-1*) Kluwer Academic.

Nonius Marcellus: Dictionary of Republican Latin. Ed. by Wallace M. Lindsay. (St. Andrews University Publications: No. 1). 120p. 1985. reprint ed. 25.87 (*3-487-01092-5*) G Olms Pubs.

Nonjudicial Foreclosures on Cooperative Apartments. (Real Estate Law & Practice Course Handbook Ser.). 224p. 1992. ring bd. 70.00 (*0-685-69468-2*) PLI.

Nonlethal Weapons: War Without Death. David A. Morehouse. LC 96-16271. 160p. 1996. 55.00 (*0-275-95170-7*, Praeger Pubs) Greenwood.

***Nonlinear: A Field Guide to Digital & Video Editing.** 4th rev. ed. Michael Rubin & Ron Diamond. (Illus.). 400p. (C). 2000. pap. 39.95 (*0-937404-85-3*) Triad Pub FL.

Nonlinear: A Guide to Digital Film & Video Editing. 3rd ed. Michael Rubin. LC 95-40791. (Illus.). 320p. (Orig.). (C). 1995. pap. 29.95 (*0-937404-84-5*) Triad Pub FL.

Nonlinear Acoustics. Robert T. Beyer. LC 97-77103. 452p. 1997. 55.00 (*1-56396-724-3*) Am Inst Physics.

Nonlinear Acoustics. K. A. Naugolnykh & L. A. Ostrovsky. (Research Trends in Physics Ser.). (Illus.). 336p. 1994. boxed set 94.95 (*1-56396-338-8*) Spr-Verlag.

Nonlinear Acoustics: Theory & Applications. Ed. by Mark F. Hamilton & David T. Blackstock. LC 97-35867. (Illus.). 455p. 1997. text 95.00 (*0-12-321860-8*) Morgan Kaufmann.

***Nonlinear Acoustics at the Turn of the Millennium: ISNA 15, 15th International Symposium.** Ed. by Werner Lauterborn & Thomas Kurz. LC 00-104855. (AIP Conference Proceedings Ser.: Vol. 524). (Illus.). xxii, 591p. 2000. 185.00 (*1-56396-945-9*) Am Inst Physics.

Nonlinear Active Microwave Circuits. T. Berceli. 1987. pap. 130.00 (*963-05-4303-6*, Pub. by Akade Kiado) St Mut.

Nonlinear Analysis. Ed. by Themistocles M. Rassias. 572p. 1988. text 99.00 (*9971-5-0140-6*) World Scientific Pub.

Nonlinear Analysis & Applications. V. Lakshmikantham. (Lecture Notes in Pure & Applied Mathematics Ser.: Vol. 109). (Illus.). 680p. 1987. pap. text 190.00 (*0-8247-7810-3*) Dekker.

Nonlinear Analysis & Applications. Ed. by S. P. Singh & J. H. Burry. (Lecture Notes in Pure & Applied Mathematics Ser.: Vol. 80). (Illus.). 488p. 1982. pap. text 165.75 (*0-8247-1790-2*) Dekker.

Nonlinear Analysis & Continuum Mechanics: Papers for the 65th Birthday of James Serrin. J. Serrin. Ed. by G. Butazzo et al. LC 97-26098. (Illus.). 160p. 1997. 49.00 (*0-387-98296-5*) Spr-Verlag.

***Nonlinear Analysis & Convex Analysis.** Ed. by Wataru Takahashi & Tamaki Tanaka. 350p. 1999. 86.00 (*981-02-4074-0*) World Scientific Pub.

Nonlinear Analysis & Microlocal Analysis: Proceedings of the International Conference at the Nankai Institute of Mathematics. K. C. Chang et al. (Nankai Series in Pure, Applied Mathematics & Theoretical Physics). 400p. 1992. text 78.00 (*981-02-0913-4*) World Scientific Pub.

Nonlinear Analysis & Optimization. Ed. by C. Vinti. (Lecture Notes in Mathematics Ser.: Vol. 1107). v, 214p. 1985. 37.95 (*0-387-13903-6*) Spr-Verlag.

Nonlinear Analysis in Soil Mechanics: Theory & Implementation. Wai-Fah Chen & E. Mizuno. (Developments in Geotechnical Engineering Ser.: No. 53). 672p. 1990. 245.50 (*0-444-43043-1*) Elsevier.

Nonlinear Analysis, 1989 Conference. Ed. by F. C. Liu & T. P. Liu. 384p. (C). 1991. text 113.00 (*981-02-0136-2*) World Scientific Pub.

Nonlinear Analysis of Physiological Data. Ed. by H. Kantz et al. LC 98-5675. 350p. 1998. 59.95 (*3-540-63481-9*) Spr-Verlag.

Nonlinear Analysis of Shell Structures. Anthony N. Palazotto & Scott T. Dennis. (Educ Ser.). 245p. (C). 1992. text 61.95 (*1-56347-033-0*, 33-0) AIAA.

Nonlinear Analysis of Shells by Finite Elements. Ed. by F. G. Rammerstorfer. (CISM International Centre for Mechanical Sciences Ser.: Vol. 328). (Illus.). v, 283p. 1992. 86.95 (*0-387-82416-2*) Spr-Verlag.

Nonlinear Analysis of Structures. M. Sathyamoorthy. LC 97-27731. (CRC Mechanical Engineering Ser.). 640p. 1997. boxed set 94.95 (*0-8493-9652-2*) CRC Pr.

Nonlinear Analysis on Manifolds: Monge-Ampere Equations. T. Aubin. (Grundlehren der Mathematischen Wissenschaften Ser.: Vol. 252). 204p. 1982. 107.95 (*0-387-90704-1*) Spr-Verlag.

Nonlinear Analytical & Applications to Abstract Economics & Variational Inequalities. G. Yuan. LC 99-17316. (Pure & Applied Mathematics Ser.). (Illus.). 648p. 1999. text 195.00 (*0-8247-0031-7*) Dekker.

Nonlinear & Adaptive Control Design. Miroslav Krstic et al. LC 95-10082. (Adaptive & Learning Systems for Signal Processing, Communications & Control Ser.). 576p. 1995. 98.95 (*0-471-12732-9*) Wiley.

Nonlinear & Chaotic Phenomena in Plasmas, Solids & Fluids, Edmonton, Alberta, Canada, July 16-27, 1990. Ed. by W. Rozmus & J. A. Tuszynski. 640p. 1991. text 118.00 (*981-02-0386-1*) World Scientific Pub.

***Nonlinear & Coherent Optics: Laser Optics '98: 22-26 June 1998, St. Petersburg, Russia** Laser Optics '98 Staff et al. LC 99-193798. (Proceedings Ser.). vi, 138 p. 1998. write for info. (*0-8194-3158-3*) SPIE.

Nonlinear & Collective Phenomena in Beam Physics: Proceedings of the 12th Advanced ICFA Beam Dynamics Workshop Held in Arcidosso, Italy, 1996. Ed. by Swapan Chattopadhyay et al. LC 97-72970. (Illus.). 448p. 1997. 115.00 (*1-56396-668-9*, CP 395, AIP Pr) Spr-Verlag.

Nonlinear & Collective Phenomena in Beam Physics-1998 WKSP: International Committee on Future Accelerators. Ed. by Swapan Chattapadhyay et al. LC 99-61288. (Conference Proceedings Ser.). (Illus.). 366p. 1999. 110.00 (*1-56396-862-2*) Am Inst Physics.

Nonlinear & Convex Analysis. 1995. 71.00 (*3-540-58767-5*) Spr-Verlag.

Nonlinear & Convex Analysis: Proceedings in Honor of Ky Fan. Lin. Ed. by Stephen Simons. (Lecture Notes in Pure & Applied Mathematics Ser.: Vol. 107). (Illus.). 320p. 1987. pap. text 165.00 (*0-8247-7777-8*) Dekker.

Nonlinear & Convex Analysis in Economic Theory. Ed. by Toru Maruyama & Wataru Takahashi. LC 94-39352. (Lecture Notes in Economics & Mathematical Systems Ser.: Vol. 419). 1995. write for info. (*0-387-58767-5*) Spr-Verlag.

An Asterisk (*) at the beginning of an entry indicates that the title is appearing for the first time.

Nonlinear & Global Analysis. Ed. by Felix E. Browder. LC 92-36618. (Reprints from the Bulletin of the American Mathematical Society Ser.: Vol. 1). 625p. 1992. pap. 73.00 (*0-8218-8500-6*, BULLRE/1) Am Math.

Nonlinear & Mixed-Integer Optimization: Fundamentals & Applications. Christodoulos A. Floudas. (Topics in Chemical Engineering Ser.). (Illus.). 480p. 1995. text 85.00 (*0-19-510056-5*) OUP.

Nonlinear & Optimal Control Systems. Thomas L. Vincent & Walter J. Grantham. LC 96-37129. 576p. 1997. 110.00 (*0-471-04235-8*) Wiley.

Nonlinear & Parametric Phenomena, Theory & Applications in Radiophysical & Mechanical Systems. 400p. 1998. 44.00 (*981-02-3051-6*) World Scientific Pub.

Nonlinear & Quantum Optical Phenomena in Nonequilibrium Media. Ed. by V. A. Shcheglov. LC 93-32492. (Proceedings of the Lebedev Physics Institute Ser.: Vol. 217). 285p. (C). 1994. lib. bdg. 195.00 (*1-56072-138-3*) Nova Sci Pubs.

Nonlinear & Quantum Optics, 10 vols., Set. Ed. by Nicolaas Bloembergen. LC 96-77141. (Research Trends in Physics Ser.). (Illus.). 620p. (C). 1996. 85.00 (*1-889545-00-7*) Stefan Univ Pr.

Nonlinear & Quantum Optics: Proceedings of the Third School of Ja Swieca. C. B. De Araujo & F. A. De Oliveira. 1994. text 75.00 (*981-02-1089-2*) World Scientific Pub.

Nonlinear & Relativistic Effects in Plasmas. V. Stefan. 784p. 1992. 99.00 (*0-88318-787-6*) Spr-Verlag.

***Nonlinear & Robust Control of PDE Systems: Methods & Applications to Transport-Reaction Problems.** Panagiotis D. Christofides. 2000. 59.95 (*0-8176-4156-4*) Spr-Verlag.

Nonlinear & Stochastic Dynamics: 1994 International Mechanical Engineering Congress & Exposition, Chicago, Illinois - November 6-11, 1994. Ed. by A. K. Bajaj. LC 94-27986. (AMD - Design Engineering Ser.: Vol. 192, Vol. 78). 348p. 1994. 92.00 (*0-7918-1441-6*, G00936) ASME.

Nonlinear & Turbulent Processes in Physics, 3 vols., Vol. 1. R. Z. Sagdeev. xx, 654p. 1984. text 421.00 (*3-7186-0216-4*) Gordon & Breach.

Nonlinear & Turbulent Processes in Physics, 3 vols., Vol. 2. R. Z. Sagdeev. xx, 477p. 1984. text 340.00 (*3-7186-0217-2*) Gordon & Breach.

Nonlinear & Turbulent Processes in Physics, 3 vols., Vol. 3. R. Z. Sagdeev. 1692p. 1984. text 864.00 (*3-7186-0212-1*); text 385.00 (*3-7186-0218-0*) Gordon & Breach.

Nonlinear Approximation Theory. D. Braess. (Computational Mathematics Ser.: Vol. 7). (Illus.). 305p. 1986. 139.95 (*0-387-13625-8*) Spr-Verlag.

Nonlinear Aspects of Telecommunication. Andrzej Borys. (Electronic Engineering Systems Ser.). 1999. write for info. (*0-8493-2571-4*) CRC Pr.

***Nonlinear Biomedical Signal Processing.** Metin Akay. LC 00-27777. 2000. write for info. (*0-7803-6011-7*) IEEE Standards.

Nonlinear Boundary Value Problems for Holomorphic Functions & Singular Integral Equations. E. Wegert. (Mathematical Research Ser.: Vol. 65). 240p. 1993. pap. 55.00 (*0-685-67850-4*, Pub. by Akademie Verlag) Wiley.

Nonlinear Circuits Handbook. Ed. by Daniel H. Sheingold. LC 75-42559. (Illus.). 1976. pap. text 5.95 (*0-916550-01-X*) Analog Devices.

Nonlinear Coherent Structures. Ed. by M. Barthes & J. Mustrede Leon. (Lecture Notes in Physics Ser.: Vol. 353). x, 280p. 1990. 44.95 (*0-387-52240-9*) Spr-Verlag.

Nonlinear Coherent Structures in Physics & Biology. K. H. Spatschek & F. G. Mertens. (NATO ASI Ser.: Vol. 329). (Illus.). 484p. (C). 1994. text 129.50 (*0-306-44803-3*, Kluwer Plenum) Kluwer Academic.

Nonlinear Coherent Structures in Physics & Biology: Proceedings of the 7th Interdisciplinary Workshop Held at Dijon, France, 4-6 June 1991. Ed. by M. Remoissenet & M. Peyrard. (Lecture Notes in Physics Ser.: Vol. 393). xii, 398p. 1991. 79.95 (*0-387-54890-4*) Spr-Verlag.

Nonlinear Commutators in Interpolation Theory. Nigel J. Kalton. LC 88-6240. (Memoirs Ser.: No. 73/385). 85p. 1988. pap. 18.00 (*0-8218-2448-1*, MEMO/73/385) Am Math.

Nonlinear Computational Mechanics: State of the Art. Ed. by P. Wriggers & William R. Wagner. xii, 750p. 1991. 234.95 (*0-387-54254-X*) Spr-Verlag.

Nonlinear Computational Structural Mechanics: New Approaches & Non-Incremental Methods of Calculation. P. Ladeveze & J. G. Simmonds. Ed. by F. F. Ling. LC 98-29990. (Mechanical Engineering Ser.). (Illus.). 240p. 1998. 59.95 (*0-387-98594-8*) Spr-Verlag.

Nonlinear Computer Modeling of Chemical & Biochemical Data. James F. Rusling & Thomas F. Kumosinski. LC 95-30376. (Illus.). 268p. 1996. text 64.95 (*0-12-604490-2*) Acad Pr.

Nonlinear Continuum Mechanics for Finite Element Analysis. Javier Bonet & Richard D. Wood. LC 97-11366. (Illus.). 266p. (C). 1997. text 52.95 (*0-521-57272-X*) Cambridge U Pr.

***Nonlinear Continuum Mechanics of Solids: Fundamental Mathematical & Physical Concepts.** Yavuz Bapsar & Dieter Weichert. LC 99-55461. x, 204p. 2000. pap. 59.95 (*3-540-66601-X*) Spr-Verlag.

Nonlinear Control: System Design, 1995. A. J. Krener & D. Q. Mayne. (IFAC Postprint Ser.). 896p. 1995. pap. write for info. (*0-08-042371-X*, Pergamon Pr) Elsevier.

***Nonlinear Control & Analytical Mechanics with Mathematica: A Computational Approach, Set.** Harry G. Kwatny & G. L. Blankenship. (Control Engineering Ser.). (Illus.). 328p. 2000. 59.95 incl. cd-rom (*0-8176-4147-5*, Pub. by Birkhauser) Spr-Verlag.

Nonlinear Control of Electric Machinery. D. M. Dawson et al. LC 98-14952. (Illus.). 464p. 1998. text 175.00 (*0-8247-0180-1*) Dekker.

Nonlinear Control Systems. Aldo Isidori. (Communications & Control Engineering Ser.). (Illus.). xii, 479p. 1994. 63.95 (*0-387-50601-2*) Spr-Verlag.

Nonlinear Control Systems. B. Naumov. 1990. 80.00 (*0-8493-7127-9*, QA402) CRC Pr.

Nonlinear Control Systems. H. Nijmeijer & A. J. Van der Schaft. LC 98-47481. 1998. pap. write for info. (*0-08-043049-X*, Pergamon Pr) Elsevier.

Nonlinear Control Systems. 3rd ed. Alberto Isidori. Ed. by B. W. Dickinson et al. LC 95-14976. (Communications & Control Engineering Ser.). (Illus.). 568p. 1995. 79.95 (*3-540-19916-0*) Spr-Verlag.

Nonlinear Control Systems: An Algebraic Setting. G. Conte et al. LC 98-52362. (Lecture Notes in Control & Information Sciences). xvi, 166p. 1999. pap. 59.00 (*1-85233-151-8*) Spr-Verlag.

Nonlinear Control Systems: An Introduction. Aldo Isidori. (Lecture Notes in Control & Information Sciences: Vol. 72). 300p. 1986. pap. 27.30 (*0-387-15595-3*) Spr-Verlag.

Nonlinear Control Systems Design. Ed. by Aldo Isidori. LC 89-71013. (IFAC Proceedings Ser.: No. 9002). 428p. 1990. 197.75 (*0-08-037022-5*, Pergamon Pr) Elsevier.

Nonlinear Control Systems Design, 1992: Selected Papers from the IFAC Symposium, Bordeaux, France, 24-26 June 1992. Ed. by M. Fliess. LC 93-3698. (IFAC Symposia Ser.: No. 7). 506p. 1993. 197.75 (*0-08-041901-1*, Pergamon Pr) Elsevier.

***Nonlinear Control Systems II.** A. Isidori. (Communications & Control Engineering Ser.). (Illus.). xii, 300p. 1999. 89.95 (*1-85233-188-7*, Pub. by Spr-Verlag) Spr-Verlag.

Nonlinear Controllability & Optimal Control. Hector J. Sussmann. (Pure & Applied Mathematics Ser.: Vol. 133). (Illus.). 488p. 1990. text 189.75 (*0-8247-8258-5*) Dekker.

Nonlinear Cooperative Phenomena in Biological Systems: Proceedings of the Adriatico Research Conference ICTP, Trieste, Italy 19-22 August 1997. Ed. by L. Matsson. LC 98-34936. 350p. 1998. 74.00 (*981-02-3454-6*) World Scientific Pub.

Nonlinear Crack Models for Nonmetallic Materials A. Carpinteri. LC 99-23128. 1999. write for info. (*0-7923-5750-7*) Kluwer Academic.

Nonlinear Deformed & Irreversible Quantum Systems: Proceedings of the International Symposium. H. D. Doebner et al. 500p. 1995. text 143.00 (*981-02-2266-1*) World Scientific Pub.

Nonlinear Differential Equations. Raimond A. Struble. LC 79-23165. 278p. 1983. reprint ed. lib. bdg. 31.50 (*0-89874-056-8*) Krieger.

***Nonlinear Differential Equations, 404.** Pavel Drabek et al. LC 99-229206. 12p. 1999. per. 49.95 (*1-58488-036-8*, Chap & Hall CRC) CRC Pr.

Nonlinear Differential Equations & Dynamical Systems. 2nd ed. F. Verhulst. LC 96-2740. (Universitext Ser.). 312p. 1996. pap. 32.50 (*3-540-60934-2*) Spr-Verlag.

***Nonlinear Differential Equations in Ordered Spaces, Vol. 111.** S. Carl & Seppo Heikkilha. LC 00-30835. (Monographs & Surveys in Pure & Applied Mathematics). 336p. 2000. boxed set 74.95 (*1-58488-068-6*, Chap & Hall CRC) CRC Pr.

Nonlinear Diffusion Equations & Their Equilibrium States 1. Ed. by W. M. Ni et al. (Mathematical Sciences Research Institute Publications: Vol. 12). (Illus.). 350p. 1988. 63.95 (*0-387-96771-0*) Spr-Verlag.

Nonlinear Diffusion Equations & Their Equilibrium States 2. Ed. by W. M. Ni et al. (Mathematical Sciences Research Institute Publications: Vol. 13). (Illus.). 350p. 1988. 63.95 (*0-387-96772-9*) Spr-Verlag.

Nonlinear Diffusion Equations & Their Equilibrium States 3: Proceedings from a Conference Held August 20-29, 1980 in Gregynog, Wales. Ed. by N. G. Lloyd et al. (Progress in Nonlinear Differential Equations & Their Applications Ser.: Vol. 7). x, 572p. 1992. 146.00 (*0-8176-3531-9*) Birkhauser.

Nonlinear Diffusion of Electromagnetic Fields. Isaak D. Mayergoyz. LC 98-12650. (Electromagnetism Ser.). (Illus.). 412p. 1998. boxed set 120.00 (*0-12-480870-0*) Acad Pr.

Nonlinear Diffusion Problems. Ed. by A. P. Fasano & M. Primicerio. (Lecture Notes in Mathematics Ser.: Vol. 1224). viii, 188p. 1987. 33.95 (*0-387-17192-4*) Spr-Verlag.

Nonlinear Digital Filters: Principles & Applications. Ioannis Pitas & Anastasios N. Venetsanopoulos. (C). 1990. text 132.50 (*0-7923-9049-0*) Kluwer Academic.

Nonlinear Dispersive Wave Systems. L. Debnath. (Advanced Series in Nonlinear Dynamics). 600p. 1992. text 121.00 (*981-02-0948-7*) World Scientific Pub.

Nonlinear Dynamic & Stochastic Mechanics. Wolfgang H. Kliemann. 560p. 1995. boxed set 94.95 (*0-8493-8333-1*, 8333) CRC Pr.

Nonlinear Dynamical Analysis of the EEG: Proceedings of the 2nd Annual Conference. B. H. Jansen & M. E. Brandt. 384p. 1993. text 95.00 (*981-02-1204-6*) World Scientific Pub.

Nonlinear Dynamical Control Systems. H. Nijmeijer & A. Van der Schaft. (Illus.). xiii, 467p. (C). 1996. 59.95 (*0-387-97234-X*) Spr-Verlag.

Nonlinear Dynamical Economics & Chaotic Motion. Hans-Walter Lorenz. (Lecture Notes in Economics & Mathematical Systems Ser.: Vol. 334). xii, 248p. 1989. pap. 28.60 (*0-387-51413-9*) Spr-Verlag.

Nonlinear Dynamical Economics & Chaotic Motion. 2nd enl. rev. ed. H. W. Lorenz. (Lecture Notes in Economics & Mathematical Systems Ser.: Vol. 334). (Illus.). 19p. 1995. reprint ed. 98.00 (*3-87568-816-3*) Spr-Verlag.

Nonlinear Dynamical Economics & Chaotic Motion. 2nd enl. rev. ed. Hans-Walter Lorenz. 1993. write for info. (*3-540-56881-6*) Spr-Verlag.

Nonlinear Dynamical Economics & Chaotic Motion. 2nd enl. rev. ed. Hans-Walter Lorenz. LC 93-5233. 1997. 98.00 (*0-387-56881-6*) Spr-Verlag.

Nonlinear Dynamical Systems. 2nd ed. P. A. Cook. LC 93-42976. (Series in Systems & Control Engineering). (C). 1994. pap. text 50.00 (*0-13-625161-7*) P-H Intl.

Nonlinear Dynamical Systems: Feedforward Neural Network Perspectives. Haykin. 256p. Date not set. 95.00 (*0-471-34911-9*) Wiley.

Nonlinear Dynamical Systems & Carleman Linearization. Kenneth L. Kowalski & W. H. Steeb. 192p. (C). 1991. text 46.00 (*981-02-0587-2*) World Scientific Pub.

Nonlinear Dynamical Systems & Chaos. Ed. by H. W. Broer et al. LC 95-47179. (Progress in Nonlinear Differential Equations & Their Applications Ser.: Vol. 19). 459p. 1996. 149.00 (*0-8176-5346-5*) Birkhauser.

Nonlinear Dynamical Systems & Chaos. Ed. by H. W. Broer et al. (Progress in Nonlinear Differential Equations & Their Applications Ser.: 19). 459p. 1996. 149.00 (*3-7643-5346-5*) Spr-Verlag.

Nonlinear Dynamics. Michael Tabor. LC 88-15516. 384p. 1989. 110.00 (*0-471-82728-2*) Wiley.

Nonlinear Dynamics. Ed. by Giorgio Turchetti. 436p. (C). 1989. text 108.00 (*9971-5-0741-2*) World Scientific Pub.

Nonlinear Dynamics: A Two-Way Trip from Physics to Math. Hernan G. Solari et al. LC 96-15831. (Illus.). 372p. 1996. 166.00 (*0-7503-0379-4*); pap. 56.00 (*0-7503-0380-8*) IOP Pub.

Nonlinear Dynamics: Exploration Through Normal Forms. Peter B. Kahn & Yair Zarmi. LC 97-9275. 401p. 1997. 89.95 (*0-471-17682-6*) Wiley.

***Nonlinear Dynamics: Techniques & Applications in Psychology.** Richard A. Heath. LC 00-32128. 2000. write for info. (*0-8058-3200-9*) L Erlbaum Assocs.

***Nonlinear Dynamics & Brain Functioning.** Ed. by Paul E. Rapp. 273p. 1999. 95.00 (*1-56072-648-2*) Nova Sci Pubs.

Nonlinear Dynamics & Chaos. LC 97-36349. (Nonlinear Science Ser.). 450p. 1997. text 54.00 (*981-02-3143-1*) World Scientific Pub.

Nonlinear Dynamics & Chaos. Ed. by R. L. Dewar et al. 450p. (C). 1992. text 99.00 (*981-02-0770-0*) World Scientific Pub.

Nonlinear Dynamics & Chaos: Geometrical Methods for Engineers & Scientists. J. M. Thompson & H. B. Stewart. LC 85-29482. 392p. 1986. 169.95 (*0-471-90960-2*) Wiley.

Nonlinear Dynamics & Chaos: With Applications in Physics, Biology, Chemistry, & Engineering. Steven H. Strogatz. LC 93-6166. 498p. (C). 1994. 59.00 (*0-201-54344-3*) Addison-Wesley.

Nonlinear Dynamics & Chaos in Astrophysics: A Festschrift in Honor of George Contopoulos. Georgios I. Kontopoulos et al. LC 98-51749. (Annals of the New York Academy of Science Ser.). 1998. write for info. (*1-57331-163-4*) NY Acad Sci.

Nonlinear Dynamics & Chaos in Astrophysics: A Festschrift in Honor of George Contopoulos. Georgios I. Kontopoulos. Ed. by J. Robert Buchler et al. LC 98-51749. (Annals of the New York Academy of Sciences Ser.). 1998. text 140.00 (*1-57331-162-6*) NY Acad Sci.

Nonlinear Dynamics & Chaos in Mechanical Systems with Discontinuities. 350p. 1997. 54.00 (*981-02-2927-5*) World Scientific Pub.

***Nonlinear Dynamics & Chaos in Semiconductors.** K. Aoki. 1999. 149.00 (*0-7503-0514-2*); pap. text 59.00 (*0-7503-0515-0*) IOP Pub.

Nonlinear Dynamics & Chaotic Phenomena: An Introduction. Bhimsen K. Shivamoggi. LC 97-29304. (Fluid Mechanics & Its Applications Ser.: No. 42). 404p. 1997. text 217.50 (*0-7923-4772-2*) Kluwer Academic.

Nonlinear Dynamics & Controls: Proceedings, ASME International Mechanical Engineering Congress & Exposition, 1996, Atlanta, Georgia. Ed. by Anil K. Bajaj et al. LC 96-78672. (DE Ser.: Vol. 91). 239p. 1996. pap. text 96.00 (*0-7918-1530-7*) ASME Pr.

Nonlinear Dynamics & Economics. Ed. by William A. Barnett et al. (International Symposia in Economic Theory & Econometrics Ser.: No. 10). (Illus.). 417p. (C). 1996. text 64.95 (*0-521-47141-9*) Cambridge U Pr.

Nonlinear Dynamics & Fractals: New Numerical Techniques for Sedimentary Data. Gerard V. Middleton et al. (Short Course Notes Ser.: No. 36). (Illus.). 180p. (Orig.). 1995. pap. 55.00 (*1-56576-021-2*) SEPM.

Nonlinear Dynamics & Particle Acceleration. Yoski H. Ichikawa & Tushiki Tajima. LC 91-55348. (AIP Conference Proceedings Ser.: No. 230). 304p. 1991. 85.00 (*0-88318-824-4*) Am Inst Physics.

Nonlinear Dynamics & Pattern Formation in Semiconductors & Devices. Ed. by F. J. Niedernostheide. (Proceedings in Physics Ser.: Vol. 79). 272p. 1995. 89.00 (*0-387-58833-7*) Spr-Verlag.

Nonlinear Dynamics & Pattern Formation in Semiconductors & Devices: Proceedings of the International Conference, Noordwijkerhout, the Netherlands, July 4-7, 1994. Ed. by F. J. Niedernostheide. LC 95-2680. (Proceedings in Physics Ser.). xi, 265p. 1995. 97.95 (*3-540-58833-7*) Spr-Verlag.

Nonlinear Dynamics & Pattern Formation in the Natural Environment. A. Doelman. 1995. lib. bdg. 79.95 (*0-582-27371-4*, Pub. by Addison-Wesley) Longman.

Nonlinear Dynamics & Predictability of Geophysical Phenomena, IUGG, 1994, Vol. 18. Ed. by William I. Newman et al. LC 94-20388. (Geophysical Monographs: Vol. 83). 107p. 1994. 28.00 (*0-87590-469-6*) Am Geophysical.

Nonlinear Dynamics & Quantum Phenomena in Optical Systems: Proceedings of the 3rd International Workshop Blanes (Gerona, Spain), October 1-3, 1991. Ed. by R. Vilaseca & R. Corbalan. (Proceedings in Physics Ser.: Vol. 55). (Illus.). x, 327p. 1992. 84.95 (*0-387-53602-7*) Spr-Verlag.

Nonlinear Dynamics & Spatial Complexity in Optical Systems. Ed. by R. G. Harrison & S. Uppal. (Scottish Universities Summer School in Physics, a NATO Advanced Study Institute Ser.: No. 41). (Illus.). 308p. 1993. 189.00 (*0-7503-0257-7*) IOP Pub.

***Nonlinear Dynamics & Statistics.** Ed. by Alistair Mees. (Illus.). 493p. 2000. 89.95 (*0-8176-4163-7*) Birkhauser.

Nonlinear Dynamics & Stochastic Mechanics. Ed. by W. H. Kliemann et al. LC 96-15175. (Fields Institute Communications Ser.: Vol. 9). 238p. 1996. text 74.00 (*0-8218-0257-7*, FIC/9) Am Math.

Nonlinear Dynamics & Structures in Biology & Medicine: Optical & Laser Technologies. Ed. by Valery V. Tuchin. LC 96-72140. 206p. 1997. pap. 59.00 (*0-8194-2468-4*) SPIE.

Nonlinear Dynamics & the Beam-Beam Interaction. Ed. by M. Month & J. C. Herrera. LC 79-57341. (AIP Conference Proceedings Ser.: No. 57). (Illus.). 340p. lib. bdg. 20.50 (*0-88318-156-8*) Am Inst Physics.

Nonlinear Dynamics & Time Series: Building a Bridge Between the Natural & Statistical Sciences. Colleen D. Cutler & Daniel Kaplan. LC 96-44411. (Fields Institute Communications Ser.: No. 11). 252p. 1996. text 79.00 (*0-8218-0521-5*) Am Math.

Nonlinear Dynamics Aspects of Particle Accelerators. Ed. by J. M. Jowett et al. (Lecture Notes in Physics Ser.: Vol. 247). viii, 583p. 1986. 76.95 (*0-387-16455-3*) Spr-Verlag.

Nonlinear Dynamics, Chaos & Econometrics. Ed. by M. Hashem Pesaran & Simon M. Potter. 256p. 1993. 140.00 (*0-471-93942-0*) Wiley.

Nonlinear Dynamics, Chaos & Instability. William A. Brock & David A. Hsieh. (Illus.). 346p. 1991. 46.50 (*0-262-02329-6*) MIT Pr.

Nonlinear Dynamics, Chaos & Instability - IBM version. David A. Hsieh & William A. Brock. 1992. pap. text 15.00 (*0-262-52173-3*) MIT Pr.

Nonlinear Dynamics, Chaos, & Instability - Unix Version. David A. Hsieh & William A. Brock. 1992. pap. text 15.00 (*0-262-52172-5*) MIT Pr.

Nonlinear Dynamics, Chaotic & Complex Systems. Ed. by E. Infeld et al. LC 97-4012. (Illus.). 349p. (C). 1997. text 85.00 (*0-521-58201-6*) Cambridge U Pr.

***Nonlinear Dynamics, Complexity & Public Policy.** Euel W. Elliott & L. Douglas Kiel. LC 99-41874. 200p. 1999. 59.00 (*1-56072-707-1*) Nova Sci Pubs.

Nonlinear Dynamics in Circuits. Ed. by T. L. Carroll & L. M. Pecora. 400p. 1995. text 102.00 (*981-02-2438-9*, N-PB2910) World Scientific Pub.

Nonlinear Dynamics in Economics: A Theoretical & Statistical Approach to Agricultural Markets. B. Finkenstadt. Ed. by Gunter U. Fandel & W. Trockel. LC 95-213509. (Lecture Notes in Economics & Mathematical Systems Ser.: Vol. 426). (Illus.). 156p. 1995. 52.00 (*3-540-59374-8*) Spr-Verlag.

Nonlinear Dynamics in Economics & Social Sciences: Proceedings of the Second Informal Workshop Held at the Certosa di Pontignano, Siena, Italy, May 27-30, 1991. Ed. by F. Gori et al. LC 93-4014. (Lecture Notes in Economics & Mathematical Systems Ser.: Vol. 399). (Illus.). viii, 367p. 1993. pap. 65.00 (*0-387-56704-6*) Spr-Verlag.

Nonlinear Dynamics in Engineering Systems. Ed. by W. O. Schiehlen. (International Union of Theoretical & Applied Mechanics Symposia Ser.). (Illus.). 385p. 1990. 93.95 (*0-387-50200-9*) Spr-Verlag.

Nonlinear Dynamics in Human Behaviour. LC 97-111986. 428p. 1996. lib. bdg. 62.00 (*981-02-2742-6*) World Scientific Pub.

***Nonlinear Dynamics in Human Behaviour.** Ed. by W. H. Sulis & A. Combs. (NATO Science Ser.: Vol. 320). 350p. 2000. 107.00 (*1-58603-020-5*) IOS Press.

Nonlinear Dynamics in Optical Systems. LC 92-80630. (Nineteen Ninety-Two Technical Digest Ser.: Vol. 16). 300p. (Orig.). 1992. pap. 75.00 (*1-55752-259-6*); pap. 48.00 (*1-55752-258-8*) Optical Soc.

Nonlinear Dynamics in Optical Terms: Proceedings of the 2nd Topical Meeting. R. G. Harrison et al. 1993. text 86.00 (*981-02-1259-3*) World Scientific Pub.

Nonlinear Dynamics in Particle Accelerators. LC 97-106685. 250p. 1996. text 27.00 (*981-02-2517-2*) World Scientific Pub.

Nonlinear Dynamics in Particle Accelerators: Theory & Experiments: Proceedings. Conference on Nonlinear Dynamics in Particle Accel et al. Ed. by Swapan Chattopadhyay et al. LC 95-78135. (AIP Conference Proceedings Ser.: Vol. 344). (Illus.). 282p. 1995. 115.00 (*1-56396-446-5*) Am Inst Physics.

Nonlinear Dynamics in Solids. Ed. by H. Thomas. (Illus.). 250p. 1992. 62.95 (*0-387-53569-1*) Spr-Verlag.

Nonlinear Dynamics, Mathematical Biology & Social Science. Joshua Epstein. LC 97-6802. (C). 1997. pap. 35.00 (*0-201-41988-2*) Addison-Wesley.

Nonlinear Dynamics, Mathematical Biology & Social Science. Joshua M. Epstein. LC 97-6802. (Santa Fe Institute Ser.). (C). 1997. 61.00 (*0-201-95989-5*) Addison-Wesley.

Nonlinear Dynamics of Active & Passive Systems of Vibration Protection. M. Z. Kolovsky et al. Tr. by A. K. Belyaev from RUS. LC 99-34626. (Foundations of Engineering Mechanics Ser.). (Illus.). 425p. 1999. 119.00 (*3-540-65661-8*) Spr-Verlag.

Nonlinear Dynamics of Compliant Offshore Structures. Patrick Bar-Avi & Haym Benaroya. LC 97-19331. (Advances in Engineering Ser.: Vol. I). (Illus.). 182p. 1997. 88.00 (*90-265-1499-9*) Swets.

An Asterisk (*) at the beginning of an entry indicates that the title is appearing for the first time.

Nonlinear Dynamics of Electronic Systems. W. Schwarz & A. C. Davies. 440p. 1994. text 109.00 (*981-02-1769-2*) World Scientific Pub.

Nonlinear Dynamics of Interacting Populations. Alexander Bazykin. LC 98-11768. (Neural Systems Ser.). 193p. 1997. text 76.00 (*981-02-1685-8*) World Scientific Pub.

Nonlinear Dynamics of Marine Vehicles. Ed. by J. M. Falzarano & F. Papoulias. LC 93-73266. 125p. pap. 40.00 (*0-7918-1030-5*) ASME.

Nonlinear Dynamics of Ocean Waves: Proceedings of the Symposium Held at the Applied Physics Laboratory, Johns Hopkins University, 30-31 May 1991. Ed. by A. Brandt et al. LC 92-16906. 228p. 1992. text 81.00 (*981-02-1071-X*) World Scientific Pub.

Nonlinear Dynamics of Reservoir Mixtures. Vladimir S. Mitlin. 272p. 1993. boxed set 129.95 (*0-8493-4416-6*, TN871) CRC Pr.

Nonlinear Dynamics of Structures. R. Z. Sagdeev et al. 432p. 1991. text 115.00 (*981-02-0429-9*) World Scientific Pub.

***Nonlinear Econometric Modeling in Time Series Analysis: Proceedings of the 11th International Symposium in Economic Theory.** Ed. by William A. Barnett et al. (International Symposia in Economic Theory & Econometrics Ser.: No. 11). (Illus.). 240p. (C). 2000. 69.95 (*0-521-59424-3*) Cambridge U Pr.

Nonlinear Economic Dynamics. Ed. by Jean-Michel Grandmont. (Economic Theory, Econometrics & Mathematical Economics Ser.). 216p. 1987. text 54.95 (*0-12-295140-9*) Acad Pr.

Nonlinear Economic Dynamics. Tonu Puu. (Lecture Notes in Economics & Mathematical Systems Ser.: Vol. 336). (Illus.). viii, 119p. 1989. pap. 17.80 (*0-387-51438-4*) Spr-Verlag.

Nonlinear Economic Dynamics. 2nd enl. rev. ed. Tonu Puu. (Illus.). x, 151p. 1991. 39.00 (*0-387-53351-6*) Spr-Verlag.

Nonlinear Economic Dynamics. 3rd enl. rev. ed. Tonu Puu. LC 92-35868. 1993. 69.95 (*0-387-56145-5*) Spr-Verlag.

Nonlinear Economic Dynamics. 4th enl. rev. ed. T. Onu Puu. LC 97-14351. (Illus.). x, 288p. 1997. 83.00 (*3-540-62768-5*) Spr-Verlag.

Nonlinear Economic Models: Cross-Sectional, Time Series & Neural Network Applications. Ed. by John Creedy & Vance L. Martin. LC 97-23224. 304p. (C). 1997. text 95.00 (*1-85898-637-0*) E Elgar.

***Nonlinear Editing.** Patrick Morris. LC 99-32801. 224p. 1999. pap. 29.95 (*0-240-51564-1*, Focal) Buttrwrth-Heinemann.

Nonlinear Editing & Visual Literacy. Roy Stafford. LC 96-158516. 1996. pap. text 12.50 (*0-85170-549-9*, Pub. by British Film Inst) Ind U Pr.

Nonlinear Editing Basics: A Primer on Electronic Film & Video Editing. Steven E. Browne. LC 98-9166. 224p. 1998. pap. 29.95 (*0-240-80282-9*, Focal) Buttrwrth-Heinemann.

Nonlinear Effects in Fluids & Solids, Vol. 45. M. M. Carroll & M. A. Hayes. (Mathematical Concepts & Methods in Science & Engineering Ser.: No. 45). (Illus.). 384p. (C). 1996. text 107.00 (*0-306-45179-4*, Kluwer Plenum) Kluwer Academic.

Nonlinear Effects in Metals in the Microwave Band, Vol. 11. G. I. Leviev. (Soviet Scientific Reviews Ser.: Vol. 11, Pt. 2). ii, 94p. 1989. pap. text 106.00 (*3-7186-4903-9*) Gordon & Breach.

Nonlinear Effects in Optical Fibers. E. M. Dianov et al. (Laser Science & Technology Ser.: Vol. 2). viii, 60p. 1989. pap. text 74.00 (*3-7186-4889-X*) Gordon & Breach.

Nonlinear Eigenvalues & Analytic-Hypoellipticity. Ching-Chau Yu. LC 98-18251. (Memoirs of the American Mathematical Society Ser.: Vol. 134, No. 636). 92p. 1998. pap. 39.00 (*0-8218-0784-6*, MEMO/134/636) Am Math.

Nonlinear Elasticity. J. J. Stoker. (Illus.). xii, 130p. (Orig.). 1968. text 190.00 (*0-677-00660-8*) Gordon & Breach.

Nonlinear Electromagnetic Systems. Ed. by A. J. Moses & Amitava Basak. LC 95-8175. (Studies in Applied Electromagnetics & Mechanics: Vol. 10). 900p. (YA). (gr. 12). 1996. 150.00 (*90-5199-251-3*, 251-3) IOS Press.

Nonlinear Electromechanical Effects & Applications. Gerard A. Maugin. (Series in Theoretical & Applied Mechanics: Vol. 1). 184p. 1986. text 47.00 (*9971-978-43-1*); pap. text 28.00 (*9971-5-0096-5*) World Scientific Pub.

Nonlinear Elliptic & Evolution Problems & Their Finite Element Approximations. Alexander Zenisek. (Computational Mathematics & Applications Ser.). 422p. 1990. text 128.00 (*0-12-779560-X*) Acad Pr.

Nonlinear Elliptic & Parabolic Equations of the Second Order. N. V. Krylov. (C). 1987. text 272.50 (*90-277-2289-7*) Kluwer Academic.

Nonlinear Elliptic Boundary Value Problems. V. I. Skrypnik. 232p. (C). 1986. 135.00 (*0-7855-4978-1*, Pub. by Collets) St Mut.

Nonlinear Equations. Barut. 1978. text 126.50 (*90-277-0936-X*) Kluwer Academic.

Nonlinear Equations & Operator Algebras. Vladimir A. Marchenko. (C). 1987. text 144.00 (*90-277-2654-X*) Kluwer Academic.

Nonlinear Evolution & Chaotic Phenomena. Ed. by G. Gallavotti et al. (NATO ASI Series B, Physics: Vol. 176). (Illus.). 338p. 1988. 95.00 (*0-306-42909-8*, Plenum Trade) Perseus Pubng.

Nonlinear Evolution Equations. V. Makankov et al. 504p. 1993. text 121.00 (*981-02-1448-0*) World Scientific Pub.

Nonlinear Evolution Equations. Niva B. Maslova. LC 93-7001. (Series on Advances in Mathematics for Applied Sciences: Vol. 10). 208p. 1993. text 74.00 (*981-02-1162-7*) World Scientific Pub.

Nonlinear Evolution Equations. Ed. by N. N. Uraltseva. LC 95-2339. (American Mathematical Society Translations Ser.: Series 2, Vol. 164). 220p. 1995. text 95.00 (*0-8218-4123-8*, TRANS2/164) Am Math.

Nonlinear Evolution Equations & Applications. Gheorghe Morosanu. (C). 1988. text 211.50 (*90-277-2486-5*) Kluwer Academic.

Nonlinear Evolution Equations & Dynamical Systems. Ed. by S. Carillo et al. (Research Reports in Physics). (Illus.). 200p. 1990. pap. 51.00 (*0-387-51983-1*) Spr-Verlag.

Nonlinear Evolution Equations & Dynamical Systems, '90. Ed. by Vladimir G. Makhankov & O. K. Pashaev. (Research Reports in Physics). (Illus.). 240p. 1991. 75.95 (*0-387-53294-3*) Spr-Verlag.

Nonlinear Evolution Equations & Dynamical Systems, '91: Proceedings of the Workshop. Ed. by M. Boiti et al. 600p. 1992. text 143.00 (*981-02-0856-1*) World Scientific Pub.

Nonlinear Evolution Equations & Dynamical Systems, '94. A. Bishop et al. 404p. 1995. text 113.00 (*981-02-2219-X*) World Scientific Pub.

Nonlinear Evolution Equations & Infinite Dimensional Dynamical Systems. 284p. 1997. text 47.00 (*981-02-3055-9*) World Scientific Pub.

Nonlinear Evolution Equations & Painleve Test. W. H. Steeb & N. Euler. 344p. 1988. text 68.00 (*9971-5-0744-7*) World Scientific Pub.

***Nonlinear Evolution Equations & Their Applications.** Ed. by T-T Li et al. 332p. 1999. 58.00 (*981-02-4048-1*) World Scientific Pub.

Nonlinear Evolution Equations That Change Type. Ed. by A. Friedman et al. (IMA Volumes in Mathematics & Its Applications Ser.: Vol. 27). (Illus.). xiv, 284p. 1990. 62.95 (*0-387-97353-2*) Spr-Verlag.

Nonlinear Evolution of Spatial Economic Systems. Ed. by Peter Nijkamp & Aura Reggiani. LC 93-34002. (Illus.). x, 285p. 1993. 119.95 (*0-387-57162-0*) Spr-Verlag.

Nonlinear Evolution of Spatio-Temporal Structures in Dissipative Continuo. Ed. by F. H. Busse & L. Kramer. (NATO ASI Ser.: Vol. 225). (Illus.). 582p. (C). 1990. text 174.00 (*0-306-43603-5*, Kluwer Plenum) Kluwer Academic.

Nonlinear Evolution Operators & Semigroups. N. H. Pavel. (Lecture Notes in Mathematics Ser.: Vol. 1260). 285p. 1987. 43.95 (*0-387-17974-7*) Spr-Verlag.

Nonlinear Evolutionary Partial Differential Equations: International Conference on Nonlinear Evolutionary Partial Differential Equations, June 21-25, 1993, Beijing, People's Republic of China. Hsia-Hsi Ting & Tai-Ping Liu. LC 96-44773. (AMS-IP Studies in Advanced Mathematics: Vol. 3). xiii, 637p. 1996. pap. write for info. (*0-8218-0661-0*, AMSIP/3) Am Math.

Nonlinear Evolutions. J. Mustrede Leon. 808p. (C). 1988. text 143.00 (*9971-5-0458-8*) World Scientific Pub.

Nonlinear Excitations in Biomolecules. Ed. by M. Peyrard. 424p. 1995. 107.95 (*3-540-59250-4*) Spr-Verlag.

Nonlinear Extensions of the Schrodinger Equation. Salomon S. Mizrahi & Viktor V. Dodonov. 250p. 1997. 48.00 (*981-02-3249-7*) World Scientific Pub.

Nonlinear Feedback Control Systems: An Operator Theory Approach. Rui J. DeFigueiredo & Guanrong Chen. LC 93-19434. (Illus.). 220p. 1993. text 36.00 (*0-12-208630-9*) Acad Pr.

Nonlinear Fiber Optics. 2nd ed. Govind P. Agrawal. LC 94-44371. (Optics & Photonics Ser.). (Illus.). 592p. 1995. text 74.00 (*0-12-045142-5*) Acad Pr.

Nonlinear Fields: Classical, Random, Semiclassical - Karpacz, 91. Ed. by P. Garbaczewski & Z. Popowicz. 550p. (C). 1991. text 124.00 (*981-02-0647-X*) World Scientific Pub.

Nonlinear Filtering & Smoothing: An Introduction to Martingales, Stochastic Integrals & Estimation. Venkatarama Krishnan. LC 83-16712. 330p. reprint ed. pap. 102.30 (*0-7837-2820-4*, 205765200006) Bks Demand.

Nonlinear Filters: Estimation & Applications. 2nd ed. Hisashi Tanizaki. LC 96-26472. 254p. 1996. 99.50 (*3-540-61326-9*) Spr-Verlag.

Nonlinear Filters for Image Processing. Edward R. Dougherty & Jaakko Astola. LC 99-17646. (Series on Imaging Science & Engineering). 16p. 1999. pap. 80.00 (*0-8194-3033-1*) SPIE.

Nonlinear Financial Forecasting: Proceedings of the 1st INFFC. Ed. by Randall B. Caldwell. 320p. (Orig.). 1997. pap. 59.95 (*0-9651332-1-4*) Finance & Technol.

Nonlinear Finite Element Analysis & Adina: Proceedings of the 3rd Adina Conference, Massachusetts, U. S. A., 10-12 June 1981. Ed. by Klaus-Jurgen Bathe. 206p. 1981. 125.00 (*0-08-027594-X*, Pergamon Pr) Elsevier.

***Nonlinear Finite Element Analysis for Continua & Structures.** Ted Belytschko et al. 300p. 2000. pap. text 69.95 (*0-471-98774-3*) Wiley.

Nonlinear Finite Element Analysis of Plates & Shells. Ed. by T. J. Hughes et al. (AMD Ser.: Vol. 48). 286p. 1981. 40.00 (*0-686-34480-4*, H00198) ASME.

***Nonlinear Finite Element for Continua & Structures.** Ted Belytschko et al. 300p. 2000. text 155.00 (*0-471-98773-5*) Wiley.

Nonlinear Finite Elements Analysis & Adina. Ed. by Klaus-Jurgen Bathe. (Computers & Structures Ser.: No. 17). 311p. 1983. 136.00 (*0-08-030566-0*, Pub. by Pergamon Repr) Franklin.

Nonlinear Fracture Mechanics. Ed. by M. P. Wnuk. (CISM International Centre for Mechanical Sciences Ser.: No. 314). (Illus.). v, 451p. 1991. 102.95 (*0-387-82246-1*) Spr-Verlag.

Nonlinear Fracture Mechanics Vol. I: Time-Dependent Fracture. Ed. by A. Saxena et al. LC 88-38147. (Special Technical Publication Ser.: No. STP 995). (Illus.). 471p. 1989. text 66.00 (*0-8031-1174-6*, STP995) ASTM.

Nonlinear Fracture Mechanics Vol. II: Elastic-Plastic Fracture. Ed. by J. D. Landes et al. LC 88-38147. (Special Technical Publication Ser.: No. STP 995). (Illus.). 625p. 1989. text 78.00 (*0-8031-1257-2*, 04-995002-30) ASTM.

Nonlinear Fracture Mechanics for Engineers. A. Saxena. LC 97-37838. 496p. 1998. boxed set 84.95 (*0-8493-9496-1*) CRC Pr.

Nonlinear Functional Analysis. P. S. Milokjevik. (Lecture Notes in Pure & Applied Mathematics Ser.: Vol. 121). (Illus.). 288p. 1989. pap. text 155.00 (*0-8247-8255-0*) Dekker.

Nonlinear Functional Analysis. Jacob T. Schwartz. viii, 236p. 1969. text 208.00 (*0-677-01500-3*) Gordon & Breach.

Nonlinear Functional Analysis, Pt. 1. Ed. by Felix E. Browder. LC 74-34154. (Proceedings of Symposia in Pure Mathematics Ser.: Vol. 18). 296p. 1970. pap. 50.00 (*0-8218-0243-7*, PSPUM/18.1) Am Math.

Nonlinear Functional Analysis, Pt. 2. Ed. by Felix E. Browder. LC 74-34154. (Proceedings of Symposia in Pure Mathematics Ser.: Vol. 18). 308p. 1970. pap. 75.00 (*0-8218-0244-5*, PSPUM/18.2) Am Math.

Nonlinear Functional Analysis, Set, Pts. 1 & 2. Ed. by Felix E. Browder. LC 74-34154. (Proceedings of Symposia in Pure Mathematics Ser., Humboldt State University, Arcata, CA, July 29-August 16, 1974: Vol. 18). 604p. 1970. pap. 110.00 (*0-8218-1418-4*, PSPUM/18) Am Math.

Nonlinear Functional Analysis & Applications to Differential Equations: Proceedings of the 2nd School ICTP, Trieste, Italy 21 April-9th May, 1997. Ed. by A. Ambrosetti et al. 400p. 1998. 84.00 (*981-02-3470-8*) World Scientific Pub.

Nonlinear Functional Analysis & Differential Equations. Ed. by Lamberto Cesari et al. (Lecture Notes in Pure & Applied Mathematics Ser.: Vol. 19). (Illus.). 368p. 1976. pap. text 175.00 (*0-8247-6452-8*) Dekker.

Nonlinear Functional Analysis & Its Applications. Ed. by S. P. Singh. 1986. text 192.00 (*90-277-2211-0*) Kluwer Academic.

Nonlinear Functional Analysis & Its Applications. 2nd ed. Eberhard Zeidler. (Illus.). 960p. 1997. 129.00 (*0-387-96499-1*) Spr-Verlag.

Nonlinear Functional Analysis & Its Applications, 2 pts., Pt. 1. Ed. by Felix E. Browder. LC 85-28725. (Proceedings of Symposia in Pure Mathematics Ser.: Vol. 45). 540p. (Orig.). 1986. text 82.00 (*0-8218-1471-0*, PSPUM/45.1) Am Math.

Nonlinear Functional Analysis & Its Applications, Pt. 1. Eberhard Zeidler. Tr. by P. Wadsack from GER. (Illus.). 800p. 1993. 144.95 (*0-387-90914-1*) Spr-Verlag.

Nonlinear Functional Analysis & Its Applications, 2 pts., Pt. 2. Ed. by Felix E. Browder. LC 85-28725. (Proceedings of Symposia in Pure Mathematics Ser.: Vol. 45). 577p. (Orig.). 1986. text 89.00 (*0-8218-1472-9*, PSPUM/45.2) Am Math.

Nonlinear Functional Analysis & Its Applications, Pt. II-A. Eberhard Zeidler. (Illus.). 480p. 1989. 119.00 (*0-387-96802-4*) Spr-Verlag.

Nonlinear Functional Analysis & Its Applications, Pt. II-B. Eberhard Zeidler. (Illus.). 760p. 1989. 156.95 (*0-387-97167-X*) Spr-Verlag.

Nonlinear Functional Analysis & Its Applications, 2 pts., Set. Ed. by Felix E. Browder. LC 85-28725. (Proceedings of Symposia in Pure Mathematics Ser.: Vol. 45). 1117p. (Orig.). 1986. text 160.00 (*0-8218-1467-2*, PSPUM/45) Am Math.

Nonlinear Functional Analysis & Its Applications III: Variational Methods & Optimization. Eberhard Zeidler. Tr. by L. L. Boron from GER. (Illus.). 600p. 1984. 118.95 (*0-387-90915-X*) Spr-Verlag.

Nonlinear Guided Waves & Their Applications. LC 95-72776. (Nineteen Ninety-Six Technical Digest Ser.: No. 15). 1996. pap. 75.00 (*1-55752-455-6*) Optical Soc.

Nonlinear Guided Waves & Their Applications. (Nineteen Ninety-Nine OSA Technical Digest Ser.). 300p. (C). 1999. pap. 75.00 (*1-55752-587-0*) Optical Soc.

Nonlinear Guided Waves & Their Applications: Technical Digest : Collocated with the Workshop on Novel Solitons & Nonlinear Periodic Structures, Integrated Photonics Research, April 1-3, 1998, Victoria Conference Centre, Victoria, British Columbia, Canada. Optical Society of America Staff. LC 98-84329. xxxvii, 300 p. 1998. write for info. (*1-55752-537-4*) Optical Soc.

Nonlinear Hydrodynamic Modeling: A Mathematical Introduction. Ed. by H. N. Shirer. (Lecture Notes in Physics Ser.: Vol. 271). xvi, 546p. 1987. 60.95 (*0-387-17557-1*) Spr-Verlag.

Nonlinear Hyperbolic Equations & Field Theory. M. K. Murthy. 1992. lib. bdg. 62.95 (*0-582-08766-X*, Pub. by Addison-Wesley) Longman.

Nonlinear Hyperbolic Problems. Ed. by C. Carasso et al. (Lecture Notes in Mathematics Ser.: Vol. 1270). 341p. 1987. pap. 47.90 (*0-387-18200-4*) Spr-Verlag.

Nonlinear Hyperbolic Problems. Ed. by C. Carasso et al. (Lecture Notes in Mathematics Ser.: Vol. 1402). 255p. 1989. 37.30 (*0-387-51746-4*) Spr-Verlag.

Nonlinear Ill-Posed Problems. Tikhonov & A. I. Leonov. 392p. 1997. ring bd. 164.90 (*0-412-78660-5*, Chap & Hall CRC) CRC Pr.

***Nonlinear Image Processing.** Sanjit K. Mitra. 450p. 2000. 89.95 (*0-12-500451-6*) Acad Pr.

Nonlinear Image Processing IX, Vol. 3304. Ed. by Edward R. Dougherty & Jaakko T. Astola. 334p. 1998. 69.00 (*0-8194-2744-6*) SPIE.

Nonlinear Image Processing VIII, Vol. 3026. Ed. by Edward R. Dougherty & Jaakko T. Astola. 358p. 1997. 69.00 (*0-8194-2437-4*) SPIE.

***Nonlinear Image Processing X.** Ed. by Edward R. Dougherty & Jaakko T. Astola. 348p. 1999. pap. text 72.00 (*0-8194-3117-6*) SPIE.

Nonlinear Infrared Generation. Ed. by Y. R. Shen et al. (Topics in Applied Physics Ser.: Vol. 16). 1977. 64.95 (*0-387-07945-9*) Spr-Verlag.

Nonlinear Instability Analysis. Ed. by L. Debnath & S. R. Choudhury. LC 97-65233. (Advances in Fluid Mechanics Ser.: Vol. 12). 336p. 1997. 169.00 (*1-85312-428-1*, 4281) Computational Mech MA.

***Nonlinear Instability Analysis, Vol. II.** Ed. by L. Debnath. (Advances in Fluid Mechanics Ser.). 300p. 2000. 145.00 (*1-85312-842-2*, Pub. by WIT Pr) Computational Mech MA.

Nonlinear Instability Analysis, Chaos & Turbulence, 2 vols. Ed. by L. Debnath & D. N. Riahi. (Advances in Fluid Mechanics Ser.). 2000. write for info. (*1-85312-731-0*, 7310) Computational Mech MA.

Nonlinear Instability Analysis, Chaos & Turbulence, Vol. 1. Ed. by Lokenath Debnath & Daniel N. Riahi. LC 97-81142. (Advances in Fluid Mechanics Ser.: Vol. 20). 368p. 1999. 185.00 (*1-85312-515-6*, 4156) Computational Mech MA.

***Nonlinear Instability Analysis, Chaos & Turbulence, Vol. 25.** Ed. by Lokenath Debnath & Daniel N. Riahi. (Advances in Fluid Mechanics Ser.: Vol. 25). 424p. 2000. 199.00 (*1-85312-730-2*, 7302) Computational Mech MA.

Nonlinear Instability of Nonparallel Flows. Ed. by S. P. Lin et al. LC 94-19338. 1994. 202.95 (*0-387-57679-7*) Spr-Verlag.

Nonlinear Integrable Equations: Recursion Operators, Group-Theoretical & Hamiltonian Structures of Soliton Equations. Boris G. Konopelchenko. (Lecture Notes in Physics Ser.: Vol. 270). viii, 361p. 1987. 44.95 (*0-387-17567-9*) Spr-Verlag.

Nonlinear Integrable Systems - Classical Theory & Quantum Theory: Proceedings of RIMS Symposium, Kyoto, Japan, May 13-16, 1981. Ed. by Michio Jimbo & Tetsuji Miwa. 296p. 1983. text 60.00 (*9971-950-32-4*) World Scientific Pub.

Nonlinear Integral Equations. Philip M. Anselone. LC 64-17771. (U. S. Army Mathematics Research Center Publication Ser.: No. 11). 390p. reprint ed. pap. 120.90 (*0-608-30938-9*, 201020500068) Bks Demand.

Nonlinear Integral Equations in Abstract Spaces, Vol. 373. Dajun Guo et al. LC 96-26714. (Mathematics & Its Applications Ser.). 352p. (C). 1996. text 191.50 (*0-7923-4144-9*) Kluwer Academic.

***Nonlinear Interactions: Analytical, Computational, & Experimental Methods.** Ali H. Nayfeh. LC 99-86738. 763p. 2000. text 110.00 (*0-471-17591-9*) Wiley.

Nonlinear Kinetic Theory & Mathematical Aspects of Hyperbolic Systems. V. C. Boffi et al. Ed. by Franco Bampi & Giuseppe Toscani. LC 92-33361. (Advances in Mathematics Ser.: Vol. 9). 284p. 1993. text 95.00 (*981-02-1087-6*) World Scientific Pub.

Nonlinear Klein-Gordon & Chroedinger Systems: Theory & Applications: El Escorial, Madrid, Spain, 25-30 September 1995. Luis Vazquez et al. LC 96-8560. 380p. 1996. write for info. (*981-02-2565-2*) World Scientific Pub.

***Nonlinear Labor Market Dynamics.** Michael Neugart. LC 00-26593. (Lecture Notes in Economics & Mathematical Systems Ser.: Vol. 486). (Illus.). x, 175p. 2000. pap. 53.00 (*3-540-67279-6*) Spr-Verlag.

Nonlinear Laser Chemistry: Multiple-Photon Excitation. V. S. Letokhov. (Chemical Physics Ser.: Vol. 22). (Illus.). 417p. 1983. 69.95 (*0-387-11705-9*) Spr-Verlag.

Nonlinear Laser Spectroscopy. V. S. Letokhov & V. P. Chebotayev. (Optical Sciences Ser.: Vol. 4). (Illus.). 1977. 46.00 (*0-387-08044-9*) Spr-Verlag.

Nonlinear Liapunov Dynamics. Ed. by J. M. Skowronski. 608p. (C). 1990. text 61.00 (*981-02-0192-3*) World Scientific Pub.

Nonlinear Long Surface Waves & Solitons. R. K. Zeytounian. 256p. 1997. 64.50 (*0-412-78420-3*, Chap & Hall NY) Chapman & Hall.

Nonlinear LP-Norm Estimation. R. Gonin & A. H. Money. (Statistics Ser.: Vol. 100). (Illus.). 320p. 1989. text 165.00 (*0-8247-8125-2*) Dekker.

Nonlinear Magnetohydrodynamics. Dieter Biskamp. (Cambridge Monographs on Plasma Physics: No. 1). (Illus.). 392p. 1997. pap. text 44.95 (*0-521-59918-0*) Cambridge U Pr.

Nonlinear Mappings of Monotone Type. D. Pascali & S. Sburlan. 351p. 1979. lib. bdg. 115.50 (*90-286-0118-X*) Kluwer Academic.

***Nonlinear Mathematical Analysis & Applications.** Ed. by Themistocles M. Rassias. 320p. 1999. pap. 75.00 (*1-57485-044-X*) Hadronic Pr Inc.

Nonlinear Mathematics. Thomas L. Saaty & Joseph Bram. 381p. (C). 1982. reprint ed. pap. text 10.95 (*0-486-64233-X*) Dover.

Nonlinear Mathematics & Its Applications: Proceedings of the EPSRC Postgraduate School in Applied Nonlinear Mathematics, University of Surrey, 1995. Ed. by Philip J. Aston. LC 96-19429. (Illus.). 264p. 1996. pap. text 26.95 (*0-521-57676-8*) Cambridge U Pr.

Nonlinear Mathematics & Its Applications: Proceedings of the EPSRC Postgraduate School in Applied Nonlinear Mathematics, University of Surrey, 1995. Ed. by Philip J. Aston. LC 96-19429. (Illus.). 264p. 1996. text 74.95 (*0-521-57190-1*) Cambridge U Pr.

Nonlinear Mechanical Vibrations. P. Srinivasan. 283p. 1996. 75.00 (*0-470-23439-3*) Wiley.

Nonlinear Mechanics. Demeter G. Fertis. LC 93-12192. 480p. 1993. lib. bdg. 94.95 (*0-8493-8933-X*, TA646) CRC Pr.

Nonlinear Mechanics. 2nd ed. Demeter G. Fertis. LC 98-29311. 560p. 1998. boxed set 94.95 (*0-8493-9002-8*) CRC Pr.

Nonlinear Mechanics, Groups & Symmetry. Yu. A. Mitropolaky & A. K. Lopatin. LC 94-48068. (Mathematics & Its Applications Ser.: Vol. 319). 377p. 1995. text 188.00 (*0-7923-3339-X*) Kluwer Academic.

Nonlinear Mechanics of Structures. Michael Kleiber & C. Wozniak. (C). 1991. text 351.50 (*0-7923-0720-8*) Kluwer Academic.

Nonlinear Methods in Numerical Analysis. Ed. by Annie Cuyt & L. Wuytack. (North-Holland Mathematics Studies: No. 136). x,278p. 1987. 114.00 (*0-444-70189-3*, North Holland) Elsevier.

Nonlinear Methods in Offshore Engineering. S. K. Chakrabarti. (Developments in Marine Technology Ser.: No. 5). xviii,544p. 1990. 228.00 (*0-444-88457-2*) Elsevier.

Nonlinear Methods in Riemannian & Kahlerian Geometry. Jurgen Jost. (DMV Seminar Ser.: No. 10). 154p. 1988. 27.00 (*0-8176-1920-8*) Birkhauser.

Nonlinear Methods of Spectral Analysis. 2nd ed. Ed. by Simon Haykin. (Topics in Applied Physics Ser.: Vol. 34). (Illus.). 280p. 1983. pap. 52.00 (*0-387-12386-5*) Spr-Verlag.

***Nonlinear MHD Waves & Turbulence: Proceedings of the Workshop Held in Nice, France, 1-4 December 1998.** Ed. by Thierry Passot & P. L. Sulem. LC 99-57894. (Lecture Notes in Physics Ser.: Vol. 536). x, 385p. 1999. 89.90 (*3-540-66697-4*) Spr-Verlag.

Nonlinear Microwave Circuits. Stephen A. Maas. LC 96-9355. 504p. 1996. 69.95 (*0-7803-3403-5*) IEEE Standards.

Nonlinear Microwave Signal Processing - Towards a New Range of Devices: Proceedings of the NATO Advanced Research Workshop, Rome, Italy, 3-6 October, 1996. Ed. by Romolo Marcelli. LC 96-52195. (NATO ASI Series: Partnership Sub-Series 3). 528p. (C). 1996. text 291.00 (*0-7923-4358-1*) Kluwer Academic.

***Nonlinear Model-Based Process Control.** Rashid Ansari & Moses O. Tade. LC 99-47343. (Advances in Industrial Control Ser.). 2000. write for info. (*1-85233-213-1*) Spr-Verlag.

Nonlinear Model Based Process Control. R. D. Berber & Costas Kravaris. LC 98-29495. (Applied Sciences Ser.). 1998. 399.00 (*0-7923-5220-3*) Kluwer Academic.

***Nonlinear Model Predictive Control.** Frank Allghower & Alex Zheng. LC 00-23622. (Progress in Systems & Control Theory Ser.). 2000. write for info. (*0-8176-6297-9*) Birkhauser.

***Nonlinear Model Predictive Control.** Ed. by Frank Allghower & Alex Zheng. (Progress in Systems & Control Theory Ser.: Vol. 26). 488p. 2000. 109.00 (*3-7643-6297-9*, Pub. by Birkhauser) Spr-Verlag.

Nonlinear Modeling: Advanced Black-Box Techniques. Johana K. Suykens & J. Vandewalle. LC 98-26531. 1998. 125.00 (*0-7923-8195-5*) Kluwer Academic.

Nonlinear Modeling & Forecasting. Martin Casdagli. (C). 1992. 63.00 (*0-201-52764-2*) Addison-Wesley.

Nonlinear Models, 2 vols. Ed. by Herman J. Bierens & A. Ronald Gallant. (International Library of Critical Writings in Econometrics: Vol. 8). 1016p. 1997. 360.00 (*1-85898-382-7*) E Elgar.

Nonlinear Models for Repeated Measurement Data. Marie Davidian. 360p. (gr. 13). 1995. boxed set 65.95 (*0-412-98341-9*, Chap & Hall CRC) CRC Pr.

Nonlinear Multiobjective Optimization. Kaisa Miettinen. LC 98-37888. (International Series in Operations Research & Management Science). 1998. write for info. (*0-7923-8278-1*) Kluwer Academic.

Nonlinear Multivariate Analysis. A. Gifi. LC 89-24944. 602p. 1990. 225.00 (*0-471-92620-5*) Wiley.

Nonlinear Narrow Optical Resonance by Laser Radiation see Progress in Quantum Electronics

Nonlinear Networks & Systems. Richard Clay. LC 76-127660. (Illus.). 296p. reprint ed. pap. 91.80 (*0-608-10234-2*, 201017900068) Bks Demand.

Nonlinear Nonequilibrium Thermodynamics I: Linear & Nonlinear Fluctuation-Dissipation Theorems. Rouslan L. Stratonovich. Ed. by H. Haken. LC 92-27990. (Synergetics Ser.: Vol. 57). (Illus.). 376p. 1992. 127.95 (*0-387-55216-2*) Spr-Verlag.

Nonlinear Nonlocal Equations in the Theory of Waves. Pavel I. Naumkin & Ilia A. Shishmarev. LC 93-8452. (Translations of Mathematical Monographs: Vol. 133).Tr. of Nelineinye Nelokalnye Uravneniia v Teorii Voln. 289p. 1994. text 149.00 (*0-8218-4573-X*, MMONO/133) Am Math.

Nonlinear Numerical Analysis of Reinforced Concrete: Presented at the Winter Annual Meeting of the American Society of Mechanical Engineers, Phoenix, Arizona, November 14-19, 1982. American Society of Mechanical Engineers Staff. Ed. by Leonard E. Schwer. LC 82-73178. (Illus.). 129p. reprint ed. pap. 40.00 (*0-8357-2850-1*, 203908500010) Bks Demand.

Nonlinear Numerical Methods & Rational Approximation. Ed. by Annie Cuyt. (C). 1988. text 206.50 (*90-277-2669-8*) Kluwer Academic.

Nonlinear Numerical Methods & Rational Approximation II. Ed. by Annie Cuyt. LC 94-20809. (Mathematics & Its Applications Ser.: Vol. 296). 464p. (C). 1994. text 276.00 (*0-7923-2967-8*) Kluwer Academic.

Nonlinear Ocean Waves. Ed. by W. Perrie. LC 97-80258. (Advances in Fluid Mechanics Ser.: Vol. 17). 272p. 1997. 135.00 (*1-85312-414-1*, 4141) Computational Mech MA.

Nonlinear Optical & Electroactive Polymers. Ed. by Paras N. Prasad & D. R. Ulrich. 448p. 1987. 125.00 (*0-306-42768-0*, Plenum Trade) Perseus Pubng.

Nonlinear Optical Communication Networks: December 27, 1994. Eugenio Iannone et al. LC 97-21332. (Series in Microwave & Optical Engineering). 472p. 1998. 89.95 (*0-471-15270-6*, Wiley-Interscience) Wiley.

Nonlinear Optical Diagnostics of Laser-Excited Semiconductor Surfaces. S. A. Khmanov et al. Ed. by V. S. Letokhov. (Laser Science & Technology Ser.: Vol. 2). ii, 76p. 1989. pap. text 106.00 (*3-7186-4891-1*) Gordon & Breach.

***Nonlinear Optical Effects & Materials.** Ed. by P. Gunter. (Series in Optical Sciences: Vol. 72). (Illus.). xii, 524p. 2000. 159.00 (*3-540-65029-6*) Spr-Verlag.

Nonlinear Optical Effects in Organic Polymers. Ed. by J. Messier et al. (C). 1989. text 202.50 (*0-7923-0132-3*) Kluwer Academic.

Nonlinear Optical Engineering, Vol. 3263. Ed. by Metin S. Mangir. 184p. 1998. 69.00 (*0-8194-2702-0*) SPIE.

Nonlinear Optical Liquids, Vol. 2853. Ed. by Christopher M. Lawson. 218p. 1996. 56.00 (*0-8194-2241-X*) SPIE.

Nonlinear Optical Liquids & Power Limiters, Vol. 3146. Ed. by Christopher M. Lawson. LC 98-122019. 194p. 1997. 59.00 (*0-8194-2568-0*) SPIE.

Nonlinear Optical Liquids for Power Limiting & Imaging, Vol. 3472. Ed. by Christopher M. Lawson. 1998. 59.00 (*0-8194-2927-9*) SPIE.

Nonlinear Optical Materials. 352p. 1991. lib. bdg. 169.00 (*0-8493-0147-5*, QC374) CRC Pr.

Nonlinear Optical Materials. Ed. by J. V. Moloney. (IMA Volumes in Mathematics & Its Applications Ser.). (Illus.). 267p. 1997. 69.95 (*0-387-98581-6*) Spr-Verlag.

Nonlinear Optical Materials: Principles & Applications, V. Degiorgio. LC 94-73355. 490p. (gr. 12). 1995. 155.00 (*90-5199-204-1*) IOS Press.

Nonlinear Optical Materials: Theory & Modeling. Ed. by Shashi P. Karna & Alan T. Yeates. (ACS Symposium Ser.: No. 628). (Illus.). 264p. 1996. text 95.00 (*0-8412-3401-9*, Pub. by Am Chemical) OUP.

Nonlinear Optical Materials & Devices for Applications in Information Technology: Proceedings of the NATO Advanced Study Institute, Erice, Sicily, Italy, July 13-26, 1993. Ed. by Arthur Miller et al. LC 95-11664. (NATO ASI Ser., Series C: Applied Sciences: Vol. 289). 372p. (C). 1995. text 202.50 (*0-7923-3457-4*) Kluwer Academic.

***Nonlinear Optical Phenomena & Coherent Optics in Information Technologies.** Ed. by Sergei S. Chesnokov et al. 484p. 1999. pap. text 103.00 (*0-8194-3207-5*) SPIE.

Nonlinear Optical Phenomena in Semiconductors & Semiconductor Microstructures. H. Huag et al. (International Series on Advanced Solid State Electronics & Technology). 400p. 1998. text 58.00 (*981-02-2297-1*) World Scientific Pub.

Nonlinear Optical Properties of LC & PDLC. Ed. by Francesco Simoni. LC 97-10522. (Liquid Crystals Ser.: Vol. 1). 310p. 1997. text 81.00 (*981-02-1751-X*) World Scientific Pub.

Nonlinear Optical Properties of Organic & Polymeric Materials. Ed. by David J. Williams. LC 83-15514. (ACS Symposium Ser.: No. 233). 251p. 1983. lib. bdg. 39.95 (*0-8412-0802-6*) Am Chemical.

Nonlinear Optical Properties of Organic & Polymeric Materials. Ed. by David J. Williams. LC 83-15514. (ACS Symposium Ser.: Vol. 233). 262p. 1983. reprint ed. pap. 81.30 (*0-608-03082-1*, 206353500007) Bks Demand.

Nonlinear Optical Properties of Organic Materials IX, Vol. 2852. Ed. by Gustaaf R. Moehlmann. 304p. 1996. 76.00 (*0-8194-2240-1*) SPIE.

Nonlinear Optical Properties of Organic Materials X, Vol. 3147. Ed. by Mark G. Kuzyk. 288p. 1997. 80.00 (*0-8194-2569-9*) SPIE.

Nonlinear Optical Properties of Polymers. Ed. by A. J. Heeger et al. (Symposium Proceedings Ser.: Vol. 109). 1988. text 17.50 (*0-931837-77-4*) Materials Res.

***Nonlinear Optical Waves** A. I. Maimistov & A. M. Basharov. LC 99-27060. (Fundamental Theories of Physics Ser.). 1999. write for info. (*0-7923-5752-3*) Kluwer Academic.

Nonlinear Optics. Robert W. Boyd. (Illus.). 439p. (C). 1991. text 75.00 (*0-12-121680-2*) Acad Pr.

Nonlinear Optics. Jerome V. Moloney & Alan C. Newell. (ATIMS Ser.). 320p. (C). 1992. 46.95 (*0-201-51014-6*) Addison-Wesley.

Nonlinear Optics. Ed. by S. G. Rautian. 537p. (C). 1992. lib. bdg. 225.00 (*1-56072-074-3*) Nova Sci Pubs.

Nonlinear Optics. E. G. Sauter. LC 96-28541. (Wiley Series in Microwave & Optical Engineering). 232p. 1996. 84.95 (*0-471-14860-1*, Wiley-Interscience) Wiley.

Nonlinear Optics. Ed. by D. V. Skobel'tsyn. Tr. by Frank L. Sinclair from RUS. LC 72-107530. (Proceedings of the P. N. Lebedev Physics Institute Ser.: No. 43). (Illus.). 211p. 1970. reprint ed. pap. 65.50 (*0-608-05510-7*, 206597800006) Bks Demand.

Nonlinear Optics. 4th ed. Nicolaas Bloembergen. LC 96-215048. 1996. 32.00 (*981-02-2598-9*); pap. text 18.00 (*981-02-2599-7*) World Scientific Pub.

Nonlinear Optics: Basic Concepts. D. L. Mills. (Illus.). viii, 184p. 1991. 39.95 (*0-387-54192-6*) Spr-Verlag.

Nonlinear Optics: Basic Concepts. 2nd ed. D. L. Mills. LC 98-6385. (Illus.). 260p. 1998. pap. 42.50 (*3-540-64182-3*) Spr-Verlag.

Nonlinear Optics: Materials, Fundamentals, & Applications. LC 95-72776. (Nineteen Ninety-Six Technical Digest Ser.: No. 11). 508p. 1996. pap. 75.00 (*1-55752-447-5*) Optical Soc.

Nonlinear Optics & Acoustics of Fluids. Ed. by F. V. Bunkin. (Proceedings of the Institute of General Physics of the Academy of Sciences of the U. S. S. R. Ser.: Vol. 6). 172p. 1989. text 165.00 (*0-941743-28-4*) Nova Sci Pubs.

Nonlinear Optics & Adaptive Laser Systems. V. I. Bespalov & G. A. Pasmanik. 147p. (C). 1993. lib. bdg. 165.00 (*1-56072-121-9*) Nova Sci Pubs.

Nonlinear Optics & Optical Physics. Ed. by Iam-Choon Khoo et al. LC 94-2413. (Series in Nonlinear Optics: Vol. 2). 492p. 1994. pap. 48.00 (*981-02-0968-1*) World Scientific Pub.

Nonlinear Optics & Optical Physics: Lecture Notes from Capri Spring School, Capri, Italy, June 1992. Francesco Simoni. Ed. by Iam-Choon Khoo et al. (Series in Nonlinear Optics: Vol. 2). 492p. 1994. text 99.00 (*981-02-0967-3*) World Scientific Pub.

Nonlinear Optics & Quantum Electronics. Max Schubert & B. Wilhelmi. LC 85-20310. (Pure & Applied Optics Ser.). 752p. 1986. 215.00 (*0-471-08807-2*) Wiley.

Nonlinear Optics III. Ed. by R. A. Fisher & J. F. Reintjes. 1992. 20.00 (*0-8194-0772-0*, 1626) SPIE.

Nonlinear Optics in Metals. K. H. Bennemann. LC 98-8282. (The International Series of Monographs on Physics: No. 98). (Illus.). 752p. 1999. text 155.00 (*0-19-851893-5*) OUP.

Nonlinear Optics in Signal Processing. Ed. by R. W. Eason & Arthur Miller. LC 92-31149. 1992. write for info. (*0-442-31658-5*) Chapman & Hall.

Nonlinear Optics in Solids: Proceedings of the International Summer School Aalborg, Denmark, July 31 - August 4, 1989. Ed. by D. Keller et al. (Wave Phenomena Ser.: Vol. 9). (Illus.). ix, 351p. 1990. 86.95 (*0-387-52647-1*) Spr-Verlag.

Nonlinear Optics '98: Materials, Fundamentals & Applications Topical Meeting, 10-14 August 1998, Princeville Hotel, Princeville, Kauai, Hawaii. Optical Society of America Staff & Lasers & Electro-Optics Society (IEEE) Staff. LC 98-85597. 468 p. 1998. pap. write for info. (*0-7803-4952-0*) IEEE Standards.

Nonlinear Optics of Free Atoms & Molecules. David Cotter et al. Ed. by David L. MacAdam. (Optical Sciences Ser.: Vol. 17). (Illus.). 1980. 78.95 (*0-387-09628-0*) Spr-Verlag.

Nonlinear Optics of Liquid & Photorefractive Crystals: 23-30 October, 1995, Ai-Danil, Crimea, Ukraine. Gertruda V. Klimusheva et al. LC 96-68051. x, 338 p. 1996. pap. write for info. (*0-8194-2182-0*) SPIE.

Nonlinear Optics of Liquid & Photorefractive Crystals II. Ed. by Gertruda V. Klimusheva. LC 99-206517. (Proceedings of SPIE Ser.: Vol. 3488). 315p. 1998. 69.00 (*0-8194-2947-3*) SPIE.

Nonlinear Optics of Organic Molecules & Polymeric Materials. Ed. by Hari S. Nalwa & Seizo Miyata. LC 96-20281. (Illus.). 896p. 1996. boxed set 199.95 (*0-8493-8923-2*) CRC Pr.

Nonlinear Optics of Organics & Semiconductors. T. Kobayashi. (Proceedings in Physics Ser.: Vol. 36). (Illus.). 360p. 1989. 83.95 (*0-387-51045-1*) Spr-Verlag.

***Nonlinear Optics of Random Media: Fractal Composites & Metal-Dielectric Films.** Vladimir M. Shalaev. LC 99-38272. (Tracts in Modern Physics Ser.: Vol. 158). (Illus.). xii, 140p. 1999. 89.95 (*3-540-65615-4*) Spr-Verlag.

Nonlinear Optics of Semiconductor Lasers. Ed. by N. G. Basov. (Proceedings of the Lebedev Physics Institute Ser.: Vol. 166). 281p. (C). 1987. text 165.00 (*0-941743-01-2*) Nova Sci Pubs.

Nonlinear Optimization & Applications: Proceedings of the International School of Mathematics "G Stampacchia" 21st Workshop Held in Erice, Italy, June 13-21, 1995. G. Di Pillo & F. Giannessi. LC 96-21924. (Illus.). 380p. (C). 1996. 132.00 (*0-306-45316-9*, Kluwer Plenum) Kluwer Academic.

***Nonlinear Optimization & Related Topics.** G. Di Pillo & F. Giannessi. LC 99-56953. (Applied Optimization Ser.). (C). 1999. text. write for info. (*0-7923-6109-1*) Kluwer Academic.

Nonlinear Ordinary Differential Equations. R. Grimshaw. 336p. 1991. boxed set 99.95 (*0-8493-8607-1*, QA) CRC Pr.

Nonlinear Ordinary Differential Equations. R. Grimshaw. 1991. 59.95 (*0-632-02708-8*, QA, CRC Reprint) Franklin.

***Nonlinear Ordinary Differential Equations: An Introduction to Dynamical Systems.** 3rd ed. D. W. Jordan et al. LC 99-17648. (Illus.). 560p. 1999. text 90.00 (*0-19-856563-1*) OUP.

Nonlinear Ordinary Differential Equations: An Introduction to Dynamical Systems. 3rd ed. Dominic Jordan & Peter Smith. LC 99-17648. (Illus.). 560p. 1999. pap. text 40.00 (*0-19-856562-3*) OUP.

Nonlinear Ordinary Differential Equations & Their Applications. P. L. Sachdev. (Pure & Applied Mathematics Ser.: Vol. 142). (Illus.). 456p. 1990. text 179.75 (*0-8247-8364-6*) Dekker.

Nonlinear Oscillation in Feedback Systems. V. Biro. 208p. (C). 1985. 140.00 (*963-05-3425-8*, Pub. by Akade Kiado) St Mut.

Nonlinear Oscillations. Ali H. Nayfeh & Dean T. Mook. LC 78-27102. (Pure & Applied Mathematics: A Wiley-Interscience Series of Texts, Monographs & Tracts). 720p. 1979. 250.00 (*0-471-03555-6*) Wiley.

Nonlinear Oscillations. Ali H. Nayfeh & Dean T. Mook. LC 78-27102. (Classics Library). 720p. 1995. pap. 76.95 (*0-471-12142-8*) Wiley.

Nonlinear Oscillations & Waves in Dynamical Systems. P. S. Landa. LC 95-48427. (Mathematics & Its Applications Ser.: Vol. 360). 556p. (C). 1996. text 254.00 (*0-7923-3931-2*) Kluwer Academic.

Nonlinear Oscillations, Dynamical Systems, & Bifurcations of Vector Fields. 3rd ed. J. Guckenheimer & P. Holmes. Ed. by F. John et al. (Applied Mathematical Sciences Ser.: Vol. 42). (Illus.). xvi, 459p. 1997. reprint ed. 45.95 (*0-387-90819-6*) Spr-Verlag.

Nonlinear Oscillations in Biology. Ed. by Frank C. Hoppensteadt. LC 79-26469. (Lectures in Applied Mathematics: Vol. 17). 253p. 1979. text 58.00 (*0-8218-1117-7*, LAM/17) Am Math.

Nonlinear Oscillations in Biology. Summer Seminar on Applied Mathematics, University. Ed. by Frank C. Hoppenstead. LC 79-26469. (Lectures in Applied Mathematics: No. 17). 263p. reprint ed. pap. 81.60 (*0-608-05982-X*, 205264800008) Bks Demand.

Nonlinear Oscillations in Biology & Chemistry. Ed. by Hans G. Othmer. (Lecture Notes in Biomathematics Ser.: Vol. 66). vi, 289p. 1986. 51.95 (*0-387-16481-2*) Spr-Verlag.

Nonlinear Oscillations in Feedback Systems. V. Biro. 208p. (C). 1985. 160.00 (*0-7855-4971-4*, Pub. by Collets) St Mut.

Nonlinear Parabolic & Elliptic Equations. C. V. Pao. LC 92-30342. (Illus.). 794p. (C). 1993. 155.00 (*0-306-44343-0*, Plenum Trade) Perseus Pubng.

Nonlinear Parabolic Equation. L. Boccardo & A. Tesei. 1987. pap. text. write for info. (*0-582-99459-4*, Pub. by Addison-Wesley) Longman.

Nonlinear Partial Differential Equation. Brezis. Date not set. text. write for info. (*0-582-02181-2*, Pub. by Addison-Wesley) Longman.

Nonlinear Partial Differential Equations. A. Benkirane. (Pitman Research Notes in Mathematics Ser.). 1996. lib. bdg. 52.95 (*0-582-29213-1*) Longman.

Nonlinear Partial Differential Equations. Ed. by Joel A. Smoller. LC 83-2844. (Contemporary Mathematics Ser.: Vol. 17). 446p. 1983. pap. 41.00 (*0-8218-5017-2*, CONM/17) Am Math.

Nonlinear Partial Differential Equations: A Volume in Honor of Xiaqi Ding. Ed. by Gui-Qiang Chen et al. 460p. 1999. 86.00 (*981-02-3664-6*) World Scientific Pub.

***Nonlinear Partial Differential Equations: International Conference on Nonlinear Partial Differential Equations & Applications, March 21-24, 1998, Northwestern University.** International Conference on Nonlinear Partial Differential Equations & Applications Staff et al. LC 99-30749. (Contemporary Mathematics Ser.). 303p. 1999. pap. write for info. (*0-8218-1196-7*) Am Math.

Nonlinear Partial Differential Equations & Applications: Proceedings of the Conference Chongqing University, Pr China 26 - 31 May 1997. Ed. by Guo Boling & Yang Dadi. 260p. 58.00 (*981-02-3659-X*) World Scientific Pub.

Nonlinear Partial Differential Equations & Their Applications. Ed. by D. Cioranescu & J. L. Lions. (Pitman Research Notes in Mathematics Ser.: No. 391). 352p. 1998. pap. 60.00 (*0-582-36926-6*, LM0646, Chap & Hall CRC) Addison-Wesley.

Nonlinear Partial Differential Equations & Their Applications: College de France Seminar, Vol. 10. Ed. by Haim Brezis & J. L. Lions. LC 90-8426. (Pitman Research Notes in Mathematics Ser.: Vol. 220). 407p. 1991. reprint ed. pap. 126.20 (*0-608-03596-3*, 206441900009) Bks Demand.

Nonlinear Partial Differential Equations for Scientists & Engineers. L. Debnath. LC 97-15710. 532p. 1997. 65.00 (*0-8176-3902-0*) Birkhauser.

Nonlinear Partial Differential Equations for Scientists & Engineers. Lokenath Debnath. LC 97-15710. 1997. write for info. (*3-7643-3902-0*) Birkhauser.

Nonlinear Partial Differential Equations in Differential Geometry. Ed. by Robert Hardt & Michael Wolf. LC 95-20571. (IAS-Park City Mathematics Ser.: Vol. 2). 339p. 1995. pap. 59.00 (*0-8218-0431-6*, PCMS/2) Am Math.

Nonlinear Partial Differential Equations in Engineering & Applied Science. Ed. by Robert L. Sternberg. (Lecture Notes in Pure & Applied Mathematics Ser.: Vol. 54). (Illus.). 504p. 1980. pap. text 155.00 (*0-8247-6996-1*) Dekker.

Nonlinear Partial Differential Equations in Geometry & Physics: The 1995 Barrett Lectures. Ed. by G. Baker & A. Freire. LC 96-51031. (Progress in Nonlinear Differential Equations & Their Applications Ser.: Vol. 29). 153p. 1997. 58.00 (*3-7643-5493-3*) Spr-Verlag.

Nonlinear Partial Differential Equations in Geometry & Physics: The 1995 Barrett Lectures. Garth Baker & Alexandre S. Freire. LC 96-51031. (Progress in Nonlinear Differential Equations & Their Applications Ser.). 1997. 58.00 (*0-8176-5493-3*) Birkhauser.

Nonlinear Partial Differential Equations of Second Order. Guangchang Dong. LC 91-27853. (Translations of Mathematical Monographs: Vol. 95). 251p. 1991. text 136.00 (*0-8218-4554-3*, MMONO/95) Am Math.

***Nonlinear PDE's, Dynamics & Continuum Physics.** Ed. by Jerry Bona et al. (CONM Ser.: Vol. 255). 264p. 2000. 65.00 (*0-8218-1052-9*) Am Math.

Nonlinear Phenomena & Chaos in Magnetic Materials. P. E. Wigen. 400p. 1994. text 71.00 (*981-02-1005-1*) World Scientific Pub.

Nonlinear Phenomena in Atmospheric & Oceanic Sciences. Ed. by A. Friedman et al. (IMA Volumes in Mathematics & Its Applications Ser.: Vol. 40). (Illus.). xiii, 267p. 1992. 78.95 (*0-387-97818-6*) Spr-Verlag.

Nonlinear Phenomena in Chemical Dynamics: Proceedings. Ed. by C. Vidal & A. Pacault. (Synergetics Ser.: Vol. 12). (Illus.). 280p. 1982. 60.95 (*0-387-11294-4*) Spr-Verlag.

Nonlinear Phenomena in Fluids, Solids & Other Complex Systems: Proceedings of the 2nd Latin American Workshop on Nonlinear Phenomena, Santiago, Chile, 6-14 September, 1990. Ed. by P. Cordero et al. (North-Holland Delta Ser.: Vol. 9). xii, 482p. 1991. 165.00 (*0-444-88791-1*, NHD 9, North Holland) Elsevier.

N

An Asterisk (*) at the beginning of an entry indicates that the title is appearing for the first time.

Nonlinear Phenomena in Physics of Fluids & Plasmas - Proceedings of the ENEA Workshops on Nonlinear Dynamics, Bologna, Italy, October 30-31, 1989. Ed. by Giuseppe Maino et al. (ENEA Workshop on Nonlinear Dynamics Ser.: Vol. 2). 208p. 1991. text 89.00 (*981-02-0363-2*) World Scientific Pub.

Nonlinear Phenomena in Solids, Modern Topics: Proceedings of the 3rd International School on Condensed Matter Physics, Yarna, Bulgaria, Sept. 21-29, 1984. Ed. by M. Borissov. 484p. 1985. 100.00 (*9971-966-72-7*) World Scientific Pub.

Nonlinear Phenomena in Stellar Variability: Proceedings of the 134th Colloquium of the International Astronomical Union Held in Mito, Japan, January 7-10, 1992. Ed. by M. Takeuti & J. Robert Buchler. LC 94-8296. 376p. (C). 1994. text 191.50 (*0-7923-2769-1*) Kluwer Academic.

Nonlinear Photonics. Ed. by H. M. Gibbs et al. (Electronics & Photonics Ser.: Vol. 30). (Illus.). xii, 210p. 1990. 75.95 (*0-387-52194-1*) Spr-Verlag.

Nonlinear Photonics: Nonlinearities in Optics, Optoelectronics & Fiber Communications. Yili Guo et al. (Illus.). 620p. (C). text 38.00 (*962-201-861-0*, Pub. by Chinese Univ) U of Mich Pr.

Nonlinear Physical Phenomena. Ed. by A. Ferraz & F. Oliveira. 272p. (C). 1990. text 101.00 (*981-02-0032-3*) World Scientific Pub.

Nonlinear Physics. Ed. by Gu Chaohao et al. (Research Reports in Physics). (Illus.). 315p. 1990. 71.95 (*0-387-52389-8*) Spr-Verlag.

Nonlinear Physics: From the Pendulum to Turbulence & Chaos. 4th ed. R. Z. Sagdeev et al. (Contemporary Concepts in Physics Ser.: Vol. 4). xxiv, 676p. 1988. text 218.00 (*3-7186-4828-8*); pap. text 71.00 (*3-7186-4829-6*); 3.5 hd 96.00 (*3-7186-4830-X*) Gordon & Breach.

Nonlinear Physics: From the Pendulum to Turbulence & Chaos, Set. 4th ed. R. Z. Sagdeev et al. (Contemporary Concepts in Physics Ser.: Vol. 4). 656p. 1988. pap. 150.00 incl. disk (*3-7186-4832-6*) Gordon & Breach.

Nonlinear Physics: Theory & Experiment. 628p. 1996. 90.00 (*981-02-2559-8*) World Scientific Pub.

Nonlinear Physics for Beginners. Ed. by Lui Lam. 250p. (C). 1997. text 55.00 (*981-02-0140-0*); pap. text 21.00 (*981-02-0141-9*) World Scientific Pub.

Nonlinear Physics of Complex Systems: Current Status & Future Trends. J. Urgen Parisi et al. LC 96-41822. (Lecture Notes in Physics Ser.: Vol. 476). xiii, 388p. 1996. 92.00 (*3-540-61734-5*) Spr-Verlag.

***Nonlinear Physics of DNA.** L. V. Iakushevich. LC 97-29529. (Wiley Series in Nonlinear Science). 218p. 1998. 175.00 (*0-471-97824-8*) Wiley.

Nonlinear Physics with MAPLE for Scientists & Engineers, 2 vols. R. Enns & Simon Fraser. 552p. 1997. write for info. (*3-7643-3977-1*) Birkhauser.

Nonlinear Physics with Maple for Scientists & Engineers. Richard H. Enns & George McGuire. LC 96-40498. Date not set. 74.50 (*0-8176-3977-2*) Birkhauser.

Nonlinear Physics with Maple for Scientists & Engineers. Richard H. Enns & George McGuire. LC 96-40498. (Illus.). 389p. 1997. 54.50 (*0-8176-3838-5*) Birkhauser.

***Nonlinear Physics with Maple for Scientists & Engineers.** 2nd ed. Richard H. Enns & G. C. McGuire. LC 99-52748. (Illus.). 656p. 1999. 69.95 incl. disk (*0-8176-4119-X*, Pub. by Birkhauser) Spr-Verlag.

***Nonlinear Physics with Maple for Scientists & Engineers.** 2nd ed. Richard H. Enns & George McGuire. LC 99-52748. 2000. write for info. (*3-7643-4119-X*) Birkhauser.

Nonlinear Poisson Brackets: Geometry & Quantization. M. V. Karasev & V. P. Maslov. LC 92-42061. (Translations of Mathematical Monographs: Vol. 119). 366p. 1993. text 170.00 (*0-8218-4596-9*, MMONO/119) Am Math.

***Nonlinear Potential Theory & Weighted Sobolev Spaces.** Bengt Ove Turesson. LC 00-40015. (Lecture Notes in Mathematics Ser.). 2000. pap. write for info. (*3-540-67588-4*) Spr-Verlag.

Nonlinear Potential Theory of Degenerate Elliptic Equations. Juha Heinonen et al. LC 92-32906. (Oxford Mathematical Monographs). 368p. (C). 1993. text 75.00 (*0-19-853669-0*, Clarendon Pr) OUP.

Nonlinear Prediction Ladder-Filters for Higher-Order Stochastic Sequences. J. Zarzycki. LC 85-12668. (Lecture Notes in Control & Information Sciences: Vol. 73). (Illus.). v, 132p. 1985. 25.95 (*0-387-15635-6*) Spr-Verlag.

Nonlinear Preference & Utility Theory. Peter C. Fishburn. LC 87-29729. (Mathematical Sciences Ser.). 288p. 1988. text 60.00 (*0-8018-3598-4*) Johns Hopkins.

Nonlinear Pricing: Published in Association with the Electric Power Research Institute. Robert B. Wilson. (Illus.). 440p. 1997. reprint ed. pap. 26.00 (*0-19-511582-1*) OUP.

Nonlinear Pricing: Theory & Applications. Christopher May. LC 98-37590. (Trading Advantage Ser.). 361p. 1999. 69.95 (*0-471-24551-8*) Wiley.

Nonlinear Problems: Proceedings of a Symposium Conducted by the Mathematics Research Center, United States Army, at the University of Wisconsin, Madison, April 30-May 2, 1962. Ed. by Rudolph E. Langer. LC 63-8971. (U. S. Army. Mathematics Research Center Publication Ser.: No. 8). 336p. reprint ed. pap. 104.20 (*0-608-10292-X*, 202113800021) Bks Demand.

Nonlinear Problems in Accelerator Physics: Proceedings of the International Workshop, Held in Berlin, Germany, 30 March-2 April 1992. Ed. by Martin Berz et al. (Institute of Physics Conference Ser.: No. 131). (Illus.). 276p. 1993. 161.00 (*0-7503-0238-0*) IOP Pub.

***Nonlinear Problems in Aviation & Aerospace.** Ed. by S. Sivasundaram. Vol. 11. 250p. 1999. text 120.00 (*90-5699-222-8*) Gordon & Breach.

Nonlinear Problems in Engineering: Proceedings of the ENEA Workshop on Nonlinear Dynamics, Rome, Italy, 6-7 May 1991. Ed. by Giuseppe Maino & C. Carmignani. (ENEA Workshop on Nonlinear Dynamics Ser.: Vol. 4). 400p. 1991. text 104.00 (*981-02-0832-4*) World Scientific Pub.

Nonlinear Problems in Future Particle Accelerators. Ed. by W. Scandale & Giorgio Turchetti. 440p. (C). 1991. text 130.00 (*981-02-0231-8*) World Scientific Pub.

Nonlinear Problems in Geometry. Ed. by D. DeTurck. LC 86-1151. (Contemporary Mathematics Ser.: Vol. 51). 130p. 1986. pap. 25.00 (*0-8218-5053-9*, CONM/51) Am Math.

Nonlinear Problems in Geometry: Proceedings of an AMS Special Session Held May 3-4, 1985. Ed. by Dennis M. DeTurck. LC 86-1151. (Contemporary Mathematics Ser.: No. 51). (Illus.). 140p. 1986. pap. 43.40 (*0-608-05567-0*, 205260400006) Bks Demand.

Nonlinear Problems in Mechanics of Continua. Applied Mathematics Symposium Staff et al. Ed. by Eric Reissner. LC 50-1183. (Proceedings of Symposia in Applied Mathematics Ser.). 219p. 1949. text 31.00 (*0-8218-1301-3*, PSAPM/1) Am Math.

Nonlinear Problems of Elasticity. Stuart S. Antman. LC 94-25684. (Applied Mathematical Sciences: 107). 750p. 1994. 69.95 (*0-387-94199-1*) Spr-Verlag.

Nonlinear Process Control. M. Chidambaram. 140p. 1995. 54.95 (*0-470-23552-7*) Wiley.

Nonlinear Process Control: Applications of Generic Model Control. Peter L. Lee. LC 93-21311. (Advances in Industrial Control Ser.). 1993. 64.95 (*0-387-19856-3*) Spr-Verlag.

Nonlinear Processes in Physics. A. S. Fokas et al. LC 92-32811. (Nonlinear Dynamics Ser.). 1993. write for info. (*3-540-55912-4*); 97.95 (*0-387-55912-4*) Spr-Verlag.

Nonlinear Programming. Olvi L. Mangasarian. LC 94-36844. (Classics in Applied Mathematics Ser.: Vol. 10). xv, 220p. 1994. pap. 33.00 (*0-89871-341-2*) Soc Indus-Appl Math.

Nonlinear Programming. 2nd ed. Dimitri P. Bertsekas. LC 99-73208. 708p. 1999. text 79.00 (*1-886529-00-0*) Athena Scientific.

Nonlinear Programming: Proceedings of the SIAM-AMS Symposia, New York, March, 1975, Vol. 9. Ed. by Richard W. Cottle & C. E. Lemke. LC 75-45471. 200p. 1980. reprint ed. pap. 27.00 (*0-8218-1329-3*, SIAMS/9) Am Math.

Nonlinear Programming: Sequential Unconstrained Minimization Techniques. A. V. Fiacco & Garth P. McCormick. LC 68-30909. (Classics in Applied Mathematics Ser.: No. 4). xvi, 210p. 1990. pap. 35.50 (*0-89871-254-8*) Soc Indus-Appl Math.

Nonlinear Programming: Theory & Algorithms. 2nd ed. Mokhtar S. Bazaraa et al. LC 92-30957. 656p. 1993. text 103.95 (*0-471-55793-5*) Wiley.

Nonlinear Programming & Variational Inequality Problems: A Unified Approach. Michael Patriksson. LC 98-45184. (Applied Optimization Ser.). 12p. 1999. 168.00 (*0-7923-5455-9*) Kluwer Academic.

Nonlinear Properties of Internal Waves: La Jolla Institute, 1981. Ed. by Bruce J. West. (AIP Conference Proceedings Ser.: No. 76). 351p. 1981. lib. bdg. 32.00 (*0-88318-175-4*) Am Inst Physics.

Nonlinear Psychophysical Dynamics. Robert A. Gregson. 232p. 1988. 49.95 (*0-8058-0015-8*) L Erlbaum Assocs.

Nonlinear Random Waves. Vladimir V. Konotop & Luis Vazquez. 308p. 1994. text 74.00 (*981-02-1725-0*) World Scientific Pub.

Nonlinear Regression. G. A. Seber & C. J. Wild. LC 88-17194. (Probability & Mathematical Statistics: Applied Probability & Statistics Section Ser.). 800p. 1989. 175.00 (*0-471-61760-1*) Wiley.

Nonlinear Regression Analysis & Its Applications. Douglas M. Bates & Donald G. Watts. LC 88-6065. (Probability & Mathematical Statistics Ser.). 384p. 1988. 114.95 (*0-471-81643-4*) Wiley.

Nonlinear Regression Modeling: A Unified Practical Approach. David A. Ratkowsky. (Statistics: Textbooks & Monographs: Vol. 48). (Illus.). 288p. 1983. text 125.00 (*0-8247-1907-7*) Dekker.

Nonlinear Renewal Theory in Sequential Analysis. M. Woodroofe. LC 81-84856. (CBMS-NSF Regional Conference Ser.: No. 39). v, 119p. 1982. pap. 29.50 (*0-89871-180-0*) Soc Indus-Appl Math.

Nonlinear Sampled-Data Systems. P. Vidal. xvi, 346p. 1969. text 391.00 (*0-677-30230-4*) Gordon & Breach.

Nonlinear Schrodinger Equations: Self-Focusing Instability & Wave Collapse. C. Sulem & P. L. Sulem. Ed. by J. E. Marsden & L. Sirov. LC 98-53840. (Applied Mathematical Sciences Ser.: Vol. 139). (Illus.). 369p. 1999. 64.95 (*0-387-98611-1*) Spr-Verlag.

Nonlinear Science. National Research Council Staff. LC 97-220788. 50p. 1997. pap. text 10.00 (*0-309-05843-0*) Natl Acad Pr.

Nonlinear Science: Emergence & Dynamics of Coherent Structures. Alwyn C. Scott. LC 99-10300. (Illus.). 492p. 1999. text 69.00 (*0-19-850107-2*) OUP.

Nonlinear Science: The Next Decade. Ed. by David K. Campbell et al. (Physica D Ser.). (Illus.). 592p. 1992. pap. text 40.00 (*0-262-53109-7*, Bradford Bks) MIT Pr.

***Nonlinear Science at the Dawn of the 21st Century.** Peter L. Christiansen et al. LC 00-26993. (Lecture Notes in Physics Ser.: Vol. 542). xxvi, 458p. 2000. 98.00 (*3-540-66918-3*) Spr-Verlag.

Nonlinear Seismic Analysis & Design of Reinforced Concrete Buildings: Workshop on Nonlinear Seismic Analysis of Reinforced Concrete Buildings Bled Slovenia Yugoslavia. Ed. by P. Fajfar & H. Krawinkler. (Illus.). 308p. (C). (gr. 13). 1992. text 200.00 (*1-85166-764-4*) Elsevier Applied Sci.

Nonlinear Semigroups. Isao Miyadera. Tr. by Choong Y. Cho. LC 92-11318. (Translations of Mathematical Monographs: Vol. 109). 230p. 1992. text 99.00 (*0-8218-4565-9*, MMONO/109) Am Math.

Nonlinear Semigroups, Partial Differential Equations & Attractors. Ed. by T. L. Gill & W. W. Zachary. (Lecture Notes in Mathematics Ser.: Vol. 1248). ix, 185p. 1987. 34.95 (*0-387-17741-8*) Spr-Verlag.

Nonlinear Semigroups, Partial Differential Equations & Attractors. Ed. by T. L. Gill & W. W. Zachary. (Lecture Notes in Mathematics Ser.: Vol. 1394). ix, 233p. 1989. 36.95 (*0-387-51594-1*) Spr-Verlag.

Nonlinear Signal & Image Analysis. J. Robert Buchler & Henry E. Kandrup. LC 96-29561. (Annals of the New York Academy of Sciences Ser.). 1997. 80.00 (*1-57331-044-1*) NY Acad Sci.

Nonlinear Signal & Image Analysis. J. Robert Buchler & Henry E. Kandrup. LC 96-29561. (Annals of The New York Academy of Sciences Ser.: Vol. 808). 1997. pap. 80.00 (*1-57331-045-X*) NY Acad Sci.

Nonlinear Simulation of Time Dependent Towing of Ocean Vehicles. Michael M. Bernitsas & Nikos S. Kekridis. LC VM0521.. (University of Michigan, Dept. of Naval Architecture & Marine Engineering, Report Ser.: No. 283). 59p. reprint ed. pap. 30.00 (*0-608-14585-8*, 202482400038) Bks Demand.

Nonlinear Singular Perturbation Phenomena: Theory & Applications. K. W. Chang & F. A. Howes. (Applied Mathematical Sciences Ser.: Vol. 56). (Illus.). viii, 180p. 1984. 58.95 (*0-387-96066-X*) Spr-Verlag.

***Nonlinear Solid Mechanics.** Wilfried B. Holzapfel. 500p. 2000. text 145.00 (*0-471-82304-X*) Wiley.

***Nonlinear Solid Mechanics: A Continuum Approach for Engineering.** Wilfried B. Holzapfel. 500p. 2000. pap. 69.95 (*0-471-82319-8*) Wiley.

Nonlinear Space Plasma Physics. Ed. by R. Z. Sagdeev. LC 93-70460. (Research Trends in Physics Ser.). (Illus.). 528p. 1993. 99.00 (*0-88318-924-0*, AIP Pr) Spr-Verlag.

***Nonlinear Spatio-Temporal Dynamics & Chaos in Semiconductors.** Eckehard Scholl. (Cambridge Nonlinear Science Ser.: Vol. 10). (Illus.). 375p. 2000. write for info. (*0-521-45186-8*) Cambridge U Pr.

***Nonlinear Spectroscopy for Molecular Structure Determination.** R. W. Field et al. (IUPAC Chemical Data Ser.). (Illus.). 1998. 87.50 (*0-632-04217-6*) Blackwell Sci.

Nonlinear Spectroscopy of Molecules see Progress in Quantum Electronics

Nonlinear Spectroscopy of Solids: Advances & Applications. B. Di Bartolo. (NATO ASI Series B: Vol. 339). (Illus.). 668p. (C). 1995. 159.50 (*0-306-44916-1*) Plenum.

Nonlinear Stability & Bifurcation Theory: An Introduction for Engineers & Applied Scientists. H. Troger & A. Steindl. (Illus.). xi, 407p. 1991. 100.95 (*0-387-82292-5*) Spr-Verlag.

Nonlinear Stability & Waves: Sixth Workshop. D. K. Callebaut & W. Malfliet. 1994. text 75.00 (*981-02-1060-4*) World Scientific Pub.

Nonlinear Stability of Shock Waves for Viscous Conservation Laws. T. Liu. LC 85-9153. (Memoirs of the AMS Ser.: No. 56/328). 109p. 1988. reprint ed. pap. 21.00 (*0-8218-2329-9*, MEMO/56/328) Am Math.

Nonlinear Stability of Structures: Theory & Computational Techniques. Ed. by W. B. Kratzig & Anthony N. Kounadis. (CISM International Centre for Mechanical Sciences Ser.: No. 342). (Illus.). ix, 415p. 1995. pap. 85.00 (*3-211-82651-3*) Spr-Verlag.

Nonlinear Statistical Model. Andrej Pazman. LC 93-7412. (Mathematics & Its Applications Ser.: Vol. 254). 1993. text 174.50 (*0-7923-2247-9*) Kluwer Academic.

Nonlinear Statistical Models. A. Ronald Gallant. LC 86-18955. 624p. 1987. 177.00 (*0-471-80260-3*) Wiley.

Nonlinear Stochastic Dynamic Engineering Systems. Ed. by G. I. Schueller & Franz Ziegler. (International Union of Theoretical & Applied Mechanics Symposia Ser.). (Illus.). x, 541p. 1988. 93.00 (*0-387-18804-5*) Spr-Verlag.

Nonlinear Stochastic Evolution Problems in Applied Sciences. N. Bellomo et al. LC 92-35069. (Mathematics & Its Applications Ser.: Vol. 82). (C). 1992. text 138.00 (*0-7923-2042-5*) Kluwer Academic.

Nonlinear Stochastic Integrators, Equations & Flows, Vol. 6. R. A. Carmona & D. Nualart. x, 160p. 1990. text 134.00 (*2-88124-733-4*) Gordon & Breach.

Nonlinear Stochastic Mechanics: IUTAM Symposium, Turin, 1991. Ed. by N. Bellomo & F. Casiati. LC 92-20009. (International Union of Theoretical & Applied Mechanics Symposia Ser.). xiii, 552p. 1992. 199.95 (*0-387-55545-5*) Spr-Verlag.

Nonlinear Stochastic PDE's: Hydrodynamic Limit & Burger's Turbulence. Ed. by Tadahisa Funaki & Wojbor A. Woyczynski. LC 95-44888. (IMA Volumes in Mathematics & Its Applications Ser.: Vol. 77). 330p. 1995. 59.95 (*0-387-94624-1*) Spr-Verlag.

Nonlinear Stochastic Problems. Ed. by Richard S. Bucy & Jose M. Moura. 1983. text 257.50 (*90-277-1590-4*) Kluwer Academic.

Nonlinear Stochastic Systems in Physics & Mechanics. Ed. by N. Bellomo & R. Riganti. 260p. 1987. text 49.00 (*9971-5-0249-6*) World Scientific Pub.

Nonlinear Stokes Phenomena. Ed. by Y. S. Il'yashenko. LC 91-640741. (Advances in Soviet Mathematics Ser.: Vol. 14). 287p. 1993. text 116.00 (*0-8218-4112-2*, ADVSOV/14C) Am Math.

Nonlinear Structures in Physical Systems: Pattern Formation, Chaos, & Waves: Proceedings of the Second Woodward Conference, San Jose State University, November 17-18, 1989. Ed. by Lui Lam & H. C. Morris. (Woodward Conference Ser.). (Illus.). x, 331p. 1990. 83.95 (*0-387-97344-3*) Spr-Verlag.

Nonlinear Structures in Physical Systems: Pattern Formation, Chaos & Waves: Proceedings of the 2nd Woodward Conference, San Jose State University, November 17-18, 1989 Woodward Conference Staff et al. LC 90-9866. x, 330p. 1990. write for info. (*3-540-97344-3*) Spr-Verlag.

Nonlinear Superconducting Devices & High-TC Materials: Proceedings of the International Conference. N. F. Pedersen. 500p. 1995. text 150.00 (*981-02-2091-X*) World Scientific Pub.

Nonlinear Superconductive Electronics & Josephson Devices. Ed. by G. Costabile et al. (Illus.). 456p. (C). 1992. text 162.00 (*0-306-44100-4*, Kluwer Plenum) Kluwer Academic.

Nonlinear Symmetries & Nonlinear Equations. Giuseppe Gaeta. (Mathematics & Its Applications Ser.). 280p. (C). 1994. text 166.50 (*0-7923-3048-X*) Kluwer Academic.

Nonlinear Synamics Structures. Virdi. (Civil Engineering Ser.). (Illus.). 288p. 1997. pap. 119.95 (*0-7514-0008-4*) Thomson Learn.

Nonlinear Synthesis: Proceedings of a IIASA Workshop Held in Sopron, Hungary, June 1989. Ed. by Christopher I. Byrnes & A. Kurzansky. (Progress in Systems & Control Theory Ser.: Vol. 9). viii, 304p. 1991. 109.50 (*0-8176-3484-3*) Birkhauser.

***Nonlinear System Vol. D, Pt. 2: Optimal Control.** Ed. by A. Isidori & C. V. Hollot. 602p. 1999. pap. 126.00 (*0-08-043218-2*) Elsevier.

***Nonlinear System Vol. F, Pt. 1: Optimal Control.** Ed. by A. Isidori et al. 560p. 1999. pap. 126.00 (*0-08-043217-4*) Elsevier.

Nonlinear System Analysis & Synthesis Vol. 1: Fundamental Principles. Ed. by J. Karl Hedrick & H. M. Paynter. 146p. 1978. pap. 15.00 (*0-685-99209-8*, G00138) ASME.

Nonlinear System Dynamics. W. Richard Kolk & Robert A. Lerman. (Illus.). 288p. 1992. text 64.95 (*0-442-00428-1*, VNR) Wiley.

***Nonlinear System Identification: Input-Output Modeling Approach, 2 vols.** Robert Haber & Lbaszlbo. Keviczky. LC 99-16508. (Mathematical Modelling--Theory & Applications Ser.). 1999. pap. write for info. (*0-7923-5857-0*) Kluwer Academic.

Nonlinear System Theory: The Volterra-Wiener Approach. Wilson J. Rugh. LC 80-8874. (Johns Hopkins Series in Information Sciences & Systems). 340p. 1981. reprint ed. pap. 105.40 (*0-608-04010-X*, 206474600011) Bks Demand.

Nonlinear Systems. P. G. Drazin. (Cambridge Texts in Applied Mathematics Ser.: No. 10). (Illus.). 331p. (C). 1992. pap. text 36.95 (*0-521-40668-4*) Cambridge U Pr.

Nonlinear Systems. 2nd ed. Hassan K. Khalil. LC 95-45804. 734p. (C). 1995. 105.00 (*0-13-228024-8*) P-H.

Nonlinear Systems: Analysis, Stability & Control. Shankar Sastry. (Illus.). 425p. (C). 1998. text. write for info. (*0-201-51481-8*) Addison-Wesley.

***Nonlinear Systems: Analysis, Stability & Control.** Shankar Sastry. Ed. by J. E. Marsden et al. LC 99-11798. (Interdisciplinary Applied Mathematics Ser.: Vol. 10). (Illus.). 721p. 1999. 79.95 (*0-387-98513-1*) Spr-Verlag.

Nonlinear Systems: The Parameter Analysis & Design. Dragoslav D. Siljak. LC 68-26853. 638p. reprint ed. pap. 197.80 (*0-608-30904-4*, 200635400058) Bks Demand.

Nonlinear Systems Vol. 1: Dynamics & Control, Vol. 1. Ronald R. Mohler. 288p. 1990. text 63.00 (*0-13-623489-5*) P-H.

Nonlinear Systems of Partial Differential Equations in Applied Mathematics, 2 pts., Pt. I. Ed. by B. Nicolaenko et al. LC 85-15107. (Lectures in Applied Mathematics: Vol. 23). 470p. 1986. text 61.00 (*0-8218-1125-8*, LAM/23.1) Am Math.

Nonlinear Systems of Partial Differential Equations in Applied Mathematics, 2 pts., Pt. II. Ed. by B. Nicolaenko et al. LC 85-15107. (Lectures in Applied Mathematics: Vol. 23). 387p. 1986. text 61.00 (*0-8218-1126-6*, LAM/23.2) Am Math.

Nonlinear Systems of Partial Differential Equations in Applied Mathematics, 2 pts., Set. Ed. by B. Nicolaenko et al. LC 85-15107. (Lectures in Applied Mathematics: Vol. 23). 858p. 1986. text 101.00 (*0-8218-1123-1*, LAM/23) Am Math.

Nonlinear Systems Techniques & Applications. 2nd ed. Julius Bendat. LC 97-11446. 474p. 1998. 105.00 (*0-471-16576-X*) Wiley.

Nonlinear Theory of Dislocations & Disclinations in Elastic Bodies. Leonid M. Zubov. Ed. by W. Beiglbock et al. LC 97-37130. (Lecture Notes in Physics Ser.: Vol. 47). vi, 205p. 1997. text 49.00 (*3-540-62684-0*) Spr-Verlag.

Nonlinear Theory of Elastic Shells. 2nd rev. ed. A. Libai & J. G. Simmonds. LC 97-13643. (Illus.). 558p. (C). 1998. text 85.00 (*0-521-47236-9*) Cambridge U Pr.

Nonlinear Theory of Generalized Functions. H. A. Biagioni. Ed. by A. Dold et al. (Lecture Notes in Mathematics Ser.: Vol. 1421). xii, 214p. 1990. 34.80 (*0-387-52408-8*) Spr-Verlag.

Nonlinear Theory of Generalized Functions. Michael Grosser. LC 98-52356. 400p. 1999. pap. text 84.95 (*0-8493-0649-3*) CRC Pr.

Nonlinear Theory of Shallow Shells, Vol. 133. I. Vorovich. LC 98-17535. (Applied Mathematical Sciences Ser.). (Illus.). 410p. 1998. 59.95 (*0-387-98339-2*) Spr-Verlag.

Nonlinear Theory of Shells Through Variational Principles: From Elemetary Algebra to Different Geometry. R. Valid. 496p. 1996. 225.00 (*0-471-95494-2*) Wiley.

An Asterisk (*) at the beginning of an entry indicates that the title is appearing for the first time.

Nonlinear Theory of Sound Beams. N. S. Bahkvalov et al. Tr. by Robert T. Beyer from RUS. LC 87-1850. (Translation Ser.). (Illus.). 184p. 1987. text 60.00 (*0-88318-520-2*) Am Inst Physics.

Nonlinear Theory of Strong Electro-Magnetic Wave Plasma. Ed. by O. N. Krokhin. (Proceedings of the Lebedev Physics Institute Ser.: Vol. 213). 315p. (C). 1994. lib. bdg. 165.00 (*1-56072-154-5*) Nova Sci Pubs.

Nonlinear Time-Discrete Systems: A General Approach by Nonlinear Superposition. M. Goessel. (Lecture Notes in Control & Information Sciences: Vol. 41). 112p. 1982. 18.95 (*0-387-11914-0*) Spr-Verlag.

Nonlinear Time Series Analysis. Holger Kantz & Thomas Schreiber. LC 96-37159. (Cambridge Nonlinear Science Ser.: Vol. 7). 320p. 1997. text 80.00 (*0-521-55144-7*) Cambridge U Pr.

Nonlinear Time Series Analysis. Holger Kantz & Thomas Schreiber. (Nonlinear Science Ser.: No. 7). (Illus.). 320p. (C). 1999. pap. text 34.95 (*0-521-65387-8*) Cambridge U Pr.

Nonlinear Time Series Analysis of Economic & Financial Data. Philip Rothman. LC 98-45191. 6p. 1999. 149.95 (*0-7923-8379-6*) Kluwer Academic.

Nonlinear Time Series & Economic Fluctuations. 200p. 1998. 27.00 (*981-02-2523-7*) World Scientific Pub.

Nonlinear Time Series & Probability Measures. Cees Diks. LC 99-16722. (Nonlinear Time Series & Chaos). (Illus.). 180p. 1998. 24.00 (*981-02-3505-4*) World Scientific Pub.

***Nonlinear Time Series Models in Empirical Finance.** Philip Hans Franses & Dick Van Dijk. LC 99-88504. (Illus.). 296p. 2000. write for info. (*0-521-77041-6*); pap. write for info. (*0-521-77965-0*) Cambridge U Pr.

***Nonlinear Time Series Workshop.** Douglas M. Patterson & Richard A. Ashley. LC 99-46691. (Dynamic Modeling & Econometrics in Economics & Finance Ser.). 1999. write for info. (*0-7923-8674-4*) Kluwer Academic.

Nonlinear Underwater Acoustics. B. K. Novikov et al. LC 87-70336.Tr. of Russian. 272p. 1987. pap. 39.00 (*0-88318-522-9*) Acoustical Soc Am.

Nonlinear Vibration. Ed. by R. A. Ibrahim. LC 93-72631. 287p. 65.00 (*0-7918-1171-9*) ASME Pr.

Nonlinear Vibrations in Mechanical & Electrical Systems. J. J. Stoker. LC 91-41112. (Classics Library: No. 1826). 296p. 1992. pap. 79.95 (*0-471-57033-8*) Wiley.

Nonlinear Vibrations, 1993. Ed. by R. A. Ibrahim et al. (DE Ser.: Vol. 54). 65.00 (*0-685-70658-3*, G00815) ASME.

Nonlinear Vibrations, 1992. Ed. by R. A. Ibrahim et al. (DE Series, Vol. 50: AMD: Vol. 144). 176p. 1993. 50.00 (*0-7918-1092-5*, G00736) ASME.

Nonlinear Vision. Robert B. Pinter & Bahram Nabet. 576p. 1992. 99.95 (*0-8493-4292-9*, QP475) CRC Pr.

Nonlinear Water Waves. Lokenath Debnath. (Illus.). 544p. 1994. text 138.00 (*0-12-208437-3*) Acad Pr.

Nonlinear Water Waves. Ed. by Kiyoshi Horikawa & H. Maruo. (Illus.). xvii, 466p. 1988. 93.00 (*0-387-18793-6*) Spr-Verlag.

Nonlinear Wave Dynamics Complexity & Simplicity. LC 97-12177. 1997. text 117.50 (*0-7923-4508-8*) Kluwer Academic.

Nonlinear Wave Equations. Satyanad Kichenassamy. (Pure & Applied Mathematics Ser.: Vol. 194). (Illus.). 296p. 1995. text 125.00 (*0-8247-9328-5*) Dekker.

Nonlinear Wave Equations. W. Strauss. LC 89-18167. (CBMS Regional Conference Series in Mathematics: No. 73). 91p. 1989. pap. 19.00 (*0-8218-0725-0*, CBMS-73) Am Math.

***Nonlinear Wave Equations: A Conference in Honor of Walter A. Strauss on the Occasion of His 16th Birthday, May 2-3, 1998, Brown University.** Walter A. Strauss & Yan Guo. LC 00-44158. (Contemporary Mathematics Ser.). 2000. write for info. (*0-8218-2071-0*) Am Math.

Nonlinear Wave Equations, Formation of Singularities. F. John. LC 90-700. (University Lectures: Vol. 2). 64p. 1990. pap. 15.00 (*0-8218-7001-7*, ULECT/2) Am Math.

***Nonlinear Wave Equations Perturbed by the Viscous Term.** V. P. Maslov & Peter Petrovich Mosolov. LC 00-43001. (Expositions in Mathematics Ser.). 2000. write for info. (*3-11-015282-7*) De Gruyter.

Nonlinear Wave Motion. T. B. Benjamin & D. J. Benney. Ed. by A. C. Newell. LC 73-19504. (Lectures in Applied Mathematics: Vol. 15). 229p. 1974. text 70.00 (*0-8218-1115-0*, LAM/15) Am Math.

Nonlinear Wave Motion. Alan C. Newell. LC 73-19504. (Lectures in Applied Mathematics: No. 15). (Illus.). 237p. reprint ed. pap. 73.50 (*0-608-05981-1*, 20526470008) Bks Demand.

Nonlinear Wave Processes in Acoustics. K. A. Naugolnykh & L. A. Ostrovsky. LC 98-2925. (Cambridge Texts in Applied Mathematics Ser.: No. 9). (Illus.). 308p. (C). 1998. text 74.95 (*0-521-39080-X*); pap. text 29.95 (*0-521-39984-X*) Cambridge U Pr.

Nonlinear Wave Processes in Excitable Media. Ed. by Arun V. Holden et al. LC 90-49843. (NATO ASI Ser.: Vol. 244). (Illus.). 578p. (C). 1990. text 174.00 (*0-306-43800-3*, Kluwer Plenum) Kluwer Academic.

Nonlinear Waves, No. 1. Ed. by A. V. Gaponov-Grekhov et al. (Research Reports in Physics). (Illus.). 260p. 1989. pap. 49.00 (*0-685-25299-X*) Spr-Verlag.

Nonlinear Waves No. 3: Physics & Astrophysics: Proceedings of the Gorky School 1989. Ed. by A. V. Gaponov-Grekhov et al. (Research Reports in Physics). (Illus.). xi, 325p. 1990. pap. 64.00 (*0-387-52024-4*) Spr-Verlag.

Nonlinear Waves & Solitons. Morikazu Toda. (C). 1989. text 278.00 (*0-7923-0442-X*) Kluwer Academic.

Nonlinear Waves & Weak Turbulence. Ed. by V. E. Zakharov. Tr. by A. B. Sossinsky from RUS. LC 91-640741. (American Mathematical Society Translations Ser. 2: Vol. 182). 197p. 1998. text 89.00 (*0-8218-4113-0*) Am Math.

Nonlinear Waves & Weak Turbulence with Applications in Oceanography & Condensed Matter Physics. Ed. by N. Fitzmaurice et al. LC 93-24471. (Progress in Nonlinear Differential Equations & Their Applications Ser.: Vol. 9). 1993. 98.00 (*0-8176-3667-6*) Birkhauser.

Nonlinear Waves in Dispersive & Dissipative Systems with Coupled Fields. Sergei Korsunsky. 1997. 85.95 (*0-582-30404-0*, Pub. by Addison-Wesley) Longman.

***Nonlinear Waves in Elastic Crystals.** Gerard A. Maugin. LC 99-44815. (Oxford Mathematical Monographs). (Illus.). 320p. 2000. text 95.00 (*0-19-853484-1*) OUP.

Nonlinear Waves in Elastic Media. A. G. Kulikovskii & Elena I. Sveshnikova. LC 95-10565. 256p. 1995. boxed set 124.95 (*0-8493-8643-8*, 8643) CRC Pr.

Nonlinear Waves in Inhomogeneous & Hereditary Media. A. A. Lokshin & E. A. Sagomonyan. (Research Reports in Physics). (Illus.). x, 121p. 1992. 79.95 (*0-387-54536-0*) Spr-Verlag.

Nonlinear Waves in Networks. Felix Ali Mehmeti. LC 94-35239. (Mathematical Research Ser.: Vol. 80). 1994. pap. text 59.85 (*3-05-501640-8*, Pub. by Akademie Verlag) Wiley.

Nonlinear Waves in Real Fluids. Ed. by A. Kluwick. (CISM International Centre for Mechanical Sciences Ser.: Vol. 315). (Illus.). v, 334p. 1991. 90.95 (*0-387-82277-1*) Spr-Verlag.

Nonlinear Waves in Solid State Physics. Ed. by Alan D. Boardman et al. LC 90-25112. (NATO ASI Ser.: Vol. 247). (Illus.). 508p. (C). 1991. text 174.00 (*0-306-43811-9*, Kluwer Plenum) Kluwer Academic.

Nonlinear Waves in Solids, 341. J. Engelbrecht & A. Jeffrey. (CISM International Centre for Mechanical Sciences Ser.). 382p. 1994. 94.95 (*0-387-82558-4*) Spr-Verlag.

Nonlinear Waves in Waveguides: With Stratification. S. B. Leble. (Research Reports in Physics). (Illus.). ix, 163p. 1991. pap. 69.00 (*0-387-52149-6*) Spr-Verlag.

Nonlinear Waves, Solitons & Chaos. E. Infeld & G. Rowlands. (Illus.). 435p. (C). 1990. pap. text 44.95 (*0-521-37937-7*) Cambridge U Pr.

***Nonlinear Waves, Solitons & Chaos.** 2nd ed. E. Infeld & George Rowlands. LC QC174.26.W28, I55. (Illus.). 450p. (C). 2000. 120.00 (*0-521-63212-9*); pap. 44.95 (*0-521-63557-8*) Cambridge U Pr.

***Nonlinear Workbook: Chaos, Fractals, Cellular Automata, Neural Networks, Genetic Algorithms, Fuz.** Willi-Hans Steeb. 1999. pap. text 38.00 (*981-02-4026-0*) WSC Inst MA Studies.

Nonlinear World - Fourth International Workshop on Nonlinear & Turbulent Processes in Physics, 2 vols., 1. V. G. Bar'Yakhtar et al. 1540p. 1990. text 298.00 (*981-02-0271-7*) World Scientific Pub.

Nonlinear World - Fourth International Workshop on Nonlinear & Turbulent Processes in Physics, 2 vols., Set. V. G. Bar'Yakhtar et al. 1540p. 1990. text. write for info. (*981-02-0272-5*) World Scientific Pub.

Nonlinearities in Action: Oscillations, Chaos, Order, Fractals. A. V. Gaponov-Grekhov & M. I. Rabinovich. LC 92-8461. (Illus.). 204p. 1993. 64.95 (*0-387-51988-2*) Spr-Verlag.

Nonlinearity & Functional Analysis. Melvyn S. Berger. 1977. text 99.00 (*0-12-090350-4*) Acad Pr.

Nonlinearity in Condensed Matter: Proceedings of the Sixth International Conference, Los Alamos, New Mexico, 5-9 May, 1986. Ed. by A. R. Bishop et al. (Solid-State Sciences Ser.: Vol. 69). (Illus.). 410p. 1987. 74.95 (*0-387-17561-X*) Spr-Verlag.

Nonlinearity in Engineering Structures: Detection, Identification & Modelling. G. R. Tomlinson. 1999. 55.00 (*0-7503-0356-5*) IOP Pub.

Nonlinearity with Disorder 2: Proceedings of the Tashkent Conference, Tashkent, U. S. S. R. October 1-7, 1990. Fatkhulla K. Abdullaev et al. Ed. by A. R. Bishop & S. N. Pnevmatikos. LC 92-19322. (Proceedings in Physics Ser.: Vol. 67). (Illus.). 350p. 1992. 108.95 (*0-387-55474-2*) Spr-Verlag.

Nonliner Image Processing 3. Ed. by J. Astola et al. 1992. 20.00 (*0-8194-0812-3*, 1658) SPIE.

Nonliner Nonequilibrium Thermodynamics II: Advanced Theory. Rouslan L. Stratonovich. LC 93-39995. 1993. write for info. (*3-540-57051-9*) Spr-Verlag.

Nonliner Nonequilibrium Thermodynamics II: Advanced Theory. Rouslan L. Stratonovich. LC 93-39995. 1994. write for info. (*0-387-57051-9*) Spr-Verlag.

Nonliteral Language: Processing & Use: A Special Issue of "Metaphor & Symbolic Activity", Vol. 10, No. 1, 1995. Ed. by Roger J. Kreuz & Shelly Dews. 56p. 1995. pap. 20.00 (*0-8058-9948-0*) L Erlbaum Assocs.

Nonliterary Influences on Science Fiction: An Essay. Algis Budrys. (Booklet Ser.: No. 9). 24p. (Orig.). 1983. pap. 1.25 (*0-936055-06-5*) C Drumm Bks.

Nonlitigation Action Guides: References & Key Words & Phrases, Summer 1992, Action Guide. Ed. by Suzanne E. Graber. 107p. 1992. pap. text 42.00 (*0-88124-565-8*, MI-11551) Cont Ed Bar-CA.

Nonlocal Acoustoelectronic Effects in Mentals & Layered Conductors, Vol. 17. V. Gokhfel'd & V. G. Peeschansky. (Soviet Scientific Reviews Series, Section D: Biology Reviews: Vol. 17, Pt. 1). 149p. 1993. pap. text 213.00 (*3-7186-5390-7*) Gordon & Breach.

Nonlocal Bifurcations. Yu Ilyashenko & Weigu Li. LC 98-40047. (Mathematical Surveys & Monographs: No. 66). 290p. 1998. 69.00 (*0-8218-0497-9*) Am Math.

Nonlocal Quantum Theory & Stochastic Quantum Mechanics. Khavtgain Namsrai. 1985. text 274.00 (*90-277-2001-0*) Kluwer Academic.

Nonlocality in Quantum Physics. Andrei A. Grib & W. A. Rodrigues. LC 99-33174. (C). 1999. text. write for info. (*0-306-46182-X*, Kluwer Plenum) Kluwer Academic.

Nonmammalian Animal Models for Biomedical Research. Ed. by Avril D. Woodhead & Katherine Vivirito. 400p. 1989. boxed set 298.00 (*0-8493-4763-7*, QL55) CRC Pr.

Nonmammalian Genomes Analysis: A Practical Guide. Ed. by Bruce W. Birren & Eric Lai. (Illus.). 353p. 1996. pap. text 39.95 (*0-12-101285-9*, QH445) Acad Pr.

Nonmechanical Dewatering of Water Plant Residuals. Carel Vandermeyden & David A. Cornwell. LC 97-46729. 163p. 1998. 195.00 (*0-89867-946-X*) Am Water Wks Assn.

Nonmetallic Containers for Waste Paper, UL 242. 3rd ed. 1993. pap. 250.00 (*1-55989-321-4*) Underwrtrs Labs.

Nonmetallic Materials & Applications see Handbook of Materials Science

Nonmetallic Materials & Composites at Low Temperatures 3. Ed. by Gunther Hartwig & David J. Evans. (Cryogenic Materials Ser.). 246p. 1986. 69.50 (*0-306-42117-8*, Plenum Trade) Perseus Pubng.

Nonmetallic Outlet Boxes, Flush-Device Boxes, & Covers, UL 514C. 3rd ed. 1996. write for info. (*0-7629-0116-0*) Underwrtrs Labs.

Nonmetallic Safety Cans for Petroleum Products, UL 1313. 2nd ed. (C). 1993. pap. text 290.00 (*1-55989-455-5*) Underwrtrs Labs.

Nonmetallic-Sheathed Cables, UL 719. 10th ed. (C). 1996. pap. text 95.00 (*0-7629-0063-6*) Underwrtrs Labs.

Nonmetallic Surface Raceways & Fittings, UL 5A. 2nd ed. (C). 1999. pap. text 95.00 (*1-55989-598-5*) Underwrtrs Labs.

Nonmetallic Underground Conduit with Conductors: UL 1990. 1998. write for info. (*0-7629-0287-6*, UL 1990) Underwrtrs Labs.

Nonmetallic Underground Piping for Flammable Liquids: UL 971. 1995. write for info. (*1-55989-910-7*, UL 971) Underwrtrs Labs.

Nonmetropolitan America in Transition. Ed. by Amos H. Hawley & Sara M. Mazie. LC 81-3511. (Institute for Research in Social Science Ser.). 853p. reprint ed. pap. 200.00 (*0-7837-2460-8*, 204261300005) Bks Demand.

Nonmilitary Defense: Chemical & Biological Defenses in Perspective: A Collection of Papers Comprising the Symposium on Nonmilitary Defense, Presented Before the Division of Industrial & Engineering Chemistry, in Participation with the Special Board Committee on Civil Defense, at the 137th Meeting of the American Chemical Society, Cleveland, OH, April 1960. American Chemical Society Staff. LC 60-50429. (Advances in Chemistry Ser.: Vol. 26). (Illus.). 108p. 1960. reprint ed. pap. 33.50 (*0-608-06895-0*, 206710300009) Bks Demand.

Nonmodular Lattice Varieties. Henry Rose. LC 83-22449. (Memoirs Ser.: No. 47/292). 76p. 1984. pap. 16.00 (*0-8218-2292-6*, MEMO/47/292) Am Math.

Nonmonetary Eligibility in State Unemployment Insurance Programs: Law & Practice. Walter Corson et al. LC 86-10985. 138p. (C). 1986. 20.00 (*0-88099-039-2*); pap. text 10.00 (*0-88099-038-4*) W E Upjohn.

Nonmonotonic & Inductive Logic: Second International Workshop, Reinhardsbrunn Castle, Germany, December 2-6, 1991, Proceedings. Gerhard Brewka et al. LC 92-46636. (Lecture Notes in Computer Science Ser.: Vol. 659). 1993. write for info. (*3-540-56433-0*) Spr-Verlag.

Nonmonotonic & Inductive Logic: 1st International Workshop Karlsruhe, Germany, December 4-7, 1990 Proceedings. Ed. by J. Dix et al. (Lecture Notes in Artificial Intelligence Ser.: Vol. 543). x, 243p. 1991. 32.95 (*0-387-54564-6*) Spr-Verlag.

Nonmonotonic Logic: Context-Dependent Reasoning. Wiktor Marek & M. Truszczynski. Ed. by D. W. Loveland. (Artificial Intelligence Ser.). x, 396p. 1993. 93.95 (*0-387-56448-9*) Spr-Verlag.

Nonmonotonic Logics: Basic Concepts, Results & Techniques, Vol. 118. Karl Schlechta. LC 96-30059. (Lecture Notes in Artificial Intelligence). 1997. 49.00 (*3-540-62482-1*) Spr-Verlag.

Nonmonotonic Reasoning. Grigoris Antoniou. (Artificial Intelligence Ser.). (Illus.). 275p. 1997. 39.50 (*0-262-01157-3*) MIT Pr.

Nonmonotonic Reasoning: An Overview. Gerhard Brewka et al. LC 96-46540. (Lecture Notes Ser.). 192p. (C). 1996. 49.95 (*1-881526-84-4*); pap. 22.95 (*1-881526-83-6*) CSLI.

Nonmonotonic Reasoning: From Theoretical Foundation to Efficient Computation. Gerhard Brewka. (Tracts in Theoretical Computer Science Ser.: No. 12). 182p. (C). 1991. text 42.95 (*0-521-38394-3*) Cambridge U Pr.

Nonmotorized Transportation. LC 92-43319. (Transportation Research Record Ser.: No. 1372). 1993. write for info. (*0-309-05413-3*) Transport Res Bd.

Nonmotorized Transportation Research & Issues (TRR 1396) Ed. by Norman Solomon. (Transportation Research Record Ser.). (Illus.). 88p. 1993. pap. text 24.00 (*0-309-05469-9*) Transport Res Bd.

Nonna's Italian Kitchen. Bryanna C. Grogan. LC 98-29142. (Illus.). 256p. 1998. pap. 14.95 (*1-57067-055-2*) Book Pub Co.

Nonnegative Matrices. Henryk Minc. LC 87-27416. (Discrete Mathematics Ser.). 206p. 1988. 160.00 (*0-471-83966-3*) Wiley.

Nonnegative Matrices & Applications. R. B. Bapat & T. E. Raghavan. (Encyclopedia of Mathematics & Its Applications Ser.: No. 64). (Illus.). 349p. (C). 1997. text 69.95 (*0-521-57167-7*) Cambridge U Pr.

Nonnegative Matrices & Other Topics in Linear Algebra. Alexander Graham. (Mathematics & Its Applications Ser.). 304p. 1987. text 65.95 (*0-470-20855-4*) P-H.

Nonnegative Matrices in Dynamic Systems. Abraham Berman et al. LC 88-33934. 192p. 1989. 160.00 (*0-471-62074-2*) Wiley.

Nonnegative Matrices in the Mathematical Sciences. Abraham Berman & Robert J. Plemmons. LC 94-37449. (Classics in Applied Mathematics Ser.: Vol. 9). xx, 340p. 1994. pap. 30.00 (*0-89871-321-8*) Soc Indus-Appl Math.

Nonnegotiable. Charles Robinson. LC 99-62089. 112p. 1999. pap. 8.95 (*1-56167-492-3*) Am Literary Pr.

Nonnegotiable Gospel. 3rd ed. Dave Hunt. 40p. 1999. pap. 2.00 (*1-928660-01-0*) Berean Call.

Nonobviousness: The Ultimate Condition of Patentability: Papers Compiled in Commemoration of the Silver Anniversary of 35 USC 103. Ed. by John F. Witherspoon. LC 79-22961. 879p. reprint ed. pap. 200.00 (*0-608-16696-0*, 202679300052) Bks Demand.

Nononcogenic Avian Viruses. Ed. by R. Pandey. (Progress in Veterinary Microbiology & Immunology Ser.: Vol. 5). (Illus.). viii, 136p. 1989. 100.00 (*3-8055-4827-3*) S Karger.

Nonoperative Orthopaedic Medicine & Manual Therapy: Diagnosis & Treatment of the Lower Extremities. Dos Winkel et al. LC 96-36871. 688p. 1997. 75.00 (*0-8342-0902-0*) Aspen Pub.

Nonoperative Orthopaedic Medicine & Manual Therapy: Diagnosis & Treatment of the Upper Extremities. Dos Winkel et al. LC 96-46879. 592p. 1997. 75.00 (*0-8342-0901-2*) Aspen Pub.

Nonoscillation, Disconjugacy & Integral Inequalities. Shmuel Friedland. LC 76-25246. 78p. 1976. pap. 21.00 (*0-8218-2176-8*, MEMO/7/176) Am Math.

Nonparametric Statistical Methods. 2nd ed. Myles Hollander & Douglas A. Wolfe. LC 98-3314. (Probability & Statistics Ser.). 787p. 1999. 94.95 (*0-471-19045-4*) Wiley.

Nonparametric & Semiparametric Methods in Econometrics & Statistics: Proceedings of the Fifth International Symposium. William A. Barnett. Ed. by James E. Powell et al. (International Symposia in Economic Theory & Econometrics Ser.: No. 5). (Illus.). 507p. (C). 1991. text 85.00 (*0-521-37090-6*) Cambridge U Pr.

Nonparametric & Semiparametric Methods in Econometrics & Statistics: Proceedings of the Fifth International Symposium. Ed. by James E. Powell et al. (International Symposia in Economic Theory & Econometrics Ser.: No. 5). (Illus.). 507p. (C). 1991. pap. text 33.95 (*0-521-42431-3*) Cambridge U Pr.

***Nonparametric Approach to Perceptions-Based Market Segmentation: Foundations.** Josef A. Mazanec & Helmut Strasser. LC 00-32194. (Interdisciplinary Studies in Economics & Mangement). 2000. write for info. (*3-211-83473-7*) Spr-Verlag.

Nonparametric Approaches to Environmental Impact Assessment. Ed. by Keith W. Hipel. LC TD0194.6.N66. (AWRA Monograph Ser.: No. 10). 94p. reprint ed. pap. 30.00 (*0-7837-1091-7*, 204162300021) Bks Demand.

***Nonparametric Comparative Statics & Stability.** James P. Quirk. LC 98-55311. 256p. 1999. 55.00 (*0-691-00690-3*, Pub. by Princeton U Pr) Cal Prin Full Svc.

Nonparametric Curve Estimation: Methods, Theory & Applications. Sam Efromovich. LC 99-13253. (Series in Statistics). 424p. 1999. 74.95 (*0-387-98740-1*) Spr-Verlag.

Nonparametric Econometrics. Adrian Pagan & Aman Ullah. LC 98-37218. (Themes in Modern Econometrics Ser.). (Illus.). 440p. (C). 1999. 74.95 (*0-521-35564-8*) Cambridge U Pr.

***Nonparametric Econometrics.** Adrian Pagan & Aman Ullah. LC 98-37218. (Themes in Modern Econometrics Ser.). (Illus.). 424p. (C). 1999. pap. 29.95 (*0-521-58611-9*) Cambridge U Pr.

Nonparametric Estimation of Probability Densities & Regression Curves. E. A. Nadaraya. (C). 1988. text 185.00 (*90-277-2757-0*) Kluwer Academic.

Nonparametric Function Estimation, Modeling & Simulation. James Thompson & Richard Tapia. LC 90-10222. (Miscellaneous Bks.: No. 21). xvi, 304p. 1990. pap. 43.00 (*0-89871-261-0*) Soc Indus-Appl Math.

Nonparametric Functional Estimation & Related Topics. Ed. by George Roussas. (C). 1991. text 341.00 (*0-7923-1226-0*) Kluwer Academic.

Nonparametric Measures of Association. Jean D. Gibbons. (Quantitative Applications in the Social Sciences Ser.: Vol. 91). (Illus.). 96p. (C). 1993. pap. text 10.95 (*0-8039-4664-3*) Sage.

Nonparametric Methods. Ed. by P. R. Krishnaiah & Pranab K. Sen. 968p. 1985. 199.00 (*0-444-86871-2*) Elsevier.

Nonparametric Methods for Quantitative Analysis. Jean D. Gibbons. LC 74-28910. (American Sciences Press Series in Mathematical & Management Sciences: Vol. 2). 1976. text 96.95 (*0-03-007811-3*) Am Sciences Pr.

Nonparametric Methods for Quantitative Analysis. 2nd ed. Jean D. Gibbons. LC 84-73390. (American Sciences Press Series in Mathematical & Management Sciences: Vol. 2). 1985. 148.00 (*0-935950-09-5*) Am Sciences Pr.

Nonparametric Methods for Quantitative Analysis. 3rd ed. Jean D. Gibbons. LC 94-70174. (Series in Mathematical & Management Sciences: Vol. 2). (Illus.). 550p. (C). 1996. 195.00 (*0-935950-37-0*) Am Sciences Pr.

Nonparametric Methods in Change Point Problems. B. E. Brodsky & B. S. Darkhovsky. LC 92-43810. (Mathematics & Its Applications Ser.: No. 243). 224p. (C). 1993. text 129.50 (*0-7923-2122-7*) Kluwer Academic.

Nonparametric Methods in Communications. Ed. by P. Papantoni-Kazakos & Dimitri Kazakos. LC 77-14049. (Electrical Engineering & Electronics Ser.: No. 2). 303p. reprint ed. pap. 94.00 (*0-7837-3347-X*, 204330500008) Bks Demand.

Nonparametric Methods in Multivariate Analysis. Madan L. Puri & Pranab K. Sen. LC 90-19772. 456p. (C). 1993. reprint ed. lib. bdg. 74.50 (*0-89464-551-X*) Krieger.

Nonparametric Probability Density Estimation. Richard A. Tapia & James R. Thompson. LC 77-17249. (Johns Hopkins Series in the Mathematical Sciences: No. 1). 192p. reprint ed. pap. 59.60 (*0-8357-8253-0*, 203411900088) Bks Demand.

Nonparametric Smoothing & Lack-of-Fit Tests. Jeffrey D. Hart. LC 97-10931. (Springer Series in Statistics). 304p. 1997. 44.95 (*0-387-94980-1*) Spr-Verlag.

Nonparametric Statistical Inference. 3rd expanded rev. ed. Ed. by Jean Gibbons & Subh Chakraborti. (Statistics: Textbooks & Monographs: Vol. 131). (Illus.). 572p. 1992. text 195.00 (*0-8247-8661-0*) Dekker.

***Nonparametric Statistical Methodology for the Design & Analysis of Final Status Decommissioning Surveys: Interim Draft Report for Comment & Use.** C. V. Gogolak. 240p. 1998. per. 20.00 (*0-16-062746-X*) USGPO.

Nonparametric Statistics. David C. Sutor & Donald B. White. LC 92-26382. (Six Sigma Research Institute Ser.). 1992. pap. 16.95 (*0-201-63415-5*) Addison-Wesley.

Nonparametric Statistics. 2nd ed. Sidney Siegel & N. J. Castellan. 384p. (C). 1988. text 77.25 (*0-07-057357-3*) McGraw.

Nonparametric Statistics: An Introduction. Jean D. Gibbons. (Quantitative Applications in the Social Sciences Ser.: Vol. 90). 1992. pap. 10.95 (*0-8039-3951-5*) Sage.

Nonparametric Statistics for Stochastic Processes: Estimation & Prediction. D. Bosq. LC 96-13588. (Lecture Notes in Statistics Ser.: Vol. 110). 169p. 1996. pap. 43.95 (*0-387-94713-2*) Spr-Verlag.

Nonparametric Statistics for Stochastic Processes: Estimation & Prediction. 2nd ed. Denis Bosq. Ed. by P. Bickel et al. LC 98-28496. (Lecture Notes in Statistics Ser.: Vol. 110). 214p. 1998. pap. 34.95 (*0-387-98590-5*) Spr-Verlag.

Nonparametric Statistics in Health Care Research: Statistics for Small Samples & Unusual Distributions. Marjorie A. Pett. LC 96-35711. 400p. (C). 1997. 58.00 (*0-8039-7038-2*, 70382); pap. 26.95 (*0-8039-7039-0*, 70390) Sage.

Nonparametric Techniques in Statistical Inference. International Symposium on Nonparametric Technique. Ed. by Madan L. Puri. LC 75-116750. 637p. reprint ed. pap. 180.00 (*0-608-15769-4*, 2031715) Bks Demand.

Nonparametric Trend Analysis. George A. Ferguson. LC 65-13086. 69p. reprint ed. pap. 25.00 (*0-7837-1038-0*, 2023830) Bks Demand.

N

***Nonparametrics.** rev. ed. Lehmann. 480p. 1998. 65.20 (*0-13-997735-X*) P-H.

Nonparametrics: Statistical Methods Based on Ranks. E. L. Lehmann. LC 72-93538. 1975. text 49.95 (*0-8162-4994-6*) Holden-Day.

Nonpartisan Elections & the Case for Party Politics. Willis D. Hawley. LC 73-3488. (Wiley Series in Urban Research). 218p. reprint ed. pap. 67.60 (*0-608-10305-5*, 200771600064) Bks Demand.

Nonpartisan League, 1915-1922: An Annotated Bibliography. Patrick K. Coleman & Charles R. Lamb. LC 85-21480. xiii, 86p. (Orig.). 1985. pap. 12.95 (*0-87351-189-1*) Minn Hist.

Nonpension Postretirement Benefits: Strategies for Colleges & Universities. National Association of College & University Busin. Ed. by Jefferson Reeder. 173p. 1992. 42.95 (*0-915164-80-9*) NACUBO.

Nonperturbative Aspects of Strings, Branes & Supersymmetry. J. Louis. LC 99-27206. 500p. 1999. 166.00 (*981-02-3785-5*) World Scientific Pub.

Nonperturbative Methods in Low Dimensional Quantum Field Theories. Ed. by G. Domokos et al. 500p. (C). 1991. text 118.00 (*981-02-0576-7*) World Scientific Pub.

Nonperturbative Methods in Quantum Field Theory: Proceedings of the Workshop Adelaide, Australia 2-13 February 1998. Ed. by A. W. Schreiber et al. 350p. 1999. 74.00 (*981-02-3665-4*) World Scientific Pub.

Nonperturbative Quantum Field Theory. Ed. by G. T. Hooft et al. (NATO ASI Series B, Physics: Vol. 185). (Illus.). 546p. 1988. 145.00 (*0-306-43027-4*, Plenum Trade) Perseus Pubng.

Nonpetroleum Vehicular Fuels I: February, 1980. (Synthetic Fuels Ser.). 371p. 1980. pap. 40.00 (*0-910091-31-5*) Inst Gas Tech.

Nonpetroleum Vehicular Fuels II. 419p. 1981. pap. 50.00 (*0-910091-30-7*) Inst Gas Tech.

Nonpetroleum Vehicular Fuels III. 491p. 1982. pap. 55.00 (*0-910091-01-3*) Inst Gas Tech.

Nonpetroleum Vehicular Fuels IV: Symposium. Institute of Gas Technology Staff. 292p. 1984. pap. 50.00 (*0-910091-51-X*) Inst Gas Tech.

Nonpetroleum Vehicular Fuels V: CNG Fuel. 459p. 1985. pap. 75.00 (*0-910091-54-4*) Inst Gas Tech.

Nonpharmacological Management of Atrial Fibrillation. Ed. by Francis D. Murgatroyd & John Camm. LC 97-4340. (Illus.). 560p. 1997. 120.00 (*0-87993-665-7*) Futura Pub.

Nonpharmacological Therapy of Arrhythmias for the 21st Century: The State of the Art. Ed. by Igor Singer et al. LC 98-4105. (Illus.). 992p. 1998. 125.00 (*0-87993-690-8*) Futura Pub.

Nonphysician & Family Health in Sub-Sahara Africa. Ed. by Ronald S. Waife & Marianne C. Burkhart. (FRE.). 141p. 1981. 7.00 (*0-933853-11-4*) Pathfinder Fund.

Nonplanar Microstrip Antennas. Kin-Lu Wong. LC 98-35003. (Wiley Series in Microwave & Optical Engineering). 372p. 1999. 105.00 (*0-471-18244-3*) Wiley.

Nonpoems. Florentin Smarandache. Ed. by Xiquan Publishing House Staff. (RUM., Illus.). 100p. (Orig.). (C). 1991. pap. 4.99 (*1-879585-01-4*) Erhus Univ Pr.

Nonpoint Pollution & Urban Stormwater Management. Ed. by J. W. Patterson et al. LC 95-61552. (Water Quality Management Library: Vol. 9). 435p. 1995. pap. 99.95 (*1-56676-305-3*) Technomic.

Nonpoint Source Pollution. Ed. by Bruce W. Vigon. LC TD0420.N65. (AWRA Monograph Ser.: No. 3). (Illus.). 61p. reprint ed. pap. 30.00 (*0-8357-3173-1*, 203943600012) Bks Demand.

Nonpoint Source Pollution Regulation - Issues & Analysis: The FEEM-KLUWER International Series on Economics, Energy & Environment. Ed. by Cesare Dosi. LC 94-32311. (Economics, Energy & Environment Ser.). 192p. (C). 1994. lib. bdg. 106.00 (*0-7923-3121-4*) Kluwer Academic.

Nonpolicy Debate. 2nd ed. Michael D. Bartanen & David A. Frank. Orig. Title: Debating Values. 220p. (C). 1994. pap. text 40.00 (*0-13-776717-X*) P-H.

Nonpositive Curvature. Jurgen Jost. LC 97-11973. 1997. write for info. (*3-7643-5736-3*) Birkhauser.

Nonpositive Curvature: Geometric & Analytic Aspects. Jurgen Jost. LC 97-11973. (Lectures in Mathematics). 1997. write for info. (*0-8176-5736-3*) Birkhauser.

Nonprescription Drug Therapy: Guiding Patient Self-Care. Ed. by Tim R. Covington. (Illus.). 1008p. 1999. ring bd. write for info. (*1-57439-048-1*) Facts & Comparisons.

Nonprescription Drugs: Value of a Pharmacist-Controlled Class Has Yet to Be Determined. 136p. (Orig.). (C). 1996. pap. text 20.00 (*0-7881-2934-1*) DIANE Pub.

NonPrescription (OTC) Medications: Counseling Guidelines on the Safe Use of Over-the-Counter Medicines. Augustine S. Aruna. Ed. by Victor A. Padron. 168p. 1997. pap. text 23.50 (*0-9677721-1-7*) Global Pubng Net.

Nonprescription Product Therapeutics. W. Steven Pray. LC 98-22505. 1999. write for info. (*0-683-30126-8*) Lppncott W & W.

Nonprescription Products: Patient Assessment Handbook. Ed. by Lynn Limon et al. LC 96-79456. (Illus.). 456p. (Orig.). 1996. pap. 42.00 (*0-917330-82-X*, T270) Am Pharm Assn.

Nonprice Predation under Section 2 of the Sherman Act. LC 91-72111. 98p. 1991. pap. 20.00 (*0-89707-683-4*, 503-0205, ABA Antitrust) Amer Bar Assn.

Nonprofessional Revolution in Mental Health. Francine Sobey. LC 71-118355. 253p. reprint ed. pap. 78.50 (*0-608-15521-7*, 202970100063) Bks Demand.

Nonprofit - For-Profit Joint Ventures in Rural Affordable Housing: Case Studies. Housing Assistance Council Staff. 53p. 1997. 5.00 (*1-58064-000-1*) Housing Assist.

Nonprofit Accounting & Auditing Disclosure Manual. Allan B. Afterman & Rowan H. Jones. 1992. ring bd. 135.00 (*0-685-69608-1*, NADM) Warren Gorham & Lamont.

Nonprofit Almanac, 1996-1997: A Publication of Independent Sector. Virginia A. Hodgkinson. 1996. pap. 25.95 (*0-7879-0345-0*) Jossey-Bass.

Nonprofit Almanac, 1992-1993: Dimensions of the Independent Sector. 4th ed. Ed. by Independent Sector Staff. 648p. pap. 54.95 (*1-55542-746-4*) Ind Sector.

Nonprofit & For-Profit HMOs: Converging Practices but Different Goals? Harry Nelson. 36p. (Orig.). 1997. pap. write for info. (*1-887748-13-X*) Milbank Memorial.

Nonprofit Answer Book: An Executive Director's Guide to Frequently Asked Questions. Ed. by Patty Oertel. 272p. 1999. pap. write for info. (*1-892233-01-0*) SCCNM.

Nonprofit Board Answer Book: Practical Guidelines for Board Members & Chief Executives. Robert C. Andringa & Ted W. Engstrom. LC 97-32835. 1998. 29.95 (*0-925299-80-4*) Natl Ctr Nonprofit.

Nonprofit Board Committees: How to Make Them Work, No. 54. Ed. by Ellen C. Hirzy. 16p. 1992. pap. text 12.00 (*0-925299-24-3*, No. 37) Natl Ctr Nonprofit.

Nonprofit Board Committees: How to Make Them Work see Comites de Conselhos Diretores de Organizacoes Sem Fins Lucrativos: Como Faze - los Funcionar

Nonprofit Boards: Roles, Responsibilities & Performances. Diane J. Duca. LC 96-23264. 192p. 1996. 29.95 (*0-471-13020-6*) Wiley.

Nonprofit Boards: What to Do & How to Do It. John E. Tropman. xiv, 247p. 1999. pap. 22.95 (*0-87868-694-0*, 6940, CWLA Pr) Child Welfare.

Nonprofit Boards & Leadership: Cases on Governance, Change, & Board-Staff Dynamics. Ed. by Miriam M. Wood. (Nonprofit Sector Ser.). 266p. 1995. text 26.95 (*0-7879-0139-3*) Jossey-Bass.

Nonprofit Board's Guide to Bylaws: Creating a Framework for Effective Governance. Kim A. Zeitlin & Susan E. Dorn. 36p. (Orig.). 1996. pap. 16.00 (*0-925299-50-2*) Natl Ctr Nonprofit.

Nonprofit Boards of Directors: Analyses & Applications. Ed. by Robert D. Herman & Jon Van Til. 256p. 1988. 39.95 (*0-88738-216-9*) Transaction Pubs.

***Nonprofit Boards That Work: The End of One-Size-Fits All Governance.** Maureen K. Robinson. 224p. 2000. text 29.95 (*0-471-35432-5*) Wiley.

Nonprofit CEOs Speak Out on Importance of Communications. International Association of Business Communicator. (Orig.). 1982. pap. 22.50 (*0-686-37162-3*) Intl Assn Busn Comm.

Nonprofit Compensation & Benefits Practices. Applied Research & Development Institute Internatl. LC 97-35611. (Nonprofit Law, Finance, & Management Ser.). 224p. 1998. 59.95 (*0-471-18089-0*) Wiley.

Nonprofit Computer Sourcebook: The Professional's Guide to Products, Services & Information Sources for Computer Systems. 91st ed. Ed. by Alex Norsworthy. 355p. 1990. 75.00 (*0-914756-97-4*, 600087) Taft Group.

Nonprofit Consultants: How to Choose Them, How to Use Them. Alison Buttenheim. 20p. 1998. pap. 10.00 (*1-892233-02-9*) SCCNM.

Nonprofit Controllers Manual. Craig R. Stevens & Morton L. Sorkin. 544p. 1996. 125.00 (*0-7913-2571-7*) Warren Gorham & Lamont.

Nonprofit Corporation Law Handbook. 2nd rev. ed. Stuart J. Faber. 295p. 1984. pap. text 36.50 (*0-89074-093-3*) Lega Bks.

Nonprofit Corporation Statutes: A Critique & Proposal. Ralph E. Boyer. LC 57-63886. (Michigan Legal Publications). 269p. 1957. 40.00 (*1-57588-343-0*, 300100) W S Hein.

Nonprofit Corporations, Organizations & Associations. 6th ed. Howard L. Oleck & Martha E. Steart. LC 93-47544. 1664p. (C). 1994. text 99.95 (*0-13-121310-5*) P-H.

***Nonprofit Corporations, Organizations, & Associations, 1997-1998 Supplement.** 6th ed. Howard L. Oleck & Martha E. Stewart. LC 93-47544. (Illus.). 478p. (C). 1998. pap. 49.95 (*0-13-911090-9*) P-H.

Nonprofit Counsel, 1990. Bruce R. Hopkins. 1990. pap. 96.00 (*0-471-52707-6*) Wiley.

Nonprofit Economy. Burton A. Weisbrod. LC 87-23718. (Illus.). 271p. 1988. 37.95 (*0-674-62625-7*) HUP.

Nonprofit Economy. Burton A. Weisbrod. 272p. 1991. pap. 22.00 (*0-674-62626-5*, WEINOX) HUP.

Nonprofit Employment Law: Compensation, Benefits, & Regulation. David G. Samuels & Howard Pianko. LC 98-22979. (Nonprofit Law, Finance, & Management Ser.). 364p. 1998. 130.00 (*0-471-19304-6*) Wiley.

Nonprofit Enterprise: Law & Taxation, 3 vols. Marilyn E. Phelan. LC 85-7870. 1990. 350.00 (*0-685-10477-X*) West Group.

Nonprofit Enterprise in Market Economics. Estelle James & Susan Rose-Ackerman. (Fundamentals of Pure & Applied Economics Ser.: Volume 9). viii, 102p. 1986. pap. text 49.00 (*3-7186-0329-2*) Gordon & Breach.

Nonprofit Enterprise in the Arts: Studies in Mission & Constraint. Ed. by Paul Dimaggio. (Illus.). 385p. 1987. text 70.00 (*0-19-504063-5*) OUP.

Nonprofit Entrepreneur: Creating Ventures to Earn Income. Ed. by Edward Skloot. LC 87-36494. 170p. (Orig.). 1988. pap. 19.95 (*0-87954-239-X*) Foundation Ctr.

Nonprofit Financial Management. Andrew S. Lang. LC 95-13206. 150p. ring bd. 119.00 (*0-8342-0430-4*, S179) Aspen Pub.

Nonprofit Governance: The Executive's Guide. Ed. by Victor Futter & George W. Overton. LC 96-79908. 350p. 1997. pap. 79.95 (*1-57073-422-4*, 507-0305) Amer Bar Assn.

***Nonprofit Guide to Compensation Policies.** Fred Kohler, Sr. & Robert Walker, Jr. Ed. by K. Kaufman. (Illus.). 113p. 1999. pap. text 29.95 (*1-891872-01-X*) Mgmt Ctr.

Nonprofit Guide to 403(b) Plans. Eleanor Lowder. 300p. 1996. 62.00 (*0-8342-0616-1*) Aspen Pub.

Nonprofit Handbook, 2 vols. 2nd ed. Ed. by Tracy D. Connors & James M. Greenfield. LC 96-54804. 576p. 1997. 240.00 (*0-471-15400-8*) Wiley.

Nonprofit Handbook. 2nd ed. Gary M. Grobman. LC 99-64921. (Illus.). 353p. 1999. pap. 29.95 (*0-9653653-2-8*, Pub. by White Hat) IPG Chicago.

Nonprofit Handbook: Fundraising, Vol. 2. 2nd ed. Ed. by James M. Greenfield. LC 96-54805. (Wiley Fund Development Ser.). 744p. 1997. 110.00 incl. disk (*0-471-15658-2*) Wiley.

Nonprofit Handbook: Management, Vol. 1. 2nd ed. Ed. by Tracy D. Connors & James M. Greenfield. LC 96-54804. 832p. 1997. 130.00 (*0-471-17967-1*) Wiley.

***Nonprofit Handbook: Management Supplement , 1998.** Connors. (Nonprofit Law, Finance, & Management Ser.). 172p. 1998. pap. 57.00 (*0-471-19594-4*) Wiley.

***Nonprofit Handbook, Fund Raising.** 2nd ed. Ed. by Tracy Daniel Connors. (Wiley Nonprofit Law, Finance, & Management Ser.). 112p. 2000. pap. 65.00 (*0-471-36133-X*) Wiley.

***Nonprofit Handbook, Management: February 2000 Supplement.** 2nd ed. Ed. by Tracy Daniel Connors. 208p. 2000. pap. 65.00 (*0-471-36142-9*) Wiley.

***Nonprofit Institutions & the 1993 System of National Accounts.** Helmut K. Anheier & Lester M. Salamon. (Working Papers of the Johns Hopkins Comparative Nonprofit Sector Project: Vol. 25). (Illus.). 26p. 1998. pap. text 6.00 (*1-886333-30-0*) JH Univ Inst Pol Studies.

Nonprofit Investment Policies: A Practical Guide to Creation & Implementation. 30th ed. Robert P. Fry, Jr. LC 97-38261. (NSFRE-Wiley Fund Development Ser.). 302p. 1998. 55.00 (*0-471-17887-X*) Wiley.

Nonprofit Law: Ten Issues in Search of Resolution. Lester M. Salamon & Susan L. Q. Flaherty. (Working Papers of the Johns Hopkins Comparative Nonprofit Sector Project: Vol. 20). (Illus.). 37p. 1996. pap. text 6.00 (*1-886333-24-6*) JH Univ Inst Pol Studies.

Nonprofit Lobbying Guide. 2nd ed. Bob Smucker. (Illus.). 158p. (C). 1999. pap. 16.00 (*0-929556-00-3*, P152) Ind Sector.

Nonprofit Management Education: U. S. & World Perspectives. Ed. by Michael O'Neill & Kathleen Fletcher. LC 98-14904. 176p. 1998. 55.00 (*0-275-96115-X*, Praeger Pubs) Greenwood.

Nonprofit Management Handbook: Operating Policies & Procedures. Tracy D. Connors. LC 92-10811. 943p. 1996. pap. 59.95 (*0-471-15177-7*) Wiley.

***Nonprofit Management Handbook: 1999 Edition.** 2nd ed. Ed. by Tracy D. Connors & James M. Greenfield. 256p. 1999. pap. 65.00 (*0-471-29907-3*) Wiley.

Nonprofit Manager's Resource Directory. Ronald A. Landskroner. LC 95-51509. (Nonprofit Law, Finance, & Management Ser.). 522p. 1996. pap. text 84.95 incl. disk (*0-471-14839-3*) Wiley.

Nonprofit Mergers: The Board Responsibility to Consider the Unthinkable, No. 56. David LaPiana. 26p. 1994. pap. text 12.00 (*0-925299-32-4*) Natl Ctr Nonprofit.

Nonprofit Mergers & Alliances: A Strategic Planning Guide. Thomas A. McLaughlin. LC 97-13384. (Nonprofit Law, Finance, & Management Ser.). 288p. 1996. 59.95 incl. disk (*0-471-18088-2*) Wiley.

***Nonprofit Mergers Workbook: The Leader's Guide to considering, negotiating & Executing a Merger.** David LaPiana. Ed. by Vincent Hyman. 240p. 2000. per. 28.00 (*0-940069-21-0*) A H Wilder.

Nonprofit News Coverage: A Guide for Journalists. Burnis R. Morris. (Illus.). 64p. (Orig.). 1993. pap. 12.00 (*0-929556-13-5*, P91) Ind Sector.

Nonprofit Organization Handbook. 2nd ed. Ed. by Tracy D. Connors. 784p. 1988. 89.50 (*0-07-012432-9*) McGraw.

Nonprofit Organization Management: Forms, Checklists & Guidelines. Ed. by Sara N. Di Lima & Lisa T. Johns. LC 95-51518. 1996. 149.00 (*0-8342-0710-9*, S191) Aspen Pub.

Nonprofit Organization Operating Manual: Planning for Survival & Growth. Arnold J. Olenick & Philip R. Olenick. LC 91-12292. 484p. (Orig.). 1991. pap. text 29.95 (*0-87954-293-4*) Foundation Ctr.

Nonprofit Organization, Statutes, Regulations & Forms. James J. Fishman & Stephen Schwarz. (University Casebook Ser.). 888p. 1995. pap. text 21.95 (*1-56662-318-9*) Foundation Pr.

Nonprofit Organization Supplement to the Corporate Counsellor's Desk Book. Phillip M. Grier. 224p. write for info. (*0-318-61826-5*) Harcourt.

***Nonprofit Organizations: Their Leadership, Management & Functions.** J. Steven Ott. 2000. pap. 38.00 (*0-8133-6787-5*) Westview.

Nonprofit Organizations: 1998 Supplement. Fishman & Schwarz. 1998. write for info. (*1-56662-646-3*) Foundation Pr.

Nonprofit Organizations & Public Policy, Vol. 14:1/2. Ed. by Robert Lowry. 140p. 1995. pap. 15.00 (*0-944285-43-0*) Pol Studies.

Nonprofit Organizations' Business Forms. (Wiley Nonprofit Law, Finance, & Management Ser.). 127p. 1997. 135.00 incl. disk (*0-471-18398-9*) Wiley.

Nonprofit Organizations, Cases & Materials. James J. Fishman & Stephen Schwarz. (University Casebook Ser.). 196p. 1996. pap. text, teacher ed. write for info. (*1-56662-340-5*) Foundation Pr.

Nonprofit Organizations Cases & Materials: 1997 Supplement. James J. Fishman & Stephan Schwarz. (University Casebook Ser.). 78p. (C). 1997. pap. text. write for info. (*1-56662-582-3*) Foundation Pr.

Nonprofit Organizations in a Market Economy: Understanding New Roles, Issues, & Trends. Ed. by David C. Hammack & Dennis R. Young. LC 92-41367. (Nonprofit Sector-Public Administration Ser.). 479p. 1993. text 45.95 (*1-55542-540-2*) Jossey-Bass.

Nonprofit Organizations in an Age of Uncertainty: A Study of Growth & Decline. Joseph Galaskiewicz & Wolfgang Bielefeld. LC 98-17049. 304p. 1998. pap. text 23.95 (*0-202-30566-X*) Aldine de Gruyter.

Nonprofit Organizations in an Age of Uncertainty: A Study of Organizational Change. Joseph Galaskiewicz & Wolfgang Bielefeld. LC 98-17049. 304p. 1998. lib. bdg. 49.95 (*0-202-30565-1*) Aldine de Gruyter.

Nonprofit Organizations, 1995: Overview & Update. (Tax Law & Estate Planning Course Handbook Ser.). 480p. 1994. pap. 99.00 (*0-614-17275-6*, J4-3681) PLI.

Nonprofit Personnel Forms & Guidelines: Compliance with Human Resource Law & Regulation, Suppl. No. 3. Matthew J. DeLuca. LC 93-49655. ring bd. 149.00 (*0-8342-0422-3*, S150) Aspen Pub.

Nonprofit Personnel Polices, Suppl. No. 4. Ed. by John Gillis. LC 96-51519. 1997. ring bd. 149.00 (*0-8342-0410-X*, S130) Aspen Pub.

Nonprofit Policy Agenda: Recommendations for State & Local Action. Deborah Koch & Sarah Boehm. 118p. (Orig.). 1992. pap. 15.00 (*1-886949-08-5*) Union Inst.

Nonprofit Problem Solver: A Management Guide. Richard Lord. LC 88-32188. 165p. 1989. 49.95 (*0-275-93125-0*, C3125, Praeger Pubs) Greenwood.

Nonprofit Report: Accounting, Taxation & Management. Ed. by Murray Dropkin. 112.00 (*0-685-69609-X*, NPR) Warren Gorham & Lamont.

Nonprofit Sector: A New Global Force. Lester M. Salamon & Helmut K. Anheier. (Working Papers of the Johns Hopkins Comparative Nonprofit Sector Project: Vol. 21). (Illus.). 19p. 1996. pap. text 6.00 (*1-886333-25-4*) JH Univ Inst Pol Studies.

***Nonprofit Sector: An Overview.** J. Steven Ott. 600p. 2000. pap. 38.00 (*0-8133-6785-9*) Westview.

***Nonprofit Sector & Democracy: Essays Exploring the Mission of the Nonprofit Sector.** Kristin L. Scotchmer & Elizabeth VanBenschoten. 28p. 2000. pap. 5.00 (*1-886949-23-9*) Union Inst.

Nonprofit Sector & the New Federal Budget. Alan J. Abramson & Lester M. Salamon. 138p. (Orig.). 1986. pap. text 19.50 (*0-87766-401-3*) Urban Inst.

Nonprofit Sector in France. Edith Archambault. (Johns Hopkins Non-Profit Sector Ser.). 200p. 1997. text 27.95 (*0-7190-4904-0*, Pub. by Manchester Univ Pr) St Martin.

Nonprofit Sector in France: C Edition. Edith Archambault. Ed. by Lester M. Salamon & Helmut K. Anheier. (Johns Hopkins Non-Profit Sector Ser.). 200p. 1997. text 45.00 (*0-7190-4903-2*, Pub. by Manchester Univ Pr) St Martin.

Nonprofit Sector in International Perspective: Studies in Comparative Culture & Policy. Ed. by Estelle James. (Yale Studies on Nonprofit Organizations). (Illus.). 400p. 1989. text 75.00 (*0-19-505629-9*) OUP.

Nonprofit Sector in Italy. Gian P. Barbetta. LC 97-12999. (Johns Hopkins Nonprofit Sector Ser.). 1997. text. write for info. (*0-7190-5086-3*) Manchester Univ Pr.

Nonprofit Sector in Italy. Gian P. Barbetta. LC 97-12999. (Johns Hopkins Nonprofit Sector Ser.). 1997. text 59.95 (*0-7190-5085-5*, Pub. by Manchester Univ Pr) St Martin.

Nonprofit Sector in Japan. Takayoshi Amenomori & Tadashi Yamamoto. LC 97-48660. (John Hopkins Nonprofit Sector Ser.). 208p. 1998. 39.95 (*0-7190-5385-4*, Pub. by Manchester Univ Pr) St Martin.

An Asterisk (*) at the beginning of an entry indicates that the title is appearing for the first time.

Nonprofit Sector in Sweden. Tommy Lundstrom & Filip Wijkstrom. LC 97-13575. (Johns Hopkins Nonprofit Sector Ser.). 1998. text. write for info. (*0-7190-5126-6*) Manchester Univ Pr.

Nonprofit Sector in Sweden. Tommy Lundstrom & Filip Wijkstrom. LC 97-13575. (Johns Hopkins Nonprofit Sector Ser.). 304p. 1998. 69.95 (*0-7190-5125-8*, Pub. by Manchester Univ Pr) St Martin.

Nonprofit Sector in the Developing World: A Comparative Analysis. Helmut K. Anheier & Lester M. Salamon. LC 97-48661. (Johns Hopkins Nonprofit Sector Ser.). 320p. 1998. 45.00 (*0-7190-5386-2*, Pub. by Manchester Univ Pr) St Martin.

Nonprofit Sector in the Mixed Economy. Ed. by Avner Ben-Ner & Benedetto Gui. LC 93-19165. 288p. (C). 1993. text 52.50 (*0-472-10429-2*, 10429) U of Mich Pr.

Nonprofit Sector in the United Nations System of National Accounts: Definition, Treatment, & Practice. Helmut K. Anheier et al. (Working Papers of the Johns Hopkins Comparative Nonprofit Sector Project: No. 4). (Illus.). 33p. 1992. pap. text 6.00 (*1-886333-03-3*) JH Univ Inst Pol Studies.

Nonprofit Sleuths: Follow the Money. Crumbley et al. 1997. pap. 22.95 (*0-87393-628-0*) Dame Pubns.

Nonprofit Start-Up Kit. Ed. by Jill Muehrcke. 88p. 1995. pap. 35.00 (*0-614-18255-7*) Soc Nonprofit Org.

Nonprofit Strategic Planning: For Quick Results. Shea Smith, 3rd. (Illus.). 196p. 1997. pap. 16.95 (*0-9660663-0-8*) Shea Smith.

Nonprofit/Government Contracting & Sectoral Relationships: An Annotated Bibliography. Kristen L. Scotchmer. 222p. (Orig.). 1995. pap. 20.00 (*1-886949-02-6*) Union Inst.

Nonprofits & Government: Collaboration & Conflict. Ed. by Elizabeth T. Boris & C. Eugene Steverle. LC 98-47103. 1999. pap. 29.50 (*0-87766-687-3*); lib. bdg. 57.50 (*0-87766-686-5*) Urban Inst.

Nonprofits for Hire: The Welfare State in the Age of Contracting. Steven Rathgeb & Michael Lipsky. (Illus.). 312p. 1995. pap. 19.50 (*0-674-62639-7*, SMINOX) HUP.

Nonprofits for Hire: The Welfare State in the Age of Contracting. Steven R. Smith & Michael Lipsky. (Illus.). 312p. (C). 1995. text 44.50 (*0-674-62638-9*) HUP.

Nonprofits for Profit: The WFP Guide to Social Entrepreneurship. 4th ed. WetFeet.com Staff. (Insider Guides Ser.). 68p. 1997. spiral bd. 25.00 (*1-58207-000-8*) WetFeet.

***Nonprofit's Guide to Executive Search: Discovering Leaders of the Future.** Families International Incorporated Staff. 32p. 1999. pap. 24.95 (*0-87304-318-9*) Manticore Pubs.

***Nonprofits in Urban America.** Ed. by Richard C. Hula & Cynthia Jackson-Elmoore. LC 00-37267. 2000. write for info. (*1-56720-376-0*) Greenwood.

Nonprofit's Internet Companion. unabridged ed. Ed. by Edward A. Tureen. 1999. pap. 19.95 (*1-892938-02-2*) S E K Pubns.

Nonproliferation & U. S. Foreign Policy. Ed. by Joseph A. Yager. LC 80-20483. 438p. 1980. 36.95 (*0-8157-9674-9*); pap. 16.95 (*0-8157-9673-0*) Brookings.

Nonproliferation Predicament. Ed. by Joseph F. Pilat. 150p. (C). 1985. 32.95 (*0-88738-047-6*) Transaction Pubs.

Nonproliferation Primer: Preventing the Spread of Nuclear, Chemical & Biological Weapons. Randall Forsberg et al. LC 95-11840. 157p. 1995. pap. text 16.50 (*0-262-56095-X*) MIT Pr.

Nonproliferation Regimes: Policies to Control the Spread of Nuclear, Chemical, & Biological Weapons & Missiles. 1994. lib. bdg. 250.95 (*0-8490-5696-9*) Gordon Pr.

Nonproliferation Role of the International Atomic Energy Agency: A Critical Assessment. Lawrence Scheinman. LC 85-42950. 72p. 1985. pap. text 8.95 (*0-915707-18-7*) Resources Future.

Nonqualified Deferred Compensation. 95th ed. Stephen Leimberg. LC 95-142978. 1995. pap. text 35.00 (*0-15-602507-8*) Harcourt.

Nonqualified Deferred Compensation & Life Insurance. Michael G. Goldstein et al. LC 98-21447. 1998. write for info. (*1-57073-574-3*) Amer Bar Assn.

***Nonqualified Deferred Compensation Answer Book.** Henry A. Smith III Esq. 448p. 1999. boxed set 136.00 (*0-7355-0503-9*) Panel Pubs.

Nonqualified Deferred Compensation Answer Book. 2nd ed. 1994. 116.00 (*1-56706-129-X*) Panel Pubs.

Nonqualified Deferred Compensation Answer Book. 3rd ed. Henry A. Smith, III et al. 496p. boxed set 118.00 (*1-56706-314-4*, S70) Panel Pubs.

Nonqualified Deferred Compensation Answer Book. annuals 3rd ed. Henry A. Smith, III et al. LC 98-114505. (Illus.). 496p. boxed set 118.00 (*1-56706-426-4*, 64264) Panel Pubs.

Nonqualified Deferred Compensation Answer Book: Forms & Checklists. 2nd ed. Michael P. Connors et al. 344p. pap. 96.00 (*1-56706-369-1*, 63691) Panel Pubs.

Nonqualified Deferred Compensation Arrangements. Neal A. Mancoff & David M. Weiner. 1990. 145.00 (*0-685-24500-4*) West Group.

Nonqualified Deferred Compensation Plans. Bruce J. McNeil. 210p. 1994. pap. text. write for info. (*0-314-04029-3*) West Pub.

Nonqualified Deferred Compensation Plans. Bruce J. McNeil. 305p. 1996. pap. text. write for info. (*0-314-20308-7*) West Pub.

Nonqualified Deferred Compensation Plans: 1997 Edition. Bruce J. McNeil. 328p. 1997. pap. text. write for info. (*0-314-22429-7*) West Pub.

Nonqualified Deferred Compensation Plans, 1995 Edition. Bruce J. McNeil. 277p. 1995. pap. text. write for info. (*0-314-07218-7*) West Pub.

Nonquitt, a Summer Album, 1872-1985. Nan Lyell. Ed. by Anne M. Lyell. LC 87-71240. (Illus.). 288p. 1987. 35.00 (*0-9618732-0-5*) Barekneed Pubs.

Nonradial & Nonlinear Stellar Pulsation: Proceedings. Ed. by H. A. Hill. (Lecture Notes in Physics Ser.: Vol. 125). 497p. 1980. 47.95 (*0-387-09994-8*) Spr-Verlag.

Nonradial Oscillation of Stars. 2nd ed. Wasaburo Unno et al. 300p. 1989. 64.50 (*0-86008-439-6*, Pub. by U of Tokyo) Col U Pr.

Nonradial Polymerization see Comprehensive Chemical Kinetics

Nonradiative Recombination in Semiconductors. V. N. Abakumov et al. (Modern Problems in Condensed Matter Sciences Ser.: Vol. 33). xviii, 320p. 1991. 232.75 (*0-444-88854-3*, North Holland) Elsevier.

Nonradioactive Analysis of Biomolecules. 2nd ed. Ed. by Christopher Kessler. LC 99-52528. (Springer Lab Manuals Ser.). (Illus.). xii, 750p. 1999. pap. 109.00 (*3-540-64601-9*) Spr-Verlag.

Nonrecursive Causal Models. William D. Berry. (Quantitative Applications in the Social Science Ser.: Vol. 37). 88p. 1984. pap. 10.95 (*0-8039-2265-5*) Sage.

Nonrefillable (Disposable) Type Fuel Gas Cylinder Assemblies, UL147A. 2nd ed. (C). 1996. pap. text 135.00 (*0-7629-0044-X*) Underwrtrs Labs.

Nonrefillable (Disposable) Type Metal Container Assemblies for Butane, UL 147B. 2nd ed. (C). 1996. pap. text 135.00 (*0-7629-0045-8*) Underwrtrs Labs.

Nonrepresentational Forms of the Comic: Humor, Irony & Jokes. Marcella Tarozzi-Goldsmith. LC 90-11766. (American University Studies: Philosophy: Ser. V, Vol. 117). X, 218p. (C). 1991. text 37.95 (*0-8204-1481-6*) P Lang Pubng.

Nonresidential Parenting: New Vistas in Family Living. Ed. by Charlene E. Depner & James H. Bray. (Focus Editions Ser.: Vol. 155). (Illus.). 240p. (C). 1993. text 59.95 (*0-8039-5050-0*); pap. text 26.00 (*0-8039-5051-9*) Sage.

Nonresonant Laser-Matter Interaction (NLMI-9), Vol. 3093. Ed. by Vitaly I. Konov & Mikhail N. Libenson. LC 98-122072. 418p. 1997. 89.00 (*0-8194-2508-7*) SPIE.

Nonresponse in Household Interview Surveys. Robert M. Groves & Mick P. Couper. LC 97-39223. (Series in Probability & Statistics). 368p. 1998. 89.95 (*0-471-18245-1*) Wiley.

Nonreusable Plastic Containers for Flammable & Combustible Liquids, UL 1853. 2nd ed. (C). 1995. pap. text 175.00 (*1-55989-177-7*) Underwrtrs Labs.

Nonroman. Florentin Smarandache. Ed. by Xiquan Publishing House Staff. (RUM.). 270p. (Orig.). (C). 1996. pap. 24.99 (*1-879585-17-0*) Erhus Univ Pr.

Nonroutine Problems: Doing Mathematics. Robert London. (Illus.). 60p. (Orig.). (YA). (gr. 10 up). 1989. pap. text 19.95 (*0-939765-30-6*, G117) Janson Pubns.

Nonsampling Error in Surveys. Judith T. Lessler & William D. Kalsbeek. LC 91-31950. (Probability & Mathematical Statistics: Applied Probability & Statistics Section Ser.). 432p. 1992. 145.00 (*0-471-86908-2*) Wiley.

Nonselective Cation Channels: Pharmacology, Physiology, & Biophysics. Ed. by D. Siemen & J. K. Hescheler. LC 93-13821. (Experientia Supplementa Ser.: Vol. 66). 1993. 110.00 (*0-8176-2888-6*) Birkhauser.

Nonselfadjoint Operator Algebras, Operator Theory, & Related Topics: The Carl M. Pearcy Anniversary Volume. Ed. by H. Bercovici & C. I. Foias. (Operator Theory Ser.: Vol. 104). 224p. 1998. 89.50 (*3-7643-5954-4*) Spr-Verlag.

Nonselfadjoint Operator Algebras, Operator Theory & Related Topics: The Carl M. Pearcy Anniversary Volume. Carl M. Pearcy et al. LC 98-22018. (Operator Theory, Advances & Applications Ser.). 1998. 89.50 (*0-8176-5954-4*) Birkhauser.

Nonselfadjoint Operators & Related Topics: Workshop on Operator Theory & Its Applications, Beersheba, February 24-28, 1992. Workshop on Operator Theory & Its Applications. Ed. by Avraham Feintuch et al. LC 94-26987. (Operator Theory, Advances & Applications Ser.: 73). 432p. 1994. 129.00 (*0-8176-5097-0*) Birkhauser.

Nonsense see Yok-Yok

Nonsense. Barry Rudner. (Illus.). 32p. (J). (gr. k-6). 1991. pap. 5.95 (*0-925928-04-6*) Tiny Thought.

Nonsense: Aspects of Intertextuality in Folklore & Literature. Susan Stewart. LC 79-4950. 240p. reprint ed. pap. 74.40 (*0-608-06289-8*, 206661800008) Bks Demand.

Nonsense & Commonsense: A Children's Book of Victorian Verse. John Grossman & Priscilla Dunhill. LC 92-50285. (Illus.). 128p. (J). 1992. 17.95 (*1-56305-313-6*, 3313) Workman Pub.

Nonsense Anthology. Ed. by Carolyn Wells. LC 76-128160. (Granger Index Reprint Ser.). 1977. 21.95 (*0-8369-6189-7*) Ayer.

Nonsense Books. Edward Lear. (BCL1-PR English Literature Ser.). 1992. reprint ed. lib. bdg. 139.00 (*0-7812-7589-X*) Rprt Serv.

Nonsense Club: Literature & Popular Culture, 1749-1764. Lance Bertelsen. (Illus.). 334p. 1986. text 75.00 (*0-19-812859-2*) OUP.

***Nonsense! He Yelled.** Roger Eschbacher. LC 00-24077. (Illus.). (J). 2002. write for info. (*0-8037-2582-5*, Dial Yng Read) Peng Put Young Read.

Nonsense in Flight. Simon Drew. (Illus.). 48p. 1987. 12.50 (*1-85149-061-2*) Antique Collect.

Nonsense of Common Sense, 1737-1738. Lady Mary Wortley Montagu. Ed. by Robert Halsband. LC 71-129373. (Northwestern University. Humanities Ser.: No. 17). reprint ed. 27.50 (*0-404-50717-4*) AMS Pr.

Nonsense: or Hits & Criticisms on the Follies of the Day. Marcus M. Pomeroy. LC 70-91091. (American Humorists Ser.). reprint ed. lib. bdg. 25.50 (*0-8398-1572-7*) Irvington.

Nonsense Poems. Edward Lear. LC 93-39193. (Illus.). 96p. (Orig.). (J). 1998. reprint ed. pap. 1.00 (*0-486-28031-4*) Dover.

Nonsense Rhyme: The Sing-Song of the Flapper-Jacker-Whacker-O. John F. Smith. LC 95-67455. (Illus.). (J). (gr. k-3). 1995. 15.95 (*1-884375-02-2*) Chinky-Po Tree.

Nonsense Songs. Edward Lear. LC 96-77401. (Illus.). 40p. (J). 1997. 16.00 (*0-689-81369-4*) McElderry Bks.

Nonsense Songs. Edward Lear & Jonathan Allen. (Illus.). 208p. (J). (gr. 4-8). 1995. 14.95 (*0-8050-2774-2*, Bks Young Read) H Holt & Co.

Nonsense upon Stilts: Bentham, Burke & Marx on the Rights of Man. Ed. by Jeremy Waldron. 224p. 1988. pap. text 14.95 (*0-416-91890-5*) Routledge.

Nonsense Verse. Ed. by Quentin Blake. LC 97-112693. 1997. pap. 12.95 (*0-14-058757-8*) Viking Penguin.

Nonsense Verse. Quentin Blake. 288p. 1999. pap. 4.99 (*0-14-036660-1*) Viking Penguin.

Nonsense Verse. Edward Lear. (Illus.). 32p. 1999. 12.95 (*1-85149-704-8*) Antique Collect.

Nonsensus, Cross-Referencing Edward Lear's Book of Nonsense. Justin Schiller. 133p. (Orig.). 1988. pap. text. write for info. (*0-904995-13-5*, Pub. by Catalpa Pr Ltd) Penguin Books.

Nonsentential Constituents: A Theory of Grammatical Structure & Pragmatic Interpretation. Ellen L. Barton. LC 90-31712. (Pragmatics & Beyond New Ser.: Vol. 2). xviii, 247p. 1990. 65.00 (*1-55619-045-X*) J Benjamins Pubng Co.

Nonsequences: Self Poems. Christopher Middleton. (Orig.). (C). 1966. pap. 2.00 (*0-393-04228-6*) Norton.

Nonsequential Processes. E. Best & C. Fernandez. (EATCS Monographs on Theoretical Computer Science: Vol. 13). vii, 112p. 1988. 43.95 (*0-387-19030-9*) Spr-Verlag.

Nonsexist Research Methods: A Practical Guide. Magrit Eichler. 144p. 1987. 29.95 (*0-04-497044-7*); pap. 9.95 (*0-04-497045-5*) Routledge.

Nonsexist Research Methods: Practical Guide. Margrite Eichler. 192p. (C). 1987. pap. 19.99 (*0-415-90605-9*) Routledge.

***Nonsilver & Alternative Process Photography.** Christopher James. (C). 2000. pap. 30.00 (*0-7668-2077-7*) Delmar.

Nonsilver Printing Processes: Four Selections, 1886-1927. Ed. by Peter C. Bunnell. LC 72-9221. (Literature of Photography Ser.). 1975. 24.95 (*0-405-04928-5*) Ayer.

Nonsmoker Solution. Lynn H. Christensen. LC 94-94331. 192p. 1994. pap. 10.95 (*0-9641059-1-8*) Crystal VA.

Nonsmooth Analysis & Control Theory. Frank H. Clarke et al. LC 97-34140. (Graduate Texts in Mathematics Ser.: Vol. 178). (Illus.). 296p. 1997. 49.95 (*0-387-98336-8*) Spr-Verlag.

Nonsmooth Analysis & Geometric Methods in Deterministic Optimal Control. Ed. by Boris Mordukhovich & Hector J. Sussmann. LC 96-13083. (IMA Volumes in Mathematics & Its Applications Ser.: Vol. 78). 264p. 1996. 54.95 (*0-387-94764-7*) Spr-Verlag.

Nonsmooth & Discontinuous Problems of Control & Optimization: A Proceedings Volume from the IFAC Workshop, Chelyabinsk, Russia, June 17-20, 1998. V. D. Batukhtin. LC 98-49283. 244p. 1999. 65.00 (*0-08-043237-9*, Pergamon Pr) Elsevier.

Nonsmooth Approach to Optimization Problems with Equilibrium Constraints: Theory, Applications & Numerical Results. Jiri V. Outrata et al. LC 98-24596. 273p. 1998. write for info. (*0-7923-5170-3*) Kluwer Academic.

Nonsmooth Impact Mechanics: Models, Dynamics, & Control. Bernard Brogliato. LC 96-26963. (Lecture Notes in Control & Information Sciences: Vol. 220). 400p. 1996. pap. 76.00 (*3-540-76079-2*) Spr-Verlag.

Nonsmooth Mechanics: Models, Dynamics & Control. 2nd ed. Bernard Brogliato. Ed. by B. W. Dickinson et al. LC 98-53322. xx, 556p. 1999. 119.00 (*1-85233-143-7*) Spr-Verlag.

Nonsmooth Mechanics & Applications. Ed. by J. J. Moreau & P. D. Panagiotopoulos. (CISM Courses & Lectures: Vol. 302). (Illus.). v, 462p. 1988. 103.95 (*0-387-82066-3*) Spr-Verlag.

Nonsmooth Optimization: Analysis & Algorithms with Applications to Optimal Control. Pekka Neittaanmaki & M. M. Makela. 300p. (C). 1992. text 48.00 (*981-02-0773-5*) World Scientific Pub.

Nonsmooth Optimization & Related Topics. Ed. by F. H. Clarke et al. (Ettore Majorana International Science Ser., Life Sciences: Vol. 43). (Illus.). 502p. (C). 1989. text 174.00 (*0-306-43247-1*, Kluwer Plenum) Kluwer Academic.

Nonstandard Analysis: Theory & Applications: Lectures Given at the NATO Advanced Study Institute, Nonstandard Analysis & Its Applications, at the International Centre for Mathematical Sciences, Edinburgh, July 1996. L. Arkeryd et al. LC 97-14127. (NATO ASI Series. Series C, Mathematical & Physical Sciences). 1997. text 197.50 (*0-7923-4586-X*) Kluwer Academic.

***Nonstandard Analysis for the Working Mathematician.** Peter A. Loeb & Manfred P. H. Wolff. LC 00-30655. (Mathematics & Its Applications Ser.). 2000. write for info. (*0-7923-6340-X*) Kluwer Academic.

Nonstandard Analysis in Practice. Ed. by Francine Diener & Marc Diener. LC 95-44955. 250p. 1995. 54.95 (*3-540-60297-6*) Spr-Verlag.

Nonstandard Asymptotic Anlysis. I. Van der Berg. (Lecture Notes in Mathematics Ser.: Vol. 1249). ix, 187p. 1987. 34.95 (*0-387-17767-1*) Spr-Verlag.

Nonstandard Finite Difference Models of Differential Equations. Ronald E. Mickens. 250p. 1993. text 61.00 (*981-02-1458-8*) World Scientific Pub.

Nonstandard Logics & Nonstandard Metrics in Physics. W. M. Honig. (Series on Knots & Everything: Vol. 10). 300p. 1995. pap. text 32.00 (*981-02-2251-3*) World Scientific Pub.

Nonstandard Logics & Nonstandard Metrics in Physics. William M. Honig. 300p. 1995. 55.00 (*981-02-2203-3*) World Scientific Pub.

Nonstandard Methods for Stochastic Fluid Mechanics. M. Capinski & N. J. Cutland. (Series on Advances in Mathematics). 248p. 1995. text 61.00 (*981-02-1710-2*) World Scientific Pub.

Nonstandard Methods in Commutative Harmonic Analysis. E. I. Gordon. LC 97-7187. (Translations of Mathematical Monographs: Vol. 164). 166p. 1997. text 99.00 (*0-8218-0419-7*, MMONO/164) Am Math.

Nonstandard Methods in Fixed Point Theory. A. G. Aksoy & M. A. Khamsi. Ed. by J. H. Ewing et al. (Universitext Ser.). (Illus.). ix, 139p. 1990. 49.95 (*0-387-97364-8*) Spr-Verlag.

Nonstandard Methods of Analysis. Anatoly G. Kusraev & S. S. Kutateladze. LC 94-16567. (Mathematics & Its Applications Ser.: Vol. 291).Tr. of Nestandartnye Metody Analiza. 448p. (C). 1994. text 251.00 (*0-7923-2892-2*) Kluwer Academic.

Nonstandard Queries & Nonstandard Answers. R. Demolombe & Tomasz Imielinski. (Illus.). 292p. 1994. text 79.00 (*0-19-853852-9*) OUP.

Nonstandard Varieties of Language. Ed. by Gunnel Melchers & Nils-Lennart Johannesson. (Stockholm Studies in English: No. 84). 220p. 1994. pap. 46.50 (*91-22-01635-X*) Coronet Bks.

***Nonstandard Work Arrangements & the Changing Labor Market: Dimensions, Causes & Institutional Responses.** Ed. by M. Ferber et al. 2000. 29.95 (*0-913447-80-3*) Indus Relations Res.

Nonstationarity & Structural Breaks in Economic Time Series: Asymptotic Theory & Monte Carlo Simulations. Antonio E. Noriega-Muro. 268p. 1993. 72.95 (*1-85628-580-4*, Pub. by Avebry) Ashgate Pub Co.

Nonstationary Flows & Shock Waves. Irvine I. Glass & J. P. Sislian. LC 93-44526. (Engineering Science Ser.: No. 39). (Illus.). 572p. 1994. text 160.00 (*0-19-859388-0*, Clarendon Pr) OUP.

Nonstationary Stochastic Processes & Their Applications: Proceedings of the Workshop. A. G. Miamee. 296p. 1992. text 95.00 (*981-02-1076-0*) World Scientific Pub.

Nonsteady Burning & Combustion Stability of Solid Propellants. Ed. by L. DeLuca & M. Summerfield. (PAAS Ser.: Vol. 143). 875p. 1992. 109.95 (*1-56347-014-4*, V-143) AIAA.

Nonsteady Fluid Dynamics: Presented at the Winter Annual Meeting of the American Society of Mechanical Engineers, San Francisco, California, December 10-15, 1978. Ed. by D. E. Crow & J. A. Miller. LC 78-59889. 258p. reprint ed. pap. 80.00 (*0-608-30891-9*, 201159000080) Bks Demand.

Nonsteady, One-Dimensional, Internal, Compressible Flows: Theory & Applications. John A. Kentfield. (Oxford Engineering Science Ser.: Vol. 31). (Illus.). 304p. 1993. text 70.00 (*0-19-507358-4*) OUP.

Nonsteroidal Anti-Inflammatory Drugs. Ed. by N. J. Lowe & C. Hensby. (Pharmacology & the Skin Ser.: Vol. 2). (Illus.). x, 158p. 1989. 129.75 (*3-8055-4898-2*) S Karger.

Nonsteroidal Anti-Inflammatory Drugs. Ed. by Joseph G. Lombardino. LC 85-12018. (Chemistry & Pharmacology of Drugs Ser.: Vol. 5). 464p. reprint ed. pap. 143.90 (*0-7837-2399-7*, 204008400006) Bks Demand.

Nonsteroidal Anti-Inflammatory Drugs: Mechanisms & Clinical Uses. 2nd ed. Ed. by Alan J. Lewis & Daniel E. Furst. LC 93-34984. (Illus.). 480p. 1993. text 240.00 (*0-8247-8856-7*) Dekker.

Nonsteroidal Anti-Inflammatory Drugs in the Treatment of Chronic Glomerulonephritis. Y. Vanrenterghem. No. 5. 137p. (Orig.). 1988. pap. 32.50 (*90-6186-281-7*, Pub. by Leuven Univ) Coronet Bks.

Nonstochastic Effects of Ionizing Radiation: ICRP Publication, No. 41. Ed. by F. D. Sowby. (Illus.). 33p. 1984. pap. 32.75 (*0-08-032333-2*, Pergamon Pr) Elsevier.

Nonstoichiometric Compounds: A Symposium Sponsored by the Division of Inorganic Chemistry at the 141st Meeting of the American Chemical Society, Washington, D.C., 1962. American Chemical Society, Non-Stoichiometric Comp. LC 63-16562. (Advances in Chemistry Ser.: 39). 261p. reprint ed. pap. 81.00 (*0-608-14816-4*, 202563100045) Bks Demand.

Nonstop Neurotic Cabaret. Robert Rhodes. 192p. 1998. pap. 14.95 (*0-85449-278-X*) Gay Mens Pr.

Nonstriatal Dopaminergic Neurons. Ed. by Erminio Costa & Gian L. Gessa. LC 76-5661. (Advances in Biochemical Psychopharmacology Ser.: No. 16). (Illus.). 728p. pap. 200.00 (*0-7837-7543-1*, 204696100005) Bks Demand.

Nonstrictly Hyperbolic Conservation Laws. Ed. by Barbara L. Keyfitz & Herbert C. Kranzer. LC 86-28690. (Contemporary Mathematics Ser.: Vol. 60). 133p. 1987. pap. 25.00 (*0-8218-5069-5*, CONM/60C) Am Math.

Nonstructural Issues of Seismic Design & Construction: A Technical Evaluation Based on a Workshop Sponsored by the National Science Foundation. Ed. by Roger E. Scholl. 122p. 1984. pap. 10.00 (*0-685-14416-X*) Earthquake Eng.

Nonsuch: Land of Water. William Beebe. 277p. Date not set. 23.95 (*0-8488-2208-0*) Amereon Ltd.

Nonsuch Professor. William Secker. 1995. 21.99 (*0-87377-191-5*) GAM Pubns.

Nonsulfide Qualitative Analysis of Cations: Separating & Identifying Representative Cations from Groups A-E. Judith C. Foster. (Modular Laboratory Program in Chemistry Ser.). 16p. (C). 1995. pap. text 1.50 (*0-87540-462-6*, ANAL 462-6) Chem Educ Res.

Nonsulfide Qualitative Analysis of Cations: Separating & Identifying Representative Group A Cations. Judith C. Foster. (Modular Laboratory Program in Chemistry Ser.). 12p. (C). 1995. pap. text 1.50 (*0-87540-463-4*, ANAL 463-4) Chem Educ Res.

Nonsuperpowers & South Africa: Implications for U. S. Policy. Richard J. Payne. LC 89-46340. 333p. 1990. reprint ed. pap. 103.30 (*0-608-01070-7*, 205937800001) Bks Demand.

Nonsurgical Management of Acute Low Back Pain: Cutting Through the AHCPR Guidelines. Ed. by Erwin G. Gonzalez & Richard S. Materson. LC 97-45695. (Illus.). 272p. 1997. 115.00 (*1-888799-13-7*) Demos Medical.

Nonsymmetric Fields Theory & Its Applications. Marek W. Kalinowski. 532p. (C). 1990. text 86.00 (*981-02-0335-7*); pap. text 40.00 (*981-02-0336-5*) World Scientific Pub.

Nonsynaptic Diffusion Neurotransmission & Late Brain Reorganization. Paul Bach-y-Rita. LC 95-2187. 232p. 1995. pap. 69.95 (*0-939957-77-9*) Demos Medical.

Nontarget Effects of Agricultural Fungicides. Ed. by Subhash C. Vyas. 272p. 1988. 153.00 (*0-8493-6889-8*, SB951, CRC Reprint) Franklin.

***Nontarget Effects of Biological Control.** Peter A. Follett & Jian J. Duan. LC 99-48110. 1999. write for info. (*0-7923-7725-7*) Kluwer Academic.

Nontariff Agricultural Trade Barriers. Jimmye S. Hillman. LC 78-16054. 254p. reprint ed. pap. 78.80 (*0-8357-3803-5*, 203653100003) Bks Demand.

Nontariff Distortions of International Trade. Robert E Baldwin. LC 78-109436. 222p. reprint ed. pap. 68.90 (*0-608-13342-6*, 205577900038) Bks Demand.

Nontech Guide/Energy Resources. Ben W. Ebenhack. LC 94-23721. 1995. 64.95 (*0-87814-434-X*) PennWell Bks.

Nontechnical Explanation of the 1994 NEHRP Recommended Provisions. Christopher Arnold. (Illus.). 82p. 1997. reprint ed. pap. text 25.00 (*0-7881-4698-X*) DIANE Pub.

Nontechnical Guide to Petroleum Geology, Exploration, Drilling, & Production. Norman J. Hyne. 536p. 1995. 64.95 (*0-87814-438-2*) PennWell Bks.

NonTheatre: One Act & Half-of-Act Dramas! Florentin Smarandache. Ed. by R. Muller. (Illus.). 130p. (C). 1995. pap. 9.99 (*1-879585-42-1*) Erhus Univ Pr.

Nonthermal Preservation of Foods. Barbosa-Canovas et al. LC 97-35932. (Food Science & Technology Ser.: Vol. 82). (Illus.). 296p. 1997. text 145.00 (*0-8247-9979-8*) Dekker.

"Nonton" - "The Search For" Anthropic Signature Particles. Jerald P. Dyrek. 320p. 1997. 37.50 (*0-9645447-6-8*); 37.50 (*0-9645447-5-X*) Dyrek-Seaways.

Nontopological Solitons. L. Wilets. (Lecture Notes in Physics Ser.: Vol. 24). 168p. 1989. text 36.00 (*9971-5-0697-1*) World Scientific Pub.

Nontoxic Baby: Reducing Harmful Chemicals from Your Baby's Life. Nancy S. Green. 90p. 1991. pap. 9.95 (*0-914955-09-8*) Lotus Pr.

Nontrade Issues see Positive Approach to the International Economic Order

Nontraditional Education: Alternative Ways to Earn Your Credentials. Kathleen Green. 14p. 1997. pap. 2.00 (*0-16-054510-2*) USGPO.

Nontraditional Families: Parenting & Child Development. Ed. by Michael E. Lamb. (Illus.). 372p. 1982. text 79.95 (*0-89859-178-3*) L Erlbaum Assocs.

Nontraditional Machining Processes. 2nd ed. Ed. by E. J. Weller. LC 83-51179. (Illus.). 285p. reprint ed. pap. 88.40 (*0-7837-6277-1*, 204599200010) Bks Demand.

Nontraditional Manufacturing Processes. Gary F. Benedict. (Manufacturing Engineering & Materials Processing Ser.: Vol. 19). (Illus.). 400p. 1987. text 170.00 (*0-8247-7352-7*) Dekker.

Nontraditional Methods in Diffusion: Proceedings of a Symposium Sponsored Jointly by the Metallurgical Society of AIME & the MSD-ASM Atomic Transport Activity Held at the Fall Meeting of the Metallurgical Society in Philadelphia, PA, October 4-5, 1983. Metallurgical Society of AIME Staff. Ed. by G. E. Murch et al. LC 84-60064. (Metallurgical Society of AIME Ser.). 321p. 1984. reprint ed. pap. 99.60 (*0-608-02386-8*, 206302800004) Bks Demand.

Nontraditional Methods of Sensing Stress, Strain & Damage in Materials & Structure. George T. Lucas & David A. Stubbs. LC 97-18165. (Illus.). 231p. 1997. pap. text 52.00 (*0-8031-2403-1*, STP1318) ASTM.

Nontraditional Organized Crime: Law Enforcement Officials' Perspectives of Five Criminal Groups. (Illus.). 62p. (Orig.). (C). 1992. pap. text 25.00 (*0-941375-19-6*) DIANE Pub.

Nontraditional Problems in Mathematical Hydrodynamics. O. V. Troshkin. LC 94-48581. (Translations of Mathematical Monographs: Vol. 144). 197p. 1995. text 39.00 (*0-8218-0285-2*, MMONO/144) Am Math.

Nontraditional Undergraduates: Trends in Enrollment from 1986 to 1992 & Persistence & Attainment Among 1989-90 Beginning Postsecondary Students. Laura J. Horn. 70p. 1996. per. 8.50 (*0-16-048914-8*) USGPO.

Nontraditional Work Programs: A Guide. 1980. 6.00 (*0-686-81343-X*) Wider Oppor Women.

Nonuniform Discrete Fourier Transform & Its Applications in Signal Processing. Sonali Bogchi & Sanjit K. Mitra. LC 98-45266. (Series in Computer Science). xiv, 208 p. 1999. write for info. (*0-7923-8281-1*) Kluwer Academic.

Nonunion Employee Representation: History, Contemporary Practice & Policy. Daniel J. B. Mitchell. Ed. by Bruce E. Kaufman & Daphne Gottlieb Taras. LC 99-32610. 592p. 2000. text 87.95 (*0-7656-0494-9*) M E Sharpe.

***Nonuniqueness in Geoscientific Inference.** P. S. Moharir. LC 99-89544. (Uncertainty Theory in Artificial Intelligence Ser.). 2000. 95.00 (*0-86380-217-6*) Research Studies Pr Ltd.

Nonvenomous Snakes. Ludwig Trutnau. 192p. 1986. 24.00 (*0-8120-5632-9*) Barron.

Nonverbal Aspects of Psychotherapy. Peter H. Waxer. LC 78-71280. 105p. 1978. 45.00 (*0-275-90321-4*, C0321, Praeger Pubs) Greenwood.

Nonverbal Assessment of Intelligence. R. McCallum & Bruce A. Bracken. (C). 1995. 32.95 (*0-205-15765-3*, Macmillan Coll) P-H.

Nonverbal Behavior: Perspectives, Applications & Intercultural Insights. Ed. by Aaron W. Wolfgang. LC 84-10899. 500p. (C). 1997. pap. text 38.00 (*0-88937-008-7*) Hogrefe & Huber Pubs.

Nonverbal Behavior & Communication. 2nd ed. Ed. by Aron W. Siegman & Stanley Feldstein. LC 86-50424. 640p. (C). 1987. pap. 59.95 (*0-8058-0018-2*) L Erlbaum Assocs.

Nonverbal Behavior & Social Psychology. Richard Heslin & Miles Patterson. (Perspectives in Social Psychology Ser.). 196p. 1982. 54.50 (*0-306-40952-6*, Plenum Trade) Perseus Pubng.

Nonverbal Communication. Abne M. Eisenberg & Ralph R. Smith. LC 77-160790. (Speech Communication Ser.: No. 9). 1971. pap. 5.50 (*0-672-61155-4*, Bobbs) Macmillan.

Nonverbal Communication. 2nd ed. Lippold. 1988. teacher ed. 16.00 (*0-07-553824-5*) McGraw.

Nonverbal Communication. 2nd ed. Loretta A. Malandro et al. 352p. (C). 1988. pap. 45.94 (*0-07-555059-8*) McGraw.

Nonverbal Communication. 3rd ed. (What Research Says to the Teacher Ser.). 1988. pap. 3.95 (*0-8106-1082-5*) NEA.

Nonverbal Communication. 4th ed. Knapp. (C). 1996. pap. text, teacher ed. 28.00 (*0-15-505321-3*) Harcourt Coll Pubs.

Nonverbal Communication. 4th ed. Virginia P. Richmond & James C. McCroskey. LC 99-45962. 356p. (C). 1999. pap. text 40.00 (*0-205-29577-0*, Longwood Div) Allyn.

Nonverbal Communication: Forms & Functions. Peter A. Andersen. LC 98-36051. 416p. 1998. pap. text 41.95 (*1-55934-726-0*) Mayfield Pub.

Nonverbal Communication: Studies & Applications. 3rd ed. Mark L. Hickson & Donald W. Stacks. 336p. (C). 1992. text. write for info. (*0-697-12925-X*) Brown & Benchmark.

Nonverbal Communication: Studies & Applications. 4th ed. Mark L. Hickson, III & Don W. Stacks. LC 98-45343. (Illus.). 420p. (C). 2000. pap. text. write for info. (*1-891487-20-5*) Roxbury Pub Co.

Nonverbal Communication: Survey, Theory, & Research. Daniel Druckman et al. LC 81-21309. (Sage Library of Social Research: No. 139). (Illus.). 264p. reprint ed. pap. 81.90 (*0-8357-4782-4*, 203771900009) Bks Demand.

Nonverbal Communication: The State of the Art. Robert G. Harper et al. LC 77-19185. (Wiley Series on Personality Processes). 375p. reprint ed. pap. 116.30 (*0-7837-2825-5*, 205764700006) Bks Demand.

Nonverbal Communication: The Unspoken Dialogue. David B. Buller et al. (Illus.). 545p. (C). 1994. pap. text 21.95 (*1-57074-093-3*) Greyden Pr.

Nonverbal Communication: The Unspoken Dialogue. 2nd ed. Judee K. Burgoon et al. 535p. (C). 1995. pap. 41.25 (*0-07-008995-7*) McGraw.

Nonverbal Communication & Human Interaction. 2nd ed. Knapp. (C). 1992. pap. text, teacher ed. 3.00 (*0-03-053224-8*) Harcourt Coll Pubs.

Nonverbal Communication & Marital Interaction. Patricia Noller. (International Series in Experimental Social Psychology: Vol. 9). (Illus.). 250p. 1984. text 104.00 (*0-08-027927-9*, CRC Reprint) Franklin.

Nonverbal Communication for Media, Library, & Information. Ellen S. McCardle. Ed. by Patrick R. Penland. LC 73-90766. (Communications Science & Technology Ser.: No. 5). (Illus.). 111p. reprint ed. pap. 34.50 (*0-7837-0650-2*, 204098900019) Bks Demand.

Nonverbal Communication in Human Interaction. 4th ed. Mark L. Knapp & Judith A. Hall. LC 96-78487. 512p. (C). 1996. pap. text 47.50 (*0-03-018023-6*, Pub. by Harcourt Coll Pubs) Harcourt.

Nonverbal Communication in Social Interaction. Ed. by Ullica Segerstrale & Peter Molnar. 288p. 1996. 29.95 (*0-8058-2179-1*) L Erlbaum Assocs.

***Nonverbal Communication in the Classroom.** Patrick W. Miller. LC 99-93528. (Illus.). 48p. 2000. pap. text 6.95 (*0-9673279-0-3*) P Miller Assoc.

***Nonverbal Communication in the Workplace.** Patrick W. Miller. LC 99-93527. (Illus.). 48p. 2000. pap. text 6.95 (*0-9673279-1-1*) P Miller Assoc.

Nonverbal Communication in Translation: New Perspectives & Challenges in Literature, Interpretation & the Media. Ed. by Fernando Poyatos. LC 97-1033. (Benjamins Translation Library: No. 17). xii, 361p. 1997. 94.00 (*1-55619-699-7*) J Benjamins Pubng Co.

Nonverbal Communication, Interaction & Gesture. Ed. by Adam Kendon. (Selections from Semiotica Ser.). 548p. 1981. pap. 26.15 (*90-279-3089-9*) Mouton.

Nonverbal Communication Reader: Classic & Contemporary Readings. 2nd rev. ed. Ed. by Laura K. Guerrero et al. (Illus.). 471p. (C). 1999. pap. 25.95 (*1-57766-040-4*) Waveland Pr.

Nonverbal Communication Skills Handbook. Ed. by Joyce M. C. Breasure. (Professional Handbook Ser.). 49p. (Orig.). 1982. pap. text 10.00 (*0-931975-13-1*) Advanced Dev Sys.

Nonverbal Communication Today. Ed. by Mary R. Key. (Contributions to the Sociology of Language Ser.: No. 33). 319p. 1982. text 74.00 (*90-279-3050-3*) Mouton.

Nonverbal Communication Workbook. Joseph A. DeVito. (Illus.). 287p. (C). 1989. pap. text 19.95 (*0-88133-393-X*) Waveland Pr.

Nonverbal Interaction. Ed. by John M. Wiemann & Randall P. Harrison. LC 82-20539. (Sage Annual Reviews of Communication Research Ser.: No. 11). 288p. 1983. reprint ed. pap. 89.30 (*0-608-01187-8*, 205948500001) Bks Demand.

Nonverbal Learning Disabilities: The Syndrome & the Model. Byron P. Rourke. LC 89-1958. 253p. 1989. lib. bdg. 35.00 (*0-89862-378-2*) Guilford Pubns.

***Nonverbal Perceptual & Cognitive Processes in Children with Language Disorders: Toward a New Framework for Clinical Intervention.** Felicie Affolter et al. LC 00-34122. 2000. pap. 34.50 (*0-8058-3213-0*) L Erlbaum Assocs.

NonVerbal Predication: Theory, Typology, Diachrony. Kees Hengeveld. LC 92-22942. (Functional Grammar Ser.: No. 15). xxiii, 321p. (C). 1992. lib. bdg. 106.15 (*3-11-013713-5*) Mouton.

Nonverbal Reasoning. Jack Rudman. (General Aptitude & Abilities Ser.: CS-27). 1994. pap. 23.95 (*0-8373-6727-1*) Nat Learn.

Nonverbal Vocal Communication: Comparative & Developmental Approaches. Ed. by H. Papousek et al. (Studies in Emotion & Social Interaction). (Illus.). 319p. (C). 1992. text 59.95 (*0-521-41265-X*) Cambridge U Pr.

Nonverbalen Ausdrucksmittel in Anton Cechovs Buhnenwerk. Christine Grafin von Bruhl. Bd. 52. 248p. 51.95 (*3-631-49062-3*) P Lang Pubng.

Nonviolence: Social & Psychological Issues. V. K. Kool. 290p. (Orig.). (C). 1993. pap. text 34.00 (*0-8191-9232-5*); lib. bdg. 57.50 (*0-8191-9231-7*) U Pr of Amer.

Nonviolence: The Gentle Persuader. Glenn Smiley. 45p. 1991. 3.50 (*0-614-05028-6*) Fellowship of Recon.

Nonviolence: The Gentle Persuader. Glenn Smiley. 1991. pap. 3.50 (*0-911810-76-5*, Fellwship Pubns) Fellowship of Recon.

Nonviolence - The Gentle Persuader. Glenn Smiley. 45p. 1991. 3.50 (*0-614-05042-1*, Fellwship Pubns) Fellowship of Recon.

Nonviolence & Community: Reflections on the Alternatives to Violence Project. Newton Garver & Eric Reitan. LC 95-69392. 1995. pap. 4.00 (*0-87574-322-6*) Pendle Hill.

Nonviolence & Israel-Palestine. Johan Galtung. 79p. 1989. pap. 5.00 (*0-8248-1264-6*) S M Matsunaga.

***Nonviolence & Its Violent Consequences.** William Meyers. 20p. 2000. pap. 2.00 (*1-886625-07-7*, Pub. by III Pub) Left Bank.

Nonviolence, Comsumption & Community among Ancient Indian Ascetics. Gail H. Sutherland. LC 98-900073. 78p. 1997. 8.00 (*81-85952-40-X*, Pub. by Indian Inst) Nataraj Bks.

***Nonviolence for the Third Millennium.** Ed. by Simon Harak. LC 99-86084. 268p. 2000. pap. 22.00 (*0-86554-660-6*) Mercer Univ Pr.

Nonviolence in America: A Documentary History. rev. ed. Ed. by Staughton Lynd & Alice Lynd. LC 94-41973. 576p. reprint ed. pap. 178.60 (*0-608-20192-8*, 207145100012) Bks Demand.

Nonviolence in America: A Documentary History. rev. ed. Ed. by Staughton Lynd & Alice Lynd. LC 94-41973. 600p. 1995. 45.00 (*1-57075-013-0*); pap. 25.00 (*1-57075-010-6*) Orbis Bks.

Nonviolence in Hawaii's Spiritual Traditions. Ed. by Glenn D. Paige & Sarah Gilliatt. LC 91-35187. 103p. 1991. pap. 5.00 (*1-880309-00-9*) S M Matsunaga.

Nonviolence in Theory & Practice. Robert L. Holmes. 208p. (C). 1989. 32.50 (*0-534-12180-2*) Wadsworth Pub.

Nonviolence on Trial. Robert Hillegass. LC 87-61440. (Orig.). 1987. pap. 1.00 (*0-87574-274-2*) Pendle Hill.

Nonviolence to Animals, Earth, & Self in Asian Traditions. Christopher K. Chapple. LC 92-25791. (SUNY Series in Religious Studies). 146p. (C). 1993. pap. text 18.95 (*0-7914-1498-1*) State U NY Pr.

Nonviolent Action: A Research Guide. Ronald McCarthy & Gene Sharp. LC 97-25316. (History Reference Ser.). 692p. 1997. text 109.00 (*0-8153-1577-5*, SS940) Garland.

Nonviolent Action & Social Change. Ed. by Severyn T. Bruyn & Paula Rayman. 320p. 1980. pap. text 15.95 (*0-8290-0271-5*) Irvington.

Nonviolent Action in the Liberation of Latvia. Olgerts Eglitis. (Monograph Ser.). 72p. 1993. 4.00 (*1-880813-06-8*) A Einstein Inst.

Nonviolent Coming of God. James W. Douglass. LC 91-23942. 250p. (Orig.). 1991. pap. 16.00 (*0-88344-753-3*) Orbis Bks.

Nonviolent Communications: A Language of Compassion. Marshall B. Rosenberg. LC 98-67231. (Illus.). 212p. 1999. pap. 17.95 (*1-892005-02-6*, BK033, Pub. by PuddleDancer) IPG Chicago.

Nonviolent Crisis Intervention: Learning to Defuse Explosive Behavior. Algene Caraulia & Linda Steiger. Ed. by Eugene T. Wyka & Sandra Christensen. LC 97-156982. 139p. 1997. text 59.00 (*0-9651733-2-1*) Crisis Prevent.

Nonviolent Insurrection in El Salvador: The Fall of Maximiliano Hernandez Martinez. Patricia Parkman. LC 88-9432. 168p. 1988. 33.50 (*0-8165-1062-8*) U of Ariz Pr.

***Nonviolent Intervention Across Borders: A Recurrent Vision.** Yeshua Moser-Puangsuwan & Thomas Weber. LC 99-88960. 2000. 20.00 (*1-880309-11-4*) S M Matsunaga.

Nonviolent National Defense: A Philosophical Inquiry into Applies Nonviolence. Norman C. Freund. Ed. by Stephen H. Rinehart. LC 87-22478. (Social Philosophy Research Institute Bks.: No. 5). 82p. (Orig.). (C). 1987. lib. bdg. 31.00 (*0-8191-6655-3*) U Pr of Amer.

Nonviolent Resistance. Cecil E. Hinshaw. (C). 1956. pap. 4.00 (*0-87574-088-X*) Pendle Hill.

Nonviolent Revolutionary: Story of a Gandhian Educator. Narayan Desai. Ed. by A. Paul Hare. LC 97-29282. (Illus.). 208p. 1997. 89.95 (*0-7734-8543-0*) E Mellen.

Nonviolent Social Movements: A Geographical Perspective. Ed. by Stephen Zunes et al. LC 99-17510. (Illus.). 320p. 1999. text 59.95 (*1-57718-075-5*) Blackwell Pubs.

***Nonviolent Social Movements: A Geographical Perspective.** Ed. by Stephen Zunes et al. LC 99-17510. (Illus.). 320p. 1999. pap. text 27.95 (*1-57718-076-3*) Blackwell Pubs.

***Nonviolent Soldier of Islam: Badshah Khan, a Man to Match His Mountains.** 2nd ed. Eknath Easwaran. (Illus.). 240p. 1999. 24.00 (*1-888314-01-X*); pap. 13.95 (*1-888314-00-1*) Nilgiri Pr.

Nonviolent Story: Narrative Conflict Resolution in the Gospel of Mark. Robert R. Beck. LC 95-42415. 210p. (Orig.). 1996. pap. 16.00 (*1-57075-061-0*) Orbis Bks.

Nonviolent Struggle & the Revolution in East Germany. Roland Bleiker. (Monograph Ser.). 53p. 1993. 3.00 (*1-880813-07-6*) A Einstein Inst.

Nonviral Vectors for Gene Therapy. Leaf Huang et al. LC 99-63092. (Illus.). 456p. 1999. 99.95 (*0-12-358465-5*) Acad Pr.

Nonvolatile Semiconductor Memories: Technologies, Design, & Applications. Chenming Hu. LC 90-29044. 464p. 1996. 79.95 (*0-87942-269-6*, PC02634) Inst Electrical.

Nonvolatile Semiconductor Memory Technology: A Comprehensive Guide to Understanding & Using NVSM Devices. Ed. by William D. Brown & Joe E. Brewer. LC 97-19691. (IEEE Press on Microelectronic Systems Ser.). 616p. 1997. 99.95 (*0-7803-1173-6*, PC5644) Inst Electrical.

***Nonvoters: America's No-Shows.** Jack C. Doppelt & Ellen Shearer. LC 99-6630. 272p. 1999. 59.95 (*0-7619-1900-7*); pap. 24.95 (*0-7619-1901-5*) Sage.

Nonwood Fibre Applications in Papermaking: A Literature Review. Graham Moore. 110p. 1996. pap. 110.00 (*1-85802-106-5*) Pira Internatl.

Nonwood Plant Fiber Pulping: Progress Report, No. 11. Technical Association of the Pulp & Paper Industry. LC TS1109.T425. 108p. 1981. reprint ed. pap. 33.50 (*0-608-08438-7*, 202281200030) Bks Demand.

Nonwood Plant Fiber Pulping: Progress Report, No. 12. Technical Association of the Pulp & Paper Industry. LC 82-80290. 96p. 1982. reprint ed. pap. 30.00 (*0-608-08437-9*, 202281800030) Bks Demand.

Nonwood Plant Fiber Pulping: Progress Report, No. 13. Technical Association of the Pulp & Paper Industry. LC TS1109.T425. 156p. 1982. reprint ed. pap. 48.40 (*0-608-08436-0*, 202282400030) Bks Demand.

Nonwood Plant Fiber Pulping: Progress Report, No. 14. Technical Association of the Pulp & Paper Industry. LC TS1109.T425. 116p. 1983. reprint ed. pap. 36.00 (*0-608-08435-2*, 202283400030) Bks Demand.

Nonwood Plant Fiber Pulping: Progress Report, No. 15. Technical Association of the Pulp & Paper Industry. LC TS1109.T425. 132p. 1975. reprint ed. pap. 41.00 (*0-608-08439-5*, 202529700043) Bks Demand.

Nonwood Plant Fiber Pulping: Progress Report, No. 16. Technical Association of the Pulp & Paper Industry. Ed. by E. Cameron Cobb & John L. Michelson. LC TS1109.T425. 71p. 1986. pap. 30.00 (*0-608-08440-9*, 202919100059) Bks Demand.

Nonwood Plant Fiber Pulping: Progress Report, No. 17. Technical Association of the Pulp & Paper Industry. (Illus.). 165p. 1987. reprint ed. pap. 47.10 (*0-608-05656-1*, 2032278) Bks Demand.

Nonwood Plant Fiber Pulping: Progress Report, No. 18. Technical Association of the Pulp & Paper Industry. LC TS1109.T425. (Illus.). 131p. 1988. reprint ed. pap. 40.70 (*0-608-05657-X*, 203227900079) Bks Demand.

Nonwood Plant Fiber Pulping: Progress Report, No. 19. Technical Association of the Pulp & Paper Industry. LC TS1109.T425. (Illus.). 287p. reprint ed. pap. 89.00 (*0-7837-1199-9*, 204173200023) Bks Demand.

Nonwood Plant Fiber Pulping Progress Reports, Vol. 21. 212p. (Orig.). 1994. pap. 72.00 (*0-89852-287-0*, 0101R242) TAPPI.

Nonwood Plant Fiber Pulping Progress Reports, Vol. 22. 270p. (Orig.). 1995. pap. 90.00 (*0-89852-296-X*, 0101R251) TAPPI.

Nonwoven Fabrics. Jack Weiner et al. Incl. Vol. 1. General & Testing, Properties & Finishing, Supplement No. 2. LC 74-100622. 1974. 15.95 Vol. 2. Forming Methods, Supplement. LC 74-100622. 1974. 15.95 Vol. 3. Chemical & Mechanical Bonding, Supplement. LC 74-100622. 1974. 15.95 Vol. 4. Uses. LC 74-100622. 1974. 15.95 LC 74-100622. 1974. 15.00 (*0-87010-027-0*) Inst Paper Sci & Tech.

Nonwoven Fibers: Properties, Characteristics & Applications Short Course, 1992: Sheraton Wayfarer Hotel, Bedford, NH, September 21-23. Technical Association of the Pulp & Paper Industry. LC TS1828.. (TAPPI Notes Ser.). (Illus.). 303p. reprint ed. pap. 94.00 (*0-7837-3878-1*, 204372300010) Bks Demand.

N

An Asterisk (*) at the beginning of an entry indicates that the title is appearing for the first time.

Nonwoven Textiles. Oldrich Jirsak & Larry Wadsworth. LC 97-68958. 144p. 1998. 39.95 (*0-89089-987-8*) Carolina Acad Pr.

Nonwovens. Ed. by M. L. Gulrajani. 1992. 45.00 (*0-7855-2825-3*, Pub. by Textile Inst) St Mut.

Nonwovens: An Advanced Tutorial. 313p. 1989. pap. 43.00 (*0-89852-457-1*, 0101R157) TAPPI.

Nonwovens: An Advanced Tutorial. Ed. by Albin F. Turbak & Tyrone L. Vigo. LC TS1818.N66. (Illus.). 319p. 1989. reprint ed. pap. 98.90 (*0-8357-6333-1*, 203560600096) Bks Demand.

Nonwovens: Theory, Process, Performance, & Testing. Ed. by A. F. Turbak. 256p. (Orig.). 1993. pap. 103.00 (*0-89852-265-X*, 0101R199) TAPPI.

Nonwovens: 1984 Symposium Notes. Technical Association of the Pulp & Paper Industry. LC TS1109.N6. 191p. 1984. reprint ed. pap. 59.30 (*0-608-08441-7*, 202279500030) Bks Demand.

Nonwovens Conference: Nashville, April 5-8, 1988. Technical Association of the Pulp & Paper Industry. LC TS1828.N5. (TAPPI Proceedings Ser.). (Illus.). 272p. 1988. reprint ed. pap. 84.40 (*0-608-08442-5*, 203227200079) Bks Demand.

Nonwovens Conference, 1989: Marriott's Marco Island Resort, Marco Island, FL, May 7-11. Technical Association of the Pulp & Paper Industry. LC TS1828.N5. (TAPPI Proceedings Ser.). (Illus.). 281p. reprint ed. pap. 87.20 (*0-8357-6334-X*, 203560700096) Bks Demand.

Nonwovens Conference, 1987: Proceedings of TAPPI, Marriott's World Center, Orlando, FL, April 20-24. Technical Association of the Pulp & Paper Industry. LC TS1828.N5. (Illus.). 235p. 1987. pap. 72.90 (*0-608-08444-1*, 202997600067) Bks Demand.

Nonwovens Conference, 1986: Proceedings of TAPPI, Marriott Hotel, Atlanta, GA, April 20-23, 1986. Technical Association of the Pulp & Paper Industry. LC TS1828.N5. 269p. 1986. pap. 83.40 (*0-608-08443-3*, 202918900059) Bks Demand.

Nonwovens Conference, 1990: Marriott's Marco Island Hotel, Marco Island, FL, May 6-10. Technical Association of the Pulp & Paper Industry. LC TS1828.N624. (TAPPI Proceedings Ser.). (Illus.). 403p. reprint ed. pap. 125.00 (*0-8357-4192-3*, 203697000006) Bks Demand.

Nonwovens Conference, 1994: Grenelefe Conference Center, Orlando, Florida, February 14-16. Technical Association of the Pulp & Paper Industry. LC 90-643703. (TAPPI Proceedings Ser.). (Illus.). 284p. 1994. reprint ed. pap. 88.10 (*0-608-05354-6*, 208240200004) Bks Demand.

Nonwovens Conference, 1991: Marriott's Marco Island Hotel, Marco Island, FL, May 12-16. Technical Association of the Pulp & Paper Industry. LC 90-643703. (TAPPI Proceedings Ser.). 407p. pap. 126.20 (*0-7837-0256-6*, 204056500017) Bks Demand.

Nonwovens Conference, 1992: Marriott's Marco Island Hotel, Marco Island, FL, May 10-14. Technical Association of the Pulp & Paper Industry. LC TS1828.N66. (TAPPI Proceedings Ser.). 268p. reprint ed. pap. 83.10 (*0-7837-3178-7*, 204278200006) Bks Demand.

Nonwovens Primer. Ed. by E. Silk & D. Durso. 30p. (Orig.). 1986. pap. 15.00 (*0-89852-434-2*, 0101R134) TAPPI.

Nonwovens Symposium, 1985: Proceedings of TAPPI, Myrtle Beach Hilton, Myrtle Beach, SC. April 21-15. Technical Association of the Pulp & Paper Industry. LC TS1828.N5. 285p. reprint ed. pap. 88.40 (*0-608-12217-3*, 202528200043) Bks Demand.

Nonzero: The Logic of Human Destiny. Robert Wright. 2000. pap. 15.00 (*0-679-75894-1*) Knopf.

Nonzero: The Logic of Human Destiny. Robert Wright. LC 99-40859. 480p. 2000. 27.50 (*0-679-44252-9*) Pantheon.

Noo-Noo Tidies Up. Ed. by Scholastic, Inc. Staff. LC 99-215206. (Lift-the-Flap Bk.). (Illus.). 24p. (J). (ps-k). 1999. 6.99 (*0-590-27855-X*) Scholastic Inc.

Noob Tawg Tau Hlub Ua Ntsoj Tsuag (Hmong) Arthur Morton. Tr. by Yer J. Thao. (J). (gr. k-3). 1994. 12.50 (*1-57842-075-X*) Delmas Creat.

***Noodle.** Terry Durack. LC 99-24105. (Illus.). 208p. 1999. 27.00 (*1-57959-053-5*, SOMA) BB&T Inc.

***Noodle: Aromatic Recipes with an Eastern Influence.** (Illus.). 64p. 2000. 11.95 (*1-85967-783-5*, Lorenz Bks) Anness Pub.

Noodle Book. K. Hayter. 128p. 1996. 12.98 (*0-7858-0553-2*) Bk Sales Inc.

***Noodle Dance! Chunky Roly Poly.** Mouseworks Staff. 16p. (J). 1999. 3.50 (*0-7364-0011-7*, Pub. by Mouse Works) Time Warner.

***Noodle Fusion: Asian Pasta Dishes for Western Palates.** Andrea Chesman & Dorothy Rankin. LC 99-33920. 224p. 2000. pap. 16.95 (*0-89594-956-3*) Crossing Pr.

Noodle Kugel. 2nd ed. Sonia Usatch. 40p. 1990. pap. 8.00 (*0-925062-00-6*) Writers Ink Pr.

Noodle Mouse Goes to Hawaii. Joyce C. Stender. LC 96-91546. (Illus.). 32p. (J). (ps-3). 1997. 9.95 (*1-890557-27-7*) Cadelle Pub.

Noodle Mouse's First Christmas. unabridged ed. Joyce C. Stender. LC 96-92959. (Illus.). v, 38p. (Orig.). (J). (ps-3). 1996. pap. 6.95 (*1-890557-25-0*) Cadelle Pub.

Noodle, Nitwit, Numskull. Zola. (Illus.). (J). 1996. 12.95 (*0-919627-87-0*, Pub. by Quarry Pr); pap. 7.95 (*0-919627-89-7*, Pub. by Quarry Pr) LPC InBook.

Noodle Shop Cookbook. 224p. 1999. 16.00 (*0-02-862935-3*, Pub. by Macmillan) S&S Trade.

Noodle Soup. Gloria Repp. LC 93-42417. (Illus.). 32p. (J). 1994. pap. 5.49 (*0-89084-582-4*, 055681) Bob Jones Univ.

Noodle Words: An Introduction to Chinese & Japanese Characters. D. M. Murray & T. W. Wong. LC 79-147179. (Illus.). 96p. (YA). (gr. 9 up). 1971. pap. 8.95 (*0-8048-0948-8*) Tuttle Pubng.

Noodles. Pam Preece-Sandoval & Bob Reese. (Ten Word Book Ser.). (Illus.). (J). (gr. k-3). 1994. pap. 3.95 (*0-89868-254-1*, Read Res); lib. bdg. 9.95 (*0-89868-253-3*, Read Res) ARO Pub.

Noodles. Pam Preece-Sandoval & Bob Reese. Tr. by Gloria Schaffer-Melendez. (Un Libro de Diaz Palabras Ser.). (SPA., Illus.). (J). (gr. k-3). 1994. pap. 3.95 (*0-89868-262-2*, Read Res); lib. bdg. 9.95 (*0-89868-261-4*, Read Res) ARO Pub.

Noodles. Michael Zulli. (Illus.). 64p. (Orig.). 1991. pap. 3.95 (*1-879450-09-7*) Kitchen Sink.

***Noodles: A Vegetarian Journey Through the World of Pasta.** Cornelia Schinharl. LC 99-31700. 96p. 2000. 14.95 (*0-7641-1278-3*) Barron.

Noodles: Essential Kitchen. Vicki Liley. LC 98-37002. (Essential Kitchen Ser.). (Illus.). 112p. 1999. 17.95 (*962-593-459-6*) Periplus.

***Noodles: The New Way.** Sri Owen. LC 00-27532. (Illus.). 144p. 2000. 24.95 (*0-375-50436-2*) Villard Books.

Noodles & Pasta. Joy Davies. LC 99-12434. (Illus.). 144p. (YA). (gr. 11). 1999. 19.95 (*0-7370-0031-7*) T-L Custom Pub.

Noodles, Chinese Home-Cooking. Lee Hwa Lin. (CHI & ENG.). 96p. 1993. 17.95 (*0-941676-35-8*) Wei-Chuan Pub.

Noodles, Classical Chinese Cooking. Lee Hwa Lin. (CHI & ENG.). 96p. 1993. 17.95 (*0-941676-42-0*) Wei-Chuan Pub.

***Noodles Express: Fast & Easy Meals in 15 to 45 Minutes.** Dana McCauley. (Illus.). 160p. 1999. pap. 14.95 (*1-55209-396-4*) Firefly Bks Ltd.

***Noodles Quick & Easy.** Kit Chan. 96p. 1999. pap. 12.95 (*0-7548-0554-9*) Anness Pub.

***Noodles to Pasta: Fresh & Easy Recipes with Noodles.** Lynne Mullins. (Illus.). 2000. pap. text. write for info. (*0-7322-6752-8*) HarpC.

Noodlin Steelhead & Salmon. Dick Swan. (Illus.). 149p. 1996. pap. text 9.95 (*1-57188-047-X*) F Amato Pubns.

Noodling: Hand Grabbing Snapping Turtles. Richard E. Faler. (Illus.). 24p. (Orig.). 1993. pap. 4.50 (*1-881399-13-3*) Beaver Pond P&P.

***Noodling for Flatheads: Moonshine, Monster Catfish & Other Southern Comforts.** Burkhard Bilger. (Illus.). 256p. 2000. write for info. (*0-684-85010-9*) Scribner.

Noog Nyob Tsua Tog Vaaj Tog Tsev (Hmong) Arthur Morton. Tr. by Yer J. Thao. (J). (gr. k-3). 1995. 12.50 (*1-57842-018-0*) Delmas Creat.

Noogamich & Other Stories. Marjorie Kendall. 1991. pap. 5.95 (*0-921054-34-3*) Nimbus Publ.

Nook Farm. Joseph S. Van Why. Ed. by Earl A. French. LC 75-20778. (Illus.). 1975. pap. 5.00 (*0-917482-02-6*) Stowe-Day.

Nooks & Crannies of New York. Yeadon. 1986. write for info. (*0-684-16083-8*, Scribners Ref) Mac Lib Ref.

Nooksack Tales & Trails. Percival R. Jeffcott. (Illus.). 448p. 1995. reprint ed. pap. 19.95 (*0-9646976-0-2*) Sincyrly Ours Pub.

***Noon.** Geoff Bouvier et al. (Illus.). 2000. pap. 9.00 (*0-9676211-0-0*) Noon Inc.

Noon. Cole Swenson. LC 97-20935. (New American Poetry Ser.: No. 24). 96p. (Orig.). 1997. pap. 10.95 (*1-55713-287-9*) Sun & Moon CA.

Noon, 22nd Century. Arkadifi N. Strugaktlskifi & Boris N. Strugaktlskifi. LC 78-17444. (Best of Soviet Science Fiction Ser.). xv, 319p. (J). 1978. write for info. (*0-02-615150-2*) Macmillan.

Noon Wine see Six Great Modern Short Novels

Noonday Exigencies. Hinton R. Helper. (Notable American Authors Ser.). 1992. reprint ed. lib. bdg. 75.00 (*0-7812-3078-0*) Rprt Serv.

Noonday Friends. Mary Stolz. (J). 1965. 10.05 (*0-606-02852-8*, Pub. by Turtleback) Demco.

Noonday Friends. Mary Stolz. LC 65-20257. (Illus.). 192p. (J). (gr. 4-7). 1965. lib. bdg. 15.89 (*0-06-025946-9*) HarpC Child Bks.

Noonday Friends. Mary Stolz. LC 65-20257. (Trophy Bk.). (Illus.). 192p. (J). (gr. 3-7). 1971. pap. 4.95 (*0-06-440009-3*, HarpTrophy) HarpC Child Bks.

Noonkanbah Story: Profile of an Aboriginal Community in Western Australia. Erich Kolig. 160p. (Orig.). (C). 1987. pap. 24.95 (*0-908569-37-8*, Pub. by Univ Otago Pr) Intl Spec Bk.

Noontide Night: A Y2K Novel. Andrew L. Burt. 314p. 1999. pap. 12.95 (*0-9672984-0-7*, NeverWrlds Pr) TechSoft.

Noontide Sun: The Field Journals of the Rev. Stephen Bowers, Arlene Benson. LC 97-29865. (Anthropological Papers: Vol. 44). (Illus.). 301p. 1997. pap. 27.50 (*0-87919-136-8*) Ballena Pr.

Noontide Sun: The Field Journals of the Rev. Stephen Bowers, Pionner Archaeologist. Arlene Benson. LC 97-29865. (Anthropological Papers: Vol. 44). (Illus.). 301p. 1997. 36.00 (*0-87919-135-X*) Ballena Pr.

Noontime Walker's Guide to Downtown Los Angeles. Janet Lendhoff. (Illus.). 16p. 1994. 5.95 (*1-883897-04-1*) River Rock CA.

Noor-un-Nisa Inayat Khan (Madeleine) George Cross MBE, Croix de Guerre with Gold Star. rev. ed. Jean O. Fuller. Orig. Title: Madeleine. (Illus.). 271p. 1988. reprint ed. pap. 11.95 (*0-85692-067-3*, Pub. by East-West) Omega Pubns NY.

Nooron Nobi. Ahmad Nawaz. LC 98-70823. (BEN.). xiv, 100p. 1998. pap. 10.00 (*1-58225-140-1*) Ananta Prakashani.

Noorps Are Coming. Robert T. Stout. (Illus.). 32p. (J). (ps-6). 1982. pap. 3.95 (*0-911049-05-3*) Yuletide Intl.

Noose at Sundown. Terrell L. Bowers. LC 96-95480. 192p. 1997. 18.95 (*0-8034-9231-6*, Avalon Bks) Bouregy.

Noose of Words: Readings of Desire, Violence, & Language in Euripides' Hippolytos. Barbara Goff. 220p. (C). 1990. text 49.95 (*0-521-36397-7*) Cambridge U Pr.

Noose Report. Ed. by Alfred Hitchcock. 1976. 20.95 (*0-8488-0529-1*) Amereon Ltd.

Nootka & Quileute Music. Frances Densmore. (Bureau of American Ethnology Bulletins Ser.). 358p. 1995. lib. bdg. 99.00 (*0-7812-4124-3*) Rprt Serv.

Nootka & Quileute Music. Frances Densmore. LC 72-1885. (Music Ser.). (Illus.). 416p. 1972. reprint ed. lib. bdg. 42.50 (*0-306-70513-3*) Da Capo.

Nootka Sound: And the Surrounding Waters of Maquinna. Heather Harbord. (Illus.). 122p. 1996. pap. 11.95 (*1-895811-03-1*) Heritage Hse.

Nootka Sound Controversy. William R. Manning. LC 65-27195. 1969. reprint ed. 22.95 (*0-405-03678-7*) Ayer.

Nootka Texts: Tales & Ethnological Narratives, with Grammatical Notes & Lexical Materials. Ed. by Edward Sapir & Morris Swadesh. LC 78-11226. reprint ed. 55.00 (*0-404-11893-3*) AMS Pr.

Noot's Toupee Day. Mrs. Kern's 1995-96 Third Grade Class. (WeWrite Kids! Ser.: No. 31). (Illus.). 50p. (J). (ps-4). 1996. pap. 3.95 (*1-57635-004-5*); lib. bdg. 18.95 (*1-57635-003-7*) WeWrite.

Noozles: New Friends. L. Spencer Humphrey. 32p. (J). 1993. pap. 2.95 (*0-8125-2320-2*, Pub. by Tor Bks) St Martin.

Noplace Like Home: The Literary Artist & Russia's Search for Cultural Identity. Amy C. Singleton. LC 97-4275. (SUNY Series, The Margins of Literature). 193p. (C). 1997. text 53.50 (*0-7914-3399-4*); pap. text 17.95 (*0-7914-3400-1*) State U NY Pr.

Nop's Hope. Donald McCaig. 240p. 1998. reprint ed. pap. 14.95 (*1-55821-574-3*) Lyons Pr.

Nop's Trials. Donald McCaig. 336p. 1992. pap. 13.95 (*1-55821-185-3*) Lyons Pr.

Nor Crystal Tears. Alan Dean Foster. 240p. 1994. reprint ed. 20.00 (*0-7278-4564-0*) Severn Hse.

Nor Is It over Yet: Florida in the Era of Reconstruction, 1863-1877. Jerrell H. Shofner. LC 70-186325. 1974. 34.95 (*0-8130-0353-9*) U Press Fla.

Nor Live So Long. Sara Woods. 224p. 1988. pap. 3.50 (*0-380-70478-1*, Avon Bks) Morrow Avon.

Nor Meekly Serve My Time: The H Block Struggle, 1976-1981. Ed. by Brian Cambell et al. (Illus.). 264p. 1994. pap. 20.95 (*0-9514229-5-2*, Pub. by Beyond the Pale) Irish Bks Media.

Nor Shall Your Glory Be Forgot. L. Kristofferson & Brian C. Pohanka. LC 99-10694. (Illus.). 128p. 1999. text 27.95 (*0-312-20473-6*) St Martin.

Nor the Battle to the Strong. Carl Jackson. LC 98-122023. 352p. 1997. pap. 16.95 (*0-948833-97-1*, Pub. by Peepal Tree Pr) Paul & Co Pubs.

Nor the Moon by Night: Across the Treacherous Tatra Mountains, the Bobov Chassidim Seek a Haven from the War. Devora Gliksman. LC 97-3087. 1997. 23.95 (*0-87306-767-3*); pap. 20.95 (*0-87306-789-4*) Feldheim.

Nor the Years Condemn. Robin Hyde. LC 96-142457. 272p. 1994. pap. 29.95 (*0-908569-83-1*, Pub. by Univ Otago Pr) Intl Spec Bk.

Nor the Years Condemn. Ted Sherrell. 225p. (C). 1988. 50.00 (*1-85200-021-X*, Pub. by United Writers Pubns) St Mut.

Nora. Diana Palmer. 1994. mass mkt. 5.99 (*0-8041-0975-3*) Ivy Books.

Nora. Diane Palmer. Date not set. pap. 8.95 (*0-449-91267-1*) Fawcett.

Nora: Maybe a Ghost Story. Constance C. Greene. LC 92-44929. 1993. pap. 3.95 (*0-685-64850-8*) Harcourt.

Nora: Maybe a Ghost Story. Constance C. Greene. LC 92-44929. (Illus.). 208p. (J). (gr. 5-9). 1993. 10.95 (*0-15-277696-6*, Gulliver Bks); pap. 3.95 (*0-15-276895-5*, Gulliver Bks) Harcourt.

***Nora: The Real Life of Molly Bloom.** Brenda Maddox. 512p. 2000. pap. 14.00 (*0-618-05700-5*) HM.

Nora Connor. Annie M. Smithson. 1990. pap. 12.95 (*0-85342-952-9*) Dufour.

Nora Ephron Collected. Nora Ephron. 224p. 1991. pap. 8.95 (*0-380-71253-9*, Avon Bks) Morrow Avon.

Nora, Nora: A Novel. Anne Rivers Siddons. 320p. 2000. 25.00 (*0-06-017613-X*) HarpC.

***Nora, Nora: A Novel.** large type ed. Anne Rivers Siddons. 432p. 2000. pap. 25.00 (*0-06-019718-8*) HarpC.

Nora Normal/Great Ghost Adventure. R. Asquith. (Illus.). (J). mass mkt. 6.95 (*0-340-68071-7*, Pub. by Hodder & Stought Ltd) Trafalgar.

Nora of Skye Aerie. Jill Morgan. (J). 1999. pap. 3.99 (*0-679-88837-3*, Pub. by Random Bks Yng Read) Random.

Nora Plays All Day: Big Book. large type ed. Joellen Hiltbrand. (Little Books & Big Bks.). (Illus.). 8p. (J). (ps-1). 1998. pap. text 19.89 (*0-8215-0855-5*) Sadlier.

***Nora Roberts: A Reader's Checklist & Reference Guide.** CheckerBee Publishing Staff. 1999. pap. text 4.95 (*1-58598-033-1*) CheckerBee.

Nora S. Unwin: Artist & Wood Engraver. Linda C. McGoldrick. LC 89-208. (Illus.). 208p. 1990. pap. 27.50 (*0-87233-097-4*) Bauhan.

Nora Was a Nurse. large type ed. Peggy Gaddis. 1990. 27.99 (*0-7089-2316-X*) Ulverscroft.

Noradrenergic Mechanisms in Parkinson's Disease. F. Colpaert. 288p. 1993. lib. bdg. 159.00 (*0-8493-8391-9*) CRC Pr.

Noradrenergic Neurons. Marianne Fillenz. (Illus.). 248p. (C). 1990. pap. text 31.95 (*0-521-28780-4*) Cambridge U Pr.

Noran Bang: The Yellow Room. M. J. Kang. 96p. (Orig.). 1999. pap. 13.95 (*0-88754-571-8*, Pub. by Theatre Comm) Consort Bk Sales.

Nora's Ark. Natalie Kinsey-Warnock. (J). 1924. write for info. (*0-688-17244-X*, Wm Morrow) Morrow Avon.

Nora's Recipes from Egypt. Nora George. LC 95-94815. (Illus.). 208p. (Orig.). 1995. pap. 23.00 (*0-9648676-0-5*) N George.

Nora's Ribbon of Memories. Stephanie G. Whitson. LC 99-36159. (Keepsake Legacies Ser.). 288p. 1999. pap. 12.99 (*0-7852-7187-2*) Nelson.

Nora's Roar. Clayton Eshleman. 32p. (Orig.). 1996. 50.00 (*1-887289-16-X*); pap. 10.00 (*1-887289-11-9*) Rodent Pr.

Nora's Room. Jessica Harper. (J). 14.95 (*0-06-029136-2*, Wm Morrow); lib. bdg. 14.89 (*0-06-029137-0*, Wm Morrow) Morrow Avon.

Nora's Stars. Satomi Ichikawa. (Illus.). 32p. (J). (ps-3). 1997. pap. 5.99 (*0-698-11596-1*, PapStar) Peng Put Young Read.

Norbert Elias. Robert Van Krieken. LC 97-27714. 224p. (C). 1998. 60.00 (*0-415-10415-7*); pap. 18.99 (*0-415-10416-5*) Routledge.

***Norbert Elias: An Introduction, 1 Vol.** Stephen Mennell. LC 99-195127. 1999. pap. text 28.95 (*1-900621-20-7*) Dufour.

Norbert Elias Reader: A Biographical Selection. Johan Goudsblom & Stephen Mennell. LC 97-8619. 320p. 1997. text 62.95 (*0-631-19308-1*); pap. text 29.95 (*0-631-19309-X*) Blackwell Pubs.

Norbert Nipkin. Robert McConnell. (J). 1994. audio 7.95 (*0-929141-24-5*) Napoleon Publ.

Norbert Nipkin: Teacher's Resource Package. Napolean. 1995. pap. text, teacher ed. 8.95 (*0-929141-44-X*) Napoleon Publ.

Norbert Nipkin & the Magic Riddle Stone see Norbert Nipkin et la Pierre aux Enigmes

Norbert Nipkin & the Magic Riddle Stone. Robert McConnell. (Illus.). 48p. 1990. 14.95 (*0-929141-03-2*) Napoleon Publ.

Norbert Nipkin & the Magic Riddle Stone. Robert McConnell. (Illus.). (J). 1995. audio 7.95 (*0-929141-25-3*) Napoleon Publ.

Norbert Nipkin & the Magic Riddle Stone: Teacher's Resource Package. Napolean. (Illus.). 1995. pap. text, teacher ed. 8.95 (*0-929141-45-8*) Napoleon Publ.

Norbert Nipkin et la Pierre aux Enigmes. Robert McConnell.Tr. of Norbert Nipkin & the Magic Riddle Stone. (FRE., Illus.). 48p. (Orig.). 1990. pap. 15.95 (*0-929141-07-5*) Napoleon Publ.

Norbert Wiener - Collected Works Vol. 4: Cybernetics, Science & Society, Ethics, Aesthetics & Literary Criticism, Book Reviews & Obituaries. Norbert Wiener. Ed. by Pesi R. Masani. (Mathematicians of Our Time Ser.). (Illus.). 383p. 1986. 90.00 (*0-262-23123-9*) MIT Pr.

Norbert Wiener, 1894-1964. Pesi R. Masani. (Vita Mathematica Ser.). 402p. 1989. 99.50 (*0-8176-2246-2*) Birkhauser.

Norbert Wiener, 1894-1964. American Mathematical Society Staff. 145p. 1988. pap. 30.00 (*0-8218-0030-2*, NW) Am Math.

Norby & the Court Jester. Janet Asimov & Isaac Asimov. 1996. mass mkt. 5.50 (*0-441-00341-9*) Ace Bks.

Norby & the Court Jester. Janet Asimov & Isaac Asimov. (Norby Ser.). 128p. (J). (gr. 3-7). 1991. 14.95 (*0-8027-8131-4*); lib. bdg. 15.85 (*0-8027-8132-2*) Walker & Co.

Norby & the Court Jester. large type ed. Janet Asimov & Isaac Asimov. 158p. 1999. 24.95 (*0-7838-8610-1*, G K Hall & Co) Mac Lib Ref.

Norby & the Invaders. Janet Asimov & Isaac Asimov. LC 85-13635. (Norby Ser.). 138p. (J). (gr. 3-5). 1985. 10.95 (*0-8027-6599-8*); lib. bdg. 10.85 (*0-8027-6607-2*) Walker & Co.

Norby & the Lost Princess. Isaac Asimov & Janet Asimov. 129p. (J). lib. bdg. 20.90 (*0-8027-6593-9*) Walker & Co.

Norby & the Oldest Dragon. Janet Asimov & Isaac Asimov. (Norby Ser.). (J). (gr. 4-9). 1990. 14.95 (*0-8027-6909-8*); lib. bdg. 15.85 (*0-8027-6910-1*) Walker & Co.

Norby & the Queen's Necklace. Janet Asimov & Isaac Asimov. LC 86-11120. (Norby Ser.). 144p. (J). (gr. 4-9). 1986. 11.95 (*0-8027-6659-5*); lib. bdg. 12.85 (*0-8027-6660-9*) Walker & Co.

Norby & the Terrified Taxi. Janet Asimov. LC 97-3583. (Norby Ser.). 144p. (J). (gr. 3-7). 1997. 15.95 (*0-8027-8642-1*) Walker & Co.

Norby & Yobo's Great Adventure. Janet Asimov & Isaac Asimov. (Norby Ser.). 224p. (J). (gr. 4-9). 1989. 12.95 (*0-8027-6893-8*); lib. bdg. 13.85 (*0-8027-6894-6*) Walker & Co.

Norby Finds a Villain. Janet Asimov & Isaac Asimov. 102p. (J). (gr. 4-9). 1987. 12.95 (*0-8027-6710-9*); lib. bdg. 13.85 (*0-8027-6711-7*) Walker & Co.

Norby, the Mixed up Robot. Janet Asimov & Isaac Asimov. LC 82-25173. 96p. (J). (gr. 5-7). 1983. lib. bdg. 10.85 (*0-8027-6496-7*) Walker & Co.

Norby the Mixed-Up Robot. unabridged ed. Janet Asimov & Isaac Asimov. (J). (gr. 1-5). 1986. audio 10.50 (*0-89845-634-7*, CP 1792, Caedmon) HarperAudio.

Norby's Other Secret. Janet Asimov & Isaac Asimov. LC 83-40417. 138p. 1984. 10.95 (*0-8027-6525-4*) Walker & Co.

NORC Bibliography of Publications, 1941-1991: A Fifty Year Cumulation. Patrick Bova & Michael P. Worley. x, 452p. 1991. pap. 15.00 (*0-932132-46-4*) Natl Opinion Res.

NORC General Social Survey: A User's Guide. James A. Davis & Tom W. Smith. (Guides to Major Social Science Data Bases Ser.: Vol. 1). 96p. (C). 1991. text 28.00 (*0-8039-4367-9*); pap. text 11.50 (*0-8039-4037-8*) Sage.

Nord. Louis-Ferdinand Celine. (FRE.). 1976. pap. 16.95 (*0-8288-3625-6*, F92041) Fr & Eur.

Nord. Louis-Ferdinand Celine. (Folio Ser.: No. 851). (FRE.). 1972. pap. 13.95 (*2-07-036851-3*) Schoenhof.

Nord Contre Sud. Jules Verne. (FRE., Illus.). 440p. 1978. pap. 18.95 (*0-7859-1220-7*, 2010050290) Fr & Eur.

Nord, Est, Belgique, Luxembourg, Suisse see Dictionnaire des Eglises de France

N

Nord (Flandres/Artois/Picardie) Map. 1996. 8.95 (*2-06-700236-8*, 236) Michelin.

Norden, Man & Environment. Ed. by U. Varjo & W. Tietze. (Illus.). 536p. 1987. lib. bdg. 82.75 (*3-443-01022-9*, Pub. by Gebruder Borntraeger) Balogh.

Nordgermanisches Obligationenrecht, 2 vols., Set. Karl Von Amira. Incl. Vol. 1. Altschwedisches Obligationenrecht. xiii, 788p. 1973. reprint ed. Vol. 2. Westnordisches Obligationenrecht. xvi, 964p. 1973. reprint ed. (C). 1973. 347.00 (*3-11-002183-8*) De Gruyter.

Nordhoff's West Coast. Charles Nordhoff. (Pacific Basin Ser.). 1998. pap. 31.00 (*0-7103-0257-6*, Pub. by Kegan Paul Intl) Col U Pr.

Nordic Approach to Labour Market Policy: Nord 1995:29. Madsen Kongshoj. 85p. 1996. pap. 25.00 (*92-9120-808-6*, NC8086, Pub. by Nordic Coun Minsters) Bernan Associates.

Nordic-Baltic Security from an International Perspective. Arne O. Brundtland & Don M. Snider. (CSIS Panel Reports). 132p. (Orig.). (C). 1994. pap. 16.95 (*0-89206-256-8*) CSIS.

Nordic Banking Crises: Pitfalls in Financial Liberization, Vol. 161. Burkhard Drees & Pazarba Sio Glu Ceyla. LC 98-14799. (Occasional Papers). 1998. 15.00 (*1-55775-700-3*) Intl Monetary.

Nordic Botanical Research in the Andes & Western Amazonia. Ed. by S. Laegaard & F. Borchsenius. (AAU Reports: No. 25). (Illus.). 88p. (C). 1990. pap. 12.95 (*87-87600-33-1*, Pub. by Aarhus Univ Pr) David Brown.

Nordic Business in the Long View: On Control & Strategy in Structural Change. Ed. by Kersti Ullenhag. LC 92-41165. 1993. 35.00 (*0-7146-4524-9*, Pub. by F Cass Pubs) Intl Spec Bk.

Nordic Energy Systems: Historical Perspectives & Current Issues. Ed. by Arne Kaijser & Marika Hedin. LC 94-44735. (Universitext Ser.). (Illus.). xi, 246p. (C). 1995. pap. 39.95 (*0-88135-164-4*, Sci Hist) Watson Pub Intl.

Nordic Environments: Comparing Political, Administrative & Policy Aspects. Ed. by Marko Joas & Ann-Sofie Hermanson. LC 98-74758. 4p. 1999. text 69.95 (*1-84014-920-5*) Ashgate Pub Co.

Nordic Experiences: Exploration of Scandinavian Cultures, 71. Berit I. Brown. LC 96-18203. (Contributions to the Study of World Literature Ser.). 336p. 1997. 75.00 (*0-313-29954-4*) Greenwood.

Nordic Eye: Proceedings from NAFA I. Ed. by Peter I. Crawford. 128p. 1993. 22.00 (*87-89825-00-4*) Smyrna.

Nordic Face: A Glimpse of Iron Age Scandinavia. J. W. Jamieson. 1996. reprint ed. pap. 6.00 (*0-941694-08-9*) Inst Study Man.

Nordic Flora: Towards the Twenty-First Century. Ed. by Ulla-Maj Hultgard et al. (Symbolae Botanicae Upsalienses Ser.: No. 31: 3). (Illus.). 364p. (Orig.). 1996. pap. 67.50 (*91-554-3707-9*) Coronet Bks.

Nordic Folklore: Recent Studies. Ed. by Reimund Kvideland & Henning K. Sehmsdorf. LC 88-45453. (Folklore Studies in Translation). 270p. 1990. 41.95 (*0-253-33125-0*) Ind U Pr.

Nordic Gods & Heroes: Padraic Column. unabridged ed. Padraic Colum. LC 95-22396. (Illus.). 304p. (Orig.). 1996. reprint ed. pap. text 8.95 (*0-486-28912-5*) Dover.

***Nordic Government & Politics.** Alistair Thomas. 256p. 2000. pap. 17.99 (*0-415-12355-0*) Routledge.

Nordic Instrumental Music for Colleges & Universities. Mark Lammers. 236p. (Orig.). (C). 1991. pap. 15.00 (*0-9630771-0-4*) M Lammers.

Nordic Knitting. Susanne Pagoldh. LC 91-28263. 120p. 1991. write for info. (*0-7136-3525-8*) A & C Blk.

Nordic Knitting. Susanne Pagoldh. Tr. by Carol Rhoades from SWE. LC 91-28263. (Illus.). 120p. 1991. 21.95 (*0-934026-68-8*) Interweave.

Nordic Labour Markets in the 1990's, 2 vols., Vol. 1. Eskil Wadensj o. LC 96-8591. 454p. 1996. write for info. (*0-444-82488-X*) Elsevier.

Nordic Labour Markets in the 1990s. Ed. by Wadensj O. Eskil. LC 96-8591. 454p. 1996. 244.00 (*0-444-82477-4*) Elsevier.

Nordic Labour Markets in the 1990s, 2 vols., Vol. 2. Ed. by Wadensj O. Eskil. LC 96-8591. 664p. 1996. write for info. (*0-444-82489-8*) Elsevier.

Nordic Labour Relations Model. Niklas Bruun et al. 250p. 1992. 78.95 (*1-85521-239-0*, Pub. by Dartmth Pub) Ashgate Pub Co.

Nordic Landscape Painting in the Nineteenth Century. Torsten Gunnarsson. Tr. by Nancy Adler. LC 98-24071. (Illus.). 296p. 1998. 65.00 (*0-300-07041-1*) Yale U Pr.

***Nordic Letters, 1870-1910.** Michael Robinson. 422p. 2000. 59.95 (*1-870041-39-9*, Pub. by Norvik Pr) Dufour.

Nordic Macromycetes, Vol. 2. Ed. by Lise Hansen & Henning Knudsen. (Illus.). 474p. 1993. pap. 63.00 (*87-983961-0-2*, NORMAC, Pub. by Nordsvamp) Mad River.

Nordic Macromycetes Vol. 3: Hetersbasidioid, Aphyllophonoid, & Gastromycetoid Basidiomycetes. Ed. by Lise Hansen & Henning Knudsen. (Illus.). 474p. 1997. pap. 67.00 (*87-983961-1-0*, NORMAC3, Pub. by Nordsvamp) Mad River.

Nordic Mind: Current Trends in Scandinavian Literary Criticism. Ed. by Frank E. Andersen & John Weinstock. LC 86-22476. 400p. (Orig.). (C). 1987. pap. text 36.00 (*0-8191-5692-2*) U Pr of Amer.

Nordic National Cinemas. Tytti Soila et al. LC 97-8287. (National Cinemas Ser.). (Illus.). 272p. (C). 1998. 75.00 (*0-415-08194-7*); pap. 24.99 (*0-415-08195-5*) Routledge.

Nordic Nations in the New Western Security Regime. Ingemar Dorfer. LC 97-8532. (Woodrow Wilson Center Press Ser.). 128p. 1997. text 32.50 (*0-943875-83-8*); pap. text 15.95 (*0-943875-82-X*) Johns Hopkins.

Nordic Nexus: A Lesson in Peaceful Security. Bruce O. Solheim. LC 93-23479. 192p. 1994. 55.00 (*0-275-94743-2*, Praeger Pubs) Greenwood.

***Nordic Nights.** Lise McClendon. (Mystery Ser.: Bk. 364). 2000. mass mkt. 5.99 (*0-373-26364-3*, 1-26364-9, Wrldwide Lib) Harlequin Bks.

Nordic Nights. Lise McClendon. LC 99-34869. (Alix Thorssen Mystery Ser.). 292p. 1999. 23.95 (*0-8027-3340-9*) Walker & Co.

Nordic Parliaments: A Comparative Analysis. David Arter. LC 84-9803. 432p. 1985. text 35.00 (*0-312-57767-2*) St Martin.

Nordic Prosody: Proceedings of the VIIth Conference, Joensuu, 1996. Ed. by Stefan Werner. LC 98-155236. 281p. 1998. pap. 48.95 (*3-631-32713-7*) P Lang Pubng.

Nordic Prosody: Proceedings of the 7th Conference, Joensu, 1996. Ed. by Stefan Werner. LC 98-155236. (Illus.). 281p. (C). 1998. pap. text 48.95 (*0-8204-3549-X*) P Lang Pubng.

Nordic Radioecology: The Transfer of Radionuclides Through Nordic Ecosystems to Man. Ed. by H. Dahlgaard. LC 95-188023. (Studies in Environmental Science: Vol. 62). 498p. 1994. 222.00 (*0-444-81617-8*) Elsevier.

Nordic Reference Soils: Characterisation & Classification of 13 Typical Nord Tema Nord 1998: 537. (Tema Nord Ser.). 1998. 18.00 (*92-893-0194-5*, NC1945) Nordic Coun Minsters.

***Nordic Region-Building in a European Perspective.** Ed. by Harald Baldersheim. LC 98-74704. 7p. 1999. text 61.95 (*0-7546-1001-2*) Ashgate Pub Co.

Nordic Regions in Profile. Tr. by Brian Turner from SWE. LC 99-183318. 264p. 1997. pap. 40.00 (*92-893-0019-1*, NC0191, Pub. by Nordic Coun Minsters) Bernan Associates.

Nordic Religions in the Viking Age. Thomas A. DuBois. LC 99-22405. 1999. 19.95 (*0-8122-1714-4*) U of Pa Pr.

Nordic Security: Issues & Prospects. Katarina Brodin. (CISA Working Papers: No. 67). 25p. (Orig.). 1989. pap. 15.00 (*0-86682-086-8*) Ctr Intl Relations.

Nordic Security at the Turn of the Twenty-First Century, 117. Ed. by Ciro E. Zoppo. LC 91-21189. (Contributions in Military Studies Ser.: No. 117). 272p. 1992. 62.95 (*0-313-27576-9*, ZSC, Greenwood Pr) Greenwood.

Nordic Security in the 1990's: Options in the Changing Europe. Ed. by Jan Berg. LC 92-11703. (C). 1992. text 59.00 (*0-86187-080-8*) St Martin.

Nordic Skiing: Steps to Success. Laurie Gullion. LC 92-20148. (Steps to Success Activity Ser.). (Illus.). 160p. 1992. pap. 14.95 (*0-87322-394-2*, PGUL0394) Human Kinetics.

Nordic Social Policy: Changing Welfare States. Mikko Hautto. LC 98-49961. 1999. pap. write for info. (*0-415-20876-9*) Routledge.

Nordic Statements on Apartheid. 53p. 1978. write for info. (*91-7106-114-2*, Pub. by Nordic Africa); suppl. ed. write for info. (*91-7106-127-4*, Pub. by Nordic Africa) Transaction Pubs.

Nordic States & European Unity. Christine Ingebritsen. LC 97-48658. (Cornell Studies in Political Economy). (Illus.). 224p. 1998. 29.95 (*0-8014-3484-X*) Cornell U Pr.

***Nordic States & European Unity.** Christine Ingebritsen. (Studies in Political Economy). (Illus.). 224p. 2000. pap. text 17.95 (*0-8014-8659-9*) Cornell U Pr.

Nordic Transputer Applications: Proceedings of the First & Second Nordic Transputer Seminars. Ed. by Lars Annell & Martin Torngren. (Transputer & Occam Engineering Ser.). 196p. (gr. 12). 1991. pap. 70.00 (*90-5199-070-7*, Pub. by IOS Pr) IOS Press.

***Nordic Warriors: SS-Panzergrenadier-Regiment 24 Danmark, Eastern Front, 1943-45.** Richard Landwehr & Holger T. Nielsen. (Armed Forces of the Third Reich). 194p. 1999. (*1-899765-07-7*, Pub. by Shelf Bks) Intl Spec Bk.

Nordic Way: A Path to Baltic Equilibrium. Edward L. Killham. (Illus.). 300p. 1993. 37.50 (*0-929590-12-0*); pap. 18.95 (*0-929590-13-9*) Compass Pr.

***Nordic Way: A Path to Baltic Equilibrium.** Edward L. Killham. (Illus.). 300p. 1999. reprint ed. pap. text 20.00 (*0-7881-6362-0*) DIANE Pub.

***Nordic Women Writers: An Anthology.** Lanae Isaacson & Inger Olsen. 400p. 2000. 105.00 (*0-8153-2775-7*) Garland.

Nordic World: Sports in Society. Ed. by Henrik Meinander et al. LC 97-43918. (Sport in the Global Society Ser.). 200p. (C). 1998. text 52.50 (*0-7146-4825-6*, Pub. by F Cass Pubs); pap. text 22.50 (*0-7146-4391-2*, Pub. by F Cass Pubs) Intl Spec Bk.

Nordic Yearbook of Folklore, 1993. Ed. by Ulrika Wolf-Knuts. 190p. (Orig.). 1993. pap. 48.00 (*91-22-01592-2*) Coronet Bks.

Nordics in America: The Future of Their Past. Intro. by Odd Sverre Lovoll. (Special Publications). (Illus.). 228p. 1993. 20.00 (*0-87732-081-0*) Norwegian-Am Hist Assn.

Nordi's Gift. Clyde Rice. LC 90-1948. 460p. 1990. 21.95 (*0-932576-77-X*) Breitenbush Bks.

Nordische und die Englische Version der Tristan-Sage, No. 1. Ed. by Eugene Koelbing. (GER.). cxlviii, 224p. 1978. reprint ed. write for info. (*3-487-06637-8*) G Olms Pubs.

Nordische und die Englische Version der Tristan-Sage, No. 2. Ed. by Eugene Koelbing. (GER.). xciii, 292p. 1985. reprint ed. write for info. (*3-487-07658-6*) G Olms Pubs.

Nordisches Plankton, 1911-42, 7 vols. Ed. by K. Brandt & C. Apstein. 1964. 720.00 (*90-6123-110-8*) Lubrecht & Cramer.

Nordish Quest. Richard McCulloch. 108p. 1989. pap. 5.00 (*0-9608928-2-6*) Towncourt Ent.

Nordisk Forvaltningsordbok. (NOR.). 283p. 1982. 75.00 (*0-8288-2263-8*, F22270) Fr & Eur.

Nordisk Musik-Tidende 1880-1892; Orkestertidende 1892-1894. Ed. by H. Robert Cohen. (Repertoire International de la Presse Musicale Ser.). (NOR.). 352p. (gr. 1). 1996. lib. bdg. 145.00 (*0-8357-2420-4*) UMI.

Nordjordanische Ortsnamen. Sultan Al-Ma'ani. (Texte und Studien Zur Orientalistik Ser.: Bd. 7). (GER.). xiv, 326p. 1992. write for info. (*3-487-09632-3*) G Olms Pubs.

***Nordland Haiku Revisited.** Joyce Metzger. (Illus.). 104p. 1999. pap. 8.95 (*1-878116-95-9*) JVC Bks.

***Nordlings.** Kathleen McDonnell. 207p. (YA). (gr. 5-9). 2000. pap. 6.95 (*1-896764-23-1*, Pub. by Sec Story Pr) Orca Bk Pubs.

***Nordstrom on Sales & Leases of Goods** 2nd ed. Robert J. Nordstrom et al. LC 99-36569. 1999. boxed set 175.00 (*0-7355-0684-1*) Panel Pubs.

***Nordstrom Way: The Inside of America's #1 Customer Service Company.** 2nd ed. Robert Spector & Patrick D. McCarthy. LC 99-15649. 244p. 1999. 24.95 (*0-471-35486-4*) Wiley.

Nordstrom Way: The Inside Story of America's #1 Customer Service Company. Robert Spector & Patrick D. McCarthy. LC 94-39182. 244p. 1995. 24.95 (*0-471-58496-7*) Wiley.

Nordstrom Way: The Inside Story of America's #1 Customer Service Company. Robert Spector & Patrick D. McCarthy. LC 94-39182. 256p. 1996. pap. 15.95 (*0-471-16160-8*) Wiley.

Nordstrom Way: The Inside Story of America's #1 Customer Service Company. Robert Spector & Patrick D. McCarthy. 256p. 1997. pap. 5.99 (*0-471-19171-X*) Wiley.

Nordwestdeutsche Feuchgruenland Gesellschaften Unter Kontrollierten Nutzungsbedingungen. Peter Schwartze. (Dissertationes Botanicae Ser.: Band 183). (GER., Illus.). xii, 204p. 1992. pap. 71.00 (*3-443-64095-8*, Pub. by Gebruder Borntraeger) Balogh.

Nordwestdeutschland im Tertiaer see Nordwestdeutschland Im Tertiaer (Northwest Germany During the Tertiary)

Nordwestdeutschland Im Tertiaer (Northwest Germany During the Tertiary) Contrib. by Heinz Tobien. (Beitrage Zur Regionalen Geologie der Erde. Ser.: Vol. 18).Tr. of Nordwestdeutschland im Tertiaer. (GER., Illus.). xxvi, 763p. 1986. 117.00 (*3-443-11018-5*, Pub. by Gebruder Borntraeger) Balogh.

Nordwestgermanisch. Ed. by Edith Marold & Christiane Zimmermann. (Ergaenzungsbaende zum Reallexikon der Germanischen Alterrumskunde: Bd. 13). (GER.). x, 299p. (C). 1995. 126.15 (*3-11-014818-8*) De Gruyter.

Noreascon 1 Proceedings. Ed. by Leslie Turek. (Illus.). 1976. 6.00 (*0-915368-00-5*) New Eng SF Assoc.

Noreascon I Program Book. 130p. 1971. pap. 2.00 (*1-886778-00-0*) New Eng SF Assoc.

Noreascon 3 Memory Book. Ed. by Laurie Mann. (Illus.). 64p. 1991. 3.00 (*0-9603146-7-9*) MA Convent Fandom.

Noreascon 3 Souvenir Book. Ed. by Greg Thokar. (Illus.). 192p. 1989. pap. 3.00 (*0-9603146-6-0*) MA Convent Fandom.

Noreascon 2 Memory Book. Suford Lewis. (Illus.). 56p. 1985. pap. text 2.00 (*0-9603146-3-6*) MA Convent Fandom.

Noreascon II Program Book. Ed. by Leslie J. Turek. (Illus.). 160p. 1980. pap. 2.00 (*0-9603146-1-X*) MA Convent Fandom.

Noreen. Richard Manton. 1992. mass mkt. 5.95 (*0-929654-89-7*, 110) Blue Moon Bks.

Noreen. Richard Manton. 192p. 1999. mass mkt. 7.95 (*1-56201-129-4*) Blue Moon Bks.

Norfolk. Margaret Knox. (Country Guide Ser.: No. 26). (Illus.). 144p. pap. 12.50 (*0-7478-0232-7*, Pub. by Shire Pubns) Parkwest Pubns.

Norfolk. Tom Pocock. (Pimlico County History Guides Ser.). (Illus.). 192p. 1997. pap. 19.95 (*0-7126-5154-3*, Pub. by Pimlico) Trafalgar.

Norfolk: A Photographic History, 1860-1960. Neil R. Storey. (Illus.). 160p. 1996. pap. 22.95 (*0-7509-1306-1*, Pub. by Sutton Pub Ltd) Intl Pubs Mktg.

Norfolk: Taxation Treatment of Interest. 2nd ed. E. C. Norfolk. 272p. 1992. boxed set 133.00 (*0-406-00285-1*, MICHIE) LEXIS Pub.

Norfolk: Taxation Treatment of Interest. 3rd ed. E. C. Norfolk. 1997. write for info. (*0-406-89073-0*, NTTI3, MICHIE) LEXIS Pub.

Norfolk: The First Four Centuries. Thomas C. Parramore et al. LC 94-9457. 480p. (C). 1994. 29.95 (*0-8139-1557-0*) U Pr of Va.

***Norfolk: The First Four Centuries.** Thomas C. Parramore et al. 2000. 17.95 (*0-8139-1988-6*) U Pr of Va.

Norfolk & Suffolk in the Great War. Gerald Gliddon. 118p. 1988. 75.00 (*0-947893-07-5*, Pub. by Gliddon Bks) St Mut.

Norfolk & Suffolk Surnames in the Middle Ages. Richard McKinley. 176p. 1975. 16.00 (*0-85033-196-X*, Pub. by Leopards Head Pr) David Brown.

Norfolk & Suffolk Walks. (Ordnance Survey Pathfinder Guides Ser.). (Illus.). 80p. 1993. pap. 14.95 (*0-7117-0551-8*) Seven Hills Bk.

Norfolk & Western: A History. rev. ed. E. F. Striplin. LC 96-71382. (Illus.). 250p. 1997. reprint ed. pap. text 21.95 (*0-9633254-6-9*) Norfolk & Wstrn HS.

Norfolk & Western: Diesel's Last Conquest. William Warden. (Illus.). 62p. 1996. pap. 14.95 (*0-9622003-6-0*) TLC VA.

Norfolk & Western: Second Generation Diesels. Paul K. Withers & Robert G. Bowers. 256p. 1989. 45.00 (*0-9618503-2-9*) Withers Pub.

Norfolk & Western Coal Cars, 1881-1997. Andrew Dow. (Illus.). 240p. 1998. 29.95 (*1-883089-36-0*) TLC VA.

***Norfolk & Western Color Guide to Freight & Passenger Equipment.** Jim Nichols. (Illus.). 128p. 2000. 54.95 (*1-58248-038-9*) Morning NJ.

***Norfolk & Western Electrics.** Mason Y. Cooper. (Illus.). (C). 2000. write for info. (*0-9633254-9-3*) Norfolk & Wstrn HS.

Norfolk & Western in Color, 1945-1964, Vol. 1. Jim Nichols. LC 96-78484. (Illus.). 128p. 1997. 49.95 (*1-878887-72-6*) Morning NJ.

Norfolk & Western in the Appalachians: From the Blue Ridge to the Big Sandy. Ed King. LC 98-112703. (Golden Years Ser.). (Illus.). 128p. (Orig.). 1997. pap. 18.95 (*0-89024-316-6*, 01083, Kalmbach Books) Kalmbach.

***Norfolk & Western Passenger Service, 1945-1971.** William Warden. (Illus.). 128p. 2000. 28.95 (*1-883089-50-6*, 130609AE, Pub. by TLC VA) Motorbooks Intl.

***Norfolk & Western Railroads; Inc. Virginian, Clinchfield RR's Vol. 18: Steam Trains & Locomotives 1938-1956.** Robert K. Durham. (Illus.). 72p. 2000. pap. 21.00 (*1-891427-07-5*) Durham Publng.

Norfolk & Western Railway. Ed. by Richard E. Cox. (Illus.). 40p. (Orig.). 1985. pap. 5.97 (*0-912935-01-4*) Vanishing Vistas.

Norfolk & Western Railway Standards Drawings. Ed. by James F. Brewer & Thomas D. Dressler. LC 92-81707. (Illus.). 120p. 1996. reprint ed. pap. text 28.50 (*0-9633254-0-X*) Norfolk & Wstrn HS.

Norfolk & Western Railway's Magnificent Mallets: The Y Class 2-8-8-2S. William E. Warden. (Illus.). 60p. 1996. pap. 14.95 (*1-883089-01-8*) TLC VA.

Norfolk & Western Signal Diagrams. Contrib. by Greever Grafix Staff. LC 99-70208. (Illus.). 65p. 1999. pap. text 19.95 (*0-9633254-8-5*) Norfolk & Wstrn HS.

Norfolk & Western's Shenandoah Valley Line. Mason Y. Cooper. LC 97-76580. (Illus.). 260p. 1998. 49.95 (*0-9633254-7-7*) Norfolk & Wstrn HS.

Norfolk Blues: The Civil War Diary of the Norfolk Light Artillery Blues. Ken Wiley. LC 96-51428. (Illus.). 326p. 1997. 30.00 (*1-57249-019-5*, Burd St Pr) White Mane Pub.

Norfolk Broads: Landscape History. Williamson. LC 96-51935. 256p. 1997. 59.95 (*0-7190-4800-1*, Pub. by Manchester Univ Pr) St Martin.

Norfolk Churches: Their Foundations, Architecture & Furnishings. H. O. Mansfield. 208p. 1994. 30.00 (*0-900963-57-3*, Pub. by T Dalton) St Mut.

Norfolk Coast Path Guide: Baggywrinkles & Birdwatchers. Richard Hayward. (British Footpath Guides Ser.: No. 4). (Illus.). 100p. pap. 6.95 (*1-880848-14-7*) Brit Footpaths.

Norfolk County Pioneer Sketches of Long Point Settlement: or Norfolk's Foundation Builders & Their Family Genealogies. E. A. Owen. (Illus.). 578p. 1996. reprint ed. lib. bdg. 59.50 (*0-8328-5157-4*) Higginson Bk Co.

Norfolk County, Virginia, Revolutionary War & War of 1812 Applications for Pensions, Bounty Land & Warrants & Heirs of Deceased Pensioners. Elizabeth B. Wingo. 200p. 1964. pap. 20.00 (*0-89308-408-5*) Southern Hist Pr.

Norfolk County, Virginia, 1706-1792, Marriages Of, Vol. 1. Elizabeth B. Wingo. 92p. 1984. reprint ed. pap. 25.00 (*0-89308-401-8*, VA 80) Southern Hist Pr.

Norfolk County, Virginia, Tithables, 1730-1750. Elizabeth B. Wingo & W. Bruce Wingo. 258p. 1979. pap. 22.50 (*0-89308-406-9*, BVA 85) Southern Hist Pr.

Norfolk County, Virginia, Tithables, 1751-1765. Elizabeth B. Wingo. 278p. 1981. pap. 26.50 (*0-89308-407-7*, BVA 86) Southern Hist Pr.

Norfolk Highlights, 1584-1881. George H. Tucker. LC 72-85451. (Illus.). 134p. 1972. 18.00 (*1-878515-67-5*) W S Dawson.

Norfolk Historical Society: The Beginnings. Ed. by Calvert W. Tazewell. LC 92-72521. (Illus.). 95p. (Orig.). 1993. pap. 11.00 (*1-878515-75-6*) W S Dawson.

Norfolk History: On the Web. Ed. by Calvert W. Tazewell. LC 95-67003. 350p. 1995. write for info. (*1-57000-039-5*) W S Dawson.

Norfolk Hunt: One Hundred Years of Sport. Norman M. Fine. Ed. by David W. Lewis, Jr. (Illus.). 212p. 1995. 95.00 (*0-9645282-0-7*) Millwood Hse.

Norfolk Island: An Outline of Its History, 1774-1981. 4th ed. Merval Hoare. (Illus.). 1988. pap. 16.95 (*0-7022-2100-7*, Pub. by Univ Queensland Pr) Intl Spec Bk.

Norfolk Rambles: Leading Businesses of 1884. abr. ed. Ed. by Calvert W. Tazewell. LC 92-74637. (Illus.). 96p. 1993. pap. 11.00 (*1-878515-77-2*) W S Dawson.

Norfolk Roll of Honour, 1914 to 1918: List of Men from Norfolk Parishes Who Fell in the Great War. H. Rider Haggard. 126p. 1988. 40.00 (*0-947893-12-1*, Pub. by Gliddon Bks) St Mut.

Norfolk Southern, 1982-1994, Motive Power Review. Robert G. Bowers & Paul K. Withers. LC 94-62162. 1995. 38.95 (*1-881411-04-4*) Withers Pub.

Norfolk Southern, 1995 Review iew. Scott Lindsey. Ed. by Dale Sanders. (Illus.). 144p. 1995. per. 36.95 (*0-945434-24-3*) Hundman Pub.

Norfolk Surnames in the Sixteenth Century. R. A. McKinley. LC 70-512957. (Department of English Local History/Occasional Papers: 2). 60p. 1969. write for info. (*0-7185-2023-8*) Continuum.

Norfolk Terrier. Joan R. Read. (Illus.). 344p. 1989. 29.95 (*0-9623261-0-0*) J R Read.

Norfolk Terrier. 2nd rev. ed. Joan R. Read. Ed. by Nat R. LaMar. 1994. write for info. (*0-9623261-1-9*) J R Read.

Norfolk Terrier No. 112: AKC Rank. Anna K. Nicholas. (Rare Breed Ser.). (Illus.). 96p. 1997. 19.95 (*0-7938-0761-1*, RX-111) TFH Pubns.

***Norfolk Ultimate Entertainment, 2000.** (Illus.). 726p. 1999. pap. 40.00 (*1-58553-044-1*, 0063) Enter Pubns.

***Norfolk, Virginia.** Ruth Rose. (Black America Ser.). 128p. (YA). 2000. pap. 18.99 (*0-7385-0564-1*) Arcadia Publng.

An Asterisk (*) at the beginning of an entry indicates that the title is appearing for the first time.

Norfolk, Virginia: The Sunrise City by the Sea: A Tribute to Photographer Carroll H. Walker, Sr. Amy W. Yarsinske. LC 94-6346. 1994. write for info. (*0-89865-883-7*) Donning Co.

***Norfolk's Church Street, Virginia: Between Memory & Reality.** Amy Waters Yarsinske. (Images of America Ser.). (Illus.). 128p. 1999. pap. 18.99 (*0-7385-0103-4*) Arcadia Publng.

Norfolk's Waters: An Illustrated Maritime History. William L. Tazewell. 1982. 22.95 (*0-89781-045-7*, 5049) Am Historical Pr.

Norfork Lake: A Cultural Resources Management Study with Implications for Prehistoric Settlement-Subsistence Patterns in the Ozarks. Thomas J. Padgett. (Illus.). 72p. 1979. pap. 1.50 (*1-56349-027-7*, RR15) AR Archaeol.

Norge og Verdenskrigen. Wilhelm Keilhau. (Verdenskrigens Okonomiske Og Sociale Historie (Skandinavisk Serie)). (GER.). 1927. 125.00 (*0-317-27530-5*) Elliots Bks.

Noriega Mess: The Drugs, the Canal, & Why America Invaded. Luis Murillo. (Illus.). 1100p. 1995. 32.00 (*0-923444-02-5*) Video Bks.

Norie's Nautical Tables. A. Blance. 636p. (C). 1991. 29.95 (*0-85288-160-6*, Pub. by Laurie Norie & Wilson Ltd) Bluewater Bks.

Norie's Nautical Tables. rev. ed. Ed. by A. G. Blance. (Illus.). 600p. (C). 1983. 100.00 (*0-85288-091-X*, Pub. by Laurie Norie & Wilson Ltd) St Mut.

Noritake Collectibles, A to Z: A Pictorial Record & Guide to Values. David H. Spain. LC 97-11385. 304p. 1997. 49.95 (*0-7643-0057-1*) Schiffer.

Noritake Dinnerware: Identification Made Easy. Robin Brewer. (Illus.). 144p. 1999. 39.95 (*0-7643-0925-0*) Schiffer.

Norito: A Translation of the Ancient Japanese Ritual Prayers. Tr. by Donald L. Philippi from JPN. 95p. (C). 1998. pap. text 15.00 (*0-7881-5459-1*) DIANE Pub.

Norka: A German Village in Russia. 2nd rev. ed. Ed. by Marie M. Olson & Anna M. Reisbick. 49p. 1986. 6.00 (*0-914222-22-8*) Am Hist Soc Ger.

NORM: A Guide to Naturally Occurring Radioactive Material. William F. Wilson. LC 93-36025. 250p. 1993. 84.95 (*0-87814-407-2*, S4539) PennWell Bks.

Norm & Context in the Social Sciences. Ed. by Sander Griffioen & Jan Verhoogt. (Christian Studies Today). 296p. (C). 1990. pap. text 29.00 (*0-8191-7802-0*); lib. bdg. 49.50 (*0-8191-7801-2*) U Pr of Amer.

Norm & Nature: The Movements of Legal Thought. Roger A. Shiner. (Clarendon Law Ser.). 368p. 1992. text 59.00 (*0-19-825719-8*) OUP.

Norm Estimations for Operator-Valued Functions & Applications. Michael I. Gil. LC 95-32196. (Monographs & Textbooks in Pure & Applied Mathematics: Vol. 192). (Illus.). 376p. 1995. text 155.00 (*0-8247-9609-8*) Dekker.

Norm Inequalities for Derivatives & Differences. Man K. Kwong & Anton Zettl. LC 92-42110. 1993. 36.95 (*0-387-56387-3*) Spr-Verlag.

Norm of Truth: An Introduction to the Philosophy of Logic. Pascal Engel. Tr. by Miriam Kochan. (Studies in Philosophy). 400p. 1992. text 55.00 (*0-8020-2775-X*); pap. text 24.95 (*0-8020-6891-X*) U of Toronto Pr.

Norm und Geschichtlichkeit der Dichtung: Klassisch-Romantische Aethetik und Moderne Literatur. Goetz Braun. 312p. 1983. 93.10 (*3-11-008238-1*) De Gruyter.

***Norm und Naturrecht Verstehen: Eine Studie Zu Herausforderungen der Fundamentalethik.** Johannes M. Schnarrer. 380p. 1999. 56.95 (*3-631-33647-0*) P Lang Pubng.

Norm und Variation. Ed. by Klaus J. Mattheier. (Forum Angewandte Linguistik Ser.: Bd. 32). (Illus.). 201p. 1997. 42.95 (*3-631-32106-6*) P Lang Pubng.

Norm, Variation & Change in Language. Ed. by Johan Falk et al. (Stockholm Studies in Modern Philology, New Ser.: No. 11). 255p. 1997. pap. 48.50 (*91-22-01714-3*, Pub. by Almqvist Wiksell) Coronet Bks.

Norma: A Biography. Tim Walker. (Illus.). 192p. 1994. 34.95 (*1-85702-063-4*) Trafalgar.

***Norma Fox Mazer: A Writer's World /** Arthea J. S. Reed. LC 00-38759. (Studies in Young Adult Literature). 2000. write for info. (*0-8108-3814-1*) Scarecrow.

Norma in Full Score. Vincenzo Bellini. 448p. pap. 19.95 (*0-486-27970-7*) Dover.

Norma Jean: The Life of Marilyn Monroe. Fred L. Guiles. (Illus.). 341p. 1994. pap. 13.95 (*1-56924-937-7*) Marlowe & Co.

Norma Jean, Jumping Bean. Joanna Cole. LC 86-15588. (Step into Reading Ser.: A Step 2 Book). (Illus.). 48p. (J). (ps-3). 1987. pap. 3.99 (*0-394-88668-2*, Pub. by Random Bks Yng Read) Random.

Norma Jean, Jumping Bean. Joanna Cole. (Step into Reading Ser.: A Step 2 Book). (J). (gr. 1-3). 1987. 9.19 (*0-606-03055-7*, Pub. by Turtleback) Demco.

Norma Libretto. Vincenzo Bellini. (ENG & ITA.). 40p. 1986. pap. 4.95 (*0-7935-2774-0*, 50340540) H Leonard.

Norma No Friends. Illus. by Paula Metcalf. 40p. (J). (gr. k-3). 1999. 15.95 (*1-902283-87-2*) Barefoot Bks NY.

Normal. Lucia Nevai. LC 96-47655. 238p. 1997. 17.95 (*1-56512-158-9*, 72158) Algonquin Bks.

Normal Accidents: Living with High-Risk Technologies. Charles Perrow. LC 83-45256. 400p. 1985. pap. 20.00 (*0-465-05142-1*, Pub. by Basic) HarpC.

***Normal Accidents: Living with High Risk Technologies.** Charles Perrow. LC 99-32990. 1999. pap. 19.95 (*0-691-00412-9*, Pub. by Princeton U Pr) Cal Prin Full Svc.

Normal Aging 1: Reports from the Duke Longitudinal Study, 1955-1969. Ed. by Erdman B. Palmore. LC 74-132028. xxiv, 431p. 1970. text 49.95 (*0-8223-0238-1*) Duke.

Normal Aging 3: Reports from the Duke Longitudinal Studies, 1975-84. Ed. by George L. Maddox et al. LC 85-1598. (Illus.). xx, 468p. (C). 1985. text 49.95 (*0-8223-0624-7*) Duke.

Normal Aging 2: Reports from the Duke Longitudinal Study, 1970-1973. Erdman B. Palmore. LC 74-132028. xix, 316p. 1974. text 49.95 (*0-8223-0311-6*) Duke.

Normal Alcoholic. William F. Kraft. LC 99-13593. 159p. 1999. pap. 9.95 (*0-8189-0853-X*) Alba.

Normal & Abnormal Development: The Influence of Primitive Reflexes on Motor Development. Mary R. Fiorentino. (Illus.). 80p. 1980. 24.95 (*0-398-02278-X*) C C Thomas.

Normal & Abnormal Development of Cortex. Ed. by Albert M. Galaburda & Yves Christen. LC 97-22615. (Research & Perspectives in Neurosciences Ser.). (Illus.). 214p. 1997. text 94.95 (*3-540-63208-5*) Spr-Verlag.

Normal & Abnormal Epidermal Keratinization. Ed. by M. S. Seigi & I. A. Bernstein. (Current Problems in Dermatology Ser.: Vol. 11). (Illus.). x, 344p. 1983. pap. 144.50 (*3-8055-3752-2*) S Karger.

Normal & Abnormal Processes in the Basic Sciences. National Medical School Review Staff. LC 96-22910. (Board Simulator Ser.). 253p. 1996. pap. 24.95 (*0-683-06331-6*) Lppncott W & W.

Normal & Abnormal Processes in the Basic Sciences: A Body Systems-Based Review for USMLE Step 1. 2nd ed. National Medical School Review (R) Staff & Gerald D. Barry. LC 97-6602. (Board Simulator Ser.). 288p. 1997. pap. 24.95 (*0-683-30297-3*) Lppncott W & W.

Normal & Abnormal Swallowing: Imaging in Diagnosis & Therapy. Ed. by B. Jones & Martin W. Donner. (Illus.). 256p. 1995. 149.00 (*0-387-97347-8*) Spr-Verlag.

Normal & Disordered Phonology in Children. Carol Stoel-Gammon & Carla Dunn. LC 84-15309. (Illus.). 238p. (Orig.). 1985. text 36.00 (*0-89079-150-3*, 1328) PRO-ED.

Normal & Disturbed Motility of the Gastrointestinal Tract. Andre J. Smout & Louis M. Akkermans. 320p. 1992. 65.00 (*1-871816-15-7*, Pub. by Wrightson Biomed) Taylor & Francis.

Normal & Handicapped Children: A Comparative Approach. Hassen Uddin. (Illus.). xv, 135p. 1995. 16.00 (*81-7024-663-6*, Pub. by Ashish Pub Hse) Nataraj Bks.

Normal & Impaired Motor Development. Ed. by C. O'Brien. (Illus.). 270p. 1994. pap. text 49.50 (*1-56593-148-3*, 0460) Singular Publishing.

Normal & Impaired Motor Development: Theory into Practice. Carolyn O'Brien & Alan Hayes. LC 94-68790. 256p. 1995. pap. 35.95 (*0-412-47890-0*) Chapman & Hall.

***Normal & Malignant Liver Cell Growth: Proceedings: International Falk Workshop (1998: Halle, Germany)** Ed. by W. E. Fleig. LC 99-188037. 247p. 1999. 180.00 (*0-7923-8748-1*) Kluwer Academic.

***Normal & Pathlogic Development of the Human Brain & Spinal Cord.** Dambska. 212p. 1999. pap. 79.00 (*0-86196-591-4*, Pub. by J Libbey Med) Bks Intl VA.

Normal & Pathological Responses to Bereavement. John Ellard et al. LC 73-10473. (Attitudes Toward Death Ser.). 238p. 1974. text 32.50 (*0-317-66456-5*) Irvington.

Normal & the Pathological. Georges Canguilhem. Tr. by Carolyn R. Fawcett & Robert S. Cohen from FRE. LC 88-20626. 327p. 1989. reprint ed. 28.95 (*0-942299-58-2*) Zone Bks.

Normal & the Pathological. Georges Canguilhem. Tr. by Carolyn R. Fawcett from FRE. LC 88-20626. 327p. 1989. reprint ed. pap. 16.95 (*0-942299-59-0*) Zone Bks.

Normal & Therapeutic Nutrition. 17th rev. ed. Corinne H. Robinson. 784p. (C). 1990. text 75.00 (*0-02-402605-0*, Macmillan Coll) P-H.

Normal Approximation & Asymptotic Expansions. R. N. Bhattacharya & Ranga R. Rao. LC 83-19559. 306p. (C). 1986. reprint ed. lib. bdg. 49.50 (*0-89874-690-6*) Krieger.

Normal Avenue. Karen Blomain. (Poetry Ser.). 48p. 1998. pap. 10.00 (*1-879205-78-5*) Nightshade Pr.

Normal Baby: The Sensorimotor Processes of the First Year. 2nd rev. ed. Cheryl Colangelo et al. (Illus.). (C). 1986. pap. text. write for info. (*0-911681-03-5*) Valhalla Rehab.

Normal Bad Boys: Public Policies, Institutions & the Politics of Client Recruitment. Prue Rains & Eli Teram. 200p. 1992. 60.00 (*0-7735-0906-2*, Pub. by McG-Queens Univ Pr) CUP Services.

***Normal Bridge Bidding: Finding Your Bid in the Modern Game.** Lawrence Kane. LC 98-90615. 1999. pap. 8.95 (*0-533-12866-8*) Vantage.

Normal Chaos of Love. Ulrich Beck & Elisabeth Beck-Gernsheim. Tr. by Mark Ritter & Jane Wiebel from GER. 227p. 1995. text 66.95 (*0-7456-1071-4*); pap. text 26.95 (*0-7456-1382-9*) Blackwell Pubs.

Normal Child: Some Problems of the Early Years & Their Treatment. 10th ed. Ronald S. Illingworth. (Illus.). 450p. (Orig.). 1991. pap. text 65.00 (*0-443-04455-4*) Church.

Normal Child & Adolescent. 11th ed. Tamhne. (C). 1999. pap. text. write for info. (*0-443-05707-9*) Church.

Normal Child & Adolescent Development. Ralph Gemelli. 596p. 1996. text 75.50 (*0-88048-258-3*, 8258) Am Psychiatric.

Normal Children Have Problems, Too: How Parents Can Understand & Help. Stanley K. Turecki. LC 95-17918. 272p. 1995. reprint ed. pap. 13.95 (*0-553-37438-9*) Bantam.

Normal Christian Birth. Stuart Pawson. 19.95 (*0-340-48972-3*, Pub. by Hodder & Stought Ltd) Trafalgar.

Normal Christian Church Life see Vida Cristiana Normal de la Iglesia

Normal Christian Church Life. Watchman Nee. 188p. 1980. per. 8.75 (*0-87083-027-9*, 08-013-001) Living Stream Ministry.

Normal Christian Faith see Fe Cristiana Normal

Normal Christian Faith. (Orthodoxy of the Church Ser.). 213p. 1994. per. 10.00 (*0-87083-748-6*, 11-010-001) Living Stream Ministry.

Normal Christian Faith. Watchman Nee. 213p. per. 8.00 (*0-87083-006-6*, 11010001) Living Stream Ministry.

***Normal Christian Life.** Watchman Nee. (Deluxe Christian Classics). 204p. 2000. 9.97 (*1-57748-915-2*) Barbour Pub.

Normal Christian Life. Watchman Nee. 1979. mass mkt. 5.95 (*0-87508-414-1*) Chr Lit.

Normal Christian Life. Watchman Nee. 285p. 1977. mass mkt. 5.99 (*0-8423-4710-0*) Tyndale Hse.

Normal Christian Life: Also Including the Overcoming Life. Watchman Nee. (Essential Christian Library Ser.). 412p. 1999. 9.97 (*1-57748-519-X*) Barbour Pub.

Normal Christian Life: Study Guide. rev. ed. H. Foster. 52p. 1993. pap. 3.25 (*0-87508-418-4*) Chr Lit.

Normal Christian Worker see Obrero Cristiano Normal

Normal Christian Worker see Vida Cristiana Normal

Normal College Knowledge: A Sometimes Humorous, Sometimes Sad but Always Loving Inside View of Western. Charles J. Flora. (Illus.). 203p. (Orig.). 1991. pap. 19.95 (*0-9631036-0-1*) Jero Enter.

Normal Course in Play. Joseph Lee. LC 72-143067. 1982. 23.95 (*0-8434-0436-1*, Pub. by McGrath NH) Ayer.

Normal Crimes: Sociological Features of the Penal Code in a Public Defender Office. David Sudnow. (Reprint Series in Sociology). (C). 1993. reprint ed. pap. text 5.00 (*0-8290-2757-2*, S-636) Irvington.

Normal Development Copybook. Marsha D. Klein et al. (Illus.). 195p. 1992. pap. text 47.50 (*0-7616-4732-5*) Commun Skill.

***Normal Development of Functional Motor Skills.** Alexander. (C). 1998. pap. text 58.00 (*0-12-784571-2*) Acad Pr.

Normal Distribution. School Mathematics Project Staff. (Mathematics Series: Ages 16-19). 96p. (C). 1990. pap. text 11.95 (*0-521-40890-3*) Cambridge U Pr.

Normal Distribution: Characterizations with Applications. Wlodzimierz Bryc. LC 95-12920. (Lecture Notes in Statistics Ser.: Vol. 100). (Illus.). 140p. 1995. 48.95 (*0-387-97990-5*) Spr-Verlag.

Normal Elliptic Functions: A Normalized Form of Weierstrass's Elliptic Functions. Archibald R. Low. LC 55-37289. 32p. reprint ed. pap. 30.00 (*0-608-15660-4*, 203192700077) Bks Demand.

Normal Families of Analytical & Meromorphic Functions. Joel L. Schiff. LC 92-35795. (Universitext Ser.). 248p. 1993. 48.95 (*0-387-97967-0*) Spr-Verlag.

Normal Families of Meromorphic Functions. C. T. Chuang. 488p. 1993. text 86.00 (*981-02-1257-7*) World Scientific Pub.

Normal Family Processes. 2nd ed. Ed. by Froma Walsh. LC 81-7197. (Family Therapy Ser.). 511p. 1993. lib. bdg. 49.00 (*0-89862-090-2*) Guilford Pubns.

***Normal Findings in CT & MRI.** Torsten B. Moeller. (Illus.). 250p. 1999. pap. 32.00 (*0-86577-864-7*) Thieme Med Pubs.

***Normal Findings in CT & MRI.** Torsten B. Moller & Emil Reif. LC 99-33663. 1999. write for info. (*3-13-116521-9*) Thieme Med Pubs.

***Normal Findings in Radiology.** Torsten B. Moller. LC 99-40799. (Illus.). 280p. 1999. pap. 32.00 (*0-86577-871-X*) Thieme Med Pubs.

Normal Forms & Bifurcation of Planar Vector Fields. Shui-Nee Chow et al. (Illus.). 480p. (C). 1994. text 74.95 (*0-521-37226-7*) Cambridge U Pr.

Normal Forms & Homoclinic Chaos. Ed. by William F. Langford & Wayne Nagata. LC 95-20344. (Fields Institute Communications Ser.: Vol. 4). 294p. 1995. text 98.00 (*0-8218-0326-3*, FIC/4) Am Math.

***Normal Girl.** Molly Jong-Fast. LC 99-57324. 208p. 2000. 21.95 (*0-375-50281-5*) Villard Books.

***Normal Heart & the Destiny of Me.** Larry Kramer. 256p. 2000. reprint ed. pap. 14.00 (*0-8021-3692-3*, Pub. by Grove-Atltic) Publishers Group.

Normal Human Anatomy. Arnold J. Smolen. 1994. text 700.00 (*1-56815-022-9*) Mosby Inc.

Normal Infant Development & Borderline Deviations: Early Diagnosis & Therapy. Ed. by Inge Flehmig. (Flexibook Ser.). (Illus.). 279p. 1992. pap. text 29.50 (*0-86577-428-5*, 92-003158) Thieme Med Pubs.

Normal Is Just a Setting on Your Dryer. Patsy Clairmont. LC 93-3380. 1993. pap. 9.99 (*1-56179-112-1*) Focus Family.

***Normal Is Just a Setting on Your Dryer: Pithy Parables about People's Perilous Pursuits of Normalcy.** Patsy Clairmont. 1998. pap. 15.99 incl. audio (*1-56179-594-1*) Focus Family.

Normal Is Just a Setting on Your Hair Dryer. Patsy Clairmont. 140p. 1999. pap. 10.99 (*1-56179-585-2*) Focus Family.

Normal Language Acquisition. Sharon L. James. 212p. (Orig.). (C). 1991. pap. text 43.00 (*0-205-13571-4*) Allyn.

Normal Life: A Study of War & Industrially Injured Pensioners. Sally Sainsbury. 230p. 1993. 66.95 (*1-85628-482-4*, Pub. by Avebury Technical) Ashgate Pub Co.

Normal Lung. 2nd ed. John R. Murray. (Illus.). 377p. 1986. text 47.00 (*0-7216-6613-2*, W B Saunders Co) Harcrt Hlth Sci Grp.

Normal Lymph Node Topography: A CT-Atlas. E. Richter & T. Feyerabend. (Illus.). 120p. 1990. 165.00 (*0-387-52549-1*) Spr-Verlag.

Normal, Malignant Hematopoiesis & New Advances: Proceedings of the Sixth Pezcoller Symposium Held in Rovereto, Italy, June 29-July 1, 1994, Vol. 6. Ed. by Enrico Mihich et al. LC 95-37107. (Pezcoller Foundation Symposium Ser.: Vol. 6). (Illus.). 260p. 1995. 95.00 (*0-306-45136-0*, Kluwer Plenum) Kluwer Academic.

Normal Man. Susie Boyt. 184p. 1997. pap. 10.95 (*1-85799-421-3*, Pub. by Weidenfeld & Nicolson) Trafalgar.

Normal Matrix & Pathological Conditions: Proceedings of 2nd International Congress of the Society for Matrix Research. Ed. by Hartmut Heine & P. Anastasiadis. (Illus.). 174p. (Orig.). 1992. pap. 45.00 (*3-437-11400-X*, Pub. by Gustav Fischer) Lubrecht & Cramer.

Normal Modes & Localization in Nonlinear Systems. Alexander F. Vakakis et al. LC 95-26004. (Series in Nonlinear Science). 552p. 1996. 84.95 (*0-471-13319-1*, Wiley-Interscience) Wiley.

Normal Prices, Technical Change, & Accumulation. Bertram Schefold. 496p. 1997. text 79.95 (*0-312-16147-6*) St Martin.

Normal Psychology of the Aging Process. enl. rev. ed. Ed. by Norman E. Zinberg & Irving Kaufman. LC 77-92178. 285p. 1978. 45.00 (*0-8236-3641-0*) Intl Univs Pr.

Normal Radiographic Anatomy. B. K. Omar. 1983. 90.00 (*0-7855-0795-7*, Pub. by Current Dist) St Mut.

Normal School Education & Efficiency in Teaching. Junius L. Meriam. LC 77-177071. (Columbia University. Teachers College. Contributions to Education Ser.: No. 1). reprint ed. 37.50 (*0-404-55001-0*) AMS Pr.

Normal School Education in Connecticut. James L. Meader. LC 74-177065. (Columbia University. Teachers College. Contributions to Education Ser.: No. 307). reprint ed. 37.50 (*0-404-55307-9*) AMS Pr.

Normal Schools, 2 vols. Henry Barnard. 1985. reprint ed. lib. bdg. 79.00 (*0-932051-87-1*) Rprt Serv.

Normal Sex. Linda Smukler. LC 94-2800. 88p. 1994. pap. 8.95 (*1-56341-042-7*); lib. bdg. 18.95 (*1-56341-043-5*) Firebrand Bks.

Normal Skin. John Burnside. 64p. 1998. pap. 12.95 (*0-224-04286-6*, Pub. by Jonathan Cape) Trafalgar.

Normal-State Properties & Laser Distribution of Semiconductor Thin Films. N. Y. Chen. 140p. 1995. pap. 57.50 (*90-407-1087-2*, Pub. by Delft U Pr) Coronet Bks.

Normal Structures & Bordism Theory, with Applications to MSP. N. Ray et al. LC 77-10134. (Memoirs Ser.: No. 12/193). 66p. 1977. pap. 21.00 (*0-8218-2193-8*, MEMO/12/193) Am Math.

Normal Table of Xenopus Laevis (Daudin) A Systematical & Chronological Survey of the Development from the Fertilized Egg till the End of Metamorphosis. Ed. by P. D. Nieuwkoop & J. Faber. LC 94-11518. (Illus.). 252p. 1994. pap. text 61.00 (*0-8153-1896-0*) Garland.

Normal Testicular Descent & the Aetiology of Cryptorchidism. John M. Hutson et al. LC 95-24947. (Advances in Anatomy, Embryology & Cell Biology Ser.: Vol. 132). 75p. 1995. 86.95 (*3-540-60283-6*) Spr-Verlag.

Normal Two-Dimensional Singularities. Henry B. Laufer. LC 78-160261. (Annals of Mathematics Studies: No. 71). (Illus.). 173p. 1971. reprint ed. pap. 53.70 (*0-608-06633-8*, 206683000009) Bks Demand.

Normal Values for Selected Physical Parameters: An Aid to Syndrome Delineation. Ed. by Daniel Bergsma. LC 75-25485. (National Foundation Ser.: Vol. 10, No. 13). 1974. write for info. (*0-686-18086-0*) March of Dimes.

Normal Values in Pregnancy. Ramsay. (C). 1996. pap. text 38.00 (*0-7020-2021-4*) Harcourt.

Normal Variant & Pitfalls. Volger. 1986. text 172.00 (*0-7216-1457-4*, W B Saunders Co) Harcrt Hlth Sci Grp.

***Normal Variation in Speech.** Krakow. 2002. pap. 44.00 (*1-56593-976-X*) Singular Publishing.

Normale und Gestorte Kindersprache: Linguistische Untersuchungen zum Erwerb von Syntax und Morphologie. Harald Clahsen. LC 87-34651. ix, 340p. (C). 1988. 74.00 (*90-272-2052-2*); pap. 22.95 (*90-272-2053-0*) J Benjamins Pubng Co.

Normalities & Abnormalities in Human Movement. Ed. by B. Kirkcaldy. (Medicine & Sport Science Ser.: Vol. 29). (Illus.). xiv, 214p. 1989. 148.75 (*3-8055-4823-0*) S Karger.

Normality: The Official Strategy Guide. Jeff Sengstack. LC 96-67259. 144p. 1996. per. 19.99 (*0-7615-0493-1*) Prima Pub.

Normality & Pathology in Childhood: Assessments of Development. Anna Freud. LC 65-17007. (Writings of Anna Freud: Vol. 6). 273p. (Orig.). 1966. 45.00 (*0-8236-6875-4*); pap. 25.95 (*0-8236-8165-3*, 26875) Intl Univs Pr.

Normality & Pathology in Cognitive Functions. Ed. by A. Ellis. 1982. text 135.00 (*0-12-237480-0*) Acad Pr.

***Normality & the Process Behavior Chart.** Donald J. Wheeler. 156p. 2000. pap. 20.00 (*0-945320-56-6*, SPC Pr) Stat Process Contrl.

Normality Is Hard Work: Trade Unions & the Politics of Community Care. Mick Carpenter. LC 97-191455. 168p. (C). 1994. pap. 29.50 (*0-85315-803-7*, Pub. by Lawrence & Wishart) NYU Pr.

Normalization, Cut-Elimination, & the Theory of Proofs. A. M. Ungar. LC 92-13877. (Center for the Study of Language & Information-Lecture Notes Ser.). 236p. (C). 1992. 54.95 (*0-937073-83-0*); pap. 19.95 (*0-937073-82-2*) CSLI.

Normalization of Soviet - Japanese Relations, 1945-1970: An Indian View. Savitri Vishwanathan. LC 70-186317. (Illus.). 190p. 1973. 15.00 (*0-910512-16-7*) Diplomatic IN.

N

An Asterisk (*) at the beginning of an entry indicates that the title is appearing for the first time.

Normalization with China: A Comparative Study of U. S. & Japanese Processes. Sadako N. Ogata. (Research Papers & Policy: No. 30). xii, 109p. (Orig.). (C). 1989. pap. 15.00 (*1-55729-013-X*) IEAS.

Normally Hyperbolic Invariant Manifolds in Dynamical Systems. Stephen Wiggins. LC 94-8078. (Applied Mathematical Sciences Ser.: Vol. 105). (Illus.). 208p. 1994. 64.95 (*0-387-94205-X*) Spr-Verlag.

Norman. Loren Spiotta-Dimare. 1998. 12.95 (*1-58021-058-9*); pap. 5.95 (*1-58021-053-8*) Benefactory.

Norman. 2nd ed. Fred E. Hanson. (Illus.). 64p. (Orig.). (J). (gr. 3-5). 1989. reprint ed. pap. 6.00 (*0-9624292-0-1*) Black Willow Pr.

Norman Bel Geddes: An Exhibition of Theatrical & Industrial Designs. Jennifer D. Roberts. (Illus.). 60p. 1979. pap. 10.00 (*0-87959-092-0*) U of Tex H Ransom Ctr.

Norman Bel Geddes, 1893-1958, Rassegna 60. (Illus.). 110p. 1994. pap. 35.00 (*88-85322-18-2*, Pub. by Birkhauser) Princeton Arch.

*__Norman Blake Anthology.__ Norman Blake. 200p. 1998. pap. 24.95 (*0-7866-4088-X*, 96641) Mel Bay.

Norman Collie - A Life in Two Worlds: Mountain Explorer & Scientist, 1859-1942. Christine Mill. (Aberdeen University Press Bks.). (Illus.). 256p. 1987. text 30.00 (*0-08-032456-8*, Pub. by Aberdeen U Pr) Macmillan.

Norman Conquest. R. Allen Brown. LC 84-142214. (Documents of Medieval History Ser.). xix, 181p. 1984. write for info. (*0-7131-6406-9*, Pub. by E A) Routldge.

Norman Conquest. N. J. Higham. LC 99-163550. (Pocket Histories Ser.). 128p. 1998. pap. 9.95 (*0-7509-1953-1*, Pub. by Sutton Pub Ltd) Intl Pubs Mktg.

Norman Conquest. Marjorie Reeves. (Then & There Ser.). (Illus.). 60p. (Orig.). (gr. 7-12). 1988. pap. text 8.60 (*0-582-00384-9*, 78110) Longman.

Norman Conquest, 10 bks., Set. David Birt. (Resource Units: Middle Ages, 1066-1485 Ser.). (Illus.). 24p. 1974. pap. text, teacher ed. 12.95 (*0-582-39372-8*) Longman.

Norman Conquest & Beyond. Frank Barlow. 318p. (C). 1983. 55.00 (*0-907628-19-2*) Hambledon Press.

Norman Conquest & Its Effects on the Economy: 1066-86. Rex Welldon Finn. LC 72-571794. xiv, 322p. 1971. write for info. (*0-582-50231-4*) Longman.

Norman Conquest & the English Coinage. M. Dolley. 1966. 5.00 (*0-685-51535-4*) S J Durst.

Norman Conquest in English Historiography. James M. Carter. 115p. (Orig.). 1980. pap. text 26.95 (*0-89126-086-2*) MA-AH Pub.

Norman Conquests: Table Manners, Living Together, Round & Round the Garden. Alan Ayckbourn. LC 78-73501. 224p. 1988. pap. 13.00 (*0-8021-3134-4*, Grove) Grove-Atltic.

Norman Corwin & Radio: The Golden Years. R. LeRoy Bannerman. LC 85-1028. (Illus.). 294p. 1986. pap. 91.20 (*0-608-05128-4*, 206568700005) Bks Demand.

Norman Corwin's Letters. Norman Corwin. Ed. by A. J. Langguth. LC 93-15898. 480p. 1993. 29.95 (*0-9623032-5-9*) Barricade Bks.

Norman Davis Collection: Ancient Coins in North American Collections 1. Hyla A. Troxell. (Illus.). 81p. 1969. pap. 15.00 (*0-89722-058-7*) Am Numismatic.

Norman Dorlaug's Green Revolution & Indias Population Problem. S. Chandrasekhar. 1997. pap. 7.50 (*1-890456-00-4*) Popl Rev Bks.

Norman Douglas. Henry Tomlinson. LC 74-1189. (English Biography Ser.: No. 31). 1974. lib. bdg. 75.00 (*0-8383-1804-5*) M S G Haskell Hse.

Norman Foster. Daniel Treiber. LC 97-179017. (Illus.). 144p. 1995. pap. 29.99 (*0-419-20320-6*, E & FN Spon) Routledge.

Norman Foster: A Global Architecture. Martin Pawley. LC 99-25469. (Illus.). 240p. 1999. pap. 25.00 (*0-7893-0263-2*, Pub. by Universe) St Martin.

*__Norman Foster: Catalogue of Work.__ Norman Foster & David Jenkins. (Illus.). 240p. 2000. pap. 29.95 (*3-7913-2401-2*) Prestel Pub NY.

Norman Foster: Sketch Book. Ed. by Werner Blaser. (Illus.). 112p. 1993. pap. 42.00 (*3-7643-2837-1*, Pub. by Birkhauser) Princeton Arch.

Norman Foster - Buildings & Projects, 1964-1973, Vol. 1. Ed. by Ian Lambot. (Norman Foster Ser.). (Illus.). 260p. 1996. 85.00 (*3-7643-5446-1*, Pub. by Birkhauser) Princeton Arch.

Norman Foster - Buildings & Projects, 1971-1978, Vol. 2. Ed. by Ian Lambot. (Norman Foster Ser.). (Illus.). 240p. 1996. 85.00 (*3-7643-5447-X*, Pub. by Birkhauser) Princeton Arch.

Norman Foster - Buildings & Projects, 1978-1982, Vol. 3. Ed. by Ian Lambot. (Norman Foster Ser.). (Illus.). 264p. 1996. 85.00 (*3-7643-5448-8*, Pub. by Birkhauser) Princeton Arch.

Norman Foster, Buildings & Projects, 1982-1989, Vol. 4. Ian Lambot. (Norman Foster Ser.). (Illus.). 256p. 1996. 85.00 (*3-7643-5428-3*, Pub. by Birkhauser) Princeton Arch.

Norman Foster, Commerzbank, Frankfurt am Main. Norman Foster. (Opus Ser.: Vol. 21). (Illus.). 72p. 1998. 48.00 (*3-930698-21-8*) Dist Art Pubs.

Norman Foster Studio: Consistency Through Diversity. Malcolm Quantrill. 232p. 1997. 85.00 (*0-419-19750-8*, E & FN Spon) Routledge.

Norman Geschwind: Selected Publications. Norman Geschwind et al. LC 96-37401. 592p. 1997. text 57.75 (*0-7506-9753-9*) Buttrwrth-Heinemann.

Norman Glossary: Glossaire Normand. C. Maze. (FRE.). 124p. 1984. pap. 39.95 (*0-8288-1716-2*, F52940) Fr & Eur.

Norman Hall's Corrections Officer Exam Preparation Book. Norman Hall. LC 97-22916. 1997. pap. 10.95 (*1-55850-793-0*) Adams Media.

Norman Hall's Police Exam Preparation Book: Guaranteed Methods to Score 80 Percent to 100 Percent or Your Money Back. Norman Hall. LC 94-183603. 280p. 1994. pap. 12.95 (*1-55850-296-3*) Adams Media.

Norman Hall's Postal Exam Preparation Book. 2nd ed. Norman Hall. LC 94-9167. 1994. pap. 10.95 (*1-55850-363-3*) Adams Media.

Norman Hall's State Trooper & Highway Patrol Exam Preparation Book. Norman S. Hall. LC 98-46211. 304p. 1999. pap. text 12.95 (*1-58062-077-9*) Adams Media.

Norman Henry Biltz: Memoirs of Duke of Nevada--Development of Lake Tahoe, California, & Nevada; Reminiscences of Nevada Political & Financial Life. Ed. by Mary E. Glass. 267p. 1968. lib. bdg. 45.50 (*1-56475-045-0*) U NV Oral Hist.

Norman Henry Biltz: Memoirs of Duke of Nevada--Development of Lake Tahoe, California, & Nevada; Reminiscences of Nevada Political & Financial Life. Ed. by Mary E. Glass. 267p. 1969. fiche. write for info. (*1-56475-046-9*) U NV Oral Hist.

Norman Impact on the Medieval World. Kathleen Gormley et al. (Irish History in Perspective Ser.). (Illus.). 1997. pap., teacher ed. 11.95 (*0-521-46602-4*) Cambridge U Pr.

Norman Impact on the Medieval World. Kathleen Gormley et al. (Irish History in Perspective Ser.). (Illus.). 64p. (C). 1997. pap. 13.95 (*0-521-46601-6*) Cambridge U Pr.

Norman Institutions. Charles H. Haskins. LC 80-2026. 1981. reprint ed. 44.00 (*0-404-18568-1*) AMS Pr.

Norman Invasion of Ireland. Richard Roche. 134p. 1995. pap. 19.95 (*0-947962-81-6*, Pub. by Anvil Books Ltd) Irish Bks Media.

Norman Kingdom of Sicily. Donald Matthew. (Medieval Textbooks Ser.). 434p. (C). 1992. text 80.00 (*0-521-26284-4*); pap. text 26.95 (*0-521-26911-3*) Cambridge U Pr.

Norman Kings. James Chambers. LC 82-112904. 224p. 1981. write for info. (*0-297-77964-8*, Pub. by Weidenfeld & Nicolson) Trafalgar.

Norman Knight, 950-1204 A. D. Chris Gravett. (Warrior Ser.: No. 1). (Illus.). 64p. pap. 12.95 (*1-85532-287-0*, 9600, Pub. by Ospry) Stackpole.

Norman Leslie: A Tale of Present Times, 2 vols. in 1. Theodore S. Fay. (C). 1972. reprint ed. lib. bdg. 45.00 (*0-8422-8044-8*) Irvington.

Norman Leslie: A Tale of Present Times, 2 vols. in 1. Theodore S. Foy. (C). 1986. reprint ed. pap. text 9.95 (*0-8290-1938-3*) Irvington.

Norman Levine & His Works. Larry Mathews. 46p. (C). 1989. pap. text 9.95 (*1-55022-034-9*, Pub. by ECW) Genl Dist Srvs.

Norman Levine Reader: Insights on Achieving Success & Fulfillment. Norman G. Levine. Ed. by Brad Ragaglia. 280p. 1998. pap. 24.99 (*1-891042-01-7*) Million Dollar.

Norman Lewis: Black Paintings, 1946-1977. David Craven et al. Ed. by Stephanie Salomon. LC 98-60258. (Illus.). 124p. 1998. pap. 29.95 (*0-942949-14-5*) Studio Mus Harlem.

Norman Lindsay on Art, Life & Literature. Keith Wingrove. 1990. pap. 16.95 (*0-7022-2227-5*, Pub. by Univ Queensland Pr) Intl Spec Bk.

Norman Linear Alg Prelim Ed. Norman. 1994. pap. text. write for info. (*0-201-44316-3*) Addison-Wesley.

Norman London. William F. Stephen. Tr. by H. E. Butler. LC 89-46223. (Historical Travel Ser.). (Illus.). 128p. (Orig.). 1990. pap. 12.00 (*0-934977-19-4*) Italica Pr.

Norman MacCaig: A Study of His Life & Work. Marjory McNeill. 154p. 1996. pap. 40.00 (*1-873644-46-9*, Pub. by Mercat Pr Bks) St Mut.

Norman MacCaig: Critical Essays. Ed. by Joy Hendry & Raymond Ross. (Modern Scottish Writers Ser.). 200p. 1991. 29.00 (*0-7486-0201-1*, Pub. by Edinburgh U Pr) Col U Pr.

Norman Maclean. Norman F. Maclean. Ed. by Ron McFarland & Hugh Nichols. LC 87-72517. (American Authors Ser.). 200p. 1988. pap. 15.00 (*0-917652-71-1*) Confluence Pr.

Norman Maclean. Ron McFarland. LC 93-70135. (Western Writers Ser.: No. 107). (Illus.). 55p. 1993. pap. 4.95 (*0-88430-106-0*) Boise St U W Writ Ser.

Norman Mailer. Michael K. Glenday. LC 95-3705. (Modern Novelists Ser.). 1995. text 39.95 (*0-312-12644-1*) St Martin.

Norman Mailer. rev. ed. Robert Merrill. (Twayne's United States Authors Ser.). 160p. 1992. 32.00 (*0-8057-3967-X*, Twyne) Mac Lib Ref.

Norman Mailer: A Collection of Critical Essays. Ed. by Leo Braudy. 1972. pap. 1.95 (*0-13-545541-3*, STC101, Spectrum IN) Macmillan Gen Ref.

Norman Mailer: Quick-Change Artist. Jennifer Bailey. LC 79-14282. 160p. 1980. text 44.00 (*0-06-490284-6*, 06324) B&N Imports.

Norman Mailer: The Radical As Hipster. Robert Ehrlich. LC 78-14849. 244p. 1978. lib. bdg. 21.00 (*0-8108-1160-X*) Scarecrow.

Norman McLaren, Manipulator of Movement: The National Film Board Years, 1947-67. Valliere T. Richard. LC 80-53998. (Illus.). 128p. 1982. 28.50 (*0-87413-192-8*) U Delaware Pr.

Norman Newman & the Werewolf of Walnut Street. Ellen Conford. LC 95-12758. (Illus.). 96p. (J). (gr. 2-5). 1995. lib. bdg. 15.35 (*0-8167-3849-1*, Little Rainbow) Troll Communs.

Norman Newman & the Werewolf of Walnut Street. Ellen Conford. (Norman Newman Ser.). 1995. 8.15 (*0-606-07958-0*, Pub. by Turtleback) Demco.

Norman Perrin's Interpretation of the New Testament. Calvin R. Mercer. Ed. by Charles Mabee. LC 84-27335. (Studies in American Biblical Hermeneutics: No. 2). 192p. 1986. 24.95 (*0-86554-219-8*, MUP-H197) Mercer Univ Pr.

Norman Plays Basketball. Clare Gault & Frank Gault. (Illus.). (J). (gr. k-3). 1978. pap. 1.50 (*0-590-05394-9*) Scholastic Inc.

*__Norman Rockwell.__ 1999. 13.95 (*0-7892-5413-1*) Abbeville Pr.

*__Norman Rockwell.__ Abrams Staff. (Illus.). 1999. 12.95 (*0-8109-5824-4*, Pub. by Abrams) Time Warner.

Norman Rockwell. Christopher Finch. (Illus.). 1996. pap. 4.95 (*0-89659-090-9*) Abbeville Pr.

Norman Rockwell. Random House Value Publishing Staff. 1999. 9.99 (*0-517-16121-4*) Random Hse Value.

*__Norman Rockwell.__ Mike Venezia. LC 99-58036. (Getting to Know the World's Greatest Artists Ser.). (Illus.). (J). 2000. 22.50 (*0-516-21594-9*) Childrens.

Norman Rockwell: A Centennial Celebration. Norman Rockwell Museum Staff. (Illus.). 120p. 1993. 15.98 (*0-7924-5761-7*, Thunder Bay) Advantage Pubs.

Norman Rockwell: A Pop-Up Art Experience. Norman Rockwell Museum Staff. (Illus.). 1999. pap. 18.95 (*0-7893-0366-3*, Pub. by Universe) St Martin.

Norman Rockwell: Address Book. Abbeville Press Staff. 1992. 16.95 (*1-55859-202-4*) Abbeville Pr.

Norman Rockwell: America's Best-Loved Illustrator. Joel H. Cohen. LC 96-35103. (First Bks.). (J). 1997. lib. bdg. 22.00 (*0-531-20266-6*) Watts.

Norman Rockwell: America's Best-Loved Illustrator. Joel H. Cohen. (First Books-Biographies Ser.). (J). 1997. pap. text 6.95 (*0-531-15840-3*) Watts.

Norman Rockwell: Artist & Illustrator. Thomas S. Buechner. (Illus.). 328p. 1996. pap. 49.98 (*0-8109-8150-5*, Pub. by Abrams) Time Warner.

Norman Rockwell: My Adventures As an Illustrator. Norman Rockwell. (Illus.). 432p. 1995. pap. 19.95 (*0-8109-2596-6*, Pub. by Abrams) Time Warner.

*__Norman Rockwell: Pictures for the American People.__ Ed. by Maureen H. Hennessey & Anne Knutson. (Illus.). 199p. 1999. 35.00 (*0-8109-6392-2*, Pub. by Abrams) Time Warner.

Norman Rockwell: Pictures for the American People. Ed. by Anne Knutson & Maureen H. Hennessey. LC 97-7635. (Library of American Art Ser.). (Illus.). 160p. 1997. 45.00 (*0-8109-3794-8*, Pub. by Abrams) Time Warner.

Norman Rockwell: Storyteller with a Brush. Beverly Gherman. LC 98-36546. (Illus.). 57p. (J). (gr. 4-8). 2000. 19.95 (*0-689-82001-1*) Atheneum Yung Read.

Norman Rockwell: The Artist & His Work. Norman Rockwell Museum Staff. LC 95-13523. 120p. 1995. 12.95 (*1-56799-209-9*, Friedman-Fairfax) M Friedman Pub Grp Inc.

Norman Rockwell: The Artist & His Work. Norman Rockwell. 1999. 19.98 (*1-56799-760-0*) M Friedman Pub Grp Inc.

Norman Rockwell: 332 Magazine Covers. Christopher Finch. (Illus.). 400p. 1990. 39.98 (*0-89660-058-0*, Artabras) Abbeville Pr.

Norman Rockwell: 332 Magazine Covers. Christopher Finch. (Tiny Folios Ser.). (Illus.). 356p. 1997. 11.95 (*0-7892-0409-6*) Abbeville Pr.

Norman Rockwell & the Saturday Evening Post: The Complete Cover Collection, 1916-1971. Starkey Flythe & Donald Stoltz. (Illus.). 672p. 1996. reprint ed. 49.98 (*1-56731-131-8*, MJF Bks) Fine Comms.

Norman Rockwell & the Saturday Evening Post Vol. 1: The Early Years. Starkey Flythe, Jr. (Illus.). 1994. 24.98 (*1-56731-061-3*, MJF Bks) Fine Comms.

Norman Rockwell & the Saturday Evening Post Vol. 2: The Middle Years. Donald Stoltz & Marshall Stoltz. (Illus.). 1994. 24.98 (*1-56731-062-1*, MJF Bks) Fine Comms.

Norman Rockwell & the Saturday Evening Post Vol. 3: The Later Years. Donald Stoltz & Marshall Stoltz. (Illus.). 1994. 24.98 (*1-56731-063-X*, MJF Bks) Fine Comms.

Norman Rockwell at Home in Vermont: The Arlington Years, 1939-1953. Stuart Murray. LC 96-35007. (Illus.). 96p. 1997. pap. 14.95 (*1-884592-02-3*) Images from the Past.

*__Norman Rockwell Christmas.__ Margaret Rockwell. (Illus.). 80p. 2000. 7.98 (*1-58663-073-3*) M Friedman Pub Grp Inc.

Norman Rockwell Illustrated Cookbook. George Mendoza. 1989. 17.95 (*0-685-33408-2*) Random Hse Value.

Norman Rockwell Postcard Book. Illus. by Norman Rockwell. (Postcard Bks.). 64p. (Orig.). 1987. pap. text 8.95 (*0-89471-554-2*) Running Pr.

Norman Rockwell Wit. William Gibson. (Illus.). 216p. 1993. 11.95 (*0-685-64987-3*, 34509) Interp Mktg Prods.

Norman Rockwell's America. Christopher Finch. (Illus.). 256p. 1985. pap. 24.98 (*0-8109-8071-1*, Pub. by Abrams) Time Warner.

Norman Rockwell's American Children: A Postcard Book. Norman Rockwell. (Postcard Bks.). (Illus.). 64p. (Orig.). 1993. pap. 8.95 (*1-56138-258-2*) Running Pr.

Norman Rockwell's American Christmas Postcard Book. Norman Rockwell. (Postcard Bks.). (Illus.). 64p. (Orig.). 1990. pap. text 8.95 (*0-89471-894-0*) Running Pr.

*__Norman Rockwell's American Memories.__ Rockwell. (Illus.). 1999. 7.98 (*1-56731-352-3*, MJF Bks) Fine Comms.

Norman Rockwell's Christmas Book. Ed. by Molly Rockwell. LC 93-9925. (Illus.). 222p. 1993. pap. 12.98 (*0-8109-8121-1*, Pub. by Abrams) Time Warner.

Norman Rockwell's Chronicles of America. Margaret Rockwell. 120p. 1996. 17.98 (*1-56799-344-3*, MetroBooks) M Friedman Pub Grp Inc.

Norman Rockwell's Faith of America. Ed. by Fred Bauer. (Illus.). 160p. 1996. 14.98 (*0-89660-066-1*, Artabras) Abbeville Pr.

Norman Rockwell's Four Freedoms. Norman Rockwell & Stuart Murray. LC 97-48769. 176p. 1998. 12.99 (*0-517-20213-1*) Random Hse Value.

Norman Rockwell's Four Freedoms: Images That Inspired a Nation. Stuart Murray & James McCabe. LC 93-3545. (Illus.). 176p. 1993. pap. 14.95 (*0-936399-42-2*) Berkshire Hse.

Norman Rockwell's Greatest Painting. large type ed. Hollis Hodges. (General Ser.). 339p. 1989. lib. bdg. 17.95 (*0-8161-4812-0*, G K Hall Lrg Type) Mac Lib Ref.

Norman Rockwell's Growing up in America. Margaret Rockwell. LC 99-18036. 120p. 1998. 17.98 (*1-56799-598-5*, Friedman-Fairfax) M Friedman Pub Grp Inc.

Norman Rockwell's Scrapbook for a Young Boy. deluxe ed. George Mendoza. (Illus.). (J). 1979. 17.95 (*0-89659-026-7*) Abbeville Pr.

Norman Rockwell's World War II: Impressions from the Homefront. Susan E. Meyer. 96p. 1991. pap. 20.00 (*0-9631011-0-2*) USAA.

*__Norman Saves the Day!__ Andrew Clements. LC 99-39637. (J). 2001. per. 15.00 (*0-689-82914-0*) S&S Childrens.

Norman Schwarzkopf see Chelsea House Library of Biography

Norman Schwarzkopf: Hero with a Heart. Libby Hughes. LC 92-13598. (People in Focus Ser.). (Illus.). 144p. (YA). (gr. 5 up). 1992. lib. bdg. 13.95 (*0-87518-521-5*, Dillon Silver Burdett) Silver Burdett Pr.

Norman Street: Poverty & Politics in an Urban Neighborhood. Ida Susser. (Illus.). 230p. 1982. pap. text 21.95 (*0-19-503049-4*) OUP.

Norman Thomas. James C. Duran. Ed. by Sylvia E. Bowman. LC 73-15831. (Twayne's United States Authors Ser.). 173p. 1974. text 20.95 (*0-8057-0727-1*) Irvington.

Norman Thomas Papers Guide, 1904-1967. Compiled by Melanie A. Yolles. 75p. 1985. pap. write for info. (*0-89887-036-4*) Chadwyck-Healey.

Norman to the Rescue. Loren Spiotta-DiMare. (Humane Society of the United States Animal Tales Ser.). (J). (gr. 1-4). 1999. pap., pap. text 9.95 incl. audio (*1-58021-055-4*) Benefactory.

Norman Van Aken's Cooking in the New World. Norman Van Aken. (Illus.). 224p. 1999. pap. 18.95 (*0-912333-82-0*, Pub. by BB&T Inc) Publishers Group.

Norman Van Aken's Feast of Sunlight: 200 Inspired Recipes from the Master of New World Cuisine. Norman Van Aken. LC 97-6625. (Illus.). 320p. 1997. reprint ed. pap. 14.95 (*1-55832-136-5*) Harvard Common Pr.

Norman Vincent Peale: An Inspiring Collection of Three Complete Books. Norman Vincent Peale. 400p. 1997. 9.99 (*0-517-18661-6*) Random Hse Value.

Norman Vincent Peale: The Inspirational Writings. Norman Vincent Peale. 416p. 1996. 12.99 (*0-88486-153-8*, Inspirational Pr) Arrowood Pr.

Norman Vincent Peale: Words That Inspired Him. 1994. 12.98 (*0-88486-100-7*) Arrowood Pr.

Normance. Louis-Ferdinand Celine. (Feerie Pour une Autre Fois Ser.: Vol. II). (FRE.). 463p. 1989. pap. 11.95 (*0-7859-1877-9*, 2070370534) Fr & Eur.

Normance: Feerie pour une Autre Fois 2. Louis-Ferdinand Celine. (FRE.). 1977. pap. 13.95 (*0-8288-3674-4*, F92050) Fr & Eur.

Normance (Feerie . . . 2) Louis-Ferdinand Celine. (Folio Ser.: No. 1053). (FRE.). 463p. (Orig.). 1954. pap. 10.95 (*2-07-037053-4*) Schoenhof.

Normand Lockwood: His Life & Music. Kay Norton. LC 93-16889. (Composers of North America Ser.: No. 11). (Illus.). 545p. 1993. 62.50 (*0-8108-2683-6*) Scarecrow.

Normandale Community College Introductory Algebra Package. rev. ed. McHale. (C). 1995. 51.00 (*0-201-89516-1*, 15887) Addison-Wesley.

*__Normandie - Cotentin: France (Guides Regionaux)__ 4th ed. (FRE.). 1998. pap. text 20.00 (*2-06-034604-5*) Michelin.

Normandie Map. 1997. 8.95 (*2-06-700231-7*, 231) Michelin.

Normandie Mission. Duncan Harding. 192p. 25.00 (*0-7278-5522-0*) Severn Hse.

Normandie Vallee de la Seine Green Guide: France (Guides Regionaux) 3rd ed. Michelin Staff. (FRE., Illus.). 1996. per. 20.00 (*2-06-034703-3*, 347) Michelin.

Normandy. (Panorama Books Collection). (FRE.). 3.95 (*0-685-35939-5*) Fr & Eur.

Normandy. K. Arnold et al. LC 94-68179. (Illustrated Travel Guides from Thomas Cook Ser.). (Illus.). 192p. (Orig.). 1994. pap. 12.95 (*0-8442-9090-4*, Passprt Bks) NTC Contemp Pub Co.

Normandy. Insight Guides Staff. (Insight Guides). 1998. pap. text 7.95 (*0-88729-551-7*); pap. text 21.95 (*0-88729-730-7*) Langenscheidt.

Normandy. William P. Mack. (Destroyer Ser.: Bk. 6). 250p. 1995. 22.95 (*1-877853-38-0*) Nautical & Aviation.

Normandy. John McNeill. (Blue Guide Ser.). (Illus.). 256p. 1993. pap. 18.95 (*0-393-30971-1*) Norton.

Normandy: Gold Beach. Chris Dunfie. (Battleground Europe Ser.). 1999. pap. text 16.95 (*1-58097-008-7*) Combined Pub.

Normandy: Omaha Beach. Kilvert Jones. 1999. pap. 16.95 (*1-58097-015-X*) Combined Pub.

Normandy: Pegasus Bridge & Merville Battery. Carl Shilleto. 1999. pap. 16.95 (*1-58097-010-9*) Combined Pub.

Normandy: The United States Army Campaigns of World War 2. William M. Hammond. 48p. 1994. pap. 2.25 (*0-16-042083-0*) USGPO.

An Asterisk (*) at the beginning of an entry indicates that the title is appearing for the first time.

Normandy & the Seine: A Guide to 700 Kilometers of Footpaths along the Seine from Paris to the Coast & Through the Gentle Normandy Countryside. French Ramblers Association Staff. Tr. by Helen McPhail from FRE. (Footpaths of Europe Ser.). (Illus.). 142p. (Orig.). 1990. pap. 19.95 (*1-85365-155-9*, Pub. by McCarta) Seven Hills Bk.

***Normandy Battles.** Bob Carruthers. (Illus.). 2000. 29.95 (*0-304-35396-5*) Continuum.

Normandy Before 1066. 2nd ed. Bates. 1996. pap. text. write for info. (*0-582-08410-5*) Longman.

Normandy Campaign, 1944: A Selected Bibliography, 9. Colin F. Baxter. LC 91-46970. (Bibliographies of Battles & Leaders Ser.: No. 9). 184p. 1992. lib. bdg. 55.00 (*0-313-28301-X*, BXN, Greenwood Pr) Greenwood.

Normandy Encore No. 16: French Entree. Patricia Fenn. (Illus.). 220p. 1996. pap. text 11.95 (*1-899163-17-4*) Cimino Pub Grp.

Normandy Green Guide: English Edition. Michelin Staff. 1996. pap. 19.95 (*0-7859-7206-4*, 2061348017) Fr & Eur.

Normandy Green Guide: France (Regional Guides) 2nd ed. Ed. by Michelin Staff. 1996. per. 20.00 (*2-06-134802-5*, 1348) Michelin.

Normandy, 1944. Stephen Badsey. (Campaign Ser.: No. 1). (Illus.). 96p. 1990. pap. 14.95 (*0-85045-921-4*, 9500, Pub. by Ospry) Stackpole.

Normandy, 1994: The Canadian Summer. Bill McAndrew et al. (Illus.). 164p. 1996. 50.00 (*2-920718-55-X*, Pub. by A4rt Global) Howell Pr VA.

Normandy Picardy & Pas de Calais. Barbara Eperon. Ed. by Arthur Eperon. (Regional Guides of France Ser.). (Illus.). 192p. 1994. reprint ed. pap. 16.95 (*0-8442-9940-5*, Passprt Bks) NTC Contemp Pub Co.

Normandy, Picardy & the Pas de Calais. 2nd rev. ed. Barbara Eperon. (Illus.). 200p. 1996. pap. 17.95 (*0-8442-9943-X*, 9943X, Passprt Bks) NTC Contemp Pub Co.

Normandy Summer. large type ed. Nerina Thorne. (Linford Romance Library). 272p. 1997. pap. 16.99 (*0-7089-5122-8*, Linford) Ulverscroft.

Normandy Summer - Love's Charade. large type ed. Joy St. Clair. 320p. 31.99 (*0-7089-4052-8*) Ulverscroft.

Normandy to the Bulge: An American Infantry GI in Europe During World War II. Richard D. Courtney. LC 96-7731. (Illus.). 208p. (C). 1996. 29.95 (*0-8093-2084-3*) S Ill U Pr.

***Normandy to the Bulge: An American Infantry GI in Europe During World War II.** Richard D. Courtney. (Illus.). 181p. 2000. pap. 19.95 (*0-8093-2102-5*) S Ill U Pr.

Normandy 1944, 1. Osprey. 1999. pap. text 17.95 (*1-85532-949-2*) Ospry.

Normannen. Rene de Goscinny & M. Uderzo. (GER., Illus.). (J). 24.95 (*0-8288-4980-3*) Fr & Eur.

***Normans.** Marjorie Chibnall. 2001. 26.95 (*0-631-18671-9*) Blackwell Pubs.

Normans. Peter Chrisp. (Look into the Past Ser.). (Illus.). 32p. (J). (gr. 4-6). 1995. lib. bdg. 22.83 (*1-56847-174-2*) Raintree Steck-V.

Normans. Hazel M. Martell. LC 91-40970. (Worlds of the Past Ser.). (Illus.). 64p. (YA). (gr. 6 up). 1992. lib. bdg. 21.00 (*0-02-762428-5*, Mac Bks Young Read) S&S Childrens.

Normans. David Nicolle. (Elite Ser.: No. 9). (Illus.). 64p. pap. 12.95 (*0-85045-729-7*, 9408, Pub. by Ospry) Stackpole.

Normans. Trevor Rowley. (Illus.). 208p. 1999. 32.50 (*0-7524-1434-8*, Pub. by Tempus Pubng) Arcadia Publng.

***Normans.** Trevor Rowley. (Illus.). 176p. 2000. pap. 24.99 (*0-7524-1496-8*, Pub. by Tempus Pubng) Arcadia Publng.

Normans. Anne Steel. 24p. 1987. write for info. (*0-86592-162-8*) Rourke Enter.

Normans. 2nd ed. R. Allen Brown. (Illus.). 190p. (C). 1995. reprint ed. pap. 29.95 (*0-85115-359-3*, Boydell Pr) Boydell & Brewer.

Normans. 2nd ed. R. Allen Brown. (Illus.). 190p. (C). 1997. reprint ed. text 29.95 (*0-85115-358-5*, Boydell Pr) Boydell & Brewer.

Normans, Vol. 9. David Nicolle. 64p. 1998. pap. 14.95 (*1-85532-944-1*) Ospry.

Normans & the Norman Conquest. Reginald A. Brown. LC 77-366379. xvi, 292p. 1969. write for info. (*0-09-456260-1*, Pub. by Constable & Co) Trafalgar.

Normans & the Norman Conquest. R. Allen Brown. 272p. (C). 1998. reprint ed. pap. 29.95 (*0-85115-367-4*, Boydell Pr) Boydell & Brewer.

Norman's Heart. Margaret Moore. (Historical Ser.). 1996. per. 4.50 (*0-373-28911-1*, 1-28911-5) Harlequin Bks.

Normans in Britain. David Walker. (Historical Association Studies). (Illus.). 160p. (C). 1995. pap. text 15.95 (*0-631-18582-8*) Blackwell Pubs.

Normans in Britain Donald Wilkinson & John Cantrell. LC 87-154588. (Documents & Debates Ser.). viii, 114 p. 1987. write for info. (*0-333-39871-8*, Pub. by Macmillan Ed) Spr-Verlag.

Normans in Scotland. Robert L. Ritchie. LC 80-2216. reprint ed. 57.50 (*0-404-18783-8*) AMS Pr.

***Normans in Sicily: The Magnificent Story of the Other Norman Conquest.** John Julius Norwich. (Illus.). 793p. 2000. pap. 35.00 (*0-14-015212-1*, Pub. by Pnguin Bks Ltd) Trafalgar.

Norman's Natchez: An Early Photographer & His Town. Joan W. Gandy & Thomas H. Gandy. LC 78-15570. (Illus.). 1978. 25.00 (*0-87805-078-7*) Myrtle Bank.

Norman's New World Cuisine. Norman Van Aken. LC 96-39675. 336p. 1997. 50.00 (*0-679-43202-7*) Random.

Normans Rare Guitars: 30 Years of Buying Selling & Collecting. David Swartz & Norman Harris. Ed. by Keith Lissale. (Illus.). 280p. 1999. 100.00 (*0-9669219-0-9*); pap. 60.00 (*0-9669219-1-7*, DS00750) Swartz Inc.

Norman's Snowball. Hazel J. Hutchins. (Toddler Ser.). (Illus.). 24p. (J). (ps-1). 1989. 12.95 (*1-55037-053-7*, Pub. by Annick) Firefly Bks Ltd.

Norman's Snowball. Hazel J. Hutchins. (Toddler Ser.). (Illus.). 24p. (J). (ps-3). 1989. pap. 4.95 (*1-55037-050-2*, Pub. by Annick) Firefly Bks Ltd.

Norman's Snowball. Hazel J. Hutchins. (Annikins Ser.: Vol. 15). (Illus.). 24p. (J). (ps-1). 1996. pap. 1.25 (*1-55037-494-X*, Pub. by Annick) Firefly Bks Ltd.

Normas Cuidados Paciente. 6th ed. Tucker. (C). 1997. text 74.80 (*84-8174-262-7*) Mosby Inc.

Normas de Interpretacion Biblica. Ernesto Trenchard. (SPA.). 164p. 1958. mass mkt. 4.99 (*0-8254-1749-X*, Edit Portavoz) Kregel.

Normas en las Necesidades Humanas. Vincent W. Kafka. 12p. 1988. pap. 3.95 (*0-913261-19-X*) Effect Learn Sys.

Normas para la Realizacion del Estudio Pelvico Femenino Por Medio de Ultrasonido. Tr. of Standards for the Performance of the Ultrasound Examination of the Female. (SPA.). 8p. 1995. pap. 10.00 (*1-930047-03-7*, GFPS) Am Inst Ultrasound.

Normas para la Realizacion del Estudio Vascular/Doppler Por Ultrasonido. Tr. of Standards for Performance of the Vascular/Doppler Ultrasound Examination. (SPA.). 16p. 1992. pap. 10.00 (*1-930047-04-5*, GVDS) Am Inst Ultrasound.

Normas para Llevar A Cabo el Examen Obstetrico Prenatal Con Ultrasonido. Tr. of Standards for Performance of the Antepartum Obstetrical Ultrasound. (SPA.). 8p. 1994. pap. 10.00 (*1-930047-05-3*, GAOBS) Am Inst Ultrasound.

Normative Approach to War: Peace, War, & Justice in Hugo Grotius. Ed. by Yasuaki Onuma & James Crawford. LC 92-2466. 440p. 1993. text 85.00 (*0-19-825709-0*, Clarendon Pr) OUP.

Normative Basis of Culture: A Philosophical Inquiry. Henry McDonald. LC 85-23795. xii, 241p. 1986. text 35.00 (*0-8071-1280-1*) La State U Pr.

Normative Basis of Fault in Criminal Law: History & Theory. Adekemi Odujirin. LC 98-215019. (History & Theory Ser.). 336p. 1998. text 55.00 (*0-8020-4304-6*); pap. text 21.95 (*0-8020-8132-0*) U of Toronto Pr.

Normative Constitution: Essays for the Third Century. Ed. by Richard Sherlock et al. LC 95-16794. 176p. (C). 1995. text 51.00 (*0-8476-8048-7*); pap. text 21.95 (*0-8476-8049-5*) Rowman.

Normative Cultures. Robert C. Neville. LC 94-33403. 280p. (C). 1995. text 49.50 (*0-7914-2577-0*); pap. text 16.95 (*0-7914-2578-9*) State U NY Pr.

Normative Dictionary & Guide to the Spanish Language: Diccionario Normative y Guia de la Lengua Espanol. 2nd ed. Francisco Marsa. (SPA.). 480p. 1990. write for info. (*0-7859-4954-2*) Fr & Eur.

Normative Ethics. Shelly Kagan. LC 97-30631. (Dimensions of Philosophy Ser.). 352p. (C). 1997. pap. 28.00 (*0-8133-0846-1*, Pub. by Westview) HarpC.

Normative Ethics & Objective Reason Vol. 1: Ethics at the Crossroads. Ed. by George F. McLean. LC 92-13187. (Cultural Heritage & Contemporary Change Series I: Vol. 7). 300p. 1997. pap. 17.50 (*1-56518-022-4*) Coun Res Values.

Normative Health Care Measures. 1995. write for info. (*1-57372-001-1*) HCIA.

Normative Health Care Measures. 1996. write for info. (*1-57372-032-1*) HCIA.

Normative Judaism. Ed. by Jacob Neusner. LC 90-13892. (Origins of Judaism Ser.: Vol. 1). 1592p. 1991. text 70.00 (*0-8240-8172-2*) Garland.

Normative Model of Physical Therapist Assistant Education: Version 99. 1999. pap. 55.95 (*1-887759-64-6*) Am Phys Therapy Assn.

Normative Model of Physical Therapist Professional Education: Version 97. Contrib. by APTA Staff. 250p. 1997. pap. 55.95 (*1-887759-38-7*, E-33) Am Phys Therapy Assn.

***Normative Political Economy: Subjective Freedom, the Market & the State.** David P. Levine. LC 00-34482. 2000. write for info. (*0-415-23529-4*) Routledge.

Normative Social Action. Ed. by David Sciulli. (Comparative Social Research Ser.: Supplement 2). 236p. 1997. 78.50 (*0-7623-0226-7*) Jai Pr.

Normative Structure of Black Nationalism. G. Matthews. 77p. 1998. pap. text 12.00 (*1-56411-171-7*) Untd Bros & Sis.

Normative Systems. C. E. Alchourron & E. Bulygin. LC 75-170895. (Library of Exact Philosophy: Vol. 5). (Illus.). 1972. 69.95 (*0-387-81019-6*) Spr-Verlag.

Normative Theory in International Relations: A Pragmatic Approach. Molly Cochran. (Cambridge Studies in International Relations: No. 68). 326p. (C). 2000. 59.95 (*0-521-63050-9*) Cambridge U Pr.

Normative Theory in International Relations: A Pragmatic Approach. Molly Cochran. (Cambridge Studies in International Relations: Vol. 68). 326p. (C). 2000. pap. 22.95 (*0-521-63965-4*) Cambridge U Pr.

***Normativity.** Jonathan Dancy. (Ratio Special Issues Ser.). 160p. 2000. pap. 22.95 (*0-631-22041-0*) Blackwell Pubs.

Normativity & Norms: Critical Perspectives on Kelsenian Themes. Ed. by Stanley L. Paulson. 682p. 1999. text 120.00 (*0-19-876315-8*) OUP.

Norms & National Security: Police & Military in Postwar Japan. Peter J. Katzenstein. LC 96-6463. (Studies in Political Economy). 328p. 1996. text 42.50 (*0-8014-3260-X*) Cornell U Pr.

***Norms & Nobility: A Treatise on Education.** David V. Hicks. LC 99-33456. 184p. 1999. pap. 26.50 (*0-7618-1467-1*) U Pr of Amer.

Norms & Nobility: A Treatise on Education. David V. Hicks. 176p. 1990. reprint ed. pap. 22.00 (*0-8476-7660-9*) Rowman.

Norms & the State in China. Ed. by Huang Chun-chieh & Erik J. Zurcher. LC 92-43011. (Sinica Leidensia Ser.: Vol. 28). xxvi, 416p. 1993. 181.00 (*90-04-09665-5*) Brill Academic Pubs.

Norms & Values: Essays on the Work of Virginia Held. Ed. by Joram G. Haber & Mark S. Halfon. LC 98-9197. 304p. 1998. 68.00 (*0-8476-8490-3*); pap. 24.95 (*0-8476-8491-1*) Rowman.

***Norm's Boy: An Amazon Adventure.** Neville George. 232p. 1999. 19.95 (*1-882897-37-4*) Lost Coast.

Norms, Deviance & Social Control: Conceptual Matters. Jack P. Gibbs. LC 80-24957. 204p. reprint ed. pap. 63.30 (*0-608-16301-5*, 202625700049) Bks Demand.

Norms for Priestly Formation, 2 vols. Catholic Church Staff. LC 97-146505. (United States Catholic Conference Publications). 1994. write for info. (*1-55586-619-0*) US Catholic.

Norms for Priestly Training in Ireland. Veritas Publications Staff. 96p. 1989. pap. 35.00 (*0-86217-276-4*, Pub. by Veritas Pubns) St Mut.

Norms for Priests & Their Third Age. National Conference of Catholic Bishops Staff. 6p. (Orig.). 1988. pap. 0.50 (*1-55586-207-1*) US Catholic.

Norms Governing Liturgical Calendars. NCCB, Secretariat of the Bishops' Committee on the. (Liturgy Documentary Ser.: No. 6). 176p. 1984. 6.95 (*1-55586-928-9*) US Catholic.

Norms in Argumentation. Ed. by Robert Maier. (Studies of Argumentation in Pragmatic & Discourse Analysis). 218p. (Orig.). (C). 1989. pap. 67.70 (*90-6765-423-X*) Mouton.

***Norms in Future International Politics: A Conference at UCLA.** (New Ser.: Vol. 21). 30p. 1998. pap. 15.00 (*0-86682-107-4*) Ctr Intl Relations.

Norms in International Relations: The Struggle against Apartheid. Audie Klotz. 1999. pap. text 16.95 (*0-8014-8603-3*) Cornell U Pr.

Norms in International Relations: The Struggle Against Apartheid. Audie J. Klotz. (Studies in Political Economy). (Illus.). 200p. 1996. text 29.95 (*0-8014-3106-9*) Cornell U Pr.

Norms of Faith & Life see Recent Studies in Early Christianity: A Collection of Scholarly Essays

Norms of Language. Renate Bartsch. (Linguistics Library). (Illus.). 348p. (C). 1987. pap. text 29.95 (*0-582-00419-5*, 70403) Longman.

Norms of Language: Theoretical & Practical Aspects. Renate Bartsch. LC 86-27515. (Longman Linguistics Library). (Illus.). 364p. 1987. pap. 112.90 (*0-608-05250-7*, 206578800001) Bks Demand.

Norms of Language Theoretical & Practical Aspects. Renate Bartsch. Ed. by Mark Anderson. (Linguistics Library). 368p. (Orig.). 1988. pap. 18.95 (*0-685-18890-6*) Longman.

***Norms of Nature: Naturalism & the Nature of Functions.** Paul S. Davies. LC 00-55403. (Life & Mind Ser.). 2001. write for info. (*0-262-04187-1*) MIT Pr.

Norms of Rhetorical Culture. Thomas B. Farrell. 1995. pap. 19.00 (*0-300-06502-7*) Yale U Pr.

***Norms on Possibilities: Forcing with Trees & Creatures.** Andrzej Roslanowski & Saharon Shelah. LC 99-27220. (Memoirs of the American Mathematical Society Ser.). 1999. write for info. (*0-8218-1180-0*) Am Math.

Norms, Values, & Society. Ed. by Herlinde Pauer-Studer. (Vienna Circle Institute Yearbook Ser.). 360p. (C). 1994. lib. bdg. 156.00 (*0-7923-3071-4*, Pub. by Kluwer Academic) Kluwer Academic.

NORP Think Factor. Dennis A. Challeen. (Illus.). 216p. 1994. pap. text 24.95 (*0-9641375-0-X*) Staige Prods.

Norplant: Guide Pratique a l'Intention des Programmes de Planification Familiale. 2nd rev. ed. Ed. by Noel McIntosh et al. (FRE., Illus.). 141p. 1993. pap. text 15.00 (*0-929817-05-2*) JHPIEGO.

Norplant Contraceptive Subdermal Implants: Managerial & Technical Guidelines. (CHI, ENG, FRE & SPA.). vi, 134p. 1990. pap. text 14.40 (*0-614-08036-3*, 1930014) World Health.

Norplant Implants Guidelines for Family Planning Service Programs. 2nd rev. ed. Ed. by Noel McIntosh et al. (RUS., Illus.). (Orig.). 1996. pap. 15.00 (*0-929817-02-8*) JHPIEGO.

Norplant Implants Guidlines for Family Planning Service Programs: A Problem-Solving Reference Manual. 2nd ed. Ed. by Noel McIntosh et al. (Illus.). 1995. pap. text 15.00 (*0-929817-09-5*) JHPIEGO.

Norris & Campbell's Anaesthetics, Resuscitation & Intensive Care. 7th ed. Donald Campbell & Alistair A. Spence. (Illus.). 254p. 1990. pap. text 29.95 (*0-443-04067-2*) Church.

Norris & Campbell's Anaesthetics, Resuscitation & Intensive Care. 8th ed. David Campbell & Alastair A. Spence. LC 96-26056. 1998. pap. text 35.95 (*0-443-04886-X*) Church.

Norris from Nebraska. John F. Kennedy. (Illus.). 32p. (Orig.). 1991. pap. text 10.00 (*0-938932-02-0*) U Nebr CFGPS.

Norris Wright Cuney: A Tribune of the Black People, Vol. 6. Cuney & Maud C. Hare. LC 94-19856. (African American Women Writers, 1910-1940 Ser.). 1995. reprint ed. 25.00 (*0-8161-1631-8*, G K Hall & Co) Mac Lib Ref.

Norris Wright Cuney: A Tribute to Black People. Maud C. Hare. Ed. by Henry Louis Gates, Jr. (African American Women Writers 1910-1940 Ser.). 1995. 15.95 (*0-7838-1397-X*, Hall Reference) Macmillan.

Norse America: Tenth Century Onward. W. R. Anderson. LC 97-207482. (Illus.). 220p. 1996. 25.00 (*0-9607070-2-6*) Valhalla Pr.

Norse Building Customs in the Scottish Isles. Aage Roussell. LC 77-87681. reprint ed. 34.50 (*0-404-16477-3*) AMS Pr.

Norse Discoveries & Explorations in America. Edward Reman. LC 76-1871. (Illus.). 201p. 1976. reprint ed. lib. bdg. 38.50 (*0-8371-8745-1*, REND, Greenwood Pr) Greenwood.

Norse Discoveries & Explorations of America. 1991. lib. bdg. 79.97 (*0-8490-4416-2*) Gordon Pr.

Norse Discoveries & Explorations of America. 1992. lib. bdg. 79.95 (*0-8490-5423-0*) Gordon Pr.

Norse Discovery of America, 2 vols., Vol. 2. 2nd ed. Helge Ingstad. (Illus.). 573p. 1986. 31.00 (*82-00-07039-5*) Scandnvan Univ Pr.

Norse Gods & Heroes. Morgan J. Roberts. LC 94-10323. (Myths of the World Ser.). (Illus.). 112p. 1994. 15.98 (*1-56799-090-8*) M Friedman Pub Grp Inc.

Norse Influence on Celtic Scotland. George Henderson. LC 77-87678. reprint ed. 49.50 (*0-404-16469-2*) AMS Pr.

Norse Lands see Traditional Tales from Around the World

Norse Magic. D. J. Conway. LC 90-6204. (Llewellyn's New World Magic Ser.). (Illus.). 240p. (Orig.). 1990. mass mkt. 4.99 (*0-87542-137-7*) Llewellyn Pubns.

Norse-Mythology: And the Modern Human Being. Ernst Uehli. Ed. by James Dewtherer & David Mitchell. Tr. by Rudolf Copple. 170p. pap. 15.00 (*1-888365-13-7*) Assn Waldorf Schls.

Norse Mythology: The Stormy Myths of the Nordic Gods. Arthur Cotterell. 1999. 12.95 (*1-85967-998-6*) Anness Pub.

Norse Mythology, Legends of Gods & Heroes. Peter A. Munch. Tr. by Sigurd B. Hustvedt. LC 74-112002. 1970. reprint ed. 49.50 (*0-404-04538-3*) AMS Pr.

Norse Myths. Ed. by Kevin Crossley-Holland. 276p. 1981. pap. 16.00 (*0-394-74846-8*) Pantheon.

Norse Myths. R. I. Page. (Legendary Past Ser.). (Illus.). 80p. 1991. pap. 12.95 (*0-292-75546-5*) U of Tex Pr.

Norse Myths & Legends. Philip Ardagh. LC 97-29439. (Illus.). (J). 1999. 23.00 (*0-382-39994-3*, Dillon Silver Burdett); pap. write for info. (*0-382-39995-1*, Dillon Silver Burdett) Silver Burdett Pr.

Norse Myths & Legends. Educational Development Corporation Staff & Carolyn B. Mitchell. (Myths & Legends Ser.). (Illus.). 48p. (J). (gr. 6-12). 1987. pap. text 7.95 (*0-7460-0010-3*) EDC.

Norse Myths & Legends. Evans. (Myths & Legends Ser.). (Illus.). 48p. (J). (gr. 6 up). 1999. lib. bdg. 15.95 (*0-88110-249-0*) EDC.

Norse Romance: Haerra Ivan, Vol. 3. Ed. by Henrick Williams et al. Tr. by Karin Palmgren. (Arthurian Archives Ser.). 320p. 1999. 75.00 (*0-85991-560-3*) Boydell & Brewer.

Norse Romance: Knights of the Round Table, Vol. 2. Ed. by Marianne E. Kalinke. (Arthurian Archives Ser.). 344p. 1999. 90.00 (*0-85991-556-5*, DS Brewer) Boydell & Brewer.

Norse Romances: The Tristan Legend, Vol. 1. Ed. by Marianne E. Kalinke. LC 99-21646. (Arthurian Archives Ser.: Vol. 3). 308p. 1999. 90.00 (*0-85991-552-2*, DS Brewer) Boydell & Brewer.

Norse Sagas Translated into English: A Bibliography. Compiled by Donald K. Fry. LC 79-8632. (Studies in the Middle Ages: No. 3). 1980. 32.50 (*0-404-18016-7*) AMS Pr.

Norse Stories. Robert Hull. LC 93-30731. (Tales from Around the World Ser.). (Illus.). 48p. (J). (gr. 4-6). 1993. lib. bdg. 24.26 (*1-56847-131-9*) Raintree Steck-V.

Norse Stories. Ed. by Hamilton W. Mabie. (Illus.). Date not set. 14.95 (*0-7818-0770-0*) Hippocrene Bks.

Norse Tradition: A Beginner's Guide. Pete Jennings. (Beginner's Guide Ser.). (Illus.). 96p. 1998. mass mkt. 11.95 (*0-340-72082-4*, Pub. by Hodder & Stought Ltd) Trafalgar.

Norsk - Engelsk Administrativ Ordbok. Patrick N. Chaffey. (ENG & NOR.). 192p. lib. bdg. 150.00 (*0-7859-3674-2*, 8200077586) Fr & Eur.

Norsk - Islandsk Ordbok. Hrobjartur Einarsson. (ICE & NOR.). 446p. lib. bdg. 300.00 (*0-7859-3671-8*, 8200075842) Fr & Eur.

Norsk - Persisk Ordbok. Mano Amarloui. (NOR & PER.). 784p. 1992. 350.00 (*0-7859-3667-X*, 8200029751) Fr & Eur.

Norsk - Serbokroatisk Ordbok. Brit Bakker et al. (CRO, NOR & SER.). 688p. 1992. lib. bdg. 275.00 (*0-7859-3672-6*, 8200075850) Fr & Eur.

Norsk - Spansk Ordbok. Kare Nilsson & Paasche Nilsson. (NOR & SPA.). 392p. lib. bdg. 150.00 (*0-7859-3673-4*, 8200075869) Fr & Eur.

Norsk - Vietnamesisk Ordbok. Quoc K. Nguyen. (NOR & VIE.). 501p. lib. bdg. 225.00 (*0-7859-3668-8*, 8200067572) Fr & Eur.

Norsk Data Ordbok. Knut Hofstad. (NOR.). 213p. lib. bdg. 125.00 (*0-7859-3665-3*, 8200025578) Fr & Eur.

Norsk-Engelsk Ordbok: Norwegian-English Dictionary. 4th ed. Einar Haugen. (NOR.). 533p. 1995. pap. 24.00 (*82-00-22722-7*) Scandnvan Univ Pr.

Norsk-Engelsk Ordbok Praktisk: Practical Norwegian-English Dictionary. W. Guy & J. Messell. (ENG & NOR.). 324p. 1979. 39.95 (*0-8288-4828-9*, M9467) Fr & Eur.

Norsk for Utlendinger, 6 cass., Set, Vol. 1. Ase-Berit & Rolf Strandskogen. (NOR.). pap. text 125.00 incl. audio (*0-88432-147-9*, AFNW01) Audio-Forum.

Norsk for Utlendinger, Vol. 2. Ase-Berit Strandskogen & Rolf Strandskogen. (NOR.). 95.00 incl. audio Audio-Forum.

Norsk-Fransk Ordbok: Norwegian-French Dictionary. M. Lesoil. (FRE.). 445p. 1978. 39.95 (*0-8288-5258-8*, M9463) Fr & Eur.

Norsk Hostfest: Heritage Comes Alive. Lori Olson & Jim Olson. (Illus.). (Orig.). 1995. pap. 8.00 (*1-56037-078-5*) Am Wrld Geog.

N

An Asterisk (*) at the beginning of an entry indicates that the title is appearing for the first time.

Norsk I Sammenheng. Margaret H. O'Leary & Frankie Shackelford. (C). 1992. text 50.00 (*0-07-056232-6*) McGraw.

Norsk, Nordmenn og Norge. Kathleen Stokker & Odd Haddal. LC 81-50827. 264p. 1981. pap., teacher ed. 17.95 (*0-299-08804-9*); text 29.95 (*0-299-08690-9*); audio 100.00 (*0-299-08809-X*) U of Wis Pr.

Norsk, Nordmenn og Norge. Kathleen Stokker et al. LC 81-50827. 184p. 1981. pap., wbk. ed. 14.95 (*0-299-08774-3*) U of Wis Pr.

Norsk, Nordmenn og Norge: Antologi (Anthology) Kathleen Stokker. LC 92-11696. (Illus.). 68p. (C). 1993. pap., teacher ed. 7.95 (*0-299-13456-3*); pap. text 19.95 (*0-299-13454-7*); lib. bdg. 35.00 (*0-299-13450-4*) U of Wis Pr.

Norsk, Nordmenn og Norge: Workbook for Second Year Anthology (Antologi) Kathleen Stokker. LC 92-11696. (Illus.). 224p. (C). 1993. wbk. ed. 10.00 (*0-299-13455-5*) U of Wis Pr.

Norsk Teknisk Fagordbok: Norwegian-English, English-Norwegian. Havard Hjulstad & Bjarne Norevik. (ENG & NOR.). 747p. 1984. pap. 350.00 (*0-7859-3669-6*, 8200071049) Fr & Eur.

Norsk-Tysk Ordbok: Norwegian-German Dictionary. G. Paulsen. (GER & NOR.). 416p. 1973. 39.95 (*0-8288-6326-1*, M-9466) Fr & Eur.

Norsk Utviklingsbistand. Olav Stokke. 218p. 1975. write for info. (*91-7106-091-X*, Pub. by Nordic Africa) Transaction Pubs.

Norska: A Viking Woman's Journey. Doris Meek & Mike MacCarthy. 260p. (Orig.). 1995. pap. 14.50 (*1-885516-01-0*) SD Writs Mnthly.

Norstad Cold War Supreme Command. Jordon. LC 99-37877. 1999. text 45.00 (*0-312-22670-5*) St Martin.

Norstedt Dictionary Italian to Swedish. (ITA & SWE.). 850p. 1994. 125.00 (*0-320-00650-6*) Fr & Eur.

Norstedt Italian/Swedish/Italian Dictionary. (ITA & SWE.). 1568p. 1994. 225.00 (*0-320-00652-2*) Fr & Eur.

Norstedts Dataordbok. (NOR.). 512p. 1985. 125.00 (*0-8288-1362-0*, F 11080) Fr & Eur.

Norstrilia. rev. ed. Cordwainer Smith. Ed. by James A. Mann. LC 94-68979. (Illus.). xiv, 248p. 1995. 22.00 (*0-915368-61-7*, NESFA Pr) New Eng SF Assoc.

Norte see Norther

Norte: The Cuisine of Northern Mexico. rev. ed. James W. Peyton. LC 95-14930. (Cookbook Ser.). (Illus.). 256p. 1995. pap. 22.50 (*1-878610-58-9*) Red Crane Bks.

***Nortel Networks: How Innovation & Vision Created a Network Giant.** Larry Macdonald. 2000. 27.95 (*0-471-64542-7*) Wiley.

Nortel Networks: The Complete Reference. James Knapp. 1295p. 1999. pap. 59.99 (*0-07-212027-4*) Osborne-McGraw.

***Nortel Networks Layer 3 Switching.** Regis J. Bates. (Networking Ser.). 352p. 2000. pap. text. write for info. (*0-07-212426-1*) Osborne-McGraw.

North. David Clark. (Battlefield Walks Ser.). (Illus.). 192p. 1996. pap. 17.95 (*0-7509-0259-0*, Pub. by Sutton Pub Ltd) Intl Pubs Mktg.

North. Seamus Heaney. LC 85-12863. 73p. (C). 1985. pap. 13.95 (*0-571-10813-X*) Faber & Faber.

North. Slade. 1996. 25.00 (*0-7869-0391-0*) TSR Inc.

North. C. P. Taylor. (Methuen New Theatrescripts Ser.). 285p. (Orig.). (C). 1988. pap. write for info. (*0-413-16470-5*, A0193, Methuen Drama) Methn.

North. Michael S. Whittington. (Collected Research Studies of the Royal Commission on the Economic Union & Development Prospects for Canada: No. 72). 208p. 1985. pap. text 16.95 (*0-8020-7320-4*) U of Toronto Pr.

North. Louis-Ferdinand Celine. Tr. by Ralph Manheim from FRE. LC 96-15668. 454p. 1996. reprint ed. pap. 13.95 (*1-56478-142-9*) Dalkey Arch.

North: Adventures in the Frozen Wild. Nicolas Vanier. Tr. by Willard Wood from FRE. LC 97-22000. (Illus.). 340p. 1997. 49.50 (*0-8109-1391-7*, Pub. by Abrams) Time Warner.

North: From down to Donegal. Ian Hill & Christopher Hill. LC 95-204021. (Illus.). 128p. 1996. 45.00 (*0-85640-546-9*, Pub. by Blackstaff Pr) Dufour.

North: North, Act of Union, Mary's Men, Soldiers. Seamus Finnegan. 160p. (Orig.). 1987. pap. 11.95 (*0-7145-2870-6*) M Boyars Pubs.

North Across the River: A Civil War Trail of Tears. Ruth B. Cook. LC 97-49449. 224p. 1999. 24.95 (*1-57587-070-3*) Crane Hill AL.

***North Across the River: A Civil War Trail of Tears.** Ruth Beaumont Cook. (Illus.). 224p. 2000. pap. 14.95 (*1-57587-166-1*, Pub. by Crane Hill AL) Blair.

North Africa: Development & Reform in a Changing Global Economy. Dirk Vandewalle. 250p. 1996. text 55.00 (*0-312-15853-X*) St Martin.

North Africa: Morocco. Christine Ronan. 1997. pap. text 9.95 (*0-673-36358-9*) Addson-Wesley Educ.

***North Africa: Morocco, Algeria & Tunisia.** Hans Van Rijn. 230p. 1999. 125.00 (*0-85288-412-5*, Pub. by Laurie Norie & Wilson Ltd) St Mut.

North Africa: Regional Tensions & Strategic Concerns. Richard B. Parker. LC 87-6954. 226p. 1987. 57.95 (*0-275-92773-3*, C2773, Praeger Pubs); pap. 16.95 (*0-275-92774-1*, B2774, Praeger Pubs) Greenwood.

North Africa: Strait of Gibraltar to Tunisia. R. C. C. Pilotage Foundation Staff. (Illus.). 198p. (C). 1995. 125.00 (*0-85288-155-X*, Pub. by Laurie Norie & Wilson Ltd) St Mut.

North Africa: Strait of Gibraltar to Tunisia. Compiled by Hans Van Rijn. (C). 1991. 200.00 (*0-7855-5948-5*, Pub. by Laurie Norie & Wilson Ltd) St Mut.

North Africa & the Desert. G. E. Woodberry. 384p. 1990. reprint ed. 125.00 (*1-85077-078-6*, Pub. by Darf Pubs Ltd) St Mut.

North Africa in Transition: State, Society, & Economic Transformation in the 1990's. Yahia H. Zoubir. LC 98-39084. 1999. 59.95 (*0-8130-1655-X*) U Press Fla.

North Africa Oil & Gas. IEA Staff. LC 97-185065. 174p. (Orig.). 1997. pap. 57.00 (*92-64-15330-6*, 61-96-33-1, Pub. by Org for Econ) OECD.

North African. 2nd rev. ed. (Handbooks of the World Ser.). (Illus.). 864p. 1994. 24.95 (*0-8442-8978-7*, Passprt Bks) NTC Contemp Pub Co.

North African Landings, 1942, a Strategic Decision. Keith Sainsbury. LC 79-52242. (Politics & Strategy of the Second World War Ser.). (Illus.). 215p. 1979. 21.50 (*0-87413-158-8*) U Delaware Pr.

North African Cooking. Hilaire Walden. 128p. 1995. 12.98 (*0-7858-0267-3*) Bk Sales Inc.

North African Handbook, 1994. Anne Mclachlan. 800p. 1994. pap. 24.95 (*0-8442-9978-2*, Passprt Bks) NTC Contemp Pub Co.

North African Jewry in the Twentieth Century: The Jews of Morocco, Tunisia, & Algeria. Michael M. Laskier. LC 93-28377. (C). 1994. text 65.00 (*0-8147-5072-9*) NYU Pr.

North African Jewry in the Twentieth Century: The Jews of Morocco, Tunisia, & Algeria. Michael M. Laskier. 1997. pap. text 20.00 (*0-8147-5129-6*) NYU Pr.

North African Odyssey: Adventures in the Mediterranean Theater of War. Norris H. Perkins. (Illus.). 134p. (Orig.). 1995. pap. 14.95 (*0-9638442-1-0*) Four Mntn Prods.

North African Provinces from Diocletian to the Vandal Conquest. Brian H. Warmington. LC 78-135615. (Illus.). 126p. 1971. reprint ed. lib. bdg. 49.50 (*0-8371-5202-X*, WAP&, Greenwood Pr) Greenwood.

North African Stones Speak. Paul L. MacKendrick. LC 79-18534. (Illus.). 456p. reprint ed. pap. 141.40 (*0-7837-6860-5*, 204668900003) Bks Demand.

North African Textiles. J. Hudson & Christopher Spring. 1995. pap. 27.00 (*0-7141-2523-7*, Pub. by Textile Inst) St Mut.

North African Textiles. Christopher Spring & Julie Hudson. (Illus.). 144p. 1996. pap. 34.95 (*1-56098-666-2*) Smithsonian.

North African Villages: Morocco, Algeria, & Tunisia. Norman F. Carver, Jr. 200p. 1989. 34.95 (*0-932076-08-4*); pap. 27.95 (*0-932076-09-2*) Documan.

North Against South: The American Illiad, 1848-1877. Ludwell H. Johnson, III. (American Republic Ser.). 301p. (C). 1995. 29.95 (*0-9623842-7-5*) Fndtn Amer Ed.

North Alaska Chronicle: Notes from the End of Time. John M. Campbell. LC 97-44708. (Illus.). 160p. 1998. 45.00 (*0-89013-353-0*); pap. 29.95 (*0-89013-354-9*) Museum NM Pr.

North Alaskan Eskimo: A Study in Ecology & Society. Robert F. Spencer. (Bureau of American Ethnology Bulletins Ser.). 490p. 1995. lib. bdg. 109.00 (*0-7812-4171-5*) Rprt Serv.

North Amerian Distributed Generation System Markets. Ed. by Frost & Sullivan Staff. 331p. 1991. spiral bd. 2950.00 (*0-7889-0673-9*, 5578-14) Frost & Sullivan.

***North America.** Bill Asikinak. (Exploration Into... Ser.). (Illus.). (J). 2000. 17.95 (*0-7910-6025-X*) Chelsea Hse.

***North America.** Allan Fowler. LC 00-27560. (Rookie Read-About Geography Ser.). (Illus.). (J). 2001. write for info. (*0-516-21671-6*) Childrens.

North America. Julia Jasmine. (Continents Ser.). 80p. (J). 1997. pap. 9.95 (*1-55734-693-3*) Tchr Create Mat.

North America. Marilyn Messik. (Welcome Directory of Selected Hotels & I Ser.). 1998. pap. text 16.95 (*0-9522508-7-X*) US Welcome.

***North America.** Jo Ellen Moore. Ed. by Marilyn Evans. (Geography Units Ser.: Vol. 1). (Illus.). 80p. (J). (gr. 3-6). 1999. pap. 12.95 (*1-55799-710-1*, 763) Evan-Moor Edu Pubs.

North America. David Petersen. LC 98-24337. (True Bks.). 47 p. (J). 1998. 21.00 (*0-516-20768-7*) Childrens.

North America. David Petersen. (True Bks.). (Illus.). 48p. (J). (gr. 3-5). 1999. pap. text 6.95 (*0-516-26437-0*) Childrens.

North America. Fran Sammis. LC 98-11755. (Mapping Our World Ser.). (J). 1998. lib. bdg. 27.07 (*0-7614-0368-X*, Benchmark NY) Marshall Cavendish.

North America. Cass R. Sandak. LC 97-5819. (Continents Ser.). 48p. (J). 1998. lib. bdg. 25.69 (*0-8172-4780-7*) Raintree Steck-V.

North America. April Pulley Sayre. LC 98-27266. (Seven Continents Ser.). (Illus.). (J). (gr. 5-8). 1998. lib. bdg. 23.40 (*0-7613-3226-X*) TFC Bks NY.

North America, 2 vols. Ed. by Bruce G. Trigger & Wilcomb E. Washburn. Incl. Pt. 1. North America., **3 vols.** LC 96-37349. (Illus.). 583p. (C). 1996. text 54.95 (*0-521-57392-0*); Pt. 2. North America., **3 vols.** LC 96-37349. (Illus.). 519p. (C). 1996. text 54.95 (*0-521-57393-9*); LC 96-37349. (Cambridge History of the Native Peoples of the Americas Ser.). (Illus.). 1349p. 1996. 110.00 (*0-521-34440-9*) Cambridge U Pr.

North America. Anthony Trollope. Ed. by Donald Smalley & Bradford A. Booth. 618p. 1986. pap. 13.95 (*0-306-80278-3*) Da Capo.

North America. Mary Tull & Sharon Franklin. LC 98-49507. (Artisans Around the World Ser.). 48p. (J). 1999. lib. bdg. 25.69 (*0-7398-0117-1*) Raintree Steck-V.

North America. 5th ed. Stephen S. Birdsall et al. LC 98-51000. (Illus.). 464p. 1999. text 87.95 (*0-471-00998-9*) Wiley.

North America see North America

North America: A Geographical Mosaic. Ed. by Frederick W. Boal & Stephen Royle. (Illus.). 352p. 2000. text 75.00 (*0-340-69262-6*) OUP.

North America: A Geography of the United States & Canada. 9th ed. John H. Paterson. (Illus.). 544p. (C). 1994. text 64.95 (*0-19-508058-0*) OUP.

North America: A Human Geography. Paul Guinness & Michael Bradshaw. LC 84-28434. (Illus.). 350p. 1985. pap. 44.00 (*0-389-20557-5*, N8119) B&N Imports.

North America: Continent of Conjecture, An Archetype Edition. Robert McAlmon. (Illus.). 44p. (Orig.). (C). 1983. reprint ed. pap. 10.00 (*0-932139-02-7*) Dark Child Pr.

North America: Environment Society. Ed. by Frederick W. Boal & Stephen Royle. (Illus.). 352p. 2000. pap. 24.95 (*0-340-69261-8*) OUP.

North America: The Historical Geography of a Changing Continent. Ed. by Robert D. Mitchell & Paul A. Groves. (Illus.). 512p. (C). 1987. pap. 34.95 (*0-8476-7549-1*, R7549) Rowman.

North America: The Historical Geography of a Changing Continent. Ed. by Robert D. Mitchell & Paul A. Groves. (Illus.). 480p. (C). 1987. 90.00 (*0-8476-7347-2*, R7347) Rowman.

North America - Classic Comparative Perspectives see Aboriginal Sign Languages of the Americas & Australia

North America & the Beginnings of European Colonization. Karen O. Kupperman. Ed. by Carla R. Phillips & David J. Weber. (Essays on the Columbian Encounter Ser.). 42p. (Orig.). (C). 1992. pap. 7.00 (*0-87229-068-9*) Am Hist Assn.

***North America & the Caribbean.** Martyn Bramwell. LC 98-48812. (The World in Maps Ser.). (Illus.). 56p. (YA). (gr. 4-7). 2000. 23.93 (*0-8225-2911-4*, Lerner Publctns) Lerner Pub.

North America Arctic Animals. Colleyan Mastin. (North American Nature Ser.). (Illus.). 32p. (J). (gr. 1 up). 1997. pap. 9.95 (*1-895910-23-4*) Grasshopper Bks.

North America Automotive Electrical System Component Aftermarkets. Ed. by Frost & Sullivan Staff. 370p. 1995. spiral bd. 2395.00 (*0-7889-0318-7*, 5171-18) Frost & Sullivan.

North America Country Studies. Randy L. Womack. (Illus.). 96p. (gr. 4 up). 1991. student ed. 10.95 (*1-56500-022-6*) Gldn Educ.

North America, 1837-1914 see British Documents on Foreign Affairs: Series C: North America

North America in Colonial Times, 4 vols. Scribner Staff. LC 98-29862. 910p. (J). 1998. 299.00 (*0-684-80538-3*) Mac Lib Ref.

North America in Colonial Times, Vol. 1. Scribner Staff. LC 98-29862. (J). 1998. 90.00 (*0-684-80534-0*) Mac Lib Ref.

North America in Colonial Times, Vol. 2. Scribner Staff. LC 98-29862. (J). 1998. 90.00 (*0-684-80535-9*) Mac Lib Ref.

North America in Colonial Times, Vol. 3. Scribner Staff. LC 98-29862. (J). 1998. 90.00 (*0-684-80536-7*) Mac Lib Ref.

North America in Colonial Times, Vol. 4. Scribner Staff. LC 98-29862. (J). 1998. 90.00 (*0-684-80537-5*) Mac Lib Ref.

North America Is the Lord's. James W. Lowry. (Christian Day School Ser.). (J). (gr. 5). 1980. 18.95 (*0-87813-916-8*) Christian Light.

North America, 1940-1945 see British Documents on Foreign Affairs: Series C: North America

North America, 1919-1939 see British Documents on Foreign Affairs: Series C: North America

North America Sales Automation Software Markets. Ed. by Frost & Sullivan Staff. 417p. 1997. spiral bd. 2450.00 (*0-7889-0702-6*, 5436-70) Frost & Sullivan.

North America Today: An Atlas of Reproducible Pages. (Illus.). 210p. 1995. ring bd. 49.95 (*0-930141-58-X*) World Eagle.

North America Wild Animals, 4 vols. Colleyan Mastin. (North American Nature Ser.). (Illus.). 32p. (J). (gr. 1 up). 1997. pap. 9.95 (*1-895910-21-8*) Grasshopper Bks.

North American Acalephae. Alexander Agassiz. (Works of Alexander Agassiz). 1989. reprint ed. lib. bdg. 79.00 (*0-7812-1581-1*) Rprt Serv.

North American Aftermarket for Specialty Performance Undercarriage Components. Frost & Sullivan. 341p. 1996. spiral bd. 1895.00 (*0-7889-0622-4*, 5559-18) Frost & Sullivan.

North American Aftermarket for Specialty Performance Underhood Components. Frost & Sullivan Staff. 450p. 1996. spiral bd. 1895.00 (*0-7889-0553-8*, 5298-18) Frost & Sullivan.

North American Air Pollution Control Equipment: Deadline 1995 - Compliance with CAAA Phase I. Market Intelligence Staff. 325p. (Orig.). 1992. 1695.00 (*1-56753-336-1*) Frost & Sullivan.

North American Air Pollution Control Equipment Markets. Market Intelligence Staff. 455p. 1994. spiral bd. 2395.00 (*0-7889-0149-4*, 5194-15) Frost & Sullivan.

North American Aircraft & Aerospace Museum Guide. 8th ed. Ed. by Ronald B. Stone. (Illus.). 246p. 1998. pap. 16.95 (*1-877687-05-7*) Bruce Beeson.

North American Aircraft, 1934-1998, Vol. 1. Norman Avery. LC 98-60468. (American Aircraft Manufacturers Ser.: No. 4). (Illus.). 200p. 1998. pap. 35.95 (*0-913322-05-9*) Jonathan T Pub.

North American Aircraft, 1934-1999, Vol. 2. Kevin Thompson. (American Aircraft Manufacturers Ser.: No. 5). (Illus.). 176p. 1999. pap. 35.95 (*0-913322-06-7*) Jonathan T Pub.

North American Airline Handbook. Ed. by Tom Norwood et al. (Illus.). 256p. (Orig.). 1997. pap. 19.95 (*0-9653993-1-1*) Airways Intnl.

***North American Airlines Handbook.** 2nd rev. ed. Tom Norwood & John Wegg. (Illus.). 248p. 1999. pap. 19.95 (*0-9653993-5-4*, A-19) Airways Intnl.

North American & Comparative Federalism: Essays for the 1990s. Berkeley Seminar on Federalism (4th, 1992) Staff. Ed. by Harry N. Scheiber. LC 91-47941. 110p. reprint ed. pap. 34.10 (*0-608-20128-6*, 207140000011) Bks Demand.

North American Animal Discovery Library, 6 bks., Set. Lynn M. Stone. (Illus.). 144p. (J). (gr. k-5). 1990. lib. bdg. 71.64 (*0-86593-040-6*); lib. bdg. 53.70 (*0-685-36336-8*) Rourke Corp.

North American Animals in Origami. John Montroll. LC 94-96743. (Illus.). 120p. (Orig.). 1995. pap. text 9.95 (*1-877656-10-0*) Antroll Pub.

North American Animals in Origami. John Montroll. LC 94-49013. 128p. (Orig.). 1995. pap. 9.95 (*0-486-28667-3*) Dover.

North American Animals Punch Out. Jan Sovak. (J). (ps-3). 1998. pap. 3.95 (*0-486-29652-0*) Dover.

North American Apples: Varieties, Rootstocks, Outlook. R. F. Carlson et al. (Illus.). 197p. 1970. text 15.00 (*0-87013-157-5*) Mich St U Pr.

North American Art since 1900. C. M. Turner. LC 97-143880. (International Encyclopedia of Art Ser.). (Illus.). 64p. (J). (gr. 5-12). 1996. 19.95 (*0-8160-3328-5*) Facts on File.

North American Art to Nineteen Hundred. C. M. Turner. Ed. by Arlene Pancza-Graham. LC 97-165195. (International Encyclopedia of Art Ser.). (Illus.). 64p. (J). (gr. 5-12). 1997. 19.95 (*0-8160-3332-3*) Facts on File.

North American Auction Markets, 1999. Ed. by Barbara O. Stephenson. Date not set. 35.00 (*0-931036-70-4*) Gordon s Art.

North American Auto Industry under NAFTA. Sidney Weintraub & Christoper Sands. LC 98-42162. (Significant Issues Ser.). 263p. 1998. pap. 24.95 (*0-89206-337-8*) CSIS.

North American Auto Unions in Crisis: Lean Production As Contested Terrain. Ed. by William C. Green & Ernest J. Yanarella. LC 95-17312. (SUNY Series in the Sociology of Work). 260p. (C). 1996. text 59.50 (*0-7914-2823-0*); pap. text 19.95 (*0-7914-2824-9*) State U NY Pr.

North American Automotive Accessory Aftermarket. Frost & Sullivan Staff. 352p. 1996. spiral bd. 2495.00 (*0-7889-0549-X*, 5365-18) Frost & Sullivan.

North American Automotive Electronic Control Module Markets. Ed. by Frost & Sullivan Staff. 288p. 1997. spiral bd. 3250.00 (*0-7889-0719-0*, 5562-18) Frost & Sullivan.

North American Automotive OEM Engine & Engine-Related Component Markets: For Overall Industry Health: Integrate or Subdivide? 434p. 1996. spiral bd. 2495.00 (*0-7889-0351-9*, 5361-18) Frost & Sullivan.

North American Automotive OEM Seating, Lighting & Trim Components Markets: Focus on Vehicle Safety & Appearance. Frost & Sullivan Staff. 438p. 1996. spiral bd. 2495.00 (*0-7889-0507-4*, 5363-18) Frost & Sullivan.

North American Automotive Sensor Markets. Frost & Sullivan Staff. 383p. 1996. spiral bd. 2495.00 (*0-7889-0539-2*, 5511-18) Frost & Sullivan.

North American Automotive Sensor Markets: Legislation Guarantees Growth, New Technologies Guarantee Battle Royale. Market Intelligence Staff. 342p. 1992. 1895.00 (*1-56753-394-9*) Frost & Sullivan.

North American B-25 Mitchell, Vol. 12. Frederick Johnsen. (Warbird Tech Ser.). 1997. pap. 16.95 (*0-933424-77-9*) Specialty Pr.

North American Bed & Breakfast Directory. Wakeman & Costine Staff. (Illus.). 48p. 1999. pap. 9.95 (*0-9670672-0-0*, 001999) Wakeman & Costine Inc.

North American Big-Game Animals. Byron W. Dalrymple. 1985. 29.95 (*0-943822-56-4*) Times Mir Mag Bk Div.

North American Biotic Communities: Book & Map Set. David E. Brown et al. 1998. pap. 34.95 (*0-87480-568-6*) U of Utah Pr.

North American Bird Folknames & Names: Comprehensive Listing with Detailed Etymology. James K. Sayre. LC 95-94257. 291p. (Orig.). 1996. pap. 24.95 (*0-9645039-0-5*) Bottlebrush Pr.

North American Boletes: A Color Guide to the Fleshy Pored Mushrooms. Alan E. Bessette et al. LC 99-21065. 1999. 95.00 (*0-8156-0588-9*) Syracuse U Pr.

North American Bows, Arrows & Quivers. Otis T. Mason. (Illus.). 216p. 31.95 (*0-8488-0037-0*, J M C & Co) Amereon Ltd.

North American Buffalo: Critical Study of the Species in Its Wild State. 2nd ed. Frank G. Roe. LC 79-18945. 1010p. reprint ed. pap. 200.00 (*0-608-12870-8*, 202366300033) Bks Demand.

North American Building Control System Markets: Digital Technologies Improves Ease-of-Use. Frost & Sullivan Staff. 413p. 1996. spiral bd. 2195.00 (*0-7889-0396-9*, 5357-15) Frost & Sullivan.

North American Cabin Crew Insignia. Roy Thompson & Bob Feld. (Illus.). 85p. (Orig.). 1990. pap. 10.00 (*1-878973-00-2*) Hse History.

***North American Campground Directory: Woodall's 2000 Campground Directory.** 2076p. 1999. pap. text 21.95 (*0-7627-0582-5*) Globe Pequot.

***North American Campground Directory 2001.** Woodalls Publishing Staff. (Illus.). 2000. pap. 21.95 (*0-7627-0857-3*) Globe Pequot.

***North American Canoe Country: The Classic Guide to Canoe Technique.** Calvin Rutstrum. (Fesler-Lampert Minnesota Heritage Bks.). (Illus.). 2000. pap. write for info. (*0-8166-3660-5*) U of Minn Pr.

North American Cattle-Ranching Frontiers: Origins, Diffusion & Differentiation. Terry G. Jordan. LC 92-36428. (Histories of the American Frontier Ser.). (Illus.). 450p. 1993. pap. 24.95 (*0-8263-1422-8*) U of NM Pr.

N

An Asterisk (*) at the beginning of an entry indicates that the title is appearing for the first time.

North American Cattle-Ranching Frontiers: Origins, Diffusion, & Differentiation. Terry G. Jordan. LC 92-36428. (Histories of the American Frontier Ser.). (Illus.). 451p. 1993. reprint ed. pap. 139.90 (*0-608-07288-5*, 206751600009) Bks Demand.

North American Cities & the Global Economy: Challenges & Opportunities. Ed. by Peter K. Kresl & Gary Gappert. (Urban Affairs Annual Review Ser.: Vol. 44). 272p. (C). 1995. 62.00 (*0-8039-7094-3*); pap. 26.00 (*0-8039-7095-1*) Sage.

North American City. 5th ed. Maurice Yeates. LC 97-2378. 352p. (C). 1997. 83.00 (*0-321-01364-6*) Addson-Wesley Educ.

*__North American Clone Brews: Homebrew Recipes for Your Favorite American & Canadian Beers.__ Scott R. Russell. LC 00-26599. (Illus.). 192p. 2000. pap. 14.95 (*1-58017-246-6*) Storey Bks.

*__North American Club & Course Index.__ Peter Georgiady. 224p. 1999. pap. 25.00 (*1-886752-12-5*) Airlie Hall Pr.

North American Club Makers. Peter Georgiady. 256p. (Orig.). 1998. pap. 50.00 (*1-886752-08-7*) Airlie Hall Pr.

*__North American Coins & Prices: A Guide to U. S., Canadian & Mexican Coins 2001.__ 10th rev. ed. David C. Harper. LC 91-76402. (Illus.). 560p. 2000. pap. 17.95 (*0-87341-928-6*, NA10) Krause Pubns.

North American Combustion Handbook Vol. I: Combustion, Fuels, Stoichiometry, Heat Transfer, Fluid Flow. 3rd ed. Richard J. Reed. LC 86-11635. 332p. 1986. 55.00 (*0-9601596-2-2*) North Am Mfg Co.

North American Combustion Handbook Vol. II: A Basic Reference on the Art & Science of Industrial Heating. 3rd unabridged ed. Richard J. Reed et al. (Illus.). 456p. 1997. 55.00 (*0-9601596-3-0*) North Am Mfg Co.

North American Conference on Insurance Taxation Proceedings Book, 1993. Ed. by Bernard B. Goodman. 247p. 1993. ring bd. 125.00 (*1-56423-031-7*) Ntl Ctr Tax Ed.

North American Contributions to the History of Linguistics. Ed. by Francis P. Dinneen & E. F. K. Koerner. (Studies in the History of the Language Sciences: No. 58). xii, 238p. 1990. 59.00 (*1-55619-353-X*) J Benjamins Pubng Co.

North American Corporate Design Review: The Annual of Corporate Design Excellence. 160p. 1994. 39.99 (*1-56496-135-4*) Rockport Pubs.

*__North American Cranes.__ Lesley A. Dutemple. LC 98-4519. 48p. (J). (gr. 2-5). 1999. 22.60 (*1-57505-302-0*, Carolrhoda) Lerner Pub.

North American Datum of 1982. Ed. by Herbert W. Stoughton. 48p. 1983. 13.00 (*0-614-06113-X*, S281) Am Congrs Survey.

North American Datum of 1983: A Collection of Papers Describing the Planning & Implementation of the Readjustment of the North American Horizontal Network. 48p. 1983. 6.40 (*0-318-42978-0*, S281) Am Congrs Survey.

North American Desert Life Coloring Book. Ruth Soffer. (Illus.). (J). pap. 2.95 (*0-486-28234-1*) Dover.

North American Deserts. Edmund C. Jaeger. (Illus.). x, 308p. 1957. 24.50 (*0-8047-0498-8*) Stanford U Pr.

North American Dictionary of the French Language. Louis-Alexandre Belisle. (FRE.). 1979. 125.00 (*0-8288-7286-4*, M8528) Fr & Eur.

North American Ducks, Geese & Swans. Soffer. 1998. pap. 2.95 (*0-486-29165-0*) Dover.

North American Dye Plants. rev. ed. Anne Bliss. (Illus.). 288p. 1994. reprint ed. pap. 8.95 (*0-934026-89-0*) Interweave.

North American Economic Integration: Monetary & Exchange Rate Aspects. Sylvia Maxfield. (Pew Case Studies in International Affairs). 50p. (C). 1995. pap. text 3.50 (*1-56927-212-3*, GU Schl Foreign) Geo U Inst Dplmcy.

North American Economic Integration: Theory & Practice. Norris C. Clement et al. LC 99-22084. 346p. 1999. 95.00 (*1-84064-102-9*) E Elgar.

*__North American Economic Integration: Theory & Practice.__ Norris C. Clement et al. 360p. 2000. text 30.00 (*1-84064-412-5*) E Elgar.

North American Elders: United States & Canadian Perspectives, 8. Ed. by Eloise Rathbone-McCuan & Betty Havens. LC 87-15048. (Contributions to the Study of Aging Ser.: No. 8). 312p. 1988. 65.00 (*0-313-25484-2*, REL/, Greenwood Pr) Greenwood.

North American Emergency Response Guidebook, 1996. (Illus.). 354p. 1996. per. 9.00 (*0-16-048562-2*, 050-000-00561-5) USGPO.

North American Endangered & Protected Species. Lusch & Wehinger. Ed. by Mark Flint. LC 94-77816. (Illus.). 180p. (C). 1995. 500.00 (*1-885743-00-9*) Internat Wildlife.

North American Endangered Species, 4 vols. Colleyan Mastin. (North American Nature Ser.). (Illus.). 32p. (J). (gr. 1 up). 1997. pap. 9.95 (*1-895910-27-7*) Grasshopper Bks.

North American Energy Measurement & Verification Protocol. Steven R. Schiller et al. (Illus.). 98p. (Orig.). 1997. pap. text 30.00 (*0-7881-4172-4*) DIANE Pub.

North American Engine Parts Aftermarket. 373p. 1996. spiral bd. 2495.00 (*0-7889-0567-8*, 5366-18) Frost & Sullivan.

North American Ergonomic Resources Guide: 1995-96 Edition. Ed. by Michael Gauf. 110p. (Orig.). 1995. pap. 48.00 (*0-9642184-1-0*) CTD News.

North American Exploration Vol. 1: A New World Disclosed. Ed. by John L. Allen. LC 96-33025. (Illus.). xvii, 540p. 1997. text 85.00 (*0-8032-1015-9*) U of Nebr Pr.

North American Exploration Vol. 2: A Continent Defined. Ed. by John L. Allen. LC 96-33025. (Illus.). ix, 474p. 1997. text 85.00 (*0-8032-1023-X*) U of Nebr Pr.

North American Exploration Vol. 3: A Continent Comprehended. Ed. by John L. Allen. LC 96-33025. (Illus.). xiii, 656p. 1997. text 85.00 (*0-8032-1043-4*) U of Nebr Pr.

*__North American F-86 Sabre.__ Duncan Curtis. (Illus.). 200p. 2000. 54.95 (*1-86126-358-9*, 130700AE, Pub. by Cro1wood) Motorbooks Intl.

North American F-86 SabreJet Day Fighters. David W. Menard. (Warbird Tech Ser.: Vol. 3). (Illus.). 100p. (Orig.). 1996. pap. 16.95 (*0-933424-66-3*) Specialty Pr.

*__North American F-86D/K/L Sabre Dog Pt. 1: Design/Structures/Testing.__ Ray Wagner. Ed. by Steve Ginter. (Air Force Legends Ser.: No. 202). (Illus.). 96p. 1999. pap. 17.95 (*0-942612-99-X*, NFAF202) Naval Fighters.

North American Falconry & Hunting Hawks. 5th ed. Ed. by Frank L. Beebe & Harold M. Webster. (Illus.). 490p. 1995. 40.00 (*0-685-66290-X*); 55.00 (*0-912510-01-3*) North Am Fal Hunt.

North American Fish Cookery. A. J. McClane. 1995. 27.95 (*0-8050-1065-3*) H Holt & Co.

North American FJ-4-4B Fury. Steve Ginter. (Naval Fighters Ser.: No. 25). (Illus.). 106p. (Orig.). 1994. pap. text 17.95 (*0-942612-25-6*) Naval Fighters.

North American FJ-1 Fury. Steven J. Ginter & Ron Picciani. (Naval Fighters Ser.: No. 7). (Illus.). 1983. pap. 7.95 (*0-942612-07-8*) Naval Fighters.

North American Fly Fishing. Bob Newman. LC 98-10432. (Illus.). 224p. 1998. pap. 15.95 (*0-89732-240-1*) Menasha Ridge.

North American Forest & Conservation History: A Bibliography. Ronald J. Fahl. vii, 408p. 1977. 25.00 (*0-89030-235-9*) Duke.

North American Forest & Conservation History: A Bibliography. Ronald J. Fahl. 408p. 1977. 31.95 (*0-87436-235-0*) Forest Hist Soc.

North American Forests: The Geography, Ecology & Silviculture. Laurence C. Walker. LC 98-3924. 1998. lib. bdg. 69.95 (*1-57444-176-0*, SL1760) St Lucie Pr.

North American Free Trade: Assessing the Impact. Ed. by Nora Lustig et al. 288p. (C). 1992. 42.95 (*0-8157-5316-0*); pap. 18.95 (*0-8157-5315-2*) Brookings.

North American Free Trade: Issues & Recommendations. Gary C. Hufbauer & Jeffrey J. Schott. LC 92-8206. (Illus.). 369p. (C). 1992. pap. 25.00 (*0-88132-120-6*) Inst Intl Eco.

North American Free Trade Agreement, 2 vols. 1994. lib. bdg. 600.00 (*0-8490-5694-2*) Gordon Pr.

North American Free Trade Agreement. Krosrow Ffatemi & Dominick Salvatore. LC 94-17295. (Series in International Security & Arms Control: No. 1). (Illus.). 366p. 1994. text 72.50 (*0-08-042404-X*, Pergamon Pr) Elsevier.

North American Free Trade Agreement, Vol. 2. (Illus.). 400p. (C). 1994. pap. text 65.00 (*0-7881-0246-X*) DIANE Pub.

North American Free Trade Agreement: A Guide to Customs Procedures. (Illus.). 44p. (C). 1994. pap. text 25.00 (*0-7881-0244-3*) DIANE Pub.

North American Free Trade Agreement: A Guide to Customs Procedures. 1994. lib. bdg. 256.75 (*0-8490-5815-5*) Gordon Pr.

North American Free Trade Agreement: A New Frontier in International Trade & Investment of the Americas. LC 94-207250. 442p. 1994. pap. 85.00 (*0-89707-977-9*, 521-0092, ABA Intl Law) Amer Bar Assn.

North American Free Trade Agreement: Background, Legislative Process, & Provisions for Agricultural Trade. C. Parr Rosson, III et al. (Illus.). 67p. (Orig.). (C). 1994. pap. text 20.00 (*0-7881-0309-1*) DIANE Pub.

North American Free Trade Agreement: Canada - U. S. A. - Mexico. George W. Grayson. Ed. by Nancy L. Hoepli. LC 93-70279. (Headline Ser.: No. 299). (Illus.). 80p. (Orig.). 1993. pap. 5.95 (*0-87124-151-X*) Foreign Policy.

North American Free Trade Agreement: Canada Schedule of Tariff Rate Reductions. (Illus.). 350p. (Orig.). (C). 1994. pap. text 75.00 (*0-7881-0248-6*) DIANE Pub.

North American Free Trade Agreement: Labor, Industry, & Government Perspectives. Ed. by Mario F. Bognanno & Kathryn J. Ready. LC 93-19113. 272p. 1993. 69.50 (*0-89930-849-X*, Q849, Quorum Bks); pap. 27.95 (*0-275-94675-4*, B4675, Praeger Pubs) Greenwood.

North American Free Trade Agreement: Legislative History of North America Free Trade Agreement Implementation Act: Public Law 103-182, Including 1996 Supplement, 29 vols. in 31, Set. Jon S. Schultz & Bernard D. Reams, Jr. LC 94-77540. 1994. 4100.00 (*0-89941-899-6*, 307340) W S Hein.

North American Free Trade Agreement: Mexico - U. S. - Canada Trade Accord. Mary E. Lassanyi. 27p. (C). 1995. pap. text 15.00 (*0-7881-1843-9*) DIANE Pub.

North American Free Trade Agreement: Mexico Schedule of Tariff Rate Reductions. (Illus.). 350p. (Orig.). (C). 1994. pap. text 75.00 (*0-7881-0249-4*) DIANE Pub.

North American Free Trade Agreement: Opportunities for United States Industries, Nafta Industry Sector Reports. 395p. 1993. per. 33.00 (*0-16-042958-7*) USGPO.

North American Free Trade Agreement: Regional Community & the New World Order. George W. Grayson. Ed. by Kenneth W. Thompson. LC 94-35271. (Miller Center Series on a New World Order: Vol. 3). 310p. (C). 1994. pap. text 24.50 (*0-8191-9714-9*, Pub. by White Miller Center); lib. bdg. 49.50 (*0-8191-9713-0*, Pub. by White Miller Center) U Pr of Amer.

North American Free Trade Agreement: Schedule of Canada, 2 vols., Set. 1995. lib. bdg. 595.00 (*0-8490-5813-9*) Gordon Pr.

North American Free Trade Agreement: Selected Annotated References, 1989-1992. Robert Howe. (Latin American Information Ser.: No. 1). 29p. (Orig.). 1992. pap. 20.00 (*0-917617-31-2*) SALALM.

North American Free Trade Agreement: Tariff Schedules of the U. S., 2 vols. 1994. lib. bdg. 595.00 (*0-8490-8532-2*) Gordon Pr.

North American Free-Trade Agreement: The Strategic Implications for Canada. Michael Hart. 1990. pap. 17.94 (*0-88645-114-0*, Pub. by Inst Res Pub) Ashgate Pub Co.

*__North American Free Trade Agreement & Specialty Air Services Operations.__ 23p. 2000. pap. 2.50 (*0-16-059014-0*) USGPO.

North American Free Trade Agreement & the European Union. Nicholas V. Gianaris. LC 97-34757. 296p. 1998. 65.00 (*0-275-96167-2*, Praeger Pubs) Greenwood.

North American Free Trade Agreement Between the Government of the U. S. of America, the Government of Canada & the Government of the United Mexican States, 6 vols. 1994. lib. bdg. 1800.00 (*0-8490-8531-4*) Gordon Pr.

North American Free Trade Agreement (NAFTA) Joseph Fitz. 7p. 1993. pap. write for info. (*1-58703-017-9*) CA St Libry.

North American Free Trade Agreement Rules of Origin & Documentation. unabridged ed. Janis F. Seal. 265p. 2000. spiral bd. 89.00 (*1-891249-08-8*) Global Train Ctr.

North American Free Trade Agreements: Assessment of Major Issues. (Illus.). 168p. (Orig.). (C). 1994. pap. text 35.00 (*0-7881-1065-9*) DIANE Pub.

North American Free Trade Agreements (Includes NAFTA: Commentary; NAFTA: Dispute Settlement & NAFTA/U. S. - CFTA Treaties), 6 vols. Ed. by James R. Holbein & Donald J. Musch. LC 92-61611. 1992. ring bd. 700.00 (*0-379-01038-0*) Oceana.

North American Free Trade Guide. 160p. (Orig.). (C). 1993. pap. text 19.50 (*1-878630-50-4*) CA Chamber Commerce.

North American Furbearers: A Contemporary Reference. Eugene F. Deems, Jr. & Duane Pursley. (Illus.). 217p. 1983. text 14.00 (*0-932108-08-3*) IAFWA.

North American Furniture Standards. Sean Fegan. LC 97-28882. (Illus.). 97p. 1997. spiral bd. 450.00 (*0-921577-73-7*) AKTRIN.

North American Game Animals. David R. Maas. LC 95-18908. (Hunting & Fishing Library). (Illus.). 128p. 1995. 19.95 (*0-86573-048-2*) Creat Pub Intl.

North American Game Birds. Chris Dorsey et al. LC 95-39431. (Hunting & Fishing Library). (Illus.). 128p. 1996. 19.95 (*0-86573-049-0*) Creat Pub Intl.

North American Game Birds of Upland & Shoreline. Paul A. Johnsgard. LC 74-15274. (Illus.). 261p. reprint ed. pap. 81.00 (*0-8357-6596-2*, 203599400001) Bks Demand.

North American Game Fishing: A Compendium of Tips, Techniques, Habitats, Species & Conservation Information for Today's Fisherman. John Buckland. 256p. 19.99 (*1-57215-242-7*, JG2427) World Pubns.

North American Global Positioning Systems Application Markets. Ed. by Frost & Sullivan Staff. 582p. 1997. spiral bd. 3950.00 (*0-7889-0681-X*, 5332-22) Frost & Sullivan.

North American Grasshoppers: Acrididae - Gomphocerinae & Acridinae, Vol. 1. Daniel Otte. (Illus.). 304p. (C). 1981. 86.95 (*0-674-62660-5*) HUP.

North American Grasshoppers: Acrididae, Oedipodinae, Vol. 2. Daniel Otte. (Illus.). 352p. 1985. 88.95 (*0-674-62661-3*) HUP.

North American Guide to Nude Recreation. 17th ed. Ed. by Arne Eriksen & Julie Bagby. (Illus.). 200p. (Orig.). 1990. pap. text 18.95 (*1-882033-03-5*) AANR.

North American Guide to Nude Recreation. 19th ed. American Association for Nude Recreation. 198p. 1997. pap. text 24.95 (*1-882033-06-X*) AANR.

North American Guide to Nude Recreation: The Most Comprehensive Listing of Nude Recreation Resorts & Clubs. 20th ed. American Association for Nude Staff. 224p. 1999. pap. 24.95 (*1-882033-08-6*) AANR.

North American Heavy-Duty Truck OEM Component Markets: Increase Demand for Heavy Trucks Brings Opportunities for Component Suppliers. 301p. 1995. spiral bd. 2195.00 (*0-7889-0383-7*, 5161-18) Frost & Sullivan.

North American Herpetology. Holbrook. LC 76-6229. 1976. write for info. (*0-916984-02-8*) SSAR.

North American Highway Atlas. rev. ed. 128p. 1985. 5.95 (*0-88098-077-X*, H M Gousha) Prntice Hall Bks.

*__North American Historical Atlases, 5 vols.__ Rebecca Stefoff. (Illus.). 2001. 121.05 (*0-7614-1055-4*, Benchmark NY) Marshall Cavendish.

North American History, 1988. (C). 1989. 295.00 (*0-8161-7107-6*, Hall Reference) Macmillan.

North American Horse Travel Guide. Bruce McAllister. LC 94-180827. (Illus.). 312p. (Orig.). 1993. pap. 19.95 (*0-9638817-2-8*) Roundup Pr.

North American Horse Travel Guide. 2nd ed. Bruce McAllister. (Illus.). 444p. (Orig.). 1995. pap. 19.95 (*0-9638817-3-6*) Roundup Pr.

North American Horse Travel Guide. 4th ed. Bruce McAllister. (Illus.). 494p. (Orig.). 1996. pap. 22.95 (*0-9638817-4-4*) Roundup Pr.

North American Horsemen's Association Safety Progam Catalog. Ed. by Linda Liestman. (NAHA Risk Reduction Ser.). 11p. 1987. pap. text 15.00 (*1-887811-00-1*) N Amer Horsemens.

North American Horsemen's Association Safety Progam Catalog. Ed. by Linda Liestman. (NAHA Risk Reduction Ser.). 25p. 1990. pap. text 15.00 (*1-887811-01-X*) N Amer Horsemens.

North American Horsemen's Association Safety Progam Catalog. Ed. by Linda Liestman. (NAHA Risk Reduction Ser.). 34p. 1991. pap. text 15.00 (*1-887811-02-8*) N Amer Horsemens.

North American Horsemen's Association Safety (Risk Management) Program Catalog. Ed. by Linda Liestman. (NAHA Risk Reduction Ser.). 56p. 1992. pap. text 15.00 (*1-887811-04-4*) N Amer Horsemens.

North American Horsemen's Association 1990 Yearbook. Ed. by Linda Liestman. (NAHA Yearbook Ser.). 47p. 1991. pap. text 3.00 (*1-887811-03-6*) N Amer Horsemens.

North American Horsemen's Association 1991 Yearbook. Ed. by Linda Liestman. (NAHA Yearbook Ser.). 54p. 1992. pap. text 3.00 (*1-887811-05-2*) N Amer Horsemens.

North American Horsemen's Association 1992-1993 Yearbook. Ed. by Linda Liestman. (NAHA Yearbook Ser.). 68p. 1994. pap. text 4.00 (*1-887811-08-7*) N Amer Horsemens.

North American Horsemen's Association 1994 Yearbook. Ed. by Linda Liestman. (NAHA Yearbook Ser.). 62p. 1994. pap. text 4.00 (*1-887811-07-9*) N Amer Horsemens.

North American Horsemen's Association 1995 Risk Reduction Programs & Contracts & Agreements. Ed. by Linda Liestman. (NAHA Risk Reduction Ser.). 109p. 1995. pap. text 20.00 (*1-887811-10-9*) N Amer Horsemens.

North American Horsemen's Association 1995 Yearbook. Ed. by Linda Liestman. (NAHA Yearbook Ser.). 78p. 1995. pap. text 4.00 (*1-887811-11-7*) N Amer Horsemens.

North American Hunting Adventures. Monte Burch. Ed. by Bill Miller. LC 87-613212. (Hunter's Information Ser.). (Illus.). 208p. 1988. write for info. (*0-914697-09-9*) N Amer Outdoor Grp.

North American Import-Car Hard-Part Aftermarket: Import/Domestic Distinction Persists. Frost & Sullivan Staff. 445p. 1996. spiral bd. 2495.00 (*0-7889-0414-0*, 5156-18) Frost & Sullivan.

North American Ind. Class System. U. S. Government Staff. 1997. pap. 36.00 (*1-57980-101-3*) Claitors.

*__North American Indian.__ David Murdoch. (Eyewitness Books). (Illus.). (J). (gr. 4-7). 2000. 19.99 (*0-7894-6609-0*) DK Pub Inc.

*__North American Indian.__ David Murdoch. (Eyewitness Books). (J). (gr. 4-7). 2000. 15.95 (*0-7894-6028-9*) DK Pub Inc.

N

North American Indian: The Complete Portfolios. Edward S. Curtis. (Klotz Ser.). (Illus.). 768p. 1997. pap. 29.99 (*3-8228-8183-X*) Taschen Amer.

North American Indian Vol. 12: Hopi. Edward S. Curtis. Ed. by Frederick W. Hodge. LC 94-71420. (Illus.). 448p. 1996. pap. 19.95 (*1-884865-00-3*) Curtis & Forrest.

North American Indian Activity Book. Winky Adam. (Illus.). 64p. (J). 1998. pap. 1.00 (*0-486-29824-8*) Dover.

North American Indian Anthropology: Essays on Society & Culture. Ed. by Raymond J. DeMallie & Alfonso Ortiz. LC 94-20618. (Illus.). 448p. 1996. pap. 18.95 (*0-8061-2808-9*) U of Okla Pr.

North American Indian Art. Jill L. Furst & Peter Furst. LC 82-40343. (Illus.). 264p. 1990. pap. 35.00 (*0-8478-0572-7*, Pub. by Rizzoli Intl) St Martin.

North American Indian Artifacts: A Collector's Identification & Value Guide. 6th ed. Lar Hothem. LC 98-84635. (Illus.). 496p. 1999. pap. 26.95 (*0-87341-554-X*, INAF6) Krause Pubns.

North American Indian Arts. Andrew Hunter Whiteford. (Golden Guide Ser.). 1990. 11.05 (*0-606-11689-3*, Pub. by Turtleback) Demco.

North American Indian Beadwork Designs. Clark Wissler. LC 99-36848. 32p. 1999. pap. text 2.95 (*0-486-40713-6*) Dover.

North American Indian Beadwork Patterns. Stanley-Millner. LC 95-23623. (Illus.). 64p. pap. 3.95 (*0-486-28835-8*) Dover.

North American Indian Ceremonies. Karen Liptak. (First Time Bks.). 1992. 11.15 (*0-606-05512-6*, Pub. by Turtleback) Demco.

North American Indian Ceremonies. Karen Liptak. Ed. by V. Mathews. LC 90-12337. (First Bks.). (Illus.). 64p. (J). (gr. 4-6). 1992. lib. bdg. 22.00 (*0-531-20100-7*) Watts.

North American Indian Chiefs. Karl Nagelfell. 64p. 1995. 16.95 (*1-57215-055-6*) World Pubns.

North American Indian Crafts. Peter F. Copeland. (J). (gr. 1-5). 1996. pap. 2.95 (*0-486-29283-5*) Dover.

North American Indian Dances & Rituals. Copeland. 1998. pap. 2.95 (*0-486-29913-9*) Dover.

North American Indian Design Coloring Book. 81st ed. Paul E. Kennedy. (Illus.). (J). (gr. 4-7). 1971. pap. 2.95 (*0-486-21125-8*) Dover.

North American Indian Designs for Artists & Craftspeople. Eva Wilson. (Pictorial Archive Ser.). 128p. 1987. reprint ed. pap. 8.95 (*0-486-25341-4*) Dover.

North American Indian Designs Iron-On Transfer Patterns, Vol. 181. Madeleine Orban-Szontagh. (Illus.). 48p. (Orig.). 1991. pap. 3.50 (*0-486-26883-7*) Dover.

North American Indian Designs/Stained Glass. John Green. 1995. pap. 3.95 (*0-486-28608-8*) Dover.

North American Indian Ecology. 2nd rev. ed. J. Donald Hughes. LC 94-61154. Orig. Title: American Indian Ecology. (Illus.). 174p. 1996. pap. 20.00 (*0-87404-220-8*) Tex Western.

*__North American Indian Games__ Madelyn K. Anderson. LC 99-30240. (Library Ser.). 2000. 24.00 (*0-531-20403-0*) Watts.

*__North American Indian Games.__ Madelyn K. Anderson. (Indians of the Americas Library). (Illus.). (YA). 2000. pap. 8.95 (*0-531-16474-8*) Watts.

North American Indian Icons. Beth Garbo.Tr. of Calander Book 2000. (Illus.). 106p. 1998. spiral bd. 12.95 (*1-892373-40-8*, 40-8); spiral bd. 12.95 (*1-892373-31-9*, 31-9) Especially Bks.

North American Indian Jewelry & Adornment: From Prehistory to the Present. Lois Sherr Dubin. LC 98-37491. (Illus.). 608p. 1999. 75.00 (*0-8109-3689-5*, Pub. by Abrams) Time Warner.

North American Indian Landmarks: A Traveler's Guide. George Cantor. (Illus.). 409p. 1999. reprint ed. pap. text 18.00 (*0-7881-6284-5*) DIANE Pub.

North American Indian Language Materials, 1890-1965: An Annotated Bibliography of Monographic Works. G. Edward Evans & Jeffrey Clark. (American Indian Bibliographic Ser.). 153p. (Orig.). 1980. pap. 5.00 (*0-935626-15-8*) U Cal AISC.

North American Indian Life: Customs & Traditions of 23 Tribes. unabridged ed. Ed. by Elsie C. Parsons. LC 92-22904. Orig. Title: American Indian Life by Several of Its Students. (Illus.). 1993. reprint ed. pap. text 10.95 (*0-486-27377-6*) Dover.

North American Indian Motifs. Dover Staff. (Electronic Clip Art Ser.). (Illus.). 64p. pap. 9.95 incl. cd-rom (*0-486-99945-9*) Dover.

North American Indian Music: A Guide to Published Sources & Selected Recordings. Richard Keeling. LC 96-41847. (Library of Music Ethnology: Vol. 5). 420p. 1997. text 75.00 (*0-8153-0232-0*, H1440) Garland.

North American Indian Orpheus Tradition: A Contribution to Comparative Religion. Ake Hultcrantz. (Ethnographical Museum of Swedem Monograph: No. 2). 340p. (Orig.). 1957. pap. 68.00 (*91-22-01352-0*) Coronet Bks.

North American Indian Portfolios. Bedmer et al. (Tiny Folios Ser.). (Illus.). 272p. 1996. pap. 11.95 (*1-55859-601-1*) Abbeville Pr.

North American Indian Sign Language. Karen Liptak. (First Time Bks.). 1992. 12.15 (*0-606-05514-2*, Pub. by Turtleback) Demco.

North American Indian Sign Language. Karen Liptak. LC 90-12336. (First Bks.). (Illus.). 64p. (J). (gr. 4-6). 1990. lib. bdg. 22.00 (*0-531-10869-4*) Watts.

North American Indian Stickers. Madeleine Orban-Szontagh. (Illus.). (J). (gr. k-3). 1991. pap. 1.00 (*0-486-26821-7*) Dover.

North American Indian Stories, 4 vols., Set. Gretchen W. Mayo. (Illus.). 256p. (J). (gr. 5 up). 1990. pap. 23.80 (*0-8027-7341-9*) Walker & Co.

North American Indian Stories: Earthmaker's Tales. Gretchen W. Mayo. (Illus.). 48p. (J). (gr. 5 up). 1990. pap. 5.95 (*0-8027-7343-5*) Walker & Co.

North American Indian Stories: More Earthmaker's Tales. Gretchen W. Mayo. (Illus.). 48p. (J). (gr. 5 up). 1990. pap. 5.95 (*0-8027-7344-3*) Walker & Co.

North American Indian Stories: More Star Tales. Gretchen W. Mayo. LC 90-12786. (Illus.). 48p. (J). (gr. 4-7). 1990. pap. 5.95 (*0-8027-7347-8*) Walker & Co.

North American Indian Stories: Star Tales. Gretchen W. Mayo. (Illus.). 48p. (J). (gr. 5 up). 1990. pap. 5.95 (*0-8027-7345-1*) Walker & Co.

North American Indian Survival Skills. Karen Liptak. LC 90-12354. (First Bks.). (Illus.). 64p. (J). (gr. 4-6). 1990. lib. bdg. 22.00 (*0-531-10870-8*) Watts.

North American Indian Tales. W. T. Larned & John Green. LC 96-48788. (Children's Thrift Classics Ser.). (Illus.). 96p. 1997. reprint ed. pap. text 1.00 (*0-486-29656-3*) Dover.

North American Indian Travel Guide. 5th rev. ed. Lisa W. Shanks & Ralph C. Shanks. (Illus.). 294p. (Orig.). 1994. pap. 17.95 (*0-930268-12-1*) Costano.

North American Indian Tribal Chiefs. Karen Liptak. (First Time Bks.). 1992. 11.15 (*0-606-05516-9*, Pub. by Turtleback) Demco.

North American Indian Wars. Richard L. Dillon. 1993. 17.98 (*1-55521-951-9*) Bk Sales Inc.

*__North American Indian Wars.__ Don Nardo. LC 98-47353. (Turning Points in World History Ser.). 220p. 1999. pap. 17.45 (*1-56510-958-9*) Greenhaven.

North American Indian Wars. Don Nardo. LC 98-47353. (Turning Points in World History Ser.). 221p. (YA). (gr. 9 up). 1999. lib. bdg. 27.45 (*1-56510-959-7*) Greenhaven.

*__North American Indian Women.__ Robin Langley Sommer. 128p. 1998. write for info. (*1-57215-159-5*) World Pubns.

North American Indians. George Catlin & Peter Matthiessen. (Illus.). 560p. 1989. pap. 13.95 (*0-14-025267-3*, Penguin Bks) Viking Penguin.

North American Indians. Edward S. Curtis & Joseph E. Brown. (Illus.). 96p. 1992. pap. 29.95 (*0-89381-492-X*) Aperture.

North American Indians. Marie Gorsline & Douglas Gorsline. LC 77-79843. (Pictureback Ser.). (Illus.). (J). (ps-2). 1978. pap. 3.25 (*0-394-83702-9*, Pub. by Random Bks Yng Read) Random.

North American Indians. Judy Nayer. (At Your Fingertips Ser.). (Illus.). 10p. (J). (ps-3). 1995. bds. 6.95 (*1-56293-548-8*, McClanahan Book) Learn Horizon.

*__North American Indians.__ Alexandra Parsons. (Make It Work! History Ser.). (Illus.). (J). (gr. 4-7). 2000. pap. 6.95 (*1-58728-301-8*) Two Can Pub.

North American Indians. Virginia Slachman. Date not set. 4.95 (*1-55708-357-6*, MCR546) McDonald Pub Co.

North American Indians. Smithsonian Institution Staff. 1974. lib. bdg. 105.00 (*0-226-76617-9*) U Ch Pr.

North American Indians. Michael Stotter. Ed. by Anness Publishing Staff. (Step into Ser.). (Illus.). 64p. (J). 1999. 12.95 (*0-7548-0216-7*, Lorenz Bks) Anness Pub.

*__North American Indians.__ Two Can Publishing Ltd. Staff. (Make It Work! History Ser.). (Illus.). 2000. 14.95 (*1-58728-308-5*) Two Can Pub.

North American Indians. Bill Yenne. 1992. 15.98 (*1-55521-802-4*) Bk Sales Inc.

North American Indians: A Comprehensive Account. 2nd ed. Alice B. Kehoe. 624p. (C). 1992. pap. text 46.00 (*0-13-624362-2*) P-H.

North American Indians: A Dissertation Index. 1976. 28.00 (*0-8357-0134-4*) Univ Microfilms.

North American Indians & Alaska Natives: Absracts of the Psychological & Behavioral Literature, 1967-1994. Ed. by Joseph E. Trimble & Weldon M. Bagwell. LC 95-17645. (Bibliographies in Psychology Ser.: No. 15). 272p. 1995. pap. 19.95 (*1-55798-311-9*) Am Psychol.

North American Indians in Historical Perspective. Ed. by Eleanor B. Leacock & Nancy O. Lurie. (Illus.). 498p. (C). 1988. reprint ed. pap. text 22.95 (*0-88133-377-8*) Waveland Pr.

North American Indians of Achievement. Incl. Cochise: Apache Chief. Nancy Schwartz. (Illus.). 116p. (YA). (gr. 5 up). 1992. pap. 8.95 (*0-7910-1694-3*); Hiawatha: Founder of the Iroquois Confederacy. Nancy Bonvillain. (Illus.). 116p. (YA). (gr. 5 up). 1994. pap. 8.95 (*0-7910-1693-5*); Pocahontas: Powhatan Peacemaker. Anne Holler. (Illus.). 116p. (YA). (gr. 5 up). 1992. pap. 8.95 (*0-7910-1952-7*); Pontiac - Ottawa Rebel. Celia Bland. (Illus.). 116p. (YA). (gr. 7 up). 1994. pap. 8.95 (*0-7910-2043-6*); Red Cloud: Sioux War Chief. Jerry Lazar. LC 94-22728. (Illus.). (YA). (gr. 5 up). 1995. pap. 7.95 (*0-7910-2044-4*); Sarah Winnemucca: Northern Paiute Writer & Diplomat. Ellen Scordato. (Illus.). 116p. (YA). (gr. 4-7). 1992. pap. 8.95 (*0-7910-1696-X*); Set pap. 79.50 (*0-7910-3757-6*) Chelsea Hse.

North American Indians of Achievement. Incl. Ben Nighthorse Campbell: Cheyenne Chief & U. S. Senator. Christopher E. Henry. (Illus.). 116p. (YA). (gr. 5 up). 1994. lib. bdg. 19.95 (*0-7910-2046-0*); Charles Eastman: Sioux Physician & Writer. Karin L. Badt. Ed. by W. David Baird. LC 94-34896. (Illus.). 116p. (YA). (gr. 5 up). 1995. lib. bdg. 19.95 (*0-7910-2048-7*); Chief Gall: Sioux War Chief. Jane Shumate. LC 94-13645. (Illus.). (YA). (gr. 5 up). 1995. lib. bdg. 19.95 (*0-7910-1713-3*); Chief Joseph: Nez Perce Leader. Clifford E. Trafzer. (Illus.). 116p. (YA). (gr. 5 up). 1994. lib. bdg. 19.95 (*0-7910-1708-7*); Cochise: Apache Chief. Melissa Schwartz. (Illus.). 116p. (YA). (gr. 5 up). 1992. lib. bdg. 19.95 (*0-7910-1706-0*); Geronimo: Apache Warrior. Melissa Schwartz. (Illus.). 116p. (YA). (gr. 5 up). 1992. lib. bdg. 19.95 (*0-7910-1701-X*); Geronimo: Apache Warrior. Melissa Schwartz. (Illus.). 116p. (YA). (gr. 5 up). 1992. pap. 8.95 (*0-7910-1691-9*); Hiawatha: Founder of the Iroquois Confederacy. Nancy Bonvillain. (Illus.). 116p. (YA). (gr. 5 up). 1992. lib. bdg. 19.95 (*0-7910-1707-9*); Joseph Brant: Mohawk Chief. Claire Wilson & Jonathan Bolton. LC 91-38917. (Illus.). 116p. (YA). (gr. 4-7). 1992. lib. bdg. 19.95 (*0-7910-1709-5*); King Philip: Wampanoag Rebel. Joseph Roman. (Illus.). 116p. (YA). (gr. 5 up). 1992. lib. bdg. 19.95 (*0-7910-1704-4*); Osceola: Seminole Rebel. Alex Zane. Ed. by W. David Baird. LC 93-21750. (Illus.). 116p. (YA). (gr. 5 up). 1994. lib. bdg. 19.95 (*0-7910-1716-8*); Peter MacDonald: Former Chairman of the Navajo Nation. Celia Bland. LC 94-21856. (Illus.). 116p. (Orig.). (YA). (gr. 5-13). 1995. lib. bdg. 19.95 (*0-7910-1714-1*); Pocahontas - Powhatan Peacemaker. Anne Holler. LC 92-9946. (Illus.). 116p. (YA). (gr. 5-13). 1996. 19.95 (*0-7910-1705-2*); Red Cloud: Sioux War Chief. Jerry Lazar. LC 94-22728. (Illus.). 116p. (YA). (gr. 5 up). 1995. lib. bdg. 19.95 (*0-7910-1718-4*); Sarah Winnemucca: Northern Paiute Writer & Diplomat. Ellen Scordato. (Illus.). 116p. (YA). (gr. 5 up). 1992. lib. bdg. 19.95 (*0-7910-1710-9*); Sequoyah: Inventor of the Cherokee Alphabet. Jane A. Shumate. LC 93-18107. (Illus.). 116p. (YA). (gr. 4-7). 1994. lib. bdg. 19.95 (*0-7910-1720-6*); Sitting Bull: Chief of the Sioux. Bob Bernotas. (Illus.). 116p. (YA). (gr. 5 up). 1992. lib. bdg. 19.95 (*0-7910-1703-6*); Tecumseh: Shawnee Rebel. Robert Cwiklik. LC 92-21656. (Illus.). 116p. (YA). (gr. 4-7). 1994. lib. bdg. 19.95 (*0-7910-1721-4*); Wilma Mankiller: Principal Chief of the Cherokees. Melissa Schwarz. (Illus.). 116p. (YA). (gr. 5 up). 1994. lib. bdg. 19.95 (*0-7910-1715-X*); 1992. 458.85 (*0-7910-1700-1*) Chelsea Hse.

North American Industrial Operator Interface Device & Software Markets. Market Intelligence Staff. 298p. 1994. 2195.00 (*0-7889-0142-7*) Frost & Sullivan.

North American Industry Classification System: United States, 1997. LC 98-203884. (NAICS Manual Ser.). 1251p. 1998. 32.50 (*0-16-049698-5*) USGPO.

North American Industry Classification System: United States, 1997. Bernan Press Staff. LC 19-981000. 1200p. 1998. 32.50 (*0-89059-097-4*) Bernan Pr.

North American Industry Classification System: United States (1997) Ed. by Jack E. Triplett. 1247p. (C). 1999. pap. text 50.00 (*0-7881-7647-1*) DIANE Pub.

North American Industry Classification System (NAICS) - United States, 1997. Jist Works Staff. 1998. pap. 34.95 (*1-56370-516-8*) JIST Works.

North American Industry Classification System (NAICS) - United States, 1997. Office Management & Budget Staff. 1200p. 1998. pap. 28.50 (*0-934213-57-7*) Natl Tech Info.

North American Industry Classification System (NAICS) - United States, 1997. Office of Management & Budget Staff. 1200p. 1998. 32.50 (*0-934213-56-9*) Natl Tech Info.

North American Industry Classification System (NAICS) - United States, 1997. U. S. Government Staff. 1997. 38.00 (*1-57980-040-8*, NAICH) Claitors.

North American Industry Classification System (NAICS) - United States, 1997. Works Jist Staff. 1247p. 1998. 37.95 (*1-56370-537-0*) JIST Works.

North American Industry Classification System, United States, 1997. LC 98-203884. (NAICS Manual Ser.). 1251p. 1998. pap. 28.50 (*0-16-049699-3*) USGPO.

North American Industry Classification System United States 1997. Bernan Press Staff. 1247p. 1998. pap. text 28.50 (*0-89059-098-2*) Bernan Pr.

North American Integrated Services Digital Network Users' Forum Agreements on ISDN. Ed. by Daniel P. Stokesberry et al. (Illus.). 250p. (Orig.). (C). 1996. pap. text 50.00 (*0-7881-2696-2*) DIANE Pub.

North American Intelligent Transportation. John Boatman. (Transportation - Related Special Reports). 1996. 695.00 (*0-7106-1500-0*) Janes Info Group.

North American ISDN Users' Forum. (Illus.). 306p. (Orig.). (C). 1995. pap. text 50.00 (*0-7881-2485-4*) DIANE Pub.

*__North American Italian Renaissance: Italian Writing in America & Canada.__ Kenneth Scambray. (Essay Ser.: No. 43). 138p. 2000. pap. 13.00 (*1-55071-107-5*, , Pub. by Guernica Editions) Paul & Co Pubs.

North American Labor Markets: A Comparative Profile. Labor Secretariat of the Commission Staff. (North American Labor Ser.). (FRE.). 200p. 1997. pap. 35.00 (*0-89059-074-5*, BPF0745) Bernan Pr.

North American Labor Markets: A Comparative Profile, 1997. LC 98-103989. 200p. (C). 1997. lib. bdg. 35.00 (*0-89059-070-2*, BP0702) Bernan Pr.

North American Locomotive Production, 1968-1989. James T. Bradley. (Illus.). 192p. 1989. 27.50 (*0-9624633-0-2*) Bradley Enterprises.

North American Maintenance of Way Equipment. James T. Bradley. (Illus.). 64p. (C). 1992. pap. 19.95 (*0-9624633-4-5*) Bradley Enterprises.

North American Manufacturing Research Conference: Proceedings of the Conference, Pennsylvania State University, May 19-22, 1981. LC 81-50696. (Manufacturing Engineering Transactions Ser.: Vol. 9). 610p. reprint ed. pap. 189.10 (*0-608-15476-8*, 202940200060) Bks Demand.

North American Manufacturing Research Conference Proceedings: May 27-29, 1987, Lehigh University, Bethlehem, PA. North American Manufacturing Research Conference (. LC 76-646280. (SME Manufacturing Technology Review Ser.: No. 2). (Illus.). 702p. reprint ed. pap. 200.00 (*0-8357-6507-5*, 203587800097) Bks Demand.

North American Manufacturing Research Conference Proceedings: May 28-30, 1986, University of Minnesota, Minneapolis, MN - Organized by the University of Minnesota Department of Mechanical Engineering, Minneapolis, MN. North American Manufacturing Research Conference (. LC 76-646280. (Manufacturing Technology Review Ser.: No. 1). (Illus.). 684p. reprint ed. pap. 200.00 (*0-8357-6475-3*, 203584600097) Bks Demand.

North American Manufacturing Research Conference Proceedings, May 18-21, 1980, University of Missouri-Rolla, Rolla, Missouri. LC 76-646280. (Manufacturing Engineering Transactions Ser.: Vol. 8). (Illus.). 439p. reprint ed. pap. 136.10 (*0-608-18432-2*, 203248400079) Bks Demand.

North American Manufacturing Research Conference Proceedings, May 19-22, 1985, University of California-Berkeley, Berkeley, CA. North American Manufacturing Research Conference (. LC 76-646280. (Manufacturing Engineering Transactions Ser.: No. 13). (Illus.). 602p. 1985. reprint ed. pap. 186.70 (*0-8357-6505-9*, 203587600097) Bks Demand.

North American Manufacturing Research Conference Proceedings, May 24-25, 1982, McMaster University, Hamilton, Ontario, Canada. LC 76-646280. (Manufacturing Engineering Transactions Ser.: Vol. 10). (Illus.). 550p. reprint ed. pap. 170.50 (*0-608-18433-0*, 203248500079) Bks Demand.

North American Manufacturing Research Conference Proceedings, May 24-26, 1983, University of Wisconsin-Madison, Madison, WI. 2nd ed. North American Manufacturing Reserach Conference (. LC 76-646280. (Manufacturing Engineering Transactions Ser.: No. 11). (Illus.). 504p. 1983. reprint ed. pap. 156.30 (*0-7837-8192-X*, 204789700008) Bks Demand.

North American Markets Directory for Artisans. Caroline R. Merriam & Kathy Borrus. (ENG & SPA.). 250p. (Orig.). 1997. pap. 25.00 (*0-9625480-2-2*) Crafts Ctr.

North American Medium & High-Voltage Switchgear Markets. Ed. by Frost & Sullivan Staff. 258p. 1997. spiral bd. 2450.00 (*0-7889-0734-4*, 5577-14) Frost & Sullivan.

North American Mentor Anthology of Poems. Ed. & Intro. by John E. Westburg. (Illus.). 48p. 1965. 10.00 (*0-87423-000-4*) Westburg.

North American Metalworking Research Conference: Proceedings, 7th, May 13-16, 1979, University of Michigan, Ann Arbor, MI. North American Metalworking Research Conference St. LC 79-63779. (Manufacturing Engineering Transactions Ser.: No. 7). (Illus.). 389p. reprint ed. pap. 120.60 (*0-608-18100-5*, 203216700078) Bks Demand.

North American Metalworking Research Conference, May 17-19, 1976: Proceedings. Ed. by Taylan Altan. LC 76-6005. (Illus.). 494p. reprint ed. pap. 153.20 (*0-608-17820-9*, 203248300079) Bks Demand.

North American Metalworking Research Conference Proceedings, Fifth, University of Massachusetts, Amherst, 1977. LC 77-75743. (Manufacturing Engineering Transactions Ser.: Vol. 5). 389p. reprint ed. pap. 120.60 (*0-608-13134-2*, 202417600035) Bks Demand.

North American Metalworking Research Conference Proceedings, Sixth, University of Florida, 1978. LC 78-51585. (Manufacturing Engineering Transactions Ser.: Vol. 6). 478p. reprint ed. pap. 148.20 (*0-608-13141-5*, 202417700035) Bks Demand.

North American Monster. Haden Blackman. LC 97-43243. 272p. 1998. pap. 15.00 (*0-609-80017-5*) Crown Pub Group.

*__North American Moose.__ Lesley A. DuTemple. LC 99-37091. (Nature Watch Bks.). (Illus.). 48p. (J). (gr. 4-7). 2000. 23.93 (*1-57505-426-4*, Carolrhoda) Lerner Pub.

North American Moose. Randolph L. Peterson. LC 56-1401. 324p. reprint ed. pap. 100.50 (*0-608-15414-8*, 202934300060) Bks Demand.

North American Myths & Legends. Philip Ardagh. LC 97-47440. (J). 1999. 23.00 (*0-382-39998-6*, Dillon Silver Burdett); pap. write for info. (*0-382-39999-4*, Dillon Silver Burdett) Silver Burdett Pr.

North American NA-16/AT-6, Vol. 11. Dan Hagadorn. (Warbird Tech Ser.). 1997. pap. text 16.95 (*0-933424-76-0*) Specialty Pr.

North American Najadicola & Unionicola: Collections & Communities. Malcolm F. Vidrine. LC 96-60323. vi, 259p. 1996. lib. bdg. 150.00 (*0-9637304-6-0*) G Q Vidrine Collect.

North American Najadicola & Unionicola: Diagnoses & Distributions. Malcolm F. Vidrine. LC 96-60320. (Illus.). vi, 355p. (C). 1996. pap. 100.00 (*0-9637304-8-7*); lib. bdg. 150.00 (*0-9637304-4-4*) G Q Vidrine Collect.

North American Najadicola & Unionicola: Photomicrographs. Malcolm F. Vidrine. LC 96-60323. (Illus.). xiv, 205p. (C). 1996. lib. bdg. 150.00 (*0-9637304-5-2*) G Q Vidrine Collect.

North American Najadicola & Unionicola: Systematics & Coevolution. Malcolm F. Vidrine. LC 96-60321. vi, 145p. (C). 1996. lib. bdg. 150.00 (*0-9637304-7-9*) G Q Vidrine Collect.

North American Native Fishes for the Home Aquarium. David M. Schleser. LC 98-20378. (Illus.). 176p. 1998. pap. 12.95 (*0-7641-0367-9*) Barron.

*__North American Natural Gas Trends, 2000.__ 114p. 2000. pap. 95.00 (*1-930497-13-X*, Pub. by A Andersen LLP) Gulf Pub.

*__North American Nature Activity Book, No. 1.__ James Kavanagh. (Nature Activity Bks.). (Illus.). 64p. (J). (ps up). 1999. pap. 6.95 (*1-889903-98-1*, Pub. by Waterford WA) Falcon Pub Inc.

*__North American Nature Activity Book, No. 2.__ James Kavanagh. (Nature Activity Bks.). (Illus.). 64p. (J). (ps up). 1999. pap. 6.95 (*1-889903-99-X*, Pub. by Waterford WA) Falcon Pub Inc.

North American Non Revenue Freight Cars. James T. Bradley. (Illus.). 64p. (C). 1993. pap. 19.95 (*0-9624633-5-3*) Bradley Enterprises.

North American Ocean Creatures, 4 vols. Colleyan Mastin. (North American Nature Ser.). (Illus.). 32p. (J). (gr. 1 up). 1997. pap. 9.95 (*1-895910-25-0*) Grasshopper Bks.

North American Official Cellular Users Guide. Judi Black. (Illus.). iv, 200p. 1988. pap. 15.95 (*0-929051-00-9*) Cellmark Pub.

North American Oil & Gas Fields. Ed. by Jules Braunstein. LC 76-258. (American Association of Petroleum Geologists. Memoir Ser.: 24). 370p. reprint ed. pap. 114.70 (*0-608-12009-X*, 202287800031) Bks Demand.

North American Owls: Biology & Natural History. Paul A. Johnsgard. LC 87-27516. (Illus.). 336p. (Orig.). (C). 1988. 45.00 (*0-87474-560-8*) Smithsonian.

North American Owls: Biology & Natural History. Paul A. Johnsgard. (Illus.). 336p. (Orig.). 1997. pap. 24.95 (*1-56098-724-3*) Smithsonian.

North American P-51 Mustang. Frederick A. Johnsen. (Warbird Tech Ser.: Vol. 5). (Illus.). 100p. (Orig.). 1996. pap. 16.95 (*0-933424-68-X*) Specialty Pr.

North American Patterns of Growth & Development: The Continental Context. W. T. Easterbrook. 336p. 1990. text 37.50 (*0-8020-5835-3*) U of Toronto Pr.

North American Payphone Markets: Niche Locations, Canadian Markets Restart Growth. 311p. 1992. 1695.00 (*1-56753-021-4*) Frost & Sullivan.

North American PBX & Key Telephone Systems Market: Manufacturers Shift Toward Wireless Systems. Frost Sullivan Staff. 476p. 1996. spiral bd. 2295.00 (*0-7889-0482-5*, 2819-62) Frost & Sullivan.

North American PC Cards Market. Ed. by Frost & Sullivan Staff. 151p. 1997. spiral bd. 2450.00 (*0-7889-0741-7*, 5434-72) Frost & Sullivan.

North American Permanent Papers. Ellen R. McCrady. 52p. (Orig.). 1995. pap. 19.50 (*0-9622071-3-6*) Abbey Pubns.

North American Permanent Papers - 1998: A Guide to Permanent Papers Available in the U. S. & Canada. Ed. by Ellen McCrady. 60p. 1998. pap. 19.50 (*0-9622071-4-4*) Abbey Pubns.

North American Perspective: Computing & Networks in Canada & the United States: Proceedings. 222p. 12.00 (*0-318-14026-8*) EDUCOM.

North American Perspectives on European Security. Ed. by Michael K. Hawes & Joel J. Sokolsky. LC 90-5693. (Studies in World Peace: Vol. 5). 300p. 1990. lib. bdg. 89.95 (*0-88946-589-4*) E Mellen.

*__North American Pictures.__ Imre Gyovai. (Illus.). 1999. 0.00 (*0-9673296-0-4*) M Dzurilla.

North American Plantfile. Gary Hightshoe et al. LC 97-218842. (Illus.). 576p. 1997. 154.95 (*0-07-028816-X*) McGraw.

North American Plantfile: A Pictorial & Photographic Essay of Native & Exotic Plants Adaptable to the United States, Canada & Northern Mexico for Use in Landscape Design. Gary L. Hightshoe & Harlen D. Groe. LC 95-9889. (Illus.). 1995. write for info. (*0-422-20760-8*, VNR) Wiley.

North American Plantlife. Gary L. Hightshoe & Harlen D. Groe. 1995. text 149.95 (*0-442-20760-3*, VNR) Wiley.

An Asterisk (*) at the beginning of an entry indicates that the title is appearing for the first time.

North American Polypores, 2 vols., Set. R. L. Gilbertson & Leif Ryvarden. (Illus.). 885p. 1987. text 160.00 (*0-945345-06-2*) Lubrecht & Cramer.

North American Porcupine. Uldis Roze. (Illus.). 224p. 1989. pap. 15.95 (*0-87474-787-2*) Smithsonian.

North American Power Semiconductor Markets: Who's Got the Power? Vendors Target Portability & Energy Efficiency. Market Intelligence Staff. 300p. 1994. 1995.00 (*0-7889-0026-9*) Frost & Sullivan.

North American Premises Wiring Sysems. Ed. by Frost & Sullivan Staff. 430p. 1997. spiral bd. 2495.00 (*0-7889-0670-4*, 2762-62) Frost & Sullivan.

North American Premises Wiring Systems Markets: A Vibrant Industry. Frost & Sullivan Staff. 343p. 1995. spiral bd. 2395.00 (*0-7889-0316-0*) Frost & Sullivan.

North American Psocoptera (Insecta) Edward L. Mockford. Ed. by Ross H. Arnett, Jr. (Flora & Fauna Handbook Ser.: No. 10). (Illus.). xii, 455p. 1993. lib. bdg. 99.95 (*1-877743-12-7*) Sandhill Crane.

North American Railroad: Its Origin, Evolution, & Geography. James E. Vance, Jr. LC 94-16306. (Creating the North American Landscape Ser.). (Illus.). 384p. 1995. 39.95 (*0-8018-4573-4*) Johns Hopkins.

North American Rails. Mayfair Games Staff. Date not set. 25.00 (*0-923763-69-4*) Mayfair Games.

North American Rain Forest Scrapbook. Virginia Wright-Frierson. LC 98-42402. (Illus.). 40p. (J). 1999. 15.95 (*0-8027-8679-0*) Walker & Co.

North American Rain Forest Scrapbook. Virginia Wright-Frierson. LC 98-42402. (Illus.). 40p. (J). (gr. 1-7). 1999. lib. bdg. 16.85 (*0-8027-8680-4*) Walker & Co.

North American Range Plants. 4th ed. Stephan L. Hatch et al. LC 91-13836. (Illus.). xvi, 493p. 1992. pap. text 25.00 (*0-8032-9205-8*, Bison Books) U of Nebr Pr.

North American Range Plants. 5th ed. James Stubbendieck et al. LC 96-37402. (Illus.). xv, 501p. 1997. text 50.00 (*0-8032-4260-3*) U of Nebr Pr.

North American Range Plants. 5th ed. James Stubbendieck et al. LC 96-37402. (Illus.). xv, 501p. 1997. pap. text 25.00 (*0-8032-9243-0*) U of Nebr Pr.

North American Rapid Evacuation & Tunneling: Proceedings of the Conference, 2nd, San Francisco, CA, June 24-27, 2 vols., 1. North American Rapid Excavation & Tunneling Confer. LC 74-84644. 968p. reprint ed. pap. 200.00 (*0-608-11783-8*, 200513000050) Bks Demand.

North American Rapid Evacuation & Tunneling: Proceedings of the Conference, 2nd, San Francisco, CA, June 24-27, 2 vols., 2. North American Rapid Excavation & Tunneling Confer. LC 74-84644. 807p. reprint ed. pap. 200.00 (*0-608-11784-6*, 200513000051) Bks Demand.

North American Religion: The Journal of the Centre for the Study of North American Religion, Vol. 1. Ed. by Thomas A. Robinson & Malcolm Greenshields. 1992. write for info. (*0-7734-9066-3*) E Mellen.

North American Religion: The Journal of the Centre for the Study of North American Religion, Vol. 2. Ed. by Thomas A. Robinson & Malcolm Greenshields. 1993. 69.95 (*0-7734-9416-2*); pap. 29.95 (*0-7734-9418-9*) E Mellen.

North American Rockwell T-2 Buckeye, No. 15. Steven J. Ginter. (Illus.). 62p. (Orig.). 1987. pap. 12.95 (*0-942612-15-9*) Naval Fighters.

North American Roll Identifier GCA Standard 129, 1995. Ed. by Alan Kotok et al. (Illus.). 20p. (Orig.). 1995. pap. 17.00 (*0-933505-34-5*) Graph Comm Assn.

North American Romance Writers. Kay Mussell & Johanna Tunon. LC 98-44836. 296p. 1999. text 39.50 (*0-8108-3604-1*) Scarecrow.

North American Shortwave Frequency Guide, Vol. 3. rev. ed. James Pickard. (Illus.). 208p. 1996. pap. 19.95 (*0-917963-09-1*) Artsci Inc.

North American Sketches of R. B. Cunninghame Graham. Ed. by John Walker. LC 86-25054. 160p. 1987. text 29.95 (*0-8173-0355-3*) U of Ala Pr.

North American Social Report: Economics, Religion, & Morality, Vol. 5. Alex C. Michalos. 1982. pap. text 84.00 (*90-277-1358-8*) Kluwer Academic.

North American Social Report Vol. 1: A Comparative Study of the Quality of Life in Canada & Theusa from 1964 to 1974: Foundations, Populations & Health. Alex C. Michalos. 280p. 1980. pap. text 101.00 (*90-277-1058-9*) Kluwer Academic.

North American Social Report Vol. 3: A Comparative Study of the Quality of Life in Canada & the U. S. A. from 1964 to 1974. Alex C. Michalos. 212p. 1981. pap. text 95.50 (*90-277-1257-3*) Kluwer Academic.

North American Species of Cuterebra, The Rabbit & Rodent Bot Flies: (Diptera: Cuterebridae) Curtis W. Sabrosky. LC 86-82263. (Thomas Say Monographs: Vol. 11). 240p. 1986. 21.00 (*0-938522-30-2*, ESATS11) Entomol Soc.

North American Species of Gymnopilus. L. R. Hesler. (Mycologia Memoirs Ser.: No. 3). (Illus.). 117p. 1969. pap. text 12.50 (*0-945345-39-9*) Lubrecht & Cramer.

North American Species of Hygrophorus. Lexemuel R. Hesler & Alexander H. Smith. LC 62-20535. 430p. reprint ed. pap. 133.30 (*0-608-11958-X*, 202316900032) Bks Demand.

North American Species of Lactarius. Lexemuel R. Hesler & Alexander H. Smith. LC 78-6744. (Illus.). 853p. reprint ed. pap. 200.00 (*0-7837-4716-0*, 205906800003) Bks Demand.

North American Species of Pholiota. A. H. Smith & L. R. Hesler. (Illus.). 1979. reprint ed. lib. bdg. 20.00 (*0-02-852470-5*) Lubrecht & Cramer.

North American Starfishes. Alexander Agassiz. (Works of Alexander Agassiz). 1989. reprint ed. lib. bdg. 79.00 (*0-7812-1584-6*) Rprt Serv.

North American Strategic Network: International Traveler Information Interchange Standard (ITIS) Locational Database. Enterprise Staff. 69p. 1993. pap. text 10.00 (*1-884508-01-4*) CO Dept Transport.

North American Sturgeons: Biology & Aquaculture Potential. Ed. by F. P. Binkowski & S. I. Doroshov. 1986. text 192.00 (*90-6193-539-3*) Kluwer Academic.

North American Sun Kings: Keepers of the Flame. Joseph B. Mahan. 300p. 1992. 30.00 (*1-880820-03-X*) ISAC Pr.

North American Survey of Geoscientists. Ed. by Nicholas H. Claudy. 132p. 1988. pap. 20.00 (*0-913312-95-9*) Am Geol.

North American T-28 Trojan. Steven J. Ginter. (Naval Fighters Ser.: No. 5). (Illus.). 68p. (Orig.). 1982. pap. 12.95 (*0-942612-05-1*) Naval Fighters.

North American Tariffs, 35 vols., Set. 1996. 1245.00 (*0-614-18408-8*, 126TFZ) Info Gatekeepers.

North American Terrestrial Orchids: Symposium II - Proceedings & Lectures. Ed. by Elmer H. Plaxton. LC 82-62805. (Illus.). 144p. 1983. pap. 17.95 (*0-9610332-0-7*) Mich Orchid Soc.

North American Terrestrial Vegetation. 2nd rev. ed. Ed. by Michael G. Barbour & William Dwight Billings. LC 97-29061. (Illus.). 621p. (C). 2000. text 120.00 (*0-521-55027-0*); pap. text 49.95 (*0-521-55986-3*) Cambridge U Pr.

North American Think Tank on Youth Gambling Issues Final Report. Elizabeth M. George. 42p. 1995. reprint ed. spiral bd. 15.00 (*1-930467-02-8*, LA Zarus) MN Coun Gambling.

North American Timber Trends Study. David Boulter & David Darr. LC 96-220706. (UN ECE/FAO Timber & Forest Studies: No. 9). 48p. 25.00 (*92-1-116637-3*, 68691) UN.

North American T1 Equipment Markets: LAN Interconnectivity, Hybrid Networks Accurate Growth. Market Intelligence Staff. 520p. (Orig.). 1992. 1695.00 (*1-56753-375-2*) Frost & Sullivan.

North American T1/T3 Equipment Markets. Frost & Sullivan. 401p. 1997. spiral bd. 2495.20 (*0-7889-0634-8*, 2642-60) Frost & Sullivan.

North American Totem Poles: Secrets & Symbols of North America. Molly Perham. (Illus.). 16p. (J). (gr. 3-8). 1999. boxed set 14.95 (*1-55209-325-5*) Firefly Bks Ltd.

North American Trade Guide: 1998 Edition. Ed. by Dianna Birnie & Tery Moran-Lever. (ISSN Ser.: No. 1071-958X). (Illus.). 2056p. 1997. pap. text 419.00 (*0-9649630-7-8*) Primedia Directories.

North American Trade Guide, 1997. Ed. by Tery Moran-Lever. (Illus.). 1984p. 1996. pap. text 399.00 (*0-9649630-3-5*) Primedia Directories.

North American Trade Guide 1999. Dianna Birnie. 2072p. 1998. pap. 475.00 (*1-891131-02-8*) Primedia Directories.

North American Trajectory: Cultural, Economic, & Political Ties among the United States, Canada, & Mexico. Ronald F. Inglehart et al. LC 96-8795. (Social Institutions & Social Change Ser.). (Illus.). 208p. 1996. lib. bdg. 41.95 (*0-202-30556-2*) Aldine de Gruyter.

North American Trajectory: Cultural, Economic & Political Ties among the United States, Canada & Mexico. Ronald F. Inglehart et al. LC 96-8795. (Social Institutions & Social Change Ser.). (Illus.). 208p. 1996. pap. text 20.95 (*0-202-30557-0*) Aldine de Gruyter.

North American Trees: A Comprehensive Guide. 3rd ed. Elias. 800p. 89.95 (*0-471-16277-9*) Wiley.

North American Trees: Exclusive of Mexico & Tropical Florida. 4th ed. Richard J. Preston, Jr. LC 89-1944. (Illus.). 436p. (C). 1989. 49.95 (*0-8138-1171-6*); pap. 26.95 (*0-8138-1172-4*) Iowa St U Pr.

North American Truck Accessory Aftermarkets. Ed. by Frost & Sullivan Staff. 366p. 1997. spiral bd. 2950.00 (*0-7889-0674-7*, 5574-18) Frost & Sullivan.

***North American Truck Fleet Directory 2000.** 1846p. 1999. pap. 335.00 (*0-88711-381-8*) Am Trucking Assns.

North American Tunneling '98: Proceedings of the North American Tunneling '98 Conference, Newport Beach, California, 21-25.02.1998. Ed. by Levent Ozdemir. LC 99-496418. (Illus.). 275p. (C). 1998. text 98.00 (*90-5410-931-9*, Pub. by A A Balkema) Ashgate Pub Co.

North American Tunneling, '96: Proceedings of the North American Conference NAT '96 & 22nd General Assembly International, vols. 2. Ed. by Levent Ozdemir. (Illus.). 863p. (C). 1996. text 188.00 (*90-5410-802-9*, Pub. by A A Balkema) Ashgate Pub Co.

North American Tunneling '96, Vol. 1. Ozdemir. 529p. 1996. 97.00 (*90-5410-803-7*) Ashgate Pub Co.

North American Tunneling '96, Vol. 2. Ozdemir. 270p. 1996. 97.00 (*90-5410-804-5*) Ashgate Pub Co.

North American Voice Processing Service. 590p. 1996. spiral bd. 2495.00 (*0-7889-0575-9*, 2517-63) Frost & Sullivan.

North American Wading Birds. John Netherton. LC 98-13105. (Illus.). 128p. 1998. pap. 16.95 (*0-89658-402-X*) Voyageur Pr.

North American Wild Game Cookbook. Bill Mabbutt & Anita Mabbutt. (Illus.). 212p. (Orig.). 1992. reprint ed. pap. 12.95 (*0-9634334-0-7*); reprint ed. spiral bd. 12.95 (*0-9634334-1-5*) B & A Mabbutt.

North American Wildlife. Joan Campbell. LC 87-63429. 1988. 8.95 (*0-916809-22-6*) Scott Pubns MI.

***North American Wildlife.** David Jones. (Illus.). 304p. 1999. 29.95 (*1-55110-900-X*) Whitecap Bks.

***North American Wildlife.** WALL-12r. 1999. 12.95 (*1-57624-489-X*) A M C A L.

***North American Wildlife: An Illustrated Guide to 2,000 Plants & Animals.** Reader's Digest Editors. 1998. 28.95 (*0-7621-0020-6*, Pub. by RD Assn) Penguin Putnam.

***North American Wildlife Realistic 3-D Scrollsaw Art.** Rick Longabaugh & Karen Longabaugh. (Illus.). 128p. 1999. pap. 14.95 (*0-9633112-8-X*) Berry Basket.

North American Wildlife Series. Bobbie Kalman. Incl. Animal Babies. (Illus.). 56p. (J). (gr. 3-10). 1987. pap. 8.95 (*0-86505-186-0*); Birds at My Feeder. LC 93-6237. (Illus.). 56p. (J). (gr. 3-10). 1987. pap. 8.95 (*0-86505-187-9*); Forest Mammals. Illus. by Glen Loates. 56p. (J). (gr. 3-10). 1987. pap. 8.95 (*0-86505-185-2*); Owls. Illus. by Glen Loates. 56p. (J). (gr. 3-4). 1987. pap. 8.95 (*0-86505-184-4*); (J). (gr. 3-4). 1987. Set pap. 35.80 (*0-86505-203-4*) Crabtree Pub Co.

North American Wildlife Series, 4 bks. Bobbie Kalman. Incl. Animal Babies. (Illus.). 56p. (J). (gr. 3-4). 1987. 21.28 (*0-86505-166-6*); Birds at My Feeder. (Illus.). 56p. (J). (gr. 3-4). 1987. 21.28 (*0-86505-167-4*); (J). 1987. write for info. (*0-86505-183-6*) Crabtree Pub Co.

North American Windmill Manufacturers' Trade Literature: A Descriptive Guide. Ed. by T. Lindsay Baker. LC 98-6908. (Illus.). 608p. 1998. 37.50 (*0-8061-3045-8*) U of Okla Pr.

North American Wireless Customer Premises Equipment. Ed. by Frost & Sullivan Staff. 176p. 1997. spiral bd. 3900.00 (*0-7889-0711-5*, 2697-62) Frost & Sullivan.

North American Wireless Office Markets. Frost & Sullivan Staff. 466p. 1996. spiral bd. 2495.00 (*0-7889-0597-X*, 2466-65) Frost & Sullivan.

North American Wolves. Barbara Keevil Parker. LC 97-41572. (J). (gr. 2-5). 1997. 19.93 (*1-57505-095-1*, Carolrhoda) Lerner Pub.

North American Women Artists of the Twentieth Century: A Biographical Dictionary. Ed. by Jules Heller & Nancy G. Heller. LC 94-49710. (Illus.). 736p. 1997. pap. text 34.95 (*0-8153-2584-3*) Garland.

North American XB-70 Valkyrie: A Photo Chronicle. Garry R. Pape & John M. Campbell. LC 94-66966. (Illus.). 288p. (YA). (gr. 10-13). 1995. pap. 9.95 (*0-88740-906-7*) Schiffer.

North American XB-70 in Color. John M. Campbell. LC 97-80704. (Illus.). 112p. 1998. pap. 19.95 (*0-7643-0507-7*) Schiffer.

North-Americans of Yesterday: A Comparative Study of North-American Indian Life, Customs, & Products, on the Theory of the Ethnic Unity of Race. Frederick Samuel Dellenbaugh. LC 74-7950. (Illus.). reprint ed. 49.50 (*0-404-11837-2*) AMS Pr.

North America's Endangered Species. David Sanger. Ed. by Don Lynch. (Illus.). 97p. (J). (gr. 4-8). 1992. pap. text 1.50 (*0-913205-17-6*) Grace Dangberg.

North America's Favorite Butterflies: A Pictorial Guide. Patti Putnam & Milt Putnam. LC 97-9334. (Illus.). 136p. 1997. pap. 9.95 (*1-57223-109-2*, 1092) Willow Creek Pr.

North America's Greatest Big Game Lodges & Outfitters: More Than 250 Hot Spots in the Unites States & Canada. John E. Ross & Jay Cassell. LC 99-31204. (Illus.). 308p. 1999. pap. 19.95 (*1-57223-147-5*, 147X) Willow Creek Pr.

***North America's Greatest Bird Hunting Lodges & Preserves: More Than 200 Hotspots in the U. S. & Canada.** John Ross. LC 00-21961. (Illus.). 278p. 2000. pap. 19.95 (*1-57223-279-X*, 279x) Willow Creek Pr.

***North America's Greatest Fishing Lodges: More Than 250 Destinations in the United States, Canada & Central America.** 2nd rev. ed. John Ross. LC 00-26389.Tr. of Aports Afield's guide to North America's Greatest Fishing Lodges. (Illus.). 352p. 2000. pap. 19.95 (*1-57223-297-8*, 2978) Willow Creek Pr.

***North America's Greatest Mountain Vacations: 100 Peak Destinations in U. S. & Canada.** Mark Williams. (Illus.). 228p. 2000. pap. 19.95 (*1-57223-287-0*) Willow Creek Pr.

***North America's Greatest Waterfowling Lodges & Outfitters: 250 Prime Destinations in the U. S., Canada & Mexico.** Chuck Petrie. (Illus.). 278p. 2000. pap. 19.95 (*1-57223-312-5*) Willow Creek Pr.

North & Central America see 1999 Political Risk Yearbook

North & South. Elizabeth Gaskell. Ed. & Intro. by Patricia Ingham. 480p. 1996. pap. 8.95 (*0-14-043424-0*) Penguin Putnam.

North & South. Elizabeth Gaskell. Ed. by Jenny Uglow. 442p. 1993. pap. 6.95 (*0-460-87257-5*, Everyman's Classic Lib) Tuttle Pubng.

North & South. Elizabeth Gaskell. (Classics Library). 1998. pap. 3.95 (*1-85326-093-2*, 0932WW, Pub. by Wrdsworth Edits) NTC Contemp Pub Co.

North & South. John Jakes. 816p. 1985. mass mkt. 7.50 (*0-440-16205-X*) Dell.

North & South. John Jakes. LC 81-47898. 752p. 1982. 24.95 (*0-15-166998-8*) Harcourt.

***North & South.** John Jakes. (North & South Trilogy Ser.: Vol. 1). 816p. 2000. mass mkt. 7.99 (*0-451-20081-0*, Sig) NAL.

North & South. large type ed. Elizabeth Gaskell. 725p. 1982. 27.99 (*0-7089-8031-7*, Charnwood) Ulverscroft.

North & South. Elizabeth Gaskell. 1988. reprint ed. lib. bdg. 49.00 (*0-7812-0038-5*) Rprt Serv.

North & South. Elizabeth Gaskell. LC 70-145039. 1971. reprint ed. 69.00 (*0-403-00985-5*) Scholarly.

North & South. 2nd ed. Elizabeth Gaskell. Ed. by Angus Easson. LC 98-13092. (Oxford World's Classics Ser.). 494p. 1998. pap. 7.95 (*0-19-283194-1*) OUP.

North & South: A Statistical View of the Conditions of the Free & Slave States. Henry Chase & Charles W. Sanbourn. LC 75-116280. 191p. 1972. reprint ed. 13.00 (*0-403-00437-3*) Scholarly.

***North & South American Indians.** George Catlin. (LC History-America-E). 99p. 1999. reprint ed. lib. bdg. 69.00 (*0-7812-4247-9*) Rprt Serv.

North & South Carolina Marriage Records from the Earliest Colonial Days to the Civil War. William M. Clemens. LC 73-1942. 295p. 1995. reprint ed. 25.00 (*0-8063-0555-X*, 1025) Genealog Pub.

***North & South Korean Political Systems: A Comparative Analysis.** rev. ed. Sung Chul Yang. LC 99-65245. 1013p. 1999. 54.95 (*1-56591-105-9*) Hollym Intl.

North & South: Slavery - Its Contrasts. Caroline E. Rush. LC 70-149877. (Black Heritage Library Collection). 1977. 28.95 (*0-8369-8757-8*) Ayer.

North & West. Michael Burwell. (Illus.). (Orig.). (C). 1989. pap. 3.95 (*0-9623693-0-6*) Heaven Bone Pr.

North & West Africa. 1996. 10.95 (*2-06-700953-2*, 953) Michelin.

North Anna Campaign "Even to Hell Itself" May 21-26, 1864. J. Michael Miller. (Virginia Civil War Battles & Leaders Ser.). (Illus.). 188p. 1989. 19.95 (*0-930919-71-8*) H E Howard.

North Apennines: United States Army Campaigns of World War 2. Dwight D. Oland. 31p. 1996. pap. 1.75 (*0-16-061321-3*) USGPO.

North Apennines & Beyond with the 10th Mountain Division. Harris Dusenbery. LC 98-72371. (Illus.). 272p. 1998. pap. 14.95 (*0-8323-0522-7*) Binford Mort.

North Arabian Desert Archaeological Survey, 1925-50. Henry Field. (HU PMP Ser.: Vol. 45, No. 2). (Orig.). 1960. 40.00 (*0-527-01319-6*) Periodicals Srv.

North Atlantic Assembly. Christian Brumter. 1986. lib. bdg. 96.00 (*90-247-3318-9*) Kluwer Academic.

North Atlantic Civilization at War: The World War II Battles of Sky, Sand, Snow, Sea & Shore. Patrick L. Hatcher. LC 97-14509. 192p. (C). (gr. 13). 1998. 28.95 (*0-7656-0135-4*, East Gate Bk) M E Sharpe.

North Atlantic Coast Fisheries Arbitration at the Hague: Argument on Behalf of the United States. Elihu Root. (Illus.). cix, 445p. 1982. reprint ed. 49.95 (*0-8377-1035-9*, Rothman) W S Hein.

***North Atlantic International General Aviation Operations Manual.** 49p. 1999. pap. 5.25 (*0-16-058879-0*) USGPO.

North Atlantic Mail Sailings, 1840-75. W. Hubbard & R. Winter. 1988. 50.00 (*0-9603548-4-0*) US Phil Classics.

North Atlantic Maritime Cultures. Ed. by Raoul Andersen. (World Anthropology Ser.). (Illus.). xviii, 365p. 1979. 63.10 (*90-279-7830-1*) Mouton.

***North Atlantic Treaty Organization (NATO) Enlargement Costs.** United States Government Printing Office Staff. LC 98-166271. (S. Hrg. Ser.). vi, 163 p. 1998. write for info. (*0-16-056524-3*) USGPO.

North Atlantic Treaty Organization vs. the Warsaw Pact Military Alliance - a Geopolitical Struggle: Essays on National Security. Joseph D. Lowe. LC 89-91186. (Illus.). 325p. 1994. 100.00 (*0-930325-13-3*) Lowe Pub.

North Atlantic Water Dependent Use Study, 3 vols., Vols. I-III. Ed. by Marine Law Institute, Staff. (Orig.). 1989. pap. 20.00 (*0-9618224-0-6*) Univ S ME Marine Law Inst.

North Atlantic Water Dependent Use Study Vol. 1: Managing the Shoreline for Water Dependent Uses. Marine Law Institute, Staff & Robinson & Cole Land Use, Staff. (Handbook of Legal Tools). (Orig.). 1989. pap. 10.00 (*0-9618224-2-2*) Univ S ME Marine Law Inst.

North Atlantic Water Dependent Use Study Vol. 2: Guidebook to the Economics of Waterfront Planning & Water Dependent Uses. Marine Law Institute, Staff & Boston University Institute for Employment Policy,. 296p. (Orig.). 1989. pap. 10.00 (*0-9618224-3-0*) Univ S ME Marine Law Inst.

North Atlantic Water Dependent Use Study Vol. 3: An Executive Summary. Marine Law Institute, Staff. 32p. (Orig.). 1989. pap. 2.00 (*0-9618224-4-9*) Univ S ME Marine Law Inst.

North Atlantic World in the Seventeenth Century. Kenneth G. Davies. LC 74-78994. (Europe & the World in the Age of Expansion Ser.: No. 4). 380p. 1974. pap. 117.80 (*0-7837-2967-7*, 205748700006) Bks Demand.

North Attleborough. Bob Lanpher. (Images of America Ser.). 1998. pap. 16.99 (*0-7524-0885-2*) Arcadia Publng.

North Australian Sea Cucumbers. L.R. Cannon & H. Silver. 1994. 86.95 (*3-540-14194-4*); 86.95 (*3-540-14193-6*) Spr-Verlag.

North Bank: Claiming a Place on the Rogue. Robin Carey. LC 98-25222. 128p. 1998. 19.95 (*0-87071-448-1*) Oreg St U Pr.

North Bank Road: The Spokane, Portland & Seattle Railway. John T. Gaertner. LC 90-39951. (Illus.). 288p. (Orig.). 1991. pap. 24.95 (*0-87422-070-X*) Wash St U Pr.

North Bay Door County, Wisconsin: From Pristine Wilderness to Viable Community. James A. Erickson. LC 98-71891. 224p. (Orig.). (C). 1998. pap. 16.95 (*1-57579-112-9*) Pine Hill Pr.

North Bay Narrative. Walter Staples. LC 98-31488. (Illus.). 210p. 1998. pap. 15.00 (*0-914339-70-2*, Pub. by P E Randall Pub) U Pr of New Eng.

North Bay Trails: Outdoor Adventures in Marin, Napa & Sonoma Counties. David Weintraub. LC 99-55952. 288p. 1999. pap. 15.95 (*0-89997-236-5*) Wilderness Pr.

***North Beach Revisited: New & Revised Poems.** A. D. Winans. LC 99-97624. 106p. 2000. pap. 12.95 (*1-891408-11-9*, GBP-11) Green Bean.

North Berwick Register, 1904 (Town History & Directory) Mitchell & Campbell. 112p. 1997. reprint ed. pap. 19.50 (*0-8328-5879-X*) Higginson Bk Co.

***North Biscay: Quessant to the Gironde Estuary.** K. Adlard Coles. 260p. 1999. 125.00 (*0-85288-416-8*, Pub. by Laurie Norie & Wilson Ltd) St Mut.

North Biscay: Quessant to the Gironde Estuary. 6th rev. ed. K. Adlard Coles. (Illus.). 224p. 1994. 125.00 (*0-85288-245-9*, Pub. by Laurie Norie & Wilson Ltd) St Mut.

North Biscay Pilot. K. Adlard Coles & A. N. Black. 1979. 49.95 (*0-8464-0072-3*) Beekman Pubs.

North Branford & Northford, 1850-1950. Totoket Historical Society Staff. (Images of America Ser.). 1998. pap. 16.99 (*0-7524-0952-2*) Arcadia Publng.

An Asterisk (*) at the beginning of an entry indicates that the title is appearing for the first time.

***North Brevard County.** John Manning & Robert Hudson. (Images of America Ser.). (Illus.). 128p. 1999. pap. 18.99 (*0-7385-0241-3*) Arcadia Publng.

North Briton: A Study in Political Propaganda. George Nobbe. LC 39-24192. reprint ed. 20.00 (*0-404-04779-3*) AMS Pr.

North Brittany: St. Malo to Quessant. 6th rev. ed. K. Adlard Coles. (Illus.). 256p. (C). 1992. 125.00 (*0-85288-162-2*, Pub. by Laurie Norie & Wilson Ltd) St Mut.

North Burgos Archaeological Survey: Bronze & Iron Age Archaeology on the Meseta del Norte (Province of Burgos, North-Central Spain) Ed. by G. A. Clark. (Anthropological Research Papers: No. 19). (Illus.). xviii, 307p. 1979. pap. 20.00 (*0-685-19302-0*) AZ Univ ARP.

North by Choice: Tahquamenon Area Poems. Ed. by Frances Alatalo & Lori Anderson. (Illus.). 112p. (Orig.). 1991. pap. 12.95 (*0-9629546-0-8*) Newberry News.

***North by Night: A Story of the Underground Railroad.** Katherine Ayres. (Illus.). 192p. (YA). 2000. pap. 4.50 (*0-440-22747-X*, YB BDD) BDD Bks Young Read.

North by Night: A Story of the Underground Railroad. Katherine Ayres. LC 98-10039. 192p. (J). (gr. 5-9). 1998. 15.95 (*0-385-32564-9*) Delacorte.

North by Northwest. Rebello Auiler. 2000. text 27.95 (*0-312-24413-4*) St Martin.

North by Northwest. Alfred Hitchcock. Ed. by James Naremore. LC 93-18283. (Films in Print Ser.: Vol. 20). (Illus.). 310p. (C). 1993. text 40.00 (*0-8135-2006-1*); pap. text 17.00 (*0-8135-2007-X*) Rutgers U Pr.

***North by Northwest.** John Leham & Ernest. (Illus.). 144p. 2000. pap. 14.00 (*0-571-20184-9*) Faber & Faber.

North by Northwest: The Screenplay. Ernest Lehman. 1976. 18.95 (*0-8488-0178-4*) Amereon Ltd.

North Cabin Gallery. John Ratzloff. 1992. pap. 12.95 (*0-934860-87-4*) Adventure Pubns.

North California. 5th ed. Insight Guides Staff. (Insight Guides). 1998. pap. text 22.95 (*0-88729-731-5*) Langenscheidt.

***North Canada - Yukon, Northwest Territories, Nunavut: The Bradt Travel Guide.** Geoffrey Roy. (Illus.). 2000. pap. 18.95 (*1-84162-003-3*) Globe Pequot.

North Carolina see From Sea to Shining Sea

North Carolina see Atlas of Historical County Boundaries

North Carolina see One Nation Series

***North Carolina.** Alliance for Safe Driving Staff. (Career Education - License to Drive Ser.). 2002. 31.50 (*0-7668-2376-8*); 10.50 (*0-7668-2377-6*) Delmar.

North Carolina. Capstone Press, Geography Department Staff. (One Nation Ser.). (Illus.). 48p. (J). (gr. 3-7). 1997. lib. bdg. 19.00 (*0-516-20932-9*) Childrens.

North Carolina. Dennis B. Fradin. LC 91-35576. (From Sea to Shining Sea Ser.). (Illus.). 64p. (J). (gr. 3-5). 1992. pap. 7.95 (*0-516-43833-6*) Childrens.

North Carolina. H. M. Gousha. 1996. 2.95 (*0-671-55091-8*) S&S Trade.

North Carolina. Carol M. Highsmith & Ted Landphair. LC 97-37125. (Photographic Tour Ser.). (Illus.). 128p. 1998. 14.99 (*0-517-18605-5*) Random.

North Carolina. Paul Joseph. LC 97-18663. (United States Ser.). (Illus.). 32p. (J). 1998. lib. bdg. 19.93 (*1-56239-869-5*, Checkerboard Library) ABDO Pub Co.

***North Carolina.** Tanya Lloyd. (Illus.). 96p. 2000. 14.95 (*1-55285-027-7*) Carlton Bks Ltd.

North Carolina. Andrea Schulz. LC 92-44846. (Illus.). 72p. 1993. lib. bdg. 19.95 (*0-8225-2744-8*, Lerner Publctns) Lerner Pub.

North Carolina. Andrea Schulz. (Hello U. S. A. Ser.). (Illus.). 72p. (J). (gr. 3-6). 1998. pap. 5.95 (*0-8225-9790-X*) Lerner Pub.

North Carolina. Kathleen Thompson. LC 95-26118. (Portrait of America Library). 48p. (J). (gr. 4-8). 1996. pap. 5.95 (*0-8114-7459-3*) Raintree Steck-V.

North Carolina. Kathleen Thompson. (Portrait of America Library). (Illus.). 48p. (YA). (gr. 3-6). 1996. lib. bdg. 22.83 (*0-8114-7378-3*) Raintree Steck-V.

North Carolina. 2nd ed. Martin Hintz & Stephen V. Hintz. LC 97-44305. (America the Beautiful Ser.). (J). 1998. lib. bdg. 32.00 (*0-516-20638-9*) Childrens.

North Carolina. 4th ed. LC 97-208867. 1997. write for info. (*0-15-309122-3*) Harcourt.

North Carolina: A Camera Profile. Ed. by Jane Corey. (Illus.). 1978. pap. 8.95 (*0-936179-06-6*) Provincial NC.

North Carolina: A Complete Tour Book in Five Languages: Four Seasons of Splendor: Spanish, French, German, Japanese, English. Catherine D. Joseph. 48p. (Orig.). 1995. pap. 7.50 (*1-880970-17-1*) Aerial Photo.

North Carolina: A Guide to Backcountry Travel & Adventure. James Bannon. LC 95-71155. (Illus.). 387p. (Orig.). 1995. pap. 16.00 (*0-9648584-0-1*) Out There Pr.

North Carolina: A Guide to the Old North State. Federal Writers' Project Staff. (American Guidebook Ser.). 649p. 1939. reprint ed. 95.00 (*0-403-02182-0*) Somerset Pub.

North Carolina: A Guide to the Old North State. Federal Writers' Project Staff & Writers Program-WPA Staff. (American Guide Ser.). 1989. reprint ed. lib. bdg. 89.00 (*0-7812-1032-1*, 1032) Rprt Serv.

***North Carolina: A Guide to Unique Places.** 5th ed. Sara Pitzer. (Off the Beaten Path Ser.). (Illus.). 2000. pap. 12.95 (*0-7627-0818-2*) Globe Pequot.

North Carolina: A History. William S. Powell. LC 88-40142. xvi, 232p. 1988. reprint ed. pap. 11.95 (*0-8078-4219-2*) U of NC Pr.

North Carolina: A Pictorial Souvenier. Carol Highsmith. 1999. 7.99 (*0-517-20484-3*) Random Hse Value.

North Carolina: Cobb's America Guyed Books. Irvin S. Cobb. (Collected Works of Irvin S. Cobb). 61p. 1998. reprint ed. lib. bdg. 88.00 (*1-58201-602-X*) Classic Bks.

North Carolina: From the Mountains to the Sea. Jim Doane. LC 80-80955. 72p. (J). (ps-12). 1980. 3.50 (*0-936672-75-7*) Aerial Photo.

North Carolina: Images of Wildness. George Humphries. 128p. 1993. 39.95 (*1-56579-042-1*); pap. 29.95 (*1-56579-043-X*) Westcliffe Pubs.

North Carolina: Off the Beaten Path: A Guide to Unique Places. 4th ed. Sara Pitzer. LC 98-35319. (Off the Beaten Path Ser.). (Illus.). 288p. 1998. pap. 12.95 (*0-7627-0272-9*) Globe Pequot.

North Carolina: Our People, Places, & Past. James D. Charlet et al. (Illus.). 320p. (J). (gr. 4 up). 1987. lib. bdg. 22.95 (*0-89089-319-5*) Carolina Acad Pr.

North Carolina: Our People, Places, & Past Student Workbook. James D. Charlet et al. (Illus.). 300p. (YA). 1988. student ed. 49.95 (*0-935911-13-8*) Cornucop Pub.

North Carolina: The Final Battles. Mark Snell. (Civil War Regiments Ser.: Vol. 6). (Illus.). 188p. 1998. pap. 12.00 (*1-882810-54-6*) Savas Pub.

North Carolina: The History of a Southern State. Hugh T. Lefler & Albert R. Newsome. LC 72-81330. (Illus.). 825p. reprint ed. pap. 200.00 (*0-8357-3869-8*, 203660100004) Bks Demand.

North Carolina: The Tar Heel State. James Killoran et al. (Illus.). 433p. (YA). (gr. 4 up). 1997. 27.95 (*1-882422-29-5*) Jarrett Pub.

North Carolina: 1870 Census Index, 3 vols., Set. Ed. by Bradley W. Steuart. 2953p. 1989. lib. bdg. 350.00 (*1-877677-00-0*) Herit Quest.

North Carolina - Collected Works of Federal Writers Project. Federal Writers' Project Staff. 1991. reprint ed. lib. bdg. 98.00 (*0-7812-5696-8*) Rprt Serv.

North Carolina - Robinson on Corporation Law: 1991 Supplement. Jack Robinson. 81p. 1996. write for info. (*0-87473-864-4*, 66662-10, MICHIE) LEXIS Pub.

***North Carolina Advance Annotation Service No. 3.** 275p. 1999. pap. Price not set. (*0-327-09733-7*, 4658515) LEXIS Pub.

North Carolina Advance Annotation Service Pamphlet, 1998, No. 2. 160p. 1998. pap. write for info. (*0-327-05077-2*, 46584-14) LEXIS Pub.

***North Carolina Advance Legislative Service, No. 1.** 150p. 1999. Price not set. (*0-327-08893-1*, 4657116) LEXIS Pub.

***North Carolina Advance Legislative Service, Vol. 4.** 510p. 1999. pap. write for info. (*0-327-09847-3*, 4657416) LEXIS Pub.

North Carolina & Old Salem Cookery. rev. ed. Beth Tartan. LC 91-50790. (Chapel Hill Bks.). (Illus.). viii, 282p. (C). 1992. 34.95 (*0-8078-2035-0*); pap. 19.95 (*0-8078-4375-X*) U of NC Pr.

North Carolina & Other State Greats (Biographies) Carole Marsh. (Carole Marsh North Carolina Bks.). (Illus.). (J). 1994. pap. 19.95 (*1-55609-938-X*); lib. bdg. 29.95 (*1-55609-937-1*); disk 29.95 (*1-55609-939-8*) Gallopade Intl.

North Carolina & the Coming of the Civil War. William C. Harris. (Illus.). xiv, 65p. 1992. reprint ed. pap. 8.00 (*0-86526-235-7*) NC Archives.

North Carolina & the New Deal. Anthony J. Badger. (Illus.). xiii, 102p. 1981. pap. 5.00 (*0-86526-186-5*) NC Archives.

North Carolina & the War of 1812. Sarah M. Lemmon. (Illus.). ix, 54p. 1984. pap. 5.00 (*0-86526-087-7*) NC Archives.

North Carolina Annotated Rules, 1999 Supplement: Pocket Part. 110p. 1999. write for info. (*0-327-08647-5*, 46489-16) LEXIS Pub.

North Carolina Aquaculture Report. Rural Economic Development Center Staff. 128p. (Orig.). 1989. pap. text 5.00 (*0-945597-12-6*) NC Biotech Ctr.

North Carolina Architecture: Published for the Historic Preservation Foundation of North Carolina Inc. Catherine W. Bishir. LC 90-30662. (Illus.). xvi, 516p. (C). 1990. 85.00 (*0-8078-1923-9*) U of NC Pr.

North Carolina Area Health Education Centers: A Brief History. Henry S. Uhl. Ed. by Karen Klein. (Illus.). 88p. (C). 1993. pap. text. write for info. (*0-9621194-6-6*) Stratford NC.

North Carolina Artists Exhibition, 1990. Ed. by Christine J. Huber. LC 84-650670. (Illus.). 102p. (Orig.). 1990. pap. 10.00 (*0-88259-959-3*) NCMA.

North Carolina Arts Council Artist Fellowships, 1993-94. Jeff Fleming et al. Ed. by Nancy H. Margolis. (Illus.). 28p. 1994. write for info. (*0-9611560-2-3*) SEC Contemp Art.

North Carolina As a Civil War Battleground, 1861-1865. John G. Barrett. (Illus.). 1998. reprint ed. pap. 8.00 (*0-86526-088-5*) NC Archives.

***North Carolina Atlas: Portrait for a New Century.** Ed. by Douglas M. Orr, Jr. & Alfred W. Stuart. LC 99-17353. (Illus.). 480p. 2000. 45.00 (*0-8078-2507-7*) U of NC Pr.

***North Carolina Atlas 2000.** 4th ed. Ed. by DeLorme Mapping Staff. (Illus.). 2000. pap. 19.95 (*0-89933-277-3*) DeLorme Map.

North Carolina Attorney's/Paralegal's/Secretary's Handbook. 3rd ed. Jean M. Walburg. (Attorney's/Paralegal's/Secretary's Handbooks Ser.). 522p. 1997. ring bd. 47.00 (*0-927573-48-2*) Mariposa Pub.

North Carolina Attorney's/Paralegal's/Secretary's Handbook. 3rd ed. Ed. by Jean M. Walburg. (Attorney's/Paralegal's/Secretary's Handbooks Ser.). 700p. 1997. ring bd. 47.00 (*0-927573-54-7*) Mariposa Pub.

North Carolina Automotive Directory. Ed. by T. L. Spelman. 1985. 24.95 (*1-55527-024-7*) Auto Contact Inc.

North Carolina Bandits, Bushwackers, Outlaws, Crooks, Devils, Ghosts, Desperadoes & Other Assorted & Sundry Characters! Carole Marsh. (Carole Marsh North Carolina Bks.). (Illus.). (J). 1994. pap. 19.95 (*0-7933-0840-2*); lib. bdg. 29.95 (*0-7933-0841-0*); disk 29.95 (*0-7933-0842-9*) Gallopade Intl.

North Carolina Barbecue. Bob Garner. LC 96-22503. (Illus.). 1996. 19.95 (*0-89587-152-1*) Blair.

North Carolina Beaches. Glenn Morris. LC 97-31528. (Illus.). 312p. 1998. pap. 18.95 (*0-8078-4683-X*) U of NC Pr.

North Carolina Biking Guide. Chris Boyce. Ed. by Barbara McCaig. 100p. (Orig.). 1989. pap. text 5.95 (*0-935201-79-3*) Affordable Adven.

North Carolina "BIO" Bingo! 24 Must Know State People for Kids to Learn about While Having Fun! Carole Marsh. (Bingo! Ser.). (Illus.). (J). (gr. 2-8). 1998. pap. 14.95 (*0-7933-8621-7*) Gallopade Intl.

North Carolina Birds. James Kavanagh. (Pocket Naturalist Ser.). (Illus.). 12p. (YA). 1997. pap. 5.95 (*1-889903-40-X*, Pub. by Waterford WA) Falcon Pub Inc.

North Carolina Bookstore Book: A Surprising Guide to Our State's Bookstores & Their Specialties for Students, Teachers, Writers & Publishers. Carole Marsh. (Carole Marsh North Carolina Bks.). (Illus.). 1994. pap. 19.95 (*0-7933-2955-8*); lib. bdg. 29.95 (*0-7933-2954-X*); disk 29.95 (*0-7933-2956-6*) Gallopade Intl.

***North Carolina Business Directory, 1999-2000.** American Business Directories Staff. 2848p. 1999. boxed set 520.00 incl. cd-rom (*0-7687-0137-6*, 1046-9060) Am Busn Direct.

***North Carolina Business Directory (2000-2001)** American Business Directories Staff et al. 2,848p. 2000. boxed set 520.00 incl. cd-rom (*0-7687-0222-4*) Am Busn Direct.

North Carolina Capital Case Law Handbook. Robert L. Farb. LC 97-128375. 248p. (Orig.). (C). 1996. pap. text 21.00 (*1-56011-289-1*, 96.09) Institute Government.

North Carolina Capital Case Law Handbook. limited ed. Robert L. Farb. LC 97-128375. 248p. (Orig.). 1996. text 31.00 (*1-56011-293-X*, 96.09HB) Institute Government.

North Carolina Census Index: 1850 Slave Schedule. (Illus.). 1988. lib. bdg. 95.00 (*0-89593-444-2*, Accel Indexing) Genealogical Srvcs.

North Carolina Census Index: 1860 Slave Schedule. (Illus.). 1990. lib. bdg. 120.00 (*0-89593-446-9*, Accel Indexing) Genealogical Srvcs.

North Carolina Census Index: 1890 Union Veterans. Ronald V. Jackson. (Illus.). 1984. lib. bdg. 79.00 (*0-89593-755-7*, Accel Indexing) Genealogical Srvcs.

North Carolina Chain Gang, a Study of County Convict Road Work. Jesse F. Steiner & Roy M. Brown. LC 69-14949. (Criminology, Law Enforcement, & Social Problems Ser.: No. 39). (Illus.). 1969. reprint ed. 24.00 (*0-87585-039-1*) Patterson Smith.

North Carolina Charters & Constitutions, 1578-1698. Mattie Parker. (Colonial Records of North Carolina Ser.: Vol. 1). xxii, 247p. 1963. 15.00 (*0-86526-022-2*) NC Archives.

North Carolina Charters & Constitutions, 1578-1698. deluxe ed. Ed. by Mattie Parker. (Colonial Records of North Carolina Ser.). xxii, 247p. 1963. lthr. 20.00 (*0-86526-021-4*) NC Archives.

North Carolina Christmas. Jan Kiefer. (Illus.). 128p. 1996. 39.95 (*1-56579-154-1*) Westcliffe Pubs.

***North Carolina City & County Privilege License Taxes.** 5th ed. William A. Campbell. (C). 2000. pap. 14.50 (*1-56011-365-0*) Institute Government.

North Carolina City Council Procedures. 2nd rev. ed. David M. Lawrence. LC 97-192212. 38p. (Orig.). 1997. pap. text 13.00 (*1-56011-301-4*, 96.22) Institute Government.

North Carolina Civil Procedure, 2 Vols. 2nd ed. G. Gray Wilson. 160.00 (*0-327-12385-0*) LEXIS Pub.

North Carolina Civil Procedure, 2 vols. 2nd ed. G. Gray Wilson. LC 95-81778. 1995. 160.00 (*1-55834-301-6*, 68480-11, MICHIE) LEXIS Pub.

North Carolina Civil Procedure: 1990 Supplement. G. Grey Wilson. 1991. write for info. (*0-87473-734-6*, 68481-10, MICHIE) LEXIS Pub.

North Carolina Civil Procedure: 1991 Cumulative Supplement. Gray Wilson. 156p. 1991. write for info. (*0-87473-861-X*, 68482-10, MICHIE) LEXIS Pub.

North Carolina Civil Procedure, 1998 Cumulative Supplement. 2nd ed. G. Gray Wilson. 75p. 1998. suppl. ed. write for info. (*0-327-00492-4*, 6848315) LEXIS Pub.

***North Carolina Civil Procedure, 1999 Cumulative Supplement: Pocketpart, 2 vols.** 2nd ed. Incl. Vol. 1. 1999. (*0-327-01746-5*, 68486-16); Vol. 2. 1999. (*0-327-01747-3*, 68487-16); 100p. 1999. suppl. ed. write for info. (*0-327-01745-7*, 68483-16) LEXIS Pub.

North Carolina Civil War Documentary. Ed. by John G. Barrett & W. Buck Yearns. LC 79-17604. (Illus.). xvi, 365p. 1980. 32.50 (*0-8078-1407-5*) U of NC Pr.

North Carolina Classic Christmas Trivia: Stories, Recipes, Activities, Legends, Lore & More. Carole Marsh. (Carole Marsh North Carolina Bks.). (Illus.). (J). 1994. pap. 19.95 (*0-7933-0843-7*); lib. bdg. 29.95 (*0-7933-0844-5*); disk 29.95 (*0-7933-0845-3*) Gallopade Intl.

North Carolina Coastales! Carole Marsh. (Carole Marsh North Carolina Bks.). (J). 1994. lib. bdg. 29.95 (*0-7933-7298-4*) Gallopade Intl.

North Carolina Code Research Guide. LC 89-85552. 1993. suppl. ed. 97.50 (*0-318-68088-2*) West Group.

North Carolina Colony. Dennis B. Fradin. LC 91-13314. (Thirteen Colonies Ser.). (Illus.). 190p. (J). (gr. 4 up). 1991. lib. bdg. 30.00 (*0-516-00396-8*) Childrens.

North Carolina Commercial Feed Law of 1973, 1998 Edition. 1999. write for info. (*0-327-08387-5*, 30345-10) LEXIS Pub.

North Carolina Confederate Militia Officers Roster: As Contained in the Adjutant-General's Officers Roster. Ed. by Stephen E. Bradley, Jr. (Illus.). 439p. 1992. 35.00 (*1-56837-044-X*) Broadfoot.

North Carolina Constitutional & Statutory Provisions with Respect to Higher Education. rev. ed. Compiled by Laurie L. Mesibov. 403p. (C). 1988. pap. text 17.00 (*1-56011-110-0*, 88.08) Institute Government.

North Carolina Continentials. Hugh F. Rankin. LC 79-135311. 440p. reprint ed. pap. 136.40 (*0-8357-3866-3*, 203659800004) Bks Demand.

***North Carolina Controlled Substances Act & Regulations: 1999 Edition.** 205p. 2000. pap. 20.00 (*0-327-10440-6*, 3055113) LEXIS Pub.

***North Carolina Cookbook.** Compiled by Janics Mancuso. (Cooking Across America Ser.). (Illus.). 94p. 1999. pap. 6.95 (*1-885590-42-3*) Golden West Pub.

North Carolina Corporation Laws, Partnership Laws & Securities Act, 1993 Edition. Ellen DeGeneres. 30.00 (*0-614-05927-5*, MICHIE) LEXIS Pub.

***North Carolina Corporations, Partnerships & Securities Laws: 1999 Edition.** annot. ed. 602p. 2000. pap. 42.00 incl. cd-rom (*0-327-10314-0*, 3051515) LEXIS Pub.

***North Carolina Corporations, Partnerships & Securities Laws Annotated Advance Legislative Service: 1999 Edition.** 109p. 1999. pap. 12.50 (*0-327-09856-2*, 3031510) LEXIS Pub.

North Carolina Corporations, Partnerships & Securities Laws Annotated, 1998 Supplement. 26p. 1999. write for info. (*0-327-07748-4*, 3051611) LEXIS Pub.

North Carolina County Maps. rev. ed. Ed. by Cy Puetz. (Illus.). 156p. 1996. pap. 16.85 (*0-916514-11-0*) Cnty Maps.

***North Carolina Court Rules: 2000 Edition.** annot. ed. LEXIS Law Publishing Editors. 1355p. 1999. pap. 47.50 (*0-327-10222-5*, 4648817) LEXIS Pub.

***North Carolina Crime in Perspective 2000.** Ed. by Kathleen O'Leary Morgan & Scott E. Morgan. 22p. 2000. spiral bd. 19.00 (*0-7401-0332-6*) Morgan Quitno Corp.

North Carolina Crime Perspective, 1998. Ed. by Kathleen O'Leary Morgan & Scott E. Morgan. 20p. 1998. pap. 19.00 (*1-56692-932-6*) Morgan Quitno Corp.

North Carolina Crime Perspective, 1999. Kathleen O'Leary Morgan. 22p. 1999. spiral bd. 19.00 (*0-7401-0132-3*) Morgan Quitno Corp.

North Carolina Crimes: A Guidebook on the Elements of Crime. 4th ed. Ed. by Thomas H. Thornburg. (Illus.). 532p. (C). 1996. text 42.00 (*1-56011-262-X*); pap. text 32.00 (*1-56011-261-1*) Institute Government.

North Carolina Criminal & Traffic Law Manual with Cd-rom: 1999 Edition. 1240p. pap. 37.00 (*0-327-10444-9*) LEXIS Pub.

North Carolina Criminal & Traffic Law Manual, 1993. 25.00 (*0-614-05928-3*, MICHIE) LEXIS Pub.

North Carolina Criminal & Traffic Law Manual, 1998 Edition. LC 99-230165. 1225p. 1999. write for info. (*0-327-07449-3*, 3054715) LEXIS Pub.

***North Carolina Criminal Code: Handbook for Law Enforcement Officers.** rev. ed. Anderson Publishing Co. Staff. 642p. 1999. pap. 14.95 (*0-87084-479-2*) Anderson Pub Co.

North Carolina Criminal Law & Motor Vehicle Handbook. annuals rev. ed. Ed. by Gould Staff. 1110p. (C). pap. 21.95 (*1-882476-00-X*) Gould.

***North Carolina Criminal Law & Procedure: 1999 Edition.** LEXIS Law Publishing Editors. 1414p. 1999. pap. 43.00 incl. cd-rom (*0-327-10149-0*, 3051916) LEXIS Pub.

***North Carolina Criminal Law & Procedure Advance Legislative Service: 1999 Edition.** 224p. 1999. pap. write for info. (*0-327-09858-9*, 3031910) LEXIS Pub.

North Carolina Criminal Law & Procedure, 1993. Patricia Ireland. 32.00 (*0-614-05929-1*, MICHIE) LEXIS Pub.

North Carolina Criminal Law & Procedure, 1998 Edition. 1298p. 1999. write for info. (*0-327-07450-7*, 3051915) LEXIS Pub.

North Carolina Criminal Procedure: With 1992 Cumulative Supplement. Irving Joyner. 991p. 1989. text 80.00 (*0-87473-458-4*, 63610, MICHIE) LEXIS Pub.

North Carolina Criminal Procedure Forms. Van Camp et al. 514p. 1989. 75.00 (*0-87473-433-9*, 68165-10, MICHIE) LEXIS Pub.

North Carolina "Crinkum-Crankum" A Funny Word Book about Our State. Carole Marsh. (Carole Marsh North Carolina Bks.). (Illus.). (J). (gr. 3-12). 1994. 29.95 (*0-7933-4907-9*); pap. 19.95 (*0-7933-4908-7*); disk 29.95 (*0-7933-4909-5*) Gallopade Intl.

North Carolina Curiosities: Jerry Bledsoe's Outlandish Guide to the Dadblamedst Things to See & Do in North Carolina. 3rd ed. Jerry Bledsoe. Ed. by Sara Pitzer. LC 98-32210. (Illus.). 288p. 1998. pap. 10.95 (*0-7627-0327-X*) Globe Pequot.

North Carolina Dingbats! Bk. 1: A Fun Book of Games, Stories, Activities & More about Our State That's All in Code! for You to Decipher. Carole Marsh. (Carole Marsh North Carolina Bks.). (Illus.). (J). (gr. 3-12). 1994. pap. 19.95 (*0-7933-3873-5*); lib. bdg. 29.95 (*0-7933-3872-7*); disk 29.95 (*0-7933-3874-3*) Gallopade Intl.

North Carolina Directory: A Listing of Tar Heel Societies & Selected Books for Sale. R. S. Spencer, Jr. (Illus.). 231p. 1992. pap. 15.00 (*0-936370-07-6*) N C Genealogical.

North Carolina During Reconstruction. Richard L. Zuber. (Illus.). viii, 67p. 1975. reprint ed. pap. 8.00 (*0-86526-089-3*) NC Archives.

North Carolina Early Census, Vol. 1. Ronald V. Jackson. (Illus.). 1980. lib. bdg. 58.00 (*0-89593-734-4*, Accel Indexing) Genealogical Srvcs.

An Asterisk (*) at the beginning of an entry indicates that the title is appearing for the first time.

North Carolina Early Census, Vol. 2. Ronald V. Jackson. (Illus.). 1980. lib. bdg. 58.00 (*0-89593-735-2*, Accel Indexing) Genealogical Srvcs.

North Carolina Early Census, Vol. 3. Ronald V. Jackson. (Illus.). 1981. lib. bdg. 58.00 (*0-89593-736-0*, Accel Indexing) Genealogical Srvcs.

North Carolina Early Census, Vol. 4. Ronald V. Jackson. (Illus.). 1981. lib. bdg. 58.00 (*0-89593-737-9*, Accel Indexing) Genealogical Srvcs.

North Carolina Early Census, Vol. 5. Ronald V. Jackson. (Illus.). lib. bdg. 58.00 (*0-89593-738-7*, Accel Indexing) Genealogical Srvcs.

North Carolina Early Census, Vol. 6. Ronald V. Jackson. (Illus.). lib. bdg. 58.00 (*0-89593-739-5*, Accel Indexing) Genealogical Srvcs.

North Carolina Early Census, Vol. 7. Ronald V. Jackson. (Illus.). lib. bdg. 58.00 (*0-89593-740-9*, Accel Indexing) Genealogical Srvcs.

North Carolina Eldercare Sourcebook: A Resource Guide for Older Adults & Caregivers. Carla S. Rogg & Oskar H. Rogg. (Orig.). 1995. spiral bd. 24.95 (*0-9631939-4-5*) Care Solutions.

North Carolina Employment Guide. 200p. 1995. pap. 36.75 (*1-881803-05-8*) Career Res.

North Carolina Employment Guide: 1998 Edition. 14th ed. Louise Hughes. 182p. 1997. pap. 36.00 (*1-881803-07-4*) Career Res.

North Carolina Employment Guide, 1997. 190p. 1996. pap. 36.00 (*1-881803-06-6*) Career Res.

North Carolina Employment Guide, 1994. (Career Resources Ser.). 169p. 1993. pap. 34.95 (*1-881803-03-1*) Career Res.

North Carolina Employment Guide, 1993. Paul Mueller & Sage Mueller. 153p. 1992. pap. 34.95 (*1-881803-01-5*); disk 69.95 (*0-685-61600-2*) Career Res.

North Carolina Employment Guide, 1995. Career Resources Staff. 170p. 1994. pap. 34.95 (*1-881803-04-X*) Career Res.

North Carolina Employment Law. C. Daniel Barrett. 90.00 (*0-327-12386-9*) LEXIS Pub.

North Carolina Employment Law. C. Daniel Barrett. LC 98-85224. 1998. text. write for info. (*0-327-00136-4*, 68493-10) LEXIS Pub.

North Carolina Employment Law, 1999 Supplement. C. Daniel Barrett. 75p. 1999. pap. write for info. (*0-327-01328-1*, 6849311) LEXIS Pub.

North Carolina Environmental Law Handbook. Carlyle, Womble, Sandridge & Rice Staff et al. 388p. 1994. pap. text 89.00 (*0-86587-306-2*) Gov Insts.

North Carolina Estate Settlement Practice Guide. John P. Huggard. Ed. by Clayton W. Davidson, III. LC 96-75935. 500p. 1996. pap. text. write for info. (*0-7620-0055-4*) West Group.

North Carolina Evidence Courtroom Manual. pap. 50.00 (*1-58360-233-X*) Anderson Pub Co.

North Carolina Evidentiary Foundation. Robert P. Mosteller et al. LC 98-85075. 1998. text 80.00 (*0-327-00114-3*, 60110-10) LEXIS Pub.

North Carolina Experience: An Interpretive & Documentary Approach. Ed. by Lindley S. Butler & Alan D. Watson. LC 83-27357. (Illus.). 475p. 1984. pap. 19.95 (*0-8078-4124-2*) U of NC Pr.

***North Carolina Experience Pocket Guide.** Carole Marsh. (North Carolina Experience! Ser.). (Illus.). (J). 2000. pap. 6.95 (*0-7933-9452-X*) Gallopade Intl.

North Carolina Faces the Freedmen: Race Relations During Presidential Reconstruction, 1865-67. Roberta S. Alexander. LC 84-28758. xvi, 238p. (C). 1985. text 38.95 (*0-8223-0628-X*) Duke.

North Carolina Facts & Factivities. Carole Marsh. (Carole Marsh State Bks.). (Illus.). (J). (gr. 4-7). 1996. pap., teacher ed. 19.95 (*0-7933-7913-X*, C Marsh) Gallopade Intl.

North Carolina Facts & Symbols. Emily McAuliffe. (States & Their Symbols Ser.). 1999. 15.00 (*0-531-12007-4*) Watts.

***North Carolina Facts & Symbols.** Shelley Swanson Sateren. LC 99-31820. (States & Their Symbols Ser.). 1999. 14.60 (*0-7368-0381-5*) Capstone Pr.

***North Carolina Family & Related Laws: 1999 Edition.** annot. ed. 1071p. 2000. pap. 53.00 incl. cd-rom (*0-327-10448-1*, 3052613) LEXIS Pub.

North Carolina Family & Related Laws Annotated, 1998 Edition. 936p. 1999. write for info. (*0-327-07642-9*, 3052612) LEXIS Pub.

North Carolina Family Law Vol. 1: 1989 Cumulative Supplement. Robert E. Lee. 1989. pap. write for info. (*0-87215-893-4*, 64277-10, MICHIE) LEXIS Pub.

North Carolina Family Law, 1998 Cumulative Supplement, Vol. 1. Suzanne Reynolds & Kenneth Craig. (Illus.). 1998. write for info. (*0-327-00648-X*, 64281-15) LEXIS Pub.

North Carolina Family Law, 1998 Cumulative Supplement, Vol. 2. Suzanne Reynolds & Kenneth Craig. (Illus.). 1998. write for info. (*0-327-00650-1*, 64282-15) LEXIS Pub.

North Carolina Family Law, 1998 Cumulative Supplement, Vol. 3. 4th ed. Suzanne Reynolds & Kenneth Craig. (Illus.). 1998. write for info. (*0-327-00651-X*, 64283-15) LEXIS Pub.

North Carolina Family Law, 1998 Cumulative Supplement, Vol. 4. 4th ed. Suzanne Reynolds & Kenneth Craig. (Illus.). 1998. write for info. (*0-327-00652-8*, 64284-15) LEXIS Pub.

North Carolina Family Law with 1991 Cumulative Supplements, 4 vols., Set. 4th ed. Robert E. Lee et al. 1987. 240.00 (*0-87215-473-4*, 64270-10, MICHIE) LEXIS Pub.

North Carolina Federal Census Index, 2 vols., Set. 1988. 400.00 (*0-89593-589-9*, Accel Indexing) Genealogical Srvcs.

North Carolina Federal Census Index, 1790 (1908) Ronald V. Jackson. (Illus.). 1978. lib. bdg. 55.00 (*0-89593-754-9*, Accel Indexing) Genealogical Srvcs.

North Carolina Federal Census Index, 1800. Ronald V. Jackson. LC 77-86111. (Illus.). lib. bdg. 65.00 (*0-89593-103-6*, Accel Indexing) Genealogical Srvcs.

North Carolina Federal Census Index, 1810. Ronald V. Jackson & Gary R. Teeples. LC 77-86112. (Illus.). lib. bdg. 79.00 (*0-89593-104-4*, Accel Indexing) Genealogical Srvcs.

North Carolina Federal Census Index, 1820. Ronald V. Jackson. LC 77-86113. (Illus.). lib. bdg. 79.00 (*0-89593-105-2*, Accel Indexing) Genealogical Srvcs.

North Carolina Federal Census Index, 1830. Ronald V. Jackson. LC 77-86114. (Illus.). lib. bdg. 83.00 (*0-89593-106-0*, Accel Indexing) Genealogical Srvcs.

North Carolina Federal Census Index, 1840. Ronald V. Jackson. LC 77-86115. (Illus.). 1978. lib. bdg. 84.00 (*0-89593-107-9*, Accel Indexing) Genealogical Srvcs.

North Carolina Federal Census Index, 1850. Ronald V. Jackson. LC 77-86109. (Illus.). 1976. lib. bdg. 125.00 (*0-89593-108-7*, Accel Indexing) Genealogical Srvcs.

North Carolina Federal Census Index, 1860, 2 vols., Set. Ed. by Ronald Vern Jackson. LC 99-198435. (Illus.). 1988. lib. bdg. 375.00 (*0-89593-445-0*, Accel Indexing) Genealogical Srvcs.

North Carolina Festival Fun for Kids! Carole Marsh. (Carole Marsh North Carolina Bks.). (Illus.). (J). (gr. 3-12). 1994. pap. 19.95 (*0-7933-4026-8*); lib. bdg. 29.95 (*0-7933-4025-X*) Gallopade Intl.

North Carolina Festival Fun for Kids! Carole Marsh. (Carole Marsh North Carolina Bks.). (Illus.). (YA). (gr. 3-12). 1994. disk 29.95 (*0-7933-4027-6*) Gallopade Intl.

North Carolina Football Mystery. Carole M. Longmeyer. (Sportsmystery Ser.). (Illus.). (Orig.). (J). (gr. 3 up). 1994. pap. 19.95 (*0-935326-29-4*) Gallopade Intl.

North Carolina Freedman's Savings & Trust Company Records. Bill Reeves. 598p. 1992. 25.00 (*0-936370-08-4*) N C Genealogical.

North Carolina Gardener's Guide: The What, Where, When, How & Why of Gardening in North Carolina. Toby Bost. LC 97-181166. (Illus.). 400p. (Orig.). 1997. pap. 19.95 (*1-888608-09-9*) Cool Springs Pr.

North Carolina Gazetteer. William S. Powell. LC 68-25916. xviii, 561p. 1985. pap. 18.95 (*0-8078-1247-1*) U of NC Pr.

North Carolina Genealogical Research. George K. Schweitzer. 169p. 1998. pap. 15.00 (*0-913857-03-3*) Genealog Sources.

***North Carolina Genealogical Society Journal, 1975-1984--Consolidated.** William D. Bennett. LC 97-228519. 600p. 1999. pap. 45.00 (*0-8063-4711-2*) Clearfield Co.

North Carolina General Practice Form Book, 1993. Wake Forest University School of Law Continuing Le. 836p. 1993. pap. text 65.00 (*0-942225-74-0*) Wake Forest Law.

North Carolina General Practice Handbook-Form Book, 1993. Wake Forest University School of Law Continuing Le. 1669p. 1993. pap. text 110.00 (*0-942225-77-5*) Wake Forest Law.

North Carolina General Practice Handbook, 1993. Wake Forest University School of Law Continuing Le. 833p. 1993. pap. text 65.00 (*0-942225-73-2*) Wake Forest Law.

***North Carolina General Statutes Softbound Sample.** 1200p. 1999. Price not set. (*0-327-09168-1*, 4630910) LEXIS Pub.

North Carolina "GEO" Bingo! 38 Must Know State Geography Facts for Kids to Learn While Having Fun! Carole Marsh. (Bingo! Ser.). (Illus.). (J). (gr. 2-8). 1998. pap. 14.95 (*0-7933-8622-5*) Gallopade Intl.

North Carolina Getaways: A Guide to Bed & Breakfasts & Inns. 2nd rev. ed. Don Vandeventer. (Getaways Ser.). (Illus.). 256p. (Orig.). 1996. pap. 14.95 (*1-886443-01-7*) Down Home Pubns.

North Carolina Ghosts & Legends. Nancy Roberts. LC 91-14469. (Illus.). 133p. 1991. reprint ed. pap. 9.95 (*0-87249-765-8*) U of SC Pr.

North Carolina Giving: The Directory of the State's Foundations. Anita G. Shirley. 900p. 1990. pap. 99.00 (*0-9624910-0-4*) Capital Consortium.

North Carolina Giving: The Directory of the State's Foundations. Anita G. Shirley. 900p. 1993. pap. 149.00 (*0-9624910-1-2*) Capital Consortium.

North Carolina Government! The Cornerstone of Everyday Life in Our State! Carole Marsh. (Carole Marsh North Carolina Bks.). (Illus.). (J). (gr. 3-12). 1996. pap. 19.95 (*0-7933-6281-4*); lib. bdg. 29.95 (*0-7933-6280-6*); disk 29.95 (*0-7933-6282-2*) Gallopade Intl.

North Carolina Government & Politics. Jack D. Fleer. LC 94-4247. (Politics & Governments of the American States Ser.). (Illus.). xxviii, 346p. 1994. pap. text 22.00 (*0-8032-6885-8*) U of Nebr Pr.

North Carolina Government & Politics. Jack D. Fleer. LC 94-4247. (Politics & Governments of the American States Ser.). (Illus.). xxviii, 346p. 1994. text 50.00 (*0-8032-1993-8*) U of Nebr Pr.

North Carolina Guidebook for Registers of Deeds. 8th ed. William A. Campbell. 2000. pap. write for info. (*1-56011-353-7*) Institute Government.

***North Carolina Health Care in Perspective 2000.** Ed. by Kathleen O'Leary Morgan & Scott E. Morgan. 21p. 2000. spiral bd. 19.00 (*0-7401-0232-X*) Morgan Quitno Corp.

North Carolina Health Care Perspective, 1998. Ed. by Kathleen O'Leary Morgan & Scott E. Morgan. 20p. 1998. pap. 19.00 (*1-56692-832-X*) Morgan Quitno Corp.

North Carolina Health Care Perspective, 1999. Kathleen O'Leary Morgan. 21p. 1999. spiral bd. 19.00 (*0-7401-0082-3*) Morgan Quitno Corp.

North Carolina Higher-Court Minutes, 1724-1730. Ed. by Robert J. Cain. (Colonial Records of North Carolina Ser.: Vol. 6). lxi, 791p. 1981. 30.00 (*0-86526-027-3*) NC Archives.

North Carolina Higher-Court Minutes, 1709-1723. Ed. by WIlliam S. Price, Jr. (Colonial Records of North Carolina Ser.: Vol. 5). xliii, 631p. 1977. 21.00 (*0-86526-026-5*) NC Archives.

North Carolina Higher-Court Records, 1697-1701. Ed. by Mattie Parker. (Colonial Records of North Carolina Ser.: Vol. 3). (Illus.). lxviii, 620p. 1971. 15.00 (*0-86526-024-9*) NC Archives.

North Carolina Higher-Court Records, 1702-1708. Ed. by William S. Price, Jr. (Colonial Records of North Carolina Ser.: Vol. 4). xxxix, 533p. 1974. 16.00 (*0-86526-025-7*) NC Archives.

North Carolina Hiking Trails. 3rd rev. ed. Allen De Hart. LC 87-31848. (Illus.). 512p. 1996. pap. 18.95 (*1-878239-48-1*) AMC Books.

North Carolina "HISTO" Bingo! 42 Must Know State History Facts for Kids to Learn While Having Fun! Carole Marsh. (Bingo! Ser.). (Illus.). (J). (gr. 2-8). 1998. pap. 14.95 (*0-7933-8623-3*) Gallopade Intl.

North Carolina Historical & Biographical Index, Vol. 1. Ronald V. Jackson. LC 78-53711. (Illus.). 1984. lib. bdg. 30.00 (*0-89593-194-X*, Accel Indexing) Genealogical Srvcs.

North Carolina Historical & Genealogical Register, No. 3. James R. Hathaway. LC 70-132931. 1760p. 1998. reprint ed. pap. 125.00 (*0-8063-0441-3*) Clearfield Co.

North Carolina Historical Review: Fifty-Year Index, 1924-1973. Ed. by Beth G. Crabtree & Ruth C. Langston. vi, 534p. 1984. pap. 30.00 (*0-86526-211-X*) NC Archives.

North Carolina Historical Review: Supplement to Fifty-Year Index, 1974-1983. Ed. by Ruth C. Langston. 243p. (Orig.). 1999. reprint ed. pap. 30.00 (*0-86526-213-6*) NC Archives.

North Carolina History: An Annotated Bibliography, 3. H. G. Jones. LC 94-37085. (Bibliographies of the States of the United States Ser.: Vol. 3). 824p. 1995. lib. bdg. 105.00 (*0-313-28255-2*) Greenwood.

North Carolina History! Surprising Secrets about Our State's Founding Mothers, Fathers & Kids! Carole Marsh. (Carole Marsh North Carolina Bks.). (Illus.). (J). (gr. 3-12). 1996. pap. 19.95 (*0-7933-6128-1*); lib. bdg. 29.95 (*0-7933-6127-3*); disk 29.95 (*0-7933-6129-X*) Gallopade Intl.

North Carolina Hot Air Balloon Mystery. Carole Marsh. (Carole Marsh North Carolina Bks.). (Illus.). (J). (gr. 2-9). 1994. 29.95 (*0-7933-2615-X*); pap. 19.95 (*0-7933-2616-8*); disk 29.95 (*0-7933-2617-6*) Gallopade Intl.

North Carolina Hot Zones! Viruses, Diseases, & Epidemics in Our State's History. Carole Marsh. (Hot Zones! Ser.). (Illus.). (J). (gr. 3-12). 1998. pap. 19.95 (*0-7933-8928-3*); lib. bdg. 29.95 (*0-7933-8927-5*) Gallopade Intl.

North Carolina in Maps. William P. Cumming. viii, 36p. 1992. pap. 30.00 (*0-86526-137-7*) NC Archives.

North Carolina in Perspective, 1998. Ed. by Kathleen O'Leary Morgan & Scott E. Morgan. 24p. 1998. pap. 19.00 (*1-56692-882-6*) Morgan Quitno Corp.

North Carolina in Perspective, 1999. Ed. by Kathleen O'Leary Morgan. 26p. 1999. spiral bd. 19.00 (*1-56692-982-2*) Morgan Quitno Corp.

***North Carolina in Perspective 2000.** Ed. by Kathleen O'Leary Morgan & Scott E. Morgan. 26p. 2000. spiral bd. 19.00 (*0-7401-0282-6*) Morgan Quitno Corp.

North Carolina in the American Revolution. Hugh F. Rankin. (Illus.). vii, 75p. 1996. reprint ed. pap. 8.00 (*0-86526-091-5*) NC Archives.

North Carolina in the Mexican War. William S. Hoffmann. (Illus.). 48p. 1969. pap. 5.00 (*0-86526-092-3*) NC Archives.

North Carolina in 1861. James H. Boykin. LC 61-15678. 237p. 1961. pap. 6.99 (*0-9603342-8-9*) Boykin.

North Carolina Indian Dictionary for Kids! Carole Marsh. (Carole Marsh State Bks.). (J). (gr. 2-9). 1995. 29.95 (*0-7933-7743-9*, C Marsh) Gallopade Intl.

North Carolina Indian Dictionary for Kids! Carole Marsh. (Carole Marsh State Bks.). (J). (gr. 2-9). 1996. pap. 19.95 (*0-7933-7744-7*, C Marsh); disk 29.95 (*0-7933-7745-5*, C Marsh) Gallopade Intl.

***North Carolina Investment & Business Guide: Business, Investment, Export-Import Opportunities, 50 vols., Vol. 33.** Global Investment Center, USA Staff. (U. S. Regional Investment & Business Library-99: Vol. 33). (Illus.). 350p. (Orig.). 1999. pap. 59.95 (*0-7397-1132-6*) Intl Business Pubns.

North Carolina Is My Home. Charles Kuralt & Loonis McGlohan. Ed. by Patty Davis. LC 86-45579. (Illus.). 104p. 1986. 31.95 (*0-88742-107-5*) Globe Pequot.

***North Carolina Is My Home.** 2nd ed. Charles Kuralt & Loomis McGlohan. Ed. by Patty Davis. LC 98-14340. (Illus.). 112p. 1998. pap. 21.95 (*0-7627-0228-1*) Globe Pequot.

***North Carolina Jeopardy.** Carole Marsh. (North Carolina Experience! Ser.). (Illus.). (J). (gr. 2-6). 2000. pap. 7.95 (*0-7933-9519-4*) Gallopade Intl.

North Carolina Jeopardy! Answers & Questions about Our State! Carole Marsh. (Carole Marsh North Carolina Bks.). (Illus.). (J). (gr. 3-12). 1994. pap. 19.95 (*0-7933-4179-5*); lib. bdg. 29.95 (*0-7933-4178-7*); disk 29.95 (*0-7933-4180-9*) Gallopade Intl.

***North Carolina Jography.** Carole Marsh. (North Carolina Experience! Ser.). (Illus.). (J). (gr. 2-6). 2000. 7.95 (*0-7933-9520-8*) Gallopade Intl.

North Carolina Jography: A Fun Run Through the Tarheel State. Carole Marsh. (Statemeant Ser.). (Illus.). 50p. (Orig.). (J). (gr. 4-8). 1994. pap. 19.95 (*0-935326-81-2*) Gallopade Intl.

North Carolina Juvenile Code & Related Statutes. annot. ed. Pref. by Janet Mason. 1999. 40.00 (*1-56011-352-9*) Institute Government.

***North Carolina Juvenile Code & Related Statutes Annotated: 1999-2000 Cumulative Supplement.** Michie Company Editorial Staff. (C). 2000. pap. 13.00 (*1-56011-371-5*) Institute Government.

North Carolina Juvenile Code & Related Statutes Annotated, 1998-99 Edition. annot. ed. 375p. 1999. write for info. (*0-327-08500-2*, 30340-10) LEXIS Pub.

North Carolina Kid's Cookbook: Recipes, How-to, History, Lore & More. Carole Marsh. (Carole Marsh North Carolina Bks.). (Illus.). (J). 1994. pap. 19.95 (*0-7933-0852-6*); lib. bdg. 29.95 (*0-7933-0853-4*); disk 29.95 (*0-7933-0854-2*) Gallopade Intl.

North Carolina Land Grants in South Carolina. Brent H. Holcomb. (Illus.). 184p. 1999. reprint ed. 20.00 (*0-8063-1164-9*, 2783) Genealog Pub.

North Carolina Land Grants Recorded in Greene County, Tennessee. 160p. 1981. 25.00 (*0-89308-204-X*) Southern Hist Pr.

North Carolina Land Surveying Law: Questions & Answers. John E. Keen. 81p. (C). 1995. pap. text 25.00 (*1-56569-036-2*) Land Survey.

North Carolina Law of Torts. Charles E. Daye & Mark W. Morris. 722p. 1991. 85.00 (*0-87473-757-5*, MICHIE); 85.00 (*0-87473-751-6*, 61170-10, MICHIE); 85.00 (*0-327-00993-4*, 61170, MICHIE) LEXIS Pub.

North Carolina Law of Torts. Charles E. Daye & Mark W. Morris. 1995. suppl. ed. 40.00 (*0-614-25254-7*, 61171-13, MICHIE) LEXIS Pub.

***North Carolina Law of Torts.** 2nd ed. Charles E. Daye & Mark W. Morris. 950p. 1999. write for info. (*0-327-04935-9*, 6117011) LEXIS Pub.

North Carolina Law of Torts: 1992 Supplement. Daye & Morris. 1992. write for info. (*0-87473-976-4*, 61171-10, MICHIE) LEXIS Pub.

North Carolina Law of Torts: 1998 Cumulative Supplement. Charles E. Daye & Mark W. Morris. LC 91-61407. 210p. 1998. write for info. (*0-327-00219-0*, 61171-16) LEXIS Pub.

North Carolina Law of Torts with 1992 Supplement. Charles E. Daye & Mark W. Morris. 722p. 1991. 75.00 (*0-685-48592-7*, MICHIE) LEXIS Pub.

North Carolina Legal Research Guide. Jean S. McKnight. LC 94-46352. xiv, 124p. 1994. 38.00 (*0-8377-0868-0*, Rothman) W S Hein.

North Carolina Legends. Richard Walser. (Illus.). viii, 76p. 1999. reprint ed. pap. 8.00 (*0-86526-139-3*) NC Archives.

North Carolina Legislation, 1996: A Summary of Legislation in the 1996 General Assembly of Interest to North Carolina Public Officials. Ed. by Joseph S. Ferrell. 170p. (Orig.). 1996. pap. text 22.00 (*1-56011-298-0*) Institute Government.

North Carolina Legislation, 1998: A Summary of Legislation in the 1998 General Assembly of Interest to North Carolina Public Officials. Ed. by John L. Saxon. 1999. pap. text 25.00 (*1-56011-338-3*, 98.22) Institute Government.

***North Carolina Legislation 1999: A Summary of Legislation in the 1999 General Assembly.** Ed. by David W. Owens. (C). 1999. pap. 30.00 (*1-56011-361-8*) Institute Government.

***North Carolina Legislation, 2000: A Summary of Legislation in the 2000 General Assembly of Interest to North Carolina Public Officials.** Ed. by David W. Owens. (C). 2000. pap. 25.00 (*1-56011-381-2*) Institute Government.

North Carolina Library Book: A Surprising Guide to the Unusual Special Collections in Libraries Across Our State for Students, Teachers, Writers & Publishers - Includes Reproducible Mailing Labels Plus Activities for Young People! Carole Marsh. (Carole Marsh North Carolina Bks.). (Illus.). 1994. pap. 19.95 (*0-7933-3105-6*); lib. bdg. 29.95 (*0-7933-3104-8*); disk 29.95 (*0-7933-3106-4*) Gallopade Intl.

North Carolina Lighthouses. David Stick. (Illus.). xi, 85p. 1999. reprint ed. pap. 8.00 (*0-86526-191-1*) NC Archives.

North Carolina Limited Liability Company Forms & Practice Manual, 2 vols. 2nd ed. Cyrus M. Johnson, Jr. LC 96-1322. 672p. 1996. ring bd. 239.90 (*1-57400-007-1*) Data Trace Pubng.

North Carolina Manufacturers Directory, 1999. 1999. 99.00 (*1-55600-629-2*) Harris InfoSource.

North Carolina Manufacturers Directory, 2000. annuals rev. ed. Harris InfoSource Staff. Ed. by Frances L. Carlsen. 1385p. 123.00 (*1-55600-668-3*) Harris InfoSource.

North Carolina Manufacturers Register. 6th rev. ed. Ed. by Frank Lambing. 1999. 106.00 (*1-58202-061-2*) Manufacturers.

North Carolina Marriage Laws & Procedures. 3rd ed. Janet Mason. 31p. (C). 1994. pap. text 2.50 (*1-56011-235-2*, 94.23) Institute Government.

North Carolina Marriages, Early to Eighteen Hundred. Liahona Research, Inc. Staff. Ed. by Jordan Dodd. 523p. 1991. lib. bdg. 95.00 (*1-877677-28-0*) Herit Quest.

North Carolina Marriages Index, 1801-1825. Liahona Research Staff. 900p. lib. bdg. 145.00 (*1-877677-33-7*) Herit Quest.

North Carolina Math! How It All Adds up in Our State. Carole Marsh. (Carole Marsh North Carolina Bks.). (Illus.). (YA). (gr. 3-12). 1996. pap. 19.95 (*0-7933-6587-2*); lib. bdg. 29.95 (*0-7933-6586-4*) Gallopade Intl.

North Carolina Media Book: A Surprising Guide to the Amazing Print, Broadcast & Online Media of Our State for Students, Teachers, Writers & Publishers - Includes Reproducible Mailing Labels Plus Activities

for Young People! Carole Marsh. (Carole Marsh North Carolina Bks.). (Illus.). 1994. pap. 19.95 (*0-7933-3261-3*); lib. bdg. 29.95 (*0-7933-3260-5*); disk 29.95 (*0-7933-3262-1*) Gallopade Intl.

North Carolina Mental Health, Developmental Disabilities & Substance Abuse Laws: 1999 Edition. 452p. pap. 27.00 (*0-327-13106-3*) LEXIS Pub.

North Carolina Mental Health, Develpomental Disabilities & Substance Abuse Laws, 1998 Supplement. 86p. 1999. pap. write for info. (*0-327-07993-2*, 30501-13) LEXIS Pub.

North Carolina Museum of Art: Catalogue of Spanish Paintings. Edward J. Sullivan. LC 86-61911. (Illus.). 132p. 1986. pap. 18.00 (*0-88259-952-6*) NCMA.

North Carolina Museum of Art: Handbook of the Collections. Virginia Burden et al. LC 97-76050. (Illus.). 288p. 1998. 50.00 (*0-88259-978-X*) NCMA.

North Carolina Mutual Life Insurance Company: Its Historical Development & Current Operations. Jesse E. Gloster. LC 75-41758. (Companies & Men: Business Enterprises in America Ser.). (Illus.). 1976. 33.95 (*0-405-08074-3*) Ayer.

North Carolina Mystery Van Takes Off! Book 1: Handicapped North Carolina Kids Sneak Off on a Big Adventure. Carole Marsh. (Carole Marsh North Carolina Bks.). (Illus.). (J). (gr. 3-12). 1994. 29.95 (*0-7933-5060-3*); pap. 19.95 (*0-7933-5061-1*); disk 29.95 (*0-7933-5062-X*) Gallopade Intl.

North Carolina Naturalist, H. H. Brimley. Herbert H. Brimley. Ed. by Eugene P. Odum. LC 78-134058. (Essay Index Reprint Ser.). 1977. 20.95 (*0-8369-2145-3*) Ayer.

North Carolina Nature Writing: Four Centuries of Personal Narratives & Descriptions. Richard Rankin. LC 96-2640. (Illus.). (Orig.). 1996. pap. 12.95 (*0-89587-151-3*) Blair.

North Carolina 1998 Advance Legislative Service, No. 4. 997p. 1999. pap. write for info. (*0-327-07436-1*, 4657415) LEXIS Pub.

North Carolina 1998 ALS, No. 3. 415p. 1998. pap. write for info. (*0-327-07064-1*, 4657315) LEXIS Pub.

***North Carolina 1998 Index Vol. 23 & 23: General Statutes of North Carolina Index.** 3216p. 1999. write for info. (*0-327-06806-X*, 4656615) LEXIS Pub.

North Carolina 1998 Replacement Pamphlets. 5000p. 1999. ring bd. write for info. (*0-327-07466-3*, 4658113) LEXIS Pub.

***North Carolina 1999 Advance Legislative Service No. 3.** 400p. 1999. pap. Price not set. (*0-327-09666-7*, 4657316) LEXIS Pub.

North Carolina 1999 Advance Annotation Service. 175p. 1999. pap. write for info. (*0-327-08414-6*, 46583-15) LEXIS Pub.

***North Carolina 1999 Advance Legislative Service No. 2.** 400p. 1999. pap. Price not set. (*0-327-09662-4*, 4657216) LEXIS Pub.

***North Carolina 1999 Advance Annotation Service, No. 2.** 210p. 1999. Price not set. (*0-327-09111-8*, 4658415) LEXIS Pub.

***North Carolina 1999 Replacement Code Index, 2 vols., Set.** 3022p. 1999. Price not set. (*0-327-19716-1*, 4656616) LEXIS Pub.

North Carolina 98 ALS Tables Supplement, No. 4. 50p. Date not set. write for info. (*0-327-07989-4*, 51641-15) LEXIS Pub.

North Carolina Notary Law Primer. National Notary Association Editors. LC 92-80094. 128p. 1992. pap. 16.00 (*0-933134-68-1*) Natl Notary.

North Carolina on My Mind. LC 99-225811. (Illus.). 120p. 1998. 29.95 (*1-56044-685-4*) Falcon Pub Inc.

North Carolina Passport. Ronald J. Reiser. (Illus.). 36p. (Orig.). (YA). (gr. 9-12). 1991. 3.95 (*0-9625515-8-9*) VJR Passports.

North Carolina Pesticide Law of 1971, 1998 Edition. 35p. 1999. pap. write for info. (*0-327-07994-0*, 30508-14) LEXIS Pub.

North Carolina Plantation & Historic Homes Cookbook. Ken Raveill. 32p. (Orig.). (C). 1992. pap. 4.50 (*0-936672-92-7*) Aerial Photo.

North Carolina Planters & Their Children, 1800-1860. Jane T. Censer. LC 83-19960. 191p. 1990. pap. text 15.95 (*0-8071-1634-3*) La State U Pr.

North Carolina Postcard Album, 1905-1925. Stephen E. Massengill & Robert M. Topkins. (Illus.). xii, 172p. 1988. 55.00 (*0-86526-236-5*) NC Archives.

North Carolina Procedure: 1990 Supplement. Irving Joyner. 1990. write for info. (*0-87473-728-1*, 63611-10, MICHIE) LEXIS Pub.

North Carolina Public Defender Manual. John Rubin & Thomasin Hughes. (C). 1998. pap. text 25.00 (*1-56011-339-1*) Institute Government.

***North Carolina Public Utilities Laws & Regulations: 1999 Edition.** 669p. 2000. pap. 50.00 (*0-327-10458-9*, 3055513) LEXIS Pub.

North Carolina Quilts. Ed. by Ruth H. Roberson. LC 88-10598. (Illus.). xviii, 214p. (C). 1988. 39.95 (*0-8078-1811-9*) U of NC Pr.

North Carolina Quiz Bowl Crash Course! Carole Marsh. (Carole Marsh North Carolina Bks.). (Illus.). (J). 1994. pap. 19.95 (*1-55609-935-5*); lib. bdg. 29.95 (*1-55609-934-7*); disk 29.95 (*1-55609-936-3*) Gallopade Intl.

North Carolina Railroad Map: A History of North Carolina Railroads, 1830-1990. 6th rev. ed. Ed. by S. David Carriker. (Illus.). 50p. (Orig.). 1998. pap. 20.00 (*0-936013-09-5*) Herit Pub NC.

North Carolina Railroads: The Common Carrier Railroads of North Carolina. 6th ed. S. David Carriker. 66p. 1998. pap. 20.00 (*0-936013-08-7*) Herit Pub NC.

North Carolina Real Estate: Principles & Practice. 4th ed. Nancy F. Keck & Ralph A. Palmer. LC 99-30171. (Illus.). 528p. (C). 1999. pap. text 35.40 (*0-13-010592-9*) P-H.

North Carolina Real Estate: 1989 Supplement. Patrick K. Hetrick. 1989. write for info. (*0-87473-588-2*, 62789-10, MICHIE) LEXIS Pub.

North Carolina Real Estate for Brokers & Salesmen. 4th ed. Patrick K. Hetrick & Larry A. Outlaw. LC 94-3515. (Illus.). 918p. 1994. 36.95 (*0-13-625104-8*) P-H.

North Carolina Real Estate Study & License Preparation Guide. George R. Bell. (Illus.). 350p. (Orig.). (C). 1989. pap. 19.95 (*0-9622772-0-7*) Sunshine NC.

North Carolina Reflections. Photos by George Humphries. LC 98-2848. (Littlebook Ser.). (Illus.). 64p. 1998. 14.95 (*1-56579-301-3*) Westcliffe Pubs.

North Carolina Regulations: Containing Insurance Department Regulations, Bulletins & Directives, & Selected Attorney General's Opinions. North Carolina. Dept. of Insurance. LC 97-67932. 1997. write for info. (*0-89246-474-7*) NILS Pub.

North Carolina Research: Genealogy & Local History. 2nd rev. ed. Helen F. Leary. (Illus.). 600p. 1996. 48.00 (*0-936370-10-6*) N C Genealogical.

North Carolina Retirement & Relocation Guide. large type ed. Bill Lyna & Detra Carter. (Retirement & Relocation Guides Ser.). (Illus.). 350p. (Orig.). Date not set. pap. 24.95 (*1-56559-112-7*) HGI-Over Fifty.

North Carolina Retirement Systems Laws: 1999 Edition. 332p. 24.00 (*0-327-10459-7*); pap. 22.00 (*0-327-11270-0*) LEXIS Pub.

North Carolina Retirement Systems Laws 1998 Edition. 344p. 1999. pap. write for info. (*0-327-07996-7*, 30511-15) LEXIS Pub.

***North Carolina Revised Rules of Professional Conduct: 2000 Edition.** 135p. 2000. pap. 18.00 (*0-327-10461-9*, 3052116) LEXIS Pub.

North Carolina Rollercoasters! Carole Marsh. (Carole Marsh North Carolina Bks.). (Illus.). (J). (gr. 3-12). 1994. pap. 19.95 (*0-7933-5324-6*); lib. bdg. 29.95 (*0-7933-5323-8*) Gallopade Intl.

North Carolina Rollercoasters! Carole Marsh. (Carole Marsh North Carolina Bks.). (Illus.). (YA). (gr. 3-12). 1994. disk 29.95 (*0-7933-5325-4*) Gallopade Intl.

***North Carolina Rules of Evidence with Objections.** 2nd ed. Anthony J. Bocchino. 187p. 2000. pap. 25.95 (*1-55681-492-5*) Natl Inst Trial Ad.

North Carolina Rules of Professional Conduct, 1999 Edition **Special Attention** 126p. 1999. pap. write for info. (*0-327-07460-4*, 3052115) LEXIS Pub.

North Carolina School Trivia: An Amazing & Fascinating Look at Our State's Teachers, Schools & Students! Carole Marsh. (Carole Marsh North Carolina Bks.). (Illus.). (J). 1994. pap. 19.95 (*0-7933-0849-6*); lib. bdg. 29.95 (*0-7933-0850-X*); disk 29.95 (*0-7933-0851-8*) Gallopade Intl.

North Carolina Security Interests. Richard A. Lord & Charles C. Lewis. 450p. 1985. 40.00 (*0-614-05931-3*, MICHIE) LEXIS Pub.

North Carolina Senior Resource Guide: A Resource Guide for Older Adults, Caregivers & Eldercare Professional. Carla S. Rogg & Oskar H. Rogg. 277p. (Orig.). 1995. pap. 19.95 (*0-9631939-7-X*) Care Solutions.

North Carolina 1790 Census: Heads of Families. pap. 30.00 (*1-877677-50-7*) Herit Quest.

North Carolina Shore & Its Barrier Islands: Restless Ribbons of Sand. Orrin H. Pilkey. LC 98-4578. (Living with the Shore Ser.). 1998. 54.95 (*0-8223-2208-0*); pap. 18.95 (*0-8223-2224-2*) Duke.

North Carolina Silly Basketball Sportsmysteries, Vol. 1. Carole Marsh. (Carole Marsh North Carolina Bks.). (Illus.). (J). 1994. pap. 19.95 (*0-7933-0846-1*); lib. bdg. 29.95 (*0-7933-0847-X*); disk 29.95 (*0-7933-0848-8*) Gallopade Intl.

North Carolina Silly Basketball Sportsmysteries, Vol. 2. Carole Marsh. (Carole Marsh North Carolina Bks.). (Illus.). (J). 1994. pap. 19.95 (*0-7933-1837-8*); lib. bdg. 29.95 (*0-7933-1836-X*); disk 29.95 (*0-7933-1838-6*) Gallopade Intl.

North Carolina Silly Football Sportmysteries, Vol. 2. Carole Marsh. (Carole Marsh North Carolina Bks.). (Illus.). (J). 1994. pap. 19.95 (*1-55609-931-2*); lib. bdg. 29.95 (*1-55609-930-4*); disk 29.95 (*1-55609-932-0*) Gallopade Intl.

North Carolina Silly Football Sportsmysteries, Vol. 1. Carole Marsh. (Carole Marsh North Carolina Bks.). (Illus.). (J). 1994. pap. 19.95 (*1-55609-928-2*); lib. bdg. 29.95 (*1-55609-927-4*); disk 29.95 (*1-55609-929-0*) Gallopade Intl.

North Carolina Silly Trivia! Carole Marsh. (Carole Marsh North Carolina Bks.). (Illus.). (J). 1994. lib. bdg. 29.95 (*1-55609-921-5*); disk 29.95 (*1-55609-922-3*) Gallopade Intl.

North Carolina Social Worker Certification Laws, 1997. 61p. 1998. pap. write for info. (*0-327-05763-7*, 30581-10) LEXIS Pub.

North Carolina-South Carolina Supplement see American Slave: A Composite Autobiography, Supplement Series 1

North Carolina Spelling Bee! Score Big by Correctly Spelling Our State's Unique Names. Carole Marsh. (Carole Marsh North Carolina Bks.). (Illus.). (YA). (gr. 3-12). 1996. pap. 19.95 (*0-7933-6740-9*); lib. bdg. 29.95 (*0-7933-6739-5*) Gallopade Intl.

North Carolina State Constitution: A Reference Guide, 16. John V. Orth. LC 92-42676. (Reference Guides to the State Constitutions of the United States Ser.: No. 16). 216p. 1993. lib. bdg. 75.00 (*0-313-27570-X*, ONC, Greenwood Pr) Greenwood.

North Carolina State Constitution: With History & Commentary. John V. Orth. LC 95-14496. (Reference Guides to the State Constitutions of the United States Ser.: No. 16). 212p. (C). 1995. text 24.95 (*0-8078-4551-5*) U of NC Pr.

***North Carolina State Credit Directory, 2000 Edition.** rev. ed. American Business Directories Staff. 736p. 1999. boxed set 175.00 incl. cd-rom (*0-7687-0315-8*) Am Busn Direct.

North Carolina State Parks. Barbara McCaig & Boyce. (Illus.). 100p. (Orig.). 1989. pap. text 5.95 (*0-935201-65-3*) Affordable Adven.

North Carolina State Parks Map Guide. (Illus.). 92p. 1997. spiral bd. 14.95 (*0-9664001-0-0*) Graphics Two-Thousnd.

North Carolina Statutes Relating to Child Support. rev. ed. Compiled by John L. Saxon. 178p. (C). 1996. pap. text 21.50 (*1-56011-288-3*, 96.08) Institute Government.

***North Carolina Student Supplement for Litigation.** Neal R. Bevans. LC 99-88903. 2000. pap. text, student ed. 21.95 (*0-7355-1327-9*) Panel Pubs.

North Carolina Survival. Betty L. Hall & Margo Perkins. 160p. (Orig.). (gr. 10-12). 1979. pap. text 5.84 (*0-03-046941-4*) Westwood Pr.

North Carolina Taproots: Courthouses of North Carolina. Paul Crane & Sophie Crane. LC 97-75414. (Illus.). 144p. 1997. 19.95 (*1-57736-042-7*, Hillsboro Pr) Providence Hse.

North Carolina Taxpayers, 1701-1786. Clarence E. Ratcliff. LC 84-80487. 228p. 1999. reprint ed. 20.00 (*0-8063-1079-0*) Genealog Pub.

North Carolina Taxpayers, 1679-1790. Clarence E. Ratcliff. 230p. 1996. reprint ed. 25.00 (*0-8063-1204-1*, 4762) Genealog Pub.

North Carolina Teachers' & State Employees' Comprehensive Major Medical Plan General Statutes, 1997. 65p. pap. 12.00 (*1-55834-908-1*) LEXIS Pub.

North Carolina Teachers' Professional Competencies Handbook. Bruce Beezer. LC 91-76030. 176p. (C). 1992. pap. 14.00 (*0-89089-443-4*) Carolina Acad Pr.

North Carolina, the Years Before Man: A Geologic History. Fred Beyer. LC 91-70197. (Illus.). 240p. (YA). (gr. 10). 1991. text 34.95 (*0-89089-400-0*) Carolina Acad Pr.

North Carolina Through Four Centuries. William S. Powell. LC 88-7691. (Illus.). xviii, 652p. (C). 1989. 37.50 (*0-8078-1846-1*); text 29.95 (*0-8078-1850-X*) U of NC Pr.

North Carolina Timeline: A Chronology of North Carolina History, Mystery, Trivia, Legend, Lore & More. Carole Marsh. (Carole Marsh North Carolina Bks.). (Illus.). (J). (gr. 3-12). 1994. pap. 19.95 (*0-7933-5975-9*); lib. bdg. 29.95 (*0-7933-5974-0*); disk 29.95 (*0-7933-5976-7*) Gallopade Intl.

North Carolina Tort Law, 2 vols. William S. Haynes. LC 89-64179. 1992. suppl. ed. 65.00 (*0-317-03795-1*) West Group.

North Carolina Tort Law. David A. Logan & Wayne A. Logan. LC 94-73844. 662p. (C). 1996. lib. bdg. 100.00 (*0-89089-844-8*) Carolina Acad Pr.

North Carolina Tort Law, 2 vols., Set. William S. Haynes. LC 89-64179. 1989. 180.00 (*0-317-03794-3*) West Group.

North Carolina Tort Law, 1992. rev. ed. Wake Forest University School of Law - CLE Staff. 597p. 1992. pap. text 65.00 (*0-942225-60-0*) Wake Forest Law.

North Carolina Traveler: A Vacationer's Guide to the Mountains, Piedmont, & Coast. 5th rev. ed. Ed. by Sunny Smith et al. LC 96-54234. (Illus.). 386p. 1999. pap. 15.95 (*0-89587-175-0*) Blair.

North Carolina Trees & Wildflowers. James Kavanagh. (Pocket Naturalist Ser.). (Illus.). 1998. 5.95 (*1-889903-56-6*, Pub. by Waterford WA) Falcon Pub Inc.

North Carolina Trial Practice. Carol B. Anderson. LC 95-82262. 845p. 1996. 95.00 (*1-55834-312-1*, 65160-10, MICHIE) LEXIS Pub.

North Carolina Trial Practice, 1998 Cumulative Supplement. Carol B. Anderson. 100p. 1998. pap. write for info. (*0-327-00616-1*, 6516111) LEXIS Pub.

North Carolina Trivia. rev. ed. Ernie Couch & Jill Couch. LC 91-2463. 192p. (Orig.). 1991. pap. 6.95 (*1-55853-112-2*) Rutledge Hill Pr.

North Carolina Troops, 1861-1865 Vol. XIV, Infantry: A Roster: 57th, 58th, 60th, & 61st Regiments. Ed. by Weymouth T. Jordan, Jr. (Illus.). xxiv, 813p. 1998. 40.00 (*0-86526-280-2*) NC Archives.

North Carolina Troops, 1861-1865: A Roster, 13 vols., Vols. I-X. Ed. by Weymouth T. Jordan, Jr. Incl. North Carolina Troops, 1861-1865 Vol. 13: A Roster, Infantry (53rd-56th Regiments) (Illus.). xx, 752p. 1993. 38.00 (*0-86526-018-4*); write for info. (*0-86526-005-2*) NC Archives.

North Carolina Troops, 1861-1865, Vol. 13, A Roster, Infantry (53rd-56th Regiments) see North Carolina Troops, 1861-1865: A Roster

North Carolina 2000! Coming Soon to a Calendar Near You - The 21st Century! - Complete Set of AL 2000 Items. Carole Marsh. (Two Thousand! Ser.). (Illus.). (J). (gr. 3-12). 1998. pap. 75.00 (*0-7933-9375-2*) Gallopade Intl.

North Carolina 2000! Coming Soon to a Calendar Near You - The 21st Century! - Complete Set of All 2000 Items. Carole Marsh. (Two Thousand! Ser.). (Illus.). (J). (gr. 3-12). 1998. lib. bdg. 85.00 (*0-7933-9376-0*) Gallopade Intl.

North Carolina 2000! Coming Soon to a Calendar near You--The 21st Century! Carole Marsh. (Two Thousand! Ser.). (Illus.). (J). (gr. 3-12). 1998. pap. 19.95 (*0-7933-8775-2*); lib. bdg. 29.95 (*0-7933-8774-4*) Gallopade Intl.

***North Carolina 2000 Rules of Civil Procedure & Evidence.** LEXIS Law Publishing Editors. 865p. 1999. pap. 45.00 (*0-327-10223-3*, 4649017) LEXIS Pub.

North Carolina UFOs: E. T. Tales from the Tar Heel State. Ed. by Daisy Roland & Sandi Goodridge. 94p. 1998. pap. 10.00 (*0-9649370-3-4*) Shadowbox.

North Carolina UFO's & Extraterrestrials! A Look at the Sightings & Science in Our State. Carole Marsh. (Carole Marsh North Carolina Bks.). (Illus.). (J). (gr. 3-12). 1997. pap. 19.95 (*0-7933-6434-5*); lib. bdg. 29.95 (*0-7933-6433-7*) Gallopade Intl.

North Carolina Unfair Business Practice. Noel L. Allen. 702p. 95.00 (*0-327-01933-6*) LEXIS Pub.

North Carolina Unfair Business Practice. Noel L. Allen. LC 95-78586. 702p. 1995. 95.00 (*1-55834-250-8*, 60095, MICHIE) LEXIS Pub.

North Carolina Unfair Business Practice, 1998 Cumulative Supplement. Noel L. Allen. 200p. 1998. suppl. ed. 42.00 (*0-327-00397-9*, 6009612) LEXIS Pub.

North Carolina Uninsured & Underinsured Motorist Coverage: A Handbook. George L. Simpson, III. Ed. by Clay Davidson. LC 95-82272. 300p. 1996. text. write for info. (*0-7620-0030-9*) West Group.

North Carolina Votes on the Constitution: A Roster of Delegates to the State Ratification Conventions of 1788 & 1789. Ed. by Stephen E. Massengill. (North Carolina & the Constitution Ser.). (Illus.). xii, 86p. (Orig.). 1988. pap. 6.00 (*0-86526-237-3*) NC Archives.

North Carolina Waterfalls: Where to Find Them, How to Photograph Them. Kevin Adams. LC 93-35021. (Illus.). 210p. (Orig.). 1994. pap. 16.95 (*0-89587-110-6*) Blair.

North Carolina Wild Places: A Closer Look. North Carolina Wildlife Resources Commission Staff. Ed. by Lawrence S. Earley. LC 92-81998. (Illus.). 82p. (Orig.). (J). (gr. 2-6). 1994. pap. 10.00 (*0-9628949-1-5*) NC Wildlife.

North Carolina Wild Places: Teacher's Guide. (Illus.). (Orig.). 1994. pap. 6.00 (*0-9628949-4-X*) NC Wildlife.

***North Carolina Wildlife Resources General Statutes: 2000 Supplement.** Institute of Government Staff. (C). 2000. write for info. (*1-56011-377-4*) Institute Government.

***North Carolina Wildlife Resources General Statutes 1999.** Institute of Government Staff. (C). 1999. ring bd. 37.00 (*1-56011-362-6*) Institute Government.

North Carolina Wildlife Viewing Guide. Charles Roe. Ed. by Chris Cauble. LC 91-58883. (Watchable Wildlife Ser.). (Illus.). 96p. (Orig.). 1992. pap. 5.95 (*1-56044-055-4*) Falcon Pub Inc.

North Carolina Women: Making History. Margaret Supplee Smith & Emily Herring Wilson. LC 98-25243. (Illus.). 420p. 1999. 29.95 (*0-8078-2463-1*) U of NC Pr.

North Carolina Workers' Compensation Law Annotated: 1994 Edition. pap. 35.00 (*0-327-11345-6*) LEXIS Pub.

***North Carolina Workers' Compensation Law Annotated with CD-ROM: 1999-2000 Edition.** 747p. 2000. write for info. (*0-327-10465-1*, 3048913) LEXIS Pub.

North Carolina Yeoman: The Diary of Basil Armstrong Thomasson, 1853-1962. Paul D. Escott. LC 95-8429. 1996. 50.00 (*0-8203-1755-1*) U of Ga Pr.

North Carolina, 1850: Mortality Schedule. 1989. 56.00 (*0-89593-590-2*, Accel Indexing) Genealogical Srvcs.

North Carolina, 1860: Mortality Schedule. 1993. 85.00 (*0-89593-591-0*, Accel Indexing) Genealogical Srvcs.

North Carolina 1998 Cumulative Supplement. 5000p. 1999. ring bd. write for info. (*0-327-07467-1*, 4656715) LEXIS Pub.

North Carolina 1999 Rules of Civil Procedure & Evidence. Lexis Law Publishing Staff. 880p. 1998. write for info. (*0-327-06651-2*) LEXIS Pub.

***North Carolina's Big Activity Book.** Carole Marsh. (North Carolina Experience! Ser.). (Illus.). (J). (gr. k-5). 2000. pap. 9.95 (*0-7933-9462-7*) Gallopade Intl.

North Carolina's Capital, Raleigh. Elizabeth C. Waugh. 1992. pap. 20.00 (*0-9631710-1-1*) Jr League Raleigh.

***North Carolina's Criminal Justice System.** Paul Knepper. 1999. pap. 25.00 (*0-89089-826-X*) Carolina Acad Pr.

North Carolina's Historic Restaurants & Their Recipes. 3rd rev. ed. Dawn O'Brien. LC 83-2831. (Illus.). 204p. 1990. 14.95 (*0-89587-067-3*) Blair.

North Carolina's Hurricane History. rev. ed. Jay Barnes. LC 98-16051. 272p. 1998. pap. 19.95 (*0-8078-4728-3*) U of NC Pr.

North Carolina's Hurricane History. rev. ed. Jay Barnes. LC 98-16051. (Illus.). 272p. 1998. 34.95 (*0-8078-2416-X*) U of NC Pr.

North Carolina's Literary Resource Guide. 5th ed. Ed. by Bobbie Collins-Perry. 92p. 1999. pap. 10.00 (*1-883314-10-0*) NC Writers Network.

North Carolina's (Most Devastating!) Disasters & (Most Calamitous!) Catastrophies! Carole Marsh. (Carole Marsh North Carolina Bks.). (Illus.). (J). 1994. pap. 19.95 (*0-7933-0837-2*); lib. bdg. 29.95 (*0-7933-0838-0*); disk 29.95 (*0-7933-0839-9*) Gallopade Intl.

North Carolina's Role in the First World War. Sarah M. Lemmon. (Illus.). viii, 91p. 1975. pap. 5.00 (*0-86526-094-X*) NC Archives.

North Carolina's Role in the Spanish-American War. Joseph F. Steelman. (Illus.). x, 39p. 1975. pap. 5.00 (*0-86526-096-6*) NC Archives.

North Carolina's Role in World War II. Sarah M. Lemmon. (Illus.). viii, 69p. 1995. reprint ed. pap. 5.00 (*0-86526-095-8*) NC Archives.

North Carolina's Scariest Swamp: The Great Dismal. Carole Marsh. (North Carolina Bks.). (Illus.). (J). (gr. 3 up). 1994. pap. 19.95 (*0-7933-1271-X*); lib. bdg. 29.95 (*0-7933-1270-1*); disk 29.95 (*0-7933-1272-8*) Gallopade Intl.

North Carolina's Unsolved Mysteries (& Their "Solutions") Includes Scientific Information & Other Activities for Students. Carole Marsh. (Carole Marsh North Carolina Bks.). (Illus.). (J). (gr. 3-12). 1994. pap. 19.95 (*0-7933-5822-1*); lib. bdg. 29.95 (*0-7933-5821-3*); disk 29.95 (*0-7933-5823-X*) Gallopade Intl.

North Cascades. 1997. lib. bdg. 250.95 (*0-8490-8175-0*) Gordon Pr.

An Asterisk (*) at the beginning of an entry indicates that the title is appearing for the first time.

North Cascades. National Park Service Staff. (Official National Park Handbook Ser.: No. 131). (Illus.). 112p. 1986. pap. 7.50 (*0-912627-31-X*) Natl Park Serv.

North Cascades: The Story Behind the Scenery. Saul Weisberg. LC 88-80121. (Illus.). 48p. (Orig.). 1988. pap. 7.95 (*0-88714-021-1*) KC Pubns.

North Cascades Crest: Notes & Images from America's Alps. Photos & Text by James Martin. LC 98-41006. (Illus.). 128p. 1999. pap. 19.95 (*1-57061-140-8*) Sasquatch Bks.

North Cascades Highway: Washington's Popular & Scenic Pass. JoAnn Roe. LC 97-24305. (Illus.). 192p. 1997. pap. 14.95 (*0-89886-517-4*) Mountaineers.

North Cascades Highway Guide. Fred T. Darvill, Jr. Ed. by Shirley T. Moore. 63p. (Orig.). 1986. pap. text 3.95 (*0-914019-10-4*) NW Interpretive.

North Cascades National Park, WA. rev. ed. Ed. by Trails Illustrated Staff. (Illus.). 1995. 8.99 (*0-925873-70-5*) Trails Illustrated.

North Caucasus: Russia's Fragile Borderland. Anna Matveeva. (Central Asian & Caucasian Prospects Ser.). 96p. 1998. pap. 12.95 (*1-86203-062-6*, Pub. by Royal Inst Intl Affairs) Brookings.

North Central see Directory of Child Day Care Centers

North Central Arkansas Death Record Index, 1914-1923: Baxter, Cleburne, Conway, Faulkner, Fulton, Independence, Izard, Jackson, Lawrence, Randolph, Sharp, Stone, Van Buren, White, & Woodruff Counties. Ed. by Desmond W. Allen. 74p. (Orig.). 1996. pap. 16.00 (*1-56546-080-4*) Arkansas Res.

North Central Arkansas Death Record Index, 1924-1933: Baxter, Cleburne, Conway, Faulkner, Fulton, Independence, Izard, Jackson, Lawrence, Randolph, Sharp, Stone, Van Buren, White & Woodruff Counties. Ed. by Desmond W. Allen. 84p. 1997. pap. 16.00 (*1-56546-114-2*) Arkansas Res.

North Central Arkansas Death Record Index, 1934-1940: Baxter, Cleburne, Conway, Faulkner, Fulton, Independence, Izard, Jackson, Lawrence, Randolph, Sharp, Stone, Van Buren, White & Woodruff Counties. Ed. by Desmond W. Allen. 55p. (Orig.). 1996. pap. 15.00 (*1-56546-088-X*) Arkansas Res.

***North Central Arkansas Death Record Index, 1941-1948: Baxter, Cleburne, Conway, Faulkner, Fulton, Independence, Izard, Jackson, Lawrence, Randolph, Sharp, Stone, Van Buren, White, & Woodruff Counties.** Compiled by Desmond Walls Allen. 97p. 1999. pap. 18.00 (*1-56546-161-4*) Arkansas Res.

North Central Arkansas 1870 Census Index: Conway, Fulton, Independence, Izard, Jackson, Lawrence, Marion, Randolph, Searcy, Sharp, Van Buren, White, & Woodruff Counties. Martha Vaughn. 182p. 1999. pap. 25.00 (*1-56546-142-8*) Arkansas Res.

North Central Association Quarterly: Directory of Accredited Institutions. write for info. (*0-318-20600-5*) NCACS.

North Central Coll 98 Freshman. B. Brodhead. 1998. pap. text 18.00 (*0-07-428955-1*) McGraw.

North Central GPS Companion: Includes Iowa, Minnesota, Wisconsin. Ed. by Clayton Wendt. 426p. 1998. pap. 13.95 (*1-891759-14-0*, 50223) Wendt Cos Inc.

North Central Oklahoma: Rooted in the Past - Growing for the Future, Vol. 1. Ed. by NCOHA Staff. (Illus.). 1008p. 1995. 70.00 (*0-9660090-4-5*) NCOHA.

North-Central Section Field Guide. Ed. by D. L. Biggs. (DNAG Centennial Field Guides Ser.: No.3). (Illus.). 490p. 1988. 21.75 (*0-8137-5403-8*) Geol Soc.

North Central Texas Legal Services Foundation, Inc., Policy Manual, 3 vols., I. 1986. 12.00 (*0-685-23183-6*, 41,240A) NCLS Inc.

North Central Texas Legal Services Foundation, Inc., Policy Manual, 3 vols., II. 1986. 9.00 (*0-685-23184-4*, 41,240B) NCLS Inc.

North Central Texas Legal Services Foundation, Inc., Policy Manual, 3 vols., III. 1986. 9.00 (*0-685-23185-2*, 41,240) NCLS Inc.

***North China at War: The Social Ecology of Revolution, 1937-1945.** Ed. by Feng Chongyi & David S. Goodman. LC 99-89422. 145p. 2000. pap. 29.95 (*0-8476-9939-0*); text 74.00 (*0-8476-9938-2*) Rowman.

North China Lover. Marguerite Duras. Tr. by Leigh Hafrey. LC 92-53729. 240p. 1992. 19.95 (*1-56584-018-6*, Pub. by New Press NY) Norton.

North China Lover. Marguerite Duras. LC 92-53729. 240p. 1993. pap. 10.00 (*1-56584-043-7*, Pub. by New Press NY) Norton.

North City Traffic, Straight Ahead. James Douglas. (Irish Play Ser.). 1968. pap. 1.25 (*0-912262-09-5*) Proscenium.

North Clyde Estuary: An Illustrated Architectural Guide. Frank A. Walker & Fiona Sinclair. (Illus.). 176p. (C). 1992. pap. 35.00 (*1-873190-07-7*, Pub. by Rutland Pr) St Mut.

North Coast of Antigua. Wilson Ltd. Staff & Imray L. Norie. (C). 1987. 53.00 (*0-7855-5932-9*, Pub. by Laurie Norie & Wilson Ltd) St Mut.

North Coast Roses. Rhonda M. Hart. (Cascadia Gardening Ser.). (Illus.). 96p. (Orig.). 1993. pap. 8.95 (*0-912365-76-5*) Sasquatch Bks.

North Country: A History Embracing Jefferson, St. Lawrence, Oswego, Lewis & Franklin Counties, 3 vols. Harry F. Landon. (Illus.). 1647p. 1997. reprint ed. lib. bdg. 165.00 (*0-8328-6887-6*) Higginson Bk Co.

North Country: A Personal Journey Through the Borderland. Howard Frank Mosher. 272p. 1998. pap. 13.00 (*0-395-90139-1*, Mariner Bks) HM.

North Country: Writing from the Upper Hudson Valley & the Adirondacks. Ed. by Joseph Bruchac et al. LC 85-70358. 472p. (Orig.). 1986. pap. 12.95 (*0-912678-65-8*, Greenfld Rev Pr) Greenfld Rev Lit.

North Country Almanac: A Seasonal Guide to the Great Outdoors. Anne Brataas. (Illus.). 192p. 1996. pap. 10.95 (*0-8362-1327-0*) Andrews & McMeel.

North Country Bassin' Ed. by Tom Zenanko. (Illus.). 227p. (Orig.). 1983. pap. 9.95 (*0-9610296-2-5*) Zenanko Outdoors.

North Country Captives: Selected Narratives of Indian Captivity from Vermont & New Hampshire. Ed. by Colin G. Calloway. LC 91-50810. (Illus.). 176p. 1992. pap. 16.95 (*0-87451-582-3*) U Pr of New Eng.

North Country Christmas. Frwd. by Susan Butcher. (Illus.). (J). (gr. 1-6). 1992. 15.95 (*0-934007-18-7*); pap. 8.95 (*0-934007-14-4*) Paws Four Pub.

North Country Cooking. Bob Igoe & Dorothy Igoe. (Illus.). 128p. 1995. pap. 12.50 (*0-925168-46-7*) North Country.

North Country Landscape. Intro. by Patricia A. Anderson. (Illus.). 23p. 1986. pap. 7.00 (*0-685-18656-3*) SUNYP R Gibson.

North Country Maid. large type unabridged ed. Mary Craddock. (Reminiscence Ser.). 240p. 1998. 24.95 (*0-7531-5072-7*, 150727) ISIS Pub.

North Country Night. Daniel San Souci. (J). 1994. mass mkt. 3.99 (*0-440-90113-8*) Dell.

North Country Night. Daniel San Souci. (Illus.). 32p. (J). 1994. pap. 7.99 (*0-440-41029-0*) Dell.

North Country Night. Daniel San Souci. 1990. 12.19 (*0-606-07060-5*, Pub. by Turtleback) Demco.

North Country Notebook. George Vukelich. (Illus.). 210p. (Orig.). 1987. 17.95 (*0-944133-00-2*); pap. 10.95 (*0-944133-01-0*) Nrth Cntry Pr.

North Country Notebook, Vol. 2. George Vukelich. LC 92-25131. (Illus.). 144p. (Orig.). 1992. 17.95 (*0-944133-09-6*); pap. 10.95 (*0-944133-10-X*) Nrth Cntry Pr.

***North Country Reader.** Jean Ervin. LC 00-37987. (Borealis Classic Stories Ser.). 2000. pap. write for info. (*0-87351-388-6*) Minn Hist.

North Country Spring. Elizabeth Kouhi. (Illus.). 54p. (J). (ps-8). 1980. 6.95 (*0-920806-10-4*, Pub. by Penumbra Pr) U of Toronto Pr.

North Country Spring. Reeve Lindbergh. LC 95-52366. (Illus.). 32p. (J). 1997. 15.95 (*0-395-82819-8*) HM.

North Country Spring. Reeve Lindbergh. LC 95-52366. (Illus.). (J). 1997. write for info. (*0-316-52710-6*) Little.

North Country Tales, Truths & Trivia. Ruth Timm. (Illus.). 168p. 1994. pap. 12.95 (*0-925168-24-6*) North Country.

North Cove Yacht Harbor. Lee Nash. Ed. by Maxine Brady. (Illus.). 50p. write for info. (*0-318-64708-7*) Watermark Assocs.

North Cross to Southern Cross. Frank Mulville. 1994. pap. text 14.95 (*1-85253-291-2*) Cimino Pub Grp.

***North Cyprus: The Bradt Travel Guide.** 3rd ed. Diana Darke. LC 99-54343. (Illus.). 2000. pap. 14.95 (*1-84162-012-2*, Pub. by Bradt Pubns) Globe Pequot.

North Dakota see Atlas of Historical County Boundaries

***North Dakota.** (Switched on Schoolhouse Ser.). (Illus.). (J). 2000. pap. 24.95 (*0-7403-0286-8*) Alpha AZ.

North Dakota. Dennis B. Fradin. (From Sea to Shining Sea Ser.). (J). 1998. pap. text 7.95 (*0-516-26281-5*) Childrens.

North Dakota. Dennis B. Fradin & Judith B. Fradin. LC 94-4871. (From Sea to Shining Sea Ser.). (Illus.). 64p. (J). (gr. 3-5). 1994. lib. bdg. 26.00 (*0-516-03834-6*) Childrens.

***North Dakota.** Martin Hintz. LC 99-42902. (America the Beautiful Ser.). (YA). 2000. 33.00 (*0-516-21072-6*) Childrens.

North Dakota. C. M. Knutson. 24p. (Orig.). (J). (gr. k-6). 1986. pap. 1.00 (*0-938451-01-4*) Selena Pr.

North Dakota. Patricia K. Kummer. LC 98-15062. (One Nation Ser.). (Illus.). 48p. (J). (gr. 3-7). 1999. 19.00 (*0-7368-0023-9*) Capstone Pr.

***North Dakota.** Melissa McDaniel. (Celebrate the States Ser.). (Illus.). (J). 2001. 35.64 (*0-7614-1069-4*, Benchmark NY) Marshall Cavendish.

North Dakota. Kathleen Thompson. LC 95-50424. (Portrait of America Library). 48p. (J). (gr. 4-8). 1996. pap. text 5.95 (*0-8114-7460-7*) Raintree Steck-V.

North Dakota. Kathleen Thompson. (Portrait of America Library). (Illus.). 48p. (J). (gr. 3-6). 1996. lib. bdg. 22.83 (*0-8114-7379-1*) Raintree Steck-V.

North Dakota. Joan M. Verba. Ed. by Lerner Geography Department Staff. (Hello U. S. A. Ser.). (Illus.). 72p. (J). (gr. 3-6). 1992. lib. bdg. 19.95 (*0-8225-2746-4*, Lerner Publctns) Lerner Pub.

North Dakota. Anne Welsbacher. LC 97-31415. (The United States Ser.). (Illus.). 32p. (J). 1998. lib. bdg. 19.93 (*1-56239-896-2*, Checkerboard Library) ABDO Pub Co.

North Dakota. rev. ed. Margaret S. Herguth. LC 89-25283. (America the Beautiful Ser.). (Illus.). 144p. (J). (gr. 5-8). 1990. lib. bdg. 28.00 (*0-516-00480-8*) Childrens.

North Dakota, 33. Capstone Press Geogra Staff. (One Nation Ser.). (J). 1998. 19.00 (*0-516-21479-9*) Childrens.

North Dakota: A Guide to the Northern Prairie State. Federal Writers' Project Staff. LC 72-84498. (American Guidebook Ser.). 1980. reprint ed. lib. bdg. 79.00 (*0-685-04694-X*) Somerset Pub.

North Dakota: A Guide to the Northern Prairie State. Federal Writers' Project Staff & Writers Program-WPA Staff. (American Guide Ser.). 1989. reprint ed. lib. bdg. 59.00 (*0-7812-1033-X*, 1033) Rprt Serv.

North Dakota: A Living Legacy. Theodore B. Jelliff. (Illus.). 400p. (YA). (gr. 8 up). 1983. 19.50 (*0-9612140-0-7*) K K Pub Co.

North Dakota: In Grateful Homage. Pauline N. Diede. Ed. by C. Jane Brandt. Tr. by New Salem Journal Printing Staff. (Pioneer Life Bks.: Vol. IV). (Illus.). 75p. (Orig.). 1987. pap. text 6.95 (*0-685-26962-0*) P Neher Diede.

North Dakota: Land of Changing Seasons. Frances M. Berg. LC 76-45874. (Old West Region Ser.: Vol. 1). (Illus.). 176p. 1977. 28.95 (*0-918532-01-9*, Flyng Diamond); pap. 17.95 (*0-918532-02-7*, Flyng Diamond) Hlthy Wght Network.

North Dakota, a Guide to the Northern Prairie State see WPA Guide to 1930s North Dakota

North Dakota Advance Code Service, Vol. 3. 60p. 1999. pap. write for info. (*0-327-07708-5*, 4689914) LEXIS Pub.

North Dakota Air Balloon Mystery. Carole Marsh. (Carole Marsh North Dakota Bks.). (Illus.). (J). (gr. 2-9). 1994. 29.95 (*0-7933-2624-9*); pap. 19.95 (*0-7933-2625-7*); disk 29.95 (*0-7933-2626-5*) Gallopade Intl.

North Dakota & Other State Greats (Biographies) Carole Marsh. (Carole Marsh North Dakota Bks.). (Illus.). (J). 1994. pap. 19.95 (*1-55609-977-0*); lib. bdg. 29.95 (*1-55609-976-2*) Gallopade Intl.

North Dakota & Other State Greats (Biographies) Carole Marsh. (Carole Marsh North Dakota Bks.). (Illus.). (J). 1997. disk 29.95 (*1-55609-978-9*) Gallopade Intl.

North Dakota Atlas & Gazetteer. Mapping Delorme. LC 99-464315. 1999. pap. text 16.95 (*0-89933-232-3*) DeLorme Map.

North Dakota Bandits, Bushwackers, Outlaws, Crooks, Devils, Ghosts, Desperadoes & Other Assorted & Sundry Characters! Carole Marsh. (Carole Marsh North Dakota Bks.). (Illus.). (J). 1994. pap. 19.95 (*0-7933-0864-X*); lib. bdg. 29.95 (*0-7933-0865-8*); disk 29.95 (*0-7933-0866-6*) Gallopade Intl.

North Dakota "BIO" Bingo! 24 Must Know State People for Kids to Learn about While Having Fun! Carole Marsh. (Bingo! Ser.). (Illus.). (J). (gr. 2-8). 1998. pap. 14.95 (*0-7933-8624-1*) Gallopade Intl.

North Dakota Bookstore Book: A Surprising Guide to Our State's Bookstores & Their Specialties for Students, Teachers, Writers & Publishers. Carole Marsh. (Carole Marsh North Carolina Bks.). (Illus.). 1994. pap. 19.95 (*0-7933-2958-2*); lib. bdg. 29.95 (*0-7933-2957-4*); disk 29.95 (*0-7933-2959-0*) Gallopade Intl.

***North Dakota Business Directory, 2000 Edition.** rev. ed. American Business Directories Staff. 480p. 1999. boxed set 375.00 (*0-7687-0170-8*) Am Busn Direct.

North Dakota Census Index, 1885, Vol. 1. (Illus.). lib. bdg. 54.00 (*0-89593-449-3*, Accel Indexing) Genealogical Srvcs.

North Dakota Census Index, 1880: Mortality Schedule. (Illus.). 1984. lib. bdg. 30.00 (*0-89593-448-5*, Accel Indexing) Genealogical Srvcs.

North Dakota Census Index, 1885: Mortality Schedule. (Illus.). 1984. lib. bdg. write for info. (*0-89593-451-5*, Accel Indexing) Genealogical Srvcs.

North Dakota Census Index, 1870: Mortality Schedule. (Illus.). lib. bdg. 30.00 (*0-89593-447-7*, Accel Indexing) Genealogical Srvcs.

North Dakota Centennial Newspaper Index. Michael M. Miller. 130p. 1991. write for info. (*0-9629777-0-5*) ND State Univ.

North Dakota Century Code. annot. ed. Prevention Magazine Health Books Staff. write for info. (*0-614-05932-1*, MICHIE) LEXIS Pub.

North Dakota Century Code Annotated, 23. 650.00 (*0-327-11919-5*) LEXIS Pub.

North Dakota Century Code Annotated. 1959. write for info. (*0-87473-011-2*, MICHIE) LEXIS Pub.

North Dakota Century Code Annotated, Court Rules: 1998-99 Edition. Michie's Editorial Staff. 1,141p. pap. 55.00 (*0-327-11944-6*) LEXIS Pub.

***North Dakota Century Code, 1999 Cumulative Supplement, 22 vols.** Incl. North Dakota Century Code, 1999 Cumulative Supplement Vol. 1A: General Provisions. 1999. (*0-327-08929-6*, 50610-13); North Dakota Century Code, 1999 Cumulative Supplement Vol. 1B: Alcoholic Beverages. 1999. (*0-327-08930-X*, 50611-13); North Dakota Century Code, 1999 Cumulative Supplement Vol. 2A: Corporations. 1999. (*0-327-08931-8*, 50612-13); North Dakota Century Code, 1999 Cumulative Supplement Vol. 2B: Corrections. 1999. (*0-327-08932-6*, 50613-13); North Dakota Century Code, 1999 Cumulative Supplement Vol. 3A: Debtor-Creditor. 1999. (*0-327-08933-4*, 50614-13); North Dakota Century Code, 1999 Cumulative Supplement Vol. 3B: Education. 1999. (*0-327-08934-2*, 50615-13); North Dakota Century Code, 1999 Cumulative Supplement Vol. 4A: Game & Fish. 1999. (*0-327-08935-0*, 50616-13); North Dakota Century Code, 1999 Cumulative Supplement Vol. 4B: Mental & Physical Illness. 1999. (*0-327-08936-9*, 50617-13); North Dakota Century Code, 1999 Cumulative Supplement Vol. 5: Judicial Branch. 1999. (*0-327-08937-7*, 50618-13); North Dakota Century Code, 1999 Cumulative Supplement Vol. 6: Judicial Procedure. 1999. (*0-327-08938-5*, 50619-13); North Dakota Century Code, 1999 Cumulative Supplement Vol. 7A: Labor & Employment. 1999. (*0-327-08939-3*, 50620-13); North Dakota Century Code, 1999 Cumulative Supplement Vol. 7B: Motor Vehicles. 1999. (*0-327-08940-7*, 50621-13); North Dakota Century Code, 1999 Cumulative Supplement Vol. 8A: Municipal Government. 1999. (*0-327-08941-5*, 50622-13); North Dakota Century Code, 1999 Cumulative Supplement Vol. 8B: Commercial Code. 1999. (*0-327-08942-3*, 50623-13); North Dakota Century Code, 1999 Cumulative Supplement Vol. 9A: Occupations. 1999. (*0-327-08943-1*, 50624-13); North Dakota Century Code, 1999 Cumulative Supplement Vol. 9B: Property. 1999. (*0-327-08944-X*, 50625-13); North Dakota Century Code, 1999 Cumulative Supplement Vol. 10A: Public Welfare. 1999. (*0-327-08945-8*, 50626-13); North Dakota Century Code, 1999 Cumulative Supplement Vol. 10B: State Government. 1999. (*0-327-08946-6*, 50627-13); North Dakota Century Code, 1999 Cumulative Supplement Vol. 11: Historical Society. 1999. (*0-327-08947-4*, 50628-13); North Dakota Century Code, 1999 Cumulative Supplement Vol. 12: Trusts. 1999. (*0-327-08948-2*, 50629-13); North Dakota Century Code, 1999 Cumulative Supplement Vol. 13A: Constitutions. 1999. (*0-327-08949-0*, 50638-13); North Dakota Century Code, 1999 Cumulative Supplement Vol. 13B: Parallel Tables. 1999. (*0-327-08950-4*, 50639-13); 5000p. 1999. write for info. (*0-327-08894-X*, 4682413) LEXIS Pub.

North Dakota Century Code, 1999 Advance Code Service Pamphlet: July 1998. (Advance Code Service, 1998 Ser.: No. 1). 60p. 1998. pap. write for info. (*0-327-05444-1*, 46897-14) LEXIS Pub.

North Dakota Century Code, 1999 Cumulative Supplement, Vol. 1A, General Provisions see North Dakota Century Code, 1999 Cumulative Supplement

North Dakota Century Code, 1999 Cumulative Supplement, Vol. 1B, Alcoholic Beverages see North Dakota Century Code, 1999 Cumulative Supplement

North Dakota Century Code, 1999 Cumulative Supplement, Vol. 2A, Corporations see North Dakota Century Code, 1999 Cumulative Supplement

North Dakota Century Code, 1999 Cumulative Supplement, Vol. 2B, Corrections see North Dakota Century Code, 1999 Cumulative Supplement

North Dakota Century Code, 1999 Cumulative Supplement, Vol. 3A, Debtor-Creditor see North Dakota Century Code, 1999 Cumulative Supplement

North Dakota Century Code, 1999 Cumulative Supplement, Vol. 3B, Education see North Dakota Century Code, 1999 Cumulative Supplement

North Dakota Century Code, 1999 Cumulative Supplement, Vol. 4A, Game & Fish see North Dakota Century Code, 1999 Cumulative Supplement

North Dakota Century Code, 1999 Cumulative Supplement, Vol. 4B, Mental & Physical Illness see North Dakota Century Code, 1999 Cumulative Supplement

North Dakota Century Code, 1999 Cumulative Supplement, Vol. 5, Judicial Branch see North Dakota Century Code, 1999 Cumulative Supplement

North Dakota Century Code, 1999 Cumulative Supplement, Vol. 6, Judicial Procedure see North Dakota Century Code, 1999 Cumulative Supplement

North Dakota Century Code, 1999 Cumulative Supplement, Vol. 7A, Labor & Employment see North Dakota Century Code, 1999 Cumulative Supplement

North Dakota Century Code, 1999 Cumulative Supplement, Vol. 7B, Motor Vehicles see North Dakota Century Code, 1999 Cumulative Supplement

North Dakota Century Code, 1999 Cumulative Supplement, Vol. 8A, Municipal Government see North Dakota Century Code, 1999 Cumulative Supplement

North Dakota Century Code, 1999 Cumulative Supplement, Vol. 8B, Commercial Code see North Dakota Century Code, 1999 Cumulative Supplement

North Dakota Century Code, 1999 Cumulative Supplement, Vol. 9A, Occupations see North Dakota Century Code, 1999 Cumulative Supplement

North Dakota Century Code, 1999 Cumulative Supplement, Vol. 9B, Property see North Dakota Century Code, 1999 Cumulative Supplement

North Dakota Century Code, 1999 Cumulative Supplement, Vol. 10A, Public Welfare see North Dakota Century Code, 1999 Cumulative Supplement

North Dakota Century Code, 1999 Cumulative Supplement, Vol. 10B, State Government see North Dakota Century Code, 1999 Cumulative Supplement

North Dakota Century Code, 1999 Cumulative Supplement, Vol. 11, Historical Society see North Dakota Century Code, 1999 Cumulative Supplement

North Dakota Century Code, 1999 Cumulative Supplement, Vol. 12, Trusts see North Dakota Century Code, 1999 Cumulative Supplement

North Dakota Century Code, 1999 Cumulative Supplement, Vol. 13A, Constitutions see North Dakota Century Code, 1999 Cumulative Supplement

North Dakota Century Code, 1999 Cumulative Supplement, Vol. 13B, Parallel Tables see North Dakota Century Code, 1999 Cumulative Supplement

North Dakota Century Code 1999 Advance Code Service. John Stoner. (Nineteen Ninety-Eight Advance Code Service Ser.). 80p. 1999. pap. 56.00 (*0-327-05445-X*, 46896-14) LEXIS Pub.

North Dakota Century Code 1999 Advance Legislative Service Pamphlet, No. 1. 1000p. 1999. pap. write for info. (*0-327-08514-2*, 46881-12) LEXIS Pub.

North Dakota Century Code 1999 Advance Legislative Service Pamphlet, No. 2. 700p. 1999. pap. write for info. (*0-327-08651-3*, 46882-12) LEXIS Pub.

North Dakota Century Code 1998 Advance Code Service No. 3: May 1998. rev. ed. 71p. 1998. pap. 35.00 (*0-327-05101-9*, 46899-13) LEXIS Pub.

North Dakota Century School Code: 1991 Edition. 649p. 40.00 (*0-327-11363-4*) LEXIS Pub.

***North Dakota Century School Code: 1999 Cumulative Supplement.** 349p. 1999. pap. write for info. (*0-327-09449-4*, 3060412) LEXIS Pub.

North Dakota Classic Christmas Trivia: Stories, Recipes, Activities, Legends, Lore & More! Carole Marsh. (Carole Marsh North Dakota Bks.). (Illus.). (J). 1994. pap. 19.95 (*0-7933-0867-4*); lib. bdg. 29.95 (*0-7933-0868-2*); disk 29.95 (*0-7933-0869-0*) Gallopade Intl.

North Dakota Coastales. Carole Marsh. (Carole Marsh North Dakota Bks.). (Illus.). (J). 1994. pap. 19.95 (*1-55609-971-1*); disk 29.95 (*1-55609-972-X*) Gallopade Intl.

N

North Dakota Coastales. Carole Marsh. (Carole Marsh North Dakota Bks.). (Illus.). (J). 1997. lib. bdg. 29.95 (*1-55609-970-3*) Gallopade Intl.

North Dakota Coastales! Carole Marsh. (Carole Marsh North Dakota Bks.). (J). 1994. lib. bdg. 29.95 (*0-7933-7299-2*) Gallopade Intl.

***North Dakota Court Rules Annotated August 1999 Supplement.** 275p. 1999. pap. write for info. (*0-327-09230-0*, 4683118) LEXIS Pub.

North Dakota Court Rules Annotated February 1999 Supplement. 75p. 1999. pap. write for info. (*0-327-07576-7*, 4683117) LEXIS Pub.

North Dakota Court Rules Annotated, 1994-95 Edition. Michie Butterworth Editorial Staff. 55.00 (*0-87473-870-9*, MICHIE) LEXIS Pub.

***North Dakota Crime in Perspective 2000.** Ed. by Kathleen O'Leary Morgan & Scott E. Morgan. 22p. 2000. spiral bd. 19.00 (*0-7401-0333-4*) Morgan Quitno Corp.

North Dakota Crime Perspective, 1998. Ed. by Kathleen O'Leary Morgan & Scott E. Morgan. 20p. 1998. pap. 19.00 (*1-56692-933-4*) Morgan Quitno Corp.

North Dakota Crime Perspectives,1999. Kathleen O'Leary Morgan. 22p. 1999. spiral bd. 19.00 (*0-7401-0133-1*) Morgan Quitno Corp.

North Dakota Criminal & Traffic Law Manual: 1999 Edition. 740p. pap. 32.50 (*0-327-09187-8*, 3060213) LEXIS Pub.

North Dakota Criminal & Traffic Law Manual, 1993 Edition. Paul D. Colford. 25.00 (*0-614-05933-X*, MICHIE) LEXIS Pub.

North Dakota "Crinkum-Crankum" A Funny Word Book about Our State. Carole Marsh. (Carole Marsh North Dakota Bks.). (Illus.). (J). (gr. 3-12). 1994. 29.95 (*0-7933-4910-9*); pap. 19.95 (*0-7933-4911-7*); disk 29.95 (*0-7933-4912-5*) Gallopade Intl.

North Dakota Dingbats! Bk. 1: A Fun Book of Games, Stories, Activities & More about Our State That's All in Code! for You to Decipher. Carole Marsh. (Carole Marsh North Dakota Bks.). (Illus.). (J). (gr. 3-12). 1994. pap. 19.95 (*0-7933-3876-X*); lib. bdg. 29.95 (*0-7933-3875-1*); disk 29.95 (*0-7933-3877-8*) Gallopade Intl.

North Dakota Facts & Factivities. Carole Marsh. (Carole Marsh State Bks.). (Illus.). (J). (gr. 4-7). 1996. pap., teacher ed. 19.95 (*0-7933-7915-6*, C Marsh) Gallopade Intl.

***North Dakota Facts & Symbols.** Karen Bush Gibson. LC 00-22922. (States & Their Symbols Ser.). (Illus.). 24p. (J). (ps-3). 2000. lib. bdg. 15.93 (*0-7368-0642-3*, Hilltop Bks) Capstone Pr.

North Dakota Festival Fun for Kids! Carole Marsh. (Carole Marsh North Dakota Bks.). (Illus.). (J). (gr. 3-12). 1994. pap. 19.95 (*0-7933-4029-2*); lib. bdg. 29.95 (*0-7933-4028-4*) Gallopade Intl.

North Dakota Festival Fun for Kids! Carole Marsh. (Carole Marsh North Dakota Bks.). (Illus.). (YA). (gr. 3-12). 1994. disk 29.95 (*0-7933-4030-6*) Gallopade Intl.

North Dakota "GEO" Bingo! 38 Must Know State Geography Facts for Kids to Learn While Having Fun! Carole Marsh. (Bingo! Ser.). (Illus.). (J). (gr. 2-8). 1998. pap. 14.95 (*0-7933-8625-X*) Gallopade Intl.

North Dakota Government! The Cornerstone of Everyday Life in Our State! Carole Marsh. (Carole Marsh North Dakota Bks.). (Illus.). (J). (gr. 3-12). 1996. pap. 19.95 (*0-7933-6284-9*); lib. bdg. 29.95 (*0-7933-6283-0*); disk 29.95 (*0-7933-6285-7*) Gallopade Intl.

North Dakota Governments Performance Standards, 1990. Ed. by Greg Michels. (Governments Performance Standards Ser.). (Illus.). 150p. 1990. text 125.00 (*1-55507-496-0*) Municipal Analysis.

***North Dakota Health Care in Perspective 2000.** Ed. by Kathleen O'Leary Morgan & Scott E. Morgan. 21p. 2000. spiral bd. 19.00 (*0-7401-0233-8*) Morgan Quitno Corp.

North Dakota Health Care Perspective, 1998. Ed. by Kathleen O'Leary Morgan & Scott E. Morgan. 20p. 1998. pap. 19.00 (*1-56692-833-8*) Morgan Quitno Corp.

North Dakota Health Care Perspective, 1999. Kathleen O'Leary Morgan. 21p. 1999. spiral bd. 19.00 (*0-7401-0083-1*) Morgan Quitno Corp.

North Dakota "HISTO" Bingo! 42 Must Know State History Facts for Kids to Learn While Having Fun! Carole Marsh. (Bingo! Ser.). (Illus.). (J). (gr. 2-8). 1998. pap. 14.95 (*0-7933-8626-8*) Gallopade Intl.

***North Dakota History: Journal of the Northern Plains Cumulative Index, 1945-1998.** Ed. by Janet Daley. 112p. 2000. pap. 16.95 (*1-891419-19-6*) State Hist ND.

North Dakota History! Surprising Secrets about Our State's Founding Mothers, Fathers & Kids! Carole Marsh. (Carole Marsh North Dakota Bks.). (Illus.). (J). (gr. 3-12). 1996. pap. 19.95 (*0-7933-6131-1*); lib. bdg. 29.95 (*0-7933-6130-3*); disk 29.95 (*0-7933-6132-X*) Gallopade Intl.

North Dakota Hot Zones! Viruses, Diseases, & Epidemics in Our State's History. Carole Marsh. (Hot Zones! Ser.). (Illus.). (J). (gr. 3-12). 1998. pap. 19.95 (*0-7933-8931-3*); lib. bdg. 29.95 (*0-7933-8930-5*) Gallopade Intl.

***North Dakota Images.** Larry Aasen. (Images of America Ser.). (Illus.). 128p. 2000. pap. 18.99 (*0-7385-0763-6*) Arcadia Publng.

North Dakota in Perspective, 1998. Ed. by Kathleen O'Leary Morgan & Scott E. Morgan. 24p. 1998. pap. 19.00 (*1-56692-883-4*) Morgan Quitno Corp.

North Dakota in Perspective, 1999. Ed. by Kathleen O'Leary Morgan. 26p. 1999. spiral bd. 19.00 (*1-56692-983-0*) Morgan Quitno Corp.

***North Dakota in Perspective 2000.** Ed. by Kathleen O'Leary Morgan & Scott E. Morgan. 26p. 2000. spiral bd. 19.00 (*0-7401-0283-4*) Morgan Quitno Corp.

North Dakota Indian Dictionary for Kids! Carole Marsh. (Carole Marsh State Bks.). (J). (gr. 2-9). 1996. 29.95 (*0-7933-7746-3*, C Marsh); pap. 19.95 (*0-7933-7747-1*, C Marsh) Gallopade Intl.

North Dakota Indians: An Introduction. 2nd ed. Mary J. Schneider. 304p. (C). 1996. pap. text, per. 25.95 (*0-8403-9615-5*) Kendall-Hunt.

***North Dakota Investment & Business Guide: Business, Investment, Export-Import Opportunities, 50, 34.** Global Investment Center, USA Staff. (U. S. Regional Investment & Business Library-99: Vol. 34). (Illus.). 350p. (Orig.). 1999. pap. 59.95 (*0-7397-1133-4*) Intl Business Pubns.

North Dakota Jeopardy! Answers & Questions about Our State! Carole Marsh. (Carole Marsh North Dakota Bks.). (Illus.). (J). (gr. 3-12). 1994. pap. 19.95 (*0-7933-4182-5*); lib. bdg. 29.95 (*0-7933-4181-7*); disk 29.95 (*0-7933-4183-3*) Gallopade Intl.

North Dakota "Jography" A Fun Run Thru Our State! Carole Marsh. (Carole Marsh North Dakota Bks.). (Illus.). (J). 1994. pap. 19.95 (*1-55609-944-4*); lib. bdg. 29.95 (*1-55609-943-6*); disk 29.95 (*1-55609-945-2*) Gallopade Intl.

North Dakota Joke Book. Mike Dalton. 160p. 1982. 8.95 (*0-8184-0336-5*) Carol Pub Group.

North Dakota Kid's Cookbook: Recipes, How-to, History, Lore & More! Carole Marsh. (Carole Marsh North Dakota Bks.). (Illus.). (J). 1994. pap. 19.95 (*0-7933-0876-3*); lib. bdg. 29.95 (*0-7933-0877-1*); disk 29.95 (*0-7933-0878-X*) Gallopade Intl.

North Dakota Lawyers: Mapping the Socio-Political Dimensions. Albert P. Melone et al. LC 75-4047. (Publisher's Social Science Report: No. 1). (Illus.). 54p. 1975. pap. 1.75 (*0-911042-20-2*) NDSU Inst Reg.

North Dakota Library Book: A Surprising Guide to the Unusual Special Collections in Libraries Across Our State for Students, Teachers, Writers & Publishers - Includes Reproducible Mailing Labels Plus Activities for Young People! Carole Marsh. (Carole Marsh North Dakota Bks.). (Illus.). 1994. pap. 19.95 (*0-7933-3108-0*); lib. bdg. 29.95 (*0-7933-3107-2*); disk 29.95 (*0-7933-3109-9*) Gallopade Intl.

North Dakota Manufacturers Register. 4th rev. ed. Ed. by Frank Lambing. 1999. 54.00 (*1-58202-062-0*) Manufacturers.

North Dakota Math! How It All Adds up in Our State. Carole Marsh. (Carole Marsh North Dakota Bks.). (Illus.). (J). (gr. 3-12). 1996. pap. 19.95 (*0-7933-6590-2*); lib. bdg. 29.95 (*0-7933-6589-9*) Gallopade Intl.

North Dakota Media Book: A Surprising Guide to the Amazing Print, Broadcast & Online Media of Our State for Students, Teachers, Writers & Publishers - Includes Reproducible Mailing Labels Plus Activities for Young People! Carole Marsh. (Carole Marsh North Dakota Bks.). (Illus.). 1994. pap. 19.95 (*0-7933-3264-8*); lib. bdg. 29.95 (*0-7933-3263-X*); disk 29.95 (*0-7933-3265-6*) Gallopade Intl.

North Dakota Mystery Van Takes Off! Book 1: Handicapped North Dakota Kids Sneak Off on a Big Adventure. Carole Marsh. (Carole Marsh North Dakota Bks.). (Illus.). (J). (gr. 3-12). 1994. 29.95 (*0-7933-5063-8*); pap. 19.95 (*0-7933-5064-6*); disk 29.95 (*0-7933-5065-4*) Gallopade Intl.

North Dakota 1999 Advance Code Service, No. 2. 60p. 1998. write for info. (*0-327-06696-2*, 4689814) LEXIS Pub.

***North Dakota 1999 Replacement Volume 10A.** 525p. 1999. Price not set. (*0-327-09789-2*, 4678611) LEXIS Pub.

***North Dakota 1999 Replacement Volume 9B.** 525p. 1999. Price not set. (*0-327-09784-1*, 4678011) LEXIS Pub.

North Dakota Quiz Bowl Crash Course! Carole Marsh. (Carole Marsh North Dakota Bks.). (Illus.). (J). 1994. pap. 19.95 (*1-55609-974-6*); lib. bdg. 29.95 (*1-55609-973-8*); disk 29.95 (*1-55609-975-4*) Gallopade Intl.

***North Dakota Related Laws to the Insurance Laws.** North Dakota. LC 97-76070. 1999. write for info. (*0-89246-491-7*) NILS Pub.

North Dakota Rollercoasters! Carole Marsh. (Carole Marsh North Dakota Bks.). (Illus.). (J). (gr. 3-12). 1994. pap. 19.95 (*0-7933-5327-0*); lib. bdg. 29.95 (*0-7933-5326-2*) Gallopade Intl.

North Dakota Rollercoasters! Carole Marsh. (Carole Marsh North Dakota Bks.). (Illus.). (YA). (gr. 3-12). 1994. disk 29.95 (*0-7933-5328-9*) Gallopade Intl.

North Dakota School Trivia: An Amazing & Fascinating Look at Our State's Teachers, Schools & Students! Carole Marsh. (Carole Marsh North Dakota Bks.). (Illus.). (J). 1994. pap. 19.95 (*0-7933-0873-9*); lib. bdg. 29.95 (*0-7933-0874-7*); disk 29.95 (*0-7933-0875-5*) Gallopade Intl.

North Dakota Silly Basketball Sportsmysteries, Vol. 1. Carole Marsh. (Carole Marsh North Dakota Bks.). (Illus.). (J). 1994. pap. 19.95 (*0-7933-0870-4*); lib. bdg. 29.95 (*0-7933-0871-2*) Gallopade Intl.

North Dakota Silly Basketball Sportsmysteries, Vol. 1. Carole Marsh. (Carole Marsh North Dakota Bks.). (Illus.). (J). 1997. disk 29.95 (*0-7933-0872-0*) Gallopade Intl.

North Dakota Silly Basketball Sportsmysteries, Vol. 2. Carole Marsh. (Carole Marsh North Dakota Bks.). (Illus.). (J). 1994. pap. 19.95 (*0-7933-1846-7*); disk 29.95 (*0-7933-1847-5*) Gallopade Intl.

North Dakota Silly Basketball Sportsmysteries, Vol. 2. Carole Marsh. (Carole Marsh North Dakota Bks.). (Illus.). (J). 1997. lib. bdg. 29.95 (*0-7933-1845-9*) Gallopade Intl.

North Dakota Silly Football Sportsmysteries, Vol. 1. Carole Marsh. (Carole Marsh North Dakota Bks.). (Illus.). (J). 1994. pap. 19.95 (*1-55609-949-5*); lib. bdg. 29.95 (*1-55609-948-7*) Gallopade Intl.

North Dakota Silly Football Sportsmysteries, Vol. 2. Carole Marsh. (Carole Marsh North Dakota Bks.). (Illus.). (J). 1994. pap. 19.95 (*1-55609-968-1*); lib. bdg. 29.95 (*1-55609-967-3*); disk 29.95 (*1-55609-969-X*) Gallopade Intl.

North Dakota Silly Trivia! Carole Marsh. (Carole Marsh North Dakota Bks.). (Illus.). (J). 1994. pap. 19.95 (*1-55609-941-X*); lib. bdg. 29.95 (*1-55609-940-1*); disk 29.95 (*1-55609-942-8*) Gallopade Intl.

North Dakota Spelling Bee! Score Big by Correctly Spelling Our State's Unique Names. Carole Marsh. (Carole Marsh North Dakota Bks.). (Illus.). (YA). (gr. 3-12). 1996. pap. 19.95 (*0-7933-6743-3*); lib. bdg. 29.95 (*0-7933-6742-5*) Gallopade Intl.

North Dakota State Capitol: Architecture & History. Ed. by Larry Remele. (Illus.). 63p. 1989. pap. 6.50 (*1-891419-09-9*) State Hist ND.

North Dakota Timeline: A Chronology of North Dakota History, Mystery, Trivia, Legend, Lore & More. Carole Marsh. (Carole Marsh North Dakota Bks.). (Illus.). (J). (gr. 3-12). 1994. pap. 19.95 (*0-7933-5978-3*); lib. bdg. 29.95 (*0-7933-5977-5*); disk 29.95 (*0-7933-5979-1*) Gallopade Intl.

North Dakota 2000! Coming Soon to a Calendar Near You - The 21st Century! - Complete Set of AL 2000 Items. Carole Marsh. (Two Thousand! Ser.). (Illus.). (J). (gr. 3-12). 1998. pap. 75.00 (*0-7933-9377-9*) Gallopade Intl.

North Dakota 2000! Coming Soon to a Calendar Near You - The 21st Century! - Complete Set of All 2000 Items. Carole Marsh. (Two Thousand! Ser.). (Illus.). (J). (gr. 3-12). 1998. lib. bdg. 85.00 (*0-7933-9378-7*) Gallopade Intl.

North Dakota 2000! Coming Soon to a Calendar near You--The 21st Century! Carole Marsh. (Two Thousand! Ser.). (Illus.). (J). (gr. 3-12). 1998. pap. 19.95 (*0-7933-8778-7*); lib. bdg. 29.95 (*0-7933-8777-9*) Gallopade Intl.

***North Dakota 2000 Advance Code Service, Vol. 1.** 25p. 1999. pap. write for info. (*0-327-09826-0*, 4689715) LEXIS Pub.

***North Dakota 2000 Replacement, Vol. 11.** 813p. 2000. write for info. (*0-327-13107-1*, 4679111) LEXIS Pub.

North Dakota UFO's & Extraterrestrials! A Look at the Sightings & Science in Our State. Carole Marsh. (Carole Marsh North Dakota Bks.). (Illus.). (J). (gr. 3-12). 1997. pap. 19.95 (*0-7933-6437-X*); lib. bdg. 29.95 (*0-7933-6436-1*) Gallopade Intl.

North Dakota Vets & Widows Census, 1890. 1986. 55.00 (*0-89593-592-9*, Accel Indexing) Genealogical Srvcs.

North Dakota Wildlife Viewing Guide. Joseph Knue. Ed. by Chris Cauble. LC 91-58879. (Watchable Wildlife Ser.). (Illus.). 96p. (Orig.). 1992. pap. 5.95 (*1-56044-120-8*) Falcon Pub Inc.

***North Dakota Workers' Compensation Law: 1999 Edition.** 184p. 1999. pap. 20.00 (*0-327-09223-8*, 3061013) LEXIS Pub.

***North Dakota 1999 Replacement, Vol. 8B.** 525p. 1999. write for info. (*0-327-09393-5*, 4677011) LEXIS Pub.

***North Dakota 1999 Replacement Index.** 826p. 1999. Price not set. (*0-327-09108-8*, 4682513) LEXIS Pub.

North Dakota's Former Governors' Mansion: Its History & Preservation. Ed. by Virginia L. Heidenreich. (Illus.). 72p. 1991. pap. 7.50 (*1-891419-10-2*) State Hist ND.

North Dakota's (Most Devastating!) Disasters & (Most Calamitous!) Catastrophies! Carole Marsh. (Carole Marsh North Dakota Bks.). (Illus.). (J). 1994. pap. 19.95 (*0-7933-0861-5*); lib. bdg. 29.95 (*0-7933-0862-3*); disk 29.95 (*0-7933-0863-1*) Gallopade Intl.

North Dakota's Unsolved Mysteries (& Their "Solutions") Includes Scientific Information & Other Activities for Students. Carole Marsh. (Carole Marsh North Dakota Bks.). (Illus.). (J). (gr. 3-12). 1994. pap. 19.95 (*0-7933-5825-6*); lib. bdg. 29.95 (*0-7933-5824-8*); disk 29.95 (*0-7933-5826-4*) Gallopade Intl.

North Dakota...Where Food Is Love. Marcella Richman. 200p. 1994. pap. 10.95 (*0-9642215-0-0*) N Dakota Ckbook.

***North Dallas Forty.** Peter Gent. 386p. 2000. pap. 14.95 (*1-892129-89-2*) Total Sprts.

North East. John W. House. LC 77-91239. (Industrial Britain Ser.). (Illus.). 256p. 1969. 29.95 (*0-678-05569-6*) Kelley.

North East: Roots of Insurgency. Profulla Roy Chowdhury. 1986. 8.50 (*0-8364-1869-7*, Pub. by Firma KLM) S Asia.

North East Arabian Dialects. Bruce Ingham. Ed. by Muhammed H. Bakalla. (Library of Arabic Linguistics). 240p. 1982. 65.00 (*0-7103-0018-2*) Routledge.

North-East Asian Regional Security: The Role of International Institutions. Ed. by Takashi Inoguchi & Grant B. Stillman. 243p. 24.95 (*92-808-0954-7*) UN.

North East Castles: Castles in the Landscape of North East Scotland. John S. Smith. (Illus.). 1990. pap. text 12.00 (*0-08-040931-8*, Pub. by Aberdeen U Pr) Macmillan.

North East England in the Middle Ages. R. A. Lomas. 200p. (C). 1989. text 66.00 (*0-7855-6986-3*, Pub. by J Donald) St Mut.

North East England in the Middle Ages. Richard A. Lomas. 200p. (C). 1996. 66.00 (*0-85976-361-7*, Pub. by J Donald) St Mut.

North East Frontier, 1837-1901. Ian Heath. (Men at Arms Ser.: Vol. 324). (Illus.). 48p. 1999. pap. text 12.95 (*1-85532-762-7*, Pub. by Ospry) Stackpole.

North-East India: The Human Interface. Ed. by M. K. Raha & A. K. Ghosh. LC 98-900829. 469p. 1998. 43.00 (*81-212-0573-5*, Pub. by Gyan Publishing Hse) Nataraj Bks.

North East Italy Map. 1997. 8.95 (*2-06-700429-8*, 429) Michelin.

North-East Song & Story: An Anthology of Narrative Verse & Song from NE Scotland. William M. Wilson. 256p. 1990. pap. 30.00 (*1-898218-81-1*) St Mut.

North East/Baleares Spain Map. 1997. 8.95 (*2-06-700443-3*, 443) Michelin.

North Eastern Accelerator Personnel: Symposium of '91, 25th. J. Benson et al. 436p. 1992. text 109.00 (*981-02-1108-2*) World Scientific Pub.

North-Eastern Economy: Problems & Prospects. A. K. Agarwal. (C). 1988. 32.00 (*81-7099-056-4*, Pub. by Mittal Pubs Dist) S Asia.

North Eastern Electrics: The History of the Tyneside Electric Passenger Services, 1904-1967. K. Hoole. 80p. (C). 1985. 39.00 (*0-85361-358-3*) St Mut.

North-Eastern England During the Wars of the Roses: Lay Society, War, & Politics, 1450-1500. A. J. Pollard. (Illus.). 464p. 1991. text 125.00 (*0-19-820087-0*) OUP.

North-Eastern Ethiopia: Society in Famine. A Study of Three Social Institutions in a Period of Severe Strain. Karl J. Lundstrom. (Research Report Ser.: No. 34). 80p. 1976. write for info. (*91-7106-098-7*, Pub. by Nordic Africa) Transaction Pubs.

North-Eastern Frontier of India: Structural Imperatives & Aspects of Change. A. C. Sinha. (C). 1994. text 28.00 (*81-7387-009-8*, Pub. by Indus Pub) S Asia.

North Eastern States see Mobil Travel Guide

North End Italian Cookbook. 4th rev. ed. Marguerite D. Buonopane. LC 96-27596. (Illus.). 256p. 1996. pap. 14.95 (*1-56440-990-2*) Globe Pequot.

North Enough: AIDS & Other Clear-Cuts. Jan Z. Grover. LC 96-75891. 150p. (Orig.). 1997. pap. 12.95 (*1-55597-235-7*) Graywolf.

North European Baroque. rev. ed. Joshua Rifkin. (New Grove Ser.). Date not set. pap. write for info. (*0-393-31594-0*) Norton.

North European Textiles until AD 1000. Lise B. Jorgensen. (Illus.). 286p. (C). 1992. text 45.00 (*87-7288-416-9*, Pub. by Aarhus Univ Pr) David Brown.

North Face. Mary Renault. 286p. 1976. reprint ed. lib. bdg. 23.95 (*0-88411-072-9*, Queens House) Amereon Ltd.

North Fights the Civil War: The Home Front. J. Matthew Gallman. LC 93-47471. (American Ways Ser.). 224p. 1994. 22.50 (*1-56663-049-5*, Pub. by I R Dee); pap. text 9.95 (*1-56663-050-9*, Pub. by I R Dee) Natl Bk Netwk.

North Foreland to Beachy Head & Boulogne. Imray, Laurie, Norie & Wilson Ltd. Staff. (Illus.). (C). 1990. text 60.00 (*0-7855-5796-2*, Pub. by Laurie Norie & Wilson Ltd) St Mut.

***North Fork.** B. Jaime Curl. Ed. by Kara L. C. Jones. (Illus.). 30p. 2000. pap. 10.00 (*1-929359-04-7*) Kota Pr.

North Fork: Photographs from Fifteen Years at the Suffolk Times. Judy Ahrens. (Illus.). 120p. 1993. write for info. (*0-9637323-0-7*) Lynn Loring Pub.

North Fork & Shelter Island Guidebook. 3rd ed. Ed. by James I. Masters. LC 81-67384. (Illus.). 320p. (YA). (gr. 9-12). 1981. pap. 4.95 (*0-89808-007-X*) Masters Pubns.

North Fork of the Coeur d'Alene. Bert Russell. (Oral History Ser.: No. 3). (Illus.). 448p. 1985. 12.95 (*0-930344-07-3*); pap. 9.95 (*0-930344-06-5*) Lacon Pubs.

North France Pilot: Cherbourg to Calais. T. Thompson & D. Thompson. (Illus.). 120p. (C). 1990. 125.00 (*0-85288-137-1*, Pub. by Laurie Norie & Wilson Ltd) St Mut.

North France Pilot, Cherbourg to Calais. T. Thompson & D. Thompson. 120p. (C). 1990. 125.00 (*0-7855-6724-0*, Pub. by Laurie Norie & Wilson Ltd) St Mut.

North Frederick. John O'Hara. 416p. 27.95 (*0-8488-2492-X*) Amereon Ltd.

North from Mexico: The Spanish-Speaking People of the United States. Carey McWilliams. Ed. by Matt S. Meier. LC 89-38043. 372p. 1990. pap. 19.95 (*0-275-93224-9*, B3224, Greenwood Pr) Greenwood.

North from Mexico: The Spanish-Speaking People of the United States, 140. Carey McWilliams. Ed. by Matt S. Meier. LC 89-17031. 376p. 1990. 65.00 (*0-313-26631-X*, MNX/, Greenwood Pr) Greenwood.

***North from Ocala: An Autobiography.** 2000. pap. write for info. (*1-892937-06-9*) Spec Pubns.

North from Rome. Helen MacInnes. LC 58-5922. 1958. 24.95 (*0-15-167001-3*) Harcourt.

North from Texas: Incidents in the Early Life of a Range Cowman in Texas, Dakota, & Wyoming, 1852-1883. James C. Shaw. Ed. by Herbert O. Brayer. LC 96-1310. Orig. Title: Pioneering in Texas & Wyoming: Incidents in the Life of James C. Shaw. (Illus.). 128p. 1996. reprint ed. pap. 9.95 (*0-89096-730-X*) Tex A&M Univ Pr.

***North from the Mountains: A Folk History of the Carmel Melungeon Settlement, Highland County, Ohio.** John S. Kessler & Donald B. Ball. 2001. pap. write for info. (*0-86554-703-3*, P208) Mercer Univ Pr.

***North from the Mountains: A Folk History of the Carmel Melungeon Settlement, Highland County, Ohio.** Ed. by John S. Kessler & Donald B. Ball. 2001. 39.95 (*0-86554-700-9*) Mercer Univ Pr.

North Georgia Journal of History, Vol. 3. Ralph O. Jackson, 3rd. 1995. 35.00 (*1-880816-02-4*) Legacy GA.

North Georgia Traveler. Olin Jackson. (Illus.). 1998. pap. 9.95 (*1-880816-08-3*) Legacy GA.

North German Church Music in the Age of Buxtehude. Geoffrey Webber. (Oxford Monographs on Music). (Illus.). 256p. 1996. text 69.00 (*0-19-816212-X*) OUP.

***North Gladiola.** James Wilcox. LC 99-86602. (Voices of the South Ser.). 280p. 2000. pap. 15.95 (*0-8071-2565-2*) La State U Pr.

North Gladiola. James Wilcox. LC 84-48633. 1994. reprint ed. lib. bdg. 21.95 (*1-56849-523-4*) Buccaneer Bks.

An Asterisk (*) at the beginning of an entry indicates that the title is appearing for the first time.

North Haven in the 19th Century: A Memorial. Sheldon B. Thorpe. 207p. 1997. reprint ed. lib. bdg. 29.00 (*0-8328-5674-6*) Higginson Bk Co.

North Heidelberg Township - History & Lore. Kathy M. Scogna. (Illus.). 175p. 1996. 25.00 (*0-9652292-0-3*) K M Scogna.

North Idaho's Lake Country. George Wuerthner. LC 95-14568. (Illus.). (Orig.). 1995. pap. 9.95 (*1-56037-079-3*) Am Wrld Geog.

North India Between Empires: Awadh, the Mughals & the British, 1720-1801. Richard B. Barnett. 1987. reprint ed. 23.50 (*81-85054-24-X*, Pub. by Manohar) S Asia.

North Indian Peasant Goes to Market. Leon Schwartzburg. 176p. 1979. text 13.95 (*0-89684-097-2*, Pub. by Motilal Bnarsidass) S Asia.

North Indian Temple Sculpture. Urmila Agarwal. (Illus.). (C). 1996. 52.50 (*81-215-0458-9*, Pub. by M Manoharial) Coronet Bks.

North into Freedom: The Autobiography of John Malvin, Free Negro, 1795-1880. 2nd ed. Ed. by Allan Peskin. 93p. 1996. reprint ed. pap. 7.95 (*0-911704-48-5*) Western Res.

North Island Designs Five: A Scrapbook of Sweaters from a Maine Island. Chellie Pingree. LC 92-72725. (Illus.). 96p. 1993. pap. 17.95 (*0-89272-329-7*) Down East.

North Island Designs Four: Sixteen New Patterns from Talented Maine Designers. Chellie Pingree. LC 93-150314. (Illus.). 96p. 1992. pap. 17.95 (*0-89272-318-1*) Down East.

North Italian Drawings. Ivan Fenyo. LC 66-14731. (Illus.). 1966. 22.50 (*0-8079-0102-4*) October.

North Jersey Country Club: Celebrating 100 Years. William L. Quirin. LC 94-47356. 1995. write for info. (*0-89865-929-9*) Donning Co.

North Jersey Trails. 5th ed. 1998. pap. 7.95 (*1-880775-14-X*) NY-NJ Trail Confer.

North Kingstown: An Historical Sketch. Patrick T. Conley. (Illus.). 1976. pap. 3.95 (*0-917012-53-4*) RI Pubns Soc.

North Korea. U. S. Government Staff. (Country Studies). 1995. 20.00 (*0-614-30807-0*, UNORTH) Claitors.

North Korea: A Country Study. Ed. by Andrea M. Savada. (Illus.). 346p. (C). 1995. 50.00 (*0-7881-2268-1*) DIANE Pub.

North Korea: A Country Study. Andrea Matles Savada. 382p. 1994. boxed set 29.00 (*0-16-061165-2*) USGPO.

North Korea: A Political Handbook. Tai-Sung An. LC 83-16307. (Illus.). 294p. (C). 1983. lib. bdg. 45.00 (*0-8420-2205-8*) Scholarly Res Inc.

***North Korea: A Strange Socialist Fortress.** Hy-Sang Lee. LC 00-29838. 2000. write for info. (*0-275-96917-7*) Greenwood.

North Korea: Major World Nations. Amy K. Nash. LC 97-21857. (Major World Nations Ser.). (Illus.). 144p. (YA). (gr. 5 up). 1999. lib. bdg. 19.95 (*0-7910-4746-6*) Chelsea Hse.

North Korea after Kim Il Sung. Ed. by Dae-Sook Suh & Chae-Jin Lee. LC 97-32958. 266p. 1998. lib. bdg. 55.00 (*1-55587-763-X*) L Rienner.

North Korea after Kim-Il Sung: Continuity or Change? Ed. by Thomas H. Henriksen & Jongryn Mo. LC 96-35055. (Publication Ser.: No. 438). 179p. 1997. pap. 19.95 (*0-8179-9462-9*) Hoover Inst Pr.

North Korea after Kim Il-Sung: Controlled Collapse?, 2 vols., Vol. 2. 3rd ed. (Research Reports: No. M219). (CHI.). 524p. 1945. student ed. 225.00 (*0-85058-827-8*, 250199) Economist Intell.

North Korea & South Korea, 2 vols. 1997. lib. bdg. 600.99 (*0-8490-6132-6*) Gordon Pr.

North Korea & the Bomb: A Case Study in Nonproliferation. Michael J. Mazarr. LC 94-34868. 290p. 1995. text 35.00 (*0-312-12443-0*) St Martin.

North Korea & the Bomb: A Case Study in Nonproliferation. Michael J. Mazarr. 290p. 1997. pap. 17.95 (*0-312-16455-6*) St Martin.

North Korea at a Crossroads. Robert A. Scalapino. LC 96-48434. (Essays in Public Policy Ser.: No. 73). 1996. pap. text 5.00 (*0-8179-5782-0*) Hoover Inst Pr.

North Korea Country Studies: Area Handbook. 4th ed. Ed. by Andrea M. Savada. LC 93-48469. (Area Handbook Ser.: No. 550-81). 1994. 20.00 (*0-8444-0794-1*) Lib Congress.

North Korea in a Regional & Global Context. Ed. by Robert A. Scalapino & Hongkoo Lee. LC 85-81190. (Korea Research Monographs: No. 11). xviii, 404p. (Orig.). 1986. pap. 20.00 (*0-912966-82-3*) IEAS.

North Korea in Transition. Ed. by Chong-Sik Lee & Se-Hee Yoo. LC 90-85946. (Korea Research Monographs: No. 16). xx, 156p. (Orig.). 1991. pap. 12.00 (*1-55729-024-5*) IEAS.

North Korea in Transition: From Dictatorship to Dynasty, 95. Tai Sung An. LC 82-15866. (Contributions in Political Science Ser.: No. 95). 212p. 1983. 62.95 (*0-313-23638-0*, ANK/, Greenwood Pr) Greenwood.

***North Korea Through the Looking Glass.** Kong D. Oh. 2000. 39.95 (*0-8157-6436-7*); pap. write for info. (*0-8157-6435-9*) Brookings.

North Korean Economic Reform & Political Stability. Bruce Bueno de Mesquita & Jongryn Mo. (Essays in Public Policy Ser.: Vol. 70). 20p. 1996. pap. 5.00 (*0-8179-5752-9*) Hoover Inst Pr.

North Korean Foreign Relations in the Post-Cold War Era. Ed. by Samuel S. Kim. LC 98-25023. (Illus.). 306p. 1998. text 19.95 (*0-19-590604-7*) OUP.

North Korean Nuclear Program: Security, Strategy & New Perspectives from Russia. James C. Moltz & Alexandre Mansourov. LC 99-20510. 1999. pap. 24.99 (*0-415-92370-0*) Routledge.

***North Korean Nuclear Program: Security Strategy & New Perspectives from Russia.** Ed. by James Moltz & Alexandre Mansourov. LC 99-20510. 288p. (C). 1999. text. write for info. (*0-415-92369-7*) Routledge.

North Korean Special Forces. 2nd ed. Joseph S. Bermudez, Jr. LC 97-36345. (Special Warfare Ser.). (Illus.). 320p. 1997. 39.95 (*1-55750-066-5*) Naval Inst Pr.

North Koreans in Japan: Language, Ideology & Identity. Sonia Ryang. (Transitions: Asia & Asian America Ser.). (C). 1996. pap. text 26.00 (*0-8133-3050-5*, Pub. by Westview) HarpC.

North Korea's Undeclared War, 1953. Wayne A. Kirkbride. (Illus.). 112p. 1995. 12.00 (*1-56591-035-4*, Pub. by Hollym Bks) Weatherhill.

North Leinster. Alistair Rowan. (Illus.). 544p. text 65.00 (*0-14-071085-X*, Pub. by Pnguin Bks Ltd) Trafalgar.

North Leitrim: The Land War & the Fall of Parnell. Prionnsios O'Duignean. (North Leitrim History Ser.). (Illus.). 77p. (Orig.). 1988. pap. 6.95 (*1-873437-06-4*, Pub. by Drumlin Pubns Ltd) Irish Bks Media.

North Leitrim in Famine Times, 1840-1850. Prionnsias O'Duignean. (North Leitrim History Ser.). (Illus.). 56p. 1986. pap. 6.95 (*1-873437-03-X*, Pub. by Drumlin Pubns Ltd) Irish Bks Media.

North Leitrim in Land League Times, 1880-1884. Prionnsias O'Duignean. (North Leitrim History Ser.). (Illus.). 52p. 1992. reprint ed. pap. 6.95 (*1-873437-04-8*, Pub. by Drumlin Pubns Ltd) Irish Bks Media.

North Light Artist's Guide to Materials & Techniques. Phil Metzger. (Illus.). 192p. 1996. 29.99 (*0-89134-675-9*, North Lght Bks) F & W Pubns Inc.

North Light Book of Acrylic Painting Techniques. Earl G. Killeen & Leah R. Killeen. (Illus.). 144p. 1998. pap. 23.99 (*0-89134-897-2*, North Lght Bks) F & W Pubns Inc.

North Light Book of Creative Paint Finishing Techniques. Ray Bradshaw. (Illus.). 144p. 1998. 29.99 (*0-89134-823-9*, North Lght Bks) F & W Pubns Inc.

North Light Illustrated Book of Painting Techniques. Elizabeth Tate. (Illus.). 208p. 1986. 29.99 (*0-89134-148-X*, 8009, North Lght Bks) F & W Pubns Inc.

North Light Illustrated Book of Watercolor Techniques. Mark Topham. (Illus.). 144p. 1997. 29.99 (*0-89134-780-1*, North Lght Bks) F & W Pubns Inc.

North Light Pocket Guide to Painting Skies. Patricia Seligman. (North Light Pocket Guides Ser.). (Illus.). 64p. 1997. 16.99 (*0-89134-779-8*, North Lght Bks) F & W Pubns Inc.

North Light Pocket Guide to Painting Trees. Patricia Seligman. (North Light Pocket Guides Ser.). (Illus.). 64p. 1997. 16.99 (*0-89134-778-X*, North Lght Bks) F & W Pubns Inc.

North Lincolnshire Words see English Dialect Society Publications, No. 32: Original Glossaries XXIII-XXVII

North London Railway. M. Robbins. (C). 1985. 39.00 (*0-85361-074-6*) St Mut.

North Louisiana to 1865 Vol. 1: Essays on the Region & Its History. Ed. by Billy H. Gilley. 214p. 1984. pap. 12.95 (*0-940231-03-4*) McGinty Pubns.

North Mexican Cattle Industry, 1910-1975: Ideology, Conflict & Change. Manuel A. Machado, Jr. LC 80-5515. (Illus.). 168p. 1981. 24.95 (*0-89096-104-2*) Tex A&M Univ Pr.

North Midland Trains in the Thirties. A. S. Denton. 64p. (C). 1985. 39.00 (*0-85361-267-6*) St Mut.

North Mkata Plain, Tanzania: A Study of Land Capability & Land Tenure. John R. Pitblado. LC HD0987.Z63P5. (University of Toronto, Department of Geography Research Publications: No. 16). (Illus.). 192p. reprint ed. pap. 59.60 (*0-608-18012-2*, 202649700049) Bks Demand.

North North, I Said, No, Wait a Minute, South, Oh I Don't Know (148 Political Poems) Anthony Barnett. 64p. (Orig.). 1985. pap. 9.00 (*0-907954-09-X*, Pub. by Allardyce Barnett) SPD-Small Pr Dist.

North Northeast: New England Poems. Rennie McQuilkin. LC 85-13343. (Illus.). 96p. (Orig.). 1985. pap. 12.00 (*0-87233-081-8*) Bauhan.

North of Athens. John Judson. LC 80-53396. 64p. 1980. pap. 3.95 (*0-933180-20-9*) Spoon Riv Poetry.

North of Death's Door. William H. Olson. LC 92-3505. (Illus.). vi, 66p. 1992. 10.00 (*0-940473-25-9*) Wm Caxton.

North of Delhi, East of Heaven. Joyce B. Sparling. LC 88-5778. 192p. 1988. 18.95 (*0-8027-5719-7*) Walker & Co.

North of Eden: An Anthology of Alaskan Writings. Ed. by Davis et al. 128p. (Orig.). 1995. pap. 7.95 (*0-9647550-0-9*) Loose Affil.

North of England Ghost Trail. L. Linahan. 1997. text 29.95 (*0-09-476910-9*, Pub. by Constable & Co) Trafalgar.

North of England in the Reign of Richard III. A. J. Pollard. LC 95-17777. 1996. text 59.95 (*0-312-12592-5*) St Martin.

North of England Words, from a "Tour of the Caves" see English Dialect Society Publications, No. 1: Glossaries I-VII

North of Gallipoli No. 343: The Black Sea Fleet at War, 1914-1917. George M. Nekrasov. 200p. 1992. text 37.50 (*0-88033-240-9*, 343, Pub. by East Eur Monographs) Col U Pr.

North of Havana. Randy Wayne White. 1998. mass mkt. 5.99 (*0-425-16294-X*, Prime Crime) Berkley Pub.

North of Hope. Jon Hassler. 448p. 1991. mass mkt. 5.99 (*0-345-36911-4*, Pub. by Ballantine Pub Grp) Random House.

North of Infinity: Futurity Visions. Ed. by Michael Magnini. LC 99-460571. 216p. 1997. pap. 12.95 (*0-88962-634-0*, 734083Q) Mosaic.

North of Intention. Steve McCaffery. LC 86-63324. (Roof Bks.). 240p. (Orig.). 1987. pap. 120.95 (*0-937804-23-1*) Segue NYC.

***North of Ireland.** 2nd ed. Catharina Day. (Country Guides Ser.). 2000. pap. text 14.95 (*1-86011-970-0*) Cadgn Bks.

North of Monadnock. Newton F. Tolman. reprint ed. lib. bdg. 21.95 (*0-89190-953-2*, Rivercity Pr) Amereon Ltd.

North of Montana. April Smith. 1996. mass mkt. 6.99 (*0-449-22502-X*) Fawcett.

North of Montana. large type ed. April Smith. LC 95-50388. (Large Print Ser.). 352p. 1995. lib. bdg. 23.95 (*1-57490-035-8*, Beeler LP Bks) T T Beeler.

North of Naples South of Rome. Tullio. 256p. 1999. pap. 13.95 (*0-312-24317-0*) St Martin.

North of Naples, South of Rome. Paolo Tullio. LC 98-33735. 240p. 1998. 22.95 (*0-312-19307-6*, Thomas Dunne) St Martin.

North of Naples, South of Rome. Paolo Tullio & Susan Morley. 234p. 1997. pap. 14.95 (*1-874675-82-1*) Dufour.

North of North: The Way, the Truth, the Life. Connelly L. Graham. (Illus.). 320p. (Orig.). 1992. pap. 10.95 (*0-932221-20-3*) Christ Action.

North of Now: A Celebration of Country & the Soon to Be Gone. W. D. Wetherell. LC 97-28166. (Illus.). 272p. 1998. 27.95 (*1-55821-651-0*) Lyons Pr.

North of Providence - Dolores - Lady of Fadima. Edward A. Baker. 1991. pap. 5.25 (*0-8222-0091-0*) Dramatists Play.

North of Reliance: A Personal Story of Living Beyond the Wilderness. David Olesen. LC 94-12981. (Illus.). 176p. 1994. pap. 12.95 (*1-55971-433-6*, NorthWord Pr) Creat Pub Intl.

North of Sioux Falls. Alec Bond. 24p. 1983. pap. 3.00 (*0-933180-58-6*) Spoon Riv Poetry.

North of Skarv Island: A Trading Adventure Between Norwegians & Lapps. Karl S. Wikstrom. Ed. by Signe M. Carlson. LC 85-63272. (Illus.). 148p. 1985. 9.95 (*0-9615948-0-2*) Midgard Pr.

North of Slavery: The Negro in the Free States, 1790-1860. Leon F. Litwack. LC 61-10869. 332p. 1965. pap. text 15.00 (*0-226-48586-2*, P179) U Ch Pr.

North of South: An African Journey. Shiva Naipaul. LC 97-106091. 352p. 1997. pap. 12.95 (*0-14-018826-6*, Penguin Bks) Viking Penguin.

North of Superior Orient Bay Ice Climber's Guide. Shaun Parent. Ed. by Don Hynek. (Illus.). 104p. (Orig.). 1993. pap. write for info. (*0-9619571-3-1*) Granite WI.

North of the Border. Judith Van Gieson. 176p. 1993. mass mkt. 4.99 (*0-671-76967-7*) PB.

North of the Narrows: Men & Women of the Upper Priest Lake Country, Idaho. Claude Simpson & Catherine Simpson. LC 82-51781. (Illus.). 305p. (Orig.). 1981. reprint ed. pap. 15.00 (*1-879628-04-X*) Keokee ID.

North of the River: A Brief History of North Fort Worth. J'nell Pate. (Chisholm Trail Ser.: No. 11). 208p. (Orig.). (C). 1994. pap. 12.95 (*0-87565-133-X*) Tex Christian.

North of the Sky. D. Harrison. 36p. 1999. pap. 6.50 (*0-9655816-0-8*) Wings of Dawn.

North of the Sun: A Memoir of the Alaskan Wilderness. Fred Hatfield. 1990. 16.95 (*1-55972-043-3*, Birch Ln Pr) Carol Pub Group.

North of the Sun: A Memoir of the Alaskan Wilderness. Fred Hatfield. 224p. 1992. pap. 9.95 (*0-8065-1317-9*, Citadel Pr) Carol Pub Group.

North of the Tees: Studies in Medieval British History. H. S. Offler. Ed. by A. I. Doyle & A. J. Piper. (Collected Studies: No. CS547). 320p. 1996. 98.95 (*0-86078-599-8*, Pub. by Variorum) Ashgate Pub Co.

North of the Word. Neil Astley & Alan Myers. 320p. 1996. pap. 18.95 (*1-85224-251-5*, Pub. by Bloodaxe Bks) Dufour.

North of Wakulla: An Anhinga Anthology. Ed. by Mary J. Ryals & Donna Decker. (Illus.). 160p. (Orig.). 1989. pap. 12.50 (*0-938078-30-5*) Anhinga Pr.

North of Wondering. Patricia Clark. Ed. by Elaine Dallman. LC 98-61315. 72p. 1999. pap. text 13.50 (*0-935634-16-9*) Women-in-Lit.

North of Yesterday. Thomas McEvilley. LC 86-33250. 288p. 1987. 20.00 (*0-914232-86-X*); pap. 12.00 (*0-914232-85-1*) McPherson & Co.

North Osetia Republic: Economy, Industry, Government, Business. 2nd rev. ed. Russian Information & Business Center, Inc. Staff. (Russian Regional Business Directories Ser.). (Illus.). 200p. 1997. pap. 99.00 (*1-57751-366-5*) Intl Business Pubns.

***North Osetian Republic Regional Investment & Business Guide.** Global Investment & Business Center, Inc. Staff. (Russian Regional Investment & Business Guides Ser.: Vol. 52). (Illus.). 350p. 1999. pap. 99.00 (*0-7397-0818-X*) Intl Business Pubns.

***North Osetian Republic Regional Investment & Business Guide.** Contrib. by Global Investment & Business Center, Inc. Staff. (Russian Regional Investment & Business Guides Ser.: Vol. 47). (Illus.). 350p. 2000. pap. 99.95 (*0-7397-3000-2*) Intl Business Pubns.

North over South: A NonWestern Perspective of International Relations. J. Bandopadhyaya. 1982. 26.00 (*0-8364-0894-2*) S Asia.

***North over South: Northern Nationalism & American Identity in the Antebellum Era.** Susan-Mary Grant. 288p. 2000. text 35.00 (*0-7006-1025-1*) U Pr of KS.

North Oxford. Tanis Hinchcliffe. (Illus.). 256p. (C). 1992. 57.50 (*0-300-05184-0*) Yale U Pr.

North Pacific Cretaceous Trigoniid Genus Yaadia. Louella R. Saul. LC 77-84990. (University of California Publications in Social Welfare: No. 119). (Illus.). 97p. reprint ed. pap. 30.10 (*0-608-18183-8*, 203290300081) Bks Demand.

North Pacific Frontiers. Richard Frederick. LC 76-53366. (Illus.). 91p. 1976. 15.00 (*0-917048-02-4*) Wash St Hist Soc.

North Pacific Lands & Waters. limited ed. Gary Snyder. (Illus.). 32p. 1994. 125.00 (*0-918116-76-7*) Brooding Heron Pr.

North Pacific Quadrangle Fifty Years After: Balance of Power & Back to the Future. Ed. by Yu Bin. LC 97-11124. 157p. (C). 1997. lib. bdg. 39.00 (*1-56072-428-5*) Nova Sci Pubs.

***North Pacific Seaweeds.** Rita M. O'Clair & Sandra C. Lindstrom. (Illus.). xii, 162p. 2000. pap. 24.95 (*0-9664245-1-4*) Plant Pr AK.

North Pacific Triangle: The United States, Japan & Canada at Century's End. Michael Fry. LC 99-168705. (Illus.). 456p. 1998. text 60.00 (*0-8020-4212-0*); pap. text 24.95 (*0-8020-8065-0*) U of Toronto Pr.

North Pakistan. Allan. 1999. text 49.95 (*0-312-12065-6*) St Martin.

North Park Faculty Publications & Creative Works. Ed. by Sarah A. Anderson et al. 101p. (Orig.). 1992. pap. text 10.00 (*0-9643677-2-6*) North Pk Coll.

North Penn Pictorial. Phil J. Ruth. (Illus.). 176p. 1988. 29.95 (*0-9619350-0-6*) P J Ruth.

***North Plainfield.** Mario Caruso. (Images of America Ser.). 128p. 1999. pap. 18.99 (*0-7385-0005-4*) Arcadia Publng.

***North Platte Vol. 6, No. 1: River Journal.** Eric A. Pettine. (Illus.). 48p. 1999. pap. 15.95 (*1-57188-149-2*) F Amato Pubns.

North Point Historic Districts - Milwaukee. Shirley D. McArthur. LC 80-83990. (Illus.). 260p. (Orig.). 1981. pap. 25.00 (*0-9606072-0-X*) N Point Hist Soc.

North Pole Chronicles, 4 bks. Illus. by Roderick K. Keitz. Incl. Christmas Eve Tradition. R. W. Thompson, Jr. (Illus.). 16p. (J). (ps-3). 1993. 8.95 (*0-9636442-1-1*); Shopping Trip. R. W. Thompson, Jr. (Illus.). 16p. (J). (ps-3). 1995. 8.95 (*0-9636442-2-X*); Star on the Pole. R. W. Thompson. LC 97-146791. (Illus.). 16p. (J). 1996. 8.95 (*0-9636442-3-8*); Wow! I Got to Go to the North Pole. R. W. Thompson, Jr. (Illus.). 16p. (J). (ps-3). 1994. 8.95 (*0-9636442-0-3*); (J). 29.95 (*0-9636442-8-9*) N Pole Chron.

North Pole, South Pole: Journeys to the Ends of the Earth. Bertrand Imbert. (Discoveries Ser.). (Illus.). 192p. 1992. pap. 12.95 (*0-8109-2881-7*, Pub. by Abrams) Time Warner.

North Pomfret Poems: Songs of Life, Love, & Death for Four Seasons. Peter F. Smith. LC 95-92725. 130p. 1995. write for info. (*0-9649612-0-2*) P Fox Smith.

North Providence. Thomas E. Greene & Barbara A. Greene. LC 97-133976. (Images of America Ser.). 1996. pap. 16.99 (*0-7524-0293-5*) Arcadia Publng.

North Providence, Vol. II. Thomas E. Greene et al. (Images of America Ser.). 1999. pap. 16.99 (*0-7524-0844-5*) Arcadia Publng.

North Puget Sound: Afoot & Afloat. 2nd rev. ed. Marge Mueller & Ted Mueller. (Afoot & Afloat Ser.). (Illus.). 224p. 1995. pap. 14.95 (*0-89886-435-6*) Mountaineers.

***North Puget Sound Entertainment, 2000.** (Illus.). 454p. 1999. pap. 35.00 (*1-880248-51-4*, 00G3) Enter Pubns.

North Reports the Civil War. J. Cutler Andrews. LC 55-6873. (Illus.). 848p. 1955. pap. 200.00 (*0-608-05161-6*, 201049700068) Bks Demand.

North Richmond: A Community in Transition. Ed. by Marjorie Beggs. 35p. (Orig.). 1995. pap. 5.00 (*0-936434-82-1*, Pub. by Zellerbach Fam Fund) Intl Spec Bk.

***North Richmond Gets Its Buses Back: How a Poor Community & an Urban Transit Agency Struck up a Partnership.** Eugene Bardach et al. LC 99-31684. 1999. 5.00 (*0-87772-389-3*) UCB IGS.

North SAR: A Novel of Navy Combat Pilots in Vietnam. Gerry Carroll. Ed. by Paul McCarthy. 416p. 1992. mass mkt. 5.99 (*0-671-73183-1*) PB.

North Sea. Mark Jarman. LC 78-67730. (CSU Poetry Ser.: No. VI). 69p. 1978. pap. 6.00 (*0-914946-77-3*) Cleveland St Univ Poetry Ctr.

North Sea: Basic Legal Documents on Regional Environmental Co-Operation. Ed. by David Freestone. (C). 1991. lib. bdg. 183.00 (*0-7923-0919-7*) Kluwer Academic.

North Sea: Estuaries Interactions, Proceedings of the 18th EBSA Symposium. Ed. by Donald S. McLusky et al. (Developments in Hydrobiology Ser.). (C). 1990. text 233.50 (*0-7923-0694-5*) Kluwer Academic.

North Sea: Perspectives on Regional Environmental Co-Operation. Ed. by David Freestone & Ton Ijlstra. 356p. 1990. pap. text 180.00 (*1-85333-413-8*) Kluwer Academic.

North Sea & the Baltic Sea. Nina Morgan. LC 96-19443. (Seas & Oceans Ser.). 48p. (J). 1997. lib. bdg. 24.26 (*0-8172-4510-3*) Raintree Steck-V.

North Sea Atlas. Oilfield Publications Limited Staff. (Illus.). 48p. 1994. pap. 145.00 (*1-870945-64-6*) Oilfield Publns.

North Sea Climate: Based on Observations from Ships & Lightvessels. C. G. Korevaar. (C). 1990. lib. bdg. 82.00 (*0-7923-0664-3*) Kluwer Academic.

***North Sea Conference on Thrombosis & Haemostasis: 1st Conference, Maastricht, The Netherlands, June 2000.** Ed. by T. Lindhout. (Haemostasis Ser.: Vol. 30). 102p. 2000. pap. 34.00 (*3-8055-7106-2*) S Karger.

***North Sea Cooperation: Linking International & Domestic Pollution Control.** Jon B. Skjrseth. LC 99-49642. (Issues in Environmental Politics Ser.). 2000. write for info. (*0-7190-5809-0*) Manchester Univ Pr.

North Sea Development: Experiences & Challenges: Proceedings of a Conference: Sponsored by the West of Scotland Branch, the Institute of Petroleum & the Norwegian Petroleum Society & Held in Glasgow, April 3-5, 1979. Institute of Petroleum (Great Britain) Staff. LC 81-196157. 276p. reprint ed. pap. 85.60 (*0-608-15402-4*, 202926200059) Bks Demand.

North Sea Earls: The Shetland Viking Archaeological Expedition. Ian Morrison & Shetland/Viking Archaeological Expedition Staff. LC 74-152952. 148p. 1973. write for info. (*0-85614-028-7*, Pub. by GT Foulis) Haynes Manuals.

N

North Sea Facts. 2nd ed. Oilfield Publications Limited Staff. (Illus.). 400p. 1993. pap. 125.00 (*1-870945-45-X*) Oilfield Publns.

North Sea Field Development Guide, 1997-1998 Vols. 1 & 2: Northern North Sea & Southern North Sea. 6th ed. Oilfield Publications Limited Staff. (Illus.). 1400p. 1997. pap. 502.00 (*1-870945-88-3*) Oilfield Publns.

North Sea Formation Waters Atlas. Ed. by E. A. Warren & P. C. Smalley. (Geological Society Memoir Ser.: No. 15). (Illus.). 200p. 1994. 333.00 (*1-897799-07-1*, 217, Pub. by Geol Soc Pub Hse) AAPG.

North Sea Oil & Gas Reservoirs. Norwegian Institute of Technology Staff. (C). 1987. lib. bdg. 281.00 (*0-86010-865-1*, Pub. by Graham & Trotman) Kluwer Academic.

North Sea Oil & Gas Reservoirs II. Ed. by A. T. Buller et al. (C). 1990. lib. bdg. 407.50 (*1-85333-283-6*, Pub. by Graham & Trotman) Kluwer Academic.

North Sea Oil & Gas Reservoirs III: Proceedings of the Third North Sea Oil & Gas Reservoirs Conference Organized by the Norweigian Institute of Technology (NTH) Trondheim, Norway, November 30 - December 2, 1992. Ed. by J. O. Aasen. LC 93-8013. 430p. (C). 1994. lib. bdg. 310.00 (*0-7923-2304-1*) Kluwer Academic.

North Sea Oil & the Environment: Developing Oil & Gas Resources Environmental Impacts & Responses. Ed. by W. J. Cairns. (Illus.). 712p. (C). (gr. 13). 1992. 375.00 (*1-85166-704-0*) Elsevier Applied Sci.

North Sea Passage Pilot. Brian Navin. 200p. 1987. 105.00 (*0-85288-102-9*, Pub. by Laurie Norie & Wilson Ltd) St Mut.

North Sea Passage Pilot. Brian Navin & Den Helder. 200p. 1998. pap. 125.00 (*0-85288-393-5*, Pub. by Laurie Norie & Wilson Ltd) St Mut.

North Sea Passage Pilot, Cromer to Dover & Calais to Den Helder. Brian Navin. (Illus.). 1991. 51.95 (*0-85288-157-6*) Bluewater Bks.

North Sea Pollution - Technical Strategies for Improvement: Proceedings of the IAWPRC International Conference, Held in Amsterdam, The Netherlands, 10-14 September 1990. Ed. by R. R. Kruize. (Water Science & Technology Ser.: No. 24). 380p. 1992. pap. 157.00 (*0-08-041836-8*, Pergamon Pr) Elsevier.

North Sea Saga, 1960s: Opera of Oil. David Wilde. (Illus.). 100p. (Orig.). 1993. pap. text 14.95 (*1-882204-14-X*) Wilde Pub.

North Sea Subsea Atlas. Oilfield Publications Limited Staff. (Illus.). 104p. (C). 1992. pap. 89.95 (*1-870945-34-4*) Oilfield Publns.

North Sea Surge: The Story of the East Coast Floods of 1953. Michael Pollard. 136p. (C). 1988. 65.00 (*0-86138-021-5*, Pub. by T Dalton) St Mut.

North Shore: A Four Season Guide to Minnesota's Favorite Destination. Shawn C. Perich. LC 92-70990. (Illus.). 208p. (Orig.). 1992. pap. 14.95 (*0-938586-67-X*) Pfeifer-Hamilton.

North Shore: A Social History of Summers among the Noteworthy, Fashionable, Rich, Eccentric & Ordinary on Boston's Gold Coast, 1823-1929. rev. ed. Joseph E. Garland. LC 98-12940. Orig. Title: Boston's North Shore - Boston's Gold Coast. (Illus.). 408p. 1998. 27.95 (*1-889833-04-5*, Commonwealth Eds) Memoirs Unltd.

North Shore Chronicles: Big-Wave Surfing in Hawaii. rev. ed. Bruce Jenkins. LC 98-53530. (Illus.). 175p. 1999. pap. 14.95 (*1-883319-90-0*) Frog Ltd CA.

North Shore Fish. Israel Horovitz. 1989. pap. 5.25 (*0-8222-0831-8*) Dramatists Play.

North Shore Memories. Ilona K. Hemperly. (Illus.). 1994. 10.00 (*0-9644185-0-9*) Kim Co.

North Shore of Lake Superior Yesterday & Today. Duane R. Lund. 112p. 1993. pap. 8.95 (*0-934860-01-7*) Adventure Pubns.

North Shore Schools: A Comprehensive Guide to Elementary & Secondary Education. Lucie J. Patrowicz & Kathryn L. Wilk. LC 95-72396. 200p. 1996. pap. write for info. (*0-9649203-2-8*) Pigeon Cove Pr.

North Shore Store. John Kennelly. 112p. (Orig.). 1997. pap. text 9.95 (*0-9649837-1-0*) Deshais Pubng.

North Shore Tourbook: An Illustrated Guide. Jeff Cornelius. (Illus.). 32p. 1998. pap. 7.95 (*1-886028-31-1*) Savage Pr.

North Shore/South Shore. Russ Porter. LC 98-75537. (Illus.). 140p. 2000. 41.95 (*0-911581-49-9*, 130235AE, Pub. by Heimburger Hse Pub) Motorbooks Intl.

North Slope Borough Government & Policymaking. Gerald A. McBeath. (ISER Reports: No. 51). (Illus.). 94p. 1981. pap. 7.50 (*0-88353-028-7*) U Alaska Inst Res.

North Slope Inupiaq Dialogues. Edna A. MacLean. 13p. (C). 1985. pap. 3.00 (*1-55500-014-2*) Alaska Native.

North Slope Inupiaq Grammar: First Year. 3rd rev. ed. Edna A. MacLean. (Illus.). xii, 279p. 1986. pap. text 18.00 (*1-55500-026-6*) Alaska Native.

North Slope Inupiaq Literacy Manual. L. Kaplan. 62p. 1981. pap. 6.00 (*0-933769-48-2*) Alaska Native.

North Slope Now. L. J. Campbell. Ed. by Penny Rennick. LC 75-79112. (Alaska Geographic Ser.: Vol. 16, No. 2). (Illus.). 96p. 1989. pap. 9.95 (*0-88240-189-0*) Alaska Geog Soc.

North-South: A Program for Survival (The Brandt Report) Ed. by William K. Brandt & Anthony Sampson. 304p. (Orig.). 1980. pap. text 13.00 (*0-262-52059-1*) MIT Pr.

North, South, & the Environmental Crisis. Rodney White. LC 92-95048. 184p. 1993. text 50.00 (*0-8020-5952-X*); pap. text 17.95 (*0-8020-6885-5*) U of Toronto Pr.

North South Co-Operation in Retrospect & Prospect. Ed. by C. J. Jepma. LC 89-101828. 252p. reprint ed. pap. 78.20 (*0-608-20350-5*, 207160300002) Bks Demand.

North South Cooperation: Gender & Development. Caroline Sweetman & Oxfam Staff. LC 96-175897. (Gender & Development Ser.). 94p. (C). 1995. pap. 12.95 (*0-85598-300-0*, Pub. by Oxfam Pub) Stylus Pub VA.

North South Cooperation & Foreign Aid in Nepal. T. Thakur. 1994. pap. 45.00 (*0-7855-0419-2*, Pub. by Ratna Pustak Bhandar) St Mut.

North-South Debate: Technology, Basic Human Needs & the New International Economic Order. Johan Galtung. 50p. 1980. pap. 17.95 (*0-685-54930-5*) Transaction Pubs.

North-South Dialogue & the United Nations. John W. McDonald, Jr. 26p. (Orig.). (C). 1985. reprint ed. pap. text 11.50 (*0-8191-5058-4*) U Pr of Amer.

North, South, East, & West. Allan Fowler. LC 92-39261. (Rookie Read-About Science Ser.). (Illus.). 32p. (J). (ps-3). 1993. pap. 4.95 (*0-516-46011-0*) Childrens.

North, South, East & West. Allan Fowler. LC 92-39261. (Rookie Read-About Science Ser.). (Illus.). 32p. (J). (ps-3). 1993. lib. bdg. 18.50 (*0-516-06011-2*) Childrens.

North, South, East, West: American Indians & the Natural World. Marsha C. Bol. LC 98-5094. (Illus.). 176p. 1998. 40.00 (*1-57098-094-2*); pap. 24.95 (*1-57098-197-3*) Roberts Rinehart.

North South Environment. Andrew Glyn & V. Bhaskar. 256p. 1996. pap. 34.00 (*1-85383-215-4*, Pub. by Escan Pubns) Island Pr.

North-South Environmental Strategies, Costs & Bargains. Patti L. Petesch. LC 92-15158. (Policy Essay Ser.: No. 5). 124p. (C). 1992. pap. text 13.95 (*1-56517-005-9*) Overseas Dev Council.

North-South Linkages & International Macroeconomic Policy. Ed. by David Vines & David Currie. (Illus.). 429p. (C). 1995. text 69.95 (*0-521-46234-7*) Cambridge U Pr.

North-South Relations: Studies of Dependency Reversal. Ed. by Charles F. Doran et al. LC 83-13657. 257p. 1983. 65.00 (*0-275-90972-7*, C0972, Praeger Pubs) Greenwood.

North-South Science & Technology Gap. A. A. Moghadam. LC 91-18135. (Developing Economies of the Third World Ser.). 342p. 1991. text 10.00 (*0-8153-0634-2*) Garland.

North-South Technology Transfer: A Case Study of Petrochemicals in Latin America. Mariluz Cortes & Peter Bocock. LC 83-49365. 184p. reprint ed. pap. 57.10 (*0-7837-4250-9*, 204394000012) Bks Demand.

North-South Technology Transfer: Financing & Institution Building. Jack Baranson. LC 81-80543. 160p. 1981. 25.75 (*0-912338-27-X*); fiche 12.75 (*0-912338-28-8*) Lomond.

North-South Trade, Employment, & Inequality: Changing Fortunes in a Skill-Dirven World. Adrian Wood. (IDS Development Studies Ser.). (Illus.). 528p. 1995. pap. text 29.95 (*0-19-829015-2*) OUP.

North-South Trade in Manufacturers. Ed. by Neelamber Hatti et al. (C). 1990. 95.00 (*81-85182-45-0*, Pub. by Indus Pub) S Asia.

North Spirit. Paulette Jiles. LC 95-193855. 288p. 1995. 27.95 (*0-385-25499-7*) Doubleday.

North Spirit: Sojourns among the Cree & Ojibway. Paulette Jiles. LC 96-76410. 291p. 1996. pap. 16.00 (*1-886913-09-9*) Ruminator Bks.

North Staffordshire Railway Locomotives & Rolling Stock. R. W. Rush. 72p. (C). 1985. 39.00 (*0-85361-275-7*) St Mut.

North Staffordshire Sketchbook. 96p. 1987. 49.00 (*0-907496-73-3*, Pub. by JNM Pubns) St Mut.

North Star. L. S. Asekoff. LC 96-19975. 96p. 1997. 20.00 (*0-914061-57-7*) Orchises Pr.

North Star. Gloria Bond Clunie. 103p. 1998. pap. 5.50 (*0-87129-831-7*, N47) Dramatic Pub.

*__North Star.__ Amanda Harte. 320p. 2000. pap. 4.99 (*0-8439-4764-0*, Leisure Bks) Dorchester Pub Co.

North Star. Peter H. Reynolds. LC 97-94615. (Illus.). 108p. 1997. 22.00 (*1-891405-01-2*) FableVision.

North Star: A Novella. Hale Chatfield. (Illus.). 76p. (Orig.). 1992. pap. 6.00 (*0-9628478-1-X*) North Star OH.

North Star: Poems. Phillips Kloss. LC 91-45521. 64p. 1992. 10.95 (*0-86534-182-6*) Sunstone Pr.

North Star & the Southern Cross. Ann Yarmal. LC 89-50222. 96p. (Orig.). 1989. pap. 8.95 (*0-938999-03-6*) Yuganta Pr.

North Star Country. Meridel Le Sueur. LC 98-21093. (Fesler-Lampert Minnesota Heritage Book Ser.). 352p. 1998. 15.95 (*0-8166-3252-9*) U of Minn Pr.

North Star Journal. Dwight Reighard & Pat Springle. 312p. 1998. 35.00 (*1-888237-19-8*) Baxter Pr.

North Star One. William C. Tinsley et al. Ed. by Hale Chatfield. 44p. (Orig.). 1996. pap. 8.00 (*0-9628478-8-7*) North Star OH.

North Star Road see Witchcraft & the Shamanic Journey: Pagan Folkways from the Burning Times

North Star Road: Shamanism, Witchcraft & the Otherworld Journey. Kenneth Johnson. LC 95-42625. (World Religion & Magic Ser.). (Illus.). 288p. 1996. pap. 14.95 (*1-56718-370-0*) Llewellyn Pubns.

North Star, Sitka Alaska, Set, Vols. 1-5. Jackson et al. (Shorey Historical Ser.). (Illus.). 244p. reprint ed. 19.95 (*0-8466-9009-8*, S208) Shoreys Bkstore.

North Star Statehouse: An Armchair Guide to the Minnesota State Capitol. Thomas O'Sullivan. LC 94-66863. (Illus.). 124p. (Orig.). 1995. pap. 16.95 (*1-880654-07-5*) Pogo Pr.

North Star to Freedom: The Story of the Underground Railroad. Gena K. Gorrell. LC 96-8552. (Illus.). 184p. (YA). (gr. 5 up). 1997. 17.95 (*0-385-32319-0*, Delacorte Pr Bks) BDD Bks Young Read.

North Star to Freedom: The Story of the Underground Railroad. Gena K. Gorrell. 192p. (YA). (gr. 5 up). 2000. 11.95 (*0-385-32607-6*, Delacorte Pr Bks) BDD Bks Young Read.

North Star to Southern Cross. Will Kyselka & Ray Lanterman. LC 75-37655. (Illus.). 160p. (C). 1976. pap. 8.95 (*0-8248-0419-8*) UH Pr.

*__North Street: Poems,__ Jonathan Galassi. LC 99-44294. 96p. 2000. 23.00 (*0-06-019540-1*) HarpC.

North Suderland Railway. A. Wright. 96p. (C). 1985. 50.00 (*0-85361-335-4*) St Mut.

North Sulawesi Language Survey. Scott Merrifield. LC 95-68478. (Publications in Sociolinguistics: No. 1). 336p. (Orig.). 1997. pap. 28.00 (*1-55671-000-3*) S I L Intl.

North Texas Eldercare Sourcebook: A Resource Guide for Older Adults, Caregivers & Eldercare Professionals. Carla S. Rogg & Oskar H. Rogg. 186p. (Orig.). 1995. pap. 14.95 (*0-9631939-3-7*) Care Solutions.

North to Abilene. large type ed. Clifford H. Fry. (Linford Western Large Print Ser.). 288p. 1998. pap. 17.99 (*0-7089-5196-1*, Linford) Ulverscroft.

North to Alaska! Fifty Years on the World's Most Remarkable Highway. Ken Coates. (Illus.). 304p. 1998. pap. text 22.00 (*0-7881-5905-4*) DIANE Pub.

North to Alaska! Fifty Years on the World's Most Remarkable Highway. Ken Coates. (Illus.). 304p. 1991. 29.95 (*0-912006-55-2*) U of Alaska Pr.

North to Alaska: Victoria BC to Glacier Bay. 3rd ed. Charles E. Wood. 220p. 1995. pap. write for info. (*0-9697265-4-6*, Pub. by Laurie Norie & Wilson Ltd) St Mut.

North to Aztlan: A History of Mexican Americans in the United States. Richard Griswold del Castillo & Arnoldo De Leon. 1996. 29.95 (*0-8057-4586-6*, Twyne) Mac Lib Ref.

North to Canada: Men & Women Against the Vietnam War. James Dickerson. LC 98-23568. 232p. 1999. 35.00 (*0-275-96211-3*, Praeger Pubs) Greenwood.

*__North to Freedom.__ Anne Holm. (Illus.). (J). 1999. pap. 13.40 (*0-8335-1289-7*) Econo-Clad Bks.

North to Freedom. Anne Holm. (J). 1965. 11.10 (*0-606-02214-7*, Pub. by Turtleback) Demco.

North to Freedom. Anne S. Holm. LC 89-27626. 192p. (J). (gr. 3-7). 1990. pap. 6.00 (*0-15-257553-7*, Odyssey) Harcourt.

North to Iron Country. Janie L. Panagopoulos. (Dream-Quest Adventure Ser.). 224p. (J). (gr. 3-7). 1998. pap. 7.95 (*0-938682-48-2*, 682-48-2) River Rd Pubns.

North to Iron Country: A Dream-Quest Adventure. Janie L. Panagopoulos. LC 96-157418. 224p. (J). 1996. 14.95 (*0-938682-40-7*, 682-40-7) River Rd Pubns.

North to Iron Country Teacher's Guide. Patricia Westfield. (Illus.). 32p. (J). (gr. 3-7). 1999. wbk. ed. 8.95 (*0-938682-52-0*) River Rd Pubns.

North to Lake Superior: Journal of Charles W. Penny, 1840. Ed. by James L. Carter & Ernest H. Rankin. LC 71-111886. 1970. 8.95 (*0-938746-02-2*) Marquette Cnty.

North to Montana! Jehus, Bullwackers, & Mule Skinners on the Montana Trail. Betty M. Madsen & Brigham D. Madsen. LC 78-60240. (University of Utah Publications in the American West: No. 13). (Illus.). 318p. reprint ed. pap. 98.60 (*0-8357-4376-4*, 203720700007) Bks Demand.

North to Montana! Jehus, Bullwhackers & Mule Skinners on the Montana Trail. Betty M. Madsen & Brigham D. Madsen. 320p. 1998. pap. 21.95 (*0-87421-259-6*) Utah St U Pr.

North to Oak Island. Dudley Bromley. (Bestsellers II Ser.). (J). 1977. 16.60 (*0-606-02423-9*, Pub. by Turtleback) Demco.

North to Paradise. Edith R. Tjepkema. 103p. (Orig.). (YA). (gr. 8-12). 1987. pap. 4.50 (*0-9620280-0-2*) Northland Pr.

North to the Artic, 3 vols., Set. M. Edward Burtt. (Illus.). xii, 735p. (Orig.). 1992. pap. write for info. (*1-888913-04-5*) M E Burtt.

North to the Artic, Vol. 1. M. Edward Burtt. (Illus.). v, 255p. (Orig.). 1992. pap. write for info. (*1-888913-01-0*) M E Burtt.

North to the Artic, Vol. 2. M. Edward Burtt. (Illus.). iv, 249p. (Orig.). 1992. pap. write for info. (*1-888913-02-9*) M E Burtt.

North to the Artic, Vol 3. M. Edward Burtt. (Illus.). iii, 231p. (Orig.). 1992. pap. write for info. (*1-888913-03-7*) M E Burtt.

North to the Bitterroot. Ralph Compton. (Sundown Riders Ser.: No. 1). 1996. mass mkt. 5.99 (*0-312-95862-5*) St Martin.

North to the Night: A Spiritual Odyssey in the Artic. Alvah Simon. LC 99-27045. 336p. 1999. reprint ed. pap. 13.00 (*0-7679-0446-X*) Broadway BDD.

North to the Night: A Year in the Arctic Ice. Alvah Simon. LC 98-12359. (Illus.). 336p. 1998. 24.95 (*0-07-058052-9*) McGraw.

North to the Orient. Anne M. Lindbergh. LC 35-27279. 168p. 1966. pap. 10.00 (*0-15-667140-9*, Harvest Bks) Harcourt.

North to the Rails. Louis L'Amour. 192p. 1987. mass mkt. 4.50 (*0-553-28086-4*) Bantam.

North to the Rio Grande: Lorenzo de Zavala, First Vice President of the Republic of Texas. Fay Venable. (Illus.). 56p. (J). (gr. 6-7). 1988. pap. 6.95 (*1-57168-080-2*) Sunbelt Media.

North to Yesterday. Robert Flynn. LC 85-4688. (Texas Tradition Ser.: No. 4). 340p. 1985. reprint ed. 19.95 (*0-87565-014-7*); reprint ed. pap. 14.95 (*0-87565-015-5*) Tex Christian.

*__North Toward Home.__ Willie Morris. LC 99-57733. 1999. 28.00 (*1-57806-266-7*) U Pr of Miss.

*__North Toward Home.__ Willie Morris. (Rediscovery Ser.). 448p. 2000. pap. 14.00 (*0-375-72460-5*) Vin Bks.

North Ulster Walk Guides. James Hamill. (Illus.). 24p. 1987. 9.95 (*0-86281-184-8*, Pub. by Appletree Pr) Irish Bks Media.

North Umpqua Angler's Guide. Doc Crawford. (Illus.). 96p. 1989. pap. 9.95 (*0-936608-84-6*) F Amato Pubns.

North Umpqua, OR. John Shewey. (River Journal Ser.: Vol. 2, No. 2). (Illus.). 48p. 1995. pap. 15.95 (*1-57188-030-5*) F Amato Pubns.

North Vietnam. Edward G. Doyle et al. 1986. 16.30 (*0-201-11276-0*) Addison-Wesley.

North Vietnam & the Pathet Lao: Partners in the Struggle for Laos. Paul F. Langer & Joseph J. Zasloff. LC 73-134326. (Rand Corporation Research Studies). (Illus.). 276p. 1970. 29.00 (*0-674-62675-3*) HUP.

North Vietnamese Answer. Zumwalt. 1950. text 27.50 (*0-8050-4072-2*) St Martin.

North Vietnam's Strategy for Survival. Jon M. Van Dyke. LC 75-88378. (Illus.). 336p. 1972. 27.95 (*0-87015-191-6*) Pacific Bks.

North Wales, Snowdon & Offa's Dyke. Jarrold Publishing Staff. (Pathfinder Guides Ser.). 1998. pap. text 16.95 (*0-7117-0993-9*, Pub. by JARR UK) Seven Hills Bk.

North Wales Transport. Jim Roberts. (Illus.). 160p. 1998. pap. 21.95 (*0-7509-1722-9*) Sutton Pub Ltd.

North Wales/Snowdonia. Insight Guides Staff. (Insight Guides). 1998. pap. text 7.95 (*0-88729-332-8*) Langenscheidt.

North Webster: A Photographic History of a Black Community. Ann Morris & Henrietta Ambrose. LC 93-9619. (Illus.). 208p. 1993. 36.95 (*0-253-33895-6*); pap. 19.95 (*0-253-28601-8*) Ind U Pr.

North-West Aerial Fronteri, 1919-1934. Edward P. Wixted. 224p. (C). 1990. 75.00 (*0-908175-89-2*, Pub. by Boolarong Pubns) St Mut.

North-West by South. large type ed. Nancy Cato. 416p. 1987. 15.95 (*0-7089-8391-X*, Charnwood) Ulverscroft.

North West Company. Gordon C. Davidson. (BCL1 - History - Canada Ser.). 349p. 1991. reprint ed. lib. bdg. 89.00 (*0-7812-6371-9*) Rprt Serv.

North-west Frontier Drama, 1945-1947: A Re-assessment Parshotam Mehra. LC 98-917046. 262p. 1998. write for info. (*81-7304-097-4*) Manohar.

North West Frontier, 1837-1947. Robert Wilkinson-Latham. (Men-at-Arms Ser.: No. 72). (Illus.). 48p. pap. 11.95 (*0-85045-275-9*, 9200, Pub. by Ospry) Stackpole.

North-West Frontier Province & Kashmir. James Douie. (C). 1994. 14.00 (*81-85557-85-3*, Pub. by Low Price) S Asia.

North-West Half-Breed Scrip. Gail Morin. 287p. 1997. pap. 40.00 (*1-886560-44-7*) Quintin Pub RI.

*__North West Highlands: Roads to the Isles, the Obvious Beauty & Hidden Delights of the Mountainous Lands from Fort William to Ullapool.__ Tom Atkinson. (Illus.). 160p. 1999. pap. 4.95 (*0-946487-54-5*, Pub. by Luath Pr Ltd) Midpt Trade.

North West Italy Map. 1997. 8.95 (*2-06-700428-X*, 428) Michelin.

North West of England. Brian Redhead. (Radio Times Around Britain Guides Ser.). (Illus.). 96p. 1994. 8.95 (*0-563-36953-1*, Pub. by BBC) Parkwest Pubns.

North West Passage: Being the Record of a Voyage of Exploration of the Ship Gjoa 1903-1907, 2 vols., Set. Roald E. Amundsen. LC 74-5824. reprint ed. 87.50 (*0-404-11625-6*) AMS Pr.

North West Spain Map. 1997. 8.95 (*2-06-700441-7*, 441) Michelin.

North West under Three Flags, 1635-1796. Charles Moore. (C). 1996. reprint ed. 62.00 (*81-206-1153-5*, Pub. by Asian Educ Servs) S Asia.

North Western: A History of the Chicago & North Western Railway System. H. Roger Grant. LC 96-12686. (Illus.). 304p. 1996. 49.95 (*0-87580-214-1*) N Ill U Pr.

North-Western Provinces of India: Their History, Ethnology, & Administration. W. Crooke. (C). 1994. 42.00 (*81-206-0088-6*, Pub. by Asian Educ Servs) S Asia.

North-Western Provinces of India: Their History, Ethnology & Administration. William Crooke. LC 98-906404. x, 361 p. 1998. write for info. (*81-206-1067-9*) Asian Educ Servs.

North Wind. Gwyneth Jones. LC 97-22178. 288p. 1997. pap. 13.95 (*0-312-86396-9*) St Martin.

North Wind & the Sun. (Bilingual Readers in Vietnamese & English Ser.). (ENG & VIE.). 1998. pap. 8.40 (*0-8442-6108-4*, E6108-4) NTC Contemp Pub Co.

*__North Wind & the Sun.__ Brian Wildsmith. (Illus.). 32p. (J). 2000. pap. 8.95 (*0-19-272404-5*) OUP.

*__North Wind in Your Spokes: A Novel of the Tour de France.__ Hans Blickensdorfer. Tr. by Marlis Cambon from GER.Tr. of Salz im Kaffee. 304p. 2000. 23.00 (*1-891369-18-0*, Pub. by Breakaway Bks) Consort Bk Sales.

North with Doc. G. Knowles. 1993. pap. 11.95 (*0-929384-40-7*) In-Fisherman.

*__North with Franklin: The Lost Journals of James Fitzjames.__ John Wilson. (Illus.). 250p. 1999. 19.95 (*1-55041-406-2*, Pub. by Fitzhenry & W Ltd) Genl Dist Srvs.

North with Lee & Jackson: The Lost Story of Gettysburg. James A. Kegel. LC 96-141. (Illus.). 480p. 1996. 34.95 (*0-8117-1128-5*) Stackpole.

North Woods: An Inside Look at the Nature of Forests in the Northeast. Peter J. Marchand. (Illus.). 160p. 1987. pap. text 10.95 (*0-910146-64-0*) AMC Books.

*__North Woods Walkabout.__ Nan Turner Waldron. LC 98-47517. 1998. pap. text 12.95 (*0-9630546-1-9*) Butterfly & Wheel.

North Writers: A Strong Woods Collection. Ed. by John Henricksson. xviii, 292p. 1991. 18.95 (*0-8166-1950-6*) U of Minn Pr.

N

An Asterisk (*) at the beginning of an entry indicates that the title is appearing for the first time.

*__North Writers: A Strong Woods Collection.__ John Henricksson. 296p. 2000. pap. 14.95 (0-8166-3671-0) U of Minn Pr.

North Writers No. 2: Our Place in the Woods. Ed. by John Henricksson. LC 97-11452. 176p. 1997. pap. 14.95 (0-8166-2903-X) U of Minn Pr.

North York Moors. Ed. by Ken Ward. (Footpath Touring Ser.). (Illus.). 64p. 1993. pap. 4.95 (0-7117-0426-0) Seven Hills Bk.

North York Moors Walks. Jarrold Printing Staff. (Ordnance Survey Pathfinder Guides Ser.). (Illus.). 80p. 1993. pap. 14.95 (0-7117-0460-0) Seven Hills Bk.

North Yorkshire Moors Challenge Walk - 24 Miles. John N. Merrill. 32p. 1986. 29.00 (0-907496-36-9, Pub. by JNM Pubns) St Mut.

Northampton. James M. Parsons. LC 97-112794. (Images of America Ser.). 1996. pap. 16.99 (0-7524-0425-3) Arcadia Publng.

Northampton: Patronage & Policy at the Court of James I. Linda L. Peck. 288p. (C). 1982. text 55.00 (0-04-942177-8) Routledge.

Northampton County Guide. Pennsylvania Writers' Project Staff. 1993. reprint ed. lib. bdg. 89.00 (0-7812-5817-0) Rprt Serv.

Northampton County in the American Revolution. Richmond E. Myers. (Publications of the Northampton County Historical & Genealogical Society: No. 6). (Illus.). vi, 90p. 1976. 10.00 (1-877701-12-2) NCH&GS.

Northampton County North Carolina Census, 1790. Courtney York & Gerlene York. 1972. pap. 12.00 (0-916660-08-7) Hse of York.

Northampton County North Carolina Census, 1810. Courtney York & Gerlene York. (Orig.). 1970. pap. 12.00 (0-916660-12-5) Hse of York.

Northampton County, Virginia, Tithables, 1662-1677. John B. Bell. 78p. (Orig.). 1994. pap. 12.00 (1-55613-893-8) Heritage Bk.

Northampton County, Virginia, Tithables, 1720-1769. John B. Bell. 411p. (Orig.). 1993. pap. text 28.50 (1-55613-823-7) Heritage Bk.

Northampton County, Virginia, Tithables, 1720-1769. John B. Bell. 393p. (Orig.). 1994. pap. text 28.50 (0-7884-0113-0) Heritage Bk.

Northampton Massachusetts of Today, Depicted by Pen & Camera. A Description in Text & Many, Many Illustrations, of Northampton at the Dawn of the 20th Century, Including a Number of Very Interesting Old Business Advertisements. Frederick Knab. Ed. by Charles F. Warner. (Illus.). 96p. 1998. reprint ed. pap. 17.50 (0-8328-7039-0); reprint ed. lib. bdg. 27.50 (0-8328-4967-7) Higginson Bk Co.

Northampton, the Meadow City: Historical Sketch of Northampton, Massachusetts, with over 250 Photographics & Illustrations. Compiled by F. N. Kneeland & L. P. Bryant. (Illus.). 108p. 1998. reprint ed. pap. 19.50 (0-8328-7038-2) Higginson Bk Co.

Northampton, the Meadow City: Historical Sketches of Northampton, Massachusetts, with over 250 Photographics & Illustrations. Compiled by F. N. Kneeland & L. P. Bryant. (Illus.). 1998. reprint ed. lib. bdg. 29.50 (0-8328-4966-9) Higginson Bk Co.

Northanger Abbey. Jane Austen. Date not set. lib. bdg. 20.95 (0-8488-1244-1) Amereon Ltd.

Northanger Abbey. Jane Austen. LC 99-215581. (Classics Ser.). 224p. 1985. mass mkt. 4.95 (0-553-21197-8) Bantam.

Northanger Abbey. Jane Austen. 320p. 1999. pap. 4.95 (0-553-21494-2, Bantam Classics) Bantam.

Northanger Abbey. Jane Austen. Ed. by Claire Grogan. 276p. (C). 1996. pap. text 7.95 (1-55111-078-4) Broadview Pr.

*__Northanger Abbey.__ Jane Austen. 2000. pap. 2.00 (0-486-41412-4) Dover.

Northanger Abbey. Jane Austen. LC 92-52895. 1992. 15.00 (0-679-41715-X) Everymns Lib.

*__Northanger Abbey.__ Jane Austen. 290p. 2000. pap. 11.95 (1-892295-92-X) Green Integer.

*__Northanger Abbey.__ Jane Austen. (Cloth Bound Pocket Ser.). 1999. 7.95 (3-8290-3001-0) Konemann.

Northanger Abbey. Jane Austen. 1995. 13.50 (0-679-60192-9) Modern Lib NY.

Northanger Abbey. Jane Austen. 1996. mass mkt. 4.95 (0-451-52636-8) NAL.

Northanger Abbey. Jane Austen. 304p. 1994. 3.95 (0-460-87434-9, Everyman's Classic Lib) Tuttle Pubng.

Northanger Abbey. Jane Austen. Ed. by Marilyn Butler. 288p. 1996. pap. 6.95 (0-14-043413-5) Viking Penguin.

Northanger Abbey. Jane Austen. (Classics Library). 167p. 1998. pap. 3.95 (1-85326-043-6, 0436WW, Pub. by Wrdsworth Edits) NTC Contemp Pub Co.

Northanger Abbey. large type ed. Jane Austen. (Isis Clear Type Classic Ser.). 234p. 1991. 24.95 (1-85089-434-5, Pub. by ISIS Lrg Prnt) Transaction Pubs.

Northanger Abbey. large type ed. Jane Austen. (Large Print Heritage Ser.). 357p. 1998. lib. bdg. 33.95 (1-58118-030-6, 22022) LRS.

Northanger Abbey. large type ed. Jane Austen. 359p. 1995. 27.99 (0-7089-8876-8, Charnwood) Ulverscroft.

Northanger Abbey. large type ed. Jane Austen. 370p. 2000. reprint ed. lib. bdg. 24.00 (0-939495-48-1) North Bks.

Northanger Abbey. Jane Austen. 220p. 1986. reprint ed. lib. bdg. 18.95 (0-89966-534-9) Buccaneer Bks.

*__Northanger Abbey.__ Jane Austen. (Twelve-Point Ser.). 230p. 2000. reprint ed. lib. bdg. 24.00 (1-58287-121-3) North Bks.

Northanger Abbey see Oxford Illustrated Jane Austen

Northanger Abbey, Lady Susan, the Watsons & Sandition. Jane Austen. Ed. & Notes by John Davie. (Oxford World's Classics Ser.). 432p. 1998. pap. 5.95 (0-19-283368-5) OUP.

*__Northborough.__ Northborough Historical Society Staff. (Images of America Ser.). (Illus.). 128p. 2000. pap. 18.99 (0-7385-0423-8) Arcadia Publng.

Northborough History. Josiah C. Kent. (Illus.). 529p. 1994. reprint ed. lib. bdg. 55.00 (0-8328-4361-X) Higginson Bk Co.

Northbound Train: Finding the Purpose, Setting the Direction, Shaping the Destiny of Your Organization. Karl Albrecht. LC 93-49388. 224p. 1994. 22.95 (0-8144-0233-X) AMACOM.

*__Northbridge Rectory.__ large type ed. Angela M. Thirkell. 480p. 1999. 31.99 (0-7505-1340-3, Pub. by Mgna Lrg Print) Ulverscroft.

Northbridge Rectory. 2nd ed. Angela M. Thirkell. LC 96-36792. 320p. 1997. pap. 12.95 (0-7867-0380-6) Carroll & Graf.

Northbrook. Poems. Frederick Morgan. LC 81-14664. 88p. 1982. 14.95 (0-252-00947-9); 9.95 (0-252-00948-7) U of Ill Pr.

Northbury Papers. Joanne Dobson. 352p. 1999. mass mkt. 5.99 (0-553-57661-5) Bantam.

Northbury Papers. Joanne Dobson. LC 98-5895. 288p. 1998. 21.95 (0-385-48693-6) Doubleday.

Northcliffe: An Intimate Biography. Henry H. Fyfe. LC 74-100527. (BCL Ser.: I). reprint ed. 37.50 (0-404-00592-6) AMS Pr.

*__Northcliffe's Legacy.__ Peter Catterall. LC 99-89311. 210p. 2000. text 65.00 (0-312-23256-X) St Martin.

Northcon 98: Conference Proceedings, Washington State Convention Center, Seattle, Washington, Occober 21-23, 1998. Northcon 98 Staff. LC 98-86795. iv, 254 p. 1998. pap. write for info. (0-7803-5077-4) IEEE Standards.

Northcon/93: Conference Record, Oregon Convention Center, Portland, Oregon, October 12-14, 1993. Northcon/93 & IEEE, Oregon Section. LC 94-184712. iv, 263 p. 1993. write for info. (0-7803-9973-0) IEEE Standards.

Northcon '95. IEEE (Oregon Section, Seattle Section) Staff. Ed. by IEEE (Institute of Electrical & Electronics Engine. LC 95-76250. 275p. 1995. pap. text. write for info. (0-7803-2639-3, 95CH35792); lib. bdg. write for info. (0-7803-2640-7, 95CH35792); mic. film. write for info. (0-7803-2641-5, 95CH35792) Inst Electrical.

Northcon '96. IEEE Staff. LC 96-75714. 400p. 1996. write for info. (0-7803-3279-2, 96CH35928); pap. write for info. (0-7803-3277-6, 96CH35928); lib. bdg. write for info. (0-7803-3278-4, 96CH35928) Inst Electrical.

Northcountry Gardening. Neil Moran. LC 95-79339. (Illus.). 214p. 1995. pap. 16.95 (0-932212-87-5) Avery Color.

Northcountry Kitchens Cookbook: Compilation of Northcountry Recipes. 8th ed. 1985. pap. 13.95 (0-932212-21-2) Avery Color.

Northeast. Eleanor Berman. (52 Weekend & Day Trips Ser.). 1996. pap. 16.00 (0-614-12771-8) Crown Pub Group.

Northeast. Jill C. Wheeler. LC 94-8806. (America, This Land Is Your Land Ser.). (YA). (gr. 5 up). 1994. lib. bdg. 15.98 (1-56239-295-6) ABDO Pub Co.

Northeast see Directory of Child Day Care Centers

Northeast Africa Map (Includes Egypt & Arabia) 1995. 10.95 (2-06-700954-0, 954) Michelin.

Northeast & Eastern Canada. Douglas S. Carmody. LC 99-18950. (Pilot's Travel & Recreation Guides). 1999. pap. 24.95 (0-07-001743-3) McGraw.

Northeast & Southeast see Gale Encyclopedia of Native American Tribes

Northeast Asia. Ed. by Takeatsu Kimura et al. LC 96-4659. (International Collation of Traditional & Folk Medicine Ser.: Vol. 1). 240p. 1996. write for info. (981-02-2589-X) World Scientific Pub.

Northeast Asia in Prehistory. Chester S. Chard. LC 73-2040. (Illus.). 231p. reprint ed. pap. 71.70 (0-8357-6236-X, 203428000089) Bks Demand.

Northeast Asian Cooperation Dialogue: Energy & Security in Northeast Asia, No. IV. Edward Fei et al. Ed. by Susan L. Shirk & Michael Stanklewicz. (IGCC Policy Papers: No. 24). 52p. (Orig.). 1996. pap. 3.50 (0-934637-39-3) U of CA Inst Global.

Northeast Asian Cooperation Dialogue No. II: Confidence-Building & Crisis Prevention. Andrew Mack et al. (IGCC Policy Papers: No. 9). 88p. (Orig.). 1994. pap. 3.50 (0-934637-24-5) U of CA Inst Global.

Northeast Asian Energy & the Global Context. 39p. 1996. pap. 9.95 (1-899658-61-0, Pub. by Royal Inst Intl Affairs) Brookings.

Northeast Asian Security: A Korean Perspective. Young K. Cha. LC 88-2842. (Significant Issues Ser.: Vol. 10, No. 1). (Illus.). 67p. (Orig.). reprint ed. pap. 30.00 (0-8357-6640-3, 203530700094) Bks Demand.

Northeast Asian Security Regime: Proposals & Prospect. David Youtz & Paul Midford. LC 92-11117. 1992. 9.85 (0-913449-31-8) Inst EW Stud.

Northeast Bioengineering Conference, 1998. IEEE, Engineering in Medicine & Biology Society St. Ed. by Institute of Electrical & Electronics Engineers, I. LC 88-646567. 120p. 1998. pap. text 110.00 (0-7803-4544-4, 98CH36210) Inst Electrical.

Northeast Boaters Almanac. rev. ed. Rocco J. Citeno. Orig. Title: Boat Owners. (Illus.). 512p. 1999. pap. 12.95 (0-9659325-0-8) Northeast Boat.

Northeast Bronx Poets & Writers Forum Anthology, Vol. 1. Ed. by Marilyn Gordon. LC 82-83783. 48p. (C). 4.50 (0-9609542-1-X) M Gordon Pub.

Northeast Coast of Puerto Rico. Wilson Ltd. Staff & Imray L. Norie. (C). 1990. 65.00 (0-7855-5941-8, Pub. by Laurie Norie & Wilson Ltd) St Mut.

Northeast Connecticut, 1. Rand McNally Staff. (Rand McNally Streetfinder Ser.). 1999. pap. text 15.95 (0-528-97885-3) Rand McNally.

Northeast Endangered Species Conference: Proceedings, 1980. 174p. 10.00 (0-318-13865-4) Ctr Action Endangered.

Northeast Folio. Ed. by J. J. White & J. V. Brindle. (Illus.). 72p. 1979. pap. 10.00 (0-913196-22-3) Hunt Inst Botanical.

*__Northeast Garden Book.__ Sunset Editors. 2001. pap. 29.95 (0-376-03524-2) Sunset Books.

Northeast Gardener's Year. Lee Reich. 1992. 20.00 (0-201-55050-4) Addison-Wesley.

Northeast Gardener's Year. Lee Reich. 1993. pap. 12.00 (0-201-62233-5) Addison-Wesley.

Northeast Gardening: The Diverse Art & Special Considerations of Gardening in the Northeast. Elvin McDonald. 160p. 1990. text 35.00 (0-02-583125-9) Macmillan.

Northeast Georgia in Vintage Postcards. Gary Doster. LC 98-86585. (Postcard History Ser.). (Illus.). 128p. 1998. pap. 18.99 (0-7524-1377-5) Arcadia Publng.

Northeast Germany Map. 1996. 8.95 (2-06-700416-6, 416) Michelin.

*__Northeast Girls.__ Cherie Bennett. (Pageant Ser.: No. 3). 183p. (gr. 7-12). 1998. mass mkt. 4.50 (0-425-16418-7) Berkley Pub.

Northeast Glacial Aquifers: Papers Presented at AWRA Symposium on Monitoring, Modeling, & Mediating Water Quality, May 17-20, 1987, Syracuse, New York. Ed. by Allan D. Randall & A. Ivan Johnson. LC TD0223.A1A87. (AWRA Monograph Ser.: Vol. 11). 160p. 1988. reprint ed. pap. 49.60 (0-7837-9277-8, 206001500005) Bks Demand.

Northeast Governments Performance Standards, 1990. Ed. by Greg Michels. (Governments Performance Standards Ser.). (Illus.). 150p. 1990. text 125.00 (1-55507-511-8) Municipal Analysis.

Northeast Guide to Saltwater Fishing & Boating. 2nd ed. Vin T. Sporano. (Illus.). 384p. 1996. pap. text 24.95 (0-07-059893-2) Intl Marine.

Northeast Indian Resource Secrets: The Buyer's Guide. Tom R. Ford. (Illus.). 127p. 1997. per. 15.95 (1-879418-77-0, 207-833-5016) Audenreed Pr.

Northeast Indians. Spizzirri Publishing Co. Staff. Ed. by Linda Spizzirri. (Illus.). 32p. (J). (gr. 1-8). pap. 4.98 incl. audio (0-86545-040-4) Spizzirri.

Northeast Indians Fact Cards: Indians of New England & the Northeast Coast. Reeve Chace. (Illus.). 70p. (J). 1998. ring bd. 29.00 (1-884925-59-6) Toucan Valley.

Northeast India's Hidden Displacement. U. S. Committee for Refugees Staff. (Issue Papers). (Illus.). 2000. 5.00 (0-936548-05-3) US Comm Refugees.

Northeast Local. Tom Donaghy. LC 98-104351. 1996. pap. 5.25 (0-8222-1550-0) Dramatists Play.

Northeast Passage: Arctic Straits. Donat Pharand. 1984. lib. bdg. 110.00 (90-247-2979-3) Kluwer Academic.

Northeast Pennsylvania Dine-a-Mate Book. 232p. 1996. pap. text 30.00 (1-57393-057-1) Dine-A-Mate.

*__Northeast Pennsylvania Entertainment, 2000.__ (Illus.). 774p. 1999. pap. 30.00 (1-58553-045-X, 00R2) Enter Pubns.

Northeast Petroleum Directory. 6th rev. ed. Ed. by Paula Jepperson. 400p. 1994. pap. text 69.00 (0-912553-50-2) Hart Pubns.

Northeast Petroleum Directory. 7th ed. Ed. by Paula Jepperson. 370p. 1995. pap. text 89.00 (0-912553-56-1) Hart Pubns.

Northeast Petroleum Directory. 8th rev. ed. Ed. by Kelly Holder. 400p. 1996. pap. text 99.00 (0-912553-64-2) Hart Pubns.

Northeast Petroleum Directory, 1991. 2nd rev. ed. Ed. by Paula Jepperson. 520p. 1991. pap. 40.00 (0-912553-23-5) Hart Pubns.

Northeast Rail Corridor: Conflicts, Challenges, & Development Opportunities. Robert L. James. LC 83-72710. 1983. pap. 6.50 (0-914193-04-X) Coalition NE Govn.

Northeast Rail Corridor: Information on Users, Funding Sources, & Expenditures. (Illus.). 45p. (Orig.). (C). 1996. pap. text 20.00 (0-7881-3368-3) DIANE Pub.

Northeast Retreat of 1759 & 1981. Joseph S. Haas. LC 81-90691. (Cathedral of the Beechwoods Ser.: No. 1). (Illus.). 148p. (Orig.). 1981. 7.00 (0-9605552-0-X) Haas Ent NH.

Northeast Shelf Ecosystem: Assessment, Sustainability & Management. Kenneth Sherman et al. LC 96-24468. (Illus.). 376p. 1996. pap. text 71.95 (0-86542-468-3) Blackwell Sci.

Northeast Treasure Hunter's Gem & Mineral Guide: Where & How to Dig, Pan & Mine Your Own Gems & Minerals. Kathy J. Rygle & Stephen F. Pedersen. LC 99-39215. (Illus.). 1999. pap. 14.95 (0-943763-27-4) GemStone Pr.

*__Northeast 2000.__ Mobil Travel Guides Staff. (Mobil Travel Guides Ser.). 2000. pap. 16.95 (0-7853-4155-2) Pubns Intl Ltd.

Northeast United States. H. M. Gousha Staff. 1991. pap. 2.50 (0-671-89699-7, H M Gousha) Prntice Hall Bks.

Northeast Waterways: A Guide to the Trent, Witham, Ouse & Associated Waterways. Derek Bowskill. (Illus.). 200p. (C). 1986. pap. 125.00 (0-85288-099-5, Pub. by Laurie Norie & Wilson Ltd) St Mut.

Northeastern Accelerator Personnel. Ed. by R. D. Krause & T. N. Tipping. 388p. (C). 1991. text 99.00 (981-02-0636-4) World Scientific Pub.

Northeastern Accelerator Personnel. Ed. by J. W. McKay & H. R. Hyder. 340p. (C). 1989. text 130.00 (9971-5-0979-2) World Scientific Pub.

Northeastern Accelerator Personnel. Ed. by N. F. Ziegler et al. 584p. (C). 1990. text 130.00 (981-02-0179-6) World Scientific Pub.

Northeastern Accelerator Personnel: Proceedings of the 20th Symposium. Ed. by C. Browne et al. 560p. 1987. text 131.00 (9971-5-0325-5) World Scientific Pub.

Northeastern Accelerator Personnel: Proceedings of the 21st Symposium. K. R. Chapman. 484p. (C). 1988. text 108.00 (9971-5-0525-8) World Scientific Pub.

Northeastern & Western Yavapai. fac. ed. E. W. Gifford. (University of California Publications in American Archaeology & Ethnology: Vol. 34: 4). (Illus.). 118p. (C). 1936. reprint ed. pap. text 13.13 (1-55567-295-7) Coyote Press.

Northeastern Caribbean: The Leeward Islands. James Henderson. (Cadogan Country Guides Ser.). (Illus.). 288p. 1994. pap. 12.95 (0-947754-82-2) Globe Pequot.

Northeastern Dictionary of Women's Biography. 3rd ed. Jennifer S. Uglow. LC 99-23227. 642p. 1999. text 49.95 (1-55553-421-X) NE U Pr.

Northeastern Indian Girl. Kathy Allert. (Little Activity Bks.). (Illus.). (J). 1996. pap. 1.00 (0-486-28977-X) Dover.

Northeastern Indian Lives, 1632-1816. Ed. & Intro. by Robert S. Grumet. LC 95-33144. (Native Americans of the Northeast Ser.). (Illus.). 408p. (C). 1996. pap. 20.95 (1-55849-001-9); text 55.00 (1-55849-000-0) U of Mass Pr.

Northeastern Landscaping Book. Sunset Editors. (Illus.). 2000. pap. 29.95 (0-376-03520-X) Sunset Books.

Northeastern Mexico: Coahuila, Nuevo Leon & Tamaulipas. 2nd rev. ed. Ed. by Mike Nelson & George Romer. (Sanborn's Travelog - Mexico by Land Ser.). 110p. 1995. pap. 9.95 (1-878166-24-7) Wanderlust Pubns.

Northeastern New Mexico. Ed. by S. G. Lucas & A. P. Hunt. (Guidebook Ser.: No. 38). (Illus.). 354p. 1987. 20.00 (1-58546-073-7) NMex Geol Soc.

Northeastern Penn Dine-a-Mate. 256p. 1994. pap. 25.00 (1-57393-014-8) Dine-A-Mate.

Northeastern Seashore Life: Labrador to Massachusetts. James Kavanagh. (Pocket Naturalist Ser.). (Illus.). 1997. 5.95 (1-889903-11-6, Pub. by Waterford WA) Falcon Pub Inc.

Northeastern Section Field Guide. Ed. by D. C. Roy. (DNAG Centennial Field Guides Ser.: No. 5). (Illus.). 517p. 1987. 21.75 (0-8137-5405-4) Geol Soc.

Northeastern Tiger Beetles: Field Guide to Tiger Beetles of New England & Eastern Canada. Jonathan G. Leonard & Ross Taylor Bell. LC 98-41599. 192p. 1998. otabind 49.95 (0-8493-1915-3, 1915) CRC Pr.

Northeastern Tour Book. 636p. 1993. reprint ed. lib. bdg. 109.00 (0-7812-5114-1) Rprt Serv.

*__NortheastOhioEconomy.com: How the Internet Can Help Northeast Ohio Businesses, Communities.__ Donald T. Iannone. Ed. by Susan Petrone. 52p. 2000. pap. 5.00 (0-9638675-2-0) CSU Urban Chld.

Northeast's Changing Forest. Lloyd C. Irland. 416p. 1999. 50.00 (0-674-62680-X) HUP.

Norther. Emilio Carballido. LC 68-54901. (Texas Pan-American Ser.). Orig. Title: El Norte. (Illus.). 101p. reprint ed. pap. 31.40 (0-8357-7753-7, 203611100002) Bks Demand.

*__Northern Africa: A Guide to Reference & Information Sources.__ Paula Youngman Skreslet. (Social Sciences Ser.). 500p. 2000. 85.00 (1-56308-684-0) Libs Unl.

Northern Africa: Islam & Modernization. Ed. by Michael Brett. 156p. 1973. 45.00 (0-7146-2972-3, Pub. by F Cass Pubs) Intl Spec Bk.

Northern Akkad Project Reports: Mesopotamian History & Environment, Vol. 1. 52p. 1987. pap. 22.00 (0-614-96312-5, Pub. by Recherches et Pubns) Eisenbrauns.

Northern Akkad Project Reports: Mesopotamian History & Environment, Vol. 2. (Illus.). 70p. 1989. pap. 30.00 (0-614-96313-3, Pub. by Recherches et Pubns) Eisenbrauns.

Northern Akkad Project Reports: Mesopotamian History & Environment, Vol. 3. (Illus.). 68p. 1989. pap. 30.00 (0-614-96314-1, Pub. by Recherches et Pubns) Eisenbrauns.

Northern Akkad Project Reports: Mesopotamian History & Environment, Vol. 4. (Illus.). 71p. 1989. pap. 30.00 (0-614-96315-X, Pub. by Recherches et Pubns) Eisenbrauns.

Northern Akkad Project Reports: Mesopotamian History & Environment, Vol. 5. (Illus.). 100p. 1991. pap. 30.00 (0-614-96316-8, Pub. by Recherches et Pubns) Eisenbrauns.

Northern Akkad Project Reports: Mesopotamian History & Environment, Vol. 6. (Illus.). 100p. 1991. pap. 30.00 (0-614-96318-4, Pub. by Recherches et Pubns) Eisenbrauns.

Northern Akkad Project Reports: Mesopotamian History & Environment, Vol. 7. (Illus.). 91p. 1991. pap. 30.00 (0-614-96317-6, Pub. by Recherches et Pubns) Eisenbrauns.

Northern Akkad Project Reports: Mesopotamian History & Environment, Vol. 8. (Illus.). 77p. 1993. pap. 30.00 (0-614-96319-2, Pub. by Recherches et Pubns) Eisenbrauns.

Northern Akkad Project Reports: Mesopotamian History & Environment, Vol. 9. (Illus.). 61p. 1996. pap. text 30.00 (0-614-96320-6) Recherches et Pubns.

Northern Algonquian Supreme Being. John M. Cooper. LC 76-43682. (Catholic University of America Anthropological Ser.: No. 2). reprint ed. 34.50 (0-404-15515-4) AMS Pr.

Northern Alphabet. rev. ed. Ted Harrison. LC 82-50244. (Illus.). 32p. (J). (ps-1). 1996. pap. 7.95 (0-88776-233-6) Tundra Bks.

Northern & Central Nootkan Tribes. Philip Drucker. (Bureau of American Ethnology Bulletins Ser.). 480p. 1995. lib. bdg. 109.00 (0-7812-4144-8) Rprt Serv.

N

Northern & Central Nootkan Tribes. fac. ed. Philip Drucker. (Smithsonian Institution, Bureau of American Ethnology Ser.: Bulletin 144). (Illus.). 492p. (C). 1951. reprint ed. pap. text 50.63 (*1-55567-680-4*) Coyote Press.

Northern & Central Nootkan Tribes. Philip Drucker. 1988. reprint ed. lib. bdg. 75.00 (*0-7812-0233-7*) Rprt Serv.

Northern & Southern Affiliations of Antillean Culture. Charlotte D. Gower. LC 28-7691. (American Anthropological Association Memoirs Ser.: No. 35). 1927. pap. 25.00 (*0-527-00534-7*) Periodicals Srv.

***Northern & Western Asia.** Martyn Bramwell. (World in Maps Ser.). (Illus.). 56p. (YA). (gr. 4-7). 2000. 23.93 (*0-8225-2915-7*, Lerner Publctns) Lerner Pub.

Northern Antiquities. Paul H. Mallet. LC 68-57868. (Bohn's Antiquarian Library). reprint ed. 56.00 (*0-404-50020-X*) AMS Pr.

Northern Appalachian Transect: Southeastern Quebec, Canada, Through Western Maine, U. S. A. Ed. by Moench. (IGC Field Trip Guidebooks Ser.). 56p. 1989. 28.00 (*0-87590-559-5*, T358) Am Geophysical.

Northern Arabia, According to the Original Investigations of Alois Musil. Alois Musil. LC 77-87092. (American Geographical Society Oriental Explorations & Studies: Map Vol.). reprint ed. 49.50 (*0-404-60237-1*) AMS Pr.

Northern Arabian Platform Transect: Across the Palmyride Mountain Belt Syrian Arab Republic. 1991. 59.85 (*0-87590-778-4*, GGT 1) Am Geophysical.

Northern Arcadia: Foreign Travelers in Scandinavia, 1765-1815. H. Arnold Barton. LC 98-15892. (Illus.). 224p. 1999. 39.95 (*0-8093-2203-X*) S Ill U Pr.

Northern Arizona Death & Burial Records, 1936-1969. Dora M. Whiteside. 62p. (Orig.). 1989. pap. 8.00 (*0-938353-09-8*) D M Whiteside.

Northern Arizona Territorial Death & Burial Records, 1870-1910. Dora M. Whiteside. 32p. (Orig.). 1988. pap. 4.50 (*0-938353-08-X*) D M Whiteside.

Northern Asia. Mary Tull et al. LC 98-49462. (Artisans Around the World Ser.). 1999. write for info. Raintree Steck-V.

***Northern Asia: Understanding Geography & History Through Art.** Mary Tull et al. LC 98-49462. (Artisans Around the World Ser.). (Illus.). 48p. (YA). (gr. 5 up). 1999. lib. bdg. 25.69 (*0-7398-0119-8*) Raintree Steck-V.

Northern Balcony Gardening. Brian Andrews. 1992. pap. 5.95 (*0-919433-98-7*) Lone Pine.

Northern Bantu. John Roscoe. (Illus.). 305p. 1966. reprint ed. 45.00 (*0-7146-1713-X*, BHA-01713, Pub. by F Cass Pubs) Intl Spec Bk.

Northern Blood, Vol. 1. large type ed. (Magna Large Print Ser.). 336p. 1996. 27.99 (*0-7505-1026-9*, Pub. by Mgna Lrg Print) Ulverscroft.

Northern Blood 2. large type ed. Ed. by Martin Edwards. (Magna Large Print Ser.). 376p. 1997. 27.99 (*0-7505-1027-7*) Ulverscroft.

Northern Boyhood. Ralph A. Casperson. 500p. 1993. 27.95 (*1-883228-00-X*) Invictus MI.

Northern Calendar. Ira Sadoff. 80p. 1982. pap. 8.95 (*0-87923-367-2*) Godine.

Northern California. Lee Foster. (Adventure Guide). 367p. 1998. pap. text 16.95 (*1-55650-821-2*) Hunter NJ.

Northern California. Insight Guides Staff. (Insight Guides). 1998. pap. text 12.95 (*0-88729-923-7*) Langenscheidt.

Northern California. Brad Olsen. (Extreme Adventure Guide). 252p. 1998. pap. text 13.95 (*1-55650-808-5*) Hunter NJ.

Northern California: Off the Beaten Path: A Guide to Unique Places. 3rd ed. Mark Williams. (Illus.). 192p. 1999. pap. text 12.95 (*0-7627-0461-6*) Globe Pequot.

***Northern California Atlas.** 5th ed. Delorme Publishing Company Staff. (Illus.). 2000. pap. 19.95 (*0-89933-287-0*) DeLorme Map.

***Northern California Atlas & Gazetteer.** 4th ed. DeLorme US Staff. (Illus.). 128p. 1998. reprint ed. 16.95 (*0-89933-267-6*) DeLorme Map.

***Northern California Best Places Cookbook: Recipes from the Region's Outstanding Restaurants & Inns.** Cynthia C. Nims & Carolyn Dille. LC 99-15349. (Best Places Ser.). 256p. 1999. pap. 19.95 (*1-57061-183-1*) Sasquatch Bks.

Northern California Book Finder. 8th ed. 1994. pap. 5.95 (*0-9625673-4-5*) J Greenblatt.

***Northern California Business Directory (2000-2001)** American Business Directories Staff et al. 4,704p. 2000. boxed set 415.00 incl. cd-rom (*0-7687-0226-7*) Am Busn Direct.

***Northern California Business Directory, 1999-2000.** American Business Directories Staff. 4704p. 1999. boxed set 415.00 incl. cd-rom (*0-7687-0141-4*, 1063-4177) Am Busn Direct.

Northern California Cheap Sleeps: Recommendations for the Budget Traveler. Ed. by Rebecca P. Foree. 320p. (Orig.). 1995. pap. 14.95 (*1-57061-025-8*) Sasquatch Bks.

Northern California Church Member Study, 1963. Charles Y. Glock & Rodney Stark. LC 79-63206. 1979. write for info. (*0-89138-980-6*) ICPSR.

Northern California Coast Best Places. 2nd ed. Matthew R. Poole. (Illus.). 208p. 1999. pap. 12.95 (*1-57061-173-4*) Sasquatch Bks.

Northern California Coast Best Places: A Destination Guide. Ed. by Matthew R. Poole. 224p. (Orig.). 1996. pap. 11.95 (*1-57061-051-7*) Sasquatch Bks.

Northern California County Forms on Hotdocs. cd-rom 105.00 (*0-8205-4291-1*) Bender.

Northern California Dog Owners Guide: The Starter Book. Bob Christiansen & Laura Christiansen. 240p. (Orig.). 1994. pap. 9.95 (*1-884421-21-0*) Canine Lrning.

***Northern California Events Calendar 2001: The Definitive Events Calendar for the Adventurous & Curious Minded.** Christine Lee. 28p. 2000. pap. 12.95 (*0-9661987-4-3*, Pub. by LT Comm) SCB Distributors.

Northern California Gardening: A Month-by-Month Guide. Katherine G. Endicott. 384p. 1996. pap. 22.95 (*0-8118-0926-9*) Chronicle Bks.

Northern California Indian Basketry see Basketry of the Indians of California

Northern California Media Resource Guide. Ed. by Fred Gillaspy. 100p. (Orig.). 1986. pap. 16.25 (*0-941529-00-2*, MR602) Inter-Sight Commns.

Northern California One Hundred Years Ago. William H. Bishop et al. (Historical Ser.). (Illus.). (Orig.). 1976. pap. 3.50 (*0-89540-032-4*, SB-032) Sun Pub.

Northern California, Oregon & the Sandwich Islands. Charles Nordhoff. (Illus.). 256p. 1992. reprint ed. pap. 7.95 (*0-89815-419-7*) Ten Speed Pr.

***Northern California Symplectic Geometry Seminar.** Ed. by Y. Eliashberg et al. (TRANS2 Ser.: Vol. 196). 258p. 1999. 95.00 (*0-8218-2075-3*) Am Math.

***Northern California Travel Adventure Guide.** Caroline H. Wessel & Stephen Stringall. 1998. 24.95 (*1-895907-96-9*) ITMP Pub.

Northern California's Best Family Campgrounds: 50 Fun, Affordable, Kid-Friendly Sites. Roland De Wolk. (Illus.). 132p. 1997. pap. 16.95 (*0-8118-1270-7*) Chronicle Bks.

Northern California's Guide for Fun, Excitement & Romance. Brian T. Borgia. 163p. (Orig.). 1995. pap. 10.95 (*0-9645476-1-9*) Valntne Pr.

***Northern Cambria.** Anne Frances Pulling. LC 00-104041. (Images of America Ser.). (Illus.). 128p. 2000. pap. 18.99 (*0-7385-0415-7*) Arcadia Publng.

Northern Cardinals. Gary Ritchison. LC 96-44268. (Wild Bird Studies). (Illus.). 112p. 1997. pap. 19.95 (*0-8117-3100-6*) Stackpole.

Northern Cheyenne Fire Fighters: Modern Indians Fighting Forest Fires. Henry Tall Bull & Tom Weist. 39p. (J). (gr. 4 up). 1973. pap. 5.95 (*0-89992-016-0*) Coun India Ed.

Northern Cheyenne Indian Reservation, 1877-1900. Orlan Svingen. LC 97-26021. 216p. 1997. pap. 22.50 (*0-87081-486-9*) Univ Pr Colo.

Northern Cheyenne Indian Reservation, 1877-1900. Orlan J. Svingen. 176p. 1993. 34.95 (*0-87081-303-X*) Univ Pr Colo.

***Northern Chihuahuan Desert Wildflowers.** Steve West. (Guide Ser.). (Illus.). 2000. pap. 24.95 (*1-56044-980-2*, Falcon) Falcon Pub Inc.

Northern Childhood. Layton. (Longman Literature Ser.). 1995. pap. text. write for info. (*0-582-25404-3*, Pub. by Addison-Wesley) Longman.

Northern Christmas. Rockwell Kent. LC 98-8211. (Illus.). 40p. 1998. reprint ed. boxed set 10.95 (*0-8195-6362-5*, Wesleyan Univ Pr) U Pr of New Eng.

Northern Colorado Business Report Book of Lists. annuals 76p. 1999. pap. 25.00 (*1-891973-04-5*) Boulder Busn.

Northern Colorado I-25 Golf Courses: 29 Golf Courses. Betty Martin. (Simplified Graphical Maps Ser.: Vol. 1). (Illus.). 45p. 1997. spiral bd. 21.50 (*1-890652-00-8*) Bettys Desktop.

Northern Columbia Plateau Landscapes Narrative & Field Guide. Ed. by Michael M. Folsom. 71p. (Orig.). 1984. pap. 4.50 (*0-910055-05-X*) East Wash Univ.

Northern Comfort: Advanced Cold Climate Home Building Techniques. Ed. by Timothy M. Sullivan et al. (Illus.). 300p. 1995. pap. 40.00 (*0-9636075-0-2*) AK Craftsman.

Northern Comfort: New England's Early Quilts 1780-1850. Jack Larkin & Lynne Z. Bassett. LC 98-5678. (Illus.). 128p. 1998. pap. 19.95 (*1-55853-655-8*) Rutledge Hill Pr.

Northern Commonwealth: Scotland & Norway. Gordon Donaldson. (C). 1993. pap. 21.00 (*0-85411-044-5*, Pub. by Saltire Soc) St Mut.

Northern Community: A Search for a Quality Environment. Ed. by Ted S. Vinson. LC 81-65629. 794p. 1981. pap. 7.00 (*0-87262-267-3*) Am Soc Civil Eng.

Northern Copper Inuit: A History. Richard G. Condon et al. LC 95-39186. (Civilization of the American Indian Ser.: Vol. 220). (Illus.). 240p. (C). 1996. 29.95 (*0-8061-2811-9*, 2811) U of Okla Pr.

Northern Copper Inuit: A History. Richard G. Condon et al. (Illus.). 240p. 1996. text 45.00 (*0-8020-0849-6*) U of Toronto Pr.

***Northern Counties from A. D. 1000.** Norman McCord & Richard Thompson. LC 97-38880. (Regional History of England Ser.). 480p. (C). 1998. pap. text 42.19 (*0-582-49334-X*) Addison-Wesley.

***Northern Counties from Ad 1000.** Norman McCord & Richard Thompson. LC 97-38880. (Regional History of England Ser.). 480p. 1998. 98.00 (*0-582-49333-1*) Longman.

Northern Crusades. Eric Christiansen. LC 98-161230. 304p. 1998. pap. 13.95 (*0-14-026653-4*) Viking Penguin.

Northern Cyprus: A Traveller's Guide. Elieen Davey. (Illus.). 256p. 1994. 19.95 (*1-85043-747-5*, Pub. by I B T) St Martin.

Northern Cyprus in the Transition from the Early to the Middle Cypriot Period: Typology, Relative & Absolute Chronology of Some Early Cypriot III to Middle Cypriot I Tombs. Ina Kehrberg. (Studies in Mediterranean Archaeology & Literature: No. 108). (Illus.). 363p. (Orig.). 1995. pap. 57.50 (*91-7081-089-3*, Pub. by P Astroms) Coronet Bks.

***Northern Dancer: The Legend & His Legacy.** Muriel A. Lennox. (Illus.). 222p. 1999. pap. 13.95 (*0-9699025-1-4*) King3gfisher Communs.

***Northern Dancer: The Legend & His Legacy.** 2nd ed. Muriel A. Lennox. (Illus.). 222p. 1998. write for info. (*0-9699025-0-6*) BEA1.

***Northern Danelaw: Its Social Structure, C. 800-1100.** D. M. Hadley. LC 99-87413. (Studies in the Early History of Britain). 2000. write for info. (*0-7185-0014-8*, Pub. by Leicester U Pr) Cassell & Continuum.

Northern Dawn & Other Poems. Jedediah V. Huntington. (Notable American Authors Ser.). 1992. reprint ed. lib. bdg. 75.00 (*0-7812-3286-4*) Rprt Serv.

Northern Delights. Virginia MacKay. (Illus.). 108p. 1994. pap. text 8.00 (*1-885781-00-8*) Soapstone Pr.

Northern D'Lights: Another Hilarious Account of "Growing up North" Jerry Harju. Ed. by Pat Green. LC 94-72584. (Illus.). 151p. 1992. pap. 12.95 (*0-9670205-2-2*, Pub. by N Harbor Pub) Partners Bk Dist.

Northern Dreamers: Interviews with Famous Canadian Science Fiction, Fantasy & Horror Writers. Edo Van Belkom. LC 98-187370. (Illus.). 272p. 1998. pap. 14.95 (*1-55082-206-3*, Pub. by Quarry Pr) LPC InBook.

Northern Drift: Sketches on the New York Frontier. John Golden. LC 98-93238. (Illus.). xv, 320p. 1998. pap. 15.95 (*0-9665357-0-7*) City Exile Co.

Northern Dynasties: Kingship & Statecraft in Chimor: Symposium at Dumbarton Oaks, October 12 & 13, 1985. Ed. by Michael E. Moseley & Alana Cordy-Collins. LC 89-23336. (Illus.). 560p. 1990. 40.00 (*0-88402-180-7*, MCND) Dumbarton Oaks.

Northern, Eastern & Central Europe see World Architecture 1900-2000: A Critical Mosaic

Northern Editorials on Secession, 2 vols., Set. Howard C. Perkins. 1990. 31.00 (*0-8446-1347-9*) Peter Smith.

Northern Editorials on Secession, 2 vols., Set. Howard C. Perkins. (History - United States Ser.). 1993. reprint ed. lib. bdg. 150.00 (*0-7812-4891-4*) Rprt Serv.

Northern English Books, Owners & Makers in the Late Middle Ages. John B. Friedman. (Illus.). 352p. (C). 1995. text 39.95 (*0-8156-2649-5*) Syracuse U Pr.

Northern Eskimo Stories. Kathleen Lynch. (Illus.). 30p. (Orig.). 1974. reprint ed. pap. 7.95 (*1-878051-30-X*, CP058) Circumpolar Pr.

Northern Europe see International Dictionary of Historic Places

Northern Europe. Rand McNally Staff. pap. 16.95 (*0-528-91490-1*) Rand McNally.

Northern European Books: Sixteenth to Early Nineteenth Centuries, Vol. 3. Harry P. Mallgrave. 1999. 90.00 (*0-8076-1459-9*) Braziller.

Northern European Paintings in the Philadelphia Museum of Art: From the Sixteenth Through the Nineteenth Century. Peter C. Sutton. LC 89-72149. (Illus.). 400p. (Orig.). 1990. pap. 20.00 (*0-87633-082-0*) Phila Mus Art.

Northern European Paintings in the Philadelphia Museum of Art from the Sixteenth Through the Nineteenth Century: From the Sixteenth Through the Nineteenth Century. Peter C. Sutton. (Illus.). 400p. (C). 1990. 62.95 (*0-8122-8239-6*) U of Pa Pr.

Northern Exposure Book: The Official Publication of the Television Series. rev. ed. Louis Chunovic. (Illus.). 224p. 1995. pap. 17.95 (*0-8065-1623-2*, Citadel Pr) Carol Pub Group.

Northern Exposure Book: The Official Publication of the Television Show. Louis Chunovic. LC 92-37592. 1993. 16.95 (*0-8065-1409-4*) Carol Pub Group.

"Northern Exposure" Cookbook. Ellis Weiner. 176p. 1993. pap. 12.95 (*0-8092-3760-1*, 376010, Contemporary Bks) NTC Contemp Pub Co.

Northern Exposures. Photos by Rob Morrow. (Illus.). 96p. (J). 1994. pap. 9.70 (*0-7868-6064-2*, Pub. by Hyperion) Time Warner.

Northern Exposures: Scholarship on Canada in the United States. Ed. by Joseph T. Jockel et al. 420p. 1993. pap. text 19.95 (*1-883027-00-4*) Assn Can Studies.

Northern Farm. Henry Beston. 1995. pap. 9.95 (*0-8050-3092-1*) H Holt & Co.

Northern Farm A Glorious Year on A Small Maine Farm. Henry Beston. LC 99-28762. 1999. 25.95 (*0-7838-8657-8*) Macmillan Gen Ref.

Northern Farmer & His Markets During the Late Colonial Period. Max G. Schumacher. LC 75-2594. (Dissertations in American Economic History Ser.). (Illus.). 1975. 23.95 (*0-405-07216-3*) Ayer.

Northern Fields: New & Selected Poems. Chuck Miller. LC 93-26007. 128p. (Orig.). 1994. pap. 11.95 (*1-56689-014-4*) Coffee Hse.

Northern Fishes: With Special Reference to the Upper Mississippi Valley. Samuel K. Eddy. LC 73-83729. 434p. reprint ed. pap. 134.60 (*0-608-13259-4*, 205585800039) Bks Demand.

Northern Flame: Studies on the Legacy of Columba. Ed. by Cormac Bourke. 256p. 1996. 45.00 (*1-85182-268-2*, Pub. by Four Cts Pr) Intl Spec Bk.

Northern Flights: Tracking the Birds & Birders of Michigan's Upper Peninsula. Sheryl DeVore. LC 99-29655. (Illus.). 166p. 1999. pap. 12.00 (*0-87842-400-8*) Mountain Pr.

Northern Foreign Policy. Franklyn Griffiths. LC 79-319693. (Wellesley Papers: No. 7). 91p. reprint ed. pap. 30.00 (*0-8357-6445-1*, 203581600097) Bks Demand.

***Northern Forest.** Greg Breining. LC 98-48644. (Ecosystems of North America Ser.). (gr. 4-7). 2000. lib. bdg. 27.07 (*0-7614-0901-7*, Benchmark NY) Marshall Cavendish.

Northern Forest. David Dobbs & Richard Ober. 288p. 1996. pap. 19.95 (*0-930031-81-4*) Chelsea Green Pub.

Northern Forest Border in Canada & Alaska. J. A. Larsen. (Ecological Studies: Vol. 70). (Illus.). 260p. 1988. 175.00 (*0-387-96753-2*) Spr-Verlag.

Northern Forested Wetland: Ecology & Management. Carl C. Trettin. LC 96-26666. 512p. 1996. lib. bdg. 85.00 (*1-56670-177-5*) Lewis Pubs.

Northern France David W. Hogan, Jr. LC 96-233405. 31p. 1994. write for info. (*0-16-045117-5*) USGPO.

Northern France & Paris Region Green Guide: France (Regional Guides) 3rd ed. Michelin Staff. (Green Guides Ser.). (Illus.). 1997. per. 20.00 (*2-06-134403-8*, 1344) Michelin.

***Northern Frights.** Don Hutchison. 1999. pap. 15.00 (*0-88962-676-6*) Midpoint Natl.

Northern Frights. Ed. by Don Hutchison. 205p. 1992. 19.95 (*0-88962-515-8*) Mosaic.

Northern Frights. Ed. by Don Hutchison. LC 96-121536. 224p. 1995. pap. 16.95 (*0-88962-589-1*) Mosaic.

Northern Frights, No. 2. Ed. by Don Hutchison. LC 94-930527. (Illus.). 200p. 1996. pap. 16.95 (*0-88962-564-6*) Mosaic.

Northern Frights: A Supernatural Ecology of the Wisconsin Headwaters. Dennis Boyer. LC 98-8584. (Illus.). 224p. 1998. pap. 14.95 (*1-879483-53-X*) Prairie Oak Pr.

Northern Frights, No. 4. Ed. by Don Hutchinson. 1997. pap. 12.95 (*0-88962-639-1*) Mosaic.

Northern Front Range Book of Lists, 1998. annuals Ed. by Chris Wood. 80p. 1998. pap. 25.00 (*1-891973-01-0*) Boulder Busn.

Northern Frontier: The Policies & Strategy of the Later Han Empire. Rafe De Crespigny. (Faculty of Asian Studies Monographs: Vol. 4). (Illus.). 650p. 1997. pap. text 60.00 (*0-86784-410-8*, Pub. by Aust Nat Univ) UH Pr.

Northern Frontier of India - The Border Dispute with China. Sahdev Vohra. (C). 1993. 20.00 (*81-7076-051-8*, Pub. by Intellectual) S Asia.

Northern Frontier Problems. Ed. by W. Tietze. 100p. (C). 1975. pap. 23.00 (*0-08-019675-6*, Pergamon Pr) Elsevier.

Northern Georgia Sketches. William N. Harben. LC 73-110194. (Short Story Index Reprint Ser.). 1977. 21.95 (*0-8369-3345-1*) Ayer.

***Northern Girl.** Elizabeth A. Lynn. (Chronicles of Tornor Ser.: Vol. 3). 470p. 2000. pap. 14.00 (*0-441-00727-9*) Berkley Pub.

Northern Gold Fleet: Twentieth-Century Gold Dredging in Alaska. Clark C. Spence. LC 95-32474. 336p. 1996. text 44.95 (*0-252-02218-1*) U of Ill Pr.

Northern Goshank. Thomas Bosakowski. Ed. by Nancy Miller. (Illus.). 80p. 1999. pap. 35.00 (*0-88839-454-3*) Hancock House.

Northern Gothic. Lois B. Hayna. 96p. 1991. pap. 10.00 (*1-880723-00-X*) Morgan Pr WI.

Northern Governments in Transition: Political & Constitutional Development in the Yukon, Nunavut & the Western Northwest Territories. Kirk Cameron & Graham White. LC 96-111285. (Illus.). 152p. 1995. pap. 14.95 (*0-88645-177-9*, Pub. by Inst Res Pub) Ashgate Pub Co.

Northern Great Plains Rural Development Commission: Overview & Recommendation. Ed. by Roger D. McKellips. (Illus.). 40p. (C). 1998. pap. text 20.00 (*0-7881-7464-9*) DIANE Pub.

Northern Gulf Islands Explorer: The Outdoor Guide. Elaine Jones. (Illus.). 208p. 1994. pap., student ed. 12.95 (*1-895099-41-2*) Whitecap Bks.

Northern Haida Songs. John Enrico & Wendy B. Stuart. LC 96-4211. (Studies in the Anthropology of North American Indians). xiv, 519p. 1996. text 50.00 (*0-8032-1816-8*) U of Nebr Pr.

Northern Hegaz: A Topographical Itinerary. Alois Musil. LC 77-87084. (American Geographical Society Oriental Explorations & Studies: No. 1). reprint ed. 55.00 (*0-404-60231-2*) AMS Pr.

***Northern Highlands: The Empty Lands, Lands of Endless Natural Beauty, Including Wester Ross, Caithness & Sutherland.** Tom Atkinson. (Guides to Scotland Ser.). (Illus.). 160p. 1999. pap. 9.95 (*0-946487-55-3*, Pub. by Luath Pr Ltd) Midpt Trade.

***Northern Horror: Canadian Fiction Anthology.** Ed. by Edo Van Belkom. 240p. 1999. pap. 14.95 (*1-55082-266-7*) Quarry Pr.

Northern Humanism Between 1469 & 1625. Fokke Akkerman et al. LC 99-17135. 250p. 1999. write for info. (*90-04-11314-2*) Brill Academic Pubs.

Northern Hungary. Sandor A. Kostya. (Illus.). 232p. (C). 1992. 15.00 (*1-882785-00-2*, HTA) Matthias Corvinus.

***Northern Identities: Historical Interpretations of "The North" & "Northerness"** Neville Kirk. LC 99-58481. 2000. write for info. (*0-7546-0039-4*, Pub. by Ashgate Pub) Ashgate Pub Co.

Northern Imagination. Allison Mitcham. 103p. 1983. 17.95 (*0-920806-46-5*, Pub. by Penumbra Pr); pap. 7.95 (*0-920806-47-3*, Pub. by Penumbra Pr) U of Toronto Pr.

Northern India: Rajasthan, Agra, Delhi. Philip Ward. LC 89-33396. (Illus.). 256p. 1989. pap. 15.95 (*0-88289-753-5*) Pelican.

Northern Indiana Railway: Bulletin No. 132. George K. Bradley. LC 98-73157. (Illus.). 244p. 1999. 55.00 (*0-915348-32-2*, B-132) Central Electric.

Northern Ireland. Robert Blair et al. LC 86-8296. (Illus.). 116p. 1986. 25.00 (*0-85640-365-2*, Pub. by Blackstaff Pr) Dufour.

Northern Ireland. Michael O. Shannon. (World Bibliographical Ser.). 1992. lib. bdg. 136.50 (*1-85109-032-0*) ABC-CLIO.

***Northern Ireland.** 2nd ed. Paul Bew & Gordon Gillespie. LC 99-48569. 384p. 1999. 45.00 (*0-8108-3735-8*) Scarecrow.

Northern Ireland. 2nd ed. Central Office of Info. LC 96-201614. (Aspects of Britain Ser.). (Illus.). 131p. 1997. pap. 12.95 (*0-11-702009-5*, Pub. by Statnry Office) Bernan Associates.

Northern Ireland: A Comparative Analysis. Frank Lloyd Wright. 1987. 53.00 (*0-389-20769-1*) Rowman.

N

Northern Ireland: A Political Directory, 1968-1993. rev. ed. W. D. Flackes & Sydney Elliott. 513p. 1995. pap. 29.00 (*0-85640-429-2*, Pub. by Blackstaff Pr) Dufour.

Northern Ireland: A Political Directory, 1968-1993. 2nd ed. Ed. by W. D. Flackes & S. Elliott. 544p. 1995. pap. 29.00 (*0-85640-527-2*, Pub. by Blackstaff Pr) Dufour.

Northern Ireland: A Political Directory 1968-88. W. D. Flackes & Sydney Elliot. LC 89-81120. 400p. 1990. pap. 19.95 (*0-85640-418-7*, Pub. by Blackstaff Pr) Dufour.

Northern Ireland: A Psychological Analysis. Ken Heskin. LC 80-13407. 192p. 1980. text 46.00 (*0-231-05138-7*) Col U Pr.

Northern Ireland: Accountability in Northern Ireland to Serve Without Favor, Policing, & Human Rights. Human Rights Watch/Helsinki Staff. LC 97-73331. 185p. 1997. pap. 15.00 (*1-56432-216-5*) Hum Rts Watch.

Northern Ireland: Conflict & Change. Johnathan Tonge. LC 97-42854. 208p. 1998. pap. text. write for info. (*0-13-534181-7*) P-H.

Northern Ireland: Faith & Faction. Maurice Irvine. 272p. (C). (gr. 13). 1991. text 89.95 (*0-415-05579-2*, A5269) Routledge.

Northern Ireland: Living with the Crisis. Ed. by Alan J. Ward. LC 86-15157. 240p. 1987. 59.95 (*0-275-92306-1*, C2306, Praeger Pubs) Greenwood.

Northern Ireland: Major World Nations. Mary Jane Cahill. LC 99-13780. (Major World Nations Ser.). (Illus.). 144p. (YA). (gr. 5 up). 1998. 19.95 (*0-7910-4764-4*) Chelsea Hse.

Northern Ireland: Politics & the Constitution. Ed. by Brigid Hadfield. 192p. 1992. 118.00 (*0-335-09963-7*); pap. 34.95 (*0-335-09962-9*) OpUniv Pr.

Northern Ireland: Society under Siege. Rona M. Fields. LC 80-80316. 267p. 1980. pap. 24.95 (*0-87855-806-3*) Transaction Pubs.

Northern Ireland: The Background to the Conflict. Ed. by John Darby. 176p. 1987. pap. 17.95 (*0-8156-2417-4*) Syracuse U Pr.

Northern Ireland: The Context for Conflict & for Reconciliation. Craig E. Seaton. LC 97-52964. 296p. (C). 1998. pap. 32.50 (*0-7618-1031-5*) U Pr of Amer.

Northern Ireland: The Orange State. 2nd ed. Michael Farrell. (C). pap. 22.95 (*0-86104-300-6*, Pub. by Pluto GBR) Stylus Pub VA.

Northern Ireland: The Thatcher Years. Mike Morrissey & Frank Gaffikin. LC 89-25027. (Illus.). 160p. (C). 1990. pap. 15.00 (*0-86232-907-8*, Pub. by Zed Books); text 45.00 (*0-86232-906-X*, Pub. by Zed Books) St Martin.

Northern Ireland: Time of Choice. Richard Rose. LC 76-10080. (Foreign Affairs Study Ser.: No. 33). (Illus.). 185p. reprint ed. pap. 57.40 (*0-8357-4515-5*, 203737300008) Bks Demand.

Northern Ireland: Troubled Land. Eric Black. LC 96-43639. (World in Conflict Ser.). 1997. lib. bdg. 25.26 (*0-8225-3552-1*, Lerner Publctns) Lerner Pub.

Northern Ireland & Beyond. Emilio Biagini. (GeoJournal Library: Vol. 33). 1996. lib. bdg. 129.00 (*0-7923-4046-9*) Kluwer Academic.

Northern Ireland & the Politics of Reconciliation. Ed. by Dermot F. Keogh & Michael H. Haltzel. (Woodrow Wilson Center Press Ser.). 279p. (C). 1994. pap. text 19.95 (*0-521-45933-8*) Cambridge U Pr.

***Northern Ireland & the Prison Ship of 1922.** Denise Kleinrichert. (Illus.). 288p. 2000. 52.50 (*0-7165-2683-2*, Pub. by Irish Acad Pr) Intl Spec Bk.

***Northern Ireland at the Crossroads.** Marc Mulholland. LC 99-46717. 272p. 2000. text 69.95 (*0-312-22835-X*) St Martin.

Northern Ireland Economy: Performance, Prospects & Policy. Esmond Birnie & David M. Hitchens. LC HC257.N58B57 1999. 210p. 1999. text 65.95 (*1-84014-848-9*) Ashgate Pub Co.

***Northern Ireland Health & Personal Social Services: Controls to Prevent & Detect Fraud in Family Practitioner Service Payments : Report.** Northern Ireland. Comptroller and Auditor General. LC 98-203521. 1998. write for info. (*0-10-251898-X*) Statnry Office.

Northern Ireland in Pictures. Ed. by Lerner Geography Department Staff. (Visual Geography Ser.). (Illus.). 64p. (YA). (gr. 5 up). 1991. reprint ed. lib. bdg. 19.95 (*0-8225-1898-8*, Lerner Publctns) Lerner Pub.

Northern Ireland in the Second World War. Brian Barton. (Illus.). 164p. (Orig.). 1996. pap. 16.95 (*0-901905-69-0*, Pub. by Ulster Hist Fnd) Irish Bks Media.

Northern Ireland Loyalty Study, 1968. Richard Rose. LC 75-32210. 1975. write for info. (*0-89138-116-3*) ICPSR.

Northern Ireland, 1921-1994. Paul Bew et al. 1995. pap. 23.95 (*1-897959-08-7*) LPC InBook.

Northern Ireland, 1921-1996: Political Forces & Social Classes. Paul Bew et al. LC 97-115439. 272p. 1998. pap. 24.95 (*1-897959-24-9*, Pub. by Serif) IPG Chicago.

Northern Ireland Peace Process, 1993-1996: A Chronology. Paul Bew & Gordon Gillespie. LC 97-124832. 192p. 1998. pap. 17.95 (*1-897959-28-1*, Pub. by Serif) IPG Chicago.

***Northern Ireland Politics.** 2000. write for info. (*0-582-40484-3*) Pearson Educ.

Northern Ireland Politics. Arthur Aughey & Duncan Morrow. LC 95-45047. 224p. (C). 1996. pap. text 23.44 (*0-582-25346-2*, Pub. by Addison-Wesley) Longman.

Northern Ireland Problem: A Study in Group Relations. Denis P. Barritt & Charles F. Carter. LC 82-15568. 163p. 1982. reprint ed. lib. bdg. 55.00 (*0-313-23262-8*, BANI, Greenwood Pr) Greenwood.

Northern Ireland Question: Myth & Reality. Patrick J. Roche & Brian Barton. 225p. 1991. text 77.95 (*1-85628-147-7*, Pub. by Avebry) Ashgate Pub Co.

***Northern Ireland Question: Nationalism, Unionism & Partition.** Ed. by Patrick J. Roche & Brian Barton. 206p. (C). 1999. text 69.95 (*1-84014-490-4*) Ashgate Pub Co.

Northern Ireland Question: Perspectives & Policies. Ed. by Brian Barton & Patrick J. Roche. 224p. 1994. 61.95 (*1-85628-881-1*, Pub. by Avebry) Ashgate Pub Co.

Northern Ireland Question in British Politics. Ed. by Peter Catterall & Sean McDougall. LC 95-53126. 256p. 1996. text 65.00 (*0-312-12982-3*) St Martin.

Northern Ireland since 1945. Sabine Wichert. 234p. (C). 1995. pap. text 41.00 (*0-582-02392-0*, 78928) Addson-Wesley Educ.

***Northern Ireland since 1945.** 2nd ed. S. Wichert. LC 99-14758. 288p. (C). 1999. pap. 32.46 (*0-582-32678-8*) Addison-Wesley.

***Northern Ireland's Troubles: The Human Costs.** Marie-Therese Fay. LC 98-45434. 1999. write for info. (*0-7453-1379-5*) Pluto GBR.

Northern Italian Cooking. rev. ed. Biba Caggiano. (Illus.). 192p. 1992. pap. 15.95 (*1-55788-051-4*, HP Books) Berkley Pub.

Northern Italy. (Insight Guides Ser.). (Illus.). 1999. pap. 22.95 (*0-88729-285-2*) Langenscheidt.

Northern Italy, Pt. 1. Ed. by Anne Schnoebelen. LC 87-750554. (Solo Motets from the Seventeenth Century Ser.). 256p. 1987. text 30.00 (*0-8240-0637-2*) Garland.

Northern Italy: A Taste of Trattoria. rev. ed. Christina Baglivi. LC 95-7028. (Illus.). 240p. (Orig.). 1995. pap. 12.95 (*0-914457-72-1*) Mustang Pub.

Northern Kentucky: Looking to the New Millennium, a 100-Year Reflection. Steve Cauthen. LC 99-49625. (Illus.). 1999. 49.95 (*1-881096-74-2*) Towery Pub.

Northern Kentucky Earthquake of July 27, 1980. R. D. Hanson et al. 105p. 1980. pap. 12.00 (*0-318-16326-8*) Earthquake Eng.

Northern Labor & Antislavery: A Documentary History, 157. Philip S. Foner & Herbert Shapiro. LC 93-44515. (Contributions in American History Ser.: No. 157). 336p. 1994. 69.50 (*0-313-27807-5*, Greenwood Pr) Greenwood.

Northern Ladies' Civil War Recipes. rev. ed. Patricia B. Mitchell. 1994. pap. text 4.00 (*0-925117-75-7*) Mitchells.

Northern Latitudes. Lawrence Millman. 1999. pap. text 16.95 (*0-9666750-2-9*, Pub. by Nocturnum Pr) Consort Bk Sales.

***Northern Latitudes: Prose Poems.** Lawrence Millman. (Marie Alexander Prose Poetry Ser.: Vol. 3). 96p. 2000. 14.95 (*0-89823-207-4*, Pub. by New Rivers Pr) Consort Bk Sales.

Northern Light. large type ed. A. J. Cronin. 432p. 1989. 27.99 (*0-7089-8500-9*, Charnwood) Ulverscroft.

Northern Light: From Mythology to Space Research. A. Brekke & Alv Egeland. (Illus.). 190p. 1983. 119.00 (*0-387-12429-2*) Spr-Verlag.

Northern Light: Nordic Art at the Turn of the Century. Kirk Varnedoe. LC 87-50644. (Illus.). 1988. pap. text 60.00 (*0-300-04146-2*) Yale U Pr.

Northern Light: Nordic Art at the Turn of the Century. Kirk Varnedoe. LC 87-50644. (Illus.). 286p. 1988. reprint ed. pap. 88.70 (*0-608-07849-2*, 205402500011) Bks Demand.

Northern Lights. (In Classical Mood Ser.: Vol. 22). (Illus.). 1998. write for info. incl. cd-rom (*1-886614-42-3*) Intl Masters Pub.

Northern Lights. Susan Canizares. LC 97-34210. (Science Emergent Readers Ser.). (J). 1998. lib. bdg. 2.50 (*0-590-76155-2*) Scholastic Inc.

***Northern Lights.** Anne Colledge. 94p. (YA). (gr. 3 up). 2000. 12.00 (*1-902628-75-6*) Pipers Ash.

Northern Lights. Desmond Holdridge. (Illus.). 244p. 1998. pap. 15.95 (*1-885031-00-9*, Capstan Pr) Merritt Communs.

Northern Lights. Charles K. Hyde. LC 85-62139. 208p. 1986. 29.95 (*0-941912-09-4*) Mich Nat Res.

***Northern Lights.** Drago Jancar. 2000. pap. 16.95 (*0-8101-1839-4*) Northwestern U Pr.

Northern Lights. Howard Norman. 240p. 1988. pap. 10.00 (*0-671-65877-8*, WSP) PB.

***Northern Lights.** Tim O'Brien. LC 99-28842. 368p. 1999. pap. 13.00 (*0-7679-0441-9*) Broadway BDD.

Northern Lights. D. M. Souza. (Illus.). 48p. (J). (gr. 1-4). 1994. pap. 7.95 (*0-87614-629-9*, Carolrhoda) Lerner Pub.

Northern Lights. Dorothy M. Souza. LC 93-3027. (Nature in Action Ser.). (J). (gr. 1-4). 1993. lib. bdg. 19.95 (*0-87614-799-6*, Carolrhoda) Lerner Pub.

***Northern Lights.** large type ed. Frances Nugent. 360p. 2000. 31.99 (*0-7089-4173-7*) Ulverscroft.

Northern Lights: A Curriculum of Minnesota, 1989, 2 bks. Rhoda R. Gilman & Stephen Sandell. 446p. 1990. student ed. 29.95 (*0-87351-243-X*); teacher ed., ring bd. 59.95 (*0-87351-244-8*) Minn Hist.

Northern Lights: A Hanukkah Story. Diana C. Conway. (Illus.). 32p. (J). (ps-3). 1994. pap. 6.95 (*0-929371-80-1*) Kar-Ben.

***Northern Lights: A Poet's Sources.** George Mackay Brown. (Illus.). 336p. 2000. 29.95 (*0-7195-5949-9*, Pub. by John Murray) Trafalgar.

Northern Lights: A Selection of New Writing from the American West. Ed. by Deborah Clow & Donald Snow. 1995. 23.00 (*0-8446-6825-7*) Peter Smith.

Northern Lights: Inuit Textile Art from the Canadian Arctic. Katharine W. Fernstrom & Anita E. Jones. LC 93-36412. 1993. 14.95 (*0-912298-66-9*) Baltimore Mus.

***Northern Lights: Lighthouses of Canada.** David Baird. 260p. 1999. pap. 21.95 (*1-894073-09-6*) Lynx Images.

Northern Lights: Lighthouses of the Upper Great Lakes. Charles K. Hyde. LC 94-45598. (Illus.). 208p. 1995. reprint ed. 34.95 (*0-8143-2554-8*, Great Lks Bks) Wayne St U Pr.

Northern Lights: Poems. fac. ed. Susan Ludvigson. LC 81-6039. 79p. 1981. reprint ed. pap. 30.00 (*0-7837-7805-8*, 204756100007) Bks Demand.

Northern Lights: The Soccer Trails. Michael A. Kusugak. (Illus.). 24p. (J). (ps-2). 1993. pap. 6.95 (*1-55037-338-2*, Pub. by Annick); lib. bdg. 16.95 (*1-55037-339-0*, Pub. by Annick) Firefly Bks Ltd.

Northern Litchfield Hills. Betsy McDermott Fecto. (Images of America Ser.). 128p. 1996. pap. 16.99 (*0-7524-0247-1*) Arcadia Publng.

Northern Lites: A Brave New Wildwoods. Don Oakland. (Illus.). 240p. (Orig.). 1990. pap. 7.95 (*0-9615242-2-7*) Oak Pr.

***Northern Lites: A Fireside Reading Companion.** Jack Kraywinkle. 150p. 1999. pap. 11.95 (*1-885061-26-9*) Adventure Pubns.

Northern Lites: Contemporary Cooking with a Twist. Rose Chaney & Connie Berghan. (Illus.). 132p. 1998. 39.95 (*0-9662467-0-5*) Northern Lites.

Northern Magick: Rune Mysteries & Shamanism. 2nd rev. ed. Edred Thorsson. LC 98-22729. (Llewellyn's World Religion & Magic Ser.). 264p. 1998. pap. 12.95 (*1-56718-709-9*, K709) Llewellyn Pubns.

Northern Maidu. Marie Potts. LC 77-10739. (Illus.). 48p. 1977. pap. 7.95 (*0-87961-070-0*) Naturegraph.

Northern Maidu. Roland B. Dixon. LC 76-43692. (AMNH. Bulletin Ser.: Vol. XVII, Pt. 3). 152p. 1983. reprint ed. 39.50 (*0-404-15523-5*) AMS Pr.

Northern Mariana Islands: Hearing Before the Committee on Energy & Natural Resources, United States Senate, One Hundred Fifth Congress, Second Session on S. 1100 ... S. 1275 ... March 31, 1998. United States. LC 98-211755. iii, 137p. 1998. write for info. (*0-16-057281-9*) USGPO.

***Northern Mariana Islands Business & Investment Opportunities Yearbook: Investment, Export-Import & Other Business Opportunities & Contacts, 110 vols.** International Business Publications, USA Staff & Global Investment Center, USA Staff. (World Business Opportunities Library Ser.: Vol. 201). 350p. 2000. pap. 99.95 (*0-7397-1087-7*) Intl Business Pubns.

***Northern Mariana Islands Business Law Handbook: Basic Business Legislation & Regulations Affecting Business & Investing Activities, 110 Vols.** International Business Publications, USA Staff & Global Investment Center, USA Staff. (World Law Handbooks Library: Vol. 201). (Illus.). 2000. pap. 99.95 (*0-7397-1086-9*) Intl Business Pubns.

***Northern Mariana Islands Investment & Business Guide: Investment, Export-Import, Foreign Economic Assistance Projects, Contacts & More.** International Business Publications, USA Staff & Global Investment Center, USA Staff. (World Investment Guides Library Ser.: Vol. 206). (Illus.). 350p. 2000. pap. 99.95 (*0-7397-1085-0*) Intl Business Pubns.

Northern-Midland Dialect Boundary in Illinois. Roger W. Shuy. (Publications of the American Dialect Society: No. 38). (Illus.). 79p. 1962. pap. text 7.90 (*0-8173-0638-2*) U of Ala Pr.

***Northern Miriana Islands: A Country Study Guide, 110 vols.** International Business Publications, USA Staff & Global Investment Center, USA Staff. (World Country Study Guides Library Ser.: Vol. 216). (Illus.). 350p. 2000. pap. 69.95 (*0-7397-1039-7*) Intl Business Pubns.

Northern Morocco: A Cultural Geography. Marvin W. Mikesell. LC 84-29028. 135p. 1985. reprint ed. lib. bdg. 57.50 (*0-313-23865-0*, MNOR, Greenwood Pr) Greenwood.

Northern Mysteries & Magick: Runes, Gods, & Feminine Powers. 2nd rev. ed. Freya Aswynn. LC 98-9832. 288p. 1999. 14.95 (*1-56718-047-7*) Llewellyn Pubns.

Northern Mythology. Friedrich Kauffman. Tr. by M. Steele Smith from GER. 1993. reprint ed. pap. 19.95 (*1-872736-43-2*, Pub. by Mandrake Pr) Holmes Pub.

Northern Nativity. William Kurelek. (Illus.). 48p. (J). (gr. 4 up). 1996. reprint ed. pap. 9.95 (*0-88776-099-6*) Tundra Bks.

Northern Nativity: Christmas Dreams of a Prairie Boy. William Kurelek. (Illus.). (J). 1976. pap. text 16.95 (*0-912766-41-7*) Tundra Bks.

Northern Navajo Frontier, 1860-1900: Expansion Through Adversity. Robert S. McPherson. LC 88-8593. (Illus.). 143p. 1988. reprint ed. pap. 44.40 (*0-608-04131-9*, 206486400011) Bks Demand.

Northern Negd: A Topographical Itinerary. Alois Musil. LC 77-87090. (American Geographical Society Oriental Explorations & Studies: No. 5). reprint ed. 55.00 (*0-404-60235-5*) AMS Pr.

Northern Nevada Retirement & Relocation Guide. large type ed. Robert Talley. (Retirement & Relocation Guides Ser.). (Illus.). 350p. (Orig.). Date not set. pap. 24.95 (*1-56559-101-1*) HGI-Over Fifty.

Northern New England. Vance Muse et al. LC 96-40541. (Smithsonian Guide to Historic America Ser.). 294p. 1998. pap. 19.95 (*1-55670-635-9*) Stewart Tabori & Chang.

Northern New England: Maine, New Hampshire, Vermont. Thomas G. Aylesworth & Virginia L. Aylesworth. LC 94-42012. (State Studies). 88p. (J). (gr. 4 up). 1995. lib. bdg. 18.95 (*0-7910-3397-X*) Chelsea Hse.

Northern New England: Maine, New Hampshire, Vermont. Thomas G. Aylesworth & Virginia L. Aylesworth. LC 94-42012. (State Studies). 88p. (J). (gr. 7 up). 1995. pap. 8.95 (*0-7910-3415-1*) Chelsea Hse.

Northern New England Color Guide to Freight & Passenger Equipment. S. Horlsey & David R. Sweetland. (Illus.). 128p. 1994. 49.95 (*1-878887-36-X*) Morning NJ.

Northern New Hampshire Graveyards & Cemeteries: Transcriptions & Indexes of Burial Sites in Clarksville, Colebrook, Columbia, Dixville, Pittsburg, Stewartstown & Stratford. Nancy L. Dodge. 443p. 1988. reprint ed. lib. bdg. 39.00 (*0-8328-0038-4*, NH0001) Higginson Bk Co.

Northern New Spain: A Research Guide. Thomas C. Barnes et al. LC 80-24860. 147p. 1981. pap. 18.95 (*0-8165-0709-0*) U of Ariz Pr.

***Northern Nights.** Theresa Scott. 400p. 2000. mass mkt. 5.99 (*0-8439-4748-9*, Leisure Bks) Dorchester Pub Co.

Northern Nilo-Hamites. George W. Huntingford. LC 77-408451. (Ethnographic Survey of Africa - East Central Africa Ser.: Pt. 6). (Illus.). 126p. reprint ed. pap. 39.10 (*0-8357-3010-7*, 205709600010) Bks Demand.

Northern Nomadic Hunter-Gatherer: A Humanistic Approach. David Riches. (Studies in Anthropology). 1982. text 95.00 (*0-12-587620-3*) Acad Pr.

Northern Nurse. Elliot Merrick. (Illus.). 336p. 1994. reprint ed. pap. 14.00 (*0-88150-299-5*, Pub. by Countryman) Norton.

Northern Odyssee. Giorgio Tripoli. Ed. by Chrishane Eisel. (Illus.). 78p. (Orig.). 1996. pap. write for info. (*0-9642840-1-4*) Cee-Gee.

Northern Ontario Outdoor Guide. Shawn C. Perich & Gord Ellis. 300p. 1995. pap. write for info. (*0-9649257-0-2*) Outdoor News.

Northern Oregon Wilderness Areas. Donna Aitkenhead. (Illus.). 112p. 1995. pap. 8.95 (*0-911518-87-8*) F Amato Pubns.

Northern Pacific: Classic Steam Era. Lorenz P. Schrenk & Robert L. Frey. (Illus.). 320p. 1997. 59.95 (*0-945434-27-8*) Hundman Pub.

Northern Pacific Color Pictorial, Vol. I. Joseph W. Shine. 128p. (Orig.). 1994. 49.95 (*0-9616874-9-5*) Four Ways.

Northern Pacific Railway. 2nd ed. Photos by Warren McGee & Ron Nixon. (Illus.). 1996. 49.95 (*0-915370-10-7*) NW Short Line.

Northern Pacific Railway Co. Papers. W. Thomas White et al. LC 88-893872. 1984. write for info. (*0-89093-730-3*) U Pubns Amer.

Northern Painting: From Purcelle to Bruegel - 14th, 15th, & 16th Centuries. Charles Cuttler. 500p. (C). 1973. pap. text 68.00 (*0-03-089476-X*, Pub. by Harcourt Coll Pubs) Harcourt.

Northern Paiute Indians of California & Nevada. fac. ed. Ruth Underhill & Velimo Herrera. (United States Dept. of the Interior, Bureau of Indian Affairs Ser.). (Illus.). 75p. (C). 1941. reprint ed. pap. text 8.75 (*1-55567-783-5*) Coyote Press.

Northern Paiute Indians of California & Nevada. Ruth M. Underhill. LC 76-43877. (Indian Life & Customs Ser.: No. 1). reprint ed. 34.50 (*0-404-15733-5*) AMS Pr.

Northern Paiute Language of Oregon. fac. ed. W. L. Marsden. (University of California Publications in American Archaeology & Ethnology: Vol. 20: 11). 19p. (C). 1923. reprint ed. pap. text 2.50 (*1-55567-247-7*) Coyote Press.

Northern Paiute Verbs. fac. ed. Gilbert Natches. (University of California Publications in American Archaeology & Ethnology: Vol. 20: 14). 18p. (C). 1923. reprint ed. pap. text 2.19 (*1-55567-250-7*) Coyote Press.

Northern Pass Book. Wesley Littleton. 88p. 1998. pap. 23.00 (*0-7487-2401-X*) St Mut.

Northern Passage: Ethnography & Apprenticeship among the Subarctic Dene. Robert Jarvenpa. LC 99-182091. (Illus.). 210p. (C). 1998. pap. text 11.95 (*0-88133-990-3*) Waveland Pr.

Northern Passages: Feisty Tales of "Growing up North" Jerry Harju. Ed. by Pat Green & Karen Murr. LC 95-79065. (Illus.). 147p. 1995. pap. 12.95 (*0-9670205-3-0*, Pub. by N Harbor Pub) Partners Bk Dist.

Northern Passages: Reflections from Lake Superior County. Michael Van Stappen. LC 98-17055. (Illus.). 192p. 1998. pap. 13.95 (*1-879483-40-8*) Prairie Oak Pr.

Northern Passion: Pt. II: Introduction, French Text, Glossary, Etc. (EETS, OS Ser.: No. 147). 1974. reprint ed. 45.00 (*0-527-00142-2*) Periodicals Srv.

Northern Passion: Supplement. (EETS, OS Ser.: No. 183). 1974. reprint ed. 40.00 (*0-527-00143-0*) Periodicals Srv.

Northern Passion Pt. I: Four Parallel Texts. (EETS, OS Ser.: No. 145). 1974. reprint ed. 45.00 (*0-527-00141-4*) Periodicals Srv.

Northern Peaks, Vol. 1. Louis W. Dawson, II. Ed. by Robert Couchman. LC 94-71273. (Dawson's Guide to Colorado's Fourteeners Ser.). (Illus.). 255p. 1994. pap. 19.95 (*0-9628867-1-8*) Blue Clover.

***Northern Pike.** Will Ryan. LC 99-54423. (Illus.). 2000. 35.00 (*1-58574-044-6*) Lyons Pr.

Northern Pike! Ed. by Tom Zenanko. (Illus.). 212p. 1983. pap. 9.95 (*0-9610296-1-7*) Zenanko Outdoors.

Northern Pike & Muskie. Dick Sternberg. LC 91-34050. (Hunting & Fishing Library). (Illus.). 160p. 1992. 19.95 (*0-86573-037-7*) Creat Pub Intl.

Northern Pines. J. Sousa. 1993. per. 55.00 (*0-7935-2970-0*) H Leonard.

Northern Plains: Minnesota, North Dakota, South Dakota. Lansing Shephard. (Illus.). 1996. pap. 19.95 (*0-614-20484-4*) Random.

Northern Poems. Robert Billings. 1986. 5.00 (*0-920806-84-8*, Pub. by Penumbra Pr) U of Toronto Pr.

Northern Pointe Bands. fac. ed. Omer C. Stewart. Ed. by Robert H. Lowie et al. (University of California Publications: No. 2:3). 29p. (C). 1939. reprint ed. pap. 3.44 (*1-55567-122-5*) Coyote Press.

Northern Poles: Breakways & Breakthroughs in Nordic Painting & Sculpture of the 1970s & 1980s. (Illus.). 486p. 1986. 117.50 (*87-88978-00-1*) Coronet Bks.

Northern Protest: Martin Luther King, Jr., Chicago, & the Civil Rights Movement. James Ralph. LC 92-45231. 352p. 1993. text 27.95 (*0-674-62687-7*) HUP.

Northern Quahog: The Biology of Mercenaria Mercenaria. Michael A. Rice. Ed. by Carole Jaworski & Malia Schwartz. (Illus.). (Orig.). 1992. pap. text 5.00 (*0-938412-33-7*) Sea Grant Pubns.

Northern Question: Italy's Participation in the European Economic Community & the Mezzogiorno's Underdevelopment. Adrian N. Carello. LC 87-40642. (Illus.). 216p. 1989. 38.50 (*0-87413-342-4*) U Delaware Pr.

Northern Railroads in Civil War, 1861-1865. Thomas Weber. LC 79-106725. 318p. 1970. reprint ed. lib. bdg. 38.50 (*0-8371-3549-4*, WERR, Greenwood Pr) Greenwood.

Northern Railroads in the Civil War, 1861-1865. Thomas Weber. LC 98-50623. 336p. 1999. pap. 15.95 (*0-253-21321-5*); text 35.00 (*0-253-33549-3*) Ind U Pr.

Northern Reflections: A Lighthearted Account of "Growing up North" Jerry Harju. Ed. by Pat Green. LC 92-75914. (Illus.). 123p. 1992. pap. 12.95 (*0-9670205-1-4*, Pub. by N Harbor Pub) Partners Bk Dist.

Northern Refuge: A Story of a Canadian Boreal Forest. Audrey Fraggalosch. LC 98-42572. (Habitat Ser.: Vol. 12). (Illus.). 36p. (J). (gr. 1-4). 1999. 15.95 (*1-56899-678-0*); 19.99 incl. audio (*1-56899-680-2*, BC7012); pap. 5.95 (*1-56899-679-9*); pap. 19.95 incl. audio (*1-56899-681-0*) Soundprints.

Northern Refuge: A Story of a Canadian Boreal Forest, Incl. toy. Audrey Fraggalosch. (Habitat Ser.: Vol. 12). (Illus.). 36p. (J). (gr. 1-4). 1999. 26.95 (*1-56899-682-9*); 31.95 incl. audio (*1-56899-684-5*); pap. 16.95 (*1-56899-683-7*); pap. 19.95 incl. audio (*1-56899-685-3*) Soundprints.

Northern Region Economy: Progress & Prospects in the North of England. Lynne Evans et al. LC 95-1435. (Illus.). 256p. 1995. 100.00 (*0-7201-2184-1*) Continuum.

Northern Renaissance. (Shorewood Art Programs for Education Ser.). 16p. 1974. teacher ed. 107.00 (*0-88185-054-3*); 143.00 (*0-685-07229-0*) Shorewood Fine Art.

Northern Renaissance. James C. Snyder. 512p. (C). 1984. text 73.33 (*0-13-623596-4*) P-H.

Northern Renaissance Art: Painting, Sculpture, the Graphic Arts from 1350 to 1575. James C. Snyder. (Illus.). 560p. (C). 1985. 60.00 (*0-8109-1081-0*, Pub. by Abrams) Time Warner.

Northern Renaissance Art, 1400-1600: Sources & Documents. Wolfgang Stechow. 187p. 1989. pap. 14.95 (*0-8101-0849-6*) Northwestern U Pr.

Northern Rhodesia Copperbelt, 1899-1962: Technological Development up to the End of the Central African Federation. Francis L. Coleman. LC 72-149805. (Illus.). xx, 206p. 1971. lib. bdg. 35.00 (*0-678-06784-8*) Kelley.

*__Northern Rockies.__ National Geographic Staff. LC 99-85986. (National Geographic Guide to America's Outdoors). (Illus.). 288p. 2000. per. 24.00 (*0-7922-7741-4*, Pub. by Natl Geog) S&S Trade.

Northern Saga. large type ed. Steven C. Lawrence. LC 97-38877. 1997. 21.95 (*0-7838-8367-6*, G K Hall & Co) Mac Lib Ref.

Northern Sandlots: A Social History of Maritime Baseball. Colin Howell. (Illus.). 368p. 1995. text 50.00 (*0-8020-5011-5*); pap. text 18.95 (*0-8020-6942-8*) U of Toronto Pr.

Northern Schools, Southern Blacks, & Reconstruction: Freedmen's Education, 1862-1875, 87. Ronald E. Butchart. LC 79-8949. (Contributions in American History Ser.: No. 87). (Illus.). 309p. 1980. 38.50 (*0-313-22073-5*, BNS/) Greenwood.

Northern Sea Route Directory of Icebreaking Ships: Reference for the Arctic & Antarctic Transport & Offshore Industries. Ed. by Leonid Tunik. (Illus.). 217p. 1994. pap. 280.00 (*0-9644311-0-6*) Backbone Pubng.

Northern Service. Doug Byer. (Illus.). 160p. (Orig.). 1997. pap. write for info. (*1-55059-149-5*) Detselig Ents.

Northern Seventeenth Century Printers, from 1642: Bulkley (Stephen & John) Broad (Thomas & Alice) John White I of York & Thomas Wayt (York Booksellers) 286p. (C). 1986. 175.00 (*1-85072-010-X*, Pub. by W Sessions) St Mut.

Northern Shadows: An Illustrated Guide to Canadian Vampires. John Arkelian. (Illus.). 1998. pap. text 14.95 (*1-55082-209-8*, Pub. by Quarry Pr) LPC InBook.

Northern Shaolin Sword. 2nd ed. Yang Jwing-Ming & Jeffery A. Bolt. (Illus.). 200p. 1985. per. 15.95 (*0-940871-01-7*, B006/017) YMAA Pubn.

*__Northern Shaolin Sword: Form, Techniques & Applications.__ 2nd rev. ed. Jwing-Ming Yang & Jeffrey A. Bolt. (Illus.). 320p. 2000. pap. 24.95 (*1-886969-85-X*, Pub. by YMAA Pubn) Natl Bk Netwk.

Northern Shoshone. Robert H. Lowie. LC 74-7983. reprint ed. 36.00 (*0-404-11871-2*) AMS Pr.

Northern Shoshoni. Brigham D. Madsen. LC 78-53138. (Illus.). 262p. 2000. pap. 18.95 (*0-87004-266-1*) Caxton.

Northern Sierra Miwok Dictionary. 2nd ed. Catherine A. Callaghan. LC 86-28908. (University of California Publications in Linguistics: No. 110). 408p. 1987. reprint ed. pap. 126.50 (*0-7837-8129-6*, 204793600008) Bks Demand.

Northern Sierra Terrane & Associated Mesozoic Magmatic Units: Implications for the Tectonic History of the Western Cordillera. Ed. by G. H. Girty et al. 92p. 1996. 9.00 (*1-878861-74-3*) Pac Section SEPM.

Northern Sil Lum Form #7: Plum Flower Fist (or Moi Fah) Kwong W. Lam & Ted Mancuso. LC 83-50020. (Illus.). 150p. 1984. pap. 8.95 (*0-86568-044-2*, 213) Unique Pubns.

Northern Solomons: United States Army Campaigns of World War 2. Stephen J. Lofgren. 35p. 1993. pap. 1.50 (*0-16-061300-0*) USGPO.

Northern Spain. Insight Guides Staff. (Insight Guides). 1998. pap. text 22.95 (*0-88729-286-0*) Langenscheidt.

Northern Spain. E. Wigram. (Spain Ser.). 1976. lib. bdg. 69.95 (*0-8490-2353-X*) Gordon Pr.

Northern Spain. 2nd ed. Dana Facaros. 1999. pap. text 18.95 (*1-86011-913-1*) Cadgn Bks.

Northern Spain Map. 1997. 8.95 (*2-06-700442-5*, 442) Michelin.

Northern Spirits Distilled: Memories of the Upper Midwest. Jack Ozegovic. Ed. by Steven H. Semken. LC 99-71800. 252p. 2000. pap. 16.95 (*1-888160-53-5*, Pub. by Ice Cube) SPD-Small Pr Dist.

Northern Spring. Frank Ormsby. 54p. 1986. pap. 12.95 (*0-904011-92-5*) Dufour.

Northern Stars. Grant Staff. 1998. pap. 15.95 (*0-312-86475-2*) St Martin.

Northern Steamboats: Timiskaming, Nipissing & Abitibi. Richard Tatley. (Illus.). 304p. 1996. 39.95 (*1-55046-165-6*, Pub. by Boston Mills) Genl Dist Srvs.

Northern Summer. Edmond B. Szekely. (Illus.). 32p. 1972. pap. 5.95 (*0-89564-030-9*) IBS Intl.

Northern Summer: New & Selected Poems, 1963-1983. John Matthias. LC 83-18199. 224p. 1984. pap. 12.95 (*0-8040-0853-1*); text 24.95 (*0-8040-0852-3*) Swallow.

Northern Suns. Ed. by David G. Hartwell & Glenn Grant. LC 99-12846. 384p. 1999. 24.95 (*0-312-86461-2*, Pub. by Tor Bks) St Martin.

*__Northern Suns.__ Ed. by David G. Hartwell & Glenn Grant. (Illus.). 384p. 2000. pap. 14.95 (*0-312-86462-0*, Pub. by Tor Bks) St Martin.

Northern Tales. Howard Norman. 343p. 1998. pap. 16.00 (*0-375-70267-9*) Random.

Northern Tales. Cas Treleaven. (Illus.). 205p. (Orig.). 1995. pap. write for info. (*1-57579-002-5*) Pine Hill Pr.

Northern Telecom E. H. & S. Field Verification Workbook. Date not set. wbk. ed. write for info. (*0-88061-181-2*) Intl Loss Cntrl.

Northern Telecom E. H. & S. Reference Manual. Date not set. ring bd. write for info. (*0-88061-180-4*) Intl Loss Cntrl.

Northern Telecom E. H. & S. Working Copy. Date not set. spiral bd. write for info. (*0-88061-182-0*) Intl Loss Cntrl.

Northern Territories & Beyond: Russian, Japanese & American Perspectives. Ed. by James E. Goodby et al. LC 94-32927. 408p. 1995. 67.95 (*0-275-95093-X*, Praeger Pubs) Greenwood.

Northern Territories Controversy: A Four-Decade Stalemate Between Japan & Russia. Gerald R. Pitzl. (Pew Case Studies in International Affairs). 50p. (C). 1994. pap. text 3.50 (*1-56927-364-2*, GU Schl Foreign) Geo U Inst Dplmcy.

Northern Territories Dispute & Russo-Japanese Relations: Vol. 1: Between War & Peace, 1697-1985; Vol. 2: Neither War nor Peace, 1985-1998, 2 vols. Tsuyoshi Hasegawa. LC 98-14623. (Research Ser.: No. 97). (Illus.). 702p. 1998. pap. text 38.50 (*0-87725-197-5*) U of Cal IAS.

Northern Territory: Experience Australia's Outback Territory. 2nd ed. Hugh Finlay & David Andrew. (Illus.). 320p. 1999. pap. 16.95 (*0-86442-791-3*) Lonely Planet.

Northern Thebaid: Monastic Saints of the Russian North. 3rd ed. Ed. by Seraphim Rose & Herman Podmoshensky. LC 75-18031. (RUS., Illus.). 308p. 1995. pap. 17.00 (*0-938635-37-9*) St Herman Pr.

Northern Traditional Dancer. C. Scott Evans. (Illus.). 50p. 1998. pap. 12.95 (*0-9624883-1-3*, Pub. by Reddick Enterp) Book Pub Co.

Northern Trails: Some Studies of Animal Life in the Far North. William J. Long. (Illus.). xxv, 390p. 1989. reprint ed. pap. 14.95 (*0-936041-05-6*) Barbary Coast Bks.

Northern Travel. Bayard Taylor. (Notable American Authors). 1999. reprint ed. lib. bdg. 125.00 (*0-7812-9758-3*) Rprt Serv.

Northern Travelers to Sixteenth-Century Italy: Drawings from New England Collections. Nicola Courtright. (Illus.). 1990. pap. 5.00 (*0-914337-14-9*) Mead Art Mus.

Northern Trawl. Ruppert Creed & Jim Hawkins. 77p. 1986. 35.00 (*0-907033-44-X*) St Mut.

*__Northern Trek, 8 vols.__ Scott Wrobel et al. (Illus.). (J). (gr. 2-7). 2000. lib. bdg. 170.40 (*1-58340-022-2*) Smart Apple.

Northern Tribes of Nigeria: Ethnographical Account of the Northern Provinces of Nigeria Together with a Report of the 1921 Decennial Census, 2 vols. Charles K. Meek. (Illus.). 1971. reprint ed. 145.00 (*0-7146-2686-4*, Pub. by F Cass Pubs) Intl Spec Bk.

Northern Tucson Basin Survey: Research Directions & Background Studies. Ed. by Fish & Fish Madsen Staff. (Archaeological Ser.: No. 182). (Illus.). 283p. 1993. pap. 19.95 (*1-889747-47-5*) Ariz St Mus.

Northern Ute Music. Frances Densmore. (Bureau of American Ethnology Bulletins Ser.). 213p. 1995. lib. bdg. 89.00 (*0-7812-4075-1*) Rprt Serv.

Northern Ute Music. Frances Densmore. LC 72-1887. (Music Ser.). (Illus.). 236p. 1972. reprint ed. lib. bdg. 27.50 (*0-306-70515-X*) Da Capo.

Northern Virginia & the Beltway Street Guide & Directory: 1999 Edition. Thomas Bros. Maps Staff. (Illus.). 304p. 1998. pap. 14.95 (*1-58174-030-1*) Thomas Bros Maps.

*__Northern Virginia & the Beltway Street Guide & Directory: 2000 Edition.__ (Illus.). 304p. 2000. pap. 14.95 (*1-58174-136-7*) Thomas Bros Maps.

Northern Virginia Carry Out. Ed. by Ann H. Waigand. 96p. (Orig.). 1987. pap. 4.95 (*0-942231-00-7*) Educ Traveler.

Northern Visions: An Anthology of Scandinavian - Nordic Poetry. Intro. by Bradley R. Strahan. (Black Dog Ser.). (Illus.). 62p. (Orig.). (C). 1991. pap. 7.00 (*0-938872-15-X*) Black Buzzard.

Northern Voice for the Dissolution of the United States of North America. Frank Stockton. (Notable American Authors Ser.). 1999. reprint ed. lib. bdg. 125.00 (*0-7812-8915-7*) Rprt Serv.

Northern Voices: Inuit Writing in English. Penny Petrone. (Illus.). 330p. 1988. 27.50 (*0-8020-5772-1*) U of Toronto Pr.

Northern Voices: Inuit Writing in English. Ed. by Penny Petrone. 332p. 1992. pap. text 19.95 (*0-8020-7717-X*) U of Toronto Pr.

*__Northern Wars: War, State & Society in Northeastern Europe, 1558-1721.__ Robert I. Frost. LC 00-24674. (Modern Wars in Perspective Ser.). 416p. 2000. pap. 24.00 (*0-582-06429-5*) Longman.

Northern Wastes (Realm) R. Maxwell. (Middle-Earth Role Playing Ser.). (Illus.). 192p. 1997. pap. 28.00 (*1-55806-296-3*, 2025) Iron Crown Ent Inc.

Northern Waters. Jan Zita Grover. 231p. 1999. pap. 14.00 (*1-55597-294-2*, Pub. by Graywolf) SPD-Small Pr Dist.

Northern Waters: Management Issues & Practice. David Symes. LC 98-25866. 1998. 115.00 (*0-85238-257-X*) Blackwell Sci.

Northern Waters: Resources & Security Issues. Ed. by Clive Archer & David Scrivener. 256p. 1986. 61.00 (*0-389-20657-1*, N8215) B&N Imports.

*__Northern Waterway Guide 2000.__ Judith Powers. (Illus.). 2000. 36.95 (*1-930188-06-4*) Intertec-Primedia.

Northern Whale Fishery. William Scoresby, Jr. Date not set. write for info. (*0-87770-274-8*) Ye Galleon.

Northern Windows: An Anthology of Ulster Autobiography. Ed. by Frank Ormsby. 256p. 1987. 22.00 (*0-85640-375-X*, Pub. by Blackstaff Pr) Dufour.

Northern Woman in the Plantation South: Letters of Tryphena Blanche Holder Fox, 1856-1876. Ed. by Wilma King-Hunter. LC 92-39173. 300p. 1997. reprint ed. pap. 14.95 (*1-57003-188-6*) U of SC Pr.

Northern Woodland Indians. Mira Bartok & Christine Ronan. (Ancient & Living Cultures Ser.). 28p. (Orig.). (J). (gr. 3 up). 1995. pap. 9.95 (*0-673-36256-6*, GoodYrBooks) Addson-Wesley Educ.

Northern Words in Modern English see Persian Words in English

Northerners: A Study in the Reign of King John. James C. Holt. (Illus.). 318p. 1992. pap. 32.00 (*0-19-820309-8*) OUP.

Northerners: A Study in the Reign of King John. James C. Holt. LC 80-27864. 272p. 1981. reprint ed. lib. bdg. 65.00 (*0-313-22764-0*, HOTN, Greenwood Pr) Greenwood.

Northern/Intermountain Regions' Fish Habitat Inventory: Grazed, Rested, & Ungrazed Reference Stream Reaches, Silver King Creek, California. C. Kerry Overton et al. (Illus.). 32p. 1997. reprint ed. 10.00 (*0-89904-600-2*, Bear Meadows Resrch Grp); reprint ed. pap. 4.20 (*0-89904-601-0*, Bear Meadows Resrch Grp) Crumb Elbow Pub.

Northfield Cemetery. M. Edward Burtt. (Illus.). ii, 17p. 1997. pap. write for info. (*1-888913-35-5*) M E Burtt.

Northfield Dreams. Keiji Emori. 55p. 1996. pap. 10.00 (*0-9633846-2-7*) Scope Pub.

Northfork Mono. fac. ed. E. W. Gifford. (University of California Publications in American Archaeology & Ethnology: Vol. 31: 2). 66p. (C). 1932. reprint ed. pap. text 7.81 (*1-55567-282-5*) Coyote Press.

Northing up the Nooksack. Alan C. Schmierer. (Illus.). 79p. (Orig.). 1983. pap. text 2.95 (*0-914019-01-5*) NW Interpretive.

Northland Stories. Jack London. Ed. by Jonathan Auerbach. LC 96-21720. 1997. pap. 10.95 (*0-14-018996-3*) Viking Penguin.

Northland Wild Flowers. John B. Moyle & Evelyn W. Moyle. LC 76-55173. (Illus.). 246p. 1984. pap. 18.95 (*0-8166-1355-9*) U of Minn Pr.

Northlands, New Art from Scandinavias. Compiled by David Elliott & Maaretta Jaaukkuri. 80p. 1990. 48.00 (*0-905836-68-5*, Pub. by Museum Modern Art) St Mut.

Northlight. Deborah Wheeler. 352p. (Orig.). 1995. mass mkt. 4.99 (*0-88677-639-2*, Pub. by DAW Bks) Penguin Putnam.

Northmen in America. H. Hermannsson. 1972. 59.95 (*0-8490-0735-6*) Gordon Pr.

Northmen Talk: A Choice of Tales from Iceland. Jacqueline Simpson. LC 65-16366. 320p. reprint ed. pap. 99.20 (*0-608-30800-5*, 200490000047) Bks Demand.

Northport, ME Vital Records of Typescript Prior to 1892. Tr. by Elizabeth M. Mosher. 207p. 1995. 65.00 (*0-89725-232-2*, 1613) Picton Pr.

Northrepps Grandchildren. Ed. by Verily Anderson. 272p. (C). 1989. 25.00 (*0-904623-97-1*, Pub. by T Dalton) St Mut.

*__Northridge, Chaps. 20 & 23.__ Weygandt. (C). 1998. pap. text 10.00 (*0-471-32941-X*) Wiley.

Northridge Earthquake: Lifeline Performance & Post-Earthquake Response. Ed. by Anshel J. Schiff. LC 95-34082. (Monograph Ser.: No. 8). 352p. 1995. 39.00 (*0-7844-0106-3*) Am Soc Civil Eng.

Northridge Earthquake: Preliminary Damage Estimate on California's Public Colleges. Kirk L. Knutsen. 4p. 1994. pap. write for info. (*1-58703-021-7*) CA St Libry.

Northridge Earthquake: Vulnerability & Disaster. Robert C. Bolin & Lois Stanford. LC 98-11099. (Illus.). 288p. (C). 1998. 110.00 (*0-415-17897-5*) Routledge.

Northridge Earthquake Vol. 2: Preliminary Damage Estimates - California Public Libraries. Liz Gibson. 4p. 1994. pap. write for info. (*1-58703-022-5*) CA St Libry.

Northridge Earthquake of January 17, 1994, Reconnaissance Report, 2 vols. Ed. by John F. Hall. (Illus.). 803p. 1996. pap. 45.00 (*0-943198-77-1*, 95-03) Earthquake Eng.

Northridge Earthquake of January 17, 1994, Reconnaissance Report, Vol. 1. Ed. by John F. Hall. (Illus.). 523p. 1995. pap. 30.00 (*0-943198-85-2*) Earthquake Eng.

Northridge Earthquake of January 17, 1994, Reconnaissance Report, Vol. 2. Ed. by John F. Hall. (Illus.). 280p. 1996. pap. 15.00 (*0-943198-86-0*) Earthquake Eng.

Northridge Earthquake 1994 - Performance of Structures, Lifelines & Fire Protection Systems. (Illus.). 130p. (Orig.). (C). 1994. pap. text 40.00 (*0-7881-1183-3*) DIANE Pub.

Northridge High Football Camp. S. Joseph Krol. Date not set. pap. 12.95 (*0-85449-225-9*, Pub. by Gay Mens Pr) LPC InBook.

Northrop: A Report on the Company's Environmental Policies & Practices. (Illus.). 30p. (C). 1994. reprint ed. pap. text 40.00 (*0-7881-0907-3*, Coun on Econ) DIANE Pub.

Northrop F-89 Scorpion: A Photo Chronicle. David R. McLaren & Marty J. Isham. (Illus.). 128p. 1996. pap. 24.95 (*0-7643-0065-2*) Schiffer.

Northrop Flying Wings. Edward T. Maloney. (Illus.). 55p. 1975. pap. 19.95 (*0-915464-00-4*, WW II Pubns) Aviation.

Northrop Flying Wings: A History of Jack Northrop's Visionary Aircraft. Garry R. Pape & John M. Campbell. (Illus.). 288p. 1994. 49.95 (*0-88740-689-0*) Schiffer.

Northrop Frye. Ian Balfour. (World Authors Ser.). 160p. 1988. 28.95 (*0-8057-8235-4*, TWAS 806 (CANADA), Twyne) Mac Lib Ref.

Northrop Frye: A Visionary Life. Joseph Adamson. LC 94-104728. (Illus.). 112p. (Orig.). 1993. pap. 9.95 (*1-55022-184-1*, Pub. by ECW) LPC InBook.

Northrop Frye: An Annotated Bibliography of Primary & Secondary Sources. Robert D. Denham. 1987. text 60.00 (*0-8020-2630-3*) U of Toronto Pr.

Northrop Frye: Anatomy of His Criticism. Hamilton. 1991. pap. 18,95 (*0-8020-6921-5*) U of Toronto Pr.

Northrop Frye: Anatomy of His Criticism. A. C. Hamilton. 316p. 1991. text 45.00 (*0-8020-2697-4*); pap. text 18.95 (*0-8020-6905-3*) U of Toronto Pr.

Northrop Frye: Myth & Metaphor, Selected Essays 1974-1988. Northrop Frye. 386p. 1992. reprint ed. pap. text 18.50 (*0-8139-1369-1*) U Pr of Va.

Northrop Frye: The Theoretical Imagination. Jonathan Hart. LC 93-28764. (Critics of the Twentieth Century Ser.). 336p. (C). 1994. pap. 27.99 (*0-415-07537-8*) Routledge.

Northrop Frye: The Theoretical Imagination. Jonathan Hart. LC 93-28764. (Critics of the Twentieth Century Ser.). 336p. (C). (gr. 13). 1994. text 59.95 (*0-415-07536-X*) Routledge.

Northrop Frye in Conversation. David Cayley. (In Conversation Ser.). 240p. 1996. pap. 13.95 (*0-88784-525-8*) Stoddart Publ.

Northrop Frye on Culture & Literature: A Collection of Review Essays. Northrop Frye. Ed. by Robert D. Denham. LC 77-12917. 272p. reprint ed. pap. 84.40 (*0-608-18239-7*, 205665300078) Bks Demand.

Northrop Frye on Myth: An Introduction. Ford Russell. LC 97-18441. (Theorists of Myth Ser.: Vol. 10). (Illus.). 245p. 1998. text 47.00 (*0-8240-3446-5*, H1166) Garland.

Northrop Frye on Shakespeare. Northrop Frye. LC 86-50485. 224p. (C). 1988. reprint ed. pap. 14.00 (*0-300-04208-6*) Yale U Pr.

Northrop Frye's student essays, 1932-1938. Northrop Frye. Ed. by Robert D. Denham. LC 98-146928. (Collected Works of Northrop Frye: Vol. 3). 576p. 1997. text 90.00 (*0-8020-4235-X*) U of Toronto Pr.

Northrop Grumman B-2 Spirit: An Illustrated History. Bill Holder. LC 98-84395. (Illus.). 80p. 1998. pap. 19.95 (*0-7643-0591-3*) Schiffer.

Northrop P-61 Black Widow, Vol. 15. Warren Thompson. (Warbird Tech Ser.). 1997. pap. text 16.95 (*0-933424-80-9*) Specialty Pr.

Northrop P-61 Black Widow: The Complete History & Combat Record. Garry R. Pape et al. LC 90-24611. (Illus.). 144p. 1995. pap. 24.95 (*0-88740-738-2*) Schiffer.

Northrop Story, 1929-1939. Richard S. Allen. LC 90-7094. (Illus.). 178p. 1993. 29.95 (*0-88740-585-1*) Schiffer.

Northrop's T-38 Talon: A Pictorial History. Don Logan. LC 95-68024. (Illus.). 152p. (Orig.). 1995. pap. 24.95 (*0-88740-800-1*) Schiffer.

Northrop's YF-17 Cobra: A Pictorial History. Don Logan. LC 95-71769. (Illus.). 64p. (YA). (gr. 12). 1996. pap. 19.95 (*0-88740-910-5*) Schiffer.

Northrup Frye in Conversation. David Cayley. 240p. (Orig.). 1992. pap. 13.95 (*0-614-17723-5*, Pub. by Hse of Anansi Pr) Genl Dist Srvs.

Northrup-Northrop Genealogy; a Record of the Known Descendants of Joseph Northrup, One of the Original Settlers of Milford, Connecticut, in 1639. A. J. Northrup. (Illus.). 473p. 1989. reprint ed. pap. 71.00 (*0-8328-0907-1*); reprint ed. lib. bdg. 79.00 (*0-8328-0906-3*) Higginson Bk Co.

Norths Meet Murder. Frances Lockeridge & Richard Lockeridge. 19.95 (*0-89190-916-8*) Amereon Ltd.

Northseamen: The Story of the Fishermen, Yachtsmen & Shipbuilders of the Colne & Blackwater Rivers. John Leather. 336p. 1990. 45.00 (*0-900963-22-0*, Pub. by T Dalton) St Mut.

Northshore. Sheri S. Tepper. (Awakeners Ser.: No. 1). (Illus.). 256p. 1988. pap. 3.50 (*0-8125-5617-8*, Pub. by Tor Bks) St Martin.

North/south Carolina. Rand McNally Staff. 1997. pap. 5.95 (*0-528-96676-6*) Rand McNally.

North/south Dakota. Rand McNally Staff. 1997. pap. 5.95 (*0-528-96699-5*) Rand McNally.

*__Northstar: Focus Listg Spkng Intrm Mid East.__ 240p. (C). 1999. pap. 0.00 (*0-201-62137-1*) HEPC Inc.

N

An Asterisk (*) at the beginning of an entry indicates that the title is appearing for the first time.

Northstar: Focus on Listening & Speaking Basic Level. Laurie Frazier. LC 97-39163. 192p. 1998. pap. text 22.33 (*0-201-57179-X*) Addison-Wesley.

Northstar: Focus on Listening & Speaking, Intermediate Level. Helen Solarzano. LC 97-41537. 240p. 1997. pap. text 23.11 (*0-201-57178-1*) Addison-Wesley.

Northstar: Focus on Reading/Writing High-Intermediate Tests. Laura Andrew. 52p. (C). 1999. pap. 13.27 (*0-201-45821-7*) Addison-Wesley.

***Northstar: Focus Readng Wrt Interm Mid East.** 240p. (C). 1999. pap. write for info. (*0-201-62136-3*) Addison-Wesley.

Northstar: Focus on Reading: Writing Advanced Tests. Judy Miller. 48p. 1999. ring bd. 13.27 (*0-201-45825-X*) Addison-Wesley.

Northstar Rising. James Axler. 1997. per. 5.99 (*0-373-89008-7*, 1-89008-6) Harlequin Bks.

Northumberland. Nikolaus Pevsner. 600p. text 65.00 (*0-14-071059-0*, Pub. by Pnguin Bks Ltd) Trafalgar.

Northumberland: The Political Career of John Dudley, Earl of Warwick & Duke of Northumberland. Barrett L. Beer. LC 73-77386. 247p. reprint ed. pap. 76.60 (*0-7837-1340-1*, 204148800020) Bks Demand.

Northumberland & Newcastle upon Tyne. Priscilla Boniface & Peter Fowler. (Country Guide Ser.: No. 30). (Illus.). 64p. pap. 8.50 (*0-85263-998-8*, Pub. by Shire Pubns) Parkwest Pubns.

Northumberland & Tyne & Wear. Brasseys Inc. Staff. (Twentieth Century Defence of Britain Ser.). 128p. 1998. pap. text 11.95 (*1-85753-234-1*, Pub. by Brasseys) Brasseys.

Northumberland Co., VA Apprenticeships, 1750-1852. Ed. by W. Preston Haynie. LC 94-178733. 99p. (Orig.). 1994. pap. 14.00 (*1-55613-947-0*) Heritage Bk.

Northumberland County Bookshelf or a Parcel of Old Books, 1650-1852. Compiled by W. Preston Haynie. 140p. (Orig.). 1994. pap. text 13.00 (*0-7884-0097-5*) Heritage Bk.

Northumberland County, Virginia, Apprenticeships, 1650-1750. W. Preston Haynie. vi, 124p. (Orig.). 1993. pap. text 15.00 (*1-55613-783-4*) Heritage Bk.

***Northumberland County Virginia Registers of Free Blacks.** Karen E. Sutton. LC 99-475371. 127p. 1999. pap. 23.00 (*0-7884-1132-2*, S877) Heritage Bk.

Northumberland County, Virginia, 1678-1713, Vol. 1. Lindsay O. Duvall. (Virginia Colonial Abstracts, Series II). 160p. 1979. reprint ed. pap. 20.00 (*0-89308-062-4*) Southern Hist Pr.

Northumberland County, Virginia, 1850 Census. Bayne P. O'Brien. 118p. (Orig.). 1972. reprint ed. pap. 15.00 (*0-89308-307-0*) Southern Hist Pr.

Northumberland Dreaming: A Past Life Remembered. Mary R. Mercker. LC 98-72214. 424p. 1998. pap. text 14.95 (*1-57174-086-4*) Hampton Roads Pub Co.

Northumbria. Insight Guides Staff. (Insight Guides). 1998. pap. text 7.95 (*0-88729-426-X*) Langenscheidt.

Northumbria: English Border Country. Rob Talbot & Robin Whiteman. (Country Ser.). (Illus.). 160p. 1998. 27.50 (*0-297-82249-7*, Pub. by Weidenfeld & Nicolson) Trafalgar.

Northumbria Walks. (Ordnance Survey Pathfinder Guides Ser.). (Illus.). 80p. 1993. pap. 14.95 (*0-7117-0552-6*) Seven Hills Bk.

Northumbrian Renaissance: A Study in the Transmission of Style. Carol L. De Vegar. LC 85-40507. (Illus.). 352p. 1987. 65.00 (*0-941664-11-2*) Susquehanna U Pr.

***Northumbria's Golden Age.** Ed. by Jane Hawkes & Susan Mills. LC 99-206574. (Illus.). 3p. 1998. 39.95 (*0-7509-1685-0*, Pub. by Sutton Pub Ltd) Intl Pubs Mktg.

***Northumbria's Golden Age, AD 547-735.** Peter Fairless. 1999. pap. 24.00 (*1-85072-138-6*, Pub. by W Sessions) St Mut.

Northward Bound: The Mexican Immigrant Experience in Ballad & Song. Maria Herrera-Sobek. LC 92-22209. 372p. 1993. 14.95 (*0-253-32737-7*) Ind U Pr.

Northward Ho. Thomas Dekker & John Webster. LC 75-133655. (Tudor Facsimile Texts. Old English Plays Ser.: No. 119). reprint ed. 59.50 (*0-404-53419-8*) AMS Pr.

Northward over the Great Ice Vols. 1-2: A Narrative of Life & Work on Greenland, 1886, 1891-97. Robert E. Peary. (Illus.). 1993. reprint ed. lib. bdg. 125.00 (*0-8328-3133-6*) Higginson Bk Co.

Northwards by Sea. Gordon Donaldson. (Illus.). 1978. 27.00 (*0-8464-0677-2*) Beekman Pubs.

Northwest. San Antonio Cartographers Staff. 1996. 2.95 (*0-671-56296-7*) Macmillan.

***Northwest.** VeraLee Wiggins. 464p. 2000. pap. 4.97 (*1-57748-644-7*) Barbour Pub.

Northwest: Alaska, Idaho, Oregon, Washington. Thomas G. Aylesworth & Virginia L. Aylesworth. LC 94-45824. (Discovering America Ser.). 88p. (J). (gr. 4 up). 1995. lib. bdg. 19.95 (*0-7910-3406-2*) Chelsea Hse.

Northwest: Alaska, Idaho, Oregon, Washington. Thomas G. Aylesworth & Virginia L. Aylesworth. LC 94-45824. (Discovering America Ser.). 88p. (J). (gr. 4 up). 1995. pap. 8.95 (*0-7910-3424-0*) Chelsea Hse.

***Northwest: Regional Map & Travel Planner, Including Washington, Oregon, Idaho, Montana & Wyoming.** National Geographic Society Staff. 1998. pap. 7.95 (*1-57262-416-7*) MapQuest.

Northwest Airlines. Geoff Jones. (ABC Ser.). (Illus.). 96p. 1998. pap. 12.95 (*1-882663-28-4*) Plymouth VT.

Northwest & Great Plains see Mobil Travel Guide

***Northwest & Great Plains.** Mobil Travel Guides Staff. (Mobil Travel Guides Ser.). 2000. pap. 16.95 (*0-7853-4154-4*) Pubns Intl Ltd.

Northwest Animal Babies. Art Wolfe. LC 98-5159. (Illus.). 32p. (J). (ps-3). 1998. 15.95 (*1-57061-144-0*) Sasquatch Bks.

Northwest Arkansas 1870 Census Index: Benton, Boone, Carroll, Crawford, Franklin, Johnson, Madison, Newton, Pope, Sebastian, & Washington Counties. Martha Vaughn. 200p. 1999. pap. 27.00 (*1-56546-143-6*) Arkansas Res.

Northwest Atlantic Groundfish: Perspectives on a Fishery Collapse. Ed. by J. S. Boreman et al. LC 97-77481. 242p. 1997. pap. text 56.00 (*1-888569-06-9*, 550.23P) Am Fisheries Soc.

Northwest Berry Cookbook: Finding, Growing, & Cooking with Berries Year-Round. Kathleen D. Stang. 144p. 1998. pap. 16.95 (*1-57061-112-2*) Sasquatch Bks.

Northwest Best Places: Restaurants, Lodgings, & Touring in Oregon, Washington, & British Columbia. 12th rev. ed. Ed. by Stephanie Irving. (Best Places Ser.). 599p. 1997. pap. 19.95 (*1-57061-111-4*) Sasquatch Bks.

Northwest Best Places Cookbook: Recipes from the Outstanding Restaurants & Inns of Washington, Oregon, & British Columbia. Cynthia Nims & Lori McKean. LC 96-13187. 280p. (Orig.). 1996. pap. 16.95 (*1-57061-075-4*) Sasquatch Bks.

Northwest Birds in Winter. Alan Contreras. LC 97-26736. (Illus.). 288p. 1997. pap. 17.95 (*0-87071-425-2*) Oreg St U Pr.

Northwest Boat Dives: 60 Ultimate Dives in Puget Sound & Hood Canal. Dave Bliss. LC 96-50999. 184p. (Orig.). 1997. pap. 16.95 (*1-57061-090-8*) Sasquatch Bks.

***Northwest Boat Travel.** Anderson Publishing Company Staff. Ed. by Gwen Cole & Phil Cole. 2000. pap. 19.95 (*0-945989-12-1*) Anderson WA.

Northwest Boat Travel, Vol. 22. (Illus.). 19.95 (*0-945989-11-3*) Todd Commns.

Northwest Boat Travel, Vol. 22. Anderson Publishing Company Staff. Ed. by Gwen Cole & Phil Cole. 344p. 1999. pap. 19.95 (*0-945989-09-1*) Anderson WA.

Northwest Bounty: The Extraordinary Foods & Wonderful Cooking of the Pacific Northwest. rev. ed. Schuyler Ingle & Sharon Kramis. 304p. 1999. pap. 16.95 (*1-57061-225-0*) Sasquatch Bks.

Northwest Budget Traveler: Cheap Eats, Cheap Sleeps, Affordable Adventure. 3rd rev. ed. Ed. by Nancy Leson. (Best Places Ser.). Orig. Title: Northwest Cheap Sleeps. (Illus.). 320p. 1998. pap. 16.95 (*1-57061-126-2*) Sasquatch Bks.

Northwest Carving Traditions. Karen Norris & Ralph Norris. LC 98-53343. (Illus.). 3p. 1999. 59.95 (*0-7643-0799-1*) Schiffer.

Northwest Cheap Sleeps see Northwest Budget Traveler: Cheap Eats, Cheap Sleeps, Affordable Adventure

Northwest Coast. large type ed. James G. Swan. 464p. 1989. reprint ed. 26.95 (*0-87770-473-2*) Ye Galleon.

Northwest Coast, Vol. 7. Wayne Suttles. (Illus.). 796p. 1990. 51.00 (*0-87474-187-4*) Smithsonian.

Northwest Coast: A Natural History. Stewart T. Schultz. LC 89-39460. (Illus.). 401p. 1990. 29.95 (*0-88192-142-4*) Timber.

Northwest Coast: A Natural History. Stewart T. Schultz. (Illus.). 401p. 1998. 19.95 (*0-88192-418-0*) Timber.

Northwest Coast: British Navigation, Trade & Discoveries to 1812. Barry M. Gough. 279p. 1992. text 65.00 (*0-7748-0399-1*) U of Wash Pr.

***Northwest Coast: Personal Narratives of Discovery, Conquest & Exploration.** Edward Eberstadt. 127p. 1999. 45.00 (*1-57898-180-8*) Martino Pubng.

Northwest Coast Indian Art: An Analysis of Form. Bill Holm. LC 65-10818. (Thomas Burke Memorial Washington State Museum Monograph: No. 1). (Illus.). 133p. 1965. pap. 16.95 (*0-295-95102-8*) U of Wash Pr.

Northwest Coast Indian Designs. Madeleine Orban-Szontagh. LC 94-19490. 48p. 1994. pap. 5.95 (*0-486-28179-5*) Dover.

Northwest Coast Indian Painting: House Fronts & Interior Screens. Edward Malin. LC 98-39230. (Illus.). 288p. 1999. 39.95 (*0-88192-471-7*) Timber.

***Northwest Coast Indians.** Mir Tamim Ansary. LC 99-13517. (Native Americans Ser.). (Illus.). 32p. (J). (gr. 2-4). 1999. 14.95 (*1-57572-921-0*) Heinemann Lib.

Northwest Coast Indians. Mira Bartok & Christine Ronan. LC 96-100915. (Big World Read Along Ser.). (Illus.). 20p. (J). (gr. k-2). 1995. bds. 4.95 (*0-673-36257-4*, GoodYrBooks) Addson-Wesley Educ.

Northwest Coast Indians: Stencils. Mira Bartok & Christine Ronan. (Ancient & Living Cultures Ser.). (Illus.). 32p. (Orig.). (J). (gr. 3 up). 1992. pap. 9.95 (*0-673-36056-3*, GoodYrBooks) Addson-Wesley Educ.

Northwest Coast Indians Coloring Book. Tom Smith & Diane Smith. (Color & Story Bks.). (Illus.). 32p. (Orig.). (J). (ps up). 1993. pap. 5.99 (*0-8431-3491-7*, Price Stern) Peng Put Young Read.

Northwest Coast Native & Native-Style Art: A Guidebook for Western Washington. Lloyd J. Averill & Daphne K. Morris. LC 95-21962. (Illus.). xxxix, 215p. (C). 1995. pap. 17.95 (*0-295-97468-0*) U of Wash Pr.

Northwest Coast: or Three Years' Residence in Washington Territory. James G. Swan. LC 70-90378. (Illus.). 460p. 1982. pap. 14.95 (*0-295-95190-7*) U of Wash Pr.

Northwest Conifers: A Photographic Key. Dale N. Bever. LC 81-65509. (Illus.). 116p. 1981. pap. 18.95 (*0-8323-0390-9*) Binford Mort.

Northwest Connecticut, CT. (Streetfinder Ser.). (Illus.). 1994. pap. 14.95 (*0-528-91324-7*) Rand McNally.

Northwest Conservation & Electric Power Plan, 1991, Vol. I, Pt. I. (Illus.). 442p. (Orig.). (C). 1995. pap. text 60.00 (*0-7881-2257-6*) DIANE Pub.

Northwest D. C. Carry Out. Ed. by Ann H. Waigand. 96p. (Orig.). 1988. pap. 4.95 (*0-942231-02-3*) Educ Traveler.

***Northwest Essentials Cookbook: Cooking with the Ingredients That Define a Regional Cuisine.** Greg Atkinson. LC 99-15346. 272p. 1999. pap. 19.95 (*1-57061-179-3*) Sasquatch Bks.

Northwest Ethiopia: Peoples & Economy. Frederick J. Simoons. LC 83-1596. (Illus.). 250p. 1983. reprint ed. lib. bdg. 59.75 (*0-313-23887-1*, SINO, Greenwood Pr) Greenwood.

Northwest European Micorpaleontology & Palymology. Ed. by David J. Batten & Michael C. Keen. 1989. text 153.00 (*0-470-21487-2*) P-H.

Northwest European Pollen Flora, Vol. 3. Ed. by W. Punt & G. C. Clarke. 138p. 1981. 136.50 (*0-444-41996-9*) Elsevier.

Northwest European Pollen Flora, Vol. 5. Ed. by W. Punt et al. 154p. 1988. 150.00 (*0-444-87268-X*) Elsevier.

Northwest European Pollen Flora, Vol. VI. W. Punt & Stephen Blackmore. 276p. 1991. 191.50 (*0-444-89164-1*) Elsevier.

Northwest European Pollen Flora, Vol. 7. Ed. by W. Punt & G. C. Clarke. (Illus.). 282p. 1995. 200.75 (*0-444-82392-1*) Elsevier.

Northwest Explorations. 2nd ed. Gordon Speck. LC 70-92541. (Illus.). 400p. 1970. 14.95 (*0-8323-0216-3*) Binford Mort.

Northwest Exposures: A Geologic Story of the Northwest. David Alt & Donald W. Hyndman. LC 95-37140. 456p. 1995. pap. text 24.00 (*0-87842-323-0*) Mountain Pr.

Northwest Ferry Tales: Collection of Stories, Poems & Anecdotes from Washington, British Columbia & Alaska. Joyce Delbridge. (Illus.). 128p. 1990. reprint ed. pap. 9.95 (*0-88839-250-8*) Hancock House.

Northwest Ferry Tales: Stories, Poems & Anecdotes from Washington, British Columbia & Alaska. Ed. by Joyce Delbridge et al. LC 88-50264. (Illus.). 128p. (Orig.). (YA). (gr. 5 up). 1989. pap. 8.95 (*0-9616103-8-7*) Vashon Pt Prod.

Northwest Florida Expeditions of Clarence Bloomfield Moore. David S. Brose. LC 99-6364. (Classics in Southeastern Archaeology Ser.). 1999. pap. 49.95 (*0-8173-0992-6*) U of Ala Pr.

Northwest Fly Fishing: Trout & Beyond. John Shewey. (Illus.). 128p. (Orig.). 1992. 34.95 (*1-878175-25-4*); pap. 21.95 (*1-878175-24-6*) F Amato Pubns.

Northwest Food & Wine: Great Food to Serve with the Wines of Washington & Oregon. Dan Taggart & Kathleen Taggart. LC 98-26355. 256p. 1998. pap. 18.95 (*1-57061-147-5*) Sasquatch Bks.

Northwest Foraging: Wild Edibles of the Pacific Northwest. Doug Benoliel. (Illus.). 1974. pap. 12.95 (*0-913140-13-9*) Signpost Bk Pub.

Northwest Forest Plan: A Report to the President & Congress. E. Thomas Tuchmann et al. (Illus.). 259p. 1998. pap. text 40.00 (*0-7881-7366-9*) DIANE Pub.

Northwest Garden Style: Ideas, Designs, & Methods for the Creative Gardener. Jan K. Whitner. (Illus.). 208p. (Orig.). 1996. pap. 19.95 (*1-57061-064-9*); pap. 39.90 incl. audio (*1-57061-086-X*) Sasquatch Bks.

Northwest Gardeners' Resource Directory. 8th rev. ed. Stephanie Feeney. 352p. 1999. pap. 19.95 (*0-9639853-5-3*) Cedarcroft Pr.

Northwest Gateway: The Story of the Port of Seattle. Archie Binns. (Illus.). 325p. 1958. 14.95 (*0-8323-0004-7*) Binford Mort.

Northwest Georgia in Vintage Postcards. Gary Doster. LC 98-86669. (Postcard History Ser.). (Illus.). 128p. 1998. pap. 18.99 (*0-7524-1376-7*) Arcadia Publng.

Northwest Germany Map. 1996. 8.95 (*2-06-700415-8*, 415) Michelin.

Northwest Glory Days. Marge Davenport. (Illus.). 208p. (Orig.). 1983. pap. 6.95 (*0-938274-02-3*) Paddlewheel.

Northwest Golfer's Almanac, 2 vols., Vol. 1: Background Basics. Ed. by Jeff Shelley. 176p. 1991. 7.95 (*0-9629329-0-6*) Fairgreens Mda.

Northwest Governments Performance Standards, 1990. Ed. by Greg Michels. (Governments Performance Standards Ser.). (Illus.). 150p. 1990. text 125.00 (*1-55507-509-6*) Municipal Analysis.

Northwest Greenland: A History. Richard Vaughan. LC 91-8114. (Illus.). 233p. 1991. 29.95 (*0-89101-072-6*) U Maine Pr.

***Northwest Herb Lover's Handbook: A Guide to Growing Herbs for Cooking, Crafts & Home Remedies.** Mary Preus. LC 99-47198. (Illus.). 224p. 2000. pap. 16.95 (*1-57061-172-6*) Sasquatch Bks.

Northwest High Tech. 6th ed. Resolution Business Press Staff. 1997. 34.95 (*0-945264-21-6*) Resolution Busn Pr.

Northwest History: Articles from the Pacific Northwest Quarterly. Jerome Peltier. LC 96-52910. 1996. pap. 14.95 (*0-87770-602-6*) Ye Galleon.

Northwest Indian Designs. 5th ed. Caren Caraway. (International Design Library). (Illus.). 48p. 1982. pap. 6.95 (*0-916144-98-4*, Naturencyclop) Stemmer Hse.

***Northwest Indiana Entertainment, 2000.** (Illus.). 614p. 1999. pap. 35.00 (*1-880248-52-2*, 0058) Enter Pubns.

Northwest Indians. Cleary & Taylor. (Illus.). 48p. (J). (gr. 3-6). 1996. pap., teacher ed. 5.95 (*1-55799-571-0*, 557) Evan-Moor Edu Pubs.

Northwest Indians. Spizzirri Publishing Co. Staff. Ed. by Linda Spizzirri. (Illus.). 32p. (J). (gr. 1-8). pap. 4.98 incl. audio (*0-86545-047-1*) Spizzirri.

Northwest Institute Language Program: Learning to Read, Write & Speak English, 3 vols. William J. Worthley & Northwest Institute for Psycholinguistic Studies Staff. LC 97-92499. xxii, 838 p. 1997. write for info. (*0-9660490-3-9*) Pacific Pl Pubs.

Northwest Journal. Date not set. pap. text 10.95 (*1-882877-05-5*) Panoply Pr.

Northwest Journal: Mountain Cover. Northwest Publishers Consortium Staff. 1996. pap. 10.95 (*1-882877-07-1*) Panoply Pr.

***Northwest Lands, Northwest Peoples: Readings in Environmental History.** Ed. by Dale D. Goble & Paul W. Hirt. LC 99-27118. (Illus.). 560p. 1999. 60.00 (*0-295-97839-2*); pap. text 29.95 (*0-295-97838-4*) U of Wash Pr.

Northwest Marine Weather: From the Columbia River to Cape Scott, Including Puget Sound, the San Juan & Gulf Islands, & the Straits of Juan de Fuca, Georgia, Johnstone, & Queen Charlotte. Jeff Renner. 144p. 1993. 10.95 (*0-89886-376-7*) Mountaineers.

Northwest Mountain Weather: Understanding & Forecasting for the Backcountry User. Jeff Renner. LC 91-46559. (Illus.). 96p. (Orig.). 1992. pap. 10.95 (*0-89886-297-3*) Mountaineers.

Northwest National Park & Forest Wit. William Gibson & Pacific Northwest National Parks & Forests Associa. (Illus.). 216p. 1992. 8.95 (*0-936023-01-5*, 34503) Interp Mktg Prods.

Northwest Native Harvest. Carol Batdorf. 96p. (Orig.). 1990. pap. 7.95 (*0-88839-245-1*) Hancock House.

Northwest Natural Hot Springs. Tom Stockley & B. G. Olson. LC 91-44972. (Umbrella Guides Ser.). (Illus.). 96p. (Orig.). 1992. pap. 10.95 (*0-945397-14-3*, Umbrella Bks) Epicenter Pr.

Northwest Necropolis of Satricum. Demetrius J. Waarsenburg. (Scrinium VIII). (Illus.). 557p. 1995. 177.00 (*90-5170-294-9*, Pub. by Thesis Pubs) D Brown Bk Co.

Northwest Nurse. large type ed. Arlene J. Fitzgerald. (Linford Romance Library). 256p. 1993. pap. 16.99 (*0-7089-7453-8*, Linford) Ulverscroft.

Northwest Oklahoma. Christy Siemsen. (Illus.). 219p. 1994. 54.50 (*0-88107-241-9*) Curtis Media.

Northwest Ordinance: Essays on Its Formation, Provisions & Legacy. Ed. by Federick D. Williams. LC 88-42857. 150p. (C). 1988. 17.95 (*0-87013-262-8*) Mich St U Pr.

Northwest Ordinance, 1787: A Bicentennial Handbook. Ed. by Robert M. Taylor, Jr. LC 87-3674. (Illus.). xxiv, 136p. 1987. 22.50 (*0-87195-016-2*); pap. 7.95 (*0-87195-008-1*) Ind Hist Soc.

Northwest Oregon Stable Guide: One Hundred Boarding, Breeding & Training Stables for Horses. Carole Devereux. LC 93-74828. 144p. 1993. pap. 15.95 (*1-884422-13-6*) Centaur Pubns.

Northwest Pacific Ocean Waters in Winter. Joseph L. Reid. LC 72-12351. (Johns Hopkins Oceanographic Studies: No. 5). (Illus.). 96p. 1973. reprint ed. pap. 30.00 (*0-608-04008-8*, 206474400011) Bks Demand.

Northwest Passage. Norman Lavers. LC 83-27484. 137p. 1984. 15.95 (*0-914590-86-3*); pap. 7.95 (*0-914590-87-1*) Fiction Coll.

Northwest Passage. Barry Lopez. (Illus.). 96p. 1996. 68.00 (*0-89381-676-0*) Aperture.

Northwest Passage. Andrew J. Lucas & Jeff Ranger. (Cyberpunk Ser.). 64p. 1996. pap. 10.00 (*1-887801-44-8*, Atlas Games) Trident MN.

Northwest Passage. Kenneth Roberts. 1983. write for info. (*0-318-56616-8*) Haas Ent NH.

Northwest Passage: The Great Columbia River. William Dietrich. 448p. 1995. 26.00 (*0-671-79650-X*) S&S Trade.

Northwest Passage: The Great Columbia River. William Dietrich. LC 96-3972. (Illus.). 448p. 1996. reprint ed. pap. 18.95 (*0-295-97546-6*) U of Wash Pr.

Northwest Passage: The Life of Ellis Scism, Pt.1. Ellis Scism & Stanley Scism. LC 94-12003. 272p. (Orig.). 1994. pap. 4.99 (*1-56722-023-1*) Word Aflame.

Northwest Passage & Apache Blood, 2 vols. in 1. David Thompson. (Wilderness Ser.: Vols. 11 & 12). 352p. 1998. mass mkt. 4.99 (*0-8439-4391-2*, Leisure Bks) Dorchester Pub Co.

Northwest Passage Solo. David S. Cowper. LC 93-34441. (Illus.). 244p. 1994. 23.95 (*0-924486-65-1*) Sheridan.

Northwest Passages: A Literary Anthology of the Pacific Northwest from Coyote Tales to Roadside Attractions. Ed. by Bruce Barcott. LC 94-2939. 320p. (Orig.). 1994. pap. 15.95 (*1-57061-005-3*) Sasquatch Bks.

Northwest Passages: From the Pen of John Muir in California, Oregon, Washington & Alaska. John Muir. LC 98-73725. (Illus.). 64p. 1998. reprint ed. 15.00 (*0-9633056-8-9*) Coldstream Pr.

Northwest Penstemons. Dee Strickler. (Illus.). 192p. 1997. 29.95 (*1-56044-572-6*, Skyhse) Falcon Pub Inc.

Northwest Perspectives: Essays on the Culture of the Pacific Northwest. Ed. by Edwin R. Bingham & Glen A. Love. LC 77-15189. 264p. 1979. 22.00 (*0-295-95594-5*); pap. 10.95 (*0-295-95805-7*) U of Wash Pr.

Northwest Portrait, 1994. 5th ed. (Illus.). 51p. (C). 1994. pap. text 25.00 (*0-7881-0727-5*) DIANE Pub.

Northwest Rail Pictorial, Vol. 3. Warren W. Wing. (Illus.). 200p. 1998. 42.95 (*0-9647521-7-4*) Oso Pubng.

Northwest Rail Pictorial I. Warren W. Wing. Ed. by Pacific Fast Mail Staff. (Illus.). 160p. 1983. 29.95 (*0-915713-06-3*) Pac Fast Mail.

Northwest Sahaptin Texts, 2 pts. Melville Jacobs. LC 70-82338. (Columbia University. Contributions to Anthropology Ser.: Vol. 19). reprint ed. 50.00 (*0-404-50569-4*) AMS Pr.

Northwest Salmon Crisis: A Documentary History. Ed. by Joseph Cone & Sandy Ridlington. (Illus.). 320p. (C). 1996. 29.95 (*0-87071-390-6*) Oreg St U Pr.

***Northwest Salmon Crisis: A Documentary History.** Ed. by Joseph Cone & Sandy Ridlington. (Illus.). 384p. 2000. pap. 22.95 (*0-87071-472-4*) Oreg St U Pr.

Northwest Style: Interior Design & Architecture in the Pacific Northwest. Ann Wall Frank. LC 99-17976. (Illus.). 204p. 1999. 40.00 (*0-8118-2536-1*) Chronicle Bks.

***Northwest Territories.** (Canada in the Twenty First Century Ser.). (Illus.). (J). 2000. 18.95 (*0-7910-6066-7*) Chelsea Hse.

N

Northwest Territories. Alaska Geographic Society Staff. Ed. by Richard Harrington. LC 72-92087. (Alaska Geographic Ser.: Vol. 12, No. 3). (Illus.). 136p. 1985. pap. 9.95 (*0-88240-204-8*) Alaska Geog Soc.

Northwest Territories. Harry Beckett. LC 97-22219. (Journey Across Canada Ser.). 24p. (J). (gr. 3-5). 1997. lib. bdg. 18.60 (*1-55916-207-4*) Rourke Bk Co.

***Northwest Territories.** Richard W. Daitch. (Hello Canada Ser.). 1999. pap. 7.95 (*1-55041-265-5*) Fitzhenry & W Ltd.

Northwest Territories. Richard W. Daitch. LC 95-4222. (Hello Canada Ser.). (Illus.). 76p. (J). (gr. 3-6). 1996. 18.95 (*0-8225-2761-8*) Lerner Pub.

Northwest Territory 1800 Census: Index of Washington County, Ohio 1791-1803 Marriages & Thomas Summers History of Marietta Index Plus Wm. P. Cutlers List of Signers of July 13, 1787 Ordinance. Fay Maxwell. 51p. 1973. 20.00 (*1-885463-20-0*) Ohio Genealogy.

***North/West Texas Business Directory, 1999-2000.** rev. ed. American Business Directories Staff. 3456p. 1999. boxed set 415.00 incl. cd-rom (*0-7687-0207-0*) Am Busn Direct.

Northwest to Fortune. Vilhjalmur Stefansson. LC 73-20881. (Illus.). 356p. (C). 1974. reprint ed. lib. bdg. 65.00 (*0-8371-5729-3*, STNF, Greenwood Pr) Greenwood.

Northwest Treasure Hunter's Gem & Mineral Guide: Where & How to Dig, Pan & Mine Your Own Gems & Minerals. Kathy J. Rygle & Stephen F. Pedersen. LC 99-39215. (Illus.). 176p. 1999. pap. 14.95 (*0-943763-24-X*) GemStone Pr.

Northwest Trees. Stephen F. Arno. LC 77-82369. (Illus.). 238p. 1977. 30.00 (*0-916890-55-4*) Mountaineers.

Northwest Trees. Stephen F. Arno. LC 77-82369. (Illus.). 238p. 1990. pap. 12.95 (*0-916890-50-3*) Mountaineers.

Northwest Trek Book. Nancy Field & Sally Machlis. (Illus.). 26p. (J). (gr. 1-6). 1977. reprint ed. pap. 3.50 (*0-941042-00-6*) Dog Eared Pubns.

Northwest Twelve-Moon Journey. Raymond L. Powis. (Illus.). 88p. (Orig.). 1995. pap. 19.95 (*1-888647-00-0*) Ray & Roo Enter.

Northwest Voices: An Anthology of Prose & Poetry. Tacoma Writers Club Staff. Ed. by Charlotte Richards. (Illus.). 96p. (Orig.). 1996. pap. 10.00 (*0-9654350-0-8*) Whispering Firs.

Northwest Weeds: The Ugly & Beautiful Villains of Fields, Gardens, & Roadsides. Ronald J. Taylor. LC 89-48817. 183p. 1990. pap. 14.00 (*0-87842-249-8*) Mountain Pr.

Northwest Weekend Gardener Organizer: A Three Year Planner. Lavon H. La Fresnaye. (Illus.). 160p. 1998. pap. 17.95 (*0-9662674-0-0*) La Fresnaye.

Northwest Wines: A Pocket Guide to the Wines of Washington, Oregon, & Idaho. 2nd rev. ed. Paul Gregutt et al. LC 96-22758. 208p. (Orig.). 1996. pap. 11.95 (*1-57061-062-2*) Sasquatch Bks.

Northwest Woman & an Evening with Thomas Condon. Dorothy Velasco. LC 82-10282. (Illus.). 84p. (Orig.). 1982. pap. 3.50 (*0-943572-00-2*) Spring Historical.

Northwest Women: An Annotated Bibliography of Sources on the History of Oregon & Washington Women 1787-1970. Ed. by Karen J. Blair. (Illus.). 150p. (Orig.). 1997. pap. 32.95 (*0-87422-145-5*) Wash St U Pr.

Northwestern Arkansas Death Record Index, 1914-1923: Benton, Boone, Carroll, Madison, Marion, Newton, Searcy, & Washington Counties. Ed. by Desmond W. Allen. 53p. (Orig.). 1996. pap. 15.00 (*1-56546-081-2*) Arkansas Res.

Northwestern Arkansas Death Record Index, 1924-1933: Benton, Boone, Carroll, Madison, Marion, Newton, Searcy, & Washington Counties. Ed. by Desmond W. Allen. 52p. 1997. pap. 15.00 (*1-56546-115-0*) Arkansas Res.

Northwestern Arkansas Death Record Index, 1934-1940: Benton, Boone, Carroll, Madison, Marion, Newton, Searcy, & Washington Counties. Ed. by Desmond W. Allen. 50p. (Orig.). 1996. pap. 15.00 (*1-56546-089-8*) Arkansas Res.

***Northwestern Arkansas Death Record Index, 1941-1948: Benton, Boone, Carroll, Madison, Marion, Newton, Searcy, & Washington Counties.** Compiled by Desmond Walls Allen. 72p. 1999. pap. 16.00 (*1-56546-160-6*) Arkansas Res.

Northwestern Fights & Fighters. Cyrus T. Brady. LC 79-15171. 431p. 1979. reprint ed. pap. 133.70 (*0-7837-8859-2*, 204956900001) Bks Demand.

***Northwestern Fights & Fighters: The Nez Perce & Modoc Wars.** 2nd unabridged ed. Cyrus T. Brady. (Illus.). 434p. 1999. reprint ed. pap. 18.95 (*0-87928-130-8*) Corner Hse.

Northwestern Indiana, from 1800 to 1900: A View of Our Region Through the Nineteenth Century. T. H. Ball. (Illus.). 570p. 1995. reprint ed. lib. bdg. 59.00 (*0-8328-5013-6*) Higginson Bk Co.

Northwestern Journal of International Law & Business, 1979-1995/96, 17 vols., Set. 1979. 707.50 (*0-8377-9125-1*, Rothman) W S Hein.

Northwestern Mutual Life: A Century of Trusteeship. Harold F. Williamson & Orange A. Smalley. LC 75-41787. (Companies & Men: Business Enterprises in America Ser.). (Illus.). 1976. reprint ed. 39.95 (*0-405-08102-2*) Ayer.

Northwestern New Jersey: A History of Somerset, Morris, Hunterdon, Warren & Sussex Counties, 5 vols. in 2. Ed. by A. V. Honeyman. (Illus.). 1997. reprint ed. lib. bdg. 165.00 (*0-8328-6035-2*) Higginson Bk Co.

Northwestern PA. Early History & Growth of Carlisle; Early Footprints of Developments & Improvements in Northwestern Pennsylvania. Theodore B. Klein & Isaac B. Brown. (Illus.). 75p. 1997. reprint ed. pap. 19.00 (*0-8328-6381-5*) Higginson Bk Co.

Northwestern Pacific Railroad & Its Successors. Wesley Fox. (Illus.). 112p. 1995. 38.95 (*1-884831-01-X*) Fox Pubns.

Northwestern Seashore Life: Alaska to Oregon. James Kavanagh. (Pocket Naturalist Ser.). (Illus.). (J). 1997. 5.95 (*1-889903-10-8*, Pub. by Waterford WA) Falcon Pub Inc.

Northwestern State University of Louisiana, 1884-1948: A History. Marietta M. LeBreton. LC 85-61932. (Illus.). 320p. 1985. 30.00 (*0-917898-10-9*) NSU Pr LA.

Northwestern University. Photos by Jack Mellott. (First Edition Ser.). (Illus.). 112p. 1988. 39.00 (*0-916509-46-X*) Harmony Hse Pub.

***Northwestern University: Celebrating 150 Years.** Jay Pridmore. LC 00-8901. 2000. write for info. (*0-8101-1829-7*) Northwestern U Pr.

Northwestern University Law Review: 1906-1994/95, 91 vols., Set. 1996. 4787.50 (*0-8377-9126-X*, Rothman) W S Hein.

Northwestern Wild Berries. J. E. Underhill. (Illus.). 96p. pap. 8.95 (*0-88839-027-0*) Hancock House.

Northwest's Own Railway - Spokane, Portland & Seattle Railway & Its Subsidiaries, 2 vols. Incl. Mainline. Walter R. Grande. 1992. (*0-9634128-0-9*); Subsidiaries. 1995. (*0-9634128-1-7*); write for info. (*0-9634128-2-5*) Grande Pr.

Northwood. Sarah Josephbuell Hale. LC 74-38652. (Black Heritage Library Collection). 1977. reprint ed. 26.95 (*0-8369-9010-2*) Ayer.

Northwood Country Girl. Patricia M. Johnson. 60p. (Orig.). 1993. pap. 8.00 (*0-9635690-1-5*) TA Pubns.

Northwood Lad. William Brashear. Ed. by Gwen Costa. LC 90-1137. (YA). (gr. 6 up). 1992. pap. 14.95 (*0-87949-333-X*) Ashley Bks.

Northwood Rambles: Seasons of Wonder. Jean E. Dohms. LC 97-73814. (Illus.). 142p. (Orig.). 1997. pap. 12.95 (*0-9645665-1-6*) Boulder Knob Bks.

Northwoods Adventures, Vols. 1-5. Lois Johnson. (Northwoods Adventures Ser.). (J). 1993. pap., boxed set 29.99 (*1-55661-775-5*, 252775) Bethany Hse.

Northwoods Adventures Series, Vols. 6-10. Lois Walfrid Johnson. (Northwoods Adventures Ser.). (J). 1995. pap., boxed set 29.99 (*1-55661-793-3*, 252793) Bethany Hse.

Northwoods Companion: Fall & Winter. John Bates. (Illus.). 240p. (Orig.). 1997. pap. 14.95 (*0-9656763-1-5*) Manitowish River.

Northwoods Companion: Spring & Summer. John Bates. LC 97-70781. (Illus.). 240p. (Orig.). 1997. pap. 14.95 (*0-9656763-0-7*) Manitowish River.

Northwoods Cradle Song: From a Menominee Lullaby. Douglas Wood. LC 95-2888. (Illus.). 32p. (J). (ps-k). 1998. pap. 5.99 (*0-689-82228-6*) Aladdin.

Northwoods Cradle Song: From a Menominee Lullaby. Douglas Wood. LC 95-2888. (Illus.). 32p. (J). (ps-k). 1996. mass mkt. 15.00 (*0-689-80503-9*) S&S Bks Yung.

***Northwoods Fish Cookery.** Ron Berg. LC 99-50532. 2000. pap. 16.95 (*0-8166-3583-8*) U of Minn Pr.

***Northwoods Pulp: Four Tales of Crime & Weirdness.** Thomas Sparrow. 320p. 1999. pap. 14.95 (*0-9672006-0-1*, 99-01) Bluestone Pr.

***Northwoods Reader: Northern Wit & Wisdom.** rev. ed. Cully Gage. 320p. 1999. pap. 16.95 (*1-892384-02-7*) Avery Color.

***Northwoods Table: Natural Cuisine Featuring Native Foods.** Henry Sinkus. LC 00-26387. (Illus.). 96p. 2000. 22.50 (*1-57223-291-9*, 2919) Willow Creek Pr.

Northwoods Wildlife Region, Vol. 1. Jay Conrader & Constance Conrader. LC 83-6257. (Illus.). 192p. (C). 1983. pap. 8.95 (*0-87961-127-8*) Naturegraph.

Northwords. Ed. by Leonard Belasco. LC 80-85225. 66p. (Orig.). 1981. pap. 12.95 (*0-915032-23-6*) Natl Poet Foun.

Northworld. David Drake. (Northworld Ser.: No. 1). 1990. mass mkt. 4.99 (*0-441-84830-3*) Ace Bks.

Northworld Trilogy. David Drake. 1999. mass mkt. 6.99 (*0-671-57787-5*) Baen Bks.

***Norton.** George Yelle & Ruth Goold. LC 99-69228. (Images of America Ser.). (Illus.). 128p. 2000. pap. 18.99 (*0-7385-0264-2*) Arcadia Publng.

Norton: A History. Mick Woolett. (Illus.). 320p. 1997. pap. 29.95 (*1-85532-700-7*, Pub. by Ospry) Stackpole.

Norton: The Complete History. Derek Magrath. (Illus.). 160p. 1997. pap. 24.95 (*1-86126-062-8*, Pub. by Cro1wood) Motorbooks Intl.

Norton: The Legend Continues. Jim Reynolds. 96p. 1995. 12.98 (*0-7858-0310-6*) Bk Sales Inc.

Norton - Grove Concise Encyclopedia of Music. 2nd enl. rev. ed. Stanley Sadie. 1994. 42.50 (*0-393-03753-3*) Norton.

Norton A People in A Nation with Atlas, 4 vols., 2. 5th ed. Mary B. Norton et al. Price not set. (*0-395-78884-6*) HM.

Norton Anthology of African American Literature. Ed. by Henry Louis Gates, Jr. et al. 2665p. 1996. 59.95 (*0-393-04001-1*) Norton.

Norton Anthology of African American Literature. Ed. by Henry Louis Gates, Jr. 1996. pap. text 55.00 (*0-393-95908-2*, Norton Paperbks) Norton.

***Norton Anthology of American Literature.** 5th ed. Nina Baym. LC 98-26885. 2700p. 1999. pap. 52.25 (*0-393-97291-7*) Norton.

Norton Anthology of American Literature Vol. 1: 1620-1865, Vol. 1. 5th ed. Ed. by Nina Baym et al. LC 97-45578. 2600p. (C). 1998. pap. text 52.25 (*0-393-95871-X*) Norton.

Norton Anthology of American Literature Vol. 2: 1865 to the Present, Vol. 2. 5th ed. Ed. by Nina Baym et al. LC 97-45578. 2950p. (C). 1998. pap. text 52.25 (*0-393-95872-8*) Norton.

***Norton Anthology of American Literature With Walden Norton Critical: Shorter Edition.** 5th ed. James M. Bayman. 1999. pap. text, boxed set 44.50 (*0-393-99019-2*) Norton.

Norton Anthology of Contemporary Fiction. R. V. Cassill. (Orig.). (C). 1987. pap. text 33.50 (*0-393-95619-9*) Norton.

Norton Anthology of Contemporary Fiction. 2nd ed. R. Cassill. (C). 1997. pap., teacher ed. write for info. (*0-393-96834-0*) Norton.

Norton Anthology of Contemporary Fiction. 2nd ed. R. V. Cassill & Joyce Carol Oates. LC 96-51171. 556p. (C). 1997. pap. text 37.50 (*0-393-96833-2*) Norton.

Norton Anthology of English Literature. 6th ed. M. Abrams. (C). 1996. text 40.00 (*0-393-96806-5*); text 55.75 (*0-393-96807-3*); text 55.75 (*0-393-96935-5*); pap. text 39.00 (*0-393-96809-X*); pap. text 39.00 (*0-393-96810-3*); pap. text 54.25 (*0-393-96812-X*); pap. text 39.00 (*0-393-96936-3*) Norton.

Norton Anthology of English Literature. 6th ed. M. Abrams. (C). 1996. text 38.00 (*0-393-96805-7*); text 40.00 (*0-393-96804-9*); pap. text 36.00 (*0-393-96811-1*) Norton.

Norton Anthology of English Literature. 6th ed. M. Abrams. 1997. pap. 52.80 (*0-393-98405-2*) Norton.

Norton Anthology of English Literature. 6th ed. Ed. by M. H. Abrams. (C). 1996. text 53.50 (*0-393-96803-0*) Norton.

Norton Anthology of English Literature. 6th ed. Ed. by M. H. Abrams. (C). 1996. pap. text 37.50 (*0-393-96808-1*) Norton.

Norton Anthology of English Literature, 001. 6th ed. Ed. by Meyer H. Abrams. LC 92-40016. (C). 1993. pap. write for info. (*0-393-96288-1*); text 50.00 (*0-393-96287-3*) Norton.

***Norton Anthology of English Literature, Vol. 1.** 7th ed. M. H. Abrams. LC 99-43298. 1999. pap. 52.25 (*0-393-97487-1*, Norton Paperbks) Norton.

***Norton Anthology of English Literature, Vol. 1.** 7th ed. M. H. Abrams. LC 99-43298. Vol. 1. 2974p. 1999. 53.50 (*0-393-97486-3*, Norton Paperbks) Norton.

Norton Anthology of English Literature, Vol. 2. 6th ed. Ed. by Meyer H. Abrams. LC 92-40016. (C). 1993. text 50.00 (*0-393-96289-X*); pap. text 36.00 (*0-393-96290-3*) Norton.

***Norton Anthology of English Literature, Vol. 2.** 7th ed. M. H. Abrams. 1999. pap. 52.25 (*0-393-97491-X*, Norton Paperbks) Norton.

***Norton Anthology of English Literature, Vol. 2.** 7th ed. M. H. Abrams. LC 99-43298. Vol. 2. 1999. 53.50 (*0-393-97490-1*, Norton Paperbks) Norton.

Norton Anthology of Literature by Women. 2nd ed. Sandra M. Gilbert. (C). Date not set. pap. text, teacher ed. write for info. (*0-393-96894-4*) Norton.

Norton Anthology of Literature by Women: The Traditions in English. 2nd ed. Ed. by Sandra M. Gilbert & Susan Gubar. 2600p. (C). 1996. pap. 53.00 (*0-393-96825-1*, Norton Paperbks) Norton.

Norton Anthology of Modern Poetry. 2nd ed. Ed. by Richard Ellmann & Robert O'Clair. 1865p. (C). 1988. pap. text, teacher ed. 53.00 (*0-393-95636-9*) Norton.

Norton Anthology of Poetry. 4th ed. Ed. by Margaret Ferguson et al. LC 96-8035. 850p. (C). 1996. pap. text 53.00 (*0-393-96820-0*, Norton Paperbks) Norton.

Norton Anthology of Poetry. 4th ed. Ed. by Margaret Ferguson et al. LC 96-3198. 1215p. (C). 1996. pap. text 32.50 (*0-393-96924-X*) Norton.

Norton Anthology of Poetry. 4th ed. James Knapp. Ed. by Margaret Ferguson. 1996. 50.00 incl. cd-rom (*0-393-96914-2*, Norton Paperbks) Norton.

Norton Anthology of Short Fiction. 5th ed. Ed. by R. V. Cassill. LC 94-42761. 1718p. (C). 1995. pap. 33.00 (*0-393-96663-1*); pap. 37.00 (*0-393-96664-X*) Norton.

Norton Anthology of Short Fiction. 5th ed. Ed. by R. V. Cassill. (C). 1995. pap. text, teacher ed. write for info. (*0-393-96703-4*) Norton.

Norton Anthology of Theory & Criticism. Vincent Leitch. (C). pap. text. write for info. (*0-393-97429-4*) Norton.

Norton Anthology of Western Music Vol. I: Ancient to Baroque, Vol. 1. 3rd ed. Ed. by Claude V. Palisca. 600p. (C). 1996. pap. 40.50 (*0-393-96906-1*, Norton Paperbks) Norton.

Norton Anthology of Western Music Vol. II: Classic to Modern, Vol. 2. 3rd ed. Ed. by Claude V. Palisca. 800p. (C). 1996. pap. text 40.50 (*0-393-96907-X*, Norton Paperbks) Norton.

Norton Anthology of World Literature, Vol. 1. 7th ed. Ed. by W. W. Norton & Company Staff. Date not set. write for info. (*0-393-97335-2*) Norton.

Norton Anthology of World Literature, Vol. 2. 7th ed. Ed. by W. W. Norton & Company Staff. Date not set. write for info. (*0-393-97342-5*) Norton.

Norton Anthology of World Masterpieces. Maynard Mack. LC 96-39009. 3052p. (C). 1997. pap. text 53.50 (*0-393-97143-0*) Norton.

Norton Anthology of World Masterpieces. 5th ed. Ed. by Maynard Mack et al. (C). 1987. pap. write for info. (*0-393-95486-2*) Norton.

Norton Anthology of World Masterpieces, Vol. 1. 6th expanded ed. Ed. by Patricia M. Spacks et al. LC 94-42732. (C). 1995. pap. 53.50 (*0-393-96346-2*) Norton.

Norton Anthology of World Masterpieces, Vol. 1. 7th ed. Sarah N. Lawall. LC 98-35047. Vol. 1. 2500p. 1998. pap. 51.50 (*0-393-97289-5*) Norton.

Norton Anthology of World Masterpieces, Vol. 2. 6th expanded ed. P. M. Pasinetti et al. LC 94-42732. Vol. 2. 2p. (C). 1995. pap. 53.50 (*0-393-96348-9*) Norton.

Norton Anthology of World Masterpieces, Vol. 2. 7th ed. Sarah N. Lawall. LC 98-35047. Vol. 2. 2500p. 1998. pap. 51.50 (*0-393-97300-X*) Norton.

Norton Anthology of World Masterpieces: Instructor's Guide. Ed. by Maynard Mack et al. (C). 1987. pap., teacher ed. 10.50 (*0-393-95489-7*) Norton.

Norton Anthology on Theory & Criticism. Vincent Leitch. (C). pap. text. write for info. (*0-393-97574-6*) Norton.

Norton Anthology to American Literature. 5th ed. Ed. by Tindall. LC 98-41989. 1999. text 53.50 (*0-393-97339-5*) Norton.

Norton Banker Forms, 2 vols., Set. William L. Norton, Jr. et al. LC 81-10028. 1992. ring bd. 195.00 (*0-685-59825-X*) West Group.

Norton Bankruptcy Code & Rules, 2 vols. William L. Norton, Jr. et al. LC 81-10028. 1981. pap. 99.75 (*0-685-44923-8*) West Group.

Norton Bankruptcy Law & Practice, 11 vols. 2nd ed. William L. Norton, Jr. et al. LC 93-71471. 1993. ring bd. 975.00 (*0-317-11808-0*) West Group.

Norton Boater's Log: An Innovative Log, Guest Register, & Boater's Data Manual. John Rousmaniere. LC 96-39784. 96p. 1997. pap. 22.00 (*0-393-31660-2*) Norton.

***Norton Book of American Autobiography.** Ed. & Intro. by Jay Parini. LC 98-43398. 704p. 1999. 32.50 (*0-393-04677-X*) Norton.

Norton Book of American Short Stories. Ed. by Peter Prescott. 1988. 29.95 (*0-393-02619-1*) Norton.

Norton Book of American Short Stories. Ed. by Peter Prescott. (Books of...Ser.). (C). 1990. pap. text. write for info. (*0-393-96092-7*) Norton.

Norton Book of Classical Literature. Ed. by Bernard M. Knox. LC 92-10378. 868p. 1993. 29.95 (*0-393-03426-7*) Norton.

Norton Book of Friendship. Ed. by Eudora Welty & Ronald A. Sharp. 608p. 1991. 27.95 (*0-393-03065-2*) Norton.

Norton Book of Ghost Stories. Ed. by Brad Leithauser. LC 94-17383. 1994. 25.00 (*0-393-03564-6*) Norton.

Norton Book of Interviews. Ed. by Christopher Silvester. LC 95-5791. Orig. Title: The Penguin Book of Interviews: An Anthology from 1859 to the Present Day. 1996. 30.00 (*0-393-03876-9*) Norton.

Norton Book of Light Verse. Ed. by Russell Baker. 1986. 29.95 (*0-393-02366-4*) Norton.

Norton Book of Modern War. Ed. by Paul Fussell, Jr. 1990. 24.95 (*0-393-02909-3*) Norton.

Norton Book of Nature Writing. Robert Finch. Ed. by John C. Elder. 1990. 35.00 (*0-393-02799-6*) Norton.

Norton Book of Personal Essays. Ed. & Intro. by Joseph Epstein. LC 96-26975. 480p. 1997. 30.00 (*0-393-03654-5*) Norton.

Norton Book of Science Fiction. Ed. by Ursula K. Le Guin & Brian Attebery. 1997. pap. text. write for info. (*0-393-97241-0*) Norton.

Norton Book of Science Fiction: North American science fiction, 1960-1990. Ed. by Ursula K. Le Guin & Brian Attebery. LC 93-16130. 869p. 1993. 29.95 (*0-393-03546-8*) Norton.

Norton Book of Sports. Ed. by George Plimpton. 500p. 1992. 24.95 (*0-393-03040-7*) Norton.

Norton Book of the Sea. John O. Coote. 1989. 22.50 (*0-393-02778-3*) Norton.

Norton Book of Travel. Ed. by Paul Fussell, Jr. 1987. 19.95 (*0-393-02481-4*) Norton.

Norton Book of Womens' Lives. Phyllis Rose. 832p. 1995. pap. 18.95 (*0-393-31290-9*, Norton Paperbks) Norton.

Norton Book of Women's Lives. Ed. by Phyllis Rose. LC 92-40015. 1993. 30.00 (*0-393-03532-8*) Norton.

Norton Commander 2.0. (C). 1989. text. write for info. (*0-201-51080-4*) Addison-Wesley.

Norton Desktop 4.0 for Windows. (Prisma Computer Courses Ser.). (Illus.). 200p. (Orig.). 1995. pap. 12.95 (*1-85365-391-8*, Pub. by Spectrum) Seven Hills Bk.

Norton Dictionary of Modern Thought. Alan Bullock. LC 99-24581. 1999. 59.95 (*0-393-04696-6*) Norton.

Norton-Grove Dictory of Woman Composers. Ed. by Julie A. Sadie & Rhian Samuel. LC 96-120482. (Illus.). 450p. 1995. 45.00 (*0-393-03487-9*) Norton.

Norton Guide to Writing. Thomas Cooley. (Illus.). 650p. (C). 1992. text 34.50 (*0-393-96232-6*); pap. text 45.25 (*0-393-95320-3*) Norton.

Norton Guide to Writing. Thomas Cooley. (Illus.). 650p. (C). 1992. pap. text. write for info. (*0-393-95324-6*) Norton.

Norton Guide to Writing with the Mac. Thomas Cooley. (C). 1992. pap. text 39.50 (*0-393-96266-0*) Norton.

Norton History of Chemistry. William H. Brock. Ed. by Roy Porter. (History of Science Ser.). (Illus.). 768p. 1993. pap. 19.95 (*0-393-31043-4*) Norton.

Norton History of Environmental Sciences. Peter J. Bowler. Ed. by Roy Porter. (History of Science Ser.). (Illus.). 652p. 1993. 35.00 (*0-393-03535-2*); pap. 17.95 (*0-393-31042-6*) Norton.

Norton History of Modern Europe, 7 vols. Incl. Age of Religious Wars, 1559-1715. 2nd ed. Richard S. Dunn. (C). 1979. pap. text 15.50 (*0-393-09021-3*); Vol. 3. Kings & Philosophies, 1689-1789. Leonard Krieger. (C). 1970. pap. text 16.00 (*0-393-09905-9*); Vol. 4. Age of Revolution & Reaction, 1789-1850. 2nd ed. Charles Breunig. (C). 1977. pap. 15.50 (*0-393-09143-0*); Vol. 5. Age of Nationalism, 1850-1890. 2nd ed. Norman M. Rich. (C). 1976. pap. text 15.50 (*0-393-09183-X*); 1981. pap. text. write for info. (*0-318-54691-4*) Norton.

Norton History of Modern Europe. Ed. by Felix Gilbert. (Illus.). (C). 1971. write for info. (*0-393-09938-5*) Norton.

Norton History of Science in Society. Lewis Pyenson & Susan Sheets-Pyenson. (Illus.). 512p. 1999. pap. 17.95 (*0-393-31736-6*) Norton.

Norton History of the Human Sciences. Roger Smith. LC 97-22287. 1000p. 1997. 50.00 (*0-393-04543-9*); pap. 29.95 (*0-393-31733-1*) Norton.

N

An Asterisk (*) at the beginning of an entry indicates that the title is appearing for the first time.

Norton History of the Mathematical Sciences. Ivor Grattan-Guinness. LC 98-7876. (Illus.). 817p. 1998. 35.00 (*0-393-04650-8*) Norton.

Norton Introduction to Fiction. 6th ed. Ed. by Jerome Beaty. LC 95-4814. (C). 1995. pap. 41.75 (*0-393-96821-9*) Norton.

***Norton Introduction to Literature.** 7th ed. Ed. by Jerome Beaty et al. LC 97-24449. 2200p. (C). 1998. text 53.00 (*0-393-97202-X*) Norton.

***Norton Introduction to Literature.** 7th ed. Jerome Beaty et al. LC 97-24451. (C). 1998. pap. text 32.50 (*0-393-97222-4*) Norton.

Norton Introduction to Literature: Drama. Ed. by Carl E. Bain. 600p. (C). 1973. pap. text 41.75 (*0-393-09366-2*) Norton.

Norton Introduction to Poetry. 7th ed. Ed. by Hunter. LC 98-23108. 1998. pap. 37.00 (*0-393-97357-3*) Norton.

Norton Introduction to Short Novels. 3rd ed. Jerome Beaty. (C). 1999. pap., teacher ed. write for info. (*0-393-96832-4*) Norton.

***Norton Introduction to Short Novels.** 3rd ed. Jerome Beaty. LC 98-41702. (C). 1999. pap. 33.00 (*0-393-96831-6*) Norton.

Norton Manual of Music Notation. George Heussenstamm. 200p. (Orig.). (C). 1987. pap. text 25.00 (*0-393-95526-5*) Norton.

Norton Matisses. Jack D. Flam. (Illus.). 24p. 1973. pap. 2.50 (*0-943411-12-2*) Norton Gal Art.

Norton Motorcycles from 1950-1986. Steve Wilson. LC 96-78554. (Illus.). 160p. 1997. 27.95 (*1-85260-573-1*) Haynes Manuals.

Norton Museum of Art: The American Collection. Christina Orr-Cahall et al. (Illus.). 293p. 1995. pap. 35.00 (*0-943411-29-7*) Norton Gal Art.

Norton Museum of Art: The European Collection. David F. Setford. (Illus.). 241p. 1996. pap. 35.00 (*0-943411-30-0*) Norton Gal Art.

Norton Poetry Workshop CD-ROM Packaged with the Norton Anthology of Poetry, Shorter. 4th ed. Ed. by James Knapp & Margaret Ferguson. 1996. pap. text 62.00 incl. cd-rom (*0-393-97081-7*, Norton Paperbks) Norton.

Norton Priory: The Archaeology of a Medieval Religious House. Patrick Greene. (Illus.). 180p. 1989. text 99.95 (*0-521-33054-8*) Cambridge U Pr.

Norton Reader. 9th ed. Arthur M. Eastman. (C). 1996. pap. text, teacher ed. write for info. (*0-393-96828-6*) Norton.

***Norton Reader.** 10th ed. Peterson. LC 99-33320. 1999. pap. 26.50 (*0-393-97384-0*) Norton.

Norton Reader: An Anthology of Expository Prose. 3rd ed. Arthur M. Eastman. LC 72-7030. xxvi, 121p. 1973. write for info. (*0-393-09875-3*) Norton.

Norton Reader: An Anthology of Expository Prose. 9th abr. ed. Ed. by Linda H. Peterson et al. LC 95-2937. (C). 1995. pap. text 24.50 (*0-393-96827-8*) Norton.

***Norton Reader: An Anthology of Expository Prose.** 10th ed. Ed. by Peterson. LC 99-33319. 1999. 28.50 (*0-393-97383-2*) Norton.

Norton Rose: Cross Border Security. Ed. by Douglas Colliver & Charles Proctor. 1997. write for info. (*0-406-05463-0*, NRCB, MICHIE) LEXIS Pub.

Norton Rose on Civil Jurisdiction & Judgments. Adrian Briggs. Ed. by Peter Rees & Norton Rose. 350p. 1993. 124.00 (*1-85044-500-1*) LLP.

Norton Sampler: Short Essays for Composition. 4th ed. Ed. by Thomas Cooley. LC 92-26173. 427p. (C). 1993. pap. text 22.25 (*0-393-95739-X*) Norton.

Norton Sampler: Short Essays for Composition. 5th ed. Ed. by Cooley. LC 96-24245. 1997. pap. write for info. (*0-393-97090-6*) Norton.

***Norton Scores Vol. 2: An Anthology for Listening: Gregorian Chant to Beethoven.** 8th ed. Ed. by Kristine Forney. 1999. pap. 32.00 (*0-393-97341-7*) Norton.

Norton Scores Vol. 2: An Anthology for Listening: Schubert to the Present. 8th ed. Ed. by Kristine Forney. pap. 32.00 (*0-393-97347-6*) Norton.

Norton Shakespeare. William Shakespeare. Ed. by Stephen Greenblatt et al. LC 97-7083. (Illus.). 3600p. (C). 1997. 55.00 (*0-393-97087-6*) Norton.

Norton Shakespeare. William Shakespeare. Ed. by Stephen Greenblatt et al. LC 97-7083. (Illus.). 3600p. (C). 1999. 65.00 (*0-393-04107-7*) Norton.

Norton Shakespeare Workshop. William Shakespeare. Ed. by Mark Rose. 1997. 51.50 incl. cd-rom (*0-393-97088-4*) Norton.

Norton Simon Museum: A Brief Guide. Sara C. Abdo & Gloria Williams. (Illus.). 64p. (Orig.). 1996. pap. 6.00 (*0-915776-12-X*) NS Mus.

Norton Textra Writer 2.5 with Online Handbook. Ann Arbor Software Staff. (C). 1992. pap. text 36.25 (*0-393-96278-4*) Norton.

Norton Textra Writer 2.5 with Online Handbook to accompany The Confident Writer: Manual with IBM 3.5 Disk. 2nd ed. Constance Gefvert. 1992. pap. 26.00 (*0-393-96256-3*) Norton.

Norton Textra Writer 2.5 with Online Handbook to Accompany Writing: A College Handbook. 4th ed. James A. Heffernan & John E. Lincoln. (C). 1994. pap. text. write for info. (*0-393-96517-1*); disk. write for info. (*0-393-96515-5*) Norton.

Norton Textra Writer 2.5 with Online Handbook to Accompany Writing: A College Handbook. 4th ed. James A. Heffernan & John E. Lincoln. (C). 1994. pap. text. write for info. incl. disk (*0-393-96516-3*); pap. text 40.50 (*0-393-96518-X*) Norton.

Norton Twin Restoration. R. Bacon. (Illus.). 256p. 1996. pap. 39.95 (*0-85045-708-4*, Pub. by Ospry) Motorbooks Intl.

Norton Utilities 5.0. H. Etzler. (C). 1990. text. write for info. (*0-201-55934-X*) Addison-Wesley.

Norton Utilities 8 for Dummies. Beth Slick. LC 94-75907. 350p. 1994. pap. 19.95 (*1-56884-166-3*) IDG Bks.

***Norton Vyse: Psychic.** Rose C. de Crespigny. Ed. by Jack Adrian. (Occult Detectives Library: Vol. 2). xx, 104p. 1999. 34.50 (*1-899562-73-7*) Ash-Tree.

Norton's Folly: Norwegian Immigrants & Yankee Neighbors on the Wisconsin Frontier. Neil Eckstein. LC 97-170915. 264p. (Orig.). 1997. pap. 8.95 (*1-57502-487-X*, P01453) Morris Pubng.

Norton's Guide to Writing Short Stories with MAC. Cooley. (C). 1992. pap. text 37.50 (*0-393-96269-5*) Norton.

Norton's Hut. John Marsden. 32p. (YA). (gr. 5 up). 1999. 13.95 (*1-887734-64-3*) Star Brght Bks.

Norton's Star Atlas. 19th ed. Ridpath. 192p. (C). 1998. pap. text 31.88 (*0-582-35655-5*) Longman.

***Nortons Star Atlas&Ref.** 19th ed. Ridpath. (C). 1998. 62.81 (*0-582-31283-3*) Longman.

***Norumbega Fault System of the Northern Appalachians** Allan Ludman & David P. West. LC 99-22075. (Special Paper Ser.). 1999. write for info. (*0-8137-2331-0*) Geol Soc.

Norwalk Vol. I: With Supplement (All Published). With Genealogical Register. Charles M. Selleck. (Illus.). 535p. 1997. reprint ed. lib. bdg. 55.00 (*0-8328-5677-0*) Higginson Bk Co.

Norwalk after Two Hundred Fifty Years: An Account of the Celebration of the 250th Anniversary of the Charter of the Town, 1651-1901. Includes Historical Sketches of Churches, Schools, Old Homes, Institutions, Eminent Men, etc., along with Military Service Records. (Illus.). 387p. 1995. reprint ed. lib. bdg. 42.50 (*0-8328-4621-X*) Higginson Bk Co.

Norwalk Cemeteries. Lester Card. 152p. 1997. reprint ed. pap. 21.00 (*0-8328-5676-2*) Higginson Bk Co.

Norwalk Inscriptions Copied from Gravestones...Arranged with Genealogical Notes & Record Revolutionary Service, Etc., in Three Parts. Francis F. Spies. 854p. 1997. reprint ed. pap. 58.50 (*0-8328-5675-4*) Higginson Bk Co.

Norwalk Potteries. Andrew L. Winton & Kate Winton. LC 81-19914. (Orig.). 1981. pap. 6.50 (*0-914016-83-0*) Phoenix Pub.

Norway. (Panorama Books Collection). (FRE.). 3.95 (*0-685-35938-7*) Fr & Eur.

Norway. (Insight Guides Ser.). 1998. 22.95 (*0-88729-136-8*) Langenscheidt.

Norway. 16.95 (*0-528-91396-4*) Rand McNally.

Norway. Jean F. Blashfield. LC 99-21552. (Enchantment of the World Ser.). (Illus.). 144p. (gr. 5-9). 2000. 32.00 (*0-516-20651-6*) Childrens.

***Norway.** Knut Heidar. 192p. 2000. text 54.95 (*0-8133-3200-1*, Pub. by Westview) HarpC.

Norway. Insight Guides Staff. (Insight Guides). 1998. pap. text 7.95 (*0-88729-430-8*) Langenscheidt.

***Norway.** Deborah L. Kopka. LC 99-50689. (Ticket to Ser.). 48p. (J). (ps-3). 2000. 22.60 (*1-57505-148-6*, Carolrhoda) Lerner Pub.

***Norway.** Deborah L. Kopka. LC 99-16665. (Globe-Trotters Club Ser.). (Illus.). 48p. (J). (gr. 4-7). 2000. lib. bdg. 22.60 (*1-57505-123-0*, Carolrhoda) Lerner Pub.

Norway. Elaine Landau. LC 98-37714. (Geography Ser.). (J). 1999. lib. bdg. 21.50 (*0-516-20985-X*) Childrens.

***Norway.** Elaine Landau. (True Bks.). (J). 2000. pap. text 6.95 (*0-516-26767-1*) Childrens.

Norway. Ed. by Sverre Lyngstad et al. (Review of National Literatures Ser.: Vol. 12). 240p. 1983. pap. 6.95 (*0-918680-17-4*) Griffon House.

Norway. Leland B. Sather. (World Bibliographical Ser.: No. 67). 320p. 1986. lib. bdg. 46.95 (*1-85109-010-X*, Pub. by Clio Pr) ABC-CLIO.

Norway see Enchantment of the World Series

***Norway.** 2nd ed. Rough Guides Staff. (Illus.). 368p. 2000. pap. 17.95 (*1-85828-524-0*, Rough Guides) Viking Penguin.

***Norway.** 5th ed. Ed. by Fodors Travel Publications, Inc. Staff. (Illus.). 192p. 2000. pap. 11.50 (*0-679-00402-5*) Fodors Travel.

Norway see Cultures of the World - Group 11

***Norway: A Country Study Guide.** Global Investment & Business Center, Inc. Staff. (World Country Study Guides Library: Vol. 128). (Illus.). 350p. 2000. pap. 59.00 (*0-7397-2426-6*) Intl Business Pubns.

Norway: A Guide to the Admission & Academic Placement of Norwegian Students in North American Colleges & Universities. Clifford F. Sjogren & Lornie G. Kerr. 93p. (Orig.). 1985. pap. 9.00 (*0-87447-204-0*) College Bd.

Norway: A History from the Vikings to Our Own Times. Rolf Danielsen et al. 486p. 1995. 41.00 (*82-00-21803-1*) Scandnvan Univ Pr.

Norway: A Study of the Educational System of Norway & A Guide to the Academic Placement of Students in Educational Institutions in the United States. Shelley M. Feagles & Karlene N. Dickey. LC 94-9985. (World Education Ser.). 1994. 50.00 (*0-929851-22-6*) Am Assn Coll Registrars.

Norway: Eighteen Seventy-Eight Issues Oscar II Krone Values. Per Gellein. Ed. by Jared H. Richter. Tr. by Harry B. Jones from NOR. (Illus.). (Orig.). 1983. pap. text 3.50 (*0-936493-01-1*) Scand Philatelic.

Norway: Eighteen Seventy-One to Eighteen Seventy-Five Issue Skilling Denominations, Shaded Posthorn. Jared H. Richter. (Illus.). 50p. (Orig.). 1984. pap. text 5.00 (*0-936493-07-0*) Scand Philatelic.

Norway: Eighteen Seventy-Seven to Eighteen Seventy-Eight Issue Ore Denominations, Shaded Posthorn. Arnstein Berntsen. Ed. by Jared H. Richter. Tr. by Gunnar Steen from NOR. (Illus.). 58p. (Orig.). 1984. pap. text 5.00 (*0-936493-03-8*) Scand Philatelic.

Norway: Eighteen Sixty-Seven to Eighteen Sixty-Eight Issue Coat of Arms Typographed. D. Thune-Larsen. Ed. by Jared H. Richter. Tr. by Harry B. Jones from NOR. (Illus.). (Orig.). 1983. pap. text 3.50 (*0-936493-02-X*) Scand Philatelic.

Norway: Major World Nations. Ralph Zickgraf. LC 97-17788. (Major World Nations Ser.). (Illus.). 144p. (YA). (gr. 5 up). 1999. lib. bdg. 19.95 (*0-7910-4747-4*) Chelsea Hse.

Norway: Welcome to the 1994 Olympic Games. Robert Wulf. 145p. 1995. 24.95 (*1-883954-00-2*) Milestone.

Norway - A Country Study Guide: Basic Information for Research & Pleasure. Global Investment Center, USA Staff. (World Country Study Guide Library: Vol. 128). (Illus.). 350p. 1999. pap. 59.00 (*0-7397-1525-9*) Intl Business Pubns.

***Norway, a Cultural Guide.** Barbara Krulik. Ed. by Russ Hoyle. (Scandinavian Cultural Guides Ser.: No. 1). (Illus.). 288p. (Orig.). 1999. pap. 24.95 (*0-9672846-1-9*, Pub. by M-K Prodns) IPG Chicago.

***Norway & National Liberation in Southern Africa.** Tore Linne Eriksen. 250p. 1999. 30.00 (*91-7106-447-8*) Almqvist Wiksell.

Norway & the European Community: The Political Economy of Integration. Ed. by Brent F. Nelsen. LC 92-45109. 264p. 1993. 57.95 (*0-275-94211-2*, C4211, Praeger Pubs) Greenwood.

Norway & the Nobel Peace Prize. Oscar J. Falnes. LC 72-168003. reprint ed. 20.00 (*0-404-02365-7*) AMS Pr.

Norway & the United States, 1905-1955: Two Democracies in Peace & War. Wayne S. Cole. LC 89-1860. (Illus.). 233p. 1989. reprint ed. pap. 72.30 (*0-608-00045-0*, 206081100006) Bks Demand.

***Norway Business Intelligence Report, 190 vols.** Global Investment & Business Center, Inc. Staff. (World Business Intelligence Library: Vol. 128). (Illus.). 350p. 2000. pap. 99.95 (*0-7397-2626-9*) Intl Business Pubns.

***Norway Business Law Handbook.** Global Investment & Business Center, Inc. Staff. (Global Business Law Handbooks Library: Vol. 128). (Illus.). 2000. pap. 99.95 (*0-7397-2026-0*) Intl Business Pubns.

***Norway Business Opportunity Yearbook.** Global Investment & Business Center, Inc. Staff. (Global Business Opportunity Yearbooks Library: Vol. 128). (Illus.). 2000. pap. 99.95 (*0-7397-2226-3*) Intl Business Pubns.

***Norway Business Opportunity Yearbook: Export-Import, Investment & Business Opportunities.** International Business Publications, U. S. A. Staff & Global Investment Center, U. S. A. Staff. (Global Business Opportunity Yearbooks Library: Vol. 128). (Illus.). 350p. 1999. pap. 99.95 (*0-7397-1326-4*) Intl Business Pubns.

***Norway Country Review 2000.** Robert C. Kelly et al. (Illus.). 60p. 1999. pap. 39.95 (*1-58310-552-2*) CountryWatch.

***Norway Foreign Policy & Government Guide.** Contrib. by Global Investment & Business Center, Inc. Staff. (World Foreign Policy & Government Library: Vol. 123). (Illus.). 350p. 1999. pap. 99.00 (*0-7397-3621-3*) Intl Business Pubns.

***Norway Foreign Policy & Government Guide.** Global Investment & Business Center, Inc. Staff. (World Foreign Policy & Government Library: Vol. 123). (Illus.). 350p. 2000. 99.95 (*0-7397-3826-7*) Intl Business Pubns.

***Norway Government & Business Contacts Handbook: Strategic Government & Business Contacts for Conducting Successful Business, Export-Import & Investment Activity, 110 vols.** International Business Publications, USA Staff & Global Investment Center, USA Staff. (World Export-Import & Business Library: Vol. 3). (Illus.). 2000. pap. 99.95 (*0-7397-6037-8*) Intl Business Pubns.

Norway in Pictures. Ed. by Lerner Publications, Department of Geography Staff. (Visual Geography Ser.). (Illus.). 64p. (YA). (gr. 5 up). 1990. lib. bdg. 19.95 (*0-8225-1871-6*, Lerner Publctns) Lerner Pub.

***Norway Investment & Business Guide.** Global Investment & Business Center, Inc. Staff. (Global Investment & Business Guide Library: Vol. 128). (Illus.). 2000. pap. 99.95 (*0-7397-1826-6*) Intl Business Pubns.

***Norway Investment & Business Guide: Export-Import, Investment & Business Opportunities.** International Business Publications, USA Staff & Global Investment Center, USA Staff. (World Investment & Business Guide Library-99: Vol. 128). (Illus.). 350p. 1999. pap. 99.95 (*0-7397-0323-4*) Intl Business Pubns.

Norway, 1940. Francois Kersaudy. LC 98-33494. (Illus.). 284p. 1998. pap. 15.00 (*0-8032-7787-3*, KERNOX) U of Nebr Pr.

Norway Salmon Yearbook, 1991. Ed. by Trond Wold. 1991. pap. 34.50 (*1-880315-00-9*) Aqua Seed.

Norway-Sweden: Union, Disunion, & Scandinavian Integration. Raymond E. Lindgren. LC 78-13451. 298p. 1979. reprint ed. lib. bdg. 38.50 (*0-313-21043-8*, LINS, Greenwood Pr) Greenwood.

Norway to America: A History of the Migration. Ingrid Semmingsen. Tr. by Einar Haugen. LC 78-3201. (Illus.). 1980. pap. 14.95 (*0-8166-1000-2*) U of Minn Pr.

Norway Visions & Verse of Vikingland Collector's Postcard Book. Illus. by Karen Jenson. (Collector's Post Card Bks.). (ENG & NOR.). 22p. (Orig.). 1996. pap. 9.95 (*1-881988-21-X*) Paulstad Inc.

Norway's Best Stories: An Introduction to Modern Norwegian Fiction. Ed. by Hanna A. Larsen. Tr. by Anders Orbeck from NOR. LC 75-169557. (Short Story Index Reprint Ser.). 1977. reprint ed. 23.95 (*0-8369-4019-9*) Ayer.

Norway's Response to the Holocaust: An Historical Perspective. Samuel Abrahamsen. LC 90-82993. (Illus.). 200p. 1991. pap. 13.95 (*0-89604-117-4*, Holocaust Library) US Holocaust.

Norweb Collection: An American Legacy. Michael Hodder & Q. David Bowers. (Illus.). 288p. 1987. text 29.95 (*0-943161-00-2*) Bowers & Merena.

Norwegian. Pimsleur Language Method Staff. 1999. 95.00 (*0-671-04398-6*) S&S Trade.

Norwegian. Margaretha D. Simons. (Illus.). 288p. 1998. pap. 24.95 incl. audio (*0-8442-3818-X*, Teach Yrslf) NTC Contemp Pub Co.

***Norwegian: A Language Map.** Kristine K. Kershul. (Language Map Ser.). (Illus.). 8p. 2000. pap. 7.95 (*0-944502-12-1*) Bilingual Bks.

Norwegian: A Practical Grammar. Ase-Berit Strardskogen. Ed. by Rolf Strardskogen. Tr. by Barbara White. LC 93-45628. (ENG & NOR.). 204p. (C). (gr. 13). 1994. pap. 22.99 (*0-415-10979-5*) Routledge.

Norwegian: LANGUAGE/30. rev. ed. Educational Services Corporation Staff. (NOR.). 1993. pap. 16.95 incl. audio (*0-910542-67-8*) Educ Svcs DC.

Norwegian-American Historical Association. Odd Sverre Lovoll & Kenneth O. Bjork. LC 75-15444. 80p. 1975. pap. 30.00 (*0-608-04840-2*, 206549700004) Bks Demand.

***Norwegian-American Studies.** Ed. by Odd Sverre Lovoll. (Illus.). 404p. 2000. 20.00 (*0-87732-089-6*) Norwegian-Am Hist Assn.

Norwegian-American Studies, Vol. 21. Ed. by Kenneth O. Bjork. 311p. 1962. 15.00 (*0-87732-043-8*) Norwegian-Am Hist Assn.

Norwegian-American Studies, Vol. 22. Ed. by Kenneth O. Bjork. 264p. 1965. 15.00 (*0-87732-045-4*) Norwegian-Am Hist Assn.

Norwegian-American Studies, Vol. 23. Ed. by Kenneth O. Bjork. 256p. 1967. 15.00 (*0-87732-048-9*) Norwegian-Am Hist Assn.

Norwegian-American Studies, Vol. 24, 1970. Norwegian-American Historical Association. LC 87-657088. (Illus.). 311p. reprint ed. pap. 96.50 (*0-608-10411-6*, 204038500024) Bks Demand.

Norwegian-American Studies, Vol. 25. Ed. by Kenneth O. Bjork. 293p. 1972. 15.00 (*0-87732-052-7*) Norwegian-Am Hist Assn.

Norwegian-American Studies, Vol. 26. Ed. by Kenneth O. Bjork. 271p. 1974. 15.00 (*0-87732-054-3*) Norwegian-Am Hist Assn.

Norwegian-American Studies, Vol. 27. Ed. by Kenneth O. Bjork. 323p. 1977. 15.00 (*0-87732-058-6*) Norwegian-Am Hist Assn.

Norwegian-American Studies, Vol. 28. Ed. by Kenneth O. Bjork. 367p. 1979. 15.00 (*0-87732-063-2*) Norwegian-Am Hist Assn.

Norwegian-American Studies, Vol. 29. Ed. by Odd Sverre Lovoll. 402p. 1983. 15.00 (*0-87732-068-3*) Norwegian-Am Hist Assn.

Norwegian-American Studies, Vol. 30. Norwegian-American Historical Association. LC 87-657088. 352p. reprint ed. pap. 109.20 (*0-7837-0108-X*, 204038500030) Bks Demand.

Norwegian-American Studies, Vol. 31. Ed. by Odd Sverre Lovoll. (Illus.). 346p. 1986. 18.00 (*0-87732-072-1*) Norwegian-Am Hist Assn.

Norwegian-American Studies, Vol. 32. Ed. by Odd Sverre Lovoll. (Illus.). 297p. 1989. 18.00 (*0-87732-076-4*) Norwegian-Am Hist Assn.

Norwegian-American Studies, Vol. 33. Ed. by Odd Sverre Lovoll. (Studies & Records). 370p. 1992. 18.00 (*0-87732-080-2*) Norwegian-Am Hist Assn.

Norwegian-American Studies, Vol. 34. Ed. by Odd Sverre Lovoll. (Illus.). 360p. 1995. 20.00 (*0-87732-084-5*) Norwegian-Am Hist Assn.

Norwegian-American Studies & Records, Vol. 4. Ed. by Theodore C. Blegen. 159p. 1929. 12.00 (*0-87732-008-X*) Norwegian-Am Hist Assn.

Norwegian-American Studies & Records, Vol. 5. Ed. by Theodore C. Blegen. 152p. 1930. 12.00 (*0-87732-009-8*) Norwegian-Am Hist Assn.

Norwegian-American Studies & Records, Vol. 6. Ed. by Theodore C. Blegen. 191p. 1932. 12.00 (*0-87732-010-1*) Norwegian-Am Hist Assn.

Norwegian-American Studies & Records, Vol. 8. Ed. by Theodore C. Blegen. 176p. 1934. 12.00 (*0-87732-014-4*) Norwegian-Am Hist Assn.

Norwegian-American Studies & Records, Vol. 9. Ed. by Theodore C. Blegen. 131p. 1936. 12.00 (*0-87732-017-9*) Norwegian-Am Hist Assn.

Norwegian-American Studies & Records, Vol. 10. Ed. by Theodore C. Blegen. 202p. 1938. 12.00 (*0-87732-019-5*) Norwegian-Am Hist Assn.

Norwegian-American Studies & Records, Vol. 11. Ed. by Theodore C. Blegen. 183p. 1940. 15.00 (*0-87732-022-5*) Norwegian-Am Hist Assn.

Norwegian-American Studies & Records, Vol. 14. Norwegian-American Historical Association. LC 26-145503. 273p. reprint ed. pap. 84.70 (*0-608-15445-8*, 202929200014) Bks Demand.

Norwegian-American Studies & Records, Vol. 16. Ed. by Theodore C. Blegen. 218p. 1950. 15.00 (*0-87732-033-0*) Norwegian-Am Hist Assn.

Norwegian-American Studies & Records, Vol. 17. Ed. by Theodore C. Blegen. 185p. 1952. 15.00 (*0-87732-035-7*) Norwegian-Am Hist Assn.

Norwegian-American Studies & Records, Vol. 18. Ed. by Theodore C. Blegen. 252p. 1952. 15.00 (*0-87732-037-3*) Norwegian-Am Hist Assn.

Norwegian-American Studies & Records, Vol. 19. Ed. by Theodore C. Blegen. 218p. 1956. 15.00 (*0-87732-039-X*) Norwegian-Am Hist Assn.

Norwegian-American Studies & Records, Vol. 20. Ed. by Theodore C. Blegen. 246p. 1959. 15.00 (*0-87732-041-1*) Norwegian-Am Hist Assn.

Norwegian Americans & the Politics of Dissent, 1880-1924. Lowell J. Soike & Odd Sverre Lovoll. (Special Publications). (Illus.). 275p. 1991. 20.00 (*0-87732-079-9*) Norwegian-Am Hist Assn.

Norwegian Book of Knowledge. Waldenbooks Publishing Company Staff. (Illus.). pap. 2.25 (*0-681-35056-3*) Waldenbooks Co Inc.

***Norwegian Cassette Packs.** Berlitz Editors. (NOR.). 192p. 2000. 18.95 (*2-8315-7744-6*) Berlitz.

Norwegian Cruising Guide. 2nd ed. John Armitage & Mark Brackenbury. (Illus.). 200p. 1996. 39.50 (*0-7136-4115-0*) Sheridan.

Norwegian Dances & Other Works for Piano. Edvard Grieg. 224p. pap. 12.95 (*0-486-26669-9*) Dover.

Norwegian Dances Waltz Caprices. E. Grieg. 1999. pap. 10.95 (*0-486-29611-3*) Dover.

Norwegian Dictionary: Norwegian-English, English-Norwegian. LC 93-48842. 560p. (C). (gr. 13). 1994. pap. 29.99 (*0-415-10801-2*) Routledge.

Norwegian-Dutch, Dutch-Norwegian Pocket Dictionary: Norsk-Nederlansk-Norsk. (DUT & NOR.). 379p. 1981. 29.95 (*0-8288-4671-5*, M9459) Fr & Eur.

Norwegian Election Study, 1965. Henry Valen. 1976. write for info. (*0-89138-155-4*) ICPSR.

Norwegian Elkhound. Nina P. Ross. Ed. by Luana Luther. LC 93-74007. (Illus.). 320p. 1995. 26.95 (*0-944875-39-4*) Doral Pub.

Norwegian Elkhound Champions, 1952-1992. Jan Linzy. (Illus.). 175p. 2000. pap. 36.95 (*1-55893-011-6*) Camino E E & Bk.

Norwegian Elkhounds. Anna K. Nicholas. (Illus.). 1997. pap. 9.95 (*0-7938-2319-6*, KW-110S) TFH Pubns.

Norwegian Emigrant Songs & Ballads. Ed. by Theodore C. Blegen et al. LC 78-15211. (Scandinavians in America Ser.). 1979. reprint ed. lib. bdg. 30.95 (*0-405-11633-0*) Ayer.

Norwegian-English: Large. 2nd ed. Willy A. Kirkeby. 1373p. 1986. 195.00 (*82-573-0275-9*) IBD Ltd.

Norwegian-English - English-Norwegian Dictionary. J. W. Dietrichson. (Skolordbok Ser.). (ENG & NOR.). 331p. 1992. 33.75 (*82-573-0484-0*, Pub. by Kunnskapsforlaget) IBD Ltd.

Norwegian-English - English-Norwegian Dictionary of Motor Vehicle & Traffic Terminology. Willy A. Kirkeby. 128p. 1978. 64.00 (*82-573-0079-9*) IBD Ltd.

Norwegian-English Commercial Dictionary. E. D. Gabrielsen. 199p. 1987. 49.50 (*82-573-0108-6*) IBD Ltd.

Norwegian-English Contract Law Dictionary. R. Craig. (ENG & NOR.). 150p. 1992. 69.00 (*0-7859-8909-9*) Fr & Eur.

Norwegian-English Contract Law Dictionary. Criag. (ENG & NOR.). 150p. 1992. 69.95 (*0-7859-7481-4*, 8200213277) Fr & Eur.

***Norwegian-English Dictionary.** Craig. (ENG & NOR.). 420p. 1999. 195.00 (*0-320-01674-9*) Fr & Eur.

Norwegian-English Dictionary. Ed. by Einar Haugen. 504p. 1974. pap. 29.95 (*0-299-03874-2*) U of Wis Pr.

Norwegian-English Dictionary. Ingvald E. Haugen. (ENG & NOR.). 1984. 195.00 (*0-8288-0476-1*, M3549) Fr & Eur.

Norwegian-English Dictionary. 5th ed. Willy A. Kirkeby & B. Berulfsen. (ENG & NOR.). 515p. 1989. 47.00 (*82-573-0301-1*) IBD Ltd.

Norwegian-English Dictionary: Norsk-Engelsk Ordbok. Willy A. Kirkeby. (ENG & NOR.). 541p. 1981. 49.95 (*0-8288-0477-X*, M9456) Fr & Eur.

Norwegian-English Dictionary: Norsk-Engelsk Ordbok. Willy A. Kirkeby & S. Utgave. (ENG & NOR.). 1400p. 1986. 150.00 (*0-8288-0478-8*, M9458) Fr & Eur.

Norwegian-English Dictionary: Norsk-Engelsk Ordbok. 3rd ed. Einar Haugen. (NOR.). 506p. 1984. 39.50 (*82-00-06546-4*) Scandnvan Univ Pr.

Norwegian-English, English-Norwegian Dictionary, Norwegian-English Dictionary. J. Meyer Myklestad & H. Soras. (ENG & NOR.). 42.50 (*0-87557-054-2*) Saphrograph.

Norwegian-English, English-Norwegian Medical Dictionary. Kass. (ENG & NOR.). 104p. 1993. 49.95 (*0-7859-7505-5*, 8257305588) Fr & Eur.

Norwegian-English, English-Norwegian Pocket Dictionary. 21st ed. (ENG & NOR.). 330p. 1992. pap. 30.00 (*0-7859-8911-0*) Fr & Eur.

Norwegian-English, English-Norwegian Pocket Dictionary. 21st ed. 330p. 1992. 36.25 (*82-517-8012-8*) IBD Ltd.

Norwegian-English Law Dictionary: Criminal Law & Procedure & Miscellaneous Terms. Patrick N. Chaffey. (ENG & NOR.). 188p. 1992. 65.00 (*0-7859-8910-2*) Fr & Eur.

Norwegian-English Legal Dictionary (Plus E-N Vocabulary) 2nd ed. P. Chaffey. (ENG & NOR.). 176p. 1997. pap. 78.00 (*82-00-22602-6*, Pub. by Scand Univ Pr) IBD Ltd.

Norwegian-English-Norwegian Dictionary. 2nd ed. Dale E. Gabrielsen. (ENG & NOR.). 568p. 1980. 14.95 (*0-8288-0475-3*, M 9432) Fr & Eur.

Norwegian-English Technical Dictionary. rev. ed. J. Ansteinsson. (ENG & NOR.). 223p. 1985. 125.00 (*0-7859-7137-8*) Fr & Eur.

Norwegian-English Technical Dictionary. 3rd ed. J. Ansteinsson. (ENG & NOR.). 1990. 88.00 (*0-7859-8965-X*) Fr & Eur.

Norwegian-English Technical Dictionary. 4th ed. J. Ansteinsson. (ENG & NOR.). 514p. 1994. 125.00 (*0-8288-0647-0*, M8480) Fr & Eur.

Norwegian-English Technical Dictionary. 4th rev. ed. J. Ansteinsson & Olav Reiersen. 514p. 1994. 85.00 (*82-7028-496-3*) IBD Ltd.

Norwegian Exile Mail, 1940-1945. Karl U. Sanne. Ed. by George B. Koplowitz. Tr. by Sigmund Meireran from NOR. (Illus.). 219p. (Orig.). 1986. pap. text 17.50 (*0-936493-10-0*) Scand Philatelic.

Norwegian Fire. Julian J. Savarin. 25.00 (*0-7278-5391-0*) Severn Hse.

Norwegian Folk Art: The Migration of a Tradition. Ed. by Marion Nelson. LC 97-175773. (Illus.). 280p. 1996. pap. 55.00 (*0-7892-0196-8*) Abbeville Pr.

Norwegian Folk Songs & Dances, 1. Edvard Grieg. 120p. 1998. pap. text 7.98 (*963-9059-28-5*) Kone Music.

Norwegian Folk Tales. Peter C. Asbjornsen & Jorgen Moe. 192p. 1982. pap. 14.00 (*0-394-71054-1*) Pantheon.

Norwegian Homesteaders see Way It Was: The North Dakota Experience

Norwegian in 10 Minutes a Day. 3rd ed. Kristine K. Kershul. LC 98-231697. (Ten Minutes a Day Ser.). (Illus.). 134p. 1998. per. 17.95 (*0-944502-39-3*) Bilingual Bks.

Norwegian in Three Months. Oivind Blom. LC 98-48007. (Hugo Ser.). 240p. 1999. pap. 14.95 (*0-7894-4428-3*) DK Pub Inc.

Norwegian Institute at Athens: The First Five Lectures. Ed. by Oivind Andersen & Helene Whittaker. (Papers from the Norwegian Institute at Athens). (Illus.). 86p. 1991. pap. 22.50 (*960-85145-0-9*, Pub. by P Astroms) Coronet Bks.

Norwegian Intelligence Service, 1945-1970: Northern Vigil. Olav Riste. LC 99-23373. (Studies in Intelligence Ser.). 352p. 1999. pap. 24.50 (*0-7146-4455-2*, Pub. by F Cass Pubs) Intl Spec Bk.

***Norwegian Intelligence Service, 1945-1970: Northern Vigil.** Olav Riste. LC 99-23373. (Studies in Intelligence Ser.). 315p. 1999. 59.50 (*0-7146-4900-7*) F Cass Pubs.

***Norwegian Invasion of England in 1066.** Kelly DeVries. LC 99-37405. (Warfare in History Ser.). 352p. 1999. 60.00 (*0-85115-763-7*) Boydell & Brewer.

Norwegian Jokes. E. C. Stangland. (Illus.). (Orig.). 1979. pap. 2.50 (*0-9602692-0-7*) Norse Pr.

Norwegian Kitchen: Recipes & Copy Provided by The Association of Norwegian Chefs. Association of Norwegian Chefs Staff. Tr. by Melody Favish. (Illus.). 1994. 45.00 (*82-90823-23-1*) Skandisk.

Norwegian Lady Smiled: A Media Antidote. Angelina Griffin. Ed. by A. K. Griffin. (Along for the Ride Ser.). 65p. 1995. reprint ed. per. write for info. (*0-9646016-0-5*) Snapnet Edits.

Norwegian Language in America: A Study in Bilingual Behavior. E. Ingvald Haugen. LC 70-85187. (Indiana University Studies in the History & Theory of Linguistics). 727p. reprint ed. pap. 200.00 (*0-608-30079-9*, 201302300083) Bks Demand.

Norwegian Literature in Medieval & Early Modern Times. Theodore Jorgenson. LC 77-27602. 208p. 1978. reprint ed. lib. bdg. 59.50 (*0-313-20073-4*, JONL, Greenwood Pr) Greenwood.

Norwegian Migration to America: The American Transition. Theodore C. Blegen. LC 31-20308. 677p. reprint ed. pap. 200.00 (*0-8357-3438-2*, 203969500013) Bks Demand.

Norwegian Migration to America: The American Transition. Theodore C. Blegen. LC 68-31271. (Illus.). 655p. (C). 1969. reprint ed. lib. bdg. 75.00 (*0-8383-1215-2*) M S G Haskell Hse.

Norwegian Migration to America, 1825-1860. Theodore C. Blegen. LC 69-18759. (American Immigration Collection. Series 1). 1969. reprint ed. 20.95 (*0-405-00507-5*) Ayer.

Norwegian Migration to America, 1825-1860. Theodore C. Blegen. LC 68-31271. 413p. (C). 1969. reprint ed. lib. bdg. 75.00 (*0-8383-0325-0*) M S G Haskell Hse.

Norwegian Migration to America, 1825-1860, 2 Vols. Theodore C. Blegen. LC 68-31271. (American History & Americana Ser.: No. 47). 1969. reprint ed. lib. bdg. 150.00 (*0-8383-0330-7*) M S G Haskell Hse.

Norwegian Minds - American Dreams: Ethnic Activism among Norwegian-American Intellectuals. Peter Thaler. LC 97-19957. (Illus.). 168p. 1998. 32.50 (*0-87413-629-6*) U Delaware Pr.

Norwegian Missions in African History Vol. 2: Madagascar. Finn Fuglestad & Jarle Simensen. 144p. (C). 1986. 32.00 (*82-00-07415-3*, Pub. by Scand Univ Pr) IBD Ltd.

Norwegian Norsk Fonetikk for Utlendinger (Norwegian Phonetics), 4 cass., Set. Ase-Berit & Rolf Strandskogen. (Norwegian Phonetics Ser.). 210p. pap. text 75.00 incl. audio (*0-88432-148-7*, AFNW98) Audio-Forum.

Norwegian North Polar Expedition, 1893-96: Scientific Results, 6 Vols. Ed. by Fridtjof Nansen. LC 68-55206. (Illus.). 1971. reprint ed. lib. bdg. 495.00 (*0-8371-3852-3*, NANO) Greenwood.

Norwegian North Polar Expedition, 1893-96: Scientific Results, 6 Vols, Vol. 1. Ed. by Fridtjof Nansen. LC 68-55206. (Illus.). 1971. reprint ed. lib. bdg. 95.00 (*0-8371-3877-9*, NANP) Greenwood.

Norwegian North Polar Expedition, 1893-96: Scientific Results, 6 Vols, Vol. 2. Ed. by Fridtjof Nansen. LC 68-55206. (Illus.). 1971. reprint ed. lib. bdg. 95.00 (*0-8371-3881-7*, NANQ) Greenwood.

Norwegian North Polar Expedition, 1893-96: Scientific Results, 6 Vols, Vol. 3. Ed. by Fridtjof Nansen. LC 68-55206. (Illus.). 1971. reprint ed. lib. bdg. 95.00 (*0-8371-3882-5*, NANR) Greenwood.

Norwegian North Polar Expedition, 1893-96: Scientific Results, 6 Vols, Vol. 4. Ed. by Fridtjof Nansen. LC 68-55206. (Illus.). 1971. reprint ed. lib. bdg. 95.00 (*0-8371-3883-3*, NANS) Greenwood.

Norwegian North Polar Expedition, 1893-96: Scientific Results, 6 Vols, Vol. 5. Ed. by Fridtjof Nansen. LC 68-55206. (Illus.). 1971. reprint ed. lib. bdg. 95.00 (*0-8371-3884-1*, NANT) Greenwood.

Norwegian North Polar Expedition, 1893-96: Scientific Results, 6 Vols, Vol. 6. Ed. by Fridtjof Nansen. LC 68-55206. (Illus.). 1971. reprint ed. lib. bdg. 95.00 (*0-8371-3885-X*, NANU) Greenwood.

Norwegian Oil Policies. T. Lind & G. A. Mackay. LC HD9575.N62L5. 158p. reprint ed. pap. 49.00 (*0-7837-1170-0*, 204169900022) Bks Demand.

Norwegian Penal Code. Tr. by Harold Schjoldager & Finn Baker from NOR. (American Series of Foreign Penal Codes: Vol. 3). xi, 167p. 1961. 25.00 (*0-8377-0023-X*, Rothman) W S Hein.

Norwegian Petroleum Directorate Seismic Data Packages Jan Mayen, North Sea, Norwegian Sea & Barents Sea. Norwegian Petroleum Directorate Staff. 320p. 1993. pap. 150.00 (*82-7257-384-9*, Pub. by Oljedirektoratet) St Mut.

***Norwegian Phrase Book.** Berlitz Editors. (Illus.). 192p. 2000. pap. 7.95 (*2-8315-7736-5*) Berlitz.

Norwegian Phrase Book. DK Publishing Staff. LC 99-21844. (Eyewitness Travel Guide Phrase Bks.). 128p. 1999. pap. 6.95 (*0-7894-4868-8*) DK Pub Inc.

Norwegian Pioneer Women: A Resource Guide. Jocelyn Riley. 114p. 1995. 45.00 incl. VHS (*1-877933-16-3*) Her Own Words.

Norwegian Proverbs: Selected from the Tales of Peter Christian Asbjornsen & Jorgen Moe. Compiled by Joanne Asala. 63p. 1994. pap. 10.95 (*0-941016-97-8*) Penfield.

Norwegian Recipes: Old Time Favorites. Norma Wangness. 160p. 1988. spiral bd. 6.95 (*0-941016-43-9*) Penfield.

Norwegian Religious Pluralism: A Trans-Atlantic Comparison. Frederick Hale. LC 92-44088. (Texts & Studies in Religion: Vol. 59). 244p. 1993. text 89.95 (*0-7734-9217-8*) E Mellen.

Norwegian Romanesque Decorative Sculpture, 1090-1210. Martin Blindheim. (Illus.). 1966. 35.00 (*0-85458-170-7*) Transatl Arts.

Norwegian Rose Painting in America: What the Immigrants Brought. Nils Ellingsgard. 96p. 1993. 18.00 (*82-00-21861-9*) Scandnvan Univ Pr.

Norwegian Sailors in American Waters. Knut Gjetset. Ed. by Franklyn D. Scott. LC 78-15186. (Scandinavians in America Ser.). (Illus.). 1979. reprint ed. lib. bdg. 25.95 (*0-405-11637-3*) Ayer.

Norwegian Sailors on the Great Lakes. Knut Gjerset. Ed. by Franklyn D. Scott. LC 78-15207. (Scandinavians in America Ser.). (Illus.). 1979. reprint ed. lib. bdg. 21.95 (*0-405-11636-5*) Ayer.

Norwegian Settlement in the United States. Carlton C. Qualey. LC 70-129409. (American Immigration Collection. Series 2). 1978. reprint ed. 23.95 (*0-405-00563-6*) Ayer.

***Norwegian Settlers (Norifte Settlementers) En Overfigt over den Norifte Indvandring til og Bebyggelfe af Umerifas Nurdveften fra Umeritas Opdagelfe til Indianerfrigen i Dveften.** Hjalmar R. Holand. (NOR.). 603p. 1999. reprint ed. lib. bdg. 65.00 (*0-8328-9815-5*) Higginson Bk Co.

Norwegian-Swedish Dictionary: Norsk-Svensk Ordbok. rev. ed. N. Beckman. (NOR & SWE.). 210p. 1985. 49.95 (*0-8288-1035-4*, M3320) Fr & Eur.

Norwegian-Swedish-Finnish Flora: Norsk-Svensk-Finsk Flora. J. Lid. (FIN, NOR & SWE.). 837p. 1985. 195.00 (*0-8288-1248-9*, F22443) Fr & Eur.

Norwegian Twins. Lucy F. Perkins. 18.95 (*0-89190-471-9*) Amereon Ltd.

Norwegian Verbs & Essentials of Grammar. Louis Janus. LC 98-43328. (ENG & NOR.). 176p. 1996. pap. 16.95 (*0-8442-8596-X*, 8596X) NTC Contemp Pub Co.

Norwegian Women's Writing 1850-1990. Sharon Wood & Janet Garton. LC 92-30594. (Women in Context Ser.). 352p. (C). 1993. pap. 29.95 (*0-485-92001-8*, Pub. by Athlone Pr); text 85.00 (*0-485-91001-2*, Pub. by Athlone Pr) Humanities.

***Norwegian Wood.** Haruki Murakami. LC 99-53821. 320p. 2000. pap. 13.00 (*0-375-70402-7*) Vin Bks.

Norwegian Yankee: Knute Nelson & the Failure of American Politics, 1860-1923. Millard Gieske & Steven Keillor. Ed. & Frwd. by Odd Sverre Lovoll. (Illus.). 426p. 1995. 30.00 (*0-87732-083-7*) Norwegian-Am Hist Assn.

Norwegian/English Dictionary. Berlitz Editors. (NOR & ENG.). 368p. 1998. pap. 7.95 (*2-8315-6382-8*) Berlitz.

Norwegians in Wisconsin. Richard J. Fapso. (Ethnic Ser.). (Illus.). 40p. 1977. pap. 3.95 (*0-87020-171-9*, NOWI) State Hist Soc Wis.

Norwegisch-Daenisches Etymologisches Woerterbuch, Vol. 1. 2nd ed. H. S. Falk & Alf Torp. (DAN & NOR.). 1960. 150.00 (*0-8288-6843-3*, M-7570) Fr & Eur.

Norwegisch-Daenisches Etymologisches Woerterbuch, Vol. 2. 2nd ed. H. S. Falk & Alf Torp. (DAN & NOR.). 1960. 150.00 (*0-8288-6842-5*, M-7571) Fr & Eur.

***Norwegische Katnersohne Als Konigliche Dragoner: Eine Abhandlung Uber Den Dragonerdienst In Norwegen und die Grenzwache In Schleswig-Holstein, 1758-1762.** Alf R. Bjercke. (GER., Illus.). 247p. 1999. 46.00 (*3-631-34727-8*) P Lang Pubng.

Norwich. Margaret Cheney McNally & Francis L. Niles. LC 98-87696. (Images of America Ser.). (Illus.). 128p. 1998. pap. 16.99 (*0-7524-1270-1*) Arcadia Publng.

Norwich Cathedral: Church, City, & Diocese, 1096-1996. Ed. by Ian Atherton et al. LC 95-49426. 1996. 60.00 (*1-85285-134-1*) Hambledon Press.

Norwich Connecticut: A Photographic Essay. German Tellez. (Illus.). 1988. 26.50 (*0-9621704-0-2*) Norwich Pubns.

Norwich Heresy Trials, 1428-31. N. P. Tanner. (Camden Fourth Ser.: Vol. 20). 233p. 27.00 (*0-901050-39-3*) David Brown.

Norwich Memorial: Annals of Norwich, New London County, in the Great Rebellion of 1861-65. Malcolm M. Dana. (Illus.). 395p. 1997. reprint ed. lib. bdg. 45.00 (*0-8328-5678-9*) Higginson Bk Co.

Norwich School. Josephine Walpole. (Illus.). 224p. 1997. 59.50 (*1-85149-261-5*) Antique Collect.

Norwich Shawl: Its History & a Catalogue of the Collection at Strangers Hall Museum, Norwich. Pamela Clabburn. (Illus.). 145p. 1995. 40.00 (*0-11-701591-1*, Pub. by Statnry Office); pap. 26.00 (*0-11-701584-9*, Pub. by Statnry Office) Balogh.

Norwich Terriers. Anna K. Nicholas. (Illus.). 192p. 1993. 9.95 (*0-86622-580-3*, KW209) TFH Pubns.

Norwich University. Photos by Brian Smith. LC 94-76305. (Illus.). 112p. 1995. 47.95 (*1-56469-023-7*) Harmony Hse Pub.

Norwood. John M. Grove. (Images of America Ser.). 1999. pap. 16.99 (*0-7524-0848-8*) Arcadia Publng.

Norwood. Charles Portis. 1994. 24.95 (*1-56849-403-3*) Buccaneer Bks.

Norwood. Charles Portis. LC 99-10234. 272p. 1999. pap. 13.95 (*0-87951-703-4*, Pub. by Overlook Pr) Penguin Putnam.

Norwood & Tux: And the Magic Mittens. Todd Hafer. Ed. by Jonna Barry & Karen A. Artl. (Illus.). 24p. (J). (gr. k-4). 1998. 8.09 (*0-944943-77-2*) Current Inc.

***Norwood: or Village in New England.** Henry Ward Beecher. 252p. 2000. pap. 9.95 (*0-594-03590-2*) Eightn Hundrd.

Norwood Park Home Cemetery in Chicago, Illinois. (Illus.). 24p. 1997. pap. 3.00 (*1-881125-16-5*) Chi Geneal Soc.

***Nory Ryan's Song.** Patricia Reilly Giff. 176p. (gr. 4-7). 2000. 15.95 (*0-385-32141-4*) Delacorte.

Nos Engano Dios? John S. Feinberg.Tr. of Deceived by God. 1998. pap. text 8.99 (*0-88113-515-1*) Caribe Betania.

Nos Freres Farouches see Oeuvres

Nos Veremos en la Cumbre. Zig Ziglar.Tr. of See You at The Top. (SPA., Illus.). 381p. 1997. pap. text 25.98 (*968-13-0131-5*) Edit Diana.

Nose. Nikolai Vasilevich Gogol. (Illus.). 32p. 1993. 17.95 (*0-87923-963-8*) Godine.

***Nose.** Katherine Goode. LC 00-8126. (Body Works Ser.). (Illus.). 32p. 2000. 16.95 (*1-56711-493-8*) Blackbirch.

Nose. Robert James. (Human Body Ser.). 1995. lib. bdg. 14.60 (*1-57103-101-4*) Rourke Pr.

Nose. Ed. by P. Van Cauwenberge et al. (Illus.). xii, 356p. 1998. 131.50 (*90-6299-147-5*) Kugler Pubns.

Nose. Arthur Yorinks. 64p. 2000. 14.99 (*0-7868-0499-8*, Pub. by Hyprn Child); lib. bdg. 15.49 (*0-7868-2429-8*, Pub. by Hyprn Child) Little.

Nose. Arthur Yorinks. 64p. Date not set. pap. 5.99 (*0-7868-1342-3*, Pub. by Hyprn Ppbks) Little.

Nose Book. Al Perkins. LC 71-117540. (Bright & Early Bks.: No. 8). (Illus.). (J). (ps-1). 1970. 7.99 (*0-394-80623-9*, Pub. by Random Bks Yng Read) Random.

Nose Brotherhood Knows: A Collection of Nothings & Non-Happenings 1926-1965. Ed. by Willum B. Long & Mary C. Long. LC 96-95419. (Illus.). 200p. (Orig.). 1997. pap. text 25.00 (*0-9617517-5-4*) Bear Hllow TX.

Nose Can Slant. Sharon Wohl. (Illus.). 8p. (J). (gr. k-2). 1998. mass mkt. 4.95 (*0-9665443-2-3*) A Better Way.

Nose Death. John M. Bennett. 10p. (C). 1984. pap. 2.50 (*0-935350-12-8*) Luna Bisonte.

Nose Death. deluxe ed. John M. Bennett. 10p. (C). 1984. pap. 7.50 (*0-935350-13-6*) Luna Bisonte.

***Nose for Adventure.** Richard Scrimger. 160p. (J). (gr. 3-6). 2000. pap. 6.95 (*0-88776-499-1*) Tundra Bks.

Nose from Jupiter. Richard Scrimger. LC 97-62178. 160p. (J). (gr. 3-6). 1998. pap. 5.95 (*0-88776-428-2*) Tundra Bks.

Nose Is a Nose. Susan Kropa. 144p. (J). (gr. 4-6). 1988. student ed. 13.99 (*0-86653-449-0*, GA1058) Good Apple.

Nose Is Not Toes. Glenn Doman. LC 81-67340. (Gentle Revolution Ser.). (Illus.). 84p. 1963. 15.95 (*0-944349-62-5*) Inst Achieve Human Pot.

Nose Is Not Toes. Glenn Doman. (Illus.). 144p. (J). Date not set. 15.95 (*0-89529-718-3*, Avery) Penguin Putnam.

Nose Knows: A Sensualist Guide to Great Joints. Lloyd M. Battista. LC 96-44558. (Illus.). 256p. (Orig.). 1996. pap. 13.00 (*1-879415-23-2*) Mtn n Air Bks.

Nose! Nose? No-Se & Other Plays. Andrei Amalrik. Tr. & Intro. by Daniel Weissbort. LC 72-90507. 228p. (Orig.). 1973. pap. 2.95 (*0-15-667350-9*, Harvest Bks) Harcourt.

Nose on My Face. large type ed. Laurence Payne. (Mystery Ser.). 560p. 1989. 27.99 (*0-7089-2031-4*) Ulverscroft.

***Nose Pickers from Outer Space.** Gordon Korman. 128p. (J). 1999. pap. 3.99 (*0-7868-1413-6*, Pub. by Disney Pr) Little.

Nose Pickers from Outer Space. Gordon Korman. LC 98-52340. (Illus.). 137p. (J). (gr. 3-4). 1999. lib. bdg. 13.49 (*0-7868-2431-X*, Pub. by Hyprn Child) Little.

Nose Pickers from Outer Space. Gordon Korman. LC 98-52340. (Illus.). 137p. 1999. pap. 3.99 (*0-7868-1343-1*, Pub. by Hyprn Ppbks) Little.

Nose Smoking, How to Help Children Avoid the Addiction of Nicotine, Rings, Spings & Thingamajigs: Old Hound Dog's Story. Troy Diamond. LC 90-61384. (Illus.). 100p. (J). 1990. pap. 17.95 (*0-945437-08-0*) MacDonald-Sward.

Nose to Nose. Gene Doty. 40p. 1998. 5.00 (*0-913719-97-8*, High Coo Pr) Brooks Books.

Nose-to-Nose Selling. Phil Kline. 135p. 1993. 25.00 (*0-9636108-0-5*); pap. 15.00 (*0-9636108-3-X*) Nose-To-Nose.

Nose to Toes. JoAnne Nelson. LC 91-34706. (Primarily Health Ser.). (Illus.). (J). (ps-2). 1995. pap. 6.00 (*0-7802-3245-3*) Wright Group.

Nose to Toes. Lilli V. Obligado. LC 98-40344. (J). 1999. pap. 3.25 (*0-679-88825-X*, Pub. by Random Bks Yng Read) Random.

Noses. Stephen Savage. (Adapting for Survival Ser.). (Illus.). 40p. (J). (gr. 2-6). 1995. lib. bdg. 5.00 (*1-56847-354-0*) Raintree Steck-V.

N

An Asterisk (*) at the beginning of an entry indicates that the title is appearing for the first time.

*Noses That Plow & Poke. Diane Swanson & Rose Cowles. LC 99-34008. (Up Close Ser.). 1999. 9.95 (1-55054-715-1) Ragged Bear.

*Noses That Poke & Plow. Diane Swanson. LC 99-34008. (Up Close Ser.). 2000. pap. 5.95 (1-55054-733-X) Sterling.

*Noses to the Grindstone: Shaping Industrial Servitude. Sharon Beder. LC 00-43285. 2000. boxed set. write for info. (1-85649-885-9, Pub. by Zed Books) St Martin.

Nosew Decorating: Fast, Fun & Fusible Craft Projects. Kunkel. (Illus.). 128p. 1998. pap. 12.95 (0-8069-8645-X) Sterling.

Nosey Notes. Frances Kirschner & Joanna Sorrentino. (Illus.). 60p. (Orig.). (J). (gr. 3-9). 1983. pap. 3.00 (0-9612696-0-X) Frantasy Wkshp.

*Nosferatu. Brian Campbell. (Clan Novel Ser.). 2000. pap. 14.95 (1-56504-266-2) White Wolf.

*Nosferatu. Gherbod Fleming. (Clan Novel Ser.). 288p. 2000. pap. 5.99 (1-56504-835-0) White Wolf.

*Nosferatu. Jim Shepard. LC 97-34371. 208p. 1998. 22.00 (0-679-44667-2) Knopf.

Noshe Djan: Afghan Food & Cookery. Helen Saberi. (Illus.). 160p. (Orig.). 1996. pap. 20.00 (0-907325-31-9, Pub. by Prospect) Food Words.

Nosin' 'Round with Peekie Petie. Helena Chung-Hawks. (Illus.). 36p. (J). (gr. 1-2). 1997. pap. 7.95 (1-887747-12-5) Legendary Pub.

Nosing for Numbers. (Ready Readers Series II Stage I). (Illus.). 32p. (J). (ps-1). 1996. pap. write for info. (1-56144-946-6, Honey Bear Bks) Modern Pub NYC.

Nosmo King. Martha R. Merritt. LC 96-83022. (Illus.). 35p. (YA). (gr. 3-12). 1996. pap. 6.95 (0-9650661-0-X) Beekman Hill Pub.

Nosography. 2nd rev. ed. Knud H. Faber. LC 75-23706. (Illus.). 1976. reprint ed. 45.00 (0-404-13258-8) AMS Pr.

Nosology & Research Methods in Psychiatry: Festschrift in Honor of Professor Jules Angst. Ed. by C. Scharfetter. (Journal Ser.: Vol. 28, No. 1, 1995). (Illus.). iv, 98p. 1995. pap. 31.50 (3-8055-6265-9) S Karger.

Nosotras: Latina Literature Today. Ed. by Maria Del Carmen Boza et al. LC 85-73396. (ENG & SPA.). 96p. 1986. pap. text 10.00 (0-916950-63-8) Biling Rev-Pr.

Nosotros: The Hispanic People of Oregon, Essays & Recollections. Ed. by Erasmo Gamboa & Carolyn M. Buan. LC 95-79043. (Illus.). 180p. (Orig.). 1995. pap. 21.95 (1-880377-01-2) Oregon Council.

Nosotros Jovenes. Harcourt Brace Staff. (SPA.). 1990. pap., teacher ed. 13.25 (0-15-388357-X) Harcourt Schl Pubs.

Nosotros Jovenes, 1990. Created by Harcourt Brace Staff. (SPA.). 1990. pap. text, teacher ed., wbk. ed. 18.00 (0-15-388354-5); pap. text, wbk. ed. 14.75 (0-15-388353-7); pap. text, wbk. ed. 15.00 (0-15-388352-9) Holt R&W.

Nosotros Jovenes, 1990. Harcourt Brace Staff. (SPA.). 1990. pap., teacher ed., wbk. ed. 14.75 (0-15-388355-3) Harcourt Schl Pubs.

Nosotros Jovenes, 1990: Testbook. Harcourt Brace Staff. (SPA.). 1990. pap. 13.25 (0-15-388356-1) Harcourt Schl Pubs.

Nosotros Podemos Compartir en la Escuela (We Can Share at School), Vol. 4096. Rozanne L. Williams. Tr. by Nora Mallernee. (Learn to Read Social Studies). (SPA., Illus.). 8p. (J). (ps-1). 1997. pap. 1.75 (1-57471-283-7, 4096) Creat Teach Pr.

Nosotros Si Podemos Hacerlo! Laura Dwight. Tr. by Maria Fiol. LC 97-69608.Tr. of We Can Do It!. (SPA., Illus.). 40p. (J). (gr. k-3). 1998. 13.95 (1-887734-37-6) Star Brght Bks.

Nosotros Somos Dios. Luis Soto-Ruiz. (C). 1998. pap. 28.95 (0-8384-3468-1) Heinle & Heinle.

Nosso Lar - A Spiritual Home. Tr. by Andrea Dessen & John Zerio from POR. pap. 10.00 (0-9649907-1-7) A Kardec Educ.

*Nostalgia. Gizella M. Csapo. LC 98-91051. 1999. pap. 5.95 (0-533-13027-1) Vantage.

Nostalgia. Paul Hallasy. 53p. (Orig.). pap. 6.95 (0-9627135-1-1) P Hallasy.

Nostalgia. Doris Rowley. 48p. 1984. 19.00 (0-7212-0693-X, Pub. by Regency Pr GBR) St Mut.

Nostalgia: An Existential Exploration of Longing & Fulfilment in the Modern Age. Ralph Harper. LC 66-19003. 146p. reprint ed. pap. 45.30 (0-608-10145-1, 200121200071) Bks Demand.

Nostalgia & Beyond: Eleven Latvian Women Writers. Inta M. Ezergailis. LC 97-39065. 280p. (C). 1997. text 57.00 (0-7618-0996-1); pap. text 36.50 (0-7618-0997-X) U Pr of Amer.

Nostalgia & Sexual Difference: The Resistance to Contemporary Feminism. Janice Doane & Devon Hodges. 160p. 1987. 27.50 (0-416-01531-X, 1180); pap. 12.95 (0-416-01541-7, 1185) Routledge.

Nostalgia Artistica: Artistic Publicity of Some of the Smaller Airlines, 1926-1936. Don Thomas. (Illus.). 48p. 1993. pap. 10.00 (0-9618642-5-7) D Thomas.

*Nostalgia Book. Boym. 2000. 30.00 (0-465-00707-4, Pub. by Basic); pap. 16.00 (0-465-00708-2, Pub. by Basic) HarpC.

Nostalgia Collection: #138. (E-Z Play Today Ser.). 248p. 1997. otabind 14.95 (0-7935-6972-9) H Leonard.

Nostalgia de la Muerte. Villaurutia. (SPA.). pap. 10.99 (968-16-4880-3, Pub. by Fondo) Continental Bk.

Nostalgia Entertainment Sourcebook: The Complete Resource Guide to Classic Movies, Vintage Music, Old Time Radio & Theatre. Ed. by Jordan R. Young. 160p. 1991. pap. 9.95 (0-940410-24-9, Moonstone Pr) Past Times.

Nostalgia Entertainment Sourcebook: The Complete Resource Guide to Classic Movies, Vintage Music, Old Time Radio & Theatre. Ed. by Jordan R. Young. (Illus.). 160p. 1991. 19.95 (0-940410-25-7, Moonstone Pr) Past Times.

*Nostalgia Favorites. 1999. pap. 8.95 (0-634-00913-3) H Leonard.

Nostalgia for Death & Hieroglyphs of Desire: Poetry. Xavier Villaurrutia & Octavio Paz. Ed. & Tr. by Eliot Weinberger from SPA. Tr. by Esther Allen from SPA. LC 92-17926. 144p. 1993. pap. 12.00 (1-55659-053-9) Copper Canyon.

Nostalgia Home Plan Collection: A New Approach to Time-Honored Design. Ed. by Carol S. Shea. LC 97-77469. 160p. 1998. pap. 9.95 (0-9647658-8-8) Design Basics.

*Nostalgia Home Plans: 100 Time-Honored Designs Updated with Today's Features. Design Basics Staff. 2000. pap. 14.95 (1-881955-69-9) Home Planners.

Nostalgia Home Plans Collection Vol. II: A New Approach to Time-Honored Design. Ed. by Carol Stratman Shea & Bruce Arant. 160p. 1999. pap. 9.95 (1-892150-04-2) Design Basics.

Nostalgia of the Infinite. Janet Hamill. (Doubles Ser.). (Illus.). 112p. 1992. pap. 11.95 (0-938075-21-7) Ocean View Bks.

Nostalgia of the Infinite. limited ed. Janet Hamill. (Doubles Ser.). (Illus.). 112p. 1992. 59.95 (0-938075-22-5) Ocean View Bks.

Nostalgia of the Solar Rings. Eddy Wilson. 28p. 1998. pap. 9.95 (1-885206-57-7) Cader Pubng.

Nostalgia of the Unknown: The Complete Prose Poetry. Clark A. Smith. Ed. by Steve Behrends et al. 40p. (Orig.). 1988. pap. 4.95 (0-940884-01-1) Necronomicon.

Nostalgia on the Right: Historical Roots of the Idealized Family. 2nd ed. Nancy Theriot. (Illus.). 50p. (Orig.). 1990. pap. 5.50 (0-915987-07-4) Political Rsch Assocs.

Nostalgia Revisted: The Works of Emmitt Thames. Illus. by Emmitt Thames. LC 84-16649. (Contemporary Realists Ser.). 64p. 1984. pap. 10.00 (0-913060-22-4) Norton Art.

Nostalgia Street Rods. O'Toole. 1998. 19.95 (0-949398-57-8, 861701Q, Pub. by Graffiti) Motorbooks Intl.

Nostalgias for a House of Cards: Poems. Byron Vazakas. Orig. Title: Poems of Byron Vazakas. 1970. 4.95 (0-8079-0159-8); pap. 1.95 (0-8079-0160-1) October.

Nostalgias y Rebeldias: Cinco Directoras Latinoamericanas de Cine en Europa. Luis Trelles-Plazaola. (Biblioteca de Autores de Puerto Rico Ser.). (Illus.). 160p. (Orig.). 1993. pap. 5.00 (1-56328-035-3) Edit Plaza Mayor.

Nostalgic Angels: Rearticulating Hypertext Writing. Johndan et al. LC 96-46981. (New Directions in Computers & Composition Studies Ser.). 373p. 1997. pap. 24.95 (1-56750-281-4); text 73.25 (1-56750-280-6) Ablx Pub.

Nostalgic Barbie: A Postcard Book. (Postcard Bks.). (Illus.). 64p. (Orig.). 1990. pap. 8.95 (0-89471-820-7) Running Pr.

Nostalgic Dreams. Diane Richards. 96p. 1993. pap. 10.50 (1-56770-273-2) S Scheewe Pubns.

*Nostalgic Drum. Femi Osofisan. LC 99-50317. 1999. pap. write for info. (0-86543-806-4) Africa World.

Nostalgic Happenings in the Three Bands of John Philip Sousa. Malcolm Heslip. (Illus.). 83p. 1992. 9.95 (0-918048-09-5) Integrity.

Nostalgic Noel: Four New Inspirational Love Stories from Christmas Gone By. Rebecca Germany et al. LC 99-161905. 352p. 1998. pap. 4.97 (1-57748-349-9) Barbour Pub.

Nostalgic Rock. 1990. pap. 5.95 (0-7935-0133-4, 00001295) H Leonard.

Nostalgic Teleology: Friedrich Schiller & the Schemata of Aesthetic Humanism. Constantin Behler. LC 95-36517. (Stanford German Studies: Vol. 26). 259p. 1995. 46.95 (3-906755-22-3) P Lang Pubng.

Nostalgic Trip into the History of the Jews of Iraq. Yusuf R. Ghanimah. Ed. by Sheila Dallal. Tr. by Reading A. Dallal from ARA. LC 98-35838. (Illus.). 252p. 1998. 57.00 (0-7618-1224-5); pap. 36.50 (0-7618-1225-3) U Pr of Amer.

*Nostalgic Trivia for Seniors. Gary Grimm & John Artman. (Illus.). 45p. 1998. pap. text 7.95 (1-56490-101-7) G Grimm Assocs.

Nostalgie Camarade. Francois Billetdoux. 49.95 incl. audio (0-685-21219-X) Fr & Eur.

Nostalgie de la Grece a l'Aube de l'Idealisme Allemand: Kant & les Grecs dans l'Itineraire de Schiller, de Holderlin & de Hegel. Jacques Taminiaux. 286p. 1967. text 85.50 (90-247-0153-8) Kluwer Academic.

Nostalgie des Origines. Mircea Eliade. (FRE.). 276p. 1991. pap. 12.95 (0-7859-2250-4, 2070326330) Fr & Eur.

Nostalgie du Desert: L'Ideal Eremitique en Castille au Siecle d'Or. Alain Saint-Saens. LC 92-47127. (FRE., Illus.). 300p. 1993. text 99.95 (0-7734-9804-4) E Mellen.

Nostalgist's Map of America. Agha S. Ali. 112p. 1992. pap. 9.95 (0-393-30924-X) Norton.

*Nostos. V. Penelope Pelizzon. LC 99-36767. 80p. 1999. 24.95 (0-8214-1298-1); pap. 12.95 (0-8214-1299-X) Ohio U Pr.

Nostradamos: Final Reckoning. Peter Lemesurier. LC 97-110464. 208p. 1997. reprint ed. pap. 12.95 (0-425-15610-9) Berkley Pub.

Nostradamus. Knut Boeser. Tr. by John Brownjohn from GER. LC 95-37244. 1996. 7.99 (0-517-14910-9) Random Hse Value.

Nostradamus. John Hogue. (Pocket Prophecy Ser.). (Illus.). 64p. 2000. text 7.95 (1-86204-490-2, Pub. by Element MA) Penguin Putnam.

Nostradamus. Sherif Mazar. (SPA., Illus.). 1997. pap. 7.98 (968-403-789-9) Selector.

Nostradamus: Biblical & Physical Prophecies for Our Times; the Middle East, Russia & America in Prophecy. Rudolph R. Windsor. Ed. by Mary L. Windsor. LC 97-90092. (Illus.). 137p. (Orig.). 1997. pap. 16.95 (0-9620881-3-7) Windsors Golden Series.

Nostradamus: Countdown to Apocalypse. Jean-Charles de Fontbrune. 512p. 1995. pap. 12.95 (0-8050-1048-3) H Holt & Co.

Nostradamus: His Key to the Centuries. Valerie Hewitt. Date not set. pap. 10.99 (0-7493-2158-X) Heinemann.

*Nostradamus: History of the Future: Year by Year, 2000-2025. Peter Lorie. 2000. 22.95 (1-86204-790-1, Pub. by Element MA) Penguin Putnam.

Nostradamus: Key to the Bible Code. Patricia Sunday. 1999. pap. text 15.95 (0-9665933-2-4) Sunday Ministries.

Nostradamus: Predictions for the 21st Century. Manfred Dimde. LC 98-18210. (Illus.). 160p. 1998. 12.95 (0-8069-0757-6) Sterling.

Nostradamus: Predictions of World War III. 2nd rev. ed. Jack Manuelian. (Illus.). 192p. (Orig.). 1996. pap. 14.95 (0-938294-52-0) Inner Light.

Nostradamus: Prophecies for Women. Peter Lorie. (Illus.). 221p. 1998. text 23.00 (0-7881-5904-6) DIANE Pub.

Nostradamus: Prophecies of the Present Times? David P. Francis. 304p. 1988. pap. 14.00 (0-85030-517-9, Pub. by Aqrn Pr) HarpC.

Nostradamus: Prophesies. Henry C. Roberts. 15.00 (0-685-22062-1) Wehman.

Nostradamus: Quien Sobrevivira? Stefan Paulus. LC 97-48469. (ENG & SPA.). 312p. 1999. pap. text 9.95 (1-56718-516-9) Llewellyn Pubns.

Nostradamus: The Man Who Saw Through Time. Lee McCann. (Illus.). 421p. 1982. pap. 9.95 (0-374-51754-1) FS&G.

Nostradamus: The Man Who Saw Through Time. Lee McCann. (Illus.). 448p. 1994. reprint ed. 9.99 (0-517-43693-0) Random Hse Value.

Nostradamus: The New Revelations. John Hogue. (Illus.). 300p. 1995. pap. 19.95 (1-85230-683-1, Pub. by Element MA) Penguin Putnam.

Nostradamus: The Next Fifty Years. Peter Lemesurier. 304p. 1994. pap. 12.95 (0-425-14433-X) Berkley Pub.

Nostradamus: The Voice That Echoes Through Time. Maurice A. LaCasse. (Illus.). 208p. (Orig.). 1992. 19.95 (1-56167-088-X) Noble Hse MD.

Nostradamus - the Complete Prophecies. John Hogue. LC 96-53641. 608p. 1997. pap. 29.95 (1-85230-959-8, Pub. by Element MA) Penguin Putnam.

Nostradamus - The Complete Prophecies. John Hogue. 1999. pap. 24.95 (1-86204-388-4, Pub. by Element MA) Penguin Putnam.

*Nostradamus & Beyond: 128 New Prophecies Based on His Techniques. Peter Lemeseurier. LC 99-39414. (Illus.). 128p. 1999. pap. 16.95 (0-8069-9911-X) Sterling.

*Nostradamus & His Prophecies. Edgar Leoni. LC 00-29513. 2000. pap. 18.95 (0-486-41468-X) Dover.

Nostradamus & His Prophecies. Edgar Leoni. LC 82-9479. (Illus.). 832p. 1988. 12.99 (0-517-38809-X) Random Hse Value.

Nostradamus & the Millenium: Last Predictions. John Hogue. LC 86-24384. (Illus.). 208p. 1987. 17.95 (0-385-24011-2) Doubleday.

*Nostradamus & the Millennium: What May Be Coming. Perry Kane. LC 99-90694. 1999. 25.00 (0-7388-0470-3); pap. 18.00 (0-7388-0471-1) Xlibris Corp.

Nostradamus & the '90s: Prophecies of Nostradamus Pertaining to the 1990's. Robert Delacroix. 150p. 1993. pap. 5.95 (0-9635358-0-3) ARS Historica.

*Nostradamus Ate My Hamster. Rankin. (J). 2000. pap. 8.95 (0-552-14355-3, Pub. by Transworld Publishers Ltd) Trafalgar.

*Nostradamus Ate My Hamster. Robert Rankin. 2000. 27.50 (0-385-40705-X, Pub. by Transworld Publishers Ltd) Trafalgar.

Nostradamus Code: The Lost Manuscript That Unlocks the Secrets of the Master Prophet. Ottavio C. Ramotti. Tr. by Tami Calliope from ITA. LC 98-16398. (Illus.). 192p. 1998. 25.00 (0-89281-666-X, Inner Trad) Inner Tradit.

Nostradamus, Countdown to Apocalypse. Jean-Charles de Fontbrune et al. LC 84-672738. xi, 453 p. 1983. write for info. (0-09-150620-4) Hutchinson.

*Nostradamus' Dream Interpretations. Dita Arzt-Wegman. Orig. Title: Umfangreiches Agyptisches Traum-Deutungs Buch by Nostradamus. (Illus.). 175p. 1999. pap. 14.95 (0-9686022-0-7, Pub. by VPI1) Allnce Hse.

Nostradamus Encyclopedia. Peter Lemesurier. LC 98-223000. (Illus.). 288p. 1997. text 29.95 (0-312-17093-9) St Martin.

Nostradamus Encyclopedia. 2nd ed. Peter Lemesurier. 1999. pap. 21.95 (0-312-19994-5) St Martin.

Nostradamus for Women: Prophecies for Women. Peter Lorie & Manuela D. Mascetti. 224p. 1995. 22.50 (0-684-81178-2) Simon & Schuster.

Nostradamus' Lost Predictions see Psychic Misfortune

Nostradamus, 1999: Who Will Survive? Stefan Paulus. Ed. by Edgar Rojas. LC 96-20696. 304p. (Orig.). 1996. pap. 14.95 (1-56718-515-0) Llewellyn Pubns.

Nostradamus' Oracles. K. Chodkiewicz & R. Christopher Abel. Ed. by R. C. Abel. (Illus.). (Orig.). 1999. pap. 7.95 (1-55818-384-1, Sure Fire) Holmes Pub.

Nostradamus Personal Forecast for All Signs: Yearly Forecast. 33p. 1999. pap. 9.95 (0-9667312-1-2) Startheme Pubns.

Nostradamus Prophecy. John S. Powell. LC 97-77857. 354p. 1998. 23.95 (0-9661922-5-7) Belladonna Pr.

*Nostradamus Prophecy. John S. Powell. 368p. 1999. mass mkt. 5.50 (0-8439-4652-0, Leisure Bks) Dorchester Pub Co.

Nostradamus Two: Into the Twenty-First Century. Jean-Charles De Fontbrune. LC 84-25342. (Illus.). 176p. 1995. pap. 10.95 (0-8050-0599-4, Owl) H Holt & Co.

Nostradamus' Unpublished Prophecies: The Untold Story. Arthur Crockett. 64p. 1983. 10.00 (0-938294-16-4) Hlth Research.

*Nostratic: Examining a Linguistic Macrofamily. Ed. by A. Colin Renfrew & Daniel Nettle. (Papers in the Prehistory of Languages). 999p. 1999. pap. 54.00 (1-902937-00-7, Pub. by McDonald Inst) David Brown.

Nostratic: Sifting the Evidence. Ed. by Joseph C. Salmons & Brian D. Joseph. LC 98-17514. (Current Issues in Linguistic Theory Ser.: Vol. 142). vi, 293p. (C). 1998. 75.00 (1-55619-597-4) J Benjamins Pubng Co.

Nostratic Macrofamily: A Study in Distant Linguistic Relationship. Allan R. Bomhard & John C. Kerns. LC 93-45587. (Trends in Linguistics, Studies & Monographs: No. 74). xii, 932p. (C). 1994. lib. bdg. 229.25 (3-11-013900-6) Mouton.

Nostratic Macrofamily & Linguistic Palaeontology. Aharon Dolgopolsky. (Papers in the Prehistory of Languages). (Illus.). 116p. 1998. pap. 36.00 (0-9519420-7-7) McDonald Inst.

Nostromo. Joseph Conrad. Ed. by Ruth Nadelhaft. 440p. 1997. pap. 12.95 (1-55111-074-1) Broadview Pr.

Nostromo. Joseph Conrad. 1992. 20.00 (0-679-41321-9) Everymns Lib.

*Nostromo. Joseph Conrad. (Cloth Bound Pocket Ser.). 400p. 1998. 7.95 (3-8290-0887-2, 520659) Konemann.

*Nostromo. Joseph Conrad. LC 99-43964. 600p. 1999. 34.95 (1-56000-469-X) Transaction Pubs.

Nostromo. Joseph Conrad. 1990. pap. 12.95 (0-14-118049-8) Viking Penguin.

Nostromo. Joseph Conrad. 4p. 1999. audio 23.95 (0-14-086453-9) Viking Penguin.

Nostromo. Joseph Conrad. Ed. & Intro. by Martin S. Smith. 480p. (C). 1999. pap. 8.95 (0-14-018371-X) Viking Penguin.

Nostromo. Joseph Conrad. (Classics Library). 1998. pap. 3.95 (1-85326-174-2, 170XWW, Pub. by Wrdsworth Edits) NTC Contemp Pub Co.

Nostromo. Joseph Conrad. 566p. 1983. reprint ed. lib. bdg. 37.95 (0-89966-311-7) Buccaneer Bks.

Nostromo. rev. ed. Joseph Conrad. Ed. by Cedric Watts. (Everyman Paperback Classics Ser.). 416p. 1995. pap. 5.95 (0-460-87191-9, Everyman's Classic Lib) Tuttle Pubng.

Nostromo: A Tale of the Seaboard. Joseph Conrad. LC 91-53185. 1992. 20.00 (0-679-40990-4) Knopf.

Nostromo: A Tale of the Seaboard. Joseph Conrad. LC 96-6289. 1996. 18.50 (0-679-60202-X) Modern Lib NY.

*Nostromo: A Tale of the Seaboard. Joseph Conrad. Ed. by Keith Carabine. (Oxford World Classics Ser.). 584p. 2000. pap. 7.95 (0-19-283556-4) OUP.

Nostrums for Fashionable Entertainments: Dining in Georgia, 1800-1850. Feay S. Coleman. LC 85-50257. 1992. pap. 19.95 (0-933075-00-6) Telfair Mus.

*Not: A Trio. David Huddle. 126p. 2000. 20.00 (0-268-03651-9, Pub. by U of Notre Dame Pr) Chicago Distribution Ctr.

*Not Always So. Shunryu Suzuki. 2000. pap. 10.00 (0-06-095754-9) HarpC.

Not a Balancing Act: Poems. Claire Needell. (Burning Deck Poetry Ser.). 64p. 1993. pap. 8.00 (0-930901-89-4) Burning Deck.

Not a Balancing Act: Poems. limited ed. Claire Needell. (Burning Deck Poetry Ser.). 64p. 1993. pap. 15.00 (0-930901-90-8) Burning Deck.

Not a Bed: Level One. Lavaun Linde & Mary Quishenberry. (Bible Stories for Early Readers Ser.: Bk. 1). (Illus.). 32p. (Orig.). (J). (gr. 1). 1986. pap. text 4.99 (0-945107-00-5) Bradshaw Pubs.

Not a Bird Will Sing. Audrey Howard. 448p. 1998. 27.00 (0-340-66608-0, Pub. by Hodder & Stought Ltd) Trafalgar.

Not a Chance. Judith Andrews Green. (Thumbprint Mysteries Ser.). 128p. 1999. pap. 5.95 (0-8092-0683-8, 068380) NTC Contemp Pub Co.

*Not a Chance. Jessica Treat. 150p. 2000. pap. 12.95 (1-57366-089-2, Pub. by Fiction Coll) Northwestern U Pr.

Not a Chance: The Myth of Chance in Modern Science & Cosmology. R. C. Sproul. LC 94-26298. (Illus.). 256p. 1999. pap. 11.99 (0-8010-5852-X) Baker Bks.

Not a Conquered People: Two Carolinians View Parliamentary Taxation. William S. Price, Jr. (Illus.). 49p. 1975. pap. 4.00 (0-86526-111-3) NC Archives.

Not a Copper Penny in My House: Poems from the Caribbean. Monica Gunning. LC 92-61631. (Illus.). 32p. (J). (gr. 2-5). 1999. pap. 8.95 (1-56397-793-1) Boyds Mills Pr.

Not a Creature Was Stirring. Fred E. Katz. LC 97-35640. (SpineChillers Mysteries Ser.: No. 6). (Illus.). 144p. (J). (gr. 3-7). 1996. pap. 5.99 (0-8499-4061-3) Tommy Nelson.

*Not a Day Goes By. E. Lynn Harris. 208p. 2000. 19.95 (0-385-49824-1) Doubleday.

Not a Family Man. Patricia McClinn. (Special Edition Ser.). 1994. per. 3.50 (0-373-09864-2, 5-09864-5) Silhouette.

Not a Game for Boys. Simon Block. 64p. (Orig.). 1996. pap. 13.95 (1-85459-234-3, Pub. by N Hern Bks) Theatre Comm.

Not a Ghost of a Chance: A Mystery. Peter Ray. 1997. pap. 3.50 (1-57514-314-3, 1177) Encore Perform Pub.

Not a Little Monkey. Charlotte Zolotow. LC 88-21457. (Charlotte Zolotow Bk.). (Illus.). 32p. (J). (ps-1). 1989. 13.00 (0-06-026980-4) HarpC Child Bks.

Not a Man, & Yet a Man. Albery A. Whitman. LC 79-83896. (Black Heritage Library Collection). 1977. 18.95 (0-8369-8688-1) Ayer.

N

Not a Man, & Yet a Man. Albery A. Whitman. LC 78-104594. 254p. reprint ed. lib. bdg. 16.50 (*0-8398-2165-4*) Irvington.

Not a Nibble. Elizabeth Honey. (Illus.). 32p. (J). (ps-1). 1997. pap. 6.95 (*1-86448-242-7*, Pub. by Allen & Unwin Pty) IPG Chicago.

Not a Paticularly Different Voice: The Jurisprudence of Sandra Day O'Connor. Robert W. Van Sickel. LC 97-42350. (Studies in Law & Politics). 199p. 1998. 45.95 (*0-8204-3914-2*) P Lang Pubng.

Not a Penny More, Not a Penny Less. Jeffrey Archer. 320p. 1994. mass mkt. 6.50 (*0-06-100735-8*, Harp PBks) HarpC.

Not a Penny More, Not a Penny Less. Jeffrey Archer. 1990. per. 4.50 (*0-671-69353-0*) PB.

Not a Pretty Picture: Ethnic Minority Views on Television. Bob Mullan. 128p. 1996. text 58.95 (*1-85972-498-1*, Pub. by Avebry) Ashgate Pub Co.

Not a Promised Dime. Marcia L. Wilson. 51p. 1993. pap. 7.95 (*0-9634526-4-9*) Bell Ruth Pr.

Not a Sign in the Sky, but a Living Person. Marc Robertson. 32p. 1975. 9.00 (*0-86690-219-8*, R1403-014) Am Fed Astrologers.

Not a Silent People: Controversies That Have Shaped Southern Baptists. Walter B. Shurden. 128p. 1995. pap. 14.00 (*1-57312-021-9*) Smyth & Helwys.

***Not a Sparrow Falls: The Philosophy of Stephen R. L. Clark.** Daniel A. Dombrowski. 352p. 2000. 39.95 (*0-87013-549-X*) Mich St U Pr.

Not a Station but a Place. Judith Clancy & M. F. K. Fisher. LC 79-20885. (Illus.). 72p. 1979. pap. 7.95 (*0-912184-02-7*); bds. 9.95 (*0-912184-08-6*) Synergistic Pr.

Not a Still Life: The Art & Writings of Rae Perlin. Rae Perlin & Marian F. White. (Illus.). 212p. 1991. pap. 9.55 (*1-895387-00-0*) Creative Bk Pub.

Not a Swan. Michelle Magorian. LC 91-19507. (Laura Geringer Bks.). 416p. (YA). (gr. 7 up). 1992. lib. bdg. 17.89 (*0-06-024215-9*) HarpC Child Bks.

Not a Tame Lion: The Spiritual Legacy of C. S. Lewis. Terry W. Glaspey. (Leaders in Action Ser.). 243p. 1996. 14.95 (*1-888952-21-0*) Cumberland Hse.

Not a Total Waste: The True Story of a Mother, a Son & AIDS. B. M. Lloyd. LC 93-93482. (Illus.). 270p. 1994. pap. 16.95 (*0-88962-540-9*) Mosaic.

Not a War: American Vietnamese Fiction, Poetry & Essays. Ed. by Dan Duffy. (Viet Nam Forum Ser.: No. 16). 316p. 1997. pap. 20.00 (*0-614-31206-X*) Yale U SE Asia.

Not a Wicked Stepmother. rev. ed. Michael P. Steiner, Sr. (Illus.). 42p. (Orig.). (J). (gr. 4 up). 1991. pap. text 12.95 (*1-879417-00-6*) Stern & Stern.

Not about Nightingales. Tennessee Williams. Ed. & Intro. by Allean Hale. LC 97-47779. 128p. 1998. pap. 12.95 (*0-8112-1380-3*, NDP860, Pub. by New Directions) Norton.

***Not Afraid of Flavor: Recipes from Magnolia Grill.** Ben Barker & Karen Barker. (Illus.). 336p. 2000. 29.95 (*0-8078-2585-9*) U of NC Pr.

Not Afraid to Change: The Remarkable Story of How One Man Overcame Homosexuality. John Paulk. LC 98-60061. (Illus.). 256p. 1998. pap. 12.95 (*1-57921-150-X*, Pub. by WinePress Pub) BookWorld.

***Not Again Anna!** Vivian French. (J). 1999. pap. text 6.95 (*1-86233-077-8*) Levinson Bks.

Not Again Anna! Vivian French & Alex Ayliffe. LC 98-213334. (Illus.). 24p. (J). (gr. k-3). 1998. 14.95 (*1-899607-96-X*) Sterling.

Not All Black & White: Affirmative Action & American Values. Christopher Edley, Jr. LC 96-21397. 1996. 25.00 (*0-8090-2955-3*) Hill & Wang.

Not All Black & White: Affirmative Action & American Values. Christopher Edley. 320p. 1998. pap. 13.00 (*0-374-52541-2*) Hill & Wang.

***Not All Dogs.** C. Kelly Robinson. LC 99-95221. 349p. 1999. pap. 14.99 (*0-9673208-0-1*) Against the Grain.

Not All Doom & Gloom. Arlene L. Hafer. LC 96-94634. (Illus.). 104p. (Orig.). 1996. pap. 9.00 (*0-9653903-0-6*) A L Hafer.

Not All Glory! True Accounts of RAF Airmen Taken Prisoner in Europe, 1939-1945. Victor F. Gammon. LC 97-178572. 288 p. 1996. write for info. (*1-85409-388-6*) Arms & Armour.

Not All Is Changed: A Life History of Hingham. Lorena L. Hart & Francis R. Hart. LC 93-79100. (Illus.). 1993. 39.50 (*0-9638083-0-3*) Hingham Hist.

Not All Israel Is Israel. Larry D. Harper. (Resurrection Theology Ser.). 1991. pap. text 12.99 (*1-880761-00-9*) Elijah Proj.

Not All of Us Are Saints: A Doctor's Journey with the Poor. David Hilfiker. LC 94-4717. 288p. 1994. 20.95 (*0-8090-3921-4*) Hill & Wang.

Not All Rhythm & Rhyme. Najwak T. Abdul-Sabur. 48p. 1999. pap. 6.95 (*0-9657247-1-9*) J & J Consultants.

Not All Rivers. Adriana Spadoni. LC 74-22816. (Labor Movement in Fiction & Non-Fiction Ser.). reprint ed. 45.00 (*0-404-58475-6*) AMS Pr.

Not All Soldiers Wore Pants: Witty World War II WAC Tells All. Rose Rosenthal. 239p. 1994. pap. 14.00 (*0-9636931-0-7*) Ryzell Bks.

Not All Warriors. William H. Baumer. LC 70-152156. (Essay Index Reprint Ser.). 1977. 21.95 (*0-8369-2180-1*) Ayer.

Not All Warriors. William Baumer. (Essay Index Reprint Ser.). 325p. 1982. reprint ed. lib. bdg. 18.00 (*0-8290-0790-3*) Irvington.

Not Always on Horseback: An Australian Correspondent at War & Peace in Asia, 1961-1993 Denis A. Warner. LC 98-156036. xiii, 266p. 1997. write for info. (*1-86448-467-5*, Pub. by Allen & Unwin Pty) IPG Chicago.

***Not Always So.** Shunryu Suzuki. 2000. 22.00 (*0-06-019785-4*) HarpC.

Not Always the Winter: The Human Side of Racial Prejudice. Jerry Lawson. 223p. 1996. 16.00 (*0-9652034-0-9*) J Lawson.

Not an Apologia for Suicide. Thomas Krampf. 74p. 1998. pap. 12.50 (*0-9616797-3-5*) Ischua Bks.

Not an Easy Choice: A Feminist Re-Examines Abortion. Kathleen McDonnell. 192p. pap. 9.95 (*0-88961-089-4*, Pub. by Womens Pr) LPC InBook.

Not an Illustration but the Equivalent: A Cognitive Approach to Abstract Expressionism. Claude Cernuschi. LC 96-37498. (Illus.). 176p. 1997. 45.00 (*0-8386-3710-8*) Fairleigh Dickinson.

Not an Ivory Tower: The Making of an Australian Vice-Chancellor. Horne. 1997. pap. 14.95 (*0-7334-0449-9*, Pub. by New South Wales Univ Pr) Intl Spec Bk.

Not Angels but Agencies: The Ecumenical Response to Poverty... A Primer. Michael Taylor. (Risk Book Ser.). 1995. pap. 17.00 (*0-334-02624-5*) TPI PA.

Not Another Meeting: A Practical Guide for Facilitating Effective Meetings. Frances Micale. LC 99-20270. (Illus.). xvi, 163p. 1999. pap. 17.95 (*1-55571-480-3*, Oasis Pr) PSI Resch.

Not Architecture but Evidence That It Exists: Lauretta Vinciarelli's Watercolors. Ed. by Brooke Hodge. (Illus.). 148p. 1999. 45.00 (*1-56898-188-0*) Princeton Arch.

Not As a Stranger. large type ed. Morton Thompson. 1976. 27.99 (*0-85456-563-9*) Ulverscroft.

Not As a Stranger. Morton Thompson. 1993. reprint ed. lib. bdg. 39.95 (*1-56849-118-2*) Buccaneer Bks.

Not As Briefed. Wright Lee. (Illus.). 240p. (Orig.). 1996. pap. text 14.95 (*1-885354-01-0*) Honoribus Pr.

Not As Far As Velma. Nicolas Freeling. 1989. 17.95 (*0-89296-380-8*, Pub. by Mysterious Pr) Little.

Not As Far As You Think: The Realities of Working Women. Lynda Moore. LC 85-40109. 224p. (C). 1986. pap. text 14.95 (*0-669-10836-7*) Free Pr.

Not As I Do: A Father's Report. Ed Lowe. 208p. 1995. pap. 9.95 (*0-8362-7045-2*) Andrews & McMeel.

Not As Long but Just As Wide: The Story of Tacoma's Municipal Belt Line Railway. John S. Ott. 300p. (Orig.). 1996. pap. write for info. (*0-9637684-2-5*) Tacoma Pub Util.

Not As the World Gives: St Francis' Message to Laymen Today see Image of Christ: Saint Francis of Assisi

Not As You Once Imagined. Alice Derry. LC 93-60592. 25p. 1993. pap. 7.00 (*0-932264-00-X*) Trask Hse Bks.

Not Ashamed. Ed Robinson. 32p. 1992. pap. 3.99 (*0-8341-1438-0*) Beacon Hill.

***Not Ashamed: The Story of Jews for Jesus.** Ruth Tucker. LC 99-49886. 320p. 1999. pap. 12.99 (*1-57673-602-4*) Multnomah Pubs.

***Not Ashamed: The Story of Jews for Jesus.** Ruth Tucker. 2000. pap. 12.99 (*1-57673-700-4*) Multnomah Pubs.

Not Ashamed of the Gospel: A Commentary on St. Paul's Epistle to the Romans. Daniel E. Cripe. (Historic, Orthodox Exposition of the Bible Ser.: Vol. VI). 684p. (Orig.). 1997. pap. 23.95 (*1-890875-00-7*) Jordan Pub Hse.

***Not at Their Mercy: A Self-Defense Book Designed to Prevent Women from Being at the Mercy of Unconscionable Sexual Predators.** David Green et al. (Illus.). 207p. 2000. pap. 19.95 (*0-9679754-0-9*) T-Comm.

***Not Automatic: Women & the Left in Forging the Auto Workers Union.** Sol Dollinger & Genora J. Dollinger. LC 99-38833. 220p. 1999. 48.00 (*1-58367-017-3*, Pub. by Monthly Rev) NYU Pr.

Not Automatic: Women & the Left in the Forging of the Auto Workers' Union. Genora J. Dollinger. LC 99-38833. 1999. pap. 18.00 (*1-58367-018-1*, Pub. by Monthly Rev) NYU Pr.

Not Before Marriage! Sandra Steffen. 1996. per. 3.99 (*0-373-24061-9*, 1-24061-3) Silhouette.

Not Better . . . Not Worse . . . Just Different. Sharon Scott. (Illus.). 118p. (Orig.). (J). (gr. k-5). 1992. pap. 7.95 (*0-87425-195-8*) HRD Press.

Not Between Brothers. D. Marion Wilkinson. 656p. 1999. reprint ed. mass mkt. 6.99 (*0-451-19686-4*, Sig) NAL.

Not Between Brothers: An Epic Novel of Texas. D. Marion Wilkinson. LC 98-19546. (Illus.). 1996. 27.95 (*0-9651879-0-X*) Boaz Pubng.

Not Between Brothers: An Epic Novel of Texas. D. Marion Wilkinson. LC 98-19546. 1998. pap. 15.95 (*0-9651879-3-4*) Boaz Pubng.

Not Black & White: Inside Words from the Bronx WritersCorps. Ed. by Mary Hebert. (New Voices Ser.). (Illus.). 246p. (Orig.). 1996. pap. 17.95 (*0-911051-83-X*) Plain View.

Not Bloody Likely, & Other Quotations from Bernard Shaw. George Bernard Shaw. Ed. by Bernard F. Dukore. LC 96-18731. 224p. 1997. 21.00 (*0-231-10478-2*) Col U Pr.

Not Born in Sin: The Return of Christ. Africanus Pontifex Staff. (Illus.). 282p. 1998. per. 24.95 (*0-9662007-0-5*) Divine Minist.

***Not by Accident: What I Learned from My Son's Untimely Death.** Isabel Fleece. 80p. 2000. pap. 5.99 (*0-8024-6583-8*) Moody.

Not by Arms ALONE: A Novel of a U. S. Navy Destroyer in the Pacific Theater, 1941-1945. Gary Zimmermann. (Illus.). 626p. 1994. pap. 22.50 (*0-9644793-0-3*) Zimmermann NY.

Not by Arms Alone: Essays on Our Time. Hans Kohn. LC 70-167374. (Essay Index Reprint Ser.). 1977. reprint ed. 18.95 (*0-8369-2461-4*) Ayer.

Not by Birth Alone: Conversion to Judaism. Jacob Homolka et al. LC 97-4967. (Jewish Studies). 256p. 1997. 44.95 (*0-304-33808-7*); pap. 24.95 (*0-304-33809-5*) Continuum.

Not by Blood Alone: Poems. Roberta Gould. Ed. by Guillermo R. Banda. 66p. (Orig.). 1990. pap. 5.00 (*0-936628-05-7*) Waterside.

Not by Bread Alone. Calvin E. Chunn. (Illus.). 86p. (Orig.). 1981. pap. 5.00 (*0-9606828-1-3*) Soc Descend Wash Army.

Not by Bread Alone. Ed. by Cookbook Committee of Holy Trinity Episcopal Churc. (Illus.). 304p. 1985. pap. 11.95 (*0-9615284-0-0*) Holy Episcopal.

Not by Bread Alone. David B. Knox. 160p. 1990. pap. 6.99 (*0-85151-565-7*) Banner of Truth.

***Not by Bread Alone.** Robert A. Sungenis. 400p. 2000. pap. 14.95 (*1-57918-124-4*, 3674) Queenship Pub.

Not by Bread Alone. Nellie Vandeman. (Outreach Ser.). 1981. pap. 0.77 (*0-8163-0452-1*) Pacific Pr Pub Assn.

Not by Bread Alone: A Guide to Creative Ministry Through Food. Ed. by Sandy Farhart & Brenda Castro. (Illus.). 286p. 1993. text, spiral bd. 18.00 (*1-56908-025-9*) Global Evang.

Not by Bread Alone: A Novel about the Price of Success. Wendell B. Will. LC 97-70381. xii, 629p. 1997. 29.95 (*0-935219-08-0*) Intl Trading Mastery.

Not by Bread Alone: Proverbs of the Bible. Wolfgang Mieder. LC 90-63099. (Illus.). 80p. (Orig.). 1990. pap. 6.95 (*0-933050-86-0*) New Eng Pr VT.

Not by Bread Alone: Recipes & Reflections for Christian Cooks. Mary A. McGivern. LC 98-70832. 160p. 1998. pap. 12.95 (*0-87946-181-0*, 271) ACTA Pubns.

Not by Bread Alone: Recipes of the Women of Palmer Church. Palmer Memorial Episcopal Churchwomen, Houston, Te. Ed. by Michele S. Roberts. (Illus.). 288p. (Orig.). pap. text 12.95 (*0-318-20648-X*) D Armstrong.

Not by Chance: Making Sense Out of Suffering. Brian H. Edwards. 1982. pap. 4.99 (*0-85234-170-9*, Pub. by Evangelical Pr) P & R Pubng.

Not by Chance: Shattering the Modern Theory of Evolution. Lee M. Spetner. LC 99-29518. 288p. (Orig.). 1999. pap. 14.95 (*1-880582-24-4*) Judaica Pr.

Not by Design: The Origin of the Universe. Victor J. Stenger. LC 88-4162. (Illus.). 203p. 1988. 29.95 (*0-87975-451-6*) Prometheus Bks.

Not by Faith Alone: A Biblical Study of the Catholic Doctrine of Justification. Robert A. Sungenis. LC 97-69045. 774p. (Orig.). 1997. 34.95 (*1-57918-008-6*, 3671H); pap. 24.95 (*1-57918-009-4*, 3671) Queenship Pub.

***Not by Fire but by Ice: Discover What Killed the Dinosaurs... And Why It Could Soon Kill Us.** 2nd ed. Robert W. Felix. LC 99-71069. (Illus.). 256p. 1999. 15.95 (*0-9648746-8-7*) Sugarhse Pub.

Not by Might. Al Lacy. (Angel of Mercy Ser.: Vol. 8). 350p. 1998. pap. 10.99 (*1-57673-242-8*, Multnomah Fiction) Multnomah Pubs.

Not by Might, nor by Power. Joyce Metzler Baker. LC 89-27002. (Illus.). 233p. 1990. pap. text 9.99 (*0-87227-135-8*, RBP5164) Reg Baptist.

Not by Might nor by Power: A Pentecostal Theology of Social Concern in Latin America. Douglas Petersen. 260p. 1996. reprint ed. pap. 20.00 (*1-870345-20-7*, Pub. by Regnum Bks) OM Literature.

***Not by Politics Alone: The Enduring Influence of the Christian Right.** Sara Diamond. LC 98-24502. 280p. 1998. lib. bdg. 29.95 (*1-57230-385-9*) Guilford Pubns.

***Not by Politics Alone: The Enduring Influence of the Christian Right.** Sara Diamond. 280p. 2000. pap. text 17.95 (*1-57230-494-4*, C0494) Guilford Pubns.

Not by Reason Alone: Religion, History, & Identity in Early Modern Political Thought. Joshua Mitchell. LC 93-3048. 272p. 1993. 34.95 (*0-226-53221-6*) U Ch Pr.

Not by Reason Alone: Religion, History, & Identity in Early Modern Political Thought. Joshua Mitchell. xii, 252p. 1996. pap. text 16.95 (*0-226-53222-4*) U Ch Pr.

Not by Schools Alone: Sharing Responsibility for America's Education Reform. Sandra A. Waddock. LC 94-33259. 256p. 1995. 55.00 (*0-275-94790-4*, Praeger Pubs) Greenwood.

Not by Scripture Alone: A Catholic Critique of the Protestant Doctrine of Sola Scriptura. Robert A. Sungenis. LC 97-76397. 1998. pap. 19.95 (*1-57918-055-8*, 3672) Queenship Pub.

Not by Strange Gods. Elizabeth Maddox Roberts. LC 76-12119. reprint ed. 39.50 (*0-404-15237-6*) AMS Pr.

***Not by Strength by Guile.** Peter Mercer. (Illus.). 16p. 2000. 26.00 (*1-85782-368-0*) Blake Publng.

Not by the Color of Their Skin: The Impact of Racial Differences on the Child's Development. Marjorie McDonald. LC 73-134334. Orig. Title: Integration & Skin Color. 242p. 1971. 37.50 (*0-8236-3690-9*); pap. 24.95 (*0-8236-8166-1*, 23690) Intl Univs Pr.

Not by the Sword. Nash Candelaria. LC 81-71731. 235p. 1982. 26.00 (*0-916950-30-1*); pap. 16.00 (*0-916950-31-X*) Biling Rev-Pr.

Not by the Sword. Kathryn Watterson. 360p. 1995. 23.00 (*0-671-86893-4*) S&S Trade.

Not by Timber Alone: Economics & Ecology for Sustaining Tropical Forests. Theodore Panayotou & Peter S. Ashton. LC 92-10222. 280p. 1992. text 45.00 (*1-55963-195-3*); pap. text 27.00 (*1-55963-196-1*) Island Pr.

Not Comin' Home to You. Lawrence Block. 224p. 1997. mass mkt. 4.95 (*0-7867-0388-1*) Carroll & Graf.

(Not) Coming Home. Nikoline Hansen. 364p. 1997. 61.95 (*3-631-31018-8*) P Lang Pubng.

Not Counting Women & Children: Neglected Stories from the Bible. Megan Mckenna. 232p. 1994. pap. 27.00 (*0-86012-230-1*, Pub. by Srch Pr) St Mut.

Not Counting Women & Children: Some Forgotten Stories from the Bible. Megan McKenna. LC 93-36627. 146p. (Orig.). 1994. pap. 12.00 (*0-88344-946-3*) Orbis Bks.

Not Crazy, Just Enlightened: A Voyage of the Soul. Debra J. Taubenslag. 192p. 2000. pap. 12.95 (*1-880090-24-4*) Galde Pr.

Not Dancing. Stephen Dunn. LC 84-70175. (Poetry Ser.). 77p. 1984. 12.95 (*0-88748-000-4*) Carnegie-Mellon.

Not Deaf Enough: Raising a Child Who Is Hard of Hearing with Hugs, Humor & Imagination. Patricia Ann Morgan Candlish. (Illus.). 242p. (Orig.). 1996. pap. 22.95 (*0-88200-201-5*) Alexander Graham.

Not Dying: A Memoir. William Saroyan. LC 96-26736. (Illus.). 256p. 1996. reprint ed. pap. 12.95 (*1-56980-081-2*) Barricade Bks.

Not Eating Enough: Overcoming Underconsumption of Military Operational Rations. Institute of Medicine, Committee on Military Nutri. Ed. by Bernadette M. Marriott. 500p. (Orig.). (C). 1995. pap. text 45.00 (*0-309-05341-2*) Natl Acad Pr.

Not Either an Experimental Doll: The Separate World of Three South African Women. Ed. by Shula Marks. LC 88-12867. (Illus.). 234p. (Orig.). 1988. 31.95 (*0-253-34843-9*); pap. 12.95 (*0-253-28640-9*) Ind U Pr.

Not Either an Experimental Doll: The Separate Worlds of Three South African Women. Ed. by Shula Marks. (Killie Campbell Africana Library Publication: No. 2). (Illus.). 236p. 1987. pap. write for info. (*0-86980-542-8*, Pub. by Univ Natal Pr) Intl Spec Bk.

***Not Enough Beds!** Lisa Bullard. LC 98-30518. (Picture Bks.). (Illus.). 32p. (J). (gr. k-3). 1999. 15.95 (*1-57505-356-X*) Lerner Pub.

Not Enough Room! Joanne Rocklin. (Hello Math Reader Ser.). (J). 1998. 8.70 (*0-606-13669-X*, Pub. by Turtleback) Demco.

Not Enough Room! Joanne Rocklin & Marilyn Burns. LC 97-12853. (Hello Math Reader Ser.). (Illus.). (J). 1998. 3.50 (*0-590-39962-4*) Scholastic Inc.

Not Entirely Benign Procedure: Four Years As a Medical Student. Perri Klass. LC 94-50781. 288p. 1994. reprint ed. pap. 12.95 (*0-452-27258-0*, Plume) Dutton Plume.

Not Entitled: A Memoir. Frank Kermode. LC 95-18335. 272p. 1995. 23.00 (*0-374-18103-9*) FS&G.

***Not Entitled: A Memoir.** Frank Kermode. 272p. 1999. pap. 13.00 (*0-374-52592-7*) FS&G.

Not Even A. Mouse: A Chris-Mouse Tale. Jerome McDonough. (Illus.). 20p. (Orig.). (J). (gr. k-9). 1984. pap. 3.00 (*0-88680-220-2*) I E Clark.

Not Even Dicta. 180p. 1997. lib. bdg. write for info. (*0-9661629-5-1*) S J McEwen.

Not Even Footprints. Marj Dunmire. (Illus.). 72p. (Orig.). (J). (gr. 2). 1987. pap. 4.95 (*0-942559-04-5*) Pegasus Graphics.

Not Even God Is Ripe Enough. Bakare Gbadanosi & Ulli Beier. (African Writers Ser.). 58p. (C). 1968. pap. 7.95 (*0-435-90048-X*, 90048) Heinemann.

***Not Even My Name: From a Death March in Turkey to a New Home in America, a Young Girl'sTrue Story of Genocide & Survival.** Thea Halo. LC 00-23536. (Illus.). 336p. 2000. text 25.00 (*0-312-26211-6*, Picador USA) St Martin.

Not Even Wrong: Margaret Mead, Derek Freeman, & the Samoans. Martin Orans. Ed. by L. L. Langness & Robert B. Edgerton. LC 95-39377. (Publications in Anthropology & Related Fields). 190p. (Orig.). (C). 1996. pap. 14.95 (*0-88316-564-3*) Chandler & Sharp.

Not Every Day an Aurora Borealis for Your Birthday: A Love Poem. Carl Sandburg. LC 96-41685. (Illus.). (YA). 1997. 13.00 (*0-679-88170-0*, Pub. by Knopf Bks Yng Read) Random.

Not Every Sea Hath Pearls. Loulie A. Mathews. 173p. (Orig.). 1986. pap. 7.95 (*0-87961-165-0*) Naturegraph.

Not Every Spirit: A Dogmatics of Christian Disbelief. Christopher Morse. LC 93-45865. 432p. (C). 1994. pap. 24.00 (*1-56338-087-0*) TPI PA.

Not Everybody's Doing It: Making Choices about Sex. Norman D. Stolpe. (LifeWise Ser.). 1995. pap., teacher ed. 7.95 (*1-56212-093-X*) CRC Pubns.

***Not Everyday an Aurora Borealis for Your Birthday: A Love Poem.** Carl Sandburg. LC 96-41685. 1998. pap. 13.00 (*0-679-88169-7*, Bullseye Bks) Random Bks Yng Read.

***Not Exactly Eden.** Linda Windsor. 2000. pap. 6.99 (*1-57673-445-5*) Multnomah Pubs.

Not Exactly Nashville. Betsy Kuhn. 1999. pap. 3.99 (*0-440-41478-4*) BDD Bks Young Read.

Not Exactly Nashville. Betsy Kuhn. LC 97-33275. 144p. (J). (gr. 4-6). 1998. 14.95 (*0-385-32589-4*) Delacorte.

Not Exactly Rocket Science. Brent Coulson. LC 98-90529. (Illus.). 112p. 1998. pap. 10.00 (*0-9665637-0-0*) Smirk Prods.

Not Exactly the Three Musketeers. Joel Rosenberg. LC 98-43785. (Guardians of the Flame Ser.). 320p. 2000. 23.95 (*0-312-85782-9*, Pub. by Tor Bks) St Martin.

***Not Exactly the Three Musketeers.** Joel Rosenberg. 384p. 2000. mass mkt. 6.99 (*0-8125-5046-3*, Pub. by Tor Bks) St Martin.

Not Exactly What I Had in Mind: An Incurable Love Story. Rosemary Breslin. 229p. 3.99 (*0-614-26976-8*) Villard Books.

Not Fade Away. Jim Dodge. 304p. 1998. reprint ed. pap. 12.00 (*0-8021-3584-6*, Grove) Grove-Atltic.

***Not Fade Away: A Backstage Pass to 20 Years of Rock & Roll.** Ben Fong-Torres. LC 99-43365. (Illus.). 384p. 1999. pap. 14.95 (*0-87930-590-8*) Miller Freeman.

Not Fade Away: A Comparison of Two Generations of Composers of Contemporary Popular Music. Walter Rimler. (Illus.). 240p. 1983. 40.00 (*0-87650-159-5*) Popular Culture.

N

An Asterisk (*) at the beginning of an entry indicates that the title is appearing for the first time.

Not Fade Away: An Exhibition of Contemporary Virginia Photography. Brooks Johnson. (Illus.). 13p. 1980. pap. 3.00 (*0-940744-27-9*) Chrysler Museum.

Not Fade Away: How the Baby Boom Grew Up. Michael Gross. Date not set. pap. 13.00 (*0-06-093124-8*) HarpC.

Not Fade Away: Poems, 1989-1994. Adrian Henri et al. 64p. 1995. pap. 15.95 (*1-85224-313-9*) Dufour.

Not Fade Away: Quality Woodwork, an American Myth. William Keisling. LC 97-21541. 558p. 1999. 24.00 (*1-882611-12-8*) Yardbird Bks.

***Not Fade Away: Quality Woodwork, In American Myth.** William Keisling. LC 97-21541. 558p. 1999. pap. 15.00 (*1-882611-13-6*) Yardbird Bks.

***Not Fade Away: The On-Line World Remembers Jerry Garcia.** Ed. by David Gans. (Illus.). 128p. 1999. reprint ed. pap. text 15.00 (*0-7881-6709-X*) DIANE Pub.

***Not Fade Away: The Rock & Roll Photography of Jim Marshall.** Jim Marshall. (Illus.). 144p. 2000. pap. 29.95 (*0-8212-2656-8*, Pub. by Bulfinch Pr) Little.

Not Fade Away: The Rock & Roll Photography of Jim Marshall. Jim Marshall. LC 97-11245. (Illus.). 144p. (gr. 8). 1997. 50.00 (*0-8212-2362-3*) Little.

***Not Falling.** Desmond Graham. 64p. 1999. pap. (*1-85411-249-X*, Pub. by Seren Bks) Dufour.

Not Far Afield: U. S. Interests & the Global Environment. Norman Myers. LC 87-50723. 84p. 1987. pap. text 10.00 (*0-915825-24-4*) World Resources Inst.

***Not Far from Everyone of Us: An Evangelical Theological Yearbook.** Ed. by Joseph Gatis. 500p. 1999. 64.95 (*1-57309-395-5*); pap. 32.95 (*1-57309-396-3*) Intl Schol Pr.

Not Far from the River: Poems from the Gatha-Saptasati. Tr. & Intro. by David Ray. LC 90-81354. 160p. (Orig.). 1990. pap. 10.00 (*1-55659-034-2*) Copper Canyon.

Not for a Billion Gazillion Dollars. Paula Danziger. (Illus.). 126p. (J). (gr. 3-7). 1998. pap. 4.99 (*0-698-11693-3*, PapStar) Peng Put Young Read.

Not for America Alone: The Triumph of Democracy & the Fall of Communism. George J. Mitchell. LC 96-50332. 320p. 1997. 25.00 (*1-56836-083-5*) Kodansha.

***Not for Attribution: A Treasury of Public Relations - Public Affairs Anecdotes.** Jon L. Allen. LC 99-91546. 1999. 25.00 (*0-7388-0870-9*); pap. 18.00 (*0-7388-0871-7*) Xlibris Corp.

Not for Babies. Donna Guthrie. (Illus.). 24p. (J). (ps-1). 1993. pap. 2.50 (*0-671-79362-4*) Aladdin.

Not for Bread Alone. Calvin E. Chuun. (Illus.). 64p. 1981. 3.00 (*0-318-16568-6*) Soc Descend Wash Army.

Not for Bread Alone. Konosuke Matsushita. 176p. (Orig.). 1994. pap. 12.00 (*0-425-14133-0*) Berkley Pub.

Not for Bread Alone. Lynda K. Taylor. 202p. 1980. pap. 19.95 (*0-8464-1429-5*) Beekman Pubs.

Not for Children Only: The Mexican Comic Book in the Late 1960s & 1970s, 30. Harold B. Hinds & Charles M. Tatum. LC 91-40319. (Contributions to the Study of Popular Culture Ser.: No. 30). 264p. 1992. 59.95 (*0-313-25467-2*, HNC, Greenwood Pr) Greenwood.

***Not for Every Eye.** 2nd ed. Gerard Bessette. Tr. by Glen Shortliffe from FRE. (Picas Ser.: No. 20). Orig. Title: Le Libraire. 92p. 1999. reprint ed. pap. 7.00 (*1-55096-549-2*, Pub. by Exile Edns) Paul & Co Pubs.

Not for Innocent Ears: Spiritual Traditions of a Desert Cahuilla Medicine Woman. rev. ed. Ruby Modesto & Guy Mount. (Illus.). 128p. 1986. per. 9.95 (*0-9604462-0-6*) Sweetlight.

Not for Johnny Only: Recollections for My American Son. Meta Cordy. LC 97-6886. Orig. Title: Nich Nur Fur Johnny. 272p. (Orig.). 1997. pap. 12.95 (*1-56474-223-7*) Fithian Pr.

Not for Love. large type ed. Pamela Hatton. 1995. 11.50 (*0-7505-0829-9*, Pub. by Mgna Lrg Print) Ulverscroft.

Not for Love. Alice D. Miller. 1994. reprint ed. lib. bdg. 21.95 (*1-56849-518-8*) Buccaneer Bks.

Not for Love Alone: A Critical Analysis. Jill Beck. (Educational Performance Collection). 30p. 1985. pap. write for info. (*0-932582-49-4*) Dance Notation.

Not for Love Alone: Labanotation Score. Buzz Miller & Jane Marriett. (Educational Performance Collection). 80p. 1986. pap. write for info. (*0-932582-50-8*) Dance Notation.

Not for Me. Fred B. Chernow & Carol Chernow. (Illus.). 36p. (J). (gr. 1-7). 1986. pap. 3.00 (*0-9610742-1-3*) Purcell Prods.

Not for Myself Alone: Memoir of a Lawyer Who Fought for Human Rights. Herman Edelsberg. LC 88-81545. (Illus.). 270p. 1988. 17.95 (*0-941325-01-6*) Interstellar Media.

***Not for Ourselves Alone: The Story of Elizabeth Cady Stanton & Susan B. Anthony.** Geoffrey C. Ward & Ken Burns. LC 99-31056. 272p. 1999. 35.00 (*0-375-40560-7*) Knopf.

Not For Profit. Johnson. (C). 1998. pap. text 24.00 (*0-471-32873-1*) Wiley.

Not-for-Profit Accounting Field Guide, 1999-2000. Richard F. Larkin & Marie DiTommaso. 248p. 1999. pap. 22.95 (*0-471-24637-9*) Wiley.

Not-for-Profit CEO: A Survivor's Manual. George B. Wright. LC 92-81341. (Illus.). 144p. (Orig.). (C). 1992. reprint ed. pap. 11.95 (*0-9632655-0-4*) CThree Pubns.

Not for Profit Corporations in Florida. 2nd ed. LC 95-60235. 198p. 1997. ring bd. 45.00 (*0-945979-70-3*, 209) FL Bar Legal Ed.

Not-for-Profit-Hospitals: Conversion Issues Prompt Increased State Oversight. Ed. by James O. McClyde. 51p. (C). 1999. reprint ed. pap. text 20.00 (*0-7881-7719-2*) DIANE Pub.

Not for Profit, Not for Sale, Vol. 6: Reshaping Local Government. Michael Starks. 280p. (C). 1991. text 39.95 (*0-946967-36-9*); pap. text 21.95 (*0-946967-37-7*) Transaction Pubs.

Not-for-Profit Organizations: With Conforming Changes as of May 1, 1997. American Institute of Certified Public Accountants Staff. LC 96-34724. 389p. Date not set. reprint ed. pap. 120.60 (*0-608-20772-1*, 207187100003) Bks Demand.

Not for Queen & Country: A No-Holds Barred Account of Life As a British Soldier. Edward Denmark. 1998. pap. text 9.95 (*1-901442-08-X*, Pub. by Pharaoh Pr) Seven Hills Bk.

Not for Revenge. Donald S. Vogel. Ed. by Peggy Goad. LC 90-71866. 240p. (Orig.). 1991. write for info. (*1-879154-03-X*); pap. write for info. (*1-879154-04-8*) Vlly Hse Gllry.

Not for Sadie. Jane Mathews. (Illus.). 48p. (Orig.). (J). (gr. k-3). 1993. pap. 9.95 (*1-880812-05-3*) S Ink WA.

***Not for Sale: Saving Your Soul & Your Sanity at Work.** J. Murray Elwood. LC 99-67506. 128p. 2000. pap. 9.95 (*1-893732-13-4*) SORIN BKS.

Not for Sale: Young People in Society. B. Henriksson. (Illus.). 224p. 1983. text 24.00 (*0-08-030364-1*, HQ769, Pergamon Pr); pap. text 13.00 (*0-08-028484-1*, Pergamon Pr) Elsevier.

Not for School, but for Life: Lessons from the Historical Archaeology of the Phoenix Indian School. Owen Lindauer. LC 97-51619. (OCRM Report Ser.). 1998. write for info. (*1-886067-15-5*) AZ State Univ Anthro.

Not for Teachers Only: Creating a Context of Joy for Learning & Growth. Patricia E. Ortman. (Orig.). 1988. pap. 4.95 (*0-317-91345-X*) P E Ortman.

Not for the Poor Alone: European Social Services. Alfred J. Kahn & Sheila B. Kamerman. LC 75-14690. 197p. 1975. 14.95 (*0-87722-045-X*) Temple U Pr.

Not for Women Only: Social Work Practice for a Feminist Future. Ed. by Mary Bricker-Jenkins & Nancy R. Hooyman. LC 85-28532. 127p. 1986. 18.95 (*0-87101-131-X*) Natl Assn Soc Wkrs.

***Not Forgotten.** E. B. Grayden. LC 99-59858. (Illus.). 144p. 2000. pap. 12.95 (*1-880090-93-7*) Galde Pr.

Not Forgotten. Nancy Holder. (Angel Ser.: No. 2). 224p. (YA). (gr. 7-12). 2000. per. 4.99 (*0-671-04145-2*, Pocket Pulse) PB.

Not Forgotten: Remembering Those Who Died in the Persian Gulf War. Daniel J. Grey. LC 95-60797. (Illus.). 210p. 1995. 32.50 (*0-9646083-0-8*) Emkell Pub.

***Not from Around Now: Poetry for a Small Choir.** A. Molotkov. (Illus.). 115p. (C). 2000. pap. 16.00 (*0-9678919-2-2*) Discord.

Not from the Apes: A History of Man's Origin & Evolution. Bjorn Kurten. LC 84-1842. 1984. pap. text 19.50 (*0-231-05815-2*) Col U Pr.

Not-God: A History of Alcoholics Anonymous. Ernest Kurtz. 436p. pap. 14.50 (*0-89486-065-8*, 1036A) Hazelden.

Not Good If Detached. Corrie Ten Boom. 1991. pap. 5.99 (*0-87508-022-7*) Chr Lit.

Not Good If Detached. Corrie Ten Boom. LC 98-46635. (Corrie Ten Boom Library Ser.). 208p. 1999. 12.99 (*0-8007-1765-1*) Revell.

Not Grass Alone. large type ed. Nelson Nye. LC 95-11095. (Nightingale Ser.). 237p. 1995. pap. 17.95 (*0-7838-1384-8*, G K Hall Lrg Type) Mac Lib Ref.

Not Guilty. James Buchanan. 1990. pap. 4.99 (*0-946462-22-4*, Pub. by Evangelical Pr) P & R Pubng.

Not Guilty. George A. Sullivan. LC 98-137434. (Illus.). (J). (gr. 3-9). 1997. mass mkt. 3.99 (*0-590-89749-7*) Scholastic Inc.

Not Guilty. George A. Sullivan. 1997. 9.09 (*0-606-13004-7*, Pub. by Turtleback) Demco.

Not Guilty: Report of the 1937-38 Commission of Inquiry into the Charges Made Against Leon Trotsky in the Moscow Trials. John Dewey et al. LC 72-87928. 422p. 1973. reprint ed. lib. bdg. 65.00 (*0-913460-00-1*) Pathfinder NY.

Not Guilty! The Good News about Working Mothers. Betty Holcomb. LC 98-16527. 224p. 1998. 25.00 (*0-684-82233-4*) S&S Trade.

***Not Guilty! The Good News for Working Mothers.** Betty Holcomb. 384p. 2000. per. 14.00 (*0-684-86725-7*) S&S Trade.

***Not Guilty: The Suprising Trial of Gerald Regan.** Stephen Kimber. 300p. 1999. 26.95 (*0-7737-3192-X*, Pub. by Stoddart Publ) Genl Dist Srvs.

***Not Guilty by Reason of Insanity: One Man's Story of Recovery.** Randy Starr. Ed. by Robert Lundin. 150p. 1999. pap. 10.95 (*0-9674794-0-1*) Recovery Bks.

Not Half the Trubles: A Letter from Virginia Reed, May 16, 1847. Virginia Reed. Ed. by Charles H. Dodd. (Illus.). iii, 54p. (Orig.). 1996. pap. 9.95 (*0-9653876-0-7*) Ninetnth Cent Pub.

Not Her Real Name. Emily Perkins. LC 97-3574. 272p. 1997. pap. 12.00 (*0-385-48664-2*, Anchor NY) Doubleday.

***Not Here.** Mike James. 28p. 2000. pap. 4.00 (*1-891408-13-5*, GBP-12) Green Bean.

Not Here by Chance Vol. II: The Story of Oakhurst Baptist Church, Decatur, Georgia, 1988-1993. Alverta S. Wright. 45p. 1993. pap. 5.00 (*0-614-29807-5*) Oakhurst Baptist.

Not Here Not There. Peter Turner. (Illus.). 112p. 1998. pap. 29.95 (*1-899235-76-0*, Pub. by Dewi Lewis) Dist Art Pubs.

Not His Death-His Overcoming of Death. Karl Roebling. 30p. 1983. pap. 5.00 (*0-942910-10-9*) Dynapress.

Not His Kind of Woman. large type ed. Roberta Leigh. 1992. reprint ed. 18.95 (*0-263-13097-5*) Mac Lib Ref.

Not His Property. Edwina Shore. (Presents Ser.: No. 437). 1992. pap. 2.79 (*0-373-11437-0*, 1-11437-0) Harlequin Bks.

Not His Wedding! Suzanne Simms. (Desire Ser.: No. 718). 1992. pap. 2.89 (*0-373-05718-0*, 5-05718-7) Harlequin Bks.

Not His Wedding! large type ed. Suzanne Simms. (Silhouette Romance Ser.). 1995. lib. bdg. 18.95 (*0-373-59414-3*) Thorndike Pr.

Not His Wife. Sally T. Hayes. (Intimate Moments Ser.). 1994. per. 3.50 (*0-373-07611-8*, 1-07611-6) Silhouette.

Not Honour More. Joyce Cary. 1976. 24.95 (*0-88411-312-4*, Queens House) Amereon Ltd.

Not Honour More: Novel. Joyce Cary. LC 85-10601. (Second Trilogy - The New Directions Classics Ser.: Bk. 3). 320p. 1985. reprint ed. pap. 7.95 (*0-8112-0966-0*, NDP608, Pub. by New Directions) Norton.

Not Husband Material! large type ed. Caroline Anderson. (Mills & Boon Large Print Ser.). 288p. 1998. 24.99 (*0-263-15328-2*, Pub. by Mills & Boon) Ulverscroft.

Not I, but Christ. Watchman Nee. Tr. by Stephen Kaung. (Basic Lesson Ser.: Vol. 4). 143p. 1974. 6.50 (*0-935008-11-X*); pap. 4.50 (*0-935008-12-8*) Christian Fellow Pubs.

Not I, but Christ. large type ed. Corrie Ten Boom. (Large Print Inspirational Ser.). 256p. 1986. pap. 10.95 (*0-8027-2528-7*) Walker & Co.

Not I, but Christ. Stephen F. Olford. LC 96-39643. 192p. 1997. reprint ed. pap. 12.99 (*0-89107-943-2*) Crossway Bks.

Not I, but Christ. Corrie Ten Boom. LC 97-15003. (Corrie Ten Boom Library Ser.). 192p. 1997. reprint ed. 12.99 (*0-8007-1742-2*, Niet ik, maar C) Revell.

Not I, but the Wind. Frieda Lawrence. 2000. reprint ed. lib. bdg. 79.00 (*0-7812-7713-2*) Rprt Serv.

Not I, Not I. Margaret Hillert. (Illus.). (J). (ps-2). 1981. pap. 5.10 (*0-8136-5563-3*); lib. bdg. 7.95 (*0-8136-5063-1*) Modern Curr.

Not Impossible Summer. unabridged ed. Sue A. Alderson. 112p. (Orig.). (YA). (gr. 3 up). 1983. pap. 4.95 (*0-7736-7286-9*) STDK.

Not in Bronxville. Rita Farrelly. 400p. 1999. pap. 6.99 (*1-886094-83-7*) Chicago Spectrum.

Not in Front of the Audience: Homosexuality on Stage. Nicholas De Jongh. (Illus.). 232p. (Orig.). (C). 1992. pap. 24.99 (*0-415-03363-2*, A5626) Routledge.

Not in Heaven: Coherence & Complexity in Biblical Narrative. Ed. by Jason P. Rosenblatt & Joseph C. Sitterson, Jr. LC 91-6317. (Indiana Studies in Biblical Literature). (Illus.). 272p. 1991. 41.95 (*0-253-35036-0*); pap. 6.95 (*0-253-20678-2*, MB-678) Ind U Pr.

Not in Heaven: The Nature & Function of Halakha. Eliezer Berkovits. LC 82-23255. 131p. 1983. pap. 11.95 (*0-88125-003-1*) Ktav.

Not in Heaven: or Beyond the Sea: Explorations in the World of Jewish Tradition. Shmuel Werzberger. 20.00 (*0-88125-128-3*) Ktav.

Not in My Back Yard: Removing Barriers to Affordable Housing. (Illus.). 264p. (Orig.). (C). 1993. pap. text 35.00 (*0-7881-0066-1*) DIANE Pub.

***Not in My Backyard.** Susan Rogers Cooper. (E. J. Pugh Mystery Ser.). 256p. 1999. mass mkt. 5.99 (*0-380-80532-4*, Avon Bks) Morrow Avon.

Not in My Backyard: The Handbook. Jane A. Morris. LC 94-8052. 300p. (Orig.). 1994. pap. 14.95 (*0-9624945-7-7*) Silvercat Pubns.

Not in My Bed! The Wrong Bed. Kate Hoffmann. (Temptation Ser.: No. 731). 1999. per. 3.75 (*0-373-25831-3*, 1-25831-8) Harlequin Bks.

Not in Our Backyards! Community Action for Health & the Environment. Nicholas Freudenberg. LC 84-10524. 320p. 1984. 26.00 (*0-85345-653-4*, Pub. by Monthly Rev); pap. 12.00 (*0-85345-654-2*, Pub. by Monthly Rev) NYU Pr.

Not in Our Family! Helping Teenagers Cope with the Drug Scene. Sherwood O. Cole. 224p. (Orig.). 1998. pap. 12.95 (*0-939497-49-2*) Promise Pub.

Not in Our Stars. Harriet Hudson. 256p. 1998. 24.00 (*0-7278-5327-9*) Severn Hse.

***Not in Our Stars.** large type ed. Harriet Hudson. 368p. 1999. 31.99 (*0-7505-1330-6*, Pub. by Mgna Lrg Print) Ulverscroft.

Not in Ourselves, nor in Our Stars Either. Malvina Reynolds. 40p. 1975. pap. 1.00 (*0-915620-03-0*) Schroder Music.

Not in Sisterhood: Edith Wharton Willa Cather Zona Gale. Deborah Lindsay Williams. text. write for info. (*0-312-22921-6*) St Martin.

Not in the House, Newton! Judith Heide & Judith Heide Gilliland. LC 94-11792. (Illus.). 32p. (J). (ps-k). 1995. 15.00 (*0-395-61195-4*, Clarion Bks) HM.

***Not in the Stars.** Buck Busfield. 44p. 1998. pap. 5.60 (*0-87129-897-X*, N48) Dramatic Pub.

Not in the Wind. Brant Day. (Illus.). 32p. (J). 1995. 12.95 (*0-910523-14-2*) Grandin Bk Co.

Not in Vain: A Rifleman Remembers World War II. Leon C. Standifer. LC 91-23154. (Illus.). 232p. 1992. 24.95 (*0-8071-1703-X*) La State U Pr.

Not in Vain: A Rifleman Remembers World War II. Leon C. Standifer. LC 91-23154. (Illus.). 296p. 1998. pap. 16.95 (*0-8071-2338-2*) La State U Pr.

Not in Vain: An Extraordinary Life. Ada Aharoni. LC 97-76404. (Illus.). 240p. 1998. pap. 14.95 (*1-889409-18-9*) Ladybug Pr CA.

Not in Your Lifetime. 2nd ed. Anthony Summers. LC 98-85501. (Illus.). 704p. 1998. pap. text 18.95 (*1-56924-739-0*) Marlowe & Co.

Not Inconsiderable: Being the Life & Times of John Major. Patrick Wright. (Illus.). 96p. 1996. pap. 13.95 (*0-233-98958-7*, Pub. by Andre Deutsch) Trafalgar.

Not June Cleaver: Women & Gender in the Postwar America, 1945-1960. Ed. by Joanne Meyerowitz. LC 93-26987. (Critical Perspectives on the Past Ser.). 368p. (C). 1994. pap. 22.95 (*1-56639-171-7*); text 69.95 (*1-56639-170-9*) Temple U Pr.

Not Just a Bag of Bones. Thomas-Cochran. (What a Wonderful World 2 Ser.). 1992. pap. text. write for info. (*0-582-90975-9*, Pub. by Addison-Wesley) Longman.

Not Just a Bed for the Night: The Story of Trust. Alice Leahy & Anne Dempsey. 192p. 1997. pap. 12.95 (*1-86023-024-5*, Pub. by Martello Bks) Irish Amer Bk.

Not Just a Passing Phase: Social Work with Gay, Lesbian & Bisexual People. George Appleby & Jeane Anastas. LC 97-37962. 496p. 1998. 52.00 (*0-231-10322-0*); pap. 29.00 (*0-231-10323-9*) Col U Pr.

***Not Just a Pretty Face: Dolls & Human Figurines in Alaska Native Cultures.** Molly C. Lee. (Illus.). 2000. pap. 17.95 (*0-931163-18-8*) U Alaska Museum.

***Not Just a Romance: A Collection of Sensual Adventurous Novellas.** Betty L'Ursula. 2000. pap. 18.00 (*0-7388-2150-0*) Xlibris Corp.

Not Just a Room with a Bath. Souter. pap. 9.95 (*0-8464-4492-5*) Beekman Pubs.

Not Just a Room with a Bath: Simple & Natural Remedies for Common Ailments that Can Be Applied in One's Own Bathroom. Keith Souter. 109p. 1995. pap. 7.95 (*0-85207-291-0*, Pub. by C W Daniel) Natl Bk Netwk.

Not Just a Secretary: Using the Job to Get Ahead. Jodie B. Morrow & Myrna Lebov. LC 82-24744. (General Trade Bks.). 182p. 1984. pap. 12.95 (*0-471-87060-9*, 1-999) Wiley.

Not Just a Shelter Kid: How Homeless Children Find Solace. rev. ed. Melanie S. Percy. LC 96-30013. (Children of Poverty Ser.). (Illus.). 104p. 1997. text 33.00 (*0-8153-2618-1*) Garland.

Not Just a Soldier's War. large type ed. Betty Burton. (Charnwood Large Print Ser.). 464p. 1997. 27.99 (*0-7089-8953-5*, Charnwood) Ulverscroft.

Not Just a Summer Crush. C. S. Adler. LC 98-11358. 128p. (J). (gr. 5-8). 1998. 15.00 (*0-395-88532-9*, Clarion Bks) HM.

Not Just Another Cowboy. Carol Finch, pseud. 1999. per. 4.25 (*0-373-24242-5*, 1-24242-9) Silhouette.

Not Just Another Day: Families, Grief & Special Days. Missy Lowery. 1992. pap. 2.95 (*1-56123-055-3*) Centering Corp.

***Not Just Another Love Story.** Wayne G. MacDowell. LC 99-62148. 370p. 1999. pap. 19.95 (*1-889131-42-3*) CasAnanda.

Not Just Another Low-Fat Recipe Book: Discovering a New Relationship with Food. Sam Martel. Ed. by Muriel Ray. (Illus.). 105p. 1995. write for info. (*0-614-23145-0*) Hlth & Food.

***Not Just Another Moose.** Illus. by Stephanie Greene & Andrea Wallace. LC 99-41355. 32p. (J). (gr. 1-5). 2000. 15.95 (*0-7614-5061-0*, Cav Child Bks) Marshall Cavendish.

Not Just Another Namebook: How & Why the Numerical Patterns Hidden Within Your Name Influence Your Daily Life, Love Life & Bank Account. Maryanna Korwitts & Jim Gash. 1995. pap. 19.95 (*1-887270-02-7*) Weve Got Your Number.

Not Just Another Nicaragua Travel Guide. Alan Holme et al. Tr. by Davi Trumann. (Illus.). 246p. 1991. pap. 14.95 (*0-9625847-0-3*) Mango Pubns.

Not Just Another Perfect Wife. Robin Elliott. (Desire Ser.). 1993. per. 2.99 (*0-373-05818-7*, 5-05818-5) Silhouette.

Not Just Another Pretty Dress: Two Centuries of Clothing & Textiles from Cherry Hill. Cornelia H. Frisbee-Houde. LC 82-81738. (Illus.). 32p. (Orig.). 1983. pap. 5.00 (*0-943366-05-4*) Hist Cherry Hill.

Not Just Another Pretty Face. Peter Filichia. 160p. 1988. pap. 2.50 (*0-380-75244-1*, Avon Bks) Morrow Avon.

Not Just Another Pretty Face: The Confessions & Confections of a Girlie Cartoonist. R. C. Harvey. (Illus.). 136p. 1996. 35.00 (*1-883847-24-9*); pap. 14.95 (*1-883847-23-0*) MU Press.

Not Just Another Science Fair: K-8. Laura Vazquez et al. (Illus.). 224p. (Orig.). 1994. pap. 12.95 (*0-673-36132-2*, GoodYrBooks) Addson-Wesley Educ.

Not Just Another Science Fair: K-8. Laura Vazquez et al. (Illus.). 224p. (Orig.). 1994. disk 18.95 (*0-673-36212-4*, GoodYrBooks) Addson-Wesley Educ.

Not Just Another Science Fair: K-8, Set. Laura Vazquez et al. (Illus.). 224p. (Orig.). 1994. pap. 18.95 incl. disk (*0-673-36134-9*, GoodYrBooks) Addson-Wesley Educ.

Not Just Another Self-Defence Book. Hugh B. Wilson & John W. Yee. (Streetproofing for Kids Ser.). (Illus.). 144p. (Orig.). (J). 1997. pap. write for info. (*1-896212-01-8*) Outgoing.

Not Just Another Szep Book. Paul M. Szep. LC 97-13916. 160p. Date not set. pap. 8.95 (*1-56554-294-0*) Pelican.

Not Just Any Medical School: The Science, Practice & Teaching of Medicine at the University of Michigan, 1850-1941. Horace W. Davenport. LC 99-6221. 400p. 1999. text 52.50 (*0-472-11076-4*, 11076) U of Mich Pr.

Not Just Any Ring. Houghton Mifflin Company Staff. (Literature Experience 1993 Ser.). (J). (gr. 2). 1992. pap. 9.48 (*0-395-61782-0*) HM.

Not-Just-Anybody Family. Betsy C. Byars. 160p. (J). (gr. k-6). 1987. pap. 4.50 (*0-440-45951-6*, YB BDD) BDD Bks Young Read.

Not-Just-Anybody Family. Betsy C. Byars. (J). 1987. 9.09 (*0-606-03059-X*, Pub. by Turtleback) Demco.

Not-Just-Anybody Family. Betsy C. Byars. 149p. (J). (gr. 4-6). pap. 4.50 (*0-8072-1429-9*) Listening Lib.

Not Just Anywhere: The Story of W. H. A. L. E. & New Bedford's Waterfront Historic District. Marsha McCabe & Joseph D. Thomas. Ed. by Arthur Bennett & Clara Stites. (Illus.). 128p. 1995. 37.95 (*0-932027-29-6*); pap. 16.95 (*0-932027-28-8*) Spinner Pubns.

Not Just Bacon & Eggs. Donna D. Jomaa. LC 91-90903. 160p. (Orig.). 1991. pap. 9.95 (*0-9619202-1-1*) Straw Hat Prodns.

***Not Just Beans: 50 Years of Frugal Family Favorites.** Tawra Jean Kellam. (Illus.). iv, 268p. 1999. 14.95 (*0-9676974-0-9*) Not Just Beans.

N

An Asterisk (*) at the beginning of an entry indicates that the title is appearing for the first time.

Not Just Cheesecake! A Yogurt Cheese Cookbook. 2nd rev. ed. Shelley Melvin. LC 97-6928. 224p. 1997. pap. 16.95 (*0-937404-45-4*) Triad Pub FL.

Not Just Deserts: A Republican Theory of Criminal Justice. John Braithwaite & Philip Pettit. 240p. 1990. 70.00 (*0-19-824233-6*) OUP.

Not Just Deserts: A Republican Theory of Criminal Justice. John Braithwaite & Philip Pettit. 238p. 1993. reprint ed. pap. text 22.00 (*0-19-824056-2*) OUP.

Not Just for CEO's: Sure Fire Success Secrets for the Leaders in Each of Us. John H. Zenger. 160p. 1995. 21.95 (*0-7863-0528-2*, Irwn Prfssnl) McGraw-Hill Prof.

Not Just for Girls: Involving Boys & Men in Teen Pregnancy Prevention. National Campaign to Prevent Teen Pregnancy Staff. 35p. 1997. pap. 15.00 (*1-58671-021-4*) Natl Cpgn Teen Preg.

Not Just for the Money: An Economic Theory of Personal Motivation. Bruno Frey. LC 96-35154. 168p. 1997. 80.00 (*1-85898-509-9*) E Elgar.

Not Just for the Money: An Economic Theory of Personal Motivation. Bruno S. Frey & Ntozake Shange. LC 96-35154. 168p. 1998. pap. 20.00 (*1-85898-845-4*) E Elgar.

Not Just Games: Strategic Uses of Experiential Learning to Drive Business Results. Dynamic Learning Staff. 86p. 1996. pap. text, per. 19.95 (*0-7872-1985-1*) Kendall-Hunt.

Not Just Gilpin County: Photographs of People & Places, Mines & Mountains, Focused on, but Not Limited to, Gilpin County, Colorado. Tyler Hall. LC 90-93510. 80p. 1991. 24.95 (*0-9637356-0-8*) V E Hall Pub.

Not Just Grammar. Amy M. Burke. 38p. (J). (gr. 4-6). 1996. pap., wbk. ed. 9.99 (*0-89824-222-3*) Royal Fireworks.

Not Just Java. 2nd ed. Peter Van der Linden. LC 99-174599. 352p. (C). 1998. pap. text 39.99 (*0-13-079660-3*, Prentice Hall) P-H.

Not Just Milk & Honey: An Anthology of Hebrew Short Stories. Haya Hoffman & National Book Trust Staff. LC 99-933214. xvi, 226 p. 1998. write for info. (*81-237-2456-X*, Pub. by Natl Bk Trust) S Asia.

***Not Just One in Eight: Stories of Breast Cancer Survivors & Their Families.** Barbara F. Stevens & Patricia A. Ganz. 380p. 2000. pap. 12.95 (*1-55874-832-6*) Health Comm.

N

Not Just Pumping Iron: On the Psychology of Lifting Weights. Edward W. Smith. (Illus.). 176p. (C). 1989. pap. text 36.95 (*0-398-05544-0*) C C Thomas.

Not Just Race Not Just Gender: Black Feminist Readings. Valerie Smith. LC 97-32082. 192p. (C). (gr. 13). 1998. 70.00 (*0-415-90325-4*) Routledge.

Not Just Race, Not Just Gender: Black Feminist Readings. Valerie Smith. LC 97-32082. 192p. (C). 1998. pap. 18.99 (*0-415-90326-2*) Routledge.

Not Just Schoolwork. Amy M. Burke & Roger Wallace. LC 76-9524. 201p. (Orig.). (J). (gr. 3-12). 1990. pap. 32.95 (*0-8290-0354-1*) NL Assocs.

Not Just Schoolwork, Vol. 2. Amy M. Burke. (Orig.). (J). (gr. 4-12). 1993. pap. 21.95 (*1-878347-24-1*) NL Assocs.

Not Just Schoolwork, Vol. 3. Amy M. Burke. (Orig.). (J). (gr. 4-12). 1993. pap. 21.95 (*1-878347-25-X*) NL Assocs.

Not Just Schoolwork, Vol. 4. rev. ed. Amy M. Burke. (Illus.). 112p. (Orig.). 1994. pap. text 21.95 (*1-878347-34-9*) NL Assocs.

Not Just Stories. Tweski & Shaar. 22.99 (*0-89906-386-1*, NOTH); pap. 19.99 (*0-89906-387-X*, NOTP) Mesorah Pubns.

Not Just the Cleaning Lady: A Hygienist's Guide to Survival. Catherine A. Schmidt. LC 97-47790. 1998. 29.95 (*0-87814-672-5*) PennWell Bks.

Not Just Trees: The Legacy of a Douglas-Fir Forest. Jane Claire Dirks-Edmunds. LC 98-46721. (Illus.). 360p. 1999. 35.00 (*0-87422-169-2*); pap. 22.95 (*0-87422-170-6*) Wash St U Pr.

Not Knot. University of Minnesota, Geometry Center Staff. 1991. pap. text 44.00 incl. VHS (*1-56881-042-3*) AK Peters.

Not-Knowing. Donald Barthelme. 2100p. 1999. pap. 15.00 (*0-679-74120-8*) Discovery.

Not Knowing Where. Oswald Chambers. 1989. pap. 8.95 (*0-87508-302-1*) Chr Lit.

Not Knowing Where: A Spiritual Journey Through the Book of Genesis. Oswald Chambers. LC 96-33343. 208p. 1989. pap. 10.99 (*0-929239-15-6*) Discovery Hse Pubs.

Not Like Any Other Children's Book. Ed. by Louisa Smith & Glen Smith. (Illus.). 40p. (Orig.). (J). (gr. 2 up). 1982. pap. 8.95 (*0-9609230-0-4*) Smith & Smith Pub.

Not Like Other Girls. Jayne Bremyer. 162p. (J). (ps up). 1982. pap. 9.95 (*0-944996-09-4*) Carlsons.

Not Like Us: How Europeans Loved, Hated & Transformed American Culture Since WWII. Richard H. Pells. 400p. 1998. pap. 18.00 (*0-465-00163-7*, Pub. by Basic) HarpC.

Not Like Us: Immigrants & Minorities in America, 1890-1924. Roger Daniels. LC 97-16117. (American Ways Ser.). 192p. 1998. pap. text 12.95 (*1-56663-166-1*) I R Dee.

Not Like Us: Immigrants & Minorities in Modern America, 1890-1924. Roger Daniels. LC 97-16117. (American Ways Ser.). 192p. 1997. 22.50 (*1-56663-165-3*, Pub. by I R Dee) Natl Bk Netwk.

Not Looking for a Texas Man. Lass Small. (Yours Truly Ser.: No. 4). 1995. per. 3.50 (*0-373-52004-2*) Harlequin Bks.

Not Lost, Just Somewhere Else. Hazel Edwards. (Illus.). 30p. (J). (gr. 1-7). 1994. 11.95 (*0-85572-203-7*, Pub. by Hill Content Pubng) Seven Hills Bk.

***Not Made by Hands.** Thomas M. Sennott. 1999. pap. text 7.95 (*0-89870-734-X*) Ignatius Pr.

Not Many Fathers: The restoration of Divine Order. Richard A. Wright. 164p. (Orig.). (C). 1993. pap. text 9.00 (*0-9632748-2-1*) Majesty Pubns.

Not Me. Eileen Myles. 202p. 1991. pap. 6.00 (*0-936756-67-5*) Autonomedia.

Not Me! The World War II Memoir of a Reluctant Rifleman, M221H. Alexander H. Hadden. (World War II Memoir Ser.: 221). (Illus.). 155p. 1997. 27.95 (*1-57638-094-7*) Merriam Pr.

***Not Me! I Scream: Poetry of Despair & Inner Peace.** M. Broughton Boone. LC 99-90207. 56p. 1999. pap. 7.95 (*0-9671203-1-4*) Cape Winds Pr.

Not Me, Said the Monkey. Colin West. LC 87-3712. (Illus.). 24p. (J). (ps-2). 1988. 10.95 (*0-397-32253-4*); lib. bdg. 12.89 (*0-397-32254-2*) HarpC Child Bks.

Not Milk...Nut Milks! 40 of the Most Original Dairy-Free Recipes Ever! Candia L. Cole. LC 97-41706. (Illus.). 128p. 1997. pap. 9.95 (*0-88007-218-0*) Woodbridge Pr.

Not Minutes, but Miles. Laverne Thomas. 40p. (Orig.). 1996. pap. 8.95 (*1-57502-158-7*, PO752) Morris Pubng.

Not More Writing?! Virginia Molino & Lyn Nadeau. (Activity Book Ser.). (Illus.). 144p. (Orig.). 1996. pap. 17.95 (*1-57022-048-4*) ECS Lrn Systs.

Not Much Fun: The Lost Poems of Dorothy Parker. Dorothy Parker. Ed. by Stuart Silverstein. 256p. 1996. 21.50 (*0-684-81855-8*) S&S Trade.

Not My Baby! Judith McWilliams. (Temptation Ser.). 1993. per. 2.99 (*0-373-25540-3*, 1-25540-5) Harlequin Bks.

Not My Child: A Mother Confronts Her Child's Sexual Abuse. Patricia Crowley. 320p. 1991. mass mkt. 4.95 (*0-380-71276-8*, Avon Bks) Morrow Avon.

Not My Child! Thirty Simple Ways to Help Prevent Your Child from Becoming Lost, Missing, Abducted, or Abused. Jan Wagner. LC 94-61259. (Illus.). 240p. (Orig.). 1994. pap. 14.95 (*0-9641842-0-6*) J A Wagner.

Not My Dog. Colby Rodowsky. (Illus.). 80p. (J). (gr. 2-5). 1999. 15.00 (*0-374-35531-2*) FS&G.

Not My Gift: A Story of Divine Empowerment. Jennifer L. Tinsman. 1999. pap. 14.95 (*1-879997-13-4*, Pub. by Mystic Child Studio) BookMasters.

***Not My Heart, But Yours: Story of a Transplant.** deluxe ed. Deryl Borders & Doug Poling. 196p. 1999. pap. 12.95 (*0-9673558-0-X*) D Borders.

Not My Kid: A Parent's Guide to Kids & Drugs. Beth Polson & Miller Newton. 224p. 1985. mass mkt. 4.50 (*0-380-69997-4*, Avon Bks) Morrow Avon.

Not My Way. Andrea L. Blair. 128p. 1996. 9.95 (*1-883520-23-1*) Jeremiah Pr.

Not My Will. Francena H. Arnold. pap. 9.99 (*0-8024-3831-8*, 232) Moody.

Not My Will. Andrew Murray. Tr. by Marian M. Schoolland. 1977. pap. 3.95 (*0-310-29722-2*, 10381P) Zondervan.

Not My Will, but Thine. Neal A. Maxwell. 1988. 14.95 (*0-88494-672-X*) Bookcraft Inc.

Not Necessarily Cervantes: Readings of the Quixote. Robert L. Hathaway. (Documentacion Cervantina Ser.: Vol. 15). 199p. 1995. pap. 14.50 (*0-936388-70-6*) Juan de la Cuesta.

Not Necessarily Christmas. Susan Bartlett. 98p. 1991. 19.95 (*0-9630473-0-2*) Quilted Cot.

Not Necessarily Nice: Stories. Daniel Curzon. LC 98-89872. 365p. 1999. 25.00 (*0-7388-0301-4*); pap. 15.00 (*0-7388-0302-2*) Xlibris Corp.

Not Necessarily the New Age: Critical Essays. Ed. by Robert Basil. LC 88-12635. 395p. 1988. 28.95 (*0-87975-490-7*) Prometheus Bks.

Not Nice on Ice. Carolyn Keene. LC 99-175566. (Nancy Drew Notebooks: No. 10). (Illus.). 80p. (J). (gr. 2-4). 1996. pap. 3.99 (*0-671-52711-8*, Pocket Books) PB.

Not Nice on Ice. Carolyn Keene. (Nancy Drew Notebooks: No. 10). (J). (gr. 2-4). 1996. 9.19 (*0-606-08579-3*, Pub. by Turtleback) Demco.

Not No Easy Business: Interviews with Prostitutes. Ed. by Maxine Alexander et al. (Southern Exposure Ser.). (Illus.). 72p. (Orig.). (C). 1983. pap. 4.00 (*0-943810-68-X*) Inst Southern Studies.

***Not Nominated: Great Films Not Nominated for the Best Picture Academy Award.** Ed. by Bruce Hershenson & Richard Allen. (Illustrated History of Movies Through Posters Ser.: Vol. 15). (Illus.). 80p. 2000. 50.00 (*1-887893-45-8*, Pub. by B Hershenson) Partners Pubs Grp.

***Not Nominated: Great Films Not Nominated for the Best Picture Academy Award, Vol. 15.** Ed. by Bruce Hershenson & Richard Allen. (Illustrated History of Movies Through Posters Ser.: Vol. 15). (Illus.). 80p. 2000. pap. 20.00 (*1-887893-44-X*, Pub. by B Hershenson) Partners Pubs Grp.

Not Now . . . I'm Having a No Hair Day: Humor & Healing for People with Cancer. Christine Clifford. LC 96-10027. (Illus.). 110p. (Orig.). 1996. pap. 9.95 (*1-57025-120-7*) Pfeifer-Hamilton.

Not Now Bernard. David McKee. (J). 1991. pap. text. write for info. (*0-05-004559-8*) Addison-Wesley.

Not Now, But Now. M. F. K. Fisher. LC 82-81499. 264p. 1982. reprint ed. pap. 12.00 (*0-86547-072-3*) N Point Pr.

***Not Now, Charlie!** (Illus.). (J). 1999. text 7.99 (*0-7112-1325-9*) F Lincoln.

Not Now, Darling. Ray Cooney & John Chapman. 1971. pap. 5.25 (*0-8222-0832-6*) Dramatists Play.

Not Now Honey I'm Watching the Game: What to Do When Sports Come Between You & Your Mate. Kevin Quirk. LC 97-19429. 256p. 1997. pap. 12.00 (*0-684-83447-2*) S&S Trade.

Not Now! Maybe Later. Peter Blackerby. Ed. by Roman Hardly. LC 97-66998. (Illus.). 48p. (J). (gr. 1-3). 1997. lib. bdg. 19.95 (*0-912495-33-2*) San Diego Pub Co.

***Not Now, Mrs. Wolf.** Shen Roddie. LC 99-49410. (Illus.). 32p. (J). (ps-3). 2000. 5.95 (*0-7894-5613-3*, D K Ink) DK Pub Inc.

***Not Now, Mrs. Wolf.** Shen Roddie. (Illus.). 32p. (J). (ps-3). 2000. 9.95 (*0-7894-6355-5*) DK Pub Inc.

"Not Now!" Said the Cow see **Bank Street Ready-to-Read Books: Levels 1, 2 & 3**

Not Now! Said the Cow-Bank Street. Joanne F. Oppenheim. 32p. (J). (ps-3). 1981. pap. 4.50 (*0-553-34691-1*) Bantam.

Not of One Mind. Ed. by Dale Taronowieski & Carla A. Graybard. LC 76-2038. 128p. reprint ed. pap. 39.70 (*0-608-30417-4*, 205043700081) Bks Demand.

Not of Our Time. Tom Morgan. Ed. by Ronald Pickup. (Illus.). 124p. (Orig.). 1989. pap. text 10.00 (*0-9623094-0-0*) GlenHill Prodns.

Not of Pure Blood: The Free People of Color & Racial Prejudice in Nineteenth-Century Puerto Rico. Jay Kinsbruner. LC 96-7908. 168p. 1996. text 44.95 (*0-8223-1836-9*); pap. text 15.95 (*0-8223-1842-3*) Duke.

Not of This World. Ministries Shepherd. 1999. 20.00 (*5-554-66320-6*); pap. text 12.00 (*0-923417-71-0*) Shepherd Minst.

Not of This World. Shepherd Ministries Staff. 1999. 10.00 (*0-923417-69-9*) Shepherd Minst.

Not of This World: The Life & Teaching of Fr Seraphim Rose. Monk D. Christensen. LC 93-83654. (Illus.). 1056p. 1994. pap. 29.95 (*0-938635-52-2*) St Herman Pr.

Not of War Only: A Novel of the Mexican Revolution. Norman Zollinger. 608p. 1995. 5.99 (*0-8125-3013-6*, Pub. by Forge NYC) St Martin.

Not of Woman Born, 1 vol. Constance Ash. 288p. 1999. mass mkt. 6.99 (*0-451-45681-5*) NAL.

Not of Woman Born: Representations of Caesarean Birth in Medieval & Renaissance Culture. Renate Blumenfeld-Kosinski. LC 89-17421. (Illus.). 216p. 1991. reprint ed. pap. text 14.95 (*0-8014-9974-7*) Cornell U Pr.

Not Old Madam, Vintage. Charis U. Frankenberg. (C). 1988. 30.00 (*0-7855-3371-0*, Pub. by T Dalton) St Mut.

Not Old, Not Full of Days. Norma Singer. Ed. by Mildred Zagury. LC 96-60415. 496p. 1996. pap. 16.95 (*1-880254-37-9*) Vista.

Not on a Silver Platter. Beatrice B. White. (Illus.). 492p. (Orig.). 1989. text 50.00 (*0-9622738-0-5*); pap. text 18.50 (*0-9622738-1-3*) M Bliss.

Not on Any Map: Essays on Postcoloniality & Cultural Nationalism. Ed. by Stuart Murray. 192p. 1997. pap. 19.95 (*0-85989-468-1*, Pub. by Univ Exeter Pr) Northwestern U Pr.

Not on the Map. Kevin Bowen & Bruce Weigl. LC 97-132788. 32p. 1996. pap. 10.95 (*1-873790-95-3*, Pub. by Dedalus) Dufour.

Not on the Screen. Henry B. Fuller. (Collected Works of Henry B. Fuller). 1988. reprint ed. lib. bdg. 59.00 (*0-7812-1212-X*) Rprt Serv.

Not on This Board You Don't: Making Your Trustees More Effective. Arthur Frantzreb. LC 96-46282. 250p. 1996. 40.00 (*1-56625-067-6*) Bonus Books.

Not On Your Own: The Power Of Learning Together. Mary Glover & Linda Sheppard. (New Directions). (J). 1993. pap. 7.95 (*0-590-73459-8*) Scholastic Inc.

***Not One Damsel in Distress: World Folktales for Strong Girls.** Jane Yolen. LC 99-18509. (Illus.). 128p. (J). (gr. 3-7). 2000. 17.00 (*0-15-202047-0*) Harcourt.

***Not One Dollar More! How To Save $3,000 to $30,000 Buying Your Next Home.** 2nd ed. Joseph E. Cummins. LC 99-23040. 286p. 1999. pap. 16.95 (*0-471-35726-X*) Wiley.

Not One Dollar More! How to Save 3000 to 30000 Dollars Buying Your Next Home. Joseph E. Cummins. LC 93-79861. 260p. (Orig.). 1995. pap. 19.95 (*0-9638215-9-8*) Kells Media.

Not One Man! Not One Penny! German Social Democracy, 1863-1914. Gary P. Steenson. LC 80-54058. (Illus.). 304p. 1981. pap. 19.95 (*0-8229-5329-3*) U of Pittsburgh Pr.

Not One Man's Work. Leland Kinsey. LC 96-4245. 96p. 1996. 25.00 (*1-55821-430-5*, 14035); pap. 16.95 (*1-55821-431-3*, 14313) Lyons Pr.

***Not One of the Boys: Living Life as a Feminist.** Brenda Feigen. (Illus.). 272p. 2000. 26.00 (*0-679-40842-8*) Knopf.

Not One Should Perish. 1997. 17.99 (*0-614-27172-X*) CEF Press.

Not One Should Perish: Devotional Inspired True Stories of Children. 9.99 (*1-55976-418-X*) CEF Press.

***Not One Shred of Decency: A Historical Novel Based on Actual Events.** Bob Brown. 2000. pap. 12.95 (*0-9675673-0-0*) River City Bks.

Not One Stone. Bob L. Ross. 1993. pap. 6.00 (*1-56186-521-4*) Pilgrim Pubns.

Not Only an Economist: Recent Essays. Mark Blaug. LC 96-26479. 416p. 1997. 100.00 (*1-85898-455-6*) E Elgar.

Not Only for Myself: Identity Politics & the Law. Martha Minow. LC 96-29578. 1997. 25.00 (*1-56584-374-6*, Pub. by New Press NY) Norton.

Not Only for Myself: Identity, Politics, & the Law. Martha Minow. 1998. pap. 14.95 (*1-56584-513-7*, Pub. by New Press NY) Norton.

Not Only I. Chris McCully. LC 97-131679. 1997. pap. 14.95 (*1-85754-255-X*, Pub. by Carcanet Pr) Paul & Co Pubs.

Not Only Passengers: How the Electric Railways Carried Freight, Express & Baggage. Roy G. Benedict & James R. McFarlane. LC 92-71563. (Bulletin Ser.: No. 129). (Illus.). 128p. 1992. 35.00 (*0-915348-29-2*) Central Electric.

Not Only the 'Dangerous Trades' Women's Work & Health in Britain, 1880-1914. Barbara Harrison. LC 97-129837. (Gender & Society Ser.). 240p. 1996. 75.00 (*0-7484-0144-X*); pap. 27.95 (*0-7484-0145-8*) Taylor & Francis.

Not Only the Market: The Role of the Market, Government & Civic Sector in the Development of Post-Communist Societies. Martin Potucek. LC 99-38542. 180p. 2000. 49.95 (*963-9116-52-1*); pap. 19.95 (*963-9116-51-3*) Ctrl Europ Univ.

Not Only War. Victor Daly. Date not set. 21.95 (*0-8434-0002-1*) Ayer.

Not Ordinary Men: The Story of the Battle of Kohima. John Colvin. (Illus.). 256p. 1995. pap. 16.95 (*0-85052-477-6*, Pub. by Leo Cooper) Trans-Atl Phila.

***Not Otherwise Specified.** Joan Fallon. 2000. pap. text 16.95 (*1-56492-286-3*) Laredo.

Not Our Baby, Vol. 1. Sharon Clark. (Illus.). 149p. 1984. 17.95 (*0-920490-43-3*) Temeron Bks.

Not Our Kind of Girl: Unravelling the Myths of Black Teenage Motherhood. Elaine B. Kaplan. LC 96-46709. 265p. 1997. pap. 16.95 (*0-520-20858-7*, Pub. by U CA Pr) Cal Prin Full Svc.

Not Out of Africa: How Afrocentrism Became an Excuse to Teach Myth As History. Mary Lefkowitz. LC 97-183099. 256p. 1997. pap. 13.00 (*0-465-09838-X*, Pub. by Basic) HarpC.

Not Out of Hate: A Novel of Burma. Ma M. Lay. Ed. by William Frederick. Tr. by Margaret Aung-Thwin from BUR. LC 90-28553. (Monographs in International Studies, Southeast Asia Ser.: No. 88). 260p. (Orig.). 1991. pap. text 20.00 (*0-89680-167-5*) Ohio U Pr.

***Not out of Mind.** Ed. by Althea Hayton. 208p. 1999. pap. 40.00 (*0-85305-441-X*, Pub. by Arthur James) St Mut.

Not Peace but a Sword. Patrick Gibbs. (Illus.). 224p. 1993. 29.95 (*0-948817-68-2*, Pub. by Grub St) Seven Hills Bk.

Not Peace but a Sword. Vincent Sheean. (American Biography Ser.). 367p. 1991. reprint ed. lib. bdg. 79.00 (*0-7812-8351-5*) Rprt Serv.

Not Peace but a Sword: John Henry Newman. Felicity O'Brien. 188p. (C). 1996. pap. 39.95 (*0-85439-327-7*, Pub. by St Paul Pubns) St Mut.

Not Playing for Celtic. David Bennie. (Illus.). 224p. 1996. 29.95 (*1-85158-757-8*, Pub. by Mainstream Pubng) Trafalgar.

***Not Proven.** Woody Hanstein. LC 00-90013. 272p. 2000. pap. 12.00 (*1-879418-61-4*) Audenreed Pr.

Not Quite a Gentleman. large type ed. Paula Marshall. 350p. 1996. 23.99 (*0-263-14528-X*, Pub. by Mills & Boon) Ulyerscroft.

Not Quite a Horsewoman. Caroline Akrill. 187p. (C). 1990. pap. 21.00 (*0-85140-727-7*, Pub. by J A Allen) St Mut.

Not Quite a Horsewoman. Caroline Akrill. 230p. 1995. pap. 35.00 (*0-85131-643-3*, Pub. by J A Allen) Trafalgar.

Not Quite an Angel. Bobby Hutchinson. 1994. per. 3.50 (*0-373-70595-6*) Harlequin Bks.

Not Quite at Home: How an American Jewish Community Lives with Itself & Its Neighbors. Marshall Sklare et al. LC 77-81092. (Institute of Human Relations Press Paperback Ser). x, 85p. (Orig.). 1969. pap. 1.00 (*0-87495-017-1*) Am Jewish Comm.

Not Quite Dead Enough. Rex Stout. 1994. reprint ed. lib. bdg. 27.95 (*1-56849-341-X*) Buccaneer Bks.

Not Quite Fiction. unabridged ed. Stephen-Paul Martin. LC 97-60474. 100p. (Orig.). 1997. pap. 8.95 (*0-9654877-2-5*) Vatic Hum Pr.

Not Quite Like Home: Small Hostels for Alcoholics & Others. Shirley Otto & Jim Orford. LC 77-12664. 234p. reprint ed. pap. 72.60 (*0-608-13422-8*, 202428200035) Bks Demand.

Not Quite Perfect. Jane King. 249p. 12.95 (*0-9640300-1-2*) Galhattan Pr.

Not Quite Perfect. Jane King. 1998. mass mkt. 11.95 (*0-9640300-2-0*) Galhattan Pr.

***Not Quite Scaramouche.** Joel Rosenberg. 2001. text 23.95 (*0-312-86897-9*) St Martin.

Not Ready for Prime Time. Brent Askari. 272p. 1999. 24.95 (*0-7867-0648-1*) Carroll & Graf.

***Not Ready for Prime Time Statistics.** 226p. (C). 2000. per. 70.00 (*0-7872-7330-9*) Kendall-Hunt.

***Not Really an Alaskan Mountain Man.** Douglas P. Fine. 2000. write for info. (*0-671-04043-X*, PB Hardcover) PB.

Not Safe after Dark & Other Stories. Peter Robinson. LC 99-167275. 227p. 1998. pap. 16.00 (*1-885941-29-3*) Crippen & Landru.

Not Safe at Home: How America's Housing Crisis Threatens the Health of Its Children. Ed. by Megan Sandel & Joshua Sharfstein. 46p. (C). 1999. pap. text 20.00 (*0-7881-7855-5*) DIANE Pub.

***Not Sally Marshall Again!** Amanda McKay. 187p. 2000. pap. 12.95 (*0-7022-3169-X*, Pub. by Univ Queensland Pr) Intl Spec Bk.

Not Schools Alone: Guidelines for Schools & Communities to Prevent the Use of Tobacco, Alcohol, & Other Drugs among Children & Youth. 40p. (Orig.). (C). 1996. pap. text 25.00 (*0-7881-2721-7*) DIANE Pub.

Not Schools Alone: Guidelines for Schools & Communities to Prevent the Use of Tobacco, Alcohol, & Other Drugs among Children & Youth. California Department of Education Staff. 40p. 1990. pap. 5.25 (*0-8011-0969-8*) Calif Education.

Not Set in Stone. Grace B. Freeman. 64p. (Orig.). 1986. 13.00 (*0-9607730-9-6*); pap. 9.00 (*0-9607730-1-0*) Johns Pr.

Not Shooting & Not Crying: Psychological Inquiry into Moral Disobedience, 85. Ruth Linn. LC 88-24720. (Contributions in Military Studies Ser.: No. 85). 174p. 1989. 52.95 (*0-313-26497-X*, LNS, Greenwood Pr) Greenwood.

Not Simply Divine: Beneath the Make-up, above the Heels & Behind the Scenes with a Cult Superstar. Bernard Jay. 1994. pap. 12.00 (*0-86369-740-2*) Hemmings.

Not Simply Divine: Beneath the Make-up, above the Heels & Behind the Scenes with a Cult Superstar. Bernard Jay. LC 94-4991. (Illus.). 256p. 1994. pap. 12.00 (*0-671-88467-0*, Fireside) S&S Trade Pap.

Not Simply with Words: The Story of Susan Ingouf Lafferty. Barbara Joiner. LC 98-170703. 118p. (YA). (gr. 9-12). 1998. pap. text 7.95 (*1-56309-234-4*, W986103) Womans Mission Union.

An Asterisk (*) at the beginning of an entry indicates that the title is appearing for the first time.

Not since Carrie: Forty Years of Broadway Musical Flops. Ken Mandelbaum. (Illus.). 384p. 1992. pap. 14.95 (*0-312-08273-8*) St Martin.

Not Sisters. Maggie Nelson & Cynthia Nelson. 56p. 1996. pap. 8.00 (*1-887128-17-4*) Soft Skull Pr.

Not Slave, Not Free: The African American Economic Experience since the Civil War. Jay R. Mandle. LC 91-27995. (Illus.). 152p. 1992. pap. text 17.95 (*0-8223-1220-4*) Duke.

Not So! Popular Myths about America from Columbus to Clinton. Paul F. Boller, Jr. 288p. 1996. reprint ed. pap. 12.95 (*0-19-510972-4*) OUP.

Not So! Popular Myths About America's Past from Columbus to Clinton. Paul F. Boller, Jr. 288p. 1995. text 30.00 (*0-19-509186-8*) OUP.

***Not So Bad As We Seem: Or Many Sides to a Character.** Edward Bulwer Lytton. 44p. 1999. reprint ed. pap. 7.00 (*0-7661-0806-6*) Kessinger Pub.

Not So Big House: A Blueprint for the Way We Really Live. Sarah Susanka. LC 98-23080. 200p. 1998. 30.00 (*1-56158-130-5*, 070259) Taunton.

Not So Buried Treasure: The Berenstain Bears. Stan Berenstain & Jan Berenstain. (Comes to Life Bks.). 16p. (J). (ps-2). 1995. write for info. (*1-57234-057-6*) YES Ent.

Not-So-dismal Science: A Broader View of Economies & Societies. Ed. by Mancur Olson & Satu Kahkohnen. LC 98-33705. (Illus.). 286p. 2000. pap. text 19.95 (*0-19-829490-5*) OUP.

Not-So-Dismal Science: A Broader View of Economies & Societies. Ed. by Mancur Olson & Satu Kahkohnen. LC 98-33705. (Illus.). 286p. 2000. text 65.00 (*0-19-829369-0*) OUP.

***Not So Dumb: "Secrets," "Schoolyard Games," "Not So Dumb" & "Night Light"** John Lazarus. 208p. (gr. 7-12). 2000. pap. 17.95 (*0-88754-578-5*) Theatre Comm.

Not So Far from Home: A Norwegian Correspondent in the Midwest. Roald Steen. (Illus.). 238p. 1993. pap. 11.95 (*0-942323-20-3*) N Amer Heritage Pr.

***Not So Fast.** Ellen Weiss. (My Very First Simba Stories Ser.). (Illus.). 32p. (J). (gr. k-2). 2000. 17.99 (*0-7868-3266-5*, Pub. by Disney Pr) Time Warner.

Not-So-Fast Rabbit. Carol B. Kaplan. Ed. by Janet L. Bolinske. LC 87-62997. (Animal Tales Ser.). (Illus.). 24p. (Orig.). (J). (ps). 1988. pap. 4.95 (*0-88335-079-3*) Milliken Pub Co.

Not So Fast, Songololo. Niki Daly. LC 94-40984. (Illus.). (J). (gr. k-3). 1996. mass mkt. 4.95 (*0-689-80154-8*) Aladdin.

Not So Fast, Songololo. Niki Daly. (J). 1998. pap. 4.95 (*0-87628-975-8*) Ctr Appl Res.

Not So Fast, Songololo. Niki Daly. LC 85-70134. (Illus.). 32p. (J). (gr. k-3). 1986. 16.00 (*0-689-50367-9*) McElderry Bks.

Not So Fast, Songololo. Niki Daly. LC 94-40984. (J). 1996. 10.15 (*0-606-09700-7*, Pub. by Turtleback) Demco.

Not So Free to Choose: The Political Economy of Milton Friedman & Ronald Reagan. Elton Raynack. LC 86-21276. 224p. 1986. 57.95 (*0-275-92363-0*, C2363, Praeger Pubs) Greenwood.

***Not So Funny When It Happened: The Best of Travel Humor & Misadventure.** Ed. by Tim Cahill et al. 224p. 2000. pap. 12.95 (*1-885211-55-4*) Trvlers Tale.

Not-So-Good Shepherd. Scott Lucas. LC 98-89473. 375p. 1998. text 25.00 (*0-7388-0281-6*); pap. text 15.00 (*0-7388-0282-4*) Xlibris Corp.

Not So Grand Jury: The Story of the Federal Grand Jury System. Blanche D. Blank. 108p. (Orig.). (C). 1993. pap. text 22.50 (*0-8191-9101-9*) U Pr of Amer.

Not So Grand Jury: The Story of the Federal Grand Jury System. Blanche D. Blank. 108p. (Orig.). (C). 1993. lib. bdg. 42.00 (*0-8191-9100-0*) U Pr of Amer.

Not-So-Great Escape. Focus on the Family Staff. (McGee & Me! Ser.: Vol. 3). (J). 1989. pap. 5.99 (*0-8423-4167-6*) Tyndale Hse.

Not-So-Great Moments in Sports. Michael J. Pellowski. (Illus.). 96p. (Orig.). 1995. pap. 5.95 (*0-8069-1257-X*) Sterling.

Not-So-Great Outdoors. Jean Waricha. (Full House Michelle Ser.: Vol. 16). 96p. (J). (gr. 2-4). 1997. per. 3.99 (*0-671-00835-8*) PB.

Not-So-Grizzly Bear Stories. Hiawyn Oram. LC 98-17388. (Illus.). 96p. (J). (ps-2). 1998. 16.95 (*1-888444-41-X*) Little Tiger.

Not-So-Humble Vegetables: Home Library Cookbooks. Home Library Editors. 120p. 1999. pap. 11.95 (*1-56426-152-2*, Pub. by Cole Group) ACCESS Pubs Network.

Not So Idle Notions. Lillian Abramson. LC 94-46356. 128p. 1995. 15.95 (*0-944957-52-8*) Rivercross Pub.

Not-So Itsy Bitsy Spider: A Pop-Up Book. Yumi Heo. 12p. (J). 1999. 12.95 (*1-58117-051-3*) Intervisual Bks.

Not-So-Jolly Roger. Jon Scieszka. (Time Warp Trio Ser.). (Illus.). 64p. (J). (gr. 2-6). 1993. pap. 4.99 (*0-14-034684-8*) Peng Put Young Read.

Not-So-Jolly Roger. Jon Scieszka. (Time Warp Trio Ser.). 1993. 8.70 (*0-606-05517-7*, Pub. by Turtleback) Demco.

Not-So-Jolly Roger. unabridged ed. Jon Scieszka. (Time Warp Trio Ser.). (J). (gr. 2-4). 1998. pap. text 15.98 incl. audio (*0-8072-0394-7*, EFTR194SP) Listening Lib.

***Not-So-Jolly Roger.** unabridged ed. Jon Scieszka. (Time Warp Trio Ser.). (J). (gr. 2-4). 1999. pap. 29.98 incl. audio (*0-8072-1302-0*, EFTR194MP) Listening Lib.

Not So Long Ago. Lloyd R. Morris. (History - United States Ser.). 504p. 1993. reprint ed. lib. bdg. 99.00 (*0-7812-4845-0*) Rprt Serv.

Not-So-Minor Leagues. Douglas Gay & Kathlyn Gay. LC 95-43848. (Illus.). 112p. (J). (gr. 5-8). 1996. lib. bdg. 22.40 (*1-56294-921-7*) Millbrook Pr.

Not-So-Normal Norman. Cynthia Stowe. Ed. by Judith Mathews. LC 94-255. (Illus.). 128p. (J). (gr. 3-6). 1994. lib. bdg. 13.95 (*0-8075-5767-6*) A Whitman.

Not-So-Perfect, Perfect Parent Bill of Rights. Leah Johnston-Rowbotham. Ed. by Kay Bensing. LC 98-61367. 168p. 1998. pap. 12.95 (*1-880254-56-5*) Vista.

Not-So-Perfect Picnic. Disney Enterprises, Inc. Staff & Pixar Animation Studios Staff. (Disney-Pixar's "A Bug's Life" Library: Vol. 11). (Illus.). 44p. (J). (gr. 1-6). 1998. 3.99 (*1-57973-027-2*) Advance Pubs.

Not-So Perfect Rosie. Patricia Reilly Giff. LC 96-36985. (Ballet Slippers Ser.: No. 4). (Illus.). 96p. (J). (gr. 2-6). 1997. 13.99 (*0-670-86968-6*) Viking Penguin.

Not So Quiet . . . Stepdaughters of War. Helen Z. Smith. LC 88-31072. 304p. 1989. 35.00 (*0-935312-97-8*); pap. 11.95 (*0-935312-82-X*) Feminist Pr.

***Not-So-Quiet Times: 240 Family Devotions Based on the Words of Jesus.** Tracy Harrast. Ed. by Lise Caldwell. LC 99-55975. 272p. (J). (gr. 1-6). 2000. pap. 12.99 (*0-7847-1041-4*) Standard Pub.

***Not-So-Quiet Times Two: Two Hundred & Forty Family Devotions from Psalms & Proverbs.** Tracy Harrast. Ed. by Laura Derico. 272p. (J). 2000. pap. 12.99 (*0-7847-1090-2*, 04299) Standard Pub.

Not So Rotten Ralph. Jack Gantos. LC 93-759. (Illus.). 32p. (J). (gr. 4 up). 1994. 15.00 (*0-395-62302-2*) HM.

Not So Rotten Ralph. Jack Gantos. LC 93-759. (Illus.). 32p. (ps-3). 1997. pap. 4.95 (*0-395-85156-4*) HM.

***Not So Rotten Ralph.** Jack Gantos. (Illus.). (J). 2000. pap. 9.95 (*0-618-08126-7*) HM.

Not So Rotten Ralph. Jack Gantos. 1997. 10.15 (*0-606-11690-7*, Pub. by Turtleback) Demco.

Not-So-Scary Breast Cancer Book: Two Sisters' Guide from Discovery to Recovery. Carolyn Ingram & Leslie Gebhart. LC 99-37875. (Illus.). 192p. 1999. 14.95 (*1-886230-29-3*) Impact Pubs CA.

Not-So-Scary Night. Blanche L. Tomaszewski. LC 97-6764. (J). 1997. write for info. (*1-56763-316-1*); pap. write for info. (*1-56763-317-X*) Ozark Pub.

Not So Silent Envoy: A Biography of Ambassador Samuel David Berger. Graenum Berger. LC 92-76083. (Illus.). 225p. 1992. pap. 13.50 (*0-9635641-0-2*) J W B Hampton.

Not-So-Silent Passage: How to Manage Your Man's Menopause Without Committing Manslaughter. Cheryl Solimini. LC 97-29018. (Illus.). 112p. 1998. pap. 8.95 (*0-87905-751-3*) Gibbs Smith Pub.

Not So Simple: The "Simple" Stories by Langston Hughes. Donna A. Harper. 280p. (C). 1995. pap. 19.95 (*0-8262-1088-0*) U of Mo Pr.

Not So Simple: The "Simple" Stories by Langston Hughes. Donna A. Harper. 280p. (C). 1996. text 34.95 (*0-8262-0980-7*) U of Mo Pr.

Not So Simple Pleasures: Content & Contentment in Contemporary Art. Dana Friis-Hansen. LC 90-50870. (Illus.). 32p. 1990. 8.00 (*0-938437-34-8*) MIT List Visual Arts.

Not-So-Still Life. Jimmy Ernst. 1992. pap. 11.50 (*0-916366-81-2*, Pub. by Pushcart Pr) Norton.

Not So Stupid: Incredible Short Stories. Malorie Blackman. (Livewire Ser.). (YA). (gr. 6-9). pap. 6.95 (*0-7043-4924-8*, Pub. by Womens Press) Trafalgar.

Not So Trivial for Science & Social Studies. Nancy M. Allen. 200p. (Orig.). (J). (gr. 2). 1996. pap. 15.95 (*0-913956-95-3*) EBSCO.

Not So Trivial for Science & Social Studies. Nancy M. Allen. 200p. (Orig.). (J). (gr. 3). 1996. pap. 15.95 (*0-913956-96-1*) EBSCO.

Not So Trivial for Science & Social Studies. Nancy M. Allen. 400p. (Orig.). (J). (gr. 4). 1996. pap. 19.95 (*0-913956-97-X*) EBSCO.

Not So Trivial for Science & Social Studies. Nancy M. Allen. 500p. (Orig.). (J). (gr. 5). 1996. pap. 19.95 (*0-913956-98-8*) EBSCO.

Not So Trivial for Science & Social Studies. Nancy M. Allen. 600p. (Orig.). (J). (gr. 6). 1996. pap. 19.95 (*0-913956-99-6*) EBSCO.

Not-So-Wicked Stepmother. Peter Matthiessen. (Illus.). (J). 1999. pap. write for info. (*0-14-054080-6*) NAL.

Not So Wicked Stepmother. Leslie Allgood Venable. (Illus.). 24p. (J). (gr. 1-7). 1999. per. 9.95 (0-9666817-0-3) L A Venable Pubg.
Olivia & Maria are two young sisters who are coping with the recent divorce of their parents. Later, when their dad begins dating again, the sisters decide to make sure he's dating someone who is right for them too. When dad does meet that someone, Olivia & Maria are happy. Then dad announces his plan to remarry. Now the girls must cope with the experience of having a stepmother. Will she be like the wicked stepmother in the story, Cinderella? As one who has experienced the role of stepmother twice, I can assure you that it is a role one must give careful consideration. You are not only making a commitment to your partner, but also to his children. As a stepmother, I had always searched unsuccessfully for a children's book depicting stepmothers in a positive way. Something to erase the indelible image of the "wicked" stepmother in the story Cinderella. I wanted them to have confirmation that not ALL stepmothers are mean & indifferent. Much to my dismay, I was never able to present them with anything tangible. And so, these frightened children were left to battle the situation with very little reassurance of a positive outcome. Finally I decided to put teaching on the back burner & do something about this dilemma. I would write a children's book on a subject I knew something about & felt that children, divorced singles with children & stepparents desperately needed. My hope is that those who read "The Not So Wicked Stepmother" will come away with a positive attitude about stepfamilies & some ideas about how to make them successful. ***Publisher Paid Annotation.***

Not So Wild a Dream. Eric Sevareid. 32.95 (*0-8488-0189-X*) Amereon Ltd.

Not So Wild a Dream. Eric Sevareid. LC 76-11538. 552p. (C). 1995. pap. 24.95 (*0-8262-1014-7*) U of Mo Pr.

Not So Wild a Dream. Eric Sevareid. 1993. reprint ed. 35.95 (*1-56849-220-0*) Buccaneer Bks.

***Not-So-Wise Man: A Christmas Story.** Alan MacDonald. LC 99-31745. (Illus.). 32p. (J). (ps-4). 1999. 15.00 (*0-8028-5196-7*, Eerdmans Bks) Eerdmans.

Not Spain. Richard Sanger. LC 98-191456. 96p. 1998. pap. 13.95 (*0-88754-551-3*) Theatre Comm.

Not Sticks, Not Stones But Words: Women's Power Potential, Self-Esteem & Spirituality. Jacquelyn Donald-Mims. 1998. pap. write for info. (*1-891809-04-0*) Pub by Devon.

Not Strictly by the Numbers. Bob Knauff. LC 90-84844. (Illus.). 114p. 1991. pap. 11.95 (*0-89278-150-5*, 91-2150) Carolina Biological.

Not Strictly Kosher: Pioneer Jews of New Zealand (1831-1901) Odeda Rosenthal. (Illus.). 208p. (Orig.). 1988. 35.00 (*0-910425-07-8*) Starchand Pr.

Not-Strictly Vegetarian Cookbook. 2nd ed. Lois Dribin & Susan Ivankovich. LC 89-16932. (Illus.). 248p. 1989. reprint ed. pap. 12.95 (*1-55561-029-3*) Fisher Bks.

Not Such an Ass see Henry Cecil Reprint Series

Not Sweet (The Snoring Poem) Ed. & Tr. by Malachi McCormick. 24p. 1986. 7.00 (*0-943984-26-2*) Stone St Pr.

Not Telling Mother. Diane Salvatore. 160p. 1993. pap. 9.95 (*1-56280-044-2*) Naiad Pr.

Not That Far. May Miller. 1973. 6.85 (*0-941490-12-2*) Solo Pr.

Not That I Care: Morgan. Rachel Vail. (The Friendship Ring Ser.). (J). (gr. 4-8). 1998. pap. text 59.88 (*0-590-95214-5*) Scholastic Inc.

Not That I Care: Morgan. Rachel Vail. (The Friendship Ring Ser.: Vol. 3). 240p. (J). (gr. 4-8). 1998. 14.95 (*0-590-03476-6*, Pub. by Scholastic Inc); pap. text 4.99 (*0-590-37453-2*) Scholastic Inc.

***Not That I Care: Morgan.** Rachel Vail. (The Friendship Ring Ser.). 240p. (J). (gr. 4-8). 1999. pap. 3.99 (*0-439-08763-5*, Pub. by Scholastic Inc) Penguin Putnam.

Not That Kind of Place. Frances Fyfield. Ed. by Jane Chelius. 256p. 1991. reprint ed. mass mkt. 5.50 (*0-671-73945-X*) PB.

Not That Sort of Girl. Mary Wesley. LC 88-31836. 320p. 1989. pap. 11.95 (*0-14-010826-2*, Penguin Bks) Viking Penguin.

Not the Buddha. Jim Gove. Ed. by Edward Mycue. (Took Modern Poetry in English Ser.: No. 2). (Illus.). 28p. (Orig.). 1990. pap. 3.00 (*0-9625855-5-6*) Norton Coker Pr.

***Not the Classical Ideal: Athens & the Construction of the Other in Greek Art.** Ed. by Beth Cohen. (Illus.). 560p. 2000. 87.00 (*90-04-11618-4*); 48.00 (*90-04-11712-1*) Brill Academic Pubs.

Not the Cross, but the Crucified. Herman-Emiel Mertens. (Louvain Theological & Pastoral Monographs). 1993. pap. text 25.00 (*0-8028-0571-X*) Eerdmans.

Not the End of the World. Rebecca Stowe. LC 92-45867. 160p. 1993. pap. 8.95 (*0-393-31006-X*) Norton.

Not the Germans Alone: A Son's Search for the Truth of Vichy. Isaac Levendel. LC 99-19628. 280p. 1999. 25.95 (*0-8101-1663-4*) Northwestern U Pr.

***Not the Germans Alone: A Son's Search for the Truth of Vichy.** Isaac Levendel. 2000. pap. 15.95 (*0-8101-1843-2*) Northwestern U Pr.

Not the Last Word: New Work from the Institute of American Indian Arts. Ed. by Pola Leonard et al. 154p. (Orig.). (C). 1997. pap. text 8.00 (*1-881396-13-4*) IOA Indian Arts.

Not the Marrying Kind. Charlotte Moore. (Romance Ser.). 1993. per. 2.75 (*0-373-08975-9*, 5-08975-0) Silhouette.

Not the Marrying Kind. large type ed. Irene Ord. (Linford Romance Library). 1991. pap. 16.99 (*0-7089-7119-9*, Linford) Ulverscroft.

Not the Monster. Anna Ross. (Sesame Street Baby Board Bks.). (Illus.). 12p. (J). (ps). 1994. 4.99 (*0-679-84739-1*, Pub. by Random Bks Yng Read) Random.

Not the Moors Murders: A Detective's Story of the Biggest Child-Killer Hunt in History. Ed. by Pat Molloy. 266p. (C). 1988. 24.00 (*0-86383-473-6*, Pub. by Gomer Pr) St Mut.

Not the Only One: Lesbian & Gay Fiction for Teens. Ed. by Tony Grima. 200p. (Orig.). (YA). (gr. 8 up). 1995. pap. 7.95 (*1-55583-275-X*) Alyson Pubns.

Not the Only Planet: Travel Stories from Science Fiction. Ed. by Damien Broderic. 350p. 1998. pap. 12.95 (*0-86442-582-1*) Lonely Planet.

Not the Piano, Mrs. Medley! Evan Levine. (Illus.). (J). (ps-3). 1996. pap. 15.95 incl. audio (*0-87499-373-3*) Live Oak Media.

Not the Piano, Mrs. Medley! Evan Levine. LC 90-29085. (Illus.). 32p. (J). (ps-2). 1991. 15.95 (*0-531-05956-1*); lib. bdg. 16.99 (*0-531-08556-2*) Orchard Bks Watts.

Not the Piano, Mrs. Medley! Evan Levine. LC 90-29085. (Illus.). 32p. (J). (ps-2). 1995. pap. text 5.95 (*0-531-07062-X*) Orchard Bks Watts.

Not the Piano, Mrs. Medley! Evan Levine. 1995. 11.15 (*0-606-08835-0*, Pub. by Turtleback) Demco.

Not the Piano, Mrs. Medley! unabridged ed. Evan Levine. (Illus.). (J). (ps-3). 1996. 24.95 incl. audio (*0-87499-374-1*) Live Oak Media.

Not the Piano, Mrs. Medley!, 4 bks., Set. Evan Levine. (Illus.). (J). (ps-3). 1996. pap., teacher ed. 33.95 incl. audio (*0-87499-375-X*) Live Oak Media.

Not the Salary but the Opportunity. Orison S. Marden. 96p. 1998. pap. write for info. (*0-89540-410-9*, SB-410) Sun Pub.

Not the Same Old Activities for Early Childhood. Moira D. Green. LC 97-13478. (Illus.). 224p. (C). 1997. mass mkt. 26.95 (*0-7668-0010-5*) Delmar.

Not the Subject of Cocktail Parties. Richard J. Weekley. 1986. 2.00 (*0-932593-03-8*) Black Bear.

Not the Way It Really Was: Constructing the Tolai Past. Klaus Neumann. LC 91-28884. (Pacific Islands Monographs: No. 10). (Illus.). 328p. (C). 1992. text 32.00 (*0-8248-1333-2*) UH Pr.

Not The Way It's Supposed to Be: A Breviary of Sin. Cornelius Plantinga. 216p. 1996. pap. 16.00 (*0-8028-4218-6*) Eerdmans.

Not Then, Not Now, Not Ever - I'll Have No Chains on Me: A Black Man's Promise. James A. Stelly. 205p. 1997. pap. 12.95 (*0-89896-397-4*) Larksdale.

Not This August. Cyril Kornbluth. 1993. reprint ed. lib. bdg. 18.95 (*0-89968-346-0*, Lghtyr Pr) Buccaneer Bks.

Not This Gal! Glenda Sanders. (Temptation Ser.: No. 641). 1997. per. 3.50 (*0-373-25741-4*, 1-25741-9) Harlequin Bks.

Not This Guy! Glenda Sanders. LC 96-616. (Temptation Ser.). 219p. 1995. per. 3.25 (*0-373-25647-7*, 1-25647-8) Harlequin Bks.

Not This Island Music. Robert Kelly. LC 87-5181. 184p. (Orig.). 1987. 20.00 (*0-87685-693-8*); pap. 10.00 (*0-87685-692-X*) Black Sparrow.

Not This Pig: Poems. Philip Levine. LC 68-16006. (Wesleyan Poetry Program Ser.: Vol. 38). 80p. 1968. pap. 12.95 (*0-8195-1038-6*, Wesleyan Univ Pr) U Pr of New Eng.

Not Til I Have Done: A Personal Testimony. Elizabeth Achtemeier. LC 98-39672. 136p. 1999. 18.00 (*0-664-22136-X*) Westminster John Knox.

Not 'Til I Have Done: A Personal Testimony. Elizabeth R. Achtemeier. LC 98-39672. 1999. 18.00 (*0-664-25809-3*) Westminster John Knox.

Not Times Fools. Stanley Jablonski. 385p. mass mkt. 4.99 (*1-896329-92-6*) Picasso Publ.

Not to Be: Essays about Integration. Mba Mbulu. 105p. 1995. pap. 8.00 (*1-883885-10-8*) ASET Pubns.

Not to Be Broadcast: The Truth about the Radio. Ruth Brindze. LC 73-19802. (Civil Liberties in American History Ser.). 310p. 1974. reprint ed. lib. bdg. 37.50 (*0-306-70598-2*) Da Capo.

Not to Be Forgotten: The Life, Death, & Hope of Police Sgt. Timothy A. Simenson. Robert B. Simenson. LC 96-84669. (Illus.). 176p. (Orig.). 1996. pap. 12.95 (*0-9651977-0-0*) Fair Haven WI.

Not to Be Forgotten Forties: A Nostalgic, Eclectic Recollection of the People Who Formed the Most Significant Decade in World History. Don Gwaltney. (Illus.). 256p. 1996. 29.95 (*0-9639591-2-3*) Apple Core Pr.

Not to Be Taken. Anthony Berkeley. 224p. 1995. 19.50 (*0-7451-8658-0*, Black Dagger) Chivers N Amer.

Not to Mention the War. Elmer H. Davis. LC 71-107692. (Essay Index Reprint Ser.). 1977. 23.95 (*0-8369-1602-6*) Ayer.

***Not to People Like Us: Domestic Abuse in Upscale Families.** Susan Weitzman. 272p. 2000. 26.00 (*0-465-09073-7*, Pub. by Basic) HarpC.

Not to Rest in Silence: A Celebration of People's Poetry. Ed. by Ted Plantos. LC 96-13124. 30p. (Orig.). 1996. pap. 5.00 (*1-884206-00-X*) Unfinish Monumnt.

Not to the Strong. Elwood McQuaid. LC 91-71438. 1991. pap. 8.95 (*0-915540-45-2*) Frnds Israel.

Not to the Swift: The "Old" Isolationists in the Cold War Era. Justus D. Doenecke. LC 76-1030. 289p. 1978. 38.50 (*0-8387-1940-6*) Bucknell U Pr.

Not to Worry, Mom, I'm Okay: Lessons in Living from a Beloved Son. Karma Smith Belnap. LC 96-13841. 1996. pap. 10.95 (*1-55503-931-6*, 01112317) Covenant Comms.

Not Tonight Dear . . . A Cornucopia of Excuses! Dakota Clark. Ed. by William A. Wrench. (Illus.). 136p. (Orig.). 1989. pap. write for info. (*0-318-65867-4*) Point View Pr.

Not Tonight Dear, I Have a Computer. Steve Scarborough. Ed. by Cliff Carle. 128p. 1999. pap. 6.95 (*1-57644-069-9*) CCC Pubns.

Not Tonite Dear, My Back Is Killing Me! Bruce A. Lepore & Chris N. Lepore. (Illus.). 52p. 1986. pap. 5.95 (*0-9613365-5-2*) Bridgeview.

Not Too Late: Aging & Psychotherapy. Ann Orbach. LC 97-100823. 160p. 1996. pap. 24.95 (*1-85302-380-9*, Pub. by Jessica Kingsley) Taylor & Francis.

Not Too Perfect Nativity Play: And Other Dramatic Resources for Christmas. 54p. 1987. pap. 4.99 (*0-8341-9518-6*, MC-269) Lillenas.

***Not Too Scary Vocabulary, Vol. 1.** abr. ed. Renee Mazer. (YA). (gr. 9 up). 1999. pap. Price not set. incl. audio (*0-9664845-0-9*, Pub. by High Score) Penton Overseas.

***Not Too Small at All.** Deborah Holt Williams. (Illus.). 16p. (J). (gr. k-2). 2000. pap. 3.75 (*1-58323-008-4*) Seedling Pubns.

***Not Trauma Alone: Therapy for Child Abuse Survivors in Family & Social Context.** Steven N. Gold. LC 00-23632. 2000. write for info. (*1-58391-027-1*) Brunner-Mazel.

Not Under Forty. Willa Cather. LC 88-14282. vii, 149p. 1988. pap. 10.00 (*0-8032-6331-7*, Bison Books) U of Nebr Pr.

N

An Asterisk (*) at the beginning of an entry indicates that the title is appearing for the first time.

Not Under Forty. Willa Cather. (Collected Works of Willa Cather). 147p. 1998. reprint ed. lib. bdg. 88.00 (1-58201-571-6) Classic Bks.

Not Under the Law. Grace Livingston Hill. 1976. reprint ed. lib. bdg. 25.95 (0-89190-022-5, Rivercity Pr) Amereon Ltd.

*Not Unlike a Madman in Cheap Sandals. James V. Anderson. 110p. 1999. pap. 11.95 (0-9675981-4-1) J V Anderson.

Not Until Christmas, Walter! Eileen Christelow. LC 96-52217. (Illus.). 40p. (J). (gr. k-3). 1997. 15.00 (0-395-82273-4) HM.

Not Until You've Done Your Practice. Philip Johnston & David Sutton. (Illus.). 80p. 1993. reprint ed. pap. 5.95 (0-86417-320-2, Pub. by Kangaroo Pr) Seven Hills Bk.

Not Vanishing. Chrystos. 1988. pap. 10.95 (0-88974-015-1, Pub. by Press Gang Pubs) LPC InBook.

Not Very Messy, Unless . . . Julia G. Boyce. (Illus.). 8p. (J). (gr. k-2). 1998. pap. 3.75 (1-880612-79-8) Seedling Pubns.

Not Vital. 112p. pap. write for info. (1-881616-47-9) Dist Art Pubs.

*Not War but Murder -- Cold Harbor, 1864. Ernest B. Furgurson. LC 99-37147. (Illus.). 309p. 2000. 27.50 (0-679-45517-5) Knopf.

Not Waving . . . Gen LeRoy. LC 98-228482. 1998. pap. 5.25 (0-8222-1612-4) Dramatists Play.

Not Wet Yet. Ian Shoales. 320p. 1997. pap. 15.00 (1-880985-45-4) Two Thirteen Sixty-one.

Not What the Doctor Ordered: How to End the Medical Monopoly in Pursuit of Managed Care. 2nd rev. ed. Jeffrey C. Bauer. LC 97-43100. (Illus.). 240p. 1997. 24.95 (0-07-006721-X) McGraw.

Not Where I Started From. Kate Wheeler. 240p. 1997. pap. 12.00 (0-395-86032-6, Mariner Bks) HM.

*Not Whether but When: The U. S. Decision to Enlarge NATO. James M. Goldgeier. LC 99-6674. 1999. 42.95 (0-8157-3172-8) Brookings.

*Not Whether but When: The U.S. Decision to Enlarge NATO James M. Goldgeier. LC 99-6674. 1999. 18.95 (0-8157-3171-X) Brookings.

*Not Who We Used to Be. David Serlin. 2000. 30.00 (0-226-74883-9) U Ch Pr.

Not with a Bang but a Whimper: Western Europe Approaches the Third Millenium. Robert A. Levine. LC 96-17907. 95p. 1996. pap. 15.00 (0-8330-2401-9, MR-765-AF/A/OSD) Rand Corp.

*Not with My Child: Combating What Predators Do to Sexually Abuse & Silence Children. Ed. by Roger Castillo. 376p. 1999. pap. 29.95 (0-9665882-9-0) United Youth Security.

Not with My Child You Don't: A Citizens' Guide to Eradicating OBE & Restoring EDU. Robert Holland. LC 96-223567. 358p. 1996. pap. 12.95 (0-9647408-0-X) Citizen Projects.

Not with Our Blood, 1870. Elizabeth Massie. (Young Founders Ser.). 1997. 10.09 (0-606-13936-2, Pub. by Turtleback) Demco.

Not with the Fist: Mexican - Americans in a Southwest City. Ruth D. Tuck. LC 73-14218. (Mexican American Ser.). 256p. 1977. reprint ed. 24.95 (0-405-05691-5) Ayer.

Not Without a Struggle: Leadership Development for African American Women in Ministry. Vashti M. McKenzie. LC 96-26237. 160p. (Orig.). 1996. pap. 15.95 (0-8298-1076-5) Pilgrim OH.

Not Without a Wife! Alexandra Sellers. 1997. per. 3.50 (0-373-52043-3, 1-52043-6) Silhouette.

*Not Without Bear. Anna Grossnickle Hines. LC 99-70679. (Illus.). 18p. (J). (ps-k). 2000. 9.95 (0-531-30205-9) Orchard Bks Watts.

Not Without Courage. T. Elizabeth Renich. (Shadowcreek Chronicles Ser.: Bk. 3). 340p. 1996. pap. 8.99 (1-883002-32-X) Emerald WA.

Not Without Dust & Heat: A Memoir. James L. Adams. LC 94-62067. xiii, 465p. 1995. text 29.95 (0-913552-55-0) Exploration Pr.

Not Without Honor: The History of American Anti-Communism. Richard G. Powers. 400p. 1996. 30.00 (0-02-925301-2); 29.50 (0-684-82427-2) Free Pr.

Not Without Honor: The History of American Anticommunism. Richard G. Powers. LC 97-80742. (Illus.). 592p. 1998. pap. 18.00 (0-300-07470-0) Yale U Pr.

Not Without Honor: The Story of Sammy Lee. Molly F. Wampler. LC 87-12385. (Illus.). 224p. (Orig.). 1987. pap. 9.95 (0-936784-37-7) J Daniel.

Not Without Laughter. Langston Hughes. 1976. 23.95 (0-8488-1055-4) Amereon Ltd.

Not Without Laughter. Langston Hughes. 320p. 1995. per. 11.00 (0-02-020985-1) Macmillan.

Not Without My Child. Rebecca Winters. (Superromance Ser.). 1996. per. 3.99 (0-373-70697-9, 1-70697-7) Harlequin Bks.

Not Without My Daughter. Betty Mahmoody & William Hoffer. 1991. reprint ed. mass mkt. 6.99 (0-312-92588-3) St Martin.

Not Without Parables: Stories of Yesterday, Today & Eternity. Catherine D. Doherty. 187p. 1989. 13.95 (0-921440-16-2) Madonna Hse.

Not Without Peril. Marguerite Allis. 414p. 1989. reprint ed. 18.95 (0-9622471-0-3) Old Fort Four.

*Not Without Peril: One Hundred & Fifty Years of Misadventure on the Presidential Range of New Hampshire. Nicholas Howe. LC 99-86536. 2000. 22.95 (1-878239-93-7) AMC Books.

Not Without Risk. Suzanne Brockmann. (Intimate Moments Ser.). 1995. per. 3.75 (0-373-07647-9, 1-07647-0) Silhouette.

*Not Without You. Janelle Taylor. 352p. 2000. mass mkt. 6.99 (0-8217-6613-9) Kensgtn Pub Corp.

Not Words Alone: Selected Speeches of Kosonike Koso-Thomas. Ed. by Olayinka Koso-Thomas. 176p. (C). 1991. 65.00 (0-7223-2430-8, Pub. by A H S Ltd) St Mut.

Not Working: State, Unemployment, & Neo-Conservatism in Canada. Stephen McBride. (State & Economic Life Ser.: No. 16). 272p. (Orig.). 1992. text 50.00 (0-8020-5998-8); pap. text 19.95 (0-8020-6929-0) U of Toronto Pr.

Not Yet: A Story of Faith & Hope John Meyer. Evangeline M. De Master. (Illus.). (Orig.). 1995. pap. write for info. (0-9643883-0-8) Meyer-DeMaster.

Not Yet: Reconsidering Ernst Bloch. Ed. by Jamie O. Daniel & Tom Moylan. 240p. 1997. pap. 20.00 (0-86091-683-9, Pub. by Verso) Norton.

Not Yet African: The Long Voyage Home. unabridged ed. Kevin Gordon. LC 97-48925. 192p. (gr. 9-12). 1998. pap., per. 14.00 (1-57889-013-6) Passeggiata.

Not Yet "Free at Last" The Unfinished Business of the Civil Rights Movement: Our Battle for School Choice. Mikel Holt. LC 99-40712. 225p. 1999. pap. 19.95 (1-55815-510-4) ICS Pr.

Not Yet over the Hump: African Americans into the 21st Century - A Primer. Ed Smith. 240p. (Orig.). 1994. pap. 14.95 (0-9641446-0-3) JAED Pubng.

Not Yet Pregnant: Infertile Couples in Contemporary America. Larry L. Greil. LC 90-21142. 250p. (C). 1991. pap. 14.95 (0-8135-1683-8); text 40.00 (0-8135-1682-X) Rutgers U Pr.

Not Yet the Yeti: Rhymes for the Times. xii, 142p. (Orig.). 1997. pap. 10.00 (0-9656805-0-9) Davro Press.

Not Yet, Tip. Alan M. Hofmeister et al. (Reading for All Learners Ser.). (Illus.). (J). pap. write for info. (1-56861-146-3) Swift Lrn Res.

Not-Yet-Transformed God: Depth Psychology & the Individual Religious Experience. Janet O. Dallett. LC 98-21648. 160p. 1998. pap. 16.95 (0-89254-042-7) Nicolas-Hays.

Not Yet, Yvette. Helen Ketteman. LC 91-19608. (J). (ps-2). 1995. pap. 4.95 (0-8075-5772-2) A Whitman.

Not Your Everyday Lady. Donna Smith. (Illus.). 96p. (Orig.). 1988. pap. 8.00 (0-318-35205-2) Batt Bks.

Not Your Father's Union Movement: Inside the AFL-CIO. Ed. by Jo-Ann Mort. 240p. 1998. 60.00 (1-85984-889-3, Pub. by Verso); pap. 20.00 (1-85984-286-0, Pub. by Verso) Norton.

Not Your Grandmother's Flower Garden: A Strip-Pieced Quilt Method. Marcia L. Baker. LC 97-146463. (Not Your Grandmother's Quilts Ser.: Vol. 1). (Illus.). 36p. (Orig.). 1996. pap. 14.95 (0-9651439-0-2) Alicias Attic.

Not Your Grandmother's Stars: A Strip-Pieced Quilt Method. Marcia L. Baker. (Not Your Grandmother's Quilts Ser.: Vol. 3). (Illus.). 48p. (Orig.). Date not set. pap. write for info. (0-9651439-2-9) Alicias Attic.

Not Your Grandmother's Tumbling Blocks: A Strip-Pieced Quilt Method. Marcia L. Baker. (Not Your Grandmother's Quilts Ser.: Vol. 2). (Illus.). 24p. (Orig.). 1997. pap. 10.00 (0-9651439-1-0) Alicias Attic.

Nota de Derecho Penal. Eduardo De Acha. LC 82-71757. (SPA.). 184p. (Orig.). 1982. 12.95 (0-89729-314-2) Ediciones.

Notable Advances in the Understanding & Treatment of Mentally Handicapped Children. J. E. Wallace. LC 58-1578. (Augustana College Library Occasional Papers, Wallin Lecture: No. 1). 20p. 1957. pap. 1.00 (0-910182-22-1) Augustana Coll.

Notable Aircraft of the 1930's: And How They Were Built, 10 vols., Set. Incl. Vol. I. Ed. by Clarence W. Sutton. LC 81-90009. 1982. lib. bdg. 45.00 (0-940300-01-X); Vol. II. Ed. by Clarence W. Sutton. LC 81-90009. 1982. lib. bdg. 45.00 (0-940300-02-8); Vol. III. Ed. by Clarence W. Sutton. LC 81-90009. 1982. lib. bdg. 45.00 (0-940300-03-6); Vol. IV. Ed. by Clarence W. Sutton. LC 81-90009. 1982. lib. bdg. 45.00 (0-940300-04-4); Vol. V. Ed. by Clarence W. Sutton. LC 81-90009. 1982. lib. bdg. 45.00 (0-940300-05-2); Vol. VI. Ed. by Clarence W. Sutton. LC 81-90009. 1982. lib. bdg. 45.00 (0-940300-06-0); Vol. VII. Ed. by Clarence W. Sutton. LC 81-90009. 1982. lib. bdg. 45.00 (0-940300-07-9); Vol. VIII. Ed. by Clarence W. Sutton. LC 81-90009. 1982. lib. bdg. 45.00 (0-940300-08-7); Vol. IX. Ed. by Clarence W. Sutton. LC 81-90009. 1982. lib. bdg. 45.00 (0-940300-09-5); Vol. X. Clarence W. Sutton. LC 81-90009. (Illus.). 140p. 1982. lib. bdg. 45.00 (0-940400-09-X); LC 81-90009. (Illus.). 140p. 1982. Set lib. bdg. 450.00 (0-940300-00-1) Sutton Avn Pr.

*Notable American Novelists. Carl Rollyson. LC 99-34407. 2000. write for info. (0-89356-162-2); write for info. (0-89356-163-0); write for info. (0-89356-164-9) Salem Pr.

*Notable American Novelists, 3 vols. Salem Press Editors. LC 99-34407. (Illus.). 1209p. 1999. lib. bdg. 175.00 (0-89356-161-4, Magills Choice) Salem Pr.

*Notable American Poets. Ed. by Barbara Morris Fischer. (Illus.). 80p. 1999. lib. bdg. 37.95 (0-912658-04-5) J Mark Pr.

Notable American Trial Series, 4 vols. Francis X. Busch. 1998. reprint ed. 240.00 (1-57588-423-2, 311330) W S Hein.

Notable American Women: The Modern Period. Ed. by Barbara Sicherman & Carol H. Green. (Illus.). 795p. 1983. pap. text 35.50 (0-674-62733-4) HUP.

Notable American Women Paper Dolls in Full Color. Tom Tierney. (Illus.). 32p. (J). 1989. pap. 4.95 (0-486-26011-9) Dover.

Notable American Women, 1607-1950: A Biographical Dictionary, 3 vols., Set. Ed. by Edward T. James & Janet W. James. LC 76-152274. 2141p. 1973. pap. 45.00 (0-674-62734-2) Belknap Pr.

Notable Americans: What They Did, from 1620 to the Present. 4th ed. Ed. by Linda S. Hubbard. 733p. 1987. 155.00 (0-8103-2534-9) Gale.

Notable Asian Americans. Ed. by Helen Zia & Susan B. Gall. LC 94-33638. 468p. (J). (gr. 6-9). 1994. 80.00 (0-8103-9623-8) Gale.

Notable Beginning: The Founding & Early Years of the CSUF Department of Music, 1959-69. Joseph W. Landon. (Illus.). 255p. 1996. text 50.00 (0-943988-04-7) Music Educ Pubns.

Notable Biographies. Incl. James Baldwin. Randall Kenan. (Illus.). 140p. (YA). (gr. 9 up). 1994. lib. bdg. 19.95 (0-7910-2301-X); James Baldwin. Randall Kenan. 140p. (YA). (gr. 9 up). 1994. pap. 9.95 (0-7910-2876-3); John Maynard Keynes. Jeffrey Escoffier. LC 94-1133. (Illus.). 140p. (YA). (gr. 9 up). 1994. lib. bdg. 19.95 (0-7910-2860-7); John Maynard Keynes. Jeffrey Escoffier. LC 94-1133. (Illus.). 140p. (YA). (gr. 9 up). 1994. pap. 9.95 (0-7910-2879-8); K. D. Lang. Paula Martinac. LC 95-14170. (Illus.). 140p. (YA). (gr. 9 up). 1996. lib. bdg. 19.95 (0-7910-2872-0); K. D. Lang. Paula Martinac. LC 95-14170. (Illus.). 140p. (YA). (gr. 9 up). 1996. pap. 9.95 (0-7910-2899-2); Liberace. Ray Mungo. Ed. by Martin Duberman. LC 94-10201. (Illus.). 140p. (YA). (gr. 9 up). 1995. lib. bdg. 19.95 (0-7910-2850-X); Liberace. Ray Mungo. Ed. by Martin Duberman. (Illus.). 140p. (YA). (gr. 9 up). 1995. pap. 9.95 (0-7910-2885-2); Marlene Dietrich. W. K. Martin. Ed. by Martin Duberman. LC 94-23518. (Illus.). 140p. (YA). (gr. 9 up). 1995. 19.95 (0-7910-2862-3); Marlene Dietrich. W. K. Martin. Ed. by Martin Duberman. LC 94-23518. (Illus.). 140p. (YA). (gr. 9 up). 1995. pap. 9.95 (0-7910-2881-X); Martina Navratilova. Gilda Zwerman. Ed. by Martin Duberman. LC 94-23326. (Illus.). 140p. (YA). (gr. 9 up). 1995. lib. bdg. 19.95 (0-7910-2303-6); Martina Navratilova. Gilda Zwerman. Ed. by Martin Duberman. LC 94-23326. (Illus.). 140p. (YA). (gr. 9 up). 1995. pap. 9.95 (0-7910-2878-X); Oscar Wilde. Jeff Nunokawa. Ed. by Martin B. Duberman. LC 93-42397. (Illus.). 140p. (YA). (gr. 9 up). 1995. pap. 9.95 (0-7910-2884-4); Oscar Wilde. Jeff Nunokawa. Ed. by Martin B. Duberman. LC 93-42397. (Illus.). 140p. (YA). (gr. 9 up). 1994. lib. bdg. 19.95 (0-7910-2311-7); Sappho. Jane M. Snyder. Ed. by Martin Duberman. LC 94-1134. (Illus.). 140p. (YA). (gr. 9 up). 1994. lib. bdg. 19.95 (0-7910-2308-7); Sappho. Jane M. Snyder. Ed. by Martin Duberman. LC 94-1134. (Illus.). 140p. (YA). (gr. 9 up). 1995. pap. 9.95 (0-7910-2883-6); T. E. Lawrence. Daniel Wolfe. LC 94-27034. (Illus.). 140p. (YA). (gr. 9 up). 1995. lib. bdg. 19.95 (0-7910-2324-9); T. E. Lawrence. Daniel Wolfe. LC 94-27034. (Illus.). 140p. (YA). (gr. 9 up). 1995. pap. 9.95 (0-7910-2891-7); Willa Cather. Sharon O'Brien. Ed. by Martin B. Duberman. LC 93-43244. (Illus.). 140p. (YA). (gr. 9 up). 1994. lib. bdg. 19.95 (0-7910-2302-8); Willa Cather. Sharon O'Brien. Ed. by Martin B. Duberman. LC 93-43244. (Illus.). 140p. (YA). (gr. 9 up). 1994. pap. 9.95 (0-7910-2877-1); 1994. Set 5.25 hd 638.40 (0-7910-2300-1); Set 5.25 hd 199.50 (0-7910-3754-1) Chelsea Hse.

Notable Black American Men. LC 98-38166. 1998. 90.00 (0-7876-0763-0, 00153584) Gale.

Notable Black American Scientists. Binkley. LC 98-36338. (Illus.). 500p. 1998. 80.00 (0-7876-2789-5, GML00298-112329) Gale.

Notable Black American Women, Bk. I. Ed. by Jessie C. Smith. 1333p. 1991. 80.00 (0-8103-4749-0) Gale.

*Notable Black Americans. Beth Button. Ed. by Kathy Rogers. (Famous Faces Ser.). (Illus.). 8p. 2000. 6.95 (1-56472-279-1) Edupress Inc.

Notable British Trials Series, 83 vol. 1997. reprint ed. write for info. (1-56169-111-9) Gaunt.

Notable Career in Finding Out. James S. Henderson et al. LC 77-160731. (Illus.). 48p. 1971. 5.00 (0-87470-016-7) Rockefeller.

Notable Children's Books, 1940-1959: Prepared by the Book Re-Evaluation Committee. American Library Association Staff. LC 66-24177. 47p. reprint ed. pap. 30.00 (0-608-12796-5, 202421300035) Bks Demand.

Notable Children's Books, 1940-1970. American Library Association Staff. LC 77-641. 94p. reprint ed. pap. 30.00 (0-7837-5965-7, 204576600007) Bks Demand.

Notable Children's Books, 1971-75. American Library Association Staff. LC 81-65981. (Illus.). 48p. 1981. reprint ed. pap. 30.00 (0-7837-9676-5, 206040400005) Bks Demand.

Notable Contributions to the Periodical International Accounting Literature, 1975-1978. International Accounting Section of AAA. 168p. 1979. 8.00 (0-86539-012-6) Am Accounting.

Notable Corporate Chronologies, 3 vols. 2nd ed. 1960p. 1998. 390.00 (0-8103-9500-2, 00000845) Gale.

Notable Corporate Chronologies. 3rd ed. 700p. 1999. 115.00 (0-7876-2465-9, GML00299-111989, Gale Res Intl) Gale.

Notable Corporate Chronologies, Vols. 1-2. Ed. by Susan B. Martin. 1994. 375.00 (0-8103-9217-8, 007660) Gale.

Notable Cross-Examinations. Ed. by Edward W. Fordham. LC 79-98759. 202p. 1970. reprint ed. lib. bdg. 65.00 (0-8371-3099-9, FOCE, Greenwood Pr) Greenwood.

Notable Discovery of Coosnage; The Second Part of Conny-Catching; Thirde & Last Parte of Conny-Catching; A Disputation Betweene a Hee & Shee Conny-Catcher see Life & Complete Works in Prose & Verse of Robert Greene

Notable Family Networks in Latin America. Diana Balmori et al. LC 84-2423. (Illus.). 264p. 1984. 32.50 (0-226-03639-1) U Ch Pr.

Notable Financial Causes Celebres. Edward Stamp et al. Ed. by Richard P. Brief. LC 80-1466. (Dimensions of Accounting Theory & Practice Ser.). 1980. lib. bdg. 25.95 (0-405-13488-6) Ayer.

Notable Hispanic American Women. Ed. by Eva M. Neito et al. 485p. 1993. 75.00 (0-8103-7578-8, 003318) Gale.

Notable Hispanic American Women. 2nd ed. 1998. 75.00 (0-7876-2068-8, 00152450) Gale.

Notable History of the Saracens. Augustine Curio. Ed. by Thomas Newton. LC 77-6870. (English Experience Ser.: No. 863). 1977. reprint ed. lib. bdg. 35.00 (90-221-0863-5) Walter J Johnson.

Notable Horoscopes. Bangalore V. Raman. (C). 1991. reprint ed. 14.00 (81-208-0900-9, Pub. by Motilal Bnarsidass) S Asia.

Notable Images of Virtues & Vices: Character Types in Sir Philip Sidney's New Arcadia & in Italian Romance Epic. Neda Jeny. (American University Studies: Comparative Literature: Ser. III, Vol. 24). 200p. (C). 1989. text 32.90 (0-8204-0740-2) P Lang Pubng.

*Notable Interlude. Bernard Capes. Ed. by Jack Adrian. 20p. 1999. pap. 7.50 (1-899562-67-2, Calabash Pr) Ash-Tree.

Notable Kin. Gary B. Roberts. LC 97-78404. 288p. 1998. 35.00 (0-936124-17-2) C Boyer.

Notable Kin, Vol. 2. Gary B. Roberts. LC 97-78404. 300p. 1998. lib. bdg. 30.00 (0-936124-20-2) C Boyer.

Notable Latin American Women: Twenty-Nine Leaders, Rebels, Poets, Battlers & Spies, 1500-1900. Jerome R. Adams. LC 94-40310. 197p. 1995. lib. bdg. 32.50 (0-7864-0022-6) McFarland & Co.

Notable Latino Americans: A Biographical Dictionary. Matt S. Meier et al. LC 96-27392. 448p. (J). (gr. 7). 1997. 65.00 (0-313-29105-5) Greenwood.

Notable Libel Case: The Criminal Prosecution of Theodore Lyman Jr. by Daniel Webster in the Supreme Judicial Court of Massachusetts November Term, 1828. Josiah H. Benton, Jr. (Illus.). 1985. reprint ed. lib. bdg. 20.00 (0-8377-0347-6, Rothman) W S Hein.

Notable Maryland Women. Ed. by Winifred G. Helmes. LC 77-966. 432p. reprint ed. pap. 134.00 (0-8357-5554-1, 203518400093) Bks Demand.

Notable Mathematicians: From Ancient Times to Present. LC 97-33662. 1998. 85.00 (0-7876-3071-3) Gale.

Notable Medical Books: From the Lilly Library Indiana University. William R. LeFanu. Ed. by S. O. Waife et al. (Illus.). 275p. (C). 1976. 20.00 (0-685-20051-5) IN Univ Lilly Library.

*Notable Men & Women of Spanish Texas. Donald E. Chipman & Harriett D. Joseph. LC 99-19906. (Illus.). 368p. 1999. 40.00 (0-292-71217-0) U of Tex Pr.

*Notable Men & Women of Spanish Texas. Donald E. Chipman & Harriett Denise Joseph. LC 99-19906. 368p. 1999. pap. 17.95 (0-292-71218-9) U of Tex Pr.

Notable Men of Tennessee, Personal & Genealogical, with Portraits, 2 vols., Set. Ed. by John Allison. (Illus.). 667p. 1995. reprint ed. lib. bdg. 71.50 (0-8328-4723-2) Higginson Bk Co.

Notable Native Americans. 2nd ed. Ed. by Sharon Malinowski & George H. J. Abrams. LC 94-36202. 492p. 1994. 80.00 (0-8103-9638-6) Gale.

Notable New Zealand Statesmen: Twelve Prime Ministers. Guy H. Scholefield. LC 72-5588. (Biography Index Reprint Ser.). 1977. reprint ed. 23.95 (0-8369-8139-1) Ayer.

Notable North Carolina Women. Jennifer Ravi. LC 92-70165. (Illus.). 156p. (Orig.). 1992. pap. 9.95 (1-878177-03-6) Bandit Bks.

Notable Numbers. rev. ed. William T. Stokes. (Illus.). 1974. pap. text 9.95 (0-914534-01-7) Stokes.

Notable or Notorious? A Gallery of Parisians. Gordon Wright. LC 90-47629. (Illus.). 160p. 1991. pap. text 10.95 (0-674-62743-1, WRINOX) HUP.

Notable Poets, 3 vols., Set. Salem Press Editors. (Illus.). 950p. (YA). (gr. 9 up). 1998. lib. bdg. 175.00 (0-89356-967-4, Magills Choice) Salem Pr.

Notable Projects from Public Utilities: Innovations & Progressive Programs in Services, Marketing, & Resources-Operations from U.S. Electric, (& Gas) Utilities. Susan K. Friedman. LC 92-90504. 183p. (Orig.). 1992. pap. 28.95 (0-9635628-0-0) S K Friedman.

Notable Quotables (A Compendium of Quotes by Salvation Army Authors) Allen Satterlee. 1985. 15.95 (0-86544-028-X) Salv Army Suppl South.

Notable Quotes. Leigh Rubin. (Orig.). 1981. pap. 5.95 (0-941364-00-3) Rubes Pubns.

Notable Quotes. Leigh Rubin. LC 81-69508. (Notable Quotes Ser.: Vol. I). (Illus.). 80p. (Orig.). (J). (gr. 4 up). 1981. pap. 5.95 (0-943384-00-1) Rubes Pubns.

Notable Selections in American Government. Mitchel Gerber. LC 95-83883. (Sources Ser.). (Illus.). 344p. 1996. pap. text 14.00 (1-56134-262-9, Dshkn McG-Hill) McGrw-H Hghr Educ.

*Notable Selections in Economics Ser. Belayneh Seyoum & Rebecca Abraham. (Sources Ser.). 384p. (C). 1999. pap. 20.94 (0-07-303590-4) McGrw-H Hghr Educ.

Notable Selections in Education. 2nd ed. Fred Schultz. (Sources Ser.). (Illus.). 384p. 1998. pap. text 14.00 (0-697-34333-2, Dshkn McG-Hill) McGrw-H Hghr Educ.

Notable Selections in Human Sexuality. Gary F. Kelly. (Sources Ser.). (Illus.). 400p. 1998. pap. text 14.00 (0-697-42263-1, Dshkn McG-Hill) McGrw-H Hghr Educ.

Notable Selections in Mass Media. Jarice Hanson & David J. Maxcy. LC 95-83882. (Sources Ser.). (Illus.). 400p. 1996. pap. text 14.00 (1-56134-764-7, Dshkn McG-Hill) McGrw-H Hghr Educ.

Notable Selections in Race & Ethnicity. 2nd ed. Adalberto Aguirre, Jr. & David V. Baker. (Sources Ser.). (Illus.). 416p. 1998. pap. text 14.00 (0-697-34332-4, Dshkn McG-Hill) McGrw-H Hghr Educ.

Notable Selections in Social Psychology. 2nd ed. Terry F. Pettijohn. (Sources Ser.). (Illus.). 368p. 1998. pap. text 14.00 (0-697-39114-0, Dshkn McG-Hill) McGrw-H Hghr Educ.

Notable Southern Families, Vol. 1. Zella Armstrong. 247p. 1997. reprint ed. pap. 25.00 (0-8063-4725-2, Pub. by Clearfield Co) ACCESS Pubs Network.

***Notable Southern Families, Vol. III.** Zella Armstrong. 369p. 2000. reprint ed. pap. 32.50 (*0-8063-4889-5*, Pub. by Clearfield Co) ACCESS Pubs Network.

***Notable Southern Families, Vol. V.** Zella Armstrong. 611p. 2000. reprint ed. pap. 48.50 (*0-8063-4891-7*, Pub. by Clearfield Co) ACCESS Pubs Network.

Notable Southern Families Vol. II: Genealogies of the Families of Bean, Boone, Borden, Bryan, Carter, Davis, Donaldson, Hardwick, Haywood, Holliday, Hollingsworth, Houston, Johnston, Kelton, Magill, Rhea, Montgomery, Shelby, Vance, Wear, & Williams. Zella Armstrong. 377p. 1997. reprint ed. pap. 32.50 (*0-8063-4726-0*, Pub. by Clearfield Co) ACCESS Pubs Network.

***Notable Southern Families Vol. 4: The Sevier Family: Antecedents & Emigration; William Sevier, the Emigrant, & His Descendants; Valentine Sevier, the Emigrant, & His Descendants; Joanna Goode Sevier, Wife of Younger Landrum, Jr., & Her Descendants; Governor John Sevier & His Descendants.** Zella Armstrong. 325p. 2000. reprint ed. pap. 28.00 (*0-8063-4890-9*) Clearfield Co.

Notable Southern Families Vol. 6: The Doak Family. Janie P. French. 98p. 1993. reprint ed. pap. 12.50 (*0-8063-4892-5*) Clearfield Co.

Notable Trees of Centre County. Ed. by Centre County Historical Society Staff. (Illus.). 40p. 1992. pap. 8.00 (*1-887315-06-3*) Centre Cty Hist Soc.

***Notable Twentieth-Century Latin American Women: A Biographical Dictionary.** Ed. by Cynthia Margarita Tompkins & David William Foster. LC 00-27631. 310p. 2000. 60.00 (*0-313-31112-9*, GR1112) Greenwood.

Notable Twentieth-Century Pianists: A Bio-Critical Sourcebook, 2 vols. John Gillespie & Anna Gillespie. LC 95-9757. (Bio-Critical Sourcebooks on Musical Performance Ser.). 1024p. 1995. lib. bdg. 125.00 (*0-313-25660-8*, Greenwood Pr) Greenwood.

Notable Twentieth-Century Pianists: A Bio-Critical Sourcebook, Vol. 1. Anna Gillespie. LC 95-9757. 1995. lib. bdg. 95.00 (*0-313-29695-2*, Greenwood Pr) Greenwood.

Notable Twentieth-Century Pianists: A Bio-Critical Sourcebook, Vol. 2. John Gillespie & Anna Gillespie. LC 95-9757. (Bio-Critical Sourcebooks on Musical Performance Ser.). 1995. lib. bdg. 95.00 (*0-313-29696-0*, Greenwood Pr) Greenwood.

Notable Twentieth-Century Scientists, 4 vols. Ed. by Emily J. McMurray & Donna Olendorf. LC 94-5263. 2397p. 1994. 305.00 (*0-8103-9181-3*) Gale.

Notable Twentieth-Century Scientists Supplement. Olendorf. LC 98-14016. 617p. 1998. 90.00 (*0-7876-2766-6*) Gale.

Notable U. S. Ambassadors since 1775: A Biographical Dictionary. Ed. by Cathal J. Nolan. LC 96-50291. 448p. 1997. lib. bdg. 95.00 (*0-313-29195-0*, Greenwood Pr) Greenwood.

Notable Women, 2 vols., 2. Mary Cullen & Maria Luddy. 1992. 47.00 (*1-85594-079-5*) St Mut.

Notable Women Authors of the Day. Helen C. Black. 342p. 1977. 26.95 (*0-8369-2637-4*) Ayer.

Notable Women Authors of the Day. Helen C. Black. 342p. reprint ed. lib. bdg. 49.00 (*0-685-10416-8*) Rprt Serv.

Notable Women in American History. 41.95 (*0-382-40676-1*) Cobblestone Pub Co.

Notable Women in American History: A Guide to Recommended Biographies & Autobiographies. Lynda G. Adamson. LC 98-55350. 464p. 1999. 49.95 (*0-313-29584-0*, GR9584, Greenwood Pr) Greenwood.

Notable Women in Mathematics: A Biographical Dictionary. Ed. by Charlene Morrow & Teri Perl. LC 97-18598. (Illus.). 320p. (YA). (gr. 9 up). 1998. 49.95 (*0-313-29131-4*, Greenwood Pr) Greenwood.

Notable Women in New Zealand Health: Te Hauora Ki Aotearoa : Eona Weahine Rongonui. Patricia A. Sargison. LC 93-234589. ix, 86 p. 1993. write for info. (*0-582-86078-4*) Longman.

Notable Women in the American Theatre: A Biographical Dictionary. Ed. by Alice M. Robinson et al. LC 89-17065. 1008p. 1989. lib. bdg. 135.00 (*0-313-27217-4*, RNW/, Greenwood Pr) Greenwood.

Notable Women in the Life Sciences: A Biographical Dictionary. Ed. by Benjamin F. Shearer & Barbara S. Shearer. LC 95-25603. 456p. 1996. 49.95 (*0-313-29302-3*, Greenwood Pr) Greenwood.

Notable Women in the Physical Sciences: A Biographical Dictionary. Ed. by Benjamin F. Shearer & Barbara S. Shearer. LC 96-9024. 496p. 1997. 49.95 (*0-313-29303-1*, Greenwood Pr) Greenwood.

***Notable Women in World Government, 2 Vols.** Ed. by Salem Press Editors. LC 99-88983. (Illus.). 640p. 2000. lib. bdg. 95.00 (*0-89356-201-7*, Magills Choice) Salem Pr.

Notable Women in World History: A Guide to Recommended Biographies & Autobiographies. Lynda G. Adamson. LC 97-33136. 416p. 1998. 49.50 (*0-313-29818-1*, Greenwood Pr) Greenwood.

Notable Women of China: Shang Dynasty to the Early Twentieth Century. Ed. by Barbara Bennett Peterson. LC 99-30322. 432p. 2000. text 74.95 (*0-7656-0504-X*, Sharpe Ref) M E Sharpe.

Notable Women of Scripture. Ken Gurley. LC 93-47482. 190p. (Orig.). 1994. pap. 8.99 (*1-56722-018-5*) Word Aflame.

Notable Women Scientists. Ed. by Pamela Proffitt. LC 99-35741. 700p. (J). 1999. 85.00 (*0-7876-3900-1*, GML00299-113696, Gale Res Intl) Gale.

Notables & Clergy in Mount Lebanon: The Khazin Sheikhs & the Maronite Church, 1736-1840. Richard Van Leeuwen. LC 94-26323. xi, 290p. 1994. 100.00 (*90-04-09978-6*) Brill Academic Pubs.

***Notables of Harrison County, Ohio.** Erving E. Beauregard. LC 99-57089. (Studies in Local & Institutional History: Vol. 2). 452p. 2000. text 109.95 (*0-7734-7841-8*) E Mellen.

Notables of the Right: The Conservative Party & Political Mobilization in Germany, 1876-1918. James N. Retallack. 224p. (C). 1988. text 55.00 (*0-04-900038-1*) Routledge.

Notably Norwegian: Recipes, Festivals, Folk Arts. Louise Roalson. LC 82-81569. (Illus.). 88p. 1982. pap. 8.95 (*0-941016-05-6*) Penfield.

Notae Latinae. Wallace M. Lindsay. xxiv, 500p. 1972. reprint ed. write for info. (*0-318-71161-3*) G Olms Pubs.

Notae Latinae: An Account of Abbreviation in Latin MSS. of the Early Minuscule Period. Wallace M. Lindsay. xxiv, 500p. 1972. reprint ed. write for info. (*0-318-72042-6*); reprint ed. suppl. ed. write for info. (*0-318-72043-4*) G Olms Pubs.

Notaire du Havre see Chronique des Pasquier

Notaire du Havre. Duhamel. (FRE.). (C). pap. 9.95 (*0-8442-1711-5*, VF1711-5) NTC Contemp Pub Co.

Notaire du Havre. Georges Duhamel. (Chronique Des Pasquier Ser.: Vol. I). (FRE.). 1972. pap. 10.95 (*0-7859-2210-5*, 2070369O3X) Fr & Eur.

Notan: The Dark-Light Principle of Design. Dorr Bothwell & Marlys Mayfield. (Illus.). 80p. 1991. reprint ed. pap. 5.95 (*0-486-26856-X*) Dover.

Notaries of French-Canada: 1626-1900: Alphabetical, Chronologically by Area Served. rev. ed. Robert J. Quintin. 93p. 1994. pap. 15.00 (*1-886560-01-3*, 09401) Quintin Pub RI.

Notaries Public in England since the Reformation. C. W. Brooke. 160p. 1998. pap. 165.00 (*1-85297-034-0*, Pub. by Erskine Press) St Mut.

Notarii & Exceptores. H. C. Teitler. (Dutch Monographs on Ancient History & Archaeology: Vol. 1). ix, 380p. (C). 1985. 74.00 (*90-70265-77-X*, Pub. by Gieben) J Benjamins Pubng Co.

***Notary Home Study Course.** rev. ed. National Notary Association Staff. 1999. pap. 48.00 (*1-891133-25-X*) Natl Notary.

Notary Law & Practice: Cases & Materials. Michael L. Closen et al. LC 97-67209. 629p. 1997. text 68.00 (*0-933134-85-1*, 5100) Natl Notary.

Notary Public. Jack Rudman. (Career Examination Ser.: C-531). 1994. pap. 19.95 (*0-8373-0531-4*) Natl Learn.

***Notary Public Guidebook for North Carolina.** 7th rev. ed. William A. Campbell. LC 99-229796. (C). 1999. pap. text 10.00 (*1-56011-348-0*, 99.04) Institute Government.

***Notary Public Guidebook for North Carolina.** 8th ed. William A. Campbell. (C). 2000. pap. write for info. (*1-56011-382-0*) Institute Government.

Notary Public Practices & Glossary. 2nd ed. Raymond C. Rothman. 1998. 22.00 (*1-891133-08-X*) Natl Notary.

Notas, No. 45. Ortega y Gasset Jose. (SPA.). 157p. 1967. write for info. (*0-8288-8550-8*) Fr & Eur.

Notas Biograficas: Hispanos Americanos, 6 bks. (J). (gr. 2-4). 1994. 72.25 (*0-8136-5292-8*) Modern Curr.

Notas Biograficas: Mujeres Norteamericanas, 6 bks. (J). (gr. 2-4). 1994. 72.25 (*0-8136-5784-9*) Modern Curr.

Notas Biograficas: Nativos Americanos, 6 bks. (J). (gr. 2-4). 1994. 72.25 (*0-8136-5812-8*) Modern Curr.

Notas para Conciertos Imaginarios. Carlos Gomez Amat. (Nueva Austral Ser.: Vol. 7). (SPA.). 1991. pap. text 24.95 (*84-239-1807-6*) Elliots Bks.

Notation. Virginia Gaburo. LC 77-75432. (Illus.). 176p. (C). 1977. pap. 14.65 (*0-939044-16-1*) Lingua Pr.

Notation Issue: A Special Issue of the Journal Choreography & Dance, Vol. 1, Part 1. Muriel Topaz. (Choreography & Dance Studies: Vol. 1, Pt. 1). 96p. 1988. pap. text 15.00 (*3-7186-0468-X*) Gordon & Breach.

Notation Musicale des Manuscrits Liturgiques Latins. Jacques Hourlier.Tr. of Musical Notation of Latin Liturgical Chants. (ENG & FRE., Illus.). 40p. (C). 1991. pap. 39.95 (*2-85274-136-9*, 4061, Pub. by Abbey St Peter Solesmes) Paraclete MA.

Notation of Medieval Music. Carl Parrish. LC 78-11831. 230p. 1978. lib. bdg. 30.00 (*0-918728-08-8*) Pendragon NY.

Notation of Polyphonic Music, 900-1600. 5th ed. Willi Apel. LC 61-12067. (Medieval Academy Bks.: No. 38). 1961. 28.00 (*0-910956-15-4*) Medieval Acad.

Notational Analysis of Sport. Hughes & Franks. LC 97-202953. 272p. (Orig.). 1997. pap. text. write for info. (*0-419-18010-9*, E & FN Spon) Routledge.

Notations. Herman Bergeijk & Deborah Hauptmann. LC 98-220735. (Illus.). 224p. 1998. pap. 30.00 (*90-5662-072-X*, Pub. by NAi Uitgevers) Dist Art Pubs.

Notations. Ed. by John M. Cage. reprint ed. lib. bdg. 49.00 (*0-685-14864-5*) Rprt Serv.

Notations & Editions. Edith Borroff. LC 76-58563. (Music Reprint Ser.). 1977. reprint ed. lib. bdg. 32.50 (*0-306-70867-1*) Da Capo.

Notations for Software Design. Loe M. Feijs et al. LC 94-29179. (Formal Approaches to Computing & Information Technology Ser.). 1994. 78.95 (*0-387-19902-0*) Spr-Verlag.

Notations in Elementary Mathematics see History of Mathematical Notations

Notations in Passing. Nathan Lyons. 121p. 1974. 23.95 (*0-262-12067-4*); pap. text 12.50 (*0-262-62028-6*) MIT Pr.

Notations Mainly in Higher Mathematics see History of Mathematical Notations

Notations of the Wild: Ecology in the Poetry of Wallace Stevens. Gyorgyi Voros. LC 96-3071. 208p. 1997. text 28.95 (*0-87745-570-8*) U of Iowa Pr.

***Notations on a Visible World.** Kathleen Wakefield. LC 00-105326. xiv, 76p. 2000. pap. 12.00 (*0-938078-66-6*) Anhinga Pr.

Notations on the Arrest. Yosef Y. Schneersohn. Ed. by Moshe C. Levin. Tr. by David A. Gurevich from HEB. LC 80-21987. (Illus.). 226p. (Orig.). 1980. 11.75 (*0-86639-100-2*) Friends Refugees.

Notations Through Verse, 3 vols. Albert Krassner. (Illus.). 135p. 1984. pap. 15.95 (*0-912061-04-9*) Veridon Edns.

Notch of the Knife. William Haggard. Date not set. lib. bdg. 19.95 (*0-88411-667-0*, Aeonian Pr) Amereon Ltd.

Notches: A Gabriel Du Pre Mystery. Peter Bowen. (Dead Letter Mysteries Ser.). 1998. mass mkt. 5.50 (*0-312-96492-7*) St Martin.

Note-Book Kept by Thomas Lechford, Esq., in Boston, Massachusetts Bay, from June 27, 1638 to July 29, 1641. Thomas Lechford. 460p. 1998. reprint ed. pap. 34.50 (*0-7884-0926-3*, L113) Heritage Bk.

Note-Book Kept by Thomas Lechford, Esq., in Boston, Massachusetts Bay, from June 27, 1638, to July 29, 1641. rev. ed. Thomas Lechford. Ed. by Edward E. Hale, Jr. et al. LC 88-30732. 512p. 1989. reprint ed. 49.50 (*0-929539-06-0*, 1106) Picton Pr.

Note Book of an Unknown Writer. Meredith. 143p. 1995. pap. text 4.99 (*1-886820-02-3*) Meredith WA.

Note Book of Elbert Hubbard. Elbert Hubbard. 1976. 34.95 (*0-8488-0598-4*) Amereon Ltd.

Note Book of Elbert Hubbard. Elbert Hubbard. 1980. reprint ed. 25.00 (*0-936128-32-1*) De Young Pr.

Note Book of Elbert Hubbard. Elbert Hubbard. 244p. 1998. reprint ed. pap. 19.95 (*0-7661-0416-8*) Kessinger Pub.

Note-Book of Medieval History, A.D. 323 - A. D. 1453. Charles R. Beazley. LC 70-160957. (Select Bibliographies Reprint Ser.). 1977. reprint ed. 20.95 (*0-8369-5824-1*) Ayer.

Note-Book of the Shelley Society. Shelley Society, London Staff. LC 74-30283. (First Ser.: No. 2). reprint ed. 34.50 (*0-404-11502-0*) AMS Pr.

Note Books of Percy Bysshe Shelley, 3 vols., Set. Percy Bysshe Shelley. (BCL1-PR English Literature Ser.). 1992. reprint ed. lib. bdg. 225.00 (*0-7812-7649-7*) Rprt Serv.

Note-Books of Samuel Butler see Shrewsbury Edition of the Works of Samuel Butler

Note Books of Samuel Butler. Samuel Butler. 1988. reprint ed. lib. bdg. 75.00 (*0-7812-0347-3*) Rprt Serv.

Note-Books of Samuel Butler, 1874-1883, Vol. I. Ed. by Hans-Peter Breuer. (Complete Note-Books of Samuel Butler). 402p. 1984. lib. bdg. 52.00 (*0-8191-4193-3*) U Pr of Amer.

Note Cards of Color-Bearers. E. Lisle Reedstrom. 9.95 (*0-685-71943-X*, J M C & Co) Amereon Ltd.

Note Conjointe: Note sur M. Bergson et la Philosophie Bergsonienne, Note Conjointe sur Descartes et la Philosophie Cartesienne. Charles Peguy. pap. 8.75 (*0-685-37030-5*) Fr & Eur.

Note de Methodologie Generale sur l'Analyse de Filiere: Utilisation de l'Analyse de Filiere pour l'Analyse Economique des Politiques. (FRE.). 116p. 1994. 15.00 (*92-5-203495-1*, FF4951, Pub. by FAO) Bernan Associates.

Note Eternelle du Present: Ecrits sur l'Art (1923-1960) Pierre Reverdy. 288p. 16.95 (*0-686-54726-8*) Fr & Eur.

Note for a Missing Friend. Dina Ben-Lev. 28p. (Orig.). 1991. pap. 8.00 (*0-9624178-2-3*, HVWC) Slapering Hol.

Note Found in a Bottle: My Life as a Drinker. Susan Cheever. 208p. 2000. per. 12.95 (*0-671-04073-1*, WSP) PB.

Note Found in a Bottle: My Life as a Drinker. Susan Cheever. LC 98-26463. 192p. 1999. 22.50 (*0-684-80432-8*) S&S Trade.

Note from Your Teacher. Scholastic, Inc. Staff. (Orig.). 1999. pap. text 3.95 (*0-439-07233-6*) Scholastic Inc.

Note from Your Teacher: More Than 450 Ready-Made Notes for Communication & Personalizing Report Cards. Kimberly Colen. Ed. by Judy Mitchell. (Illus.). 240p. (Orig.). (J). (gr. k-6). 1995. pap., teacher ed. 19.95 (*1-57310-033-1*) Teachng & Lrning Co.

Note Grouping: A Method for Achieving Expression & Style in Musical Performance. James M. Thurmond. LC 81-90711. (Illus.). 144p. (C). 1982. text 24.95 (*0-942782-00-3*) Meredith Music.

Note Integrative per l'Insegnante 1. (GER.). 28p. 1997. pap. write for info. (*3-468-96819-1*) Langenscheidt.

Note of an Anatomist. Frank Gonzalez-Crussi. 144p. 1986. pap. 4.95 (*0-15-667430-0*, Harvest Bks) Harcourt.

Note of Parting. L. Ryan. 1996. mass mkt. 13.95 (*0-340-62458-2*, Pub. by Hodder & Stought Ltd) Trafalgar.

Note on Charlotte Bronte. Algernon Charles Swinburne. LC 75-119440. (English Biography Ser.: No. 31). (C). 1970. reprint ed. lib. bdg. 75.00 (*0-8383-1068-0*) M S G Haskell Hse.

Note on Degeneracy & Multiple Optima in Linear Programs. Ronald E. Miller & Nazir G. Dossani. (Discussion Papers: No. 17). 1967. pap. 10.00 (*1-55869-080-8*) Regional Sci Res Inst.

Note on Literary Criticism. James T. Farrell. LC 92-43765. 236p. (C). 1993. reprint ed. 52.50 (*0-231-08256-8*, Mrngside); reprint ed. pap. 19.00 (*0-231-08257-6*, Mrngside) Col U Pr.

Note on the Mirror: Pregnant Teenagers Tell Their Stories. Julia Loren. 160p. 1990. pap. 6.99 (*0-310-53531-X*) Zondervan.

Note on the Proceedings: Tripartite Meeting on Social & Labour Issues Concerning Migrant Workers in the Construction Industry, Geneva, 4-8 March 1996. Tripartite Meeting on Social and Labour Issues Concerning Migrant Workers in the Construction Industry Staff & International Labour Office Staff. LC 98-228258. 1996. write for info. (*92-2-110243-2*) Intl Labour Office.

Note on the Usefulness, Even in the Computer Age, of the "Round-by-Round" Method of Performing Input-Output Impact Calculations. Benjamin H. Stevens. (Discussion Papers: No. 132). 17p. (C). 1988. pap. 10.00 (*1-55869-135-9*) Regional Sci Res Inst.

Note Puppet Pattern. Dave Privett & Keann Brown. (Illus.). 18p. 1998. pap. 15.00 (*1-58302-052-7*) One Way St.

***Note Reading Color Cards.** large type unabridged ed. Terilyn Taylor & Toni Milleret. (Color Connection Ser.). (Illus.). 117p. 1999. pap. text 29.95 (*0-9671719-1-1*) T & T Pubg.

***Note Reading Color Cards - Cello: A Colorful Method to Musical Note Reading.** Terilyn Taylor & Toni Milleret. (Color Connection Ser.). (Illus.). 78p. 2000. pap. 24.95 (*0-9671719-9-7*) T & T Pubg.

***Note Reading Color Cards - Viola: A Colorful Method of Musical Note Reading.** Terilyn Taylor. (Color Connection Ser.). (Illus.). 78p. 2000. pap. 24.95 (*0-9671719-5-4*) T & T Pubg.

***Note Reading for the Rock Guitarist.** Ben Bolt. 32p. 1998. pap. 9.95 (*0-7866-3463-4*, 94813BCD) Mel Bay.

Note Reading for Violin. Shinichi Suzuki. Tr. by Kyoko Selden from JPN. (Suzuki Viola School Ser.). 112p. (J). (gr. 1-6). 1985. reprint ed. pap. text 14.95 (*0-87487-213-8*, Suzuki Method) Summy-Birchard.

Note Reading Studies for Bass. Arnold Evans. 80p. 1994. pap. 9.95 (*0-7866-0247-3*, 95297) Mel Bay.

***Note Slipped under the Door: Teaching from Poems We Love.** Nick Flynn & Shirley McPhillips. LC 00-30814. 2000. write for info. (*1-57110-320-1*) Stenhse Pubs.

Note sur les lectures de stries journalieres observees sur les otolithes de poissons see Notes on Observations of Daily Rings on Otoliths of Deepwater Snappers

Note Taking & Outlining Skills, LS01A. 4th rev. ed. James Scott. 32p. (YA). (gr. 7-12). 1994. pap., wbk. ed. 2.50 (*1-58049-801-9*) Prestwick Hse.

Note-Taking Made Easy. Judi Kesselman-Turkel & Franklynn Peterson. 108p. 1982. pap. 8.69 (*0-8092-5653-3*, 565330, Contemporary Bks) NTC Contemp Pub Co.

Notebook. Robb Hawks & Rick Berlin. (Illus.). 74p. 1993. pap. 14.00 (*1-58302-053-5*, BRE-08) One Way St.

Notebook. Robert Lowell. 265p. 1995. pap. 12.00 (*0-374-50947-6*) FS&G.

Notebook. Nicholas Sparks. LC 96-33815. 224p. 1996. 16.95 (*0-446-52080-2*, Pub. by Warner Bks) Little.

***Notebook.** Nicholas Sparks. 240p. 1999. mass mkt. 12.00 (*0-446-67609-8*, Pub. by Warner Bks) Little.

Notebook. large type ed. Nicholas Sparks. 1996. 25.95 (*0-7862-0821-X*, G K Hall Lrg Type) Mac Lib Ref.

Notebook. Nicholas Sparks & Bobbie Kalman. 256p. 1998. reprint ed. mass mkt. 6.99 (*0-446-60523-9*, Pub. by Warner Bks) Little.

***Notebook: Reading Group Guide.** Nicholas Sparks. 2000. pap. write for info. (*0-446-79043-5*) Warner Bks.

Notebook Atlas, 12. Insight Guides Staff. 1998. pap. text 35.40 (*0-8416-9609-8*) Am Map.

***Notebook Dictionary.** Ed. by Websters New World Staff. 112p. 2000. pap. 3.99 (*0-7645-6149-9*) IDG Bks.

Notebook Dictionary: Webster. (FRE.). 75p. 1996. 3.95 (*0-88729-073-6*) Langenscheidt.

Notebook Dictionary: Webster. 75p. 1996. 3.95 (*0-88729-077-9*) Langenscheidt.

Notebook Dictionary: Webster. (SPA.). 75p. 1996. 3.95 (*0-88729-072-8*) Langenscheidt.

Notebook Dictionary & Thesaurus. Webster's New World Staff & Joyce L. Vedral. 128p. 1997. 4.95 (*0-02-862056-9*) Macmillan.

Notebook Dividers to Accompany Real Writing. Lois Hassan. 1997. pap. text 0.01 (*0-312-15771-1*) St Martin.

Notebook for Realwrite & Realtime. McCormick. 272p. 1997. pap. text 11.60 (*0-13-621947-0*) P-H.

***Notebook for Saint Nicholas: From Renaissance to Swing 15 Intermediate Christmas Carols.** Peter Jancewicz. 32p. 1999. pap. 6.95 (*0-7390-0394-1*, 18076) Alfred Pub.

Notebook for Teachers: Making Changes in the Elementary Curriculum. rev. ed. Ruth S. Charney et al. LC 87-126317. (Illus.). 78p. 1993. pap. 19.95 (*0-9618636-0-9*) NE Found Child.

Notebook for the Rest of Your Life. Jane Anderson et al. (Illus.). 95p. 1995. ring bd. 20.00 (*0-9634836-2-5*) Sheep Shoppe.

Notebook Leaflets. fac. ed. Ellen Gould Harmon White. LC 97-80672. 144p. 1998. reprint ed. per. 7.95 (*1-57258-127-1*) Teach Servs.

Notebook of a Colonial Clergyman. Ed. by Doberstein. Tr. by Tappert. 1998. pap. 16.00 (*0-8006-3148-X*, Fortress Pr) Augsburg Fortress.

***Notebook of a Footsoldier & Other Stories.** Randhir Khare. LC 99-937990. 1999. 14.00 (*81-7223-335-3*, Pub. by CE25) S Asia.

Notebook of a Return to a Native Land. Aime Cesaire. 86p. 1997. pap. text 14.95 (*1-56886-046-3*) Marsilio Pubs.

Notebook of a Sixties Lawyer: An Unrepentant Memoir & Selected Writings. Michael S. Smith. 300p. 1991. 19.95 (*0-918266-26-2*); pap. 9.95 (*0-918266-25-4*) Smyrna.

Notebook of a Ten Square Rush-mat Sized World. Kamo N. Chomei. 1979. 10.95 (*0-85105-343-2*, Pub. by Smyth) Dufour.

Notebook of an Agitator: From the Wobblies to the Fight Against the Korean War & McCarthyism. 2nd ed. James P. Cannon. LC 73-79782. (Illus.). 379p. 1974. lib. bdg. 55.00 (*0-87348-304-9*) Pathfinder NY.

Notebook of an Agitator: From the Wobblies to the Fight Against the Korean War & McCarthyism. 3rd ed. James P. Cannon. LC 93-84144. (Illus.). 379p. 1993. pap. 21.95 (*0-87348-770-2*) Pathfinder NY.

Notebook of Bass Otis: Philadelphia Portrait Painter. Thomas Knoles. (Illus.). 74p. (Orig.). 1993. pap. text 13.95 (*0-944026-48-6*) Am Antiquarian.

Notebook of Lost Things: A Novel. Megan Staffel. LC 98-43484. 240p. 1999. 23.00 (*1-56947-160-6*) Soho Press.

Notebook of Memories. Illus. by Cheryl A. Benner. (Blank Notebook Ser.). 96p. 1990. pap. 5.95 (*1-56148-004-5*) Good Bks PA.

Notebook of Shadows: Selected Poems, 1974-1980. Philippe Denis. Tr. by Mark Irwin from FRE. LC 82-82907. (Contemporary European Poetry Ser.). Orig. Title: Cahier d'ombres. 68p. (Orig.). 1982. pap. 5.00 (*0-910321-00-0*) Globe Pr.

Notebook of Stone. Vivian Darroch-Lozowski. 71p. 1987. 9.95 (*0-920806-92-9*, Pub. by Penumbra Pr) U of Toronto Pr.

Notebook of Techniques for a Flute Recital. James J. Pellerite. 1967. pap. text 3.50 (*0-931200-50-4*) Zalo.

Notebook of the Reverend John Fiske, 1644 to 1675. Ed. by Robert G. Pope. LC 74-81447. 256p. 1974. 17.50 (*0-88389-052-6*, PEMP185, Essx Institute) Peabody Essex Mus.

Notebook of Trigorin. Tennessee Williams. 1998. pap. 5.25 (*0-8222-1597-7*) Dramatists Play.

Notebook of Trigorin: A Free Adaptation of Anton Chekov's The Sea Gull. Tennessee Williams. LC 97-25480. 128p. 1997. 19.95 (*0-8112-1371-4*, Pub. by New Directions); pap. 9.95 (*0-8112-1362-5*, NDP850, Pub. by New Directions) Norton.

Notebook of William Blake: A Photographic & Typographic Facsimile. rev. ed. Ed. by David V. Erdman & Donald K. Moore. 1977. pap. 35.00 (*0-918414-01-6*) Readex Bks.

Notebook on Time. Richard Zybert. LC 80-50741. (Illus.). 60p. (Orig.). 1982. pap. 4.95 (*0-9604260-0-0*) Zybert.

Notebook Physiofinder. P. George Simone. (C). 1995. ring bd. 10.31 (*0-673-55735-9*) Addson-Wesley Educ.

Notebook Progress. Robert Nevins. 336p. (C). 1995. spiral bd. 44.95 (*0-7872-1011-0*) Kendall-Hunt.

Notebook, the Proof, the Third Lie: Three Novels. Agota Kristof. Tr. by Alan Sheridan et al from FRE. LC 97-14269. 496p. 1997. reprint ed. pap. 15.00 (*0-8021-3506-4*, Grove) Grove-Atltic.

Notebook Tracker: Maps for Tracking Dogs. Betty A. Mueller. 100p. 1996. spiral bd. 11.95 (*1-888994-04-5*) Howln Moon.

Notebook U. S. Atlas. V. Nichols. (Illus.). 16p. 1993. pap. 1.95 (*1-879424-44-4*) Nickel Pr.

Notebook World Atlas. V. Nichols. (Illus.). 16p. (YA). (gr. 5-12). 1993. reprint ed. pap. 1.95 (*1-879424-25-8*) Nickel Pr.

Notebooks. Samuel Taylor Coleridge. Ed. by Kathleen Coburn. Incl. Vol. 1. Notebooks of Samuel Taylor Coleridge, 1794-1804. LC 56-13196. 1161p. 1957. text 175.00 (*0-691-09802-6*, Pub. by Princeton U Pr); Vol. 2. Notebooks of Samuel Taylor Coleridge, 1804-1808., **2 pts.** LC 56-13196. 1026p. 1981. text 165.00 (*0-691-09803-4*, Pub. by Princeton U Pr); Vol. 3. Notebooks of Samuel Taylor Coleridge, 1808-1819. LC 56-13196. 1652p. 1974. text 210.00 (*0-691-09804-2*, Pub. by Princeton U Pr); LC 56-13196. (Bollingen Ser.: Vol. 50). (Illus.). write for info. (*0-318-55361-9*) Princeton U Pr.

Notebooks. Jerome Rothenberg. (Illus.). 1977. pap. 8.00 (*0-87924-033-4*) Membrane Pr.

Notebooks. limited ed. Elmore Leonard. 60p. 1990. 50.00 (*0-935716-52-1*) Lord John.

Notebooks: Selections from the A. M. Klein Papers. A. M. Klein. Ed. by Zailig Pollock & Usher Caplan. (Collected Works of A. M. Klein). (Illus.). 296p. (C). 1994. text 55.00 (*0-8020-2990-6*) U of Toronto Pr.

Notebooks for an Ethics. Jean-Paul Sartre. Tr. by David Pellauer. 608p. 1992. 57.50 (*0-226-73511-7*) U Ch Pr.

Notebooks for the Grandchildren: Recollections of a Trotskyist Who Survived the Stalin Terror. Mikhail Baitalsky. Ed. & Tr. by Marilyn Vogt-Downey from RUS. LC 93-25175. (Historical Memories Ser.). 460p. (C). 1995. text 75.00 (*0-391-03829-X*) Humanities.

Notebooks for the Idiot. Fyodor Dostoyevsky. LC 67-25513. 1973. pap. text 2.95 (*0-226-15962-0*, P559) U Ch Pr.

Notebooks, Nineteen Fourteen to Nineteen Sixteen. 2nd ed. Ludwig Josef Johann Wittgenstein. Ed. by George H. Von Wright. Ed. & Tr. by G. E. Anscombe. LC 79-15686. 1980. reprint ed. 20.00 (*0-226-90429-6*) U Ch Pr.

Notebooks, Nineteen Fourteen to Nineteen Sixteen. 2nd ed. Ludwig Josef Johann Wittgenstein. Ed. by George H. Von Wright & G. E. Anscombe. LC 79-15685. (Illus.). 234p. 1984. reprint ed. pap. text 15.00 (*0-226-90447-4*) U Ch Pr.

Notebooks, 1960 to 1977. Athol Fugard. LC 83-49025. 248p. 1990. reprint ed. pap. 10.95 (*1-55936-012-7*) Theatre Comm.

Notebooks, 1935-1942. Albert Camus. Tr. by Philip M. Thody & Justin O'Brien. LC 98-162086. 225p. 1994. pap. 12.95 (*1-56924-993-8*) Marlowe & Co.

Notebooks, 1935 to 1951. Albert Camus. Tr. by Philip M. Thody & Justin O'Brien. LC 98-27433. 1998. 16.95 (*1-56924-666-1*) Marlowe & Co.

Notebooks of a Lyric Poet: Avetik S. Isahakian, 1875-1957. Avetik S. Isahakian. Tr. by Leon D. Megrian. 418p. (C). 1991. lib. bdg. 46.50 (*0-8191-8051-3*) U Pr of Amer.

Notebooks of a Naked Youth. Billy Childish. LC 98-9601. 244p. pap. 14.00 (*0-941543-21-8*) Sun Dog Pr.

Notebooks of a Naked Youth. deluxe ed. Billy Childish. LC 98-9601. 192p. 1998. 35.00 (*0-941543-22-6*) Sun Dog Pr.

Notebooks of Andre Walter. Andre Gide. 136p. 1986. 30.00 (*0-7206-5700-8*, Pub. by P Owen Ltd) Dufour.

Notebooks of Captain Coignet: Soldier of the Empire, 1799-1816. Jean-Roch Coignet. (Illus.). 292p. 1998. pap. 18.95 (*1-85367-313-7*, Pub. by Greenhill Bks) Stackpole.

Notebooks of David Ignatow. David Ignatow. Ed. by Ralph J. Mills, Jr. LC 73-13213. 395p. 1973. reprint ed. pap. 14.95 (*0-935296-22-0*, Pub. by Sheep Meadow) U Pr of New Eng.

Notebooks of Don Rigoberto. Mario Vargas Llosa. Tr. by Edith Grossman. 272p. 1999. pap. 12.95 (*0-14-028359-5*) Viking Penguin.

Notebooks of Don Rigoberto. Mario Vargas Llosa & Edith Grossman. LC 98-70961. (Illus.). 400p. 1998. 25.00 (*0-374-22327-0*) FS&G.

***Notebooks of Don Rigoberto Readers.** Alvaro Vargas Llosa. 1998. text 23.00 (*0-374-96121-2*) FS&G.

Notebooks of Edgar Degas: A Catalogue of the Thirty-Eight Note-Books in the Bibliotheque Nationale & Other Collections., 2 vols. 2nd rev. ed. Theodore Reff. LC 84-82426. (Illus.). 167p. 1985. reprint ed. lib. bdg. 195.00 (*0-87817-304-8*) Hacker.

Notebooks of Henry James. Henry James. Ed. by F. O. Matthiessen & Kenneth B. Murdock. xxviii, 455p. 1981. pap. text 34.00 (*0-226-51104-9*) U Ch Pr.

Notebooks of Lana Skimnest. Anselm Atkins. 240p. 1992. pap. 11.95 (*0-916288-33-1*) Micah Pubns.

Notebooks of Lazarus Long. Robert A. Heinlein. LC 95-21900. (Illus.). 64p. 1995. pap. 15.95 (*0-87654-473-1*) Pomegranate Calif.

Notebooks of Leonardo da Vinci. Leonardo da Vinci. Ed. & Selected by Irma A. Richter. LC 99-186641. (Illus.). 432p. 1999. pap. 9.95 (*0-19-283897-0*) OUP.

Notebooks of Leonardo Da Vinci, 1. Leonardo da Vinci. (Illus.). 860p. 1970. reprint ed. pap. 18.95 (*0-486-22572-0*) Dover.

Notebooks of Leonardo Da Vinci, 2. Leonardo da Vinci. (Illus.). 860p. 1970. reprint ed. pap. 19.95 (*0-486-22573-9*) Dover.

Notebooks of Leonardo da Vinci, Vols. 1 & 2. Leonardo da Vinci. Ed. by Jean-Paul Richter. (Illus.). 1970. 61.00 (*0-8446-4535-4*) Peter Smith.

Notebooks of Malte Laurids Brigge. Rainer Maria Rilke. Tr. by M. D. Norton. 240p. 1992. pap. 12.00 (*0-393-30881-2*) Norton.

Notebooks of Malte Laurids Brigge. Rainer Maria Rilke. Tr. by Stephen Mitchell. LC 90-50272. (Vintage International Ser.). 304p. 1990. pap. 14.00 (*0-679-73245-4*) Vin Bks.

Notebooks of Paul Brunton: Pt. 1, Human Experience; Pt. 2, The Arts in Culture, Vol. 9. Paul Brunton. LC 87-81537. (Notebooks of Paul Brunton Ser.). (Illus.). 400p. 1987. 29.95 (*0-943914-30-2*); pap. 16.95 (*0-943914-31-0*) Larson Pubns.

Notebooks of Paul Brunton: The Orient - Its Legacy to the West, Vol. 10. Paul Brunton. (Notebooks of Paul Brunton Ser.). (Illus.). 272p. 1987. 25.00 (*0-943914-32-9*); pap. 14.95 (*0-943914-33-7*) Larson Pubns.

Notebooks of Paul Brunton: The Sensitives-Dynamics & Dangers of Mysticism, Vol. 11. Paul Brunton. (Notebooks of Paul Brunton Ser.). (Illus.). 352p. 1987. 29.95 (*0-943914-35-3*); pap. 16.95 (*0-943914-34-5*) Larson Pubns.

Notebooks of Paul Brunton Vol. 1: Perspectives (Posthumous) Paul Brunton. Ed. by Paul Cash et al. LC 84-47752. 408p. 1984. 25.00 (*0-943914-09-4*); pap. 16.95 (*0-943914-12-4*) Larson Pubns.

Notebooks of Paul Brunton Vol. 1: Perspectives (Posthumous) limited ed. Paul Brunton. Ed. by Paul Cash et al. LC 84-47752. 408p. 1984. 30.00 (*0-943914-10-8*) Larson Pubns.

Notebooks of Paul Brunton, Vol. 2: The Quest. Paul Brunton. Ed. by Paul Cash & Timothy Smith. LC 85-81507. (Illus.). 384p. 1986. 29.95 (*0-943914-13-2*); pap. 16.95 (*0-943914-14-0*) Larson Pubns.

Notebooks of Paul Brunton, Vol. 3: Part 1, Practices for the Quest; Part 2, Relax & Retreat. Paul Brunton. Ed. by Paul Cash & Timothy Smith. LC 86-81030. 392p. 1986. 29.95 (*0-943914-15-9*); pap. 16.95 (*0-943914-16-7*) Larson Pubns.

Notebooks of Paul Brunton, Vol. 4: Pt. 1 - Meditation; Pt. 2 - The Body. Paul Brunton. Ed. by Paul Cash & Timothy Smith. LC 86-81949. 432p. 1986. 29.95 (*0-943914-18-3*) Larson Pubns.

Notebooks of Paul Brunton, Vol. 4: Pt. 1 - Meditation; Pt. 2 - The Body, Pt. 1: Meditation. Paul Brunton. Ed. by Paul Cash & Timothy Smith. LC 86-81949. 272p. 1986. pap. 14.95 (*0-943914-19-1*) Larson Pubns.

Notebooks of Paul Brunton, Vol. 4: Pt. 1 - Meditation; Pt. 2 - The Body, Pt. 2: The Body. Paul Brunton. Ed. by Paul Cash & Timothy Smith. LC 86-81949. 160p. 1986. pap. 12.50 (*0-943914-20-5*) Larson Pubns.

Notebooks of Paul Brunton, Vol. 5: Pt. 1 - Emotions & Ethics; Pt. 2 - The Intellect. Paul Brunton. Ed. by Paul Cash & Timothy Smith. LC 86-82480. (Illus.). 432p. 1986. 29.95 (*0-943914-21-3*); pap. 16.95 (*0-943914-22-1*) Larson Pubns.

Notebooks of Paul Brunton, Vol. 6: Pt. 1 - The Ego; Pt. 2 - From Birth to Rebirth. Paul Brunton. Ed. by Paul Cash & Timothy Smith. LC 86-82481. (Illus.). 320p. 1987. 29.95 (*0-943914-24-8*); pap. 16.95 (*0-943914-25-6*) Larson Pubns.

Notebooks of Paul Brunton, Vol. 7: Healing of the Self; Pt. 2 the Negatives, Pt. 1. Paul Brunton. Ed. by Paul Cash & Timothy Smith. LC 87-80403. (Illus.). 320p. 1987. 29.95 (*0-943914-26-4*); pap. 16.95 (*0-943914-27-2*) Larson Pubns.

Notebooks of Paul Brunton, Vol. 8: Reflections on My Life & Writings. Paul Brunton. Ed. by Timothy Smith. LC 87-80402. (Illus.). 272p. 1987. 25.00 (*0-943914-28-0*); pap. 14.95 (*0-943914-29-9*) Larson Pubns.

Notebooks of Samuel Taylor Coleridge. 1989. write for info. (*0-318-64059-7*) Princeton U Pr.

Notebooks of Samuel Taylor Coleridge, Vol. 5. Samuel Taylor Coleridge. Vol. 5. 1989. 100.00 (*0-691-09907-3*, Pub. by Princeton U Pr) Cal Prin Full Svc.

Notebooks of Samuel Taylor Coleridge, Vol. 6. 1989. 100.00 (*0-691-09908-1*) Princeton U Pr.

Notebooks of Samuel Taylor Coleridge, 1804-1808 see Notebooks

Notebooks of Samuel Taylor Coleridge, 1808-1819 see Notebooks

Notebooks of Samuel Taylor Coleridge, 1819-1826: 1819-1826, Vol. 4. Ed. by Kathleen Coburn & Merton Christensen. (Bollingen Ser.: Vol. 50, No. 4). (Illus.). 538p. (C). 1989. text 175.00 (*0-691-09906-5*, Pub. by Princeton U Pr) Cal Prin Full Svc.

Notebooks of Samuel Taylor Coleridge, 1794-1804 see Notebooks

Notebooks of the Mind: Explorations of Thinking. Vera John-Steiner. (Illus.). 288p. 1997. reprint ed. pap. 13.95 (*0-19-510896-5*) OUP.

Notebooks, 1942-1951. Albert Camus. Tr. by Philip M. Thody & Justin O'Brien. LC 98-162086. 288p. 1994. pap. 12.95 (*1-56924-967-9*) Marlowe & Co.

***Notecards.** Tova Roseman. (Tova's Garden Ser.). (Illus.). 4p. 1999. mass mkt. 2.50 (*0-943674-03-4*) Roseman Publng.

Noted Negro Women. Monroe A. Majors. LC 73-138341. (Black Heritage Library Collection). 1977. 29.95 (*0-8369-8733-0*) Ayer.

Noted Negro Women. Monroe A. Majors. 1972. 99.95 (*0-8490-0737-2*) Gordon Pr.

Noted Prophecies: Predictions, Omens, & Legends. Countess Zalinski. 168p. 1996. reprint ed. spiral bd. 15.50 (*0-7873-0983-4*) Hlth Research.

Noteforms for Surveying Measurements. Russell C. Brinker et al. LC 80-13406. (Illus.). 63p. 1981. pap. 15.00 (*0-910845-09-3*, 441) Landmark Ent.

Notemaking & Study Skills, Superwrite. 2nd ed. A. James Lemaster. (KB - Notemaking Ser.). 1995. text 37.95 (*0-538-63276-3*) S-W Pub.

Notemaking & Study Skills, Superwrite. 2nd ed. A. James Lemaster. (KB - Notemaking Ser.). 1996. wbk. ed. 12.00 (*0-538-63277-1*) S-W Pub.

Notemaking Superwrite: Alphabetic Writing System. A. James Lemaster. (KB - Notemaking Ser.). 1989. mass mkt. 15.00 (*0-538-60763-7*) S-W Pub.

Notemaking, Superwrite Alpha Writing System. 2nd ed. A. James Lemaster. (KB - Notemaking Ser.). 1995. 240.25 (*0-538-63080-9*) S-W Pub.

Notemaking, Superwrite Alpha Writing System. 2nd ed. A. James Lemaster. (KB - Notemaking Ser.). 1995. text 15.00 (*0-538-63079-5*) S-W Pub.

Noter Up. Donald J. Dunn. 1986. ring bd. 80.00 (*0-89941-439-7*, 303800) W S Hein.

Noter-Up. Ed. by J. C. Van Der Walt & F. R. Malan. (Index to Southern African Law Reports, 1828-1946: Vol. 7). 1994. write for info. (*0-409-04118-1*, MICHIE) LEXIS Pub.

Noter-Up to the Industrial Law Journal. Ed. by Frans Rautenbach. 34p. 1992. pap. write for info. (*0-7021-2813-9*, Pub. by Juta & Co) Gaunt.

Notes. (Believer's Life System Women's Edition Ser.). 1998. ring bd. 3.50 (*0-8024-6974-4*) Moody.

***Notes.** Marcel Duchamp. Ed. & Tr. by Paul Matisse from FRE. (Illus.). 128p. 2000. reprint ed. pap. 13.95 (*1-878972-34-0*, Pub. by Exact Change) Consort Bk Sales.

Notes: For Applications of Relaxed Training & Feeling Training, Set-AS. Russell E. Mason. 1975. pap. 10.00 (*0-89533-025-3*) F I Comm.

Notes: On the Making of Apocalypse Now. Eleanor Coppola. LC 91-24001. (Illus.). 292p. 1991. reprint ed. pap. 17.95 (*0-87910-150-4*) Limelight Edns.

Notes Vols. 1-50: An Index. Karen R. Little. LC 95-6324. 1995. write for info. (*0-914954-50-4*) Music Library Assn.

Notes about the United States. Edward R. Ward. 340p. 1995. write for info. (*0-9645578-0-0*) E R Ward.

Notes Algologiques: Recueil d'Observation sur les Algues, 2 parts in 1 vol. E. Bornet & G. Thuret. (Bibliotheca Phycologica Ser.: Vol. 9). (Illus.). 1969. 150.00 (*3-7682-0601-7*) Lubrecht & Cramer.

Notes & Abstracts: International Neutron Therapy Workshop. Yosh Maruyama. (Nuclear Science Applications Ser.). 56p. 1991. pap. text 101.00 (*3-7186-5122-X*, Harwood Acad Pubs) Gordon & Breach.

Notes & Anecdotes of Many Years. Joseph B. Bishop. LC 78-128210. (Essay Index Reprint Ser.). 1977. 20.95 (*0-8369-1904-1*) Ayer.

Notes & Comments - Ramesses II, Royal Inscriptions, Vol. II. K. A. Kitchen. (Ramesside Inscriptions Ser.). 684p. 1999. 150.00 (*0-631-18435-X*) Blackwell Pubs.

Notes & Comments on Cases in International Law, Commercial Law, & Arbitration. F. A. Mann. LC 92-15318. 304p. (C). 1993. text 75.00 (*0-19-825798-8*, Clarendon Pr) OUP.

Notes & Comments on "Robert's Rules" rev. ed. Jon L. Ericson. LC 90-46549. 168p. (C). 1991. pap. 14.95 (*0-8093-1704-4*) S Ill U Pr.

Notes & Comments on Scripture, 7 vols., Set. J. N. Darby. 37.00 (*0-88172-068-2*) Believers Bkshelf.

Notes & Conjectural Emendations of Certain Doubtful Passages in Shakespeare's Plays. Peter A. Daniel. LC 78-163665. reprint ed. 22.50 (*0-404-01919-6*) AMS Pr.

Notes & Essays on Shakespeare. John W. Hales. LC 72-1098. reprint ed. 45.00 (*0-404-03027-0*) AMS Pr.

Notes & Illustrations Concerning the Family History of James Smith. Lady Durning-Lawrence. (Illus.). 156p. 1991. reprint ed. pap. 24.00 (*0-8328-2170-5*) Higginson Bk Co.

***Notes & Illustrations Covering the Family History of James Smith of Coventry (b. 1731-d. 1794) & His Descendants.** fac. ed. Lady Durning-Lawrence. 156p. 1999. reprint ed. 34.00 (*0-8328-9968-2*) Higginson Bk Co.

Notes & Index to Sir Herbert Grierson's Edition of the Letters of Sir Walter Scott. Ed. by James C. Corson. 716p. 1979. text 135.00 (*0-19-812718-9*) OUP.

Notes & Jottings on Scripture. J. N. Darby. 7.95 (*0-88172-069-0*) Believers Bkshelf.

Notes & Journal of Travel in Europe, 3 vols. in 1. Washington Irving. 1991. 69.00 (*0-403-00385-7*) Scholarly.

Notes & Observations on Army Surgery: A Treatise on Gunshot Wounds. Morris Schuppert & Felix Formento. (American Civil War Surgery Ser.: No. 9). 109p. 1990. reprint ed. 75.00 (*0-930405-18-8*) Norman SF.

Notes & Problems in Applied General Equilibrium Economics. P. B. Dixon et al. (Advanced Textbooks in Economics Ser.: Vol. 32). xvi,392p. 1992. 84.75 (*0-444-88449-1*, North Holland); 170.00 incl. disk (*0-444-89379-2*) Elsevier.

Notes & Queries, Vol. 3. Compiled by Brian Whitaker. (Illus.). 192p. 1993. pap. 13.95 (*1-85702-052-9*) Fourth Estate.

Notes & Resources for Teaching "The Bedford Reader" 6th ed. 1997. 6.66 (*0-312-14496-2*) St Martin.

Notes & Reviews. Henry James. LC 68-22100. (Essay Index Reprint Ser.). 1977. reprint ed. 18.95 (*0-8369-0565-2*) Ayer.

Notes & Tones: Musician-to-Musician Interviews. rev. ed. Arthur Taylor. (Illus.). 318p. 1993. reprint ed. pap. 15.00 (*0-306-80526-X*) Da Capo.

Notes & Views of the Purple Emperor. T. R. Heslop et al. 260p. 1964. 35.00 (*0-7855-0667-5*) St Mut.

Notes Around Meadow Rise. Ed. by Heidi Beaumont. 114p. (Orig.). 1996. pap. 15.95 (*0-943025-93-1*) Cummngs & Hath.

Notes by a Naturalist. rev. ed. Henry N. Moseley. LC 72-1710. Orig. Title: Notes by a Naturalist on the Challenger. (Illus.). reprint ed. 65.00 (*0-404-08159-2*) AMS Pr.

Notes by a Naturalist on the Challenger see Notes by a Naturalist

Notes, Criticisms, & Correspondence upon Shakespeare's Plays & Actors. James H. Hackett. LC 68-21216. (Illus.). 1972. reprint ed. 24.95 (*0-405-08586-9*, Pub. by Blom Pubns) Ayer.

Notes de Voyage. Prosper Merimee & Pierre M. Auzas. (FRE.). 785p. 1989. 89.95 (*0-7859-1560-5*, 2876600366) Fr & Eur.

Notes Drawn from the River of Ecstasy. William Kistler. 96p. 1998. pap. 12.00 (*1-57178-068-8*) Coun Oak Bks.

Notes d'Un Voyage en Corse, 1840. Prosper Merimee. (FRE.). 110p. 1989. pap. 19.95 (*0-7859-1559-1*, 2876600358) Fr & Eur.

Notes et Contre-Notes. Eugene Ionesco. (Coll. Pratique de theatre). (FRE.). 1966. pap. 10.95 (*0-8288-9825-1*, F105950) Fr & Eur.

Notes et Contre-Notes. Eugene Ionesco. (Idees Ser.). (FRE.). 384p. 1970. pap. 9.95 (*2-07-035107-6*) Schoenhof.

Notes for a Late-Blooming Martyr: Poems by Marlys West. Marlys West. LC 99-31368. (Akron Series in Poetry). 80p. 1999. 24.95 (*1-884836-55-0*); pap. 13.95 (*1-884836-56-9*) U Akron Pr.

Notes for Another Life. Sue E. Bridgers. 258p. (YA). 1998. lib. bdg. 29.95 (*0-7351-0044-6*) Replica Bks.

***Notes for Friends.** Robert Adams. LC 99-29077. 80p. 1999. pap. 29.95 (*0-87081-545-8*) Univ Pr Colo.

Notes for General Physics. Gabriel Weinreich. (Illus.). 250p. (C). 1972. 12.00 (*0-911014-16-0*); pap. 6.00 (*0-911014-17-9*) Neo Pr.

Notes for Music Catalogers. Ralph Hartsock. (Soldier Creek Music Ser.: No. 3). 373p. 1994. pap. 50.00 (*0-936996-63-3*) Soldier Creek.

Notes for Parents: On the Teaching of Reading. Caleb Gattegno. 52p. 1977. pap. 3.00 (*0-87825-021-2*) Ed Solutions.

Notes for Potters in Australia. Ivan McMeekin. (Illus.). 310p. 1985. pap. 27.95 (*0-86840-209-5*, Pub. by New South Wales Univ Pr) Intl Spec Bk.

Notes for Professor Singell 's Economics 201. Larry Singell. 118p. (C). 1998. spiral bd. 25.95 (*0-7872-5101-1*, 41510101) Kendall-Hunt.

Notes for Serials Cataloging. 2nd ed. Beverley Geer et al. LC 97-36865. 200p. 1998. 38.50 (*1-56308-449-X*) Libs Unl.

Notes for Strings Bk. 1: Violin. George Zepp. Ed. by Thom Proctor. 24p. (C). 1979. pap. text 5.50 (*0-7692-1768-0*, EL02664) Wrner Bros.

Notes for the DRCOG. 3rd ed. J. Anthony & P. Kaye. (Illus.). 215p. 1995. pap. write for info. (*0-443-04713-8*) Church.

Notes for the MRCGP. 2nd ed. K. T. Palmer. (Illus.). 336p. 1992. pap. 42.95 (*0-632-02909-9*) Blackwell Sci.

Notes for the MRCGP. 3rd ed. K. T. Palmer. LC 97-46538. 1998. 39.95 (*0-86542-777-1*) Blackwell Sci.

Notes for the New Chief: A Police Chief's Manual from Law & Order Magazine. W. Cleon Skousen. (Illus.). 306p. 1972. 12.95 (*0-910558-45-0*) Ensign Pub.

Notes for the Practising Midwife. 5th rev. ed. (SEARO Regional Health Papers: No. 5). 134p. 1985. pap. text 7.00 (*92-9022-174-7*, 1930014) World Health.

Notes from a Bottle Found on the Beach at Carmel. Evan S. Connell. LC 94-43666. 1995. pap. 13.00 (*0-88001-407-5*) HarpC.

Notes from a Ceramics Laboratory. Anna O. Shepard. (Illus.). 1977. pap. 7.00 (*0-87279-952-2*) Carnegie Inst.

Notes from a Conscious Teaching. Girard Haven. 164p. Date not set. text 10.00 (*0-9645782-1-2*) Ulysses Bks.

***Notes from a Dark Street.** 2nd ed. Edward Adler. iii, 219p. 2000. per. 18.95 (*0-931642-31-0*) Lintel.

Notes from a Friend: A Quick & Simple Guide to Taking Control of Your Life. Anthony Robbins. LC 95-19436. 112p. 1995. per. 8.95 (*0-684-80056-X*) S&S Trade.

An Asterisk (*) at the beginning of an entry indicates that the title is appearing for the first time.

Notes from a Jewish Nun. Nikki Stiller. Ed. by Stanley H. Barkan. (Review Jewish Writers Chapbook Ser.: No. 7). 48p. 1992. 15.00 (*0-89304-316-8*); pap. 5.00 (*0-89304-317-6*) Cross-Cultrl NY.

Notes from a Jewish Nun: Mini Book. Nikki Stiller. Ed. by Stanley H. Barkan. (Review Jewish Writers Chapbook Ser.: No. 7). 48p. 1992. 15.00 (*0-89304-318-4*); pap. 5.00 (*0-89304-319-2*) Cross-Cultrl NY.

Notes from a Journey to Nepal. I. H. Burkill. (C). 1977. text 100.00 (*0-89771-572-1*, Pub. by Intl Bk Distr) St Mut.

Notes from a Journey to Nepal. Ed. by I. H. Burkill. x, 81p. 1977. reprint ed. 41.00 (*0-7855-3067-3*, Pub. by Intl Bk Distr) St Mut.

Notes from a Kidwatcher: Selected Writings of Yetta M. Goodman. Wilde. LC 96-11841. 316p. 1996. text 55.00 (*0-435-07212-9*) Heinemann.

Notes from a Kidwatcher: Selected Writings of Yetta M. Goodman. Ed. by Sandra Wilde. LC 96-11841. 316p. 1996. pap. text 27.00 (*0-435-08868-8*) Heinemann.

Notes from a Mother to Her Children on Getting, Being & Staying Married. Jo Lief. LC 98-45947. 1999. 0.00 (*0-8362-7867-4*) Andrews & McMeel.

***Notes from a Narrow Ridge: Religion & Bioethics.** Ed. by Dena S. Davis & Laurie Zoloth. 302p. 1999. pap. 24.95 (*1-55572-052-8*); lib. bdg. 55.00 (*1-55572-077-3*) Univ Pub Group.

Notes from a Native Son: Essays on the Appalachian Experience. Garry Barker. LC 95-4356. 216p. (Orig.). 1995. pap. 16.95 (*0-87049-900-9*) U of Tenn Pr.

Notes from a Ring Theory Conference. I. N. Herstein. LC 72-165202. (CBMS Regional Conference Series in Mathematics: Vol. 9). 38p. 1971. pap. 16.00 (*0-8218-1658-6*, CBMS/9C) Am Math.

Notes from a Sealed Room: An Israeli View of the Gulf War. Robert Werman. LC 92-1319. 224p. (C). 1992. 26.95 (*0-8093-1830-X*) S Ill U Pr.

Notes from a Small Island. Bill Bryson. LC 95-43437. 324p. 1996. 25.00 (*0-688-14725-9*, Wm Morrow) Morrow Avon.

Notes from a Small Island. Ellen Kort. (Fox Sense Collection). (Illus.). 25p. (Orig.). 1994. pap. 24.95 (*1-885520-00-X*) Fox Print.

Notes from a Small Island. Bill Bryson. LC 95-43437. 324p. 1997. reprint ed. pap. 13.50 (*0-380-72750-1*, Avon Bks) Morrow Avon.

Notes from a Thankful Heart. Contrib. by Marilynn Ham. 68p. 1990. 9.99 (*0-8341-9075-3*, MB-615) Lillenas.

Notes from a Therapist. Dorothy Wagner. 1999. pap. write for info. (*0-449-90475-X*) Fawcett.

Notes from a Traveling Childhood: Readings for Internationally Mobile Parents & Children. Ed. by Karen C. McCluskey. (Illus.). x, 122p. (Orig.). 1994. pap. 5.95 (*0-9658538-1-0*) Foreign Serv Youth.

Notes from a Wayfarer: The Autobiography of Helmut Thielicke. Helmut Thielicke. Tr. by David R. Law from GER. 416p. 1995. 24.95 (*1-55778-708-5*) Paragon Hse.

Notes from an Incomplete Revolution: Real Life since Feminism. Meredith Maran. 272p. 1998. pap. 12.95 (*0-553-37489-3*) Bantam.

Notes from an Upstairs Room. Richard F. Gillum. 63p. (Orig.). 1994. pap. 8.00 (*0-9635690-5-8*) TA Pubns.

Notes from Another India. Seabrook. LC 95-5828. 44.95 (*0-7453-0840-6*, Pub. by Pluto GBR) Stylus Pub VA.

Notes from Another India. Seabrook. 1996. pap. 13.95 (*0-7453-0839-2*, Pub. by Pluto GBR) Stylus Pub VA.

Notes from Baby Angel Grace. 2nd ed. Marian Behnke. (Illus.). 64p. (Orig.). 1995. spiral bd. 10.00 (*0-9646614-0-3*) Azure Pub.

Notes from Blue Mountain. Linda Lowery Keep. (Hannah & the Angels Ser.: No. 4). (J). (gr. 3-6). 1998. pap. 3.99 (*0-679-89161-7*, Pub. by Random Bks Yng Read) Random.

Notes from China. Joan (Maurice) Robinson. LC 64-23734. 46p. reprint ed. pap. 30.00 (*0-608-30848-X*, 200170700004) Bks Demand.

***Notes from Exile: On Being Acadian.** Clive Doucet. 320p. 1999. text 21.95 (*0-7710-2839-3*) McCland & Stewart.

Notes from Hampstead: The Writer's Notes, 1954-1971. Elias Canetti. Tr. by John Hargraves from GER. LC 97-26918. 224p. 1998. 23.00 (*0-374-22326-2*) FS&G.

Notes from Home: The Ultimate Reference Book for Homeowners. rev. ed. Lisa Hegland. 2p. 1998. pap. 24.95 (*0-9649502-4-3*) Litrlly Lisa.

***Notes from Indian Country.** Tim Giago. LC 84-91699. (Illus.). 419p. 1999. pap. 25.54 (*0-9673938-0-9*) Giago Bk.

Notes from Little Lakes: The Story of a Family & Fifteen Acres. Mel Ellis. Ed. by Ted J. Rulseh. LC 96-85950. (Illus.). 261p. 1996. 23.95 (*0-9653381-0-X*) Cabin Bkshelf.

***Notes from Madoo: Making a Garden in the Hamptons.** Robert Dash. LC 00-20062. 256p. 2000. 24.00 (*0-618-01692-9*) HM.

Notes from Midlife & Other Poems. Lyman K. Randall. LC 86-800088. 70p. 1986. pap. 5.95 (*0-317-52124-1*) Freeman Farms.

***Notes from Millennium Beach: Encouraging, Inspiring & Amusing Words & Pictures to Ease You into the Coming 1,000 Years.** Bob Young. LC 98-31264. (Illus.). 64p. 1999. pap. 22.00 (*0-932727-11-5*, N Paradigm Bks) Hope Pub Hse.

Notes from Mom. Josie Stewart & Lynn Salem. (Seedlings Ser.). (Illus.). 16p. (J). (gr. k-1). 1992. pap. 3.75 (*1-880612-01-1*) Seedling Pubns.

Notes from Myself: A Guide to Creative Journal Writing. Anne Hazard Aldrich. LC 97-6786. 160p. 1998. pap. 11.95 (*0-7867-0433-0*) Carroll & Graf.

Notes from New Zealand: A Book of Travel & Natural History. Edward Kanze. 88p. 1995. pap. 12.95 (*0-8050-2665-7*) H Holt & Co.

Notes from New Zealand: A Book of Travel & Natural History. Edward Kanze. (Illus.). 288p. 1995. 24.95 (*0-8050-1990-1*, J Macrae Bks) H Holt & Co.

***Notes from New Zealand: A Book of Travel & Natural History.** Edward Kanze. 236p. 1999. reprint ed. pap. text 13.00 (*0-7881-6246-2*) DIANE Pub.

Notes from Rome. R. Lanciani. (Illus.). 464p. 1988. pap. 30.00 (*0-904152-12-X*, Pub. by British Schl Rome) David Brown.

Notes from Sick Rooms. Julia Stephen. 65p. 1980. pap. 3.50 (*0-913006-16-5*) Puckerbrush.

***Notes from Skinner's Elbow.** Michael Koehler. Ed. by Gary C. Busha. 36p. 1999. pap. 5.00 (*1-891725-08-4*) Wolfsong Pubns.

Notes from Temuco see Cuadernos de Temuco

Notes from the Boundless Frontier: Reflections on the Macrobiotic Diet. Philosophy & Way of Life. Edward Esko. 112p. 1993. pap. 7.95 (*0-9628528-8-0*) One Peaceful World.

***Notes from the Closet.** Barbara Roseman. 2000. pap. 9.95 (*1-56167-564-4*) Am Lit Soc.

Notes from the Coach Vol. 1: The Power of a Pro-Vision Life. Ed Cerny. Ed. by Margaret Locklair. (Illus.). 105p. 1997. pap. 12.00 (*0-9661020-0-2*) Coachs Corner.

Notes from the Colorado Rockies: Living in a Small Town, Today & Yesterday. large type ed. Annie Cass. 93p. 1996. pap. 9.95 (*0-9649137-0-4*) Oldham Pubng.

Notes from the Commentary of Chandrakanta see Vaisesika Sutras of Kanada: With Commentary of Sankara Misra & Extracts from Gloss, of Jayanarayana & Notes from Commentary of Candrakanta

Notes from the Cosmos: A Futurist's Insights into the World of Dream Prophecy & Intuition. Gordon-Michael Scallion. LC 97-73762. (Illus.). 346p. (Orig.). 1997. pap. 16.95 (*0-9619709-0-1*) Matrix Inst.

Notes from the Countries of Blood-Red Flowers. Macdara Woods. LC 94-153292. 96-p. 1994. pap. 11.95 (*1-873790-44-9*) Dufour.

Notes from the Exile. David Barton. LC 82-84118. 70p. (Orig.). 1983. pap. 3.95 (*0-941692-05-1*) Elysian Pr.

Notes from the Field in Commmunication for Child Survival. Ed. by Renata E. Seidel. LC 93-17710. 1993. 15.00 (*0-89492-102-9*) Acad Educ Dev.

Notes from the Green Room: Coping with Stress & Anxiety in Musical Performance. Paul G. Salmon & Robert G. Meyer. LC 98-17775. (Health & Psychology Ser.). 240p. 1998. reprint ed. pap. 24.95 (*0-7879-4378-9*) Jossey-Bass.

Notes from the Guatemalan Highlands. rev. ed. Parmer Snider. pap. 9.95 (*1-884062-00-8*) Zotz Pr.

Notes from the Heart: A Celebration of Traditional Irish Music. P.J. Curtis. (Illus.). 180p. 1995. pap. 13.95 (*1-898142-07-6*, Pub. by Torc) Dufour.

Notes from the Hidden Years: Reflections on Spirituality, Politics & Other Stuff. Chuck Cutolo. LC 99-93215. 230p. 1999. pap. 16.95 (*0-9672093-0-7*) Denise Pubns.

Notes from the M. O. B. (Mother of the Bride) Planning Tips & Advice from a Wedding Day Veteran. Sherri Goodall. LC 99-90197. (Illus.). 114p. 1999. pap. 12.95 (*0-9671235-0-X*) Pennythought Pr.

Notes from the Margins of an Old Preacher's Bible. Dun Gordy. 93p. 1997. pap. 9.95 (*1-884707-67-X*) Lifestyles.

Notes from the Material World: Contemporary Photomontage. Contrib. by Nancy Bless. LC 92-44897. (Illus.). 36p. 1992. pap. 14.95 (*0-932718-34-5*) Kohler Arts.

Notes from the Minefield: United States Intervention in Lebanon & the Middle East. Irene Gendzier. (Illus.). 400p. 1996. 44.50 (*0-231-10474-X*) Col U Pr.

***Notes from the Minefield: United States Intervention in Lebanon & the Middle East, 1945-1958.** Irene Gendzier. (Interventions Ser.). 504p. 1998. pap. text 29.00 (*0-8133-6689-5*, Pub. by Westview) HarpC.

Notes from the Nest. 2nd ed. Kurt Brecht. (Illus.). 41p. 1988. pap. 4.00 (*1-879188-00-7*) Dirty Rotten Pr.

Notes from the Netshed. Armor de Comos. (Illus.). 256p. 1997. pap. 17.95 (*1-55017-172-0*) Harbour Pub Co.

***Notes from the New Chitlin Circuit.** Kwasi Ramsey. iv, 124p. 1999. pap. 11.95 (*0-9671082-1-7*, Division of Wrds) Black Alchemist.

***Notes from the North: Incorporating a Brief History of the Scots & the English.** Emma Wood. 192p. 1999. pap. 14.95 (*0-946487-46-4*, Pub. by Luath Pr Ltd) Midpt Trade.

Notes from the Nursing Home. Adele Kenny. (Xtras Ser.: No. 10). vi, 32p. (Orig.). 1982. pap. 2.50 (*0-89120-023-1*) From Here.

Notes from the Other Side of Night. Juliana G. Pilon. LC 94-7701. 1994. reprint ed. pap. text 14.95 (*0-8191-9510-3*) U Pr of Amer.

Notes from the Periphery: Marginality in North American Literature & Culture, Vol. 63. Susan Castillo. (American University Studies: American Literature: No. XXIV). XIII, 196p. (C). 1995. pap. 29.95 (*0-8204-2757-8*) P Lang Pubng.

***Notes from the Pianist's Bench.** Boris Berman. LC 00-36514. (Illus.). 288p. 2000. 30.00 (*0-300-08375-0*) Yale U Pr.

Notes from the Road: Adventure & Commentary Through the Inner Space of America by a Homeless on Wheels. Karin Zirk. (Illus.). 42p. (Orig.). 1993. pap. text 4.00 (*0-9635540-4-2*) Mutant Species.

Notes from the Shore. Jennifer Ackerman. 208p. 1996. pap. 11.95 (*0-14-017788-4*, Penguin Bks) Viking Penguin.

Notes from the Song of Life: A Spiritual Companion. rev. ed. Tolbert McCarroll. LC 77-7135. (Illus.). 144p. (Orig.). 1995. reprint ed. pap. 8.95 (*0-89087-200-7*) Celestial Arts.

Notes from the Underground see Three Short Novels of Dostoyevsky

Notes from the Underground. Fyodor Dostoyevsky. 1976. 20.95 (*0-8488-0347-7*) Amereon Ltd.

Notes from the Underground. Fyodor Dostoyevsky. (Thrift Editions Ser.). 96p. 1992. reprint ed. pap. 1.00 (*0-486-27053-X*) Dover.

Notes from the Underground: The Ralph de Toledano-Whittaker Chambers Letters, 1949-1960. Ralph De Toledano & Whittaker Chambers. LC 97-27563. 332p. 1997. 24.95 (*0-89526-425-0*) Regnery Pub.

Notes from the Underground & A Confession. Fyodor Dostoyevsky & Leo Tolstoy. Ed. by A. D. Briggs. 256p. 1994. pap. text 6.50 (*0-460-87448-9*, Everyman's Classic Lib) Tuttle Pubng.

Notes from the Underground & The Double. Fyodor Dostoyevsky. 1991. pap. 10.95 (*0-452-01093-4*, Mer) NAL.

Notes from the Underground & The Double. large type ed. Fyodor Dostoyevsky. 515p. 1997. reprint ed. lib. bdg. 24.00 (*0-939495-15-5*) North Bks.

Notes from the Underground & The Gambler. Fyodor Dostoyevsky. Tr. by Jane Kentish. (Oxford World's Classics Ser.). 320p. 1999. pap. 7.95 (*0-19-283626-9*) OUP.

Notes from the Underground Notes. James L. Roberts. (Cliffs Notes Ser.). 72p. 1970. pap. 4.95 (*0-8220-0900-5*, Cliff) IDG Bks.

***Notes from the Underground; The Double.** Fyodor Dostoyevsky. 323p. 1998. reprint ed. lib. bdg. 24.00 (*1-58287-053-5*) North Bks.

Notes from the Wild. Bernie Krause. (Illus.). 80p. 1996. 18.95 incl. audio compact disk (*1-55961-385-8*, Ellipsis Arts) Relaxtn Co.

Notes from under Burbia. T. Thrasher. ix, 46p. 1995. pap. 6.00 (*1-888662-00-X*) Vinegar Hill.

Notes from Underground. Eric Bogosian. LC 97-40724. 176p. 1997. pap. text 11.95 (*1-55936-142-5*) Theatre Comm.

Notes from Underground. Fyodor Dostoyevsky. Tr. by Mirra Ginsburg from RUS. 192p. 1983. mass mkt. 4.95 (*0-553-21144-7*, Bantam Classics) Bantam.

Notes from Underground. Fyodor Dostoyevsky. Tr. by Richard Pevear & Larissa Volokhonsky. LC 92-32581. 160p. 1994. pap. 10.00 (*0-679-73452-X*) Knopf.

Notes from Underground. Fyodor Dostoyevsky. Ed. & Tr. by Michael R. Katz. LC 88-1062. (Critical Editions Ser.). 256p. (C). 1989. pap. text 11.25 (*0-393-95744-6*) Norton.

Notes from Underground: Rock Music Counterculture in Russia. Thomas Cushman. LC 95-1541. (SUNY Series in the Sociology of Culture). 403p. (C). 1995. text 59.50 (*0-7914-2543-6*); pap. text 19.95 (*0-7914-2544-4*) State U NY Pr.

Notes from Underground: Zines & the Politics of Alternative Culture. Stephen Duncombe. LC 97-29603. 1997. pap. 19.00 (*1-85984-158-9*, Pub. by Verso) Norton.

Notes from Underground & Selected Stories: White Nights, Dream of a Ridiculous Man, House of the Dead. Fyodor Dostoyevsky. Tr. by Andrew R. MacAndrew. 1961. mass mkt. 4.95 (*0-451-52376-8*, CE1823, Sig Classics) NAL.

Notes from Underground & the Double. Fyodor Dostoyevsky. Tr. by Jessie Coulson. (Classics Ser.). 288p. 1972. pap. 11.99 (*0-14-044252-9*, Penguin Classics) Viking Penguin.

Notes from Within: A Souls Awakening. Mark Conrad. 240p. 1998. 18.95 (*1-891569-22-8*, 00041198) Pura Vida.

Notes froma Ring Theory Conference. I. N. Herstein. LC 72-165202. (Regional Conference Series in Mathematics: Vol. 9). 43p. reprint ed. pap. 30.00 (*0-608-10504-X*, 205278700009) Bks Demand.

Notes, Historical & Biographical, Concerning Elizabeth-Town: Its Eminent Men, Churches & Ministers. Nicholas Murray. (Illus.). 174p. 1997. reprint ed. lib. bdg. 26.50 (*0-8328-6048-4*) Higginson Bk Co.

Notes Historical & Biographical, Concerning Elizabeth-Town, New Jersey: Its Eminent Men, Churches & Ministers. Nicholas Murray. xviii, 179p. 1991. reprint ed. pap. 17.50 (*1-55613-392-8*) Heritage Bk.

Notes, Historical, Descriptive & Personall, of Livermore in Androscoggin (Formerly in Oxford) County. (Illus.). 169p. 1997. reprint ed. lib. bdg. 25.00 (*0-8328-5869-2*) Higginson Bk Co.

Notes Illustrating the Military Geography of the Unites States, 1813-1880. United States Adjutant-General's Office. Ed. by Raphael P. Thian & John M. Carroll. LC 79-63158. 242p. reprint ed. pap. 75.10 (*0-8357-7731-6*, 203608800002) Bks Demand.

Notes in Geometry. E. G. Rees. (Universitext Ser.). (Illus.). 109p. 1993. 42.95 (*0-387-12053-X*) Spr-Verlag.

Notes in the Lunchbox: How to Help Your Child Succeed at School. Barbara E. Reider. Ed. by Kathleen Reimer & Mary Ritter. (Illus.). 144p. (Orig.). 1993. pap. 9.95 (*0-9621156-1-4*) Sierra Hse Pub.

Notes in Verse. Melvin Diamond. Ed. & Illus. by Donna Norton. LC 96-4627. 1996. pap. 6.95 (*0-910733-03-1*) ICTL Pubns.

***Notes, 1998.** Paul Nervy. 102p. 1999. pap. 6.00 (*0-9670613-6-9*) Protean Pub.

***Notes, 1999.** Paul Nervy. 80p. 2000. pap. 6.00 (*0-9670613-8-5*) Protean Pub.

Notes of a Busy Life, 2 vols., Set. Joseph B. Foraker. 1993. reprint ed. lib. bdg. 150.00 (*0-7812-5364-0*) Rprt Serv.

Notes of a Christian: A Book of the Apostocate. John L. Kelleher. 74p. 1984. 6.95 (*0-89697-209-7*) Intl Univ Pr.

Notes of a Crucian Son. Richard A. Schrader, Sr. & Richard A. Schrader, Jr. LC 89-90972. (Illus.). 90p. (Orig.). 1989. pap. 7.65 (*0-9622987-0-0*) R A Schrader.

Notes of a Daughter from the Old Country. Melanie Perish. 15p. (Orig.). (C). 1978. pap. 1.75 (*0-934238-04-9*) Motheroot.

Notes of a Desolate Man. Zhu Tianwen. LC 98-32400. 10p. 1999. 19.95 (*0-231-11608-X*) Col U Pr.

***Notes of a Desolate Man.** Chu Tien-Wen. Tr. by Howard Goldblatt & Sylvia Li-chun Lin. 2000. reprint ed. pap. 14.95 (*0-231-11609-8*) Col U Pr.

Notes of a Director. Alexander Tairov. LC 68-31042. (Books of the Theatre: No. 7). 1983. pap. 19.95 (*0-87024-309-8*) U of Miami Pr.

Notes of a Dirty Old Man. 2nd ed. Charles Bukowski. LC 73-84226. 1973. pap. 12.95 (*0-87286-074-4*) City Lights.

Notes of a Dreamer. Dave Schultz. LC 92-73022. (Illus.). 300p. (Orig.). 1992. pap. 10.00 (*0-937393-16-9*) Fred Pr.

Notes of a Happy Sociologist. Jack N. Porter. 30p. (Orig.). 1980. pap. 5.00 (*0-932270-04-2*) Spencer Pr.

Notes of a Hunter. unabridged ed. Ivan Sergeevich Turgenev. (World Classic Literature Ser.). (RUS.). pap. 8.95 (*2-87714-278-7*, Pub. by Bookking Intl) Distribks Inc.

Notes of a Jewish Convert to the LDS Church: Conversion of a Soul. Marlena Tanya Muchnick. 83p. 1998. mass mkt. 12.95 (*0-89716-803-8*, Peanut Btr Pubng) Elton-Wolf Pub.

Notes of a Journey from Cornhill to Grand Cairo. William Makepeace Thackeray. (Illus.). 160p. (Orig.). 1994. pap. 29.95 (*1-873054-01-7*) Seven Hills Bk.

Notes of a Journey in America & Letters from Illinois. 3rd ed. Morris Birkbeck. LC 71-119545. 1971. reprint ed. 45.00 (*0-678-00686-5*) Kelley.

Notes of a Moscow Pianist. Dmitry I. Paperno. LC 97-21882. (Illus.). 238p. 1998. 27.95 (*1-57467-034-4*, Amadeus Pr) Timber.

Notes of a Native Son. 2nd ed. James Baldwin. LC 90-52598. (African-American Studies). 176p. 1984. reprint ed. pap. 13.00 (*0-8070-6431-9*) Beacon Pr.

Notes of a Nervous Man. James Lileks. Ed. by Jane Chelius. 240p. 1992. reprint ed. pap. 10.00 (*0-671-73702-3*) PB.

Notes of a Pianist. Louis M. Gottschalk. LC 79-1260. (Music Reprint Ser.). 1979. reprint ed. 55.00 (*0-306-79508-6*) Da Capo.

Notes of a Pianist. Louis M. Gottschalk. (American Biography Ser.). 420p. 1991. reprint ed. lib. bdg. 89.00 (*0-7812-8150-4*) Rprt Serv.

Notes of a Piano Tuner. Denele P. Campbell. LC 96-49856. 160p. 1997. 16.95 (*1-56164-127-8*) Pineapple Pr.

Notes of a Provincial Wildfowler. Sergei Aksakov. Tr. by Kevin Windle from RUS. LC 98-16062. (Studies in Russian Literature & Theory). (Illus.). 216p. 1998. text 29.95 (*0-8101-1391-0*) Northwestern U Pr.

Notes of a Racial Caste Baby: Color Blindness & the End of Affirmative Action. Bryan K. Fair. 224p. 1999. reprint ed. pap. 17.95 (*0-8147-2652-6*) NYU Pr.

Notes of a Racial Caste Baby: Colorblindness & the End of Affirmative Action. Bryan K. Fair. LC 96-25394. 272p. (C). 1997. text 45.00 (*0-8147-2651-8*) NYU Pr.

Notes of a Red Guard. Eduard M. Dune. Ed. & Tr. by Diane P. Koenker & S. A. Smith from RUS. LC 92-18937. (Illus.). 328p. (C). 1993. text 37.50 (*0-252-01972-5*); pap. text 16.95 (*0-252-06277-9*) U of Ill Pr.

Notes of a Refugee: Poems. Harvey M. Plotnick. LC 92-14940. 64p. 1992. pap. 14.95 (*0-7734-0002-8*, Mellen Poetry Pr) E Mellen.

Notes of a Seaplane Instructor: An Instructional Guide to Seaplane Flying. Burke Mees. LC 97-39177. (Focus Series Book). (Illus.). 1998. pap. 19.95 (*1-56027-310-0*, ASA-NSI) ASA Inc.

Notes of a Son & Brother see Works of Henry James Jr.: Collected Works

Notes of a Soviet Doctor. 2nd ed. Gravrill S. Pondoey. Tr. by Basil Haigh. LC 59-9232. 248p. reprint ed. pap. 76.90 (*0-608-30200-7*, 202065200018) Bks Demand.

Notes of a Soviet Master. A. Ilyin-Genevsky. Ed. by D. A. Brandreth. Tr. by B. Cafferty from RUS. (Great Masters Ser.).Tr. of Zapiski Sovetskogo Mastera. 54p. 1986. 24.00 (*0-939433-00-1*) Caissa Edit.

Notes of a Tour in the Manufacturing Districts of Lancashire. 2nd ed. William C. Taylor. LC 67-131562. (Reprints of Economic Classics Ser.). viii, 331p. 1968. reprint ed. 27.50 (*0-678-05088-0*) Kelley.

Notes of a Twenty-Five Years' Service in the Hudson's Bay Territory, Vol. 19. John McLean. Ed. by W. S. Wallace. LC 68-28607. 402p. 1968. reprint ed. lib. bdg. 65.00 (*0-8371-5057-4*, MCNS, Greenwood Pr) Greenwood.

Notes of a Villager: A Mexican Poet's Youth & Revolution. Jose R. Romero. Tr. by John Mitchell & Ruth M. de Aguilar from SPA. LC 88-4042. 222p. 1988. 15.95 (*0-917635-04-3*); pap. 9.95 (*0-917635-05-1*) Plover Pr.

Notes of a Voyage to California Via Cape Horn, Together with Scenes in el Dorado, in the Years 1849-50. Samuel C. Upham. LC 72-9472. (Far Western Frontier Ser.). (Illus.). 598p. 1973. reprint ed. 40.95 (*0-405-04999-4*) Ayer.

Notes of a White Black Woman: Race, Color, Community. Judy Scales-Trent. LC 94-45176. 206p. 1995. 22.50 (*0-271-01430-X*) Pa St U Pr.

Notes of an Aircraft Designer. Alexander Yakovlev. Tr. by Albert Zdornykh. LC 72-169445. (Literature & History of Aviation Ser.). 1972. reprint ed. 32.95 (*0-405-03788-0*) Ayer.

Notes of an Anatomist. Frank Gonzalez-Crussi. LC 85-776. 96p. 1985. 12.95 (*0-15-167285-7*) Harcourt.

Notes of an Itinerant Policeman. Josiah Flynt. LC 72-5504. (Select Bibliographies Reprint Ser.). 1977. reprint ed. 23.95 (*0-8369-6907-3*) Ayer.

Notes of Debates in the Federal Convention of 1787. James Madison. 720p. 1987. reprint ed. pap. 19.95 (*0-393-30405-1*) Norton.

N

Notes of Debates in the Federal Convention of 1787. rev. ed. James Madison. LC 84-5080. 718p. 1985. text 50.00 (*0-8214-0777-5*) Ohio U Pr.

Notes of Departure. Katherine Soniat. LC 85-51607. 1985. pap. 6.95 (*0-317-47689-0*) Walt Whitman.

Notes of Infinite Permutation Groups. M. Bhattacharjee. LC 98-39226. (Lecture Notes in Mathematics Ser.: Vol. 169). 1999. pap. write for info. (*3-540-64965-4*) Spr-Verlag.

Notes of Jane Heap. 158p. 1994. 20.00 (*0-89756-019-1*) Two Rivers.

Notes of Seven Decades. rev. ed. Antal Dorati. LC 80-27568. (Illus.). 379p. reprint ed. pap. 117.50 (*0-608-10523-6*, 205443400009) Bks Demand.

Notes of Sixty Years: The Autobiography of Florence Kelley. Florence Kelley. LC 85-82668. (Illus.). 100p. 1985. pap. 17.50 (*0-88286-093-3*) C H Kerr.

Notes of Some Wanderings. Nivedita. 3.00 (*0-87481-185-6*) Vedanta Pr.

Notes of the Bacon-Shakespeare Question. Charles Allen. 1973. 59.95 (*0-8490-0738-0*) Gordon Pr.

Notes of the Terry Family in the United States: Mainly Descendants from Samuel of Springfield, Massachusetts, but Including Some Descendants from Stephen of Windsor, Connecticut, Thomas of Freetown, Massachusetts, Etc. S. Terry. 351p. 1989. reprint ed. pap. 52.50 (*0-8328-1161-0*); reprint ed. lib. bdg. 60.50 (*0-8328-1160-2*) Higginson Bk Co.

Notes of the Treaty Carried on at Ripon Between King Charles First & the Covenanters of Scotland, A. D. 1640. John Borough. Ed. by John Bruce. (Camden Society, London. Publications, First Ser.: No. 100). reprint ed. 30.00 (*0-404-50200-8*) AMS Pr.

Notes of Travel: Recollections of Majunga, Zanzibar, Musca, Aden, Mocha, & Other Eastern Ports. Joseph B. Osgood. LC 72-5546. (Black Heritage Library Collection). 1977. reprint ed. 28.95 (*0-8369-9146-X*) Ayer.

***Notes on a Broken Chandelier (Poems by Kjersti A. Reed)** Kjersti A. Reed. 33p. 2000. pap. 6.00 (*1-882983-45-9*) March Street Pr.

***Notes on a Cowardly Lion: The Biography of Bert Lahr.** John Lahr. LC 99-43657. (Illus.). 417p. 2000. pap. 16.95 (*0-520-22304-7*, Pub. by U CA Pr) Cal Prin Full Svc.

Notes on a Dream. Maxwell Anderson. Ed. by Laurence G. Avery. LC 70-633716. (Illus.). 1971. 10.00 (*0-87959-056-4*) U of Tex H Ransom Ctr.

Notes on a House in Westconnaug, It's People & History. Edward H. Balfour. LC 98-92911. (Illus.). 114p. 1998. pap. 9.95 (*1-57502-818-2*) Morris Pubng.

Notes on a Journey in America: From the Coast of Virginia to the Territory of Illinois. Morris Birkbeck. (American Biography Ser.). 156p. 1991. reprint ed. lib. bdg. 59.00 (*0-7812-8020-6*) Rprt Serv.

***Notes on a Mandala.** Laurie L. Patten & David L. Haberman. 312p. 2000. 40.00 (*1-889119-56-3*) Seven Bridges.

Notes on a Refrigerator Door. Jo H. Haring. LC 92-61665. 1992. pap. 11.95 (*0-9634369-0-2*) Tincup Pr.

Notes on a Tour in America, August 7th to November 17th, 1877. Vivian H. Hussey. LC 73-13154. (Foreign Travelers in America, 1810-1935 Ser.). (Illus.). 276p. 1974. reprint ed. 21.95 (*0-405-05476-9*) Ayer.

Notes on ACI 318-95 Building Code Requirements for Structural Concrete with Design Applications. 5th rev. ed. Portland Cement Association Staff. Ed. by S. K. Ghosh & Basile G. Rabbat. (Illus.). 920p. 1996. pap. 30.00 (*0-89312-144-4*, EB070D) Portland Cement.

Notes on ACI 318-83. 1989. 52.00 (*0-317-99890-0*, EB070D) ACI.

Notes on Active Pedagogy: A Supplement to the Active Learning Modules Produce by the AAG/CCG2. Susanne Moser & Susan Hanson. (Active Learning Modules on the Human Dimensions of Global Change Ser.). (Illus.). 30p. (C). 1997. pap. text 3.00 (*0-89291-228-6*) Assn Am Geographers.

Notes on an Important Nineteenth Century Collection of Central & North American Birds Made by N. S. Goss. Marion A. Jenkinson & Robert M. Mengel. (Occasional Papers: No. 81). 10p. 1979. pap. 1.00 (*0-317-04603-9*) U KS Nat Hist Mus.

Notes on an Unhurried Journey. John A. Taylor. LC 91-13368. 225p. 1991. 17.95 (*0-941423-63-8*) FWEW.

Notes on an Unhurried Journey. large type ed. John A. Taylor. LC 92-40878. (General Ser.). 352p. 1993. lib. bdg. 19.95 (*0-8161-5716-2*, G K Hall Lrg Type) Mac Lib Ref.

Notes on an Urban Ecology. Robert R. Ward. 180p. 1998. pap. write for info. (*1-891239-01-5*) Primeval Pr.

Notes on Anchor Work. D. E. Walsh. (Illus.). 97p. 1985. pap. 27.95 (*1-879778-71-8*, BK-490) Marine Educ.

Notes on Architecture. Information Design, Inc. (Illus.). 548p. pap. 8.95 (*1-56052-057-4*) Crisp Pubns.

Notes on Asylums for the Insane in America. John C. Bucknill. LC 73-2391. (Mental Illness & Social Policy; the American Experience Ser.). 1973. reprint ed. 14.95 (*0-405-05199-9*) Ayer.

Notes on Blood Meridian. John Sepich & Shelby Foote. (Illus.). 191p. (Orig.). 1993. pap. 12.50 (*0-9638927-0-3*) Bellarmine Coll.

Notes on C. J. Sauthier & Lord Percy. Mark Babinski et al. LC 98-183871. 50p. 1997. write for info. (*0-9656301-0-2*) Krinder Peak.

Notes on C. J. Sauthier & Lord Percy: With Listing of Maps of the State of New York Drawn by Simeon De Witt & David H. Burr. expanded ed. Mark Babinski et al. LC 97-76636. 65p. 1997. write for info. (*0-9656301-3-7*) Krinder Peak.

Notes on Central America. Ephraim G. Squier. LC 70-172443. (Illus.). reprint ed. 62.50 (*0-404-06221-0*) AMS Pr.

Notes on Chasta Costa Phonology & Morphology. Edward Sapir. (Anthropological Publications: Vol. II/2). (Illus.). 72p. 1914. pap. 15.00 (*0-686-24092-8*) U Museum Pubns.

Notes on Chaucer: A Commentary on the Prologue & Six of the Canterbury Tales. Henry B. Hinckley. LC 79-146829. (Studies in Chaucer: No. 6). 1972. reprint ed. lib. bdg. 75.00 (*0-8383-0569-5*) M S G Haskell Hse.

Notes on Child Study. Edward Lee Thorndike. LC 74-21432. (Classics in Child Development Ser.). 162p. 1979. reprint ed. 21.95 (*0-405-06481-0*) Ayer.

Notes on Chopin. Andre Gide. Tr. by Bernard Frechtman from FRE. LC 78-3640. 126p. 1978. reprint ed. lib. bdg. 35.00 (*0-313-20371-7*, GINC, Greenwood Pr) Greenwood.

Notes on Clinical Biochemistry. J. K. Candlish & M. J. Crook. 272p. 1993. text 55.00 (*981-02-1065-5*); pap. text 28.00 (*981-02-1066-3*) World Scientific Pub.

Notes on Cochiti, New Mexico. Noel Dumarest. LC 20-23196. (American Anthropological Association Memoirs Ser.: No. 27). 1919. 25.00 (*0-527-00526-6*) Periodicals Srv.

Notes on Complex Function Theory. Donald Sarason. (Illus.). ix, 145p. (Orig.). (C). 1994. pap. text 17.00 (*0-9655211-2-5*) H Helson.

Notes on Conductors & Conducting. T. R. Croger. 76p. 1991. reprint ed. lib. bdg. 59.00 (*0-7812-9359-6*) Rprt Serv.

Notes on Corresponding Symbols in Various Parts of the World see Study of Navajo Symbolism

Notes on Cuba. John G. Wurdemann. 359p. Date not set. 45.95 (*0-405-01720-0*) Arno Press.

Notes on Cuba. John G. Wurdemann. 12.95 (*0-405-18976-1*, 16893) Ayer.

Notes on Double Knitting. rev. ed. Beverly Royce. Ed. by Meg Swansen. (Illus.). 85p. 1994. pap. 17.00 (*0-942018-06-0*) Schoolhouse WI.

***Notes on Drowning.** Rob McLennan. LC 98-215213. 80p. 1998. pap. 10.50 (*0-921411-75-8*) Genl Dist Srvs.

Notes on Dryden's Virgil (1698) Luke Milbourne. LC 74-16036. (Life & Times of Seven Major British Writers Ser.). 232p. 1974. write for info. (*0-8240-1236-4*) Garland.

Notes on Duels & Duelling: Alphabetically Arranged with a Preliminary Historical Essay. Lorenzo Sabine. 1977. text 22.95 (*0-8369-8191-X*, 8329) Ayer.

Notes on Eastern Cretan Phonology: A Corpus-Based Study. Kimmo Granqvist. LC 97-165132. (Acta Universitatis Stockholmiensis Ser.: Vol. VIII). (Illus.). 150p. 1997. pap. 47.50 (*91-22-01758-5*, Pub. by Almqvist Wiksell) Coronet Bks.

Notes on Educational Problems in Communist China, 1941-47. Michael Lindsay et al. LC 77-10962. 194p. 1977. reprint ed. lib. bdg. 55.00 (*0-8371-9815-1*, LINE, Greenwood Pr) Greenwood.

Notes on Eight Papago Songs. fac. ed. E. G. Stricklen. (University of California Publications in American Archaeology & Ethnology: Vol. 20: 17). 6p. (C). 1923. reprint ed. pap. text 0.94 (*1-55567-253-1*) Coyote Press.

Notes on Elizabethan Dramatists with Conjectural Emendations of the Text. Karl Elze. LC 70-166027. reprint ed. 31.50 (*0-404-02327-4*) AMS Pr.

Notes on Epistemology. Walter F. Cunningham. LC 59-33496. (Fordham Philosophy Ser.). 204p. reprint ed. pap. 63.30 (*0-7837-5574-0*, 204535600005) Bks Demand.

Notes on Exposure Limits for Non-Ionising Radiations. Donald Hughes. 69p. 1997. pap. 150.00 (*0-948237-24-4*, Pub. by H&H Sci Cnslts) St Mut.

Notes on Fallacies of American Protectionists. Francis Lieber. (Neglected American Economists Ser.). 1974. lib. bdg. 61.00 (*0-8240-1018-3*) Garland.

Notes on Fermat's Last Theorem. Alf Van Der Poorten. LC 95-46319. (Canadian Mathematical Society Series & Advanced Texts). 240p. 1996. 54.95 (*0-471-06261-8*) Wiley.

Notes on First Corinthians. W. Kelly. 9.95 (*0-88172-094-1*) Believers Bkshelf.

Notes on Fishing. Sergei Aksakov. Tr. by Thomas P. Hodge. LC 97-14128. 280p. 1997. 30.00 (*0-8101-1366-X*) Northwestern U Pr.

Notes on Fugue for Beginners. Edward J. Dent. (Music Book Index Ser.). 47p. 1992. reprint ed. lib. bdg. 59.00 (*0-7812-9504-1*) Rprt Serv.

Notes on Geometric Transformations. Ali R. Amir-Moez. LC 97-45226. (Illus.). 127p. 1998. text 20.00 (*0-936428-16-3*) Polygonal Pub.

Notes on Giant Fasciolarias see Palaeontographica Americana: Vol. 2

Notes on Grammar. Dee A. Holisky. LC 92-28791. 544p. (Orig.). 1997. pap. 49.95 (*0-914061-31-3*) Orchises Pr.

Notes on Graphic Design & Visual Communications. rev. ed. Gregg Berryman. LC 90-21563. (Illus.). 46p. (C). 1990. pap. 8.95 (*1-56052-044-2*) Crisp Pubns.

Notes on Greek Philosophy from Thales to Aristotle. Anthony Preus. 306p. 1996. pap. 17.00 (*1-883058-09-0*, SAG&IP) Global Pubns.

***Notes on Hampton Mansion.** 2nd rev. ed. Charles E. Peterson & Sally Sims Stokes. LC 00-34853. (Illus.). 2000. pap. write for info. (*0-9655233-4-9*) Univ MD Coll Pk.

Notes on Hessian Soldiers Surname Z. Clifford N. Smith. 1992. pap. 20.00 (*0-915162-89-X*) Westland Pubns.

Notes on Hessian Soldiers Surnames A-F. Clifford N. Smith. 1992. pap. 20.00 (*0-915162-96-2*) Westland Pubns.

Notes on Hessian Soldiers Surnames F-H. Clifford N. Smith. 1992. pap. 20.00 (*0-915162-97-0*) Westland Pubns.

Notes on Hessian Soldiers Surnames M. Clifford N. Smith. 1992. pap. 20.00 (*0-915162-98-9*) Westland Pubns.

Notes on Hessian Soldiers Surnames S. Clifford N. Smith. 1992. 20.00 (*0-915162-99-7*) Westland Pubns.

Notes on Hessian Soldiers Who Remained in Canada & the United States after the American Revolution, 1775-1784 Pt. 1: Deserters by Regiment & Company. rev. ed. Clifford N. Smith. (German-American Genealogical Research Monographs: No. 28, Pt. 2). 30p. 1992. pap. 20.00 (*0-915162-94-6*) Westland Pubns.

Notes on Hessian Soldiers Who Remained in Canada & the United States aftr the American Revolution, 1775-1784, Part 1: Deserters by Places of Origin. rev. ed. Clifford N. Smith. (German-American Genealogical Research Monographs: No. 28, Pt. 1). ii, 35p. 1992. pap. 20.00 (*0-915162-93-8*); pap. 20.00 (*0-915162-95-4*) Westland Pubns.

Notes on Historical Evidence in Reference to Adverse Theories of the Origin & Nature of the Government of the United States of America. John B. Dillon. 141p. 1985. reprint ed. 32.50 (*0-8377-0521-5*, Rothman) W S Hein.

Notes on Hopi Clans. Robert H. Lowie. LC 74-7984. (Anthropological Papers of the American Museum of Natural History: Vol. 30, Pts. 6-7). 34.50 (*0-404-11873-9*) AMS Pr.

Notes on Hopi Economic Life. Ernest Beaglehole. LC 76-43655. (Yale Univ. Publications in Anthropology: No. 15). reprint ed. 24.50 (*0-404-15489-1*) AMS Pr.

Notes on Hospitals. Florence Nightingale. 1976. lib. bdg. 150.00 (*0-8490-2357-2*) Gordon Pr.

Notes on Human Physiology: By an Experienced Teacher. 3rd ed. 539p. 1977. 65.00 (*0-7855-0820-1*, Pub. by Current Dist) St Mut.

Notes on Humanity: Faith, Reason, Certainty. R. W. Carstens. 142p. (Orig.). 1985. pap. text 15.00 (*0-8191-4885-7*) U Pr of Amer.

Notes on Identifying & Assessing Hazards. ICHEM Engineers Staff. (Institution of Chemical Engineers Symposium Ser.). 1983. pap. 19.00 (*0-08-031415-5*, Pergamon Pr) Elsevier.

Notes on India. Robert Bohm. LC 81-51390. 244p. 1982. pap. 7.50 (*0-89608-125-7*) South End Pr.

Notes on Interdesign. rev. ed. ICSID Staff & M. Mullin. 1977. 7.00 (*0-08-021484-3*, Pub. by Pergamon Repr) Franklin.

Notes on Interior Design. Information Design, Inc. Staff. LC 92-24453. (Illus.). 48p. (C). 1992. reprint ed. pap. text 8.95 (*1-56052-154-6*) Crisp Pubns.

Notes on Introductory Combinatorics. George Polya et al. (Progress in Computer Science Ser.: Vol. 4). 1990. 21.95 (*3-7643-3123-2*); 36.50 (*0-8176-3170-4*) Birkhauser.

Notes on Ionising Radiation: Biological Effects, Quantities, Dose Limits & Regulations. D. Hughes. 1991. pap. 150.00 (*0-948237-07-4*, Pub. by H&H Sci Cnslts) St Mut.

Notes on Iqbal's Asrar-i Khudi. Ed. by Arthur J. Arberry. 46p. 1996. pap. 4.00 (*0-614-21234-0*, 909) Kazi Pubns.

Notes on Iroquois Archaeology. Alanson B. Skinner. LC 76-43827. (MAI. Indian Notes & Monographs. Miscellaneous: No. 18). 1977. reprint ed. 52.00 (*0-404-15679-7*) AMS Pr.

Notes on Jonah. Robert Brown. 24p. (Orig.). 1994. pap. 2.50 (*1-880573-06-7*) Bible Search Pubns.

Notes on Joseph Conrad: With Some Unpublished Letters. Arthur Symons. 1925. 20.00 (*0-685-13669-8*) Kelly.

Notes on Joseph Conrad: With Some Unpublished Letters. Arthur Symons. LC 71-148899. (Select Bibliographies Reprint Ser.). 1977. reprint ed. 13.95 (*0-8369-5662-1*) Ayer.

Notes on Land Tenure & Local Institutions in Old Japan. John H. Wigmore & D. B. Simmons. LC 79-52919. (Studies in Japanese History & Civilization). 270p. 1979. lib. bdg. 62.50 (*0-313-27027-9*, U7027, Greenwood Pr) Greenwood.

Notes on Language & Style. T. E. Hulme. LC 74-1105. (Studies in Comparative Literature: No. 35). (C). 1974. lib. bdg. 39.00 (*0-8383-2017-1*) M S G Haskell Hse.

Notes on Lie Algebras. rev. ed. H. Samelson. (Universitext Ser.). xii, 162p. 1990. reprint ed. 43.95 (*0-387-97264-1*) Spr-Verlag.

Notes on Life & Letters. Joseph Conrad. LC 72-1327. (Essay Index Reprint Ser.). 1977. reprint ed. 18.95 (*0-8369-2842-3*) Ayer.

***Notes on Linear Algebra.** James Edmondson. 100p. (C). 2000. per. 19.95 (*0-7872-7287-6*) Kendall-Hunt.

Notes on Logic & Set Theory. Peter T. Johnstone. 126p. 1987. pap. text 21.95 (*0-521-33692-9*) Cambridge U Pr.

Notes on Love in a Tamil Family. Margaret Trawick. 1990. pap. 17.95 (*0-520-07894-2*, Pub. by U CA Pr) Cal Prin Full Svc.

Notes on Mada Phonology. Norman Price. LC 88-63673. (Language Data, African Ser.: No. 23). 51p. 1989. pap. text 4.15 (*0-88312-600-1*) S I L Intl.

Notes on Makihan Ethnology. Alanson B. Skinner. (Illus.). 34p. (C). 1925. pap. text 3.75 (*1-55567-890-4*) Coyote Press.

Notes on Malthus's Measure of Value. David Ricardo. Ed. by Pier L. Porta. 84p. (C). 1992. text 39.95 (*0-521-40298-0*) Cambridge U Pr.

Notes on Mechanism Analysis. Allen S. Hall, Jr. 196p. 1986. reprint ed. pap. text 19.95 (*0-88133-270-4*) Waveland Pr.

Notes on Medical Bacteriology. 5th ed. Sleigh. (C). 1998. pap. text 29.95 (*0-443-05847-4*) Church.

Notes on Medical Bacteriology. 5th ed. J. Douglas Sleigh & Morag C. Timbury. LC 97-39910. 1998. write for info. (*0-443-05848-2*) Church.

Notes on Medical Virology. 11th ed. Morag C. Timbury. LC 97-8837. 1998. pap. text 21.95 (*0-443-05845-8*) Church.

Notes on Meteorology. J. F. Kemp & P. Young. (Illus.). 112p. 1971. pap. text 36.95 (*0-7506-1736-5*) Buttrwrth-Heinemann.

Notes on Microwave Circuits, Vol. 2. Darko Kajfez. LC 84-223799. (Illus.). 296p. (Orig.). (C). 1986. pap. text 32.00 (*0-930071-02-6*) Vector Forum.

Notes on Microwave Circuits, Vol. 3. Darko Kajfez. LC 84-223799. (Illus.). 350p. (Orig.). (C). 1988. pap. text 39.00 (*0-930071-03-4*) Vector Forum.

Notes on Middle American Archaeology & Ethnology, 5 vols. Nos. 1-131, Set. Carnegie Institute of Washington Staff. reprint ed. 362.50 (*0-685-78166-6*) AMS Pr.

Notes on Music in Old Boston. William A. Fisher. LC 74-27340. xvi, 100p. 1976. reprint ed. 29.50 (*0-404-12914-5*) AMS Pr.

Notes on Nebraska. Robert Manley. LC 91-66158. 80p. 1997. reprint ed. pap. 7.99 (*1-886225-24-9*, 500) Dageforde Pub.

Notes on Nepal with an Introduction by H. H. Risley. Eden Vansittart. (C). 1992. reprint ed. 26.00 (*81-206-0774-0*, Pub. by Asian Educ Servs) S Asia.

Notes on Ninety Fourth Street. D. H. Melhem. 66p. 1972. write for info. (*0-318-64125-9*) Poets Pr.

Notes on Notes. Jean Osborne. 101p. (C). 1974. write for info. (*0-915631-01-6*) Osborne.

Notes on Novelists see Works of Henry James Jr.: Collected Works

Notes on Novelists: With Some Other Notes. Henry James. LC 68-56451. 1969. reprint ed. pap. 25.00 (*0-8196-0233-7*) Biblo.

Notes on Nowhere: Feminist Utopian Logic & Social Transformation. Jennifer Burwell. LC 96-31507. (American Culture Ser.). 1997. pap. 19.95 (*0-8166-2639-1*); text 49.95 (*0-8166-2638-3*) U of Minn Pr.

Notes on Nursing. Florence Nightingale. 140p. 18.95 (*0-8488-2535-7*) Amereon Ltd.

Notes on Nursing, 2 bks., Set. Incl. Bk. 1. Science & the Art. Florence Nightingale. 50p. 1980. Bk. 2. What It Is & What It Is Not. Muriel Skeet. 75p. 1980. 1980. write for info. (*0-443-02130-9*) Church.

Notes on Nursing: What It Is, & What It Is Not. Florence Nightingale. LC 79-79233. 140p. 1969. pap. 4.95 (*0-486-22340-X*) Dover.

Notes on Nursing: What It Is, & What It Is Not. Florence Nightingale & Barbara S. Barnum. LC 92-15476. 168p. 1992. text 28.00 (*0-397-55007-3*) Lppncott W & W.

Notes on Nursing: What It Is, & What It Is Not. Florence Nightingale. 140p. 1987. reprint ed. lib. bdg. 21.95 (*0-89966-604-3*) Buccaneer Bks.

Notes on Nursing Notes. Fay Yocum. 200p. 1999. pap. write for info. (*0-9637649-5-0*) Awareness Prods.

Notes on Nursing, Replica Edition: What It Is & What It Is Not. Florence Nightingale. 79p. 1946. text 17.95 (*0-397-54000-0*, 64-01046, Lippnctt) Lppncott W & W.

Notes on Observations of Daily Rings on Otoliths of Deepwater Snappers. F. Brouard et al. (ICLARM Translations Ser.: No. 3). Orig. Title: Note sur les lectures de stries journalieres observees sur les otolithes de poissons. (Illus.). 8p. (Orig.). 1984. pap. 2.00 (*971-10-2207-9*, Pub. by ICLARM) Intl Spec Bk.

Notes on Paediatrics: Cardiorespiratory Disease. Alex Habel & Rod Scott. LC 98-23207. (Paediatric Notes Ser.). (Illus.). 160p. 1998. pap. text 25.00 (*0-7506-2444-2*) Buttrwrth-Heinemann.

Notes on Paediatrics: Neonatology. Alex Habel & Rod Scott. LC 98-23206. (Paediatric Notes Ser.). (Illus.). 144p. 1998. pap. text 25.00 (*0-7506-2446-9*) Buttrwrth-Heinemann.

Notes on Paint. Merrill Wagner. (Illus.). 80p. 1990. pap. text 15.00 (*0-9627794-0-7*) M Wagner.

Notes on Pathology, Part II. Ed. by Current Dist Staff. 260p. 1976. 80.00 (*0-7855-0799-X*, Pub. by Current Dist) St Mut.

Notes on Pathology Pt. 1: By an Experienced Teacher. 298p. 1976. 69.00 (*0-7855-0744-2*, Pub. by Current Dist) St Mut.

Notes on Pediatric Neurology. Alex Habel & Rod Scott. LC 98-23208. (Paediatric Notes Ser.). (Illus.). 104p. 1998. pap. text 25.00 (*0-7506-2445-0*) Buttrwrth-Heinemann.

Notes on Pharmaco-Therapeutics: By an Experienced Teacher. 3rd ed. 284p. 1974. 59.00 (*0-7855-0821-X*, Pub. by Current Dist) St Mut.

Notes on "Pilgrimage" Dorothy Richardson Annotated. George H. Thomson. (British Authors 1880-1920 Ser.: Vol. 13). 352p. 1999. lib. bdg. 40.00 (*0-944318-12-6*) ELT Pr.

Notes on Political Economy. Jacob N. Cardozo. LC 72-187225. (Reprints of Economic Classics Ser.). xiv, 273p. 1972. reprint ed. 45.00 (*0-678-00860-4*) Kelley.

Notes on Political Economy, As Applicable to the United States: By a Southern Planter. Nathaniel A. Ware. LC 66-19698. (Reprints of Economic Classics Ser.). viii, 304p. 1967. reprint ed. 45.00 (*0-678-00235-5*) Kelley.

Notes on Pomo Ethnogeography. fac. ed. Omer C. Stewart. Ed. by A. L. Kroeber et al. (University of California Publications in American Archaeology & Ethnology: No. 40:2). 37p. (C). 1943. reprint ed. pap. 4.06 (*1-55567-313-9*) Coyote Press.

Notes on Practice in Civil Courts. I. A. Abbasi. 15p. 1977. pap. 45.00 (*0-7855-1428-7*) St Mut.

Notes on Prayer. Elliot. 1992. pap. text 1.50 (*0-8474-1192-3*) Back to Bible.

Notes on Protection Against Laser Radiation in the Laboratory, No. 10. D. Hughes. 62p. (C). 1994. pap. 125.00 (*0-948237-09-0*, Pub. by H&H Sci Cnslts) St Mut.

Notes on Prout & Hunt & Other Art Criticisms see Complete Works of John Ruskin

Notes on Puget Sound. Samuel Wilkeson. 1994. pap. 6.95 (*0-87770-528-3*) Ye Galleon.

Notes on Quantum Mechanics. Enrico Fermi. LC 64-9447. 1962. pap. text 10.00 (*0-226-24361-3*) U Ch Pr.

An Asterisk (*) at the beginning of an entry indicates that the title is appearing for the first time.

Notes on Quantum Mechanics: A Course Given by Enrico Fermi at the University of Chicago. 2nd ed. Enrico Fermi. LC 95-3363. 191p. 1995. pap. text 14.95 (0-226-24381-8) U Ch Pr.

Notes on Radiological Diagnosis. Laurence S. Lau & John F. DeCampo. 216p. 1985. pap. text 46.00 (0-7216-1936-3, W B Saunders Co) Harcrt Hlth Sci Grp.

Notes on Railroad Accidents. Charles F. Adams, Jr. (Works of Charles Francis Adams Jr. (1835-1915)). 1989. reprint ed. lib. bdg. 79.00 (0-7812-1407-6) Rprt Serv.

Notes on Reindeer Nomadism. Gudmund Hatt. LC 20-5783. (American Anthropological Association Memoirs Ser.: No. 26). 1919. pap. 25.00 (0-527-00525-8) Periodicals Srv.

Notes on Relative Clauses see Society's Work

Notes on Romans. W. Kelly. 8.95 (0-88172-107-7) Believers Bkshelf.

Notes on Romans. Arthur Pridham. 461p. 1977. 15.99 (0-8254-3519-6, Kregel Class) Kregel.

Notes on Russian America Pt. I: Novo-Arkhangel'sk, Vol. 1. Kirill T. Khlebnikov. Tr. by Serge Lecomte & R. A. Pierce from RUS. LC 96-30255. (Alaska History Ser.: No. 43). (Illus.). 1994. 30.00 (1-895901-04-9) Limestone Pr.

Notes on Russian America Pts. II-V: Kad'iak, Unalashka, Atkha, Pribylov Islands, No. 42. Tr. by Marina Ramsay from RUS. LC 96-30255. (Alaska History Ser.). (Illus.). 1994. 30.00 (1-895901-02-2) Limestone Pr.

Notes on Science Technology & Science Education in the Development of the South. Abdus Salam. 264p. 1991. pap. text 9.00 (0-9625118-6-2) World Scientific Pub.

Notes on Scripture. Jonathan Edwards & Stephen J. Stein. LC 97-25895. (Works of Jonathan Edwards Ser.). 640p. 1998. 80.00 (0-300-07198-1) Yale U Pr.

Notes on Set Theory. Yiannis N. Moschovakis. LC 93-35825. (University Texts in Mathematics Ser.). (Illus.). 272p. 1994. 39.95 (0-387-94180-0) Spr-Verlag.

Notes on Shakespeare's Versification. 4th ed. George H. Browne. LC 78-39547. reprint ed. 20.00 (0-404-01138-1) AMS Pr.

Notes on Social Measurement: Historical & Critical. Otis D. Duncan. LC 83-62503. (Russell Sage Foundation 75th Anniversary Ser.). 272p. 1984. 34.95 (0-87154-219-6) Russell Sage.

Notes on Some Bushman Implements. B. Van Rippen. LC 19-15013. (American Anthropological Association Memoirs Ser.: No. 23). 1918. pap. 25.00 (0-527-00522-3) Periodicals Srv.

Notes on Southside Virginia. Walter A. Watson. (Bulletin of the Virginia State Library: Vol. 15, Nos. 2-4). 346p. 1973. reprint ed. 9.95 (0-88490-069-X) Library of VA.

*Notes on Sovereignty: From the Standpoint of the State & of the World. Robert Lansing & Carnegie Endowment for International Peace Staff. LC 99-47540. 1999. write for info. (1-57588-591-3) W S Hein.

Notes on Space-Time. Donna Brook. 1977. pap. 5.00 (0-914610-11-2) Hanging Loose.

Notes on Spoken Cornish. Rod Lyon & John Pengilly. (C). 1989. 30.00 (1-85022-034-4, Pub. by Dyllansow Truran) St Mut.

Notes on Surgery: By an Experienced Teacher. 2nd ed. 379p. 1987. reprint ed. 75.00 (0-7855-0822-8, Pub. by Current Dist) St Mut.

Notes on Surigao Culture & Personalities. Eulogio V. Eleazar. (Illus.). 129p. (Orig.). (C). 1990. pap. 9.50 (971-10-0405-4, Pub. by New Day Pub) Cellar.

Notes on Symptom Control in Hospice & Palliative Care: U. S. A. Version. rev. ed. Peter Kaye. (Illus.). 427p. 1995. pap. text 28.95 (0-9623438-1-1) Hospice Education.

Notes on Teaching the Bible (Old Testament & Mark) Robert A. Moss & David Wertheimer. (YA). (gr. 9-12). 1981. teacher ed. 16.25 (1-881678-12-1) CSEE.

Notes on Technology & the Moral Order. Alvin W. Gouldner & Richard A. Peterson. LC 62-20957. 1962. 19.95 (0-672-51159-2) Irvington.

Notes on the Animals of North America, 1793. Benjamin S. Barton. Ed. & Intro. by Keir B. Sterling. LC 73-17801. (Natural Sciences in America Ser.). 150p. 1974. 15.95 (0-405-05719-9) Ayer.

Notes on the Archaeology of the Kaibito & Rainbow Plateaus in Arizona. Noel Morss. (Harvard University Peabody Museum of Archaeology & Ethnology Papers: Vol. 12, No. 3). 1974. reprint ed. pap. 30.00 (0-527-01225-4) Periodicals Srv.

Notes on the Bacon-Shakespeare Question. Charles Allen. LC 75-113542. reprint ed. 52.50 (0-404-00326-5) AMS Pr.

Notes on the Bella Bella Kwakiutl. fac. ed. Ronald L. Olson. Ed. by R. F. Heizer et al. (University of California Publications: No. 14:5). 33p. (C). 1955. reprint ed. pap. 3.75 (1-55567-138-1) Coyote Press.

Notes on the Bhagavad-Gita. William Q. Judge. 1972. 69.95 (0-8490-0739-9) Gordon Pr.

Notes on the Bhagavad-Gita. William Q. Judge & Robert Crosbie. 237p. 1918. reprint ed. 5.00 (0-938998-10-2) Theosophy.

Notes on the Bhagavad-Gita. T. Subba Row. LC 77-88628. 182p. 1978. reprint ed. 15.95 (0-911500-81-2); reprint ed. pap. 10.95 (0-911500-82-0) Theos U Pr.

Notes on the Birds of Cley Norfolk. H. N. Pashley. 127p. (C). 1992. pap. text 95.00 (0-9512263-3-9, Pub. by Enchanted Abiary) St Mut.

Notes on the Buffalo-Head Dance of the Bear Gens of the Fox Indians. Truman Michelson. reprint ed. 29.00 (0-403-03668-2) Scholarly.

Notes on the Buffalo-Head Dance of the Thunder Gens of the Fox Indians. Truman Michelson. (Bureau of American Ethnology Bulletins Ser.). 94p. 1995. lib. bdg. 79.00 (0-7812-4087-5) Rprt Serv.

Notes on the Catechism: An Outline of the Faith. James C. Thompson. 96p. 1979. pap. 5.95 (0-8192-1249-0) Morehouse Pub.

Notes on the Celebration of the Eucharist: A Supplement to the Ceremonial Directions of the Book of Common Prayer, 1979. Bruce E. Ford. LC 86-21523. 48p. (Orig.). 1986. pap. 7.50 (0-942466-10-1) Hymnary Pr.

Notes on the Chilula Indians of Northwestern California. fac. ed. Pliny E. Goddard. (University of California Publications in American Archaeology & Ethnology: Vol. 10: 6). 23p. (C). 1914. reprint ed. pap. text 2.81 (1-55567-192-6) Coyote Press.

Notes on the Cinematographer. Robert Bresson. Tr. by Jonathan Griffin. (Green Integer Ser.: No. 2). 144p. 1997. pap. 8.95 (1-55713-365-4) Green Integer.

Notes on the Classification of Mushrooms. John Minot. LC 88-63668. 210p. 1989. 35.00 (0-88000-145-3) Quarterman.

Notes on the Collection of Transfers. William J. Sidis. LC 80-50701. 305p. reprint ed. lib. bdg. 75.00 (0-88000-115-1) Quarterman.

Notes on the Constitution of the United States: Showing the Construction & Operation of the Constitution As Determined by the Federal Supreme Court. William A. Sutherland. xv, 973p. 1991. reprint ed. 75.00 (0-8377-2644-1, Rothman) W S Hein.

Notes on the Construction of the Violin, 1902. W. B. Coventry. 75p. 1899. pap. 15.00 (0-87556-358-9) Saifer.

Notes on the Cultivation of Choral Music & the Oratorio Society of New York. Henry E. Krehbiel. LC 75-137315. reprint ed. 27.50 (0-404-03782-8) AMS Pr.

Notes on the Culture of the Yana. fac. ed. E. W. Gifford et al. Ed. by Robert H. Lowie et al. (University of California Publications: No. 3:3). 64p. (C). 1943. reprint ed. pap. 7.50 (1-55567-077-6) Coyote Press.

Notes on the Development of the Linguistic Society of America, 1924 to 1950. Martin Joos. 170p. (Orig.). 1986. pap. 20.00 (0-87950-725-X) Spoken Lang Serv.

Notes on the Development of the Prinicpal Sounds of Indo-European Through Proto-Germanic & West Germanic into Old English. Matthew H. Scargill. LC PE0124.S3. 42p. reprint ed. pap. 30.00 (0-608-30162-0, 205121700005) Bks Demand.

Notes on the Distribution of Pennsylvania Plants Based on Specimens in The Carnegie Museum of Natural History Herbarium. Sue A. Thompson et al. (Special Publications: No. 14). 55p. (Orig.). 1989. pap. 11.00 (0-911239-30-8) Carnegie Mus.

Notes on the Early Settlement of the North-Western Territory. Jacob Burnet. LC 75-90. (Mid-American Frontier Ser.). 1975. reprint ed. 41.95 (0-405-06857-3) Ayer.

Notes on the Eastern Cree & Northern Salteaux. Alanson B. Skinner. LC 76-43828. (AMNH. Anthropological Papers: Vol. 9, Pt. 1). reprint ed. 15.50 (0-404-15682-7) AMS Pr.

Notes on the Ethnology of the Indians of Puget Sound. fac. ed. T. T. Waterman. (Indian Notes & Monographs - Miscellaneous Ser.: Vol. 59). (Illus.). 141p. (Orig.). (C). 1973. reprint ed. pap. text 15.63 (1-55567-681-2) Coyote Press.

Notes on the Floridian Peninsula. Daniel G. Brinton. LC 69-19548. reprint ed. 31.50 (0-404-01084-9) AMS Pr.

Notes on the Floridian Peninsula. Daniel G. Brinton. (Works of Daniel Garrison Brinton). 1989. reprint ed. lib. bdg. 79.00 (0-7812-2055-6) Rprt Serv.

Notes on the Folk-Lore of the North-East of Scotland. Walter Gregor. (Folk-Lore Society, London Monographs: Vol. 7). 1974. reprint ed. pap. 28.00 (0-8115-0502-2) Periodicals Srv.

Notes on the Folk-Lore of the Northern Counties of England & the Borders. William Henderson. (Folk-Lore Society, London Monographs: Vol. 2). 1974. reprint ed. pap. 40.00 (0-8115-0500-6) Periodicals Srv.

Notes on the Folklore of the Fjort. Richard E. Dennett. LC 78-67705. (Folktale Ser.). reprint ed. 29.50 (0-404-16078-6) AMS Pr.

Notes on the Fox Wapanowiweni. Truman Michelson. (Bureau of American Ethnology Bulletins Ser.). 195p. 1995. lib. bdg. 79.00 (0-7812-4105-7) Rprt Serv.

Notes on the Gattegno Approach to Math. Caleb Gattegno. 31p. 1973. ring bd. 2.00 (0-87825-043-3) Ed Solutions.

Notes on the Gynecology & Obstetrics of the Arikara Tribe of Indians, Vol. 14, No. 1. Melvin Gilmore. 1980. reprint ed. pap. 2.50 (0-686-69103-2) Acoma Bks.

Notes on the Heart: Affective Issues in the Writing Classroom. Susan H. McLeod. LC 96-17771. 1997. 39.95 (0-8093-1738-9); pap. 19.95 (0-8093-2106-8) S Ill U Pr.

Notes on the History of Military Medicine. Fielding H. Garrison. v, 206p. 1970. reprint ed. 37.70 (0-685-66466-X, 05102809) G Olms Pubs.

Notes on the History of Religion in the Himalaya of the N. W. P., India. Edwin F. Atkinson. LC 78-72374. reprint ed. 37.50 (0-404-17224-5) AMS Pr.

Notes on the History of Waterford. Ed. by Thomas H. Gage, Jr. (Illus.). 87p. 1997. reprint ed. pap. 16.50 (0-8328-5924-9) Higginson Bk Co.

Notes on the Human Ecology of Glen Canyon. Angus M. Woodbury. (Glen Canyon Ser.: No. 26). reprint ed. 20.00 (0-404-60674-1) AMS Pr.

Notes on the Interpretation of Twenty-Four Famous Piano Sonatas by Beethoven. J. Alfred Johnstone. 205p. 1991. reprint ed. lib. bdg. 79.00 (0-7812-9336-7) Rprt Serv.

Notes on the Iroquois. Henry R. Schoolcraft. LC 74-9006. reprint ed. 49.50 (0-404-11898-4) AMS Pr.

Notes on the Iroquois, or Contributions to American History, Antiquities, & General Ethnology. Henry Schoolcraft. (Illus.). 498p. 1998. reprint ed. lib. bdg. 52.50 (0-8328-9587-3) Higginson Bk Co.

Notes on the Islands of the Unalashka District. Ivan Veniaminov. Ed. by Richard A. Pierce. Tr. by Lydia T. Black from RUS. (Alaska History Ser.: No. 27). 1984. 35.00 (0-919642-03-9) Limestone Pr.

Notes on the Isthmus of Panama & Darien, Also on the River San Juan, Lakes of Nicaragua, Etc.... George Peacock. (Illus.). vii, 96p. 1988. reprint ed. pap. 9.00 (0-913129-20-8) La Tienda.

Notes on the Joint Housing Conference. 1988. pap. 3.75 (0-685-30167-2, 44,285) NCLS Inc.

Notes on the Kitchen Table: Families Offer Messages of Hope for Generations to Come. Bob Greene & D. G. Fulford. LC 97-44309. 176p. 1998. 16.95 (0-385-49061-5) Doubleday.

Notes on the Lectures of L. Ron Hubbard. L. Ron Hubbard. 256p. 1989. 28.00 (0-88404-422-X) Bridge Pubns Inc.

Notes on the Life & Works of Bernard Romans. P. Lee Phillips. Ed. by John Ware. LC 74-20757. (Floridiana Facsimile & Reprint Ser.). (Illus.). 138p. 1975. reprint ed. 19.95 (0-8130-0413-6) U Press Fla.

Notes on the Literature of Charities. Herbert B. Adams. (Works of Herbert B. Adams). 48p. 1985. reprint ed. lib. bdg. 39.00 (0-318-03786-6) Rprt Serv.

Notes on the Literature of the Piano. Albert Lockwood. LC 67-30400. (Music Ser.). 1968. reprint ed. lib. bdg. 32.50 (0-306-70983-X) Da Capo.

Notes on the McCloud River Winter & Selected Excerpts from Alexander S. Taylor's Indianology of California. fac. ed. Ed. by Robert F. Heizer. (University of California Archaeological Research Facility). 82p. (C). 1973. reprint ed. pap. text 8.44 (1-55567-656-1) Coyote Press.

Notes on the Mental Health Act, 1983. Ralph L. Kilby. (C). 1983. 30.00 (0-7219-0204-9, Pub. by Scientific) St Mut.

Notes on the Nature of Man. Tom Mooney. 1985. pap. 3.00 (0-317-28508-4) T Mooney.

Notes on the Nicomachean Ethics of Aristotle, 2 vols. J. A. Stewart. LC 72-9306. (Philosophy of Plato & Aristotle Ser.). (ENG & GRE.). 1974. reprint ed. 59.95 (0-405-04863-7) Ayer.

Notes on the People of Siwah & el Garah in the Libyan Desert. Walter B. Cline. LC 76-44706. reprint ed. 44.50 (0-404-15916-8) AMS Pr.

Notes on the Piano. Ernst Bacon. LC 63-13887. (Illus.). 175p. 1963. reprint ed. pap. 54.30 (0-608-06969-8, 206717700009) Bks Demand.

Notes on the Plague Years: AIDS in Marseilles. Bernard Paillard. Tr. by Berkeley Frank from FRE. LC 98-28154. (Social Problems & Social Issues Ser.). 313p. 1998. pap. text 24.95 (0-202-30555-4); lib. bdg. 51.95 (0-202-30554-6) Aldine de Gruyter.

Notes on the Principles & Practices of Baptist Churches. Francis Wayland. Ed. by Edwin S. Gaustad. LC 79-52610. (Baptist Tradition Ser.). 1980. reprint ed. lib. bdg. 30.95 (0-405-12475-9) Ayer.

Notes on the Progress of the Colored People of Maryland Since the War. Jeffrey R. Brackett. LC 76-170689. (Black Heritage Library Collection). 1977. reprint ed. 20.95 (0-8369-8879-5) Ayer.

*Notes on the Psalms by Marie Olson. Marie Olson. Ed. by Louise Dick. 500p. (Orig.). 1999. pap. 19.95 (0-935899-09-X) LeTourneau Pr.

Notes on the Psychology of Learning. John F. Wakefield. iv, 70p. 1999. ring bd. 10.00 (0-943465-55-9) Honors Pr.

Notes on the Puerto Rican Revolution: An Essay on American Dominance & Caribbean Resistance. Gordon Lewis. LC 74-7791. 288p. 1976. pap. 10.00 (0-85345-371-3, Pub. by Monthly Rev) NYU Pr.

Notes on the Pumpkin. Ellen Levine. 16p. (Orig.). 1979. pap. 3.00 (0-89924-020-8) Lynx Hse.

Notes on the Quantum Theory of Angular Momentum. Eugene Feenberg. LC 99-35679. 1999. pap. 7.95 (0-486-40923-6) Dover.

Notes on the Quantum Theory of Angular Momentum. Eugene Feenberg & George E. Pake. LC 59-13223. 65p. reprint ed. pap. 30.00 (0-608-30270-8, 200078900044) Bks Demand.

Notes on the Royal Academy Exhibition, 1868. William M. Rossetti. LC 75-144681. reprint ed. 27.50 (0-404-05418-8) AMS Pr.

Notes on the Science of Government & the Relation of the States to the United States, 1913. Raleigh C. Minor. LC 99-47233. x, 192p. 1995. reprint ed. 40.00 (1-886363-09-9, 310570) Lawbk Exchange.

Notes on the Settlement & Indian Wars. annot. ed. Joseph Doddridge. 1824. reprint ed. pap. 14.95 (0-87012-001-8) McClain.

Notes on the Settlement & Indian Wars of the Western Parts of VA & PA from 1763 to 1783, Inclusive, Together with a Review of the State of Society & Manners of the First Settlers of the Western Country. Joseph Doddridge. 320p. 1991. reprint ed. pap. 22.50 (1-55613-127-5) Heritage Bk.

*Notes on the Settlement & Indian Wars of the Western Parts of Virginia: Inclusive, Together with a Review of the State of Society & Manners of the First Settlers of the West Country. Joseph Doddridge. 320p. 1998. reprint ed. pap. 28.50 (0-8063-4767-8, 9316) Clearfield Co.

Notes on the Seven Churches: (Of the Revelation) Kingdom Quotes Staff. pap. write for info. (0-930179-19-6) Johns Enter.

Notes on the Seven Seals: (From the Book of Revelation) Kingdom Quotes Staff. pap. write for info. (0-930179-39-0) Johns Enter.

Notes on the Social Organizations & Customs of the Mandan, Hidatsa, & Crow Indians. Robert H. Lowie. LC 74-7985. 1976. reprint ed. 34.50 (0-404-11874-7) AMS Pr.

Notes on the Sounds & Vocabulary of Gullah. Lorenzo D. Turner. (Publications of the American Dialect Society: No. 3). 28p. 1945. pap. 3.00 (0-8173-0603-X) U of Ala Pr.

Notes on the Southern Maidu. fac. ed. Paul-Louis Faye. (University of California Publications in American Archaeology & Ethnology: Vol. 20: 3). 22p. (C). 1923. reprint ed. pap. text 2.81 (1-55567-239-6) Coyote Press.

Notes on the Spiritual Exercises of St. Ignatius of Loyola. Ed. by David L. Fleming. (Best of the Review Ser.: Bk. 1). 331p. (Orig.). 1980. pap. text 10.95 (0-924768-01-0) Review Relig.

Notes on the Spirituality of the Society of Jesus Christ the Priest. Alfonso Galvez. Tr. by Lope Pascual from SPA. LC 94-66009. 89p. (Orig.). 1994. pap. write for info. (0-9641108-0-6) Shoreless Lake.

Notes on the State of Virginia. Thomas Jefferson. 1990. 16.50 (0-8446-2321-0) Peter Smith.

Notes on the State of Virginia. Thomas Jefferson. Ed. & Intro. by William Peden. LC 95-47378. 342p. (C). 1996. pap. 16.95 (0-8078-4588-4) U of NC Pr.

Notes on the State of Virginia. Thomas Jefferson. LC 98-28819. 400p. 1998. pap. 12.95 (0-14-043667-7) Viking Penguin.

Notes on the State of Virginia. Thomas Jefferson. Ed. by William Peden. 1994. reprint ed. lib. bdg. 37.95 (1-56849-296-0) Buccaneer Bks.

Notes on the Study of Central Asia. Yuri Bregel. (Papers on Inner Asia: No. 28). 1995. 4.50 (0-614-14924-X) Res Inst Inner Asian Studies.

Notes on the Synthesis of Form. Christopher W. Alexander. LC 64-13417. (Illus.). 216p. 1964. pap. text 16.50 (0-674-62751-2) HUP.

Notes on the Thadou Kukis. William Shaw. Ed. by J. H. Hutton. LC 77-87080. (Illus.). 1977. reprint ed. 34.50 (0-404-16868-X) AMS Pr.

Notes on the Theory of Choice. David M. Kreps. (Underground Classics in Economics Ser.). 207p. (C). 1988. pap. 30.00 (0-8133-7553-3, Pub. by Westview) HarpC.

Notes on the Tillamook. fac. ed. Franz Boas. (University of California Publications in American Archaeology & Ethnology: Vol. 20: 1). 14p. (C). 1923. reprint ed. pap. text 1.88 (1-55567-237-X) Coyote Press.

Notes on the United States of North America During a Phrenological Visit in 1838-1940, 2 vols. George Combe. LC 73-13125. (Foreign Travelers in America, 1810-1935 Ser.). 780p. 1974. reprint ed. 58.95 (0-405-05448-3) Ayer.

Notes on the War in the South: With Biographical Sketches of the Lives of Montgomery, Jackson, Sevier, Late Governor Claiborne & Others. Nathaniel H. Claiborne. LC 76-146382. (First American Frontier Ser.). 1977. reprint ed. 24.95 (0-405-02833-4) Ayer.

Notes on the Way. Mother.Tr. of Notes sur le Chemin. (FRE.). 347p. 1995. pap. 6.50 (81-7058-376-4, Pub. by SAA) E-W Cultural Ctr.

Notes on the Way. Margaret H. Rhondda. LC 68-8488. (Essay Index Reprint Ser.). 1977. 19.95 (0-8369-0822-8) Ayer.

Notes on Thermodynamics & Statistics. Enrico Fermi. 190p. (Orig.). 1988. pap. text 11.95 (0-226-24379-6) U Ch Pr.

Notes on Things Korean. Suzanne C. Han. LC 95-76496. (Illus.). 248p. 1995. 22.95 (1-56591-019-2) Hollym Intl.

Notes on Thomas Jefferson, 1885. Lloyd Simpson. 182p. 1998. reprint ed. pap. text 25.00 (0-87556-850-5) Saifer.

Notes on Thought & Vision & The Wise Sappho. H. D., pseud. LC 82-17903. 44p. 1983. pap. 7.95 (0-87286-141-4) City Lights.

Notes on Time Decay & Scattering for Some Hyperbolic Problems. Cathleen S. Morawetz. (CBMS-NSF Regional Conference Ser.: No. 19). v, 81p. 1975. pap. text 23.50 (0-89871-016-2) Soc Indus-Appl Math.

Notes on Titus. Glen Burch. 36p. (Orig.). 1995. pap. 3.00 (1-880573-25-3) Bible Search Pubns.

Notes on Tour in the Manufacturing Districts of Lancashire. 3rd ed. William C. Taylor. 331p. 1968. reprint ed. 28.50 (0-7146-1408-4, BHA-01408, Pub. by F Cass Pubs) Intl Spec Bk.

Notes on Training. Tsutomu Ohshima. LC 99-158941. 252 p. 1998. 40.00 (0-937663-32-8) Idyll Arbor.

Notes on Training. Tsutomu Ohshima. 252p. 1998. 40.00 (1-882883-36-5, Pine Winds Pr) Idyll Arbor.

Notes on Turquois in the East, 1913-1914: Field Museum of Natural History. Berthold Laufer. (Field Museum Monographs: Vol. 13). 1913. 50.00 (0-527-01873-2) Periodicals Srv.

Notes on Wall Vegetation. Segal. 1972. pap. text 126.50 (90-6193-254-8, Pub. by M Nijhoff) Kluwer Academic.

Notes on Walt Whitman As Poet & Person. John Burroughs. LC 68-24932. (Studies in Whitman: No. 28). 1969. reprint ed. lib. bdg. 75.00 (0-8383-0922-4) M S G Haskell Hse.

Notes on Walt Whitman As Poet & Person. John Burroughs. (Works of John Burroughs). 1989. reprint ed. lib. bdg. 79.00 (0-7812-2177-3) Rprt Serv.

Notes on Wenham History, 1643-1943. Ed. by Adeline P. Cole. (Illus.). 155p. 1993. reprint ed. lib. bdg. 25.00 (0-8328-3135-2) Higginson Bk Co.

Notes on Western Nevada Archaeology & Ethnology. fac. ed. Sonia Ragir et al. (Reports of the University of California Archaeological Survey: No. 66). (Illus.). 138p. 1966. reprint ed. pap. 15.00 (1-55567-380-5) Coyote Press.

Notes on Woman Printers in Colonial America & the United States, 1639-1975. Marjorie D. Barlow. LC 76-46686. 103p. reprint ed. pap. 32.00 (0-7837-4344-0, 204405400012) Bks Demand.

Notes on Zuni, 2 pts., Pt. I. Elsie C. Parsons. (American Anthropological Association Memoirs Ser.: No. 20). 1917. 15.00 (0-527-00518-5) Periodicals Srv.

N

An Asterisk (*) at the beginning of an entry indicates that the title is appearing for the first time.

Notes on Zuni, 2 pts., Pt. II. Elsie C. Parsons. (American Anthropological Association Memoirs Ser.: No. 20). 1917. 25.00 (*0-527-00519-3*) Periodicals Srv.

Notes Pour Servir a L'histoire, a la Bibliographie et a la Cartographie De la Nouvelle-France et Des pays adjacents, 1545-1700. Henry Harrisse. (French-Canadian Civilization Ser.). (FRE.). reprint ed. lib. bdg. 50.00 (*0-697-00006-0*) Irvington.

Notes, Quotes & Advice: Wit, Wisdom & Insight on Success. Ed. by Lee T. Silber. 100p. (Orig.). (C). 1993. pap. 6.95 (*0-9628771-2-3*) Tales From Tropics.

Notes sur la Technique Poetique. Georges Duhamel & Charles Vildrac. (FRE.). 50p. 1925. pap. 36.95 (*0-7859-5423-6*) Fr & Eur.

Notes sur l'Affaire Dominici. Jean Giono. (FRE.). 160p. 1955. 27.95 (*0-8288-9784-0*, F103550) Fr & Eur.

Notes sur le Chemin see Notes on the Way

Notes Sur le Classement Chronologique Des Monnaies D'athenes (Series Avec Noms De Magistrats) M. L. Kambanis. (FRE., Illus.). 1980. pap. 5.00 (*0-916710-78-5*) Obol Intl.

Notes sur le Rire. Marcel Pagnol. (FRE.). 127p. 1987. pap. 13.95 (*0-7859-1549-4*, 2826308203) Fr & Eur.

Notes Surgical Nursing. 3rd ed. Fream. 1986. pap. text 27.00 (*0-443-03380-3*, W B Saunders Co) Harcrt Hlth Sci Grp.

Notes That Tickled Me. Laurie Z. Wieder. (Illus.). 100p. (Orig.). 1996. pap. write for info. (*1-57502-256-7*, PO939) Morris Pubng.

Notes to Dad. Josie Stewart & Lynn Salem. (Illus.). 12p. (J). (gr. k-1). 1994. pap. 3.75 (*1-880612-46-1*) Seedling Pubns.

Notes to Literature, Vol. 1. Theodor W. Adorno. Ed. by Lawrence D. Kritzman & Richard Wolin. Tr. by Shierry W. Nicholsen from GER. (European Perspectives Ser.). 284p. (C). 1991. text 46.00 (*0-231-06332-6*) Col U Pr.

Notes to Literature, Vol. 1. Theodor W. Adorno. Ed. by Lawrence D. Kritzman & Richard Wolin. Tr. by Shierry W. Nicholsen from GER. (European Perspectives Ser.). 284p. (C). 1993. pap. 19.50 (*0-231-06333-4*) Col U Pr.

Notes to Literature, Vol. 2. Theodor W. Adorno. Ed. by Rolf Tiedemann & Shierry W. Nicholsen. (European Perspectives Ser.). 350p. (C). 1992. text 57.50 (*0-231-06912-X*) Col U Pr.

Notes to Literature, Vol. 2. Theodor W. Adorno. LC 90-27732. 350p. 1994. pap. 19.50 (*0-231-06913-8*) Col U Pr.

Notes to My Becca: A Father's Thoughts on Welcoming His Long-Awaited Child. C. Stephen Fouquet. LC 95-6540. 224p. 1995. pap. 11.95 (*0-925190-40-3*) Fairview Press.

***Notes to My Children on Getting, Being & Staying Married.** Jo Lief. 64p. 1999. 8.95 (*0-7407-0038-3*) Andrews & McMeel.

Notes to My Self. Slightly Off Center Writers Group Staff. (Orig.). 1995. pap. 8.95 (*1-56721-102-X*) Twnty-Fifth Cent Pr.

Notes to Myself. Hugh Prather. 176p. 1983. mass mkt. 6.99 (*0-553-27382-5*, Bantam Classics) Bantam.

***Notes to Myself: A Guided Journal.** Photos by Solomon M. Skolnick. (Guided Journals). (Illus.). 128p. 1999. 11.99 (*0-88088-223-9*) Peter Pauper.

Notes to Nancy. Ecomae Baunach. LC 96-92445. (Illus.). 144p. (J). (ps-6). 1996. 9.95 (*0-9651202-4-4*) Park Publishing.

Notes to Teachers see Miquon Math Lab Series: Complete Home School

Notes to the Heart. Caryn L. Wolf. (Illus.). 64p. (Orig.). 1986. pap. 5.95 (*0-9616870-0-2*) DBJ Pub.

Notes Toward a Family Tree. John Barton. 112p. 1994. pap. 10.95 (*1-55082-066-4*, Pub. by Quarry Pr) LPC InBook.

Notes Toward the Truth about the Self. Siva Prem. 16p. 1997. pap. 2.00 (*0-938075-72-1*, Permanence Pr) Ocean View Bks.

Notes Towards the Definition of Culture see Christianity & Culture

Notes upon Some of Shakespeare's Plays. Frances A. Kemble. LC 77-144644. reprint ed. 31.50 (*0-404-03645-7*) AMS Pr.

Notes upon Some of Shakespeare's Plays. Frances A. Kemble. (Notable American Authors Ser.). 1999. reprint ed. lib. bdg. 125.00 (*0-7812-3662-2*) Rprt Serv.

Notes Used on Catalog Cards: A List of Examples. 2nd ed. Compiled by Olive Swain. LC 81-13247. 82p. 1982. reprint ed. lib. bdg. 55.00 (*0-313-23225-3*, SWNC, Greenwood Pr) Greenwood.

Notes While Preparing Sketch Book & C. 1817. Washington Irving. (BCL1-PS American Literature Ser.). 97p. 1992. reprint ed. lib. bdg. 59.00 (*0-7812-6754-4*) Rprt Serv.

***Notes 1988-1997.** Paul Nervy. 545p. 1999. spiral bd. 10.00 (*0-9670613-3-4*) Protean Pub.

Notes 4.5 Administrator's Guide. Bret Swedeen. 1997. pap. 44.99 (*0-614-28535-6*, Network Pr) Sybex.

Notes/Notizen. Robert Lax. Tr. by Alfred Kuoni from GER. 93p. (Orig.). 1995. pap. text 15.00 (*3-85842-295-9*) Franciscan Inst.

***Notespeller for Piano: Hal Leonard Student Piano Library, Vol. 1.** Karen Harrington. 32p. 1999. pap. 4.95 (*0-634-00477-8*) H Leonard.

***Notespeller for Piano BK.2: Hal Leonard Student Piano Library.** Karen Harrington. 32p. 2000. pap. 4.95 (*0-634-01283-5*) H Leonard.

***Notespeller for Piano 1 International.** 32p. 1999. pap. 4.95 (*0-634-01037-9*) H Leonard.

Notetaking & Outlining Skills see Ready-to-Use Writing Workshop Activities Kits

Notetaking & Report Writing. rev. ed. Herman Ohme & Jean Ohme. (Illus.). 56p. 1989. pap. 5.00 (*0-936047-11-9*) CA Educ Plan.

Noteworthy. Phyllis L. Lim & William Smalzer. (J). 1990. audio 14.95 (*0-8384-2949-1*) Heinle & Heinle.

Noteworthy. Phyllis L. Lim & William Smalzer. (J). 1990. audio 62.95 (*0-8384-2948-3*) Heinle & Heinle.

Noteworthy. Phyllis L. Lim & William Smalzer. (J). 1991. pap. 17.50 (*0-8384-2946-7*) Heinle & Heinle.

Noteworthy. 2nd ed. Phyllis L. Lim. (College ESL Ser.). 230p. (J). 1996. pap. 28.95 (*0-8384-5009-1*) Heinle & Heinle.

Noteworthy. 2nd ed. Lim & Smalzer. 1996. pap. text, teacher ed. 4.75 (*0-8384-5011-3*) Heinle & Heinle.

Noteworthy: A Collection of Recipes from the Ravinia Festival. Ed. by Joan Freehling. LC 85-62782. (Illus.). 457p. 1986. 20.00 (*0-9615803-0-5*) Ravinia Fest.

Noteworthy Vol. 2: A New Recipe Collection from the Ravinia Festival. Ed. by Joan Freehling & Jan Weil. (Illus.). 473p. 1986. 20.00 (*0-9615803-1-3*) Ravinia Fest.

Noteworthy Philadelphia: A City's Musical Heritage, 1750-1915 - An Exhibition May 15 Through December 31, 1997. Contrib. by Sarah J. Weatherwax. (Illus.). 44p. 1997. pap. 7.50 (*0-914076-92-2*) Lib Co Phila.

Noteworthy Publications by African-American Surgeons: In Commemoration of the 100th Anniversary of the National Medical Association. limited ed. Vernon J. Henderson & Claude H. Organ, Jr. (Illus.). 414p. 1995. 75.00 (*0-9617380-2-2*) C H Organ.

Noteworthy Pubs, Taverns & Saloons of Colorado. Karen O. Earley. 128p. 1995. pap. 12.95 (*0-9647300-5-7*) CO Advent Pubns.

Noteworthy Species of Grammitidaceae from South-East Asia. B. S. Parris. (Illus.). 129p. 1990. pap. 20.00 (*0-9504876-8-6*, Pub. by Royal Botnic Grdns) Balogh.

Noteworthy Tale. Brenda Mutchnick & Ron Casden. LC 97-70933. (Illus.). 32p. (J). (gr. 1-4). 1997. 17.95 (*0-8109-1386-0*, Pub. by Abrams) Time Warner.

NoteWriter. Rita S. Conway. (Illus.). 328p. 1996. vinyl bd. 29.95 (*0-9655195-3-8*) Sandpiper Pubs Inc.

Notez Bien: Teacher's Edition. Kulik & Toner. 1992. text, teacher ed. 34.00 (*0-8384-2435-X*) Thomson Learn.

Nothiger Vorrath Zur Geschichte der Deutschen Dramatischen Dichtkunst. Johann C. Gottsched. 414p. 1970. reprint ed. write for info. (*0-318-71786-7*) G Olms Pubs.

***Nothin' but a Champion.** Tom A. Savage. (Illus.). 240p. 2000. 22.95 (*0-9676751-2-X*) Harman Sports.

Nothin' but Fine: The Music & the Gospel According to Jake Hess. Jake Hess & Richard Hyatt. 257p. 1995. 19.95 (*0-9647237-1-9*) Buckland Pr.

Nothin' but Good Times Ahead. Molly Ivins. 304p. 1994. pap. 13.00 (*0-679-75488-1*) Vin Bks.

Nothin' but Good Times Ahead. large type ed. Molly Ivins. LC 93-43545. (General Ser.). 464p. 1994. lib. bdg. 24.95 (*0-8161-5925-4*, G K Hall Lrg Type) Mac Lib Ref.

Nothin' but Muffins. Cyndi Duncan & Georgie Patrick. (Colorado Collection: No. 2). (Illus.). 96p. (Orig.). 1991. pap., spiral bd. 12.95 (*0-9626335-1-8*) C&G Pub CO.

Nothin' but the 'Boo. Donald Ransom. (Illus.). 20p. (Orig.). 1981. pap. text 2.50 (*0-686-32817-5*) Skydog OR.

Nothin' But the Truth: More Yankee Yarns. Deane C. Davis. LC 82-80343. (Illus.). 224p. 1982. 10.95 (*0-933050-10-0*) New Eng Pr VT.

***Nothin' Fancy.** Betty Young. (Illus.). vi, 48p. 1998. pap. 11.95 (*0-9676140-0-7*) B Young.

Nothin' Finer. Chapel Hill Service League Staff. (Illus.). 254p. 1993. spiral bd. 15.95 (*0-9633052-0-4*) CH Srv Leag.

Nothin' Left to Lose. Carl T. Smith. LC 99-30233. 308p. 1999. 22.00 (*1-887714-47-2*, Pub. by Summerhse Pr) Koen Bk Distributors.

***Nothin Personal Doc, but I Hate Dentists! The Feel Good Guide to Going to the Dentist.** McHenry Lee et al. (Illus.). 165p. 1999. pap. 16.95 (*0-9674851-0-X*) IHD.

Nothin' Strange, Mum. Velma Van Buskirk. (Illus.). 48p. (Orig.). 1996. pap. text 12.00 (*1-887196-03-X*) Wells Col Pr.

Nothing. Greg Evason. 60p. (Orig.). 1991. pap. 7.00 (*0-926935-53-4*) Runaway Spoon.

***Nothing.** Henry Green, pseud. 203p. 2000. pap. 11.95 (*1-56478-260-3*) Dalkey Arch.

Nothing. Mick Inkpen. LC 97-30898. (Illus.). 32p. (J). (ps-2). 1998. 14.95 (*0-531-30076-5*) Orchard Bks Watts.

Nothing. Henry Green, pseud. LC 72-122052. 250p. 1970. reprint ed. 25.00 (*0-678-03160-6*) Kelley.

Nothing about Us Without Us: Developing Innovative Technologies for, by, & with Disabled Persons. David Werner. (Illus.). (Orig.). 1997. pap. 15.00 (*0-9655585-3-3*) HealthWrights.

***Nothing about Us Without Us: Disability Oppression & Empowerment.** James I. Charlton. 213p. 2000. pap. 16.95 (*0-520-22481-7*, Pub. by U CA Pr) Cal Prin Full Svc.

Nothing about Us, Without Us: The Dialectics of Disability Oppression & Empowerment. James I. Charlton. LC 97-1661. 247p. 1998. 27.50 (*0-520-20795-5*, Pub. by U CA Pr) Cal Prin Full Svc.

Nothing at All. Denys Cazet. LC 93-25204. (Illus.). 32p. (J). (ps-1). 1993. 15.95 (*0-531-06822-6*) Orchard Bks Watts.

Nothing at All. Denys Cazet. LC 93-25204. (Illus.). 32p. (J). (ps-1). 1994. lib. bdg. 16.99 (*0-531-08672-0*) Orchard Bks Watts.

Nothing at All. Cid Corman. (Poetry New York Pamphlet Ser.: Vol. 11). 16p. 1999. pap. 5.00 (*0-923389-23-7*) Meet Eyes Bind.

***Nothing at All.** Wanda Ga'g. LC 98-60770. (Wanda Ga'g Classic Collection). (Illus.). 32p. (J). (ps-3). 1998. 9.98 (*0-7651-0859-3*) Smithmark.

Nothing at All Sand. Wanda Ga'g. pap. 5.95 (*0-698-20675-4*) Putnam Pub Group.

Nothing Bad Happens, Ever. Joan Fountain. 1998. write for info. (*0-446-52341-0*) Warner Bks.

Nothing Bad Happens, Ever. Joan Fountain et al. LC 96-26296. 204p. 1996. 18.00 (*1-882723-14-7*) Gold Leaf Pr.

Nothing Bad Happens to Good Girls: Fear of Crime in Women's Lives. Esther Madriz. LC 96-37659. 192p. 1997. 40.00 (*0-520-20291-0*, Pub. by U CA Pr); pap. 15.95 (*0-520-20855-2*, Pub. by U CA Pr) Cal Prin Full Svc.

Nothing Basically Wrong. Patrick Oliphant. (Illus.). 160p. (Orig.). 1988. pap. 8.95 (*0-8362-1833-7*) Andrews & McMeel.

Nothing Begins with N: New Investigations of Freewriting. Ed. by Pat Belanoff et al. LC 89-26290. 304p. (C). 1991. 36.95 (*0-8093-1657-9*); pap. 21.95 (*0-8093-1658-7*) S Ill U Pr.

***Nothing Better Than a Good Laugh.** Maria T. Grado. LC 99-64077. 96p. 1999. pap. 9.95 (*1-56167-524-5*) Am Literary Pr.

Nothing Beyond the Necessary: Roman Catholicism & the Ecumenical Future. Jon Nilson. LC 95-11964. 120p. (Orig.). 1995. pap. 7.95 (*0-8091-3576-0*) Paulist Pr.

Nothing Book (Wanna Make Something of It?) Ed. by Bruce Harris. 160p. 1974. 8.00 (*0-517-51648-9*) Harmony Bks.

Nothing Burns in Hell. Philip Jose Farmer. LC 98-10259. 288p. 1998. text 22.95 (*0-312-86470-1*) St Martin.

***Nothing Burns in Hell.** Philip Jose Farmer. 288p. 1999. mass mkt. 6.99 (*0-8125-6495-2*, Pub. by Tor Bks) St Martin.

Nothing but a Pig. Brock Cole. 32p. 1990. pap. 3.95 (*0-374-45541-4*) FS&G.

Nothing but Big Band Music Bk. 9: Piano. 64p. (Orig.). Date not set. pap. 8.95 (*0-7692-1139-9*, PF0261) Wrner Bros.

Nothing but Blue Skies. Thomas McGuane. 1994. pap. 14.00 (*0-679-74778-8*) Random.

Nothing But... Borders! Reproducible Borders for All Occasions. Karen Sevaly. (Illus.). 80p. (J). 1999. pap. 9.95 (*1-57882-020-0*, TF-1652) Teachers Friend Pubns.

Nothing But Christ: Rufus Anderson & Ideology of Protestant Foreign Missions. Paul Harris. LC 99-19369. (Religion in America Ser.). (Illus.). 216p. 2000. text 39.95 (*0-19-513172-X*) OUP.

Nothing but Christmas Songs Bk. 5: Piano. 64p. (Orig.). Date not set. pap. 7.95 (*0-7692-1140-2*, PF0418) Wrner Bros.

Nothing But... Clip Art! Reproducible Clip Art for All Occasions! Karen Sevaly. (Illus.). 80p. (J). 1999. pap. 9.95 (*1-57882-019-7*, TF-1651) Teachers Friend Pubns.

Nothing But Freedom: Emancipation & Its Legacy. Eric Foner. LC 83-7906. (Walter Lynwood Fleming Lectures). (Illus.). 142p. 1983. pap. text 11.95 (*0-8071-1189-9*) La State U Pr.

Nothing but Glory: Pickett's Division at Gettysburg. Kathleen G. Harrison & John W. Busey. LC 87-80902. (Illus.). 618p. (C). 1994. reprint ed. text 29.95 (*0-939631-56-3*) Thomas Publications.

Nothing but Gossip. Marne Davis Kellogg. 304p. 1999. mass mkt. 5.99 (*0-553-58046-9*) Bantam.

Nothing but Gossip: A Lilly Bennett Mystery. Marne D. Kellogg. LC 98-24037. 288p. 1998. 21.95 (*0-385-48860-2*) Doubleday.

***Nothing but Heather: Scottish Nature in Poems, Photographs & Prose.** Gerry Cambridge. 2000. pap. 24.95 (*0-946487-49-9*) Luath Pr Ltd.

Nothing but History: Reconstruction & Extremity after Metaphysics. David D. Roberts. LC 94-43786. 342p. 1995. 45.00 (*0-520-20080-2*, Pub. by U CA Pr) Cal Prin Full Svc.

***Nothing but Mountain State Fishing.** Andy Hansroth. (Illus.). 197p. 2000. pap. 8.95 (*0-941147-03-7*) Charleston Gazette.

***Nothing But My Sword: The Life of James Keith.** Sam Coull. 224p. 2000. pap. 19.95 (*1-84158-024-4*, Pub. by Birlinn Ltd) Dufour.

Nothing but Net! An Essay on the Culture of Pickup Basketball. Michael Moran. LC 91-76837. 118p. (Orig.). 1991. pap. 7.95 (*0-9631597-0-4*) Full Ct TX.

***Nothing But Net: Business the Cisco Way: Secrets of the World's Fastest-Growing Company Ever.** David M. Stauffer. 328p. 2000. write for info. (*1-84112-087-1*, Pub. by Capstone Pub NH) LPC Group.

***Nothing but Net: How I Generated $750,000 in Internet Revenues with Virtually No Advertising Costs.** Michael Campbell. 97p. 1999. ring bd. 68.00 (*1-930336-04-7*) Adnet Intl.

Nothing But... Patterns! Reproducible Patterns for All Occasions! Karen Sevaly. (Illus.). 80p. (J). 1999. pap. 9.95 (*1-57882-021-9*, TF-1653) Teachers Friend Pubns.

Nothing but Prairie & Sky: Life on the Dakota Range in the Early Days. Contrib. by Walker D. Wyman & Bruce Siberts. LC 54-5930. (Western Frontier Library: Vol. 45). (Illus.). 248p. 1988. pap. 11.95 (*0-8061-2122-X*) U of Okla Pr.

Nothing But... Shape Books! Reproducible Shape Book Patterns for All Occasions! Karen Sevaly. (Illus.). 80p. (J). 1999. pap. 9.95 (*1-57882-022-7*, TF-1654) Teachers Friend Pubns.

Nothing but the Best. Thomas Girtin. 1960. 12.95 (*0-8392-1078-7*) Astor-Honor.

Nothing but the Best. Joy Haney. 1997. pap. 7.95 (*1-880969-23-8*) Schl Prophet.

Nothing but the Best. University of Alabama Staff. 292p. 1996. 24.95 (*0-9654540-0-2*, Pub. by U AL Coll Hum Envn) Wimmer Bk Dist.

Nothing but the Best Southern Recipes. Ed. by Kathleen L. Sloan. LC 77-23793. (Illus.). 1977. spiral bd. 7.00 (*0-915114-02-X*) Lewis-Sloan.

Nothing but the Blues. Bert Konowitz. Date not set. pap. write for info. incl. audio compact disk (*0-7390-0700-9*, 19354); pap. write for info. (*0-7390-0871-4*, 14484) Alfred Pub.

Nothing but the Blues: Postcard Book. (Postcard Bks.). (Illus.). 1995. pap. 7.95 (*1-55859-829-4*) Abbeville Pr.

Nothing But the Blues: The Music & the Musicians. Ed. by Lawrence Cohn. LC 93-2791. (Illus.). 432p. 1993. 45.00 (*1-55859-271-7*) Abbeville Pr.

Nothing but the Blues The Music & the Musicians. Lawrence Cohn. 1999. pap. text 35.00 (*0-7892-0607-2*) Abbeville Pr.

Nothing But the Blues: The Music & the Musicians. limited deluxe ed. Ed. by Lawrence Cohn. (Illus.). 432p. 1995. 100.00 incl. cd-rom (*1-55859-698-4*) Abbeville Pr.

Nothing but the Girl: The Blatant Lesbian Image. Susie Bright. Ed. by Jill Posener. 1996. 29.95 (*0-304-33482-0*, Pub. by Cassell) LPC InBook.

Nothing but the Girl: The Blatant Lesbian Image. Susie Bright. 1996. pap. 29.95 (*1-86047-001-7*, Pub. by Cassell) LPC InBook.

Nothing but the Girl: The Blatant Lesbian Image. Susie Bright. 1997. pap. text 24.95 (*1-86047-002-5*) Continuum.

Nothing but the Marvelous: The Wisdoms of Henry Miller. 2nd rev. expanded ed. Henry Miller. Ed. by Blair Fielding. (Illus.). 143p. 1999. pap. 12.95 (*0-88496-440-X*, Pub. by Capra Pr) Consort Bk Sales.

Nothing but the Night. Bill Pronzini. LC 98-43720. 272p. 1999. 23.95 (*0-8027-3330-1*) Walker & Co.

***Nothing but the Night.** large type ed. Bill Pronzini. 2000. 24.95 (*1-57490-266-0*, Beeler LP Bks) T T Beeler.

***Nothing but the Night.** Bill Pronzini. 272p. 2000. reprint ed. pap. 8.95 (*0-8027-7582-9*) Walker & Co.

Nothing but the Night. John Williams. LC 89-9131. 128p. 1990. reprint ed. pap. 14.00 (*1-55728-113-0*) U of Ark Pr.

Nothing but the Rent. Sharon Mitchell. LC 97-34068. 336p. 1998. 23.95 (*0-525-94306-4*) NAL.

Nothing but the Rent. Sharon Mitchell. 348p. 1999. mass mkt. 6.99 (*0-451-19260-5*, Sig) NAL.

Nothing but the Truth. (Assessment Packs Ser.). 15p. 1998. pap. text 15.95 (*1-58303-053-0*) Pthways Pubng.

Nothing but the Truth. Raz Autry. (Illus.). 250p. 1988. pap. 7.95 (*0-934145-61-X*) Airborne Pr.

Nothing But The Truth. Avon Staff. 1993. mass mkt. 4.99 (*0-380-26539-7*, Avon Bks) Morrow Avon.

Nothing but the Truth. Brian H. Edwards. 1993. pap. 16.99 (*0-85234-305-1*, Pub. by Evangelical Pr) P & R Pubng.

***Nothing But the Truth.** Phyllis A. Green. 36p. 1999. 9.95 (*1-56137-740-6*) Novel Units.

***Nothing but the Truth.** Karl Keating. 158p. 2000. pap. 11.95 (*1-888992-12-3*) Catholic Answers.

***Nothing But the Truth.** John Lescroart. 2000. mass mkt. 7.99 (*0-440-22664-3*) Dell.

***Nothing but the Truth.** John T. Lescroart. 1999. mass mkt. 7.50 (*0-440-29574-2*) Bantam Dell.

***Nothing but the Truth.** Samuel Lock. 232p. 1999. pap. 17.95 (*0-224-05084-2*, Pub. by Jonathan Cape) Trafalgar.

Nothing but the Truth. Ronn Smith. 1997. 10.09 (*0-606-11691-5*, Pub. by Turtleback) Demco.

***Nothing but the Truth.** large type ed. John T. Lescroart. LC 99-59449. 2000. 26.95 (*1-56895-813-7*) Wheeler Pub.

Nothing but the Truth: A Documentary Novel. Avi. 224p. (YA). (gr. 5 up). 1993. mass mkt. 4.99 (*0-380-71907-X*, Avon Bks) Morrow Avon.

Nothing but the Truth: A Documentary Novel. Avi. LC 91-9200. 192p. (YA). (gr. 6 up). 1991. 16.95 (*0-531-05959-6*) Orchard Bks Watts.

Nothing but the Truth: A Documentary Novel. Avi. (J). 1991. 9.60 (*0-606-05518-5*, Pub. by Turtleback) Demco.

Nothing but the Truth: A Documentary Novel. large type ed. Avi. LC 93-42497. (J). 1994. pap. 16.95 (*0-7862-0131-2*) Thorndike Pr.

***Nothing but the Truth: A Novel.** John T. Lescroart. LC 99-32584. 435p. 2000. 24.95 (*0-385-33353-6*) Delacorte.

Nothing but the Truth: A Play by Ronn Smith Based on the Award-Winning Novel by Avi. Ronn Smith. 256p. (YA). 1997. mass mkt. 4.99 (*0-380-78715-6*, Avon Bks) Morrow Avon.

Nothing but the Truth: A Student Response Journal. rev. ed. James Scott. 14p. (YA). (gr. 7-12). 1998. ring bd. 19.95 (*1-58049-719-5*, RJ13R) Prestwick Hse.

Nothing but the Truth: A Study Guide. Toni Albert. Ed. by J. Friedland & R. Kessler. (Novel-Ties Ser.). (J). (gr. 5-7). 1994. pap. text 15.95 (*1-56982-071-6*) Lrn Links.

***Nothing But the Truth: An Anthology of Native American Literature.** John L. Purdy & James Ruppert. 800p. 2000. pap. 37.33 (*0-13-011642-4*) P-H.

Nothing but the Truth: Defending the Gospel in a Disturbing Age. John F. MacArthur. LC 99-37022. 192p. 1999. pap. 10.99 (*1-58134-090-7*) Crossway Bks.

Nothing but theworldtheworldtheworld & Family Practice. Heather Laymon & Mark Yasenchack. 44p. (Orig.). 1989. pap. text 3.00 (*0-9623107-0-0*) Mybrothers Pr.

Nothing but Trouble. Beverly Barton. (Desire Ser.). 1994. per. 2.99 (*0-373-05881-0*, 1-05881-7) Silhouette.

Nothing but Trouble. Laura Bradley. (Scarlet Ser.). 1998. mass mkt. 3.99 (*1-85487-568-X*, Pub. by Scarlet Bks) London Brdge.

Nothing but Trouble. Gus Clarke. (Illus.). 32p. 1998. pap. 9.95 (*0-86264-841-6*, Pub. by Andersen Pr) Trafalgar.

Nothing but Trouble. Patricia Hermes. 160p. (J). (gr. 4-7). 1995. pap. 3.50 (*0-590-44876-5*) Scholastic Inc.

Nothing but Trouble. Betty R. Wright. (Illus.). 128p. (J). (gr. 2-5). 1997. pap. text 3.50 (*0-590-84912-3*) Scholastic Inc.

Nothing but Trouble, Trouble, Trouble. Patricia Hermes. LC 93-13968. 160p. (J). (gr. 3-7). 1994. 13.95 (*0-590-43499-3*) Scholastic Inc.

Nothing but Velvet. Kat Martin. 1997. mass mkt. 6.50 (*0-312-96243-6*) St Martin.

Nothing but Wedding Music Bk. 6: Piano. 64p. (Orig.). 1984. pap. 8.95 (*0-7692-1141-0*, PF0271) Wrner Bros.

An Asterisk (*) at the beginning of an entry indicates that the title is appearing for the first time.

Nothing But You. Roger Angell. LC 98-12965. 1998. pap. 15.00 (0-375-75150-5) Modern Lib NY.

Nothing by Chance. Richard Bach. 240p. 1990. mass mkt. 7.50 (0-440-20656-1) Dell.

Nothing by Chance: A Gypsy Pilot's Adventures in Modern America. Richard Bach. (Illus.). 194p. 1983. text 18.95 (0-02-504690-X) Macmillan.

***Nothing Can Possibly Go Wrong!** Chuck Harman. Ed. by Sandra J. Payne. (Adventures of Artie the Airplane & His Friends Ser.). (Illus.). 32p. (J). (gr. k-6). 1999. pap. 6.99 (1-891736-07-8) Studio Five.

Nothing Can Rescue Me. large type ed. Elizabeth Daly. 315p. 1991. reprint ed. lib. bdg. 20.95 (1-56054-217-9) Thorndike Pr.

Nothing Changes Love. Jacqueline Baird. LC 95-13706. (Presents Ser.). 188p. 1995. per. 3.25 (0-373-11757-4, 1-11757-1) Harlequin Bks.

Nothing Could Be Finer: Canden Polo 1898-1948. John H. Daniels. 200p. 1997. 49.95 (1-887269-27-4) J Culler & Sons.

Nothing Daunted: The Story of Isobel Kuhn. Gloria Repp. Ed. by Manda Cooper. LC 94-15531. (Light Line Ser.). 168p. 1994. pap. 6.49 (0-89084-753-3, 080481) Bob Jones Univ.

Nothing Diplomatic: Five Decades of True & Witty Tales from a Globetrotting Diplomat. Richard G. Leonard. LC 96-86103. (Illus.). 128p. (Orig.). 1997. pap. 14.00 (1-885884-84-2) Cormorant Pr.

Nothing Down: Dynamic New High-Profit, Low-Risk Strategies for Building Real Estate Wealth in the '90s - The New Revised Edition for the All-Time Bestselling Real Estate Book. Robert G. Allen. 368p. 1990. 23.50 (0-671-72558-0) S&S Trade.

Nothing Echoes Like an Empty Mailbox. Charles M. Schulz. (Peanuts Classics Ser.). (Illus.). 128p. 1995. pap. 7.95 (0-8050-3936-8, Owlet BYR) H Holt & Co.

Nothing Echoing Endlessly. Sam L. Vulgaris. Ed. by SA-DE Publications Staff. (Illus.). 132p. (Orig.). 1990. per. write for info. (0-9620417-5-0) SA-DE Pubns.

Nothing Else Matters: A Sam Casey Mystery. S. D. Tooley. 288p. 2000. 22.95 (0-9666021-2-9) Full Moon Pub.

Nothing Ever Happened. David Godman. (Illus.). 1308p. 1998. pap. 45.00 (0-9638022-5-9) Avadhuta Fnd.

Nothing Ever Happens Here. Patricia Sealey. (Junior African Writers Ser.). (Illus.). 80p. (J). (gr. 3 up). 1992. pap. 3.88 (0-7910-2903-4) Chelsea Hse.

Nothing Ever Happens on 90th Street. Roni Schotter. LC 96-4000. (Illus.). 32p. (J). (gr. k-5). 1997. 16.95 (0-531-09536-3); lib. bdg. 17.99 (0-531-08886-3) Orchard Bks Watts.

Nothing Ever Happens on 90th Street. Roni Schotter. LC 96-4000. (Illus.). 32p. (J). (gr. k-5). 1999. pap. 5.95 (0-531-07136-7) Orchard Bks Watts.

Nothing Exists That Is Not Shiva: Commentaries on the Shiva Sutra, Vijnanabhairava, Gurugita, & Other Sacred Texts. Swami Muktananda. LC 97-22811. 160p. (Orig.). 1997. pap. 12.95 (0-911307-56-7) SYDA Found.

Nothing Face Voivod: With Tablature. 1992. 16.95 (0-89524-710-0, 02507064) Cherry Lane.

Nothing Fancy: Recipes & Recollections of Soul-Satisfying Food. Diana Kennedy. 262p. 1998. 14.95 (0-89815-991-1) Ten Speed Pr.

Nothing Friendly in the Vicinity: My Patrols on the Submarine USS Guardfish in World War II. Claude C. Conner. LC 99-63652. (Illus.). 240p. 1999. 24.95 (1-882810-41-4) Savas Pub.

Nothing Gold Can Stay. Rosemary Matteson. Ed. by Donna Ingham. LC 98-61620. 260p. 1999. pap. 17.95 (1-881636-73-9) Windsor Hse Pub Grp.

***Nothing Gold Can Stay.** Casey Nelson. LC 00-26233. 256p. 2000. pap. 12.95 (1-55583-492-2, Pub. by Alyson Pubns) Consort Bk Sales.

***Nothing Gold Can Stay: A Liam Campbell Mystery.** Dana Stabenow. 288p. 2000. 23.95 (0-525-94559-8, Dutt) Dutton Plume.

Nothing Good Ever Happens to Me: An Adoption Love Story. Caroline H. Lindsay. 128p. 1996. pap. text 9.95 (0-87868-601-0) Child Welfare.

Nothing Grows by Moonlight. Torborg Nedreaas. Tr. by Bibbi Lee from NOR. LC 87-5000. (European Women Writers Ser.).Tr. of Av Maneskinn Gror det Ingenting. vi, 198p. 1987. text 30.00 (0-8032-3313-2) U of Nebr Pr.

Nothing Grows in One Place Forever: Poems of a Sicilian-American. Leo L. Marcello. LC 98-11360. 119p. 1998. 22.00 (1-56809-036-6); pap. 14.50 (1-56809-037-4) Time Being Bks.

Nothing Happened. Bill Harley. LC 94-10266. (Illus.). 32p. (J). (gr. 1 up). 1995. 14.95 (1-883672-09-0) Tricycle Pr.

Nothing Happened. Ebba Haslund & Barbara Wilson. LC 98-55440.Tr. of Det/Hendte Ingenting. (Illus.). 200p. 1999. 12.95 (1-879679-13-2, Pub. by Women Translation) Consort Bk Sales.

Nothing Happened & Besides I Wasn't There. Mark Wallace. 56p. 1997. pap. 9.50 (1-890311-01-4) Edge Bks.

Nothing Happens: Chantal Akerman's Hyperrealist Everyday. Ivone Margulies. LC 95-30516. (Illus.). 288p. 1996. text 49.95 (0-8223-1726-5); pap. text 17.95 (0-8223-1723-0) Duke.

Nothing Happens Next: Responses to Questions about Meditation. Cheri Huber. Orig. Title: The Perils & Pitfalls of Practice. (Illus.). 122p. 1995. pap. 8.00 (0-9636255-3-5, 2097280859) Keep it Simple.

Nothing Here But Trees. Jean Van Leeuwen. LC 97-34318. (Illus.). 32p. (J). (gr. k-4). 1998. 15.99 (0-8037-2178-1, Dial Yng Read) Peng Put Young Read.

Nothing If Not Critical: Selected Essays on Art & Artists. Robert Hughes. 488p. 1992. pap. 15.95 (0-14-016524-X, Penguin Bks) Viking Penguin.

Nothing in Common. Barbara Bottner. LC 85-45834. 176p. (YA). (gr. 7 up). 1986. 12.95 (0-06-020604-7) HarpC Child Bks.

***Nothing in Itself: Complexions of Fashion.** Herbert Blau. LC 99-19964. (Theories of Contemporary Culture Ser.). 352p. 1999. 49.95 (0-253-33587-6) Ind U Pr.

Nothing in Itself: Complexions of Fashion. Herbert Blau. LC 99-19964. (Theories of Contemporary Culture Ser.). (Illus.). 352p. 1999. pap. 24.95 (0-253-21333-9) Ind U Pr.

Nothing in Nature Is Private. Claudia Rankine. Ed. by Nuala Archer. (CSU Poetry Ser.: Vol. XLIV). 88p. (Orig.). 1994. pap. 10.00 (1-880834-09-X) Cleveland St Univ Poetry Ctr.

Nothing in Nature Is Private. Claudia Rankine. Ed. by Nuala Archer. (CSU Poetry Ser.: Vol. XLIV). 88p. (Orig.). 1995. 15.00 (1-880834-10-3) Cleveland St Univ Poetry Ctr.

Nothing in the Mailbox see Nada en el Buzon

Nothing in the Mailbox. Carolyn Ford. (Books for Young Learners). (Illus.). 12p. (J). (gr. k-2). 1996. pap. text 5.00 (1-57274-022-1, A2483) R Owen Pubs.

Nothing in This Book Is True, but It's Exactly How Things Are: The Esoteric Meaning of the Monuments on Mars. Bob Frissell. LC 94-19400. (Illus.). 230p. (Orig.). 1994. pap. 14.95 (1-883319-01-3) Frog Ltd CA.

Nothing in Your Hands. William Andris. LC 86-82253. 200p. (Orig.). 1986. pap. 6.95 (0-9604278-1-3) St Basil Pr.

Nothing Is Altogether Trivial: An Anthology of Writing from the Edinburgh Review. Murdo MacDonald. (Illus.). 240p. 1996. pap. 22.00 (0-7486-0698-X, Pub. by Edinburgh U Pr) Col U Pr.

Nothing Is As It Seems: The Tragedy of the Implicit in Euripides' "Hippolytus" Hanna M. Roisman. LC 98-36863. (Greek Studies). 304p. 1998. 68.00 (0-8476-9092-X); pap. 24.95 (0-8476-9093-8) Rowman.

Nothing Is As It Should Be: A North American Woman in Chile. Carol Andreas. LC 76-7836. (Illus.). 140p. 1976. pap. text 16.95 (0-87073-779-1) Schenkman Bks Inc.

Nothing Is Beatleproof: Advanced Beatles Trivia for Fab Four Fanciers. Michael J. Hockinson. LC 89-92311. (Rock & Roll Trivia Ser.: No. 1). (Illus.). 250p. 1990. 34.50 (1-56075-006-5) Popular Culture.

Nothing Is for Free. large type ed. William Newton. (Linford Mystery Library). 1991. pap. 16.99 (0-7089-7132-6) Ulverscroft.

***Nothing Is Forever.** Created by Francine Pascal. (Sweet Valley High Senior Year Ser.: No. 20). 192p. (YA). (gr. 7 up). 2000. pap. 4.50 (0-553-49336-1, Sweet Valley) BDD Bks Young Read.

Nothing Is Funny: The True Costs of Political Corrections. Jon C. Caldara. 11p. 1993. pap. text 8.00 (1-57655-101-6) Independ Inst.

***Nothing Is Hidden: Essays on Zen Master Dogen's Instructions for the Cook.** Ed. by Shohaku Okumura & Jisho Warner. 2000. pap. 14.95 (0-8348-0478-6) Weatherhill.

Nothing Is Impossible. Drumbeat Publishing Staff. Date not set. pap. text. write for info. (0-582-78570-7, Pub. by Addison-Wesley) Longman.

Nothing Is Impossible, Said Nelly Bly. Judy Carlson. (Real Readers Ser.: Level Blue). (Illus.). 32p. (J). (gr. 1-4). 1989. pap. 4.95 (0-8114-6721-X) Raintree Steck-V.

Nothing Is Impossible with God. Kathryn Kuhlman. (Illus.). 323p. 1992. reprint ed. pap. 10.99 (0-88270-656-X) Bridge-Logos.

Nothing is Sacred. Mark Espinoza. 50p. (Orig.). 1992. pap. 3.95 (1-880537-00-1) Dimension.

Nothing Is Sacred. Josephine Herbst. Ed. by Elizabeth Hardwick. LC 76-51671. (Rediscovered Fiction by American Women Ser.). 1977. reprint ed. lib. bdg. 27.95 (0-405-10050-7) Ayer.

***Nothing Is Terrible.** Matthew Sharpe. LC 99-39236. 288p. 2000. 23.95 (0-375-50197-5) Villard Books.

Nothing Is the Number When You Die. Joan Fleming. 1996. 19.50 (0-7451-8695-5, Black Dagger) Chivers N Amer.

Nothing Is Too Good to Be True: Seven Steps to Personal Freedom & Creative Fulfillment. Leona E. Stefanko & Carol Keefer. 180p. (Orig.). 1992. pap. 9.95 (0-9633732-0-X) Inst Self-Awareness.

Nothing Is Too Wonderful to Be True. Philip Morrison. LC 94-17906. (Masters of Modern Physics Ser.). 1994. 34.95 (1-56396-363-9) Spr-Verlag.

Nothing Is Worth More Than This Day. Mary Engelbreit. 1998. 10.95 (0-8362-6395-2) Andrews & McMeel.

Nothing Larger Than Life: A Novel. Ed. by Brynmill Press Ltd. Staff. 240p. (C). 1989. 85.00 (0-907839-46-0, Pub. by Brynmill Pr Ltd) St Mut.

Nothing Lasts Forever. Sidney Sheldon. 400p. 1995. reprint ed. mass mkt. 7.99 (0-446-35473-2, Pub. by Warner Bks) Little.

Nothing Lasts Forever - Roman Pompeii: World History Unit for the Middle Grades. rev. ed. Lyn Reese. Ed. by Mary A. Dougherty & Jean B. Wilkinson. (Illus.). 37p. (YA). (gr. 6-9). 1990. spiral bd. 10.00 (0-9625880-5-9) Wom Wrld Hist.

Nothing Left to Give. large type ed. Caroline Anderson. 288p. 1995. 23.99 (0-263-14175-6, Pub. by Mills & Boon) Ulverscroft.

Nothing Less Than Love. large type ed. Vanessa Grant. (Harlequin Ser.). 1993. reprint ed. lib. bdg. 18.95 (0-263-13263-3) Mac Lib Ref.

Nothing Less Than Victory. Russell Miller. 1998. pap. 15.00 (0-688-16845-0, Quil) HarperTrade.

Nothing Like Blood. Leo Bruce. (Carolus Deene Mystery Ser.). 192p. 1985. 15.00 (0-89733-128-1) Academy Chi Pubs.

***Nothing Like It in the World: The Men Who Built the Transcontinental Railroad 1865-1869.** Stephen E. Ambrose. (Illus.). 416p. 2000. 28.00 (0-684-84609-8) S&S Trade.

***Nothing Like It in the World: The Men Who Built the Transcontinental Railroad 1865-1869.** large type ed. Stephen E. Ambrose. 416p. 2000. 28.00 (0-7432-0430-1) S&S Trade.

Nothing Like the Sun: A Magnificent, Bawdy Telling of Shakespeare's Love. Anthony Burgess. 240p. 1996. pap. 12.00 (0-393-31507-X) Norton.

Nothing Man. 1991. mass mkt. 4.50 (0-445-77442-8, Pub. by Warner Bks) Little.

Nothing Man. Jim Thompson. LC 97-26239. 1997. pap. 10.00 (0-375-70031-5) Vin Bks.

Nothing Mat(t)ers: A Feminist Critique of Postmodernism. Somer Brodribb. 208p. 1992. text 50.00 (1-875559-10-8) NYU Pr.

Nothing Mat(t)ers: A Feminist Critique of Postmodernism. Somer Brodribb. 208p. (C). 1992. text 50.00 (0-87555-910-7, 559108) NYU Pr.

Nothing Matters, & Other Stories. Herbert B. Tree. LC 70-132130. (Short Story Index Reprint Ser.). 1977. 19.95 (0-8369-3687-6) Ayer.

Nothing More Agreeable: Music in George Washington's Family. Judith S. Britt. LC 84-20735. (Illus.). 120p. 1984. pap. 4.95 (0-931917-10-7) Mt Vernon Ladies.

***Nothing More Heroic: A Pioneer Missionary Memoir of Courage & Faith** R. Lanier Britsch. LC 99-35842. 1999. write for info. (1-57345-565-2) Deseret Bk.

Nothing More, Nothing Less. Jane McFann. 176p. (Orig.). (YA). (gr. 5 up). 1993. pap. 3.50 (0-380-76636-1, Avon Bks) Morrow Avon.

Nothing More Than Murder. Jim Thompson. LC 90-50630. 240p. 1991. pap. 11.00 (0-679-73309-4) Vin Bks.

***Nothing More Than Question Marks.** Billi Caye. 24p. 1999. 3.50 (1-57688-016-8, 80168) Branch & Vine.

Nothing Much Happened at School Today. Danny Gordon. 24p. (J). (gr. k-6). 1992. pap. 5.00 (1-886210-01-2) Tyketoon Yng Author.

Nothing, Nobody: The Voices of the Mexico City Earthquake. Elena Poniatowska. Tr. by Aurora de Camacho Schimidt & Arthur Schimidt. (Voices of Latin America Life Ser.). (Illus.). (Orig.). (C). 1995. pap. 22.95 (1-56639-345-0); lib. bdg. 69.95 (1-56639-344-2) Temple U Pr.

Nothing on My Mind: An Intimate Account of American Zen. Erik Storlie. LC 96-16432. 208p. (Orig.). 1996. pap. 14.00 (1-57062-183-7, Pub. by Shambhala Pubns) Random.

Nothing Out There: Poems by Paul B. Roth. Paul B. Roth. LC 96-60530. 80p. 1996. pap. 9.95 (0-9632547-6-6) Vida Pub.

Nothing Personal. Eileen Dreyer. 480p. 1997. mass mkt. 6.50 (0-06-104275-7, Harp PBks) HarpC.

***Nothing Personal.** Jason Starr. 256p. 2000. pap. 14.00 (1-56858-161-0, Pub. by FWEW) Publishers Group.

Nothing Real Can Be Threatened. Tara Singh. LC 89-35821. 285p. (Orig.). 1989. pap. 13.95 (1-55531-230-6) Life Action Pr.

Nothing Remains but to Fight: The Defence of Rorke's Drift, 1879. Ian Knight. LC 92-41770. 168p. 1993. 45.00 (1-85367-137-1, 5565) Stackpole.

***Nothing Risque Nothing Gained.** S. Leaderer. 1998. pap. 100.00 (81-86982-61-2, Pub. by Business Pubns) St Mut.

Nothing Risque, Nothing Gained: Ribald Riddles, Lascivious Limericks, Carnal Corn & Other Good, Clean, Dirty Fun. Richard Lederer. LC 95-12959. (Illus.). 294p. (Orig.). 1995. pap. 12.00 (1-55652-243-6) Chicago Review.

Nothing Sacred. Al Cairns. 1998. mass mkt. 6.99 (0-7704-2766-9) Bantam.

***Nothing Sacred.** Michael Vollbracht. (Illus.). 156p. 2000. text 85.00 (0-8478-2245-1) Rizzoli Intl.

Nothing Sacred: Nazi Espionage Against the Vatican, 1939-1945. David J. Alvarez & Robert A. Graham. LC 97-11657. (Studies in Intelligence). 190p. 1997. 52.50 (0-7146-4744-6, Pub. by F Cass Pubs); pap. 24.50 (0-7146-4302-5, Pub. by F Cass Pubs) Intl Spec Bk.

***Nothing Scares Us.** Frieda Wishinsky. LC 00-8022. (Picture Bks.). 32p. (J). (ps-3). 2000. 15.95 (1-57505-490-6, Carolrhoda) Lerner Pub.

Nothing Sensible: Erotic Haiku. Sue Dering. 12p. (Orig.). 1994. pap. 6.95 (0-9644532-0-7) S Dering Pub.

Nothing Serious, Just a Little Chat with the Boss. Ann E. Weeks. 52p. 1994. pap. 7.00 (1-886036-01-2) Passages Pbg.

Nothing Serious...The Best of Jack Cowan. Jack Cowan. LC 87-91343. 200p. 1987. 12.95 (0-9617335-2-7); pap. write for info. (0-9617335-3-5) San Angelo Standard Times.

Nothing Short of a Miracle. Patricia Thayer. (Special Edition Ser.: No. 1116). 1997. per. 3.99 (0-373-24116-X, 1-24116-5) Silhouette.

Nothing Short of a Miracle. Patricia Treece. LC 93-87105. 264p. 1994. pap. 9.95 (0-87973-741-7, 741) Our Sunday Visitor.

Nothing Special: Living Zen. Charlotte J. Beck & Steve Smith. LC 92-56131. 288p. 1994. reprint ed. pap. 13.00 (0-06-251117-3, Pub. by Harper SF) HarpC.

Nothing Sticks Like a Shadow. Ann Tompert. LC 83-18554. (Illus.). 32p. (J). (gr. k-3). 1988. pap. 7.95 (0-395-47950-9) HM.

Nothing Stops a Determined Being! write for info. (0-918430-04-6) Happy History.

Nothing Stops a Determined Being! Aron Breslow. 2000. write for info. (0-918430-03-8) Happy History.

Nothing Succeeds Like Success. Christian D. Larson. 80p. 1997. pap. 35.00 (0-89540-385-4) Sun Pub.

***Nothing Tastes Quite Like a Gerbil: And Other Vile Verses.** David Orme. (Illus.). 64p. (J). 2000. mass mkt. 4.99 (0-330-34632-9) Mcm Child Bks.

Nothing That Is: A Natural History of Zero. Robert Kaplan. LC 99-29000. (Illus.). 240p. 1999. 22.00 (0-19-512842-7) OUP.

***Nothing That Is: A Natural History of Zero, 6 vols.** Robert Kaplan. (Illus.). 1999. pap. 176.00 (0-19-521568-0) OUP.

Nothing the Sun Could Not Explain: New Brazilian Poetry. Ed. by Regis Bonvicino et al. (Sun & Moon Classics Ser.: Vol. 82). 200p. 1998. pap. 15.95 (1-55713-366-2) Sun & Moon CA.

Nothing Things. P. N. Dedeaux. 1998. mass mkt. 6.95 (1-56333-653-7) Masquerade.

Nothing to Be Afraid Of. Jan Mark. LC 81-48064. 128p. (J). (gr. 6 up). 1982. 12.95 (0-06-024087-3) HarpC Child Bks.

Nothing to Be Ashamed Of: Growing up with Mental Illness in Your Family. Sherry H. Dinner. 160p. (J). (ps-3). 1989. lib. bdg. 12.93 (0-688-08482-6) Lothrop.

***Nothing to Be Ashamed of: Growing up with Mental Illness in Your Family.** Sherry H. Dinner. 212p. (YA). (gr. 6-7). 2000. reprint ed. text 22.00 (0-7881-9093-8) DIANE Pub.

Nothing to Declare: A Memoir. Taki. LC 91-10724. (Illus.). 224p. 1992. pap. 10.00 (0-87113-484-5, Atlntc Mnthly) Grove-Atltic.

Nothing to Declare: Memoirs of a Woman Traveling Alone. Mary Morris. LC 98-46693. 304p. 1998. pap. 13.00 (0-312-19941-4) St Martin.

Nothing to Declare: Memoirs of a Woman Traveling Alone. large type ed. Mary Morris. (General Ser.). 355p. 1989. lib. bdg. 19.95 (0-8161-4730-2, G K Hall Lrg Type) Mac Lib Ref.

Nothing to Do. Horatio Alger, Jr. (Works of Horatio Alger Jr.). 1989. reprint ed. lib. bdg. 79.00 (0-685-27581-7) Rprt Serv.

Nothing to Do: A Tilt at Our Best Society. Horatio Alger, Jr. (Illus.). 45p. 1978. reprint ed. 18.00 (0-686-37021-X) G K Westgard.

Nothing to Do but Stay: My Pioneer Mother. large type ed. Carrie Young. LC 93-30413. 184p. 1993. lib. bdg. 19.95 (0-7862-0072-3) Thorndike Pr.

Nothing to Do but Stay: My Pioneer Mother. Carrie Young. LC 90-49401. (Bur Oak Original Ser.). (Illus.). 127p. 2000. reprint ed. pap. 12.95 (0-87745-329-2) U of Iowa Pr.

Nothing to Do but to Save Souls: John Wesley's Charge to His Preachers. Robert E. Coleman. LC 90-50723. 107p. 1994. reprint ed. pap. 8.00 (0-915143-05-4) Evangel Indiana.

N

Nothing to Do but to Save Souls...John Wesley: John Wesley's Charge to His Preachers. Robert E. Coleman. 112p. 1990. 9.95 (0-310-75480-1); pap. 7.99 (0-310-75481-X) Zondervan.

Nothing To Do with Dionysos: Athenian Drama in Its Social Context. Ed. by John J. Winkler & Froma I. Zeitlin. (Illus.). 396p. 1990. pap. text 21.95 (0-691-01525-2, Pub. by Princeton U Pr) Cal Prin Full Svc.

Nothing to Fear. Jackie F. Koller. Ed. by Karen Grove. LC 90-39344. 288p. (YA). (gr. 5 up). 1991. 14.95 (0-15-200544-7, Gulliver Bks) Harcourt.

Nothing to Fear. Jackie F. Koller. LC 90-39444. 288p. (YA). (gr. 5 up). 1993. pap. 8.00 (0-15-257582-0, Gulliver Bks) Harcourt.

Nothing to Fear. Jackie French Koller. 1991. 13.10 (0-606-05956-3, Pub. by Turtleback) Demco.

***Nothing to Fear.** Jefferey Modic & Bayard Stockton. vii, 224p. 1999. 16.00 (0-9672508-0-3) Tres Pinos.

Nothing to Fear. Franklin D. Roosevelt, Jr. LC 76-128302. (Essay Index Reprint Ser.). 1977. 30.95 (0-8369-1845-2) Ayer.

***Nothing to Fear: Devotions for the End Time.** Morris L. Venden. Ed. by Kenneth Wade. LC 98-37464. 144p. 1999. pap. 9.99 (0-8163-1695-3) Pacific Pr Pub Assn.

Nothing to Fear: Jesus Walks on Water. Marilyn Lashbrook. (J). (gr. k-4). 1998. pap. 5.95 (0-933657-82-X) Rainbow Studies.

Nothing to Fear: Jesus Walks on Water. Marilyn Lashbrook. LC 90-61060. (Me Too! Bks.). (Illus.). 32p. (J). (gr. k-3). 1991. 6.95 (0-86606-443-5, 3000958) Treasure Pub.

Nothing to Fear: Risks & Hazards in American Society. Ed. by Andrew Kirby. LC 90-11011. 301p. 1990. 39.95 (0-8165-1185-3) U of Ariz Pr.

Nothing to Lose. Frances J. Beard. LC 97-90378. 224p. 1997. pap. 13.95 (0-9658370-1-7) FJ Co.

Nothing to Lose. Clifton A. Cross. 192p. (Orig.). 1995. pap., per. 9.95 (1-885951-13-2) Pprbck Writer.

Nothing to Lose. Lisa K. Friedman. LC 98-83083. 256p. 2000. pap. 14.95 (0-88739-243-1) Creat Arts Bk.

Nothing to Lose. large type ed. Robert Charles. (Linford Mystery Library). 416p. 1998. pap. 17.99 (0-7089-5208-9, Linford) Ulverscroft.

Nothing to Lose. large type ed. Isobel Neill. (Romance Ser.). 1994. pap. 16.99 (0-7089-7610-7, Linford) Ulverscroft.

Nothing to Lose. David Fennario. 144p. 1977. reprint ed. pap. 12.95 (0-88922-121-9, Pub. by Talonbks) Genl Dist Srvs.

Nothing to Lose but Our Lives: Empowerment to Oppose Industrial Hazards in a Transitional World. Ed. by David Dembo et al. 208p. (Orig.). (C). 1988. pap. 13.50 (0-936876-38-7) LRIS.

Nothing to Pay. Caradoc Evans. LC 95-1773. (New Directions Classics Ser.). 240p. 1995. pap. 11.95 (0-8112-1290-4, NDP800, Pub. by New Directions) Norton.

Nothing to Prove: The Jim Abbott Story. Bob Bernotas. Ed. by John Urda. (Illus.). 192p. (YA). 1995. 18.00 (1-56836-064-9) Kodansha.

Nothing to Read: Newspapers & Elections in a Social Experiment. Jeffrey J. Mondak. LC 95-16976. 200p. 1995. text 44.50 (0-472-09599-4, 09599); pap. text 19.95 (0-472-06599-8, 06599) U of Mich Pr.

Nothing to Remember. Julia Holland. LC 99-204592. 1998. pap. 12.95 (*0-7022-3062-6*, Pub. by Univ Queensland Pr) Intl Spec Bk.

Nothing Too Good for a Cowboy. Richmond P. Hobson. 254p. 1996. pap. 9.95 (*0-7710-1862-2*) McCland & Stewart.

Nothing Unusual: The Torture of Children in Turkey. Ed. by Human Rights Watch Staff. 80p. (Orig.). 1992. pap. 7.00 (*1-56432-052-9*) Hum Rts Watch.

Nothing Venture. Patricia Wentworth. 256p. 1990. mass mkt. 5.50 (*0-446-35908-4*, Pub. by Warner Bks) Little.

Nothing Venture. Patricia Wentworth. 1994. pap. write for info. (*0-318-70048-4*) Warner Bks.

Nothing Ventured: The Perils & Payoffs of the Great American Venture Capital Game. Robert J. Kunze. 224p. 1991. 22.95 (*0-88730-461-3*, HarpBusn) HarpInfo.

Nothing Ventured, Nothing Gained: The Seattle JOA & Newspaper Preservation. Tim A. Pilgrim. LC 97-15997. (Illus.). 288p. 1997. pap. 39.50 (*1-56750-050-1*); text 78.50 (*0-89391-886-5*) Ablx Pub.

***Nothing Ventured Nothing Gained: Thrills & Spills in Venture Capital.** Bill Ferris. (Illus.). 152p. 2000. pap. 24.95 (*1-86508-281-3*, Pub. by Allen & Unwin Pty) Paul & Co Pubs.

Nothing Wakes Her. Faye Kicknosway. (Illus.). 1979. 12.50 (*0-933114-01-X*); pap. 3.50 (*0-933114-00-1*) Oyster Pr.

Nothing Was Ever Said. Ellen Mahaffy. (Illus.). 116p. 1993. 25.00 (*0-89822-109-9*) Visual Studies.

***Nothing We Lose Can Be Replaced.** Tom Meschery. (Rainshadow Editions Ser.). xii, 67p. 1999. pap. 12.00 (*1-891033-15-8*) Black Rock Pr.

Nothing Will Be As Sweet As the Taste. Elana Dykewomon. 1995. pap. 9.99 (*0-906500-57-5*) LPC InBook.

Nothing Without Christ: Some Current Problems in Religious Thought in the Light of Seventeenth Century Thought & Experience. Dean Freiday. LC 84-70040. 1984. pap. 3.95 (*0-913342-44-0*) Barclay Pr.

Nothing Without Providence. Michael Yates. (Illus.). 160p. (Orig.). 1993. pap. 9.95 (*0-9635793-1-2*) Green Hse Pr.

Nothing/Doing. Cid Corman. LC 99-31894. 160p. 1999. pap. 13.95 (*0-8112-1425-7*, Pub. by New Directions) Norton.

Nothingness: The Science of Empty Space. Henning Genz. LC 98-87966. (Illus.). 352p. 1998. text 30.00 (*0-7382-0061-1*, Helix Bks) Perseus Pubng.

***Nothingness & Emptiness: A Buddhist Engagement with the Ontology of Jean-Paul Sartre.** Steven W. Laycock. (C). 2001. pap. text. write for info. (*0-7914-4910-6*) State U NY Pr.

N

***Nothingness & Emptiness: A Buddhist Engagement with the Ontology of Jean-Paul Sartre.** Steven W. Laycock. (C). 2001. text. write for info. (*0-7914-4909-2*) State U NY Pr.

Nothingness Beyond God: An Introduction to the Philosophy of Nishida Kitaro. 2nd expanded rev. ed. Robert E. Carter. LC 97-32790. (Illus.). 256p. (C). 1998. pap. text 16.95 (*1-55778-761-1*) Paragon Hse.

***Nothings: Poems from Hollywood.** Mark Dunster. 11p. 1999. pap. 5.00 (*0-89642-985-7*) Linden Pubs.

Nothing's Fair in Fifth Grade see Best-Selling Apples

Nothing's Fair in Fifth Grade. Barthe DeClements. 137p. (J). (gr. 3-5). pap. 4.50 (*0-8072-1413-2*) Listening Lib.

Nothing's Fair in Fifth Grade. Barthe DeClements. LC 80-54195. 144p. (J). (gr. 4-7). 1981. 15.99 (*0-670-51741-0*, Viking Child) Peng Put Young Read.

Nothing's Fair in Fifth Grade. Barthe DeClements. LC 89-48757. (Illus.). 137p. (J). (gr. 3-7). 1990. pap. 4.99 (*0-14-034443-8*, PuffinBks) Peng Put Young Read.

Nothing's Fair in Fifth Grade. Barthe DeClements. (J). 1981. 9.09 (*0-606-04491-4*, Pub. by Turtleback) Demco.

Nothings Gonna Stop Us Now. 144p. (Orig.). (YA). 1991. pap. 16.95 (*0-7692-1058-9*, VF1738) Wrner Bros.

Nothing's Impossible. large type ed. Brian Blessed. 288p. 1996. 22.95 (*1-85695-113-8*, Pub. by ISIS Lrg Prnt) Transaction Pubs.

***Nothing's Impossible: Leadership Lessons from Inside & Outside the Classroom.** Lorraine Monroe. LC 99-19298. 240p. 1999. pap. 12.00 (*1-891620-20-7*, Pub. by PublicAffairs NY) HarpC.

Nothing's Impossible-Everything's Possible. Chuck Taylor. 45p. 1986. pap. 4.95 (*0-941720-27-6*); lib. bdg. 10.95 (*0-941720-28-4*) Slough Pr TX.

Nothing's the End of the World. Sara Holbrook. LC 93-61164. (Illus.). 48p. (J). (gr. 3-7). 1995. 14.95 (*1-56397-249-2*, Wordsong) Boyds Mills Pr.

Nothin's Funnier Than Golf in Texas. Joe James. LC 98-37662. 1998. pap. 9.95 (*0-88415-294-4*, 5294) Gulf Pub.

Nothin's Funnier Than Golf in Texas. Joe James. LC 94-202316. (Illus.). 96p. 1994. pap. 9.95 (*0-9631584-1-4*) Rocking J Pr.

Nothlove. William A. Hamilton. (Illus.). 67p. 1994. pap. 20.00 (*0-9658638-0-8*) Imagineering.

Nothstein: The First Nothstein Family History, 1750-1950, Descendants of Peter Nothstein of Pa. xxvi, 119p. 1992. reprint ed. pap. 22.50 (*0-8328-2699-5*); reprint ed. lib. bdg. 32.50 (*0-8328-2698-7*) Higginson Bk Co.

Notice & Think. Barbara L. McCombs & Linda Brannan. (Skills for Job Success Ser.). (Illus.). 32p. (Orig.). (YA). (gr. 7-12). 1990. teacher ed. 1.95 (*1-56119-002-0*); disk 39.95 (*1-56119-101-9*) Educ Pr MD.

Notice & Think. Barbara L. McCombs & Linda Brannan. (Skills for Job Success Ser.). (Illus.). 32p. (Orig.). 1990. pap., student ed. 5.95 (*1-56119-001-2*) Educ Pr MD.

Notice & Think, Set. Barbara L. McCombs & Linda Brannan. (Skills for Job Success Ser.). (Illus.). 32p. (Orig.). (YA). (gr. 7-12). 1990. teacher ed., wbk. ed. 54.95 (*1-56119-059-4*) Educ Pr MD.

Notice Concerning the Assessment of Cooperative Joint Ventures Pursuant to Article 85 of the EEC Treaty: An Assessment. Matthew P. Downs. (Leuven Law Ser.: Vol. 3). 60p. (Orig.). 1995. pap. 26.00 (*90-6186-690-1*, Pub. by Leuven Univ) Coronet Bks.

Notice Me! Ric Masten. LC 85-82615. 100p. 1986. pap. 6.00 (*0-931104-17-3*) SunInk Pubn.

Notice of Death. large type ed. John Penn. 1983. 27.99 (*0-7089-1060-2*) Ulverscroft.

Notice Sur Divers Manuscrits Grecs Relatifs A la Musique, Comprenant une Traduction Francaise et Des Commentaires. Alexandre J. Vincent. 600p. reprint ed. write for info. (*0-318-71444-2*) G Olms Pubs.

Notice sur les Collections Musicales de la Bibliotheque de Cambrai. Charles Coussemaker, pseud. 180p. 1975. reprint ed. 50.00 (*3-487-05857-X*) G Olms Pubs.

Notices & Documents Illustrative of the Literary History of Glasgow During the Greater Part of Last Century. Ed. by William J. Duncan. (Maitland Club, Glasgow. Publications: No. 14). reprint ed. 41.50 (*0-404-52947-X*) AMS Pr.

Notices from New Jersey Newspapers, 1781-1790. Thomas B. Wilson. (Records of New Jersey Ser.: Vol. 1). 561p. 1988. lib. bdg. 30.00 (*0-912606-32-0*) Hunterdon Hse.

Notices from the Local Records of Dysart. Ed. by William Muir. LC 73-164819. (Maitland Club, Glasgow. Publications: No. 73). reprint ed. 27.50 (*0-404-53110-5*) AMS Pr.

Notices from the New Hampshire Gazette, 1765-1800. Otis G. Hammond. 1985. lib. bdg. 15.00 (*0-912606-01-0*) Hunterdon Hse.

Notices Genealogical & Historical of the Martin Family of New England, Who Settled at Weymouth & Hingham in 1635, with Some Account of Their Descendants. H. J. Martin. 358p. 1989. reprint ed. pap. 53.50 (*0-8328-0859-8*); reprint ed. lib. bdg. 61.50 (*0-8328-0858-X*) Higginson Bk Co.

Notices of British Fungi: Eighteen Forty-One to Eighteen Forty-Five, 35 papers bd. in 1 vol., Vol. 1. M. J. Berkeley & C. E. Broome. 1967. 120.00 (*3-7682-0456-1*) Lubrecht & Cramer.

Notices of East Florida, with an Account of the Seminole Nation of Indians. William H. Simmons. Ed. by George E. Buker. LC 73-2820. (Floridiana Facsimile & Reprint Ser.). 123p. 1973. reprint ed. 17.95 (*0-8130-0400-4*) U Press Fla.

Notices of Original Unprinted Documents. Ed. by Joseph Stevenson. LC 70-176442. (Maitland Club, Glasgow. Publications: No. 56). reprint ed. 34.50 (*0-404-53045-1*) AMS Pr.

Notices of the Indian Archipelago & Adjacent Countries. J. H. Moor. 398p. 1968. reprint ed. 85.00 (*0-7146-2020-3*, Pub. by F Cass Pubs) Intl Spec Bk.

Notices of the Jews & Their Country by the Classic Writers of Antiquity. Ed. by John Gill. LC 70-97281. (Judaica Ser.). 180p. 1972. reprint ed. lib. bdg. 55.00 (*0-8371-2603-7*, GINJ, Greenwood Pr) Greenwood.

Notices Relative to the Bannatyne Club. James Maidment. LC 70-172715. (Bannatyne Club, Edinburgh. Publications). reprint ed. 37.50 (*0-404-52887-2*) AMS Pr.

Notices to Airmen. Government Printing Office Staff. 1996. per. 91.00 (*0-16-011826-3*) USGPO.

Noticia de un Secuestro - Notice of a Kidnapping. Gabriel Garcia Marquez. 1996. pap. 13.95 (*0-14-026247-4*) Viking Penguin.

Noticias de Nutka: An Account of Nootka Sound in 1792. Jose M. Mozino. LC 84-45542. (American Ethnological Society Monographs: No. 50). 1988. reprint ed. 35.00 (*0-404-62948-2*) AMS Pr.

Noticias de Nutka: An Account of Nootka Sound in 1792. 2nd ed. Jose M. Mozino. Ed. & Tr. by Iris H. Engstrand from SPA. LC 90-50981. 200p. 1991. reprint ed. pap. 14.95 (*0-295-97103-7*) U of Wash Pr.

Noticias de Seguridad. 52p. 56.00 (*0-318-59936-8*) Inter-Am Safety.

Noticias Mundiales y la Profecia Biblica. C. Dyers.Tr. of World News & Bible Prophecy. (SPA.). 274p. pap. 9.99 (*1-56063-950-4*, 498210) Editorial Unilit.

Notification of Communicable Diseases: A Survey of Existing Legislation. WHO Staff. (International Digest of Health Legislation Offprints: Vol. 9, No. 4). 51p. 1958. 3.00 (*92-4-169094-1*) World Health.

Notification of New Chemical Substances in Accordance With Directive 67/548/eec On The Classification, Packaging, & Labelling of Dangerous Substances: No-longer Polymers List. European Commission. LC 97-203092. 75p. 1997. 18.00 (*92-827-8995-0*, Pub. by Comm Europ Commun) Bernan Associates.

Notification of New Chemical Substances in Accordance with Directive 67/548/eec on the Classification, Packaging, & Labelling of Dangerous Substances: No-Longer Polymers List. European Commission. LC 98-120608. 121 p. 1997. 30.00 (*92-828-0196-9*, Pub. by Comm Europ Commun) Bernan Associates.

Notification of New Chemical Substances in Accordance with Directive 67/548/EEC on the Classification, Packaging & Labelling of Dangerous Substances: Technical Guidance for the Completion of a Summary Notification Dossier for a New Chemical Substance Utilising the Structured Notification Interchange Format (SNIF), Base-Set & Levels 1 & 2. European Commission. LC 98-120627. 81 p. 1997. 19.00 (*92-828-0195-0*, Pub. by Comm Europ Commun) Bernan Associates.

***Notion of an Ideal Audience in Legal Argument.** George C. Christie. 232p. 2000. 104.00 (*0-7923-6283-7*, Kluwer Plenum) Kluwer Academic.

***Notion of Equality.** Mane Hajdin. LC 00-38100. (International Research Library of Philosophy). 2000. write for info. (*0-7546-2104-9*, Pub. by Ashgate Pub) Ashgate Pub Co.

***Notion of Family.** Eleanor Mallet. LC 99-32222. (Illus.). 80p. 2000. 18.00 (*1-882203-57-7*) Orange Frazer.

Notional Theory of Syntactic Categories. John M. Anderson. LC 96-21789. (Cambridge Studies in Linguistics: No. 82). 365p. 1997. text 69.95 (*0-521-58023-4*) Cambridge U Pr.

***Notions: Over 50 Great Gadgets You Can't Live Without.** Jolynn Gower. (Illus.). 2000. pap. 24.95 (*1-56158-415-0*) Taunton.

Notions & Perspectives of Nonlinear Optics: Proceeding of the Third International Aalborg Summer School. LC 97-125993. 630p. 1996. 61.00 (*981-02-2627-6*) World Scientific Pub.

Notions & Potions: A Safe, Pracctical Guide to Creating Magic & Miracles. Susan Bowes. LC 96-40136. (Illus.). 112p. 1997. pap. 14.95 (*0-8069-9602-1*) Sterling.

Notions & Reforms: In the Coming of Age. Richard E. Petitti. (Self Realization Bks.: Bk. III). (Illus.). 100p. 1986. pap. 10.00 (*0-938582-07-0*) Sensitive Man.

Notions of a Mirror: Poems Previously Uncollected, 1964-1982. Anthony Howell. 56p. 1983. pap. 13.95 (*0-85646-104-0*, Pub. by Anvil Press) Dufour.

Notions of Convexity. Lars Hormander. LC 94-32572. (Progress in Mathematics Ser.: Vol. 127). viii, 414p. 1994. 54.50 (*0-8176-3799-0*) Birkhauser.

Notions of Nationalism. Ed. by Sukumar Periwal. LC 95-233799. (Central European University Press Bks.). 258p. (C). 1995. text 51.95 (*1-85866-021-1*); pap. text 21.95 (*1-85866-022-X*) Ctrl Europ Univ.

Notions of the Americans: Picked up by a Travelling Bachelor. James Fenimore Cooper. Ed. by Gary Williams. LC 89-4493. (Writings of James Fenimore Cooper). 807p. (C). 1991. pap. text 24.95 (*0-7914-0214-2*) State U NY Pr.

Notions of the Americans: Picked up by a Travelling Bachelor. James Fenimore Cooper. Ed. by Gary Williams. LC 89-4493. (Writings of James Fenimore Cooper). 807p. (C). 1991. text 59.50 (*0-7914-0213-4*) State U NY Pr.

Notions of the Americans: Picked up by a Travelling Bachelor. James Fenimore Cooper. (Works of James Fenimore Cooper). 1990. reprint ed. lib. bdg. 79.00 (*0-7812-2377-6*) Rprt Serv.

Notions of the Deaf & Dumb Before Instruction. Harvey P. Peet. 1973. 59.95 (*0-8490-0740-2*) Gordon Pr.

Notions on Gregorian Rhythmics. Dom Gajard. (FRE.). 80p. (C). 1944. text 13.95 (*1-55725-033-2*, 4051, Pub. by Abbey St Peter Solesmes) Paraclete MA.

Notions Philosophiques Dictionnaire, 2 vols. Sylvain Auroux. (FRE.). 3344p. 1992. 995.00 (*0-7859-9268-5*) Fr & Eur.

Notitia Dignitatum. Ed. by Ireland. (LAT.). 1998. 37.50 (*3-8154-1552-7*, T1552, Pub. by B G Teubner) U of Mich Pr.

Notitia Dignitatum. Ed. by R. I. Ireland. (Illus.). 96p. (C). text 42.50 (*3-519-01552-8*) B G Teubner.

Notizen zum Unterricht. (Schriften Ser.: Bd. 3). Date not set. write for info. (*3-487-08381-7*) G Olms Pubs.

Notonemouridae (Insecta: Plecoptera) see Fauna of New Zealand Series

Notorious. Janet Dailey. 1995. 24.00 (*0-614-96256-0*) HarpC.

Notorious. Miller. 1987. mass mkt. 3.95 (*0-445-73484-1*, Pub. by Warner Bks) Little.

Notorious. Herb Ritts. LC 92-53227. (Illus.). 168p. 1992. 125.00 (*0-8212-1911-1*, Pub. by Bulfinch Pr) Little.

Notorious. large type ed. Janet Dailey. LC 96-16390. 1996. lib. bdg. 26.95 (*0-7862-0707-8*) Thorndike Pr.

Notorious. large type ed. Janet Dailey. LC 96-16390. 550p. 1997. pap. 24.95 (*0-7862-0706-X*) Thorndike Pr.

Notorious Abbess. Vera Chapman. Ed. by Ken Zahorski. LC 93-15629. 239p. 1997. 22.50 (*0-89733-387-X*) Academy Chi Pubs.

Notorious Abbess. Vera Chapman. 1998. pap. text 12.95 (*0-89733-447-7*) Academy Chi Pubs.

Notorious & Noble, 1. Janice Bennett. (Zebra Regency Romance Ser.). 288p. 1999. mass mkt. 4.99 (*0-8217-6266-4*) Kensgtn Pub Corp.

Notorious & Notable New Englanders. Peter F. Stevens. LC 96-52201. (Illus.). 288p. (Orig.). 1997. pap. 14.95 (*0-89272-397-1*) Down East.

Notorious Angel. Jennifer Blake. 384p. 1996. 24.00 (*0-7278-4992-1*) Severn Hse.

***Notorious Dr. August: His Real Life & Crimes.** Christopher Bram. LC 99-55805. 512p. 2000. 26.00 (*0-688-17569-4*, Wm Morrow) Morrow Avon.

Notorious Groom. Caroline Cross. (Desire Ser.). 1998. per. 3.75 (*0-373-76143-0*, 0-76143-7) Silhouette.

Notorious Identity: Materializing the Subject in Shakespeare. Linda Charnes. 232p. (Orig.). (C). 1995. pap. text 19.95 (*0-674-62781-4*) HUP.

Notorious Literary Attacks. Ed. by Albert Mordell. LC 69-18932. (Essay Index Reprint Ser.). 1977. 18.95 (*0-8369-0047-2*) Ayer.

***Notorious Physician of London.** Barbara Howard Traister. 1999. 26.00 (*0-226-81140-9*) U Ch Pr.

Notorious Victoria: The Life of Victoria Woodhull-Uncensored. Mary Gabriel. LC 97-27151. (Illus.). 336p. 1998. 24.95 (*1-56512-132-5*, 72132) Algonquin Bks.

Notorious Voices: Feminist Biblical Interpretation, 1500-1920. Marla J. Selvidge. LC 79-48075. 256p. 1996. 29.95 (*0-8264-0913-X*) Continuum.

Notorius Identity: Materializing the Subject in Shakespeare. Linda Charnes. LC 93-9755. 256p. 1993. text 44.50 (*0-674-62780-6*) HUP.

Notre Ami le Roi. Gilles Perrault. (Folio-Actuel Ser.). (FRE.). 1990. pap. 14.95 (*2-07-032695-0*) Schoenhof.

Notre Charge Apostolique see Our Apostolic Mandate: Letter to the French Archbishops & Bishops on the "Sillon"

Notre Coeur. Guy de Maupassant. (FRE.). 1993. pap. 10.95 (*0-7859-3176-7*, 2253062553) Fr & Eur.

Notre-Dame & Related Conductus. Ed. by Gordon A. Anderson. (Gesamtausgaben - Collected Works: Vol. X). 140p. lib. bdg. 94.00 (*0-937902-27-6*) Inst Mediaeval Mus.

Notre-Dame & Related Conductus, Pt. 1. Ed. by Gordon A. Anderson. (Gesamtausgaben - Collected Works: Vol. X). 140p. 1981. lib. bdg. 85.00 (*0-931902-20-7*) Inst Mediaeval Mus.

Notre-Dame & Related Conductus, Pt. 3. Ed. by Gordon A. Anderson. (Gesamtausgaben - Collected Works: Vol. X). 140p. 1981. lib. bdg. 94.00 (*0-912024-17-8*) Inst Mediaeval Mus.

Notre-Dame & Related Conductus, Pt. 4. Ed. by Gordon A. Anderson. (Gesamtausgaben - Collected Works: Vol. X). 140p. lib. bdg. 94.00 (*0-937902-22-5*) Inst Mediaeval Mus.

Notre-Dame & Related Conductus, Pt. 5. Ed. by Gordon A. Anderson. (Gesamtausgaben - Collected Works: Vol. X). 140p. 1981. lib. bdg. 60.00 (*0-931902-11-8*) Inst Mediaeval Mus.

Notre-Dame & Related Conductus, Pt. 6. Ed. by Gordon A. Anderson. (Gesamtausgaben - Collected Works: Vol. X). 140p. 1981. lib. bdg. 94.00 (*0-912024-18-6*) Inst Mediaeval Mus.

Notre-Dame & Related Conductus, Vol. 10/7. (Gesamtausgaben - Collected Works). Date not set. write for info. (*0-931902-23-1*) Inst Mediaeval Mus.

Notre Dame Conductus: A Study of the Repertory. Robert Falck. (Wissenschaftliche Abhandlungen-Musicological Studies: Vol. 33). 300p. 1981. lib. bdg. 100.00 (*0-912024-35-6*) Inst Mediaeval Mus.

Notre-Dame de Paris. Alain Erlande-Brandenburg. Tr. by John Goodman. LC 97-35370. (Illus.). 256p. 1998. 75.00 (*0-8109-1394-1*, Pub. by Abrams) Time Warner.

***Notre-Dame de Paris.** Alain Erlande-Brandenburg & Caroline Rose. Tr. by John Goodman. (Illus.). 256p. 2000. 34.98 (*0-8109-8179-3*, Pub. by Abrams) Time Warner.

Notre-Dame de Paris. Victor Hugo. (Coll. GF). (FRE.). pap. 9.95 (*0-685-34919-5*) Fr & Eur.

Notre-Dame de Paris. Victor Hugo. Ed. by Jean Guyard. (Class. Garnier Ser.). (FRE.). pap. 29.95 (*0-685-34918-7*) Fr & Eur.

Notre-Dame de Paris. Victor Hugo. (FRE.). 704p. 1989. pap. 12.95 (*0-7859-2337-3*, 2070365492) Fr & Eur.

Notre-Dame de Paris. Victor Hugo. (FRE.). (C). 1972. pap. 11.95 (*0-8442-1983-5*, VF1983-5) NTC Contemp Pub Co.

***Notre-Dame de Paris.** Victor Hugo. (Oxford World's Classics Ser.). 592p. 1999. pap. 10.95 (*0-19-283701-X*) OUP.

Notre-Dame de Paris. Victor Hugo. (Folio Ser.: No. 549). (FRE.). 704p. 1974. pap. 12.95 (*2-07-036549-2*) Schoenhof.

Notre-Dame de Paris. unabridged ed. Victor Hugo. (FRE.). pap. 7.95 (*2-87714-124-1*, Pub. by Bookking Intl) Distribks Inc.

Notre Dame de Paris: Advanced Level. text 7.95 (*0-8219-1216-X*) EMC-Paradigm.

Notre-Dame de Paris: Avec: Gohin, Yves. Les Travailleurs de la Mer. Victor Hugo. Ed. by Jacques Seebacher. (FRE.). 704p. 1989. pap. 15.95 (*0-7859-4761-2*) Fr & Eur.

Notre-Dame de Paris: Les Travailleurs de la Mer. Victor Hugo. (Pleiade Ser.). (FRE.). 1749p. 1975. 84.95 (*2-07-010678-0*) Schoenhof.

Notre-Dame de Paris: Les Travailleurs de la Mer. deluxe ed. Victor Hugo. Ed. by Jacques Seebacher & Yves Gohin. (FRE.). 1776p. 1975. 125.00 (*0-7859-3815-X*, 2070106780) Fr & Eur.

Notre-Dame-des-Fleurs. Jean Genet. (FRE.). 1976. pap. 10.95 (*0-7859-2380-2*, 2070368602) Fr & Eur.

Notre-Dame des Fleurs. Jean Genet. (Folio Ser.: No. 860). (FRE.). pap. 9.95 (*2-07-036860-2*) Schoenhof.

Notre Dame des Fleurs. Jean Genet. (FRE.). 1976. pap. 11.95 (*0-8288-3675-2*, M5695) Fr & Eur.

Notre Dame Football Encyclopedia: The Ultimate Guide to America's Favorite College Team. Marder et al. LC 99-20317. (Illus.). 288p. 1999. pap. 19.95 (*0-8065-2108-2*, Citadel Pr) Carol Pub Group.

Notre Dame Football Today. Joseph Guise. 1982. 39.95 (*0-918223-00-8*) Pindar Pr.

***Notre Dame Gameday Book.** Todd Tucker. 2000. pap. 19.95 (*1-888698-30-6*) Diamond Communications.

Notre Dame Lab Report. (C). 1990. write for info. (*0-201-87010-X*) Addison-Wesley.

Notre-Dame of Paris. Victor Hugo. Tr. & Intro. by John Sturrock. (Classics Ser.). 496p. 1978. pap. 11.95 (*0-14-044353-3*, Penguin Classics) Viking Penguin.

Notre-Dame of Paris: The Biography of a Cathedral. Allan Temko. 1990. pap. 14.95 (*0-393-30664-X*) Norton.

Notre Dame Review No. 1: Inaugural Voyage. Ed. by Valerie Sayers. (Illus.). 155p. 1995. pap. 8.00 (*1-892492-00-8*, 1082-1864-01) Notre Dame Rev.

Notre Dame Review No. 2: Dangerous Times. Ed. by Valerie Sayers. (Illus.). 129p. 1996. pap. 8.00 (*1-892492-01-6*, 1082-1864-02) Notre Dame Rev.

Notre Dame Review No. 4: Public Life/Private Lives. Ed. by Valerie Sayers et al. (Illus.). 153p. 1997. pap. 8.00 (*1-892492-03-2*, 1082-1864-04) Notre Dame Rev.

Notre Dame Review No. 5: Age & Envy. Ed. by Valerie Sayers et al. (Illus.). 163p. 1998. pap. 8.00 (*1-892492-04-0*, 1082-1864-05) Notre Dame Rev.

Notre Dame Review No. 6: Is It Art? Is It Politics? Ed. by Valerie Sayers et al. (Illus.). 165p. 1998. pap. 8.00 (*1-892492-05-9*, 1082-1864-06) Notre Dame Rev.

Notre Dame Review Vol. 3: Eros & the Skull. Ed. by Valerie Sayers et al. (Illus.). 141p. 1996. pap. 8.00 (*1-892492-02-4*, 1082-1864-03) Notre Dame Rev.

Notre Dame Review Vol. 7: Work. Ed. by William O'Rourke & John Matthias. (Illus.). 1998. pap. 8.00 (*1-892492-06-7*) Notre Dame Rev.

Notre Dame Review Vol. 8: Place-Displacement. Ed. by William O'Rourke & John Matthias. (Illus.). 1999. pap. 8.00 (*1-892492-07-5*) Notre Dame Rev.

***Notre Dame Review Vol. 9: Soft Millennium.** Illus. by William O'Rourke et al. 176p. 2000. pap. 8.00 (*1-892492-08-3*) Notre Dame Rev.

***Notre Dame Review Vol. 10: Body & Soul.** Illus. by William O'Rourke et al. 176p. 2000. pap. 8.00 (*1-892492-09-1*) Notre Dame Rev.

Notre Dame, the Official Campus Guide. Damaine Vonada. LC 98-18607. (Illus.). 228p. 1998. 24.95 (*0-268-01486-8*); pap. 19.95 (*0-268-01484-1*) U of Notre Dame Pr.

Notre Dames des Hirondelles: Contes de Noel. Marguerite Yourcenar. (FRE.). 32p. 1982. 14.95 (*0-7859-0464-6*, 2070581195) Fr & Eur.

Notre Dame's Era of Ara. Tom Pagna & Bob Best. LC 94-16378. (Illus.). 310p. 1994. reprint ed. pap. 14.95 (*0-912083-74-3*) Diamond Communications.

Notre Dame's Greatest Coaches. Moose Krause & Stephen Singular. Ed. by Paul McCarthy. (Illus.). 256p. 1994. reprint ed. per. 5.99 (*0-671-86702-4*) PB.

Notre Dame's Greatest Coaches: Rockne, Leahy, Parseghian, Holtz. Moose Krause & Stephen Singular. (Illus.). 249p. 1999. reprint ed. text 22.00 (*0-7881-6440-6*) DIANE Pub.

Notre Jeunesse de la Raison. Charles Peguy. (Folio Essais Ser.: No. 232). (FRE.). pap. 15.95 (*2-07-032786-8*) Schoenhof.

Notre Langue Louisianaise: Our Louisiana Language, Bk. 1. Patrick Gelhay & David E. Marcantel. LC 85-81018. (ENG & FRE., Illus.). 180p. (J). (gr. 4). 1985. teacher ed. 14.95 (*0-935085-01-7*); text 14.95 (*0-935085-00-9*); write for info. (*0-935085-03-3*) Ed Francaises.

Notre Langue Louisianaise: Our Louisiana Language, Set. Patrick Gelhay & David E. Marcantel. LC 85-81018. (ENG & FRE., Illus.). 180p. (J). (gr. 4). 1985. audio 49.95 (*0-935085-02-5*) Ed Francaises.

Notre Monde, Level 2. Remunda Cadoux. (FRE.). 1971. write for info. (*0-02-268580-4*) Macmillan.

Notre Planete dans l'Univers. (Gallimard - Encyclopedie Benjamin Ser.). (FRE.). 77p. (J). 1990. 24.95 (*2-07-035901-8*) Schoenhof.

Notre's Gardens. 2nd expanded rev. ed. Photos by Michael Kenna. (ENG & FRE., Illus.). 80p. 1999. 49.95 (*0-9630785-3-4*) RAM Publications.

Nots. Mark C. Taylor. LC 92-38702. (Religion & Postmodernism Ser.). (Illus.). 296p. (C). 1993. pap. text 16.95 (*0-226-79131-9*); lib. bdg. 45.00 (*0-226-79130-0*) U Ch Pr.

Notter's Essentials of Nursing Research. 6th ed. Jacqueline R. Hott & Wendy C. Budin. LC 98-39259. 1999. 29.95 (*0-8261-1599-3*) Springer Pub.

Notting Hill. Richard Curtis. 1999. pap. 15.00 (*0-340-73844-8*, Pub. by Hodder & Stought Ltd) Trafalgar.

Notting Hill in the 60s. Phillips. (C). 1991. pap. 25.00 (*0-85315-751-0*, Pub. by Lawrence & Wishart) NYU Pr.

Notting Hill Mystery. Charles Felix. LC 75-32744. (Literature of Mystery & Detection Ser.). 1976. reprint ed. 15.95 (*0-405-07870-6*) Ayer.

Nottingham: An Illustrated History. J. V. Beckett & Ken Brand. LC 96-46265. (Illus.). 1997. write for info. (*0-7190-4002-7*, Pub. by Manchester Univ Pr) St Martin.

Nottingham & the Great War. David Marcombe. (C). 1984. text 40.00 (*0-7855-3207-2*, Pub. by Univ Nottingham) St Mut.

Nottingham in Focus: The Photographs of Frank Stephenson. Ralph Gee. 128p. (C). 1989. 59.00 (*1-85563-011-7*, Pub. by Quoin Pub Ltd) St Mut.

Nottingham Labour Movement, 1880-1939. Peter Wyncoll. (Illus.). 256p. (C). 1985. pap. 19.50 (*0-85315-613-1*, Pub. by Lawrence & Wishart) NYU Pr.

Nottinghamshire. Jeff Hopewell & Margaret Hopewell. (Country Guide Ser.: No. 35). (Illus.). 120p. pap. 12.50 (*0-7478-0194-0*, Pub. by Shire Pubns) Parkwest Pubns.

Nottinghamshire Adult Numeracy Pack. Univ. of Nottingham. (C). 1984. text 40.00 (*0-7855-3176-9*, Pub. by Univ Nottingham) St Mut.

Nottinghamshire at Work. David J. Ottewell. LC 97-172902. (Britain in Old Photographs Ser.). (Illus.). 125p. 1996. write for info. (*0-7509-1278-2*) Sutton Pub Ltd.

Nottinghamshire Coal Field & the British Miners Strike, 1984-85. K. Coates & W. John Morgan. (C). 1989. 40.00 (*0-7855-6426-8*, Pub. by Univ Nottingham) St Mut.

Nottinghamshire Constabulary: One Hundred & Fifty Years in Photographs. Bill Withers. (Illus.). 80p. (C). 1989. 59.00 (*1-85563-008-7*, Pub. by Quoin Pub Ltd) St Mut.

Nottinghamshire in the Eighteenth Century. Jonathan D. Chambers. 377p. 1966. 35.00 (*0-7146-1285-5*, Pub. by F Cass Pubs) Intl Spec Bk.

Nottinghamshire Miners between the Wars. C. Griffin. 1984. pap. 21.00 (*1-85041-024-0*) U of Nottingham.

Nottoway Artillery & Barr's Battery Virginia Light Artillery. Jeffrey C. Weaver. (Virginia Regimental Histories Ser.). (Illus.). 142p. 1994. 19.95 (*1-56190-063-X*) H E Howard.

Nottoway River Survey Pt. 1: Clovis Settlement Patterns, Vol. 28. Joseph M. McAvoy. 171p. 1992. pap. 22.50 (*1-884626-01-7*) Notto Way.

Notts Coalfield & the British Miners Strike. W. John Morgan & Ken Coates. 1989. pap. 21.00 (*1-85041-034-8*) U of Nottingham.

Notts Miners Between the Wars: The Spencer Union Revisited. C. P. Griffin. (C). 1984. text 40.00 (*0-7855-3215-3*, Pub. by Univ Nottingham) St Mut.

Notturno for Viola & Piano Centennial Edition. Ludwig van Beethoven. 1992. pap. 7.95 (*0-7935-2022-3*) H Leonard.

Notule of Grossteste & Nichomachaen Ethics. S. H. Thomson. 1970. reprint ed. pap. 39.95 (*0-8383-0122-3*) M S G Haskell Hse.

Notwendigkeit und Freiheit im Weltengeschehen und im Menschlichen Handeln see Necessity & Freedom

***Nou Tip De Profesor: Profesorul de Reevaluare Prin Consiliere.** Tr. by Ileana Vajda & Anamaria Kilyeni. Orig. Title: A New Kind of Communicator. (RUM.). 96p. 1999. pap. 4.00 (*1-58429-055-2*) Rational Isl.

N'Oubliez Pas l'Artiste. Gerard Delteil. (FRE.). 248p. 1991. pap. 12.95 (*0-7859-2159-1*, 2070383393) Fr & Eur.

Noughts & Crosses. Arthur T. Quiller-Couch. LC 77-103527. (Short Story Index Reprint Ser.). 1977. 19.95 (*0-8369-3269-2*) Ayer.

Noun + Verb Compounding in Western Romance. Kathryn Klingebiel. (UC Publications in Linguistics). 1989. 40.00 (*0-520-09729-7*, Pub. by U CA Pr) Cal Prin Full Svc.

Noun Chart Bulletin Board: Visuals. Susan F. Gabriele. (Illus.). (Orig.). 1990. pap. text 24.95 (*0-937354-23-6*) Delta Systems.

Noun Classes & Categorization: Proceedings of a Symposium on Categorization & Noun Classification, Eugene, Oregon, October 1983. Ed. by Colette Craig. LC 86-3651. (Typological Studies in Language: Vol. 7). vii, 481p. 1986. 115.00 (*0-915027-33-X*) J Benjamins Pubng Co.

***Noun in Biblical Armenian: Origin & Word Formation: with Special Emphasis on the Indo-European Heritage.** Birgit A. Olsen. LC 99-11550. (Trends in Linguistics Ser.). xiiv, 1100p. 1999. 125.35 (*3-11-016483-3*) De Gruyter.

Noun-Modifying Constructions in Japanese: A Frame-Semantic Approach. Yoshiko Matsumoto. LC 97-5309. (Studies in Language Companion Ser.: Vol. 35). 300p. 1997. lib. bdg. 74.00 (*1-55619-846-9*) J Benjamins Pubng Co.

Noun Phrase in Bengal. Malaya Gangopadhyay. (C). 1991. 56.00 (*81-208-0377-9*, Pub. by Motilal Bnarsidass) S Asia.

Noun Phrase Licensing. rev. ed. Jeffrey T. Runner. LC 98-21435. (Outstanding Dissertations in Linguistics Ser.). 264p. 1998. 62.00 (*0-8153-3134-7*) Garland.

Noun Phrases & Nominalizations: The Syntax of DPS. Tal Siloni. LC 97-15607. (Studies in Natural Language & Linguistic Theory). 1997. text 107.00 (*0-7923-4608-4*) Kluwer Academic.

Nounours-Lapin - Teddy Rabbit. Kathy Stinson. (Picture Bks.). (FRE., Illus.). 32p. (J). 1996. pap. 4.95 (*1-55037-030-8*, Pub. by Les Editions) Firefly Bks Ltd.

Nouns. Mary Ellen Pierce. 1992. 4.95 (*1-55708-221-9*, MCR315) McDonald Pub Co.

Nouns & Pronouns. S. Harold Collins. (Straight Forward English Ser.). (Illus.). 35p. (Orig.). (J). (gr. 4-6). 1990. pap. 3.95 (*0-931993-33-4*, GP-033) Garlic Pr OR.

Nouns & Pronouns. rev. ed. Contrib. by Beth Bridgman. (Horizons Grammar Ser.). (Illus.). 24p. (J). (gr. 4-6). 1998. pap. 5.95 (*1-58086-065-6*, Usborne) EDC.

Nouns, Singular & Plural, IBM see Grammar Lab

***Nouns Swarm a Verb.** Chris Vitiello. 87p. 1999. pap. 10.00 (*0-9649033-2-6*, Pub. by Xurban) SPD-Small Pr Dist.

Nountown. Cindy Iutzi. (Illus.). 16p. (Orig.). (J). (gr. 5-8). 1996. pap. 15.95 (*1-56490-015-0*) G Grimm Assocs.

***Nourish: Sustenance for Body & Soul.** Holly Davis. (Illus.). 192p. 2000. pap. 19.95 (*1-58008-181-9*) Ten Speed Pr.

Nourish & Flourish: How to Feast Nutritiously. Janet Lake & Sandra Zilker. 174p. 1990. text 12.50 (*0-9640010-1-2*) Peace Pubng.

Nourish the People: The State Civilian Granary System in China, 1650-1850. Pierre-Etienne Will & R. Bin Wong. LC 91-18781. (Michigan Monographs in Chinese Studies: No. 60). 631p. 1992. text 75.00 (*0-89264-090-1*); pap. text 40.00 (*0-89264-091-X*) Ctr Chinese Studies.

Nourished by the Word: Reading the Bible Contemplatively. Wilfrid Stinissen. LC 98-43683. 1999. pap. 11.95 (*0-7648-0384-0*) Liguori Pubns.

Nourishing a Happy Affair: Nutrition Alternatives for Individual & Family Needs. Leslie Cohen. LC 82-16226. (Illus.). 150p. (Orig.). 1983. pap. 5.95 (*0-943914-02-7*) Larson Pubns.

***Nourishing Destiny: The Inner Tradition of Chinese Medicine.** Lonny S. Jarrett et al. xxvi, 492p. 1999. text 75.00 (*0-9669916-0-5*) Spirit Path Pr.

***Nourishing Life.** Katharine P. Riddle. LC 99-74223. (Illus.). 256p. 1999. pap. 16.95 (*1-57197-183-1*) Pentland Pr.

Nourishing Self-Esteem: A Parent Handbook for Nurturing Love. Earl White. LC 80-54439. (Illus.). 80p. (Orig.). 1981. pap. 6.95 (*0-9603656-1-3*) Whitenwife Pubns.

Nourishing the Body Temple. Simone Gabbay. LC 98-56084. 1999. 12.95 (*0-87604-423-2*) ARE Pr.

***Nourishing the Caregives, BCRI-7.** Beth Kephart et al. Ed. by Aubrey Lande. 40p. 1999. 20.00 incl. audio compact disk (*1-893601-06-4*) Belle Curve.

Nourishing the Roots. Bhikkhu Bodhi. 64p. 1990. 3.75 (*955-24-0072-4*, Pub. by Buddhist Pub Soc) Vipassana Res Pubns.

Nourishing the Seeds of Self-Esteem: A Handbook of Group Activities for Nurturing Esteem in Self & Others. Earl White. LC 79-56144. (Illus.). 220p. (Orig.). 1980. per. 12.00 (*0-9603656-0-5*) Whitenwife Pubns.

Nourishing Traditions: The Cookbook That Challenges Politically Correct Nutrition. Sally Fallon. LC 97-143385. 1995. pap. text 22.95 (*1-887314-15-6*) Pro Perkins Pubng.

***Nourishing Traditions: The Cookbook That Challenges Politically Correct Nutrition & the Diet Dictocrats.** 2nd rev. ed. Sally Fallon & Mary G. Enig. (Illus.). 680p. 1999. pap. 25.00 (*0-9670897-2-7*) New Trends Pubg.

Nourishing Words: Bridging Private Reading & Public Teaching. Wendy Atwell-Vasey. LC 97-45757. (SUNY Series in Feminist Theory in Education). 246p. (C). 1998. text 59.50 (*0-7914-3631-4*); pap. text 19.95 (*0-7914-3632-2*) State U NY Pr.

Nourishment for Life Cookbook. Don Matesz & Rachel Albert-Matesz. Ed. by Danielle Williams. LC 94-66937. (Illus.). 500p. (Orig.). 1994. pap. 20.00 (*0-9641267-0-2*) Nourish For Life.

Nourishment Home Grown: How to Grow Real Nutritious Foods in Your Back Yard. A. F. Beddoe. 300p. 1992. 25.00 (*1-881201-04-X*); pap. 20.00 (*1-881201-02-3*) S & J Unltd.

Nourritures Terrestres: Nouvelles Nourritures. Andre Gide. (FRE.). 1989. pap. 10.95 (*0-8288-3683-3*, F102721) Fr & Eur.

Nourritures Terrestres et les Nouvelles Nourritures: Poesies. Andre Gide. (Folio Ser.: No. 117). (FRE.). 1960. pap. 9.25 (*2-07-036117-9*) Schoenhof.

Nourse: James Nourse & His Descendants. M. C. Lyle. (Illus.). 167p. 1991. reprint ed. pap. 22.50 (*0-8328-1823-2*); reprint ed. lib. bdg. 32.50 (*0-8328-1822-4*) Higginson Bk Co.

Nous. Matthew Lipman. (Philosophy for Children Ser.). 77p. 1997. 10.50 (*0-916834-30-1*) Inst Advncmnt Philos Child.

Nous. Claude Roy. (FRE.). 576p. 1980. pap. 15.95 (*0-7859-4141-X*, 2070372472) Fr & Eur.

Nous Autres Francais: Essai. Georges Bernanos. pap. 38.95 (*0-685-37223-5*, F87800) Fr & Eur.

Nous Autres les Sanchez. Catherine Paysan. (FRE.). 1976. pap. 8.95 (*0-7859-4061-8*) Fr & Eur.

Nous Avons Tue Darlan see We Killed Darlan: Algiers 1942: A Personal Account of the French Resistance in North Africa, 1940-1942

Nous Deux, 1947-1997. E. Peters. 1998. 17.95 (*90-6831-957-4*, Pub. by Peeters Pub) Bks Intl VA.

Nous et les Autres see On Human Diversity: Nationalism, Racism, & Exoticism in French Thought

Nous le Peuple. Lonnelle Aikman. 1982. pap. 2.50 (*0-916200-01-9*) US Capitol Hist.

Nous les Jeunes. Harcourt Brace Staff. (FRE.). 1990. pap. text, wbk. ed. 14.75 (*0-15-381753-4*) Holt R&W.

Nous les Jeunes. Created by Harcourt Brace Staff. (FRE.). 1990. pap. text, teacher ed., wbk. ed. 18.00 (*0-15-381754-2*) Holt R&W.

Nous les Jeunes: Activity Workbook. Created by Harcourt Brace Staff. (FRE.). 1990. pap., wbk. ed. 15.00 (*0-15-381752-6*) Holt R&W.

Nous, les Jeunes: Level Two. Emmanuel D'Usseau. 1990. text 58.50 (*0-15-381750-X*) Harcourt.

Nous les Vivants. Erskine Caldwell. (FRE.). 1979. pap. 11.95 (*0-7859-1892-2*, 2070371131) Fr & Eur.

Nous N'Avons Jamais Ete Modernes see We Have Never Been Modern

Nous Ne Sommes Pas Nes/Oeuf!, Big Bk. large type ed. Ruth Heller. (FRE., Illus.). (J). pap. 29.99 (*0-590-73029-0*) Scholastic Inc.

Nous Nous Sommes Tant Aimes . . . Carole Buck. (Rouge Passion Ser.: Vol. 471). 1998. mass mkt. 3.50 (*0-373-37471-2*, 1-37471-9) Harlequin Bks.

Nous Sommes Tous des Apprentis Sages. Luce Bertrand. LC 96-941040. (FRE.). 147p. 1996. 19.95 (*2-89466-003-0*) Edns Roseau.

Nous Tous, 1990. Jarvis. 1992. teacher ed. 238.50 (*0-03-022748-8*) Harcourt Schl Pubs.

Nous Vivons Plus d'Une Fois. 306p. 1990. 18.50 (*2-920083-47-3*) Edns Roseau.

Nous Vous/French 2. Jarvis. 1990. text, teacher ed. 71.25 (*0-03-014944-4*) Holt R&W.

Noussance de l'Aube see Birth at Dawn

Nouveau Allemand sans Pier. Albert O. Cherel. 24.95 (*0-685-10990-9*); audio. write for info. (*0-318-51925-9*) Fr & Eur.

Nouveau Anglais Sans Peine. Albert O. Cherel. 24.95 (*0-685-11001-X*) Fr & Eur.

Nouveau Anglais Sans Peine, Set. Albert O. Cherel. audio 125.00 (*0-685-11003-6*) Fr & Eur.

Nouveau Bescherelle: L'Art de Conjuguer. Louis Bescherelle. 15.95 (*0-685-11014-1*) Fr & Eur.

Nouveau Bloc-Notes (II, 1958-1960) Francois Mauriac. 11.50 (*0-685-34281-6*) Fr & Eur.

Nouveau Bloc-Notes (III, 1961-1964) Francois Mauriac. 15.95 (*0-685-34282-4*) Fr & Eur.

Nouveau Bloc-Notes (IV, 1965-1967) Francois Mauriac. 22.50 (*0-685-34283-2*) Fr & Eur.

Nouveau Creve-Coeur. Louis Aragon. (FRE.). 192p. 1980. pap. 12.95 (*0-8288-3810-0*, 2070321894) Fr & Eur.

Nouveau Dans la Ville, Maigret et la Vielle Dame, l'Amie de Madame Maigret, l'Enterrement de Monsieur Bouvet, Maigret et les Petits Cochons Sans Queue, les Voles Verts, Tante Jeanne, les Memoires de Maigret, 23 vols., Set. Georges Simenon. (FRE.). 860p. 1988. 49.95 (*0-7859-0554-5*, 225802353X) Fr & Eur.

Nouveau Dictionary Medicaments. G. Huchon. (FRE.). 1998. 27.95 (*0-320-00361-2*) Fr & Eur.

Nouveau Dictionnaire: Francais-Chinois: French-Chinese. deluxe ed. Commercial Press Staff. (CHI & FRE.). 846p. 1980. 24.95 (*0-8288-4711-8*, M9278) Fr & Eur.

Nouveau Dictionnaire Astrologique. Hades. (FRE.). 256p. 1990. pap. 55.00 (*0-7859-8062-8*, 2850763322) Fr & Eur.

Nouveau Dictionnaire Breton-Francais. Roparz Hemon. (BRE & FRE.). 848p. 1985. pap. 26.95 (*0-7859-7998-0*, 2736800060) Fr & Eur.

Nouveau Dictionnaire de Droit et de Sciences Economiques. Raymond Barraine. (FRE.). 540p. 1974. 59.95 (*0-8288-6203-6*, M6023) Fr & Eur.

Nouveau Dictionnaire de Droit et de Sciences Economiques. 4th ed. Raymond Barraine. (FRE.). 540p. 1974. pap. 32.95 (*0-7859-0937-0*, M6023) Fr & Eur.

Nouveau Dictionnaire de la Micro-Informatique. Ilya Virga. (FRE.). 416p. 1990. pap. 22.95 (*0-7859-7886-0*, 2501011864) Fr & Eur.

Nouveau Dictionnaire de la Musique. Roland De Cande. (FRE.). 680p. 1983. text 165.00 (*0-7859-7623-X*, 2020065754) Fr & Eur.

Nouveau Dictionnaire de la Peche. Jean Schreiner et al. (FRE.). 384p. 1975. 35.95 (*0-8288-5942-6*, M6505) Fr & Eur.

Nouveau Dictionnaire de la Peinture Moderne. (FRE.). 416p. 1963. 47.50 (*0-8288-9198-2*, F10800) Fr & Eur.

Nouveau Dictionnaire de la Sculpture Moderne: New Dictionary of Modern Sculpture. (FRE.). 328p. 1970. 75.00 (*0-8288-6551-5*, M-6431) Fr & Eur.

Nouveau Dictionnaire de Prenoms. Jean-Maurice Barbe. (FRE.). 448p. 1985. pap. 45.00 (*0-7859-8112-8*, 2858827958) Fr & Eur.

Nouveau Dictionnaire de Theologie. 2nd ed. Bernard Lauret. (FRE.). 1136p. 1996. 250.00 (*0-7859-9493-9*) Fr & Eur.

Nouveau Dictionnaire des Aliments. 2nd ed. S. Monette. (FRE.). 638p. 1997. 95.00 (*0-320-00483-X*) Fr & Eur.

Nouveau Dictionnaire des Difficultes du Francais Moderne. 2nd rev. ed. Joseph Hanse. (FRE.). 1991. lib. bdg. 160.00 (*0-685-58983-8*, F140240) Fr & Eur.

Nouveau Dictionnaire des Difficultes du Francais Moderne. 3rd ed. Daniel Blampain. 983p. 1994. 95.00 (*0-7859-8750-9*) Fr & Eur.

Nouveau Dictionnaire des Girouettes. Sophie Coignard. (FRE.). 245p. 1993. pap. 45.00 (*0-7859-7812-7*, 2221074793) Fr & Eur.

Nouveau Dictionnaire des Huiles Vegetales. Ucciani. (FRE.). 652p. 1995. 350.00 (*0-7859-9850-0*) Fr & Eur.

Nouveau Dictionnaire des Synonymes. Emile Genouvrier et al. (FRE.). 656p. 1992. 59.95 (*0-8288-5503-X*, M6266) Fr & Eur.

Nouveau Dictionnaire des Synonymes. Laure-Diane Pernon. (FRE.). 289p. 1986. 32.95 (*0-7859-8658-8*, 285882925x) Fr & Eur.

Nouveau Dictionnaire des Synonymes, 1, 1. (FRE.). 1999. 27.95 (*2-03-710229-1*) LKC.

Nouveau Dictionnaire Etymologique: New Etymological Dictionary. 6th ed. Albert Dauzat. (FRE.). 805p. 1991. pap. 33.95 (*0-7859-4627-6*) Fr & Eur.

Nouveau Dictionnaire Francais-Neerlandais, Nederlands-Francais: The New Dutch - French, French - Dutch Dictionary. 18th ed. Ludovic Grootaers. (DUT & FRE.). 826p. 1982. 85.00 (*0-7859-5122-9*) Fr & Eur.

Nouveau Dictionnaire Hebreu-Francais. rev. ed. Marc M. Cohn. (FRE & HEB.). 266p. 1934. pap. 12.95 (*0-7859-4714-0*) Fr & Eur.

Nouveau Dictionnaire Larousse: Mars French - English, English - French. Jean Mergault. (ENG & FRE.). 478p. 1989. 49.95 (*0-7859-7651-5*, 2034016211) Fr & Eur.

Nouveau Dictionnaire Larousse des Mots Croises. Larousse Staff. (FRE.). 1981. 24.95 (*0-8288-2340-5*, F 136830) Fr & Eur.

Nouveau Dictionnaire Larousse des Synonymes. Emile Genouvrier. (FRE.). 510p. 1992. pap. 28.95 (*0-7859-7678-7*, 2037102194) Fr & Eur.

Nouveau Dictionnaire Larousse Francais-Hebreu. Marc Honegger & P. Prevost. 2576p. 1991. 185.00 (*0-7859-4742-6*) Fr & Eur.

Nouveau Dictionnaire Medical. Edmond Schuller. (FRE.). 349p. 1987. 39.95 (*0-7859-8011-3*, 2737300495) Fr & Eur.

Nouveau French for Business: Le Francais des Affaires. Claude Le Goff. (FRE.). 191p. 1994. teacher ed. 37.95 (*2-278-04408-7*, U0975) Hatier Pub.

Nouveau French for Business: Teacher's Guide, Answer Key. Claude Le Goff. (FRE.). 47p. 1995. pap., teacher ed. 14.95 (*2-278-04410-9*, Pub. by Edns Didier) Hatier Pub.

Nouveau Genre ou le Cafe d'un Theatre: Scenes I a X. Gerard De Nerval. 112p. 1969. 6.95 (*0-686-54816-7*) Fr & Eur.

Nouveau Glossaire Nautique, Lettre C: Revision de l'Edition Publiee en 1848. Augustin Jal. (FRE.). 1978. pap. 73.85 (*90-279-7538-8*) Mouton.

Nouveau Guide France: Manuel de Civilisation Francaise. G. Michaud. (Hachette Ser.). (FRE.). pap. 26.95 (*2-01-015387-1*) Schoenhof.

Nouveau Guide France: Manuel de Civilization Francaise. G. Michaud. write for info. (*0-318-63623-9*) Fr & Eur.

Nouveau Guide France: Manuel de Civilization Francaise. 2nd rev. ed. G. Michaud. 1992. 34.95 (*0-8288-7899-4*, F695) Fr & Eur.

Nouveau Italien Sans Peine. Albert O. Cherel. 24.95 (*0-685-11264-0*); audio 125.00 (*0-685-01737-0*) Fr & Eur.

Nouveau Japonais Sans Peine, Level 1. (FRE & JPN.). 1997. pap. 75.00 incl. audio (*2-7005-1044-5*, Pub. by Assimil) Distribks Inc.

Nouveau Japonais Sans Peine, Level 2. (FRE & JPN.). Date not set. pap. 75.00 incl. audio (*2-7005-1045-3*, Pub. by Assimil) Distribks Inc.

Nouveau Larousse de la Medecine, No. 2. Ed. by Andre Domart & Jacques Bourneuf. (FRE.). 515p. 150.00 (*0-686-56993-8*, M-6333) Fr & Eur.

Nouveau Larousse de la Medecine, No. 2. Andre Domart & Jacques Bourneuf. 1152p. 1988. 155.00 (*0-7859-4827-9*) Fr & Eur.

Nouveau Larousse Dictionnaire Analogique. George Niobet. (FRE.). 856p. 1980. pap. 31.95 (*0-8288-1942-4*, M14296) Fr & Eur.

Nouveau Larousse du Scrabble. M. Pialat. (FRE.). 880p. 1981. 52.50 (*0-8288-2344-8*, F82270) Fr & Eur.

Nouveau Larousse Elementaire. Larousse Staff. 35.00 (*0-317-45759-4*) Fr & Eur.

N

Nouveau Larousse Encyclopedique, 2 vols. Ed. by Larousse Staff. 1895p. Date not set. 395.00 (*0-7859-9802-0*) Fr & Eur.

Nouveau Larousse Medical. deluxe ed. Maurice Fontaine. (FRE.). 1956p. 1969. 135.00 (*0-7859-4550-4*) Fr & Eur.

Nouveau Livre de Scenarios Sociaux, 1994. Ed. by Carol Gray. (FRE.). 158p. 1997. pap. 34.95 (*1-885477-42-2*) Fut Horizons.

Nouveau Locataire see Theatre

Nouveau Locataire. Eugene Ionesco. (Theatre Populaire Ser.). pap. 6.95 (*0-685-34256-5*) Fr & Eur.

Nouveau Micro Robert. Paul Robert et al. (FRE.). 1376p. 1988. 69.95 (*0-8288-1947-5*, M4457) Fr & Eur.

Nouveau Neerlandais sans Peine: Dutch for French Speakers. Assimil Staff. (DUT & FRE.). 28.95 (*0-8288-4344-9*, M14878) Fr & Eur.

Nouveau Paris, 6 pts. in 3. Louis-Sebastien Mercier. xxxviii, 1486p. reprint ed. write for info. (*0-318-71379-9*) G Olms Pubs.

Nouveau Petit Larousse. Larousse Staff. write for info. (*0-8288-7835-8*) Fr & Eur.

Nouveau Petit Robert: Dictionnaire Alphabetique & Analogique de la Langue Francaise. (FRE.). Date not set. 195.00 incl. audio compact disk (*0-7859-9538-2*) Fr & Eur.

Nouveau Petit Robert: Dictionnaire Alphabetique & Analogique de la Langue Francaise. Josette Rey-Debove. (FRE.). 2551p. 1995. 150.00 (*0-7859-9206-5*) Fr & Eur.

Nouveau Recueil. Francis Ponge. (FRE.). 240p. 1992. pap. 24.95 (*0-7859-1386-6*, 2070722880) Fr & Eur.

Nouveau Roman, les Raison de l'Ensemble. J. Ricardou. (FRE.). 1990. pap. 16.95 (*0-7859-2718-2*) Fr & Eur.

Nouveau Roman Reader. Ed. by John Calder & John Fletcher. LC 85-18353. 256p. (Orig.). 1986. pap. 11.95 (*0-7145-3720-9*) Riverrun NY.

Nouveau Systeme de Musique Theorique. fac. ed. Jean-Philippe Rameau. (Monuments of Music & Music Literature in Facsimile, II Ser.: Vol. 7). (Illus.). 1965. lib. bdg. 35.00 (*0-8450-2207-5*) Broude.

Nouveau Theatre Choisi. Eugene Labiche. 9.95 (*0-686-54235-5*) Fr & Eur.

Nouveau Theologien, M. Laudet. Charles Peguy. pap. 3.95 (*0-685-37044-5*) Fr & Eur.

Nouveau Visage de Saint Bernard see Second Look at Saint Bernard

Nouveau Vouage aux Isles de l'Amerique see Nuevo Viaje a Islas de la America

Nouveaux Amis de Pit. Marcus Pfister.Tr. of Penguin Pete's New Friends. (FRE., Illus.). 32p. (J). (gr. k-3). 1992. 15.95 (*3-314-20632-1*, Pub. by North-South Bks NYC) Chronicle Bks.

Nouveaux Carnets du Major Thompson. Pierre Daninos. (FRE.). 226p. 1973. 17.95 (*0-8288-9176-1*, M3358) Fr & Eur.

Nouveaux Contes d'Amadou Koumba. Birago Diop. (FRE.). 188p. 1967. pap. 12.95 (*0-7859-3455-3*) Fr & Eur.

Nouveaux Contes de Fees pour les Petits. De Segur. (Folio - Junior Ser.: No. 149). (FRE., Illus.). 216p. (J). (gr. 5-10). 1980. pap. 9.95 (*2-07-033149-0*) Schoenhof.

Nouveaux Contes d'Hiver. Isak Dinesen. (FRE.). 416p. 1987. pap. 11.95 (*0-7859-2060-9*, 2070378217) Fr & Eur.

Nouveaux Convertis. Pierre Assouline. (FRE.). 316p. 1982. pap. 17.95 (*0-7859-2187-7*, 2226014071) Fr & Eur.

Nouveaux Copains. Harcourt Brace Staff. (FRE.). 1989. pap. text, teacher ed., wbk. ed. 16.75 (*0-15-381706-2*); pap. text, teacher ed., wbk. ed. 18.00 (*0-15-381707-0*) Holt R&W.

Nouveaux Copains: Level One. Emmanuel D'Usseau. 1989. text 56.50 (*0-15-381700-3*) Harcourt.

Nouveaux Copains: Testbook. Harcourt Brace Staff. (FRE.). 1989. pap. text, student ed. 15.00 (*0-15-381708-9*) Holt R&W.

Nouveaux Copains: Testbook. Harcourt Brace Staff. (FRE.). 1989. pap. text, teacher ed. 15.00 (*0-15-381710-0*) Holt R&W.

Nouveaux Copains 89. Harcourt Brace Staff. 1989. text 32.75 (*0-15-381690-2*); text 32.75 (*0-15-381692-9*) Holt R&W.

Nouveaux Discours du Docteur O'Grady. Andre Maurois. pap. 9.95 (*0-685-36950-1*) Fr & Eur.

Nouveaux Exercices Francais. 2nd ed. Maurice Grevisse. (FRE.). 320p. 1968. pap. 24.95 (*0-8288-3321-4*, F134896) Fr & Eur.

Nouveaux Gites Ruraux, 1996. (FRE.). 614p. 1996. 39.95 (*0-7859-9763-6*) Fr & Eur.

Nouveaux Gites Ruraux, 1997. 620p. 1997. 39.95 (*0-7859-9450-5*) Fr & Eur.

Nouveaux Gites Ruraux 1998. Gites de France Staff. (ENG & FRE.). 432p. 1998. pap. 39.95 (*0-7859-9661-3*) Fr & Eur.

***Nouveaux Gites Ruraux 2000.** annuals Ed. by Gites de France Staff. (FRE.). 2000. pap. 39.95 (*0-320-03694-4*) Fr & Eur.

Nouveaux Memoires Interieurs. Francois Mauriac. 13.50 (*0-685-34297-2*) Fr & Eur.

Nouveaux Memoires Interieurs (More Reflections from the Soul) Francois Mauriac. Tr. by Mary Kimbrough from FRE. LC 91-33023. 228p. 1992. lib. bdg. 89.95 (*0-7734-9616-5*) E Mellen.

Nouvel Allemand sans Peine: German for French Speakers. Assimil Staff. (FRE & GER.). 28.95 (*0-8288-4308-2*, M12664) Fr & Eur.

Nouvel Anglais des Affaires. (ENG & FRE., Illus.). (Orig.). 1997. pap. 75.00 incl. audio (*2-7005-1362-2*, Pub. by Assimil) Distribks Inc.

Nouvel Anglais des Affaires. Assimil Staff. 1999. 95.00 (*2-7005-1088-7*, Pub. by Assimil) Distribks Inc.

Nouvel Anglais Sans Peine: English for French Speakers. Assimil Staff. (ENG & FRE.). 1992. 28.95 (*0-685-52979-7*, M14907) Fr & Eur.

Nouvel Armorial du Bibliophile: Guide to the Provenance of Heraldic Arms on Book Bindings, 2 vols., Vols. 1 & 2. Joannis Guigard. (FRE., Illus.). 922p. 1999. reprint ed. 250.00 (*1-55660-177-8*) A Wofsy Fine Arts.

Nouvel Art de Vivre Tome I, Week 1-26: Cours d'un an d'Hygiene Physique, Intellectuelle et Spirituelle. K. O. Schmidt. 442p. 1987. 19.95 (*2-920083-26-0*) Edns Roseau.

Nouvel Art de Vivre Tome I, Week 1-26: Cours d'un an d'Hygiene Physique, Intellectuelle et Spirituelle, Tome II. K. O. Schmidt. 381p. 1987. 19.95 (*2-920083-31-7*) Edns Roseau.

Nouvel Espagnol Sans Peine. (FRE & SPA., Illus.). (Orig.). 1997. pap. 75.00 incl. audio (*2-7005-1025-9*, Pub. by Assimil) Distribks Inc.

Nouvel Espagnol sans Peine: Spanish for French Speakers. Assimil Staff. (FRE & SPA.). 28.95 (*0-8288-4315-5*, S28993) Fr & Eur.

Nouvel Examen de l'usage General des Fiefs en France Pendant le XIe, le XIIe, le XIIIe & XIVe Siecle, 2 vols., Set. Nicolas Brussel & Thomas N. Bisson. LC 79-8359. reprint ed. 175.00 (*0-404-18337-9*) AMS Pr.

Nouvel Italien Sans Peine. (FRE & ITA., Illus.). (Orig.). 1997. pap. 75.00 incl. audio (*2-7005-0100-4*, Pub. by Assimil) Distribks Inc.

Nouvel Italien sans Peine: Italian for French Speakers. Assimil Staff. (FRE & ITA.). 28.95 (*0-8288-4346-5*, F63240) Fr & Eur.

Nouvel Observateur: Arts, Idees, Spectacles. Ed. by Annie Monnerie. (FRE.). 109p. 1994. pap. 17.25 (*0-8442-1786-7*, Natl Textbk Co) NTC Contemp Pub Co.

Nouvel Ordre Ecologique see New Ecological Order

Nouvel Ordre Monetaire pour L'Europe. Karl O. Pohl. LC HG0930.5.P64. (Conference Per Jacobsson Ser.: Vol. 1992). (FRE.). 34p. reprint ed. pap. 30.00 (*0-608-08740-8*, 206937900004) Bks Demand.

Nouvell Espagnol Sans Peine. Albert O. Cherel. 24.95 (*0-685-11166-0*); audio 125.00 (*0-685-01711-7*) Fr & Eur.

***Nouvelle Angleterre.** 6th ed. Michelin Travel Publication Staff. (Michelin Green Guides Ser.). 1999. pap. text 20.00 (*2-06-056806-4*) Michelin.

Nouvelle Angleterre Green Guide: French Edition. Michelin Staff. (FRE.). 1997. pap. 19.95 (*0-7859-7213-7*, 2060056829) Fr & Eur.

Nouvelle Biographie Generale, 46 vols. bd. in 23, Set. Ed. by J. C. Hoefer. (FRE.). 22000p. 1981. reprint ed. 2000.00 (*0-915346-75-3*) A Wofsy Fine Arts.

***Nouvelle Chance de Bonheur.** Christine Rimmer. 1999. mass mkt. 3.99 (*0-373-39534-5*) Silhouette.

Nouvelle Encyclopedie Autodidactique Quillet, 6 vols., Set. Quillet Staff. (FRE.). 668p. 1977. 695.00 (*0-8288-5504-8*, M6434) Fr & Eur.

Nouvelle Encyclopedie du Cheval. Maloine Staff. (FRE.). 784p. 1992. 225.00 (*0-8288-9443-4*) Fr & Eur.

***Nouvelle France: The Making of French Canada - A Cultural History.** Peter M. Moogk. (Illus.). 320p. 2000. pap. 25.95 (*0-87013-528-7*) Mich St U Pr.

Nouvelle Grammaire Communicative: Answer Key. Phil Turk & Genevieve G. Vandaele. (FRE.). 48p. (C). pap. 4.95 (*0-8442-1453-1*, VF1453-1) NTC Contemp Pub Co.

Nouvelle Grammaire Communicative: Comminicative Grammar Worktext with Written & Oral Practice. Phil Turk & Genevieve Garcia Vendaele. (New Communicative Ser.). (FRE & ENG., Illus.). 320p. 1997. pap. 12.95 (*0-8442-1452-3*, 14523) NTC Contemp Pub Co.

Nouvelle Grammaire Francaise. 2nd rev. ed. Maurice Grevisse & Andre Goosse. (FRE.). 378p. 1989. lib. bdg. 31.95 (*0-8288-3322-2*) Fr & Eur.

Nouvelle Heloise, 2 vols., 1. Jean-Jacques Rousseau. (FRE.). 1993. pap. 19.95 (*0-7859-2932-0*) Fr & Eur.

Nouvelle Heloise, 2 vols., 2. Jean-Jacques Rousseau. (FRE.). 1993. pap. 19.95 (*0-7859-2933-9*) Fr & Eur.

Nouvelle Heloise: Julie, or the New Eloise. Jean-Jacques Rousseau. Tr. by Judith H. McDowell. LC 67-27114. (FRE.). 428p. 1986. reprint ed. pap. 14.95 (*0-271-00602-1*) Pa St U Pr.

Nouvelle Histoire de Mouchette. Georges Bernanos. 1960. 8.95 (*0-7859-0604-5*, F87810) Fr & Eur.

Nouvelle Justine, 2 vols., 1. Marquis De Sade, pseud. (FRE.). 448p. 1978. pap. 16.95 (*0-686-55369-1*) Fr & Eur.

Nouvelle Justine, 2 vols., 2. Marquis De Sade, pseud. (FRE.). 448p. 1978. pap. 16.95 (*0-7859-1479-X*, 2264009101) Fr & Eur.

Nouvelle of Henry James in Theory & Practice. Lauren T. Cowdery. LC 85-24619. (Studies in Modern Literature: No. 47). 146p. reprint ed. pap. 45.30 (*0-8357-1623-6*, 207048000096) Bks Demand.

Nouvelle-Orleans. Richard Bizier. (Illus.). 264p. 1997. pap. text 14.95 (*1-56554-351-3*) Pelican.

***Nouvelle-Orleans.** Richard Bizier. (Travel Guide (French Guides) Ser.). 1998. pap. text 17.95 (*2-89464-065-X*) Ulysses Travel.

***Nouvelle Soul.** Barbara Summers. 256p. 1999. 22.95 (*1-56743-003-1*, Amistad) HarperTrade.

Nouvelle Soul: Short Stories. Barbara Summers. 352p. 1994. reprint ed. pap. 8.95 (*1-56743-043-0*, Amistad) HarperTrade.

Nouvelle Yenta Cookbook. Jeannie Sakol. LC 91-40777. 192p. 1992. pap. 12.95 (*0-942637-48-8*) Barricade Bks.

Nouvelles. Stephen King. 1999. pap. 13.95 (*2-266-07186-6*) Presses Pocket.

Nouvelles. Genevieve Serreau. (POR.). 24.95 incl. audio (*0-685-21220-3*) Fr & Eur.

Nouvelles Aventures du Brave Soldat Chveik. Jaroslav Hasek. (FRE.). 309p. 1985. pap. 11.95 (*0-7859-2647-X*, 207037663X) Fr & Eur.

Nouvelles Completes, Vol. 1. Paul Morand. Ed. by Michel Collomb. (FRE.). 1992. lib. bdg. 160.00 (*0-7859-3900-8*) Fr & Eur.

Nouvelles Completes: Carmen et 10 Autres Nouvelles, 2 vols. Prosper Merimee. Ed. by Pierre Josserand. 1974. pap. 12.95 (*0-7859-2880-4*) Fr & Eur.

Nouvelles Completes Vol. 1: Colomba et 10 Autres Nouvelles. Prosper Merimee. (FRE.). 1976. pap. 12.95 (*0-7859-3387-5*) Fr & Eur.

Nouvelles Conferences d'Introduction a la Psychanalyse. Sigmund Freud. (FRE.). 1989. pap. 12.95 (*0-7859-2818-9*) Fr & Eur.

Nouvelles Conventions de la Haye: Leur Application par les Juges Nationauxtome. 1996. lib. bdg. 129.00 (*90-411-0320-1*) Kluwer Academic.

Nouvelles Conventions de la Haye leur Application par leur Application les Juges Nationaux Tome IV: Jurisprudence - Situation Actuelle - Bibliographie. Mathilde Sumampouw. 384p. (C). 1994. lib. bdg. 136.50 (*0-7923-2945-7*, Pub. by M Nijhoff) Kluwer Academic.

Nouvelles du Quebec. 2nd ed. K. Brearley & R. Bruce McBride. 1977. pap. text 19.95 (*0-13-625467-5*) P-H.

Nouvelles du Sombre Empire. Georges Duhamel. (FRE.). 208p. 1960. pap. 16.95 (*0-7859-5424-4*) Fr & Eur.

Nouvelles et Textes pour Rien. Samuel Beckett. (FRE.). 208p. 1955. pap. 28.95 (*0-7859-0605-3*, F86090) Fr & Eur.

Nouvelles Etudes et Nouveaux Documents Photographiques sur Wolff. Christian Wolff. Ed. by Jean Ecole. (Gesammelte Werke III. Abteilung: Bd. 35). 1997. write for info. (*3-487-10194-7*) G Olms Pubs.

Nouvelles Exemplaires. Miguel De Cervantes Saavedra. (FRE.). 640p. 1981. pap. 13.95 (*0-7859-1929-5*, 2070372561) Fr & Eur.

Nouvelles Frances (France in America) 1500-1815: An Imperial Perspective. Philip P. Boucher. (Illus.). 143p. (Orig.). 1989. pap. 25.00 (*0-916617-32-7*, Pub. by J C Brown) Oak Knoll.

***Nouvelles Histoires Extraordinaires.** Edgar Allan Poe. 1999. pap. 9.95 (*2-266-08285-X*) Midwest European Pubns.

Nouvelles Instructions Sur L'usage De Daguerreotype et Melanges Photographiques, 2 vols. Charles Chevalier. Ed. by Peter C. Bunnell & Robert A. Sobieszek. LC 76-23036. (Sources of Modern Photography Ser.). (Illus.). 1979. reprint ed. lib. bdg. 15.95 (*0-405-09599-6*) Ayer.

Nouvelles Lectures Libres. Rebecca M. Valette. (FRE.). 190p. (C). 1982. pap. text 31.96 (*0-669-04753-8*) HM Trade Div.

Nouvelles Lettres et Opuscules Inedits de Leibniz. Gottfried Wilhelm Leibniz. ccxix, 440p. 1971. reprint ed. write for info. (*3-487-04179-0*) G Olms Pubs.

Nouvelles Nourritures: Les Nouritures Terrestres. Andre Gide. (FRE.). 256p. 1989. 10.95 (*0-7859-1150-2*, 2070361179) Fr & Eur.

Nouvelles Orientales. Marguerite Yourcenar. (FRE.). 149p. 1978. 15.95 (*0-7859-0457-3*, 2070299732) Fr & Eur.

Nouvelles Orientales. Marguerite Yourcenar. (Imaginaire Ser.). (FRE.). 149p. 1963. pap. 12.95 (*2-07-029973-2*) Schoenhof.

Nouvelles Pieces Grincantes. Jean Anouilh. Incl. Boulanger. Boulangere et le Petit Mitron. Grotte. Hurluberlu: Ou, le Reactionnaire Amoureux. Orchestre. Poissons Rouges. 19.50 (*0-685-37154-9*, F81779) Fr & Eur.

Nouvelles Pieces Noires: Jezabel, Antigone, Romeo et Jeanette, Medee. Incl. Antigone. Jezabel. Jean Anouilh. Medee. Jean Anouilh. Romeo & Jeannette. Jean Anouilh. 45.00 (*0-685-37155-7*, F81781) Fr & Eur.

Nouvelles Reflexions sur sa demonstration du principe de l'harmonie. fac. ed. Jean-Philippe Rameau. (Monuments of Music & Music Literature in Facsimile, II Ser.: Vol. 138). (Illus.). 1969. lib. bdg. 35.00 (*0-8450-2338-1*) Broude.

Nouvelles Revolutionnaires. Honore de Balzac. (FRE.). 1989. pap. 12.95 (*0-7859-3431-6*) Fr & Eur.

Nouvelles Suites de Pieces de Clavecin. fac. ed. Jean-Philippe Rameau. (Monuments of Music & Music Literature in Facsimile, I Ser.: Vol. 13). (Illus.). 1967. lib. bdg. 35.00 (*0-8450-2013-7*) Broude.

Novell's CNE Study Guide for Version 4.11: For Version 4.11. David J. Clarke. 2532p. 1997. pap. text 148.99 incl. cd-rom (*0-7645-4533-7*) IDG Bks.

Nouville: Un Village Francais. Denise Bernot & Blancard. (Ordres Sociaux Ser.). 464p. 1996. pap. text 71.00 (*2-88449-058-2*) Gordon & Breach.

Nouwen Then. Christopher De Vinck. LC 99-18862. 176p. 1999. 16.99 (*0-310-22462-4*) Zondervan.

Nov. 1, 1881-Mar. 27, 1882 see Germans to America: Lists of Passengers Arriving at U. S. Ports, 1850-1893

Nov. 1, 1883-Apr. 14, 1884 see Germans to America: Lists of Passengers Arriving at U. S. Ports, 1850-1893

Nov. 1, 1864-Nov. 2, 1865 see Germans to America: Lists of Passengers Arriving at U. S. Ports, 1850-1893

Nov. 4, 1865-June 12, 1866 see Germans to America: Lists of Passengers Arriving at U. S. Ports, 1850-1893

Nov. 2, 1857-July 29, 1859 see Germans to America: Lists of Passengers Arriving at U. S. Ports, 1850-1893

Nov. 16, 1882-Apr. 19, 1883 see Germans to America: Lists of Passengers Arriving at U. S. Ports, 1850-1893

Nova. Baron J. Ashanti. 137p. 1991. pap. 9.95 (*0-86316-137-5*) Writers & Readers.

Nova. Baron J. Ashanti. 137p. 1991. 19.95 (*0-86316-138-3*) Writers & Readers.

***Nova, Vol. 36.** Standard Schaefer. (New American Poetry Ser.: Vol. 36). 96p. 2000. pap. 10.95 (*1-55713-404-9*) Sun & Moon CA.

Nova: Adventures in Science. LC 82-16306. (Illus.). 288p. 1982. pap. 16.95 (*0-201-05359-4*) Addison-Wesley.

***Nova Acta Paracelsica.** Alois M. Haas. 1999. 20.95 (*3-906764-00-1*, Pub. by P Lang) P Lang Pubng.

Nova Affair. unabridged ed. Thomas Bloom. LC 99-93050. 216p. 1999. pap. 9.95 (*0-9659845-2-4*) Ravenhaus Pub.

Nova Britannia: Offring Fruites by Planting in Virginia. Robert Johnson. LC 71-26324. (English Experience Ser.: No. 111). 40p. 1969. reprint ed. 20.00 (*90-221-0111-8*) Walter J Johnson.

***Nova, Chevy II & Monte Carlo Parts Locating Guide.** David R. Gimbel & Adam Gimbel. 100p. 1999. reprint ed. pap. 18.95 (*1-891752-21-9*) Jalopy Joe.

Nova Command. Brad Strickland. (Starfleet Academy Ser.: No. 9). (J). (gr. 3-6). 1995. pap. 3.99 (*0-671-51009-6*) PB.

Nova Command. Brad Strickland. (Star Trek Ser.). 1995. 9.09 (*0-606-08617-X*, Pub. by Turtleback) Demco.

Nova Doctrina Vetusque: Essays on Early Christianity in Honor of Fredric W. Schlatter, S. J. Ed. by Douglas Kries & Catherine B. Tkacz. LC 98-26795. (American University Studies: Vol. 207, No. VII). XI, 291p. (C). 1999. text 49.95 (*0-8204-4136-8*) P Lang Pubng.

Nova et Vetera: Informal Mediations. George Tyrrell. LC 72-913. reprint ed. 12.50 (*0-404-07861-3*) AMS Pr.

Nova et Vetera: Patristic Studies in Honor of Thomas Patrick Halton. Thomas P. Halton. Ed. by John Petruccione. LC 97-40251. xxxv, 277p. (C). 1998. text 54.95 (*0-8132-0900-5*) Cath U Pr.

Nova et Vetera: The Theology of Tradition in American Catholicism. Gerald Fogarty. LC 87-60584. (Pere Marquette Lectures: No. 18). 80p. (C). 1987. 15.00 (*0-87462-542-4*) Marquette.

Nova Evangelizacao: Perspectiva dos Oprimidos see New Evangelization: Good News to the Poor

Nova Express. William S. Burroughs. LC 92-18339. 192p. 1992. pap. 12.00 (*0-8021-3330-4*, Grove) Grove-Atltic.

Nova 57 Minor: The Waxing & Waning of the Sixty-First Adventure of Sherlock Holmes. Jon L. Lellenberg. LC 89-80834. (Illus.). 109p. 1990. 19.00 (*0-934468-26-5*, Pub. by Gaslight) Empire Pub Srvs.

Nova Four. Ed. by Harry Harrison. 21.95 (*0-88411-699-9*) Amereon Ltd.

Nova Francia, or the Description of That Part of New France, Which Is One Continent with Virginia. Marc Lescarbot. Tr. by Pierre E. Erondelle. LC 77-7415. (English Experience Ser.: No. 877). 1977. reprint ed. lib. bdg. 31.00 (*90-221-0877-5*) Walter J Johnson.

Nova Genera Ac Species Plantarum Quas in Regno Chilensi, Peruviano & in Terra Amazonica Annis 1827-32: 1835-45. E. Poeppig & S. Endlicher. 1968. 450.00 (*3-7682-0549-5*) Lubrecht & Cramer.

Nova Genera & Species Plantarum Quas in Peregrinatione Orbis Collegerunt: 1815-25, 7 vols. in 3. A. Von Humbolt et al. 1963. 780.00 (*3-7682-0165-1*) Lubrecht & Cramer.

Nova Genera of Species Plantarum Quae Sub Itinere in Indiam Occidentalem Digessit. O. Swartz. 1962. reprint ed. 50.00 (*3-7682-0120-1*) Lubrecht & Cramer.

Nova Grammatica Ungarica. Albertus M. Szenciensis. LC 68-65315. (Uralic & Altaic Ser.: Vol. 98). 202p. 1969. reprint ed. pap. text 12.00 (*0-87750-042-8*) Res Inst Inner Asian Studies.

Nova Hedwigia, Neih. Michael Wynne. LC 98-196603. 156p. 1998. pap. 72.00 (*3-443-51038-8*, Pub. by Gebruder Borntraeger) Balogh.

Nova Hibernia, Irish Poets & Dramatists of Today & Yesterday. Michael Monahan. LC 67-23249. (Essay Index Reprint Ser.). 1977. 21.95 (*0-8369-0713-2*) Ayer.

"Nova Musica" & "De Proportionibus" Johannes Ciconia. Ed. by Oliver B. Ellsworth. LC 93-34080. (Greek & Latin Music Theory Ser.: Vol. 8). (Illus.). x, 532p. 1993. text 50.00 (*0-8032-1465-0*) U of Nebr Pr.

Nova, 1965-1979. Ed. by ADP Hollander Interchange Staff. (Illus.). 312p. 1998. pap. 19.95 (*1-58132-005-1*) ADP-Hollander.

Nova Reader: Science at the Turn of the Millennium. Sandra Hackman. (Illus.). 8p. 1999. 24.95 (*1-57500-105-5*, Pub. by TV Bks) HarpC.

***Nova Scotia.** (Canada in the Twenty First Century Ser.). (Illus.). (J). 2000. 18.95 (*0-7910-6067-5*) Chelsea Hse.

Nova Scotia. Harry Beckett. LC 97-6136. (Journey Across Canada Ser.). 24p. (J). (gr. 3-5). 1997. lib. bdg. 18.60 (*1-55916-199-X*) Rourke Bk Co.

***Nova Scotia.** A. Thompson. (Hello Canada Ser.). 1999. pap. 7.95 (*1-55041-272-8*) Fitzhenry & W Ltd.

Nova Scotia. Alex Thompson. LC 94-24101. (Hello Canada Ser.). (Illus.). 72p. (J). (gr. 3-6). 1995. lib. bdg. 14.21 (*0-8225-2759-6*) Lerner Pub.

Nova Scotia. 2nd ed. Stephen Poole. (Illus.). 200p. 1998. pap. 16.95 (*0-88780-436-5*, Pub. by J Lorimer) Formac Dist Ltd.

Nova Scotia: A Color Guidebook. Stephen Poole. (Illus.). 192p. 1995. pap. 19.95 (*0-88780-268-0*) Formac Dist Ltd.

***Nova Scotia: Shaped by the Sea: A Living History.** Lesley Choyce. (Illus.). 304p. 1999. text 30.00 (*0-7881-6781-2*) DIANE Pub.

Nova Scotia & Confederation, 1864-74. Kenneth G. Pryke. LC 79-322022. (Canadian Studies in History & Government: No. 15). 252p. reprint ed. pap. 78.20 (*0-608-15418-0*, 202934500060) Bks Demand.

Nova Scotia & the Maritimes by Bike: 21 Tours Geared for Discovery. Walter Sienko. LC 95-23634. (Illus.). 240p. 1995. pap. 14.95 (*0-89886-442-9*) Mountaineers.

Nova Scotia Conference on Early Identification of Hearing Loss, Halifax, Nova Scotia, September 9-11, 1974. Nova Scotia Conference on Early Identification of. Ed. by Georges T. Mencher. 1976. 42.75 (*3-8055-2296-7*) S Karger.

Nova Scotia Duck Tolling Retriever. Gail MacMillan & Alison Strang. LC 95-8602. (Illus.). 288p. 1996. 49.95 (*0-931866-73-1*) Alpine Pubns.

An Asterisk (*) at the beginning of an entry indicates that the title is appearing for the first time.

Nova Scotia Immigrants to 1867. Leonard H. Smith. 560p. 1994. 37.50 (*0-8063-1343-9*, 5474) Genealog Pub.

Nova Scotia Immigrants to 1867, Vol. II. Leonard H. Smith. LC 79-52060. 304p. 1994. 30.00 (*0-8063-0845-1*) Genealog Pub.

***Nova Scotia, New Brunswick, Prince Edward Island.** 5th ed. Fodors Travel Publications, Inc. Staff. (Illus.). 2000. pap. 12.00 (*0-679-00413-0*) Fodors Travel.

Nova Scotia Patchwork Patterns: Full-Size Templates & Instructions for 12 Quilts. Carter Houck. (Illus.). 64p. (Orig.). 1982. pap. 5.95 (*0-486-24145-9*) Dover.

Nova Scotia Pictorial Country Inns. 6th ed. Sherman Hines. (Illus.). 128p. 1991. pap. 12.95 (*0-921128-35-5*) Nimbus Publ.

Nova Scotia Statutes: Statutes at Large, Set, Vols. 1-4. Richard J. Uniacke. LC 76-612783. 1970. reprint ed. lib. bdg. 195.00 (*0-912004-06-1*) Gaunt.

Nova Scotia Wildlife Viewing Guide. Julie Tower & Anne Camozzi. (Illus.). 126p. 1999. pap. text 12.95 (*1-55109-256-5*) Nimbus Publ.

Nova Scotian Boletes. D. W. Grund & K. A. Harrison. (Bibliotheca Mycologica Ser.: No. 47). 1976. text 48.00 (*3-7682-1062-6*) Lubrecht & Cramer.

Nova Scotia's Massachusetts: A Study of Massachusetts - Nova Scotia Relations, 1630 to 1784. George A. Rawlyk. (Illus.). 256p. (C). 1973. 49.95 (*0-7735-0142-8*, Pub. by McG-Queens Univ Pr) CUP Services.

Nova SS: Nova & Chevy II 1962-79. Steve Statham. LC 97-26965. (Muscle Car Color History Ser.). (Illus.). 128p. 1997. pap. 21.95 (*0-7603-0285-5*) MBI Pubg.

Nova Three. Ed. by Harry Harrison. 22.95 (*0-88411-698-0*) Amereon Ltd.

Nova Two. Ed. by Harry Harrison. 21.95 (*0-88411-697-2*) Amereon Ltd.

Novae & Related Stars. Ed. by Michael Friedjung. (Astrophysics & Space Science Library: No. 65). 1977. lib. bdg. 104.50 (*90-277-0793-6*) Kluwer Academic.

Novae Hollandiae Plantarum Specimen, 1894-06: 1894-06, 2 vols. in 1. Jean J. De La Billardiere. 1966. 156.00 (*3-7682-0344-1*) Lubrecht & Cramer.

Novaia Nepodtsenzurnaia Chastushka. Ed. by Vladimir Kozlovsky. LC 81-52027. (RUS.). 405p. 1982. 20.00 (*0-89830-060-6*); pap. 15.00 (*0-89830-046-0*) Russica Pubs.

Novak's Gynecology. 12th ed. Jonathan S. Berek et al. LC 96-16316. (Illus.). 1360p. 1996. 95.00 (*0-683-00593-6*) Lppncott W & W.

Novak's Gynecology Self-Assessment & Review: Study Guide for Novak's Gynecology. David L. Olive et al. LC 97-50305. 369p. 1997. 32.00 (*0-683-00589-8*) Lppncott W & W.

Novak's Textbook of Gynecology. 11th ed. Howard W. Jones. Ed. by Jones, 3rd & Anne C. Wentz. (Illus.). 919p. 1988. 82.00 (*0-683-04469-9*) Lppncott W & W.

Novalis: German Poet, European Thinker, Christian Mystic. Friedrich Hiebel. LC 54-62201. (North Carolina. University. Studies in the Germanic Languages & Literatures: No. 10). reprint ed. 27.00 (*0-404-50910-X*) AMS Pr.

Novalis: Hymns to the Night. Georg P. Friedrich von Hardenberg. Tr. by Jeremy Reed from GER. 32p. 1989. reprint ed. 23.00 (*1-870612-65-5*, Pub. by Enitha Pr); reprint ed. pap. 11.95 (*1-870612-60-4*, Pub. by Enitha Pr) Dufour.

Novalis: Philosophical Writings. Ed. & Tr. by Margaret M. Stoljar from GER. LC 96-16782. 194p. (C). 1997. pap. text 16.95 (*0-7914-3272-6*) State U NY Pr.

Novalis: Philosophical Writings. Ed. & Tr. by Margaret M. Stoljar from GER. LC 96-16782. 194p. (C). 1997. text 39.50 (*0-7914-3271-8*) State U NY Pr.

Novalis: Signs of Revolution. Wm. Arctander O'Brien. LC 94-19760. (Post-Contemporary Interventions Ser.). 384p. 1994. text 54.95 (*0-8223-1509-2*); pap. text 18.95 (*0-8223-1519-X*) Duke.

Novalis & Mathematics. Martin Dyck. LC 76-164817. (North Carolina. University. Studies in the Germanic Languages & Literatures: No. 27). reprint ed. 37.50 (*0-404-50927-4*) AMS Pr.

Novantiqua: Rhetorics As a Contemporary Theory. Paolo Valesio. LC 79-9632. (Advances in Semiotics Ser.). 336p. 1980. 10.95 (*0-253-11055-6*) Ind U Pr.

Novantrone Mitoxantrone for Injection Concentrate: Initial Therapy of Acute Nonlymphocytic Leukemia. Ed. by Chris Fellner. (Orig.). 1995. pap. write for info. (*1-57130-014-7*) Medicine Grp USA.

Novara: Isabella Leonarda, Motetti a Voce Sola, Op. 14. Bologna, 1687, Isabella Leonarda, Motetti a Voce Sola, Op. 15. Bologna, 1690, Isabella Leonarda, Motetti, a Voce Sola, Op. 17 Bologna, 1695. Ed. by Anne Schnoebelen. (Solo Motets from the Seventeenth Century Ser.: Vol. 5). 336p. 1988. text 40.00 (*0-8240-0640-2*) Garland.

Novarits Foundation Symposium 215: Immumnological Tolerance, Vol. 215. Gregory Bock & Jamie Goode. LC 98-14471. (Novartis Foundation Symposium Ser.). 248p. 1998. 128.00 (*0-471-97843-4*) Wiley.

Novarodok: A Movement That Lived in Struggle & Its Unique Approach to the Problem of Man. Meir Levin. LC 96-11264. 216p. 1997. pap. 30.00 (*1-56821-603-3*) Aronson.

***Novartis Foundation Symposium.** Novartis staff. LC 98-46843. 296p. 1999. 128.00 (*0-471-98259-8*) Wiley.

Novartis Foundation Symposium. Novartis staff. LC 99-204533. 292p. (C). 1999. 128.00 (*0-471-98540-6*) Wiley.

Novartis Foundation Symposium. Novartis staff. LC 99-32328. 290p. 1999. 125.00 (*0-471-98815-4*) Wiley.

Novartis Foundation Symposium. Novartis staff. 528p. 2000. text 125.00 (*0-471-97978-3*) Wiley.

Novartis Foundation Symposium 217 Genetics & Tuberculosis, Vol. 217. Derek Chadwick & Gail Cardew. LC 98-23836. (Novartis Foundation Symposium Ser.). 280p. 1998. 128.00 (*0-471-98261-X*) Wiley.

Novartis Foundation Symposium 227. Novartis staff. LC 99-57033. 280p. 2000. 125.00 (*0-471-99918-0*) Wiley.

Novartis Foundation Symposium 229. Novartis staff. 300p. 2000. text 125.00 (*0-471-62744-5*) Wiley.

Nova's Ark. David Kirk. LC 97-48410. (Illus.). 40p. (J). (ps-3). 1999. 17.95 (*0-590-28208-5*) Scholastic Inc.

Novas Travessias: Contemporary Photography in Brazil. Maria L. Carvalho. LC 96-163458. (Illus.). 224p. 1996. pap. 25.00 (*1-85984-088-4*, Pub. by Verso) Norton.

Novas Travessias: Contemporary Photography in Brazil. Maria Luiza Melo Carvalho. LC 96-163458. (Illus.). 224p. (C). (gr. 13 up). 1996. 65.00 (*1-85984-963-6*, Pub. by Verso) Norton.

Novatian: The Trinity, The Spectacle, Jewish Foods, In Praise of Purity, Letters. LC 73-9872. (Fathers of the Church Ser.: Vol. 67). 223p. 1974. 19.95 (*0-8132-0067-9*) Cath U Pr.

Novato Township: Land Grant to World War II. May R. Ungemach. LC F869.N68U54 1989. (Illus.). 497p. 1991. reprint ed. text 28.50 (*0-9619810-0-8*) M R Ungemach.

Noveaux Memoires Interieurs. Francois Mauriac. (Folio Ser.: No. 566). (FRE.). pap. 8.95 (*2-07-036566-2*) Schoenhof.

***Novecento Americano: The Ballad.** L. Raginhart. 32p. 1999. pap. 6.00 (*0-9659095-1-4*) Conewago Hse.

Novel. 250p. 25.00 (*0-685-53108-2*) Soft Teach Inc.

Novel. Paul Hoover. LC 90-33381. 80p. 1990. 19.95 (*0-8112-1148-7*, Pub. by New Directions); pap. 9.95 (*0-8112-1153-3*, NDP706, Pub. by New Directions) Norton.

Novel. James A. Michener. 448p. 1992. mass mkt. 5.99 (*0-449-22143-1*, Crest) Fawcett.

Novel. Miller. Date not set. 23.00 (*0-8050-6012-X*) H Holt & Co.

Novel: Language & Narrative from Cervantes to Calvino. Andre Philippus Brink. LC 97-48400. 388p. 1998. text 30.00 (*0-8147-1330-0*) NYU Pr.

Novel: Level 3. Jane Ehlers. (International Reader's Library). (J). 1993. mass mkt. 6.95 (*0-8384-3804-0*) Heinle & Heinle.

Novel: What It Is. Francis M. Crawford. LC 79-75506. (Select Bibliographies Reprint Ser.). 1977. 18.95 (*0-8369-5003-8*) Ayer.

Novel: What It Is. Francis M. Crawford. LC 73-98831. 108p. 1971. reprint ed. lib. bdg. 49.50 (*0-8371-2924-9*, CRTN, Greenwood Pr) Greenwood.

Novel: What It Is. Francis M. Crawford. LC 76-104434. reprint ed. pap. text 10.50 (*0-89197-869-0*); reprint ed. lib. bdg. 16.75 (*0-8398-0280-3*) Irvington.

Novel: What It Is. Francis M. Crawford. (Works of Francis Marion Crawford). 1990. reprint ed. lib. bdg. 79.00 (*0-7812-2562-0*) Rprt Serv.

Novel According to Cervantes. Stephen Gilman. 1989. 45.00 (*0-520-06231-0*, Pub. by U CA Pr) Cal Prin Full Svc.

Novel Adsorbents & Their Environmental Applications. Ed. by Y. Cohen & R. W. Peters. 82p. 1995. 75.00 (*0-8169-0689-0*, S-309) Am Inst Chem Eng.

Novel & Authenticity. David Holbrook. LC 86-32027. (Critical Studies). 1987. 53.00 (*0-389-20711-X*, N8269) B&N Imports.

Novel & Contemporary Experience in Africa. Shatto A. Gakwandi. LC 77-1273. 140p. (C). 1981. pap. 19.95 (*0-8419-0642-4*, Africana) Holmes & Meier.

Novel & Film: Essays in Two Genres. Bruce Morrissette. LC 85-995. (Illus.). xii, 182p. 1985. pap. text 10.95 (*0-226-54024-3*) U Ch Pr.

Novel & Film: Essays in Two Genres. Bruce Morrissette. LC 85-995. (Illus.). xii, 194p. 1985. lib. bdg. 31.50 (*0-226-54023-5*) U Ch Pr.

Novel & Nation: Studies in the New Irish Fiction. Smyth. LC 97-2948. 1997. 44.95 (*0-7453-1220-9*, Pub. by Pluto GBR) Stylus Pub VA.

Novel & Romance: The Odyssey to Tom Jones. M. Hubert McDermott. 192p. 1989. text 53.50 (*0-389-29869-7*, N8427) B&N Imports.

***Novel & Short Story Writer's Market.** Ed. by Barbara Kurfoff. 688p. 2001. pap. 24.99 (*1-58297-009-2*) F & W Pubns Inc.

Novel & Society: Defoe to George Eliot. Grahame Smith. LC 83-22286. 240p. 1984. 44.00 (*0-389-20440-4*, N8002) B&N Imports.

Novel & Society in Elizabethan England. David Margolies. LC 84-20369. 204p. 1985. 38.50 (*0-389-20538-9*, BNB-08100) B&N Imports.

Novel & the Cinema. Geoffrey Wagner. LC 74-20939. (Illus.). 394p. (C). 1975. 38.50 (*0-8386-1618-6*) Fairleigh Dickinson.

Novel & the Globalization of Culture. Michael V. Moses. 272p. 1995. pap. text 24.95 (*0-19-508952-9*) OUP.

Novel & the Modern World. rev. ed. David Daiches. LC 60-11134. xii, 220p. 1984. reprint ed. pap. text 13.00 (*0-226-13470-9*, Midway Reprint) U Ch Pr.

Novel & the Nation: Studies in the New Irish Fiction. Gerry Smyth. (Contemporary Irish Studies Ser.). 192p. 1997. pap. 14.95 (*0-7453-1215-2*, Pub. by Pluto GBR) Stylus Pub VA.

Novel & the Nazi Past. Donna K. Reed. LC 83-49004. (American University Studies: Germanic Languages & Literature: Ser. I, Vol. 28). X, 216p. (C). 1984. text 26.50 (*0-8204-0064-5*) P Lang Pubng.

Novel & the Police. D. A. Miller. 1988. pap. 15.95 (*0-520-06746-0*, Pub. by U CA Pr) Cal Prin Full Svc.

Novel Antipsychotic Drugs. Ed. by Herbert Y. Meltzer. LC 92-3453. (Illus.). 284p. 1992. reprint ed. pap. 88.10 (*0-608-05808-4*, 205977300007) Bks Demand.

Novel Application of Anomalous (Resonance) X-ray Scattering for Structural Characterization of Disordered Materials. Yoshio Waseda. (Lecture Notes in Physics Ser.: Vol. 204). vi, 183p. 1984. 22.95 (*0-387-13359-3*) Spr-Verlag.

Novel Applications of Lasers: Proceedings of a Symposium, 9-10 January 1992, New Delhi. H. B. Bohidar. (C). 1994. 22.00 (*81-224-0627-0*, Pub. by Wiley Estrn) Franklin.

Novel Approach: Being There. Elisabeth Gareis et al. LC 96-61976. 100p. (Orig.). 1997. pap. text 16.95 (*0-472-08411-9*, 08411) U of Mich Pr.

Novel Approach: Being There. Elisabeth Gareis et al. LC 96-61976. 100p. (Orig.). 1997. pap., teacher ed. 16.95 (*0-472-08417-8*, 08417) U of Mich Pr.

***Novel Approach: Field of Dreams.** Elisabeth Gareis. (Illus.). 170p. (C). 2000. pap. text, student ed. 21.95 (*0-472-08545-X*, 08545) U of Mich Pr.

Novel Approach: Fried Green Tomatoes. Elisabeth Gareis et al. LC 97-61975. 104p. (C). 1998. pap. text 16.95 (*0-472-08495-X*, 08495) U of Mich Pr.

Novel Approach: Fried Green Tomatoes. Elisabeth Gareis et al. LC 97-61975. 104p. (C). 1998. pap., teacher ed. 18.95 (*0-472-08499-2*, 08499) U of Mich Pr.

Novel Approach: The Color Purple. Elisabeth Gareis. (Illus.). (C). student ed. write for info. (*0-472-08544-1*); pap. text, student ed. write for info. (*0-472-08543-3*) U of Mich Pr.

Novel Approach: The Shawshank Redemption. Elisabeth Gareis et al. LC 97-60881. 112p. (C). 1998. pap. text 16.95 (*0-472-08483-6*, 08483) U of Mich Pr.

Novel Approach: The Shawshank Redemption. Elisabeth Gareis et al. LC 97-60881. 112p. (C). 1998. pap. text, teacher ed. 18.95 (*0-472-08484-4*, 08484) U of Mich Pr.

Novel Approach to Sexuality & Disability. Georgie Maxfield. Ed. by Fanny Toner. (Illus.). 195p. (Orig.). 1996. pap. 7.95 (*0-9654069-0-3*) Nrthrn NV Amputee.

Novel Approach to Theatre: From Adams to Zola. Linda Sarver & Tom Markus. LC 96-42086. (Illus.). 320p. 1997. 48.00 (*0-8108-3251-8*) Scarecrow.

Novel Approaches for Bioremediation of Organic Pollution. Ed. by R. Fass et al. LC 99-11925. (Illus.). 312p. (C). 1999. 139.50 (*0-306-46102-1*, Kluwer Plenum) Kluwer Academic.

Novel Approaches in Anticancer Drug Design: Molecular Modelling - New Treatment Strategies. Ed. by W. J. Zeller et al. (Beitraege Zur Onkologie, Contributions to Oncology Ser.: Vol. 49). (Illus.). viii, 196p. 1995. 143.50 (*3-8055-6043-5*) S Karger.

Novel Approaches to Integrated Pest Management. Reuven Reuveni. 384p. 1995. boxed set 94.95 (*0-87371-881-X*, L881) Lewis Pubs.

Novel Approaches to Selective Treatments of Human Solid Tumors: Laboratory & Clinical Correlation. Y. M. Rustum. (Advances in Experimental Medicine & Biology Ser.: Vol. 339). (Illus.). 332p. (C). 1994. text 95.00 (*0-306-44592-1*, Kluwer Plenum) Kluwer Academic.

Novel Approaches to the Treatment of Alzheimer's Disease. Ed. by E. M. Meyer et al. LC 89-26615. (Advances in Behavioral Biology Ser.: No. 36). (Illus.). 400p. 1989. 110.00 (*0-306-43402-4*, Plenum Trade) Perseus Pubng.

***Novel Approaches to Treatment of Osteoporosis.** Ed. by R. G. Russell. Vol. 25. (Illus.). 264p. 1999. 99.00 (*3-540-64813-5*) Spr-Verlag.

Novel Arguments: Reading Innovative American Fiction. Richard Walsh. (Studies in American Literature & Culture: Vol. 91). 199p. (C). 1995. text 59.95 (*0-521-47145-1*) Cambridge U Pr.

Novel As Archive: Or the Genesis, Reception & Criticism of Goethe's Wilhelm Meister's Wanderjahre. Ehrhard Bahr. LC 98-35703. (Studies in German Literature & Culture). 224p. 1998. 55.00 (*1-57113-096-9*) Camden Hse.

Novel As Family Romance: Language, Gender, & Authority from Fielding to Joyce. Christine Van Boheemen. LC 87-47553. (Illus.). 256p. (C). 1987. 37.50 (*0-8014-1928-X*) Cornell U Pr.

Novel As Performance: The Fiction of Ronald Sukenick & Raymond Federman. Jerzy Kutnik. LC 85-22280. (Crosscurrents-Modern Critiques, Third Ser.). 303p. 1986. text 26.95 (*0-8093-1249-2*) S Ill U Pr.

Novel As Transformation Myth: A Study of the Novels of Mongo Beti & Ngugi wa Thiong'o. Kandioura Drame. LC 89-14005. (Foreign & Comparative Studies Program, African Ser.: No. 43). (Orig.). (C). 1990. pap. text 14.00 (*0-915984-68-7*) Syracuse U Foreign Comp.

Novel Aspect of Electron-Molecule Collisions. Kurt H. Becker. 1998. 78.00 (*981-02-3469-4*) World Scientific Pub.

Novel Aspects of Insect-Plant Interactions. Ed. by Pedro Barbosa & Deborah K. Letourneau. LC 88-5494. 362p. 1988. 150.00 (*0-471-83276-6*) Wiley.

Novel Aspects of Pain Management: Opioids & Beyond. jana sawynod & Alan Cowan. LC 98-32316. 373p. 1999. 119.95 (*0-471-18017-3*) Wiley.

Novel Aspects of Plant Lipid Metabolism, or Simply, Plant Lipid Metabolism: Proceedings of the Eleventh International Meeting on Plant Lipids, Held in Paris, France, June 26-July 1, 1994. Eleventh International Meeting on Plant Lipids Sta. Ed. by Jean-Claude Kader & Paul Mazliak. LC 94-40633. 1995. text 268.50 (*0-7923-3250-4*) Kluwer Academic.

Novel Aspects of the Biology of Chrysomelidae. Ed. by Pierre H. Jolivet et al. LC 93-3085. (Series Entomologica: Vol. 50). 1994. text 468.50 (*0-7923-2185-5*) Kluwer Academic.

Novel Associations: Theodor Fontane & George Eliot Within the Context of 19th Century Realism. Gabriele A. Wittig Davis. LC 83-48180. (Stanford German Studies: Vol. 19). 170p. (C). 1983. pap. text 17.90 (*0-8204-0018-1*) P Lang Pubng.

Novel Before the Novel: Essays & Discussions about the Beginnings of Prose Fiction in the West. Arthur R. Heiserman. LC 76-8102. 248p. reprint ed. pap. 76.90 (*0-608-18213-3*, 205661700078) Bks Demand.

Novel Biodegradable Microbial Polymers. Ed. by Edwin A. Dawes. (Nato Advanced Science Institutes, Applied Sciences Ser.: Series E). (C). 1990. text 236.50 (*0-7923-0949-9*) Kluwer Academic.

Novel Calcium-Binding Proteins: Fundamentals & Clinical Implications. Ed. by C. W. Heizmann. (Illus.). 640p. 1991. 184.00 (*0-387-53277-3*) Spr-Verlag.

Novel Chemotherapeutic Agents: Preactivation in the Treatment of Cancer & AIDS. K. S. Gulliya. LC 96-17729. (Medical Intelligence Unit Ser.). 233p. 1996. 99.00 (*1-57059-350-7*) Landes Bioscience.

Novel Configurations: A Study of French Fiction. 2nd ed. Allan Pasco. LC 86-63079. 1994. pap. 24.95 (*1-883479-00-2*) Summa Pubns.

Novel Cosmetic Delivery Systems. Ed. by Shlomo Magdassi & Elka Touitou. LC 98-31683. (Cosmetic Science & Technology Ser.: Vol. 19). (Illus.). 376p. 1998. text 165.00 (*0-8247-1703-1*) Dekker.

Novel Cuisine: Recipes That Recreate the Culinary Highlights of Famous Novels. Elaine Borish. 1999. pap. 16.95 (*0-9524881-3-2*) FID1 UK.

***Novel Cytokine Inhibitors.** Ed. by G. A. Higgs & B. Henderson. (Progress in Inflammation Research Ser.). (Illus.). 400p. 2000. 155.00 (*3-7643-5942-0*, Pub. by Birkhauser) Spr-Verlag.

Novel Defense of Scientific Realism. Jarrett Leplin. LC 96-29086. (Illus.). 224p. 1997. text 39.95 (*0-19-511363-2*) OUP.

Novel Delivery Systems for Oral Vaccines. Ed. by Derek T. O'Hagan. LC 93-40167. 288p. 1994. lib. bdg. 189.00 (*0-8493-4866-8*, 4866) CRC Pr.

***Novel Design & Information Technology Applications for Civil & Structural Engineering.** Ed. by B. Kumar & B. H. V. Topping. 242p. 1999. pap. 295.00 (*0-948749-63-6*, Pub. by Civil-Comp) St Mut.

Novel Diarrhea Viruses: Symposium. CIBA Foundation Staff. LC 86-32597. (CIBA Foundation Symposium Ser.: No. 128). 280p. 1987. 128.00 (*0-471-91094-5*) Wiley.

Novel Drug Delivery & Its Therapeutic Application. Ed. by Walter S. Nimmo & L. F. Prescott. LC 89-14662. (Illus.). 383p. 1989. reprint ed. pap. 118.80 (*0-608-02598-4*, 206325600004) Bks Demand.

Novel Drug Delivery Systems. 2nd enl. rev. ed. Yie W. Chien. (Drugs & the Pharmaceutical Sciences Ser.: Vol. 50). (Illus.). 816p. 1991. text 225.00 (*0-8247-8520-7*) Dekker.

Novel Epics: Gogol, Dostoevsky, & National Narrative. Frederick T. Griffiths & Stanley J. Rabinowitz. (Studies in Russian Literature & Theory). 184p. 1990. pap. 14.95 (*0-8101-0901-8*) Northwestern U Pr.

Novel Experimental Techniques in Fracture Mechanics. Ed. by A. Shukla. LC 93-73592. 247p. pap. 65.00 (*0-7918-1039-9*) ASME.

Novel Extenders: African-American Collection. Natalie Lewis. (ECS Think & Learn Activity Bks.). (Illus.). 128p. (Orig.). 1996. pap., teacher ed. 14.95 (*1-57022-050-6*) ECS Lrn Systs.

Novel Extenders: Multicultural Collection, Grade 4-6. Natalie Lewis. (ECS Think & Learn Activity Bks.). (Illus.). 112p. 1996. pap. text, teacher ed. 14.95 (*1-57022-078-6*, ECS0786) ECS Lrn Systs.

Novel Extenders IV. Natalie Lewis. (ECS Think & Learn Activity Bks.). 128p. 1994. pap. 15.95 (*1-57022-007-7*) ECS Lrn Systs.

Novel Extenders, Grade 1-3: Multicultural Collection. Natalie Lewis. (ECS Think & Learn Activity Bks.). (Illus.). 112p. 1996. pap. text, teacher ed. 14.95 (*1-57022-060-3*, ECS0603) ECS Lrn Systs.

Novel Extenders I. Natalie Lewis. (ECS Think & Learn Activity Bks.). 128p. 1994. pap., teacher ed. 15.95 (*1-57022-000-X*) ECS Lrn Systs.

Novel Extenders III. Natalie Lewis. (ECS Think & Learn Activity Bks.: Vol. 3). (Illus.). 128p. 1994. pap., teacher ed. 15.95 (*1-57022-006-9*, ECS:0069) ECS Lrn Systs.

Novel Extenders II. Natalie Lewis. (ECS Think & Learn Activity Bks.). (Illus.). 144p. 1994. pap., teacher ed. 16.95 (*1-57022-001-8*, ECS0018) ECS Lrn Systs.

Novel Food Technologies & Ingredients: Fat & Cholesterol-Reduced Foods & Balking Agents & High-Intensity Sweeteners for Reduced-Calorie Foods. Ed. by Shelley A. Minden. (Illus.). (Orig.). 1997. pap. write for info. (*1-57936-046-7*) IBC USA.

Novel Forms of Carbon. Ed. by D. Cox et al. (Materials Research Society Symposium Proceedings Ser.: Vol. 270). 521p. 1992. text 30.00 (*1-55899-165-4*) Materials Res.

Novel Forms of Carbon II Vol. 349: Materials Research Society Symposium Proceedings. Ed. by Y. Achiba et al. LC 95-122054. 557p. 1994. text 30.00 (*1-55899-249-9*) Materials Res.

Novel Frames: Literature As Guide to Race, Sex, & History in American Culture. Joseph R. Urgo. LC 91-17627. 1991. pap. text 16.95 (*0-87805-539-8*) U Pr of Miss.

Novel Gazing: Queer Readings in Fiction. Eve K. Sedgwick. LC 97-7608. (Series Q). 1997. pap. text 21.95 (*0-8223-2040-1*); lib. bdg. 59.95 (*0-8223-2028-2*) Duke.

Novel Histories: The Fiction of Biblical Criticism. Roland Boer. (Playing the Texts Ser.: Vol. 2). 224p. 1997. 74.00 (*1-85075-835-2*, Pub. by Sheffield Acad); pap. 24.50 (*1-85075-836-0*, Pub. by Sheffield Acad) CUP Services.

Novel Histories of Galdos. Diane F. Urey. LC 88-27626. 277p. 1989. reprint ed. pap. 85.90 (*0-608-02582-8*, 206322800004) Bks Demand.
Novel Idea. Lewis. 1986. 13.12 (*0-07-040717-7*) McGraw.
Novel Ideas - A Writer's Workbook. LaNell Seay. (Illus.). 35p. 1997. ring bd., wbk. ed. 15.95 (*1-891797-10-7*) Silver Fox TX.
Novel Imaging Systems: Proceedings, Two-Day Seminar. Society of Photographic Scientists & Engineers Sta. Ed. by Richard D. Murray. LC 80-509790. 194p. reprint ed. pap. 60.20 (*0-608-14984-5*, 202570000046) Bks Demand.
***Novel Immunological Aspects of CMV-Related Diseases: Pathogenesis, Diagnosis & Therapy.** Ed. by C. A. Bruggeman et al. (Intervirology Ser.: Vol. 42, Nos. 5-6). (Illus.). 158p. 2000. pap. 39.25 (*3-8055-7049-X*) S Karger.
Novel in Antiquity. Tomas Hagg. (Illus.). 276p. 1991. reprint ed. pap. 18.95 (*0-520-07638-9*, Pub. by U CA Pr) Cal Prin Full Svc.
Novel in England. Caserio. LC 98-35176. 441p. 1998. 33.00 (*0-8057-1662-9*, Twyne) Mac Lib Ref.
Novel in France: Mme. de Lafayette, Laclos, Constant, Stendhal, Balzac, Flaubert, Proust. Martin Turnell. LC 72-297. (Essay Index Reprint Ser.). 1977. reprint ed. 33.95 (*0-8369-2831-8*) Ayer.
Novel in Japanese: Aspects of Its Social & Literary Character. George Quinn. (KITLV Verhandelingen Ser.: No. 148). (Illus.). 330p. (Orig.). 1992. pap. 33.50 (*90-6718-033-5*, Pub. by KITLV Pr) Cellar.
Novel in the Americas. Ed. by Raymond L. Williams. LC 92-26248. 208p. 1992. 29.95 (*0-87081-271-8*) Univ Pr Colo.
Novel in the Ancient World. Ed. by Gareth L. Schmeling. LC 96-33697. (Mnemosyne, Bibliotheca Classica Batava, Supplementum, 0169-8958 Ser.: No. 159). 1996. 251.50 (*90-04-09630-2*) Brill Academic Pubs.
Novel in the Balance. Arthur M. Saltzman. LC 93-14192. 198p. 1993. text 29.95 (*0-87249-960-X*) U of SC Pr.
Novel in the Lusophone World. Charles M. Kelley. 320p. 1998. write for info. (*0-7083-1455-4*, Pub. by Univ Wales Pr) Paul & Co Pubs.
Novel Infectious Agents & the Central Nervous System. CIBA Foundation Staff. LC 87-31740. (CIBA Foundation Symposium Ser.: No. 135). 288p. 1988. 128.00 (*0-471-91512-2*) Wiley.
Novel Inhibitors of Leukotrienes. Bengt Samuelsson et al. LC 99-25656. (Progress in Inflammation Research Ser.). 400p. 1999. 180.00 (*3-7643-5884-X*, Pub. by Birkhauser) Spr-Verlag.
Novel into Film. write for info. (*0-614-10492-0*) U Delaware Pr.
Novel into Film: The Case of la Familia de Pascual Duarte & los Santos Inocentes. Patricia J. Santoro. LC 95-45570. 216p. 1996. 36.50 (*0-87413-574-5*) U Delaware Pr.
***Novel Laser Methods in Medicine & Biology.** Ed. by Alexander M. Prokhorov et al. 188p. 1999. pap. text 62.00 (*0-8194-3315-2*) SPIE.
Novel Laser Sources & Applications: Proceedings of a Workshop Held November 12-13, 1993, San Jose, California, USA. Joseph F. Becker et al. LC 94-29108. 1994. 30.00 (*0-8194-1512-X*, PM16) SPIE.
Novel Lasers, Devices & Applications. (Nineteen Ninety-Nine OSA Technical Digest Ser.). 200p. (C). 1999. pap. 66.00 (*1-55752-608-7*) Optical Soc.
Novel Lives: The Fictional Autobiographies of Guillermo Cabrera Infante & Mario Vargas Llosa. Rosemary G. Feal. LC 86-2561. (North Carolina Studies in the Romance Languages & Literatures: No. 226). 175p. reprint ed. pap. 54.30 (*0-608-20066-2*, 207133800011) Bks Demand.
Novel-Machine: The Theory & Fiction of Anthony Trollope. fac. ed. Walter M. Kendrick. LC 79-18294. 160p. 1980. pap. 49.60 (*0-7837-7639-X*, 204739200007) Bks Demand.
Novel Materials - Design & Properties. B. K. Rao & S. N. Behera. LC 98-21481. 1998. 115.00 (*1-56072-559-1*) Nova Sci Pubs.
***Novel Materials & Crystal Growth Techniques for Nonlinear Optical Devices: Proceedings of a Conference Held 23 January 2000, San Jose, California.** R. B. Lal. Ed. by SPIE Staff. LC 00-20243. (Critical Reviews of Optical Science & Technology Ser.). 2000. pap. write for info. (*0-8194-3543-0*) SPIE.
Novel Materials in Heterogeneous Catalysis. Ed. by R. Terry Baker & Larry L. Murrell. LC 90-1209. (Symposium Ser.: No. 437). (Illus.). 376p. 1990. 98.00 (*0-8412-1863-3*, Pub. by Am Chemical) OUP.
Novel Methods in Molecular & Cellular Biochemistry of Muscle. William C. Claycomb. Ed. by Grant N. Pierce. LC 96-39968. (Developments in Molecular & Cellular Biochemistry Ser.). 304p. (C). 1997. text 289.50 (*0-7923-4387-5*) Kluwer Academic.
Novel Molecular Approaches to Anti-Inflammatory Therapy. Ed. by W. Pruzanski & P. Vadas. LC 95-1382. (Agents & Actions Supplements Ser.: Vol. 46). 1995. 69.50 (*0-8176-5096-2*) Birkhauser.
Novel NDE Methods for Materials: Proceedings of a Symposium. AIME, Metallurgical Society Staff. Ed. by Bhakta B. Rath. LC 83-62891. (Conference Proceedings - The Metallurgical Society of AIME Ser.). (Illus.). 205p. reprint ed. pap. 63.60 (*0-8357-5543-6*, 203515800093) Bks Demand.
***Novel News.** 1999. 9.95 (*1-58130-596-6*) Novel Units.
Novel of Entertainment During the Gallant Era: A Study of the Novels of August Bohse, Vol. 13. Elizabeth Brewer. (Arbeiten zur Mittelern Deutschen Literatur und Sprache Ser.). 145p. 1983. 10.00 (*3-261-03241-3*) P Lang Pubng.
Novel of Manners in America. James W. Tuttleton. 320p. (C). 1974. reprint ed. pap. 5.00 (*0-393-00717-0*) Norton.
Novel of Thank You. 2nd ed. Gertrude Stein. LC 93-21209. 240p. 1994. reprint ed. pap. 11.95 (*1-56478-049-X*) Dalkey Arch.
Novel of Thank You, Vol. Eight Of Unpubl. Gertrude Stein. LC 73-103664. (Select Bibliographies Reprint Ser.). 1980. 30.95 (*0-8369-5164-6*) Ayer.
Novel of the American West. John R. Milton. LC 79-17713. 359p. 1980. reprint ed. pap. 111.30 (*0-608-02679-4*, 206333200004) Bks Demand.
Novel of the Future. Anais Nin. LC 86-1895. 212p. 1986. reprint ed. pap. 10.95 (*0-8040-0879-5*) Swallow.
Novel of the Spanish Civil War, 1936-1975. Gareth Thomas. (Illus.). 285p. (C). 1990. text 69.95 (*0-521-37158-9*) Cambridge U Pr.
Novel of Violence in America. 2nd enl. rev. ed. Wilbur M. Frohock. LC 57-14767. 250p. pap. 77.50 (*0-8357-8973-X*, 203341600086) Bks Demand.
Novel of Worldliness: Crebillon, Marivaux, Laclos, Stendhal. Peter Brooks. LC 68-56303. 305p. reprint ed. pap. 94.60 (*0-608-17854-3*, 203264100080) Bks Demand.
Novel on Yellow Paper. Stevie Smith. (New Directions Classics Ser.). 256p. 1994. reprint ed. pap. 10.95 (*0-8112-1239-4*, NDP778, Pub. by New Directions) Norton.
Novel Openers: First Sentences of over 11,000 Fictional Works, Topically Arranged with Subject, Keyword, Author & Title Indexing. Bruce L. Weaver. LC 94-41653. 996p. 1995. lib. bdg. 95.00 (*0-7864-0050-1*) McFarland & Co.
Novel Optical Materials & Applications. Francesco Simoni. Ed. by Iam-Choon Khoo & C. Umeton. LC 96-38379. 352p. 1996. 96.95 (*0-471-12793-0*) Wiley.
Novel Optical Systems & Large-Aperture Imaging, Vol. 3430. Ed. by Jose M. Sasian et al. LC 99-192228. 1998. 80.00 (*0-8194-2885-X*) SPIE.
Novel Peripheral Neurotransmitters. Ed. by Christopher Bell. (International Encyclopedia of Pharmacology & Therapeutics Ser.: No. 135). (Illus.). 388p. 1991. 127.25 (*0-08-040691-2*, Pub. by PPI) Elsevier.
Novel Pharmacological Interventions for Alcoholism. Ed. by C. A. Naranjo & Edward M. Sellers. (Illus.). xv, 378p. 1991. 82.95 (*0-387-97741-4*) Spr-Verlag.
Novel Phytoplankton Blooms. Ed. by E. M. Cosper et al. (Coastal & Estuarine Studies: Vol. 35). (Illus.). xi, 799p. 1990. 132.00 (*0-387-51961-0*) Spr-Verlag.
Novel Possibilities: Fiction & the Formation of Early Victorian Culture. Joseph W. Childers. 240p. 1995. text 32.95 (*0-8122-3324-7*) U of Pa Pr.
Novel Powder Processing, Vol. 7. 512p. 1992. 130.00 (*1-878954-26-1*) Metal Powder.
Novel Production Methods for Ethylene, Light, Hydrocarbons & Aromatics. Ed. by Lyle F. Albright et al. (Chemical Industries Ser.: Vol. 46). (Illus.). 576p. 1991. text 250.00 (*0-8247-8588-6*) Dekker.
Novel Radiation Sources Using Relativistic Electrons from Infrared to X-Rays. LC 97-44643. 202p. 1998. 62.00 (*981-02-3050-8*) World Scientific Pub.
Novel Refractory Semiconductors. Ed. by D. Emin et al. (MRS Symposium Proceedings Ser.: Vol. 97). 1987. text 17.50 (*0-931837-64-2*) Materials Res.
Novel Results in Particle Physics. Ed. by R. S. Panvini et al. LC 82-73954. (AIP Conference Proceedings Ser.: No. 93). 384p. 1982. lib. bdg. 35.00 (*0-88318-192-4*) Am Inst Physics.
Novel Secrets: Ten Secrets Novelists Need to Know. Lary Crews. Ed. by George J. Haborak. 80p. (Orig.). 1996. pap. 9.95 (*0-9656132-0-8*) Sarasota Bay Pub.
Novel Sentence: Creative Writing Hints from the Prose. Robert C. Goodspeed. (Orig.). (C). 1991. pap. text 10.95 (*0-9637355-0-0*) Goodspeed Pubns.
Novel Sentence: Creative Writing Hints from the Prose (Elementary Edition) 4th ed. Robert C. Goodspeed. (J). (gr. 5-6). 1995. pap. text 4.95 (*0-9637355-3-5*) Goodspeed Pubns.
Novel Sentence: Creative Writing Hints from the Prose (Junior High Edition) 3rd ed. Robert C. Goodspeed. (J). (gr. 7-9). 1995. pap. text 6.95 (*0-9637355-2-7*) Goodspeed Pubns.
Novel Sentence: Creative Writing Hints from the Prose (Senior High Edition) 2nd ed. Robert C. Goodspeed. (YA). (gr. 10-12). 1995. pap. text 8.95 (*0-9637355-1-9*) Goodspeed Pubns.
Novel Silicon Based Technologies. Ed. by R. A. Levy. (C). 1991. text 146.50 (*0-7923-1112-4*) Kluwer Academic.
***Novel, Spirituality & Modern Culture.** Ed. by Paul Fiddes. 200p. 2000. 49.95 (*0-7083-1598-4*, Pub. by U Wales Pr); pap. 29.95 (*0-7083-1599-2*, Pub. by U Wales Pr) Paul & Co Pubs.
Novel Strategies in the Design & Production of Vaccines: Proceedings of the 39th OHOLO Conference Held in Eilat, Israel, May 7-11, 1995. Ed. by Sara Cohen & Avigdor Shafferman. (Illus.). 214p. 1996. 85.00 (*0-306-45211-1*, Kluwer Plenum) Kluwer Academic.
Novel Study Based on James & the Giant Peach. Roald Dahl. Ed. by Diane Brookes. (J). 1998. pap. text, teacher ed. 7.95 (*0-9683234-9-9*) RRP.
Novel Study for Grade Three Based on Stone Fox. Diane Brookes & John R. Gardiner. 1998. pap. text, teacher ed. 7.95 (*0-9683449-1-7*) RRP.
Novel Study for Grade Two Based on Dolphins at Daybreak. Diane Brookes & Mary Pope Osborne. (Illus.). 1998. pap. text, teacher ed. 7.95 (*0-9683640-1-2*) RRP.
***Novel Study for Grades One & Two Based on a Tale of Antarctica.** Diane Brookes & Ulco Glimmerveen. 1998. pap. text, teacher ed. 7.95 (*0-9683449-0-9*) RRP.
Novel Study for Grades One & Two Based on Esio Trot. Diane Brookes & Roald Dahl. 1998. pap. text, teacher ed. 7.95 (*0-9683449-3-3*) RRP.
Novel Study for Grades One & Two Based on Fantastic Mr. Fox. Diane Brookes & Roald Dahl. 1998. pap. text, teacher ed. 7.95 (*0-9683449-5-X*) RRP.
***Novel Study for Grades One & Two Based on Frog & Toad Are Friends.** Diane Brookes & Arnold Lobel. 1998. pap. text, teacher ed. 7.95 (*0-9683234-2-1*) RRP.
***Novel Study for Grades One & Two Based on Little Penguin's Tale.** Diane Brookes & Audrey Wood. 1998. pap. text, teacher ed. 7.95 (*0-9683234-3-X*) RRP.
Novel Study for Grades One & Two Based on the Twits. Diane Brookes & Roald Dahl. 1998. pap. text, teacher ed. 7.95 (*0-9683449-6-8*) RRP.
***Novel Study for Grades One & Two Based on When the Giants Came to Town.** Diane Brookes & Marcia Leonard. 1998. pap. text, teacher ed. 7.95 (*0-9683234-5-6*) RRP.
***Novel Study for Grades One or Grades Three & Four Based on Mr. Popper's Penguins.** Diane Brookes et al. 1998. pap. text, teacher ed. 7.95 (*0-9683449-7-6*) RRP.
***Novel Study for Grades Three & Four Based on Playing with Penguins & Other Adventures in Antarctica.** Diane Brookes & Ann McGovern. 1998. pap. text, teacher ed. 7.95 (*0-9683449-2-5*) RRP.
***Novel Study for Grades Three & Four Based on The Dragon's Egg.** Diane Brookes & Alison Baird. 1998. pap. text, teacher ed. 7.95 (*0-9683234-7-2*) RRP.
***Novel Study for Grades Two & Three Based on Cam Jensen & the Mystery of the Dinosaur Bones.** Diane Brookes & David A. Adler. 1998. pap. text, teacher ed. 7.95 (*0-9683234-8-0*) RRP.
Novel Study for Grades Two & Three Based on Cam Jensen & the Mystery of the Dinosaur Bones, 23 vols. Diane Brookes & Franz J. Brandenburg. (Raven Rock Primary Novel Study Collection). 1998. pap. 7.95 (*0-9683640-3-9*) Raven Rocks Pr.
***Novel Study for Grades Two & Three Based on Dinosaurs Before Dark.** Diane Brookes & Mary Pope Osborne. 1998. pap. text, teacher ed. 7.95 (*0-9683234-6-4*) RRP.
Novel Study for Grades Two & Three Based on the Magic Finger. Diane Brookes & Roald Dahl. 1998. pap. text, teacher ed. 7.95 (*0-9683449-4-1*) RRP.
Novel Superconductivity. Ed. by Stuart A. Wolf & Vladimir Z. Kresin. LC 87-25731. (Illus.). 1154p. 1987. 165.00 (*0-306-42691-9*, Plenum Trade) Perseus Pubng.
Novel Surfactants. Holmberg. LC 98-29985. (Illus.). 376p. 1998. text 165.00 (*0-8247-0203-4*) Dekker.
Novel Synergy of Auriculotherapy. Kinesiology & Temporomandibular Dysfunction (TMD) Treatment Protocols for the Quantitative Characterization & Treatment Of: Hyperacusis - a Pain-Causing Ultra-Sensitivity to Normal Sounds. Meyer R. Rosen. LC 94-77159. 112p. 1994. pap. 60.00 (*0-9641617-0-2*) Interact Cnslting.
Novel Synthesis & Processing of Ceramics. Ed. by F. R. Sale. (British Ceramics Proceedings Ser.: No. 53). 278p. 1995. 150.00 (*0-901716-70-7*, Pub. by Inst Materials) Ashgate Pub Co.
Novel Synthesis & Processing of Ceramics: Proceedings of the International Symposium on Novel Synthesis & Processing of Ceramics, Kurume, Japan, October 1997. Ed. by Hiroshige Suzuki et al. (Key Engineering Materials Ser.: Vols. 159 & 160). (Illus.). 452p. (C). 1998. text 162.00 (*0-87849-814-1*, Pub. by Trans T Pub) Enfield Pubs NH.
Novel Systems for the Study of Human Disease. OECD Staff. LC 98-146020. 400p. 1998. pap. 26.00 (*92-64-16011-6*, 93-98-02-1-P, Pub. by Org for Econ) OECD.
Novel Techniques in Fossil Fuel Mass Spectrometry. Ed. by Terrence R. Ashe & Karl V. Wood. LC 89-352. (Special Technical Publication Ser.: No. STP 1019). (Illus.). 225p. 1989. pap. text 49.00 (*0-8031-1198-3*, STP1019) ASTM.
Novel Techniques in Metal Deformation Testing: Proceedings of a Symposium Sponsored by the Shaping & Forming Committee of the Metallurgical Society of AIME & the Process Modeling Committee of the American Society for Metals, Held at the Fall Meeting, St. Louis, Missouri, October 25-26, 1982. Metallurgical Society of AIME Staff. Ed. by R. H. Wagoner. LC 83-60514. (Conference Proceedings Ser.). 432p. reprint ed. pap. 134.00 (*0-7837-1440-8*, 205241400016) Bks Demand.
Novel Techniques in Synthesis & Processing Advanced Materials: Proceedings Symposium on Novel Techniques in Synthesis & Processing of Advanced Materials (1994: Rosemont, IL) Ed. by Jogender Singh & Steve M. Copley. (Illus.). 456p. 1995. 10.00 (*0-87339-288-4*, 2884) Minerals Metals.
***Novel Theology: Nikos Kazantzakis' Encounter with Whiteheadian Process Theism.** Darren J. N. Middleton. 2000. 39.95 (*0-86554-624-X*, H521) Mercer Univ Pr.
Novel Therapeutic Agents for the Treatment of Autoimmune Diseases. Ed. by Vibeke Strand & David L. Scott. LC 96-18671. (Illus.). 332p. 1996. text 150.00 (*0-8247-9748-5*) Dekker.
Novel Therapeutic Strategies in the Treatment of Sepsis. Ed. by Donald C. Morrison & John L. Ryan. (Infectious Disease & Therapy Ser.: Vol. 19). (Illus.). 392p. 1995. text 165.00 (*0-8247-9661-6*) Dekker.
Novel Therapeutics from Modern Biotechnology: From Laboratory to Human Testing. A. Abuchowski. 1998. 299.00 (*3-540-65025-3*) Spr-Verlag.
***Novel Therapeutics from Modern Biotechnology: From Laboratory to Human Testing.** Ed. by D. L. Oxender & L. E. Post. LC 99-16259. (Illus.). 250p. 1999. pap. 106.00 (*3-540-65927-7*) Spr-Verlag.
Novel Therapies for CNS Injuries: Rationales & Results. Ed. by Patti L. Peterson & John W. Phillis. 416p. 1995. boxed set 264.95 (*0-8493-7652-1*, 7652) CRC Pr.
Novel to Film: An Introduction to the Theory of Adaptation. Brian McFarlane. (Illus.). 288p. (C). 1996. text 70.00 (*0-19-871151-4*) OUP.
Novel to Film: An Introduction to the Theory of Adaptation. Brian McFarlane. (Illus.). 288p. 1996. pap. text 21.00 (*0-19-871150-6*) OUP.
Novel to 1900 see St. James Reference Guide to English Literature
Novel Trends in Electroorganic Synthesis. Ed. by S. Torii. xxii, 462p. 1998. 139.00 (*4-431-70221-0*) Spr-Verlag.
Novel Verdicts: A Guide to Courtroom Fiction. 2nd ed. Jon L. Breen. LC 99-35315. 293p. 1999. text 39.50 (*0-8108-3674-2*) Scarecrow.
***Novel Vocabulary: Anne Frank: The Diary of a Young Girl.** 40p. 2000. pap. text 21.95 (*1-58303-104-9*) Pthways Pubng.
***Novel Vocabulary: Out of the Dust.** 40p. 2000. pap. text 21.95 (*1-58303-105-7*) Pthways Pubng.
***Novel Vocabulary: Roll of Thunder, Hear My Cry.** 40p. 2000. pap. text 21.95 (*1-58303-108-1*) Pthways Pubng.
***Novel Vocabulary: The Cay.** 40p. 2000. pap. text 21.95 (*1-58303-102-2*) Pthways Pubng.
***Novel Vocabulary: The Giver.** 40p. 2000. pap. text 21.95 (*1-58303-103-0*) Pthways Pubng.
***Novel Vocabulary: The Outsiders.** 40p. 1999. pap. text 21.95 (*1-58303-106-5*) Pthways Pubng.
***Novel Vocabulary: The Pigman.** 40p. 2000. pap. text 21.95 (*1-58303-107-3*) Pthways Pubng.
***Novel Vocabulary: The Westing Game.** 40p. 2000. pap. text 21.95 (*1-58303-109-X*) Pthways Pubng.
Novel vs. Fiction. Ed. by Jackson I. Cope & Geoffrey Green. 166p. 1981. 8.50 (*0-937664-56-1*) Pilgrim Bks OK.
Novel with Cocaine. M. Agieev & Michael H. Heim. LC 98-22090. (European Classics). 1998. 11.95 (*0-8101-1709-6*) Northwestern U Pr.
Novel with Cocaine. unabridged ed. M. Ageyev. (World Classic Literature Ser.). (RUS.). pap. 6.95 (*2-87714-279-5*, Pub. by Bookking Intl) Distribks Inc.
Novel Without a Name. Duong T. Huong. 304p. 1996. pap. 12.95 (*0-14-025510-9*, Penguin Bks) Viking Penguin.
Novel Without a Name. Duong Thu-Huong. Tr. by Phan Huy-Duong & Nina McPherson. LC 94-33673. 320p. 1995. 23.00 (*0-688-12782-7*, Wm Morrow) Morrow Avon.
***Novel Without Lies.** Anatoly Mariengof. (Glas Ser.: Vol. 23). (Illus.). 192p. 2000. pap. 14.95 (*1-56663-302-8*, Pub. by I R Dee) Natl Bk Netwk.
Novela Antioquena. Enrique C. De La Casa. 100p. 2.00 (*0-318-14294-5*) Hispanic Inst.
Novela Caballeresca. (SPA.). 7.95 (*84-241-5617-X*) E Torres & Sons.
Novela Centroamericana: Desde el Popol-vuh Hasta los Umbrales de la Novela Actual. Ramon L. Acevedo. LC 81-10316. (Coleccion Mente y Palabra). 503p. 1981. 15.00 (*0-8477-0584-6*); pap. 12.00 (*0-8477-0585-4*) U of PR Pr.
Novela Chicana Escrita en Espanol: Cinco Autores Comprometidos. Salvador Rodriguez del Pino. LC 81-71730. (SPA.). iv, 159p. 1982. pap. 18.00 (*0-916950-28-X*) Biling Rev-Pr.
Novela Colombiana Hacia Finales del Siglo Veinte: Una Nueva Aproximacion a la Historia. Lucia Ortiz. (Wor(l)ds of Change Ser.: Vol. 27). (SPA.). X, 173p. (C). 1998. text 41.95 (*0-8204-3352-7*) P Lang Pubng.
Novela de la Revolucion Mexicana (Novel of the Mexican Revolution) 3rd ed. Adalbert Dessau. (SPA.). 478p. 1986. reprint ed. pap. 10.99 (*968-16-0542-X*, Pub. by Fondo) Continental Bk.
Novela del Tranvia. Gutierrez Najera. (SPA.). pap. 8.99 (*968-16-5097-2*, Pub. by Fondo) Continental Bk.
Novela Dominicana en N. Y. Hector Amarante. (SPA.). 122p. 1998. pap. 8.00 (*0-938693-12-3*) Maya Pubns.
Novela Ecuatoriana Contemporanea de 1970-1985, Vol. 14. Jimmy J. Chica. (Wor(l)ds of Change Ser.). (SPA.). X, 193p. (C). 1996. text 45.95 (*0-8204-2698-9*) P Lang Pubng.
Novela Femenina, Critica Feminista. Katica Urbanc. (SPA.). 103p. (Orig.). 1996. pap. 14.95 (*0-9643576-1-5*) Textos toledanos.
Novela Moderna en Venezuela, Vol. 1. Amarilis Hidalgo De Jesus. (Wor(l)ds of Change Ser.). (SPA.). 192p. (C). 1996. text 45.95 (*0-8204-2312-2*) P Lang Pubng.
Novela Picaresca. (SPA.). 7.95 (*84-241-5614-5*) E Torres & Sons.
Novela Social En Chile (1900-1925) Ideologia y Disyuntiva Historica. Walter Fuentes. (Series Towards a Social History of Hispanic & Luso-Brazilian Literatures). 170p. (Orig.). 1990. pap. 10.00 (*1-877660-06-X*) IFTSOIL.
Novela y el Cuento Psicologicos Demiquel de Carrion (Estudio Psico-Social Cubano) Mirza Gonzalez. LC 76-42900. 1979. pap. 9.95 (*0-89729-102-6*) Ediciones.
Novelas de Ciro Alegria see Novelistica de Ciro Alegria
Novelas de las Companias: Textos Polisemicos de la Cuenca del Caribe. Angel T. Santiago-Soto. LC 92-36951. (American University Studies: Romance Languages & Literature: Ser. II, Vol. 188). XVIII, 244p. (C). 1993. text 47.95 (*0-8204-1744-0*) P Lang Pubng.
Novelas de Torquemada: Torquemada en la Hoguera, Torquemada en la Cruz. Benito Perez Galdos. (SPA.). 1989. 18.50 (*0-8288-2584-X*) Fr & Eur.
Novelas de Unamuno. Rosendo D. Peterson. 104p. 1990. 30.00 (*0-916379-44-2*) Scripta.
Novelas Ejemplares see Three Exemplary Novels
Novelas Ejemplares. Miguel De Cervantes Saavedra. (SPA.). 7.95 (*84-241-5613-7*) E Torres & Sons.
Novelas Ejemplares. Miguel De Cervantes Saavedra. (SPA.). pap. 8.95 (*968-432-190-2*, Pub. by Porrua) Continental Bk.
Novelas Ejemplares. Miguel de Saaverdra Cervantes. (SPA.). 1997. pap. text 8.98 (*968-15-0585-9*) Ed Mex.

N

Novelas Ejemplares, No. 29. Miguel De Cervantes Saavedra. (SPA.). 234p. 1981. write for info. (*0-8288-8551-6*) Fr & Eur.

Novelas Ejemplares, Vol. I. unabridged ed. Miguel De Cervantes Saavedra & Carmen M. Cervantes. (SPA.). pap. 7.95 (*84-410-0040-9*, Pub. by Bookking Intl) Distribks Inc.

Novelas Ejemplares, Vol. II. unabridged ed. Miguel De Cervantes Saavedra. (SPA.). pap. 7.95 (*84-410-0041-7*, Pub. by Bookking Intl) Distribks Inc.

Novelas Ejemplares, I. Miguel De Cervantes Saavedra. Ed. by Florencio Sevilla Arroyo. (Nueva Austral Ser.: Vol. 199). (SPA.). 1991. pap. text 19.95 (*84-239-7199-6*) Elliots Bks.

Novelas Ejemplares, II. Miguel De Cervantes Saavedra. Ed. by Florencio Sevilla Arroyo. (Nueva Austral Ser.: Vol. 200). (SPA.). 1991. pap. text 19.95 (*84-239-7200-3*) Elliots Bks.

Novelas en Verso. Cristobal de Tamariz. Ed. by Donald McGrady. LC 75-135055. 476p. 1974. pap. 14.00 (*84-399-2183-7*) Biblio Siglo.

Novelas Mas Famosas Del Mundo. Ed. by Maria E. Alvarez del Real. (SPA., Illus.). 400p. (Orig.). (C). 1991. pap. 4.95 (*1-56259-001-4*) Editorial Amer.

***Novelist Adventure Booklight & Flashlight.** Lumatec Industries Staff. 1999. pap. 14.95 (*1-884595-28-6*) Lumatec Industries Inc.

Novelist & Mammon: Literary Responses to the World of Commerce in the Nineteenth Century. Norman Russell. (Illus.). 288p. 1986. 65.00 (*0-19-812851-7*) OUP.

Novelist As Critic. (Review of Contemporary Fiction Ser.: Vol. 8, No. 3). 1993. pap. 8.00 (*1-56478-111-9*) Dalkey Arch.

Novelist As Historian: Essays on the Victorian Historical Novel. James Simmons. 1973. pap. text 16.95 (*90-279-2528-3*) Mouton.

Novelist As Philosopher: Studies in French Fiction, 1935-1960. Ed. by John Cruickshank. LC 77-28882. 257p. 1978. reprint ed. lib. bdg. 35.00 (*0-313-20271-0*, CRNP, Greenwood Pr) Greenwood.

Novelist As Playwright: Cervantes & the Entremes Nuevo. Cory A. Reed. LC 92-25216. (Studies on Cervantes & His Times: Vol. 4). 222p. (C). 1993. text 43.95 (*0-8204-1989-3*) P Lang Pubng.

Novelist to a Generation: The Life & Thought of Winston Churchill. Robert W. Schneider. LC 76-4643. 333p. 1976. pap. 8.95 (*0-87972-117-0*) Bowling Green Univ Popular Press.

Novelistas Como Criticos (Novelists As Critics), Vol. I. Norma Klahn. (SPA.). 744p. 1991. pap. 29.99 (*968-16-3636-8*, Pub. by Fondo) Continental Bk.

Novelistas Como Criticos (Novelists As Critics), Vol. II. Norma Klahn. (SPA.). 720p. 1991. pap. 29.99 (*968-16-3637-6*, Pub. by Fondo) Continental Bk.

Novelistas Espanoles Modernos. 8th enl. rev. ed. Jose A. Balseiro. LC 76-27662. (SPA.). 403p. 1977. 8.00 (*0-8477-3173-1*) U of PR Pr.

***Novelistic Approach to the Utopian Question: Platonov's Cevengur in the Light of Dostoevskiji's Anti Utopian Legacy.** Audun J. Morch. (Acta Humaniora). 216p. 1998. pap. 28.00 (*82-00-12995-0*) Scandnvan Univ Pr.

Novelistic Love in the Platonic Tradition: Fielding, Faulkner, & the Postmodernists. Jennie Wang. LC 97-25282. 240p. 1997. 58.00 (*0-8476-8622-1*); pap. 22.95 (*0-8476-8623-X*) Rowman.

Novelistic World of Juan Benet. David K. Herzberger. (C). 1976. pap. 6.95 (*0-89217-002-6*) American Hispanist.

Novelistica Cubana de la Revolucion. Antonio Fernandez-Vazquez. LC 79-52159. (SPA.). 157p. 1980. pap. 10.00 (*0-89729-228-6*) Ediciones.

Novelistica de Ciro Alegria. 2nd enl. ed. Matilde Vilarino De Olivieri. LC 79-22294. (Coleccion Mente y Palabra). Orig. Title: Las Novelas de Ciro Alegria. (SPA.). 231p. 1980. 5.00 (*0-8477-0566-8*); pap. 4.00 (*0-8477-0567-6*) U of PR Pr.

Novelistica Espanola de los Sesenta. Edenia Guillermo & J. A. Hernandez. 1971. 12.45 (*0-88303-002-0*); pap. 9.00 (*0-685-73208-8*) E Torres & Sons.

Novelists: We Are Seven. Patrick Braybrooke. LC 67-22075. (Essay Index Reprint Ser.). 1977. 20.95 (*0-8369-1320-5*) Ayer.

Novelists & Prose Writers see Great Writers of the English Language

***Novelist's Essential Guide to Crafting Scenes.** Raymond Obstfeld. LC 00-36797. (Novelist's Essential Guide Ser.). 208p. 2000. pap. 14.99 (*0-89879-973-2*, Wrtrs Digest Bks) F & W Pubns Inc.

***Novelist's Essential Guide to Creating Plot.** J. Madison Davis. LC 00-36798. (Novelist's Essential Guide Ser.). 208p. 2000. pap. 14.99 (*0-89879-984-8*, Wrtrs Digest Bks) F & W Pubns Inc.

Novelist's Guide: Powerful Techniques for Creating Character, Dialogue & Plot. Margret Geraghty. 240p. (Orig.). 1997. pap. 14.95 (*0-7499-1653-2*, Pub. by Piatkus Bks) London Brdge.

Novelists in Interview. Ed. by John Haffenden. 250p. (Orig.). 1985. 12.95 (*0-416-37590-1*, 9555) Routledge.

Novelist's Notebook. Laurie Henry. LC 98-52050. 144p. 1999. 18.99 (*1-884910-42-4*, 48039, Story Press) F & W Pubns Inc.

Novelita Rosa. rev. ed. Yanitzia Canetti. (SPA.). 192p. 1997. pap. 16.00 (*1-58018-023-X*) Versal Ed Grp.

Novell Certification Handbook. 2nd ed. John Mueller & Robert Williams. LC 96-5711. (Illus.). 1996. pap. 24.95 (*0-07-044365-3*) McGraw.

Novell Certification Handbook. 2nd ed. John Mueller & Robert A. Williams. 1996. pap. write for info. (*0-07-044265-7*) McGraw.

Novell Certified Internet Professional. James Chellis. 1664p. 1997. student ed. 99.99 (*0-7821-2035-0*) Sybex.

Novell Certified Internet Professional Study Guide. Anthony Garlin. 448p. 1997. pap. text, student ed. 39.95 (*0-471-17938-8*) Wiley.

Novell Certified Internet Professional Testing Guide. Frank Cabiroy. 1997. pap. text 69.99 incl. cd-rom (*0-7821-2107-1*) Sybex.

Novell CNE 4 Study Guide. Debra Niedermiller-Chaffins. 1379p. (Orig.). 1995. pap., student ed. 90.00 (*1-56205-512-7*) New Riders Pub.

Novell Companion: A Complete on-the-Job Reference & Troubleshooting Guide for LAN Managers. Ed. by John E. Johnston. (Illus.). 600p. 1993. ring bd. 89.00 (*0-929321-07-3*) WEKA Pub.

***Novell Directory Services.** David Kearns. (Mastering Ser.). 768p. 2000. pap. 39.99 (*0-7821-2632-4*) Sybex.

Novell Directory Services: From the Instructors at Productivity Point. 270p. 2000. pap. 24.95 (*1-888232-35-8*) Knwldg Univ.

Novell Groupwise 4.1 Introduction. Computer Confidence Staff. (Illus.). xvi, 136p. 1996. spiral bd. 29.00 incl. disk (*1-57533-085-7*, 09601) Comput Confidence.

***Novell Intranetware 4.11 Sistema y Clientas: Manual Practico.** ENI Publishing Ltd. Staff. (Mega Plus Ser.). 2000. pap. 24.95 (*2-84072-675-0*) ENI Publng.

Novell Intranetware Professional Reference. New Riders Publishing Staff. LC 97-21526. 1000p. 1997. 69.99 incl. cd-rom (*1-56205-729-4*) New Riders Pub.

Novell Master CNE: Study Guide. Alan Frayer. (Illus.). 448p. 1997. pap., pap. text, student ed. 49.95 incl. cd-rom (*0-07-912981-1*) McGraw.

Novell Netware. (Prisma Computer Courses Ser.). (Illus.). 200p. (Orig.). 1995. pap. 12.95 (*1-85365-321-7*, Pub. by Spectrum) Seven Hills Bk.

Novell Netware for Users. Gary B. Shelly et al. LC 95-35306. (Shelly Cashman Ser.). 1995. mass mkt. 10.00 (*0-7895-0000-0*) Course Tech.

Novell Netware Lite: Simplified Network Solutions: A Practical Guide to Installing & Running a Peer-to-Peer Local Area Network. Thom Duncan. (Illus.). 272p. 1992. pap. 24.95 (*1-55958-186-7*) Prima Pub.

Novell Netware Smartstart. John Preston. LC 93-86488. 179p. 1994. 25.99 (*1-56529-411-4*) Que.

Novell Netware Story, Vol. 1. Mike Becker. (C). 1992. text. write for info. (*0-201-55974-9*) Addison-Wesley.

Novell Netware Story Vol. 2: Novell Netware 286. Mike Becker. (C). 1992. text. write for info. (*0-201-55995-1*) Addison-Wesley.

Novell Netware Story Vol. 3: Novell Netware 386. Eric Tierling. (C). 1992. text. write for info. (*0-201-55996-X*) Addison-Wesley.

Novell Netware Story Vol. 4: Novell Netware C Compiler. Mike Becker. (C). 1992. text. write for info. (*0-201-55997-8*) Addison-Wesley.

Novell Netware Story Vol. 5: Novell Netware Datenbankprodukte. Mike Becker. (GER.). (C). 1993. text. write for info. (*0-201-55998-6*) Addison-Wesley.

***Novell Netware 5 Basics.** Lindberg. LC 99-31810. 368p. 1999. pap. 29.99 (*0-7645-4563-9*) IDG Bks.

Novell Perfect Office. Speers et al. (DF - Computer Applications Ser.). 1056p. 1996. pap. 52.95 (*0-7895-0570-3*) Course Tech.

Novella: A Novel Poem. Chris Bendon. LC 98-105255. 1997. pap. 14.95 (*3-7052-0086-0*, Pub. by Poetry Salzburg) Intl Spec Bk.

Novella Box. Incl. Invisibles. Hugh Fox. 106p. pap. 10.00 (*1-882986-05-9*); Same Thing Happening over & Over. Leonard Chabrowe. 60p. pap. 5.00 (*1-882986-06-7*); Teak. Robert Reinhold. 36p. pap. 4.00 (*1-882986-07-5*); 202p. Set pap., boxed set 15.00 (*0-912292-40-7*) Smith.

Novella Collection, Vol. 1. Charles Hebert et al. 1998. pap. 16.95 (*1-891643-01-0*) Pontalba Pr.

Novellas & Other Writings: Madame de Treymes; Ethan Frome; Summer; Old New York; The Mother's Recompense; A Backward Glance. Edith Wharton. Ed. by Cynthia G. Wolff. LC 89-62930. (Illus.). 1137p. 1990. 45.00 (*0-940450-53-4*, Pub. by Library of America) Penguin Putnam.

Novellas of Hortense Calisher. Hortense Calisher. LC 97-18519. 1997. 20.00 (*0-679-60249-6*) Modern Lib NY.

Novellas of John O'Hara. large type ed. John O'Hara. 608p. 1995. 19.00 (*0-679-60167-8*) Random.

Novellas of Ludwig Tieck & E. T. A. Hoffmann. Tr. by Thomas Carlyle et al. (GERM Ser.: Vol. 58). xiv, 3178p. 1992. reprint ed. 55.00 (*0-938100-90-4*) Camden Hse.

Novellas of Martha Gellhorn. Martha E. Gellhorn. LC 93-42194. 1994. pap. 15.00 (*0-679-74369-3*) Vin Bks.

Novellas of Valentin Rasputin: Genre, Language & Style. Teresa Polowy. (Middlebury Studies in Russian Language & Literature: Vol. 1). X, 262p. (C). 1989. text 42.50 (*0-8204-0643-0*) P Lang Pubng.

Novelle. Johann Wolfgang Von Goethe. (GER.). (C). 1986. 3.95 (*0-8442-2770-6*, X2770-6) NTC Contemp Pub Co.

Novelle de Ramon Gomez de la Serna. Herlinda C. Saitz. (Monagrafias A Ser.: No. CXXXV). 190p. (C). 1990. 58.00 (*0-7293-0285-7*, Pub. by Tamesis Bks Ltd) Boydell & Brewer.

Novelle del Novecento. Intro. by Brian Moloney. (Italian Texts Ser.). (ITA.). 150p. (Orig.). 1988. reprint ed. text 16.95 (*0-7190-0200-1*, Pub. by Manchester Univ Pr) St Martin.

Novelle per un Anno: An Anthology. Luigi Pirandello. Ed. by C. A. McCormick. (Italian Texts Ser.). (ITA.). 240p. (C). 1988. pap. 19.95 (*0-7190-0469-1*, Pub. by Manchester Univ Pr) St Martin.

Novellen: C Level. Arnold Zweig. 8.95 (*0-88436-042-3*) EMC-Paradigm.

Novellen und Erzahlungen, 1888-1900. Paul Heyse. (Gesammelte Werke (Gesamtausgabe) Ser.: Reihe 4, Bd. 2). (GER.). 120.00 (*3-487-09835-0*) G Olms Pubs.

Novellen und Erzahlungen, 1850-1886: Im Anhang: Aus der Zweiten Fassung des "Jungbrunnens" (1878) Paul Heyse. (Gesammelte Werke (Gesamtausgabe) Ser.: Reihe 4, Bd. 1). (GER.). 120.00 (*3-487-09834-2*) G Olms Pubs.

Novellen und Erzahlungen, 1900-1906. Paul Heyse. (Gesammelte Werke (Gesamtausgabe) Ser.: Reihe 4, Bd. 3). (GER.). 120.00 (*3-487-09836-9*) G Olms Pubs.

Novellen und Erzahlungen, 1906-1909. Paul Heyse. (Gesammelte Werke (Gesamtausgabe) Ser.: Reihe 4, Bd. 4). (GER.). write for info. (*3-487-09837-7*) G Olms Pubs.

Novellino. Tr. by Roberta L. Payne from ITA. LC 94-36773. (Studies in Italian Culture: Vol. 19). XVII, 154p. (C). 1995. text 42.95 (*0-8204-2676-8*) P Lang Pubng.

Novellino or One Hundred Ancient Tales: A Edition & Translation Based on the 1525 Gualteruzzi Editio Princeps. Ed. by Joseph P. Consoli & James J. Wilhelm. LC 96-41562. (Garland Library of Medieval Literature: Vol. 105A). 224p. 1997. text 50.00 (*0-8153-1080-3*) Garland.

***Novello: Ten Years of Great American Writing.** Ed. by Amy Rogers et al. 300p. 2000. pap. 16.95 (*1-878086-87-1*, Pub. by Down Home NC) Blair.

Novello-Contemporary Keyboard. (YA). 1993. pap. 49.95 (*0-89898-651-6*, F3316P9X) Wrner Bros.

Novell's Bordermanager Administrator's Handbook. Laura Y. Pan. LC 99-15720. 350p. 1999. pap. 34.99 (*0-7645-4565-5*) IDG Bks.

Novell's CIP Internet Business Strategist. Jim Bowman. LC HD30.37.B69 1998. 456p. 1996. pap. 39.99 (*0-7645-4549-3*) IDG Bks.

***Novell's CIP Web Authoring & Design Study.** Jim Bowman. LC 98-70589. 752p. 1998. pap. 49.99 (*0-7645-4548-5*) IDG Bks.

Novell's CNA Study Guide for IntranetWare. David J. Clarke, 4th. LC 96-79590. 700p. 1997. 69.99 incl. cd-rom (*0-7645-4513-2*) IDG Bks.

Novell's CNASM Study Guide for NetWare 5. David J. Clarke, IV. LC TK5105.5.C555 1999. (Illus.). 944p. 1999. student ed. 74.99 incl. cd-rom (*0-7645-4542-6*) IDG Bks.

***Novell's CNE Clarke Notes for NetWare 5 Advanced Administration & Design & Implementation: Course 570 & 575.** David James Clarke. LC 99-86386. (Illus.). 400p. 2000. pap. text 34.99 (*0-7645-4578-7*) IDG Bks.

***Novell's CNE Clarke Notes for NetWare 5 Networking Technologies & Service & Support: Course 5.** David James Clarke. (Illus.). 400p. 2000. pap. 34.99 (*0-7645-4576-0*) IDG Bks.

***Novell's CNE Clarke Notes Update to NetWare 5.** David James Clarke. LC 99-48098. 264p. 1999. pap. 24.99 (*0-7645-4575-2*) IDG Bks.

***Novell's CNE Study Guide for Netware 5.** David J. Clarke, IV. LC 99-60654. (Novell Press Ser.). 1552p. 1999. student ed., boxed set 99.99 incl. cd-rom (*0-7645-4543-4*) IDG Bks.

Novell's CNE Study Guide for Netware 4.11. David J. Clarke, IV. LC 96-78781. 1600p. 1997. pap. 89.99 (*0-7645-4512-4*) IDG Bks.

Novell's CNE Study Guide to Core Technologies. David J. Clarke, 4th. 900p. 1996. pap., student ed. 74.99 incl. cd-rom (*0-7645-4501-9*) IDG Bks.

Novell's CNE Study Set for NetWare 5. David James Clarke. 2700p. 1999. pap. text 174.99 (*0-7645-4554-X*) IDG Bks.

Novell's CNE Update to Netware 5. Clarke. LC QA76.3.C62 1999. 696p. 1998. pap., student ed. 49.99 (*0-7645-4559-0*) IDG Bks.

Novell's Critical Server Issues. Richard Jensen. LC QA76.9.C55D39 1998. 720p. 1998. pap. 59.99 (*0-7645-4550-7*) IDG Bks.

Novell's Dictionary of Networking. 2nd ed. Kevin Shafer et al. LC 97-74810. 656p. 1997. pap. 24.99 (*0-7645-4528-0*, Novell Pr) IDG Bks.

Novell's GroupWise 5.5 User's Handbook. Shawn B. Rogers & Richard H. McTague. LC HF5548.4.N68R636. 288p. 1998. 24.99 (*0-7645-4552-3*) IDG Bks.

Novell's Groupwise 5 User's Handbook. Shawn B. Rogers. LC 96-78235. (Illus.). 300p. 1996. pap. 24.99 (*0-7645-4509-4*) IDG Bks.

Novell's GroupWise "X" Administrator's Guide. Shawn B. Rogers & Richard H. McTague. 750p. 1999. pap. 44.99 incl. cd-rom (*0-7645-4556-6*) IDG Bks.

Novell's Groupwise 5 Administrator's Guide. Shawn B. Rogers. LC 97-70944. 736p. 1997. pap. 44.99 incl. cd-rom (*0-7645-4521-3*) IDG Bks.

Novell's Guide to Bordermanager. J. D. Marymee & Sandy Stevens. LC 97-77817. 400p. 1998. pap. 49.99 (*0-7645-4540-X*) IDG Bks.

Novell's Guide to Creating Intranetwork Intranet. Karanjit Siyan. LC 97-72190. 816p. 1997. pap. 39.99 (*0-7645-4531-0*) IDG Bks.

***Novell's Guide to Integrating Linux & NetWare.** Doug Bierer. (Illus.). 700p. 2000. pap. text 49.99 (*0-7645-4725-9*) IDG Bks.

Novell's Guide to Integrating NetWare 5 & NT. J. D. Marymee. LC 99-31811. 480p. 1999. pap. 44.99 (*0-7645-4580-9*) IDG Bks.

Novell's Guide to Internet Access Solutions. Robert L. Spicer. LC 96-78230. 400p. 1996. pap. 39.99 incl. cd-rom (*0-7645-4515-9*) IDG Bks.

Novell's Guide to IntranetWare Networks. Jeffrey F. Hughes & Thomas. LC 96-78234. 1200p. 1996. 59.99 incl. cd-rom (*0-7645-4516-7*) IDG Bks.

***Novell's Guide to NDS Solutions.** Jeffrey F. Hughes. (Illus.). 2000. pap. text 59.99 (*0-7645-4675-9*) IDG Bks.

Novell's Guide to NetWare 5 Networks. Jeffrey F. Hughes & Blair W. Thomas. LC TK5105.8.N65H843. 1600p. 1999. 74.99 incl. cd-rom (*0-7645-4544-2*) IDG Bks.

Novell's Guide to NetWare 3.12 Networks. Currid, Cheryl C., & Company, Staff. LC 93-60632. 842p. 1993. 34.99 (*0-7821-1093-2*) Sybex.

Novell's Guide to Netware 4.1 Networks. Jeffrey F. Hughes & Novell Staff. LC 95-82357. 1200p. 1996. 59.99 (*1-56884-736-X*) IDG Bks.

Novell's Guide to Networking Hardware. Kevin Shafer. LC TK7887.5.S484 1998. 1392p. 1998. pap. 69.99 (*0-7645-4553-1*) IDG Bks.

Novell's Guide to Small Intranetwork Networks. Eric Harper. LC 97-78377. 408p. 1998. 34.99 (*0-7645-4504-3*) IDG Bks.

Novell's Guide to TCP/IP & Internetwork. Drew Heywood. LC 97-72194. 816p. 1997. pap. 49.99 (*0-7645-4532-9*) IDG Bks.

Novell's Guide to TCP/IP & Netware 5. Drew Heywood. LC 99-60193. (Novell Press Ser.). (Illus.). 900p. 1999. pap. 49.99 (*0-7645-4564-7*) IDG Bks.

***Novell's Guide to Troubleshooting NDS.** Peter Kuo. LC 99-34587. 624p. 1999. pap. 44.99 (*0-7645-4579-5*) IDG Bks.

***Novell's Guide to Troubleshooting NetWare 5.** Rick Santangelo. LC TK5105.8.N65S26 1999. (Illus.). 840p. 1999. pap. 49.99 incl. cd-rom (*0-7645-4558-2*) IDG Bks.

***Novell's Guide to Troubleshooting TCP/IP.** Stephanie Lewis. LC 99-33557. 1056p. 1999. pap. 59.99 (*0-7645-4562-0*) IDG Bks.

Novell's Internet Plumbing Handbook. Peter Rybaczyk. LC 97-77540. 336p. 1998. pap. 34.99 (*0-7645-4537-X*) IDG Bks.

Novell's Intranetware Administrator's Handbook. Kelley J. Lindberg. LC 96-78238. 576p. 1996. pap. 39.99 incl. disk (*0-7645-4517-5*) IDG Bks.

Novells Introduction to Networking. Cheryl C. Currid. LC 96-79758. 350p. 1997. pap. 19.99 (*0-7645-4525-6*) IDG Bks.

***Novell's Introduction to Networking.** 2nd ed. Cheryl C. Currid. (Illus.). 360p. 2000. pap. 24.99 (*0-7645-4700-3*) IDG Bks.

***Novell's LDAP Developer's Guide.** Roger Harrison. (Illus.). 600p. 2000. pap. text 59.99 (*0-7645-4720-8*) IDG Bks.

Novell's ManageWise Administrator's Handbook: Networks with Management. Randi E. Constable. LC 96-80451. 300p. 1997. pap. 29.99 (*1-56884-817-X*) IDG Bks.

***Novell's NDS Basics.** Peter Kuo. (Illus.). 300p. 2000. pap. text 29.99 (*0-7645-4726-7*) IDG Bks.

Novell's NDS Developer's Guide. Andrews. 744p. 1999. 59.99 (*0-7645-4557-4*) IDG Bks.

Novell's NetWare 5 Administrator's Handbook. Kelley J. Lindberg. LC TK5105.8.N65L565. 560p. 1999. pap. 39.99 (*0-7645-4546-9*) IDG Bks.

***Novells Netware 5 Resource Kit.** Jeffrey F. Hughes & Blair W. Thomas. 2048p. 1999. 99.99 (*0-7645-4545-0*) IDG Bks.

Novell's Z.E.N. Works Administrator's Handbook. Ron Tanner. LC 99-22684. 416p. 1999. pap. 39.99 (*0-7645-4561-2*) IDG Bks.

***Novell's ZENworks for Servers Administrator's Handbook.** Ron Tanner. (Illus.). 400p. 2000. pap. text 39.99 (*0-7645-4732-1*) IDG Bks.

Novels. Wilhelm Raabe. Ed. by Volkmar Sander. LC 82-22097. (German Library: Vol. 45). 320p. 1992. 39.50 (*0-8264-0280-1*) Continuum.

Novels. Wilhelm Raabe. Ed. by Volkmar Sander. LC 66-28139. (German Library: Vol. 45). 320p. (C). 1992. 19.95 (*0-8264-0281-X*) Continuum.

Novels, 6 vols. Charles W. Williams. Incl. Descent into Hell. 1965. pap. 12.00 (*0-8028-1220-1*); Many Dimensions. 1965. pap. 10.00 (*0-8028-1221-X*); War in Heaven. 1965. pap. 10.00 (*0-8028-1219-8*); 1965. Set pap. 55.00 (*0-8028-1215-5*) Eerdmans.

Novels: Complete & Unabridged, 19 vols., Set. Samuel Richardson. (BCL1-PR English Literature Ser.). 1992. reprint ed. lib. bdg. 1425.00 (*0-7812-7396-X*) Rprt Serv.

Novels: Fanshawe; The Scarlet Letter; The House of the Seven Gables; The Blithedale Romance; The Marble Faun. Nathaniel Hawthorne. Ed. by Millicent Bell. LC 82-18031. (Library of America Ser.). 1272p. 1983. 39.50 (*0-940450-08-9*, Pub. by Library of America) Penguin Putnam.

Novels: The House of Mirth; The Reef; The Custom of the Country; The Age of Innocence. Edith Wharton. Ed. by R. W. B. Lewis. LC 85-19816. 1328p. 1986. 35.00 (*0-940450-31-3*, Pub. by Library of America) Penguin Putnam.

Novels - Hannah Thurston. Bayard Taylor. (Notable American Authors). 1999. reprint ed. lib. bdg. 125.00 (*0-7812-8996-3*) Rprt Serv.

Novels - The Gilded Age (With Mark Twain) Charles D. Warner. (Notable American Authors Ser.). 1999. reprint ed. lib. bdg. 125.00 (*0-7812-9905-5*) Rprt Serv.

Novels & Arguments: Inventing Rhetorical Criticism. Zahava K. McKeon. LC 82-2677. 270p. 1982. lib. bdg. 27.00 (*0-226-56034-1*) U Ch Pr.

Novels & Essays: Vandover & the Brute; McTeague; The Octopus; Essays. Frank Norris. Ed. by Donald Pizer. LC 85-23133. 1232p. 1986. 35.00 (*0-940450-40-2*, Pub. by Library of America) Penguin Putnam.

Novels & Memoirs, 1941-1951: The Real Life of Sebastian Knight; Bend Sinister; Speak, Memory. Vladimir Nabokov. Ed. by Brian Boyd. LC 96-15257. (Illus.). 710p. 1996. 35.00 (*1-883011-18-3*, Pub. by Library of America) Penguin Putnam.

Novels & Miscellaneous Works of Daniel Defoe, 20 vols. Daniel Defoe. LC 79-154120. reprint ed. write for info. (*0-404-09300-0*) AMS Pr.

Novels & Novelists. Katherine Mansfield. reprint ed. 49.00 (*0-403-02290-8*) Somerset Pub.

N

An Asterisk (*) at the beginning of an entry indicates that the title is appearing for the first time.

Novels & Other Writings: The Dream Life of Balso Snell; Miss Lonelyhearts; A Cool Million; The Day of the Locust; Other Writings. Nathanael West. Ed. by Sacvan Bercovitch. LC 96-49007. 829p. 1997. 35.00 (*1-883011-28-0*, Pub. by Library of America) Penguin Putnam.

Novels & Plays: 30 Creative Teaching Guides for Grades 6-12. Albert B. Somers & Janet E. Worthington. LC 97-20283. 250p. 1997. pap. 24.50 (*1-56308-489-9*) Libs Unl.

Novels & Plays of Eduardo Manet: An Adventure in Multiculturalism. Phyllis Zatlin. LC 98-54792. (Studies in Romance Literatures). 1999. 43.00 (*0-271-01949-2*) Pa St U Pr.

Novels & Plays of Saki. Saki, pseud. 1988. reprint ed. lib. bdg. 49.00 (*0-7812-0544-1*) Rprt Serv.

Novels & Plays of Saki. Saki, pseud. LC 71-145199. 1971. reprint ed. 39.00 (*0-403-01123-X*) Scholarly.

Novels & Related Works of Charles Brockden Brown: Clara Howard & Jane Talbot. Charles Brockden Brown. Ed. by Sydney J. Krause & S. W. Reid. LC 85-8102. (C.S.E. Edition Ser.: Vol. 5). 539p. 1986. 35.00 (*0-87338-320-6*) Kent St U Pr.

Novels & Related Works of Charles Brockden Brown: Edgar Huntly; or, Memoirs of a Sleep-Walker. Charles Brockden Brown. Ed. by Sydney J. Krause & S. W. Reid. LC 84-4376. (C.S.E. Edition Ser.: No. 4). 510p. 1985. 35.00 (*0-87338-305-2*) Kent St U Pr.

Novels & Selected Works of Mary Shelley, 8 vols., Set. Mary Wollstonecraft Shelley. Ed. by Nora Crook & Pamela Clemit. LC 96-1536. 3000p. 1996. 795.00 (*1-85196-076-7*, Pub. by Pickering & Chatto) Ashgate Pub Co.

Novels & Selected Writings of Daniel Defoe: Shakespeare Head Edition, 14 vols., Set. Daniel Defoe. 300p. 1974. reprint ed. 417.50 (*0-87471-521-0*); reprint ed. 417.50 (*0-87471-500-8*) Rowman.

Novels & Social Writings: The People of the Abyss; The Road; The Iron Heel; Martin Eden; John Barleycorn; Essays. Jack London. Ed. by Donald Pizer. LC 82-6940. 1192p. 1982. 40.00 (*0-940450-06-2*, Pub. by Library of America) Penguin Putnam.

Novels & Stories: Deephaven; A Country Doctor; The Country of the Pointed Firs; Dunnet Landing Stories; Selected Stories & Sketches. Sarah Orne Jewett. Ed. by Michael D. Bell. LC 93-24167. (Library of America Ser.). 937p. 1994. 35.00 (*0-940450-74-7*, Pub. by Library of America) Penguin Putnam.

Novels & Stories: Deephaven; A Country Doctor; The Country of the Pointed Firs; Stories & Sketches. Sarah Orne Jewett. Ed. by Michael D. Bell. LC 93-24167. (Library of America College Editions). 937p. (C). 1996. pap. text 11.95 (*1-883011-34-5*, Pub. by Library of America) Penguin Putnam.

Novels & Stories: Jonah's Gourd Vine; Their Eyes Were Watching God; Moses, Man of the Mountain; Seraph on the Suwanee, Vol. I. Zora Neale Hurston. Ed. by Cheryl A. Wall. LC 94-25757. Vol. 1. 1041p. 1995. 35.00 (*0-940450-83-6*, Pub. by Library of America) Penguin Putnam.

Novels & Stories: The Call of the Wild; White Fang; The Sea-Wolf; Klondike Stories. Jack London. Ed. by Donald Pizer. LC 82-249. 1021p. 1982. 30.00 (*0-940450-05-4*, Pub. by Library of America) Penguin Putnam.

Novels & Stories, 1905-1918: The Troll Garden; O Pioneers; The Song of Lark; My Antonia. Willa Cather. LC 99-20131. (Library of America College Editions Ser.). 975p. (C). 1999. pap. text 13.95 (*1-883011-74-4*, Pub. by Library of America) Penguin Putnam.

Novels & Stories, 1932-1937: The Pastures of Heaven; To a God Unknown; Tortilla Flat; In Dubious Battle; Of Mice & Men. John Steinbeck. Ed. by Robert DeMott & Elaine A. Steinbeck. 1994. 35.00 (*1-883011-01-9*, Pub. by Library of America) Penguin Putnam.

Novels & Stories of Frank R. Stockton. Frank Stockton. (Notable American Authors Ser.). 1999. reprint ed. lib. bdg. 125.00 (*0-7812-8938-6*) Rprt Serv.

Novels & Tales of Goethe. Johann Wolfgang Von Goethe. 1976. lib. bdg. 69.95 (*0-8490-2360-2*) Gordon Pr.

Novels & Tales of Henry James, 26 vols., Set. Henry James. (BCL1-PS American Literature Ser.). 1992. reprint ed. lib. bdg. 1950.00 (*0-7812-6761-7*) Rprt Serv.

Novels Behind Glass: Commodity Culture & Victorian Narrative. Andrew H. Miller. (Literature, Culture, Theory Ser.: No. 17). (Illus.). 254p. (C). 1995. text 59.95 (*0-521-47133-8*) Cambridge U Pr.

Novels, 1881-1886: Washington Square; The Portrait of a Lady; The Bostonians. Henry James. Ed. by William T. Stafford. LC 85-5207. 1249p. 1985. 40.00 (*0-940450-30-5*, Pub. by Library of America) Penguin Putnam.

Novels, 1886-1888: The Minister's Charge; April Hopes; Annie Kilburn. William Dean Howells. Ed. by Don L. Cook. LC 88-82728. 881p. 1989. 40.00 (*0-940450-51-8*, Pub. by Library of America) Penguin Putnam.

Novels, 1886-1890: The Princess Casamassima; The Reverberator; The Tragic Muse. Henry James. Ed. by Daniel M. Fogel. LC 88-82724. 1296p. 1989. 40.00 (*0-940450-56-9*, Pub. by Library of America) Penguin Putnam.

Novels, 1875-1886: A Foregone Conclusion; A Modern Instance; Indian Summer; The Rise of Silas Lapham. William Dean Howells. Ed. by Edwin H. Cady. LC 82-112. 1217p. 1982. 40.00 (*0-940450-04-6*, Pub. by Library of America) Penguin Putnam.

Novels, 1871-1880: Watch & Ward; Roderick Hudson; The American; The Europeans; Confidence. Henry James. Ed. by William T. Stafford. LC 83-5475. 1287p. 1983. 37.50 (*0-940450-13-5*, Pub. by Library of America) Penguin Putnam.

***Novels for Students.** 5th ed. Ed. by Marie Rose Napierkowski & Sheryl Ciccarelli. 350p. 1999. text 60.00 (*0-7876-2115-3*) Gale.

***Novels for Students.** 6th ed. Ed. by Marie Rose Napierkowski & Deborah A. Stanley. 350p. 1999. text 60.00 (*0-7876-2116-1*) Gale.

***Novels for Students.** 8th ed. Vol. 8. 350p. 2000. text 60.00 (*0-7876-3827-7*) Gale.

***Novels for Students, Vol. 3.** 350p. 1998. text 60.00 (*0-7876-2113-7*, 00157669) Gale.

***Novels for Students, Vol. 4.** Telgen. 350p. 1998. text 60.00 (*0-7876-2114-5*, GML00298-111632) Gale.

***Novels for Students, Vol. 7.** Gale Group Publishing Staff. 350p. 1999. text 60.00 (*0-7876-3826-9*) Gale.

***Novels for Students, Vol. 9.** 350p. 2000. text 60.00 (*0-7876-3828-5*, UXL) Gale.

Novels for Students: Presenting Analysis, Context & Criticism on Commonly Studied Novels, Vol. 1. Ed. by Diane Telgen. 350p. (YA). (gr. 9 up). 1997. text 60.00 (*0-7876-1686-9*) Gale.

Novels for Students: Presenting Analysis, Context & Criticism on Commonly Studied Novels, Vol. 2. Ed. by Diane Telgen. 350p. (YA). 1997. text 60.00 (*0-7876-1687-7*, GML00198-111088) Gale.

Novels from Reagan's America: A New Realism. Joseph Dewey. LC 99-36889. 1999. write for info. (*0-8130-1714-9*) U Press Fla.

Novels from Richard Bentley's Standard Novels Series, 12 vols. Richard Bentley. reprint ed. write for info. (*0-404-54400-2*) AMS Pr.

Novels in English: The Eighteenth & Nineteenth-Century Holdings at Schloss Corvex, Hoxter, Germany. John Graham. (American University Studies: English Language & Literature: Ser. IV, Vol. 2). XII, 141p. (Orig.). (C). 1983. pap. text 18.95 (*0-8204-0030-0*) P Lang Pubng.

Novels into Film: The Encyclopedia of Movies Adapted from Books. John C. Tibbetts & James M. Walsh. LC 99-10009. (Illus.). 320p. 1999. pap. 16.95 (*0-8160-3961-5*, Checkmark) Facts on File.

Novels, Mont Saint Michel, the Education: Democracy; Esther; Mont Saint Michel & Chartres; Education of Henry Adams. Henry (Brooks) Adams. Ed. by Ernest Samuels & Jayne N. Samuels. LC 83-5448. 1246p. 1983. 40.00 (*0-940450-12-7*, Pub. by Library of America) Penguin Putnam.

Novels, 1955-1962: Lolita; Pnin; Pale Fire; Lolita: A Screenplay. Vladimir Nabokov. Ed. by Brian Boyd. LC 96-15256. 925p. 1996. 35.00 (*1-883011-19-1*, Pub. by Library of America) Penguin Putnam.

Novels, 1957-1962: The Town; The Mansion; The Reivers. William Faulkner. LC 99-18348. (Library of America). 102p. 1999. 35.00 (*1-883011-69-8*, Pub. by Library of America) Penguin Putnam.

Novels, 1942-1954: Go down Moses; Intruder in the Dust; Requiem for a Nun; A Fable. William Faulkner. Ed. by Joseph Blotner & Noel Polk. LC 94-2942. 1115p. 1994. 35.00 (*0-940450-85-2*, Pub. by Library of America) Penguin Putnam.

Novels, 1969-1974: Ada, or Ardor; Transparent Things; Look at the Harlequins! Vladimir Nabokov. Ed. by Brian Boyd. LC 96-15255. 824p. 1996. 35.00 (*1-883011-20-5*, Pub. by Library of America) Penguin Putnam.

Novels, 1930-1935: As I Lay Dying, Sanctuary, Light in August, Pylon. William Faulkner. Ed. by Joseph Blotner & Noel Polk. LC 84-23424. 1034p. 1985. 35.00 (*0-940450-26-7*, Pub. by Library of America) Penguin Putnam.

Novels, 1936-1940: Absalom, Absalom!; If I Forget Thee; Jerusalem (The Wild Palms); The Unvanquished; The Hamlet. William Faulkner. Ed. by Joseph Blotner & Noel Polk. LC 89-62931. 1117p. 1990. 37.50 (*0-940450-55-0*, Pub. by Library of America) Penguin Putnam.

Novels, Novelists, & Readers: Toward a Phenomenological Sociology of Literature. Mary F. Rogers. LC 90-9890. (SUNY Series in the Sociology of Culture). 332p. (C). 1991. pap. text 21.95 (*0-7914-0603-2*) State U NY Pr.

Novels of Alex La Guma: The Representation of a Political Conflict. Ed. by Kathleen Balutanski. LC 86-51304. 142p. 1990. reprint ed. 25.00 (*0-89410-557-4*, Three Contnts); reprint ed. pap. 12.50 (*0-89410-558-2*, Three Contnts) L Rienner.

Novels of Alfred De Vigny: A Study of Their Form & Composition. Elaine Shwimer. LC 91-12043. (Harvard Romance Languages Ser.). 336p. 1991. reprint ed. text 20.00 (*0-8240-0482-5*) Garland.

***Novels of Amitav Ghosh.** R. K. Dhawan. LC 98-915589. 296p. 1999. write for info. (*81-7551-011-0*, Pub. by Prestige) Advent Bks Div.

Novels of Anita Desai. Usha Bande. 191p. 1988. text 25.00 (*81-85218-01-3*, Pub. by Prestige) Advent Bks Div.

Novels of Anthony Trollope - 1996. Skilton. 1996. 168.00 (*1-870587-49-9*) Ashgate Pub Co.

Novels of Anthony Trollope - 1997. Skilton. 1997. 168.00 (*1-870587-55-3*) Ashgate Pub Co.

Novels of Anthony Trollope - 1998. Skilton. 165.00 (*1-870587-61-8*) Ashgate Pub Co.

Novels of Anthony Trollope - 1999. Skilton. 168.00 (*1-870587-67-7*) Ashgate Pub Co.

Novels of Arun Joshi. Ed. by R. K. Dhawan. 288p. 1992. 32.50 (*81-85218-62-5*, Pub. by Prestige) Advent Bks Div.

Novels of August Strindberg: A Study in Theme & Structure. Eric O. Johannesson. LC 68-29156. 335p. reprint ed. pap. 103.90 (*0-608-15841-0*, 203143700074) Bks Demand.

Novels of Ayi Kwei Armah. K. Damodar Rao. 1993. 15.95 (*81-85218-75-7*, Pub. by Prestige) Advent Bks Div.

Novels of Bernard Malamud. M. Rajagopalachari. 222p. 1988. text 27.50 (*81-85218-02-1*, Pub. by Prestige) Advent Bks Div.

Novels of Bhabani Bhattacharya. Balram S. Sorot. 1991. text 25.00 (*81-85218-32-3*, Pub. by Prestige) Advent Bks Div.

Novels of C. P. Snow: A Critical Introduction. Suguna Ramanathan. LC 79-300490. xi, 125p. 1978. write for info. (*0-333-23480-4*) Macmillan.

Novels of Charles Dickens: A Bibliography & Sketch. Frederic G. Kitton. LC 75-148806. reprint ed. 41.50 (*0-404-08874-0*) AMS Pr.

Novels of Chinua Achebe. G. D. Killam. LC 75-455903. 106p. 1969. write for info. (*0-435-18500-4*) Buttrwrth-Heinemann.

Novels of Christiane: Countering the Culture. Margaret-Anne Hutton. 288p. 1999. pap. text 21.95 (*0-85989-586-6*, Pub. by Univ Exeter Pr) Northwestern U Pr.

Novels of Christiane Rochefort: Countering the Culture. Margaret-Anne Hutton. 288p. 1999. 70.00 (*0-85989-585-8*, Pub. by Univ Exeter Pr) Northwestern U Pr.

Novels of Colin Wilson. Nicolas Tredell. LC 82-13913. (Critical Studies). 158p. (C). 1982. text 44.00 (*0-389-20280-0*, N7098) B&N Imports.

Novels of Dorothy M. Richardson: Streams of Consciousness & Beyond. H. G. Chauhan. 1991. text 25.00 (*81-85151-37-7*, Pub. by Harman Pub Hse) Advent Bks Div.

Novels of Everyday Life: The Series in English Fiction, 1850-1930. Laurie Langbauer. LC 98-39544. 304p. 1999. 47.50 (*0-8014-3497-1*); pap. 18.95 (*0-8014-8501-0*) Cornell U Pr.

***Novels of Fernando Del Paso.** Robin W. Fiddian. LC 00-32586. 2000. write for info. (*0-8130-1806-4*) U Press Fla.

Novels of Flaubert: A Study of Themes & Techniques. Victor H. Brombert. LC PQ2247.B68. 311p. pap. 96.50 (*0-8357-8974-8*, 205228500085) Bks Demand.

Novels of Frank Norris. Donald Pizer. LC 72-6785. (Studies in Fiction: No. 34). 1972. reprint ed. lib. bdg. 75.00 (*0-8383-1666-2*) M S G Haskell Hse.

Novels of George Eliot. Robert Liddell. LC 77-366420. 193 p. 1977. write for info. (*0-7156-0992-0*) G Duckworth.

Novels of George Eliot. Jerome Thale. LC 59-8377. 187p. reprint ed. 58.00 (*0-8357-9069-X*, 201611900099) Bks Demand.

Novels of George Eliot. 4th ed. Barbara Hardy. xii, 242 p. (C). 1985. pap. 10.95 (*0-485-12005-4*, Pub. by Athlone Pr) Humanities.

Novels of George Meredith. Elmer J. Bailey. LC 75-163892. (Studies in George Meredith: No. 21). 1971. reprint ed. lib. bdg. 75.00 (*0-8383-1312-4*) M S G Haskell Hse.

Novels of George Meredith & Some Notes on the English Novel. Osbert Sitwell. LC 72-10858. (Studies in Fiction: No. 34). (C). 1970. reprint ed. pap. 19.95 (*0-8383-0070-7*) M S G Haskell Hse.

Novels of Graham Greene: Impact of Childhood on Adult Life. P. N. Pandit. 208p. 1990. text 27.50 (*81-85218-17-X*, Pub. by Prestige) Advent Bks Div.

Novels of Henry James: A Study. Elizabeth L. Cary. LC 72-10933. (Studies in Henry James: No. 17). (C). 1969. reprint ed. lib. bdg. 75.00 (*0-8383-0520-2*) M S G Haskell Hse.

Novels of Henry James: A Study of Culture & Consciousness. Brian Lee. LC 78-323943. viii, 123p. 1978. write for info. (*0-7131-6115-9*) Arnld Pub.

Novels of Henry Mackenzie, 4 vols. Henry MacKenzie. Incl. 2. Man of the World. 1976. reprint ed. 30.00 (*0-404-04092-6*); 3. Man of the World. 1976. reprint ed. 30.00 (*0-404-04093-4*); Vol. 1. Man of Feeling. 1976. 30.00 (*0-404-04091-8*); Vol. 4. Julia de Roubigne. 1976. reprint ed. 30.00 (*0-404-04094-2*); 1976. write for info. (*0-318-50676-9*) AMS Pr.

Novels of Henry Mackenzie, 4 vols., Set. Henry MacKenzie. Incl. 2. Man of the World. 1976. reprint ed. 30.00 (*0-404-04092-6*); 3. Man of the World. 1976. reprint ed. 30.00 (*0-404-04093-4*); Vol. 1. Man of Feeling. 1976. 30.00 (*0-404-04091-8*); Vol. 4. Julia de Roubigne. 1976. reprint ed. 30.00 (*0-404-04094-2*); 1976. 120.00 (*0-404-04090-X*) AMS Pr.

Novels Of Hugh Maclennan. Robert H. Cockburn. LC 76-109579. 165 P.p. 1970. write for info. (*0-88772-108-7*) HAR Davenport.

Novels of Hugh MacLennan. Robert H. Cockburn. LC 76-109579. 165p. reprint ed. pap. 51.20 (*0-608-13578-X*, 202228800026) Bks Demand.

Novels of Initiation: A Guidebook for Teaching Literature to Adolescents. David Peck. 224p. 1989. pap. text 17.95 (*0-8077-2951-5*) Tchrs Coll.

Novels of Jacinto Octavio Picon. Noel M. Valis. LC 84-45456. (Illus.). 224p. 1986. 38.50 (*0-8387-5082-6*) Bucknell U Pr.

Novels of Jack London: A Reappraisal. Charles N. Watson, Jr. LC 82-70548. 324p. 1982. 25.00 (*0-299-09300-X*) U of Wis Pr.

Novels of Jane Austen: An Interpretation. Darrel Mansen. LC 73-166540. xiv, 226p. 1973. write for info. (*0-333-14661-1*) Macmillan.

Novels of Johann Karl Wezel: Satire, Realism & Social Criticism in Late 18th Century Literature. Phillip S. McKnight. (New York University Ottendorfer Series: Neue Folge: Vol. 14). 312p. 1981. pap. 54.00 (*3-261-04797-6*) P Lang Pubng.

Novels of Joseph Conrad. R. K. Dhawan. 224p. 1992. text 27.50 (*81-85218-07-2*, Pub. by Prestige) Advent Bks Div.

Novels of Kamala Markandaya & Ruth Jhabvala. Rekha Jha. 180p. 1990. text 25.00 (*81-85218-15-3*, Pub. by Prestige) Advent Bks Div.

Novels of Manohar Malgaonkar, a Study. Ashok K. Sharma. LC 95-910281. (Indian Writers Ser.). viii, 122p. 1995. write for info. (*81-7018-852-0*) BR Pub.

Novels of Manohar Malgonkar. M. Rajagopalachari. 104p. 1990. text 18.95 (*81-85218-16-1*, Pub. by Prestige) Advent Bks Div.

Novels of Margaret Drabble: Equivocal Figures. Ellen C. Rose. (Illus.). 141p. 1980. 44.00 (*0-389-20006-9*, N6783) B&N Imports.

Novels of Margaret Drabble: "this Freudian family nexus" Nicole S. Bokat. LC 97-44504. (Sexuality & Literature Ser.: Vol. 7). 274p. (C). 1998. 51.95 (*0-8204-3980-0*) P Lang Pubng.

Novels of Martin Walser: A Critical Introduction. Frank Pilipp. (GERM Ser.: Vol. 64). (Illus.). xii, 196p. 1991. 60.00 (*0-938100-98-X*) Camden Hse.

Novels of Mrs. Aphra Behn. Aphra Behn. LC 72-98812. 380p. 1970. reprint ed. lib. bdg. 65.00 (*0-8371-2824-2*, BENB, Greenwood Pr) Greenwood.

Novels of Mrs. Aphra Behn. Aphra Behn. (BCL1-PR English Literature Ser.). 380p. 1992. reprint ed. lib. bdg. 89.00 (*0-7812-7320-X*) Rprt Serv.

Novels of Mrs. Oliphant: A Subversive View of Traditional Themes. Margarete Rubik. LC 93-13111. (Writing about Women: Feminist Literary Studies: Vol. 8). 343p. (C). 1994. text 54.95 (*0-8204-2209-6*) P Lang Pubng.

Novels of Mulk Raj Anand. Ed. by R. K. Dhawan. 288p. (C). 1992. 27.50 (*81-85218-63-3*, Pub. by Prestige) Advent Bks Div.

Novels of Nadine Gordimer: History from the Inside. Stephen Clingman. 296p. (C). 1986. text 39.95 (*0-04-800082-5*) Routledge.

Novels of Nadine Gordimer: History from the Inside. 2nd ed. Stephen Clingman. LC 92-4691. 320p. 1992. pap. 18.95 (*0-87023-802-7*) U of Mass Pr.

Novels of Philip K. Dick. Kim Stanley Robinson. Ed. by Robert Scholes. LC 84-2621. (Studies in Speculative Fiction: No. 9). 162p. reprint ed. pap. 50.30 (*0-8357-1589-2*, 207062300008) Bks Demand.

Novels of Pierre Loti. Clive Wake. LC 73-80224. (De Proprietatibus Litterarum, Ser. Practica: No. 82). 1974. pap. text 26.15 (*90-279-2660-3*) Mouton.

Novels of Rex Warner: An Introduction. N. H. Reeve. 190p. 1990. text 45.00 (*0-312-03703-1*) St Martin.

Novels of Robert Surtees, 10 vols. Robert S. Surtees. LC 73-148311. reprint ed. 240.00 (*0-404-08900-3*) AMS Pr.

Novels of Salman Rushdie. Ed. by R. K. Dhawan & G. R. Taneja. 225p. 1991. text 30.00 (*81-85218-33-1*, Pub. by Prestige) Advent Bks Div.

Novels of Samuel Beckett. 2nd ed. John Fletcher. LC 72-178537. 252p. 1970. write for info. (*0-7011-0695-6*) Chatto & Windus.

Novels of Samuel Richardson, 19 vols. Samuel Richardson. LC 75-114357. 1970. reprint ed. 1282.50 (*0-404-05310-6*) AMS Pr.

Novels of Saul Bellow: An Introduction. Keith Opdahl. LC 67-16197. 1967. 30.00 (*0-271-73118-4*) Pa St U Pr.

Novels of Shashi Deshpande: A Study in the Image of Woman. Sarabjit K. Sandhu. 80p. 1991. text 15.95 (*81-85218-28-5*, Pub. by Prestige) Advent Bks Div.

Novels of Simone De Beauvoir. Elizabeth Fallaize. 240p. 1988. text 45.00 (*0-415-02294-0*) Routledge.

Novels of Simone de Beauvoir. Elizabeth Fallaize. LC 89-101656. 208p. reprint ed. pap. 64.50 (*0-608-20339-4*, 207159200002) Bks Demand.

Novels of Testimony & Resistance from Central America. Linda J. Craft. LC 96-45381. 240p. 1997. 39.95 (*0-8130-1508-1*) U Press Fla.

Novels of the 1840s. Kathleen Tillotson. 1983. reprint ed. pap. 12.95 (*0-19-871109-3*) OUP.

Novels of the Past but Not Forgotten. John O. Eidson. 252p. 1985. pap. 9.95 (*0-87921-076-1*) Attic Pr.

Novels of Theodore Dreiser: A Critical Study. Donald Pizer. LC 75-20769. 394p. reprint ed. pap. 122.20 (*0-8357-6536-9*, 203589800097) Bks Demand.

Novels of Thomas Deloney. Thomas Deloney. Ed. by Merritt E. Lawlis. LC 77-18010. (Illus.). 462p. 1978. reprint ed. lib. bdg. 79.50 (*0-313-20105-6*, DENO, Greenwood Pr) Greenwood.

Novels of Thomas Hardy: Illusion & Reality. Penelope Vigar. LC 75-305166. 226 p. 1974. write for info. (*0-485-11147-0*) Athlone Pr.

Novels of Thomas Love Peacock. Bryan Burns. LC 84-19905. 256p. 1985. 53.00 (*0-389-20532-X*, 08094) B&N Imports.

Novels of Tobias Smollett. Paul-Gabriel Bouce. Tr. by Antonia White. LC 75-31687. ix, 405p. 1976. write for info. (*0-582-50023-0*) Addison-Wesley.

Novels of Toni Morrison: The Search for Self & Place Within the Community. Patrick B. Bjork. LC 91-24571. (American Univ. Studies, XXIV, Am. Lit.: Vol. 31). 172p. (C). 1994. pap. text 29.95 (*0-8204-2569-9*) P Lang Pubng.

Novels of V. S. Naipaul: A Study in Theme & Form. Shashi P. Kamra. 176p. 1990. text 25.00 (*81-85218-12-9*, Pub. by Prestige) Advent Bks Div.

Novels of Virginia Woolf. B. Sudipta. 176p. 1990. text 27.50 (*81-85218-14-5*, Pub. by Prestige) Advent Bks Div.

Novels of Virginia Woolf: Fact & Vision. Alice V. Kelley. LC 73-77134. 1976. pap. 4.95 (*0-226-42986-5*, P698) U Ch Pr.

Novels of V.S. Naipaul: Quest for Order & Identity. N. Ramadevi. LC 96-905450. 152p. 1996. write for info. (*81-7551-006-4*, Pub. by Prestige) Advent Bks Div.

Novels of William Faulkner: A Critical Interpretation. rev. ed. Olga W. Vickery. LC 64-23150. 318p. 1995. pap. text 19.95 (*0-8071-2006-5*) La State U Pr.

Novels of William Godwin & Those of His Contemporaries. Mona Scheuermann. Ed. by Devendra P. Varma. LC 79-8477. (Gothic Studies & Dissertations). 1980. lib. bdg. 31.95 (*0-405-12678-6*) Ayer.

An Asterisk (*) at the beginning of an entry indicates that the title is appearing for the first time.

Novels of William Styron. S. Laxmana Murthy. 204p. 1988. text 27.50 (*81-85218-03-X*, Pub. by Prestige) Advent Bks Div.

Novels of William Styron: From Harmony to History. Gavin Cologne-Brookes. LC 94-19731. (Southern Literary Studies). 288p. (C). 1995. text 40.00 (*0-8071-1900-8*) La State U Pr.

Novels of Wole Soyinka. M. Rajeshwar. 96p. 1990. text 17.95 (*81-85218-21-8*, Pub. by Prestige) Advent Bks Div.

Novels of World War II: An Annotated Bibliography of World War Two Fiction. Michael Paris. LC 90-176799. 196p. 1990. reprint ed. pap. 60.80 (*0-7837-9271-9*, 206000900004) Bks Demand.

Novels of Wright Morris: A Critical Interpretation. Gail B. Crump. LC 77-15796. 266p. 1978. reprint ed. pap. 82.50 (*0-608-01851-1*, 206250100003) Bks Demand.

Novels, Readers, & Reviewers: Responses to Fiction in Antebellum America. Nina Baym. LC 84-5033. 288p. 1984. pap. text 17.95 (*0-8014-9466-4*) Cornell U Pr.

Novel's Seductions: Stael's Corinne in Critical Inquiry. Karyna Szmurlo. LC 98-7650. 1999. write for info. (*0-8387-5337-X*) Bucknell U Pr.

Novels, 1705 to 1714, 7 Vols. in Two, Set. Mary D. Manley. LC 75-161934. 1816p. 1971. 200.00 (*0-8201-1094-9*) Schol Facsimiles.

Novels, Stories, Sketches & Poems of Thomas Nelson Page, 18 vols., Set. Thomas N. Page. (BCL1-PS American Literature Ser.). 1992. reprint ed. pap. text 990.00 (*0-685-51403-X*); reprint ed. lib. bdg. 1350.00 (*0-7812-6821-4*) Rprt Serv.

***Novelties in String Theory: Proceedings of the Johns Hopkins Workshop on Current Problems in Particle Theory 22, Ghoteborg, 1998 (August 20-22)** Lars Brink & R. Marnelius. LC 99-41242. 370p. 1999. write for info. (*981-02-4084-8*) World Scientific Pub.

Novelties in the Heavens: Rhetoric & Science in the Copernican Controversy. Jean D. Moss. LC 92-21608. 368p. (C). 1993. pap. text 17.95 (*0-226-54235-1*) U Ch Pr.

Novelties in the Heavens: Rhetoric & Science in the Copernican Controversy. Jean D. Moss. LC 92-21608. 368p. (C). 1993. lib. bdg. 49.95 (*0-226-54234-3*) U Ch Pr.

Novelty & Sing along Songs. Ed. by Tony Esposito. 96p. 1997. pap. 12.95 (*0-7692-0040-0*, FB9703) Wrner Bros.

Novelty Cakes. 1. 1999. pap. text 8.95 (*1-85391-490-8*) Merehurst Ltd.

Novelty Cakes: 35 Imaginative Cakes for All Occasions. Carol Deacon. LC 99-230134. (Quick & Easy Ser.). (Illus.). 95p. 1999. pap. 14.95 (*1-85368-735-9*, Pub. by New5 Holland) Sterling.

Novelty Slipper Orchids. Harold Koopowitz. (Illus.). 142p. 1991. 25.00 (*0-685-40998-8*) HarpC.

Novelty Songbook, Vol. 166. 120p. 1982. per. 9.95 (*0-7935-0546-1*, 00101809) H Leonard.

Novelty Trimmings: Millinery. (Illus.). 50p. 1998. reprint ed. pap. 8.95 (*0-9669077-0-1*) Judith M Pubg.

Novelty Unicycling. Jack Wiley. (Illus.). 27p. (gr. 7 up). 1989. pap. 6.95 (*0-913999-25-3*) Solipaz Pub Co.

***November.** (Monthly Patterns & Projects Ser.). (Illus.). 80p. (J). (ps-2). 2000. pap. 7.95 (*1-58273-127-6*) Newbridge Educ.

November. Gustave Flaubert. 164p. 1987. pap. 7.95 (*0-88184-334-2*) Carroll & Graf.

November. Derek Henderson. Ed. by Derek Pollard. 10p. 1997. pap. 3.00 (*0-9665407-1-9*) Bl Nght Pr.

November. Daniel Parker. (Countdown Ser.: No. 11). 128p. (YA). (gr. 7-12). 1999. mass mkt. 3.99 (*0-689-81829-7*) Aladdin.

November. Georges Simenon. Tr. by Jean Stewart. LC 78-6067. 185p. 1978. pap. 2.95 (*0-15-667582-X*, Harvest Bks) Harcourt.

November. David Trinidad. 86p. (Orig.). 1986. pap. 5.95 (*0-937815-01-2*) Hanuman Bks.

***November: Full Color Monthly Activities fro Grades 1-3.** (Monthly Bks.). (Illus.). 64p. (J). (gr. 1-3). 2000. pap. 12.95 (*0-88724-550-1*, CD-2092) Carson-Dellos.

November - December. Barbara Gruber. (Instant Idea Bks.). (Illus.). 64p. 1988. 7.95 (*0-86734-074-6*, FS-8312) Schaffer Pubns.

November & Thanksgiving. Nancy M. Davis et al. (Davis Teaching Units Ser.: Vol. 1, No. 3). (Illus.). 31p. (Orig.). (J). (ps-2). 1986. pap. 4.95 (*0-937103-02-0*) DaNa Pubns.

November Boots. Nancy Hundal. (Illus.). 1996. 12.95 (*0-00-223893-4*) Collins SF.

***November Boughs.** Walt Whitman. (Notable American Authors Ser.). 1999. reprint ed. lib. bdg. 125.00 (*0-7812-9950-0*) Rprt Serv.

***November Chill.** Mary Casanova. 144p. (J). (gr. 3-7). 2000. 14.99 (*0-7868-0547-1*, Pub. by Disney Pr) Time Warner.

November Days: A Love Story. Bonnie Ruth. 299p. (Orig.). 1995. pap. 12.95 (*0-9645378-7-7*) F Scott Pr.

November 18: What Your Birth Date Reveals about You. (Birth Date Book Ser.). (Illus.). 80p. 1998. 4.95 (*0-8362-6345-6*) Andrews & McMeel.

November 8: What Your Birth Date Reveals about You. (Birth Date Book Ser.). (Illus.). 80p. 1998. 4.95 (*0-8362-6334-0*) Andrews & McMeel.

November 11: What Your Birth Date Reveals about You. (Birth Date Book Ser.). (Illus.). 80p. 1998. 4.95 (*0-8362-6337-5*) Andrews & McMeel.

November Essentials: Idea Booklet & Pocket Folder Organizer. Karen Sevaly. (Illus.). 16p. 1997. pap., teacher ed., wbk. ed. 3.99 (*1-57882-010-3*, TF-1261) Teachers Friend Pubns.

November Ever After. Laura Torres. LC 99-17697. 171p. (YA). (gr. 7 up). 1999. 16.95 (*0-8234-1464-7*) Holiday.

November 15: What Your Birth Date Reveals about You. (Birth Date Book Ser.). (Illus.). 80p. 1998. 4.95 (*0-8362-6341-3*) Andrews & McMeel.

November 5: What Your Birth Date Reveals about You. (Birth Date Book Ser.). (Illus.). 80p. 1998. 4.95 (*0-8362-6331-6*) Andrews & McMeel.

November 1: What Your Birth Date Reveals about You. (Birth Date Book Ser.). (Illus.). 80p. 1998. 4.95 (*0-8362-6327-8*) Andrews & McMeel.

November 14: What Your Birth Date Reveals about You. (Birth Date Book Ser.). (Illus.). 80p. 1998. 4.95 (*0-8362-6340-5*) Andrews & McMeel.

November 4: What Your Birth Date Reveals about You. (Birth Date Book Ser.). (Illus.). 80p. 1998. 4.95 (*0-8362-6330-8*) Andrews & McMeel.

November Haggard: Uncollected Prose & Verse. Patrick Kavanagh. (Illus.). 230p. 1971. 50.00 (*0-914612-03-4*) Kavanagh.

November Idea Book: A Creative Idea Book for the Elementary Teacher, Ps-6. rev. ed. Karen Sevaly. (Illus.). 144p. (Orig.). 1997. pap. 10.95 (*0-943263-02-6*, TF-1100) Teachers Friend Pubns.

November Man. 1988. mass mkt. 3.95 (*0-446-73751-8*, Pub. by Warner Bks) Little.

November Man. Bill Granger. 1979. pap. 1.95 (*0-449-14245-0*, GM) Fawcett.

November Man. Bill Granger. 352p. 1988. mass mkt. 5.99 (*0-446-32473-6*, Pub. by Warner Bks) Little.

November Monthly Activities. Rice. (Illus.). 80p. (J). (ps-1). 1996. pap., wbk. ed. 9.95 (*1-55734-862-6*) Tchr Create Mat.

November Monthly Activities. Sterling & Susan S. Nowlin. (Monthly Activities Ser.). (Illus.). 80p. (J). (gr. 6-8). 1996. pap., wbk. ed. 9.95 (*1-55734-153-2*) Tchr Create Mat.

November Monthy Activities. Dona H. Rice. (Illus.). 80p. 1996. pap., teacher ed. 9.95 (*1-55734-872-3*, TCM872) Tchr Create Mat.

November, 1948: A Memoir. Carl Dawson. 176p. 1990. text 20.00 (*0-8139-1258-X*) U Pr of Va.

November, 1975: The Inside Story of Australia's Greatest Political Crisis. Paul Kelly. (Illus.). 256p. 1996. pap. 19.95 (*1-86373-987-4*, Pub. by Allen & Unwin Pty) Paul & Co Pubs.

November 1916: The Red Wheel: Knot II. Aleksandr Solzhenitsyn. Tr. by H. T. Willetts from RUS. LC 98-14263. Vol. 2. 1040p. 1999. 35.00 (*0-374-22314-9*) FS&G.

***November 1916: The Second Knot of the Red Wheel.** Aleksandr Solzhenitsyn. Tr. by H. T. Willetts from RUS. LC 98-14263. Vol. 2. 1040p. 2000. pap. 17.00 (*0-374-52703-2*) FS&G.

November, 1938: From the Reichskristallnacht to Genocide. Ed. by Walter H. Pehle. Tr. by William Templer. 269p. 1991. 37.50 (*0-85496-687-0*) Berg Pubs.

November 19: What Your Birth Date Reveals about You. (Birth Date Book Ser.). (Illus.). 80p. 1998. 4.95 (*0-8362-6346-4*) Andrews & McMeel.

November 9: What Your Birth Date Reveals about You. (Birth Date Book Ser.). (Illus.). 80p. 1998. 4.95 (*0-8362-6335-9*) Andrews & McMeel.

November of the Heart. LaVyrle Spencer. 432p. 1994. mass mkt. 7.50 (*0-515-11331-X*, Jove) Berkley Pub.

November Patriots: The Murder of John Kennedy. unabridged ed. Constance Kritzberg & Larry Hancock. (Illus.). 562p. 1998. pap. 16.50 (*0-9667281-0-6*) UnderCover Pr.

November Patterns, Projects & Plans. Imogene Forte. 80p. (J). (ps-1). 1989. pap. text 9.95 (*0-86530-127-1*, IP 166-9) Incentive Pubns.

November Propertius. Norm Sibum. LC 99-203095. 96p. 1998. pap. 14.95 (*1-85754-303-3*, Pub. by Carcanet Pr) Paul & Co Pubs.

November Rain. Myungkark Park. (Illus.). 100p. 1997. pap. write for info. (*1-877974-30-7*) Prompter Pubns.

November 2: What Your Birth Date Reveals about You. (Birth Date Book Ser.). (Illus.). 80p. 1998. 4.95 (*0-8362-6328-6*) Andrews & McMeel.

Nov. 2, 1891-May 31, 1892 see Germans to America: Lists of Passengers Arriving at U. S. Ports, 1850-1893

November 17: What Your Birth Date Reveals about You. (Birth Date Book Ser.). (Illus.). 80p. 1998. 4.95 (*0-8362-6344-8*) Andrews & McMeel.

November 7: What Your Birth Date Reveals about You. (Birth Date Book Ser.). (Illus.). 80p. 1998. 4.95 (*0-8362-6333-2*) Andrews & McMeel.

November 16: What Your Birth Date Reveals about You. (Birth Date Book Ser.). (Illus.). 80p. 1998. 4.95 (*0-8362-6342-1*) Andrews & McMeel.

November 6: What Your Birth Date Reveals about You. (Birth Date Book Ser.). (Illus.). 80p. 1998. 4.95 (*0-8362-6332-4*) Andrews & McMeel.

November Surprise: Read the Fine Print Before You Vote. Dinesh Shah. 32p. (Orig.). 1992. pap. 3.95 (*0-9634764-5-9*, We The People) Fnding Fathers.

November 10: What Your Birth Date Reveals about You. (Birth Date Book Ser.). (Illus.). 80p. 1998. 4.95 (*0-8362-6336-7*) Andrews & McMeel.

November 10, 1736-June 7, 1739 see Journal of the Commons House of Assembly: Series One

November 3: What Your Birth Date Reveals about You. (Birth Date Book Ser.). (Illus.). 80p. 1998. 4.95 (*0-8362-6329-4*) Andrews & McMeel.

November 13: What Your Birth Date Reveals about You. (Birth Date Book Ser.). (Illus.). 80p. 1998. 4.95 (*0-8362-6339-1*) Andrews & McMeel.

November 30: What Your Birth Date Reveals about You. (Birth Date Book Ser.). (Illus.). 80p. 1998. 4.95 (*0-8362-6358-8*) Andrews & McMeel.

November 3 - 3 Delta: Helicopter Watch over New York. Lou Timolat. LC 74-81422. (Illus.). 128p. 1974. pap. 12.95 (*0-85699-116-3*) Chatham Pr.

November Tree. large type ed. Margaret Maddocks. 1989. 27.99 (*0-7089-2058-6*) Ulverscroft.

***November Tree.** large type ed. Ann Stevens. 368p. 1999. 31.99 (*0-7089-4078-1*, Linford) Ulverscroft.

November 12: What Your Birth Date Reveals about You. (Birth Date Book Ser.). (Illus.). 80p. 1998. 4.95 (*0-8362-6338-3*) Andrews & McMeel.

November 20: What Your Birth Date Reveals about You. (Birth Date Book Ser.). (Illus.). 80p. 1998. 4.95 (*0-8362-6347-2*) Andrews & McMeel.

November 28: What Your Birth Date Reveals about You. (Birth Date Book Ser.). (Illus.). 80p. 1998. 4.95 (*0-8362-6355-3*) Andrews & McMeel.

November 25: What Your Birth Date Reveals about You. (Birth Date Book Ser.). (Illus.). 80p. 1998. 4.95 (*0-8362-6352-9*) Andrews & McMeel.

November 21: What Your Birth Date Reveals about You. (Birth Date Book Ser.). (Illus.). 80p. 1998. 4.95 (*0-8362-6348-0*) Andrews & McMeel.

November 24: What Your Birth Date Reveals about You. (Birth Date Book Ser.). (Illus.). 80p. 1998. 4.95 (*0-8362-6351-0*) Andrews & McMeel.

November 29: What Your Birth Date Reveals about You. (Birth Date Book Ser.). (Illus.). 80p. 1998. 4.95 (*0-8362-6356-1*) Andrews & McMeel.

November 22: What Your Birth Date Reveals about You. (Birth Date Book Ser.). (Illus.). 80p. 1998. 4.95 (*0-8362-6349-9*) Andrews & McMeel.

November 22 - The Day Remembered. Morning News Staff Dallas 1. LC 89-71363. 160p. 1990. pap. 11.95 (*0-87833-711-3*) Taylor Pub.

***November 22, 1968: A Reference Guide to the JFK Assassination.** William E. Scott. LC 98-54261. 296p. 1999. 38.00 (*0-7618-1336-5*) U Pr of Amer.

November 27: What Your Birth Date Reveals about You. (Birth Date Book Ser.). (Illus.). 80p. 1998. 4.95 (*0-8362-6354-5*) Andrews & McMeel.

November 26: What Your Birth Date Reveals about You. (Birth Date Book Ser.). (Illus.). 80p. 1998. 4.95 (*0-8362-6353-7*) Andrews & McMeel.

November 23: What Your Birth Date Reveals about You. (Birth Date Book Ser.). (Illus.). 80p. 1998. 4.95 (*0-8362-6350-2*) Andrews & McMeel.

November Veil. Linda Hall. LC 97-143865. (Royal Canadian Mouted Police Ser.). 247p. 1996. pap. 9.99 (*0-934998-68-X*) Evangel Indiana.

***November Wedding & Other Poems.** Ted McCarthy. LC 98-204407. 2000. pap. 13.95 (*1-901866-21-1*, Pub. by Lilliput Pr) Dufour.

November, 1792-February, 1793 see Papers of Alexander Hamilton

November 1834 - June 1836 see Diary of Charles Francis Adams

Novemberfest. Theodore Weesner. LC 96-15042. (Hardscrabble Bks.). 397p. 1996. pap. 15.95 (*0-87451-766-4*) U Pr of New Eng.

Novemberland: Selected Poems 1956-1993. Gunter Grass. Tr. by Michael Hamburger. LC 95-38418. (ENG & GER.). 176p. 1996. pap. 15.00 (*0-15-600331-7*, Harvest Bks) Harcourt.

Novena: The Power of Prayer. Barbara Calamari. (Illus.). 156p. 1999. text 24.95 (*0-670-88444-8*) Penguin Books.

***Novena for Forgiveness.** (Scripture Novenas Ser.). 24p. 2001. pap. write for info. (*0-8198-5141-8*) Pauline Bks.

***Novena for Health.** (Scripture Novenas Ser.). 24p. 2001. pap. write for info. (*0-8198-5140-X*) Pauline Bks.

Novena for Justice & Peace. Campaign for Human Development Staff. LC 98-191022. 13 p. 1998. 1.00 (*1-57455-237-6*) US Catholic.

***Novena in a Time of Difficulty.** (Scripture Novenas Ser.). 24p. 2001. pap. write for info. (*0-8198-5142-6*) Pauline Bks.

***Novena in Praise of the Father.** (Scripture Novenas Ser.). 24p. 2001. pap. write for info. (*0-8198-5143-4*) Pauline Bks.

Novena in Praise of the Holy Spirit. (Scripture Novenas Ser.). 24p. pap. write for info. (*0-8198-5145-0*) Pauline Bks.

***Novena in Praise of the Son.** (Scripture Novenas Ser.). 24p. 2001. pap. write for info. (*0-8198-5144-2*) Pauline Bks.

Novena of Forgiveness. (Scripture Novenas Ser.). 24p. pap. write for info. (*0-8198-5146-9*) Pauline Bks.

Novena of Holy Communions. Lawrence G. Lovasik. 51p. 1995. pap. 2.00 (*0-89555-519-0*) TAN Bks Pubs.

***Novena of Hope in Suffering.** (Scripture Novenas Ser.). 24p. 2001. pap. write for info. (*0-8198-5147-7*) Pauline Bks.

***Novena of Thanksgiving.** (Scripture Novenas Ser.). 24p. 2001. pap. write for info. (*0-8198-5148-5*) Pauline Bks.

Novena Prayers to St. Theresa, the Little Flower. Daughters of St. Paul Staff. 22p. (J). 1985. pap. 1.25 (*0-8198-5123-X*) Pauline Bks.

***Novena to Find Employment.** (Scripture Novenas Ser.). 24p. 2001. pap. write for info. (*0-8198-5149-3*) Pauline Bks.

***Novena to Obtain Patience.** (Scripture Novenas Ser.). 24p. 2001. pap. write for info. (*0-8198-5150-7*) Pauline Bks.

***Novena to Overcome Fear.** (Scripture Novenas Ser.). 24p. 2001. pap. write for info. (*0-8198-5151-5*) Pauline Bks.

Novena to St. Anthony. Veritas Publications Staff. 1989. pap. 22.00 (*1-85390-032-X*, Pub. by Veritas Pubns) St Mut.

Novena to St. Benedict. 40p. 1987. pap. 2.95 (*0-8146-0803-5*) Liturgical Pr.

Novena to St. Joseph. Veritas Publications Staff. 1989. pap. 22.00 (*1-85390-041-9*, Pub. by Veritas Pubns) St Mut.

Novenas Favoritas A los Santos. Lawrence G. Lovasik. (SPA., Illus.). 64p. 1995. pap. 2.50 (*0-89942-658-1*, 658/S) Catholic Bk Pub.

Novenas Favoritas a Maria. Lawrence G. Lovasik. (SPA.). 1993. pap. 2.50 (*0-89942-061-3*, 159/04S) Catholic Bk Pub.

Noventa Millas. Auristela Soler. LC 80-68772. (Coleccion Caniqui). (SPA.). 140p. (Orig.). 1982. pap. 9.95 (*0-89729-270-7*) Ediciones.

Noves et l'Ete. Albert Camus. (Folio Ser.: No. 16). (FRE.). 1959. pap. 6.95 (*2-07-036016-4*) Schoenhof.

Novgorod: Art Treasures & Architectural Monuments: 11th to 18th Centuries. Vladimir Gormin & Liudmila Yarosh. 1984. 250.00 (*0-7855-1582-8*) St Mut.

Novgorod in Focus: Selected Essays. Henrik Birnbaum. 192p. 1996. 24.95 (*0-89357-261-6*) Slavica.

Novgorod Mint During the Swedish Occupation, 1611-1617. Anders R. Berglund & Vasilii V. Zakharov. (Illus.). v, 56p. (Orig.). 1983. pap. 13.00 (*0-912671-03-3*) Russian Numis.

Novgorod Oblast: Economy, Industry, Government, Business. 2nd rev. ed. Russian Information & Business Center, Inc. Staff. (Russian Regional Business Directories Ser.). (Illus.). 200p. 1997. pap. 99.00 (*1-57751-401-7*) Intl Business Pubns.

***Novgorod Oblast Regional Investment & Business Guide.** Global Investment & Business Center, Inc. Staff. (Russian Regional Investment & Business Guides Ser.: Vol. 53). (Illus.). 350p. 1999. pap. 99.00 (*0-7397-0852-X*) Intl Business Pubns.

***Novgorod Oblast Regional Investment & Business Guide.** Contrib. by Global Investment & Business Center, Inc. Staff. (Russian Regional Investment & Business Guides Ser.: Vol. 11). (Illus.). 350p. 2000. pap. 99.95 (*0-7397-3001-0*) Intl Business Pubns.

Novgorodian Icon-Painting. V. N. Lazarev. (Illus.). 210p. (C). 1976. text 180.00 (*0-569-08320-6*, Pub. by Collets) St Mut.

Novi. Barbara G. Louie. LC 98-87869. (Images of America Ser.). 1998. write for info. (*0-7385-0012-7*) Arcadia Publng.

Novi Vol. 2: The Legendary Indianapolis Race Car, 1961-1966. George Peters & Henri Greuter. (Illus.). 222p. (Orig.). 1998. pap. 32.95 (*0-9630227-1-7*) Bar Jean Enter.

Novi Engleski bez Muke: English for Serbo-Croatian Speakers. Assimil Staff. (ENG & SER.). 28.95 (*0-8288-4321-X*, M12724) Fr & Eur.

Novi Francuski Bez Muke: French for Serbo-Croatian Speakers. Assimil Staff. (FRE & SER.). 28.95 (*0-8288-4333-3*, F62317) Fr & Eur.

Novi Nemacki Bez Muke: German for Serbo-Croatian Speakers. Assimil Staff. (GER & SER.). 28.95 (*0-8288-4324-4*, F17130) Fr & Eur.

Novi Spanski Bez Muke: Spanish for Serbo-Croatian Speakers. Assimil Staff. (SER & SPA.). 28.95 (*0-8288-4325-2*, F30860) Fr & Eur.

Novia de Medianoche: Midnight Bride. Barbara McCauley. (Deseo Ser.).Tr. of Midnight Bride. (SPA.). 1997. per. 3.50 (*0-373-35209-3*, 1-35209-5) Harlequin Bks.

***Novia de Sherbrooke.** Catherine Coulter. (SPA.). 1998. pap. 10.95 (*84-01-50700-6*) Plaza.

Novia de Ultramar. Lectorum Publications Staff. 1997. pap. text 10.50 (*84-01-50801-0*) Lectorum Pubns.

***Novia del Sabado.** Kate Walker.Tr. of Saturday's Bride. (SPA.). 2000. per. 3.50 (*0-373-33549-0*) Harlequin Bks.

***Novia Especial: (A Special Bride)** Barbara McCauley. (Deseo Ser.: No. 151).Tr. of A Special Bride. (SPA.). 1999. per. 3.50 (*0-373-35281-6*, 1-35281-4) Harlequin Bks.

Novia Huida. Joan Johnston. (Deseo Ser.: No. 215).Tr. of Fugitive Bride. (SPA.). 1997. per. 3.50 (*0-373-35215-8*, 1-35215-2) Harlequin Bks.

Novia Indecisa: The Bride Wore Tie-Dye. Pamela Ingraham. (Deseo Ser.: Vol. 126). (SPA.). 1998. per. 3.50 (*0-373-35256-5*, 1-35256-6) Harlequin Bks.

***Novia Maliciosa.** Catherine Coulter. (SPA.). 368p. 2000. pap. 9.50 (*0-553-06126-7*) Bantam.

Novia Mas Bella (The Most Beautiful Bride) Cindy Gerard. (Deseo Ser.). (SPA.). 1998. per. 3.50 (*0-373-35231-X*, 1-35231-9) Harlequin Bks.

Novia Obstinada: The Disobedient Bride. Joan Johnston. (Deseo Ser.). (SPA.). 1996. per. 3.50 (*0-373-35168-2*, 1-35168-3) Harlequin Bks.

Novia Por Correspondencia - Correspondence Girlfriend. Cindy Gerard. (Deseo Ser.). (SPA.). 1998. per. 3.50 (*0-373-35234-4*, 1-35234-3) Harlequin Bks.

Novia Triste: The Bride in Blue. Miranda Lee. (Bianca Ser.).Tr. of Sad Bride. (SPA.). 1997. per. 3.50 (*0-373-33432-X*, 1-33432-5) Harlequin Bks.

Novia Vestia De Rojo. Diana Hamilton. (Bianca Ser.: Vol.157).Tr. of Bride Wore Red. (SPA.). 1999. per. 3.50 (*0-373-33507-5*, 1-33507-4) Harlequin Bks.

Novia y Dos Bodas. Anne Eames. (Deseo Ser.: No. 35182).Tr. of Two Weddings & a Bride. (SPA.). 1997. per. 3.50 (*0-373-35182-8*, 1-35182-4) Harlequin Bks.

Noviazago. C. Fabio Filho.Tr. of All about Dating. (SPA.). 78p. 1988. pap. 4.99 (*0-8297-0422-1*) Vida Pubs.

Noviazgo Fingido (False Engagement), No. 136. Pamela Macaluso. (Harlequin Deseo Ser.). (SPA.). 1998. mass mkt. 3.50 (*0-373-35266-2*, 1-35266-5) Harlequin Bks.

Novice Class Radio Amateur FCC Test Manual. Martin Schwartz. LC 89-81078. 1997. pap. 9.95 (*0-912146-21-4*, 27-01) Ameco.

Novice Duncan's Useful Guide for Starting Herbs from Seed. Lois M. Duncan. (Illus.). 34p. (Orig.). 1997. pap. 20.00 (*0-9635410-1-3*) Beginnings.

Novice Insomniac: Poems. Emily Warn. 125p. 1996. pap. 12.00 (*1-55659-112-8*) Copper Canyon.

Novice Nomad. Brian L. Lewis. (Illus.). 84p. pap. 9.95 (*1-928693-00-8*) Novice Nomad.

Novice to Advanced Dressage. Leonie Marshall. 1990. pap. 21.00 (*0-85131-373-6*, Pub. by J A Allen) St Mut.

Novice to Advanced Dressage. Leonie Marshall. 1996. pap. 40.00 (*0-85131-631-X*, Pub. by J A Allen) Trafalgar.

Novices: A Study of Poetic Apprenticeship. Clayton Eshleman. 80p. (Orig.). (C). 1996. pap. 14.95 (*1-56886-036-6*) Marsilio Pubs.

N

Novice's Tale. Margaret Frazer. 240p. (Orig.). 1992. mass mkt. 5.99 (*0-425-14321-X*) Berkley Pub.

Novice's Tale. Margaret Frazer et al. (Orig.). 1992. pap. 4.50 (*0-515-10900-2*, Jove) Berkley Pub.

Novikov Conjectures, Index Theorems & Rigidity, Vol. 1. Ed. by Jonathan Rosenberg et al. (London Mathematical Society Lecture Note Ser.: No. 226). (Illus.). 382p. (C). 1996. pap. text 47.95 (*0-521-49796-5*) Cambridge U Pr.

Novikov Conjectures, Index Theorems & Rigidity, Vol. 2. Ed. by Jonathan Rosenberg et al. (London Mathematical Society Lecture Note Ser.: No. 227). (Illus.). 374p. (C). 1996. pap. text 47.95 (*0-521-49795-7*) Cambridge U Pr.

Novio Boy: A Play. Gary Soto. LC 96-32605. 96p. (J). (gr. 7). 1997. pap. 7.00 (*0-15-201531-0*) Harcourt.

Novio de Alquiler (Hiring Boyfriend), No. 135. Kim Lawrence. (Harlequin Bianca Ser.). (SPA.). 1998. mass mkt. 3.50 (*0-373-33485-0*, 1-33485-3) Harlequin Bks.

***Novio de Alta Sociedad.** Mary Lyons. Vol. 209.Tr. of High Society Groom. (SPA.). 2000. per. 3.50 (*0-373-33559-8*, 1-33559-5) Harlequin Bks.

Novio Dificil, Vol. 161. Anne McAllister. (Silhouette Deseo Ser.). (SPA.). 156p. 1999. mass mkt. 3.50 (*0-373-35291-3*) Harlequin Bks.

Novio Perdido: The Prodigal Groom. Karen Leabo. (SPA.). 1997. per. 3.50 (*0-373-35175-5*, 1-35175-8) Harlequin Bks.

Novio Robado: Teacher's guide. EMC-Paradigm Publishing Staff & Fabiola Franco. text 5.95 (*0-8219-0035-8*) EMC-Paradigm.

Novio Robado: Textbook. EMC-Paradigm Publishing Staff & Fabiola Franco. text 5.95 (*0-8219-0033-1*) EMC-Paradigm.

Novio Robado: Workbook. Fabiola Franco. text, wbk. ed. 4.95 (*0-8219-0034-X*) EMC-Paradigm.

Novios - Conversemos Sobre Cosas Que Apenas Se Hablan: Before You Marry, Things That Make a Difference. Jose L. Martinez. (SPA.). 80p. 1984. reprint ed. pap. 6.99 (*0-311-46104-2*) Casa Bautista.

Novitas Mundi: Perception of the History of Being. David G. Leahy. LC 93-45673. 422p. (C). 1994. text 59.50 (*0-7914-2137-6*); pap. text 19.95 (*0-7914-2138-4*) State U NY Pr.

Novo Alemao sem Custo: German for Portuguese Speakers. Assimil Staff. (GER & POR.). 28.95 (*0-8288-4314-7*, F10158) Fr & Eur.

Novo Dicionario Tecnico de Informatica Ingles - Portuguese. Enzo Paladino. (ENG & POR.). 1986. pap. 75.00 (*0-8288-3965-4*, F119705) Fr & Eur.

Novo Frances Sem Custo. Albert O. Cherel. 24.95 (*0-685-11200-4*); audio 125.00 (*0-685-01714-1*) Fr & Eur.

Novo Ingles Sem Custo. Albert O. Cherel. 24.95 (*0-685-11249-7*); audio 125.00 (*0-685-01732-X*) Fr & Eur.

Novo Ingles sem Custo: English for Portuguese Speakers. Assimil Staff. (ENG & POR.). 28.95 (*0-8288-4307-4*, M14924) Fr & Eur.

Novopokolentsy. Boris Prianishnikoff. (Illus.). 320p. 1986. write for info. (*0-9616413-1-2*) Multilingual.

Novosibirsk Oblast: Economy, Industry, Government, Business. 2nd rev. ed. Russian Information & Business Center, Inc. Staff. (Russian Regional Business Directories Ser.). (Illus.). 200p. 1997. pap. 99.00 (*1-57751-402-5*) Intl Business Pubns.

***Novosibirsk Oblast Regional Investment & Business Guide.** Global Investment & Business Center, Inc. Staff. (Russian Regional Investment & Business Guides Ser.: Vol. 54). (Illus.). 350p. 1999. pap. 99.00 (*0-7397-0853-8*) Intl Business Pubns.

***Novosibirsk Oblast Regional Investment & Business Guide.** Contrib. by Global Investment & Business Center, Inc. Staff. (Russian Regional Investment & Business Guides Ser.: Vol. 12). (Illus.). 350p. 2000. pap. 99.95 (*0-7397-3002-9*) Intl Business Pubns.

Novum Dictionarii Genus. Erasmus Alberus. (Documenta Linguistica, Reihe I: Worterbucher Des Vol. 15 & 16. Jahrhunderts Ser.). (GER.). 840p. 1975. reprint ed. 240.00 (*3-487-05602-X*) G Olms Pubs.

Novum Organum. Francis Bacon. Ed. & Tr. by John Gibson & Peter Urbach. LC 93-39277. 362p. 1994. pap. 16.00 (*0-8126-9245-4*) Open Court.

***Novum Testamentum Greece.** 27th ed. Aland Nestle. 1999. 33.99 (*5-550-00786-X*) Nairi.

Novus Ordo Seclorum. 2nd rev. ed. Raghavan N. Iyer. (Institute of World Culture Ser.). 76p. (Orig.). 1983. pap. 12.75 (*0-88695-014-7*) Concord Grove.

Novus Ordo Seclorum: The Intellectual Origins of the Constitution. Forrest McDonald. LC 85-13544. xiv, 362p. 1985. 29.95 (*0-7006-0284-4*); pap. 14.95 (*0-7006-0311-5*) U Pr of KS.

Novye Metody Statisticheskogo Analiza Istoricheskikh Tekstov: Prilozhenikila K Khronologii , 2 vols. A. T. Fomenko. LC 99-28224. (Rossifiskie Matematicheskie I Nauchnye Issledovanikila Ser.). 1999. write for info. (*0-7734-3196-9*) E Mellen.

Novye Stansy K. Avguste: Stikhotvoreniia K. M. B. Joseph Brodsky. (RUS.). 144p. 1983. pap. 15.95 (*0-88233-776-9*) Ardis Pubs.

Novyi Gulliver (New Gulliver) Andrei Bitov. LC 97-6900. (RUS.). 220p. 1997. 15.00 (*1-55779-089-2*) Hermitage Pubs.

Now. Lauren Bacall. 1996. mass mkt. 6.99 (*0-345-40232-4*) Ballantine Pub Grp.

Now. Lauren Bacall. LC 94-9819. (Illus.). 224p. 1994. 25.50 (*0-394-57412-5*) Knopf.

Now. Judith Baumel. 1996. 16.95 (*1-881163-14-8*); pap. 10.95 (*1-881163-15-6*) Miami Univ Pr.

***Now.** Alan Cohen. 2000. 40.00 (*0-226-11294-2*) U Ch Pr.

Now. Mark Dischinger et al. Ed. by Shawn Sprvill. (Illus.). 128p. 1998. pap. 9.00 (*0-9652528-5-X*, 002) Neshui Pubng.

Now. Gabriel Josipovici. LC 99-199602. 180p. 1998. pap. 17.95 (*1-85754-367-X*, Pub. by Carcanet Pr) Paul & Co Pubs.

Now. Merikay McLeod. 32p. (J). (ps-12). 1995. pap. 0.99 (*1-57258-060-7*) Teach Servs.

Now a Bridge: Poems from Central America. Marilyn Peretti. (Illus.). 8p. 1997. pap. 4.00 (*0-9673333-1-8*, 2) Splendid Pr.

Now-a-Day Poems. Philander C. Johnson. LC 70-37307. (Black Heritage Library Collection). (Illus.). 1977. reprint ed. 20.95 (*0-8369-8944-9*) Ayer.

Now-a-Days. Laura J. Curtis Bullard. LC 76-48580. 309p. 1980. reprint ed. pap. 8.95 (*0-89101-042-4*) U Maine Pr.

Now All We Need Is a Title: Famous Book Titles & How They Got That Way. Andre Bernard. 128p. 1996. pap. 11.00 (*0-393-31436-7*, Norton Paperbks) Norton.

Now Ancetres see Our French Canadian Ancestors

Now & Always/Para Siempre. Caridad Cordato. (Encanto Ser.). (SPA & ENG.). 1999. mass mkt. 5.99 (*0-7860-0666-8*) Kensgtn Pub Corp.

Now & at Other Times. Irwin Siegel. 32p. (Orig.). 1997. pap. write for info. (*1-886094-60-8*) Chicago Spectrum.

Now & Forever see Danielle Steel

***Now & Forever.** Elizabeth Doyle. 2000. mass mkt. 4.99 (*0-8217-6528-0*, Zebra Kensgtn) Kensgtn Pub Corp.

Now & Forever. Elizabeth Sherwood. 1995. mass mkt. 4.99 (*0-7860-0209-3*, Pinncle Kensgtn) Kensgtn Pub Corp.

Now & Forever. Danielle Steel. 432p. 1985. mass mkt. 6.99 (*0-440-11743-7*) Dell.

Now & Forever, Bk. 65. Kimberly Raye. (Shadows Ser.). 1996. per. 3.50 (*0-373-27065-8*, 1-27065-1) Silhouette.

Now & Forever: A Novel. Anita Stansfield. 304p. 1996. pap. 11.95 (*1-55503-910-3*, 01112236) Covenant Comms.

Now & Forever - Let's Make Love. Joan E. Lloyd. LC 97-7016. 256p. (Orig.). 1997. mass mkt. 12.99 (*0-446-67279-3*, Pub. by Warner Bks) Little.

***Now & Later Tales & Short Stories.** Al Schalow. LC 99-70423. 112p. 2000. pap. 12.95 (*0-9654963-3-3*) Medwag Pub.

Now & Long Ago. Glenn D. Lough. (Illus.). 720p. (C). 1969. reprint ed. 40.00 (*0-87012-513-3*) McClain. NOW & LONG AGO is a collection of colorful & informative stories of the pioneers of the Monogahela Valley & those men & women in whom the spirit of the Old Defenders ("the spirit of fire") continued, & continues to exist, even now. Explorers, traders, settlers, & citizens relate the thrilling, informative & authentic story of the discovery & settlement of the Monogahela country in this masterwork of researched regional history. Reprinted, 1991.
Publisher Paid Annotation.

Now & on Earth. Jim Thompson. 1994. pap. 11.00 (*0-679-74013-9*) Random.

Now & Then. Penny Hayes. 240p. (Orig.). 1996. pap. 11.95 (*1-56280-121-X*) Naiad Pr.

Now & Then. Neil Reich. 196p. 1996. pap. text 29.95 (*0-312-14783-X*) St Martin.

Now & Then. Naomi J. Thompson. Ed. by Beryl Lumpkin. 1992. 9.95 (*0-9622568-5-4*) Earthtide Pubns.

Now & Then. 2nd ed. William Corlett. LC 98-148577. 300p. 1998. reprint ed. pap. 11.95 (*1-55583-424-8*) Alyson Pubns.

Now & Then, Vol. 8. Le R. Perry. (Illus.). 60p. 1998. pap. 10.50 (*1-56770-428-X*) S Scheewe Pubns.

Now & Then: A Memoir of Vocation. Frederick Buechner. LC 91-55091. 128p. 1991. reprint ed. pap. 12.00 (*0-06-061182-0*, Pub. by Harper SF) HarpC.

Now & Then: From Coney Island to Here. Joseph Heller. LC 97-49658. 259p. 1998. 24.00 (*0-375-40062-1*) Knopf.

Now & Then: From Coney Island to Here. Joseph Heller. 1998. pap. 7.00 (*0-375-70251-2*) Random.

Now & Then: From Coney Island to Here. Joseph Heller. 259p. 1999. pap. 13.00 (*0-375-70055-2*) Vin Bks.

***Now & Then: From Coney Island to Here.** large type ed. Joseph Heller. 368p. 1999. 31.99 (*0-7089-9066-5*, Linford) Ulverscroft.

Now & Then: More Hilltown Stories. Porter W. Wright. (Illus.). 66p. 1999. pap. 12.00 (*0-9666270-2-4*) Stiles Studio.

Now & Then: More Views of Sutton Old & New: A Photographic Record & Commentary on Sutton Away from the High Street. Frank Burgess. (C). 1985. pap. 25.00 (*0-907335-13-6*, Pub. by Sutton Libs & Arts) St Mut.

***Now & Then: Poems from Hollywood.** Mark Dunster. 11p. 1999. pap. 5.00 (*0-89642-740-4*) Linden Pubs.

Now & Then: Reading & Writing about the American Immigrant Experience. Neil Reich. 240p. (C). 1996. pap. text 18.95 (*0-521-65756-3*) Cambridge U Pr.

Now & Then: Reading & Writing about the American Immigrant Experience: Instructor's Manual. Neil Reich. 32p. (C). 1996. pap., teacher ed. 6.00 (*0-521-65755-5*) Cambridge U Pr.

Now & Then & Long Ago in Rockland County, New York. 2nd ed. Compiled by Cornelia F. Bedell. LC 92-36972. (Illus.). 399p. 1992. reprint ed. 25.00 (*0-911183-45-0*) Rockland County Hist.

Now & Then & Other Tales from Ome. Richard W. Seltzer, Jr. LC 76-12138. (Illus.). (J). (gr. 5). 1976. 10.00 (*0-915232-03-0*); pap. 4.50 (*0-915232-02-2*) B & R Samizdat.

Now & Then in the U. P. Amy J. VanOoyen. (Woodpecker Ser.: Vol. 1). (Illus.). 170p. (Orig.). 1993. pap. 11.95 (*1-889363-01-4*) Woodpecker Bks.

Now & Then Poems (Almost Six Decades of Poetry) Frances Towne. (Illus.). 1985. 12.95 (*0-935497-00-5*) Fountainhead.

Now Anyone Can . . . Teach Revelation. C. S. Lovett. (Illus.). 128p. 1993. pap., teacher ed. 5.95 (*0-938148-46-X*) Prsnl Christianity.

Now Are We in Christ Jesus. Kenneth Copeland. 26p. 1980. pap. 1.00 (*0-938458-03-5*) K Copeland Pubns.

Now Back to You, Dick. Dick Irvin. 249p. 1996. mass mkt. 2.99 (*0-7710-4354-6*) McCland & Stewart.

Now Breathe: A Very Personal Journal of Breast Cancer. Claudia Sternbach. LC 98-83286. 156p. 1999. pap. 13.95 (*0-9653800-4-1*) Whiteaker Pr.

***Now Choose Life: Theology & Ethics in Deuteronomy.** Gary J. Millar. LC 99-28294. (New Studies in Biblical Theology). 216p. 1999. pap. 24.00 (*0-8028-4407-3*) Eerdmans.

***Now City Guide to Toronto: The Insider's Handbook.** Now Magazine Staff. (Illus.). 256p. 1999. pap. 15.95 (*0-7710-6818-2*) McCland & Stewart.

Now-Consciousness: Exploring the World Beyond Thought. Albert Blackburn. LC 83-82540. 154p. 1983. reprint ed. pap. 8.95 (*0-9613054-0-1*) Idylwild Bks.

Now Dare Everything: Tales of HIV-Related Psychotherapy. Steven Dansky. LC 92-48376. 1994. pap. 17.95 (*1-56023-037-1*, Harrington Park) Haworth Pr.

Now Dare Everything: Tales of HIV-Related Psychotherapy. Steven F. Dansky. LC 92-48376. (Illus.). 332p. 1994. lib. bdg. 49.95 (*1-56024-398-8*) Haworth Pr.

Now Distributing the Following Volumes in the Serial: Adenylyl Cyclases. Ed. by Dermont M. F. Cooper. Vol. 32. 240p. 99.95 (*0-12-036132-9*) Acad Pr.

Now Don't Try to Reason with Me: Essays & Ironies for a Credulous Age. Wayne Booth. LC 73-12359. 1970. lib. bdg. 9.50 (*0-226-06579-0*) U Ch Pr.

Now Don't Try to Reason with Me: Essays & Ironies for a Credulous Age. Wayne Booth. LC 73-12359. 1972. pap. text 2.95 (*0-226-06580-4*, P461) U Ch Pr.

Now Don't Try to Reason with Me: Essays & Ironies for a Credulous Age. Wayne Booth. LC 73-123359. 397p. Date not set. reprint ed. pap. 123.10 (*0-608-20598-2*, 205456300003) Bks Demand.

Now Everybody Really Hates Me. Jane R. Martin & Patricia Marx. LC 92-13075. (Illus.). 32p. (J). (ps-3). 1993. 14.95 (*0-06-021293-4*) HarpC Child Bks.

Now Everybody Really Hates Me. Jane R. Martin & Patricia Marx. LC 92-13075. (Trophy Picture Bk.). (Illus.). 32p. (J). (gr. k-3). 1996. pap. 6.95 (*0-06-443440-0*, HarpTrophy) HarpC Child Bks.

Now Everybody Really Hates Me. Jane Read Martin & Pam Ryan. LC 92-13075. (J). 1993. 10.15 (*0-606-09701-5*, Pub. by Turtleback) Demco.

Now Face to Face. Karleen Koen. 608p. 1997. mass mkt. 6.99 (*1-57566-177-2*, Knsington) Kensgtn Pub Corp.

Now Faith: If It Be Thy Will. Sharon Nutt. 32p. 1999. pap. 4.95 (*0-9640801-2-5*, 8012-5) Jireh Pubns.

Now Faith Is. Frederick K. Price. 32p. 1984. pap. 1.00 (*0-89274-302-6*, HH-302) Harrison Hse.

Now for Reality. Austin O. Spare & Aleister Crowley. (Illus.). 1990. text 47.50 (*1-872736-01-7*, Pub. by Mandrake Pr) Holmes Pub.

Now Get Out There & Sell Something. Harris DeWese. 272p. 34.00 (*0-614-25577-5*, 00SM44703) Print Indus Am.

Now Habit. Neil A. Fiore. 224p. 1988. pap. 13.95 (*0-87477-504-3*, Tarcher Putnam) Putnam Pub Group.

Now He Is Legend. Gordon D. Shirreffs. 192p. 1996. reprint ed. mass mkt. 3.99 (*0-8439-4124-3*) Dorchester Pub Co.

Now He Thinks He's Dead. Ron Goulart. 144p. 1992. 18.95 (*0-8027-3220-8*) Walker & Co.

***Now Hear This.** Contrib. by Glenn J. Gray. 1999. pap. 7.95 (*1-56794-199-0*) Star Bible.

Now Hear This. Edwin P. Hoyt. (Illus.). 298p. 1994. 24.95 (*1-56924-893-1*) Marlowe & Co.

Now Hear This. Lisa Radon. 20p. (Orig.). 1994. pap. 3.00 (*0-916397-36-X*) Manic D Pr.

Now Hear This! 2nd ed. Barbara H. Foley. LC 93-41028. (College ESL Ser.). 160p. (J). 1994. mass mkt. 20.95 (*0-8384-5270-1*) Heinle & Heinle.

Now Hear This!: Histories of U. S. Ships in World War II. John J. Motley & Philip R. Kelly. LC 79-18703. 1980. reprint ed. 30.00 (*0-89201-057-6*) Zenger Pub.

Now Hear This: The Life of Hugh S. Knowles: Acoustical Engineer & Entrepreneur. Susan Goodwillie. LC 99-36211. (Illus.). 196p. 1999. 24.00 (*0-9665051-2-3*) Francis Pr.

Now Hear This: The Memoir of a Junior Naval Officer in the Great Pacific War. fac. ed. Douglas E. Leach. LC 87-3905. (Illus.). 202p. 1987. pap. 62.70 (*0-7837-7630-6*, 204738200007) Bks Demand.

***Now Hear This! Language Arts: Activities to Improve Language Arts & Listening Skills: Grades 4-6.** Ann R. Fisher & Betsy Fisher. Ed. by Judy Mitchell. (Illus.). 96p. 1999. pap., teacher ed. 9.95 (*1-57310-180-X*) Teachng & Lrning Co.

***Now Hear This! Math: Activities to Improve Math & Listening Skills: Grades 4-6.** Ann R. Fisher & Bryce A. Fisher. Ed. by Judy Mitchell. (Illus.). 96p. 1999. pap., teacher ed. 9.95 (*1-57310-181-8*) Teachng & Lrning Co.

***Now Hear This! Science: Science Activities to Improve Science & Listening Skills: Grades 4-6.** Ann R. Fisher. Ed. by Judy Mitchell. (Illus.). 96p. 1999. pap., teacher ed. 9.95 (*1-57310-182-6*) Teachng & Lrning Co.

Now Here's a Man Who Knows His Shit Vol. 1: The Guide to Scatology. Santa Barbara Sun Bulletin Staff. Ed. by Jim Harter & Dover Publications, N. Y. C. Staff. (Illus.). 114p. 1999. pap. 9.95 (*0-9666605-9-5*) Possum Press.

Now Here's My Plan. Shel Silverstein. 1976. pap. 2.95 (*0-671-22280-5*, Fireside) S&S Trade Pap.

Now Hiring: Film. Michael Serrian. 1994. pap. 5.95 (*0-382-24748-5*, Crstwood Hse) Silver Burdett Pr.

Now Hiring: Finding & Keeping Good Help for Your Entry-Wage Jobs. Steve Lauer et al. LC 96-20824. 192p. (Orig.). 1996. 17.95 (*0-8144-7912-X*) AMACOM.

Now Hiring: Government Jobs for Lawyers. LC 90-55866. 180p. 1990. 14.95 (*0-89707-581-1*, 527-0034) Amer Bar Assn.

Now Hiring: The Feminization of Work in the United States, 1900-1995. Julia Kirk Blackwelder. LC 97-15922. (Illus.). 320p. 1997. 39.95 (*0-89096-776-8*); pap. 17.95 (*0-89096-798-9*) Tex A&M Univ Pr.

Now Hiring! Destination Resort Jobs: The Insider's Guide to Seasonal & Year-Round Employment at America's Top Vacation Resorts. Mark Connley & Jennifer Dubois. (Illus.). 274p. (Orig.). (C). 1994. pap. 17.95 (*1-881199-56-8*) Perptual Pr.

Now Hiring! Jobs in Asia: The Insider's Guide to Gaining Seasonal & Year-round Employment Throughout Asia. Jennifer Dubois et al. LC 93-84884. (Illus.). 280p. (Orig.). (C). 1993. pap. 17.95 (*1-881199-23-1*) Perptual Pr.

Now Hiring! Jobs in Eastern Europe: The Insider's Guide to Working & Living in the Czech Republic, Hungary, Poland & Slovakia. Clarke Canfield. LC 94-74013. (Illus.). 260p. 1996. pap. 14.95 (*1-881199-62-2*) Perptual Pr.

Now Hiring! Outdoor Jobs: The Insider's Guide to Gaining Seasonal & Year-Round Employment in America's National Parks & Forests. Jennifer Dubois & Steve Gutmann. Ed. by Elliot Veith. (Illus.). 297p. (C). 1993. pap. 17.95 (*1-881199-50-9*) Perptual Pr.

Now Hiring! Ski Resort Jobs: The Insider's Guide to Seasonal & Year-Round Employment at North America's Top Ski Resorts. Steve Giordano & George Thomas. LC 95-70183. (Illus.). 400p. (C). 1994. pap. 14.95 (*1-881199-51-7*) Perptual Pr.

Now I Am Big. Meryl Doney. (Illus.). 16p. (J). 1983. reprint ed. 0.99 (*0-86683-705-1*, AY8301) Harper SF.

Now I Am Civilized. Eugene H. Huffman. LC 73-18579. (Illus.). reprint ed. 31.50 (*0-404-11390-7*) AMS Pr.

Now I Am Thee. (Yoni Gold Board Book Ser.). bds. 4.95 (*1-58330-153-4*) Feldheim.

Now I Can Fly! Jane McWhorter. 1985. pap. 7.15 (*0-89137-437-X*) Quality Pubns.

Now, I Can Fly! Simple Words for the Complex Journey Through Life. Vera R. Chitty. 80p. 1998. pap. 13.95 (*0-9663459-0-8*) Chitty Ents.

Now I Get. 2nd ed. Beason. 1999. pap. text 24.95 (*0-312-20135-4*) St Martin.

Now I Get It. Beason. 1997. pap. text 5.00 (*0-312-15287-6*) St Martin.

Now I Get It. 5th ed. Beason. 1996. pap. text 31.45 incl. audio compact disk (*0-312-15743-6*) St Martin.

***Now I Get It! Thirty-Six Ten-Minute Skits about Science, Math, Language & Social Studies for Fun & Learning.** L. E. McCullough. 256p. (J). (gr. k-2). 2000. pap., teacher ed. 16.95 (*1-57525-161-2*) Smith & Kraus.

Now I Have Two Homes. Sharon C. Hare. LC 95-79687. (Illus.). 20p. (Orig.). (J). (ps-3). 1995. pap. 5.00 (*0-9639450-2-5*) Joy Ent.

Now I Know Better: Kids Tell Kids about Safety. Children's Hospital at Yale New-Haven Staff. (Illus.). 96p. (J). (gr. 4 up). 1996. pap. 7.95 (*0-7613-0149-6*); lib. bdg. 21.90 (*0-7613-0109-7*) Millbrook Pr.

***Now I Know Better, Too: Kids Tell Kids about Safety.** Illus. by Douglas Baker et al. 111p. (J). (gr. k-12). 1999. pap. 7.95 (*0-9676469-0-1*) Yale-New Haven.

Now I Know Why Tigers Eat Their Young: How to Survive Your Teenagers - with Wisdom & a Little Humor. Peter Marshall. LC 93-48110. 136p. 1994. pap. 12.95 (*1-55958-499-8*) Prima Pub.

Now I Lay Me Down: Suicide & the Elderly. Ed. by David Lester & Margot Tallmer. LC 93-25814. 252p. (Orig.). 1994. pap. 22.95 (*0-914783-65-3*) Charles.

Now I Lay Me down to Dream: Understanding Your Dreams. Arnie Wallace. 100p. (Orig.). 1991. pap. write for info. (*0-9625341-3-7*) Challenger CA.

Now I Lay Me down to Sleep. Frank Lambirth. 240p. 1989. mass mkt. 3.95 (*0-445-20672-1*, Pub. by Warner Bks) Little.

Now I Lay Me down to Sleep. Lurlene McDaniel. 160p. (YA). 1991. mass mkt. 4.50 (*0-553-28897-0*) Bantam.

Now I Lay Me Down to Sleep. Lurlene McDaniel. (J). 1995. 9.60 (*0-606-07960-2*) Turtleback.

Now I Lay Me down to Sleep. Patricia H. Rushford. LC 96-45848. (Helen Bradley Mysteries Ser.: No. 1). 24p. 1997. pap. 8.99 (*1-55661-730-5*) Bethany Hse.

Now I Lay Me down to Sleep: Action Prayers, Poems, & Songs for Bedtime. Debbie T. O'Neal. LC 94-71213. (Illus.). 32p. (J). (ps-k). 1994. pap. 6.99 (*0-8066-2602-X*, 9-2602, Augsburg) Augsburg Fortress.

NOW I Remember: Recovered Memories of Sexual Abuse. Charles R. Kelley & Eric C. Kelley. LC 94-96158. 140p. 1994. 20.00 (*1-885643-00-4*) K-R Pubns.

Now I See see Puedo Ver: La Historia Del Hombre Que Nacio Ciego

Now I See. deluxe limited ed. Charley Boswell. 212p. 1991. reprint ed. 39.95 (*0-9630273-1-X*) Highland AL.

Now I See. Charley Boswell. 212p. 1991. reprint ed. 18.50 (*0-9630273-0-1*) Highland AL.

Now I See: The Story of the Man Born Blind. Marilyn Lashbrook. (Me Too! Bks.). (J). (ps-2). 1998. 5.95 (*0-933657-62-5*, 3000842) Rainbow Studies.

Now I See: The Story of the Man Born Blind. Marilyn Lashbrook. LC 88-62520. (Me Too! Bks.). (Illus.). 32p. (J). (ps). 1989. 7.95 (*0-86606-437-0*, 869) Treasure Pub.

Now I See Why Life Is Like Baseball after All: Rhymeo Game Plans for Baseball Fans. Cyrano De Words-u-lac. (Illus.). 212p. (Orig.). 1995. pap. 6.95 (*0-9636177-6-1*) Rhymeo Ink.

An Asterisk (*) at the beginning of an entry indicates that the title is appearing for the first time.

Now I Understand: Evangelist & Disciple see Ahora Entiendo: Evang. & Discipulado

Now I Will Never Go to Sleep. Marx. (Illus.). (J). 14.95 (*0-06-027483-2*); lib. bdg. 14.89 (*0-06-027482-4*) HarpC.

Now I Will Never Leave the Dinner Table. Jane R. Martin & Patricia Marx. LC 94-3209. (Illus.). 32p. (J). (ps-3). 1996. lib. bdg. 14.89 (*0-06-024795-9*) HarpC Child Bks.

Now I Will Never Leave the Dinner Table. Jane Read Martin & Patricia Marx. LC 94-3209. (Illus.). 32p. (J). (ps-3). 1999. pap. 5.95 (*0-06-443556-3*) HarpC Child Bks.

Now I Will Never Leave the Dinner Table. 80th ed. Jane R. Martin & Patricia Marx. LC 94-3209. (Illus.). 32p. (J). (ps-3). 1996. 14.95 (*0-06-024794-0*) HarpC Child Bks.

Now I'm Big. Margaret Miller. LC 95-17774. (Illus.). 32p. (J). (ps up). 1996. 15.00 (*0-688-14077-7*, Grenwillow Bks); lib. bdg. 14.93 (*0-688-14078-5*, Grenwillow Bks) HarpC Child Bks.

Now I'm Going Quality, a Guide for New Business Owners: New Business Owner Quality System Guide. Gunther B. Gumpp. Ed. by Brisitte Gumpp. (Illus.). 60p. 1998. pap. 28.00 (*1-881006-32-8*) Qual Cont Systs Srvs.

Now I'm One. Pamela Kennedy. Ed. by Sue Reck. LC 93-79573. (God Made Me Special Bks.). (Illus.). 10p. (J). (ps). 1994. bds. 4.29 (*0-7814-0151-8*, Chariot Bks) Chariot Victor.

Now I'm Three. Pamela Kennedy. Ed. by Sue Reck. LC 93-79575. (God Made Me Special Bks.). (Illus.). 10p. (J). (ps). 1994. bds. 4.29 (*0-7814-0153-4*, Chariot Bks) Chariot Victor.

Now I'm Two. Pamela Kennedy. Ed. by Sue Reck. LC 93-79574. (God Made Me Special Bks.). (Illus.). 10p. (J). (ps). 1994. bds. 4.29 (*0-7814-0152-6*, Chariot Bks) Chariot Victor.

Now in My Day . . . Milton Caniff. (Illus.). 48p. 1992. 28.00 (*0-88014-083-6*) Mosaic Pr OH.

Now in November. Josephine W. Johnson. 1991. lib. bdg. 21.95 (*1-56849-058-5*) Buccaneer Bks.

Now in November. Josephine W. Johnson. 231p. 1985. mass mkt. 4.50 (*0-88184-174-9*) Carroll & Graf.

Now in November. Josephine W. Johnson. LC 90-26975. 288p. 1991. reprint ed. 29.95 (*1-55861-033-2*); reprint ed. pap. 10.95 (*1-55861-035-9*) Feminist Pr.

Now in Our Fourth Century: Some American Families: A Documentary & Pictorial History of More Than Twenty Families Who Were Well Settled in the American Colonies Before the Year 1700, & Many of Their Ancestors, Kin, & Descendants. Paul Drake. (Illus.). 586p. (Orig.). 1995. pap. text 61.50 (*0-7884-0146-7*) Heritage Bk.

***Now in Our Hands: Caring for California[0012]s Abused & Neglected Children.** (Illus.). 132p. 2000. pap. text 30.00 (*0-7881-8955-7*) DIANE Pub.

Now! Instant Keyboard Fun I. Nancy Poffenberger. 32p. (J). (gr. 4 up). 1985. reprint ed. pap. 4.95 (*0-938293-39-7*) Fun Pub OH.

Now Is Eternity see Now Is... Eternity: Comfort & Wisdom for Difficult Hours

***Now Is... Eternity: Comfort & Wisdom for Difficult Hours.** 2nd ed. Johann Christoph Blumhardt & Christoph Friedrich Blumhardt. LC 99-50833. Orig. Title: Now Is Eternity. 100p. 2000. pap. 8.00 (*0-87486-993-5*) Plough.

Now Is the Hour: Native American Prophecies & Guidance for Earth Changes. Elisabeth Dietz & Shirley Jonas. LC 98-30958. (Illus.). 108p. 1998. pap. 10.00 (*1-57733-029-3*) B Dolphin Pub.

Now Is the Thing to Praise. Dolores Kendrick. LC 83-82774. 116p. 1984. pap., per. 7.00 (*0-916418-54-5*) Lotus.

Now Is the Time. Fred L. Fifer & Cynthia E. Ledbetter. (Do It Now Ser.). 210p. (J). 1992. 8.95 (*1-885568-09-6*) SCE Assocs.

Now Is the Time. 2nd ed. Katherine Cain. Ed. by Kay Cain. (Illus.). 40p. (Orig.). 1979. reprint ed. pap. 3.95 (*0-9603188-1-X*) K Tolson.

Now Is the Time: A Personal Account of South Africa's Historic Transition from Apartheid to Democracy. Marius Benson. LC 95-103688. 156p. 1994. write for info. (*0-7333-0357-9*) ABC Ent.

***Now Is the Time: Spiritual Reflections.** Stanislaus Kennedy. LC 98-210500. 164p. 1999. 14.95 (*1-86059-087-X*, Pub. by Town Hse) Roberts Rinehart.

Now Is the Time for Mercy. George W. Kosicki. 104p. 1991. 4.95 (*0-940535-41-6*, UP141) Franciscan U Pr.

Now Is the Time for Mercy: The Message & Devotion to the Divine Mercy. Ed. by Marians of the Immaculate Conception Staff. LC 87-62981. 114p. 1988. pap. text 8.00 (*0-944203-05-1*) Marian Pr.

Now Is the Time to Advance Pedagogical Education. B. Othanel Smith. (DeGarmo Lectures: No. 5). 1980. 10.00 (*0-933669-29-1*) Soc Profs Ed.

Now Is What Counts: Are You Listening? Do We Know How? Trisha M. Hamid. 1999. pap. 14.95 (*0-9671299-0-7*) Hendrix Pubg.

Now Is Your Time! The African-American Struggle for Freedom. Walter Dean Myers. LC 91-314. (Trophy Nonfiction Bk.). (Illus.). 320p. (YA). (gr. 6 up). 1992. pap. 11.95 (*0-06-446120-3*, HarpTrophy) HarpC Child Bks.

Now Is Your Time! The African-American Struggle for Freedom. Walter Dean Myers. 1991. 16.05 (*0-606-01107-2*, Pub. by Turtleback) Demco.

Now It Can Be Told. Ogese T. McKay. 60p. 1991. pap. text 10.00 (*0-9629807-0-6*) Ogese T McKay.

Now It Can Be Told: The Story of the Manhattan Project. Leslie Groves. LC 75-1001. (FDR & the Era of the New Deal Ser.). 465p. 1975. reprint ed. lib. bdg. 39.50 (*0-306-70738-1*) Da Capo.

Now It Can Be Told: The Story of the Manhattan Project. Leslie Groves. (Quality Paperbacks Ser.). (Illus.). 464p. 1983. reprint ed. pap. 16.00 (*0-306-80189-2*) Da Capo.

Now It Is Morning. Candace Whitman. LC 98-17120. (Illus.). 32p. (J). (ps-2). 1999. 15.00 (*0-374-35527-4*) FS&G.

***Now It's Fall.** Lois Lenski. (Illus.). (J). 2000. 9.95 (*0-375-81069-2*) Random.

***Now It's Fall.** Lois Lenski. (Illus.). (J). 2000. 11.99 (*0-375-91069-7*) Random Bks Yng Read.

***Now It's Jazz: Writings on Kerouac & the Sounds.** Clark Coolidge. 136p. 1999. 14.00 (*0-945953-09-7*, Pub. by Living Batch Bks) SPD-Small Pr Dist.

Now It's Time to Say Goodbye: A Novel. Dale Peck. LC 97-26688. 480p. 1998. 25.00 (*0-374-22271-1*) FS&G.

***Now It's Time to Say Goodbye: A Novel.** Dale Peck. LC 98-53918. 464p. 1999. pap. 15.95 (*0-688-16841-8*, Wm Morrow) Morrow Avon.

Now It's Time to Say Goodbye Readers Guide. Dale Peck. student ed. write for info. (*0-374-96122-0*) FS&G.

Now It's Your Move: A Guide for the Outplaced Employee. Frederick W. DeRoche & Mary A. McDougall. (Illus.). 224p. (C). 1984. pap. 16.95 (*0-13-625426-8*) P-H.

Now It's Your Turn: How Women Can Transform Their Lives & Save the Planet. Alana Lyons. LC 98-26346. 1998. pap. 13.95 (*0-9663694-0-8*) Jaguar Bks Inc.

Now Its Your Turn for Success: A Training & Motivational Book Specifically Designed for the Direct Sales & Multi-Level Marketing Industries. 2nd ed. Richard Houghton & Janet Kelly. 270p. 1998. reprint ed. pap. 16.95 (*1-899836-21-7*, Pub. by Crown Hse) LPC Group.

Now Johnny Can Do Arithmetic. Caleb Gattegno. 82p. 1971. pap. 4.95 (*0-87825-018-2*) Ed Solutions.

Now Let Me Fly. Johnson. 1998. pap. 5.99 (*0-87628-977-4*) Ctr Appl Res.

Now Let Me Fly. Delores Johnson. 1997. mass mkt. 5.99 (*0-689-80966-2*) S&S Bks Yung.

Now Let Me Fly: The Story of a Slave Family. Dolores Johnson. LC 92-33683. (Illus.). 32p. (J). (gr. k-5). 1993. lib. bdg. 15.00 (*0-02-747699-5*, Mac Bks Young Read) S&S Childrens.

Now Let Me Fly, the Story of a Slave Family. Dolores Johnson. 1997. 11.19 (*0-606-11692-3*, Pub. by Turtleback) Demco.

***Now Let's Say Alphabet Coloring Book.** Lavearne Phillips. (Illus.). 15p. (J). (ps-1). 1998. pap. 3.00 (*1-930058-01-2*) Lave Phillips.

Now Let's Talk about Music. Gordon Merrick. LC 97-7282. 256p. 1997. reprint ed. pap. 12.95 (*1-55583-293-8*) Alyson Pubns.

Now Let's Talk of Graves. Sarah Shankman. Ed. by Jane Chelius. 320p. 1991. reprint ed. per. 5.99 (*0-671-68457-4*) PB.

Now Look at Numbers. Judith Conaway. (J). 1997. pap. 3.99 (*0-679-88167-0*) McKay.

***Now More Than Ever.** Aldous Huxley. Ed. by David Bradshaw & James Sexton. LC 99-58286. (HRHRC Imprint Ser.). 144p. 2000. 19.95 (*0-292-73122-1*) U of Tex Pr.

Now More Than Ever: Proceedings, Aldous Huxley Centenary Symposium, University of Munster, 1994. Ed. by Bernfried Nugel. LC 96-33951. (Illus.). XV, 379p. 1996. 63.95 (*0-8204-2963-5*, PR6015) P Lang Pubng.

Now My Soul Is Hardened: Abandoned Children in Soviet Russia, 1918-1930. Alan M. Ball. LC 92-46236. 1994. 60.00 (*0-520-08010-6*, Pub. by U CA Pr) Cal Prin Full Svc.

Now My Soul Is Hardened: Abandoned Children in Soviet Russia, 1918-1930. Alan M. Ball. (Illus.). 356p. 1996. pap. 19.95 (*0-520-20694-0*, Pub. by U CA Pr) Cal Prin Full Svc.

Now of Our Human Destiny. John M. McMath. LC 88-71529. 1990. 12.95 (*0-8158-0453-9*) Chris Mass.

Now One Foot, Now the Other. Tomie De Paola. LC 80-22239. (Illus.). 48p. (J). (ps-3). 1981. 13.95 (*0-399-20774-0*, G P Putnam) Peng Put Young Read.

Now or Never. Elizabeth A. Adler. 448p. 1997. mass mkt. 6.99 (*0-440-22464-0*) Dell.

Now or Never. Carmen Green. 224p. 1996. mass mkt. 4.99 (*0-7860-0327-8*, Pinncle Kensgtn) Kensgtn Pub Corp.

Now or Never. Bruce Hart & Carole Hart. 256p. 1991. mass mkt. 3.50 (*0-380-75963-2*, Avon Bks) Morrow Avon.

Now or Never. Melissa Lowell. (Silver Blades Ser.: No. 2). 160p. (J). (gr. 4-7). 1997. pap. 3.50 (*0-553-48519-9*) BDD Bks Young Read.

Now or Never. Joyce Vedral. 1993. 14.99 (*0-446-77813-3*) Warner Bks.

***Now or Never: How Companies Must Change to Win the Battle for Internet Consumers, Set.** unabridged ed. Mary Modahl. 2000. audio 25.95 (*0-694-52311-9*) HarperAudio.

Now or Never: How Companies Must Change Today to Win the Battle for Internet Consumers. Mary Modahl. LC 99-49437. (Illus.). 272p. 2000. 27.00 (*0-06-662012-0*) HarpC.

***Now or Never: How Companies Must Change Today to Win the Battle for Internet Consumers.** Mary Modahl. 2001. write for info. (*0-06-662013-9*) HarpC.

Now or Never: Keep Your Body Young, Fit & Firm - With the Weight Training Program That Works Even As You Age. Joyce L. Vedral. 256p. 1986. mass mkt. 14.99 (*0-446-37010-X*, Pub. by Warner Bks) Little.

Now or Never: Rafe's Revenge, Hand in Glove, Partners in Crime, 3 bks. in 1. Anne Stuart et al. (By Request Ser.). 1999. per. 6.99 (*0-373-20166-4*, 1-20166-4) Harlequin Bks.

Now or Neverland: Peter Pan & the Myth of Eternal Youth. Ann Yeoman. (Illus.). 192p. 1999. pap. 18.00 (*0-919123-83-X*) Inner City Bks.

Now Pitching, Bob Feller: A Baseball Memoir. Bob Feller & Bill Gilbert. (Illus.). 1990. 18.95 (*1-55972-005-0*, Birch Ln Pr) Carol Pub Group.

***Now Playing Games Leader Manual: Grades 1-6.** (Holyword Studios VBS Ser.). 2000. pap., teacher ed. 9.99 (*0-7644-2176-X*) Group Pub.

Now Poof She Is Gone. Wendy Rose. LC 94-29772. 104p. (Orig.). 1994. pap. 8.95 (*1-56341-048-6*); lib. bdg. 18.95 (*1-56341-049-4*) Firebrand Bks.

Now Presenting: Classic Tales for Readers Theatre. Merrily P. Hansen. 1997. pap. 20.00 (*0-201-29066-9*) Addison-Wesley.

Now Read On: A Guide to Contemporary Popular Fiction. 2nd ed. Mandy Hicken & Raymond John Prytherch. LC 93-47276. 456p. 1994. 61.95 (*1-85928-008-0*, Pub. by Scolar Pr) Ashgate Pub Co.

Now Read On: A Multicultural Anthology of Literature in English. John McRae & Malachi E. Vethamani. LC 98-38478. 1999. 65.00 (*0-415-18216-6*); pap. 21.99 (*0-415-18217-4*) Routledge.

***Now Read This: A Guide to Mainstream Fiction, 1978-1998.** Nancy Pearl et al. LC 99-15280. (Genreflecting Advisory Ser.). 500p. 1999. 65.00 (*1-56308-659-X*) Libs Unl.

Now Sheba Sings the Song. Maya Angelou. (Illus.). 56p. 1994. pap. 13.95 (*0-452-27143-6*, Plume) Dutton Plume.

Now Soon Later. Lisa Grunwald. LC 95-35845. (Illus.). 24p. (J). (ps-3). 1996. 15.00 (*0-688-13946-9*, Grenwillow Bks) HarpC Child Bks.

Now, Swim. Harold Witt. 72p. 1974. pap. 6.00 (*0-912592-22-2*) Ashland Poetry.

Now Techniques for Today's Poets. Eddie C. Cole. 76p. 1977. pap. 10.95 (*0-317-17453-3*) World Poetry Pr.

Now That Baby Can Crawl, Walk & Run, Bk. 1. 100p. 2000. pap. 14.95 (*0-9654700-1-6*) F R Parker.

Now That Baby Is Home: From Infant to Toddler. William Sears & Martha Sears. LC 97-47385. 288p. 1998. mass mkt. 5.99 (*0-7852-7207-0*) Nelson.

Now That Forever Has Ended. Tom Steinbach. 400p. (Orig.). 1995. 23.95 (*0-9649219-1-X*); pap. 13.95 (*0-9649219-0-1*) Times Ten.

Now That Forever Has Ended. Tom Steinbach. 384p. (Orig.). 1996. pap. 10.95 (*0-9649219-2-8*) Times Ten.

Now That I Am in the Light I See. Jane Blue. (Orig.). 1996. pap. write for info. (*0-914134-11-6*) Konocti Bks.

Now That I Am Old: Meditations on the Meaning of Life. Maria Reilly. LC 92-63179. 128p. (Orig.). 1994. pap. 7.95 (*0-89622-559-3*) Twenty-Third.

Now That I Believe see Ahora que Creo

Now That I Believe. Robert A. Cook. mass mkt. 4.99 (*0-8024-5983-8*, 233) Moody.

Now That I Have Cancer . . . I Am Whole: Meditations for Cancer Patients & Those Who Love Them. 2nd rev. ed. 1997. reprint ed. pap. 10.95 (*0-9658625-1-8*) Nght Song.

Now That I'm a Christian. 1996. pap. 2.89 (*0-8344-0129-0*) Sweet Pub.

Now That I'm a Christian, Vol. 1. Chuck Miller. 64p. (Orig.). 1974. pap. 5.95 (*0-8307-0425-6*, 5201918, Regal Bks) Gospel Lght.

Now That I'm Out What Do I Do. Brian McNaught. LC 96-53513. 240p. 1997. text 22.95 (*0-312-15616-2*) St Martin.

Now That I'm Out What Do I Do. Brian McNaught. 224p. 1998. pap. 12.95 (*0-312-19518-4*) St Martin.

Now That I'm Saved . . . 16 Ways to Experience God. Paul D. Rusnak. LC 95-77538. 142p. (Orig.). 1996. pap. 6.99 (*0-88270-684-5*) Bridge-Logos.

Now That Is Amazing Grace. William MacDonald. 96p. (Orig.). 1995. pap. 3.95 (*1-882701-21-6*) Uplook Min.

Now That I've Cast It. Maxine Taylor. 96p. 1975. 11.00 (*0-86690-203-1*, T1473-014) Am Fed Astrologers.

Now That Makes Sense! Relating to People with Wit & Wisdom. rev. ed. Mark Ortman. 232p. (Orig.). 1993. pap. 11.95 (*0-9634699-9-1*) Wise Owl Bks & Mus.

Now That Mom's Not Around Cookbook. 2nd rev. ed. Dawn DePew. 343p. 1998. pap. 16.95 (*0-9628409-1-2*) D DePew.

***Now That My Father Lies Down Beside Me: New & Selected Poems, 1970-2000.** Stanley Plumly. LC 99-57297. 176p. 2000. 23.00 (*0-06-019659-9*, Ecco Press) HarperTrade.

Now That Never Was. Perry Mafi. 119p. (Orig.). 1992. pap. text 7.95 (*0-9631372-1-2*) P Mafi Writs.

Now That Retirement Has Come. Albert F. Harper. (Christian Living Ser.). 40p. 1988. pap. 3.50 (*0-8341-1243-4*) Beacon Hill.

Now That the Buffalo's Gone: A Study of Today's American Indians. Alvin M. Josephy, Jr. LC 84-40283. (Illus.). 316p. (Orig.). 1984. reprint ed. pap. 18.95 (*0-8061-1915-2*) U of Okla Pr.

Now That the Night Ends: Tanka of Gerard John Conforti. Ed. by Cor Van den Heuvel. 90p. (Orig.). 1996. pap. 10.00 (*0-944676-40-5*) AHA Bks.

Now That We Are Free: Coloured Communities in a Democratic South Africa. Ed. by Wilmot James et al. LC 96-27365. 142p. (Orig.). 1996. pap. text 15.95 (*1-55587-693-5*, 876935) L Rienner.

Now That We Have to Walk: Exploring the Out-of-Doors. Raymond T. Fuller. LC 72-37921. (Essay Index Reprint Ser.). 1977. reprint ed. 21.95 (*0-8369-2590-4*) Ayer.

Now That You Are a Catholic: An Informal Guide to Catholic Customs, Traditions & Practices. enl. rev. ed. John Kenny. 108p. 1986. pap. 4.95 (*0-8091-2974-4*) Paulist Pr.

***Now That You Are Free... How to Maintain Spiritual Victories.** Jerry Sproull. 19p. 1999. pap. 1.59 (*0-87509-843-6*) Chr Pubns.

Now That You Are Grandparents. Marylou Cook. (Christian Living Ser.). 40p. 1988. pap. 3.50 (*0-8341-1242-6*) Beacon Hill.

Now That You Are His see Agora Que Voce e de Cristo

Now That You Are His. David Shibley. 64p. 1985. pap. 2.95 (*0-88144-081-7*) Christian Pub.

Now That You Are His: First Steps in the Christian Walk. David Shibley. LC 93-84142. 96p. 1993. pap. 5.95 (*0-89221-236-5*) New Leaf.

Now That You Are 18: Legal Rights & Citizenship Education. LC 88-46207. 36p. 1989. pap. 5.00 (*0-89707-433-5*, 549-0087-01) Amer Bar Assn.

Now That You Can Walk, Go Get Me a Beer. Cartoon Bank Staff. 128p. 1994. pap. 9.00 (*0-671-87962-6*, Fireside) S&S Trade Pap.

Now That You Know: A Journey Toward Earth Literacy. McGregor Smith, Jr. 187p. 1997. pap. 10.00 (*0-9644659-7-3*) Earth Knows Publ.

Now That You Know: A Parent's Guide to Understanding Their Gay & Lesbian Children. 3rd ed. Betty Fairchild & Nancy Hayward. LC 98-16373. xiii, 281p. (C). 1998. pap. 13.00 (*0-15-600605-7*) Harcourt.

Now That You Know: What Every Parent Should Know about Homosexuality. Betty Fairchild & Nancy Hayward. LC 78-22251. 240p. 1981. pap. 6.95 (*0-15-667702-4*, Harvest Bks) Harcourt.

Now That Your Are Publicly Owned: Designed to Acquaint Directors & Officers with the New Responsibilities Applicable to Their Companies. 3rd ed. Carl W. Schneider & Jason M. Shargel. 30p. 1995. pap. write for info. (*0-936093-09-9*) Packard Pr Fin.

Now That Your Job Has Gone. Spak Vee. (Illus.). 176p. 1996. pap. 27.95 (*0-644-36117-4*, Pub. by Aust Gov Pub) Accents Pubns.

Now That You're a Deacon. Howard B. Foshee. LC 74-79488. 128p. 1975. 11.99 (*0-8054-3506-9*, 4235-06) Broadman.

Now That You're All Grown up, What Do You Want to Be? A Career Transition Guide. Betsy Newman. 280p. 1996. pap., per. 21.95 (*0-7872-2250-X*) Kendall-Hunt.

Now that You're in the Military Service. David Grosse. 64p. 1978. pap. 3.25 (*0-8341-0484-9*) Beacon Hill.

Now That You're Out of the Closet - What about the Rest of the House. Linda Handel. LC 97-46453. 244p. 1998. 20.95 (*0-8298-1244-X*) Pilgrim OH.

***Now That You're Out of the Closet, What about the Rest of the House.** Linda Handel. 2000. reprint ed. pap. 14.95 (*1-57071-652-8*) Sourcebks.

Now That You're Pregnant. Louise Edeiken & Johanna Antar. 192p. 1992. pap. 12.00 (*0-02-079031-7*) Macmillan.

Now That You're Saved. Richard Kennedy. 1977. pap. 1.95 (*0-89265-046-X*) Randall Hse.

Now That You're Saved. Lyle Pointer. (Christian Living Ser.). 40p. (Orig.). 1987. pap. 3.50 (*0-8341-1157-8*) Beacon Hill.

Now That You're 21 (Or Thereabouts) Notes on Making Life Work Better. Grand-pere. LC 98-92610. (Illus.). 158p. 1998. pap. 14.95 (*0-9663542-0-6*, Pub. by DAssociates) ACCESS Pubs Network.

***Now That You've Asked Her Out: Straight Talk for Guys.** Gary Hunt. 132p. (Orig.). (gr. 7-12). 2000. pap. 9.95 (*0-595-09225-X*) iUniversecom.

Now, That's a Good Question! R. C. Sproul. LC 95-26112. 325p. 1996. pap. 12.99 (*0-8423-4711-9*) Tyndale Hse.

Now That's a Hat! Linda R. Wexler. Ed. by Howard B. Raff. (Illus.). 64p. (Orig.). 1997. pap. 4.95 (*1-888230-05-3*) Chelsea St Prods.

Now, That's a Miracle! Reflections on Faith & Life. Richard Stoll Armstrong. LC 96-7630. (Illus.). 1996. 9.25 (*0-7880-0762-9*) CSS OH.

Now, That's Profound Charlie Brown. Charles M. Schulz. LC 99-216590. (Illus.). 176p. 1999. pap. 8.95 (*0-06-107561-2*, Pub. by Harper SF) HarpC.

Now the Day Is Over. Joan Fiset. (Women's Poetry Ser.). (Illus.). 160p. (Orig.). 1997. pap. 12.95 (*0-911287-22-1*) Blue Begonia.

Now the Dog Is Quiet: Romain Will Knock. George K. Dreher. LC 95-77979. 72p. (Orig.). 1995. pap. 4.95 (*0-9601000-4-0*) Longshanks Bk.

Now the Good News: Director's Manual. Kenneth Gleason. Ed. by Kieran Sawyer. (Developing Faith Ser.). 16p. 1997. pap. text, teacher ed. 16.95 (*0-87793-611-0*) Ave Maria.

Now the Good News: Participant Book. Kenneth Gleason. Ed. by Kieran Sawyer. (Developing Faith Ser.). 80p. (YA). (gr. 9-12). 1997. pap. text 5.95 (*0-87793-610-2*) Ave Maria.

Now, the Memory. Paul Gotro. 74p. 1987. pap. 6.95 (*0-86492-049-0*, Pub. by Goose Ln Edits) Genl Dist Srvs.

Now the Men's Voices. Martha L. Ice. LC 94-42838. 208p. 1995. 59.95 (*0-275-94968-0*, Praeger Pubs) Greenwood.

Now the Moon Appears among the Lilies. Susan Ingersoll. LC 98-227442. 62p. 1998. 14.95 (*1-55081-112-6*, Pub. by Breakwater Bks) Genl Dist Srvs.

Now the News: The Story of Broadcast Journalism. Edward Bliss, Jr. 575p. (C). 1992. pap. 25.50 (*0-231-04403-8*) Col U Pr.

Now the News in Detail: A Guide to Broadcast Journalism in Australia. 2nd ed. Murray Masterton & Roger Patching. 293p. (C). 1995. pap. 56.00 (*0-7300-1441-X*, Pub. by Deakin Univ) St Mut.

Now the Synthesis: Capitalism, Socialism & the New Social Contract. Ed. by Richard Noyes. 247p. 1991. 36.00 (*0-8419-1300-5*) Holmes & Meier.

***Now the Time!** George Bendall. LC 00-130313. 200p. 2000. pap. 15.95 (*0-87516-733-0*) DeVorss.

Now the Wolf Has Come: The Creek Nation in the Civil War. Christine S. White & Benton R. White. LC 95-40697. 216p. 1996. 29.95 (*0-89096-689-3*) Tex A&M Univ Pr.

Now the Woman Shall Conquer. John M. Haffert. 106p. 1997. pap. 6.00 (*1-890137-04-9*) One Hund-One Fnd.

N

Now They Lay Me down to Sleep: What You Don't Know about Anesthesia & Surgery May Harm You. William G. Pace & Frederick W. Ernst. LC 96-19515. 180p. 1996. pap. 12.00 (*0-9651454-0-9*, Pub. by F W Ernst) Partners Pubs Grp.

Now This: A May Morrison Mystery. Nancy Star & Jack Gourlay. 352p. 1999. 24.00 (*0-671-00895-1*) PB.

*__Now This: Radio, Television... And the Real World.__ Judy Muller. LC 99-87257. 256p. 2000. 23.95 (*0-399-14619-9*) Putnam Pub Group.

Now, This Day. Elise N. Morgan. 1948. pap. 6.95 (*0-87516-330-0*) DeVorss.

Now Through a Glass Darkly: Specular Images of Being & Knowing from Virgil to Chaucer. Edward P. Nolan. 364p. 1991. text 47.50 (*0-472-10170-6*, 10170) U of Mich Pr.

*__Now-Time/Image-Space: Temporization of Politics in Walter Benjamin's Philosophy of History & Art.__ Kia Lindroos. 303p. 1999. pap. 24.95 (*951-39-0341-9*, Pub. by SoPhi Academic) Intl Spec Bk.

Now, Voyager. Olive H. Prouty. 340p. 1991. reprint ed. lib. bdg. 25.95 (*0-89966-791-0*) Buccaneer Bks.

*__Now Voyager: A Film Score Guide, 1.__ Kate Daubney. LC 99-88601. (Film Score Guides Ser.: Vol. 1). 128p. 2000. lib. bdg. 45.00 (*0-313-31253-2*, Greenwood Pr) Greenwood.

Now Wait for Last Year. Philip K. Dick. LC 92-50645. 1993. pap. 12.00 (*0-679-74220-4*) Vin Bks.

Now We Are Civilized: A Study of the World View of the Zapotec Indians of Mitla, Oaxaca. Charles M. Leslie. LC 60-7651. 133p. reprint ed. pap. 38.00 (*0-7837-3686-X*, 2043560) Bks Demand.

Now We Are Civilized: A Study of the World View of the Zapotec Indians of Mitla, Oaxaca. Charles M. Leslie. LC 81-14. (Illus.). 108p. 1981. reprint ed. lib. bdg. 55.00 (*0-313-22847-7*, LENW, Greenwood Pr) Greenwood.

Now We Are Seven. Margaret Woodward. 1997. mass mkt. 5.99 (*0-8041-1659-8*) Ivy Books.

Now We Are Six see Treasury of Winnie-the-Pooh

Now We Are Six. A. A. Milne, pseud. (Illus.). 112p. (J). (ps up). 1988. 10.99 (*0-525-44446-7*, Dutton Child) Peng Put Young Read.

Now We Are Six. A. A. Milne, pseud. (Illus.). 112p. (J). (ps-3). 1992. pap. 4.99 (*0-14-036124-3*, PuffinBks) Peng Put Young Read.

Now We Are Six. deluxe ed. A. A. Milne, pseud. (Illus.). 112p. (J). (ps-6). 1992. 22.50 (*0-525-44960-4*, Dutton Child) Peng Put Young Read.

Now We Are Six. unabridged ed. A. A. Milne, pseud. (J). 1997. pap. 10.95 incl. audio (*0-14-086680-9*, Png AudioBks) Viking Penguin.

Now We Are Sixty. Felicity Hoffecker. 1998. pap. text 9.75 (*1-881907-20-1*) Two Bytes Pub.

Now We Can Have a Wedding! Judy Cox. LC 97-11103. (Illus.). 32p. (J). (ps-3). 1998. lib. bdg. 15.95 (*0-8234-1342-X*) Holiday.

Now We Have a New Baby. Ed. by Meryl Doney. (Illus.). 16p. (J). 1983. reprint ed. 0.99 (*0-86683-707-8*, AY8302) Harper SF.

Now We're Getting Somewhere. David Clewell. LC 94-10665. (Felix Pollak Prize in Poetry Ser.). 96p. 1994. pap. 11.95 (*0-299-14414-3*) U of Wis Pr.

*__Now We're Going to Have to Spray for Politicians.__ Pat Oliphant. 160p. 2000. pap. 12.95 (*0-7407-0614-4*) Andrews & McMeel.

Now! We're Having Fun: Humorous Anecdotes of Life on the Last Frontier. Ted H. Leonard. (Illus.). 160p. 1994. pap. 9.50 (*0-9641553-0-3*) Alaska Wrd Wrks.

Now! We're Having Fun: Humorous Anecdotes of Life on the Last Frontier. rev. ed. Ted H. Leonard. (Illus.). 160p. 1997. pap. 10.00 (*0-9641553-1-1*) Alaska Wrd Wrks.

Now We're Talking. Dean Hughes. LC 98-44733. (Scrappers Ser.: No. 4). 128p. (J). (gr. 3-7). 1999. 14.00 (*0-689-81927-7*) S&S Childrens.

*__Now We're Talking.__ Dean Hughes. LC 98-44733. (Scrappers Ser.: No. 4). 128p. (J). (gr. 3-7). 1999. pap. 4.50 (*0-689-81937-4*, 076714003996) S&S Childrens.

Now We're Talking: Questions that Bring You Closer to Your Kids. Robert C. Crosby. LC 96-21531. 1996. pap. 8.99 (*1-56179-472-4*) Focus Family.

Now We're Talking: Questions to Build Intimacy with Your Spouse. Robert C. Crosby & Pamela Crosby. LC 96-21530. 1996. pap. 8.99 (*1-56179-473-2*) Focus Family.

Now What? A Guidebook for the New Christian. Ralph W. Harris. 24p. 1964. pap. 0.69 (*0-88243-558-2*, 02-0558) Gospel Pub.

Now What? A Step-by-Step Explanation of What to Do After You Have Completed the Forms for a Restraining Order. 1988. pap. write for info. (*0-318-66438-0*, 44,215) NCLS Inc.

*__Now What? A User's Guide to Troubleshooting Laser Printer Problems.__ Don S. Thompson et al. (Illus.). 120p. 1998. pap. 19.95 (*0-9669486-0-2*, TR440) Genl Rib.

Now What? How to Discover Your Destiny. Roger A. Faber. 98p. 1998. pap. 8.00 (*1-880122-02-2*) White Stone.

Now What! Resting in the Lord When Life Doesn't Make Sense. Gary R. Mayes. LC 95-14652. 176p. 1995. pap. 9.99 (*0-89107-856-8*) Crossway Bks.

Now What Do I Do for Fun? W. Anne. 20p. (Orig.). 1985. pap. 1.50 (*0-89486-297-9*, 1269B) Hazelden.

Now What, Lord? Bible Devotions for Girls. Barbara O. Webb. LC 85-22884. (Augsburg Young Readers Ser.). 112p. (Orig.). (J). (gr. 3-7). 1996. pap. 6.99 (*0-8066-2182-6*, 9-2182, Augsburg) Augsburg Fortress.

Now What's a Christian to Do? Ed. by David P. Polk. 144p. (Orig.). 1993. pap. 10.99 (*0-8272-2510-5*) Chalice Pr.

Now, When I Was a Kid. Don Rodabaugh. (Illus.). 127p. 1998. pap. 10.95 (*1-890622-40-0*) Leathers Pub.

Now, Where Were We? Back to Basic Truths That We Have Lost Sight of Through No Fault of My Own. Roy Blount, Jr. 1989. 17.95 (*0-685-24552-7*) Villard Books.

Now! with Emotion. William H. Bohnsack. 80p. (Orig.). 1996. pap. 5.95 (*1-57502-327-X*, P01098) Morris Pubng.

Now with His Love. large type ed. Hilda Nickson. (Linford Romance Library). 317p. 1984. pap. 16.99 (*0-7089-6027-8*, Linford) Ulverscroft.

Now You Are Sara: A Memoir. Caroline Alexander. Tr. by John Sandys-Wunsch. LC 93-72362. 78p. 1993. pap. 9.95 (*0-914539-07-8*) Ben-Simon.

Now You Can . . . Peggy M. Olson. 42p. 1995. pap. text, spiral bd. 7.95 (*1-887414-02-9*) PMO Pubns.

Now You Can Dance. J. Cassini. (Ballroom Dance Ser.). 1986. lib. bdg. 69.95 (*0-8490-3264-4*) Gordon Pr.

Now You Have Time: Evangelist & Disciple see Ahora que Aun Hay Tiempo...Esperanza para los Que Han Quedado Atras: Evang. & Discipulado

Now You Know. Michael Frayn. 1995. pap. 10.95 (*0-413-70010-0*) Methn.

"Now You Know" Reactions after Seeing "Saving Private Ryan" Ed. by Jesse Kornbluth & Linda Sunshine. LC 99-23579. 1999. 15.00 (*1-55704-384-1*, Pub. by Newmarket) Norton.

Now You Know: The Story of the Four Freshmen (Golden Anniversary Edition) 2nd anniversary ed. Ross Barbour. LC 98-29601. (Illus.). 320p. 1998. pap. 24.95 (*0-936653-83-3*) Tiare Pubns.

Now You Know about . . . Celtic. Bob Crampsey. 160p. 1994. pap. write for info. (*0-7855-2704-4*, Pub. by Argyll Pubng) St Mut.

Now You Know about . . . Rangers. Bob Crampsey. 160p. 1994. pap. write for info. (*1-874640-11-4*, Pub. by Argyll Pubng) St Mut.

Now You See Her. Eileen Dewhurst. 256p. 1995. 20.00 (*0-7278-4733-3*) Severn Hse.

Now You See Her. Linda Howard. LC 99-166541. 325p. 1998. 23.00 (*0-671-56882-5*, Pocket Books) PB.

Now You See Her. Whitney Otto. 320p. 1995. pap. 12.00 (*0-345-37826-1*) Ballantine Pub Grp.

Now You See Her. large type ed. Eileen Dewhurst. (Large Print Ser.). 432p. 1996. 27.99 (*0-7089-3550-8*) Ulverscroft.

Now You See Her. large type ed. Linda Howard. Date not set. 28.95 (*0-7862-1727-8*, G K Hall Lrg Type) Mac Lib Ref.

Now You See Her. large type ed. Linda Howard. (Paperback Bestsellers Ser.). 1999. pap. 26.95 (*0-7862-1728-6*) Thorndike Pr.

Now You See Her. large type ed. Whitney Otto. LC 94-18646. 388p. 1994. lib. bdg. 23.95 (*0-8161-7407-5*, G K Hall Lrg Type) Mac Lib Ref.

Now You See Her. Linda Howard. 362p. 1999. reprint ed. mass mkt. 6.99 (*0-671-03405-7*) PB.

Now You See Her, Now You Don't. Diana G. Gallagher. (Sabrina, the Teenage Witch Ser.: No. 16). 160p. (YA). (gr. 7-12). 1998. per. 4.50 (*0-671-02120-6*, Archway) PB.

Now You See Her, Now You Don't. William Murray. LC 94-13433. 1995. 22.00 (*0-8050-2971-0*) H Holt & Co.

Now You See Him... Anne Stuart. (Intimate Moments Ser.: No. 429). 1992. per. 3.39 (*0-373-07429-8*, 5-07429-9) Harlequin Bks.

Now You See Him... large type ed. Anne K. Stuart. LC 93-144. (Romance Ser.). 359p. 1993. reprint ed. lib. bdg. 18.95 (*1-56054-679-4*) Thorndike Pr.

Now You See It. Richard Matheson. 1996. mass mkt. write for info. (*0-614-05531-8*); mass mkt. 6.99 (*0-8125-4811-6*, Pub. by Tor Bks) St Martin.

Now You See It: Studies on Lesbian & Gay Film. Richard Dyer. (Illus.). 352p. (C). 1990. pap. 22.99 (*0-415-03556-2*, A4864) Routledge.

*__Now You See It: Using Illusion to Present the Gospel.__ Keith Wills. 216p. 1999. reprint ed. pap. 16.99 (*1-898938-74-1*, Pub. by Alpha GBR) OM Literature.

Now You See It & Pig in a Poke. Georges Feydeau. Tr. by Kenneth McLeish. 160p. 1998. pap. 16.95 (*0-948230-77-0*, Pub. by N Hern Bks) Consort Bk Sales.

Now You See It, Now You Don't: Lessons in Sleight-of-Hand. Bill Tarr & Barry Ross. 1976. pap. 18.00 (*0-394-72202-7*, V202) Vin Bks.

Now You See It, Now You Don't: Optical Illusion Book. Seymour Simon. LC 97-49855. 96p. (J). (gr. 3 up). 1998. mass mkt. 5.95 (*0-688-16153-7*, Wm Morrow) Morrow Avon.

Now You See It, Now You Don't: Optical Illusion Book. Seymour Simon. LC 97-49855. (Illus.). 96p. (J). (gr. 3-7). 1998. 17.00 (*0-688-16152-9*, Wm Morrow) Morrow Avon.

Now You See It, Now You Don't! Sequential Tricks for Developing Language. Carol Esterreicher. (Illus.). 120p. (J). (gr. 2-6). 1996. spiral bd., wbk. ed. 26.95 (*1-58650-048-1*, BK-244) Super Duper.

Now You See Me . . . Now You Don't. Dan Greenburg. LC 97-49511. (Zack Files: No. 12). (Illus.). 64p. (J). (gr. 2-5). 1998. mass mkt. 3.99 (*0-448-41738-3*, G & D) Peng Put Young Read.

Now You See Me . . . Now You Don't. Dan Greenburg. (Zack Files: No. 12). (J). (gr. 2-5). 1998. 9.15 (*0-606-12852-2*, Pub. by Turtleback) Demco.

Now You See Them, Now You Don't. Francois Caumartin. Tr. by David Homel. (Illus.). 24p. (J). (ps-3). 1996. pap. 4.95 (*1-55209-007-8*) Firefly Bks Ltd.

Now You're Cooking! Friends of the Part School Staff. Ed. by Laura W. Hunter. (Illus.). 300p. (Orig.). 1996. pap. 12.00 (*1-57502-196-X*, Cookbks by Morris) Morris Pubng.

Now You're Cooking: A Guide to Cooking for Boys & Girls. Barbara K. Feig. LC 75-10991. (Illus.). 144p. (YA). (gr. 7 up). 1975. pap. 4.95 (*0-916836-01-0*) J B Pal.

Now You're Cooking: Everything a Beginner Needs to Know to Start Cooking Today. Elaine Corn. LC 94-19208. (Illus.). 320p. 1994. 24.95 (*1-883791-00-6*, Astolat Bks) Harlow & Ratner.

Now You're Cooking: Everything a Beginner Needs to Know to Start Cooking Today. Elaine Corn. LC 94-19208. (Illus.). 320p. 1997. reprint ed. pap. 16.95 (*1-883791-05-7*, Astolat Bks) Harlow & Ratner.

*__Now You're Cooking for Company: Everything a Beginner Needs to Know to Have People Over.__ Elaine Corn. 318p. 2000. text 25.00 (*0-7881-9090-3*) DIANE Pub.

Now You're Cooking for Company: Everything a Beginner Needs to Know to Have People Over. Elaine Corn. LC 96-18683. (Illus.). 320p. 1996. 24.95 (*1-883791-03-0*, Astolat Bks) Harlow & Ratner.

Now You're Learning Espanol: Bilingual Verse. Dick Hayman. (Illus.). 32p. (J). (gr. 4-6). 1997. pap. 3.00 (*1-881791-02-5*) In One EAR.

Now You're Talking. Joan R. Keyes. (Illus.). (J). (gr. 4-9). 1988. student ed. 5.95 (*1-55737-067-2*) Ed Activities.

Now You're Talking: All You Need to Get Your First Ham License. Ed. by Larry D. Wolfgang. LC 97-175057. 1997. pap. 19.00 (*0-87259-597-8*) Am Radio.

Now You're Talking: Arabic in No Time. (ENG & ARA.). 1986. pap. 13.95 incl. audio (*0-8120-7428-9*) Barron.

Now You're Talking: Chinese in No Time. (ENG & CHI.). 48p. 1986. 14.95 incl. audio (*0-8120-7405-X*) Barron.

Now You're Talking: French in No Time. 2nd ed. Now You're Talking Staff. (Now You're Talking! Ser.). (FRE & ENG.). 48p. 1992. pap. 13.95 incl. audio (*0-8120-7880-2*) Barron.

*__Now You're Talking: French in No Time.__ 3rd ed. Gail Stein. (FRE.). 2000. pap. text 14.95 incl. audio (*0-7641-7355-3*) Barron.

Now You're Talking: German in No Time. 2nd ed. (GER & ENG.). 48p. 1992. pap. 13.95 incl. audio (*0-8120-7881-0*) Barron.

*__Now You're Talking: German in No Time.__ 3rd ed. Henry Strutz. (GER.). 2000. pap. text 14.95 incl. audio (*0-7641-7354-5*) Barron.

Now You're Talking: Italian in No Time. 2nd ed. (ITA & ENG.). 48p. 1992. pap. 13.95 incl. audio (*0-8120-7882-9*) Barron.

*__Now You're Talking: Italian in No Time.__ 3rd ed. Mario Costantino. (ITA.). 2000. pap. text 14.95 incl. audio (*0-7641-7356-1*) Barron.

Now You're Talking: Japanese in No Time. 2nd ed. Nobuo Akiyama et al. (ENG & JPN.). 1998. pap. 15.95 incl. audio (*0-7641-7165-8*) Barron.

Now You're Talking: Russian in No Time. (Now Your Talking in No Time Ser.). (ENG & RUS.). 1991. pap. 13.95 incl. audio (*0-8120-7733-4*) Barron.

Now You're Talking: Spanish in No Time. 2nd ed. (SPA & ENG.). 48p. 1992. pap. 13.95 incl. audio (*0-8120-7884-5*) Barron.

*__Now You're Talking: Spanish in No Time.__ 3rd ed. Heywood Wald. (SPA.). 2000. pap. text 14.95 incl. audio (*0-7641-7358-8*) Barron.

Now You've Got It! Math Problem Solving. Laurie Steding. (Great Beginnings Ser.: Level 2). (J). 1997. pap. 1.95 (*0-8167-3251-5*) Troll Communs.

Now You've Got Your Period. rev. ed. Ellen V. Mahoney. Ed. by Roger Rosen. (Coping Ser.). (YA). (gr. 7-12). 1993. lib. bdg. 17.95 (*0-8239-1662-6*) Rosen Group.

*__Now Zoey's Alone.__ Katherine Applegate. LC 99-96352. (Making Out Ser.: No. 24). 176p. (YA). (gr. 7-12). 2000. mass mkt. 5.95 (*0-380-81528-1*, Avon Bks) Morrow Avon.

Nowa Encyklopedia Powszechna PWN, 6 vols. Ed. by Jan Kofman. (POL.). 1995. 590.00 (*0-614-25057-9*) Szwede Slavic.

Nowadays. George Middleton. Ed. by Walter J. Meserve & Mollie A. Meserve. (When Conscience Trod the Stage Ser.). 1998. pap., spiral bd. 4.95 (*0-937657-46-8*) Feedbk Theabks & Prospero.

Nowadays, & Other Stories. George A. Hibbard. LC 74-142885. (Short Story Index Reprint Ser.). 1977. 20.95 (*0-8369-3748-1*) Ayer.

Nowell Codex see Early English Manuscripts in Facsimile

NowHere: Space, Time, & Modernity. Ed. by Roger Friedland & Dierdre Boden. 1994. 55.00 (*0-520-08017-3*, Pub. by U CA Pr); pap. 19.95 (*0-520-08018-1*, Pub. by U CA Pr) Cal Prin Full Svc.

Nowhere & a Man with Women. Reine Barteve. Tr. by Lorraine Alexander et al from FRE. 90p. (Orig.). (C). 1987. pap. text 8.95 (*0-913745-27-8*) Ubu Repertory.

Nowhere City. Alison Lurie. LC 97-796. 1997. pap. 12.00 (*0-8050-5179-1*, Owl) H Holt & Co.

Nowhere City. Alison Lurie. 336p. 1986. mass mkt. 4.50 (*0-380-70070-0*, Avon Bks) Morrow Avon.

Nowhere City. Alison Lurie. 336p. 1992. pap. 9.00 (*0-380-71936-3*, Avon Bks) Morrow Avon.

*__Nowhere Else on Earth.__ Josephine Humphreys. LC 00-36666. 320p. 2000. 24.95 (*0-670-89176-2*, Viking) Viking Penguin.

*__Nowhere Except San Francisco: Memoirs of a Resident Tourist.__ Frederick T. Harper. 239p. 1999. pap. write for info. (*0-7392-0356-8*, PO3547) Morris Pubng.

Nowhere Fast. Margoe Jane. Ed. by Craig H. Hastings. LC 80-85061. (Illus.). 64p. (Orig.). 1980. pap. 4.00 (*0-9602330-1-6*) Margoe Jane.

Nowhere in America: The Big Rock Candy Mountain & Other Comic Utopias. Hal Rammel. (Folklore & Society Ser.). (Illus.). 184p. 1990. text 25.95 (*0-252-01717-X*) U of Ill Pr.

Nowhere Left to Go. Bruce Green. 136p. 1998. pap. 13.00 (*0-8059-4347-1*) Dorrance.

Nowhere Man. John D. Schuetze. 78p. (Orig.). 1994. pap., teacher ed. 7.50 (*0-8100-0519-0*, 22N0856); pap., student ed. 4.00 (*0-8100-0520-4*, 22N0855) Northwest Pub.

*__Nowhere Man: The Final Days of John Lennon.__ Robert Rosen. 212p. 2000. 22.50 (*1-887128-46-8*) Soft Skull Pr.

Nowhere Man: 43 Light St. Rebecca York. (Intrigue Ser.: Vol. 473). 1998. per. 3.99 (*0-373-22473-7*, 1-22473-2) Harlequin Bks.

*__Nowhere Near.__ 56p. 1999. pap. 28.00 (*0-9675404-0-2*) Barth Studios.

*__Nowhere, Now Here.__ Ann Howard Creel. LC 99-86219. (J). 2000. pap. write for info. (*1-58485-200-3*) Pleasant Co.

Nowhere Steps. Mark Rudman. LC 90-30054. 139p. 1990. pap. 13.95 (*0-935296-90-5*, Pub. by Sheep Meadow); text 27.50 (*0-935296-93-X*, Pub. by Sheep Meadow) U Pr of New Eng.

Nowhere to Be Found. Alan Marks. LC 87-32729. (Illus.). 28p. (J). (ps up). 1991. pap. 14.95 (*0-88708-062-6*, Picture Book Studio) S&S Childrens.

*__Nowhere to Call.__ Cynthia C. DeFelice. 2001. pap. 4.95 (*0-380-73306-4*, Wm Morrow) Morrow Avon.

Nowhere to Call Home. Cynthia DeFelice. LC 98-36602. 208p. (YA). (gr. 5 up). 1999. 16.00 (*0-374-35552-5*) FS&G.

Nowhere to Go. Sigmund Stoler. LC 93-34151. 1994. 17.95 (*0-8453-4851-5*, Cornwall Bks) Assoc Univ Prs.

Nowhere to Go: The Tragedy of Runaway & Throwaway Kids. Nancy O. Wilson. 104p. (YA). 1991. pap. 6.95 (*1-57515-012-3*) PPI Pubng.

Nowhere to Go but Down? Andrew S. MacDonald. 232p. 1989. text 44.95 (*0-04-445408-2*) Routledge.

Nowhere to Go but In. Osho. LC 97-220014. 373p. 1995. 15.95 (*81-7261-017-3*, Pub. by Rebel Pub) Oshos.

Nowhere to Grow: Homeless & Runaway Adolescents & Their Families. Les B. Whitbeck & Danny R. Hoyt. LC 99-19051. (Social Institutions & Social Change Ser.). 216p. 1999. pap. text 23.95 (*0-202-30584-8*); lib. bdg. 47.95 (*0-202-30583-X*) Aldine de Gruyter.

Nowhere to Hide. Jasmine Cresswell. (Intrigue Ser.). 1992. per. 2.89 (*0-373-22194-0*, 1-22194-4) Harlequin Bks.

Nowhere to Hide. James Elliott. 400p. 1998. mass mkt. 5.99 (*0-7860-0538-6*, Pinncle Kensgtn) Kensgtn Pub Corp.

Nowhere to Hide. James Elliott. LC 96-6565. 1997. 22.50 (*0-684-82362-4*) S&S Trade.

Nowhere to Hide. large type ed. Susan Francis. 560p. 1994. 27.99 (*0-7089-3110-3*) Ulverscroft.

Nowhere to Run. Robert Daley. 1997. mass mkt. 188.73 (*0-446-16416-X*) Warner Bks.

Nowhere to Run. Gay G. Gunn. LC 97-216921. 261p. 1997. pap. 10.95 (*1-885478-13-5*, Pub. by Genesis Press) BookWorld.

Nowhere to Run. Rochelle Majer Krich. 304p. (Orig.). 1994. mass mkt. 4.99 (*0-380-76534-9*, Avon Bks) Morrow Avon.

Nowhere to Run. Pat Warren. 320p. 1993. mass mkt. 4.50 (*0-8217-4132-2*, Zebra Kensgtn) Kensgtn Pub Corp.

Nowhere to Run. Kate William. (Sweet Valley High Ser.: No. 25). (YA). (gr. 7 up). 1986. 9.09 (*0-606-00732-6*, Pub. by Turtleback) Demco.

Nowhere to Run. large type ed. Rochelle M. Krich. (Niagara Large Print Ser.). 448p. 1997. 29.50 (*0-7089-5866-4*) Ulverscroft.

Nowhere to Run: The Story of Soul Music. Gerri Hirshey. LC 94-15454. (Illus.). 416p. 1994. reprint ed. pap. 14.95 (*0-306-80581-2*) Da Capo.

Nowhere to Run: The Wilderness, May 4th & 5th, 1864, Vol. I. John M. Priest. LC 95-2000. (Illus.). 316p. 1995. 29.95 (*0-942597-74-5*) White Mane Pub.

Nowhere to Run, Nowhere to Hide! Kathleen Duey. (Alone in the Dark Ser.). (Illus.). 32p. (J). 2000. pap. text 3.95 (*1-891100-14-9*) Smart Kids Publ.

Nowhere to Turn. Lisa Fann. (Orig.). 1998. mass mkt. 11.95 (*1-57532-113-0*) Press-Tige Pub.

Nowhere to Turn. Rhonda Graham. LC 92-33210. 1993. pap. 2.97 (*0-8163-1128-5*) Pacific Pr Pub Assn.

Nowle's Passing. Edith Forbes. 272p. 1997. pap. 12.00 (*1-878067-99-0*) Seal Pr WA.

Nowlin - Stone Genealogy: Record of the Descendants of James Nowlin, Who Came to Pittsylvania County, Virginia, from Ireland about 1700; Also a Record of the Descendants of George Stone & of James Hoskin Stone Who Was born in Pittsylvania County in 1778. James E. Nowlin. (Illus.). 548p. 1993. reprint ed. pap. 82.00 (*0-8328-3727-X*); reprint ed. lib. bdg. 92.00 (*0-8328-3726-1*) Higginson Bk Co.

*__Nowottny: Shells & Corridors.__ Marianne Nowottny. (Illus.). 74p. 1998. pap. 10.00 (*0-9677326-1-1*) Abaton Bk.

*__Now's the Time: The Complete Resnick Short Stories.__ John Harvey. 1999. 29.95 (*1-871033-58-6*, Pub. by Slow Dancer); pap. 14.95 (*1-871033-53-5*, Pub. by Slow Dancer) Dufour.

*__Now's the Time: The Complete Resnick Short Stories.__ num. aut. ed. Ed. by John Harvey. 272p. 1999. 34.95 (*0-8023-9075-7*) Dufour.

Nowy Slownik Angielsko-Polsk & Polsko-Angielski. Tadeusz Piotrowski & Zygmunt Saloni. 688p. 1995. pap. 24.00 (*0-614-25053-6*) Szwede Slavic.

*__Nox: Prima's Official Strategy Guide.__ Greg Kramer. LC 99-64227. (Illus.). 489p. 2000. pap. 19.99 (*0-7615-2323-5*) Prima Pub.

Noyau et Enjeux de l'Eschatologie Paulinienne: De l'Apocalyptique Juive et de l'Eschatologie Hellenistique dans Quelques Argumentations de l'Apotre Paul. Jean-Bosco M. Bulembat. xx, 338p. 1997. 118.00 (*3-11-015387-4*) De Gruyter.

Noyes-Gilman Ancestry: Being a Series of Sketches with a Chart of the Ancestry of Charles Phelps Noyes & Emily H. (Gilman) Noyes, His Wife. C. P. Noyes.

An Asterisk (*) at the beginning of an entry indicates that the title is appearing for the first time.

(Illus.). 478p. 1989. reprint ed. pap. 72.00 (*0-8328-0909-8*); reprint ed. lib. bdg. 80.00 (*0-8328-0908-X*) Higginson Bk Co.

Noyes' Oral Histology & Embryology. 7th rev. ed. Frederick B. Noyes. Ed. by Isaac Schour. LC 53-9573. 448p. reprint ed. pap. 138.90 (*0-608-14006-6*, 205544200023) Bks Demand.

Noyesism Unveiled. Hubbard Eastman. LC 72-134402. reprint ed. 55.00 (*0-404-08446-X*) AMS Pr.

Nozieres Thry Quan Liq. Nozieres. pap. (*0-201-40841-4*) Addison-Wesley.

Nozione Di Proairesis in Gregorio Di Nissa: Analisi Semiotico-Linguistica E Prospettive Antropologiche. Giampietro Dal Toso. X, 348p. 1998. 51.95 (*3-631-33700-0*) P Lang Pubng.

Nozze di Figaro: Libretto. Composed by Wolfgang Amadeus Mozart.Tr. of Marriage of Figaro. (ITA.). 96p. 1986. pap. 4.95 (*0-7935-2592-6*, 50340080) H Leonard.

Nozze di Lammermoor, Vol. 2. Michelle Carafa. (Italian Opera 1810-1840 Ser.). 378p. 1986. text 30.00 (*0-8240-6551-4*) Garland.

Nozze di Teti, e di Peleo: Azione Coro-Drammatica by Angelo Maria Ricci, Vol. 3. Gioachino Rossini. Ed. by Guido J. Joerg. 451p. 1994. lib. bdg. 75.00 (*0-226-72847-1*) U Ch Pr.

N.P. Banana Yoshimoto. Ed. by Jane Rosenman. 208p. 1995. pap. 10.00 (*0-671-89826-4*, WSP) PB.

NP Color Guide to Freight & Passenger Equipment. Todd Sullivan. (Illus.). 1995. 49.95 (*1-878887-49-1*) Morning NJ.

NP Inet Using Netscape Communicator Software. Carey. (New Perspectives Ser.). (C). 1997. pap. 21.95 (*0-7600-5764-8*) Course Tech.

NP Internet Using NTSCP Communicator Software. Poindexter. (C). 1997. pap. 18.95 (*0-7600-5501-7*) Course Tech.

***NP on Advanced VBA.** Parsons. (New Perspectives Ser.). (C). 2000. pap. 48.95 (*0-619-01936-0*) Course Tech.

***NP on Dynamic HTML.** Carey. (New Perspectives Ser.). (C). 2000. pap. 33.95 (*0-619-01918-2*) Course Tech.

***NP on Microsoft Window NT 4.0 Workstation.** Oja Parsons. (New Perspectives Ser.). (C). 1999. spiral bd. 14.00 (*0-619-01912-3*) Course Tech.

NP On Ms Access97-comprehensiv. 10th ed. Joseph Adamski et al. (NEW PERSPECTIVES). 552p. (C). 1997. pap. 31.50 (*0-7600-5259-X*) Course Tech.

***NP on MS Win 98.** Parsons et al. (C). 1998. per. 21.95 (*0-7600-5447-9*) Course Tech.

***NP on MS Windows 2000 for Power Users.** Phillips. (New Perspectives Ser.). (C). 2000. pap. 48.95 (*0-619-01935-2*) Course Tech.

***NP On Office 97 "Millenium Edition"** ed. Oja Parsons. (C). 1999. pap. 58.95 (*0-7600-6505-5*) Thomson Learn.

***NP on Publisher 2000.** Parsons. (New Perspectives Ser.). (C). 2000. pap. 31.95 (*0-619-01932-8*) Course Tech.

NPA Guide to National Parks of Northern New South Wales. Peter Wright. 342p. (C). 1992. text 110.00 (*0-9599160-8-3*, Pub. by Surrey Beatty & Sons) St Mut.

***Npd: Entwicklung, Ideologie und Struktur.** Uwe Hoffmann. (Europaische Hochschulschriften Politikwissenschaft Ser.). 496p. 1999. 63.95 (*3-631-35439-8*) P Lang Pubng.

NPDES Best Management Practices Manual. Environmental Protection Agency Staff. 208p. 1995. pap. text 69.00 (*0-86587-466-2*) Gov Insts.

NPDES Compliance Inspection Manual. 3rd ed. EPA Staff. 564p. 1995. pap. text 89.00 (*0-86587-465-4*) Gov Insts.

NPDES Permit Handbook. 2nd ed. Swidler & Berlin Staff. 323p. 1992. pap. text 78.00 (*0-86587-303-8*) Gov Insts.

NPEA Daggers & Associated Knives. R. J. Weinand. (Illus.). 151p. 1988. pap. 19.95 (*0-614-10614-1*) Johnson Ref Bks.

NPIB Companion Reader (in Braille) Ed. by Alan J. Koenig et al. 39p. 1994. pap. 10.50 (*0-9634229-6-0*) SCALARS Pub.

NPK Fertilizer Production Alternatives. Ed. by E. D. Frederick & J. J. Schultz. LC 88-35781. (Special Publications: No. SP-9). (Illus.). 176p. (Orig.). 1988. pap. text 50.00 (*0-88090-072-5*) Intl Fertilizer.

NPM Cook Book: With Lyre, Harp, & Spatula. Richard Gibala. 96p. (Orig.). 1995. pap., spiral bd. 5.95 (*0-614-08606-X*) NPM Pubns.

NPM Workbook: Job Descriptions, Contracts, Salary. rev. ed. Virgil C. Funk. viii, 136p. 1996. pap. text 15.00 (*1-888360-01-1*) NPM Pubns.

NPO Volunteer Management Manual. Jeff Stratton. 120p. ring bd. 99.00 (*0-8342-0515-7*, S134) Aspen Pub.

NPR Classical Music Companion: Terms & Concepts from A-Z. Miles Hoffman. LC 97-10479. 306p. 1997. pap. 15.00 (*0-395-70742-0*, HD10080, Mariner Bks) HM.

NPR Guide to Building a Classical CD Collection. Ted Libbey. LC 92-50292. (Illus.). 496p. 1994. pap. 15.95 (*1-56305-051-X*, 3051) Workman Pub.

***NPR Guide to Building a Classical CD Collection: The 300 Essential Works.** 2nd rev. ed. Ted Libbey. (Illus.). 528p. 1999. pap. 15.95 (*0-7611-0487-9*) Workman Pub.

NPSH for Rotodynamic Pumps. European Association for Pump Manufacturers. LC 99-10806. 88p. 1999. 82.00 (*1-85617-356-9*) Elsevier.

NPT: The Main Political Barrier to Nuclear Weapon Proliferation. Stockholm International Peace Research Institute S. 64p. 1980. pap. 21.00 (*0-85066-205-2*) Taylor & Francis.

***NRC: Regulator of Nuclear Safety.** 24p. 1999. pap. 3.75 (*0-16-063011-8*) USGPO.

NRC Antitrust Licensing Actions, 1978-1996. S. J. Mayer. 144p. 1997. per. 14.00 (*0-16-062862-8*) USGPO.

***NRC Collection of Abbreviations.** 147p. 1998. per. 13.00 (*0-16-062752-4*) USGPO.

***NRC Comprehensive Records Disposition Schedule.** 412p. 1998. ring bd. 33.00 (*0-16-062726-5*) USGPO.

***NRC Enforcement Manual.** 594p. 1998. ring bd. 52.00 (*0-16-063005-3*) USGPO.

***NRC Enforcement Manual, Change Notice No. 1, November 1998.** 48p. 1998. ring bd. 4.75 (*0-16-063009-6*) USGPO.

NRC Enforcement Manual, Change Notice No. 3, November 1996. 364p. 1996. ring bd. 35.00 (*0-16-062994-2*) USGPO.

***NRC Enforcement Policy Review: July 1995-July 1997.** J. Ben Lieberman. 64p. 1998. pap. 5.50 (*0-16-062737-0*) USGPO.

NRC High-level Radioactive Waste Program: Annual Progress Report Fiscal Year 1996. Budhi Sagar. 332p. 1997. per. 46.00 (*0-16-062807-5*) USGPO.

NRC Information Notices, Bulletins & Administrative Letters. 1989. pap. 144.00 (*0-16-015186-4*) USGPO.

***NRC Occupational Safety & Health Program for Managers & Supervisors: What You Should Know.** 14p. 1998. pap. 1.75 (*0-16-063001-0*) USGPO.

***NRC Regulatory Agenda: Semiannual Report, January-June 1998.** 58p. 1998. pap. 6.00 (*0-16-062756-7*) USGPO.

***NRC Regulatory Agenda: Semiannual Report July-December 1997.** 58p. 1998. pap. 6.00 (*0-16-062725-7*) USGPO.

NRC Regulatory Agenda, Semiannual Report, January - June 1997. 57p. 1997. pap. 7.00 (*0-16-062708-7*) USGPO.

***NRC Regulatory Agenda, Semiannual Report, July-December 1999.** 68p. 2000. pap. 8.00 (*0-16-059111-2*) USGPO.

NRC Telephone Directory. Government Printing Office Staff. 1989. per. 9.50 (*0-16-012187-6*) USGPO.

NRC TLD Direct Radiation Monitoring Network. Government Printing Office Staff. 1984. per. 20.00 (*0-16-012065-9*) USGPO.

NRCA Roofing & Waterproofing Manual, 2 vols., Set. 4th rev. ed. (Illus.). 1858p. 1996. 295.00 (*0-934809-08-9*, ML104) Natl Roofing Cont.

NREL Photovoltaic Program Review, 12th Proceedings. Ed. by Rommel Noufi & Harin S. Ullah. LC 94-70748. (AIP Conference Proceedings Ser.: No. 306). 624p. 1994. text 150.00 (*1-56396-315-9*) Am Inst Physics.

NREL/SNL Photovoltaics Program Review Vol. 394: Proceedings of the 14th Conference: A Joint Meeting. Ed. by C. Edwin Witt et al. LC 97-72645. (Illus.). xiii, 918p. 1997. 225.00 (*1-56396-687-5*) Am Inst Physics.

NRF Retail Industry Buying Guide: Suppliers of Retail Services & Products. 1997. pap. 50.00 (*0-87102-101-3*, 80-1014) Nat Retail Fed.

NRF/Annual Specialty Store Wage & Benefit Survey. 1997. 825.00 (*0-87102-104-8*, 55-4531) Nat Retail Fed.

NRI Investment Policy & Procedures. Ed. by Jay N. Vyas. (C). 1988. 250.00 (*0-7855-4772-X*) St Mut.

NROTC Supplement to the Principles of Naval Weapons Systems Workbook. Ed. by Gary Harrell. (Illus.). 76p. 1985. wbk. ed. 5.95 (*0-87021-540-X*) Naval Inst Pr.

NRSV Analytical Concordance to the New Testament. Ed. by Richard E. Whitaker & John R. Kohlenberger, III. 800p. 2000. text 60.00 (*0-19-528443-7*) OUP.

NRTC Programme Guide. NRTC Staff. (Competent Retail Manager Ser.). 1992. pap. text 34.00 (*0-08-042095-8*). Elsevier.

***NS: Natural Sex.** 2000. 25.00 (*0-7388-0872-5*); 18.00 (*0-7388-0873-3*) Xlibris Corp.

NS 100 Fundamentals of Naval Science. 6th ed. USNA Staff & Taylor. 256p. 1998. per. 13.50 (*0-7872-4629-8*) Kendall-Hunt.

NS-Presseanweisungen der Vorkriegszeit Edition und Dokumentation 1933-1939, Vol. 1, 1933. Hans Bohrmann & Gabriele Toepser-Ziegert. 351p. 1984. lib. bdg. 60.00 (*3-598-10552-5*) K G Saur Verlag.

NS-Presseanweisungen der Vorkriegszeit Edition und Dokumentation 1933-1939, Vol. 2, 1934. Ed. by Hans Bohrmann. xxvi, 694p. 1985. lib. bdg. 90.00 (*3-598-10553-3*) K G Saur Verlag.

NS-Presseanweisungen der Vorkriegszeit Edition und Dokumentation 1935-1939, 2 vols., Vol.3, 1935. Ed. by Hans Bohrmann. 1112p. 1987. lib. bdg. 190.00 (*3-598-10554-1*) K G Saur Verlag.

NS-Presseanweisungen der Vorkriegszeit, 1936, Bd. 4. Ed. by Hans Bohrmann. (NS-Presseanweisungen der Vorkriegszeit Edition und Dokumentation Ser.). (GER.). 1993. lib. bdg. 286.00 (*3-598-11004-9*) K G Saur Verlag.

***NSA Cryptologic Documents.** Contrib. by National Archives Staff. (Cryptographic Ser.). vi, 134p. 1999. pap. 26.80 (*0-89412-277-0*, C-83) Aegean Park Pr.

NSAID-Induced Gastroduodenal Damage Vol. 12, Supplement 1, 1994: Prevention & Treatment. Ed. by C. Scarpignato. (Journal: Digestive Diseases: Vol. 13, Supplement 1, 1994). (Illus.). iv, 106p. 1995. pap. 34.00 (*3-8055-6068-0*) S Karger.

NSAIDs: A Profile of Adverse Effects. Ed. by Ivan Borda & Raymond Koff. (Illus.). 240p. 1992. text 39.00 (*1-56053-018-9*) Hanley & Belfus.

***NSC- First Aid & CPR Standard Web Enhanced.** 2nd ed. National Safety Council Staff. (Illus.). 160p. (C). 1998. pap. text 5.70 (*0-7637-0897-6*) JB Pubns.

NSC First Aid & CPR: Advanced. 3rd ed. National Safety Council Staff. LC 96-21029. 1996. pap. 35.75 (*0-7637-0183-1*) Jones & Bartlett.

NSC Sixty-Eight: Blueprint for American Strategy in the Cold War. Ed. by Ernest R. May. 176p. 1993. text 35.00 (*0-312-09445-0*); pap. text 15.95 (*0-312-06637-6*) St Martin.

NSCA Quick Series Guide to Aerobic Training. Seven Hills Publishing Staff. 1998. pap. text 5.95 (*2-922164-08-X*) Seven Hills Pubs.

NSCA Quick Series Guide to Basic Weight Training. Seven Hills Publishing Staff. 1998. pap. text 5.95 (*2-922164-09-8*) Seven Hills Pubs.

NSCA Quick Series Guide Training Log. Seven Hills Publishing Staff. 1998. pap. text 5.95 (*2-922164-10-1*) Seven Hills Pubs.

NSDA Legal Briefing Conference: Proceedings - September 23-25, 1985, Four Seasons Hotel, Washington, D.C. National Soft Drink Association Staff. 287p. write for info. (*0-318-61971-7*) Natl Soft Drink.

NSDAP & the Crisis of Agrarian Conservatism in Lower Bavaria: National Socialism & the Peasants' Road to Modernity. Kim R. Holmes. LC 91-13392. (Modern European History II Ser.). 248p. 1991. text 15.00 (*0-8153-0414-5*) Garland.

NS404 Marines. USNA (Taylor) Staff. 88p. 1996. pap. text, per. 8.10 (*0-7872-3365-X*) Kendall-Hunt.

NS402 Submarines. USNA (Taylor) Staff. 104p. 1996. pap. text, per. 12.90 (*0-7872-3363-3*) Kendall-Hunt.

NSFRE Fund-Raising Dictionary. National Society of Fund Raising Executives Staff. Ed. by Barbara R. Levy & R. L. Cherry. LC 95-44594. (NSFRE-Wiley Fund Development Ser.). 240p. 1996. 29.95 (*0-471-14916-0*) Wiley.

Nside Nsync. Nsync et al. LC 99-71280. (Illus.). 144p. (gr. 4-7). 1999. pap. 25.00 (*0-7893-0380-9*, Pub. by Universe) St Martin.

***NSNA, NCLEX-RN Review.** 4th ed. Alice M. Stein. LC 99-12882. (Illus.). 1008p. 1999. 38.95 (*0-7668-1443-2*) Delmar.

NSNA Review Series: Critical Care Nursing. VEC Staff. (NSNA Review Ser.). 224p. (C). 1996. pap. 31.95 (*0-8273-7642-1*) Delmar.

NSNA's NCLEX - RN Review 1992. Alice M. Stein. 1992. text 29.95 (*0-8273-4836-3*) Delmar.

Nsong' a Lianja: L'Epopee Nationale des Nkundo. Edmond Boelaert. (B. E. Ser.: No. 126). 1949. pap. 18.00 (*0-8115-3054-X*) Periodicals Srv.

NSP Training Handbook: Movers, Space Explorer, Science Wonder. Dale McCreedy et al. (National Science Partnership for Girl Scouts & Science Museums Ser.). (Illus.). 52p. 1996. pap. 12.00 (*1-889939-00-5*) Franklin PA.

NSP Training Handbook: Science Sampler. Dale McCreedy & Kate Tabachnick. (National Science Partnership for Girl Scouts & Science Museums Ser.). (Illus.). 32p. 1996. pap. 8.00 (*1-889939-01-3*) Franklin PA.

NSP Training Handbook: Water Wonders, Weather Watch, Science Sleuth, Science in the Worlds. Dale McCreedy et al. (National Science Partnership for Girl Scouts & Science Museums Ser.). (Illus.). 68p. 1996. pap. 12.00 (*1-889939-02-1*) Franklin PA.

NSPW 96: New Security Paradigms Workshop. Date not set. text. write for info. (*0-89791-944-0*, 537961) Assn Compu Machinery.

NSRV Bible. Philip H. Pfattiecher. 1998. 15.99 (*0-8066-0392-5*) Augsburg Fortress.

NSTA Pathways to the Science Standards: Guidelines for Moving the Vision into Practice, Elementary School Edition. Ed. by Lawrence F. Lowry. (Illus.). 152p. 1997. pap. text 29.95 (*0-87355-161-3*, PB124X) Natl Sci Tchrs.

NSTA Pathways to the Science Standards: Guidelines for Moving the Vision into Practice, High School Edition. (Pathways Ser.). (Illus.). 196p. 1996. pap., teacher ed. 29.95 (*0-87355-144-3*, PB126X) Natl Sci Tchrs.

NSTA Pathways to the Science Standards: Guidelines for Moving the Vision into Practice, Middle School Edition. Ed. by Steven J. Rakow. LC 98-170616. (Illus.). 1998. pap. text 29.95 (*0-87355-166-4*, PB125X) Natl Sci Tchrs.

NS310: Strategy & Tactics. 5th ed. USNA Staff & Taylor. 304p. 1998. per. 16.00 (*0-7872-5119-4*) Kendall-Hunt.

***NS310: Strategy & Tactics.** 6th ed. USNA (Pinnix) Staff. 268p. 1999. per. 16.00 (*0-7872-6265-X*) Kendall-Hunt.

***Nsu & You...making the Campus ConnectionCollege Strategies Handbook: College Strategies Handbook.** 2nd ed. Eddie Jackson. 138p. (C). 1999. per. 28.95 (*0-7872-6101-7*, 41610101) Kendall-Hunt.

NSUCO Oculomotor Test. W. C. Maples. Ed. by Willard Bleything. (Illus.). 60p. (Orig.). (C). 1994. lib. bdg. 18.00 (*0-943599-74-1*) OEPF.

NSW Sniper Log Book. Stephen J. Leung. (Model 9600 - Waterproof Ser.). 268p. 1996. 85.00 (*1-885633-05-X*) Iron Brigade.

***N'Sync.** Andrews McMeel Publishing Staff. (Illus.). 1999. pap. 9.95 (*0-7407-0434-6*) Andrews & McMeel.

***N'Sync.** Ed. by Anne Raso. (Celebrity Ser.: No. 22). 2000. pap. 4.99 (*0-88013-014-8*, Pub. by Starlog Grp Inc) Kable News Co Inc.

***N'Sync.** Ed. by Anne Raso. (Teen Girl Power Poster Special Ser.: No. 1). 2000. pap. 3.99 (*0-88013-025-3*, Pub. by Starlog Grp Inc) Kable News Co Inc.

***N'Sync Back to School.** Ed. by Anne Raso. (Celebrity Ser.: No. 27). 2000. pap. 4.99 (*0-88013-027-X*, Pub. by Starlog Grp Inc) Kable News Co Inc.

NT: A Strategic Review. Cliff Leach. 400p. (C). 1993. pap. text 75.00 (*0-13-045261-0*) P-H.

NT Bible Stories. (Illus.). (ps-3). 1993. pap. 3.49 (*0-7696-0052-2*) Amer Educ Pub.

NT Enterprise Network Design. Morgan Stern et al. LC 97-69206. 624p. 1997. pap. text 54.99 (*0-7821-2156-X*) Sybex.

NT Fat FAQs. Steve Scoggins. (Illus.). 556p. 1997. pap., pap. text 39.95 incl. cd-rom (*0-07-913244-8*) McGraw.

Windows 2000 Server Systems Administrator's Black Book With CDROM. Paul Taylor et al. 600p. 1999. 39.99 (*1-57610-268-8*) Coriolis Grp.

Windows 2000 Systems Programming Black Book With CDROM. Al Williams. LC 99-42701. 700p. 2000. 49.99 incl. cd-rom (*1-57610-280-7*) Coriolis Grp.

NT 5: The Next Revolution. Ari Kaplan. LC 98-25094. 400p. 1998. pap. 29.99 (*1-57610-288-2*) Coriolis Grp.

NT 5 Network Migration. Stewart Miller. 1998. pap. 49.99 (*0-7645-3212-X*) IDG Bks.

NT 5.0 Secrets. Harry M. Brelsford. LC 99-19196. 1500p. 1999. 59.99 (*0-7645-3130-1*) IDG Bks.

***NT 4 Max Box.** Mark Minasi. 6608p. 1999. boxed set 94.98 (*0-7821-2527-1*) Sybex.

NT 4 Network Security. 2nd ed. Matthew Strebe et al. LC 98-88332. (Illus.). 976p. 1998. pap. 49.99 (*0-7821-2425-9*) Sybex.

NT Gilty. David Gordon. LC 95-77238. 340p. 1996. 21.95 (*0-944435-36-X*) Glenbridge Pub.

NT Network Plumbing: Routers, Proxies & Web Services. Anthony Northrup. LC QA76.76.O63N673 1998. 624p. 1998. pap. 39.99 (*0-7645-3209-X*) IDG Bks.

NT Network Printing. 400p. 1997. 29.99 (*0-7821-2007-5*) Sybex.

NT Network Solutions Kit. Lisa Donald. 1997. 59.99 incl. cd-rom (*0-7821-2122-5*) Sybex.

NT Networking Programming Toolkit. John Murphy. LC 98-31978. (Microsoft Technology Ser.). 256p. 1998. pap. text 49.99 (*0-13-081324-9*) P-H.

NT Server 4. Matthew Strebe. LC 99-61308. (24seven Ser.). 480p. 1999. pap. 34.99 (*0-7821-2507-7*) Sybex.

NT Server 4 Administrator's Handbook. 448p. 1997. 29.99 (*0-7821-1980-8*) Sybex.

***NT Server 4 in the Enterprise Study Guide.** 3rd ed. Lisa Donald. (MCSE Exam Preparation Guide Ser.). (Illus.). 720p. 1999. pap., student ed. 49.99 (*0-7821-2697-9*) Sybex.

***NT Server 4 Study Guide.** 3rd ed. James Chellis. (MCSE Exam Preparation Guide Ser.). (Illus.). 816p. 1999. pap., student ed. 49.99 (*0-7821-2696-0*) Sybex.

NT Server Management & Control. 2nd ed. Kenneth L. Spencer. LC 97-46924. 576p. (C). 1997. pap. text 49.95 (*0-13-856568-6*) P-H.

***NT Workstation 4 Study Guide.** 3rd ed. James Chellis. (MCSE Exam Preparation Guide Ser.). (Illus.). 768p. 1999. pap., student ed. 49.90 (*0-7821-2698-7*) Sybex.

NTA Trapping Handbook: A Guide for Better Trapping. Tom Krause. Ed. by Norman Gray et al. (Illus.). 206p. 1984. text 9.00 (*0-9620698-1-7*); pap. text 5.00 (*0-9620698-0-9*) Natl Trap Assn.

NTA Trapping Handbook: A Guide for Better Trapping. Tom Krause. Ed. by Norman Gray et al. (Illus.). 206p. 1984. reprint ed. 12.00 (*0-685-37388-6*); reprint ed. pap. 8.00 (*0-685-37389-4*) Natl Trap Assn.

NTC Al Corriente: Everyday Expressions Needed to Communicate in Simple Spanish. Robert J. Johnson. LC 95-217354. (SPA., Illus.). 160p. 1994. pap. 16.95 (*0-8442-7309-0*, 73090) NTC Contemp Pub Co.

NTC Book of Advertising & Marketing Checklists. Ron Kaatz. 192p. 1993. pap. 19.95 (*0-8442-3198-3*, NTC Business Bks) NTC Contemp Pub Co.

NTC Dictionary of Word Origins. Adrian Room. (Illus.). 194p. 1994. pap. 12.95 (*0-8442-5179-8*, 51798, Natl Textbk Co) NTC Contemp Pub Co.

NTC Language Learning Flash Cards. (Illus.). 1989. teacher ed. 5.60 (*0-8442-8353-3*) NTC Contemp Pub Co.

NTC Thesaurus of Everyday American English. Anne Bertram. LC 95-174468. 496p. 1994. 16.95 (*0-8442-5825-3*, 58253) NTC Contemp Pub Co.

NTC Thesaurus of Everyday American English. Anne Bertram. 340p. 1994. pap. 12.95 (*0-8442-5826-1*, 58261) NTC Contemp Pub Co.

NTC Vocabulary Builders Level 1: Red Book. 1995. pap., teacher ed. 14.06 (*0-8442-5842-3*) NTC Contemp Pub Co.

NTC Vocabulary Builders Level 2: Blue Book. LC 94-65416. 200p. (J). pap., student ed. 12.00 (*0-8442-5843-1*) NTC Contemp Pub Co.

NTC Vocabulary Builders Level 2: Blue Book. 1995. pap., teacher ed. 14.06 (*0-8442-5845-8*) NTC Contemp Pub Co.

NTC Vocabulary Builders Level 3: Green Book. pap., teacher ed. 14.06 (*0-8442-5847-4*) NTC Contemp Pub Co.

NTC Vocabulary Builders Level 3: Green Book. LC 94-65416. 200p. (J). pap., student ed. 12.00 (*0-8442-5846-6*) NTC Contemp Pub Co.

NTC Vocabulary Builders Level 4: Yellow Book. pap., teacher ed. 14.06 (*0-8442-5849-0*) NTC Contemp Pub Co.

NTC Vocabulary Builders Level 4: Yellow Book. LC 94-65416. 200p. (J). pap., student ed. 12.00 (*0-8442-5848-2*) NTC Contemp Pub Co.

NTC's American English Learner's Dictionary. 30.00 (*0-8442-2425-1*) NTC Contemp Pub Co.

***NTC's American English Learner's Dictionary.** NTC Publishing Group Staff. 2000. pap. 45.00 (*0-658-00131-0*, 001310); pap. 30.00 (*0-658-00156-6*, 001566) NTC Contemp Pub Co.

NTC's American English Learners's Dictionary: The Essential Vocabulary of American Language & Culture. Ed. by Richard A. Spears. (Illus.). 1104p. 1998. pap. 24.95 (*0-8442-5860-1*, 58601) NTC Contemp Pub Co.

NTC's American Idioms Dictionary. 20.00 (*0-658-00129-9*) NTC Contemp Pub Co.

***NTC's American Idioms Dictionary.** NTC Publishing Group Staff. 2000. pap. 30.00 (*0-658-00130-2*, 001302); audio compact disk 20.00 (*0-658-00160-4*, 001604) NTC Contemp Pub Co.

NTC's American Idioms Dictionary. 2nd ed. Richard A. Spears. (Illus.). 432p. 1995. 16.95 (*0-8442-0825-6*, 08256); pap. 12.95 (*0-8442-0826-4*, 08264) NTC Contemp Pub Co.

NTC's Anthology of Nonfiction. Jane B. Gordon & Karen Kuchner. pap., teacher ed. 14.06 (*0-8442-5809-1*); pap., student ed. 28.19 (*0-8442-5808-3*) NTC Contemp Pub Co.

NTC's Basic Japanese Level 1: Beginning. Lynn Williams. (JPN.). 208p. (YA). 1994. pap., student ed. 12.65 (*0-8442-8433-5*, Natl Textbk Co) NTC Contemp Pub Co.

NTC's Basic Japanese Level 1: Beginning. Lynn Williams. (JPN.). 320p. (YA). 1994. teacher ed. 25.35 (*0-8442-8432-7*, Natl Textbk Co) NTC Contemp Pub Co.

NTC's Basic Japanese Level 1: Beginning. Lynn Williams. (JPN.). 360p. (YA). 1995. text 32.50 (*0-8442-8430-0*, Natl Textbk Co) NTC Contemp Pub Co.

NTC's Basic Japanese Level 1: Beginning, 3 cass., Set. Lynn Williams. (JPN.). (YA). 1994. audio 31.95 (*0-8442-8378-9*, Natl Textbk Co) NTC Contemp Pub Co.

NTC's Basic Japanese Level 2: Intermediate. Lynn Williams. (JPN.). 320p. (YA). 1993. teacher ed. 25.35 (*0-8442-8441-6*, Natl Textbk Co) NTC Contemp Pub Co.

NTC's Basic Japanese Level 2: Intermediate. Lynn Williams. (JPN.). 336p. (YA). 1994. text 32.25 (*0-8442-8440-8*, Natl Textbk Co) NTC Contemp Pub Co.

NTC's Basic Japanese Level 2: Intermediate. Lynn Williams. (JPN.). 160p. (YA). 1995. student ed. 12.65 (*0-8442-8442-4*, Natl Textbk Co) NTC Contemp Pub Co.

NTC's Basic Japanese Level 2: Intermediate, 3 cass., Set. Lynn Williams. (JPN.). (YA). 1993. audio 31.95 (*0-8442-8382-7*, Natl Textbk Co) NTC Contemp Pub Co.

NTC's Beginners French & English Dictionary. Jacqueline Winders et al. LC 98-16229. (Illus.). 512p. 1995. 12.95 (*0-8442-1475-2*, 14752, Natl Textbk Co) NTC Contemp Pub Co.

NTC's Beginners German & English Dictionary. Moya Brennan & Sarah Briggs. LC 97-49442. (Here's How Ser.). (Illus.). 192p. 1998. pap. 12.95 (*0-8442-2479-0*) NTC Contemp Pub Co.

NTC's Beginners German & English Dictionary. Erick P. Byrd. Ed. by Frank R. Abate. (Illus.). 496p. 1995. pap. 8.95 (*0-8442-2497-9*) NTC Contemp Pub Co.

NTC's Beginners German & English Dictionary. Erick P. Byrd. Ed. by Frank R. Abate. (ENG & GER., Illus.). 496p. 1995. 12.95 (*0-8442-2496-0*) NTC Contemp Pub Co.

NTC's Beginners Italian & English Dictionary. Raffaele A. Dioguardi. Ed. by Frank R. Abate. LC 95-147735. (ENG & ITA., Illus.). 464p. 1995. 12.95 (*0-8442-8443-2*, 84432, Natl Textbk Co) NTC Contemp Pub Co.

NTC's Beginners Italian & English Dictionary. Raffaele A. Dioguardi & Frank R. Abate. LC 97-47729. (Illus.). 464p. 1995. pap. 9.95 (*0-8442-8444-0*, 84440, Natl Textbk Co) NTC Contemp Pub Co.

NTC's Beginner's Spanish & English Dictionary. National Textbook Company Staff. (SPA & ENG., Illus.). 488p. 1995. pap. 7.95 (*0-8442-7699-5*, 76995, Natl Textbk Co) NTC Contemp Pub Co.

NTC's Bulgarian & English Dictionary. Elena Stankova & Ivanka Harlakova. (ENG & BUL., Illus.). 288p. 1994. 23.95 (*0-8442-4979-3*, 49793, Natl Textbk Co) NTC Contemp Pub Co.

NTC's Business Writer's Handbook. Arthur H. Bell. 736p. Date not set. pap. 22.95 (*0-8442-5913-6*, VGM Career) NTC Contemp Pub Co.

NTC's Business Writer's Handbook. Arthur H. Bell. LC 94-80055. (Illus.). 736p. 1995. 35.00 (*0-8442-5912-8*, NTC Business Bks) NTC Contemp Pub Co.

NTC's Classical Dictionary. Adrian Room. 252p. 1994. 29.95 (*0-8442-5473-8*, Natl Textbk Co) NTC Contemp Pub Co.

NTC's Compact Dutch & English Dictionary: The Most Practical & Concise Dutch & English Dictionary. Ed. by NTC Publishing Group Staff. LC 97-48917. (DUT., Illus.). 592p. 1998. 24.95 (*0-8442-8351-7*) NTC Contemp Pub Co.

NTC's Compact Dutch & English Dictionary: The Most Practical & Convenient Dutch & English Dictionary. NTC Publishing Group Staff. (DUT & ENG.). 584p. 1999. pap. 19.95 (*0-8442-0101-4*, 01014, Natl Textbk Co) NTC Contemp Pub Co.

NTCs Compact English Dictionary: The Core Vocabulary for Learners. Richard Spears. 700p. Date not set. pap. 12.95 (*0-8442-0107-3*, 01073) NTC Contemp Pub Co.

NTC's Compact Finnish & English Dictionary. NTC Publishing Group Staff. LC 98-26853. (ENG & FIN.). 800p. 1998. 27.95 (*0-8442-0147-2*, 01472) NTC Contemp Pub Co.

NTC's Compact Finnish & English Dictionary: The Most Practical & Convenient Finnish & English Dictionary. NTC Publishing Group Staff. (FIN & ENG.). 800p. 1999. pap. 21.95 (*0-8442-0325-4*, 03254, Natl Textbk Co) NTC Contemp Pub Co.

NTC's Compact Korean & English Dictionary. Ed. by B. J. Jones et al. (ENG & KOR., Illus.). 800p. (C). 1996. 29.95 (*0-8442-8360-6*, 83606) NTC Contemp Pub Co.

NTC's Compact Korean & English Dictionary. Ed. by B. J. Jones & Gene S. Rhie. LC 97-43326. (ENG & KOR., Illus.). 800p. 1996. pap. 22.95 (*0-8442-8361-4*, 83614) NTC Contemp Pub Co.

NTC's Compact Portuguese & English Dictionary. Christopher Naylor. LC 95-35949. (POR., Illus.). 816p. 1995. pap. 19.95 (*0-8442-4691-3*, 46913) NTC Contemp Pub Co.

NTC's Compact Russian & English Dictionary. National Textbook Company Staff & L. P. Popova. LC 98-16230. (RUS & ENG., Illus.). 448p. 1994. pap. 12.95 (*0-8442-4284-5*, 42845, Natl Textbk Co) NTC Contemp Pub Co.

NTC's Compact Russian & English Dictionary. National Textbook Company Staff et al. LC 94-150421. (RUS & ENG., Illus.). 448p. 1994. 17.95 (*0-8442-4283-7*, 42837) NTC Contemp Pub Co.

NTC's Compact Swedish & English Dictionary. LC 97-2621. (ENG & SWE.). 800p. 1997. pap. 18.95 (*0-8442-4960-2*, 49602, Natl Textbk Co) NTC Contemp Pub Co.

NTC's Compact Swedish & English Dictionary. Passport Books Staff. LC 97-2621. (ENG & SWE., Illus.). 800p. 1997. 24.95 (*0-8442-4959-9*, 49599, Natl Textbk Co) NTC Contemp Pub Co.

NTC's Dictionary for Doubtful Spellers. David Downing. LC 90-63166. (Illus.). 336p. 1995. pap. 5.95 (*0-8442-5474-6*, Natl Textbk Co) NTC Contemp Pub Co.

NTC's Dictionary of Acronyms & Abbreviations. Steven R. Kleinedler. (Illus.). 320p. 1995. pap. 12.95 (*0-8442-5376-6*, 53766, Natl Textbk Co) NTC Contemp Pub Co.

NTC's Dictionary of Acronyms & Abbreviations: Intermediate Through Advanced. Steven R. Kleinedler. Ed. by Richard A. Spears. (Illus.). 320p. 1995. 16.95 (*0-8442-5160-7*, 51607, Natl Textbk Co) NTC Contemp Pub Co.

NTC's Dictionary of Advertising. 2nd ed. Jack G. Wiechmann. (Illus.). 288p. 1993. pap. 19.95 (*0-8442-3487-7*, NTC Business Bks) NTC Contemp Pub Co.

NTC's Dictionary of American English Phrases. Richard A. Spears. (Illus.). 560p. 1995. 17.95 (*0-8442-0847-7*, 08477, Passprt Bks) NTC Contemp Pub Co.

NTC's Dictionary of American English Pronunciation. Bernard Silverstein. LC 97-46675. (Illus.). 400p. 1994. pap. 14.95 (*0-8442-0727-6*, Natl Textbk Co) NTC Contemp Pub Co.

NTC's Dictionary of American English Pronunciation. Bernard Silverstein. LC 94-130290. (Illus.). 400p. 1994. 16.95 (*0-8442-0726-8*, 07268, Natl Textbk Co) NTC Contemp Pub Co.

NTC's Dictionary of American English Pronunciation. Bernard Silverstein. 260p. 1995. audio 9.95 (*0-8442-0728-4*, Natl Textbk Co) NTC Contemp Pub Co.

NTC's Dictionary of American English Pronunciation, Set. Bernard Silverstein. 400p. 1994. pap. 26.15 incl. audio (*0-8442-0725-X*, 0725X, Natl Textbk Co) NTC Contemp Pub Co.

NTC's Dictionary of American Idioms. Richard A. Spears. Ed. by Linda Schinke-Llano. 480p. 1993. pap. 12.95 (*0-8442-5450-9*, Natl Textbk Co) NTC Contemp Pub Co.

NTC's Dictionary of American Idioms. Richard A. Spears. Ed. by Linda Schinke-Llano. 480p. 1993. 16.95 (*0-8442-5452-5*, Natl Textbk Co) NTC Contemp Pub Co.

NTC's Dictionary of American Slang & Colloquial Expressions. 20.00 (*0-658-00124-8*) NTC Contemp Pub Co.

***NTC's Dictionary of American Slang & Colloquial Expressions.** NTC Publishing Group Staff. 2000. pap. 30.00 (*0-658-00087-X*, 00087X); audio compact disk 20.00 (*0-658-00157-4*, 001574) NTC Contemp Pub Co.

NTC's Dictionary of American Slang & Colloquial Expressions. Richard A. Spears. 544p. 1993. 16.95 (*0-8442-5461-4*, Natl Textbk Co) NTC Contemp Pub Co.

NTC's Dictionary of American Slang & Colloquial Expressions. 2nd ed. Richard A. Spears. LC 95-149319. (Illus.). 568p. 1994. 16.95 (*0-8442-0827-2*, Passprt Bks) NTC Contemp Pub Co.

NTC's Dictionary of American Slang & Colloquial Expressions. 2nd ed. Richard A. Spears. LC 98-8058. 556p. 1995. pap. 12.95 (*0-8442-0828-0*, Passprt Bks) NTC Contemp Pub Co.

NTC's Dictionary of British Slang. Ed. by Ewart James. (Illus.). 576p. 1996. 17.95 (*0-8442-0838-8*, 08388) NTC Contemp Pub Co.

NTC's Dictionary of Canadian French. Ed. by Sinclair Robinson & Donald Smith. LC 97-51184. 300p. 1995. 17.95 (*0-8442-1486-8*, 14868, Natl Textbk Co) NTC Contemp Pub Co.

NTC's Dictionary of Changes in Meaning: A Comprehensive Reference to the Major Changes in Meanings in English Words. Adrian Room. (Illus.). 304p. 1994. 29.95 (*0-8442-5136-4*) NTC Contemp Pub Co.

NTC's Dictionary of Changes in Meaning: A Comprehensive Reference to the Major Changes in Meanings in English Words. Adrian Room. (Illus.). 304p. 1995. pap. text 14.95 (*0-8442-5135-6*) NTC Contemp Pub Co.

NTC's Dictionary of China's Cultural Code Words. Boye L. Demente. LC 95-42218. (BBC Phrase Bks.). (CHI., Illus.). 488p. 1995. 17.95 (*0-8442-8480-7*, 84807, Passprt Bks) NTC Contemp Pub Co.

NTC's Dictionary of Common Mistakes in Spanish. John Pride. (BBC Phrase Bks.). (SPA & ENG., Illus.). 256p. 1995. 14.95 (*0-8442-7255-8*, 72558, Passprt Bks) NTC Contemp Pub Co.

NTC's Dictionary of Common Mistakes in Spanish: Common Errors of English Speakers in Spanish & How to Avoid Them. John Pride. (ENG & SPA.). 256p. 1998. pap. 10.95 (*0-8442-7252-3*, 72523) NTC Contemp Pub Co.

NTC's Dictionary of Commonplace Words in Real-Life Contexts: An Essential Guide to the Everyday Objects in American Life. Anne Bertram. LC 96-26183. (Illus.). 400p. 1998. pap. 14.95 (*0-8442-0846-9*, 08469) NTC Contemp Pub Co.

NTC's Dictionary of Debate. Jim Hanson. (Illus.). 208p. 1994. 14.95 (*0-8442-5458-4*, Natl Textbk Co) NTC Contemp Pub Co.

NTC's Dictionary of Debate. Jim Hanson. (Illus.). 208p. 1994. pap. 11.95 (*0-8442-5459-2*, 54592, Natl Textbk Co) NTC Contemp Pub Co.

NTC's Dictionary of Easily Confused Words. Deborah K. Williams. LC 95-149480. (Illus.). 340p. 1994. 16.95 (*0-8442-5786-9*, 57869, Passprt Bks) NTC Contemp Pub Co.

NTC's Dictionary of Easily Confused Words. Deborah K. Williams. (Illus.). 340p. 1996. pap. 14.95 (*0-8442-5787-7*, 57877) NTC Contemp Pub Co.

NTC's Dictionary of Euphemisms: The Most Practical Guide to Unraveling Euphemisms. Anne Bertram. LC 97-49341. 320p. 1998. 16.95 (*0-8442-0842-6*, 08426) NTC Contemp Pub Co.

NTC's Dictionary of Euphemisms: The Most Practical Guide to Unraveling Euphemisms. Anne Bertram. 320p. 1999. pap. 14.95 (*0-8442-0843-4*, 08434) NTC Contemp Pub Co.

NTC's Dictionary of Everyday American English Expressions. Richard A. Spears. LC 95-139741. (Illus.). 415p. 1994. 16.95 (*0-8442-5778-8*, 57788) NTC Contemp Pub Co.

NTC's Dictionary of Everyday American English Expressions. Richard A. Spears. (Illus.). 415p. 1995. pap. 12.95 (*0-8442-5779-6*, 57796) NTC Contemp Pub Co.

NTC's Dictionary of Faux Amis. C. W. Kirk-Greene. (ENG & FRE.). 204p. 1996. 16.95 (*0-8442-1503-1*, 15031, Natl Textbk Co); pap. 12.95 (*0-8442-1494-9*, 14949) NTC Contemp Pub Co.

NTC's Dictionary of Folksy, Regional & Rural Sayings: A Practical Guide to Down-Home Expressions & the Way They Are Used. Anne Bertram. Ed. by Richard A. Spears. (Illus.). 400p. 1996. pap. 16.95 (*0-8442-5834-2*, 58342) NTC Contemp Pub Co.

NTC's Dictionary of French Faux Pas. Anne Crowe. (FRE & ENG., Illus.). 256p. 1994. 14.95 (*0-8442-1465-5*, 14655) NTC Contemp Pub Co.

NTC's Dictionary of German False Cognates. Ed. by Geoff Parkes & Alan Cornell. (ENG & GER., Illus.). 226p. 1996. pap. 12.95 (*0-8442-2494-4*) NTC Contemp Pub Co.

NTC's Dictionary of German False Cognates. Ed. by Geoffrey Parkes & Alan Cornell. (ENG & GER., Illus.). 226p. 1996. 16.95 (*0-8442-2495-2*, Natl Textbk Co) NTC Contemp Pub Co.

NTC's Dictionary of Grammar Terminology. Richard A. Spears. LC 90-63164. (Illus.). 224p. 1995. 16.95 (*0-8442-5468-1*, 54681, Natl Textbk Co) NTC Contemp Pub Co.

NTC's Dictionary of Japan's Cultural Code Words. Boye L. De Mente. (JPN., Illus.). 384p. 1996. pap. 15.95 (*0-8442-8315-0*, 83150, Natl Textbk Co) NTC Contemp Pub Co.

NTC's Dictionary of Korea's Business: The Complete Guide to Key Words That Express How the Koreans Think, Communicate, & Behave. Boye L. De Mente. LC 97-49357. (Illus.). 416p. 1998. 22.95 (*0-8442-8362-2*, 83622) NTC Contemp Pub Co.

NTC's Dictionary of Latin American Spanish. Rafael A. Olivares. (ENG & SPA.). 384p. 1999. pap. 17.95 (*0-8442-7964-1*, 79641) NTC Contemp Pub Co.

NTC's Dictionary of Latin American Spanish. Raphael Oliveres. LC 97-22112. (SPA., Illus.). 384p. Date not set. 19.95 (*0-8442-7963-3*, 79633) NTC Contemp Pub Co.

NTC's Dictionary of Latin & Greek Origins. Ed. by Bob Moore & Maxine Moore. LC 96-25819. (Illus.). 400p. 1996. 19.95 (*0-8442-8320-7*, 83207, Natl Textbk Co) NTC Contemp Pub Co.

NTC's Dictionary of Latin & Greek Origins. Bob Moore et al. LC 96-25819. (LAT, GRE & ENG., Illus.). 400p. 1996. pap. 15.95 (*0-8442-8321-5*, 83215, Natl Textbk Co) NTC Contemp Pub Co.

NTC's Dictionary of Literary Terms. Kathleen Morner & Ralph Rausch. (Illus.). 304p. 1993. 16.95 (*0-8442-5465-7*, 54657, Natl Textbk Co) NTC Contemp Pub Co.

NTC's Dictionary of Literary Terms. Kathleen Morner & Ralph Rausch. LC 98-7223. (Illus.). 304p. 1995. pap. 12.95 (*0-8442-5464-9*, 54649, Natl Textbk Co) NTC Contemp Pub Co.

NTC's Dictionary of Mailing List Terminology & Techniques. Nat G. Bodian. (Illus.). 320p. 1994. 49.95 (*0-8442-3188-6*, Natl Textbk Co) NTC Contemp Pub Co.

NTC's Dictionary of Mexican Cultural Code Words. Boye L. De Mente. (Illus.). 352p. 1996. 18.95 (*0-8442-7959-5*, 79595) NTC Contemp Pub Co.

NTC's Dictionary of Phrasal Verbs. 20.00 (*0-658-00125-6*) NTC Contemp Pub Co.

***NTC's Dictionary of Phrasal Verbs & Other Idiomatic Verbal Phrases.** NTC Publishing Group Staff. 2000. pap. 30.00 (*0-658-00090-X*, 00090X); audio compact disk 20.00 (*0-658-00159-0*, 001590) NTC Contemp Pub Co.

NTC's Dictionary of Phrasal Verbs & Other Idiomatic Verbal Phrases: Intermediate Through Advanced. Richard A. Spears. (Illus.). 896p. 1994. 22.95 (*0-8442-5463-0*, 54630, Natl Textbk Co) NTC Contemp Pub Co.

NTC's Dictionary of Phrasal Verbs & Other Idiomatic Verbal Phrases: Intermediate Through Advanced. Richard A. Spears et al. (Illus.). 896p. 1994. pap. 16.95 (*0-8442-5462-2*, 54622, Natl Textbk Co) NTC Contemp Pub Co.

NTC's Dictionary of Proverbs & Cliches. Anne Bertram. (Illus.). 320p. 1996. pap. 12.95 (*0-8442-5158-5*, 51585, Natl Textbk Co) NTC Contemp Pub Co.

NTC's Dictionary of Proverbs & Cliches: Intermediate Through Advanced. Anne Bertram. Ed. by Richard A. Spears. (Illus.). 320p. 1994. pap. 16.95 (*0-8442-5159-3*, 51593, Natl Textbk Co) NTC Contemp Pub Co.

NTC's Dictionary of Quotations. Robin Hyman. (Illus.). 520p. 1994. 19.95 (*0-8442-5753-2*, 57532); pap. 15.95 (*0-8442-5754-0*, 57540, Natl Textbk Co) NTC Contemp Pub Co.

NTC's Dictionary of Shakespeare: A Comprehensive Guide to Shakespeare's Plays, Characters, & Contemporaries. Sandra Clark. (Illus.). 304p. 1994. 27.95 (*0-8442-5755-9*, 57559, Natl Textbk Co) NTC Contemp Pub Co.

NTC's Dictionary of Shakespeare: A Comprehensive Guide to Shakespeare's Plays, Characters, & Contemporaries. Sandra Clark. (Illus.). 304p. 1996. pap. 12.95 (*0-8442-5756-7*, 57567, Natl Textbk Co) NTC Contemp Pub Co.

NTC's Dictionary of Spanish Cognates: Thematically Organized. Rose Nash. (SPA.). 320p. 1999. pap. 15.95 (*0-8442-7962-5*) NTC Contemp Pub Co.

NTC's Dictionary of Spanish Cognates Thematically Arranged. Rose Nash. LC 97-16771. (SPA & ENG., Illus.). 320p. 1997. 19.95 (*0-8442-7961-7*, 79617) NTC Contemp Pub Co.

NTC's Dictionary of Spanish False Cognales. Ed. by Marcial Prado. LC 97-49455. (ENG & SPA., Illus.). 280p. 1996. pap. 12.95 (*0-8442-7977-3*, 79773, Natl Textbk Co) NTC Contemp Pub Co.

NTC's Dictionary of the U. S. A. A Practical Guide to American Language & Culture. George Thomas Kurian. LC 97-24618. (Illus.). 256p. 1998. 16.95 (*0-8442-5862-8*, 58628) NTC Contemp Pub Co.

NTC's Dictionary of the United Kingdom: The Most Practical Guide to British Language & Culture. Ewart James. (Illus.). 416p. 1997. pap. 16.95 (*0-8442-5856-3*, 58563) NTC Contemp Pub Co.

***NTC's Dictionary of the United States: A Practical Guide to American Language & Culture.** George Kurian. LC 97-24618. (Illus.). 256p. 1998. pap. 14.95 (*0-8442-5863-6*, 58636) NTC Contemp Pub Co.

NTC's Dictionary of Theatre & Drama Terms. Jonnie P. Mobley. (Illus.). 176p. 1993. 19.95 (*0-8442-5345-6*, 53456, Natl Textbk Co) NTC Contemp Pub Co.

NTC's Dictionary of Theatre & Drama Terms. Jonnie P. Mobley. LC 98-13124. (Illus.). 176p. 1994. pap. 14.95 (*0-8442-5333-2*, 53332, Natl Textbk Co) NTC Contemp Pub Co.

NTC's Dictionary of Tricky Words: A Practical & Complete Guide to Choosing the Right Word. Deborah K. Williams. LC 96-21920. 208p. (Orig.). 1996. pap. 9.95 (*0-8442-5764-8*, 57648) NTC Contemp Pub Co.

NTC's Dictionary of Tricky Words: With Complete Examples of Correct Usage. Deborah K. Williams. LC 97-26865. (Illus.). 208p. 1996. 7.95 (*0-8442-5472-X*) NTC Contemp Pub Co.

NTC's Dictionary of World Origins. Adrian Room. (Illus.). 194p. 1993. 19.95 (*0-8442-5137-2*, 51372, Natl Textbk Co) NTC Contemp Pub Co.

NTC's EFL Bookshelf. 50.00 (*0-658-00128-0*) NTC Contemp Pub Co.

***NTC's EFL Bookshelf.** NTC Publishing Group Staff. 2000. cd-rom 50.00 (*0-658-00161-2*, 001612) NTC Contemp Pub Co.

NTC's English Idioms Dictionary: Imtermediate Through Advanced. Richard A. Spears & Betty Kirkpatrick. (Illus.). 471p. 1993. 16.95 (*0-8442-5478-9*, C5478-9, Natl Textbk Co) NTC Contemp Pub Co.

NTC's English Idioms Dictionary: Imtermediate Through Advanced. Richard A. Spears & Betty Kirkpatrick. LC 98-7224. (Illus.). 471p. 1994. pap. 12.95 (*0-8442-5479-7*, Natl Textbk Co) NTC Contemp Pub Co.

NTC's French - English Business Dictionary. Michael Marcheteau. (ENG & FRE., Illus.). 600p. 1994. 39.95 (*0-8442-1479-5*, 14795, Natl Textbk Co) NTC Contemp Pub Co.

NTC's French Grammar. Isabelle Fournier. LC 97-38273. (NTC's...Grammar Ser.). (ENG & FRE., Illus.). 192p. 1997. pap. 7.95 (*0-8442-1493-0*, 14930) NTC Contemp Pub Co.

NTC's German Grammar. Richard Tenberg & Guido Rings. LC 97-39935. (NTC's...Grammar Ser.). (ENG & GER., Illus.). 192p. 1997. pap. 7.95 (*0-8442-2503-7*) NTC Contemp Pub Co.

NTC's Guide to Grammar Terms: With Complete Examples of Correct Usage. Richard A. Spears & Steven R. Kleinedler. LC 96-51180. (Illus.). 256p. 1997. pap. 12.95 (*0-8442-5749-4*, 57494) NTC Contemp Pub Co.

NTC's Gulf Arabic - English Dictionary: A Compact Dictionary of the Contemporary Arabic of the Mideast. Hamdi A. Qafisheh. (ARA & ENG., Illus.). 672p. 1997. 34.95 (*0-8442-4606-9*, 46069, Natl Textbk Co) NTC Contemp Pub Co.

NTC's Gulf Arabic-English Dictionary: A Compact Dictionary of the Contemporary Arabic of the Mideast. Hamdi A. Qafisheh. (ARA & ENG.). 672p. 1999. pap. 27.95 (*0-8442-0299-1*, 02991) NTC Contemp Pub Co.

NTC's Handbook for Writers. Martin Steinmann & Michael Keller. LC 94-66704. (Illus.). 368p. 1994. 27.95 (*0-8442-5810-5*, 58105) NTC Contemp Pub Co.

***NTC's Hebrew & English Dictionary.** Aribe Comay & Naomi Tsur. LC 99-27862. 1280p. 1999. 39.95 (*0-658-00065-9*, 000659) NTC Contemp Pub Co.

NTC's Hungarian & English Dictionary. Tamas Magay & Laszlo Kiss. LC 96-12536.Tr. of Angol-Magyar Kisszotar. (ENG & HUN., Illus.). 840p. 1996. 29.95 (*0-8442-4968-8*, 49688, Natl Textbk Co) NTC Contemp Pub Co.

An Asterisk (*) at the beginning of an entry indicates that the title is appearing for the first time.

NTC's Hungarian & English Dictionary. Tamas Magay & Laszlo Kiss. LC 96-12536.Tr. of Angol-Magyar Kisszotar. (HUN & ENG.). 848p. 1998. pap. 23.95 (0-8442-4969-6, 49696, Natl Textbk Co) NTC Contemp Pub Co.

NTC's Italian Grammar. Alwena Lamping. LC 97-34565. (Grammar Ser.). (ENG & ITA., Illus.). 192p. 1997. pap. 10.95 (0-8442-8080-1, 80801) NTC Contemp Pub Co.

NTC's Mass Media Dictionary. R. Terry Ellmore. (Illus.). 608p. 1995. pap. 24.95 (0-8442-3186-X, NTC Business Bks) NTC Contemp Pub Co.

NTC's Multilingual Dictionary of American Sign Language. Claude O. Proctor. (FRE, ENG, DUT, CHI & ARA., Illus.). 767p. 1994. 49.95 (0-8442-0731-4) NTC Contemp Pub Co.

NTC's Multilingual Dictionary of American Sign Language. Claude O. Proctor. LC 98-16218. (Illus.). 767p. 1996. pap. 29.95 (0-8442-0732-2, 07322, Natl Textbk Co) NTC Contemp Pub Co.

NTC's New College Greek & English Dictionary. LC 97-42245. (ENG & GRE., Illus.). 560p. (C). 1996. pap. 21.95 (0-8442-8482-3, 84823, Natl Textbk Co) NTC Contemp Pub Co.

NTC's New College Russian & English Dictionary. A. M. Taube et al. (ENG & RUS., Illus.). 1136p. 1996. 27.95 (0-8442-4280-2, 42802) NTC Contemp Pub Co.

NTC's New Japanese & English Character Dictionary. National Textbook Company Staff & Jack Halpern. (JPN & ENG., Illus.). 2220p. 1995. 49.95 (0-8442-8434-3, 84343, Natl Textbk Co) NTC Contemp Pub Co.

NTC's Practice Test Kit for the TOEFL. Milada Broukal & Enid Nolan-Woods. 160p. 1994. pap. 9.95 (0-8442-0743-8, Natl Textbk Co) NTC Contemp Pub Co.

NTC's Practice Test Kit for the TOEFL. 2nd ed. Milada Broukal. (Illus.). 168p. 1997. pap. text 13.95 (0-8442-0495-1, 04951) NTC Contemp Pub Co.

NTC's Practice Test Kit for the TOEFL. 2nd ed. Milada Broukal & Enid Nolan-Woods. 168p. 1997. pap. 39.95 incl. audio (0-8442-0496-X, 0496X) NTC Contemp Pub Co.

NTC's Preparation Book for the TOEFL. 2nd ed. Milada Broukal. (Illus.). 352p. 1997. pap. text 15.95 (0-8442-0483-8, 04838) NTC Contemp Pub Co.

NTC's Preparation Kit for the TOEFL. Milada Broukal & Enid Nolan-Woods. 352p. 1994. pap. 11.95 (0-8442-0738-1, Natl Textbk Co) NTC Contemp Pub Co.

NTC's Preparation Kit for the TOEFL, Set. Milada Broukal & Enid Nolan-Woods. 352p. 1995. 39.95 incl. audio (0-8442-0739-X, Natl Textbk Co) NTC Contemp Pub Co.

NTC's Preparation Kit for the TOEFL, 3 cass., Set. 2nd ed. Milada Broukal & Enid Nolan-Woods. 352p. 1997. pap. 39.95 incl. audio (0-8442-0482-X, 0482X) NTC Contemp Pub Co.

NTC's Romanian & English Dictionary. Andrei Bantas. LC 97-49454. (ENG & RUM., Illus.). 672p. 1997. 29.95 (0-8442-4976-9, 49769, Natl Textbk Co) NTC Contemp Pub Co.

NTC's Spanish Grammar. Rosa M. Martin. LC 97-36713. (Grammar Ser.). (ENG & SPA., Illus.). 192p. 1997. pap. 7.95 (0-8442-7225-6, 72256) NTC Contemp Pub Co.

NTC's Spell It Right Dictionary. David Downing. (Illus.). 336p. 1994. pap. 6.95 (0-8442-5477-0, 54770, Natl Textbk Co) NTC Contemp Pub Co.

NTC's Super-Mini American Idioms Dictionary. Ed. by Richard A. Spears. LC 96-15028. (Illus.). 256p. 1996. pap. 5.95 (0-8442-0916-3, 09163) NTC Contemp Pub Co.

NTC's Super-Mini American Slang Dictionary. Ed. by Richard A. Spears. LC 96-15029. (Illus.). 248p. 1996. pap. 5.95 (0-8442-0917-1, 09171) NTC Contemp Pub Co.

NTC's Thematic Dictionary of American Idioms. Richard A. Spears. LC 97-24440. (Illus.). 432p. 1997. 18.95 (0-8442-0830-2, 08302) NTC Contemp Pub Co.

NTC's Thematic Dictionary of American Idioms. Richard A. Spears. 432p. 1999. pap. 15.95 (0-8442-0831-0, 08310) NTC Contemp Pub Co.

NTC's Thematic Dictionary of American Slang. Richard A. Spears. LC 97-24459. (Illus.). 560p. 1997. 18.95 (0-8442-0832-9, 08329) NTC Contemp Pub Co.

NTC's Thematic Dictionary of American Slang. Richard A. Spears. 560p. 1999. pap. 15.95 (0-8442-0833-7, 08337) NTC Contemp Pub Co.

NTC's Vietnamese - English Dictionary. Ed. by Nguyen Dinh-Hoa. (ENG & VIE., Illus.). 704p. (C). 1996. 24.95 (0-8442-8356-8, 83568) NTC Contemp Pub Co.

NTC's Vietnamese - English Dictionary. rev. ed. Ed. by Nguyen Dinh-Hoa. LC 95-18670. (ENG & VIE., Illus.). 704p. (YA). (gr. 3). 1995. pap. 17.95 (0-8442-8357-6, 83576) NTC Contemp Pub Co.

NTC's Vocabulary Builders. LC 94-65416. 200p. (J). 1995. pap. 12.00 (0-8442-5841-5) NTC Contemp Pub Co.

NTC's Yemeni Arabic-English Dictionary. Hamdi A. Qafisheh. 672p. 1999. 34.95 (0-8442-2597-5) NTC Contemp Pub Co.

NTE - Core Battery with Cassettes. rev. ed. Research & Education Association Staff. LC 97-68606. (Illus.). 768p. 2000. pap. text 23.95 incl. audio (0-87891-851-5) Res & Educ.

NTE Core Battr; St, 1 vol. Warner Books Staff. 1998. 9.95 (0-446-77729-3) Warner Bks.

NTE (New Technology English) Bk. 1: Handling Social Conventions. Edwin T. Cornelius, Jr. (New Technology English Ser.: Vol. 4). (Illus.). 147p. 1984. text 8.95 (0-89209-109-6); pap. text 6.25 (0-89209-403-6) Pace Grp Intl.

NTE (New Technology English) Bk. 1: Handling Social Conventions, Set of 6. Edwin T. Cornelius, Jr. (New Technology English Ser.: Vol. 4). (Illus.). 147p. 1984. audio 25.00 (0-89209-113-4) Pace Grp Intl.

NTE (New Technology English) Bk. 2: Interacting in Social & Business Settings. Edwin T. Cornelius, Jr. (New Technology English Ser.: Vol. 5). (Illus.). 150p. 1984. text 8.95 (0-89209-110-X); pap. text 6.25 (0-89209-404-4) Pace Grp Intl.

NTE (New Technology English) Bk. 2: Interacting in Social & Business Settings, 6 cass., Set. Edwin T. Cornelius, Jr. (New Technology English Ser.: Vol. 5). (Illus.). 150p. 1984. audio 25.00 (0-89209-114-2) Pace Grp Intl.

NTE (New Technology English) Bk. 3: Expressing & Finding Out Attitudes. Edwin T. Cornelius, Jr. (New Technology English Ser.: Vol. 6). (Illus.). 151p. 1984. text 8.95 (0-89209-111-8); pap. text 6.25 (0-89209-405-2) Pace Grp Intl.

NTE (New Technology English) Bk. 3: Expressing & Finding Out Attitudes, 6 cass., Set. Edwin T. Cornelius, Jr. (New Technology English Ser.: Vol. 6). (Illus.). 151p. 1984. audio 25.00 (0-89209-115-0) Pace Grp Intl.

NTE (New Technology English) Bk. 4: Extending Personal Abilities. Edwin T. Cornelius, Jr. (New Technology English Ser.: Vol. 7). (Illus.). 152p. 1984. text 8.95 (0-89209-112-6); pap. text 6.25 (0-89209-406-0) Pace Grp Intl.

NTE (New Technology English) Bk. 4: Extending Personal Abilities, 6 cass., Set. Edwin T. Cornelius, Jr. (New Technology English Ser.: Vol. 7). (Illus.). 152p. 1984. audio 25.00 (0-89209-116-9) Pace Grp Intl.

NTE Progress & Performance. Edwin T. Cornelius, Jr. (New Technology English Ser.: Vol. 10). (Illus.). 249p. 1984. text 8.95 (0-685-09168-6); pap. text 6.95 (0-89209-409-5) Pace Grp Intl.

NTE Progress & Performance, 8 cass., Set. Edwin T. Cornelius, Jr. (New Technology English Ser.: Vol. 10). (Illus.). 249p. 1984. audio 36.00 (0-89209-158-4) Pace Grp Intl.

Nth Degree. Randolph Howes. 200p. pap. 5.95 (1-885458-00-2) Free Radical.

Nth Whoopee of Sight: Recent Paintings & Pastels by Richard Merkin. (Illus.). 10p. 1980. pap. 2.50 (0-940744-26-0) Chrysler Museum.

NTIA Telecom 2000: Charting the Course for a New Century in the Communications & Information Sectors of the Economy, 2 vols., Set. 1995. lib. bdg. 603.95 (0-8490-6749-9) Gordon Pr.

NTL Managers' Handbook. Alice G. Sargent. Ed. by Roger A. Ritvo. LC 83-61458. (Orig.). (C). 1983. pap. 16.95 (0-9610392-0-5) NTL Inst.

Ntozake Shange: A Critical Study of the Plays. Neal A. Lester & Ntozake Shange. LC 94-36113. (Critical Studies in Black Life & Culture: Vol. 21). 336p. 1995. text 58.00 (0-8153-0314-9, H1441) Garland.

NTP Workshop on Validation & Regulatory Acceptance of Alternative Toxicological Test Methods: Final Report. Ed. by Kenneth Olden. (Illus.). 41p. (C). 1997. pap. text 30.00 (0-7881-4233-X) DIANE Pub.

Ntsoj Tsuag Xyoob Ntoo Tsua Koj Thab Kuv (Hmong) Arthur Morton. Tr. by Yer J. Thao. (J). (gr. k-3). 1994. 12.50 (1-57842-071-7) Delmas Creat.

Ntsuag Nos: Ib Tug Cinderella Hmoob. Jewell R. Coburn et al. Tr. by Jean Moua. LC 95-36353. (VIE., Illus.). 32p. (J). (gr. 2-6). 1996. 15.95 (1-885008-03-1) Shens Bks.

NTW/2.5. (C). Date not set. pap. write for info. (0-393-96393-4) Norton.

N'Tzor L'Shoncha: Guard Your Tongue in Yiddish. Zelig Pliskin. Tr. by M. G. Rosenbaum. (YID.). xxxxiii, 284p. 1996. 14.00 (0-9654702-0-2) M Birnhack.

Nu. Fred Aufray. 96p. 2000. 19.95 (1-893263-07-X) Ipso Facto.

Nu Naybahood: Funetic Ebonic Dictionary. D. Munyungo Jackson & Darryl Jackson. (Illus.). 185p. 1998. pap. 13.95 (1-881524-39-6) Milligan Bks.

Nu Perdu & Retour Amont, Dans la Pluie Giboyeuse, le Chien de Coeur, l'Effroi la Joie, Contres une Maison Seche. Rene Char. (Poesie Ser.). (FRE.). 143p. 1971. pap. 9.95 (2-07-032178-9) Schoenhof.

Nu Perdu et Autres Poemes, 1964-1975. Rene Char. (FRE.). 1978. pap. 10.95 (0-8288-3822-4, F83180) Fr & Eur.

***Nu Wache UF, Sunder Trage.** Martina Probst. 186p. 1999. 37.95 (3-631-34562-3) P Lang Pubng.

Nuala & Her Secret Wolf: Drumshee Timeline Series Book 1. Cora Harrison. (Drumshee Timeline Ser.: Bk. 1). (Illus.). 128p. (J). (gr. 4-8). 1998. pap. 6.95 (0-86327-585-0, Pub. by Wolfhound Press) Irish Amer Bk.

Nuances: The Soul of Hospice. John W. Abbott. 122p. 1997. pap. 14.95 (0-936479-01-9) Connecticut Hospice Inc.

Nuances of Technique in Dynamic Psychotherapy. Mardi J. Horowitz. LC 89-30865. 288p. 1989. 50.00 (0-87668-859-8) Aronson.

Nuanua: Pacific Writings in English since 1980. Ed. by Albert Wendt. LC 94-45613. (Talanoa Ser.). 405p. 1995. pap. text 17.00 (0-8248-1731-1) UH Pr.

Nuat Thai: Traditional Thai Medical Massage. Anthony B. James. 148p. 1991. pap. 16.95 (1-886338-02-7) Meta Jrnl Pr.

Nuat Thai the Northern Style. Anthony B. James. 144p. (Orig.). 1993. pap. text 16.95 (1-886338-01-9) Meta Jrnl Pr.

Nuat Thai, Traditional Thai Medical Massage. 2nd rev. ed. Anthony B. James. (Illus.). 140p. 1991. reprint ed. 37.00 (1-886338-03-5) Meta Jrnl Pr.

Nuaulu Ethnozoology: A Systematic Inventory. Roy Ellen. (Illus.). 217p. (Orig.). 1993. pap. 30.00 (0-904938-20-4, Pub. by CSEAS) Cellar.

Nuba: An Anthropological Study of the Hill Tribes in Kordofan. Siegfried F. Nadel. LC 76-44768. reprint ed. 67.50 (0-404-15957-5) AMS Pr.

***Nubby's Quiz Show: Math.** McGraw-Hill Book Company Staff. 1999. 14.95 (1-57768-321-8) MG-Hill OH.

***Nubecita Panza de Agua (Water Belly, the Little Cloud) Cuentos Bilingues (Bilingual Stories)** Tito A. Brovelli. Tr. by Kirk Anderson. (ENG & SPA., Illus.). 24p. (J). (ps-6). 2000. 14.00 (0-9673032-0-6, Pub. by Sweet Dreams Bilingual Pubs) IPG Chicago.

Nubecitas. Frances Sainz. (Foundations Ser.). 23p. (J). (ps-1). 1992. pap. text 23.00 (1-56843-046-9); pap. text 4.50 (1-56843-093-0) EMG Networks.

Nubes Oscuras con Interiores de Plata - Dark Clouds Silver Linings. Hart. (SPA.). 264p. 1996. write for info. (1-56063-570-3) Editorial Unilit.

Nubia & Abyssinia. Michael Russell. 440p. 1990. 135.00 (1-85077-052-2, Pub. by Darf Pubs Ltd) St Mut.

Nubia Deserts & Outside Egypt. Porter. (Topographical Bibliography of Ancient Egyptian Hieroglyphic Texts Ser.: Reliefs & Paintings, Vol. 7). 1983. 91.50 (0-900416-04-1, Pub. by Aris & Phillips) David Brown.

Nubian: A Novel. Duane Smith. Ed. by Myra B. Moon. LC 92-8885. 392p. 1992. 19.95 (0-9632074-4-X) Azimuth GA.

Nubian: A Novel. Duane Smith. 1994. 12.95 (0-9632074-0-7) Azimuth GA.

Nubian Ceremonial Life. John G. Kennedy. 300p. 1996. 18.50 (0-614-21629-X, 910) Kazi Pubns.

Nubian Cousins: Adventures in Verse. Marcellus J. Leonard. (Illus.). 35p. 1999. pap. 5.00 (1-928795-00-5, Glass Cage) M Leonard IL.

Nubian Culture: Past & Present. Ed. by Tomas Hagg. (Kungl Vitterhets Historie Ser.: No. 17). (Illus.). 438p. (Orig.). 1987. pap. text 55.00 (91-7402-188-5) Coronet Bks.

Nubian Ethnographies. Elizabeth W. Fernea & Robert A. Fernea. 203p. (C). 1991. pap. text 12.50 (0-88133-480-4) Waveland Pr.

Nubian Kingdoms. Edna Russman. LC 97-29389. (African Civilizations Ser.). 64p. (J). 1998. 22.00 (0-531-20283-6) Watts.

***Nubian Princess.** Patrice Cathey. 4p. 1999. pap. 3.00 (0-9673501-0-7) Onya Pubg.

Nubian Wedding Book. Ingrid Strugis. (Illus.). 192p. 1998. pap. 15.00 (0-609-80185-6, Crown) Crown Pub Group.

Nubiana, Vol. I. B. J. Ashanti. 48p. 1977. pap. 2.00 (0-917886-01-1) Shamal Bks.

Nubians & the Nubian Language in Contemporary Egypt: A Case of Cultural & Linguistic Contact. Aleya Rouchdy. LC 90-19286. (Studies in Semitic Languages & Linguistics: No. 15). xiv, 83p. 1991. 64.50 (90-04-09197-1) Brill Academic Pubs.

Nubians of West Aswan: Village Women in the Midst of Change. Anne M. Jennings. 1995. pap. text 17.95 (1-55587-592-0); lib. bdg. 42.00 (1-55587-570-X) L Rienner.

Nubile Nostalgia: A Teenage Wasteland. Ed. by John Wood. (Illus.). 64p. 1999. pap. 25.00 (0-85449-288-7) LPC InBook.

Nuckolls Family: Extract "Pioneer Settlers of Grayson County, Virginia" Benjamin F. Nuckolls. 32p. 1994. reprint ed. pap. 6.50 (0-8328-4168-4) Higginson Bk Co.

Nucla Circulating Atmospheric Fluidized Bed Demonstration: Final Report. Ed. by Raymond E. Keith. (Illus.). 482p. (C). 1998. pap. text 60.00 (0-7881-7507-6) DIANE Pub.

Nuclear- & Radiochemistry: Fundamentals & Applications. K. H. Lieser. LC 98-113375. 472p. 1997. 260.00 (3-527-29453-8, Wiley-VCH) Wiley.

Nuclear Accident. Christopher Lampton. LC 91-43564. (Disaster! Ser.). (Illus.). 64p. (J). (gr. 4-6). 1992. pap. 5.95 (1-56294-782-6) Millbrook Pr.

Nuclear Accident Dosimetry Systems. IAEA Staff. (Panel Proceedings Ser.). (Illus.). 200p. 1970. pap. 25.00 (92-0-021070-8, ISP241, Pub. by IAEA) Bernan Associates.

Nuclear Accidents: Harmonization of the Public Health Response. (Euro Reports & Studies Ser.: No. 110). 111p. 1989. pap. text 10.00 (92-890-1276-5) World Health.

Nuclear Age. Tim O'Brien. 368p. 1993. mass mkt. 6.99 (0-440-21586-2, LE) Dell.

Nuclear Age. Tim O'Brien. 320p. 1996. pap. 13.95 (0-14-025910-4) Viking Penguin.

Nuclear Age: A. D. 1950 - 1990 see TimeFrame Series

Nuclear Age: Time Frame AD, 1950-1990. Time-Life Books Editors. (Time Frame Ser.). 1990. lib. bdg. 28.60 (0-8094-6476-4) Time-Life.

Nuclear Age at Fifty. David Krieger. 99p. (Orig.). (C). 1995. pap. text 35.00 (0-7881-1884-6) DIANE Pub.

Nuclear Age Reader. WGBH Educational Foundation Staff. Ed. by Carl Kaysen et al. 650p. (C). 1988. pap. text 44.00 (0-07-554004-5); pap. text, student ed. 20.50 (0-07-554020-7) McGraw.

Nuclear Air Cleaning Handbook. ERDA Technical Information Staff et al. LC 76-52974. (ERDA Technical Information Center Ser.). 302p. 1976. pap. 15.50 (0-87079-103-6, ERDA-76-21); fiche 9.00 (0-87079-296-2, ERDA-76-21) DOE.

Nuclear Alert: The Strategic Bomber Forces of the Cold War. Robert Jackson. LC 97-44902. 1998. 42.95 (1-85753-256-2, Pub. by Brasseys) Brasseys.

Nuclear Analytical Methods in the Life Sciences. Ed. by Rolf Zeisler & Vincent P. Guinn. (Illus.). 792p. 1991. 150.00 (0-89603-202-7) Humana.

Nuclear Analytical Methods in the Life Sciences, 1994. Ed. by Jan Kucera et al. (Illus.). 768p. 1994. 150.00 (0-89603-300-7) Humana.

Nuclear & Atomic Physics at One Gigaflop, Vol. 16. Ed. by C. Bottcher et al. (Nuclear Science Research Conference Ser.: Vol. 6). xiv, 326p. 1989. pap. text 107.00 (3-7186-0492-2) Gordon & Breach.

Nuclear & Chemical Dating Techniques. Ed. by Lloyd A. Currie. LC 81-20649. (ACS Symposium Ser.: No. 176). 1982. 54.95 (0-8412-0669-4) Am Chemical.

Nuclear & Chemical Dating Techniques: Interpreting the Environmental Record. Ed. by Lloyd A. Currie. LC 81-20649. (ACS Symposium Ser.: No. 176). (Illus.). 528p. 1982. reprint ed. pap. 163.70 (0-608-03242-5, 206376100007) Bks Demand.

***Nuclear & Condensed Matter Physics: VI Regional CRRNSM Conference.** Ed. by Antonino Messina. LC 00-100717. (AIP Conference Proceedings Ser.: Vol. 513). (Illus.). 442p. 2000. 130.00 (1-56396-929-7, Pub. by Am Inst Physics) Spr-Verlag.

Nuclear & Conventional Forces in Europe: Implications for Arms Control & Security: 1987 Colloquium Reader. Ed. by W. Thomas Wander. LC UA0646.3.N8. (AAAS Publication: No. 87-18). 219p. reprint ed. pap. 67.90 (0-7837-0055-5, 204030200016) Bks Demand.

Nuclear & Partcl Physics. W. E. Burcham & M. Jobes. LC 94-13700. (C). 1995. pap. text 61.95 (0-582-45088-8, Pub. by Addison-Wesley) Longman.

Nuclear & Particle Astrophysics. Ed. by J. G. Hirsch & D. Page. LC 98-7170. (Cambridge Contemporary Astrophysics Ser.). (Illus.). 300p. (C). 1998. 69.95 (0-521-63010-X) Cambridge U Pr.

Nuclear & Particle Physics. 1992. 1012.95 (0-387-55143-3) Spr-Verlag.

Nuclear & Particle Physics. Ed. by C. J. Burden & B. A. Robson. 468p. (C). 1990. text 113.00 (981-02-0235-0) World Scientific Pub.

Nuclear & Particle Physics. W. S. Williams. (Illus.). 398p. 1991. pap. text 54.90 (0-19-852046-8) OUP.

Nuclear & Particle Physics: The Changing Interface. Mira Dey & Jishnu Day. LC 93-14273. (Series in Nuclear & Particle Physics). 1994. 86.95 (0-387-56790-9) Spr-Verlag.

Nuclear & Particle Physics: The Changing Interface. Mira Dey & J. Dey. (Series in Nuclear & Particle Physics). (Illus.). 120p. 1993. write for info. (3-540-56790-9) Spr-Verlag.

Nuclear & Particle Physics, 1993: Proceedings of the Conference Held in Glasgow, U. K., 30 March-1 April 1993. Ed. by I. J. MacGregor & A. T. Doyle. (Institute of Physics Conference Ser.: No. 133). (Illus.). 288p. 1993. 200.00 (0-7503-0289-5) IOP Pub.

Nuclear & Particle Physics on the Light Cone. Ed. by Mikkel B. Johnson & L. S. Kisslinger. 532p. (C). 1989. text 125.00 (9971-5-0803-6) World Scientific Pub.

Nuclear & Particle Physics Simulations: The Consortium of Upper-Level Physics Software. Roberta Bigelow et al. LC 95-35662. 240p. 1995. pap., pap. text 46.95 incl. disk (0-471-54883-9) Wiley.

Nuclear & Particle Physics with High Intensity Proton Accelerators. Ed. by T. K. Komatsubara et al. LC 98-206066. 511p. 1997. text 61.00 (981-02-3108-3) World Scientific Pub.

Nuclear & Practice Physics Source Book. McGraw-Hill Editors. (Science Reference Ser.). 529p. 1988. 64.95 (0-07-045509-0) McGraw.

Nuclear & Quark Matter. 500p. 1997. lib. bdg. 61.00 (981-02-2745-0) World Scientific Pub.

Nuclear & Radiochemistry. 3rd ed. G. Friedlander et al. LC 81-1000. 704p. 1981. pap. 99.95 (0-471-86255-X) Wiley.

Nuclear & Radiochemistry Applications. Ed. by Richard M. Lambrecht & Nabil Morcos. LC 82-9111. (Illus.). 592p. 1982. 68.00 (0-08-029389-1, Pub. by Pergamon Repr) Franklin.

Nuclear & Relativistic Astrophysics & Nuclidic Cosmochemistry, 1963-1967, 4 vols., Vol. 1. B. Kuchowicz. xiv, 366p. 1976. text 421.00 (0-677-02760-5) Gordon & Breach.

Nuclear & Relativistic Astrophysics & Nuclidic Cosmochemistry, 1963-1967, 4 vols., Vol. 3. B. Kuchowicz. 200p. 1982. text 161.00 (0-677-02780-X) Gordon & Breach.

***Nuclear & Toxic Waste.** Thomas Streissguth. LC 00-30905. (At Issue Ser.). 2001. pap. write for info. (0-7377-0476-4) Greenhaven.

Nuclear Annihilation & Contemporary American Poetry: Ways of Nothingness. John Gery. 240p. (C). 1996. 49.95 (0-8130-1417-4) U Press Fla.

Nuclear Arms: Ethics, Strategy, Politics. Ed. by R. James Woolsey & Michael Quinlan. LC 83-26580. 289p. 1984. 24.95 (0-917616-56-1); pap. 19.95 (0-917616-55-3) ICS Pr.

Nuclear Arms: Technologies in the 1990's. Ed. by Dietrich Schroeer & David Hafemeister. LC 88-83262. (AIP Conference Proceedings Ser.: No. 178). 493p. 1988. lib. bdg. 70.00 (0-88318-378-1) Am Inst Physics.

Nuclear Arms Control: Background & Issues. National Academy of Sciences, U. S. Committee on I. LC 84-62287. 378p. 1985. pap. text 24.95 (0-309-03491-4) Natl Acad Pr.

Nuclear Arms in the Third World: U. S. Policy Dilemma. Ernest W. Lefever. LC 78-24810. 168p. reprint ed. pap. 52.10 (0-608-12715-9, 202538800043) Bks Demand.

Nuclear Arms Race. William Gay & Michael Pearson. LC 86-32087. (Last Quarter Century Ser.: No. 1). 304p. 1987. reprint ed. pap. 94.30 (0-7837-9679-X, 206040700005) Bks Demand.

Nuclear Arms Race. 2nd ed. Craig. 1989. teacher ed. 25.62 (0-07-013348-4) McGraw.

Nuclear Arms Race: Technology & Society. 2nd ed. P. P. Craig & J. A. Jungerman. 576p. (C). 1990. pap. 50.94 (0-07-013347-6) McGraw.

Nuclear Astrophysics. Ed. by W. Hillebrandt & R. Kuhfuss. (Lecture Notes in Physics Ser.: Vol.287). ix, 347p. 1987. 53.95 (0-387-18279-9) Spr-Verlag.

N

An Asterisk (*) at the beginning of an entry indicates that the title is appearing for the first time.

Nuclear Astrophysics. Ed. by M. Lozano et al. (Research Reports in Physics). (Illus.). 350p. 1989. pap. 66.00 (*0-387-50751-5*) Spr-Verlag.

Nuclear Astrophysics Summer School Proceedings: Nankai Institute of Mathematics 17-27 June 1991. G-Z He et al. Ed. by X-Q Li & Da-Hsuan Feng. 350p. 1993. text 98.00 (*981-02-0857-X*) World Scientific Pub.

Nuclear Asymptote: On Containing Nuclear Proliferation. Peter A. Wilson & Roger C. Molander. LC 93-28969. 1993. pap. 15.00 (*0-8330-1435-8*, MR-214-CC) Rand Corp.

Nuclear Attack - Civil Defense: Aspects of Civil Defense in the Nuclear Age. Royal United Services Institute Staff. (Illus.). 292p. 1983. 28.00 (*0-08-027041-7*, Pergamon Pr); pap. 13.95 (*0-08-027042-5*, Pergamon Pr) Elsevier.

*Nuclear Axis: Germany, Japan & the Atom Bomb Race, 1939-1945.** Philip Henshall. (Illus.). 256p. 2000. 32.95 (*0-7509-2293-1*) Sutton Publng.

Nuclear "Balance" in Europe: Status, Trends, Implications. Donald R. Cotter et al. (USSI Report Ser.: No. 83-1). (Illus.). 48p. (Orig.). 1983. pap. 5.00 (*0-913187-01-1*) U S Strat Inst.

Nuclear Beta Decays & the Neutrino: Proceedings of the International Symposium on Neutrino Mass & VTA Interactions in Particle & Nuclear Physics, Osaka Japan, June 11-13, 1986. Ed. by T. Kotani et al. 600p. 1986. text 124.00 (*9971-5-0164-3*) World Scientific Pub.

Nuclear, Biological, & Chemical Defense. 1991. lib. bdg. 250.00 (*0-8490-4062-0*) Gordon Pr.

Nuclear, Biological & Chemical Reconnaisance & Decontamination Operations. 1990. lib. bdg. 250.00 (*0-87700-890-6*) Revisionist Pr.

Nuclear, Biological, & Chemical Reconnaisance & Decontamination Operations. 1991. lib. bdg. 250.00 (*0-8490-4082-5*) Gordon Pr.

Nuclear, Biological & Chemical Warfare. L. W. McNaught. (Brassey's Battlefield Weapons Systems & Technology Ser.: Vol. 4). 60p. 1984. text 35.95 (*0-08-028328-4*, Pergamon Pr); pap. text 19.95 (*0-08-028329-2*, Pergamon Pr) Elsevier.

Nuclear, Biological, Chemical Contamination Avoidance. 1991. lib. bdg. 250.00 (*0-8490-4129-5*) Gordon Pr.

N

Nuclear Black Market: Global Organized Crime Project. Ed. by Frank Cilluffo et al. LC 96-20400. (CSIS Report Ser.). 49p. (C). 1996. pap. text 16.95 (*0-89206-287-8*) CSIS.

Nuclear Blackmail: The 1994 U. S. Democratic People's Republic of Korea Agreed Framework on North Korea's Nuclear Program. Victor Gilinsky. LC 97-5228. (Essays in Public Policy Ser.: No. 76). 1997. pap. 5.00 (*0-8179-5812-6*) Hoover Inst Pr.

Nuclear Blackmail & Nuclear Balance. Richard K. Betts. LC 87-13384. 240p. 1987. 36.95 (*0-8157-0936-6*); pap. 16.95 (*0-8157-0935-8*) Brookings.

*Nuclear Byproduct Material Risk Review: Results of Survey of NRC & Agreement State Materials Licensing & Inspection Personnel, Final Report.** D. Serig. 126p. 2000. per. 12.00 (*0-16-059231-3*) USGPO.

Nuclear California: An Investigative Report. Ronald V. Dellums et al. Ed. by David E. Kaplan. LC 82-1213. (Illus.). 144p. (Orig.). 1982. pap. 5.95 (*0-9607166-0-2*) Greenpeace-Ctr Invest Re.

Nuclear Cardiac Imaging: Equilibrium & Gated First Pass Radionuclide Angiocardiography. Frans J. Wackers et al. (C). 1992. text 500.00 incl. disk (*1-56815-013-X*) Mosby Inc.

Nuclear Cardiac Imaging: Principles & Applications. 2nd ed. Ami S. Iskandrian & Mario S. Verani. LC 95-31109. (Illus.). 464p. (C). 1996. text 180.00 (*0-8036-0071-2*) OUP.

Nuclear Cardiology. Ed. by Manuel D. Cerqueira. LC 93-31087. (Practical Cardiac Diagnosis Ser.). (Illus.). 280p. 1993. pap. 44.95 (*0-86542-248-6*) Blackwell Sci.

Nuclear Cardiology: State of the Art & Future Directions. 2nd ed. Zaret Beller. LC 98-33551. (Illus.). 668p. (C). (gr. 13). 1998. text 129.00 (*0-8151-1740-X*, 30422) Mosby Inc.

Nuclear Cardiology & Cardiac Magnetic Resonance. Ernst E. Van Der Wall. LC 92-15313. 285p. (C). 1992. text 185.00 (*0-7923-1780-7*) Kluwer Academic.

Nuclear Cardiology in Everyday Practice. Ed. by J. Candell-Riera & D. Ortega-Alcalde. LC 93-24826. (Developments in Cardiovascular Medicine Ser.: Vol. 146). 396p. (C). 1994. text 243.00 (*0-7923-2374-2*) Kluwer Academic.

Nuclear Cardiovascular Imaging: Current Clinical Practice. Ed. by Milton J. Guiberteau. (Illus.). 248p. 1989. text 105.00 (*0-443-08577-3*) Church.

Nuclear Carriers. Kyle Carter. (Seguridad Ser.). (Illus.). 24p. (J). (gr. k-4). 1989. lib. bdg. 10.95 (*0-86625-084-0*) Rourke Pubns.

Nuclear Carriers. Jon Rawlinson. (Sea Power Library). (Illus.). 48p. (J). (gr. 3-8). 1989. 13.95 (*0-685-58646-4*) Rourke Corp.

Nuclear Catholics & Other Essays. James M. Cameron. LC 89-28096. 277p. reprint ed. pap. 85.90 (*0-7837-3184-1*, 204278800006) Bks Demand.

*Nuclear Challenge.** Christoph Bluth. 184p. 2000. 69.95 (*1-85521-896-8*) Ashgate Pub Co.

Nuclear Chemical Engineering. 2nd ed. Manson Benedict et al. (Illus.). 1024p. (C). 1981. 116.25 (*0-07-004531-3*) McGraw.

Nuclear Chemistry: Theory & Applications. Ed. by G. Choppin & J. Ryberg. (Illus.). 1980. 294.00 (*0-08-023826-2*, Pergamon Pr) Elsevier.

Nuclear Chemistry: Theory & Applications. Ed. by Gregory R. Choppin & J. Ryberg. (Illus.). 1980. pap. 275.00 (*0-08-023823-8*, Pergamon Pr) Elsevier.

Nuclear Choices: A Citizen's Guide to Nuclear Technology. rev. ed. Richard Wolfson. LC 93-8494. (New Liberal Arts Ser.). 467p. 1993. pap. text 27.50 (*0-262-73108-8*) MIT Pr.

Nuclear Chromodynamics: Topical Conference on Nuclear Chromodynamics, Argonne National Lab., USA, May 19-21, 1988. Ed. by J-W. Qiu & D. Sivers. 312p. 1988. text 84.00 (*9971-5-0652-1*) World Scientific Pub.

Nuclear Chromodynamics, Quarks & Gluons in Particles & Nuclei: Proceedings of the Workshop on Nuclear Chromodynamics, Santa Barbara, California, August 12-23, 1985. Ed. by S. Brodsky & E. Moniz. 532p. 1986. pap. 52.00 (*9971-5-0056-6*); text 131.00 (*9971-5-0055-8*) World Scientific Pub.

*Nuclear Clustering.** Hisashi Horiuchi. (Illus.). 2000. 66.00 (*1-86094-212-1*) Imperial College.

Nuclear Coexistence: Rethinking U. S. Policy to Promote Stability in an Era of Proliferation. William C. Martel & William T. Pendley. 178p. (C). 1998. reprint ed. pap. text 35.00 (*0-7881-4663-7*) DIANE Pub.

Nuclear Coexistence: Rethinking United States Policy to Promote Stability in an Era of Proliferation. William C. Martel. 192p. 1994. per. 15.00 (*0-16-061362-0*) USGPO.

Nuclear Collective Dynamics: Proceedings of the 1982 International Summer School of Nuclear Physics, Poiana Brasov, Romania, Aug. 26-Sept. 7, 1983. Ed. by D. Bucurescu et al. 522p. 1983. 91.00 (*9971-950-69-3*); pap. 41.00 (*9971-950-73-1*) World Scientific Pub.

Nuclear Collective Motion & Nuclear Reaction Dynamics. Ed. by K. L. Kubo et al. 544p. (C). 1990. pap. 44.00 (*981-02-0415-9*); text 118.00 (*981-02-0327-6*) World Scientific Pub.

Nuclear Command & Control in NATO, Shaun Gregory. (Illus.). 224p. 1995. 50.00 (*0-08-041791-4*) Elsevier.

Nuclear Command & Control in NATO: Nuclear Weapons Operations & the Strategy of Flexible Response. Shaun R. Gregory. 256p. 1996. text 69.95 (*0-312-12914-9*) St Martin.

Nuclear Computerized Library for Assessing Reactor Reliability: A User's Guide, 3 vols., Set. 1990. lib. bdg. 955.75 (*0-8490-4006-X*) Gordon Pr.

Nuclear Condensed Matter Physics: Nuclear Methods & Applications. Gunter Schatz & Alois Weidinger. Tr. by John A. Gardner from GER. LC 95-4911.Tr. of Nukleare Festkorperphysik. 290p. 1996. 185.00 (*0-471-95479-9*) Wiley.

Nuclear Confrontation in Europe. Ed. by Jeffrey Boutwell et al. LC 85-14062. 247p. 1985. 59.95 (*0-86569-128-2*, Auburn Hse) Greenwood.

Nuclear Connection: A Reassessment of Nuclear Power & Nuclear Proliferation. Ed. by Jack N. Barkenbus et al. LC 84-26786. (Illus.). 295p. (C). 1985. 19.95 (*0-88702-204-9*) Washington Inst Pr.

Nuclear Contamination of Water Resources. Institution of Civil Engineers Staff. 268p. 1990. text 105.00 (*0-7277-1527-5*, Pub. by T Telford) RCH.

Nuclear Crisis Management: A Dangerous Illusion. Richard N. Lebow. LC 86-16767. (Cornell Studies in Security Affairs). 232p. 1987. 35.00 (*0-8014-1989-1*); pap. 14.95 (*0-8014-9531-8*) Cornell U Pr.

Nuclear Crisis Management: A Dangerous Illusion. Richard N. Lebow. LC 86-16767. (Cornell Studies in Security Affairs). 227p. reprint ed. pap. 70.40 (*0-608-20918-X*, 207201700003) Bks Demand.

Nuclear Criticality Safety: Theory & Practice. Ronald Allen Knief. 236p. 1985. pap. 43.00 (*0-89448-028-6*, 300020) Am Nuclear Soc.

Nuclear Criticism. Ken Ruthven. (Interpretations Ser.). 144p. (Orig.). 1993. pap. 19.95 (*0-522-84491-X*, Pub. by Melbourne Univ Pr) Paul & Co Pubs.

Nuclear Cytology in Relation to Development. Francesco D'Amato. LC 76-46045. (Developmental & Cell Biology Ser.: No. 6). 291p. reprint ed. pap. 83.00 (*0-608-15709-0*, 2031636) Bks Demand.

Nuclear Data Evaluation Methodology: Proceedings of the Symposium. Charles L. Dunford. 700p. 1993. text 178.00 (*981-02-1285-2*) World Scientific Pub.

Nuclear Data for Basic & Applied Science: Proceedings of the International Conference, Santa Fe, U. S. A., May 1985 - A Special Issue of the Journal Radiation Effects, 2 vols., Set. Ed. by P. G. Young et al. xxxviii, 1,744p. 1986. text 1021.00 (*0-677-21360-3*) Gordon & Breach.

*Nuclear Data for Neutron & Proton Radiotherapy & for Radiation Protection.** International Commission on Radiation Units & Measurements Staff. LC 99-57272. (Report Ser.). 2000. write for info. (*0-913394-62-9*) Intl Comm Rad Meas.

Nuclear Data for Reactors, Vol. 1. IAEA Staff. (Proceedings Ser.). (Illus.). 1702p. 1970. pap. 95.00 (*92-0-030070-7*, ISP259-1, Pub. by IAEA) Bernan Associates.

Nuclear Data for Reactors, Vol. 2. IAEA Staff. (Proceedings Ser.). (Illus.). 1702p. 1970. pap. 110.00 (*92-0-030170-3*, ISP259-2, Pub. by IAEA) Bernan Associates.

Nuclear Data for Science & Technology. Ed. by K. H. Bockhoff. 1983. text 389.50 (*90-277-1560-2*) Kluwer Academic.

Nuclear Data for Science & Technology: Proceedings of an International Conference Held at the Forschungszentrum Julich, FRG, 13-17 May 1991. Ed. by S. M. Qaim. (Research Reports in Physics). 1100p. 1992. 198.00 (*0-387-55100-X*) Spr-Verlag.

Nuclear Data Guide for Reactor: Neutron Metrology. J. H. Baard et al. (C). 1989. text 266.50 (*0-7923-0486-1*) Kluwer Academic.

Nuclear Debate: Deterrence & the Lapse of Faith. Robert W. Tucker. LC 85-14007. 1985. 29.95 (*0-8419-1038-3*); pap. 16.50 (*0-8419-1039-1*) Holmes & Meier.

Nuclear Decay Modes. Dorin N. Poenaru. LC 95-45782. (Fundamental & Applied Nuclear Physics Ser.). 577p. 1996. 353.00 (*0-7503-0338-7*) IOP Pub.

Nuclear Defense Weapon. T. J. Saber. Ed. & Illus. by Tom Scionti. 20p. (Orig.). 1992. reprint ed. 4.50 (*1-880537-50-8*) Dimension.

Nuclear Density Functional Theory. I. Z. Petkov & M. V. Stoitsov. (Studies in Nuclear Physics: No. 14). (Illus.). 376p. 1991. 79.00 (*0-19-851731-9*) OUP.

Nuclear Desalination of Sea Water: Proceedings of an International Symposium. Internatinal Atomic Energy Agency Staff. 557p. 1998. pap. 170.00 (*92-0-104097-0*, STI/PUB/1025, Pub. by IAEA) Bernan Associates.

Nuclear Designs: Great Britain, France, & China in the Global Governance of Nuclear Arms. Bruce D. Larkin. 354p. (C). 1996. text 39.95 (*1-56000-239-5*) Transaction Pubs.

Nuclear Deterrence: Ethics & Strategy. Ed. by Russell Hardin et al. LC 85-8423. viii, 404p. 1985. pap. text 16.00 (*0-226-31704-8*) U Ch Pr.

Nuclear Deterrence: Ethics & Strategy. Ed. by Russell Hardin et al. LC 85-8423. viii, 404p. 1985. lib. bdg. 36.00 (*0-226-31702-1*) U Ch Pr.

Nuclear Deterrence: Problems & Perspectives in the 1990s. 173p. 36.00 (*92-9045-084-3*, E.GV.93.0.16) UN.

Nuclear Deterrence & Moral Restraint. Ed. by Henry Shue. (Cambridge Studies in Philosophy & Public Policy). 448p. (C). 1989. text 85.00 (*0-521-38063-4*); pap. text 27.95 (*0-521-38967-4*) Cambridge U Pr.

Nuclear Deterrence in a Regional Context. Dean Wilkening et al. LC 94-36395. 90p. 1995. pap. text 15.00 (*0-8330-1596-6*, MR-500-A/AF) Rand Corp.

Nuclear Deterrence, Morality & Realism. John Finnis et al. (Illus.). 434p. 1988. pap. text 24.95 (*0-19-824791-5*) OUP.

Nuclear Deterrence Theory: The Search for Credibility. Robert Powell. (Illus.). 238p. (C). 1990. text 74.95 (*0-521-37527-4*) Cambridge U Pr.

Nuclear Dilemma: The Greatest Moral Problem of All Time. Theodore M. Hesburgh. (Eighth Morgenthau Memorial Lectures). 22p. 1989. pap. 4.00 (*0-87641-230-4*) Carnegie Ethics & Intl Affairs.

Nuclear Diplomacy & Crisis Management: An International Security Reader. Ed. by Sean M. Lynn-Jones et al. 364p. 1990. 36.00 (*0-262-12152-2*); pap. text 18.00 (*0-262-62078-2*) MIT Pr.

Nuclear Diplomacy & the Special Relationship: Britain's Deterrent & America, 1957-1962. Ian Clark. LC 93-30705. 470p. 1994. text 85.00 (*0-19-827370-3*, Clarendon Pr) OUP.

Nuclear Disarmament: How Much Have the Five Nuclear Powers Promised in the Non-Proliferation Treaty? George Bunn et al. (Global Security Issues Ser.). 32p. 1994. pap. text 10.00 (*1-884179-01-0*) Lawyers Alliance.

*Nuclear Disarmament: Obstacles to Banishing the Bomb.** Jozef Goldblat. 2000. text 55.00 (*1-86064-576-3*, Pub. by I B T) St Martin.

Nuclear Disarmament & Global Order. David Fischer et al. (SIPRI Pubns.). 270p. 1994. text 45.00 (*0-19-829155-8*) OUP.

Nuclear Disarmament & Non-Proliferation in Northeast Asia. LC 96-216397. (UNIDIR Research Papers: No. 33). 83p. pap. 15.00 (*92-9045-100-9*, E.GV.95.0.3) UN.

Nuclear Disarmament in International Law. Haralambos Athanasopulos. LC 99-53082. (Illus.). 237p. 2000. lib. bdg. 48.50 (*0-7864-0587-2*) McFarland & Co.

Nuclear Disaster at Chernobyl. Robin Cruise. Ed. by Liz Parker. (Take Ten Bks.). 46p. (YA). (gr. 6-12). 1993. pap. text 3.95 (*1-56254-099-8*) Saddleback Pubns.

*Nuclear Disaster at Chernobyl.** rev. ed. Robin Cruise. (Take Ten Ser.). (Illus.). 46p. (YA). (gr. 4-12). 1999. pap. 3.95 (*1-58659-022-7*) Artesian.

*Nuclear Disasters.** Rob Alcraft. LC 99-27879. (World's Worst Ser.). 1999. lib. bdg. write for info. (*1-57572-989-X*) Heinemann Lib.

Nuclear Disasters & the Built Environment: A Report to the Royal Institute of British Architects. Philip Steadman & Simon Hodgkinson. (Illus.). 134p. 1990. pap. text 110.00 (*0-408-50061-1*, Butterwrth Archit) Buttrwrth-Heinemann.

Nuclear Disengagement in Europe. Ed. by Sverre Lodgaard & Marek Thee. 272p. 1983. 63.00 (*0-85066-244-3*) Taylor & Francis.

Nuclear Disengagement in Europe. Stockholm International Peace Research Institute S. Ed. by Sverre Lodgaard & Marek Thee. 272p. 1983. 63.00 (*0-8002-3088-4*) Taylor & Francis.

Nuclear Dynamics & Nuclear Disassembly. Ed. by J. B. Natowitz. 552p. (C). 1989. text 151.00 (*9971-5-0945-8*) World Scientific Pub.

Nuclear Dynamics at Long & Short Distances: Proceedings of the First International Conference. Ed. by Anibal Gattone et al. LC 97-29362. 180p. 1997. pap. 48.00 (*981-02-3293-4*) World Scientific Pub.

Nuclear Dynamics in Phase Space. 400p. 1998. lib. bdg. 46.00 (*981-02-2664-0*) World Scientific Pub.

*Nuclear Dynamics in the Nucleonic Regime.** D. Durand. (Fundamental & Applied Nuclear Physics Ser.). 1999. 200.00 (*0-7503-0537-1*) IOP Pub.

Nuclear Dynamite: The Peaceful Nuclear Explosions Fiasco. Trevor Findlay. (Illus.). 350p. 1990. text 39.00 (*0-08-034436-4*, Pergamon Pr) Elsevier.

Nuclear-Electric Power in the Asia-Pacific Region: Proceedings of the Workshop Held in Honolulu, Hawaii, 23-28 January 1983. Ed. by D. J. Rose. 265p. 1985. pap. 61.00 (*0-08-031654-9*, Pergamon Pr) Elsevier.

Nuclear Electrodynamics. A. I. Akhiezer et al. Tr. by J. Gribkova. (Series in Nuclear & Particle Physics). (Illus.). 420p. 1993. write for info. (*3-540-54906-4*) Spr-Verlag.

Nuclear Electrodynamics. A. I. Akhiezer et al. Tr. by J. Gribkova from RUS. LC 92-43795. (Series in Nuclear & Particle Physics). (Illus.). 480p. 1994. 137.95 (*0-387-54906-4*) Spr-Verlag.

Nuclear Electronics. Paul W. Nicholson. LC 73-8196. 402p. reprint ed. 124.70 (*0-608-15236-6*, 202667700051) Bks Demand.

Nuclear Emergency - How to Protect Your Family from Nuclear Radiation, Fallout & Terrorism. Ken Larson. 144p. 1997. pap. 10.95 (*0-9642497-2-3*) Rhema Pubng.

Nuclear Emergency - Terrorism Response Plan. (Illus.). 72p. (Orig.). (C). 1994. pap. text 25.00 (*0-941375-83-8*) DIANE Pub.

Nuclear Emergency Data Management. NEA Staff. LC 98-145150. (Proceedings Ser.). 480p. 1998. pap. 79.00 (*92-64-16037-X*, 66-98-02-1-P, Pub. by Org for Econ) OECD.

Nuclear Employee Safety Concerns: Allegation System Offers Better Protection, but Important Issues Remain. Larry Horinko & Bob Sampson. (Illus.). 69p. (Orig.). (C). 1997. pap. text 30.00 (*0-7881-4634-3*) DIANE Pub.

Nuclear Endings: Stopping War on Time. Stephen J. Cimbala. LC 88-27441. 318p. 1989. 65.00 (*0-275-93165-X*, C3165, Praeger Pubs) Greenwood.

Nuclear Energy see Inventors & Inventions - Group 2

Nuclear Energy. Raymond L. Murray. LC 74-8685. 296p. 1975. text 28.00 (*0-685-04008-9*, Pergamon Pr); pap. text 16.50 (*0-685-04009-7*, Pergamon Pr) Elsevier.

*Nuclear Energy.** Pat Ward & Barb Ward. (Illus.). 64p. (YA). (gr. 5). 1999. pap. text 8.95 (*1-58037-087-X*, Pub. by M Twain Media) Carson-Dellos.

Nuclear Energy: A Sensible Alternative. Ed. by Karl O. Ott & Bernard I. Spnrad. 408p. 1985. 49.50 (*0-306-41441-4*, Plenum Trade) Perseus Pubng.

*Nuclear Energy: An Introduction to the Concepts, Systems & Applications of Nuclear Processes.** 5th ed. Raymond Murray. 400p. 2000. pap. text 59.95 (*0-7506-7136-X*, Newnes) Buttrwrth-Heinemann.

Nuclear Energy: In SI Metric Units. 2nd ed. Raymond L. Murray. 1980. text 52.00 (*0-08-024751-2*, Pergamon Pr); pap. text 22.00 (*0-08-024750-4*, Pergamon Pr) Elsevier.

Nuclear Energy: Principles, Practices & Prospects. David Bodansky. (Illus.). 416p. 1996. text 65.00 (*1-56396-244-6*) Am Inst Physics.

*Nuclear Energy: Promise or Peril?** C R Hill. LC 99-35359. 1999. 70.00 (*981-02-4011-2*) WSC Inst MA Studies.

Nuclear Energy: Salvation or Suicide? Ed. by Carol C. Collins. LC 84-5943. (Editorials on File Bk.). (Illus.). 255p. reprint ed. pap. 79.10 (*0-7837-5331-4*, 204507100005) Bks Demand.

Nuclear Energy - Nuclear Waste. Anne Galperin. (Earth at Risk Ser.). (Illus.). 128p. (YA). (gr. 5 up). 1992. lib. bdg. 19.95 (*0-7910-1585-8*) Chelsea Hse.

Nuclear Energy & Insurance. James Dow. 465p. (C). 1989. 525.00 (*0-948691-58-1*, Pub. by Witherby & Co) St Mut.

Nuclear Energy & Nuclear Weapon Proliferation. 462p. 1979. 45.00 (*0-85066-184-6*) Taylor & Francis.

Nuclear Energy & Public Safety: A Bibliography of Popular Literature, Part I. Michael Gabriel. (CPL Bibliographies Ser.: No. 73). 73p. 1982. 10.00 (*0-86602-073-X*, Sage Prdcls Pr) Sage.

Nuclear Energy & Security in the Former Soviet Union. Ed. by David R. Marples. LC 97-14352. (C). 1997. pap. 69.00 (*0-8133-9013-3*, Pub. by Westview) HarpC.

Nuclear Energy at War: The Implications of Israel's Reactor Strike. Bennett Ramberg. (CISA Working Papers: No. 34). 34p. (Orig.). 1992. pap. 15.00 (*0-86682-045-0*) Ctr Intl Relations.

Nuclear Energy Conversion. rev. ed. M. M. El-Wakil. LC 78-6169. 682p. 1982. 53.00 (*0-89448-015-4*) Am Nuclear Soc.

Nuclear Energy Data, 1998. NEA Staff. 48p. 1998. pap. 20.00 (*92-64-05762-5*, 66 98 11 3 P, Pub. by European Conference Ministers Transp) OECD.

*Nuclear Energy Data 1999.** NEA Staff. 48p. 1999. pap. 21.00 (*92-64-05856-7*, 66 1999 08 3 P, Pub. by Org for Econ) OECD.

Nuclear Energy Data 1997. NEA Staff. 52p. 1997. pap. 20.00 (*92-64-05520-7*, 66-97-05-3, Pub. by Org for Econ) OECD.

Nuclear Energy for Peaceful Uses: Status & Salient Issues for Regional Co-Operation. (Energy Resources Development Ser.: No. 29). 62p. 1986. 10.50 (*92-1-119405-9*, E.86.II.F.4) UN.

Nuclear Energy in Germany. Karl Winnacker & Wirtz. LC 79-88088. 356p. 1979. 50.00 (*0-89448-018-9*, 690003) Am Nuclear Soc.

Nuclear Energy Policy: A Reference Handbook. Earl R. Kruschke & Byron M. Jackson. LC 89-18132. (Contemporary World Issues Ser.). 246p. (YA). 1989. lib. bdg. 39.50 (*0-87436-238-5*) ABC-CLIO.

Nuclear Energy Progression, ser. vol. 4. Williams. (Progress in Nuclear Energy Ser.). 1980. pap. 43.00 (*0-08-026002-0*, no. 2, Pergamon Pr) Elsevier.

Nuclear Energy Simplified. 2nd ed. Frank L. Bouquet. (Illus.). 137p. 1994. 75.00 (*1-56216-219-5*); pap. 45.00 (*1-56216-220-9*) Systems Co.

Nuclear Energy Simplified: An Overview of the Nuclear Technology of Reactors, Space & Medicine. Frank L. Bouquet. (Illus.). 130p. (Orig.). 1992. pap. 40.00 (*1-56216-074-5*); text 70.00 (*1-56216-073-7*) Systems Co.

Nuclear Energy Synergetics: An Introduction to Conceptual Models of Integrated Nuclear Energy Systems. A. A. Harms & M. Heindler. LC 82-16175. 252p. 1982. 65.00 (*0-306-40951-8*, Plenum Trade) Perseus Pubng.

An Asterisk (*) at the beginning of an entry indicates that the title is appearing for the first time.

Nuclear Engineering: An Introduction, Set. K. Almenas & R. Lee. (Illus.). 568p. 1992. 118.95 incl. 5.25 hd (*0-387-53960-3*) Spr-Verlag.

Nuclear Engineering: Theory & Technology of Commercial Nuclear Power. 2nd ed. Ronald A. Knief. 650p. 1992. pap. 74.95 (*1-56032-089-3*) Hemisp Pub.

Nuclear Engineering: Theory & Technology of Commercial Nuclear Power. 2nd ed. Ronald A. Knief. 650p. 1992. 200.00 (*1-56032-088-5*) Hemisp Pub.

Nuclear Engineering Division, 1998, CFD & Thermal Hydraulic Analysis in Nuclear Reactors: Proceedings International Mechanical Engineering Congress & Exposition, Anaheim, CA. Ed. by Yassin A. Hassan et al. LC 99-183114. (NE Ser.: Vol. 22). 57p. 1998. 80.00 (*0-7918-1608-7*) ASME.

Nuclear Engineering Sourcebook: A Compilation of Documents for Nuclear Equipment Qualification. LC 92-10967. 1992. write for info. (*1-55937-206-0*) IEEE Standards.

Nuclear Environmental Chemical Analysis. E. H. Klehr & I. J. Tolgyessy. (Analytical Chemistry Ser.). 224p. 1987. text 68.95 (*0-470-20834-1*) P-H.

Nuclear EQ Sourcebook: A Compilation of Documents for Nuclear Equipment Qualification & Supplement Set. 1856p. per. 299.00 (*1-55937-361-X*, SP67-QOE-QOE) IEEE Standards.

Nuclear EQ Sourcebook, Supplement to. 416p. 1993. per. 89.00 (*1-55937-358-X*, SP59-QOE) IEEE Standards.

Nuclear Equation of State. 424p. 1996. lib. bdg. 58.00 (*981-02-2675-6*) World Scientific Pub.

Nuclear Equation of State Pt. A: Discovery of Nuclear Shock Waves & The EOS. Ed. by Walter Greiner & H. Stocker. (NATO ASI Ser.: Vol. 216A). (Illus.). 820p. (C). 1990. text 210.00 (*0-306-43486-5*, Kluwer Plenum) Kluwer Academic.

Nuclear Equation of State Pt. B: QCD & the Formation of the Quark-Gluon Plasma. Ed. by Walter Greiner & H. Stocker. LC 89-171006. (NATO ASI Ser.: Vol. 216B). (Illus.). 610p. (C). 1990. text 198.00 (*0-306-43487-3*, Kluwer Plenum) Kluwer Academic.

Nuclear Ethics. Joseph S. Nye, Jr. 130p. 1988. pap. 12.95 (*0-02-923091-8*) Free Pr.

Nuclear Evolution: Discovery of the Rainbow Body. Christopher Hills. Ed. by Norah Hills. LC 76-53180. (Illus.). 1010p. (Orig.). 1977. pap. 39.95 (*0-916438-09-0*) Dr Hills Technol.

Nuclear-Explosion Seismology. Howard C. Rodean. LC 73-170333. (AEC Critical Review Ser.). 168p. 1971. pap. 12.00 (*0-87079-288-1*, TID-25572); fiche 9.00 (*0-87079-289-X*, TID-25572) DOE.

Nuclear Facilities Siting. Compiled by American Society of Civil Engineers Staff. LC 82-73507. 64p. 1982. pap. 14.00 (*0-87262-344-0*) Am Soc Civil Eng.

Nuclear Fact Book. Ed. by A. M. Platt et al. xvi, 176p. 1985. text 82.00 (*3-7186-0273-3*) Gordon & Breach.

Nuclear Fallacies: How We Have Been Misguided since Hiroshima. Robert W. Malcolmson. 128p. 1985. pap. 24.95 (*0-7735-0586-5*, Pub. by McG-Queens Univ Pr) CUP Services.

Nuclear Fallacies: How We Have Been Misguided since Hiroshima. Robert W. Malcolmson. 128p. 1985. 60.00 (*0-7735-0585-7*, Pub. by McG-Queens Univ Pr) CUP Services.

Nuclear Fallacy: Dispelling the Myth of Nuclear Strategy. Morton H. Halperin. LC 86-32255. 192p. 1987. 24.95 (*0-88730-114-2*, HarpBusn) HarpInfo.

Nuclear Fallout. Douglas M. Baker. 1982. pap. 9.00 (*0-906006-68-6*, Pub. by Baker Pubns) New Leaf Dist.

Nuclear Fan. Louise O. Neaderland. (Illus.). 1984. 10.00 (*0-942561-02-3*) Bone Hollow.

Nuclear Fear: A History of Images. Spencer R. Weart. LC 87-25995. 544p. 1988. 49.95 (*0-674-62835-7*) HUP.

Nuclear Fear: A History of Images. Spencer R. Weart. 544p. 1989. reprint ed. pap. text 14.95 (*0-674-62836-5*) HUP.

Nuclear Fission: Reaction to the Discovery in 1939. Lawrence Badash et al. (IGCC Research Papers Ser.: No. 1). 58p. (Orig.). 1985. pap. text 3.50 (*0-934637-01-6*) U of CA Inst Global.

Nuclear Fission & Fission-Product Spectroscopy: Second International Workshop. Ed. by G. Fioni et al. LC 98-87501. (Conference Proceedings Ser.: Vol. 447). (Illus.). 475p. 1998. 130.00 (*1-56396-823-1*) Am Inst Physics.

Nuclear Fission & Heavy-Ion-Induced Reactions, Festschrift & Proceedings of the International Symposium on Nuclear Fission & Heavy-Ion-Induced Reactions, Vol. 11. W. U. Schroder. xxi, 521p. 1987. pap. text 209.00 (*3-7186-0366-7*) Gordon & Breach.

Nuclear Fission Process. Cyriel Wagemans. 528p. 1991. lib. bdg. 249.00 (*0-8493-5434-X*, QP790) CRC Pr.

Nuclear Fission Reactors. I. R. Cameron. LC 82-18128. 398p. 1982. 85.00 (*0-306-41073-7*, Plenum Trade) Perseus Pubng.

Nuclear Fission Reactors: Potential Role & Risk of Converters & Breeders. Gary C. Kessler. (Topics in Energy Ser.). (Illus.). 257p. 1983. 74.95 (*0-387-81713-1*) Spr-Verlag.

Nuclear Fission Safety, 1994-1998: Synopsis of the Research Projects, EUR 16980. 250p. 1996. pap. 45.00 (*92-827-8195-X*, CGNA-16980-ENC, Pub. by Comm Europ Commun) Bernan Associates.

Nuclear Fission Safety Programme Radiation Protection Research Action Final Report EUR 16769 GER/EN/FR, 3 vols. 1997. 270.00 (*92-827-7982-3*, CG-NA-16769-3Ac, Pub. by Comm Europ Commun) Bernan Associates.

Nuclear Forces in Europe: Enduring Dilemmas, Present Prospects. Leon V. Sigal. LC 83-45960. 181p. 1984. 29.95 (*0-8157-7904-6*); pap. 10.95 (*0-8157-7903-8*) Brookings.

Nuclear Free & Independent Pacific Movement: After Mururoa. Roy Smith. LC 97-148465. (Library of International Relations). (Illus.). 256p. 1997. text 59.50 (*1-86064-101-6*, Pub. by I B T) St Martin.

Nuclear Free Zones. Ed. by David Pitt & Gordon Thompson. 160p. 1987. lib. bdg. 55.00 (*0-7099-4076-9*, Pub. by C Helm) Routldge.

Nuclear Freeze Campaign: Rhetoric & Foreign Policy in the Telepolitical Age. J. Michael Hogan. LC 94-26660. (Rhetoric & Public Affairs Ser.). 1994. 39.95 (*0-87013-367-5*) Mich St U Pr.

Nuclear Freeze Controversy. Ed. by Keith B. Payne & Colin S. Gray. LC 84-20835. 194p. 1985. pap. text 17.50 (*0-8191-4365-0*); lib. bdg. 57.00 (*0-8191-4364-2*) U Pr of Amer.

Nuclear Fuel Cycle see Nuclear Power & Its Fuel Cycle

Nuclear Fuel Cycle see Nuclear Power Experience: Nuclear Safety

Nuclear Fuel Cycle see Nuclear Power & Its Fuel Cycle

Nuclear Fuel Cycle: Analysis & Management. 2nd ed. R. G. Cochran & Nicholas Tsoulfanidis. 392p. 1999. 58.00 (*0-89448-451-6*, 350015) Am Nuclear Soc.

Nuclear Fuel Cycle: From Ore to Waste. P. D. Wilson. (Illus.). 342p. (C). 1996. text 55.00 (*0-19-856540-2*) OUP.

Nuclear Fuel Cycle & Reactor Strategies: Adjusting to New Realities. International Atomic Energy Agency Staff. LC 98-153288. 311p. 1998. pap. 100.00 (*92-0-103797-X*, STI/PUB/1026, Pub. by IAEA) Bernan Associates.

Nuclear Fuel Cycle Information System: A Directory of Nuclear Fuel Cycle Facilities, 1996 Edition. IAEA Staff. 307p. 1996. pap. 100.00 (*92-0-101096-6*, STI/PUB/978, Pub. by IAEA) Bernan Associates.

Nuclear Fuel Fabrication. 2nd ed. C. Ganguly. 464p. 1989. text 245.00 (*0-87849-598-3*, Pub. by Trans T Pub) Enfield Pubs NH.

Nuclear Fuel Fabrication: Proceedings of European Nuclear Conference Paris, 1975. P. Zaleski & R. Sher. (Nuclear Energy Maturity Ser.: No. 7). 1976. 89.00 (*0-08-021128-3*, Pub. by Pergamon Repr) Franklin.

***Nuclear Fuel of Pressurized Water Reactors & Fast Reactors.** Ed. by H. C. Bailly et al. (Illus.). 660p. 1999. 253.00 (*1-898298-57-2*, Pub. by Intercept UK) Spr-Verlag.

Nuclear Fuel Quality Assurance. (Proceedings Ser.). (Illus.). 488p. 1976. pap. 85.00 (*92-0-050276-8*, ISP435, Pub. by IAEA) Bernan Associates.

Nuclear Fueled Plants see ASME Standard Number TWDPS-1: Recommended Practices for the Prevention of Water Damage to Steam Turbines Used for Electric Power Generation

Nuclear Fusion. H. R. Hulme. (Wykeham Science Ser.: No. 4). 164p. 1970. pap. 18.00 (*0-85109-050-8*) Taylor & Francis.

Nuclear Fusion & Plasma Physics. C. S. Liu & F. Wagner. 400p. 1995. text 106.00 (*981-02-2151-7*) World Scientific Pub.

Nuclear Fusion by Inertial Confinement. Guillermo Velaide. 768p. 1992. lib. bdg. 375.00 (*0-8493-6926-6*, QC791) CRC Pr.

Nuclear Future. Michael Mandelbaum. LC 82-74068. (Cornell Studies in Security Affairs). 131p. 1983. pap. 12.95 (*0-8014-9254-8*) Cornell U Pr.

Nuclear Geochemistry. Natalia A. Titaeva.Tr. of Iadernaia Geokhimiia. 460p. 1993. 99.95 (*0-685-67835-0*) CRC Pr.

Nuclear Geochemistry. Natalia A. Titaeva. Tr. by G. Egorov from RUS. LC 94-6352. (Advances in Science & Technology in the U. S. S. R. Ser.).Tr. of Iadernaia Geokhimiia. 304p. 1994. 99.95 (*0-8493-7545-2*) CRC Pr.

Nuclear Geophysics: Selected Papers on Applications of Nuclear Techniques in Minerals Exploration, Mining & Process Control. Ed. by C. G. Clayton. (Illus.). 479p. 1983. 55.00 (*0-08-029158-9*, 82-24570, Pergamon Pr) Elsevier.

Nuclear Geophysics & Its Applications. (Technical Report Ser.: No. 393). 200p. 1999. pap. 75.00 (*92-0-100699-3*, STI/DOC/393, Pub. by IAEA) Bernan Associates.

Nuclear Handbook for Medical Service Personnel. 1991. lib. bdg. 79.95 (*0-8490-4125-2*) Gordon Pr.

Nuclear Handbook for Medical Service Personnel. 1995. lib. bdg. 255.75 (*0-8490-6554-2*); lib. bdg. 256.75 (*0-8490-6629-8*) Gordon Pr.

Nuclear Health & Safety: More Can Be Done to Better Control Environmental Restoration Costs. 46p. pap. text 30.00 (*0-7881-4074-4*) DIANE Pub.

Nuclear Heartland: A Guide to the One Thousand Missile Silos of the United States. Nukewatch Staff. Ed. by Samuel H. Day, Jr. (Illus.). 96p. (Orig.). (C). 1988. pap. 10.00 (*0-942046-01-3*) Prog Found.

Nuclear Heat Transport. rev. ed. M. M. El-Wakil. LC 78-61691. 514p. 1981. 46.00 (*0-89448-014-6*) Am Nuclear Soc.

***Nuclear Hepatology: A Textbook of Hepatobiliary Diseases.** Gerbail Krishnamurthy & Shakuntala Krishnamurthy. LC 00-21831. (Illus.). 330p. 2000. 169.00 (*3-540-65917-X*) Spr-Verlag.

Nuclear Holocausts: Atomic War in Fiction, 1895-1984. Paul Brians. LC 86-10685. 410p. 1987. 29.50 (*0-87338-335-4*) Kent St U Pr.

Nuclear Holocausts: Atomic War in Fiction, 1895-1984. Paul Brians. LC 86-10685. 410p. reprint ed. pap. 127.10 (*0-608-10528-7*, 207114800009) Bks Demand.

Nuclear Hormone Receptors: Molecular Mechanisms, Cellular Functions Clinical Abnormalities. Ed. by Malcolm G. Parker. 404p. 1991. text 125.00 (*0-12-545072-9*) Acad Pr.

Nuclear Imaging in Clinical Cardiology. M. L. Simmons & Johan H. Reiber. (Developments in Cardiovascular Cardiology Ser.). 254p. 1984. text 174.50 (*0-89838-599-7*) Kluwer Academic.

Nuclear Imaging in Drug Discovery, Development, & Approval. Ed. by H. Donald Burns et al. LC 92-48930. x, 339p. 1992. 63.50 (*0-8176-3601-3*) Birkhauser.

Nuclear Imaging of the Chest. Yong W. Bahk et al. LC 97-29699. (Illus.). 320p. 1997. write for info. (*3-540-62766-9*) Spr-Verlag.

Nuclear Imperatives & Public Trust: Dealing with Radioactive Waste. Luther J. Carter. LC 87-4706. 473p. 1987. pap. 22.95 (*0-915707-47-0*) Resources Future.

Nuclear Issues in the South Pacific: Hearing Before the Committee on International Relations, U. S. House of Representatives. Ed. by Doug Bereuter. (Illus.). 152p. 1998. reprint ed. pap. text 30.00 (*0-7881-4227-5*) DIANE Pub.

Nuclear Landscapes. Peter Goin. LC 90-38591. (Creating the North American Landscape Ser.). (Illus.). 172p. 1991. pap. 32.50 (*0-8018-4078-3*) Johns Hopkins.

Nuclear Law Bulletin, 1997, No. 59. 100p. 1997. pap. 33.00 (*92-64-15394-2*, Pub. by Org for Econ) OECD.

Nuclear Law Bulletin, 1997 No. 59: Supplement: Romania - Law on the Safe Conduct of Nuclear Activities. 23p. 1997. pap. write for info. (*92-64-15571-6*, Pub. by Org for Econ) OECD.

***Nuclear Legacy: Students of Two Atomic Cities.** Maureen McQuerry & Tetyana Tetyana. LC 99-58585. 328p. 2000. boxed set 22.50 (*1-57477-087-X*) Battelle.

Nuclear Legislation: Analytical Study - Regulatory & Institutional Framework for Nuclear Activities, 1996. 168p. 1997. ring bd. 190.00 (*92-64-15499-X*, Pub. by Org for Econ) OECD.

Nuclear Legislation Analytical Study: Regulatory & Institutional Framework for Nuclear Activities. NEA Staff. (ENG & FRE.). 582p. 1995. 190.00 (*92-64-14586-9*, Pub. by Org for Econ) OECD.

Nuclear Lemons. 5th ed. James Riccio & Lisa Brooks. 75p. 1996. pap. 15.00 (*0-937188-58-1*) Pub Citizen.

Nuclear Level Densities: Proceedings of the OECD Meeting. Giuseppe Maino et al. 350p. 1992. text 95.00 (*981-02-1077-9*) World Scientific Pub.

Nuclear Localization of Growth Factors & of Monoclonal Antibodies. Ed. by Ewa M. Rakowicz-Szulczynska. LC 93-12471. 224p. 1993. lib. bdg. 179.00 (*0-8493-4713-0*, QP552) CRC Pr.

Nuclear Madness: What You Can Do! rev. ed. Helen Caldicott. LC 94-5016. 1994. pap. 10.95 (*0-393-31011-6*) Norton.

Nuclear Magnetic Double Resonance: Proceedings of the International School of Physics "Enrico Fermi," Course CXXIII, 13-21 October, 1992. Ed. by B. Maraviglia. LC 93-48564. (Enrico Fermi International School of Physics Ser.: Vol. 123). 518p. 1993. 259.25 (*0-444-81823-5*, North Holland) Elsevier.

Nuclear Magnetic Double Resonance. Principles & Applications in Solid State Physics. Incl. Factor Group Analysis. J. Remlinger. 1973. Vibrational Absorption of Electron & Hydrogen Centers in Tonic Crystals. Dieter Bauerle. 1973. (Tracts in Modern Physics Ser.: Vol. 68). (Illus.). 200p. 1973. 53.40 (*0-387-06341-2*) Spr-Verlag.

Nuclear Magnetic Resonan. Robin K. Harris. (C). 1993. pap. text 61.88 (*0-582-44653-8*, Pub. by Addison-Wesley) Longman.

Nuclear Magnetic Resonance. P. J. Hore. (Oxford Chemistry Primers Ser.: No. 32). (Illus.). 96p. 1995. pap. text 12.95 (*0-19-855682-9*) OUP.

Nuclear Magnetic Resonance. Ed. by H. F. Linskens et al. (Modern Methods of Plant Analysis Ser.: Vol. 2). (Illus.). 215p. 1986. 152.95 (*0-387-15910-X*) Spr-Verlag.

Nuclear Magnetic Resonance. Francis A. Rushworth & David P. Tunstall. LC 72-89713. xii, 254p. 1973. text 306.00 (*0-677-04820-3*) Gordon & Breach.

Nuclear Magnetic Resonance, No. 23. G. A. Webb. 522p. 1994. 293.00 (*0-85186-462-7*, R6462) CRC Pr.

Nuclear Magnetic Resonance, Pt. C. Ed. by John N. Abelson et al. (Methods in Enzymology Ser.: Vol. 239). (Illus.). 813p. 1994. text. write for info. (*0-12-182140-4*) Acad Pr.

Nuclear Magnetic Resonance, Vol. 10. Webb. 1990. 197.00 (*0-85186-332-9*) CRC Pr.

Nuclear Magnetic Resonance, Vol. 11. Webb. 1989. 208.00 (*0-85186-342-6*) CRC Pr.

Nuclear Magnetic Resonance, Vol. 12. Webb. 1989. 252.00 (*0-85186-352-3*) CRC Pr.

Nuclear Magnetic Resonance, Vol. 13. Webb. 1989. 219.00 (*0-85186-362-0*) CRC Pr.

Nuclear Magnetic Resonance, Vol. 17. Webb. 1988. 296.00 (*0-85186-402-3*) CRC Pr.

Nuclear Magnetic Resonance, Vol. 18. G. A. Webb. 570p. 1989. 296.00 (*0-85186-412-0*) CRC Pr.

Nuclear Magnetic Resonance, Vol. 19. Webb. 1990. 308.00 (*0-85186-422-8*) CRC Pr.

Nuclear Magnetic Resonance, Vol. 20. Webb. 1991. 384.00 (*0-85186-432-5*) CRC Pr.

Nuclear Magnetic Resonance, Vol. 21. Webb. 1992. 320.00 (*0-85186-442-2*) CRC Pr.

Nuclear Magnetic Resonance, Vol. 22. Webb. 1993. 273.00 (*0-85186-452-X*) CRC Pr.

Nuclear Magnetic Resonance, Vol. 24. Webb. 636p. 1995. 279.00 (*0-85404-302-0*) CRC Pr.

Nuclear Magnetic Resonance, Vol. 26. G. A. Webb. (Specialist Periodical Reports). xii, 604p. 1997. 407.00 (*0-85404-312-8*) Am Chemical.

Nuclear Magnetic Resonance, Vols. 1-8. Incl. Vol. 2. 1971-72 Literature. LC 72-78527. 1973. 38.00 (*0-85186-262-4*); Vol. 3. 1972-73 Literature. LC 72-78527. 1974. 43.00 (*0-85186-272-1*); Vol. 4. 1973-74 Literature. LC 72-78527. 1975. 45.00 (*0-85186-282-9*); Vol. 5. 1974-75 Literature. LC 72-78527. 1976. 52.00 (*0-85186-292-6*); Vol. 6. 1975-76 Literature. LC 72-78527. 1977. 54.00 (*0-85186-302-7*); Vol. 8. R. J. Abraham. LC 72-78527. 1979. 73.00 (*0-85186-322-1*); Vol. 1. 1970-71 Literature. LC 72-78527. 1972. 34.00 (*0-85186-252-7*); Vol. 7. 1976-77 Literature. LC 72-78527. 1978. 65.00 (*0-85186-312-4*); LC 72-78527. write for info. (*0-318-50475-8*) Am Chemical.

Nuclear Magnetic Resonance: Basic Principles. Atta-ur-Rahman. (Illus.). 260p. 1986. 89.00 (*0-387-96243-3*) Spr-Verlag.

Nuclear Magnetic Resonance: Concepts & Methods. D. Canet. LC 95-39900. 270p. 1996. pap. 79.95 (*0-471-96145-0*) Wiley.

Nuclear Magnetic Resonance Pt. A: Spectral Techniques & Dynamics. Ed. by John N. Abelson et al. (Methods in Enzymology Ser.: Vol. 176). 530p. 1989. text 125.00 (*0-12-182077-7*) Acad Pr.

Nuclear Magnetic Resonance Pt. B: Structure & Mechanism. Ed. by Norman J. Oppenheimer et al. (Methods in Enzymology Ser.: Vol. 177). 550p. 1989. text 125.00 (*0-12-182078-5*) Acad Pr.

Nuclear Magnetic Resonance & Relaxation. Brian Cowan. LC 96-46614. 457p. 1997. text 99.95 (*0-521-30393-1*) Cambridge U Pr.

Nuclear Magnetic Resonance Data Subvolume B: Chemical Shifts & Coupling Constants for Fluorine-19, Nitrogen-15, Vol. III/35. Ed. by R. R. Gupta & M. D. Lechner. (Numerical Data & Functional Relationships in Science & Technology Ser.). vii, 242p. 1998. 1348.00 (*3-540-63275-1*) Spr-Verlag.

Nuclear Magnetic Resonance in Agriculture. Ed. by Philip E. Pfeffer & Walter V. Gerasimowicz. 400p. 1989. lib. bdg. 259.00 (*0-8493-6864-2*, S540) CRC Pr.

Nuclear Magnetic Resonance in Biology & Medicine: A Special Issue of the Journal Life Chemistry Reports, Vol. 1, Part 4. Jack Cohen et al. (Life Chemistry Reports: Vol. 1, No. 4). ii, 176p. 1983. pap. text 171.00 (*3-7186-0170-2*) Gordon & Breach.

Nuclear Magnetic Resonance in Modern Technology: Proceedings of the NATO Advanced Study Institute, Sarigerme Park (Dalaman), Turkey, August 16-September 4, 1992. Ed. by Gary E. Maciel. (NATO ASI, Series C, Mathematical & Physical Sciences: Vol. 447). 620p. (C). 1995. text 374.00 (*0-7923-3167-2*) Kluwer Academic.

N

Nuclear Magnetic Resonance in Solid Polymers. Vincent J. McBrierty & Kenneth J. Packer. LC 92-45158. (Solid State Science Ser.). (Illus.). 370p. (C). 1993. text 99.95 (*0-521-30140-8*) Cambridge U Pr.

Nuclear Magnetic Resonance of Liquid Crystals. James W. Emsley. 1984. text 264.50 (*90-277-1878-4*) Kluwer Academic.

Nuclear Magnetic Resonance of Liquid Crystals. 2nd ed. Ronald Y. Dong. LC 97-10095. (Partially Ordered Systems Ser.). (Illus.). 328p. 1997. 69.95 (*0-387-98230-2*) Spr-Verlag.

Nuclear Magnetic Resonance of Liquid Crystals: Partially Ordered Systems. Ronald Y. Dong. LC 93-5261. 1993. 64.95 (*0-387-94121-5*) Spr-Verlag.

Nuclear Magnetic Resonance of Paramagnetic Macromolecules. Ed. by Gerd N. La Mar. LC 94-48061. (NATO ASI Ser.: Series C, Mathematical & Physical Sciences: Vol. 457). 1995. text 213.50 (*0-7923-3348-9*) Kluwer Academic.

Nuclear Magnetic Resonance Probes of Molecular Dynamics. Ed. by Robert Tycko. LC 94-9737. (Understanding Chemical Reactivity Ser.). 568p. (C). 1994. lib. bdg. write for info. (*0-7923-2795-0*) Kluwer Academic.

Nuclear Magnetic Resonance Spectroscopy, 3 vols., Set. Ed. by Pal Sohar. 312p. 1983. 373.00 (*0-8493-5631-8*, QD272, CRC Reprint) Franklin.

Nuclear Magnetic Resonance Spectroscopy, Vol. I. Pal Sohar. LC 82-9524. 312p. 1983. 171.00 (*0-8493-5632-6*) CRC Pr.

Nuclear Magnetic Resonance Spectroscopy, Vol. II. Ed. by Pal Sohar. 360p. 1983. 197.00 (*0-8493-5633-4*, QD272, CRC Reprint) Franklin.

Nuclear Magnetic Resonance Spectroscopy, Vol. III. Ed. by Pal Sohar. 368p. 1984. 202.00 (*0-8493-5634-2*, QD272, CRC Reprint) Franklin.

Nuclear Magnetic Resonance Spectroscopy in Environment Chemistry. Ed. by Mark A. Nanny et al. LC 95-47215. (Topics in Enviornmental Chemistry). (Illus.). 344p. 1997. text 70.00 (*0-19-509751-3*) OUP.

Nuclear Magnetic Resonance Spectroscopy of Cement-Based Materials. Ed. by Pierre Colombet et al. LC 97-43419. (Illus.). 300p. 1997. 129.00 (*3-540-63134-8*) Spr-Verlag.

Nuclear Magnetic Shieldings & Molecular Structure: Proceedings of the NATO ARW on "The Calculation of NMR Shielding Constants & Their Use in the Geometric & Electronic Structures of Molecules & Solids" College Park, MD, U. S. A. July 20-24, 1992. Ed. by John A. Tossell. LC 92-43816. (NATO Advanced Science Institutes Series C: Mathematical & Physical Sciences: No. 386). 600p. (C). 1993. text 294.00 (*0-7923-2119-7*) Kluwer Academic.

Nuclear Magnresonance. Alberte Pullman. (The Jerusalem Symposia on Quantum Chemistry & Biochemistry Ser.). 1978. text 184.00 (*90-277-0932-7*) Kluwer Academic.

Nuclear Materials: Accountability Management Safeguards. James E. Lovett. LC 74-78611. (ANS Monographs). 310p. 1974. 32.00 (*0-89448-001-4*, 300007) Am Nuclear Soc.

Nuclear Materials: Plutonium Processing in the Nuclear Weapons Complex. (Illus.). 37p. (Orig.). (C). 1993. pap. text 20.00 (*1-56806-568-X*) DIANE Pub.

Nuclear Materials Management. (Proceedings Ser.). (Illus.). 888p. 1966. 95.00 (*92-0-050066-8*, ISP110, Pub. by IAEA) Bernan Associates.

An Asterisk (*) at the beginning of an entry indicates that the title is appearing for the first time.

*Nuclear Materials Safety Management. L. J. Jardine & Mikhail M. Moshkov. LC 99-43054. (NATO ASI Ser.). 1999. write for info. (0-7923-5890-2) Kluwer Academic.

Nuclear Materials Safety Management. K. L. Peddicord et al. LC 98-26191. (NATO Science Ser.). 378p. 1998. write for info. (0-7923-5191-6) Kluwer Academic.

Nuclear Matrix: Structural & Functional Organization, Vols. 162A & 162B. Ed. by Ronald Berezney & Kwang W. Jeon. LC 97-135683. (Illus.). 1047p. 1997. pap. text 69.00 (0-12-384620-X) Morgan Kaufmann.

Nuclear Matrix & Spatial Organization of Chromosomal DNA Domains. Sergey V. Razin. LC 96-29884. (Molecular Biology Intelligence Unit Ser.). 198p. 1997. 99.00 (1-57059-425-2) Landes Bioscience.

Nuclear Matter & Heavy Ion Collisions. Ed. by M. Soyeur et al. LC 89-22901. (NATO ASI Series B, Physics: Vol. 205). (Illus.). 511p. 1989. 135.00 (0-306-43372-9, Plenum Trade) Perseus Pubng.

Nuclear Matter in Different Phases & Transitions: Proceedings of the Workshop Nuclear Matter in Different Phases & Transitions, March 31-april 10, 1998, Les Houches, France. Workshop Nuclear Matter in Different Phases and Transitions et al. LC 99-18971. (Fundamental Theories of Physics Ser.). 1999. write for info. (0-7923-5660-8) Kluwer Academic.

Nuclear Measurements in Industry. Sandor Rozsa. 310p. (C). 1989. 150.00 (963-05-5219-1, Pub. by Akade Kiado) St Mut.

Nuclear Medical Physics, 3 vols., Set. Ed. by Lawrence E. Williams. 1987. 357.00 (0-8493-4677-0, R895, CRC Reprint) Franklin.

Nuclear Medical Physics, 3 vols., Vol. I. Ed. by Lawrence E. Williams. 256p. 1987. write for info. (0-318-62590-3, CRC Reprint) Franklin.

Nuclear Medical Physics, Vol. 1. L. Williams. LC 87-10262. 256p. 1987. reprint ed. 130.00 (0-8493-4678-9, CRC Reprint) Franklin.

Nuclear Medical Physics, 3 vols., Vol. II. Ed. by Lawrence E. Williams. 192p. 1987. write for info. (0-318-62591-1, CRC Reprint) Franklin.

Nuclear Medical Physics, Vol. 2. L. Williams. LC 87-10262. 200p. 1987. reprint ed. 116.00 (0-8493-4679-7, CRC Reprint) Franklin.

Nuclear Medical Physics, 3 vols., Vol. III. Ed. by Lawrence E. Williams. 224p. 1987. write for info. (0-318-62592-X, CRC Reprint) Franklin.

Nuclear Medical Physics, Vol. 3. L. Williams. LC 87-10262. 192p. 1987. reprint ed. 112.00 (0-8493-4680-0, CRC Reprint) Franklin.

Nuclear Medicine see Handbook of Nuclear Medicine

Nuclear Medicine. Wendy B. Murphy & Jack Murphy. Ed. by Dale C. Garell & Solomon H. Snyder. (Encyclopedia of Health Ser.). (Illus.). 116p. (YA). (gr. 7 up). 1994. lib. bdg. 19.95 (0-7910-0070-2) Chelsea Hse.

Nuclear Medicine: Clinical & Technological Bases. J. T. Andrews et al. LC 91-46493. 241p. reprint ed. pap. 74.80 (0-608-08654-1, 206917700003) Bks Demand.

Nuclear Medicine: Diagnosis & Therapy. Ed. by John C. Harbert et al. LC 95-20599. (Illus.). 1200p. (Orig.). 1995. text 199.00 (0-86577-570-2) Thieme Med Pubs.

Nuclear Medicine: Factors Influencing the Choice & Use of Radionuclides in Diagnosis & Therapy. LC 81-84121. (Report Ser.: No. 70). 175p. 1982. 45.00 (0-913392-57-X) NCRP Pubns.

Nuclear Medicine: Principles & Practice, 2 Vols. Mark A. Boles et al. Ed. by Robert E. Henkin. (Illus.). 1852p. (C). (gr. 13). 1995. text 309.00 (0-8016-7701-7, 07701) Mosby Inc.

Nuclear Medicine: Quantitative Procedures. Heinz W. Wahner. 1983. 49.50 (0-316-91748-6, Little Brwn Med Div) Lppncott W & W.

*Nuclear Medicine: Science & Safety. Alan C. Perkins. 192p. 2000. 49.00 (0-86196-605-8, Pub. by John Libby) Buttrwrth-Heinemann.

Nuclear Medicine: Self-Study Program 2: Instrumentation. Peter T. Kirchner & Barry A. Siegel. LC 95-48204. 70p. (Orig.). 1996. pap. 63.00 (0-932004-44-X) Soc Nuclear Med.

Nuclear Medicine: Teaching File. Habibian. LC 98-45018. 912p. 1999. 179.00 (0-683-30122-5) Lppncott W & W.

Nuclear Medicine: Technology & Techniques. 4th ed. Donald R. Bernier et al. LC 97-6999. (Illus.). 544p. (C). (gr. 13). 1997. text 91.00 (0-8151-1991-7, 30346) Mosby Inc.

Nuclear Medicine: The Requisites. 2nd ed. James H. Thrall. (Radiology Requisites Ser.). 415p. 2000. text. write for info. (0-323-00537-3) Mosby Inc.

Nuclear Medicine: Therapy. Alan C. Perkins & D. M. Lewis. 200p. 2001. 49.00 (0-86196-570-1, Pub. by John Libby) Buttrwrth-Heinemann.

Nuclear Medicine Vol. IV, Unit 1: Self-Study Program 3: Oncology Overview & Monitoring Cancer Therapy. Thomas P. Haynie et al. LC 97-153510. (Illus.). 50p. (Orig.). 1997. pap. 15.00 (0-932004-51-2) Soc Nuclear Med.

Nuclear Medicine--The Requisites. James H. Thrall & Harvey A. Ziessman. (Illus.). 384p. (C). (gr. 13). 1994. text 79.00 (0-8016-6674-0, 06674) Mosby Inc.

Nuclear Medicine & Biology Advances: Proceedings of the Third World Congress on Nuclear Medicine & Biology, August 29 - September 2, 1982, Paris, France, 7 vols. Ed. by C. Raynaud. 3685p. 1983. 1672.00 (0-08-026405-0, Pub. by Pergamon Repr) Franklin.

Nuclear Medicine & Lung Disease. J. L. Baulieu et al. (Illus.). xii, 124p. 1993. 167.00 (0-387-59605-4) Spr-Verlag.

Nuclear Medicine Annual, 1980. fac. ed. Ed. by Leonard M. Freeman. LC 80-645231. (Illus.). 440p. 1980. pap. 136.40 (0-7837-7250-5, 204705500005) Bks Demand.

Nuclear Medicine Annual, 1982. Ed. by Leonard M. Freeman. LC 80-645231. (Illus.). 420p. 1982. reprint ed. pap. 130.20 (0-7837-9511-4, 206026000005) Bks Demand.

Nuclear Medicine Annual, 1983. Ed. by Leonard M. Freeman. LC 80-645231. (Illus.). 407p. 1983. reprint ed. pap. 126.20 (0-7837-9512-2, 206026100005) Bks Demand.

Nuclear Medicine Annual, 1984. Ed. by Leonard M. Freeman. LC 80-645231. (Illus.). 360p. 1984. reprint ed. pap. 111.60 (0-7837-9513-0, 206026200005) Bks Demand.

Nuclear Medicine Annual, 1985. Ed. by Leonard M. Freeman & Heidi S. Weissman. LC 80-645231. (Illus.). 362p. 1985. reprint ed. pap. 112.30 (0-7837-9514-9, 206026300005) Bks Demand.

Nuclear Medicine Annual, 1986. Ed. by Leonard M. Freeman & Heide S. Weissmann. LC 80-645231. 317p. 1986. reprint ed. pap. 98.30 (0-608-00395-6, 206110900007) Bks Demand.

Nuclear Medicine Annual, 1988. Nuclear Medicine Annual Staff. Ed. by Leonard M. Freeman & Heidi S. Weissmann. LC 80-645231. 352p. 1988. reprint ed. pap. 109.20 (0-608-04720-1, 206544100004) Bks Demand.

Nuclear Medicine Annual, 1991. Ed. by Leonard M. Freeman. LC 80-645231. 238p. 1991. reprint ed. pap. 73.80 (0-608-05816-5, 205978100007) Bks Demand.

Nuclear Medicine Annual, 1993. Ed. by Leonard M. Freeman. LC 80-645231. 281p. 1993. reprint ed. pap. 87.20 (0-608-05829-7, 205979400007) Bks Demand.

Nuclear Medicine Annual, 1994. Nuclear Medicine Annual Staff. Ed. by Leonard M. Freeman. LC 80-645231. 304p. 1994. reprint ed. pap. 94.30 (0-608-04729-5, 206545000004) Bks Demand.

Nuclear Medicine Annual 1995. Nuclear Medicine Annual Staff. Ed. by Leonard M. Freeman. LC 80-645231. (Illus.). 298p. reprint ed. pap. 92.40 (0-608-09643-1, 205441900001) Bks Demand.

Nuclear Medicine Annual 1996. Nuclear Medicine Annual Staff. Ed. by Leonard M. Freeman. LC 80-645231. 304p. reprint ed. pap. 94.30 (0-608-09736-5, 206989900007) Bks Demand.

Nuclear Medicine Annual, 1996, Vol. 199. Leonard Freeman. 304p. 1996. text 115.00 (0-397-51774-2) Lppncott W & W.

Nuclear Medicine Annual, 1995, Vol. 199. Ed. by Leonard M. Freeman. (Illus.). 304p. 1995. text 112.00 (0-7817-0285-2) Lppncott W & W.

Nuclear Medicine Annual, 1997, Vol. 199. Leonard M. Freeman. (Illus.). 300p. 1997. text 115.00 (0-397-58464-4) Lppncott W & W.

Nuclear Medicine Annual 1998, Vol. 199. Leonard M. Freeman. 300p. 1998. text 112.00 (0-7817-1608-X) Lppncott W & W.

Nuclear Medicine Annual, 1999. Leonard M. Freeman. 368p. 112.00 (0-7817-1961-5) Lppncott W & W.

Nuclear Medicine Annual, 2000. Leonard M. Freeman. 288p. text 112.00 (0-7817-2573-9) Lppncott W & W.

Nuclear Medicine Board Review: Questions & Answers for Self-Assessment. C. Richard Goldfarb. LC 97-41323. 1997. write for info. (3-13-107871-5) Thieme Med Pubs.

Nuclear Medicine Board Review: Questions & Answers for Self-Assessment. Richard Goldfarb et al. LC 97-41323. 176p. 1997. pap. 19.95 (0-86577-703-9) Thieme Med Pubs.

Nuclear Medicine for Technicians. Robert C. Lange. LC 72-95732. 180p. reprint ed. pap. 55.80 (0-608-12353-6, 202426600036) Bks Demand.

Nuclear Medicine Handbook for Achieving Compliance with NRC Regulations. Katherine M. Elliott et al. LC 97-9525. 159p. 1997. pap. text 40.00 (0-932004-50-4) Soc Nuclear Med.

Nuclear Medicine Imaging. Owens. 1999. text. write for info. (0-7216-6089-4, W B Saunders Co) Harcrt Hlth Sci Grp.

Nuclear Medicine in Clinical Diagnosis & Treatment, 2 vols. Ed. by I. P. Murray & P. J. Ell. LC 94-34613. (Illus.). 1388p. 1995. text 270.00 (0-443-04710-3) Church.

*Nuclear Medicine in Clinical Diagnosis & Treatment. 2nd ed. I. P. Murray & P. J. Ell. 1999. 495.00 (0-443-05861-X) Church.

Nuclear Medicine in Clinical Practice: 100 Self-Assessment Case Studies. P. Ryan et al. LC 97-67752. (Illus.). 224p. 1997. pap. text 29.95 (0-412-45830-6, Pub. by E A) OUP.

Nuclear Medicine in Clinical Urology & Nephrology. W. Newlon Tauxe & Eva V. Dobovsky. (Illus.). 358p. (C). 1992. pap. text 110.00 (0-8385-6983-8, A6983-9, Apple Lange Med) McGraw.

Nuclear Medicine in Gastroenterology. Ed. by Hans J. Biersack & Peter H. Cox. (Developments in Nuclear Medicine Ser.). 264p. 1991. text 180.50 (0-7923-1074-8) Kluwer Academic.

Nuclear Medicine in Oncology. Steven M. Larson & William Kaplan. (Illus.). 500p. 1997. text 135.00 (0-397-51375-5) Lppncott W & W.

Nuclear Medicine in Pharmaceutical Research. A. C. Perkins. 1999. 99.00 (0-7484-0688-3) Taylor & Francis.

Nuclear Medicine Physics: The Basics. 5th ed. Ramesh Chandra. LC 97-15681. (Illus.). 240p. 1998. pap. 39.00 (0-683-30092-X) Lppncott W & W.

Nuclear Medicine Science & Safety. Perkins. 200p. 49.00 (0-86196-470-5, Pub. by J Libbey Med) Bks Intl VA.

Nuclear Medicine Self-Study Program: Nuclear Medicine Oncology: PET Tumor Imaging, 8 vols. Sudha Challa & Carl K. Hoh. Ed. by Thomas P. Haynie. LC 99-34619. 1999. write for info. (0-932004-62-8, Pub. by Soc Nuclear Med) Matthews Medical Bk Co.

Nuclear Medicine Self-Study Program, Cardiology Vol. III, Unit 1: Physical & Technical Aspects of Nuclear Cardiology. Elias H. Botvinick et al. LC 97-25005. (Nuclear Medicine Self-Study Program III). (Illus.). 96p. 1997. pap. 35.00 (0-932004-52-0) Soc Nuclear Med.

Nuclear Medicine: Self-Study Program IV: Oncology. Patrice K. Rehm. LC 97-41360. (Conventional Tumor Imaging Ser.: No. 2). (Illus.). 1997. pap. text 35.00 (0-932004-53-9) Soc Nuclear Med.

*Nuclear Medicine Self-Study Program Oncology, Vol. IV. Nabi H. Abdel. LC 98-49229. (Nuclear Medicine Self-Study Program IV Ser.: Unit 3). 49p. 1999. pap. 20.00 (0-932004-61-X) Soc Nuclear Med.

*Nuclear Medicine Technology: Procedures & Quick Reference. Pete Shackett. LC 99-52131. 1999. write for info. (0-7817-1981-X) Lppncott W & W.

Nuclear Medicine Technology Review. Sheila D. Rosenfeld & Susan A. White. LC 76-57458. (Illus.). 264p. reprint ed. pap. 81.90 (0-8357-7601-8, 205692300096) Bks Demand.

Nuclear Meditations. Cathy McFann. (Fastbook 1985 Ser.). 20p. 1985. 6.00 (0-911051-16-3) Plain View.

Nuclear Mentalities. Heuser. LC 97-45487. 277p. 1998. text 69.95 (0-312-21321-2) St Martin.

Nuclear Mentality: A Psychosocial Analysis of the Arms Race. Lynn Barnett. Ed. by Ian Lee. 192p. (C). pap. 21.00 (0-7453-0393-5, Pub. by Pluto GBR) Stylus Pub VA.

Nuclear Methods & Nuclear Equations of State. M. Baldo. LC 99-30643. 600p. 1997. text 109.00 (981-02-2165-7) World Scientific Pub.

Nuclear Methods for Transmutation of Nuclear Waste: Problems, Perspectives, Cooperative Research. LC 97-140856. 250p. 1996. 41.00 (981-02-3011-7) World Scientific Pub.

Nuclear Methods in Mineralogy & Geology: Techniques & Applications. Ed. by Attila Vertes et al. LC 98-6343. (Illus.). 570p. (C). 1998. text 135.00 (0-306-45832-2, Kluwer Plenum) Kluwer Academic.

Nuclear Methods in Science & Technology. Iu M. Tsipenluk & David A. Bradley. LC 97-40151. (Fundamental & Applied Nuclear Physics Ser.). 1997. 180.00 (0-7503-0422-7) IOP Pub.

Nuclear Methods of Dating. Ed. by Etienne Roth & Bernard Poty. (C). 1990. text 567.00 (0-7923-0188-9) Kluwer Academic.

Nuclear Middle East: Infrastructure, Likely Military Postures & Prospects for Strategic Stability. Paul Jabber. (CISA Working Papers: No. 6). 47p. (Orig.). 1977. pap. 15.00 (0-86682-005-1) Ctr Intl Relations.

Nuclear Missiles & a Justification for a Crazy Life. Bob Madden. 170p. (Orig.). 1982. pap. 2.50 (0-9608256-0-6) R Madden.

Nuclear Models. Walter Greiner & J. A. Maruhn. LC 95-46048. (Illus.). 375p. 1996. reprint ed. 59.95 (3-540-59180-X) Spr-Verlag.

Nuclear Molecular. Walter Greiner et al. 496p. 1995. text 86.00 (981-02-1723-4) World Scientific Pub.

*Nuclear Monopoly. George H. Quester. 234p. 2000. 44.95 (0-7658-0022-5) Transaction Pubs.

*Nuclear Muse: Literature, Physics & the First Atomic Bombs. John Canaday. LC 99-52229. (Illus.). 2000. pap. 22.95 (0-299-16854-9) U of Wis Pr.

Nuclear Nativity: Rituals of Renewal & Empowerment in the Marshall Islands. Laurence M. Carucci. LC 96-30262. 210p. (C). 1997. lib. bdg. 32.00 (0-87580-217-6) N Ill U Pr.

Nuclear Negotiations: Reassessing Arms Control Goals in U. S.-Soviet Relations. Alan F. Neidle. LC 82-83390. (Tom Slick World Peace Ser.). 204p. 1982. pap. 5.00 (0-89940-004-3) LBJ Sch Pub Aff.

Nuclear Neighborhoods. Ed. by J. Richard Eiser. LC 96-203314. 220p. 1995. text 80.00 (0-85989-455-X, Pub. by Univ Exeter Pr); pap. text 39.95 (0-85989-456-8, Pub. by Univ Exeter Pr) Northwestern U Pr.

Nuclear Nightmare. Don Pendleton. LC 95-22341. (Stony Man Ser.). 349p. 1995. per. 4.99 (0-373-61903-0, 1-61903-0, Wrldwide Lib) Harlequin Bks.

Nuclear Non-Proliferation: A Guide to the Debate. Jozef Goldblat. 100p. 1985. 45.00 (0-85066-310-5) Taylor & Francis.

Nuclear Non-Proliferation: Towards a Universal NPT Regime. D. Shyam Babu. 1993. 27.50 (81-220-0292-7, Pub. by Konark Pubs Pvt Ltd) Advent Bks Div.

Nuclear Non-Proliferation & the Non-Proliferation Treaty. Ed. by M. Fry et al. (Illus.). 216p. 1990. 61.00 (0-387-51756-1) Spr-Verlag.

*Nuclear Non-Proliferation & the Problem of Threshold States. Shibashis Chatterjee. LC 99-936951. 1999. 17.50 (81-85195-89-7, Pub. by Minerva Assocs) S Asia.

Nuclear Non-Proliferation in India & Pakistan: South Asian Perspectives. Ed. by P. R. Chari et al. LC 96-904933. 1996. 29.00 (81-7304-153-9, Pub. by Manohar) S Asia.

Nuclear Non-Proliferation Treaty. Ed. by Ian Bellany et al. 142p. 1985. 35.00 (0-7146-3250-3, Pub. by F Cass Pubs) Intl Spec Bk.

Nuclear Nonproliferation: A Primer. Gary T. Gardner. LC 93-23571. 146p. (C). 1994. pap. text 13.95 (1-55587-489-4) L Rienner.

Nuclear Nonproliferation: Export Licensing Procedures for Dual-Use Items Need to Be Strengthened. (Illus.). 69p. (Orig.). (C). 1995. pap. text 25.00 (0-7881-1727-0) DIANE Pub.

Nuclear Nonproliferation: Implementation of the U. S. - North Korean Agreed Framework on Nuclear Issues. Gene Aloise. (Illus.). 66p. (C). 1998. pap. text 20.00 (0-7881-3858-8) DIANE Pub.

Nuclear Nonproliferation: Implications of the U. S./North Korean Agreement on Nuclear Issues. (Illus.). 63p. (Orig.). (C). 1997. pap. text 30.00 (0-7881-3817-0) DIANE Pub.

Nuclear Nonproliferation: Information on Nuclear Exports Controlled by U. S. - Euratom Agreement. (Illus.). 45p. (C). 1996. reprint ed. pap. text 25.00 (0-7881-3663-1) DIANE Pub.

Nuclear Nonproliferation: Status of U. S. Efforts to Improve Nuclear Material Controls in Newly Independent States. (Illus.). 46p. (Orig.). (C). 1996. pap. text 25.00 (0-7881-2862-0) DIANE Pub.

Nuclear Nonproliferation: Uncertainties with Implementing IAEA's Strengthened Safeguards System. F. James Shafer, Jr. 40p. 1999. pap. text 20.00 (0-7881-7973-X) DIANE Pub.

Nuclear Nonproliferation & Safety: Challenges Facing the International Atomic Energy Agency (IAEA) 76p. pap. text 30.00 (0-7881-4122-8) DIANE Pub.

*Nuclear Nonproliferation: Concerns with DOE[0012]s Efforts to Reduce the Risks Posed by Russia[0012]s Unemployed Weapons Scientists. Victor S. Rezendes. (Illus.). 105p. (C). 2000. pap. text 25.00 (0-7567-0014-0) DIANE Pub.

Nuclear North: The People, the Regions, & the Arms Race. Carole Giangrande. 231p. (Orig.). 1983. pap. 9.95 (0-88784-136-8, Pub. by Hse of Anansi Pr) Genl Dist Srvs.

Nuclear Oncogenes. Ed. by Frederick W. Alt et al. (Illus.). 194p. (Orig.). 1987. pap. text 30.00 (0-87969-305-3) Cold Spring Harbor.

Nuclear Oncology. C. Aktolun & W. Newlon Tauxe. LC 99-10449. 500p. 1999. 189.00 (3-540-64760-0) Spr-Verlag.

Nuclear Oncology: Diagnosis & Therapy. Iraj Khalkhali et al. 500p. text 135.00 (0-7817-1990-9) Lppncott W & W.

Nuclear Oracles: A Political History of the General Advisory Committee of the Atomic Energy Commission, 1947-1977. Richard T. Sylves. LC 87-2845. (Illus.). 353p. 1987. reprint ed. pap. 109.50 (0-608-00116-3, 206088100006) Bks Demand.

Nuclear Organization, Chromatin Structure & Gene Expression. Ed. by Roel Van Driel & Arie P. Otte. LC 97-15623. (Illus.). 308p. 1998. text 115.00 (0-19-854923-7); pap. text 55.00 (0-19-854922-9) OUP.

Nuclear Overhauser Effect in Stereochemical & Conformational Analysis. David Neuhaus & Michael Williamson. LC 88-33963. 522p. 1989. lib. bdg. 110.00 (1-56081-616-3, Wiley-VCH) Wiley.

Nuclear Overhauser Effect in Stereochemical & Conformational Analysis. David Neuhaus & Michael Williamson. LC 88-33963. 522p. 1989. 170.00 (0-471-18684-8, Wiley-VCH) Wiley.

Nuclear Overhauser Effect in Structural & Conformational Analysis. D. Neuhaus & M. P. Williamson. (Methods in Stereochemical Analysis Ser.). 522p. 1992. pap. 89.95 (0-471-18851-4, Wiley-VCH) Wiley.

*Nuclear Overhauser Effect in Structural & Conformational Analysis. 2nd ed. David Neuhaus & Michael P. Williamson. LC 99-49630. 640p. 2000. 125.00 (0-471-24675-1) Wiley.

Nuclear Pakistan. M. G. Chitkara. LC 96-903071. xv, 332p. 1996. 35.00 (81-7024-767-5, Pub. by Ashish Pub Hse) Nataraj Bks.

Nuclear Particles & Physics: Group I, Vols. 1-6. Incl. Elastic & Charge Exchange Scattering of Elementary Particles: Nucleon Nucleon & Kaon Nucleon Scattering. H. Schopper. (Illus.). 750p. 1980. 1188.95 (0-387-09382-6); Magnetic & Other Properties of Oxides & Related Compounds. F. Bonnenberg. LC 62-53136. (Illus.). xvi, 666p. 1970. 1067.95 (0-387-05176-7); Production of Radionuclides at Intermediate Energies Subvol. E: Interaction of Pions & Antiprotons with Nuclei. H. Schoper. (Illus.). 270p. 1994. 979.95 (0-387-57540-5); Q-Values & Excitation Functions of Nuclear Reactions Vol. 5, Pt. B: Excitation Functions for Charged-Particle Induced Nuclear Reactions. K. A. Keller. Ed. by K. H. Hellwege. 1973. 792.95 (0-387-06167-3); Structure Data of Elements & Intermetallic Phases. P. Eckerlin & H. Kandler. LC 62-53136. 1971. 1485.00 (0-387-05500-2); Pt. 2. Elastic & Charge Exchange Scattering of Elementary Particles Subvol. B; Pion Nucleon Scattering-Methods & Results of Phenomenological Analyses. Ed. by H. Schopper. (Illus.). 610p. 1982. 1441.95 (0-387-11282-0); Set. Structure Data of Organic Crystals., **2 vols.** E. Schudt & G. Weitz. LC 62-53136. (Illus.). 1971. 2365.00 (0-387-05177-5); Suppl. B, Pt. 1. Elastic & Charge Exchange - Scattering of Elementary Particles Subvol. B: Pion Nucleon Scattering. G. Hoehler. (Illus.). 420p. 1981. 979.95 (0-387-09694-9); Vol. 1. Energy Levels of Nuclei. Ed. by K. H. Hellwege. (Illus.). 814p. 1961. 1303.95 (0-387-02715-7); Vol. 2. Nuclear Radii. H. R. Collard. Ed. by H. Schopper & K. H. Hellwege. (Illus.). viii, 54p. 1967. 88.95 (0-387-03894-9); Vol. 3. Numerical Tables for Angular Correlation Computations in Alpha, Beta & Gamma Spectroscopy. H. Appel. Ed. by H. Schopper & K. H. Hellwege. vi, 1202p. 1968. 1919.95 (0-387-04218-0); Vol. 4. Numerical Tables for Beta-Decay & Electron Capture. H. Behrens & J. Jaenecke. Ed. by H. Schopper & K. H. Hellwege. (Illus.). viii, 316p. 1968. 506.95 (0-387-04593-7); Vol. 4, Pt. A. Magnetic & Other Properties of Oxides & Related Compounds. J. B. Goodenough. LC 62-53136. (Illus.). xv, 367p. 1970. 588.95 (0-387-04898-7); Vol. 5, Pt. C. Estimation of Unknown Excitation Functions & Thick-Target Yields for p, d, He & Reactions. A. N. Diddens. Ed. by K. H. Hellwege. 1974. 412.95 (0-387-06723-X); Vol. 5, Pt. A. Q-Values & Excitation Functions of Nuclear Reactions: Q-Values. K. A. Keller. Ed. by K. H. Hellwege. 1972. 1067.95 (0-387-06031-6); Vol. 6. Properties & Production Spectra of Elementary Particles. A. N. Diddens. Ed. by H. Schopper & K. H. Hellwege. 1972. 264.95 (0-387-06047-2); Vol. 7. Elastic & Charge Exchange Scattering of Elementary Particles. Ed. by H. Schopper & K. H. Hellwege. 1973. 863.95

An Asterisk (*) at the beginning of an entry indicates that the title is appearing for the first time.

(0-387-06248-3); Vol. 8. Photoproduction of Elementary Particles. H. Genzel & P. J. Joos. Ed. by K. H. Hellwege. 1973. 544.95 (0-387-06249-1); LC 62-53136. (Landolt-Bornstein - Numerical Data & Functional Relationships in Science & Technology, Series Group I). write for info. (0-318-55789-4) Spr-Verlag.

Nuclear Particles in Cancer Treatment. John F. Fowler. (Medical Physics Handbook Ser.: No. 8). (Illus.). 190p. 1981. 19.00 (0-85274-521-4) IOP Pub.

Nuclear Peninsula. Francoise Zonabend. Tr. by J. A. Underwood from FRE. LC 92-17481. (Illus.). 150p. (C). 1993. text 47.95 (0-521-41321-4) Cambridge U Pr.

Nuclear Pharmacy. 2nd ed. Chilton. 244p. 1998. text 45.00 (0-397-55400-1) Lppncott W & W.

Nuclear Pharmacy: An Introduction to the Clinical Application of Radiopharmaceuticals. Henry M. Chilton & Richard L. Witcofski. LC 85-23910. (Illus.). 190p. 1986. text 35.00 (0-8121-1021-8) Lppncott W & W.

Nuclear Phase Transitions & Heavy Ion Reactions: Proceedings of the International Conference, Crete, Greece. T. T. Kuo et al. Ed. by G. Aragnostatos. 480p. (C). 1987. text 138.00 (9971-5-0223-2) World Scientific Pub.

***Nuclear Physical Methods in Radioecological Investigations of Nuclear Test Sites: Advanced Research Workshop.** Siegfried S. Hecker. LC 00-41093. (Nato Science Ser.). 2000. write for info. (0-7923-6447-3) Kluwer Academic.

Nuclear Physics. (Advanced Health Physics Training Ser.). (Illus.). 258p. 1983. ring bd. 95.00 (0-87683-178-1) GP Courseware.

Nuclear Physics. C. A. Bertulani et al. LC 98-161797. 350p. 1997. text 74.00 (981-02-3230-6) World Scientific Pub.

Nuclear Physics. M. G. Bowler. 444p. (C). 1973. 191.00 (0-08-018990-3, Pub. by Pergamon Repr) Franklin.

Nuclear Physics. Huchinings. (UK - Science Ser.). 1990. pap. 26.95 (0-17-448208-6) S-W Pub.

Nuclear Physics. annot. ed. Harry Henderson. LC 97-17380. (Milestones in Discovery & Invention Ser.). 128p. 1998. 19.95 (0-8160-3567-9) Facts on File.

Nuclear Physics. rev. ed. Enrico Fermi. LC 50-6826. (Midway Reprint Ser.). 258p. 1974. reprint ed. pap. text 22.00 (0-226-24365-6) U Ch Pr.

Nuclear Physics. 2nd ed. Irving Kaplan. 1962. write for info. (0-201-03602-9) Addison-Wesley.

Nuclear Physics: An Introduction. Shriprakas B. Patel. 346p. 1991. text 74.95 (0-470-21130-X) Halsted Pr.

Nuclear Physics: An Introduction. 2nd ed. W. E. Burcham. LC 73-164480. (Longman Text Ser.). 706p. reprint ed. pap. 200.00 (0-608-10172-9, 201190400080) Bks Demand.

Nuclear Physics: First European Biennial Workshop, Megeve, France 25-29 March 1991. Ed. by D. Guinet & J. R. Pizzi. 380p. 1991. text 104.00 (981-02-0839-1) World Scientific Pub.

Nuclear Physics: Proceedings of the International Conference on the Occasion of the Golden Jubilee of the Indian National Science Academy, Bombay, December, 1984. Ed. by B. K. Jain. 1985. 128.00 (9971-978-28-8) World Scientific Pub.

Nuclear Physics: Proceedings of the Ninth Workshop, Buenos Aire, Argentina June 23-July 4, 1986. Ed. by A. Macchiavelli et al. 608p. 1987. text 138.00 (9971-5-0204-6) World Scientific Pub.

Nuclear Physics: Proceedings of the Second European Bienniеal Conference. D. Guinet. 444p. 1995. text 121.00 (981-02-1478-2) World Scientific Pub.

Nuclear Physics: Proceedings of the 12th Workshop. M. C. Cambiaggio et al. 396p. (C). 1990. text 113.00 (981-02-0158-3) World Scientific Pub.

Nuclear Physics: Proceedings of the 15th Workshop. J. F. Niello et al. 400p. 1993. text 114.00 (981-02-1374-3) World Scientific Pub.

Nuclear Physics: Proceedings of the 20th Brazilian Meeting Brazil 31 August - 4 September 1997. Ed. by C. L. Lima et al. LC 98-8802. 467p. 1998. 86.00 (981-02-3429-5) World Scientific Pub.

Nuclear Physics: SERC School Series, Jaipur, India, 28 Sept.-11 Oct. 1987. Ed. by B. K. Jain. 408p. 1988. text 108.00 (9971-5-0633-5, ZB0633PP) World Scientific Pub.

Nuclear Physics: The Collected Works of Eugene Paul Wigner. Ed. by A. S. Wightman. (Scientific Papers: Vol. II). 560p. 1995. 159.95 (0-387-56972-3) Spr-Verlag.

Nuclear Physics: The Core of Matter, the Fuel of Stars. National Research Council Staff. LC 98-89539. 222p. (C). 1999. pap. 42.00 (0-309-06276-4) Natl Acad Pr.

Nuclear Physics: XIV Symposium. Ed. by M. E. Brandan. 264p. (C). 1991. text 89.00 (981-02-0601-1) World Scientific Pub.

Nuclear Physics - Energy & Matter: Special Student Edition. J. M. Pearson. (Illus.). 264p. 1986. 42.00 (0-85274-804-3) IOP Pub.

Nuclear Physics - Recent Trends & Developments: Proceedings of the XVIIth Mikolajki Summer School on Nuclear Physics Held in Mikolajki, Poland, September 2-4, 1985. Z. Wilhelmi et al. (Nuclear Science Research Conference Ser.). xiv, 1000p. 1987. 365.00 (3-7186-0351-9) Gordon & Breach.

Nuclear Physics & Fundamental Particles. Roger Muncaster. 160p. 1998. pap. 34.50 (0-7487-1805-2) St Mut.

Nuclear Physics Applications on Materials Science. Ed. by E. Recknagel & J. C. Soares. (C). 1988. text 271.50 (90-247-3703-6) Kluwer Academic.

Nuclear Physics at Intermediate Energy. Ed. by T. Nagae. 484p. (C). 1989. text 151.00 (981-02-0000-5) World Scientific Pub.

***Nuclear Physics at Storage Rings: Fourth International Conference: STORI99.** Ed. by Hans-Otto Meyer & Peter Schwandt. LC 00-102026. (AIP Conference Proceedings Ser.: Vol. 512). (Illus.). xv, 436p. 2000. 130.00 (1-56396-928-9, Pub. by Am Inst Physics) Spr-Verlag.

Nuclear Physics at the Borderlines: Proceedings of the Fourth International Summer School, Sponsored by the Universidad Hispano-Americana, Santa Maria de la Rapida, La Rapida, Huelva, Spain, June 17-29, 1991. Ed. by J. M. Arias et al. (Research Reports in Physics). (Illus.). xii, 268p. 1992. 79.95 (0-387-55074-7) Spr-Verlag.

Nuclear Physics Conference. Ed. by O. Sala et al. 832p. (C). 1990. pap. 53.00 (981-02-0036-6); text 173.00 (981-02-0035-8) World Scientific Pub.

Nuclear Physics: Electronuclear Physics with Internal Targets & the Blast Detector. Richard Milner. 1999. 122.00 (981-02-4004-X) World Scientific Pub.

Nuclear Physics for Engineers & Scientists: Low Energy Theory with Applications Including Reactors & Their Environmental Impact. Stanley E. Hunt. (Mechanical Engineering Ser.). 376p. 1987. text 136.00 (0-470-20841-4) P-H.

Nuclear Physics in Retrospect: Proceedings of a symposium on the 1930's. Symposium on the History of Nuclear Physics Staff. Ed. by Roger H. Stuewer. LC 78-8192. 358p. 1979. reprint ed. pap. 111.00 (0-7837-2917-0, 205753700006) Bks Demand.

Nuclear Physics in the Soviet Union: Current Status & Future Prospects. Sergei Polikanov. Ed. by Steven Jones. 120p. (Orig.). 1984. pap. text 75.00 (1-55831-035-5) Delphic Associates.

Nuclear Physics in the Universe: Proceedings of the First Symposium on Nuclear Physics in the Universe Held in Oak Ridge, Tennessee, U. S. A., 24-26 September, 1992. Ed. by Michael W. Guidry & M. R. Strayer. (Illus.). 491p. 1993. 234.00 (0-7503-0279-8) IOP Pub.

Nuclear Physics, Neutron Physics & Nuclear Energy: Proceedings of the 9th International School. Ed. by W. Andrejtscheff & D. Elenkov. 492p. (C). 1990. text 151.00 (981-02-0253-9) World Scientific Pub.

Nuclear Physics, 1929-1952. Ed. by R. Peierls. (Niels Bohr Collected Works). 694p. 1986. 350.75 (0-444-86929-8, North Holland) Elsevier.

Nuclear Physics of Our Times. A. V. Ramayya & Walter Greiner. 584p. 1993. text 114.00 (981-02-1358-1) World Scientific Pub.

Nuclear Physics with Effective Field Theory: Proceedings of the Joint Caltech/INT Workshop California Institute of Technology, U. S. A. 26-27 February 1998. Ed. by Ryoichi Seki et al. (Proceedings from the Institute for Nuclear Theory Ser.). 230p. 1998. 58.00 (981-02-3596-8) World Scientific Pub.

***Nuclear Physics with Effective Field Theory II: University of Washington, Seattle, U. S. A. 25-26 Feb.** Paulo F. Bedaque. 1999. 75.00 (981-02-4181-X) World Scientific Pub.

Nuclear Physics with Heavy Ions. D. Braun et al. Tr. by Kenneth J. Ivin from GER. (MMI Press Polymer Monographs: Vol. 4). (C). 1984. 118.95 (0-685-42165-1) Gordon & Breach.

Nuclear Physics with Heavy Ions. Ed. by Peter B. Braun-Munzinger. (Nuclear Science Research Conference Ser.: Vol. 6). 1984. text 477.00 (3-7186-0196-6) Gordon & Breach.

Nuclear Physics with Stored, Cooled Beams (McCormick's Creek State Park, Indiana, 1984) Ed. by P. Schwandt & H. O. Meyer. LC 85-71167. (AIP Conference Proceedings Ser.: No. 128). 349p. 1985. lib. bdg. 45.60 (0-88318-327-7) Am Inst Physics.

Nuclear Pion Photoproduction. A. Nagl et al. (Tracts in Modern Physics Ser.: Vol. 120). viii, 174p. 1991. 107.95 (0-387-50671-3) Spr-Verlag.

Nuclear Planning in NATO: Pitfalls of First Use. Daniel Charles. LC 86-17233. 200p. 1986. text 29.95 (0-88730-137-1, HarpBusn) HarpInfo.

Nuclear Plant Aging Research. 1995. lib. bdg. 251.99 (0-8490-6741-3) Gordon Pr.

Nuclear Plant Instrumentation, Oak Ridge, TN, April 18-21, 1993: Control & Man-Machine Interface Technologies. 644p. 1994. 77.00 (0-89448-185-1, 700192) Am Nuclear Soc.

Nuclear Policies in Europe. Bruno Tertais. (Adelphi Papers: 327). (Illus.). 96p. 2000. pap. 24.95 (0-19-922427-7) OUP.

Nuclear Policies in Northeast Asia. LC 96-125283. 265p. 32.00 (92-9045-101-7, E.GV.95.0.8) UN.

Nuclear Policy & World Order: Why Denuclearization? Richard A. Falk. 30p. 1978. pap. 17.95 (0-87855-755-5) Transaction Pubs.

Nuclear Policy of India. K. K. Pathak. 276p. 1980. 24.95 (0-318-37256-8) Asia Bk Corp.

Nuclear Policy of India. K. K. Pathak. 1983. 18.50 (0-8364-1024-6, Pub. by Gitanjali Prakashan) S Asia.

Nuclear Politics: Energy & the State in the United States, Sweden & France. James M. Jasper. (Illus.). 323p. (C). 1990. text 52.50 (0-691-07841-6, Pub. by Princeton U Pr) Cal Prin Full Svc.

Nuclear Politics in America: A History & Theory of Government Regulation. Robert J. Duffy. LC 97-19146. (Studies in Government & Public Policy). 336p. 1997. 45.00 (0-7006-0852-4); pap. 22.50 (0-7006-0853-2) U Pr of KS.

Nuclear Politics in South Asia: In Search of an Alternative Paradigm. B. M. Jain. (C). 1994. 26.00 (81-7033-256-7, Pub. by Rawat Pubns) S Asia.

Nuclear Power. Diane Gibson. LC 99-55893. (Sources of Energy Ser.). (Illus.). 24p. (J). (gr. 2-7). 2001. lib. bdg. 21.30 (1-887068-80-5) Smart Apple.

Nuclear Power. Jonathan F. Gosse. (Illus.). 202p. 1990. 20.96 (0-8269-3406-4) Am Technical.

***Nuclear Power.** Ian Graham. LC 98-38725. (Energy Forever Ser.). (J). 1999. 25.69 (0-8172-5763-2) Raintree Steck-V.

Nuclear Power. Nigel Hawkes. (World Issues Ser.). (Illus.). 48p. (J). (gr. 5 up). 1990. lib. bdg. 13.95 (0-685-36380-5) Rourke Corp.

Nuclear Power. Richard K. Miller & Christy H. Gunter. (Market Research Survey Ser.: No. 346). 50p. 1997. pap. 200.00 (1-55865-361-9) Future Tech Surveys.

Nuclear Power. Nina Morgan. LC 97-20302. (Twentieth Century Inventions Ser.). (Illus.). 48p. (J). (gr. 4-9). 1998. 24.26 (0-8172-4818-8) Raintree Steck-V.

Nuclear Power. James J. Duderstadt. LC 79-12776. (Energy, Power & Environment Ser.: No. 3). (Illus.). 400p. reprint ed. pap. 124.00 (0-7837-4321-1, 204400700012) Bks Demand.

Nuclear Power. Ed. by Richard V. Moore. LC 77-142962. (Institution of Electrical Engineers Monograph Ser.: Vol. 6). (Illus.). 208p. reprint ed. pap. 64.50 (0-8357-8975-6, 203345300086) Bks Demand.

Nuclear Power, Set II. Nigel Hawkes. (World Issues Ser.). (Illus.). 48p. (J). (gr. 5 up). 1990. lib. bdg. 25.27 (0-86592-098-2) Rourke Enter.

***Nuclear Power: A Reference Handbook.** Harry Henderson. 2000. lib. bdg. 45.00 (1-57607-128-6) ABC-CLIO.

Nuclear Power: Both Sides. Michio Kaku & Jennifer Trainer. (Illus.). 288p. 1983. pap. 11.95 (0-393-30128-1) Norton.

Nuclear Power: Policy & Prospects. Ed. by P. M. Jones. LC 86-26714. (World Energy Options Ser.). 434p. reprint ed. pap. 134.60 (0-7837-3225-2, 204324200007) Bks Demand.

Nuclear Power: Promise or Peril? Michael J. Daley. LC 96-19085. (Pro/Con Ser.). (J). 1996. lib. bdg. 21.27 (0-8225-2611-5, Lerner Publctns) Lerner Pub.

Nuclear Power: Siting & Safety. Stan Openshaw. (Illus.). 337p. 1986. text 45.00 (0-7102-0183-4, Routledge Thoemms) Routledge.

Nuclear Power: Sustainability, Climate Change & Competition. NEA Staff. 88p. 1998. pap. 60.00 (92-64-16954-7, 6198291P) OECD.

Nuclear Power: Technical & Institutional Options for the Future. National Research Council Staff. 234p. (C). 1992. pap. text 27.00 (0-309-04395-6) Natl Acad Pr.

Nuclear Power: Technology on Trial. James J. Duderstadt & Chihiro Kikuchi. 240p. 1979. pap. text 19.95 (0-472-06312-X, 06312) U of Mich Pr.

Nuclear Power: The Fifth Horseman. Denis Hayes. 1976. pap. write for info. (0-916468-05-4) Worldwatch Inst.

Nuclear Power: The Market Test. Christopher Flavin. 1983. pap. write for info. (0-916468-56-9) Worldwatch Inst.

Nuclear Power - Accidental Releases - Practical Guidance for Public Health Action: Report on a WHO Meeting. (WHO Regional Publications, European Ser.: No. 21). 53p. 1987. pap. text 10.00 (92-890-1112-2) World Health.

Nuclear Power - Accidental Releases - Principles of Public Health Action: Report on a WHO Meeting. (Who Regional Publications, European Ser.: No. 16). 62p. 1984. pap. text 12.00 (92-890-1107-6) World Health.

Nuclear Power - Health Implications of Transuranium Elements: Report on a Working Group. (WHO Regional Publications, European Ser.: No. 11). 88p. 1982. pap. text 14.00 (92-890-1102-5) World Health.

Nuclear Power - Management of High-Level Radioactive Waste: Report on a Working Group. (WHO Regional Publications, European Ser.: No. 13). 63p. 1982. pap. text 10.00 (92-890-1104-1) World Health.

Nuclear Power & Health: The Implications for Health of Nuclear Power Production. (WHO Regional Publications: No. 51). xviii, 145p. 1994. pap. text 26.00 (92-890-1315-X, 1310051) World Health.

Nuclear Power & Its Fuel Cycle. Incl. Vol. 1. Nuclear Power Prospects & Plans. 1977. pap. 155.00 (92-0-050077-3, ISP465-1); Vol. 2, Pt. 2. Nuclear Fuel Cycle. 1977. pap. 155.00 (92-0-050177-X, ISP465-2); Vol. 3, Pt. 2. Nuclear Fuel Cycle. 1977. pap. 155.00 (92-0-050277-6, ISP465-3); Vol. 5. Nuclear Safety. 1978. pap. 155.00 (92-0-050477-9, ISP465-5); Vol. 6. Nuclear Power in Developing Countries. 1978. pap. 155.00 (92-0-050577-5, ISP465-6); Vol. 7. Nuclear Power & Public Opinion, Safeguards. 1978. pap. 155.00 (92-0-050677-1, ISP465-7); Vol. 8. Indexes & Lists. 1978. pap. 65.00 (92-0-050777-8, ISP465-8); Set pap. 890.00 (0-685-12766-4, ISP465SET) Bernan Associates.

Nuclear Power & Its Regulation in the United States, Vol. 7, Pt. 2. Ed. by L. Manning Muntzing. (Illus.). 125p. 1981. pap. 36.00 (0-08-027139-1, Pergamon Pr) Elsevier.

Nuclear Power & National & International Security: The Politics & Economic Implications of Closing the Nuclear Fuel Cycle. Ed. by Aspen Institute Staff. 28p. (Orig.). 1984. pap. text 8.50 (0-8191-5854-2) U Pr of Amer.

Nuclear Power & Public Opinion, Safeguards see Nuclear Power & Its Fuel Cycle

Nuclear Power & Social Power. Rick Eckstein. LC 96-23908. 208p. (C). 1996. lib. bdg. 69.95 (1-56639-485-6) Temple U Pr.

Nuclear Power & Social Power. Rick Eckstein. LC 96-23908. 208p. (C). 1996. pap. 19.95 (1-56639-486-4) Temple U Pr.

Nuclear Power & the Public. Ed. by Harry Foreman. LC 78-139961. 291p. reprint ed. pap. 90.30 (0-608-14623-4, 205586800039) Bks Demand.

Nuclear Power at the Crossroads: Challenges & Prospects for the Twenty-First Century. Ed. by Thomas C. Lowinger & George W. Hinman. LC 93-81259. (Illus.). 218p. 1994. 24.00 (0-918714-42-7) Intl Res Ctr Energy.

Nuclear Power Controversy. Ed. by Arthur W. Murphy. LC 76-40017. (American Assembly Guides Ser.). 1976. 9.95 (0-13-625582-5); pap. 3.95 (0-13-625574-4) Am Assembly.

Nuclear Power Controversy. American Assembly Staff. Ed. by Arthur W. Murphy. LC 76-40017. 192p. reprint ed. pap. 59.60 (0-608-11007-8, 201539800093) Bks Demand.

Nuclear Power Debate. Desaix Myers. 153p. 1977. 25.95 (0-275-56440-1) Greenwood.

Nuclear Power Debate: Issues & Choices. Scott A. Fenn. LC 80-28065. 199p. 1981. 52.95 (0-275-90622-1, C0622, Praeger Pubs) Greenwood.

Nuclear Power Deception: U. S. Nuclear Mythology from Electricity "Too Cheap to Meter" to "Inherently Safe" Reactors. Arjun Makhijani & Scott Saleska. LC 98-36673. (Illus.). 240p. 1999. 38.50 (0-945257-75-9); pap. 17.50 (0-945257-92-9) Apex Pr.

Nuclear Power Development: Prospects in the 1990s. Stanley M. Nealey. LC 89-38237. 1990. pap. text 19.95 (0-935470-53-0) Battelle.

Nuclear Power Development in the U. S. to 1960: A New Pattern in Innovation & Technological Change. Alfred G. Dale. Ed. by Stuart Bruchey. LC 78-22670. (Energy in the American Economy Ser.). (Illus.). 1979. lib. bdg. 18.95 (0-405-11974-7) Ayer.

Nuclear Power Dictionary, Vol. 63. E. Brandenberger & F. Stattmann. (ENG & GER.). 456p. 1978. pap. 95.00 (0-8288-5259-6, M7572) Fr & Eur.

Nuclear Power Economics 1964, Vol. 2. IAEA Staff. Ed. by Valence Ionescu & L. Dimitrov. (Bibliographical Ser.: No. 30). 303p. 1968. pap. 35.00 (92-0-054068-6, ISP21 30, Pub. by IAEA) Bernan Associates.

Nuclear Power, Energy & the Environment. P. E. Hodgson. 350p. 1998. 48.00 (1-86094-088-9, Pub. by Imperial College); pap. 24.00 (1-86094-101-X, Pub. by Imperial College) World Scientific Pub.

Nuclear Power Engineering in the CMEA Countries. S. Sytchev. (C). 1985. 50.00 (0-7855-6300-8, Pub. by Collets) St Mut.

Nuclear Power Experience: Nuclear Safety, 6 vols., Vols. 2-4. Incl. Vol. 3. Nuclear Fuel Cycle. 893p. 1983. pap. 250.00 (92-0-050283-0, ISP627 3, Pub. by IAEA); Vol. 4. Nuclear Safety. (Illus.). 873p. 1993. pap. 235.00 (92-0-050383-7, ISP627 4); (Proceedings Ser.). (Illus.). 1983. 570.00 (0-318-60567-8, Pub. by IAEA) Bernan Associates.

Nuclear Power for Beginners. C. Croall & S. Sempler. 1990. pap. 35.00 (0-7855-7026-8, Pub. by Northcote House) St Mut.

Nuclear Power from Underseas to Outer Space. John W. Simpson. 468p. 1994. 50.00 (0-89448-559-8) Am Nuclear Soc.

Nuclear Power Game. Ronald Babin. Tr. by Ted Richmond from FRE. Orig. Title: L'Option Nucleaire. 236p. 1985. 43.99 (0-920057-30-6, Pub. by Black Rose); pap. 14.99 (0-920057-31-4, Pub. by Black Rose) Consort Bk Sales.

Nuclear Power Generation see Modern Power Station Practice

Nuclear Power Generation & Fuel Cycle Report, 1997. 133p. 1997. per. 13.00 (0-16-063492-X) USGPO.

Nuclear Power Goes On-Line: A History of Shippingport, 105. William Beaver. LC 89-26065. (Contributions in Economics & Economic History Ser.: No. 105). 208p. 1990. 55.00 (0-313-27244-1, BVS/, Greenwood Pr) Greenwood.

Nuclear Power Hazard Control Policy. John C. Chicken. LC 80-40992. (Illus.). 300p. 1982. 126.00 (0-08-023254-X, Pub. by Pergamon Repr) Franklin.

Nuclear Power in Developing Countries see Nuclear Power & Its Fuel Cycle

Nuclear Power in Japan. Ed. by Kent F. Hansen. (JTEC Panel Reports). xxiv, 277p. 1990. pap. write for info. (1-883712-11-4, JTEC) Intl Tech Res.

Nuclear Power in Japan: Executive Summary. Ed. by Kent F. Hansen. 12p. 1990. pap. write for info. (1-883712-04-1, JTEC) Intl Tech Res.

Nuclear Power Industry in America. Pope. 1999. 22.95 (0-8057-4629-3, Twyne); per. 14.95 (0-8057-4630-7, Twyne) Mac Lib Ref.

Nuclear Power Issue: A Guide to Who's Doing What in the U. S. & Abroad. Kimberly J. Mueller. LC 79-52430. (Who's Doing What Ser.: No. 8). (Illus.). 106p. (Orig.). 1981. pap. 25.00 (0-912102-44-6) Cal Inst Public.

Nuclear Power, Its History. R. F. Pocock. 280p. 1984. 60.00 (0-905418-15-8, Pub. by Gresham Bks) St Mut.

Nuclear Power, Man & the Environment. R. J. Pentreath. (Wykeham Science Ser.: No. 51). 268p. 1977. pap. 18.00 (0-85109-840-1) Taylor & Francis.

Nuclear Power, Man & the Environment. R. J. Pentreath. LC 80-20173. (Wykeham Science Ser.: No. 51). 250p. (C). 1981. pap. 18.00 (0-8448-1381-8, Crane Russak) Taylor & Francis.

Nuclear Power, Nuclear Fuel Cycle & Waste Management: Status & Trends 1992. IAEA Staff. 85p. 1992. pap. 19.00 (92-0-102192-5, STI/PUB/919, Pub. by IAEA) Bernan Associates.

Nuclear Power, Nuclear Fuel Cycle & Waste Management Pt. C: Status & Trends, 1994. International Atomic Energy Agency Staff. 97p. 1994. pap. 25.00 (92-0-102494-0, STI/PUB/956, Pub. by IAEA) Bernan Associates.

Nuclear Power, Nuclear Weapons, & Japanese Policy see Japan's Nuclear Future: The Plutonium Debate & East Asian Security

Nuclear Power Option: Proceedings of an International Conference on the Nuclear Power Option. IAEA Staff. LC 95-218864. 763p. 1995. pap. 235.00 (92-0-100395-1, STI/PUB/946, Pub. by IAEA) Bernan Associates.

N

An Asterisk (*) at the beginning of an entry indicates that the title is appearing for the first time.

Nuclear Power Plant Aging, Availability Factor & Reliability Analysis. International Conference on Nuclear Power Plant Ag. Ed. by V. S. Goel. LC 85-73459. (Illus.). 670p. reprint ed. pap. 200.00 (*0-608-17322-3*, 205640000065) Bks Demand.

Nuclear Power Plant & Facility Maintenance Topical Meeting, Salt Lake City, UT, April 7-11, 1991, 2 vols., Set. 910p. 1991. 100.00 (*0-89448-164-9*, 700164) Am Nuclear Soc.

Nuclear Power Plant Design Analysis. AEC Technical Information Center Staff & Alexander Sesonske. LC 73-600245. 497p. 1973. pap. 20.25 (*0-87079-009-9*, TID-26241); fiche 9.00 (*0-87079-287-3*, TID-26241) DOE.

Nuclear Power Plant Generic Aging Lessons Learned (GALL) Appendix A: Main Report. K. E. Kasza. 444p. 1996. per. 36.00 (*0-16-062794-X*) USGPO.

Nuclear Power Plant Generic Aging Lessons Learned (GALL) Appendix B. K. E. Kasza. 280p. 1996. per. 22.00 (*0-16-062795-8*) USGPO.

Nuclear Power Plant Life Extension Topical Meeting, Snow Bird, UT, July 31-Aug. 3, 1988. 692p. 1988. 75.00 (*0-89448-139-8*, 700142) Am Nuclear Soc.

Nuclear Power Plant Maintenance International Marketing, Salt Lake City, UT March 23-27, 1986, 2 vols. 1212p. 1986. pap. 96.00 (*0-89448-129-0*, 700116) Am Nuclear Soc.

Nuclear Power Plant Personnel Training & Its Evaluation: A Guidebook. IAEA Staff. (Technical Reports: No. 380). 138p. 1996. pap. 55.00 (*92-0-101496-1*, STI/DOC/380, Pub. by IAEA) Bernan Associates.

Nuclear Power Plant Thermodynamics & Heat Transfer: A Primer. Charles E. Tomlinson. LC 89-2169. (Illus.). 225p. 1989. reprint ed. pap. 69.80 (*0-608-00050-7*, 206081600006) Bks Demand.

Nuclear Power Prospects & Plans see Nuclear Power & Its Fuel Cycle

Nuclear Power Reactor Instrumentation Systems Handbook, 2 vols. AEC Technical Information Center Staff. Ed. by Joseph M. Harrer & James G. Beckerley. LC 72-600355. fiche 9.00 (*0-87079-299-7*, TID-25952-P1); fiche 9.00 (*0-87079-300-4*, TID-25952-P2) DOE.

Nuclear Power Reactor Instrumentation Systems Handbook, 2 vols., Vol. 1. AEC Technical Information Center Staff. Ed. by Joseph M. Harrer & James G. Beckerley. LC 72-600355. 313p. 1973. pap. 16.00 (*0-87079-005-6*, TID-25952-P1) DOE.

Nuclear Power Reactor Instrumentation Systems Handbook, 2 vols., Vol. 2. AEC Technical Information Center Staff. Ed. by Joseph M. Harrer & James G. Beckerley. LC 72-600355. 285p. 1974. pap. 15.00 (*0-87079-144-3*, TID-25952-P2) DOE.

N

***Nuclear Power Reactors in the World, April 1999.** International Atomic Energy Agency. (Illus.). 78p. 1999. pap. 14.00 (*92-0-101599-2*, Pub. by IAEA) Bernan Associates.

Nuclear Power Safety: Industry Concerns with Federal Whistleblower Protection System. Larry Horinko et al. (Illus.). 51p. 1998. pap. text 25.00 (*0-7881-7077-5*) DIANE Pub.

Nuclear Power: Villain or Victim? Our Most Misunderstood Source of Electricity. Max W. Carbon. LC 97-91918. (Illus.). xii, 100p. 1997. pap. 13.95 (*0-9658096-0-9*) Pebble Beach.

Nuclear Predicament. Donna Gregory. 1986. teacher ed. 8.95 (*0-317-52488-7*) St Martin.

***Nuclear Predicament.** 3rd ed. Beckman. LC 99-47280. 340p. 1999. pap. text 33.60 (*0-13-680638-4*) P-H.

Nuclear Present: A Guide to Recent Books on Nuclear War, Weapons, the Peace Movement, & Related Issues, with a Chronology of Nuclear Events, 1789-1991. Grant Burns. LC 92-32440. 654p. 1992. 73.00 (*0-8108-2619-4*) Scarecrow.

Nuclear Profiles of the Soviet Successor States. William C. Potter et al. (Orig.). 1993. 9.95 (*0-9633859-5-X*) Ctr Nonproliferation.

Nuclear Proliferation. Glenn A. Cheney. LC 98-4526. (Impact Bks.). 144 p. (J). 1999. 24.00 (*0-531-11431-7*) Watts.

***Nuclear Proliferation: An Annotated Biography.** A. M. Babkina. 239p. 1999. 49.00 (*1-56072-646-6*) Nova Sci Pubs.

Nuclear Proliferation: Breaking the Chain. Ed. by George H. Quester. LC 80-53960. 255p. 1981. reprint ed. pap. 79.10 (*0-608-01972-0*, 206262700003) Bks Demand.

Nuclear Proliferation: Phase II. Ed. by Robert M. Lawrence & Joel Larus. LC 74-11724. viii, 256p. (Orig.). (C). 1974. pap. 12.95 (*0-7006-0128-7*) U Pr of KS.

Nuclear Proliferation: The Post-Cold-War Challenge. Ronald J. Bee. Ed. by Nancy L. Hoepli-Phalon. LC 94-61086. (Headline Ser.: No. 303). (Illus.). 72p. (Orig.). 1995. pap. 5.95 (*0-87124-160-9*, HS 303) Foreign Policy.

Nuclear Proliferation after the Cold War. Ed. by Mitchell Reiss & Robert S. Litwak. (Woodrow Wilson Center Press Ser.). 320p. (C). 1994. text 45.00 (*0-943875-64-1*); pap. text 16.95 (*0-943875-57-9*) Johns Hopkins.

Nuclear Proliferation & International Security. K. Subrahmanyam. 310p. 1986. 29.95 (*0-318-37250-9*) Asia Bk Corp.

Nuclear Proliferation & National Security. M. Abdel-Aziz. 238p. 1980. 21.95 (*0-318-37212-6*) Asia Bk Corp.

Nuclear Proliferation & Safeguards. 1991. lib. bdg. 250.00 (*0-8490-4923-7*) Gordon Pr.

Nuclear Proliferation & the Legality of Nuclear Weapons. William M. Evan & Ved P. Nanda. 436p. (Orig.). (C). 1995. pap. text 48.00 (*0-7618-0089-1*); lib. bdg. 69.50 (*0-7618-0088-3*) U Pr of Amer.

Nuclear Proliferation Factbook. 1986. lib. bdg. 250.00 (*0-8490-3497-3*) Gordon Pr.

***Nuclear Proliferation in the Indian Subcontinent: The Self-Exhausting 'Superpowers' & Emerging Alliances.** Hooman Peimani. LC 99-88509. 2000. write for info. (*0-275-96704-2*, Praeger Pubs) Greenwood.

Nuclear Proliferation in the 1980s: Perspectives & Proposals. William H. Kincade & Christopher Bertram. write for info. (*0-333-32304-1*) Macmillan.

Nuclear Pursuits: The Scientific Biography of Wilfrid Bennett Lewis. Ruth Fawcett. (Illus.). 232p. 1994. 55.00 (*0-7735-1186-5*, Pub. by McG-Queens Univ Pr) CUP Services.

Nuclear Quadrupole Resonance Spectroscopy Data: Supplement. H. Chihara & N. Nakamura. (Numerical Data & Functional Relationships in Science & Technology Ser.: Vol. 39). viii, 424p. 1997. 1869.00 (*3-540-62428-7*) Spr-Verlag.

Nuclear Quagmire. Gregory L. Harrigan. LC 84-50400. 125p. (Orig.). 1991. pap. 5.95 (*0-916403-02-5*) Shanty Pr.

Nuclear Quality Systems Auditor Training Handbook. 2nd ed. ASQ Energy Division Staff. (Audit Quality Ser.). 194p. 1986. 38.00 (*0-87389-008-6*, H0520) ASQ Qual Pr.

Nuclear Radiation: Risks & Benefits. Edward E. Pochin. (Monographs on Science, Technology & Society). (Illus.). 204p. 1985. pap. text 18.95 (*0-19-858337-0*) OUP.

Nuclear Radiation: What It Is, How to Detect It, How to Protect Yourself from It. Gregory H. Piesinger. LC 80-24001. (Illus.). 127p. (Orig.). (C). 1980. pap. 9.95 (*0-937224-00-6*) Dyco Inc.

Nuclear Radiation Detection--Lab Manual. Geoffrey G. Eichholz & J. W. Poston. 181p. (Orig.). (C). 1985. lib. bdg. 26.00 (*0-87371-063-0*, CRC Reprint) Franklin.

Nuclear Radiation in Warfare. 150p. 1981. 45.00 (*0-85066-217-6*) Taylor & Francis.

Nuclear Radii see Nuclear Particles & Physics: Group I

Nuclear Radiology (Fourth Series) Test & Syllabus. James H. Thrall et al. (Professional Self-Evaluation & Continuing Education Program Ser.: Vol. 30). (Illus.). 750p. 1990. 190.00 (*1-55903-030-5*) Am Coll Radiology.

Nuclear Reaction Data & Nuclear Reactors: Physics, Design & Safety: Proceedings of the Workshop: ICTP, Trieste, Italy, 15 April-17 May, 1996, 2 vols. A. Gandini et al. LC 98-204418. 1998. write for info. (*981-02-3978-5*) World Scientific Pub.

Nuclear Reaction Data & Nuclear Reactors: Physics, Design & Safety Proceedings of the Workshop ICTP, Trieste, Italy 23 Feb - 27 Mar 1998. Ed. by P Oblozinsky & A. Gandini. LC 99-29343. 560p. 1999. 94.00 (*981-02-3916-5*) World Scientific Pub.

Nuclear Reaction Dynamics of Nucleon-Hadron Many Body System: Proceedings of the 14th RCNP Osaka International Symposium. LC 97-101645. 512p. 1996. lib. bdg. 69.00 (*981-02-2750-7*) World Scientific Pub.

Nuclear Reaction Mechanism. Ed. by S. Mukherjee et al. 636p. (C). 1989. text 161.00 (*9971-5-0882-6*) World Scientific Pub.

Nuclear Reaction Mechanisms: Proceedings of the 20th International Symposium on Nuclear Physics. Ed. by D. Seeliger. 312p. (C). 1991. text 104.00 (*981-02-0691-7*) World Scientific Pub.

Nuclear Reactions. Ian E. McCarthy. 1970. pap. 120.00 (*0-08-006629-1*, Pub. by Pergamon Repr) Franklin.

Nuclear Reactions: Science & Trans-Science. Alvin M. Weinberg. LC 92-16086. (Masters of Modern Physics Ser.). 1992. 34.95 (*0-88318-861-9*) Spr-Verlag.

Nuclear Reactions & Charged-Particle Accelerators. Ed. by D. V. Skobel'tsyn. Tr. by J. George Adashko from RUS. LC 76-161. (Proceedings of the P. N. Lebedev Physics Institute Ser.: No. 69). 150p. 1976. reprint ed. pap. 46.50 (*0-608-05528-X*, 206599600006) Bks Demand.

Nuclear Reactions & Interaction of Neutrons & Matter. Ed. by D. V. Skobel'tsyn. Tr. by Joachim R. Buchner from RUS. LC 74-32059. (Proceedings of the P. N. Lebedev Physics Institute Ser.: No. 63). (Illus.). 169p. 1975. reprint ed. pap. 52.40 (*0-608-05523-9*, 206599100006) Bks Demand.

Nuclear Reactions in Stellar Surfaces & Their Relations with Stellar Evolution. Hubert Reeves. (Illus.). xii, 88p. 1971. text 142.00 (*0-677-02960-8*); pap. text 101.00 (*0-677-02965-9*) Gordon & Breach.

Nuclear Reactor Analysis. James J. Duderstadt & Louis J. Hamilton. 672p. (C). 1976. text 117.95 (*0-471-22363-8*) Wiley.

Nuclear Reactor Engineering. 3rd ed. Samuel Glasstone & Alexander Sesonske. 824p. (C). 1991. reprint ed. lib. bdg. 99.50 (*0-89464-567-6*) Krieger.

Nuclear Reactor Engineering. 4th ed. Samuel Glasstone & Alexander Sesonske. LC 93-9732. 1993. text 54.95 (*0-442-00932-1*); text 54.95 (*0-442-00935-6*) Chapman & Hall.

Nuclear Reactor Kinetics & Control. Jeffery D. Lewins. LC 77-8107. 1978. 129.00 (*0-08-021682-X*, Pub. by Pergamon Repr) Franklin.

Nuclear Reactor Materials & Applications. Benjamin Ma. 592p. (gr. 13). 1982. text 84.95 (*0-442-22559-8*) Chapman & Hall.

***Nuclear Reactor Physics.** Weston M. Stacey. 640p. 2001. 120.00 (*0-471-39127-1*) Wiley.

Nuclear Reactor Safety: On the History of the Regulatory Process. David Okrent. LC 80-53958. 389p. 1981. reprint ed. pap. 120.60 (*0-608-01888-0*, 206254000003) Bks Demand.

Nuclear Reactor Safety Heat Transfer. O. C. Jones. 1981. text 120.00 (*0-07-032873-0*) McGraw.

Nuclear Reactor Safety Heat Transfer: Presented at the Winter Meeting of the ASME. Ed. by A. A. Bishop & Frank A. Kulacki. LC 77-87329. 68p. reprint ed. pap. 30.00 (*0-608-10290-3*, 201690400005) Bks Demand.

Nuclear Reactor Theory. George I. Bell & Samuel Glasstone. LC 78-22102. 638p. 1979. reprint ed. lib. bdg. 79.50 (*0-88275-790-3*) Krieger.

Nuclear Reactor Theory: Proceedings. Ed. by Garrett D. Birkhoff & E. P. Wigner. LC 50-1183. (Proceedings of Symposia in Applied Mathematics Ser.: Vol.11). 339p. 1961. reprint ed. pap. 51.00 (*0-8218-1311-0*, PSAPM/11) Am Math.

Nuclear Reactor Theory: Proceedings of the Eleventh Symposium in Applied Mathematics of the American Mathematical Society, Held at the Hotel New Yorker, April 23-25, 1959. fac. ed. Ed. by Garrett D. Birkhoff & Eugene P. Wigner. LC 50-1183. (Proceedings of Symposia in Applied Mathematics Ser.: No. 11). 345p. 1961. reprint ed. pap. 107.00 (*0-608-01007-3*, 206186500012) Bks Demand.

Nuclear Reactors - Physics, Design & Safety: Proceedings of the Workshop. Ed. by A. Gandini et al. 1128p. 1995. text 168.00 (*981-02-2425-7*, P-P2897) World Scientific Pub.

***Nuclear Reality.** Elaine Landau. LC 99-40023. 128p. (J). (gr. 7). 2000. lib. bdg. 22.90 (*0-7613-1555-1*) TFC Bks NY.

Nuclear Receptor Superfamily. 2nd ed. Ed. by Didier Picard. LC 99-24782. (Practical Approach Ser.: 207). (Illus.). 304p. 1999. pap. text 55.00 (*0-19-963742-3*) OUP.

Nuclear Receptors: A Practical Approach. 2nd ed. Ed. by Didier Picard. LC 99-24782. (The Practical Approach Ser.: No. 207). (Illus.). 304p. 1999. text 110.00 (*0-19-963743-1*) OUP.

***Nuclear Receptors & Genetic Disease.** Thomas P. Burris. 400p. 2000. 129.95 (*0-12-146160-2*) Acad Pr.

Nuclear Regulation: Action Needed to Control Radioactive Contamination. (Illus.). 34p. 1994. pap. text 30.00 (*1-57979-082-8*) DIANE Pub.

Nuclear Regulation: Action Needed to Control Radioactive Contamination at Sewage Treatment Plants. (Illus.). 33p. (Orig.). (C). 1995. pap. text 20.00 (*0-7881-1683-5*) DIANE Pub.

Nuclear Regulation: Better Criteria & Data Would Help Ensure Safety of Nuclear Materials. Ed. by James E. Wells, Jr. et al. (Illus.). 73p. (C). 1997. reprint ed. pap. text 30.00 (*0-7881-4125-2*) DIANE Pub.

Nuclear Regulation: Preventing Problem Plants Requires More Effective NRC Action. Gary Boss. (Illus.). 77p. (C). 1998. pap. text 20.00 (*0-7881-4131-7*) DIANE Pub.

Nuclear Regulation: Testimony. 8p. 1994. pap. text 10.00 (*1-57979-124-7*) DIANE Pub.

Nuclear Regulatory Commission Issuances. Government Printing Office Staff. pap. 71.00 (*0-16-012070-5*) USGPO.

Nuclear Regulatory Commission Rules & Regulations for Medical Licensees. Government Printing Office Staff. 1984. ring bd. 354.00 (*0-16-017543-7*) USGPO.

Nuclear Regulatory Commission Rules & Regulations, Title 10, Code of Federal Regulations. Government Printing Office Staff. 1983. ring bd. 584.00 (*0-16-017533-X*) USGPO.

***Nuclear Regulatory Legislation, 104th Congress.** Government Printing Office Staff. 585p. 1998. per. 29.00 (*0-16-049426-5*); per. 26.00 (*0-16-049427-3*) USGPO.

***Nuclear Regulatory Legislation, 105th Congress.** 532p. 2000. per. 28.00 (*0-16-059106-6*) USGPO.

***Nuclear Regulatory Legislation, 105th Congress.** 556p. 2000. per. 30.00 (*0-16-059109-0*) USGPO.

Nuclear Renewal. Richard Rhodes. 1999. pap. 10.95 (*0-14-024134-5*) Viking Penguin.

Nuclear Research U. S. A. Knowledge for the Future. Albert V. Crewe & Joseph J. Katz. (Illus.). 1990. 13.00 (*0-8446-0564-6*) Peter Smith.

Nuclear Risks in Tribal Communities: Scoping Report by the Confederated Tribes of the Umatilla Indian Reservation. (Illus.). 110p. (Orig.). (C). 1995. pap. text 30.00 (*0-7881-2586-9*) DIANE Pub.

Nuclear Rites: A Weapons Laboratory at the End of the Cold War. Hugh Gusterson. LC 96-7234. (Illus.). 392p. 1996. 45.00 (*0-520-08147-1*, Pub. by U CA Pr) Cal Prin Full Svc.

Nuclear Rites: A Weapons Laboratory at the End of the Cold War. Hugh Gusterson. 392p. 1998. pap. text 19.95 (*0-520-21373-4*, Pub. by U CA Pr) Cal Prin Full Svc.

Nuclear Rivalry & International Order. Ed. by Jorn Gjelstad & Olav Njolstad. (Peace Research Institute, Oslo Ser.). 256p. (C). 1996. 75.00 (*0-8039-7753-0*) Sage.

Nuclear Rivals in the Middle East. Shyam Bhatia. 160p. 1988. lib. bdg. 57.50 (*0-415-00479-9*) Routledge.

Nuclear Safeguards & the International Atomic Energy Agency. (Illus.). 147p. (Orig.). (C). 1995. pap. text 35.00 (*0-7881-2443-9*) DIANE Pub.

Nuclear Safety. M. M. Williams. (Illus.). 1979. pap. 22.00 (*0-08-024752-0*, Pergamon Pr) Elsevier.

Nuclear Safety see Nuclear Power Experience: Nuclear Safety

Nuclear Safety see Nuclear Power & Its Fuel Cycle

Nuclear Safety: A Human Factors Perspective. Jyuji Misumi. LC 99-179121. 350p. 1999. 110.00 (*0-7484-0818-5*) Taylor & Francis.

Nuclear Safety: Concerns with Nuclear Facilities & Other Sources of Radiation in the Soviet Union. (Illus.). 41p. (Orig.). (C). 1996. pap. text 20.00 (*0-7881-2952-X*) DIANE Pub.

Nuclear Safety: International Assistance Effprst to Make Soviet-Designed Reactors Safer. (Illus.). 48p. 1994. pap. text 35.00 (*1-57979-083-6*) DIANE Pub.

Nuclear Safety: International Assistance Efforts to Make Soviet-Designed Reactors Safer. (Illus.). 43p. (Orig.). (C). 1994. pap. text 25.00 (*0-7881-1507-3*) DIANE Pub.

Nuclear Safety: Risks & Regulation. William C. Wood. LC 82-22730. (AEI Studies: No. 370). (Illus.). 96p. reprint ed. pap. 30.00 (*0-8357-4516-3*, 203737400008) Bks Demand.

Nuclear Safety: Status of U. S. Assistance to Improve the Safety of Soviet-Designed Reactors. Bernice Steinhardt. (Illus.). 72p. (C). 1998. reprint ed. pap. text 30.00 (*0-7881-3930-4*) DIANE Pub.

Nuclear Safety: U. S. Assistance to Upgrade Soviet-Designed Nuclear Reactors in the Czech Republic. (Illus.). 31p. (C). 1996. reprint ed. pap. text 25.00 (*0-7881-3664-X*) DIANE Pub.

Nuclear Safety Research in OECD Countries: Areas of Agreement, Areas for Further Action, Increasing Need for Further Collaboration. NEA Staff. LC 97-182172. 80p. (Orig.). 1996. pap. 20.00 (*92-64-15336-5*, 66-96-15-1, Pub. by Org for Econ) OECD.

Nuclear Safety Research in OECD Countries: Capabilities & Facilities. 104p. 1997. pap. 28.00 (*92-64-15509-0*, Pub. by Org for Econ) OECD.

Nuclear Safety Review for 1996. (Yearbook Ser.: Pt. D). 64p. 1996. pap. 16.00 (*92-0-103496-2*, STI/PUB/1019, Pub. by IAEA) Bernan Associates.

Nuclear Safety Review for 1992 Pt. D: IAEA Yearbook. IAEA Staff. 130p. 1992. pap. 25.00 (*92-0-102292-1*, STI/PUB/920, Pub. by IAEA) Bernan Associates.

Nuclear Safety Review for (Yr.) (Part D of the IAEA Yearbook) 1994. International Atomic Energy Agency Staff. 107p. 1994. pap. 15.00 (*92-0-102594-7*, STI/PUB/957, Pub. by IAEA) Bernan Associates.

Nuclear Science & Technology: State-of-the-Art Review on Technology for Measuring & Controlling Very Low Level Radioactivity in Relation to the Decommissioning of Nuclear Power Plants. M. Hulot et al. (Illus.). 126p. (Orig.). (C). 1995. pap. text 40.00 (*0-7881-2590-7*) DIANE Pub.

Nuclear Seasons. Espinet. 96p. 1995. per. write for info. (*0-920813-61-5*) Sister Vis Pr.

***Nuclear Security.** Helen Cothran. LC 00-30904. (At Issue Ser.). (Illus.). 2001. lib. bdg. write for info. (*0-7377-0478-0*) Greenhaven.

Nuclear Seduction: Why the Arms Race Doesn't Matter - And What Does. William A. Schwartz et al. 1989. 38.00 (*0-520-06134-9*, Pub. by U CA Pr); pap. 15.95 (*0-520-08283-4*, Pub. by U CA Pr) Cal Prin Full Svc.

Nuclear Shapes & Nuclear Structure at Low Excitation Energies. M. Vergnes et al. (NATO ASI Ser.: Vol. 289). (Illus.). 472p. (C). 1992. text 140.00 (*0-306-44195-0*, Kluwer Plenum) Kluwer Academic.

Nuclear Shell Model. K. Heyde. Ed. by M. K. Gaillard et al. (Series in Nuclear & Particle Physics). (Illus.). 392p. 1990. 91.95 (*0-387-51581-X*) Spr-Verlag.

Nuclear Shell Model. 2nd ed. K. Heyde. 400p. 1994. 79.95 (*0-387-58072-7*) Spr-Verlag.

Nuclear Shell Models: Proceedings of the Nuclear Shell Models Symposium in Honor of the 60th Birthday of Igal Talmi, Philadelphia, 1984. Ed. by M. Vallieres & B. H. Wildenthal. 754p. 1985. 114.00 (*9971-978-23-7*) World Scientific Pub.

Nuclear Simulation: Second European Nuclear Simulation Symposium Schliersee, October, 1990 Proceedings. M. R. Heller. (Illus.). viii, 240p. 1990. 79.95 (*0-387-53085-1*) Spr-Verlag.

Nuclear Spectroscopy, 2 pts. Ed. by Fay Ajzenberg-Selove. 1960. write for info. (*0-318-50319-0*) Acad Pr.

Nuclear Spectroscopy & Nuclear Interactions: Proceedings of the International Symposium Held at Osaka, Japan, March 1984. Hiroyasu Ejiri & T. Fukuda. 776p. 1984. 89.00 (*9971-966-54-9*) World Scientific Pub.

Nuclear Spectroscopy of Astrophysical Sources. Ed. by Neil Gehrels & Gerald H. Share. LC 88-71625. (AIP Conference Proceedings Ser.: No. 170). 400p. 1988. 65.00 (*0-88318-370-6*) Am Inst Physics.

Nuclear Spectroscopy of Fission Products: Thirty-Five Papers from a Workshop on the Nuclear Spectroscopy of Fission Products Held at the Institut Laue- Langevin, Grenoble, 21-23 May 1979. Institute of Physics, Great Britain Electron Micro. Ed. by Till Von Egidy. LC 80-511666. (Conference Ser.: No. 51). 344p. reprint ed. pap. 106.70 (*0-7837-3249-X*, 204326800007) Bks Demand.

Nuclear Spectroscopy on Charge Density Wave Systems. Ed. by Tilman Butz. LC 92-12827. (Physics & Chemistry of Materials with Low-Dimensional Structures Ser.: Vol. 15). 332p. (C). 1992. text 208.00 (*0-7923-1779-3*) Kluwer Academic.

Nuclear Spring. Georgiana Hart. (Illus.). (Orig.). 1987. pap. 10.95 (*0-9617820-0-5*) Material Press.

Nuclear Strategizing: Deterrence & Reality. Stephen J. Cimbala. LC 87-38496. 316p. 1988. 59.95 (*0-275-92987-6*, C2987, Praeger Pubs) Greenwood.

Nuclear Strategy & European Security Dilemmas. Panayiotis Ifestos. (Towards an Autonomous European Defence System? Ser.). 496p. 1988. text 96.95 (*0-566-05641-0*, Pub. by Dartmth Pub) Ashgate Pub Co.

Nuclear Strategy & National Security: Points of View. Ed. by Robert J. Pranger & Roger P. Labrie. LC 77-15624. (AEI Studies: No. 175). 526p. reprint ed. pap. 163.10 (*0-8357-4517-1*, 203737500008) Bks Demand.

Nuclear Strategy & National Style. Colin S. Gray. LC 86-4665. 364p. 1986. lib. bdg. 29.95 (*0-8191-5333-8*) U Pr of Amer.

Nuclear Strategy & Strategic Planning. Colin S. Gray & William R. Van Cleave. LC 83-20800. (Philadelphia Policy Papers). 130p. (Orig.). (C). 1984. pap. 5.95 (*0-910191-07-7*) For Policy Res.

An Asterisk (*) at the beginning of an entry indicates that the title is appearing for the first time.

Nuclear Strategy & the Code of the Warrior: Faces of Mars & Shiva in the Crisis of Human Survival. Ed. by Richard Grossinger & Lindy Hough. (Io Ser.: No. 33). 300p. (Orig.). 1984. 25.00 (*0-938190-50-4*); pap. 12.95 (*0-938190-49-0*) North Atlantic.

Nuclear Strategy & World Order: The U. S. Imperative. Louis R. Beres. 52p. 1982. pap. 14.95 (*0-911646-12-4*) Transaction Pubs.

***Nuclear Strategy for India.** Rajan Menon. LC 00-38744. 2000. pap. write for info. (*0-7619-9450-5*) Sage.

Nuclear Strategy in a Dynamic World: American Policy in the 1980s. Donald M. Snow. LC 80-13634. 298p. 1981. pap. 92.40 (*0-7837-8405-8*, 205921600009) Bks Demand.

***Nuclear Strategy in the Twenty-first Century.** Stephen J. Cimbala. LC 99-52984. 224p. 2000. 65.00 (*0-275-96869-3*, Praeger Pubs) Greenwood.

Nuclear Strike: Official Game Secrets. Prima Publishing Staff. LC 97-69327. 112p. 1997. per. 12.99 (*0-7615-1214-4*) Prima Pub.

Nuclear Structure. Aage Bohr & Ben R. Mottelson. LC 97-51929. 1998. 86.00 (*981-02-3979-3*); 86.00 (*981-02-3980-7*) World Scientific Pub.

Nuclear Structure: Single-Particle Motion, Nuclear Deformations. Aage Bohr & Ben R. Mottelson. LC 97-51929. 1256p. 1997. text 86.00 (*981-02-3197-0*) World Scientific Pub.

Nuclear Structure & Function. Ed. by James R. Harris & I. B. Zbarsky. LC 90-14252. (Illus.). 500p. 1990. 135.00 (*0-306-43731-7*, Plenum Trade) Perseus Pubng.

Nuclear Structure & Nuclear Reactions at Low & Intermediate Energies: Proceedings of the International Conference Held at the Jinr, Dubna, Russia in Sept., 1992. Ed. by R. Jolos. (Illus.). 400p. 1993. pap. text. write for info. (*0-911767-81-9*) Hadronic Pr Inc.

Nuclear Structure at High Spin, Excitation, & Momentum Transfer. Ed. by Hermann Nann. LC 86-70837. (AIP Conference Proceedings Ser.: No. 142). 488p. 1986. lib. bdg. 70.00 (*0-88318-341-2*) Am Inst Physics.

Nuclear Structure from a Simple Perspective. Richard F. Casten. (Oxford Studies in Nuclear Physics). (Illus.). 400p. 1990. text 85.00 (*0-19-504599-8*) OUP.

***Nuclear Structure from a Simple Perspective.** 2nd ed. Richard F. Casten. (Oxford Studies in Nuclear Physics: Vol. 23). (Illus.). 432p. 2000. pap. text 60.00 (*0-19-850724-0*) OUP.

Nuclear Structure Models. R. Bengtsson et al. 520p. 1993. text 109.00 (*981-02-1131-7*) World Scientific Pub.

***Nuclear Structure 98.** Ed. by Cyrus Baktash. (Conference Proceedings Ser.: Vol. 481). (Illus.). 632p. 1999. 165.00 (*1-56396-858-4*, Pub. by Am Inst Physics) Spr-Verlag.

Nuclear Structure of the Zirconium Region. J. Eberth et al. (Illus.). 450p. 1988. 104.95 (*0-387-50120-7*) Spr-Verlag.

Nuclear Structure, Reactions & Symmetries: Proceedings of the International Conference on Nuclear Structure, Reactions & Symmetries Dubrovink, Yugoslavia 5-14 June 1986, 2 vols. Ed. by R. A. Meyer & Vladimir Paar. 309p. 1986. text 164.00 (*9971-5-0141-4*) World Scientific Pub.

Nuclear Structure Study with Neutrons. International Conference on Nuclear Structure Staf. Ed. by J. Ero & J. Szucs. LC 73-17651. (Illus.). 514p. 1974. reprint ed. pap. 159.40 (*0-608-05475-5*, 206594400006) Bks Demand.

Nuclear Structure, 1985: Proceeding of the Niels Bohr Centennial Conference, Copenhagen, Denmark, May 20-25, 1985, Set. Ed. by Ricardo A. Brogila et al. 614p. 1985. 146.00 (*0-317-38671-9*, North Holland) Elsevier.

Nuclear Sub-Benzene Hydrocarbons see Rodd's Chemistry of Carbon Compounds

Nuclear Submarine Decommissioning & Related Problems: Proceedings of the NATO Advanced Research Workshop, Moscow, Russia, June 19-22, 1995. A. A. Sarkisov. Ed. by L. G. LeSage. LC 96-9885. (NATO ASI Series, Partnership SubSeries 1: Disarmament Technologies). 368p. (C). 1996. text 217.50 (*0-7923-4189-9*) Kluwer Academic.

Nuclear Submarine Decontamination: Proceedings of the International Seminar on Nuclear War & Peace. K. Goebel. (Science & Culture Ser.). 1998. 68.00 (*981-02-3526-7*) World Scientific Pub.

Nuclear Submicroscopy. G. Jasmin & R. Simard. (Methods & Achievements in Experimental Pathology Ser.: Vol. 12). (Illus.). viii, 300p. 1986. 249.75 (*3-8055-4137-6*) S Karger.

Nuclear Summer: The Clash of Communities at the Seneca Women's Peace Encampment. Louise Krasniewicz. LC 91-55538. (Anthropology of Comtemporary Issues Ser.). (Illus.). 280p. 1992. pap. text 17.95 (*0-8014-9938-0*) Cornell U Pr.

Nuclear Survival: Effects of Radiation & Principles of Detection. 1986. lib. bdg. 250.00 (*0-8490-3522-8*) Gordon Pr.

Nuclear Systems, I. Neil E. Todreas & Mujid S. Kazimi. LC 66-56045. 700p. 1989. 154.00 (*0-89116-935-0*); pap. 69.95 (*1-56032-051-6*) Hemisp Pub.

Nuclear Systems, Vol. II. Neil E. Todreas & Mujid S. Kazimi. LC 66-56045. 700p. 1990. pap. 85.00 (*1-56032-079-6*) Hemisp Pub.

Nuclear Systems, Vol. II. Neil E. Todreas & Mujid S. Kazimi. LC 66-56045. 700p. 1990. 159.00 (*0-89116-936-9*) Hemisp Pub.

Nuclear Techniques for Analytical & Industrial Applications. G. Vourvopoulos & T. Paradellis. 1993. text 78.00 (*981-02-1322-0*) World Scientific Pub.

Nuclear Techniques in Diagnostic Medicine. Ed. by P. P. van Rijk. 1986. text 401.00 (*0-89838-744-2*) Kluwer Academic.

Nuclear Techniques in Soil - Plant Studies for Agriculture & Environmental Preservation. (Illus.). 735p. (Orig.). (C). 1995. pap. text 250.00 (*0-7881-2608-3*) DIANE Pub.

Nuclear Techniques in Soil - Plant Studies for Sustainable Agriculture & Environment. I.A.E.A. Staff. LC 96-167541. 735p. 1995. pap. 255.00 (*92-0-100895-3*, STI/PUB/947, Pub. by IAEA) Bernan Associates.

Nuclear Techniques in Structural Chemistry. Ed. by Attila Vertes & Bela Levay. 266p. 1991. 50.00 (*1-56081-510-8*, Wiley-VCH) Wiley.

Nuclear Technologies for Space Exploration Proceedings, Jackson Hole, WY, August 1992, 3 vols., Set. 940p. 103.00 (*0-89448-174-6*, 700177) Am Nuclear Soc.

Nuclear Technology see Woerterbuch Kerntechnik: English-German-French-Russian

Nuclear Terrorism & Countermeasures: Hearing Before the Military Research & Development Subcommittee of the Committee on National Security, House of Representatives, One Hundred Fifth Congress, First Session : Hearings Held October 1 & 2, 1997. United States Government. LC 98-143774. iv, 297 p. 1998. write for info. (*0-16-056199-X*) USGPO.

Nuclear Test Ban. Languages Service Staff. (ARA, ENG & FRE.). 300p. 30.00 (*92-1-000057-9*, JX1974) UN.

***Nuclear Test Explosions.** Frederick Warner. LC 99-35805. 306p. 2000. 180.00 (*0-471-97848-5*, Wiley Heyden) Wiley.

Nuclear Tests: Long-Term Consequences in the Semipalatinsk/Altai Region. NATO Staff. Ed. by Charles S. Shapiro et al. LC 97-39008. (NATO ASI Ser.: Vol. 36). 202p. 1998. 110.00 (*3-540-63805-9*) Spr-Verlag.

Nuclear Theme As a Determinant of Pa Tet in Javanese Music. Mantle Hood. LC 77-5680. (Music Reprint Ser.). 1977. reprint ed. lib. bdg. 45.00 (*0-306-77419-4*) Da Capo.

Nuclear Theology. Kevin Little. 80p. 1999. pap. 8.00 (*0-8059-4540-7*) Dorrance.

Nuclear Theory Vol. 1: Nuclear Models. 3rd enl. rev. ed. Judah M. Eisenberg & W. Greiner. 918p. 1987. pap. 105.50 (*0-444-87073-3*) Elsevier.

Nuclear Theory Vol. 2: Excitation Mechanisms of the Nucleus. 2nd ed. Judah M. Eisenberg & Walter Greiner. 422p. 1976. pap. 44.75 (*0-7204-0483-5*, North Holland) Elsevier.

Nuclear Theory Vol. 2: Excitation Mechanisms of the Nucleus. 3rd rev. ed. Judah M. Eisenberg & W. Greiner. 516p. 1988. pap. 108.25 (*0-444-87082-2*, North Holland) Elsevier.

Nuclear Theory, 1981: Proceedings of the Nuclear Theory Summer Workshop Institute of Theoretical Physics, Santa Barbara, CA, August 1981. George F. Bertsch. 309p. 1982. 52.00 (*9971-950-06-5*); pap. 30.00 (*9971-950-07-3*) World Scientific Pub.

Nuclear Thermal Hydraulics Conference, 5th, San Francisco, CA, Nov. 26-30, 1989. 520p. 1989. 39.00 (*0-89448-150-9*, 700148) Am Nuclear Soc.

Nuclear Thermal Hydraulics Conference, 6th, Washington, DC, Nov. 11-16, 1990, Set. 240p. 1990. 40.00 (*0-89448-156-8*, 700156) Am Nuclear Soc.

Nuclear Thermal Hydraulics, 4th Topical Meeting, Washington, D. C., Oct. 30-Nov. 4, 1988, 2 vols. 4th ed. 166p. 1988. 30.00 (*0-89448-147-9*, 700140) Am Nuclear Soc.

Nuclear Thermal Hydraulics, 3rd Topical Proceedings, Los Angeles, CA: Nov. 15-19, 1987. 139p. 1987. 30.00 (*0-89448-135-5*, 700126) Am Nuclear Soc.

Nuclear Threshold: The Global Spread of Nuclear Weapons, 1990-1991. Leonard S. Spector & Jacqueline R. Smith. 145p. (C). 2000. text 29.95 (*0-8133-1468-2*); pap. text 9.95 (*0-8133-1469-0*) Westview.

Nuclear Tibet. John Ackerly. 64p. pap. 7.50 (*1-879245-06-X*) Intl Campaign Tibet.

Nuclear Track Registration: Proceedings of the Pacific Northwest Conference, 5th, Hanford Engineering Development Laboratory, Westinghouse Hanford Company, Richland, WA, July 28-29, 1982. Ed. by E. V. Benton et al. 96p. 1983. pap. 61.00 (*0-08-030274-2*, Pergamon Pr) Elsevier.

Nuclear Tracks & Radiation Measurements, Vol. 15, Nos. 1-4 see Solid State Nuclear Track Detectors: Proceedings of the 14th International Conference, Lahore, Pakistan, 2-6 April, 1988

Nuclear Tracks in Solids: Principles & Applications. Robert L. Fleischer et al. LC 73-90670. (Illus.). 627p. reprint ed. pap. 194.40 (*0-7837-4845-0*, 204449200003) Bks Demand.

Nuclear Transmutation: The Reality of Cold Fusion. Tadahiko Mizuno. Ed. by Eugene Mallove. Tr. by Jed Rothwell from JPN. LC 98-88301. (Illus.). 152p. 1998. 29.95 (*1-892925-00-1*) Cold Fusion Tech.

Nuclear Turning Point: A Blueprint for Deep Cuts & De-Alerting of Nuclear Weapons. Bruce Blair et al. LC 98-58149. 420p. 1999. 52.95 (*0-8157-0954-4*); pap. 22.95 (*0-8157-0953-6*) Brookings.

Nuclear (II), Solar, & Geothermal Energy see 1997 Annual Book of ASTM Standards: Nuclear, Solar, & Geothermal Energy, Section 12

Nuclear Volume & Cellular Metabolism. R. Hildebrand. (Advances in Anatomy, Embryology & Cell Biology Ser.: Vol. 60). (Illus.). 60p. 1980. 28.00 (*0-387-09796-1*) Spr-Verlag.

Nuclear War: The Aftermath - Special Ambio Publication, Vol. 11. 3rd ed. Royal Swedish Academy of Sciences Staff. Ed. by J. Peterson & D. Hinrichsen. (Illus.). 204p. 1982. pap. text 98.00 (*0-08-028176-1*, Pub. by Pergamon Repr) Franklin.

Nuclear War: The Moral Dimension. James E. Child. (Studies in Social Philosophy & Policy: No. 6). 150p. (Orig.). 1986. 16.95 (*0-912051-09-4*); pap. 8.95 (*0-912051-10-8*) Soc Phil Pol.

Nuclear War: The Moral Dimension. Ed. by James E. Child. 160p. (Orig.). 1985. pap. 18.95 (*0-912051-05-1*) Transaction Pubs.

Nuclear War: The Moral Dimension. James W. Child. 224p. (Orig.). 1986. 39.95 (*0-912051-04-3*) Transaction Pubs.

Nuclear War & Nuclear Strategy: Unfinished Business, 68. Stephen J. Cimbala. LC 87-12003. (Contributions in Military Studies Ser.: No. 68). 299p. 1987. 59.95 (*0-313-26015-X*, CNW/, Greenwood Pr) Greenwood.

Nuclear War & Radioactive Fallout: Index of New Information with Authors, Subjects & References. Henry A. Reddy. 150p. 1997. 47.50 (*0-7883-1320-7*); pap. 44.50 (*0-7883-1321-5*) ABBE Pubs Assn.

Nuclear War & You: Before, During, After. Jerrold Richards. LC 84-70562. 272p. (Orig.). 1984. pap. 8.95 (*0-9613278-0-4*) CFPR Pubns.

Nuclear War Survival Skills. 2nd rev. ed. Cresson H. Kearny. LC 87-60790. (Illus.). 282p. 1988. pap. text 12.50 (*0-942487-01-X*) Oregon Inst Sci Med.

Nuclear Warfare: Science & Medical Subject Analysis with Reference Bibliography. American Health Research Institute Staff. LC 85-48095. 150p. 1987. 47.50 (*0-88164-462-5*); pap. 44.50 (*0-88164-463-3*) ABBE Pubs Assn.

Nuclear Waste: Change in Test Strategy Sound, but D. O. E. Overstated Savings. 48p. 1994. pap. text 20.00 (*1-57979-084-4*) DIANE Pub.

Nuclear Waste: Change in Test Strategy Sound, but DOE Overstated Savings. 40p. pap. text 15.00 (*0-7881-1590-1*) DIANE Pub.

Nuclear Waste: Defense Waste Processing Facility-Cost, Schedule, & Technical Issues. (Illus.). 62p. (Orig.). (C). 1993. pap. text 25.00 (*1-56806-389-X*) DIANE Pub.

Nuclear Waste: Foreign Countries' Approaches to High-Level Waste Storage & Disposal. 60p. (Orig.). 1994. pap. text 45.00 (*1-57979-085-2*) DIANE Pub.

Nuclear Waste: Foreign Countries' Approaches to High-Level Waste Storage & Disposal. 59p. (Orig.). (C). 1994. pap. text 25.00 (*0-7881-1329-1*) DIANE Pub.

***Nuclear Waste: Further Actions Needed to Increase the Use of Innovative Cleanup Technologies.** James Noel. 65p. (C). 1999. pap. text 20.00 (*0-7881-8274-9*) DIANE Pub.

Nuclear Waste: Greater Use of Removal Actions Could Cut Time & Cost for Cleanup. (Illus.). 22p. (Orig.). (C). 1996. pap. text 20.00 (*0-7881-3148-6*) DIANE Pub.

Nuclear Waste: Nevada's Use of Nuclear Waste Grant Funds. 35p. (Orig.). (C). 1996. pap. text 20.00 (*0-7881-3017-X*) DIANE Pub.

Nuclear Waste: The Problem That Won't Go Away. Nicholas Lenssen. 70p. (Orig.). 1991. pap. 5.00 (*1-878071-07-6*) Worldwatch Inst.

Nuclear Waste: Uncertainties about Opening Waste Isolation Pilot Plan. (Illus.). 64p. (Orig.). (C). 1996. pap. text 25.00 (*0-7881-3398-5*) DIANE Pub.

Nuclear Waste: Yucca Mountain Project Behind Schedule & Facing Major Scientific Uncertainties. 56p. (Orig.). (C). 1993. pap. text 25.00 (*1-56806-496-9*) DIANE Pub.

Nuclear Waste Cleanup Technology & Opportunities. Robert Noyes. LC 95-22674. (Illus.). 456p. 1995. 129.00 (*0-8155-1381-X*) Noyes.

Nuclear Waste Disposal: Gambling on Yucca Mountain. Sarah Ginsburg. 176p. 1994. pap. 18.80 (*0-89412-247-9*) Aegean Park Pr.

Nuclear Waste Disposal: Geophysical Safety. Alexei V. Byalko. 304p. 1994. lib. bdg. 159.00 (*0-8493-4469-7*, TD868) CRC Pr.

Nuclear Waste Disposal Crisis. David Lochbaum. 192p. 1995. 34.95 (*0-87814-463-3*) PennWell Bks.

Nuclear Waste Handling & Storage. Ed. by Ralph A. Kohl. (Sessions Proceedings Ser.). 76p. 1986. 3.00 (*0-87262-562-1*) Am Soc Civil Eng.

Nuclear Waste Instrumentation Engineering, Vol. 3536. Ed. by David E. Robertson. 192p. 1999. 59.00 (*0-8194-2997-X*) SPIE.

Nuclear Waste Management. Compiled by American Society of Civil Engineers Staff. LC 82-73506. 52p. 1982. pap. 3.00 (*0-87262-343-2*) Am Soc Civil Eng.

Nuclear Waste Management, No. III. Ed. by George B. Mellinger. (Ceramic Transactions Ser.: Vol. 9). (Illus.). 595p. 1990. 10.00 (*0-944904-24-6*, CT009) Am Ceramic.

Nuclear Waste Management: The Ocean Alternative-Edited Proceedings of a Public Policy Forum Sponsored by the Oceanic Society in the GeorgetownUniversity Law Center, DC, February 6, 1980. Ed. by Thomas Jackson. (Policy Studies on Energy). (Illus.). 100p. 1981. 42.00 (*0-08-027204-5*, Pergamon Pr) Elsevier.

Nuclear Waste Management Abstracts. Richard A. Heckman & Camille Minichino. LC 81-19868. (IFI Data Base Library). 111p. 1982. 85.00 (*0-306-65202-1*, Kluwer Plenum) Kluwer Academic.

Nuclear Waste Management Technology, Vol. 1. Ed. by P. William Tedder & A. M. Platt. 680p. 1989. 126.00 (*0-685-30333-0*) Gordon & Breach.

Nuclear Waste Policy: Siting the High-Level Nuclear Waste Repository. Ed. by David Pijawka & Alvin H. Mushkatel. (Orig.). 1991. pap. 15.00 (*0-944285-27-9*) Pol Studies.

Nuclear Waste Policy Act of 1997: Hearing Before the Committee on Energy & Natural Resources, U. S. Senate. Ed. by Frank H. Murkowski. 119p. (C). 1998. pap. text 25.00 (*0-7881-7297-2*) DIANE Pub.

Nuclear Waste Primer: A Handbook for Citizens. rev. ed. League of Women Voters Staff. (Illus.). 176p. 1994. pap. 10.95 (*1-55821-226-4*, 448) Lyons Pr.

Nuclear Waste Reprocessing. Ed. by G. R. Plumb. (Illus.). 72p. 1984. pap. 44.00 (*0-08-031509-7*, Pergamon Pr) Elsevier.

***Nuclear Waste Storage & Disposal Policy: Congressional Hearing.** Ed. by Frank Murkowski. 99p. 2000. pap. text 20.00 (*0-7567-0144-9*) DIANE Pub.

Nuclear Wastelands: A Global Guide to Nuclear Weapons Production & Its Health & Environmental Effects. Ed. by Arjun Makhijani et al. LC 95-945. 666p. 1995. 65.00 (*0-262-13307-5*) MIT Pr.

***Nuclear Wastelands: A Global Guide to Nuclear Weapons Production & Its Health & Environmental Effects.** Ed. by Arjun Makhijani et al. (Illus.). 696p. (C). 2000. reprint ed. pap. 42.00 (*0-262-63204-7*) MIT Pr.

Nuclear Wastes: Technologies for Separations, Transmutation. National Research Council Staff. 592p. (Orig.). (C). 1996. text 79.95 (*0-309-05226-2*) Natl Acad Pr.

Nuclear Weak Process & Nuclear Structure. Ed. by M. Morita et al. 622p. (C). 1989. text 151.00 (*981-02-0007-2*) World Scientific Pub.

Nuclear-Weapon-Free Zone in the Middle East: Problems & Prospects, 65. Mahmoud Karem. LC 87-7531. (Contributions in Military Studies Ser.: No. 65). 202p. 1988. 52.95 (*0-313-25628-4*, KMW/, Greenwood Pr) Greenwood.

Nuclear Weapons. Adam Brown. (World Issues Ser.). (Illus.). 48p. (J). (gr. 5 up). 1987. 13.95 (*0-685-67572-6*) Rourke Corp.

Nuclear Weapons, Set II. Adan Brown. (World Issues Ser.). (Illus.). 48p. (J). (gr. 5 up). 1987. lib. bdg. 25.27 (*0-86592-278-0*) Rourke Enter.

Nuclear Weapons: A Comprehensive Study. 169p. pap. 19.95 (*92-1-142172-1*, 91.IX.10) UN.

***Nuclear Weapons: More Countries, More Threats.** Tom Streissguth. LC 99-50599. (Issues in Focus Ser.). (Illus.). 112p. (YA). (gr. 6 up). 2000. lib. bdg. 20.95 (*0-7660-1248-4*) Enslow Pubs.

Nuclear Weapons: Principles, Effects & Survivability. Charles S. Grace. Ed. by Geoffrey Lee. (Land Warfare: Brassey's New Battlefield Weapons & Technology Ser.: Vol. 10). (Illus.). 146p. 1993. 40.00 (*0-08-040991-1*, Pub. by Brasseys); pap. 25.00 (*0-08-040992-X*, Pub. by Brasseys) Brasseys.

Nuclear Weapons: The Balance of Terror, the Quest for Peace. A. J. Edwards. LC 85-17383. 275p. (C). 1986. text 64.50 (*0-88706-185-0*); pap. text 21.95 (*0-88706-186-9*) State U NY Pr.

Nuclear Weapons: The Road to Zero. Joseph Rotblat. LC 98-140971. 344p. (C). 1998. text 79.00 (*0-8133-3517-5*, Pub. by Westview) HarpC.

Nuclear Weapons after the Comprehensive Test Ban: Implications for Modernization & Proliferation. Ed. by Eric H. Arnett. LC 96-222615. (SIPRI Publication). (Illus.). 160p. 1996. text 39.95 (*0-19-829194-9*) OUP.

Nuclear Weapons & Arms Control in South Asia after the Test Ban. Ed. by Eric Arnett. (SIPRI Research Reports Ser.: No. 14). (Illus.). 108p. 1998. text 47.50 (*0-19-829412-3*); pap. text 24.50 (*0-19-829411-5*) OUP.

Nuclear Weapons & Arms Control in the Middle East. Shai Feldman. LC 96-44081. (CSIA Studies in International Security). 350p. 1996. 40.00 (*0-262-06189-9*); pap. text 20.00 (*0-262-56108-5*) MIT Pr.

Nuclear Weapons & British Strategic Planning, 1955-1958. Martin S. Navias. (Nuclear History Program Ser.). 280p. 1991. text 65.00 (*0-19-827754-7*, 12190) OUP.

Nuclear Weapons & Contemporary International Law. 2nd rev. ed. Nagendra K. Singh & Edward J. McWhinney. (C). 1988. lib. bdg. 228.00 (*90-247-3637-4*) Kluwer Academic.

Nuclear Weapons & International Law. Istvan S. Pogany. LC 86-31342. 226p. 1987. text 39.95 (*0-312-57986-1*) St Martin.

***Nuclear Weapons & International Law in the Post Cold War World.** Charles J. Moxley, Jr. LC 00-29866. 832p. 2000. write for info. (*1-57292-152-8*, Pub. by Austin & Winfield) U Pr of Amer.

Nuclear Weapons & Law, 31. Ed. by Arthur S. Miller & Martin Feinrider. LC 84-4482. (Contributions in Legal Studies: No. 31). (Illus.). 415p. 1984. 79.50 (*0-313-24206-2*, MNW/, Greenwood Pr) Greenwood.

Nuclear Weapons & Nuclear War: A Source Book for Health Professionals. Henry Abraham. Ed. by Christine Cassel et al. LC 83-24511. 553p. 1984. 65.00 (*0-275-91423-2*, C1423, Praeger Pubs) Greenwood.

Nuclear Weapons & Scientific Responsibility. C. G. Weeramantry. LC 87-2804. 225p. 1987. 25.00 (*0-89341-542-1*, Longwood Academic) Hollowbrook.

***Nuclear Weapons & Scientific Responsibility.** C. G. Weeramantry. 450p. 1999. pap. text 114.00 (*90-411-1289-8*) Kluwer Law Intl.

Nuclear Weapons & the Future of Humanity: The Fundamental Questions. Ed. by Avner Cohen & Steven Lee. LC 84-18362. (Philosophy & Society Ser.). (Illus.). 512p. (C). 1986. pap. 31.00 (*0-8476-7258-1*) Rowman.

Nuclear Weapons & the National Interest: The Early Years. Michael O. Wheeler. (Illus.). 111p. (C). 1996. reprint ed. pap. text 25.00 (*0-7881-2950-3*) DIANE Pub.

***Nuclear Weapons & the World Court.** Ved P. Nanda. LC 98-20697. 1998. 95.00 (*1-57105-051-5*) Transnatl Pubs.

Nuclear Weapons Are Illegal: The Historic Opinion of the World Court & How It Will Be Enforced. Ed. by Ann F. Ginger. LC 98-13353. (Illus.). 558p. 1998. pap. 28.50 (*0-945257-86-4*) Apex Pr.

Nuclear Weapons Are Illegal: The Historic Opinion of the World Court & How It Will Be Enforced. Ed. by Ann F. Ginger. LC 98-13353. 558p. 1998. 49.50 (*0-945257-87-2*) Apex Pr.

Nuclear Weapons, Arms Control & the Threat of Thermonuclear War: 7th Supplement, 1993-1995. 7th ed. Blair D. Hydrick. LC 96-41845. (Special Studies). 1996. suppl. ed. 1655.00 (*1-55655-539-3*) U Pubns Amer.

N

An Asterisk (*) at the beginning of an entry indicates that the title is appearing for the first time.

Nuclear Weapons Complex: Management for Health, Safety & the Environment. National Research Council Staff. 156p. 1989. pap. text 19.00 (*0-309-04179-1*) Natl Acad Pr.

Nuclear Weapons Databook Vol. 2: U. S. Nuclear Warhead Production. Thomas B. Cochran et al. LC 82-24376. 240p. 1987. text 39.95 (*0-88730-124-X*, HarpBusn); pap. text 40.00 (*0-88730-125-8*, HarpBusn) HarpInfo.

Nuclear Weapons Databook Vol. II: U. S. Nuclear Warhead Production. Thomas B. Cochran et al. 1987. 40.00 (*0-318-23279-0*); pap. 25.00 (*0-318-23280-4*) Natl Resources Defense Coun.

Nuclear Weapons Databook Vol. III: U. S. Nuclear Warhead Facility Profiles. Thomas B. Cochran et al. 132p. 1987. 39.95 (*0-318-39810-9*); pap. 24.95 (*0-318-39811-7*) Natl Resources Defense Coun.

Nuclear Weapons Databook Vol. 3: U. S. Nuclear Warhead Facility Profiles. Thomas Cochran et al. LC 87-14552. (Nuclear Weapons Databook Ser.). 160p. 1987. pap. 29.95 (*0-88730-146-0*, HarpBusn); text 39.95 (*0-88730-126-6*, HarpBusn) HarpInfo.

Nuclear Weapons Databook Vol. 4: Soviet Nuclear Weapons. Thomas B. Cochran et al. 364p. 1989. pap. text 40.00 (*0-88730-049-9*, HarpBusn) HarpInfo.

Nuclear Weapons Employment Doctrine & Procedures. 1995. lib. bdg. 256.95 (*0-8490-6559-3*) Gordon Pr.

Nuclear Weapons-Free Zones. Ramesh C. Thakur. LC 98-23639. 1998. text 69.95 (*0-312-21745-5*) St Martin.

Nuclear Weapons in a Changing Europe. Ed. by Vilho Harle & Pekka Sivonen. (Tapri Studies in International Relations). 256p. 1991. text 59.00 (*0-86187-094-8*) St Martin.

Nuclear Weapons in Israel. Taysir N. Nashif. viii, 124p. 1996. 15.00 (*81-7024-753-5*, Pub. by Ashish Pub Hse) Nataraj Bks.

Nuclear Weapons in the Changing World: Perspectives from Europe, Asia, & North America. P. J. Garrity & S. Maaranen. (Issues in International Security Ser.). (Illus.). 304p. (C). 1992. 45.00 (*0-306-43472-5*, Plenum Trade) Perseus Pubng.

Nuclear Weapons in the University Classroom: An Interdisciplinary Teaching Reference. Michael S. Hamilton et al. 164p. (Orig.). (C). 1990. pap. text 19.00 (*0-8191-7742-3*) U Pr of Amer.

Nuclear Weapons Industry. Kenneth A. Bertsch & Linda S. Shaw. 405p. 1984. pap. text 10.00 (*0-931035-75-9*) IRRC Inc DC.

Nuclear Weapons of the United States: An Illustrated History. James N. Gibson. (Illus.). 240p. 1996. 49.95 (*0-7643-0063-6*) Schiffer.

Nuclear Weapons, Policies & the Test Ban Issue. William R. Van Cleave & S. T. Cohen. LC 86-25221. 118p. 1987. 45.00 (*0-275-92312-6*, C2312, Praeger Pubs) Greenwood.

Nuclear Weapons Safety & Trident. John Harvey & Stefan Michalowski. 104p. (Orig.). 1993. pap. 12.00 (*0-935371-28-1*) CFISAC.

Nuclear Weapons Tests: Prohibition or Limitation? Ed. by Jozef Goldblat & David Cox. (SIPRI Publication). (Illus.). 446p. 1988. text 95.00 (*0-19-829120-5*) OUP.

Nuclear Winter. Mark A. Harwell. (Illus.). xxi, 179p. 1986. 71.95 (*0-387-96093-7*) Spr-Verlag.

Nuclear Winter. Ed. by Gary E. McCuen. (Ideas in Conflict Ser.). (Illus.). 140p. (YA). (gr. 7-12). 1987. lib. bdg. 15.95 (*0-86596-062-3*) G E M.

Nuclear Winter & the New Defense Systems: Problems & Perspectives, the 4th International Seminar on Nuclear War. W. S. Newman & S. Stipcich. (Science & Culture Ser.). 532p. 1992. text 123.00 (*981-02-1187-2*) World Scientific Pub.

Nuclear Winter, Deterrence & the Prevention of Nuclear War. Ed. by Peter C. Sederberg. LC 86-9412. 210p. 1986. 49.95 (*0-275-92160-3*, C2160, Praeger Pubs) Greenwood.

Nuclear Winter Man. Terry Deary. LC 96-30163. (Classified Ser.). 96p. (J). (gr. 5 up). 1997. pap. 5.95 (*0-7534-5044-5*) LKC.

***Nuclease Methods & Protocols.** Ed. by Catherine H. Schein. LC 00-23797. (Methods in Molecular Biology Ser.: Vol. 160). 575p. 2000. 99.50 (*0-89603-679-0*) Humana.

Nucleases. Ed. by Stuart M. Linn & Richard J. Roberts. LC 85-9653. (Cold Spring Harbor Monographs: No. 14). 402p. reprint ed. pap. 124.70 (*0-7837-2004-1*, 204227800002) Bks Demand.

Nucleases, Monograph 25. 2nd ed. Ed. by Richard J. Roberts et al. (Illus.). 300p. (C). 1994. pap. 38.00 (*0-87969-426-2*) Cold Spring Harbor.

Nucleation. A.L. Greer & K.F. Kelton. 1999. write for info. (*0-08-042147-4*, Pergamon Pr) Elsevier.

Nucleation. Ed. by Albert C. Zettlemoyer. LC 70-77144. (Illus.). 618p. reprint ed. pap. 191.60 (*0-608-30246-5*, 205502900008) Bks Demand.

***Nucleation: Basic Theory with Applications.** Dimo Kashchiev. LC 99-51578. (Illus.). 544p. 2000. 149.95 (*0-7506-4682-9*) Buttrwrth-Heinemann.

Nucleation & Atmospheric Aerosols. Ed. by N. Fukuta & P. E. Wagner. LC 92-25348. 523p. 1992. 63.00 (*0-937194-26-3*) A Deepak Pub.

Nucleation & Atmospheric Aerosols, 1996: Proceedings of the Fourteenth International Conference on Nucleation & Atmospheric Aerosols. Wagner & Markku Kulmala. LC 96-26489. 966p. 1996. 368.75 (*0-08-042030-3*, Pergamon Pr) Elsevier.

Nucleation & Crystallization in Glasses. Ed. by J. H. Simmons et al. LC 83-125327. (Advances in Ceramics Ser.: Vol. 4). 367p. (Orig.). 1982. reprint ed. pap. 113.80 (*0-608-00720-X*, 206149400009) Bks Demand.

Nucleation & Crystallization in Liquids & Glasses. Ed. by Michael C. Weinberg. LC 92-42210. (Ceramic Transactions Ser.: Vol. 30). 386p. 1993. 74.00 (*0-944904-57-2*, CT030) Am Ceramic.

***Nucleation & Growth Process in Materials Vol. 580: Materials Research Society Symposium Proceedings.** Ed. by A. Gonis et al. 2000. text 93.00 (*1-55899-488-2*) Materials Res.

Nucleation in Papua New Guinea Cultures. Ed. by Marvin K. Mayers & Daniel D. Rath. LC 88-81188. (International Museum of Cultures Publications: No. 23). 120p. (Orig.). 1988. pap. 22.00 (*0-88312-177-8*) S I L Intl.

Nuclei Far from Stability: Fifth International Conference. Ed. by Ian S. Towner. LC 87-73214. (Conference Proceeding Ser.: No. 164). 912p. 1988. lib. bdg. 90.00 (*0-88318-364-1*) Am Inst Physics.

Nuclei Far from Stability & Atomic Masses & Fundamental Constants, 1992: The Proceedings of the 6th International Conference on Nuclei Far from Stability & the 9th International Conference on Atomic Masses & Fundamental Constants Held in Mainz, Germany, 19-24 July 1992. R. Neugart & A. Wohr. (Institute of Physics Conference Ser.: No. 132). 1040p. 1993. 373.00 (*0-7503-0262-3*) IOP Pub.

Nuclei in the Cosmos. H. Oberhummer. Ed. by J. L. Birman et al. (Graduate Texts in Contemporary Physics Ser.). (Illus.). xii, 236p. 1991. 79.95 (*0-387-54198-5*) Spr-Verlag.

Nuclei in the Cosmos: Proceedings of the Second International Symposium on Nuclear Astrophysics Held in Karlsruhe, Germany 6-10 July, 1992. Ed. by F. Kappeler & K. Wisshak. 664p. 1993. 300.00 (*0-7503-0260-7*) IOP Pub.

Nuclei in the Cosmos: Third International Symposium on Nuclear Astrophysics. Maurizio Busso et al. (AIP Conference Proceedings Ser.: No. 327). (Illus.). 650p. 1995. boxed set 135.00 (*1-56396-436-8*, AIP Pr) Spr-Verlag.

Nuclei, Neutrons & Energy: Proceedings of the VIII International School. Ed. by W. Andrejtscheff et al. 492p. 1988. text 117.00 (*9971-5-0692-0*) World Scientific Pub.

Nuclei of Normal Galaxies - Lessons from the Galactic Center: Proceedings of the NATO Advanced Research Workshop, Schloss Ringberg, Kreuth, Bavaria, Germany, July 25-30, 1993. Ed. by R. Genzel. LC 94-32556. (NATO Advanced Science Institutes: Vol. 445). 528p. (C). 1994. text 281.00 (*0-7923-3158-3*) Kluwer Academic.

Nuclei off the Line of Stability. Ed. by Richard A. Meyer & Daeg S. Brenner. LC 86-25905. (ACS Symposium Ser.: No. 324). (Illus.). xvi, 518p. 1986. 104.95 (*0-8412-1005-5*, PA 414) Am Chemical.

Nuclei off the Line of Stability. Ed. by Richard A. Meyer & Daeg S. Brenner. LC 86-25905. (ACS Symposium Ser.: Vol. 324). 552p. 1986. reprint ed. pap. 171.20 (*0-608-03528-9*, 206424700008) Bks Demand.

Nucleic Acid Amplification Techniques for Virus Detection in Transfusion Medicine. Ed. by Gregor Caspari. (Infusionstherapie und Transfusionsmedizin Ser.: Vol. 25, No. 2-3). (Illus.). 140p. 1998. pap. 58.25 (*3-8055-6717-0*) S Karger.

Nucleic Acid Amplification Technologies. H. Lee et al. write for info. (*0-8176-3921-7*) Birkhauser.

Nucleic Acid Amplification Technologies: Application to Disease Diagnosis. Ed. by H. Lee et al. (Molecular & Laboratory Medicine Ser.). (Illus.). 300p. 1997. pap. text 39.95 (*1-881299-04-X*, BioTechniques) Eaton Pub Co.

Nucleic Acid Analysis: Principles & Bioapplications. Ed. by Charles A. Dangler. LC 95-47202. 284p. 1996. 119.95 (*0-471-10358-6*) Wiley.

Nucleic Acid & Molecular Biology, Vol. 8. Ed. by F. Eckstein & David M. Lilley. 255p. 1994. 199.95 (*0-387-57485-9*) Spr-Verlag.

Nucleic Acid & Protein Sequence Analysis. Ed. by M. J. Bishop & C. J. Rawlings. (Practical Approach Ser.). 436p. 1987. 75.00 (*1-85221-007-9*); pap. 49.95 (*1-85221-006-0*) OUP.

Nucleic Acid-Based Diagnosis. S. Jeffery et al. (Medical Perspectives Ser.). (Illus.). 176p. 1997. pap. 38.95 (*0-387-91511-7*) Spr-Verlag.

Nucleic Acid-Binding Protein FactsBook. Rhodes. 192p. 1997. write for info. (*0-12-587078-7*) Acad Pr.

Nucleic Acid Biosynthesis. Ed. by Allen I. Laskin & Jerold A. Last. LC 72-89529. (Methods in Molecular Biology Ser.: No. 4). (Illus.). 288p. reprint ed. pap. 89.30 (*0-7837-0781-9*, 204109500019) Bks Demand.

Nucleic Acid Chemistry: Improved & New Synthetic Procedures, Methods & Techniques, Vol. 4. Ed. by Leroy B. Townsend & R. Stuart Tipson. 432p. 1991. 165.00 (*0-471-54281-4*) Wiley.

Nucleic Acid Electrophoresis. Ed. by Dietmar Tietz. LC 98-7474. (Lab Manual Ser.). (Illus.). ix, 275p. 1998. 79.95 (*3-540-63959-4*) Spr-Verlag.

Nucleic Acid Hybridization. M. L. M. Andersen. 1998. pap. 34.95 (*0-387-91556-7*) Spr-Verlag.

Nucleic Acid Hybridization: Essential Data. Ed. by P. M. Gilmartin. 150p. 1996. pap. 37.00 (*0-471-95084-X*) Wiley.

Nucleic Acid Hybridization: Essential Techniques. Ed. by Jeff Ross. LC 97-19726. (Essential Techniques Ser.). 176p. 1998. pap. 49.95 (*0-471-97125-1*) Wiley.

Nucleic Acid-Metal Ion Interactions. Ed. by Thomas G. Spiro. LC 79-13808. 268p. 1985. reprint ed. 55.95 (*0-471-04399-0*) Krieger.

Nucleic Acid Probes. Ed. by Robert H. Symons. 224p. 1989. lib. bdg. 195.00 (*0-8493-4942-7*, QP624) CRC Pr.

***Nucleic Acid Protocols Handbook.** Ed. by Ralph Rapley. 1072p. 2000. spiral bd. 110.00 (*0-89603-841-6*) Humana.

Nucleic Acid Protocols Handbook. Ed. by Ralph Rapley. LC 98-43385. (Illus.). 1050p. 2000. 149.50 (*0-89603-459-3*) Humana.

Nucleic Acid Sequence Database, Vol 1. Margaret O. Dayhoff et al. LC 81-84122. (Illus.). xiv, 214p. (Orig.). 1981. pap. text 25.00 (*0-686-79304-8*) Natl Biomedical.

Nucleic Acid Sequence Database, Vol 1. Margaret O. Dyahoff et al. LC 81-84122. (Illus.). xiv, 214p. (Orig.). 1981. text 35.00 (*0-912466-09-X*) Natl Biomedical.

Nucleic Acid Sequences Handbook, Vol. I. Christian Gautier et al. LC 81-19904. 320p. 1982. 75.00 (*0-275-90798-8*, C07981, Praeger Pubs) Greenwood.

Nucleic Acid Sequences Handbook, Vol. 2. Christian Gautier et al. LC 81-19904. 320p. 1982. 75.00 (*0-275-90799-6*, C07992, Praeger Pubs) Greenwood.

Nucleic Acid Structure, Pt. 3. Ed. by Stephen Neidle. LC 87-6137. (Topics in Molecular & Structural Biology Ser.). 230p. 1987. 130.00 (*0-89573-606-3*, Wiley-VCH) Wiley.

Nucleic Acid Targeted Drug Design. Ed. by C. Propst & Thomas Perun. LC 92-17585. (Illus.). 644p. 1992. text 225.00 (*0-8247-8662-9*) Dekker.

Nucleic Acid Techniques in Bacterial Systematics. Erko Stackebrandt & Michael Goodfellow. LC 90-12998. (Modern Microbiological Methods Ser.). 370p. 1991. 360.00 (*0-471-92906-9*) Wiley.

Nucleic Acids. Ed. by John M. Walker. LC 84-15696. (Methods in Molecular Biology Ser.: Vol. 2). 375p. 1984. 79.50 (*0-89603-064-4*); pap. 39.50 (*0-89603-107-1*) Humana.

Nucleic Acids see Methods in Enzymology

Nucleic Acids, Vol. 65, Pt. I. Ed. by Sidney P. Colowick et al. LC 54-9110. (Methods in Enzymology Ser.). 1980. text 179.00 (*0-12-181965-5*) Acad Pr.

Nucleic Acids: Structures, Properties, & Functions. Victor A. Bloomfield et al. LC 98-45268. (Illus.). 794p. (C). 2000. text 85.00 (*0-935702-49-0*) Univ Sci Bks.

Nucleic Acids & Biotechnology. H. D. Kumar. (Illus.). viii, 152p. 1990. text 27.95 (*0-7069-4829-7*) Advent Bks Div.

Nucleic Acids & Molecular Biology, Vol. 1. (Illus.). 255p. 1987. 129.00 (*0-387-17595-4*) Spr-Verlag.

Nucleic Acids & Molecular Biology, Vol. 2. Ed. by G. Eckstein & David M. Lilley. (Illus.). 235p. 1988. 141.95 (*0-387-18953-X*) Spr-Verlag.

Nucleic Acids & Molecular Biology, Vol. 3. Ed. by F. Eckstein & David M. Lilley. (Illus.). 255p. 1989. 152.95 (*0-387-50808-2*) Spr-Verlag.

Nucleic Acids & Molecular Biology, Vol. 4. Ed. by F. Eckstein & David M. Lilley. 336p. 1990. 182.95 (*0-387-52407-X*) Spr-Verlag.

Nucleic Acids & Molecular Biology, Vol. 5. Ed. by F. Eckstein & David M. Lilley. (Illus.). 256p. 1991. 158.95 (*0-387-53121-1*) Spr-Verlag.

Nucleic Acids & Molecular Biology, Vol. 6. Ed. by F. Eckstein & David M. Lilley. (Illus.). 288p. 1992. 185.95 (*0-387-55238-3*) Spr-Verlag.

Nucleic Acids & Molecular Biology, Vol. 7. Ed. by F. Eckstein & David M. Lilley. (Illus.). 300p. 1993. 196.95 (*0-387-56218-4*) Spr-Verlag.

Nucleic Acids & Molecular Biology, Vol. 9. Ed. by F. Eckstein & David M. Lilley. (Illus.). 344p. 1995. 195.95 (*3-540-58824-8*) Spr-Verlag.

Nucleic Acids & Molecular Biology: Cataytic RNA, Vol. 10. Ed. by F. Eckstein & David M. Lilley. 376p. 1996. 197.00 (*3-540-60795-1*) Spr-Verlag.

Nucleic Acids & Protein Synthesis see Methods in Enzymology

Nucleic Acids & Proteins in Plants I: Structure, Biochemistry & Physiology of Proteins. Ed. by D. Boulter. (Encyclopedia of Plant Physiology Ser.: Vol. 14A). (Illus.). 760p. 1982. 336.95 (*0-387-11008-9*) Spr-Verlag.

Nucleic Acids & Proteins in Plants II: Structure, Biochemistry & Physiology of Nucleic Acids. Ed. by B. Parthier & D. Boulter. (Encyclopedia of Plant Physiology Ser.: Vol. 14 B). (Illus.). 774p. 1982. 336.95 (*0-387-11140-9*) Spr-Verlag.

Nucleic Acids & Proteins Synthesis, Pt. G, Moldave see Methods in Enzymology

Nucleic Acids Clong & Protein Purification. 434p. (C). 1996. text 61.00 (*0-536-59489-9*) Pearson Custom.

Nucleic Acids in Chemistry & Biology. 2nd ed. Ed. by G. Michael Blackburn & Michael J. Gait. (Illus.). 538p. (C). 1996. pap. text 59.95 (*0-19-963533-1*) OUP.

Nucleic Acids in the Environment. Ed. by J. T. Trevors & Jan D. Van Elsas. LC 94-47364. (Laboratory Ser.). (Illus.). 256p. 1995. write for info. (*3-540-58069-7*) Spr-Verlag.

Nucleic Acids in the Environment. Ed. by J. T. Trevors & Jan D. Van Elsas. LC 94-47364. (Laboratory Ser.). (Illus.). 272p. 1995. 86.95 (*0-387-58069-7*) Spr-Verlag.

Nucleic Acids to Parasympatholytics see Ullmann's Encyclopedia of Industrial Chemistry

Nucleic Acids Vectors. Alberte Pullman. (The Jerusalem Symposia on Quantum Chemistry & Biochemistry Ser.). 1983. text 261.50 (*90-277-1655-2*) Kluwer Academic.

Nucleo-Cytoplasmic Transport. Ed. by Reiner Peters & M. Trendelenburg. (Illus.). 315p. 1986. 79.95 (*0-387-17050-2*) Spr-Verlag.

Nucleo-Cytoplastic Transport. Ed. by Reiner Peters. 184p. 1989. pap. text 52.00 (*0-12-552100-6*) Acad Pr.

Nucleo del Poder: The Power Point. Michael E. Gerber. 224p. 1994. pap. 11.50 (*0-06-633704-6*) Addson-Wesley Educ.

Nucleolus During the Cell Cycle. Marc Thiry & Guy Goessens. LC 96-22639. (Molecular Ser.). 149p. 1996. 99.00 (*1-57059-361-2*) Landes Bioscience.

Nucleolus Ribosome Biogenesis. A. A. Hadjiolov. (Cell Biology Monographs: Vol. 12). (Illus.). 290p. 1985. 123.95 (*0-387-81790-5*) Spr-Verlag.

Nucleon Compton Effect at Low & Medium Energies. Ed. by D. V. Skobel'tsyn. LC 69-12521. (Proceedings of the P. N. Lebedev Physics Institute Ser.: No. 41). (Illus.). 225p. 1969. reprint ed. pap. 69.80 (*0-608-05508-5*, 206597600006) Bks Demand.

Nucleon Correlations in Nuclei. A. N. Antonov et al. LC 92-27020. (Series in Nuclear & Particle Physics). 1993. 141.95 (*0-387-55911-6*) Spr-Verlag.

Nucleon-Hadron Many-Body Systems: From Hadron-Meson to Quark-Lepton Nuclear Physics. Ed. by Hiroyasu Ejiri & Hiroshi Toki. LC 99-19980. (Oxford Studies in Nuclear Physics: No. 22). (Illus.). 370p. 1999. text 140.00 (*0-19-851900-1*) OUP.

Nucleon Momentum & Density Distributions in Nuclei. Ed. by T. J. Kennie et al. (Oxford Studies in Nuclear Physics: No. 9). (Illus.). 176p. 1988. text 75.00 (*0-19-851726-2*) OUP.

Nucleon-Nucleon & Nucleon-Antinucleon Interactions. Ed. by H. Mitter & W. Plessas. (Acta Physica Austriaca Ser.: Suppl. 27). (Illus.). 724p. 1986. 136.95 (*0-387-81900-2*) Spr-Verlag.

Nucleon-Nucleon Interaction & Nuclear Many-Body Problems: Proceedings of the International Summer School, Changchun, China, July 25-Aug. 1983. S. S. Wu & T. T. Kuo. 1984. 121.00 (*9971-966-35-2*) World Scientific Pub.

Nucleon-Nucleon Interaction & Nuclear Many-Body Problems: Proceedings of the International Summer School, Changchun, China, July 25, 1983. S. S. Wu & T. T. Kuo. xv, 748p. 1984. pap. 46.00 (*9971-966-46-8*) World Scientific Pub.

Nucleon-Nucleon Interactions, 1977. International Conference on Nucleon-Nucleon Intera. LC 78-54249. (AIP Conference Proceedings Ser., 2nd, University of British Columbia, June 1978: No. 41). (Illus.). 1978. lib. bdg. 23.50 (*0-88318-140-1*) Am Inst Physics.

Nucleon Optical Model. P. E. Hodgson. 400p. 1994. text 91.00 (*981-02-1722-6*) World Scientific Pub.

Nucleon Resonances & Nucleon Structures: Institute for Nuclear Theory 1st Summer School. G. A. Miller. 400p. 1992. text 95.00 (*981-02-0954-1*) World Scientific Pub.

Nucleophilic Addition to Carbonyl: Gringnard Reaction with an Aldehyde. Jan W. Simek. Ed. by J. Jeffers. (Modular Laboratory Program in Chemistry Ser.). 12p. (C). 1998. pap. text 1.75 (*0-87540-718-8*, SYNT 718) Chem Educ Res.

Nucleophilic Aromatic Displacement: The Influence of the Nitro Group. F. Terrier. (Organic Nitro Chemistry Ser.). 460p. 1991. 198.00 (*0-471-18697-X*, Wiley-VCH) Wiley.

Nucleophilic Aromatic Displacement: The Influence of the Nitro Group. Francois Terrier. 460p. 1991. 125.00 (*0-89573-312-9*, Wiley-VCH) Wiley.

Nucleophilic Aromatic Substitution of Hydrogen. Oleg N. Chupakhin et al. (Illus.). 367p. 1994. text 111.00 (*0-12-174640-2*) Acad Pr.

Nucleophilicity. Ed. by J. Milton Harris & Samuel P. McManus. LC 86-28843. (Advances in Chemistry Ser.: No. 215). (Illus.). xiii, 494p. 1987. 94.95 (*0-8412-0952-9*) Am Chemical.

Nucleophilicity. Ed. by J. Milton Harris & Samuel P. McManus. LC 86-28843. (Advances in Chemistry Ser.: Vol. 215). 512p. 1987. reprint ed. pap. 158.80 (*0-608-03894-6*, 206434100008) Bks Demand.

Nucleoside Analogs in Cancer Therapy. Bruce D. Cheson et al. LC 97-11276. (Basic & Clinical Oncology Ser.). (Illus.). 488p. 1997. text 175.00 (*0-8247-9850-3*) Dekker.

Nucleoside Triphosphotases in Energy Transduction, Cellular Regulation & Information Transfer in Biological Systems. Ed. by J. F. Eccleston et al. 120p. (C). 1992. text 35.00 (*1-85578-032-1*, Pub. by Portland Pr Ltd) Ashgate Pub Co.

Nucleosides & Nucleotides As Antitumor & Antiviral Agents. C. K. Chu & D. C. Baker. LC 93-13432. (Illus.). 346p. (C). 1993. text 95.00 (*0-306-44520-4*, Kluwer Plenum) Kluwer Academic.

Nucleosomes. Ed. by Paul M. Wasserman et al. (Methods in Enzymology Ser.: Vol. 170). 683p. 1989. text 136.00 (*0-12-182071-8*) Acad Pr.

Nucleosynthesis: Challenges & New Developments. Ed. by W. David Arnett & James W. Truran. LC 85-1160. (Illus.). x, 308p. 1985. pap. text 21.00 (*0-226-02788-0*) U Ch Pr.

Nucleosynthesis: Challenges & New Developments. Ed. by W. David Arnett & James W. Truran. LC 85-1160. (Illus.). x, 308p. 1995. lib. bdg. 43.50 (*0-226-02787-2*) U Ch Pr.

Nucleosynthesis: Challenges & New Developments. Ed. by W. David Arnett & James W. Truran. LC 85-1160. (Illus.). 316p. reprint ed. pap. 98.00 (*0-608-09263-0*, 205406500002) Bks Demand.

Nucleosynthesis & Chemical Evolution of Galaxies. Bernard E. Pagel. (Illus.). 392p. (C). 1997. text 74.95 (*0-521-55061-0*); pap. text 30.95 (*0-521-55958-8*) Cambridge U Pr.

Nucleosynthesis & Its Implications on Nuclear & Particle Physics. Ed. by Jean Audouze & Nicole Mathieu. 1986. text 220.00 (*90-277-2173-4*) Kluwer Academic.

Nucleotide Analogues As Antiviral Agents. Ed. by John C. Martin. LC 89-15114. (Symposium Ser.: No. 401). (Illus.). 175p. 1989. text 49.95 (*0-8412-1659-2*, Pub. by Am Chemical) OUP.

Nucleotide Antagonists As Anticancer Drugs. Richard I. Christopherson & Stephen D. Lyons. 2000. boxed set 95.00 (*0-8493-4309-7*) CRC Pr.

***Nucleotides & Their Receptors in the Nervous System.** P. Illes & Herbert Zimmermann. LC 99-23832. (Progress in Brain Research Ser.). 452p. 1999. 193.00 (*0-444-50082-0*) Elsevier.

Nucleus, Vol. 2. Ed. by Alan P. Wolffe. Date not set. 128.50 (*0-7623-0399-9*) Jai Pr.

N

An Asterisk (*) at the beginning of an entry indicates that the title is appearing for the first time.

Nucleus: A History of Atomic Energy of Canada Limited. Robert Bothwell. (Illus.). 576p. 1988. 34.95 (*0-8020-2670-2*) U of Toronto Pr.

Nucleus Vol. 1: The Nucleosome. Ed. by Alan P. Wolffe. 264p. 1995. 128.50 (*1-55938-940-0*) Jai Pr.

***Nucleus - New Physics for the New Millennium.** F. D. Smit et al. LC 99-55325. 536p. 2000. 139.50 (*0-306-46302-4*, Kluwer Plenum) Kluwer Academic.

Nucleus & Cytoplasm. 3rd ed. Henry Harris. (Illus.). 1974. text 18.95 (*0-19-854124-4*) OUP.

Nucleus Emblematum Selectissimorum. Gabriel Rollenhagen. (GER.). 45p. 1985. reprint ed. write for info. (*3-487-07505-9*) G Olms Pubs.

Nucleus of the Solitary Tract. Ed. by Robin A. Barraco. LC 93-26818. 448p. 1993. lib. bdg. 212.50 (*0-8493-4707-6*, QP377) CRC Pr.

Nuctemeron of Apollonius Tyana. Jan Van Rijckenborgh. (DUT.). 125p. (Orig.). 1987. pap. 12.00 (*90-70053-24-1*) Rosycross Pr.

Nude. Monica Bohm-Duchen. (Artists & Themes Ser.). (Illus.). 64p. (Orig.). 1992. pap. 9.95 (*1-85759-004-X*) Scala Books.

Nude. Kenneth Clark. (Illus.). 458p. 1996. reprint ed. 17.98 (*1-56731-123-7*, MJF Bks) Fine Comms.

Nude: A Study in Ideal Form. Kenneth M. Clark. (A. W. Mellon Lectures in the Fine Arts, 1989: Vol. 34, No. 2). (Illus.). 458p. 1956. pap. text 27.95 (*0-691-01788-3*, Pub. by Princeton U Pr) Cal Prin Full Svc.

Nude: Creative Photography Workshop. Bruce Pinkard. LC 99-14005. (Illus.). 192p. 1999. pap. 29.95 (*1-883403-60-X*, Pub. by Saunders Photo) Sterling.

Nude: Perception & Personality. Pavel Machotka. (Illus.). 352p. (C). 1979. text 39.50 (*0-8290-0868-3*) Irvington.

Nude: Theory. Jain Kelly. LC 79-2427. (Illus.). 176p. 1979. 35.00 (*0-912810-24-6*); pap. 19.95 (*0-912810-33-5*) Lustrum Pr.

***Nude Vol. 2, Vol. 3.** Nippan Books Staff. (Combat Action Pose Collection). (Illus.). 1999. pap. 39.95 (*4-906436-97-8*, Pub. by Ginga Shuppan) Bks Nippan.

***Nude & Beauty Photography.** Nancy Brown. LC 99-87076. (Kodak Pro Workshop Ser.). (Illus.). 2000. pap. write for info. (*0-87985-774-9*, Kodak) Saunders Photo.

Nude Before God. Shiv K. Kumar. 1985. 18.95 (*0-318-36912-5*) Asia Bk Corp.

***Nude Body Nude.** Howard Schatz & Beverly J. Ornstein. LC 00-38296. 320p. 2000. 75.00 (*0-06-019552-5*, E Burlingame Bks) HarpC.

Nude Colony: Alexander Kaletski. Michiel Van Der Wal. (Illus.). 1997. 20.00 (*0-9648340-5-7*) Dillon Gallery.

Nude Descending a Staircase. X. J. Kennedy. LC 94-70470. (Classic Contemporaries Ser.). 64p. 1994. reprint ed. pap. 12.95 (*0-88748-204-X*) Carnegie-Mellon.

Nude Figure: A Visual Reference for the Artist. Mark E. Smith. LC 98-3379. (Illus.). 208p. 1998. pap. 29.95 (*0-8230-3232-9*) Watsn-Guptill.

Nude Formalism: With Susan Bee. Charles Bernstein. 20p. 1989. pap. 5.00 (*1-55713-092-2*) Sun & Moon CA.

Nude in American Painting, 1950-1980. David McCarthy. LC 97-27042. (Illus.). 272p. (C). 1998. text 70.00 (*0-521-59316-6*) Cambridge U Pr.

Nude in Black & White. Lucille Khornak. (Illus.). 144p. 1993. pap. 22.50 (*0-8174-5088-2*, Amphoto) Watsn-Guptill.

Nude in Contemporary Art. David McCarthy. 1999. pap. 19.95 (*1-888332-10-7*) Lebhar Friedman.

Nude in Tub: Stories of Quillifarkeag, Maine. G. K. Wuori. LC 98-41977. 294p. 1999. 18.95 (*1-56512-223-2*, 72223) Algonquin Bks.

***Nude Memoir.** Laura Moriarty. 88p. 2000. pap. 9.00 (*1-928650-07-4*, Pub. by Krupskaya) SPD-Small Pr Dist.

Nude Men. Amanda Filipacchi. 304p. 1994. pap. 9.95 (*0-14-017892-9*, Penguin Bks) Viking Penguin.

Nude Modelling for the Afterlife. Henry Normal. 64p. 1994. pap. 12.95 (*1-85224-279-5*, Pub. by Bloodaxe Bks) Dufour.

Nude Mouse in Oncology Research. Epie Boven & Benjamin Winograd. (Illus.). 352p. 1991. lib. bdg. 229.00 (*0-8493-6531-7*, RC267) CRC Pr.

Nude, Naked, Stripped. Dana Friis-Hansen & Carrie Rickey. LC 85-63327. (Illus.). 76p. (Orig.). 1985. pap. 7.50 (*0-938437-13-5*) MIT List Visual Arts.

Nude Photography: Masterpieces from the Past 150 Years. Ed. by Peter-Cornell Richter. LC 98-234099. (Illus.). 144p. 1998. pap. 29.95 (*3-7913-1998-1*) te Neues.

***Nude Sculpture: 5,000 Years.** Photos by David Finn. LC 00-25152. (Illus.). 208p. 2000. 39.95 (*0-8109-3346-2*, Pub. by Abrams) Time Warner.

Nude World. Robbert Broekstra. Ed. by Don Bensen & Bernard J. Loibl. (Illus.). 120p. (Orig.). 1997. pap. text 29.95 (*0-9636805-2-8*) Events Unltd.

Nudes. Greg Gorman. (Illus.). 128p. 1998. 65.00 (*3-908161-42-8*) Abbeville Pr.

Nudes. Irina Ionesco. (Illus.). 144p. 1996. 49.95 (*3-908162-52-1*, Pub. by Edit Stemmle) Dist Art Pubs.

***Nudes.** Jose M. Parramon. (Workbooks for Painting Ser.). (Illus.). 32p. 1999. pap. 5.95 (*0-7641-1210-4*) Barron.

Nudes. Paolo Roversi. (Illus.). 144p. 1997. 45.00 (*3-931141-57-8*) Dist Art Pubs.

Nudes. David Seidner. (Illus.). 64p. 1998. 19.95 (*3-929078-20-1*, Kehayoff) te Neues.

Nudes. Lee Friedlander. (Illus.). 96p. 1996. reprint ed. pap. 39.95 (*0-224-03217-8*, Pub. by Jonathan Cape) Trafalgar.

Nudes: Egon Schiele. Alessandra Comini. LC 95-166232. (Illus.). 64p. 1995. 25.00 (*0-8478-1841-1*, Pub. by Rizzoli Intl) St Martin.

Nudes & Nikes: Champions & Legends of the First Olympics. Dyan Blacklock. (True Stories Ser.). (Illus.). 100p. (Orig.). (J). (gr. 3-8). 1997. pap. 6.95 (*1-86448-455-1*, Pub. by Allen & Unwin Pty) IPG Chicago.

Nudes & Nonsense. J. Ronald York. 64p. (Orig.). 1993. pap. 14.95 (*0-916078-33-7*) Iris Pr.

***Nudes from Nowhere: Utopian Sexual Landscapes.** Darby Lewes. 240p. 2000. 67.00 (*0-8476-9814-9*); pap. 26.95 (*0-8476-9815-7*) Rowman.

***Nudes from the Polaroid Collections.** Ed. & Text by Barbara Hitchcock. (Illus.). 2000. 75.00 (*3-908163-32-3*, Pub. by Edit Stemmle) Abbeville Pr.

Nudes Index. Contrib. by Koenemann Inc. Staff. (Indexes Ser.). (Illus.). 312p. 1999. 39.95 (*3-8290-0501-6*, 810145) Konemann.

Nudes Index I. Knickerbocker Press Staff. (Indexes Ser.). (Illus.). 312p. 1999. 39.95 (*3-8290-0502-4*, 810144) Konemann.

Nudes, 1986-1991: Beyond the Boundaries. Photos by Ron Terner. (Illus.). 72p. 1991. pap. 30.00 (*0-317-04093-6*) Focal Point Pr.

Nudes, 1975 to 1985. Photos by Ron Terner. LC 85-81663. (Illus.). 58p. 1986. 30.00 (*0-317-01360-2*) Focal Point Pr.

Nudes, Prudes & Attitudes: Pornography & Censorship. Avedon Carol. LC 95-137372. 208p. pap. 18.95 (*1-873797-13-3*, Pub. by New Clarion) Paul & Co Pubs.

Nudes, Prudes & Attitudes: Pornography & Censorship. Avedon Carol. LC 95-137372. 208p. 1994. 45.00 (*1-873797-14-1*, Pub. by New Clarion) Paul & Co Pubs.

Nudes 3. B. Martin Pedersen. 256p. 1999. text 70.00 (*1-888001-66-6*) Graphis US.

Nudge Blue: A Rifleman's Chronicle of World War II. 2nd rev. ed. Donald E. Lavender. (World War II Monograph: Vol. 222). (Illus.). 82p. 1997. reprint ed. 25.95 (*1-57638-096-3*, M222H); reprint ed. pap. 15.95 (*1-57638-095-5*, M222S) Merriam Pr.

Nudi. Paolo Roversi. (Illus.). 128p. 1999. 49.95 (*3-88243-662-X*, Pub. by Steidl) Dist Art Pubs.

***Nudibranchs of Heron Island, Great Barrier Reef: A Survey of the Opisthobranchia (Sea Slugs) of Heron & Wistari Reefs.** J. G. Marshall & R. C. Willan. (Illus.). 268p. 1999. 60.00 (*90-5782-033-1*, Pub. by Backhuys Pubs) Balogh.

Nudibranchs of Southern Africa: A Guide to Opisthobranch Molluscs of South Africa. Terrence Gosliner. LC 86-62429. 136p. 1987. pap. 37.95 (*0-930118-13-8*, 117G) Sea Chall.

Nudism Comes to America. Frances Merrill & Mason Merrill. LC 72-9773. reprint ed. 45.00 (*0-404-57476-9*) AMS Pr.

Nudist Magazines of the '50s & '60s, Bk. 1. Stan Sohler & Ed Lange. (Nudist Nostalgia Ser.). (Illus.). 100p. 1992. pap. 24.95 (*1-55599-046-0*) Events Unltd.

Nudist Magazines of the '50s & '60s, Bk. 1. Stan Sohler & Ed Lange. (Nudist Nostalgia Ser.). (Illus.). 96p. 1993. 29.95 (*1-55599-045-2*) Events Unltd.

Nudist Magazines of the '50s & '60s, Bk. 2. Ed Lange & Stan Sohler. Ed. by Iris Bancroft. (Nudist Nostalgia Ser.). (Illus.). 96p. 1993. 29.95 (*1-55599-047-9*); pap. 24.95 (*1-55599-048-7*) Events Unltd.

Nudist Magazines of the '50s & '60s, Bk. 3. Ed Lange. Ed. by Iris Bancroft. (Nudist Nostalgia Ser.). (Illus.). 100p. (C). 1994. 29.95 (*1-55599-050-9*) Events Unltd.

Nudist Magazines of the '50s & '60s, Bk. 3. Ed Lange. Ed. by Iris Bancroft. (Nudist Nostalgia Ser.). (Illus.). 96p. (C). 1995. pap. 24.95 (*1-55599-051-7*) Events Unltd.

Nudist Magazines of the '50s & '60s, Bk. 4. Ed Lange & Stan Sohler. Ed. by Iris Bancroft & Chris Moran. (Illus.). 96p. 1996. 29.95 (*1-55599-053-3*); pap. 24.95 (*1-55599-054-1*) Events Unltd.

Nudist Nudes. Ed Lange. LC 91-9296. (Illus.). 1991. pap. 14.95 (*1-55599-043-6*) Events Unltd.

***Nudist on the Late Shift.** Po Bronson. LC 00-27416. 256p. 2000. pap. 14.95 (*0-7679-0603-9*) Broadway BDD.

Nudist on the Late Shift: And Other True Tales of Silicon Valley. Po Bronson. LC 98-32381. 288p. 1999. 25.00 (*0-375-50277-7*) Random.

Nudo & Crudo. Claudia Gian Ferrari. 1996. pap. 19.95 (*88-8158-062-4*, Pub. by Charta) Dist Art Pubs.

Nuer: A Description of the Modes of Livelihood & Political Institutions of a Nilotic People. Edward E. Evans-Pritchard. (Illus.). 284p. 1969. text 22.95 (*0-19-500322-5*) OUP.

Nuer Conquest: The Structure & Development of an Expansionist System. Raymond C. Kelly. (Illus.). 328p. 1985. pap. text 21.95 (*0-472-08056-3*, 08056) U of Mich Pr.

Nuer Customs & Folklore. Ray Huffman. LC 32-11476. 136p. reprint ed. pap. 42.20 (*0-8357-3009-3*, 205709500011) Bks Demand.

Nuer Dilemmas: Coping with Money, War, & the State. Sharon E. Hutchinson. LC 95-1248. (Centennial Bk.). (Illus.). 420p. (C). 1996. pap. 19.95 (*0-520-20284-8*, Pub. by U CA Pr); text 55.00 (*0-520-08869-7*, Pub. by U CA Pr) Cal Prin Full Svc.

Nuer English Dictionary. Ray Huffman. 22.50 (*0-87559-060-8*) Shalom.

***Nuer Journeys, Nuer Lives: Sudanese Refugees in Minnesota.** Holtzman & Foner. 141p. 1999. pap. text 20.00 (*0-205-29679-3*) Allyn.

Nuer Prophets: A History of Prophecy from the Upper Nile in the Nineteenth & Twentieth Centuries. Douglas H. Johnson. (Oxford Studies in Social & Cultural Anthropology). (Illus.). 428p. 1997. pap. text 21.00 (*0-19-823367-1*) OUP.

Nuer Religion. Edward E. Evans-Pritchard. (Illus.). 348p. 1971. pap. text 22.95 (*0-19-874003-4*) OUP.

Nuer View of Biological Life: Nature & Sexuality in the Experience of the Ethiopian Nuer. Aster Akalu. (Regiae Societatis Humaniorum: Scripta Minora, Ser. 1988-1989: Pt. 1). (Illus.). 60p. (Orig.). 1989. pap. 32.50 (*91-22-01283-4*) Coronet Bks.

Nuernberger Tagebuch. 10th ed. Gustave M. Gilbert. (GER.). 1997. pap. 22.50 (*3-596-21885-3*, Pub. by Fischer Tasch) Intl Bk Import.

Nuestra America Latina. Aline Frambes-Buxeda. (SPA., Illus.). 520p. 1989. pap. 25.00 (*0-9623590-0-9*) Libros-Ediciones.

Nuestra Aventura Literaria: Los Ismos en la Poesia Puertorriquena, 1913-1940. 2nd rev. ed. Luis Hernandez Aquino. 270p. (C). 1980. reprint ed. pap. 4.50 (*0-8477-3134-0*) U of PR Pr.

Nuestra Busqueda de la Felicidad: Una Invitacion Para Conocer la Iglesia De Jesucristo De los Santos De los Ultimos Dias. M. Russell Ballard. (SPA.). xii, 141p. 1994. pap. 6.95 (*0-87579-915-9*) Deseret Bk.

Nuestra Calabaza, Vol. 4080. Renee Keeler. Ed. by Christine Hood. Tr. by Rancho Park Publishing Staff. (Math Spanish Learn to Read Ser.).Tr. of Our Pumpkin. (SPA., Illus.). 8p. (J). (ps-2). 1996. pap. 1.75 (*1-57471-154-7*, 4080) Creat Teach Pr.

***Nuestra Esperanza en Cristo.** Nav Press Staff.Tr. of Our Hope in Christ. (SPA.). 48p. (YA). 2000. pap. 3.99 (*0-311-13662-1*, Edit Mundo) Casa Bautista.

Nuestra Evolucion. Waldo Vieira. Tr. by Luis Minero from POR. (SPA., Illus.). 172p. 1997. pap. 11.95 (*85-86019-21-6*) Intl Inst Proj.

Nuestra Fantastica Tierra. Nicola Baxter. (Biblioteca de Descubrimientos Ser.).Tr. of Our Wonderful Earth. (SPA., Illus.). (J). (gr. 3-6). 1997. 11.95 (*0-915741-84-9*, SY7075) C D Stampley Ent.

Nuestra Gente. Tomas Sarramia. (SPA.). 220p. 1993. pap. write for info. (*0-929441-14-1*) Pubns Puertorriquenas.

Nuestra Literatura Maya: Kotz'ib' Gaspar P. Gonzalez. (SPA., Illus.). 175p. (Orig.). 1997. pap. 14.95 (*1-886502-17-X*) Yax Te Found.

Nuestra Senora de Guadalupe. Tomie De Paola. LC 79-19609. (SPA., Illus.). 48p. (J). (ps-3). 1980. pap. 8.95 (*0-8234-0404-8*); lib. bdg. 16.95 (*0-8234-0374-2*) Holiday.

***Nuestra Senora de la Soledad.** Marcela Serrano. (SPA.). 2000. pap. 16.95 (*968-19-0600-4*) Aguilar.

Nuestra Tierra Violenta. Tr. by Maria T. Sanz & Maia Larios S. (Explora y Aprende Ser.). (SPA., Illus.). 96p. (YA). (gr. 3-8). 1994. 15.00 (*0-915741-55-5*) C D Stampley Ent.

Nuestra Victoria (Our Victory) F. Carver. (SPA.). 0.35 (*0-685-74963-0*, 540525) Editorial Unilit.

Nuestra Voz: Poblacion y Desarrollo: Perspectiva de Latinamerica y el Caribe. Ed. by Patricia Ardila et al. (SPA., Illus.). 44p. (C). 1994. pap. text 5.95 (*1-879358-05-0*) Panos Inst.

Nuestras Aventuras. Lyn Swanson-Natsnes. (SPA., Illus.). (J). (ps-3). 1998. pap. 4.95 (*1-57255-496-7*) Mondo Pubng.

Nuestras Constituciones Federal y Estatal. rev. ed. Alex Schmidt & Steve Schmidt. Ed. & Illus. by Dennis Schmidt.Tr. of Our Federal & State Constitution. (ENG & SPA.). 64p. 1996. pap. text 6.00 (*1-892291-05-3*) RJS Pubns.

***Nuestro Andar Diario.** Jack W. Hayford. (SPA.). 1999. pap. 5.99 (*0-7899-0588-4*) Spanish Hse Distributors.

Nuestro Bebe. Nancy C. Akmon.Tr. of Our Baby. (SPA., Illus.). 56p. 1997. 33.95 (*1-884807-23-2*) Blushing Rose.

Nuestro Bebe: Regalo. Mackenzie.Tr. of Our Baby Book: Gift. (SPA.). write for info. (*0-614-27087-1*) Editorial Unilit.

Nuestro Bebe (Our Baby Book) C. Mackenzie. (SPA.). 10.99 (*1-56063-613-0*, 494014) Editorial Unilit.

Nuestro Dios Es Maravilloso: Encuentrese Cara a Cara Con el Poder y la Gloria de Neustro Dios. Tony Evans. Tr. by Luis M. Alvarez.Tr. of Our god Is Awesome. (SPA., Illus.). 384p. 1998. pap. text 11.99 (*0-311-46151-4*) Casa Bautista.

Nuestro Espiritu Humano. Witness Lee.Tr. of OUR HUMAN SPIRIT. (SPA.). 82p. 1986. per. 4.50 (*0-87083-259-X*, 07-013-002) Living Stream Ministry.

Nuestro Hogar en el Espacio. Jose F. Valdes. (Ciencia para Todos Ser.). (SPA.). pap. 6.99 (*968-16-2919-1*, Pub. by Fondo) Continental Bk.

Nuestro Libro de Oracion Familiar. Ed. by Bernard McWilliams. (SPA., Illus.). 405p. 1967. 29.95 (*0-915741-28-8*) C D Stampley Ent.

Nuestro Mundo. 3rd ed. Ed. by Ana C. Jarvis et al. 260p. (C). 1991. pap. text. write for info. (*0-318-68394-6*) HM Trade Div.

Nuestro Mundo. 3rd ed. Ana C. Jarvis et al. (SPA.). 192p. (C). 1991. pap. text 30.76 (*0-669-20893-0*) HM Trade Div.

Nuestro Mundo: Su Historia, Sus Culturas. 2nd ed. James Killoran et al. (SPA., Illus.). 420p. (YA). (gr. 9-10). 1996. 19.95 (*1-882422-23-6*) Jarrett Pub.

Nuestro Mundo Pertenece a Dios. 58p. pap. 4.50 (*1-56212-021-2*) CRC Pubns.

Nuestro Nuevo Testamento. Merrill C. Tenney. Orig. Title: New Testament Survey. (SPA.). 512p. 1973. pap. 15.99 (*0-8254-1716-3*, Edit Portavoz) Kregel.

Nuestro Pacto Con Dios. Kenneth Copeland. Tr. by Luis Gonzales. (ENG & SPA.). 39p. 1984. pap. 2.95 (*0-88114-302-2*) K Copeland Pubns.

Nuestro Padre San Daniel. Ferrer G. Miro. 1989. pap. text 14.95 (*84-85866-18-5*) Ediciones Torre.

Nuestro Padre San Daniel: El Obispo Leproso. Gabriel Miro. Ed. by Miguel A. Lozano Marcos. (Nueva Austral Ser.: Vol. 224). (SPA.). 1991. pap. text 34.95 (*84-239-7224-0*) Elliots Bks.

Nuestro Planeta Tierra. Lisa Trumbauer. Ed. by Don Curry. Tr. by Leyla Torres from ENG. (Spanish Discovery Links Ser.). (SPA.). 8p. (J). (gr. k). 1997. pap. text 2.75 (*1-56784-998-9*) Newbridge Educ.

Nuestro Satelite - la Luna see Our Satellite: The Moon

Nuestro Trabajo Es Importante para Dios. Doug Sherman. (Serie Realidades - Realities Ser.).Tr. of God Cares about Your Work. (SPA.). 25p. 1995. 1.99 (*1-56063-280-1*, 498133) Editorial Unilit.

Nuestros Cuentos Favoritos: De Diversas Partes Del Mundo. Ed. by Miriam Farbey. Tr. by Roselma Zubizarreta. (Children Just Like Me Ser.). (ENG & SPA., Illus.). 48p. (J). (gr. 2-5). 1997. 24.95 (*0-9628720-3-2*, MI72032) Mariuccia Iaconi Bk Imports.

***Nuestros Cuerpos, Nuestras Vidas: Our Bodies, Ourselves.** Boston Women's Health Collective Staff.Tr. of Our Bodies, Ourselves. (SPA.). 704p. 2000. pap. 24.00 (*1-58322-024-0*) Seven Stories.

Nuestros Santos entre Nosotros see Our Saints among Us: 400 Years of New Mexican Devotional Art

Nueva Antologia Poetica. Jorge L. Morales. 368p. 1975. pap. 5.00 (*0-8477-3217-7*) U of PR Pr.

***Nueva Biblia Ilustrada.** New Kids Media Staff. (SPA., Illus.). (J). 2000. 10.99 (*0-7899-0653-8*) Editorial Unilit.

Nueva Burguesia (The New Bourgeoisie) 2nd ed. Mariano Azuela. (SPA.). 140p. 1985. pap. 7.99 (*968-16-1853-X*, Pub. by Fondo) Continental Bk.

***Nueva Cocina para la Mujer.** Choly Berreteaga. (SPA.). 1999. pap. 21.50 (*84-241-2256-9*) Everest SP.

Nueva Dimension. Michael Green.Tr. of New Dimension. (SPA.). 80p. 1989. pap. write for info. (*0-614-27153-3*) Editorial Unilit.

Nueva Dimension. Michael Warr. (Serie Bolsilibros - Pocket Bks.).Tr. of New Dimension. (SPA.). 80p. pap. 1.50 (*0-945792-91-3*, 490253) Editorial Unilit.

Nueva Dimension Mundial de las Finanzas. Yusuke Kashiwagi. LC HG3881.K37. (Conferencia Per Jacobsson de 1986 Ser.). (SPA.). 31p. reprint ed. pap. 30.00 (*0-608-08767-X*, 206940600004) Bks Demand.

Nueva en el Zoologica. Frank B. Edwards. (New Reader Ser.).Tr. of New at the Zoo. (SPA., Illus.). 24p. (J). (ps-1). 1998. pap. 5.95 (*0-921285-71-X*, Pub. by Bungalo Books) Firefly Bks Ltd.

Nueva Enciclopedia Cumbre, 15 vols. 32nd ed. (Illus.). 5026p. (YA). (gr. 7 up). 2000. lib. bdg. 345.00 (*0-7172-5114-4*) Grolier Educ.

Nueva Enciclopedia de Medicina y Salud: Para el Hogar Moderno. Richard J. Wagman. Tr. by Maria T. Sanz & Pedro Larios A. (SPA., Illus.). 1390p. 1992. 59.95 (*0-915741-35-0*) C D Stampley Ent.

Nueva Era. John Ankerberg & John Weldon. (Hechos Acerca de...Ser.).Tr. of New Age Movement. (SPA.). 46p. 1994. pap. 3.29 (*1-56063-773-0*, 498429) Editorial Unilit.

Nueva Era. Russell Chandler. Tr. by Moises Chavez from ENG.Tr. of Understanding the New Age. (SPA.). 288p. 1992. pap. 10.50 (*0-311-05045-X*) Casa Bautista.

Nueva Era. Walter Martin.Tr. of New Age. (SPA.). 144p. (Orig.). 1991. pap. 8.99 (*0-88113-055-9*) Caribe Betania.

Nueva Era Del Ocultismo. Marcos Richards. (SPA.). 55p. 1998. pap. 1.50 (*1-885630-47-6*) HLM Producciones.

Nueva Familia de Rut. P. Frank.Tr. of Ruth's New Family. (SPA.). (J). 1.99 (*1-56063-785-4*, 490315) Editorial Unilit.

Nueva Ficcion Hispanoamericana a Traves de Miguel Angel Asturias y Gabriel Garcia Marquez. L. Gonzalez Del Valle & Vicente Cabrera. 1972. 9.95 (*0-88303-008-X*); pap. 6.95 (*0-685-73212-6*) E Torres & Sons.

Nueva Gramatica Comunicativa. Phil Turk & Mike Zollo. (SPA., Illus.). 224p. Date not set. pap., wbk. ed. 12.95 (*0-8442-7105-5*, 71055) NTC Contemp Pub Co.

Nueva Gramatica Comunicativa: Answer Key. Phil Turk & Mike Zollo. (SPA.). 48p. 1995. pap. 8.40 (*0-8442-7109-8*) NTC Contemp Pub Co.

Nueva Granada: Paul Horgan & the Southwest, 6. Robert F. Gish. LC 94-29267. (Tarleton State University Southwestern Studies in the Humanities: No. 6). 160p. 1995. 22.50 (*0-89096-640-0*) Tex A&M Univ Pr.

***Nueva Guia De Ginecologia.** Garcia Del Real Eduardo. 1999. pap. text 18.95 (*84-7880-977-5*) Planeta.

Nueva Hermanita de Francisca. Russell Hoban. 1997. 11.15 (*0-606-10859-9*, Pub. by Turtleback) Demco.

Nueva Historia de la Novela Hispanoamericana. Fernando Alegria. (Rama Ser.). (SPA.). 450p. 1986. pap. 22.50 (*0-910061-29-7*, 1505) Ediciones Norte.

Nueva Internacional No. 3: El Ascenso y el Ocaso de la Revolucion Nicaraguense. (SPA.). 363p. pap. 15.00 (*0-87348-772-9*) Pathfinder NY.

Nueva Jerusalem. Lorenzo Florian. (ENG, SPA & TAG.). 36p. 1997. pap. 6.00 (*0-937690-41-4*) Wrld Lib Pubns.

Nueva Llamada. Jan Van Rijckenborgh. (SPA.). 1987. pap. 1.50 (*90-70196-34-4*) Rosycross Pr.

***Nueva Luz.** Ed. by Charles Biasing Rivera & Betty Wilde. (SPA.). (YA). (gr. 9 up). 2000. 5.00 En Foco.

Nueva Manera de Llevar a Cabo el Aumento y la Extension de la Iglesia. Witness Lee.Tr. of NEW WAY TO CARRY OUT THE INCREASE AND SPREAD OF THE CHURCH. (SPA.). 67p. 1987. per. 5.25 (*0-87083-368-5*, 12-013-002) Living Stream Ministry.

Nueva Mirada a la Consejeria Biblica. John F. MacArthur, Jr.Tr. of Introduction to Biblical Counselling. (SPA.). 384p. 1996. 13.99 (*0-89922-572-1*, C008-5721) Caribe Betania.

Nueva Nutricion: Una Medicina para el Proximo Milenio. Michael Colgan. 1998. pap. text 17.95 (*84-7808-197-6*) Sirio Editorial.

Nueva Oportunidad. Paul D. Riggs. (Deseo Ser.).Tr. of New Opportunity. (SPA.). 1999. per. 3.50 (*0-373-35308-1*, 1-35308-5) Harlequin Bks.

Nueva Sintaxis del Griego Antiguo. F. R. Abrados. (SPA.). 840p. 1993. 200.00 (*84-249-1480-5*) Elliots Bks.

N

Nueva Sociedad. 4th ed. Edward H. Carr. (Ciencias Sociales Ser.: No. 39). (SPA.). 185p. 1984. pap. 3.00 (*0-8477-0039-9*) U of PR Pr.

Nueva Tolerancia. Josh McDowell.Tr. of New Tolerance. write for info. (*0-7899-0604-X*, 497781) Editorial Unilit.

Nueva Vida Con Ingles. 3rd ed. Esther L. Esparza. (Illus.). 180p. (Orig.). 1990. reprint ed. pap. text 12.50 (*1-879817-00-4*) Star Light Pr.

Nueva Vida Con Ingles: Teacher's Edition. Esther L. Esparza. (Illus.). 40p. (Orig.). 1990. reprint ed. 19.95 (*1-879817-01-2*) Star Light Pr.

Nueva Vida (New Life) rev. ed. A. R. Knight & Gordon H. Schroeder. (SPA.). 47p. 1971. pap. 4.00 (*0-8170-0696-6*) Judson.

Nueva York. Luis Barolome. 1998. pap. 59.95 (*84-03-59430-5*) Routledge.

Nueva York. Michelin Staff. 1999. pap. text 9.95 (*2-06-661101-8*) Michelin.

Nueva York: Guia Completa Para Viajeros. 1991. pap. 39.95 (*0-7859-9032-1*) Fr & Eur.

Nueva York: Guia Completa Para Viajeros. Luis Barolome. (SPA.). 182p. 1993. pap. 39.95 (*0-7859-7562-4*, 8420749001) Fr & Eur.

Nueva York Alive. Nancye White. (SPA.). 1980. pap. 5.95 (*0-935572-05-8*) Alive Pubns.

Nueva York, Ciudad del Misterio. Jose A. Figueroa-Sanchez. 1984. pap. 12.00 (*84-499-7421-6*) Edit Mensaje.

Nueva York en Espanol: Tourist Guides. 4th rev. ed. (Travel Guides Ser.: Vol. 4). (SPA., Illus.). 200p. 1999. reprint ed. pap. 16.95 (*0-940788-06-3*) Modern Guides.

Nueva York en Vivo. Martin Dunford. (SPA.). 375p. 1992. pap. 39.95 (*0-7859-7561-6*, 84207459600) Fr & Eur.

Nueva York en Vivo (Anaya) 373p. 1992. pap. 39.95 (*0-7859-9030-5*) Fr & Eur.

Nueva York Guia Turistica. Berlitz Editors. (Pocket Guides Ser.). (SPA., Illus.). 144p. 1998. pap. 8.95 (*2-8315-6562-6*) Berlitz.

Nueva York Guiarama. C. Atkins & D. Wickers. 128p. 1991. pap. 15.95 (*0-7859-9031-3*) Fr & Eur.

Nueva York Guias Visuales. 2nd ed. (SPA.). 1995. vinyl bd. 59.95 (*0-7859-9174-3*) Fr & Eur.

Nuevas Alternativas en la Predicacion Biblica: Variety in Biblical Preaching. Harold Freeman. Tr. by Ruben A. Zorzoli. (SPA.). 176p. (Orig.). 1991. pap. 8.50 (*0-311-42086-9*) Casa Bautista.

Nuevas Aventuras de Hank El Perro Vaquero. John R. Erickson. (J). 1992. 12.05 (*0-606-08761-3*, Pub. by Turtleback) Demco.

***Nuevas Aventuras de Hank el Perro Vaquero.** John R. Erickson. (SPA., Illus.). (J). 2000. 10.34 (*0-606-18416-3*) Turtleback.

***Nuevas Aventuras de Hank, el Perro Vaquero, Vol. 2.** John R. Erickson. (Hank the Cowdog Ser.: Vol. 2). (SPA., Illus.). 144p. (J). (gr. 3-7). 2000. pap. 6.99 (*0-14-130700-5*, PuffinBks) Peng Put Young Read.

Nuevas Aventuras de Paddington (More about Paddington) Michael Bond. 1996. pap. text 7.50 (*84-279-3704-0*) Lectorum Pubns.

Nuevas Dimensiones. 2nd ed. Hendrickson. (College Spanish Ser.). (C). 1992. pap., suppl. ed. 36.95 (*0-8384-2330-2*) Heinle & Heinle.

Nuevas Dimensiones. 2nd ed. Hendrickson. (College Spanish Ser.). (C). 1992. pap., teacher ed. 21.95 (*0-8384-2636-0*) Heinle & Heinle.

Nuevas Dimensiones. 2nd ed. Angela Labarca & Hendrickson. (C). 1992. pap., student ed. 30.75 (*0-8384-2336-1*) Heinle & Heinle.

Nuevas Dimensiones. 2nd ed. Angela Labarca & Hendrickson. (C). 1992. pap., student ed. 32.95 (*0-8384-2334-5*) Heinle & Heinle.

Nuevas Dimensiones. 2nd ed. Angela Labarca & James M. Hendrickson. (C). 1992. pap. 40.95 (*0-8384-2335-3*) Heinle & Heinle.

Nuevas Dimensions. Angela Labarca. (College Spanish Ser.). (C). 1988. pap., teacher ed. 19.00 (*0-8384-1588-1*) Wadsworth Pub.

Nuevas Fabulas Infantiles. Antonio Salgado.Tr. of New Children's Fables. (SPA.). (ps-3). 1997. pap. text 7.98 (*968-403-902-6*) Selector.

Nuevas Fronteras. 3rd ed. Levy-Ko. (SPA.). (C). 1996. 35.50 incl. audio (*0-03-017233-0*) Harcourt.

Nuevas Frontieras. 3rd ed. Levy-Ko. (C). 1996. 51.00 (*0-03-013403-X*) Harcourt.

Nuevas Frontieras. 5th ed. Levy-Ko. 1995. 246.00 (*0-03-015708-0*) Harcourt Coll Pubs.

Nuevas Memorias Sobre las Antiguedades Neogranadinas: De la Cronologia en la Arqueologia Colombiana y Otros Asuntos. Santiago Mora & Franz Florez. (SPA., Illus.). 175p. 1997. pap. 22.00 incl. disk (*958-608-131-1*, UC14, Pub. by Guadalupe) UPLAAP.

Nuevas Minucias del Lenguaje (New Details of the Language) Jose G. Moreno De Alba. (SPA.). 435p. 1996. 30.99 (*968-16-4856-0*, Pub. by Fondo) Continental Bk.

Nuevas Odas Elementales. Pablo Neruda. (SPA.). 1964. 9.95 (*0-8288-2535-1*, S20092) Fr & Eur.

Nuevas Perspectivas en Atencion Primaria de Salud. J. M. Aranda Regules. (SPA.). 399p. 1994. pap. 31.50 (*84-7978-114-9*, Pub. by Ediciones Diaz) IBD Ltd.

Nuevas Perspectivas Sobre La Generacion Del 27: Ensayos Literaries. Hector H. Romero. LC 81-69021. (SPA.). 169p. (Orig.). 1983. pap. 14.95 (*0-89729-299-5*) Ediciones.

Nuevas Profecias Nostradamus Hasta el Ano 2025. Jean-Charles De Fontbrune. pap. text 22.95 (*84-270-2098-8*) E Martinez Roca.

Nuevas Reflexiones Respecto Al Terrorismo Y el Terrorismo En America (Conexiones Internacionales) see New Reflections on Terrorism & Terrorism in America: International Connections

Nuevas Tendencias en el Teatro Espanol: Matilla-Nieva-Ruibal. Anje C. Van Der Naald. LC 79-56765. (SPA., Illus.). 162p. (Orig.). 1982. pap. 12.95 (*0-89729-246-4*) Ediciones.

Nuevas Voces Hispanas. Silvia Burunat & Julio Burunat. (C). text. write for info. (*0-318-69172-8*) Harcourt Coll Pubs.

Nuevas Voces Hispanas: Contextos Literarios para el Debate y la Composicion. Guijarro-Cou. LC 99-49454. 169p. 1999. pap. text 29.33 (*0-13-938077-9*) P-H.

***Nueve Caras de Cristo: La Busqueda del Verdadero Iniciado.** Eugene E. Whitworth. Tr. by Juan M. Castro. Orig. Title: Nine Faces of Christ. (SPA.). 380p. 1998. pap. 19.00 (*0-9632573-7-4*) Sin Limites.

Nueve Siglos de Literatura Espanola: Nine Centuries of Spanish Literature: A Dual-Language Anthology. unabridged ed. Seymour Resnick & Jeanne Pasmantier. LC 94-19769. 480p. 1994. pap. text 9.95 (*0-486-28271-6*) Dover.

Nuevo Aleman Sin Esfuerzo, 4 cass. (SPA.). pap. 75.00 incl. audio (*2-7005-1019-4*, Pub. by Assimil); pap. 69.95 incl. audio compact disk (*2-7005-1067-4*, Pub. by Assimil) Distribks Inc.

Nuevo Aleman Sin Esfuerzo. Hilde Schneider. Tr. by Instituto Vikingo Staff from FRE. (Sin Esfuerzo Ser.). (Illus.). 415p. 1988. 24.95 (*2-7005-0138-1*, Pub. by Assimil) Distribks Inc.

Nuevo Aleman Sin Esfuerzo: German for Spanish Speakers. Assimil Staff. (GER & SPA.). audio 125.00 (*0-685-54621-7*) Fr & Eur.

Nuevo Aleman sin Esfuerzo: German for Spanish Speakers. Assimil Staff. (GER & SPA.). 28.95 (*0-8288-4312-0*, S4667) Fr & Eur.

Nuevo Aliento. Charles R. Swindoll.Tr. of Second Wind. (SPA.). 96p. 1996. pap. 5.99 (*0-8297-1858-3*) Vida Pubs.

Nuevo Atlas Biblico. Pat Wise.Tr. of New Bible Atlas. (SPA.). 1986. 21.99 (*0-8423-6325-4*, 490405) Editorial Unilit.

Nuevo Comentario Biblico. Guthrie et al.Tr. of New Bible Commentary. (SPA.). 972p. 1986. reprint ed. pap. 61.99 (*0-311-03001-7*) Casa Bautista.

Nuevo Comentario Biblico Siglo XXI. G. J. Wenham. (Comentario del Nuevo Testamento Ser.).Tr. of New Bible Commentary XXI Century. (SPA.). 1040p. (C). 1999. 62.50 (*0-311-03071-8*, Edit Mundo) Casa Bautista.

Nuevo Comienzo (A New Beginning) Emma Darcy. (Deseo Ser.). (SPA.). 1998. per. 3.50 (*0-373-33449-4*, 1-33449-9) Harlequin Bks.

Nuevo Conquistador de Mexico: Una Fabula? Guy Odom. LC 98-44929. 223p. 1999. 21.95 (*0-8253-0502-0*) Beaufort Bks NY.

Nuevo Cubano Cooking. Sue Mullin. 128p. 1993. 12.98 (*1-55521-906-3*) Bk Sales Inc.

Nuevo Destino: The Life Story of a Shipibo Bilingual Educator. Lucille Eakin. LC 79-91447. (International Museum of Cultures Ser.: No. 9). (Illus.). 56p. (Orig.). 1980. pap. 3.92 (*0-88312-159-X*) S I L Intl.

Nuevo Diccionario Biblico. A. Lockward.Tr. of New Bible Dictionary. (SPA.). 24.99 (*0-7899-0389-X*, 490258) Editorial Unilit.

Nuevo Diccionario de Religiones, Denominaciones y Sectas. Marcos A. Ramos.Tr. of New Dictionary of Religions, Denominations & Cults. (SPA.). 1997. 12.99 (*0-89922-284-6*, C100-315X) Caribe Betania.

Nuevo Diccionario de Sinonimos y Antonimos, Spa., 2 vols. Claude-Francois Achard. 1425p. 1983. reprint ed. 350.00 (*0-8288-1719-7*, F8013) Fr & Eur.

Nuevo Diccionario de Teologia. Tr. of New Dictionary of Theology. (SPA.). 35.99 (*0-311-09135-0*) Casa Bautista.

Nuevo Diccionario Enciclopedico Larousse, 9 vols. Ed. by Larousse Staff. (SPA.). 2680p. 1995. 1495.00 (*0-7859-9772-5*) Fr & Eur.

Nuevo Diccionario Ilustrado de la Biblia. Wilton M. Nelson.Tr. of New Illustrated Bible Dictionary. (SPA., Illus.). 1392p. 1998. 39.99 (*0-89922-285-4*, C010-2854) Caribe Betania.

Nuevo Diccionario Ingles-Espanol y Espanol-Ingles: New Spanish-English & English-Spanish Dictionary. 5th ed. Esteban Mac Cragh. 1990. 29.95 (*0-7859-5037-0*) Fr & Eur.

Nuevo Empresario en Mexico (Mexico's New Entrepeneur) Carlos L. Cifuentes. (SPA.). 322p. 1994. pap. 11.99 (*968-16-4507-3*, Pub. by Fondo) Continental Bk.

Nuevo Ensayo de una Biblioteca Espanola de Libros Raros y Curiosos Formada En Presencia de los Ejemplares de la Biblioteca De the Hispanic Society of America y de la Ticknor Collection En la Boston Public Library, Fascicula Segundo, C-f. Homero Seris. (SPA.). 1969. 8.00 (*0-87535-111-5*) Hispanic Soc.

Nuevo Frances Sin Esfuerzo, 3 CDs. (SPA.). pap. 95.00 incl. audio compact disk (*2-7005-1065-8*, Pub. by Assimil) Distribks Inc.

Nuevo Frances Sin Esfuerzo. Anthony Bulger & Jean L. Cherel. Tr. by Felix J. Martinez. (Sin Esfuerzo Ser.). (Illus.). 436p. 1983. 24.95 (*2-7005-0103-9*, Pub. by Assimil) Distribks Inc.

Nuevo Frances Sin Esfuerzo. Jean L. Cherel. (FRE & SPA.). 1983. 28.95 (*0-685-11201-2*) Fr & Eur.

Nuevo Frances Sin Esfuerzo, 3 cass., Set. Anthony Bulger & Jean L. Cherel. Tr. by Felix J. Martinez. (Sin Esfuerzo Ser.). 1983. 75.00 incl. audio (*2-7005-1146-8*, Pub. by Assimil) Distribks Inc.

Nuevo Frances Sin Esfuerzo, 4 cass., Set. Jean L. Cherel. (FRE & SPA.). 1983. audio 125.00 (*0-7859-5546-1*, 2700501039) Fr & Eur.

Nuevo Frances sin Esfuerzo: French for Spanish Speakers. Assimil Staff. (FRE & SPA.). 28.95 (*0-8288-4332-5*, S9342) Fr & Eur.

Nuevo Glosario, Diccionario Poliglota de la Arquitectura. Buenaventura Bassegoda Muste. (CAT, ENG, FRE, GER & ITA.). 366p. 1976. pap. 75.00 (*0-8288-5745-8*, S50134) Fr & Eur.

Nuevo Ingles Sin Esfuerzo, 4 CDs. (SPA.). pap. 95.00 incl. audio compact disk (*2-7005-1066-6*, Pub. by Assimil); pap. 75.00 incl. audio (*2-7005-1301-0*, Pub. by Assimil) Distribks Inc.

Nuevo Ingles Sin Esfuerzo. Anthony Bulger. Tr. by Jose G. Vasquez from FRE. (Sin Esfuerzo Ser.). (Illus.). 585p. 1991. 24.95 (*2-7005-0099-7*, Pub. by Assimil) Distribks Inc.

Nuevo Ingles Sin Esfuerzo. Albert O. Cherel. 24.95 (*0-685-11250-0*); audio 125.00 (*0-685-01733-8*) Fr & Eur.

Nuevo Ingles sin Esfuerzo: English for Spanish Speakers. Assimil Staff. (ENG & SPA.). 28.95 (*0-8288-4306-6*, S27285) Fr & Eur.

Nuevo Italiano Sin Esfuerzo, 4 CDs. (SPA.). pap. 95.00 incl. audio compact disk (*2-7005-1068-2*, Pub. by Assimil); pap. 75.00 incl. audio (*2-7005-1302-9*, Pub. by Assimil) Distribks Inc.

Nuevo Italiano Sin Esfuerzo. Giovanna Galdo & Ena Marchi. (Sin Esfuerzo Ser.). (Illus.). 429p. 1986. 24.95 (*2-7005-0118-7*, Pub. by Assimil) Distribks Inc.

Nuevo Italiano sin Esfuerzo: Italian for Spanish Speakers. Assimil Staff. (ITA & SPA.). 28.50 (*0-8288-4336-8*, F13320) Fr & Eur.

Nuevo Latino: Recipes That Celebrate the New Latin-American Cuisine. Douglas Rodriguez & John Harrisson. (Illus.). 168p. 1995. 29.95 (*0-89815-752-8*) Ten Speed Pr.

Nuevo Lexico Griego Espanol: Greek-Spanish Lexicon of the New Testament. McKibben-Stockwell. (SPA.). 316p. 1985. reprint ed. pap. 12.99 (*0-311-42072-9*, Edit Mundo) Casa Bautista.

Nuevo Libro de Cocina Diete. Robert C. Atkins. (SPA.). 224p. 1997. per. 12.95 (*0-684-84195-9*, Libros) S&S Trade Pap.

Nuevo Manual Biblico: Indice. Tr. of Bible Handbook: Index. (SPA.). 34.99 (*0-685-74965-7*, 490409); pap. 26.99 (*0-685-74964-9*, 490407) Editorial Unilit.

Nuevo Manual Biblico de Unger. Merrill F. Unger. Orig. Title: New Unger's Bible Handbook. (SPA., Illus.). 720p. 1987. 39.99 (*0-8254-1779-1*, Edit Portavoz); pap. 34.99 (*0-8254-1781-3*, Edit Portavoz) Kregel.

Nuevo Manual Biblico Ilustrado. Tr. of New Illustrated Bible Handbook. (SPA., Illus.). 29.99 (*0-685-74966-5*, 490410) Editorial Unilit.

Nuevo Manual Biblico Ilustrado. David Alexander & Pat Alexander.Tr. of New Illustrated Bible Handbook. (SPA., Illus.). 1993. 29.99 (*0-8423-6289-4*, 490410) Editorial Unilit.

Nuevo Manual de Usos y Costumbres de los Tiempos Biblicos. Ralph Gower. Orig. Title: New Manners & Customs of Bible Times. (SPA., Illus.). 400p. 1990. pap. 32.99 (*0-8254-1280-3*, Edit Portavoz) Kregel.

***Nuevo Milenio: Preguntas y Respuestas.** Joao de Dues Gois. (SPA.). 32p. 1998. pap. 1.00 (*0-7648-0278-X*, Libros Liguori) Liguori Pubns.

Nuevo Momento en Nuestra America. Ed. by Robert S. Leiken. (SPA.). 168p. (C). 1994. pap. 19.95 (*0-935501-89-4*, Pub. by U Miami N-S Ctr) L Rienner.

Nuevo Nacimiento. Kenneth E. Hagin.Tr. of New Birth. (SPA.). 1983. pap. 1.00 (*0-89276-150-4*) Faith Lib Pubns.

Nuevo Order Monetario para Europa. Karl O. Pohl. LC HG0930.5.P64. (Conferencia Per Jacobsson de 1992 Ser.). (SPA.). 34p. reprint ed. pap. 30.00 (*0-608-08741-6*, 206938000004) Bks Demand.

Nuevo Regalo. Patron Lujan Roger. (SPA.). 1997. pap. text 14.98 (*968-409-918-5*) Edamex.

Nuevo Regalo Excepcional. Patron Lujan Roger. (SPA.). 1997. pap. text 18.98 (*968-409-762-X*) Edamex.

Nuevo Teatro Latinoamericano: Una Lectura Historica. Beatriz J. Rizk. (Towards a Social History of Hispanic & Luso-Brazilian Literature Ser.). (SPA.). 144p. (Orig.). (C). 1987. pap. 9.95 (*0-910235-25-2*) Prisma Bks.

***Nuevo Testamento.** Broadman & Holman Publishing Staff. (SPA.). 2000. pap. 5.95 (*0-8054-9425-1*) Broadman.

Nuevo Testamento - "Venid a Mi" Rva: Come unto Me Rva N. T. (SPA.). 288p. (Orig.). 1986. pap. 1.40 (*0-311-48752-1*) Casa Bautista.

Nuevo Testamento de Estudio. Charles C. Ryrie.Tr. of Ryrie Study New Testament. (SPA.). 512p. 1996. 9.99 (*0-8254-1647-7*, Edit Portavoz) Kregel.

Nuevo Testamento en Cuadros para Ninos. Kenneth N. Taylor. Orig. Title: The New Testament in Pictures for Little Eyes. (SPA., Illus.). 160p. (J). 1991. pap. 7.99 (*0-8254-1708-2*, Edit Portavoz) Kregel.

***Nuevo Testamento Ilustrado.** Cook Communication Ministry Staff.Tr. of Illustrated New Testament. (SPA., Illus.). 256p. (J). 1999. pap. 8.99 (*0-311-38642-3*, Edit Mundo) Casa Bautista.

Nuevo Testamento, Version Recobro, Black. Living Street Ministry Staff.Tr. of New Testament, Recovery Version. (SPA.). 1338p. 1994. boxed set, lthr. 65.00 (*0-87083-801-6*, 01-013-002) Living Stream Ministry.

Nuevo Testamento, Version Recobro, Edicion Economica en Rustica (Black) Living Street Ministry Staff.Tr. of NEW TESTAMENT, RECOVERY VERSION (ECONOMY BLACK, 6 3/4. (SPA.). 1368p. 1994. per. 15.00 (*0-87083-804-0*, 01-018-002) Living Stream Ministry.

Nuevo Testamento, Version Recobro, Edicion Economica en Rustica (Maroon) Living Street Ministry Staff.Tr. of NEW TESTAMENT, RECOVERY VERSION (ECONOMY BURGUNDY, 6 3/4. (SPA.). 1368p. 1994. per. 15.00 (*0-87083-803-2*, 01-019-002) Living Stream Ministry.

Nuevo Testamento, Version Recobro, Maroon. Living Street Ministry Staff.Tr. of NEW TESTAMENT, RECOVERY VERSION. (SPA.). 1338p. 1994. boxed set, lthr. 65.00 (*0-87083-802-4*, 01-014-002) Living Stream Ministry.

Nuevo Testamento el Camino de Vida 1960. Tr. of Come unto Me New Testament. 1984. pap. 1.45 (*0-311-48574-X*) Baptist Spanish.

Nuevo Tex-Mex: Festive New Recipes from Just North of the Border. David Garrido & Rob Walsh. LC 97-30796. 1998. 19.95 (*0-8118-1612-5*) Chronicle Bks.

Nuevo Viaje a Islas de la America, Vol. 1. Jean B. Labat. Ed. by Manuel Cardenas-Ruiz. LC 83-3591. Orig. Title: Nouveau Vouage aux Isles de l'Amerique. (SPA., Illus.). 279p. 1984. pap. 6.50 (*0-8477-0876-4*) U of PR Pr.

Nuevos Amigos. Harcourt Brace Staff. (SPA.). 1989. pap. text, teacher ed. 15.00 (*0-15-388309-X*); pap. text, teacher ed., wbk. ed. 16.75 (*0-15-388305-7*); pap. text, teacher ed., wbk. ed. 18.00 (*0-15-388306-5*); pap. text, wbk. ed. 14.00 (*0-15-388304-9*) Holt R&W.

Nuevos Amigos: Testbook. Harcourt Brace Staff. (SPA.). 1989. pap. text 15.00 (*0-15-388307-3*) Holt R&W.

Nuevos Amigos Spanish, 1989. Harcourt Brace Staff. 1989. text 56.50 (*0-15-388300-6*) Holt R&W.

Nuevos Amigos Spanish, 1989, Pt. 3. Harcourt Brace Staff. 1989. text 32.75 (*0-15-388292-1*) Holt R&W.

Nuevos Amigos Spanish 1989. Harcourt Brace Staff. 1989. text 66.00 (*0-15-388301-4*, Pub. by Harcourt Coll Pubs) Harcourt.

Nuevos Destinos 384p. 1997. pap. 56.56 (*0-07-059333-7*) McGraw.

***Nuevos Destinos** 1998. mass mkt., teacher ed. 47.96 (*0-07-027514-9*) McGraw.

***Nuevos Destinos** 288p. 1998. pap., student ed. 24.69 (*0-07-027515-7*) McGraw.

***Nuevos Destinos** 1998. mass mkt. 53.32 (*0-07-027522-X*) McGraw.

***Nuevos Destinos: Spanish in Review.** Cynthia Medina. 112p. (C). 1999. pap. 20.63 (*0-07-233815-6*) McGrw-H Hghr Educ.

Nuevos Enfoques en el Estudio de la Litica. Ed. by Maria D. Soto. 442p. 1990. pap. 10.20 (*968-36-1415-9*, UN026) UPLAAP.

***Nuevos Mundos: Lectura, Cultura y Comunicacion: Curso de Espanol Para Estudiates Bilingues.** Ana Roca. (SPA.). 254p. 1998. pap. 40.95 (*0-471-19205-8*) Wiley.

Nuevos Rumbos: A Short Course for Elementary Spanish. 2nd ed. Ronni L. Gordon & David M. Stillman. LC 85-60977. (ENG & SPA.). 405p. (C). 1986. student ed. 29.96 (*0-669-08964-8*); text 57.96 (*0-669-08962-1*); audio 2.66 (*0-669-08965-6*); audio 31.16 (*0-669-08966-4*) HM Trade Div.

Nuevos Senderos: Reflections on Hispanics & Philanthropy. Ed. by Diana Campoamor et al. LC 98-38439. 224p. 1998. pap. 19.95 (*1-55885-263-8*) Arte Publico.

Nuevos Sofistas: La Subversion Cultural de Nietzsche a Beckett. Ludwig Schajowicz. LC 78-9541. 584p. 1979. 9.60 (*0-8477-2823-4*); pap. 8.00 (*0-8477-2817-X*) U of PR Pr.

Nuevos Umbrales de Fe. Kenneth E. Hagin.Tr. of New Thresholds of Faith. (SPA.). 1988. pap. 5.95 (*0-89276-185-7*) Faith Lib Pubns.

Nuff Respect. D. J. Edwards. 308p. 1996. mass mkt. 10.95 (*0-7472-4860-5*, Pub. by Headline Bk Pub) Trafalgar.

Nuff Respect. large type ed. D. J. Edwards. 480p. 31.50 (*0-7089-3684-9*) Ulverscroft.

Nuffield Desgin & Technology. Barlex et al. 1995. pap. text, student ed. write for info. (*0-582-21266-9*, Pub. by Addison-Wesley) Longman.

Nuffield Design & Technology. Barlex et al. 1995. pap. text, student ed. write for info. (*0-582-21265-0*, Pub. by Addison-Wesley) Longman.

Nugae Antiquae, 2 vols. John Harington. Ed. by Thomas Park. LC 02-21609. reprint ed. 125.00 (*0-404-03125-0*) AMS Pr.

Nugae Antiquae, 3 vols., Set. John Harington. Ed. by Henry Harington. (Anglistica & Americana Ser.: No. 14). 1968. reprint ed. 122.20 (*0-685-66475-9*, 05102017) G Olms Pubs.

Nugget & Darling. Barbara M. Joosse. LC 94-17011. (Illus.). 32p. (J). (gr. k-3). 1997. 14.95 (*0-395-64571-9*, Clarion Bks) HM.

Nugget City. Wayne D. Overholser. 224p. 1998. mass mkt. 4.40 (*0-8439-4454-4*, Leisure Bks) Dorchester Pub Co.

Nugget City. Wayne D. Overholser. LC 96-43959. (Five-Star Western Ser.). 218p. 1997. 17.95 (*0-7862-0733-7*) Five Star.

Nugget City. large type ed. Wayne D. Overholser. LC 97-45667. 1998. 18.95 (*0-7862-0756-6*) Thorndike Pr.

Nuggets: Recipes Good As Gold. Junior League of Colorado Springs Staff. LC 82-83706. (Illus.). 189p. 1983. text 13.95 (*0-9609930-4-5*) Jr League Colo Spgs.

Nuggets & Dust Panned Out in California. Ambrose Bierce. (Principle Works of Ambrose Gwinett Bierce). 1989. reprint ed. lib. bdg. 79.00 (*0-7812-1955-8*) Rprt Serv.

Nuggets from King Solomon's Mine. John B. Schmalz. LC 94-79886. (Astro-Cards Reprints Ser.). (Illus.). 60p. 1996. reprint ed. pap. text 9.00 (*1-885500-06-8*, AR3) Astro-Cards.

Nuggets from King Solomon's Mine. John B. Schmalz. (Illus.). 66p. 1996. reprint ed. pap. 7.95 (*1-56459-465-3*) Kessinger Pub.

Nuggets from 1949. Owen Hannant. 70p. 1985. pap. 9.95 (*0-87770-364-7*) Ye Galleon.

Nuggets from the Scriptures. Berenice M. Shotwell. LC 89-92092. 1990. 11.50 (*0-9603026-2-X*) Shadwold.

An Asterisk (*) at the beginning of an entry indicates that the title is appearing for the first time.

Nuggets in the Ground: A Beginner's Guide to Aoinagi Karate. Raymnond R. Castilonia. LC 96-75886. (Illus.). 175p. 1996. pap., lab manual ed. write for info. (*0-9636817-4-5*) Intl Univ Line.

Nuggets of Faith. Jack Hartman. 78p. 1984. pap. 4.00 (*0-915445-01-8*) Lamplight FL.

Nuggets of Gold. Claudia N. Tynes. (Illus.). 64p. 1998. pap. 8.95 (*0-9665517-0-2*) Write FourU.

Nuggets of Gold: Surgeons Quotes. George B. Burch. 1999. pap. text 9.99 (*1-889893-29-3*) Emerald House Group Inc.

***Nuggets of Goldrush History.** Mildred Forester & Roy Pence. Ed. by Mantle Hood. (Illus.). x, 99p. 1999. pap. 12.95 (*0-9661065-2-0*) Tale Spin.

Nuggets of Life. Dave Meyer. 160p. (Orig.). 1996. mass mkt. 5.99 (*0-89274-974-1*, HH-974) Harrison Hse.

Nuggets of Nevada County History. Juanita K. Browne. LC 83-23781. (Illus.). xii, 143p. (Orig.). 1983. pap. 10.50 (*0-915641-00-3*) Nevada County Hist Society.

Nuggets of Truth. Charles Hunter & Frances Hunter. 1975. pap. 4.95 (*0-917726-01-4*) Hunter Bks.

Nuggets of Truth from God's Word. Rodney M. Howard-Browne. 178p. 1998. pap. text 10.00 (*1-884662-11-0*) Revival Minst Intl.

Nuggets on the Diamond: Professional Baseball in the Bay Area from the Gold Rush to the Present. Dick Dobbins & Jon Twichell. Ed. by Jon Rochmis. LC 94-60296. (Illus.). 304p. (Orig.). 1994. 32.95 (*0-942627-00-8*); pap. 29.95 (*0-942627-01-6*) Woodford Pubng.

Nuh (Noah) Siddiqia Juma. (Illus.). 16p. (J). (ps-1). 1997. 10.00 (*1-879402-44-0*) Tahrike Tarsile Quran.

Nuisance. Frank Endersby. 12p. (J). (gr. 4 up). 1981. 2.99 (*0-85953-233-X*) Childs Play.

Nuisance. Lass Small. (Desire Ser.). 1995. per. 2.99 (*0-373-05901-9*, 1-05901-3) Silhouette.

Nuisance Animals: Backyard Pests to Free-Roaming Killers. John Trout, Jr. Ed. by Jim Casada. (Illus.). 192p. (C). 1997. pap. 14.95 (*0-9636526-1-3*) Wild Trails Pubng.

Nuisance Publik. Marie Decary. (Novels in the Roman Plus Ser.). (FRE., Illus.). 160p. (YA). (gr. 8 up). 1995. pap. 8.95 (*2-89021-249-1*, Pub. by La Courte Ech) Firefly Bks Ltd.

Nuit see Nights

Nuit. Marie Balka. (FRE.). 1978. pap. 12.95 (*0-7859-1875-2*, 2070370380) Fr & Eur.

Nuit Americaine. Roger Crittenden. LC 98-215545. (Film Classics Ser.). (Illus.). 80p. 1998. pap. 10.95 (*0-85170-672-X*) Ind U Pr.

Nuit & Brouillard: On the Making, Reception & Functions of a Major Documentary Film. Richard Raskin. (Illus.). 186p. (C). 1987. pap. 23.00 (*87-7288-100-3*, Pub. by Aarhus Univ Pr) David Brown.

Nuit Avec Eve. Elda Minger. (Rouge Passion Ser.: Bk. 489). 1999. mass mkt. 3.50 (*0-373-37489-5*, 1-37489-1) Harlequin Bks.

Nuit Bengali. Mircea Eliade. (FRE.). 1979. pap. 10.95 (*0-7859-2412-4*, 2070370879) Fr & Eur.

Nuit Blancues - Le sous Sol. Fyodor Dostoyevsky. (FRE.). 1982. pap. 11.95 (*0-7859-1951-1*, 2070373525) Fr & Eur.

Nuit d'Ambre. Sylvie Germain. (FRE.). 434p. 1989. pap. 13.95 (*0-7859-2572-4*, 2070381617) Fr & Eur.

Nuit de la Saint-Jean see Chronique des Pasquier

Nuit de Mai (A Night in May) Alfred De Musset. Tr. & Intro. by Claire N. White. (Illus.). 28p. (Orig.). 1989. pap. 20.00 (*0-930126-27-0*) Typographeum.

Nuit de Saint-Jean. Georges Duhamel. (Chronique Des Pasquier Ser.: Vol. IV). (FRE.). 192p. 1973. pap. 10.95 (*0-7859-1754-3*, 2070364402) Fr & Eur.

Nuit des Fantomes. Julien Green. (FRE.). 1990. pap. 16.95 (*0-7859-2716-6*) Fr & Eur.

Nuit des Grands Chiens Malades. A. D. G. (FRE.). 217p. 1990. pap. 10.95 (*0-7859-2155-9*, 2070383253) Fr & Eur.

Nuit D'Ivresse. Roseanne Williams. (Rouge Passion Ser.: No. 521). (FRE.). 1999. mass mkt. 3.99 (*0-373-37521-2*, 1-37521-1) Harlequin Bks.

Nuit d'Orage. Georges Duhamel. (FRE.). 262p. 1928. 14.95 (*0-7859-0040-3*, F99350) Fr & Eur.

Nuit du Serail. Michel D. Grece. (FRE.). 1984. pap. 13.95 (*0-7859-2490-6*, 2070375560) Fr & Eur.

Nuit du Vampire. Denis Cote. (Novels in the Roman Jeunesse Ser.). (FRE.). 96p. (J). (gr. 4-7). 1990. pap. 7.95 (*2-89021-117-7*, Pub. by La Courte Ech) Firefly Bks Ltd.

Nuit Est le Manteau des Pauvres. Claude Roy. (FRE.). 1976. pap. 10.95 (*0-7859-4053-7*) Fr & Eur.

Nuit Glacee. Pa Kin. (FRE.). 1983. pap. 15.95 (*0-7859-4195-9*) Fr & Eur.

Nuit, le Jour et Toutes les Autres Nuits. Michel Audiard. (FRE.). 1980. pap. 10.95 (*0-7859-1917-1*, 2070372014) Fr & Eur.

Nuit sans Nuit see Nights As Day, Days As Night

Nuit Sera Calme. Romain Gary. (FRE.). 1976. pap. 11.95 (*0-7859-2365-9*, 2070367193) Fr & Eur.

Nuit Sera Calme. Romain Gary. (Folio Ser.: No. 719). (FRE.). 264p. 1974. pap. 9.95 (*2-07-036719-3*) Schoenhof.

Nuit Talismanique. Rene Char. (FRE.). 1983. pap. 16.95 (*0-7859-3403-0*) Fr & Eur.

Nuit Tres Longue. Chrystine Brouillet. (Novels in the Roman Plus Ser.). (FRE.). 160p. (YA). (gr. 8 up). 1992. pap. 8.95 (*2-89021-174-6*, Pub. by La Courte Ech) Firefly Bks Ltd.

Nuits. Alfred De Musset. 5.95 (*0-686-55550-3*) Fr & Eur.

***Nuits de Chine.** Daphne Clair. (Azur Ser.: No. 796). (FRE.). 1999. mass mkt. 3.99 (*0-373-34796-0*, 1-34796-2, Harlequin French) Harlequin Bks.

Nuits de Malaisie. Karen Van Der Zee. (Azur Ser.). (FRE.). 1997. pap. 3.50 (*0-373-34660-3*, 1-34660-0) Harlequin Bks.

Nuits de Montmartre - Basfonds de Berlin. Joseph Kessel. (FRE.). 1990. pap. 16.95 (*0-7859-3201-1*, 2264014741) Fr & Eur.

Nuits de Paris. Nicholas E. Restif de la Bretonne. (Folio Ser.: No. 1739). (FRE.). 1986. pap. 14.95 (*2-07-037739-3*) Schoenhof.

Nuits d'Ivresse. Madeline Harper. (Rouge Passion Ser.). (FRE.). 1997. pap. 3.50 (*0-373-37434-8*, 1-37434-7) Harlequin Bks.

Nuits d'Octobre see Oeuvres

Nuits d'Octobre. Gerard Enerval. Ed. by Lemaitre. (Class. Garnier Ser.). pap. write for info. Schoenhof.

Nuk Tessli: The Life of a Wilderness Dweller. Chris Czajkowski. (Illus.). 224p. 1999. pap. 14.95 (*1-55143-133-5*) Orca Bk Pubs.

Nuke Chronicles: Writers & Artists on the Future. 2nd rev. ed. Ed Sanders et al. Ed. by Josh Gosciak. (Illus.). 48p. 1985. pap. 4.00 (*0-936556-00-5*) Contact Two.

***Nuke Down.** Chet Cunningham. 2000. mass mkt. 5.99 (*0-553-58077-9*) Bantam.

Nuke Hill. Steven Spetz. 272p. 1987. per. 3.95 (*0-373-62110-8*) Harlequin Bks.

Nuke-Rebuke: Writers & Artists Against Nuclear Energy & Weapons. Ed. by Morty Sklar. LC 83-20140. (Contemporary Anthology Ser.: No. 5). (Illus.). 208p. 1984. 12.00 (*0-930370-16-3*); pap. 6.00 (*0-930370-17-1*) Spirit That Moves.

Nuke-Rebuke: Writers & Artists Against Nuclear Energy & Weapons, Signed A-Z. limited ed. Ed. by Morty Sklar. LC 83-20140. (Contemporary Anthology Ser.: No. 5). (Illus.). 208p. (C). 1984. 25.00 (*0-930370-15-5*) Spirit That Moves.

Nukes: Four Horror Writers on the Ultimate Horror. Mort Castle et al. Ed. & Intro. by John Maclay. LC 85-63719. 100p. (Orig.). 1986. pap. 4.95 (*0-940776-22-7*) Maclay Assoc.

Nukespeak, the Media & the Bomb. Crispin Aubrey. LC 83-101127. (Comedia/Minority Press Group Ser.). vii, 135p. 1982. write for info. (*0-906890-26-8*) Routledge.

Nukleare Festkorperphysik see Nuclear Condensed Matter Physics: Nuclear Methods & Applications

Nukleare Mitwirkung: Die Bundesrepublik Deutschland in der atlantischen Allianz 1954-1970. Dieter Mahncke. (Beitraege zur Auswaertigen und Internationalen Politik Ser.: Vol. 6). xvi, 274p. (C). 1972. 79.25 (*3-11-001820-9*) De Gruyter.

Nul N'est Cense Ignorer la Loi: Petit Dictionnaire Juridique. 3rd ed. Jacqueline Bromberger. (FRE.). 494p. 1977. pap. 39.95 (*0-7859-7937-9*, 2711100588) Fr & Eur.

Nulce/Nulse Families in America: Descendants of Elisha Nulce/Nulse, 1725-1796, Goshen, NY, Vol. 1. Lynn C. Harper. LC 98-70463. 400p. 1998. pap. 40.00 (*1-57502-756-9*, P02095) Morris Pubng.

Nulce/Nulse Families in America: Descendants of Elisha Nulce/Nulse, 1725-1796 Goshen, NY, Vol. 2. Lynn C. Harper. LC 98-70463. 324p. 1998. pap. 40.00 (*1-57502-757-7*, P02096) Morris Pubng.

Nulce/Nulse Families in America: Descendants of James Nulce/Nulst, 1791-1875 Somerset County, NJ, Vol. 3. Lynn C. Harper. LC 98-70463. 70p. 1998. pap. 40.00 (*1-57502-758-5*) Morris Pubng.

Null - Ohler. Descendants of Jacob Null & Lucy Ohler. Rachel S. Tefft. 103p. 1997. pap. 16.00 (*0-8328-9481-8*); lib. bdg. 26.00 (*0-8328-9480-X*) Higginson Bk Co.

Null-Additive Set Functions. Endre Pap. (Mathematics & Its Applications Ser.: Vol. 337). 324p. (C). 1995. text 154.50 (*0-7923-3658-5*) Kluwer Academic.

Null Bock Auf High Tech: Arbeitsplatz-Export: Nurweil die Loehne Zu Hosh Sind? Reimer Hartenstein. (GER.). 1996. write for info. (*0-9639887-3-5*) IT Press.

Null Models in Ecology. Nicholas J. Gotelli & Gary R. Graves. (Illus.). 400p. 1996. pap. text 32.95 (*1-56098-645-X*) Smithsonian.

Null Models in Ecology. Nicholas J. Gotelli & Gary R. Graves. (Illus.). 400p. 1996. text 65.00 (*1-56098-657-3*) Smithsonian.

Null Set. George Chambers. LC 76-47788. 1977. 15.95 (*0-914590-34-0*); pap. 6.95 (*0-914590-35-9*) Fiction Coll.

Null Subject Parameter. Ed. by Osvaldo Jaeggli & Ken Safir. (C). 1989. pap. text 58.50 (*1-55608-087-5*); lib. bdg. 151.00 (*1-55608-086-7*) Kluwer Academic.

Nullity of Marriage in the Catholic Church. Veritas Publications Staff. 1989. 15.00 (*0-86217-296-9*, Pub. by Veritas Pubns) St Mut.

Numb Toes & Aching Soles: Coping with Peripheral Neuropathy. John A. Senneff. LC 99-62350. 336p. 1999. pap. 19.95 (*0-9671107-1-8*) MedPress.

Numb Toes & Aching Soles: Coping with Peripheral Neuropathy. John A. Senneff. LC 99-62350. 336p. 1999. 29.95 (*0-9671107-2-6*) MedPress.

Numbah One Day of Christmas: The Hawaii Version of the 12 Days. Eaton B. Magoon, Jr. et al. LC 94-77955. (Illus.). 20p. 1994. 9.95 (*1-880188-91-0*) Bess Pr.

Numbat-His Magic Quest. Mark Pearson. (C). 1990. 45.00 (*0-947333-14-2*, Pub. by Pascoe Pub) St Mut.

Numbears: A Counting Book. Kathleen Hague. LC 85-27006. (Illus.). 32p. (J). (ps-2). 1995. 13.95 (*0-8050-0309-6*, Bks Young Read); pap. 4.95 (*0-8050-1679-1*) H Holt & Co.

***Number: From Ahmes to Cantor.** Midhat J. Gazale. LC 99-36677. 2000. 29.95 (*0-691-00515-X*, Pub. by Princeton U Pr) Cal Prin Full Svc.

Number: Manuscript Edition. Arthur Carter. 1952. pap. 13.00 (*0-8222-0833-4*) Dramatists Play.

Number: The Language of Science. 4th rev. ed. Tobias Dantzig. (Illus.). 340p. 1967. pap. 18.95 (*0-02-906990-4*) Free Pr.

Number & Letter Games. S. Harold Collins. (Beginning Sign Language Ser.). (Illus.). 29p. (J). 1995. pap. 3.95 (*0-931993-72-5*, GP-072) Garlic Pr OR.

Number & Operations: A "Hands On" Approach to Teaching . . . Linda-Sue Brisby et al. (Illus.). 218p. 1991. teacher ed. 17.95 (*0-927726-07-6*) Hands On CA.

Number & Time: Reflections Leading Toward a Unification of Depth, Psychology & Physics. Marie-Louise Von Franz. Tr. by Andrea Dykes from GER. LC 73-86467. (Studies in Jungian Thought). 332p. 1974. 34.95 (*0-8101-0429-6*); pap. 22.95 (*0-8101-0532-2*) Northwestern U Pr.

Number & Timing of Paleoseismic Events on the Nephi & Levan Segments, Wasatch Fault Zone, Utah. Michael D. Jackson. LC TN24.U8 A322. (Special Study Ser.: Vol. 78). (Illus.). 23p. 1991. pap. 6.50 (*1-55791-197-5*, SS-78) Utah Geological Survey.

Number Art: Thirteen 123s from Around the World. Leonard Everett Fisher. LC 82-5050. (Illus.). 64p. (J). (gr. 3-7). 1984. mass mkt. 16.95 (*0-02-735240-4*, Four Winds Pr) S&S Childrens.

Number Bingo. Jock Gunter & Carla Clason. (Technical Notes Ser.: No. 7). 15p. (Orig.). 1973. 2.00 (*0-932288-16-2*) Ctr Intl Ed U of MA.

***Number Books, Bk. 1.** Andrew Parker & Jane Stamford. (J). (ps-2). 1999. pap., wbk. ed. 15.00 (*0-7217-2341-1*, Pub. by Schofield) St Mut.

***Number Books, Bk. 2.** Andrew Parker & Jane Stamford. (J). (gr. 1-3). 1999. pap., wbk. ed. 15.00 (*0-7217-2342-X*, Pub. by Schofield) St Mut.

***Number Books, Bk. 3.** Andrew Parker & Jane Stamford. (J). (ps-2). 1999. pap., wbk. ed. 15.00 (*0-7217-2343-8*, Pub. by Schofield) St Mut.

***Number Books, Bk. 4.** Andrew Parker & Jane Stamford. (J). (ps-2). 1999. pap., wbk. ed. 15.00 (*0-7217-2344-6*, Pub. by Schofield) St Mut.

***Number Books, Bk. 5.** Andrew Parker & Jane Stamford. (J). (ps-2). 1999. pap., wbk. ed. 15.00 (*0-7217-2345-4*, Pub. by Schofield) St Mut.

Number by Colors: A Guide to Using Color to Understand Technical Data. Brand Fortner & T. H. Meyer. 349p. 1996. 44.95 (*0-387-94685-3*) Spr-Verlag.

Number-Cell Challenges: A Collection of Ingenious Number Puzzles. Wilson Ransome. 36p. (YA). (gr. 4 up). 1997. pap. 8.50 (*1-899618-07-4*, Pub. by Tarquin Pubns) Parkwest Pubns.

Number Chomp. Susan Pagnucci. (Illus.). 48p. (Orig.). (J). (gr. 1-2). 1984. pap. 4.50 (*0-929326-04-0*) Bur Oak Pr Inc.

Number Circus. (Fisher-Price Little People Concept Bks.: Vol. 3). (Illus.). 24p. (J). 1998. pap. write for info. (*0-7666-0321-0*, Honey Bear Bks) Modern Pub NYC.

Number Concepts & Operations in the Middle Grades: The Research Agenda for Mathematics Education, Vol. 2. Ed. by Merlyn Behr & J. Hiebert. 280p. 1988. text 59.95 (*0-8058-0353-X*) L Erlbaum Assocs.

***Number Concepts & Relationships: Inventive Exercises to Sharpen Skills & Raise Achievement.** Imogene Forte et al. Ed. by Jennifer Streams. (Basic Not Boring Ser.). (Illus.). 64p. (J). (gr. 2-3). 2000. pap. text 6.95 (*0-86530-443-2*, IP 4-5-X) Incentive Pubns.

***Number Devil: A Mathematical Adventure.** Hans Enzensberger. LC 97-42448. (Illus.). 264p. (gr. 5-9). 2000. pap. 17.00 (*0-8050-6299-8*) St Martin.

Number Devil: A Mathmatical Adventure. Hans Magnus Enzensberger. Tr. by Michael Henry Heim. LC 97-42448. (Illus.). 262p. (YA). (gr. 5-9). 1998. 25.00 (*0-8050-5770-6*, Metropol Bks) H Holt & Co.

Number Drills. Carolee Freer. 56p. 1997. text 15.00 (*1-890458-11-2*) Prof Educ Dist.

***Number Eight.** David Collins. (Numberlies Ser.). 24p. (J). 2000. pap. text 3.25 (*0-7894-5304-5*, D K Ink) DK Pub Inc.

Number Field Sieve. Ed. by H. W. Lenstra, Jr. (Lecture Notes in Mathematics Ser.: Vol. 1554). (Illus.). vii, 132p. 1993. pap. write for info. (*3-540-57013-6*) Spr-Verlag.

Number Fields, Vol. VIII. rev. ed. Daniel A. Marcus. LC 77-21467. 279p. (C). 1997. 39.00 (*0-387-90279-1*) Spr-Verlag.

***Number Five.** David Collins. (Numberlies Ser.). 24p. (J). 2000. pap. text 3.25 (*0-7894-5326-6*, D K Ink) DK Pub Inc.

Number 5 Jungle Carbine. Alan M. Petrillo. (British Firearms Ser.: Vol. 5). (Illus.). 32p. (Orig.). 1994. pap. 7.95 (*1-880677-06-7*) Excalibur AZ.

This book covers the rifles that collectors have come to call "Jungle Carbine" - the Lee Enfield Number 5 Mark 1. It focuses on the Mark 1 model & its variant parts, the never-issued Mark 2 version, the grenade-firing model & contemporary competitors from commonwealth countries. The book has a general history of the rifles & a chapter on the problem of the "wandering zero." The book has 15 photographs to illustrate the text. Contact Excalibur Publications, PO Box 35369, Tucson, AZ 85740-5369. Voice (520) 575-9057. Fax: (520) 575-9068.

Publisher Paid Annotation.

Number for Your Thoughts: Facts & Speculations about Numbers from Euclid to the Latest Computers. Malcolm E. Lines. LC 86-183277. (Illus.). 220p. 1986. pap. 26.00 (*0-85274-495-1*) IOP Pub.

Number Forty-Four: The Mysterious Stranger. Mark Twain, pseud. LC 81-40326. (Mark Twain Library: No. 3). 200p. 1982. 45.00 (*0-520-04544-0*, Pub. by U CA Pr); pap. 14.95 (*0-520-04545-9*, Pub. by U CA Pr) Cal Prin Full Svc.

Number Forty-Four & Other Football Stories, Vol. 1. Harold M. Sherman. LC 72-4408. (Short Story Index Reprint Ser.). 1977. reprint ed. 21.95 (*0-8369-4188-8*) Ayer.

***Number Four.** David Collins. (Numberlies Ser.). 24p. (J). 2000. pap. text 3.25 (*0-7894-5325-8*, D K Ink) DK Pub Inc.

Number Games. Rick Detorie. (Magic Answer Bks.). 1989. pap. 1.95 (*0-8125-7318-8*, Pub. by Tor Bks) St Martin.

Number Games. Ray Gibson. (You & Your Child Ser.). (Illus.). 32p. (J). (ps-2). 1993. pap. text 5.95 (*0-7460-1294-2*, Usborne); lib. bdg. 14.95 (*0-88110-651-8*, Usborne) EDC.

Number Games & Story Problems: Addition & Subtraction. Marlene Kliman & Susan J. Russell. Ed. by Catherine Anderson & Beverly Cory. (Investigations in Number, Data, & Space Ser.). (Illus.). 234p. (J). (gr. 1 up). 1997. pap. text 22.95 (*1-57232-470-8*, 43707) Seymour Pubns.

***Number Hunt.** (Pooh Learning Ser.). (ps-3). 2000. pap. 6.98 incl. audio (*0-7634-0473-5*) W Disney Records.

Number Ideas Through Pictures. Mannis Charosh. LC 73-4370. (Young Math Ser.). (Illus.). 40p. (J). (gr. 1-5). 1974. lib. bdg. 12.89 (*0-690-00156-8*) HarpC Child Bks.

Number in Preschool & Kindergarten: Educational Implications of Piaget's Theory. Constance Kamii. LC 82-81943. 92p. 1982. pap. text 6.00 (*0-912674-80-6*, NAEYC #103) Natl Assn Child Ed.

Number in Scripture. Ethelbert W. Bullinger. LC 67-26498. 320p. 1980. pap. 12.99 (*0-8254-2238-8*, Kregel Class) Kregel.

Number Jugglers: Math Game Book & Math Game Cards. Ruth B. Alexander. LC 98-16542. 64p. 1998. pap. 12.95 (*0-7611-0882-3*) Workman Pub.

Number-Key Practice for Use on Typewriter, Ten-Key & Keypunch Keyboards. R. Bloomquist et al. (C). 1975. text 12.24 (*0-07-006105-X*) McGraw.

Number Magazine, Nos. 1-8. reprint ed. 37.50 (*0-404-19538-5*) AMS Pr.

Number Magnets: Learning to Count with Ally & Zack. Jennifer Glossop & Val Taylor. (Learn 'n' Play Magnetic Adventure Bks.). (Illus.). 48p. (J). (ps up). 1998. spiral bd. 21.99 (*1-894042-35-2*) Somerville Hse.

Number Mosaics. Adi R. Kanga. 376p. 1995. text 60.00 (*981-02-1888-5*) World Scientific Pub.

Number Munch! Charles Reasoner. LC 95-122272. (Illus.). 34p. (J). (ps-k). 1993. pap. 9.95 (*0-8431-3674-X*, Price Stern) Peng Put Young Read.

Number Munch! Charles Reasoner. (Mini Bites Ser.). (Illus.). 32p. (J). (ps-k). 1998. pap. 4.99 (*0-8431-7821-3*, Price Stern) Peng Put Young Read.

***Number Nine.** David Collins. (Numberlies Ser.). 24p. (J). 2000. pap. text 3.25 (*0-7894-5305-3*, D K Ink) DK Pub Inc.

Number Nine: The Search for the Sigma Code. Cecil Balmond. LC 98-11906. (Illus.). 220p. 1998. 19.98 (*3-7913-1933-7*) te Neues.

Number Ninety-One: The Adventures of a New York Telegraph Boy. Horatio Alger, Jr. (Illus.). 205p. 1977. reprint ed. 24.00 (*0-686-37022-8*) G K Westgard.

Number of Animals. Christopher Wormell & Kate Green. (Illus.). 32p. (J). (ps-12). 1993. 26.60 (*1-56846-083-X*, Creat Educ) Creative Co.

Number of Members As Determining the Sociological: Form of the Group, Pt. I. Georg Simmel. (Reprint Series in Social Sciences). (C). 1993. reprint ed. pap. text 5.00 (*0-8290-2696-7*, S-267) Irvington.

Number of the Beast. Robert A. Heinlein. 512p. 1986. mass mkt. 6.99 (*0-449-13070-3*, GM) Fawcett.

Number of the Beast. Snoo Wilson. 208p. (Orig.). 1984. pap. 9.95 (*0-7145-3959-7*) Riverrun NY.

Number of Things: Baldy Russell, Estey City, & the Ozanne Stage; History Ranching & Mining on the U. S. Army White Sands Missile Range. unabridged ed. Peter L. Eidenbach & Robert Hart. LC 97-77832. (Illus.). 170p. 1997. pap. 12.00 (*1-887523-07-3*) Human Systs Res.

Number of Things: The Year with Nature. Margaret D. Elliott. (Illus.). 244p. (Orig.). 1988. pap. 9.95 (*0-9620788-0-8*) Gillette Natl Hist.

Number of Things You Can Count On. Phillips Winslow. (Foundations Ser.). 16p. (J). (ps). 1992. pap. text 23.00 (*1-56843-007-8*); pap. text 4.50 (*1-56843-057-4*) EMG Networks.

Number on My Grandfather's Arm. David A. Adler. (Illus.). 28p. (J). (gr. 1-3). 1987. 10.95 (*0-8074-0328-8*, 103641) UAHC.

***Number One.** David Collins. (Numberlies Ser.). 24p. (J). 2000. pap. text 3.25 (*0-7894-5322-3*, D K Ink) DK Pub Inc.

Number One: The World's Best Batsmen & Bowlers, 1800-1996. Simon Wilde. 224p. 1998. 40.00 (*0-575-06453-6*, Pub. by V Gollancz) Trafalgar.

#1 Adult Contemporary Hits of the 80s. 152p. 1995. otabind 14.95 (*0-7935-3789-4*) H Leonard.

#1 Adult Contemporary Hits of the 90s. 176p. 1995. otabind 14.95 (*0-7935-3792-4*) H Leonard.

Number One All Time Adult Contemporary Hits for Easy Piano. (Easy Play Ser.). 176p. 1995. otabind 14.95 (*0-7935-4500-5*, 00222588) H Leonard.

***#1 Black Mail Order Directory, 1999: Specializing in Afrocentric Products by Mail.** (Illus.). 1999. pap. 9.95 (*1-885716-04-4*) JAK Prods.

Number 1 Country Hits of the 90's. (Decade Ser.). 152p. 1994. otabind 12.95 (*0-7935-3560-3*, 00311699) H Leonard.

#1 Country Songs of the 80's. Leonard, Hal, Corporation Staff. 168p. 1997. otabind 12.95 (*0-7935-8552-X*) H Leonard.

No. 111 2/7/93-10.20.96. Kenneth Goldsmith. 1997. pap. 17.50 (*0-935724-87-7*) Figures.

Number One in the U. S. A. Records & Wins in Sports, Entertainment, Business, & Science with Sources Cited. 2nd ed. Thomas P. Slavens. LC 90-42090. 175p. 1990. 26.50 (*0-8108-2350-0*) Scarecrow.

Number One Key to Success: Meditation. Marilyn Hickey. pap. 4.95 (*1-56441-017-X*) M Hickey Min.

Number One Number Fun. Kay Chorao. LC 94-9926. (Illus.). 32p. (J). (gr. k-3). 1995. lib. bdg. 15.95 (*0-8234-1142-7*) Holiday.

Number One Price Guide to M. I. Hummel. 5th ed. Robert L. Miller. 1992. pap. 15.95 (*0-88486-068-X*) Arrowood Pr.

Number 1 Problem. Jeanne K. Grieser. LC 96-34562. (Illus.). (J). 1997. write for info. (*1-56763-300-5*); pap. write for info. (*1-56763-301-3*) Ozark Pub.

***#1 Rock Hits.** 96p. 1999. otabind 12.95 (*0-7935-9978-4*) H Leonard.

***#1 Search Engine Primer.** Paul J. Bruemmer. xvii, 82p. 1999. pap. 95.00 (*0-9677579-0-8*) Web Ignite Corp.

Number 1 Songs of the 80's. (Piano-Vocal-Guitar Ser.). 256p. 1991. otabind 14.95 (*0-7935-0426-0*, 00311503) H Leonard.

Number 1 Songs of the 80's: 46 No. 1 Hits As Listed on the Hot 100 Singles Chart, No. 239. 192p. 1991. otabind 12.95 (*0-7935-0646-8*, 00243005) H Leonard.

Number One Songs of the 90's: Alto Saxophone. 32p. 1994. pap. 4.95 (*0-7935-3246-9*, 00849934) H Leonard.

Number One Songs of the 90's: Clarinet. 32p. 1994. pap. 4.95 (*0-7935-3245-0*, 00849933) H Leonard.

Number One Songs of the 90's: Flute. 32p. 1994. pap. 4.95 (*0-7935-3244-2*, 00849932) H Leonard.

Number One Songs of the 90's: Trombone. 32p. 1994. pap. 4.95 (*0-7935-3248-5*, 00849936) H Leonard.

Number One Songs of the 90's: Trumpet. 32p. 1994. pap. 4.95 (*0-7935-3247-7*, 00849935) H Leonard.

***Number One, Tickle Your Tum.** John Prater. (Baby Bear Ser.). (Illus.). 24p. (J). 1999. bds. 6.95 (*0-7641-5185-1*) Barron.

Number One Way to Fight the Devil. Norvel Hayes. 32p. 1978. pap. 1.00 (*0-89274-094-9*, HH-094) Harrison Hse.

Number Our Days. Barbara Myerhoff. 318p. 1980. pap. 12.00 (*0-671-25430-8*, Touchstone) S&S Trade Pap.

Number Pal. Robin Q. Buschemeyer. (Professor Elly Fun's Back to Basics Ser.). (Illus.). 40p. (Orig.). (J). (ps-3). 1986. pap. 2.99 (*0-935609-02-4*) Eduplay.

***Number Parade: A Wildlife Counting Book.** Jakki Wood. (Illus.). 32p. (J). (ps-1). 1999. pap. 7.99 (*0-7112-0863-8*) F Lincoln.

Number Patterns see Let's Investigate - Group 1

Number Play. David Kirkby. LC 95-33557. (Mini Math Ser.). (Illus.). (J). 1998. (*1-57572-005-1*) Heinemann Lib.

Number, Please! History of the London Telephone. D. Occomore. 1995. pap. 20.00 (*0-88734-913-7*) Players Pr.

Number Poems. Irving Weiss. 70p. 1997. pap. 5.00 (*1-57141-037-6*) Runaway Spoon.

Number Power: A Cooperative Approach to Mathematics & Social Development. Laurel Robertson. (J). (gr. 2). 1993. pap. text 21.95 (*0-201-45520-X*) Addison-Wesley.

Number Power: A Cooperative Approach to Mathematics & Social Development. Laurel Robertson. (J). (gr. 3). 1993. pap. text 21.95 (*0-201-45522-6*) Addison-Wesley.

Number Power: A Cooperative Approach to Mathematics & Social Development. Laurel Robertson. (J). (gr. 4). 1993. pap. text 21.95 (*0-201-45523-4*) Addison-Wesley.

Number Power: A Cooperative Approach to Mathematics & Social Development. Laurel Robertson. LC 95-127107. 1994. pap. text 21.95 (*0-201-45525-0*) Addison-Wesley.

Number Power: A Cooperative Approach to Mathematics & Social Development. Laurel Robertson. (J). (gr. 5). 1994. pap. text 21.95 (*0-201-45524-2*) Addison-Wesley.

Number Power: A Cooperative Approach to Mathematics & Social Development. Laurel Robertson. (J). (gr. k). 1995. teacher ed. 29.00 (*0-201-49320-9*) Addison-Wesley.

Number Power: A Cooperative Approach to Mathematics & Social Development. Laurel Robertson. (J). (gr. 1). 1996. pap. text 21.95 (*0-201-49323-3*) Addison-Wesley.

***Number Power: A Cooperative Approach to Mathematics & Social Development: Grade 1.** Laurel Robertson et al. 214p. 1999. pap. 19.95 (*1-57621-197-5*, NPT011) Develop Studies.

***Number Power: A Cooperative Approach to Mathematics & Social Development: Grade 4.** Laurel Robertson et al. 208p. 1999. pap. 19.95 (*1-57621-202-5*, NPT041) Develop Studies.

***Number Power: A Cooperative Approach to Mathematics & Social Development: Grade 5.** Laurel Robertson et al. 212p. 1999. pap. 19.95 (*1-57621-203-3*, NPT051) Develop Studies.

***Number Power: A Cooperative Approach to Mathematics & Social Development: Grade 6.** Laurel Robertson et al. 222p. 1999. pap. 19.95 (*1-57621-204-1*, NPT061) Develop Studies.

***Number Power: A Cooperative Approach to Mathematics & Social Development: Kindergarten.** Laurel Robertson et al. 208p. 1999. pap. 19.95 (*1-57621-196-7*, NPT0K1) Develop Studies.

Number Power: Analyzing Data: The Real World of Adult Math, No. 8. Ellen Frechette. LC 92-28285. (Number Power Ser.: Vol. 8). (Illus.). 186p. 1992. pap. 10.60 (*0-8092-4213-3*) NTC Contemp Pub Co.

***Number Power Vol. 1: A Cooperative Approach to Mathematics & Social Development: Grade 2.** Laurel Robertson et al. 192p. 1999. pap. 19.95 (*1-57621-198-3*, NPT021) Develop Studies.

***Number Power Vol. 1: A Cooperative Approach to Mathematics & Social Development: Grade 3.** Laurel Robertson et al. 226p. 1999. pap. 19.95 (*1-57621-200-9*, NPT031) Develop Studies.

***Number Power Vol. 2: A Cooperative Approach to Mathematics & Social Development: Grade 2.** Laurel Robertson et al. 192p. 1999. pap. 19.95 (*1-57621-199-1*, NPT022) Develop Studies.

***Number Power Vol. 2: A Cooperative Approach to Mathematics & Social Development: Grade 3.** Laurel Robertson et al. 196p. 1999. pap. 19.95 (*1-57621-201-7*, NPT032) Develop Studies.

Number Power 1: Addition, Subtraction, Multiplication & Division: The Real World of Adult Math. Jerry Howett. Ed. by Benita Somerfield & Brian Schenk. LC 76-27723. (Number Power Ser.: No. 1). 154p. (Orig.). 1976. pap., wbk. ed. 10.60 (*0-8092-8011-6*) NTC Contemp Pub Co.

Number Power Review. Robert Mitchell. LC 93-8627. 1993. pap. 10.60 (*0-8092-3805-5*) NTC Contemp Pub Co.

Number Power 7: Problem Solving & Test Taking Strategies: The Real World of Adult Math, Vol. 7. Ellen Frechette. (Number Power Ser.: No. 7). 1990. pap. 10.60 (*0-8092-4195-1*) NTC Contemp Pub Co.

Number Power 2: Fractions, Decimals, & Percents: The Real World of Adult Math, No. 2. Jerry Howett. (Number Power Ser.: Vol. 2). 154p. 1977. pap. 10.60 (*0-8092-8010-8*) NTC Contemp Pub Co.

Number Power 3: Algebra: The Real World of Adult Math, Vol. 3. Robert Mitchell. (Number Power Ser.: No. 3). 154p. 1982. pap. 10.60 (*0-8092-5714-9*) NTC Contemp Pub Co.

Number Power 4: Geometry: The Real World of Math, Vol. 1. Robert Mitchell. (Number Power Ser.: Vol. 4). 154p. (Orig.). 1983. pap. 10.60 (*0-8092-5583-9*) NTC Contemp Pub Co.

Number Power 5: Graphs, Tables, Schedules & Maps: The Real World of Adult Math, Vol. 1. Robert Mitchell. (Number Power Ser.: Vol. 5). 1983. pap. 10.60 (*0-8092-5644-4*) NTC Contemp Pub Co.

Number Power 6: Word Problems, Vol. 6. rev. ed. Kenneth Tamarkin. (Number Power Ser.: No. 6). 1990. pap. 10.60 (*0-8092-4024-6*) NTC Contemp Pub Co.

Number Problem Visual Masters: With BASIC Program Solutions. Donald D. Spencer. 96p. 1988. pap. 15.95 (*0-89218-156-7*, NO. 3055) Camelot Pub.

Number Problem Visual Masters: With Pascal Program Solutions. Donald D. Spencer. 96p. 1988. pap. 15.95 (*0-89218-157-5*, NO. 3056) Camelot Pub.

Number Problems & Computers: With BASIC & Pascal Program Solutions. 2nd ed. Donald D. Spencer. LC 96-4024. 1996. pap. 18.95 (*0-89218-270-9*) Camelot Pub.

Number Puzzles see First Step Math

Number Puzzles. Deni Bown. (Jigsaw Puzzles Ser.). 8p. 1996. 4.95 (*0-7894-0616-0*) DK Pub Inc.

Number Puzzles. Dorling Kindersley Staff. (Math Sticker Work Bk.). (Illus.). 16p. (J). (ps-2). 1997. pap. 4.95 (*0-7894-1515-1*) DK Pub Inc.

Number Puzzles. Barrie Henderson. (J). (gr. 4-7). 1994. pap. 2.95 (*0-590-20839-X*) Scholastic Inc.

Number Puzzles. Ken A. Russell. 224p. 1994. pap. 7.95 (*0-572-01890-8*, Pub. by W Foulsham) Trans-Atl Phila.

Number Puzzles. Jenny Tyler. (Brain Benders Ser.). (J). (gr. 3 up). 1980. pap. 4.95 (*0-86020-435-9*, Usborne) EDC.

Number Puzzles. Jenny Tyler. (Brain Benders Ser.). 32p. (J). (gr. 3 up). 1999. lib. bdg. 12.95 (*0-88110-050-1*, Usborne) EDC.

***Number Recognition & Counting & Quantity Workbook.** 2nd ed. Melissa Del 'Homme. (Tutor Bks.). (Illus.). 160p. (YA). (gr. k up). 2000. pap., wbk. ed. 12.95 (*0-7373-0454-5*, 04545W, Pub. by Lowell Hse Juvenile) NTC Contemp Pub Co.

Number Recognition Workbook. Melissa Del'Homme. (Tutor Bks.). (Illus.). 80p. (YA). (gr. k up). 1998. pap., wbk. ed. 8.95 (*1-56565-849-3*, 08493W, Pub. by Lowell Hse Juvenile) NTC Contemp Pub Co.

Number Rhymes. Carol Thompson. (Little Barron's Toddler Bks.). (Illus.). 20p. (J). (ps). 1999. pap. 4.95 (*0-7641-0863-8*) Barron.

Number Search: Travel Games with Press & Peel Clings. (J). (ps-3). 1997. pap. 4.99 (*0-88743-732-X*) Sch Zone Pub Co.

***Number Sense.** Carol Greenes. (Illus.). (J). (gr. 1). 1999. pap. 12.95 (*0-7690-0013-4*) Seymour Pubns.

Number Sense. Allan Suter. 1990. pap., teacher ed. 9.50 (*0-8092-4218-4*) NTC Contemp Pub Co.

Number Sense, 16 Pieces. Allan D. Suter. 1990. pap. 60.00 (*0-8092-4190-0*) NTC Contemp Pub Co.

Number Sense: Answer Key. Allan Suter. 1990. pap. 5.25 (*0-8092-4191-9*) NTC Contemp Pub Co.

Number Sense: Decimals - Addition & Subtraction. Allan D. Suter. 1990. pap. 7.00 (*0-8092-4230-3*) NTC Contemp Pub Co.

Number Sense: Fraction - Addition & Subtraction. Allan D. Suter. 1990. pap. 7.00 (*0-8092-4225-7*) NTC Contemp Pub Co.

Number Sense: Fractions - Multiplication & Divison. Allan D. Suter. 1990. pap. 7.00 (*0-8092-4224-9*) NTC Contemp Pub Co.

Number Sense: How the Mind Creates Mathematics. Stanislas Dehaene. LC 96-53840. (Illus.). 288p. 1997. 30.00 (*0-19-511004-8*) OUP.

Number Sense: How the Mind Creates Mathematics. Stanislas Dehaene. (Illus.). 288p. 1999. pap. 16.95 (*0-19-513240-8*) OUP.

Number Sense: Meaning of Fractions. Allan D. Suter. 1990. pap. 7.00 (*0-8092-4226-5*) NTC Contemp Pub Co.

Number Sense: Meaning of Percents. Allan D. Suter. 1990. pap. 7.00 (*0-8092-4221-4*) NTC Contemp Pub Co.

Number Sense: Percent Application. Allan D. Suter. 1990. pap. 7.00 (*0-8092-4220-6*) NTC Contemp Pub Co.

Number Sense: Ratios, Proportions, & Percentages. Allan D. Suter. 1990. pap. 7.00 (*0-8092-4222-2*) NTC Contemp Pub Co.

Number Sense: Simple Effective Number Sense Experiences. Barbara J. Reys et al. Ed. by Joan Gideon & Catherine Anderson. (Illus.). 238p. (Orig.). (J). (gr. 4-6). 1996. pap. text, teacher ed. 18.95 (*1-57232-263-2*, 21802) Seymour Pubns.

Number Sense: Simple Effective Number Sense Experiences. Barbara J. Reys et al. Ed. by Joan Gideon. (Number Sense Ser.). (Illus.). 214p. (Orig.). (J). (gr. 3-4). 1996. pap. text 18.95 (*1-57232-262-4*, 21801) Seymour Pubns.

Number Sense: Simple Effective Number Sense Experiences. Barbara J. Reys et al. Ed. by Joan Gideon. (Illus.). 182p. (Orig.). 1997. pap. text, teacher ed. 18.95 (*1-57232-261-6*, 21800) Seymour Pubns.

Number Sense: Whole Numbers - Addition & Subtraction. Allan D. Suter. 1990. pap. 7.00 (*0-8092-4234-6*) NTC Contemp Pub Co.

Number Sense: Whole Numbers - Multiplication & Division. Allan D. Suter. 1990. pap. 7.00 (*0-8092-4233-8*) NTC Contemp Pub Co.

Number Sense & Operations. Grace Burton et al. LC 92-41880. (Curriculum & Evaluation Standards for School Mathematics Addenda Ser.: Grades K-6). (Illus.). 56p. 1993. pap. 13.95 (*0-87353-319-4*) NCTM.

Number Sense Now: Guidebook. 128p. 1993. 15.00 (*0-87353-361-5*) NCTM.

Number Sense Now: Videotapes & Guidebook. 128p. 1993. 98.00 (*0-87353-393-3*) NCTM.

***Number Seven.** David Collins. (Numberlies Ser.). 24p. (J). 2000. pap. text 3.25 (*0-7894-5303-7*, D K Ink) DK Pub Inc.

Number Seven: Alexander Hamilton's Secret Attempts to Control American Foreign Policy, with Supporting Documents. Julian P. Boyd. LC 64-8515. 184p. 1964. reprint ed. pap. 57.10 (*0-7837-9303-0*, 206004300004) Bks Demand.

***Number Six.** David Collins. (Numberlies Ser.). 24p. (J). 2000. pap. text 3.25 (*0-7894-5302-9*, D K Ink) DK Pub Inc.

Number Six Hundred Sixty-Six. W. W. Westcott. 1993. reprint ed. pap. 6.95 (*1-55818-235-7*) Holmes Pub.

Number Skills. Golden Staff. (Step Ahead Plus Workbks.). (Illus.). 64p. (J). (ps-3). 1993. pap., wbk. ed. 3.49 (*0-307-03665-0*, 03665, Goldn Books) Gldn Bks Pub Co.

Number Skills. E. Mareth & R. Kelly. 1980. text 8.85 (*0-07-040341-4*) McGraw.

Number Stories of Long Ago. David E. Smith. (Illus.). 150p. (J). (gr. k-3). 1995. reprint ed. pap. 10.95 (*0-87353-408-5*) NCTM.

Number Systems. 2nd ed. S. V. Fomin. Tr. by Joan W. Teller & Thomas P. Branson from RUS. LC 73-89787. (Popular Lectures in Mathematics). 48p. (C). 1994. pap. text 10.00 (*0-226-25669-3*) U Ch Pr.

Number Systems: Constructions & Properties. Inder K. Rana. LC 97-52724. 370p. 1998. 36.00 (*981-02-3304-3*) World Scientific Pub.

Number Systems: Foundations of Algebra & Analysis. 2nd ed. Solomon Feferman. LC 88-63518. xii, 418p. (C). 1989. text 23.95 (*0-8284-0333-3*, 333) Chelsea Pub.

Number Systems, Addition & Personal Communication: Subtraction & Recreation. Learning Achievement Corp. Staff. (MATCH Ser.: Bk. 1). (Illus.). 128p. 1981. text 13.96 (*0-07-037111-3*) McGraw.

***Number Ten.** David Collins. (Numberlies Ser.). 24p. (J). 2000. pap. text 3.25 (*0-7894-5332-0*, D K Ink) DK Pub Inc.

Number the Stars. 44p. (J). 1998. student ed. 11.95 (*1-56137-605-1*, NU6051SP) Novel Units.

***Number the Stars.** Phyllis A. Green. 36p. 1998. 9.95 (*1-56137-254-4*) Novel Units.

Number the Stars. Lois Lowry. 144p. (YA). (gr. 5 up). 1990. pap. 5.50 (*0-440-40327-8*, YB BDD) BDD Bks Young Read.

Number the Stars. Lois Lowry. (J). 1992. pap. 3.50 (*0-440-80291-1*) BDD Bks Young Read.

Number the Stars. Lois Lowry. 144p. (J). 1994. pap. 3.99 (*0-440-91002-1*) Dell.

Number the Stars. Lois Lowry. LC 98-104337. (J). 1996. pap. 5.50 (*0-87129-711-6*, N45) Dramatic Pub.

Number the Stars. Lois Lowry. LC 88-37134. 160p. (J). (gr. 4-7). 1989. 16.00 (*0-395-51060-0*) HM.

Number the Stars. Lois Lowry. (Literature Experience 1993 Ser.). (J). (gr. 6). 1992. pap. 11.04 (*0-395-61834-7*) HM.

Number the Stars. Lois Lowry. (J). (gr. 6). 1995. 9.28 (*0-395-73270-0*) HM.

Number the Stars. Lois Lowry. (J). 1989. 10.09 (*0-606-04493-0*, Pub. by Turtleback) Demco.

Number the Stars. Lois Lowry. (J). 1998. 10.09 (*0-606-13670-3*, Pub. by Turtleback) Demco.

Number the Stars. Pathways Publishing Staff. (Assessment Packs Ser.). 15p. 1998. pap. text, teacher ed. 15.95 (*1-58303-054-9*) Pthways Pubng.

Number the Stars. large type ed. Lois Lowry. 172p. (J). (gr. 6). 43.00 (*0-614-20609-X*, L-38209-00 APHB) Am Printing Hse.

Number the Stars. Lois Lowry. 144p. (J). (gr. 5-9). 1998. reprint ed. mass mkt. 5.50 (*0-440-22753-4*, LLL BDD) BDD Bks Young Read.

Number the Stars: A Literature Unit. Kathy Jordan. (Literature Units Ser.). (Illus.). 48p. (Orig.). 1993. student ed. 7.95 (*1-55734-424-8*) Tchr Create Mat.

Number the Stars: A Study Guide. Barbara Reeves. Ed. by Joyce Friedland & Rikki Kessler. (Novel-Ties Ser.). (J). (gr. 5-7). 1991. pap. text 15.95 (*0-88122-579-7*) Lrn Links.

Number the Stars: A Unit Plan. Janine Sherman. 191p. 1996. teacher ed., ring bd. 26.95 (*1-58337-171-0*) Teachers Pet Pubns.

Number the Stars: L-I-T Guide. Charlotte Jaffe & Barbara Roberts. (J). (gr. 4-10). Date not set. pap. 8.95 (*1-56644-983-9*, 983-9AP) Educ Impress.

Number the Stars: Literature Guide. Scholastic, Inc. Staff. (Literature Guide Ser.). 16p. (J). 1997. pap. text 3.95 (*0-590-36650-5*) Scholastic Inc.

***Number the Stars - Musical.** Lois Lowry. 33p. 1998. pap. 5.95 (*0-87129-834-1*, N03) Dramatic Pub.

Number the Stars & Friedrich: Curriculum Unit. Center for Learning Network Staff et al. (Novel Ser.). 96p. (YA). (gr. 6-9). 1994. spiral bd. 18.95 (*1-56077-315-4*) Ctr Learning.

Number the Stars Study Guide. Lisa Leep. 54p. (J). (gr. 5-7). 1996. student ed., ring bd. 12.99 (*1-58609-146-8*) Progeny Pr WI.

Number Theoretic & Algebraic Methods in Computer Science: Proceedings of the International Conference. Alf J. Van De Poorten & Igor E. Shparlinski. 200p. 1995. text 64.00 (*981-02-2334-X*) World Scientific Pub.

Number Theoretic Methods in Cryptography Complexity Lowerbounds. I. Spharlinski. LC 99-200367. (Progress in Computer Science Ser.: Vol. 17). 184p. 1999. 95.00 (*3-7643-5888-2*) Birkhauser.

Number Theory. Ed. by K. Alladi. (Lecture Notes in Mathematics Ser.: Vol. 1122). vii, 217p. 1985. 37.95 (*0-387-15222-9*) Spr-Verlag.

Number Theory. George E. Andrews. LC 94-5243. (Illus.). 259p. 1998. pap. text 7.95 (*0-486-68252-8*) Dover.

***Number Theory.** Ed. by R. P. Bambah & R. J. Hans-Gill. (Trends in Mathematics Ser.). 536p. 2000. 115.00 (*3-7643-6259-6*) Birkhauser.

***Number Theory.** R. P. Bambah et al. LC 00-21717. (Trends in Mathematics Ser.). (Illus.). 2000. write for info. (*0-8176-6259-6*) Birkhauser.

Number Theory. Ed. by D. V. Chudnovsky et al. (Lecture Notes in Mathematics Ser.: Vol. 1240). v, 324p. 1987. 47.95 (*0-387-17669-1*) Spr-Verlag.

***Number Theory.** Jones Staff & Holt. 2002. pap. text. write for info. (*0-7167-3688-8*) W H Freeman.

Number Theory. Wladyslaw Narkiewicz. Tr. by S. Kanemitsu. 371p. 1984. text 54.00 (*9971-950-13-8*); pap. text 30.00 (*9971-950-26-X*) World Scientific Pub.

Number Theory. Melvyn B. Nathanson et al. (Lecture Notes in Mathematics Ser.: Vol. 1135). v, 283p. 1985. 42.95 (*0-387-15649-6*) Spr-Verlag.

Number Theory. Andre Weil. 384p. (C). 1988. 54.50 (*0-8176-3141-0*) Birkhauser.

Number Theory. Ed. by William J. LeVeque & E. G. Straus. LC 70-78057. (Proceedings of Symposia in Pure Mathematics Ser.). 98p. 1970. reprint ed. pap. 34.00 (*0-8218-1412-5*, PSPUM/12) Am Math.

Number Theory: A Programmers Guide. Mark A. Herkommer. (Illus.). 432p. 1998. 65.00 incl. disk (*0-07-913074-7*) McGraw.

Number Theory: A Seminar Held at the Graduate School & University Center of the City University of N.Y. 1982. D. V. Chudnovsky et al. (Lecture Notes in Mathematics Ser.: Vol. 1052). v, 309p. 1984. 38.70 (*0-387-12909-X*) Spr-Verlag.

***Number Theory: Algebraic Numbers & Functions.** Helmut Koch. LC 00-22320. (Graduate Studies in Mathematics: Vol. 24). 392p. 2000. 59.00 (*0-8218-2054-0*) Am Math.

Number Theory: An Introduction. Don Redmond. (Monographs & Textbooks in Pure & Applied Mathematics: Vol. 201). (Illus.). 772p. 1996. text 175.00 (*0-8247-9696-9*) Dekker.

Number Theory: Diophantine, Computational & Algebraic Aspects: Proceedings of the International Conference Held in Eger, Hungary, July 29-August 2, 1996. Kalman Gyory et al. LC 98-15973. 596p. 1998. 158.95 (*3-11-015364-5*) De Gruyter.

Number Theory: Discrete Mathematics & Number Theory, January 3-6, 1996, Tiruchirapalli, India. Ed. by V. Kumar Murty & Michel Waldschmidt. LC 97-30207. (Contemporary Mathematics Ser.: Vol. 210). 399p. 1997. pap. 69.00 (*0-8218-0606-8*) Am Math.

Number Theory: New York Seminar, 1989-1900. Ed. by Melvyn B. Nathanson et al. (Illus.). viii, 275p. 1991. 40.95 (*0-387-97670-1*) Spr-Verlag.

Number Theory: New York Seminar, 1991-1995. D. V. Chudnovsky et al. LC 96-24221. 272p. 1996. pap. 49.95 (*0-387-94826-0*) Spr-Verlag.

Number Theory: Proceedings: Fourth Conference of the Canadian Number Theory Association, July 2-8, 1994, Dalhousie University, Halifax, Nova Scotia. Ed. by Karl Dilcher. LC 95-30722. (Canadian Mathematical Society Conference Proceedings Ser.: Vol. 15). 431p. 1995. pap. 89.00 (*0-8218-0312-3*, CMSAMS/15) Am Math.

Number Theory: (Proceedings of the Canadian Mathematical Society) H. Kisilevsky & J. Labute. LC 87-1307. (Conference Proceedings of the Canadian Mathematical Society Ser.: Vol. 7). 466p. 1987. pap. 67.00 (*0-8218-6012-7*, CMSAMS/7) Am Math.

Number Theory: Proceedings of the First Conference of the Canadian Number Theory Association Held at the Banff Center, Banff, Alberta, April 17-27, 1988. Richard A. Mollin. xiv, 659p. (C). 1990. lib. bdg. 129.95 (*3-11-011723-1*) De Gruyter.

Number Theory: Seminaire de Theorie des Nombres de Paris 1993-94. Sinnou David. (London Mathematical Society Lecture Note Ser.: No. 235). 223p. 1996. pap. text 44.95 (*0-521-58549-X*) Cambridge U Pr.

Number Theory: The Theory of Partitions. George E. Andrews. LC 76-41770. (Encyclopedia of Mathematics & Its Applications Ser.: Vol. 2). (Illus.). 1976. text. write for info. (*0-201-13501-9*) Addison-Wesley.

Number Theory - Theorie des Nombres: Proceedings of the International Number Theory Conference Held at Universite Laval in 1987. Ed. by Jean-Marie De Koninck & Claude Levesque. xxii, 1002p. (C). 1989. lib. bdg. 179.95 (*3-11-011791-6*) De Gruyter.

An Asterisk (*) at the beginning of an entry indicates that the title is appearing for the first time.

Number Theory, Algebra, Mathematical Analysis, & Their Applications: Dedicated to the 100th Anniversary of the Birth of Ivan Matveevich Vinogradov: Collected Papers. Ed. by V. S. Vladimirov et al. LC 93-17807. (Proceedings of the Steklov Institute of Mathematics Ser.: Vol. 200). 373p. 1993. pap. 245.00 (*0-8218-3150-X*) Am Math.

Number Theory & Analysis. N. G. Cudakov et al. LC 88-19373. (Translations Ser.: Series 1, Vol. 2). 532p. 1962. reprint ed. 44.00 (*0-8218-1602-0*, TRANS1/2) Am Math.

Number Theory & Analysis, Vol. 207. Ed. by A. A. Karatsuba & V. I. Blagodat. 351p. 1996. 269.00 (*0-8218-0467-7*, STEKLO/207C) Am Math.

Number Theory & Analysis: A Collection of Papers in Honor of Edmund Landau (1877-1938) Ed. by Paul Turan & E. Bombieri. LC 68-8991. 355p. reprint ed. pap. 110.10 (*0-608-30065-9*, 201939300011) Bks Demand.

Number Theory & Applications. Ed. by Richard A. Mollin. (C). 1989. text 298.50 (*0-7923-0149-8*) Kluwer Academic.

Number Theory & Combinatorics: Proceedings of the Conference on Number Theory Okayama, Japan, 30-31 January 1984. Ed. by Masao Ito et al. 456p. 1985. 89.00 (*9971-978-77-6*) World Scientific Pub.

Number Theory & Its Applications: Proceedings of a Summer School at Bilkent Univeristy. Ed. by Cem Y. Yildirim & Serguei A. Stepanov. LC 98-45745. (Illus.). 360p. 1998. pap. text 150.00 (*0-8247-1969-7*) Dekker.

Number Theory & Its Applications in China. W. Yuan et al. LC 88-19373. (Contemporary Mathematics Ser.: No. 77). 170p. 1988. pap. 26.00 (*0-8218-5084-9*, CONM/77) Am Math.

Number Theory & Its History. Oystein Ore. (Illus.). 380p. 1988. reprint ed. pap. text 10.95 (*0-486-65620-9*) Dover.

Number Theory & Operator Theory. fac. ed. American Mathematical Society Staff. LC QA0003.A4. (Translations Ser.: Vol. 13, No. 2). 350p. 1960. reprint ed. pap. 108.50 (*0-7837-8297-7*, 204908300013) Bks Demand.

Number Theory & Physics. Ed. by J. M. Luck et al. (Proceedings in Physics Ser.: Vol. 47). (Illus.). xiii, 311p. 1990. 74.95 (*0-387-52129-1*) Spr-Verlag.

Number Theory & Related Topics. R. Askey. (Illus.). 262p. 1990. pap. 24.95 (*0-19-562367-3*) OUP.

Number Theory for Beginners. Andre Weil. 1985. pap. 29.50 (*0-387-90381-X*) Spr-Verlag.

***Number Theory for Computing.** S. Y. Yan. LC 99-58845. 250p. 1999. 42.00 (*3-540-65472-0*) Spr-Verlag.

Number Theory I: Fundamental Problems, Ideas & Theories. Ed. by A. N. Parshin et al. LC 94-46819. (Encyclopedia of Mathematical Sciences Ser.: Vol. 49).Tr. of Teoriia Chisel 1. (Illus.). 344p. 1995. 107.95 (*0-387-53384-2*) Spr-Verlag.

Number Theory I: Fundamental Problems, Ideas & Theories. Ed. by A. N. Parshin & I. R. Shafarevich. (Encyclopedia of Mathematical Sciences Ser.: Vol. 49).Tr. of Teoriia Chisel 1. 308p. 1996. 98.00 (*3-540-53384-2*) Spr-Verlag.

Number Theory III: Diophantine Geometry. Serge A. Lang. (Encyclopedia of Mathematical Sciences Ser.: Vol. 60). (Illus.). 304p. 1991. 118.95 (*0-387-53004-5*) Spr-Verlag.

***Number Theory in Progress, 2 vols.** Ed. by Kalman Gyory et al. LC 99-19358. xvi, 1185p. 1999. 237.00 (*3-11-015715-2*) De Gruyter.

Number Theory in Science & Communication. 2nd enl. ed. M. R. Schroeder. (Information Sciences Ser.: Vol. 7). (Illus.). xix, 374p. 1991. 49.50 (*0-387-15800-6*) Spr-Verlag.

Number Theory in Science & Communication: With Applications in Cryptography, Physics, Digital Information, Computing & Self-Similarity. 3rd ed. M. R. Schroeder. LC 96-53994. (Springer Series in Information Sciences). 420p. 1997. pap. 49.95 (*3-540-62006-0*) Spr-Verlag.

Number Theory in the Quadratic Field with Golden Section Unit. Fred W. Dodd. LC 83-17799. (Examples of Mathematical Structures Ser.: Vol. 3). 159p. 1984. 8.50 (*0-936428-08-2*) Polygonal Pub.

Number Theory Institute, 1969: Proceedings of Symposia in Pure Mathematics, 20th, Stony Brook, N. Y., 1969. Ed. by Donald J. Lewis. LC 76-125938. (Proceedings of Symposia in Pure Mathematics Ser.: Vol. 20). 451p. 1971. text 60.00 (*0-8218-1420-6*, PSPUM/20) Am Math.

Number Theory IV: Transcendental Numbers. Ed. by A. N. Parshin et al. Tr. & Contrib. by Yu V. Nesterenko. (Encyclopaedia of Mathematical Sciences Ser.: No. 44). (Illus.). 345p. 1997. 95.00 (*3-540-61467-2*) Spr-Verlag.

Number Theory, Madras, 1987. Ed. by K. Alladi. (Lecture Notes in Mathematics Ser.: Vol. 1395). vii, 234p. 1989. 36.95 (*0-387-51595-X*) Spr-Verlag.

Number Theory, New York, 1986-1988. Ed. by D. V. Chudnovsky et al. (Lecture Notes in Mathematics Ser.: Vol. 1383). v, 256p. 1989. 41.95 (*0-387-51549-6*) Spr-Verlag.

Number Theory Noordwijkerhout, 1983: Proceedings of the Journees Arithmetiques Held at Noordwijkerhout, The Netherlands July 11-15, 1983. H. Jager. (Lecture Notes in Mathematics Ser.: Vol. 1068). v, 296p. 1984. 46.95 (*0-387-13356-9*) Spr-Verlag.

***Number Theory 1: Fermat's Dream.** Kazuya Kato et al. Tr. by Masato Kuwata from JPN. LC 99-33556. (Translations of Mathematical Monographs: Vol. 186). 154p. 1999. 25.00 (*0-8218-0863-X*) Am Math.

Number Theory 2: Algebraic Number Theory. H. Koch. Ed. by A. N. Parshin et al. (Encyclopedia of Mathematical Sciences Ser.: Vol. 62). 308p. 1992. 118.95 (*0-387-53386-9*) Spr-Verlag.

Number Theory, Ulm, 1987. Ed. by H. P. Schlickewei & E. Wirsing. (Lecture Notes in Mathematics Ser.: Vol. 1380). v, 266p. 1989. 41.95 (*0-387-51397-3*) Spr-Verlag.

Number Theory with an Emphasis on the Markoff Spectrum. Ed. by Andrew Pollington & William Moran. LC 93-18075. (Lecture Notes in Pure & Applied Mathematics Ser.: Vol. 147). (Illus.). 352p. 1993. pap. text 150.00 (*0-8247-8902-4*) Dekker.

Number Theory with Applications. James A. Anderson & James M. Bell. LC 96-25134. 566p. 1996. 89.33 (*0-13-190190-7*) P-H.

Number Theory with Applications. W. C. Li. LC 95-49001. (Series on University Mathematics: Vol. 7). 300p. 1996. 53.00 (*981-02-2226-2*) World Scientific Pub.

Number Theory with Computer Applications. Ramanujachary Kumanduri & Christina Romero. LC 97-16756. 543p. 1997. 89.33 (*0-13-801812-X*) P-H.

Number Theory with Its Mathematical Philosophy. Li-Chung Wang. LC 94-90271. 207p. (Orig.). (C). 1994. pap. text 16.95 (*0-9624242-2-6*) L C Wang Pr.

Number Theory 1992-3: Seminaire de Theorie des Nombres. Ed. by Sinnou David. (London Mathematical Society Lecture Note Ser.: No. 215). 301p. (C). 1995. pap. text 47.95 (*0-521-55911-1*) Cambridge U Pr.

***Number Three.** David Collins. (Numberlies Ser.). 24p. (J). 2000. pap. text 3.25 (*0-7894-5324-X*, D K Ink) DK Pub Inc.

No. 3 Templeton Place. Francis H. De Sbuzo. 301p. 1998. pap. write for info. (*1-86106-879-4*, Pub. by Minerva Pr) Unity Dist.

***Number to Sound: The Musical Way to the Scientific Revolution.** Paolo Gozza. LC 99-51945. (Western Ontario Series in the Philosophy of Science). 1999. write for info. (*0-7923-6069-9*) Kluwer Academic.

No. 25 see Shoemaker's Best Selections: For Readings & Recitations

No. 26 Jayne Street. Mary H. Austin. (Collected Works of Mary Hunter Austin). 353p. 1998. reprint ed. lib. bdg. 98.00 (*1-58201-527-9*) Classic Bks.

***Number Two.** David Collins. (Numberlies Ser.). 24p. (J). 2000. pap. text 3.25 (*0-7894-5323-1*, D K Ink) DK Pub Inc.

Number Vibration in Questions & Answers. L. Dow Balliett. 104p. 1983. pap. 9.00 (*0-89540-139-8*, SB-139) Sun Pub.

Number Words. Leonard C. Duncan. 148p. 1984. spiral bd. 25.00 (*0-941414-07-8*) LCD.

Number Words & Number Symbols: A Cultural History of Numbers. Karl Augustus Menninger. Tr. by Paul Broneer from GER. (Illus.). xiii, 480p. 1992. reprint ed. pap. 14.95 (*0-486-27096-3*) Dover.

Numbered Account. Christopher Reich. 768p. 1998. mass mkt. 7.99 (*0-440-22529-9*) Dell.

Numbered Account. large type ed. Christopher Reich. LC 98-19325. 1998. 28.95 (*0-7862-1505-4*) Thorndike Pr.

Numbered Days: Poems by Dagmar Nick. Dagmar Nick. Tr. by Jim Barnes from GER. LC 98-8816.Tr. of Gezahlte Tage. (Illus.). 134p. 1998. 22.00 (*0-943549-54-X*); pap. 15.00 (*0-943549-53-1*) Truman St Univ.

Numbered Motion Offense. Mel Hankinson. 110p. (Orig.). 1993. pap. 14.95 (*1-56404-052-6*) Championship Bks & Vid Prodns.

Numbered Voices: How Opinion Polling Has Shaped American Politics. Susan Herbst. (Illus.). xii, 240p. 1995. pap. text 14.95 (*0-226-32743-4*) U Ch Pr.

Numbered Voices: How Opinion Polls Shape American Politics. Susan Herbst. LC 92-14256. (American Politics & Political Economy Ser.). (Illus.). 240p. (C). 1993. 24.95 (*0-226-32742-6*) U Ch Pr.

Numberical Analysis, 1993. D. F. Griffiths. 1994. lib. bdg. 79.95 (*0-582-22568-X*, Pub. by Addison-Wesley) Longman.

Numbering in American Sign Language: Number Signs for Everyone. Ed. by Dawn Sign Press Production Staff. LC 98-25013. 142p. 1998. pap. text 19.95 (*0-915035-72-3*) Dawn Sign.

Numbering of Our Days. Anthony F. Perrino. (Mediation Manuals Ser.). (Illus.). (Orig.). 1988. pap. 3.00 (*0-933840-33-0*) Unitarian Univ.

Numbering of the Victories of the Emperor Gallienus & the Loyalty of His Legions. Andreas Alfoldi. (Illus.). 1977. 4.75 (*0-915018-28-4*) Attic Bks.

Numbering the Stars: A Phraseological Analysis of Genesis 15. Hallvard Hagelia. (Coniectanea Biblica Old Testament Ser.: No. 39). 252p. (Orig.). 1994. pap. 53.50 (*91-22-01591-4*) Coronet Bks.

***Numbering Your Genealogy: Basic Systems, Complex Families & International Kin.** Joan F. Curran et al. LC 00-25929. (Special Publications). 2000. pap. write for info. (*0-915156-64-4*) Natl Genealogical.

Numberland. Auriel W. Livezey. LC 95-175314. 160p. 1995. pap. 9.95 (*0-9642628-1-9*) Mtntop Pubng.

Numberlies. (Illus.). 24p. (J). 1996. write for info. (*0-7894-1112-1*) DK Pub Inc.

Numberlies: Number Eight. Colin Hawkins & Jacqui Hawkins. (Illus.). 32p. (J). (ps). 1993. 8.95 (*0-370-31513-8*, Pub. by Bodley Head) Trafalgar.

Numberlies: Number Seven. Colin Hawkins & Jacqui Hawkins. (Illus.). 32p. (J). (ps). 1993. 8.95 (*0-370-31512-X*, Pub. by Bodley Head) Trafalgar.

Numberlies: Number Six. Colin Hawkins & Jacqui Hawkins. (Illus.). 32p. (J). (ps). 1993. 8.95 (*0-370-31511-1*, Pub. by Bodley Head) Trafalgar.

Numbermagnets: Counting Your Way to the Perfect Party! Jennifer Glossop. (J). (ps up). 1999. 21.99 (*0-525-46082-9*, Dutton Child) Peng Put Young Read.

Numbers see Daily Study Bible for the Old Testament

Numbers see Let's Investigate - Group 1

Numbers see Discovering Math

Numbers see Science Works!

Numbers see Little Mouse's Learn-&-Play

***Numbers.** (Look & Learn Ser.). (J). 2000. 7.95 (*1-84215-170-3*) Anness Pub.

Numbers. (People's Bible Commentary Ser.). 264p. 1996. pap. 10.99 (*0-570-04868-0*, 12-8046) Concordia.

Numbers. (Butterfly Bks.). (ARA., Illus.). 11.95 (*0-86685-614-5*, LDL6164, Pub. by Librairie du Liban) Intl Bk Ctr.

Numbers. (Honey Bear Shaped Ser.). (Illus.). 12p. (J). (gr. k-2). 1982. bds. 3.95 (*0-87449-021-9*) Modern Pub NYC.

Numbers. (Write & Wipe Bks.). (Illus.). 6p. (J). (gr. k-2). 1997. pap. write for info. (*1-56144-988-1*, Honey Bear Bks) Modern Pub NYC.

Numbers. (Active Minds Ser.). (Illus.). 24p. (J). 1993. 4.98 (*1-56173-483-7*) Pubns Intl Ltd.

Numbers. Timothy R. Ashley. LC 96-28743. (New International Commentary on the Old Testament Ser.). 683p. 1995. 42.00 (*0-8028-2523-0*) Eerdmans.

Numbers. C. Beylon. 1997. pap. text 1.00 (*0-486-29775-6*) Dover.

Numbers. Karen Bryant-Mole. (First Learning Ser.). (Illus.). 24p. (J). (ps-3). 1992. pap. 4.50 (*0-7460-1042-7*) EDC.

***Numbers.** Karen Bryant-Mole. (First Learning Ser.). (Illus.). 24p. (YA). (ps up). 2000. pap. 4.95 (*0-7460-3802-X*, Usborne) EDC.

Numbers. Philip J. Budd. (Biblical Commentary Ser.: Vol. 5). 29.99 (*0-8499-0204-5*) Word Pub.

Numbers. Christopher Carrie. (Crayola Kinder Art BKs.). (Illus.). 12p. (Orig.). (J). (ps). 1987. pap. 4.70 (*0-86696-203-4*) Binney & Smith.

***Numbers.** Dennis R. Cole. (New American Commentary Ser.: Vol. 3B). 2000. 27.99 (*0-8054-9503-7*) Broadman.

Numbers. Eryl W. Davies. 378p. 1995. pap. 19.95 (*0-551-02835-1*, Pub. by Sheffield Acad) CUP Services.

Numbers. Nancy M. Davis et al. (Davis Teaching Units Ser.: Vol. 2, No. 5). (Illus.). 26p. (Orig.). (J). (ps-2). 1986. pap. 4.95 (*0-937103-14-4*) DaNa Pubns.

Numbers. Devlin. 224p. (C). 1999. pap. 18.95 (*0-471-32822-7*) Wiley.

Numbers. DK Editors. (Bath Bks.). (Illus.). 10p. (J). (ps). 1998. 4.95 (*0-7894-2922-5*) DK Pub Inc.

Numbers. Heinz-Dieter Ebbinghaus et al. Ed. by J. H. Ewing. (Graduate Texts in Mathematics Ser.). (Illus.). 376p. 1990. 54.00 (*0-387-97202-1*) Spr-Verlag.

Numbers. Monique Felix. (Mouse Bks.). (Illus.). 32p. (J). (gr. k-3). 1993. 10.60 (*1-56846-001-5*, Creative Eds) Creative Co.

Numbers. Josep M. Fite & Luis Rizo. LC 96-44408. (Math for Children Ser.). (J). 1997. pap. 5.95 (*0-382-39882-3*, Silver Pr NJ); lib. bdg. 15.95 (*0-382-39881-5*, Silver Pr NJ) Silver Burdett Pr.

Numbers. Frank Schaffer Publications, Inc. Staff. (Back-to-Basics Ser.). 32p. 1996. wbk. ed. 3.95 (*0-86734-968-9*, FS-30004) Schaffer Pubns.

Numbers. Gerald Hawksley. LC 98-67334. (Touch & Feel Concepts Ser.). 14p. (J). (ps). 1999. 6.95 (*0-7613-0980-2*, Copper Beech Bks) Millbrook Pr.

Numbers. Sally Hewitt. LC 95-18462. (Take off With Ser.). (Illus.). 32p. (J). (gr. 1-3). 1996. lib. bdg. 21.40 (*0-8172-4116-7*) Raintree Steck-V.

Numbers. David Kirkby. (Mini Math Ser.). (J). 1998. (*1-57572-001-9*) Heinemann Lib.

Numbers. David Kirkby. LC 95-20566. (Math Live Ser.). (Illus.). (J). 1998. 19.92 (*1-57572-042-6*) Heinemann Lib.

Numbers. Paul W. Kuske. LC 90-60486. (People's Bible Ser.). 32p. 1990. student ed. 4.00 (*0-8100-0345-7*, 22N2222); pap. 10.99 (*0-8100-0327-9*, 15N0492) Northwest Pub.

Numbers. Helen K. Mainelli. (Bible Commentary - Old Testament Ser.). 136p. 1985. pap. 4.95 (*0-8146-1373-X*) Liturgical Pr.

***Numbers.** Gordon Massman. Ed. by David Baratier. 88p. 2000. pap. 12.00 (*1-886350-88-4*, Pub. by Pavement Saw); lib. bdg. 75.00 (*1-886350-89-2*, Pavemnt Saw) Pavement Saw.

Numbers. J. Vernon McGee. (Thru the Bible Commentary: Vol. 8). 1997. pap. 6.97 (*0-7852-0332-X*) Nelson.

Numbers. NCPTA Staff. (Home Learning Ser.). (J). 1996. mass mkt. 6.96 (*0-340-64658-6*, Pub. by Hodder & Stought Ltd) Trafalgar.

Numbers. Dennis T. Olson. (Interpretation Ser.). 208p. 1996. 24.95 (*0-8042-3104-4*) Westminster John Knox.

Numbers Peter Patilla. LC 99-20369. (Math Links Ser.). 1999. lib. bdg. write for info. (*1-57572-966-0*) Heinemann Lib.

***Numbers.** Gayle Perry. Ed. by Stacey Wolkoff. (Primary Theme Ser.: Vol. 2431). (Illus.). 32p. (J). (gr. k-2). 2000. pap. 6.98 (*1-57471-683-2*) Creat Teach Pr.

Numbers. James Philip. (Mastering the Old & New Testament Ser.: Vol. 4). 1993. pap. 14.99 (*0-8499-3543-1*) Word Pub.

Numbers. James Philip. (Communicator's Commentary Ser.: Vol. 4). 364p. 1997. 22.99 (*0-8499-0409-9*) Word Pub.

Numbers. Henry Pluckrose. (Math Counts Ser.). (Illus.). 32p. (J). 1995. pap. 4.95 (*0-516-45454-4*) Childrens.

Numbers. Anna Pomaska. (Illus.). 32p. (J). (ps-1). pap. 1.00 (*0-486-29545-1*) Dover.

Numbers. Bern Porter. (Illus.). 52p. (Orig.). 1989. pap. 3.00 (*0-926935-20-8*) Runaway Spoon.

Numbers. John Rechy. LC 83-49450. 272p. 1990. pap. 13.00 (*0-8021-5198-1*, Groye) Grove-Atltic.

Numbers. Walter Riggans. 264p. 1993. pap. 22.00 (*0-7152-0522-6*, Pub. by St Andrew) St Mut.

Numbers. Shereen G. Rutman. (Toddler Time Ser.). (Illus.). 16p. (J). 1992. pap., student ed. 2.95 (*1-56293-191-1*, McClanahan Book) Learn Horizon.

Numbers. Schaffer, Frank, Publications Staff. (Help Your Child Learn Ser.). (Illus.). 24p. (J). (ps-2). 1978. student ed. 3.98 (*0-86734-002-9*, FS-3003) Schaffer Pubns.

Numbers. Pamela J. Schroeder & Jean M. Donisch. LC 96-7312. (What's the Big Idea? Ser.). (Illus.). 32p. (J). (gr. k-2). 1996. lib. bdg. 12.95 (*0-86625-580-X*) Rourke Pubns.

Numbers. Annette Taulbee. (Be Smart Bks.). (Illus.). 24p. (J). (ps). 1986. 3.98 (*0-86734-061-4*, FS-3053) Schaffer Pubns.

Numbers. Gordon J. Wenham. Ed. by Donald J. Wiseman. LC 81-11806. (Tyndale Old Testament Commentary Ser.). 240p. 1981. pap. 12.99 (*0-87784-254-X*, 254) InterVarsity.

Numbers. Gordon J. Wenham. Ed. by Donald J. Wiseman. LC 81-11806. (Tyndale Old Testament Commentary Ser.: Vol. 4). 240p. 1981. 19.99 (*0-87784-891-2*, 891) InterVarsity.

Numbers. Gordon J. Wenham. (Old Testament Guides Ser.: Vol. 5). 130p. 1997. pap. 12.50 (*1-85075-801-8*, Pub. by Sheffield Acad) CUP Services.

Numbers. R. S. Yeoman. 48p. 1985. 14.95 (*0-307-19861-8*) Gldn Bks Pub Co.

Numbers. rev. ed. Sara Anderson. (Illus.). 10p. (J). (ps-1). 1997. pap. 9.00 (*1-56021-274-8*) W J Fantasy.

Numbers. 3rd ed. Ed. by J. H. Ewing et al. Tr. by H. L. Orde from GER. (Graduate Texts in Mathematics Ser.: Vol. 123). (Illus.). 395p. 1996. reprint ed. pap. 39.95 (*0-387-97497-0*) Spr-Verlag.

Numbers: A Practical Commentary. B. Maarsingh. LC 86-29263. (Text & Interpretation Ser.). 128p. reprint ed. pap. 39.70 (*0-7837-3189-2*, 204279300006) Bks Demand.

Numbers: Active Minds. Photos by George Siede & Donna Preis. (Active Minds-English Ser.). (Illus.). 24p. (J). (ps-3). 1992. lib. bdg. 11.95 (*1-56674-003-7*, HTS Bks) Forest Hse.

Numbers: Barney's Number Circus. Margie Larsen & Mary A. Dudko. (Barney's Beginnings Ser.). (Illus.). 16p. (J). (ps-k). 1996. pap., wbk. ed. 2.95 (*1-57064-092-0*) Lyrick Pub.

Numbers: Barney's Number Circus. Margie Larsen & Mary A. Dudko. (Barney's Beginnings Ser.). (Illus.). 32p. (J). (ps-k). 1997. pap., wbk. ed. 2.95 (*1-57064-175-7*) Lyrick Pub.

Numbers: Beginning Skills. Dona H. Rice. (Basic Skills Ser.). 32p. (J). (gr. k-1). 1997. pap. 2.95 (*1-57690-238-2*) Tchr Create Mat.

Numbers: Bible Study Commentary. F. B. Huey, Jr. (Bible Study Commentary Ser.). 144p. (Orig.). 1981. pap. 6.99 (*0-310-36073-0*, 11064P) Zondervan.

Numbers: Facts, Figures & Fiction. Richard Phillips. (Illus.). 96p. (C). 1994. 22.95 (*0-521-46481-1*) Cambridge U Pr.

Numbers: Flip-&-Find. Candlewick Press Staff. (Illus.). 24p. (J). (ps-1). 1999. 7.99 (*0-7636-0893-9*) Candlewick Pr.

***Numbers: Foil Fun Board Book.** Salina Yoon. (Foil Fun Board Bks.). (Illus.). (J). 2000. 4.95 (*1-58117-062-9*, Piggy Toes Pr) Intervisual Bks.

Numbers: Individual Sets. Marion W. Stuart. text. write for info. (*0-943343-13-5*) Lrn Wrap-Ups.

Numbers: Journey to God's Rest-Land. Irving L. Jensen. (Everyman's Bible Commentary Ser.). 1968. pap. 9.99 (*0-8024-2004-4*) Moody.

Numbers: Numbers. (Fit-A-Shape Ser.). (Illus.). 10p. (J). 1998. bds. 5.95 (*1-56138-797-5*) Running Pr.

Numbers: Pull & Look Sliding Board Book. Willabel L. Tong. LC 99-186253. (Pull & Look Sliding Board Bks). 12p. (J). 1998. bds. 4.95 (*1-888443-86-3*, Piggy Toes Pr) Intervisual Bks.

Numbers: Rational & Irrational. Ivan Niven. LC 61-6226. (New Mathematical Library: No. 1). 140p. 1961. pap. text 20.95 (*0-88385-601-8*, NML-01) Math Assn.

***Numbers: The Little That Could, 1 vol.** Cristina Ong. (Illus.). 24p. (ps). 1999. bds. 1.99 (*0-448-41972-6*) Putnam Pub Group.

Numbers: The Universal Language. Denis Guedj. Tr. by Lory Frankel from ENG. LC 97-7637. (Discoveries Ser.). (Illus.). 176p. 1997. 12.95 (*0-8109-2845-0*, Pub. by Abrams) Time Warner.

Numbers: Their Occult Power & Mystic Virtue. W. Wynn Wescott. 127p. 1983. pap. 12.00 (*0-89540-128-2*, SB-128) Sun Pub.

Numbers: Their Occult Power & Mystic Virtues. W. Wynn Westcott. 127p. 1993. reprint ed. pap. 10.95 (*1-56459-316-9*) Kessinger Pub.

Numbers: Their Occult Power & Mystic Virtues. 2nd ed. W. Wynn Westcott. 125p. 1996. reprint ed. spiral bd. 13.50 (*0-7873-1314-9*) Hlth Research.

Numbers: With Over 50 Reusable Stickers. Books Lorenz. 1998. pap. text 5.95 (*1-85967-772-X*, Lorenz Bks) Anness Pub.

***Numbers - Pre-K.** Brighter Vision Publishing Staff. (Primary Skills Ser.). (Illus.). (J). (ps-3). 2000. pap. 2.25 (*1-55254-173-8*) Brighter Vision.

Numbers-a-Minute Timing Copy for Ten-Key Adding & Calculating Machines. George S. Rhodes. 36p. (Orig.). (C). 1980. pap. text 6.95 (*0-89420-219-7*, 126000); audio 19.25 (*0-89420-226-X*, 126004) Natl Book.

Numbers All Around. Susan Canizares & Betsey Chessen. LC 98-54205. (Learning Center Emergent Readers Ser.). 1998. 2.50 (*0-439-04598-3*) Scholastic Inc.

Numbers All Around Me, Vol. 4470. Trisha Callella-Jones. Ed. by Joel Kupperstein. (Learn to Read Math Ser.). (Illus.). 16p. (J). 1998. pap. 2.75 (*1-57471-377-9*, 4470) Creat Teach Pr.

Numbers & Age. John M. Patten, Jr. (Read All about Numbers Ser.). 24p. (J). (gr. 1-4). 1996. lib. bdg. 12.95 (*0-86593-437-1*) Rourke Corp.

Numbers & Colors: Early Learning Workbooks. Peter M. Spizzirri. Ed. by Linda Spizzirri. (Illus.). 32p. (J). (ps-2). 1997. pap. 2.95 (*0-86545-237-7*) Spizzirri.

Numbers & Counting. (Wipe-Off Book Ser). (Illus.). 24p. (J). (ps-k). 1998. 4.99 (*0-7681-0090-9*, McClanahan Book) Learn Horizon.

Numbers & Counting. American Education Publishing Staff. (Brighter Child Ser.). (Illus.). (J). 1993. pap. text 3.49 (*1-56189-293-9*) Amer Educ Pub.

Numbers & Counting. John M. Patten, Jr. (Read All about Numbers Ser.). 24p. (J). (gr. 1-4). 1996. lib. bdg. 12.95 (*0-86593-438-X*) Rourke Corp.

Numbers & Counting: Grades K-1. Troll Books Staff. (Teacher Time-Savers Ser.). 80p. (J). (gr. k-1). 1999. pap. text 11.95 (*0-8167-3946-3*) Troll Communs.

***Numbers & Counting Activity Book.** Brighter Vision Publishing Staff. (Illus.). (J). 2000. pap. 1.39 (*1-55254-150-9*) Brighter Vision.

***Numbers & Cycles in Ancient Astronomy.** Charles William Johnson. (Science in Ancient Artwork Ser.). (Illus.). 87p. 1999. pap. 20.00 (*1-58616-180-6*, 180-6) Earth Matrix.

Numbers & Deuteronomy see Torah Commentary for Our Times

Numbers & Functions: Steps to Analysis. R. P. Burn. (Illus.). 352p. (C). 1992. text 80.00 (*0-521-41086-X*) Cambridge U Pr.

Numbers & Functions: Steps to Analysis. R. P. Burn. (Illus.). 350p. (C). 1994. pap. text 30.95 (*0-521-45773-4*) Cambridge U Pr.

***Numbers & Functions: Steps to Analysis.** R. P. Burn. 350p. 2000. pap. write for info. (*0-521-78836-6*) Cambridge U Pr.

Numbers & Geometry. John Stillwell. Ed. by F. W. Gehring & P. R. Halmos. LC 97-22858. (Undergraduate Texts in Mathematics Ser.). 272p. 1997. 34.95 (*0-387-98289-2*) Spr-Verlag.

Numbers & Ideals. Abraham Robinson. LC 65-16747. (Illus.). 1965. 16.00 (*0-8162-7234-4*) Holden-Day.

Numbers & Letters: or The Thirty-Two Paths of Wisdom. Margaret B. Peeke. 191p. 1986. reprint ed. pap. 21.00 (*0-7873-0666-5*) Hlth Research.

Numbers & Letters: or The Thirty-Two Paths of Wisdom, 1908. Margaret B. Peeke. 215p. 1996. reprint ed. pap. 17.95 (*1-56459-816-0*) Kessinger Pub.

Numbers & Losses in the Civil War in America, 1861-65. fac. ed. Thomas L. Livermore. Ed. & Intro. by John D. Kallmann. 160p. 1996. 24.95 (*0-9650926-0-7*, L-1001) J Kallmann.

Numbers & Measuring. John M. Patten, Jr. (Read All about Numbers Ser.). 24p. (J). (gr. 1-4). 1996. lib. bdg. 12.95 (*0-86593-434-7*) Rourke Corp.

Numbers & Money. John M. Patten, Jr. (Read All about Numbers Ser.). 24p. (J). (gr. 1-4). 1996. lib. bdg. 12.95 (*0-86593-439-8*) Rourke Corp.

Numbers & Nationhood: Writing Statistics in Nineteenth-Century Italy. Silvana Patriarca. LC 95-4328. (Studies in Italian History & Culture). 292p. (C). 1996. text 59.95 (*0-521-46296-7*) Cambridge U Pr.

Numbers & Number Values see Early Learning Mastery Masters

Numbers & Numerals see Basic Mathematics

Numbers & Other One-Act Plays. Grover Theis. LC 79-50032. (One-Act Plays in Reprint Ser.). 1980. reprint ed. 20.00 (*0-8486-2056-9*) Roth Pub Inc.

Numbers & Proofs. R. Allenby. (An Arnold Publication). (Illus.). x288p. 1998. pap. text 24.95 (*0-340-67653-1*, Pub. by E A) OUP.

Numbers & Shapes. (Let's Have Fun Spanish-English Coloring & Activity Bks.). (Illus.). 32p. (J). (ps-1). 1992. pap. 2.95 (*1-56144-106-6*, Honey Bear Bks) Modern Pub NYC.

Numbers & Shapes Revisited: More Problems for Young Mathematicians. J. Corfman. (Illus.). 320p. 1995. pap. text 29.95 (*0-19-853460-4*) OUP.

Numbers & Speed. John M. Patten. LC 96-12625. (Read All about Numbers Ser.). 24p. (J). (gr. 1-4). 1996. lib. bdg. 12.95 (*0-86593-436-3*) Rourke Corp.

Numbers & Sports. John M. Patten, Jr. (Read All about Numbers Ser.). 24p. (J). (gr. 1-4). 1996. lib. bdg. 12.95 (*0-86593-435-5*) Rourke Corp.

Numbers & Symmetry: An Introduction to Algebra. Bernard L. Johnston & Fred Richman. LC 96-45224. 272p. 1997. lib. bdg. 31.95 (*0-8493-0301-X*) CRC Pr.

Numbers & Tempers: Selected Early Poems, 1966-1986. Ray DiPalma. (Sun & Moon Classics Ser.: No. 24). 176p. 1992. pap. 11.95 (*1-55713-099-X*) Sun & Moon CA.

Numbers & Words: A Problem Per Day. Marcy Cook. (J). (gr. 4-7). 1995. pap. 9.50 (*0-201-48002-6*) Addison-Wesley.

Numbers & Words: A Problem Per Day. Marcy Cook. (Illus.). 64p. 1987. pap. text 9.50 (*0-914040-52-9*) Cuisenaire.

Numbers & You: A Numerology Guide for Everyday Living. Lloyd Strayhorn. 352p. 1987. mass mkt. 5.99 (*0-345-34593-2*) Ballantine Pub Grp.

Numbers & You: A Numerology Guide for Everyday Living. Lloyd Strayhorn. 1997. pap. 12.00 (*0-345-41911-1*) Ballantine Pub Grp.

Numbers & You: A Numerology Guide for Everyday Living. Lloyd Strayhorn. LC 80-18386. 154p. 1980. 9.95 (*0-937290-02-5*); pap. 7.00 (*0-937290-61-0*) Yama Pub.

Numbers Are Everywhere. Margie Burton et al. Ed. by Susan Evento. (Early Connections Ser.). 16p. (J). (gr. k-2). 1998. pap. 4.25 (*1-892393-39-5*) Benchmark Educ.

Numbers at the Beach. (Super Sticker Bks.). (Illus.). 16p. (J). (gr. k-2). 1996. pap. write for info. (*1-56144-455-3*, Honey Bear Bks) Modern Pub NYC.

Numbers at Work & at Play. Stephen P. Richards. (Illus.). 213p. (Orig.). (YA). (gr. 10-12). 1987. pap. 8.95 (*0-9608224-2-9*) S P Richards.

Numbers Book: Student Syllabus, 2 vols. Sue C. Cook. (J). (gr. k-2). 1974. audio 19.95 (*0-89420-208-1*, 193000) Natl Book.

Numbers Book: Student Syllabus, 2 vols., 1. Sue C. Cook. (J). (gr. k-2). 1974. pap. text 19.95 (*0-89420-081-X*, 193050) Natl Book.

Numbers Book: Student Syllabus, 2 vols., 2. Sue C. Cook. (J). (gr. k-2). 1974. pap. text 19.95 (*0-89420-082-8*, 193051) Natl Book.

***Numbers Bubble Gum Board Book.** Eckard. 2000. bds. 7.99 (*0-307-10299-8*) Gldn Bks Pub Co.

Numbers Count. Bob Bernstein. 96p. (J). (gr. 2-7). 1990. 11.99 (*0-86653-542-X*, GA1151) Good Apple.

***Numbers Count: The Secrets of Numerology.** Paul Warwick. 2000. pap. text 10.95 (*1-902809-21-1*) Allison & Busby.

Numbers, Deuteronomy, Introduction to Narrative Literature, Joshua, Judges, Ruth, 1 & 2 Samuel. (The New Interpreter's Bible: Vol. 2). 1998. 81.50 (*0-687-27815-5*) Abingdon.

Numbers Dot-to-Dot: Activity Book. Barbara Allman. (J). 1997. pap. text 2.29 (*0-7647-0251-3*) Schaffer Pubns.

Numbers Every Day. Kari Jenson Gold. Ed. by Jenni Whitfield. (Early Math Big Bks.). (Illus.). 16p. (J). (ps-2). 1997. pap. 16.95 (*1-56784-953-9*) Newbridge Educ.

Numbers Every Day: Mini Book. Kari J. Gold. Ed. by Jenni Whitfield. (Early Math Ser.). (Illus.). 16p. (J). (ps-1). 1997. pap. 3.16 (*1-56784-978-4*) Newbridge Educ.

Numbers (Everyman's Bible Commentary) see Numeros: Viaje a la Tierra de Reposo

Numbers for Blood Bankers. Ed. by Joy L. Fridey et al. LC 95-44611. (Illus.). 107p. (C). 1995. 40.00 (*1-56395-045-6*) Am Assn Blood.

Numbers from Nowhere: The American Indian Contact Population Debate. David P. Henige. LC 97-50252. 544p. 1998. 47.95 (*0-8061-3044-X*) U of Okla Pr.

Numbers Fun. (Fisher-Price Little People Toddler Workbooks Ser.). (Illus.). 32p. (J). (ps-1). 1997. pap. write for info. (*1-56144-933-4*, Honey Bear Bks) Modern Pub NYC.

Numbers Game. Graham Perry. 128p. (Orig.). 1993. mass mkt. 3.99 (*0-446-60040-7*, Pub. by Warner Bks) Little.

Numbers Game: Ensuring Quantity & Quality in the Teaching Work Force. NASBE Study Group on Teacher Development, Supply, & Demand Staff. 48p. 1998. pap. 12.00 (*1-58434-039-8*) NASBE.

Numbers, Groups & Codes. J. F. Humphreys & M. Y. Prest. 304p. (C). 1990. pap. text 28.95 (*0-521-35938-4*) Cambridge U Pr.

***Numbers in Our Lives: A Course in ACP Numerology.** Amie Angeli. LC 97-94774. (ACP Oracles Ser.: Vol. 1). (Illus.). 96p. 1998. pap. 19.50 (*1-891333-00-3*) AngeLines Pub.

Numbers in Presence & Absence: A Study of Husserl's Philosophy of Mathematics. J. P. Miller. (Phaenomenologica Ser.: Vol. 90). 157p. 1982. lib. bdg. 99.50 (*90-247-2709-X*, Pub. by M Nijhoff) Kluwer Academic.

Numbers in the Bible see Numeros en la Biblia

***Numbers in the Bible.** Robert Johnston. (Illus.). 2000. pap. 6.99 (*0-8254-2965-X*) Kregel.

Numbers in the Bible: God's Unique Design in Biblical Numbers. Robert D. Johnston. LC 90-36538. Orig. Title: The Arithmetic of Heaven. 112p. 1990. reprint ed. pap. 4.99 (*0-8254-3628-1*) Kregel.

Numbers in the Dark. Italo Calvino. 288p. 1996. pap. 12.00 (*0-679-74353-7*) Random.

***Numbers, Information & Complexity.** Ingo Althoumlfer et al. 672p. 2000. 155.00 (*0-7923-7765-6*) Kluwer Academic.

Numbers (Los Numeros), Vol. 5. large type ed. Illus. by Clare Beaton. (English-Spanish Bilingual First Bks.). (ENG & SPA.). 24p. (J). (ps up). 1998. lib. bdg. 14.45 (*1-56674-251-X*) Forest Hse.

Numbers Mean More Than You Think. Elsie M. Knapp & Denise Faithful. 51p. 1974. pap. 3.00 (*0-686-05514-4*) Sandollar Pr.

Numbers, Number Words, & Sets see Let's Learn Set

Numbers of Alexander. William H. Toel. Ed. by Lisa M. Toel. LC 89-84973. 272p. (Orig.). 1989. write for info. (*0-9623490-1-1*); pap. write for info. (*0-9623490-0-3*) ICA Pr.

Numbers of Generators of Ideals in Local Rings. Judith D. Sally. LC 77-19016. (Lecture Notes in Pure & Applied Mathematics Ser.: No. 35). 107p. reprint ed. pap. 33.20 (*0-8357-6237-8*, 202901200058) Bks Demand.

Numbers of Heaven. unabridged ed. Roy H. Hart. LC 97-93089. (Illus.). 159p. (Orig.). 1997. pap. 12.50 (*0-935688-01-3*) Menta Pubns.

Numbers of Ordinary Arithmetic & Algebra. rev. ed. Mervin L. Keedy & Marvin L. Bittinger. (Algebra, a Modern Introduction Ser.). (gr. 7-9). 1981. pap. text. write for info. (*0-201-03982-6*) Addison-Wesley.

Numbers 1. Richard Kostelanetz. 1974. 300.00 (*0-932360-34-3*) Archae Edns.

Numbers 1 to 10. (Home Workbooks Ser.). (Illus.). 64p. (Orig.). (J). (ps-1). 1995. pap., wbk. ed. 2.49 (*0-88724-339-8*, CD-6836) Carson-Dellos.

Numbers 1 to 10. Ed. by Lois Bottoni & Patti Reynolds. (Golden Step Ahead Workbooks Ser.). (Illus.). 36p. (ps-3). 1985. 2.09 (*0-307-23537-8*, 03537, Goldn Books) Gldn Bks Pub Co.

Numbers 1 to 12. Joan Hoffman. (I Know It! Book Ser.). (Illus.). 32p. (J). (ps-3). 1987. student ed. 2.49 (*0-938256-26-2*, 02026) Sch Zone Pub Co.

Numbers 1 to 20. (Home Workbooks Ser.). (Illus.). 64p. (Orig.). (J). (ps-1). 1995. pap., wbk. ed. 2.49 (*0-88724-340-1*, CD-6837) Carson-Dellos.

Numbers 1 to 20: A New Translation with Introduction & Commentary. Baruch Levine. LC 92-12262. (Anchor Bible Ser.: Vol. 4). 544p. 1993. 42.50 (*0-385-15651-0*) Doubleday.

Numbers 1 to 20: The Circus & the Bees. William R. Johnson. Ed. by Pauline D. Johnson. (BLIP Production Reference Board Bks.). (Illus.). 48p. (J). (ps-2). 1986. pap. 4.95 (*0-936917-03-2*, B605) Blip Prods.

Numbers 1 to 20 Dot-to-Dot. (Be Smart Bks.). (Illus.). 24p. (J). (ps). 1986. 3.98 (*0-86734-063-0*, FS-3055) Schaffer Pubns.

Numbers Puzzles & Games. Frank Schaffer Publications, Inc. Staff. (Homework Helpers Ser.). (Illus.). 56p. 1996. 2.29 (*0-86734-944-1*, FS-11058) Schaffer Pubns.

Numbers, Seasons, Months & Days. 2nd ed. Nancy N. Bijan. (First Ser.). (PER., Illus.). 21p. (J). (ps-6). 1998. pap. 5.95 (*1-880710-11-0*) Monterey Pacific.

Numbers, Sequences & Series. Keith E. Hirst. (Modular Mathematics Ser.). 208p. 1995. pap. text 18.95 (*0-340-61043-3*, Pub. by E A) Routldge.

Numbers, Sets & Axioms: The Apparatus of Mathematics. A. G. Hamilton. LC 82-4206. 265p. 1983. pap. text 33.95 (*0-521-28761-8*) Cambridge U Pr.

Numbers, Shapes & Sizes, No. 3209. Roberta Schomburg & Hedda B. Sharapan. Ed. by Joellyn T. Cicciarelli. (Grow & Learn with Mister Rogers Ser.). (Illus.). 32p. (J). (gr. k-3). 1999. pap. 6.98 (*1-57471-545-3*) Creat Teach Pr.

***Numbers Sticker Activity Book.** 12p. (J). 1999. pap. 2.99 (*0-7214-2943-2*, Ladybrd) Penguin Putnam.

***Numbers Sticker Workbooks.** School Zone Publishing Staff. (Illus.). (J). 1998. pap. 3.59 (*0-88743-119-4*) Sch Zone Pub Co.

Numbers Teacher's Manual. Vivian D. Gunderson. (Bible Learn & Do Ser.). (Illus.). 96p. 1981. pap. text 4.00 (*0-915374-29-3*) Rapids Christian.

Numbers 10 to 100. Lois Bottoni. (Step Ahead Workbooks Ser.). (Illus.). 32p. (J). (ps-3). 1985. pap. 2.09 (*0-307-03586-7*, 03586, Goldn Books) Gldn Bks Pub Co.

***Numbers 21-36.** Baruch A. Levine. LC 99-28025. (Anchor Bible Ser.: Vol. 4). 496p. 2000. 45.00 (*0-385-41256-8*) Doubleday.

Numbers 2. Richard Kostelanetz. 1977. pap. 4.00 (*0-935350-84-5*) Luna Bisonte.

Numbers with Small Prime Factors & the Least Kth Power Non-Residue. Karl K. Norton. LC 52-42839. (Memoirs Ser.: No. 1/106). 106p. 1971. pap. 16.00 (*0-8218-1806-6*, MEMO/1/106) Am Math.

Numbers with Small Prime Factors & the Least kth Power Non-Residue. Karl K. Norton. LC 52-42839. (American Mathematical Society Ser.: No. 106). 110p. reprint ed. pap. 34.10 (*0-608-09213-4*, 205271700005) Bks Demand.

***Numbers Workbook.** Landoll. (Beginners Bible Ser.). 2000. pap. text 14.95 (*1-56189-619-5*) Amer Educ Pub.

Numbers You Need. Nigel J. Hopkins & John W. Mayne. 349p. 1993. 55.00 (*0-8103-8373-X*) Gale.

Numbers 0 to 10, 5 bks. Cynthia Muller et al. (Apples for Teachers Ser.). 96p. 11.99 (*0-8224-0457-5*, FE0457) Fearon Teacher Aids.

Numbers 0 to 10. Lynette Pyne. (Basic Skills Ser.). (Illus.). 32p. (J). (gr. k-1). 1997. pap. text 4.95 (*0-88724-387-8*, CD-2122) Carson-Dellos.

Numbers 0 to 20. Cindy Barden. (Basic Skills Ser.). (Illus.). 32p. (J). (gr. 1-2). 1997. pap. text 4.95 (*0-88724-388-6*, CD-2123) Carson-Dellos.

Numbers/English-French. Clare Beaton. LC 96-85799. (Bilingual First Bks.). (FRE & ENG., Illus.). 24p. (J). (ps up). 1997. pap. 3.95 (*0-7641-0034-3*) Barron.

Numbers/English-Spanish. Clare Beaton. LC 96-85834. (Bilingual First Bks.). (SPA & ENG., Illus.). 24p. (J). (ps up). 1997. pap. 3.95 (*0-7641-0035-1*) Barron.

Numbersense & Place Value, Vol. 2655. Ed. by Janet Bruno. (Child-Centered Math Ser.: Vol. 5). (Illus.). 80p. 1997. pap. 4.98 (*1-57471-238-1*, 2655) Creat Teach Pr.

Numbskull Factor: The Decline of Common Sense in America. Robert J. Samuelson. LC 92-56845. 320p. 1993. 23.00 (*0-8129-2207-7*, Times Bks) Crown Pub Group.

Numbskulls. William Taylor. LC 94-43618. 160p. (J). (gr. 3-7). 1995. 14.95 (*0-590-22629-0*, Scholastic Hardcover) Scholastic Inc.

Numen: Poems. limited ed. Cole Swenson. (Poetry Ser.). 80p. 1994. pap. 15.00 (*1-886224-01-3*) Burning Deck.

Numerabilia Romana Uno ad Duo Mila see Roman Numerals I to MM: Numerabilia Romana Uno Ad Duo Mila

***Numeracy & Mathematics Across the Primary Curriculum: Building Confidence & Understanding.** David Coles. 2000. pap. 26.95 (*1-85346-640-9*) David Fulton.

Numeracy Development: A Guide for Adult Educators. Ed. by Iddo Gal. (Literacy Research, Policy & Practice Ser.). 336p. 1999. text 67.50 (*1-57273-232-6*); pap. text 27.50 (*1-57273-233-4*) Hampton Pr NJ.

Numeral Classifier Systems: The Case of Japanese. Pamela A. Downing. LC 96-9444. (Studies in Discourse & Grammar: No. 4). xx, 336p. Date not set. 79.00 (*1-55619-370-X*) J Benjamins Pubng Co.

Numeral Philosophy. Albert Christy. 82p. 1983. pap. 8.00 (*0-89540-141-X*, SB-141) Sun Pub.

Numeral Philosophy. Albert Christy. 30p. 1993. reprint ed. spiral bd. 8.00 (*0-7873-0170-1*) Hlth Research.

Numeral Types & Changes Worldwide. Jadranka Gvozanovibc. LC 98-52394. (Trends in Linguistics Ser.). 1999. 127.25 (*3-11-016113-3*) De Gruyter.

Numeral Words. Melius De Villiers. 124p. 1996. reprint ed. spiral bd. 11.50 (*0-7873-0272-4*) Hlth Research.

Numercal Methods in Geomechanics, Vol. 4. 3rd ed. 1979. 162.00 (*90-6191-044-7*, Pub. by A A Balkema) Ashgate Pub Co.

Numercial Combustion. Ed. by A. Dervieux & Bernard Larrouturou. (Lecture Notes in Physics Ser.: Vol. 351). vii, 481p. 1989. 70.95 (*0-387-51968-8*) Spr-Verlag.

Numeric Analysis, 1991. Griffiths. 1992. pap. 48.95 (*0-582-08908-5*, Pub. by Addison-Wesley) Longman.

Numeric Databases. Ed. by Ching-Chin Chen & Peter Hernon. LC 83-25761. 304p. 1984. 73.25 (*0-89391-247-6*) Ablx Pub.

Numeric Filing: A Guideline. ARMA International Staff. 14p. 1989. pap. 29.00 (*0-933887-32-9*, A4531) ARMA Intl.

Numeric Keyboarding. Jackson et al. (PB - Keyboarding Ser.). (J). (gr. k-8). 1990. 71.95 (*0-538-60580-4*) S-W Pub.

Numerica: A Modeling Language for Global Optimization. Pascal Van Hentenryck et al. LC 97-990. 232p. 1997. pap. text 25.00 (*0-262-72027-2*) MIT Pr.

Numerical Adventures with Geochemical Cycles. James C. Walker. (Illus.). 210p. 1990. text 55.00 (*0-19-504520-3*) OUP.

Numerical Air Flow Modelling. Ed. by G. E. Whittle. (C). 1987. 115.00 (*0-86022-124-5*, Pub. by Build Servs Info Assn) St Mut.

Numerical Algorithms. Ed. by J. L. Mohammed & J. Walsh. (Illus.). 368p. 1987. text 60.00 (*0-19-853364-0*) OUP.

Numerical Algorithms for Modern Parallel Computer Architectures. Ed. by M. Schultz. (IMA Volumes in Mathematics & Its Applications Ser.: Vol. 13). (Illus.). xi, 232p. 1988. 35.00 (*0-387-96733-8*) Spr-Verlag.

Numerical Algorithms with C. G. Engeln-Mullges & Frank Uhlig. LC 96-23158. 624p. 1996. pap. text 49.95 incl. cd-rom (*3-540-60530-4*) Spr-Verlag.

Numerical Algorithms with Fortran. G. Engeln-Mullges & Frank Uhlig. 1996. 49.50 incl. cd-rom (*0-614-14506-6*) Spr-Verlag.

Numerical Algorithms with Fortran. Gisela Engeln-Mullges & Frank Uhlig. LC 96-32380. 602p. 1996. 49.95 (*3-540-60529-0*) Spr-Verlag.

Numerical Analysis. Applied Mathematics Symposium Staff. Ed. by J. H. Curtiss. LC 50-1183. (Proceedings of Symposia in Applied Mathematics Ser.). 303p. 1956. text 49.00 (*0-8218-1306-4*, PSAPM/6) Am Math.

Numerical Analysis. Richard L. Burden et al. 1978. pap. text 22.00 (*0-87150-243-7*) PWS Pubs.

Numerical Analysis. Walter Gautschi. LC 97-186. 500p. 1997. 64.50 (*0-8176-3895-4*) Birkhauser.

Numerical Analysis. Griffiths & Watson. 1986. pap. text. write for info. (*0-582-98897-7*, Pub. by Addison-Wesley) Longman.

Numerical Analysis. B. D. Gupta. 588p. 1990. text 45.00 (*81-220-0125-4*, Pub. by Konark Pubs Pvt Ltd) Advent Bks Div.

Numerical Analysis. Ian Jacques & C. J. Judd. 300p. 1987. text 75.00 (*0-412-27950-9*); pap. text 34.50 (*0-412-27960-6*) Chapman & Hall.

Numerical Analysis. R. Kress. Ed. by S. Axler et al. LC 97-43748. (Graduate Texts in Mathematics Ser.: Vol. 181). (Illus.). 336p. 1998. text 39.00 (*0-387-98408-9*) Spr-Verlag.

Numerical Analysis. Kalyan K. Mukherjee. (C). 1989. 60.00 (*0-89771-396-6*, Pub. by Current Dist) St Mut.

Numerical Analysis. Vithal A. Patel. LC 93-86061. 652p. (C). 1993. text 93.00 (*0-03-098330-4*) SCP.

Numerical Analysis. Peter R. Turner. (Macmillan College Work Out Ser.). 265p. (C). 1994. pap. text 20.00 (*0-333-58665-4*) Scholium Intl.

Numerical Analysis. 2nd ed. Douglas J. Faires et al. LC 80-29558. 598p. (C). 1981. mass mkt. 27.75 (*0-87150-314-X*, 33L 2511) PWS Pubs.

Numerical Analysis. 2nd ed. Lee W. Johnson & R. Dean Riess. LC 81-15019. (Mathematics Ser.). (Illus.). 448p. (C). 1982. text. write for info. (*0-201-10392-3*) Addison-Wesley.

Numerical Analysis. 3rd ed. Burden. (Mathematics Ser.). 1985. teacher ed. 14.00 (*0-87150-858-3*) PWS Pubs.

Numerical Analysis. 3rd ed. Richard L. Burden & J. Douglas Faires. (C). 1985. mass mkt. 41.50 (*0-87150-857-5*) PWS Pubs.

Numerical Analysis. 3rd ed. Maron. (Mathematics Ser.). 1991. teacher ed. 23.25 (*0-534-12373-2*) Brooks-Cole.

Numerical Analysis. 4th ed. Richard L. Burden & J. Douglas Faires. (Math). 784p. (C). 1988. mass mkt. 51.00 (*0-534-91585-X*) PWS Pubs.

Numerical Analysis. 5th ed. Richard L. Burden & J. Douglas Faires. LC 92-32192. 784p. 1993. text 78.95 (*0-534-93219-3*) PWS Pubs.

Numerical Analysis. 6th ed. Richard L. Burden & Douglas J. Faires. LC 96-27594. (Mathematics Ser.). 776p. (C). 1996. mass mkt. 106.95 (*0-534-95532-0*) Brooks-Cole.

Numerical Analysis: A Comprehensive Introduction. Hans R. Schwarz. LC 89-5538. (Illus.). 531p. 1989. reprint ed. pap. 164.70 (*0-608-02603-4*, 206326100004) Bks Demand.

Numerical Analysis: A First Course in Scientific Computation. Peter Deuflhard & Andreas Hohmann. Tr. by F. A. Potra & F. Schulz from GER. LC 94-46993. (C). 1995. pap. text 42.95 (*3-11-013882-4*); lib. bdg. 69.95 (*3-11-014031-4*) De Gruyter.

Numerical Analysis: A. R. Mitchell 75th Birthday Volume. 380p. 1996. lib. bdg. 61.00 (*981-02-2719-1*) World Scientific Pub.

Numerical Analysis: A Second Course. James M. Ortega. LC 89-48562. (Classics in Applied Mathematics Ser.: No. 3). xiii, 201p. 1990. pap. 34.50 (*0-89871-250-5*) Soc Indus-Appl Math.

Numerical Analysis: An Introduction. Walter Gautschi. LC 97-186. 500p. 1997. write for info. (*3-7643-3895-4*) Birkhauser.

Numerical Analysis: Approximation of Some Partial Differential Equations. Roger Temam. Tr. by J. W. Neinhuys from FRE. LC 73-75643. 163p. 1973. text 138.50 (*90-277-0308-6*) Kluwer Academic.

Numerical Analysis: Instructor's Solution Manual. 6th ed. Richard L. Burden & Douglas J. Faires. (C). 1997. text, teacher ed. write for info. (*0-534-95366-2*) Brooks-Cole.

Numerical Analysis: Proceedings of the Fourth IIMAS Workshop Held at Guanajuanto, Mexico, July 23-27, 1984. Ed. by J. P. Hennart. (Lecture Notes in Mathematics Ser.: Vol. 1230). x, 234p. 1987. pap. 28.50 (*0-387-17200-9*) Spr-Verlag.

Numerical Analysis: Proceedings of the 10th Biennial Conference Held at Dundee, Scotland, June 28-July 1, 1983. Ed. by D. F. Griffiths. (Lecture Notes in Mathematics Ser.: Vol. 1066). ix, 275p. 1984. 42.95 (*0-387-13344-5*) Spr-Verlag.

Numerical Analysis: Study Guide. 6th ed. Richard L. Burden & Douglas J. Faires. (Mathematics Ser.). (C). 1997. text, mass mkt., student ed. 30.00 incl. disk (*0-534-95533-9*) Brooks-Cole.

Numerical Analysis: Symposia in Applied Mathematics, Vol. 22. Ed. by Gene H. Golub & Joseph Oliger. LC 78-11096. (Proceedings of Symposia in Applied Mathematics Ser.). 135p. 1978. reprint ed. pap. 21.00 (*0-8218-0122-8*, PSAPM/22) Am Math.

Numerical Analysis: The Mathematics of Scientific Computing. David R. Kincaid & Ward Cheney. 700p. (C). 1991. text 55.00 (*0-534-13014-3*) Brooks-Cole.

Numerical Analysis: Theory & Practice. Asaithambi. (C). 1995. text 87.50 (*0-03-030983-2*) Harcourt Coll Pubs.

Numerical Analysis Algorithm. Murphy. 1990. pap. write for info. (*0-318-68279-6*) P-H.

Numerical Analysis & Computation Theory & Practice. Edward K. Blum. LC 79-150574. (Addison-Wesley Series in Mathematics). 624p. reprint ed. pap. 193.50 (*0-608-15178-5*, 205608000046) Bks Demand.

Numerical Analysis & Graphic Visualization with MATLAB. Shoichiro Nakamura. LC 95-32597. 496p. (C). 1995. 90.00 (*0-13-051518-3*) P-H.

Numerical Analysis & Its Applications: First International Workshop, WNAA '96, Rousse, Bulgaria, June 24-26, 1996: Proceedings. Lubin Vulkov et al. LC 97-6969. (Lecture Notes in Computer Science Ser.: Vol. 119). 1997. pap. 91.00 (*3-540-62598-4*) Spr-Verlag.

Numerical Analysis & Modelling of Soil Structure Interaction. Ed. by John W. Bull. 1993. write for info. (*1-85861-014-1*) Elsevier.

Numerical Analysis & Parallel Processing. Ed. by P. R. Turner. (Lecture Notes in Mathematics Ser.: Vol. 1397). vi, 264p. 1989. 41.95 (*0-387-51645-X*) Spr-Verlag.

Numerical Analysis for Applied Mathematics, Science & Engineering. Donald Greenspan. LC 87-37391. (C). 1993. pap. 52.00 (*0-201-40692-6*) Addison-Wesley.

Numerical Analysis for Applied Science. Myron B. Allen, III & Eli L. Isaacson. LC 97-16688. (Pure & Applied Mathematics: A Wiley-Interscience Series of Texts, Monographs & Tracts). 492p. 1997. 84.95 (*0-471-55266-6*) Wiley.

Numerical Analysis for Integral & Related Operator Equations. Siegfried Probdorf & Bernd Silbermann. (Mathematische Lehrbucher und Monographien: Abt. II, Band 84). 540p. 1991. text 236.25 (*3-05-500696-8*, Pub. by Akademie Verlag) Wiley.

Numerical Analysis for Integral & Related Operator Equations. S. Prossdorf & Bernd Silbermann. (Operator Theory Ser.: Vol. 52). 560p. 1991. 234.00 (*0-8176-2620-4*) Birkhauser.

Numerical Analysis for Statisticians. Kenneth Lange. Ed. by J. Chambers et al. LC 98-16688. (Statistics & Computing Ser.). 360p. 1999. 69.95 (*0-387-94979-8*) Spr-Verlag.

Numerical Analysis for the Geological Sciences. James R. Carr. (Illus.). 592p. (C). 1994. 67.00 (*0-02-319511-8*, Macmillan Coll) P-H.

Numerical Analysis, Lancaster, 1984. Ed. by P. R. Turner. (Lecture Notes in Mathematics Ser.: Vol. 1129). xiv, 179p. 1985. 34.95 (*0-387-15234-2*) Spr-Verlag.

Numerical Analysis Mathematics of Scientific Computing. 2nd ed. David Kincaid & Ward Cheney. (Mathematics Ser.). 804p. 1996. mass mkt. 94.95 (*0-534-33892-5*) Brooks-Cole.

Numerical Analysis, 1989: Proceedings of the 13th Dundee Conference, June 1989. Dundee Conference on Numerical Analysis Staff. Ed. by D. F. Griffiths & G. A. Watson. LC 89-13163. (Pitman Research Notes in Mathematics Ser.: Vol. 228). 295p. 1990. reprint ed. pap. 91.50 (*0-608-03597-1*, 206442000009) Bks Demand.

***Numerical Analysis 1999.** D. F. Griffiths & G. A. Watson. (C&H/CRC Research Notes in Mathematics Series). 288p. 2000. per. 74.95 (*1-58488-020-1*, Chap & Hall CRC) CRC Pr.

Numerical Analysis of Electromagnetic Fields. Pei-bai Zhou. LC 92-39200. (Electric Energy Systems & Engineering Ser.). 1993. 149.95 (*0-387-54722-3*) Spr-Verlag.

Numerical Analysis of Forming Processes. Ed. by J. F. Pittman et al. LC 83-21600. (Wiley Series in Numerical Methods in Engineering). 462p. reprint ed. pap. 143.30 (*0-7837-4012-3*, 204384200011) Bks Demand.

Numerical Analysis of Ordinary Differential Equations & Its Applications. T. Mitsui & Y. Shinohara. 250p. 1995. text 55.00 (*981-02-2229-7*) World Scientific Pub.

Numerical Analysis of Parameterized Nonlinear Equations. Werner C. Rheinboldt. LC 84-21974. (Lecture Notes in the Mathematical Sciences Ser.). 299p. 1986. pap. 150.00 (*0-471-88814-1*) Wiley.

Numerical Analysis of Reinforced Concrete Structures. Constantin Avram et al. LC 92-46460. (Developments in Civil Engineering Ser.: Vol. 41). (Illus.). 510p. 1993. 238.00 (*0-444-98842-4*) Elsevier.

Numerical Analysis of Selected Semilinear Differential Equations. Ed. by Collet's Holdings, Ltd. Staff. 1986. 63.00 (*0-7855-1182-2*, Pub. by Collets) St Mut.

Numerical Analysis of Selected Semilinear Differential Equations. C. Gorssmann. 204p. (C). 1984. 90.00 (*0-7855-4977-3*, Pub. by Collets) St Mut.

Numerical Analysis of Spectral Methods: Theory & Applications. David Gottlieb & Steven A. Orszag. (CBMS-NSF Regional Conference Series in Applied Mathematics: No. 26). v, 170p. 1977. reprint ed. pap. text 33.00 (*0-89871-023-5*) Soc Indus-Appl Math.

Numerical Analysis of Systems of Ordinary & Stochastic Differential Equations. S. S. Artemiev & T. A. Averina. (Illus.). 184p. 1997. 129.50 (*90-6764-250-9*, Pub. by VSP) Coronet Bks.

Numerical Analysis of Viscoelastic Problems. P. V. Le Tallec. Ed. by P. G. Ciarlet & J. L. Lions. (Recherches en Mathematiques Appliquees Ser.: Vol. 15). iv, 136p. 1990. 44.95 (*0-387-52450-9*) Spr-Verlag.

Numerical Analysis Problem Solver. rev. ed. Research & Education Association Staff. LC 83-62277. (Illus.). 896p. 1994. pap. text 29.95 (*0-87891-549-4*) Res & Educ.

Numerical Analysis Via Derive. Steven Schonefeld. (Illus.). 525p. 1994. pap. text 44.95 (*0-9623629-2-1*) MathWare.

Numerical Analysis, 1987. Griffiths & Watson. 1988. pap. text. write for info. (*0-582-02157-X*, Pub. by Addison-Wesley) Longman.

Numerical Analysis, 1995. D. F. Griffiths. (Pitman Research Notes in Mathematics Ser.). 1996. pap. 52.00 (*0-582-27633-0*) Longman.

Numerical-Analytic Methods in the Theory of Boundary Value Problems. M. Ronto & A. M. Samoilenko. 360p. 1999. 58.00 (*981-02-3676-X*) World Scientific Pub.

Numerical & Alphabetical Progressions & Abstract Reasoning. Jack Rudman. (General Aptitude & Abilities Ser.: CS-30). 1994. pap. 23.95 (*0-8373-6730-1*) Nat Learn.

Numerical & Physical Aspect of Aerodynamic Flows III. Ed. by T. Cebeci. 490p. 1986. 118.95 (*0-387-96281-6*) Spr-Verlag.

Numerical & Physical Aspects of Aerodynamic Flows, Pt. II. Ed. by T. Cebeci. (Illus.). 500p. 1983. 131.00 (*0-387-12659-7*) Spr-Verlag.

Numerical & Physical Aspects of Aerodynamic Flows IV. Ed. by T. Cebeci. (Illus.). xii, 420p. 1990. 121.95 (*0-387-52259-X*) Spr-Verlag.

Numerical Approaches to Combustion Modeling. Ed. by Elaine S. Oran & Jay P. Boris. (PAAS Ser.: Vol. 135). (Illus.). 825p. 1991. 109.95 (*1-56347-004-7*, V-135) AIAA.

Numerical Approximation Jozef Kacur. text. write for info. (*0-471-49001-6*) Wiley.

Numerical Approximation of Hyperbolic Systems of Conservation Laws. E. Godlewski. (Applied Mathematical Sciences Ser.: Vol. 118). 528p. 1996. 64.95 (*0-387-94529-6*) Spr-Verlag.

Numerical Approximation of Partial Differential Equations. A. Quarteroni & A. Valli. LC 94-21763. (Computational Mathematics Ser.: Vol. 23). 1997. 108.95 (*0-387-57111-6*) Spr-Verlag.

Numerical Approximation of Partial Differential Equations 2nd ed. Alfio Quarteroni & A. Valli. LC 97-160884. (Series in Computational Mathematics). xvi, 543p. 1997. write for info. (*3-540-57111-6*) Spr-Verlag.

***Numerical Astrophysics.** Ed. by Shoken M. Miyama et al. LC 98-53211. (Astrophysics & Space Science Library). 1999. 225.00 (*0-7923-5566-0*) Kluwer Academic.

Numerical BASIC. Bruce P. Douglass. 1984. write for info. (*0-318-57974-X*) Macmillan.

Numerical Bayesian Methods Applied to Signal Processing. W. J. Fitzgerald & Joseph J. O'Ruanaidh. (Statistics & Computing Ser.). (Illus.). 1996p. 1996. 52.95 (*0-387-94629-2*) Spr-Verlag.

Numerical Bayesian Methods Applied to Signal Processing. Joseph J. O'Ruanaidh & William J. Fitzgerald. LC 95-44635. 1996. write for info. (*0-614-09506-9*) Spr-Verlag.

Numerical Bible, 7 vols., Set. Incl. Vol. 1. Genesis to Deuteronomy. Ed. by F. W. Grant. 623p. 1990. 18.99 (*0-87213-262-5*); Vol. 2. Joshua to Second Samuel. Ed. by F. W. Grant. 489p. 1990. 18.99 (*0-87213-263-3*); Vol. 3. Psalms. F. W. Grant. 548p. 1990. 18.99 (*0-87213-264-1*); Vol. 4. Ezekiel. F. W. Grant. 339p. 1990. 18.99 (*0-87213-265-X*); Vol. 5. Matthew to John. Ed. by F. W. Grant. 626p. 1990. 18.99 (*0-87213-266-8*); Vol. 6. Acts to Second Corinthians. Ed. by F. W. Grant. 1990. 18.99 (*0-87213-267-6*); Vol. 7. Hebrews Through Revelations. F. W. Grant. 1990. 18.99 (*0-87213-268-4*); 1990. 134.99 (*0-87213-261-7*) Loizeaux.

Numerical Bible: Hebrews to Revelation (1932) Loizeaux. 520p. 1998. reprint ed. pap. 35.00 (*0-7661-0123-1*) Kessinger Pub.

***Numerical Bifurcation Analysis for Reaction-Diffusion Equations.** Zhen Mei. LC 00-41043. (Series in Computational Mathematics: Vol. 28). xiv, 414p. 2000. 84.00 (*3-540-67296-6*) Spr-Verlag.

Numerical Calculus: Approximations, Interpolation, Finite Differences, Numerical Integration & Curve Fitting. William E. Milne. LC 49-7739. 403p. reprint ed. pap. 125.00 (*0-7837-1421-1*, 204177600023) Bks Demand.

Numerical-Chronological-Author Index 1979 to 1985-86, Vol. II. Ed. by Horace Jacobs & Robert H. Jacobs. 350p. 1987. pap. text 45.00 (*0-87703-251-3*); lib. bdg. 60.00 (*0-87703-250-5*) Univelt Inc.

Numerical Cognition. Ed. by Stanislas Dehaene. (Cognition Ser.). 316p. (Orig.). 1993. pap. 22.95 (*1-55786-444-6*) Blackwell Pubs.

Numerical Computation in Science & Engineering. C. Pozrikidis. LC 97-38185. (Illus.). 640p. (C). 1998. text 84.95 (*0-19-511253-9*) OUP.

Numerical Computation of Electric & Magnetic Fields. Charles W. Steele. LC 85-22659. (Illus.). 256p. 1987. text 54.95 (*0-442-27841-1*, VNR) Wiley.

Numerical Computation of Electric & Magnetic Fields. 2nd ed. Steele. (Electrical Engineering Ser.). 1993. text 69.95 (*0-442-01434-1*, VNR) Wiley.

Numerical Computation of Internal & External Flows, Vol. 1. 2nd ed. Hirsch. 121.00 (*0-471-95652-X*); pap. 60.00 (*0-471-95653-8*) Wiley.

Numerical Computation of Internal & External Flows, Vol. 2. 2nd ed. Hirsch. 121.00 (*0-471-95654-6*); pap. 61.00 (*0-471-95655-4*) Wiley.

Numerical Computation of Internal & External Flows, Vol. 1, Fundamentals of Numerical Discretization, Vol. 1, Fundamentals of Numerical Discretization. Charles Hirsch. LC 87-23116. 538p. 1989. pap. 120.00 (*0-471-92385-0*) Wiley.

Numerical Computation of Internal & External Flows, Vol. 2, Computational Methods for Inviscid & Viscous Flows, Vol. 2, Computational Methods for Inviscid and Vis. Charles Hirsch. LC 87-23116. 714p. 1990. pap. 140.00 (*0-471-92452-0*) Wiley.

Numerical Computation of Stress Waves in Solids. X. Lin. 317p. 1996. 205.00 (*3-05-501725-0*) Wiley.

Numerical Computation of Stress Waves in Solids. Xiao Lin. 317p. 1996. 170.00 (*3-527-40094-X*) Wiley.

Numerical Computation 1 Vol. XVI: Methods, Software, & Analysis, Vol. XVI. C. Ueberhuber. LC 96-46772. (Illus.). 504p. 1997. pap. 44.95 (*3-540-62058-3*) Spr-Verlag.

Numerical Computation 2 Vol. XVI: Methods, Software, & Analysis, Vol. 2. C. Ueberhuber. LC 96-46772. (Illus.). 495p. 1997. pap. 49.95 (*3-540-62057-5*) Spr-Verlag.

Numerical Computer Methods. Ed. by John N. Abelson et al. (Methods in Enzymology Ser.: Vol. 210). (Illus.). 718p. 1992. text 125.00 (*0-12-182111-0*) Acad Pr.

Numerical Computer Methods, Pt. B. Ed. by Michael L. Johnson et al. (Methods in Enzymology Ser.: Vol. 240). (Illus.). 857p. 1994. text. write for info. (*0-12-182141-2*) Acad Pr.

Numerical Computing for Engineers. Harris Schilling. LC 99-28210. (Electrical Engineering Ser.). 715p. 1999. pap. text 92.95 (*0-534-37014-4*) Brooks-Cole.

Numerical Continuation Methods: An Introduction. E. Allgower & K. Georg. Ed. by R. L. Graham et al. (Computational Mathematics Ser.: Vol. 13). (Illus.). xiv, 388p. 1990. 123.95 (*0-387-12760-7*) Spr-Verlag.

Numerical Control, Vol. 1. Ed. by Jack Moorhead. LC 80-52723. (Illus.). 250p. 1980. reprint ed. pap. 77.50 (*0-7837-9733-8*, 206046200001) Bks Demand.

Numerical Control, Vol. 2. Ed. by Jack Moorhead. LC 80-52723. (Illus.). 270p. 1980. reprint ed. pap. 83.70 (*0-7837-9734-6*, 206046200002) Bks Demand.

Numerical Control: Making a New Technology. J. Francis Reintjes. (Oxford Series on Advanced Manufacturing: No. 9). (Illus.). 240p. (C). 1991. text 57.00 (*0-19-506772-X*) OUP.

Numerical Control: Mathematics & Applications. Pierre Bezier. LC 70-39230. (Wiley Series in Computing). 256p. reprint ed. 79.40 (*0-8357-9944-1*, 201490000094) Bks Demand.

Numerical Control: Supplies, Accessories, Programmable Controllers, Computer Numerical Control, Direct Numerical Control, Components, Retrofitting. Society of Manufacturing Engineers Staff. LC 82-62969. (Productivity Equipment Ser.). (Illus.). 417p. reprint ed. pap. 129.30 (*0-8357-3044-1*, 203929900012) Bks Demand.

Numerical Control Explained Two Axis Milling Machine. John Kastius. LC 79-730903. 1978. student ed. 7.00 (*0-8064-0237-7*, 510) Bergwall.

Numerical Control Part Programming. James J. Childs. LC 73-9766. (Illus.). 354p. 1973. 26.95 (*0-8311-1099-6*) Indus Pr.

Numerical Data & Functional Relationships in Science & Technology. B. Predel. Ed. by O. Madelung. (Group IV Ser.: Vol. 5, Subvolume I: Ni-Np . . . Pt-Zr). xxix, 397p. 1998. 1752.00 (*3-540-61712-4*) Spr-Verlag.

***Numerical Data & Functional Relationships in Science & Technology.** B. Predel. Ed. by W. Martienssen. (Landolt-Bornstein Ser.: Group IV, Vol. 5, Subvol. J). (Illus.). xxxi, 365p. 1998. 1839.00 (*3-540-61742-6*) Spr-Verlag.

Numerical Data & Functional Relationships in Science & Technology Group 4, Vol. 8, Pt. E: Physical Chemistry. Landolt-Bornstein. (Thermodynamic Properties of Organic Compounds & Their Mixtures Ser.: Vol. 8). viii, 373p. 1998. 2215.00 incl. cd-rom (*3-540-62510-0*) Spr-Verlag.

Numerical Dating in Stratigraphy, Pt. 1. Ed. by Gilles S. Odin. LC 81-14792. (Wiley-Interscience Publications). 658p. reprint ed. pap. 200.00 (*0-7837-3198-1*, 204324500001) Bks Demand.

Numerical Dating in Stratigraphy, Pt. 2. Ed. by Gilles S. Odin. LC 81-14792. (Wiley-Interscience Publications). 438p. reprint ed. pap. 135.80 (*0-7837-3199-X*, 204324500002) Bks Demand.

Numerical Derivatives & Nonlinear Analysis. Harriet Kagiwada et al. (Mathematical Concepts & Methods in Science & Engineering Ser.: Vol. 31). (Illus.). 212p. (C). 1986. 78.00 (*0-306-42178-X*, Plenum Trade) Perseus Pubng.

Numerical Determination of the Electronic Structure of Atoms, Diatomic & Polyatomic Molecules. Mireille Defranceschi & Joseph Delhalle. (C). 1989. text 186.00 (*0-7923-0170-6*) Kluwer Academic.

Numerical Developments in CFD - 1995. Ed. by M. N. Dhaubhadel et al. LC 95-78824. (1995 ASME/JSME Fluids Engineering Conference Ser.: FED-Vol. 215). 120p. 1995. 76.00 (*0-7918-1470-X*, G00965) ASME.

***Numerical Discources of the Buddha.** Nyanaponika Thera & Bhikkhu Bodhi. 352p. 2000. 65.00 (*0-7425-0404-2*) AltaMira Pr.

***Numerical Discourses of the Buddha: An Anthology of Suttas from the Anguttara Nikaya.** Bhikkhu Bodhi. 352p. 2000. pap. 19.95 (*0-7425-0405-0*) AltaMira Pr.

***Numerical Discourses of the Buddha: An Anthology of Suttas from the Anguttara Nikaya.** Ed. by Bhikkhu Bodhi & Nyanaponika Thera. LC 99-21076. (Sacred Literature Ser.). 344p. 2000. 65.00 (*0-7619-4808-2*) AltaMira Pr.

***Numerical Discourses of the Buddha: An Anthology of Suttas from the Anguttara Nikaya.** Ed. by Bhikkhu Bodhi & Nyanaponika Thera. LC 99-21076. (Sacred Literature Ser.). 344p. 2000. pap. 24.95 (*0-7619-4809-0*) AltaMira Pr.

***Numerical Distance Protection: Principles & Applications.** Gerhard Ziegler. 321p. 2000. 59.95 (*3-89578-142-8*) Wiley.

Numerical Distinction of Sins According to the Franciscan School of the Seventeenth & Eighteenth Centuries. Bonaventure A. Brown. xviii, 114p. 1948. pap. 3.50 (*1-57659-112-3*) Franciscan Inst.

***Numerical Ecology.** 2nd ed. Pierre Legendre. (Developments in Environmental Modelling Ser.). 1998. 150.00 (*0-444-89249-4*) Elsevier.

Numerical Ecology. 2nd ed. Pierre Legendre & Louis Legendre. LC 98-45198. (Developments in Environmental Modelling Ser.: Vol. 20). 853p. 1998. pap. 73.50 (*0-444-89250-8*) Elsevier.

***Numerical Experiments in Stratigraphy: Recent Advances in Stratigraphic & Sedimentologic Computer Simulations.** Ed. by John W. Harbaugh et al. (Special Publications: Vol. 62). (Illus.). 362p. 1999. 170.00 (*1-56576-061-1*) SEPM.

Numerical Exploration of Community Patterns. Laszlo Orloci & O. Wildi. (Ecological Computations Ser.: No. 1). (Illus.). 124p. 1990. 32.00 (*90-5103-037-1*, Pub. by SPB Acad Pub) Balogh.

Numerical Exploration of Community Patterns: A Guide to the Use of Mulva-5. 2nd rev. ed. O. Wildi et al. 171p. 1996. 45.00 (*90-5103-114-9*, Pub. by SPB Acad Pub) Balogh.

***Numerical Formulation for Masonry Creep, Shrinkage & Cracking.** G. P. A. G. van Zijl. (Engineering Mechanisms Ser.: Vol. 01). 90p. 1999. pap. 20.00 (*90-407-1892-X*, Pub. by Delft U Pr) Coronet Bks.

***Numerical Formulation for Moisture Migration in Masonry.** G. P. A. G. van Zijl. (Engineering Mechanisms Ser.: Vol. 02). (Illus.). 90p. 1999. pap. 20.00 (*90-407-1893-8*, Pub. by Delft U Pr) Coronet Bks.

Numerical Fracture Mechanics. M. H. Aliabadi & D. P. Rooke. 280p. 1991. 104.00 (*1-85312-057-X*) Computational Mech MA.

Numerical Fracture Mechanics. M. H. Aliabadi & D. P. Rooke. LC 91-70200. 280p. (C). 1991. text 104.00 (*0-945824-39-4*, 057X) Computational Mech MA.

Numerical Fracture Mechanics. M. H. Aliabadi & D. P. Rooke. (C). 1991. text 185.50 (*0-7923-1175-2*) Kluwer Academic.

Numerical Geology. N. M. Rock. (Lecture Notes in Earth Sciences Ser.: Vol. 18). xi, 427p. 1988. 52.95 (*0-387-50070-7*) Spr-Verlag.

Numerical Grid Generation: Foundations & Applications. J. F. Thompson et al. 504p. 1985. pap. 45.50 (*0-444-00985-X*) P-H.

Numerical Grid Generation in Computational Field Simulations: Proceedings of the 5th International Conference, Held at Mississippi State University, April 1-April 5, 1996. B. K. Soni. LC 98-118536. 1996. write for info. (*0-9651627-1-0*) MSU Eng Res Ctr.

Numerical Grid Methods & Their Application to Schrodinger's Equation: Proceedings of the NATO Advanced Research Workshop on Grid Methods in Atomic & Molecular Quantum Calculations, Corte, Corsica, France, September 27 - October 3, 1992. Ed. by C. Cerjan. LC 93-27854. (NATO Advanced Study Institutes Series C, Mathematical & Physical Sciences: Vol. 412). 272p. (C). 1993. text 174.50 (*0-7923-2423-4*) Kluwer Academic.

Numerical Groundwater Modeling: Flow & Contaminant Migration, 3 disks, Set. William Clarence Walton. (Illus.). 272p. 1989. lib. bdg. 129.00 incl. disk (*0-87371-196-3*, L196) Lewis Pubs.

Numerical Heat Transfer. Tien-Mo Shih. 563p. 1984. pap. 73.95 (*0-89116-919-9*) Hemisp Pub.

Numerical Heat Transfer. 2nd ed. W. J. Minkowycz. text 150.00 (*0-471-34878-3*) Wiley.

Numerical Heat Transfer & Fluid Flow. Suhas V. Patankar. 197p. 1980. 66.95 (*0-89116-522-3*) Hemisp Pub.

Numerical Implementation & Application of Constitutive Models in the Finite Element Method: Proceedings of the ASME International Mechanical Engineering Congress & Exposition, 1995, San Francisco, CA. Ed. by James A. Sherwood & Michael Sheh. LC 96-194148. (1995 ASME International Mechanical Engineering Congress & Exposition Ser.: AMD-Vol. 213/MD-Vol. 63). 160p. 1995. 72.00 (*0-7918-1733-4*, H01015) ASME.

Numerical Index of Air Force Publications, 2 vols., Set. 1995. lib. bdg. 625.99 (*0-8490-8373-7*) Gordon Pr.

Numerical Initial Value Problems in Ordinary Differential Equations. C. William Gear. (Automatic Computation Ser.). (Illus.). 1971. text 72.00 (*0-13-626606-1*) P-H.

Numerical Insights into Dynamic Systems: Interactive Dynamic System Simulation with Microsoft Windows 95 & NT. G. A. Korn. (Numerical Insights Ser.: Vol. 1). 232p. 1998. text 32.00 (*90-5699-156-6*, ECU46, Harwood Acad Pubs) Gordon & Breach.

Numerical Integration: Recent Developments, Software & Applications. Ed. by Terje O. Espelid & Alan Genz. (C). 1992. text 185.00 (*0-7923-1583-9*) Kluwer Academic.

N

An Asterisk (*) at the beginning of an entry indicates that the title is appearing for the first time.

Numerical Integration: Recent Developments, Software & Applications. Ed. by Patrick Keast & Graeme Fairweather. (C). 1987. text 233.00 (*90-277-2514-4*) Kluwer Academic.

Numerical Integration IV: Proceedings of the Conference at the Mathematical Research Institute at Oberwolfach, November 8-14, 1992. Ed. by H. Brass & Gunther Hammerlin. LC 93-5106. (International Series of Numerical Mathematics: Vol. 112). 400p. 1993. 119.00 (*0-8176-2922-X*) Birkhauser.

Numerical Integration of Stochastic Differential Equations. G. N. Milstein. (Mathematics & Its Applications Ser.: Vol. 313). 169p. (C). 1994. text 115.00 (*0-7923-3213-X*) Kluwer Academic.

Numerical Integration on Advanced Computer Systems. Arnold R. Krommer & Christopher W. Ueberhuber. LC 94-33285. 1994. 52.00 (*0-387-58410-2*) Spr-Verlag.

Numerical Integration on Advanced Computer Systems. Arnold R. Krommer & Christopher W. Ueberhuber. (Lecture Notes in Computer Science Ser.: Vol. 848). 341p. 1994. 55.95 (*3-540-58410-2*) Spr-Verlag.

Numerical Integration Three. Ed. by Gunther Hammerlin & H. Brass. (International Series of Numerical Mathematics: Vol. 85). 344p. 1988. 112.00 (*0-8176-2205-5*) Birkhauser.

Numerical Intrigue: The Secret Life of Numbers. Laurence Urdang. LC 84-8095. xxxi, 334p. 1999. write for info. (*0-930454-16-2*) Verbatim Bks.

Numerical Library in C for Scientists & Engineers. H. T. Lau. 816p. 1994. boxed set 94.95 (*0-8493-7376-X*, 7376) CRC Pr.

Numerical Linear Algebra. Willy Brandal. Ed. by Charles O. Christenson & Bryan A. Smith. LC 91-73640. (Illus.). 210p. (Orig.). (C). 1991. pap. 30.00 (*0-914351-05-2*) BCS Assocs.

Numerical Linear Algebra. Lloyd N. Trefethen & David Bau, III. LC 96-52458. (Miscellaneous Bks.: No. 50). xii, 361p. 1997. pap. text 37.00 (*0-89871-361-7*, OT 50) Soc Indus-Appl Math.

Numerical Linear Algebra: Proceedings of the Conference in Numerical Linear Algebra & Scientific Computation, Kent (Ohio), March 13-14, 1992. Ed. by Lothar Reichel et al. LC 93-8437. ix, 199p. 1993. lib. bdg. 95.95 (*3-11-013784-4*) De Gruyter.

Numerical Linear Algebra & Applications. Biswa N. Datta. LC 94-30071. 750p. 1995. pap. 110.95 (*0-534-17466-3*) Brooks-Cole.

Numerical Linear Algebra & Optimisation. P. G. Ciarlet. (Cambridge Texts in Applied Mathematics Ser.: No. 2). 452p. 1989. pap. text 44.95 (*0-521-33984-7*) Cambridge U Pr.

Numerical Linear Algebra & Optimization, Vol. 1. Philip E. Gill et al. (Illus.). 448p. (C). 1991. 46.95 (*0-201-12649-4*) Addison-Wesley.

Numerical Linear Algebra, Digital Signal Processing & Parallel Algorithms. Ed. by Gene H. Golub & Paul Van Dooren. (NATO ASI Series F: Computer & Systems Sciences, Special Programme AET: Vol. 70). (Illus.). xiii, 729p. 1991. 172.95 (*0-387-52300-6*) Spr-Verlag.

Numerical Linear Algebra for High-Performance Computers. Jack Dongarra et al. LC 98-44444. (Software, Environments & Tools Ser.: Vol. 7). (Illus.). xviii, 342p. 1998. pap. 37.00 (*0-89871-428-1*, BKSE0007) Soc Indus-Appl Math.

Numerical Linear Algebra Techniques for Systems & Control. Ed. by R. V. Patel et al. LC 93-27006. (Illus.). 736p. 1993. text 99.95 (*0-7803-0443-8*, PC3400) Inst Electrical.

Numerical Linear Algebra with Applications in Statistics. J. E. Gentle. Ed. by J. Chambers et al. (Statistics & Computing Ser.). 232p. 1998. 59.95 (*0-387-98542-5*) Spr-Verlag.

Numerical List of Manufactured & Mineral Products. 1995. lib. bdg. 255.99 (*0-8490-8362-1*) Gordon Pr.

Numerical Lists & Schedule of Volumes of the U. S. Congressional Serial Set: 73rd Congress Through the 96th Congress, 3 vols., Set. Carol J. Gray & Bernard D. Reams, Jr. LC 34-28260. 1983. reprint ed. lib. bdg. 195.00 (*0-89941-277-7*, 303040) W S Hein.

Numerical Math & Computing. 2nd ed. Ward Cheney & David Kincaid. LC 84-27420. (Math). 512p. (C). 1985. mass mkt. 59.50 (*0-534-04356-9*) Brooks-Cole.

Numerical Math & Computing. 3rd ed. Cheney. (Mathematics Ser.). 1994. mass mkt., teacher ed. write for info. (*0-534-20113-X*) Brooks-Cole.

Numerical Mathematical Analysis. 6th ed. James B. Scarborough. 608p. 1966. 65.00 (*0-8018-0575-9*) Johns Hopkins.

Numerical Mathematics. Gunther Hammerlin & K. H. Hoffmann. Ed. by J. H. Ewing et al. (Undergraduate Texts in Mathematics Ser.). (Illus.). xi, 424p. 1991. 49.95 (*0-387-97494-6*) Spr-Verlag.

*__Numerical Mathematics.__ Alfio Quarteroni et al. LC 99-59414. (Texts in Applied Mathematics Ser.). 677p. 2000. 59.95 (*0-387-98959-5*) Spr-Verlag.

Numerical Mathematics: A Laboratory Approach. Shlomo Breuer & Gideon Zwas. LC 92-36528. (Illus.). 283p. (C). 1993. text 54.95 (*0-521-44040-8*) Cambridge U Pr.

Numerical Mathematics: Proceedings of the 1st China-Japan Seminar. Zhong-Ci Shi & T. Ushijima. 300p. 1993. text 95.00 (*981-02-1340-9*) World Scientific Pub.

Numerical Mathematics: Theory & Computer Applications. 3rd ed. Carl-Erik Froberg. (C). 1985. 49.95 (*0-8053-2530-1*) Addison-Wesley.

Numerical Mathematics & Computing. 3rd ed. Ward Cheney & David Kincaid. LC 93-43850. 1994. mass mkt. 67.50 (*0-534-20112-1*) Brooks-Cole.

Numerical Mathematics, Singapore, 1988. Ed. by Ravi P. Agarwal & Y. M. Chow. (International Series of Numerical Mathematics: Vol. 86). 540p. 1988. 142.00 (*0-8176-2255-1*) Birkhauser.

Numerical Method of Lines: Integration of Partial Differential Equations. William E. Schiesser. (Illus.). 326p. 1991. text 88.00 (*0-12-624130-9*) Acad Pr.

Numerical Methods. Wolfgang Boehm & Hartmut Prautzsch. (Illus.). 196p. (C). 1993. pap. text 39.95 (*1-56881-020-2*) AK Peters.

Numerical Methods. J. Douglas Faires. (Mathematics Ser.). 1993. teacher ed. 24.25 (*0-534-93295-9*) Brooks-Cole.

Numerical Methods. D. Greenspan & P. Rozsa. (Colloquia Mathematica Societatis Janos Bolyai Ser.: Vol. 59). 378p. 1991. 234.50 (*0-444-98694-4*, North Holland) Elsevier.

Numerical Methods. Robert W. Hornbeck. (Illus.). 320p. (C). 1982. pap. text 50.00 (*0-13-626614-2*) P-H.

Numerical Methods. Ed. by V. Pereyra. (Lecture Notes in Mathematics Ser.: Vol. 1005). 296p. 1983. 42.95 (*0-387-12334-2*) Spr-Verlag.

Numerical Methods. E. A. Volkov. 250p. 1989. 76.95 (*1-56032-011-7*) Hemisp Pub.

Numerical Methods. 2nd ed. Burden. LC 97-47340. 511p. 1998. mass mkt. 98.95 (*0-534-35187-5*) Brooks-Cole.

Numerical Methods. 2nd ed. Burden. 1998. pap. 25.00 (*0-534-35185-9*) Brooks-Cole.

Numerical Methods: Study Manual. Paul Hultquist. (Illus.). 350p. (C). 1988. pap. text 10.75 (*0-8053-4653-8*) Addison-Wesley.

Numerical Methods & Analysis. James L. Buchanan & Peter R. Turner. 640p. (C). 1992. 70.31 (*0-07-008717-2*) McGraw.

Numerical Methods & Constitutive Modelling in Geomechanics. C. S. Desai & G. Gioda. (CISM Ser.: Vol. 311). (Illus.). v, 407p. 1990. 86.95 (*0-387-82215-1*) Spr-Verlag.

Numerical Methods & Error Bounds. Jurgen Herzberger. Ed. by Gotz Alefeld. 305p. 1996. pap. 94.95 (*3-527-40076-1*) Wiley.

Numerical Methods & Error Bounds: Proceedings of the IMACS-GAMM International Symposium on Numerical Methods & Errors Bounds Held in Oldenburg, Germany, July 9-12, 1995. Ed. by Gotz Alefeld & Jurgen Herzberger. (Mathematical Research Ser.: Vol. 89). (Illus.). 305p. 1996. pap. 83.95 (*3-05-501696-3*, Wiley-VCH) Wiley.

Numerical Methods & Inequalities in Functional Spaces: Proceedings. Ed. by V. N. Faddeeva. (Proceedings of the Steklov Institute of Mathematics Ser.: Vol. 84). 194p. 1968. pap. 60.00 (*0-8218-1884-8*, STEKLO/84) Am Math.

Numerical Methods & Scientific Computing: Using Software Libraries for Problem Solving. Norbert Kockler. LC 94-8064. (Illus.). 346p. 1994. text 65.00 (*0-19-859698-7*, Clarendon Pr) OUP.

Numerical Methods & Software Tools in Industrial Mathematics. Ed. by Morten Daehlen & Aslak Tveito. LC 97-185. (Illus.). 400p. 1997. 69.95 (*0-8176-3973-X*) Birkhauser.

Numerical Methods & Software Tools in Industrial Mathematics. Morten Dhlen & Aslak Tveito. LC 97-185. 416p. 1997. write for info. (*3-7643-3973-X*) Birkhauser.

Numerical Methods Based on Sinc & Analytic Functions. Frank Stenger. LC 93-9403. (Computational Mathematics Ser.: Vol. 20). 1993. 89.95 (*0-387-94008-1*) Spr-Verlag.

*__Numerical Methods for Bifurcations of Dynamical Equilibria.__ Willy J. F. Govaerts. LC 99-44796. (Miscellaneous Titles in Applied Mathematics Ser.: No. 66). xxii, 362p. 2000. pap. 61.00 (*0-89871-442-7*, OT0066) Soc Indus-Appl Math.

*__Numerical Methods for Bifurction Problems & Large-Scale Dynamical Systems.__ Ed. by E. Doedel & L. S. Tuckerman. LC 99-88039. (Illus.). 496p. 2000. 89.95 (*0-387-98970-6*) Spr-Verlag.

Numerical Methods for Conservation Laws. Randall J. LeVeque. (Lectures in Mathematics ETH Zurich: Vol. 1). 232p. 1990. 24.50 (*0-8176-2464-3*) Birkhauser.

Numerical Methods for Conservation Laws. 2nd ed. R. J. Le Veque. (Lectures in Mathematics ETH Zurich). 232p. 1996. 34.50 (*0-8176-2723-5*) Birkhauser.

Numerical Methods for Differential Equations: A Computational Approach. John R. Dormand. Ed. by Alan Jeffrey. (Library of Engineering Mathematics). 384p. 1996. lib. bdg. 94.95 incl. 3.5 hd, 5.25 hd, 3.5 ld (*0-8493-9433-3*, 9433) CRC Pr.

Numerical Methods for Differential Equations: Fundamental Concepts for Scientific & Engineering Applications. Michael A. Celia & William G. Gray. 464p. (C). 1991. 69.80 (*0-13-626961-3*, 540801) P-H.

Numerical Methods for Differential Equations & Applications. Liviu Ixaru. 1984. text 232.00 (*90-277-1597-1*) Kluwer Academic.

Numerical Methods for Elliptic Problems with Singularities: Boundary Methods & Non-Conforming Combinations. Z. C. Li. 276p. (C). 1990. text 48.00 (*981-02-0292-X*) World Scientific Pub.

Numerical Methods for Engine-Airframe Integration. Ed. by S. N. Murthy & G. C. Paynter. LC 86-10920. (PAAS Ser.: Vol. 102). (Illus.). 544p. 1986. 79.95 (*0-930403-09-6*, V-102) AIAA.

Numerical Methods for Engineering Application. 2nd ed. Joel H. Ferziger. LC 97-35864. 378p. 1998. 69.95 (*0-471-11621-1*, Wiley-Interscience) Wiley.

Numerical Methods for Engineering Applications. Edward R. Champion, Jr. LC 93-1189. (Mechanical Engineering Ser.: Vol. 84). (Illus.). 464p. 1993. text 189.00 (*0-8247-9135-5*) Dekker.

Numerical Methods for Engineers. Bilal M. Ayyub & Richard H. McCuen. LC 95-20132. 362p. 1995. 97.00 (*0-13-337361-4*, Pub. by P-H) S&S Trade.

Numerical Methods for Engineers. D. V. Griffiths. 352p. 1991. boxed set 89.95 (*0-8493-8610-1*, QA) CRC Pr.

Numerical Methods for Engineers. 2nd ed. Steven C. Chapra. LC 88-523. (C). 1988. text 27.50 (*0-07-010674-6*) McGraw.

Numerical Methods for Engineers. 3rd ed. Steve Chapra & Ray Canale. 800p. (C). 1998. 80.50 (*0-07-561254-2*) McGraw-Hill Prof.

Numerical Methods for Engineers: With Programming & Software Applications. 3rd ed. Steven C. Chapra & Raymond P. Canale. LC 97-37136. 1997. write for info. (*0-07-010938-9*) McGraw.

Numerical Methods for Engineers & Scientists. J. Douglas Faires & Richard L. Burden. LC 92-37392. 512p. 1993. mass mkt. 73.50 (*0-534-93136-7*) PWS Pubs.

Numerical Methods for Engineers & Scientists. Joe Hoffman. 704p. (C). 1992. 92.50 (*0-07-029213-2*) McGraw.

Numerical Methods for Engineers & Scientists. Harbans S. Sidhu. (Illus.). 352p. (C). 1992. pap. text 50.00 (*0-9633826-0-8*) H S Sidhu.

Numerical Methods for Engineers & Scientists: A Students' Course Book. Avi C. Bajpai et al. LC QA0297.B32. (Series of Programmes on Mathematics for Engineers & Scientists). 392p. reprint ed. pap. 121.60 (*0-7837-4021-2*, 204385100011) Bks Demand.

*__Numerical Methods for Engineers with Mathcad.__ Khyruddin Akbar Ansari. LC 99-69302. (Illus.). vi, 349p. 1999. 90.00 (*0-9645727-6-1*, Ulyssian Pubns) Pine Orchard.

Numerical Methods for Engineers with Personal Computer Applications. 2nd rev. ed. Steven C. Chapra & Raymond P. Canale. (C). 1988. text 67.74 (*0-07-909944-0*) McGraw.

Numerical Methods for Euler Equations of Fluid Dynamics. Ed. by F. Angrand et al. LC 85-62674. (Proceedings in Applied Mathematics Ser.: No. 21). xii, 508p. 1985. text 56.25 (*0-89871-200-9*) Soc Indus-Appl Math.

Numerical Methods for Fluid Dynamics II. 2nd ed. K. W. Morton & M. J. Baines. (Institute of Mathematics & Its Applications Conference Series, New Ser.: New Series 7). (Illus.). 679p. 1986. 95.00 (*0-19-853610-0*) OUP.

Numerical Methods for Fluid Dynamics III. Ed. by K. W. Morton & M. J. Baines. (Institute of Mathematics & Its Applications Conference Series, New Ser.: New Series 17). (Illus.). 552p. 1989. 98.00 (*0-19-853632-1*) OUP.

Numerical Methods for Fluid Dynamics IV. Ed. by M. J. Baines & K. W. Morton. (Illus.). 622p. 1994. text 115.00 (*0-19-853696-8*) OUP.

Numerical Methods for Fluid Dynamics V. K. W. Morton & M. J. Baines. LC 95-49215. (Illus.). 650p. (C). 1996. text 90.00 (*0-19-851480-8*, Clarendon Pr) OUP.

Numerical Methods for Fluid Transient Analysis: Presented at Applied Mechanics, Bioengineering & Fluids Engineering Conference, Houston, Texas, June 20-22, 1983. Applied Mechanics, Bioengineering & Fluids Enginee. Ed. by C. S. Martin & M. Hanif Chaudhry. LC 83-71317. (FED Ser.: Vol. 4). 87p. pap. 30.00 (*0-7837-0202-7*, 204049800017) Bks Demand.

Numerical Methods for Free Boundary Problems. Ed. by P. Neittaanmaki. (International Series of Numerical Mathematics: Vol. 99). 439p. 1991. 59.00 (*3-7643-2641-7*) Birkhauser.

Numerical Methods for Free Boundary Problems. Ed. by Pekka Neittaanmaki. (International Series of Numerical Mathematics: Vol. 99). xv, 439p. 1991. 137.00 (*0-8176-2641-7*) Birkhauser.

Numerical Methods for Geophysical Fluid Dynamics. D. R. Durran. Ed. by J. E. Marsden & L. Sirov. LC 98-24739. (Applied Mathematical Sciences Ser.). 460p. 1998. 49.95 (*0-387-98376-7*) Spr-Verlag.

Numerical Methods for Grid Equations, 2 vols., Set. E. S. Nikolaev & A. A. Samarskii. 744p. 1989. 415.50 (*0-8176-2278-0*) Birkhauser.

Numerical Methods for Grid Equations, 2 vols., Vol. 1. E. S. Nikolaev & A. A. Samarskii. 242p. 1989. 165.00 (*0-8176-2276-4*) Birkhauser.

Numerical Methods for Grid Equations, 2 vols., Vol. 2. E. S. Nikolaev & A. A. Samarskii. 502p. 1989. 313.50 (*0-8176-2277-2*) Birkhauser.

Numerical Methods for Lattice Quantum Many-Body Problems. Douglas J. Scalapino. 1998. write for info. (*0-201-15692-X*) Addison-Wesley.

*__Numerical Methods for Lattice Quantum Many-Body Problems.__ Ed. by Douglas J. Scalapino. (Frontiers in Physics Ser.). 400p. 1999. 70.00 (*0-7382-0119-7*, Pub. by Perseus Pubng) HarpC.

Numerical Methods for Least Squares Problems. Ake Bjorck. LC 96-3908. (Miscellaneous Bks.: No. 51). xvii, 408p. 1996. pap. 51.00 (*0-89871-360-9*, OT51) Soc Indus-Appl Math.

Numerical Methods for Linear Control Systems & Analysis. Datta. 450p. 1997. write for info. (*0-12-203590-9*) Acad Pr.

Numerical Methods for Non-Newtonian Fluid Dynamics. Ed. by G. C. Vradis & D. A. Siginer. LC 94-71258. (Fluid Engineering Division Conference Ser.: Vol. 179). 111p. 1994. pap. 35.00 (*0-7918-1362-2*) ASME.

Numerical Methods for Nonlinear Algebraic Equations. Ed. by Philip Rabinowitz. LC 78-115963. (Illus.). xii, 200p. 1970. pap. text 77.00 (*0-677-14235-8*) Gordon & Breach.

Numerical Methods for Nonlinear Variational Problems. Roland Glowinski. (Computational Physics Ser.). (Illus.). 475p. 1984. 168.95 (*0-387-12434-9*) Spr-Verlag.

Numerical Methods for Nuclear Reactor Calculations. Gurii I. Marchuk. LC 59-9229. (Soviet Journal of Atomic Energy: Nos. 3-4, 1958). 300p. reprint ed. pap. 93.00 (*0-608-30741-6*, 202065300018) Bks Demand.

*__Numerical Methods for Optimal Control Problems with State Constraints.__ R. Pytlak. LC 99-16712. (Lecture Notes in Mathematics Ser.: Vol. 1707). (Illus.). xv, 215p. 1999. pap. 41.00 (*3-540-66214-6*) Spr-Verlag.

Numerical Methods for Ordinary Differential Equations. Ed. by A. Bellen et al. (Lecture Notes in Mathematics Ser.: Vol. 1386). vii, 136p. 1989. 29.95 (*0-387-51478-3*) Spr-Verlag.

Numerical Methods for Ordinary Differential Systems: The Initial Value Problem. J. D. Lambert. LC 90-28513. 304p. 1991. 99.95 (*0-471-92990-5*) Wiley.

*__Numerical Methods for Partial Differential Equations.__ G. A. Evans et al. (Undergraduate Mathematics Ser.). (Illus.). xii, 290p. 1999. pap. 36.95 (*3-540-76125-X*) Spr-Verlag.

Numerical Methods for Partial Differential Equations. Ed. by Zhu You-lan & Guo Ben-yu. (Lecture Notes in Mathematics Ser.: Vol. 1297). 244p. 1988. 44.95 (*0-387-18730-8*) Spr-Verlag.

Numerical Methods for Partial Differential Equations. 3rd ed. William F. Ames. (Computer Science & Scientific Computing Ser.). (Illus.). 451p. 1992. text 71.00 (*0-12-056761-X*) Acad Pr.

Numerical Methods for Partial Differential Equations: Proceedings of 2nd Conference. L. A. Ying & B. Y. Guo. 200p. 1992. text 81.00 (*981-02-0929-0*) World Scientific Pub.

Numerical Methods for Physics. 2nd ed. Garcia. (C). 2000. pap. text. write for info. (*0-13-016129-2*) P-H.

Numerical Methods for Physics. 2nd ed. Alejandro Garcia. LC 99-28552. 423p. (C). 1999. 76.00 (*0-13-906744-2*, Macmillan Coll) P-H.

Numerical Methods for Polymeric Systems. Ed. by Stuart G. Whittington. LC 98-7728. (IMA Volumes in Mathematics & Its Applications Ser.: Vol. 102). (Illus.). 237p. 1998. 69.95 (*0-387-98557-3*) Spr-Verlag.

Numerical Methods for Problems in Infinite Domains. Dan Givoli. LC 92-15438. (Studies in Applied Mechanics: Vol. 33). xvi,300p. 1992. 191.00 (*0-444-88820-9*) Elsevier.

Numerical Methods for Problems with Moving Fronts. Bruce A. Finlayson. LC 92-93277. 605p. (C). 1992. text 60.00 (*0-9631765-0-1*) Ravenna Pk.

Numerical Methods for Scientists & Engineers. 2nd ed. Richard W. Hamming. (Illus.). 721p. 1987. reprint ed. pap. 15.95 (*0-486-65241-6*) Dover.

Numerical Methods for Scientists & Engineers Using Matlab. Garold G. Borse. LC 96-39300. 656p. 1996. mass mkt. 94.95 (*0-534-93822-1*) PWS Pubs.

Numerical Methods for Shallow-Water Flow. Cornelis B. Vreugdenhil. LC 94-32557. (Water Science & Technology Library). 276p. (C). 1994. text 156.00 (*0-7923-3164-8*) Kluwer Academic.

Numerical Methods for Simulation of Industrial Metal Forming Processes. Ed. by M. J. Saran et al. (CED Series, Vol. 5: AMD: Vol. 156). 112p. 1992. 37.50 (*0-7918-1133-6*, G00777) ASME.

Numerical Methods for Singularly Perturbed Differential Equations: Convection-Diffusion & Flow Problems. H. G. Roos et al. LC 96-1184. (Springer Series in Computational Mathematics: Vol. 24). (Illus.). 368p. 1996. 98.00 (*3-540-60718-8*) Spr-Verlag.

Numerical Methods for Stiff Equations & Singular Perturbation Problems. Willard L. Miranker. (Mathematics & Its Applications Ser.: No. 5). 216p. 1980. text 104.50 (*90-277-1107-0*) Kluwer Academic.

Numerical Methods for Stochastic Control Problems in Continuous Time. Harold J. Kushner & Paul Dupuis. LC 92-10350. (Applications of Mathematics Ser.: Vol. 24). (Illus.). ix, 439p. 1992. 65.95 (*0-387-97834-8*) Spr-Verlag.

Numerical Methods for Stochastic Processes. Nicolas Bouleau & Dominique Lepingle. LC 93-10302. (Series in Probability & Mathematical Statistics). 384p. 1993. 115.00 (*0-471-54641-0*) Wiley.

Numerical Methods for the Simulation of Multi-Phase & Complex Flow. Ed. by T. M. Verheggen. (Lecture Notes in Physics Ser.: Vol. 398). 153p. 1992. 59.95 (*0-387-55278-2*) Spr-Verlag.

Numerical Methods for the Solution of Ill-Posed Problems. A. N. Tikhonov. (Mathematics & Its Applications Ser.). 264p. 1995. text 137.00 (*0-7923-3583-X*) Kluwer Academic.

Numerical Methods for Two-Point Boundary Value Problems. Herbert B. Keller. (Illus.). 192p. 1993. reprint ed. pap. 9.95 (*0-486-66925-4*) Dover.

Numerical Methods for Unconstrained Optimization & Nonlinear Equations. J. E. Dennis, Jr. & Robert B. Schnabel. LC 95-51776. (Classics in Applied Mathematics Ser.: Vol. 16). xvi, 378p. 1996. pap. 37.00 (*0-89871-364-1*) Soc Indus-Appl Math.

Numerical Methods for Wave Propagation: Selected Contributions from the Workshop Held in Manchester, U. K. Containing the Harten Memorial Lecture. E. F. Toro & J. F. Clarke. LC 98-22284. (Fluid Mechanics & Its Applications Ser.). 1998. 170.00 (*0-7923-5125-8*) Kluwer Academic.

Numerical Methods Geomechanics 5th Edition, Vol. 1. 1985. 149.00 (*90-6191-581-3*) Ashgate Pub Co.

Numerical Methods in Applied Sciences. Ed. by Wei Cai et al. (Illus.). 296p. 1996. 45.45 (*1-880132-15-X*) Sci Pr NY.

Numerical Methods in Approximation Theory, Vol. 9. Ed. by D. Braess & Larry L. Schumaker. LC 92-34850. (International Series of Numerical Mathematics: Vol. 105). xiv, 357p. 1992. 122.00 (*0-8176-2746-4*) Birkhauser.

Numerical Methods in Coupled Systems. fac. ed. Ed. by R. W. B. Lewis et al. LC 82-24809. (Wiley Series in Numerical Methods in Engineering). (Illus.). 632p. 1984. reprint ed. pap. 196.00 (*0-608-00958-X*, 206180600011) Bks Demand.

Numerical Methods in Economics. Kenneth L. Judd. LC 98-13591. (Illus.). 644p. 1998. 55.00 (*0-262-10071-1*) MIT Pr.

N

An Asterisk (*) at the beginning of an entry indicates that the title is appearing for the first time.

***Numerical Methods in Electromagnetism.** Sheppard J. Salon. (Electromagnetics Ser.). (Illus.). 1999. 79.95 (*0-12-615760-X*) Acad Pr.

Numerical Methods in Engineering, 2 vols. Ed. by R. Gruber et al. xxvi, 1426p. 1989. 446.00 (*0-387-51589-5*) Spr-Verlag.

Numerical Methods in Engineering & Applied Science: Numbers Are Fun. Bruce Irons & Nigel Shrive. (Mathematics & Its Applications Ser.). 248p. 1987. text 41.95 (*0-470-20803-1*) P-H.

Numerical Methods in Engineering Practice. Amir W. Al-Khafaji & John R. Tooley. (Illus.). 656p. 1995. text 76.95 (*0-03-001757-2*) OUP.

Numerical Methods in Engineering Practice. Amir W. Al-Khafaji & John R. Tooley. 642p. 1986. student ed. write for info. (*0-03-001753-X*) SCP.

Numerical Methods in Engineering Simulation. Ed. by M. Cerrolaza et al. LC 96-83299. 424p. 1996. 175.00 (*1-85312-475-3*, 4753) Computational Mech MA.

Numerical Methods in Engineering & Science. Graham De Vahl Davis. (Illus.). 288p. 1986. text 70.00 (*0-04-515002-8*); pap. text 24.95 (*0-04-515003-6*) Routledge.

Numerical Methods in Finance. Ed. by L. C. Rogers & D. Talay. 336p. 1997. text 57.95 (*0-521-57354-8*) Cambridge U Pr.

Numerical Methods in Fluid Dynamics. Ed. by F. Brezzi. (Lecture Notes in Mathematics Ser.: Vol. 1127). vii, 333p. 1985. 46.95 (*0-387-15225-3*) Spr-Verlag.

Numerical Methods in Fluid Dynamics. M. Holt. (Computational Physics Ser.). (Illus.). 290p. 1989. 59.95 (*0-387-12799-2*) Spr-Verlag.

Numerical Methods in Fluid Dynamics: 8th International Conference Proceedings, Aachen, FRG, 1982. Ed. by E. Krause. (Lecture Notes in Physics Ser.: Vol. 170). 569p. 1982. 55.95 (*0-387-11948-5*) Spr-Verlag.

Numerical Methods in Fluid Mechanics. Alain P. Vincent. LC 98-15581. (CRM Proceedings & Lecture Notes Ser.: Vol. 16). xiv, 199p. 1998. pap. 59.00 (*0-8218-0813-3*, CRMP/16) Am Math.

Numerical Methods in Fluids Dynamics. Ed. by Hans J. Wirz & J. J. Smolderen. LC 77-18145. (Series in Thermal & Fluids Engineering). 415p. reprint ed. pap. 128.70 (*0-608-10247-4*, 201669700005) Bks Demand.

Numerical Methods in Geomechanics. Ed. by J. B. Martins. 1982. text 226.00 (*90-277-1461-4*) Kluwer Academic.

Numerical Methods in Geomechanics: Innsbruck, 1988, 4 vols. 1988. 511.00 (*90-6191-809-X*, Pub. by A A Balkema) Ashgate Pub Co.

Numerical Methods in Geomechanics: Papers Presented & Discussed at the Second International Conference on Numerical Methods in Geomechanics Held at Virginia Polytechnic Institute & State University, Blacksburg, VA., June, 1976, 3 vols., 1. LC 76-151157. 606p. reprint ed. pap. 187.90 (*0-608-11357-3*, 201955100001) Bks Demand.

Numerical Methods in Geomechanics: Papers Presented & Discussed at the Second International Conference on Numerical Methods in Geomechanics Held at Virginia Polytechnic Institute & State University, Blacksburg, VA., June, 1976, 3 vols., 2. LC 76-151157. 687p. reprint ed. pap. 200.00 (*0-608-11358-1*, 201955100002) Bks Demand.

Numerical Methods in Geomechanics: Papers Presented & Discussed at the Second International Conference on Numerical Methods in Geomechanics Held at Virginia Polytechnic Institute & State University, Blacksburg, VA., June, 1976, 3 vols., 3. LC 76-151157. 270p. reprint ed. pap. 83.70 (*0-608-11359-X*, 201955100003) Bks Demand.

Numerical Methods in Geomechanics: Proceedings of the International Conference, Aachen, 2-6 April 1979, 4 vols., Set. Ed. by W. Wittke. 1580p. (C). 1979. text 621.00 (*90-6191-040-4*, Pub. by A A Balkema) Ashgate Pub Co.

Numerical Methods in Geomechanics 6th Edition, Vol. 1. 1988. 129.00 (*90-6191-810-3*) Ashgate Pub Co.

Numerical Methods in Geomechanics 6th Edition, Vol. 2. 1988. 100.00 (*90-6191-811-1*) Ashgate Pub Co.

Numerical Methods in Geomechanics 6th Edition, Vol. 3. 1988. 129.00 (*90-6191-812-X*) Ashgate Pub Co.

Numerical Methods in Geomechanics 6th Edition, Vol. 4. 1989. 129.00 (*90-6191-830-8*) Ashgate Pub Co.

Numerical Methods in Geomechanics, Nagoya, 1985: Proceedings of the 5th International Conference, Nagoya, 1-5 April 1985, 4 vols. Ed. by T. Kawamoto & Yoski H. Ichikawa. 1960p. (C). 1985. text 576.00 (*90-6191-580-5*, Pub. by A A Balkema) Ashgate Pub Co.

Numerical Methods in Geotechnical Engineering: Proceedings of the 3rd European Conference, Manchester, 7-9 September 1994. Ed. by I. M. Smith. (Illus.). 444p. (C). 1994. text 123.00 (*90-5410-510-0*, Pub. by A A Balkema) Ashgate Pub Co.

***Numerical Methods in Geotechnical Engineering: Recent Developments: Proceedings of Sessions of Geo-Denver 2000, August 5-8, 2000, Denver, Colorado.** Geo-Denver 2000 Staff et al. LC 00-34250. (Geotechnical Special Publication Ser.). 2000. pap. write for info. (*0-7844-0502-6*) Am Soc Civil Eng.

Numerical Methods in Heat Transfer, Vol. 1. Roland W. Lewis. LC 80-49973. (Wiley Series in Numerical Methods in Engineering). 552p. reprint ed. pap. 171.20 (*0-7837-6553-3*, 204413100001) Bks Demand.

Numerical Methods in Heat Transfer, Vol. 3. Roland W. Lewis. LC 80-49973. (Wiley Series in Numerical Methods in Engineering). (Illus.). 308p. reprint ed. pap. 95.50 (*0-7837-4391-2*, 204413100003) Bks Demand.

Numerical Methods in Mechanics. C. Conca. (Pitman Research Notes in Mathematics Ser.). 1997. pap. 47.95 (*0-582-31320-1*, Pub. by Addison-Wesley) Longman.

Numerical Methods in Multibody Dynamics. Edda Eich-Soellner & Claus Fhuhrer. LC 98-200281. (European Consortium for Mathematics in Industry Ser.). 290 p. 1998. write for info. (*3-519-02601-5*) B G Teubner.

Numerical Methods in Multiphase Flows, 1994. Ed. by T. C. Crowe. LC 90-55409. (Fluids Engineering Division Conference Ser.: Vol. 185). 315p. 1994. pap. text 55.00 (*0-7918-1368-1*) ASME.

Numerical Methods in Offshore Engineering. fac. ed. Ed. by O. C. Zienkiewicz et al. LC 77-12565. (Wiley Series in Numberical Methods in Engineering). 594p. pap. 184.20 (*0-7837-7370-6*, 204718000005) Bks Demand.

Numerical Methods in Offshore Piling: 3rd International Conference, Nantes, May 21-22, 1986. Institute Francais du Petrole & Laboratoire des Po. (Colloques & Seminaires Ser.: Vol. 43). (Illus.). 544p. (C). 1986. 605.00 (*2-7108-0500-6*, Pub. by Edits Technip) Enfield Pubs NH.

Numerical Methods in Quarternary Pollen Analysis. H. J. Birks & A. D. Gordon. 1985. text 142.00 (*0-12-101250-6*) Acad Pr.

Numerical Methods in Structural Mechanics. Zdenek Bittnar & Jiri Sejnoha. LC 96-14306. 480p. 1996. 72.00 (*0-7844-0170-5*) Am Soc Civil Eng.

Numerical Methods in the Biomedical Sciences. E. H. Twizell. (Mathematics & Its Applications Ser.). 300p. 1988. text 73.95 (*0-470-21002-8*) P-H.

Numerical Methods in the Theory of Neutron Transport. Gurii I. Marchuk & V. I. Lebedev. xx, 601p. 1986. text 421.00 (*3-7186-0182-6*); pap. text 75.00 (*3-7186-0210-5*) Gordon & Breach.

Numerical Methods of Approximation Theory. Ed. by Lothar Collatz et al. (International Series of Numerical Mathematics: No. 81). 264p. 1987. 84.00 (*0-8176-1855-4*) Birkhauser.

Numerical Methods of Approximation Theory, Vol. 7. Ed. by Lothar Collatz et al. (International Series of Numerical Mathematics: Vol. 67). (ENG & GER.). 148p. 1984. 42.50 (*3-7643-1580-6*) Birkhauser.

Numerical Methods of DSP Systems in C. Don Morgan. LC 97-1744. 352p. 1997. pap. 54.99 (*0-471-13232-2*) Wiley.

Numerical Methods of Geomechanics, 1982: Fourth International Conference, Edmonton, Canada, 31. 05-4.06 1982, 3 vols. Ed. by Z. Eisenstein. 1302p. (C). 1982. text 621.00 (*90-6191-246-6*, Pub. by A A Balkema) Ashgate Pub Co.

Numerical Methods of Nonlinear Programming: Implementations. Ed. by C. Richter et al. (Mathematical Research Ser.). 135p. 1991. 29.00 (*3-05-500883-9*, Pub. by Akademie Verlag) Wiley.

***Numerical Methods of Statistics.** John F. Monahan. (Cambridge Series in Statistical & Probabilistic Mathematics: Vol. 7). (Illus.). 450p. 2001. write for info. (*0-521-79168-5*) Cambridge U Pr.

Numerical Methods Programming Projects Book. Thomas A. Grandine. (Illus.). 154p. 1990. pap. text 22.50 (*0-19-853387-X*) OUP.

Numerical Methods Software: Computational Software Library (CSL) Shoichiro Nakamura. 178p. (Orig.). (C). 1990. pap. text 35.00 (*0-9626943-8-X*) Compu Methods.

Numerical Methods, Software, & Analysis. 2nd ed. John R. Rice. (Illus.). 720p. 1992. text 71.00 (*0-12-587755-2*) Acad Pr.

Numerical Methods That Work. rev. ed. Forman S. Acton. (Spectrum Ser.). 560p. 1990. pap. text 41.95 (*0-88385-450-3*, NMTW) Math Assn.

Numerical Methods Using MATLAB. George Linfield & John Penny. 250p. 1995. pap. 50.00 (*0-13-030966-4*) P-H.

Numerical Methods Using MATLAB. 2nd ed. G. R. Lindfield. LC 99-36536. 482p. 1999. pap. 56.00 (*0-13-012641-1*) Allyn.

Numerical Methods with FORTRAN IV Case Studies. William S. Dorn & Daniel D. McCracken. LC 86-20125. 462p. (C). 1987. reprint ed. text 53.95 (*0-89874-982-4*) Krieger.

Numerical Methods with MATLAB. 3rd ed. Mathews. 680p. 1998. 89.33 (*0-13-270042-5*) P-H.

***Numerical Methods with Matlab: Implementations & Applications.** Gerald W. Recktenwald. LC 00-42758. 2000. write for info. (*0-13-030802-1*) P-H.

Numerical Modeling in Applied Physics & Astrophysics. Richard L. Bowers. 512p. 1991. 75.00 (*0-86720-123-1*) Jones & Bartlett.

Numerical Modeling in Combustion. Ed. by T. J. Chung. (Series in Computational Methods & Physical Processes in Mechanics & Thermal Sciences). 532p. 1993. 229.00 (*0-89116-822-2*) Hemisp Pub.

Numerical Modeling of Explosives & Propellants. 2nd ed. Charles L. Mader. LC 97-21340. 464p. 1997. boxed set 119.95 (*0-8493-3149-8*) CRC Pr.

Numerical Modeling of Manufacturing Processes: Presented at the Winter Annual Meeting of the American Society of Mechanical Engineers, Atlanta, Georgia, November 27-December 2, 1977. American Society of Mechanical Engineers Staff. Ed. by R. F. Jones, Jr. et al. LC 77-87324. (Illus.). 188p. reprint ed. pap. 58.30 (*0-8357-2851-X*, 203908600010) Bks Demand.

Numerical Modeling of Ocean Dynamics. Z. Kowalik & T. S. Murty. (Advanced Series in Ocean Engineering). 496p. 1993. text 78.00 (*981-02-1333-6*); pap. text 44.00 (*981-02-1334-4*) World Scientific Pub.

Numerical Modeling of Seismic Wave Propagation. Ed. by K. R. Kelly & K. J. Marfurt. (Geophysics Reprint Ser.: No. 13). 525p. 1990. text 75.00 (*1-56080-011-9*, 186A) Soc Expl Geophys.

Numerical Modeling of Silicon Photodiodes for High-Accuracy Applications. Jon Geist et al. (Illus.). 30p. (Orig.). (C). 1993. pap. text 15.00 (*0-7881-0059-9*) DIANE Pub.

***Numerical Modeling of the Global Atmosphere in the Climate System.** Philip W. Mote & Alan O'Neill. LC 00-37056. (NATO ASI Ser.). 2000. write for info. (*0-7923-6301-9*, Kluwer Plenum) Kluwer Academic.

Numerical Modelling & Capacity Design of Earthquake-Resistant Reinforced Concrete Walls. Peter Linde. LC 93-37013. (Report of the Institute of Structural Engineering ETH Zurich Ser.: No. 200). 236p. 1994. 76.00 (*0-8176-2968-8*) Birkhauser.

Numerical Modelling & Design of Electrical Machines & Devices. Kay Hameyer & Ronnie Belmanns. (Advances in Electrical & Electronic Engineering Ser.: Vol. 1). 336p. 1999. text 159.00 (*1-85312-626-8*, Pub. by WIT Pr) Computational Mech MA.

Numerical Modelling in Geodynamics: With Applications. Josef Nedoma. LC 97-20322. 990p. 1998. 160.00 (*0-471-97461-7*) Wiley.

Numerical Modelling of Eddy Currents. Andrzej Krawczyk & John A. Tegopoulos. LC 93-28868. (Monographs in Electrical & Electronic Engineering: No. 32). (Illus.). 124p. 1993. text 39.95 (*0-19-859382-1*) OUP.

Numerical Modelling of Hydrogen Transport in Steel. Alfons Krom. (Illus.). 106p. 1998. pap. 39.50 (*90-407-1647-1*, Pub. by Delft U Pr) Coronet Bks.

Numerical Modelling of Material Deformation Processes: Research, Development, & Application. Ed. by P. Hartley et al. (Illus.). 480p. 1992. 142.95 (*0-387-19584-X*) Spr-Verlag.

Numerical Modelling of Nonlinear Stellar Pulsations: Problems & Prospects: Proceedings of the NATO Advanced Research Workshop Held in Les Arcs, France, March 20-24, 1989. Ed. by J. Robert Buchler. (C). 1990. text 201.00 (*0-7923-0598-1*) Kluwer Academic.

Numerical Modelling of Random Processes & Fields: Algorithms & Applications. V. A. Ogorodnikovv & S. M. Prigarin. 250p. 1996. 155.00 (*90-6764-199-5*, Pub. by VSP) Coronet Bks.

Numerical Models in Fracture Mechanics of Concrete. Ed. by Folker H. Wittman. 304p. 1994. 110.00 (*90-5410-353-1*, Pub. by A A Balkema) Ashgate Pub Co.

Numerical Models in Geomechanics, Vol. 1. G. N. Pande. 1992. 116.00 (*90-5410-089-3*) Ashgate Pub Co.

Numerical Models in Geomechanics, Vol. 2. 1992. 116.00 (*90-5410-090-7*, Pub. by A A Balkema) Ashgate Pub Co.

Numerical Models in Geomechanics: International Symposium, Zurich, 13-17 September 1982. Ed. by R. Dungar et al. 831p. (C). 1982. text 252.00 (*90-6191-225-3*, Pub. by A A Balkema) Ashgate Pub Co.

Numerical Models in Geomechanics: Proceedings of the Fourth International Symposium - NUMOG IV - Swansea, U. K. 24-27 August 1992, 2 vols., Set. Ed. by G. N. Pande & S. Pietruszczak. (Illus.). 1032p. (C). 1992. text 239.00 (*90-5410-088-5*, Pub. by A A Balkema) Ashgate Pub Co.

Numerical Models in Geomechanics: Proceedings of the 6th International Symposium, NUMOG VI, Montreal, Canada, 2-4 July 1997. Ed. by S. Pietruszczak & G. N. Pande. 766p. (C). 1997. text 146.00 (*90-5410-886-X*, Pub. by A A Balkema) Ashgate Pub Co.

***Numerical Models in Geomechanics: Proceedings of the 7th International Symposium, NUMOG VII, Graz, Austria, 1-3 September 1999.** Ed. by G. N. Pande et al. (Illus.). 690p. (C). 1999. text 115.00 (*90-5809-095-7*) A A Balkema.

Numerical Models in Geomechanics NUMOG V: Proceedings of the Fifth International Symposium on Numerical Models in Geomechanics-Numog V, Davos, Switzerland, 6-8 September 1995. Ed. by G. N. Pande & S. Pietruszczak. (Illus.). 720p. (C). 1995. text 194.00 (*90-5410-568-2*, Pub. by A A Balkema) Ashgate Pub Co.

Numerical Models of Oceans & Oceanic Processes. Lakshmi H. Kantha. 1168p. 1999. 129.95 (*0-12-434068-7*) Acad Pr.

Numerical Ocean Acoustic Propagation in Three Dimensions. Ding Lee & Martin H. Schultz. LC 95-32946. 250p. 1995. 54.00 (*981-02-2303-X*) World Scientific Pub.

Numerical Ocean Circulation Modeling. Dale B. Haidvogel & Aike Beckmann. LC 99-19666. (Series on Environmental Science & Management). 300p. 1998. 38.00 (*1-86094-114-1*) World Scientific Pub.

Numerical Operations: Answer Key. Jocelyn Walton & Cheryl Klein. 149p. 1995. text, teacher ed. 19.95 (*1-886292-18-3*) CEO Sftware.

Numerical Operations: Series E. Jocelyn C. Walton & Sheryl Klein. 149p. (J). (gr. 7-10). 1995. text, wbk. ed. 19.95 (*1-886292-12-4*) CEO Sftware.

Numerical Operations with Polynomial Matrices: Application to Multi-Variable Dynamic Compensator Design. P. Stefanidis et al. (Lecture Notes in Control & Information Sciences: Vol. 171). (Illus.). 212p. 1992. 63.95 (*0-387-54992-7*) Spr-Verlag.

Numerical Optimization. Jorge Nocedal & Stephen J. Wright. LC 99-13263. (Series in Operations Research). 600p. 1999. 64.95 (*0-387-98793-2*) Spr-Verlag.

Numerical Optimization, 1984. Ed. by Paul T. Boggs et al. LC 85-50611. (Proceedings in Applied Mathematics Ser.: No. 20). xi, 287p. 1985. text 38.75 (*0-89871-054-5*) Soc Indus-Appl Math.

Numerical Optimization of Computer Models. Hans-Paul Schwefel. LC 81-173223. (Illus.). 397p. reprint ed. pap. 123.10 (*0-8357-8518-1*, 203481500091) Bks Demand.

Numerical Optimization Techniques. Y. G. Evtushenko. xiv, 558p. 1985. 159.95 (*0-387-90949-4*) Spr-Verlag.

Numerical Optimization Techniques. Ed. by Yu. G. Evtushenko et al. LC 85-7230. (Translations Series in Mathematics & Engineering). 472p. 1985. text 98.00 (*0-911575-07-3*) Optimization Soft.

***Numerical Optimization Techniques for Engineering Design.** 3rd ed. Garrett N. Vanderplaats. (Illus.). 441p. (C). 1999. reprint ed. pap. text. write for info. (*0-944956-00-9*) Vanderplaats Resrch.

***Numerical Palaeobiology Computer-Based Modelling & Analysis of Fossils & Their Distribution.** D.A.T. Harper. LC 98-47325. 478p. 1999. 99.00 (*0-471-97405-6*) Wiley.

Numerical Partial Differential Equations: Conservation Laws & Elliptic Equations. J. W. Thomas. 1999. 49.95 (*0-387-98346-5*) Spr-Verlag.

Numerical Partial Differential Equations: Finite Difference Methods. J. W. Thomas. LC 95-17143. (Texts in Applied Mathematics Ser.: Vol. 22). (Illus.). 472p. 1995. 54.95 (*0-387-97999-9*) Spr-Verlag.

Numerical Prediction & Dynamic Meteorology. 2nd ed. George J. Haltiner & Roger T. Williams. LC 79-25544. 496p. 1980. text 108.95 (*0-471-05971-4*) Wiley.

Numerical Problems in Physical Chemistry (with Solutions & Hints) Amalendu Ghosal. (C). 1989. 40.00 (*0-89771-409-1*, Pub. by Current Dist) St Mut.

Numerical Problems in Thermodynamics & Kinetics of Chemical Engineering Processes. Stanislaw Wronski et al. Tr. & Contrib. by Andrzej K. Bin. 1995. write for info. (*1-56700-045-2*) Begell Hse.

Numerical Properties & Methodologies in Heat Transfer: Proceedings of the Second Annual Symposium. Ed. by Tien-Mo Shih. LC 82-6187. (Computational Methods in Mechanics & Thermal Sciences Ser.). (Illus.). 554p. 1983. text 140.00 (*0-89116-309-3*) Hemisp Pub.

Numerical Proportions of the Sexes at Birth. John B. Nichols. LC 07-23967. (American Anthropological Association Memoirs Ser.: No. 4). 1906. 25.00 (*0-527-00503-7*) Periodicals Srv.

Numerical Range: The Field of Values of Linear Operators & Matrices. Karl E. Gustafson & Duggirala K. Rao. LC 96-23980. (Universitext Ser.). 189p. 1996. pap. 34.95 (*0-387-94835-X*) Spr-Verlag.

Numerical Recipes Examples for the Macintosh. 2nd ed. William T. Vetterling et al. 1990. pap. 29.95 (*0-521-38767-1*) Cambridge U Pr.

Numerical Recipes in C: The Art of Scientific Computing. 2nd ed. William H. Press et al. 1020p. (C). 1992. text 57.95 (*0-521-43108-5*) Cambridge U Pr.

Numerical Recipes in C: The Art of Scientific Computing. 2nd ed. William H. Press et al. (C). 1992. disk 39.95 (*0-521-43724-5*) Cambridge U Pr.

Numerical Recipes in C: The Art of Scientific Computing. 2nd ed. William H. Press et al. (C). 1993. disk 39.95 (*0-521-43715-6*) Cambridge U Pr.

Numerical Recipes in FORTRAN: The Art of Scientific Computing. 2nd ed. William H. Press et al. 92p. (C). 1992. disk 39.95 (*0-521-43717-2*) Cambridge U Pr.

Numerical Recipes in FORTRAN: The Art of Scientific Computing. 2nd ed. William H. Press et al. (C). 1993. disk 39.95 (*0-521-43716-4*) Cambridge U Pr.

Numerical Recipes in FORTRAN 90: The Art of Parallel Scientific Computing. 2nd ed. William H. Press et al. (Fortran Numerical Recipes Ser.: Vol. 2). (Illus.). 571p. (C). 1996. text 47.95 (*0-521-57439-0*) Cambridge U Pr.

Numerical Recipes in FORTRAN 77: The Art of Scientific Computing. 2nd ed. William H. Press et al. 992p. (C). 1992. text 57.95 (*0-521-43064-X*) Cambridge U Pr.

Numerical Recipes in FORTRAN 77 Example Book: The Art of Scientific Computing. 2nd ed. William H. Press et al. 256p. (C). 1992. pap. text 29.95 (*0-521-43721-0*) Cambridge U Pr.

Numerical Recipes in Pascal: The Art of Scientific Computing. rev. ed. William H. Press et al. (Illus.). 781p. (C). 1989. text 57.95 (*0-521-37516-9*) Cambridge U Pr.

Numerical Recipes in Pascal Example Book: The Art of Scientific Computing. rev. ed. William H. Press et al. (Illus.). 231p. (C). 1989. pap. text 29.95 (*0-521-37675-0*) Cambridge U Pr.

Numerical Recipes in Pascal Example Book: The Art of Scientific Computing. 2nd ed. William H. Press et al. 336p. (C). 1992. pap. text 29.95 (*0-521-43720-2*) Cambridge U Pr.

Numerical Recipes Routines & Examples in BASIC. Julien C. Sprott. 410p. (C). 1991. pap. text 37.95 (*0-521-40689-7*) Cambridge U Pr.

Numerical Schemes for Conservation Laws. Dietmar Kroner. LC 97-133929. 516p. 1997. 125.00 (*0-471-96793-9*) Wiley.

***Numerical Secrets of the Bible: Rediscovering the Bible Codes.** C. J. Labuschagne. LC 00-9699. 2000. write for info. (*0-941037-67-3*, BIBAL Press) D & F Scott.

Numerical Simulation in Fluid Dynamics: A Practical Introduction. Michael Griebel et al. LC 97-40624. (SIAM Monographs on Mathematical Modeling & Computation). (Illus.). xvi, 217p. 1997. pap. 59.50 (*0-89871-398-6*, MM03) Soc Indus-Appl Math.

Numerical Simulation in Oil Recovery. Ed. by M. F. Wheeler. (IMA Volumes in Mathematics & Its Applications Ser.: Vol. 11). (Illus.). xi, 283p. 1987. 54.95 (*0-387-96653-6*) Spr-Verlag.

Numerical Simulation of Canopy Flows. Gunter Gross. LC 93-2799. (Physical Environment Ser.: Vol. 12). 1993. write for info. (*3-540-52520-3*); 139.95 (*0-387-52520-3*) Spr-Verlag.

Numerical Simulation of Casting Solidification in Automotive Applications: Proceedings of the 18th Annual Automotive Materials Symposium Sponsored by the Detroit Section of TMS, Held on May 1-2, Kellogg Center, Michigan State University. Automotive Materials Symposium Staff. Ed. by

N

An Asterisk (*) at the beginning of an entry indicates that the title is appearing for the first time.

Chongmin Kim & Chung-Whee Kim. LC 91-51008. (Illus.). 364p. 1991. reprint ed. pap. 112.90 (*0-608-05692-8*, 206620700007) Bks Demand.

Numerical Simulation of Chemical Reactions in Point-Source Plumes. J. P. Meeder. (Illus.). 117p. 1998. pap. 39.50 (*90-407-1639-0*, Pub. by Delft U Pr) Coronet Bks.

Numerical Simulation of Combustion Phenomena. Roger Temam et al. Ed. by Bernard Larrouturou. (Lecture Notes in Physics Ser.: Vol. 241). ix, 404p. 1985. pap. 44.00 (*0-387-16073-6*) Spr-Verlag.

Numerical Simulation of Fluid Flow & Heat Mass Transfer Processes. Ed. by N. C. Markatos et al. (Lecture Notes in Engineering Ser.: Vol. 18). 505p. 1986. 58.95 (*0-387-16377-8*) Spr-Verlag.

Numerical Simulation of Magnetospheric Electron Transport Phenomena. Michel Blanc et al. (Applied Mathematics Ser.: Vol. 1). xvii, 62p. 1987. pap. text 82.00 (*2-88124-165-4*) Gordon & Breach.

Numerical Simulation of Non-Newtonian Flow. M. J. Crochet et al. (Rheology Ser.: Vol. 1). xiv, 352p. 1991. reprint ed. 183.00 (*0-444-42291-9*) Elsevier.

Numerical Simulation of Plasmas. Y. N. Dnestrovskii & D. P. Kostomarov. Tr. by N. V. Deyneka from RUS. (Computational Physics Ser.). (Illus.). 320p. 1986. 135.95 (*0-387-15835-9*) Spr-Verlag.

Numerical Simulation of Reactive Flow. Elaine S. Oran & J. P. Boris. 550p. 1987. 59.75 (*0-444-01251-6*) P-H.

Numerical Simulation of Unsteady Flows, Transition to Turbulence. Ed. by W. Rodi et al. (Illus.). 528p. (C). 1992. text 74.95 (*0-521-41618-3*) Cambridge U Pr.

Numerical Simulation of Viscous Shock Layer Flows. Yuri P. Golovachov. LC 95-30329. (Fluid Mechanics & Its Applications Ser.: Vol. 33). 360p. (C). 1995. text 184.00 (*0-7923-3626-7*) Kluwer Academic.

Numerical Simulations in the Environmental & Earth Sciences: Proceedings of the Second UNAM-CRAY Supercomputing Conference. Ed. by Fernando G. Garcia et al. LC 96-39291. (Illus.). 298p. (C). 1997. text 80.00 (*0-521-58047-1*) Cambridge U Pr.

Numerical Simulations in Turbomachinery. Ed. by A. Hamed. LC 94-77599. (1995 ASME/JSME Fluids Engineering Conference Ser.: FED-Vol. 227). 192p. 1995. 96.00 (*0-7918-1482-3*, G00977) ASME.

Numerical Simulations of Heat Transfer & Fluid Flow on a Personal Computer. Susumu Kotake & Kunio Hijikata. LC 92-39908. (Transport Processes in Engineering Ser.: Vol. 3). 241p. 1992. 232.25 (*0-444-89811-5*); pap. 104.50 (*0-444-89812-3*) Elsevier.

Numerical Solution of Algebraic Equations. R. A. Wait. LC 78-21869. 168p. reprint ed. pap. 52.10 (*0-8357-3400-5*, 203965700013) Bks Demand.

Numerical Solution of Boundary Value Problems for Ordinary Differential Equations. Uri M. Ascher et al. LC 95-33340. (Classics in Applied Mathematics Ser.: Vol. 13). xxv, 595p. 1995. pap. 42.50 (*0-89871-354-4*, CL13) Soc Indus-Appl Math.

Numerical Solution of Elliptic Equations. Garrett D. Birkhoff. (CBMS-NSF Regional Conference Series in Applied Mathematics: No. 1). xi, 82p. 1971. pap. text 21.00 (*0-89871-001-4*) Soc Indus-Appl Math.

Numerical Solution of Elliptic Problems. Garrett D. Birkhoff & Robert E. Lynch. LC 84-51823. (Studies in Applied Mathematics: No. 6). (Illus.). ix, 319p. 1984. text 52.00 (*0-89871-197-5*) Soc Indus-Appl Math.

Numerical Solution of Field Problems in Continuum Physics: Proceedings of the SIAM-AMS Symposia, North Carolina, April, 1968. Ed. by Garrett D. Birkhoff & R. S. Varga. LC 75-92659. (SIAM-AMS Proceedings Ser.: Vol. 2). 280p. 1970. text 38.00 (*0-8218-1321-8*, SIAMS/2) Am Math.

Numerical Solution of Initial-Value Problems in Differential-Algebraic Equations. K. E. Brenan et al. 210p. 1989. 44.95 (*0-444-01511-6*) P-H.

Numerical Solution of Initial-Value Problems in Differential-Algebraic Equations. Kathryn E. Brenan et al. LC 95-46482. (Classics in Applied Mathematics Ser.: Vol. 14). x, 256p. 1995. pap. 32.00 (*0-89871-353-6*) Soc Indus-Appl Math.

Numerical Solution of Integral Equations. Ed. by L. M. Delves & J. Walsh. (Illus.). 1974. 45.00 (*0-19-853342-X*) OUP.

Numerical Solution of Integral Equations. M. A. Golberg. LC 90-7210. (Mathematical Concepts & Methods in Science & Engineering Ser.: Vol. 42). (Illus.). 430p. (C). 1990. text 110.00 (*0-306-43262-5*, Kluwer Plenum) Kluwer Academic.

Numerical Solution of Integral Equations of the Second Kind. Kendall E. Atkinson. (Cambridge Monographs on Applied & Computational Mathematics: No. 4). 568p. 1997. text 74.95 (*0-521-58391-8*) Cambridge U Pr.

Numerical Solution of Markov Chains. Ed. by William J. Stewart. (Textbooks & Reference Ser.: No. 8). (Illus.). 728p. 1991. text 215.00 (*0-8247-8405-7*) Dekker.

Numerical Solution of Nonlinear Structural Problems: A Symposium Presented at the Winter Annual Meeting of ASME, Detroit, MI, November 11-15, 1973. Ed. by R. F. Hartung. LC 73-87732. (ASME Applied Mechanics Division Ser.: Vol. 6). 228p. reprint ed. pap. 70.70 (*0-608-30909-5*, 205609200047) Bks Demand.

Numerical Solution of Ordinary & Partial Differential Equations: Based on a Summer School, Oxford, August- September, 1961. L. Fox. LC 62-12993. 1962. 232.00 (*0-08-009660-3*, Pub. by Pergamon Repr) Franklin.

Numerical Solution of Partial Differential Equations. Dirk P. Laurie. (International Series of Numerical Mathematics: Vol. 66). 334p. (C). 1983. text 54.95 (*3-7643-1561-X*) Birkhauser.

Numerical Solution of Partial Differential Equations. K. W. Morton & D. F. Mayers. (Illus.). 239p. (C). 1995. text 69.95 (*0-521-41855-0*); pap. text 25.95 (*0-521-42922-6*) Cambridge U Pr.

Numerical Solution of Partial Differential Equations. 3rd ed. Gordon D. Smith. (Oxford Applied Mathematics & Computing Science Ser.). (Illus.). 350p. 1986. pap. text 45.95 (*0-19-859650-2*) OUP.

Numerical Solution of Partial Differential Equations: Proceedings of the NATO Advanced Study Institute, Kjeller, Norway, August, 1973. NATO Advanced Study Institute Staff. Ed. by J. Gram. LC 73-91204. (NATO Advanced Study Institutes Ser.: No. C-2). 1973. text 162.50 (*90-277-0413-9*) Kluwer Academic.

Numerical Solution of Partial Differential Equations in Science & Engineering. Leon Lapidus & George F. Pinder. LC 81-16491. 696p. 1982. 199.50 (*0-471-09866-3*) Wiley.

Numerical Solution of Partial Differential Equations in Science & Engineering. Leon Lapidus & George F. Pinder. 677p. 1999. pap. 79.95 (*0-471-35944-0*) Wiley.

Numerical Solution of SDE Through Computer Experiments. Peter E. Kloeden et al. LC 97-27732. (Universitext Ser.). 1997. write for info. (*3-540-57074-8*) Spr-Verlag.

Numerical Solution of SDE Through Computer Experiments: Universitext. Peter E. Kloeden et al. (Illus.). 308p. 1997. 54.95 (*0-387-57074-8*) Spr-Verlag.

Numerical Solution of Stochastic Differential Equations. Peter E. Kloeden & Eckhard Platen. LC 95-463. (Applications of Mathematics Ser.: No. 23). 1995. write for info. (*3-540-54062-8*) Spr-Verlag.

Numerical Solution of Stochastic Differential Equations. Peter E. Kloeden & Eckhard Platen. Ed. by A. V. Balakrishnan et al. LC 92-15916. (Applications of Mathematics Ser.: Vol. 23). (Illus.). 632p. 1997. 86.95 (*0-387-54062-8*) Spr-Verlag.

Numerical Solution of Sturm-Liouville Problems. John D. Pryce. (Monographs on Numerical Analysis). (Illus.). 336p. 1994. text 59.00 (*0-19-853415-9*) OUP.

Numerical Solution of the Helmholtz Equation. Richard A. Marschall. 110p. (C). 1993. text 142.00 (*0-9636418-0-8*) Marschall Acoustics.

Numerical Solution of the Incompressible Navier-Stokes Equations. L. Quartapelle. LC 93-28305. (International Series of Numerical Mathematics: Vol. 113). 1993. 100.00 (*3-7643-2935-1*); 118.00 (*0-8176-2935-1*) Birkhauser.

Numerical Solution of Two Point Boundary Problems I: Ordinary Differential Equations. L Fox. 371p. 1990. pap. 9.95 (*0-486-66495-3*) Dover.

Numerical Solution of Two Point Boundary Value Problems. Herbert B. Keller. (CBMS-NSF Regional Conference Ser.: No. 24). viii, 61p. 1976. reprint ed. pap. text 21.00 (*0-89871-021-9*) Soc Indus-Appl Math.

Numerical Solutions for Partial Differential Equations: Problem Solving Using Mathematica. Victor G. Ganzha & Evgenii V. Vorozhtsov. Ed. by R. Fateman & R. Grossman. LC 95-48195. (Symbolic & Numeric Computation Ser.). 368p. 1996. pap. 94.95 (*0-8493-7379-4*) CRC Pr.

Numerical Solutions of the N-Body Problem. Andrzej Marciniak. 1985. text 155.50 (*90-277-2058-4*) Kluwer Academic.

Numerical Structure Factor Tables. Martin J. Buerger. LC QD0908.B8. (Geological Society of America, Special Paper: No. 33). 127p. reprint ed. pap. 39.40 (*0-7837-0356-2*, 204067600018) Bks Demand.

Numerical Studies. B. M. Herbst. 1996. pap. write for info. (*0-582-01481-6*, Pub. by Addison-Wesley) Longman.

Numerical Syntaxology: Proceedings of Part of the Symposium "Numerical Syndynamics" Held in Unovce Near Galanta, Slovakia, May 18-23, 1983. Ed. by L. Mucina & M. B. Dale. (Advances in Vegetation Science Ser.). (C). 1989. reprint ed. text 266.50 (*0-7923-0388-1*) Kluwer Academic.

Numerical Tables for Angular Correlation Computations in Alpha, Beta & Gamma Spectroscopy see Nuclear Particles & Physics: Group I

Numerical Tables for Beta-Decay & Electron Capture see Nuclear Particles & Physics: Group I

Numerical Taxonomy of Birth Defects & Polygenic Disorders. Ed. by Daniel Bergsma. (Alan R. Liss Ser.: Vol. 13, No. 3a). 1977. 28.00 (*0-686-23124-4*) March of Dimes.

Numerical Techniques. Spilling. 1989. 52.50 (*0-901462-68-3*) Institute of Management Consultants.

Numerical Techniques for Engineering Analysis & Design, Set. Ed. by G. N. Pande & J. Middleton. (C). 1987. lib. bdg. 156.50 (*90-247-3597-1*) Kluwer Academic.

Numerical Techniques for Engineering Analysis & Design, Vol. 1. Ed. by G. N. Pande & J. Middleton. (C). 1987. text 316.50 (*90-247-3565-3*) Kluwer Academic.

Numerical Techniques for Engineering Analysis & Design, Vol. 1: Engineering. Ed. by G. N. Pande & J. Middleton. (C). 1987. text 294.00 (*90-247-3564-5*) Kluwer Academic.

Numerical Techniques for Microwave & Millimeter-Wave Passive Structures. Ed. by Tatsuo Itoh. LC 88-28620. 720p. 1989. 225.00 (*0-471-62563-9*) Wiley.

Numerical Techniques for Stochastic Optimization. Ed. by Roger J. Wets & Y. Ermoliev. (Computational Mathematics Ser.: Vol. 10). (Illus.). 590p. 1988. 165.95 (*0-387-18677-8*) Spr-Verlag.

Numerical Techniques in Electromagnetics. Matthew N. Sadiku. 720p. 1992. boxed set 104.95 (*0-8493-4232-5*) CRC Pr.

***Numerical Techniques in Electromagnetics.** 2nd ed. Matthew N. O. Sadiku. LC 00-26823. (Illus.). 2000. 99.95 (*0-8493-1395-3*) CRC Pr.

Numerical Techniques in Finance. Simon Benninga. 256p. (Orig.). 1989. pap. text 26.00 (*0-262-52141-5*) MIT Pr.

Numerical Techniques in Finance. Simon Benninga. 256p. (Orig.). 1989. 42.00 (*0-262-02286-9*) MIT Pr.

Numerical Thermal Analysis. Satish P. Ketkar. LC 98-32285. 14p. 1999. write for info. (*0-7918-0073-3*) ASME Pr.

Numerical Toolbox for Verified Computing: With Algorithms & PASCAL-XSC Programs. R. Hammer. LC 93-39210. 1994. 103.95 (*0-387-57118-3*) Spr-Verlag.

Numerical Treatment of Eigenvalue Problems. Ed. by Lothar Collatz. (International Series of Numerical Mathematics: No. 83, Vol. 4). 264p. 1987. 84.00 (*0-8176-1856-2*) Birkhauser.

Numerical Treatment of Eigenvalue Problems, Vol. 3. Julius Albrecht et al. (International Series of Numerical Mathematics: Vol. 69). (ENG & GER.). 216p. 1984. 49.95 (*3-7643-1605-5*) Birkhauser.

Numerical Treatment of Eigenvalue Problems Vol. 5: Workshop in Oberwolfach, February 25 - March 3, 1990. Ed. by Julius Albrecht et al. (International Series of Numerical Mathematics: Vol. 96). (ENG & GER.). 256p. 1991. 96.00 (*0-8176-2575-5*) Birkhauser.

Numerical Trigonometry: Syllabus. Carlton W. Bryson & Allan W. Gray. 1973. pap. text 10.95 (*0-89420-050-X*, 355110); audio 70.70 (*0-89420-164-6*, 355000) Natl Book.

Numerically Exceptive Logic: A Reduction of the Classical Syllogism. Wallace A. Murphree. LC 90-23023. (American University Studies: Philosophy: Ser. V, Vol. 112). (Illus.). 222p. (C). 1991. text 32.95 (*0-8204-1449-2*) P Lang Pubng.

Numerische Behandlung von Differentialbleichungen, 2 vols., Vol. 2. Ed. by Gunther Hammerlin et al. (International Series of Numerical Mathematics: Nos. 27 & 31). (GER.). 276p. 1980. pap. 37.95 (*0-8176-0853-2*) Birkhauser.

Numerische Behandlung von Differentialgleichungen Mit Besonderer Berucksichtigung Freier Randwertaufgaben. Julius Albrecht. Ed. by Lothar Collatz & Gunther Hammerlin. (International Series of Numerical Mathematics: No. 39). (GER., Illus.). 280p. 1980. 55.50 (*0-8176-0986-5*) Birkhauser.

Numerische Behandlung von Eigenwertaufgaben. Ed. by Julius Albrecht & Lothar Collatz. (International Series of Numerical Mathematics: Vol. 2, No. 43). (GER., Illus.). 203p. pap. 38.95 (*3-7643-1067-7*) Birkhauser.

Numerische Methoden bei Optimierungsaufgaben, 3 vols., Vol. 2. Ed. by Lothar Collatz et al. (International Series of Numerical Mathematics: Nos. 17, 23 & 36). (GER., Illus.). 166p. 1980. 32.95 (*0-8176-0732-3*) Birkhauser.

Numerische Methoden der Approximationstheorie, 4 vols., Vol. 3. Ed. by Lothar Collatz & Gunter Meinardus. (International Series of Numerical Mathematics: Nos. 16, 26, 30 & 42). (GER., Illus.). 334p. 1980. 54.00 (*0-8176-0824-9*) Birkhauser.

Numerische Prozeduren aus Nachlass und Lehre Heinz Rutishauser. Ed. by W. Gander et al. (GER.). 127p. 1980. 55.50 (*0-8176-0874-5*) Birkhauser.

Numero Uno Gang Mysteries, 5 novels, Set. Elaine Pageler. (Illus.). 240p. (Orig.). (J). (gr. 3-9). 1988. pap. 17.00 (*0-87879-550-2*) High Noon Bks.

Numero XXIV Invenzioni Teatrali. Gaspare Galliari. LC 68-21215. (ITA., Illus.). 1972. reprint ed. 18.95 (*0-405-08547-8*, Pub. by Blom Pubns) Ayer.

***Numerologia: Manual Practico.** Anthony Alessandrini. 1999. pap. text 6.95 (*84-270-2140-2*) E Martinez Roca.

Numerologia: With Tantra, Ayurveda, & Astrology. Harish Johari.Tr. of Numerology. (SPA., Illus.). 194p. 1994. pap. 12.95 (*0-89281-463-2*) Inner Tradit.

***Numerologia (Compatibilidad y Amistad)** Margaret Arnold. (ENG & SPA.). 240p. 2000. pap. 9.95 (*1-56718-041-8*, Llewellyn Esp) Llewellyn Pubns.

Numerology see Numerologia: With Tantra, Ayurveda, & Astrology

Numerology. David V. Barrett. LC 95-11680. (Predictions Library). (Illus.). 56p. 1995. 8.95 (*0-7894-0307-2*, 6-70513) DK Pub Inc.

Numerology. Harish Johari. 200p. 1990. pap. 12.95 (*0-89281-258-3*, Destiny Bks) Inner Tradit.

Numerology. New Holland Publishing Ltd. Staff. LC 99-168287. (Ancient Wisdom for the New Age Ser.). (Illus.). 72p. 1998. 9.95 (*1-85368-983-1*, Pub. by New5 Holland) Sterling.

Numerology. Clifford W. Cheasley. 80p. 1996. reprint ed. spiral bd. 10.50 (*0-7873-1144-8*) Hlth Research.

Numerology. Malcolm Madison. 23p. 1985. reprint ed. spiral bd. 8.00 (*0-7873-1243-6*) Hlth Research.

Numerology: As Taught by Yogi Bhajan, Bk. 1. Guruchander S. Khalsa. Ed. by Gurujivan K. Khalsa. 86p. (Orig.). 1993. pap. 14.95 (*0-9636752-0-6*) Radiant Lght.

Numerology: Enrich Your Life Through Numbers: Numerology Can Guide You in Your Search for the Answers, Vol. I. Alana Lotharius. 120p. 1992. text 24.95 (*0-9629732-9-7*) Quintile.

***Numerology: Intro Guide to the Power of Numbers as a Guide for Life.** Rodford Barrat. (New Perspectives Ser.). 2000. pap. 9.95 (*1-86204-625-5*, Pub. by Element MA) Penguin Putnam.

Numerology: Its Facts & Secrets. Ariel Y. Taylor. 1977. pap. 5.00 (*0-87980-109-3*) Wilshire.

Numerology: Key to Tarot. Sandor Konraad. LC 83-60062. 240p. 1983. pap. 13.95 (*0-914918-45-1*, Whitford) Schiffer.

Numerology: Key to Your Inner Self. Hans Decoz & Tom Monte. LC 93-30671. 276p. pap. 12.95 (*0-89529-566-0*, Avery) Penguin Putnam.

Numerology: Nuances in Relationships. rev. ed. Lynn M. Buess. 310p. (Orig.). 1997. pap. 13.75 (*0-929385-23-3*) Light Tech Pubng.

Numerology: The Power to Know. Jason D. Cooper. 1988. 5.95 (*0-85030-472-5*, Pub. by Aqrn Pr) Harper SF.

Numerology: The Romance in Your Name. Juno Jordan. 348p. 1977. reprint ed. pap. 16.95 (*0-87516-227-4*) DeVorss.

Numerology: The Universal Vibrations of Numbers. Barbara J. Bishop. LC 89-77886. (Self-Help Ser.). (Illus.). 224p. (Orig.). 1999. pap., wbk. ed. 12.95 (*0-87542-056-7*) Llewellyn Pubns.

Numerology: Theory & Outline of a Literary Mode. Jack MacQueen. 163p. 1985. 25.00 (*0-85224-492-4*, Pub. by Edinburgh U Pr) Col U Pr.

Numerology: Your Character & Future Revealed in Numbers. Norman Shine. LC 94-19091. (Illus.). 128p. 1995. per. 14.00 (*0-671-50303-0*, Fireside) S&S Trade Pap.

Numerology: Your Love & Relationship Guide. Sonia Ducie. LC 98-55287. 208p. 1999. pap. 10.95 (*1-86204-331-0*, Pub. by Element MA) Penguin Putnam.

Numerology: Your Personal Guide for Life. Sonia Ducie. 178p. 1999. pap. 10.95 (*1-86204-502-X*, Pub. by Element MA) Penguin Putnam.

Numerology Vol. 1: The Complete Guide: The Personality Reading, Vol. 1. Matthew O. Goodwin. 400p. 1981. pap. 14.95 (*0-87877-053-4*) Newcastle Pub.

Numerology Vol. 2: The Complete Guide: Advanced Personality Analysis & Reading the Past, Present & Future, Vol. 2. Matthew O. Goodwin. 428p. 1981. pap. 14.95 (*0-87877-054-2*) Newcastle Pub.

Numerology - Spiritual Light Vibrations. Jeanne. (Illus.). 380p. (Orig.). 1986. pap. text 39.95 (*0-9617877-0-8*) Your Ctr for Truth.

Numerology, a Step-by-Step Guide: A Number of Your Friends Are Animals. Jackie Suggs. Ed. by Judith L. Powell & Leslie C. Bodtke. LC 88-12346. (Illus.). 256p. (Orig.). 1988. pap. 9.95 (*0-914295-67-5*) Top Mtn Pub.

***Numerology & Relationships: A Beginner's Guide.** John C. Burford. (Headway Guides for Beginners Ser.). (Illus.). 96p. 2000. pap. 11.95 (*0-340-77487-8*, Pub. by Headway) Trafalgar.

Numerology & the Divine Triangle. Faith Javane & Dusty Bunker. (Illus.). 273p. 1979. pap. 14.95 (*0-914918-10-9*, Whitford) Schiffer.

Numerology & the English Cabalah: Translating Numbers into Words & Words into Numbers. Shirley B. Lawrence. Ed. by William L. Lammey & Gina Misiroglu. (Illus.). 224p. (Orig.). 1994. pap. 18.95 (*0-87877-188-3*) Newcastle Pub.

Numerology & Vibration. Joe S. Riley et al. 1996. reprint ed. spiral bd. 10.00 (*0-7873-0726-2*) Hlth Research.

Numerology & Your Future. Dusty Bunker. 256p. 1980. pap. 16.95 (*0-914918-18-4*, Whitford) Schiffer.

Numerology Asks: Who Do You Think You Are Anyway? rev. ed. Karen David. 167p. 1982. reprint ed. pap. text 9.95 (*0-87500-009-6*) RKM Pub Co.

Numerology, Astrology & Dreams. Dusty Bunker. Ed. by Julie Lockhart. LC 87-62095. (Illus.). 236p. 1987. pap. 19.95 (*0-914918-74-5*, Whitford) Schiffer.

Numerology Cards: Expand Your Knowledge of Yesterday, Today & Tomorrow. Alana Lotharius. (Illus.). 106p. (Orig.). 1991. 7.95 (*0-9629732-0-3*) Quintile.

Numerology Cards & Guide. Alana Lotharius. (Illus.). 106p. 1991. 23.95 (*0-9629732-2-X*) Quintile.

Numerology for Baby Names. Phyllis Vega. 336p. 1998. mass mkt. 5.99 (*0-440-22611-2*) Dell.

Numerology for Beginners. Kristyna Arcarti. (Headway Guide for Beginners Ser.). 108p. 1995. pap. 11.95 (*0-340-59551-5*, Pub. by Headway) Trafalgar.

***Numerology for Beginners: Easy Guide to Love, Money, Destiny.** Gerie Bauer. 2000. pap. 9.95 (*1-56718-057-4*) Llewellyn Pubns.

Numerology for Newlyweds, Vol. 1. Urna Gray & Marlow Gray. 1997. mass mkt. 6.99 (*0-312-96289-4*) St Martin.

Numerology for Personal Transformation: Easy As A B C 1 2 3, Empower the Real You & All You Are to Become by Understanding & Manifesting the Potential in Your Name & Birthdate to Bring Out Your Best! Roberleigh H. Claigh. (Illus.). 163p. 1997. reprint ed. pap. 13.95 (*0-9631405-1-5*) Liv Wellness.

Numerology for the New Age. Lynn M. Buess. 262p. 1991. pap. 11.00 (*0-929385-31-4*) Light Tech Pubng.

Numerology Has Your Number. Ellin Dodge. 352p. 1988. pap. 12.00 (*0-671-64243-X*, Fireside) S&S Trade Pap.

Numerology Kit. Carol Adrienne. 192p. 1988. pap. 17.95 (*0-452-26081-7*, Plume) Dutton Plume.

Numerology Kit. Carol Adrienne. 1989. pap. 12.95 (*0-317-02807-3*) NAL.

Numerology Made Easy. M. Mykian. 1979. pap. 10.00 (*0-87980-376-2*) Wilshire.

Numerology Magic: Use Number Squares for Love, Luck & Protection. 2nd rev. ed. Richard Webster. LC 98-35459. (Illus.). 192p. 1999. 9.95 (*1-56718-813-3*, K813) Llewellyn Pubns.

***Numerology of Birthdays.** Ariel. 272p. 1999. 5.95 (*0-7407-0100-2*) Andrews & McMeel.

Numerology of Names. Laureli Blyth. 152p. (Orig.). 1996. pap. 9.95 (*0-7137-2636-9*, Pub. by Blandford Pr) Sterling.

***Numerology of the I Ching: A Sourcebook of Symbols, Structures & Traditional Wisdom.** Alfred Huang. (Illus.). 192p. 2000. pap. 14.95 (*0-89281-811-5*, Inner Trad) Inner Tradit.

***Numerology of the I Ching: A Sourcebook of Symbols, Structures, & Traditional Wisdom.** Alfred Huang. 2000. 24.95 (*0-89281-824-7*, Inner Trad) Inner Tradit.

Numerology: or What Pythagoras Wrought. Underwood Dudley. LC 97-74345. 329p. 1997. pap. 29.95 (*0-88385-524-0*) Math Assn.

Numerology Palmistry & Prosperity. M. Katakkar. (C). 1993. 9.00 (*81-85674-52-3*, Pub. by UBS Pubs Dist) S Asia.

An Asterisk (*) at the beginning of an entry indicates that the title is appearing for the first time.

Numerology, the Power in Numbers: A Right & Left Brain Approach. rev. ed. Ruth Drayer. LC 95-100125. 221p. (Orig.). 1994. pap. 14.95 (*0-9640321-0-4*) Jewels of Light.
Numerology Up-to-Date: A Key to Your Fortune. Karen Adams. 64p. 1996. reprint ed. spiral bd. 9.00 (*0-7873-1274-6*) Hlth Research.
Numerology Workbook. Paul Rodrigo. 192p. 1996. pap. text, wbk. ed. 22.50 (*0-572-02214-X*, Pub. by W Foulsham) Trans-Atl Phila.
Numerology Workbook: Understanding & Using the Powers of Numbers. Julie Line. (Illus.). 224p. 1997. reprint ed. pap. 14.95 (*0-8069-9763-X*) Sterling.
Numerorum Mysteria. Petrus Bungus. (GER.). 1983. reprint ed. write for info. (*3-487-07297-1*) G Olms Pubs.
Numeros: Grupos Y Anillos. (C). 1996. pap. 13.33 (*0-201-65395-8*) HEPC Inc.
Numeros: Viaje a la Tierra de Reposo. Irving L. Jensen. (Comentario Biblico Portavoz Ser.). Orig. Title: Numbers (Everyman's Bible Commentary). (SPA.). 112p. 1980. pap. 6.99 (*0-8254-1355-9*, Edit Portavoz) Kregel.
***Numeros, Conceptos y Figuras Geometricas.** Portavoz Editorial Staff. 64p. 1999. pap. 4.99 (*0-8254-0997-7*, Edit Portavoz) Kregel.
Numeros en la Biblia. Robert Johnston. Orig. Title: Numbers in the Bible. 112p. 1994. mass mkt. 3.99 (*0-8254-1364-8*, Edit Portavoz) Kregel.
Numeros Inteiros e Criptografia see Mathematics of Ciphers: Number Theory & RSA Cryptography
Numeros Numbers. Illus. by Ricardo Sanchez. (ENG & SPA.). 32p. (Orig.). (J). (gr. k-2). 1994. pap. 4.95 (*0-922852-30-8*, V009) Another Lang Pr.
Numerous Avalanches. Geraldine Kudaka. LC 79-55230. 1979. 3.00 (*0-912678-39-9*, Greenfld Rev Pr) Greenfld Rev Lit.
Numerous Choirs: A Chronicle of Elizabeth Bayley Seton & Her Spiritual Daughters, Volume 1: the Seton Years 1774-1821. Ed. by Ellin M. Kelly. LC 81-80304. (Illus.). x, 296p. 1981. 15.00 (*0-9605784-0-4*) Mater Dei Provincialate.
Numerous Choirs Vol. II: A Chronicle of Elizabeth Bayley Seton & Her Spiritual Daughters: Expansion, Division, & War 1821-1865. Ed. by Ellin M. Kelly. (Illus.). 278p. 1996. 20.00 (*0-9605784-1-2*) Mater Dei Provincialate.
Numeta 85, Numerical Methods in Engineering, Theory & Applications: Proceedings of an International Conference Swansea, UK, 7-11 January 1985, 2 vols., Set. Ed. by J. Middleton & G. N. Pande. 1084p. (C). 1985. text 388.00 (*90-6191-577-5*, Pub. by A A Balkema) Ashgate Pub Co.
Numiform 89: Numerical Methods in Industrial Forming Processes. Ed. by E. G. Thompson et al. 619p. (C). 1989. text 220.00 (*90-6191-897-9*, Pub. by A A Balkema) Ashgate Pub Co.
Numiform 92: Numerical Methods in Industrial Forming Processes. Ed. by Jean-Loup Chenot et al. (Illus.). 928p. (C). 1992. text 188.00 (*90-5410-087-7*, Pub. by A A Balkema) Ashgate Pub Co.
Numiform 86: Proceedings of the International Conference on Numerical Methods in Industrial Forming Processes, Gothenburg, 25-29 August 1986. Ed. by K. Mattiasson et al. 404p. (C). 1986. text 220.00 (*90-6191-659-3*, Pub. by A A Balkema) Ashgate Pub Co.
Numinoses und Heiliges in der Osterreichischen Literatur. Karlheinz F. Auckenthaler. (GER.). 1995. 62.95 (*3-906753-88-3*) P Lang Pubng.
Numinous Site: The Poetry of Luis Pales Matos. Julio Marzan. LC 94-47234. 200p. 1995. 35.00 (*0-8386-3581-4*) Fairleigh Dickinson.
Numinous Universe. Daniel Liderbach. 1989. pap. 9.95 (*0-8091-3060-2*) Paulist Pr.
Numismatic Archaeology. Ed. by K. A. Sheedy & Ch. Papageorgiadou-Banis. (Oxbow Monographs in Archaeology: No. 75). (Illus.). 180p. 1997. pap. 33.00 (*1-900188-23-6*, Pub. by Oxbow Bks) David Brown.
Numismatic Bibliography & Libraries. Francis D. Campbell. 39p. 1994. pap. 4.00 (*1-889172-19-7*) Numismatic Intl.
Numismatic Dictionary. Heinz Fengler. (RUS.). 328p. 1982. 19.95 (*0-8288-1341-8*, M 15137) Fr & Eur.
Numismatic History of Ireland: History of Irish Coinage 1000 A. D. to the Present - Coins from a Private Collection: Exhibition Catalogue. Ed. by Olga K. Preisner. (Illus.). 28p. 1984. pap. 2.50 (*0-911209-32-8*) Palmer Mus Art.
Numismatic History of Mexico. Alberto F. Pradeau. LC 77-93447. (Illus.). 1978. reprint ed. lib. bdg. 25.00 (*0-915262-20-7*) S J Durst.
Numismatic Terms of Spain & Spanish America. G. Beals. (Illus.). 1966. pap. 15.00 (*0-932106-05-6*) S J Durst.
Numismatics. M. P. Sotnikova & I. G. Spasskii. 238p. 1985. 65.00 (*0-7855-0808-2*) St Mut.
Numismatics of Massachusetts. Malcolm Storer. LC 80-52820. 317p. 1981. reprint ed. 35.00 (*0-88000-117-8*) Quarterman.
Numismatique Grecque Falsifications Moyens pour les Reconnaitre. O. E. Ravel. (FRE.). 105p. 1980. reprint ed. 20.00 (*0-916710-71-8*) Obol Intl.
Numismatist Index, 1888-1978 Vols. 1-91. 1980. 4.95 (*0-686-75364-X*) American Numismatic.
Numismatist's Bedside Companion, Vol. I. Q. David Bowers et al. (Illus.). 224p. (Orig.). 1988. pap. 9.95 (*0-943161-02-9*) Bowers & Merena.
Numismatist's Countryside Companion, Vol. V. Ed. by Q. David Bowers. 192p. 1994. pap. text 12.95 (*0-943161-51-7*) Bowers & Merena.
Numismatist's Downtown Companion, Vol. VII. Ed. by Q. David Bowers. 192p. 1994. pap. text 12.95 (*0-943161-53-3*) Bowers & Merena.
Numismatist's Fireside Companion, Vol. 2. Ed. by Q. David Bowers. 224p. (Orig.). 1988. pap. text 9.95 (*0-943161-10-X*) Bowers & Merena.
Numismatist's Lakeside Companion. Ed. by Q. David Bowers. 224p. (Orig.). 1990. pap. text 9.95 (*0-943161-25-8*) Bowers & Merena.
Numismatist's Topside Companion, Vol. VIII. Ed. by Q. David Bowers. 192p. 1994. pap. text 12.95 (*0-943161-54-1*) Bowers & Merena.
Numismatist's Traveling Companion, Vol. 6. Ed. by Q. David Bowers. 192p. 1994. pap. text 12.95 (*0-943161-52-5*) Bowers & Merena.
Numismatist's Weekend Companion, Vol. IV. Ed. by Q. David Bowers. 224p. (Orig.). 1992. pap. text 9.95 (*0-943161-41-X*) Bowers & Merena.
***Numunwari.** Ed. by Surrey Beatty Staff. 256p. 1999. pap. 100.00 (*0-949324-83-3*, Pub. by Surrey Beatty & Sons) St Mut.
Nun. Denis Diderot. Tr. by Leonard W. Tancock. (Classics Ser.). 192p. 1981. pap. 15.99 (*0-14-044300-2*, Penguin Classics) Viking Penguin.
Nun. Sandra Shwayder. 1992. pap. 11.95 (*0-911051-60-0*) Plain View.
Nun & an Officer: Love History Tragedy, Bosnia-Hercegovina Yugoslavia. Radmila Johnson. 300p. 1994. pap., per. 24.95 (*1-57087-042-X*) Prof Pr NC.
Nun & Other Stories. Pedro Antonio De Alarcon. Tr. by Robert M. Fedorchek from SPA. LC 98-39220. (Illus.). 184p. 1999. 35.00 (*0-8387-5415-5*) Bucknell U Pr.
Nun-Ayin: Hebrew-English Dictionary. (Complete Biblical Library: Vol. 5). (ENG & HEB.). 639p. 1999. 49.95 (*1-884642-45-4*) World Library.
Nun Better: Tastes & Tales from Around a Cajun Table. Ed. by Dierdre D. Boese. (Illus.). 288p. 1996. 18.95 (*0-9655106-0-3*) St Cecilia Schl.
Nun but the Brave. Jean M. Warner. 176p. 1996. pap. 39.95 (*0-85439-443-5*, Pub. by St Paul Pubns) St Mut.
Nun in the Closet. Dorothy Gilman. 1986. mass mkt. 5.99 (*0-449-21167-3*, Crest) Fawcett.
Nun in the Closet. Joanne Michaels. LC 94-2197. 200p. (Orig.). 1994. pap. 9.95 (*0-934678-43-X*) New Victoria Pubs.
Nun Like It: Favorite Recipes from St. Gabriel's Retreat House & All Saints Convent. Ed. by Sister Mary Charles & Sister Julia Mary. (Illus.). 102p. 1987. pap. text 10.00 (*1-878919-00-8*) Scriptorm MD.
Nun (L'Isolee) Rene Bazin. 243p. 1995. pap. 10.95 (*1-887548-02-5*) St Michael NC.
Nun Plussed: A Sister Mary Teresa Mystery. Monica Quill. LC 95-2321. 250p. 1995. per. 3.99 (*0-373-26187-X*, Wrldwide Lib) Harlequin Bks.
Nun, the Infidel, & the Superman: The Remarkable Friendships of Dame Laurentia McLachlan with Sydney Cockerell, Bernard Shaw & Others. Felicitas Corrigan. LC 84-52822. (Illus.). viii, 152p. 1985. 21.00 (*0-226-11589-5*) U Ch Pr.
Nun Who Escaped: A True Story. abr. rev. ed. Josephine M. Bunkley. LC 98-67306. Orig. Title: Miss Bunkley's Book: The Testimony of an Escaped Novice. 106p. 1998. reprint ed. pap. 11.95 (*1-889298-84-0*) Rhwymbooks.
Nun, Witch, Playmate: The Americanization of Sex. 2nd ed. Herbert W. Richardson. xii, 147p. 1977. reprint ed. lib. bdg. 69.95 (*0-88946-950-4*) E Mellen.
***Nunavat.** (Canada in the Twenty First Century Ser.). (Illus.). (J). 2000. 18.95 (*0-7910-6073-X*) Chelsea Hse.
***Nunavut.** L. Hancock. (Hello Canada Ser.). 1999. pap. 7.95 (*1-55041-271-X*) Fitzhenry & W Ltd.
Nunavut. Lyn Hancock. (Hello Canada Ser.). (Illus.). 76p. 1995. lib. bdg. 14.21 (*0-8225-2758-8*) Lerner Pub.
Nunavut. Lyn Hancock. (Hello Canada Ser.). (Illus.). 76p. (J). (gr. 3-6). 1997. pap. 6.95 (*0-8225-9800-0*) Lerner Pub.
Nunc Dimittis: Night Prayer of the Church. Margaret Daly. 72p. 1991. pap. 7.95 (*1-85390-103-2*, Pub. by Veritas Pubns) St Mut.
Nunc Primum Typis Mandatum, Curante Thoma Stapleton. Chronicon Petroburgense Staff. (Camden Society, London. Publications, First Ser.: No. 47). reprint ed. 49.00 (*0-404-50147-8*) AMS Pr.
Nunc Pro Tunc, a Country Lawyer's Essays on Estate Planning & Aging. rev. ed. Richard M. Enders. 110p. (Orig.). 1991. pap. 12.95 (*0-9627964-1-7*) SOS Clinton.
Nunca. Lynn Salem & Josie Stewart. Tr. by Mariana Robles. (SPA., Illus.). 8p. (J). (gr. k-1). 1994. pap. 3.75 (*1-880612-25-9*) Seedling Pubns.
Nunca Bese a los Sapos! (Never Kiss Frogs!) Robert Leeson. Tr. by Monica Mansour. (SPA., Illus.). (J). (gr. 3-4). 1993. pap. 5.99 (*968-16-4235-X*, Pub. by Fondo) Continental Bk.
Nunca Es Tarde para Amar. Marie Ferrarella. (Bianca Ser.).Tr. of Never Is Late to Love. (SPA.). 1999. per. 3.50 (*0-373-33530-X*, 1-33530-6) Harlequin Bks.
Nunca Me Casare. Suzanne Simms. (Deseo Ser.: No. 216).Tr. of I Will Never Get Married. (SPA.). 1997. per. 3.50 (*0-373-35216-6*, 1-35216-0) Harlequin Bks.
Nunca Se de Por Vencido (Cast down but Not Destroyed) Bayless Conley. Tr. by Juan Hernandez. (SPA.). 32p. 1994. pap. text 2.95 (*1-57139-027-8*) Hernandez Translat.
Nunchaku: Karate Weapon of Self-Defense. Fumio Demura. 1999. pap. text 35.95 (*1-58133-143-6*) Black Belt Mag.
Nunchaku: The Complete Guide. Jiro Shiroma. LC 87-50403. 200p. (Orig.). 1989. pap. 12.95 (*0-86568-091-4*, 121) Unique Pubns.
Nunchaku for Self-Defense. Hansel S. Kaneshiro. LC 74-169956. (Illus.). 82p. 1971. pap. 3.95 (*0-9600670-1-9*) Kaneshiro.
Nunchaku in Action: For Kobudo & Law Enforcement. Joseph C. Hess. LC 83-60124. (Weapons Ser.). (Illus.). 224p. (Orig.). (YA). 1983. reprint ed. pap. 17.95 (*0-89750-086-5*, 423) Ohara Pubns.
Nunchaku Karate Weapon of Self-Defense. Fumio Demura. LC 78-183341. (Weapons Ser.). (Illus.). 1971. pap. text 10.95 (*0-89750-006-7*, 111) Ohara Pubns.
Nunchaku, Karate's Deadliest Fighting Sticks. 3rd ed. Andrew S. Linick. LC 75-6144. (Illus.). 240p. 1982. reprint ed. 29.95 (*0-917098-01-3*); reprint ed. pap. 17.95 (*0-917098-00-5*) LKA Inc.
Nunco de Mi Te Vas: Poemas. Matias M. Huidobro. 1997. pap. 16.00 (*0-89729-843-8*) Ediciones.
Nunda Irish: A Story of Irish Immigrants: the Joys & Sorrows of Their Life in America & Dakota. Bill McDonald. (Illus.). 275p. (Orig.). 1991. pap. 10.00 (*0-9629033-0-2*) Farmstead MN.
Nundinas Instituere et Habere. Johannes Nolle. (Subsidia Epigraphica Ser.). 172p. 1982. write for info. (*3-487-07259-9*) G Olms Pubs.
Nunn's Applied Respiratory Physiology. 4th ed. J. F. Nunn. (Illus.). 608p. 1999. text 100.00 (*0-7506-1336-X*) Buttrwrth-Heinemann.
***Nunn's Applied Respiratory Physiology.** 5th ed. Andrew Lumb & J. F. Nunn. LC 99-40687. 687p. 1999. text 115.00 (*0-7506-3107-4*) Buttrwrth-Heinemann.
Nunquam. Lawrence Durrell. (FRE.). 448p. 1980. pap. 11.95 (*0-7859-1910-4*, 2070371719) Fr & Eur.
***Nunquam.** Lawrence Durrell. 1999. per. 119.85 (*0-671-78072-7*, Pocket Books) PB.
Nuns & Soldiers. Iris Murdoch. 1990. pap. 12.95 (*0-14-005757-9*) Viking Penguin.
Nuns As Artists: The Visual Culture of a Medieval Convent. Jeffrey Hamburger. LC 96-6145. (Illus.). 370p. (C). 1997. 55.00 (*0-520-20386-0*, Pub. by U CA Pr) Cal Prin Full Svc.
Nuns in Nineteenth-Century Ireland. Caitriona Clear. LC 87-27767. (Illus.). 234p. 1988. reprint ed. pap. 72.60 (*0-7837-9108-9*, 204991000004) Bks Demand.
Nuns Looking Anxious, Listening to Radios. Helen Humphreys. 80p. 1990. pap. 9.95 (*0-919626-47-5*, Pub. by Brick Bks) Genl Dist Srvs.
Nun's Priest's Prologue & Tale. Geoffrey Chaucer. Ed. & Intro. by Maurice Hussey. (Selected Tales from Chaucer Ser.). 104p. 1966. pap. text 10.95 (*0-521-04626-2*) Cambridge U Pr.
Nun's Priest's Tale. Geoffrey Chaucer. Ed. by Derek Pearsall. LC 83-5760. (Variorum Edition of the Works of Geoffrey Chaucer, The Canterbury Tales Ser.: Vol. II, Pt. 9). 300p. 1984. 49.95 (*0-8061-1779-6*) U of Okla Pr.
Nunsense Country Western Jamboree. Ed. by Jeannette Delisa. 92p. (Orig.). (C). 1996. pap. text 16.95 (*1-57623-605-6*, PF9632) Wrner Bros.
Nunzio, Martin Puryear: Forma Lignea. Martha Boyden & American Academy in Rome Staff. LC 98-202561. 119 p. 1997. write for info. (*88-435-6285-1*) Electa.
Nuova Enciclopedia della Letteratura Garzanti. (ITA.). 1296p. 1989. pap. 82.00 (*0-913298-82-4*) S F Vanni.
Nuova Enciclopedia della Musica Garzanti. (ITA.). 1064p. 1989. pap. 75.00 (*0-913298-83-2*) S F Vanni.
Nuova Enciclopedia dell'Arte Garzanti. (ITA.). 1120p. 1990. pap. 72.00 (*0-913298-86-7*) S F Vanni.
Nuova Enciclopedia Geografica Garzanti. (ITA.). 1245p. 1991. pap. 72.00 (*0-913298-81-0*) S F Vanni.
Nuova Encyclopedia Medica Garzanti. (ITA.). 1328p. 1993. pap. text 82.00 (*0-913298-94-8*) S F Vanni.
Nuova Grammatica Communicativa: Answer Key, Answer Key. Derek Aust & Mike Zello. (ITA.). pap. 4.95 (*0-8442-8090-9*, X8090-9) NTC Contemp Pub Co.
Nuova Grammatica Comunicativa: A Communicative Grammar Worktext with Written & Oral Practice. Derek Aust et al. LC 97-69975. (ITA.). 416p. (C). 1998. pap., student ed. 14.95 (*0-8442-8089-5*, 80895) NTC Contemp Pub Co.
Nuova Raccolta di Lettere Sulla Pittura, Scultura Ed Architettura, 3 vols., Set. Michelangelo Gualandi. 1138p. 1975. reprint ed. write for info. (*3-487-05358-6*) G Olms Pubs.
Nuove Letture di Cultura. Carolina D. Lawson. (SPA.). 296p. 1990. pap. 20.95 (*0-8442-8000-3*) NTC Contemp Pub Co.
Nuovi Amici Per Pit. Marcus Pfister.Tr. of Penguin Pete's New Friends. (ITA., Illus.). (J). (gr. k-3). 1992. 15.95 (*88-8203-131-4*, Pub. by North-South Bks NYC) Chronicle Bks.
Nuovi Studi Sul Pensiero di Christian Wolff. Christian Wolff. (Christian Wolff, Gesammelte Werke, Three. Abt., Materialien und Dokumente Ser.: Vol. 31). iv, 284p. 1992. reprint ed. write for info. (*3-487-09536-X*) G Olms Pubs.
Nuovo Boch: Dizionario Francese-Italiano/Italiano-Francese. Ed. by R. Boch. (FRE & ITA.). 2178p. 1992. 125.00 (*0-913298-54-9*) S F Vanni.
Nuovo Dizionario di Elettrotecnic e di Elettronica: Italiano-Inglese, Inglese-Italiano. A. Colella. (ENG & ITA.). 541p. 1977. 125.00 (*0-8288-5505-6*, M9296) Fr & Eur.
Nuovo Dizionario di Terminologia Giuridica: New Dictionary of Legal Terms. A. Menghi. (ITA.). 1979. pap. 49.95 (*0-8288-4830-0*, M9654) Fr & Eur.
Nuovo Dizionario Francese Garzanti. Garzanti. (FRE & ITA.). 1040p. 1991. 150.00 (*0-8288-3372-9*, 8811192855) Fr & Eur.
Nuovo Dizionario Garzanti. (ITA.). 1088p. 1991. lib. bdg. 65.00 (*0-8288-3369-9*, M9188) Fr & Eur.
Nuovo Dizionario Garzanti. Garzanti. 65.00 (*0-8288-8199-5*, M9188) Fr & Eur.
Nuovo Dizionario Inglese Garzanti see New Garzanti English Dictionary
Nuovo Dizionario Italiano Garzanti. (ITA.). 1088p. 59.95 (*0-7859-8877-7*) Fr & Eur.
Nuovo Dizionario Italiano-Inglese, Inglese-Italiano. Caselli. (ENG & ITA.). 2427p. 1990. 125.00 (*0-7859-7476-8*, 8811103215) Fr & Eur.
Nuovo Francese Senza Sforzo. (FRE & ITA., Illus.). (Orig.). 1997. pap. 75.00 incl. audio (*2-7005-1330-4*, Pub. by Assimil) Distribks Inc.
Nuovo Francese senza Sforzo. Albert O. Cherel. 24.95 (*0-685-11202-0*); audio 125.00 (*0-685-01716-8*) Fr & Eur.
Nuovo Francese senza Sforzo: French for Italian Speakers. Assimil Staff. (FRE & ITA.). 28.50 (*0-8288-4330-9*, F9000) Fr & Eur.
Nuovo Ingles senza Sforzo: English for Italian Speakers. Assimil Staff. (ENG & ITA.). 28.95 (*0-8288-4305-8*, M14923) Fr & Eur.
Nuovo Inglese Senza Sforzo. Assimil Staff. 1999. pap. text 29.95 (*2-7005-0096-2*, Pub. by Assimil) Distribks Inc.
Nuovo Inglese senza Sforzo. Albert O. Cherel. 24.95 (*0-685-11251-9*); audio 125.00 (*0-685-01734-6*) Fr & Eur.
Nuovo Manuale Di Stile see Italian Style Manual
Nuovo Ragazzini - Biagi Concise Dizionario Inglese e Italiano: Italian English. 2nd ed. Giuseppe Ragazzini. 1991. 85.00 (*0-685-49364-4*, F10010) Fr & Eur.
Nuovo Ragazzini Dizionario Inglese-Italiano Italiano-Inglese. 2nd ed. Giuseppe Ragazzini. (ENG & ITA.). 2144p. 1989. lib. bdg. 150.00 (*0-685-48307-X*, F9072) Fr & Eur.
Nuovo Ragazzini Gigante. 2nd ed. Giuseppe Ragazzini. (ITA.). 2128p. 250.00 (*0-8288-9420-5*, F9073) Fr & Eur.
Nuovo Ragazzini Rossi. 2nd ed. Giuseppe Ragazzini. (ENG & ITA.). 2352p. 195.00 (*0-8288-9424-8*) Fr & Eur.
Nuovo Spagnolo Senza Sforzo. (ITA & SPA., Illus.). (Orig.). 1997. pap. 75.00 incl. audio (*2-7005-1333-9*, Pub. by Assimil) Distribks Inc.
Nuovo Spagnolo senza Sforzo: Spanish for Italian Speakers. Assimil Staff. (ITA & SPA.). 28.95 (*0-8288-4320-1*, S844) Fr & Eur.
Nuovo Tedesco senza Sforzo. Albert O. Cherel. 24.95 (*0-685-11582-8*); audio 125.00 (*0-685-01770-2*) Fr & Eur.
Nuovo Tedesco senza Sforzo: German for Italian Speakers. Assimil Staff. (GER & ITA.). 28.95 (*0-8288-4313-9*, F10246) Fr & Eur.
Nuovo Zingarelli Minore: Vocabolario Della Lingua Italiana. Nicola Zingarelli et al. (ITA.). 1186p. 1987. 49.95 (*0-8288-1990-4*, M14535) Fr & Eur.
Nuovo Zingarelli Vocabolario della Lingua Italiana. 11th ed. Nicola Zingarelli. (ITA.). 2272p. 1988. lib. bdg. 175.00 (*0-8288-3334-6*, F9071) Fr & Eur.
Nuptial Arithmetic: Marsilio Ficino's Commentary on the Fatal Number in Book VIII of Plato's Republic. Michael J. Allen. LC 92-26074. 1994. 60.00 (*0-520-08143-9*, Pub. by U CA Pr) Cal Prin Full Svc.
Nuptiality in Sub-Saharan Africa: Contemporary Anthropological & Demographic Perspectives. Ed. by Caroline Bledsoe & Gilles Pison. (International Studies in Demography). (Illus.). 342p. 1994. text 72.00 (*0-19-828761-5*) OUP.
Nur eine Rose als Stuetze, Gedichte. Hilde Domin. (GER.). 96p. 1994. pap. 11.75 (*3-596-12207-4*, Pub. by Fischer Tasch) Intl Bk Import.
Nuraghe Noeddos & the Bonu Ighinu Valley. David Trump. (Oxbow Monographs in Archaeology: No. 3). (Illus.). 136p. 1990. pap. 18.00 (*0-946897-20-4*, Pub. by Oxbow Bks) David Brown.
Nuragic Sardinia in Its Mediterranean Setting: Some Recent Advances. Fulvia Lo Schiavo. 42p. 1985. pap. 7.00 (*0-614-21829-2*) David Brown.
NURBS: From Projective Geometry to Practical Use. 2nd rev. ed. Gerald Farin. LC 99-12045. (Illus.). 266p. (C). 1999. 49.00 (*1-56881-084-9*) AK Peters.
Nurbs Book. Les Piegl & Wayne Tiller. LC 95-32273. (Monographs in Visual Communication). 1995. write for info. (*3-540-55069-0*) Spr-Verlag.
Nurbs Book. 2nd ed. Les A. Piegl & Wayne Tiller. LC 96-48140. (Monographs in Visual Communication). (Illus.). 650p. 1997. pap. 54.95 (*3-540-61545-8*) Spr-Verlag.
NURBS for Curve & Surface Design. Ed. by G. Farin. LC 91-35169. (Miscellaneous Bks.: No. 26). ix, 161p. 1991. pap. 44.50 (*0-89871-286-6*) Soc Indus-Appl Math.
Nuremberg. Richard Norton-Taylor. LC 97-182455. (Nick Hern Bks.). 96p. 1997. pap. 14.95 (*1-85459-332-3*, Pub. by N Hern Bks) Theatre Comm.
Nuremberg: German Views of the War Trials. Ed. by Wilbourn E. Benton & George Grimm. LC 55-5739. 240p. reprint ed. pap. 74.40 (*0-8357-8976-4*, 203341000086) Bks Demand.
***Nuremberg: Infamy on Trial.** Joseph Persico. 2000. pap. 15.95 (*0-14-029815-0*) Penguin Putnam.
Nuremberg: Infamy on Trial. Joseph E. Persico. 544p. 1995. pap. 15.95 (*0-14-016622-X*, Penguin Bks) Viking Penguin.
Nuremberg: The Last Battle. unabridged ed. David Irving. (Illus.). 377p. 1996. 35.00 (*1-872197-16-7*, Pub. by Focal Pt) WW Two Bks.
Nuremberg Diary. Gustave M. Gilbert. (Illus.). 488p. 1995. reprint ed. pap. 16.95 (*0-306-80661-4*) Da Capo.
Nuremberg 1896 International Chess Tournament. Ed. by John C. Owen. (Great Tournaments Ser.: Vol. 9). (Illus.). 413p. Date not set. 45.00 (*0-939433-54-0*) Caissa Edit.
Nuremberg, 1893 Proceedings see International Congress on the History of Art
Nuremberg Fallacy. expanded ed. Eugene Davidson. LC 98-8048. 352p. 1998. pap. 19.95 (*0-8262-1201-8*) U of Mo Pr.
Nuremberg Forty Years Later: The Struggle against Injustice in Our Time. Ed. by Irwin Cotler. LC 95-191527. 304p. 1995. 65.00 (*0-7735-1239-X*, Pub. by McG-Queens Univ Pr); pap. 22.95 (*0-7735-1250-0*, Pub. by McG-Queens Univ Pr) CUP Services.

N

An Asterisk (*) at the beginning of an entry indicates that the title is appearing for the first time.

Nuremberg Funnel: Idaho-German Tales. George M. Klein. Ed. by Jean Terra. LC 96-76373. (Illus.). 182p. 1996. pap. 16.95 (*1-887747-01-X*, 297-231X) Legendary Pub.

Nuremberg in the Sixteenth-Century: City Politics & Life Between the Middle Ages & Modern Times. rev. ed. Gerald Strauss. LC 76-12379. 315p. reprint ed. pap. 97.70 (*0-608-13231-4*, 205606300044) Bks Demand.

***Nuremberg Nazi War Crimes Trials: A Headline Court Case.** Harvey Fireside. LC 99-50926. (Headline Court Cases Ser.). (Illus.). 112p. (YA). (gr. 6 up). 2000. lib. bdg. 20.95 (*0-7660-1384-7*) Enslow Pubs.

Nuremberg Trial. Joe Heydecker & Johannes Leeb. LC 75-9111. 398p. 1975. reprint ed. lib. bdg. 69.50 (*0-8371-8131-3*, HENT, Greenwood Pr) Greenwood.

Nuremberg Trial & International Law. Ed. by George K. Ginsburgs & V. N. Kudriavtsev. (Law in Eastern Europe Ser.). 304p. 1990. lib. bdg. 146.00 (*0-7923-0798-4*) Kluwer Academic.

Nuremberg Trials. Earle Rice, Jr. (Famous Trials Ser.). (Illus.). 112p. (J). (gr. 6). 1996. lib. bdg. 22.45 (*1-56006-269-X*) Lucent Bks.

Nuremberg War Crimes, 1945-46. Michael R. Marrus. LC 96-86777. 276p. 1997. pap. 12.95 (*0-312-13691-9*) St Martin.

Nuremburg Chronicle: A Facisimile of Hartmann Schedel's Buch der Chroniken, Printed by Anton Koberger in 1943. Hartmann Schedel. 1980. 90.95 (*0-405-12490-2*) Ayer.

Nuremburg Laws. Amy Newman. LC 98-27778. (Words That Changed History Ser.). (Illus.). (YA). (gr. 4-12). 1998. lib. bdg. 23.70 (*1-56006-354-8*) Lucent Bks.

Nurenberg Funnel: Designing Minimalist Instruction for Practical Computer Skill. John M. Carroll. (Technical Communication Ser.). 362p. 1990. 48.50 (*0-262-03163-9*) MIT Pr.

NURETH Five: Fifth International Conference on Nuclear Reactor Thermal Hydraulics Proceedings, Salt Lake City, UT, September 21-24, 1992, Set. 2098p. 1993. 220.00 (*0-89448-178-9*, 700188) Am Nuclear Soc.

Nureyev. Clive Barnes & Kaye. 1996. 24.50 (*0-02-874114-5*) Free Pr.

Nureyev. Ed. by Howard Brown. (Illus.). 208p. (C). 1993. text 49.95 (*0-7148-2966-8*, Pub. by Phaidon Press) Phaidon Pr.

Nureyev. Peter Watson. LC 96-19636. 1999. 30.00 (*0-679-43903-X*) Random.

Nureyev. limited ed. Clive Barnes. (Illus.). 240p. 1982. 35.00 (*0-9609736-2-1*) Helene Obolensky Ent.

Nureyev. rev. ed. Ed. by Howard Brown. (Illus.). 208p. 1995. reprint ed. pap. 29.95 (*0-7148-3470-X*, Pub. by Phaidon Press) Phaidon Pr.

Nureyev: His Life. Diane Solway. LC 98-13483. (Illus.). 625p. 1999. 27.50 (*0-688-12873-4*, Wm Morrow) Morrow Avon.

***Nureyev: His Life.** Diane Solway. 640p. 1999. reprint ed. pap. 16.00 (*0-688-17220-2*, Wm Morrow) Morrow Avon.

Nuristan. Hakim M. Said. 563p. (Orig.). 1992. pap. 49.00 (*1-56744-464-4*) Kazi Pubns.

Nuristani Buildings. Lennart Edelberg. (Jutland Archaeological Society Publications: No. 18). (Illus.). 225p. (C). 1984. 36.00 (*87-88415-28-7*, Pub. by Aarhus Univ Pr) David Brown.

Nurmi: Or The Journey to the Trout. Gerhard Kopf. Tr. by Leslie Willson. LC 98-17521. (Studies in German Literature, Linguistics, & Culture). 165p. 1998. 39.95 (*1-57113-277-5*) Camden Hse.

Nurnberger Hexenhammer, 1491. Heinrich Kramer. (Rechtsgeschichte, Zivilisationsprozess, Psychohistorie - Quellen und Studien Ser.: Bd. 2). (GER.). ix, 146p. 1992. reprint ed. write for info. (*3-487-09380-4*) G Olms Pubs.

Nurnbergisches Gelehrten-Lexicon, 8 vols., Set. Georg A. Will. 1983. write for info. incl. fiche (*0-318-71951-7*) G Olms Pubs.

NURS ASST 4 WKBK. 4th ed. Relda Kelly. 1995. pap. text, wbk. ed. 17.95 (*0-8151-5057-1*) Mosby Inc.

Nurse. Peggy Anderson. 1990. mass mkt. 6.99 (*0-425-12286-7*, Berkley-Pacer) Berkley Pub.

Nurse. Jack Rudman. (Career Examination Ser.: C-532). 1994. pap. 27.95 (*0-8373-0532-2*) Nat Learn.

Nurse. 7th ed. Ed. by Sanchez. 288p. 1986. pap. 9.95 (*0-317-52680-4*, Arco) Macmillan Gen Ref.

Nurse: Hearts & Hands. William H. Hull. 235p. 1991. pap. 9.95 (*0-939330-04-0*) W H Hull.

Nurse Abuse: Impact & Resolution. 2nd rev. ed. Ed. by Laura G. Vonfrolio et al. 300p. 1996. pap. 15.00 (*1-888315-02-4*) Power NY.

Nurse Administrator. Jack Rudman. (Career Examination Ser.: C-2913). 1994. pap. 34.95 (*0-8373-2913-2*) Nat Learn.

Nurse Against the Town. large type ed. Jane Converse. (Linford Romance Library). 208p. 1993. pap. 16.99 (*0-7089-7456-2*, Linford) Ulverscroft.

Nurse Aide in Long Term Care. Betty J. Walston & Keith E. Walston. 352p. 1995. 38.60 (*0-8273-8787-3*) Delmar.

Nurse Aide in Long-Term Care. 2nd ed. Betty J. Walston. 324p. 1995. pap. 42.95 (*0-8273-5470-3*) Delmar.

Nurse Aide in Long-Term Care: Instructor's Guide. 3rd ed. Betty J. Walston & Keith E. Walston. 298p. 1994. teacher ed. 19.00 (*0-8273-5471-1*) Delmar.

Nurse Aide Test Study Guide. Patty Leary et al. Ed. by Sandra Balkema et al. (Illus.). 200p. (Orig.). 1989. pap. 10.00 (*0-685-44697-2*) Matthew Scott.

Nurse Alice in Love. large type ed. Theresa Charles. 1990. 27.99 (*0-7089-2281-3*) Ulverscroft.

Nurse & the Crystal Ball. large type ed. Florence Stuart. (Linford Romance Library). 256p. 1995. pap. 16.99 (*0-7089-7671-9*, Linford) Ulverscroft.

Nurse & the Star. large type ed. Peggy Gaddis. (Dales Romance Ser.). 1992. pap. 13.95 (*1-85389-303-X*, Dales) Ulverscroft.

Nurse Anesthesia: Clinical Textbook. John J. Nagelhout & Karen L. Zaglaniczny. Ed. by Maura Connor. (Illus.). 1375p. 1996. pap. text 130.00 (*0-7216-6479-2*, W B Saunders Co) Harcrt Hlth Sci Grp.

Nurse Anesthesia: Pretest Self-Assessment & Review. Ed. by Francis R. Gerbasi. LC 97-21700. (Pretest Specialty Level Ser.). (Illus.). 264p. 1997. pap. text 39.95 (*0-07-052080-1*) McGraw-Hill HPD.

***Nurse Apprentice, 1860-1977.** 286p. 2000. 79.95 (*0-7546-0172-2*) Ashgate Pub Co.

Nurse As Caregiver for the Dying Patient & His Family. Ed. by Ann M. Earle & Nina Arson-Dizzo. LC 76-14441. 252p. 1976. 12.50 (*0-930194-31-4*) Ctr Thanatology.

Nurse As Educator: Principle of Teaching & Learning. Susan B. Bastable. LC 97-7066. (Nursing Ser.). 432p. 1997. pap. 40.00 (*0-7637-0310-9*) Jones & Bartlett.

Nurse As Executive. 4th ed. Barbara Stevens-Barnum & Darlene M. Kerfoot. 369p. 1995. 52.00 (*0-8342-0571-8*, 20571) Aspen Pub.

Nurse As Group Leader. 3rd ed. Carolyn C. Clark. LC 94-3104. (Teaching of Nursing Ser.: Vol. 3). 304p. (C). 1994. text 32.95 (*0-8261-2333-3*) Springer Pub.

Nurse As Healer. Lynn Keegan. LC 93-26361. (Real Nursing Ser.). 228p. (C). 1993. mass mkt. 21.50 (*0-8273-6156-4*) Delmar.

Nurse As Manager. Joyce L. Schweiger. LC 80-17456. 194p. 1989. pap. text 32.20 (*0-8273-4360-4*) Delmar.

Nurse As Manager Handbook. Joyce L. Schweiger. LC 86-9126. (Red Bks.). 600p. 1989. pap. text 33.95 (*0-8273-4361-2*) Delmar.

Nurse As Therapist: A Behavioural Model. Ed. by Philip J. Barker & Douglas Fraser. LC 85-10935. 250p. (Orig.). 1985. pap. 25.00 (*0-7099-3253-7*, Pub. by C Helm) Routldge.

Nurse Assistant. Quinlan. LC 98-17782. (Careers Without College Ser.). (Illus.). 48p. (J). (gr. 4-7). 1998. 19.00 (*0-7368-0036-0*) Capstone Pr.

***Nurse Assistant.** Kathryn A. Quinlan. (Careers Without College Ser.). (J). 1998. 19.00 (*0-516-21398-9*) Childrens.

Nurse Assistant in Long-Term Care: A Rehabilitative Approach. Hazel M. Castillo. (Illus.). 528p. (gr. 13). 1992. pap. text 27.00 (*0-8016-0945-3*, 00945) Mosby Inc.

Nurse Assistant Test Preparation. Wanda Smith. LC 94-35572. (Test Prep Ser.). 192p. 1994. pap. 22.00 (*0-8359-4925-7*, Arco) Macmillan Gen Ref.

Nurse Assisting Challenge. Delmar Staff. (Home Care Aide Ser.). 1996. 16.95 (*0-8273-7870-X*) Delmar.

Nurse at Burford's Landing. large type ed. Peggy Dern. (Linford Romance Library). 304p. 1993. pap. 16.99 (*0-7089-7335-3*, Linford) Ulverscroft.

Nurse at Crag House. large type ed. Alison Bray. (Dales Large Print Ser.). 235p. 1997. pap. 18.99 (*1-85389-780-9*, Dales) Ulverscroft.

Nurse at Deer Cottage. large type ed. Mary J. Warmington. (Dales Large Print Ser.). 212p. 1997. pap. 18.99 (*1-85389-726-4*) Ulverscroft.

Nurse at Guale Farms. large type ed. Georgia Craig. (Romance Ser.). 288p. 1992. 27.99 (*0-7089-2709-2*) Ulverscroft.

Nurse at High Hedges. large type ed. Jane Lester. 288p. 1988. 27.99 (*0-7089-1882-4*) Ulverscroft.

Nurse at Kelvin Abbey. large type ed. Quenna Tilbury. 304p. 1989. 27.99 (*0-7089-2000-4*) Ulverscroft.

Nurse at Large. large type ed. Holly North. 245p. 1992. 27.99 (*0-7505-0323-8*, Pub. by Mgna Lrg Print) Ulverscroft.

***Nurse at Pinewood.** large type ed. Janita Cleve. 320p. 2000. 18.99 (*1-84137-004-5*, Pub. by Mgna Lrg Print) Ulverscroft.

***Nurse at Smokey River.** large type ed. Denise Conway. 272p. 1999. pap. 20.99 (*1-85389-967-4*, Dales) Ulverscroft.

Nurse at Spanish Cay. large type ed. Peggy Gaddis. 1990. pap. 16.99 (*0-7089-6921-6*, Linford) Ulverscroft.

Nurse Betrayed. large type ed. Jeanne Bowman. (Linford RomanceLarge Print Ser.). 256p. 1995. pap. 16.99 (*0-7089-7678-6*, Linford) Ulverscroft.

Nurse Brenda's Husband. large type ed. Quenna Tilbury. 1989. 27.99 (*0-7089-2082-9*) Ulverscroft.

Nurse Case Management in the 21st Century. Ed. by Elaine L. Cohen. LC 95-41096. (Illus.). 288p. (C). (gr. 13). 1995. text 43.95 (*0-8151-1518-0*, 25106) Mosby Inc.

Nurse Christine. large type ed. Peggy Gaddis. (Romance Ser.). 304p. 1992. 27.99 (*0-7089-2660-6*) Ulverscroft.

Nurse-Client Interaction: Implementing the Nursing Process. 6th ed. Sandra J. Sundeen. LC 97-42735. (Illus.). 376p. (C). (gr. 13). 1997. pap. text 29.00 (*0-8151-2605-0*, 31075) Mosby Inc.

Nurse Communicates. April Sieh & Louise Brentin. Ed. by Maura Connor. LC 96-30276. (Illus.). 352p. 1997. pap. text 26.00 (*0-7216-4173-3*, W B Saunders Co) Harcrt Hlth Sci Grp.

Nurse Consultant's Handbook. Belinda Puetz & Linda J. Shinn. LC 96-47041. 248p. 1997. 39.95 (*0-8261-9520-2*) Springer Pub.

***Nurse Courageous.** large type ed. Donna Rix. 320p. 2000. 20.99 (*1-84137-022-3*, Pub. by Mgna Lrg Print) Ulverscroft.

Nurse Dawes Is Dead. large type ed. Stella Shepherd. 1995. 27.99 (*0-7505-0792-6*, Pub. by Mgna Lrg Print) Ulverscroft.

Nurse Drake's Dilemma. large type ed. Kay Winchester. 288p. 1989. 27.99 (*0-7089-2019-5*) Ulverscroft.

Nurse Education. write for info. (*0-340-55786-9*, Pub. by E A) Routldge.

Nurse Education: A Practice-Reflective Based Approach. Reed. 216p. 1993. pap. 51.50 (*1-56593-212-9*, 0540) Singular Publishing.

Nurse Educator in Academia: Strategies for Success. Theresa M. Valiga & Helen J. Streubert. LC 90-10437. (Teaching of Nursing Ser.: Vol. 13). 240p. 1991. 34.95 (*0-8261-7150-8*) Springer Pub.

Nurse Educators, 1997: Findings from the RN & LPN Faculty Census. Delroy Louden & Dawnette Jones. 150p. 1997. 26.95 (*0-88737-755-6*, 19-7556, NLN Pr) Natl League Nurse.

***Nurse Educators, 1997: Findings from the RN & LPN Faculty Census.** NLN Staff. (Illus.). 72p. (C). 1999. pap. text 32.50 (*0-7637-1011-3*) JB Pubns.

Nurse Ellen. large type ed. Peggy Gaddis. (Linford Romance Library). 1996. pap. 16.99 (*0-7089-7836-3*, Linford) Ulverscroft.

Nurse Elsa. large type ed. Jeanne Bowman. (Ulverscroft). 224p. 1994. 27.99 (*0-7089-3054-9*) Ulverscroft.

Nurse Entrepreneur: Building the Bridge of Opportunity. rev. ed. Carolyn S. Zagury et al. Ed. by Mary A. Liotta. LC 94-61762. 176p. 1995. pap., wbk. ed. 21.95 (*1-880254-28-X*) Vista.

Nurse Executives Business Plan Manual. Joyce Y. Johnson. 216p. 1988. 155.00 (*0-87189-761-X*, 89761) Aspen Pub.

Nurse for Apple Valley. large type ed. Peggy Gaddis. (Linford Romance Library). 1995. pap. 16.99 (*0-7089-7786-3*, Linford) Ulverscroft.

Nurse for the Season. large type ed. Pauline Ash. (Linford Romance Library). 320p. 1986. pap. 6.95 (*0-7089-6169-X*, Linford) Ulverscroft.

Nurse Foster. large type ed. Rhona Uren. (Linford Romance Library). 336p. 1998. pap. 17.99 (*0-7089-5243-7*, Linford) Ulverscroft.

Nurse from Newstone. large type ed. Jill Murray. 1991. 27.99 (*0-7089-2522-7*) Ulverscroft.

Nurse GS4-GS7. Jack Rudman. (Career Examination Ser.: C-533). 1994. pap. 27.95 (*0-8373-0533-0*) Nat Learn.

Nurse Hilary. large type ed. Peggy Gaddis. (Romance Ser.). 288p. 1992. 27.99 (*0-7089-2624-X*) Ulverscroft.

Nurse Hopeful. large type ed. Freda Fenton. (Dales Large Print Ser.). 219p. 1997. pap. 18.99 (*1-85389-754-X*, Dales) Ulverscroft.

Nurse in Arabia. large type ed. Julia Davis. 240p. 1992. pap. 16.99 (*0-7089-7187-3*, Linford) Ulverscroft.

Nurse in Blue. Taber. 22.95 (*0-8488-1195-X*) Amereon Ltd.

***Nurse in Conflict.** large type ed. Lorna Page. 336p. 1999. pap. 20.99 (*1-85389-940-2*, Dales) Ulverscroft.

Nurse in Confusion. large type ed. Ivy Preston. (Linford Romance Library). 288p. 1996. pap. 16.99 (*0-7089-7904-1*) Ulverscroft.

Nurse in Izbah. large type ed. Jill Murray. (Linford Romance Library). 320p. 1985. pap. 16.99 (*0-7089-6070-7*, Linford) Ulverscroft.

***Nurse in Love.** Karla Benton. 336p. 1999. 20.99 (*1-85389-954-2*) Ulverscroft.

Nurse in Love. large type ed. Louie Williams. (Dales Large Print Ser.). 256p. 1998. pap. 19.99 (*1-85389-822-8*, Dales) Ulverscroft.

***Nurse in Need.** large type ed. Sharon Court. 336p. 1999. pap. 20.99 (*1-85389-944-5*, Dales) Ulverscroft.

Nurse in Panic. large type ed. Jane Converse. LC 93-27183. 204p. 1994. lib. bdg. 14.95 (*0-7862-0046-4*) Thorndike Pr.

Nurse in Rome. large type ed. Jane Converse. (Linford Romance Library). 240p. 1994. pap. 16.99 (*0-7089-7523-2*, Linford) Ulverscroft.

Nurse in South America. large type ed. Jean Alexander. 320p. 1992. pap. 16.99 (*0-7089-7139-3*, Linford) Ulverscroft.

Nurse in the Clouds. large type ed. Valerie Scott. (Linford Romance Library). 320p. 1998. pap. 17.99 (*0-7089-5231-3*, Linford) Ulverscroft.

Nurse in the East. large type ed. Jane Lester. (Linford Romance Library). 336p. 1985. pap. 16.99 (*0-7089-6098-7*, Linford) Ulverscroft.

Nurse in the Shadows. large type ed. Peggy Gaddis. (Linford Romance Library). 288p. 1993. pap. 16.99 (*0-7089-7332-9*, Linford) Ulverscroft.

Nurse in the Valley. large type ed. Grace Goodwin. (Romance Ser.). 272p. 1992. 27.99 (*0-7089-2661-4*) Ulverscroft.

Nurse in Torment. large type ed. Olive Patterson. (Dales Large Print Ser.). 237p. 1998. pap. 19.99 (*1-85389-797-3*, Dales) Ulverscroft.

Nurse Instructor. Jack Rudman. (Career Examination Ser.: C-2108). 1994. reprint ed. pap. 34.95 (*0-8373-2108-5*) Nat Learn.

***Nurse Investigates.** large type ed. Lorna Page. 288p. 2000. pap. 20.99 (*1-85389-994-1*, Dales) Ulverscroft.

Nurse Leadership Development: A Training Program for Developing Nurse Intrapreneurs. Laura J. McCarthy & Carolyn S. Zagury. Ed. by Mary L. Diecker et al. LC 91-75022. (Illus.). 346p. 1997. 79.00 (*1-880254-00-X*) Vista.

Nurse Liza Hale. large type ed. Jane Corby. 1991. pap. 16.99 (*0-7089-6972-0*) Ulverscroft.

Nurse Log. large type ed. Aurelia J. DeBolt. (Illus.). 64p. 1998. pap. 9.95 (*0-9664595-0-4*) Minute Pr WA.

Nurse Lugton's Curtain. Virginia Woolf. Ed. by Liz VanDoren. LC 90-5087. (Illus.). 32p. (J). (gr. 2 up). 1991. 14.95 (*0-15-200545-5*, Gulliver Bks) Harcourt.

Nurse Magda's Dilemma. large type ed. Mary-Beth Williams. (Dales Large Print Ser.). 317p. 1997. pap. 18.99 (*1-85389-777-9*, Dales) Ulverscroft.

***Nurse Maitland.** large type ed. Sonia Deane. 336p. 1999. pap. 20.99 (*1-85389-961-5*, Dales) Ulverscroft.

Nurse Manager: A Practical Guide to Better Employee Relations. 2nd ed. June B. Pugh & Mary A. Woodard-Smith. Ed. by Thomas Eoyang. (Illus.). 125p. 1996. pap. text 14.95 (*0-7216-6445-8*, W B Saunders Co) Harcrt Hlth Sci Grp.

Nurse Manager & the Law. Carmelle P. Cournoyer. 388p. (C). 1989. 69.00 (*0-8342-0049-X*) Aspen Pub.

Nurse Manager's Answer Book. Ruth I. Hansten & Marilynn J. Washburn. 256p. 1994. 33.00 (*0-8342-0501-7*, 20501) Aspen Pub.

Nurse Manager's Problem Solver. Tim Porter-O'Grady. (Illus.). 322p. (C). (gr. 13). 1994. pap. text 33.95 (*0-8016-7945-1*, 07945) Mosby Inc.

Nurse Manager's Survival Guide: Practical Answers to Everyday Problems. 2nd ed. Tina M. Marrelli. LC 96-37670. (Illus.). 400p. (C). (gr. 13). 1997. pap. text 29.95 (*0-8151-5672-3*, 28206) Mosby Inc.

Nurse-Midwife Discusses Pregnancy & Childbirth. Barbara Graves. 1994. 6.00 (*0-910304-14-9*) Budlong.

Nurse of Green. large type ed. Jane Corby. (Linford Romance Library). 272p. 1994. pap. 16.99 (*0-7089-7519-4*, Linford) Ulverscroft.

Nurse of Polka Dot Island. large type ed. Jeanne Bowman. (Linford Romance Library). 1991. pap. 16.99 (*0-7089-7104-0*) Ulverscroft.

Nurse on Forest Island. large type ed. Kay Winchester. (Romance Suspense Ser.). 288p. 1992. 27.99 (*0-7089-2707-6*) Ulverscroft.

Nurse on Loan. large type ed. Ann Jennings. (Linford Romance Library). 304p. 1995. pap. 16.99 (*0-7089-7794-4*, Linford) Ulverscroft.

Nurse on Neuro. large type ed. Ann Jennings. (Romance Ser.). 336p. 1995. pap. 16.99 (*0-7089-7661-1*, Linford) Ulverscroft.

Nurse on the Move. large type ed. Frances Crowne. 269p. 1993. 27.99 (*0-7505-0470-6*, Pub. by Mgna Lrg Print) Ulverscroft.

***Nurse on the Riviera.** large type ed. Marjorie Vernon. 256p. 1999. pap. 20.99 (*1-85389-910-0*) Ulverscroft.

Nurse on the Scene. large type ed. Lindsay Hicks. (Linford Romance Library). 336p. 1993. pap. 16.99 (*0-7089-7407-4*, Linford) Ulverscroft.

Nurse on Vacation. large type ed. Jane Burdall. (Dales Large Print Ser.). 262p. 1997. pap. 18.99 (*1-85389-713-2*) Ulverscroft.

Nurse, Pharmacology & Drug Therapy. Marshal Shlafer. Ed. by Debra Hunter. 1432p. (C). 1989. text 55.95 (*0-201-12796-2*); trans. 175.00 (*0-201-57837-9*); disk. write for info. (*0-318-67273-1*) Addison-Wesley.

Nurse, Pharmacology & Drug Therapy. 3rd ed. Marshall Shlafer. (C). 2001. text. write for info. (*0-8053-7247-4*) Addison-Wesley.

Nurse-Physician Collaboration: Care of Adults & the Elderly. Eugenia L. Siegler & Fay W. Whitney. LC 94-19260. (Advanced Practice Nursing & Geriatric Nursing Ser.). (Illus.). 264p. 1994. 35.95 (*0-8261-8500-2*) Springer Pub.

Nurse Practitioner Protocols. rev. ed. Matthew M. Cohen & Anni Lanigan. 264p. 1991. disk. write for info. (*0-924381-14-0*) Sunbelt Med Pubs.

Nurse Practitioner Protocols. 2nd rev. ed. Matthew M. Cohen & Anni Lanigan. 264p. 1995. pap. 55.00 (*0-924381-24-8*); ring bd. 85.00 (*0-924381-23-X*) Sunbelt Med Pubs.

***Nurse Practitioners: Clinical Skills & Professional Issues.** Mike Walsh et al. LC 99-15486. 320p. 1999. pap. text 45.00 (*0-7506-3990-3*) Buttrwrth-Heinemann.

***Nurse Practitioners: Developing the Role in the Hospital Setting.** Shirley Reveley et al. 256p. 2000. pap. 40.00 (*0-7506-4761-2*) Buttrwrth-Heinemann.

Nurse Practitioners: Medical Subject Analysis with Reference Bibliography. Ralphette P. Kaline. LC 85-48085. 150p. 1987. 39.50 (*0-88164-442-0*); pap. 34.50 (*0-88164-443-9*) ABBE Pubs Assn.

Nurse Practitioner's Business Practice & Legal Guide. Carolyn Buppert. LC 98-39952. 496p. 1999. 79.00 (*0-8342-1185-8*, 11858) Aspen Pub.

***Nurse Practitioner's Clinical Companion.** Springhouse Publishing Staff. (Illus.). 480p. 2000. pap. text 39.95 (*1-58255-006-9*) Springhouse Corp.

***Nurse Practitioner's Drug Handbook.** 3rd ed. Ed. by Springhouse Publishing Staff. (Illus.). 2000. pap. 39.95 (*0-87434-997-4*) Springhouse Corp.

Nurse Practitioners in Primary Care. Naomi Chambers. LC 98-198331. 130 p. 1998. write for info. (*1-85775-298-8*) Scovill Paterson.

Nurse Remembers. Eula A. Sforza. (Illus.). 233p. 1991. pap. 22.50 (*0-9636567-0-8*) E A Sforza.

Nurse Rita's Request. large type ed. Jane Lester. 281p. 1989. 27.99 (*0-7089-1933-2*) Ulverscroft.

Nurse Rowan's Return. large type ed. Kay Winchester. 1991. 27.99 (*0-7089-2359-3*) Ulverscroft.

Nurse Saver: An Organizational Too! Kevan J. Burns & Caroline E. Burns. (Illus.). 24p. 1998. wbk. ed. 25.00 (*0-9663913-0-6*) Nurse Saver.

Nurse Shark. John F. Provost. LC 95-1173. (Sharks Ser.). (Illus.). 24p. (J). (ps-4). 1995. lib. bdg. 18.60 (*1-56239-472-X*, Checkerboard Library) ABDO Pub Co.

Nurse Sharks see Tiburones Nodrizas

Nurse Sharks. Sarah Palmer. (Shark Discovery Library). (Illus.). 24p. (J). (gr. k-5). 1988. 8.95 (*0-685-58311-2*) Rourke Corp.

Nurse Sharks. Sarah Palmer. (Shark Discovery Library). (Illus.). 24p. (J). (gr. k-4). 1988. lib. bdg. 14.60 (*0-86592-459-7*) Rourke Enter.

Nurse Smith, Cook. large type ed. Joyce Dingwell. 304p. 1984. 27.99 (*0-7089-1085-8*) Ulverscroft.

Nurse-Social Worker Collaboration in Managed Care: A Model of Community Case Management. Joellen W. Hawkins et al. LC 97-22490. (Illus.). 240p. 1997. 37.95 (*0-8261-9830-9*) Springer Pub.

***Nurse Staffing & Patient Outcomes in the Inpatient Hospital Setting.** 52p. 2000. pap. 24.95 (*1-55810-151-9*) Am Nurses Pub.

Nurse Teachers As Researchers: A Reflective Approach. Ed. by Sally Thomson. (Illus.). 256p. (Orig.). 1997. pap. 45.00 (*1-56593-759-7*, 1476) Singular Publishing.

*Nurse Trent. large type ed. Sonia Deane. 384p. 2000. pap. 20.99 (1-85389-998-4, Dales) Ulverscroft.

*Nurse Trivia Calendar 2000. Rebecca Rayman. 300p. 1999. boxed set 12.95 (1-56930-104-2) Skidmore Roth Pub.

Nurse under Fire. large type ed. Florence Stuart. (Dales Romance Ser.). 1992. pap. 13.95 (1-85389-328-5, Dales) Ulverscroft.

Nurse under Suspicion. large type ed. Carol Marsh. 287p. 1989. 27.99 (0-7089-1962-6) Ulverscroft.

Nurse Verena at Weirwater. large type ed. Leslie Lance. 1991. 27.99 (0-7089-2463-8) Ulverscroft.

Nurse Victoria. large type ed. Mary J. Warmington. (Linford Romance Library). 240p. 1992. pap. 16.99 (0-7089-7214-4, Linford) Ulverscroft.

Nurse Was Juliet. large type ed. Peggy Gaddis. 1991. pap. 16.99 (0-7089-6977-1) Ulverscroft.

Nurse Weston's New Job. large type ed. Clare Lavenham. (Dales Large Print Ser.). 205p. 1997. pap. 18.99 (1-85389-756-6, Dales) Ulverscroft.

Nurse Who Shocked the Matron. large type ed. Ursula Bloom & Sheila Burns. 264p. 1989. 22.95 (0-7451-0983-7, G K Hall Lrg Type) Mac Lib Ref.

Nurse with the Red-Gold Hair. large type ed. Jane Corby. (Linford Romance Library). 256p. 1993. pap. 16.99 (0-7089-7457-0, Linford) Ulverscroft.

Nurse Wore Black. Richard H. Brawer. Ed. by Diane Dettmore. LC 94-60684. (Illus.). 180p. 1994. pap. 10.95 (1-880254-17-4) Vista.

Nurse Yourself: Self Help from A-Z. Darlene Sredl. (Nursing Self Help Ser.: Vol. 1). 89p. (Orig.). 1997. mass mkt. 12.95 (0-614-27162-2, 777-97) Med Res Assocs.

NurseNotes: Maternal-Newborn Nursing. Irene M. Bobak. LC 96-9117. 304p. 1997. pap. text 29.95 (0-7817-1128-2) Lppncott W & W.

NurseNotes: Medical-Surgical Nursing. Nelson. LC 96-23717. 464p. 1997. pap. text 31.95 (0-7817-1130-4) Lppncott W & W.

NurseNotes: Pediatric Nursing. Geraldine C. Colombrari & Diane M. Billings. LC 96-20788. 256p. 1997. pap. text 29.95 (0-7817-1129-0) Lppncott W & W.

NurseNotes: Psychiatric-Mental Health Nursing. Diane M. Billings. LC 96-9116. 272p. 1997. pap. text 29.95 (0-7817-1127-4) Lppncott W & W.

*Nurseries. Cathy Nelson Price. LC 00-20492. (For Your Home Ser.). (Illus.). 72p. 2000. pap. 12.95 (1-56799-919-0, Friedman-Fairfax) M Friedman Pub Grp Inc.

Nurseries & More: The Complete Manual of Baby Accessory Patterns. Linda W. Storm. (Illus.). 128p. (Orig.). 1988. pap. 12.95 (0-934679-02-9); spiral bd. 14.95 (0-934679-01-0) Babies Storm.

Nurseries Now: A Fair Deal for Parents & Children Martin Hughes. LC 81-484384. 284 P. :p. 1980. 1.95 (0-14-022056-9) Viking Penguin.

Nursery. LC PZ8.3.N9368 1998. 96p. (J). 1998. 14.95 (0-7868-3178-2) Little.

Nursery Activities. 32p. (J). 1997. pap., wbk. ed. 2.79 (1-57405-285-3) CharismaLife Pub.

*Nursery Activity Book, Bk. 1. Kathryn Linaker. (J). (ps). 1999. pap., wbk. ed. 15.00 (0-7217-6500-9, Pub. by Schofield) St Mut.

*Nursery Activity Book, Bk. 2. Kathryn Linaker. (J). (ps). 1999. pap., wbk. ed. 15.00 (0-7217-6501-7, Pub. by Schofield) St Mut.

*Nursery Activity Book, Bk. 3. Kathryn Linaker. (J). (ps). 1999. pap., wbk. ed. 15.00 (0-7217-6502-5, Pub. by Schofield) St Mut.

*Nursery Activity Book, Bk. 4. Kathryn Linaker. (J). 1999. pap., wbk. ed. 15.00 (0-7217-6503-3, Pub. by Schofield) St Mut.

*Nursery Activity Book, Bk. 5. Kathryn Linaker. (J). 1999. pap., wbk. ed. 15.00 (0-7217-6504-1, Pub. by Schofield) St Mut.

*Nursery Activity Book, Bk. 6. Kathryn Linaker. (J). 1999. pap., wbk. ed. 15.00 (0-7217-6505-X, Pub. by Schofield) St Mut.

Nursery & Landscape Weed Control Manual. Bob Rice. 264p. 1992. pap. 29.95 (0-913702-42-0) Thomson Pubns.

Nursery & Plantation Practices in Forestry. Vinod Kumar. 525p. 1995. 550.00 (0-7855-2748-6, Pub. by Scientific Pubs) St Mut.

Nursery & Seed Catalogs: A Directory of Collections. Pref. by June Rogier & MaryLou Wolfe. 87p. (Orig.). 1989. pap. write for info. (0-9621791-2-4) CBHL Inc.

Nursery Bedtime Book. Linda J. Sattgast. (Illus.). 48p. (J). 1995. 7.99 (0-88070-749-6, Gold n Honey) Zondervan.

Nursery Bible. Mack Thomas. (Illus.). 48p. (J). (ps). 1994. 7.99 (0-88070-665-1, Gold n Honey) Zondervan.

Nursery Board: Homes. Sian Tucker. (Illus.). 14p. (J). (ps-k). 1994. pap. 2.95 (0-671-88261-9) Litle Simon.

Nursery Board: Let's Go. Sian Tucker. (Illus.). 14p. (J). (ps-k). 1994. pap. 2.95 (0-671-88263-5) Litle Simon.

Nursery Board: Shopping. Sian Tucker. (Illus.). 14p. (J). (ps-2). 1994. 2.95 (0-671-88262-7) Litle Simon.

*Nursery Crimes. Ayelet Waldman. LC 99-46909. 224p. 2000. 21.95 (0-425-17469-7) Berkley Pub.

Nursery Crimes: Sexual Abuse in Day Care. David Finkelhor et al. 320p. (C). 1988. text 49.95 (0-8039-3399-1); pap. text 23.50 (0-8039-3400-9) Sage.

Nursery Cross Stitch. Julie Hasler. (Illus.). 1996. 18.95 (1-870586-20-4, D Porteous-Parkwest) Parkwest Pubns.

*Nursery Decor for Beginners. Creative Publishing International, Inc. Staff. LC 99-88292. (Coats & Clark Ser.). (Illus.). 128p. 2000. 17.95 (0-86573-866-1) Creat Pub Intl.

Nursery Food Book. write for info. (0-340-55935-7, Pub. by E A) Routldge.

Nursery Food Book. Whiting. 176p. 1992. pap. 47.50 (1-56593-551-9, 0530) Singular Publishing.

Nursery Management. Hay. 1997. pap. text 26.95 (0-7020-2044-3) Bailliere Tindall.

*Nursery Management: Administration & Culture. 4th ed. Davidson. LC 99-25857. (Illus.). 529p. 1999. 93.00 (0-13-857996-2) P-H.

Nursery Question. J. M. Bennett. 1991. pap. 5.00 (0-936128-75-5) De Young Pr.

Nursery Quiet & Noisy Book. Scharlotte Rich. (Illus.). 48p. (J). 1995. 7.99 (0-88070-770-4, Gold n Honey) Zondervan.

Nursery Realms: Children in the Worlds of Science Fiction, Fantasy, & Horror. Ed. by Gary Westfahl & George E. Slusser. LC 98-47940. (Illus.). 240p. 1999. pap. 40.00 (0-8203-2095-1) U of Ga Pr.

Nursery Realms: Children in the Worlds of Science Fiction, Fantasy, & Horror. Ed. by Gary Westfahl & George E. Slusser. LC 98-47940. (Proceedings of the J. Lloyd Eaton Conference of Science Fiction & Fantasy Literature Ser.). (Illus.). 223p. 1999. pap. 20.00 (0-8203-2144-3) U of Ga Pr.

Nursery Rhyme Book. (Illus.). 64p. 1979. pap. 9.95 (0-8256-9337-3, AM26824) Music Sales.

Nursery Rhyme Book. Ed. by Andrew Lang. 23.95 (0-89190-082-9) Amereon Ltd.

*Nursery Rhyme Quilt. Bonnie Kaster. LC 99-10297. 1999. 14.95 (1-56477-261-6) Martingale & Co.

Nursery Rhyme Songbook. Caroline Hooper. (Songbooks Ser.). (Illus.). 48p. (J). (ps up). 1997. pap. 9.95 (0-7460-1703-0, Usborne); lib. bdg. 17.95 (0-88110-914-2, Usborne) EDC.

Nursery Rhyme Songbook: With Easy Music to Play for Piano & Guitar. Sally Emerson. LC 92-53106. (Illus.). 72p. (J). (ps). 1995. pap. 14.95 (1-85697-635-1) LKC.

Nursery Rhyme Songs. (Let's Sing & Learn Ser.). (Illus.). 24p. (J). 1997. pap. 7.95 incl. audio (0-8092-3045-3, 304530, Contemporary Bks) NTC Contemp Pub Co.

Nursery Rhyme Sticker Book. Caroline Hooper. (Songbooks Ser.). (Illus.). 20p. (J). (ps-3). 1998. text 6.95 (0-7460-3008-8, Usborne) EDC.

Nursery Rhyme Tape Pack/Songbook. Caroline Hooper. Ed. by Emma Danes. (Songbooks Ser.). (Illus.). 48p. (Orig.). (J). (ps up). 1997. pap. 19.95 (0-7460-2862-8, Usborne) EDC.

Nursery Rhyme Theme-a-Saurus: The Great Big Book of Nursery Rhyme Teaching Themes. Jean Warren. Ed. by Kathleen Cubley. LC 92-60926. (Illus.). 160p. (Orig.). (J). (ps-1). 1993. pap. 14.95 (0-911019-55-3, WPH 1005) Totline Pubns.

*Nursery Rhyme Time. Julia M. Maro. (Eloquence Ser.: Vol. 2). (Illus.). 94p. 1999. pap. 19.95 (0-9677129-0-4) AAC Intervent.

Nursery Rhyme Time. Ru Story-Huffman. LC 95-36064. (Illus.). 90p. 1996. pap., teacher ed. 14.95 (0-917846-56-7, 34004, Alleyside) Highsmith Pr.

Nursery Rhymes see Critter Sitters Board Books

Nursery Rhymes see Learn to Read with Phonetic & Non-Phonetic Words

Nursery Rhymes. 160p. (J). (ps-k). 1994. 9.98 (1-85854-539-0) Brimax Bks.

*Nursery Rhymes. 24p. 1999. pap. 7.95 (0-634-00081-0) H Leonard.

Nursery Rhymes. (J). (gr. k up). 1991. pap. 1.47 (1-56297-093-3, GS-32) Lee Pubns KY.

Nursery Rhymes. (Modern Ser.). (Illus.). 24p. (J). (gr. k-2). 1988. 3.95 (0-87449-499-0) Modern Pub NYC.

Nursery Rhymes. (My First Sing-Alongs Ser.). (J). text 7.99 incl. audio (1-55723-603-8) W Disney Records.

Nursery Rhymes. Dorling Kindersley Staff. (Baby's Bk.). (J). 1994. write for info. (1-56458-827-0) DK Pub Inc.

Nursery Rhymes. Ladybird Series. (First Bks.: No. S808-5). (Illus.). (J). (ps). pap. 3.95 (0-7214-5056-3, Ladybrd) Penguin Putnam.

Nursery Rhymes. Illus. by Doreen McGuinness. (My Big Little Fat Bks.). 20p. (J). (ps). 1996. bds. 3.49 (1-85854-402-5) Brimax Bks.

Nursery Rhymes. Illus. by Katy Rhodes. (Carousel Ser.). (J). (ps-1). 1994. boxed set 7.95 (1-884628-09-5, Flyng Frog) Allied Pub MD.

Nursery Rhymes. Illus. by Amye Rosenberg. (Happytime Ser.). 24p. (J). (ps-1). 1987. pap. 1.25 (0-7214-9550-8, S871-6, Ladybrd) Penguin Putnam.

Nursery Rhymes. Scholastic, Inc. Staff. 1998. 7.95 (0-590-04138-X) Scholastic Inc.

Nursery Rhymes. Kim Thompson et al. (Early Childhood Ser.). (Illus.). 24p. (J). (ps-2). 1995. pap. 9.98 incl. audio (1-882331-83-4, Twin415) Twin Sisters.

Nursery Rhymes. Illus. by Eloise Wilkin. LC 78-64606. (Board Bks.). (J). (ps). 1979. 4.99 (0-394-84129-8, Pub. by Random Bks Yng Read) Random.

Nursery Rhymes. unabridged ed. Rock & Learn, Inc. Staff. (Rock n' Learn Ser.). (Illus.). 30p. (J). (ps-k). 1995. pap. 12.99 incl. audio (1-878489-53-4, RL953) Rock N Learn.

Nursery Rhymes: A Collection from Mother Goose. Random House Value Publishing Staff. (c). (Illus.). 1999. 5.99 (0-517-20330-8) Random Hse Value.

Nursery Rhymes: Easy Readers Tales & Rhymes. Teacher Created Materials Staff. (Easy Readers Ser.). 16p. (J). (ps-1). 1997. pap. 2.49 (1-57690-285-4) Tchr Create Mat.

Nursery Rhymes: Interactive Storybook. (Illus.). 8p. (J). (ps-6). 1997. 12.50 (1-890647-03-9) Lrning Curve.

*Nursery Rhymes: Music & Dance. Lynn Brunelle. (Illus.). 20p. (J). 1999. 5.95 (1-892374-25-0) Weldon Owen.

Nursery Rhymes & Fairy Tales. Margaret Tarrant. (J). 1984. 5.98 (0-671-06535-1) S&S Trade.

Nursery Rhymes & Songs. (Illus.). 64p. pap. 10.95 (0-8256-2443-6, AM60211) Music Sales.

Nursery Rhymes for All Keyboards. Selected by Daniel Scott. 48p. 1992. pap. 14.95 (0-7119-3167-4, AM90033) Music Sales.

*Nursery Rhymes for Cats. Hope. (J). 2000. pap. 10.95 (0-553-50720-6, Pub. by Transworld Publishers Ltd) Trafalgar.

Nursery Rhymes for Modern Times. Horatio Hotchpotch. LC 75-43129. (Illus.). 64p. 1976. 4.95 (0-915010-13-5) Sutter House.

Nursery Rhymes for Nursery Times. Mary L. Thompson. (Illus.). 1993. 6.50 (0-8378-5445-8) Gibson.

Nursery Rhymes for the Dead. Sue Owen. LC 80-18778. 61p. 1980. pap. 4.00 (0-87886-112-2, Greenfld Rev Pr) Greenfld Rev Lit.

Nursery Rhymes from Mother Goose. Random House Staff. LC 94-11973. (Illus.). 96p. (J). (gr. 2-8). 1994. 8.99 (0-517-11857-2) Random Hse Value.

Nursery Rhymes from Mother Goose: Told in Signed English. Harry Bornstein & Karen L. Saulnier. (Awareness & Caring Ser.). (Illus.). 48p. (J). (gr. k-3). 1992. lib. bdg. 17.95 (1-56674-034-7) Forest Hse.

Nursery Rhymes from Mother Goose: Told in Signed English. Harry Bornstein & Karen L. Saulnier. LC 91-42409. (Signed English Ser.). (Illus.). 48p. (J). (ps-2). 1992. 14.95 (0-930323-99-8, Pub. by K Green Pubns) Gallaudet Univ Pr.

Nursery Rhymes in Meher's Time. Mehera J. Irani. (Illus.). (J). (gr. 3 up). 1977. pap. text 5.95 (0-913078-29-8) Sheriar Pr.

Nursery Rhymes, North of the Border. Frwd. by Celia Barker Lottridge. (Illus.). 63p. (J). (ps-1). 1996. 18.95 (0-88899-213-0) Publishers Group.

*Nursery Rhymes of Winnie the Pooh. (Books Are Fun Ser.). 96p. (J). 2000. 14.95 (0-7868-3263-0, Pub. by Disney Pr) Time Warner.

Nursery Rhymes Pillow Book. (J). 1990. pap. 19.95 (1-55923-045-2) Wicklow Ltd.

Nursery Rhymes Series, Big bk. (J). (gr. k-2). 1991. pap. 23.00 (1-56843-036-1) EMG Networks.

Nursery Rhymes Series, Little bk. (J). (gr. k-2). 1991. 4.50 (0-685-62344-0) EMG Networks.

Nursery Rhymes Story. Michael Foreman. 1996. pap. 4.99 (0-7636-0174-8) Candlewick Pr.

Nursery School & Day Care Center Management Guide. 2nd ed. Clare Cherry et al. 1987. ring bd. 31.99 (0-8224-4793-2) Fearon Teacher Aids.

Nursery Songs. (I-See-You-Bks.). (Illus.). 8p. (J). (gr. k up). 1997. 3.50 (1-56293-984-X, McClanahan Book) Learn Horizon.

Nursery Songs & Lap Games. Compiled by Pamela Kennedy & Joan Covell. LC 90-36506. (Illus.). 32p. (J). 1990. 13.95 (0-8249-8486-2, Ideals Child) Hambleton-Hill.

Nursery Songs & Lap Games, Set. Compiled by Pamela Kennedy & Joan Covell. LC 90-36506. (Illus.). 32p. (J). (gr. 1-5). 1990. 17.95 incl. audio (0-8249-7399-2, I73992, Ideals Child) Hambleton-Hill.

Nursery Songs & Lullabies. Francine Lancaster. (Francine Sings Keepsake Collection). (J). (gr. k up). 1984. 16.95 incl. audio (0-930647-00-9); audio. write for info. (0-318-58469-7) Lancaster Prodns.

Nursery Supervisor. Jack Rudman. (Career Examination Ser.: C-3575). 1994. pap. 29.95 (0-8373-3575-2) Nat Learn.

Nursery Tales Around the World. Ed. by Judy Sierra. LC 93-2068. (Illus.). 114p. (J). 1996. 20.00 (0-395-67894-3, Clarion Bks) HM.

Nursery Tales, Traditions, & Histories of the Zulus: In Their Own Words, with a Translation into English & Notes, Vol. 1. Henri Callaway. (B. E. Ser.: No. 36). 1868. 40.00 (0-8115-2987-8) Periodicals Srv.

Nursery Teacher in Action. Margaret Lally. 194p. 1991. pap. 27.00 (1-85396-131-0, Pub. by P Chapman) Taylor & Francis.

Nursery Technology for Agroforestry: Application in Arid & Semi-Arid Regions. S. Puri & P. K. Khosla. (Winrock Ser.). 392p. (C). 1993. text 75.00 (1-881570-11-8) Science Pubs.

Nursery Treasury. Sanduik Bokforlag. (Illus.). 1997. pap. 12.98 (1-58048-004-7) Sandvik Pub.

Nursery Treasury: A Collection of Rhymes, Poems, Lullabies & Games. Illus. by Moira Maclean & Colin Maclean. 128p. (J). 1988. 24.95 (0-385-24650-1) Doubleday.

Nursery World of Dr. Blatz. Jocelyn M. Raymond. 280p. 1991. text 35.00 (0-8020-2793-8) U of Toronto Pr.

*Nursery Writing Book, Bk. 1. Kathryn Linaker. (J). (ps). 1999. pap., wbk. ed. 19.00 (0-7217-6512-2, Pub. by Schofield) St Mut.

*Nursery Writing Book, Bk. 2. Kathryn Linaker. (J). (ps). 1999. pap., wbk. ed. 19.00 (0-7217-6513-0, Pub. by Schofield) St Mut.

*Nursery Writing Book, Bk. 3. Kathryn Linaker. (J). (ps). 1999. pap., wbk. ed. 19.00 (0-7217-6514-9, Pub. by Schofield) St Mut.

*Nursery Writing Book, Bk. 4. Kathryn Linaker. (J). (ps). 1999. pap., wbk. ed. 19.00 (0-7217-6515-7, Pub. by Schofield) St Mut.

*Nursery Writing Book, Bk. 5. Kathryn Linaker. (J). (ps). 1999. pap., wbk. ed. 19.00 (0-7217-6516-5, Pub. by Schofield) St Mut.

*Nursery Writing Book, Bk. 6. Kathryn Linaker. (J). (ps). 1999. pap., wbk. ed. 19.00 (0-7217-6517-3, Pub. by Schofield) St Mut.

Nurses see Community Helpers Series

Nurses see Enfermeros y Enfermeras

Nurses. Robert James. LC 95-18940. (People Who Care for Our Health Discovery Library). 24p. (J). (gr. k-4). 1995. lib. bdg. 15.93 (1-55916-167-1) Rourke Bk Co.

Nurses. Dee Ready. (Community Helpers Ser.). (J). 1997. lib. bdg. 14.00 (0-516-20504-8) Childrens.

Nurses. Marcia Rose. 1997. mass mkt. 6.99 (0-345-39001-6) Ballantine Pub Grp.

Nurses: The Human Touch. Michael Brown. 1992. mass mkt. 5.99 (0-8041-0800-5) Ivy Books.

Nurse's Aide. Jack Rudman. (Career Examination Ser.: C-535). 1994. pap. 23.95 (0-8373-0535-7) Nat Learn.

Nurses & Consumers: Partners in Assuring Quality Care in the Home. Laura Reif & Karen S. Martin. 60p. 1995. pap. text 20.95 (1-55810-120-9, CH-49) Am Nurses Pub.

Nurses & Doctors at Work: Rethinking Professional Boundaries. Deidre Wicks. LC 99-178837. 1998. 95.00 (0-335-20274-8); pap. text 29.95 (0-335-20273-X) Taylor & Francis.

Nurses & Families: A Guide to Family Assessment & Intervention. 3rd ed. Lorraine M. Wright & Maureen Leahey. LC 93-43430. (Illus.). 358p. (C). 1999. pap. text 23.95 (0-8036-0371-1) Davis Co.

Nurses & Family Health Promotion: Concepts, Assessment & Interventions. 2nd ed. Ed. by Perri J. Bomar. LC 95-19486. (Illus.). 429p. 1995. pap. text 38.95 (0-7216-3795-7, W B Saunders Co) Harcrt Hlth Sci Grp.

Nurses & Health Care. Ed. by Elizabeth Lucas. 1976. pap. 24.95 (0-8464-0679-9) Beekman Pubs.

Nurses & Physicians in Transition. Janice A. Buehler. Ed. by Philip Kalisch & Beatrice Kalisch. LC 82-10940. (Studies in Nursing Management: No. 10). 163p. 1982. reprint ed. pap. 50.60 (0-8357-1379-2, 207007100063) Bks Demand.

Nurses & Work Satisfaction: An Index for Measurement. 2nd ed. Paula L. Stamps. LC 97-18700. 1997. 42.00 (1-56793-061-1) Health Admin Pr.

Nurses as Consultants: Essential Concepts & Processes. Susan Norwood. LC 97-22981. 336p. 1997. pap. text 41.00 (0-8053-5427-1, Prentice Hall) P-H.

*Nurses at War, 1939-45. Penny Starns. (Illus.). 224p. 2000. text 34.95 (0-7509-2387-3) Sutton Publng.

Nurse's Atlas of Dermatology. Theodore Rosen et al. 203p. 1983. 25.50 (0-316-75705-5, Little Brwn Med Div) Lppncott W & W.

Nurse's Book of Courage. Helene K. Nawrocki. 61p. 1993. pap. 14.95 (0-9636792-0-1); audio 14.95 (0-9636792-1-X) Ctr Nursing Excell.

Nurse's Clinical Guide to Dosage Calculations. 2nd rev. ed. Belle Erickson & Catherine M. Todd. LC 94-3506. 224p. 1994. spiral bd. 27.95 (0-87434-703-3) Springhouse Corp.

Nurse's Clinical Guide to Maternity Care. 2nd ed. Springhouse Publishing Company Staff. LC 97-42636. 512p. 1998. pap. text 29.95 (0-87434-883-8) Springhouse Corp.

Nurse's Clinical Guide to Neonatal Care. 2nd ed. Springhouse Publishing Company Staff. LC 97-42704. 400p. 1998. pap. text 29.95 (0-87434-884-6) Springhouse Corp.

Nurse's Clinical Guide to Psychiatric & Mental Health Care. Linda C. Copel. LC 95-32425. (Illus.). 384p. 1995. pap. 27.95 (0-87434-720-3) Springhouse Corp.

*Nurse's Clinical Guide to Psychiatric & Mental Health Care. 2nd ed. Linda Copel. LC 99-35195. 1999. write for info. (0-87434-986-9) Springhouse Corp.

Nurse's Clinical Pocket Manual: Nursing Diagnoses, Care Planning & Documentation. Mary F. Moorhouse & Marilynn E. Doenges. 477p. (C). 1990. spiral bd. 18.95 (0-8036-6314-5) Davis Co.

Nurses, Computers & Information Technology. Procter. 118p. 1992. pap. 34.95 (1-56593-019-3, 0262) Thomson Learn.

Nurses Counselling: The View from the Practitioners. Ed. by Philip Burnard & Ian Hulatt. LC 96-14626. 192p. 1996. pap. text 40.00 (0-7506-2004-8) Buttrwrth-Heinemann.

Nurse's Diary. large type ed. Louie Williams. (Linford Romance Large Print Ser.). 304p. 1998. pap. 17.99 (0-7089-5249-6, Linford) Ulverscroft.

Nurse's Directory of Capitol Connections. 4th rev. ed. 90p. 1997. ring bd. 25.00 (0-9659713-0-9) Sharp Legis.

Nurse's Dosage Calculator. Springhouse Publishing Company Staff. (Illus.). 24p. 1998. boxed set 24.95 incl. disk (0-87434-974-5) Springhouse Corp.

Nurses Drug Facts Reference Set, 1997, 2 bks. write for info. incl. cd-rom (1-57439-010-4) Facts & Comparisons.

Nurses Drug Guide 2000. Wilson & Shannon. 1999. pap. text 32.95 (0-8385-7115-8) Appleton & Lange.

Nurse's Drug Handbook. 6th ed. Suzanne Loebl & George R. Spratto. 1991. pap. 33.95 (0-8273-4527-5) Delmar.

Nurse's Drug Reference, 1990. 2nd ed. George R. Spratto. (Professional Reference - Nursing Ser.). 1990. pap. 25.95 (0-8273-4277-2) Delmar.

Nurse's Fast Facts: The Only Book You Need for Clinicals. 2nd ed. Brenda W. Holloway. (Illus.). 592p. 23.95 (0-8036-0599-4) Davis Co.

Nurse's Guide for Teaching Patients Undergoing Cancer Chemotherapy. 1984. lib. bdg. 250.00 (0-87700-543-5) Revisionist Pr.

Nurse's Guide to Cancer Care. Constance S. Kirkpatrick. LC 86-17666. 304p. 1986. 65.00 (0-8476-7500-9); pap. 27.95 (0-8476-7501-7) Rowman.

Nurse's Guide to Cardiac Monitoring. Peter J. B. Hubner. LC 74-501980. ix, 66 p. 1971. write for info. (0-7020-0378-6, W B Saunders Co) Harcrt Hlth Sci Grp.

Nurse's Guide to Cardiac Monitoring. 2nd ed. Peter J. B. Hubner. LC 76-358596. ix, 66 p. 1975. write for info. (0-7020-0592-4, W B Saunders Co) Harcrt Hlth Sci Grp.

Nurse's Guide to Cardiac Rhythm Interpretation: Implications for Patient Care. Sara Paul & Jennifer D. Hebra. Ed. by Barbara N. Cullen. LC 97-36629. (Illus.). 405p. (C). 1998. pap. text 27.95 (0-7216-5906-3, W B Saunders Co) Harcrt Hlth Sci Grp.

N

An Asterisk (*) at the beginning of an entry indicates that the title is appearing for the first time.

Nurse's Guide to Caring for Elders. Mary Carroll & L. Jane Brue. 240p. (C). 1987. pap. 29.95 (*0-8261-5520-0*) Springer Pub.

Nurses' Guide to Clinical Procedures. 3rd ed. Anthelyn Jean Smith-Temple. LC 99-86649. 768p. 1997. spiral bd. write for info. (*0-7817-1455-9*) Lppncott W & W.

Nurses' Guide to Clinical Procedures. 3rd ed. Jean Smith-Temple & Joyce Y. Johnson. LC 97-15075. (Illus.). 768p. 1997. spiral bd. 26.00 (*0-397-55464-8*) Lppncott W & W.

Nurse's Guide to Diet Therapy. 2nd ed. Lois H. Bodinski. 1989. pap. text 33.50 (*0-8273-4209-8*) Delmar.

Nurse's Guide to Home Care of the Elderly. Sheryl Zang. LC 98-22344. 500p. 1998. spiral bd. 29.95 (*0-7817-1542-3*) Lppncott W & W.

Nurses' Guide to Home Care Procedures. Ed. by Joyce Y. Johnson et al. LC 97-19139. (Illus.). 640p. 1997. spiral bd. 26.00 (*0-397-55468-0*) Lppncott W & W.

Nurse's Guide to Home Health Care. Tina M. Marrelli. LC 97-18701. (Illus.). 448p. (C). (gr. 13). 1997. spiral bd. 26.95 (*0-8151-5558-1*, 29633) Mosby Inc.

Nurse's Guide to Infection Control see Healthcare Worker's & Professional Provider's Guide to Preventitive Measures of Infection Control/ Epidemiology

Nurse's Guide to Managed Care. Turner. LC 98-44092. 288p. 1999. pap. 34.00 (*0-8342-1235-8*, 12358) Aspen Pub.

Nurse's Guide to Marketing. Ruth R. Alward. (Home Care Aide Ser.). 1990. pap. 43.45 (*0-8273-4203-9*) Delmar.

Nurse's Guide to Public Speaking. Barry Kaplan. LC 96-53471. 126p. 1997. pap. 23.95 (*0-8261-9590-3*) Springer Pub.

***Nurse's Guide to Successful Management.** Jo A. McGuffin. LC 98-43530. 1999. spiral bd. 29.95 (*0-323-00388-5*) Mosby Inc.

Nurses' Guide to Understanding Laboratory & Diagnostic Tests. Denise D. Wilson. LC 98-3764. 550p. 1998. pap. text 24.95 (*0-7817-1834-1*) Lppncott W & W.

Nurse's Handbook for High-Dose Chemotherapy. Sakurai. 1997. pap. text. write for info. (*0-7216-6958-1*, W B Saunders Co) Harcrt Hlth Sci Grp.

Nurses Handbook for Home Care Procedures. Marie S. Jaffe. (Nursing Education Ser.). 1992. pap. 31.50 (*0-8273-4508-9*) Delmar.

Nurse's Handbook of Complementary & Alternative Therapies. Springhouse Publishing Company Staff. LC 98-21445. 416p. 1998. 29.95 (*0-87434-898-6*) Springhouse Corp.

Nurses' Handbook of Complementary Therapies. Ed. by Denise F. Rankin-Box. LC 94-41151. 1995. pap. text 17.95 (*0-443-05180-1*) Church.

Nurse's Handbook of Complementary Therapies: U. S. A. Edition. Ed. by D. Rankin-Box & V. Slater. (Illus.). 190p. 1996. pap. write for info. (*0-443-07791-6*) Church.

Nurses' Handbook of Health Assessment. 3rd ed. Janet Weber. LC 96-21001. 480p. 1996. spiral bd. 23.95 (*0-397-55326-9*) Lppncott W & W.

Nurses' Handbook of Health Assessment. 4th ed. Janet Weber. 512p. spiral bd. 24.95 (*0-7817-2331-0*) Lppncott W & W.

Nurse's Handbook of Home Infusion Therapy. SPC Staff. Ed. by Patricia Schull. LC 97-65077. (Illus.). 224p. 1997. 24.95 (*0-87434-908-7*) Springhouse Corp.

Nurses' Handbook of Intravenous Medications. Sharon Weinstein. LC 90-6684. 658p. 1991. reprint ed. pap. 200.00 (*0-608-07304-0*, 206753200009) Bks Demand.

Nurse's Handbook of Patient Education. Shirin F. Pestonjee. LC 99-36721. 274p. 1999. text 29.95 (*1-58255-018-2*) Springhouse Corp.

Nurse's Homecare Companion. Springhouse Publishing Company Staff. LC 97-50211. 512p. 1998. pap. text 29.95 (*0-87434-894-3*) Springhouse Corp.

Nurses' Illustrated Physiology. 4th rev. ed. Ann B. McNaught & Robin Callander. (Illus.). 158p. 1989. pap. text 15.95 (*0-443-02703-X*) Church.

Nurses in Family Planning: Counseling, Patient Advocacy & Clinical Care. Mickey Gillmor-Kahn et al. LC 82-84278. (Illus.). 300p. 1982. pap. text 19.95 (*0-8290-0927-2*) Irvington.

Nurses in Managed Care. Stutz. (C). 1999. pap. text. write for info. (*0-7216-8147-6*, W B Saunders Co) Harcrt Hlth Sci Grp.

Nurses in Nazi Germany: Moral Choice in History. Bronwyn Rebekah McFarland-Icke. LC 99-18151. 335p. 1999. 35.00 (*0-691-00665-2*, Pub. by Princeton U Pr) Cal Prin Full Svc.

Nurses in Texas: Nurse Aides to Advanced Nurse Practitioners, 1971-1991. Olive Roen. (Working Paper Ser.: No. 62). 84p. 1992. pap. 5.50 (*0-89940-544-4*) LBJ Sch Pub Aff.

Nurses in the Courtroom: Cases & Commentary for Concerned Professionals. Barbara E. Calfee. 250p. (Orig.). 1992. pap. text 25.00 (*0-9633540-2-7*) ARC Pub.

***Nurses in the Political Arena: The Public Face of Nursing.** Harriet R. Feldman & Sandra B. Lewenson. LC 00-30090. (Illus.). 2000. pap. write for info. (*0-8261-1331-1*) Springer Pub.

Nurses in the Workplace. Ed. by Marie E. Cowart & William J. Serow. (Illus.). 304p. 1992. 39.95 (*0-8039-4313-X*) Sage.

***Nurse's Legal Handbook.** 4th ed. Springhouse Publishing Staff. 2000. pap. text 36.95 (*0-87434-991-5*) Springhouse Corp.

Nurse's Liability for Malpractice: A Programmed Course. 6th ed. Eli P. Bernzweig. LC 95-30160. (Illus.). 496p. (C). (gr. 13). 1995. pap. text 37.00 (*0-8151-0702-1*, 26104) Mosby Inc.

Nurse's Love Affair. large type ed. Louie Williams. (Dales Large Print Ser.). 243p. 1997. pap. 18.99 (*1-85389-753-1*, Dales) Ulverscroft.

Nurses Manage: Issues of Nurses & Management in the General Hospital. Carol Hawley et al. 368p. 1995. 91.95 (*1-85972-107-9*, Pub. by Avebry) Ashgate Pub Co.

Nurse's Managed Care Manual. Ed. by David B. Nash & Patricia Carroll. (Illus.). 260p. (Orig.). 1997. spiral bd. 54.95 (*1-890045-01-2*) T L C Med Pub.

Nurse's Manual of Infectious Diseases: Little, Brown's Infectious Diseases Fact Finder. Kathy Moss & Susanne L. Arbogast. LC 96-28013. 258p. 1996. spiral bd. 34.95 (*0-316-58513-0*, Little Brwn Med Div) Lppncott W & W.

Nurse's Manual of Laboratory & Diagnostic Tests. 3rd rev. ed. Bonita M. Cavanaugh. LC 98-50920. (Illus.). 1056p. 1999. pap. 35.95 (*0-8036-0363-0*) Davis Co.

Nurse's Manual of Laboratory Test & Diagnostic Procedures. 2nd ed. Louise M. Malarkey & Mary E. McMorrow. Ed. by Thomas Eoyang. LC 99-11885. (Illus.). 895p. 1999. pap. text. write for info. (*0-7216-7812-2*, W B Saunders Co) Harcrt Hlth Sci Grp.

Nurse's Manual of Laboratory Tests & Diagnostic Procedures. Louise M. Malarkey & Mary E. McMorrow. Ed. by Ton Eoyang. LC 95-17715. (Illus.). 1005p. 1996. pap. text 31.50 (*0-7216-3774-4*, W B Saunders Co) Harcrt Hlth Sci Grp.

Nurse's Masquerade. large type ed. Jean Carew. (Linford Romance Library). 256p. 1994. pap. 16.99 (*0-7089-7518-6*, Linford) Ulverscroft.

Nurse's Med Deck. 6th ed. Judith H. Deglin. 432p. 1998. ring bd. 28.95 (*0-8036-0367-3*) Davis Co.

Nurse's Med Deck. 6th ed. Judith H. Deglin & April H. Vallerand. (C). 1998. boxed set 33.95 (*0-8036-0368-1*) Davis Co.

***Nurse's Med Deck.** 7th ed. Judith Hopfer Deglin. (Illus.). 2000. 33.95 (*0-8036-0587-0*); pap. 28.95 (*0-8036-0588-9*) Davis Co.

Nurses' Medication Errors: An Interpretative Study of Experiences. Marianne Arndt. LC 95-167614. (Illus.). XVIII, 408p. 1994. pap. 59.95 (*3-631-47209-9*) P Lang Pubng.

Nurse's Meditative Journal. Sherry Kahn. LC 94-36263. (Nurse as Healer Ser.). (C). 1995. mass mkt. 21.95 (*0-8273-7109-8*) Delmar.

Nurses Never Cry. large type ed. Valerie Benson. (Dales Large Print Ser.). 282p. 1995. pap. 18.99 (*1-85389-550-4*, Dales) Ulverscroft.

***Nurses Notes.** Linda Strangio. Ed. by Carolyn S. Zagury. LC 99-72874. 288p. 1999. pap. 14.95 (*1-880254-63-8*) Vista.

Nurses' Notes to God. Marian Wilcox. LC 87-36141. 64p. (Orig.). 1988. pap. 4.99 (*0-8361-3464-8*) Herald Pr.

Nurses, Nurse Practitioners: Evolution to Advanced Practice. Ed. by Mathy D. Mezey & Diane O. McGivern. LC 93-13719. 400p. 1993. 32.95 (*0-8261-7770-0*) Springer Pub.

Nurses, Nurse Practitioners: Evolution to Advanced Practice. 2nd ed. Mathy D. Mezey & Diane O'Neill-McGivern. LC 98-26293. (Series on Advanced Practice Nursing). 1998. 39.95 (*0-8261-7771-9*) Springer Pub.

Nurses of a Different Stripe: A History of the Columbia University School of Nursing, 1892-1992. Gary Goldenberg. LC 91-77490. (Illus.). 288p. 1992. 20.00 (*0-9631670-0-6*) Col U Sch Nursing.

Nurses of All Nations: A History of the International Council of Nurses, 1899-1999. Barbara L. Brush. LC 98-37564. 1999. write for info. (*0-7817-1904-6*) Lppncott W & W.

Nurses' Perceptions of Spiritual Care. Linda Ross. LC 97-70635. (Developments in Nursing & Health Care). (Illus.). 224p. (C). 1997. text 69.95 (*1-85972-618-6*, Pub. by Ashgate Pub) Ashgate Pub Co.

Nurse's Photolibrary, Vol. 1. Springhouse Corporation Staff. LC 92-48480. 1993. 23.95 (*0-87434-511-1*) Springhouse Corp.

Nurse's Place. large type ed. Barbara Parkins. (Dales Large Print Ser.). 351p. 1998. pap. 19.99 (*1-85389-802-3*, Dales) Ulverscroft.

Nurse's Pocket Companion. 2nd ed. Springhouse Publishing Company Staff. Ed. by Patricia Schull. (Illus.). 672p. 1996. 34.95 (*0-87434-859-5*) Springhouse Corp.

Nurse's Pocket Guide: Nursing Diagnoses with Interventions. 6th ed. Marilynn E. Doenges & Mary F. Moorhouse. LC 97-29009. 670p. (C). 1997. spiral bd. 23.95 (*0-8036-0319-3*) Davis Co.

***Nurse's Pocket Guide: Nursing Diagnoses with Interventions.** 7th ed. Marilynn E. Doenges & Mary F. Moorhouse. LC 97-29009. 710p. (C). 2000. spiral bd. 24.95 (*0-8036-0525-0*) Davis Co.

Nurse's Quest for a Professional Identity. Helen A. Cohen. 1981. pap. write for info. (*0-201-01157-3*) Addison-Wesley.

Nurse's Questions/Women's Questions: The Impact of the Demographic Revolution & Feminism on United States Working Women, 1946-1986. Susan Leighow. (American University Studies Series XXVII: Vol. 5). VIII, 209p. (C). 1996. text 39.95 (*0-8204-2755-1*) P Lang Pubng.

Nurse's Quick Reference to Common Laboratory & Diagnostic Tests. 2nd ed. Frances T. Fischbach. LC 97-8629. 528p. 1997. spiral bd. 19.95 (*0-7817-1031-6*) Lppncott W & W.

Nurse's Research Library. Delmar Publishers Staff et al. 48p. pap. 48.95 (*0-7668-0587-5*, Pub. by Delmar) Thomson Learn.

Nurse's Shift Work Handbook. Ruth R. Alward & Timothy H. Monk. (Illus.). 147p. (Orig.). (C). 1993. pap. text 21.95 (*1-55810-087-3*, NP-82) Am Nurses Pub.

Nurses Story. rev. ed. Carol Gino. LC 96-95308. 336p. 1997. pap. 14.95 (*1-889853-03-8*) Aah-ha Bks.

Nurse's Survival Handbook. 3rd ed. Barbara Acello. Ed. by Molly Sullivan. 350p. (Orig.). (C). 1997. per. 39.95 (*1-56930-040-2*) Skidmore Roth Pub.

Nurses Taking the Lead: Personal Qualities of Effective Leadership. Fay L. Bower. LC 99-31083. (Illus.). 315p. (C). 2000. pap. text. write for info. (*0-7216-8169-7*, W B Saunders Co) Harcrt Hlth Sci Grp.

Nurses Work: An Analysis of the U. K. Nursing Labour Market. Ed. by James Buchan et al. LC 98-771462. (Developments in Nursing & Health Care Ser.). 160p. 1998. text 55.95 (*1-84014-386-X*, Pub. by Ashgate Pub) Ashgate Pub Co.

Nurses' Work, the Sacred & the Profane. Zane R. Wolf. LC 87-35770. (Studies in Health, Illness, & Caregiving). (Illus.). 324p. (C). 1988. pap. text 21.50 (*0-8122-1266-5*) U of Pa Pr.

***Nurses's Clinical Guide: Medication Administration.** Springhouse Publishing Staff. LC 99-57636. 2000. pap. text 29.95 (*1-58255-024-7*) Springhouse Corp.

Nurses's Illustrated Handbook of Home Health Procedures. Springhouse Publishing Company Staff. LC 98-11706. (SPA & ENG., Illus.). 608p. 1998. 32.95 (*0-87434-960-5*) Springhouse Corp.

Nursing. (Quick Study Academic Ser.). 4p. pap. 3.95 (*1-57222-174-7*) Barcharts.

Nursing. Blythe Camenson. LC 94-42628. (VGM Career Portraits Ser.). (Illus.). 96p. (J). (gr. 7 up). 1995. 13.95 (*0-8442-4369-8*, 43698, VGM Career) NTC Contemp Pub Co.

Nursing. Terence J. Sacks. LC 98-10328. (Careers in...Ser.). (Illus.). 128p. 1998. 17.95 (*0-8442-4554-2*, 45542, VGM Career); pap. 13.95 (*0-8442-4555-0*, 45550, VGM Career) NTC Contemp Pub Co.

Nursing. 2nd ed. write for info. (*0-340-63188-0*, Pub. by E A) Routldge.

Nursing: A Human Needs Approach. 5th ed. Albert Ellis & Elizabeth A. Nowlis. (Illus.). 1056p. (C). 1994. pap. text 41.95 (*0-397-55004-9*, Lippnctt) Lppncott W & W.

Nursing: A Knowledge Base for Practice. write for info. (*0-340-51492-2*, Pub. by E A) Routldge.

Nursing: A Knowledge Base for Practice. 2nd ed. Abigayl Perry. (Illus.). 400p. 1997. pap. 34.95 (*1-56593-819-4*, 1610) Singular Publishing.

Nursing: Art & Science. Ed. by Alison L. Kitson. LC 92-32252. 156p. 1992. pap. 47.75 (*1-56593-063-0*, 0369) Singular Publishing.

Nursing: Concepts of Practice. 5th ed. Dorothea E. Orem. LC 94-47916. (Illus.). 448p. (C). (gr. 13). 1995. pap. text 39.00 (*0-8151-6552-8*, 24728) Mosby Inc.

Nursing: From Education to Practice, Rx for Success. Helen Hodges et al. 432p. (C). 1988. pap. text 31.95 (*0-8385-7019-4*, A7019-1) Appleton & Lange.

Nursing: Human Science & Human Care. Jean Watson. 128p. 1988. pap. 24.95 (*0-88737-417-4*, 15-2236) Natl League Nurse.

***Nursing: Human Science & Human Care.** Jean Watson & NLN Staff. (Illus.). 128p. (C). 1999. pap. text 32.50 (*0-7637-1111-X*) JB Pubns.

Nursing: Its Hidden Agendas. write for info. (*0-340-55726-5*, Pub. by E A) Routldge.

Nursing: Its Hidden Agendas. Jolley. 186p. 1993. pap. 59.50 (*1-56593-237-4*, 0541) Singular Publishing.

Nursing: Its Principles & Practice for Hospital & Private Use. Isabel A. Hampton. (Illus.). 500p. 1993. text 49.00 (*0-7216-5156-9*, W B Saunders Co) Harcrt Hlth Sci Grp.

Nursing: Reflecting on an Evolving Practice. Judy Lumby. (C). 1991. pap. 65.00 (*0-7300-1263-8*, NPR300, Pub. by Deakin Univ) St Mut.

Nursing: The Career of a Lifetime. Shirley H. Fondiller & Barbara J. Nerone. 1995. 19.95 (*0-88737-655-X*) Natl League Nurse.

Nursing: The Fine Art: An Illustrated History. 2nd ed. M. Patricia Donahue. (Illus.). 560p. (C). (gr. 13). 1995. text 56.95 (*0-8151-2727-8*, 26817) Mosby Inc.

Nursing: The Philosophy & Science of Caring. Jean Watson. LC 78-71220. 1985. pap. 27.50 (*0-87081-154-1*) Univ Pr Colo.

Nursing: The Reflective Approach to Adult Nursing Practice. 2nd ed. A. Faulkner. (Illus.). 576p. (C). 1996. pap. text 47.99 (*1-56593-432-6*, 1101) Singular Publishing.

Nursing - Power Through Excellence: Proceedings of the West Virginia Nurses' Association Research Symposium. Ed. by Janet F. Wang et al. (Illus.). 305p. 1988. write for info. (*0-318-64877-6*) Morgantown Print & Bind.

Nursing a Problem. Lesley MacKay. 1989. 110.00 (*0-335-09902-5*); pap. 32.95 (*0-335-09901-7*) OpUniv Pr.

Nursing Administration. Jack Rudman. (Certified Nurse Examination Ser.: CN-16). 1994. pap. 23.95 (*0-8373-6116-8*) Nat Learn.

Nursing Administration: From Concepts to Practice. Laura C. Young & Arlene N. Hayne. (Illus.). 400p. 1988. text 52.00 (*0-7216-1810-3*, W B Saunders Co) Harcrt Hlth Sci Grp.

Nursing Administration: Managing Patient Care. 2nd ed. Ed. by Jaqueline A. Dienemann. LC 97-14107. 544p. (C). 1997. pap. text 49.95 (*0-8385-6986-2*, A-6986-2) Appleton & Lange.

Nursing Administration: Micro Macro Approach. Phillip J. Decker & Eleanor J. Sullivan. (Illus.). 704p. (C). 1992. pap. text 59.95 (*0-8385-7073-9*, A7073-8) Appleton & Lange.

Nursing Administration (Advanced) Jack Rudman. (Certified Nurse Examination Ser.: CN-17). 1994. pap. 23.95 (*0-8373-6117-6*) Nat Learn.

Nursing Administration Handbook. 4th ed. Howard S. Rowland & Beatrice L. Rowland. LC 96-39566. 768p. 1997. 80.00 (*0-8342-0926-8*, 20926) Aspen Pub.

Nursing Administration in the 21st Century. Sarah E. Allison & Kathie M. Renpenning. LC 98-25382. 1998. 48.00 (*0-7619-1455-2*); pap. 22.50 (*0-7619-1456-0*) Sage.

Nursing Administration Manual for Long-Term Care Facilities. 2nd ed. Charlotte K. Eliopoulos. 435p. 1996. 95.00 (*1-882515-00-5*) Hlth Educ Netwk.

Nursing Administration Quarterly Series, 3 vols., Set. Ed. by Barbara J. Brown. (Brown Ser.). 736p. 1993. 100.00 (*0-8342-0386-3*, 20386) Aspen Pub.

Nursing Administration Quarterly Series: Operations & the Working Environment, Vol. 2. Brown. 224p. 1993. 42.00 (*0-8342-0508-4*, 20508) Aspen Pub.

Nursing Adolescents: Psychology, Research & Practice. Jayne Taylor & Dave Muller. (Illus.). 224p. 1994. pap. 21.95 (*0-632-03625-7*, Pub. by Blckwll Scitfc UK) Blackwell Sci.

Nursing & Allied Health School Entrance Examinations. 13th ed. Marion F. Gooding. LC 95-36421. 496p. 1995. 15.95 (*0-02-860578-0*, Arco) Macmillan Gen Ref.

Nursing & Anthropology: Two Worlds to Blend. Madeleine Leininger. 196p. (C). 1994. pap. text 17.95 (*1-57074-113-1*) Greyden Pr.

Nursing & Care Home Care Plans. Linda Faber-Czingula. 150p. 1996. ring bd. write for info. (*1-890118-07-9*, QualityCare Pub) Convalescnt Cnslts.

Nursing & Computers: An Anthology. Ed. by K. A. Rieder et al. (Computers & Medicine Ser.). (Illus.). 345p. 1989. 68.00 (*0-387-96937-3*) Spr-Verlag.

Nursing & Computers: An Anthology, 1987-1996. Ed. by Virginia K. Saba et al. LC 97-12462. (Computers & Medicine Ser.). (Illus.). 600p. 1997. 79.00 (*0-387-94955-0*) Spr-Verlag.

Nursing & Health Care for the Homeless. Ed. by Juanita K. Hunter. LC 92-2172. 235p. (C). 1993. text 64.50 (*0-7914-1349-7*); pap. text 21.95 (*0-7914-1350-0*) State U NY Pr.

Nursing & Malpractice Risks: Understanding the Law. 3rd ed. Becky Colgan & Barbara J. Youngberg. 160p. (C). 1996. pap. text 49.95 (*1-878025-91-0*) Western Schls.

***Nursing & Mental Disorder: Clinical Practice.** Lorraine Conlon. (Illus.). 256p. 2000. pap. text 45.00 (*0-7506-4309-9*) Buttrwrth-Heinemann.

Nursing & Nursing Education: Public Policies & Private Actions. Institute of Medicine Staff. 336p. 1983. pap. text 24.95 (*0-309-03346-2*) Natl Acad Pr.

Nursing & Philosophy. Jan Reed & Ian Ground. LC 96-167803. 1997. write for info. (*0-340-61028-X*, Pub. by E A) Routldge.

***Nursing & Politics Power Thru Practice.** Abigail Masterson. LC 98-31647. 1999. write for info. (*0-443-05991-8*) Church.

Nursing & Thanatolgy. 1982. 17.95 (*0-405-13095-3*) Ayer.

Nursing & the American Health Care Delivery System. 4th ed. Joellen B. Hawkins & Loretta P. Higgins. (Illus.). 224p. (Orig.). 1993. pap. text 16.00 (*0-913292-46-X*) Tiresias Pr.

Nursing & the Continuum of Care. M. Patricia Donahue & American Organization of Nurse Executives Staff. LC 98-9874. (AONE Leadership Ser.). 138p. 1998. 36.00 (*1-55648-235-3*) AHPI.

Nursing & the Continuum of Care. M. Patricia Donahue & American Organization of Nurse Executives Staff. LC 98-9874. (AONE Leadership Ser.). 1998. write for info. (*1-55664-823-5*) Mosby Inc.

Nursing & the Disabled. Ardella M. Fraley. (Nursing-Health Science Ser.). 1991. 52.50 (*0-86720-314-5*) Jones & Bartlett.

***Nursing & the Experience of Illness: Phenomenology in Practice.** Irena Madjar. LC 98-33321. 1999. 85.00 (*0-415-20782-7*); pap. 25.99 (*0-415-20783-5*) Routledge.

Nursing & the Injustices of the Law. Megan-Jane Johnstone. (Illus.). 349p. 1994. pap. text 52.00 (*0-7295-1418-8*) Bailliere Tindall.

Nursing & the Law. T. Verschoor et al. LC 97-162542. 120p. 1997. 35.00 (*0-7021-3542-9*, Pub. by Juta & Co) Gaunt.

Nursing & the Law. 5th ed. Darlene M. Trandel-Korenchuk & Keith M. Trandel-Korenchuk. LC 97-36619. 400p. 1997. 45.00 (*0-8342-0570-X*, 20570) Aspen Pub.

Nursing & the Older Patient. 3rd ed. Lynne Swiatczak & Steve Wright. (Illus.). 224p. 1998. pap. 49.50 (*0-7487-3353-1*, Pub. by S Thornes Pubs) Trans-Atl Phila.

Nursing As a Therapeutic Activity: An Ethnography. Steven J. Ersser. LC 97-70634. (Developments in Nursing & Health Care). (Illus.). 392p. (C). 1997. text 83.95 (*1-85972-658-5*, Pub. by Ashgate Pub) Ashgate Pub Co.

Nursing As Caring: A Model for Transforming Practice. Anne Boykin & Savina Schoenhofer. LC 93-23021. 1993. 26.95 (*0-88737-601-0*) Natl League Nurse.

Nursing As Therapy. McMahon. 234p. 1991. pap. 43.25 (*1-56593-012-6*, 0253) Singular Publishing.

Nursing As Therapy. 2nd ed. Richard McMahon & Alan Pearson. (Illus.). 336p. 1998. pap. 47.50 (*0-7487-3326-4*, Pub. by S Thornes Pubs) Trans-Atl Phila.

Nursing Assessment - Bloodborne Valuepack. National Safety Council Staff et al. (Nursing-Health Science Ser.). (C). 1993. text 57.50 (*0-86720-690-X*) Jones & Bartlett.

Nursing Assessment & Diagnosis. 2nd ed. Janis P. Bellack & Barbara J. Edlind. (Nursing-Health Science Ser.). 864p. (C). 1992. 54.95 (*0-86720-436-2*) Jones & Bartlett.

Nursing Assessment of the Pregnant Woman: Antepartal Screening & Laboratory Evaluation. Mary L. Barron et al. LC 98-20272. 1998. 15.00 (*0-86525-081-2*) March of Dimes.

Nursing Assistance: Spanish Version. McCarthy. (SPA.). 1995. pap., wbk. ed. 13.60 (*0-8359-4947-8*) P-H.

An Asterisk (*) at the beginning of an entry indicates that the title is appearing for the first time.

Nursing Assistant. Marian Edmiston. Ed. by Kelly Gorham. (Nursing Ser.). 24p. (C). 1994. student ed. 7.00 (*0-8064-0024-2*, N10) Bergwall.

Nursing Assistant. Joan F. Needham. (Home Care Aide Ser.). 1999. teacher ed. 18.00 (*0-8273-6488-1*); wbk. ed. 12.95 (*0-8273-6487-3*); pap. 27.95 (*0-8273-6486-5*) Delmar.

Nursing Assistant. Perspective Press Staff. 304p. 1995. write for info. (*0-8151-6698-2*) Mosby Inc.

Nursing Assistant. Perspective Press Staff. (Illus.). 304p. (gr. 13). 1995. write for info. (*0-8151-4747-3*, 24904) Mosby Inc.

Nursing Assistant. Jack Rudman. (Career Examination Ser.: C-534). 1994. pap. 23.95 (*0-8373-0534-9*) Nat Learn.

Nursing Assistant. 2nd ed. Pulliam. 1997. pap., teacher ed. 23.20 (*0-8359-5161-8*); pap., wbk. ed. 13.27 (*0-8359-5162-6*) P-H.

Nursing Assistant. 6th ed. Barbara R. Hegner & Esther Caldwell. 1991. teacher ed. 25.50 (*0-8273-4799-5*) Delmar.

Nursing Assistant. 6th ed. Barbara R. Hegner & Esther Caldwell. 1992. pap. 31.00 (*0-8273-4800-2*) Delmar.

Nursing Assistant. 6th ed. Barbara R. Hegner & Esther Caldwell. 1992. pap., student ed. 19.95 (*0-8273-4802-9*) Delmar.

Nursing Assistant. 8th ed. Barbara R. Hegner. LC 98-9510. (Home Care Aide Ser.). (C). 1998. mass mkt. 50.95 (*0-8273-9063-7*) Delmar.

Nursing Assistant. 8th ed. Barbara R. Hegner. (Home Care Aide Ser.). (C). 1998. pap., wbk. ed. 18.50 (*0-8273-9062-9*) Delmar.

Nursing Assistant. 8th abr. rev. ed. Barbara R. Hegner et al. (Home Care Aide Ser.). 720p. (C). 1998. pap. text 44.95 (*0-8273-9058-0*) Delmar.

Nursing Assistant: A Nursing Process Approach. 7th ed. Barbara R. Hegner. 768p. 1995. pap. 31.00 (*0-8273-6223-4*) Delmar.

Nursing Assistant: A Nursing Process Approach. 7th ed. Barbara R. Hegner. (Home Care Aide Ser.). 786p. (C). 1995. text 35.50 (*0-8273-6286-2*) Delmar.

Nursing Assistant: A Nursing Process Approach. 7th rev. ed. B. R. Hegner & Esther Caldwell. 168p. 1997. teacher ed. write for info. (*0-8273-8499-8*) Delmar.

Nursing Assistant: A Nursing Process Approach. 7th rev. ed. Barbara Hegner & Esther Caldwell. (HOME CARE AIDE). 768p. 1996. mass mkt. 32.00 (*0-8273-8394-0*) Delmar.

Nursing Assistant: A Nursing Process Approach. 7th rev. ed. Barbara R. Hegner & Ester Caldwell. (HOME CARE AIDE). 768p. 1996. mass mkt. 34.50 (*0-8273-8414-9*) Delmar.

Nursing Assistant: Acute, Subacute, & Long-Term Care. 2nd ed. Jolynn Pulliam. LC 97-12604. 336p. 1997. pap. text 30.00 (*0-8359-5141-3*) P-H.

Nursing Assistant: CTB IBM 3.5/5.25. Barbara R. Hegner. (Home Care Aide Ser.). 1995. 68.25 (*0-8273-6289-7*) Delmar.

Nursing Assistant: Laser Disc User Manual. 7th ed. Barbara R. Hegner. (Home Care Aide Ser.). 1994. pap. 12.95 (*0-8273-7045-8*, VNR) Wiley.

Nursing Assistant: Nursing Procedures & Application. 7th ed. Barbara R. Hegner. (Home Care Aide Ser.). 164p. (C). 1995. teacher ed. 25.50 (*0-8273-6288-9*) Delmar.

Nursing Assistant: Nursing Procedures Approach. 5th ed. Doyle. (Home Care Aide Ser.). 1989. wbk. ed. 18.95 (*0-8273-3369-2*) Delmar.

Nursing Assistant: Nursing Procedures Approach. 5th ed. Doyle. (Home Care Aide Ser.). 1989. pap. 25.95 (*0-8273-3370-6*) Delmar.

Nursing Assistant: Spanish Edition Instructor's Guide. 6th ed. Barbara R. Hegner & Esther Caldwell. 106p. 1993. pap., teacher ed. 21.00 (*0-8273-5800-8*) Delmar.

Nursing Assistant: Spanish Edition Workbook. 6th ed. Barbara R. Hegner. 297p. 1993. pap. 18.00 (*0-8273-5801-6*) Delmar.

Nursing Assistant: Spanish Version. McCarthy. (SPA.). 304p. (C). 1995. pap. text 22.00 (*0-8359-4920-6*) P-H.

Nursing Assistant Level 5 Workbook. 5th ed. Kelly. 1999. pap. text, wbk. ed. write for info. (*0-323-01046-6*) Mosby Inc.

Nursing Assistant Complete Test Bank (IBM) 6th ed. Barbara R. Hegner. (Home Care Aide Ser.). 1992. 64.95 (*0-8273-4842-8*) Delmar.

Nursing Assistant Exam. Ed. by Jim Gish. LC 97-33319. (National Standards Ser.). 256p. (Orig.). 1997. pap. 20.00 (*1-57685-053-6*) LrningExprss.

Nursing Assistant Fundamentals: A Patient-Centered Approach. June Eastmond et al. 704p. (gr. 6-12). student ed. 15.00 (*0-02-802425-7*) Glencoe.

Nursing Assistant Fundamentals: A Patient-Centered Approach. June Eastmond et al. (gr. 6-12). 1998. text, student ed. 39.75 (*0-02-802441-9*) Glencoe.

Nursing Assistant Fundamentals: A Patient-Centered Approach Instructor's Annotated. annot. ed. June Eastmond et al. 704p. teacher ed. 38.15 (*0-02-802426-5*) Glencoe.

Nursing Assistant Instructors Resource Kit. 6th ed. Barbara R. Hegner. 1992. pap. 74.95 (*0-8273-4875-4*) Delmar.

Nursing Assistant IRK. 7th ed. Barbara R. Hegner. 528p. 1995. teacher ed. 78.95 (*0-8273-7046-6*) Delmar.

Nursing Assistant Procedures Viewer's Manual. Barbara Kast. 241p. 1993. 16.75 (*0-8273-5557-2*) Delmar.

Nursing Assistant Review for Competency Evaluation. 2nd ed. SheilaA. Sorrentino. (Illus.). 176p. (C). (gr. 13). 1996. pap. text 15.00 (*0-8151-8625-8*, 28734) Mosby Inc.

Nursing Assistant Review for Competency Evaluation: Textbook for Nursing Assistants & Reviews. 4th ed. Sheila A. Sorrentino. (Illus.). 160p. 1996. write for info. (*0-8151-8626-6*) Mosby Inc.

Nursing Assistant Workbook. 7th ed. Barbara R. Hegner. 560p. 1995. student ed. 19.45 (*0-8273-6287-0*) Delmar.

Nursing Assistants. 4th ed. Sheila A. Sorrentino. (Illus.). 800p. (gr. 13). 1995. text 34.00 (*0-8151-8030-6*, 25744) Mosby Inc.

Nursing Assistants: A Basic Study Guide. 5th rev. ed. Beverly Robertson. (Illus.). 184p. 1998. pap. text 13.95 (*1-880246-09-0*) First Class Bks.

Nursing Assistant's Casebook of Elder Care. George H. Weber & George J. McCall. LC 87-12434. 238p. 1987. pap. 18.95 (*0-86569-166-5*, Auburn Hse) Greenwood.

***Nursing Assistant's Survival Guide: Tips & Techniques for the Most Important Job in America.** Karl Pillemer et al. (Illus.). 100p. 1999. 11.95 (*0-9653629-2-2*) Frontline Pub.

Nursing Assisting: A Nursing Process Approach. 7th rev. ed. Barbara Hegner. 560p. 1996. wbk. ed. 20.00 (*0-8273-8426-2*) Delmar.

Nursing Assisting: Essentials for Long Term Care. Acello. LC 98-17776. 384p. (C). 1998. pap. 30.95 (*0-8273-8450-5*) Delmar.

Nursing Assisting: Essentials for Long-Term Care - IML. Acello. 224p. 1998. teacher ed. 13.95 (*0-8273-8451-3*) Delmar.

Nursing Assisting in Long-Term Care. Barbara R. Hegner. (Home Care Aide Ser.). 1988. pap. 29.95 (*0-8273-2959-8*); pap., teacher ed. 17.00 (*0-8273-2960-1*) Delmar.

Nursing Attendants: Your Role Working in Psychiatry. Gloria Elliott. (Illus.). 60p. (Orig.). 1994. pap. text 8.00 (*0-9640929-5-6*) Good Sign NY.

Nursing Beyond the Year 2000: Report of a WHO Study Group. LC 95-103037. (Technical Reports: No. 842). (ENG, FRE & SPA.). iv, 21p. 1994. pap. text 6.00 (*92-4-120842-2*, 1100842) World Health.

Nursing Boards Review: American Journal of Nursing. 10th ed. Ajn & C. V. Mosby. (Illus.). 624p. (C). (gr. 13). 1996. pap. text 30.95 (*0-8151-0080-9*, 27082) Mosby Inc.

Nursing Book. College. 1984. 6.95 (*0-316-15182-3*, Little Brwn Med Div) Lppncott W & W.

Nursing Calculations. 2nd ed. John D. Gatford. LC 86-17145. 106p. (Orig.). 1987. pap. text. write for info. (*0-443-03533-4*) Church.

Nursing Calculations. 3rd ed. John D. Gatford. 128p. (Orig.). 1990. pap. text. write for info. (*0-443-04347-7*) Church.

Nursing Calculations. 4th ed. Gatford. 1994. pap. text 7.95 (*0-443-04920-3*, W B Saunders Co) Harcrt Hlth Sci Grp.

Nursing Care. Ed. by Moya Jolley & Brykczynska Gosia. 272p. 1992. pap. 56.00 (*0-340-53920-8*) Thomson Learn.

Nursing Care: Summary of a European Study. 1987. pap. text 13.00 (*92-890-1040-1*) World Health.

Nursing Care: The Challenge to Change. Jolley. 286p. 1992. pap. 69.95 (*1-56593-536-5*, 0531) Singular Publishing.

Nursing Care Coordinator. Jack Rudman. (Career Examination Ser.: C-3735). 1994. pap. 39.95 (*0-8373-3735-6*) Nat Learn.

Nursing Care During the Labor Process. 3rd ed. Janet S. Malinowski. LC 88-30981. (Illus.). 433p. (C). 1989. pap. text 26.95 (*0-8036-5803-6*) Davis Co.

Nursing Care for Children. 2nd ed. Sandra R. Mott. Ed. by Debra Hunter. 1907p. (C). 1990. pap. text 9.95 (*0-201-52924-6*) Addison-Wesley.

Nursing Care for Myocardial Infarction: Physiological Basis of Cardiovascular Nursing. Marilyn B. Rubin. LC 76-6218. (Illus.). 200p. 1977. 14.50 (*0-87527-151-0*) Green.

Nursing Care for Older Adults: Theory & Practice. 2nd ed. Carol A. Miller. LC 94-10140. 624p. 1994. pap. text 34.95 (*0-397-55086-3*) Lppncott W & W.

Nursing Care in an Aging Society. Ed. by Domma Corr & Charles A. Corr. LC 90-9601. 368p. 1990. 38.95 (*0-8261-6630-X*) Springer Pub.

Nursing Care in Radiation Oncology. 2nd ed. Karen H. Dow et al. Ed. by Barnara N. Cullen. (Illus.). 400p. 1997. text 72.50 (*0-7216-2347-6*, W B Saunders Co) Harcrt Hlth Sci Grp.

Nursing Care of Adolescents. Jeanne Howe. (Illus.). 1979. text 31.95 (*0-07-030585-4*) McGraw.

Nursing Care of Adults. Ed. by Frances D. Monahan et al. (Illus.). 1994. teacher ed. write for info. (*0-7216-4926-2*, W B Saunders Co) Harcrt Hlth Sci Grp.

Nursing Care of Adults. Ed. by James P. Smith. (Advanced Nursing Ser.). 1995. pap. 29.95 (*0-632-03994-9*) Blackwell Sci.

Nursing Care of Adults, Test Manual. Ed. by Frances D. Monahan et al. (Illus.). 1994. write for info. (*0-7216-3504-0*, W B Saunders Co) Harcrt Hlth Sci Grp.

Nursing Care of Adults with Orthopaedic Conditions. 2nd ed. Mourad. LC 87-279. 576p. 1989. text 41.95 (*0-8273-4315-9*) Delmar.

Nursing Care of Cardiothoracic Surgery Patients. Betsy A. Finkelmeier. 528p. 1994. text 69.95 (*0-397-54796-X*) Lppncott W & W.

Nursing Care of Children. Jean W. Ashwill. 1997. pap. text, student ed. 16.50 (*0-7216-7285-X*, W B Saunders Co) Harcrt Hlth Sci Grp.

Nursing Care of Children. Ed. by James P. Smith. (Advanced Nursing Ser.). 1995. pap. 24.95 (*0-632-03995-7*) Blackwell Sci.

Nursing Care of Children: Principles & Practice. Ed. by Jean W. Ashwill & Susan C. Droske. 1997. teacher ed. write for info. (*0-7216-6502-0*, W B Saunders Co) Harcrt Hlth Sci Grp.

Nursing Care of Children: Principles & Practice. Jean W. Ashwill & Susan C. Droske. Ed. by Ilze Rader. LC 96-16728. (Illus.). 1264p. 1997. pap. text 61.95 (*0-7216-6488-1*, W B Saunders Co) Harcrt Hlth Sci Grp.

Nursing Care of Children & Families. 2nd ed. Sandra R. Mott. Ed. by Debra Hunter. 1907p. (C). 1990. text 78.75 (*0-201-12923-X*); student ed. write for info. (*0-201-12924-8*) Addison-Wesley.

Nursing Care of Geriatric Emergencies. Christine W. Bradway. (Springer Series on Geriatric Nursing). (Illus.). 304p. 1996. 44.95 (*0-8261-9010-3*) Springer Pub.

Nursing Care of Infants & Children. 2nd ed. Lucille F. Whaley. 1987. text 25.00 (*0-8016-5461-0*) Mosby Inc.

Nursing Care of Infants & Children. 4th ed. Lucille F. Whaley. 2096p. 1991. write for info. (*0-8016-5387-8*); write for info. (*0-8016-5381-9*); write for info. (*0-8016-5403-3*) Mosby Inc.

***Nursing Care of Infants & Children.** 6th ed. Anne R. Rentfro & Linda McCampbell. 352p. (C). 1998. text, student ed. write for info. (*0-323-00104-1*) Mosby Inc.

Nursing Care of Older Adults: Theory & Practice. 3rd ed. Carol A. Miller. LC 98-45982. 19p. 1998. pap. text. write for info. (*0-7817-1623-3*) Lppncott W & W.

Nursing Care of Survivors of Family Violence. Jacquelyn Campbell. (Illus.). 416p. (C). (gr. 13). 1993. pap. text 35.00 (*0-8016-6378-4*, 06378) Mosby Inc.

Nursing Care of the Addicted Client. Karen Allen et al. LC 95-50020. 384p. 1996. pap. text 36.95 (*0-397-55204-1*) Lppncott W & W.

Nursing Care of the AIDS/HIV Patient. Carol R. Kneisl. (Nursing Education Ser.). 1997. text 41.95 (*0-8273-6737-6*) Delmar.

Nursing Care of the Burn-Injured Patient. Rita B. Trofino. LC 90-15722. (Illus.). 466p. 1991. 49.95 (*0-8036-8658-7*) Davis Co.

Nursing Care of the Child with Cancer. 2nd ed. Association of Pediatric Oncology Nurses Staff. Ed. by Genevieve V. Foley et al. (Illus.). 548p. 1993. text 70.00 (*0-7216-4006-0*, W B Saunders Co) Harcrt Hlth Sci Grp.

Nursing Care of the Clients with Substance Abuse. Eleanor J. Sullivan. (Illus.). 528p. (C). (gr. 13). 1995. pap. text 37.95 (*0-8016-7881-1*, 07881) Mosby Inc.

Nursing Care of the Critically Ill Child. 2nd ed. Mary F. Hazinski. (Illus.). 1152p. (C). (gr. 13). 1991. text 64.95 (*0-8016-5312-6*, 05312) Mosby Inc.

Nursing Care of the Elderly. 4th rev. ed. Joan Cagley-Knight. Ed. by John Lantz. (Illus.). 277p. 1998. pap. 39.95 (*1-57801-031-4*) Western Schls.

***Nursing Care of the General Pediatric Surgical Patient.** McKenna & Wise. 544p. 2000. 79.00 (*0-8342-1170-X*) Aspen Pub.

Nursing Care of the HIV Positive Patient. 2nd rev. ed. Lori A. DeLorenzo. Ed. by Barbara Halliburton. 199p. 1997. pap. 59.95 (*1-57801-014-4*) Western Schls.

***Nursing Care of the HIV Positive Patient.** 3rd ed. Lori DeLorenzo. (Illus.). 238p. 1999. pap. write for info. (*1-57801-043-8*) Western Schls.

Nursing Care of the Immunocompromised Patient. M. Linda Workman et al. (Illus.). 320p. 1992. pap. text 33.00 (*0-7216-3213-0*, W B Saunders Co) Harcrt Hlth Sci Grp.

Nursing Care of the Older Person. Jane Farrell. LC 89-12662. (Illus.). 336p. 1990. reprint ed. pap. 104.20 (*0-608-07302-4*, 206753000009) Bks Demand.

Nursing Care of the Organ-Tissue Transplant Recipient. Sigardson-Poor & Haggerty. (Illus.). 384p. 1990. text 70.00 (*0-7216-2882-6*, W B Saunders Co) Harcrt Hlth Sci Grp.

Nursing Care of the Person Who Smokes. Patricia G. Rienzo. 216p. 1992. 33.95 (*0-8261-7620-8*) Springer Pub.

***Nursing Care of the Skin.** Penzer. 256p. 2000. pap. text 35.00 (*0-7506-2834-0*) Buttrwrth-Heinemann.

Nursing Care Plans: Nursing Diagnosis & Intervention. 4th ed. Meg Gulanick. LC 97-41319. 1248p. (C). (gr. 13). 1997. pap. text 37.95 (*0-8151-2471-6*, 31214) Mosby Inc.

***Nursing Care Plans & Documentation: Nursing Diagnoses & Collaborative Problems.** 3rd ed. Lynda J. Carpenito. LC 98-46595. 825p. 1998. pap. write for info. (*0-7817-1742-6*) Lppncott W & W.

Nursing Care Report Card for Acute Care. American Nurses Association Staff. 1995. pap. text 34.95 (*1-55810-112-8*, NP-101) Am Nurses Pub.

Nursing Care Studies. Riddle. 1989. pap. text 11.00 (*0-443-03939-9*, W B Saunders Co) Harcrt Hlth Sci Grp.

Nursing Care Studies. Riddle. 1993. pap. text 58.95 (*0-443-04995-5*, W B Saunders Co) Harcrt Hlth Sci Grp.

Nursing Care Studies, Vol. 3. Riddle. 1988. pap. text 11.00 (*0-443-03936-4*, W B Saunders Co) Harcrt Hlth Sci Grp.

Nursing Care Studies, Vol. 4. Riddle. 1989. pap. text 11.00 (*0-443-03937-2*, W B Saunders Co) Harcrt Hlth Sci Grp.

Nursing Care Studies, Vol. 5. Riddle. 1989. pap. text 11.00 (*0-443-03938-0*, W B Saunders Co) Harcrt Hlth Sci Grp.

Nursing Case Management. Olga Cotera. 131p. 1998. spiral bd. 125.00 (*1-879575-94-9*) Acad Med Sys.

Nursing Case Management: A Practical Guide to Success in Managed Care. Suzanne K. Powell. LC 95-32575. (Illus.). 416p. 1995. pap. text 38.00 (*0-397-55234-3*) Lppncott W & W.

Nursing Case Management: An Evolving Practice. Ed. by Phyllis K. More & Sandy Mandell. LC 96-13465. (Illus.). 304p. 1996. text 24.00 (*0-07-105481-2*) McGraw-Hill HPD.

Nursing Case Management: From Concept to Evaluation. 2nd ed. Elaine L. Cohen & Toni G. Cesta. (Illus.). 368p. (C). (gr. 13). 1996. text 41.95 (*0-8151-1906-2*, 28201) Mosby Inc.

Nursing Centers: The Time Is Now. Ed. by Barbara Murphy. 279p. 1995. 20.95 (*0-88737-623-1*, 41-2629, NLN Pr) Natl League Nurse.

Nursing Children: Psychology, Research, & Practice. 2nd ed. Dave J. Muller et al. LC 92-20109. 1992. 41.50 (*1-56593-023-1*, 0266) Thomson Learn.

***Nursing Children: Psychology, Research & Practice.** 3rd ed. Jayne Taylor et al. (Illus.). 276p. 1999. pap. 34.95 (*0-7487-3327-2*) Standard Pub.

Nursing, Communication & Education in an Information Age. Anderson. (Nursing Education Ser.). 1990. pap., teacher ed. 12.75 (*0-8273-3434-6*) Delmar.

Nursing Communication Skills: Workbook. Anne K. Roe et al. LC 75-8753. (Wiley Biomedical-Health Publication Ser.). (Illus.). 90p. reprint ed. pap. 30.00 (*0-608-10330-6*, 201258400083) Bks Demand.

Nursing Competence. write for info. (*0-340-51841-3*, Pub. by E A) Routldge.

Nursing Comprehensive Examination Review. 2nd ed. George Horemis. LC 76-14832. 1976. pap. 6.00 (*0-668-02499-2*) P-H.

Nursing Curriculum: A Curricular Model. Fred Greaves. 108p. (Orig.). 1987. pap. 17.95 (*0-7099-3871-3*, Pub. by C Helm) Routldge.

Nursing Curriculum Outline Study Guide. Peggy J. Walton. (C). 19.95 (*0-911067-00-0*) Health Ed Train.

Nursing Data Review - (Annual) 272p. 1997. 32.95 (*0-88737-530-8*, 19-2419) Natl League Nurse.

Nursing Data Review, 1997. (Illus.). 256p. 1997. 37.95 (*0-88737-732-7*, 19-7327, NLN Pr) Natl League Nurse.

***Nursing Datasource.** NLN Staff. (Illus.). 48p. (C). 1998. pap. text 42.50 (*0-7637-0939-5*) JB Pubns.

***Nursing Datasource 1997, Vol. 3.** NLN Staff. (Illus.). (C). 1999. pap. text 41.25 (*0-7637-0940-9*) JB Pubns.

***Nursing Datasource 1998.** NLN Research Division Staff. (Illus.). 64p. (C). 1999. pap. text 41.25 (*0-7637-1113-6*) JB Pubns.

***Nursing Datasource 1998, Vol. 2.** NLN Research Division Staff. (Illus.). 64p. (C). 1999. pap. text 41.25 (*0-7637-1114-4*) JB Pubns.

***Nursing Datasource 1998, Vol. 3.** NLN Research Division Staff. (Illus.). 64p. (C). 1999. pap. text 41.25 (*0-7637-1115-2*) JB Pubns.

Nursing Department Forms Manual. Howard S. Rowland & Beatrice L. Rowland. 500p. 1993. 199.00 (*0-8342-0334-0*, S58) Aspen Pub.

Nursing Department Report, 1992-93. 1992. pap. 195.00 (*0-939326-73-6*) Hosp & Hlthcare.

Nursing Diagnoses & Process in Psychiatric-Mental Health Nursing. Gertrude K. McFarland & Evelyn L. Wasli. LC 64-5161. 308p. 1986. text 17.95 (*0-397-54598-3*, Lippnctt) Lppncott W & W.

Nursing Diagnoses in Psychiatric Nursing: A Pocket Guide to Care Plan Construction. 4th ed. Mary C. Townsend. LC 96-45615. (Illus.). 498p. (C). 1997. pap. text 26.95 (*0-8036-0290-1*) Davis Co.

Nursing Diagnoses Reference Manual. 4th ed. Sheila Sparks & Cynthia Taylor. LC 97-39482. 704p. 1997. 35.95 incl. disk (*0-87434-897-8*) Springhouse Corp.

Nursing Diagnosis. Kathy V. Gettrust & Paula D. Brabec. (C). 1992. pap. 37.50 (*0-8273-4852-5*) Delmar.

Nursing Diagnosis. Schonlau. 1999. pap. text. write for info. (*0-7216-4992-0*, W B Saunders Co) Harcrt Hlth Sci Grp.

***Nursing Diagnosis: Application to Clinical Practice.** 8th ed. Lynda Juall Carpenito. LC 99-36287. 1,232p. 2000. pap. text 36.95 (*0-7817-1970-4*) Lppncott W & W.

Nursing Diagnosis: Process & Application. 3rd ed. Marjorie Gordon. LC 93-31601. (Illus.). 416p. (C). (gr. 13). 1993. text 42.00 (*0-8016-6053-X*, 06053) Mosby Inc.

Nursing Diagnosis & Care Planning. 2nd ed. Barbara J. Taptich et al. 336p. 1994. pap. text 18.95 (*0-7216-5196-8*, W B Saunders Co) Harcrt Hlth Sci Grp.

Nursing Diagnosis & Intervention. 3rd ed. Gertrude K. McFarland & Elizabeth A. McFarlane. LC 97-223430. (Illus.). 896p. (C). (gr. 13). 1996. pap. text 38.00 (*0-8151-7026-2*, 27464) Mosby Inc.

Nursing Diagnosis & Interventions for the Elderly. Meridean Maas et al. Ed. by Mark McCormick. 736p. (C). 1991. pap. text 45.25 (*0-201-12679-6*) Addison-Wesley.

Nursing Diagnosis & Process in Psychiatric Mental Health Nursing. 3rd ed. Gertrude K. McFarland. LC 96-41727. 480p. 1996. pap. text 23.95 (*0-397-55317-X*) Lppncott W & W.

Nursing Diagnosis for Wellness: Supporting Strengths. Houldin. (Illus.). 238p. 1987. pap. text 15.95 (*0-397-54645-9*) Lppncott W & W.

***Nursing Diagnosis Handbook.** 4th ed. Betty J. Ackley. (C). 1999. text 27.95 (*0-323-00786-4*) Mosby Inc.

Nursing Diagnosis Handbook. 7th ed. Judith M. Wilkinson. 664p. (C). 1999. spiral bd. 29.95 (*0-8053-8094-9*) Benjamin-Cummings.

Nursing Diagnosis Handbook: A Guide to Planning Care. 3rd ed. Gail B. Ladwig. Ed. by Betty J. Ackley. LC 96-47933. (Illus.). 528p. (C). (gr. 13). 1997. pap. text 27.00 (*0-8151-0912-1*, 28737) Mosby Inc.

Nursing Diagnosis Manual for the Well & Ill Client. T. Audean Duespohl. 312p. 1986. pap. text 26.00 (*0-7216-1825-1*, W B Saunders Co) Harcrt Hlth Sci Grp.

Nursing Diagnosis Pocket Manual. Sheila Sparks et al. 512p. 1995. spiral bd. 23.95 (*0-87434-827-7*) Springhouse Corp.

Nursing Diagnosis Reference Disk. Ed. by Michael Shaw. (Orig.). 1997. 39.95 incl. disk (*0-87434-895-1*) Springhouse Corp.

Nursing Diagnosis, "Swallowing Impaired" The Bedside Assessment of Swallowing in Neurologically-Involved Cases. Jimmie R. Rankin. 150p. 1993. pap. 19.95 (*1-883938-06-6*) Dry Bones Pr.

Nursing Documentation. 3rd ed. Patricia W. Iyer & Nancy Camp. LC 98-47696. (Illus.). 426p. 1999. pap. text 36.95 (*0-323-00223-4*) Mosby Inc.

Nursing Documentation: Charting, Recording, & Reporting. Ellen T. Eggland & Denise S. Heinemann. LC 93-6172. (Illus.). 288p. (C). 1994. pap. text 21.95 (*0-397-55010-3*, Lippncott) Lppncott W & W.

N

An Asterisk (*) at the beginning of an entry indicates that the title is appearing for the first time.

Nursing Documentation: Legal Focus Across Practice Settings. Sue Meiner. LC 99-10239. 17p. 1999. 65.00 (*0-7619-1071-9*) Sage.

*__Nursing Documentation: Legal Focus Across Practice Settings.__ Sue Meiner. LC 99-10239. 1999. pap. write for info. (*0-7619-1072-7*) Sage.

Nursing Documentation Handbook. 2nd ed. Tina M. Marrelli. (Illus.). 384p. (Orig.). (C). (gr. 13). 1995. spiral bd. 28.95 (*0-8151-6405-X*, 26130) Mosby Inc.

Nursing Documentation Resource Guide. Eleen Thomas Eggland. 356p. 1993. 155.00 (*0-8342-0385-5*, S114) Aspen Pub.

*__Nursing Drug Handbook 2001.__ Billie A. Wilson & Margaret Shannon. 1616p. 2000. 24.71 (*0-13-028292-8*) P-H.

Nursing Education. Cox. (International Journal of Nursing Studies). 1985. pap. 30.00 (*0-08-031849-5*, Pergamon Pr) Elsevier.

Nursing Education: An International Perspective. Ed. by T. G. Mashaba & H. I. Brink. 332p. (Orig.). (C). 1994. pap. text 46.15 (*0-7021-2620-9*, Pub. by Juta & Co) Intl Spec Bk.

Nursing Education in a Changing Society. Mary Q. Innis. LC RT0090.. (Illus.). 256p. reprint ed. pap. 79.40 (*0-608-30287-2*, 202050100018) Bks Demand.

Nursing Education in Thanatology: A Curriculum Continuum. Ed. by Florence E. Selder. LC 90-4470. (Loss, Grief & Care Ser.: Vol. 4, Nos. 1 & 2). 134p. 1991. text 39.95 (*0-86656-996-0*) Haworth Pr.

Nursing Education in the Middle East: Community Health Needs & Curriculum Development. Ed. by Myrna E. Mathia & Lorena S. Yamine. 244p. 1983. text 24.95 (*0-8156-6066-9*, Pub. by Am U Beirut) Syracuse U Pr.

Nursing Ethics Through the Life Span. 4th ed. (C). 2000. write for info. (*0-8385-6976-5*, Medical Exam) Appleton & Lange.

Nursing Elderly People. 2nd ed. Ed. by Sally J. Redfern. (Illus.). 600p. (Orig.). 1991. pap. text 54.00 (*0-443-04138-5*) Church.

Nursing Ethics. Bishop. (Philosophy Ser.). (C). 1996. 35.95 (*0-534-54245-X*) Wadsworth Pub.

Nursing Ethics. 3rd ed. Ian E. Thompson et al. LC 94-5561. 1994. pap. text 25.95 (*0-443-04811-8*) Church.

Nursing Ethics & Law. Jacqulyn K. Hall. Ed. by Tom Eoyang. (Illus.). 516p. 1996. pap. text 29.50 (*0-7216-4991-2*, W B Saunders Co) Harcrt Hlth Sci Grp.

Nursing Ethics Through the Life Span. 3rd ed. Elsie L. Bandman. (C). 1995. pap. text 32.95 (*0-8385-6638-3*, A6638-9) Appleton & Lange.

Nursing Exam Review in Basic Sciences. George Horemis & Clemencia Matomors. LC 72-96307. 200p. (Orig.). 1973. pap. 4.00 (*0-668-02946-3*, Arco) Macmillan Gen Ref.

Nursing Experience: Trends, Challenges, & Transitions. 3rd ed. Lucie Y. Kelly & Lucille A. Joel. LC 95-36827. 1996. pap. text 28.50 (*0-07-105483-9*) McGraw-Hill HPD.

Nursing Father: Moses As a Political Leader. Aaron Wildavsky. LC 83-1099. (Illus.). 280p. 1984. pap. text 19.95 (*0-8173-0169-0*) U of Ala Pr.

Nursing Fathers: American Colonists' Conception of English Protestant Kingship: 1688-1776. Benjamin Lewis Price. LC 98-53034. 272p. 1999. 45.00 (*0-7391-0051-3*) Lxngtn Bks.

Nursing for a Multi-Ethnic Society. Gerrish et al. LC 96-24395. (Race, Health, & Social Care Ser.). 192p. 1996. pap. 27.95 (*0-335-19615-2*) OpUniv Pr.

Nursing for a Night. large type ed. Barbara Thorn. (Dales Large Print Ser.). 261p. 1997. pap. 18.99 (*1-85389-719-1*) Ulverscroft.

Nursing for Continence. Katherine F. Jeter et al. 320p. 1990. text 42.00 (*0-7216-2892-3*, W B Saunders Co) Harcrt Hlth Sci Grp.

Nursing for Women's Health see Caring for Women through the Life Cycle

Nursing for Women's Health. Linda B. Chitwood. LC 94-60085. (Illus.). 232p. (Orig.). (C). 1992. pap. 49.95 (*1-878025-34-1*) Western Schls.

Nursing Foundations: Canadian Perspectives. Beverly W. Dugas. 1993. text. write for info. (*0-8385-7064-X*) Appleton & Lange.

Nursing, from Whence to Where? Professorial Lecture. Alan Pearson. (C). 1991. pap. 21.00 (*0-7300-1448-7*, Pub. by Deakin Univ) St Mut.

*__Nursing Frontiers: Accountability & the Boundaries of Care.__ Mike Walsh. LC 99-58096. (Illus.). 192p. 2000. pap. 33.00 (*0-7506-4316-1*) Buttrwrth-Heinemann.

Nursing Fundamentals. 2nd ed. Sharon Golub. LC 93-25831. (Notes Ser.). 192p. 1993. pap. 18.95 (*0-87434-615-0*) Springhouse Corp.

Nursing Guide to Drugs. 3rd ed. Margaret Havard. (Illus.). 344p. 1990. pap. text 25.00 (*0-443-04142-3*) Church.

Nursing Guide to Drugs. 4th ed. Havard. 1994. pap. text 19.95 (*0-443-04762-6*, W B Saunders Co) Harcrt Hlth Sci Grp.

Nursing, Health, & the Environment. Institute of Medicine Staff. Ed. by Andrew M. Pope et al. 304p. 1995. text 37.95 (*0-309-05298-X*) Natl Acad Pr.

Nursing Health Assessment: Concepts & Activities. Ed. by Margaret A. Fitzgerald et al. (Illus.). 359p. (C). 1995. pap. text 21.95 (*0-8036-0118-2*) Davis Co.

Nursing Health Care. Jack Rudman. (Regents External Degree (REDP) Ser.: Vol. 19). 43.95 (*0-8373-5669-5*) Nat Learn.

Nursing Health Care. Jack Rudman. (ACT Proficiency Examination Program (PEP) Ser.: Vol. 46). 43.95 (*0-8373-5596-6*) Nat Learn.

Nursing Health Care. Jack Rudman. (Regents External Degree Ser.: REDP-19). 1994. pap. 23.95 (*0-8373-5619-9*) Nat Learn.

Nursing Health Care. Jack Rudman. (ACT Proficiency Examination Program (PEP) Ser.: Vol. PEP-46). 1994. pap. 23.95 (*0-8373-5546-X*) Nat Learn.

Nursing History: New Perspectives, New Possibilities. Ed. by Ellen C. Lagemann. LC 82-10320. 229p. 1983. pap. 71.00 (*0-7837-8950-5*, 204966200002) Bks Demand.

Nursing History: The State of the Art. Ed. by Christopher J. Maggs. LC 86-32802. 208p. pap. 25.00 (*0-7099-4637-6*, Pub. by C Helm) Routldge.

Nursing History & the Politics of Welfare. Anne M. Rafferty et al. LC 96-19933. 296p. (C). 1997. 80.00 (*0-415-13835-3*); pap. 25.99 (*0-415-13836-1*) Routledge.

Nursing History Review, Vol. 1. 279p. 1992. pap. 35.00 (*0-8122-1450-1*) U of Pa Pr.

Nursing History Review: Official Journal of the American Association for the History of Nursing, Vol. 2. Ed. by Joan E. Lynaugh. (Illus.). 208p. 1993. pap. text 35.00 (*0-8122-1451-X*) U of Pa Pr.

Nursing History Review: Official Journal of the American Association for the History of Nursing, Vol. 3. Ed. by Joan E. Lynaugh. (Illus.). 312p. 1994. pap. text 35.00 (*0-8122-1452-8*) U of Pa Pr.

Nursing History Review: Official Journal of the American Association for the History of Nursing, Vol. 4. Ed. by Joan E. Lynaugh. (Illus.). 224p. 1995. pap. text 36.00 (*0-8122-1453-6*) U of Pa Pr.

Nursing History Review: Official Journal of the American Association for the History of Nursing, Vol. 5. Ed. by Joan E. Lynaugh. (Illus.). 256p. 1996. pap. text 36.00 (*0-8122-1454-4*) U of Pa Pr.

Nursing Home. Ira Eaton. LC 97-67418. 300p. 1997. pap. 12.95 (*1-888725-01-X*) Sci & Human Pr.

Nursing Home. large type ed. Ira Eaton. LC 98-96944. 332p. 1999. pap. 18.95 (*1-888725-23-0*, MacroPrintBks) Sci & Human Pr.

*__Nursing Home: A Necessary Evil? Not Evil Necessarily!__ Stephen G. Sinykin. 260p. 2000. pap. 19.95 (*0-9636766-3-6*) Ultimate Pr.

Nursing Home: The Complete Guide. fac. ed. Mary B. Forrest. LC 90-40851. (Illus.). 299p. 1990. reprint ed. pap. 92.70 (*0-7837-8142-3*, 204795000008) Bks Demand.

Nursing Home Abuse Investigations: New Trend in Private Investigative Practice Identified. Kelly Riddle. 120p. 1997. 19.95 (*1-891247-04-2*) Kelmar & Assocs.

Nursing Home Activities for the Handicapped. Mark Laker. 98p. 1980. pap., spiral bd. 23.95 (*0-398-04074-5*) C C Thomas.

Nursing Home Activities Specialist. (Career Examination Ser.: C-3642). pap. 27.95 (*0-8373-3642-2*) Nat Learn.

Nursing Home Adjustment & Satisfaction. Charles M. Joiner. LC 91-808. (Studies on the Elderly in America). 174p. 1991. text 25.00 (*0-8153-0518-4*) Garland.

Nursing Home Administration. 3rd ed. James E. Allen. LC 96-33640. (Illus.). 632p. 1997. 69.95 (*0-8261-5392-5*) Springer Pub.

Nursing Home Administrator. Jack Rudman. (Career Examination Ser.: C-3205). 1994. pap. 39.95 (*0-8373-3205-2*) Nat Learn.

Nursing Home Administrators: Their Influence on Quality of Care. rev. ed. Douglas A. Singh. LC 96-46551. (Studies on the Elderly in America). (Illus.). 208p. 1996. text 56.00 (*0-8153-2614-9*) Garland.

Nursing Home & Its Organizational Climate: An Ethnography. Bonnie C. Farmer. LC 95-43040. 176p. 1996. 52.95 (*0-86569-262-9*, Auburn Hse) Greenwood.

Nursing Home & Resident's Relatives. Marylou Hughes. 137p. (C). 1987. 17.50 (*1-877735-13-2*, 2119PP) Prof Prnting & Pub.

Nursing Home & You: Partners in Caring for a Relative with Alzheimer's Disease. Edna L. Blevins et al. 48p. (Orig.). 1987. pap. text 8.95 (*0-943774-37-3*) Am Assn Homes.

Nursing Home Choice: How to Choose the Ideal Nursing Home. Marian R. Kranz. Ed. by Adolph Caso. LC 97-40534. (Illus.). 280p. 1998. pap. 14.95 (*0-8283-2030-6*) Branden Bks.

Nursing Home Companion. Pauline B. Innis. 174p. 1993. 9.95 (*0-941402-10-X*) Devon Pub.

Nursing Home Connection: A Handbook for Visitors. Anne Sharp. LC 89-92775. (Illus.). 80p. (Orig.). 1990. pap. 4.95 (*0-9625382-0-5*) A Sharp.

Nursing Home Decision: Easing the Transition for Everyone. Lawrence M. Martin. 175p. 1999. pap. 14.95 (*0-471-34804-X*) Wiley.

Nursing Home Design: Consequences of Employing the Medical Model. rev. ed. Benyamin Schwarz. LC 95-50344. (Studies on the Elderly in America). (Illus.). 320p. 1996. text 88.00 (*0-8153-2400-6*) Garland.

Nursing Home Federal Requirements & Guidelines to Surveyors. 3rd ed. James E. Allen. LC 96-48423. 312p. 1997. 44.95 (*0-8261-8122-8*) Springer Pub.

*__Nursing Home Handbook: A Guide to Living Well.__ Ruth Davis. LC 99-28127. 220p. 1999. pap. 10.95 (*1-58062-208-9*) Adams Media.

Nursing Home Handbook: North Central Texas Region, 1992-1993 Edition. Amy Crawley & Cynthia O'Keafe. 300p. 1992. pap. 19.95 (*0-9634276-0-1*) Smart Choices.

Nursing Home in American Society. Colleen L. Johnson & Leslie A. Grant. LC 84-21811. (Illus.). 232p. 1985. reprint ed. pap. 72.00 (*0-608-07337-7*, 206756500009) Bks Demand.

Nursing Home Leadership. Wayne D. Ford. 317p. 1997. pap. 69.95 (*1-879876-00-0*, 30201) Mgmt Advantage.

Nursing Home Life: The Silver Lining. Helen F. Glazer. 160p. 1990. pap. 9.95 (*0-938823-05-1*) Pogment Pr.

Nursing Home Life: What It Is & What It Could Be. Clifford Bennett. LC 80-52650. (Illus.). 192p. 1980. pap. text 12.00 (*0-913292-19-2*) Tiresias Pr.

*__Nursing Home Litigation: Investigation & Case Preparation.__ Ed. by Patricia W. Iyer. LC 99-21688. (Illus.). 490p. 1999. kivar 99.00 (*0-913875-64-3*, 5643-N) Lawyers & Judges.

Nursing Home Manual. Texas Legal Services Center Staff. 438p. 1985. 27.00 (*0-685-23179-8*, 39,904) NCLS Inc.

Nursing Home Market: Supply & Demand for the Elderly. Jeffrey A. Rhoades. LC 98-29802. (Studies on the Elderly in America). (Illus.). 160p. 1998. 42.00 (*0-8153-3201-7*) Garland.

Nursing Home Ministry. Tom McCormick & Penny McCormick. 128p. 1987. pap. 9.95 (*0-310-34571-5*, 18418P) Zondervan.

Nursing Home Ministry: A Manual. Ed. by Tom McCormick & Penny McCormick. (Orig.). 1982. pap. text 6.95 (*0-934688-08-7*) Great Comm Pubns.

Nursing Home Murder. Ngaio Marsh. 240p. 1994. mass mkt. 4.50 (*0-425-14242-6*, Prime Crime) Berkley Pub.

Nursing Home Murder. Ngaio Marsh. 1999. mass mkt. 5.99 (*0-312-96999-6*) St Martin.

Nursing Home Murder. Ngaio Marsh. 1976. reprint ed. lib. bdg. 22.95 (*0-88411-491-0*) Amereon Ltd.

Nursing Home Options: Getting Quality Care for the Elderly. James N. Fisher. Ed. by Betty McBride. LC 91-73498. 112p. (Orig.). 1991. pap. 9.25 (*0-9629201-7-7*) Collective Creations.

Nursing Home Rates in the Upper Midwest: A Program Evaluation Report. Susan Von Mosch et al. (Illus.). 86p. (C). 1998. pap. text 20.00 (*0-7881-4938-5*) DIANE Pub.

Nursing Home Regulations. LC 96-233538. 304p. 1995. pap. 35.00 (*0-8080-0066-7*, 4915) CCH INC.

Nursing Home Renovation Designed for Reform. Lorraine G. Hiatt. (Illus.). 240p. 1991. text 54.95 (*0-7506-9126-3*, Butterwrth Archit) Buttrwrth-Heinemann.

*__Nursing Home Requirements & Guidelines to Surveyors.__ 4th ed. James E. Allen. LC 99-55521. 440p. 2000. pap. 46.95 (*0-8261-8123-6*) Springer Pub.

Nursing Home Salary & Benefit Report, 1991. 14th ed. Zabka, John R. Associates Inc. Staff. 204p. 1992. pap. 250.00 (*0-939326-65-5*) Hosp & Hlthcare.

Nursing Home Salary & Benefits Report, 1992. Hospital Compensation Service Staff. 1992. pap. 250.00 (*0-939326-69-8*) Hosp & Hlthcare.

Nursing Home Salary & Benefits Report, 1993. 225p. 1994. pap. 250.00 (*0-939326-76-0*) Hosp & Hlthcare.

Nursing Home Statistical Yearbook, 1995. Ed. by C. McKeen Cowles. 256p. (C). 1996. text 45.00 (*0-8018-5378-8*) Johns Hopkins.

Nursing Home Statistical Yearbook, 1996. Ed. by C. McKeen Cowles. 256p. 1997. text 50.00 (*0-8018-5638-8*) Johns Hopkins.

Nursing Home Task Force Report. Nursing Home Task Force National Hospice Organizat. LC 99-181747. 88p. 1998. write for info. (*0-931207-56-8*) Natl Hospice.

Nursing Home Volunteer Services Guide. Harold E. Knight, III & Carol J. Wortham. 60p. (Orig.). 1988. pap. 34.95 (*0-945253-03-6*) Thornsbury Bailey Brown.

*__Nursing Homes: Additional Steps Needed to Strengthen Enforcement of Federal Quality Standards.__ Ed. by William J. Scanlon. 65p. (C). 2000. pap. text 20.00 (*0-7881-8637-X*) DIANE Pub.

*__Nursing Homes: Complaint Investigation Processes Often Inadequate to Protect Residents.__ Ed. by William J. Scanlon. (Illus.). 77p. (C). 2000. pap. text 20.00 (*0-7881-8644-2*) DIANE Pub.

Nursing Homes: Getting Good Care There. Sarah G. Burger et al. LC 95-52755. (Working Caregiver Ser.). 176p. 1996. pap. 14.95 (*0-915166-97-6*, Amrcn Source Bks) Impact Pubs CA.

*__Nursing Homes: Proposal to Enhance Oversight of Poorly Performing Homes Has Merit.__ William J. Scanlon. 68p. (C). 2000. pap. text 20.00 (*0-7881-8817-8*) DIANE Pub.

Nursing Homes & Nursing Care: Lessons from the Teaching Nursing Homes. Ed. by Mathy D. Mezey et al. 176p. 1988. 23.95 (*0-8261-6210-X*) Springer Pub.

Nursing Homes & Older People: Issues of Continuing Care. Ed. by Pauline Ford & Hazel Heath. 288p. 1996. pap. text 37.50 (*0-7506-2438-8*) Buttrwrth-Heinemann.

Nursing Homes for the Elderly: Questions of Quality & Policy. Helen Bartlett. LC 92-27857. 225p. 1993. text 61.00 (*3-7186-5331-1*) Gordon & Breach.

Nursing Homes Statistical Yearbook, 1997. C. McKeen Cowles. 260p. text 50.00 (*0-8018-5802-X*) Johns Hopkins.

*__Nursing Homes That Seniors Love.__ Marilyn Rantz et al. 2000. pap. 14.95 (*1-57749-099-1*) Fairview Press.

Nursing Implications in Seizure Management. Daniel Therriault. (Illus.). 1994. pap. 22.95 (*1-928752-08-X*) Mc Gowan Pubns.

Nursing in a Violent Society: Issues & Research. Ed. by Harriet Feldman. LC 95-31624. 128p. 1995. 28.95 (*0-8261-9080-4*) Springer Pub.

Nursing in Action: Strengthening Nursing & Midwifery to Support Health for All. Jane Salvage. (WHO Regional Publications: No. 48). 128p. 1993. pap. text 21.60 (*92-890-1312-5*, 1310048) World Health.

Nursing in Ambulatory Care: The Future Is Here. American Nurses Association Staff & American Academy of Ambulatory Care Nursing Staff. LC 97-145420. 54p. 1997. 18.95 (*1-55810-135-7*, ST-2) Am Nurses Pub.

Nursing in America. Lewis Miller. (C). 1989. 32.00 (*0-7223-2389-1*, Pub. by A H S Ltd) St Mut.

Nursing in Families. Suzanne L. Feetham et al. (Illus.). 320p. (C). 1992. 49.95 (*0-8039-4715-1*); pap. 23.50 (*0-8039-4716-X*) Sage.

Nursing in Gastroenterology. Bruce. 1997. text 33.00 (*0-443-05484-3*, W B Saunders Co) Harcrt Hlth Sci Grp.

Nursing in General Practice. M. Smith & S. Luft. 272p. 1994. 37.50 (*1-56593-187-4*, 0502) Singular Publishing.

Nursing in Hospice & Terminal Care: Research & Practice. Ed. by Barbara M. Petrosino. LC 86-12015. (Hospice Journal: Vol. 2, No. 1). 138p. 1986. 39.95 (*0-86656-567-1*) Haworth Pr.

Nursing in Nursing Homes. Linda Nazarko. LC 94-49058. 1995. pap. 21.95 (*0-632-03987-6*) Blackwell Sci.

Nursing in Society. 15th ed. Dolan. (Illus.). 417p. 1983. pap. text 45.00 (*0-7216-3135-5*, W B Saunders Co) Harcrt Hlth Sci Grp.

*__Nursing in the Community.__ Kay Saucier Lundy et al. (Illus.). 832p. (C). 2000. text 52.50 (*0-7637-0706-6*) Jones & Bartlett.

Nursing in the Community. 2nd ed. Mary J. Clark. LC 95-11594. (Illus.). 1160p. (C). 1995. pap. text 49.95 (*0-8385-7091-7*, A7091-0) Appleton & Lange.

Nursing in the Community: Dimensions of Community Health Nursing. 3rd ed. Mary Jo Dummer Clark. 1103p. (C). 1998. pap. text 51.95 (*0-8385-6984-6*) Appleton & Lange.

Nursing in the Year 2000. Ed. by Joan Bilitski & Margaret C. Taylor. 70p. (Orig.). 1984. pap. 7.95 (*0-937058-20-3*) West Va U Pr.

Nursing in Today's World: Challenges, Issues, & Trends. 5th ed. Janice R. Ellis & Celia L. Hartley. LC 94-32255. 544p. 1994. pap. text 28.00 (*0-397-55177-0*) Lppncott W & W.

Nursing in Today's World: Challenges, Issues & Trends. 6th ed. Janice R. Ellis & Celia L. Hartley. LC 97-22036. 560p. 1997. pap. text 26.95 (*0-397-55428-1*) Lppncott W & W.

Nursing in Today's World: Challenges, Issues, & Trends. 7th ed. Janice Rider Ellis & Celia Love Hartley. 528p. pap. text 29.95 (*0-7817-2455-4*) Lppncott W & W.

Nursing Informatics. Ed. by M. J. Ball et al. (Computers in Health Care Ser.). (Illus.). 450p. 1993. 44.00 (*0-387-96639-0*) Spr-Verlag.

Nursing Informatics. Ed. by Paul Wainwright. LC 93-36803. 1994. pap. text 56.00 (*0-443-04705-7*) Church.

Nursing Informatics: An International Overview for Nursing in a Technological Era; Proceedings of the Fifth IMIA International Conference on Nursing Use of Computers & Information Science, San Antonio, Texas, USA, June 17-22, 1994. International Conference on Nursing Use of Compute. Ed. by Susan J. Grobe & Elly S. Pluyter-Wenting. LC 94-16514. 876p. 1994. 272.25 (*0-444-81851-0*) Elsevier.

Nursing Informatics: When Caring & Technology Meet. 2nd ed. Ed. by S. K. Newbold et al. LC 95-6681. (Computers in Health Care Ser.). (Illus.). 452p. 1995. 49.95 (*0-387-94476-1*) Spr-Verlag.

*__Nursing Informatics: Where Caring & Technology Meet.__ 3rd ed. Ed. by M. J. Ball et al. (Illus.). 456p. 2000. 59.00 (*0-387-98923-4*) Spr-Verlag.

Nursing Informatics Vol. 46: The Impact of Nursing Knowledge on Health Care Information. Ed. by U. Gerdin et al. LC 97-75048. 600p. Date not set. 119.00 (*90-5199-362-5*, 362-5) IOS Press.

Nursing Interventions. 2nd ed. Gloria M. Bulechek. (Illus.). 641p. 1992. text 61.50 (*0-7216-3802-3*, W B Saunders Co) Harcrt Hlth Sci Grp.

Nursing Interventions: Effective Nursing Treatments. 3rd ed. Gloria M. Bulechek & Joanne C. McCloskey. Ed. by Thomas Eoyang. LC 98-43443. (Illus.). 685p. 1999. text. write for info. (*0-7216-7724-X*, W B Saunders Co) Harcrt Hlth Sci Grp.

Nursing Interventions & Clinical Skills. Martha K. Elkin et al. (Illus.). 1996. teacher ed. write for info. (*0-8151-3030-9*, Pub. by Harcrt Hlth Sci Grp) Harcourt.

Nursing Interventions & Clinical Skills. Martha K. Elkin et al. (Illus.). 832p. (C). (gr. 13). 1995. pap. text 50.00 (*0-8151-3045-7*, 24832) Mosby Inc.

Nursing Interventions & Clinical Skills. Martha K. Elkin et al. (Illus.). 832p. 1996. write for info. (*0-8151-3043-0*) Mosby Inc.

*__Nursing Interventions & Clinical Skills.__ 2nd ed. Martha K. Elkin. (C). 1999. teacher ed. write for info. (*0-323-00803-8*); text. write for info. (*0-323-00802-X*) Mosby Inc.

Nursing Interventions Classification (NIC) 2nd ed. Joanne C. McCloskey et al. Ed. by Gloria M. Bulechek. (Illus.). 768p. (C). (gr. 13). 1995. pap. text 37.95 (*0-8151-6302-9*, 26018) Mosby Inc.

Nursing Interventions for Infants & Children. Craft-Denehy. (Illus.). 416p. 1989. text 58.00 (*0-7216-2129-5*, W B Saunders Co) Harcrt Hlth Sci Grp.

*__Nursing Interventions for Infants, Children & Families.__ Martha Craft-Rosenberg & Janice Ann Denehy. LC 00-8361. (Illus.). 2000. write for info. (*0-7619-0725-4*) Sage.

Nursing Is My Bag. Marian George. (Illus.). 131p. (Orig.). 1989. pap. 9.95 (*0-9623843-0-5*) M George.

Nursing Issues for the Nineties & Beyond. Ed. by Bonnie Bullough & Vern Bullough. LC 92-49817. 248p. (C). 1994. text 29.95 (*0-8261-8050-7*) Springer Pub.

Nursing Issues in Leading & Managing Change. Jeanette Lancaster. LC 98-26134. 544p. 1998. pap. text 34.95 (*0-323-00250-1*) Mosby Inc.

Nursing Issues, Trends & Portents. Castillo. (Nursing Education Ser.). 1997. pap. 26.50 (*0-8273-6270-6*) Delmar.

Nursing Job Guide, 1986-87: Annual Hospital Directory of Nursingworld Journal. 699p. 1987. pap. 48.00 (*0-317-56976-7*) Prime Natl Pub.

Nursing Jurisprudence. Mary Cushing. 534p. (C). 1988. pap. text 48.95 (*0-8385-7039-9*, A7039-9) Appleton & Lange.

Nursing Knowledge & Nursing Science. Prentice-Hall Staff. (C). 2000. text 39.95 (*0-8385-7116-6*, Medical Exam) Appleton & Lange.

N

An Asterisk (*) at the beginning of an entry indicates that the title is appearing for the first time.

Nursing Knowledge & Practice: A Decision-Making Approach. Maggie Mallik. 1997. pap. text 39.95 (*0-7020-1991-7*, Pub. by W B Saunders) Saunders.

Nursing Law & Ethics. John Tingle & A. Cribb. (Illus.). 256p. 1995. pap. 34.95 (*0-632-03617-6*, Pub. by Blckwll Scitfc UK) Blackwell Sci.

Nursing Leadership & Management: An Experiential Approach. Elaine L. La Monica. LC 82-20193. 300p. (C). 1983. reprint ed. pap. 40.00 (*0-86720-377-3*) Jones & Bartlett.

Nursing Leadership & Management: Concepts & Practice. 3rd ed. Ruth M. Tappen. LC 94-27741. 508p. 1994. pap. 31.95 (*0-8036-8337-5*) Davis Co.

Nursing Leadership & Management: Contemporary Strategies. Gertrude K. McFarland et al. LC 83-16724. 349p. (C). 1989. text 34.95 (*0-8273-4309-4*) Delmar.

Nursing Leadership & Management Skills. Mary Keenan & Joseph B. Hurst. 276p. 1995. text 17.95 (*0-8151-5207-8*) Mosby Inc.

Nursing Leadership, Management & Economics. Donna B. Jensen. 512p. 1998. pap. text 31.95 (*0-397-55359-5*) Lppncott W & W.

Nursing Leadership, Management, & Professional Practice for the LPN/LVN. Mary Ann Anderson et al. LC 96-52836. (Illus.). 252p. (C). 1997. pap. text 22.95 (*0-8036-0209-X*) Davis Co.

Nursing Leadership, Management & Research. Ann B. Grant & Veta H. Massey. LC 98-49376. (Notes Ser.). 256p. 1999. pap. 24.95 incl. disk (*0-87434-968-0*) Springhouse Corp.

Nursing Licensure Guidelines, 1999 Ed. American Hospital Association Staff. 1999. pap. text 65.00 (*1-887617-62-0*) St Bart Pr Ltd.

Nursing Made Easy. Sylvia Rayfield & Loretta Manning. (Illus.). 304p. 1997. pap. 24.95 (*0-9643622-2-8*) ICAN LA.

Nursing Malpractice. Ed. by Patricia W. Iyer. LC 96-22776. (Illus.). 1085p. 1996. 115.00 (*0-913875-10-4*, 5104-N) Lawyers & Judges.

Nursing Malpractice: Implications for Clinical Practice & Nursing Education. J. Beckmann. LC 94-10802. 298p. 1994. pap. 22.50 (*0-295-97373-0*) U of Wash Pr.

Nursing Malpractice: Liability & Risk Management. Charles C. Sharpe. LC 98-31027. 240p. 1999. 65.00 (*0-86569-280-7*, Auburn Hse); pap. 22.95 (*0-86569-286-6*, Auburn Hse) Greenwood.

Nursing Management. Barter. (Nursing Education Ser.). 1998. 24.95 (*0-8273-7853-X*) Delmar.

Nursing Management: A Systems Approach. 3rd ed. Dee A. Gillies. (Illus.). 1994. pap., teacher ed. write for info. (*0-7216-6597-7*, W B Saunders Co) Harcrt Hlth Sci Grp.

Nursing Management: A Systems Approach. 3rd ed. Dee A. Gillies. LC 93-23585. 1994. pap. text 33.00 (*0-7216-6588-8*, W B Saunders Co) Harcrt Hlth Sci Grp.

Nursing Management: An Experimental Skill Building Workbook. 3rd ed. Eleanor J. Sullivan. 272p. (C). 1992. pap. text 24.38 (*0-8053-7863-4*) Addison-Wesley.

Nursing Management: Concepts & Issues. 2nd ed. Ed. by Katherine W. Vestal. LC 94-9624. 400p. 1994. pap. text 29.95 (*0-397-55012-X*) Lppncott W & W.

Nursing Management: Issues & Ideas. Ed. by Montague Brown. (Health Care Management Review Ser.). 220p. 1992. 41.00 (*0-8342-0301-4*, 20301) Aspen Pub.

Nursing Management Desk Reference: Concepts, Strategies & Skills. Ed. by Roxane Spitzer-Lehmann. LC 93-35928. (Illus.). 764p. 1994. text 55.00 (*0-7216-4346-9*, W B Saunders Co) Harcrt Hlth Sci Grp.

Nursing Management for the Elderly. 3rd ed. Doris L. Carnevali. Ed. by Maxine Patrick. LC 92-20793. (Illus.). 688p. 1993. text 53.00 (*0-397-54898-2*) Lppncott W & W.

Nursing Management Handbook. Ken Hyett. (Illus.). 224p. 1988. write for info. (*0-443-03626-8*) Church.

Nursing Management in Canada. Judith M. Hibberd & Mavis E. Kyle. (Illus.). 1994. teacher ed. write for info. (*0-920513-20-4*, Pub. by Saulnders) Saunders.

Nursing Management in Canada. Judith M. Hibberd & Mavis E. Kyle. (Illus.). 692p. 1994. text 43.00 (*0-920513-18-2*, Pub. by Saulnders) Saunders.

Nursing Management in the New Paradigm. Catherine E. Loveridge & Susan H. Cummings. 350p. 1997. 49.00 (*0-8342-0620-X*, 20620) Aspen Pub.

Nursing Management in the 90's - An OBRA Guide for DON's. Mattie Locke. 224p. (C). 1991. 18.00 (*1-877735-31-0*, 2176PP) Prof Prnting & Pub.

Nursing Management of Diabetes Mellitus: A Guide to the Pattern Approach. 4th ed. Diana W. Guthrie & Richard A. Guthrie. LC 97-4384. (Illus.). 434p. 1997. 56.95 (*0-8261-7261-X*) Springer Pub.

Nursing Management of Multiple Birth Families: Preconception Through Postpartum. Joan E. Dauphinee et al. LC 96-40371. 1997. write for info. (*0-86525-076-6*) March of Dimes.

Nursing Math Simplified: Math Magic. Susan G. Moore. Ed. by Joseph W. Howland & Katherine Savige. (Illus.). 60p. (Orig.). (C). 1986. pap. text 7.50 (*0-943202-22-1*) H & H Pubs.

Nursing Math Simplified: Math Magic. 3rd ed. Sue Moore. Ed. & Illus. by Tom Howland. 70p. (Orig.). (C). 1992. pap. text 11.95 (*0-943202-58-2*) H & H Pub.

*__Nursing, Medicine & Primary Care.__ Anne Williams. LC 99-49874. 192p. 2000. pap. 27.95 (*0-335-20167-9*) Taylor & Francis.

Nursing Models for Practice. 2nd ed. Alan Pearson & Barbara Vaughan. 264p. 1996. pap. text 45.00 (*0-7506-1597-4*, Focal) Buttrwrth-Heinemann.

Nursing Mother, Working Mother: The Essential Guide for Breastfeeding & Staying Close to Your Baby after You Return to Work. Gale Pryor. LC 96-46491. (Illus.). 208p. 1997. 19.95 (*1-55832-116-0*); pap. 10.95 (*1-55832-117-9*) Harvard Common Pr.

Nursing Mother's Companion. 4th rev. ed. Kathleen Huggins. LC 98-51793. (Illus.). 256p. 1999. 24.95 (*1-55832-151-9*); pap. 12.95 (*1-55832-152-7*) Harvard Common Pr.

Nursing Mother's Guide to Weaning. Kathleen Huggins & Linda Ziedrich. LC 94-30070. (Illus.). 208p. 1994. 18.95 (*1-55832-066-0*) Harvard Common Pr.

Nursing Mother's Guide to Weaning. Linda Ziedrich & Kathleen Huggins. LC 94-30070. (Illus.). 208p. 1994. pap. 10.95 (*1-55832-065-2*) Harvard Common Pr.

*__Nursing Mother's Problem Solver.__ Ed. by Claire Martin & Nancy Funnemark Krebs. 320p. 2000. pap. 13.00 (*0-684-85784-7*, Fireside) S&S Trade Pap.

Nursing NCLEX-RN Pearls of Wisdom. Gossman. (Pearls of Wisdom Ser.). 1998. pap. 26.00 (*1-890369-20-9*) Boston Medical.

Nursing Negligence: Analyzing Malpractice in the Hospital Setting. Janet P. Beckmann. LC 95-41787. (Illus.). 400p. 1996. 55.00 (*0-7619-0225-2*); pap. 25.95 (*0-7619-0226-0*) Sage.

Nursing 97 Drug Handbook. 2nd rev. ed. Springhouse Publishing Company Staff. Ed. by June Norris. (Illus.). 1360p. 1996. 31.95 incl. disk (*0-87434-867-6*) Springhouse Corp.

*__Nursing Now: Today's Issues, Tomorrow's Trends.__ 2nd ed. Joseph T. Catalano. LC 99-40516. (Illus.). 536p. 1999. pap. text 31.95 (*0-8036-0496-3*) Davis Co.

Nursing Now Notes. Deborah Stewart. Date not set. spiral bd. 14.00 (*0-9678177-0-6*) D L Stewart.

Nursing Observation. 2nd ed. Virginia B. Byers. LC 73-76772. 106p. 1973. write for info. (*0-697-05536-1*) Brown & Benchmark.

Nursing Outcomes Classification. Ed. by Marion Johnson & Meridean Maas. LC 96-50091. (Illus.). 448p. (C). (gr. 13). 1997. pap. text 37.95 (*0-8151-4546-2*, 30588) Mosby Inc.

*__Nursing Outcomes Classification (NOC)__ 2nd ed. Marion Johnson et al. LC 99-40690. 1999. text. write for info. (*0-323-00893-3*) Mosby Inc.

Nursing Partnership: A Model for Nursing Practice. Judith Christensen. LC 93-12698. 272p. 1993. pap. text. write for info. (*0-443-04934-3*) Church.

Nursing Perspective on Severe Mental Illness. Ed. by Linda Chafetz. LC 87-646993. (New Directions for Mental Health Services Ser.: No. MHS 58). 107p. (Orig.). 1993. pap. 25.00 (*1-55542-695-6*) Jossey-Bass.

Nursing Perspectives & Issues. 4th ed. Gloria M. Grippando. 442p. 1989. pap. 25.90 (*0-8273-3466-4*) Delmar.

Nursing Perspectives & Issues. 5th ed. Paula R. Mitchell & Gloria M. Grippando. (C). 1992. mass mkt. 31.25 (*0-8273-4983-1*) Delmar.

*__Nursing Perspectives & Issues.__ 6th ed. Mitchell Grippando. (C). 2002. text 25.50 (*0-7668-0271-X*) Delmar.

Nursing Perspectives & Issues: Instructor's Guide. 5th ed. Paula R. Mitchell & Gloria M. Grippando. 1993. pap., teacher ed. 14.95 (*0-8273-4985-8*) Delmar.

Nursing Pharmacology. Ed. by Norma L. Pinnell. (Illus.). 1996. teacher ed. write for info. (*0-7216-5154-2*, W B Saunders Co) Harcrt Hlth Sci Grp.

Nursing Pharmacology. Norma L. Pinnell. Ed. by Dan Ruth. LC 94-20441. (Illus.). 1248p. 1996. text 57.50 (*0-7216-6482-2*, W B Saunders Co) Harcrt Hlth Sci Grp.

Nursing Pharmacology. Norma L. Pinnell. 1996. pap. text, student ed. 17.95 (*0-7216-6783-X*, W B Saunders Co) Harcrt Hlth Sci Grp.

Nursing Pharmacology. Paulette D. Rollant & Karen Hill. LC 95-36828. (Mosby's Review Ser.). (Illus.). 400p. (C). (gr. 13). 1995. pap. text 24.95 incl. 3.5 hd (*0-8151-7245-1*, 24858) Mosby Inc.

Nursing Pharmacology. 2nd ed. Lane J. Wallace. (Nursing-Health Science Ser.). 1120p. (C). 1992. 57.50 (*0-86720-429-X*) Jones & Bartlett.

Nursing Pharmacology. 3rd ed. April H. Vallerand. LC 96-48153. (Springhouse Notes Ser.). 304p. 1997. 22.95 (*0-87434-903-6*) Springhouse Corp.

Nursing Pharmacology: A Comprehensive Approach to Drug Therapy. Sandra Wardell & Lorraine Bousard. 1200p. (C). 1985. text 46.25 (*0-534-01338-4*) Jones & Bartlett.

Nursing Pharmacology: A Systems Approach to Drug Therapy & Nursing Practice. Alvin K. Swonger. 1978. 13.00 (*0-316-82553-0*, Little Brwn Med Div) Lppncott W & W.

Nursing Pharmacology: An Integrated Approach to Drug Therapy & Nursing Practice. Alvin K. Swonger & Myrtle P. Matejski. (C). 1988. text 62.33 (*0-673-39752-1*) Addson-Wesley Educ.

Nursing Pharmacology & Clinical Management. Leah Cleveland et al. LC 98-25822. 1114p. 1998. text 51.95 (*0-397-55244-0*) Lppncott W & W.

Nursing Pharmacology Value Pack. Wallace. 1992. 57.50 (*0-86720-625-X*) Jones & Bartlett.

Nursing Power & Social Judgement: An Interpretive Ethnography of a Hospital Ward. Martin Johnson. LC 97-71457. (Developments in Nursing & Health Care Ser.). (Illus.). 211p. 1997. text 64.95 (*1-85972-651-8*, Pub. by Ashgate Pub) Ashgate Pub Co.

Nursing Practice: High, Hard Ground, Messy Swamps, & the Pathways in Between. Annette F. Street. (C). 1995. pap. 40.00 (*0-7300-0750-2*, Pub. by Deakin Univ) St Mut.

Nursing Practice: Hospital & Home; the Adult. Ed. by Margaret F. Alexander et al. LC 94-16626. 1995. pap. text 40.00 (*0-443-04338-8*) Church.

Nursing Practice: Report of a WHO Expert Committee. (Technical Reports: Vol. 860).Tr. of Soins Infirmiers, Enfermeria. (ENG, FRE & SPA.). 33p. (Orig.). 1996. pap. 10.80 (*92-4-120860-0*, 1100860) World Health.

Nursing Practice - Teaching Roles: Faculty-Clinician; Clinician-Faculty. Marian Pettengill & Lu A. Young. 150p. (Orig.). 1987. pap. 12.50 (*0-942146-13-1*) Midwest Alliance Nursing.

Nursing Practice & Health Care. 2nd ed. write for info. (*0-340-55788-5*, Pub. by E A) Routldge.

Nursing Practice & Health Care. 2nd ed. Hinchcliffe. 864p. 1993. pap. 63.75 (*1-56593-534-9*, 0538) Singular Publishing.

Nursing Practice & Health Care: A Foundation Text. 3rd ed. Ed. by Sue Hinchliff et al. (An Arnold Publication). (Illus.). 736p. 1998. pap. text 34.50 (*0-340-69230-8*, Pub. by E A) OUP.

Nursing Practice & Outcomes Measurement. Joint Commission on Accreditation of Healthcare St. LC 96-43897. 193p. 1997. 50.00 (*0-86688-499-8*, OM-100) Joint Comm Hlthcare.

Nursing Practice & the Law. 2nd ed. Milton Lesnik & Bernice E. Anderson. LC 75-45453. 400p. 1976. reprint ed. lib. bdg. 75.00 (*0-8371-8729-X*, LENP, Greenwood Pr) Greenwood.

Nursing Practice & the Law: Avoiding Malpractice & Other Legal Risks. Mary E. O'Keefe. (Illus.). 432p. 2000. 29.95 (*0-8036-0602-8*) Davis Co.

Nursing Practice in the U. K. & North America. Eugene Levine et al. LC 92-12312. 1993. 49.50 (*1-56593-024-X*, 0267) Thomson Learn.

Nursing Praxis: Knowledge & Action. Ed. by Sally Thorne & Virginia E. Hayes. LC 96-35661. 320p. 1996. 52.00 (*0-7619-0010-1*); pap. 24.95 (*0-7619-0011-X*) Sage.

*__Nursing Procedures.__ 3rd ed. Springhouse Publishing Staff. 2000. 49.95 (*0-87434-978-8*) Springhouse Corp.

Nursing Procedures Manual for Skin Diseases. Leok & Associates Staff et al. 1995. pap. text. write for info. (*0-07-113835-8*) McGraw.

Nursing Process: A Critical Thinking Approach. 2nd rev. ed. Judith M. Wilkinson. LC 95-37177. 402p. (C). 1995. pap. text 30.20 (*0-8053-9366-8*) Addison-Wesley.

Nursing Process: Theory, Application & Related Processes. Norma N. Pinnell & Mary De Meneses. 432p. (C). 1986. pap. text 33.95 (*0-8385-7036-4*, A7036-5) Appleton & Lange.

Nursing Process & Nursing Diagnosis. 3rd ed. Patricia W. Iyer et al. LC 94-17892. 576p. 1994. pap. text 24.00 (*0-7216-5614-5*, W B Saunders Co) Harcrt Hlth Sci Grp.

Nursing Process & Quality Care. write for info. (*0-340-58112-3*, Pub. by E A) Routldge.

*__Nursing Process for LPN'S.__ Seaback. (C). 2000. pap. 32.95 (*0-7668-2045-9*) Delmar.

Nursing Process in Collaborative Practice. 2nd ed. Carol V. Allen. LC 96-8018. 264p. (Orig.). (C). 1996. pap. text 26.95 (*0-8385-1467-7*, A1467-8) Appleton & Lange.

Nursing Process in Psychiatry. 2nd ed. Ward. (Illus.). 256p. (Orig.). 1992. pap. text 29.95 (*0-443-04225-X*) Church.

*__Nursing Profession: Tomorrow & Beyond.__ Norma L. Chaska. LC 00-9517. 2000. write for info. (*0-7619-1943-0*) Sage.

Nursing Quality & Productivity: Practical Management Tools. Roey Kirk. 112p. 1986. 67.00 (*0-87189-366-5*, 89366) Aspen Pub.

Nursing Quality Assurance Handbook: Developing - Updating Your Program for the 1990's. Ed. by Laurie Marx & Joy Haskin. LC 90-63404. 251p. 1991. pap. 39.95 (*0-944496-19-9*) Precept Pr.

Nursing Quality Assurance in Long-Term Care. Joan LeSage & Diana Y. Barhyte. 288p. 1989. 58.00 (*0-8342-0066-X*, 20066) Aspen Pub.

Nursing Quality Indicators: Definitions & Implications. American Nurses Association Staff et al. LC 96-19465. 88p. 1996. pap. 29.95 (*1-55810-125-X*, NP-108, Am Nurses Fnd) Am Nurses Pub.

*__Nursing Quality Indicators Beyond Acute Care: Literature Review.__ 156p. 2000. pap. write for info. (*1-55810-149-7*) Am Nurses Pub.

*__Nursing Quality Indicators Beyond Acute Care: Measurement Instruments.__ 220p. 2000. pap. write for info. (*1-55810-150-0*) Am Nurses Pub.

Nursing Quality Measurement: A Review of Nursing Studies. Marilyn J. Rantz. 198p. (Orig.). 1995. pap. 33.95 (*1-55810-105-5*, NP-93) Am Nurses Pub.

*__Nursing Reflections: A Century of Caring.__ C. V. Mosby Company Staff. LC 00-29218. 176p. 2000. pap. 34.95 (*0-323-01173-X*) Mosby Inc.

Nursing Replay. Street. 1995. text 24.95 (*0-443-04761-8*, W B Saunders Co) Harcrt Hlth Sci Grp.

Nursing Research. 1996. 12.00 (*92-871-3112-0*, Pub. by Council of Europe) Manhattan Pub Co.

Nursing Research. write for info. (*0-340-66194-1*, Pub. by E A) Routldge.

Nursing Research. Ed. by M. Hardey & A. Mulhall. 240p. 1994. 41.50 (*1-56593-188-2*, 0503) Singular Publishing.

Nursing Research. 2nd ed. Morse. 208p. 1995. pap. 37.95 (*1-56593-586-1*, 1194) Singular Publishing.

Nursing Research. 5th ed. Denise F. Polit. 304p. 1994. pap. text, student ed. 18.95 (*0-397-55139-8*) Lppncott W & W.

Nursing Research: A Qualitative Perspective. 2nd ed. Ed. by Patricia L. Munhall & Carolyn O. Boyd. LC 93-20494. 1993. 30.95 (*0-88737-590-1*) Natl League Nurse.

*__Nursing Research: A Qualitative Perspective.__ 3rd ed. Patricia L. Munhall & NLN Staff. (Illus.). 288p. (C). 1999. pap. text 32.50 (*0-7637-1135-7*) JB Pubns.

Nursing Research: A Quantitative & Qualitative Approach. Carol A. Roberts & Sharon O. Burke. 400p. 1989. 46.25 (*0-86720-415-X*) Jones & Bartlett.

Nursing Research: Ethical & Legal. De Raeve. 1996. pap. text 40.95 (*0-7020-1888-0*, W B Saunders Co) Harcrt Hlth Sci Grp.

Nursing Research: Methods, Critical Appraisal & Utilization. 4th ed. Geri Lobiondo-Wood & Judith Haber. LC 97-33347. (Illus.). 624p. (C). (gr. 13). 1997. pap. text 36.00 (*0-8151-2390-6*, 31043) Mosby Inc.

*__Nursing Research: Methods, Critical Appraisal & Utilization.__ 4th ed. Geri LoBiondo-Wood & Judith Haber. (Illus.). (C). 1998. teacher ed. write for info. (*1-55664-431-0*) Mosby Inc.

Nursing Research: Principles & Methods. 5th ed. Denise F. Polit & Bernadette P. Hungler. LC 94-30403. 720p. 1994. text 45.95 (*0-397-55138-X*) Lppncott W & W.

Nursing Research: Principles & Methods. 6th ed. Denise F. Polit & Bernadette P. Hungler. LC 98-39678. 768p. 1998. text 42.95 (*0-7817-1562-8*) Lppncott W & W.

Nursing Research: Scholarship for Practice: Proceeding of a Conference Held at Deaking University in July 1992. 407p. 1992. pap. 90.00 (*0-7855-2668-4*, Pub. by Deakin Univ) St Mut.

Nursing Research: Text & Workbook. 4th ed. Patricia A. Dempsey & Arthur D. Dempsey. LC 95-40104. 250p. 1996. pap. text 29.95 (*0-316-18188-9*) Lppncott W & W.

Nursing Research & Its Utilization: International State of the Science. Ed. by Joyce J. Fitzpatrick et al. LC 94-183. 256p. 1994. 41.95 (*0-8261-8090-6*) Springer Pub.

Nursing Research for Nursing Practice: An International Perspective. Ed. by Rebecca Bergman. 250p. 1990. pap. 37.50 (*0-412-33500-X*, A4439) Chapman & Hall.

Nursing Roles: Evolving or Recycled? Ed. by Sue Moorhead & Diane G. Huber. LC 96-35619. (Series on Nursing Administration: Vol. 9). 245p. 1997. 39.95 (*0-7619-0149-3*) Sage.

Nursing School & Allied Health Entrance Exams. 14th ed. Marion Gooding. LC 97-80791. (Illus.). 423p. 1997. pap. 16.95 (*0-02-862193-X*, Arc) IDG Bks.

Nursing School & Allied Health Entrance Exams. 15th ed. Arco. (Arco Nursing & Allied Health Programs Ser.). 432p. 1999. pap. text 16.95 (*0-02-863542-6*, Arco) Macmillan Gen Ref.

Nursing School Entrance Examinations. 13th ed. Gooding. 1996. per. 15.95 (*0-671-52029-6*) S&S Trade.

Nursing School Entrance Examinations for Practical Nurse (PN) Jack Rudman. (Admission Test Ser.: Vol. 20). 43.95 (*0-8373-5120-0*) Nat Learn.

Nursing School Entrance Examinations for Practical Nurse (PN) Jack Rudman. (Admission Test Ser.: ATS-20). 1994. pap. 23.95 (*0-8373-5020-4*) Nat Learn.

Nursing School Entrance Examinations for Registered & Graduate Nurses (RN) Jack Rudman. (Admission Test Ser.: ATS-19). 1994. pap. 23.95 (*0-8373-5019-0*) Nat Learn.

Nursing School Entrance Exams. 1998. 29.95 incl. disk (*0-02-860603-5*) Macmillan.

Nursing Science: Major Paradigms, Theories & Critiques. Rosemarie R. Parse. (Illus.). 224p. 1987. text 48.00 (*0-7216-1803-0*, W B Saunders Co) Harcrt Hlth Sci Grp.

Nursing Service in Transition: A Description of Organization for Classification & Utilization of Nurse Practitioners. Rachel Ayers. 124p. 1972. pap. 5.00 (*0-940876-03-5*) City Hope.

Nursing Service Procedure Manual. W. H. Heaton. 975p. ring bd. 149.95 (*1-881057-07-0*) Heaton Pubns.

Nursing Service Training Coordinator. (Career Examination Ser.: C-3398). 1994. pap. 39.95 (*0-8373-3398-9*) Nat Learn.

Nursing Shortage: New Approaches to an Old Problem. Melvin I. Krasner. (Papers: No. 12). 36p. 1989. 5.00 (*0-934459-61-4*) United Hosp Fund.

Nursing Skills for the Management of Head, Spinal, Chest, Abdominal & Orthopedic Trauma. Linda B. Chitwood. Ed. by Barbara Halliburton. 99p. (C). 1991. pap. text 24.95 (*1-878025-94-5*) Western Schls.

Nursing Spectrum of Lasers. Judith I. Pfister et al. (Illus.). 156p. (Orig.). (C). 1988. pap. text 32.50 (*0-9622255-0-9*) ED Inc.

Nursing Spinal Cord Injuries. Ed. by Nalzina M. Woll. LC 85-26285. (Nursing Research Ser.). 176p. (C). 1986. 44.00 (*0-8476-7380-4*); pap. 20.00 (*0-8476-7387-1*) Rowman.

Nursing, Sr. H. S. Jack Rudman. (Teachers License Examination Ser.: T-44). 1994. pap. 27.95 (*0-8373-8044-8*) Nat Learn.

Nursing Staff Development. Russell C. Swansburg. 416p. (C). 1995. 50.00 (*0-86720-658-6*) Jones & Bartlett.

Nursing Staff Development: Current Competence, Future Focus. Karen J. Kelly. (Illus.). 320p. 1992. pap. text 41.95 (*0-397-54810-9*) Lppncott W & W.

Nursing Staff Development: Strategies for Success. 2nd ed. Ed. by Roberta S. Abruzzese. LC 95-49884. (Illus.). 368p. (C). (gr. 13). 1996. text 49.95 (*0-8151-0053-1*, 26131) Mosby Inc.

Nursing Staff in Hospitals & Nursing Homes: Is It Adequate? Institute of Medicine Staff. Ed. by Gooloo S. Wunderlich et al. 560p. 1996. text 59.95 (*0-309-05398-6*) Natl Acad Pr.

Nursing Staff Trends in California Hospitals, 1977 Through 1995. Joanne Spetz. LC 97-29808. (Illus.). vii, 24p. 1996. pap. 7.00 (*0-9653184-9-4*) Pub Policy Inst.

Nursing Standards: The Guide to a Marker Model. Carolyn G. Smith-Marker. 1987. write for info. (*0-932491-81-2*) Res Appl Inc.

Nursing Station Clerk Trainee. Jack Rudman. (Career Examination Ser.: C-3158). 1994. pap. 23.95 (*0-8373-3158-7*) Nat Learn.

Nursing Student to Nursing Leader: The Critical Path to Leadership Development. Anderson. LC 98-2907. 384p. 1998. text 29.95 (*0-7668-0255-8*) Delmar.

Nursing the Critically Ill Adult. 2nd ed. Nancy M. Holloway. LC 78-21153. 1984. write for info. (*0-201-12640-0*, 002665, Health Sci) Addison-Wesley.

An Asterisk (*) at the beginning of an entry indicates that the title is appearing for the first time.

Nursing the Critically Ill Adult. 3rd ed. Nancy M. Holloway. 640p. (C). 1988. teacher ed. write for info. (0-318-69192-2); text 51.75 (0-201-12271-5) Addison-Wesley.
Nursing the Elderly: A Care Plan Approach. Ed. by Virginia Burggraf & Mickey Stanley. LC 87-37937. (Illus.). 461p. 1989. reprint ed. pap. 143.00 (0-608-07305-9, 206753300009) Bks Demand.
Nursing the Neonate. Helen Yeo. LC 98-5744. 324p. 1998. pap. write for info. (0-632-05049-7) Blackwell Sci.
Nursing the Neurological & Neurotrauma Patient. Maria J. Kruse. LC 85-27837. (Nursing Research Ser.). 144p. 1986. 55.00 (0-8476-7451-7) Rowman.
Nursing the Nurse-Affirmations. Gail A. Staudt. (Illus.). 112p. Date not set. write for info. (0-9678555-1-9) G Staudt.
Nursing the Orthopaedic Patient. Ed. by Peter S. Davis. LC 93-43058. 1995. pap. text 37.95 (0-443-04461-9) Church.
Nursing the Psychiatric Emergency. Martin F. Ward. 224p. 1995. pap. text 35.00 (0-7506-1592-3) Buttrwrth-Heinemann.
Nursing the Whole Person. Dallalis. (LPN/LVN Nursing Ser.). 1995. text 59.95 (0-8273-5459-2) Delmar.
Nursing the Whole Person: Concept to Practice. White. (LPN/LVN Nursing Ser.). 1997. 36.75 (0-8273-7453-4); 16.95 (0-8273-7447-X); teacher ed. 12.95 (0-8273-7446-1) Delmar.
Nursing Theories. 5th ed. George. 512p. 1999. pap. 37.95 (0-8385-7110-7, Medical Exam) Appleton & Lange.
Nursing Theories: Conceptual & Philosophical Foundations. Ed. by Hesook S. Kim & Ingrid Kollak. LC 99-27969. (Illus.). 208p. 1999. 34.95 (0-8261-1287-0) Springer Pub.
Nursing Theories: The Base for Professional Nursing Practice. 4th ed. Julia B. George. LC 94-41658. (C). 1995. pap. text 37.95 (0-8385-7056-9, A7056-3) Appleton & Lange.
Nursing Theories & Models. Hugh McKenna. (Routledge Essentials for Nurses). (Illus.). 288p. (C). 1997. 80.00 (0-415-14222-9); pap. 24.99 (0-415-14223-7) Routledge.
Nursing Theories & Models. 2nd ed. Ruby L. Wesley. LC 94-22849. (Notes Ser.). 176p. 1994. pap. 18.95 (0-87434-744-0) Springhouse Corp.
Nursing Theories & Nursing Practice. Marilyn E. Parker. (Illus.). 512p. 2000. pap. text 36.95 (0-8036-0604-4) Davis Co.
Nursing Theories & Quality of Care. Hugh P. McKenna. LC 94-6399. (Developments in Nursing & Health Care Ser.: Vol. 23). 272p. 1994. 72.95 (1-85628-670-3, Pub. by Avebry) Ashgate Pub Co.
Nursing Theories in Practice. Ed. by Marilyn E. Parker. 320p. 1991. 24.95 (0-88737-497-2) Natl League Nurse.
Nursing Theorists & Their Work. 4th ed. Ann Marriner-Tomey & Martha R. Alligood. LC 97-11533. (Illus.). 576p. (C). (gr. 13). 1997. pap. text 38.00 (0-8151-4421-0, 30903) Mosby Inc.
Nursing Theory: Analysis, Application, Evaluation. 3rd ed. Barbara S. Barnum. (Illus.). 350p. 1990. text 32.50 (0-673-39920-6) Lppncott W & W.
Nursing Theory: Analysis, Application, Evaluation. 5th ed. Barbara J. S. Barnum. LC 97-30274. 304p. 1998. pap. text 35.95 (0-7817-1104-5) Lppncott W & W.
Nursing Theory: Utilization & Application. Ed. by Martha R. Alligood & Ann Marriner-Tomey. (Illus.). 256p. (C). (gr. 13). 1996. pap. text 35.00 (0-8151-0812-5, 27759) Mosby Inc.
Nursing Today: Transition & Trends. Ed. by JoAnn Zerwekh & Jo C. Claborn. (Illus.). 1994. pap., teacher ed. write for info. (0-7216-3646-2, W B Saunders Co) Harcrt Hlth Sci Grp.
Nursing Today: Transition & Trends. 2nd ed. Ed. by JoAnn Zerwekh & Jo C. Claborn. (Illus.). 1997. pap., teacher ed. write for info. (0-7216-6901-8, W B Saunders Co) Harcrt Hlth Sci Grp.
Nursing Today: Transition & Trends. 2nd ed. JoAnn Zerwekh & Jo Carol Claborn. Ed. by Ilze Rader. LC 96-15370. (Illus.). 544p. 1996. pap. text 26.00 (0-7216-6899-2, W B Saunders Co) Harcrt Hlth Sci Grp.
Nursing Today: Transition & Trends. 3rd ed. JoAnn Zerwekh & Jo Carol Claborn. (Illus.). 575p. Date not set. pap. text. write for info. (0-7216-8685-0, W B Saunders Co) Harcrt Hlth Sci Grp.
Nursing Twenty-Twenty. 172p. 1988. pap. 7.95 (0-88737-397-6, 41-2217) Natl League Nurse.
Nursing 2000 Drug Handbook. 1999. pap. 36.95 incl. cd-rom (0-87434-993-1) Springhouse Corp.
Nursing 2000 Drug Handbook. Springhouse Corporation Staff. 1999. cd-rom 49.95 (0-87434-994-X) Springhouse Corp.
Nursing Unit Organization: Its Effects on Staff Professionalism. Jeffrey A. Alexander. Ed. by Philip Kalisch & Beatrice Kalisch. LC 82-13485. (Studies in Nursing Management: No. 4). 166p. 1982. reprint ed. pap. 51.50 (0-8357-1369-5, 207003800063) Bks Demand.
Nursing with the "Third Ear" Reading What Patients Write - a Basic Course. Jimmie R. Rankin. (Literature of Patient Response Ser.). 100p. 1994. pap. 29.95 (1-883938-16-3) Dry Bones Pr.
Nursing Workforce Planning. Hurst. 1993. pap. text. write for info. (0-582-21322-3, Pub. by Addison-Wesley) Longman.
Nursing Wounds: Nurse Practitioners, Doctors, Women Patients, & the Negotiation of Meaning. Sue Fisher. 275p. (C). 1995. text 45.00 (0-8135-2180-7); pap. text 17.00 (0-8135-2181-5) Rutgers U Pr.
Nursing Your Adopted Baby. Kathryn Anderson. (Illus.). 32p. 1986. pap. 2.50 (0-912500-15-8) La Leche.
Nursing Your Baby. Karen Pryor. 1991. mass mkt. 6.99 (0-671-74548-4) PB.
***Nursing 101: Nursing Fundamentals Module.** 974p. (C). 1999. pap. text 52.95 (0-7872-6196-3, 41619601) Kendall-Hunt.
***Nursing 201: Advanced Nursing.** 1124p. (C). 1999. pap. text 58.95 (0-7872-6197-1, 41619701) Kendall-Hunt.
Nursing99 Drug Handbook (Australasian Edition) Springhouse Publishing Company Staff. 1056p. 1998. 43.95 (0-87434-963-X) Springhouse Corp.
Nursing's Vision for Primary Care in the 21st Century. Lucy N. Marion & American Nurses Association Staff. LC 96-10795. 47p. (Orig.). 1996. pap. 23.95 (1-55810-124-1, CH-30) Am Nurses Pub.
Nutrition: Pre- & Postnatal Development. M. Winick. LC 78-26941. (Human Nutrition Ser.). (Illus.). 516p. (C). 1979. text 110.00 (0-306-40132-0, Kluwer Plenum) Kluwer Academic.
Nurture. Sheila Griffin. LC 98-52343. 200p. 1999. pap. 14.00 (0-9659346-7-5) Mystic Moon NM.
Nurture & Torture. Lois Hirshkowitz. Ed. by Kathleen Iddings. LC 91-66343. 74p. 1992. pap. text, per. 10.00 (0-931289-09-2) San Diego Poet Pr.
Nurture Assumption: Why Children Turn Out the Way They Do. Judith Rich Harris. LC 98-34824. 352p. 1998. 25.50 (0-684-84409-5) Free Pr.
***Nurture Assumption: Why Children Turn Out the Way They Do.** Judith Rich Harris. 480p. 1999. per. 15.00 (0-684-85707-3) S&S Trade Pap.
Nurture by Nature: Parenting Our Children in Their Natural Style Through the Insights of Personality Type. Paul D. Tieger & Barbara Barron-Tieger. LC 96-41866. 304p. 1997. pap. 16.95 (0-316-84513-2) Little.
Nurture Me, Baby: Poems by James Mannion. James Mannion. 36p. (Orig.). 1995. pap. 5.00 (1-887775-06-4) Cryptic NY.
Nurture of Human Behavior: The Biopsychology of Human Behavioral Development. Lawrence V. Harper. LC 88-22243. 280p. (C). 1989. text 73.25 (0-89391-511-4) Ablx Pub.
Nurture That Is Christian: Developmental Perspectives on Christian Education. Ed. by James C. Wilhoit & John M. Dettoni. LC 95-36641. 288p. (gr. 12). 1995. pap. 18.99 (0-8010-2132-4, Bridgept Bks) Baker Bks.
***Nurture Your Child's Gift: Inspired Parenting.** Caron B. Goode. 224p. 2000. pap. 14.95 (1-58270-040-0) Beyond Words Pub.
Nurture Your Spirits. Hua-Ching Ni. LC 90-60827. 176p. 1991. pap. 12.95 (0-937064-32-7) SevenStar Comm.
Nurtured by Knowledge: Learning to Do Participatory Action-Research. Ed. by Susan E. Smith & Dennis G. Willms. LC 97-5888. (Illus.). 296p. (Orig.). 1997. 39.50 (0-945257-82-1); pap. 18.50 (0-945257-81-3) Apex Pr.
Nurtured by Love. Shinichi Suzuki. 108p. 1983. pap. text 12.95 (0-87487-584-6) Summy-Birchard.
Nurtured by Love: The Classic Approach to Talent Education. 2nd ed. Shinichi Suzuki. Tr. by Waltraud Suzuki. 121p. 1996. pap. 12.95 (0-8488-1767-2); lib. bdg. 17.95 (0-8488-0639-5) Amereon Ltd.
***Nurtured for Fraud, 1.** Dan Thomas. LC 98-87175. 1998. pap. 11.95 (0-9666741-9-7) Collins Mtn Pr.
***Nurturing a Passion for Prayer: A Discipleship Journal Bible Study.** Ed. by Discipleship Journal Staff. 96p. 2000. pap. text 6.00 (1-57683-165-5) NavPress.
Nurturing a Teacher Advisory Program. Claire G. Cole. 54p. (C). 1992. pap. text 10.00 (1-56090-064-4) Natl Middle Schl.
Nurturing Advanced Technology Enterprises: Emerging Issues in State & Local Economic Development Policy. David N. Allen & Victor Levine. LC 86-9411. 285p. 1986. 49.95 (0-275-92136-0, C2136, Praeger Pubs) Greenwood.
Nurturing an Endangered Generation: Empowering Youth with Critical Social, Emotional, & Cognitive Skills. Rosemary Thompson. LC 97-30458. 358p. 1998. 59.95 (1-56032-668-9); pap. 24.95 (1-56032-669-7) Hemisp Pub.
Nurturing & Developing Creativity: The Emergence of a Discipline. Ed. by Scott G. Isaksen et al. LC 93-29992. (Creativity Research Ser.: Vol. 2). 1993. pap. 42.50 (1-56750-007-2); text 78.50 (1-56750-008-0) Ablx Pub.
Nurturing At-Risk Youth in Math & Science: Curriculum & Teaching Considerations. Randolf Tobias. LC 98-160763. 147p. (Orig.). 1992. pap. 19.95 (1-879639-20-3) Natl Educ Serv.
***Nurturing Change Through Your Human Assets: Optimising Organisational Challenges in the New Millennium.** Madhurendra K. Varma. LC 00-33273. 2000. pap. write for info. (0-7619-9467-X) Sage.
Nurturing Children. 95p. 1996. pap. 8.00 (0-16-061603-4) USGPO.
Nurturing Children: A History of Pediatrics. A. R. Colon & P. A. Colon. LC 99-25000. 344p. 1999. lib. bdg. 69.50 (0-313-31080-7, GR1080, Greenwood Pr) Greenwood.
Nurturing Children in the Lord. Jack Fennema. 220p. 1995. reprint ed. pap. 7.25 (0-932914-30-6) Dordt Coll Pr.
Nurturing Classroom: Developing Thinking Skills, Self-Esteem, Responsibility through Simple Cooperation. Margaret E. McCabe & Jacqueline Rhoades. LC 85-80102. (Illus.). 363p. (Orig.). (ps up). 1989. pap. 26.00 (0-933935-09-9) ITA Pubns.
Nurturing Contemplation. Carol R. Murphy. LC 88-62745. (C). 1983. pap. 4.00 (0-87574-251-3) Pendle Hill.
Nurturing Development: Aid & Cooperation in Today's Changing World. Ismail Serageldin. LC 95-6432. (Directions in Development Ser.). 168p. 1995. 22.00 (0-8213-3184-1, 13184) World Bank.
Nurturing Doubt: From Missionary to Anthropologist in the Argentine Chaco. Elmer S. Miller. LC 94-30791. 248p. (C). 1995. pap. text 17.50 (0-252-06455-0) U of Ill Pr.
Nurturing Doubt: From Missionary to Anthropologist in the Argentine Chaco. Ed. by Elmer S. Miller. LC 94-30791. 248p. 1995. text 44.95 (0-252-02155-X) U of Ill Pr.
Nurturing Early Promise: Creative Thinking & Doing Activities for Young Children. Rita H. Blocksom. LC 89-62690. (Illus.). 112p. (Orig.). 1989. pap. 10.95 (0-939705-03-6) Pinnaroo.
Nurturing Evolution: The Family As a Social Womb. Richard B. Carter. LC 92-33099. 248p. (C). 1993. pap. text 26.50 (0-8191-8909-X); lib. bdg. 54.00 (0-8191-8908-1) U Pr of Amer.
Nurturing Faith Through the Book of Mormon: The 24th Annual Sidney B. Sperry Symposium. LC 95-46999. xxxviii, 194p. 1995. 15.95 (1-57345-159-2) Deseret Bk.
Nurturing Father's Journal: Developing Attitudes & Skills for Male Nurturance. Mark Perlman. (Illus.). x, 125p. 1998. pap. text 12.00 (0-9662927-0-7) CGD Inc.
***Nurturing Father's Journal: The Workbook for Strengthening Men's Parenting Skills & Attitudes.** 2nd rev. ed. Mark Perlman. (Illus.). 152p. 2000. pap., wbk. ed. 22.00 (0-9662927-2-3) CGD Inc.
Nurturing Father's Program: Facilitator Manual. Mark Perlman. (Illus.). xvii, 98p. 1998. pap. text 45.00 (0-9662927-1-5) CGD Inc.
Nurturing Giftedness in Young Children. C. June Maker et al. LC 96-20045. 58p. 1996. pap. text 15.00 (0-86586-282-6, P5156) Coun Exc Child.
***Nurturing Good Children Now: 10 Basic Skills to Strenghten & Protect Your Child's Core Self.** Ron Taffel & Melinda Blau. 304p. 2000. pap. 13.95 (0-312-26364-3, St Martin Griffin) St Martin.
Nurturing Happiness: Natural Ways to Relieve & Prevent Depression. Linda H. App. LC 97-90954. 200p. 1997. pap. 11.95 (0-9659879-5-7) Windmill Pr Alex.
Nurturing Independent Learners: Helping Students Take Charge of Their Learning. Donald Meichenbaum & Andrew Biemiller. LC 97-50477. 256p. 1997. pap. text 24.95 (1-57129-047-8) Brookline Bks.
Nurturing Inquiry: Real Science for the Elementary Classroom. Charles R. Pearce. LC 98-52475. 5p. 1999. pap. text 21.00 (0-325-00135-9) Heinemann.
Nurturing Intelligences. Brian Haggerty. vi, 162 p. (YA). 1994. pap. 24.95 (0-201-49056-0) Addison-Wesley.
Nurturing Neighborhood: The Brownsville Boys Club & Jewish Community in Urban America, 1940-1990. Gerald Sorin. (American Social Experience Ser.: No. 15). (C). 1990. text 55.00 (0-8147-7897-6) NYU Pr.
Nurturing Neighborhood: The Brownsville Boys' Club & Jewish Community in Urban America, 1940-1990. Gerald Sorin. (American Social Experience Ser.). (Illus.). 256p. (C). 1992. pap. text 19.00 (0-8147-7939-5) NYU Pr.
Nurturing New Ideas: Legal Rights & Economic Roles. Ed. by Louis J. Harris. LC 76-8377. 659p. reprint ed. pap. 200.00 (0-608-14109-7, 202430400037) Bks Demand.
Nurturing New Life. Marilyn Ganskow. 94p. 1973. pap., wbk. ed. 10.00 (1-928712-08-8) New Life Series.
***Nurturing Our Children to Succeed: A Guide for Helping Parents & Teachers Understand & Address the Emotional & Academic Challenges Facing Our Early Childhood Students.** unabridged ed. Susan Lipper. LC 99-90403. (Illus.). xviii, 154p. (Orig.). 1999. pap. 14.95 (0-9674865-0-5) Budding Self.
Nurturing Peace: Why Peace Settlements Succeed or Fail. Fen O. Hampson. LC 96-16488. 1996. 32.95 (1-878379-55-0); pap. text 19.95 (1-878379-57-7) US Inst Peace.
Nurturing Pentecostal Families. Ed. by John K. Vining. 230p. 1996. pap. 9.99 (0-87148-633-4) Pathway Pr.
Nurturing Program for Parents & Children: Activities Manual for Children 4 to 7 Years. 2nd ed. Stephen J. Bavolek & Christine M. Comstock. 195p. 1985. pap. text 23.00 (0-934309-05-1) Family Dev Res.
Nurturing Program for Parents & Children: Activities Manual for Children 8 to 12 Years. 2nd ed. Stephen J. Bavolek & Christine M. Comstock. 195p. 1985. pap. text 23.00 (0-934309-06-X) Family Dev Res.
Nurturing Program for Parents & Children: Activities Manual for Parents. 2nd ed. Stephen J. Bavolek & Christine M. Comstock. 174p. 1985. pap. text 23.00 (0-934309-01-9) Family Dev Res.
Nurturing Program for Parents & Children: Parent Handbook. Stephen J. Bavolek & Christine M. Comstock. (Illus.). 173p. (Orig.). 1985. pap. text 11.00 (0-934309-00-0) Family Dev Res.
Nurturing Program for Parents & Children: Program Implementation Manual. Stephen J. Bavolek & Christine M. Comstock. 74p. 1985. pap. text 11.00 (0-934309-04-3) Family Dev Res.
Nurturing Program for Parents & Young Children (Birth to Five Years Old) Activities Manual for Home-Based Family Parenting Curriculum. Stephen J. Bavolek & Juliana D. Bavolek. 533p. 1985. ring bd. 45.00 (0-934309-08-6) Family Dev Res.
Nurturing Program for Parents & Young Children (Birth to Five Years Old) Family Resource Handbook. Stephen J. Bavolek & Juliana D. Bavolek. (Illus.). 189p. 1985. ring bd. 10.00 (0-934309-09-4) Family Dev Res.
***Nurturing Readiness in Early Childhood Education: A Whole-Child Curriculum for Ages 2-5.** Ellen Cromwell. LC 98-56042. 278p. 1999. pap. text 24.95 (0-205-28863-4) Allyn.
Nurturing Reflective Christians to Teach: A Valiant Role for the Nation's Church Colleges & Universities: The Proceedings from the First National Symposium, April 7-9, 1994, Trinity Christian College. Ed. by Daniel C. Elliott. LC 94-47063. (Proceedings from the First National Symposium for Nurturing Reflective Christian Teachers Ser.). 150p. (C). 1995. pap. 21.00 (0-8191-9870-6); text 42.00 (0-8191-9869-2) U Pr of Amer.
Nurturing Silence in a Noisy Heart: How to Find Inner Peace. Wayne E. Oates. 128p. 1996. pap. 11.99 (0-8066-2037-4, 9-2037) Augsburg Fortress.
Nurturing Spiritual Development: Stages, Structure, Style. Kenneth H. Ives. (Studies in Quakerism: No. 8). 60p. (Orig.). 1982. pap. 4.00 (0-89670-011-9) Progresiv Pub.
Nurturing Spirituality in Children: Simple Hands-on Activities. 3rd rev. ed. Peggy J. Jenkins. LC 95-14596. (Illus.). 160p. 1995. pap. 12.95 (1-885223-23-4) Beyond Words Pub.
***Nurturing Success: Successful Women of Color & Their Daughters.** Essie E. Lee. LC 99-37530. 312p. 2000. write for info. (0-275-96033-1, Praeger Pubs) Greenwood.
***Nurturing the Gifts & Talents of Primary Grade Students.** Ed. by Susan M. Baum et al. 370p. 1998. pap. 32.95 (0-936386-71-1) Creative Learning.
Nurturing the Nurse on the Path to Success. Carolyn T. Laskey. Ed. by Jerena B. Rezvan. LC 93-61664. 210p. 1994. pap. 16.95 (1-880254-11-5) Vista.
Nurturing the Premature Infant: Developmental Intervention in the Neonatal Intensive Care Nursery. Edward Goldson. LC 98-7850. (Illus.). 216p. 1999. text 49.95 (0-19-508570-1) OUP.
***Nurturing the Soul of the Youth Worker: 8 Ways to Energize Your Life & Ministry.** Tim Smith. LC 99-36408. 1999. 14.99 (0-7644-2135-2) Group Pub.
Nurturing the Spirit: In Non-Sectarian Classrooms. Aline D. Wolf. LC 96-68468. (Illus.). 196p. (Orig.). 1996. pap., per. 13.95 (0-939195-17-8, 097) Parent-Child Pr.
Nurturing the Unborn Child: A Nine-Month Program for Soothing, Stimulating & Communicating. Thomas R. Verny & Pamela Weintraub. 213p. pap. write for info. (1-58754-104-1, Pub. by Olmstead Pr) LPC Group.
Nurturing Touch at Birth: A Labor Support Handbook. Paulina Perez. LC 97-91542. (Illus.). 84p. 1997. pap. 11.95 (0-9641159-8-0) Doubleday.
Nurturing Young Black Males: Challenges to Agencies, Programs, & Social Policy. Ed. by Ronald B. Mincy. 260p. 1994. 24.50 (0-87766-598-2) Urban Inst.
Nurturing Young Catholics: A Guide for Confirmation Sponsors, & Other Caring Adults. Joseph Moore. LC 95-7826. 64p. (Orig.). 1995. pap. 4.95 (0-8091-3575-2) Paulist Pr.
Nurturing Young Minds & Bodies. Judi Davis. 186p. 1995. pap. text 24.95 (1-885477-16-3) Fut Horizons.
Nurturing Your Baby's Soul: A Spiritual Guide for Expectant Parents. Elizabeth Clare Prophet. LC 98-60410. 1998. pap. 12.95 (0-922729-39-5) Summit Univ.
***Nurturing Your Child with Music: How Sound Awareness Creates Happy, Smart & Confident Children.** John M. Ortiz. LC 99-40897. 238p. 2000. pap. 14.95 (1-58270-021-4, Pub. by Beyond Words Pub) Publishers Group.
Nurturing Your Child's Spirit: A Montessorian Approach. 3rd ed. Jeannine L. Schmid. 1997. pap. 12.95 (1-886510-10-5) Treehaus Bks.
Nurturing Your Newborn: A Young Parent's Guide to Baby's First Month. Jeanne Warren Lindsay. LC 99-25877. 1999. pap. 7.95 (1-885356-58-7) Morning Glory.
Nurturing Your Newborn: Young Parent's Guide to Baby's First Month Teacher Guide. Jeanne W. Lindsay & Jean Brunelli. 20p. 1999. pap., teacher ed. 2.00 (1-885356-60-9) Morning Glory.
Nurturing Your Newborn: Young Parent's Guide to Baby's First Month Workbook. Jeanne W. Lindsay & Jean Brunelli. 24p. 1999. pap., wbk. ed. 2.00 (1-885356-61-7) Morning Glory.
Nurturing Your Soul. Rory Noland. LC 99-18211. 2000. pap. 14.99 (0-310-22471-3) Zondervan.
***Nurturing Yourself & Others.** Lee Schnebly. 160p. 2000. pap. 14.00 (1-55561-291-1) Fisher Bks.
Nurtz! Nurtz! Paul L. Dilsaver. 206p. 1989. pap. 13.00 (0-9637000-2-2) Acad & Arts.
Nuruddin Farah. Patricia Alden & Louis Tremaine. LC 98-33279. (World Authors Ser.). 15p. 1999. write for info. (0-8057-1667-X, Twyne) Mac Lib Ref.
Nusa Tenggara. Ed. by Kal Muller. 296p. 1991. pap. 37.50 (0-945971-36-2) Periplus.
Nusantara: A History of the East Indian Archipelago. Bernard H. Vlekke. Ed. by Mira Wilkins. LC 76-29761. (European Business Ser.). (Illus.). 1977. reprint ed. lib. bdg. 42.95 (0-405-09776-X) Ayer.
Nushagak River. Alaska Geographic Society Staff. (Alaska Geographic Ser.: Vol. 17, No. 1). (Illus.). 96p. pap. 19.95 (0-88240-192-0) Alaska Geog Soc.
***NuSpeak: Become a Powerful Speaker.** Geoffrey Lane. 144p. 1999. pap. 19.95 (1-894499-00-X) Berkana.
***Nussances et Baptemes St. Paul le la Craine: Notre-Dame-des-Sept-Douleurs.** Jean-Claude Ovellet. (FRE.). 140p. 1999. pap. 29.00 (2-921848-10-4) SGEQ.
Nussknacker & Mausek Onig see Nutcracker & the Golden Pot
Nut Between Two Blades: The Novels of Charles Robert Maturin. Peter M. Henderson. Ed. by Devendra P. Varma. LC 79-8457. (Gothic Studies & Dissertations). 1980. lib. bdg. 31.95 (0-405-12672-7) Ayer.
Nut Lover's Cookbook. Shirl Carder. LC 84-70857. 160p. 1984. pap. 6.95 (0-89087-405-0) Celestial Arts.
Nut Milk Chocolate Gang. Marie Mahood. (Illus.). 92p. 1997. pap. 15.95 (1-875998-23-3, Pub. by Central Queensland) Accents Pubns.

N

An Asterisk (*) at the beginning of an entry indicates that the title is appearing for the first time.

Nut Salad: Bompa & Me. Gayle M. Pyle. Ed. by Thomas Shaw & Anita Klemke. LC 94-68040. (Illus.). 116p. (Orig.). 1994. pap. 12.95 (*0-9633371-1-4*) Carson St Pub.

Nutation & the Earth's Rotation: Proceedings of the I.A.U. Symposium, No. 78, Kiev, U.S.S.R., May 23-28, 1977. International Astronomical Union Staff et al. Ed. by M. L. Smith & P. L. Bender. 284p. 1980. lib. bdg. 88.00 (*90-277-1113-5*) Kluwer Academic.

Nutation & the Earth's Rotation: Proceedings of the I.A.U. Symposium, No. 78, Kiev, U.S.S.R., May 23-28, 1977. International Astronomical Union Staff et al. Ed. by M. L. Smith & P. L. Bender. 284p. 1980. pap. text 55.00 (*90-277-1114-3*) Kluwer Academic.

Nutbread & Nostalgia. (Illus.). 214p. 1979. reprint ed. 18.95 (*0-9607120-0-3*) Jr League S Bend.

Nutcrack. Mark Dunster. 11p. (Orig.). (J). (gr. 1-7). 1990. pap. 4.00 (*0-89642-190-2*) Linden Pubs.

Nutcracker see Casse-Noisette

Nutcracker. (J). 2000. per. write for info. (*0-689-83285-0*) S&S Childrens.

Nutcracker. (Little Golden Books Book 'n Tape Ser.). (Illus.). (J). (ps-2). 1995. 6.99 incl. audio (*0-307-14461-5*, 14461, Goldn Books) Gldn Bks Pub Co.

***Nutcracker.** (J). 2000. 150.00 (*0-689-84107-8*) Litle Simon.

Nutcracker. (Christmas Fun-to-Read Fairy Tales Ser.). (Illus.). 24p. (J). (gr. k-3). 1992. pap. 2.50 (*1-56144-162-7*, Honey Bear Bks) Modern Pub NYC.

Nutcracker. Rita Balducci. (Little Golden Storybks.). (J). 1997. 3.99 (*0-307-16177-3*, 16177, Goldn Books) Gldn Bks Pub Co.

Nutcracker. David Brownell. (J). (gr. 1-9). 1992. pap. 4.95 (*0-88388-052-0*) Bellerophon Bks.

Nutcracker. Victoria Crenson. (Classic Christmas Sticker Storybook Ser.). (Illus.). 16p. (J). (ps-3). 1996. 3.50 (*0-689-80257-9*) Aladdin.

Nutcracker. Carin Dewhirst. LC 96-32661. (Life, Times, & Music Ser.). (Illus.). (J). 1996. write for info. (*1-56799-361-3*, Friedman-Fairfax) M Friedman Pub Grp Inc.

***Nutcracker.** Carolyn Ewing. (Little Activity Bks.). (Illus.). (J). 1998. pap. 1.00 (*0-486-40254-1*) Dover.

Nutcracker. Illus. by Linda Graves & Susan Spellman. (Favorite Christmas Tales Ser.). 24p. (J). 1993. 4.98 (*1-56173-713-5*) Pubns Intl Ltd.

Nutcracker. E. T. A. Hoffmann. (Children's Classics Ser.). (Illus.). 32p. (J). 1991. 6.95 (*0-8362-4934-8*) Andrews & McMeel.

Nutcracker. E. T. A. Hoffmann. LC 92-24140. (Illus.). 16p. (J). 1992. 4.95 (*0-8362-3026-4*) Andrews & McMeel.

Nutcracker. E. T. A. Hoffmann. Tr. by Ralph Manheim. (Illus.). 28p. (J). (ps up). 1991. 16.00 (*0-88708-051-0*, Crown) Crown Pub Group.

***Nutcracker.** E. T. A. Hoffmann. LC 99-34274. (Eyewitness Classics Ser.). 64p. (J). 1999. 14.95 (*0-7894-4766-5*) DK Pub Inc.

Nutcracker. E. T. A. Hoffmann. (J). 35.00 (*0-614-19305-2*) Harcourt.

Nutcracker. E. T. A. Hoffmann. LC 95-43873. (Illus.). (J). 1996. 35.00 (*0-15-201314-8*) Harcourt.

Nutcracker. E. T. A. Hoffmann. Tr. by E. T. Brodmann. LC 96-69108. (Illus.). 112p. (J). (ps-3). 1996. 24.95 (*1-55670-530-1*) Stewart Tabori & Chang.

Nutcracker. E. T. A. Hoffmann. LC 97-22346. (Illus.). 40p. (J). 1999. 19.95 (*0-06-027814-5*) HarpC.

Nutcracker. E. T. A. Hoffmann. (Illus.). 48p. (J). (ps-2). 1985. 6.95 (*0-8249-8095-6*, Ideals Child) Hambleton-Hill.

Nutcracker. E. T. A. Hoffmann. LC 98-12890. (Illus.). 32p. (J). (ps-3). 1998. 14.95 (*0-8109-1393-3*, Pub. by Abrams) Time Warner.

Nutcracker. E. T. A. Hoffmann. LC 91-24400. 1991. pap. 20.00 (*0-517-58659-2*) Crown Pub Group.

Nutcracker. Illus. by Naomi Howland. LC 97-10919. 24p. (J). 1997. 14.98 (*1-56799-538-1*, Friedman-Fairfax) M Friedman Pub Grp Inc.

Nutcracker. L. Spencer Humphrey. 32p. (J). 1994. pap. 2.95 (*0-8125-2322-9*, Pub. by Tor Bks) St Martin.

Nutcracker Geraldine McCaughrean. 28p. (YA). 1999. 17.95 (*0-19-279969-X*) OUP.

***Nutcracker.** Marty Noble. (Little Activity Bks.). (Illus.). (J). 1999. pap. 1.00 (*0-486-40516-8*) Dover.

Nutcracker. June W. Rogers. 1975. 3.75 (*0-87129-543-1*, N22) Dramatic Pub.

Nutcracker. Illus. by Jerry Smath. (Pudgy Pal Board Bks.). 18p. (J). (ps). 1994. bds. 3.95 (*0-448-40546-6*, G & D) Peng Put Young Read.

Nutcracker. David Walker. (Illus.). 1987. 45.00 (*0-7855-3787-2*, Pub. by Moonstone Bks) St Mut.

Nutcracker. Patricia Whitehead. LC 87-10916. (Illus.). 32p. (J). (gr. k-4). 1988. lib. bdg. 15.85 (*0-8167-1063-5*) Troll Communs.

Nutcracker. Patricia Whitehead. LC 87-10916. (Illus.). 32p. (J). (gr. k-4). 1996. pap. 3.95 (*0-8167-1064-3*) Troll Communs.

Nutcracker. abr. large type ed. Illus. by Lucy Newmark. (NanaBanana Classics Ser.). 32p. (Orig.). (J). (gr. k up). 1995. 14.95 (*1-886201-06-4*) Nana Banana.

Nutcracker: A Jewel Sticker Stories Book. Bull Schuyler. (Jewel Sticker Stories Ser.). (Illus.). 24p. (J). (ps-2). 1998. mass mkt. 3.99 (*0-448-41852-5*, G & D) Peng Put Young Read.

Nutcracker: A Young Reader's Edition of the Holiday Classic. E. T. A. Hoffmann. LC 96-67159. (Illus.). 56p. (J). 9.98 (*1-56138-764-9*, Courage) Running Pr.

***Nutcracker: Mini Edition.** Running Press Staff. 1999. 4.95 (*0-7624-0604-6*) Running Pr.

***Nutcracker: Mini Edition.** Running Press Staff. 1999. 7.95 (*0-7624-0629-1*) Running Press Min.

Nutcracker: Story & Music. Jonathan McPhee & Suzanne Burakoff. (Boston Ballet Presents Ser.: Vol. 1). (Illus.). 32p. (Orig.). (J). (gr. k-6). 1996. pap. 12.95 (*0-9640792-1-6*) Hare & Hatter.

Nutcracker: With Nutcracker CD. Illus. by Wendy W. Malinow. LC 99-181954. (BookNotes Ser.). 56p. 1998. 13.99 incl. cd-rom (*0-88088-406-1*) Peter Pauper.

Nutcracker - the Musical. Debbie Meyer. (Illus.). 26p. (Orig.). 1996. pap. 4.50 (*0-88680-418-3*) I E Clark.

***Nutcracker Activity Book.** Victoria Fremont & Cathy Beylon. (Illus.). (J). (ps-3). 1999. pap. 1.00 (*0-486-40494-3*) Dover.

Nutcracker & Other Tales: Nutcracker & Mouse King - The Fir Tree - The Real Santa. E. T. A. Hoffmann et al. (Look-Compare-Understand Ser.: Vol. 5). (Illus.). 336p. (YA). (gr. 5 up). 1999. 28.50 (*1-879870-62-2*, Pub. by Pro Lingua Pr) Baker & Taylor.

Nutcracker & the Golden Pot. E. T. A. Hoffmann. LC 93-4884. (Thrift Editions Ser.).Tr. of Nussknacker & Mausek Onig. 128p. 1993. reprint ed. pap. text 1.00 (*0-486-27806-9*) Dover.

Nutcracker Ballet. Illus. by Carolyn S. Ewing. LC 92-3320. (Step into Reading Ser.: A Step 2 Book). 48p. (J). (gr. 1-3). 1992. pap. 3.99 (*0-679-82385-9*, Pub. by Random Bks Yng Read) Random.

Nutcracker Ballet. Illus. by Stephen T. Johnson. LC 92-20654. 32p. (J). 1992. 14.95 (*0-8362-4501-6*) Andrews & McMeel.

Nutcracker Ballet. Illus. by Darcy May. (Read with Me Paperback Ser.). 32p. (J). (ps-3). 1994. pap. 2.99 (*0-590-48197-5*, Cartwheel) Scholastic Inc.

Nutcracker Ballet. Vladimir Vagin. LC 94-30716. (Illus.). 32p. (J). (gr. 1-8). 1995. 14.95 (*0-590-47222-4*) Scholastic Inc.

Nutcracker Ballet. Illus. & Retold by Vladimir Vagin. LC 94-30716. 32p. (J). (ps-3). 1995. 14.95 (*0-590-47220-8*, Scholastic Hardcover) Scholastic Inc.

Nutcracker Ballet Mystery. Carolyn Keene. (Nancy Drew Mystery Stories Ser.: No. 110). (J). (gr. 3-6). 1992. 9.09 (*0-606-02782-3*, Pub. by Turtleback) Demco.

Nutcracker Ballet Mystery. rev. ed. Carolyn Keene. Ed. by Ellen Winkler. LC 94-135959. (Nancy Drew Mystery Stories Ser.: No. 110). 160p. (J). (gr. 4-7). 2000. pap. 3.99 (*0-671-73056-8*, Minstrel Bks) PB.

***Nutcracker Company.** Provo Craft Designers Staff. (Illus.). 24p. 1998. write for info. (*1-58050-066-8*, 40-6197) Provo Craft.

Nutcracker Is Already Dancing: The HIVs & the HIV-Nots. Cary Savitch. Ed. by Ruth Orr et al. LC 96-90495. 204p. 1996. 23.95 (*0-9653697-5-7*) Teague Hse Pr.

***Nutcracker Keepsake With Nutcracker Figurine.** Running Press Staff. 1999. 17.98 (*0-7624-0667-4*) Running Pr.

***Nutcracker Keepsake Kit.** E. T. A. Hoffmann. (Illus.). 2000. 19.98 (*0-7624-0882-0*) Running Pr.

Nutcracker Keepsake Set: With Nutcracker Figurine. E. T. A. Hoffmann. (Children's Illustrated Classics Ser.). (Illus.). 56p. 1997. 17.98 (*0-7624-0207-5*, Courage) Running Pr.

Nutcracker Learn-by-Coloring Book: Scenes from the Best Loved Ballet of All Times. Ellen Jacob. (Learn-by-Coloring Ser.). (Illus.). 48p. (Orig.). (J). (ps-7). 1991. pap. 4.95 (*0-937180-09-2*) Variety Arts.

Nutcracker Magic. Rachel N. Luna. (Illus.). 20p. (J). (ps-3). pap. write for info. (*1-886551-04-9*) E Howard Bks.

Nutcracker Noel. Kate McMullan. LC 93-77115. (Michael di Capua Bks.). (Illus.). 32p. (J). (ps up). 1996. pap. 5.95 (*0-06-205910-6*, HarpTrophy) HarpC Child Bks.

Nutcracker Noel. Kate McMullan. LC 93-77115. 1993. 11.15 (*0-606-10271-X*, Pub. by Turtleback) Demco.

Nutcracker Prince: (Kids & Kisses Christmas) Rebecca Winters. LC 97-10538. (Romance Ser.). 187p. 1994. per. 2.99 (*0-373-03340-0*, 1-03340-6) Harlequin Bks.

Nutcracker Stained Glass Coloring Book. Stewart. (Illus.). (J). pap. 1.00 (*0-486-40260-6*) Dover.

Nutcracker, Story Book Set & Advent Calendar. Illus. by Nan Brooks. 4p. 1993. bds. 16.95 (*1-56305-503-1*, 3503) Workman Pub.

Nutcracker Suite. 24p. 1993. pap. 8.95 (*0-7935-2122-X*, 00110010) H Leonard.

Nutcracker Suite, No. 330. 24p. 1993. pap. 5.95 (*0-7935-2159-9*, 00102275) H Leonard.

Nutcracker Suite: Simplified Piano. Ed. by Tony Esposito. 40p. (Orig.). (YA). 1993. pap. text 5.95 (*0-7692-0035-4*) Wrner Bros.

Nutcracker Suite - Advanced: Piano. 40p. (Orig.). 1991. pap. 7.95 (*0-7692-1142-9*, F3151P1X) Wrner Bros.

Nutcracker Suite & Other Xmas. 72p. (Orig.). (YA). 1990. pap. 10.95 (*0-7692-1059-7*, VF1639) Wrner Bros.

Nutcracker Suite for Easy Guitar with Tab. 24p. 1997. pap. 5.95 (*0-7935-8610-0*) H Leonard.

Nutcracker Suite in Full Score. Peter Illich Tchaikovsky. 128p. 1987. pap. 8.95 (*0-486-25379-1*) Dover.

Nuteeriat. David Noel. 200p. 1989. pap., per. 5.00 (*0-9593205-4-7*) Bonsall Pub.

Nuthatches. Erik Matthysen. (Poyser Bird Bks.). (Illus.). 303p. 1998. text 39.95 (*0-85661-101-8*) Acad Pr.

***Nutik & Amaroq Play Ball.** George. LC 99-10505. 32p. (J). (gr. k-3). 2000. pap. 5.95 (*0-06-443523-7*) HarpC Child Bks.

***Nutik & Amaroq Play Ball.** Jean Craighead George. LC 99-10505. 32p. (J). (gr. k-3). 2000. 15.95 (*0-06-028166-9*) HarpC Child Bks.

Nutley. John Demmer. LC 97-191449. (Images of America Ser.). 1999. pap. 16.99 (*0-7524-0835-6*) Arcadia Publng.

Nutmeg Adventure. Lisa A. Reinhard. (Illus.). 40p. (J). (ps-2). 1994. 9.95 (*0-87935-099-7*) Colonial Williamsburg.

***Nutmeg & the Mutu.** Andrea Ross. (Illus.). 60p. (J). (gr. 3-5). 2000. lib. bdg. 9.95 (*1-887683-29-1*) Strybook Pr.

Nutmeg of Consolation. Patrick O'Brian. LC 91-3975. 320p. 1991. 24.00 (*0-393-03032-6*) Norton.

Nutmeg of Consolation. Patrick O'Brian. 320p. 1993. pap. 13.95 (*0-393-30906-1*) Norton.

Nutmeg of Consolation. large type ed. Patrick O'Brian. 1950. 30.00 (*0-7862-1938-6*) Mac Lib Ref.

Nutmeg Princess see Misterio de la Isla de las Especias

Nutmeg Princess. Richardo Keens Douglas. 1992. 11.15 (*0-606-05519-3*, Pub. by Turtleback) Demco.

Nutmeg Princess. Richardo Keens-Douglas. (Illus.). 32p. (J). (ps-2). 1992. pap. 5.95 (*1-55037-236-X*, Pub. by Annick); lib. bdg. 15.95 (*1-55037-239-4*, Pub. by Annick) Firefly Bks Ltd.

Nutquacker. Mary Jane Auch. LC 99-18347. (Illus.). 32p. (J). (gr. k-3). 1999. 16.95 (*0-8234-1524-4*) Holiday.

Nutraceutical Revolution: 20 Cutting-Edge Nutrients to Help You Design Your Own Perfect Whole-Life Program. Richard N. Firshein. LC 98-38675. 384p. 1998. 24.95 (*1-57322-081-7*, Riverhead Books) Putnam Pub Group.

***Nutraceutical Revolution: 20 Cutting-Edge Nutrients to Help You Design Your Own Perfect Whole-Life Program.** Richard N. Firshein. 1999. pap. text 13.95 (*1-57322-808-7*, Riverhd Trade) Berkley Pub.

Nutraceuticals: Developing, Claiming, & Marketing Medical Foods. Ed. by Stephen L. DeFelice. LC 97-31840. (Illus.). 128p. 1997. text 85.00 (*0-8247-0107-0*) Dekker.

Nutraceuticals - Designer Foods III: Garlic, Soy & Licorice. Ed. by Paul A. Lachance. LC 97-60572. (Illus.). 375p. 1997. 110.00 (*0-917678-40-0*, 3308) Food & Nut Pr.

Nutri-System Flavor Set Point Cookbook for Weight Loss. Susan S. Schiffman & Joan Scobey. 1990. 19.95 (*0-685-28259-7*) Little.

Nutrias de Mar. Sarah Palmer. (Mamifero Marino Ser.).Tr. of Sea Otters. 24p. (J). (gr. k-4). 1991. lib. bdg. 14.60 (*0-86592-681-6*) Rourke Enter.

Nutribase Complete Book of Food Counts. Arthur Ulene. 738p. 1996. pap. 6.95 (*0-89529-667-5*, Avery) Penguin Putnam.

Nutribase Complete Fast Food Restaurant Nutrtion Counter. Arthur Ulene. 432p. Date not set. mass mkt. 5.95 (*0-89529-666-7*, Avery) Penguin Putnam.

Nutribase Guide to Carbohydrates, Calories & Fat in Your Food. Arthur Ulene. 704p. 1995. mass mkt. 7.95 (*0-89529-632-2*, Avery) Penguin Putnam.

Nutribase Guide to Fat & Cholesterol in Your Food. Arthur Ulene. LC 94-48661. 720p. 1995. mass mkt. 5.95 (*0-89529-633-0*, Avery) Penguin Putnam.

Nutribase Guide to Fat & Fiber in Your Food. Arthur Ulene. 737p. 1995. mass mkt. 5.95 (*0-89529-652-7*, Avery) Penguin Putnam.

Nutribase Guide to Sodium, Calories & Fat in Your Food. Arthur Ulene. 724p. mass mkt. 5.95 (*0-89529-651-9*, Avery) Penguin Putnam.

Nutribase Nutrition Facts Desk Reference. Arthur Ulene. LC 94-2205. 816p. pap. 18.95 (*0-89529-623-3*, Avery) Penguin Putnam.

***Nutribase Nutrition Facts Desk Reference: Over 40,000 Food Product Listings Including Brand Name.** 2nd rev. ed. Art Ulene. 816p. 2000. pap. 19.95 (*1-58333-001-1*, Avery) Penguin Putnam.

Nutricide: The Rise & Fall of Saturated Fat in the Affairs of Man. Michael D. Wagoner. LC 91-90351. 74p. (Orig.). 1991. pap. 7.95 (*0-9629675-0-5*) Low Fat Pr.

***Nutricines: Food Components in Health & Nutrition.** Clifford A. Adams. 128p. 1999. pap. 80.00 (*1-897676-90-5*, Pub. by Nottingham Univ Pr) St Mut.

Nutricion, la Salud y la Educacion para Todos. Beryl Levinger. Tr. by Fauvette Vanderschoot. (C). 1993. pap. write for info. (*0-9637044-4-3*) PACT Pubns.

Nutricion y Salud. F. Grande Covian. 1999. pap. text 10.95 (*84-7880-758-6*) Planeta.

Nutrient Additions to Food: Nutritional, Technological & Regulatory Aspects. Ed. by J. Christopher Bauernfeind & Paul A. Lachance. 622p. 1991. 135.00 (*0-917678-29-X*) Food & Nut Pr.

Nutrient Adequacy: Assessment Using Food Consumption Surveys. National Research Council Staff. 160p. 1986. pap. text 19.95 (*0-309-03634-8*) Natl Acad Pr.

Nutrient Availability, No. 72. D. A. T. Southgate & John. 1989. 132.00 (*0-85186-856-8*) CRC Pr.

Nutrient Content of Food Portions. Jill Davies & John Dickerson. (Royal Society of Chemistry Publications). 64p. 1991. 37.00 (*0-85186-426-0*, R6426, CRC Reprint) Franklin.

Nutrient Control. (Manual of Practice, Facilities Development Ser.: No. 7). (Illus.). 205p. (Orig.). 1983. pap. text 35.00 (*0-943244-44-7*, MFD7PA) Water Environ.

Nutrient Cycling & Retention in Natural & Constructed Wetlands. Ed. by J. Vymazal. (Illus.). 208p. 1999. pap. 65.00 (*90-5782-022-6*, Pub. by Backhuys Pubs) Balogh.

Nutrient Cycling in Tropical Forest Ecosystems: Principles & Their Application in Management & Conservation. Carl F. Jordan. LC 85-6457. 200p. reprint ed. pap. 62.00 (*0-7837-6386-7*, 204609900010) Bks Demand.

***Nutrient Deficiencies & Toxicities CD-ROM.** (Digital Images Collection). (Illus.). 2000. cd-rom 59.00 (*0-89054-255-4*) Am Phytopathol Soc.

Nutrient Deficiencies & Toxicities in Crop Plants. Ed. by William F. Bennett. LC 93-71744. (Illus.). 202p. 1993. 69.00 (*0-89054-151-5*) Am Phytopathol Soc.

Nutrient Deficiency Symptoms in Container-Grown Douglas-Fir & White Spruce Seedlings. R. Van den Driessche & Canada BC Economic & Regional Development Agreement Staff. LC 90-221730. (FRDA Report Ser.). 29 p. 1989. write for info. (*0-7726-1057-6*) GovofBC.

Nutrient Disequilibria in Agroecosystems: Concepts & Case Studies. Ed. by E.M.A. Smaling et al. LC 99-14039. (CABI Publishing Ser.). 336p. 2000. 110.00 (*0-85199-268-4*) OUP.

Nutrient-Drug Interactions. Ethel Best. Ed. by Lorraine S. Boykin. (Illus.). 121p. (Orig.). (C). 1988. pap. text 20.00 (*0-317-91261-5*); lib. bdg. 10.00 (*0-317-91260-7*) E Best Pubg.

Nutrient Dynamics & Biological Structure in Shallow Freshwater & Brackish Lakes. Ed. by E. Mortensen. LC 93-47528. (Developments in Hydrobiology Ser.: No. 94). 528p. (C). 1994. text 403.50 (*0-7923-2677-6*) Kluwer Academic.

Nutrient Dynamics & Retention in Land - Water Ecotones of Lowland, Temperate Lakes, & Rivers. Ed. by A. Hillbricht-Ilkowska & E. Pieczynska. LC 92-46548. (Developments in Hydrobiology Ser.: No. 82). 1993. text 267.50 (*0-7923-2124-3*) Kluwer Academic.

Nutrient Elements & Toxicants. M. Rechcigi. (Comparative Animal Nutrition Ser.: Vol. 2). (Illus.). 1977. 85.25 (*3-8055-2351-3*) S Karger.

Nutrient Gene Interactions, 001. Naima Moussa. 2000. ring bd. write for info. (*0-8493-2216-2*) CRC Pr.

Nutrient Interactions. C. E. Bodwell & John W. Erdman. (IFT Basic Symposium Ser.: Vol. 3). (Illus.). 408p. 1988. text 125.00 (*0-8247-7868-5*) Dekker.

Nutrient Management for Sustainable Crop Production in Asia. Ed. by A. E. Johnston & J. K. Syers. LC 97-43258. (A CAB Internatioanl Publication). 416p. 1998. 120.00 (*0-85199-240-4*) OUP.

Nutrient Management of Food Animals to Enhance & Protect the Environment. Ed. by E. T. Kornegay. LC 95-47437. 368p. 1996. lib. bdg. 95.00 (*1-56670-199-6*, L1199) Lewis Pubs.

Nutrient Management Practices in Crops & Cropping Systems. C. P. Ghonsikar & V. S. Shinde. LC 97-913669. 1997. pap. 135.00 (*81-7233-168-1*, Pub. by Scientific Pubs) St Mut.

Nutrient Management Software: Proceedings from the Nutrient Management Software Workshop, December 11, 1996. Ed. by Natural Resource, Agriculture & Engineering Service Conference Staff. (NRAES Ser.: Vol. 100). 60p. 1996. pap. text 11.00 (*0-935817-16-6*, NRAES-100) NRAES.

Nutrient Modulation of the Immune Response. Ed. by Susanna Cunningham-Rundle. LC 92-49727. (Illus.). 576p. 1992. text 215.00 (*0-8247-8448-0*) Dekker.

Nutrient Points of Common Foods: Nutrition for the Nation. rev. ed. Virginia T. Stucky & Clara L. Gerwick. 62p. 1991. pap. text 7.90 (*0-915187-01-9*) Nutrition Ed.

Nutrient Regulation During Pregnancy, Lactation & Infant Growth. L. Allen et al. LC 94-6848. (Advances in Experimental Medicine & Biology Ser.: Vol. 352). (Illus.). 308p. (C). 1994. text 89.50 (*0-306-44719-3*, Kluwer Plenum) Kluwer Academic.

Nutrient Regulation of Insulin Secretion. Ed. by P. R. Flatt. (Portland Press Research Monographs: Vol. 1). 415p. 1992. 102.00 (*1-85578-004-6*, Pub. by Portland Pr Ltd) Ashgate Pub Co.

Nutrient Remobilization from Sediments & Its Limnological Effects. (Advances in Limnology Ser.: Vol. 18). (GER., Illus.). 113p. 1982. pap. text 34.00 (*3-510-47016-8*, Pub. by E Schweizerbartsche) Balogh.

Nutrient Removal from Wastewaters: Proceedings from the European Conference Held September 2-4, 1992, Wakefield, UK. Ed. by N. J. Horan. 385p. 1994. 179.95 (*1-56676-099-2*) Technomic.

Nutrient Requirements of Beef Cattle. 7th rev. ed. National Research Council Staff. (Nutrient Requirements of Domestic Animals Ser.). 250p. 1996. pap. text 29.95 (*0-309-05426-5*) Natl Acad Pr.

Nutrient Requirements of Beef Cattle: Update 2000. National Research Council. 248p. 1996. pap. 34.95 (*0-309-06934-3*) Natl Acad Pr.

Nutrient Requirements of Dairy Cattle: Update 1989. 6th rev. ed. National Research Council, Staff. 168p. 1989. pap. text 19.95 (*0-309-03826-X*) Natl Acad Pr.

Nutrient Requirements of Dogs, 1985. rev. ed. National Research Council Staff. 88p. 1985. reprint ed. pap. text 24.95 (*0-309-03496-5*) Natl Acad Pr.

Nutrient Requirements of Fish. National Research Council, Board on Agriculture St. LC 93-39031. (Nutrient Requirements of Domestic Animals Ser.). 124p. (C). 1993. pap. text 24.95 (*0-309-04891-5*) Natl Acad Pr.

Nutrient Requirements of Goats: Angora, Dairy, & Meat Goats in Temperate & Tropical Countries. National Research Council, Committee on Vision Sta. (Nutrient Requirements of Domestic Animals Ser.). 84p. (C). 1981. pap. text 24.95 (*0-309-03185-0*) Natl Acad Pr.

Nutrient Requirements of Horses, Set. 5th rev. ed. National Research Council Staff. 112p. 1989. pap. text 24.95 (*0-309-03989-4*) Natl Acad Pr.

Nutrient Requirements of Laboratory Animals. 4th rev. ed. National Research Council Staff. (Nutrient Requirements of Domestic Animals Ser.). 176p. (C). 1995. pap. text 29.95 (*0-309-05126-6*) Natl Acad Pr.

Nutrient Requirements of Laboratory Animals: Rat, Mouse, Gerbil, Guinea Pig, Hamster, Vole, Fish. 3rd rev. ed. National Research Council Staff. LC 78-15118. (Nutrient Requirements of Domestic Animals Ser.: No. 10). (Illus.). 104p. reprint ed. pap. 32.30 (*0-7837-5983-5*, 204579000007) Bks Demand.

Nutrient Requirements of Mink & Foxes. 2nd rev. ed. National Research Council Staff. LC 82-14486. (Nutrient Requirements of Domestic Animals Ser.: Vol. 7). 80p. 1982. reprint ed. pap. 30.00 (*0-608-03814-8*, 206466400009) Bks Demand.

Nutrient Requirements of Non-Human Primates. National Research Council Staff. LC 78-60949. (Nutrient Requirements of Domestic Animals Ser.: No. 14). 93p. reprint ed. pap. 30.00 (*0-7837-2778-X*, 204316900006) Bks Demand.

Nutrient Requirements of Poultry. 9th rev. ed. Subcommittee on Poultry Nutrition Staff, Committee. LC 94-3084. (Nutrient Requirements of Domestic Animals Ser.). 176p. (C). 1994. pap. text 24.95 (*0-309-04892-3*) Natl Acad Pr.

Nutrient Requirements of Rabbits. 2nd fac. rev. ed. National Research Council U. S. Staff. LC 77-6318. 36p. 1977. pap. 30.00 (*0-7837-7562-8*, 204731500007) Bks Demand.

Nutrient Requirements of Ruminant Livestock. Agricultural Research Council Staff. 351p. (Orig.). 1980. pap. text 72.00 (*0-85198-459-2*) C A B Intl.

Nutrient Requirements of Ruminant Livestock Supplement, No. 1. Agricultural Research Council Staff. 45p. (Orig.). 1984. pap. text 30.00 (*0-85198-528-9*) OUP.

Nutrient Requirements of Sheep. 6th rev. ed. National Research Council Staff. (Nutrient Requirements of Domestic Animals Ser.). 112p. 1985. pap. text 19.95 (*0-309-03596-1*) Natl Acad Pr.

Nutrient Requirements of Swine. 10th rev. ed. National Research Council Staff. LC 98-9007. 210p. (C). 1998. pap. text 39.95 (*0-309-05993-3*) Natl Acad Pr.

Nutrient Requirements of Swine, 1988. 9th rev. ed. National Research Council Staff. 104p. 1988. pap. text 14.95 (*0-309-03779-4*) Natl Acad Pr.

Nutrient Uptake & Cycling in Forest Ecosystems: CEC-IUFRO Symposium, Halmstad, Sweden, June 7-10, 1993. Ed. by Reinhard F. Huttl et al. LC 95-8175. (Developments in Plant & Soil Sciences Ser.: Vol. 62). 696p. (C). 1995. text 294.00 (*0-7923-3030-7*) Kluwer Academic.

***Nutrient Use in Crop Production.** Ed. by Zdenko Rengel. LC 98-39020. 267p. 1998. 79.95 (*1-56022-061-9*, Food Products) Haworth Pr.

***Nutrient Use in Crop Production.** Ed. by Zdenko Rengel. 267p. 2000. pap. 39.95 (*1-56022-076-7*, Food Products) Haworth Pr.

***Nutrient Value of Some Common Foods.** Health Canada Staff. 36p. 1999. pap. 11.95 (*0-660-17784-6*, Pub. by Canadian Govt Pub) Intl Spec Bk.

Nutrients: Superstars of Good Health. Barbara J. Patten. LC 95-33536. (Read All about Food for Good Health Ser.). 24p. (J). (gr. 1-4). 1996. lib. bdg. 12.95 (*0-86593-402-9*) Rourke Corp.

***Nutrients A to Z: A User's Guide to Foods, Herbs, Vitamins, Minerals & Supplements.** Michael Sharon. 344p. 1999. pap. 14.95 (*1-85375-325-4*, Pub. by Prion) Trafalgar.

Nutrients A-Z: A User's Guide to Foods, Herbs, Vitamins, Minerals & Supplements. Michael Sharon. 224p. 1998. pap. 13.95 (*1-85375-261-4*, Pub. by Prion) Trafalgar.

Nutrients & Brain Function. Ed. by Walter B. Essman. (Illus.). viii, 252p. 1987. 190.50 (*3-8055-4566-5*) S Karger.

Nutrients & Cancer Prevention. Ed. by Kedar N. Prasad & Frank L. Meyskens, Jr. LC 90-4677. (Experimental Biology & Medicine Ser.: Vol. 23). (Illus.). 353p. 1990. 125.00 (*0-89603-171-3*) Humana.

Nutrients & Energy. Ed. by Geoffrey H. Bourne. (World Review of Nutrition & Dietetics Ser.: Vol. 42). (Illus.). xii, 228p. 1983. 172.25 (*3-8055-3710-7*) S Karger.

Nutrients & Foods in AIDS. Ronald R. Watson. LC 97-48635. (Series in Modern Nutrition). 256p. 1998. boxed set 94.95 (*0-8493-8561-X*) CRC Pr.

Nutrients & Gene Expression: Clinical Aspects. Ed. by Carolyn D. Berdanier. LC 96-14781. (Modern Nutrition Ser.). 240p. 1996. boxed set 139.95 (*0-8493-9485-6*) CRC Pr.

***Nutrients & Narragansett Bay: A Workshop on Nutrient Removal for Wastewater Treatment Facilities.** Ed. by Meg Kerr. (Sustainable Coastal Communities Reports: Vol. 4401). 64p. 1999. pap. write for info. (*1-885454-13-9*) Coastal Res.

Nutrients As Ergogenic Aids for Sports & Exercise. Luke R. Bucci. 192p. 1993. boxed set 104.95 (*0-8493-4223-6*, QP176) CRC Pr.

Nutrients as Ergogenic Aids for Sports & Exercise. 2nd ed. Luke R. Bucci. (Nutrition in Exercise & Sport Ser.). 1999. 89.95 (*0-8493-7922-9*) CRC Pr.

Nutrients Catalog: Vitamins, Minerals, Amino Acids, Macronutrients - Beneficial Use, Helpers, Inhibitors, Food Sources, Intake Recommendations, & Symptoms of over or under Use. Harvey Newstrom. LC 92-56671. 558p. 1993. lib. bdg. 75.00 (*0-89950-784-0*) McFarland & Co.

Nutrients in Cancer Prevention & Treatment. Ed. by Kedar N. Prasad et al. LC 95-15205. (Experimental Biology & Medicine Ser.: Vol. 27). (Illus.). 405p. 1995. 140.00 (*0-89603-318-X*) Humana.

***Nutrients in Food.** Elizabeth S. Hands. LC 99-17028. 315p. 1999. 48.00 (*0-683-30705-3*) Lppncott W & W.

Nutrients in Profile. Henry Osiecki. 120p. (C). 1990. pap. 45.00 (*1-875239-04-9*, Pub. by Bio Concepts) St Mut.

Nutrients in the Control of Metabolic Diseases. Ed. by A. P. Simopoulos. LC 92-49666. (World Review of Nutrition & Dietetics Ser.: Vol. 69). (Illus.). xii, 170p. 1992. 204.50 (*3-8055-5594-6*) S Karger.

Nutrifacts: A Quick Reference for Nutrition in HIV Care. Jeanette M. Dunn. Ed. by Camle A. Mutzabaugh et al. (Illus.). 1997. pap. write for info. (*1-891814-02-8*) Found Care Mgmt.

Nutrion Care. 4th ed. Moore. 2000. write for info. (*0-323-00843-7*) Mosby Inc.

Nutripoints Program for Optimal Nutrition: Value Pack - Multimedia Package. 4th ed. Roy E. Vartabedian. 608p. 1999. pap. 49.95 incl. audio, VHS (*0-9641952-1-6*) Designs for Wellness.

Nutrition see Ghizaouna

Nutrition. (Illus.). 61p. 1997. write for info. (*0-945100-40-X*) Parlay Intl.

Nutrition. Carol C. Caldwell. (Illus.). 160p. 14.95 (*0-8442-8187-5*) NTC Contemp Pub Co.

***Nutrition.** Farrell & Nicoteri. (Quick Look Nursing Ser.). 2000. 18.95 (*1-889325-22-8*, Pub. by Fence Crk Pubng) Blackwell Sci.

Nutrition. Anne Galperin. (Encyclopedia of Health Ser.). (Illus.). 116p. (YA). (gr. 7 up). 1991. lib. bdg. 19.95 (*0-7910-0024-9*) Chelsea Hse.

***Nutrition.** Paul Insel. (Illus.). 960p. (C). 2000. text 75.00 (*0-7637-0910-7*) Jones & Bartlett.

***Nutrition.** Lisa Newman. LC 99-37372. (Crossing Press Pocket Ser.). 96p. 1999. pap. 6.95 (*1-58091-004-1*) Crossing Pr.

Nutrition. Reed. Date not set. pap. text, teacher ed. write for info. (*0-314-53518-7*) West Pub.

Nutrition. Annette Spence et al. (Encyclopedia of Good Health Ser.). (Illus.). 128p. (YA). 1988. 18.95 (*0-8160-1670-4*) Facts on File.

Nutrition. 2nd ed. Smolin. (C). 1996. pap. text, teacher ed. 28.00 (*0-03-018633-1*) Harcourt.

Nutrition. 4th ed. Wardlaw. LC 99-18616. 1999. 44.00 (*0-07-109368-0*) McGraw.

Nutrition. 6th ed. Frances S. Sizer. Date not set. pap. text, teacher ed. write for info. (*0-314-03425-0*); pap. text, teacher ed. write for info. (*0-314-03632-6*) West Pub.

Nutrition. 6th ed. Frances S. Sizer. 1994. pap., student ed. 19.50 (*0-314-03641-5*) West Pub.

Nutrition. 7th ed. Whitney. (Political Science Ser.). Date not set. student ed. 52.00 (*0-314-22399-1*) West Pub.

Nutrition, No. 2446. JoAnne Kato & Kimberlee Graves. Ed. by Susan Friedman. (Primary Theme Ser.). (Illus.). 32p. (J). (gr. 2-3). 1999. pap. 6.98 (*1-57471-542-9*) Creat Teach Pr.

Nutrition, Unit 3. Brown. Date not set. 2.75 (*0-314-06267-X*) West Pub.

Nutrition, Unit 4. Brown. Date not set. 2.75 (*0-314-06268-8*) West Pub.

Nutrition, Unit 5. Brown. Date not set. 2.75 (*0-314-06269-6*) West Pub.

Nutrition, Unit 6. Brown. Date not set. 2.75 (*0-314-06270-X*) West Pub.

Nutrition, Unit 7. Brown. Date not set. 2.75 (*0-314-06271-8*) West Pub.

Nutrition, Unit 8. Brown. Date not set. 3.00 (*0-314-06272-6*) West Pub.

Nutrition, Unit 9. Brown. Date not set. 2.75 (*0-314-06273-4*) West Pub.

Nutrition, Unit 10. Brown. Date not set. 2.75 (*0-314-06274-2*) West Pub.

Nutrition, Unit 11. Brown. Date not set. 2.75 (*0-314-06275-0*) West Pub.

Nutrition, Unit 13. Brown. Date not set. 2.75 (*0-314-06277-7*) West Pub.

Nutrition, Unit 14. Brown. Date not set. 3.00 (*0-314-06278-5*) West Pub.

Nutrition, Unit 15. Brown. Date not set. 2.00 (*0-314-06279-3*) West Pub.

Nutrition, Unit 16. Brown. Date not set. 2.00 (*0-314-06280-7*) West Pub.

Nutrition, Unit 17. Brown. Date not set. 2.75 (*0-314-06281-5*) West Pub.

Nutrition, Unit 18. Brown. Date not set. 2.00 (*0-314-06282-3*) West Pub.

Nutrition, Unit 19. Brown. Date not set. 2.00 (*0-314-06283-1*) West Pub.

Nutrition, Unit 20. Brown. Date not set. 2.75 (*0-314-06284-X*); 2.75 (*0-314-06285-8*) West Pub.

Nutrition, Unit 22. Brown. Date not set. 3.00 (*0-314-06286-6*) West Pub.

Nutrition, Unit 23. Brown. Date not set. 2.00 (*0-314-06287-4*) West Pub.

Nutrition, Unit 24. Brown. Date not set. 3.50 (*0-314-06288-2*) West Pub.

Nutrition, Unit 25. Brown. Date not set. 2.00 (*0-314-06289-0*) West Pub.

Nutrition, Unit 26. Brown. Date not set. 2.00 (*0-314-06290-4*) West Pub.

Nutrition, Unit 27. Brown. Date not set. 2.75 (*0-314-06291-2*) West Pub.

Nutrition, Unit 28. Brown. Date not set. 2.75 (*0-314-06292-0*) West Pub.

Nutrition, Unit 29. Brown. Date not set. 3.50 (*0-314-06293-9*) West Pub.

Nutrition, Unit 30. Brown. Date not set. 2.75 (*0-314-06294-7*) West Pub.

Nutrition, Unit 31. Brown. Date not set. 2.00 (*0-314-06295-5*) West Pub.

Nutrition, Unit 32. Brown. Date not set. 2.75 (*0-314-06296-3*) West Pub.

Nutrition, Unit 33. Brown. Date not set. 2.00 (*0-314-06297-1*) West Pub.

Nutrition, Unit 34. Brown. Date not set. 2.00 (*0-314-06298-X*) West Pub.

Nutrition: A Development Approach. LaQuatra. (Nursing Education Ser.). 1990. pap., teacher ed. 12.00 (*0-8273-3076-6*) Delmar.

Nutrition: A Health Promotion Approach. large type ed. Geoffrey P. Webb. 384p. 1995. pap. 34.95 (*1-56593-641-8*, 1330) Singular Publishing.

***Nutrition: A Key to Good Health.** rev. ed. Ed. by Mei Ling Rein. (Information Plus Reference Ser.). (Illus.). 1999. pap. text 25.95 (*1-57302-101-6*) Info Plus TX.

Nutrition: A Reference Handbook. David A. Bender & Arnold E. Bender. (Illus.). 612p. 1996. text 110.00 (*0-19-262368-0*) OUP.

***Nutrition: Applications in Biology & Chemistry.** 2nd ed. Cord. 1998. pap. 7.25 (*1-57837-077-9*) Thomson Learn.

Nutrition: Codata Directory of Data Sources for Science & Technology, Chapter Twelve. Ed. by CODATA Staff. (CODATA Bulletin Ser.). 93p. 1985. pap. 11.00 (*0-08-032489-4*, Pub. by PPL) Elsevier.

Nutrition: Concepts & Controversies. California College for Health Sciences Staff. (Illus.). 226p. (C). 1993. spiral bd. 25.00 (*0-933195-04-4*) CA College Health Sci.

Nutrition: Concepts & Controversies. Sizer. (Adaptable Courseware-Hardside Ser.). Date not set. 34.25 (*0-534-15982-6*) Wadsworth Pub.

Nutrition: Concepts & Controversies. 5th ed. Eva M. Hamilton et al. Ed. by Marshall. 354p. (C). 1991. pap. text 49.25 (*0-314-81091-9*) West Pub.

Nutrition: Concepts & Controversies. 7th ed. Sizer & Whitney. 1997. student ed. 17.50 (*0-314-20995-6*) Wadsworth Pub.

Nutrition: Concepts & Controversies. 8th ed. Sizer. (Health Sciences Ser.). 1999. pap. text, student ed. 19.75 (*0-534-56468-2*) Wadsworth Pub.

***Nutrition: Concepts & Controversies.** 8th ed. Sizer & Whitney. (Health Sciences Ser.). 1999. pap. 1.50 (*0-534-56474-7*) Wadsworth Pub.

Nutrition: Concepts & Controversies. 8th ed. Sizer et al. LC 99-36374. (Health Sciences Ser.). 567p. 1999. pap. 67.95 (*0-534-56466-6*) Wadsworth Pub.

Nutrition: Eating for Good Health. 1995. lib. bdg. 251.95 (*0-8490-6686-7*) Gordon Pr.

Nutrition: Essentials & Diet Therapy. 7th ed. Nancy J. Peckenpaugh & Charlotte M. Poleman. (Illus.). 642p. 1995. pap., teacher ed. write for info. (*0-7216-5131-3*, W B Saunders Co) Harcrt Hlth Sci Grp.

Nutrition: Essentials & Diet Therapy. 7th ed. Nancy J. Peckenpaugh & Charlotte M. Poleman. LC 94-21254. 560p. 1995. pap. text 31.00 (*0-7216-5130-5*, W B Saunders Co) Harcrt Hlth Sci Grp.

Nutrition: Metabolic & Clinical Applications, Vol. 4. R. E. Hodges et al. LC 78-27208. (Human Nutrition Ser.). (Illus.). 500p. (C). 1979. text 110.00 (*0-306-40203-3*, Kluwer Plenum) Kluwer Academic.

Nutrition: On the Road to Good Health. 3rd rev. ed. Ed. by Virginia Peterson et al. (Information Plus Compact Ser.). (Illus.). 84p. (YA). 1998. pap. text 14.95 (*1-57302-081-8*) Info Plus TX.

***Nutrition: Principles & Practices.** Applegate. 2002. pap. text. write for info. (*0-7167-3727-2*) W H Freeman.

Nutrition: Proteins & Amino Acids. Ed. by A. Yoshida et al. 300p. 1990. 96.00 (*0-387-52223-9*) Spr-Verlag.

Nutrition: Science & Application. 2nd ed. Smolin. LC 95-72725. (C). 1996. text 66.50 (*0-03-017708-1*) Harcourt.

Nutrition: Science & Applications. Smolin. (C). 1998. pap. text. write for info. (*0-03-025702-6*) Harcourt Coll Pubs.

***Nutrition: Science & Applications.** 3rd ed. Lori A. Smolin. 1999. pap. text 73.00 (*0-03-025893-6*) HarBrace.

Nutrition: The Cancer Answer. Maureen K. Salaman. 1983. 15.95 (*0-913087-00-9*) MKS Inc.

Nutrition: The Cancer Answer. Maureen K. Salaman. LC 83-61514. 1984. pap. 14.95 (*0-913087-01-7*) MKS Inc.

Nutrition: The Cancer Answer II. Maureen K. Salaman. 1995. 19.95 (*0-913087-20-3*); pap. 16.95 (*0-913087-19-X*) MKS Inc.

Nutrition 1999-2000 Edition. 11th ed. Cook-Fuller. 1999. pap., student ed. 16.56 (*0-07-040354-6*) McGraw.

Nutrition Across the Life Span: The Life Cycle. Ed. by Mary Kay Mitchell. (Illus.). 512p. 1997. pap., teacher ed. write for info. (*0-7216-5031-7*, W B Saunders Co) Harcrt Hlth Sci Grp.

Nutrition Across the Lifespan: The Life Cycle. Mary K. Mitchell. Ed. by Maura Connor. 432p. 1997. pap. text 51.00 (*0-7216-3784-1*, W B Saunders Co) Harcrt Hlth Sci Grp.

Nutrition Action Themes for the United States: A Report in Response to the International Conference on Nutrition. Jay Hirschman et al. 63p. (Orig.). (C). 1997. pap. text 25.00 (*0-7881-4621-1*) DIANE Pub.

Nutrition Activities for Preschoolers. D. Cryer et al. (Illus.). 288p. (Orig.). (J). (ps). 1996. pap. 31.20 (*0-201-49452-3*) Addison-Wesley.

Nutrition Adequacy: Nutrients Available & Needs. Ed. by Jean Mauron. (Experientia Supplementa Ser.: Vol. 44). 384p. (C). 1983. text 52.95 (*3-7643-1479-6*) Birkhauser.

Nutrition, Aging, & Immune Function Vol. 53, No. 4, Pt. 2: A Foundation for Nutritional Advancement Symposium (Boston, MA) 110p. 1995. pap. 20.00 (*0-614-22651-1*) ILSI.

Nutrition, Aging & the Elderly Vol. 6. H. N. Munro & D. B. Danford. LC 88-39816. (Human Nutrition Ser.). (Illus.). 414p. 1989. 110.00 (*0-306-43047-9*, Kluwer Plenum) Kluwer Academic.

Nutrition Alive: A Basic Approach. 2nd ed. Elaine A. Johnson & Susan M. Houston. 300p. 1993. per. 30.95 (*0-8403-7645-6*) Kendall-Hunt.

***Nutrition Almanac.** Gayla J. Kirschmann. 1999. pap. 17.95 (*0-07-134548-5*) McGraw.

Nutrition Almanac. 4th ed. John D. Kirschmann & Gayla J. Kirschmann. (Illus.). 494p. 1996. pap. 19.95 (*0-07-034922-3*) McGraw.

Nutrition & Aerobic Exercise. Ed. by Donald K. Layman. LC 85-26872. (ACS Symposium Ser.: No. 294). 160p. reprint ed. pap. 49.60 (*0-7837-1967-1*, 205244500001) Bks Demand.

Nutrition & Aging. Ed. by Myron Winick. LC 75-34225. (Current Concepts in Nutrition Ser.: Vol. 4). 219p. reprint ed. 67.90 (*0-8357-9945-X*, 205527700012) Bks Demand.

Nutrition & AIDS. 1994. lib. bdg. 250.75 (*0-8490-5632-2*) Gordon Pr.

Nutrition & Alcohol. Ronald R. Watson. 496p. 1992. boxed set 157.95 (*0-8493-7933-4*, RC565) CRC Pr.

Nutrition & Behavior. Ed. by S. A. Miller. 320p. 1981. pap. 65.00 (*0-89859-735-8*) L Erlbaum Assocs.

Nutrition & Behavior. Alexander G. Schauss. (Good Health Guide Ser.). (Orig.). 1985. pap. 2.95 (*0-87983-374-2*, Keats Publng) NTC Contemp Pub Co.

Nutrition & Behavior Vol. 5. J. R. Galler et al. LC 83-27035. (Human Nutrition Ser.). (Illus.). 532p. (C). 1984. text 132.00 (*0-306-41435-X*, Kluwer Plenum) Kluwer Academic.

Nutrition & Behavior in Dogs & Cats: Proceedings of the First Nordic Symposium on Small Animal Veterinary Medicine, Oslo, Norway, September 15-18, 1982. Ed. by R. S. Anderson. LC 83-17281. 246p. 1984. 113.00 (*0-08-029778-1*, Pub. by Pergamon Repr) Franklin.

Nutrition & Biotechnology in Heart Disease & Cancer: Proceedings of a Conference Held in Research Triangle Park, North Carolina, December 5-7, 1993. J. B. Longenecker et al. LC 95-7574. (Advances in Experimental Medicine & Biology Ser.: Vol. 369). (Illus.). 278p. (C). 1995. 95.00 (*0-306-44994-3*, Kluwer Plenum) Kluwer Academic.

Nutrition & Body Image. Susan J. Laing. (Comprehensive Health for Middle Grades Ser.). (J). (gr. 6-9). 1996. 24.00 (*1-56071-470-0*, H572) ETR Assocs.

Nutrition & Body Image: Health Facts. Lucas Stang & Kathleen R. Miner. LC 93-41014. 1994. 12.95 (*1-56071-186-8*, H306) ETR Assocs.

Nutrition & Bone Development. Jean-Philippe Bonjour & Reginald C. Tsang. LC 98-22556. 240p. 1998. text. write for info. (*0-7817-1753-1*) Lppncott W & W.

Nutrition & Bone Development. Ed. by David J. Simmons. (Illus.). 400p. 1990. text 59.95 (*0-19-504376-6*) OUP.

Nutrition & Brain Development. Govind A. Dhopeshwarkar. LC 83-8139. (Illus.). 210p. 1983. 55.00 (*0-306-41060-5*, Plenum Trade) Perseus Pubng.

Nutrition & Cancer Prevention. Erica T. Goode et al. Ed. by Sheila Mahoney & Nancy Wiltsek. (Illus.). 17p. 1984. pap. 2.50 (*0-933161-01-8*) Better H Prog.

Nutrition & Cancer Prevention. Thomas E. Moon & Marc S. Micozzi. (Illus.). 608p. 1988. text 225.00 (*0-8247-7993-2*) Dekker.

Nutrition & Cancer Prevention. Ed. by Ronald R. Watson et al. LC 95-21177. (CRC Modern Nutrition Ser.). 384p. 1995. boxed set 149.95 (*0-8493-8503-2*, 8503) CRC Pr.

Nutrition & Candida Albicans. Galland. 1989. pap. 4.95 (*0-87983-446-3*, Keats Publng) NTC Contemp Pub Co.

Nutrition & Cardiovascular Disease. Ed. by Ruth J. Hegyeli. (Progress in Biochemical Pharmacology Ser.: Vol. 19). (Illus.). x, 316p. 1982. 201.00 (*3-8055-3571-6*) S Karger.

Nutrition & Cardiovascular Risks. Ed. by J. C. Somogyi et al. (Bibliotheca Nutritio et Dieta Ser.: No. 49). (Illus.). viii, 154p. 1992. 146.25 (*3-8055-5554-7*) S Karger.

Nutrition & Care of Animals. Nancy Irlbeck. 384p. (C). 1996. pap., per. 31.95 (*0-7872-1818-9*) Kendall-Hunt.

Nutrition & Central Nervous System Function. John D. Fernstrom. 224p. 1993. boxed set 120.95 (*0-8493-4466-2*, QP136) CRC Pr.

***Nutrition & Chemical Toxicity.** Costas Ioannides. LC 98-24067. (Current Toxicology Ser.). 398p. 1998. 225.00 (*0-471-97453-6*) Wiley.

Nutrition & Cookery. Jones Staff. 1988. pap. text. write for info. (*0-582-41385-0*, Pub. by Addison-Wesley) Longman.

Nutrition & Dental Health. A. J. Rugg-Gunn. LC 92-49776. (Illus.). 488p. 1993. 87.50 (*0-19-262109-2*) OUP.

Nutrition & Dental Health. 2nd ed. Ann Ehrlich. LC 93-43043. 243p. (C). 1994. mass mkt. 29.75 (*0-8273-5716-8*) Delmar.

Nutrition & Development. Ed. by Myron Winick. LC 72-5097. (Current Concepts in Nutrition Ser.: Vol. 1). 255p. reprint ed. 79.10 (*0-8357-9946-8*, 201362800086) Bks Demand.

Nutrition & Diagnosis-Related Care. 3rd ed. Sylvia Escott-Stump. LC 91-42187. (Illus.). 617p. 1992. pap. text 39.95 (*0-8121-1556-2*) Lppncott W & W.

Nutrition & Diagnosis-Related Care. 4th ed. Sylvia Escott-Stump. LC 97-6842. 785p. 1997. pap., spiral bd. 49.00 (*0-683-30120-9*) Lppncott W & W.

Nutrition & Diet. 2nd ed. Cataldo. Date not set. pap. text, student ed. 18.50 (*0-314-50888-0*) West Pub.

Nutrition & Diet Logic. Charla Devereaux. 160p. (Orig.). 1995. pap. 7.95 (*0-572-01801-0*, Pub. by Foulsham UK) Assoc Pubs Grp.

Nutrition & Diet Therapy. Vec Staff & Delmar Staff. Ed. by Winifred A. Morse. (NSNA Review Ser.). 224p. 1995. pap. 31.95 (*0-8273-7073-3*) Delmar.

Nutrition & Diet Therapy. Wardlaw. Date not set. 53.25 (*0-07-234648-5*) McGraw.

Nutrition & Diet Therapy. 2nd ed. Carroll A. Lutz & Karen R. Przytulski. LC 97-4030. (Illus.). 630p. 1997. pap. 39.95 (*0-8036-0231-6*) Davis Co.

Nutrition & Diet Therapy. 2nd ed. Susan M. Quillman. (Notes Ser.). 208p. 1993. pap. 18.95 (*0-87434-612-6*) Springhouse Corp.

***Nutrition & Diet Therapy.** 5th ed. Cataldo et al. LC 98-42478. (Health Sciences Ser.). 1998. pap. 69.95 (*0-534-54594-7*) Wadsworth Pub.

Nutrition & Diet Therapy. 5th ed. Carolynn E. Townsend. 350p. 1989. pap. 33.25 (*0-8273-3456-7*) Delmar.

Nutrition & Diet Therapy. 6th ed. E. Carolynn Townsend. LC 93-38517. 519p. (C). 1994. mass mkt. 36.00 (*0-8273-5745-1*) Delmar.

***Nutrition & Diet Therapy.** 7th ed. Carolynn E. Townsend & Ruth Roth. LC 99-20354. (Allied Health Ser.). 480p. (C). 1999. pap. 48.95 (*0-7668-0296-5*) Delmar.

Nutrition & Diet Therapy. 8th ed. Sue Rodwell Williams. teacher ed. write for info. (*0-8151-9485-4*) Mosby Inc.

Nutrition & Diet Therapy. 8th ed. Sue Rodwell Williams. (Illus.). 880p. (C). (gr. 13). 1997. text 64.00 (*0-8151-9273-8*, 28383) Mosby Inc.

Nutrition & Diet Therapy: A Nursing Approach. Michele Grodner et al. (Illus.). 768p. (C). (gr. 13). 1995. pap. text 43.00 (*0-8151-4041-X*, 24638) Mosby Inc.

Nutrition & Diet Therapy: Instructor's Guide. 6th ed. Carolynn E. Townsend. 39p. 1994. teacher ed. 14.95 (*0-8273-6295-1*) Delmar.

N

An Asterisk (*) at the beginning of an entry indicates that the title is appearing for the first time.

Nutrition & Diet Therapy: Principles & Practice. 3rd ed. Corinne B. Cataldo et al. Ed. by Marshall. 613p. (C). 1992. pap. 52.50 (*0-314-93359-X*) West Pub.

Nutrition & Diet Therapy: Principles & Practice. 4th ed. Corinne B. Cataldo et al. LC 95-16288. 750p. (C). 1995. 57.95 (*0-314-04448-5*) West Pub.

Nutrition & Diet Therapy: Self-Instructional Modules. 3rd ed. Peggy S. Stanfield & Y. H. Hui. LC 96-28764. (Nursing Ser.). 576p. 1996. pap. 45.00 (*0-7637-0154-8*) Jones & Bartlett.

Nutrition & Diet Therapy Seven Prospectus. Sue Rodwell Williams. 1993. write for info. (*0-8016-8033-6*) Mosby Inc.

Nutrition & Diet with Chinese Cooking. 6th rev. ed. Christine Liu. (Illus.). 338p. 1985. pap. 16.95 (*0-9610566-1-4*, A837797) Graphique Pubs.

Nutrition & Dietetics for Health. 9th ed. Barker. 1996. pap. text 33.00 (*0-443-05252-2*, W B Saunders Co) Harcrt Hlth Sci Grp.

Nutrition & Dietetics for Nurses. 7th ed. Mary E. Beck. (Churchill Livingstone Nursing Text Ser.). (Illus.). 1984. pap. text 24.00 (*0-443-03121-5*) Church.

Nutrition & Dietetics for Nurses. 8th ed. Mary E. Beck. (Illus.). 221p. 1991. pap. text. write for info. (*0-443-03557-1*) Church.

Nutrition & Disease: An Annotated Bibliography. Karen Lieberman-Nissen. LC 90-14114. 190p. 1991. text 10.00 (*0-8240-7977-9*, 548) Garland.

Nutrition & Disease Update: Cancer. Ed. by David Kritchevsky & Kenneth K. Carroll. LC 93-49456. 304p. 1994. pap. 55.00 (*0-935315-49-7*) Am Oil Chemists.

Nutrition & Disease Update: Heart Disease. Ed. by David Kritchevsky & Kenneth K. Carroll. LC 93-49457. 288p. 1994. pap. 50.00 (*0-935315-50-0*) Am Oil Chemists.

Nutrition & Drugs. Ed. by Myron Winick. LC 83-1187. (Current Concepts in Nutrition Ser.: No. 12). 216p. 1983. reprint ed. pap. 67.00 (*0-7837-2799-2*, 205767400006) Bks Demand.

Nutrition & Economic Development in the Eighteenth-Century Habsburg Monarchy: An Anthropometic History. John Komlos. LC 89-30637. (Illus.). 343p. 1989. reprint ed. pap. 106.40 (*0-608-07650-3*, 205996800010) Bks Demand.

Nutrition & Environmental Health: The Influence of Nutritional Status on Pollutant Toxicity & Carcinogenicity. Edward J. Calabrese. LC 79-21089. (Illus.). 607p. reprint ed. pap. 188.20 (*0-8357-6238-6*, 205644800001) Bks Demand.

Nutrition & Environmental Health: The Influence of Nutritional Status on Pollutant Toxicity & Carcinogenicity, Vol. 2. Edward J. Calabrese. LC 79-21089. (Illus.). 488p. reprint ed. pap. 151.30 (*0-8357-6239-4*, 205644800002) Bks Demand.

***Nutrition & Exercise Immunology.** David C. Nieman & Bente Klarlund Pedersen. LC 00-21954. (Nutrition in Exercise & Sport Ser.). 2000. write for info. (*0-8493-0741-4*) CRC Pr.

Nutrition & Exercise in Obesity Management. Ed. by Jean Storlie & Henry A. Jordan. LC 87-22620. (La Crosse Exercise & Health Ser.). (Illus.). 167p. reprint ed. pap. 51.80 (*0-608-07046-7*, 206725300009) Bks Demand.

Nutrition & Feeding of Fish. T. Lovell. (Illus.). 224p. (C). (gr. 13). 1988. text 72.95 (*0-412-12291-X*) Chapman & Hall.

Nutrition & Feeding of Fish. Tom Lovell. 1998. 150.00 (*0-7923-8311-7*) Kluwer Academic.

***Nutrition & Feeding of Fish.** 2nd ed. Tom Lovell. LC 98-44242. 280p. 1999. 150.00 (*0-412-07701-9*) Kluwer Academic.

Nutrition & Feeding of Infants & Toddlers. Rosanne B. Howard & Harland S. Winter. 448p. 1984. 43.00 (*0-316-37473-3*, Little Brwn Med Div) Lppncott W & W.

Nutrition & Feeding of Poultry from Larbier & Leclerq's: Nutrition et Alimentation des Volailles. Ed. & Tr. by J. Wiseman. 305p. 1999. 200.00 (*1-897676-52-2*, Pub. by Nottingham Univ Pr) St Mut.

Nutrition & Fitness. 3rd ed. Cindy Wolff et al. 312p. (C). 1997. pap. text, per. 39.95 (*0-7872-3389-7*, 41338901) Kendall-Hunt.

Nutrition & Fitness: Evolutionary Aspects, Children's Health, Programs & Policies: 3rd International Conference on Nutrition & Fitness, Athens, May 1996. Ed. by Artemis P. Simopoulos. LC 97-17102. (World Review of Nutrition & Dietetics Ser.: Vol. 81, 1997). (Illus.). xiv, 172p. 1997. 172.25 (*3-8055-6452-X*) S Karger.

Nutrition & Fitness: Lifestyle Choices for Wellness. Dorothy F. Westbrook. LC 98-51411. (Illus.). 400p. (YA). (gr. 9-12). 1999. text 45.28 (*1-56637-510-X*) Goodheart.

Nutrition & Fitness: Metabolic & Behavioral Aspects in Health & Disease: 3rd International Conference on Nutrition & Fitness, Athens, May 1996. Ed. by Artemis P. Simopoulos & Konstantinos N. Pavlou. LC 97-19727. (World Review of Nutrition & Dietetics Ser.: Vol. 82, 1997). (Illus.). xiv, 266p. 1997. 198.25 (*3-8055-6474-0*) S Karger.

Nutrition & Fitness for Athletes, Pt. I. Ed. by Artemis P. Simopoulos & Konstantinos N. Pavlou. LC 93-18147. (World Review of Nutrition & Dietetics Ser.: Vol. 71). (Illus.). xvi, 200p. 1993. 257.50 (*3-8055-5707-8*) S Karger.

Nutrition & Fitness for Athletes, Nutrition & Fitness in Health & Disease & in Growth & Development Pts. I & II: Complete Set. Ed. by A. P. Simopoulos & Konstatinos N. Pavlou. (World Review of Nutrition & Dietetics Ser.: Vol. 71 & 72). (Illus.). xxx, 444p. 1993. 505.25 (*3-8055-5709-4*) S Karger.

Nutrition & Fitness in Health & Disease & in Growth & Development, Pt. II. Ed. by A. P. Simpoulos. (World Review of Nutrition & Dietetics Ser.: Vol. 72). (Illus.). xiv, 244p. 1993. 304.50 (*3-8055-5706-X*) S Karger.

Nutrition & Food Deficiencies Animals. Ed. by Miroslav Rechcigl. 1978. 307.00 (*0-8493-2797-0*, RC620, CRC Reprint) Franklin.

Nutrition & Food Deficiencies Animals, Vol. III. Ed. by Miroslav Rechcigl. 388p. 1978. 70.50 (*0-8493-2798-9*, CRC Reprint) Franklin.

Nutrition & Food Preparation & Preventive Care & Maintenance. S. C. Lehman. (Lifeworks Ser.). 1981. text 13.96 (*0-07-037094-X*) McGraw.

Nutrition & Food Services for Integrated Health Care: A Handbook for Leaders. Rita Jackson. LC 96-3075. 336p. 1996. 59.00 (*0-8342-0760-5*) Aspen Pub.

Nutrition & Food Supplementary Notes. 2nd ed. Stanley R. Wilfong. 324p. (C). 1996. spiral bd. 37.95 (*0-7872-2382-4*, 41238201) Kendall-Hunt.

Nutrition & Gene Expression. Ed. by Carolyn D. Berdanier & James L. Hargrove. 592p. 1992. lib. bdg. 169.00 (*0-8493-6961-4*, QP144) CRC Pr.

Nutrition & Growth Vol. 2. D. B. Jelliffe & E. F. Jelliffe. LC 78-27076. (Human Nutrition). (Illus.). 472p. (C). 1979. text 110.00 (*0-306-40128-2*, Kluwer Plenum) Kluwer Academic.

Nutrition & Growth in Infancy & Early Childhood. Nancy E. Hitchcock et al. (Monographs in Pediatrics: Vol. 19). (Illus.). xii, 92p. 1986. 68.75 (*3-8055-4223-2*) S Karger.

Nutrition & Growth of Norway Spruce Forests in a Nordic Climatic & Depositio Tema Nord 1998: 566. (Tema Nord Ser.). 254p. 1998. 25.00 (*92-893-0228-3*, NC2283) Nordic Coun Minsters.

Nutrition & Health: Topics & Controversies. Ed. by Felix Bronner. LC 95-16297. (Illus.). 272p. 1995. boxed set 74.95 (*0-8493-7849-4*, 7849) CRC Pr.

Nutrition & Health Campaign for Women Slide Set & Script Narratives. American Dietetic Association Staff. 66p. 1994. ring bd. 45.95 incl. sl. (*0-88091-141-7*) Am Dietetic Assn.

Nutrition & Health Care. Whitney. 1996. student ed. 15.75 (*0-314-07585-2*) West Pub.

Nutrition & Health Habits: Discussion. Richard L. Crews & Richard L. Kozlenko. 80p. (C). 1988. student ed. write for info. (*0-945864-20-5*); pap. text. write for info. (*0-945864-13-2*) Columbia Pacific U Pr.

Nutrition & Health HSCI 337. Deborah Forman-Petoyan. 1998. text 14.52 (*1-56870-329-5*) RonJon Pub.

***Nutrition & Health in Developing Countries.** Ed. by Richard Semba & Martin W. Bloem. 400p. 2000. 99.50 (*0-89603-806-8*) Humana.

Nutrition & Healthy Living. 2nd ed. Leeds. 2001. 40.50 (*0-07-230078-7*) McGraw.

Nutrition & Heart Disease. Ed. by H. Naito. (Monographs of the American College of Nutrition: Vol. 5). 365p. 1982. text 37.50 (*0-88331-168-2*) R B Luce.

Nutrition & Heart Disease, 2 vols., Set. Ed. by Ronald R. Watson. LC 87-8070. 1987. 188.00 (*0-8493-4640-1*, RC682, CRC Reprint) Franklin.

Nutrition & Heart Disease, 2 vols., Vol. 1. Ed. by Ronald R. Watson. LC 87-8070. 176p. 1987. 94.00 (*0-8493-4641-X*, CRC Reprint) Franklin.

Nutrition & Heart Disease, 2 vols., Vol. 2. Ed. by Ronald R. Watson. LC 87-8070. 192p. 1987. 94.00 (*0-8493-4642-8*, CRC Reprint) Franklin.

Nutrition & HIV: A New Model for Treatment. Mary Romeyn. 353p. 1998. pap. text 19.00 (*0-7881-5711-6*) DIANE Pub.

Nutrition & HIV: A New Model for Treatment. rev. ed. Mary Romeyn. LC 97-41330. 384p. 1998. mass mkt. 19.95 (*0-7879-3964-1*) Jossey-Bass.

Nutrition & Hydration: Moral & Pastoral Reflections. Committee for Pro-Life Activities Staff & NCCB Staff. 16p. 1992. pap. 1.95 (*1-55586-516-X*) US Catholic.

Nutrition & Hydration in Hospice Care: Needs, Strategies, Ethics. Ed. by Charlette R. Gallagher-Allred & Madalon O. Amenta. LC 93-50675. (Hospice Journal: Vol. 9, Nos. 2/3). (Illus.). 157p. (C). 1994. 39.95 (*1-56024-659-6*) Haworth Pr.

Nutrition & Hydration in Hospice Care: Needs, Strategies, Ethics. Ed. by Charlette R. Gallagher-Allred & Madalon O. Amenta. LC 93-50675. (Hospice Journal: Vol. 9, Nos. 2/3). 157p. (C). 1997. pap. 14.95 (*0-7890-0216-7*) Haworth Pr.

Nutrition & Immunology: Principles & Practice. Ed. by M. Eric Gershwin et al. LC 99-10901. 520p. 1999. 149.50 (*0-89603-719-3*) Humana.

Nutrition & Immunology Vol. 8, Vol. 8. D. M. Klurfeld. (Human Nutrition Ser.). (Illus.). 378p. (C). 1993. 110.00 (*0-306-44366-X*, Plenum Trade) Perseus Pubng.

Nutrition & Lactation in the Dairy Cow. P. G. Garnsworthy. (Illus.). 429p. 1988. 240.00 (*0-408-00717-6*) Buttrwrth-Heinemann.

Nutrition & Life. Robert C. Sandness. 300p. 1995. 17.95 (*0-9614076-3-8*) Sandness.

Nutrition & Managed Care Handbook. Ellyn C. Silverman. 250p. 1998. 55.00 (*0-8342-0985-3*, 09853) Aspen Pub.

Nutrition & Management of Ducks. M. L. Scott & W. F. Dean. (Illus.). 177p. 1991. text 28.00 (*0-317-03047-7*) Scott & Assocs.

Nutrition & Meal Planning in Child Care Programs: Practical Guide. Sari Edelstein. LC 92-355. 1992. spiral bd. 15.00 (*0-88091-103-4*) Am Dietetic Assn.

Nutrition & Mental Illness: An Orthomolecular Approach to Balancing Body Chemistry. Carl C. Pfeiffer. 128p. 1988. pap. 12.95 (*0-89281-226-5*, Heal Arts VT) Inner Tradit.

Nutrition & Metabolism in Patient Care. John M. Kinney et al. (Illus.). 736p. 1988. text 195.00 (*0-7216-1156-7*, W B Saunders Co) Harcrt Hlth Sci Grp.

Nutrition & Metabolism in Renal Disease. Ed. by Shaul G. Massry et al. (Journal: Mineral & Electrolyte Metabolism Ser.: Vol. 18, Nos. 2-5, 1992). (Illus.). 268p. 1992. pap. 250.50 (*3-8055-5691-8*) S Karger.

Nutrition & Metabolism in Renal Disease: Proceedings of the 8th International Congress on Renal Nutrition & Metabolism, Naples, October, 1996. Ed. by J. D. Kopple et al. (Mineral & Electrolyte Metabolism Ser.: Vol. 23, Nos. 3-6, 1997). (Illus.). iv, 194p. 1997. pap. 86.25 (*3-8055-6586-0*) S Karger.

Nutrition & Metabolism in Renal Disease Vol. 22, No. 1-3: International Society of Renal Nutrition & Metabolism. Ed. by Shaul G. Massry et al. (Journal: Mineral & Electrolyte Metabolism Ser.: Vol. 22, No. 1-3, 1996). (Illus.). 202p. 1995. pap. 129.75 (*3-8055-6249-7*) S Karger.

Nutrition & Metabolism in the Surgical Patient. 2nd rev. ed. Ed. by Josef E. Fischer. LC 95-31028. 704p. 1996. text 189.00 (*0-316-28390-8*) Lppncott W & W.

Nutrition & Metabolism of the Fetus & Infant. Ed. by H. K. Visser. (Nutricia Symposium Ser.: No. 5). 1979. text 171.00 (*90-247-2202-0*) Kluwer Academic.

Nutrition & National Policy. Ed. by Beverly Winikoff. 1978. 45.00 (*0-262-23087-9*) MIT Pr.

Nutrition & Nervous System: Proceedings of the European Nutritionists Group Symposium, 9th, Chianciano, 1970. European Nutritionists Group Symposium Staff. Ed. by J. C. Somogyi & F. Fidanza. (Bibliotheca Nutritio et Dieta Ser.: No. 17). (Illus.). 202p. 1972. pap. 68.00 (*3-8055-1309-7*) S Karger.

Nutrition & Neurobiology. Ed. by J. C. Somogyi. (Bibliotheca Nutritio et Dieta Ser.: No. 38). (Illus.). viii, 224p. 1986. 155.75 (*3-8055-4246-1*) S Karger.

Nutrition & Performance, Vol 7/1-2. C. F. Consolazio. (Illus.). 200p. 1983. pap. 92.00 (*0-08-031013-3*, 38, Pergamon Pr) Elsevier.

Nutrition & Physical Activity to Optimize Performance & Well-Being Vol. 54, No. 4, Pt. 2: 3rd International Conference Series on Nutrition & Health Promotion (Atlanta, GA) 183p. 1996. pap. 35.00 (*0-614-22655-4*) ILSI.

Nutrition & Physical Degeneration. 6th ed. Weston A. Price. LC 97-41920. 528p. 1997. pap. 20.95 (*0-87983-816-7*, 38167K, Keats Publng) NTC Contemp Pub Co.

Nutrition & Physical Degeneration. 9th ed. Weston A. Price. (Illus.). 560p. 1977. 34.95 (*0-916764-00-1*) Price-Pottenger.

Nutrition & Poverty. Ed. by Siddiqur R. Osmani. (WIDER Studies in Development Economics). (Illus.). 382p. 1993. text 69.00 (*0-19-828396-2*) OUP.

Nutrition & Pregnancy: A Complete Guide from Preconception to Postdelivery. Judith E. Brown. LC 97-38624. 240p. 1998. 25.00 (*1-56565-790-X*, 07909W, Pub. by Lowell Hse) NTC Contemp Pub Co.

Nutrition & Pregnancy: A Complete Guide from Preconception to Postdelivery. Judith E. Brown. LC 97-38624. (Illus.). 288p. 1998. reprint ed. pap. 16.00 (*0-7373-0018-3*, 00183W) NTC Contemp Pub Co.

Nutrition & Psychotropic Drugs in the Elderly. David A. Smith. (Geriatric Psychopathology Ser.). (Orig.). Date not set. pap. 29.95 (*1-884937-29-2*) Manisses Communs.

Nutrition & Reproduction. Ed. by George A. Bray & Donna H. Ryan. LC 98-10771. (Pennington Center Nutrition Ser.: Vol. 8). 460p. 1998. text 95.00 (*0-8071-2306-4*) La State U Pr.

Nutrition & Restaurants: A Consumer Perspective. 206p. 1993. pap. 75.00 (*0-614-31132-2*, CS972) Natl Restaurant Assn.

Nutrition & Stress. Harold S. Rosenberg. Ed. by Richard A. Passwater & Earl R. Mindell. (Good Health Guide Ser.). 32p. (Orig.). 1983. pap. 3.95 (*0-87983-298-3*, 32983K, Keats Publng) NTC Contemp Pub Co.

Nutrition & Stroke. M. Hennerici et al. LC 96-36757. (Nestle Nutrition Workshop Ser.). 192p. 1997. text 63.00 (*0-397-58770-8*) Lppncott W & W.

Nutrition & Technology of Foods for Growing Humans: Proceedings of the European Nutritionists Group Symposium, Zurich, 1971. European Nutritionists Group Symposium Staff. Ed. by J. C. Somogyi. (Bibliotheca Nutritio et Dieta Ser.: No. 18). (Illus.). 200p. 1972. pap. 80.00 (*3-8055-1317-8*) S Karger.

Nutrition & the Adult: Macronutrients, Vol. 3A. R. B. Alfin-Slater & D. Kritchevsky. LC 79-25119. (Human Nutrition Ser.). (Illus.). 308p. (C). 1980. text 110.00 (*0-306-40287-4*, Kluwer Plenum) Kluwer Academic.

Nutrition & the Adult Vol. 3B: Micronutrients. R. B. Alfin-Slater & D. Kritchevsky. LC 79-25119. (Human Nutrition Ser.). (Illus.). 450p. (C). 1980. text 110.00 (*0-306-40288-2*, Kluwer Plenum) Kluwer Academic.

Nutrition & the Cell: The Inside Story. Marion Mason et al. LC 72-95734. (Illus.). 92p. reprint ed. 30.00 (*0-8357-9636-1*, 201310400085) Bks Demand.

Nutrition & the Diabetic Child: Proceedings of the 4th Beilinson Symposium, Herzlya, May 21-24, 1978. International Beilinson Symposium Staff. Ed. by Laron Zvi & Karp Moshe. (Pediatric & Adolescent Endocrinology Ser.: Vol. 7). 1980. pap. 159.25 (*3-8055-3019-6*) S Karger.

Nutrition & the Feeding of Horses. Beth Maloney. (Illus.). 216p. 1998. pap. 32.95 (*1-85310-744-1*, Pub. by Swan Hill Pr) Voyageur Pr.

Nutrition & the Female Athlete. Jaime S. Ruud. LC 96-11966. (Nutrition in Exercise & Sport Ser.). 176p. 1996. boxed set 69.95 (*0-8493-7917-2*) CRC Pr.

Nutrition & the Immune Response. Ed. by J. Dwight Stinnett. LC 82-17708. 160p. 1983. 119.00 (*0-8493-5650-4*, RC623, CRC Reprint) Franklin.

Nutrition & the Killer Diseases. Myron Winick. LC 81-3317. (Current Concepts in Nutrition Ser.: No. 10). (Illus.). 199p. reprint ed. pap. 61.70 (*0-608-17423-8*, 205645900067) Bks Demand.

Nutrition & the Mind. Gary Null. LC 94-46982. 303p. (Orig.). 1995. pap. 14.95 (*1-888363-24-X*) Seven Stories.

Nutrition & the Quality of Life. Ed. by Geoffrey H. Bourne. (World Review of Nutrition & Dietetics Ser.: Vol. 49). (Illus.). x, 218p. 1987. 168.75 (*3-8055-4450-2*) S Karger.

Nutrition & Utilization Technology in Aquaculture. Ed. by C. E. Lim & D. J. Sessa. 288p. 1995. 70.00 (*0-935315-54-3*) Am Oil Chemists.

Nutrition & Ventilatory Function. Ed. by R. D. Ferranti et al. LC 92-2313. (Current Topics in Rehabilitation Ser.). 1992. 69.95 (*0-387-19776-1*) Spr-Verlag.

Nutrition & Weight Control Study Guide. Patricia A. Eisenman et al. (American Coaching Effectiveness Program Ser.). (Illus.). 208p. 1991. student ed., spiral bd. 32.00 (*0-88011-385-5*, ACEP0207) Human Kinetics.

Nutrition & Women's Cancers. Barbara C. Pence & Dale M. Dunn. (Modern Nutrition Ser.). 192p. 1998. boxed set 84.95 (*0-8493-8562-8*) CRC Pr.

Nutrition & You with Readings. 4th ed. William A. Forsythe, III. (Illus.). 224p. 1998. pap. text 25.00 (*0-89892-167-8*) Contemp Pub Co of Raleigh.

Nutrition & Your Health: Dietary Guidelines for Americans. 43p. 1995. pap. 58.00 (*0-16-060806-6*, Agriculture Dept) USGPO.

Nutrition Appendices. Brown. 1995. pap. text. write for info. (*0-314-06299-8*) West Pub.

Nutrition Applied to Injury Rehabilitation & Sports Medicine. Luke R. Bucci. 304p. 1994. boxed set 131.95 (*0-8493-7913-X*, 7913) CRC Pr.

***Nutrition Aspects Of HIV Infection.** Ed. by Tracie L. Miller & Sherwood L. Gorbach. (Illus.). 224p. 1999. text 69.50 (*0-340-74195-3*) OUP.

Nutrition Assessment: A Comprehensive Guide for Planning Intervention. 2nd ed. Margaret D. Simko et al. 400p. 1994. 48.00 (*0-8342-0557-2*, 20557) Aspen Pub.

Nutrition Assistant. Jack Rudman. (Career Examination Ser.: C-3303). 1994. pap. 23.95 (*0-8373-3303-2*) Nat Learn.

Nutrition Bible: A Comprehensive, No-Nonsense Guide to Foods, Nutrients, Additives, Preservatives, Pollutants, & Everything Else We Eat & Drink. Jean Anderson & Barbara Deskins. LC 94-38080. 544p. 1996. 30.00 (*0-688-11619-1*, Wm Morrow) Morrow Avon.

Nutrition Bible: A Comprehensive, No-Nonsense Guide to Foods, Nutrients, Additives, Preservatives, Pollutants & Everything Else We Eat & Drink. Jean Anderson & Barbara Deskins. (Illus.). 480p. 1997. reprint ed. pap. 17.00 (*0-688-15559-6*, Quil) HarperTrade.

Nutrition Bibliography of Indonesia. Ed. by Simon Postmus. LC 55-10494. 146p. reprint ed. pap. 45.30 (*0-608-11249-6*, 200135700076) Bks Demand.

Nutrition Bibliography of Malaya. Peng C. Leong. LC 52-40995. 32p. reprint ed. pap. 30.00 (*0-608-11254-2*, 200135900076) Bks Demand.

Nutrition, Cancer & You: What You Need to Know, & Where to Start. Susan Calhoun & Jane Bradley. Ed. by Michael McKenzie. LC 96-85765. 192p. 1996. pap. 12.95 (*1-886110-06-9*, Pub. by Addax Pubng) Midpt Trade.

Nutrition Care in Nursing Facilities. 2nd rev. ed. Clara L. Gerwick & Consultant Dietitians in Health Care Facilities St. LC 92-49942. 1992. pap. text 28.00 (*0-88091-105-0*) Am Dietetic Assn.

Nutrition Care of People with Diabetes Mellitus: A Nutrition Reference for Health Professionals. Penelope S. Easton et al. 1991. 89.95 (*1-56022-004-X*) Haworth Jrnl Co-Edits.

Nutrition Care of People with Diabetes Mellitus: A Nutrition Reference for Health Professionals. Penelope S. Easton et al. LC 90-13936. 263p. 1991. pap. 39.95 (*1-56022-007-4*) Haworth Jrnl Co-Edits.

Nutrition Care of the Older Adult: A Handbook for Dietetics Professionals Working Throughout the Continuum of Care. Consultant Dietitians in Health Care Facilities St. LC 98-42196. 250p. 1998. 34.95 (*0-88091-167-0*) Am Dietetic Assn.

Nutrition Case Management of Diabetes: User's Manual. Mary Litchford et al. (C). 1997. pap. 7.00 (*1-880989-56-5*) Case Sftware.

Nutrition Casebook on Developmental Disabilities. Ninfa S. Springer. LC 81-21383. 1982. 39.95 (*0-8156-2266-X*); pap. 16.95 (*0-8156-2259-7*) Syracuse U Pr.

Nutrition Challenge for Women. Louise Lambert-Lagace. 192p. 1990. pap. 12.95 (*0-923521-06-2*) Bull Pub.

Nutrition Chemistry & Biology. 2nd ed. Julian F. Spallholz & Mallory Boylan. LC 98-34621. (Modern Nutrition Ser.). 368p. 1998. boxed set 64.95 (*0-8493-8504-0*) CRC Pr.

Nutrition Compendium. Ed. by Sharlene Sherwin et al. 32p. 0.50 (*0-318-03051-9*) Sant Bani Ash.

***Nutrition Concepts.** 2nd ed. Bernard Frye. 346p. (C). 2000. per. 38.95 (*0-7872-7113-6*) Kendall-Hunt.

Nutrition Counseling & Comunication Skills. Katharine Curry & Amy Jaffe. Ed. by Maura Connor. LC 97-34828. (Illus.). 384p. 1997. pap. text 32.95 (*0-7216-7298-1*, W B Saunders Co) Harcrt Hlth Sci Grp.

Nutrition Counseling Skills for Medical Nutrition Therapy. Linda G. Snetselaar. LC 96-53385. 375p. 1997. 49.00 (*0-8342-0755-9*) Aspen Pub.

Nutrition Count Cookbook. Doris J. Kuchar. LC 89-91320. (Illus.). 326p. (Orig.). 1989. pap. 12.95 (*0-9621355-0-X*) D J Kuchar.

Nutrition Curriculum: Activities Kit, Level 1, Grades 5-8. Paul Bell et al. (Illus.). 288p. 1986. pap. text 27.95 (*0-87628-617-1*) Ctr Appl Res.

Nutrition Curriculum: Activities Kit, Level 2, Grades 9-12. Paul Bell et al. (Illus.). 352p. 1986. pap. text 27.95 (*0-87628-618-X*) Ctr Appl Res.

N

Nutrition Debate: Sorting Out Some Answers. Joan D. Gussow & Paul Thomas. LC 86-21616. 400p. (Orig.). 1986. pap. 8.00 (*0-915950-66-9*) Bull Pub.

Nutrition Desk Reference. Robert H. Garrison, Jr. & Elizabeth Somer. LC 84-26098. 264p. (C). 1985. 34.95 (*0-87983-523-0*, Keats Publng) NTC Contemp Pub Co.

Nutrition Desk Reference. 3rd ed. Robert H. Garrison & Elizabeth Somer. LC 95-32741. (Orig.). 1995. 27.95 (*0-87983-665-2*, Keats Publng) NTC Contemp Pub Co.

Nutrition Desk Reference. 3rd ed. Robert Garrison, Jr. & Elizabeth Somer. 664p. 1997. 19.95 (*0-87983-826-4*, 38264K, Keats Publng) NTC Contemp Pub Co.

Nutrition, Diet & Dental Health: Concepts & Methods. Carole Palmer et al. 78p. 1981. 32.00 (*0-318-17799-4*) Am Dental Hygienists.

Nutrition, Diet & Oral Health. Andrew J. Rugg-Gunn & June H. Nunn. LC 99-11561. (Illus.). 208p. 1999. pap. text 59.50 (*0-19-262937-9*) OUP.

Nutrition, Diet Modifications & Meal Patterns. Ruby P. Puckett & Sherryl Danks. 356p. (C). 1996. pap. text, per. 52.95 (*0-7872-2638-6*) Kendall-Hunt.

Nutrition, Disease Resistance & Immune Function. Ed. by Ronald R. Watson. LC 84-1812. (Clinical & Experimental Nutrition Ser.: No. 1). 422p. 1984. reprint ed. pap. 130.90 (*0-608-01307-2*, 206205200001) Bks Demand.

Nutrition Disorders: Subject, Reference & Research Guidebook. Eva Saint Gompert. LC 87-47647. 160p. 1987. 47.50 (*0-88164-594-X*); pap. 44.50 (*0-88164-595-8*) ABBE Pubs Assn.

Nutrition Doctor's A to Z Food Counter. Ed Blonz. LC 99-182511. 288p. 1999. mass mkt. 6.50 (*0-451-19587-6*, Sig) NAL.

Nutrition During Lactation. Institute of Medicine, Committee on Nutritional St. 326p. 1991. 34.95 (*0-309-04391-3*) Natl Acad Pr.

Nutrition During Pregnancy: Part I: Weight Gain, Part II: Nutrient Supplements, Pts. 1 & 2. Ed. by Committee on Nutritional Status During Pregnancy &. 480p. 1990. 34.95 (*0-309-04138-4*) Natl Acad Pr.

Nutrition During Pregnancy & Lactation: An Implementation Guide. Institute of Medicine, Subcommittee for a Clinical. LC 92-19175. 144p. (Orig.). (C). 1992. pap. 14.95 (*0-309-04738-2*) Natl Acad Pr.

Nutrition Education: Study Guide. Ed. by Deakin University Press Staff. (C). 1988. pap. 75.00 (*0-7300-0621-2*, SHN770, Pub. by Deakin Univ) St Mut.

Nutrition Education & Modern Concepts of Food Assimilation. Ed. by Geoffrey H. Bourne. (World Review of Nutrition & Dietetics Ser.: Vol. 40). (Illus.). xii, 192p. 1982. 141.75 (*3-8055-3519-8*) S Karger.

Nutrition Education Consultant. Jack Rudman. (Career Examination Ser.: C-2740). 1994. pap. 34.95 (*0-8373-2740-7*) Nat Learn.

Nutrition Education for the Public: Discussion Papers of the FAO Expert Consultation. LC 98-110864. (Food & Nutrition Papers: No. 62). 212p. 1997. pap. 25.00 (*92-5-103936-4*, F39364, Pub. by FAO) Bernan Associates.

Nutrition Education in Public Elementary & Secondary Schools. Carin Celebuski. 65p. 1996. pap. 4.25 (*0-16-048755-2*) USGPO.

Nutrition Education in Public Elementary & Secondary Schools. Carin Celebuski & Elizabeth Farris. (Illus.). 57p. (C). 1998. pap. text 20.00 (*0-7881-4839-7*) DIANE Pub.

***Nutrition Education in Public Elementary School Classrooms, K-5.** Carin Celebuski. 76p. 2000. pap. 7.00 (*0-16-050280-2*) USGPO.

Nutrition Education in U. S. Medical Schools. National Research Council (U. S.), Committee on Nutrition in Medical Education Staff. LC 85-61572. 151p. 1985. reprint ed. pap. 46.90 (*0-608-02335-3*, 206297600004) Bks Demand.

Nutrition Education Materials & Audiovisuals for Grades 7 Through 12. Shirley K. Evans. 44p. 1996. reprint ed. pap. text 25.00 (*0-7881-3355-1*) DIANE Pub.

Nutrition Education Materials & Audiovisuals for Grades 7 Through 12. Shirley K. Evans. 52p. 1998. reprint ed. pap. text 20.00 (*0-7881-4345-X*) DIANE Pub.

Nutrition, Endocrinology, & Disease. Ed. by George A. Bray & Donna H. Ryan. (Pennington Center Nutrition Ser.: Vol. 4). (Illus.). 232p. 1995. text 45.00 (*0-8071-1954-7*) La State U Pr.

Nutrition Essentials & Diet Therapy. 8th ed. Nancy J. Peckenpaugh & Charlotte M. Poleman. Ed. by Maura Connor. (Illus.). 635p. (C). 1998. pap. text 32.95 (*0-7216-7707-X*, W B Saunders Co) Harcrt Hlth Sci Grp.

Nutrition, Exercise & Weight Control. Summerfield. (Health Sciences Ser.). 2000. pap. 42.00 (*0-534-54153-4*) Wadsworth Pub.

Nutrition, Exercise & Weight Training Journal: A 12-Week Record. Karen M. Ditchey & Pamela K. Novak. Ed. by Arik T. Ohnstad. (Illus.). 208p. 1997. ring bd. 9.95 (*0-9659908-0-X*) My Place Pub.

Nutrition Factor: Its Role in National Development. Alan Berg. LC 73-1081. 290p. 1973. pap. 16.95 (*0-8157-0913-7*) Brookings.

Nutrition Facts for Better Bodies. Robert S. Wennik. LC 95-7324. 1995. write for info. (*1-56796-097-9*) WRS Group.

Nutrition Facts Manual: A Quick Reference. Bloch. 352p. 1996. pap. text 34.75 (*0-683-07719-8*) Lppncott W & W.

Nutrition Facts Manual: A Quick Reference. Ed. by Maurice E. Shils et al. LC 95-36795. 1995. write for info. (*0-614-08567-5*) Lppncott W & W.

Nutrition, Fitness & Sports. 6th ed. Williams. 2001. 40.00 (*0-07-228804-3*) McGraw.

Nutrition, Fitness, & Sports. 6th ed. Williams. 2001. pap., wbk. ed. 15.50 (*0-07-228805-1*) McGraw.

Nutrition-Fitness Link: How Diet Can Help Your Body & Mind. Charles A. Salter. LC 92-35146. (Teen Nutrition Book). (Illus.). 96p. (YA). (gr. 7 up). 1993. lib. bdg. 22.40 (*1-56294-260-3*) Millbrook Pr.

Nutrition, Food, & Man: An Interdisciplinary Perspective. Ed. by Paul B. Pearson & J. Richard Greenwell. LC 80-10297. (Illus.). 175p. 1980. pap. 54.30 (*0-608-05644-8*, 206609800006) Bks Demand.

Nutrition, Food, & the Environment. Vincent Hegarty. 1995. 55.00 (*0-9624407-4-4*) Eagan Pr.

Nutrition for a Healthy Heart. Robert J. Peshek. (Illus.). 1979. 20.00 (*0-9605902-2-6*) Color Coded Charting.

Nutrition for a Healthy Pregnancy, 6 Vols. American Dietetic Association Staff. 1998. pap. 41.70 (*1-56561-161-6*) Wiley.

Nutrition for a Healthy Pregnancy: The Complete Guide to Eating Before, During, & After Your Pregnancy. Elizabeth Somer. LC 94-42167. 256p. 1995. pap. 14.95 (*0-8050-3775-6*, Owl) H Holt & Co.

Nutrition for Climbers. Beth Bennett. (How to Rock Climb Ser.). 32p. 1995. pap. 4.95 (*0-934641-76-5*) Falcon Pub Inc.

Nutrition for Dummies. 2nd ed. Carol A. Rinzler. LC 97-70747. (For Dummies Ser.). (Illus.). 410p. 1996. pap. 19.99 (*0-7645-5032-2*) IDG Bks.

***Nutrition for Dummies.** 2nd ed. Carol A. Rinzler. (For Dummies Ser.). 416p. 1999. pap. 19.99 (*0-7645-5180-9*, Dummies Trade Pr) IDG Bks.

Nutrition for Fitness. 4th ed. Williams. 1995. 13.43 (*0-697-25546-8*, WCB McGr Hill) McGrw-H Hghr Educ.

Nutrition for Fitness & Sport. 4th ed. Melvin H. Williams. 480p. (C). 1995. text 39.00 (*0-697-23052-X*) Brown & Benchmark.

Nutrition for Fitness & Sport. 4th ed. Melvin H. Williams. 160p. (C). 1995. text, student ed. 15.00 (*0-697-25548-4*) Brown & Benchmark.

Nutrition for Fitness & Sport. 4th ed. Melvin H. Williams. 480p. (C). 1997. per. write for info. (*0-07-114865-5*) McGraw.

Nutrition for Fitness & Sport. 5th ed. Williams. LC 97-41026. 512p. 1998. pap. 52.50 (*0-697-29510-9*) McGraw.

***Nutrition for Foodservice & Culinary Professionals.** 4th ed. Drummond. 656p. 2000. text 59.95 (*0-471-34777-9*) Wiley.

Nutrition for Foodservice Managers: Concepts, Application & Management. Mahmood A. Khan. LC 97-36348. 416p. 1998. 59.95 (*0-471-12951-8*) Wiley.

Nutrition for God's Temple. Dick Couey. LC 93-20409. (Studies in Health & Human Services: Vol. 22). 664p. 1993. pap. 109.95 (*0-7734-9288-7*); text 129.95 (*0-7734-9286-0*) E Mellen.

Nutrition for Health & Healthcare. 2nd ed. Whitney et al. (Health Sciences Ser.). 2000. mass mkt. 45.00 (*0-534-51552-5*) Wadsworth Pub.

***Nutrition for Life.** Bill Phillips. 2000. 26.00 (*0-06-019768-4*) HarpC.

***Nutrition for Life Guide to Personal Wealth.** 1999. write for info. (*0-02-863703-8*) IDG Bks.

Nutrition for Living: Study Guide. 3rd ed. Janet L. Christian & Janet Greger. (Illus.). 736p. 1991. pap. text, student ed. 19.95 (*0-8053-1004-5*) Benjamin-Cummings.

Nutrition for Nurses. O. L. Oke & Ojofeitimi. 1985. pap. text. write for info. (*0-582-77705-4*, Pub. by Addison-Wesley) Longman.

Nutrition for Pregnancy: Focus on Healthy Outcomes. Carol A. Hickey et al. LC 93-49591. (Maternal Nutrition Ser.: No. 3). 1994. write for info. (*0-86525-057-X*) March of Dimes.

Nutrition for Primary Care. Heber. 1999. text. write for info. (*0-7216-4300-0*, W B Saunders Co) Harcrt Hlth Sci Grp.

***Nutrition for Professionals: The Nutrition Specialist Course.** 5th unabridged ed. Jane Pentz. Ed. by Elaine Greenwood & Lindy Bonczek. (Illus.). 220p. 1999. pap. text 75.00 (*1-892426-03-X*) LMA Publishing.

Nutrition for Professionals: The Nutrition Specialist Manual. 4th unabridged ed. Jane Pentz. Ed. by Elaine Greenwood & Lindy Bonczek. (Illus.). 175p. 1998. ring bd. 75.00 (*1-892426-00-5*) LMA Publishing.

Nutrition for Recovery: A Patient's Guide. Kathryn J. Reichert. 1993. 36.95 (*0-8493-8652-7*, RC552) CRC Pr.

Nutrition for Recovery: Eating Disorders. Kathryn J. Reichert. 144p. 1993. 65.00 (*0-8493-8651-9*, RC552) CRC Pr.

Nutrition for Serious Athletes. Dan Benardot. LC 99-46572. 352p. 1999. pap. 16.95 (*0-88011-833-4*) Human Kinetics.

Nutrition for Special Needs in Infancy: Protein Hydrolysates. Ed. by Fima Lifshitz. LC 85-25288. (Clinical Disorders in Pediatric Nutrition Ser.: No. 4). 336p. 1985. reprint ed. pap. 104.20 (*0-608-01305-6*, 206205000001) Bks Demand.

Nutrition for Sport. Wilf Paish. (Illus.). 128p. 1991. pap. 22.95 (*1-85223-380-X*, Pub. by Crolwood) Trafalgar.

Nutrition for Sport. Steve Wootton. LC 87-530. (Illus.). 207p. 1988. reprint ed. pap. 64.20 (*0-7837-9917-9*, 206064300006) Bks Demand.

Nutrition for Sport & Exercise. 2nd ed. Jacqueline R. Berning & Suzanne N. Steen. LC 98-11758. 300p. 1998. 52.00 (*0-8342-0882-2*) Aspen Pub.

Nutrition for the Food Service Professional. 3rd ed. Karen Eich Drummond. (Hospitality, Travel & Tourism Ser.). 642p. 1996. text 41.95 (*0-442-02114-3*, VNR) Wiley.

Nutrition for the Food Service Professional. 3rd ed. Karen Eich Drummond. (Hospitality, Travel & Tourism Ser.). 642p. 1996. 49.95 (*0-471-28719-9*, VNR) Wiley.

Nutrition for the Foodservice Manager: Student Manual. Educational Foundation of the National Restaurant. 80p. (Orig.). 1991. pap. write for info. (*0-915452-58-8*) Educ Found.

Nutrition for the Foodservice Profession. 2nd ed. Drummond. (Hospitality, Travel & Tourism Ser.). 1996. pap., teacher ed. write for info. (*0-442-01866-5*, VNR) Wiley.

Nutrition for the Foodservice Professional. Drummond. (Hospitality, Travel & Tourism Ser.). 1997. pap. write for info. (*0-442-02474-6*, VNR) Wiley.

Nutrition for the Hospitalized Patient: Basic Science & Principles of Practice. Ed. by Michael H. Torosian. LC 94-43115. (Illus.). 712p. 1995. text 165.00 (*0-8247-9292-0*) Dekker.

Nutrition for the 90s. Judy Rainwater. 1992. pap., spiral bd. 13.50 (*0-9622066-1-X*) Ranrai Pub.

Nutrition for the Recreational Athlete. Ed. by Catherine G. Ratzin-Jackson. LC 94-19402. (Nutrition in Exercise & Sport Ser.). 272p. 1995. boxed set 94.95 (*0-8493-7914-8*) CRC Pr.

***Nutrition for Today.** Applegate. 2002. pap. text, student ed. write for info. (*0-7167-3954-2*) W H Freeman.

Nutrition for Vegetarians. Agatha Thrash & Calvin L. Thrash. (Illus.). 155p. 1982. pap. 7.95 (*0-942658-03-5*) NLB.

Nutrition for Women: The Complete Guide. Elizabeth Somer. 496p. 1995. 27.50 (*0-8050-2389-5*); pap. 14.95 (*0-8050-3563-X*) H Holt & Co.

Nutrition, Genetics, & Heart Disease. Ed. by George A. Bray & Donna H. Ryan. LC 96-9007. (Pennington Center Nutrition Ser.: Vol. 6). (Illus.). 408p. (C). 1996. text 60.00 (*0-8071-2051-0*) La State U Pr.

Nutrition, Genetics, & Obesity. Ed. by George A. Bray & Donna H. Ryan. LC 98-50606. (Pennington Center Nutrition Ser.: Vol. 9). (Illus.). 574p. 1999. text 95.00 (*0-8071-2407-9*) La State U Pr.

Nutrition God's Way. Gwendolyn A. Arthur. 96p. 1987. pap. 4.25 (*0-88144-115-5*) Christian Pub.

Nutrition, Growth & Development: Proceedings of the International Symposium, Valencia, May, 1973. Ed. by C. A. Canosa et al. (Modern Problems in Pediatrics Ser.: Vol. 14). (Illus.). 1974. 85.25 (*3-8055-1757-2*) S Karger.

Nutrition Guide for the Restaurateur. 72p. 1986. pap. 36.00 (*0-317-57890-1*, CS983) Natl Restaurant Assn.

Nutrition Handbook for AIDS. 2nd ed. Jean E. Schreiner. LC 91-118966. (Illus.). 134p. 1990. ring bd. 34.95 (*0-9622157-1-6*) Carrot Top Nutrition.

Nutrition Handbook for HIV/AIDS. 3rd rev. ed. Jean E. Schreiner. (Illus.). 165p. 1999. ring bd. 42.95 (*0-9622157-3-2*, HB301) Carrot Top Nutrition.

Nutrition Handbook for Nursing Practice. 3rd ed. Susan G. Dudek. LC 96-26302. 864p. 1997. pap. text 31.95 (*0-397-55364-1*, Lippncott) Lppncott W & W.

Nutrition Handbook for Nursing Practice. 4th ed. Susan G. Dudek. 800p. pap. text 33.00 (*0-7817-2344-2*) Lppncott W & W.

Nutrition Handbook Teacher's Manual. Joan E. Pizzo. 28p. 1983. pap. 5.95 (*0-939126-15-X*) Back Bay Bks.

Nutrition, Health & Harmony: A Handbook of Natural Health. rev. ed. Jonathon D. Miller. (Illus.). (Orig.). 1980. pap. 5.98 (*0-935815-00-7*) Lifecircle.

Nutrition, Health, & Safety for Preschool Children. Roberta L. Duyff et al. LC 94-4626. 1994. 22.00 (*0-02-802089-8*) Glencoe.

Nutrition, Health, Fitness, & Sports. 5th ed. Williams. 1998. wbk. ed. 13.00 (*0-697-37782-2*, WCB McGr Hill) McGrw-H Hghr Educ.

Nutrition Improvement Projects in Tanzania: Implementation, Determinants of Performance & Policy Implications. John M. Msuya. LC 99-25012. (Development Economics & Policy Ser.: Vol. 11). (Illus.). XX, 206p. 1999. pap. text 45.95 (*0-8204-3639-9*) P Lang Pubng.

***Nutrition in a Nutshell: Build Health & Slow Down the Aging Process.** Bonnie Minsky. 164p. 2000. 12.95 (*1-890612-17-0*) Vital Health.

Nutrition in Aging. 4th ed. Schlenker. 2001. 32.25 (*0-07-228812-4*) McGraw.

Nutrition in Arabian Gulf Countries: Malnutrition & Minerals. Ed. by Geoffrey H. Bourne. (World Review of Nutrition & Dietetics Ser.: Vol. 54). (Illus.). xii, 292p. 1987. 226.75 (*3-8055-4682-3*) S Karger.

Nutrition in Cancer & Trauma-Sepsis. Ed. by F. Bozzetti & R. Dionigi. (Illus.). viii, 204p. 1985. pap. 64.50 (*3-8055-3959-2*) S Karger.

Nutrition in Cancer Care: A Quick Reference for Nutritional Oncology. Jeanette M. Dunn & Carole A. Mutzebaugh. Ed. by Brenda Garritson & Lizbeth Adams. (Illus.). viii, 132p. 1997. pap. write for info. (*1-891814-03-6*) Found Care Mgmt.

Nutrition in Catering: Study Guide. Deakin University Press Staff. (C). 1991. pap. 75.00 (*0-7300-1240-9*, SHN 795, Pub. by Deakin Univ) St Mut.

Nutrition in Clinical Care. 2nd ed. Rosanne B. Howard. Ed. by Nancy H. Herbold. (Illus.). 800p. (C). 1982. text 42.95 (*0-07-030514-5*) McGraw.

Nutrition in Clinical Dentistry. 3rd ed. Abraham E. Nizel & Papas. 400p. 1989. pap. text 48.50 (*0-7216-2423-5*, W B Saunders Co) Harcrt Hlth Sci Grp.

Nutrition in Clinical Nursing. Idamarie Laquatra. (Nursing Education Ser.). 1990. pap. 31.50 (*0-8273-3075-8*) Delmar.

Nutrition in Clinical Practice. Marion Nestle. LC 85-60806. 330p. (Orig.). 1986. pap. 19.95 (*0-930010-11-6*) Jones Med.

Nutrition in Clinical Practice: Proceedings of the Congress of the European Society of Parenteral & Enteral Nutrition (ESPEN), Leipzig, August 1988, 10th. Ed. by G. Dietze et al. (Illus.). x, 308p. 1989. 101.75 (*3-8055-4894-X*) S Karger.

Nutrition in Developmental Transition in South-East Asia. C. Gopalan. (SEARO Regional Health Papers: No. 21). xi, 130p. 1992. pap. text 10.00 (*92-9022-190-9*, 1580021) World Health.

Nutrition in Disease & Development. Ed. by Geoffrey H. Bourne. (World Review of Nutrition & Dietetics Ser.: Vol. 39). (Illus.). x, 194p. 1982. 139.25 (*3-8055-3459-0*) S Karger.

Nutrition in Early Childhood & Its Effects in Later Life. Ed. by J. C. Somogyi. (Bibliotheca Nutritio et Dieta Ser.: No. 31). (Illus.). viii, 144p. 1982. pap. 92.25 (*3-8055-3527-9*) S Karger.

Nutrition in Europe. Ed. by Leif Hambraeus. 150p. 1981. text 53.50 (*0-86598-059-4*) Rowman.

Nutrition in Exercise & Sport. 3rd ed. Ira Wolinsky. LC 97-8495. (Nutrition in Exercise & Sport Ser.). 704p. 1997. boxed set 159.95 (*0-8493-8560-1*) CRC Pr.

Nutrition in Exercise & Sports. Ed. by James F. Hickson, Jr. & Ira Wolinsky. 448p. 1989. 110.00 (*0-8493-4759-9*, TX361, CRC Reprint) Franklin.

Nutrition in Exercise & Sports. 2nd ed. Contrib. by Wolinsky. 528p. 1993. lib. bdg. 149.00 (*0-8493-7911-3*, TX361) CRC Pr.

Nutrition in Forest Trees in Plantations. Glyn D. Bowen & E. K. Nambiar. 1985. text 184.00 (*0-12-120980-6*) Acad Pr.

Nutrition in Gastrointestinal Disease. Ed. by Luigi Barbara et al. LC 86-31316. 320p. 1987. reprint ed. pap. 99.20 (*0-608-04685-X*, 206540600004) Bks Demand.

Nutrition in Gastrointestinal Disease. Ed. by Robert C. Kurtz. LC 81-10271. (Contemporary Issues in Clinical Nutrition Ser.: No. 1). 160p. reprint ed. pap. 49.60 (*0-7837-2577-9*, 204273600006) Bks Demand.

Nutrition in General Practice: Giving Advice to Women. Nicola Seabrook. LC 97-24706. 208p. 1997. pap. text 37.50 (*0-7506-3464-2*) Buttrwrth-Heinemann.

Nutrition in Health Maintenance & Health Promotion for Primary Care Providers: A Self-Instructional Module. Yolanda M. Gutierrez. 262p. (Orig.). 1994. pap. 45.00 (*0-943671-10-8*) UCSF Schl Nursing.

Nutrition in Industry, 1946. (I.L.O. Studies & Reports: Nos. 4 & 5). 1974. reprint ed. 60.00 (*0-317-16638-7*) Periodicals Srv.

Nutrition in Infancy & Childhood. 7th ed. Trahms. 2000. 32.25 (*0-07-228813-2*) McGraw.

Nutrition in Kitchen: A Cookbook. Suzzanne N. Myer & Teresa K. Enslin. (Illus.). (Orig.). 1988. pap. 7.95 (*0-317-91385-9*) Cooking Concepts.

Nutrition in Major Metabolic Diseases. Ed. by C. Gopalan & Kamala Krishnaswamy. (Illus.). 252p. 1997. text 29.95 (*0-19-564100-0*) OUP.

Nutrition in Oral Health & Disease. Robert L. Pollack & Edward Kravitz. LC 84-27804. 499p. reprint ed. pap. 154.70 (*0-7837-2739-9*, 204311900006) Bks Demand.

Nutrition in Pediatrics. W. Allan Walker & John B. Watkins. 830p. 1985. 120.00 (*0-316-91831-8*, Little Brwn Med Div) Lppncott W & W.

Nutrition in Pediatrics. 2nd ed. W. Allan Walker & John B. Watkins. LC 97-222636. 850p. 1996. boxed set 99.95 (*1-55009-026-7*) DEKR.

Nutrition in Pregnancy. 7th ed. Worthington. 2000. 32.25 (*0-07-230083-3*) McGraw.

Nutrition in Pregnancy & Growth. Ed. by P. J. Walter & M. Porrini. LC 96-19370. (Bibliotheca Nutritio et Dieta Ser.: No. 53, 1996). (Illus.). viii, 138p. 1996. 160.00 (*3-8055-6300-0*) S Karger.

Nutrition in Preventive Pediatrics. Ed. by R. Di Toro. (Contributions to Infusion Therapy Ser.: Vol. 22). (Illus.). vi, 168p. 1989. 65.25 (*3-8055-4852-4*) S Karger.

Nutrition in Primary Care. David L. Katz. 350p. (Orig.). pap. text 39.95 (*0-683-30638-3*) Lppncott W & W.

Nutrition in Primary Care. Briony Thomas. 256p. (Orig.). 1996. pap. text 34.95 (*0-632-03981-7*) Blackwell Sci.

Nutrition in Public Health: A Handbook for Developing Programs & Services. Mildred Kaufman. LC 90-51. 592p. (C). 1990. 73.00 (*0-8342-0144-5*) Aspen Pub.

Nutrition in Space Flight & Weightlessness Models. Helen W. Lane & Dale A. Schoeller. LC 99-51978. (Modern Nutrition Ser.). 328p. 1999. boxed set 89.95 (*0-8493-8567-9*) CRC Pr.

Nutrition in Sport. Ronald J. Maughan et al. LC 99-12066. (Olympic Encyclopaedia of Sports Medicine Ser.: Vol. VII). (Illus.). 704p. 2000. 125.00 (*0-632-05094-2*) Blackwell Sci.

Nutrition in the Community: A Critical Look at Nutrition. 2nd ed. Ed. by Donald S. McLaren. LC 82-6992. (Wiley-Interscience Publications). 480p. reprint ed. pap. 148.80 (*0-7837-4517-6*, 204429600001) Bks Demand.

Nutrition in the Elderly. Ed. by A. Horwitz et al. (Illus.). 312p. 1989. 75.00 (*0-19-261793-1*) OUP.

Nutrition in the Infant: Practice & Procedures. Ed. by Victor Preedy & Ronald Watson. (Greenwich Medical Media Ser.). (Illus.). 500p. 2000. text 195.00 (*1-900151-62-6*) OUP.

Nutrition in the 90s: Current Controversies & Analysis. Ed. by Gerald E. Gaull et al. (Illus.). 136p. 1991. text 45.00 (*0-8247-8525-8*) Dekker.

Nutrition in the 90s: Current Controversies in Nutrition. Frank N. Kotsonis & M. A. Mackey. Date not set. write for info. (*0-8247-9980-1*) Dekker.

Nutrition in the 90s: Policy Issues. Ed. by Margaret R. Biswas & Madouh Gabr. (Illus.). 220p. (C). 1994. 18.95 (*0-19-563393-8*) OUP.

Nutrition in the 90s Vol. 2: Current Controversies & Analysis. Frank N. Kotsonis & M. MacKey. (Illus.). 192p. 1994. text 45.00 (*0-8247-9212-2*) Dekker.

Nutrition in the Prevention of Disease. Ed. by J. C. Somogyi & S. Hejda. (Bibliotheca Nutritio et Dieta Ser.: No. 44). (Illus.). v, 187p. 1989. 147.00 (*3-8055-4962-8*) S Karger.

An Asterisk (*) at the beginning of an entry indicates that the title is appearing for the first time.

Nutrition in Women's Health. Debra Krummel & Penny M. Kris-Etherton. 608p. 1995. 52.00 (*0-8342-0682-X*) Aspen Pub.

Nutrition in Zimbabwe. Julia Tagwireyi & Ted Greiner. LC 94-16144. (Directions in Development Ser.). 140p. 1994. pap. 22.00 (*0-8213-2731-3*, 12731) World Bank.

Nutrition Issues in Developing Countries: Part I: Diarrheal Diseases, Part II: Diet & Activity During Pregnancy & Lactation, Pts. 1 & 2. Ed. by Subcommittee on Nutrition & Diarrheal Control, Ins. 206p. 1992. pap. text 28.00 (*0-309-04092-2*) Natl Acad Pr.

Nutrition Labeling: Issues & Directions for the 1990s. Institute of Medicine, Committee on the Health Eff. 372p. 1990. pap. 34.95 (*0-309-04326-3*) Natl Acad Pr.

Nutrition Labeling Handbook. Ed. by Ralph Shapiro. LC 95-21838. (Food Science & Technology Ser.: Vol. 69). (Illus.). 712p. 1995. text 225.00 (*0-8247-9285-8*) Dekker.

Nutrition Learning Packages: Joint WHO-UNICEF Nutrition Support Programme. (ENG, FRE & SPA.). vii, 170p. 1989. pap. text 30.00 (*92-4-154251-9*, 1150328) World Health.

Nutrition Lecture Guide. Cynthia L. Gonzalez. 136p. (C). 1997. pap. text, per. 14.95 (*0-7872-3421-4*) Kendall-Hunt.

Nutrition, Lipids & Coronary Heart Disease: A Global View. fac. ed. Ed. by Robert I. Levy et al. LC 78-67020. (Nutrition in Health & Disease Ser.: No. 1). (Illus.). 578p. pap. 179.20 (*0-7837-7529-6*, 204697500005) Bks Demand.

Nutrition, Lipids, Health & Disease. E. Niki & A. S. Ong. 384p. 1995. 95.00 (*0-935315-64-0*) Am Oil Chemists.

Nutrition Made Simple at a Glance. Daphne Jordan-Joseph. LC 98-46921. 1999. write for info. (*1-886433-00-3*) A&B Bks.

Nutrition Management for Food Services. Leslie Cummings. (Food & Hospitality Ser.). 1989. text 44.25 (*0-8273-3522-9*) Delmar.

Nutrition Management for Food Services. Leslie Cummings. (Food & Hospitality Ser.). 1990. pap., teacher ed. 11.95 (*0-8273-3523-7*) Delmar.

Nutrition Management of the Cancer Patient: A Practical Guide for Professionals. Abby S. Bloch. 431p. (C). 1990. text 82.00 (*0-8342-0132-1*) Aspen Pub.

Nutrition Manual for At-Risk Infants & Toddlers. rev. ed. Ed. by Janice H. Cox. LC 96-49613. 248p. 1997. 59.95 (*0-944496-47-4*) Precept Pr.

Nutrition Matters: People, Food & Famine. Helen Young & Susanne Jaspers. LC 96-176128. 144p. (Orig.). 1995. pap. 17.50 (*1-85339-243-X*, Pub. by Intermed Tech) Stylus Pub VA.

Nutrition Model. Jean Carpenter. Ed. by Diane Fusaro. 64p. (J). (gr. 5-8). 1998. pap. text. write for info. (*0-614-22244-3*) Hubbard Sci.

Nutrition Monitoring: Data Serve Many Purposes; Users Recommend Improvements. (Illus.). 62p. (Orig.). (C). 1996. pap. text 20.00 (*0-7881-3247-4*) DIANE Pub.

Nutrition Monitoring: Establishing a Model Program. (Illus.). 88p. (C). 1996. reprint ed. pap. text 20.00 (*0-7881-3370-5*) DIANE Pub.

Nutrition Monitoring: Progress in Developing a Coordinated Program. (Illus.). 51p. (Orig.). (C). 1995. pap. text 30.00 (*0-7881-2215-0*) DIANE Pub.

Nutrition Monitoring in the U. S., Chartbook: Selected Findings from the National Nutrition Monitoring & Related Research Program, No. 1. 1994. lib. bdg. 250.00 (*0-8490-8405-9*) Gordon Pr.

Nutrition Monitoring in the United States Chartbook I: Selected Findings from the National Nutrition Monitoring & Related Research Program. 160p. 1993. per. 12.00 (*0-16-042026-1*) USGPO.

Nutrition, 1996-1997. annuals 8th ed. Charlotte Cook-Fuller & Stephen Barrett. 256p. (C). 1996. text. write for info. (*0-697-31606-8*) Brown & Benchmark.

Nutrition, 98-99. 10th ed. Charlotte Cook-Fuller & Stephen Barrett. (Annual Ser.). (Illus.). 240p. 1998. pap. text 12.25 (*0-697-39176-0*, Dshkn McG-Hill) McGrw-H Hghr Educ.

Nutrition Notes: Musical Nutrition Education to Sing & Color. 3rd rev. ed. Barbara J. Mayfield. (Illus.). 88p. (Orig.). (J). (ps-2). 1997. pap. 17.95 incl. audio (*1-883983-04-5*) Noteworthy Creat.

Nutrition Now. Judith E. Brown. LC 94-42869. 712p. (C). 1995. 49.95 (*0-314-04447-7*) West Pub.

Nutrition Now. 2nd ed. Brown. (Health Sciences Ser.). 1998. 59.95 (*0-534-56439-9*) Wadsworth Pub.

Nutrition Now. 2nd ed. Brown. (Health Sciences Ser.). 1999. pap. text 27.00 (*0-534-76796-6*) Wadsworth Pub.

*__Nutrition Now.__ 3rd ed. Brown. (Health Sciences Ser.). 2001. 43.00 (*0-534-58005-X*) Wadsworth Pub.

Nutrition Nuggets & More: A Companion to Lowfat Lifestyle. Ronda Gates. (Illus.). 256p. (Orig.). 1990. pap. 10.95 (*1-878319-00-0*) Lifestyles Four.

Nutrition of Animals of Agricultural Importance, 2 vols., Set. D. Cuthbertson & H. Sinclair. LC 69-14229. 1969. 629.00 (*0-08-006943-6*, Pub. by Pergamon Repr) Franklin.

Nutrition of Eucalypts. Ed. by P. M. Attiwill & M. A. Adams. (Illus.). 448p. 1996. 150.00 (*0-643-05757-9*, Pub. by CSIRO) Accents Pubns.

Nutrition of Florida Citrus Trees. (Illus.). 61p. 1995. pap. 10.00 (*0-916287-11-4*, SP169) Univ Fla Food.

Nutrition of Fruit Crops: Tropical, Sub-Tropical, Temperate: Tree & Small Fruits. 2nd ed. Ed. by Norman F. Childers et al. LC 66-63534. (Illus.). 904p. 1966. reprint ed. pap. 200.00 (*0-608-04329-X*, 206510900012) Bks Demand.

Nutrition of Goats No. 10. AFRC Technical Committee on Responses to Nutrients. (A CAB International Publication). 136p. 1998. pap. text 40.00 (*0-85199-216-1*) OUP.

Nutrition of Grazing Ruminants in Warm Climates. Ed. by Lee R. McDowell. (Animal Feeding & Nutrition Ser.). 1985. text 125.00 (*0-12-483370-5*) Acad Pr.

Nutrition of Older Adults. write for info. (*0-340-60156-6*, Pub. by E A) Routldge.

Nutrition of Older Adults. Geoffrey P. Webb & June Copeman. (Illus.). 238p. (Orig.). 1996. pap. 39.95 (*1-56593-768-6*, 1494) Singular Publishing.

Nutrition of Pigs & Poultry: Proceedings. Easter School in Agricultural Science (8th 1961, U. Ed. by J. T. Morgan & D. H. Lewis. LC SF0396.G7E3. 387p. reprint ed. pap. 120.00 (*0-608-15033-9*, 202575400046) Bks Demand.

Nutrition of Sows & Boars. Ed. by W. H. Close & D. J. A. Cole. 200p. 1999. 160.00 (*1-897676-53-0*, Pub. by Nottingham Univ Pr) St Mut.

Nutrition of the Chicken. 3rd ed. Malden C. Nesheim et al. 555p. 1982. 32.00 (*0-9602726-2-3*, 76-49249) Scott & Assocs.

Nutrition of the Elderly. Ed. by Hamish Munro & Gunter Schlierf. LC 91-40901. (Nestle Nutrition Workshop Ser.: No. 29). (Illus.). 247p. 1992. reprint ed. pap. 76.60 (*0-608-05806-8*, 205977100007) Bks Demand.

Nutrition of the Low Birthweight Infant. Ed. by Bernard L. Salle & Paul R. Swyer. LC 93-7903. (Nestle Nutrition Workshop Ser.: Vol. 32). 240p. 1993. text 69.00 (*0-7817-0098-1*) Lppncott W & W.

Nutrition of the Rabbit. C. Blas & J. Wiseman. LC 98-7573. 352p. 1999. text 100.00 (*0-85199-279-X*) OUP.

Nutrition of the Turkey. M. L. Scott. (Illus.). 180p. (C). 1987. 15.00 (*0-317-67786-1*) Scott & Assocs.

*__Nutrition of the Very Low Birthweight Infant, Vol. 43.__ Ekhard E. Ziegler et al. LC 99-37293. 288p. 2000. write for info. (*0-7817-2215-2*) Lppncott W & W.

Nutrition Outline. Harry Sitren. 208p. (C). 1995. spiral bd. 30.95 (*0-7872-1064-1*) Kendall-Hunt.

Nutrition Outline. 4th ed. Michael D. Sitren. 244p. (C). 1999. spiral bd. 38.95 (*0-7872-5696-X*, 41569601) Kendall-Hunt.

Nutrition, Physical Activity, & Health in Early Life: Studies in Preschool Children. Jana Parizkova. LC 95-41134. (Nutrition in Exercise & Sport Ser.). 320p. 1996. boxed set 94.95 (*0-8493-7919-9*) CRC Pr.

Nutrition, Physiology & Micro Biology of Plant Cell. Carlo Leifert. 1999. 65.00 (*0-8493-8943-7*) CRC Pr.

Nutrition, Physiology & Obesity. Rachel Schemmel. 240p. 1980. 140.00 (*0-8493-5471-4*, RC628, CRC Reprint) Franklin.

Nutrition Policy for Food-Rich Countries: A Strategic Analysis. Nancy Milio. LC 89-43482. 240p. reprint ed. pap. 74.40 (*0-608-08796-3*, 206943500004) Bks Demand.

Nutrition Policy Implementation: Issues & Experience. Ed. by Nevin S. Schrimshaw & Mitchel B. Wallerstein. (Illus.). 572p. 1982. 110.00 (*0-306-40858-9*, Plenum Trade) Perseus Pubng.

Nutrition Policy in Public Health. Ed. by Felix Bronner. LC 97-3392. (Illus.). 336p. 1997. 52.95 (*0-8261-9660-8*) Springer Pub.

Nutrition Power Talks: Over 1,000 Nutrition Ideas for Health Professionals. Linda Marcoux. (Illus.). 157p. (Orig.). Date not set. pap. write for info. (*0-9633536-0-8*) Hlth TREND.

Nutrition Problems & Programmes in South-East Asia. C. Gopalan. (SEARO Regional Health Papers). 174p. 1987. pap. text 17.00 (*92-9022-184-4*) World Health.

Nutrition Program Representative. Jack Rudman. (Career Examination Ser.: Vol. C-3808). 1997. pap. 29.95 (*0-8373-3808-5*) Nat Learn.

Nutrition Requirements of Man: A Conspectus of Research. Journal of Nutrition Staff & Nutrition Foundation Staff. LC 80-50451. 592p. 1980. 15.00 (*0-685-11736-7*) ILSI.

Nutrition Research: Future Directions & Applications. Ed. by Jonathan E. Fielding & H. I. Frier. LC 91-18292. (Illus.). 127p. 1991. reprint ed. pap. 39.40 (*0-608-05851-3*, 205981800007) Bks Demand.

Nutrition Research & the Elderly Vol. 52, No. 8, Pt. 2: U. S. Administration on Aging Symposium (Washington, D. C.) 183p. 1994. pap. 20.00 (*0-614-22650-3*) ILSI.

Nutrition Research & the Elderly II Vol. 54, No. 1, Pt. 2: Nutrition in Long-Term Care: U. S. Administration on Aging Symposium (Washington, D. C.) 65p. 1996. pap. 20.00 (*0-614-22653-8*) ILSI.

Nutrition Research in South-East Asia: The Emerging Agenda of the Future. C. Gopalan. (WHO Regional Publications: No. 23). 1994. pap. text 15.00 (*92-9022-166-6*, 1560023) World Health.

Nutrition Screening, Assessment, & Guidance During Pregnancy. Carolyn O. Sharbaugh & Carol W. Suitor. LC 93-49497. (Maternal Nutrition Ser.: No. 7). 1994. write for info. (*0-86525-043-X*) March of Dimes.

Nutrition Second Metabolism in Pregnancy: Mother & Fetus. Pedro Rosso. (Illus.). 336p. 1990. text 59.95 (*0-19-503928-9*) OUP.

Nutrition Secrets: Questions You Will Be Asked in the Clinic, at the Bedside, on Exams. Charles W. Van Way. LC 98-21357. (Secrets Ser.). 1998. 35.00 (*1-56053-206-8*) Hanley & Belfus.

Nutrition Secrets for Optimal Health. Betsey Kurleto & Beverly Price. LC 96-61269. 1996. pap. 19.95 (*0-9654080-0-0*) Tall Tree Pubng.

Nutrition Secrets of the Ancients: Foods & Recipes for Optimum Health in the New Millenium. Gene F. Spiller & Rowena Hubbard. LC 95-42384. 416p. 1996. 22.95 (*0-7615-0340-4*) Prima Pub.

Nutrition Secrets of the Ancients: Foods & Recipes for Optimum Health in the New Millennium. Gene F. Spiller. 416p. 1997. per. 16.00 (*0-7615-0999-2*) Prima Pub.

Nutrition Secrets of the Ancients: Foods & Recipes for Optimum Health in the New Millennium. Gene Spiller & Rowena Hubbard. (Illus.). 402p. 1998. text 23.00 (*0-7881-5425-7*) DIANE Pub.

Nutrition Services Consultant. Jack Rudman. (Career Examination Ser.: C-2836). 1994. pap. 34.95 (*0-8373-2836-5*) Nat Learn.

Nutrition Services in Perinatal Care. National Research Council (U. S.), Committee on Bi. LC RG0559.N86. 82p. reprint ed. pap. 30.00 (*0-8357-7702-2*, 203605600002) Bks Demand.

Nutrition Services in Perinatal Care. 2nd ed. Institute of Medicine, Food & Nutrition Board Staff. 128p. (C). 1992. pap. text 19.00 (*0-309-04694-7*) Natl Acad Pr.

Nutrition Services Supervisor. Jack Rudman. (Career Examination Ser.: C-1384). 1994. pap. 29.95 (*0-8373-1384-8*) Nat Learn.

Nutrition Society, 1941-1991: Presidents & Honorary Members - Their Stories & Recollections. Ed. by Elsie M. Widdowson. 140p. (Orig.). 1991. pap. text 40.00 (*0-85198-716-8*) OUP.

Nutrition, Stress & Aging: An Holistic Approach. Donald R. Morse & Robert L. Pollack. LC 87-45805. (Stress in Modern Society Ser.: No. 17). 1988. 32.50 (*0-404-63268-8*) AMS Pr.

Nutrition Support: Theory & Therapeutics. Scott A. Shikora & George L. Blackburn. LC 96-28658. (Clinical Nutrition Ser.). 598p. 1997. 79.00 (*0-412-06681-5*) Kluwer Academic.

Nutrition Support Dietetics Core Curriculum, 1993. 2nd ed. Ed. by Eva P. Shronts et al. (Illus.). 515p. (Orig.). 1993. reprint ed. pap. text 70.00 (*1-889622-00-1*, 343) Am Soc Parenteral.

Nutrition Support Handbook. Laura E. Matarese et al. (Illus.). 111p. (Orig.). 1997. 20.00 (*0-9615424-5-4*) Cleveland Clinic.

Nutrition Support in the Critically Ill: A Handbook. Alexa Scott et al. 250p. 1997. 34.95 (*1-56593-874-7*, 1712) Singular Publishing.

Nutrition Support Nursing Core Curriculum. 3rd rev. ed. Ed. by Kathryn A. Hennessy & Marsha E. Orr. (Illus.). 412p. (Orig.). 1996. pap. text 90.00 (*1-889622-02-8*, 306) Am Soc Parenteral.

Nutrition Support Policies, Procedures, Forms & Formulas. Annalynn Skipper. 500p. 1995. ring bd. 135.00 (*0-8342-0716-8*) Aspen Pub.

*__Nutrition Support to Elderly Women: Influence on Diet Quality.__ Michelle B. Pierce. LC 99-55080. (Studies on the Elderly in America). 2000. write for info. (*0-8153-3812-0*) Garland.

Nutrition Survival Kit: A Wholefoods Recipe & Reference Guide. Kathy Dinaburg & D'Ann Akel. LC 76-28772. (Illus.). 256p. (C). 1976. 16.95 (*0-915572-18-4*); pap. 7.95 (*0-915572-17-6*) Panjandrum.

Nutrition, the Environment & the Food Chain: Who's Kidding Who . . . ? rev. ed. Eddy H. Pevovar. (Therapeutic Nutrition Ser.). (Illus.). 200p. (Orig.). 1995. pap. text 350.00 (*0-9645077-1-4*, 001-95); lib. bdg. 380.00 (*0-9645077-2-2*, 001-95) Nutr Res Proj.

Nutrition, the Environment & the Food Chain: Who's Kidding Who . . . ? rev. ed. Eddy H. Pevovar. (Therapeutic Nutrition Ser.: Vol. 1). (Illus.). 200p. (Orig.). 1995. pap. text 350.00 (*0-9645077-0-6*, 001-95) Nutr Res Proj.

Nutrition Therapy: Advanced Counseling Skills. Ed. by Kathy K. Helm. (Illus.). 256p. (Orig.). (C). 1995. pap., wbk. ed. 14.95 (*0-9631033-3-4*); pap. text, student ed. 65.00 (*0-9631033-2-6*) Helm Seminars.

Nutrition Therapy: Advanced Counseling Skills. Ed. by Kathy K. Helm & Bridget Klawitter. (Illus.). 256p. (Orig.). (C). 1995. pap. 39.95 (*0-9631033-1-8*) Helm Seminars.

Nutrition Through the Life Cycle: Case Studies for the Dietary Manager. Litchford. 136p. 1997. spiral bd. 21.00 (*0-7872-3604-7*) Kendall-Hunt.

Nutrition Through the Lifecycle I: User's Guide. Mary D. Litchford et al. 1994. 139.00 (*1-880989-30-1*); 139.00 (*1-880989-31-X*); 139.00 (*1-880989-32-8*); 139.00 (*1-880989-33-6*); pap., teacher ed. 6.00 (*1-880989-35-2*) Case Sftware.

Nutrition Through the Lifecycle I: User's Guide. Mary D. Litchford et al. (C). 1997. pap., student ed. 7.00 (*1-880989-34-4*) Case Sftware.

Nutrition Through the Lifecycle II. Mary D. Litchford et al. 1995. 139.00 (*1-880989-46-8*); 139.00 (*1-880989-47-6*); 139.00 (*1-880989-48-4*); 139.00 (*1-880989-49-2*) Case Sftware.

Nutrition Through the Lifecycle II. Mary D. Litchford et al. (C). 1995. pap., student ed. 7.00 (*1-880989-50-6*) Case Sftware.

Nutrition Throughout the Lifecycle. 4th ed. Worthington. LC 99-26466. 464p. 1999. pap. 61.25 (*0-07-292732-1*) McGraw.

Nutrition Throughout the Lifecycle. 5th ed. Roberts. 2002. 48.00 (*0-07-231615-2*) McGraw.

Nutrition, Toxicity & Cancer. Ian R. Rowland. 464p. 1991. lib. bdg. 159.00 (*0-8493-8812-0*, QP141) CRC Pr.

Nutrition, Toxicity & Cancer. Ian R. Rowland. 450p. 1990. 62.50 (*0-936923-47-4*) Telford Pr.

Nutrition 21st Century. William L. Kyle. 312p. 1995. pap. 12.95 (*0-9662880-0-9*) Kyle Pub.

Nutrition Two-Thousand, 2 vols., Set. Ed. by John A. Weyl. (Illus.). 824p. (Orig.). 1992. pap. 69.90 (*0-9623293-9-8*) Pacific Odyssey.

Nutrition Two-Thousand, Vol. 1. Ed. by John A. Weyl. (Illus.). 609p. (Orig.). 1992. pap. 39.95 (*0-9623293-5-5*) Pacific Odyssey.

Nutrition Two-Thousand, Vol. 2. Ed. by John A. Weyl. (Illus.). 215p. (Orig.). 1992. pap. 29.95 (*0-9623293-6-3*) Pacific Odyssey.

Nutrition Unit 1 & 2, Unit 1&2. Brown. Date not set. write for info. (*0-314-06266-1*) West Pub.

Nutrition Unit Twelve, Unit 12. Brown. Date not set. 2.75 (*0-314-06276-9*) West Pub.

Nutrition Workbook. 11th ed. Lane. 1992. pap. 11.96 (*0-314-01328-8*) Wadsworth Pub.

Nutrition Workshop Guide. rev. ed. Eriann Hullquist. (Illus.). 32p. (Orig.). 1995. 1.50 (*0-945383-38-X*, 945-5831) Teach Servs.

Nutrition 1996/97. 8th annot. ed. Cook & Fuller. 1996. teacher ed. (*0-697-31607-6*, WCB McGr Hill) McGrw-H Hghr Educ.

Nutrition 94 & 95. 6th ed. Cook-Fuller Barrett. 1993. 12.74 (*1-56134-256-4*) McGraw.

Nutritional Abnormalities in Infectious Diseases: Effects on Tuberculosis & AIDS. Ed. by Christopher E. Taylor. LC 96-51894. (Journal of Nutritional Immunology Monograph Ser.: Vol. 5, No. 1). 58p. (C). 1997. 17.95 (*0-7890-0019-9*) Haworth Pr.

Nutritional Adaptation of the Gastrointestinal Tract of the Newborn. Ed. by Norman Kretchmer & Alexandre Minkowski. LC 83-48665. (Nestle Nutrition Workshop Ser.: No. 3). (Illus.). 244p. 1983. reprint ed. pap. 75.70 (*0-608-00626-2*, 206121300007) Bks Demand.

Nutritional Adaptation to New Life Styles. Ed. by J. C. Somogyi & E. H. Koskinen. (Bibliotheca Nutritio et Dieta Ser.: No. 45). (Illus.). viii, 220p. 1990. 182.75 (*3-8055-5183-5*) S Karger.

Nutritional Anaemias: Proceedings of the WHO Scientific Group, Geneva, 1967. WHO Staff. (Technical Reports: No. 405). 1968. pap. text 5.00 (*92-4-120405-2*, 1100405) World Health.

Nutritional & Acid-Base Aspects of Amino Acid Metabolism: 7th International Ammoniagenesis Workshop, Galway, May 1996. Ed. by Daniel J. O'Donovan. LC 97-23206. (Contributions to Nephrology Ser.: Vol. 121, 1997). (Illus.). x, 172p. 1997. 198.25 (*3-8055-6490-2*) S Karger.

Nutritional & Environmental Influences on the Eye. Allen Taylor. LC 98-49170. (Modern Nutrition Ser.). 304p. 1999. boxed set 129.95 (*0-8493-8565-2*) CRC Pr.

Nutritional & Health Aspects of Sugars: Evaluation of New Findings. LC 95-232372. (Concise Monographs). (Illus.). 23p. 1995. pap. 12.50 (*0-944398-65-0*, 398650) ILSI.

Nutritional & Pharmacological Strategies in Chronic Renal Failure. Ed. by A. Albertazzi et al. (Contributions to Nephrology Ser.: Vol. 81). (Illus.). x, 290p. 1991. 29.75 (*3-8055-5189-4*) S Karger.

Nutritional & Safety Aspects of Food Processing. Ed. by Steven R. Tannenbaum. LC 78-31276. (Food Science Ser.: No. 6). (Illus.). 464p. 1979. reprint ed. pap. 143.90 (*0-608-00205-4*, 206098800006) Bks Demand.

Nutritional & Toxicological Aspects of Food Processing. Ed. by R. Walker & E. Quadrucci. 300p. 1988. 126.00 (*0-85066-417-9*) Taylor & Francis.

Nutritional & Toxicological Consequences of Food Processing. Ed. by M. Friedman. (Advances in Experimental Medicine & Biology Ser.: Vol. 289). (Illus.). 552p. (C). 1991. text 174.00 (*0-306-43891-7*, Kluwer Plenum) Kluwer Academic.

Nutritional & Toxicological Significance of Enzyme Inhibitors in Foods. Ed. by Mendel Friedman. LC 86-15151. (Advances in Experimental Medicine & Biology Ser.: Vol. 199). 584p. 1986. 125.00 (*0-306-42368-5*, Plenum Trade) Perseus Pubng.

Nutritional Anemias. LC 92-10892. (Nestle Nutrition Workshop Ser.: Vol. 30). (Illus.). 232p. 1992. reprint ed. pap. 72.00 (*0-608-07261-3*, 206748900009) Bks Demand.

*__Nutritional Anthropology: Biocultural Perspectives on Food & Nutrition.__ Alan H. Goodman et al. LC 99-16016. viii, 392p. 1999. pap. text 42.95 (*1-55934-074-6*) Mayfield Pub.

*__Nutritional Applications in Exercise & Sport.__ Ira Wolinsky & Judy A. Driskell. LC 00-42904. (Nutrition in Exercise & Sport Ser.). (Illus.). 2000. write for info. (*0-8493-8199-1*) CRC Pr.

Nutritional Approaches to Aging Research. Gairdner B. Moment. 280p. 1982. 157.00 (*0-8493-5831-0*, QP86, CRC Reprint) Franklin.

Nutritional Aspects of Aging, 2 vols., Vol. I. Linda H. Chen. LC 85-9720. 336p. 1986. 171.00 (*0-8493-5737-3*, QP86, CRC Reprint) Franklin.

Nutritional Aspects of Aging, 2 vols., Vol. II. Linda H. Chen. LC 85-9720. 288p. 1986. 144.00 (*0-8493-5738-1*, QP86, CRC Reprint) Franklin.

Nutritional Aspects of Fats. Ed. by J. C. Somogyi. (Bibliotheca Nutritio et Dieta Ser.: No. 25). (Illus.). 230p. 1977. 95.75 (*3-8055-2655-5*) S Karger.

Nutritional Aspects of Human Physical & Athletic Performance. 2nd ed. Melvin H. Williams. (Illus.). 576p. 1985. pap. 68.95 (*0-398-06499-7*) C C Thomas.

Nutritional Aspects of Human Physical & Athletic Performance. 2nd ed. Melvin H. Williams. (Illus.). 576p. (C). 1985. 94.95 (*0-398-05060-0*) C C Thomas.

Nutritional Aspects of Osteoporosis. Ed. by P. Burckhardt et al. LC 98-13311. (Serono Symposia, U. S. A. Ser.). (Illus.). 296p. 1998. 135.00 (*0-387-98494-1*) Spr-Verlag.

Nutritional Aspects of Physical Performance. Ed. by J. C. Somogyi. (Bibliotheca Nutritio et Dieta Ser.: No. 27). (Illus.). 1979. pap. 66.50 (*3-8055-2913-9*) S Karger.

*__Nutritional Assessment.__ 3rd ed. Lee. 2001. 18.74 (*0-07-292731-3*) McGraw.

Nutritional Assessment: A Laboratory Manual. Rosalind S. Gibson. (Illus.). 208p. (C). 1993. spiral bd., lab manual ed. 37.95 (*0-19-508547-7*) OUP.

Nutritional Assessment & Support. Anne Grant & Susan DeHoog. (Illus.). 400p. (C). 1991. pap. text 30.00 (*0-9627678-0-8*) Grant-DeHoog.

Nutritional Assessment & Support: A Primer. 2nd ed. Carey P. Page & Thomas C. Hardin. (Illus.). 256p. (Orig.). 1994. pap. 19.00 (*0-683-06705-2*) Lppncott W & W.

N

An Asterisk (*) at the beginning of an entry indicates that the title is appearing for the first time.

Nutritional Assessment in Health Programs. Ed. by George Christakos. LC 74-120960. 90p. 1973. 7.50 (0-87553-116-4, 070) Am Pub Health.

Nutritional Assessment in Malnutrition & Stress. Mary D. Litchford et al. 1994. 139.00 (1-880989-36-0); 139.00 (1-880989-37-9); 139.00 (1-880989-38-7); 139.00 (1-880989-39-5) Case Sftware.

Nutritional Assessment in Malnutrition & Stress. Mary D. Litchford et al. (C). 1994. pap. 6.00 (1-880989-44-1) Case Sftware.

Nutritional Assessment of Elderly Populations: Measure & Function. Ed. by Irwin H. Rosenberg et al. LC 94-26017. (Bristol-Myer Squibb/Mead Johnson Nutrition Symposia Ser.: No. 13). (Illus.). 335p. 1995. reprint ed. pap. 103.90 (0-608-05802-5, 205976700007) Bks Demand.

Nutritional Assessment of Elderly Populations: Measure & Function: Proceedings of the 13th Annual Bristol-Myers Squibb/Mead Johnson Symposium on Nutrition Research, Held in Boston on Oct. 11-13, 1993, No. 13. Ed. by Irwin H. Rosenberg. LC 94-26017. (Bristol-Meyers Squibb-Mead Johnson Nutrition Symposia Ser.: Vol. 13). 336p. 1995. 65.00 (0-7817-0232-1) Random.

Nutritional Assessment of Malnutrition & Stress User's Manual. Mary D. Litchford et al. (C). 1994. pap. 7.00 (1-880989-20-4) Case Sftware.

Nutritional Balancing & Hair Mineral Analysis. 2nd rev. ed. Lawrence D. Wilson. LC 98-90604. (Illus.). 400p. 1998. pap. 24.95 (0-9628657-4-5) L D Wilson Cnstls.

Nutritional Bioavailability of Calcium. Ed. by Constance V. Kies. LC 85-3931. (ACS Symposium Ser.: No. 275). (Illus.). 208p. 1985. reprint ed. pap. 64.50 (0-608-03265-4, 206378400007) Bks Demand.

Nutritional Bioavailability of Iron. Ed. by Constance V. Kies. LC 82-16391. (ACS Symposium Ser.: No. 203). 204p. 1982. lib. bdg. 34.95 (0-8412-0746-1) Am Chemical.

Nutritional Bioavailability of Iron. Ed. by Constance V. Kies. LC 82-16391. (ACS Symposium Ser.: No. 203). (Illus.). 215p. 1982. reprint ed. pap. 66.70 (0-608-03216-6, 206373500007) Bks Demand.

Nutritional Bioavailability of Manganese. Ed. by Constance V. Kies. LC 87-19553. (ACS Symposium Ser.: No. 354). (Illus.). ix, 155p. 1987. 39.95 (0-8412-1433-6) Am Chemical.

Nutritional Bioavailability of Manganese. Ed. by Constance V. Kies. LC 87-19553. (ACS Symposium Ser.: Vol. 354). 168p. 1987. reprint ed. pap. 52.10 (0-608-03877-6, 206432400008) Bks Demand.

Nutritional Bioavailability of Zinc. Ed. by George E. Inglett. LC 82-22706. (ACS Symposium Ser.: No. 210). 280p. 1983. lib. bdg. 39.95 (0-8412-0760-7) Am Chemical.

N

Nutritional Bioavailability of Zinc: Based on a Symposium. Ed. by George E. Inglett. LC 82-22706. (ACS Symposium Ser.: No. 210). (Illus.). 290p. 1983. reprint ed. pap. 89.90 (0-608-04334-6, 206511400001) Bks Demand.

Nutritional Biochemistry. Tom Brody. (Food Science & Technology Ser.). (Illus.). 658p. 1994. text 83.00 (0-12-134835-0) Acad Pr.

Nutritional Biochemistry. 2nd ed. Tom Brody. LC 98-40384. (Illus.). 1006p. (C). 1998. text 79.95 (0-12-134836-9) Acad Pr.

Nutritional Biochemistry of the Vitamins. David A. Bender. (Illus.). 451p. (C). 1992. text 105.00 (0-521-38144-4) Cambridge U Pr.

Nutritional Care & the HIV Positive Persons: A Manual for Individuals & Their Caregivers. James F. Hickson Jr. 208p. 1995. boxed set 74.95 (0-8493-7843-5) CRC Pr.

***Nutritional Care for High-Risk Newborns.** Sharon Groh-Wargo. (Illus.). 2000. 79.95 (1-56625-133-8) Bonus Books.

Nutritional Care for Older People: A Handbook. June Copeman. 160p. pap. 45.00 (0-86242-284-1, Pub. by Age Concern Eng) St Mut.

Nutritional Care of the Terminally Ill. Charlette R. Gallagher-Allred. LC 89-381. 304p. (C). 1989. 59.00 (0-8342-0060-0) Aspen Pub.

Nutritional Cereal Counter. Paul J. Montgomery. (Illus.). 102p. (Orig.). (YA). (gr. 9 up). 1998. pap. 3.50 (0-9621865-1-1) Prod Info Analysis.

Nutritional Communications in Vitamin A Programs. International Vitamin A Consultative Group Staff. (Illus.). 124p. 1992. pap. 3.50 (0-944398-08-1) ILSI.

Nutritional Concerns for Women. Ed. by Ira Wolinsky et al. LC 95-42174. (Modern Nutrition Ser.). 352p. 1996. boxed set 69.95 (0-8493-8502-4) CRC Pr.

Nutritional Concerns Quarterly. (C). 1994. 223.75 (0-03-009364-3) Harcourt Coll Pubs.

Nutritional Conditions (Good, Bad & Diseased) Found in the Health of Americans: Index of Authors & Subjects. Onetta L. Stafford. 180p. 1993. 47.50 (1-55914-944-2); pap. 44.50 (1-55914-945-0) ABBE Pubs Assn.

Nutritional Considerations in a Changing World. Ed. by Geoffrey H. Bourne. (World Review of Nutrition & Dietetics Ser.: Vol. 44). (Illus.). x, 218p. 1984. 143.50 (3-8055-3837-5) S Karger.

Nutritional Cooking with Tofu. 2nd rev. ed. Christine Liu. LC 83-32385. (Illus.). 168p. 1992. pap. 12.95 (0-9610566-8-1) Graphique Pubs.

***Nutritional Cost of Prescription Drugs.** Ross Pelton. Ed. by James B. Lavalle. 262p. 2000. pap. 14.95 (0-89582-548-1) Morton Pub.

Nutritional Defects, Deficiency & Diseases in Local & Global Populations: Index of New Information & Research Reference Book. Nelson M. Ferris. 150p. 1996. 47.50 (0-7883-1168-9); pap. 44.50 (0-7883-1169-7) ABBE Pubs Assn.

Nutritional Deficiencies in Industrialized Countries. Ed. by J. C. Somogyi & G. Varela. (Bibliotheca Nutritio et Dieta Ser.: Vol. 30). (Illus.). viii, 172p. 1981. 111.50 (3-8055-1994-X) S Karger.

Nutritional Diseases. Jon Zonderman & Laurel Shader. (Bodies in Crisis Ser.). (Illus.). 64p. (J). (gr. 5-8). 1995. lib. bdg. 18.90 (0-8050-2601-0) TFC Bks NY.

Nutritional Disorders & Requirements. Ed. by Geoffrey H. Bourne. (World Review of Nutrition & Dietetics Ser.: Vol. 50). (Illus.). xii, 272p. 1987. 208.75 (3-8055-4506-1) S Karger.

Nutritional Disorders of American Women. Ed. by Myron Winick. LC 76-54393. (Current Concepts in Nutrition Ser.: Vol. 5). 190p. reprint ed. pap. 58.90 (0-608-30491-3, 205527600012) Bks Demand.

Nutritional Disorders of Grain Sorghum. N. J. Grundon et al. (Illus.). 99p. (Orig.). 1986. pap. 69.00 (0-949511-33-1) St Mut.

Nutritional Ecology of the Ruminant. 2nd ed. Peter J. Van Soest. LC 94-7001. (Comstock Bk.). (Illus.). 488p. 1994. text 69.50 (0-8014-2772-X) Cornell U Pr.

Nutritional Education Materials & Audiovisuals for Grades Preschool Through 6. Shirley K. Evans. (Illus.). 68p. (Orig.). (C). 1996. pap. text 25.00 (0-7881-3153-2) DIANE Pub.

Nutritional Energetics. Leonard S. Bull. 1999. 60.00 (0-8493-8750-7) CRC Pr.

Nutritional Energetics of Domestic Animals & Glossary of Energy Terms. 2nd rev. ed. National Research Council Staff. LC 80-28912. 60p. (Orig.). reprint ed. pap. 30.00 (0-8357-4998-3, 203793100009) Bks Demand.

Nutritional Engineering: How to Keep Your Bad Habits & Still Avoid Flame-Out. David A. Keiper. LC 85-17605. (Illus.). 184p. 1988. 24.95 (0-931375-21-5) Hinsdale Pr.

Nutritional Epidemiology. 2nd ed. Walter Willett. (Monographs in Epidemiology & Biostatistics: Vol. 30). (Illus.). 528p. 1998. text 67.50 (0-19-512297-6) OUP.

Nutritional Epidemiology: Possibilities & Limitations. (Concise Monographs). (Illus.). 28p. 1996. pap. 12.50 (0-944398-87-1, 398871) ILSI.

Nutritional Guide. 2nd ed. Louise Tenney. 260p. 1998. pap. text 14.95 (1-885670-87-7) Woodland UT.

Nutritional Guide for the Problem Drinker. Ruth Guenther. (Good Health Guide Ser.). 32p. (Orig.). 1983. pap. 2.50 (0-87983-295-9, 32959K, Keats Publng) NTC Contemp Pub Co.

Nutritional Guide with Food Combining. Louise Tenney. 237p. (Orig.). 1991. pap. 14.95 (0-913923-90-7) Woodland UT.

Nutritional Guidelines for Correcting Behavior. rev. ed. Barbara Reed. 1984. pap. 10.00 (0-939956-07-1) Natural Pr.

Nutritional Healing. Denise Mortimore. LC 98-20386. (In a Nutshell Ser.). (Illus.). 64p. 1998. 7.95 (1-86204-245-4, Pub. by Element MA) Penguin Putnam.

Nutritional Healing: A Complete Guide to Vitamins, Minerals, Food Supplements & Herbs for over Two Hundred Common Ailments & Disorders. 1991. lib. bdg. 79.95 (0-8490-5121-5) Gordon Pr.

***Nutritional Healing: Body, Mind, & Spirit.** Douglas Wyeth Morrison. 300p. 2001. pap. 27.50 (1-55643-362-X) North Atlantic.

***Nutritional Healing Premium One.** 1999. 9.95 (0-13-018393-8) P-H.

Nutritional Healing with Color: Includes Diets & Recipes for Optimum Health. Suzy Chiazzari. LC 98-52358. (Illus.). 208p. 1999. pap. 16.95 (1-86204-393-0, Pub. by Element MA) Penguin Putnam.

Nutritional Health Bible. Linda Lazarides. 336p. 1998. pap. 16.00 (0-7225-3424-8) Thorsons PA.

***Nutritional Health Premium Two.** 1999. 9.95 (0-13-018394-6) P-H.

Nutritional, Herbal, & Homeopathic Guide to Healing. Ra Un Nefer Amen I. 52p. (Orig.). 1988. pap. 6.00 (0-317-93992-0) Kamit Pubns.

Nutritional Herbology: A Reference Guide to Herbs. rev. ed. Mark Pedersen. LC 94-60830. 336p. 1994. pap. text 19.95 (1-885653-03-4) W W Whitman.

Nutritional Herbology: A Reference Guide to Herbs. 3rd rev. ed. Mark Pedersen. 352p. 1998. pap. 21.95 (1-885653-07-7) W W Whitman.

Nutritional Immunology. Jau-Fei Chen. Ed. by Taig D. Stewart et al. Date not set. pap. 9.95 (0-9651025-0-5) Bright Ideas Pr.

Nutritional Impact of Food Processing: Symposium Nutritional Impact of Food Processing, Reykjavik, September, 1987. Ed. by J. C. Somogyi. (Bibliotheca Nutritio et Dieta Ser.: No. 43). (Illus.). viii, 344p. 1989. 252.25 (3-8055-4848-6) S Karger.

***Nutritional Implications of Macronutrient Substitutes.** G. Harvey Anderson. 1999. pap. text 24.95 (0-8018-6212-4) Johns Hopkins.

Nutritional Implications of Macronutrient Substitutes. G. Harvey Anderson et al. LC 97-19405. (Annals of the New York Academy of Sciences Ser.: Vol. 819). 1997. pap. 95.00 (1-57331-085-9) NY Acad Sci.

Nutritional Implications of Macronutrient Substitutes, Vol. 819. Ed. by G. Harvey Anderson et al. LC 97-19405. 1997. 95.00 (1-57331-084-0) NY Acad Sci.

Nutritional Influences on Illness: A Sourcebook of Clinical Research. Melvin R. Werbach. 508p. 1990. pap. 24.95 (0-87983-531-1, 35311K, Keats Publng) NTC Contemp Pub Co.

Nutritional Influences on Illness: A Sourcebook of Clinical Research. 2nd ed. Melvyn R. Werbach. 700p. 1993. text 64.95 (0-9618550-3-7) Third Line Pr.

Nutritional Influences on Illness: A Sourcebook of Clinical Research. 2nd ed. Melvyn R. Werbach. LC 96-60020. 700p. 1996. pap. text 37.95 (0-9618550-5-3) Third Line Pr.

Nutritional Influences on Mental Illness: A Sourcebook of Clinical Research. Melvyn R. Werbach. LC 91-65076. 360p. 1991. text 39.95 (0-9618550-1-0) Third Line Pr.

Nutritional Influences on Mental Illness: A Sourcebook of Clinical Research. 2nd ed. Melvyn R. Werbach. LC 99-70757. 454p. 1999. text 59.99 (0-9618550-8-8) Third Line Pr.

Nutritional Intervention in the Aging Process. Ed. by H. J. Armbrecht et al. (Illus.). 330p. 1984. 87.00 (0-387-96025-2) Spr-Verlag.

***Nutritional Leverage for Great Golf.** Nina Anderson et al. Ed. by Neil Orenstein. LC 99-72917. 152p. (Orig.). 1999. pap. 9.95 (1-884820-53-0) ATN Grp Pub.

***Nutritional Lifestyles 4-Copy Slipcase.** 1999. 29.95 (1-86204-565-8, Pub. by Element MA) Penguin Putnam.

Nutritional Management of Genetic Disorders. Ed. by Myron Winick. LC 79-16192. (Current Concepts in Nutrition Ser.: Vol. 8). 245p. reprint ed. pap. 76.00 (0-608-30853-6, 205560400029) Bks Demand.

***Nutritional Management of Inflammatory Disorders: Assessing Toxic Susceptibility - Improving Glycemic Balance.** (Illus.). 128p. 1998. pap. 45.00 (0-9624859-2-6) HealthComm Intl.

Nutritional Management of Renal Disease. Ed. by Joel D. Kopple & Shaul G. Massry. LC 96-17372. (Illus.). 929p. 1997. 99.00 (0-683-04740-X) Lppncott W & W.

Nutritional Medicine: The Drug-Free Guide to Better Family Health. Stephen Davies & Alan Stewart. 640p. (Orig.). 1990. pap. 12.95 (0-380-70733-0, Avon Bks) Morrow Avon.

Nutritional Medicine: The Drug-Free Guide to Better Family Health. Stephen Davies & Alan Stewart. Ed. by Andrew Stanway. 543p. (Orig.). 1987. pap. 24.00 (0-330-28833-4, Pub. by Pan) Trans-Atl Phila.

Nutritional Methods of Blood Regeneration. Raymond W. Bernard. 1996. spiral bd. 14.00 (0-7873-1011-5) Hlth Research.

Nutritional Methods of Intestinal Regeneration, Pts. I & II. Raymond W. Bernard. 1996. spiral bd. 14.00 (0-7873-1010-7) Hlth Research.

Nutritional Needs & Assessment of Normal Growth. Ed. by Michael Gracey & Frank Falkner. LC 84-27526. (Nestle Nutrition Workshop Ser.: No. 7). (Illus.). 240p. 1985. reprint ed. pap. 74.40 (0-608-00652-1, 206124000007) Bks Demand.

Nutritional Needs in Cold & High-Altitude Environments: Applications for Military Personnel in Field Operations. Institute of Medicine, Military Nutrition Research. Ed. by Bernadette M. Marriott et al. 568p. (Orig.). 1996. pap. text 39.00 (0-309-05484-2) Natl Acad Pr.

Nutritional Needs in Hot Environments: Applications for Military Personnel in Field Operations. Institute of Medicine Staff. Ed. by Bernadette M. Mariott. 392p. (Orig.). (C). 1993. pap. text 39.00 (0-309-04840-0) Natl Acad Pr.

Nutritional Needs of Athletes. Fred Brouns. LC 93-11818. 174p. 1994. 75.00 (0-471-94079-8) Wiley.

Nutritional Needs of the Preterm Infant. Ed. by Reginald C. Tsang et al. LC 92-49242. (Illus.). 450p. 1993. 55.00 (0-683-08425-9) Lppncott W & W.

Nutritional Needs of the Six to Twelve Month Old Infant. Ed. by William C. Heird. LC 91-10416. (Carnation Nutrition Education Ser.: No. 2). (Illus.). 352p. reprint ed. pap. 109.20 (0-608-05814-9, 205977900007) Bks Demand.

Nutritional Oncology. Ed. by David Heber et al. LC 98-86561. xix, 632 p. (C). 1998. text 149.95 (0-12-335960-0) Acad Pr.

Nutritional Outline for the Professional & the Wise Man. 7th rev. ed. James F. Balch, Jr. & Phyllis Balch. 329p. 1987. pap. 21.95 (0-942023-25-0) P A B Bks.

Nutritional Pathobiology. Ed. by E. Bajusz & C. Jasmin. (Methods & Achievements in Experimental Pathology Ser.: Vol. 6). (Illus.). 1972. 104.50 (3-8055-1343-7) S Karger.

Nutritional Pathology: Pathobiochemistry of Dietary Imbalances. Herschel Sidransky. (Biochemistry of Disease Ser.: Vol. 10). (Illus.). 416p. 1985. text 189.50 (0-8247-7303-9) Dekker.

Nutritional Physiology of Minerals. Richard C. Ewan. 1999. 65.00 (0-8493-8752-3) CRC Pr.

Nutritional Physiology of Vitamins. Ewan. 1994. write for info. (0-8493-8753-1) CRC Pr.

Nutritional Planning in India. Rajaram Dasgupta. (C). 1989. 27.50 (81-7013-049-2, Pub. by Navarang) S Asia.

Nutritional Problems & Education: Selected Topics. Ed. by Geoffrey H. Bourne. (World Review of Nutrition & Dietetics Ser.: Vol. 47). (Illus.). xii, 208p. 1986. 161.00 (3-8055-4214-3) S Karger.

Nutritional Problems of the Elderly. Ed. by J. C. Somogyi & F. Fidanza. (Bibliotheca Nutritio et Dieta Ser.: No. 33). (Illus.). viii, 200p. 1983. pap. 138.50 (3-8055-3700-X) S Karger.

Nutritional, Psychological & Social Aspects of Obesity. Ed. by J. C. Somogyi. (Bibliotheca Nutritio et Dieta Ser.: No. 26). (Illus.). 1977. 75.00 (3-8055-2764-0) S Karger.

Nutritional Quality of Cereal Grains: Genetic & Agronomic Improvement. R. A. Olson & K. J. Frey. (Agronomy Monograph Ser.: No. 28). 512p. 1987. 37.50 (0-89118-092-3) Am Soc Agron.

Nutritional Relation of Soils. N. Kanta Dutta. 176p. 1990. 85.00 (81-7041-457-1, Pub. by Scientific Pubs) St Mut.

Nutritional Requirements of Infants & Young Children: Practical Guidelines. Joyce M. Thompson & Gillian Howard. LC 97-22822. 1997. pap. 32.95 (0-632-04891-3) Blackwell Sci.

Nutritional Requirements of Lactarius Species, & Cultural Characters in Relation to Taxonomy. A. J. P. Oort. (Verhandelingen der Koninklijke Nederlandse Akademie van Wetenschappen, Afd. Natuurkunde Ser.: No. 76). 96p. 1981. pap. text 47.00 (0-444-85533-5) Elsevier.

Nutritional Self Defense: A Reference Manual for the Health Professional & the Educated Layperson. 4th rev. ed. Lily Splane. (Illus.). 248p. (C). 1993. pap. text 27.95 (0-945962-04-5) Anaphase II.

Nutritional Self-Defense: Protecting Yourself from Yourself. Frances S. Goulart. LC 85-40581. 302p. 1990. pap. 10.95 (0-8128-6246-5, Scrbrough Hse) Madison Bks UPA.

Nutritional Sex Control & Rejuvenation. Raymond W. Bernard. 1996. spiral bd. 10.50 (0-7873-1009-3) Hlth Research.

Nutritional Status Assessment of the Individual. Ed. by G. E. Livingston. 479p. 1989. 125.00 (0-917678-25-7) Food & Nut Pr.

Nutritional Status in Ghana & Its Determinants. Harold Alderman. (Working Papers). (C). 1990. pap. text 7.00 (1-56401-101-1) Cornell Food.

Nutritional Status of Rwandan Households: Survey Evidence on the Role of Household Consumpiton Behavior. CFNPP Staff & Randall Schnepf. (Working Papers). (C). 1992. pap. 7.00 (1-56401-123-2) Cornell Food.

Nutritional Strategies & Management of Aquaculture Waste, Vol. 10. C. B. Cowey. (Water Science & Technology Ser.: Vol. 31). 262p. 1995. pap. write for info. (0-08-042662-X, Pergamon Pr) Elsevier.

Nutritional Supplements & Chronic Fatigue Syndrome: A Guide. 1992. lib. bdg. 75.95 (0-8490-5315-3) Gordon Pr.

***Nutritional Supplements Buyer's Guide.** Daniel Gastelu. LC 99-59792. 2000. pap. 16.00 (0-609-80464-2, Three Riv Pr) Crown Pub Group.

***Nutritional Supplements in United Kingdom: A Strategic Entry Report, 1996.** Compiled by Icon Group International Staff. (Illus.). 99p. 1999. ring bd. 990.00 incl. audio compact disk (0-7418-1216-9) Icon Grp.

Nutritional Support for Sick Children. Ed. by R. Di Toro. (Contributions to Infusion Therapy Ser.: Vol. 19). (Illus.). vi, 150p. 1988. 51.50 (3-8055-4705-6) S Karger.

Nutritional Support in Nursing. Grant Staff & Kennedy-Caldwell. 1987. text 66.00 (0-8089-1889-3, Grune & Strat) Harcrt Hlth Sci Grp.

Nutritional Therapy. Frances A. Cannon. Ed. by Richard Petz. pap. write for info. (0-318-62235-1) RAPCOM Enter.

***Nutritional Therapy: An Introductory Guide to the Healing Power of Food.** Jeannette Ewim. (New Perspectives (Element) Ser.). (Illus.). 128p. 2000. pap. 9.95 (1-86204-740-5, Pub. by Onewrld Pubns) Penguin Putnam.

Nutritional Therapy for Cat Diseases. Shawn Messonnier. (Pet Care Naturally Ser.). 64p. 1998. pap. 4.95 (0-87983-923-6, Keats Publng) NTC Contemp Pub Co.

Nutritional Therapy for Dog Diseases. Shawn Messonnier. (Pet Care Naturally Ser.). 64p. 1998. pap. 4.95 (0-87983-922-8, Keats Publng) NTC Contemp Pub Co.

Nutritional Treatment of Chronic Renal Failure. Ed. by Sergio Giovannetti. (Topics in Renal Medicine Ser.). (C). 1989. text 232.00 (0-7923-0086-6) Kluwer Academic.

Nutritional Triggers for Health & in Disease. Ed. by Artemis F. Simopoulos. (World Review of Nutrition & Dietetics Ser.: Vol. 67). (Illus.). x, 202p. 1991. 197.50 (3-8055-5265-3) S Karger.

Nutritional Value of Cereal Products, Beans & Starches. Ed. by Geoffrey H. Bourne. (World Review of Nutrition & Dietetics Ser.: Vol. 60). (Illus.). viii, 260p. 1989. 200.00 (3-8055-4992-X) S Karger.

Nutritional Value of Indigenous Wild Plants: An Annotated Bibliography. Compiled by Joel N. Elias & John R. K. Robson. LC 76-51040. vi, 232p. 1978. 38.50 (0-87875-112-2) Whitston Pub.

Nutritional Yeast Cookbook: Recipes Using Red Star Vegetarian Support Formula Flakes. Joanne Stepaniak. LC 96-51983. 144p. (Orig.). 1997. pap. 9.95 (1-57067-038-2) Book Pub Co.

Nutritionally Beneficial Ingredients & Additives for Processed Foods & Beverages. Dorothy Kroll. LC 97-144906. 359p. 1997. 2850.00 (1-56965-115-9, GA-074R) BCC.

Nutritionally Incorrect: Defending Yourself from the Dangerous American Diet. Alan Spreen. 1999. pap. 12.95 (1-58054-043-0) Woodland UT.

Nutritionist. Jack Rudman. (Career Examination Ser.: C-2326). 1994. pap. 27.95 (0-8373-2326-6) Nat Learn.

Nutritionist I. Jack Rudman. (Career Examination Ser.: C-3004). 1994. pap. 27.95 (0-8373-3004-1) Nat Learn.

Nutritionist II. Jack Rudman. (Career Examination Ser.: C-3005). 1994. pap. 29.95 (0-8373-3005-X) Nat Learn.

Nutritive Quality & Mineral Content of Potential Desert Tortoise Food Plants. E. Durant McArthur et al. (Illus.). 36p. 1998. reprint ed. pap. 5.00 (0-89904-546-4, Wildlife Resrch Grp) Crumb Elbow Pub.

Nutritive Value of Foods. Susan E. Gebhardt & Ruth H. Matthews. (Illus.). 72p. (C). 1994. pap. text 20.00 (0-7881-0634-1) DIANE Pub.

Nutritive Value of Foods. Susan E. Gebhardt & Ruth H. Matthews. (Illus.). 72p. 1997. reprint ed. pap. text 25.00 (0-7881-4459-6) DIANE Pub.

Nuts! see **Yok-Yok**

Nuts. Catherine Chambers. (Would You Believe It! Ser.). (Illus.). 32p. (J). (gr. 1-6). 1996. lib. bdg. 21.40 (0-8172-4104-3) Raintree Steck-V.

Nuts! Kevin Freiberg & Jackie Freiberg. LC 97-50102. (Illus.). 384p. 1998. pap. 16.00 (0-7679-0184-3) Broadway BDD.

An Asterisk (*) at the beginning of an entry indicates that the title is appearing for the first time.

Nuts: A Cookbook. (Illus.). 128p. 1997. 12.98 (*0-7858-0789-6*) Bk Sales Inc.

***Nuts: A Russian Fairy Tale.** Ralph Bunch. (Illus.). 84p. (YA). (gr. 3 up). 2000. 19.95 (*1-58151-058-6*, Pub. by BookPartners) Midpt Trade.

***Nuts: Poems from Hollywood.** Mark Dunster. 11p. 1999. pap. 5.00 (*0-89642-722-6*) Linden Pubs.

Nuts! Southwest Airlines' Crazy Recipe for Business & Personal Success. Kevin Freiberg & Jackie Freiberg. (Illus.). 364p. 1996. 24.95 (*1-885167-18-0*) Bard Press.

Nuts! - The Battle of the Bulge: The Story & Photographs. Donald M. Goldstein et al. (World War II Commemorative, Association of the U. S. Army Book Ser.). (Illus.). 208p. 1994. 31.95 (*0-02-881069-4*) Brasseys.

Nuts! - The Battle of the Bulge: The Story & Photographs. Donald M. Goldstein et al. (World War II Commemorative, Association of the U. S. Army Book Ser.). (Illus.). 208p. 1997. pap. 21.95 (*1-57488-039-X*) Brasseys.

Nuts, a Play in Three Acts. Tom Topor. LC 81-135048. 1981. pap. text 5.50 (*0-573-61325-7*) S French Trade.

Nuts about Nuts. rev. ed. Diane Wilmer. (Quality Time Easy Readers Ser.). (Illus.). 32p. (J). (gr. 1-3). 1990. reprint ed. lib. bdg. 12.95 (*1-878363-09-3*) Forest Hse.

***Nuts about Squirrels: A Guide to Coexisting with - And Even Appreciating - Your Bushy-Tailed Friends.** Richard E. Mallery. LC 99-86730. 192p. 2000. pap. 11.95 (*0-446-67576-8*) Warner Bks.

Nuts & Bolts: A Practical Guide for Implementing a Junior High-Middle School Enrichment Program. Sharen Hilliard & Jan Sattler. 1987. pap. 14.95 (*0-936386-47-9*) Creative Learning.

Nuts & Bolts: A Practical Guide to Teaching College Composition. Ed. by Thomas Newkirk. LC 92-42069. 216p. (C). 1993. pap. text 22.50 (*0-86709-321-8*, 0321, Pub. by Boynton Cook Pubs) Heinemann.

Nuts & Bolts: Organization & Management Techniques for an Interest Centered Pre-School Classroom. Marilyn Segal & Len Tomasello. LC 80-83444. (Illus.). 78p. 1981. pap. 14.95 (*0-89334-063-4*) Humanics Ltd.

Nuts & Bolts: Survival Guide for Teachers. Cindy J. Christopher. LC 91-6691. 140p. 1997. pap. text 24.95 (*0-87762-858-0*) Scarecrow.

Nuts & Bolts: Youth Ministry Between the Meetings. Duffy Robbins. 192p. 1991. pap. 12.99 (*0-310-52571-3*) Zondervan.

Nuts & Bolts a Novice Needs to Wire His New Home: The Bundle Saved Will Be His. Joe Miller. (Illus.). 65p. (Orig.). 1986. pap. 9.95 (*0-9616542-0-1*) Joe Miller Pub.

Nuts-&-Bolts Approach to Teaching Nursing. Victoria Schoolcraft. LC 89-11517. (Teaching of Nursing Ser.: Vol. 11). 224p. 1989. 32.95 (*0-8261-6600-8*) Springer Pub.

***Nuts-&-Bolts Approach to Teaching Nursing.** 2nd ed. Victoria Schoolcraft & Jeanne Novotny. (Series on the Teaching of Nursing). (Illus.). 212p. 2000. text 42.95 (*0-8261-6601-6*) Springer Pub.

Nuts & Bolts for the Social Sciences. Jon Elster. (Illus.). 192p. (C). 1989. pap. text 18.95 (*0-521-37606-8*) Cambridge U Pr.

Nuts & Bolts Guide to Rigging: A Step by Step Handbook for Empaches, Kaschper, Pocock, Schgenbrod & Vespoli. Michael L. Davenport. LC 92-91056. 306p. 1992. 28.95 (*0-9639300-0-1*) Mouse Hse Bks.

***Nuts-&-Bolts Guide to Writing Your Life Story.** large type ed. Jan E. Seale. (Illus.). 336p. 1998. pap. 26.95 (*0-936927-25-9*) Knowing Pr.

Nuts & Bolts Issues for Small Groups. rev. ed. William J. McKay. LC 96-69489. 160p. (C). 1996. pap. 8.95 (*0-9633831-6-7*) Stephen Minist.

Nuts & Bolts Marketing - The Fundamentals You Need. 1995. 52.95 (*0-924050-06-3*) K & A Pr.

Nuts & Bolts of Civil Litigation Practice. Jennifer Dwight. LC 93-48681. (Paralegal Ser.). (C). 1995. ring bd. 51.50 (*0-87632-987-3*) Thomson Learn.

Nuts & Bolts of Cooperative Learning. David W. Johnson et al. LC 95-233203. (Illus.). 158p. (Orig.). 1994. pap. text, teacher ed. 20.00 (*0-939603-21-7*) Interaction Bk Co.

Nuts & Bolts of Copyright. Deborah B. Mastin & Timothy Hushion. Ed. by Marilyn Stevens. (Art Calendar Guide Ser.). 43p. 1999. pap. 9.95 (*0-945388-07-1*) Art Calendar.

***Nuts & Bolts of Facilitation: Tools for the Art of Facilitation.** Frank A. Prince & David C. Morrison. (Illus.). 75p. 1998. pap. 12.95 (*1-893013-00-6*) Unleash Your Mind.

Nuts & Bolts of Financial Products: The Evolving World of Capital Market & Investment Management Products. Roger D. Blanc et al. LC 98-112539. (Corporate Law & Practice Course Handbook Ser.). 640 p. 1997. 129.00 (*0-87224-357-5*) PLI.

Nuts & Bolts of Financial Products: Understanding the Evolving World of Capital Market & Investment Management Products. Clifford E. Kirsch et al. LC 98-134447. (Corporate Law & Practice Course Handbook Ser.). 728 p. 1998. 129.00 (*0-87224-413-X*) PLI.

Nuts & Bolts of Helping. (C). 1999. pap. text. write for info. (*0-205-31454-6*) Allyn.

***Nuts & Bolts of Helping.** Jeffrey A. Kottler. LC 99-34604. 145p. 1999. pap. 34.00 (*0-205-30888-0*) Allyn.

Nuts & Bolts of Learning. Shari Soza. (Study Skills Ser.). 43p. (Orig.). 1984. pap. text 2.50 (*0-931711-00-2*) S Soza Enters.

Nuts & Bolts of NTO: How to Help Women Enter Nontraditional Occupations. 2nd ed. Jo S. Sanders. LC 86-20369. 204p. (Orig.). 1986. reprint ed. pap. 26.50 (*0-8108-1943-0*) Scarecrow.

Nuts & Bolts of Open Adoption. Catholic Human Services Staff. 1995. 150.00 (*0-9641035-3-2*) R-Squared Pr.

Nuts & Bolts of Reengineering. Dean H. Stamatis. LC 96-53193. 176p. (Orig.). 1997. pap. 29.95 (*0-9650445-1-3*) Paton Pr.

Nuts & Bolts of Running an Astrological Practice. Wendy Hawks. 1996. 13.00 (*0-86690-418-2*, H3285-014) Am Fed Astrologers.

Nuts & Bolts of Securities Law. Larry D. Soderquist & Practising Law Institute. LC 95-165993. 624p. 1995. 129.00 (*0-87224-184-X*) PLI.

Nuts & Bolts of Securities Laws. (Corporate Law & Practice Course Handbook, 1985-86 Ser.). 624p. 1994. pap. 99.00 (*0-614-17188-1*, B4-7104) PLI.

Nuts & Bolts of Surviving the Loss or Illness of a Loved One: A Step by Step Guide That Will Save Time & Money. Barbara T. Cochrane & Helen F. McGrane. LC 89-64320. 140p. (Orig.). 1990. pap. 14.95 (*0-9625863-3-1*) Regenesis CA.

Nuts & Meats. (Food Markets in Review Ser.). 186p. 1999. pap. 300.00 (*0-614-10658-3*) Food Inst.

Nuts, Bolts & Carnations: 3-Act Comedy. Don Rausch. 58p. 1977. pap. 4.00 (*0-88680-143-5*) I E Clark.

Nuts, Bolts & Greens of a Healthy Back: A Blending of American & Chinese Theory. Marcia Schmidt. 172p. 1999. pap. 16.95 (*1-880439-06-9*) PERQ Pubns.

***Nuts, Bolts & Magnetrons: A Practical Guide for Industrial Marketers.** Millier. 320p. 2000. pap. 39.95 (*0-471-85325-9*) Wiley.

Nuts in May. Frederick Bratton. 63p. 1984. 25.00 (*0-7855-1068-0*, Pub. by Regency Pr GBR) St Mut.

Nuts in the Woodwork: Chicken Soup for the Hangover. Tommy Kirchhoff. Ed. by Kat Wood et al. 123p. (Orig.). (C). 1999. pap. 16.00 (*0-9666422-0-1*) Transcending Mun.

Nuts 'n Bolts Outfitting Your Kayak. Charlie Walbridge. 32p. 1997. pap. 4.95 (*0-89732-220-7*) Menasha Ridge.

Nuts-'n-Bolts, Preventing Traveler's Diarrhea. Donald Sullivan. (Nuts-N-Bolts Guides Ser.). (Illus.). 32p. 1995. pap. 4.95 (*0-89732-176-6*) Menasha Ridge.

Nuts! Nuts! Nuts! M. Mosley. (Illus.). 176p. 1997. spiral bd. 5.95 (*1-57166-091-7*) Hearts N Tummies.

Nuts to You! Lois Ehlert. 1998. pap. 6.00 (*0-15-201600-7*) Harcourt.

Nuts to You! abr. ed. Lois Ehlert. LC 92-19441. (Illus.). 32p. (J). (ps-3). 1993. 16.00 (*0-15-257647-9*, Harcourt Child Bks) Harcourt.

Nutshell California Gift Set, 3 vols., Set. Leslie D. Cole. (Illus.). 1996. pap. 17.49 (*0-614-17781-2*) Nutshell TourMaps.

Nutshell Classics: A Doll's House. Suzanne Mustacich. 1988. pap. text 40.00 (*0-938735-50-0*) Classic Theatre Schl.

Nutshell Classics: As You Like It, Set. Annabelle Howard. 1988. pap. text 130.00 (*0-938735-79-9*); pap. text 110.00 (*0-938735-87-X*) Classic Theatre Schl.

Nutshell Classics: Cyrano de Bergerac, Set. Suzanne Mustacich. 1988. pap. text 150.00 (*0-938735-52-7*); pap. text 100.00 (*0-938735-53-5*) Classic Theatre Schl.

Nutshell Classics: Hamlet. Forrest Stone. 1988. pap. text 160.00 (*0-938735-91-8*); pap. text 90.00 (*0-938735-92-6*) Classic Theatre Schl.

Nutshell Classics: Julius Caesar. William Ruhlmann. 1988. pap. text 140.00 (*0-938735-95-0*); pap. text 90.00 (*0-938735-96-9*) Classic Theatre Schl.

Nutshell Classics: Mare & Pear Ubu. Annabelle Howard. 1988. text 55.00 (*0-938735-90-X*); pap. text 145.00 (*0-938735-82-9*) Classic Theatre Schl.

Nutshell Classics: Romeo & Juliet. Julie Schonfeld. 1988. pap. text 130.00 (*0-938735-97-7*); pap. text 95.00 (*0-938735-98-5*) Classic Theatre Schl.

Nutshell Classics: The Clouds, Set. Steve Kang. 1989. pap. text 145.00 (*0-938735-57-8*); pap. text 80.00 (*0-938735-58-6*) Classic Theatre Schl.

Nutshell Classics: The Government Inspector, Set. Forrest Stone. 1989. pap. text 135.00 (*0-938735-55-1*); pap. text 85.00 (*0-938735-56-X*) Classic Theatre Schl.

Nutshell Classics: The Haunted House. Joshua Malina. 1988. pap. text 80.00 (*0-938735-99-3*) Classic Theatre Schl.

Nutshell Classics: The Importance of Being Earnest. Joshua Malina. 1988. pap. text 55.00 (*0-938735-51-9*) Classic Theatre Schl.

Nutshell Classics: The Second Shepherd's Play. Julie Schonfeld. 1988. pap. text 45.00 (*0-938735-54-3*) Classic Theatre Schl.

Nutshell Classics: The Tempest. Forrest Stone. 1988. pap. text 105.00 (*0-938735-93-4*); pap. text 80.00 (*0-938735-94-2*) Classic Theatre Schl.

Nutshell Library, Set. Maurice Sendak. Incl. Alligators All Around. LC 62-13315. (Illus.). 1962. (*0-318-52919-X*); Chicken Soup with Rice. LC 62-13315. 1962. One Was Johnny. LC 62-13315. 1962. Pierre. LC 62-13315. (Illus.). 1962. (*0-318-52922-X*); LC 62-13315. (Illus.). (J). (ps-3). 1962. 15.95 (*0-06-025500-5*) HarpC Child Bks.

Nutshell Oregon Gift Set. Leslie D. Cole. (In a Nutshell Tourmaps Ser.). (Illus.). 6p. 1994. pap. 17.49 (*1-884497-99-3*) Nutshell TourMaps.

Nutshells. Stephen P. Lindeman. 12p. (Orig.). 1994. pap. write for info. (*1-885206-05-4*, Iliad Pr) Cader Pubng.

Nutt Family Tree. Victoria J. Malyurek. (Illus.). ii, 10p. (Orig.). (J). (ps-3). 1996. pap. write for info. (*1-889294-06-3*) Victorias Pub.

Nuttall's Travels into the Arkansas Territory, 1819 see Early Western Travels, 1748-1846

Nuttis Schell: Essays on the Scots Language Presented to a J Aitken. Caroline Macafee. 240p. 1987. text 39.00 (*0-08-034530-1*, Pergamon Pr) Elsevier.

Nutty & the Case of the Ski-Slope Spy. Dean Hughes. LC 85-7962. 144p. (J). (gr. 4-6). 1985. text 15.00 (*0-689-31126-5*) Atheneum Yung Read.

Nutty As a Fruitcake. Mary R. Daheim. LC 96-96422. 272p. 2000. mass mkt. 5.99 (*0-380-77879-3*) Morrow Avon.

Nutty Challenges & Zany Dares. Bob Longe. LC 93-32391. (Illus.). 128p. (J). 1994. pap. 4.95 (*0-8069-0454-2*) Sterling.

Nutty Delights. Dale Johnson & Faye Oberg. (Illus.). 28p. 1984. pap. 5.95 (*0-9605904-6-3*) Hot off Pr.

Nutty Footy Book. Martin Chatterton. (Illus.). (J). 1995. pap. 7.95 (*0-14-037057-9*, Pub. by Pnguin Bks Ltd) Trafalgar.

Nutty from Nut. Mohamed S. Ladak. 82p. 1986. pap. 15.00 (*0-7855-1716-2*, Pub. by A H S Ltd) St Mut.

Nutty Knock Knocks! Joseph Rosenbloom. LC 85-27626. (Illus.). 128p. (J). (gr. 4-7). 1986. pap. 4.95 (*0-8069-6304-2*) Sterling.

Nutty Knock Knocks! Joseph Rosenbloom. (J). 1986. 10.05 (*0-606-04286-5*, Pub. by Turtleback) Demco.

Nutty, the Movie Star. Dean Hughes. LC 88-36614. 144p. (J). (gr. 3-7). 1989. 15.00 (*0-689-31509-0*) Atheneum Yung Read.

Nutty, the Movie Star. Dean Hughes. LC 91-15517. 144p. (J). (gr. 3-7). 1991. reprint ed. mass mkt. 3.95 (*0-689-71524-2*) Aladdin.

Nutty World of Animals. Martin Chatterton. (Illus.). 96p. (J). pap. 7.95 (*0-14-038988-1*, Pub. by Pnguin Bks Ltd) Trafalgar.

Nutty's Ghost. Dean Hughes. (J). 1998. 3.95 (*0-689-71550-1*) Aladdin.

Nutty's Ghost. Dean Hughes. LC 92-8530. 144p. (J). (gr. 3-7). 1993. 13.95 (*0-689-31743-3*) Atheneum Yung Read.

***Nuturing a Child's Soul.** Timothy K. Jones. 2000. 16.99 (*0-8499-1656-9*) Word Pub.

Nutzpflanzen der Tropen und Subtropen (Useful Plants of the Tropics & Subtropics) Band 1: Allgemeiner Pflanzenbau (General Cultivation) G. Franke. (GER., Illus.). 359p. 1995. 27.00 (*3-8001-2687-7*, Pub. by Eugen Ulmer) Balogh.

Nutzpflanzen der Tropen und Subtropen (Useful Plants of the Tropics & Subtropics) Band 3: Spezieller Pflanzenbau. Genussmittel Liefernde Pflanzen, Kautschuk Liefernde Pflanzen, Gummi Liefernde Pflanzen, Oel und Fett Liefernde Pflanzen, Knollenpflanzen, Zucker Liefernde Pflanzen (Special Cultivation. Condiments, India Rubber, Rubber, Oil & Fat Plants, Tuberous Plants, Sugar Plants) G. Franke. (GER., Illus.). 479p. 1994. 25.00 (*3-8001-2667-2*, Pub. by Eugen Ulmer) Balogh.

Nutzplflanzen der Tropen und Subtropen (Useful Plants of the Tropics & Subtropics) Band 2: Spezieller Pflanzenbau. Getreide, Obst, Faserpflanzen (Special Cultivation. Cereals, Grains, Fruits, Fiber Plants) G. Franke. (GER., Illus.). 403p. 1994. 24.00 (*3-8001-2666-4*, Pub. by Eugen Ulmer) Balogh.

Nutzungsausfallersatz ein Notwendiges Ubel? Versuch einer Dogmatischen Begrundung und Alternativlosungen. Sonke-Peter Nehlsen. (Aivilrechtliche Schriften Ser.: Bd. 11). (GER.). 237p. 1996. pap. 44.95 (*3-631-30773-X*) P Lang Pubng.

Nuwisha: Changing Breeds Book. Ethan Skemp & James Moore. (Werewolf Ser.). (Illus.). 72p. (Orig.). 1997. pap. 12.00 (*1-56504-336-7*, 3076) White Wolf.

Nuyorasian Anthology: Asian American Writings on New York City. Ed. by Bino A. Realuyo et al. (Illus.). 472p. 1999. pap. 19.95 (*1-889876-07-0*) Asian Am Writers.

Nuyorican Experience: Literature of the Puerto Rican Minority, 62. Eugene V. Mohr. LC 82-9282. (Contributions in American Studies: No. 62). 137p. 1982. 45.00 (*0-313-23334-9*, MNE/, Greenwood Pr) Greenwood.

***Nuzi at Seventy-Five.** Ed. by David I. Owen & Gernot Wilhelm. LC 99-52665. (Studies on the Civilization & Culture of Nuzi & the Hurrians: Vol. 10). (Illus.). 454p. 2000. 60.00 (*1-883053-50-1*) CDL Pr.

Nuzi Dialect of Akkadian: Orthography & Phonology. M. Berkooz. (LD Ser.: No. 23). 1937. pap. 25.00 (*0-527-00769-2*) Periodicals Srv.

Nuzi-Studien I: Die Archive des Palastes und die Prosopographie der Berufe. Walter Mayer. (Alter Orient und Altes Testament Ser.: Vol. 205). (GER.). xiii, 221p. 1978. text 17.50 (*3-7887-0574-4*) NeukirchenerV.

***Nuzul-E-Quran.** Ahmad Nawaz. LC 00-133579. 80p. 2000. pap. 10.00 (*1-58225-382-X*) Ananta Prakashani.

Nuzum Family History. rev. ed. Charles E. Haggerty. LC 82-99940. (Illus.). 400p. 1983. lib. bdg. 30.00 (*0-686-43327-0*) D G Nuzum.

NVA & Viet Cong. K. Conboy & K. Bowra. (Elite Ser.: No. 38). (Illus.). 64p. pap. 12.95 (*1-85532-162-9*, 9453, Pub. by Ospry) Stackpole.

Nvision Catalog of Products, Vol. 1. Nigel Spratling. (Illus.). 60p. (Orig.). (C). 1997. pap. 12.95 (*0-9640361-5-0*) NVision.

NVL's Guide to LAN/WAN Analysis: IPX/SPX. Laura A. Chappell. LC 97-77228. 912p. 1998. pap. 59.99 (*0-7645-4508-6*) IDG Bks.

NVQ Workbooks on Management Skills, in Association with ISM 1-7, No. 1. George Edwards. LC 66-17540. 72p. 1999. spiral bd. 24.95 (*0-304-70429-6*) Continuum.

NVQ Workbooks on Management Skills, in Association with ISM 1-7, No. 2. George Edwards. 72p. 1999. spiral bd. 24.95 (*0-304-70430-X*) Continuum.

NVQ Workbooks on Management Skills, in Association with ISM 1-7, No. 3. George Edwards. Book 3. 72p. 1999. spiral bd. 24.95 (*0-304-70431-8*) Continuum.

NVQ Workbooks on Management Skills, in Association with ISM 1-7, No. 4. George Edwards. LC 77-6950. (ENG & GER.). 72p. 1999. spiral bd. 24.95 (*0-304-70432-6*) Continuum.

NVQ Workbooks on Management Skills, in Association with ISM 1-7, No. 5. George Edwards. LC 77-6949. B. (ENG & GER.). 72p. 1999. spiral bd. 24.95 (*0-304-70433-4*) Continuum.

NVQ Workbooks on Management Skills, in Association with ISM 1-7, No. 6. George Edwards. LC 76-15645. (ENG & GER.). 72p. 1999. spiral bd. 24.95 (*0-304-70434-2*) Continuum.

NVQ Workbooks on Management Skills, in Association with ISM 1-7, No. 7. George Edwards. LC 60-53363. 72p. 1999. spiral bd. 24.95 (*0-304-70435-0*) Continuum.

NW Free/Historic Places OR/WA: The Best Free Historic Attractions in Oregon & Washington. Kiki Canniff. 189p. 1995. pap. 5.95 (*0-941361-13-6*, KFH1) F Amato Pubns.

NW Golfer. rev. ed. Kiki Canniff. 254p. 1996. pap. 9.95 (*0-941361-12-8*, KNWG) F Amato Pubns.

NW Naiad: Scuba Diving Poetry. Lia La Mer. (Illus.). 118p. 1998. 14.00 (*1-58486-008-1*) LyricLine Pr.

Nwanyibu: Womanbeing & African Literature. Phanuel A. Egejuru et al. LC 97-9795. 1997. write for info. (*0-86543-617-7*); pap. write for info. (*0-86543-618-5*) Africa World.

Nwhrc Book of Women's Health: Your Complete Guide To Health And Well-Being. Ed. by Anthony R. Scialli. LC 98-43590. (Illus.). 704p. 1999. 35.00 (*0-688-12434-8*, Wm Morrow) Morrow Avon.

NWMP & Law Enforcement, Eighteen Seventy-Three to Nineteen Hundred Five. R. C. Macleod. LC 76-3709. 230p. reprint ed. pap. 71.30 (*0-8357-8254-9*, 203401100088) Bks Demand.

***NxLevel Business Plan Workbook & Resource Guide, Vol. 3.** Helen L. Sumner & George H. Gault. 2000. wbk. ed. write for info. (*1-890730-11-4*) NxLevel Train.

NxLevel Establishing a Shaved-Use Commercial Kitchen. Ed. by Cameron Wold. (Illus.). 380p. (Orig.). 1997. pap. 58.00 (*1-890730-04-1*) NxLevel Train.

NxLevel Guide for Business Start-Ups: Western, 2 vols. 2nd ed. Ed. by David P. Wold. (Illus.). 666p. 1996. pap. 45.00 (*1-890730-00-9*) NxLevel Train.

NxLevel Guide for Entrepreneurs: Western. 2nd ed. Ed. by David P. Wold. (Illus.). 708p. 1995. pap. 65.00 (*1-890730-01-7*) NxLevel Train.

***NxLevel Guide for Entrepreneurs - Business Plan Workbook & Resource Guide.** 3rd ed. David Wold. 600p. 2000. write for info. (*1-890730-09-2*) NxLevel Train.

***NxLevel Program Manager's Manual.** Robert Horn. Ed. by Zoe Taylor Guynn. 1999. write for info. (*1-890730-07-6*) NxLevel Train.

NxLevel Small Business Guide to International Trade: Business Without Borders. Julia R. Prais. (Illus.). 248p. (Orig.). 1997. pap. 35.00 (*1-890730-03-3*) NxLevel Train.

NxLevel Tourism Entrepreneurial Handbook. 2nd ed. Ed. by John Sem. (Illus.). 199p. 1995. pap. 25.00 (*1-890730-02-5*) NxLevel Train.

N'y a Pas de Fumee (Where There's Smoke) Janet Munsil. (FRE., Illus.). 32p. (J). (ps-2). 1996. pap. 4.95 (*1-55037-311-0*, Pub. by Les Editions) Firefly Bks Ltd.

***Ny Folding Map.** Tub. 2005. pap. 4.95 (*0-06-263508-5*, Pub. by Harper SF) HarpC.

***NY 411 2000: A Reference Guide for Film & Television Production.** Ed. by Anne Boyd. 450p. 2000. pap. 49.00 (*1-879930-15-3*, Pub. by Media Pub Intl) SCB Distributors.

NY Giants. Historical Briefs, Inc. Staff. Ed. by Thomas Antonucci & Michael Antonucci. 176p. 1995. pap. 19.95 (*0-89677-062-1*) Hist Briefs.

NY Kitchen Employers' Network. Ken Krol. Ed. by Christine Krol. 148p. 1995. pap. 39.95 (*0-9646399-0-4*) Kitchen Empl Network.

NY Kitchen Employers' Network: NY Ken. 2nd ed. Contrib. by Ken Krol & Christine Krol. (Illus.). 225p. 1996. pap. 39.95 (*0-9646399-1-2*); lib. bdg. 39.95 (*0-9646399-2-0*) Kitchen Empl Network.

NY Public Library. RSI Promotions. 1997. 72.00 (*0-15-100379-3*) Dryden Pr.

NY State Corporation Tax Law & Regulations. CCH Editorial Staff. 484p. 1998. pap. 99.95 (*0-8080-0258-9*) CCH INC.

NY State Sales & Use Tax Law & Regulations. CCH Editorial Staff. LC 98-174985. 952p. 1998. pap. 89.95 (*0-8080-0259-7*) CCH INC.

NY World's Fair Collectibles, 1964-1965. Joyce Grant. LC 98-88338. (Illus.). 160p. (Orig.). 1999. pap. 29.95 (*0-7643-0732-0*) Schiffer.

NY Yankees 1903-1961. Historical Briefs, Inc. Staff. Ed. by Thomas Antonucci & Michael Antonucci. 176p. 1995. pap. 19.95 (*0-89677-061-3*) Hist Briefs.

NY 411, 1. LA 411 Pub Co Staff. 1999. pap. text 49.00 (*1-879930-11-0*) LA Four-Eleven.

***Nyae Nyae Kung: Beliefs & Rites.** Lorna J. Marshall. LC 99-74169. (Peabody Museum Monographs: Vol. 8). (Illus.). 362p. 2000. pap. 25.00 (*0-87365-908-2*); text 45.00 (*0-87365-909-0*) Peabody Harvard.

Nyaishes, or Zoroastrian Litanies. Ed. by Maneckji N. Dhalla. LC 70-164829. (Columbia University. Indo-Iranian Ser.: No. 6). reprint ed. 37.50 (*0-404-50476-0*) AMS Pr.

Nyali Means Change: The June 14, 1993 Referendum in Malawi: IFES Monitoring, Voter Education & Pollworker Training Projects. Laurie Cooper. vi, 100p. 1993. pap. text 12.00 (*1-879720-23-X*) Intl Fndt Elect.

Nyamwezi Today: A Tanzanian People in the 1970s. R. G. Abrahams. LC 80-41012. (Changing Cultures Ser.). 159p. reprint ed. pap. 45.40 (*0-608-15687-6*, 2031613) Bks Demand.

Nyarlathotep Cycle: Stories about the God of a Thousand Forms. Robert Bloch et al. Ed. by Robert M. Price. (Call of Cthulhu Roleplaying Ser.). 256p. 1997. pap. 10.95 (*1-56882-092-5*) Chaosium.

N

NYAT! (National Yiddish Art Theater) Philip Lamb. 120p. 1987. pap. 6.95 (*0-918537-02-9*) Justin Bks.

Nyaya Philosophy of Language. John Vattanky. LC 95-906553. (C). 1995. 54.00 (*81-7030-435-0*, Pub. by Sri Satguru Pubns) S Asia.

***Nyaya-Sutras of Gautama: With the Bhasya of Vatsyayana & the Vartika of Uddyotakara, 4 Vols.** Tr. by Ganganatha Jha. 1999. 98.00 (*81-208-1264-6*, Pub. by Motilal Bnarsidass) S Asia.

Nyaya Sutras of Gotama. Gotama. Tr. by Chandra V. Satisa. LC 73-3795. (Sacred Books of the Hindus: No. 8). reprint ed. 42.50 (*0-404-57808-X*) AMS Pr.

Nyaya Sutras of Gotama. Tr. by M. M. Vidyabhusana. (C). 1990. reprint ed. 20.00 (*81-208-0748-0*, Pub. by Motilal Bnarsidass) S Asia.

Nyaya Sutras of Maharshi Aautama. Ed. & Tr. by Peter Freund. (Darshanas of the Vedic Literature Ser.). (SAN.). 77p. (Orig.). 1996. pap. 12.00 (*0-614-30243-9*, D-09) Maharishi U Mgmt Pr.

Nyaya Sutras of Maharshi Guatama. Ed. by Peter Freund. (SAN.). 77p. 1997. pap. 12.00 (*0-923569-20-0*) Maharishi U Mgmt Pr.

Nyaya Theory of Linguistic Performance: A New Interpretation of Tattvacintamani. Pradyot K. Mukhopadhyay. (Jadavpur Studies in Philosophy, Second Ser.). 1992. 25.00 (*81-7074-095-9*, Pub. by KP Bagchi) S Asia.

Nyayabhasyavarttika of Bharadvaja Uddyotakara. Ed. by Anantalal Thakur. (C). 1997. 54.00 (*81-85636-31-1*, Pub. by M Manoharial) S Asia.

Nyayalaya Karya (Court Work in Hindi) V. M. Shukla. 307p. 1968. 40.00 (*0-7855-7565-0*) St Mut.

Nyayanukha of Dignaga. Ed. by Giuseppe Tucci. LC 78-72427. reprint ed. 27.50 (*0-404-17288-1*) AMS Pr.

Nyayasara of Bhasarvajna: A Critical Study. T. K. Narayanan. (C). 1992. text 20.00 (*81-7099-391-1*, Pub. by Mittal Pubs Dist) S Asia.

Nyayavarttikatatparyatika of Vaspatinisra. Ed. by Anantalal Thakur. (C). 1997. 62.00 (*81-85636-26-5*, Pub. by M Manoharial) S Asia.

NYC A-Z, Vol. II. Mary Pratt. Ed. by Jerome Poynton. LC 98-183313. (Illus.). 100p. 1998. spiral bd. 16.95 (*0-9663561-0-1*) M Pratt.

NYC A-Z, Vol. 3. Mary Pratt. (Illus.). 140p. 1999. write for info. (*0-9663561-1-X*) M Pratt.

***NYC Arts Unfolds, 2001.** (NYC Unfolds Ser.). (Illus.). 1999. 8.95 (*0-931141-83-4*) VanDam Inc.

NYC Bar & Club Guide see Gotham Guide - 1999 Bars, Clubs, Lounges - NYC: 1999 Bars, Clubs & Lounges NYC

NYC Color Guide to Freight & Passenger Equipment. David R. Sweetland & R. J. Yanssey. (Illus.). 128p. 1994. 49.95 (*1-878887-30-0*) Morning NJ.

NYC Culture Guide: Culture of NYC. deluxe ed. (Streetsmart Ser.). (Illus.). 1998. 7.95 (*0-931141-99-0*) VanDam Inc.

***NYC Dining Unfolds, 2001.** deluxe ed. (NYC Unfolds Ser.). (Illus.). 1999. 8.95 (*0-931141-96-6*) VanDam Inc.

NYC Downtown Manhattan (DoMa) Unfolds. (NYC Unfolds Ser.). (Illus.). 1998. 2.95 (*0-931141-79-6*) VanDam Inc.

***NYC Entertainment Unfolds, 2001.** deluxe ed. (NYC Unfolds Ser.). (Illus.). 1999. 7.95 (*0-931141-98-2*) VanDam Inc.

NYC for Free. Christopher Sulavik. Ed. by Emily Church & Stephen B. Sulavik. LC 98-90099. 168p. 1998. pap. 12.95 (*0-9661847-0-X*) Tatra Pr.

NYC for Free, Revised Edition. Christopher Sulavik. 1999. pap. text 12.95 (*0-9661847-3-4*) Tatra Pr.

NYC Get a Grip Gripe Book see Get a Grip New York, Bk. 2, How to Complain Effectively & Get Satisfaction

***NYC Marketplace 2001.** Ed. by Zagat Publishers Staff. (Illus.). 2000. pap. 10.95 (*1-57006-233-1*) Zagat.

NYC Midtown Manhattan Unfolds. (NYC Unfolds Ser.). (Illus.). 1998. 2.95 (*0-931141-80-X*) VanDam Inc.

NYC Multi-Lingual Unfolds. deluxe ed. (NYC Unfolds Ser.). (Illus.). 1998. 7.95 (*0-931141-67-2*) VanDam Inc.

NYC Restaurants. 2nd ed. Andre Gayot. (Illus.). 352p. 1999. pap. text 14.00 (*1-881066-44-4*) Gault Millau.

***NYC Shopping Unfolds, 2001.** deluxe ed. (NYC Unfolds Ser.). (Illus.). 1999. 7.95 (*0-931141-97-4*) VanDam Inc.

NYC Subway Unfolds. (NYC Unfolds Ser.). 1998. 2.95 (*0-931141-72-9*) VanDam Inc.

Nyce: The Abraham & Leanna (Godshall) Nyce Family: Their Ancestors & Descendants. Gladys P. Mease & Gwendolyn P. Hartzel. (Illus.). 109p. 1995. reprint ed. pap. 19.50 (*0-8328-4932-4*); reprint ed. lib. bdg. 29.50 (*0-8328-4931-6*) Higginson Bk Co.

NYCLEX, 1997. Princeton Review Publishing Staff. (Princeton Review Ser.). 1997. pap. 20.00 (*0-679-76915-3*) Random Ref & Info.

Nye & Riley's Railway Guide (With J. W. Riley) Edgar W. Nye. (Notable American Authors Ser.). 1999. reprint ed. lib. bdg. 125.00 (*0-7812-4657-1*) Rprt Serv.

***Nyeayakusumeadnjali: Hindu Rational Enquiry into the Existance of God: Interpretative Exposition of Udayaneacearya's Auto-Commentary with Translation of Kearikeas** Udayaneacearya Staff & Bhaswati Bhattacharya. LC 99-931896. xiv, 343p. 1999. write for info. (*81-7305-151-8*, Pub. by Aryan Bks Intl) S Asia.

***NYIF Guide to Mutual Funds.** Kazanjian. 1999. pap. 20.00 (*0-13-013781-2*) Prntice Hall Bks.

NYIF Vest-Pocket Guide to Stock Brokerage Math. William A. Rini. LC 92-15201. 208p. (C). 1992. text 16.95 (*0-13-847690-X*) P-H.

Nyingma Edition of the sDe-dge bKa-gyur & bsTan-gyur, 120 vols., Set. Ed. by Tarthang Tulku. (Tibetan Buddhist Canon Ser.). 65000p. 1981. write for info. (*0-89800-129-3*) Dharma Pub.

Nyingma School of Tibetan Buddhism: Its Fundamentals & History, 2 vols., Set. Dudjom Rinpoche & Jigdrel Y. Dorje. Ed. & Tr. by Matthew Kapstein & Gyurme Dorje. (Illus.). 1568p. 1991. 240.00 (*0-86171-087-8*) Wisdom MA.

Nyla & the White Crocodile. Norma R. Youngberg. (Illus.). 128p. 1978. pap. 4.99 (*0-8163-1724-0*) Pacific Pr Pub Assn.

Nylexadorian Theory. Mickey Clarke. Ed. by Bill Halbert & Mary Barnes. 125p. 1998. per. 15.00 (*1-929326-02-5*) Hal Bar Pubg.

***Nylon: The Story of a Fashion Revolution.** Susannah Handley. LC 99-34205. 2000. 29.95 (*0-8018-6325-2*) Johns Hopkins.

Nylon Frog Goes for a Swim. Mariah Downey. 1998. pap. 6.95 (*0-533-12725-4*) Vantage.

Nylon Plastics Handbook. Ed. by Melvin I. Kohan. LC 95-17083. 631p. 1995. 199.50 (*1-56990-189-9*) Hanser-Gardner.

NYLS Guide to New York: 1999 Edition. (Illus.). 368p. 1998. pap. 16.95 (*1-892768-02-X*) Inside NY.

***NYLS Guide to New York: 2000 Edition.** 320p. 1999. pap. 16.95 (*1-892768-13-5*, Pub. by Inside NY) BookWorld.

Nyman's: The Story of a Sussex Garden. Shirley Nicholson. (Illus.). 192p. 1994. pap. 17.95 (*0-7509-0615-4*, Pub. by Sutton Pub Ltd) Intl Pubs Mktg.

***Nymph.** Francesca Lia Block. 128p. 2000. 16.95 (*1-885865-30-9*) Circlet Pr.

Nymph Errant: Vocal Selections. Ed. by Carol Cuellar. 36p. (Orig.). (C). 1991. pap. text 9.95 (*0-7692-0776-6*, VF1712) Wrner Bros.

Nymph Fishing. Dave Hughes. 56p. 1995. pap. 19.95 (*1-57188-002-X*) F Amato Pubns.

Nymph Fishing for Larger Trout. Charles E. Brooks. (Illus.). 192p. 1988. pap. 18.95 (*0-941130-90-8*) Lyons Pr.

Nymphen: Untersuchungen zum Dios-Begriff 2. Harald Zusanek. (Untersuchungen zum dios-Begriff 2). 368p. 1998. 67.95 (*3-631-32099-X*) P Lang Pubng.

Nymphenburg Porcelain: The Bauml Collection. Alfred Ziffer. (Illus.). 400p. 1997. 110.00 (*3-925369-61-9*, Pub. by Arnoldsche Art Pubs) Antique Collect.

Nymphing: A Basic Book. Gary A. Borger. LC 78-11358. (Illus.). 192p. 1979. 18.95 (*0-8117-1010-6*) Stackpole.

Nympholepsy. Rodger Kamenetz. (Orig.). 1985. 12.95 (*0-931848-66-0*); pap. 8.95 (*0-931848-67-9*) Dryad Pr.

***Nymphomania: A History.** Carol Groneman. 256p. 2000. 24.95 (*0-393-04838-1*) Norton.

Nymphs: Tying & Fishing. Larry Tullis. (Illus.). 39p. 1996. pap. 12.95 (*1-57188-085-2*) F Amato Pubns.

Nymphs of the Genus Ixodes: (Acari: Ixodidae) of the United States: Taxonomy, Identification Key, Distribution, Hosts, & Medical/Veterinary Importance. Ed. by L. A. Darden & J. E. Keirans. (Thomas Say Publications in Entomology). 95p. 1996. pap. 35.00 (*0-938522-57-4*; ESATSP9) Entomol Soc.

Nyolcadik Torzs Nyomban. unabridged ed. Andrew J. Erdely. Ed. by Charlotte Erdely.Tr. of Struggle for Human Rights. (ENG & HUN., Illus.). v, 244p. 1996. write for info. (*0-9653686-0-2*) A J Erdely.

NYPD. Andrew Cocker. 11.95 (*962-217-658-5*) China Guides.

***NYPD: The Inside Story of New York's Legendary Police Department.** Thomas A. Reppetto & James Lardner. (Illus.). 384p. 2000. 27.50 (*0-8050-5578-9*, J Macrae Bks) H Holt & Co.

NYPD--On the Street with the New York City Police Department's Emergency Service Unit. Samuel M. Katz. (Illus.). 127p. 1995. pap. 19.95 (*0-7603-0186-7*) MBI Pubg.

NYPD Battles Crimes: Innovative Strategies in Policing. Eli B. Silverman. LC 99-17514. 1999. text 50.00 (*1-55553-402-3*) NE U Pr.

***NYPD Battles Crimes: Innovative Strategies in Policing.** Eli B. Silverman. LC 99-17514. 243p. 1999. pap. text 22.00 (*1-55553-401-5*) NE U Pr.

NYPD Blue Pt. 1: Blue Beginning. Max Allan Collins. 48p. 1998. pap. 7.00 (*0-14-081644-5*) Viking Penguin.

***NYPD Blue Pt. 1: Blue Beginning.** rev. ed. Max Allan Collins. (Penguin Readers : Level 3). 1p. (YA). 1999. pap. text 7.00 (*0-582-40170-4*) Longman.

NYPL Book of American History. Melinda Corey & George Ochoa. 240p. 1993. pap. 11.00 (*0-671-79634-8*, Fireside) S&S Trade Pap.

Nyra. Marjorie B. Ramsay. (Illus.). (J). (gr. 4-7). 1979. 4.95 (*0-917182-10-3*) Triumph Pub.

NYROCKS, '97: Proceedings from the 36th U. S. Rock Mechanics Symposium, Columbia University, New York, U. S. A., 30 June-2 July, 1997. Ed. by Kunsoo Kim. LC 99-223705. 370p. 1997. 795.00 incl. cd-rom (*0-08-042844-4*, Pergamon Pr) Elsevier.

***NYS Felony Sentencing Guidelines.** Bonnie Cohen-Gallet. 24p. 2000. 8.95 (*1-889031-33-X*) Looseleaf Law.

NYS Waterways Project Child Poet Supplement. Ed. by Richard A. Spiegel & Barbara Fisher. (Illus.). 7p. (Orig.). (J). (gr. 1-5). 1979. pap. 0.50 (*0-934830-17-7*) Ten Penny.

NYSPCC Professionals' Handbook Identifying & Reporting Child Abuse & Neglect. 7th rev. ed. Anne Reiniger et al. Ed. by Marlene Charnizon. (Illus.). 80p. 1997. pap. text 12.95 (*0-9628247-0-4*) NYSPCC.

***NYSPCC Professionals' Handbook on Providing Supervised Visitation.** Anne Reiniger et al. 158p. 2000. pap. 15.00 (*0-9628247-1-2*) NYSPCC.

Nystagmus As a Resultant in Accordance with the Theoretical Principals of the Physical Mechanisms of the Normal Human Labrinths. R. Grohmann. (Advances in OtoRhinoLaryngology Ser.: Vol. 18). (Illus.). 1972. 64.50 (*3-8055-1357-7*) S Karger.

NYSTCE - The New York State Teacher Certification Exam. Research & Education Association Staff. LC 97-65091. 592p. 1999. pap. text 30.95 (*0-87891-866-3*) Res & Educ.

Nystrom Atlas of Our Country. LC 96-675048. (J). (gr. 5-9). 1996. pap. 7.95 (*0-7825-0589-9*) Nystrom.

Nystrom Block Buddy Atlas. (J). (gr. 1). 1998. pap. 6.95 (*0-7825-0657-7*) Nystrom.

Nystrom Canadian Desk Atlas. LC 95-19646. (Illus.). 166p. (YA). (gr. 7 up). 1995. pap. 13.95 (*0-7825-0587-2*) Nystrom.

Nystrom Desk Atlas. LC 94-675638. (YA). (gr. 7 up). 1994. pap. 13.95 (*0-7825-0349-7*) Nystrom.

Nystrom Map Champ Atlas. (J). (gr. 3). 1997. pap. 6.95 (*0-7825-0637-2*) Nystrom.

Nystrom Nystronaut Atlas. (J). (gr. 2). 1998. pap. 6.95 (*0-7825-0662-3*) Nystrom.

Nystuen-Dacey Nodal Analysis. Keith J. Tinkler. (Monographs: No. 7). (Illus.). 110p. (Orig.). (C). 1988. pap. 15.95 (*1-877751-14-6*); pap. text 15.95 (*1-877751-15-4*) Inst Math Geo.

***NYT Analyzing Financial Statements: 25 Keys to Understanding the Numbers.** Eric Press. LC 99-37749. (Illus.). 104p. 1999. pap. 12.95 (*0-86730-771-4*) Lebhar Friedman.

NYT Business Planning: 25 Keys to a Sound Business Plan. Ed Williams et al. LC 99-44632. (Illus.). 104p. 1999. pap. 12.95 (*0-86730-775-7*) Lebhar Friedman.

***NYT Daily Awards Vol. 53.** Will Shortz. 1999. 9.95 (*0-8129-3209-9*, Times Bks) Crown Pub Group.

NYT Forecasting Budgets: 25 Keys to Successful Planning. Norman Moore. LC 99-44631. (Illus.). 104p. 1999. pap. 12.95 (*0-86730-776-5*) Lebhar Friedman.

***NYT General Psychology.** 1999. write for info. (*0-13-013997-1*) P-H.

NYT Growing & Managing a Business: 25 Keys to Building Your Company. Kathleen R. Allen. LC 99-37755. 104p. 1999. pap. 12.95 (*0-86730-774-9*) Lebhar Friedman.

***NYT Human Sexuality.** 1998. write for info. (*0-13-973462-7*) P-H.

***NYT Human Sexuality.** 1999. write for info. (*0-13-013999-8*) P-H.

***NYT Sales & Marketing: 25 Keys to Selling Your Products.** Anthony Di Benedetto & Michael A. Kamins. Ed. by Tom Redburn. LC 99-27702. 104p. 1999. pap. 12.95 (*0-86730-773-0*) Lebhar Friedman.

***NYT Tracking & Controlling Costs: 25 Keys to Cost Management.** Mohammed Hussein. LC 99-27689. (Illus.). 104p. 1999. pap. 12.95 (*0-86730-777-3*) Lebhar Friedman.

Nyung Na: The Means of Achievement of the Eleven-Faced Great Compassionate One, Avalokiteshvara of the (Bhikshuni) Lakshmi Tradition. Dalai Lama XIV. Ed. by Constance Miller & Sarah Thresher. Tr. by Lama Thubten Zopa Rinpoche & George Churinoff from TIB. (Illus.). 208p. 1995. pap. 16.00 (*0-86171-250-1*) Wisdom MA.

Nzayilu N'ti: Guide des Arbres et Arbustes de la Region de Kinshasa-Brazzaville. L. Pauwels. (Scripta Botanica Belgica Ser.: Vol. 4). (Illus.). 495p. 1992. 57.00 (*90-72619-10-2*, Pub. by Natl Botanic Grdn Belgium) Balogh.

Nzinga. Ramla Bandele. (J). 1992. pap. 6.95 (*0-88378-023-2*) Third World.

Nzinga: Developing Determination & Persistence, Set. AESOP Enterprises, Inc. Staff & Gwendolyn J. Crenshaw. (Heroes & Sheroes Ser.). 16p. (J). (gr. 3-12). 1991. pap. write for info. incl. audio (*1-880771-14-4*) AESOP Enter.

***Nzingha: Warrior Queen of Matamba, Angola, Africa, 1595.** Patricia McKissack. LC 00-24216. (Royal Diaries Ser.). (Illus.). 208p. (YA). (gr. 4-7). 2000. write for info. (*0-439-11210-9*) Scholastic Inc.

O

***O: Cirque du Soleil at the Bellagio.** Photos by Veronique Vial. 2000. 45.00 (*1-57687-094-4*) Powerhouse.

O - Becoming One: Transformation Beyond Survival. Lisa Raphael. (Illus.). 127p. 1998. pap. 15.95 (*0-9662582-9-0*) Cadence Pub.

O Africa, Where I Baked My Bread. Lance Jeffers. LC 77-75581. (Illus.). 77p. (YA). (gr. 9-12). 1977. pap. 5.00 (*0-916418-11-1*) Lotus.

O Alienista see Alienist

O Amor Cobre Todo. Paul E. Billheimer.Tr. of Love Covers. (POR.). 192p. 1990. pap. 8.95 (*0-8297-1633-5*) Vida Pubs.

O Amor das Letras e das Gentes: In Homage to Maria de Lourdes Belchior Pontes. Ed. by Joao C. Dos Santos & Frederick G. Williams. LC 95-74795. (Publication Ser.: No. 9). (FRE & POR.). 504p. (Orig.). (C). 1995. pap. 35.00 (*0-942208-28-5*) Bandanna Bks.

O & an Empty Room. Sandra Key-Aberg. (Orig.). 1985. pap. 7.95 (*0-7145-0736-9*) Riverrun NY.

***O & W: The Long Life & Slow Death of the New York, Ontario & Western Railway.** 40th ed. William F. Helmer. (Illus.). 224p. 2000. pap. 15.95 (*1-883789-25-7*) Blk Dome Pr.

O Apostolo. John Pollock.Tr. of Apostle. (POR.). 304p. 1990. pap. 11.95 (*0-8297-1621-1*) Vida Pubs.

O. B. Perkins & the Southern Oratorical Preaching Tradition. Gary Holloway. LC 92-34965. (Studies in American Religion: Vol. 58). 196p. 1992. text 79.95 (*0-7734-9173-2*) E Mellen.

O Barao see Baron

***O Bed! O Breakfast!** Rob Dalby. 2000. pap. 14.95 (*1-58571-021-0*, 909-098, Pub. by Genesis Press) BookWorld.

O Beulah Land. Mary Lee Settle. LC 96-2226. (Beulah Quintet Ser.: Bk. II). 368p. 1996. pap. 14.95 (*1-57003-115-0*) U of SC Pr.

O Blessed Night: Theological Underpinnings for Recovery from Addiction. OMI Staff et al. LC 90-19635. 205p. (Orig.). 1991. pap. 9.95 (*0-8189-0587-5*) Alba.

***O Blessed Spring: An Easter Journey in the Catechism.** Ed. by Bill Hurst. (Illus.). 64p. 1999. pap. 5.00 (*0-9661326-1-0*) Metrop NY Mission.

"O" Book: The Other Sixteen Hours: The Social & Emotional Problems of Dyslexia. Michael Ryan. (Orton Emeritus Ser.). 1994. pap. 5.00 (*0-89214-008-9*) Intl Dyslexia.

O Brave New People: The European Image of Native Americans. John F. Moffitt & Santiago Sebastian. LC 94-48680. (Illus.). 413p. 1996. 55.00 (*0-8263-1639-5*) U of NM Pr.

O Brave New People: The European Invention of the American Indian. John F. Moffitt & Santiago Sebastian. (Illus.). 399p. 1998. pap. 24.95 (*0-8263-1989-0*) U of NM Pr.

O Brave New Words! Native American Loanwords in Current English. Charles L. Cutler. LC 94-15764. (Illus.). 304p. 1994. 19.95 (*0-8061-2655-8*) U of Okla Pr.

***O Brave New Words! Native American Loanwords in Current English.** Charles L. Cutler. 304p. 2000. pap. text 13.95 (*0-8061-3246-9*) U of Okla Pr.

***O Brother, Where Art Thou?** Joel Coen & Ethan Coen. (Screenplays Ser.). (Illus.). 160p. 2000. pap. 14.00 (*0-571-20518-6*) Faber & Faber.

O Bruadair: Translations from the Irish. Michael Hartnett. 54p. 1985. 18.95 (*0-904011-91-7*) Dufour.

O Burma! rev. ed. Chin Aung. Ed. by Win Aung. LC 00-91503. 200p. 2000. pap. 20.00 (*0-9652612-6-3*) Yoma Pubng.

O. C. Marsh: Pioneer in Paleontology. Charles Schuchardt & Clara M. Levene. Ed. by Keir B. Sterling. LC 77-81133. (Biologists & Their World Ser.). (Illus.). 1978. reprint ed. lib. bdg. 51.95 (*0-405-10733-1*) Ayer.

O, Call Back Yesterday. John Sampson. LC 88-50915. (Illus.). 197p. 1989. 7.95 (*0-9613075-3-6*) Thornfield Pr.

O Canaan! Waters E. Turpin. 1977. 18.95 (*0-8369-9179-6*, 9052) Ayer.

O Canaan! Waters E. Turpin. LC 73-18610. reprint ed. 37.50 (*0-404-11420-2*) AMS Pr.

O Canada. Illus. by Ted Harrison. 32p. (J). 1992. 16.95 (*1-55074-087-3*) Kids Can Pr.

O Canada. Ted Harrison. LC 92-39800. 32p. (J). (gr. k-2). 1993. 14.95 (*0-395-66075-0*) Ticknor & Flds Bks Yng Read.

O, Canada. Ed. by Francine Ringold. 160p. 1994. pap. 6.95 (*0-685-66039-7*) Art & Human Council Tulsa.

O Canada: Essays on Canadian Literature & Culture. Ed. by Jorn Carlsen. (The Dolphin Ser.: No. 25). (Illus.). 256p. (C). 1995. pap. 19.95 (*87-7288-376-6*, Pub. by Aarhus Univ Pr) David Brown.

***O Careless Love.** Susan Dodd. 2000. pap. write for info. (*0-688-17773-5*, Perennial) HarperTrade.

O Careless Love: Stories & a Novella. Susan Dodd. LC 99-11468. 288p. 1999. 22.00 (*0-688-16999-6*, Wm Morrow) Morrow Avon.

***O Careless Love: Stories & a Novella.** large type ed. Susan Dodd. (G. K. Hall Core Ser.). 2000. 27.95 (*0-7838-8976-3*, G K Hall Lrg Type) Mac Lib Ref.

O Cesar o Nada. Manuel Vazquez Montalban. LC 98-186802. (Autores Espanoles E Iberoamericanos Ser.). 1998. 24.95 (*84-08-02505-8*) Planeta.

O-Chloronitrobenzene. Ed. by GDCh-Advisory Committee on Existing Chemicals of E. (BUA Report Ser.: No. 2). 19p. 1992. pap. 21.00 (*3-527-28450-8*, Wiley-VCH) Wiley.

O Christmas Three! Doug Larche. 1995. 5.50 (*0-87129-535-0*, O54) Dramatic Pub.

O Christmas Tree. (Lights & Music of Christmas Ser.). (Illus.). 16p. (J). 1993. 12.98 (*1-56173-708-9*) Pubns Intl Ltd.

O Christmas Tree. Leisure Arts Staff. 96p. 1992. 24.95 (*0-942237-15-3*) Leisure AR.

O Christmas Tree! Ed. by Holly P. McConnaughy. (Illus.). 64p. 1996. 4.98 (*0-614-29844-X*) DoveTail Bks.

O Christmas Tree. Vashanti Rahaman. LC 95-83193. (Illus.). 32p. (J). (ps-3). 1996. 14.95 (*1-56397-237-9*) Boyds Mills Pr.

O Christmas Tree! A Celebration. Jack Maguire. (Illus.). 112p. (Orig.). 1992. pap. 7.00 (*0-380-77070-9*, Avon Bks) Morrow Avon.

O Come Emmanuel: Scripture Verses for Advent Worship. William Marshal. LC 94-12745. 100p. 1994. pap. 7.95 (*0-8192-1629-1*) Morehouse Pub.

***O Come Let Us Adore Him.** Melody Carlson. (Illus.). 96p. 2000. 12.99 (*1-58134-200-4*) Crossway Bks.

O Come Rejoicing Music Collection. Ed. by Steven Warner & Chripogonus Waddell. 1999. pap. 17.00 (*1-58459-008-4*, 3352) Wrld Lib Pubns.

O Come Ye Back to Ireland: Our First Year in County Clare. Niall Williams & Christine Breen. LC 87-12420. 233p. 1989. reprint ed. pap. 12.00 (*0-939149-22-2*) Soho Press.

O. D. T. Escape or Die Trying: Prima's Official Strategy Guide. Jeremiah Marinas. (Games Ser.). 96p. 1998. per. 12.99 (*0-7615-1876-2*) Prima Pub.

O Dammit! A Lexicon & a Lecture from William Cowper Brann, the Iconoclast. Jerry Flemmons. LC 98-24591. (Illus.). 176p. 1998. 27.95 (*0-89672-405-0*) Tex Tech Univ Pr.

An Asterisk (*) at the beginning of an entry indicates that the title is appearing for the first time.

O Days of Wind & Moon. M. Nona McGlashan. LC 97-11702. (Illus.). 128p. (Orig.). 1997. pap. 10.95 (*1-56474-232-6*) Fithian Pr.

O-De-Jit-Wa-Win-Ning: or Contes du Temps Passe: The Memoirs of Elizabeth T. Baird. Dennis Fredrick. LC 97-77869. (Illus.). 134p. 1998. pap. 9.95 (*0-9666048-0-6*) Heritage Hill Fnd.

O Design: A Model-Based Approach. Patrick H. Garrett. 1994. pap. 39.95 (*0-7803-1053-5*) Inst Electrical.

O Deus de Toda Consolacao. Hannah Whitall Smith.Tr. of God of All Comfort. (POR.). 224p. 1991. pap. 8.95 (*0-8297-1639-4*) Vida Pubs.

O Deus Dos Pobres. Abraao De Almeida.Tr. of Liberation Theo.: God of ... Poor. (POR.). 160p. 1990. pap. 7.95 (*0-8297-1666-1*) Vida Pubs.

O Didn't He Ramble. James Koller. Tr. by Stefan Hyner from ENG. (GER.). (Orig.). 1980. pap. 4.00 (*0-940556-02-2*) Coyote.

O Discipulado de Timoteo. William J. Petersen. Orig. Title: The Discipling of Timothy. (POR.). 192p. 1986. pap. 5.95 (*0-8297-0685-2*) Vida Pubs.

O. E. Berninghaus - Taos, N. M. Master Painter of American Indians & Frontier West. Gordon E. Sanders. LC 85-25015. (Illus.). 152p. 1985. 40.00 (*0-9615177-1-9*) Taos Heritage.

O. E. S. Floor Work. Ottillie S. Brunke. 16p. 1993. reprint ed. pap. 3.00 (*0-88053-331-5*, S-241) Macoy Pub.

O Encontro: Poemas. unabridged ed. Emilia Lopes. Ed. by Peregrinacao Publications Staff. (POR.). 96p. 1998. boxed set 12.00 (*1-889358-10-X*, 08) Peregrinacao.

O Enviado do Pai see Sent from the Father: Meditations on the Fourth Gospel

O Espirito Santo e a Libertacao see Holy Spirit & Liberation

O. Eugene Pickett: Borne on a Wintry Wind. Tom Owen-Towle. 240p. (Orig.). 1996. pap. 14.00 (*1-55896-344-8*, 5231, Skinner Hse Bks) Unitarian Univ.

***O (Excerpts)** Cole Swensen. 30p. 1999. 9.00 (*0-9667655-3-2*, Pub. by Beautifulswimmer) SPD-Small Pr Dist.

O. F. Harmon: A Reluctant Hero. Roger D. Pavey. LC 99-71020. (Illus.). 201p. 2000. 30.00 (*0-9654976-3-1*) Vermil.

O Felix Culpa . . . O Happy Fault: How Bad Guys Keep Good Guys Going. Tom Peters. (Illus.). 200p. (Orig.). 1991. pap. write for info. (*1-879516-04-7*) Betterpub Pr.

O for a Thousand Tongues. 1989. pap. 1.30 (*0-8341-9695-6*) Nazarene.

O for a Thousand Tongues: The History, Nature, & Influence of Music in the Methodist Tradition. James I. Warren, Jr. 320p. 1988. 17.95 (*0-310-51530-0*, 17196) Zondervan.

O Freedom! Afro-American Emancipation Celebrations. William H. Wiggins, Jr. LC 86-14597. (Illus.). 232p. 1987. pap. 17.00 (*0-87049-665-4*) U of Tenn Pr.

O. G. Rejlander: Photography As Art. Stephanie Spencer. Ed. by Diane Kirkpatrick. LC 85-1067. (Studies in Photography: No. 8). 224p. reprint ed. 69.50 (*0-8357-1634-1*, 207043800089) Bks Demand.

O Gauge Railroading the Primer. Biggar, Myron J., Group Inc. Staff. 96p. 1997. per. 9.95 (*0-9650291-0-7*) O Gauge Railrd.

O, Genteel Lady! Esther Forbes. (Cassandra Edition Ser.). 297p. 1986. pap. 9.00 (*0-89733-234-2*) Academy Chi Pubs.

O God! Comfort My Soul! Linda C. Hoxtell & Lyle Hoxtell. 224p. (Orig.). 1995. pap. 9.95 (*0-9650408-0-1*) Fools For Christ.

O God, Guide Me! A Selection of Prayers Revealed. Bab Baha'u'llah & Abdu'l-Baha. (Illus.). 41p. (J). (gr. k-6). 1985. pap. 5.95 (*0-87743-202-3*) Bahai.

O Going Out. Linda V. Russo. 46p. 1998. 7.00 (*0-937013-86-2*, Pub. by Potes Poets) SPD-Small Pr Dist.

O Golden Land. Aaron Kramer. LC 76-56921. 1976. pap. 1.50 (*0-917428-03-X*, Dowling College) Global Pubns.

O Guardador de Rabanhos see Keeper of Sheep: Bilingual Edition

***'O Haloa, Ka Hawai'i Mua Loa.** William H. Wilson. (HAW., Illus.). 28p. (J). (gr. k). 1999. pap. 6.95 incl. audio (*1-58191-084-3*) Aha Punana Leo.

O Happy Fault: Personal Recovery Through Spiritual Growth. Robert M. Garrity. LC 94-3724. 240p. 1994. pap. 11.95 (*0-8091-3501-9*) Paulist Pr.

***O Healing Light of Christ.** Composed by Carey Landry. 112p. 1999. pap. 9.95 (*1-57992-019-5*) OR Catholic.

O. Henry. Ed. by Eugene Current-Garcia. (United States Authors Ser.: No. 77). 192p. (C). 1965. 32.00 (*0-8057-0368-3*, Twyne) Mac Lib Ref.

O. Henry. Eugene Current-Garcia. LC 93-776. (Studies in Short Fiction: No. 49). 170p. 1993. 29.00 (*0-8057-0859-6*, Twyne) Mac Lib Ref.

O. Henry. O. Henry. Ed. & Intro. by Harold Bloom. LC 98-37753. (Bloom's Short Story Writers Ser.). 112p. (YA). (gr. 11 up). 1999. lib. bdg. 18.95 (*0-7910-5123-4*) Chelsea Hse.

O. Henry: Author Kit. O. Henry. (Jamestown Classics). (J). (gr. 1-7). 1980. pap. 353.33 (*0-89061-605-1*) NTC Contemp Pub Co.

O. Henry: Great American Short Stories II. Illus. by James Balkovek. LC 94-75030. (Classic Short Stories Ser.). 80p. 1994. pap. 5.95 (*0-7854-0587-9*, 40029) Am Guidance.

O. Henry Almanac. Emilie Toepperwein & Fritz A. Toepperwein. pap. 1.75 (*0-910722-07-2*) Highland Pr.

O. Henry & the Theory of the Short Story. B. M. Ejxenbaum. Tr. by I. R. Titunik from RUS. (Michigan Slavic Contributions Ser.: No. 1). 41p. 1968. pap. 4.00 (*0-930042-09-3*) Mich Slavic Pubns.

O. Henry Biography. Charles A. Smith. (BCL1-PS American Literature Ser.). 258p. 1992. reprint ed. lib. bdg. 79.00 (*0-7812-6837-0*) Rprt Serv.

O. Henry Christmas. Howard Burman. 64p. 1998. pap. 5.00 (*0-87440-066-X*) Bakers Plays.

O. Henry Reader. O. Henry. write for info. (*0-318-58797-1*) S&S Trade.

O. Henry Stories. O. Henry. 1987. 6.98 (*0-671-08619-7*) S&S Trade.

O. Henry's New York. O. Henry. 20.95 (*0-89190-313-5*) Amereon Ltd.

O. Henry's Short Stories. O. Henry. 1976. 22.95 (*0-8488-0525-9*) Amereon Ltd.

O Hoere, Gedanken, die Immer Wieder Auferstehen: Poems & Prose. Edward Kaufmann. 1953. pap. 9.00 (*0-917324-04-8*) German Bk Ctr.

O Holy Cow. Phil Rizzuto. 128p. 1997. reprint ed. pap. 10.00 (*0-88001-533-0*) HarpC.

O Holy Cow! The Selected Verse of Phil Rizzuto. Phil Rizzuto. Ed. by Hart Seely & Tom Peyer. LC 92-40352. 1993. pap. 8.95 (*0-88001-325-7*) HarpC.

***O Holy Mary.** 1999. 10.95 (*5-559-05850-5*); 15.95 (*5-559-05852-1*) Oregon Bks.

O Holy Night see Cantique de Noel: High E Flat Voice & Piano

O Holy Night see Cantique de Noel: Medium High D Flat Voice & Piano

O Holy Night see Cantique de Noel: Medium Low in C Voice & Piano

O Holy Night see Cantique de Noel: Low B Flat Voice & Piano

O Holy Night. 1983. pap. 2.50 (*0-687-28722-7*) Abingdon.

O Holy Night. 1996. pap. 1.30 (*0-8341-9485-6*, AG-1015) Lillenas.

O Holy Night. Illus. by Bradley Clarke. (J). (ps-3). 1994. 16.99 (*1-56476-419-2*, 6-3419, Victor Bks) Chariot Victor.

***O Holy Night.** Ed. by Julie Hogan. LC 99-48355. (Illus.). 2000. 24.95 (*0-8249-4179-9*) Ideals.

O Holy Night: A Christmas Program. Fred Scheffel. 16p. 1995. pap. 3.95 (*0-7880-0633-9*, Fairway Pr) CSS OH.

O Holy Night: Timeless Meditations on Christmas. A. Jean Lesher. Ed. by Carl Koch. LC 99-179987. (Illus.). 168p. 1998. pap. 16.95 (*0-88489-534-3*) St Marys.

O' How I Love Jesus. Andy Holmes. (J). (ps). 1992. 5.99 (*0-929216-57-1*) KindrVision.

***O, How Much Heavenly Music Is Heard!** Leonard Manevich. (RUS.). 16p. 1999. pap. 12.99 (*0-9679201-0-8*) Kolobok.

O Imensuravel Amor de Deus. Floyd McClung.Tr. of Father Heart of God. (POR.). 96p. 1991. pap. 5.95 (*0-8297-1649-1*) Vida Pubs.

O Inward Traveller. Carol R. Murphy. LC 77-91637. 31p. (Orig.). 1977. pap. 1.00 (*0-87574-216-5*) Pendle Hill.

O Is for Orca: A Pacific Northwest Alphabet Book. Andrea Helm. LC 94-43908. (Illus.). 32p. (J). (ps up). 1995. 14.95 (*1-57061-038-X*) Sasquatch Bks.

***O Is for Outlaw.** Sue Grafton. 2001. mass mkt. 7.99 (*0-449-00378-7*) Ballantine Pub Grp.

"O" Is for Outlaw. Sue Grafton. LC 99-14967. 336p. 1999. 26.00 (*0-8050-5955-5*, Marian Wood) H Holt & Co.

***"O" Is for Outlaw.** large type ed. Sue Grafton. LC 99-16581. (Thorndike Basic Ser.). 537p. 1999. 30.95 (*0-7862-2044-9*) Thorndike Pr.

O. J. Files: Evidentiary Issues in a Tactical Context. Gerald F. Uelman. LC 98-106322. (Paralegal). 255p. (C). 1998. pap. text 18.00 (*0-314-22921-3*) West Pub.

O. J. Jokes Book: How Many O. J. Jokes Does It Take to Turn a Stomach. Barricade Books Staff. 1994. pap. 4.95 (*1-56980-026-X*) Barricade Bks.

O. J. Simpson: American Hero, American Tragedy. Marc A. Cerasini. LC 94-197868. 352p. 1994. mass mkt. 4.99 (*0-7860-0118-6*, Pinncle Kensgtn) Kensgtn Pub Corp.

O. J. Simpson: Not Guilty by Reason of Insanity: How the LAPD Guaranteed His Acquittal. Robert R. Ogle, Jr. LC 97-75597. iv, 204p. 1997. pap. 24.95 (*0-9661174-3-3*) R R Ogle.

O. J. Simpson: The Trial of the Century. Felicia Okeke-Ibezim. LC 97-94874. (Illus.). 124p. 1997. pap. 9.95 (*0-9661598-0-2*) Ekwike Bks & Pub.

O. J. Simpson: The Trial vs. Ol' Man River's Saga of the Raft. William Mitchum. (Illus.). 203p. 19.95 (*0-9612120-8-X*) Para-Bk-Pr.

O. J. Simpson Case, DNA Findings. 1996. 65.00 (*0-614-13040-9*) Genelex.

O. J. Simpson Conspiracy. Fred Hughes. (Illus.). 160p. (Orig.). 1995. pap. text 10.00 (*0-9647568-0-3*) Action Acad.

O. J. Simpson Facts & Fictions: News Rituals in the Construction of Reality. Darnell M. Hunt. LC 98-38422. (Illus.). 368p. (C). 1999. text 59.95 (*0-521-62456-8*); pap. text 22.95 (*0-521-62468-1*) Cambridge U Pr.

O. J. Simpson Murder Case: The Story of the Mystery Woman. Tara Persaud. LC 97-147716. 168p. 1997. pap. 10.99 (*1-56043-280-2*, Treasure Hse) Destiny Image.

O. J. Simpson Trial. Earle Rice, Jr. (Famous Trials Ser.). (Illus.). (YA). 1996. lib. bdg. 22.45 (*1-56006-271-1*) Lucent Bks.

O. J. Simpson Trial: What It Shows Us about Our Legal System. Nathan Aaseng. (Illus.). 128p. (YA). (gr. 7 up). 1996. 15.95 (*0-8027-8404-6*); lib. bdg. 16.85 (*0-8027-8405-4*) Walker & Co.

O. J. Simpson Trials: Rhetoric, Media & the Law. Ed. by Janice E. Schuetz & Lin S. Lilley. LC 99-20621. 224p. 1999. 29.95 (*0-8093-2281-1*) S Ill U Pr.

O. J. Syndrome: Confessions of an Abuser. Richard Bean & Karen Crane. (Illus.). 120p. 1995. pap. 11.95 (*0-933025-39-4*) Blue Bird Pub.

O. J. the Last Word. Gerry Spence. LC 97-38336. 256p. 1997. text 22.95 (*0-312-18009-8*) St Martin.

O. J. Unmasked: The Trial, the Truth, & the Media. M. L. Rantala. 286p. 1996. pap. 18.95 (*0-8126-9328-0*) Open Court.

O. J. Whodunit Book. Larry-Wolfe Horwitz. 1994. pap. text 4.99 (*0-9624895-2-2*) L W Horwitz.

O Jerusalem. Stanley H. Barkan. LC 97-170911. (Illus.). 48p. 1996. 15.00 (*0-89304-469-5*); pap. 7.50 (*0-89304-470-9*) Cross-Cultrl NY.

O Jerusalem! Larry Collins & Dominique Lapierre. 704p. 1988. pap. 16.00 (*0-671-66241-4*, Touchstone) S&S Trade Pap.

O Jerusalem. Jane Yolen. (J). (gr. 2 up). Date not set. 15.95 (*0-614-14861-8*, Blue Sky Press) Scholastic Inc.

O Jerusalem. Jane Yolen. (Illus.). (J). (gr. 2 up). 1996. 15.95 (*0-614-15770-6*, Blue Sky Press) Scholastic Inc.

O Jerusalem. deluxe limited ed. Stanley H. Barkan. LC 97-170911. (Illus.). 48p. 1996. 400.00 (*0-89304-472-5*) Cross-Cultrl NY.

O Jerusalem. limited ed. Stanley H. Barkan. LC 97-170911. (Illus.). 48p. 1996. 50.00 (*0-89304-471-7*) Cross-Cultrl NY.

***O Jerusalem: A Mary Russell novel.** Laurie R. King. 448p. 2000. mass mkt. 6.50 (*0-553-58105-8*) Bantam.

O Jerusalem: A Mary Russell novel. Laurie R. King. LC 98-56124. 352p. 1999. 23.95 (*0-553-11093-4*) Broadway BDD.

O, Jerusalem! The Contested Future of the Jewish Covenant. Marc H. Ellis. LC 99-24378. 200p. 1999. pap. 20.00 (*0-8006-3159-5*, 1-3159, Fortress Pr) Augsburg Fortress.

O Jesus, Make It Stop: Poetry of the Great War. (C). 1989. 45.00 (*1-871014-00-X*, Pub. by Desk Top Bks) St Mut.

O. J.'s Double Jeopardy Revenge Lynching: For the Love of a White Woman. H. Khalif Khalifah & Marsha Stewart. 150p. (Orig.). 1997. pap. 10.00 (*1-56411-164-4*) Untd Bros & Sis.

O. J.'s Trial of the Century: You Be the Juror. Robert J. Walton & F. Lagard Smith. LC 94-73459. (Illus.). 1994. pap. 19.95 (*1-886547-00-9*) Marcon Three Ltd.

O. K. Corral Inquest. Alford E. Turner. LC 81-5397. (Early West Ser.). (Illus.). 256p. 1981. 21.95 (*0-932702-14-7*) Creative Texas.

O Kamehameha Nui. Julie S. Williams. Ed. by Ipo Wong. Tr. by Hana Pau. (HAW., Illus.). 135p. (Orig.). (YA). (gr. 7-12). 1995. pap. 7.95 (*0-87336-021-4*) Kamehameha Schools.

O Kamehameha V: Lot Kapuaiwa. Rosalin U. Comeau. Ed. by Hana Pau. Tr. by Ipo Wong. (HAW., Illus.). 127p. (Orig.). (YA). (gr. 7-12). 1996. pap. 7.95 (*0-87336-036-2*) Kamehameha Schools.

O-Kee-Pa, a Religious Ceremony & Other Customs of the Mandans. George Catlin. (Works of George Catlin). 1990. reprint ed. lib. bdg. 79.00 (*0-7812-2253-2*) Rprt Serv.

***'O Kelekolio Ka Manini Li'ili'i.** Lilinoe Andrews. (HAW., Illus.). 33p. (J). (gr. k). 1999. pap. 6.95 incl. audio (*1-58191-070-3*) Aha Punana Leo.

O Lando! The Secret Doctrine Unveiled. Harvey Tordoff. (Illus.). 120p. 1999. pap. 14.95 (*1-899171-62-2*) Words Distrib.

***'O Lepeamoa.** Kawika Napoleon. (HAW., Illus.). 25p. (J). (gr. 2-3). 1999. pap. 6.95 incl. audio (*1-58191-057-6*) Aha Punana Leo.

O Lili'uokalani. Ruby H. Lowe. Ed. by Hannah H. Pau. Tr. by Kamoa'elehua Walk. (HAW., Illus.). 111p. (Orig.). (YA). (gr. 7-12). 1994. pap. 7.95 (*0-87336-027-3*) Kamehameha Schools.

O, Little Town: One-Act Christmas Drama. Jerome McDonough. (Illus.). 27p. 1978. pap. 3.25 (*0-88680-144-3*) I E Clark.

O Little Town of Bagels, Teacakes & Hamburger Buns. Jeannette Clift George. 80p. 1993. pap. write for info. (*0-9616513-4-2*) Manor of Grace.

O' Little Town of Bethlehem. Andy Holmes. (J). (ps-3). 1992. 5.99 (*0-929216-51-2*) KindrVision.

O Little Town of Bethlehem: Tree Ornament Book. Lion Publishing Staff. 8p. (J). (gr. 1 up). 1992. 1.99 (*0-7814-0766-4*, Lion) Chariot Victor.

O Little Town of Glory. Judith Bowen. 1998. per. 4.25 (*0-373-70814-9*) Silhouette.

O Logice Matematycznej i Metodzie Dedukcyjnej see Introduction to Logic & to the Methodology of Deductive Sciences

O Loma! Constituting a Self, 1977-1984. Kurt H. Wolff. (Illus.). 204p. (Orig.). 1990. pap. 9.00 (*0-9605008-8-X*) Hermes Hse Pr.

O Lord Most Holy: High Voice & Piano in A. C. Franck. Orig. Title: Panis Angelicus. (ENG & LAT.). 8p. 1986. pap. 3.95 (*0-7935-5352-0*, 50289520) H Leonard.

O Lord Most Holy: Medium Voice & Piano in G. C. Franck. Orig. Title: Panis Angelicus. (ENG & LAT.). 8p. 1986. pap. 3.95 (*0-7935-5351-2*, 50289530) H Leonard.

O Lord, Move This Mountain: Racism & Christian Ethics. E. Hammond Oglesby. 128p. 1998. pap. 12.99 (*0-8272-2710-8*) Chalice Pr.

O Lord, Teach Me to Pray: A Catechetical Prayer Book for Personal Use. Richard F. Bansemer. (Illus.). 96p. (YA). (gr. 7 up). 1995. 7.50 (*0-9633142-8-9*) Am Luth Pub Bur.

***O Lost: A Story of the Buried Life, Centenary Edition.** Thomas Wolfe. 736p. 2000. 29.95 (*1-57003-369-2*) U of SC Pr.

O Lovely Night see O Schone Nacht

O Lunalilo. Peter Galuteria. Ed. by Hannah H. Pau. Tr. by Kerry L. Wong. (HAW., Illus.). 94p. (Orig.). (YA). (gr. 7-12). 1994. pap. 7.95 (*0-87336-025-7*) Kamehameha Schools.

O Lutefisk. E. C. Stangland. 1985. pap. 8.95 (*0-9613274-5-3*) Norse Pr.

O. M. Ungers: The Dialectic City. Oswald M. Ungers & Stefan Vieths. (Illus.). 120p. 1999. 24.95 (*88-8118-210-6*, Pub. by Skira IT) Abbeville Pr.

O. M. Ungers: Works & Projects, 1990-1998. Notes by Francesco Dal Co & Marco De Micelis. LC 99-23548. (Illus.). 368p. 1999. 85.00 (*1-58093-030-1*, Pub. by Monacelli Pr) Penguin Putnam.

O Magnum Mysterium: A Capella. De Victoria. 12p. 1986. pap. 1.10 (*0-7935-5474-8*, 50305150) H Leonard.

'O Maile, Ka Pua'a. Aha Punana Leo Curriculum Development Committee. (HAW., Illus.). 28p. (J). (gr. k-1). 1989. pap. 5.95 incl. audio (*1-890270-06-7*) Aha Punana Leo.

O Maker of Canoes: An Anthology of Poems from the White Eagle Lodge. White Eagle Staff. (Illus.). 29p. 1987. pap. (*0-85487-076-8*) White Eagle.

O Marvellous Exchange: Daily Reflections for Christmas & Epiphany. John J. McIlhon. 80p. (Orig.). 1992. pap. 5.95 (*0-8146-2013-2*) Liturgical Pr.

O Marvelous Model T! A Diary of a Great Model T Ford Expedition in 1928 from Pittsburgh to the West Coast & Back. John Gerber. (Illus.). 128p. 1991. pap. 9.95 (*0-944266-13-4*) Maecenas Pr.

O Meu Portugal Antigo e Distante: Textos. unabridged ed. Eduardo M. Dias. Ed. by Peregrinacao Publications Staff. (Prosa Ser.: No. 4). (POR.). 128p. 1997. 12.00 (*1-889358-09-6*, 07) Peregrinacao.

O Mistress Mine. Terence Rattigan. 116p. 1949. 16.95 (*0-910278-43-1*) Boulevard.

O Monashestvje. John Vostorgov.Tr. of On Monasticism. 48p. 1969. pap. 2.00 (*0-317-29004-5*) Holy Trinity.

O Mosaico de Zuruan. Jerry W. Hardin. Tr. by Camilo De Andrade. 95p. 1992. 8.95 (*1-882446-04-6*); pap. 5.95 (*1-882446-05-4*) I p e Alliance.

O Mundo do Novo Testamento. J. I. Packer et al.Tr. of World of the New Testament. (POR.). 192p. 1990. pap. 8.95 (*0-8297-1590-8*) Vida Pubs.

O My America! A Novel. Johanna Kaplan. LC 95-19987. (Library of Modern Jewish Literature). 286p. 1995. pap. 17.95 (*0-8156-0328-2*) Syracuse U Pr.

O My Generation & Other Poems. Aram Saroyan. LC 74-5449. 46p. 1976. pap. 4.00 (*0-9606772-0-8*) Blackberry Bks.

O My Generation & Other Poems. deluxe ed. Aram Saroyan. LC 74-5449. 46p. 1976. lib. bdg. 20.00 (*0-9606772-1-6*) Blackberry Bks.

O My Land, My Friends: The Selected Letters of Hart Crane. Hart Crane. Ed. by Brom Weber & Langdon Hammer. LC 88-21303. 562p. 1997. 35.00 (*0-941423-18-2*) FWEW.

O My Soul: The Inside Story. Tom Peters. Ed. by William Scrivo. (Illus.). 250p. (Orig.). 1991. pap. 15.00 (*1-879516-00-4*) Betterpub Pr.

O Na Holoholona Wawae Eha O Ka Lama Hawaii: The Four-Footed Animals of Ka Lama Hawaii. Ed. & Tr. by Esther T. Mookini. Tr. by William Richards. LC 84-72886. (Illus.). 129p. (Orig.). 1985. pap. 8.00 (*0-910043-09-4*) Bamboo Ridge Pr.

O Narodzinach Lotnictwa Polskiego. Czeslaw Zbieranski. 131p. 1958. 2.50 (*0-940962-15-2*) Polish Inst Art & Sci.

O Navmachos: A Play in Three Acts. Menelaos Pagoulatos. LC 88-62480. (GRE.). 71p. (Orig.). 1988. pap. text 5.00 (*0-918618-38-X*) Pella Pub.

O-Net Dictionary of Occupational Titles. U. S. Department of Labor Staff. LC 98-18600. 672p. 1998. pap. 39.95 (*1-56370-510-9*, J5109) JIST Works.

O-Net Dictionary of Occupational Titles. U. S. Department of Labor Staff. LC 98-18600. 672p. 1998. 49.95 (*1-56370-509-5*, J5095) JIST Works.

***'O Ni'i Ka Polewao.** Na'ilima Gaison. (HAW., Illus.). 20p. (J). (gr. k). 1999. pap. 6.95 incl. audio (*1-58191-024-X*) Aha Punana Leo.

O None Can Be Loved Like Jesus. M. Basilea Schlink. 1974. pap. 1.25 (*3-87209-651-6*) Evang Sisterhood Mary.

O Novo Frances sem Custo: French for Portuguese Speakers. Assimil Staff. (FRE & POR.). 28.95 (*0-8288-4331-7*, F10470) Fr & Eur.

O Novo Ingles Sem Custo. Assimil Staff. 1999. pap. text 29.95 (*2-7005-0125-X*, Pub. by Assimil) Distribks Inc.

O. O. Howard, Union General. Gerarld Weland. LC 95-10937. (Illus.). 199p. 1995. lib. bdg. 29.95 (*0-7864-0133-8*) McFarland & Co.

O o'a'a Bird. Justin Quinn. 64p. 1995. pap. 14.95 (*1-85754-125-1*, Pub. by Carcanet Pr) Paul & Co Pubs.

O One - An Anthology. Ed. by Leslie Scalapino. LC 87-90687. 192p. 1988. 10.50 (*0-917588-18-5*) O Bks.

O. P. McMains & the Maxwell Land Grant Conflict. Morris F. Taylor. LC 78-14227. 381p. 1979. reprint ed. pap. 118.20 (*0-608-02355-8*, 206299600004) Bks Demand.

O. P. P. Naomi King. 1997. pap. text 9.95 (*1-874509-01-8*, Pub. by X Pr) LPC InBook.

***'O Pa'ao.** Kekoa Roback. (HAW., Illus.). 21p. (J). (gr. 3-4). 1999. pap. 6.95 incl. audio (*1-58191-064-9*) Aha Punana Leo.

O Papel do Conselho Diretor nas Relacoes Publicas e Comunicacoes. Joyce L. Fitzpatrick.Tr. of Board's Role in Public Relations & Communications. (POR.). 16p. (Orig.). 1996. pap. write for info. (*0-925299-67-7*) Natl Ctr Nonprofit.

O Papel do Director Executivo no Desenvoluimento do Conselho Director. Nancy R. Axelrod.Tr. of Chief Executive's Role in Developing the Nonprofit Board. (POR.). 16p. (Orig.). 1996. pap. write for info. (*0-925299-66-9*) Natl Ctr Nonprofit.

O Papel do Presidente do Conselho Diretor. Eugene C. Dorsey.Tr. of Role of the Board Chairperson. (POR.). 20p. (Orig.). 1996. pap. write for info. (*0-925299-63-4*) Natl Ctr Nonprofit.

O Paradise. William Trowbridge. LC 94-32342. 105p. 1995. pap. 16.00 (*1-55728-342-7*) U of Ark Pr.

O Pays Mon Beau Peuple. Ousmane Sembene. (FRE.). 1991. pap. 9.95 (*0-7859-3228-3*, 2266031767) Fr & Eur.

O Peso da Sombra see Shadow's Weight

O

O Pioneer! Frederik Pohl. 1999. mass mkt. 6.99 (*0-8125-4544-3*, Pub. by Tor Bks) St Martin.

O Pioneer! large type ed. Frederik Pohl. LC 98-42375. 1998. 23.95 (*0-7838-0397-4*, G K Hall & Co) Mac Lib Ref.

O Pioneer! A Tom Doherty Associates Book. Frederik Pohl. LC 98-9726. 256p. 1998. text 21.95 (*0-312-86164-8*) St Martin.

O Pioneers! Willa Cather. lib. bdg. 24.95 (*0-8488-0454-6*) Amereon Ltd.

O Pioneers! Willa Cather. 224p. 1989. mass mkt. 4.95 (*0-553-21358-X*, Bantam Classics) Bantam.

O Pioneers!, 001. Willa Cather. 208p. 1988. pap. 4.95 (*0-395-08365-6*) HM.

***O Pioneers!** Willa Cather. Ed. by Marilee Lindemann. LC 98-35944. (Oxford World's Classics Ser.). 224p. 1999. pap. 7.95 (*0-19-283216-6*) OUP.

O Pioneers! Willa Cather. (Illus.). 544p. 1992. write for info. (*0-614-32001-1*) Random Hse Value.

O Pioneers! Willa Cather. 1992. mass mkt. 3.99 (*0-8125-2076-9*, Pub. by Tor Bks) St Martin.

O Pioneers! Willa Cather. (Signet Classics). 1988. 10.05 (*0-606-04107-9*, Pub. by Turtleback) Demco.

O Pioneers! Willa Cather. 1989. 10.05 (*0-606-13671-1*, Pub. by Turtleback) Demco.

O Pioneers! Willa Cather. Ed. by Susan J. Rosowski et al. LC 96-47330. (Willa Cather Scholarly Edition Ser.). (Illus.). vii, 295p. 1997. pap. 12.95 (*0-8032-6371-6*, Bison Books) U of Nebr Pr.

O Pioneers! Willa Cather. 224p. 1994. pap. 8.95 (*0-14-018775-8*, Penguin Classics) Viking Penguin.

O Pioneers! Willa Cather. LC 92-53878. (Vintage Classics Ser.). 176p. 1992. pap. 9.00 (*0-679-74362-6*) Vin Bks.

O Pioneers! Willa Cather. 1998. lib. bdg. write for info. (*1-56723-027-X*) Yestermorrow.

O Pioneers ! Willa Cather. (C). 1989. mass mkt. 4.95 (*0-451-52285-0*) NAL.

O Pioneers! abr. ed. Willa Cather. (Classics on Cassette Ser.). 1994. 16.00 incl. audio (*0-453-00876-3*, 391292, Pub. by Penguin-HghBrdg) Penguin Putnam.

O Pioneers! large type ed. Willa Cather. (Large Print Heritage Ser.). 259p. 1997. lib. bdg. 28.95 (*1-58118-018-7*, 21493) LRS.

O Pioneers! Willa Cather. 1992. reprint ed. lib. bdg. 25.95 (*0-89966-976-X*) Buccaneer Bks.

O Pioneers! Willa Cather. (Collected Works of Willa Cather). 308p. 1998. reprint ed. lib. bdg. 98.00 (*1-58201-572-4*) Classic Bks.

O Pioneers! Willa Cather. 128p. 1993. reprint ed. pap. text 1.00 (*0-486-27785-2*) Dover.

O Pioneers! Willa Cather. Ed. by Susan J. Rosowski et al. LC 91-31149. (Willa Cather Scholarly Edition Ser.). (Illus.). xi, 392p. 1992. reprint ed. text 55.00 (*0-8032-1457-X*) U of Nebr Pr.

O Pioneers: Reproducible Teaching Unit. James Scott. 42p. (YA). (gr. 7-12). 1999. ring bd. 29.50 (*1-58049-138-3*, TU106) Prestwick Hse.

O Pioneers! - Musical. Willa Cather. 77p. 1996. pap. 5.95 (*0-87129-617-9*, O07) Dramatic Pub.

O Pioneers! - The Country of the Pointed Firs: Curriculum Unit. Center for Learning Network Staff. (Novel - Drama Ser.). 118p. 1997. teacher ed., spiral bd. 18.95 (*1-56077-524-6*) Ctr Learning.

O

O Plano de Deus para a Familia. Elvin Irwin. Orig. Title: Living on God's Family Plan. (POR.). 176p. 1986. pap. 4.95 (*0-8297-0708-5*) Vida Pubs.

O+ Factor: Stories of People Who Have Overcome Obstacles on the Road to Success. Angela D. Akers. 150p. 1998. pap. 7.95 (*0-936497-49-1*) Seven Worlds.

O-Po see Milton Encyclopedia

***O Poder de Libertacao Da Voz.** Rosana Nassar Zolin. 176p. 1999. pap. write for info. (*0-7392-0485-8*, PO3831) Morris Pubng.

***O Powerful Western Star: Poetry & Art in California.** Jack Foley. 229p. 2000. pap. 12.00 (*1-880766-25-6*, Pub. by Pantograph Pr) SPD-Small Pr Dist.

O Profeta da Esperanca. F. B. Meyer. Orig. Title: The Prophet of Hope. (POR.). 112p. 1987. pap. 5.95 (*0-8297-1607-6*) Vida Pubs.

O Proximo Passo: Para Cristaos em Crescimento. Jack T. Chick. (POR., Illus.). 64p. 1997. pap. 3.50 (*0-937958-54-9*) Chick Pubns.

O Que Voce Sabe Pode Nao Estar. David Downing.Tr. of What You Know Might Not Be So. (POR.). 136p. 1991. pap. 6.95 (*0-8297-1652-1*) Vida Pubs.

O. R. Competencies. Johns Hopkins Hospital OR Nursing Staff. 180p. 1994. spiral bd. 125.00 (*0-614-23271-6*) Acad Med Sys.

O. R. Competencies. Johns Hopkins Hospital O.R. Nursing Staff. 180p. 1994. spiral bd. 125.00 (*1-879575-52-3*) Acad Med Sys.

O Redeemed. Uzee Brown. Ed. by Scott Foss. 46p. (C). 1994. pap. 9.95 (*0-89328-128-X*, 30/1067); pap. text 9.95 (*0-89328-129-8*, 30/1072) Lorenz Corp.

O Retorno das Cigarras. Jerry W. Hardin. Tr. by Camilo De Andrade. (POR.). 147p. 1992. 9.95 (*1-882446-32-1*); pap. 6.95 (*1-882446-31-3*) I p e Alliance.

O-Ridge-Inals. Virginia Ridge. 66p. 1998. pap. write for info. (*1-57502-934-0*, PO2573) Morris Pubng.

O Romanceiro Portugues e Brasileiro: Indice Tematico e Bibliografico, 2 vols. Manuel Da Costa Fontes et al.Tr. of Portuguese & Brazilian Balladry: A Thematic & Bibliographic Index. v, 695p. 1997. 60.00 (*1-56954-063-2*) Hispanic Seminary.

O, Rosie. Lusk Daniel. LC 78-23579. (Illus.). (Orig.). 1979. pap. 12.50 (*0-914140-04-3*) Carpenter Pr.

O Rugged Land of Gold. Martha Martin. (Illus.). 226p. 1989. pap. 12.95 (*0-940055-00-7*) Vanessapress.

O Rus! Studia Litteraria Slavica in Honorem Hugh McLean. Czeslaw Milosz. Ed. by Simon Karlinsky et al. 530p. (Orig.). (C). 1995. pap. 50.00 (*1-57201-008-8*) Berkeley Slavic.

O. S. S. in Italy, 1942-1945: A Personal Memoir. Max Corvo. LC 89-3801. 334p. 1989. 39.95 (*0-275-93333-4*, C3333, Praeger Pubs) Greenwood.

O. S. S. Norwegian Special Operations Group in World War II. Bruce H. Heimark. LC 94-8383. 200p. 1994. 55.00 (*0-275-94860-9*, Praeger Pubs) Greenwood.

O Sacred Head. Nicholas Kilmer. LC 96-44301. 288p. 1997. 23.00 (*0-8050-5033-7*) H Holt & Co.

***O Sacred Head, Vol. 24.** Nicholas Kilmer. (Missing Mysteries Ser.: Vol. 24). 2000. pap. 14.95 (*1-890208-48-5*) Poisoned Pen.

O Say, Can You See: American Photographs, 1839-1939, One Hundred Years of American Photography from the Collection of George R. Rinhart. Thomas W. Fels. (Illus.). 144p. 1989. 50.00 (*0-262-06120-1*) MIT Pr.

O Schone Nacht. J. Brahms.Tr. of O Lovely Night. (ENG & GER.). 12p. 1986. pap. 1.25 (*0-7935-5469-1*, 50316790) H Leonard.

O Segundo Grande Mandamento. William M. Fletcher. Orig. Title: Second Greatest Commandment. (POR.). 176p. 1986. pap. 4.95 (*0-8297-0721-2*) Vida Pubs.

0755: Pearl Harbor Heroes: Heroism of 250 Men & Women 7 December 1941. Donald K. Ross & Helen L. Ross. (Illus.). 158p. 1988. pap. 11.95 (*0-930942-15-9*) Rokalu Pr.

O Solo Homo: The New Queer Performance. Ed. by Holly Hughes & David Roman. LC 98-5203. 496p. 1998. pap. 17.50 (*0-8021-3570-6*, Grove) Grove-Atltic.

O Strange New World: American Culture: The Formative Years. Howard M. Jones. LC 82-9161. 464p. 1982. reprint ed. lib. bdg. 52.50 (*0-313-23494-9*, JOOS, Greenwood Pr) Greenwood.

O Susan! Looking Forward with Hope after the Death of a Child. rev. ed. James W. Angell. LC 90-4699. 114p. 1990. reprint ed. pap. 9.95 (*0-932727-39-5*) Hope Pub Hse.

O Susan! Looking Forward with Hope after the Death of a Child. 2nd rev. ed. James W. Angell. LC 90-4699. 114p. 1990. reprint ed. lib. bdg. 15.95 (*0-932727-40-9*) Hope Pub Hse.

O Susanne: Ja Konjugier fur Mich! Uwe Kind & Ursula Meyer. (GER., Illus.). 116p. 1996. spiral bd. 26.00 (*0-942017-44-7*, 04-64413) Amer Assn Teach German.

O, Suzanne, Ja Konjugier Fur Mich! Uwe Kind & Ursula Meyer. (gr. 7-12). 1980. pap. text 5.25 (*0-88345-359-2*, 18601); audio 25.00 (*0-686-66262-8*, 58690) Prentice ESL.

O Taste & See . . . Edna B. Stigger. (Illus.). 160p. (Orig.). 1996. pap. 9.99 (*1-889208-04-3*) Glad Tidngs Pub.

O Taste & Sing. (Illus.). 288p. 1995. 16.95 (*0-9647438-0-9*) St Stephens.

O-Team. unabridged ed. Duanne Jahns & Darcy Jahns. 208p. (J). (gr. 3-6). 1992. mass mkt. 5.95 (*0-7736-7378-4*) STDK.

O Temps Divers, Scais-Tu Dir l'Ave, Quand un Cordier, Qui Bien Se Mire see Florilege du Concert Vocal de la Renaissance

O the Red Rose Tree. Patricia Beatty. 1994. 10.05 (*0-606-06629-2*, Pub. by Turtleback) Demco.

O, These Men, These Men: A Novel. Angela M. Thirkell. LC 96-18424. (Illus.). 224p. 1996. reprint ed. pap. 12.95 (*1-55921-173-3*) Moyer Bell.

O Thou Kind Lord: Prayers & Roadings for Children from the Baha'i Writings. Baha'u'llah & Abdul-Baha. (Illus.). 57p. (J). (gr. 1-6). Date not set. 5.50 (*1-870989-38-4*) Bahai.

O-Tolidine (3,3'-Dimenthyl-Biphenyl-4,4'-Diyldiamine) Ed. by GDCh-Advisory Committee on Existing Chemicals of E. (BUA Report Ser.: No. 26). 77p. 1993. pap. 48.00 (*3-527-28465-6*, Wiley-VCH) Wiley.

O Two - An Anthology: What Is the Inside, What Is Outside? Ed. by Leslie Scalapino. LC 90-63840. 190p. 1991. 10.50 (*1-882022-09-2*) O Bks.

O. U. I. Operating under the Influence. Robert F. Pease. 199p. 1993. per. 12.95 (*0-9637154-0-2*) Flagg Mtn Pr.

O U Women: Undoing Educational Obstacles. Patricia Lunneborg. LC 98-119889. (Cassell Education Ser.). 160p. 1994. 79.50 (*0-304-33161-9*); pap. 24.95 (*0-304-33163-5*) Continuum.

O un Amy! Essays on Montaigne in Honor of Donald M. Frame. Ed. by Raymond C. La Charite. LC 76-47501. (French Forum Monographs: No. 5). (ENG & FRE.). 341p. (Orig.). 1977. pap. 16.95 (*0-917058-04-6*) French Forum.

O Vinho do Mistico (Wine of the Mystics) (POR.). 35.00 (*0-87612-228-4*) Self Realization.

O Vous, Freres Humaines. Albert Cohen. (FRE.). 213p. 1988. pap. 10.95 (*0-7859-2084-6*, 2070379159) Fr & Eur.

O. W. Duncan Family. James K. Griggs & Carol B. Porta. (Illus.). 1977. pap. text 25.00 (*0-918292-04-2*) Griggs Print.

O Wartosciach Spolecznych: Studia I Szkice. Feliks Gross. 211p. 1961. pap. 3.00 (*0-940962-16-0*) Polish Inst Art & Sci.

'O Wau Kekahi I Ke Alualu Holoholona. Tr. by Aha Punana Leo Staff. (HAW., Illus.). 12p. (J). (gr. k). 1992. pap. 5.95 incl. audio (*1-890270-08-3*) Aha Punana Leo.

***O Wheel: Poems.** Peter M. Sacks. LC 99-40055. 104p. 2000. pap. 15.95 (*0-8203-2184-2*) U of Ga Pr.

***O. Whillikers in the Hall of Champions.** Jay Carty et al. LC 00-24523. (Illus.). (J). 2000. pap. 12.99 (*0-8307-2634-9*, Gospel Light) Gospel Lght.

O. Whillikers in the Hall of Champions: Portraits of Character. rev. ed. Jay Carty. (Illus.). 113p. (J). (gr. 3-6). 1999. pap. 14.95 (*0-9652089-1-5*) Yes Ministries.

O Wojnie Partyzanckiej (1835 Polish); Ueber den Partheiganger-Krieg (1839 Old German Translation) see On Partisan War

O Wonderful, Wonderful & Most Wonderful, Wonderful! Again Wonderful . . . Peter Arnell. 96p. 1992. write for info. (*0-9631817-0-X*) Sidney Pr.

O Wonderful, Wonderful & Most Wonderful, Wonderful! Again Wonderful . . . Peter Arnell. (Illus.). 90p. 1992. pap. write for info. (*0-9631817-1-8*) Sidney Pr.

***O Worship the King: Hymns of Assurance & Praise to Encourage Your Heart.** Joni Eareckson Tada et al. 96p. 2000. 19.99 incl. cd-rom (*1-58134-215-2*) Crossway Bks.

O Ye Jigs & Juleps! Virginia C. Hudson. 64p. 1962. 14.95 (*0-02-555340-2*) Macmillan.

O Ye Jigs & Juleps! Ed. by Don Musselman. (J). 1993. pap. 7.00 (*0-87602-315-4*) Anchorage.

O Ye Legendary Texas Horned Frog! June R. Welch. (Illus.). 102p. (Orig.). 1993. pap. 10.95 (*0-912854-17-0*) Yellow Rose Pr.

O Zebron Falls! Charles Ferry. LC 94-67373. 212p. (YA). (gr. 7 up). 1994. reprint ed. pap. 11.95 (*1-882792-04-1*) Proctor Pubns.

O Zhizni o Vjere o Tzerkvje, 2 vols. Protopresbyter Michael Pomazansky.Tr. of On Life, Faith & the Church. 650p. 1976. pap. 23.00 (*0-317-29072-X*) Holy Trinity.

Oafie the Clown. Joan Sawyer. (J). (gr. k-2). 1993. pap. 8.95 incl. audio (*0-7608-0496-6*); pap. 4.95 (*1-56801-173-3*) Sundance Pub.

Oafie the Clown, Big bk. Joan Sawyer. (J). (gr. k-2). 1993. pap. 17.95 (*1-56801-172-5*) Sundance Pub.

Oahe Sub-District: A Case Study in Water Resources Administration. Donald J. Mendel. 1963. 1.00 (*1-55614-074-6*) U of SD Gov Res Bur.

Oahspe: A New Bible in the Words of Jehovihand & His Angel Ambassadors. John B. Newbrough & David A. Cardone. LC 98-92796. (Illus.). xxvii, 923p. 1998. reprint ed. pap. 45.00 (*0-9665065-0-2*) OAHSPE.

Oahspe Bible: A New Bible in the Words of Jehovih & His Angel Embassadors (1882) Anonymous. 1016p. 1998. reprint ed. pap. 36.00 (*0-7661-0729-9*) Kessinger Pub.

Oahu - The Gathering Place. (Illus.). pap. 4.95 (*0-930492-48-X*) Hawaiian Serv.

Oahu Trails: Walks, Strolls & Treks on the Capital Isle. 2nd rev. ed. Wilderness Press Staff & Kathy Morey. LC 99-24824. (Hawaiian Trails Hiking Guides Ser.). 212p. 1999. pap. 13.95 (*0-89997-245-4*) Wilderness Pr.

Oahu Traveler's Guide. Bill Gleasner & Diana Gleasner. (Illus.). pap. 3.95 (*0-681-02784-3*) Booklines Hawaii.

O'ahu's Hidden History. William H. Dorrance. (Illus.). 240p. 1998. pap. 13.95 (*1-56647-211-3*) Mutual Pub HI.

Oak see My First Nature Books

Oak above the Kings: A Book of the Keltiad. Patricia Kennealy-Morrison. 432p. 1995. mass mkt. 5.99 (*0-451-45451-0*, ROC) NAL.

Oak & Ivy. Paul Laurence Dunbar. (Notable American Authors Ser.). 1992. reprint ed. lib. bdg. 75.00 (*0-7812-2707-0*) Rprt Serv.

Oak Anthology of Blues Guitar: Texas Blues Guitar. Stefan Grossman. (Illus.). 144p. 1984. pap. 19.95 (*0-8256-0295-5*, OK64287, Oak) Music Sales.

***Oak Apples & Heavenly Kisses.** Jeremy Dufflied. 63p. 2000. pap. 11.95 (*1-902096-61-4*, Pub. by Headland Pubns) Intl Spec Bk.

Oak Creek. Anita Rowe & Larry Rowe. LC 98-88259. (Images of America Ser.). 1998. write for info. (*0-7524-1373-2*) Arcadia Publng.

Oak Furniture: The British Tradition. 2nd ed. Victor Chinnery. (Illus.). 620p. 1986. 99.50 (*1-85149-013-2*) Antique Collect.

Oak Grove Cemetery. Rose Yaniga & John J. Yanik, Jr. LC 96-85272. 163p. 1996. pap. text 20.00 (*1-55856-231-1*, 280) Closson Pr.

Oak Hill Cemetery: Mt. Carmel, Northumberland Co., Pa. Compiled by Schuylkill Roots Staff. 27p. 1989. pap. text 5.00 (*1-55856-030-0*, 060) Closson Pr.

Oak Hybridization at the University of Utah. Walter P. Cottam et al. (State Arboretum of Utah Ser.: Publication No. 1, 1982). (Illus.). 96p. 1982. 15.00 (*0-942830-00-8*); pap. 10.00 (*0-942830-01-6*) State Arbor.

Oak in the Acorn: On Remembrance of Things Past & on Teaching Proust, Who Will Never Learn. Howard Nemerov. LC 86-21087. 168p. 1987. text 27.50 (*0-8071-1385-9*) La State U Pr.

***Oak Island & Its Lost Treasure.** Graham Harris & Les MacPhie. (Illus.). 200p. 2000. pap. 14.95 (*0-88780-492-6*, Pub. by Formac Publ Co) Seven Hills Bk.

Oak Island Gold: One of the World's Most Baffling Mysteries. William S. Crooker. (Illus.). 228p. 1993. pap. 14.95 (*1-55109-049-X*) Nimbus Publ.

Oak Island Secrets. Mark Finnan. LC 95-225814. (Illus.). 178p. 1997. pap. 12.95 (*0-88780-312-1*, Pub. by Formac Publ Co) Seven Hills Bk.

Oak Island Secrets. Mark Finnan. 178p. 1997. pap. 12.95 (*0-88780-414-4*, Pub. by Formac Publ Co) Seven Hills Bk.

Oak Knoll Historic Data Recovery Project: Sites CA-SIS-1143 & CA-SIS-1144, Klamath National Forest. K. R. Winthrop et al. (Illus.). 111p. (C). 1987. reprint ed. pap. text 12.19 (*1-55567-434-8*) Coyote Press.

Oak Leaf. Dorothy Swygert. (YA). (gr. 9 up). 1997. 20.00 (*0-9648737-1-0*, RCT01) Rekindling Heart.

Oak-Mot. deluxe limited ed. Crispin H. Glover. (Illus.). 1990. 25.00 (*0-9622997-1-5*) Volcanic Eruptions.

Oak Openings. James Fenimore Cooper. 520p. 1984. reprint ed. 40.00 (*0-938190-33-4*) North Atlantic.

Oak Park Home & Studio of Frank Lloyd Wright. Ann Abernathy & John G. Thorpe. LC 88-10649. (Illus.). 48p. (Orig.). (gr. 6 up). 1988. pap. 8.95 (*0-945635-00-1*) F Lloyd Wright.

***Oak Park, Illinois.** David M. Sokol. (Images of America Ser.). (Illus.). 128p. 2000. pap. 18.99 (*0-7385-0712-1*) Arcadia Publng.

Oak Park Strategy: Community Control of Racial Change. Carole Goodwin. LC 78-13651. (Studies of Urban Society). (Illus.). 253p. reprint ed. pap. 78.50 (*0-608-09312-2*, 205418600004) Bks Demand.

Oak Ridge & Me: From Youth to Maturity. Joanne S. Gailar. (Illus.). 140p. (Orig.). 1991. pap. 8.95 (*0-9606832-6-7*) Chldrns Mus.

Oak Ridge National Laboratory: The First Fifty Years. Leland Johnson & David Schaffer. LC 94-7667. (Illus.). 288p. (C). 1994. pap. 16.00 (*0-87049-854-1*) U of Tenn Pr.

Oak Ridge Technical Information Center: A Trailblazer in Federal Documentation. William M. Vaden. LC 92-30529. 380p. 1992. pap. 30.00 (*0-87079-596-1*, DE92018247) DOE.

Oak Ridges Moraine. Boston Mills Press Staff. LC 98-111728. 1997. 28.00 (*1-55046-191-5*, Pub. by Boston Mills) Genl Dist Srvs.

Oak Spring Flora: Flower Illustration from the Fifteenth Century to the Present Time. Lucia T. Tomasi & Julia Blakely. Tr. by Lisa Chien from ITA. LC 96-71751. (Illus.). 415p. 1997. 75.00 (*0-9654508-0-5*) Oak Spring Grdn.

Oak Spring Pomona. Sandra Raphael. LC 90-62575. (Oak Spring Garden Library: Vol. 2). (Illus.). 300p. (C). 1991. 65.00 (*0-300-04936-6*) Yale U Pr.

Oak Spring Sylva. Sandra Raphael. LC 89-61800. (Oak Spring Garden Library: Vol. 1). (Illus.). 160p. 1989. text 50.00 (*0-300-04652-9*) Yale U Pr.

Oak Sprint Flora: Flower Illustration from the Fifteenth Century to the Present Time. Lucia T. Tomasi. (Oak Spring Garden Library: Vol. 3). (Illus.). 432p. 1997. 75.00 (*0-300-07139-6*) Yale U Pr.

Oak Street Beach. Howard Rose. 120p. 1990. 16.00 (*1-878352-06-7*); pap. 9.00 (*1-878352-07-5*) R Saroff Pub.

Oak Street Chonicles & the Good News: Everyday Life & Christian Faith. Delia T. Halverson. Ed. by M. Franklin Dotts. (Illus.). 48p. (Orig.). (J). pap., teacher ed. 4.95 (*0-687-75340-6*) Abingdon.

Oak Street Chonicles & the Good News: Everyday Life & Christian Faith. Delia T. Halverson. Ed. by M. Franklin Dotts. (Illus.). 40p. (Orig.). (J). 1989. pap., student ed. 3.75 (*0-687-75339-2*) Abingdon.

Oak Tree see Webs of Life

Oak Tree. Gordon Morrison. LC 98-55148. 32p. (J). 1999. 16.00 (*0-395-95644-7*) HM.

Oak Tree & Olive Tree, 2 vols., Set. R. Barone. 1994. pap. 37.50 (*0-7165-2479-1*, Pub. by Irish Acad Pr) Intl Spec Bk.

Oak Tree with Apples. Mary W. Soergel. (Illus.). 30p. (Orig.). 1989. pap. write for info. (*0-9622512-0-8*) Ashippun Air Corps.

Oak Trees. Marcia S. Freeman. LC 98-7182. (Trees Ser.). (Illus.). 24p. (J). 1998. write for info. (*0-7368-0093-X*, Pebble Bks) Capstone Pr.

Oak Trees. Marcia S. Freeman. (Trees (Captstone) Ser.). (J). 1998. 13.25 (*0-516-21505-1*) Childrens.

Oak Wilt Perspectives: The Proceedings of the National Oak Wilt Symposium. Ed. by David N. Appel & Ronald F. Billings. (Illus.). 320p. (Orig.). (C). 1995. pap. text 30.00 (*0-9644015-0-9*) Info Develop.

Oakdale Affair. Edgar Rice Burroughs. 18.95 (*0-8488-1255-7*) Amereon Ltd.

Oakdale Affair. Edgar Rice Burroughs. 1976. reprint ed. lib. bdg. 25.95 (*0-89966-041-X*) Buccaneer Bks.

Oakdale Church Record: Berrysburg Circuit East Pennsylvania Conference Evangelical Association, 1863-1968. Schuylkill Roots Staff & Phillip A. Rice. 64p. 1992. per. 8.00 (*1-55856-110-2*, 388) Closson Pr.

Oakdale Detention Center: The First Year of Operation. Minnesota Lawyers International Human Rights Commi. 55p. 1987. pap. 3.00 (*0-929293-17-7*) MN Advocates.

Oaken Heart. large type ed. Margery Allingham. 368p. 1991. 21.95 (*1-85089-344-6*, Pub. by ISIS Lrg Prnt) Transaction Pubs.

Oakes Ames: Jottings of a Harvard Botanist. Pauline A. Plimpton. LC 79-52949. (Illus.). 401p. 1980. text 12.95 (*0-674-62921-3*) HUP.

Oakes Diaries Vol. I: Business, Politics & the Family in Bury St. Edmunds, 1778-1827, Introduction & James Oakes' Diaries, 1778-1800. Ed. by Jane Fiske. (Suffolk Records Society Ser.: No. 32). (Illus.). 417p. 1990. 45.00 (*0-85115-275-9*) Boydell & Brewer.

***Oakeshott & His Contemporaries: St. Augustine, Hegel, Et Al.** Wendell John Coats, Jr. LC 99-87913. 144p. 2000. 31.50 (*1-57591-038-1*) Susquehanna U Pr.

Oakfield: or Fellowship in the East; Or, Fellowship in the East. W. D. Arnold. xi, 442p. reprint ed. 59.00 (*0-932051-74-X*) Rprt Serv.

Oakham. Oakham Historical Society Staff. LC 98-88256. (Images of America Ser.). (Illus.). 1998. pap. 16.99 (*0-7524-1391-0*) Arcadia Publng.

Oakland Athletics. Paul Joseph. LC 96-22381. (America's Game Ser.). (Illus.). 32p. (J). (gr. 3-8). 1997. lib. bdg. 16.48 (*1-56239-668-4*) ABDO Pub Co.

Oakland Ballet: The First Twenty-Five Years. William Huck. (Journals: No. 3). 80p. 1990. pap. 15.00 (*1-881106-02-0*) SF Perf Arts Lib.

***Oakland Cemetery: St. Paul Minnesota, 1 Aug. 1885-31 December 1889.** Comment by Sharon Bruckner. 90p. 1999. pap. 15.00 (*0-915709-73-2*) Pk Geneal Bk.

Oakland Cemetery, St. Paul Minnesota Vol. 4: Interment Records from 1 June 1878 to 30 July 1885. Compiled by Sharon Bruckner. (Illus.). 80p. 1997. pap. 15.00 (*0-915709-33-3*) Pk Geneal Bk.

Oakland City Business Profiles: Oakland, CA. Cherie Emery. 1996. pap. text 19.95 (*1-885352-29-8*) Community Comm.

An Asterisk (*) at the beginning of an entry indicates that the title is appearing for the first time.

Oakland County Genealogical Society: Surname Directory, Vol. V. Society Members. Ed. by Joan Pate. 244p. (Orig.). 1995. pap. 12.00 (*1-879766-22-1*) OCG Society.

***Oakland Glimmer (a Novella) & Tales of the Want Ads (Stories)** Joe Cohen. 231p. 2000. pap. 14.95 (*1-889059-83-8*) Regent Pr.

Oakland Raiders. Bob Italia. LC 95-887. (Inside the NFL Ser.). (Illus.). 32p. (J). (gr. 3-8). 1995. lib. bdg. 15.98 (*1-56239-456-8*) ABDO Pub Co.

Oakland Raiders. Oakland Raiders Staff. Ed. by CWC Sports Inc. (NFL Team Yearbooks Ser.). (J). (gr. 1-12). 1998. pap. 9.99 (*1-891613-18-9*) Everett Sports.

***Oakland Raiders.** 3rd rev. ed. Julie Nelson. LC 99-23742. (Pro Football Today Ser.). (Illus.). 32p. (YA). (gr. 3-12). 2000. lib. bdg. 22.60 (*1-58341-054-6*, Creat Educ) Creative Co.

Oakland Register, 1903 (Town History & Directory) Compiled by H. E. Mitchell. 115p. 1997. reprint ed. pap. 19.50 (*0-8328-5881-1*) Higginson Bk Co.

Oakland Rhapsody: The Secret Soul of an American Downtown. Richard Nagler. (Illus.). 112p. (Orig.). (C). 1995. 35.00 (*1-55643-197-X*); pap. 22.95 (*1-55643-196-1*) North Atlantic.

Oakland Roadster Show: 50 Years of Hot Rods & Customs. Dain Gingerelli. LC 98-42470. 128p. 1998. pap. 21.95 (*0-7603-0608-7*) MBI Pubg.

Oakland, the Story of a City. Beth Bagwell. (Illus.). 292p. Date not set. reprint ed. 22.50 (*0-9640087-1-8*); reprint ed. pap. 11.95 (*0-9640087-0-X*) Oakland Herit.

Oakland to Shelton, the Sawdust Trail. rev. ed. Michael Fredson. (Illus.). 54p. reprint ed. pap. 4.00 (*0-935693-16-5*) Mason Cty Hist.

Oakland Welcomes the World. Mary E. Butler. 136p. 1996. 45.00 (*1-885352-27-1*) Community Comm.

Oakland/Alameda Counties Map Book. G. M. Johnson Associates Staff. (Orig.). 1999. pap. 9.95 (*0-9696979-3-7*) GM Johnson Assocs.

Oaklawn Manor. Lucile Thomas Holmes. (Illus.). 84p. 1983. reprint ed. pap. 9.95 (*0-88289-418-8*) Pelican.

Oaks. Logan. Date not set. write for info. (*0-393-04773-3*) Norton.

Oaks of California. Bruce M. Pavlik et al. (Illus.). 184p. (Orig.). 1992. pap. 21.95 (*0-9628505-1-9*) Cachuma Pr.

Oaks of India, Nepal & Bhutan. S. S. Negi & H. B. Naithani. LC 95-911159. 1995. pap. 90.00 (*81-7089-233-3*, Pub. by Intl Bk Distr) St Mut.

Oaks of North America. Howard A. Miller & Samuel H. Lamb. LC 83-25042. (Illus.). 328p. 1984. pap. 12.95 (*0-87961-137-5*) Naturegraph.

Oakseeds: Stories from the Land. Gary W. Cook. LC 92-43364. (Outdoor Tennessee Ser.). (Illus.). 208p. (C). 1993. pap. 17.95 (*0-87049-802-9*); text 30.00 (*0-87049-801-0*) U of Tenn Pr.

Oaktree Security. Adams. 1997. 30.00 (*0-8212-2420-4*) Little.

***Oakville: Jewel on the Lake.** Ron Edwards & Adrianna Edwards. (Canadian Enterprise Ser.). (Illus.). 96p. 2000. 38.00 (*1-58192-020-2*) Community Comm.

Oakwood Salt Dome, East Texas: Geologic Framework, Growth History, & Hydrocarbon Production. A. B. Giles & D. H. Wood. (Geological Circular Ser.: GC 83-1). (Illus.). 55p. 1983. pap. 2.50 (*0-318-03156-6*) Bur Econ Geology.

OALA Directory of Assisted Living Residences in Ohio, 1998. 3rd ed. (Illus.). 235p. 1998. pap. 20.00 (*0-9665610-0-7*) Ohio Assisted.

Oamaru Diatoms. T. V. Desikachary & P. M. Sreelatha. (Bibliotheca Diatomologica Ser.: Vol. 19). (Illus.). 330p. 1989. pap. text 130.00 (*3-443-57010-0*, Pub. by Gebruder Borntraeger) Balogh.

O&CB Streetcars of Omaha & Council Bluffs. Richard Orr. (Illus.). viii, 348p. 1996. 59.95 (*0-9653505-0-9*) R Orr.

Oar. Moya Cannon. 48p. 1995. reprint ed. pap. 11.95 (*1-897648-24-3*) Dufour.

Oarless Boats, Vacant Lots. Jon Veinberg. LC 98-12927. 64p. 1999. pap. 12.95 (*0-914061-74-7*) Orchises Pr.

Oars for Pleasure Rowing: Their Design & Use. Andrew B. Steever. (Illus.). 110p. 1992. pap. 15.00 (*0-913372-65-X*) Mystic Seaport.

OAS & the Promotion & Protection of Human Rights. Leblanc. 1977. pap. text 70.50 (*90-247-1943-7*) Kluwer Academic.

Oases: Poems & Prose Alastair Reid. LC 98-145218. 328 p. 1997. write for info. (*0-86241-717-1*) Canongate Books.

***Oasis.** Pauline Gedge. (Lords of the Two Lands Ser.: Vol. 2). 536p. 2000. 26.00 (*1-56947-219-X*) Soho Press.

Oasis. Gregory Maguire. LC 98-11991. 170p. (J). (gr. 4-7). 1998. pap. 4.95 (*0-7868-1293-1*, Pub. by Disney Pr) Time Warner.

Oasis. Gregory Maguire. LC 94-42891. 176p. (J). (gr. 6-9). 1996. 14.95 (*0-395-67019-5*, Clarion Bks) HM.

Oasis. Patricia Matthews. 352p. (Orig.). 1988. pap. 4.50 (*0-373-97094-3*) Harlequin Bks.

Oasis. Ed. by Timothy M. Simone. 116p. Date not set. 8.00 (*0-936756-40-3*) Autonomedia.

Oasis. large type ed. Patricia Matthews. LC 88-36823. 503p. (Orig.). 1989. reprint ed. lib. bdg. 7.95 (*0-89621-857-0*) Thorndike Pr.

Oasis: Lost Inside. Paul Moody. (Illus.). 80p. (Orig.). 1996. pap. 19.95 (*1-873884-50-8*, VX 05000, Pub. by UFO Books) Music Sales.

***Oasis: Poems from Hollywood.** Mark Dunster. 11p. 1999. pap. 5.00 (*0-89642-902-4*) Linden Pubs.

Oasis: Revealed. Lee Henshaw. (Illus.). 128p. pap. 14.95 (*0-7525-1859-3*, Pub. by Parragon Pub) Music Sales.

Oasis: Round Their Way. Mick Middles. 126p. (Orig.). (YA). pap. 17.95 (*1-897783-10-8*, MRSS627, Pub. by Indep Music Pr) Music Sales.

Oasis: The Illustrated Story. Paul Lester. (Illus.). 80p. pap. 14.95 (*0-600-58761-4*, HL00330020) H Leonard.

Oasis: The Illustrated Story. Paul Lester. 80p. 1995. pap. 14.95 (*0-7935-4729-6*, 00330020) H Leonard.

Oasis--Was, There, Then: A Photographic Journey. Jill Furmanovsky & Daniela Soave. (Illus.). 144p. (Orig.). 1998. pap. 24.95 (*0-09-186318-X*) Ebury Pr.

Oasis & Obqi: A Guide for Education & Implementation. Randa L. Sperling & Carolyn J. Humphrey. LC 98-36724. 279p. 1998. 49.95 (*0-7817-1955-0*) Lppncott W & W.

Oasis be Here Now. 88p. 1997. otabind 19.95 (*0-7935-8932-0*); otabind 16.95 (*0-7935-8933-9*) H Leonard.

Oasis Chronicles. Cimino. 1997. pap. text 24.95 (*1-901674-02-9*) Arrowhead Bks.

Oasis Chronicles. David H. Richter. 1998. pap. text 12.95 (*1-901674-42-8*) Arrowhead.

Oasis Definitely Maybe - Guitar Tablature. 80p. 1996. per. 19.95 (*0-7935-6962-1*) H Leonard.

Oasis Identities: Uyghur Nationalism along China's Silk Road. Justin Rudelson. LC 97-11066. (Illus.). 224p. 1998. pap. 17.50 (*0-231-10787-0*) Col U Pr.

Oasis Identities: Uyghur Nationalism along China's Silk Road. Justin Rudelson. LC 97-11066. (Illus.). 224p. 1998. 45.00 (*0-231-10786-2*) Col U Pr.

***Oasis in the City: The History of the Desert Botanical Garden.** Tara A. Blanc. Ed. by Susan Zelozniecki. 88p. 2000. 22.00 (*0-929690-51-6*) Herit Pubs AZ.

Oasis in the Heart: Haiku with Exposition. Toshimi Horiuchi. 152p. 1995. pap. 10.95 (*0-8348-0330-5*) Weatherhill.

Oasis in Time: Jerusalem. Asenath Petrie. 120p. (Orig.). 1994. pap. text 9.95 (*965-229-109-9*, Pub. by Gefen Pub Hse) Gefen Bks.

Oasis of Fire. Cassandra Fleming. 150p. 1996. mass mkt. 5.00 (*0-9634431-4-3*) C Y Pub Grp.

Oasis of Order: The Core Curriculum at Columbia College. Timothy P. Cross. (Illus.). 127p. (Orig.). 1995. pap. 15.00 (*0-9649084-0-9*) Columb Coll.

Oasis of Peace: A Hiroshima Story. Walter Enloe. LC 98-72515. 220 p. 1998. write for info. (*0-9633686-5-6*) Hamline Univ.

Oasis of the North. Dawn MacLeod. 276p. (C). 1985. pap. 39.00 (*0-906664-02-0*, Pub. by Mercat Pr Bks) St Mut.

Oasis of White Palm. P. Meyers & T. R. Hickman. 1983. 6.00 (*0-394-53153-1*) Random Bks Yng Read.

***OASIS Orientation & Training Video.** Tellens, Inc. Staff. 1998. 79.00 incl. VHS (*0-8342-1184-X*, 1184X) Aspen Pub.

Oasis Papers: Proceedings from the First International Symposium of the Dakhleh Oasis Project. Ed. by Mandy Marlow. (Oxbow Monographs: Vol. 97 & 6). (Illus.). 300p. 1999. 81.00 (*1-900188-54-6*, Pub. by Oxbow Bks) David Brown.

Oasis Supersonic Supernova. Michael Krugman. LC 96-37419. (Illus.). 160p. 1997. pap. 10.95 (*0-312-15376-7*) St Martin.

Oasis Technique. William H. Lindsey & Bruce Quint. 91p. 1986. 15.00 (*0-317-01541-9*) Fla Atlantic.

OAT - Optometry Admission Test: Comprehensive Manual Self Study. 2nd rev. ed. David M. Tarlow. 140p. (C). 1999. pap. text 19.95 (*1-57732-100-6*) Datar Pub.

OAT - Optometry Admission Test No. 1: Practice Exam Annotated Answers. 2nd rev. ed. David M. Tarlow. 20p. (C). 1999. pap. text 6.95 (*1-57732-102-2*) Datar Pub.

OAT - Optometry Admission Test No. 1: Practice Examination. 2nd rev. ed. David M. Tarlow. 40p. (C). 1999. pap. text 18.95 (*1-57732-101-4*) Datar Pub.

OAT - Optometry Admission Test No. 2: Practice Exam Annotated Answers. 2nd rev. ed. David M. Tarlow. 20p. (C). 1999. pap. text 6.95 (*1-57732-104-9*) Datar Pub.

OAT - Optometry Admission Test No. 2: Practice Examination, Vol. 2. 2nd rev. ed. David M. Tarlow. 40p. (C). 1999. pap. text 18.95 (*1-57732-103-0*) Datar Pub.

OAT - Optometry Admission Test No. 3: Practice Exam Annotated Answers. 2nd rev. ed. David M. Tarlow. 20p. (C). 1999. pap. text 6.95 (*1-57732-106-5*) Datar Pub.

OAT - Optometry Admission Test No. 3: Practice Examination. 2nd rev. ed. David M. Tarlow. (C). 1999. pap. text 18.95 (*1-57732-105-7*) Datar Pub.

OAT - Optometry Admission Test No. 4: Practice Exam Annotated Answers. 2nd rev. ed. David M. Tarlow. 20p. (C). 1999. pap. text 6.95 (*1-57732-108-1*) Datar Pub.

OAT - Optometry Admission Test No. 4: Practice Examination. 2nd rev. ed. David M. Tarlow. 40p. (C). 1999. pap. text 18.95 (*1-57732-107-3*) Datar Pub.

OAT - Optometry Admission Test No. 5: Practice Exam Annotated Answers. 2nd rev. ed. David M. Tarlow. 20p. (C). 1999. pap. text 6.95 (*1-57732-110-3*) Datar Pub.

***OAT - Optometry Admission Test No. 5: Practice Examination.** 2nd rev. ed. David M. Tarlow. 40p. (C). 1999. pap. text 18.95 (*1-57732-109-X*) Datar Pub.

OAT - Optometry Admission Test - Core Content. 2nd rev. ed. David M. Tarlow. (Illus.). 400p. 1999. pap. 49.95 (*1-57774-007-6*) Educ Tsting Cnslts.

OAT & AV2 Markings: A Work in Progress. Murray Heifetz & American Air Mail Society. LC 97-77651. (Illus.). 1997. write for info. (*0-939429-18-7*) Am Air Mail.

Oat Bran. Pref. by Peter J. Wood. LC 92-75520. (Illus.). 164p. 1993. 99.00 (*0-913250-77-5*) Am Assn Cereal Chem.

OAT Exam No. 1: Annotated Answers (Optometry Admissions Test) 7th ed. David M. Tarlow. (Orig.). 1996. pap. 5.95 (*1-57732-028-X*) Datar Pub.

OAT Exam No. 1: (Optometry Admissions Test) 7th ed. David M. Tarlow. (Orig.). 1996. pap. 19.95 (*1-57732-023-9*) Datar Pub.

OAT Exam No. 2: Annotated Answers (Optometry Admissions Test) David M. Tarlow. 1996. pap. write for info. (*1-57732-029-8*) Datar Pub.

OAT Exam No. 2: (Optometry Admissions Test) 7th ed. David M. Tarlow. 1996. pap. 19.95 (*1-57732-024-7*) Datar Pub.

OAT Exam No. 3: Annotated Answers (Optometry Admissions Test) 7th ed. David M. Tarlow. (Illus.). (Orig.). 1996. pap. 5.95 (*1-57732-030-1*) Datar Pub.

OAT Exam No. 3: (Optometry Admissions Test) 7th ed. David M. Tarlow. (Orig.). 1996. pap. write for info. (*1-57732-025-5*) Datar Pub.

OAT Exam No. 4: Annotated Answers (Optometry Admissions Test) 7th ed. David M. Tarlow. (Orig.). 1996. pap. 5.95 (*1-57732-031-X*) Datar Pub.

OAT Exam No. 4: (Optometry Admissions Test) 7th ed. David M. Tarlow. (Orig.). 1996. pap. 19.95 (*1-57732-026-3*) Datar Pub.

OAT Exam No. 5: Annotated Answers (Optometry Admissions Test) 7th ed. David M. Tarlow. (Orig.). 1996. pap. 5.95 (*1-57732-032-8*) Datar Pub.

OAT Exam No. 5: (Optometry Admissions Test) 7th ed. David M. Tarlow. (Illus.). 1996. pap. 19.95 (*1-57732-027-1*) Datar Pub.

OAT (Optometry Admission Test) For Comprehensive Review. 7th ed. David M. Tarlow. (Orig.). 1996. pap., student ed. 19.95 (*1-57732-022-0*) Datar Pub.

Oat Science & Technology. Ed. by H. G. Marshall & M. E. Sorrells. LC 92-19551. (Agronomy Ser.: No. 33). 846p. 1992. 48.00 (*0-89118-110-5*) Am Soc Agron.

Oaten Reeds & Trumpets: Pastoral & Epic in Virgil, Spenser, & Milton. D. N. Rosenberg. LC 80-17974. 288p. 1981. 38.50 (*0-8387-5002-8*) Bucknell U Pr.

Oath see Juramento

Oath. Frank Peretti. 1995. audio 23.00 (*0-8499-6214-5*, 6146) Word Pub.

Oath. Frank E. Peretti. 560p. 1996. pap. 12.99 (*0-8499-3863-5*) Word Pub.

Oath: Inside: Exclusive excerpt from Peretti's 1999 Novel, Sneak Preview Edition. Frank E. Peretti. 1998. pap. write for info. (*0-8499-3723-X*) Word Pub.

Oath & Perjury in Ancient Greece. Joseph Plescia. LC 73-13540. 124p. reprint ed. pap. 38.50 (*0-7837-4903-1*, 204456800004) Bks Demand.

Oath & the Measure. Michael Williams. (DragonLance Meetings Sextet: Vol. 4). (Illus.). 320p. (Orig.). 1992. pap. 5.99 (*1-56076-336-1*, Pub. by TSR Inc) Random.

Oath of Fealty. Larry Niven & Jerry Pournelle. Ed. by Dave Stern. 1984. per. 5.99 (*0-671-53227-8*) PB.

Oath of Gold. Elizabeth Moon. (Deed of Paksenarrion Ser.: Bk. III). 512p. 1989. mass mkt. 5.99 (*0-671-69798-6*) Baen Bks.

***Oath of Office.** large type ed. Max Brand. 1998. 19.95 (*1-57490-158-3*, Sagebrush LP West) T T Beeler.

Oath of Stonekeep, 1 vol. Troy Denning. 264p. 1999. mass mkt. 6.99 (*0-425-17065-9*) Blvd Books.

Oath of Swords. David Weber. 512p. (Orig.). 1995. per. 6.99 (*0-671-87642-2*) Baen Bks.

Oathbound. Mercedes Lackey. (Vows & Honor Ser.: Bk. 1). 302p. 1988. mass mkt. 5.99 (*0-88677-414-4*, Pub. by DAW Bks) Penguin Putnam.

Oathbreakers. Mercedes Lackey. (Vows & Honor Ser.: Bk. 2). 1989. mass mkt. 5.99 (*0-88677-454-3*, Pub. by DAW Bks) Penguin Putnam.

Oaths & Miracles. Nancy Kress. 1997. mass mkt. 6.99 (*0-8125-4473-0*, Pub. by Tor Bks) St Martin.

***Oaths of Allegiance in Colonial New England.** Charles Evans. (Illus.). 64p. 1998. reprint ed. pap. 11.50 (*0-8063-4826-7*) Clearfield Co.

Oaths of Office for the Use of City, County & State Officials in North Carolina. James Lung & C. E. Hinsdale. 42p. 1975. 4.00 (*1-56011-121-6*) Institute Government.

Oatmeal. Evelyn Marie. (Illus.). 24p. (J). (gr. k-3). 1997. pap. 3.50 (*1-890579-00-9*) Berry Bks.

Oatmeal & Kisses. Murray Schisgal. 1990. pap. 5.25 (*0-8222-0834-2*) Dramatists Play.

Oatmeal & the Catechism: Scottish Gaelic Settlers in Quebec. Margaret Bennett. 330p. 1998. pap. 66.00 (*0-85976-461-3*, Pub. by J Donald) St Mut.

Oatmeal & the Catechism: Scottish Gaelic Settlers in Quebec. Margaret Bennett. (Illus.). 352p. 1998. 65.00 (*0-7735-1810-X*) McG-Queens Univ Pr.

Oatmeal on My Blazer: Having It All & Other Myths. Rochelle L. Wallach & Linda M. Koe. 173p. 1992. pap. 9.95 (*0-9633304-0-3*) Panache Pr WI.

Oatmeal Sandwiches: A History of the Will T. Austin Family. limited ed. Doris Mayes. 160p. 1998. pap. write for info. (*1-887303-18-9*) Blu Lantern Pub.

Oats! A Tribute to Our Favorite Comfort Food. Shirley Streshinsky & Maria Streshinsky. (Illus.). 80p. 1996. pap. text 5.95 (*0-89087-808-0*) Celestial Arts.

Oats: Chemistry & Technology. F. Webster. LC 86-71926. 433p. 1986. 159.00 (*0-913250-30-9*) Am Assn Cereal Chem.

Oats & Apples. Horace. Ed. by Charles E. Bennett. (College Classical Ser.). 1992. pap. 17.50 (*0-89241-371-9*); lib. bdg. 32.50 (*0-89241-024-8*) Caratzas.

Oats, Peas, Beans, & Barley Cookbook: A Complete Vegetarian Cookbook Using Nature's Most Economical Foods. rev. ed. Edyth Y. Cottrell. LC 80-80794. (Illus.). 283p. (Orig.). 1989. pap. 12.95 (*0-912800-85-2*) Woodbridge Pr.

OAU after Twenty Years: An SAIS Study on Africa. Ed. by Yassin El-Ayouty et al. LC 83-24676. 406p. 1984. 75.00 (*0-275-91149-7*, C1149, Praeger Pubs) Greenwood.

OAU & the U. N. Relations Between the Organization of African Unity & the United Nations. Berhanykun Andemicael. LC 74-84658. 350p. 1976. 49.50 (*0-8419-0186-4*, Africana) Holmes & Meier.

Oaxaca. 112p. pap. text 12.95 (*88-8029-150-5*, Pub. by Bonechi) Eiron.

Oaxaca: Valley of Myth & Magic. Jennifer Fiore & Stevie Mack. 1995. teacher ed. 89.95 incl. VHS (*0-945666-32-2*) Crizmac.

Oaxacan Ceramics: Traditional Folk Art by Oaxacan Women. Lois Wasserspring. LC 99-17684. (Illus.). 132p. 2000. pap. 18.95 (*0-8118-2358-X*) Chronicle Bks.

Oaxacan Woodcarving: The Magic in the Trees. Shephard Barbash. (Illus.). 120p. 1993. 27.50 (*0-8118-0316-3*); pap. 18.95 (*0-8118-0250-7*) Chronicle Bks.

Oaxacans in Mesoamerica. John Paddock. Date not set. pap. write for info. (*0-939923-23-8*) M & W Pub Co.

***Ob.** Peter Reading. 64p. 1999. pap. (*1-85224-490-9*, Pub. by Bloodaxe Bks) Dufour.

Ob-Gyn Intern Pocket Survival Guide. Andrew Engel. 78p. (Orig.). (C). 1998. pap. 7.50 (*1-883205-00-X*) Intl Med Pub.

OB-GYN Secrets. 2nd ed. Helen L. Frederickson & Louise Wilkins-Haug. LC 92-70987. 368p. 1996. pap. 39.00 (*1-56053-205-X*) Hanley & Belfus.

***Obaasima.** Kwame Okoampa-Ahoofe, Jr. 104p. 2000. pap. 8.95 (*0-938999-13-3*) Yuganta Pr.

O'Baby: The Irish Baby Name Book. Geoffrey Johnson. LC 99-192683. 176p. 1999. mass mkt. 5.99 (*0-425-16818-2*) Berkley Pub.

Obadiah: A New Translation with Introduction & Commentary. Paul R. Raabe. LC 95-36913. (Anchor Bible Ser.). (Illus.). 336p. 1996. 34.95 (*0-385-41268-1*, Anchor NY) Doubleday.

Obadiah & Jonah: A Continental Commentary. Hans W. Wolff. Tr. by Margaret Kohl from GER. LC 86-22256. Orig. Title: Obadja, Jona. 192p. (C). 1986. text 38.00 (*0-8006-9511-9*, 1-9511, Fortress Pr) Augsburg Fortress.

Obadiah Coffee & the Music Contest. Valerie Poole. LC 89-49548. (Illus.). 32p. (J). (ps-3). 1991. 14.95 (*0-06-021619-0*); lib. bdg. 14.89 (*0-06-021620-4*) HarpC Child Bks.

Obadiah, Jonah: Introduction & Commentary. Ed. by Mordechai Cogan & Uriel Simon. (HEB.). 96p. 1992. text 12.00 (*965-13-0834-6*, Pub. by Magnes Pr) Eisenbrauns.

Obadiah, Jonah, Micah. David W. Baker et al. LC 88-9041. (Tyndale Old Testament Commentary Ser.). 208p. (Orig.). (C). 1989. pap. 12.99 (*0-87784-275-2*, 275) InterVarsity.

Obadiah, Jonah, Micah. David W. Baker et al. LC 88-9041. (Tyndale Old Testament Commentary Ser.: Vol. 23a). 208p. (Orig.). (C). 1989. 19.99 (*0-8308-1425-6*, 1425) InterVarsity.

Obadiah, Jonah, Micah. Cyril W. Spaude. LC 96-224523. 176p. 1994. pap. 9.99 (*0-570-04661-0*, 12-8026) Concordia.

Obadiah, Jonah, Micah. Cyril W. Spaude. LC 87-60176. (People's Bible Ser.). 170p. 1987. pap. 9.99 (*0-8100-0262-0*, 15N0448) Northwest Pub.

Obadiah, Jonah, Micah. Cyril W. Spaude. (The People's Bible Ser.). 60p. 1988. pap. text, student ed. 5.00 (*0-938272-67-5*, 22-2211) WELS Board.

Obadiah Through Malachi. William P. Brown. LC 96-17773. (Westminster Bible Companion Ser.). 200p. 1996. pap. 17.00 (*0-664-25520-5*) Westminster John Knox.

Obadja, Jona see Obadiah & Jonah: A Continental Commentary

Obadzeng Goes to Town. Saka Acquaye. (Evans Africa Plays Ser.). 30p. 1991. pap. write for info. (*0-237-49520-1*) EVN1 UK.

Obagi Skin Health Restoration & Rejuvenation. Z. E. Obagi. (Illus.). 250p. 1998. 135.00 (*0-387-98469-0*) Spr-Verlag.

Obake: Ghost Stories in Hawaii. Glen Grant. (Illus.). 192p. 1994. pap. 12.95 (*1-56647-072-2*) Mutual Pub HI.

***Obake: Ghost Stories in Hawaii.** Glen Grant. 274p. 2000. mass mkt. 6.95 (*1-56647-320-9*) Mutual Pub HI.

Obake Files: Ghostly Encounters in Supernatural Hawaii. Glen Grant. 448p. 1999. mass mkt. 8.95 (*1-56647-224-5*) Mutual Pub HI.

Obake Files: Ghostly Stories from the Supernatural of Hawaii. Glen Grant. LC 96-78339. 320p. 1996. pap. 15.95 (*1-56647-100-1*) Mutual Pub HI.

***Obaku Zen: The Emergence of the Third Sect of Zen in Tokugawa, Japan.** Helen J. Baroni. LC 99-355256. 294p. 2000. text 60.00 (*0-8248-2195-5*); pap. text 32.95 (*0-8248-2243-9*) UH Pr.

Oban Line. Picton Publishing Staff & Tom Weir. (Illus.). (C). 1987. 22.00 (*0-7855-2191-7*, Pub. by Picton) St Mut.

Oban, Mull & Kintyre. Jarrold Publishing Staff. (Pathfinder Guides Ser.). 1998. pap. 16.95 (*0-7117-0992-0*, Pub. by JARR UK) Seven Hills Bk.

Obasan. Joy Kogawa. LC 93-26081. 320p. 1993. pap. 11.95 (*0-385-46886-5*) Doubleday.

Obatala: IFA & the Spirit of the Chief of the White Cloth. Fa'lokun Fatunmbi. 32p. 1993. pap. 4.95 (*0-942272-30-7*) Original Pubns.

Obata's Yosemite: The Art & Letters of Chiura Obata from His Trip to the High Sierra in 1927. Ed. by Janice T. Driesbach & Susan Landauer. LC 93-8320. (Illus.). 1993. 44.95 (*0-939666-66-9*); pap. 24.95 (*0-939666-67-7*) Yosemite Assn.

Obayd Zakani: Collected Works. Ed. by Mohammad-Ja'far Mahjoub. (Persian Text Ser.: No. 2). 544p. 1999. text 48.00 (*0-933273-30-4*, Pub. by Bibliotheca Persica) Eisenbrauns.

Obdurate Brilliance: Exteriority & the Modern Long Poem. Peter Baker. 252p. (C). 1991. 49.95 (*0-8130-1064-0*) U Press Fla.

O

An Asterisk (*) at the beginning of an entry indicates that the title is appearing for the first time.

Obeah. Colin Moone. 1997. pap. 9.95 (*1-874509-18-2*, Pub. by X Pr) LPC InBook.

***Obeah.** Carlton Rapp & Kati Rapp. LC 99-65314. 192p. 2000. pap. 11.95 (*1-56315-215-0*, Pub. by SterlingHse) Natl Bk Netwk.

Obeah Man. Ismith Khan. LC 95-192915. 168p. Date not set. pap. 12.95 (*0-920661-46-7*, Pub. by TSAR Pubns) LPC InBook.

Obeah Woman May: A Caribbean Novel of Mystery & Magic. Andrew A. Munroe. 181p. 1998. pap. 12.95 (*0-9643010-1-6*) Golden Grove.

Obedience. Raniero Cantalamessa & Board of St. Paul Editorial Staff. 78p. (C). 1996. pap. 39.95 (*0-85439-281-5*, Pub. by St Paul Pubns) St Mut.

Obedience. Archimandrite Chrysostomos & Hieromonk Ambrosios. Ed. by Alexey Young & Vladimir Derugin. 90p. 1984. pap. text 3.00 (*0-916586-23-5*) Holy Cross Orthodox.

Obedience. Joseph Hansen. LC 88-40072. 208p. 1988. 16.45 (*0-89296-296-8*, Pub. by Mysterious Pr) Little.

Obedience. Joseph Hansen. 1989. mass mkt. 4.95 (*0-445-40844-8*, Mysterious Paperbk) Warner Bks.

Obedience. S. J. Hulshizer. 69p. pap. 4.95 (*0-88172-156-5*) Believers Bkshelf.

***Obedience.** Warner Press Staff. (Lion Cub Upside-Down Books Ser.). (Illus.). (J). 2000. pap. 5.95 (*0-87162-820-1*) Warner Pr.

Obedience: The Key to God's Divine Favor. Charles Mellette. 96p. (Orig.). 1996. pap. 9.99 (*1-889389-05-6*) End-Time Wave.

Obedience: The Road to Reality. Kathy Hendershot. 176p. (Orig.). 1982. pap. 3.50 (*0-911567-00-3*) Christian Mini.

Obedience & Civilization: The Origins of Authorized Crime. Don Mixon. 208p. 1989. text 34.95 (*0-7453-0331-5*) Routledge.

Obedience & Tracking Today. deluxe ed. Mardee F. Edelstein. (Illus.). 280p. 1995. pap. 35.00 (*0-614-04523-1*) Donald R Hoflin.

Obedience Experiments: A Case Study of Controversy in Social Science. Arthur Miller. LC 85-25738. 305p. 1986. 65.00 (*0-275-92012-7*, C2012, Praeger Pubs) Greenwood.

Obedience in Finances. Kenneth E. Hagin. 1983. pap. 1.00 (*0-89276-259-4*) Faith Lib Pubns.

Obedience of a Christen Man & How Christe Rulers Ought to Governe. William Tyndale. LC 77-7436. (English Experience Ser.: No. 897). 1977. reprint ed. lib. bdg. 35.00 (*90-221-0897-X*) Walter J Johnson.

***Obedience of a Christian Man.** Richard Lovett. 320p. 1999. pap. 60.00 (*1-57074-377-0*) Greyden Pr.

***Obedience of a Christian Man.** William Tyndale. (Penguin Classics Ser.). 272p. 2000. pap. 13.00 (*0-14-043477-1*, Penguin Bks) Viking Penguin.

Obedience of Faith. Morris L. Venden. LC 83-13934. 95p. (Orig.). reprint ed. pap. 30.00 (*0-7837-6431-6*, 204642900012) Bks Demand.

Obedience of Faith: A Pauline Phrase in Historical Context. Don B. Garlington. (WissUNT Neuen Testament Ser.: No. 2-38). 320p. (Orig.). 1992. pap. 71.50 (*3-16-145506-1*, Pub. by JCB Mohr) Coronet Bks.

Obedience, Suspicion & the Gospel of Mark: A Mennonite-Feminist Exploration of Biblical Authority. Lydia Neufeld Harder. (Studies in Women & Religion: Vol. 5). 168p. 1998. pap. 26.95 (*0-88920-305-9*) Wilfrid Laurier.

Obedience to Authori. Stanley Milgram. 256p. 1983. pap. 14.50 (*0-06-131983-X*, TB1983, Torch) HarpC.

Obedience to Authority: Current Perspectives on the Milgram Paradigm. Ed. by Thomas Blass. LC 99-30504. 300p. 1999. write for info. (*0-8058-2737-4*) L Erlbaum Assocs.

Obedience Training. Bruce Bartley & Bronwyn Bartley. (Illus.). 112p. 1995. 35.00 (*1-85223-799-6*, Pub. by Cro1wood) Trafalgar.

***Obedience Training.** Dennis Kelsey-Wood. (Illus.). 1999. 12.95 (*0-7938-3017-6*) TFH Pubns.

Obedience Training for Your Dog. Cecil Wimhurst. (Illus.). 70p. 1955. pap. 3.50 (*0-486-20938-5*) Dover.

Obedience, Who Wants It? The Baptized Christian's Call to Perfection. 2nd ed. David M. Knight. 33p. 1990, reprint ed. pap. 4.00 (*0-942971-19-1*) His Way.

Obedience Will Bring the Rain. Sandra A. Brooks. 38p. 1997. pap. 2.00 (*0-9665108-0-1*) Keeping Word.

Obedient & Patient Faith: An Exposition of 1st Peter. Robert Leighton. 1999. pap. text 16.95 (*1-879737-15-9*) Calvary Press.

***Obedient Father.** Akhil Sharma. LC 99-86589. 240p. 2000. text 23.00 (*0-374-10501-4*) FS&G.

Obedient Germans? A Rebuttal: A New View of German History. Peter Blickle. Tr. by Thomas A. Brady, Jr. from GER. LC 97-26222. (Studies in Early Modern German History Ser.).Tr. of Deutsche Untertanen. 145p. 1998. text 45.00 (*0-8139-1745-X*); pap. text 16.00 (*0-8139-1809-X*) U Pr of Va.

Obedient Sons: The Discourse of Youth & Generations in American Culture, 1630-1860. Glenn Wallach. LC 96-18193. (Illus.). 288p. (C). 1997. 29.95 (*1-55849-057-4*) U of Mass Pr.

Obedient to God's Word. J. C. Provost. LC 92-75258. 200p. (Orig.). 1992. pap. 7.95 (*1-879667-11-8*) Dove Pr TX.

Obedient to the Heavenly Vision see Obediente a la Vision Celestial

Obedient to the Heavenly Vision. Billy D. Murray, Sr. 250p. (Orig.). 1996. pap. 9.95 (*0-934942-97-8*) White Wing Pub.

Obedient to the Heavenly Vision. 2nd rev. ed. Billy Murray. (Illus.). 280p. 1997. pap. 9.95 (*1-889505-07-2*) White Wing Pub.

Obediente a la Vision Celestial. Billy Murray.Tr. of Obedient to the Heavenly Vision. (SPA., Illus.). 260p. (Orig.). 1996. pap. 9.95 (*1-889505-03-X*) White Wing Pub.

Obee & Mungedeech. Trude Martin. (Illus.). 112p. (J). (gr. 3-7). 1996. mass mkt. 3.99 (*0-689-80725-2*) Aladdin.

Obee & Mungedeech. Trude Martin. LC 95-43531. (Illus.). 112p. (J). (gr. 4-8). 1996. 15.00 (*0-689-80644-2*) Aladdin.

Obee & Mungedeech. Trude Martin. LC 95-43531. (J). 1996. 9.09 (*0-606-09702-3*, Pub. by Turtleback) Demco.

***Obee & Mungedeech.** Trude Martin. 107p. (J). (gr. 3-6). 1999. reprint ed. text 15.00 (*0-7881-6639-5*) DIANE Pub.

Obelisco (Diosa-Madre-Poesia) Jorge L. Morales. (Poetry Ser.). 128p. 1990. 50.00 (*0-317-05414-7*); pap. 25.00 (*0-317-05415-5*) Instit Nacional.

Obelisk: A Novel. Judith Jones. 400p. 1996. mass mkt., per. 5.99 (*0-7615-0419-2*) Prima Pub.

Obelisk & Freemasonry: Egyptian Symbols Compared with Those Discovered in America. John A. Weisse. 178p. 1993. reprint ed. pap. 18.95 (*1-56459-384-3*) Kessinger Pub.

Obelisk Conspiracy. George Martin & Michael Burren. 224p. 1976. 7.95 (*0-8065-0513-3*, Citadel Pr) Carol Pub Group.

Obelists Fly High. C. Daly King. 288p. 1986. reprint ed. pap. 5.95 (*0-486-25036-9*) Dover.

Obelix & Co. Rene de Goscinny & A. Uderzo. 1992. 24.95 (*0-7859-1041-7*, 0-340-227095) Fr & Eur.

Obelix & Company. Rene de Goscinny. (Adventures of Asterix Ser.). (Illus.). 44p. (J). 1995. reprint ed. pap. 9.95 (*0-917201-70-1*, Pub. by Dargaud) Distribks Inc.

Obelix et Compagnie. Rene de Goscinny & M. Uderzo. (FRE., Illus.). (J). 1990. 24.95 (*0-8288-5479-3*) Fr & Eur.

Obelix GMBH Co. Rene de Goscinny & A. Uderzo. (GER.). 1992. 24.95 (*0-7859-1021-2*, 3770400232) Fr & Eur.

Oberammergau: A Decade of Experiences in a Bavarian Village. Donald P. Crivellone. 112p. (Orig.). 1994. pap. 9.95 (*0-9643005-0-8*) Dobin Enter.

***Oberammergau: Child's Play: The Passion Play 2000.** Ed. by Prestel-Verlag Staff. 2000. 14.95 (*3-7913-2351-2*) Prestel Pub NY.

***Oberammergau: The Passion Play 2000.** Ed. by Prestel-Verlag Staff. 2000. 25.00 (*3-7913-2327-X*) Prestel Pub NY.

***Oberammergau: The Troubling Story of the World's Most Famous Passion Play.** James Shapiro. LC 99-89135. (Illus.). 256p. 2000. 24.00 (*0-375-40926-2*) Pantheon.

Oberbergisches Land: Zwischen Wupper und Sieg. Hellmut Grabert. (Sammlung Geologischer Fuehrer Ser.: Band 68). (GER., Illus.). viii, 178p. 1980. spiral bd. 23.00 (*3-443-15027-6*, Pub. by Gebruder Borntraeger) Balogh.

Oberer, Hanslowe & Heinsz' Statutory Supplement to Labor Law. 4th ed. Walter E. Oberer et al. (American Casebook Ser.). 866p. (C). 1994. pap. text 22.50 (*0-314-03247-9*) West Pub.

Oberheim Matrix-Six: Getting the Most Out of Your. Jeff Burger. Ed. by Peter L. Alexander. (Illus.). 102p. (C). 1987. pap. text 19.95 (*0-939067-17-X*) Alexander Pub.

Oberlin Alumni Collect: Modern & Contemporary Art. Intro. by W. J. Chiego. (Illus.). 1989. pap. 20.00 (*0-942946-04-9*) Ober Coll Allen.

Oberlin Architecture, College & Town: A Guide to Its Social History. Geoffrey Blodgett. LC 84-18987. (Illus.). 260p. 1985. pap. 11.00 (*0-87338-309-5*) Kent St U Pr.

Oberlin Book of Bandstands. Ed. by S. Frederick Starr. LC 87-22570. (Illus.). 100p. (Orig.). 1987. pap. 15.00 (*0-89133-128-X*) Ober Coll Allen.

***Oberlin Colony (Oltio) The Story of a Century.** Wilbur H. Phillips. (Illus.). 328p. 2000. pap. 24.86 (*0-7884-1491-7*, 1491) Heritage Bk.

Obermann. Etienne P. De Senancour. (FRE.). 1984. pap. 19.95 (*0-7859-4205-X*, 2070375668) Fr & Eur.

Obernberg: A Quantitative Analysis of a Peasant Tirolean Economy. Leopold Pospisil. LC 95-69512. (Memoirs of the Connecticut Academy of Arts & Sciences Ser.: Vol. 24). (Illus.). 416p. 1995. text 60.00 (*1-878508-09-1*) CT Acad Arts & Sciences.

***Obernewtyn.** Isobelle Carmody. LC 99-38130. 256p. 1999. 22.95 (*0-312-86958-4*, Pub. by Tor Bks) St Martin.

***Obernewtyn.** Isobelle Carmody. 2000. mass mkt. 6.99 (*0-8125-8422-8*) Tor Bks.

Oberon-2 Programming with Windows. J. R. Muhlbacher et al. LC 97-8043. 376p. 1997. pap. 49.95 incl. cd-rom (*3-540-62522-4*) Spr-Verlag.

Oberonia (Orchidaceae) rev. ed. R. Ansari & N. P. Balakrishnan. Ed. by E. F. De Vogel. (Orchid Monographs: Vol. 4). (Illus.). vi, 82p. 1990. pap. 25.00 (*90-71236-06-4*, Pub. by Rijksherbarium) Balogh.

Oberrheinische Kardiologen-Symposium. Ed. by R. Voegtlin. (Cardiology Ser.: Vol. 68, Suppl. 1). (Illus.). 136p. 1981. pap. 35.75 (*3-8055-3436-1*) S Karger.

Oberrheinisches Kardiologen-Symposium, Freiburg, May, 1982: Journal: Cardiology, Vol. 70, Suppl. 1, 1983. Ed. by H. Loellgen. (Illus.). iv, 140p. 1983. pap. 41.75 (*3-8055-3688-7*) S Karger.

Obersalzberg & the Third Reich. Anton Plenk. (Illus.). 87p. 1982. pap. 20.00 (*3-922590-13-6*) Johnson Ref Bks.

***Oberschlesische Literatur 1900, 1925: Historischer Umbruch und literarische Reflexion.** Bernd Witte. 2000. 48.95 (*3-631-34635-2*) P Lang Pubng.

Obervational Cosmology: Proceedings of the 124th Symposium of the International Astronomical Union, Held in Beijing, China, August 25-30, 1986 International Astronomical Union Members et al. LC 87-9561. xxiii, 854 p. 1987. write for info. (*90-277-2476-8*, Pub. by Kluwer Academic) Kluwer Academic.

Obese Child. Ed. by P. L. Giorgi et al. (Pediatric & Adolescent Medicine Ser.: Vol. 2). (Illus.). viii, 256p. 1992. 201.00 (*3-8055-5463-X*) S Karger.

Obesidad Es un Problema Familiar. Judi Hollis.Tr. of Fat Is a Family Affair. (SPA.). 172p. pap. 15.00 (*968-39-0517-X*) Hazelden.

Obesities. rev. ed. J. Vague. 172p. 35.00 (*0-86196-582-5*, Pub. by J Libbey Med) Bks Intl VA.

***Obesity.** Charlene Akers. LC 99-46398. (Overview Ser.). 128p. (YA). (gr. 4-12). 2000. 18.96 (*1-56006-662-8*) Lucent Bks.

Obesity: Advances in Understanding & Treatment. Leslie Weston. (Biomedical Library). 500p. 1996. pap. 795.00 (*1-57936-010-6*) IBC USA.

Obesity: Basic Concepts & Clinical Aspects. Ed. by F. Belfiore et al. (Frontiers in Diabetes Ser.: Vol. 11). (Illus.). viii, 220p. 1991. 214.00 (*3-8055-5405-2*) S Karger.

***Obesity: Impact on Cardiovascular Disease.** Ed. by Gerald F. Fletcher et al. LC 99-34125. (American Heart Association Monograph Ser.). (Illus.). 392p. 1999. 69.00 (*0-87993-418-2*) Futura Pub.

Obesity: New Directions in Assessment & Management. Ed. by Artemis Simopoulos & Theodore Van Itallie. LC 94-29964. (Illus.). 294p. 1995. text 42.95 (*0-914783-74-2*) Charles.

***Obesity: Pathology & Therapy.** P. Bjhorntorp et al. LC 00-44025. (Handbook of Experimental Pharmacology Ser.). 2000. write for info. (*3-540-66133-6*) Spr-Verlag.

***Obesity: The Report of the British Nutrition Foundation Task Force.** British Nutrition Foundation Staff. LC 99-88087. 2000. pap. write for info. (*0-632-05298-8*) Blackwell Sci.

Obesity: Theory & Therapy. 2nd ed. Albert J. Stunkard & Thomas A. Wadden. 394p. 1992. text 68.00 (*0-88167-884-8*) Lppncott W & W.

***Obesity & Depression in the Enlightenment: The Life & Times of George Cheyne.** Anita Guerrini. LC 99-35909. (Oklahoma Project for Discourse & Theory Ser.). 304p. 1999. 15.95 (*0-8061-3201-9*) U of Okla Pr.

***Obesity & Depression in the Enlightenment Vol. 3: The Life & Times of George Cheyne.** Anita Guerrini. LC 99-35909. (Series for Science & Culture of the Oklahoma Project for Discourse & Theory). (Illus.). 283p. (C). 2000. 25.95 (*0-8061-3159-4*) U of Okla Pr.

Obesity & Diabetes Mellitus. E. I. Sokolov. (Illus.). 331p. 1997. 115.00 (*90-6764-212-6*, Pub. by VSP) Coronet Bks.

Obesity & Medical Student Education. Ed. by Walter Futterweit et al. 110p. (Orig.). 2000. pap. 18.95 (*0-930194-89-6*) Ctr Thanatology.

Obesity & Niddm: Lessons from the Oletf Rat. Kenji Shima. LC 99-14144. 258p. 1999. 139.50 (*0-444-50112-6*) Elsevier.

***Obesity & Poverty: A New Public Health Challenge.** (Scientific Publication Ser.: Vol. 576). 135p. 2000. pap. 22.00 (*92-75-11576-1*) PAHO.

Obesity & Related Diseases. J. S. Garrow. LC 87-14631. (Illus.). 340p. 1988. text 108.00 (*0-443-03798-1*) Church.

Obesity & the Family. Ed. by David J. Kallen & Marvin B. Sussman. LC 84-4639. (Marriage & Family Review Ser.: Vol. 7, Nos. 1-2). 157p. 1984. text 49.95 (*0-86656-162-5*) Haworth Pr.

Obesity, Diabetes, & How to Eat to Live. Kevin Muhammad. LC 97-61410. (Within the Pulse Ser.: Vol. 1). (Illus.). 110p. 1997. pap. 10.95 (*0-9658864-0-9*) Crescent Pub Grp.

Obesity in Children & Youth: Measurement, Characteristics, Causes & Treatment. Anthony F. Rotatori & Robert A. Fox. (Illus.). 188p. 1989. 52.95 (*0-398-05594-7*) C C Thomas.

Obesity Management. 124p. pap. text 39.95 (*0-86471-068-2*, Pub. by Adis Intl) Lppncott W & W.

***Obesity Sourcebook: Basic Consumer Health Information about Diseases & Other Problems Associated with Obesity.** Ed. by Wilma Caldwell. (Health Reference Ser.). 400p. 2000. lib. bdg. 48.00 (*0-7808-0333-7*) Omnigraphics Inc.

Obesity Treatment: Establishing Goals, Improving Outcomes & Reviewing the Research Agenda: Proceedings of a NATO ARW Held in New York City, June 2-5, 1993. Ed. by David B. Allison & Xavier F. Pi-Sunyer. (NATO ASI Ser.: Vol. 278). (Illus.). 290p. (C). 1995. text 95.00 (*0-306-45115-8*, Kluwer Plenum) Kluwer Academic.

Obession of Oscar Oswald & Warrant of Distress. Frank Hardy. 212p. (C). 1990. 60.00 (*0-9592104-0-7*, Pub. by Pascoe Pub) St Mut.

Obey God Rather Than Man. Henry Ciszek. 322p. 1993. pap. 14.95 (*1-56794-030-7*, C2290) Star Bible.

Obey the Moon. large type ed. Vicky Martin. 545p. 1989. 27.99 (*0-7089-1963-4*) Ulverscroft.

Obey Your Signal Only: A Poetry Book. Bibliotheca Press Staff. 7.95 (*0-939476-20-7*) Prosperity & Profits.

Obeying God Is . . . Easy. John Chisolm. 90p. 1998. pap. 12.00 (*1-57502-982-0*, PO2683) Morris Pubng.

Obeying God's Word: Twelve Active Learning Experiences for Ages 4 to 12. Joette Whims & Melody Hunskor. Ed. by Henrietta Gambill. (Interactive Object Lessons Ser.). (Illus.). 64p. 1999. pap. text 7.99 (*0-7847-0938-6*, 03522) Standard Pub.

Obeying Orders: Atrocity, Military Discipline & the Law of War. Mark J. Osiel. LC 98-38647. 398p. 1999. 34.95 (*1-56000-407-X*) Transaction Pubs.

Obeying the Truth: A Study of Paul's Ethics in Galatians. John M. Barclay. Ed. by John E. Riches. (Studies of the New Testament & Its World). 320p. text 49.95 (*0-567-09493-6*, Pub. by T & T Clark) Bks Intl VA.

Obfuscated C & Other Mysteries, Set. Don Libes. LC 92-17028. (Illus.). 432p. 1992. pap. 39.95 incl. disk (*0-471-57805-3*) Wiley.

Ob/Gyn. Philippe H. Girerd. (Clerkship Ser.). 2000. pap. text 25.95 (*1-889325-08-2*, Pub. by Fence Crk Pubng) Blackwell Sci.

OB/GYN Medical Student Pearls of Wisdom. Smith. (Pearls of Wisdom Ser.). 1999. pap. 32.00 (*1-58409-001-4*) Boston Medical.

OB/GYN Nurse Practitioner. Rudman. (Certified Nurse Examination Ser.: CN-19). pap. 23.95 (*0-8373-6119-2*) Nat Learn.

OB/GYN Pearls of Wisdom. Smith. (Pearls of Wisdom Ser.). 1999. pap. 88.00 (*1-890369-06-3*) Boston Medical.

OB/GYN Ultrasound Triage & Evaluation for Advanced Practice Nurses. Cydney A. Menihan. LC 97-24741. 224p. 1997. spiral bd. 37.00 (*0-397-55383-8*) Lppncott W & W.

Obi. John Munonye. (African Writers Ser.). 210p. (C). 1969. pap. 8.95 (*0-435-90045-5*, 90045) Heinemann.

Obi. Compiled by William Earle. LC 76-38012. (Black Heritage Library Collection). 1977. reprint ed. 18.95 (*0-8369-8980-5*) Ayer.

Obikhod of Sacred Music see Obikhod Tserkovnago Penija

Obikhod Tserkovnago Penija. Tr. of Obikhod of Sacred Music. 167p. 1959. 20.00 (*0-317-30405-4*) Holy Trinity.

Obiter Dicta. Augustine Birrell. LC 17-21084. (First & Second Ser.). 1969. reprint ed. 9.00 (*0-403-00131-5*) Scholarly.

***Obiter Scripta: Essays, Lectures, Articles, Interviews & Reviews on Music & Other Subjects.** Albi Rosenthal & Jaqueline Gray. LC 00-32948. (FRE, GER, ITA & ENG.). 2000. write for info. (*0-8108-3861-3*) Scarecrow.

Obits & Murders: A Newspaper Story Set in Chicago. Jerry Crimmins. LC 90-91570. 519p. 1992. 20.00 (*0-9626047-0-4*) Ozanam Pr.

Obituaries. 2nd ed. William Saroyan. LC 78-27719. 368p. 1979. pap. 15.00 (*0-916870-17-0*) Creat Arts Bk.

Obituaries, a Guide to Sources. 2nd deluxe enl. expanded ed. Betty M. Jarboe. 1992. 175.00 (*0-7838-1001-6*, G K Hall & Co) Mac Lib Ref.

Obituaries & Death Related Items Abstracted from the Hendon Dispatch of Mendon, Adams County, Illinois, 1877-1905. Beals & Sandy Kirchner. LC 97-222196. vi, 465p. 1997. pap. 25.50 (*0-7884-0748-1*, B104) Heritage Bk.

Obituaries, Death Notices, & Genealogical Gleanings from the "Saugerties Telegraph", Vol. 3. Audrey M. Klinkenberg. 407p. (Orig.). 1994. pap. text 29.00 (*0-7884-0080-0*) Heritage Bk.

Obituaries, Death Notices & Genealogical Gleanings from the Saugerties Telegraph, 1853-60, Vol. 2. Compiled by Audrey M. Klinkenberg. 252p. (Orig.). 1991. pap. 20.00 (*1-55613-406-1*) Heritage Bk.

Obituaries for the London Times, 1961-1970. Ed. by Frank C. Roberts. 951p. 1977. lib. bdg. 235.00 (*0-313-28138-6*, ROK/, Greenwood Pr) Greenwood.

Obituaries from Barbour County Newspapers, 1890-1905. Helen S. Foley. 146p. 1976. pap. 15.00 (*0-89308-182-5*) Southern Hist Pr.

Obituaries from Ontario's Christian Guardian, 1861-1870. Donald A. McKenzie. 405p. 1988. lib. bdg. 25.00 (*0-912606-33-9*) Hunterdon Hse.

Obituaries from the London Times, 1971-1975. Ed. by Frank C. Roberts. 647p. 1978. lib. bdg. 175.00 (*0-313-28137-8*, ROG/, Greenwood Pr) Greenwood.

Obituaries from the Records of Clarence W. Love Undertaker, 1905-1915. Phelps County Genealogical Society Staff. 90p. 1989. pap. 25.00 (*1-893474-06-2*) Phelps Cnty Gene.

Obituaries from The Times, 1951-1960. Ed. by Frank C. Roberts. 896p. 1979. lib. bdg. 195.00 (*0-313-28136-X*, ROE/, Greenwood Pr) Greenwood.

***Obituaries in American Culture.** Janice Hume. LC 99-52868. 240p. 2000. pap. 18.00 (*1-57806-242-X*); text 45.00 (*1-57806-241-1*) U Pr of Miss.

Obituaries in the Performing Arts, 1995: Film, Television, Radio, Theatre, Dance, Music, Cartoons & Pop Culture. Harris M. Lentz, III. (Illus.). 218p. 1996. pap. 30.00 (*0-7864-0253-9*) McFarland & Co.

Obituaries in the Performing Arts, 1994: Film, Television, Radio, Theatre, Dance, Music, Cartoons & Pop Culture. Harris M. Lentz, III. (Illus.). 207p. 1996. pap. 30.00 (*0-7864-0254-7*) McFarland & Co.

Obituaries in the Performing Arts, 1996: Film, Television, Radio, Theatre, Dance, Music, Cartoons & Pop Culture. Harris M. Lentz, III. (Illus.). 221p. 1997. pap. 30.00 (*0-7864-0302-0*) McFarland & Co.

***Obituaries in the Performing Arts 1998: Film, Television, Radio, Theatre, Dance, Music, Cartoons & Pop Culture.** Harris M. Lentz, III. (Illus.). 255p. 1999. pap. 30.00 (*0-7864-0748-4*) McFarland & Co.

***Obituaries in the Performing Arts, 1999: Film, Television, Radio, Theatre, Dance, Music, Cartoons & Pop Culture.** Harris M. Lentz, III. 254p. 2000. 30.00 (*0-7864-0919-3*) McFarland & Co.

Obituaries in the Performing Arts, 1997: Film, Television, Radio, Theatre, Dance, Music, Cartoons & Pop Culture. Harris M. Lentz, III. (Illus.). 206p. 1998. pap. 30.00 (*0-7864-0460-4*) McFarland & Co.

***Obituaries, 1999: Clinton, Franklin & Essex County, New York.** iii, 529p. 2000. 30.00 (*0-9662895-6-0*) C M Rabideau.

Obituaries of Benton County, Arkansas, Vol. 1, 1884-1898. Barbara P. Easley. Ed. by Verla P. McAnelly. 490p. (Orig.). 1994. pap. text 33.00 (*1-55613-975-6*) Heritage Bk.

Obituaries of Benton County, Arkansas, Vol. 3 1905-1909. Barbara P. Easley. Ed. by Verla P. McAnelly. 513p. (Orig.). 1995. pap. text 33.00 (*0-7884-0196-3*) Heritage Bk.

Obituaries of Benton County, Arkansas, Vol. 8. Barbara P. Easley & Verla P. McAnelly. 418p. (Orig.). 1996. pap. 32.50 (*0-7884-0470-9*, E084) Heritage Bk.

Obituaries of Benton County, Arkansas, 1928-1929. Barbara P. Easley & Verla P. McAnelly. 504p. (Orig.). 1996. pap. 37.00 (*0-7884-0486-5*, E085) Heritage Bk.

An Asterisk (*) at the beginning of an entry indicates that the title is appearing for the first time.

Obituaries of Benton County, Arkansas, 1930-1931, Vol. 1. Barbara P. Easley & Verla P. McArielly. iv, 455p. 1997. pap. 35.00 (*0-7884-0671-X*, E088) Heritage Bk.

Obituaries of Benton County, Arkansas, 1910-1913, Vol. 4. Barbara P. Easley. Ed. by Verla P. McAnelly. 559p. (Orig.). 1995. pap. 38.00 (*0-7884-0265-X*) Heritage Bk.

Obituaries of Benton County, Arkansas, 1914-1918, Vol. 5. Barbara P. Easley. Ed. by Verla P. McAnelly. 539p. (Orig.). 1995. pap. 36.50 (*0-7884-0284-6*) Heritage Bk.

Obituaries of Benton County, Arkansas, 1919-1922, Vol. 6. Barbara P. Easley. 518p. 1996. pap. 37.00 (*0-7884-0407-5*, E081) Heritage Bk.

Obituaries of Benton County, Arkansas, 1899-1904, Vol. 2. Ed. by Barbara P. Easley & Verla P. McAnelly. 440p. (Orig.). 1995. pap. text 30.00 (*0-7884-0171-8*) Heritage Bk.

Obituaries of University of Washington Presidents, 1861-1958. Ed. by Kathryn S. Cullen. (Illus.). 150p. 1989. 22.50 (*0-685-27005-X*) NW Ctr Study Ed.

Obituaries of Washington County, Arkansas, Vol. 3, 1903-1908. Barbara P. Easley. Ed. by Verla P. McAnelly. LC 96-145926. v, 456p. (Orig.). 1996. pap. 34.50 (*0-7884-0595-0*, E087) Heritage Bk.

Obituaries of Washington County, Arkansas, 1841-1892, Vol. 1. Barbara P. Easley & Verla P. McAnelly. 466p. (Orig.). 1996. pap. 33.00 (*0-7884-0415-6*, E082) Heritage Bk.

Obituaries of Washington County, Arkansas, 1893-1902, Vol. 2. Barbara P. Easley & Verla P. McAnelly. vi, 509p. (Orig.). 1996. pap. 38.00 (*0-7884-0499-7*, E086) Heritage Bk.

Obituaries of Washington County Arkansas, 1909-1912, Vol. 4. Barbara P. Easley. LC 96-145926. 558p. 1998. pap. 33.50 (*0-7884-0936-0*, E091) Heritage Bk.

Obituary Dates from the Denni Hlasatel, 1891-1899. Ed. by Joe Novak et al. 22p. (Orig.). 1995. pap. 3.00 (*1-881125-18-1*) Chi Geneal Soc.

Obituary Dates from the Denni Hlasatel, 1930-1939. Ed. by Joe Novak et al. 105p. (Orig.). 1995. pap. 4.00 (*1-881125-15-7*) Chi Geneal Soc.

Obituary Dates from the Denni Hlasatel, 1940-1949. Ed. by Joe Novak et al. 130p. (Orig.). 1995. pap. 4.00 (*1-881125-19-X*) Chi Geneal Soc.

Obituary Notices from the Alexandria Gazette, 1784-1915. rev. ed. Lloyd House Staff. 220p. 1997. pap. 21.00 (*1-888265-20-5*) Willow Bend.

Obituary of Richard Smyth. Richard Smith. Ed. by Henry Ellis. (Camden Society, London. Publications, First Ser.: No. 44). reprint ed. 37.00 (*0-404-50144-3*) AMS Pr.

Obituary Quilt. Mary Toliver. LC 98-96691. (Bea Ellis Mysteries Ser.: Vol. 1). 156p. 1998. pap. 9.95 (*0-9666880-0-7*) Burgundy Bks.

***Obituary Rites of Freemasonry.** Robert Macoy. 106p. 1999. reprint ed. pap. 14.95 (*0-7661-0742-6*) Kessinger Pub.

***Obituary Writer.** Porter Shreve. LC 99-46759. 224p. 2000. pap. 12.00 (*0-395-98132-8*) HM.

Object Advantage: Business Process Reengineering with Object Technology. Ivar Jacobson. 368p. (C). 1995. 29.95 (*0-201-42289-1*) Addison-Wesley.

Object Advantage: Business Process Reengineering with Object Technology. 2nd ed. Ivar Jacobson. (C). 2000. text. write for info. (*0-201-40348-X*) Addison-Wesley.

Object Affection. Stephen McCauley. 316p. 1991. mass mkt. 14.00 (*0-671-74350-3*) S&S Trade.

Object Analysis & Design: Comparison of Methods. Ed. by Andrew T. Hutt. (Illus.). 224p. 1994. pap. 54.99 (*0-471-05276-0*) Wiley.

Object Analysis & Design: Descriptions of Methods. Ed. by Andrew T. Hutt. 202p. 1994. pap. 54.99 (*0-471-62366-0*) Wiley.

***Object & Action Naming Battery.** Judit Druks. 1999. pap. text. write for info. (*0-86377-888-7*) L Erlbaum Assocs.

Object & Economy in Medieval Winchester, 2 vols. Martin Biddle. (Winchester Studies: Vol. 7, Pt. 2). (Illus.). 1990. text 295.00 (*0-19-813175-5*) OUP.

Object & Property. Arda Denkel. (Studies in Philosophy). 274p. (C). 1996. text 54.95 (*0-521-55010-6*) Cambridge U Pr.

Object As Subject: Studies in the Interpretation of Still Life. Ed. by Anne W. Lowenthal. LC 95-45798. 204p. 1996. 49.50 (*0-691-03354-4*, Pub. by Princeton U Pr) Cal Prin Full Svc.

Object-Based Concurrent Programming: ECOOP '91 Workshop, Geneva, Switzerland, July 15-16, 1991 Proceedings. Ed. by G. Goose et al. LC 92-18409. (Lecture Notes in Computer Science Ser.: Vol. 612). x, 265p. 1992. 47.00 (*0-387-55613-3*) Spr-Verlag.

Object-Based Distributed Programming: ECOOP '93 Workshop, Kaiserslautern, Germany, July 1993, Proceedings. Michel Riveill. Ed. by Rachid Guerraoui et al. LC 94-10103. (Lecture Notes in Computer Science Ser.: Vol. 791). 1994. 44.95 (*0-387-57932-X*) Spr-Verlag.

Object-Based Models & Languages for Concurrent Systems: ECOOP '94 Workshop on Models & Languages for Coordination of Parallelism & Distribution, Bologna, Italy, July 5, 1994: Selected Papers. Paolo Ciancarini. Ed. by Akinori Yonezawa et al. (Lecture Notes in Computer Science Ser.: Vol. 924). 1995. write for info. (*0-387-59450-7*) Spr-Verlag.

Object-Based Models & Languages for Concurrent Systems: ECOOP '94 Workshop on Models & Languages for Coordination of Parallelism & Distribution, Bologna, Italy, July 5, 1994: Selected Papers. Ed. by Paolo Ciancarini et al. (Lecture Notes in Computer Science Ser.: Vol. 924). 193p. 1995. 36.00 (*3-540-59450-7*) Spr-Verlag.

Object-Based Parallel & Distributed Computation: France-Japan Workshop, OBPDC '95, Tokyo. Akinori Yonezawa. Ed. by Jean-Pierre Briot & Jean-Marc Geib. LC 96-27905. (Lecture Notes in Computer Science Ser.: Vol. 110). 349p. 1996. pap. 62.00 (*3-540-61487-7*) Spr-Verlag.

Object Box Framing. Ed. by Vivian C. Kistler. (Illus.). 32p. 1990. pap. text 14.00 (*0-938655-34-5*) Columba Pub.

Object-Choice: All You Need Is Love. Klaus Theweleit. Tr. by Malcolm Green. LC 94-4665. 180p. (gr. 13). 1994. pap. 18.00 (*0-86091-642-1*, Pub. by Verso) Norton.

Object Concept. Decker. (Computer Science Ser.). 1995. mass mkt., lab manual ed. 16.95 (*0-534-20500-3*) PWS Pubs.

Object Concept. 2nd ed. Decker. (Computer Science Ser.). (C). 2000. mass mkt. 52.95 (*0-534-95087-6*) PWS Pubs.

Object Concept: An Introduction to Computer Programming Using C. Rick Decker & Stuart Hirshfield. LC 94-14279. 1994. pap. 36.95 (*0-534-20499-6*) PWS Pubs.

Object Concept: An Introduction to Computer Programming Using C+s. Rick Decker & Stuart Hirshfield. LC 94-41156. 454p. 1995. 74.95 (*0-534-20496-1*) PWS Pubs.

Object Constraint Language: Precise Modeling with UML. Jos Warmer. LC 98-29492. (Addison-Wesley Technology Ser.). 144p. (C). 1998. pap. 29.95 (*0-201-37940-6*) Addison-Wesley.

Object Data Management: Object-Oriented & Extended Relational Database Systems. R. G. G. Cattell. LC 93-39690. 416p. (C). 1994. 47.95 (*0-201-54748-1*) Addison-Wesley.

Object Database Handbook: How to Select, Implement, & Use Object-Oriented Databases. Douglas K. Barry. LC 96-10800. 352p. 1996. pap. 49.99 (*0-471-14718-4*) Wiley.

Object Database Implementations: Comlex Data. Douglas K. Barry. 34p. Date not set. pap. 85.00 (*1-884842-41-0*) SIGS Bks & Multimedia.

***Object Database Standard: ODMG.** Rick Cattell. 288p. (C). 2000. pap. text 39.95 (*1-55860-647-5*) Morgan Kaufmann.

Object Database Standard: ODMG 2.0. Ed. by R.G.G. Cattell et al. LC 97-17031. 200p. (C). 1997. pap. text 36.95 (*1-55860-463-4*) Morgan Kaufmann.

Object Databases in Practice. Mary Loomis. LC 97-40480. 336p. (C). 1997. 53.00 (*0-13-899725-X*) P-H.

Object Detection, Collision Warning & Avoidance Systems. Ron Jurgen. LC 98-84889. (Automotive Electronic Series). 300p. 1998. 79.00 (*0-7680-0226-5*, PT-70) Soc Auto Engineers.

Object Developer's Professional Reference. Bill Green. (McGraw Hill Series on Object Technology). (Illus.). 432p. 1997. pap. text 49.95 (*0-07-913652-4*) McGraw.

Object Development Methods. Ed. by Andy Carmichael. LC 93-87695. (Advances in Object Technology Ser.: No. 3). 374p. 1994. pap. 39.95 (*0-13-131591-9*) Cambridge U Pr.

***Object Discovery & Invention.** Anthony Simons. (C). 1999. text. write for info. (*0-201-36064-0*) Addison-Wesley.

Object Engineering: Designing Large Scale Object-Oriented Systems. Gary Sullo. 325p. 1994. 64.99 (*0-471-62369-5*) Wiley.

Object Engineering: Managing Object Technology. Richard Due. (C). 1997. pap. text. write for info. (*0-8053-3118-2*) Addison-Wesley.

Object, Image, Inquiry: The Art Historian at Work. Getty Art History Information Program Staff. Ed. by Elizabeth Bakewell et al. LC 88-1101. 212p. 1988. pap. 14.95 (*0-89236-135-2*, Pub. by J P Getty Trust) OUP.

***Object Lessons.** Oz D. du Soleil. (Illus.). iii, 97p. 1999. pap. 9.50 (*0-9674109-0-8*) Two-Two-B.

Object Lessons. Anna Quindlen. 1997. pap. 12.00 (*0-449-00101-6*) Fawcett.

Object Lessons. Anna Quindlen. 336p. 1992. mass mkt. 6.99 (*0-8041-0946-X*) Ivy Books.

Object Lessons. Anna Quindlen. 1998. pap. 6.99 (*0-8041-9727-X*) Ivy Books.

Object Lessons: Central Saint Martins Art & Design Archive. Ed. by Sylvia Backemeyer. 1996. pap. 29.95 (*0-85331-712-7*, Pub. by Lund Humphries) Antique Collect.

Object Lessons: Cleveland Creates an Art Museum. Ed. by Evan H. Turner. LC 91-3397. (Illus.). 214p. 1991. pap. 21.50 (*0-940717-08-5*) Cleveland Mus Art.

Object Lessons: Cleveland Creates an Art Museum, Set. Ed. by Evan H. Turner. LC 91-3397. (Illus.). 214p. 1991. pap., boxed set 38.50 (*0-940717-10-7*) Cleveland Mus Art.

Object Lessons: How to Do Things with Fetishism. E. L. McCallum. LC 98-13179. (Series in Psychoanalysis & Culture). 192p. (C). 1998. text 59.50 (*0-7914-3979-8*); pap. text 19.95 (*0-7914-3980-1*) State U NY Pr.

Object Lessons: Lessons Learned in Object-Oriented Development Projects. Tom Love. (Advances in Object Technology Ser.: No. 1). 281p. (Orig.). 1993. pap. 32.95 (*0-13-472432-1*) Cambridge U Pr.

Object Lessons: Old Testament, Series C. Edward C. Grube. 128p. 1994. pap. 8.99 (*0-570-04648-3*, 12-3230) Concordia.

Object Lessons: Old Testament, Series B. Edward C. Grube. LC 92-42405. 128p. 1993. pap. 8.99 (*0-570-04606-8*, 12-3192) Concordia.

Object Lessons: The Life of the Woman & the Poet in Our Time. Eavan Boland. LC 94-32195. 254p. 1995. 23.00 (*0-393-03716-9*) Norton.

Object Lessons: The Life of the Woman & the Poet in Our Time. Eavan Boland. 254p. 1996. pap. 13.00 (*0-393-31437-5*, Norton Paperbks) Norton.

Object Lessons: The Role of Museums in Scotland. Stationery Office. 105p. 1996. pap. 30.00 (*0-11-495756-8*, HM57568, Pub. by Statnry Office) Bernan Associates.

Object Lessons: 100 Lessons from Everyday Life. expanded rev. ed. Charles C. Ryrie. pap. 5.99 (*0-8024-6029-1*, 234) Moody.

Object Lessons Based on Bible Characters. William C. Hendricks. (Object Lessons Ser.). 136p. (Orig.). (gr. 10). 1993. pap. 7.99 (*0-8010-4373-5*) Baker Bks.

Object Lessons for a Year: 52 Talks for the Children's Sermon Time. David J. Claassen. (Object Lesson Ser.). 114p. (gr. 11). 1986. pap. 6.99 (*0-8010-2514-1*) Baker Bks.

Object Lessons for Family Devotions. Sheryl Bruinsma. LC 97-1659. (Object Lessons Ser.). 80p. (Orig.). (gr. 10 up). 1997. pap. 7.99 (*0-8010-5762-0*) Baker Bks.

Object Lessons for Very Young Children. Sheryl Bruinsma. (Object Lesson Ser.). 128p. (YA). (gr. 11). 1988. pap. 7.99 (*0-8010-0956-1*) Baker Bks.

Object Lessons from Nature. Joanne De Jonge. (Object Lessons Ser.). (Illus.). 128p. (YA). (gr. 10). 1989. pap. 7.99 (*0-8010-2989-9*) Baker Bks.

Object Lessons from Paper Projects. Sheryl Bruinsma. LC 97-28456. (Object Lessons Ser.). 96p. (gr. 10). 1997. pap. 7.99 (*0-8010-5776-0*) Baker Bks.

Object Lessons from Pebbles & Paper Clips. Joanne De Jonge. (Object Lessons Ser.). 176p. (Orig.). (J). (gr. 10). 1995. pap. 7.99 (*0-8010-5041-3*) Baker Bks.

Object Lessons from the Bible. Wesley T. Runk. (Object Lessons Ser.). 96p. (YA). (gr. 10). 1980. pap. 6.99 (*0-8010-7698-6*) Baker Bks.

Object Lessons That Teach Bible Truths. William C. Hendricks & Merle D. Bleyker. (Object Lessons Ser.). 112p. (Orig.). (gr. 10). 1977. pap. 6.99 (*0-8010-4172-4*) Baker Bks.

Object Lessons That Teach Bible Verses. William C. Hendricks. LC 97-220257. (Object Lesson Ser.). 128p. (Orig.). (gr. 12 up). 1997. pap. 7.99 (*0-8010-4278-X*) Baker Bks.

Object Life Cycles: Modeling the World in States. Stephen J. Mellor & Sally Shalaer. LC 91-13591. (Yourdon Press Computing Ser.). 251p. 1991. pap. 61.00 (*0-13-629940-7*, Yourdon) P-H.

Object Love & Reality: An Introduction to a Psychoanalytic Theory of Object Relations. Arnold H. Modell. LC 68-24219. 181p. 1968. 30.00 (*0-8236-3720-4*) Intl Univs Pr.

Object Management. Ed. by Roger Tagg. (BCS Data Management Specialist Group Ser.: Vol. 5). 128p. 1992. pap. 72.95 (*1-85742-065-9*, Pub. by Ashgate Pub) Ashgate Pub Co.

Object Management Architecture Guide. 3rd ed. Object Management Group Staff et al. LC 95-49983. 164p. 1995. pap. 54.99 (*0-471-14193-3*) Wiley.

***Object Modeling.** (C). 1998. text. write for info. (*0-201-39754-4*) Addison-Wesley.

Object Modeling & Design Strategies: Tips & Techniques. Sanjiv Gossain. LC 98-146934. (Advances in Object Technology Ser.: No. 15). 336p. 1998. pap. text 39.95 (*0-521-64822-X*) Cambridge U Pr.

Object Models: Strategies, Patterns, & Applications. 2nd ed. Peter Coad et al. LC 97-109726. (Illus.). 544p. (C). 1996. pap. 58.00 (*0-13-840117-9*) P-H.

Object Models & PC Application Development in C++ Julio Sanchez. LC 97-26398. 448p. 1997. boxed set 74.95 (*0-8493-3102-1*) CRC Pr.

Object of Labor: Commodification of Agrarian Life in Socialist Hungary. Martha Lampland. LC 95-11554. 410p. 1995. pap. text 17.95 (*0-226-46830-5*); lib. bdg. 39.95 (*0-226-46829-1*) U Ch Pr.

Object of Literature. Pierre Macherey. (Literature, Culture, Theory Ser.: No. 14). 254p. (C). 1995. text 64.95 (*0-521-41955-7*); pap. text 19.95 (*0-521-47678-X*) Cambridge U Pr.

Object of Memory: Arab & Jew Narrate the Palestinian Village. Susan Slyomovics. LC 98-5346. (Illus.). 296p. 1998. pap. 19.95 (*0-8122-1525-7*) U of Pa Pr.

Object of Memory: Arab & Jew Narrate the Palestinian Village. Susan Sylomovics. LC 98-5346. (Illus.). 296p. 1998. 45.00 (*0-8122-3215-1*) U of Pa Pr.

Object of My Affection. Stephen McCauley. 1998. per. 6.99 (*0-671-02066-8*) PB.

Object of Performance: The American Avant-Garde since 1970. Henry M. Sayre. LC 88-27481. (Illus.). 324p. 1991. pap. 21.95 (*0-226-73558-3*) U Ch Pr.

Object of Performance: The American Avant-Garde since 1970. Henry M. Sayre. (Illus.). 328p. 1999. 46.95 (*0-226-73557-5*) U Ch Pr.

Object of Your Love. Speak. LC 98-18657. 208p. 1998. text 21.95 (*0-312-18638-X*) St Martin.

Object of Your Love. Dorothy Speak. 230p. pap. 19.95 (*1-895897-72-6*) Somerville Hse.

Object of Your Love. Dorothy Speak. 1999. pap. 12.95 (*0-312-20665-8*, St Martins Paperbacks) St Martin.

Object Orientation: Concepts, Analysis & Design, Languages, Databases, Graphical User Interfaces, Standards. 2nd ed. Setrag Khoshafian & Razmik Abnous. LC 95-22368. 528p. 1995. pap. 34.95 (*0-471-07834-4*) Wiley.

Object Orientation: Technology, Techniques, Management & Migration. John S. Hares & John D. Smart. LC 93-30490. (Series in Software Engineering Practice). (Illus.). 352p. reprint ed. pap. 109.20 (*0-608-20236-3*, 207149500012) Bks Demand.

Object Orientation & Prototyping in Software Engineering. Gustav Pomberger & Gunther Blaschek. 350p. 1996. pap. 60.00 (*0-13-192626-8*, Prentice Hall) P-H.

Object Orientation FAQ's. Robert Hathaway. 400p. (C). 1998. pap. 32.95 (*0-201-89541-2*) Addison-Wesley.

Object Orientation in Visual FoxPro. Savannah Brentnall. 224p. (C). 1996. pap. 19.95 (*0-201-47943-5*) Addison-Wesley.

Object Orientation in Z. Ed. by Susan Stepney et al. LC 92-21736. (Workshops in Computing Ser.). vii, 144p. 1992. 61.95 (*0-387-19778-8*) Spr-Verlag.

Object Orientation with Parallelism & Persistence. Burkhard Freitag. LC 96-31699. (International Series in Engineering & Computer Science, Natural Language Processing & Machine Translation). 248p. (C). 1996. text 127.00 (*0-7923-9770-3*) Kluwer Academic.

Object-Oriented Analysis. Coad. 1989. 19.95 (*0-07-158645-8*) McGraw.

Object-Oriented Analysis. 2nd ed. Brown. text. write for info. (*0-471-37137-8*) Wiley.

Object Oriented Analysis. 2nd ed. Peter Coad. 233p. 1990. 62.00 (*0-13-629981-4*) P-H.

Object-Oriented Analysis & Design: Selected Readings. Ed. by Eric J. Braude. 500p. 1997. pap. 49.95 (*0-7803-2341-6*, SR107) Inst Electrical.

Object-Oriented Analysis & Design with Applications. 3rd ed. Grady Booch et al. (Object Technology Ser.). 704p. 2001. 64.95 (*0-201-89551-X*) Addison-Wesley.

Object Oriented Analysis & Simulation Modelling. David Hill. LC 96-223620. 312p. 1996. pap. 39.95 (*0-201-87759-7*) Addison-Wesley.

Object Oriented Analysis Design & Application. 2nd ed. Grady Booch. 608p. (C). 1993. 62.95 (*0-8053-5340-2*) Benjamin-Cummings.

Object-Oriented & Classical Software Engineering. 4th ed. Stephen R. Schach. LC 98-15171. 1998. 58.25 (*0-07-290168-3*) McGraw.

Object-Oriented & Mixed Programming Paradigms: New Directions in Computer Graphics. Ed. by Peter Wisskrichen. LC 95-51356. (Focus on Computer Graphics Ser.). 196p. 1996. 62.00 (*3-540-60481-2*) Spr-Verlag.

Object-Oriented Approach: Concepts, Modeling, & System Development. John W. Satzinger & Tore U. Orvik. 1995. mass mkt., teacher ed. 18.50 (*0-7895-0582-7*) Course Tech.

Object-Oriented Approach: Concepts, Modeling, & Systems Development. John W. Satzinger & Tore U. Orvik. LC 95-215377. (DC - Introduction to Computing Ser.). 160p. (C). 1995. mass mkt. 21.95 (*0-7895-0110-4*) Course Tech.

***Object-Oriented Approach: Introduction.** Ekedahl. (Programming Ser.). (C). 2000. text 29.25 (*0-619-01661-2*) Course Tech.

Object-Oriented Approach to Spatial Data Processing. Jack A. Orenstein & Marius S. Vassiliou. (C). 2001. 39.00 (*0-13-119876-9*, Macmillan Coll) P-H.

Object Oriented Artificial Intelligence Using C++ Kim W. Tracy. LC 96-33964. 476p. (C). 1996. pap. text 70.95 (*0-7167-8294-4*) W H Freeman.

Object-Oriented Assembly Language. Len Dorfman. 1991. 29.95 (*0-8306-6754-7*) McGraw-Hill Prof.

Object-Oriented Behavioral Specification. William Harvey. Ed. by Haim Kilov. LC 96-32228. (International Series in Engineering & Computer Science, Natural Language Processing & Machine Translation). 336p. (C). 1996. text 120.50 (*0-7923-9778-9*) Kluwer Academic.

Object Oriented Business Engineerng. Robert E. Shelton. (C). 1997. pap. text. write for info. (*0-201-89546-3*) Addison-Wesley.

Object Oriented C++ 2nd ed. Myers. 1999. teacher ed. 24.95 (*0-07-023928-2*) McGraw.

Object-Oriented C++ Primer. Leon Poskar. (Illus.). 764p. (Orig.). (C). 1997. pap. text 25.95 (*1-890005-00-2*) MBSL Commun Co.

Object-Oriented Client-Server Application Development: Using ObjectPal & C. Steve Ayer. 1995. text 40.00 (*0-07-002861-3*) McGraw.

Object-Oriented Client/Server Internet Environments. Amjad Umar. LC 96-38139. 560p. (C). 1997. 63.00 (*0-13-375544-4*) P-H.

Object-Oriented Cobol. Edmund C. Arranga & Frank P. Coyle. (Advances in Object Technology Ser.: No. 13). 525p. (C). 1996. 39.95 (*0-13-261140-6*) Cambridge U Pr.

Object-Oriented Common Lisp. Stephen Slade. LC 97-22732. 800p. (C). 1997. pap. 62.00 (*0-13-605940-6*) P-H.

Object-Oriented Computer-Aided Engineering. Hojjat Adeli & George Yu. (C). 2001. 44.00 (*0-13-630872-4*, Macmillan Coll) P-H.

Object-Oriented Computer Simulation of Discrete-Event Systems. Jerzy Tyszer. LC 99-14418. (International Series on Discrete Event Dynamic Systems). 1999. write for info. (*0-7923-8506-3*) Kluwer Academic.

Object Oriented Computer Systems Engineering. Derrick Morris et al. LC 96-5191. (Applied Computing Ser.). 320p. 1996. pap. 34.95 (*3-540-76020-2*) Spr-Verlag.

Object-Oriented Data Structures. Saumyendra Sengupta & Carl P. Korobkin. LC 93-40950. (Illus.). 708p. 1994. 59.95 (*0-387-94194-0*) Spr-Verlag.

***Object-Oriented Data Structures for Real Programmers.** Jan L. Harrington. (Real Programmers Ser.). (Illus.). 2000. pap. 39.95 (*0-12-326429-4*) Morgan Kaufmann.

Object-Oriented Database Design Clearly Explained. Jan L. Harrington. (Clearly Explained Ser.). 350p. 1999. pap. 39.95 (*0-12-326428-6*, Pub. by Acad Pr) Harcourt.

Object-Oriented Database Programming. S. Alagic. (Texts & Monographs in Computer Science). (Illus.). 320p. 1988. 75.95 (*0-387-96754-0*) Spr-Verlag.

Object-Oriented Database System: Design & Implementation for Advanced Applications. Hiroshi Ishikawa. LC 93-28895. (Computer Science Workbench Ser.). 1993. 69.00 (*0-387-70128-1*) Spr-Verlag.

Object Oriented Databases. Setrag Khoshafian. 384p. 1993. 64.99 (*0-471-57056-7*); pap. 39.95 (*0-471-57058-3*) Wiley.

O

Object-Oriented Databases: Technology, Applications & Products (McGraw Hill Database Experts') Bindu R. Rao. 1994. pap. 40.00 (*0-07-051279-5*) McGraw.
Object Oriented Design. Peter Coad & Edward Yourdan. (Yourdon Press Computing Ser.). 197p. 1991. 46.60 (*0-13-630070-7*, Yourdon) P-H.
Object-Oriented Design & Analysis with C++, Set. Peter Henderson. 288p. 1994. pap. text 43.00 incl. disk (*0-07-707585-4*) McGraw.
***Object-Oriented Design & Programming in C++** Andy Yao. 140p. (C). 1999. 25.00 (*1-930360-12-6*) Unitd Tech.
***Object-Oriented Design for Temporal GIS.** John M. Wachowicz. 2000. 69.95 (*0-7484-0831-2*, Pub. by Tay Francis Ltd) Taylor & Francis.
Object Oriented Design Made Easy! Byron E. Miller. LC 93-78275. (Illus.). 1993. pap. 19.95 (*0-9636637-6-3*) Impatience Pubns.
Object-Oriented Design Measurement. Scott A. Whitmire. LC 97-11380. 452p. 1997. 59.99 (*0-471-13417-1*) Wiley.
Object-Oriented Design Through Heuristics. Arthur Riel. 400p. (C). 1996. text 44.95 (*0-201-63385-X*) Addison-Wesley.
Object-Oriented Development. W. Gregory Wojtkowski. (DM - Machine Language Programming Ser.). 1994. text 30.95 (*0-87709-234-6*) Course Tech.
Object Oriented Development, 4. Jackson. (Miscellaneous/Catalogs Ser.). 1999. mass mkt. 15.00 (*0-7600-5882-2*) Course Tech.
Object-Oriented Development: The Fusion Method. Derek Coleman et al. LC 93-2015. (Object-Oriented Ser.). 350p. (C). 1993. 70.00 (*0-13-338823-9*) P-H.
Object-Oriented Development C++ W. Gregory Wojtkowski. (DM - Machine Language Programming Ser.). 1994. text 28.95 (*0-87709-236-2*) Course Tech.
Object-Oriented Development Small Talk. W. Gregory Wojtkowski. (DM - Machine Language Programming Ser.). 1994. text 28.95 (*0-87709-235-4*) Course Tech.
Object Oriented Eiffel I. Thomas & Weedon. Ed. by Katherine Harutunian & Simon Plumtree. 1995. pap. text 16.80 (*0-201-87737-6*) Addison-Wesley.
***Object-Oriented Enterprise Modelling with MERODE.** Monique Snoeck et al. (Illus.). 238p. 1999. pap. 45.00 (*90-6186-977-3*, Pub. by Leuven Univ) Coronet Bks.
Object-Oriented Forth. Dick Pountain. 119p. (Orig.). 1987. text 41.00 (*0-12-563570-2*) Acad Pr.
***Object-Oriented Frameworks Using C++ & Corba Gold Book.** Vishwajit Aklecha. LC 99-23782. 574p. 1999. pap. 39.99 (*1-57610-403-6*) Coriolis Grp.
Object-Oriented Graphics: From GKS & PHIGS to Object-Oriented Systems. P. Wisskirchen. Ed. by Jose L. Encarnacao et al. (Symbolic Computation - Computer Graphics Ser.). (Illus.). xiii, 236p. 1990. 56.00 (*0-387-52859-8*) Spr-Verlag.
Object Oriented GUI Design. Mark Smith & Susan L. Fowler. LC 97-75529. (Illus.). 318p. 1997. pap. 42.95 (*0-07-059274-8*) McGraw.
Object Oriented Information Systems: Planning & Implementation. David A. Taylor. LC 91-38263. 384p. 1992. pap. 39.95 (*0-471-54364-0*) Wiley.
Object-Oriented Introduction to Computer Science Using Eiffel. Richard S. Wiener. (Prentice Hall Object-Oriented Ser.). 408p. (C). 1996. 48.80 (*0-13-183872-5*) P-H.
Object-Oriented Introduction to Data Structures Using Eiffel. Richard S. Wiener. LC 96-46763. 528p. (C). 1997. 62.00 (*0-13-185588-3*) P-H.
Object-Oriented I/O Using C++ IOSTREAMS. Cameron Hughes et al. LC 95-933. 384p. 1995. pap. 34.95 (*0-471-11809-5*) Wiley.
Object-Oriented Languages. Ed. by Gerald Masini et al. (APIC Ser.: No. 34). (Illus.). 512p. (C). 1991. text 65.00 (*0-12-477390-7*) Acad Pr.
Object-Oriented Languages: Basic Principles & Programming Techniques. M. Beaudouin-Lafon. 140p. 1994. mass mkt. 35.95 (*0-412-55800-9*, Chap & Hall NY) Chapman & Hall.
Object-Oriented Metamethods. Brian Henderson-Sellers & A. Bulthuis. LC 97-16662. 160p. 1997. 34.95 (*0-387-98257-4*) Spr-Verlag.
Object-Oriented Methodologies & Systems: Proceedings of the International Symposium ISOOMS '94, Palermo, Italy, September 21-22, 1994. Ed. by Elisa Bertino & S. Urban. LC 95-236647. (Lecture Notes in Computer Science Ser.: Vol. 858). x, 386p. 1994. 55.95 (*3-540-58451-X*) Spr-Verlag.
Object Oriented Methods. 2nd ed. (C). 1995. text. write for info. (*0-201-59479-X*) S&S Trade.
Object-Oriented Methods. 2nd ed. James Martin & James J. Odell. LC 97-39040. 432p. (C). 1997. 68.00 (*0-13-905597-5*) P-H.
***Object-Oriented Methods.** 3rd ed. Ian Graham. (C). 1999. text. write for info. (*0-201-61913-X*) Addison-Wesley.
Object-Oriented Methods: A Practical Introduction. Ian Graham. 1991. text 38.75 (*0-201-56521-8*) Addison-Wesley.
***Object Oriented Methods for Interoperable Scientific & Engineering Computing: SIAM Workshop Yorktown Heights, NY 1998.** Ed. by Michael E. Henderson et al. (Proceedings in Applied Mathematics Ser.: No. 99). (Illus.). xiv, 321p. 1999. pap. 45.00 (*0-89871-445-1*, RP0099) Soc Indus-Appl Math.
Object-Oriented Methods for Software Development. Jag Sodhi & Prince Sodhi. LC 96-15421. (Illus.). 277p. 1996. 45.00 (*0-07-059574-7*) McGraw.
Object-Oriented Metrics: Measures of Complexity. Brian Henderson-Sellers. LC 95-35148. (Object-Oriented Ser.). 252p. 1995. 39.00 (*0-13-239872-9*) P-H.
***Object-Oriented Middle Wave for Distributed Transaction.** Lane Gorton. 336p. (C). 2000. pap. text 49.95 (*0-201-39859-1*) Addison-Wesley.
Object-Oriented Modeling. Ed. by Jean-Michel Berge. LC 96-41149. (Current Issues in Electronic Modeling Ser.). 168p. (C). 1996. lib. bdg. 125.00 (*0-7923-9688-X*) Kluwer Academic.
Object Oriented Modeling & Design. James Rumbaugh & Stephen Blaha. 1991. pap. text, student ed. 31.60 (*0-13-629858-3*) P-H.
Object-Oriented Modeling & Design. Jim Rumbaugh. 528p. 1990. 69.00 (*0-13-629841-9*) P-H.
Object-Oriented Modeling & Design for Database Applications. Michael Blaha & William Premerlain. LC 97-27029. 484p. (C). 1997. 60.00 (*0-13-123829-9*) P-H.
Object-Oriented Multithreading Using C++ Cameron Hughes & Tracey Hughes. LC 97-15129. 512p. 1997. pap. 54.99 incl. disk (*0-471-18012-2*) Wiley.
Object-Oriented Network Programming in C. Douglas C. Schmidt. 608p. (C). Date not set. pap. 49.95 (*0-201-63356-6*) Addison-Wesley.
Object-Oriented Neural Networks in C++ Joey Rogers. LC 96-28409. (Illus.). 310p. 1996. pap. text 29.95 (*0-12-593115-8*) Acad Pr.
Object Oriented Perl. Damian Conway. LC 99-27793. 490p. 1999. pap. 42.95 (*1-884777-79-1*, Pub. by Manning Pubns) IPG Chicago.
Object Oriented Programming. Karen E. Bender. (C). 1990. text. write for info. (*0-201-52310-8*) Addison-Wesley.
Object Oriented Programming. D. Parsons. 328p. 1994. pap. 59.95 (*1-85805-089-8*, Pub. by DP Publns) St Mut.
Object-Oriented Programming. Toppan Japan Staff. (C). 1988. text. write for info. (*0-201-41683-2*) Addison-Wesley.
Object-Oriented Programming. Ann L. Winblad et al. (Illus.). 320p. (C). 1990. pap. text 39.95 (*0-201-50736-6*) Addison-Wesley.
Object Oriented Programming: A Unified Foundation. G. Castagna. 355p. 1996. 69.50 (*0-8176-3905-5*) Birkhauser.
Object Oriented Programming: A Unified Foundation. Giuseppe Castagna. LC 96-33163. (Progress in Theoretical Computer Science Ser.). 394p. 1996. write for info. (*3-7643-3905-5*) Birkhauser.
Object-Oriented Programming: An Evolutionary Approach. Brad C. Cox. LC 85-22921. 300p. 1986. text 31.25 (*0-201-10393-1*) Addison-Wesley.
Object-Oriented Programming: An Evolutionary Approach. 2nd ed. Brad J. Cox & Andrew Novobilski. (Illus.). 320p. (C). 1991. pap. 44.95 (*0-201-54834-8*) Addison-Wesley.
Object-Oriented Programming: Proceedings of the 8th European Conference ECOOP '94, Bologna, Italy, July 1994. Ed. by Mario Tokor & Remo Pareschi. LC 94-25835. (Lecture Notes in Computer Science Ser.: Vol. 821). 1994. 73.95 (*0-387-58202-9*) Spr-Verlag.
Object-Oriented Programming: Systems, Languages & Applications Oopsla '91 Conference. ACAM Press Staff. 1991. pap. text 35.50 (*0-201-55417-8*) Addison-Wesley.
Object-Oriented Programming: The Rest of the Story. Peter Coad & Jill Nicola. 582p. (C). 1993. 65.00 (*0-13-032616-X*) P-H.
***Object-Oriented Programming & Java.** D. C. Poole & D. B. Kiong. LC 98-18558. 250p. 1998. pap. 24.95 (*981-3083-96-4*, Pub. by Spr-Verlag) Spr-Verlag.
Object-Oriented Programming for AS/400 Programmers: An Introduction with Examples in C++ Jennifer Hamilton. LC 93-48185. 114p. 1994. pap. 44.00 (*1-882419-05-7*) News Four-Hund.
Object-Oriented Programming for Graphics. Ed. by C. Laffra et al. (Focus on Computer Graphics Ser.). 278p. 1996. 74.95 (*0-387-58314-9*) Spr-Verlag.
Object-Oriented Programming in C++ Richard Johnsonbaugh & Martin Kalin. LC 94-1540. 547p. (C). 1994. pap. 53.00 (*0-02-360682-7*, Macmillan Coll) P-H.
***Object-oriented Programming in C++** 2nd ed. Richard Johnsonbaugh & Martin Kalin. LC 99-45282. 615p. 1999. pap. 58.00 (*0-13-015885-2*) P-H.
Object-Oriented Programming in C++ 2nd rev. ed. Robert Lafore. 912p. 1995. 34.99 (*1-878739-73-5*) Sams.
Object-Oriented Programming in C Plus, Plus. 2nd ed. 128p. (C). 1999. pap. text. write for info. (*0-13-017031-3*) P-H.
Object-Oriented Programming in Eiffel - Ise Version. 2nd ed. Pete Thomas. LC 97-34030. 624p. (C). 1997. pap. text 57.00 (*0-201-33131-4*) Addison-Wesley.
Object Oriented Programming in Java. Brook Conner. (C). 1998. pap. text. write for info. (*0-201-87013-4*) Addison-Wesley.
Object-Oriented Programming in Java. Bill McCarty & Steve Gilbert. LC 97-9501. (Mitchell Waite Signature Ser.). 1000p. 1997. 59.99 incl. cd-rom (*1-57169-086-7*) Mac USA.
Object-Oriented Programming in Java. Mark C. Reynolds. (Illus.). 336p. 1997. pap., pap. text 39.95 incl. cd-rom (*0-07-913250-2*) McGraw.
Object-Oriented Programming in Oberon-2. Hanspeter Mossenbock. Tr. by Robert Bach from GER. LC 93-10033.Tr. of Objektorientierte Programmierung in Oberon-2. (Illus.). 278p. 1993. pap. text 39.00 (*0-387-56411-X*) Spr-Verlag.
Object-Oriented Programming in Oberon-2. 2nd ed. Tr. by Robert Bach. 1995. write for info. (*0-387-60062-0*) Spr-Verlag.
Object-Oriented Programming in Oberon-2. 2nd ed. Hanspeter Mossenbock. Tr. by Robert Bach. (Illus.). 280p. 1995. 49.95 (*3-540-60062-0*) Spr-Verlag.
Object-Oriented Programming in Pascal: A Graphical Approach. David A. Higuidula et al. LC 94-48465. 750p. (C). 1995. pap. text 52.00 (*0-201-62883-X*) Addison-Wesley.
Object-Oriented Programming in Turbo Pascal 5.5. Ben R. Ezzell. 500p. 1989. pap. text 22.95 (*0-201-52375-2*) Addison-Wesley.
Object-Oriented Programming in Visual BASIC. James W. Cooper & Steve Wilent. LC 96-27179. (Special Reports). 1996. write for info. (*1-880935-49-X*) Pinnacle WA.
Object-Oriented Programming Systems. Ed. by J. J. Florentin. (UNICOM Applied Information Technology Ser.: No. 10). (Illus.). 192p. 1991. mass mkt. 127.50 (*0-412-37960-0*) Chapman & Hall.
Object-Oriented Programming Systems. Z. Zafar. 1990. pap. write for info. (*0-318-63379-5*) Meghan-Kiffer.
Object-oriented Programming under MS-DOS. A. Dusko Savic. 1992. pap. text 39.95 (*0-07-707467-X*) McGraw.
Object-Oriented Programming Using C++ Ira Pohl. (Object-Oriented Software Engineering Ser.). 512p. (C). 1993. pap. 42.95 (*0-8053-5382-8*) Benjamin-Cummings.
***Object Oriented Programming Using C++** 2nd ed. Farrell. (C). 2001. pap. 35.00 (*0-619-03361-4*) Course Tech.
Object-Oriented Programming Using C++ 2nd ed. Ira Pohl. LC 96-48514. 576p. (C). 1996. pap. 41.95 (*0-201-89550-1*) Addison-Wesley.
Object-Oriented Programming Using C Plus Plus. (C). 1992. write for info. (*0-201-93793-X*); write for info. (*0-201-93794-8*) Addison-Wesley.
Object-Oriented Programming Using SOM & DSOM. Christina Lau. 288p. 1995. pap. text 44.95 incl. disk (*0-471-13123-7*) Wiley.
Object-Oriented Programming with C++ & Smalltalk. Caleb Drake. LC 97-18141. 1010p. (C). 1997. pap. 74.00 (*0-13-103797-8*) P-H.
Object Oriented Programming with C++ & OSF Motif. 2nd ed. Douglas A. Young. LC 95-15034. 464p. (C). 1995. pap. 58.00 (*0-13-209255-7*) P-H.
Object Oriented Programming with dBASE for Windows. Adam Green. 1994. pap. 34.50 (*0-679-74741-9*) Knopf.
***Object Oriented Programming with Java.** 2000. write for info. (*0-13-018288-5*) P-H.
***Object Oriented Programming with Java: A First Programming Text.** D. Barnes. LC 99-57040. 800p. 2000. write for info. (*0-13-086900-7*) P-H.
Object-Oriented Programming with Prototypes in Omega. Gunther Blaschek. LC 93-39557. (Illus.). 335p. 1994. 59.00 (*0-387-56469-1*) Spr-Verlag.
Object-Oriented Programming with REXX. Thomas G. Ender. LC 96-45983. 272p. 1997. 39.95 incl. disk (*0-471-11844-3*) Wiley.
Object Oriented Programming with Smalltalk. Michele Marchesi. 352p. 1994. pap. 66.00 (*0-13-630294-7*, Prentice Hall) P-H.
Object Oriented Programming with Turbo Pascal. Namir C. Shammas. LC 89-29768. 301p. 1990. pap. 22.95 (*0-471-51702-X*) Wiley.
Object-Oriented Programming with Visual FoxPro: Special Report. David Frankenbach. LC 96-3192. 1996. write for info. (*1-880935-44-9*) Pinnacle WA.
Object-Oriented Programming with Windows 95 & NT. Stephen Morris. LC 98-39800. 450p. 1999. pap. text 44.95 (*1-55558-193-5*, Digital DEC) Buttrwrth-Heinemann.
Object-Oriented Project Management with UML. Murray Cantor. LC 98-16413. 368p. 1998. 39.99 (*0-471-25303-0*) Wiley.
Object Oriented Rapid Prototyping. John L. Connell & Linda I. Shafer. LC 94-5264. 224p. (C). 1994. 37.60 (*0-13-629643-2*, Yourdon) P-H.
Object Oriented Ray Tracing in C++ abr. ed. Nicholas P. Wilt. 441p. 1993. pap. 36.95 (*0-471-30415-8*) Wiley.
Object Oriented Ray Tracing in C++, Set. Nicholas P. Wilt. 441p. 1993. pap. 69.95 incl. disk (*0-471-30414-X*) Wiley.
Object-Oriented Real-Time Dependable Systems: Proceedings of the 3rd Workshop on Object-Oriented Real-Time Dependable Systems, Newport Beach, CA, 1997. LC 97-71357. 300p. 1997. pap. 115.00 (*0-8186-8046-6*) IEEE Comp Soc.
Object-Oriented Real-Time Dependable Systems: 2nd Workshop on WORDS '96. LC 96-83326. 256p. 1996. pap. 50.00 (*0-8186-7570-5*) IEEE Comp Soc.
Object-Oriented Real-Time Distributed Computing (ISORC'99) Proceedings, IEEE International Symposium on Object-Oriented Real-Time Distributed Computing, ISORC'99 (2d: 1999: Saint Malo, France) Contrib. by IEEE Computer Society Staff. LC 99-61702. 351p. 1999. pap. 125.00 (*0-7695-0207-5*) IEEE Comp Soc.
Object-Oriented Real-Time Distributed Computing (ISROC, '98), 1st International Symposium On. IEEE Staff. LC 98-84578. 400p. 1998. pap. 130.00 (*0-8186-8430-5*, PR8430, IEEE Inst Elec) IEEE Comp Soc.
Object-Oriented Requirements Analysis & Logical Design: A Software Engineering Approach. Donald G. Firesmith. LC 92-15453. 592p. 1993. 74.99 (*0-471-57806-1*) Wiley.
Object-Oriented Requirements Analysis & Logical Design: A Software Engineering Approach. Donald G. Firesmith. LC 92-15453. 592p. 1996. pap. 44.95 (*0-471-57807-X*) Wiley.
Object-Oriented Reuse, Concurrency, & Distribution: An Ada-Based Approach. Colin Atkinson. 288p. (C). 1991. 39.95 (*0-201-56527-7*) Addison-Wesley.
Object-Oriented Simulation: Reusability, Adaptability, & Maintainability. George W. Zobrist & James V. Leonard. LC 96-2228. 344p. 1996. 89.95 (*0-7803-1061-6*, PC4150) Inst Electrical.
Object Oriented Simulation Conference. Ed. by Robert Beaumariage et al. (Illus.). 148p. (Orig.). 1995. pap. 80.00 (*1-56555-043-9*, OOS-95) Soc Computer Sim.
Object-Oriented Simulation Conference: Mission Earth: Modeling & Simulation for a Sustainable Global System. Ed. by Chell Roberts et al. 256p. 1996. pap. 100.00 (*1-56555-086-2*, OOS-96) Soc Computer Sim.
Object-Oriented Simulation Conference (OOS '94) Ed. by Herring et al. 190p. 1994. 80.00 (*1-56555-067-6*, SS-26-2) Soc Computer Sim.
***Object-Oriented Simulation Conference (OOS '97) Held in Phoenix, Arizona - January 1997.** Ed. by Jeffrey W. Wallace et al. 191p. 1998. pap. 100.00 (*1-56555-107-9*, OOS-97) Soc Computer Sim.
***Object-Oriented Simulation Conference 1998/1998 International Conference on Simulation in Engineering Education.** Ed. by Jeffrey W. Wallace et al. 321p. 1998. 50.00 (*1-56555-142-7*) Soc Computer Sim.
Object-Oriented Simulation, 1992. Ed. by Raymond Ege & Terrence Beaumariage. 106p. 1992. 50.00 (*1-56555-002-1*, MC92-3) Soc Computer Sim.
Object Oriented Softw Engrg W/uml& Patterns. (C). 2000. cd-rom 0.00 (*0-13-026314-1*) S&S Trade.
Object Oriented Software. Ann L. Winblad et al. (Illus.). 352p. (C). 1990. pap. text. write for info. (*0-318-66837-8*) Addison-Wesley.
Object-Oriented Software: Design & Maintenance. Luiz F. Capretz & Miriam A. Capretz. LC 96-21637. (Series on Software Engineering & Knowledge). 288p. 1996. write for info. (*981-02-2731-0*) World Scientific Pub.
Object-Oriented Software Composition. Oscar M. Nierstrasz & Dennis Tsichritzis. 362p. 1995. pap. 69.00 (*0-13-220674-9*) P-H.
Object-Oriented Software Construction. 2nd ed. Bertrand Meyer. LC 97-2407. 1296p. (C). 1997. pap. 70.00 (*0-13-629155-4*) P-H.
Object-Oriented Software Design & Construction with C++ Dennis Kafura. 440p. (C). 1998. pap. 51.00 (*0-13-901349-0*) P-H.
***Object-Oriented Software Design & Construction with Java.** Dennis Kafura. LC 99-88967. 450p. 2000. pap. text 51.00 (*0-13-011264-X*) P-H.
Object-Oriented Software Design with C++ Steven P. Reiss. LC 98-38753. (Worldwide Series in Computer Science). 544p. 1998. pap. 67.95 (*0-471-24213-6*) Wiley.
Object-Oriented Software Development: A Practical Guide. Mark Lorenz. LC 92-18566. 250p. 1992. text 41.20 (*0-13-726928-5*) Brady Pub.
Object-Oriented Software Development in Java. Xiaoping Jia. LC 99-14184. 507p. (C). 1999. 50.00 (*0-201-35084-X*) Addison-Wesley.
***Object Oriented Software Development with Uml: Process & Products.** 2nd ed. Putnam Texel & Charles Williams. (C). 1999. pap. text 60.00 (*0-13-016237-X*) P-H.
Object Oriented Software Engineering. Steve Halladay & Michael Wiebel. 358p. 1993. pap. 29.95 (*0-87930-446-4*) C M P Books.
Object-Oriented Software Engineering. Ivar Jacobson. 552p. (C). 1992. 54.95 (*0-201-54435-0*) Addison-Wesley.
Object-Oriented Software Engineering. 2nd ed. Ivar Jacobson. (C). 2000. text. write for info. (*0-201-40347-1*) Addison-Wesley.
***Object Oriented Software Engineering: Conquering Complex & Changing Systems.** Bruegge. LC 99-42746. 553p. 1999. 50.00 (*0-13-489725-0*) P-H.
Object-Oriented Software in Ada. Smith. 1995. pap. write for info. (*0-412-57830-1*) Thomson Learn.
Object-Oriented Software in ADA '95. M. A. Smith. 460p. 1995. pap. 37.95 (*1-85032-185-X*) ITCP.
***Object-Oriented Software in ANSI C++** (C). 2000. pap., student ed. 61.25 (*0-07-709504-9*) McGrw-H Hghr Educ.
Object-Oriented Software in C++ M. A. Smith. 352p. 1993. mass mkt. 37.95 (*0-412-55380-5*) Chapman & Hall.
Object-Oriented Software Management. James Callan. 1997. pap. text 44.95 (*1-55622-574-1*) Wordware Pub.
Object-Oriented Software Metrics. Mark Lorenz. 146p. 1994. 55.00 (*0-13-179292-X*) P-H.
Object-Oriented Software Systems in Manufacturing. S. Adiga. 1992. 69.50 (*0-442-31562-7*) Chapman & Hall.
***Object Oriented Software Technologies in Telecommunications: From Theory to Practice.** Iakovos Venieris et al. LC 00-23094. (Illus.). 294p. 2000. 99.95 (*0-471-62379-2*) Wiley.
Object-Oriented Software Testing: A Hierarchical Approach. Shel Siegel. LC 95-30078. 528p. 1996. pap. 59.99 (*0-471-13749-9*) Wiley.
Object Oriented SSADM. 350p. 1994. pap. 48.00 (*0-13-309444-8*) P-H.
Object Oriented System Development. Dennis Champeaux. 560p. 1993. 59.95 (*0-201-56355-X*) Addison-Wesley.
Object-Oriented Systems Analysis: A Model-Driven Approach. Barry D. Kurtz et al. 352p. 1991. text 38.00 (*0-685-50517-0*) P-H.
Object Oriented Systems Analysis: Modeling the World in Data. Stephen J. Mellor & Sally Shlaer. (Yourdon Press Computing Ser.). (Illus.). 144p. (C). 1988. pap. 58.00 (*0-13-629023-X*) P-H.
Object-Oriented Systems Analysis & Design. Ronald J. Norman. LC 95-36248. (Series in Information Management Ser.). 430p. (C). 1996. text 99.00 (*0-13-122946-X*) P-H.
Object-Oriented Systems & Applications (Readings In) Ed. by David C. Rine. LC 94-10044. 256p. 1994. 19.95 (*0-8186-6222-0*, BP06222) IEEE Comp Soc.
Object-Oriented Systems Development. Bahrami. 1997. pap. 13.50 (*0-256-25382-X*) McGraw.
***Object Oriented Systems Development.** Ali Bahrami. LC 98-43126. 432p. 1999. 52.74 (*0-256-25348-X*) Dorsey.

Object-Oriented Systems Development: An Integrated Approach. Edward Yourdon. LC 93-6098. (Yourdon Press Computing Ser.). 400p. 1993. text 64.00 (*0-13-636325-3*) Prntice Hall Bks.

***Object Oriented Technologies: Opportunities & Challenges.** Ed. by Rick Gibson. LC 99-46092. (Illus.). 187p. 2000. pap. 69.95 (*1-878289-67-5*) Idea Group Pub.

Object-Oriented Technology. David Conrad Taylor. (C). 1993. pap. text. write for info. (*0-201-42020-1*) Addison-Wesley.

Object-Oriented Technology: A Manager's Guide. David A. Taylor. (Illus.). 160p. (C). 1991. pap. 29.95 (*0-201-56358-4*) Addison-Wesley.

***Object-Oriented Technology: ECOOP' 99 Workshop Reader: ECOOP '99 Workshops, Panels & Posters, Lisbon, Portugal, June 14-18, 1999, Proceedings.** ECOOP '99 Staff. Ed. by Ana Moreira & Serge Demeyer. LC 99-89304. (Lecture Notes in Computer Science Ser.: Vol. 1743). xvii, 389p. 2000. pap. 69.00 (*3-540-66954-X*) Spr-Verlag.

Object-Oriented Technology: ECOOP'97 Workshops, Jyvsskyls, Finland, June 9-13, 1997, Proceedings, Vol. 135. Ed. by Jan Bosch et al. LC 98-2587. (Lecture Notes in Computer Science Ser.: Vol. 1361). xiv, 555p. 1998. pap. 79.00 (*3-540-64039-8*) Spr-Verlag.

Object-Oriented Technology: Proceedings of the Ecoop '98 Workshop Reader: Ecoop '98 Workshops, Demos & Posters: Brussels, Belgium, July 20-24, 1998. Ed. by Jan Bosch & Serge Demeyer. LC 98-53820. xxi, 568p. 1999. pap. 79.00 (*3-540-65460-7*) Spr-Verlag.

***Object-Oriented Technology & Computing Systems Re-Engineering.** Hussein Zedan & A. Cau. 200p. 1999. 49.95 (*1-898563-56-X*, Pub. by Horwood Pub) Paul & Co Pubs.

Object-Oriented Technology for Database & Software Systems. V. S. Alagar & R. Missaoui. LC 95-33010. 300p. 1995. 74.00 (*981-02-2170-3*) World Scientific Pub.

Object-Oriented Technology for Real-Time Systems. Maher Awad. 320p. (C). 1996. 59.00 (*0-13-227943-6*) P-H.

Object-Oriented Test & Measurement Software Development in C++ Lee Atchison & Hewlett-Packard Company Staff. LC 96-219351. 352p. (C). 1996. pap. 59.00 (*0-13-227950-9*) P-H.

***Object-Oriented Thought Process.** 240p. 2000. 29.99 (*0-672-31853-9*) Sams.

Object Oriented Turbo Pascal: A New Paradigm for Problem Solving & Programming/Book & Disk. HAIDUK. 1990. 16.74 (*0-07-909611-5*) McGraw.

Object Oriented Type Systems. Jens Palsberg & Michael J. Schwartzbach. 192p. 1994. 95.00 (*0-471-94128-X*) Wiley.

Object-Oriented User Interface Design Mechanics. Scott Isensee et al. LC 97-23767. (ITCP-US Computer Science Ser.). 400p. 1997. pap. 49.99 (*1-85032-887-0*) ITCP.

Object Perception: Structure & Process. Bryan E. Shepp & S. Ballesteros. 456p. 1989. 99.95 (*0-8058-0060-3*); pap. 59.95 (*0-8058-0333-5*) L Erlbaum Assocs.

Object Persistence. Roger Sessions. LC 96-161436. 272p. (C). 1996. 34.99 (*0-13-192436-2*) P-H.

***Object Primer: The Application Developer's Guide to Object-Orientation.** Scott W. Ambler. (Managing Object Technology Ser.: No. 3). 250p. 2000. pap. 39.95 (*0-521-78519-7*) Cambridge U Pr.

***Object-Process Methodology: A Comprehensive Systems Development Approach.** Dov Dori. 300p. 1999. 59.95 (*3-540-65471-2*) Spr-Verlag.

Object Recognition in Man, Monkey & Machine. Ed. by Michael J. Tarr & Heinrich H. Bulthoff. LC 98-31766. (Cognition Special Issues Ser.). (Illus.). 220p. 1999. pap. text 25.00 (*0-262-70070-0*, Bradford Bks) MIT Pr.

Object Recognition Through Invariant Indexing. C. A. Rothwell. (Illus.). 272p. 1995. text 85.00 (*0-19-856512-7*) OUP.

***Object-Relational Database Development: A Plumber's Guide.** Paul Brown. 600p. 2000. pap. 49.99 (*0-13-019460-3*) P-H.

***Object-Relational Database Management: With Oracle Examples.** George Feuerlicht. (Illus.). 350p. 2000. pap. 42.95 (*1-85233-194-1*) Spr-Verlag.

Object-Relational DBMSs: The Next Great Wave. Michael Stonebraker. LC 95-48896. 216p. (Orig.). 1996. pap. text 39.95 (*1-55860-397-2*) Morgan Kaufmann.

Object-Relational DBMSs: The Next Great Wave. 2nd expanded rev. ed. Michael Stonebraker & Dorothy Moore. LC 99-223526. (Morgan Kaufmann Series in Data Management Systems). 350p. (Orig.). 1998. pap. 39.95 (*1-55860-452-9*) Morgan Kaufmann.

Object Relations: A Dynamic Bridge Between Individual & Family Treatment. Samuel Slipp. LC 83-15557. 288p. 1984. 45.00 (*0-87668-747-8*) Aronson.

Object Relations: A Dynamic Bridge Between Individual & Family Treatment. Samuel Slipp. LC 83-15557. 288p. 1993. pap. 40.00 (*0-87668-527-0*) Aronson.

Object Relations & Self Psychology. 3rd ed. Michael St. Clair. LC 99-31827. (Counseling Ser.). 205p. 1999. pap. text 39.95 (*0-534-36280-X*) Brooks-Cole.

Object Relations & Self Psychology: An Introduction. Michael St. Clair. LC 86-8251. (Counseling-Psychology Ser.). 196p. (C). 1987. pap. 18.25 (*0-534-06708-5*) Brooks-Cole.

Object Relations & Self Psychology: An Introduction. 2nd ed. Michael St. Clair. LC 95-20177. 240p. 1995. text 24.25 (*0-534-33855-0*) Brooks-Cole.

Object Relations & the Developing Ego in Therapy. Althea J. Horner. 1995. pap. text 50.00 (*1-56821-708-0*) Aronson.

Object Relations & the Family Process. Randall S. Klein. LC 89-16226. 201p. 1990. 62.95 (*0-275-93268-0*, C3268, Praeger Pubs) Greenwood.

Object Relations Assessment in Younger Children: Rorschach & Tat Measures. Francis D. Kelly. 178p. 1996. pap. 26.95 (*0-398-06562-4*); text 41.95 (*0-398-06561-6*) C C Thomas.

Object Relations Brief Therapy: The Therapeutic Relationship in Short-Term Work. Michael Stadter. LC 95-20678. 376p. 1996. 60.00 (*1-56821-660-2*) Aronson.

Object Relations Couple Therapy. Jill S. Scharff & David E. Scharff. LC 90-19182. 328p. 1991. 60.00 (*0-87668-647-1*) Aronson.

Object Relations Family Therapy. David E. Scharff & Jill S. Scharff. LC 87-1755. 503p. 1987. 65.00 (*0-87668-938-1*) Aronson.

Object Relations Group Psychotherapy: The Group As an Object, a Tool, & a Training Base. Ramon Ganzarain. 390p. 1989. 55.00 (*0-8236-3725-5*) Intl Univs Pr.

Object Relations in Psychoanalytic Theory. Jay R. Greenberg & Stephen A. Mitchell. 456p. 1983. 43.50 (*0-674-62975-2*) HUP.

Object Relations in Severe Trauma: Psychotherapy of the Sexually Abused Child. Stephen Prior. LC 95-32752. 200p. 1996. 40.00 (*1-56821-554-1*) Aronson.

Object Relations Individual Therapy. Jill S. Scharff & David E. Scharff. LC 97-23357. (Illus.). 656p. 1998. 70.00 (*0-7657-0117-0*) Aronson.

Object Relations Psychotherapy: An Individualized & Interactive Approach to Diagnosis & Treatment. Cheryl Glickauf-Hughes & Marolyn C. Wells. LC 97-8531. 504p. 1997. text 55.00 (*0-7657-0069-7*) Aronson.

Object Relations, the Self & the Group. Charles Ashbach & Victor L. Schermer. LC 94-9884. (International Library of Group Psychotherapy & Group Process Ser.). 328p. (C). 1994. pap. 27.99 (*0-415-11217-6*, B4262) Routledge.

Object Relations, the Self & the Group: A Conceptual Paradigm. Charles Asbach & Victor C. Schermer. 288p. 1987. 55.00 (*0-7100-9839-1*, Routledge Thoemms) Routledge.

Object-Relations Theory & Clinical Psychoanalysis. Otto F. Kernberg. LC 75-42548. 304p. 1995. pap. 50.00 (*1-56821-612-2*) Aronson.

Object Relations Theory & Clinical Psychoanalysis. Otto F. Kernberg. LC 75-42548. 304p. 1990. reprint ed. 55.00 (*0-87668-247-6*) Aronson.

Object Relations Theory & Practice: An Introduction. David E. Scharff. LC 94-24240. 584p. 1995. 60.00 (*1-56821-419-7*) Aronson.

Object Relations Theory & Psychopathology: A Comprehensive Text. Frank L. Summers. LC 93-39264. 424p. 1994. text 55.00 (*0-88163-155-8*) Analytic Pr.

Object Relations Theory & Religion: Clinical Applications. Ed. by Mark Finn & John Gartner. LC 91-42787. 208p. 1992. 55.00 (*0-275-93518-3*, C3518, Praeger Pubs) Greenwood.

Object Relations Theory in Perspective. Ed. by Bornstein. (Psychoanalytic Inquiry Ser.: Vol. 10, No. 2). 1990. 20.00 (*0-88163-954-0*) Analytic Pr.

***Object Relations Therapy.** 2000. 95.00 (*0-205-33217-X*) Allyn.

Object Relations Therapy: Using the Relationship. Sheldon Cashdan. 1988. 25.00 (*0-393-70059-3*) Norton.

Object Relations Therapy of Physical & Sexual Trauma. Jill S. Scharff & David E. Scharff. LC 94-13945. (Library of Object Relations). 392p. 1994. 55.00 (*1-56821-292-5*) Aronson.

Object Relations Therapy with Dotors Jill & David Scharff. Carlson. 1998. VHS 95.00 (*0-205-28354-3*) Allyn.

Object Representation in Computer Vision: ECCV '96 International Workshop, Cambridge, U. K., April 13-15, 1996 - Proceedings. Ed. by J. Ponce et al. (Lecture Notes in Computer Science Ser.: Vol. 1144). viii, 403p. 1996. pap. 68.00 (*3-540-61750-7*) Spr-Verlag.

Object Representation in Computer Vision: International NSF-ARPA Workshop, New York City, NY, U. S. A., December 5-7, 1994: Proceedings. Ed. by Martial H. Hebert et al. (Lecture Notes in Computer Science Ser.: Vol. 994). 359p. 1995. 62.00 (*3-540-60477-4*) Spr-Verlag.

Object Request Brokers for Webmasters. Tom Dell. 350p. (C). 1999. pap. 39.95 (*0-12-209069-1*) Morgan Kaufmann.

Object REXX for Windows NT & Windows 95. Ulrich Wahli. LC 97-178364. 576p. (C). 1997. 45.95 incl. cd-rom (*0-13-858028-6*) P-H.

Object Rhymes. Jean Warren. Ed. by Gayle Bittinger & Kathleen Cubley. LC 98-61313. (Reproducible Rhyme Book Ser.). (Illus.). 96p. (J). (ps). 1998. pap. 8.95 (*1-57029-278-7*, 48002) Totline Pubns.

Object Security. Robert Blakely. LC 99-40091. 128p. (C). 1999. pap. 29.95 (*0-201-32565-9*) Addison-Wesley.

Object Solutions: Managing the Object-Oriented Project. Grady Booch. LC 95-24671. 669p. (C). 1995. pap. 36.95 (*0-8053-0594-7*) Addison-Wesley.

Object Stares Back: On the Nature of Seeing. James Elkins. LC 97-15949. 272p. 1997. pap. 13.00 (*0-15-600497-6*) HUP.

Object Structures: Building Object-Oriented Software Components with Fiffel. Jacob Gore. (Addison-Wesley Eiffel in Practice Series). 496p. (C). 1996. pap. 36.95 (*0-201-63480-5*) Addison-Wesley.

Object Success: A Manager's Guide to Object Orientation, It's Impact on the Corporation, & It's Use for Re-engineering. Bertrand Meyer. 250p. 1995. 63.00 (*0-13-192833-3*) P-H.

Object Talks That Teach the Gospels: 25 Lessons for Elementary Kids. Zach Hapeman. Ed. by Henrietta Gambill. (Illus.). 48p. 1999. pap. 4.99 (*0-7847-0941-6*, 02851) Standard Pub.

Object Talks That Teach the Psalms: 25 Lessons for Elementary Kids. Zach Hapeman. Ed. by Henrietta Gambill. (Illus.). 48p. 1999. pap. 4.99 (*0-7847-0942-4*, 02852) Standard Pub.

Object Technologies for Advanced Software: First JSSST International Symposium, Kanazawa, Japan, November 4-6, 1993: Proceedings. Ed. by Shojiro Nishio & Akinori Yonezawa. LC 93-32466. (Lecture Notes in Computer Science Ser.: Vol. 742). 1993. 79.95 (*0-387-57342-9*) Spr-Verlag.

Object-Technologies for Advanced Software: Second International Symposium, ISOTAS '96, Ishikawa, Japan, March 11-15, 1996 Proceedings. Ed. by Kokichi Futatsugi & Satoshi Matsuoka. (Lecture Notes in Computer Science Ser.: Vol. 1049). x, 309p. 1996. pap. 56.00 (*3-540-60954-7*) Spr-Verlag.

Object Technology: A Manager's Guide. 2nd ed. David A. Taylor. LC 97-35870. 224p. (C). 1997. pap. 29.95 (*0-201-30994-7*) Addison-Wesley.

Object Technology: Concepts & Methods. Mokrane Bouzeghoub et al. (ITCP-UK Computer Science Ser.). (C). 1997. pap. 39.99 (*1-85032-301-1*) Thomson Learn.

Object Technology: The New Approach to Application Development. Jerry Cashin. LC 96-30867. (Illus.). 231p. 1996. pap. 270.00 (*1-56607-977-2*) Comput Tech Res.

Object Technology Casebook: Lessons from Award-Winning Business Applications. Paul Harmon & William Morrisey. LC 96-12158. 377p. 1996. pap. 34.95 (*0-471-14717-6*) Wiley.

Object Technology Centers of Excellence. Timothy D. Korson. 208p. (C). 1996. 45.00 (*0-13-261231-3*) P-H.

Object Technology in Application Development. 2nd ed. Daniel Tkach & Richard Puttick. 232p. (C). 1995. pap. 29.95 (*0-201-49833-2*) Addison-Wesley.

Object Technology Made Simple. unabridged ed. Mory Bahar. Ed. by Ann Waterman. (Illus.). x, 78p. (Orig.). 1996. pap. 14.95 (*0-9652457-0-5*) Smple Sftwre.

Object Technology Strategies & Tactics. Gilbert L. Singer. (Managing Object Technology Ser.: No. 7). 377p. 1996. pap. 39.95 (*0-13-261132-5*) Cambridge U Pr.

Object Thinking CD-ROM: Development Before the Fact. Margaret Hamilton. 1996. text 50.00 (*0-07-911802-X*) McGraw.

Object to Be Destroyed: The Work of Gordon Matta-Clark. Pamela M. Lee & Gordon Matta-Clark. LC 99-17978. (Illus.). 240p. 1999. 35.00 (*0-262-12220-0*) MIT Pr.

Object Web Survival Guide. Robert Orfali et al. 672p. 1998. pap. 39.99 (*0-471-24546-1*) Wiley.

Object Windows Reference Guide, Vol. 5. 1996. 45.00 (*0-672-30927-0*) Sams.

***Objectarx Primer.** Bill Kramer. LC 99-32454. 165p. 1999. 23.95 (*0-7668-1127-1*, AutoDesk Pr) Delmar.

Objected-Oriented Data Warehousing Design: Building Star Schema. Ed. by Prentice-Hall Staff. LC 99-89100. 368p. (C). 2000. 49.00 (*0-13-085081-0*) P-H.

Objectif France. annot. ed. Alan Rosenthal. (College French Ser.). (C). 1993. mass mkt., teacher ed. 58.95 (*0-8384-3738-9*) Heinle & Heinle.

Objectif Lune see Destination Moon

Objectif Lune. Herge.Tr. of Destination Moon. (FRE., Illus.). (J). (gr. 7-9). ring bd. 19.95 (*0-8288-5051-8*) Fr & Eur.

Objectifying Motif. Charles F. Bowman. (Advances in Object Technology Ser.: No. 10). 516p. (Orig.). 1995. pap. 39.95 (*0-13-234436-X*) Cambridge U Pr.

Objectifying Real-Time Systems. John R. Ellis. (Advances in Object Technology Ser.: No. 2). 542p. (Orig.). 1994. pap. 44.95 (*0-13-125550-9*) Cambridge U Pr.

Objection: A Tennis Novel. Marvin Cohen. 256p. (Orig.). 1996. pap. 14.95 (*0-9647940-8-X*) Adventura Pubng.

Objections at Trial. 2nd ed. Ronald L. Carlson & Myron H. Bright. LC 93-25116. 280p. 1993. pap. 29.95 (*1-56257-349-7*, MICHIE) LEXIS Pub.

Objections at Trial. 3rd ed. Edward A. Imwinkelried et al. LC 98-86950. 300p. 1998. 35.00 (*0-327-00308-1*, 8219111) LEXIS Pub.

Objections at Trial: National Edition. Myron Bright. 1993. 29.95 (*0-614-06016-8*, 31105) Natl Prac Inst.

Objections Sustained: Subversive Essays on Evolution, Law & Culture. Phillip E. Johnson. LC 98-6866. 108p. 1998. 15.99 (*0-8308-1941-X*, 1941) InterVarsity.

***Objections Sustained: Subversive Essays on Evolution, Law & Culture.** Phillip E. Johnson. 188p. 2000. pap. 10.99 (*0-8308-2288-7*) InterVarsity.

Objections to Astrology. Bart J. Bok & Lawrence E. Jerome. LC 75-29798. (Science & the Paranormal Ser.). 62p. 1975. 8.95 (*0-87975-059-6*) Prometheus Bks.

Objections to Calvinism As It Is. Randolph Sinks Foster. LC 98-206078. 216p. 1998. 11.99 (*0-88019-374-3*) Schmul Pub Co.

Objections to Humanism. H. J. Blackham et al. LC 73-16796. 128p. 1974. reprint ed. lib. bdg. 49.50 (*0-8371-7235-7*, BLOH, Greenwood Pr) Greenwood.

Objections to Physicalism. Ed. by Howard Robinson. (Illus.). 332p. 1997. reprint ed. pap. text 24.95 (*0-19-823677-8*) OUP.

Objections to the Abolition of the Slave Trade with Answers. James Ramsey. LC 73-83873. (Black Heritage Library Collection). 1977. 14.95 (*0-8369-8644-X*) Ayer.

Objective - Prism & Other Surveys. Ed. by A. G. Davis Philip & A. R. Upgren. 202p. 1991. 32.00 (*0-933485-15-8*) L Davis Pr.

Objective Bajor. John Peel. (Star Trek: Deep Space Nine Ser.: No. 15). 288p. 1996. per. 5.99 (*0-671-56811-6*) S&S Trade.

Objective-Based Safety Training. Kenneth L. Miller. LC 97-52715. 269p. 1998. boxed set 59.95 (*1-56670-286-0*) Lewis Pubs.

Objective Description of the Self: The Literary Theory of Iwano Homei. Yoichi Nagashima. LC 98-153773. 240p. 1997. 29.95 (*87-7288-611-0*, Pub. by Aarhus Univ Pr) David Brown.

Objective Determination of Stories & Poems for the Primary Grades. Mary E. Nesmith. LC 78-117102. (Columbia University. Teachers College. Contributions to Education Ser.: No. 255). reprint ed. 37.50 (*0-404-55255-2*) AMS Pr.

Objective Diagnosis of Minimal Brain Dysfunction. Richard A. Gardner. LC 79-11054. xxvi, 452p. 1979. text 20.00 (*0-933812-00-0*) Creative Therapeutics.

Objective for Living. (ENG & IND.). 1993. pap. write for info. (*0-934920-55-9*, T-96IN) Derek Prince.

Objective for Living: To Do God's Will. Derek Prince. 64p. 1996. mass mkt. 4.99 (*0-88368-464-0*) Whitaker Hse.

Objective for Living: To Do God's Will see Proposito en la Vida: Hacer la Voluntad de Dios

Objective Idealism, Ethics, & Politics. Vittorio Hosle. LC 98-8563. 235p. 1998. 30.00 (*1-890318-52-3*) St Augustines Pr.

Objective Knowledge: An Evolutionary Approach. Karl R. Popper. (Illus.). 390p. (C). 1972. pap. text 26.95 (*0-19-875024-2*) OUP.

Objective Measurement: Theory into Practice, Vol. 1. Ed. by Mark Wilson. 368p. 1992. pap. 39.50 (*0-89391-814-8*); text 78.50 (*0-89391-727-3*) Ablx Pub.

Objective Measurement: Theory into Practice, Vol. 2. Ed. by Mark Wilson. 352p. (C). 1994. pap. 39.50 (*0-89391-843-1*); text 78.50 (*0-89391-842-3*) Ablx Pub.

Objective Measurement: Theory into Practice, Vol. 3. George Engelhard, Jr. et al. Ed. by Mark Wilson. 471p. 1996. pap. 39.50 (*1-56750-183-4*) Ablx Pub.

Objective Measurement: Theory into Practice, Vol. 3. Larry H. Ludlow et al. Ed. by George Engelhard, Jr. & Mark Wilson. 471p. 1996. text 78.50 (*1-56750-182-6*) Ablx Pub.

Objective Measurement: Theory into Practice, Vol. 4. Ed. by Mark Wilson & Karen Draney. 364p. 1997. pap. 39.50 (*1-56750-334-9*); text 78.50 (*1-56750-333-0*) Ablx Pub.

Objective Medical Decision Making: Systems Approach in Acute Disease. Ed. by J. E. Beneken & S. M. Lavelle. (Lecture Notes in Medical Informatics Ser.: Vol. 22). 243p. 1983. 42.95 (*0-387-12671-6*) Spr-Verlag.

Objective Mental Measurement: Individual & Program Evaluation Using the Rasch Model. Robert M. Hashway. LC 78-19739. 105p. 1978. 45.00 (*0-275-90297-8*, C0297, Praeger Pubs) Greenwood.

Objective Methods in Food Quality Assessment. John G. Kapsalis. 288p. 1986. 162.00 (*0-8493-5549-4*, TX546, CRC Reprint) Franklin.

Objective, 1995: The Intergovernmental Programme of the Activities of the Council of Europe. 1995. 18.00 (*92-871-2730-1*, Pub. by Council of Europe) Manhattan Pub Co.

Objective, 1997: The Intergovernmental Programme of Activities of the Council of Europe. 1997. 18.00 (*92-871-3298-4*, Pub. by Council of Europe) Manhattan Pub Co.

Objective, 1996: The Intergovernmental Programme of Activities of the Council of Europe. 1996. 18.00 (*92-871-3014-0*, Pub. by Council of Europe) Manhattan Pub Co.

Objective Prescriptions: And other Essays. R. M. Hare. LC 98-45922. 236p. 1999. text 65.00 (*0-19-823853-3*) OUP.

Objective Psychodiagnostic Inventories. 99th ed. Green & Henry A. Millon. 1995. 1.00 (*0-471-88315-8*) Wiley.

Objective Psychology of Grammar. J. R. Kantor. 1936. 15.00 (*0-911188-57-6*) Principia Pr.

Objective Questions in Medical Physiology. Deshpande. 304p. 1995. pap. 14.95 (*0-07-462358-3*) McGraw.

Objective Selection of Supervisors: A Study of Informal Industry Practice & Two Models for Improved Supervisor Selection. Herbert R. Northrup et al. LC 78-61998. (Manpower & Human Resources Studies: No. 8). 247p. 1978. 22.50 (*0-89546-006-8*) U PA Ctr Hum Res.

Objective, Strategy, Tactic: A Management Technique. Albert M. Juergens, Jr. & Albert M. Juergens, III. LC 92-75910. (Illus.). 119p. (Orig.). 1993. pap. 19.95 (*0-9635010-1-1*) Huntersfld Mtn.

***Objective Structured Clinical Examination in Obstetrics & Gynaecology.** Justin C. Konje & D. J. Taylor. (Illus.). 1998. pap. 49.95 (*0-632-04764-X*) Blackwell Sci.

Objective Tests in Economics. 3rd ed. Stanlake. 1983. pap. text. write for info. (*0-582-35444-7*, Pub. by Addison-Wesley) Longman.

***Objective Uine.** Herge. 1999. 19.95 (*2-203-00115-1*) Midwest European Pubns.

Objectives: The New Sculpture. Paul Schimmel et al. (Illus.). 196p. 1990. pap. 29.95 (*0-917493-15-X*) Orange Cnty Mus.

Objectives & Concepts Underlying Financial Statements. 41p. pap. 8.00 (*92-1-104325-5*, 89.II.A.18) UN.

Objectives-Based Approach to Military Campaign Analysis. Bruce Pirnie. LC 96-14140. (Illus.). 141p. (Orig.). 1996. pap. text 15.00 (*0-8330-2397-7*, MR-656-JS) Rand Corp.

Objectives, Methods, & Evaluation for Secondary Teaching. 4th ed. Michael A. Lorber. LC 95-33143. 304p. (C). 1995. pap. text 58.00 (*0-205-19392-7*) Allyn.

Objectives of Accounting & Financial Reporting by Governmental Units: A Research Study, 2 vols. Ed. by Allan R. Drebin et al. Incl. Vol. I. (Illus.). 128p. 1981. pap. Vol. II. (Illus.). 200p. 1981. pap. 7.50 1981. pap. write for info. (*0-318-56852-7*) Municipal.

O

An Asterisk (*) at the beginning of an entry indicates that the title is appearing for the first time.

Objectives of Federal Financial Reporting: Federal Financial Accounting Concepts. 1997. lib. bdg. 253.99 (*0-8490-7681-1*) Gordon Pr.

Objectives of Political Science. Milton Hobbes. 110p. (Orig.). (C). 1993. pap. text 19.50 (*0-8191-8950-2*) U Pr of Amer.

Objectives of Political Science. Milton Hobbs. LC 92-36975. 110p. (C). 1993. lib. bdg. 39.50 (*0-8191-8949-9*) U Pr of Amer.

Objectivism: The Philosophy of Ayn Rand. Leonard Peikoff. 512p. 1993. pap. 16.95 (*0-452-01101-9*, Mer) NAL.

Objectivist Newsletter, 1962-1966, Vols. 1-4. 4th ed. Ayn Rand. LC 90-61904. 224p. 1994. reprint ed. lib. bdg. 39.95 (*1-56114-149-6*) Second Renaissance.

***Objectivist Nexus: Essays in Cultural Poetics.** Rachel B. DuPlessis. (Modern & Contemporary Poetics Ser.). 376p. 1999. text 49.95 (*0-8173-0974-8*) U of Ala Pr.

***Objectivist Nexus: Essays in Cultural Poetics.** Rachel B. DuPlessis & Peter Quartermain. LC 98-58047. (Modern & Contemporary Poetics Ser.). 380p. 1999. pap. text 24.95 (*0-8173-0973-X*) U of Ala Pr.

Objectivist, 1966-1971, Vols. 5-10. 4th ed. Ayn Rand. LC 90-61907. 400p. 1994. reprint ed. lib. bdg. 54.95 (*1-56114-148-8*) Second Renaissance.

Objectivity: The Obligations of Impersonal Reason. Nicholas Rescher. LC 96-26431. 264p. (C). 1997. text 35.00 (*0-268-03701-9*); pap. text 16.00 (*0-268-03703-5*) U of Notre Dame Pr.

Objectivity & Historical Understanding. Andrew Beards. (Series in Philosophy). 184p. 1997. 64.95 (*1-85972-521-X*, Pub. by Avebry) Ashgate Pub Co.

***Objectivity & Insight.** Mark Sacks. 360p. 2000. text 55.00 (*0-19-825058-4*) OUP.

Objectivity & Its Other. Ed. by Wolfgang Natter et al. 214p. 1995. pap. text 18.95 (*0-89862-545-9*) Guilford Pubns.

Objectivity & Liberal Scholarship. Noam Chomsky. 142p. 1997. pap. 6.00 (*0-934868-33-6*) Black & Red.

Objectivity & Subjectivism in the Philosophy of Science with Special Reference to India. Dale Riepe. 232p. 1986. 27.50 (*0-8364-1655-4*, Pub. by KP Bagchi) S Asia.

Objectivity, Communication, & the Foundation of Understanding. Bruce W. McKinzie. 168p. (Orig.). (C). 1994. pap. text 24.50 (*0-8191-9537-5*); lib. bdg. 47.00 (*0-8191-9536-7*) U Pr of Amer.

Objectivity, Empiricism & Truth. R. W. Newell. (Studies in Philosophical Psychology). 126p. 27.50 (*0-7102-0897-9*, 08979, Routledge Thoemms) Routledge.

Objectivity in Law. Nicos Stavropoulos. 228p. 1996. text 65.00 (*0-19-825899-2*) OUP.

***Objectivity in Law & Morals.** Ed. by Brian Leiter. (Cambridge Studies in Philosophy & Law). 424p. 2000. write for info. (*0-521-55430-6*) Cambridge U Pr.

Objectivity in Social Research. Gunnar Myrdal. LC H 0062.M9. 125p. 1983. reprint ed. pap. 38.80 (*0-7837-8198-9*, 204790300008) Bks Demand.

Objectivity in the Making: Francis Bacon & the Politics of Inquiry. Julie R. Solomon. LC 97-19115. 321p. 1997. text 49.95 (*0-8018-5675-2*) Johns Hopkins.

Objectivity Is Not Neutrality: Explanatory Schemes in History. Thomas L. Haskell. LC 97-18956. 320p. 1997. text 35.95 (*0-8018-5681-7*) Johns Hopkins.

***Objectivity Is Not Neutrality: Explanatory Schemes in History.** Thomas L. Haskell. 440p. 2000. pap. 19.95 (*0-8018-6535-2*) Johns Hopkins.

Objectivity, Method & Point of View: Essays in the Philosophy of History. W. J. Van der Dussen & Lionel Rubinoff. LC 91-11888. (Philosophy of History & Culture Ser.: No. 6). viii, 205p. 1991. 79.00 (*90-04-09411-3*) Brill Academic Pubs.

Objectivity, Rationality & the Third Realm: Justification & the Grounds of Psychologism: A Study of Frege & Popper. Mark A. Notturno. (Nijhoff International Philosophy Ser.: No. 16). 268p. 1985. pap. text 46.00 (*90-247-3129-1*); lib. bdg. 127.50 (*90-247-2956-4*) Kluwer Academic.

Objectivity, Relativism, & Truth Vol. 1: Philosophical Papers, 2 vols. Richard McKay Rorty. (Illus.). 236p. (C). 1990. pap. text 20.95 (*0-521-35877-9*) Cambridge U Pr.

Objectivity, Science & Society: Interpreting Nature & Society in the Age of the Crisis of Science. Paul A. Komesaroff. 448p. (C). 1986. 65.00 (*0-7102-0381-0*, Routledge Thoemms) Routledge.

Objectivity, Simulation & the Unity of Consciousness: Current Issues in the Philosophy of Mind. Ed. by Christopher A. Peacocke. (Proceedings of the British Academy Ser.: Vol. 83). (Illus.). 188p. 1996. reprint ed. pap. text 16.95 (*0-19-726167-1*) OUP.

Objects. Parramon Editorial Team Staff. LC 97-21413. (Illus.). 48p. (J). (gr. 4). 1997. 12.95 (*0-7641-5042-1*) Barron.

Objects Affecting Navigable Airspace. 1997. lib. bdg. 250.95 (*0-8490-8159-9*); lib. bdg. 250.95 (*0-8490-8102-5*) Gordon Pr.

Objects & Drawings from the Sanford M. & Diane Besser Collection. Marcia Y. Manhart. 94p. 1992. pap. 20.00 (*1-884240-01-1*) Arkansas Art Ctr.

Objects & Identity: An Examination of the Relative Identity Thesis & Its Consequences. Harold W. Noonan. (Melbourne International Philosophy Ser.: Vol. 6). 192p. 1980. text 126.50 (*90-247-2292-6*) Kluwer Academic.

Objects & Others: Essays on Museums & Material Culture. Ed. by George W. Stocking, Jr. LC 85-40379. (History of Anthropology Ser.: No. 3). 240p. 1988. pap. 18.95 (*0-299-10324-2*) U of Wis Pr.

Objects & Systems: Principled Design with C++ Implementation. Bernard P. Zeigler. LC 96-18350. (Undergraduate Texts in Computer Science Ser.). 221p. 1997. 39.95 (*0-387-94781-7*) Spr-Verlag.

Objects, Components, & Frameworks with UML. Desmond D'Souza. LC 98-31109. 816p. (C). 1998. pap. text 49.95 (*0-201-31012-0*) Addison-Wesley.

Objects for Business. Dennis Minium & Keith Short. (C). 2001. text 38.00 (*0-13-241043-5*) P-H.

Objects for Concurrent Constraint Programming. Martin Henz. LC 97-34942. (The Kluwer International Series in Engineering & Computer Science). 200p. 1997. text 126.50 (*0-7923-8038-X*) Kluwer Academic.

Objects for OS/23. Scott Danforth et al. 500p. 1995. pap. 39.95 (*0-471-13126-1*) Wiley.

Objects from a Romance. Jeffrey Norman. (Illus.). 56p. (Orig.). 1991. pap. write for info. (*0-9628082-1-0*) EyeDea Bks.

Objects in Mirror Are Closer Than They Appear. Max Layton. 200p. 1994. pap. 14.95 (*0-88962-541-7*) Mosaic.

Objects in Mirror Are Closer Than They Appear. Katharine Weber. 1996. pap. 12.00 (*0-614-97768-1*, Picador USA) St Martin.

Objects in Mirror Are Closer Than They Appear. Katherine Weber. LC 96-59. 272p. 1996. pap. 12.00 (*0-312-14383-4*) St Martin.

Objects in the Mirror May Be Closer Than They Appear: Don't Let Change Run You Over. Brenda Jernigan. 1999. pap. 4.95 (*0-9658659-7-5*) Kaleidoscope.

Objects in the Southern Sky. (Illus.). 10p. 1988. 31.95 (*0-387-91316-5*) Spr-Verlag.

Objects in the Terrifying Tense Longing from Taking Place. Leslie Scalapino. LC 94-65017. (Roof Bks.). 80p. 1993. text 9.95 (*0-937804-54-1*) Segue NYC.

Objects of All Sorts: A Philosophical Grammar. Vincent Descombes. Tr. by Lorna Scott-Fox & Jeremy Harding from FRE. LC 86-164.Tr. of Grammaire d'objets en tous genres. 272p. 1987. text 38.50 (*0-8018-2551-2*) Johns Hopkins.

Objects of All Sorts: A Philosophical Grammar. Vincent Descombes. LC 86-164.Tr. of Grammaire d'objets en tous genres. 239p. reprint ed. pap. 74.10 (*0-608-08802-1*, 206944100004) Bks Demand.

Objects of Code & Desire. LeeAnn Heringer. Ed. by Wlodzimierz Holsztynski & Marek Lugowski. LC 97-208413. (Illus.). 44p. 1997. pap. 3.00 (*1-888431-11-3*) ASGP.

Objects of Concern: Canadian Prisoners of War Through the Twentieth Century. Jonathan Vance. LC 95-171880. (Illus.). 336p. 1997. 39.95 (*0-7748-0504-8*); pap. 25.95 (*0-7748-0520-X*) U of Wash Pr.

Objects of Desire. Jessica Bayer. 24p. (Orig.). 1991. pap. 4.00 (*0-945926-26-X*) Paradigm RI.

Objects of Desire. Feldman. 1999. text. write for info. (*0-312-21656-4*) St Martin.

Objects of Desire. Pamela Holm. 182p. 1998. pap. 19.95 (*1-86066-043-6*, Pub. by R Cohen Bks) Trafalgar.

Objects of Desire: Conversations with Luis Bunuel. Jose De La Colina & Tomas P. Turrent. Tr. by Paul Lenti from SPA. LC 92-82642. (Illus.). 280p. 1993. 24.00 (*0-941419-68-1*) Marsilio Pubs.

Objects of Desire: Conversations with Luis Bunuel. Jose De la Colina & Tomas P. Turrent. Tr. by Paul Lenti from SPA. LC 92-82642. (Illus.). 280p. 1994. pap. 12.95 (*0-941419-69-X*) Marsilio Pubs.

Objects of Desire: Design & Society, 1750-1980. Adrian Forty. LC 91-67302. (Illus.). 256p. 1992. reprint ed. pap. 18.95 (*0-500-27412-6*, Pub. by Thames Hudson) Norton.

Objects of Desire: The Lives of Antiques & Those Who Pursue Them. Thatcher Freund. 304p. 1995. pap. 13.95 (*0-14-024480-8*, Penguin Bks) Viking Penguin.

***Objects of Desire: The Madonnas of Modernism.** Beryl Schlossman. LC 99-32826. 1999. 39.95 (*0-8014-3649-4*) Cornell U Pr.

Objects of Desire: The Modern Still Life. Margit Rowell. (Illus.). 232p. 1997. 49.50 (*0-8109-6172-5*, Pub. by Abrams) Time Warner.

Objects of Desire: The Modern Still Life. Margit Rowell. (Illus.). 232p. 1997. 50.00 (*0-87070-111-8*, 0-8109-6172-5, Pub. by Mus of Modern Art); pap. 24.95 (*0-87070-110-X*) Mus of Modern Art.

Objects of Enquiry: The Life, Contributions, & Influence of Sir William Jones (1746-1794) Ed. by Garland Cannon & Kevin Brine. (Illus.). 176p. (C). 1995. text 45.00 (*0-8147-1517-6*) NYU Pr.

Objects of High Redshift: I. A. U. Symposium Los Angeles, Aug. 28 to 31, 1979. Ed. by George O. Abell & P. J. Peebles. (International Astronomical Union Symposia Ser.: No. 92). 328p. 1980. lib. bdg. 104.50 (*90-277-1118-6*) Kluwer Academic.

***Objects of Hope: Exploring Possibility & Limit in Psychoanalysis.** Steven Cooper. LC 00-26949. Vol. 18. 344p. 2000. 49.95 (*0-88163-271-6*) Analytic Pr.

Objects of Inspiration. Wilhelmina A. Kamas. 1998. pap. write for info. (*1-57553-931-4*) Watermrk Pr.

Objects of Knowledge. Ed. by Susan M. Pearce. LC 90-1021. (New Research in Museum Studies: An International Ser.: Vol. 1). 224p. (C). 1990. text 85.00 (*0-485-90001-7*, Pub. by Athlone Pr) Humanities.

***Objects of My Affection.** Sarah Lugg. 64p. 2000. 10.95 (*0-7407-1248-9*) Andrews & McMeel.

Objects of Myth & Memory. Diana Fane et al. (Illus.). 320p. 1991. pap. 39.95 (*0-87273-122-7*) Bklyn Mus.

Objects of Personal Significance. Janet Marquardt-Cherry. Ed. by David Conrads & Deni M. McHenry. (Illus.). 56p. (Orig.). 1996. pap. 20.00 (*1-882603-03-6*) Mid Am Arts.

***Objects of Provenance Not Known: Index to Parts 1 & 2, 3 vols.** Jaromir Malek. (Topographical Bibliography of Ancient Egyptian Hieroglyphic Ser.: Vol. VIII). 100p. (C). 2000. pap. 350.00 (*0-900416-70-X*, Pub. by Griffith Inst) David Brown.

***Objects of Provenance Not Known: Private Statues (Dynasty XVIII to the Roman Period) - Deities, 3 vols.** Jaromir Malek et al. (Topographical Bibliography of Ancient Egyptian Hieroglyphic Ser.: Vol. VIII). 700p. (C). 2000. 350.00 (*0-900416-69-6*, Pub. by Griffith Inst) David Brown.

***Objects of Provenance Not Known: Royal Statues. Private Statues, 3 vols.** Jaromir Malek et al. (Predynastic to Dynasty Ser.: Vol. XVII, Pt. 1). 500p. 2000. 350.00 (*0-900416-67-X*, Pub. by Griffith Inst) David Brown.

***Objects of Provenance Not Known: Royal Statues, Private Statues (Predynastic to Dynasty XVII)** Jaromir Malek et al. (Topographical Bibliography of Ancient Egyptian Hieroglyphic Ser.: Vol. VIII). 500p. (C). 2000. 350.00 (*0-900416-68-8*, Pub. by Griffith Inst) David Brown.

Objects of Special Devotion: Fetishes & Fetishism in Popular Culture. Ed. by Ray B. Browne. LC 81-85521. 1982. 22.95 (*0-87972-191-X*) Bowling Green Univ Popular Press.

Objects of Thought. Arthur N. Prior. Ed. by Peter T. Geach. 1971. 49.95 (*0-19-824354-5*) OUP.

Objects on a Table: Harmonious Disarray in Art & Literature. Guy Davenport. LC 98-35507. (Illus.). 144p. 1998. 27.50 (*1-887178-85-6*, Pub. by Counterpt DC) HarpC.

***Objects on a Table: Harmonious Disarray in Art & Literature.** Guy Davenport. 136p. 1999. pap. text 17.50 (*1-58243-035-7*, Pub. by Counterpt DC) HarpC.

Object Primer: The Application Developer's Guide to Object-Orientation. Sigs Books Staff & Scott W. Ambler. (Managing Object Technology Ser.: No. 3). 270p. (C). 1995. 34.95 (*0-13-242496-7*) Cambridge U Pr.

Objects Performance Video Sound. Marina Abramovic. 144p. 1996. pap. 35.00 (*0-905836-88-X*, Pub. by Museum Modern Art) St Mut.

***Objects to Components with the Java Platform.** Art Gittleman. (Illus.). 589p. (C). 1999. pap. text 67.87 (*1-57676-035-9*) Scott Jones Pubng.

Objects Unencapsulated: Java, Eiffel & C++ Ian Joyner. LC 99-15199. (Object & Component Technology Ser.). (Illus.). 416p. 1999. pap. 49.00 (*0-13-014269-7*, Prentice Hall) P-H.

Objectvision. Paul Harmon & Brian Sawyer. (Illus.). 256p. (C). 1990. pap. text 19.50 (*0-201-51049-9*) Addison-Wesley.

ObjectVision Programming for Windows. Donald R. Read. (Illus.). 352p. 1993. text 34.95 (*0-8306-4194-7*, 4258, Windcrest) TAB Bks.

Objektorienterte Analyse und Design. 2nd ed. (C). 1994. (*3-89319-673-0*) Addison-Wesley.

Objektorientierte Programmierung in Oberon-2 see Object-Oriented Programming in Oberon-2

Objektorientierte Programmierung mit Turbo Pascal 6.0. 2nd ed. Josef Mittendorfer. (GER.). (C). 1991. text. write for info. (*0-201-55956-0*) Addison-Wesley.

Objektreferenzen in Beschreibungen und Instruktionen: Eine Empirische Untersuchung Zum Zusammenhang Von Textstruktur, Referentieller Bewegung und Formen Von Objektreferenzen. Ute Kohlmann. (Europaische Hochschulschriften, Reihe 21 Ser.: No. 187). (Illus.). 214p. 1997. 42.95 (*3-631-31423-X*) P Lang Pubng.

Objet de la Psychanalyse et l'Objet en Psychanalyse. Ed. by J. R. Freymann & A. Michels. (Apertura Ser.: Vol. 2). 200p. 1989. 34.95 (*0-387-18085-0*) Spr-Verlag.

Objetivo: La Luna. Herge. (SPA., Illus.). 62p. (J). 19.95 (*0-8288-5052-6*) Fr & Eur.

Objetivos Educacionales: Criterios Basicos para la Evaluacion del Aprendizaje. Lydia Diaz De Grana. LC 76-8191. (SPA.). 94p. (Orig.). (C). 1983. pap. 4.50 (*0-8477-2721-1*) U of PR Pr.

Objetos Que Ensenan de Dios: Objects That Teach about God. Cecilio McConnell & Mary McConnell. (SPA.). 96p. 1986. pap. 7.99 (*0-311-44007-X*) Casa Bautista.

Objetos y Palabras Tabu. James George Frazer. (Fondo 2000 Ser.). (SPA.). pap. 2.99 (*968-16-5049-2*, Pub. by Fondo) Continental Bk.

Objets Familiers - Everyday Things. (Gallimard - Encyclopedie Vis. Bilingue Ser.). (ENG & FRE.). 63p. (J). 1991. 19.95 (*2-07-057513-6*) Schoenhof.

Oblagon Vol. 2: Concepts of Syd Mead. 2nd ed. Syd Mead. Tr. by Mieko Ichikawa. (ENG & JPN., Illus.). 168p. 1996. reprint ed. per. 50.00 (*4-06-201525-0*) Oblagon.

Oblaka V Kontse Veka. Naiman Anatoly. LC 93-11885. (RUS.). 100p. (Orig.). 1993. pap. 9.00 (*1-55779-069-8*) Hermitage Pubs.

Oblat. J. K. Huysmans. Ed. by Denise Cogny. (Conversion Trilogy Ser.: Vol. 3). (FRE., Illus.). 472p. 1995. pap. 74.95 (*2-86808-066-9*) Intl Scholars.

Oblate. Joris K. Huysmans. Tr. by Edward Perceval from FRE. LC 77-11670. 1978. reprint ed. 45.00 (*0-86527-284-0*) Fertig.

Oblate of St. Benedict. J. K. Huysmans. Ed. by Terry Hale. Tr. by Edward Perceval from FRE. LC 96-59432. (European Classics).Tr. of L'Oblate. 310p. 1997. pap. 11.99 (*1-873982-57-7*, Pub. by Dedalus) Hippocrene Bks.

Oblates of St Benedict: An Introduction for Inquirers & Candidates. 8p. 1989. pap. 0.20 (*0-8146-1037-4*) Liturgical Pr.

Obligaciones Contractuales. Pedro F. Silva-Ruiz. 597p. 1993. pap. 22.95 (*0-8477-3034-4*) U of PR Pr.

***Obligation & Opportunity: Single Maritime Women in Boston, 1870-1930.** Betsy Beattie-, 192p. 2000. 60.00 (*0-7735-2018-X*, Pub. by McG-Queens Univ Pr) CUP Services.

***Obligation & Opportunity: Single, Maritime Women in Boston, 1870-1930.** Mary E. Beattie. 192p. 2000. pap. 22.95 (*0-7735-2019-8*, Pub. by McG-Queens Univ Pr) CUP Services.

Obligation of Contracts Clause of the United States Constitution. Warren B. Hunting. LC 75-41148. reprint ed. 29.50 (*0-404-14674-0*) AMS Pr.

Obligation to Disobey. Michael Walzer. (Reprint Series in Political Science). (C). 1993. reprint ed. pap. text 1.00 (*0-8290-2616-9*, P-575) Irvington.

Obligation to Obey in Legal Theory. Hilaire McCoubrey. LC 96-8163. 240p. 1997. text 78.95 (*1-85521-825-9*, Pub. by Dartmth Pub) Ashgate Pub Co.

Obligations. Ward Pafford. 100p. (Orig.). 1994. pap., per. 10.00 (*1-883199-03-4*) St U W Georgia.

Obligations: Essays on Disobedience, War, & Citizenship. Michael Walzer. LC 70-111489. 260p. 1970. pap. 18.00 (*0-674-63025-4*) HUP.

Obligations Erga Omnes & International Crimes: A Theoretical Inquiry into the Implementation & Enforcement of the International Responsibility of States. Andre De Hoogh. 1996. 180.50 (*90-411-0232-9*) Kluwer Law Intl.

***Obligations of Citizenship & Demands of Faith: Religious Accomodation in Pluralist Democracies.** Nancy L. Rosenblum. LC 99-48917. 2000. pap. text 19.95 (*0-691-00708-X*, Pub. by Princeton U Pr) Cal Prin Full Svc.

***Obligations of Citizenship & Demands of Faith: Religious Accomodation in Pluralist Democracies.** Nancy L. Rosenblum. LC 99-48917. (Illus.). 400p. 2000. text 70.00 (*0-691-00707-1*, Pub. by Princeton U Pr) Cal Prin Full Svc.

Obligations of Society in the Twelfth & Thirteenth Centuries: The Ford Lectures Delivered in the University of Oxford in Michaelmas Term. Austin L. Poole. LC 80-2007. reprint ed. 37.50 (*0-404-18587-8*) AMS Pr.

Obligations of the Educated Man. Charles H. Whitmore. LC 62-29139. (Augustana College Library Occasional Papers, Wallin Lecture: No. 4). 13p. 1958. pap. 0.50 (*0-910182-25-6*) Augustana Coll.

Obligations to Future Generations. Ed. by R. I. Sikora & Brian Barry. LC 78-5495. (Philosophical Monographs: Second Annual Ser.). 272p. 1978. pap. 14.95 (*0-87722-128-6*) Temple U Pr.

Obligations to Future Generations. Ed. by R. I. Sikora & Brian Barry. 250p. 1997. 39.95 (*1-874267-31-6*, Pub. by White Horse Pr) Paul & Co Pubs.

Obligato: Untold Tales from a Life with Music. Ira Hirschmann. LC 93-49051. (Illus.). 224p. 1994. 25.00 (*0-88064-154-1*) Fromm Intl Pub.

Obliged by Nature: Photographs by Paul Rosin. Contrib. by Lisa K. Erf. (Illus.). 24p. 1993. 10.00 (*0-945558-20-1*) ISU Univ Galls.

***Obliged to Be Difficult: Nugget Coombs' Legacy in Indigenous Affairs.** Tim Rowse. LC 99-55004. 272p. (C). 2000. 64.95 (*0-521-77353-9*); pap. 24.95 (*0-521-77410-1*) Cambridge U Pr.

Obliging Need: Rural Petty Industry in Mexican Capitalism. Scott Cook & Leigh Binford. (Illus.). 336p. 1990. text 37.50 (*0-292-76032-9*) U of Tex Pr.

Oblique Approach. David Drake & Eric Flint. 480p. 1998. per. 6.99 (*0-671-87865-4*) Baen Bks.

Oblique Contexts. Leonard Linsky. LC 82-23825. (C). 1995. lib. bdg. 30.00 (*0-226-48439-4*) U Ch Pr.

***Oblique Derivative Problem: The Poncare Problem (Paneath)** 348p. 2000. 125.00 (*3-527-40113-X*) Wiley.

Oblique Derivative Problem of Potential Theory. A. I. Yanushauakas. (Contemporary Soviet Mathematics Ser.). (Illus.). 260p. (C). 1989. text 110.00 (*0-306-11023-7*, Kluwer Plenum) Kluwer Academic.

Oblique Light. Lynn Emanuel. LC 79-11007. 32p. 1979. pap. 4.00 (*0-918366-13-5*) Slow Loris.

Oblique Litanies: Nine Conversations & an Afterthought. Paul Davies. 48p. (Orig.). 1992. pap. 12.00 (*1-55022-157-4*, Pub. by ECW) Genl Dist Srvs.

Oblique Prayers: New Poems with Fourteen Translations from Jean Joubert. Denise Levertov. LC 84-1103. 96p. 1984. 9.95 (*0-8112-0909-1*, NDP578, Pub. by New Directions) Norton.

Obliquely Wild. Wayne M. Mann. Ed. by Susan M. Hammack & Edie Hammack. (Illus.). 476p. 1982. pap. 9.95 (*0-9608904-0-8*) Mann Found.

Obliterate. Richard Kostelanetz. 32p. (Orig.). 1974. pap. text 10.00 (*0-932360-64-5*) Archae Edns.

Oblivian Ha-Ha. James Tate. (Carnegie Mellon Classic Contemporary Ser.). 1998. pap. text 12.95 (*0-88748-190-6*) Carnegie-Mellon.

Oblivion. Wolf White Wolf Publishing Staff. (Mind's Eye Theatre Ser.). 192p. 1996. pap. 18.00 (*1-56504-501-7*, 5400) White Wolf.

Oblivion: On Writers & Writing. Donald Justice. LC 98-5727. 148p. 1998. pap. 14.00 (*1-885266-60-X*) Story Line.

Oblivion: Poems. Stephen Berg. 152p. 1995. 12.95 (*0-252-06457-7*) U of Ill Pr.

Oblivion: The Mystery of West Point Cadet Richard Cox. Harry J. Maihafer. LC 96-25098. 256p. 1996. 24.95 (*1-57488-043-8*) Brasseys.

***Oblivion: The Mystery of West Point Cadet Richard Cox.** Harry J. Maihafer. 1999. pap. 16.95 (*1-57488-224-4*) Brasseys.

Oblivion: There's No Escape. Norman Thales. Ed. by H. N. Badalian. 200p. (Orig.). 1987. pap. 11.95 (*0-9619610-0-7*) Expert Translation.

Oblivion & Stone: A Selection of Contemporary Bolivian Poetry & Fiction. Ed. by Sandra Reyes. Tr. by John DuVal et al from SPA. LC 97-51161. 256p. 1998. 38.00 (*1-55728-511-X*); pap. 22.00 (*1-55728-512-8*) U of Ark Pr.

O

An Asterisk (*) at the beginning of an entry indicates that the title is appearing for the first time.

Oblivion Ha-Ha. James Tate. LC 97-65566. (Classic Contemporaries Ser.). 94p. 1997. pap. 12.95 (*0-88748-215-5*) Carnegie-Mellon.

Oblivion Ha-Ha. James Tate. 112p. 1984. 24.95 (*0-87775-170-6*); pap. 14.95 (*0-87775-171-4*) Unicorn Pr.

Oblivion Seekers & Other Writings. Isabelle Eberhardt. Tr. by Paul Bowles from FRE. LC 75-12962. (Illus.). 88p. (Orig.). 1975. pap. 7.95 (*0-87286-082-5*) City Lights.

Oblomov. Ivan A. Goncharov. 560p. Date not set. 32.95 (*0-8488-2637-X*) Amereon Ltd.

Oblomov. Ivan A. Goncharov. LC 92-52923. (Everyman's Library of Children's Classics). 560p. 1992. 20.00 (*0-679-41729-X*) Everymns Lib.

Oblomov. Ivan A. Goncharov. Tr. by David Magarshack from RUS. (Classics Ser.). 496p. 1978. pap. 12.95 (*0-14-044040-2*, Penguin Classics) Viking Penguin.

Oblomov. Ivan Gontcharov. (FRE.). 288p. 1982. pap. 10.95 (*0-7859-2462-0*, 2070373924) Fr & Eur.

Oblomov. Ivan A. Goncharov. Tr. by C. J. Hogarth from RUS. LC 79-19061. 1980. reprint ed. lib. bdg. 22.00 (*0-8376-0451-6*) Bentley Pubs.

Oblomov. Ivan A. Goncharov. Tr. by Natalie Duddington. 1990. reprint ed. lib. bdg. 28.95 (*0-89966-685-X*) Buccaneer Bks.

Oblomov. unabridged ed. Goncharov. (World Classic Literature Ser.). (RUS.). pap. 8.95 (*2-87714-261-2*, Pub. by Bookking Intl) Distribks Inc.

Oblomov & His Creator: The Life & Art of Ivan Goncharov. Milton Ehre. LC 72-5378. (Studies of the Russian Institute, Columbia University & Harvard Series in Ukrainian Studies). 310p. reprint ed. pap. 96.10 (*0-8357-2779-3*, 203990500014) Bks Demand.

OBM in Multiple Business Environments: New Applications for Organizational Behavior Management. Ed. by Brandon Hall. LC 82-15417. (Journal of Organizational Behavior Management: Vol. 4, Nos. 1 & 2). 163p. 1983. text 49.95 (*0-86656-189-7*) Haworth Pr.

Obnoxiously Gross Jokes. Julius Alvin. 128p. 1999. mass mkt. 4.99 (*0-8217-6177-3*, Zebra Kensgtn) Kensgtn Pub Corp.

Obo. Bob Anderson. LC 98-73916. (Illus.). 48p. (J). (gr. 2-6). 1999. bds. 16.00 (*1-57174-124-0*) Hampton Roads Pub Co.

Oboe. Bruce Pearson. (Standard of Excellence Ser.: Bk. 1). 1993. 6.45 (*0-8497-5927-7*, W21OB) Kjos.

Oboe. Bruce Pearson. (Standard of Excellence Ser.: Bk. 2). 1993. 6.45 (*0-8497-5952-8*, W22OB) Kjos.

Oboe. Bruce Pearson. (Standard of Excellence Ser.: Bk. 3). 1996. 6.45 (*0-8497-5976-5*, W23OB) Kjos.

Oboe, Bk. 1. (Breeze Easy Method Ser.). 32p. (Orig.). 1994. pap. 6.50 (*0-89724-370-6*, BE0011) Wrner Bros.

Oboe Concerto: Piano Reduction. 9.95 (*0-7935-4029-1*, 50482228) H Leonard.

Oboe Concertos of Sir William Herschel. Ed. by Davis Jerome. LC 96-96245. (Memoirs Ser.: Vol. 225). 100p. 1998. 40.00 (*0-87169-225-2*, M225-jed) Am Philos.

Oboe Reed Styles: Theory & Practice. David A. Ledet. LC 80-8152. (Illus.). 224p. 1981. 36.95 (*0-253-37891-5*) Ind U Pr.

***Oboe Reed Styles: Theory & Practice.** David A. Ledet. (Illus.). 224p. 2000. pap. 21.95 (*0-253-21392-4*) Ind U Pr.

Oboe Solos, EFS99. Jay Arnold. (Illus.). 160p. 1958. pap. 14.95 (*0-8256-2099-6*, AM40387) Music Sales.

Oboist's Memo Pad: A Gathering Place for Reed Tips. Harvey R. Snitkin. Orig. Title: The Oboist's Scrapbook. (Illus.). 100p. 1987. reprint ed. spiral bd., wbk. ed. 7.95 (*1-888732-04-0*) HMS Pubns CT.

Oboist's Pocket Memo. Harvey R. Snitkin. (Illus.). 100p. 1987. reprint ed. spiral bd., wbk. ed. 4.25 (*1-888732-07-5*) HMS Pubns CT.

Oboist's Scrapbook see Oboist's Memo Pad: A Gathering Place for Reed Tips

Obra Animalista e Monumental de Anna Hyatt-Huntington. Emile Schaub-Koch. Tr. by Antonio Gomes da Rocha Madahil. (Illus.). 98p. 1955. 10.00 (*0-87535-140-9*) Hispanic Soc.

Obra Completa en Castellano. Pedro Corominas. (SPA.). 640p. 1993. 100.00 (*84-249-3319-2*) Elliots Bks.

Obra de Agricultura, Traducida y Comentada en 1385 por Ferrer Sayol. Palladius R. Aemilianus. Ed. by Thomas M. Capuano. (Dialect Ser.: No. 10). xxviii, 282p. 1990. 20.00 (*0-940639-45-9*) Hispanic Seminary.

Obra del Espiritu Santo. M. Ramos. (Serie Creciendo - Growing Ser.).Tr. of Work of the Holy Spirit. (SPA.). 39p. 2.50 (*1-56063-961-X*, 493035) Editorial Unilit.

***Obra en Marcha: El Manejo de la Ira Cuaderno del Participante.** Edmund F. Benson & Susan Benson. (SPA., Illus.). 64p. (J). (gr. 3-4). 1999. pap. text 12.95 (*1-58614-079-5*) Arise Found.

***Obra en Marcha: El Manejo de la Ira Manual del Instructor.** Edmund F. Benson & Susan Benson. (SPA., Illus.). 32p. 1999. pap. text, teacher ed. write for info. (*1-58614-078-7*) Arise Found.

***Obra en Marcha: Violencia & Conflicto Cuaderno del Participante.** Edmund F. Benson & Susan Benson. (SPA., Illus.). 64p. (gr. 3-4). 1999. pap. 12.95 (*1-58614-081-7*) Arise Found.

***Obra en Marcha: Violencia & Conflicto Manual del Instructor.** Edmund F. Benson & Susan Benson. (SPA., Illus.). 32p. 1999. pap. text, teacher ed. write for info. (*1-58614-080-9*) Arise Found.

***Obra en Marcha Cuaderno de Pruebas.** Edmund F. Benson & Susan Benson. (SPA., Illus.). 32p. (J). (gr. 3-4). 1999. pap. text 7.49 (*1-58614-082-5*) Arise Found.

OBRA Guidelines for Quality Improvement. 3rd rev. ed. Marie S. Jaffe. LC 98-232099. (Illus.). 400p. (C). 1998. ring bd. 149.95 (*1-56930-047-X*) Skidmore Roth Pub.

Obra Literaria de Vicente Pales Matos. Juan E. Lopez-Roman. LC 83-17123. (Coleccion Mente y Palabra). (SPA.). 293p. (Orig.). 1984. pap. 8.00 (*0-8477-0587-0*) U of PR Pr.

Obra Narrativa de Carlos Montenegro. Enrique J. Pujals. LC 79-52537. (SPA., Illus.). 153p. (Orig.). 1980. pap. 9.95 (*0-89729-231-6*) Ediciones.

Obra Narrativa de Segundo Serrano Poncela: Cronica Del Desarraigo, Vol. 1. Gerardo Pina Rosales. LC 98-53356. (Spanish Studies: No. 1). 186p. 1999. text 79.95 (*0-7734-8162-1*) E Mellen.

OBRA Nurse Aide Skills Manual. Stephanie Vaughn & Sheila A. Sorrentino. 176p. 1992. pap. text 14.95 (*0-8016-6072-6*) Mosby Inc.

Obra Poetica. Jorge Luis Borges. (SPA.). pap. 17.50 (*84-206-3048-9*, Pub. by Alianza Editorial) Continental Bk.

Obra Poetica. Laura Gallego & Luis De Arrigoitia. (UPREX, Poesia Ser.: No. 19). 177p. (C). 1972. pap. 1.50 (*0-8477-0019-4*) U of PR Pr.

Obra Poetica. Evaristo Ribera Chevremont. (SPA.). xix, 568p. 1980. 15.00 (*0-8477-3227-4*); 15.00 (*0-8477-3228-2*); pap. 12.50 (*0-8477-3231-2*) U of PR Pr.

Obra Poetica, 2 vols., Set. Chevremont E. Ribera. LC 76-41873. (SPA., Illus.). cii, 1665p. (Orig.). 1976. 30.00 (*0-8477-3218-5*); pap. 25.00 (*0-8477-3233-9*) U of PR Pr.

Obra Poetica Completa. Cesar Vallejo. (SPA.). 241p. 1983. pap. 10.00 (*0-317-46766-2*, 3401) Ediciones Norte.

Obra Poetica de Eugenio Florit. Maria Vega de Febles. LC 86-72366. (SPA.). 104p. (Orig.). 1988. pap. 12.00 (*0-89729-421-1*) Ediciones.

Obra Poetica de Felix Franco Oppenheimer: Estudio Tematico-Analitico-Estilistico. Rafael A. Gonzalez Torres. LC 79-17993. (UPREX, Estudios Literarios Ser.: No. 59). (SPA.). 246p. (Orig.). 1981. pap. 1.50 (*0-8477-0059-3*) U of PR Pr.

Obra Poetica, 1923-1967. 6th ed. Jorge Luis Borges. (SPA.). 560p. 1990. pap. 49.95 (*0-7859-4972-0*) Fr & Eur.

Obra Poetica I (1935-1970) (Poetic Works I (1937-1970) Octavio Paz. (Complete Works of Octavio Paz: Vol. XI). (SPA.). 588p. 1997. 45.99 (*968-16-3905-7*, Pub. by Fondo) Continental Bk.

Obra Postuma de Pablo Neruda. Osvaldo Rodriguez & Pablo Neruda. LC 95-82060. (SPA.). 128p. (Orig.). 1996. pap. 12.00 (*0-935318-22-4*) Edins Hispamerica.

***Obra Reunida: Narrativa Breve.** Mario Vargas Llosa. 2000. pap. 21.95 (*968-19-0496-6*) Aguilar.

Obra Selecta. Jose A. Balseiro. LC 89-46602. (SPA.). 760p. 1990. 75.00 (*0-8477-3643-1*) U of PR Pr.

Obraized Quality Assurance Through Auditing. Linda Faber-Czingula & Virginia Toby. 133p. 1996. ring bd. 49.00 (*1-890118-04-4*, QualityCare Pub) Convalescnt Cnslts.

Obrando como si el Dios en todo lo creado fuera importante. Machelle S. Wright. Tr. by Maria Siccardi. LC 95-92821.Tr. of Behaving as if the God in All Life Mattered. (SPA., Illus.). 220p. 1996. pap. 10.95 (*0-927978-22-9*) Perelandra Ltd.

Obras, 2 vols. in 3. Luis De Gongora y Argote. (Illus.). 1358p. reprint ed. write for info. (*0-318-71621-6*) G Olms Pubs.

Obras: Luis Pales Matos, Nineteen Fourteen to Nineteen Fifty-Nine, 2 vols., Set. Luis Pales Matos. Ed. by Margot Arce de Vazquez. LC 79-16469. (SPA.). 609p. 1984. 25.00 (*0-8477-3219-3*) U of PR Pr.

Obras: Luis Pales Matos, Nineteen Fourteen to Nineteen Fifty-Nine, 2 vols., Vol. I: Poetry. Luis Pales Matos. Ed. by Margot Arce de Vazquez. LC 79-16469. (SPA.). 609p. 1984. 15.00 (*0-8477-3220-7*) U of PR Pr.

Obras: Luis Pales Matos, Nineteen Fourteen to Nineteen Fifty-Nine, 2 vols., Vol. II: Prose. Luis Pales Matos. Ed. by Margot Arce de Vazquez. LC 79-16469. (SPA.). 609p. 1984. 10.00 (*0-8477-3221-5*) U of PR Pr.

Obras - Ruiz de Alarcon, Vol. I. Ruiz De Alarcon. (SPA.). 36.99 (*968-16-4974-5*, Pub. by Fondo) Continental Bk.

Obras - Ruiz de Alarcon, Vol. II. Ruiz De Alarcon. (SPA.). 36.99 (*968-16-0238-2*, Pub. by Fondo) Continental Bk.

Obras - Ruiz de Alarcon, Vol. III. Ruiz De Alarcon. (SPA.). 36.99 (*968-16-0239-0*, Pub. by Fondo) Continental Bk.

Obras Castellanas Tomo I: Poemas Menores, 2. Fray F. Moner. Ed. by Peter Cocozeella. LC 91-20691. (Hispanic Literature Ser.: Vols. 2 & 3).Tr. of SPA. 1991. 99.95 (*0-88946-388-3*) E Mellen.

Obras Castellanas Tomo I: Poemas Menores, Vol. 3. Fray F. Moner. Ed. by Peter Cocozeella. LC 91-20691. (Hispanic Literature Ser.: Vols. 2 & 3).Tr. of SPA. 1991. 99.95 (*0-88946-389-1*) E Mellen.

Obras Completas. Sor Juana Ines De la Cruz. (SPA.). pap. 19.95 (*968-432-650-5*, Pub. by Porrua) Continental Bk.

Obras Completas. Federico Garcia Lorca. write for info. (*0-318-63625-5*) Fr & Eur.

Obras Completas. Federico Garcia Lorca. 1990. 395.00 (*0-7859-9790-3*) Fr & Eur.

Obras Completas, No. 1. William Shakespeare. (ENG & SPA., Illus.). 662p. 1955. pap. 2.00 (*0-88470-717-2*) U of PR Pr.

Obras Completas, Vol. V. Eugenio Florit. Ed. by Luis Gonzalez-del-Valle & Roberto Esquenazi-Mayo. LC 80-53822. (SPA.). 470p. (Orig.). 1991. pap. 60.00 (*0-89295-062-5*) Society Sp & Sp-Am.

Obras Completas: Missa Pro Defunctis, Pt. 1. Cristobal Galan. Ed. by J. Baron. (Gesamtausgaben - Collected Works: Vol. 12, Pt. 1). (ENG & SPA.). 100p. 1982. lib. bdg. 4.00 (*0-912024-59-3*) Inst Mediaeval Mus.

Obras Completas: Prosa Critica, Vol. IV. Eugenio Florit. Ed. by Luis Gonzalez-del-Valle & Roberto Esquenazi-Mayo. LC 80-53822. (SPA.). 181p. 1989. pap. 60.00 (*0-89295-060-9*) Society Sp & Sp-Am.

Obras Completas: Versos Nuevos y Algunas Prosas de Ayer y de Hoy, Vol. III. Eugenio Florit. Ed. by Luis Gonzalez-del-Valle & Roberto Esquenazi-Mayo. LC 80-53822. (SPA.). 371p. 1982. pap. 36.00 (*0-89295-017-X*) Society Sp & Sp-Am.

Obras Completas Pt. 2: Obras Liturgicas. Cristobal Galan. Ed. by J. Baron & Daniel L. Heiple. (Gesamtausgaben - Collected Works: Vol. XII, Pt. 2). (ENG & SPA.). 252p. 1991. lib. bdg. 90.00 (*0-931902-69-X*) Inst Mediaeval Mus.

Obras Completas Pt. 3: Obras Liturgicas. Cristobal Galan. Ed. by J. Baron & Daniel L. Heiple. (Gesamtausgaben - Collected Works: Vol. XII, Pt. 3). (ENG & SPA.). 331p. 1992. lib. bdg. 130.00 (*0-931902-70-3*) Inst Mediaeval Mus.

Obras Completas (Complete Works), 3 vols., Vol. 1. Mariano Azuela. (SPA.). 1132p. 34.99 (*968-16-4093-4*, Pub. by Fondo) Continental Bk.

Obras Completas (Complete Works), 3 vols., Vol. 2. Mariano Azuela. (SPA.). 1132p. 34.99 (*968-16-4095-0*, Pub. by Fondo) Continental Bk.

Obras Completas (Complete Works), 3 vols., Vol. 3. Mariano Azuela. (SPA.). 1134p. 34.99 (*968-16-4284-8*, Pub. by Fondo) Continental Bk.

Obras Completas de Damaso Alonso: Comentarios de Textos, Vol. 8. Damaso Alonso. (SPA.). 732p. 1993. pap. 150.00 (*84-249-1012-5*) Elliots Bks.

Obras Completas de Martin Luis Guzman (Complete Works of Martin Luis Guzman), Vol. I. 3rd ed. Martin L. Guzman. (SPA.). 130p. 1995. 35.99 (*968-16-1840-8*, Pub. by Fondo) Continental Bk.

Obras Completas de Martin Luis Guzman (Complete Works of Martin Luis Guzman), Vol. II. 3rd ed. Martin L. Guzman. (SPA.). 132p. 1995. 35.99 (*968-16-2015-1*, Pub. by Fondo) Continental Bk.

Obras Completas (Libros de Poesia, 1920-1944), Vol. I. Eugenio Florit. Ed. by Luis Gonzalez-del-Valle & Roberto Esquenazi. LC 85-50415. (SPA.). 256p. 1985. pap. 30.00 (*0-89295-038-2*) Society Sp & Sp-Am.

Obras Completas (Libros de Poesia, 1946-1974), Vol. II. Eugenio Florit. Ed. by Luis Gonzalez-del-Valle & Roberto Esquenazi-Mayo. LC 82-60407. (SPA., Illus.). 168p. 1983. pap. 28.00 (*0-89295-021-8*) Society Sp & Sp-Am.

Obras Completas, Solos, Duos y Trios, Pt. 4. Cristobal Galan. Ed. by John H. Baron & Daniel L. Heiple. (Gesamtausgaben - Collected Works: Vol. XII, Pt. 4). (ENG & SPA.). 110p. 1993. lib. bdg. 140.00 (*0-931902-78-9*) Inst Mediaeval Mus.

Obras (Complete Works) Juan Rulfo. (SPA.). 341p. 1987. 16.99 (*968-16-2174-3*, Pub. by Fondo) Continental Bk.

Obras de Lope de Vega: Segunda Serie: Obras Dramaticas del Fenix, 13 vols. Intro. by E. Cotarelo y Mori et al. (Real Academia Ser.). (SPA.). 1968. 1000.00 (*0-614-00128-5*) Elliots Bks.

Obras de Wesley, 14 vols. Incl. Vol. IX. Works of John Wesley. Ed. by Justo L. Gonzalez. (SPA.). 1998. 34.95 (*1-57736-064-8*); Vol. X. Works of John Wesley. Justo L. Gonzalez. (SPA.). 1998. 34.95 (*1-57736-065-6*); Vol. XI. Works of John Wesley. Ed. by Justo L. Gonzalez. (SPA.). 1998. 34.95 (*1-57736-066-4*); Vol. XII. Works of John Wesley. Ed. by Justo L. Gonzalez. (SPA.). 1998. 34.95 (*1-57736-067-2*); Vol. XIII. Works of John Wesley. Ed. by Justo L. Gonzalez. (SPA.). 1998. 34.95 (*1-57736-068-0*); Vol. XIV. Works of John Wesley. Ed. by Justo L. Gonzalez. (SPA.). 1998. 34.95 (*1-57736-069-9*); Vol. I. Ed. by Justo L. Gonzalez. LC 96-69128. (SPA.). 422p. 1996. 34.95 (*1-57736-001-X*); Vol. II. Ed. by Justo L. Gonzalez. LC 96-69128. (SPA.). 408p. 1996. 34.95 (*1-57736-002-8*); Vol. III. Ed. by Justo L. Gonzalez. LC 96-69128. (SPA.). 344p. 1996. 34.95 (*1-57736-003-6*); Vol. IV. Ed. by Justo L. Gonzalez. LC 96-69128. (SPA.). 408p. 1996. 34.95 (*1-57736-004-4*); Vol. V. Ed. by Justo L. Gonzalez. LC 97-65646. (SPA.). 395p. 1997. 34.95 (*1-57736-034-6*); Vol. VI. Ed. by Justo L. Gonzalez. LC 97-65647. (SPA.). 472p. 1997. 34.95 (*1-57736-035-4*); Vol. VII. Ed. by Justo L. Gonzalez. LC 98-65086. (SPA.). 1998. 34.95 (*1-57736-062-1*); Vol. VIII. Ed. by Justo L. Gonzalez. LC 97-68659. (SPA.). 1998. 34.95 (*1-57736-063-X*); write for info. (*1-57736-000-1*) Providence Hse.

Obras Escogidas. San Juan De La Cruz. (SPA.). 148p. 1979. 5.95 (*0-8288-7170-1*, S7768) Fr & Eur.

Obras Escogidas (Selected Works) Francisco L. Urquiza. (SPA.). 1109p. 1987. 26.99 (*968-16-2631-1*, Pub. by Fondo) Continental Bk.

Obras Ineditas de 1992. Cristina M. Higuero. LC 92-97188. (SPA.). 50p. (Orig.). 1992. pap. 10.00 (*0-9605082-3-6*) Allied Ent.

Obras Maestras de la Literatura Universal. 9th ed. (SPA.). 502p. (Orig.). (C). 1995. pap. text 15.95 (*1-56328-007-8*) Edit Plaza Mayor.

Obras Maestras del J. Paul Getty Museum: Antiguedades: Spanish-Language Edition. (Getty Trust Publications). (SPA., Illus.). 128p. 1997. pap. 22.50 (*0-89236-422-X*, Pub. by J P Getty Trust) OUP.

Obras Maestras del J. Paul Getty Museum: Artes Decorativas: Spanish-Language Edition. (Getty Trust Publications). (SPA., Illus.). 128p. 1997. pap. 22.50 (*0-89236-456-4*, Pub. by J P Getty Trust) OUP.

Obras Maestras del J. Paul Getty Museum: Dibujos: Spanish-Language Edition. (SPA., Illus.). 128p. 1997. pap. 22.50 (*0-89236-439-4*, Pub. by J P Getty Trust) OUP.

Obras Maestras del J. Paul Getty Museum: Fotografias. Ed. by J. Paul Getty Museum Staff. (SPA., Illus.). 128p. 1999. pap. 22.50 (*0-89236-518-8*, Pub. by J P Getty Trust) OUP.

Obras Maestras del J. Paul Getty Museum - Manuscritos Iluminados. (SPA., Illus.). 128p. 1997. pap. 22.50 (*0-89236-447-5*, Pub. by J P Getty Trust) OUP.

Obras Maestras del J. Paul Getty Museum - Pinturas. (SPA., Illus.). 128p. 1997. pap. 22.50 (*0-89236-429-7*, Pub. by J P Getty Trust) OUP.

Obras Maestras del Siglo XVIII en la Galeria de Pinturas de Dresde see Dresden in the Ages of Splendor & Enlightenment: Eighteenth-Century Paintings from the Old Masters Picture Gallery

Obras I (Complete Works I) Narrativa (Prose) Rosario Castellanos. (SPA.). 983p. 1989. 31.99 (*968-16-3213-3*, Pub. by Fondo) Continental Bk.

Obras Poeticas. Luis De Gongora y Argote. (SPA.). 1970. reprint ed. 12.00 (*0-87535-008-9*) Hispanic Soc.

Obras Poeticas de Don Antonio Hurtado de Mendoza, 3 vols. Antonio Hurtado de Mendoza. Ed. by Rafael Benitez Claros. (SPA.). 1066p. 1968. pap. 250.00 (*0-614-00222-2*) Elliots Bks.

Obras Publicadas e Ineditas. Cristina M. Higuero. LC 90-85602. (SPA., Illus.). 123p. (Orig.). 1990. pap. 12.00 (*0-9605082-1-X*) Allied Ent.

Obrazkovy Slovnik Slovenciny (Pictorial Dictionary of the Slovak Language) O. Skvareninova. (SLO.). 240p. 1997. pap. write for info. (*80-08-00913-6*, Pub. by Slov Pegagog Naklad) IBD Ltd.

***Obreras: Chicana Politics of Work & Family.** Ed. by Vicki L. Ruiz. (Aztlan Anthology Ser.: Vol. 1). 328p. 2000. reprint ed. pap. 25.00 (*0-89551-094-4*) UCLA Chicano Studies.

Obrero Cristiano Normal. T. S. Nee. Orig. Title: The Normal Christian Worker. (SPA.). 112p. 1992. mass mkt. 3.99 (*0-8254-1503-9*, Edit Portavoz) Kregel.

O'Brian's Bride. Colleen Faulkner. 416p. 1995. mass mkt. 4.99 (*0-8217-4895-5*, Zebra Kensgtn) Kensgtn Pub Corp.

O'Brien & Fitzgerald Walk into a Bar . . . The Worlds Best Irish Jokes. Mr. O's & Cynthia MacGregor. LC 95-4827. (Illus.). 1995. pap. 7.95 (*0-8065-1663-1*, Citadel Pr) Carol Pub Group.

O'Briens & the O'Flahertys: A National Tale, 4 vols., 2 bks., Set. Sydney O. Morgan. LC 79-8175. reprint ed. 84.50 (*0-404-62055-8*) AMS Pr.

***O'Brien's Collecting Toy Cars & Trucks: Identification & Value Guide.** 3rd ed. Ed. by Elizabeth Stephan. LC 99-68143. (Illus.). 640p. 2000. pap. 27.95 (*0-87341-580-9*, TCT3) Krause Pubns.

***O'Brien's Collecting Toy Trains.** 5th ed. Ed. by Elizabeth A. Stephan. LC 99-63749. (Illus.). 448p. 1999. pap. 24.95 (*0-87341-769-0*) Krause Pubns.

O'Brien's Collecting Toys. 9th ed. Ed. by Elizabeth Stephan. LC 99-61890. (Illus.). 768p. 1999. per. 28.95 (*0-87341-749-6*) Krause Pubns.

O'Brien's Original Guide to Cape Cod & the Islands. 3rd rev. ed. Ed. by Greg O'Brien. LC 96-1855. Orig. Title: Insider's Guide to Cape Cod & the Islands. (Illus.). 268p. 1996. pap. 14.95 (*0-940160-66-8*) Parnassus Imprints.

Obrigado, Ayrton: Simply the Best. Paolo D'Alessio. (Illus.). 160p. 1996. 34.95 (*88-7911-141-8*, Pub. by Giorgio Nada Editore) Howell Pr VA.

Obscene Bird of Night. Jose Donoso. Tr. by Hardie St. Martin & Leonard Marcus from SPA. (Verba Mundi Ser.). 448p. 1979. reprint ed. pap. 15.95 (*1-56792-046-2*) Godine.

Obscene Literature & Constitutional Law. Theodore A. Schroeder. 1973. 59.95 (*0-8490-0745-3*) Gordon Pr.

Obscene Literature & Constitutional Law. Theodore A. Schroeder & Jerold S. Averbach. LC 72-116913. (Civil Liberties in American History Ser.). 440p. 1972. reprint ed. lib. bdg. 35.00 (*0-306-70156-1*) Da Capo.

***"Obscene" Literature & Constitutional Law: A Forensic Defense of Freedom of the Press.** Theodore Schroeder. 439p. 2000. reprint ed. 110.00 (*1-56169-601-3*) Gaunt.

***Obscene Profits: The Entrepreneurs of Pornography in the Cyber Age.** Frederick S. Lane. LC 99-35383. 272p. 2000. 27.50 (*0-415-92096-5*) Routledge.

Obscenity: An Account of Censorship Laws & Their Enforcement in England & Wales. Geoffrey Robertson. (Law in Context Ser.). xviii, 364p. 1979. 40.50 (*0-297-77213-9*) W S Hein.

Obscenity: Social Control & Artistic Creation in the European Middle Ages. Ed. by Jan M. Ziolkowski. LC 98-11433. (Cultures, Beliefs & Traditions, Medieval & Early Modern Peoples Ser.). (Illus.). 344p. 1997. 103.75 (*90-04-10928-5*) Brill Academic Pubs.

Obscenity, Anarchy, Reality. Crispin Sartwell. LC 95-406. 199p. (C). 1996. text 59.50 (*0-7914-2907-5*); pap. text 19.95 (*0-7914-2908-3*) State U NY Pr.

***Obscenity & Pornography Decisions of the United States Supreme Court.** Ed. by Maureen Harrison & Steve Gilbert. 240p. 2000. pap. 16.95 (*1-880780-23-2*) Excellent Bks.

Obscenity & Public Morality: Censorship in a Liberal Society. Harry M. Clor. LC 69-16772. 1985. pap. text 16.00 (*0-226-11035-4*, Midway Reprint) U Ch Pr.

Obscenity & the Law. Norman St. John-Stevas. LC 74-8011. (Civil Liberties in American History Ser.). 289p. 1974. reprint ed. lib. bdg. 29.50 (*0-306-70602-4*) Da Capo.

Obscenity Law Reporter, 3 vols., Set, incl. 4 suppls. National Obscenity Law Center Staff. 1996. ring bd. 300.00 (*0-9614159-1-6*) Natl Obscenity.

Obsceno Pajaro de la Noche: Ejercicio de Creacion. Maria Del C. Cerezo. LC 87-82100. (SPA.). 192p. (Orig.). 1988. pap. 19.00 (*0-89729-456-4*) Ediciones.

Obscure Destinies. Willa Cather. 1976. 21.95 (*0-8488-0453-8*) Amereon Ltd.

***Obscure Destinies: Willa Cather Scholarly Edition.** Willa Cather. LC 98-13549. (Illus.). 424p. 1998. text 65.00 (*0-8032-1430-8*) U of Nebr Pr.

Obscure Kingdoms. large type ed. Edward Fox. 512p. 1995. 27.99 (*0-7089-3259-2*) Ulverscroft.

Obscure Menace. Maggie Shayne. (Amours d'Aujourd'Hui Ser.: No. 334). (FRE.). 1999. mass mkt. 5.50 (*0-373-38334-7*, 1-38334-8) Harlequin Bks.

O

An Asterisk (*) at the beginning of an entry indicates that the title is appearing for the first time.

Obscure Religious Cults. Shashibhusan Das Gupta. 1995. reprint ed. 28.00 (*81-7102-020-8*, Pub. by Firma KLM) S Asia.

Obscure Religious Practices among Some Vaisnavas of Assam. Narendra N. Dutta. (C). 1990. text 28.50 (*0-8364-2590-1*, Pub. by Punthi Pus) S Asia.

Obscure Voices from the Past. Sylvia L. Camp. 1990. pap. 5.80 (*0-89137-458-2*) Quality Pubns.

Obscured Catastrophe of SWIFT II & Its Lessons: The Emperor's New Clothes or the Eclipse in Technology. Ed. by Olga I. Dyba et al. LC 93-90808. (Illus.). 108p. (Orig.). 1997. per. 138.00 (*0-9638406-0-6*) Comp Res & Innovat.

***Obscures Intentions.** Christy Lockhart. (FRE.). 2000. mass mkt. 3.99 (*0-373-37543-3*) Harlequin Bks.

Obseruatione Ciborum see On the Observance of Foods

Observa-Story: Portland to Cut & Color. Nancy K. Lightbody & Sarah H. Malley. LC 76-54460. (Illus.). (J). (gr. 1-4). 1976. pap. 1.25 (*0-9600612-5-8*) Greater Portland.

Observability & Observation in Physical Science. Peter Kosso. 176p. (C). 1989. lib. bdg. 101.50 (*0-7923-0389-X*, Pub. by Kluwer Academic) Kluwer Academic.

Observability in School Systems: A Problem of Inter-System Integration. Nathalie S. Friedman. Ed. by Harriet Zuckerman & Robert K. Merton. LC 79-8997. (Dissertations on Sociology Ser.). 1980. lib. bdg. 26.95 (*0-405-12968-8*) Ayer.

Observable Standard Model Physics at the SSC: Monte Carlo Simulation & Detector Capabilities - University of California, Los Angeles, January 15-24, 1986. Ed. by C. D. Buchanan et al. 420p. 1986. text 59.00 (*9971-5-0125-2*) World Scientific Pub.

Observaciones Astronomicas. Eva Arzola de Calero. LC 86-7068. (Illus.). x, 75p. 1992. pap. 5.00 (*0-8477-2327-5*) U of PR Pr.

Observadores en el Cielo. Anthony Aveni. (SPA.). 20.99 (*968-16-2702-4*, Pub. by Fondo) Continental Bk.

Observando. 2nd ed. Servando Gonzalez. LC 85-70752. (Essay Ser.). (SPA.). 116p. (Orig.). 1986. pap. 7.95 (*0-932367-06-2*) Ed El Gato Tuerto.

Observation & Analysis of Stellar Photospheres. 2nd ed. David F. Gray. (Cambridge Astrophysics Ser.: No. 20). 470p. (C). 1992. text 130.00 (*0-521-40320-0*) Cambridge U Pr.

Observation & Fantasy: The Art of Arthur Spear. Sarah R. Roberts. LC 94-74016. (Illus.). 40p. (Orig.). Date not set. pap. write for info. (*0-945506-18-X*) DeCordova Mus.

Observation & Inference: An Introduction to the Methods of Epidemiology. Alexander M. Walker. (Illus.). 173p. (Orig.). (C). 1991. pap. text 23.00 (*0-917227-07-7*) Epidemiology.

Observation & Modeling in Numerical Analysis & Model Tests in Dynamic Soil-Structure Interaction: Proceedings of Sessions Held in Conjunction with Geo-Logan, Logan, UT, July 16-17. Ed. by Toyoaki Nogami. LC 97-19515. (Geotechnical Special Publication Ser.). 152p. 1997. 22.00 (*0-7844-0252-3*) Am Soc Civil Eng.

Observation & Participation in Early Childhood Birth Through Age Five. Jean B. Billman & Janice Sherman. LC 98-121623. 186p. 1996. pap. text 31.00 (*0-205-26474-3*) Allyn.

Observation & Participation in Early Childhood Settings: A Practicum Guide. Jean B. Billman & Janice Sherman. 256p. 1995. pap. text 38.00 (*0-205-15993-1*) Allyn.

Observation & Recording: Tools for Decision Making. 116p. 1996. pap. 11.00 (*0-16-042682-0*) USGPO.

Observation Deck: A Tool Kit for Writers. Naomi Epel. 160p. 1998. pap. 19.95 (*0-8118-1481-5*) Chronicle Bks.

Observation Drawing with Children: A Framework for Teachers. Nancy R. Smith. LC 97-37995. 1997. 40.00 (*0-8077-3692-9*); pap. 18.95 (*0-8077-3691-0*) Tchrs Coll.

Observation Evaulation Report: A Model. Doris K. Williams. 1980. pap. 4.00 (*0-87972-154-5*) Bowling Green Univ Popular Press.

Observation, Experiment, & Hypothesis in Modern Physical Science. Ed. by Peter Achinstein & Owen Hannaway. 1985. 47.50 (*0-262-01083-6*, Bradford Bks) MIT Pr.

Observation Guide Children Development. 5th ed. Berk. 1999. pap. text 1.50 (*0-205-30275-0*) Allyn.

Observation Medicine. Louis G. Graff. (Illus.). 440p. 1992. text 84.00 (*1-56372-010-8*) Buttrwrth-Heinemann.

Observation of the Continental Crust Through Drilling II. Ed. by H. J. Behr et al. (Exploration of the Deep Continental Crust Ser.). (Illus.). 230p. 1987. 60.00 (*0-387-17348-X*) Spr-Verlag.

Observation of the Earth & Its Environment: Survey of Missions & Sensors. 2nd ed. H. J. Krammer. LC 94-14205. 1994. pap. write for info. (*3-540-57858-7*) Spr-Verlag.

Observation of the Earth & Its Environment: Survey of Missions & Sensors. 2nd ed. H. J. Krammer. LC 94-14205. 1994. 122.95 (*0-387-57858-7*) Spr-Verlag.

Observation of the Earth & Its Environment: Survey of Missions & Sensors. 3rd ed. Ed. by H. J. Kramer. 992p. 1996. 189.00 (*3-540-60933-4*) Spr-Verlag.

Observation, Prediction & Simulation of Phase Transitions in Complex Fluids: Proceedings of the NATO ASI, Varenna, Italy, July 25 - August 5, 1994. Ed. by Marc Baus et al. LC 95-9887. (NATO Advanced Science Institutes Ser.: No. 460). 684p. (C). 1995. text 327.50 (*0-7923-3439-6*) Kluwer Academic.

Observation Seismology: A Centennial Symposium for the Berkeley Seismographic Stations. Ed. by Joe J. Litehiser. 1990. 65.00 (*0-520-06582-4*, Pub. by U CA Pr) Cal Prin Full Svc.

Observation Series. Alan C. Walter. Ed. by Beverly Miles. 28p. (Orig.). 1995. pap. text 3.69 (*1-57569-020-9*) Wisdom Pubng.

Observation Skills for Effective Teaching. 3rd ed. Gary D. Borich & Deborah L. Bayles. LC 98-22994. 302p. 1998. pap. text 36.00 (*0-13-860396-0*, Merrill Coll) P-H.

Observation sur les Principes de l'Harmonie. fac. ed. Jean-Adams Serre. (Monuments of Music & Music Literature in Facsimile, II Ser.: Vol. 53). (Illus.). 1967. lib. bdg. 37.50 (*0-8450-2253-9*) Broude.

Observation Survey: Of Early Literacy Achievement. Marie M. Clay. LC 92-46100. 120p. (C). 1993. pap. text 19.50 (*0-435-08763-0*, 08763) Heinemann.

Observational Amateur Astronomer. Patrick Moore. (Practical Astronomy Ser.). (Illus.). 288p. 1995. 24.95 (*0-387-19899-7*) Spr-Verlag.

Observational Amateur Astronomer. Ed. by Patrick Moore. (Practical Astronomy Ser.). 1995. pap. 24.95 (*3-540-19899-7*) Spr-Verlag.

Observational & Physical Cosmology: Second Canary Islands Winter School of Astrophysics. Ed. by M. Collados et al. (Illus.). 352p. (C). 1992. text 80.00 (*0-521-41996-4*) Cambridge U Pr.

Observational & Theoretical Aspects of Relativistic Astrophysics & Cosmology: Proceedings of the International Course on Observational & Theoretical Aspects Relativistic Astrophysics & Cosmology, Spain, 1984. Ed. by J. L. Sanz. 364p. 1985. 52.00 (*9971-978-19-9*) World Scientific Pub.

Observational Astronomy for Amateurs. J. B. Sidgwick. (Illus.). 384p. 1981. reprint ed. pap. 8.95 (*0-486-24033-9*) Dover.

Observational Astrophysics. P. Lena. (Astronomy & Astrophysics Library). (Illus.). 340p. 1988. 79.95 (*0-387-18433-3*) Spr-Verlag.

Observational Astrophysics. Robert C. Smith. (Illus.). 467p. (C). 1995. text 85.00 (*0-521-26091-4*); pap. text 39.95 (*0-521-27834-1*) Cambridge U Pr.

Observational Astrophysics. Ed. by R. E. White. (Graduate Series in Astronomy). (Illus.). 360p. 1992. 168.00 (*0-7503-0201-1*) IOP Pub.

Observational Astrophysics. 2nd enl. rev. ed. Pierre Lena & Francoise Lebrun. LC 97-47092. (Astronomy & Astrophysics Library). (Illus.). xiii, 518p. 1998. 62.00 (*3-540-63482-7*) Spr-Verlag.

Observational Before-After Studies in Road Safety: Estimating the Effect of Highway & Traffic Engineering Measures. Ezra Hauer. LC 97-19181. 300p. pap. 80.25 (*0-08-043053-8*, Pergamon Pr) Elsevier.

Observational Cosmology. Ed. by Adelaide Hewitt et al. (C). 1987. lib. bdg. 296.00 (*90-277-2475-X*) Kluwer Academic.

***Observational Cosmology: The Development of Galaxy Systems.** Ed. by Giuliano Giuriein et al. (Conference Series Proceedings: Vol. 176). 497p. 1999. text 52.00 (*1-58381-000-5*) Astron Soc Pacific.

Observational Cosmology Symposium. Ed. by G. Chincarini et al. (ASP Conference Series Proceedings: Vol. 51). 746p. 1993. 34.00 (*0-937707-70-8*) Astron Soc Pacific.

Observational Cosmology with the New Radio Surveys. Ed. by M. N. Bremer et al. LC 97-39047. 345p. 1998. lib. bdg. 142.00 (*0-7923-4885-0*) Kluwer Academic.

Observational Evaluation of Severely Multi-Handicapped Children. W. S. Curtis & E. T. Donlon. (Modern Approaches to the Diagnosis & Instruction of Multi-Handicapped Children Ser.: Vol. 18). viii, 204p. 1985. 36.25 (*90-265-0595-7*) Swets.

Observational Evidence for Black Holes in the Universe. Sandip Chakrabarti. LC 98-41434. (Astrophysics & Space Science Library). 1998. 162.00 (*0-7923-5298-X*) Kluwer Academic.

Observational Evidence of Activity in Galaxies. Ed. by E. Y. Khachikian et al. (C). 1987. lib. bdg. 212.00 (*90-277-2473-3*) Kluwer Academic.

Observational Foundations of Physics. Alan Cook. LC 93-36901. (Illus.). 176p. (C). 1994. text 64.95 (*0-521-45450-6*); pap. text 22.95 (*0-521-45597-9*) Cambridge U Pr.

Observational Guide for Child Study. Ligaya Paguio et al. (Illus.). 64p. (Orig.). (C). 1990. pap. text 7.95 (*0-918772-20-6*) Daye Pr.

Observational Method in Geotechnical Engineering. LC 96-212639. 232p. 1996. 77.00 (*0-7277-2036-8*) Am Soc Civil Eng.

Observational Methods. Pellegrini. (C). 1995. pap. text. write for info. (*0-15-501217-7*) Harcourt Coll Pubs.

Observational Neutrino Astronomy. Ed. by D. B. Cline. 304p. (C). 1988. text 85.00 (*9971-5-0823-0*) World Scientific Pub.

Observational Plasma Astrophysics: Five Years of Yohkoh & Beyond. T. Watanabe et al. LC 98-11764. (Astrophysics & Space Science Library). 416p. 1998. 188.00 (*0-7923-4985-7*) Kluwer Academic.

Observational Research Handbook: Understanding How Consumers Live with Your Product. Bill Abrams & American Marketing Association Staff. LC 99-44308. 304p. Date not set. 49.95 (*0-658-00073-X*, 00073X) NTC Contemp Pub Co.

Observational Strategies. Irwin. 1997. mass mkt. 53.00 (*0-03-045726-2*) Harcourt Coll Pubs.

Observational Strategies Child Study. 2nd ed. Irwin. (C). 1997. pap. text 31.00 (*0-03-032948-5*) Harcourt Coll Pubs.

Observational Studies. Paul R. Rosenbaum. LC 95-2178. (Springer Series in Statistics). (Illus.). 230p. 1995. 54.95 (*0-387-94482-6*) Spr-Verlag.

Observational Tests of Cosmological Inflation. Ed. by Tom Shanks et al. 504p. (C). 1991. text 234.00 (*0-7923-1431-X*) Kluwer Academic.

Observational Tests of the Stellar Evolution Theory. Ed. by Andre Maeder & Alvio Renzini. 1984. pap. text 84.50 (*90-277-1775-3*); lib. bdg. 186.00 (*90-277-1774-5*) Kluwer Academic.

Observational Theory. J. M. Houtkooper. viii, 124p. 1983. pap. 23.50 (*90-265-0437-3*) Swets.

Observationes Botanicae: Six Fascicmles, 1779-1791. A. J. Retzii. 1987. 160.00 (*0-7855-2032-5*, Pub. by Scientific) St Mut.

Observations see Three Prose Works

Observations. Ernest Holmes. Ed. by Willis H. Kinnear. 64p. 1968. pap. 5.95 (*0-911336-12-5*) Sci of Mind.

Observations. Edward G. Klemm. 105p. 1990. 6.95 (*0-89697-339-5*) Intl Univ Pr.

Observations. Tom Martin. (Illus.). 155p. (Orig.). 1998. pap. 6.95 (*0-930871-04-9*) Search.

Observations. Idries Shah. 45p. 1982. pap. 9.00 (*0-86304-013-6*, Pub. by Octagon Pr) ISHK.

Observations. Max Beerbohm. LC 71-163891. (English Literature Ser.: No. 33). 1971. reprint ed. lib. bdg. 75.00 (*0-8383-1249-7*) M S G Haskell Hse.

Observations: Selected Speeches & Essays, 1982-1984. Henry A. Kissinger. 1985. 17.95 (*0-316-49664-2*) Little.

Observations - In Poetry. Nancy J. Sigler. LC 89-92176. (Illus.). 60p. (Orig.). 1989. pap. 6.50 (*0-9622800-0-3*) Regard Pub.

Observations - Thoughts - Feelings. Heidi Rimanich. (Orig.). 1997. pap. write for info. (*1-57553-466-5*) Watermrk Pr.

Observations & Conjectures upon Some Passages of Shakespeare. Thomas Tyrwhitt. LC 74-177546. reprint ed. 32.50 (*0-404-06574-0*) AMS Pr.

Observations & Essays on the Statistics of Insanity. John Thurnam. LC 75-16734. (Classics in Psychiatry Ser.). 1976. reprint ed. 30.95 (*0-405-07455-7*) Ayer.

***Observations & Predictions of Eclipse Times by Early Civilizations.** John M. Steele. 336p. 2000. 132.00 (*0-7923-6298-5*) Kluwer Academic.

Observations & Remarks Made During a Voyage to the Islands of Teneriffe, Amsterdam, Maria's Islands near Van Dieman's Land, Otaheita, Sandwich Islands, Owyhee, the Fox Islands on the Northwest Coast of America, Tinian, & From Thence to Canton, in the Brig. George Mortimer. 80p. 1989. 22.50 (*0-87770-456-2*) Ye Galleon.

Observations, Botanical & Physiological on the Potato Murrain. M. J. Berkeley. (Phytopathological Classics Ser.). 108p. 1948. 22.00 (*0-89054-009-8*) Am Phytopathol Soc.

Observations by Mr. Dooley. Finley P. Dunne. 1973. 250.00 (*0-8490-0746-1*) Gordon Pr.

Observations Concerning the Distinction of Ranks in Society. John Millar. LC 78-67536. reprint ed. 34.50 (*0-404-17199-0*) AMS Pr.

Observations Concerning the Planet Venus. Tr. by Sally Beaumont & Peter Fay. LC 95-46763. 172p. 1995. 99.95 (*3-540-19980-2*) Spr-Verlag.

Observations del Tiempo Meteorologico. Dale McCreedy & Elizabeth McAndrew. (National Science Partnership para Girl Scouts y Museos de Ciencia Ser.). Orig. Title: Weather Watch. (ENG & SPA., Illus.). 60p. 1997. pap. 8.00 (*1-889939-07-2*) Franklin PA.

Observations for Young Architects. Cesar Pelli. LC 98-52134. 207p. 1999. pap. 35.00 (*1-58093-031-X*, Pub. by Monacelli Pr) Penguin Putnam.

Observations 4. Richard Kieninger. (Orig.). 1979. pap. 3.00 (*0-685-73445-5*) Stelle.

Observations from the Edge: Deeper Than Deep Thoughts. Michelle A. Bakhit & Kevin J. Shay. (Illus.). 24p. (Orig.). 1995. pap. 3.95 (*1-881365-68-9*) Shay Pubns.

Observations from the Stern. Dale C. Wheaton. LC 94-90879. 150p. 1995. pap. 13.95 (*0-9645098-0-6*) Timbrdoodle.

Observations, in a Series of Letters Written During a Visit to Austin's Colony in 1831. Mary A. Holley. 1993. reprint ed. lib. bdg. 75.00 (*0-7812-5883-9*) Rprt Serv.

Observations in Lower California. Johann J. Baegert. Tr. by M. M. Brandenburg & Carl L. Baumann from GER. 1979. reprint ed. 48.00 (*0-520-03873-8*, Pub. by U CA Pr) Cal Prin Full Svc.

Observations in the Art of English Poesie. Thomas Campion. LC 78-38164. (English Experience Ser.: No. 441). 52p. 1972. reprint ed. 15.00 (*90-221-0441-9*) Walter J Johnson.

Observations in the Twenty-One-CM Neutral Hydrogen Line. E. Bajada & F. R. Colomb. LC QB0790.02. (Carnegie Institution of Washington Publication Ser.: No. 632). 77p. reprint ed. pap. 30.00 (*0-608-10160-5*, 200790000067) Bks Demand.

Observations Made During a Voyage Round the World. Johann R. Forster. Ed. by Nicholas Thomas et al. LC 95-582. 526p. 1996. text 55.00 (*0-8248-1725-7*) UH Pr.

Observations of a Short Cowboy. Bob LaVelle. (Illus.). 1997. mass mkt. 12.95 (*0-9663247-0-6*) LaVelle.

Observations of a Simple Man: In Poetry Form. (Orig.). 1995. pap. 4.95 (*0-9645180-2-3*) Fam Val Pub.

Observations of a Skeptic: How to Prosper in a Hostile World. L. M. Lowell. LC 97-60042. (Illus.). x, 396p. (Orig.). 1997. pap. 15.95 (*0-9656292-4-4*) Tableau Pub.

Observations of an Uppity Woman: Poems & Word Pictures. Alyce P. Nadeau. LC 99-10423. 64p. 1999. pap. 10.00 (*1-887905-15-4*) Pkway Pubs.

Observations of Anomalous Atmospheric Phenomena in the U. S. S. R., Statistical Analysis: Results of Processing First Sample of Observational Data. L. M. Gindilis et al.Tr. of Nablyudeniya anomal'nykh atmosfernykh yavleniy V S S R. (Illus.). 94p. (C). 1980. reprint ed. pap. 4.00 (*0-929343-54-9*) J A Hynek Ctr UFO.

Observations of Earth from Space: Proceedings of Symposium A1 & the Topical Meetings of the COSPAR Interdisciplinary Scientific Commission B, Meetings B7 & B9 of the COSPAR Twenty-Ninth Plenary Meeting Held in Washington, D. C., U. S. A., 28 August - 5 September 1992. Ed. by R. P. Singh et al. (Advances in Space Research Ser.: Vol. 13). (Illus.). 362p. 1993. pap. 190.25 (*0-08-042347-7*, Pergamon Pr) Elsevier.

Observations of Henry. Jerome K. Jerome. LC 72-94734. (Short Story Index Reprint Ser.). 1977. 18.95 (*0-8369-3114-9*) Ayer.

Observations of Professor Maturin. Clyde Furst. LC 70-126700. reprint ed. 34.50 (*0-404-02665-6*) AMS Pr.

Observations of Rossby Waves Near Site D. see Progress in Oceanography

Observations of Surface-to-Atmosphere Interactions in the Tropics. Michael Garstang & David R. Fitzjarrald. LC 97-44049. (Illus.). 416p. 1999. text 75.00 (*0-19-511270-9*) OUP.

Observations of the Ethnology of the Sauk Indians, Vol. 5--5. Alanson B. Skinner. LC 79-111400. 180p. 1970. reprint ed. lib. bdg. 38.50 (*0-8371-4632-1*, SKSI, Greenwood Pr) Greenwood.

Observations of the Outer Heliosphere: Proceedings of the Symposium D2 of the COSPAR 29th Plenary Meeting Held in Washington, D. C., U. S. A., 28 August-5 September, 1992. Ed. by D. E. Page. (Advances in Space Research Ser.: Vol. 13). 312p. 1993. pap. 190.25 (*0-08-042208-X*, Pergamon Pr) Elsevier.

Observations on a Collection of Papuan Crania with Notes on Preservation & Decorative Features by William H. Holmes. 2nd ed. George A. Dorsey. LC 04-12212. (Field Columbian Museum Anthropological Ser.: Vol. 2, No. 1). (Illus.). 67p. reprint ed. pap. 30.00 (*0-608-02716-2*, 206338100004) Bks Demand.

Observations on Archaeological Sites in Topanga Canyon, California. fac. ed. R. F. Heizer & E. M. Lemert. Ed. by Beals et al. (University of California Publications in American Archaeology & Ethnology: No. 44:2). (Illus.). 25p. (C). 1947. reprint ed. pap. 2.81 (*1-55567-322-8*) Coyote Press.

Observations on Birds of Southeastern Brazil. Margaret K. Mitchell. LC 57-58538. 280p. reprint ed. pap. 86.80 (*0-608-16323-6*, 202653800050) Bks Demand.

Observations on Borzoi, Called in America Russian Wolfhounds. Joseph B. Thomas. LC 75-42030. 1976. reprint ed. 15.00 (*0-686-17807-6*) Dehack.

Observations on Congregational Chanting. Ivan Von Gardner. Tr. by Isaac E. Lambertsen from RUS. 12p. (Orig.). 1993. pap. 1.00 (*0-912927-52-6*, D015) St John Kronstadt.

Observations on Cumberland & Westmoreland. William Gilpin. LC 96-19694. (Revolution & Romanticism, 1789-1834 Ser.). 268p. 1996. 135.00 (*1-85477-207-4*) Continuum.

Observations on Distribution, Ecology & Cultivation of the Tuber-Bearing Legume Genus: Pachyrhizus Rich. M. Sorensen. (Wageningen Agricultural University Papers: No. 90-3). 48p. 1990. pap. 13.00 (*90-6754-168-0*, Pub. by Backhuys Pubs) Balogh.

Observations on "Hamlet" James Plumptre. LC 71-144672. reprint ed. 20.00 (*0-404-05066-2*) AMS Pr.

***Observations on International Tourism.** Francesco Frangialli. 1999. 30.00 (*92-844-0291-3*, WT00291, Pub. by Wrld Tourism Org) Bernan Associates.

Observations on Language: Timothy Dwight; on Light. Timothy Dwight; Demonstrations of Stewart's Properties of the Circle Theodore Strong, Vol. 1, Pt. 4. Timothy Dwight et al. 1816. pap. 300.00 (*0-685-22876-2*) Elliots Bks.

Observations on Life. William E. Blackwell. 132p. 1991. 17.95 (*0-9630477-0-1*) W E Blackwell.

Observations on Madness & Melancholy: Including Practical Remarks on Those Diseases Together with Cases, & an Account of the Morbid Appearances on Dissection. 2nd enl. ed. John Haslam. LC 75-16707. (Classics in Psychiatry Ser.). 1976. reprint ed. 30.95 (*0-405-07432-8*) Ayer.

Observations on Man, 2 vols. 6th ed. David Hartley. 1986. reprint ed. pap. 34.95 (*0-935005-43-9*); reprint ed. lib. bdg. 51.95 (*0-935005-42-0*) Lincoln-Rembrandt.

Observations on Man, His Frame, His Duty & His Expectations, 2 vols. David Hartley. LC 66-11026. (History of Psychology Ser.). 1040p. 1966. reprint ed. 100.00 (*0-8201-1025-6*) Schol Facsimiles.

Observations on Man, His Frame, His Duty & His Expectations, 2 vols., Set. David Hartley. 1967. reprint ed. 122.20 (*0-685-66476-7*, 05101727) G Olms Pubs.

Observations on Man, 1791, 2 vols. David Hartley. LC 96-19694. (Revolution & Romanticism Ser.). 1004p. 1998. 165.00 (*1-85477-205-8*) Continuum.

Observations on Maniacal Disorders. William Pargeter. Ed. & Intro. by Stanley W. Jackson. LC 88-18630. (Tavistock Classics in the History of Psychiatry Ser.). 188p. reprint ed. pap. 58.30 (*0-608-20349-1*, 207160200002) Bks Demand.

Observations on Maniacal Disorders: (1792) William Pargeter. Ed. by Stanley Jackson. (Tavistock Classic Reprints in the History of Psychiatry Ser.). 208p. 1989. 37.50 (*0-415-00638-4*) Routledge.

Observations on Mental Derangement: Being an Application of the Principles of Phrenology to the Elucidation of the Causes, Symptoms, Nature, Treatment of Insanity. Andrew Combe. LC 72-161928. (History of Psychology Ser.). 352p. 1972. reprint ed. 50.00 (*0-8201-1089-2*) Schol Facsimiles.

Observations on Military Law & the Constitution & the Practice of Courts Martial. William C. DeHart. Ed. by Roy M. Mersky & J. Myron Jacobstein. (Classics in Legal History Reprint Ser.: Vol. 18). 433p. 1973. reprint ed. lib. bdg. 47.50 (*0-89941-017-0*, 300240) W S Hein.

An Asterisk (*) at the beginning of an entry indicates that the title is appearing for the first time.

Observations on Modernity. Niklas Luhmann. Tr. by William Whobrey from GER. LC 97-40908. (Writing Science Ser.). 1998. write for info. (*0-8047-3234-5*); pap. write for info. (*0-8047-3235-3*) Stanford U Pr.

Observations on Professions: Literature, Manners, & Emigration in the United States & Canada 1832. Isaac Fidler. LC 73-13129. (Foreign Travelers in America, 1810-1935 Ser.). 446p. 1974. reprint ed. 34.95 (*0-405-05452-1*) Ayer.

Observations on Some of the Manuscript Emendations of the Text of Shakespeare. James O. Halliwell-Phillipps. LC 75-168229. reprint ed. 29.50 (*0-404-03082-3*) AMS Pr.

Observations on Some Tendencies of Sentiment & Ethics in 18th Century Poetry. Johannes H. Harder. LC 68-886. (Studies in Poetry: No. 38). 1969. reprint ed. lib. bdg. 75.00 (*0-8383-0564-4*) M S G Haskell Hse.

Observations on the Archaeology & Ethnology of Nicaragua. Ephraim G. Squier. LC 88-82906. (Illus.). 64p. 1990. pap. 20.00 (*0-911437-08-8*) Labyrinthos.

Observations on the Bolbitiaceae 27: Preliminary Account of the Bolbitiaceae of New Zealand. Roy Watling & G. M. Taylor. (Bibliotheca Mycologica: Vol. 117). (GER., Illus.). 104p. 1987. 30.00 (*3-443-59018-7*, Pub. by Gebruder Borntraeger) Balogh.

Observations on the Charter & Conduct of the Society for the Propagation of the Gospel in Foreign Parts, Designed to Show Their Non-Conformity to Each Other. Jonathan Mayhew. LC 72-38456. (Religion in America, Series 2). 180p. 1972. reprint ed. 18.95 (*0-405-04077-6*) Ayer.

Observations on the Colony of Louisiana from 1796 to 1802. James Pitot. LC 79-14897. 231p. reprint ed. pap. 71.70 (*0-7837-8695-6*, 204944100011) Bks Demand.

Observations on the Commerce of American States. John B. Sheffield. LC 68-58014. (Reprints of Economic Classics Ser.). 287p. 1970. reprint ed. 49.50 (*0-678-00612-1*) Kelley.

Observations on the Criminal Responsibility of the Insane. Caleb Williams. (Historical Foundations of Forensic Psychiatry & Psychology Ser.). 148p. 1983. reprint ed. lib. bdg. 19.50 (*0-306-76178-5*) Da Capo.

Observations on the Deranged Manifestations of the Mind, or Insanity. Johann C. Spurzheim. LC 78-81359. (History of Psychology Ser.). (Illus.). 268p. 1970. reprint ed. 50.00 (*0-8201-1078-7*) Schol Facsimiles.

Observations on the Ecology & Biology of Western Cape Cod Bay, Massachusetts. Ed. by J. D. Davis & D. Merriman. (Lecture Notes on Coastal & Estuarine Studies: Vol. 11). x, 289p. 1984. pap. 44.00 (*0-387-96084-8*) Spr-Verlag.

Observations on the Establishment of the Bank of England. Francis Baring. LC 66-21659. 81p. 1967. reprint ed. 29.50 (*0-678-00281-9*) Kelley.

Observations on the Fairy Queen of Spenser, 2 vols., Set. Thomas Warton. LC 68-31011. (Illus.). 1969. reprint ed. lib. bdg. 65.00 (*0-8371-0741-5*, WAFQ) Greenwood.

Observations on the Fairy Queen of Spenser, 2 vols., Set. Thomas Warton. (BCL1-PR English Literature Ser.). 1992. reprint ed. lib. bdg. 150.00 (*0-7812-7229-7*) Rprt Serv.

Observations on the Fairy Queen of Spenser, 2 vols., Vol. 1. Thomas Warton. LC 68-31011. (Illus.). 1969. reprint ed. lib. bdg. 45.00 (*0-8371-1784-4*, WAFA) Greenwood.

Observations on the Fairy Queen of Spenser, 2 vols., Vol. 2. Thomas Warton. LC 68-31011. (Illus.). 1969. reprint ed. lib. bdg. 45.00 (*0-8371-0862-4*, WAFB) Greenwood.

Observations on the Fairy Queene of Spenser, 2 Vols. Thomas Warton. LC 68-24925. (Studies in Spenser: No. 26). 1969. reprint ed. lib. bdg. 150.00 (*0-8383-0193-2*) M S G Haskell Hse.

Observations on the Feeling of the Beautiful & Sublime. Immanuel Kant. Ed. & Tr. by John T. Goldthwait. 126p. 1991. pap. 14.95 (*0-520-07404-1*, Pub. by U CA Pr) Cal Prin Full Svc.

Observations on the Financial Position & Credit of Such of the States of the North American Union As Have Contracted Public Debts. Alexander Trotter. LC 67-21885. (Reprints of Economic Classics Ser.). viii, 455p. 1968. reprint ed. 57.50 (*0-678-00378-5*) Kelley.

Observations on the Form & Proportions of the Endocranial Casts of "Sinanthropus Pekinensis" Other Hominids & the Great Apes: A Comparative Study of Brain Size. Franz Weidenreich. LC 77-86449. (China. Geological Survey. Palaeontologia Sinica. New Ser. D: Vol. 7, Fasc. 4). (Illus.). reprint ed. 13.50 (*0-404-16692-X*) AMS Pr.

Observations on the Gaelic Language. P. McElligott. 1996. reprint ed. pap. 10.00 (*0-89979-085-2*) British Am Bks.

Observations on the Geology of the United States of America. W. Maclure. 1966. reprint ed. text 44.00 (*0-934454-67-1*) Lubrecht & Cramer.

Observations on the Growth of the Mind Including GENIUS. 5th ed. Sampson Reed. LC 72-4971. (Romantic Tradition in American Literature Ser.). 110p. 1972. reprint ed. 20.95 (*0-405-04641-3*) Ayer.

Observations on the Growth of the Mind with Remarks on Other Subjects. Sampson Reed. LC 78-100126. 200p. 1970. reprint ed. 50.00 (*0-8201-1070-1*) Schol Facsimiles.

Observations on the Importance of the American Revolution & the Means of Making It a Benefit to the World. Richard Price. LC 75-31129. reprint ed. 37.50 (*0-404-13607-9*) AMS Pr.

Observations on the Influence of Religion upon the Health & Physical Welfare of Mankind. Amariah Brigham. LC 73-2389. (Mental Illness & Social Policy; the American Experience Ser.). 1973. reprint ed. 23.95 (*0-405-05197-2*) Ayer.

Observations on the Influence of Religion upon the Health & Physical Welfare of Mankind, 1835: Remarks on the Influence of Mental Cultivation & Mental Excitement Upon Health, 2 vols. in 1. Amariah Brigham. LC 73-17271. (History of Psychology Ser.). 478p. 1973. 75.00 (*0-8201-1125-2*) Schol Facsimiles.

Observations on the Inhabitants, Climate, Soil, River Productions, Animals & Other Matters Worthy of Notice. John Bartram. 1993. reprint ed. lib. bdg. 89.00 (*0-7812-5425-6*) Rprt Serv.

Observations on the Intellectual Culture of the Caribou Eskimos. Knud J. Rasmussen. LC 76-22536. (Fifth Thule Expedition Ser.: Vol. 7, No. 2 & No. 3). reprint ed. write for info. (*0-404-58322-9*) AMS Pr.

Observations on the Language of Chaucer's "House of Fame" Henry C. Ford. LC 76-168118. reprint ed. 27.50 (*0-404-02511-0*) AMS Pr.

Observations on the Language of Chaucer's Troilus. George L. Kittredge. 1972. 59.95 (*0-8490-0747-X*) Gordon Pr.

Observations on the Means of Exciting a Spirit of National Industry. James Anderson. LC 68-25541. (Reprints of Economic Classics Ser.). xii, 526p. 1968. reprint ed. 67.50 (*0-678-00391-2*) Kelley.

Observations on the Nature, Kinds, Causes, & Prevention of Insanity: Containing Observations on the Nature, & Various Kinds of Insanity & the Appearances on Dissection, 2 vols. 2nd ed. Thomas Arnold. LC 75-16680. (Classics in Psychiatry Ser.). 1976. reprint ed. 56.95 (*0-405-07412-3*) Ayer.

Observations on the Popular Antiquities of Great Britain, 3 vols. 3rd ed. John Brand. Ed. by Henry Ellis. LC 71-136368. (Bohn's Antiquarian Library). reprint ed. 125.00 (*0-404-50005-6*) AMS Pr.

Observations on the Practice of Counterfeiting Coins & Medals. Lyman H. Low. 1979. reprint ed. pap. 2.00 (*0-915262-25-8*) S J Durst.

Observations on the President's Fiscal Year, 1999 Federal Science & Technology Budget. National Academy of Sciences Staff et al. LC 99-165073. 32p. 1998. pap. text 10.00 (*0-309-06127-X*) Natl Acad Pr.

***Observations on the President's Fiscal Year 2000 Federal Science & Technology Budget.** National Academy of Science Staff et al. 24p. 1999. pap. 12.00 (*0-309-06487-2*) Natl Acad Pr.

***Observations on the President's Fiscal Year 2001 Federal Science & Technology Budget.** Science, Engineering Committee & National Academy of Sciences Staff. 22p. 2000. pap. 12.00 (*0-309-06984-X*) Natl Acad Pr.

Observations on the River Wye. William Gilpin. LC 91-3942. 156p. 1991. reprint ed. 55.00 (*1-85477-068-3*) Continuum.

Observations on the Rust of Grain. Felice Fontana. Tr. by P. P. Pirone. (Phytopathological Classics Ser.). 40p. 1932. 22.00 (*0-89054-003-9*) Am Phytopathol Soc.

Observations on the Soviet-Canadian Transporar Ski Trek. Ed. by R. J. Shephard & A. Rode. (Medicine & Sport Science Ser.: Vol. 33). (Illus.). x, 190p. 1992. 170.50 (*3-8055-5410-9*) S Karger.

Observations on the "Spiritual Situation of the Age" Ed. by Jurgen Habermas. Tr. by Andrew Buchwalter. (Studies in Contemporary German Social Thought). 424p. 1985. pap. text 17.50 (*0-262-58074-8*) MIT Pr.

Observations on the Subjects Treated of in Dr. Smith's Inquiry into the Nature & Causes of the Wealth of Nations. 2nd ed. David Buchanan. LC 65-26360. (Reprints of Economic Classics Ser.). xvi, 318p. 1966. reprint ed. 49.50 (*0-678-00191-X*) Kelley.

Observations on the Thunder Dance of the Bear Gens of the Fox Indians. Ed. by Truman Michelson. (Bureau of American Ethnology Bulletins Ser.). 73p. 1995. lib. bdg. 79.00 (*0-7812-4089-1*) Rprt Serv.

Observations on the Wisconsin Territory. William Robertson Smith. LC 75-122. (Mid-American Frontier Ser.). 1975. reprint ed. 18.95 (*0-405-06887-5*) Ayer.

Observations on the Writings of Thomas Jefferson. Henry Lee. (Notable American Authors Ser.). 1999. reprint ed. lib. bdg. 125.00 (*0-7812-3787-4*) Rprt Serv.

Observations on the Yurok: Childhood & World Image. fac. ed. Erik H. Erikson. Ed. by Robert H. Lowie et al. (University of California Publications in American Archaeology & Ethnology: Vol. 35: 10). 53p. (C). 1943. reprint ed. pap. text 6.56 (*1-55567-303-1*) Coyote Press.

Observations on This 'n' That by Old Al Aska - The Sourdough Sage & Bard of the Boondocks. Leslie J. Klebesadel. (Illus.). 48p. (Orig.). 1989. pap. 5.00 (*0-9624117-0-1*) Kilderkin Prodns.

Observations on Time in Ancient Egypt. Gerlad Kadish. 21p. 1993. 3.00 (*1-883058-10-4*, Studies Global) Global Pubns.

Observations sur Notre Instinct pour la Musique. fac. ed. Jean-Philippe Rameau. (Monuments of Music & Music Literature in Facsimile, II Ser.: Vol. 54). (Illus.). 1967. lib. bdg. 35.00 (*0-8450-2254-7*) Broude.

Observations 3. Richard Kieninger. (Orig.). 1974. pap. 3.00 (*0-9600308-4-0*) Stelle.

Observations 2. Richard Kieninger. (Orig.). 1974. pap. 3.00 (*0-9600308-3-2*) Stelle.

Observations upon Liberal Education. George Turnbull. LC 78-67545. (Scottish Enlightenment Ser.). reprint ed. 44.00 (*0-404-17208-3*) AMS Pr.

Observations upon the Conduct of Sir William Howe at the White Plains: As Related in the Gazette of December 30, 1776. Israel Mauduit. LC 71-140874. (Eyewitness Accounts of the American Revolution Ser.). 1971. reprint ed. 14.95 (*0-405-01219-5*) Ayer.

Observations upon the Floridas. Charles B. Vignoles. Ed. by John H. Moore. LC 76-39956. (Floridiana Facsimile & Reprint Ser.). 1977. reprint ed. 17.95 (*0-8130-0421-7*) U Press Fla.

Observations upon the Prophecies of Daniel, & the Apocalypse of St. John. Sir Isaac Newton. LC 91-74116. 323p. 1991. reprint ed. 19.95 (*0-942487-02-8*) Oregon Inst Sci Med.

Observations upon the State of Negro Slavery in the Island of Santa Cruz. Ed. & Intro. by Arnold R. Highfield. 154p. reprint ed. pap. write for info. (*0-916611-17-5*) Antilles Pr.

Observations upon the Windward Coast of Africa: Religion, Character, Customs, Etc., of the Natives. Joseph Corry. (Illus.). 163p. 1968. reprint ed. 45.00 (*0-7146-1800-4*, Pub. by F Cass Pubs) Intl Spec Bk.

Observatories in Earth Orbit & Beyond. Ed. by Yoji Kondo. (C). 1991. text 137.50 (*0-7923-1133-7*) Kluwer Academic.

Observatories of the Canaries: On the Occasion of Their Inauguration, June 28-29, 1985. Ed. by P. Beers & P. Murdin. (Illus.). 168p. 1985. pap. 44.00 (*0-08-033676-0*, C150, Pub. by PPL) Elsevier.

***Observatory.** Daragh Carville. 2000. pap. 10.95 (*0-413-73910-4*, Methuen Drama) Methn.

Observatory. 2nd ed. Dimitris Tsaloumas. Tr. by Philip Grundy from GRE. LC 82-17455. 169p. 1983. pap. 16.95 (*0-7022-1765-4*) Intl Spec Bk.

***Observatory: A Novel.** Emily Grayson. LC 99-54751. 192p. 2000. 20.00 (*0-688-17439-6*, Wm Morrow) Morrow Avon.

Observatory in Islam. Aydin Sayili. Ed. by I. Bernard Cohen. LC 80-2144. (Development of Science Ser.). (Illus.). 1981. lib. bdg. 49.95 (*0-405-13951-9*) Ayer.

***Observatory Mansions.** Edward Carey. 2001. 23.00 (*0-609-60680-8*) Crown Pub Group.

Observatory Operations to Optimize Scientific Return. Ed. by Peter J. Quinn. LC 99-192205. (Proceedings of SPIE Ser.: Vol. 3349). 490p. 1998. 107.00 (*0-8194-2796-9*) SPIE.

Observe Eclipses. Michael D. Reynolds & Richard A. Sweetsir. pap. write for info. (*1-886336-10-5*) Chabot Observ.

Observe the Sons of Ulster Marching Towards the Somme. Frank McGuinness. 72p. (Orig.). 1986. pap. 9.95 (*0-571-14611-2*) Faber & Faber.

Observed Minima Timings of Eclipsing Binaries, No. 1. Compiled by Marvin E. Baldwin & Gerard Samolyk. (Illus.). 58p. 1993. pap. text 3.00 (*1-878174-10-X*) Am Assn Var Star.

Observed Minima Timings of Eclipsing Binaries, No. 2. Compiled by Marvin E. Baldwin & Gerard Samolyk. (Illus.). 58p. 1995. pap. text 3.00 (*1-878174-26-6*) Am Assn Var Star.

Observed Minima Timings of Eclipsing Binaries, No. 3. Compiled by Marvin E. Baldwin & Gerard Samolyk. (Illus.). 58p. 1996. pap. text 3.00 (*1-878174-27-4*) Am Assn Var Star.

Observed Minima Timings of Eclipsing Binaries, No. 4. Compiled by Marvin E. Baldwin & Gerard Samolyk. (Illus.). 58p. 1997. pap. text 3.00 (*1-878174-24-X*) Am Assn Var Star.

***Observed Minima Timings of Eclipsing Binaries, No. 5.** Marvin E. Baldwin. (Illus.). 59p. 1999. pap. text 3.00 (*1-878174-31-2*) Am Assn Var Star.

Observer. Aino K. Kabe. LC 96-68193. (Illus.). 96p. 1996. 14.95 (*1-56167-301-3*) Noble Hse MD.

Observer of the Dance, 1958-1982. Alexander Bland. 250p. 1986. 49.95 (*0-903102-91-9*, Pub. by Dance Bks) Princeton Bk Co.

Observer Profiles. Observer Staff. Ed. by Ivor Brown. LC 78-117330. (Biography Index Reprint Ser.). 1977. reprint ed. 23.95 (*0-8369-8022-0*) Ayer.

Observers & Macroeconomic Systems: Computation of Policy Trajectories with Separate Model Based Control. Ric D. Herbert. LC 98-36004. (Advances in Computational Economics Ser.). 1998. write for info. (*0-7923-8239-0*) Kluwer Academic.

Observers for Linear Systems. Ed. by John O'Reilly. (Mathematics in Science & Engineering Ser.). 1983. text 116.00 (*0-12-527780-6*) Acad Pr.

Observer's Good Gardening Guide. Christopher Lloyd. 1983. 25.95 (*0-03-063261-7*) Holt R&W.

Observer's Guide to Astronomy, 2 vols. Ed. by Patrick Martinez. Tr. by Storm Dunlop. LC 93-29830. (Practical Astronomy Handbooks Ser.). (Illus.). (C). 1992. write for info. (*0-521-38088-X*); write for info. (*0-521-38075-8*) Cambridge U Pr.

Observer's Guide to Astronomy, Vol. 1. Ed. by Patrick Martinez. Tr. by Storm Dunlop. (Practical Astronomy Handbooks Ser.: No. 4). (Illus.). 610p. (C). 1994. pap. 39.95 (*0-521-37945-8*); text 85.00 (*0-521-37068-X*) Cambridge U Pr.

Observer's Guide to Astronomy, 2 vols., Vol. 2. Ed. by Patrick Martinez. Tr. by Storm Dunlop. LC 93-29830. (Practical Astronomy Handbooks Ser.). (Illus.). 569p. (C). 1994. pap. 37.95 (*0-521-45898-6*); text 85.00 (*0-521-45265-1*) Cambridge U Pr.

Observer's Guide to the Geology of Prince William Sound. Jim Lethcoe. (Illus.). 190p. (Orig.). 1989. pap. 19.95 (*1-877900-00-1*) Prince W Sound.

Observers Guide to the Glaciers of Prince William Sound, Alaska. 1987. 15.95 (*0-9613146-6-4*) Prince W Sound.

Observer's Guide to the Whales of Prince William Sound. Craig Matkin. (Illus.). 112p. (Orig.). 1994. pap. 12.95 (*1-877900-03-6*) Prince W Sound.

Observers Observed: Essays on Ethnographic Fieldwork. Ed. by George W. Stocking, Jr. LC 83-47771. (History of Anthropology Ser.: Vol. 1). (Illus.). 248p. 1985. reprint ed. pap. text 18.95 (*0-299-09454-5*) U of Wis Pr.

Observer's Sky Atlas. E. Karkoschka. (Illus.). 128p. 1995. 15.95 (*0-387-51588-7*) Spr-Verlag.

Observer's Sky Atlas. 2nd ed. Erich Karkoschka. LC 98-29450. (Illus.). 136p. 1998. pap. 19.95 (*0-387-98606-5*) Spr-Verlag.

Observer's Year. Patrick Moore. LC 97-42028. (Illus.). 400p. 1997. pap. 29.95 (*3-540-76147-0*) Spr-Verlag.

Observing. Shereen G. Rutman. (Toddler Time Ser.). (Illus.). 16p. (J). 1992. pap., student ed. 2.95 (*1-56293-189-X*, McClanahan Book) Learn Horizon.

Observing Advanced Research on Biomolecular Development & Evolution, EUR 16784. W. Hebel. 97p. 1996. pap. 25.00 (*92-827-6046-4*, CGNA-16784-ENC, Pub. by Comm Europ Commun) Bernan Associates.

Observing America's Jews. Marshall Sklare. Ed. & Frwd. by Jonathan D. Sarna. LC 92-59964. (Brandeis Series in American Jewish History, Culture, & Life). 318p. 1993. 40.00 (*0-87451-623-4*) U Pr of New Eng.

Observing & Recording the Behavior of Young Children. 4th ed. Dorothy Cohen et al. LC 96-35584. 264p. (C). 1996. pap. text 19.95 (*0-8077-3575-2*) Tchrs Coll.

Observing at a Distance: Proceedings of the International Workshop on Remote Observing. D. Emerson & R. Clowes. 356p. 1993. text 95.00 (*981-02-1132-5*) World Scientific Pub.

***Observing Australia, 1959-1999.** K. S. Inglis. Ed. & Intro. by Craig S. Wilcox. 250p. 2000. pap. 29.95 (*0-522-84866-4*, Pub. by Melbourne Univ Pr) Paul & Co Pubs.

***Observing Children.** 2nd ed. Carole Sharman et al. (Illus.). 144p. 2000. pap. 18.95 (*0-304-70627-2*) Continuum.

Observing Children: A Practical Guide. Carole Sharman et al. LC 94-47130. 1995. 70.00 (*0-304-33263-1*); pap. 19.95 (*0-304-33261-5*) Continuum.

Observing Children in the Primary Classroom: All in a Day. rev. ed. Richard W. Mills. Orig. Title: Classroom Observation of Primary School Children. (Illus.). 170p. 1988. pap. text 16.95 (*0-04-445176-8*) Routledge.

Observing Children in Their Natural Worlds: A Methodological Primer. Anthony D. Pellegrini. 232p. 1996. pap. 29.95 (*0-8058-2152-X*) L Erlbaum Assocs.

Observing Children in Their Natural Worlds: A Primer in Quantitative Observational Methods. Anthony D. Pellegrini. 272p. 1996. text 55.00 (*0-8058-2151-1*) L Erlbaum Assocs.

Observing Comets, Asteroids, Meteors, & the Zodiacal Light. Stephen J. Edberg & David H. Levy. LC 93-44922. (Practical Astronomy Handbooks Ser.: No. 5). (Illus.). 259p. (C). 1994. 20.95 (*0-521-42003-2*) Cambridge U Pr.

***Observing Complexity: Systems Theory & Postmodernity.** William Rasch. 2000. pap. 19.95 (*0-8166-3298-7*) U of Minn Pr.

Observing Development of the Young Child. 4th ed. Janice J. Beaty. LC 97-2909. 402p. (C). 1997. pap. text 38.00 (*0-13-801986-X*) P-H.

Observing Dimensions of Learning in Classrooms & Schools. John L. Brown. LC 95-32520. 143p. 1995. pap. 16.95 (*0-87120-255-7*, 195209) ASCD.

***Observing Double Replacement Reactions.** M. L. Gillette et al. (Modular Laboratory in Chemistry Ser.). 12p. (C). 1999. pap. text 1.50 (*0-87540-611-4*, REAC 611-4) Chem Educ Res.

Observing Dr. Freud: A Sonnet Sequence. John Gurney. 101p. pap. write for info. (*3-7052-0446-7*, Pub. by Poetry Salzburg) Intl Spec Bk.

Observing for the Fun of It: Backyard Astronomy for the Whole Family. Melanie Melton. Ed. by Terry Spohn. LC 96-153916. (Illus.). 104p. (Orig.). 1996. per. 14.95 (*0-913135-26-7*, 18545) Kalmbach.

Observing Global Climate Change. K. Ya Kondratyev & A. P. Cracknell. LC 98-204453. 544p. 1997. 98.00 (*0-7484-0124-5*, Pub. by Tay Francis Ltd) Taylor & Francis.

Observing Handbook & Catalogue of Deep Sky Objects. 2nd ed. Christian B. Luginbuhl & Brian A. Skiff. (Illus.). 364p. (C). 1998. pap. 34.95 (*0-521-62556-4*) Cambridge U Pr.

Observing Interaction: An Introduction to Sequential Analysis. 2nd ed. Roger Bakeman & John M. Gottman. LC 96-26084. (Illus.). 220p. (C). 1997. text 69.95 (*0-521-45008-X*); pap. text 24.95 (*0-521-57427-7*) Cambridge U Pr.

Observing Marine Invertebrates: Drawings from the Laboratory. Donald P. Abbott. Ed. by Galen H. Hilgard. LC 87-9931. (Illus.). 408p. 1987. kivar 35.00 (*0-8047-1426-6*) Stanford U Pr.

Observing Marine Invertebrates: Drawings from the Laboratory. fac. ed. Donald P. Abbott. Ed. by Galen H. Hilgard. LC 87-9931. (Illus.). 408p. 1987. pap. 30.00 (*0-7837-7266-1*, 204703900005) Bks Demand.

Observing Noctilucent Clouds. M. Gadsden & P. Parviainen. (Illus.). 40p. 1995. pap. 24.95 (*0-9650686-0-9*) Intl Assn Geomag.

Observing Ourselves: Essays in Social Research. Earl Babbie. (Illus.). 189p. (C). 1998. reprint ed. pap. text 12.95 (*1-57766-019-6*) Waveland Pr.

Observing, Recording, Interpreting Child Behavior: Guide & Workbook. 2nd rev. ed. John M. Carlevale. 120p. 1990. pap. text 15.95 (*0-940139-15-4*) Consortium RI.

Observing, Recording, Interpreting Child Behavior: Guide & Workbook. 3rd rev. ed. John M. Carlevale, Sr. 124p. 1997. pap. text 14.95 (*0-940139-44-8*) Consortium RI.

Observing Schools: A Methodical Guide. Peter Foster. 208p. 1996. pap. 24.95 (*1-85396-266-X*, Pub. by P Chapman) Taylor & Francis.

Observing Self: Mysticism & Psychotherapy. Arthur J. Deikman. LC 81-70486. 208p. 1983. reprint ed. pap. 14.50 (*0-8070-2951-3*) Beacon Pr.

***Observing Signs of Chemical Reaction.** M. L. Gillette & H. Anthony Neidig. (Modular Laboratory in Chemistry Ser.). 12p. (C). 1999. pap. text 1.50 (*0-87540-604-1*, REAC 604-1) Chem Educ Res.

***Observing Single Replacement Reactions.** M. L. Gillette et al. (Modular Laboratory in Chemistry Ser.). 12p. (C). 1999. pap. text 1.50 (*0-87540-610-6*, REAC 610-6) Chem Educ Res.

O

Observing Students & Teachers Through Objective Strategies. Sharon L. McNeely. LC 96-49745. 256p. 1997. pap. text 30.00 (*0-205-26434-4*) Allyn.

Observing Systems. Heinz Von Foerster. (Systems Inquiry Ser.). 425p. (Orig.). (C). 1982. pap. text 15.95 (*0-914105-19-1*) Intersystems Pubns.

Observing Teaching & Learning: Principles & Practice. Christina Tilstone. LC 99-161359. viii, 135 p. 1998. pap. write for info. (*1-85346-334-5*, Pub. by David Fulton) Taylor & Francis.

***Observing the Caldwell Objects.** David Ratledge. LC 99-57027. (Illus.). 225p. 2000. 34.95 (*1-85233-628-5*, Pub. by Spr-Verlag) Spr-Verlag.

Observing the Economy. C. A. Gregory. 240p. 1989. 47.50 (*0-415-01754-8*, A3637); pap. 15.95 (*0-415-01755-6*, A3641) Routledge.

Observing the Erotic Imagination. Robert J. Stoller. 239p. (C). 1992. reprint ed. pap. 16.00 (*0-300-05473-4*) Yale U Pr.

Observing the Language Learner. Ed. by Angela Jaggar & M. Trika Smith-Burke. LC 84-12986. (Illus.). 255p. (Orig.). reprint ed. pap. 79.10 (*0-7837-4590-7*, 204430900002) Bks Demand.

***Observing the Moon: A Practical Guide for Amateur Astronomers.** Peter Wlasuk. LC 00-33820. (Practical Astronomy Ser.). 2000. write for info. (*1-85233-193-3*) Spr-Verlag.

***Observing the Moon: The Modern Astronomer's Guide.** Gerald North. LC QB581.N67 2000. (Illus.). 356p. 2000. 39.95 (*0-521-62274-3*) Cambridge U Pr.

***Observing The Reactionso of Household Chemicals.** 5th ed. James M. Postma et al. 2000. pap. text, lab manual ed. 1.95 (*0-7167-9413-6*) W H Freeman.

Observing the Sky. Carole Stott. LC 90-11018. (Exploring the Universe Ser.). (Illus.). 32p. (J). (gr. 4-6). 1991. pap. 4.95 (*0-8167-2133-5*); lib. bdg. 18.60 (*0-8167-2132-7*) Troll Communs.

***Observing the Sun.** Chris Kitchin. 1999. pap. 24.95 (*1-85233-035-X*) Spr-Verlag.

Observing the Sun. Peter O. Taylor. (Practical Astronomy Handbooks Ser.: No. 3). (Illus.). 173p. (C). 1992. text 35.95 (*0-521-40110-0*) Cambridge U Pr.

Observing Variable Stars: A Guide for the Beginner. 2nd ed. David H. Levy. (Illus.). 224p. (C). 1998. reprint ed. pap. 16.95 (*0-521-62755-9*) Cambridge U Pr.

Observing Young Readers: Selected Papers. Marie M. Clay. LC 82-12047. 242p. (C). (gr. 1). 1982. pap. text 23.00 (*0-435-08208-6*, 08208) Heinemann.

Obsesion. Catherine Cookson. 1999. pap. text 9.95 (*84-08-02526-0*) Planeta Edit.

Obsesion Indecente. Colleen McCullough. (SPA.). 320p. 1992. pap. 4.95 (*1-56780-235-4*) La Costa Pr.

Obsesion Secreta: Secret Obsession. Charlotte Lamb. (Bianca Ser.). (SPA.). 1996. per. 3.50 (*0-373-33375-7*, 1-33375-6) Harlequin Bks.

Obsessed. Susan Andersen. 320p. 1993. mass mkt. 4.50 (*0-8217-4330-9*, Zebra Kensgtn) Kensgtn Pub Corp.

Obsessed. Liu Heng. Tr. by David Kwan. 340p. 1991. pap. 8.95 (*0-8351-2083-X*) China Bks.

Obsessed. Liu Heng. 340p. 1991. pap. 6.45 (*7-5071-0072-3*) Cypress Co.

Obsessed! Amanda Stevens. (Intimate Moments Ser.). 1993. per. 3.39 (*0-373-07488-3*, 5-07488-5) Silhouette.

Obsessed. abr. ed. Megan Stine. Ed. by Lisa Clancy. (Real Life Ser.). 160p. (Orig.). (J). (gr. 6 up). 1994. mass mkt. 3.50 (*0-671-87271-0*, Archway) PB.

***Obsessed: A Flesh & the Word Collection of Gay Erotic Memoirs.** Michael Lowenthal. LC 98-50411. 256p. 1999. pap. 12.95 (*0-452-27999-2*, Plume) Dutton Plume.

Obsessed: The Anatomy of a Stalker. Ronald Markman & Ron LaBrecque. (Illus.). 304p. 1995. reprint ed. mass mkt. 5.99 (*0-380-76650-7*, Avon Bks) Morrow Avon.

***Obsessed by Dress: An Assemblage of Quotations.** Tobi Tobias. LC 00-9021. (Illus.). 2000. 20.00 (*0-8070-0606-8*) Beacon Pr.

***Obsessed to Fly.** Harry C. Armstrong. 1999. pap. 7.95 (*0-533-13177-4*) Vantage.

Obsessed with Mud. Larry Schug. 28p. (Orig.). 1997. pap. 4.95 (*1-886895-10-4*) Poetry Harbor.

Obsession. Louis Begley & David Bradley. (Illus.). 1994. boxed set 100.00 (*1-883060-02-8*) Quill & Brush Pr.

Obsession. Louis Begley et al. (Illus.). 116p. 1994. pap. 15.00 (*1-883060-03-6*) Quill & Brush Pr.

Obsession. Jackie Collins. 114p. 1998. mass mkt. 3.99 (*0-671-02459-0*) S&S Trade.

Obsession. Catherine Cookson. 529p. 1996. 29.95 (*0-593-03479-1*) Bantam.

Obsession. Catherine Cookson. 1996. mass mkt. 7.99 (*0-552-14157-7*) Bantam.

Obsession. Catherine Cookson. (Mira Bks.). 1998. mass mkt. 5.99 (*1-55166-454-2*, 1-66454-9, Mira Bks) Harlequin Bks.

Obsession. Catherine Cookson. LC 97-18688. 320p. 1997. 22.50 (*0-684-84241-6*) S&S Trade.

Obsession. Cathryn Cooper. mass mkt. 6.95 (*0-7472-5288-2*, Pub. by Headline Bk Pub) Trafalgar.

***Obsession.** Kay David. (Superromance Ser.: Bk. 945). 2000. mass mkt. 4.50 (*0-373-70945-5*, 1-70945-0) Harlequin Bks.

Obsession. Gwynne Forster. 320p. 1998. pap. 4.99 (*0-7860-0502-5*, Pinncle Kensgtn) Kensgtn Pub Corp.

Obsession. Arthur Guirdham. 186p. (Orig.). pap. 20.95 (*0-8464-4262-0*) Beekman Pubs.

Obsession. Arthur Guirdham. 109p. (Orig.). 1972. pap. 13.95 (*0-85435-271-6*, Pub. by C W Daniel) Natl Bk Netwk.

Obsession. Lisa Jackson. (Family Continuity Program Ser.: No. 9). 1999. mass mkt. 4.50 (*0-373-82157-3*, 1-82157-8) Harlequin Bks.

***Obsession.** Kathi Mills. 2001. pap. 12.99 (*0-8054-2149-1*) Broadman.

Obsession. Wendy Morgan. 320p. 1996. mass mkt. 4.99 (*0-8217-5120-4*, Zebra Kensgtn) Kensgtn Pub Corp.

Obsession. Terence Munsey. LC 97-92895. 208p. (Orig.). 1997. mass mkt. 5.99 (*0-9697066-5-0*) Munsey Music.

Obsession. MARIA DEL REY. 1999. mass mkt. 6.95 (*0-352-33375-8*) Nexus.

Obsession. Paolo E. Serpieri. 1996. 14.95 (*1-882931-23-8*) Heavy Metal Magazine.

Obsession. Ramsey Campbell. 320p. 1986. reprint ed. pap. 3.95 (*0-8125-1656-7*) Tor Bks.

Obsession: How Evil Spirits Influence Mortals. 4th ed. William B. Faraday. 23p. 1996. reprint ed. spiral bd. 8.00 (*0-7873-0320-8*) Hlth Research.

Obsession: Reflections on the Tyranny of Slenderness. Kim Chernin. LC 93-40213. 224p. 1994. reprint ed. pap. 13.00 (*0-06-092505-1*, Perennial) HarperTrade.

Obsession: (Secret Fantasies) Debra Carroll. LC 95-7075. (Temptation Ser.). 219p. 1995. per. 3.25 (*0-373-25630-2*, 1-25630-4) Harlequin Bks.

Obsession: The Beloved. limited ed. Terence Sellers. LC 86-91324. (Illus.). 112p. 1987. pap. 25.00 (*0-930635-55-8*) Vitriol Pubns.

Obsession: The FBI's Legendary Profiler Probes the Psyches of Killers, Rapists & Stalkers, & Their Victims & Tells How to Fight Back. John E. Douglas & Mark Olshaker. 1998. mass mkt. 6.99 (*0-671-01704-7*) PB.

Obsession: The FBI's Legendary Profiler Probes the Psyches of Killers, Rapists & Stalkers, & Their Victims & Tells How to Fight Back. John E. Douglas & Mark Olshaker. LC 97-48654. 384p. 1998. 25.50 (*0-684-84560-1*) Scribner.

Obsession: The Lives & Times of Calvin Klein. Steven S. Gaines. LC 94-70741. 1994. 22.50 (*1-55972-235-5*, Birch Ln Pr) Carol Pub Group.

Obsession: The Lives & Times of Calvin Klein. Steven S. Gaines & Sharon Churcher. 464p. 1995. mass mkt. 5.99 (*0-380-72500-2*, Avon Bks) Morrow Avon.

Obsession & Culture: A Study of Sexual Obsession in Modern Fiction. Andrew Brink. LC 95-30472. 256p. (C). 1996. 39.50 (*0-8386-3596-2*) Fairleigh Dickinson.

Obsession & Release: Rereading the Poetry of Louise Bogan. Lee Upton. LC 96-2101. 176p. 1996. 32.50 (*0-8387-5321-3*) Bucknell U Pr.

Obsession de Jerome Delisle. Guy Lavigne. (Novels in the Roman Plus Ser.). (FRE., Illus.). 160p. (YA). (gr. 8 up). 1993. pap. 8.95 (*2-89021-190-8*, Pub. by La Courte Ech) Firefly Bks Ltd.

Obsession of Victoria Gracen. large type ed. Grace Livingston Hill. LC 98-3720. 1998. 25.95 (*0-7862-1475-9*) Thorndike Pr.

Obsession of Victoria Gracen. Grace Livingston Hill. reprint ed. lib. bdg. 23.95 (*0-89190-029-2*, Rivercity Pr) Amereon Ltd.

Obsession or How Evil Spirits Influence Mortals. Michael Faraday. 50p. 1996. reprint ed. pap. 7.95 (*1-56459-653-2*) Kessinger Pub.

Obsession with Anne Frank: Meyer Levin & The "Diary" Lawrence Graver. LC 94-48123. (Centennial Book Ser.). (Illus.). 238p. 1995. 35.00 (*0-520-20124-8*, Pub. by U CA Pr) Cal Prin Full Svc.

Obsession with Anne Frank: Meyer Levin & the "Diary" Lawrence Graver. 238p. 1997. pap. text 16.95 (*0-520-21220-7*, Pub. by U CA Pr) Cal Prin Full Svc.

Obsession with History: Russian Writers Confront the Past. Andrew B. Wachtel. LC 93-14174. 274p. (C). 1994. 45.00 (*0-8047-2246-3*) Stanford U Pr.

Obsession with History: Russian Writers Confront the Past. Andrew B. Wachtel. 274p. 1995. pap. 14.95 (*0-8047-2594-2*) Stanford U Pr.

Obsession with Justice: The Story of the Deuteronomists. William J. Doorly. LC 94-15328. 224p. 1994. pap. 12.95 (*0-8091-3487-X*) Paulist Pr.

Obsessional Neuroses: Developmental Psychopathology. Humberto Nagera. LC 84-45012. 240p. 1993. pap. 40.00 (*1-56821-151-1*) Aronson.

Obsessions. Carol Dawis. (Quantam Leap Ser.: No. 13). 320p. 1997. pap. 6.50 (*1-57297-241-6*) Blvd Books.

Obsessions. Anthony S. Magistrale. (Illus.). 40p. 1989. pap. 3.95 (*0-910619-05-0*) Niekas Pubns.

Obsessions. Jessica March. 1990. mass mkt. 5.95 (*0-446-35227-6*) Warner Bks.

***Obsessions.** Joseph Mills. 2000. pap. text 12.95 (*1-873741-31-6*) Millivres Bks.

Obsessions: Tony Ward. George Pitts. (Illus.). 132p. 1998. 70.00 (*3-908162-99-8*) Abbeville Pr.

Obsessions Die Hard: Motorcycling the Pan-American Highway's Jungle Gap. 2nd ed. Ed Culberson. LC 97-180134. (Incredible Journeys Ser.). (Illus.). 272p. (Orig.). 1996. reprint ed. pap. 19.95 (*1-884313-06-X*, CULB) Whitehorse NH.

Obsessions et la Psychasthenie, 2 vols., Set. Pierre M. Janet. LC 75-16709. (Classics in Psychiatry Ser.). (FRE., Illus.). 1976. reprint ed. 108.95 (*0-405-07434-6*) Ayer.

Obsessions et la Psychasthenie, 2 Vols., Vol. 1. Pierre M. Janet. LC 75-16709. (Classics in Psychiatry Ser.). (FRE., Illus.). 1976. reprint ed. 54.95 (*0-405-07436-0*) Ayer.

Obsessions et la Psychasthenie, 2 vols., Vol. 1. Pierre M. Janet. LC 75-16709. (Classics in Psychiatry Ser.). (FRE., Illus.). 1976. reprint ed. 54.95 (*0-405-07435-2*) Ayer.

***Obsessions of an Extraordinary Executive: The Four Disciplines at the Heart of Making Any Organi.** Patrick M. Lencioni. 180p. 2000. 22.00 (*0-7879-5403-9*) Jossey-Bass.

Obsessive-Compulsive & Related Disorders in Adults: A Comprehensive Clinical Guide. Lorrin M. Koran. LC 98-42347. (Illus.). 400p. (C). 1999. pap. 59.95 (*0-521-55975-8*) Cambridge U Pr.

Obsessive Compulsive Anonymous: Recovering from Obsessive Compulsive Disorder. 2nd ed. LC 99-93043. 200p. 1999. pap. 19.00 (*0-9628066-2-5*, 4155) OCA.

Obsessive-Compulsive Disorder. 1997. lib. bdg. 250.95 (*0-8490-8142-4*) Gordon Pr.

Obsessive-Compulsive Disorder. Maj. Date not set. text. write for info. (*0-471-87163-X*) Wiley.

Obsessive Compulsive Disorder. Todd Schemmel. Ed. by Carl Steketee & Teresa Pigott. LC 99-19852. (Condensed Reviews for Professionals Ser.). 104p. 1999. pap. 14.95 (*1-887537-12-0*) Compact Clinicals.

Obsessive-Compulsive Disorder. Margaret Strock. 16p. 1994. pap. 30.00 (*0-16-045238-4*) USGPO.

Obsessive Compulsive Disorder: A Cognitive & Neuropsychological Perspective. Tallis. 222p. 1995. pap. text 46.50 (*0-471-95772-0*) Wiley.

Obsessive Compulsive Disorder: A Cognitive & Neuropsychological Perspective. Frank Tallis. LC 95-220406. (Wiley Series in Clinical Psychology). (Illus.). 223p. 1995. reprint ed. pap. 69.20 (*0-608-04002-9*, 206473900011) Bks Demand.

Obsessive Compulsive Disorder: A Guide. 6th rev. ed. John H. Greist. 65p. 1997. pap. 4.50 (*1-890802-03-4*) Madison Inst of Med.

Obsessive Compulsive Disorder: A Survival Guide for Family & Friends. Roy Cohen. LC 93-83800. 90p. 1993. pap. 9.95 (*0-9628066-1-7*) OCA.

Obsessive Compulsive Disorder: Contemporary Issues in Treatment. Ed. by Wayne K. Goodman et al. LC 98-56188. (Personality & Clinical Psychology Ser.). 661p. 1999. 69.95 (*0-8058-2837-0*) L Erlbaum Assocs.

***Obsessive-Compulsive Disorder: Help for Children & Adolescents.** Mitzi Waltz. Ed. by Linda Lamb. LC 99-86990. (Illus.). 400p. 2000. pap. 24.95 (*1-56592-758-3*) OReilly & Assocs.

Obsessive Compulsive Disorder: New Help for the Family. Herbert L. Gravitz. LC 98-70141. 224p. 1998. pap. 19.95 (*0-9661104-4-7*) Healing Visions.

Obsessive-Compulsive Disorder: Pastoral Care for the Road to Change. Robert M. Collie. LC 99-23094. 267p. 1999. pap. 19.95 (*0-7890-0862-9*, Haworth Pastrl) Haworth Pr.

***Obsessive-Compulsive Disorder: Pastoral Care for the Road to Change.** Robert M. Collie. LC 99-23094. 267p. 1999. 49.95 (*0-7890-0707-X*, Haworth Pastrl) Haworth Pr.

Obsessive-Compulsive Disorder: Psychological & Pharmacological Treatment. Ed. by Samuel M. Turner et al. (Illus.). 272p. (C). 1985. text 78.00 (*0-306-41850-9*, Kluwer Plenum) Kluwer Academic.

Obsessive-Compulsive Disorder: The Facts. 2nd ed. Padmal De Silva & Stanley Rachman. (The Facts Ser.). (Illus.). 152p. 1998. pap. 19.95 (*0-19-262860-7*) OUP.

Obsessive-Compulsive Disorder: Theory, Research, & Treatment. Ed. by Richard P. Swinson et al. LC 98-14388. 478p. 1998. lib. bdg. 52.00 (*1-57230-335-2*) Guilford Pubns.

Obsessive-Compulsive Disorder Casebook. 2nd rev. ed. Ed. by John H. Greist & James W. Jefferson. 336p. 1995. text 41.95 (*0-88048-729-1*, 8729) Am Psychiatric.

Obsessive-Compulsive Disorder in Children & Adolescents. Ed. by Judith L. Rapoport. LC 88-24262. 355p. 1989. text 47.50 (*0-88048-282-6*, 8282) Am Psychiatric.

Obsessive Compulsive Disorder in Children & Adolescents: A Guide. Hugh F. Johnston. 54p. 1993. pap. 4.50 (*1-890802-11-5*) Madison Inst of Med.

Obsessive Compulsive Disorder in Children & Adolescents: A Guide. rev. ed. Hugh F. Johnston. 58p. 1997. pap. 4.50 (*1-890802-13-1*) Madison Inst of Med.

Obsessive-Compulsive Disorder Spectrum: Pathogenesis, Diagnosis, & Treatment. Jose A. Yaryura-Tobias & Fugen A. Neziroglu. 337p. 1996. text 69.50 (*0-88048-707-0*, 8707) Am Psychiatric.

Obsessive-Compulsive Disorders. 1996. lib. bdg. 250.75 (*0-8490-5902-X*) Gordon Pr.

Obsessive-Compulsive Disorders. Bruce Goldberg. 1993. 12.00 incl. audio (*1-885577-46-X*) B Goldberg.

Obsessive-Compulsive Disorders. Ed. by Eric Hollander & Dan J. Stein. LC 97-11363. (Medical Psychiatry Ser.). (Illus.). 416p. 1997. text 145.00 (*0-8247-9856-2*) Dekker.

Obsessive-Compulsive Disorders. 3rd ed. Michael A. Jenike. LC 97-48499. (Illus.). 886p. (C). (gr. 13). 1998. text 75.00 (*0-8151-3840-7*, 30957) Mosby Inc.

***Obsessive-Compulsive Disorders: Getting Well & Staying Well.** Fred Penzel. (Illus.). 448p. 2000. 30.00 (*0-19-514092-3*) OUP.

Obsessive-Compulsive Disorders: Pathogenesis, Diagnosis, Treatment. Jose A. Yaryura-Tobias & Fugen A. Neziroglu. LC 83-7233. (Experimental & Clinical Psychiatry Ser.: Vol. 8). 294p. reprint ed. pap. 91.20 (*0-608-09002-6*, 206963700005) Bks Demand.

Obsessive Compulsive Disorders: Theory & Management. Ed. by Michael A. Jenike et al. LC 86-4887. 208p. reprint ed. pap. 64.50 (*0-8357-7863-0*, 203628000002) Bks Demand.

Obsessive-Compulsive Disorders: Treating & Understanding Crippling Habits. Steven Levenkron. 1992. mass mkt. 14.99 (*0-446-39348-7*, Pub. by Warner Bks) Little.

Obsessive-Compulsive-Related Disorders. Ed. by Eric Hollander. LC 92-10541. 286p. 1993. text 23.50 (*0-88048-402-0*, 8402) Am Psychiatric.

Obsessive Compulsive Spectrum Disorders (Norton Professional Books) Biobehavioral Treatment & Management. Fugen A. Neziroglu & Jose A. Yaryura-Tobias. LC 97-8564. 224p. (C). 1997. 29.00 (*0-393-70245-6*) Norton.

Obsessive Images. Joseph W. Beach. Ed. by William V. O'Connor. LC 73-11620. 396p. 1973. reprint ed. lib. bdg. 69.50 (*0-8371-7079-6*, BEOI, Greenwood Pr) Greenwood.

Obsessive Love. large type ed. Sarah Holland. 288p. 1996. 23.99 (*0-263-14479-8*, Pub. by Mills & Boon) Ulverscroft.

Obsessive Love: When It Hurts Too Much to Let Go. Susan Forward. 336p. 1992. mass mkt. 7.99 (*0-553-29674-4*) Bantam.

Obsessive Sex: Resolving the Conflict of Loving Sex & Loving God. Jacquelyn Donald-Mims. 264p. (YA). 1999. pap. 21.95 (*1-891809-06-7*) Pub by Devon.

***Obsessive Sex: Resolving the Conflict of Loving Sex & Loving God.** Jacquelyn Donald. (YA). (gr. 8). 1998. reprint ed. 23.95 (*1-891809-07-5*) Pub by Devon.

Obshchje-zhitel'naya Sarovskaja Pustin'Tr. of Sarov Monastery. (Illus.). 241p. reprint ed. pap. 10.00 (*0-317-29243-9*) Holy Trinity.

***Obsidian: The Age of Judgement.** Micah Skaritka et al. (Illus.). 250p. (C). 1999. 28.00 (*0-9671263-0-4*) Apophis Consort.

Obsidian Butterfly. Laurell K. Hamilton. LC 99-33253. 400p. 2000. 21.95 (*0-441-00684-1*) Ace Bks.

***Obsidian Butterfly.** Laurell K. Hamilton. 2000. mass mkt. 7.50 (*0-441-00781-3*, Jove) Berkley Pub.

Obsidian Fate. Diana G. Gallagher. (Buffy the Vampire Slayer Ser.: No. 7). 304p. (YA). (gr. 7-12). 1999. per. 5.99 (*0-671-03929-6*) PB.

Obsidian Mirror. James Norman. LC 77-72806. (Illus.). (Orig.). 1977. pap. 12.50 (*0-914140-03-5*) Carpenter Pr.

Obsidian Mirror: An Adult Healing from Incest. 2nd ed. Louise M. Wisechild. LC 88-18395. (New Leaf Ser.). 278p. 1993. pap. 12.95 (*1-878067-39-7*) Seal Pr WA.

Obsidian Ranfla. Anthony Vigil. LC 98-70393. (Imagination Ser.). 88p. (Orig.). 1999. pap. 12.00 (*1-880834-43-X*) Cleveland St Univ Poetry Ctr.

Obsidian Sky. Guy Garcia. 1994. 23.00 (*0-671-86479-3*) S&S Trade.

Obsidian Studies in the Great Basin. Ed. by Richard E. Hughes. LC 84-622938. (Contributions of the University of California Archaeological Research Facility Ser.: Vol. 45). (Illus.). 243p. 1984. reprint ed. pap. 75.40 (*0-608-01711-6*, 206236600003) Bks Demand.

Obsidian Trials: Seven Spiritual Steps for Overcoming Our Fears. Pamela S. Meunier. 194p. 1999. pap. 14.95 (*0-9669095-0-X*, Pub. by Galactica Pr) ACCESS Pubs Network.

Obsolescence & Professional Career Development. H. G. Kaufman. LC 73-85187. (Illus.). 207p. reprint ed. pap. 64.20 (*0-608-10867-7*, 205130700094) Bks Demand.

Obsolete Banknotes & Scrip of Michigan, 2 bks. R. L. Bowen. LC 84-70009. (Illus.). 1984. reprint ed. lib. bdg. 50.00 (*0-942666-37-2*) S J Durst.

Obsolete Banknotes of New York. D. C. Wismer. LC 83-71379. 1985. reprint ed. pap. 20.00 (*0-942666-27-5*) S J Durst.

Obsolete Banknotes of North Carolina. R. Pennell. LC 83-71430. 1985. reprint ed. pap. 10.00 (*0-942666-29-1*) S J Durst.

Obsolete Banknotes of Ohio. D. C. Wismer. LC 83-71378. 1985. reprint ed. pap. 10.00 (*0-942666-25-9*) S J Durst.

Obsolete Banknotes of Pennsylvania. D. C. Wismer. 1985. reprint ed. pap. 12.00 (*0-942666-45-3*) S J Durst.

Obsolete Man: Man of the Month. Lass Small. (Desire Ser.). 1994. per. 2.99 (*0-373-05895-0*, 1-05895-7) Silhouette.

Obsolete Necessity: America in Utopian Writings, 1888-1900. Kenneth M. Roemer. LC 75-17279. 254p. reprint ed. pap. 78.80 (*0-608-15860-7*, 203072900070) Bks Demand.

Obsolete Youth. Bruno Bettelheim. 1970. pap. 5.00 (*0-911302-11-5*) San Francisco Pr.

Obstacle Avoidance in Multi-Robot Systems: Experiments in Parallel Genetic Algorithms. Mark A. Gill & Albert Y. Zomaya. LC 97-52397. (Series in Robotics & Intelligent System). 1998. 34.00 (*981-02-3423-6*) World Scientific Pub.

Obstacle Course. J. F. Freedman. 1999. pap. 12.95 (*0-452-27911-9*, Plume) Dutton Plume.

Obstacle Course. Yvonne Montgomery. 192p. (Orig.). 1990. pap. 3.50 (*0-380-75992-6*, Avon Bks) Morrow Avon.

Obstacle Illusions. Elana Aron. LC 92-70695. 176p. 1992. 13.95 (*1-56062-123-0*); pap. 10.95 (*1-56062-124-9*) CIS Comm.

Obstacle Race: Aborigines in Sport. Colin Tatz. 422p. 1995. pap. 39.95 (*0-86840-349-0*, Pub. by New South Wales Univ Pr) Intl Spec Bk.

***Obstacles, Miracles & Love.** Inge Fernback Rabe. 191p. 1999. per. 25.00 (*1-893365-03-4*) Barefooted Friar.

Obstacle's Overcome. Wilbur F. Pell. LC 98-90864. 1999. 18.95 (*0-533-12953-2*) Vantage.

Obstacles to International Macroeconomic Coordination. Jeffrey A. Frankel. LC 88-29619. (Studies in International Finance: No. 64). 46p. 1988. pap. text 13.50 (*0-88165-236-9*) Princeton U Int Finan Econ.

Obstacles to Mystical Experience. Scott Crom. LC 63-23067. (C). 1963. pap. 4.00 (*0-87574-132-0*) Pendle Hill.

Obstacles to Peace. Kenneth Wapnick. 295p. (Orig.). 1987. pap. 12.00 (*0-933291-05-1*) Foun Miracles.

Obstacles to Recovery in Vietnam & Kampuchea. Joel Charny & John Spragens, Jr. (Impact Audit Ser.: No. 3). 150p. (C). 1984. pap. 5.00 (*0-910281-02-5*) Oxfam Am.

***Obstacles to Reform: Exceptional Courts, Police Impunity & Persecution of Human Rights Defenders in Turkey.** Ed. by George Black. 129p. 1999. pap. 15.00 (*0-934143-92-7*) Lawyers Comm Human.

Obstacles to the Liberalization of Trade in Insurance. Robert L. Carter et al. 208p. 1992. text 49.50 (*0-472-10318-0*, 10318) U of Mich Pr.

***Obstetric & Gynecologic Care in Physical Therapy.** 2nd ed. Rebecca A. Stephenson & Linda J. O'Connor. LC 99-59223. 322p. 2000. pap. text 35.00 (*1-55642-415-9*) SLACK Inc.

O

An Asterisk (*) at the beginning of an entry indicates that the title is appearing for the first time.

Obstetric & Gynecologic Emergencies. Ed. by Guy I. Benrubi. (Illus.). 464p. 1993. text 73.00 (*0-397-51352-6*) Lppncott W & W.

Obstetric & Gynecologic Infectious Disease. Ed. by Joseph G. Pastorek, II. LC 93-24716. 858p. 1993. text 129.00 (*0-7817-0023-X*) Lppncott W & W.

Obstetric & Gynecologic Infectious Disease. Ed. by Joseph G. Pastorek, II. LC 93-24716. (Illus.). 824p. reprint ed. pap. 200.00 (*0-608-09764-0*, 206993700007) Bks Demand.

Obstetric & Gynecologic Milestones: Illustrated. Harold Speert. (Illus.). 702p. 1996. 145.00 (*1-85070-698-0*) Prthnon Pub.

Obstetric & Gynecologic Nursing. Meg Gulanick et al. Ed. by Kathy V. Gettrust. LC 93-5045. 581p. (C). 1993. pap. 32.75 (*0-8273-5468-1*) Delmar.

Obstetric & Gynecology: A Problem Based Approach. M. C. James et al. LC 98-40973. (Illus.). 410p. 1999. pap. write for info. (*0-7020-2251-9*) W B Saunders.

Obstetric & Gynecology Oral Practice Handbook. D. Dawn. (C). 1984. 45.00 (*0-7855-4657-X*, Pub. by Current Dist) St Mut.

Obstetric & Neonatal Malpractice: Legal & Medical Handbook, 2, Vol. 2. 2nd ed. Michael D. Volk. LC 96-5646. (Medical Malpractice Library). 1800p. 1996. boxed set 255.00 (*0-471-12896-1*) Wiley.

Obstetric & Perinatal Infections. Ed. by David Charles & Maxwell Finland. LC 79-170731. (Illus.). 668p. reprint ed. 200.00 (*0-8357-9412-1*, 201453000093) Bks Demand.

Obstetric Anesthesia. Norris. (Illus.). 600p. 1993. text 99.00 (*0-397-51115-9*) Lppncott W & W.

Obstetric Anesthesia. Sivam Ramanathan. LC 87-17293. 432p. reprint ed. pap. 134.00 (*0-7837-2742-9*, 204312200006) Bks Demand.

Obstetric Anesthesia. 2nd ed. Mark C. Norris. LC 98-27543. 750p. 1998. text 125.00 (*0-7817-1017-0*) Lppncott W & W.

***Obstetric Anesthesia: Principles & Practice.** 2nd ed. David H. Chestnut. LC 99-25600. (Illus.). 1056p. (C). 1999. text. write for info. (*0-323-00383-4*) Mosby Inc.

Obstetric Anesthesia & Uncommon Disorders. David R. Gambling & M. Joanne Douglas. Ed. by Leslie Day. LC 97-1435. (Illus.). 400p. 1997. text 89.00 (*0-7216-6157-2*, W B Saunders Co) Harcrt Hlth Sci Grp.

Obstetric Anesthesia Handbook, Vol. 2E. 2nd ed. Sanjay Datta. LC 95-788. (Illus.). 368p. (C). (gr. 13). 1995. pap. text 46.95 (*0-8151-2349-3*, 24719) Mosby Inc.

Obstetric Anesthesia Pearls. William E. Ackerman & Mushtaque M. Juneja. (Illus.). 280p. (C). 1992. pap. 37.95 (*0-8385-7173-5*, A7173-6, Apple Lange Med) McGraw.

***Obstetric Anesthesia Pocket Reference.** Edward T. Riley & Shelia E. Cohen. (Illus.). 144p. 2000. pap. text 25.00 (*0-7506-7166-1*) Buttrwrth-Heinemann.

Obstetric Care: Standards of Prenatal, Intrapartum, & Postpartum Management. Kathryn M. Andolsek. LC 89-8359. (Illus.). 293p. 1989. pap. text 46.50 (*0-8121-1250-4*) Lppncott W & W.

Obstetric Decision Making. Miller. (C). 2000. pap. text. write for info. (*0-7216-8274-X*, W B Saunders Co) Harcrt Hlth Sci Grp.

Obstetric Emergencies. Ed. by Guy I. Benrubi. (Illus.). 216p. 1989. text 66.00 (*0-443-08614-1*) Church.

Obstetric Fistula. R. F. Zacharin. (Illus.). 320p. 1988. 196.00 (*0-387-82005-1*) Spr-Verlag.

Obstetric Forceps: Its History & Evolution. Kedarnath Das. (Illus.). 903p. 1993. boxed set 125.00 (*1-897849-00-1*) Norman SF.

Obstetric Genetics. Zoltan Papp & Richard H. Lindenbaum. 627p. (C). 1990. 207.00 (*963-05-5689-8*, Pub. by Akade Kiado) St Mut.

Obstetric Infections: Amnionitis & Endometritis. Valerian A. Catanzarite & W. Patrick Duff. 1989. write for info. (*0-683-17956-X*) Lppncott W & W.

Obstetric Infections: Clinical Cases. Valerian A. Catanzarite & W. Patrick Duff. 1989. write for info. (*0-683-17958-6*) Lppncott W & W.

Obstetric Intensive Care: A Practice Manual. Michael R. Floey & Thomas H. Strong, Jr. Ed. by William Schmitt. LC 96-41406. 464p. 1997. pap. text 34.00 (*0-7216-1317-9*, W B Saunders Co) Harcrt Hlth Sci Grp.

***Obstetric Litigation: A Trial Lawyer's Guide.** Elliott B. Oppenheim. 300p. 1999. 300.00 (*1-930263-02-3*) Terra Firma NM.

Obstetric Myths vs. Research Realities: A Guide to the Medical Literature. Henci Goer. LC 94-17337. 400p. 1995. 79.50 (*0-89789-427-6*, Bergin & Garvey); pap. 29.95 (*0-89789-427-8*, Bergin & Garvey) Greenwood.

Obstetric Myths vs. Research Realities: A Guide to the Medical Literature. Hency Goer. 1995. pap. text. write for info. (*0-614-32038-0*, Bergin & Garvey) Greenwood.

Obstetric Survival Handbook. Yondel Masten. LC 98-229378. (Illus.). 300p. 1998. per. 39.95 (*1-56930-083-6*) Skidmore Roth Pub.

Obstetric Syndromes & Conditions. John P. O'Grady et al. LC 97-33562. (Clinical Handbook Ser.). (Illus.). 408p. 1998. pap. 78.00 (*1-85070-754-5*) Prthnon Pub.

Obstetric Ultrasonography: Gynecologic Oncology. fac. ed. Ed. by Richard L. Berkowitz et al. LC 88-18141. (Contemporary Issues in Obstetrics & Gynecology Ser.: No. 3). (Illus.). 260p. 1988. reprint ed. pap. 80.60 (*0-7837-7890-2*, 204764600007) Bks Demand.

Obstetric Ultrasound. 2nd ed. Patricia Chudleigh. 323p. (Orig.). 1992. pap. text 65.00 (*0-443-04207-1*) Church.

Obstetric Ultrasound. 3rd ed. Chudleigh. 2000. pap. text 65.00 (*0-443-05471-1*, W B Saunders Co) Harcrt Hlth Sci Grp.

Obstetric Ultrasound, Vol. 1. Ed. by James P. Neilson & S. E. Chambers. (Illus.). 320p. 1993. 79.00 (*0-19-262224-2*) OUP.

Obstetric Ultrasound, Vol. 2. Ed. by James P. Neilson & S. E. Chambers. (Illus.). 258p. 1995. text 79.00 (*0-19-262373-7*) OUP.

Obstetrical Emergencies. Denise Wjite & Judith H. Poole. Ed. by Karla Damus et al. LC 96-1652. 1996. write for info. (*0-86525-070-7*) March of Dimes.

Obstetrical Events & Developmental Sequelae. Ed. by Nergesh Tejani. 224p. 1989. lib. bdg. 142.00 (*0-8493-5762-4*, RG627) CRC Pr.

Obstetrical Events & Developmental Sequelae. 2nd ed. Ed. by Nergesh Tejani. 240p. 1994. lib. bdg. 139.00 (*0-8493-4974-5*, 4974) CRC Pr.

Obstetrical Intervention & Technology in the 1980s. Ed. by Diony Young. LC 82-21301. (Women & Health Ser.: Vol. 7, Nos. 3-4). 203p. 1983. text 49.95 (*0-86656-143-9*) Haworth Pr.

Obstetrical Measurements: Used in a Routine Examination. A. B. Kurtz. 1997. pap. write for info. (*1-930047-40-1*, OBM) Am Inst Ultrasound.

***Obstetrical Pearls: A Practical Guide for the Efficient Resident.** 3rd ed. Michael D. Benson. LC 99-24043. 226p. (Orig.). 1999. pap. 19.99 (*0-8036-0432-7*) Davis Co.

Obstetrical Transfusion Practice. Ed. by Ronald A. Sacher & Mark E. Brecher. (Illus.). 138p. (C). 1993. text 35.00 (*1-56395-024-3*) Am Assn Blood.

Obstetrician. Lee Jacobs. LC 98-9877. (Doctors in Action Ser.). (Illus.). 24p. (J). (gr. 3-5). 1998. lib. bdg. 15.95 (*1-56711-235-8*) Blackbirch.

***Obstetrician's Armamentarium: Historical Obstetric Instruments & Their Inventors.** Bryan M. Hibbard. LC 99-36288. 2000. 225.00 (*0-930405-80-3*) Norman SF.

Obstetrics. David James & Mary Pillai. LC 93-8274. (Colour Guide Ser.). (Illus.). 152p. 1994. pap. text 19.95 (*0-443-04777-4*) Harcrt Hlth Sci Grp.

Obstetrics. Ed. by Alec Turnbull & Geoffrey Chamberlain. (Illus.). 1201p. 1989. text 165.00 (*0-443-03539-3*) Church.

Obstetrics. 2nd ed. D. K. James & Mary Pillai. LC 97-22824. (Colour Guide Ser.). 2000. text. write for info. (*0-443-05773-7*) Harcrt Hlth Sci Grp.

Obstetrics. 2nd ed. Ed. by William F. Rayburn. (House Officer Ser.). (Illus.). 272p. 1988. pap. text 20.00 (*0-683-07159-9*) Lppncott W & W.

Obstetrics: A Practical Manual. Roger Neuberg. (Illus.). 302p. 1995. pap. text 49.95 (*0-19-263007-5*) OUP.

Obstetrics: Colour Aids. D. K. James & M. Pillai. (Illus.). 144p. 1990. pap. text 19.00 (*0-443-04011-7*) Church.

Obstetrics: Essentials of Clinical Practice. 2nd ed. Kenneth R. Niswander. 379p. 1981. 34.95 (*0-316-61147-6*, Little Brwn Med Div) Lppncott W & W.

Obstetrics: Normal & Problem Pregnancies. Ed. by Steven G. Gabbe et al. LC 86-17516. (Illus.). 1166p. reprint ed. pap. 200.00 (*0-8357-4663-1*, 203759300008) Bks Demand.

Obstetrics: Normal & Problem Pregnancies. 3rd ed. George J. Annas. Ed. by Steven G. Gabbe et al. LC 96-20732. 1348p. 1996. text 117.00 (*0-443-07690-1*) Church.

Obstetrics: Psychological & Psychiatric Syndromes. J. O'Grady & M. Rosenthal. (Current Topics in Obstetrics & Gynecology Ser.). (Illus.). 383p. (C). (gr. 13). 1991. text 74.95 (*0-412-04601-6*) Chapman & Hall.

Obstetrics: Textbook for Students & Practitioners. abr. ed. Whitridge J. Williams et al. LC 96-28900. 845p. (C). 1997. 150.00 (*0-8385-7199-9*, A7199-1, Apple Lange Med) McGraw.

Obstetrics & Gyn on Call. 2nd ed. Horowitz. 1999. pap. text 28.95 (*0-8385-7141-7*, Medical Exam) Appleton & Lange.

Obstetrics & Gynaecology. Lawrence Impey. LC 98-28847. 1999. write for info. (*0-632-04901-4*) Blackwell Sci.

Obstetrics & Gynaecology. McCarthy. 1998. pap. text 24.95 (*0-443-05244-1*) Church.

Obstetrics & Gynaecology. 5th ed. James Willocks & Kevin Phillips. LC 97-2285. 1997. pap. 29.95 (*0-443-04850-9*) Church.

Obstetrics & Gynaecology: A Critical Approach to the Clinical Problems. G. J. Jarvis. (Illus.). 744p. 1994. text 135.00 (*0-19-262058-4*) OUP.

Obstetrics & Gynecologic Physical Therapy. Ed. by Elaine Wilder. LC 88-18950. (Clinics in Physical Therapy Ser.: Vol. 20). (Illus.). 239p. reprint ed. pap. 74.10 (*0-7837-1612-5*, 204190400024) Bks Demand.

Obstetrics & Gynecological Pharmaceutical Markets: New Delivery Systems for Changing Lifestyles. Market Intelligence Staff. 288p. 1993. 1995.00 (*1-56753-453-8*) Frost & Sullivan.

Obstetrics & Gynecology. Mark A. Frederiksen. LC 99-40518. (Rypins' Intensive Reviews Ser.). 1999. pap. text. write for info. (*0-397-51557-X*) Lppncott W & W.

Obstetrics & Gynecology. Lawrence Impey. LC 98-28847. 1997. pap. text 39.95 (*0-86542-704-6*) Blackwell Sci.

Obstetrics & Gynecology. Pamela S. Miles et al. LC 94-3805. (Oklahoma Notes Ser.). (Illus.). 240p. 1994. 16.95 (*0-387-94184-3*) Spr-Verlag.

Obstetrics & Gynecology. William F. Rayburn & J. Christopher Carey. LC 95-23109. (House Officer Ser.). (Illus.). 512p. 1996. pap. 23.95 (*0-683-07181-5*) Lppncott W & W.

Obstetrics & Gynecology. Elmar Sakala. LC 96-23240. (Board Review Ser.). 389p. 1997. write for info. (*0-683-07498-9*) Lppncott W & W.

Obstetrics & Gynecology. Arthur D. Sorosky. 1998. pap. text. write for info. (*0-7216-6345-1*, W B Saunders Co) Harcrt Hlth Sci Grp.

Obstetrics & Gynecology. Arthur D. Sorosky. 1998. pap. text. write for info. (*0-7216-5082-1*, W B Saunders Co) Harcrt Hlth Sci Grp.

Obstetrics & Gynecology. 2nd ed. Charles R. Beckmann et al. LC 94-40390. (Illus.). 560p. 1995. (*0-683-00503-0*) Lppncott W & W.

Obstetrics & Gynecology. 2nd ed. Mimi C. Berman & Harris L. Cohen. LC 96-39954. (Diagnostic Medical Sonography Ser.). 732p. 1997. text 105.00 (*0-397-55261-0*, Lippnctt) Lppncott W & W.

Obstetrics & Gynecology. 2nd rev. ed. Pamela S. Miles et al. (Oklahoma Notes Ser.). (Illus.). 218p. 1996. pap. text 17.95 (*0-387-94632-2*) Spr-Verlag.

Obstetrics & Gynecology. 3rd ed. (National Medical Ser.). 1993. 27.00 (*0-685-75179-1*) Lppncott W & W.

Obstetrics & Gynecology. 3rd ed. William W. Beck, Jr. LC 92-48888. (National Medical Series for Independent Study). (Illus.). 504p. 1993. pap. 27.00 (*0-683-06241-7*) Lppncott W & W.

Obstetrics & Gynecology. 3rd ed. Charles R. Beckmann et al. LC 97-49309. 1998. 37.00 (*0-683-30391-0*) Lppncott W & W.

Obstetrics & Gynecology. 4th ed. William W. Beck. LC 96-29165. (National Medical Series for Independent Study). 510p. 1996. write for info. (*0-683-18015-0*) Lppncott W & W.

Obstetrics & Gynecology: A History & Iconography. rev. ed. Harold Speert. LC 93-44107.Tr. of Iconographia Gyniatrica. (Illus.). 540p. 1994. 245.00 (*0-930405-62-5*) Norman SF.

Obstetrics & Gynecology: Digging up the Bones, Vol. 7. Nikos M. Linardakis & Sonia Lott. LC 98-10207. (Digging Up the Bones Medical Review Ser.). (Illus.). 1998. pap. 18.95 (*0-07-038220-4*) McGraw-Hill HPD.

Obstetrics & Gynecology: PreTest Self-Assessment & Review. 8th ed. Ed. by Mark Evans. LC 97-26207. (Pretest Clinical Science Ser.). (Illus.). 200p. 1997. pap. text 18.95 (*0-07-052529-3*) McGraw-Hill HPD.

***Obstetrics & Gynecology: PreTest Self Assessment & Review.** 9th ed. Mark I. Evans. (Illus.). 240p. 2000. Price not set. (*0-07-135961-3*) McGraw.

Obstetrics & Gynecology: Principles for Practice. Frank Ling & Patrick Duff. (C). 2000. 135.00 (*0-8385-7201-4*) Appleton & Lange.

Obstetrics & Gynecology: Resident Survival Guide & Handbook for Clinicians. 4th ed. John D. Gordon et al. 177p. 1995. 12.95 (*0-9638338-0-4*) Stanford Bkstore.

Obstetrics & Gynecology: Review for New National Boards. Ralph L. Kramer. LC 96-75429. 1996. pap. text 25.00 (*0-9632873-9-7*) J & S Pub VA.

Obstetrics & Gynecology: The Clinical Core. 5th ed. Ralph M. Wynn. (Illus.). 400p. 1992. text 36.00 (*0-8121-1565-1*) Lppncott W & W.

Obstetrics & Gynecology Drug Handbook. 2nd ed. Gerald I. Zatuchni & Ramona I. Slupik. LC 95-224950. 560p. (C). (gr. 13). 1996. pap. text 33.95 (*0-8151-9894-9*, 24742) Mosby Inc.

Obstetrics & Gynecology for Medical Students. Charles R. Beckmann et al. (Illus.). 496p. 1992. pap. 33.00 (*0-683-00500-6*) Lppncott W & W.

Obstetrics & Gynecology On-Call. Ira R. Horowitz. (Illus.). 640p. (C). 1996. pap. text 27.95 (*0-8385-7174-3*, A7174-4) McGraw.

Obstetrics & Gynecology Recall. F. John Bourgeois et al. LC 97-10753. (Recall Ser.). (Illus.). 256p. 1997. pap. 27.00 (*0-683-18214-5*) Lppncott W & W.

Obstetrics & Gynecology Review. Arthur D. Sorosky. 1998. pap. text. write for info. (*0-7216-5083-X*, W B Saunders Co) Harcrt Hlth Sci Grp.

Obstetrics & Gynecology Review, 1996. Harrison H. Sheld. (Illus.). 656p. 1996. pap. text 48.00 (*0-07-057741-2*) McGraw-Hill HPD.

Obstetrics & Gynecology Two Thousand. Mishell. 2000. 79.00 (*0-8151-2200-4*, 31734) Mosby Inc.

Obstetrics & Gynecology Two Thousand & Two. Mishell. 2002. 79.00 (*0-8151-2207-1*, 31736) Mosby Inc.

Obstetrics & Newborn: Illustrated Text. 3rd ed. Norman A. Beischer. (Illus.). 1997. pap. text 55.00 (*0-7020-2123-7*) Bailliere Tindall.

Obstetrics & Perinatology: Current Topics. V. I. Kulakov. 1990. 81.00 (*0-8493-7125-2*, RG572) CRC Pr.

***Obstetrics Anesthesia.** David J. Birnbach et al. LC 99-462024. (Illus.). 795p. Date not set. text. write for info. (*0-443-06560-8*, W B Saunders Co) Harcrt Hlth Sci Grp.

Obstetrics by Ten Teachers. 16th ed. Ed. by Geoffrey V.P. Chamberlain. (Illus.). 384p. 1995. pap. text 29.50 (*0-340-57313-9*, Pub. by E A) OUP.

Obstetrics, Contraception & Gynecology. David Brown. 208p. 1976. pap. 42.95 (*0-8464-1430-9*) Beekman Pubs.

Obstetrics, Gynecology, & Infant Mortality. Wrynn Smith. LC 86-32838. (Profile of Health & Disease in America Ser.). 160p. 1987. reprint ed. pap. 49.60 (*0-608-02831-2*, 206389800007) Bks Demand.

***Obstetrics, Gynecology & Infertility: Handbook for Clinicians - Resident Survival Guide.** 5th ed. John David Gordon et al. (Illus.). 325p. 2000. pap. 14.95 (*0-9645467-6-0*) Scrub Hill.

Obstetrics Illustrated. 5th ed. Alistair W. Miller & Kevin P. Hanretty. LC 97-28645. 1997. pap. text 42.00 (*0-443-05041-4*) Church.

Obstetrics in Outline. Michael D. Read & Stuart Mellor. LC 85-9367. (Illus.). 264p. reprint ed. pap. 81.90 (*0-8357-3828-0*, 203655200004) Bks Demand.

***Obstetrics Manual.** 2nd ed. Michael Humphrey. (Illus.). 220p. 1999. pap. 49.95 (*0-07-470750-7*) McGraw.

***Obstinate Bear.** Clarine Morris. (Illus.). 12p. (J). 2000. pap. 3.00 (*0-9650312-8-4*) Cosmo Starr.

Obstructed Nasal Airway: Evaluation & Treatment. Thomas V. McCaffrey & Eugene B. Kern. 350p. 1997. text. write for info. (*0-7817-0193-7*) Lppncott W & W.

***Obstruction of Justice.** large type ed. Perri O'Shaughnessy. LC 99-86696. 2000. 26.95 (*1-56895-845-5*, Compass) Wheeler Pub.

Obstruction of Justice. Perri O'Shaughnessy. 512p. 1998. reprint ed. mass mkt. 7.50 (*0-440-22472-1*) Dell.

Obstruction of Justice by Religion: A Treatise on Religious Barbarities of the Common Law, & a Review of Judicial Oppressions of the Non-Religious in the U. S. Frank Swancara. LC 70-139581. (Civil Liberties in American History Ser.). (Illus.). 1971. reprint ed. lib. bdg. 35.00 (*0-306-71964-9*) Da Capo.

Obstruction of Peace: The U. S., Israel & the Palestinians. Naseer H. Aruri. 350p. 1995. text 29.95 (*1-56751-055-8*) Common Courage.

Obstruction of Peace: The U. S., Israel & the Palestinians. Naseer H. Aruri. 350p. 1995. pap. text 18.95 (*1-56751-054-X*) Common Courage.

Obstructive Lung Disease. Ed. by Stephen G. Jenkinson. (Contemporary Management in Internal Medicine Ser.: Vol. 2, No. 3). (Illus.). 150p. 1992. text 32.50 (*0-443-08872-1*) Church.

Obstructive Sleep Apnea Syndrome: Diagnosis & Treatment. B. Tucker Woodson et al. LC 96-28959. (Self-Instructional Package Ser.). (Illus.). 69p. (Orig.). 1996. pap. text 25.00 (*1-56772-050-1*) AAO-HNS.

Obstsorten Atlas (Fruit Atlas) R. Silbereisen et al. (GER., Illus.). 420p. 1996. 117.00 (*3-8001-5537-0*, Pub. by Eugen Ulmer) Balogh.

Obstsorten. 500 Obstsorten in Wirt und Bild. (Fruits. 500 Fruits in Words & Pictures) G. Friedrich & H. Petzold. (GER., Illus.). 624p. 1993. 40.00 (*3-7402-0134-7*, Pub. by Eugen Ulmer) Balogh.

Obtain the Power of God. Andrew Murray. 104p. 1997. mass mkt. 5.99 (*0-88368-501-9*) Whitaker Hse.

Obtaining a Writ of Attachment - Action Guide - Fall 1997. Peter M. Rehon. Ed. by Kay E. Tindel. 84p. 1997. ring bd. 58.00 (*0-7626-0155-8*, CP-11124) Cont Ed Bar-CA.

Obtaining a Writ of Possession Pts. 1 & 2: Summer, 1992, Action Guide. Peter M. Rehon. Ed. by Ellen C. Lester & Suzanne E. Graber. 70p. 1992. pap. text 52.00 (*0-88124-554-2*, CP-11352) Cont Ed Bar-CA.

Obtaining ABA Approval: A Reference Manual for Legal Assistant Educators. LC 89-80685. 99p. 1989. pap. 25.00 (*0-89707-474-2*, 423-0024) Amer Bar Assn.

Obtaining Agreement on Standards in the Accounting Profession. Maurice Moonitz. (Studies in Accounting Research: Vol. 8). 93p. 1974. 12.00 (*0-86539-020-7*) Am Accounting.

Obtaining & Using Medical Records in Massachusetts. Karen R. Stafford. LC 94-75468. 94p. 1994. pap. text 45.00 (*0-944490-62-X*) Mass CLE.

Obtaining Answers to Prayer see Praying That Receives Answers

Obtaining Answers to Prayer. E. M. Bounds. 140p. 1984. mass mkt. 5.99 (*0-88368-142-0*) Whitaker Hse.

Obtaining Appointment of a Receiver (And Monitoring the Receivership) Winter, 1993, Action Guide. Edythe L. Bronston. Ed. by Carolyn J. Stein. 142p. 1993. pap. text 52.00 (*0-88124-605-0*, CP-11242) Cont Ed Bar-CA.

Obtaining Bible Promises: A Different Approach for Every Promise. Roy H. Hicks. 105p. 1986. pap. 6.99 (*0-89274-426-X*) Harrison Hse.

Obtaining Credit Fast & Easy. Robert Lightfoot. 79p. 1992. pap. 10.95 (*0-939427-73-7*) Alpha Pubns OH.

Obtaining Discovery Pts. 1-2: Initiating & Responding to Discovery Procedures - Spring 1997 Action Guide, 2 vols. Jeffrey A. Tidus. Ed. by Norma Piatt. 158p. 1997. ring bd. 58.00 (*0-7626-0121-3*, CP-11463) Cont Ed Bar-CA.

Obtaining Discovery Pts. 1 & 2: Initiating & Responding to Discovery Procedures, Winter 1993, Action Guide. Jeffrey A. Tidus. Ed. by Deborah Magers-Rankin. 149p. 1993. pap. text 52.00 (*0-88124-592-5*, CP-11462) Cont Ed Bar-CA.

Obtaining, Enforcing & Defending Against Sanctions in State & Federal Court, Spring 1997 Action Guide, Pts. 1 & 2. William H. Slocumb et al. Ed. by Deborah Magers-Rankin. 124p. 1997. ring bd. 58.00 (*0-7626-0091-8*, CP-11731) Cont Ed Bar-CA.

Obtaining, Enforcing & Defending 209A Restraining Orders in Massachussetts. Andrea J. Cabral. LC 97-70632. 570p. 1997. ring bd. 75.00 (*1-57589-067-4*, 97-10.24-BK) Mass CLE.

Obtaining Evidence in Another Jurisdiction in Business Disputes. 2nd ed. Ed. by Charles Platto. (International Bar Association Ser.). 208p. (C). 1993. lib. bdg. 114.00 (*1-85333-758-7*, Pub. by Graham & Trotman) Kluwer Academic.

Obtaining Motor Vehicle Evidence from Tire Tracks & Tread Marks: A Complete Reference for Collecting, Recording, & Analyzing Track & Tread Evidence. Bruce W. Given et al. LC 77-78931. (Illus.). 96p. reprint ed. pap. 30.00 (*0-608-18152-8*, 203284100081) Bks Demand.

Obtaining Patents. Thomas A. Turano. Ed. by Stephanie Ostrove. 1997. 173.61 (*1-58012-000-8*) James Pub Santa Ana.

***Obtaining PRC Approvals for Foreign investment Enterprises & Infrastructure Projects.** 2nd ed. Asia Law & Practice Staff. 350p. 1999. pap. text 330.00 (*962-936-066-7*, Pub. by Asia Law & Practice) Am Educ Systs.

Obtaining Priesthood Power. Blaine Yorgenson & Brenton G. Yorgenson. (Gospel Power Ser.). 43p. 1990. pap. text 3.50 (*0-929985-14-1*) Jackman Pubng.

Obtaining Technical Assistance Module, PACE Level 1: A Program for Acquiring Competence in Entrepreneurship, 3 levels. rev. ed. National Center for Research in Vocational Educati. 1983. 2.50 (*0-317-06073-2*, RD240AB4) Ctr Educ Trng Employ.

O

An Asterisk (*) at the beginning of an entry indicates that the title is appearing for the first time.

Obtaining Technical Assistance Module, PACE Level 2: A Program for Acquiring Competence in Entrepreneurship, 3 levels. rev. ed. National Center for Research in Vocational Educati. 1983. 2.50 (*0-317-06074-0*, RD240BB4) Ctr Educ Trng Employ.

Obtaining Technical Assistance Module, PACE Level 3: A Program for Acquiring Competence in Entrepreneurship, 3 levels. rev. ed. National Center for Research in Vocational Educati. 1983. 2.50 (*0-317-06075-9*, RD240CB4) Ctr Educ Trng Employ.

Obtaining the Highest Price for Your Home. Jan Dickinson. 60p. 1986. 4.95 (*0-934701-05-9*) Wheatherstone Pr.

Obtaining, Using & Protecting Trademarks. Julie O. Petrini & Lawrence R. Robins. Ed. by Anne W. Hulecki. LC 97-70623. 96p. 1997. pap. text 65.00 (*1-57589-060-7*) Mass CLE.

Obtaining Venture Financing: Principles & Practices. James W. Henderson. 366p. 1991. pap. 17.95 (*0-669-27670-7*) Lxngtn Bks.

Obtaining Your Private Investigator's License. Orion Agency, Inc. Staff. 64p. (Orig.). 1986. pap. 10.00 (*0-87364-390-9*) Paladin Pr.

Obtenga Lo Mejor de Sus Hijos, Antes Que Acaben Con Usted. Kevin Leman.Tr. of Getting the Best out of Your Kids, Before They Get the Best of You. (SPA.). 192p. 1996. 8.99 (*0-88113-141-5*, B023-1415) Caribe Betania.

Obuda Jewish Census of 1850: Original Census with Alphabetical Index. Ed. & Tr. by Richard Panchyk. 100p. (Orig.). 1996. pap. 11.50 (*0-9622473-1-6*) No Ink.

Obviation in Romance: Diachronic & Synchronic Perspectives. Deborah L. Arteaga. 218p. (C). 1994. lib. bdg. 39.50 (*0-8191-9767-X*) U Pr of Amer.

Obvious Adams: The Story of a Successful Businessman. rev. ed. Robert R. Updegraff. 38p. 1980. pap. 3.50 (*0-9613203-0-3*) Updegraff.

***Obvious Enchantment.** Tucker Malarkey. LC 99-55334. 224p. 2000. 23.95 (*0-375-50409-5*) Random.

Obvious Letters: The Associative Alphabet Every Child Will Remember. Illus. by Ozzie Pardillo. 34p. (J). (ps-1). 1998. pap. 10.95 (*0-9664217-0-1*) Educ-Easy.

Obvious Proof. Gershon Robinson & Mordechai Steinman. LC 92-76188. (Illus.). 141p. (C). 1993. 13.95 (*1-56062-175-3*) CIS Comm.

Obyknovennaia Istoriia see Ordinary Story

Ocaho Indexed Decisions. Government Printing Office Staff. 1991. pap. 305.00 (*0-16-030567-5*) USGPO.

Ocana, Cadiz, Bussaco, Torres Vedras, Sept.-Dec., 1810 see History of the Peninsular War

O'Carolan Harp Tunes Dlcmr. Shelley Stevens. 40p. 1993. 15.95 incl. audio (*0-7866-1166-9*, 94885P); audio 9.98 (*1-56222-902-8*, 94885C) Mel Bay.

O'Carolan Harp Tunes Mountain. Shelley Stevens. 40p. 1993. pap. 6.95 (*1-56222-657-6*, 94885) Mel Bay.

O'Casey & Expressionism, Set. Nesta Jones. (Theatre in Focus Ser.). 1988. pap. write for info. incl. sl. (*0-85964-163-5*) Chadwyck-Healey.

O'Casey the Dramatist. Heinz Kosok. (Irish Literary Studies: Vol. # 19). 410p. 1985. 50.00 (*0-86140-168-9*, Pub. by Smyth) Dufour.

O'Casey's Satiric Vision. Bobby L. Smith. LC 78-10853. 210p. reprint ed. pap. 65.10 (*0-7837-1348-7*, 204149600020) Bks Demand.

OCAT: Optometry College (Admission Test) Practice Examination, No. 3. David M. Tarlow. (Practice Examination Ser.). 40p. 1992. pap. text 16.95 (*0-931572-47-9*) Datar Pub.

OCAT (Optometry College Admission Test) Practice Examination, No. 1. David M. Tarlow. (Practice Examination Ser.). 40p. 1992. pap. 16.95 (*0-931572-19-3*) Datar Pub.

OCAT (Optometry College Admission Test) Practice Examination, No. 2. David M. Tarlow. (Practice Examination Ser.). 40p. 1992. pap. 16.95 (*0-931572-20-7*) Datar Pub.

OCAT (Optometry College Admission Test) Practice Examination, No. 4. David M. Tarlow. (Practice Examination Ser.). 40p. 1992. pap. 16.95 (*0-931572-17-7*) Datar Pub.

OCAT (Optometry College Admission Test) Practice Examination, No. 5. David M. Tarlow. (Practice Examination Ser.). 40p. 1992. pap. 16.95 (*0-931572-18-5*) Datar Pub.

OCAT Practice Examination: Annotated Master Answer Guide, No. 1. David M. Tarlow. 1992. 4.95 (*0-931572-42-8*) Datar Pub.

OCAT Practice Examination: Annotated Master Answer Guide, No. 2. David M. Tarlow. 1992. 4.95 (*0-931572-43-6*) Datar Pub.

OCAT Practice Examination: Annotated Master Answer Guide, No. 3. David M. Tarlow. 1992. 4.95 (*0-931572-44-4*) Datar Pub.

OCAT Practice Examination: Annotated Master Answer Guide, No. 4. David M. Tarlow. 1992. 4.95 (*0-931572-45-2*) Datar Pub.

OCAT Practice Examination: Annotated Master Answer Guide, No. 5. David M. Tarlow. 1992. 4.95 (*0-931572-46-0*) Datar Pub.

Occam & the Transputer: Current Developments. Ed. by Janet Edwards. (Transputer & Occam Engineering Ser.). 248p. (gr. 12). 1991. 75.00 (*90-5199-063-4*, Pub. by IOS Pr) IOS Press.

Occam & the Transputer: Research & Applications. Ed. by C. Askew. (Transputer & Occam Engineering Ser.). 176p. (gr. 12). 1988. pap. 50.00 (*90-5199-010-3*, Pub. by IOS Pr) IOS Press.

Occam-2. 2nd ed. John Galletly. 288p. (Orig.). 1996. pap. 37.95 (*1-85728-362-7*, Pub. by UCL Pr Ltd) Taylor & Francis.

Occam's Razor. Bill Jay. (Illus.). 144p. 17.95 (*3-923922-13-2*, Pub. by Nazraeli Pr) Dist Art Pubs.

Occam's Razor. Bill Jay. 1996. 26.95 (*3-923922-12-4*, Pub. by Nazraeli Pr) Dist Art Pubs.

Occam's Razor. Archer Mayor. LC 99-26221. 352p. 1999. 23.95 (*0-89296-682-3*, Pub. by Mysterious Pr) Little.

***Occam's Razor.** Archer Mayor. 2000. mass mkt. 6.99 (*0-446-60887-4*) Warner Bks.

Occasion Fleeting: The Story of the 33rd Fighter Group in WW II As Told in the Diary of the Flight Surgeon. (Illus.). 320p. 1997. pap. 24.95 (*0-9661587-0-9*) Appaguag.

Occasion for War: Ethnic Conflict in Lebanon & Damascus in 1860. Leila T. Fawaz. LC 94-1941. 300p. 1995. pap. 18.95 (*0-520-20086-1*, Pub. by U CA Pr) Cal Prin Full Svc.

Occasion Manquee? 1922 (A Missed Opportunity?) La Reconstruction de l'Europe (The Reconstruction of Europe) Ed. by Marta Petricioli. (FRE.). 512p. 1995. 55.95 (*3-906754-15-4*, Pub. by P Lang) P Lang Pubng.

Occasion of Sin. Andrew M. Greeley. 336p. 1992. mass mkt. 5.99 (*0-515-10894-4*, Jove) Berkley Pub.

Occasion of Sin. John Montague. LC 94-176670. 200p. 1992. pap. 12.00 (*1-877727-21-0*) White Pine.

Occasion of Sin. large type ed. Rachel Billington. 512p. 1984. 11.50 (*0-7089-1123-4*) Ulverscroft.

Occasion of Sin. large type ed. Andrew M. Greeley. LC 91-29255. 557p. 1992. lib. bdg. 14.95 (*1-56054-954-8*) Thorndike Pr.

Occasion Setting: Associative Learning & Cognition in Animals. Ed. by Nestor Schmajuk & Peter C. Holland. LC 97-47677. 440p. 1998. 49.95 (*1-55798-490-5*) Am Psychol.

Occasional Address (with William Carey) Laurence Hutton. (Notable American Authors Ser.). 1992. reprint ed. lib. bdg. 75.00 (*0-7812-3309-7*) Rprt Serv.

Occasional Addresses, 1893 to 1916. Herbert H. Asquith. LC 76-99715. (Essay Index Reprint Ser.). 1977. reprint ed. 20.95 (*0-8369-1368-X*) Ayer.

Occasional Cow. Polly Horvath. (Illus.). 112p. (J). (gr. 3-7). 1991. pap. 3.95 (*0-374-45573-2*, Sunburst Bks) FS&G.

Occasional Form: Henry Fielding & the Chains of Circumstance. J. Paul Hunter. LC 75-11337. 280p. reprint ed. pap. 86.80 (*0-608-06102-6*, 206643400008) Bks Demand.

Occasional Hell. Randall Silvis. LC 92-31129. 256p. 1993. 22.00 (*1-877946-24-9*) Permanent Pr.

***Occasional Paper: Energy E-Commerce.** Peter C. Fusaro & Jeremy Wilcox. 20p. 2000. pap. 10.00 (*0-918714-58-3*) Intl Res Ctr Energy.

Occasional Paper Series - Entire Series - Through 1992, 152 papers, Set. 1992. 75.00 (*0-685-66555-0*) U KS Nat Hist Mus.

Occasional Papers & Addresses of an American Lawyer. Henry W. Taft. xxiii, 331p. 1997. reprint ed. 95.00 (*1-56169-303-0*) Gaunt.

Occasional Papers in Sociology & Anthropology, Vol. 5. Ratna Pustak Bhandar. 1996. pap. 27.00 (*0-7855-7468-9*, Pub. by Ratna Pustak Bhandar) St Mut.

Occasional Readings: Lectionary Texts for Various Occasions & Occasional Services in the New Revised Standard Version of the Bible. Episcopal Church Staff. LC 98-199779. 264 p. 1992. write for info. (*0-89869-234-2*) Church Pub Inc.

Occasional Thoughts on Universities in the German Sense: With an Appendix Regarding a University Soon to Be Established (1808) Tr. by Terrence N. Tice & Edwina Lawler from GER. LC 91-24690. 108p. 1991. pap. 39.95 (*0-7734-9899-0*) E Mellen.

Occasional Trainer's Handbook. Rebecca Bullard et al. LC 93-36515. 264p. 1994. 39.95 (*0-87778-270-9*) Educ Tech Pubns.

***Occasional Vegetarian.** Karen Lee & Diane Porter. 272p. 1998. mass mkt. 15.99 (*0-446-67452-4*, Pub. by Warner Bks) Little.

Occasional Vegetarian: More Than 200 Robust Dishes to Satisfy Both Full & Part-time Vegetarians. Karen Lee & Diana Porter. 272p. 1995. 24.95 (*0-446-51792-5*, Pub. by Warner Bks) Little.

***Occasionally Yours (& Others) The Occasional Verse of Kevin Di Camillo, 1990-99.** Kevin Di Camillo. (Illus.). 32p. 1999. pap. 20.00 (*0-930126-58-0*) Typographeum.

Occasione fa il Ladro, Ossia il Cambio della Valigia. Gioachino Rossini. Ed. by Giovanni C. Ballola et al. 168p. 1995. lib. bdg. 135.00 (*0-226-72849-8*) U Ch Pr.

Occasions. Holbrook Jackson. LC 77-93347. (Essay Index Reprint Ser.). 1977. 19.95 (*0-8369-1299-3*) Ayer.

Occasions. Eugenio Montale. Tr. & Pref. by William Arrowsmith. LC 86-16269.Tr. of Le/Occasion. 169p. 1987. pap. 9.95 (*0-393-30324-1*) Norton.

Occasions for Joy: Poems. Winifred Rawlins. LC 95-67768. 49p. 1995. pap. 4.50 (*0-938875-34-5*) Pittenbruach Pr.

Occasions for Philosophy. 2nd ed. James C. Edwards & Douglas M. MacDonald. 608p. (C). 1984. pap. text 31.60 (*0-13-629262-3*) P-H.

Occasions of Grace. Roger White. 200p. 1992. 21.95 (*0-85398-345-3*); pap. 11.95 (*0-85398-346-1*) G Ronald Pub.

Occasions of Grace: An Historical & Theological Study of the Pastoral Offices & Episcopal Services in the Book of Common Prayer. Byron D. Stuhlman. LC 95-83254. 381p. 1995. 29.95 (*0-89869-238-5*) Church Pub Inc.

Occasions of Grace: Poems by David Glotzer. David Glotzer. (Illus.). 1978. boxed set 75.00 (*0-685-27834-4*) Heron Pr.

Occasions of Grace: Poems by David Glotzer. deluxe ed. David Glotzer. (Illus.). 1978. 110.00 (*0-685-27835-2*) Heron Pr.

Occasions of Identity: A Study in the Metaphysics of Persistence, Change, & Sameness. Andre Gallois. LC 97-24226. 310p. 1998. text 65.00 (*0-19-823744-8*) OUP.

Occasions of Poetry: Essays in Criticism & Autobiography. Thom Gunn. LC 98-53787. (Poets on Poetry Ser.). 192p. 1999. pap. 14.95 (*0-472-08583-2*, 08583) U of Mich Pr.

Occasions of Prayer: Resources for Prayerful Life. Lisa Withrow. 128p. 1999. pap. 15.95 (*0-8298-1365-9*) Pilgrim OH.

Occassions of Faith: An Anthropology of Irish Catholics. Lawrence J. Taylor. LC 95-3032. (Contemporary Ethnography Ser.). (Illus.). 282p. 1995. text 39.95 (*0-8122-3295-X*); pap. text 17.95 (*0-8122-1520-6*) U of Pa Pr.

Occhiali e Lenti a Contatto Nello Sport see Eyewear & Contact Lenses for Sports

Occidental Gleanings: Sketches & Essays, 2 Vols. Lafcadio Hearn. Ed. by Albert Mordell. LC 67-30217. (Essay Index Reprint Ser.). 1977. 35.95 (*0-8369-0525-3*) Ayer.

Occidental Ideographs: Image, Sequence, & Literary History. Franklin R. Rogers. LC 89-45972. 288p. 1991. 39.50 (*0-8387-5179-2*) Bucknell U Pr.

Occidental Petroleum Corp. A Report on the Company's Environmental Policies & Practices. (Illus.). 39p. (C). 1994. reprint ed. pap. text 40.00 (*0-7881-0981-2*, Coun on Econ) DIANE Pub.

Occidental Poetics: Tradition & Progress. Lubomir Dolezel. LC 89-32798. 271p. 1990. reprint ed. pap. 84.10 (*0-608-03491-6*, 206420600008) Bks Demand.

Occidentalism: A Theory of Counter-Discourse in Post-Mao China. Xiaomei Chen. LC 93-44883. (Illus.). 256p. 1995. text 45.00 (*0-19-508579-5*) OUP.

Occidentalism: Images of the West. Ed. by James G. Carrier. 282p. 1995. pap. text 19.95 (*0-19-827979-5*) OUP.

Occidentalism: Islamic Art in the 19th Century. Stephen Vernoit. (The Nasser D. Khalili Collection of Islamic Art: Vol. XXIII). (Illus.). 256p. 1998. text 260.00 (*0-19-727620-2*) OUP.

Occipital Seizures & Epilepsies in Children. Frederick Andermann. 256p. 68.00 (*0-86196-385-7*, Pub. by J Libbey Med) Bks Intl VA.

Occitan sans Peine: Occidental for French Speakers. Assimil Staff. (FRE.). 28.95 (*0-8288-4471-2*, F48570) Fr & Eur.

Occitan Translations of John XII & XIII-XVII from a Fourteenth-Century Franciscan Codex. M. Roy Harris. LC 84-45905. (Transactions Ser.: Vol. 75, Pt. 4). 1985. pap. 20.00 (*0-87169-754-8*, T754-HAR) Am Philos.

Occlusal Correction: Principles & Practice. Albert J. Solnit & Curnette. (Illus.). 413p. 1988. text 136.00 (*0-86715-161-7*) Quint Pub Co.

Occlusal Guidance in Pediatric Dentistry. M. Nakata & Stephen H. Wei. (Illus.). 100p. 1988. 30.00 (*0-912791-63-2*, Ishiyaku EuroAmerica) Med Dent Media.

Occlusal Registration in Edentulous Patients. Toshio Hosoi. LC 95-79130. (Dental Technique Ser.: Vol. 5). (Illus.). 56p. (C). 1995. pap. text 30.00 (*1-56386-024-4*, Ishiyaku EuroAmerica) Med Dent Media.

Occlusal Treatment: Preventive & Corrective Occlusal Adjustment. Norman R. Arnold & Sanford C. Frumker. LC 75-1306. 174p. reprint ed. pap. 54.00 (*0-608-17754-7*, 205650000069) Bks Demand.

Occlusion. unabridged ed. Margeaux Herman. 219p. 1999. pap. 11.95 (*1-893667-02-2*) Sugar Mtn.

Occlusion. 4th ed. Sigurd P. Ramfjord & Major M. Ash. LC 94-7653. 1994. text 75.00 (*0-7216-5591-2*, W B Saunders Co) Harcrt Hlth Sci Grp.

Occlusion: Principles & Assessment. Iven Klineberg. (Illus.). 263p. 1992. pap. text 85.00 (*0-7236-0990-X*) Buttrwrth-Heinemann.

Occlusion: Principles & Concepts. 2nd ed. Jose Dos Santos. LC 96-77392. (Illus.). xi, 147p. 1996. pap. 34.50 (*1-56386-035-X*, Ishiyaku EuroAmerica) Med Dent Media.

Occlusion: Principles & Concepts. 2nd rev. ed. Jose Dos Santos, Jr. (Illus.). xi, 147p. 1996. pap. text 34.50 (*1-891949-00-4*) Med Dent Media.

Occu-Facts: Facts on over 565 Occupations. Ed. by Elizabeth Handville. 624p. (Orig.). (J). (gr. 6 up). 1989. pap. text 38.00 (*0-9623657-0-X*) Careers Inc.

Occular Pathology. 4th ed. Myron Yanoff & Ben S. Fine. 1995. text 227.00 (*0-7234-2199-4*) Wolfe Pubng AZ.

Occult see Ocultismo

Occult, 34 vols. James H. Webb, Jr. write for info. (*0-318-59759-4*, 490) Ayer.

Occult ABC. Kurt E. Koch. LC 78-5066. Orig. Title: Satan's Devices. 348p. 1981. pap. 14.99 (*0-8254-3031-3*) Kregel.

Occult Anatomy & the Bible. Corinne Heline. 365p. (Orig.). 1991. reprint ed. pap. text 20.00 (*0-933963-20-3*) New Age Bible.

Occult & Curative Powers of Precious Stones. William T. Fernie. 496p. 1987. pap. 17.95 (*0-89345-230-0*, Steinerbks) Garber Comm.

***Occult & the New Age Movement: A Devil's Brew.** J. D. Kallmyer. 144p. 2000. pap. 10.95 (*0-9657682-5-2*) Moriah Pr.

Occult Arts. J. W. Frings. 236p. 1981. pap. 20.00 (*0-89540-108-8*, SB-108) Sun Pub.

Occult Arts: An Examination of the Claims Made for the Existence & Practice of Supernormal Powers. J. W. Frings. 236p. 1996. reprint ed. pap. 18.95 (*1-56459-620-6*) Kessinger Pub.

Occult Arts of Ancient Egypt. Bernard Bromage. 205p. 1996. pap. 17.00 (*0-89540-219-X*, SB-219) Sun Pub.

Occult Bibliography. Jill Phillips. 1975. lib. bdg. 250.00 (*0-8490-0748-8*) Gordon Pr.

Occult Bibliography: An Annotated List of Books Published in English, 1971 Through 1975. Thomas C. Clarie. LC 78-17156. 482p. 1978. 37.00 (*0-8108-1152-9*) Scarecrow.

Occult Bondage & Deliverance. Kurt E. Koch. LC 72-160691. 208p. 1972. pap. 9.99 (*0-8254-3006-2*) Kregel.

Occult Causes of Disease. E. Wolfram & B. Von Hohenheim. 1991. lib. bdg. 79.00 (*0-8490-4134-1*) Gordon Pr.

Occult Causes of Disease. E. Wolfram. 269p. 1996. reprint ed. spiral bd. 18.50 (*0-7873-0978-8*) Hlth Research.

Occult Causes of Disease Being a Compendium of the Teachings of Paracelsus. E. Wolfram. 296p. 1995. reprint ed. pap. 17.95 (*1-56459-506-4*) Kessinger Pub.

Occult Causes of the Present War. Lewis Spence. 144p. 1997. reprint ed. pap. 19.95 (*0-7661-0051-0*) Kessinger Pub.

Occult Chemistry. 3rd ed. Annie W. Besant & C. W. Leadbeater. 397p. 1998. reprint ed. pap. 34.50 (*0-7873-0106-X*) Hlth Research.

Occult Chemistry: Clairvoyant Observations on the Chemical Elements. rev. ed. Annie W. Besant & Charles W. Leadbeater. 170p. 1996. reprint ed. spiral bd. 16.50 (*0-7873-0108-6*) Hlth Research.

Occult Chemistry: Investigations by Clairvoyant Magnification into the Structure of the Atoms of the Periodic Table & of Some Compounds. 3rd ed. Annie W. Besant & C. W. Leadbeater. 404p. 1996. reprint ed. pap. 29.95 (*1-56459-678-8*) Kessinger Pub.

Occult Christ: Angelic Mysteries: The Divine Feminine. Ted Andrews. LC 93-3724. (Illus.). 224p. 1999. pap. 12.95 (*0-87542-019-2*) Llewellyn Pubns.

Occult Conspiracy: Secret Societies - Their Influence & Power in World History. Michael Howard. LC 97-72753. (Illus.). 224p. 1997. 6.98 (*1-56731-225-X*, MJF Bks) Fine Comms.

Occult Conspiracy: Secret Societies - Their Influence & Power in World History. Michael Howard. LC 88-35174. (Illus.). 206p. 1989. pap. text 12.95 (*0-89281-251-6*, Destiny Bks) Inner Tradit.

Occult Crime: A Law Enforcement Primer. 50p. (Orig.). (C). 1993. pap. text 20.00 (*1-56806-860-3*) DIANE Pub.

Occult Exercises & Practices: Gateways to the Four Worlds of Occultism. Gareth Knight. (Illus.). 92p. (Orig.). 1997. pap. 9.95 (*0-9650839-6-9*) Sun Chalice.

Occult Explosion. David Marshall. 1998. pap. 10.99 (*1-873796-68-4*) Review & Herald.

Occult Family Physician & Botanic Guide to Health. Antonette Matteson. 1992. lib. bdg. 89.95 (*0-8490-8744-9*) Gordon Pr.

Occult Family Physician & Botanic Guide to Health. Antonette Matteson. 317p. 1996. reprint ed. spiral bd. 22.50 (*0-7873-0587-1*) Hlth Research.

Occult Family Physician & Botanic Guide to Health: A Description of American & Foreign Plants & Their Medical Virtues. enl. rev. ed. Antonette Matteson. (Illus.). 327p. 1993. reprint ed. pap. 12.50 (*0-916638-24-3*) Meyerbooks.

Occult Family Physician & Botanic Guide to Health, 1894. Antonette Matteson. 324p. 1996. reprint ed. pap. 24.95 (*1-56459-709-1*) Kessinger Pub.

Occult Geometry & Hermetic Science of Motion & Number. A. S. Raleigh. 208p. 1991. reprint ed. pap. 11.95 (*0-87516-639-3*) DeVorss.

Occult Glossary: A Compendium of Oriental & Theosophical Terms. 2nd ed. G. De Purucker. LC 96-41435. 204p. 1996. reprint ed. 17.95 (*1-55700-050-6*); reprint ed. pap. 11.95 (*1-55700-051-4*) Theos U Pr.

Occult History: Historical Personalities & Events in the Light of Spiritual Science. Rudolf Steiner. Tr. by Dorothy S. Osmond et al from GER. 127p. 1982. reprint ed. pap. 9.95 (*0-85440-371-X*, Pub. by R Steiner Pr) Anthroposophic.

Occult Hypnotism. Robert G. Chaney. (Adventures in Esoteric Learning Ser.). 46p. 1958. pap. 4.95 (*0-918936-15-2*) Astara.

Occult in America: New Historical Perspectives. Ed. by Howard Kerr & Charles L. Crow. LC 82-24770. (Illus.). 256p. 1986. pap. 11.95 (*0-252-01360-3*) U of Ill Pr.

Occult in Early Modern Europe: A Documentary History. P. G. Maxwell-Stuart. LC 98-7748. (Documents in History Ser.). 264p. 1999. pap. 21.95 (*0-312-21753-6*); text 65.00 (*0-312-21752-8*) St Martin.

Occult in Russian & Soviet Culture. Ed. by Bernice G. Rosenthal. LC 96-37566. (Illus.). 480p. 1996. pap. 24.95 (*0-8014-8331-X*); text 59.95 (*0-8014-3258-8*) Cornell U Pr.

Occult Interpretation of the Book of Revelation. 76p. (Orig.). 1993. reprint ed. spiral bd. 11.00 (*0-7873-0035-7*) Hlth Research.

Occult Interpretations. John P. Scott. 68p. 1999. reprint ed. pap. 7.50 (*0-7661-0817-1*) Kessinger Pub.

Occult Invasion: The Subtle Seduction of the World & the Church. Dave Hunt. LC 94-22653. 450p. 1997. pap. 14.99 (*1-56507-269-3*) Harvest Hse.

Occult Japan. Percival Lowell. (Illus.). 400p. 1990. pap. 12.95 (*0-89281-306-7*) Inner Tradit.

***Occult Laboratory: Magic, Science & Second Sight in Late Seventeenth-Century Scotland.** Michael C. W. Hunter & Robert Kirk. LC 00-44469. (Illus.). 2001. write for info. (*0-85115-801-3*) Boydell & Brewer.

Occult Lines Behind Life. M. P. Pandit. 100p. (Orig.). 1992. reprint ed. pap. 7.95 (*0-941524-35-3*) Lotus Pr.

Occult Methods of Healing. Jane K. Adams. 54p. 1997. reprint ed. pap. 9.95 (*0-7661-0066-9*) Kessinger Pub.

Occult Movement in the 19th Century. Rudolf Steiner. 190p. 1973. 16.95 (*0-85440-280-2*, Pub. by R Steiner Pr) Anthroposophic.

Occult Nodal Metastasis in Solid Carcinomata: Second International Symposium on Celluar Oncology, 5. Ed. by Peter Moloy & Garth L. Nicolson. LC 87-15764. 267p. 1987. 75.00 (*0-275-92665-6*, C2665, Praeger Pubs) Greenwood.

An Asterisk (*) at the beginning of an entry indicates that the title is appearing for the first time.

Occult-Paranormal Bibliography: An Annotated List of Books Published in English, 1976-1981. Thomas C. Clarie. LC 83-20319. 579p. 1984. 45.00 (0-8108-1674-1) Scarecrow.

***Occult Phenomena.** Alois Wiesinger. 294p. 1999. reprint ed. 24.95 (0-912141-80-8) Roman Cath Bks.

Occult Phenomena, Mysteries & Philosophy. Mary Elsnau. 67p. 1996. reprint ed. spiral bd. 10.00 (0-7873-0314-3) Hlth Research.

Occult Philosophy. Isabella Ingalese. 321p. 1996. reprint ed. spiral bd. 17.50 (0-7873-1201-0) Hlth Research.

Occult Philosophy. Isabella Ingalese. 336p. 1997. reprint ed. pap. 16.95 (0-7661-0030-8) Kessinger Pub.

Occult Philosophy Bk. 4: Of Geomancy, Magical Elements, Astrological Geomancy, the Nature of Spirits, Magic of the Ancients. Henry Cornelius Agrippa. 217p. 1992. reprint ed. pap. 19.95 (1-56459-170-0) Kessinger Pub.

Occult Philosophy Elizabethan. Frances Amelia Yates. 1985. 20.00 (0-7100-0320-X, Routledge Thoemms) Routledge.

***Occult Philosophy in the Elizabethan Age, Vol. 7.** Frances A. Yates. LC 99-15954. (Selected Works). 1999. write for info. (0-415-22050-5) Routledge.

***Occult Power of Gems.** Manik C. Jain. 1998. 30.00 (0-8364-5512-6) S Asia.

Occult Power of Numbers. W. Westcott. 1998. pap. text 9.95 (0-87877-243-X) Newcastle Pub.

Occult Powers & Hypotheses: Cartesian Natural Philosophy under Louis XIV. Desmond M. Clarke. 276p. 1989. text 85.00 (0-19-824812-1) OUP.

Occult Powers in Nature & in Man. Hodson. 1988. 5.50 (0-8356-7085-6, Quest) Theos Pub Hse.

Occult Practices & Beliefs. Kurt E. Koch. LC 76-160692. 160p. 1972. pap. 8.99 (0-8254-3004-6) Kregel.

Occult Reading & Occult Hearing. Rudolf Steiner. Tr. by Dorothy S. Osmond from GER. 79p. 1975. pap. 7.95 (0-85440-286-1, Pub. by Steiner Book Centre) Anthroposophic.

Occult Review. Ed. by Ralph Shirley. 82p. 1998. reprint ed. pap. 12.95 (0-7661-0470-2) Kessinger Pub.

Occult Roots of Nazism: Secret Aryan Cults & Their Influence on Nazi Ideology. Nicholas Goodrick-Clarke. (Illus.). 293p. (C). 1992. text 45.00 (0-8147-3054-X) NYU Pr.

Occult Roots of Nazism: Secret Aryan Cults & Their Influence on Nazi Ideology. Nicholas Goodrick-Clarke. (Illus.). 293p. (C). 1993. pap. 17.95 (0-8147-3060-4) NYU Pr.

Occult Science & Occult Development: Christ at the Time of the Mystery of Golgotha & Christ in the Twentieth Century. Rudolf Steiner. 36p. 1983. pap. 8.95 (0-85440-413-9, Pub. by R Steiner Pr) Anthroposophic.

Occult Science in India & among the Ancients with an Account of Their Mystic Initiations & the History of Spiritism. Louis Jacolliot. Tr. by William L. Felt. 276p. 1994. reprint ed. pap. 17.95 (1-56459-452-1) Kessinger Pub.

Occult Science in Medicine. Franz Hartmann. 1991. lib. bdg. 79.95 (0-8490-4996-2) Gordon Pr.

Occult Science in Medicine. Franz Hartmann. 100p. 1996. reprint ed. spiral bd. 11.00 (0-7873-0380-1) Hlth Research.

Occult Science in Medicine. Franz Hartmann. 100p. 1993. reprint ed. pap. 9.95 (1-56459-355-X) Kessinger Pub.

Occult Science of Jewels: The Symbolism of Precious Stones. Grand Orient. Ed. by J. D. Holmes. 1995. pap. 6.95 (1-55818-316-7, Sure Fire) Holmes Pub.

Occult Science or Hidden Forces. L. H. Anderson et al. 271p. 1955. 9.95 (0-932785-35-2) Philos Pub.

Occult Science or Hidden Forces. deluxe ed. L. H. Anderson et al. 271p. 1955. lthr. 20.00 (0-932785-97-2) Philos Pub.

Occult Sciences: A Compendium of Transcendental Doctrine & Experiment. Arthur E. Waite. 292p. 1996. reprint ed. spiral bd. 22.50 (0-7873-0918-4) Hlth Research.

Occult Sciences: A Compendium of Transcendental Doctrine & Experiment. Arthur E. Waite. 300p. 1993. reprint ed. pap. 19.95 (1-56459-369-X) Kessinger Pub.

Occult Sciences in Atlantis. Lewis Spence. 136p. 1996. reprint ed. pap. 14.00 (0-7873-1292-4) Hlth Research.

Occult Sciences in Atlantis. Lewis Spence. 136p. 1996. reprint ed. pap. 12.95 (1-56459-585-4) Kessinger Pub.

Occult Significance of Blood. Rudolf Steiner. 44p. 1996. reprint ed. spiral bd. 9.50 (0-7873-0836-6) Hlth Research.

Occult Significance of Blood, 1907. Rudolf Steiner. 50p. 1996. reprint ed. pap. 8.25 (1-56459-911-6) Kessinger Pub.

Occult Significance of Forgiveness. 3rd ed. Sergei O. Prokofieff. Tr. by Simon B. De Lange from RUS. 208p. 1995. 31.95 (0-904693-71-6, Pub. by Temple Lodge) Anthroposophic.

Occult Significance of UFO's. Douglas M. Baker. 1979. pap. 12.50 (0-906006-43-0, Pub. by Baker Pubns) New Leaf Dist.

Occult Tales. Helena P. Blavatsky & W. Q. Judge. 226p. 1996. reprint ed. pap. 19.95 (1-56459-694-X) Kessinger Pub.

Occult Teachings Extracted from the Mahatma Letters to A. P. Sinnett. Ed. by J. R. Zulueta & Trevor A. Barker. LC 94-27007. 360p. 1995. 23.50 (0-944957-24-2) Rivercross Pub.

Occult Technology of Power. Alpine Enterprises Staff. 62p. (Orig.). 1974. pap. text 8.00 (1-55950-009-3) Loompanics.

Occult Technology of Power. 4th ed. (Ruling Class Expose Ser.). 1978. 8.95 (0-317-01977-5) A-albionic Res.

Occult Theocracy. Edith S. Miller, pseud. 741p. 1933. 25.00 (0-913022-37-3) CPA Bk Pub.

Occult Theocracy, 2 vols. Lady Queenborough. 1972. 500.00 (0-8490-0751-8) Gordon Pr.

Occult Theocracy. unabridged ed. Lady Queenborough. 741p. 1933. reprint ed. 30.00 (0-945001-23-1) GSG & Assocs.

Occult Theocrasy. Lady Queenborough & Edith Starr Miller. 741p. 1995. 25.00 (0-944379-15-X) CPA Bk Pub.

Occult Training of the Hindus see Seven Schools of Yoga: An Introduction

Occult Traumatic Lesions of the Cervical & Thoraco-Lumbar Vertebrae. 2nd ed. Martin S. Abel. 392p. 1983. 42.50 (0-87527-312-2) Green.

Occult View of Health & Disease. Geoffrey Hodson. 31p. 1996. reprint ed. spiral bd. 10.00 (0-7873-0411-5) Hlth Research.

Occult View of Health & Disease (1925) Geoffrey Hodson. 64p. 1999. reprint ed. pap. 14.95 (0-7661-0835-X) Kessinger Pub.

Occult View of the War. C. W. Leadbeater. 24p. 1997. reprint ed. pap. 9.95 (0-7661-0057-X) Kessinger Pub.

Occult Way. Bowen. 1978. pap. 14.95 (0-7229-5071-3) Theos Pub Hse.

Occult Way. Bowen. 1978. 14.95 (0-7229-5096-9) Theos Pub Hse.

Occult World. 4th ed. A. P. Sinnett. 160p. 1996. reprint ed. spiral bd. 15.00 (0-7873-0798-X) Hlth Research.

Occult World. 9th ed. A. P. Sinnett. 1969. pap. 12.95 (0-7229-0080-5) Theos Pub Hse.

Occult World, 1884. A. P. Sinnett. 176p. 1996. reprint ed. pap. 11.00 (1-56459-736-9) Kessinger Pub.

Occult World of Madame Blavatsky: Reminiscences & Impressions by Those Who Knew Her. Ed. by Daniel H. Caldwell. (Illus.). 336p. (Orig.). 1991. pap. 13.95 (0-941657-04-3) Impossible Dream.

Occultism. 4th ed. Sri Aurobindo & Mother. Ed. by Vijay. 28p. 1997. pap. 1.00 (81-7060-108-8, Pub. by SAA) E-W Cultural Ctr.

Occultism: An Alternative to Scientific Humanism. Cyril Scott. 16p. 1996. reprint ed. spiral bd. 8.00 (0-7873-1289-4) Hlth Research.

Occultism Applied to Daily Life: How to Increase Your Happiness, Usefulness & Spirituality, Lessons 141-50. C. C. Zain. (Brotherhood of Light Home Study Ser.: Course 14). (Illus.). 1996. pap. 16.95 (0-87887-354-6) Church of Light.

Occultism in Avant-Garde Art: The Case of Joseph Beuys. John F. Moffitt. Ed. by Stephen Foster. LC 88-5774. (Studies in the Fine Arts: The Avant-Garde: No. 63). 238p. reprint ed. 73.80 (0-8357-1881-6, 207067400016) Bks Demand.

Occultism in the Shakespeare Plays. L. W. Rogers. 50p. 1993. reprint ed. pap. 6.00 (1-56459-401-7) Kessinger Pub.

Occultism Simplified: The Mystic Thesaurus. Willis F. Whitehead. 96p. 1996. reprint ed. spiral bd. 11.50 (0-7873-0964-8) Hlth Research.

Occultism Simplified: or the Mystic Thesaurus. Willis F. Whitehead. (Illus.). 96p. 1994. reprint ed. pap. 9.95 (1-56459-467-X) Kessinger Pub.

Occultism, Witchcraft, & Cultural Fashion: Essays in Comparative Religions. Mircea Eliade. LC 75-12230. 158p. 1978. reprint ed. pap. text 18.00 (0-226-20392-1, P755) U Ch Pr.

Occultismus des Altertums, 2 vols. Karl Kiesewetter. LC 75-36846. (Occult Ser.). (GER.). 1976. reprint ed. 76.95 (0-405-07958-3) Ayer.

Occultismus des Altertums. Karl Kiesewetter. xxiv, 921p. 1987. reprint ed. write for info. (3-487-06056-6) G Olms Pubs.

Occultists & Mystics of All Ages. Ralph Shirley. 175p. 1981. pap. 15.00 (0-89540-083-9, SB-083) Sun Pub.

Occupancy Director. Jack Rudman. (Career Examination Ser.: C-3736). 1994. pap. 39.95 (0-8373-3736-4) Nat Learn.

Occupancy Sensors. Richard K. Miller & Marcia E. Rupnow. LC 89-85424. (Survey on Technology & Markets Ser.: No. 116). 50p. 1991. pap. text 200.00 (1-55865-139-X) Future Tech Surveys.

Occupant Containment & Methods of Assessing Occupant Protection in the Crash Development: SAE International Congress & Exposition 1994, 12 papers. (Special Publications). 103p. 1994. pap. 40.00 (1-56091-497-1, SP-1045) Soc Auto Engineers.

Occupant Control of Supply Air Diffusers. P. J. Fishwick. 1993. pap. 60.00 (0-86022-335-3, Pub. by Build Servs Info Assn) St Mut.

Occupant Protection. (Special Publications). 230p. 1999. pap. 95.00 (0-7680-0364-4, SP-1432) Soc Auto Engineers.

Occupant Protection & Injury Assessment in the Automotive Crash Environment. 1997. 94.00 (1-56091-943-4) Soc Auto Engineers.

Occupant Protection Technologies for Frontal Impact: Current Needs & Expectations for the 21st Century-1996 International Congress & Exposition. LC 96-207934. (Special Publications). 113p. 1996. pap. 49.00 (1-56091-774-1, SP-1144) Soc Auto Engineers.

Occupation. Shehadeh. 1997. pap. text 30.00 (90-411-0618-9) Kluwer Academic.

Occupation. Arnold Skemer. LC 96-67250. 112p. (Orig.). 1996. pap. 10.00 (0-932155-03-0) Phrygian Pr.

Occupation: Casanova. Alexandra Sellers. (Desire Ser.). 2000. per. 3.75 (0-373-76264-X, 1-76264-0) Silhouette.

Occupation: Housewife. Helena Z. Lopata. LC 80-23658. (Illus.). 387p. 1980. reprint ed. lib. bdg. 69.50 (0-313-22697-0, LOOH, Greenwood Pr) Greenwood.

Occupation: Israel over Palestine. 2nd rev. ed. Ed. by Naseer H. Aruri. (Monographs: No. 18). 728p. 1989. pap. 29.00 (0-937694-64-9) Assn Arab-Amer U Grads.

Occupation: Millionaire. Alexandra Sellers. 1998. per. 3.50 (0-373-52065-4, 1-52065-9) Silhouette.

***Occupation: The Ordeal of France, 1940-1944.** Ian Ousby. LC 00-22779. 2000. 18.95 (0-8154-1043-3) Cooper Sq.

Occupation: The Ordeal of France, 1940-1944. Ian Ousby. LC 98-11229. 352p. 1998. text 25.95 (0-312-18148-5) St Martin.

Occupation: The Policies & Practices of Military Conquerors. Eric Carlton. 200p. (C). 1992. text 58.50 (0-389-20981-3) B&N Imports.

Occupation - Nazi-Hunter: The Continuing Search for the Perpetrators of the Holocaust. Efraim Zuroff. LC 94-20205. 1994. 35.00 (0-88125-489-4) Ktav.

Occupation & Career Education Legislation. Dennis C. Nystrom. LC 79-12548. pap. 3.40 (0-672-97133-X, Bobbs); pap. 10.50 (0-685-00789-8, Bobbs) Macmillan.

Occupation & Class Consciousness in America, 27. Douglas M. Eichar. LC 88-35822. (Contributions in Labor Studies: No. 27). 148p. 1989. 47.95 (0-313-26111-3, EOC/, Greenwood Pr) Greenwood.

Occupation & Disease: How Social Factors Affect the Conception of Work-Related Disorders. Allard E. Dembe. LC 95-39781. 344p. 1996. 40.00 (0-300-06436-5) Yale U Pr.

Occupation & Hobby Patterns for Cake Decorating. Roland A. Winbeckler. (Illus.). 24p. (Orig.). 1986. pap. 5.95 (0-930113-05-5) Winbeckler.

Occupation & Ideology of the Salaried Employee. Carl Dreyfuss. Ed. by Leon Stein. LC 77-70490. 1977. reprint ed. lib. bdg. 46.95 (0-405-10162-7) Ayer.

Occupation & Resistance: American Impressions of the Intifada. Alternative Museum Staff. LC 90-80547. (Illus.). 80p. (Orig.). 1990. pap. 15.00 (0-932075-30-4) Alternative Mus.

Occupation & Resistance: The Greek Agony, 1941-1944. John L. Hondros. 340p. 1983. text 25.00 (0-918618-24-X); pap. text 12.00 (0-918618-19-3) Pella Pub.

Occupation As a Substitute for Restraint in the Treatment of the Mentally Ill: A History of the Passage of Two Bills Through the Massachusetts Legislature. L. Vernon Briggs. LC 72-2387. (Mental Illness & Social Policy; the American Experience Ser.). 1973. reprint ed. 21.95 (0-405-05195-6) Ayer.

Occupation of Alcatraz Island: Indian Self-Determination & the Rise of Indian Activism. Troy R. Johnson. 304p. 1996. text 49.95 (0-252-02254-8) U of Ill Pr.

Occupation of Alcatraz Island: Indian Self-Determination & the Rise of Indian Activism. Troy R. Johnson. (Illus.). 304p. 1996. 19.95 (0-252-06585-9) U of Ill Pr.

Occupation of Celtic Sites in Medieval Ireland by the Canons Regular of St Augustine & the Cistercians. Geraldine Carville. (Cistercian Studies: Nbr. 56). (Illus.). 1983. pap. 9.00 (0-87907-856-1) Cistercian Pubns.

Occupation of Chios by the Genoese & Their Administration of the Island, 1346-1566, 3 vols., Set. Philip P. Argenti. LC 78-63339. (Crusades & Military Orders Ser.: Second Series). reprint ed. 120.00 (0-404-17000-5) AMS Pr.

Occupation of Japan: Arts & Culture. Ed. by Thomas W. Burkman. 262p. (C). 1984. lib. bdg. 19.25 (0-9606418-5-8) Genl D MacArthur Fnd.

Occupation of Japan: Grass Roots Level. Ed. by William F. Nimmo. 193p. (C). 1992. lib. bdg. 19.25 (0-9606418-7-4) Genl D MacArthur Fnd.

Occupation of Japan: The Impact of the Korean War. Ed. by William F. Nimmo. 189p. (C). 1986. lib. bdg. 19.25 (0-9606418-6-6) Genl D MacArthur Fnd.

Occupation of Japan: The International Context. Ed. by Thomas W. Burkman. 308p. (C). 1984. lib. bdg. 19.25 (0-9606418-4-X) Genl D MacArthur Fnd.

Occupation of Japan, Policy & Progress. U. S. Department of State Staff. LC 76-90728. 173p. 1970. reprint ed. lib. bdg. 55.00 (0-8371-2528-6, OCJA, Greenwood Pr) Greenwood.

Occupation of Japan, 2nd Phase, 1948-1950. Robert A. Fearey. LC 72-176133. 239p. 1972. reprint ed. lib. bdg. 35.00 (0-8371-6271-8, FEOJ, Greenwood Pr) Greenwood.

Occupation of Namibia: Afrikanerdom's Attack on the British Empire. Allan D. Cooper. 226p. (Orig.). (C). 1990. pap. text 26.50 (0-8191-7955-8) U Pr of Amer.

Occupation of New York City by the British. Ewald G. Schaukirk. LC 70-77112. (Eyewitness Accounts of the American Revolution Ser.). 1969. reprint ed. 14.95 (0-405-01179-2) Ayer.

Occupation Without Troops: America's Japan Lobby & Its Puppets in Japan's Government. Glenn Davis & John G. Roberts. (Illus.). 232p. (Orig.). 1996. pap. 12.95 (4-900737-45-3) Tuttle Pubng.

Occupational: Evaluzaton Reasoning & Selected Assessment Tools. (C). 2000. 34.95 (0-8385-7221-9, Medical Exam) Appleton & Lange.

Occupational Analyst. Jack Rudman. (Career Examination Ser.: C-2548). 1994. pap. 29.95 (0-8373-2548-X) Nat Learn.

Occupational & Environmental Cancers of the Urinary System. Wilhelm C. Hueper. LC 77-76741. (Illus.). 465p. 1969. 55.00 (0-300-01126-1) Yale U Pr.

Occupational & Environmental Chemical Hazards: Cellular & Biochemical Indices for Monitoring Toxicity. V. Foa et al. LC 86-27801. (Chemical Science Ser.). 588p. 1987. text 92.95 (0-470-20802-3) P-H.

***Occupational & Environmental Infectious Diseases: Epidemiology, Prevention & Clinical Management.** Alain J. Couturier. LC 00-37443. 2000. write for info. (1-883595-27-4, OEM Pr) OEM Health.

Occupational & Environmental Medicine. 2nd ed. Joseph Ladou. 864p. (C). 1997. pap. text 49.95 (0-8385-7216-2, A-7216-3, Apple Lange Med) McGraw.

Occupational & Environmental Medicine. 3rd ed. Composed by Ladou. (C). 2001. 42.95 (0-8385-7219-7) Appleton & Lange.

Occupational & Environmental Medicine Self-Assessment & Review. Robert J. McCunney & Paul P. Rountree. LC 98-5990. 150p. 1998. pap. text 49.95 (0-7817-1612-8) Lppncott W & W.

Occupational & Environmental Neurotoxicology. Robert G. Feldman. LC 98-13524. 600p. 1998. text 95.00 (0-7817-1739-6) Lppncott W & W.

Occupational & Environmental Reproductive Hazards. Ed. by Maureen Paul. LC 92-13719. (Illus.). 448p. 1993. 85.00 (0-683-06801-6) Lppncott W & W.

Occupational & Environmental Respiratory Disease. Philip Harber et al. (Illus.). 1232p. (C). (gr. 13). 1995. text 155.00 (0-8016-7728-9, 07728) Mosby Inc.

Occupational & Environmental Safety Engineering & Management. H. R. Kavianian & C. A. Wentz. 400p. 1990. 98.95 (0-471-28912-4, VNR) Wiley.

Occupational & Environmental Safety Engineering & Management. Hamid R. Kavianian & Charles A. Wentz, Jr. 400p. 1990. text 81.95 (0-442-23822-3, VNR) Wiley.

Occupational & Industrial Hygiene: Concepts & Methods. Ed. by Nurtan A. Esmen & Myron A. Mehlman. (Advances in Modern Environmental Toxicology Ser.: Vol. 8). (Illus.). 259p. 1984. text 65.00 (0-911131-09-4) Specialist Journals.

Occupational & Physical Therapy in Educational Environments. Ed. by Irene R. McEwen. 1995. 39.95 (1-56024-777-0) Haworth Pr.

Occupational & Professional Regulation of the States: A Comprehensive Compilation. 122p. 1990. 20.00 (0-87292-958-2, C-179) Coun State Govts.

Occupational & Residential Exposure. Franklin. text. write for info. (0-471-48989-1) Wiley.

Occupational Asthma. Ed. by Emil J. Bardana, Jr. et al. LC 91-58457. 328p. 1991. text 69.00 (1-56053-017-0) Hanley & Belfus.

Occupational Biomechanics 3e. 3rd ed. Don B. Chaffin et al. LC 98-28797. 600p. 1999. 74.95 (0-471-24697-2) Wiley.

Occupational Cancer in Developing Countries. Ed. by Harri Vainio et al. (IARC Scientific Publications: No. 129). (Illus.). 202p. 1995. pap. text 40.00 (92-832-2129-X) OUP.

***Occupational Cancer in Europe: Environmental Tobacco Smoke Exposure.** Ed. by Paolo Boffetta & Enzo Merler. (Illus.). 161p. (C). 2000. pap. text 30.00 (0-7881-8534-9) DIANE Pub.

Occupational Case Analysis Interview & Rating Scale (OCAIRS) Kathy L. Kaplan & Gary Kielhofner. LC 88-43518. 160p. 1989. pap. 22.00 (1-55642-090-0) SLACK Inc.

Occupational Choice: An Approach to a General Theory. Eli Ginzberg et al. LC 51-10961. 287p. reprint ed. pap. 89.00 (0-608-12789-2, 202348400033) Bks Demand.

Occupational Clinical Psychology. James S. Manuso. LC 82-19065. 336p. 1983. 67.95 (0-275-91041-5, C1041, Praeger Pubs) Greenwood.

Occupational Commitment & the Mystique of Self-Employment among Lagos. Yahya H. Affinnih. LC 91-44506. 308p. 1992. lib. bdg. 99.95 (0-7734-9951-2) E Mellen.

Occupational Compensation Survey: National Summary, 1993. (Illus.). 279p. (C). 1997. reprint ed. pap. text 50.00 (0-7881-3888-X) DIANE Pub.

Occupational Compensation Survey: National Summary, (1994) (Illus.). 325p. (C). 1998. reprint ed. pap. text 50.00 (0-7881-3549-X) DIANE Pub.

Occupational Compensation Survey: National Summary, 1995. Government Printing Office Staff. 258p. 1997. pap. text 21.00 (0-16-049103-7) USGPO.

Occupational Compensation Survey: National Summary, 1996. Ed. by Gerald L. Perrins. (Illus.). 256p. (C). 1998. pap. text 50.00 (0-7881-7560-2) DIANE Pub.

Occupational Compensation Survey: Pay in the U. S. & Regions, Pt. 1. (Illus.). 132p. (Orig.). (YA). (gr. 12 up). 1994. pap. text 40.00 (0-7881-0792-5) DIANE Pub.

Occupational Compensation Survey Pts. II & III: Pay Comparisons, 1992, Locality Pay, 1992. Bruce J. Bergman et al. (Illus.). 171p. (Orig.). (C). 1996. pap. text 50.00 (0-7881-3550-3) DIANE Pub.

Occupational Competency Examination - General Examination (OCE) Jack Rudman. (Occupational Competency Examination (OCE) Ser.: Vol. ATS-33). 49.95 (0-8373-5133-2) Nat Learn.

Occupational Competency Examination - General Examination (OCE) Jack Rudman. (Admission Test Ser.: ATS-33). 1994. pap. 29.95 (0-8373-5033-6) Nat Learn.

Occupational Competency Examination Series. Jack Rudman. 1994. pap. write for info. (0-8373-5700-4) Nat Learn.

Occupational Crime. Mars. 112.95 (1-85521-382-6) Ashgate Pub Co.

Occupational Disease. 115p. 1987. 15.00 (0-932387-14-4) Insur Info.

Occupational Diseases: A Guide to Their Recognition, 2 vols. 1991. lib. bdg. 995.00 (0-8490-5110-X) Gordon Pr.

Occupational Diseases in Relation to Compensation & Health Insurance. Rosamond W. Goldberg. LC 68-58581. (Columbia University. Studies in the Social Sciences: No. 345). reprint ed. 32.50 (0-404-51345-X) AMS Pr.

Occupational Disorders: A Treatment Guide for Therapists. Martin D. Kantor. LC 96-28536. 272p. 1997. 69.50 (0-275-95529-X, Praeger Pubs) Greenwood.

Occupational Disorders of the Upper Extremity. Ed. by Lewis H. Millender et al. (Illus.). 308p. 1991. text 83.00 (0-443-08797-0) Church.

Occupational Dose Reduction at Nuclear Power Plants: An Annotated Bibliography. 1997. lib. bdg. 250.95 (0-8490-7711-7) Gordon Pr.

O

Occupational Earnings, 1967-1981: Returns to Occupational Choice, Schooling & Physician Specialization. Stephen Dresch. LC 86-63. (Contemporary Studies in Economic & Financial Analysis: Vol. 49). 296p. 1986. 78.50 (*0-89232-596-8*) Jai Pr.

Occupational Employee Assistance Programs for Substance Abuse & Mental Health Problems. Andrea E. Foote & John C. Erfurt. 1977. pap. 7.00 (*0-87736-327-7*) U of Mich Inst Labor.

Occupational Employment & Wages, 1996. 36p. 1998. pap. 5.00 (*0-16-049704-3*) USGPO.

***Occupational Employment & Wages, 1997.** Rebecca S. Shaw. 120p. 1999. per. 11.00 (*0-16-050136-9*) USGPO.

Occupational Employment in Manufacturing Industries. 1995. lib. bdg. 250.00 (*0-8490-5859-7*) Gordon Pr.

Occupational Employment in Mining, Construction, Finance & Services, 1990. 128p. 1992. per. 7.00 (*0-16-037928-8*) USGPO.

Occupational English 85. 4th ed. Ann A. Laster & Nell A. Pickett. 576p. (C). 1997. pap. text 70.00 (*0-06-043858-4*) Addson-Wesley Educ.

Occupational Environment - Its Evaluation & Control. Ed. by Salvatore R. DiNardi. LC 98-108720. 1997. 125.00 (*0-932627-82-X*) Am Indus Hygiene.

Occupational Epidemiology. Richard R. Monson. 232p. 1986. 132.00 (*0-8493-5793-4*, RC964, CRC Reprint) Franklin.

Occupational Epidemiology. 2nd ed. Richard R. Monson. 312p. 1990. boxed set 146.95 (*0-8493-4927-3*, RC964) CRC Pr.

Occupational Ergonomics Handbook. Waldemar Karwowski & William S. Marras. LC 98-22336. 2088p. 1998. boxed set 139.95 (*0-8493-2641-9*, 2641) CRC Pr.

Occupational Estimates & Projections for the Omaha SMSA. David W. Hinton. 53p. (Orig.). 1973. pap. text 4.00 (*1-55719-065-8*) U NE CPAR.

Occupational Experience of Residential Child & Youth Care Workers: Caring & Its Discontents. Mordecai Arieli. LC 97-7841. (Child & Youth Services Monograph Ser.: Vol. 18, No. 2). 125p. (C). 1997. 39.95 (*1-56024-784-3*); pap. 14.95 (*0-7890-0306-6*) Haworth Pr.

Occupational Exposure & Injury: Disclosure & Coverage in a Changing Workplace. LC 90-85035. 258p. 1990. pap. 54.95 (*0-89707-626-5*, 519-0134, ABA Tort) Amer Bar Assn.

Occupational Exposure Limits for Airborne Toxic Substances. 3rd ed. (Occupational Safety & Health Ser.: No. 37). xiv, 455p. 1991. pap. 42.75 (*92-2-107293-2*) Intl Labour Office.

Occupational Exposure to Silica & Cancer Risk. Lorenzo Simonato et al. (IARC Scientific Publications: No. 97). (Illus.). 144p. 1990. pap. 45.00 (*92-832-1197-9*) OUP.

Occupational Exposure, Toxic Properties, & Work Practice Guidelines for Fiber Glass. J. R. Bender et al. 48p. 1992. 22.00 (*0-932627-47-1*) Am Indus Hygiene.

Occupational Exposures in Insecticide Application & Some Pesticides. (IARC Monographs on the Evaluation of Carcinogenic Risks to Humans: Vol. 53). 612p. 1991. pap. text 105.00 (*92-832-1253-3*, 1720053) World Health.

Occupational Exposures in Petroleum Refining - Crude Oil & Major Petroleum Fuels: The Evaluation of Carcinogenic Risks to Humans. (IARC Monograph: No. 45). 322p. 1989. text 72.00 (*92-832-1245-2*) World Health.

Occupational Exposures of Hairdressers & Barbers & Personal Use of Hair Colourants, Some Hair Dyes, Cosmetic Colourants, Industrial Dyestuffs & Aromatic Amines. Ed. by World Health Organization Staff. (IARC Monographs on the Evaluation of Carcinogenic Risks to Humans: Vol. 57). 427p. 1993. pap. text 75.00 (*92-832-1257-6*, 1720057) World Health.

Occupational Exposures to Mists & Vapours from Strong Inorganic Acids, & Other Industrial Chemicals. (IARC Monographs on the Evaluation of Carcinogenic Risks to Humans: Vol. 54). 336p. 1992. pap. text 72.00 (*92-832-1254-1*, 1720054) World Health.

***Occupational Guidance, Unit 1H.** Finney Company Staff. LC 75-20074. 1999. spiral bd. 112.00 (*0-912486-84-8*, OG 1-H) Finney Co.

***Occupational Guidance, Unit 2H.** Finney Company Staff. LC 75-20074. 2000. spiral bd. 112.00 (*0-912486-85-6*, OG-2H) Finney Co.

Occupational Guidance, Unit 3G. Finney Company Staff. LC 75-20074. 1996. spiral bd. 112.00 (*0-912486-74-0*) Finney Co.

Occupational Guidance, Unit 4G. Finney Company Staff. LC 75-20074. 1997. spiral bd. 112.00 (*0-912486-81-3*) Finney Co.

***Occupational Guidance, Unit 5G.** Finney Company Staff. LC 75-20074. 1998. spiral bd. 112.00 (*0-912486-83-X*, OG 5-G) Finney Co.

Occupational Hand & Upper Extremity Injuries & Diseases. 2nd ed. Morton L. Kasdan. LC 97-27831. 1997. 88.00 (*1-56053-221-1*) Hanley & Belfus.

Occupational Hazard: Critical Writing on Recent British Art. Ed. by Duncan McCorquodale et al. (Illus.). 256p. 1997. pap. 24.95 (*0-9521773-8-2*, Pub. by Black Dog Pubg) RAM Publications.

Occupational Hazards & Reproduction. Ed. by Kari Hemminki et al. LC 84-4545. (Illus.). 333p. 1985. 132.00 (*0-89116-281-X*) Hemisp Pub.

Occupational Hazards in the Health Professions. Ed. by Dag K. Brune & Christer Edling. 416p. 1989. lib. bdg. 143.00 (*0-8493-6931-2*, RC965) CRC Pr.

Occupational Hazards of Pesticide Exposure: Sampling, Monitoring, Measuring. Ed. by Donald J. Ecobichon. LC 98-21964. 320p. 1998. text 94.95 (*1-56032-706-5*); pap. text 36.95 (*1-56032-707-3*) Hemisp Pub.

Occupational Hazards, Risks & Solutions. Paul Swuste. 217p. (Orig.). 1996. pap. 43.50 (*90-407-1356-1*, Pub. by Delft U Pr) Coronet Bks.

Occupational Health. Ed. by Stuart Pantry. 304p. 1995. 39.95 (*1-56593-415-6*, 1081) Singular Publishing.

Occupational Health. 4th ed. J. M. Harrington et al. LC 98-16050. (Pocket Consultant Ser.). (Illus.). 1998. pap. 46.95 (*0-632-04832-8*) Blackwell Sci.

Occupational Health: For the Nurse & Other Health Workers. 2nd ed. Ed. by A. J. Kotze. 278p. 1994. pap. text 46.15 (*0-7021-2668-3*, Pub. by Juta & Co) Intl Spec Bk.

Occupational Health: Recognizing & Preventing Work-Related Disease. 3rd ed. Ed. by Barry Levy & David H. Wegman. LC 94-13146. 800p. 1995. pap. text 50.00 (*0-316-52271-6*, Little Brwn Med Div) Lppncott W & W.

***Occupational Health: Recognizing & Preventing Work-Related Disease & Injury.** Barry S. Levy & David H. Wegman. LC 99-35194. 842p. 1999. pap. write for info. (*0-7817-1954-2*) Lppncott W & W.

***Occupational Health: Risk Assessment & Management.** Stephen Sadhra & Krishna G. Rampal. LC 98-28848. xii, 492p. 1999. 165.00 (*0-632-04199-4*) Blackwell Sci.

***Occupational Health: The Soldier & the Industrial Base.** Ed. by David P. Deeter & Joel C. Gaydos. (Illus.). 643p. (C). 1999. reprint ed. text 75.00 (*0-7881-8259-5*) DIANE Pub.

***Occupational Health & Hygiene.** John R. Ridley & John Channing. LC 99-35498. (Safety at Work Ser.). 241p. 1999. write for info. (*0-7506-4557-1*) Buttrwrth-Heinemann.

Occupational Health & Hygiene: Physical, Chemical & Biological Hazards. Jeremy Stranks. (Health & Safety in Practice Ser.). 192p. (Orig.). 1994. pap. 47.50 (*0-273-60908-4*, Pub. by Pitman Pub) Trans-Atl Phila.

***Occupational Health & Safety.** 3rd ed. Gary R. Krieger & Marci Z. Balge. LC 99-30897. (Occupational Safety & Health Ser.). 540p. 2000. 99.95 (*0-87912-203-X*) Natl Safety Coun.

***Occupational Health & Safety: Guide for Michigan Employers.** Brent D. Rector & Elizabeth M. McIntyre. 172p. 2000. pap. 99.00 (*1-893318-05-2*) Michigan Cham Com.

Occupational Health & Safety: Terms, Definitions, & Abbreviations. 2nd ed. Robert G. Confer & Thomas R. Confer. LC 99-12086. 500p. 1999. 29.95 (*1-56670-361-1*) Lewis Pubs.

Occupational Health & Safety Act: 85 of 1993. Paul Benjamin & Clive Thompson. 335p. 1994. ring bd. 33.00 (*0-7021-2832-5*, Pub. by Juta & Co); ring bd. 27.50 (*0-7021-3265-9*, Pub. by Juta & Co) Gaunt.

Occupational Health & Safety Act Legislation Manual. M. S. Alexander. 1995. ring bd. write for info. (*0-409-01063-4*, MICHIE) LEXIS Pub.

Occupational Health & Safety in American Industry. (Orig.). 1991. pap. 12.00 (*0-89834-116-7*, 0263) US Chamber DC.

Occupational Health & Safety in the Care & Use of Research Animals. NRC, Committee on Occupational Health & Safety of. LC 97-4794. 250p. (Orig.). 1997. pap. text 39.95 (*0-309-05299-8*) Natl Acad Pr.

Occupational Health & Safety Law & Policy: Text & Materials. Richard Johnstone. 500p. 1997. pap. 75.00 (*0-455-21497-2*, 14606, Pub. by LawBk Co) Gaunt.

Occupational Health & Safety Law in Victoria. 2nd ed. Breen Creighton & Peter Rozen. 213p. 1996. pap. 49.00 (*1-86287-239-2*, Pub. by Federation Pr) Gaunt.

Occupational Health & Safety Management. Ed. by Seymour S. Chissick & R. Derricott. LC 79-41218. (Properties of Materials Safety & Environmental Factors Ser.). (Illus.). 723p. reprint ed. pap. 200.00 (*0-8357-6240-8*, 203421700089) Bks Demand.

Occupational Health & Safety Management System: An AIHA Guidance Document. American Industrial Hygiene Association. LC 96-231697. 31 p. 1996. write for info. (*0-932627-74-9*) Am Indus Hygiene.

Occupational Health & Safety Technologist Home Study Workbook, 2 vols. rev. ed. Joseph LeBlanc. Ed. by Marvin Becker. Incl. Vol. I. Occupational Health & Safety Technologist Home Study Workbook. rev. ed. Ed. by James W. Watts. 352p. 2000. Not sold separately (*1-891017-32-2*); Vol. II. Occupational Health & Safety Technologist Home Study Workbook. rev. ed. Ed. by James Watts. (Illus.). 244p. 2000. Not sold separately (*1-891017-33-0*); wbk. ed. write for info. (*1-891017-18-7*) SRS Safety Wrkshops.

Occupational Health & Safety Technologist Home Study Workbook, 2 vols. rev. ed. Joseph LeBlanc. Ed. by James Watts & Marvin Becker. (Illus.). 590p. 1999. 155.00 (*1-891017-08-X*) SRS Safety Wrkshops.

***Occupational Health & Safety Technologist Home Study Workbook, 2 vols.** rev. ed. Joseph LeBlanc. Ed. by Marvin Becker. Incl. Vol. I. Occupational Health & Safety Technologist Home Study Workbook. rev. ed. Ed. by James W. Watts. 352p. 2000. Not sold separately (*1-891017-32-2*); Vol. II. Occupational Health & Safety Technologist Home Study Workbook. rev. ed. Ed. by James Watts. (Illus.). 244p. 2000. Not sold separately (*1-891017-33-0*); (Illus.). 596p. 2000. 155.00 (*1-891017-31-4*) SRS Safety Wrkshops.

Occupational Health & Safety Technologist Home Study Workbook see Occupational Health & Safety Technologist Home Study Workbook

Occupational Health & Safety Technologist Home Study Workbook, Vol. I. rev. ed. Joseph LeBlanc. Ed. by James Watts & Marvin Becker. (Illus.). 355p. 1999. write for info. (*1-891017-06-3*) SRS Safety Wrkshops.

Occupational Health & Safety Technologist Home Study Workbook, Vol. I. rev. ed. James Watts. Ed. by Marvin Becker & Joseph LeBlanc. (Illus.). 360p. 1998. wbk. ed. write for info. (*1-891017-19-5*) SRS Safety Wrkshops.

Occupational Health & Safety Technologist Home Study Workbook, Vol. II. rev. ed. Joseph LeBlanc. Ed. by James Watts & Marvin Becker. (Illus.). 235p. 1999. write for info. (*1-891017-07-1*) SRS Safety Wrkshops.

Occupational Health & Safety Technologist Home Study Workbook, Vol. II. rev. ed. James Watts. Ed. by Marvin Becker & Joseph LeBlanc. (Illus.). 234p. 1998. wbk. ed. write for info. (*1-891017-20-9*) SRS Safety Wrkshops.

Occupational Health & Safety Terms, Definitions, & Abbreviations. Ed. by Robert G. Confer & Thomas R. Confer. 224p. 1994. lib. bdg. 65.00 (*1-56670-077-9*, L1077) Lewis Pubs.

Occupational Health & Working Women in France: Phossy-Jaw & the Match Workers, 1890-1898. Bonnie Gordon. (Studies in Historical Demography). 200p. 1989. reprint ed. text 15.00 (*0-8240-3363-9*) Garland.

Occupational Health Aspects of Construction Work. P. Grandjean. (Euro Reports & Studies Ser.: No. 86). 28p. 1983. pap. text 4.00 (*92-890-1252-8*) World Health.

***Occupational Health for Health Care Workers.** Hans M. Hasselhorn et al. LC 99-40681. 248p. 1999. 45.00 (*0-444-50335-8*) Elsevier.

Occupational Health for the Nurse & Other Health Workers. 2nd ed. A. J. Kotze. LC 98-135328. x, 414p. 1997. write for info. (*0-7021-3557-7*) Juta & Co.

Occupational Health Guide to Violence in the Workplace. Thomas D. Schneid. LC 98-38656. (Occupational Safety & Health Guide Ser.: Vol. 1). 544p. 1999. 59.95 (*1-56670-322-0*) Lewis Pubs.

Occupational Health Hazards of Solvents. rev. ed. Ed. by Myron A. Mehlman et al. LC 86-61325. (Advances in Modern Environmental Toxicology Ser.: Vol. 2). (Illus.). 259p. 1986. text 60.00 (*0-911131-02-7*) Specialist Journals.

Occupational Health in America. Henry B. Selleck. LC 61-16777. (Illus.). 632p. reprint ed. pap. 196.00 (*0-7837-3582-0*, 204344100009) Bks Demand.

Occupational Health in Aviation: Maintenance & Support Personnel. Ed. by Russell B. Rayman et al. LC 94-25272. (Illus.). 238p. 1995. text 63.00 (*0-12-583560-4*) Acad Pr.

Occupational Health in Developing Countries. J. Jeyaratnam. 576p. 1992. 93.00 (*0-19-262122-X*) OUP.

Occupational Health in Developing Countries. J. Jeyaratnam. (Illus.). 520p. 1992. text 98.00 (*0-19-261799-0*) OUP.

Occupational Health in National Development. LC 95-135376. 492p. 1994. text 43.00 (*981-02-1465-0*) World Scientific Pub.

Occupational Health in National Development. J. Jeyaratnam & Chia Kee Seng. 576p. 1994. text 109.00 (*981-02-1464-2*) World Scientific Pub.

Occupational Health Law. 2nd ed. Diana M. Kloss. LC 94-6710. 320p. 1994. 75.00 (*0-632-03651-6*, Pub. by Blckwll Scitfc UK) Blackwell Sci.

Occupational Health Law. 3rd ed. Diana M. Kloss. LC 98-52410. 1999. write for info. (*0-632-04263-X*) Blackwell Sci.

Occupational Health Nursing: Concepts & Practice. Bonnie Rogers. LC 93-48841. (Illus.). 543p. 1994. text 60.00 (*0-7216-7588-3*, W B Saunders Co) Harcrt Hlth Sci Grp.

Occupational Health Nursing Care Guidelines. Ed. by Debra Daly-Gawenda et al. LC 96-8187. (Illus.). 336p. 1996. 49.95 (*0-8261-9350-1*) Springer Pub.

Occupational Health Pocket Consultant. 3rd ed. J. M. Harrington & F. S. Gill. (Pocket Consultant Ser.). (Illus.). 368p. 1992. pap. 39.95 (*0-632-03189-1*) Blackwell Sci.

Occupational Health Practice. 4th ed. H. A. Waldron & Christer Edling. LC 97-24662. 384p. 1997. text 99.50 (*0-7506-2720-4*) Buttrwrth-Heinemann.

Occupational Health Problems of Young Workers. S. Forssman & G. H. Coppee. (Occupational Safety & Health Ser.: No. 26). v, 143p. 1984. 9.00 (*92-2-101051-1*) Intl Labour Office.

Occupational Health Safety Technologist Home Study Workbook, 2 vols., Set. James P. Watts. (Illus.). 1991. 145.00 (*0-9630668-8-9*) SRS Tech.

Occupational Health Safety Technologist Home Study Workbook, Vol. I. James P. Watts. (Illus.). 316p. 1991. write for info. (*0-9630668-6-2*) SRS Tech.

Occupational Health Safety Technologist Home Study Workbook, Vol. II. James P. Watts. (Illus.). 216p. 1991. write for info. (*0-9630668-7-0*) SRS Tech.

Occupational Health Services: Practical Strategies for Improving Quality & Controlling Costs. Ed. by William L. Newkirk. LC 93-26520. 332p. 1993. pap. 56.95 (*1-55648-108-X*, 155400) AHPI.

Occupational Health Workbook. D. Jeff Burton. 300p. 1997. spiral bd., wbk. ed. 59.95 (*1-883992-10-9*) IVE Inc.

Occupational Hearing Loss. 2nd rev. ed. Robert T. Sataloff & Joseph Sataloff. LC 92-48421. (Occupational Safety & Health Ser.: Vol. 24). (Illus.). 856p. 1993. text 255.00 (*0-8247-8814-1*) Dekker.

Occupational Hygiene. 2nd ed. Ed. by J. M. Harrington & K. Gardiner. LC 94-45425. 576p. 1995. 135.00 (*0-632-03734-2*) Blackwell Sci.

Occupational Hygiene. 2nd ed. Ed. by Johannes Schoeman & Harald Schroder. (Illus.). 511p. (C). 1994. pap. text 84.50 (*0-7021-2877-5*, Pub. by Juta & Co) Intl Spec Bk.

Occupational Hygiene Management Guide. Stanley E. Jones et al. (Illus.). 145p. 1990. lib. bdg. 79.95 (*0-87371-255-2*, L255) Lewis Pubs.

Occupational Hygiene of Chemical & Biological Agents. J. S. Boleij et al. 298p. 1995. 161.50 (*0-444-81997-5*) Elsevier.

Occupational, Industrial & Environmental Toxicology. Michael Greenberg. LC 96-44661. (Illus.). 624p. (C). (gr. 13). 1997. text 89.95 (*0-8151-3929-2*, 26883) Mosby Inc.

***Occupational Information.** Mary Lum & Beth Tauke. (Illus.). 48p. 1999. pap. 10.00 (*0-936739-25-8*) Hallwalls Inc.

Occupational Information System for the 21st Century: The Development of O*NET. Ed. by Norman Peterson et al. LC 98-44293. 336p. 1999. pap. 39.95 (*1-55798-556-1*) Am Psychol.

Occupational Injuries: Evaluation, Management & Prevention. Ed. by Thomas N. Herington & Linda H. Morse. (Illus.). 592p. (C). (gr. 13). 1994. text 98.00 (*0-8016-6805-0*, 06805) Mosby Inc.

Occupational Injuries & Illness, 3 vols. Daniel J. Stone. 1992. ring bd. 390.00 (*0-8205-1884-0*) Bender.

Occupational Injuries & Illnesses: Counts, Rates & Characteristics. 1996. lib. bdg. 252.95 (*0-8490-6036-2*) Gordon Pr.

Occupational Injuries & Illnesses: Counts, Rates & Characteristics, 1992. Government Printing Office Staff. 273p. 1995. pap. text 18.00 (*0-16-048041-8*) USGPO.

Occupational Injuries & Illnesses: Counts, Rates & Characteristics, 1993. Government Printing Office Staff. 388p. 1996. pap. text 32.00 (*0-16-048751-X*) USGPO.

Occupational Injuries & Illnesses: Counts, Rates & Characteristics, 1994. 374p. 1997. per. 34.00 (*0-16-049067-7*) USGPO.

***Occupational Injuries & Illnesses: Counts, Rates & Characteristics, 1995.** 406p. 1998. per. 37.00 (*0-16-061767-7*) USGPO.

***Occupational Injuries & Illnesses: Counts, Rates & Characteristics, 1996.** 517p. 1999. per. 48.00 (*0-16-050092-3*) USGPO.

Occupational Injuries & Illnesses in the United States by Industry. 1994. lib. bdg. 250.75 (*0-8490-8511-X*) Gordon Pr.

Occupational Injuries & Their Cost: Canada, 1988-1990 = Les accidents du travail et leur cocut : Canada, 1988-1990. Canada. LC 93-156749. (ENG.). ix, 114p. 1992. write for info. (*0-662-59193-3*) Stat Can Mktg.

Occupational Injury: Risk, Prevention & Injury. Ed. by Anne-Marie Feyer & Ann Williamson. LC 98-140392. 277p. 1998. text 79.95 (*0-7484-0646-8*, Pub. by Tay Francis Ltd); pap. text 29.95 (*0-7484-0647-6*, Pub. by Tay Francis Ltd) Taylor & Francis.

Occupational Job Evalution: A Research-Based Approach to Job Classification. Wilfredo R. Manese. LC 87-32280. 177p. 1988. 55.00 (*0-89930-261-0*, MOL/, Quorum Bks) Greenwood.

Occupational Licensing Enforcement: Guidelines for the Investigator. 56p. 1982. 10.00 (*0-87292-029-1*, C-1) Coun State Govts.

Occupational Licensing Specialist. Jack Rudman. (Career Examination Ser.: C-3737). 1994. pap. 27.95 (*0-8373-3737-2*) Nat Learn.

Occupational Literacy Education. R. Timothy Rush et al. LC 86-778. (Illus.). 167p. reprint ed. pap. 51.80 (*0-8357-4305-5*, 203710200007) Bks Demand.

***Occupational Low Back Pain: Aggresive Nonsurgical Care.** Ed. by Bryan D. Kaplansky. 263p. 2000. 69.95 (*0-8493-0089-4*) CRC Pr.

Occupational Low Back Pain: Assessment, Treatment & Prevention. Malcom H. Pope et al. (Illus.). 348p. (C). (gr. 13). 1990. text 94.00 (*0-8016-6252-4*, 06252) Mosby Inc.

Occupational Low Back Pain: Assessment, Treatment & Prevention. 2nd ed. Malcolm H. Pope et al. 395p. (C). (gr. 13). 2000. text 79.95 (*0-8151-4349-4*, 30028) Mosby Inc.

Occupational Low Back Pain Aggressive Nonsurgical Care. Bryan D. Kaplansky. 1999. 69.95 (*1-56670-244-5*) Lewis Pubs.

***Occupational Lung Disease.** Daniel E. Banks. LC 99-21662. (Illus.). 538p. 1999. text 110.00 (*0-412-73630-6*) OUP.

Occupational Lung Diseases. 3rd ed. S. Keith Morgan & Anthony Seaton. LC 94-19777. (Illus.). 624p. 1995. text 97.00 (*0-7216-4671-9*, W B Saunders Co) Harcrt Hlth Sci Grp.

Occupational Lung Diseases: Prevention & Control. (Occupational Safety & Health Ser.: No. 67). ix, 85p. (Orig.). 1991. pap. 15.75 (*92-2-106463-8*) Intl Labour Office.

Occupational Lung Diseases: Research Approaches & Methods. Margaret E. Turner-Warwick & Weill. (Lung Biology in Health & Disease Ser.: Vol. 18). (Illus.). 544p. 1981. text 199.00 (*0-8247-1362-1*) Dekker.

Occupational Lung Disorders. 3rd ed. W. Raymond Parkes. (Illus.). 912p. 1994. text 300.00 (*0-7506-1403-X*) Buttrwrth-Heinemann.

Occupational Mathematics. Gannon. (MB - Business/Vocational Math Ser.). 1985. mass mkt. 41.95 (*0-538-13900-5*) S-W Pub.

Occupational Medical Management. Jean Felton. 1989. 145.00 (*0-316-27775-4*, Little Brwn Med Div) Lppncott W & W.

Occupational Medicine: Principles & Practical A. 3rd ed. Carl Zenz et al. LC 93-40227. (Illus.). 1312p. (C). (gr. 13). 1993. text 200.00 (*0-8016-6676-7*, 06676) Mosby Inc.

Occupational Medicine: Quick Reference Guides for Family Physicians. James D. Lomax & Eckhardt Johanning. (The Academy Collection Ser.). 208p. pap. text 29.95 (*0-7817-2053-2*) Lppncott W & W.

Occupational Medicine Practice Guidelines: A Quick Reference. Ed. by Jeffrey S. Harris. LC 99-14497. 262p. 1999. pap. text 55.00 (*1-883595-26-6*, OEM Pr) OEM Health.

Occupational Medicine Secrets. Ed. by James Cone & Rosemarie Bowler. LC 99-19893. (Secrets Ser.). (Illus.). 400p. 1999. pap. text 39.00 (*1-56053-161-4*) Hanley & Belfus.

An Asterisk (*) at the beginning of an entry indicates that the title is appearing for the first time.

Occupational Mobility in American Business & Industry, 1928-1952. W. Lloyd Warner & James C. Abegglen. Ed. by Lewis A. Coser & Walter W. Powell. LC 79-7029. (Perennial Works in Sociology). (Illus.). 1980. reprint ed. lib. bdg. 26.95 (*0-405-12127-X*) Ayer.

Occupational Mobility in the United States, 1930-1960. A. Jaffe & R. O. Carleton. LC 73-16947. (Illus.). 105p. 1974. reprint ed. lib. bdg. 59.75 (*0-8371-7248-9*, JAOM, Greenwood Pr) Greenwood.

Occupational Musculoskeletal Diseases. Nortin M. Hadler. LC 92-49724. 288p. 1992. text 79.00 (*0-88167-959-3*) Lppncott W & W.

Occupational Musculoskeletal Disorders. 2nd ed. Nortin M. Hadler. LC 98-51593. 14p. 1999. write for info. (*0-7817-1495-8*) Lppncott W & W.

Occupational Mycoses. Ed. by Arthur F. DiSalvo. LC 83-765. 261p. reprint ed. pap. 81.00 (*0-7837-2700-3*, 204307900006) Bks Demand.

Occupational Neurology & Clinical Neurotoxicology. Ed. by Margit L. Bleecker & John A. Hansen. LC 93-13454. (Illus.). 384p. 1994. 75.00 (*0-683-00848-X*) Lppncott W & W.

Occupational Neurotoxicology. Lucio G. Costa & Luigi Manzo. LC 98-5973. 296p. 1998. boxed set 139.95 (*0-8493-9231-4*) CRC Pr.

Occupational Orientation. Ryan. Date not set. pap. text, teacher ed. write for info. (*0-314-09470-9*) West Pub.

Occupational Orthopaedics. Gunnar B. J. Andersson et al. Ed. by Margareta Nordin. (Illus.). 688p. (C). (gr. 13). 1996. text 125.00 (*0-8016-7984-2*, 07984) Mosby Inc.

Occupational Outlook: A Handbook. 1991. lib. bdg. 250.00 (*0-8490-4919-9*) Gordon Pr.

Occupational Outlook Handbook. text. write for info. (*0-8205-2424-7*) Bender.

Occupational Outlook Handbook. 1996. pap. 32.00 (*0-16-043045-3*) Claitors.

Occupational Outlook Handbook. 23.95 (*0-8239-3030-0*); pap. 18.95 (*0-8239-3029-7*) Rosen Group.

***Occupational Outlook Handbook.** JIST Staff. 2000. pap. 18.95 (*1-56370-676-8*) JIST Works.

Occupational Outlook Handbook. U. S. Department of Labor Staff. 528p. 1998. 22.95 (*1-56370-475-7*) Park Ave.

Occupational Outlook Handbook: 1994-1995. 20 Bks. (512p. 1994. pap. 28.00 (*0-16-043046-1*) USGPO.

Occupational Outlook Handbook: 1998-1999 Edition. U. S. Department of Labor Staff. 528p. 1998. pap. 17.95 (*1-56370-464-1*) Park Ave.

Occupational Outlook Handbook: 1998-99 Edition. U. S. Department of Labor, Bureau of Labor Statist. 560p. 1998. 22.95 (*0-8442-4557-7*); pap. 18.95 (*0-8442-4581-X*) NTC Contemp Pub Co.

Occupational Outlook Handbook, 1996-1997. (Illus.). 502p. (Orig.). 1996. boxed set 38.00 (*0-16-048451-0*, 029-001-03221-8) USGPO.

Occupational Outlook Handbook, 1996-97 Edition. (Labor Statistics Bureau Bulletin Ser.: No. 2350). (Illus.). 502p. (Orig.). 1996. per. 32.00 (*0-16-048450-2*, 029-001-03220-0) USGPO.

Occupational Outlook Handbook, 1994-95. Contrib. by Labor Department, Labor Statistics Bureau Staff. (Illus.). 282p. 1998. per. 23.00 (*0-16-049346-3*) USGPO.

Occupational Outlook Handbook, 1990-91. U. S. Department of Labor, Bureau of Labor Statist. 504p. 1990. 25.95 (*0-910164-13-4*); pap. 21.95 (*0-910164-12-6*) Assoc Bk Pubs.

Occupational Outlook Handbook, 1994-95. U. S. Department of Labor, Bureau of Labor Statist. (Illus.). 1994. 21.95 (*0-910164-22-3*); pap. 18.95 (*0-910164-21-5*) Assoc Bk Pubs.

Occupational Outlook Handbook, 1994-1995. U. S. Department of Labor, Bureau of Labor Statist. 476p. 1994. pap. 18.95 (*0-8442-8732-6*, VGM Career) NTC Contemp Pub Co.

Occupational Outlook Handbook, 1994-1995. U. S. Department of Labor, Bureau of Labor Statist. 476p. 1994. 22.95 (*0-8442-8731-8*, VGM Career) NTC Contemp Pub Co.

Occupational Outlook Handbook, 1994-1995. U. S. Department of Labor Staff. 510p. (Orig.). 1994. pap. 15.95 (*1-878172-40-9*, Wintergreen-Orchard) Riverside Pub Co.

Occupational Outlook Handbook, 1996-1997. U. S. Department of Labor Staff. 1996. 38.00 (*1-57980-072-6*, UOC96H) Claitors.

Occupational Outlook Handbook, 1996-1997. U. S. Dept. of Labor Staff. (Illus.). 473p. 1994. reprint ed. pap. 15.95 (*1-56370-277-0*, OOH4) JIST Works.

Occupational Outlook Handbook, 1996-1997 Edition. rev. ed. U. S. Dept. of Labor, Bureau of Statistics Staff. 500p. 1996. pap. 18.95 (*0-8442-4530-5*, VGM Career) NTC Contemp Pub Co.

Occupational Outlook Handbook, 1996-1997. 22nd ed. (Illus.). 507p. (Orig.). 1996. pap. text 50.00 (*0-7881-2905-8*) DIANE Pub.

Occupational Outlook Handbook, 1996-1997: 1996-97 Edition. 520p. 1996. 21.95 (*1-878172-81-6*, 397OOHH, Wintergreen-Orchard); pap. 15.95 (*1-878172-78-6*, 397OOH, Wintergreen-Orchard) Riverside Pub Co.

Occupational Outlook Handbook, 1996-97 Edition Set. 20 Bks. (574p. 1996. pap. 34.00 (*0-16-061762-6*) USGPO.

Occupational Outlook Handbook, 1998-99. 1998. pap. 42.00 (*1-57980-182-X*) Claitors.

Occupational Outlook Handbook, 1998-99. 1998. 46.00 (*1-57980-183-8*) Claitors.

Occupational Outlook Handbook, 1998-99. (Labor Statistics Bureau Bulletin Ser.: No. 2350). (Illus.). 502p. 1996. pap. 31.00 (*0-16-020044-X*, S/N029001032200) USGPO.

Occupational Outlook Handbook, 1998-99. 23rd ed. Contrib. by Labor Dept., Labor Statistics Bureau Staff. (Illus.). 540p. 1998. per. 42.00 (*0-16-049348-X*); boxed set 46.00 (*0-16-049347-1*) USGPO.

Occupational Outlook Handbook, 06/97. rev. ed. U. S. Department of Labor Staff. 1997. pap. text 16.95 (*0-8239-2544-7*) Rosen Group.

***Occupational Outlook Handbook, 2000-01.** 568p. 2000. per. 51.00 (*0-16-050249-7*); per. 49.00 (*0-16-050250-0*); per. 49.00 (*0-16-050248-9*) USGPO.

***Occupational Outlook Handbook 2000-01.** United States Dept. of Labor Staff. 576p. 2000. pap. 18.95 (*0-658-00227-9*, 002279) NTC Contemp Pub Co.

***Occupational Outlook Handbook 2000-2001.** United States Dept. of Labor Staff. 576p. 2000. 22.95 (*0-658-00226-0*, 002260) NTC Contemp Pub Co.

***Occupational Outlook Handbook 2000-2001.** U. S. Department of Labor Staff. 528p. 2000. pap. 16.95 (*0-89434-351-3*) Ferguson.

***Occupational Outlook Handbook 2000-2001 ed.** U. S. Department of State Staff. 2000. 23.95 (*1-56370-677-6*) JIST Works.

Occupational Outlook Quarterly. Government Printing Office Staff. pap. 8.00 (*0-16-011468-3*) USGPO.

Occupational Outlooks Handbook, 1996-1997. U. S. Dept. of Labor Staff. (Illus.). 473p. 1994. reprint ed. 21.95 (*1-56370-278-9*, OOHH4) JIST Works.

Occupational Perspective of Health. Ann Wilcock. LC 98-5746. (Illus.). 272p. 1998. pap. text 36.00 (*1-55642-358-6*, 33586) SLACK Inc.

Occupational Projections & Training Data. 1997. lib. bdg. 250.99 (*0-8490-7663-3*) Gordon Pr.

Occupational Projections & Training Data, 1994. (Illus.). 82p. (Orig.). (C). 1995. pap. text 25.00 (*0-7881-2389-0*) DIANE Pub.

Occupational Projections & Training Data, 1996. Alan Eck. (Illus.). 76p. (Orig.). (C). 1996. pap. text 25.00 (*0-7881-3055-2*) DIANE Pub.

Occupational Projections & Training Data, 1996. Alan Eck. (Orig.). 1996. pap. 6.00 (*0-16-048522-3*, 029-001-03247-1) USGPO.

Occupational Projections, '96: OOH Supplement. U. S. Department of Labor Staff. 1996. pap. 6.00 (*0-614-30808-9*, UOP96P) Claitors.

Occupational Psychology. Murray Porteous. LC 96-53841. 1997. 27.57 (*0-13-227810-3*) P-H.

Occupational Radiation Exposure at Commercial Nuclear Power Reactors & Other Facilities. 1997. lib. bdg. 250.95 (*0-8490-7704-4*) Gordon Pr.

Occupational Radiation Exposure at Commercial Nuclear Power Reactors & Other Facilities, 1995: Twenty-eighth Annual Report. M. L. Thomas. 304p. 1997. per. 29.00 (*0-16-062684-6*) USGPO.

***Occupational Radiation Exposure at Commercial Nuclear Power Reactors & Other Facilities 1996: Twenty-ninth Annual Report.** M. L. Thomas. 292p. 1998. per. 24.00 (*0-16-062727-3*) USGPO.

***Occupational Radiation Exposure at Commercial Nuclear Power Reactors & Other Facilities 1997: Thirtieth Annual Report.** M. L. Thomas. 304p. 1998. per. 25.00 (*0-16-062778-8*) USGPO.

***Occupational Radiation Exposure at Commercial Nuclear Power Reactors & Other Facilities, 1998: Thirty-first Annual Report.** M. I. Thomas. 182p. 1999. per. 17.00 (*0-16-059022-1*) USGPO.

Occupational Safety & Health: A Directory of State Approaches. Alliance of American Insurers Staff. 110p. 1993. pap. text 35.00 (*1-887271-09-0*) Alliance Am Insurers.

Occupational Safety & Health: Changes Needed in the Combined Federal-State Approach. 72p. pap. text 30.00 (*0-7881-4082-5*) DIANE Pub.

Occupational Safety & Health: Employers' Experiences in Complying with the Hazard Communication Standard (HCS) (Illus.). 64p. (Orig.). (C). 1993. pap. text 20.00 (*0-7881-0172-2*) DIANE Pub.

Occupational Safety & Health: Fir Technologists, Engineers, & Managers. 3rd ed. David L. Goetsch. LC 97-44002. 749p. (C). 1998. 99.00 (*0-13-924085-3*) P-H.

Occupational Safety & Health: OSHA Action Needed to Improve Compliance with Hazard Communication Standard. (Illus.). 120p. (Orig.). (C). 1993. pap. text 30.00 (*1-56806-337-7*) DIANE Pub.

Occupational Safety & Health: The Prevention & Control of Work-Related Hazards. Frank Goldsmith & Lorin E. Kerr. LC 81-20034. 320p. 1982. 45.95 (*0-89885-092-4*, Kluwer Acad Hman Sci) Kluwer Academic.

Occupational Safety & Health: Uneven Protections Provided to Congressional Employees. 104p. (Orig.). (C). 1993. pap. text 30.00 (*1-56806-673-2*) DIANE Pub.

Occupational Safety & Health: Violations of Safety & Health Regulations by Federal Contractors. (Illus.). 144p. (Orig.). (C). 1996. pap. text 35.00 (*0-7881-3590-2*) DIANE Pub.

Occupational Safety & Health Act, 3 vols. Ben Hogan & Robert Moran. 1977. ring bd. 490.00 (*0-8205-1534-5*) Bender.

Occupational Safety & Health Administration's Proposed Revision on Occupational Injury & Illness Recording & Reporting Requirements: Hearing Before the Committee on Small Business, House of Representatives, 105th Congress, 1st Session, Washington, D. C., September 17, 1997. LC 98-161386. iv, 192p. 1997. pap. write for info. (*0-16-055994-4*) USGPO.

Occupational Safety & Health Guidance Manual for Hazardous Waste Site Activities. 1991. lib. bdg. 300.00 (*0-8490-5024-3*) Gordon Pr.

Occupational Safety & Health Guidance Manual for Hazardous Waste Site Activities. 1995. lib. bdg. 253.95 (*0-8490-7544-0*) Gordon Pr.

Occupational Safety & Health Guidance Manual for Hazardous Waste Site Activities. (Illus.). 144p. 1986. pap. 11.00 (*0-16-002525-7*, 017-033-00419-6) USGPO.

Occupational Safety & Health Guidance Manual for Hazardous Waste Site Activities. Ed. by Gail Kleiner. (Illus.). 180p. 1996. reprint ed. pap. text 30.00 (*0-7881-7399-5*) DIANE Pub.

Occupational Safety & Health Guidelines for Chemical Hazards, 2 vols. 1995. lib. bdg. 600.00 (*0-8490-8351-6*) Gordon Pr.

Occupational Safety & Health Guidelines for Chemical Hazards, 3. 360p. 1993. ring bd. 32.00 (*0-16-061555-0*) USGPO.

Occupational Safety & Health Guidelines for Chemical Hazards, Supplement 4, OHG. 290p. 1995. ring bd. 22.00 (*0-16-048381-6*) USGPO.

Occupational Safety & Health Handbook. 2nd rev. ed. Joan Hirsh. 1998. ring bd. 115.00 (*0-327-00198-4*, 82196-11) LEXIS Pub.

Occupational Safety & Health Handbook: An Employer's Guide to OSHA Laws, Regulations & Practices. Jeffrey Hirsch. 1992. ring bd. 95.00 (*0-327-00975-6*, 82196-10, MICHIE) LEXIS Pub.

Occupational Safety & Health Handbook: An Employer's Guide to OSHA Laws, Regulations, & Practices, Issue 3. Jeffrey L. Hirsh. 520p. 1995. ring bd. 95.00 (*0-409-25711-7*, 82197-13, MICHIE) LEXIS Pub.

Occupational Safety & Health in the Emergency Services. Angle. LC 98-28536. 320p. 1998. pap. text 46.95 (*0-8273-8359-2*) Delmar.

Occupational Safety & Health in the Emergency Services: Instructor's Guide. Angle. 128p. 1999. teacher ed. 24.00 (*0-8273-8360-6*) Delmar.

Occupational Safety & Health Law. 3rd ed. Mark A. Rothstein. (Handbook Ser.). 722p. (C). 1990. text. write for info. (*0-314-76669-3*) West Pub.

Occupational Safety & Health Law, Cumulative Supplement 2. Stephen A. Bokat & Horace A. Thompson, 2nd. LC 88-7252. 1995. text, suppl. ed. 65.00 (*0-87179-882-4*) BNA Books.

Occupational Safety & Health Law Handbook see Safety & Health Set

Occupational Safety & Health Law, 1988, includes the 1999 supplement. Stephen A. Bokat & Horace A. Thompson, 2nd. LC 88-7252. 1034p. 1988. suppl. ed. 100.00 incl. trans. (*0-87179-527-2*, 9147-PR9) BNA Books.

***Occupational Safety & Health Law, 1999 Cumulative Supplement.** Ed. by Randy S. Rabinowitz. 684p. 1999. 105.00 (*1-57018-147-0*, 1147-PR9) BNA Books.

Occupational Safety & Health Management. 2nd ed. Thomas J. Anton. 432p. (C). 1989. 88.44 (*0-07-002108-2*) McGraw.

Occupational Safety & Health Standards Course Guide Book. LC 98-83203. (Illus.). 660p. 1998. ring bd. 199.95 (*0-9669664-0-6*) Am Safety.

Occupational Safety & Health Standards for General Industry: With Amendments As of February 1, 1999. CCH Editorial Staff. (Illus.). 864p. 1999. pap. 42.95 (*0-8080-0350-X*) CCH INC.

Occupational Safety & Health Standards for General Industry - As of February 1, 1998. rev. ed. CCH Editorial Staff. (Safety Professional Ser.). 850p. 1998. pap. 39.50 (*0-8080-0245-7*) CCH INC.

Occupational Safety & Health Standards for General Industry with Amendments. 803p. 1997. pap. 34.00 (*0-614-26843-5*, 4720) CCH INC.

Occupational Safety & Health Standards for the Construction Industry. 546p. 1997. pap. 24.00 (*0-318-33186-1*, 4721) CCH INC.

Occupational Safety & Health Standards for the Construction Industry: With Amendments As of February 1, 1999. CCH Editorial Staff. 615p. 1999. pap. 34.95 (*0-8080-0351-8*) CCH INC.

Occupational Safety & Health Standards for the Construction Industry - As of February 1, 1998. Ed. by CCH Editorial Staff. LC 98-160157. (Safety Professional Ser.). 560p. 1998. pap. 29.50 (*0-8080-0246-5*) CCH INC.

Occupational Safety & Health Symposium for Gas Operating Personnel. 58p. 1979. pap. 3.00 (*0-318-12662-1*, J10279) Am Gas Assn.

Occupational Safety & Industrial Hygiene Markets. 3rd ed. 429p. 1997. 485.00 (*0-614-29519-X*) R K Miller Assocs.

Occupational Safety & Industrial Hygiene Markets. 3rd rev. ed. Richard K. Miller & Terri C. Walker. 426p. 1997. 485.00 (*1-881503-77-1*) R K Miller Assocs.

***Occupational Safety Calculations: A Professional Reference.** James H. Stewart et al. 165p. (YA). 2000. 119.95 (*0-9671934-1-9*) Millennium Assocs.

Occupational Safety, Health, & Fire Index: A Source Guide to Voluntary & Obligatory Regulations, Codes Standards & Publications. David E. Miller. LC 76-12285. (Occupational Safety & Health Ser.: Vol. 1). 224p. reprint ed. pap. 69.50 (*0-608-16736-3*, 202782300054) Bks Demand.

Occupational Safety Health Management. 2nd ed. Anton. 1989. student ed. 28.12 (*0-07-002109-0*) McGraw.

Occupational Safety Management & Engineering. 4th ed. Willie Hammer. 480p. 1988. text, boxed set 91.00 (*0-13-629379-4*) P-H.

***Occupational Safety Management & Engineering.** 5th ed. Hammer. 584p. 2000. 91.00 (*0-13-896515-3*) P-H.

Occupational Science: The Evolving Discipline. Ruth Zemke. LC 96-10611. 466p. 1996. pap. 44.95 (*0-8036-0138-7*) Davis Co.

Occupational Science: The Foundation for New Models of Practice. Ed. by Jerry A. Johnson & Elizabeth J. Yerxal. LC 89-26933. (Occupational Therapy in Health Care Ser.: Vol. 6, No. 4). 112p. (C). 1990. text 39.95 (*0-86656-960-X*) Haworth Pr.

Occupational Skin Disease. 2nd ed. Robert M. Adams. 624p. 1990. text 156.00 (*0-7216-2926-1*, 790026, W B Saunders Co) Harcrt Hlth Sci Grp.

Occupational Skin Disease. 3rd ed. Robert M. Adams. Ed. by Judy Fletcher. LC 98-25698. (Illus.). 830p. 1999. text 125.00 (*0-7216-7037-7*, W B Saunders Co) Harcrt Hlth Sci Grp.

Occupational Skin Disorders. Daniel J. Hogan. LC 94-1678. (Topics in Clinical Dermatology Ser.). (Illus.). 184p. 1994. 82.50 (*0-89640-248-7*) Igaku-Shoin.

Occupational Social Work Today. Pref. by Shulamith Lala Ashenberg Straussner. LC 89-27967. (Employee Assistance Quarterly Ser.: Vol. 5, No. 1). (Illus.). 118p. 1990. pap. text 14.95 (*0-86656-998-7*) Haworth Pr.

Occupational Social Work Today. Pref. by Shulamith Lala Ashenberg Straussner. LC 89-27967. (Employee Assistance Quarterly Ser.: Vol. 5, No. 1). (Illus.). 118p. 1990. text 39.95 (*0-86656-995-2*) Haworth Pr.

Occupational Socialization & Working Lives. Amanda Coffey & Paul Atkinson. LC 94-12176. (Cardiff Papers in Qualitative Research). 160p. 1994. 72.95 (*1-85628-574-X*, Pub. by Avebry) Ashgate Pub Co.

Occupational Strategy, Nursing. Jack Rudman. (ACT Proficiency Examination Program (PEP) Ser.: Vol. 47). 43.95 (*0-8373-5597-4*) Nat Learn.

Occupational Strategy, Nursing. Jack Rudman. (ACT Proficiency Examination Program Ser.: PEP-47). 1994. pap. 23.95 (*0-8373-5547-8*) Nat Learn.

Occupational Strategy, Nursing. Jack Rudman. (Regents External Degree Ser.: REDP-20). 1994. pap. 23.95 (*0-8373-5620-2*) Nat Learn.

Occupational Strategy (Nursing) Jack Rudman. (Regents External Degree (REDP) Ser.: Vol. 20). 43.95 (*0-8373-5670-9*) Nat Learn.

Occupational Stress: A Handbook. 2nd ed. Ed. by Rick Crandall & Pamela L. Perrewe. (Health Psychology & Behavioral Medicine Ser.). 280p. 1995. pap. 39.95 (*1-56032-367-1*) Taylor & Francis.

Occupational Stress: A Practical Approach. Ken Addley. LC 97-27644. 256p. 1997. text 68.00 (*0-7506-2948-7*) Buttrwrth-Heinemann.

Occupational Stress: Proceedings of the Conference on Occupational Stress, 1977. Ed. by Rosalind M. Schwartz. 78p. 1993. reprint ed. 8.00 (*0-89215-096-3*) U Cal LA Indus Rel.

Occupational Stress & Organizational Effectiveness. Ed. by Anne W. Riley & Stephen J. Zaccaro. LC 86-25250. 287p. 1987. 59.95 (*0-275-92281-2*, C2281, Praeger Pubs) Greenwood.

Occupational Stress & Productivity. John Sweetland. (Studies in Productivity: Highlights of the Literature Ser.: Vol. 8). 44p. 1979. pap. 55.00 (*0-08-029489-8*) Work in Amer.

Occupational Stress & the Mental & Physical Health of Factory Workers. James S. House. LC 80-18749. (Institute for Social Research, Research Report). 357p. (Orig.). reprint ed. pap. 110.70 (*0-7837-5245-8*, 204498000005) Bks Demand.

Occupational Stress Guide to Control. T. Reed. 1993. text 34.95 (*0-442-00189-4*, VNR) Wiley.

Occupational Stress Management. 64p. 1986. pap. text 14.95 (*0-9610026-8-9*) Perf Resource Pr.

Occupational Subcultures in the Workplace. Harrison M. Trice. (Cornell Studies in Industrial & Labor Relations: No. 26). 304p. (Orig.). 1993. pap. text 16.95 (*0-87546-303-7*, ILR Press) Cornell U Pr.

Occupational Therapist. Jack Rudman. (Career Examination Ser.: C-558). 1994. pap. 29.95 (*0-8373-0558-6*) Nat Learn.

Occupational Therapist Aide. Jack Rudman. (Career Examination Ser.: C-1380). 1994. pap. 27.95 (*0-8373-1380-5*) Nat Learn.

Occupational Therapist Assistant. Jack Rudman. (Career Examination Ser.: C-1381). 1994. pap. 27.95 (*0-8373-1381-3*) Nat Learn.

Occupational Therapy. Marguerite Abbott et al. (Opportunities in...Ser.). (Illus.). 160p. 1990. 13.95 (*0-8442-6561-6*, VGM Career) NTC Contemp Pub Co.

Occupational Therapy. Marguerite Abbott et al. (Opportunities in...Ser.). (Illus.). 160p. 1993. pap. 10.95 (*0-8442-6562-4*, VGM Career) NTC Contemp Pub Co.

Occupational Therapy. Simme Cynkin. 1979. 17.00 (*0-316-16610-3*, Little Brwn Med Div) Lppncott W & W.

Occupational Therapy. 2nd ed. Simme Cynkin & Anne M. Robinson. 384p. 1989. text 48.00 (*0-316-16611-1*) Lppncott W & W.

Occupational Therapy. 2nd ed. Tr. by Karen Folger M. S. Jacobs. 300p. 1991. text 58.00 (*0-316-45549-0*) Lppncott W & W.

Occupational Therapy: Approaches to Psychosocial & Behavioral Healthcare. (C). 2000. 55.00 (*0-8385-7220-0*, Medical Exam) Appleton & Lange.

Occupational Therapy: Configuration of a Profession. Anne C. Mosey. 186p. 1986. text 50.00 (*0-89004-699-9*) Lppncott W & W.

Occupational Therapy: Enabling Function & Well-Being. 2nd ed. Charles Christiansen & Carolyn M. Baum. 672p. 1997. 61.00 (*1-55642-361-6*, 33616) SLACK Inc.

Occupational Therapy: Enabling Function & Well-Being. 2nd ed. Charles Christiansen & Carolyn M. Baum. LC 97-9050. (Illus.). 664p. 1997. pap. 54.00 (*1-55642-248-2*, 32482) SLACK Inc.

Occupational Therapy: Foundations for Practice. 2nd ed. Hagedom. 1996. pap. text 26.95 (*0-443-05292-1*, H1258) Church.

Occupational Therapy: Making a Difference in School System Practice: a Self-Paced Clinical Course Jane Case-Smith. LC 99-178436. 1998. 463.00 (*1-56900-095-6*) Am Occup Therapy.

O

Occupational Therapy: Perspectives & Processes. Rosemary Hagedorn. LC 95-20028. 1995. pap. text 32.00 (*0-443-04978-5*) Church.

Occupational Therapy: Practice Skills for Physical Dysfunction. 4th ed. Ed. by Lorraine W. Pedretti. (Illus.). 896p. (C). (gr. 13). 1995. text 64.00 (*0-8151-6812-8*, 25289) Mosby Inc.

Occupational Therapy: Practice Skills for Physical Dysfunction. 4th ed. Lorraine W. Pedretti. (Illus.). 384p. (gr. 13). 1995. pap. text, student ed. 20.95 (*0-8151-7214-1*, 27650) Mosby Inc.

Occupational Therapy: Principles & Practice. 2nd ed. Alice J. Punwar. LC 92-48838. (Illus.). 304p. 1994. 35.00 (*0-683-06975-6*) Lppncott W & W.

Occupational Therapy: Principles & Practice. 3rd ed. Alice Punwar & Suzanne Peloquin. 312p. pap. text 37.95 (*0-683-30453-4*) Lppncott W & W.

Occupational Therapy: Program Development for Health Promotion & Preventive Services. Ed. by Jerry A. Johnson & Evelyn Jaffe. LC 89-15460. (Occupational Therapy in Health Care Ser.: Vol. 5, No. 4). (Illus.). 135p. 1989. text 4.95 (*0-86656-952-9*) Haworth Pr.

Occupational Therapy: The First 30 Years 1900 to 1930. Virginia A. Quiroga. LC 95-161107. 290p. (C). 1995. pap. 25.00 (*1-56900-025-5*) Am Occup Therapy.

Occupational Therapy: Transition from Classroom to Clinic - Physical Disability Fieldwork Applications. Vicki Smith. LC 94-228038. (Illus.). 212p. (C). 1994. pap. text 42.00 (*1-56900-003-4*) Am Occup Therapy.

Occupational Therapy: Work-Related Programs & Assessments. Karen Jacobs. 330p. 1985. 26.50 (*0-316-45547-4*) Little.

Occupational Therapy Across Cultural Boundaries: Theory, Practice & Professional Development. Ed. by Susan C. Merrill. LC 91-36744. (Occupational Therapy in Health Care Ser.). 116p. 1992. lib. bdg. 39.95 (*1-56024-223-X*) Haworth Pr.

Occupational Therapy Activities from Clay to Computers: Theory & Practice. Estelle B. Breines. (Illus.). 245p. pap. text 39.95 (*0-8036-0544-7*) Davis Co.

Occupational Therapy Activities from Clay to Computers: Theory & Practice. Estelle B. Breines. LC 94-6968. (Illus.). 245p. 1994. pap. 41.95 (*0-8036-1145-5*) Davis Co.

Occupational Therapy Aide. Kathryn A. Quinlan. LC 98-7184. (Careers Without College Ser.). (J). 1998. 19.00 (*0-7368-0037-9*, Cpstone High Low) Capstone Pr.

Occupational Therapy Aide. Kathryn A. Quinlan. (Careers Without College Ser.). (J). 1998. 19.00 (*0-516-21399-7*) Childrens.

Occupational Therapy & Adolescents with Disability. Ed. by Florence S. Cromwell. LC 85-13954. (Occupational Therapy in Health Care Ser.: Vol. 2, No. 3). 158p. 1985. text 39.95 (*0-86656-447-0*); pap. text 19.95 (*0-86656-455-1*) Haworth Pr.

***Occupational Therapy & Chronic Fatigue Syndrome.** Diane Cox. 2000. pap. 34.95 (*1-86156-155-5*) Whurr Pub.

Occupational Therapy & Mental Health: Principles, Skills & Practice. Ed. by Jennifer Creek. (Illus.). 569p. 1990. pap. text 49.95 (*0-443-03758-2*) Church.

Occupational Therapy & Mental Health: Principles, Skills & Practice. 2nd ed. Creek. 1996. pap. text 58.00 (*0-443-05202-6*, C8637) Church.

Occupational Therapy & Physical Dysfunction: Principles, Skills & Practice. 4th ed. Ed. by Ann Turner et al. LC 95-40799. 896p. 1996. pap. text 55.95 (*0-443-05177-1*) Church.

Occupational Therapy & Physical Therapy: A Resource & Planning Guide. Patricia A. Bober & Sandra L. Corbett. 204p. (Orig.). (C). 1996. pap. text 27.00 (*1-57337-035-5*, 7040) WI Dept Pub Instruct.

Occupational Therapy & Psychosocial Dysfunction. Intro. by Susan C. Merrill. LC 92-30263. (Occupational Therapy in Health Care Ser.: Vol. 8, Nos. 2 & 3). (Illus.). 247p. 1993. pap. text 19.95 (*1-56024-331-7*); lib. bdg. 39.95 (*1-56024-330-9*) Haworth Pr.

Occupational Therapy & the Elderly. Ed. by Marjorie Helm. (Illus.). 288p. (Orig.). 1987. pap. text 34.00 (*0-443-03469-9*) Church.

Occupational Therapy & the Patient with Pain. Ed. by Florence S. Cromwell. LC 84-10496. (Occupational Therapy in Health Care Ser.: Vol. 1, No. 3). 135p. 1984. text 39.95 (*0-86656-306-7*) Haworth Pr.

Occupational Therapy & the Patient with Pain. Ed. by Florence S. Cromwell. LC 84-10496. (Occupational Therapy in Health Care Ser.: Vol. 1, No. 3). 135p. 1985. pap. text 19.95 (*0-86656-454-3*) Haworth Pr.

Occupational Therapy Approaches to Stroke. Anne A. Wilcock. (Illus.). 235p. (Orig.). 1985. pap. text 50.00 (*0-443-03267-X*) Church.

Occupational Therapy Approaches to Traumatic Brain Injury. Ed. by Jerry A. Johnson & Laura Krefting. (Occupational Therapy in Health Care Ser.). 249p. 1990. text 39.95 (*1-56024-064-4*) Haworth Pr.

Occupational Therapy As a Career: An Introduction to the Field & a Structured Method for Observation. Laura Anderson & Christine Malaski. LC 98-28653. (Illus.). 156p. (C). 1998. pap. text 18.95 (*0-8036-0387-8*) Davis Co.

Occupational Therapy Assessment As the Keystone to Treatment Planning. Ed. by Florence Cromwell. LC 84-697. (Occupational Therapy in Health Care Ser.: Vol. 1, No. 2). 114p. 1984. text 39.95 (*0-86656-305-9*) Haworth Pr.

Occupational Therapy Assessment As the Keystone to Treatment Planning. Ed. by Florence Cromwell. LC 84-697. (Occupational Therapy in Health Care Ser.: Vol. 1, No. 2). 114p. 1985. pap. text 19.95 (*0-86656-453-5*) Haworth Pr.

Occupational Therapy Assessment Tools: An Annotated Index. 2nd ed. Ina Asher. LC 97-147652. 332p. 1996. pap. 40.00 (*1-56900-034-4*, 1020) Am Occup Therapy.

Occupational Therapy Assistant: A Primer. Haru Hirama. 297p. (Orig.). (C). 1996. pap. text 29.95 (*0-935273-00-X*) Chess Pub.

Occupational Therapy Assistant Career Profile. Naomi S. Greenberg. (Allied Health Professions Monograph). (Illus.). 236p. 1990. pap. 37.50 (*0-87527-270-3*) Green.

***Occupational Therapy Careers.** rev. ed. Zona R. Weeks. (Opportunities in . . . Ser.). 2000. 14.95 (*0-658-00472-7*, VGM Career) NTC Contemp Pub Co.

Occupational Therapy Consultation: Theory, Principles & Practice. Evelyn Jaffe-Epstein. (Illus.). 809p. (C). (gr. 13). 1992. text 54.00 (*0-8016-6204-4*, 06204) Mosby Inc.

Occupational Therapy Consultation: Theory, Principles & Practice. Evelyn Jaffe & Cynthia Epstein. 809p. (C). (gr. 13). 1992. text 49.95 (*0-8016-7509-X*) Mosby Inc.

Occupational Therapy Evaluation for Adults: A Pocket Guide. Maureen E. Neistadt. 256p. spiral bd. 34.95 (*0-7817-2495-3*) Lppncott W & W.

Occupational Therapy Examination Review: 800 Multiple-Choice Questions with Referenced, Explanatory Answers. 5th ed. H. Dwyer Dundon. 245p. (C). 1988. pap. text 26.95 (*0-8385-7204-9*, A7204-9) Appleton & Lange.

Occupational Therapy Examination Review Guide. Debra N. Anderson et al. LC 95-46117. (Illus.). 212p. (C). 1996. pap. text 28.95 (*0-8036-0029-1*) Davis Co.

Occupational Therapy Fieldwork Manual for Assessing Professional Skills. Judith Palladino & Ruth Jeffries. 80p. 2000. pap. text 24.95 (*0-8036-0556-0*) Davis Co.

Occupational Therapy for Children. 3rd ed. Ed. by Jane Case-Smith et al. (Illus.). 864p. (C). (gr. 13). 1995. text 63.00 (*0-8151-1541-5*, 24845) Mosby Inc.

Occupational Therapy for Children with Special Needs, 1. Elaine Wilson. LC 99-186943. 1998. pap. 37.95 (*1-86156-061-3*) Singular Publishing.

Occupational Therapy for Chronic Pain. Strong. 1997. pap. text 29.95 (*0-443-05251-4*, S2269) Church.

Occupational Therapy for Orthopaedic Conditions. Dina Penrose. LC 92-49578. (Therapy in Practice Ser.: Vol. 36). 219p. 1992. 44.75 (*1-56593-044-4*, 0292) Singular Publishing.

Occupational Therapy for People with Eating Dysfunctions. Ed. by Florence S. Cromwell. LC 86-12016. (Occupational Therapy in Health Care Ser.: Vol. 3, No. 2). 161p. 1986. text 4.95 (*0-86656-588-4*) Haworth Pr.

Occupational Therapy for Physical Dysfunction. 4th ed. Ed. by Catherine A. Trombly. (Illus.). 941p. 1995. 59.00 (*0-683-08390-2*) Lppncott W & W.

Occupational Therapy for Stroke Rehabilitation. Simon B. Thompson & Maryanne Morgan. Ed. by Jo Campling. (Therapy in Practice Ser.: No. 11). 192p. 1990. pap. 25.00 (*0-412-33530-1*, A4472) Chapman & Hall.

Occupational Therapy for the Energy Deficient Patient. Ed. by Florence S. Cromwell. LC 85-27277. (Occupational Therapy in Health Care Ser.: Vol. 3, No. 1). 119p. 1986. text 39.95 (*0-86656-550-7*); pap. text 19.95 (*0-86656-551-5*) Haworth Pr.

Occupational Therapy Foundations for Practice: Models, Frames of Reference & Core Skills. Rosemary Hagedorn. (Illus.). 105p. (Orig.). 1991. pap. text 20.95 (*0-443-04540-2*) Church.

Occupational Therapy in Long-Term Psychiatry. 2nd ed. Moya Willson. LC 86-29931. (Illus.). 222p. 1987. pap. text 34.00 (*0-443-03565-2*) Church.

Occupational Therapy in Oncology & Palliative Care. Cooper. 1997. pap. 36.00 (*1-86156-015-X*) Thomson Learn.

Occupational Therapy in Oncology & Palliative Care. Jill Cooper. (Illus.). 200p. 1997. pap. 45.00 (*1-56593-884-4*, 1732) Singular Publishing.

Occupational Therapy in Psychosocial Practice. Roann Barris et al. LC 88-43104. 150p. 1988. pap. 24.00 (*1-55642-072-2*) SLACK Inc.

Occupational Therapy in Rheumatology: An Holistic Approach. Lynne Sandles. (Therapy in Practice Ser.: No. 19). 172p. 1990. mass mkt. 26.00 (*0-412-31560-2*, A4426) Chapman & Hall.

Occupational Therapy in Short Term Psychiatry. 3rd ed. Ed. by Moya Willson. LC 96-1651. 269p. (Orig.). 1996. pap. text 21.95 (*0-443-05396-0*) Church.

Occupational Therapy in the Treatment of Adult Hemiplegia. Ortrud Eggers & Bobath. 160p. 1983. reprint ed. pap. text 44.00 (*0-7506-0128-0*) Buttrwrth-Heinemann.

Occupational Therapy Leadership: Marketing Yourself, Your Profession, & Your Organization. Grace E. Gilkeson. LC 96-53182. 344p. 1997. pap. 28.95 (*0-8036-0253-7*) Davis Co.

Occupational Therapy Manager. rev. ed. American Occupational Therapy Association Staff. Ed. by Jeanette Bair. 685p. (C). 1996. pap. text 55.00 (*0-910317-76-3*) Am Occup Therapy.

Occupational Therapy Manager's Survival Handbook. Chestina Brollier & Florence S. Cromwell. LC 87-37486. (Occupational Therapy in Health Care Ser.: Vol. 5, No. 1). (Illus.). 221p. 1988. text 39.95 (*0-86656-686-4*) Haworth Pr.

Occupational Therapy Practice Guidelines for Adults with Alzheimer's Disease. AOTA Staff. (AOTA Practice Guidelines Ser.). (Illus.). 21p. 1999. pap. 22.00 (*1-56900-133-2*, 1191) Am Occup Therapy.

***Occupational Therapy Practice Guidelines for Adults with Alzheimer's Disease.** AOTA Staff. (AOTA Practice Guidelines Ser.). (Illus.). 2000. pap. write for info. (*1-56900-146-4*) Am Occup Therapy.

Occupational Therapy Practice Guidelines for Adults with Carpal Tunnel Syndrome. AOTA Staff. (AOTA Practice Guidelines Ser.). (Illus.). 13p. 1999. pap. 22.00 (*1-56900-121-9*, 1188) Am Occup Therapy.

***Occupational Therapy Practice Guidelines for Adults with Carpal Tunnel Syndrome.** AOTA Staff. (AOTA Practice Guidelines Ser.). (Illus.). 2000. pap. write for info. (*1-56900-147-2*) Am Occup Therapy.

***Occupational Therapy Practice Guidelines for Adults with Hip Fracture Replacement.** AOTA Staff. (AOTA Practice Guidelines Ser.). (Illus.). 2000. pap. write for info. (*1-56900-148-0*) Am Occup Therapy.

Occupational Therapy Practice Guidelines for Adults with Hip Fracture/Replacement. AOTA Staff. (AOTA Practice Guidelines Ser.). (Illus.). 11p. 1999. pap. 22.00 (*1-56900-122-7*, 1153) Am Occup Therapy.

Occupational Therapy Practice Guidelines for Adults with Low Back Pain. AOTA Staff. (AOTA Practice Guidelines Ser.). (Illus.). 15p. 1999. pap. 22.00 (*1-56900-123-5*, 1155) Am Occup Therapy.

***Occupational Therapy Practice Guidelines for Adults with Low Back Pain.** AOTA Staff. (AOTA Practice Guidelines Ser.). (Illus.). 2000. pap. write for info. (*1-56900-149-9*) Am Occup Therapy.

Occupational Therapy Practice Guidelines for Adults with Low Vision. AOTA Staff. (AOTA Practice Guidelines Ser.). (Illus.). 25p. 1999. pap. 22.00 (*1-56900-124-3*, 1192) Am Occup Therapy.

***Occupational Therapy Practice Guidelines for Adults with Low Vision.** AOTA Staff. (AOTA Practice Guidelines Ser.). (Illus.). 2000. pap. write for info. (*1-56900-150-2*) Am Occup Therapy.

***Occupational Therapy Practice Guidelines for Adults with Mood Disorders.** AOTA Staff. (AOTA Practice Guidelines Ser.). (Illus.). 2000. pap. write for info. (*1-56900-142-1*) Am Occup Therapy.

Occupational Therapy Practice Guidelines for Adults with Neurodegenerative Diseases. AOTA Staff. (AOTA Practice Guidelines Ser.). (Illus.). 19p. 1999. pap. 22.00 (*1-56900-125-1*, 1194) Am Occup Therapy.

***Occupational Therapy Practice Guidelines for Adults with Rheumatoid Arthritis.** AOTA Staff. (AOTA Practice Guidelines Ser.). (Illus.). 2000. pap. write for info. (*1-56900-152-9*) Am Occup Therapy.

Occupational Therapy Practice Guidelines for Adults with Schizophrenia. AOTA Staff. (AOTA Practice Guidelines Ser.). (Illus.). 25p. 1999. pap. 22.00 (*1-56900-126-X*, 1189) Am Occup Therapy.

***Occupational Therapy Practice Guidelines for Adults with Schizophrenia.** AOTA Staff. (AOTA Practice Guidelines Ser.). (Illus.). 2000. pap. write for info. (*1-56900-153-7*) Am Occup Therapy.

Occupational Therapy Practice Guidelines for Adults with Spinal Cord Injury. AOTA Staff. (AOTA Practice Guidelines Ser.). (Illus.). 33p. 1999. pap. 22.00 (*1-56900-129-4*, 1154) Am Occup Therapy.

***Occupational Therapy Practice Guidelines for Adults with Spinal Cord Injury.** AOTA Staff. (AOTA Practice Guidelines Ser.). (Illus.). 2000. pap. write for info. (*1-56900-154-5*) Am Occup Therapy.

Occupational Therapy Practice Guidelines for Adults with Stroke. AOTA Staff. (AOTA Practice Guidelines Ser.). (Illus.). 15p. 1999. pap. 22.00 (*1-56900-127-8*, 1152) Am Occup Therapy.

***Occupational Therapy Practice Guidelines for Adults with Stroke.** AOTA Staff. (AOTA Practice Guidelines Ser.). (Illus.). 2000. pap. write for info. (*1-56900-155-3*) Am Occup Therapy.

Occupational Therapy Practice Guidelines for Adults with Traumatic Brain Injury. AOTA Staff. (AOTA Practice Guidelines Ser.). (Illus.). 18p. 1999. pap. 22.00 (*1-56900-128-6*, 1151) Am Occup Therapy.

***Occupational Therapy Practice Guidelines for Adults with Traumatic Brain Injury.** AOTA Staff. (AOTA Practice Guidelines Ser.). (Illus.). 2000. pap. write for info. (*1-56900-156-1*) Am Occup Therapy.

Occupational Therapy Practice Guidelines for Attention-Deficit/Hyperactivity Disorders. AOTA Staff. (AOTA Practice Guidelines Ser.). (Illus.). 13p. 1999. pap. 22.00 (*1-56900-130-8*, 1159) Am Occup Therapy.

***Occupational Therapy Practice Guidelines for Attention-Deficit/Hyperactivity Disorders.** AOTA Staff. (AOTA Practice Guidelines Ser.). (Illus.). 2000. pap. write for info. (*1-56900-157-X*) Am Occup Therapy.

Occupational Therapy Practice Guidelines for Cerebral Palsy. AOTA Staff. (AOTA Practice Guidelines Ser.). (Illus.). 13p. (Orig.). 1999. pap. 22.00 (*1-56900-131-6*, 1156) Am Occup Therapy.

***Occupational Therapy Practice Guidelines for Cerebral Palsy.** AOTA Staff. (AOTA Practice Guidelines Ser.). (Illus.). (Orig.). 2000. pap. write for info. (*1-56900-158-8*) Am Occup Therapy.

Occupational Therapy Practice Guidelines for Chronic Pain. AOTA Staff. (AOTA Practice Guidelines Ser.). (Illus.). 15p. 1999. pap. 22.00 (*1-56900-132-4*, 1193) Am Occup Therapy.

***Occupational Therapy Practice Guidelines for Chronic Pain.** AOTA Staff. (AOTA Practice Guidelines Ser.). (Illus.). 2000. pap. write for info. (*1-56900-159-6*) Am Occup Therapy.

Occupational Therapy Practice Guidelines for Substance Use Disorders. AOTA Staff. (AOTA Practice Guidelines Ser.). (Illus.). 23p. 1999. pap. 22.00 (*1-56900-134-0*, 1190) Am Occup Therapy.

***Occupational Therapy Practice Guidelines for Substance Use Disorders.** AOTA Staff. (AOTA Practice Guidelines Ser.). (Illus.). 2000. pap. write for info. (*1-56900-160-X*) Am Occup Therapy.

Occupational Therapy Practice Guidelines for Tendon Injuries. AOTA Staff. (AOTA Practice Guidelines Ser.). (Illus.). 13p. 1999. pap. 22.00 (*1-56900-135-9*, 1157) Am Occup Therapy.

***Occupational Therapy Practice Guidelines for Tendon Injuries.** AOTA Staff. (AOTA Practice Guidelines Ser.). (Illus.). 2000. pap. write for info. (*1-56900-161-8*) Am Occup Therapy.

Occupational Therapy Practice Guidelines for Young Children with Delayed Development. AOTA Staff. (AOTA Practice Guidelines Ser.). (Illus.). 15p. 1999. pap. 22.00 (*1-56900-136-7*, 1158) Am Occup Therapy.

***Occupational Therapy Practice Guidelines for Young Children with Delayed Development.** AOTA Staff. (AOTA Practice Guidelines Ser.). (Illus.). 2000. pap. write for info. (*1-56900-162-6*) Am Occup Therapy.

Occupational Therapy Protocol Management in Adult Physical Dysfunction. Marilyn S. Daniel & Randy Strickland. 464p. 1992. ring bd. 93.00 (*0-8342-0314-6*, 20314) Aspen Pub.

Occupational Therapy Quick Coding Guide. AOTA Staff. (Illus.). 20p. 1999. pap. 18.00 (*1-56900-115-4*, 1199) Am Occup Therapy.

Occupational Therapy Services for Children & Youth under the Individuals with Disabilities Education Act. Elizabeth Maruyama et al. LC 97-172030. iv, 240 p. 1997. 50.00 (*1-56900-069-7*) Am Occup Therapy.

***Occupational Therapy Services for Children & Youth under the Individuals with Disabilities Education Act.** 2nd ed. AOTA Staff. (Illus.). 1999. pap. write for info. (*1-56900-137-5*) Am Occup Therapy.

Occupational Therapy Stories: Psychosocial Interaction in Practice. Barbara Borg & Mary A. Bruce. LC 96-53891. 192p. (C). 1997. pap. 29.00 (*1-55642-313-6*, 33136) SLACK Inc.

Occupational Therapy Strategies & Adaptations for Independent Daily Living. Ed. by Florence S. Cromwell. LC 84-19157. (Occupational Therapy in Health Care Ser.: Vol. 1, No. 4). 186p. 1985. text 39.95 (*0-86656-350-4*); pap. text 2.95 (*0-86656-380-6*) Haworth Pr.

Occupational Therapy Student Primer: A Guide to College Success. Karen Sladyk. LC 97-7852. (Illus.). 348p. 1997. pap. 29.00 (*1-55642-318-7*, 33187) SLACK Inc.

Occupational Therapy Treatment Goals for the Physically & Cognitively Disabled. Claudia K. Allen et al. 350p. (C). 1992. pap. text 58.00 (*0-910317-72-0*) Am Occup Therapy.

Occupational Therapy with Borderline Patients. Ed. by Diane Gibson. LC 83-13008. (Occupational Therapy in Mental Health Ser.: Vol. 3, No. 3). 91p. 1983. text 39.95 (*0-86656-262-1*) Haworth Pr.

Occupational Therapy with Children. Helen Clancy. (Illus.). 320p. 1990. pap. text 35.00 (*0-443-03437-0*) Church.

Occupational Toxicants: Critical Data Evaluation for MAK Values & Classification of Carcinogens, Vol. 1. Ed. by Commission for the Investigation of Health Hazards & Dietrich Henschler. (Illus.). 398p. 1990. 165.00 (*3-527-27019-1*, Wiley-VCH) Wiley.

Occupational Toxicants: Critical Data Evaluation for MAK Values & Classification of Carcinogens, Vol. 2. Ed. by Commission for the Investigation of Health Hazards & Dietrich Henschler. (Illus.). 349p. 1991. 165.00 (*3-527-27022-1*, Wiley-VCH) Wiley.

Occupational Toxicants: Critical Data Evaluation for MAK Values & Classification of Carcinogens, Vol. 3. Ed. by Commission for the Investigation of Health Hazards & Dietrich Henschler. (Illus.). 380p. 1992. 165.00 (*3-527-27023-X*, Wiley-VCH) Wiley.

Occupational Toxicants: Critical Data Evaluation for MAK Values & Classification of Carcinogens, Vol. 4. Ed. by Commission for the Investigation of Health Hazards & Dietrich Henschler. (Illus.). 385p. 1992. 165.00 (*3-527-27025-6*, Wiley-VCH) Wiley.

Occupational Toxicants: Critical Data Evaluation for MAK Values & Classification of Carcinogens, Vol. 5. Ed. by Commission for the Investigation of Health Hazards & Dietrich Henschler. (Illus.). 390p. 1993. 165.00 (*3-527-27030-2*, Wiley-VCH) Wiley.

Occupational Toxicants: Critical Data Evaluation for MAK Values & Classification of Carcinogens, Vol. 6. Ed. by Commission for the Investigation of Health Hazards & Dietrich Henschler. (Illus.). 368p. 1994. 165.00 (*3-527-27031-0*, Wiley-VCH) Wiley.

Occupational Toxicants: Critical Data Evaluation for Mak Values & Classification of Carcinogens, Vol. 8. Ed. by H. Greim. 364p. 1997. 195.00 (*3-527-27038-8*) Wiley.

Occupational Toxicants: Critical Data Evaluation for MAK Values & Classification of Carcinogens, Vol. 9. Greim. 352p. 1998. pap. 195.00 (*3-527-27039-6*) Wiley.

***Occupational Toxicants: Critical Data Evaluation for Mak Values & Classification of Carcinogens, Vol. 11.** Ed. by D. Henschler. 364p. 1998. 155.00 (*3-527-27042-6*) Wiley.

***Occupational Toxicants: Critical Data Evaluation For Mak Values & Classification of Carcinogens, Vol. 12.** Helmut Greim. 358p. 1999. 160.00 (*3-527-27043-4*) Wiley.

***Occupational Toxicants: Critical Data Evaluation for Mak Values & Classification of Carcinogens, Vol. 13.** Ed. by D. Henschler. 349p. 1999. text 135.00 (*3-527-27047-7*) Wiley.

Occupational Toxicants Vol. 7: Critical Data Evaluation for MAK Values & Classification of Carcinogens, Vol. 7. Ed. by Dietrich Henschler & H. Greim. (Illus.). 350p. 1996. 195.00 (*3-527-27037-X*, Wiley-VCH) Wiley.

Occupational Toxicology. Ed. by Neill H. Stacey. LC 93-13852. 420p. 1993. 45.00 (*0-85066-830-1*, Pub. by Tay Francis Ltd); pap. 45.00 (*0-85066-831-X*, Pub. by Tay Francis Ltd) Taylor & Francis.

An Asterisk (*) at the beginning of an entry indicates that the title is appearing for the first time.

Occupational Training Program Guide. Robert W. Skarlinski. 42p. 1997. 39.95 (*1-58532-000-5*) Basic Ed Materials.

***Occupational Training Program Workbook: Student Edition.** Robert W. Skarlinski. 1998. student ed., wbk. ed. 39.95 (*1-58532-016-1*) Basic Ed Materials.

***Occupational Training Program Workbook: Teacher's Edition.** Robert W. Skarlinski. 82p. 1998. teacher ed., wbk. ed. 39.95 (*1-58532-001-3*) Basic Ed Materials.

Occupational Values & Post-College Career Change. Ralph Underhill. (Report Ser.: No. 120). 1967. 15.00 (*0-932132-12-X*) Natl Opinion Res.

Occupations & Social Status. Albert J. Reiss, Jr. et al. Ed. by Leon Stein. LC 77-70525. (Illus.). 1977. reprint ed. lib. bdg. 33.95 (*0-405-10193-7*) Ayer.

Occupations & Values. Morris Rosenberg. Ed. by Harriet Zuckerman & Robert K. Merton. LC 79-9020. (Dissertations on Sociology Ser.). 1980. reprint ed. lib. bdg. 18.95 (*0-405-12989-0*) Ayer.

Occupations in the Tourist Sector: A Comparative Analysis in Nine Community States. Duccio Guerra et al. LC 96-110253. 1994. 25.00 (*92-826-8367-2*, Pub. by Comm Europ Commun) Bernan Associates.

Occupations of Migrants in Ghana. Polly Hill. (Anthropological Papers Ser.: No. 42). 1970. pap. 2.00 (*0-932206-40-9*) U Mich Mus Anthro.

Occupations Theme Set, 6 bks. (Beginners Ser.). 1991. 290.72 (*0-8123-7214-X*); pap. 10.52 (*0-8123-6988-2*); pap. 10.52 (*0-8123-6951-3*); pap. 10.52 (*0-8123-6974-2*); pap. 10.52 (*0-8123-6991-2*); pap. 10.52 (*0-8123-6995-5*); pap. 10.52 (*0-8123-6958-0*) McDougal-Littell.

***Occupied America.** 4th ed. Rodolfo Acuna. LC 99-42046. 554p. (C). 1999. pap. text 46.00 (*0-321-04485-1*) Addison-Wesley.

Occupied America: A History of Chicanos. 3rd ed. Rodolfo Acuna. 475p. (C). 1997. pap. 49.00 (*0-06-040163-X*) Addson-Wesley Educ.

Occupied France: Resistance & Collaboration, 1900-1944. Roderick Kedward. (Historical Association Studies). 96p. 1985. pap. 15.95 (*0-631-13927-3*) Blackwell Pubs.

Occupied Haiti. Emily G. Balch. LC 75-14988. 186p. 1970. reprint ed. lib. bdg. 45.00 (*0-8371-2785-8*, BAL&) Greenwood.

Occupied Japan Collectibles. Florence Archambault. LC 91-67013. (Illus.). 208p. 1992. text 49.95 (*0-88740-378-6*) Schiffer.

***Occupied Japan for the Home.** Florence Archambault. (Illus.). 160p. 2000. pap. 24.95 (*0-7643-1133-6*) Schiffer.

Occupied Japan Toys. David Gould & Donna Crevar-Donaldson. (Illus.). 95p. (Orig.). 1993. pap. 14.95 (*0-89538-053-6*) L-W Inc.

Occupied Latvia Today. Ed. by Karlis Streips. LC 86-51374. 100p. 1987. 10.00 (*0-317-61420-7*) World Fed Free Latvians.

Occupied Reading: Critical Foundations for Ecological Theory. Alan A. Block. LC 94-22358. (Critical Education Practice Ser.: Vol. 3). 264p. 1995. pap. text 23.95 (*0-8153-1925-8*, SS860) Garland.

Occupied Reading: Critical Foundations for Ecological Theory. Alan A. Block. LC 94-22358. (Critical Education Practice Ser.: Vol. 3). 264p. 1995. text 47.00 (*0-8153-0932-5*, SS860) Garland.

Occupied Territory. Lynne Cohen. (Illus.). 112p. 1988. 37.95 (*0-89381-313-3*) Aperture.

Occupied Territory. Evelyn Wexler. 72p. (Orig.). 1994. pap. 10.00 (*0-932412-06-8*) Mayapple Pr.

Occupied Winchester, 1861 to 1865. 142p. 1976. pap. write for info. (*0-318-64332-4*) Winchester-Frederick Cty Hist Soc.

Occupier's Law: Israel & the West Bank. 2nd ed. Raja Shehadeh. LC 88-13301. 259p. 1989. 17.95 (*0-88728-200-8*) Inst Palestine.

Occupier's Liability Act, 1957 & Liability of Hospitals. Ravenswood Publ. Ltd. Staff. (C). 1957. 135.00 (*0-901812-20-X*); pap. 110.00 (*0-901812-19-6*) St Mut.

Occupiers' Liability in Singapore & Malaysia. Michael F. Rutter. 320p. 1986. 99.00 (*0-409-99513-4*, MICHIE) LEXIS Pub.

***Occupying & Connecting.** Frei Otto. (Illus.). 112p. 2001. 29.90 (*3-932565-11-8*) Edition A Menges.

Occurence at Owl Creek. abr. ed. Ambrose Bierce. LC 73-750986. 1973. audio 14.00 (*0-694-50220-0*, SWC 1525, Caedmon) HarperAudio.

Occurence, Properties & Utilization of Natural Zeolites: Papers of the 2nd International Conference on the Occurence, Properties & Utilization of Natural Zeolites August 12-16, 1985. D. Kallo & H. S. Sherry. (Illus.). 856p. (C). 1988. 207.00 (*963-05-4862-3*, Pub. by Akade Kiado) St Mut.

Occurences of Duke Snyder. Lee Dejasu. 1979. 3.50 (*0-614-18200-X*) Visual Studies.

Occurrence & Analysis of Organometallic Compounds in the Environment. T. R. Crompton. LC 97-28546. 248p. 1998. 150.00 (*0-471-97607-5*) Wiley.

Occurrence & Distribution of Selenium. Ed. by Milan Ihnat. 384p. 1989. lib. bdg. 252.95 (*0-8493-4932-X*, QD181) CRC Pr.

Occurrence & Pathways of Lead, Mercury, Cadium & Arsenic in the Environment: Scope 31. Thomas C. Hutchinson & K. M. Meema. LC 86-9199. 384p. 1987. 550.00 (*0-471-91126-7*) Wiley.

Occurrence & Petrophysical Properties of Carbonate Reservoirs in the Rocky Mountain Region. Ed. by Steven M. Goolsby & Mark W. Longman. 500p. 1988. 20.00 (*0-933979-11-8*) Rocky Mtn Assoc Geol.

Occurrence & Significance of Erosion, Deposition & Flooding in Great Britain. (Illus.). 202p. 1995. pap. 50.00 (*0-11-753118-9*, Pub. by Statnry Office) Balogh.

***Occurrence at Owl Creek Bridge.** Ambrose Bierce. 2000. pap. 3.95 (*1-86092-006-3*, Pub. by Travelman Pub) IPG Chicago.

Occurrence at Owl Creek Bridge. Christopher Sergel. 22p. (YA). (gr. 10 up). 1967. pap. 3.50 (*0-87129-343-9*, O10) Dramatic Pub.

Occurrence, Characteristics, & Genesis of Carbonde Gypsum & Silica Accumulations in Soils. (SSSA Special Publications: No. 26). 149p. 1991. 18.00 (*0-89118-794-4*) Soil Sci Soc Am.

Occurrence, Diagnosis, & Sources of Hospital-Associated Infections. Ed. by Willson J. Fahlberg & Dieter Groschel. LC 78-8320. (Handbook on Hospital-Associated Infections Ser.: No. 1). 152p. reprint ed. pap. 47.20 (*0-7837-0623-5*, 204096700019) Bks Demand.

Occurrence of Faults in Heating & Ventilating Equipment. A. Hasan. (C). 1972. 53.00 (*0-7855-4408-9*, Pub. by Build Servs Info Assn) St Mut.

***Occurrence of Herbicides/Pesticides in Drinking Water.** Michelle Frey. LC 99-462189. 2000. write for info. (*1-58321-060-1*) Am Water Wks Assn.

Occurrence of Tune. Charles Bernstein. (Segue Bks.). (Illus.). 24p. (Orig.). 1983. pap. text 60.00 (*0-937804-08-8*) Segue NYC.

***OCD in Children & Adolescents: A Cognitive-Behavioral Treatment Manual.** John S. March & Karen Mulle. LC 98-2637. 298p. 1998. lib. bdg. 35.00 (*1-57230-242-9*) Guilford Pubns.

***OCD Workbook: Your Guide to Breaking Free from Obsessive-Compulsive Disorder.** Bruce M. Hyman & Cherry Pedrick. 198p. 1999. pap. 18.95 (*1-57224-169-1*) New Harbinger.

Ocean see Biomes of the World - Group 1

Ocean. (Pop Into Nature Ser.). 12p. 1999. 6.99 (*0-7681-0099-2*, McClanahan Book) Learn Horizon.

Ocean. Pam Adams. (Panorama Ser.). 32p. (J). (ps). 1984. 9.99 (*0-85953-193-7*, Pub. by Childs Play) Random House.

Ocean. Gilda Berger. (Smart Science Ser.). (Illus.). 16p. (J). (gr. 2-5). Date not set. pap. 5.95 (*1-58273-507-7*) Newbridge Educ.

***Ocean.** Moira Butterfield. (Where Am I? Ser.). (Illus.). 32p. (J). (gr. 2-6). 1999. lib. bdg. 15.95 (*1-929298-36-6*, Pub. by Thameside Pr) Smart Apple.

Ocean Susan Canizares & Pamela Chanko. LC 98-23226. (Science Emergent Readers Ser.). 1998. 2.50 (*0-590-63886-6*) Scholastic Inc.

***Ocean.** James Hanley. 160p. 2000. pap. 15.00 (*1-86046-675-3*, Pub. by Harvill Press) FS&G.

Ocean. Mel Higginson. LC 94-9404. (This Earth of Ours Discovery Library). 24p. (J). (gr. k-4). 1994. lib. bdg. 10.95 (*0-86593-379-0*) Rourke Corp.

***Ocean.** Judith Jango-Cohen. (HighQ First Activity Bks.). (Illus.). 48p. (J). (ps-1). 2000. mass mkt. 3.99 (*0-7681-0218-9*, McClanahan Book) Learn Horizon.

Ocean. Mirand A. MacQuitty. LC 97-18889. (Inside Guides Ser.). (J). 1997. write for info. (*0-7894-2035-X*) DK Pub Inc.

***Ocean.** Miranda MacQuitty. (Eyewitness Books). (Illus.). (J). (gr. 4-7). 2000. 19.99 (*0-7894-6611-2*) DK Pub Inc.

***Ocean.** Miranda MacQuitty. (Eyewitness Books). (J). (gr. 4-7). 2000. 15.95 (*0-7894-6034-3*) DK Pub Inc.

Ocean. Miranda MacQuitty. (Illus.). 64p. (J). (gr. 5). 1995. 19.00 (*0-679-87331-7*); lib. bdg. 20.99 (*0-679-97331-1*) Random.

Ocean. Cari Meister. LC 98-11751. (Going Places Ser.). (Illus.). 24p. (J). 2000. lib. bdg. 18.60 (*1-57765-027-1*, Checkerboard Library) ABDO Pub Co.

Ocean. Sayre. 1996. write for info. (*0-8050-5259-3*) H Holt & Co.

Ocean. April P. Sayre. LC 96-2419. (Exploring Earth's Biomes Ser.). 80p. (J). (gr. 5-8). 1995. lib. bdg. 20.40 (*0-8050-4084-6*) TFC Bks NY.

Ocean: A Science Workbook. Mary K. Bozanksy & Bonnie Pettifor. (Illus.). 64p. (J). (ps). 1998. pap., wbk. ed. 5.95 (*1-56565-672-5*, 06725W, Pub. by Lowell Hse Juvenile) NTC Contemp Pub Co.

Ocean: An Introduction to Jodo-Shinshu Buddhism in America. Kenneth K. Tanaka. LC 97-90710. 288p. (Orig.). 1997. pap. 14.95 (*0-9658062-0-0*) WisdomOcean.

Ocean: Consider the Connections. Center for Environmental Education Staff. Ed. by Linda Maraniss & Rose Bierce. (Illus.). 104p. (Orig.). (J). (gr. 2-6). 1985. pap., student ed. 8.95 (*0-9615294-0-7*) Ctr Env Educ.

***Ocean: Hands-On Minds-On Science.** Mary Ellen Sterling. (Illus.). 96p. (J). 1999. pap., teacher ed. 11.95 (*1-57690-388-5*, TCM2388) Tchr Create Mat.

Ocean: The Living World. Barbara Taylor et al. (Illus.). 80p. (J). (gr. 1-7). 1994. write for info. (*1-56458-775-4*) DK Pub Inc.

Ocean - My Railroad, Diary of an Artist, 1973-1997. Era Gregersen. LC 99-70440. 256p. 1999. pap. 25.00 (*1-57197-176-9*) Pentland Pr.

Ocean Acoustic Propagation by Finite Difference Methods. D. Lee & S. T. McDaniel. (International Series in Modern Applied Mathematics & Computer Science: No. 15). 121p. 1988. 36.00 (*0-08-034871-8*, Pergamon Pr) Elsevier.

Ocean Acoustic Tomography. Walter Munk et al. (Monographs on Mechanics). (Illus.). 447p. (C). 1995. text 69.95 (*0-521-47095-1*) Cambridge U Pr.

Ocean Acoustics: Theory & Experiment in Underwater Sound. Ivan S. Tolstoy & Clarence S. Clay. LC 87-70798. 381p. 1987. reprint ed. pap. text 26.00 (*0-88318-527-X*) Acoustical Soc Am.

Ocean Almanac. Robert Hendrickson. LC 81-43584. (Illus.). 480p. 1984. pap. 21.95 (*0-385-14077-0*) Doubleday.

Ocean Alphabet Book. Jerry Pallotta. LC 89-60424. (Jerry Pallotta's Alphabet Bks.). (Illus.). 32p. (J). (ps-3). 1989. 15.95 (*0-88106-458-0*); pap. 6.95 (*0-88106-452-1*) Charlesbridge Pub.

Ocean Alphabet Book. Jerry Pallotta. (J). 1986. 12.15 (*0-606-03878-7*, Pub. by Turtleback) Demco.

Ocean & Marine Dictionary. David F. Tver. LC 79-1529. 368p. 1979. reprint ed. pap. 114.10 (*0-7837-9067-8*, 204981600003) Bks Demand.

Ocean & Pebbles. large type ed. Basia Hoffman. LC 97-92475. (Illus.). 32p. (J). (ps-2). 1997. 15.95 (*1-890582-01-8*) Creat by Basia.

Ocean & Pebbles. large type ed. Basia Hoffman. LC 97-92475. (Illus.). 32p. (J). (ps-2). 1999. pap. write for info. (*1-890582-02-6*) Creat by Basia.

Ocean & Seabed Acoustics. George V. Frisk. 500p. (C). 1994. text 46.60 (*0-13-630112-6*) P-H.

Ocean & the Boy. Giuseppe Conte. Tr. by Laura Stortoni from ITA. 208p. (Orig.). 1997. pap. 15.00 (*0-9641003-0-4*) Hesperia Pr.

Ocean & the Poles: Grand Challenges for European Cooperations. Ed. by Gotthilf Hempel. (Illus.). 300p. 1996. pap. 60.00 (*3-334-61023-3*, Wiley-VCH) Wiley.

Ocean Animal Clue Game: Six Playful Nature Card Games about Animals & Their Lives. Joseph Cornell. (Illus.). 60p. (YA). (gr. 2 up). 1995. boxed set 11.95 (*1-883220-27-0*) Dawn CA.

Ocean Animals. Margie Burton et al. Ed. by Alison Adams. (Early Connections Ser.). 16p. (J). (gr. k-2). 1999. pap. text 4.50 (*1-58344-074-7*) Benchmark Educ.

Ocean Animals. Arthur Morton. (Illus.). (J). (gr. k-3). 1993. 12.50 (*1-57842-061-X*) Delmas Creat.

Ocean Animals. Arthur Morton. Tr. by Suon Thach. (CAM.). (J). (gr. k-3). 1995. 12.50 (*1-57842-064-4*) Delmas Creat.

Ocean Animals, Hat Patterns & Activities. Patt Newbold & Anne Diebel. (Illus.). 46p. (J). (ps-4). 1996. pap. text 9.95 (*1-56422-985-8*) Start Reading.

Ocean Animals in Danger. Gary Turbak. LC 94-13131. (Survivors Series for Children). (Illus.). 32p. (J). (gr. 1-3). 1994. lib. bdg. 14.95 (*0-87358-574-7*, Rising Moon Bks) Northland AZ.

Ocean Apart. Robin Pilcher. LC 98-11664. 470p. 1998. text 24.95 (*0-312-19995-3*, Thomas Dunne) St Martin.

Ocean Apart: A Novel. Robin Pilcher. LC 99-19828. 1999. 29.95 (*0-7862-1911-4*) Mac Lib Ref.

Ocean Apart: A Novel. Robin Pilcher. 512p. 1999. pap. 6.99 (*0-312-97184-2*, St Martins Paperbacks) St Martin.

Ocean Apart: Explaining Three Decades of U. S.-Japanese Trade Frictions. Stephen D. Cohen. LC 97-22802. 272p. 1998. 65.00 (*0-275-95686-5*, Praeger Pubs) Greenwood.

Ocean Apart: The Relationship Between Britain & America in the Twentieth Century. David Dimbleby. 1989. 9.95 (*0-07-558699-1*) McGraw.

Ocean Apart: Vietnamese Contemporary Art from the United States & Vietnam. Lois Tarlow. LC 95-40345. Orig. Title: Nghin Trung Xa Cach. (ENG & VIE., Illus.). 128p. 1996. pap. 22.95 (*1-57098-055-1*) Roberts Rinehart.

Ocean at the Window: Hungarian Prose & Poetry since 1945. Ed. by Albert Tezla. LC 80-39770. 524p. reprint ed. pap. 162.50 (*0-7837-2915-4*, 205753900006) Bks Demand.

Ocean-Atmosphere Interaction & Climate Modeling. Boris A. Kagan. (Cambridge Atmospheric & Space Science Ser.: No. 11). (Illus.). 391p. (C). 1995. text 95.00 (*0-521-44445-4*) Cambridge U Pr.

Ocean-Atmosphere System. J. M. Walker & Allen H. Perry. LC 76-44276. 172p. reprint ed. pap. 53.40 (*0-608-13077-X*, 202521100043) Bks Demand.

***Ocean Avenger: Voyage into the Millennium.** Harold Thurston. Ed. by Marthalie Thurston-Lee. 300p. 1999. pap. 17.95 (*0-7392-0375-4*, P03591) Morris Pubng.

Ocean Avenue. Malena Morling. LC 98-66495. 1999. 22.00 (*0-932826-70-9*) New Issues MI.

Ocean Avenue. Margaret Wilkinson. LC 90-60293. 256p. (Orig.). 1991. pap. 14.95 (*1-85242-195-9*) Serpents Tail.

Ocean Avenue: (Poems) Malena Morling. LC 98-66595. (Poetry Ser.). 64p. 1999. pap. 12.00 (*0-932826-68-7*) WMU Poetry & Prose.

Ocean Basins. Open University Team Staff. (Open University Oceanography Ser.). 1988. pap. text 11.75 (*0-08-036930-8*, Pergamon Pr) Elsevier.

Ocean Basins: Structure. 2nd ed. Open University Program Staff. 1998. pap. text 37.95 (*0-7506-3983-0*) Buttrwrth-Heinemann.

Ocean Basins: Their Structure & Evolution. Ed. by Open University Team Staff. (Open University Oceonography Ser.). (Illus.). 120p. (C). 1988. pap. text 34.95 (*0-08-036365-2*, Prgamon Press) Buttrwrth-Heinemann.

Ocean Basins & Margins. Ed. by Alan E. Nairn & Francis G. Stehli. Incl. Vol. 1, The South Atlantic. LC 72-83046. 600p. 1973. (*0-306-37771-3*, Kluwer Plenum); Vol. 2, The North Atlantic. LC 72-83046. 662p. 1974. (*0-306-37772-1*, Kluwer Plenum); Vol. 3, The Gulf of Mexico & The Caribbean. LC 72-83046. 722p. 1975. (*0-306-37773-X*, Kluwer Plenum); Vol. 4A, The Eastern Mediterranean. LC 72-83046. 520p. 1977. (*0-306-37774-8*, Kluwer Plenum); Vol. 4B, The Western Mediterranean. LC 72-83046. 462p. 1978. (*0-306-37779-9*, Kluwer Plenum); Vol. 5, The Arctic Ocean. LC 72-83046. 686p. 1981. (*0-306-37775-6*, Kluwer Plenum); LC 72-83046. (Illus.). 125.00 (*0-685-04080-1*, Plenum Trade) Perseus Pubng.

Ocean Basins & Margins Vol. 6: The Indian Ocean. Ed. by Alan E. Nairn & Francis G. Stehli. LC 72-83046. 794p. 1982. 125.00 (*0-306-37776-4*, Plenum Trade) Perseus Pubng.

Ocean Basins & Margins Vol. 7A: The Pacific Ocean. A. E. Naim & F. G. Stehli. (Illus.). 748p. (C). 1985. 135.00 (*0-306-37777-2*, Plenum Trade) Perseus Pubng.

Ocean Basins & Margins Vol. 7B: The Pacific Ocean. A. E. Naim et al. (Illus.). 656p. (C). 1988. 135.00 (*0-306-37778-0*, Plenum Trade) Perseus Pubng.

Ocean Basins & Margins Vol. 8: The Tethys Ocean, Vol 8. A. E. Naim et al. (Illus.). 517p. (C). 1996. 150.00 (*0-306-45156-5*, Plenum Trade) Perseus Pubng.

***Ocean Between.** William D. Becher. xiv 672p. 2000. 27.95 (*0-9677283-4-7*) Barton.

Ocean Between. Margaret B. Edwards. (Illus.). 168p. (J). (gr. 5-8). 1993. pap. 6.95 (*0-929141-19-9*) Napoleon Publ.

Ocean Bills of Lading: Traditional Forms, Substitutes, & EDI Systems. Ed. by A. N. Yiannopoulos. LC 95-5126. 1995. lib. bdg. 105.50 (*0-7923-3361-6*, Pub. by M Nijhoff) Kluwer Academic.

Ocean Black. Hank Bostrum. 1995. mass mkt. 5.50 (*0-7860-0196-8*, Pinncle Kensgtn) Kensgtn Pub Corp.

Ocean Black. Ed. by Nal-Dutton Staff. 1993. pap. 4.50 (*0-8217-4329-5*) NAL.

Ocean Book: Aquarium & Seaside Activities & Ideas for All Ages. Center for Marine Conservation Staff. 113p. 1989. 22.95 (*0-471-50973-6*) Wiley.

Ocean Book: Aquarium & Seaside Activities & Ideas for All Ages. Center for Marine Conservation Staff. 128p. (J). (gr. k-6). 1989. pap. 12.95 (*0-471-62078-5*) Wiley.

Ocean Born. Chris Griscom. (Illus.). 95p. 1989. 25.00 (*99911-628-3-6*) Light Inst Fndtn.

Ocean Boundary Making: Regional Issues & Developments. Ed. by Douglas M. Johnston & Phillip M. Saunders. 304p. 1987. lib. bdg. 82.50 (*0-7099-1495-4*, Pub. by C Helm) Routldge.

Ocean Bridge: The History of RAF Ferry Command. Carl A. Christie. (Illus.). 458p. 1995. reprint ed. 39.95 (*0-8020-0638-8*) U of Toronto Pr.

Ocean Bridge: The History of RAF Ferry Command. Carl A. Christie. (Illus.). 458p. 1997. reprint ed. pap. 19.95 (*0-8020-8131-2*) U of Toronto Pr.

Ocean Buddies: Life in the Salty Seas. Dabney M. Philabaum & Nancy L. Alegret. (Illus.). 32p. (Orig.). (J). (gr. 2-6). 1996. pap. 7.95 (*0-9639215-1-7*) Earth Buddies.

Ocean Characteristics & Their Changes. Tr. by P. R. Kanade from JPN. (C). 1991. 142.00 (*81-7087-062-3*, Pub. by A A Balkema) Ashgate Pub Co.

Ocean Characteristics & Their Changes: Special Research Project - Newsletter No. 1-17. Tr. by P. R. Kanade from JPN. 425p. (C). 1991. text 142.00 (*90-6191-470-1*, Pub. by A A Balkema) Ashgate Pub Co.

Ocean Chemistry. Open University Team Staff. (Open University Oceanography Ser.). 1989. pap. text 11.70 (*0-08-036934-0*, Pergamon Pr) Elsevier.

Ocean Chemistry & Deep-Sea Sediments, Vol. 5. Ed. by Open University Course Team Staff. (Illus.). 128p. 1989. pap. text 39.95 (*0-08-036373-3*, Prgamon Press) Buttrwrth-Heinemann.

Ocean Circulation. Open University Program Staff. 1989. pap. text 39.95 (*0-7506-3716-1*) Buttrwrth-Heinemann.

Ocean Circulation. Open University Team Staff. (Open University Oceanography Ser.). 1989. pap. text 11.70 (*0-08-036932-4*, Pergamon Pr) Elsevier.

Ocean Circulation Inverse Problem. Carl Wunsch. (Illus.). 458p. (C). 1996. text 59.95 (*0-521-48090-6*) Cambridge U Pr.

Ocean Circulation Theory. Joseph Pedlosky. LC 96-13298. 1996. write for info. (*0-387-60489-8*); 89.95 (*3-540-60489-8*) Spr-Verlag.

Ocean City. Frank Esposito & Robert Esposito. LC 97-133978. (Images of America Ser.). 1999. pap. 16.99 (*0-7524-0478-4*) Arcadia Publng.

***Ocean City, Vol. I.** Nan DeVincent-Hayes & John E. Jacob. (Images of America Ser.). (Illus.). 128p. 1999. pap. 18.99 (*0-7385-0122-0*) Arcadia Publng.

***Ocean City, Vol. II.** Nan DeVincent-Hayes & John E. Jacob. (Images of America Ser.). (Illus.). 128p. 1999. pap. 18.99 (*0-7385-0123-9*) Arcadia Publng.

Ocean City, MD. 260p. 1998. pap. 10.95 (*0-9661994-0-5*) Palmer & Stewart.

Ocean City Postcards. Mark McLaughlin. (Postcard History Ser.). 128p. 1999. pap. 18.99 (*0-7524-0960-3*) Arcadia Publng.

Ocean City II. Frank J. Esposito & Robert J. Esposito. (Images of America Ser.). (Illus.). 128p. 1998. pap. 16.99 (*0-7524-0984-0*) Arcadia Publng.

Ocean Color - Theory & Applications in a Decade of CZCS Experience: Based on the Lectures Given During the Eurocourse Held at the Joint Research Centre Ispra, Italy, October 21, 1991. Ed. by Vittorio Barale & Peter M. Schlittenhardt. LC 92-46130. (Eurocourses: Remote Sensing Ser.: No. 3). 384p. (C). 1993. text 188.00 (*0-7923-1586-3*) Kluwer Academic.

***Ocean Community Conference 99: Celebrating 1998 International Year of the Ocean, 2 vols., Set.** 1195p. 1998. 100.00 (*0-933957-21-1*) Marine Tech Soc.

Ocean Container Transportation: An Operations Perspective. Mark L. Chadwin et al. (Illus.). 300p. (C). 1990. text 90.00 (*0-8448-1628-0*) Taylor & Francis.

Ocean Counting Book. Jerry Pallotta. LC 98-46035. (Illus.). (J). Date not set. 15.95 (*0-88106-151-4*); pap. 6.95 (*0-88106-150-6*) Charlesbridge Pub.

Ocean County see Hagstrom Atlases

Ocean Court. Arlaine Rockey. LC 98-83190. 365p. 1999. 25.00 (*0-7388-0351-0*); pap. 15.00 (*0-7388-0352-9*) Xlibris Corp.

Ocean Creatures. Sharon Shi. (Illus.). (J). (gr. k-1). 1998. write for info. (*1-892800-00-4*) Temp Tattoo.

Ocean Crisis. Linda MacRae-Campbell et al. (Our Only Earth Ser.). 104p. (J). (gr. 4-12). 1990. pap. 25.00 (*0-913705-53-5*) Zephyr Pr AZ.

Ocean Cruising on a Budget. Anne Hammick. (Illus.). 192p. 1991. pap. 19.95 (*0-87742-300-8*) Intl Marine.

Ocean Cruising on a Budget. Anne Hammick. 192p. 1991. pap. 19.95 (*0-07-158012-3*) McGraw.

***Ocean Currents: Marine Science Activities.** Craig Strang. (Illus.). 2000. pap. 21.00 (*0-924886-44-7*, GEMS) Lawrence Science.

Ocean Day. Shelley Rotner & Ken Kreisler. LC 92-6114. (Illus.). 32p. (J). (ps-1). 1993. text 14.95 (*0-02-777886-X*, Mac Bks Young Read) S&S Childrens.

O

Ocean Deep. Frances Dipper. LC 95-40835. (Mysteries Of-- Ser.). (J). 1996. 12.15 (*0-606-09658-2*, Pub. by Turtleback) Demco.

Ocean Deep. Francis Dipper. (Mysteries of...Ser.). (Illus.). 40p. (J). (gr. 4-6). 1996. lib. bdg. 22.90 (*0-7613-0454-1*, Copper Beech Bks) Millbrook Pr.

Ocean Deep. Yan Nascimbene. LC 98-50011. (J). 1999. 23.95 (*1-56846-161-5*, Creative Eds) Creative Co.

***Ocean Deep: For the Right Hand or Left Hand Alone.** Kathleen Massoud. 1999. pap. 2.50 (*0-7390-0314-3*, 18991) Alfred Pub.

***Ocean Detectives: Solving the Mysteries of the Sea.** Mary M. Cerullo. LC 99-20406. (Turnstone Ocean Explorer Bks.). 64p. (J). 1999. 27.12 (*0-7398-1236-X*) Raintree Steck-V.

Ocean Detectives: Solving the Mysteries of the Sea. Mary M. Cerullo. (Turnstone Ocean Explorer Ser.). 64p. (YA). (gr. 5-9). 1999. pap. 8.95 (*0-7398-1237-8*) Raintree Steck-V.

Ocean Disposal of Waste. I. R. Wood. 300p. 1993. text 74.00 (*981-02-0956-8*); pap. text 36.00 (*981-02-1044-2*) World Scientific Pub.

Ocean Disposal Systems for Sewage Sludge & Effluent. National Research Council (U. S.), Committee on Bi. LC 84-61848. 136p. reprint ed. pap. 42.20 (*0-8357-2695-9*, 204023200015) Bks Demand.

Ocean Ecology of North Pacific Salmonids. William G. Pearcy. LC 92-6564. (Books in Recruitment Fishery Oceanography). (Illus.). 190p. 1992. 25.00 (*0-295-97192-4*) U of Wash Pr.

Ocean Energies: Resources for the Future. Roger H. Charlier & J. R. Justus. LC 92-32795. (Elsevier Oceanography Ser.: No. 56). 554p. 1992. 268.00 (*0-444-88248-0*) Elsevier.

Ocean Energy Recovery. Ed. by Hans-Jurgen Krock. LC 90-42265. 376p. 1990. pap. text 275.00 (*0-87262-778-0*) Am Soc Civil Eng.

Ocean Energy Recovery: The State of the Art. Ed. by Richard J. Seymour. LC 92-38823. 320p. 1992. pap. 29.00 (*0-87262-894-9*) Am Soc Civil Eng.

Ocean Energy Resources: Presented at the Energy Technology Conference, Houston, Texas, Sept. 18-23, 1977. Ed. by Neil T. Monney. LC 77-82206. Vol. 4. (Illus.). 110p. reprint ed. pap. 31.40 (*0-317-09776-8*, 2016806) Bks Demand.

Ocean Engineering Division: Proceedings, ASME International Mechanical Engineering Congress & Exposition, Dallas, TX, 1997. Ed. by Daniel T. Valentine & Craig C. Jahnke. LC 98-166448. (OED Ser.: Vol. 14). 258p. 1997. pap. 110.00 (*0-7918-1853-5*, TC330) ASME Pr.

Ocean Engineering for OTEC: Presented at the 1980 Energy-Sources Technology Conference & Exhibition, New Orleans, Louisiana, February 3-7, 1980. Energy Sources Technology Conference & Exhibition. Ed. by Owen M. Griffin & Julio G. Giannotti. LC 79-57424. (OED Ser.: Vol. 9). (Illus.). 93p. reprint ed. pap. 30.00 (*0-8357-2894-3*, 203913000011) Bks Demand.

Ocean Engineering Power Systems. Alexander D. Carmichael. LC 74-4343. (Massachusetts Institute of Technology, Sea Grant Program Ser.: Report No. MITSG 74-15). (Illus.). 206p. 1974. reprint ed. pap. 63.90 (*0-7837-9068-6*, 204981700003) Bks Demand.

Ocean Environmental Management: A Primer on the Role of the Oceans & How to Maintain their Contributions to Life on Earth. Ernst G. Frankel. LC 94-33448. 350p. (C). 1995. 53.20 (*0-13-184557-8*) P-H.

***Ocean Explorer, 4 vols.** Ed. by Raintree Steck-Vaughn Publishing Staff. (Illus.). 2000. pap. 75.92 (*0-7398-1711-6*) Raintree Steck-V.

Ocean Facts. B. Gibbs. (Facts & Lists Ser.). (Illus.). 48p. (J). (gr. 3-7). 1991. pap. 5.95 (*0-7460-0621-7*, Usborne) EDC.

Ocean Floor: Bruce Heezen Commemorative Volume. Bruce C. Heezen. Ed. by R. A. Scrutton & Manik Talwani. LC 81-14700. (Illus.). 363p. reprint ed. pap. 112.60 (*0-8357-3084-0*, 203934100012) Bks Demand.

Ocean Floor Mysteries Vol. 1: The Amazing Mystery of the Great Face on the Pacific Ocean Floor. unabridged ed. Lloyd S. Carpenter. LC 97-92205. (Illus.). x, 244p. 1997. pap. write for info. (*0-9659627-0-9*) Spiral Ent Publ.

Ocean Freight Forwarder, the Exporter, & the Law. Gerald H. Ullman. LC 67-25958. 140p. 1967. reprint ed. pap. 43.40 (*0-608-02457-0*, 206310100004) Bks Demand.

Ocean Governance: Strategies & Approaches for the 21st Century. Contrib. by Thomas A. Mensah. LC 96-46528. (Proceedings of the Annual Conference of the Law of the Sea Institute Ser.: No. P28). 1996. 58.00 (*0-911189-31-9*) Law Sea Inst.

Ocean Governance: Strategies & Approaches for the 21st Century. Ed. by Thomas A. Mensah. (Proceedings of the Law of the Sea Institute's Annual Conference Ser.: Vol. 28). 700p. 1996. write for info. (*0-614-23966-4*) Law Sea Inst.

Ocean Governance for Hawaii. Contrib. by Thomas A. Mensah. (Law of the Sea Institute Ser.: Vol. 3). 1995. pap. 15.00 (*0-911189-29-7*) Law Sea Inst.

***Ocean Grove.** Wayne Bell. LC 00-102556. (Images of America Ser.). (Illus.). 128p. 2000. pap. 18.99 (*0-7385-0425-4*) Arcadia Publng.

Ocean Highway. Federal Writers' Project Staff. LC 72-10937. (American Guidebook Ser.). 1980. reprint ed. lib. bdg. 59.00 (*0-685-04695-8*) Somerset Pub.

Ocean Highway. Federal Writers' Project Staff & Writers Program-WPA Staff. (American Guide Ser.). 1989. reprint ed. lib. bdg. 59.00 (*0-7812-1069-0*, 1069) Rprt Serv.

Ocean, Ice, & Atmosphere: Interactions at the Antarctic Continental Margin. Ed. by Stanley S. Jacobs & Ray F. Weiss. LC 98-22203. (Antarctic Research Ser.: Vol. 75). 1998. 75.00 (*0-87590-910-8*) Am Geophysical.

Ocean in Iowa: A Novel. Peter Hedges. LC 97-40354. 248p. (J). 1998. 22.95 (*0-7868-6404-4*, Pub. by Hyperion) Time Warner.

Ocean in Iowa: A Novel. Peter Hedges. 256p. 1999. per. 11.00 (*0-684-85970-X*) S&S Trade Pap.

Ocean in Mind. Will Kyselka. LC 87-19171. (Illus.). 176p. 1987. pap. 16.95 (*0-8248-1112-7*, Kolowalu Bk) UH Pr.

Ocean Inside Kenji Takezo. Rick Noguchi. LC 96-10143. (Poetry Ser.). 75p. 1996. pap. 10.95 (*0-8229-5613-6*); text 24.95 (*0-8229-3959-2*) U of Pittsburgh Pr.

Ocean Law & Policy. Lorne K. Kriwoken. LC 98-112167. 1996. lib. bdg. 119.00 (*90-411-0937-4*) Kluwer Academic.

Ocean Life see Under the Microscope

Ocean Life. (Discover Ser.). (Illus.). 48p. (J). 1993. 9.98 (*1-56173-103-X*) Pubns Intl Ltd.

***Ocean Life.** Brighter Vision Publishing Staff. (Kindergarten Learning Adventure Bks.). (J). 1999. pap. 2.25 (*1-55254-056-1*) Brighter Vision.

Ocean Life. Nicholas Harris. (Big Book of Mobiles). (Illus.). 24p. (J). (gr. 1 up). 1999. pap. 12.95 (*0-7835-4889-3*) Time-Life.

Ocean Life. R. Morris. (Mysteries & Marvels Ser.). (Illus.). 32p. (J). (gr. 3-7). 1983. text 5.95 (*0-86020-753-6*, Usborne) EDC.

Ocean Life. R. Morris. (Mysteries & Marvels Ser.). (Illus.). 32p. (J). (gr. 3-7). 1999. lib. bdg. 14.95 (*0-88110-149-4*, Usborne) EDC.

Ocean Life. Steve Parker. 1995. 7.98 (*0-7858-0418-8*) Bk Sales Inc.

***Ocean Life.** Time-Life Books Editors. LC 99-29720. (Student Library). (gr. 3). 1999. 14.99 (*0-7835-1357-7*) Time-Life.

Ocean Life: A Theme Unit Developed with the New Jersey State Aquarium. Lisa Rudy. 1994. pap. 9.95 (*0-590-49508-9*) Scholastic Inc.

Ocean Life: Tide Pool Creatures. Alice Leonhardt. 40p. (J). (gr. 2-4). 1999. pap. 5.95 (*0-7398-1481-8*) Raintree Steck-V.

Ocean Life Activity Book. Linda Milliken. Ed. by Kathy Rogers. (Hands-On Science Ser.). (Illus.). 48p. 1998. pap., wbk. ed. 6.95 (*1-56472-116-7*) Edupress Inc.

Ocean Life Photo Fun Activities. Mary Jo Keller & Kathy Rogers. (Science Photo Fun Activities Ser.). (Illus.). 8p. 1997. 6.95 (*1-56472-080-2*) Edupress Inc.

Ocean Life Sticker Book. C. Bloch. (Illus.). 32p. (Orig.). (J). (gr. 6). 1993. pap. 3.95 (*1-879424-61-4*) Nickel Pr.

Ocean Liner Collectibles. Myra Yellin Outwater. LC 98-84404. 160p. 1998. pap. 29.95 (*0-7643-0581-6*) Schiffer.

Ocean Liner Postcards in Marine Art. Robert Wall. (Illus.). 192p. 1998. 29.50 (*1-85149-275-5*) Antique Collect.

Ocean Liners, Vol. 1. Oliver LeGoff. 1999. 19.99 (*0-7858-1086-2*) Bk Sales Inc.

Ocean Liners of the World. William Miller, Jr. 1984. pap. 11.50 (*0-915276-43-7*) Quadrant Pr.

Ocean Magic Book of Masks. Wilfred Spoon. LC 90-62142. (Ocean Magic Ser.). (Illus.). (J). (ps-1). 1991. 5.95 (*1-877779-13-X*) Schneider Educational.

Ocean Magic "Press 'n Peel" Game Board. Illus. by Wilfred Spoon. LC 90-62146. (Ocean Magic Ser.). (J). (ps-1). 1991. bds. 7.95 (*1-877779-14-8*) Schneider Educational.

Ocean Mammals. Elaine Landau. LC 96-17885. (True Bk.). 48p. (J). 1996. lib. bdg. 21.00 (*0-516-20041-0*) Childrens.

Ocean Mammals. Elaine Landau. (True Bks.). 48p. (J). 1997. pap. 6.95 (*0-516-26110-X*) Childrens.

Ocean Mammals. Arthur Morton. (Illus.). (J). (gr. k-3). 1993. 12.50 (*1-57842-065-2*) Delmas Creat.

Ocean Management in Global Change: Proceedings of the Conference on Ocean Management in Global Change Genoa 2226 June 1992. Ed. by P. Fabbri. (Illus.). 622p. (C). (gr. 13). 1992. 410.00 (*1-85166-868-3*) Elsevier Applied Sci.

Ocean Margin Drilling Program Atlases, Vol. 1. Laverne D. Kulm. (Regional Atlas Ser.). 1984. pap. 295.00 (*0-86720-251-3*) Jones & Bartlett.

Ocean Margin Drilling Program Atlases, Vol. 2. Alexander N. Shor & Elazar Uchipi. (Regional Atlas Ser.). 1984. pap. 295.00 (*0-86720-252-1*) Jones & Bartlett.

Ocean Margin Drilling Program Atlases, Vol. 3. Alexander N. Shor & Elazar Uchipi. (Regional Atlas Ser.). 1984. pap. 295.00 (*0-86720-253-X*) Jones & Bartlett.

Ocean Margin Drilling Program Atlases, Vol. 4. John I. Ewing & Philip D. Rabinowitz. (Regional Atlas Ser.). 1984. pap. 295.00 (*0-86720-254-8*) Jones & Bartlett.

Ocean Margin Drilling Program Atlases, Vol. 5. George M. Bryan & James R. Heirtzler. (Regional Atlas Ser.). 1984. pap. 295.00 (*0-86720-255-6*) Jones & Bartlett.

Ocean Margin Drilling Program Atlases, Vol. 6. Richard T. Buffler. (Regional Atlas Ser.). 1984. pap. 295.00 (*0-86720-256-4*) Jones & Bartlett.

Ocean Margin Drilling Program Atlases, Vol. 7. John W. Ladd & Richard T. Buffler. (Regional Atlas Ser.). 1p. 1986. pap. 295.00 (*0-86720-257-2*) Jones & Bartlett.

Ocean Margin Drilling Program Atlases, Vol. 8. Marcus G. Langseth & Jacqueline Mammerickx. (Regional Atlas Ser.). 1986. pap. 295.00 (*0-86720-258-0*) Jones & Bartlett.

Ocean Margin Drilling Program Atlases, Vol. 9. Ed. by Donald M. Hussong. (Regional Atlas Ser.). 1986. pap. 295.00 (*0-86720-259-9*) Jones & Bartlett.

Ocean Margin Drilling Program Atlases, Vol. 10. Robert C. Speed. (Regional Atlas Ser.). 1985. pap. 295.00 (*0-86720-260-2*) Jones & Bartlett.

Ocean Margin Drilling Program Atlases, Vol. 11. Philip D. Rabinowitz & Hans Schouten. (Regional Atlas Ser.). 1986. pap. 295.00 (*0-86720-261-0*) Jones & Bartlett.

Ocean Margin Drilling Program Atlases, Vol. 12. Ed. by Dennis E. Hayes & Philip D. Rabinowitz. (Regional Atlas Ser.). 1986. pap. 295.00 (*0-86720-262-9*) Jones & Bartlett.

Ocean Margin Drilling Program Atlases Vol. 13. Ed. by John L. LaBrecque. (Regional Atlas Ser.). 1986. pap. 295.00 (*0-86720-263-7*) Jones & Bartlett.

Ocean Marine Insurance, 2 vols. 2nd ed. Arthur L. Flitner & Arthur E. Brunck. LC 92-71747. 466p. 1994. 41.00 (*0-89462-071-1*, 12102/12103) IIA.

Ocean Messages. Dezia-Lehr Guthrie. 2000. write for info. (*1-881542-59-9*) Blue Star Prodns.

Ocean Modeling & Parameterization. Eric P. Chassignet et al. LC 98-34113. (NATO ASI Ser.). 1998. write for info. (*0-7923-5228-9*) Kluwer Academic.

Ocean Navigator. 6th rev. ed. Kenneth Wilkes. (Illus.). 208p. 1994. 40.00 (*0-7136-3924-5*) Sheridan.

Ocean, Ocean in the Shell. Emily Tibbetts. 24p. (J). (gr. k-6). 1992. pap. 5.00 (*1-886210-02-0*) Tyketoon Yng Author.

***Ocean of Adventure.** Eric I. Soyland. 140p. 2000. 15.00 (*0-9656278-1-0*, 102) dnalyos Pub.

Ocean of Air. David I. Blumenstock. LC 59-7509. 471p. reprint ed. pap. 146.10 (*0-608-11660-2*, 205047200083) Bks Demand.

Ocean of Bitter Dreams: Maritime Relations Between China & the United States, 1850-1915. Robert J. Schwendinger. (Illus.). 1988. 29.95 (*0-87026-067-7*) Westernlore.

Ocean of Colors. Paul S. Auerbach. (Illus.). 144p. (Orig.). 1996. pap. 24.95 (*0-87850-114-2*) Darwin Pr.

Ocean of Dreams: Forty-Three Poems. Mona Saudi & Tania Tamari Nasir. LC 99-13942. 1999. pap. 12.00 (*1-57889-096-9*) Passeggiata.

Ocean of Dreams: Forty-Three Poems by Mona Saudi. Mona Saudi. Tr. by Tamir T. Nasir from ARA. LC 98-27112. 90p. 1998. 18.00 (*1-57889-090-X*) Passeggiata.

Ocean of Eloquence: Tsong Kha Pa's Commentary on the Yogacara Doctrine of Mind. Tr. by Gareth Sparham & Shotaro Iida. LC 92-24974. (SUNY Series in Buddhist Studies). 260p. (C). 1993. text 19.50 (*0-7914-1479-5*) State U NY Pr.

Ocean of His Words: A Reader's Guide to the Art of Bahaullah. John Hatcher. LC 97-7036. 1997. 12.95 (*0-87743-259-7*) Bahai.

Ocean of Life: Visions of India & the Himalayan Kingdoms. Photos by Marilyn Silverstone. (Illus.). 72p. 1985. 37.95 (*0-89381-195-5*) Aperture.

Ocean of Love. Ari Frankel. LC 96-84992. (Illus.). 24p. (J). (ps-3). 1996. pap. 12.98 incl. audio (*1-888509-00-7*, BMR1001) Baby Matters.

Ocean of Love. Ari Frankel. LC 96-84992. (Illus.). 28p. (ps-3). 1997. pap. 9.98 incl. audio (*1-888509-02-3*, BMR1001) Baby Matters.

Ocean of Love. Ari Frankel. (ps-3). 1997. 14.98 (*1-888509-01-5*, BMR1001) Baby Matters.

Ocean of Love: Anurag Sagar of Kabir. Kabir. Ed. by Russell Perkins. Tr. by Raj K. Bagga et al. LC 82-50369. (Illus.). 252p. (Orig.). 1982. pap. 15.00 (*0-89142-039-8*) Sant Bani Ash.

Ocean of Love: My Life with Meher Baba. Delia DeLeon. (Illus.). 240p. (Orig.). 1991. pap. 10.00 (*0-913078-68-9*) Sheriar Pr.

***Ocean of Mercy.** Atoma Zim. LC 99-67732. (Illus.). 143p. 2000. pap. 19.95 (*0-9674765-2-6*) Oxygentribe Pr.

Ocean of My Words: The Importance of Deepening Our Knowledge & Understanding of the Faith. Universal House of Justice Staff. 52p. 1989. pap. 4.25 (*0-909991-21-9*) Bahai.

Ocean of Nectar: Wisdom & Compassion in Mahayana Buddhism. Geshe K. Gyatso. LC 96-147363. (Illus.). 600p. 1995. 34.95 (*0-948006-08-0*, Pub. by Tharpa Pubns); pap. 29.95 (*0-948006-23-4*, Pub. by Tharpa Pubns) ACCESS Pubs Network.

Ocean of Oil: A Century of Political Struggle over Petroleum off the California Coast. Robert Sollen. LC 97-33453. 1998. pap. 35.00 (*0-938737-34-1*) Denali Press.

Ocean of Sound: Aether Talk, Ambient Sound & Imaginary Worlds. David Toop. LC 95-69746. (Illus.). 224p. (Orig.). 1996. pap. 16.99 (*1-85242-382-X*) Serpents Tail.

Ocean of Story: Fairy Tales from India. Caroline Ness. Ed. by Neil Philip. LC 95-76366. (Illus.). 128p. (J). (gr. 2 up). 1996. 17.00 (*0-688-13584-6*) Lothrop.

Ocean of Theosophy see Oceano de la Teosofia

Ocean of Theosophy. William Q. Judge. 1972. 69.95 (*0-8490-0752-6*) Gordon Pr.

Ocean of Theosophy. William Q. Judge. LC 73-78147. 209p. 1973. pap. 11.95 (*0-911500-26-X*) Theos U Pr.

Ocean of Theosophy. William Q. Judge. (Illus.). 153p. 1915. reprint ed. 6.00 (*0-938998-07-2*) Theosophy.

Ocean of Theosophy (1910) William Q. Judge. 168p. 1998. reprint ed. pap. 12.95 (*0-7661-0544-X*) Kessinger Pub.

Ocean of Time: Alzheimer's: Tales of Hope & Forgetting. Patrick Mathiasen. LC 96-29679. 1997. 22.50 (*0-684-82252-0*) S&S Trade.

Ocean of Truth: A Defence of Objective Theism. Brian L. Hebblethwaite. 176p. 1988. pap. text 18.95 (*0-521-35975-9*) Cambridge U Pr.

Ocean of Truth: A Personal History of Global Tectonics. Henry W. Menard. LC 85-43300. (Princeton Series in Geology & Paleontology). (Illus.). 368p. 1986. reprint ed. pap. 114.10 (*0-608-06472-6*, 206676900009) Bks Demand.

Ocean of Truth: The Story of Sir Isaac Newton. Joyce McPherson. (Illus.). 144p. (Orig.). (J). (gr. 5-12). 1997. pap. 7.95 (*1-882514-50-5*) Greenleaf TN.

Ocean of Wisdom: Guidelines for Living by the Dalai Lama of Tibet. Photos by Marcia Keegan. LC 89-61093. (Illus.). 86p. 1989. 14.95 (*0-940666-09-X*) Clear Light.

Ocean of Words. Ha Jin. LC 98-11008. 1998. pap. 12.00 (*0-375-70206-7*) Vin Bks.

Ocean of Words: A Dictionary of Nautical Words & Phrases. Peter D. Jeans. LC 97-44144. (Illus.). 192p. 1998. 15.95 (*1-55972-450-1*, Birch Ln Pr) Carol Pub Group.

Ocean Optics. Ed. by Rochard W. Spinrad et al. (Oxford Monographs on Geology & Geophysics: No. 25). (Illus.). 304p. (C). 1994. text 95.00 (*0-19-506843-2*) OUP.

Ocean Optics Research in the U. S. S. R. Leopold Bayuel. Ed. by Jonathan Gallant. Tr. by Peter Sargent from RUS. iv, 141p. (Orig.). 1989. pap. text 75.00 (*1-55831-095-9*) Delphic Associates.

Ocean Optics XIII, Vol. 2963. Ed. by Steven G. Ackleson. 922p. 1997. 141.00 (*0-8194-2367-X*) SPIE.

Ocean, Our Future. Independent World Commission on the Oceans Staff. LC 98-226229. (Illus.). 248p. (C). 1998. text 59.95 (*0-521-64286-8*); pap. text 22.95 (*0-521-64465-8*) Cambridge U Pr.

***Ocean Pacific: Fresh Modern Flavors from North America's Pacific Coast.** Marjie Lambert. (Illus.). 160p. 2000. 29.95 (*962-593-815-X*) Tuttle Pubng.

Ocean Paper Chains. Stewart Walton. (J). (ps-3). 1996. pap. 7.95 (*0-688-13741-5*, Wm Morrow) Morrow Avon.

***Ocean Pilot, 4 vols.** Ed. by Raintree Steck-Vaughn Publishing Staff. (Illus.). 2000. pap. 71.92 (*0-7398-1712-4*) Raintree Steck-V.

Ocean Politics & Law: An Annotated Bibliography, 16. James C. Wang. LC 91-30202. (Bibliographies & Indexes in Law & Political Science Ser.: No. 16). 272p. 1991. lib. bdg. 75.00 (*0-313-27925-X*, WOP/, Greenwood Pr) Greenwood.

Ocean Pollution: Effects on Living Resources & Humans. Carl J. Sindermann. LC 95-16809. (CRC Press Marine Science Ser.). 304p. 1995. boxed set 104.95 (*0-8493-8421-4*, 8421) CRC Pr.

Ocean Pollution in the Arctic North & the Russian Far East: Proceedings from the Ocean Pollution Session of the Conference "Bridges of Science Between North America & the Russian Far East", Vladivostok, Russia, September 1, 1994. Ed. by Elizabeth J. Kirk. LC 95-36616. 1995. pap. write for info. (*0-87168-575-2*) AAAS.

Ocean Power: Poems from the Desert. Ofelia Zepeda. LC 94-18732. (Sun Tracks Ser.: Vol. 32). 89p. 1995. pap. 10.95 (*0-8165-1541-7*); lib. bdg. 23.95 (*0-8165-1517-4*) U of Ariz Pr.

Ocean Processes in Climate Dynamics - Global & Mediterranean Examples: Proceedings of the NATO Advanced Study Institute, Erice, Italy, January 20-February 2, 1993. Ed. by Paola Malanotte-Rizzoli & Allan R. Robinson. LC 93-38824. (NATO Advanced Study Institutes Series C, Mathematical & Physical Sciences). 460p. (C). 1995. text 259.00 (*0-7923-2624-5*) Kluwer Academic.

Ocean Processes: U. S. Southeast Continental Shelf: A Summary of Research Conducted in the South Atlantic Bight under the Auspices of the U. S. Department of Energy from 1977 to 1991. Ed. by David W. Menzel. LC 93-13553. 112p. 1993. pap. 27.00 (*0-87079-598-8*, DE93010744); fiche 12.50 (*0-87079-599-6*, DE93010744) DOE.

Ocean Pulse: A Critical Diagnosis. Ed. by John T. Tanacredi & John Loret. LC 98-4350. (Illus.). 216p. (C). 1998. text 79.50 (*0-306-45800-4*, Kluwer Plenum) Kluwer Academic.

Ocean Remembers It Is Visible: Poems 1966-1989. Craig Powell. (QRL Poetry Bks.: Vols. XXVIII-XXIX). 1989. 20.00 (*0-614-06430-9*) Quarterly Rev.

Ocean Resources see Images

Ocean Reverberation. Ed. by Dale D. Ellis. LC 93-27852. 416p. (C). 1993. text 200.50 (*0-7923-2420-X*) Kluwer Academic.

***Ocean Sailing: Celestial Navigation, Weather, Passage Planning.** Tom Cunliffe. (Illus.). 96p. 1999. pap. text 18.95 (*1-898660-61-1*, 12940SAE) Fernhurst Bks.

Ocean Sailing Yacht, Vol. 1. D. M. Street, Jr. (C). 1989. 205.00 (*0-7855-5904-3*, Pub. by Laurie Norie & Wilson Ltd) St Mut.

Ocean Science. 2nd ed. Hopkins. 1998. lab manual ed. 20.00 (*0-07-229491-4*) McGraw.

Ocean Science. 2nd ed. Keith S. Stowe. LC 82-16120. 687p. reprint ed. pap. 200.00 (*0-7837-2408-X*, 204009300006) Bks Demand.

Ocean Science: Lecture Guide. Hopkins. 1998. 13.25 (*0-07-229490-6*) McGraw.

Ocean Sciences, Resources & Technology: A Guide to the Sea. Bernard L. Gordon et al. (Illus.). 362p. 1998. pap. 20.00 (*0-910258-25-2*) Book & Tackle.

Ocean Sea. Alessandro Baricco. Tr. by Alastair McEwen from ITA. LC 98-14213. 241p. 1999. 23.00 (*0-375-40423-6*) Knopf.

Ocean Sea. Alessandro Baricco. (International Ser.). 256p. 2000. pap. 12.00 (*0-375-70395-0*) Vin Bks.

Ocean Sea Divers Worldwide Diving Directory. 2nd ed. Louis A. Karambis. (ENG, FRE, GER, ITA & JPN.). 1993. pap. 40.00 (*0-9635480-1-8*, 051826212) Ocean Sea Pubs.

Ocean Secret. Peggy Sands. 1989. 4.95 (*0-945603-03-7*) Dinnerman Bks.

Ocean Seismo-Acoustics: Low-Frequency Underwater Acoustics. Ed. by Tuncay Akal & Jonathon M. Berkson. (NATO Conference Series IV, Marine Sciences: Vol. 16). 896p. 1986. 165.00 (*0-306-42266-2*, Plenum Trade) Perseus Pubng.

An Asterisk (*) at the beginning of an entry indicates that the title is appearing for the first time.

Ocean Shipping in the Evolution of Hong Kong. Baruch Boxer. LC 61-16294. (University of Chicago, Department of Geography, Research Paper Ser.: No. 72). 111p. reprint ed. pap. 34.50 (*0-7837-0386-4*, 204070700018) Bks Demand.

Ocean Space Utilization, '85, 2 vols., Set. Ed. by W. Kato. (Illus.). 1400p. 1985. 143.95 (*0-387-70008-0*) Spr-Verlag.

Ocean States: Archipelagic Regimes in the Law of the Sea. Mohamed Munavvar. LC 94-13947. (Publications on Ocean Development: Vol. 22). 240p. (C). 1995. lib. bdg. 112.00 (*0-7923-2882-5*) Kluwer Academic.

Ocean Sunsets. Violet Parkhurst. (How to Draw & Paint Ser.). (Illus.). 32p. (Orig.). 1989. pap. 6.95 (*0-929261-63-1*, HT101) W Foster Pub.

Ocean Surface. Ed. by Yoshiaki Toba & H. Mitsuyasu. 1985. text 258.50 (*90-277-2021-5*) Kluwer Academic.

Ocean Thermal Energy Conversion. William H. Avery & Chih Wu. (Johns Hopkins Applied Physics Laboratory Series in Science & Engineering). (Illus.). 480p. (C). 1994. text 90.00 (*0-19-507199-9*, 6185) OUP.

Ocean Thermal Energy Conversion. A. Lavi. 80p. 1981. pap. 36.00 (*0-08-026705-X*, Pergamon Pr) Elsevier.

Ocean Thermal Energy Conversion: A Source Guide. 1991. lib. bdg. 250.00 (*0-8490-4843-5*) Gordon Pr.

Ocean Thermal Energy Conversion: Presented at the Energy Technology Conference & Exhibition, Houston, Texas, November 6-9, 1978. Energy Technology Conference & Exhibition Staff. Ed. by Owen M. Griffin. LC 78-67976. 11p. reprint ed. pap. 34.50 (*0-608-15365-6*, 205637400061) Bks Demand.

Ocean Tide Pool. Arthur J. Lhommedieu. LC 97-17674. (Habitats Ser.). (Illus.). 32p. (gr. 2-3). 1997. lib. bdg. 24.00 (*0-516-20740-7*) Childrens.

Ocean Tide Pool. Arthur J. Lhommedieu. LC 97-17674. (Habitats Ser.). (J). 1998. pap. text 6.95 (*0-516-20373-8*) Childrens.

Ocean Tides: Mathematical Models & Numerical Experiments. Gurii I. Marchuk & B. A. Kagan. Tr. by D. E. Cartwright. LC 82-18898. (Illus.). 240p. 1984. 131.00 (*0-08-026236-8*, Pub. by Pergamon Repr) Franklin.

Ocean to Alpine: A British Columbia Nature Guide. Cam Finlay & Joy Finlay. 1992. pap. 11.95 (*1-55105-013-7*) Lone Pine.

*__Ocean to Cross: A Paraplegic Couple Date Dares the Atlantic & Claims a New Life.__ Liz Fordred. (Illus.). 256p. 2000. 22.95 (*0-07-135504-9*) McGraw.

Ocean to Cynthia: Poems. Walter Raleigh. (Illus.). 1984p. 20.00 (*0-317-40774-0*) Abattoir.

Ocean Traders: From the Portuguese Discoveries to the Present Day. fac. ed. Michael W. Marshall. LC 89-48361. (Illus.). 192p. 1990. reprint ed. pap. 59.60 (*0-7837-8135-0*, 204794200008) Bks Demand.

Ocean Tribe. Charlotte Prentiss. 384p. 1999. mass mkt. 6.50 (*0-06-101011-1*, Harp PBks) HarpC.

Ocean Variability & Acoustic Propagation: Proceedings of the Workshop Held in La Spezia, Italy, June 4-8, 1990. Ed. by John Potter & Alex Warn-Varnas. (C). 1991. lib. bdg. 238.00 (*0-7923-1079-9*) Kluwer Academic.

Ocean View, Virginia. Amy Waters Yarsinske. (Images of America Ser.). (Illus.). 128p. 1998. pap. 16.99 (*0-7524-0931-X*) Arcadia Publng.

Ocean Wave Kinematics, Dynamics & Loads on Structures: Proceedings of the 1998 International OTRC Symposium, Houston, Texas, April 30-May 1, 1998. Jun Zhang. LC 98-15974. 526p. 1998. 69.00 (*0-7844-0336-8*) Am Soc Civil Eng.

Ocean Wave Measurement & Analysis, 2 vols. 935p. 1974. pap. 68.00 (*0-87262-116-2*) Am Soc Civil Eng.

Ocean Wave Measurement & Analysis: Proceedings of the Second International Symposium, Honoring Robert L. Wiegel, New Orleans, Louisiana, July 25-28, 1993. Ed. by Orville T. Magoon & J. Michael Hemsley. LC 94-7190. 1064p. 1994. 86.00 (*0-87262-922-8*) Am Soc Civil Eng.

*__Ocean Wave Measurement & Analysis: Proceedings of the 3rd International Symposium Waves 97: November 3-7, 1997, Ramada Plaza Resort Virginia Beach, Virginia, U. S. A., 2.__ Billy L. Edge et al. LC 98-4271. 1576p. 1998. 175.00 (*0-7844-0346-5*) Am Soc Civil Eng.

Ocean Wave Modeling. Ed. by Swamp Group Staff. 262p. 1985. 75.00 (*0-306-41685-9*, Plenum Trade) Perseus Pubng.

Ocean Waves: The Stochastic Approach. Michel K. Ochi. LC 97-16355. (Ocean Technology Ser.: No. 6). (Illus.). 332p. (C). 1998. text 110.00 (*0-521-56378-X*) Cambridge U Pr.

Ocean Waves: Their Physics & Prediction. Stanislaw R. Massel. (Advanced Series in Ocean Engineering). 350p. 1996. pap. text 36.00 (*981-02-2109-6*) World Scientific Pub.

Ocean Waves: Their Physics & Prediction. R. Massel Stanislaw. (Advanced Series in Ocean Engineering). 350p. 1996. text 74.00 (*981-02-1686-6*) World Scientific Pub.

Ocean Waves & Progressive Oscillatory Waves: Syllabus. E. H. Sluyter & Ethel Raddon. 1977. pap. text 6.95 (*0-89420-015-1*, 234011); audio 39.30 (*0-89420-165-4*, 234000) Natl Book.

Ocean Waves Engineering. Ed. by M. Rahman. 240p. 1994. 117.00 (*1-85312-285-8*) Computational Mech MA.

Ocean Waves Engineering. Ed. by M. Rahman. LC 94-70414. (Advances in Fluid Mechanics Ser.: Vol. 2). 240p. 1994. 117.00 (*1-56252-209-4*, 2858) Computational Mech MA.

*__Ocean Within.__ V. M. Caldwell. LC 99-13418. (Illus.). 236p. (J). (gr. 3-8). 1999. pap. 6.95 (*1-57131-624-8*) Milkweed Ed.

*__Ocean Within.__ V. M. Caldwell. LC 99-13418. (Illus.). 273p. (J). (gr. 6-9). 1999. 15.95 (*1-57131-623-X*) Milkweed Ed.

Ocean Without Shore: Ibn Arabi, the Book, & the Law. Michel Chodkiewicz. LC 92-35813. 184p. (C). 1993. text 21.50 (*0-7914-1625-9*) State U NY Pr.

Ocean Without Shore: Ibn Arabi, the Quran, & the Shariah. Michel Chodkiewicz. 250p. 1996. pap. 19.95 (*0-614-21324-X*, 915) Kazi Pubns.

Ocean World see Mundo Marino

Ocean World. Francesca Baines. (Launch Pad Library). (Illus.). 32p. (J). (gr. k-4). 1997. 11.95 (*0-915741-81-4*) C D Stampley Ent.

Ocean World. Illus. by Peter Sis. LC 89-11692. 24p. (J). (ps-3). 1992. lib. bdg. 15.93 (*0-688-09068-0*, Grenwillow Bks) HarpC Child Bks.

*__Ocean World.__ Illus. by Peter Sis. LC 89-11692. 24p. (J). (ps-3). 2000. pap. 5.95 (*0-688-17518-X*, Grenwillow Bks) HarpC Child Bks.

Ocean World: A Duplo Carousel Playbook. Reed Consumer Group Staff. (J). 1997. write for info. (*0-316-85336-4*) Little.

Ocean Yachtmaster: Celestial Navigation. rev. ed. Pat L. Price & Philip Ouvry. (Illus.). 215p. 1996. 40.00 (*0-7136-4553-9*) Sheridan.

Ocean Yachtmaster Exercises. Pat L. Price & Philip Ouvry. (Illus.). 128p. 1997. pap. 30.00 (*0-7136-4830-9*) Sheridan.

Ocean Yearbook, 11. Ed. by Elisabeth M. Borgese et al. 692p. 1995. lib. bdg. 77.00 (*0-226-06614-2*) U Ch Pr.

Ocean Yearbook, 12. Elisabeth M. Borgese et al. 650p. 1996. lib. bdg. 77.00 (*0-226-06615-0*) U Ch Pr.

Ocean Yearbook, No. 2. Ed. by Elisabeth M. Borgese & Norton S. Ginsburg. LC 79-642855. 724p. 1981. lib. bdg. 48.00 (*0-226-06603-7*) U Ch Pr.

Ocean Yearbook, No. 3. Elisabeth M. Borgese & Norton S. Ginsburg. LC 79-642855. 598p. 1982. lib. bdg. 59.00 (*0-226-06604-5*) U Ch Pr.

Ocean Yearbook, No. 4. Ed. by Elisabeth M. Borgese & Norton S. Ginsburg. LC 79-642855. 640p. 1984. lib. bdg. 59.00 (*0-226-06605-3*) U Ch Pr.

Ocean Yearbook, No. 5. Ed. by Elisabeth M. Borgese & Norton S. Ginsburg. LC 79-642855. 570p. 1985. lib. bdg. 59.00 (*0-226-06606-1*) U Ch Pr.

Ocean Yearbook, No. 6. Ed. by Elisabeth M. Borgese & Norton S. Ginsburg. LC 79-642855. Vol. 6. 696p. 1987. lib. bdg. 66.00 (*0-226-06608-8*) U Ch Pr.

Ocean Yearbook, No. 7. Elisabeth M. Borgese et al. 634p. 1989. lib. bdg. 71.00 (*0-226-06609-6*) U Ch Pr.

Ocean Yearbook, No. 8. Ed. by Elisabeth M. Borgese et al. LC 79-642855. 702p. 1990. lib. bdg. 78.00 (*0-226-06611-8*) U Ch Pr.

Ocean Yearbook, No. 9. Ed. by Elisabeth M. Borgese et al. 544p. 1992. lib. bdg. 78.00 (*0-226-06612-6*) U Ch Pr.

Ocean Yearbook, Vol. 10. Ed. by Elisabeth M. Borgese et al. 568p. (C). 1993. lib. bdg. 64.95 (*0-226-06613-4*) U Ch Pr.

Ocean Yearbook, Vol. 13. Aldo Chircop. 2000. lib. bdg. 87.00 (*0-226-06616-9*) U Ch Pr.

Ocean Yearbook, Vol. 14. Ed. by Elisabeth Mann Borgese et al. 1999. lib. bdg. 77.00 (*0-226-06617-7*) U Ch Pr.

*__Ocean Yearbook, Vol. 15.__ Elisabeth M. Borgese. (Illus.). 1999. lib. bdg. 77.00 (*0-226-06618-5*) U Ch Pr.

Ocean Yearbook 1, No. 1. Ed. by Elisabeth M. Borgese & Norton S. Ginsburg. 908p. 1979. lib. bdg. 36.00 (*0-226-06602-9*) U Ch Pr.

Oceana County Pioneers & Business Men of Today, 1890: History, Biography, Statistics & Humorous Incidents. L. M. Hartwick & W. H. Tuller. (Illus.). 432p. 1997. reprint ed. lib. bdg. 46.00 (*0-8328-6782-9*) Higginson Bk Co.

Oceana: or England & Her Colonies. James A. Froude. LC 72-3974. (Black Heritage Library Collection). 1977. reprint ed. 30.95 (*0-8369-9096-X*) Ayer.

Oceangoing Vessels of North German Lloyd, 1857-1919 (Die Seeschiffe des Norddeutschen Lloyd, 1857-1919), Vol. I. Arnold Kludas. Tr. by John D. Kallmann. (Illus.). 166p. 2000. pap. 24.95 (*0-9650926-5-8*, L-1006) J Kallmann.

Oceangoing Vessels of North German Lloyd, 1920-1970, Vol. II. unabridged ed. Arnold Kludas. Tr. by John D. Kallmann from GER. Orig. Title: Die Seeschiffe des Norddeutschen Lloyd, 1920-1970. (Illus.). 166p. 2000. pap. 24.95 (*0-9650926-6-6*, L-1007) J Kallmann.

Oceania: A Regional Study. Frederica M. Bunge. 588p. 1985. boxed set 22.00 (*0-16-023928-1*) USGPO.

Oceania: The Geography of Australia, New Zealand & the Pacific Islands. Tom L. McKnight. (C). 1994. text 42.00 (*0-13-123639-3*) P-H.

Oceania: The Native Cultures of Australia & the Pacific Islands, 2 vols. Douglas L. Oliver. LC 88-29551. (Illus.). 1264p. 1988. text 95.00 (*0-8248-1019-8*) UH Pr.

Oceania & Beyond: Essays on the Pacific since 1945. Ed. by Frank P. King. LC 76-5261. (Illus.). 265p. (Orig.). 1976. 35.00 (*0-8371-8904-7*, KOB/, Greenwood Pr) Greenwood.

Oceanic. Ed. by Wolfgang Hageney. (Graphic Spirit of Native Designs Ser.). (Illus.). 112p. (Orig.). 1993. pap. 24.95 (*88-7070-116-6*) Belvedere USA.

Oceanic, American Indian, & African Myths of Snaring the Sun. K. Luomala. (BMB Ser.: No. 168). 1974. reprint ed. 25.00 (*0-527-02276-4*) Periodicals Srv.

Oceanic & Anthropogenic Controls of Life in the Pacific Ocean: Proceedings of the 2nd Pacific Symposium on Marine Sciences, Nakhodka, Russia, August 11-19, 1988. Ed. by V. I. Ilyichev & V. V. Anikiev. LC 92-17798. (GeoJournal Library: Vol. 21). 345p. (C). 1992. text 185.00 (*0-7923-1854-4*) Kluwer Academic.

Oceanic Art. Adrienne L. Kaeppler et al. LC 97-8127. (Illus.). 642p. 1997. 195.00 (*0-8109-3693-3*, Pub. by Abrams) Time Warner.

Oceanic Art, 2 Vols. Anthony J. P. Meyer. LC 97-137042. (ENG, FRE & GER., Illus.). 640p. 1998. boxed set 49.95 (*3-89508-080-2*, 810033) Konemann.

Oceanic Art. Nicholas Thomas. LC 94-61059. (World of Art Ser.). (Illus.). 216p. (Orig.). 1995. pap. 14.95 (*0-500-20281-8*, Pub. by Thames Hudson) Norton.

Oceanic Basalts. Ed. by P. A. Floyd. 288p. (C). (gr. 13). 1991. mass mkt. 148.95 (*0-442-30411-0*) Chapman & Hall.

Oceanic Circle. Elisabeth Borgese. LC 98-40090. 1998. write for info. (*92-808-1013-8*); pap. 19.95 (*92-808-1028-6*) Brookings.

Oceanic Circulation Models: Combining Data & Dynamics. Ed. by David L. Anderson & Jurgen Willebrand. (C). 1989. text 298.50 (*0-7923-0394-6*) Kluwer Academic.

Oceanic Collection III: Beluga Whale, Harp Seal, Walrus & Lobster Books, 4 micro bks. Ed. by Soundprints Staff. (Smithsonian Oceanic Collection). (Illus.). 128p. (J). (ps-2). 18.95 (*1-56899-633-0*) Soundprints.

Oceanic Crust: From Accretion to Mantle Recycling. Thierry Juteau & R. C. Maury. LC 98-50711. 385p. 1999. 149.00 (*1-85233-116-X*) Spr-Verlag.

Oceanic Feeling: The Origins of Religious Sentiment in Ancient India. J. Moussaieff Masson. (Studies of Classical India: No. 3). 228p. 1980. text 140.50 (*90-277-1050-3*, D Reidel) Kluwer Academic.

Oceanic Hydraulics. Ed. by R. L. Hughes. (PAGEOPH Ser.). 184p. 1990. 27.50 (*0-8176-2498-8*) Birkhauser.

Oceanic Islands. Patrick Nunn. LC 92-28002. (Natural Environment Ser.). 360p. 1994. pap. 50.95 (*0-631-18967-X*) Blackwell Pubs.

Oceanic Micropalaeontology, Vol. 1. A. T. Ramsay. 1977. text 209.00 (*0-12-577301-3*) Acad Pr.

Oceanic Micropalaeontology, Vol. 2. Ed. by T. S. Ramsay. 1978. text 209.00 (*0-12-577302-1*) Acad Pr.

Oceanic Mixing. Akira Okubo. LC 73-133442. 151p. 1970. 19.00 (*0-403-04523-1*) Scholarly.

Oceanic Origin of the Kwakiutl-Nootka & Salish Stocks of British Columbia. Charles Hill-Tout. LC 97-582. 1997. pap. 9.95 (*0-87770-603-4*) Ye Galleon.

Oceanic Remote Sensing. Ed. by F. V. Bunkin & K. I. Voliak. (Proceedings of the Institute of General Physics of the Academy of Sciences of the U. S. S. R. Ser.: Vol. 1). 222p. (C). 1988. text 165.00 (*0-941743-12-8*) Nova Sci Pubs.

Oceanic Whitecaps & Their Role in Air-Sea Exchange Processes. Ed. by Edward C. Monahan & Gearoid M. Niocaill. 1986. text 169.50 (*90-277-2251-X*) Kluwer Academic.

Oceano - Ocean. (Eyewitness Books). (SPA.). (YA). (gr. 5 up). 1996. 14.95 (*0-614-20251-5*) Santillana.

Oceano de la Teosofia. William Q. Judge. Tr. by Bermudez Y. Polanco from ENG.Tr. of Ocean of Theosophy. (SPA.). 128p. 1983. pap. 5.00 (*0-938998-28-5*) Theosophy.

Oceano y Sus Recursos VIII: Approvechamiento de Recursos. Juan L. Cifuentes. (Ciencia para Todos Ser.). (SPA.). pap. 6.99 (*968-16-2864-0*, Pub. by Fondo) Continental Bk.

Oceano y Sus Recursos XI: Acuicultura. Juan L. Cifuentes. (Ciencia para Todos Ser.). (SPA.). pap. 6.99 (*968-16-3433-0*, Pub. by Fondo) Continental Bk.

Oceano y Sus Recursos V: Plancton. Juan L. Cifuentes. (Ciencia para Todos Ser.). (SPA.). pap. 6.99 (*968-16-2653-2*, Pub. by Fondo) Continental Bk.

Oceano y Sus Recursos I: Panorama Oceanico. Juan L. Cifuentes. (Ciencia para Todos Ser.). (SPA.). pap. 6.99 (*968-16-2389-4*, Pub. by Fondo) Continental Bk.

Oceano y Sus Recursos IV: Bilogia. Juan L. Cifuentes. (Ciencia para Todos Ser.). (SPA.). pap. 6.99 (*968-16-2539-0*, Pub. by Fondo) Continental Bk.

Oceano y Sus Recursos IX: La Pesca. Juan L. Cifuentes. (Ciencia para Todos Ser.). (SPA.). pap. 6.99 (*968-16-4815-3*, Pub. by Fondo) Continental Bk.

Oceano y Sus Recursos II: Geologia y Quimica. Juan L. Cifuentes. (Ciencia para Todos Ser.). (SPA.). pap. 6.99 (*968-16-2455-6*, Pub. by Fondo) Continental Bk.

Oceano y Sus Recursos VII: Flujos de Energia. Juan L. Cifuentes. (Ciencia para Todos Ser.). (SPA.). pap. 6.99 (*968-16-2863-2*, Pub. by Fondo) Continental Bk.

Oceano y Sus Recursos VI: Bentos y Necton. Juan L. Cifuentes. (Ciencia para Todos Ser.). (SPA.). pap. 6.99 (*968-16-2704-0*, Pub. by Fondo) Continental Bk.

Oceano y Sus Recursos X: Pesquerias. Juan L. Cifuentes. (Ciencia para Todos Ser.). (SPA.). pap. 6.99 (*968-16-3429-2*, Pub. by Fondo) Continental Bk.

Oceano y Sus Recursos III: Fisica, Matematicas & Ingenieria. Juan L. Cifuentes. (Ciencia para Todos Ser.). (SPA.). pap. 6.99 (*968-16-2456-4*, Pub. by Fondo) Continental Bk.

Oceano y Sus Recursos XII: El Futuro. Juan L. Cifuentes. (Ciencia para Todos Ser.). (SPA.). pap. 6.99 (*968-16-3434-9*, Pub. by Fondo) Continental Bk.

Oceanographer. Jack Rudman. (Career Examination Ser.: C-550). 1994. pap. 27.95 (*0-8373-0550-0*) Nat Learn.

Oceanographers & Explorers of the Sea. Kirk Polking. LC 98-36135. (Collective Biographies Ser.). 128p. (YA). (gr. 6 up). 1999. lib. bdg. 20.95 (*0-7660-1113-5*) Enslow Pubs.

Oceanographic Applications of Remote Sensing. Ed. by Motoyoshi Ikeda et al. LC 95-40927. 512p. 1995. boxed set 104.95 (*0-8493-4525-1*, 4525) CRC Pr.

Oceanographic Atlas of the International Indian Ocean Expedition. Klaus Wyrtki. (Illus.). 542p. (C). 1988. text 440.00 (*90-6191-416-7*, Pub. by A A Balkema) Ashgate Pub Co.

Oceanographic Atlases: A Guide to Their Geographic Coverage & Contents. Henry Stommel & Michele Fieux. LC 78-70786. 1978. 15.00 (*0-915176-22-X*); pap. 7.50 (*0-915176-21-1*) Woods Hole Pr.

Oceanographic Cartography. Kerr. (International Cartographic Association Ser.). 1985. pap. 48.25 (*1-85166-206-5*, Pergamon Pr) Elsevier.

Oceanographic Index: Author Cumulation, 1946-1970: Woods Hole Oceanographic Institution, Mass., 3 vols, Set. Compiled by Mary Sears. 1972. 345.00 (*0-8161-0931-1*, G K Hall & Co) Mac Lib Ref.

Oceanographic Index: Regional Cumulation, 1946-1970: Woods Hole Oceanographic Institution, Mass. Compiled by Mary Sears. 1972. 115.00 (*0-8161-0117-5*, G K Hall & Co) Mac Lib Ref.

Oceanographic Index Cumulation, 1946 to 1973: Marine Organisms, Chiefly Planktonic. Mary Sears. 1981. 275.00 (*0-8161-1324-6*, G K Hall & Co) Mac Lib Ref.

Oceanographic Index of Regional Cumulation, 1971, 1974. 1994. 175.00 (*0-7838-2254-5*, G K Hall & Co) Mac Lib Ref.

Oceanographic Index Subject Cumulation, 1946 to 1971. Mary Sears. 1980. 485.00 (*0-8161-1263-0*, G K Hall & Co) Mac Lib Ref.

Oceanographic Index, Woods Hole Oceanographic Institution Author Cumulation, 1971-1974: Woods Hole Oceanographic Institution Author Cumulation, 1971-1974. Compiled by Mary Sears. 1976. 135.00 (*0-8161-0029-2*, G K Hall & Co) Mac Lib Ref.

Oceanographic Index, Woods Hole Oceanographic Institution, Subject Cumulation 1971-1974, 2 vols, Set. Compiled by Mary Sears. 1977. 305.00 (*0-8161-0030-6*, G K Hall & Co) Mac Lib Ref.

Oceanographic Research, South Pacific Region, Agreement Between the U. S. of America & Other Governments. 1994. lib. bdg. 250.00 (*0-8490-8533-0*) Gordon Pr.

Oceanographic Tables. T. Beer. 1989. 222.00 (*1-85312-306-4*) Computational Mech MA.

Oceanography. Boy Scouts of America. (Illus.). 72p. (YA). (gr. 6-12). 1983. pap. 2.90 (*0-8395-3306-3*, 33306) BSA.

Oceanography. Robert E. Boyer. 1984. pap. 9.95 (*0-8331-1707-6*, 6611) Hubbard Sci.

Oceanography. Lorraine Conway. 64p. (J). (gr. 5 up). 1982. 7.99 (*0-86653-066-5*, GA401) Good Apple.

Oceanography. William Corso & Paul S. Joyce. (Applied Science Review Ser.). (Illus.). 192p. 1994. pap. 12.95 (*0-87434-608-8*) Springhouse Corp.

Oceanography. Wallace. (C). 1995. pap. text, student ed. 26.25 (*0-673-46939-5*) Addson-Wesley Educ.

*__Oceanography.__ 3rd ed. Pipkin. 2000. pap. text, lab manual ed. write for info. (*0-7167-3742-6*) W H Freeman.

Oceanography. 7th ed. Gross. 1996. pap. text, student ed. 24.80 (*0-13-237454-4*) P-H.

Oceanography. 7th ed. M. Grant Gross & Elizabeth Gross. LC 95-41075. 472p. 1995. 78.67 (*0-13-231788-5*) P-H.

*__Oceanography: An Earth Science Perspective.__ S. Kerhsaw. (Illus.). 304p. 2000. pap. 42.50 (*0-7487-5442-3*, Pub. by S Thornes Pubs) Intl Spec Bk.

Oceanography: An Illustrated Guide. Summerhayes. 1999. pap. text 54.95 (*0-470-34537-3*) Halsted Pr.

Oceanography: An Illustrated Text. Ed. by S. A. Thorpe & C. P. Summerhayes. LC 95-38712. (Illus.). 352p. 1996. text 82.50 (*0-470-23574-8*) Halsted Pr.

Oceanography: An Intro. 4th ed. Ingmanson. (Environmental Science Ser.). 1989. teacher ed. write for info. (*0-534-09554-2*) Wadsworth Pub.

Oceanography: An Introduction. 3rd ed. Dale E. Ingmanson & William J. Wallace. 530p. (C). 1984. pap. 30.25 (*0-534-03849-2*) Wadsworth Pub.

Oceanography: An Introduction. 4th ed. Dale E. Ingmanson & William J. Wallace. 511p. (C). 1988. pap. 36.25 (*0-534-09552-6*) Wadsworth Pub.

Oceanography: An Introduction. 5th ed. Dale E. Ingmanson & William J. Wallace. LC 94-13153. 495p. 1994. 78.95 (*0-534-24258-8*) Wadsworth Pub.

Oceanography: An Introduction to the Marine Science. Chamberlain. 480p. 1994. 48.50 (*0-8016-6344-X*) Mosby Inc.

Oceanography: An Invitation to Marine Science. Tom S. Garrison. 540p. (C). 1993. mass mkt. 49.25 (*0-534-15600-2*) Wadsworth Pub.

Oceanography: An Invitation to Marine Science. 2nd ed. Garrison. (Environmental Science Ser.). 1997. pap. 59.50 (*0-534-25727-5*) Wadsworth Pub.

Oceanography: An Invitation to Marine Science. 2nd ed. Tom S. Garrison. LC 95-35233. 567p. (C). 1995. pap. 59.50 (*0-534-25728-3*) Wadsworth Pub.

*__Oceanography: An Invitation to Marine Science.__ 3rd ed. Tom S. Garrison. (Illus.). 592p. 1999. write for info. (*0-534-81868-4*) Brooks-Cole.

Oceanography: An Understanding of the Ocean Environment. (Learning Guides Ser.). (Illus.). 30p. Date not set. pap. text 5.79 (*1-891148-10-9*) US Power.

Oceanography: Contemporary Readings in Ocean Sciences. 3rd ed. R. Gordon Pirie. LC 95-3650. (Illus.). 448p. 1996. pap. text 44.95 (*0-19-508768-2*, GC26) OUP.

Oceanography: Introduction Marine. Chamberlain. 1999. 16.50 (*0-697-21704-3*) McGraw.

Oceanography: Introduction to Marine Science. Chamberlain. 1999. 43.50 (*0-697-21702-7*) McGraw.

Oceanography: Introduction to Planet Oceanus. Paul R. Pinet. Ed. by Pullins. (Earth Science Ser.). 572p. (C). 1992. 51.25 (*0-314-77008-9*) Jones & Bartlett.

*__Oceanography: Invitation to Marine Science.__ 3rd ed. Garrison. (Environmental Science Ser.). (C). 2000. text 19.00 (*0-534-76653-6*) Brooks-Cole.

Oceanography: Invitation to Marine Science. 3rd ed. Garrison. (Environmental Science Ser.). 1998. pap. 59.75 (*0-534-53091-5*) Wadsworth Pub.

*__Oceanography: Invitation to Marine Science.__ 4th ed. Garrison. 2001. pap. 60.25 (*0-534-37557-X*) Thomson Learn.

O

An Asterisk (*) at the beginning of an entry indicates that the title is appearing for the first time.

Oceanography: Invitation to Marine Science with Infotrac. 3rd ed. Garrison. LC 98-7402. (Environmental Science Ser.). 1998. pap. 59.75 (*0-534-53082-6*) Wadsworth Pub.
Oceanography: Ocean Environment. Moore. (C). 1997. pap. text, teacher ed. 12.00 (*0-03-097379-1*) Harcourt Coll Pubs.
Oceanography: Ocean Environment. Moore. (C). 1999. text 61.50 (*0-03-097346-5*) Harcourt Coll Pubs.
Oceanography: The Past. Ed. by M. Sears & D. Merriman. (Illus.). 812p. 1980. 141.00 (*0-387-90497-2*) Spr-Verlag.
Oceanography & Acoustics: Prediction & Propagation Models. Allan R. Robinson & Ping Lee. (AIP Series on Modern Acoustics & Signal Processing). (Illus.). 300p. 1994. text 69.95 (*1-56396-203-9*, AIP Pr) Spr-Verlag.
Oceanography & Marine Biology. H. Barnes. 1959. 14.00 (*0-08-026258-9*, Pergamon Pr) Elsevier.
Oceanography & Marine Biology, 14 vols., Vol. 3. Margaret Barnes & M. Barnes. 1978. 84.00 (*0-08-023643-X*, Pergamon Pr); 84.00 (*0-08-023650-2*, Pergamon Pr) Elsevier.
Oceanography & Marine Biology, Vol. 17. 65.00 (*0-685-07572-9*, Pergamon Pr) Elsevier.
Oceanography & Marine Biology: An Annual Review. Ed. by Alan D. Ansell. LC 98-150574. 599p. 1997. 165.00 (*1-85728-716-9*) Taylor & Francis.
Oceanography & Marine Biology: An Annual Review. Margaret Barnes. (Oceanography & Marine Biology Ser.: No. 25). 664p. 1987. 135.00 (*0-08-035065-8*, Pub. by Aberdeen U Pr) Macmillan.
Oceanography & Marine Biology: An Annual Review. Ed. by Margaret Barnes. LC 64-1930. (Oceanography & Marine Biology Ser.: Vol. 22). (Illus.). 590p. 1984. 135.00 (*0-08-030392-7*, Pergamon Pr) Elsevier.
Oceanography & Marine Biology: An Annual Review, Vol. 18. Ed. by Margaret Barnes & Harold Barnes. (Illus.). 528p. 1980. 135.00 (*0-08-025732-1*, Pergamon Pr) Elsevier.
Oceanography & Marine Biology: An Annual Review, Vol. 20. Margaret Barnes. (Illus.). 778p. 1982. 135.00 (*0-08-028460-4*, Pergamon Pr) Elsevier.
Oceanography & Marine Biology: An Annual Review, Vol. 21. Ed. by Margaret Barnes. (Oceanography & Marine Biology Ser.). (Illus.). 590p. 1983. 135.00 (*0-08-030360-9*, Pergamon Pr) Elsevier.
Oceanography & Marine Biology: An Annual Review, Vol. 23. Ed. by Margaret Barnes. (Oceanography & Marine Biology Ser.). (Illus.). 656p. 1985. 135.00 (*0-08-030397-8*, Pub. by Aberdeen U Pr) Macmillan.
Oceanography & Marine Biology: An Annual Review, Vol. 24. Ed. by Margaret Barnes. (Oceanography & Marine Biology Ser.). 650p. 1986. 135.00 (*0-08-032458-4*, Pub. by Aberdeen U Pr) Macmillan.
Oceanography & Marine Biology: An Annual Review, Vol. 26. Margaret Barnes. (Oceanography & Marine Biology Ser.). (Illus.). 650p. 1988. 135.00 (*0-08-036397-0*, Pub. by Aberdeen U Pr) Macmillan.
Oceanography & Marine Biology: An Annual Review, Vol. 27. Margaret Barnes. (Illus.). 550p. 1989. 135.00 (*0-08-037718-1*, Pub. by Aberdeen U Pr) Macmillan.
Oceanography & Marine Biology: An Annual Review, Vol. 28. Ed. by Margaret Barnes. (Oceanography & Marine Biology Ser.). (Illus.). 1990. 135.00 (*0-08-037981-8*, Pub. by Aberdeen U Pr) Macmillan.
Oceanography & Marine Biology: An Annual Review, Vol. 29. Ed. by Margaret Barnes. (Illus.). 560p. 1992. text 135.00 (*0-08-040934-2*, Pub. by Aberdeen U Pr) Macmillan.
Oceanography & Marine Biology: An Annual Review, Vol. 30. Ed. by Margaret Barnes et al. 635p. 1992. 150.00 (*1-85728-071-7*, Pub. by UCL Pr Ltd) Taylor & Francis.
Oceanography & Marine Biology: An Annual Review, Vol. 31. Ed. by Alan D. Ansell et al. 640p. 1993. 150.00 (*1-85728-085-7*, Pub. by UCL Pr Ltd) Taylor & Francis.
Oceanography & Marine Biology: An Annual Review, Vol. 32. Ed. by Alan D. Ansell et al. 624p. 1994. 150.00 (*1-85728-236-1*, Pub. by UCL Pr Ltd) Taylor & Francis.
Oceanography & Marine Biology: An Annual Review, Vol. 34. Ed. by Alan D. Ansell et al. 600p. 1996. 160.00 (*1-85728-581-6*, Pub. by UCL Pr Ltd) Taylor & Francis.
Oceanography & Marine Biology: An Annual Review, Vol.19. (Illus.). 655p. 1981. 135.00 (*0-08-028439-6*, Pergamon Pr) Elsevier.
***Oceanography & Mine Warfare.** Ocean Studies Board Staff & National Research Council Staff. 2000. pap. 26.25 (*0-309-06798-7*) Natl Acad Pr.
Oceanography & Naval Special Warfare: Opportunities & Challenges. Ocean Studies Board National Research Council Staf. 100p. 1997. pap. text 39.00 (*0-309-05930-5*) Natl Acad Pr.
Oceanography & Seamanship. 2nd ed. William G. Van Dorn. LC 92-39150. (Illus.). 453p. 1993. 44.95 (*0-87033-434-4*) Cornell Maritime.
Oceanography in the Former Soviet Union. (Illus.). 51p. (Orig.). (C). 1993. pap. text 30.00 (*1-56806-447-0*) DIANE Pub.
Oceanography in the Next Decade: Building New Partnerships. National Research Council Staff. LC 92-34458. 216p. (C). 1992. pap. text 39.95 (*0-309-04794-3*) Natl Acad Pr.
Oceanography Internet Booklet. 2nd ed. Garrison. 1996. mass mkt. 4.75 (*0-534-52587-3*) Course Tech.
***Oceanography Laboratory Manual.** 4th ed. Ronald Johnson. 356p. (C). 1999. spiral bd. 31.95 (*0-7872-6098-3*, 41609801) Kendall-Hunt.
***Oceanography Laboratory Manual: Instructor's Guide.** 4th ed. Ronald Johnson. 148p. (C). 1999. pap. text, teacher ed., lab manual ed. write for info. (*0-7872-6575-6*) Kendall-Hunt.
Oceanography Marine Biology: An Annual Review, Vol. 33. Ansell. (Illus.). 500p. 1995. 150.00 (*1-85728-363-5*, Pub. by UCL Pr Ltd) Taylor & Francis.
Oceanography of Asian Marginal Seas. Kazue Takano. (Oceanography Ser.: Vol. 54). 432p. 1991. 183.50 (*0-444-88805-5*) Elsevier.
Oceanography of the Bering Sea: With Emphasis on Renewable Resources. Ed. by D. W. Hood & E. J. Kelley. (Occasional Publications: No. 2). 100p. 2.00 (*0-914500-04-X*) U of AK Inst Marine.
Oceanography of the Indian Ocean. Ed. by B. N. Desai. (Illus.). 788p. (C). 1993. text 149.00 (*90-5410-228-4*, Pub. by A A Balkema) Ashgate Pub Co.
Oceanography of the Ross Sea, Antarctica. Giancarlo Spezie. Ed. by Giuseppe M. R. Manzella. LC 98-51402. (Illus.). 288p. 1998. (*88-470-0039-4*) Spr-Verlag.
Oceanography of the Southeastern U. S. Continental Shelf. Ed. by L. P. Atkinson et al. (Coastal & Estuarine Sciences Ser.: Vol. 2). 200p. 1985. 20.00 (*0-87590-251-0*) Am Geophysical.
Oceanography Text Flash Card. Heyward Mathews. 320p. (C). 1995. pap. text, spiral bd. 18.95 (*0-7872-1120-6*) Kendall-Hunt.
Oceanograpy. 2nd ed. Tom Garrison. (Biology Ser.). 1996. pap., suppl. ed. 2.00 (*0-534-25732-1*) Wadsworth Pub.
Oceanology, 1988: Advances in Underwater Technology, Ocean Science & Offshore Engineering, Vol. 16. Ed. by Society for Underwater Technology Staff. (C). 1988. lib. bdg. 265.00 (*0-86010-984-4*, Pub. by Graham & Trotman) Kluwer Academic.
Oceanology, 1986. (Advances in Underwater Technology & Offshore Engineering Ser.: Vol. 6). (Illus.). 700p. 1986. lib. bdg. 212.00 (*0-86010-772-8*) G & T Inc.
Oceanology of China Seas. Ed. by Zhou Di & Zeng Cheng-Kui. LC 93-39781. 360p. (C). 1994. lib. bdg. 194.00 (*0-7923-2618-0*); lib. bdg. 155.50 (*0-7923-2616-4*) Kluwer Academic.
Oceanology of China Seas, Vol. 2. Ed. by Zhou Di. 240p. (C). 1994. lib. bdg. 111.50 (*0-7923-2617-2*) Kluwer Academic.
Oceans see Wonders of Our World Series
Oceans see Psyched for Science
Oceans see Read-&-Discover Science Series
Oceans see PowerKids Readers Set 2: Nature Books
Oceans. (C). 1992. 30.00 (*81-7023-212-0*, Pub. by Allied Pubs) S Asia.
***Oceans.** Lucy Baker. (Interfact Ser.). (Illus.). (J). (gr. 2-7). 2000. spiral bd. 14.95 (*1-58728-459-6*) Two Can Pub.
Oceans. Lucy Baker. LC 98-6814. (Interfact Ser.). (Illus.). 48p. (J). (gr. 2-8). 1997. spiral bd. 15.00 incl. cd-rom (*0-7166-7212-X*) World Bk.
***Oceans.** Maria Butterfield. (On the Spot Ser.). 16p. (gr. 4-6). 2000. 7.99 (*1-57584-377-3*) Rdrs Digest.
Oceans. Katharine J. Carter. LC 81-17093. (New True Books Ser.). (Illus.). 48p. (J). (gr. 2-4). 1982. pap. 5.50 (*0-516-41639-1*) Childrens.
Oceans. Brad Caudle & Melissa Caudle. (Rock 'n Learn Ser.). (J). 7.98 incl. audio NewSound.
***Oceans.** Patricia Daniels. LC 99-44330. (Nature Library). (Illus.). (J). 1999. write for info. (*0-7922-7545-4*) Natl Geog.
Oceans. Trevor Day. LC 98-18110. (Ecosystem Ser.). 1999. 45.00 (*0-8160-3647-0*) Facts on File.
Oceans. Frank Schaffer Publications, Inc. Staff. (Science Notes Ser.). (Illus.). 8p. 1996. 2.49 (*0-86734-890-9*, FS-62027) Schaffer Pubns.
***Oceans.** Susan H. Gray. (First Reports). (Illus.). 48p. (J). (gr. 2-3). 2000. write for info. (*0-7565-0022-2*) Compass Point.
Oceans. Callie Oldershaw. LC 91-45079. (Our Planet Ser.). (Illus.). 32p. (J). (gr. 4-6). 1993. pap. 4.95 (*0-8167-2754-6*) Troll Communs.
Oceans. Callie Oldershaw. LC 91-45079. (Our Planet Ser.). (Illus.). 32p. (J). (gr. 4-6). 1997. lib. bdg. 17.25 (*0-8167-2753-8*) Troll Communs.
Oceans. Anna O'Mara. (Read-&-Discover Bks.). (Illus.). 24p. (J). (gr. k-3). 1996. lib. bdg. 14.00 (*0-516-20126-3*) Childrens.
Oceans. Joy A. Palmer. 32p. (J). (gr. 1-4). 1993. pap. 4.95 (*0-8114-4915-7*) Raintree Steck-V.
***Oceans.** Jane Parker. LC 99-35801. 1999. 21.90 (*0-7613-3259-6*) Millbrook Pr.
***Oceans.** Ellen J. Prager & Sylvia A. Earle. 314p. 2000. 24.95 (*0-07-135253-8*) McGraw.
Oceans. Rand McNally Staff & Nicholas Harris. LC 96-8342. (Fold-Out Book Ser.). (Illus.). 16p. (J). 1996. 14.95 (*0-528-83835-0*) Penguin Putnam.
***Oceans.** Kathy Ross. (Illus.). (J). 1998. 14.40 (*0-606-18284-5*) Turtleback.
Oceans. Jim Rothaus. LC 96-11468. (Biomes of Nature Ser.). (Illus.). 32p. (J). (gr. 2-6). 1996. lib. bdg. 22.79 (*1-56766-286-2*) Childs World.
Oceans. Philip Sauvain. LC 96-14810. (Geography Detective Ser.). (J). 1997. lib. bdg. 19.95 (*1-57505-043-9*, Carolrhoda) Lerner Pub.
Oceans. Seymour Simon. LC 89-28452. (Illus.). 32p. (J). (gr. k up). 1990. lib. bdg. 15.93 (*0-688-09454-6*, Wm Morrow) Morrow Avon.
Oceans. Seymour Simon. LC 89-28452. (Illus.). 32p. (J). (ps-2). 1990. 16.00 (*0-688-09453-8*, Wm Morrow) Morrow Avon.
Oceans. Seymour Simon. LC 89-28452. (Illus.). 40p. (J). 1997. mass mkt. 5.95 (*0-688-15478-6*, Wm Morrow) Morrow Avon.
Oceans. Seymour Simon. (Wiley Nature Editions Ser.). 1997. 11.15 (*0-606-11694-X*, Pub. by Turtleback) Demco.
Oceans. Brian Hunter Smart. LC 98-47320. (Closer Look at Ser.). 32p. (J). (gr. 4-6). 1999. lib. bdg. 20.90 (*0-7613-0903-9*, Copper Beech Bks) Millbrook Pr.
Oceans. Darlene R. Stille. LC 98-53857. (Ecosystems Ser.). (J). 1999. 21.50 (*0-516-21510-8*) Childrens.
***Oceans.** Darlene R. Stille. (True Bks.). (J). 2000. pap. text 6.95 (*0-516-26768-X*) Childrens.
***Oceans.** Barbara Taylor. (Make It Work! Geography Ser.). (Illus.). (J). 2000. pap. 6.95 (*1-58728-251-8*) Two Can Pub.
Oceans. Lisa A. Wroble. LC 97-27275. (Overview Ser.). (Illus.). (YA). (gr. 4-12). 1997. lib. bdg. 22.45 (*1-56006-464-1*) Lucent Bks.
Oceans. unabridged ed. Brad Caudle & Melissa Caudle. (Rock 'N Learn Ser.). (Illus.). 32p. (J). (gr. 2 up). 1998. pap. 12.99 incl. audio (*1-878489-75-5*, RL975) Rock N Learn.
Oceans. 2nd ed. Karl K. Turekian. (Illus.). 160p. 1976. 15.95 (*0-13-630426-5*) P-H.
Oceans: A Book of Questions & Answers. Donald G. Groves. LC 88-32625. (Illus.). 224p. 1989. pap. 14.95 (*0-471-60712-6*) Wiley.
Oceans: Hands on Elementary School Science. Linda Poore. 57p. 1994. teacher ed. 35.00 (*1-883410-10-X*) L Poore.
Oceans: Life in the Deep. Beverly McMillan & Jack Musick. LC 97-8125. (Illus.). 176p. 1997. 27.98 (*1-56799-471-7*, MetroBooks) M Friedman Pub Grp Inc.
Oceans: Looking at Beaches & Coral Reefs, Tides & Currents... unabridged ed. Adrienne Mason. (Illus.). 80p. (J). (gr. 3-7). 1997. pap. 16.95 (*1-55074-147-0*, Pub. by Kids Can Pr) Genl Dist Srvs.
Oceans: Our Endangered Planet. Mary K. Hoff. (J). (gr. 4 up). 1993. pap. 8.95 (*0-8225-9628-8*, Lerner Publctns) Lerner Pub.
Oceans: Physical-Chemical Dynamics & Human Impact. Ed. by Shyamal K. Majumdar et al. LC 94-67523. (Illus.). x, 498p. (C). 1994. 45.00 (*0-945809-10-7*) Penn Science.
Oceans: Sea Life, Exploration, & World Geography. Amanda Bennett. (Unit Study Adventures Ser.). 179p. 1996. pap. 13.99 (*1-888306-08-4*, Home School Pr) Holly Hall.
Oceans - Thematic Unit. Mary E. Sterling. 1990. 9.95 (*1-55734-284-9*) Tchr Create Mat.
Oceans & Arctic. Compass Productions Staff. (Vanishing Animal Pop-Up Ser.). (Illus.). 10p. (J). (gr. k-4). 1993. 5.95 (*0-694-00441-3*) HarpC Child Bks.
Oceans & Climate. Grant R. Bigg. 256p. 1996. pap. text 27.95 (*0-521-58268-7*) Cambridge U Pr.
Oceans & Environmental Security: Shared U. S. & Russian Perspectives. James Broadus & Raphael Vartanov. LC 93-48894. 320p. 1994. text 60.00 (*1-55963-235-6*); pap. text 40.00 (*1-55963-236-4*) Island Pr.
Oceans & Other Fun Things. Richard Scarry. (Busy World of Richard Scarry Ser.). (Illus.). 24p. (J). 1998. pap. 3.25 (*0-689-81635-9*) S&S Childrens.
Oceans & Public Policy. Ed. by Timothy Hennessey & Maynard E. Silva. 224p. (Orig.). 1986. pap. 15.00 (*0-918592-88-7*) Pol Studies.
Oceans & Rivers. Michael W. Carroll. LC 98-42132. (J). 1999. 13.99 (*0-7814-3068-2*) Chariot Victor.
Oceans & Rivers, 6 vols. unabridged ed. Frances Dipper. LC 96-5009. (Changing World Ser.). (Illus.). 80p. (J). (gr. 3-7). 1996. 12.95 (*1-57145-027-0*, Silver Dolph) Advantage Pubs.
Oceans & Sea Life: An Integrated Unit. Kathy Rogers. (Primary Thematic Units Ser.). (Illus.). 96p. (Orig.). 1993. pap. 12.95 (*0-944459-82-X*) ECS Lrn Systs.
Oceans & Seas. Chris Arvetis & Carole Palmer. LC 93-33674. (Where Are We? Ser.). (Illus.). (J). 1994. 3.95 (*0-528-83675-7*) Rand McNally.
***Oceans & Seas.** Catherine Chambers. LC 99-44189. (Mapping Earthforms Ser.). (Illus.). 2000. lib. bdg. write for info. (*1-57572-526-6*) Heinemann Lib.
Oceans & Seas. Neil Morris. LC 96-27638. (World's Top Ten Ser.). (Illus.). 32p. (J). 1997. lib. bdg. 22.83 (*0-8172-4343-7*) Raintree Steck-V.
Oceans & Seas. Alex Voglino. (Deep Blue Planet Ser.). (Illus.). 56p. (J). (gr. 6 up). 1997. 27.12 (*0-8172-4650-9*) Raintree Steck-V.
Oceans & Seas Library, 6 bks. & 6 cass., Set. 39.95 incl. audio (*0-86545-164-8*) Spizzirri.
***Oceans & Skies.** Fran Sammis. LC 98-40835. (Mapping Our World Ser.). (J). (gr. 4-7). 1999. 27.07 (*0-7614-0374-4*) Marshall Cavendish.
Oceans & the Environment: A Pacific Island Perspective. 110p. (Orig.). (C). 1994. pap. text 35.00 (*0-7881-0726-7*) DIANE Pub.
Oceans & the Jungles. Chris Moore. (J). 1988. write for info. (*0-318-62377-3*, PuffinBks) Peng Put Young Read.
Oceans Apart. Colin Morton. LC 95-183786. 192p. 1995. pap. 16.95 (*1-55082-136-9*, Pub. by Quarry Pr) LPC InBook.
Oceans Are Emptying: Fish Wars & Sustainability. Raymond A. Rogers. LC 95-79350. 176p. 1995. 48.99 (*1-55164-031-7*, Pub. by Black Rose); pap. 19.99 (*1-55164-030-9*, Pub. by Black Rose) Consort Bk Sales.
Oceans Atlas. Anita Ganeri. LC 93-28724. (Illus.). 64p. (J). (gr. 4 up). 1994. 19.95 (*1-56458-475-5*) DK Pub Inc.
Ocean's Bounty. 2nd rev. ed. Sherri Eldridge. (Illus.). 32p. 1997. pap. 2.95 (*1-886862-21-4*, MN OCN) Harv Hill ME.
Ocean's Call. A. D. Stonecipher. LC 91-62027. (Illus.). 16p. (J). (ps-4). 1992. lib. bdg. 9.95 (*0-9621759-2-7*) Rochester Pub Lib Dist.
***Oceans' End: Travels Through Endangered Seas.** Colin Woodard. LC 99-51771. 320p. 2000. 26.00 (*0-465-01570-0*, Pub. by Basic) HarpC.
***Oceans Governance & Maritime Strategy.** Ed. by David Wilson & Dick Sherwood. 264p. 2000. pap. 39.95 (*1-86508-184-1*, Pub. by Allen & Unwin Pty) Paul & Co Pubs.
Ocean's Lure. Diane Conrad. (Illus.). vi, 52p. (Orig.). 1996. pap. 8.00 (*0-614-32388-6*) Phantsml Pr.
Oceans, '95 MTS/IEEE: Challenges of Our Changing Global Environment, 3 vols., Set. 1995. 150.00 (*0-933957-14-9*) Marine Tech Soc.
***Oceans '99 MTS/IEEE: Riding the Crest into the 21st Century, 1999, 3 vols.** 1602p. 1999. pap. 80.00 (*0-933957-24-6*) Marine Tech Soc.
Oceans 97 MTS/IEEE: 500 Years of Ocean Exploration, 2 vols., Set. IEEE (Oceanic Engineering Society) Staff. LC 97-72643. 1510p. 1997. 130.00 (*0-7803-4108-2*, 97CH36105) Inst Electrical.
Oceans 96 MTS/IEEE: Progress for the 21st Century Coastal Ocean, 3 vols., Set. IEEE (Oceanic Engineering Society) Staff. Ed. by IEEE (Institute of Electrical & Electronics Engine. LC 96-77050. 1360p. 1996. 130.00 (*0-7803-3519-8*, 96CH35967) Inst Electrical.
Oceans of Consolation: Personal Accounts of Irish Migration to Australia. David Fitzpatrick. (Illus.). 664p. 1994. text 57.50 (*0-8014-2606-5*); pap. text 25.00 (*0-8014-8230-5*) Cornell U Pr.
Oceans of Consolation: Personal Accounts of Irish Migration to Australia. Ed. by David Fitzpatrick. 656p. 1996. 69.95 (*0-522-84580-0*, Pub. by Melbourne Univ Pr) Paul & Co Pubs.
***Oceans of Emotions-3D.** large type ed. Nicole K. Clark & John T. Clark. (Illus.). 32p. (J). (ps-4). 1999. 17.95 (*1-892176-13-0*) PremaNations.
Oceans of Invisibles: Hidden Picture Funbook. Malcolm Whyte. 32p. 1995. pap. 3.99 (*0-8431-3883-1*, Price Stern) Peng Put Young Read.
Oceans of Light. Bob Talbot. pap. write for info. (*1-882501-51-9*) Talbot Prods.
Oceans of Light. Bob Talbot. 1998. 100.00 (*1-882501-50-0*) Talbot Prods.
Oceans of the World: Syllabus. Robert E. Adam. 1978. pap. text 7.75 (*0-89420-041-0*, 233021); audio 70.85 (*0-89420-166-2*, 233000) Natl Book.
Oceans of Wealth: The Hidden Riches. Robert Evans. 104p. (C). 1990. pap. 110.00 (*1-85609-003-5*, Pub. by Witherby & Co) St Mut.
Oceans Policy: New Institutions, Challenges & Opportunities. Myron H. Nordquist et al. LC 99-22756. 1999. 147.00 (*90-411-1182-4*) Kluwer Law Intl.
Oceans, Rivers, & Lakes: Energy & Substance Transfers at Interfaces. J. C. Amiard. LC 98-34666. (Developments in Hydrobiology Ser.). 1998. write for info. (*0-7923-5233-5*) Kluwer Academic.
Ocean's Role in Global Change: Progress of Major Research Programs. Ocean Studies Board, National Research Council Sta. 96p. (Orig.). (C). 1994. pap. text 25.00 (*0-309-05043-X*) Natl Acad Pr.
Oceans Special Issue. Sasi. 1998. pap. text. write for info. (*0-7167-3486-9*) W H Freeman.
***Oceans with Book & Puzzle.** (ps-3). 2000. 9.95 (*1-878427-80-6*) Cimino Pub Grp.
Oceans Without Continents. Geoff Meads. LC 97-9200. 1997. write for info. (*1-85775-270-8*, Radcliffe Med Pr) Scovill Paterson.
Oceans '98: Conference Proceedings : 28 September-1 October, 1998, Nice, France, Acropoils Convention Center. Oceans '98 & Oceanic Engineering Society (U.S.). LC 98-86363. 1853 p. 1998. write for info. (*0-7803-5048-0*) IEEE Standards.
***Oceanspace.** Allen M. Steele. LC 99-43139. 384p. 2000. 21.95 (*0-441-00685-X*) Ace Bks.
Oceanul (The Ocean) Silvia Circa. 160p. 1993. pap. 14.95 (*0-9623183-0-2*) Moonfall Pr VA.
Oceanus. 3rd ed. Ingmanson & Garrison. (Biology Ser.). 1985. pap., student ed. 13.00 (*0-534-03850-6*) Wadsworth Pub.
Oceanus: The Marine Environment. 5th ed. Lebow. (Biology Ser.). 1993. mass mkt., student ed. 14.25 (*0-534-20562-3*) Wadsworth Pub.
Oceanus: The Marine Environment. 6th ed. Tom Garrison. (Biology Ser.). 1994. pap., student ed. 14.25 (*0-534-25704-6*) Wadsworth Pub.
Oceanus: The Marine Environment. 7th ed. Tom Garrison. (Biology Ser.). 1995. pap., student ed. 18.00 (*0-534-51270-4*) Wadsworth Pub.
Oceanus Telecourse Guide. 9th ed. Lebow Garrison. (Biology Ser.). 2001. pap. 18.75 (*0-534-37563-4*) Brooks-Cole.
Oceanus Telecourse Study Guide. 8th ed. Garrison. (Environmental Science Ser.). 1998. pap., student ed. 18.00 (*0-534-53084-2*) Wadsworth Pub.
Oceanwatcher. Susan Scott. pap. 9.95 (*0-9620712-0-X*) Grn Turtle Pr.
Oceanwatcher: An Above-Water Guide to Hawaii's Marine Life. Susan Scott. (Illus.). 128p. (C). 1988. write for info. (*0-318-63363-9*) Grn Turtle Pr.
Ocellus Lucanus "On the Nature of the Universe" Thomas Taylor. 15.95 (*0-89314-403-7*) Philos Res.
Oceti Wakan. Pete S. Catches, Sr. & Retek V. Catches. Ed. by Cynthia L. Catches.Tr. of Sacred Fireplace. (Illus.). xi, 214p. (Orig.). 1997. pap. 28.00 (*0-9658626-7-4*) Oceti Wakan.
Och Vi Tog Till Vapen: Kvinna i Angola. Birgitta Lagerstrom. (Kvinna i U-Land Ser.). 144p. 1980. write for info. (*91-7106-171-1*, Pub. by Nordic Africa) Transaction Pubs.
Ocherki po Ethnografii Aleutov (Konets XVIII-per Vaia Polovina XIX v.) see Essays on the Ethnography of the Aleuts (at the End of the Eighteenth & First Half of the Nineteenth Century)
Ocherki po Teorii Stoimosti Marksa see Essays on Marx's Theory of Value
Ochlocknee: Land of Crooked Waters. Georgia B. Griffin. (Illus.). 276p. 1982. 16.00 (*0-318-11704-5*) Ochlocknee.
Ocho Casos Extranos y Dos Casos Mas: Cuentos, 1930-1970. Gustavo Agrait. (UPREX, Ficcion Ser.: No. 4). 153p. (C). 1972. pap. 1.50 (*0-8477-0004-6*) U of PR Pr.

An Asterisk (*) at the beginning of an entry indicates that the title is appearing for the first time.

OCHO MUNDOS 4/E. 4th ed. Brenda Wegmann. (ENG & SPA.). 224p. (C). 1990. pap. text 37.50 (*0-03-021824-1*) Harcourt Coll Pubs.

Ocho Pasos Hacia la Intimidad. John Trent. (Hombres de Integridad Ser.).Tr. of Eight Steps to Intimacy. (SPA.). 48p. 2.99 (*1-56063-677-7*, 495678) Editorial Unilit.

Ocho Siglos de Cuentos y Narraciones de Espana. Nancy C. Brooks et al. (gr. 12 up). 1976. pap. text 5.95 (*0-88345-280-4*, 18465) Prentice ESL.

Ochoco - Big Pine Country. Rick Steber. (Illus.). 130p. (Orig.). 1990. 32.00 (*0-945134-98-3*); pap. 22.50 (*0-945134-99-1*) Bonanza Pub.

Ochosi: Ifa & the Spirit of the Tracker. Falokum Fatuumbi. 30p. 1993. pap. 4.95 (*0-942272-29-3*) Original Pubns.

Ochre People. Noni Jabavu. LC 95-198558. (Writers Ser.). 261p. 1995. reprint ed. pap. text 12.95 (*0-86975-472-6*, Pub. by Ravan Pr) Ohio U Pr.

Ochsner Guide to the Finest Restaurants & Hotels in the World, 1997-98. 13th rev. ed. Othon H. Ochsner, II. Orig. Title: Ochsner Pocket Guide to the Finest Restaurants in the World. (Illus.). 1997. per. 20.00 (*1-881546-03-9*) Ochsner Intl.

Ochsner Pocket Guide to the Finest Restaurants in the World see Ochsner Guide to the Finest Restaurants & Hotels in the World, 1997-98

Ochsner Pocket Guide to the Finest Restaurants in the World, 1992-93. 9th ed. Othon H. Ochsner, II. (Illus.). 199p. (Orig.). 1992. pap. write for info. (*1-881546-00-4*) Ochsner Intl.

Ochsner Pocket Guide to the Finest Restaurants in the World, 1993-94. 10th ed. Othon H. Ochsner, II. (Illus.). 248p. 1993. pap. 20.00 (*1-881546-01-2*) Ochsner Intl.

Ochsner Pocket Guide to the Finest Restaurants in the world, 1994-95. 11th ed. Othon H. Ochsner, II. (Illus.). 256p. 1994. pap. 20.00 (*1-881546-02-0*) Ochsner Intl.

Ochsner's: An Informal History of the South's Largest Private Medical Center. fac. ed. John Wilds. LC 85-5779. (Illus.). 262p. (Orig.). 1985. reprint ed. pap. 81.30 (*0-7837-7767-1*, 204752300007) Bks Demand.

Ocio. Sue Roger. (Breviarios Ser.). (SPA.). pap. 6.99 (*968-16-3944-8*, Pub. by Fondo) Continental Bk.

Ociosidad Entretenida, en Varios Entremeses, Bailes, Loas y Jacaras. xvi, 129p. reprint ed. write for info. (*0-318-71626-7*) G Olms Pubs.

Ocke, Nutta Och Pillerill see Woody, Hazel & Little Pip

Ockeghem's Missa Cuiusvis Toni: In Its Original Notation & Edited in All the Modes. Intro. by George Houle. LC 91-753671. (Publications of the Early Music Institute). 152p. 1992. pap. text 19.95 (*0-253-32854-3*) Ind U Pr.

Ockelton: Equity & Trusts. Mark Ockelton. (Butterworths Core Text Ser.). 1997. pap. write for info. (*0-406-03313-7*, OET, MICHIE) LEXIS Pub.

Ockerki po Istoriji Russkoi Literaturi XIX Vjeka. I. M. Andreyev.Tr. of Essays on the History of Russian Literature of the XIX Century. 316p. 1968. pap. text 10.00 (*0-317-30303-1*) Holy Trinity.

Ockham Algebras. T. S. Blyth & J. C. Varlet. (Illus.). 250p. 1994. text 115.00 (*0-19-859938-2*) OUP.

Ockham on Aristotle's Physics: A Translation of Ockham's Brevis Summa Libri Physicorum. Tr. by Julian A. Davies. 170p. 1989. pap. 12.00 (*1-57659-060-7*) Franciscan Inst.

Ockham on the Virtues. Rega Wood. LC 96-39436. (History of Philosophy Ser.). 272p. 1997. 35.95 (*1-55753-096-3*); pap. 17.95 (*1-55753-097-1*) Purdue U Pr.

Ockham's Theory of Propositions Pt. II: Summa Logicae. William of Ockham. Tr. by A. J. Freddoso & Henry Schuurman. LC 97-37768. 220p. 1997. 35.00 (*1-890318-51-5*) St Augustines Pr.

Ockham's Theory of Terms Pt. I: Summa Logicae. unabridged ed. William of Ockham. Tr. & Intro. by Michael J. Lonx. LC 97-37876. 235p. 1997. reprint ed. 35.00 (*1-890318-50-7*) St Augustines Pr.

OCLC Authority Control Service Planning Guide. 2nd ed. OCLC Staff. LC 98-156286. iii, 30p. 1997. write for info. (*1-55653-234-2*) OCLC Online Comp.

OCLC Dial TCP/IP Access: A Guide for System Administrators. OCLC Staff. LC 98-161003. 1997. write for info. (*1-55653-237-7*) OCLC Online Comp.

OCLC, Its Governance, Function, Financing, & Technology. Albert F. Maruskin. LC 80-23417. (Books in Library & Information Science: No. 32). 157p. reprint ed. pap. 48.70 (*0-7837-0761-4*, 204107500019) Bks Demand.

OCLC, 1967-1997: Thirty Years of Furthering Access to the World's Information. Ed. by K. Wayne Smith. LC 98-15155. (Journal of Library Administration Ser.: Vol. 25, Nos. 2-4). 289p. 1998. pap. 19.95 (*0-7890-0542-5*) Haworth Pr.

OCLC, 1967-1997: Thirty Years of Furthering Access to the World's Information. Ed. by K. Wayne Smith. LC 98-15155. (Journal of Library Administration Ser.: Vol. 26, Nos. 1-2). 289p. 1998. 45.00 (*0-7890-0536-0*) Haworth Pr.

OClinical Gynecologic Endocrinology & Infertility. 6th ed. Leon Speroff et al. LC 98-36104. 1999. 120.00 (*0-683-30379-1*) Lppncott W & W.

***O'Clock.** Mary Rising Higgins. 97p. 2000. pap. 13.00 (*1-893541-25-8*, Pub. by Potes Poets) SPD-Small Pr Dist.

O'Clock. Fanny Howe. 104p. 1995. 10.95 (*1-874400-07-5*, Pub. by Reality St Edits) SPD-Small Pr Dist.

Ocmulgee Archaeology, 1936-1986. Ed. by David J. Hally. LC 93-2482. (Illus.). 264p. 1994. 45.00 (*0-8203-1606-7*) U of Ga Pr.

Ocona. Sarah Gilbert. 1995. write for info. (*0-446-51690-2*) Warner Bks.

Oconee County, South Carolina. Piper Peters Aheron. (Images of America Ser.). (Illus.). 128p. 1998. pap. 18.99 (*0-7524-0895-X*) Arcadia Publng.

Oconee River: Tales to Tell. Compiled by Katherine B. Walters. LC 93-48600. 1995. 35.00 (*0-87152-479-1*) Reprint.

O'Connors. Karen Young. (By Request Ser.). 1999. pap. 4.99 (*0-373-83413-6*, 1-83413-4) Harlequin Bks.

***O'Connor's Annotated CPRC Plus, 1999.** annot. ed. Ed. by David Beck. (Texas Annotated Codes Plus Ser.). 1018p. 1999. pap. 34.95 (*1-884554-31-8*) J McClure Pubng.

***O'Connor's Annotated Criminal Codes Plus 1999.** annot. rev. ed. George M. Secrest, Jr. (Texas Annotated Codes Plus Ser.). 1126p. 1999. pap. 49.95 (*1-884554-32-6*) J McClure Pubng.

***O'Connor's Annotated Texas Employment Codes Plus 2000.** annot. ed. Ed. by Jeffrey C. Londa. (Texas Annotated Codes Plus Ser.). 2000. pap. 49.95 (*1-884554-38-5*) J McClure Pubng.

***O'Connor's Business Organization Codes Plus 1999.** Larry Schoenbrun & Richard Tulli. (Texas Annotated Codes Plus Ser.). 1044p. 1999. pap. 49.95 (*1-884554-33-4*) J McClure Pubng.

***O'Connor's Classic Movie Guide: The Finest Films Through Seven Decades, 1930-1998.** unabridged ed. Charles O'Connor. 306p. 1998. pap. 15.95 (*1-893877-03-5*) OConnor Hannon.

***O'Connor's Federal Forms - Civil Trials, 1999.** Michol O'Connor. Ed. by D. Bryan Hughes et al. (O'Connor's Litigation Ser.). 1032p. 1999. pap. 49.95 (*1-884554-28-8*) J McClure Pubng.

***O'Connor's Federal Rules - Civil Trials, 2000.** Michol O'Connor. Ed. by Michael C. Smith & Gregory S. Coleman. (O'Connor's Litigation Ser.). 1068p. 2000. pap. 54.95 (*1-884554-36-9*) J McClure Pubng.

***O'Connor's Movie Star Treasury Vol. I: 1930-1959.** unabridged ed. Charles O'Connor. 272p. 1998. pap. 15.95 (*1-893877-01-9*) OConnor Hannon.

***O'Connor's Movie Star Treasury Vol. II: 1960-1998.** unabridged ed. Charles O'Connor. 274p. 1998. pap. 15.95 (*1-893877-02-7*) OConnor Hannon.

O'Connor's Texas Causes of Action, 2000. Leslie C. Taylor. Date not set. pap. 75.00 (*1-884554-26-1*) J McClure Pubng.

***O'Connor's Texas Forms - Civil Trials, 2000.** Michol O'Connor. Ed. by Jones McClure Publishing, Inc., Staff. (O'Connor's Litigation Ser.). 1140p. 2000. pap. 54.95 (*1-884554-35-0*) J McClure Pubng.

***O'Connor's Texas Rules - Civil Appeals, 2000.** Michol O'Connor. Ed. by Jessie Amos & Diane M. Guariglia. (O'Connor's Litigation Ser.). 2000. pap. 59.95 (*1-884554-37-7*) J McClure Pubng.

O'Connor's Texas Rules - Civil Trials, 1991: Civil Trial 1991. Michol O'Connor. Ed. by Tracie M. Burns. (Texas Lawyer Litigation Ser.). 760p. (Orig.). (C). 1991. pap. 49.95 (*1-879590-00-X*) Amer Law Media.

***O'Connor's Texas Rules - Civil Trials, 2000.** Michol O'Connor. Ed. by Diane M. Guariglia & Byron P. Davis. (O'Connor's Litigation Ser.). 1018p. 1999. pap. 54.95 (*1-884554-34-2*) J McClure Pubng.

O'Connor's Texas Rules Civil Appeals, 1998. Michael O'Connor et al. (O'Connor's Litigation Ser.). 1024p. (C). 1998. pap. 59.95 (*1-884554-20-2*) J McClure Pubng.

O'Connor's Textbook of Arthroscopic Surgery. 2nd ed. Heshmat Shahriaree. (Illus.). 880p. (C). 1992. text 185.00 (*0-397-51015-2*) Lppncott W & W.

***Oconomowoc: Barons to Bootleggers.** Barbara Barquist & David Barquist. (Illus.). x, 335p. 1999. 40.00 (*0-9675179-0-7*) Barquist.

Ocotillo Poetry. Joseph D. Island. LC 97-90376. (Illus.). 99p. (Orig.). 1998. pap. 9.95 (*0-533-12373-9*) Vantage.

***OCP: Oracle8i DBA Architecture & Administration & Backup & Recovery Study Guide.** Gregg K. Hobbs. (Ocp Ser.). 608p. 2000. pap. 49.99 (*0-7821-2683-9*, Network Pr) Sybex.

***Ocp: Oracle8i DBA Certification Kit with CD-ROM.** Chip Dawes et al. 2000. pap. 109.97 incl. cd-rom (*0-7821-2685-5*) Sybex.

***OCP: Oracle8i DBA Performance Tuning & Network Administration Study Guide.** Joe Johnson. (Ocp Ser.). 2000. pap. 49.99 (*0-7821-2684-7*, Network Pr) Sybex.

***OCP: Oracle8i DBA SQL & PL/SQL Study Guide.** Chip Dawes. (Illus.). 2000. 49.99 (*0-7821-2682-0*) Sybex.

***OCP, Oracle8i DBO Study Guide.** Lance Mortensen. 512p. 2000. 49.99 (*0-7821-2686-3*) Sybex.

OCP Training Guide: Oracle DBA. Willard Baird. LC 98-84813. (OCP Training Guide Ser.). 800p. 1998. 59.99 (*1-56205-891-6*) New Riders Pub.

OCR with a Smile! The Most Comprehensive Reference to Operating Any OCR System. Fred F. Ross. Ed. by Judy French. LC 98-96352. (Illus.). 205p. 1998. pap. 28.50 (*0-9665904-0-6*, SMILE01) Hse Scan.

Ocracoke. Carl Goerch. (Illus.). 223p. 1984. pap. 9.95 (*0-89587-031-2*) Blair.

Ocracoke: Its History & People. David Shears. LC 89-61108. (Illus.). 180p. (Orig.). 1989. pap. 10.95 (*0-9622806-2-3*) Starfish Pr.

Ocracoke: Its History & People. 2nd rev. ed. David Shears. LC 91-75665. (Illus.). 185p. (Orig.). 1992. pap. 12.95 (*0-9622806-3-1*) Starfish Pr.

Ocracoke Odyssey: A Naturalist's Reflections on Her Home by the Sea. Pat Garber. (Illus.). 150p. 1999. pap. 14.95 (*1-878086-70-7*, Pub. by Down Home NC) Blair.

Ocracoke Wild: A Naturalist's Year on an Outer Banks Island. Pat Garber. (Illus.). 166p. 1995. pap. 13.95 (*1-878086-37-5*, Pub. by Down Home NC) Blair.

Ocracokers. Alton Ballance. LC 89-4886. (Illus.). xvi, 255p. (C). 1989. 27.50 (*0-8078-1878-X*); pap. 13.95 (*0-8078-4265-6*) U of NC Pr.

Ocracy, Pts. 5-7. Peter Ganick & Sheila E. Murphy. 31p. 1995. pap. 5.00 (*1-57141-050-3*) Runaway Spoon.

Oct. 1, 1878-Dec. 31, 1879 see Germans to America: Lists of Passengers Arriving at U. S. Ports, 1850-1893

Oct. 2, 1871-April 30, 1872 see Germans to America: Lists of Passengers Arriving at U. S. Ports, 1850-1893

Oct. 2, 1876-Sept. 30, 1878 see Germans to America: Lists of Passengers Arriving at U. S. Ports, 1850-1893

Oct. 2, 1868-May 31, 1869 see Germans to America: Lists of Passengers Arriving at U. S. Ports, 1850-1893

OCT Superbase Advanced Workbook. Ian C. Cunningham & Hugh Simpson-Wells. 672p. (Orig.). 1993. pap. 49.95 (*1-873664-07-9*, Pub. by Oxford Comp Trning) Cromland.

OCT Superbase Developer's Workbook. Ian C. Cunningham & Hugh Simpson-Wells. 672p. (Orig.). 1993. pap. 49.95 (*1-873664-08-7*, Pub. by Oxford Comp Trning) Cromland.

OCT Superbase Intermediate Workbook. Ian C. Cunningham & Hugh Simpson-Wells. (Illus.). 672p. (Orig.). 1993. pap. 49.95 (*1-873664-06-0*, Pub. by Oxford Comp Trning) Cromland.

OCT Superbase Version 2: Introductory Workbook. Ian C. Cunningham & Hugh Simpson-Wells. Ed. by Eric Alexander. (Illus.). 640p. (Orig.). 1992. pap. 49.95 incl. disk (*1-873664-05-2*, Pub. by Oxford Comp Trning) Cromland.

Oct. 24, 1853-May 4, 1854 see Germans to America: Lists of Passengers Arriving at U. S. Ports, 1850-1893

Octacosanol, Carnitine, & Other "Accessory" Nutrients, Vol. 2. Earl R. Mindell & Jeffrey S. Bland. (Good Health Guide Ser.). 32p. 1982. pap. text 2.95 (*0-87983-316-5*, 33165K, Keats Publng) NTC Contemp Pub Co.

Octagon for the Curriers. Melanie Meyers & Frank Angelo. (Illus.). 112p. (Orig.). 1995. pap. 29.95 (*0-8143-2643-9*) Wayne St U Pr.

Octagon for the Curriers Melanie Meyers & Frank Angelo. LC 95-69824. 111p. 1995. write for info. (*0-9645916-0-X*) Post Pub.

Octagon House. Phoebe A. Taylor. 1999. lib. bdg. 22.95 (*1-56723-139-X*, 148) Yestermorrow.

Octagon House. Phoebe Atwood Taylor. (Asey Mayo Cape Cod Mystery Ser.). 296p. 1991. pap. 6.95 (*0-88150-194-8*, Foul Play) Norton.

***Octagonal Raven.** L. E. Modesitt, Jr. 2001. write for info. (*0-312-87720-X*) Tor Bks.

Octandre for 8 Instruments. E. Varese. 32p. 1989. pap. 12.00 (*0-7935-3366-X*, 50481068) H Leonard.

Octane-Enhancing Zeolitic FCC Catalysis: Scientific & Technical Aspects. Alfred L. Scherzer. (Chemical Industries Ser.: Vol. 42). (Illus.). 192p. 1990. text 155.00 (*0-8247-8399-9*) Dekker.

Octane Requirements of the Motor Vehicle Fleet & Gasoline Grade Sales. Rayola S. Dougher & Thomas F. Hogarty. (Illus.). 51p. (C). 1998. reprint ed. pap. text 25.00 (*0-7881-3816-2*) DIANE Pub.

Octanol-Water Partition Coefficients: Fundamentals & Physical Chemistry. J. Sangster. LC 96-52451. (Series in Solution Chemistry). 178p. 1997. 160.00 (*0-471-97397-1*) Wiley.

Octateuchs: A Study of Illustrated Byzantine Manuscripts. John Lowden. (Illus.). 246p. 1992. text 55.00 (*0-271-00771-0*) Pa St U Pr.

Octave above Thunder: New & Selected Poems. Carol Muske. LC 97-10066. (Poetry Ser.). 200p. 1997. 24.95 (*0-88748-263-5*) Carnegie-Mellon.

Octave above Thunder: New & Selected Poems. Carol Muske. LC 97-10066. 207p. 1997. pap. 16.95 (*0-14-058794-2*) Viking Penguin.

Octave & His Flute. Gerard Moncomble. (Finding Out about Music Ser.). (Illus.). 275p. (Orig.). (J). (gr. 1-5). 1994. pap. 19.95 (*0-572-01965-3*, Pub. by W Foulsham) Trans-Atl Phila.

Octave & His Piano. Gerard Moncomble. (Finding Out about Instruments Ser.). (Illus.). 275p. (J). (gr. 1-5). 1993. pap. 19.95 (*0-572-01966-1*, Pub. by W Foulsham) Trans-Atl Phila.

Octave & His Violin. Gerard Moncomble. (Finding Out about Instruments Ser.). (Illus.). (Orig.). (J). (gr. 1-5). 1994. pap. 19.95 (*0-572-01967-X*, Pub. by W Foulsham) Trans-Atl Phila.

***Octave Mirbeau's Literary & Intellectual Evolution as a French Writer, 1880-1914.** Edna McCaffrey. LC 99-58809. (Studies in French Literature: Vol. 39). 260p. 2000. text 89.95 (*0-7734-7792-6*) E Mellen.

***Octaves: Poems from Hollywood.** Mark Dunster. 11p. 1999. pap. 5.00 (*0-89642-960-1*) Linden Pubs.

***Octavia.** Jilly Cooper. 2000. pap. 8.95 (*0-552-10717-4*, Pub. by Transworld Publishers Ltd) Trafalgar.

Octavia & Univibe. 1993. pap. 24.95 incl. audio compact disk (*0-7935-1403-7*, 00660275) H Leonard.

Octavia & Univibe. 1993. pap. 19.95 incl. audio (*0-7935-1404-5*, 00660276) H Leonard.

Octavia Hill & the Social Housing Debate: Essays & Letters by Octavia Hill. Ed. by Robert Whelan. (Rediscovered Riches Ser.: No. 3). 142p. 1998. pap. 19.95 (*0-255-36431-8*, Pub. by Inst Economic Affairs) Coronet Bks.

Octavia Warms Up. Barbara Beak. LC 91-31644. (Illus.). 24p. (J). 1992. 1.99 (*0-85953-786-2*) Childs Play.

Octavian: Prolog to Actium, Antony, Pt. 10. Mark Dunster. 50p. (Orig.). 1981. pap. 4.00 (*0-89642-074-4*) Linden Pubs.

Octavian's Campsite Memorial for the Actian War. William M. Murray. LC 89-84932. (Transactions Ser.: Vol. 79, Pt. 4). (Illus.). 161p. 1989. pap. 18.00 (*0-87169-794-7*, T794-MUW) Am Philos.

Octavio Paz: A Study of His Poetics. Jason Wilson. LC 78-18108. 200p. reprint ed. pap. 57.00 (*0-608-16980-3*, 2027265) Bks Demand.

Octavio Paz: Homage to the Poet. Ed. by Kosrof Chantikian. LC 80-82167. 248p. (C). 1981. 25.95 (*0-916426-03-3*); pap. 15.95 (*0-916426-04-1*) KOSMOS.

Octavio Paz: Mexican Poet & Critic. Joseph Roman. LC 92-47051. (Hispanics of Achievement Ser.). (Illus.). 120p. (YA). (gr. 5 up). 1994. lib. bdg. 19.95 (*0-7910-1249-2*) Chelsea Hse.

Octavio Paz: Trayectoria y Visiones (Trajectory & Vision) Maya Scharer-Nussberger. (SPA.). 201p. 1989. pap. 10.99 (*968-16-3232-X*, Pub. by Fondo) Continental Bk.

Octavio Paz & the Language of Poetry: A Psycholinguistic Approach. L. Iliana Underwood. LC 90-41215. (American University Studies: Latin American Literature: Ser. XXII). XIV, 268p. (C). 1992. text 53.95 (*0-8204-1257-0*) P Lang Pubng.

Octavio Paz en Sus Obras Completas (Octavio Paz in His Complete Works) Octavio Paz. (SPA.). 77p. 1994. pap. 7.99 (*968-16-4498-0*, Pub. by Fondo) Continental Bk.

Octavius of Marcus Minucius Felix. Ed. by Thomas C. Lawler & Johannes Burghart. Tr. by G. W. Clarke from LAT. (Ancient Christian Writers Ser.: No. 39). 1974. 26.95 (*0-8091-0189-0*) Paulist Pr.

Octet Clarinet, Bassoon, Horn, 2 Violins, Viola, Cello, & Bass: Score Only. Gunther Schuller. 124p. 1992. pap. 35.00 (*0-7935-1485-1*, 50481311) H Leonard.

Octet Set of Parts. Gunther Schuller. 1992. per. 75.00 (*0-7935-1486-X*) H Leonard.

***October.** (Monthly Patterns & Projects Ser.). (Illus.). 80p. (J). (ps-2). 2000. pap. 7.95 (*1-58273-126-8*) Newbridge Educ.

October. Christopher Isherwood. (Illus.). 89p. 1983. pap. 30.00 (*0-942642-02-3*) Twelvetrees Pr.

October. Daniel Parker. LC 99-16429. (Countdown Ser.: No. 10). 128p. (YA). (gr. 5 up). 1999. mass mkt. 3.99 (*0-689-81828-9*) Aladdin.

***October: Full Color Monthly Activities for Grades 1-3.** (Monthly Bks.). (Illus.). 64p. (J). (gr. 1-3). 2000. pap. 12.95 (*0-88724-549-8*, CD-2091) Carson-Dellos.

October: The Second Decade, 1986-1996. Ed. by Rosalind E. Krauss et al. LC 97-19453. 476p. 1998. 40.00 (*0-262-11226-4*) MIT Pr.

October & Halloween. Nancy M Davis et al. (Davis Teaching Units Ser.: Vol. 1, No. 2). (Illus.). 28p. (Orig.). (J). (ps-4). 1986. pap. 4.95 (*0-937103-01-2*) DaNa Pubns.

October Cities: The Redevelopment of Urban Literature. Carlo Rotella. LC 97-27980. 384p. 1998. 50.00 (*0-520-20763-7*, Pub. by U CA Pr); pap. 18.95 (*0-520-21144-8*, Pub. by U CA Pr) Cal Prin Full Svc.

October Classic. Bill Borst. 124p. 1989. pap. 7.95 (*0-9612260-7-2*) Krank Pr.

October Country. Ray Bradbury. 1985. mass mkt. 5.99 (*0-345-32448-X*, Del Rey) Ballantine Pub Grp.

***October Country.** Ray Bradbury. LC 99-94881. (Illus.). 352p. 1999. 16.00 (*0-380-97387-1*, Avon Bks) Morrow Avon.

October Country. aut. limited ed. Ray Bradbury. (Illus.). 337p. 1997. 65.00 (*1-887368-15-9*) Gauntlet.

October Dawn: Poems. Dorothy C. Raemsch. 32p. (Orig.). 1980. pap. 5.00 (*0-9605398-0-8*) D C Raemsch.

October Earthquake Yom Kipper, 1973. Zeev Schiff. 319p. 1974. 34.95 (*0-87855-244-8*) Transaction Pubs.

October, Eight O'Clock: Stories. Norman Manea. LC 91-36377. 224p. 1993. pap. 12.00 (*0-8021-3371-1*, Grove) Grove-Atltic.

October 1864 - March 1869 see Briefwechsel: Kritische Gesamtausgabe

October 18: What Your Birth Date Reveals about You. (Birth Date Book Ser.). (Illus.). 80p. 1998. 4.95 (*0-8362-6311-1*) Andrews & McMeel.

October 8: What Your Birth Date Reveals about You. (Birth Date Book Ser.). (Illus.). 80p. 1998. 4.95 (*0-8362-6297-2*) Andrews & McMeel.

October 11: What Your Birth Date Reveals about You. (Birth Date Book Ser.). (Illus.). 80p. 1998. 4.95 (*0-8362-6300-6*) Andrews & McMeel.

October Essentials: Idea Booklet & Pocket Folder Organizer. Karen Sevaly. (Illus.). 16p. 1997. pap., teacher ed., wbk. ed. 3.99 (*1-57882-009-X*, TF-1260) Teachers Friend Pubns.

October 15: What Your Birth Date Reveals about You. (Birth Date Book Ser.). (Illus.). 80p. 1998. 4.95 (*0-8362-6307-3*) Andrews & McMeel.

October 5: What Your Birth Date Reveals about You. (Birth Date Book Ser.). (Illus.). 80p. 1998. 4.95 (*0-8362-6294-8*) Andrews & McMeel.

October 1: What Your Birth Date Reveals about You. (Birth Date Book Ser.). (Illus.). 80p. 1998. 4.95 (*0-8362-6289-1*) Andrews & McMeel.

October 1, 1778 to January 31, 1779 see Letters of Delegates to Congress, 1774-1789, Vol. 25, March 1, 1788-July 25, 1789, with Supplement, 1774-87

October 1, 1779 to March 31, 1780 see Letters of Delegates to Congress, 1774-1789, Vol. 25, March 1, 1788-July 25, 1789, with Supplement, 1774-87

October for Idas. Star Black. LC 96-45638. 1997. pap. 12.00 (*0-9651558-1-1*) Painted Leaf.

October 14: What Your Birth Date Reveals about You. (Birth Date Book Ser.). (Illus.). 80p. 1998. 4.95 (*0-8362-6306-5*) Andrews & McMeel.

October 4: What Your Birth Date Reveals about You. (Birth Date Book Ser.). (Illus.). 80p. 1998. 4.95 (*0-8362-6292-1*) Andrews & McMeel.

October Heroes: Great World Series Games Remembered by the Men Who Played Them. Donald Honig. LC 96-2375. (Illus.). iv, 285p. 1996. pap. 15.00 (*0-8032-7286-3*, Bison Books) U of Nebr Pr.

October Idea Book: A Creative Idea Book for the Elementary Teacher, Ps-6. rev. ed. Karen Sevaly. (Illus.). 144p. (Orig.). 1997. pap. 10.95 (*0-943263-01-8*, TF-1000) Teachers Friend Pubns.

October in Cairo. M. Cruz. LC 86-2807. 253p. 1988. 22.00 (*0-932966-84-5*) Permanent Pr.

October Journey. Margaret Walker. LC 73-82444. 38p. 1973. pap. 7.00 (*0-910296-96-0*) Broadside Pr.

O

An Asterisk (*) at the beginning of an entry indicates that the title is appearing for the first time.

October Light. Jeff Tagami. 1990. pap. 8.95 (*0-9609630-3-0*) Kearny St Wkshop.

October Monthly Activities. Rice. (Monthly Activities Ser.). (Illus.). 80p. (J). (ps-1). 1996. pap., wbk. ed. 9.95 (*1-55734-861-8*) Tchr Create Mat.

October Monthly Activities. Dona H. Rice. (Illus.). 80p. 1996. pap., teacher ed. 9.95 (*1-55734-871-5*, TCM871) Tchr Create Mat.

October Monthly Activities. Sterling & Susan S. Nowlin. (Monthly Activities Ser.). (Illus.). 80p. (J). (gr. 6-8). 1996. pap., wbk. ed. 9.95 (*1-55734-152-4*) Tchr Create Mat.

October Moon. Michael Scott. 160p. (J). (gr. 7-9). 1995. pap. 3.50 (*0-590-26591-1*) Scholastic Inc.

October Moon. Michael Scott. (J). 1995. 8.60 (*0-606-07961-0*, Pub. by Turtleback) Demco.

October, 1990 Elections in Pakistan. National Democratic Institute for International Af. 236p. 1991. pap. 10.00 (*1-880134-04-7*) Natl Demo Inst.

October, 1973: The Arab-Israeli War. Frank Aker. LC 85-751. (Illus.). ix, 185p. (C). 1985. lib. bdg. 27.50 (*0-208-02066-7*, Archon Bks) Shoe String.

October, 1964. David Halberstam. 400p. 1995. pap. 12.95 (*0-449-98367-6*) Fawcett.

October, 1964. large type ed. David Halberstam. (Niagara Large Print Ser.). 1996. 29.50 (*0-7089-5822-2*) Ulverscroft.

October 19: What Your Birth Date Reveals about You. (Birth Date Book Ser.). (Illus.). 80p. 1998. 4.95 (*0-8362-6313-8*) Andrews & McMeel.

October 9: What Your Birth Date Reveals about You. (Birth Date Book Ser.). (Illus.). 80p. 1998. 4.95 (*0-8362-6298-0*) Andrews & McMeel.

October Obsession. Meredith More. 192p. 1988. pap. 8.95 (*0-941483-18-5*) Naiad Pr.

October Palace. Jane Hirshfield. LC 93-21302. 112p. 1994. pap. 12.00 (*0-06-096997-0*, Perennial) HarperTrade.

October Patterns, Projects & Plans. Imogene Forte. (Illus.). 80p. (J). (ps-3). 1989. pap. text 9.95 (*0-86530-126-3*, IP 166-8) Incentive Pubns.

October Rain. Ray Smith. 28p. 1969. 3.00 (*0-686-12083-3*) Kirk Pr.

October Revolution. Tom Lamarr. LC 98-26116. 168p. 1998. 19.95 (*0-87081-501-6*) Univ Pr Colo.

October Revolution: A BBC Correspondent's Eye-Witness Account of the Storming of the Russian Parliament. Lawrence McDonnell. LC 96-138798. (Illus.). 200p. (C). 1997. pap. 16.95 (*1-873376-07-3*, Pub. by Spellmnt Pubs) St Mut.

October Revolution: A Collection of Articles & Speeches. Joseph V. Stalin. LC 76-42700. reprint ed. 32.50 (*0-404-15372-0*) AMS Pr.

October Scenario. Kevin D. Randle. LC 88-1669. (Illus.). 176p. (Orig.). pap. 9.95 (*0-934523-35-5*) Middle Coast Pub.

October 2: What Your Birth Date Reveals about You. (Birth Date Book Ser.). (Illus.). 80p. 1998. 4.95 (*0-8362-6290-5*) Andrews & McMeel.

October 17: What Your Birth Date Reveals about You. (Birth Date Book Ser.). (Illus.). 80p. 1998. 4.95 (*0-8362-6310-3*) Andrews & McMeel.

October 7: What Your Birth Date Reveals about You. (Birth Date Book Ser.). (Illus.). 80p. 1998. 4.95 (*0-8362-6296-4*) Andrews & McMeel.

October 16: What Your Birth Date Reveals about You. (Birth Date Book Ser.). (Illus.). 80p. 1998. 4.95 (*0-8362-6308-1*) Andrews & McMeel.

October 6: What Your Birth Date Reveals about You. (Birth Date Book Ser.). (Illus.). 80p. 1998. 4.95 (*0-8362-6295-6*) Andrews & McMeel.

October Sky. Homer H. Hickam, Jr. Orig. Title: Rocket Boys. 448p. 1999. mass mkt. 6.99 (*0-440-23550-2*, Dell Trade Pbks) Dell.

October Smiled Back. Lisa W. Peters. LC 95-43681. (Illus.). 32p. (J). (ps-2). 1995. 14.95 (*0-8050-1776-3*, B Martin BYR) H Holt & Co.

October Sun: A Year of Haiku. Joseph Gustafson. 64p. (Orig.). 1988. pap. 5.95 (*0-9620313-0-5*) Leicester Hill Bks.

October Swimmer. Valery Nash. (Chapbook Ser.: No. 2). 40p. (Orig.). 1996. pap. 8.95 (*0-9649463-1-9*) Folly Cove.

October 10: What Your Birth Date Reveals about You. (Birth Date Book Ser.). (Illus.). 80p. 1998. 4.95 (*0-8362-6299-9*) Andrews & McMeel.

October 3: What Your Birth Date Reveals about You. (Birth Date Book Ser.). (Illus.). 80p. 1998. 4.95 (*0-8362-6291-3*) Andrews & McMeel.

October 13: What Your Birth Date Reveals about You. (Birth Date Book Ser.). (Illus.). 80p. 1998. 4.95 (*0-8362-6305-7*) Andrews & McMeel.

October 13th, 1991 Legislative & Municipal Elections in Bulgaria. National Democratic Institute for International Af & International Republican Institute Staff. 136p. 1992. pap. 9.95 (*1-880134-12-8*) Natl Demo Inst.

October 30: What Your Birth Date Reveals about You. (Birth Date Book Ser.). (Illus.). 80p. 1998. 4.95 (*0-8362-6324-3*) Andrews & McMeel.

October 31: What Your Birth Date Reveals about You. (Birth Date Book Ser.). (Illus.). 80p. 1998. 4.95 (*0-8362-6325-1*) Andrews & McMeel.

October 31st, 1991 Presidential & Legislative Elections in Zambia. National Democratic Institute for International Af & Carter Center of Emory University Staff. 167p. 1992. pap. 9.95 (*1-880134-14-4*) Natl Demo Inst.

October 12: What Your Birth Date Reveals about You. (Birth Date Book Ser.). (Illus.). 80p. 1998. 4.95 (*0-8362-6301-4*) Andrews & McMeel.

October Twelve. Phil Rizzuto & Tom Horton. 320p. 1995. 5.99 (*0-8125-3480-8*, Pub. by Forge NYC) St Martin.

October Twelve: The Story of the Legendary Team. Phil Rizzuto & Tom Horton. 288p. 1999. pap. 14.95 (*0-312-86991-6*, Pub. by Forge NYC) St Martin.

October 20: What Your Birth Date Reveals about You. (Birth Date Book Ser.). (Illus.). 80p. 1998. 4.95 (*0-8362-6314-6*) Andrews & McMeel.

October 28: What Your Birth Date Reveals about You. (Birth Date Book Ser.). (Illus.). 80p. 1998. 4.95 (*0-8362-6322-7*) Andrews & McMeel.

October 25: What Your Birth Date Reveals about You. (Birth Date Book Ser.). (Illus.). 80p. 1998. 4.95 (*0-8362-6319-7*) Andrews & McMeel.

October 21: What Your Birth Date Reveals about You. (Birth Date Book Ser.). (Illus.). 80p. 1998. 4.95 (*0-8362-6315-4*) Andrews & McMeel.

October 24: What Your Birth Date Reveals about You. (Birth Date Book Ser.). (Illus.). 80p. 1998. 4.95 (*0-8362-6318-9*) Andrews & McMeel.

October 29: What Your Birth Date Reveals about You. (Birth Date Book Ser.). (Illus.). 80p. 1998. 4.95 (*0-8362-6323-5*) Andrews & McMeel.

October 22: What Your Birth Date Reveals about You. (Birth Date Book Ser.). (Illus.). 80p. 1998. 4.95 (*0-8362-6316-2*) Andrews & McMeel.

October 27: What Your Birth Date Reveals about You. (Birth Date Book Ser.). (Illus.). 80p. 1998. 4.95 (*0-8362-6321-9*) Andrews & McMeel.

October 26: What Your Birth Date Reveals about You. (Birth Date Book Ser.). (Illus.). 80p. 1998. 4.95 (*0-8362-6320-0*) Andrews & McMeel.

October 23: What Your Birth Date Reveals about You. (Birth Date Book Ser.). (Illus.). 80p. 1998. 4.95 (*0-8362-6317-0*) Andrews & McMeel.

October War. Mohammed Heikal. 1980. mass mkt. write for info. (*0-394-59596-3*) Random.

October Wind: A Novel of Christopher Columbus. Susan Wiggs. 576p. (Orig.). 1991. mass mkt. 4.99 (*0-8125-1681-8*) Tor Bks.

***Octoberland.** Adam Lee. LC 99-11213. (Dominions of Irth Ser.: Vol. 3). 320p. 2000. mass mkt. 6.50 (*0-380-80628-2*, Avon Bks) Morrow Avon.

***Octoberland: Book Three of the Dominions of Irth.** Adam Lee. LC 99-11213. (Dominions of Irth Ser.: Bk. 3). 320p. 1999. pap. 13.50 (*0-380-79072-6*, Eos) Morrow Avon.

October's Child. 1995. write for info. (*1-56476-917-8*, Victor Bks) Chariot Victor.

October's Child. Donald Joseph. 1993. reprint ed. lib. bdg. 75.00 (*0-7812-5940-1*) Rprt Serv.

October's Ghost. Ryne D. Pearson. 464p. 1995. reprint ed. mass mkt. 5.99 (*0-380-72227-5*, Avon Bks) Morrow Avon.

October's Quest. Charles D. Taylor. 16p. (Orig.). 1995. pap. write for info. (*1-885206-15-1*, Iliad Pr) Cader Pubng.

Octoechos: or The Book of the Eight Tones see Horologion: A Primer for Elementary Village Schools

Octoginta Emblemata Moralia Nova e Sacris Literis Petita, Formandis Ad Veram Pietatem Accomodata Et Elegantibus Picturis. Daniel Cramer. (GER.). xxxii, 317p. 1981. reprint ed. 80.00 (*3-487-05356-X*) G Olms Pubs.

Octonaires de la Vanite et Inconstance du Monde (I-VIII) see Monuments de la Musique Francaise au Temps de la Renaissance

Octonaires de la Vanite et Inconstance du Monde (IX-XII): Pseaumes, Dialogue see Monuments de la Musique Francaise au Temps de la Renaissance

Octonion Planes Defined by Quadratic Jordan Algebras. John R. Faulkner. LC 52-42839. (Memoirs Ser.: No. 1/104). 71p. 1970. pap. 16.00 (*0-8218-1804-X*, MEMO/1/104) Am Math.

***Octonions, Jordan Algebras & Exceptional Groups.** T. A. Springer & F. D. Veldkamp. (Monographs in Mathematics). 170p. 2000. 87.00 (*3-540-66337-1*) Spr-Verlag.

Octopooh Saves the Day. Terry Page. (Illus.). 24p. (J). (gr. 2-6). 1995. pap. text 4.00 (*1-887864-54-7*); lib. bdg. 7.00 (*1-887864-08-3*) Boo Bks.

Octopooh Saves the Day Coloring Book. Terry Page. (Illus.). 32p. (J). (ps-5). 1995. pap. 3.00 (*1-887864-09-1*) Boo Bks.

Octopus see Living Things - Group 1

***Octopus.** 12p. (J). 2000. 6.95 (*0-8109-5655-1*, Pub. by Abrams) Time Warner.

Octopus. Mary M. Cerullo. LC 96-13971. (Illus.). 64p. (YA). (gr. 5). 1997. 16.99 (*0-525-65199-3*) NAL.

Octopus. Frank Norris. 1976. lib. bdg. 25.95 (*0-89968-070-4*, Lghtyr Pr) Buccaneer Bks.

Octopus! Richard Powell. (Eye Spy Ser.). 10p. 1999. pap. 6.99 (*0-8431-7531-1*, Price Stern) Peng Put Young Read.

Octopus: A History of the Construction, Conspiracies, Extortions, Robberies & Villainous Acts of Subsidized Railroads. John R. Robinson. Ed. by Stuart Bruchey. LC 80-1340. (Railroads Ser.). 1981. reprint ed. lib. bdg. 15.95 (*0-405-13812-1*) Ayer.

Octopus: A Story of California. Frank Norris. 496p. 1994. pap. 14.95 (*0-14-018770-7*, Penguin Classics) Viking Penguin.

Octopus: A Story of California. Frank Norris. (BCL1-PS American Literature Ser.). 361p. 1992. reprint ed. lib. bdg. 89.00 (*0-7812-6812-5*) Rprt Serv.

Octopus: Europe in the Grip of Organized Crime. Brian Freemantle. 422p. 1996. 24.95 (*1-85797-609-6*, Pub. by Orion Pubng Grp) Trafalgar.

Octopus: Secret Government & the Death of Danny Casolaro. Kenn Thomas & Jim Keith. (Illus.). 340p. (Orig.). 1996. 19.95 (*0-922915-39-3*) Feral Hse.

Octopus & Squid. James L. Hunt. LC 96-44014. (Natural History Ser.). (Illus.). 64p. 1996. pap. 9.95 (*1-878244-16-7*) Monterey Bay Aquarium.

Octopus & Squid. Homer Seward. LC 98-24059. (Sea Monsters Ser.). (J). 1998. 18.60 (*1-57103-238-X*) Rourke Pr.

Octopus' Den. Deirdre Langeland. LC 97-8676. (Smithsonian Oceanic Collection). (Illus.). 32p. (J). (ps-2). 1997. 15.95 (*1-56899-473-7*); 4.95 (*1-56899-474-5*); 19.95 incl. audio (*1-56899-475-3*, BC4014); 9.95 incl. audio (*1-56899-481-8*) Soundprints.

Octopus' Den, Incl. large toy. Deirdre Langeland. (Smithsonian Oceanic Collection). (Illus.). 32p. (J). (ps-2). 1997. 29.95 (*1-56899-477-X*); 34.95 incl. audio (*1-56899-479-6*) Soundprints.

Octopus' Den, Incl. Sm. & Lg. Plush Toy. Deirdre Langeland. LC 97-8676. (Smithsonian Oceanic Collection). (Illus.). 32p. (J). (ps-2). 1997. 38.95 incl. audio (*1-56899-649-7*) Soundprints.

Octopus' Den, Micro bk., incl. small toy. Deirdre Langeland. (Smithsonian Oceanic Collection). (Illus.). 32p. (J). (ps-2). 1997. 14.95 incl. audio (*1-56899-480-X*) Soundprints.

Octopus' Den: Incl. small toy. Deirdre Langeland. (Smithsonian Oceanic Collection). (Illus.). 32p. (J). (ps-2). 1997. 9.95 (*1-56899-478-8*) Soundprints.

Octopus Followed Me Home. Dan Yaccarino. 32p. (J). 2000. pap. 5.99 (*0-14-056532-9*, PuffinBks) Peng Put Young Read.

Octopus Followed Me Home. Dan Yaccarino. LC 97-8821. 32p. (J). (ps-3). 1997. 15.99 (*0-670-87401-9*) Viking Penguin.

Octopus Goes to School. Carolyn Bordelon. (Illus.). 8p. (J). (gr. k-1). 1995. pap. 3.75 (*1-880612-36-4*) Seedling Pubns.

Octopus Hug. Laurence Pringle. LC 92-73830. (Illus.). 32p. (J). (ps-3). 1996. pap. 6.95 (*1-56397-559-9*) Boyds Mills Pr.

Octopus Is Amazing. Patricia Lauber. LC 89-29300. (Trophy Let's-Read-&-Find-Out Bk., Stage 2). (Illus.). 32p. (J). (gr. k-4). 1996. pap. 4.95 (*0-06-445157-7*, HarpTrophy) HarpC Child Bks.

Octopus is Amazing. Patricia Lauber. (Let's Read-&-Find-Out Science Ser.). 1990. 10.15 (*0-606-08999-3*, Pub. by Turtleback) Demco.

***Octopus Magnus: An Allegoric Play.** Gerardus Ramc. 2000. pap. text 14.95 (*1-889534-42-0*) Jay St Pubs.

Octopus Pie. Susan Terris. LC 83-11517. 166p. (J). (gr. 5 up). 1983. 11.95 (*0-374-35571-1*) FS&G.

Octopus Who Wanted to Juggle. Robert Pack. (Illus.). (Orig.). (J). (ps-7). 1990. text 13.95 (*0-913123-26-9*) Galileo.

Octopuses. Ron Hirschi. LC 98-55098. (Nature Watch Ser.). (Illus.). 48p. (J). (gr. 2-7). 2000. 22.60 (*1-57505-386-1*, Carolrhoda) Lerner Pub.

Octopuses. Jenny Markert. (Nature Books Ser.). (Illus.). 32p. (J). (gr. 2-6). 1992. lib. bdg. 22.79 (*0-89565-836-4*) Childs World.

Octopuses. Lola M. Schaefer. LC 98-31444. (J). 1999. write for info. (*0-7368-0246-0*, Pebble Bks) Capstone Pr.

Octopuses. Lola M. Schaefer. 1999. 13.25 (*0-516-21834-4*) Capstone Pr.

Octopuses: Underwater Jet Propulsion see Secrets of the Animal World

Octopussy. Ian Fleming. 1976. 17.95 (*0-8488-1006-6*) Amereon Ltd.

Octopussy. Ian Fleming. pap. 9.95 (*0-685-11431-7*); pap. 9.95 (*0-685-11430-9*) Fr & Eur.

Octoroon: or Life in Louisiana: A Play in Five Acts. Dion Boucicault. LC 77-93418. (Black Heritage Library Collection). 1977. 13.95 (*0-8369-8521-4*) Ayer.

Octo's Coral Reef. Elisa B. Karnofsky. (Illus.). 32p. 1997. pap. 7.95 (*0-9659603-0-7*) AquaCritters.

Octovian: Medieval Studies. Ed. by Frances McSparran. (OS 289 Ser.). (Illus.). 244p. 1986. 29.95 (*0-19-722291-9*) OUP.

Octopus's Garden. Cindy L. Van Dover. LC 97-27056. 183p. (C). 1997. pap. 12.00 (*0-201-15498-6*) Addison-Wesley.

Ocular Accommodation, Convergence & Fixation Disparity: A Manual of Clinical Analysis. 2nd ed. David A. Goss. LC 95-13935. (Illus.). 222p. 1995. pap. text 34.00 (*0-7506-9497-1*) Buttrwrth-Heinemann.

Ocular Allergies. Barbara J. Jennings. 208p. 1999. pap. 45.00 (*0-7506-9794-6*) Buttrwrth-Heinemann.

Ocular Anatomy & Histology. David Pipe & Linda Rapley. (C). 1989. 130.00 (*0-900099-19-4*, Pub. by Assn Brit Dispen Opticians) St Mut.

***Ocular Anatomy & Physiology.** Tammy Langley et al. LC 99-19851. (Basic Bookshelf for Eyecare Professionals Ser.). (Illus.). 160p. 1999. pap. 30.00 (*1-55642-348-9*, 63489) SLACK Inc.

Ocular Anatomy & Physiology. Trygve Saude. Tr. by Robert Fletcher. LC 92-48827. 184p. 1993. pap. 49.95 (*0-632-03599-4*) Blackwell Sci.

Ocular Anesthesia. Scott Greenbaum. Ed. by Richard Lampert. (Illus.). 256p. 1997. text 74.00 (*0-7216-5955-1*, W B Saunders Co) Harcrt Hlth Sci Grp.

Ocular Blood Flow. Ed. by H. J. Kaiser et al. (Illus.). viii, 226p. 1996. 145.25 (*3-8055-6238-1*) S Karger.

Ocular Blood Flow in Glaucoma: Means, Methods & Measurements. Ed. by G. N. Lambrou & E. L. Greve. LC 89-19833. (Illus.). 295p. 1989. lib. bdg. 86.00 (*90-6299-053-3*, Pub. by Kugler) Kugler Pubns.

Ocular Circulation & Neovascularization. Ed. by D. Benezra et al. (Documenta Ophthalmologica Proceedings Ser.). (C). 1987. lib. bdg. 285.50 (*0-89838-892-9*) Kluwer Academic.

Ocular Differential Diagnosis. 5th ed. Frederick H. Roy. LC 92-10384. 900p. 1992. pap. text 62.50 (*0-8121-1594-5*) Lppncott W & W.

Ocular Differential Diagnosis. 6th ed. Frederick H. Roy. LC 96-13229. (Illus.). 768p. 1996. pap. 65.00 (*0-683-07415-6*) Lppncott W & W.

Ocular Disease Manual. John Meyler & Geoffrey Roberson. (Manual Ser.). (Illus.). 224p. 1998. pap. 60.00 (*0-7506-1816-7*) Buttrwrth-Heinemann.

Ocular Disease Update Manual. Ed. by Louis J. Catania. 180p. 1991. 39.95 (*1-879040-12-3*) Scovill Paterson.

Ocular Disease Update 2. Ed. by Louis J. Catania. 296p. 1991. 49.95 (*1-879040-13-1*) Scovill Paterson.

Ocular Diseases: Diagnosis & Treatment. 2nd ed. Daniel K. Roberts & Jack E. Terry. (Illus.). 637p. 1996. text 99.95 (*0-7506-9062-3*) Buttrwrth-Heinemann.

Ocular Disorders Proven or Suspected to Be Hereditary in Dogs. American College of Veterinary Ophthalmologists, G. (Illus.). 296p. (Orig.). 1992. pap. text 10.00 (*0-9635163-0-2*) Canine Eye Reg.

Ocular Drug Handbook. Mosby Staff & Gaston Mauger. 320p. (C). (gr. 13). 1996. text 35.95 (*0-8151-6910-8*, 27119) Mosby Inc.

Ocular Examination: Measurements. Karla Zadnik. Ed. by Richard Lampert. LC 96-6968. 416p. 1996. pap. text 52.00 (*0-7216-5209-3*, W B Saunders Co) Harcrt Hlth Sci Grp.

Ocular Fluorophotometry & the Future. Ed. by J. G. Cunha-Vaz & E. B. Leite. LC 89-19845. (Illus.). 167p. 1989. pap. text 57.50 (*90-6299-054-1*, Pub. by Kugler) Kugler Pubns.

Ocular Histopathology: A Guide to Differential Diagnosis. Curtis Margo & Grossniklaus. (Illus.). 352p. 1990. text 130.00 (*0-7216-3291-2*, W B Saunders Co) Harcrt Hlth Sci Grp.

Ocular Immune Responses: Proceedings of the International Symposium on Immunology & Immunopathology of the Eye, 1st, Strasbourg, 1974. International Symposium on Immunology & Immunopath. Ed. by W. R. Boeke. (Modern Problems in Ophthalmology Ser.: Vol. 16). 300p. 1976. 86.25 (*3-8055-2192-8*) S Karger.

Ocular Immunology. Foster. 1999. text. write for info. (*0-7216-6339-7*, W B Saunders Co) Harcrt Hlth Sci Grp.

Ocular Immunology in Health & Disease. Steven B. Koevary. 200p. 1998. pap. text 40.00 (*0-7506-9900-0*) Buttrwrth-Heinemann.

Ocular Infections & Immunity. Gary Holland et al. Ed. by Jay S. Pepose. (Illus.). 1584p. (C). (gr. 13). 1995. text 210.00 (*0-8016-6757-7*, 06757) Mosby Inc.

***Ocular Inflammation: Basic & Clinical Concepts.** Ed. by David BenEzra. 512p. 1999. 199.95 (*1-85317-507-2*, Pub. by Martin Dunitz) Blackwell Sci.

Ocular Inflammatory Disease. Foster. Date not set. text. write for info. (*0-7216-6338-9*, W B Saunders Co) Harcrt Hlth Sci Grp.

Ocular Lens: Structure, Function, & Pathology. Ed. by Hary Maisel. 496p. 1985. text 190.00 (*0-8247-7297-0*) Dekker.

Ocular Manifestations of Neurologic Disease. Bernard H. Blaustein. LC 95-50441. (Optometric Problem Solving Ser.). (Illus.). 304p. (C). (gr. 13). 1996. pap. text 39.95 (*0-8151-0507-X*, 24391) Mosby Inc.

Ocular Microsurgery. Ed. by Arthur S. Lim. (Developments in Ophthalmology Ser.: Vol. 1). (Illus.). viii, 96p. 1981. 43.50 (*3-8055-1106-X*) S Karger.

***Ocular Molecular Biology Protocols.** Ed. by Piroska Elizabeth Rakoczy. (Methods in Molecular Medicine Ser.: Vol. 47). 350p. 2000. 99.50 (*0-89603-837-8*) Humana.

Ocular Needs in Africa. F. M. Mburu. 147p. 1984. pap. 25.00 (*0-08-031299-3*, Pergamon Pr) Elsevier.

***Ocular Pathology.** John Harry & Gary Misson. (Illus.). 250p. 2000. 125.00 (*0-7506-2171-0*) Buttrwrth-Heinemann.

Ocular Pathology. 5th ed. David J. Apple & Rabb. LC 97-41914. (Illus.). 718p. (C). (gr. 13). 1997. text 189.00 (*0-8151-0592-4*, 27523) Mosby Inc.

Ocular Pathology: A Color Atlas. Myron Yanoff & Ben S. Fine. LC 65-40033. 1988. text 95.00 (*0-397-44659-4*, Lippncott) Lppncott W & W.

Ocular Prostheses. W. Warren. (C). 1989. 25.00 (*0-89771-747-3*, Pub. by Assn Brit Dispen Opticians) St Mut.

Ocular Radiation Risk Assessment in Populations Exposed to Environmental Radiation Contamination Proceedings of the NATO Advanced Research: Workshop on Ocular Radiation Risk Assessment in Populations Exposed to Environmental Radiation Contamination, Kiev, Ukraine, July 1997. Junk, A. K. Ed Research Workshop on Ocular Radiation Risk Assessment in Populations Exposed to Environmental Radiation Contamination Staff. LC 98-31134. (NATO Science Ser.). 10p. 1998. 119.00 (*0-7923-5310-2*) Kluwer Academic.

Ocular Surgery Comanagment. (C). 2000. 110.00 (*0-8385-7211-1*, Medical Exam) Appleton & Lange.

Ocular Syndromes. 3rd ed. Walter J. Gearaets. LC 75-6708. 667p. reprint ed. pap. 200.00 (*0-608-12673-X*, 205600000043) Bks Demand.

Ocular Therapeutics: Pharmacology & Clinical Application. Paul U. Fechner & Klaus D. Teichmann. LC 97-23207. (Illus.). 700p. 1997. pap. 55.00 (*1-55642-312-8*, 63128) SLACK Inc.

Ocular Therapeutics & Drug Delivery: A Multi-Disciplinary Approach. Ed. by Indra K. Reddy. LC 94-60709. 525p. 1995. text 179.95 (*1-56676-213-8*) Technomic.

***Ocular Therapeutics & Pharmacology: A Primary & Shared Care Guide.** Michael Doughty. (Illus.). 224p. 2000. pap. 70.00 (*0-7506-4520-2*) Buttrwrth-Heinemann.

Ocular Therapeutics Handbook: A Clinical Manual. Bruce E. Onofrey et al. LC 97-25437. 400p. 1997. spiral bd. 49.95 (*0-397-51392-5*) Lppncott W & W.

Ocular Toxicity of Intraoperatively Used Drugs & Solutions. R. M. Nuijts. (Illus.). 150p. 1995. text 46.00 (*90-6299-141-6*, Pub. by Kugler) Kugler Pubns.

An Asterisk (*) at the beginning of an entry indicates that the title is appearing for the first time.

Ocular Toxicology. Sidney Lerman & Ramesh C. Tripathi. LC 91-5822. (Illus.). 410p. 1989. text 160.00 (*0-8247-8309-3*) Dekker.

Ocular Toxicology: Proceedings of the 4th Congress of the International Society of Ocular Toxicology Held in Annecy, France, October 9-13, 1994. Ed. by Keith Green et al. 388p. 1995. 115.00 (*0-306-45133-6*, Kluwer Plenum) Kluwer Academic.

Ocular Tumors. Shields. 1993. 39.00 (*0-316-78579-2*, Little Brwn Med Div) Lppncott W & W.

***Ocular Tumours.** Bertil Damato. (Illus.). 288p. 2000. 99.00 (*0-7506-2220-2*) Buttrwrth-Heinemann.

Oculo-Auditory Syndromes. Ed. by Lucian S. Regenbogen & Gabriel J. Coscas. (Illus.). 368p. (gr. 13). 1985. 86.50 (*0-89352-225-2*) Mosby Inc.

Oculocutaneous Manifestations of Rheumatic Diseases. George E. Ehrlich. (Rheumatology Ser.: Vol. 4). 150p. 1973. 52.25 (*3-8055-1594-4*) S Karger.

Oculomotor Control & Cognitive Processes: Normal & Pathological Aspects: Selected-Edited Papers from the 5th European Conference on Eye Movements, Pavia, Italy, 10-13 Sept., 1989. Ed. by R. D. Schmid & D. Zambarbieri. (Studies in Visual Information Processing Ser.). 526p. 1991. 110.00 (*0-685-40079-4*, North Holland) Elsevier.

Oculomotor Imbalance in Binocular Vision & Fixation Disparity. Kenneth N. Ogle et al. LC 67-19139. 384p. reprint ed. pap. 119.10 (*0-608-12683-7*, 205600500043) Bks Demand.

Oculoplastic & Orbital Emergencies. John V. Linberg. (Illus.). 237p. (C). 1992. pap. text 65.00 (*0-8385-3626-3*, A3626-7) McGraw.

Oculoplastic Surgery. Francis L. Tse. (Illus.). 400p. 1992. text 107.00 (*0-397-51070-5*) Lppncott W & W.

Oculoplastic Surgery. 3rd ed. Ed. by Clinton D. McCord, Jr. et al. LC 94-11199. (Illus.). 672p. 1994. text 144.00 (*0-7817-0192-9*) Lppncott W & W.

Ocultismo. John Ankerberg & John Weldon. (Hechos Acerca de...Ser.).Tr. of Occult. (SPA.). 73p. pap. 3.29 (*1-56063-517-7*, 497697) Editorial Unilit.

Ocultismo en Valle-Inclan. Emma S. Speratti-Pinero. (Monagrafias A Ser.: No. 34). (SPA.). 202p. (C). 1974. pap. 51.00 (*0-900411-79-1*, Pub. by Tamesis Bks Ltd) Boydell & Brewer.

Ocultismo y Brujeria Frente a Dios. Luis Palau. (Serie Cruzada - Crusade Ser.).Tr. of Witchcraft & Occult Before God. (SPA.). 1987. 1.99 (*0-8423-6518-4*, 498007); pap. write for info. (*0-614-27088-X*) Editorial Unilit.

Ocupacion Norteamericana y la Ley Foraker: Como Reaccionaron los Puertorriquenos. Maria D. Luque De Sanchez. LC 77-10859. 197p. 1986. pap. 7.00 (*0-8477-0851-9*) U of PR Pr.

Ocx Developers Guide. 1998. 45.00 (*0-672-30847-9*) Sams.

Od Bialego do Czerwonego Caratu. abr. ed. Jan Kucharzewski. 485p. 1958. 8.00 (*0-685-04109-3*) Polish Inst Art & Sci.

Od Force: Letters on a Newly Discovered Power in Nature. Baron Von Reichenbach. 144p. 1993. reprint ed. spiral bd. 11.00 (*0-7873-0912-5*) Hlth Research.

Od Force: Letters on a Newly Discovered Power in Nature (1854) Baron Von Reichenbach. 144p. 1996. reprint ed. pap. 9.95 (*1-56459-675-3*) Kessinger Pub.

OD Source Book: A Practitioner's Guide. Robert M. Frame et al. LC 81-70786. 208p. 1982. ring bd. 89.95 (*0-88390-172-2*, Pfffr & Co) Jossey-Bass.

Od Wikingow do Indian. Edmund Urbanski. (POL., Illus.). 246p. (Orig.). 1987. pap. 12.95 (*0-930401-09-3*) Artex Pub.

Oda a Joan Miro. limited ed. Joan Brossa. (Ediciones Especiales y de Bibliofilo Ser.). (CAT., Illus.). 1993. 1000.00 (*84-343-0183-0*) Elliots Bks.

***Oda al Perro Bombo.** Sandy Scruggs. Tr. by Laura Chavez-Davalos. LC 99-62846. (SPA., Illus.). 48p. (J). (gr. 4-7). 1999. pap. 11.95 (*0-9660239-8-6*) Azro Pr.

***Odalisque.** Richard Manton. 256p. 2000. pap. 7.95 (*1-56201-177-4*, Pub. by Blue Moon Bks) Publishers Group.

Odalisque. Fleur Reynolds. (Black Lace Ser.). 1995. mass mkt. 5.95 (*0-352-32887-8*, Pub. by Virgin Bks) London Brdge.

Odas Elementales. Pablo Neruda. (SPA.). pap. 12.95 (*84-376-0366-8*, Pub. by Ediciones Catedra) Continental Bk.

Odas Elementales. 3rd ed. Pablo Neruda. (SPA.). 276p. 1988. pap. 12.95 (*0-7859-4999-2*) Fr & Eur.

Oda's Web. Charles C. Wehrenberg. (Illus.). 496p. 1995. pap. 15.00 (*1-886163-01-4*) SoloZone.

ODBC Driver Technical Report: User's Guide & Programmer's Reference, Release 6.11. 60p. 1997. pap. 12.00 (*1-55544-236-6*, BR55272) SAS Publ.

ODBC Solution: Open Database Connectivity in Distributed Environments. Michael Stegman et al. LC 94-22950. 288p. 1995. 50.00 (*0-07-911880-1*) McGraw.

ODBC 3.5 Developer's Guide. Roger Sanders. LC 98-24785. 974p. 1998. 59.95 incl. cd-rom (*0-07-058087-1*) McGraw.

Odd & Curious. F. Morton Reed. (Illus.). 1979. pap. 10.00 (*0-915262-37-1*) S J Durst.

Odd & Eccentric People. (Library of Curious & Unusual Facts). 1992. write for info. (*0-8094-7723-8*); lib. bdg. write for info. (*0-8094-7724-6*) Time-Life.

Odd & Peculiar: The Most Unused Name of a Town or Village or City in Each of the Fifty States. Neil Swanson. (Illus.). 64p. 1996. pap. 5.50 (*0-9653988-1-1*) Wainsley Pr.

Odd Bestiary. Illus. by Alan J. Robinson. LC 86-6941. 160p. 1986. 29.95 (*0-252-01353-0*) U of Ill Pr.

Odd Bodkins. Bert Young. Ed. by D. M. Jenkins. 342p. 1989. pap. 13.95 (*0-9623867-1-5*) Prattle Pub.

***Odd Body: Church, Witness & Culture in 1 & 2 Corinthians.** Teresa Moser. (Good Ground Ser.: No. 2, Pt. 7). 47p. 2000. pap. 5.95 (*0-87303-366-3*) Faith & Life.

Odd Brain, 1. Stephen Juan. 1999. pap. 11.95 (*0-7322-5724-7*, Pub. by HarpC) Consort Bk Sales.

***Odd Cookie.** Robert Jones. (Illus.). 28p. (YA). (gr. 5-13). 1999. pap. 9.00 (*1-881524-53-1*) Milligan Bks.

Odd Cookie. Shadow. LC 95-92507. (Illus.). 24p. (Orig.). (J). (gr. 1 up). 1995. pap. 6.95 (*0-9647298-9-X*) Childrens Classics.

Odd Corners of the Southern from the Days of Steam. Alan Postlethwaite. LC 99-494966. 1999. 36.00 (*0-7509-1939-6*) A Sutton.

Odd Couple, Vol. 3. Neil Simon. LC 99-52814. 256p. 2000. pap. 14.00 (*0-684-85925-4*) S&S Trade.

Odd Couple Syndrome: Resolving the Neat-Sloppy Dilemma. Selwyn Mills & Max Weisser. Ed. by Catherine McNally. (Illus.). 160p. 1988. 14.95 (*0-944748-00-7*); pap. 10.95 (*0-944748-01-5*) Jameison Pub.

Odd Dates Only: The Bizarre Birthday Book. William Hartston. 1999. 14.95 (*0-285-63466-6*) IPG Chicago.

Odd Destiny: The Life of Alexander Hamilton. Anthony Hecht. 1985. 19.95 (*0-02-550180-1*) Macmillan.

Odd Drink: Poems from Hollywood. Mark Dunston. 14p. 1998. pap. 5.00 (*0-89642-452-9*) Linden Pubs.

Odd Duck: A Story for Odd People of All Ages. Tom O'Connell. LC 93-84633. 60p. (Orig.). 1993. pap. 7.00 (*0-9620318-3-6*) Sanctuary Unltd.

Odd-Egg Editor. Kathryn T. Windham. LC 90-12131. 160p. 1990. 17.95 (*0-87805-438-3*) U Pr of Miss.

Odd Fellows Cemetery Located at Pottsville, Schuylkill County, Pennsylvania. Schuylkill Roots Staff & Phillip A. Rice. 156p. 1993. pap. 16.50 (*1-55856-152-8*, 386) Closson Pr.

Odd Fellows, I. O. O. F. Cemetery: Shenandoah Heights, West Mahonoy Township, Schuylkill County, Pennsylvania. Schuylkill Roots Staff & Phillip A. Rice. 135p. 1993. pap. 14.50 (*1-55856-148-X*, 387) Closson Pr.

Odd Fellows in the Politics of Religion: Modernism, National Socialism, & German Judaism. Gary Lease. LC 94-23869. (Religion & Society Ser.: No. 35). 325p. (C). 1994. lib. bdg. 121.55 (*3-11-014323-2*) Mouton.

Odd Fellow's Rest, Vol. 6. Jan Villarrubia. (Zavier Review Occasional Publication: No. 6). (Illus.). x, 67p. (Orig.). pap. 7.95 (*1-883275-05-9*) Xavier Rev.

Odd Fish. Stacy Aumonier & George F. Belcher. LC 71-116929. (Short Story Index Reprint Ser.). 1977. 16.95 (*0-8369-3431-8*) Ayer.

Odd Fish: A Play. Pamela Boyd. LC 94-18974. 96p. 1994. pap. 8.95 (*0-88734-281-7*, Pub. by Red Deer) Empire Pub Srvs.

Odd Flamingo. Nina Bawden. 22.95 (*0-88411-126-1*) Amereon Ltd.

Odd Flowers & Short Eared Owls. Vi Gale. LC 84-22886. (Illus.). 1984. 20.00 (*0-915986-20-5*); pap. 8.50 (*0-915986-21-3*) Prescott St Pr.

Odd Flowers & Short Eared Owls. limited ed. Vi Gale. LC 84-22886. (Illus.). 1984. boxed set 35.00 (*0-915986-19-1*) Prescott St Pr.

Odd Genre: A Study in Imagination & Evolution, 60. John J. Pierce. LC 93-29100. (Contributions to the Study of Science Fiction & Fantasy Ser.: No. 60). 240p. 1994. 62.95 (*0-313-26897-5*, Greenwood Pr) Greenwood.

Odd Girl Out. Elizabeth J. Howard. 304p. 1996. per. 12.00 (*0-671-00025-X*, Pub. by P-H) S&S Trade.

***Odd Girl Out.** Simmons. 2002. write for info. (*0-15-100604-0*) Harcourt.

Odd Girl Out. Ann Dannon. Ed. by Jonathan N. Katz. LC 75-13735. (Homosexuality Ser.). 1975. reprint ed. 17.95 (*0-405-07405-0*) Ayer.

Odd Girls & Twilight Lovers: A History of Lesbian Life in Twentieth-Century America. Lillian Faderman. LC 90-26327. 373p. 1991. 41.00 (*0-231-07488-3*) Col U Pr.

***Odd Gods: New Religions & the Cult Controversy.** James R. Lewis. 395p. 2001. 33.00 (*1-57392-842-9*) Prometheus Bks.

Odd Job. Charlotte MacLeod. 272p. 1996. mass mkt. 5.99 (*0-446-40397-0*, Pub. by Warner Bks) Little.

Odd Jobs. John Light. (ITA.). (J). 1991. pap. 3.99 (*0-85953-603-3*) Childs Play.

Odd Jobs. John Light. LC 90-34354. (Light Reading Ser.). 24p. (J). (gr. 4 up). 1991. 1.99 (*0-85953-339-5*) Childs Play.

Odd Jobs. Time-Life Books Editors. LC 92-30493. (Library of Curious & Unusual Facts). 1993. write for info. (*0-8094-7767-X*); lib. bdg. write for info. (*0-8094-7768-8*) Time-Life.

***Odd Jobs: The Wackiest Jobs You Ever Heard Of.** Ellen Weiss. LC 99-27371. (Illus.). 64p. (J). (gr. 4-6). 2000. per. 8.99 (*0-689-82934-5*) Aladdin.

Odd John & Sirius. Olaf Stapledon. LC 72-77999. 309p. 1972. reprint ed. pap. 8.95 (*0-486-21133-9*) Dover.

***Odd Kind of Fame: Stories of Phineas Gage.** Malcolm Macmillan. LC 99-56640. (Illus.). 526p. 2000. 37.50 (*0-262-13363-6*) MIT Pr.

Odd Last Thing She Did: Poems. Brad Leithauser. LC 98-14565. 96p. 1998. 22.00 (*0-375-40141-5*) Knopf.

***Odd Last Thing She Did: Poems.** Brad Leithauser. LC 98-14565. 96p. 2000. pap. 15.00 (*0-375-70849-9*) Knopf.

Odd Leaves from the Life of a Louisiana Swamp Doctor. Henry C. Lewis. LC 96-54030. (Library of Southern Civilization). (Illus.). 240p. 1997. 24.95 (*0-8071-2185-1*); pap. 12.95 (*0-8071-2167-3*) La State U Pr.

***Odd Lot: Raising Unusual Animals.** L. C. Beattie Inlow. (Illus.). 112p. 2000. pap. 14.95 (*0-9619634-5-X*) Kopacetic Ink.

Odd-Lot Couple. Marsha J. Becker. 10p. 1992. write for info. (*1-881124-10-X*) Ctr Creat Endeavors.

Odd-Lot Trading on the New York Stock Exchange. Charles O. Hardy. LC 75-2639. (Wall Street & the Security Market Ser.). 1975. reprint ed. 23.95 (*0-405-06964-2*) Ayer.

Odd Man In: Norton Simon & the Pursuit of Culture. Suzanne Muchnic. LC 98-2981. 339p. 1998. 29.95 (*0-520-20643-6*, Pub. by U CA Pr) Cal Prin Full Svc.

Odd Man Out. Dia Vaughan. (BFI Film Classics). 79 p. 1995. pap. text 10.95 (*0-85170-493-X*, Pub. by British Film Inst) Ind U Pr.

Odd Man Out: A Memoir of the Hollywood Ten. Edward Dmytryk. LC 94-39958. (Illus.). 224p. (C). 1995. 34.95 (*0-8093-1998-5*); pap. 14.95 (*0-8093-1999-3*) S Ill U Pr.

Odd Man Out: James Mason. large type ed. Sheridan Morley. 316p. 1990. 19.95 (*1-85089-376-4*, Pub. by ISIS Lrg Prnt) Transaction Pubs.

Odd Man Out: Readings of the Work & Reputation of Edgar Degas. Carol M. Armstrong. (Illus.). 310p. 1991. 46.00 (*0-226-02695-7*) U Ch Pr.

***Odd Man Out: Truman, Stalin, Mao & the Origin of the Korean War.** Richard C. Thornton. LC 99-86272. 2000. 29.95 (*1-57488-240-6*) Brasseys.

Odd Markets in Japanese History: Law & Economic Growth. J. Mark Ramseyer. (Political Economy of Institutions & Decisions Ser.). (Illus.). 205p. (C). 1996. text 54.95 (*0-521-56386-0*) Cambridge U Pr.

Odd Mercy: Poems. Gerald Stern. LC 95-5390. 128p. 1995. 18.95 (*0-393-03879-3*) Norton.

Odd Mercy: Poems. Gerald Stern. LC 95-5390. 128p. 1997. pap. 11.00 (*0-393-31630-0*) Norton.

Odd Meters: Music Sight Reading Exercises, Vol. 1. Bruce Arnold. (Illus.). 150p. 1997. pap. 31.50 (*0-9648632-9-4*) Muse Eek.

***Odd Moments in Baseball.** Joel Cohen. (Odd Sports Stories Ser.: Vol. 1). (Illus.). 96p. (J). (gr. 3-6). 2000. mass mkt. 4.50 (*0-590-37066-9*) Scholastic Inc.

***Odd Moments in Sports, Vol. 2.** Joel Cohen. (Odd Sports Stories Ser.: Vol. 2). (Illus.). 96p. (YA). (gr. 4-7). 2000. pap. text 4.50 (*0-590-37067-7*) Scholastic Inc.

Odd Nerdrum. Ed. by Howard Fox. (Illus.). 20p. 1988. 10.00 (*0-685-30644-5*) CA St U LB Art.

***Odd Nerdrum: Postcard Book.** Ed. by Forum Gallery Staff. (Illus.). 24p. 2000. pap. 14.00 (*0-9675826-0-1*, Pub. by Forum Gal) Dist Art Pubs.

Odd Nerdrum: The Drawings. Richard Vine & E. John Bullard. (Illus.). 64p. 1994. 24.95 (*0-89494-047-3*) New Orleans Mus Art.

Odd Nerdrum, Paintings. Jan-erik E. Hansen. 1995. 65.00 (*82-03-26063-2*, Pub. by Aschehong) Dist Art Pubs.

Odd One. Marion Bowler. LC 77-86486. 1979. pap. 19.95 (*0-87949-092-6*, 77-86486) Ashley Bks.

Odd One Out. J. Tyler. (First Learning Ser.). (ps-3). 1989. pap. 3.95 (*0-7460-0268-8*, Usborne) EDC.

***Odd Ones Never Quit: 2500 Miles Solo on the Mighty Mississippi.** Eugene Osmondson. (Illus.). 336p. 1999. 20.00 (*0-8059-4720-5*) Dorrance.

Odd Pairs: A Book of Tales. Laurence Housman. LC 78-169555. (Short Story Index Reprint Ser.). 1977. reprint ed. 17.95 (*0-8369-4017-2*) Ayer.

Odd Pairs & False Friends Dizionario di False Analogie e Ambigue Affinta Fra Inglese e Italiano. Virginia Browne. (ENG & ITA.). 272p. 1987. lib. bdg. 75.00 (*0-8288-3333-8*, F120170) Fr & Eur.

Odd Perceptions. Richard L. Gregory. (Illus.). 280p. 1986. 27.50 (*0-416-90100-X*, 1005) Routledge.

Odd Primary Infinite Families in Stable Homotopy Theory. Ralph L. Cohen. LC 80-28537. (Memoirs Ser.: No. 30/242). 92p. 1981. pap. 16.00 (*0-8218-2242-X*, MEMO/30/242) Am Math.

Odd Quantum. Sam B. Treiman. LC 99-24123. 280p. 1999. 24.95 (*0-691-00926-0*, Pub. by Princeton U Pr) Cal Prin Full Svc.

Odd Sea. Frederick Reiken. 224p. 1999. pap. 9.95 (*0-385-33338-2*, Delta Trade) Dell.

Odd Sea. Frederick Reiken. LC 97-40675. 224p. 1998. 22.00 (*0-15-100360-2*) Harcourt.

Odd Tales of Irene Orgel. Irene Orgel. LC 67-14531. 116p. 1966. 30.00 (*0-87130-015-X*) Eakins.

Odd Velvet. Mary E. Whitcomb. LC 98-10966. (Illus.). 32p. (J). (gr. k-2). 1998. 13.95 (*0-8118-2004-1*) Chronicle Bks.

Odd Woman. Gail Godwin. 416p. 1995. pap. 12.00 (*0-345-38991-3*) Ballantine Pub Grp.

Odd Women. George R. Gissing. Ed. by Arlene Young. LC 97-932742. (Illus.). 340p. 1998. pap. text 12.95 (*1-55111-111-X*) Broadview Pr.

Odd Women. George R. Gissing. 416p. 1994. pap. 12.95 (*0-14-043379-1*, Penguin Classics) Viking Penguin.

***Odd Women.** George R. Gissing. 432p. 2000. pap. 13.95 (*0-19-283312-X*) OUP.

Odd Women. Rachel Perez. (Orig.). 1997. mass mkt. 6.50 (*1-56333-526-3*, Rosebud) Masquerade.

Odd Women, 3 vols. in 1. George R. Gissing. LC 70-75986. reprint ed. 94.50 (*0-404-02788-1*) AMS Pr.

Odd Women. George R. Gissing. 1971. reprint ed. pap. 9.95 (*0-393-00610-7*) Norton.

Odd Women: A Play Michael L. Meyer & George R. Gissing. LC 94-204567. 68 p. 1993. pap. write for info. (*0-573-01852-9*) French.

***Oddball.** (Friendly Tales Ser.). 5p. (J). (ps-k). 2000. 6.99 (*1-57584-722-1*, Pub. by Rdrs Digest) S&S Trade.

***Oddball Illinois: A Guide to Some Really Strange Places.** Jerome Pohlen. 2000. pap. 12.95 (*1-55652-371-8*, Pub. by Chicago Review) IPG Chicago.

Oddballs. Ed. by Al Greenier. LC 87-51641. (Showcase Comic Ser.: No. 3). 158p. (Orig.). 1988. pap. 7.95 (*0-917976-77-0*) Thunder Baas Pr.

Oddballs. Bruce Shlain. 1999. pap. 17.95 (*0-670-82268-X*) Viking Penguin.

Oddballs. William Sleator. 144p. (YA). (gr. 5 up). 1995. pap. 4.99 (*0-14-037438-8*, PuffinBks) Peng Put Young Read.

Oddballs Stories. William Sleator. 1995. 9.09 (*0-606-07962-9*, Pub. by Turtleback) Demco.

***Odder Than Ever.** Bruce Coville. LC 98-51102. 160p. (YA). (gr. 7 up). 1998. 16.00 (*0-15-201747-X*, Harcourt Child Bks) Harcourt.

***Odder Than Ever.** Bruce Coville. 144p. (YA). (gr. 8-12). 2000. pap. 6.00 (*0-15-202465-4*, Harcourt Child Bks) Harcourt.

Oddies: Poems from Hollywood. Mark Dunster. 11p. 1999. pap. 5.00 (*0-89642-759-5*) Linden Pubs.

Oddingley Murders. Carlos Flick. LC 90-50573. (Illus.). 168p. 1991. 32.50 (*0-87413-417-X*) U Delaware Pr.

Oddities: Poems from Hollywood. Mark Dunster. 11p. 1998. pap. 5.00 (*0-89642-450-2*) Linden Pubs.

Oddities in Modern Japan: Observations of an Outsider. Peter Milward. (Illus.). 187p. 1997. pap. 17.95 (*4-590-00628-6*, Pub. by Hokuseido Pr) Book East.

Oddities of the Law. Franklin F. Heard. 192p. 1983. reprint ed. lib. bdg. 35.00 (*0-8377-0648-3*, Rothman) W S Hein.

Oddities of the Law: Addresses Before Juries & Fact-Finding Tribunals. Franklin F. Heard. vii, 1181p. 1990. reprint ed. 85.00 (*0-8377-0683-1*, Rothman) W S Hein.

Oddity Odyssey. Michael D. Allred. (Madman Adventures Ser.). (Illus.). 144p. (YA). 1994. pap. 12.95 (*0-87816-315-8*) Kitchen Sink.

Oddity Odyssey: A Journey Through New England's Colorful Past. James Chenoweth. LC 96-3713. (Illus.). 88p. 1995. pap. 9.95 (*0-8050-3671-7*) H Holt & Co.

Oddly Enough. Bruce Coville. LC 94-16286. (Illus.). 176p. (YA). (gr. 7 up). 1994. 15.95 (*0-15-200093-3*, Harcourt Child Bks) Harcourt.

Oddly Enough. Bruce Coville. (YA). 1997. per. 3.99 (*0-671-51693-0*) PB.

Oddly Enough. Bruce Coville. LC 94-16286. 1997. 9.09 (*0-606-11695-8*, Pub. by Turtleback) Demco.

Oddly Enough. Russ Miller. (Illus.). 64p. 1998. pap. 8.95 (*0-941613-99-2*, Caliber Comics) Stabur Pr.

Oddo-Matic Teacher Manual. Oddo Editorial Staff. 1977. ring bd. 26.60 (*0-87783-140-8*) Oddo.

Oddo Safety Series, 4 vols., Set. Richard G. Boyer. (Illus.). (J). (ps-6). lib. bdg. 44.60 (*0-87783-170-X*) Oddo.

Oddo Sound Series, 1968, 1974, 1978, 10 vols., Set. Pape et al. (Illus.). (J). (gr. 2-5). 1978. lib. bdg. 109.50 (*0-87783-165-3*) Oddo.

***Odds.** Patty Friedmann. 256p. 2000. 24.00 (*1-58243-087-X*, Pub. by Counterpt DC) HarpC.

***Odds Against.** Dick Francis. 288p. 2000. mass mkt. 6.99 (*0-515-12551-2*, Jove) Berkley Pub.

Odds Against. Dick Francis. 320p. 1987. mass mkt. 5.99 (*0-449-21269-6*, Crest) Fawcett.

Odds Against. Dick Francis. 1987. pap. 3.50 (*0-317-56654-7*) PB.

Odds Against Him. Horatio Alger, Jr. (Works of Horatio Alger Jr.). 1989. reprint ed. lib. bdg. 79.00 (*0-685-27580-9*) Rprt Serv.

Odds Against Survival: Gaining Insight. Odette M. Fischer. 296p. 1996. pap. 14.95 (*0-9643276-8-6*) Bourget Pubng.

Odds Against Tomorrow. William P. McGivern. 208p. 1996. mass mkt. 4.95 (*0-7867-0339-3*) Carroll & Graf.

Odds Against Tomorrow: The Critical Edition. Abraham Polonsky. Ed. by John Schultheiss. LC 98-74816. (Film As Literature Ser.). (Illus.). 328p. 1999. 30.00 (*0-9635823-4-8*, Pub. by Sadanlaur Pubns) SCB Distributors.

Odds Against Us. Peter Townsend. (Illus.). 320p. 1988. mass mkt. 4.50 (*0-8217-2495-9*, Zebra Kensgtn) Kensgtn Pub Corp.

Odds & Ends: Poems from Hollywood. Mark Dunster. 11p. 1999. pap. 5.00 (*0-89642-772-2*) Linden Pubs.

Odds & Evens. Thomas C. O'Brien. (Young Math Ser.). (Illus.). (J). (gr. 1-4). 1973. pap. 1.45 (*0-690-00207-6*) HarpC Child Bks.

Odds, Ends, Bits & Pieces. William R. Woods, Jr. 1998. pap. write for info. (*1-57553-788-5*) Watermrk Pr.

Odds Must Be Crazy. Len Ragozin et al. LC 96-37632. 320p. (gr. 8). 1997. 23.95 (*0-316-60497-6*) Little.

***Odds Off.** Matt Madden. 2000. pap. 9.95 (*0-9665363-9-8*) Highwater Bks.

Odds on Your Side: The Logic of Racetrack Investing. Mark Cramer. 240p. (Orig.). 1987. pap. 24.95 (*0-9614168-4-X*) Cynthia Pub Co.

Odds Ratios in the Analysis of Contingency Tables. Tamas Rudas. LC 97-33790. (Sage University Papers). 1997. pap. write for info. (*0-7619-0362-3*) Sage.

Odds, Sods & Racing Certs: Horse Laughs, Winning One-Liners & Off-Beat Tales of the Turf. Graham Sharpe. 106p. 1999. pap. 11.95 (*1-86105-142-5*, Pub. by Robson Bks) Parkwest Pubns.

Oddsplayer. Joe Rodriguez. LC 88-10484. 180p. (Orig.). 1989. pap. 9.50 (*0-934770-88-3*) Arte Publico.

Oddworld: Abe's Exxodus: Prima's Unauthorized Game Secrets. 96p. 1998. per. 12.99 (*0-7615-1896-7*) Prima Pub.

Oddworld: Abe's Odyssee: The Official Strategy Guide. Rusel DeMaria. LC 97-69033. 144p. 1997. per. 12.99 (*0-7615-1086-9*) Prima Pub.

Oddworld 2. Gameswizards Press Staff. 1998. pap. 12.95 (*1-56893-913-2*) GT Interactive Software.

Ode: Recited at Commemoration of the Living & Dead Soldiers of Harvard University. James Russell Lowell. (Notable American Authors Ser.). 1999. reprint ed. lib. bdg. 125.00 (*0-7812-3884-6*) Rprt Serv.

Ode a Charles Fourier. Andre Breton. Ed. by Gaulmier. 12.95 (*0-685-37233-2*, F89540) Fr & Eur.

Ode & the Odic: Essays on Mandelstam, Pasternak, Tsvetaeva & Mayakovksy. Ilya Kutik. (Stockholm Studies in Russian Literature: No. 30). 213p. 1994. pap. 46.50 (*91-22-01650-3*) Coronet Bks.

O

***Ode Architect Companion.** 288p. 1998. text, lab manual ed. 22.00 (*0-471-17007-0*) Wiley.

Ode, Inscribed to John Howard, Repr. of 1780. William Hayley. Ed. by Donald H. Reiman. LC 75-31207. (Romantic Context: Poetry 1789-1830 Ser.: Vol. 58). 1979. lib. bdg. 57.00 (*0-8240-2157-6*) Garland.

Ode, of a Happy Man or Chicken Every Sunday. W. E. Thorn. (Illus.). 399p. (Orig.). 1996. pap. 15.00 (*0-943639-26-3*) Anchor Pub Co.

Ode on Visiting the Belosaraisk Spit, on the Sea of Azov. Ed. by Ilya Kutik. Tr. by Kit Robinson from RUS. (Alef Series of Poetry & Translation). 72p. (Orig.). 1995. pap. 14.00 (*1-882509-03-X*) Alef Bks.

Ode Setl'oghwnh Da' Long after I Am Gone, Stories by Teddy Charlie Told in Lower Tanana Athabaskan of Minto, Alaska. Michael Krauss & Teddy Charlie. Ed. by James Kari. (Illus.). x, 30p. 1992. pap. 6.50 (*1-55500-045-2*) Alaska Native.

Ode to a Celtic King: Design an Heirloom of Your Own. AnnMarie Allaire. (Illus.). 1998. pap. 10.00 (*0-9660393-2-7*) Rambling Hse.

Ode to an Ailing Marriage. Ruth Kaufman. (Illus.). 36p. (Orig.). 1995. 6.95 (*0-940861-58-5*) Poetry Ctr Pr.

Ode to Anna Moffo & Other Poems. Wayne Koestenbaum. LC 90-7641. 80p. 1990. 17.95 (*0-89255-154-2*) Persea Bks.

Ode to Anna Moffo & Other Poems. Wayne Koestenbaum. LC 90-7641. 80p. 1991. reprint ed. pap. 9.95 (*0-89255-155-0*) Persea Bks.

***Ode to Bass & Trout: An Illustrated Treasury of the Best Angling Literature.** Ed. by Alan James Robinson. LC 98-47631. (Illus.). 160p. 1999. 14.98 (*0-7651-0909-3*) Smithmark.

Ode to Brasstown Bald. Sylvia D. Turnage. 10p. (Orig.). 1995. pap. text 3.75 (*1-880726-07-6*) Turnage Pub.

Ode to Joy. Kozik. 1999. pap. 29.95 (*0-86719-457-X*) Last Gasp.

Ode to Joy: Homilies for Sundays & Holy Days (Cycle C) Harold A. Buetow. (Orig.). 1997. pap. 14.95 (*0-8189-0729-0*) Alba.

Ode to Minoa. Theresa Dintino. LC 98-88534. 192p. 1999. pap. 11.95 (*1-56315-143-X*) SterlingHse.

Ode to Napoleon Buonaparte & Don Juan Canto VIII & Stanzas from III & IX: Illustrating Byron's Attitudes Toward Napoleon, Wellington, & War. George Gordon Byron et al. Ed. by Cheryl F. Giuliano. LC 97-36880. (Manuscripts of the Younger Romantics Ser.: Vol. 11). 232p. 1998. text 125.00 (*0-8153-1148-6*) Garland.

Ode to Oliver: The Adventures of a Sea Otter. Lane Dowlen. LC 95-71191. (Illus.). 160p. (Orig.). (YA). (gr. 4 up). 1996. pap. 9.95 (*1-885884-99-0*) Cormorant Pr.

Ode to Patricia. 10p. 1999. mass mkt. 5.00 (*0-9657234-3-7*, 99-001) W & M Pub.

Ode to Precious, Priceless & Irreplaceable African-American Men: A Collection of Poems. Yolanda Miller. 70p. (Orig.). 1996. pap. 8.95 (*0-9650852-0-1*) Victory WI.

Ode to Satire: Criminal Justice in the O. J. Trials. Clarence G. Hanley. 179p. 1996. text 27.95 (*1-885309-08-2*) SpellBound Pr.

Ode to Splendor. Dolores P. Tata. 96p. 1988. 8.95 (*0-8187-0107-2*) Harlo Press.

Ode to Stone. Shiro Hara. Tr. by James Morita. (Cornell East Asia Ser.). 96p. 1990. pap. 8.50 (*0-939657-52-X*) Cornell East Asia Pgm.

Ode to Sucanat: The First Sucanat Cookbook. Linda J. Forristal. 48p. 1993. pap. 5.00 (*0-9639182-0-6*, Pub. by Sunrise Pine) Nutri-Books Corp.

Ode to the Chinaberry Tree & Other Poems. James Applewhite. LC 85-19707. 62p. 1986. reprint ed. pap. 30.00 (*0-608-00861-3*, 206165200010) Bks Demand.

Ode to the Cold War: Poems New & Selected. Dick Allen. LC 96-25051. 160p. (Orig.). 1997. 25.00 (*0-9641151-9-0*); pap. 14.95 (*1-889330-00-0*) Sarabande Bks.

Ode to the Lost Dutchman Mine. unabridged ed. Artus Ritter. (Illus.). 72p. 1997. pap. 9.00 (*0-9660719-0-5*) A Ritter.

***Ode to the Wart Hog.** Sandy Scruggs. LC 98-74749. (Illus.). 56p. (YA). (gr. 3 up). 1999. pap. 11.95 (*0-9660239-7-8*) Azro Pr.

***Ode to the Welsh Leek: And Other 17th Century Tales.** 23p. 1998. reprint ed. pap. 4.25 (*1-889298-42-5*) Rhwymbooks.

Ode to Walt Whitman & Other Poems. Federico Garcia Lorca. Tr. by Carlos Bauer from SPA. 160p. (Orig.). 1988. pap. 9.95 (*0-87286-212-7*) City Lights.

Ode to Yahshua: Collective Works of Thomas J. Richburg. large type ed. Thomas J. Richburg. Ed. by P. M. Johnson. (Illus.). 75p. 1996. 15.95 (*1-889466-33-6*, PB001002); pap. 10.95 (*1-889466-34-4*, PB001002) One Way Intl.

Oded Halahmy: In Retrospect: Sculpture from 1962-1997. Oded Halahmy. LC 97-94212. (Illus.). 240p. 1997. 35.00 (*0-9659838-0-3*); pap. 20.00 (*0-9659838-1-1*) O H Gallery.

Odella: A Hidden Survivor. Carlota Duarte. (Illus.). 56p. (Orig.). 1990. pap. text 17.95 (*0-9624109-0-X*) C Duarte.

Oden. Robert Goodin et al. (Illus.). 72p. 1998. pap. 18.00 (*0-9661081-0-8*) Robot Publ.

***Oden Salomos: Text, Ubersetzung, Kommentar.** Michael Lattke. (Novum Testamentum et Orbis Antiquus Ser.: Vol. 41/1). xii, 301p. 1999. text 63.00 (*3-7278-1245-1*, Pub. by Ed Univ Fri) Eisenbrauns.

Oden Salomos in Ihrer Bedeutung fur Neues Testament und Gnosis. Michael Lattke. (Orbis Biblicus et Orietalis Ser.: Vol. 25/4). (GER.). xii, 272p. 1998. text 58.25 (*3-7278-1164-1*, Pub. by Ed Univ Fri) Eisenbrauns.

***Oder Antiqua: Der Schriftstreit von 1881 Bis 1941 2., Uberarbeitete Auflage.** Silvia Hartmann-Kent. (Theorie und Vermittlung der Sprache Ser.). 438p. 1999. 52.95 (*3-631-35090-2*) P Lang Pubng.

Oder-Neisse Boundary & Poland's Modernization: The Socioeconomic & Political Impact. Z. Anthony Kruszewski. LC 74-159411. (Special Studies in International Politics & Government). 1972. 40.50 (*0-275-28292-9*) Irvington.

Oder-Neisse Line. Z. Jordan. 139p. 1952. 2.50 (*0-940962-18-7*) Polish Inst Art & Sci.

Oder-Neisse Line: A Reappraisal under International Law. Phillip A. Buhler. (East European Monographs). 160p. 1990. text 44.50 (*0-88033-174-7*, Pub. by East Eur Monographs) Col U Pr.

Odes. Horace. (Essential Poets Ser.: Vol. 82). (LAT.). 200p. Date not set. 18.00 (*1-55071-070-2*) Guernica Editions.

Odes: A Variety of Poems. David Thompson. 94p. 1985. 5.95 (*0-89697-259-3*) Intl Univ Pr.

Odes & Epodes. Tr. by C. E. Bennett. (Loeb Classical Library: No. 33). 460p. 1927. 18.95 (*0-674-99037-4*) HUP.

Odes & Epodes. Joseph P. Clancy. LC 60-10659. 262p. 1960. pap. text 17.95 (*0-226-10679-9*, P47) U Ch Pr.

Odes & Epodes of Horace. Horace. Tr. by John Marshall. LC 74-158319. (Temple Greek & Latin Classics: No. 4). reprint ed. 27.00 (*0-404-07904-0*) AMS Pr.

Odes & Fragments. Peter Pindar. (Loeb Classical Library: No. 56). 682p. 1915. 19.95 (*0-674-99062-5*) HUP.

Odes, Epodes et Chant Seculaire. Horace. lxxviii, 396p. 1966. reprint ed. write for info. (*0-318-71146-X*); reprint ed. write for info. (*0-318-71355-1*) G Olms Pubs.

Odes et Ballades: Avec: Les Orientales. Victor Hugo. Ed. by Jean Gaudon. (Poesie Ser.). 14.95 (*2-07-032190-8*) Schoenhof.

Odes et Ballades: Les Orientales. Victor Hugo. Ed. by Jean Gaudon. (FRE.). 1985. pap. 16.95 (*0-7859-2888-X*) Fr & Eur.

Odes et Prieres. Jules Romains, pseud. (FRE.). 176p. 1923. pap. 10.95 (*0-7859-1304-1*, 2070255026) Fr & Eur.

Odes, n' Odes & Scolds. F. C. Wunderlich. LC 96-96403. 1996. pap. 8.00 (*0-9649293-0-9*) Belle Terre.

Odes of Bello, Olmedo, & Heredia. Jose-Maria De Heredia. Tr. by Elijah J. Hills. 1977. lib. bdg. 59.95 (*0-8490-2365-3*) Gordon Pr.

Odes of Bello, Olmedo, & Heredia. Elijah Hills. 1920. 10.00 (*0-87535-003-8*) Hispanic Soc.

Odes of Hafiz, Poetical Horoscope. Tr. by Abbas A. Kashani from PER. LC 84-61304. (Illus.). 288p. (Orig.). 1984. pap. 10.00 (*0-939214-25-3*) Mazda Pubs.

Odes of Horace. David Ferry. (ENG & LAT.). 368p. 1998. pap. 15.00 (*0-374-52572-2*) FS&G.

Odes of Horace. Horace. Tr. by David Ferry. LC 97-9483. 288p. 1997. 35.00 (*0-374-22425-0*) FS&G.

Odes of Horace: A Critical Study. Steele Commager. LC 94-39638. 384p. 1995. pap. 15.95 (*0-8061-2729-5*) U of Okla Pr.

Odes of Horace: The Centennial Hymn. Horace. Tr. by James Michie. 1965. pap. 5.00 (*0-672-60444-2*, LLA202, Bobbs) Macmillan.

Odes of John Keats. Helen H. Vendler. 344p. 1985. pap. text 16.95 (*0-674-63076-9*) Belknap Pr.

Odes of John Keats. Helen H. Vendler. (Illus.). 344p. 1983. 40.00 (*0-674-63075-0*) HUP.

Odes of Keats & Their Earliest Known Manuscripts. John Keats. Ed. by Robert Gittings. LC 70-109442. 79p. reprint ed. pap. 30.00 (*0-8357-9370-2*, 201007900068) Bks Demand.

Odes of Pindar. Peter Pindar. Tr. & Intro. by C. M. Bowra. 256p. 1982. pap. 11.95 (*0-14-044209-X*, Penguin Classics) Viking Penguin.

Odes of Pindar. Ed. by Roy A. Swanson. LC 72-90908. (Library of Liberal Arts). (Illus.). (C). 1974. write for info. (*0-672-51543-1*, LLA178, Bobbs); pap. text 7.50 (*0-672-61245-3*, Bobbs) Macmillan.

Odes of Pindar. 2nd ed. Peter Pindar. Tr. by Richmond Lattimore from GRE. LC 75-22336. 184p. 1976. reprint ed. pap. 8.00 (*0-226-66845-2*, P33) U Ch Pr.

Odes of Roba. Clark Coolidge. 1991. 12.00 (*0-935724-46-X*) Figures.

Odes of Roba. deluxe limited ed. Clark Coolidge. 1991. 25.00 (*0-935724-47-8*) Figures.

Odes of Solomon: An Analysis of the Poetical Structure & Form. Majella Franzmann. (Novum Testamentum et Orbis Antiquus Ser.: Vol. 20). 460p. 1991. text 96.75 (*3-7278-0780-6*, Pub. by Presses Univ Fribourg) Eisenbrauns.

Odes of Solomon: An Authentic 1st Century Book of Christian Psalms. Intro. by Wayne F. Monbleau. 89p. 1989. pap. 7.00 (*0-944648-04-5*) Loving Grace Pubns.

Odes on Various Subjects. Joseph Warton. LC 92-1599. (Augustan Reprints Ser.: No. 197). 1979. reprint ed. 14.50 (*0-404-70197-3*, PR3759) AMS Pr.

Odes on Various Subjects. Joseph Warton. LC 77-8452. 64p. 1977. reprint ed. 40.00 (*0-8201-1291-7*) Schol Facsimiles.

Odes, Pastorals, Masques. John Milton. Ed. by John Broadbent et al. LC 73-94355. (Milton for Schools & Colleges Ser.). 252p. 1975. pap. text 26.95 (*0-521-20456-9*) Cambridge U Pr.

Odes to a Cockroach, Vol. 1. Pref. by Carolyn E. Cardwell. (Illus.). 250p. (Orig.). 1984. pap. 10.95 (*0-916395-00-6*, OC-1) Hieroglyphics.

Odes to a Cockroach, Vol. 2. Ed. by Carolyn E. Cardwell. (Illus.). 250p. (Orig.). 1985. pap. 10.95 (*0-916395-03-0*, OC-2) Hieroglyphics.

Odes to Chili & Chili Lovers. Madeleine S. Gary. 230p. (Orig.). pap. 9.95 (*0-913459-06-2*) New Writers Guild.

Odes to Common Things. Pablo Neruda. Tr. by Kenneth Krabbenhoft. LC 93-39665. (ENG & SPA., Illus.). 152p. 1994. 23.95 (*0-8212-2080-2*, Pub. by Bulfinch Pr) Little.

Odes to Opposites. Pablo Neruda. Tr. by Kenneth Krabbenhoft. LC 95-22412. (SPA., Illus.). 152p. 1995. 22.95 (*0-8212-2227-9*, Pub. by Bulfinch Pr) Little.

Odessa. Frederick Forsyth. (SPA.). 320p. 1992. pap. 4.95 (*1-56780-255-9*) La Costa Pr.

Odessa. Frederick Forsyth. 1998. pap. 6.95 (*84-01-49424-9*) Lectorum Pubns.

Odessa: A History, 1794-1914. Patricia Herlihy. LC 86-82703. (Harvard Ukrainian Research Institute Monograph). (Illus.). 432p. 1990. text 29.00 (*0-916458-15-6*) Harvard Ukrainian.

Odessa: A History, 1794-1914. Patricia Herlihy. (Monograph Ser.). (Illus.). 432p. (C). 1991. reprint ed. pap. text 18.00 (*0-916458-43-1*) Harvard Ukrainian.

***Odessa: Un Periodista Se Enfrenta Con Una Organizacion Secreta Nazi.** Frederick Forsyth. 1999. mass mkt. 10.95 (*84-01-46414-5*) Plaza.

Odessa Beach. Robert Leuci. LC 85-20716. 240p. 1985. 15.95 (*0-88191-029-5*) Freundlich.

***Odessa Beach.** Robert Leuci. LC 99-48429. 288p. 2000. pap. 10.95 (*1-55921-242-X*, Pub. by Moyer Bell) Publishers Group.

Odessa File. Frederick Forsyth. 368p. 1983. mass mkt. 7.50 (*0-553-27198-9*) Bantam.

Odessa, 1941-1944: A Case Study of Soviet Territory under Foreign Rule. Alexander Dallin. LC 98-208730. 296p. 1998. 48.00 (*973-98391-1-8*, Pub. by Ctr Romanian Studies) Intl Spec Bk.

Odet Philippe: Peninsular Pioneer. J. Allison DeFoor, II. (Illus.), viii, 69p. 1998. 17.95 (*0-9659395-0-2*) Safety Harbor Mus.

Odets the Playwright. 2nd ed. Gerald Weales. (Modern Theatre Profiles Ser.). 205p. (C). 1988. pap. write for info. (*0-413-58020-2*, A0195, Methuen Drama) Methn.

O.D.Hall's Men in Praise Collection. O. D. Hall. 1997. pap. 6.99 (*0-8341-9686-7*) Nazarene.

Odi Otter. Dave Sargent & Pat Sargen. LC 97-27201. (Illus.). (J). 1998. write for info. (*1-56763-380-3*) Ozark Pub.

Odi Otter. Dave Sargent & Pat Sargent. LC 97-27201. (Illus.). (J). 1998. pap. write for info. (*1-56763-381-1*) Ozark Pub.

O'Diddy: A Study Guide. Laurie Diamond. Ed. by Joyce Friedland & Rikki Kessler. (Novel-Ties Ser.). (J). (gr. 2-4). 1991. pap. text 15.95 (*0-88122-570-3*) Lrn Links.

Odidere Orunmila: A Quarterly Newspaper of the Orisas. Chief FAMA Aina Adewale Staff. (YOR.). 7p. (Orig.). 1997. pap. text 2.50 (*0-9644247-4-6*) ILE Orunmila.

Odile. Raymond Queneau. (FRE.). 196p. 1992. pap. 14.95 (*0-686-54679-2*, 2070725472) Fr & Eur.

Odile. Raymond Queneau. (Imaginaire Ser.). (FRE.). 1992. pap. 13.95 (*2-07-072547-2*) Schoenhof.

Odile. Raymond Queneau. Tr. & Intro. by Carol Sanders. LC 88-25051. 128p. 1999. reprint ed. pap. 10.95 (*1-56478-209-3*) Dalkey Arch.

Odile Decq Benoit Cornette. Clare Melhnish. LC 97-112985. (Illus.). 160p. 1996. 49.95 (*0-7148-3343-6*, Pub. by Phaidon Press) Phaidon Pr.

Odile Decq Benoit Cornette. Clare Melhuish. (Illus.). 160p. 1998. pap. 29.95 (*0-7148-3771-7*, Pub. by Phaidon Press) Phaidon Pr.

Odilon Redon: Prince of Dreams. Ed. by Douglas W. Druick. LC 94-10379. (Illus.). 472p. 1994. pap. 39.95 (*0-86559-126-1*) Art Inst Chi.

Odilon Redon: Prince of Dreams. Ed. by Douglas W. Druick. LC 94-10379. (Illus.). 472p. 1997. 60.00 (*0-8109-3769-7*) Art Inst Chi.

Odin Brotherhood: A Non-Fiction Account of Contact with an Ancient Brotherhood. Mark L. Mirabello. 1992. pap. text 9.95 (*1-55818-198-9*, Sure Fire) Holmes Pub.

Odin's Family: Myths of the Vikings. Illus. by Maryclare Foa. LC 96-1965. 128p. (J). (gr. 5 up). 1996. 19.95 (*0-531-09531-2*) Orchard Bks Watts.

Odin's Inheritor - The Myths, the Essays: The Pomeranians & Other Teutons. Myron E. Gruenwald. (Illus.). 135p. 1987. pap. 10.50 (*0-9601536-7-5*) G J OConnell.

***Odio Se Cura: Un Programa Nacional para la Prevencion de los Crimenes de Odio para las Escuelas Intermedias.** Karen A. McLaughlin & Kelly J. Brilliant. Ed. by Lorena Martinez Diaz. Tr. by Eduardo H. Berinstein.Tr. of Healing the Hate: A National Bias Crime Prevention Curriculum for Middle Schools. (SPA.). 164p. 1999. pap. write for info. (*0-89292-273-7*, Pub. by Educ Dev Ctr) Juvenile Justice.

Odio y Amor (Hate & Love) Miranda Lee. (SPA.). 1999. mass mkt. 3.50 (*0-373-33492-3*, 1-33492-9) Harlequin Bks.

Odious Mud. Sigmund A. Boloz. Ed. by Susan Stropko. (Illus.). 36p. (Orig.). 1995. pap. text 6.00 (*1-886635-09-9*) Wooded Hill AZ.

Odisea. Homer. (SPA.). 1997. pap. 5.98 (*968-15-0814-9*) Ed Mex.

Odisea. Homer. Ed. by Antonio Lopez Eire. (Nueva Austral Ser.: Vol. 70). (SPA.). 1991. pap. text 19.95 (*84-239-1870-X*) Elliots Bks.

Odisea. Homer. 1998. pap. 11.95 (*84-08-01866-3*) Planeta.

Odisea. Stella Sands. (SPA., Illus.). 32p. (J). (gr. k-4). 1992. lib. bdg. 13.95 (*1-879567-18-0*, Valeria Bks) Wonder Well.

Odisea de Penelope. Maricarmen Ohara. (SPA.). 112p. 1997. 23.00 (*0-944356-16-8*) Alegria Hispana Pubns.

Odisea del Norte. Mario Bencastro. (SPA.). 195p. 1999. pap. 12.95 (*1-55885-266-2*) Arte Publico.

Odisea 1874 o el Primer Viaje Internacional. Marco A. Moreno. (Ciencia para Todos Ser.). (SPA.). pap. 6.99 (*968-16-4809-9*, Pub. by Fondo) Continental Bk.

Odiyan Country Cookbook. Bill Farthing. (Illus.). 224p. 1977. pap. 14.95 (*0-913546-19-4*) Dharma Pub.

Odlin-Eliot Collection of Early American Silver. Frank L. Green & Milton Holland. (Illus.). 12p. 1973. pap. 2.00 (*0-917048-21-0*) Wash St Hist Soc.

Odnodnevnye Gazety SSSR, 1917-1984 - One-Day Newspapers of the U. S. S. R., 1917-1983: Po Fondam Gosudarstvennoi Publichnoi Biblioteki Im. M. E. Saltykova-Shchedrina: Alfavitnyi Katalog, 3 vols., Set. T. S. Grigoriants et al. LC 94-13431. (RUS.). 1994. lib. bdg. 174.00 (*0-88354-136-X*) N Ross.

Odnodnevnye Gazety SSSR, 1917-1984 - One-Day Newspapers of the U. S. S. R., 1917-1983: Po Fondam Gosudarstvennoi Publichnoi Biblioteki Im. M. E. Saltykova-Shchedrina: Alfavitnyi Katalog, Vol. 1. T. S. Grigoriants et al. (RUS.). 1994. lib. bdg. write for info. (*0-88354-122-X*) N Ross.

Odnodnevnye Gazety SSSR, 1917-1984 - One-Day Newspapers of the U. S. S. R., 1917-1983: Po Fondam Gosudarstvennoi Publichnoi Biblioteki Im. M. E. Saltykova-Shchedrina: Alfavitnyi Katalog, Vol. 2. T. S. Grigoriants et al. LC 94-13431. (RUS.). 1994. lib. bdg. write for info. (*0-88354-123-8*) N Ross.

Odnodnevnye Gazety SSSR, 1917-1984 - One-Day Newspapers of the U. S. S. R., 1917-1983: Po Fondam Gosudarstvennoi Publichnoi Biblioteki Im. M. E. Saltykova-Shchedrina: Alfavitnyi Katalog, Vol. 3. T. S. Grigoriants et al. LC 94-13431. (RUS.). 1994. lib. bdg. write for info. (*0-88354-124-6*) N Ross.

***Odoevskii: Kosmorama.** V. Odoevskii. Ed. by Roger Cockrell. (Modern Language Ser.). (RUS.). 85p. (C). 1998. pap. text 16.95 (*1-85399-534-7*, Pub. by Brist Class Pr) Focus Pub-R Pullins.

Odoevsky: The Salamander & Other Gothic Tales. Tr. by N. Cornwell. (ENG & RUS.). 221p. 1992. pap. 22.95 (*1-85399-227-5*, Pub. by Brist Class Pr) Focus Pub-R Pullins.

Odometer Law see Automobile Fraud: Odometer Tampering, Lemon Laundering & Concealment of Salvage History

O'Donaghue Book. Michael C. O'Laughlin. (Irish Family Histories Ser.). 50p. 1981. 15.00 (*0-940134-16-0*) Irish Genealog.

Odonata: Cordulegasteridae, Aeshnidae, Labellulidae, Vol. 3. F. C. Fraser. (Fauna of British India Ser.). (Illus.). xii, 472p. 1977. reprint ed. 30.00 (*0-88065-088-5*) Scholarly Pubns.

Odonata Vol. 1: Coenagriidae. F. C. Fraser. (Fauna of British India Ser.). (Illus.). xiv, 424p. 1977. reprint ed. 30.00 (*0-88065-086-9*) Scholarly Pubns.

Odonata Vol. 2: Agriidae & Gomphida. F. C. Fraser. (Illus.). xxiv, 416p. 1977. reprint ed. 30.00 (*0-88065-087-7*) Scholarly Pubns.

Odonata of Canada & Alaska Vol. 3, Pt. 3: Anisoptera-Three Families by Edmund M. Walker & Philip S. Corbet. Edmund M. Walker. LC 54-4344. (Illus.). 326p. reprint ed. pap. 101.10 (*0-7837-4278-9*, 204397000003) Bks Demand.

O'Donnel: A National Tale, 3 vols., 2 bks., Set. Sydney O. Morgan. LC 79-8176. reprint ed. 84.50 (*0-404-62060-4*) AMS Pr.

***O'Donoghue.** Charles Lever. 252p. 2000. pap. 9.95 (*0-594-00621-X*) Eightn Hundrd.

***Odontologia Pediatrica.** Cameron. (C). 1998. text 42.50 (*84-8174-337-2*) Mosby Inc.

O'Dooles of Reseda: A Year in the Life of America's Most Dysfunctional Family. Tim Ballou & Linda Higgins. 224p. 1995. pap. 14.95 (*0-8065-1609-7*, Citadel Pr) Carol Pub Group.

Odor & Corrosion Control in Sanitary Sewerage Systems & Treatment Plants. P. G. Bowker et al. 132p. 1989. 49.95 (*0-89116-067-1*) Hemisp Pub.

Odor & Corrosion Control in Sanitary Sewerage Systems & Treatment Plants. Robert P. Bowker et al. LC 88-38435. (Pollution Technology Review Ser.: No. 165). (Illus.). 130p. 1989. 39.00 (*0-8155-1192-2*) Noyes.

Odor & VOC Handbook. Ed. by Harold J. Rafson. LC 98-4211. (Illus.). 800p. 1998. 105.00 (*0-07-052523-4*) McGraw.

Odor Control in Wastewater Treatment Plants. Water Environment Federation Staff & American Society of Civil Engineers Staff. LC 95-16391. (Manual of Practice Ser.: No. 22). 304p. 1995. 92.00 (*0-7844-0085-7*) Water Environ.

Odor of Love: And Other Aromas. Michael D. Sage. (Illus.). 96p. (Orig.). 1997. pap. 8.00 (*0-9658977-0-2*, Teddy Bear) Camels Back Bks.

Odor Quality & Chemical Structure. Ed. by H. R. Moskowitz & Craig Warren. LC 80-28633. (ACS Symposium Ser.: No. 148). 1981. 38.95 (*0-8412-0607-4*) Am Chemical.

Odor Quality & Chemical Structure: Based on a Symposium. Ed. by Howard R. Moskowitz & Craig B. Warren. LC 80-28633. (ACS Symposium Ser.: Vol. 148). 252p. 1981. reprint ed. pap. 78.20 (*0-608-03034-1*, 206348700007) Bks Demand.

Odor Sensation & Memory. Trygg Engen. LC 91-21067. 168p. 1991. 47.95 (*0-275-94111-6*, C4111, Praeger Pubs) Greenwood.

Odor Thresholds for Chemicals with Established Occupational Health Standards. TRC. 95p. 1989. 48.00 (*0-932627-34-X*) Am Indus Hygiene.

Odoratus Sexualis: A Scientific & Literary Study of Sexual Scents & Erotic Perfumes. Iwan Bloch. LC 72-9620. reprint ed. 42.50 (*0-404-57414-9*) AMS Pr.

Odoratus Sexualis: Smell & Sex. I. Bloch. (Studies in the Psychopathology of Sex). 1992. lib. bdg. 88.00 (*0-8490-5365-X*) Gordon Pr.

Odoriferous Molecules. Paolo Pelosi. 1999. 74.95 (*0-8493-8965-8*) CRC Pr.

Odorization Vol. 2: Proceedings of a Conference Held in 1987. Ed. by Gerald G. Wilson & Amir A. Attari. viii, 582p. 1987. 75.00 (*0-910091-71-4*) Inst Gas Tech.

Odorization Symposium, August, 1980. 319p. 1980. pap. 40.00 (*0-910091-32-3*) Inst Gas Tech.

Odorization III. A. A. Attari. Ed. by G. G. Wilson. x, 676p. 1993. 80.00 (*0-910091-89-7*) Inst Gas Tech.

Odors & Deodorization in the Environment. Ed. by Guy Martin & Paul Laffort. LC 94-5422. 1994. 145.00 (*1-56081-666-X*, Wiley-VCH) Wiley.

O

Odors & Deodorization in the Environment: English Language Edition. rev. ed. Ed. by G. Martin & Paul Laffort. 486p. 1994. 199.00 (0-471-18595-7) Wiley.

Odors from Golden Vials. C. E. Orr. 78p. pap. 2.00 (0-686-29131-X) Faith Pub Hse.

Odors from Stationary & Mobile Sources. Assembly of Life Sciences (U. S.), Committee on Ni. LC 79-9068. (Illus.). 509p. reprint ed. pap. 157.80 (0-8357-6808-2, 203549100095) Bks Demand.

Odour Detection by Mobile Robots. R. Andrew Russell. LC 98-52909. 217p. 1999. 42.00 (981-02-3791-X) World Scientific Pub.

Odour Nuisances & Their Control. Denise Artis. 1984. pap. 90.00 (0-7219-1000-9, Pub. by Scientific) St Mut.

Odprawa Poslow Greckich see Dismissal of the Grecian Envoys

Odrysian Kingdom of Thrace: Orpheus Unmasked. Z. H. Archibald. LC 97-22110. (Oxford Monographs on Classical Archaeology). (Illus.). 394p. 1998. text 150.00 (0-19-815047-4) OUP.

***Odu Ifa: The Ethical Teachings.** Maulana Karenga. 426p. 1999. pap. 24.95 (0-943412-22-6) Univ Sankore Pr.

ODU IFA Bk. 1: Sacred Scriptures of IFA. Conrad E. Mauge. 48p. 1994. pap. 6.95 (0-9637516-2-X) Hse of Providence.

ODU IFA Bk. 2: Sacred Scriptures of IFA. Conrad E. Mauge. 48p. 1995. pap. 6.95 (0-9637516-3-8) Hse of Providence.

ODU IFA Bk. 3: Iwori Meji. Conrad E. Mauge. (ODU IFA Ser.). (YOR.). 54p. 1997. pap. 6.95 (0-9637516-6-2) Hse of Providence.

ODU IFA Bk. 4: Idi Meji. Conrad E. Mauge. (ODU IFA Ser.). (YOR.). 36p. 1997. pap. text 6.95 (0-9637516-7-0) Hse of Providence.

Odus of Eji Ogbe: How Man Created His Own God. unabridged ed. C. Osamaro Ibie. (Ifism - The Complete Works of Orunmila Ser.: Vol. 2). (Illus.). 242p. 1987. pap. 40.00 (1-890157-05-8) Athelia-Henrietta.

Odus of Idi. C. Osamaro Ibie. (Ifism - The Complete Works of Orunmila Ser.: Vol. 5). 144p. 1994. pap. 30.00 (1-890157-08-2) Athelia-Henrietta.

Odus of Irosun & Owanrin. C. Osamaro Ibie. (IFISM - The Complete Works of Orunmila Ser.: Vol. 8 & 9). 178p. 1998. pap. 34.95 (1-890157-09-0, Pub. by Athelia-Henrietta) BookWorld.

Odus of Iworl. unabridged ed. C. Osamaro Ibie. (Ifism - The Complete Works of Orunmila Ser.: Vol. 4). 172p. 1992. pap. 30.00 (1-890157-07-4) Athelia-Henrietta.

Odus of Obara & Okonron. C. Osamaro Ibie. (Ifism - The Complete Works of Orunmila Ser.: Vols. 6 & 7). (Illus.). 153p. 1999. pap. 34.95 (0-9638787-6-X, Pub. by Athelia-Henrietta) BookWorld.

Odus of Oyeku. unabridged ed. C. Osamaro Ibile. (Ifism - The Complete Works of Orunmila Ser.: Vol. 3). 101p. 1990. pap. 30.00 (1-890157-06-6) Athelia-Henrietta.

O'Dwyer's Directory of Corporate Communications, 1988. O'Dwyer, J. R., Co., Inc. Staff. (Annual Ser.). 400p. 1999. pap. 130.00 (0-318-32475-X) J R ODwyer.

O'Dwyer's Directory of Public Relations Executives, 2000. O'Dwyer Co. Staff. 664p. 2000. pap. 120.00 (0-941424-02-2) J R ODwyer.

O'Dwyer's Directory of Public Relations Executives, 2000. Jack O'Dwyer. 470p. 2000. 175.00 (0-317-62316-8) J R ODwyer.

***Odyssea, Vol. 2.** Homer. Ed. by A. Ludwich. (GRE., Illus.). (C). 1998. text 57.50 (3-519-04289-4) B G Teubner.

Odyssea. Stella Sands. (Illus.). 32p. (J). (gr. k-4). 1991. pap. text 7.95 (1-879567-03-2, Valeria Bks); lib. bdg. 13.95 (1-879567-04-0, Valeria Bks) Wonder Well.

***Odyssea.** 12th ed. Homer. Ed. by A. Ludwich. (Illus.). (C). 1998. text 49.50 (3-519-04288-6) U of Mich Pr.

Odyssea Astergis. Rene de Goscinny & A. Uderzo. (LAT.). 1992. 24.95 (0-7859-1030-1, 3770400607) Fr & Eur.

Odyssee. Rene de Goscinny & A. Uderzo. (GER.). 1992. 24.95 (0-7859-1023-9, 3770400267) Fr & Eur.

Odyssee. Homer. (FRE.). 1973. pap. 11.95 (0-7859-2630-5, 207036254X) Fr & Eur.

Odyssee d'Asterix. Rene de Goscinny & A. Uderzo. (FRE.). (J). 1992. 24.95 (0-7859-1076-X, 286497004X) Fr & Eur.

Odyssee d'Asterix. Rene de Goscinny & M. Uderzo. (FRE.). (J). 1990. 24.95 (0-8288-8596-6) Fr & Eur.

Odysseus. Jane Yolen. 192p. (gr. 3-7). mass mkt. 4.95 (0-06-440847-7) HarpC.

Odysseus: Onstage. Gail Erwin. 18p. (Orig.). (J). (gr. k-6). 1992. pap. 3.00 (1-57514-255-4, 1129) Encore Perform Pub.

Odysseus: The Complete Adventures. Dennis J. Hartzell. (Illus.). 92p. (Orig.). (gr. 7-9). 1978. pap. text 5.95 (0-88334-110-7) Longman.

Odysseus: The Deeds & Sufferings of the Hero in Ancient Greek Art & Literature. Frank Brommer. (Illus.). 192p. text 50.00 (0-89241-433-2) Caratzas.

***Odysseus & Penelope: An Ordinary Marriage.** unabridged ed. Inge Merkel & Renate Latimer. LC 95-53237. (Studies in Austrian Literature, Culture, & Thought Ser.).Tr. of Eine ganz gewohnliche Ehe. 391p. 2000. pap. 29.50 (1-57241-075-2) Ariadne CA.

Odysseus & the Cyclops. Homer. LC 83-14236. (Tales from the Odyssey Ser.). (Illus.). 32p. (J). (gr. 4-8). 1984. pap. 3.95 (0-8167-0008-7); lib. bdg. 18.60 (0-8167-0007-9) Troll Communs.

Odysseus & the Cyclops. Illus. & Retold by Warwick Hutton. LC 95-31303. 32p. (J). (ps-3). 1995. pap. 15.00 (0-689-80036-3) McElderry Bks.

Odysseus & the Giants. Homer. LC 83-14233. (Tales from the Odyssey Ser.). (Illus.). 32p. (J). (gr. 4-8). 1984. pap. 3.95 (0-8167-0010-9) Troll Communs.

Odysseus & the Great Challenge. Homer. LC 83-14232. (Tales from the Odyssey Ser.). (Illus.). 32p. (J). (gr. 4-8). 1984. pap. 3.95 (0-8167-0014-1) Troll Communs.

Odysseus & the Magic of Circe. Homer. LC 83-14237. (Tales from the Odyssey Ser.). (Illus.). 32p. (J). (gr. 4-8). 1984. pap. 3.95 (0-8167-0012-5) Troll Communs.

Odysseus Elytis: From the Golden to the Silver Poem. Andonis Decavalles. LC 94-67648. 218p. (Orig.). 1994. pap. text 14.00 (0-918618-61-4) Pella Pub.

Odysseus Goes Through Hell. Robinson & Cutis. (Illus.). (J). 1996. mass mkt. 8.95 (0-340-66498-3, Pub. by Hodder & Stought Ltd) Trafalgar.

Odysseus' Homecoming & the New Adam: Poems of Renewal. Bahman Sholevar. LC 82-73948. (Literature-Poetry Ser.). (Illus.). 60p. (Orig.). 1982. pap. 5.95 (0-911323-05-8) Concourse Pr.

***Odysseus in the Serpent Isle.** Jane Yolen. 192p. (J). (gr. 3-7). 2001. 14.95 (0-06-028734-9); lib. bdg. 14.89 (0-06-028735-7) HarpC Child Bks.

Odysseus Polutropos: Intertextual Readings in the "Odyssey" & the "Iliad" Pietro Pucci. (Studies in Classical Philology). 264p. 1995. pap. text 17.95 (0-8014-8270-4) Cornell U Pr.

Odysseus Superhero. Robinson & Cutis. (Illus.). (J). 1996. mass mkt. 8.95 (0-340-66497-5, Pub. by Hodder & Stought Ltd) Trafalgar.

***Odysseus 2000/2001: The International Gay Travel Planner.** 15th rev. ed. Eli Angelo & Joseph H. Bain. (Illus.). 730p. 1999. pap. 29.00 (1-881536-05-X, Pub. by Odysseus Ent) PDC-LPI.

Odyssey. 44p. (YA). 1998. 9.95 (1-56137-760-0, NU7600); 11.95 (1-56137-761-9, NU7619SP) Novel Units.

***Odyssey.** Samuel Butler. 2000. pap. write for info. (1-930142-21-8) Write Together.

***Odyssey.** Ed. by Cliffs Notes Staff. LC 00-35076. (Cliffs Notes Ser.). 96p. 2000. pap. 4.99 (0-7645-8599-1) IDG Bks.

Odyssey. Tr. by Robert Fagles. 560p. 1996. 35.00 (0-670-82162-4) Viking Penguin.

Odyssey. Tr. by Robert Fagles. (C). 1999. pap. 14.95 (0-14-026886-3) Viking Penguin.

Odyssey. Gregory A. Falls & Kurt Beattie. (J). 1978. 6.50 (0-87602-238-7) Anchorage.

Odyssey. Gray. 2000. text. write for info. (0-312-18639-8) St Martin.

Odyssey. Homer. (Illustrated Classics Collection 5). 64p. 1994. pap. 4.95 (0-7854-0782-0, 40565) Am Guidance.

Odyssey. Homer. (Cyber Classics Ser.). 1997. pap. text 14.95 (1-55701-203-2) BNI Pubns.

Odyssey. Homer. 560p. 1991. mass mkt. 5.95 (0-553-21399-7, Bantam Classics) Bantam.

***Odyssey.** Homer. LC 99-43280. (Classics Ser.). (Illus.). 64p. (J). (gr. 2-5). 2000. 14.95 (0-7894-5455-6, D K Ink) DK Pub Inc.

Odyssey. Homer. 62p. 1998. pap. 5.50 (0-87129-861-9, 059) Dramatic Pub.

Odyssey. Homer. Tr. by Robert Fitzgerald. LC 92-52903. (ENG & GRE.). 1992. 20.00 (0-679-41047-3) Everymns Lib.

***Odyssey.** Homer. Tr. by Robert Fitzgerald. (Illus.). 528p. 1998. 30.00 (0-374-22438-2) FS&G.

Odyssey. Homer. Tr. by Robert Fitzgerald. (Illus.). 528p. 1998. pap. 10.00 (0-374-52574-9); pap., teacher ed. 10.00 (0-374-96138-7) FS&G.

Odyssey. Homer. Tr. by Ennis Rees. LC 76-55800. (Library of Liberal Arts: 225). 1977. pap. 6.50 (0-672-61415-4, Bobbs) Macmillan.

***Odyssey, 1 vol.** Homer. Tr. by W.H.D. Rouse from GEC. LC 99-17203. (Signet Classics Ser.). 352p. 2000. mass mkt. write for info. (0-451-52736-4) NAL.

Odyssey. Homer. Tr. by Walter Shewring. (Oxford World's Classics Ser.). (Illus.). 372p. 1998. pap. 8.95 (0-19-283375-8) OUP.

***Odyssey.** Homer. (Oxford Illustrated Classics Ser.). (Illus.). 96p. (YA). 1999. pap. 12.95 (0-19-274183-7) OUP.

Odyssey. Homer. 1997. per. 5.99 (0-671-01548-6) PB.

Odyssey. Homer. (YA). 1997. pap. 5.99 (0-671-15448-6, Pocket Books) PB.

Odyssey. Homer. (Now Age Illustrated V Ser.). (Illus.). 64p. (J). (gr. 4-12). 1979. student ed. 1.25 (0-88301-417-3); pap. text 2.95 (0-88301-393-2) Pendulum Pr.

***Odyssey.** Homer. (Dover Thrift Editions Ser.). 1999. write for info. (0-04-864065-4) Routledge.

Odyssey. Homer. (Penguin Classics). 1991. 11.05 (0-606-02838-2, Pub. by Turtleback) Demco.

Odyssey. Homer. (Illus.). 320p. (YA). (gr. 5 up). 1997. pap. 4.99 (0-14-038309-3) Viking Penguin.

Odyssey. Homer. Tr. by Robert Fagles. 1999. pap. 9.95 (0-14-044529-3) Viking Penguin.

Odyssey. Homer. pap. text 5.75 (0-471-37759-7) Wiley.

Odyssey. Homer. (Classics of World Literature Ser.). 245p. pap. 3.95 (1-85326-025-8, 0258WW, Pub. by Wrdsworth Edits) NTC Contemp Pub Co.

***Odyssey.** Homer. Tr. by Stanley Lombardo. LC 99-54175. 512p. (C). 2000. pap. 9.95 (0-87220-484-7); lib. bdg. 34.95 (0-87220-485-5) Hackett Pub.

Odyssey. Ed. by Robin Lister. LC 93-49856. (Illus.). 96p. (J). (gr. 4 up). 1994. pap. 15.95 (1-85697-522-3) LKC.

Odyssey. Robin Lister & Homer. LC 90-172937. 96p. 1987. write for info. (0-86272-285-3) Kingfisher GBR.

Odyssey. Joanne Mattern. (Wishbone Classics Ser.). 1996. 9.09 (0-606-10365-1, Pub. by Turtleback) Demco.

Odyssey. Geraldine McCaughrean. (Illus.). 100p. (J). (gr. 4 up). 1993. 14.95 (1-56288-433-6) Checkerboard.

***Odyssey.** Bill Morison & Melissa Morison. (Illus.). 48p. (YA). (gr. 3 up). 1998. pap. write for info. (0-88388-207-8) Bellerophon Bks.

Odyssey. Brian Pulido. LC 98-134116. (Lady Death Ser.). 1997. pap. text 9.95 (0-9642260-5-7) Chaos Comics.

***Odyssey, 5 vols.** Steck-Vaughn Company Staff. (Illus.). (J). 2000. pap. 26.95 (0-8114-6971-9) Raintree Steck-V.

Odyssey. Katrina V. Thyne. (Black Lace Ser.). 300p. 1997. mass mkt. 5.95 (0-352-33111-9, Pub. by Virgin Bks) London Brdge.

Odyssey. Barbara E. Walton. (Quantum Leap Ser.: No. 10). 288p. (Orig.). 1996. mass mkt. 5.99 (1-57297-092-8) Blvd Books.

Odyssey. large type ed. Homer. 1997. pap. 19.95 (1-55701-217-2) BNI Pubns.

Odyssey. Homer. Tr. by Robert Fitzgerald. 524p. 1992. reprint ed. lib. bdg. 30.95 (0-89966-890-9) Buccaneer Bks.

Odyssey. Homer. Tr. by William Cowper. 384p. 1995. reprint ed. pap. text 8.95 (0-460-87155-2, Everyman's Classic Lib) Tuttle Pubng.

Odyssey. rev. ed. Homer. Tr. by E. V. Rieu. (Penguin Classics Ser.). 394p. 1992. pap. 9.95 (0-14-044556-0, Penguin Classics) Viking Penguin.

***Odyssey.** unabridged ed. Homer. Tr. by George H. Palmer from GEC. LC 98-50940. 256p. 1999. pap. 2.00 (0-486-40654-7) Dover.

Odyssey. unabridged ed. Diane Redmond. (Curtain Up! Ser.: Vol. 8). (Illus.). 48p. (J). (gr. 2-6). 1998. pap. 16.95 (0-7136-4628-4, Pub. by A & C Blk) Midpt Trade.

***Odyssey.** 2nd ed. 624p. (C). 1999. write for info. (0-205-31872-X) Allyn.

Odyssey. 3rd rev. ed. Menelaos Stefanidis. (Greek Mythology Pocket Ser.: Vol. 7). (Illus.). 256p. 1996. pap. 14.25 (960-425-062-0, Pub. by Sigma Publns) Cosmos.

Odyssey, Bks. VI-VIII. Homer. Ed. by A. F. Garvie. (Cambridge Greek & Latin Classics Ser.). 376p. (C). 1995. pap. text 24.95 (0-521-33840-9) Cambridge U Pr.

Odyssey, Bks. XIX & XX. Homer. Ed. by R. B. Rutherford. (Greek & Latin Classics Ser.). 260p. (C). 1992. pap. text 22.95 (0-521-34760-2) Cambridge U Pr.

Odyssey, Vol. 1. Homer. Tr. by A. T. Murray. LC 93-37392. (Loeb Classical Library: Vol. 104). (ENG & GRE.). 504p. 1994. text 19.95 (0-674-99561-9, L104) HUP.

Odyssey, 2 vols., Vol. 1, Bks. 1-12. Homer. (Loeb Classical Library: No. 104-105). 1919. 18.95 (0-674-99116-8) HUP.

Odyssey, Vol. 2. Homer. Tr. by A. T. Murray. LC 93-37392. (Loeb Classical Library: Vol. 105). (ENG & GRE.). 480p. 1994. text 19.95 (0-674-99562-7, L105) HUP.

Odyssey, 2 vols., Vol. 2, Bks. 13-24. Homer. (Loeb Classical Library: No. 104-105). 462p. 1919. 18.95 (0-674-99117-6) HUP.

Odyssey see Greek Mythology

Odyssey: A Communicative Course in English. Kimbrough et al. (Illus.). 1988. write for info. (0-318-65577-2) Longman.

***Odyssey: A Guide to Better Writing.** 2nd ed. 32p. 1999. write for info. (0-205-31797-9) Allyn.

Odyssey: A Guide to Better Writing. 2nd ed. Homer. 568p. (C). 1999. pap. text 44.00 (0-205-31457-0) Allyn.

***Odyssey: A Guide to Better Writing.** 2nd ed. Kelly & Lawton. 2000. 41.00 (0-205-32876-8) Allyn.

Odyssey: A Journey Back Home. Fernando Uribe & Dan Engler. (Illus.). 36p. (J). 1992. pap. text 1.95 (1-56814-007-X) CCC of America.

Odyssey: A New Verse Translation. Homer. Ed. & Tr. by Albert Cook. (C). 1968. pap. 14.00 (0-393-00744-8) Norton.

Odyssey: A New Verse Translation, Backgrounds, the Odyssey in Antiquity, Criticism. 2nd ed. Homer. Ed. & Tr. by Albert Cook. LC 92-39868. 415p. (C). 1993. pap. text 16.75 (0-393-96405-1) Norton.

Odyssey: A Psychotherapist's Journey along the Cutting Edge. Victor Bogart. LC 92-76171. 348p. (Orig.). 1993. pap. 24.95 (0-9635500-1-2) Baskin Pub OR.

Odyssey: A Stage Version. Derek Walcott. 164p. 1993. pap. 12.00 (0-374-52387-8, Noonday) FS&G.

Odyssey: A Stage Version. Derek Walcott. 159p. 1993. 25.00 (0-374-17249-8, Noonday) FS&G.

Odyssey: An Epic of Return. William G. Thalmann. LC 92-11677. (Twayne's Masterwork Studies: No. 100). 170p. 1992. 25.95 (0-8057-9424-7, Twyne) Mac Lib Ref.

Odyssey: Curriculum Unit. Center for Learning Network Staff & Homer. (Novel Ser.). 104p. (YA). (gr. 9-12). 1990. spiral bd. 18.95 (1-56077-112-7) Ctr Learning.

Odyssey: Quayle,&Anthony, Set. abr. ed. Homer. 1996. audio 18.00 (0-694-51764-X) HarperAudio.

Odyssey: Reproducible Teaching Unit. James Scott. 61p. (YA). (gr. 7-12). 1999. teacher ed., ring bd. 29.50 (1-58049-128-6, TU101) Prestwick Hse.

***Odyssey: Structure, Narration, & Meaning.** Bruce Louden. LC 98-41521. 200p. 1999. 35.95 (0-8018-6058-X) Johns Hopkins.

Odyssey: T. E. Lawrence's Translation of Homer's Odyssey. Homer. Ed. by Bernard M. Knox. Tr. by T. E. Lawrence. 352p. 1991. 30.00 (0-19-506818-1) OUP.

Odyssey: Tales of the Universe. Paul Liebhardt. 224p. 1991. 60.00 (0-9628861-0-6) Inst Shipboard.

Odyssey & the Iliad. Tr. by Robert Fagles. 1996. pap. 75.00 (0-670-77964-4) Viking Penguin.

***Odyssey Atlas of the World.** 4th ed. Hammond Staff. 1999. pap. text 7.95 (0-8437-1211-2) Hammond Pub.

Odyssey Book of Houseplants. Liddy Rich. 1990. pap. 19.95 (0-9625702-0-6) Plant Odyssey Pr.

Odyssey Continues. Judd Biasiotto. Ed. & Illus. by Tom Foote. 250p. (Orig.). 1987. pap. 10.00 (0-933079-06-0) World Class Enterprises.

Odyssey (Homer) Tessa Krailing. (Barron's Book Notes Ser.). (C). 1984. pap. 3.95 (0-8120-3429-5) Barron.

Odyssey, I-XII see Opera

Odyssey in a Downeast Outhouse. (Illus.). 110p. 1998. pap. 10.00 (0-9657018-1-6) B Carter.

Odyssey in Athens: Myths of Cultural Origins. Erwin F. Cook. (Myth & Poetics Ser.). 232p. 1995. text 37.50 (0-8014-3121-2) Cornell U Pr.

Odyssey in Gray: A Diary of Confederate Service, 1863-1865. Douglas F. Forrest. Ed. by William N. Still. LC 78-31757. ix, 352p. 1979. 24.95 (0-88490-005-3) Library of VA.

Odyssey in Learning & Perception. Eleanor J. Gibson. (Learning, Development & Conceptual Change Ser.). (Illus.). 656p. 1994. pap. text 22.00 (0-262-57103-X, Bradford Bks) MIT Pr.

Odyssey in Time: The Dinosaurs of North America. Dale A. Russell. (Illus.). 256p. 1992. pap. text 24.95 (0-8020-7718-8) U of Toronto Pr.

***Odyssey Interactive Companion with Cdrom: Users Guide.** 2nd ed. 2000. write for info. (0-205-32932-2) Allyn.

Odyssey into Greek Cooking. June Marinos. Ed. by Barbara Terzopoulos. (Illus.). 168p. 1997. pap. 16.25 (960-7220-20-X, Pub. by Terzopoulos) Cosmos.

***Odyssey-Literatute Unit.** Stacy Mantle. 48p. 2000. pap. 7.95 (1-57690-633-7) Tchr Create Mat.

Odyssey Notes. Robert J. Milch. (Cliffs Notes Ser.). 72p. 1963. pap. 4.95 (0-8220-0921-8, Cliff) IDG Bks.

Odyssey Now. Nicola Grove & Keith Park. LC 95-16493. 128p. 1995. pap. 29.95 (1-85302-315-9, Pub. by Jessica Kingsley) Taylor & Francis.

Odyssey of a Collector. Charles H. Carpenter et al. Ed. by Phil Freshman. (Illus.). 160p. (Orig.). 1996. pap. 29.95 (0-88039-032-8) Mus Art Carnegie.

Odyssey of a Film-Maker: Robert Flaherty's Story. Frances H. Flaherty. LC 77-169343. (Arno Press Cinema Program Ser.). (Illus.). 66p. 1975. reprint ed. 15.95 (0-405-03918-2) Ayer.

Odyssey of a Friend: Letters to William F. Buckley Jr. rev. ed. Whittaker Chambers & William F. Buckley. Ed. & Notes by William F. Buckley, Jr. LC 87-23252. 312p. 1987. pap. 9.95 (0-89526-788-8); lib. bdg. 17.95 (0-89526-567-2) Regnery Pub.

Odyssey of a Humanitarian: Emily Howland, 1827-1929. Judith C. Breault. 1981. 38.95 (0-405-14076-2) Ayer.

Odyssey of a New Religion: The Holy Order of MANS from New Age to Orthodoxy. Philip C. Lucas. LC 94-12587. (Religion in North America Ser.). 1995. 25.00 (0-253-33612-0) Ind U Pr.

Odyssey of a Nice Girl. Ruth Suckow. (Collected Works of Ruth Suckow). 364p. 1999. reprint ed. lib. bdg. 98.00 (1-58201-839-1) Classic Bks.

Odyssey of a Nursing Home Administrator. Richard C. Schriever. Ed. by Oma Whitcomb. LC 90-70581. 1990. 15.95 (0-9626978-1-8) Whitcomb Pub.

Odyssey of a Philippine Scout. Arthur K. Whitehead. (Illus.). 315p. (Orig.). 1989. pap. text 11.95 (0-9624089-0-5) Whitehead Pub.

Odyssey of a Physician: A Life of Adventure & Exploration. Eugene L. Coodley. LC 93-40536. (Illus.). 128p. (Orig.). 1994. pap. 9.95 (1-56474-092-7) Fithian Pr.

Odyssey of a Public Intellectual: Andri Gorz in Perspective. Andrea T. Levy. 320p. 2000. 53.99 (1-55164-155-0, Pub. by Black Rose) Consort Bk Sales.

Odyssey of a Public Intellectual: Andri Gorz in Perspective. Andrea T. Levy. 320p. 2000. pap. 24.99 (1-55164-154-2) Consort Bk Sales.

Odyssey of a Russian Scientist: I. G. Voznesenskii in Alaska, California & Siberia, 1839-1849. Aleksandr I. Alekseev. Ed. by Richard A. Pierce. Tr. by Wilma Follette from RUS. (Alaska History Ser.: No. 30). (Illus.). 1987. 22.00 (0-919642-05-5) Limestone Pr.

Odyssey of a Small Town Piano Teacher. Louise Guhl. 40p. 1994. 5.45 (0-8497-9548-6, WP347) Kjos.

Odyssey of a Southerner: The Life & Times of Gustavus Woodson Smith. Leonne M. Hudson. 288p. 1998. 32.00 (0-86554-589-8) Mercer Univ Pr.

Odyssey of a U-Boat Commander: Recollections of Erich Topp. Erich Topp. Tr. by Eric C. Rust. LC 91-47593. 258p. 1992. 55.00 (0-275-93898-0, C3898, Praeger Pubs) Greenwood.

Odyssey of a Veterinary Vagabond. Lewis Forbes. LC 98-92405. 356p. 1998. pap. 16.00 (1-57502-721-6, PO2026) Morris Pubng.

Odyssey of a Young Fighter Pilot. Fred Nichol. LC 96-60146. (Illus.). 236p. 1996. reprint ed. pap. 13.50 (1-882194-18-7) TN Valley Pub.

***Odyssey of Burt Alvord: Lawman, Train Robber, Fugitive.** Don Chaput. (Mining Camp Chronicles Ser.: Vol. 5). 1999. per. 18.95 (0-87026-111-8) Westernlore.

Odyssey of Chief Standing Buffalo (And the Northern Sisseton Sioux) Mark Diedrich. LC 87-73501. (Illus.). 118p. (Orig.). 1988. pap. 18.95 (0-9616901-2-7) Coyote Bks MN.

Odyssey of Exile: Jewish Women Flee the Nazis for Brazil. Ed. by Katherine Morris. LC 95-39736. (Illus.). 264p. 1996. 39.95 (0-8143-2562-9); pap. 19.95 (0-8143-2563-7) Wayne St U Pr.

Odyssey of Farah Antun: A Syrian Christian's Quest for Secularism. Donald M. Reid. LC 74-80598. (Studies in Middle Eastern History: No. 2). 1975. 25.00 (0-88297-009-7) Bibliotheca.

Odyssey of Flora Tristan. Laura Strumingher. (University of Cincinnati Studies in Historical & Contemporary Europe: Vol. 2). XVIII, 162p. (C). 1988. text 26.50 (0-8204-0888-3) P Lang Pubng.

Odyssey of Gold. Aaron A. Gold. Ed. by Peter Binzen. LC 95-11976. (Illus.). 240p. 1995. 24.95 (0-8453-4853-1) Assoc Univ Prs.

Odyssey of Hearing Loss: Tales of Triumph. Michael A. Harvey. LC 98-8086. 240p. 1998. 23.95 (1-58121-006-X) Dawn Sign.

Odyssey of Homer. Ed. by S. H. Butcher & A. Lang. 25.00 (0-8196-2881-6) Biblo.

Odyssey of Homer. Richmond Lattimore. (Perennial Classics Ser.). 384p. 1999. pap. 13.00 (0-06-093195-7) HarpC.

Odyssey of Homer. Barbara L. Picard. (Oxford Myths & Legends Ser.). (Illus.). 284p. (YA). (gr. 5-12). 1991. pap. 12.95 (0-19-274146-2) OUP.

Odyssey of Homer. Tr. by T. E. Shaw. 20.00 (0-8196-2012-2) Biblo.

O

*Odyssey of Homer, 6 cass., Vol. 4, Bks. 19-24. Homer. Ed. by Stephen G. Daitz. (Living Voice of Greek & Latin Ser.). (GRE.). 48p. 1998. 59.50 incl. audio (*1-57970-030-6*, S23880) Audio-Forum.

Odyssey of Homer: A New Verse Translation. Allen Mandelbaum. (Illus.). 1990. 48.00 (*0-520-07021-6*, Pub. by U CA Pr) Cal Prin Full Svc.

Odyssey of Homer, Done into English Verse see Collected Works of William Morris

Odyssey of Human Society see Evolution of Human Society

Odyssey of Human Society. Nathaniel I. Korman. LC 96-92646. 206p. (Orig.). 1996. pap. 9.95 (*0-9654300-0-6*) Runamiro Bks.

Odyssey of Jeremy Jack. Mark Medoff & Carleene Johnson. 1973. pap. 5.25 (*0-8222-0835-0*) Dramatists Play.

Odyssey of John Anderson. Patrick Brode. (Publications of the Osgoode Society). 176p. 1989. pap. 15.95 (*0-8020-6748-4*); text 35.00 (*0-8020-5840-X*) U of Toronto Pr.

Odyssey of Katinou Kalokovich. Natalie L. Petesch. 199p. (C). 1979. reprint ed. pap. 5.00 (*0-934238-01-4*) Motheroot.

Odyssey of Korean Democracy: Korean Politics, 1987-1990. Manwoo Lee. LC 90-7393. 184p. 1990. 52.95 (*0-275-93660-0*, C3660, Praeger Pubs) Greenwood.

***Odyssey of Love.** Germana F. Storey. 2000. pap. 12.00 (*0-8059-4955-0*) Dorrance.

Odyssey of Masquers: The Everyman Players. Orlin Corey. (Illus.). 296p. 1990. text 50.00 (*1-878281-09-7*) Rivendell Hse Ltd.

Odyssey of New Religions Today. rev. ed. John T. Biermans. LC 88-1631. (Illus.). 388p. 1988. lib. bdg. 109.95 (*0-88946-035-3*) E Mellen.

Odyssey of New Religious Movements: Persecution, Struggle, Legitimation - a Case Study of the Unification Church. John T. Biermans. LC 87-5476. (Symposium Ser.: Vol. 19). 240p. 1986. lib. bdg. 99.95 (*0-88946-710-2*) E Mellen.

Odyssey of Old Bill the Berkshire Moose. Walter P. Eaton. (Illus.). 32p. (Orig.). 1996. pap. 5.00 (*0-941583-25-2*) Attic Rev Pr.

***Odyssey of Political Theory: The Politics of Departure & Return.** Patrick Deneen. 288p. 2000. 35.00 (*0-8476-9622-7*) Rowman.

Odyssey of Primary Care Research: Historical Perspectives. Edward J. Bujold. Ed. by Thomas McGowen. LC 96-69743. 140p. 1997. pap. 24.95 (*0-9654202-0-5*) Speck Pub.

Odyssey of Revenge. Bernard Diamond. 204p. 1983. pap. 10.95 (*0-914366-21-1*) Columbia Pub.

Odyssey of Science, Culture & Consciousness. Ed. by Kishore Gandhi. 1990. 31.00 (*81-7017-269-1*, Pub. by Abhinav) S Asia.

Odyssey of Shen Congwen. Jeffrey C. Kinkley. LC 87-2276. (Illus.). 488p. 1987. 55.00 (*0-8047-1372-3*) Stanford U Pr.

Odyssey of the Abraham Lincoln Brigade: Americans in the Spanish Civil War. Peter N. Carroll. LC 93-21131. xviii, 440p. (C). 1994. 57.50 (*0-8047-2276-5*); pap. 18.95 (*0-8047-2277-3*) Stanford U Pr.

Odyssey of the Apocalypse. Elizabeth M. Burrows. 176p. 1994. 29.95 (*1-57087-091-8*) Prof Pr NC.

Odyssey of the Buddhist Mind: The Allegory of the Later Journey to the West. Xiaolian Liu. 336p. (C). 1994. lib. bdg. 54.00 (*0-8191-9670-3*) U Pr of Amer.

***Odyssey of the Gods: The Alien History of Ancient Greece.** Erich Von Daniken. (Illus.). 160p. 2000. 24.95 (*1-86204-749-9*, Pub. by Element MA) Penguin Putnam.

Odyssey of the Heart. John H. Harvey. LC 94-30159. (Illus.). 320p. 1994. pap. text 23.95 (*0-7167-2599-1*) W H Freeman.

Odyssey of the Heart. John H. Harvey. LC 94-30159. (Illus.). 320p. (C). 1994. pap. text 16.95 (*0-7167-2589-4*) W H Freeman.

Odyssey of the Heart. Elsie Pond. LC 96-70113. (Illus.). 116p. 1997. 9.95 (*0-9654936-2-8*) Redwood Retreat Pr.

Odyssey of the Mind. Eugene T. Woolf. LC 97-66546. 90p. 1997. 15.00 (*0-935615-11-3*) S Utah U Pr.

Odyssey of the Psyche: Jungian Patterns in Joyce's "Ulysses" Jean Kimball. LC 96-27129. 256p. 1997. 39.95 (*0-8093-2110-6*) S Ill U Pr.

Odyssey of the Soul. Artemus Lamb. 96p. (Orig.). 1995. pap. 11.95 (*0-85398-401-8*) G Ronald Pub.

Odyssey of the Soul: Apocatastasis. Pamela Chilton et al. LC 97-92477. (Illus.). 286p. 1998. pap. 15.00 (*0-9659891-0-0*) Quick Bk Pub.

Odyssey of the Soul: Light: The Act of Creation. Light. (Illus.). 151p. 2000. pap. 12.00 (*0-9659891-1-9*) Quick Bk Pub.

Odyssey of the Soul: Shelley's Alastor. Harold L. Hoffman. LC 33-17558. reprint ed. 20.00 (*0-404-03304-0*) AMS Pr.

***Odyssey of the Soul: When Gods Walk the Earth.** Pamela Chilton et al. 2000. pap. 12.00 (*0-9659891-2-7*) Quick Bk Pub.

Odyssey of the Western Spirit: An Account of Human Reality. Jack Meyer. (Illus.). 365p. 1998. pap. 30.00 (*0-9631727-3-5*) CSU Pubns.

Odyssey of Thomas Condon: Irish Immigrant - Frontier Missionary - Oregon Geologist. Robert D. Clark. (Illus.). 592p. 1989. 29.95 (*0-87595-200-3*) Oregon Hist.

Odyssey of Thomas Ranny. Brooks Ranny. LC 94-92014. (Illus.). 420p. 1994. 15.00 (*0-9618939-3-1*); pap. 12.00 (*0-9618939-4-X*) B Ranney.

Odyssey or Calvary? large type ed. Julio A. Concepcion. LC 97-92297. (Illus.). 120p. 1998. pap. 12.95 (*0-9659592-0-1*) Nadir Pubn.

Odyssey: Pepsi to Apple: A Journey of Adventure, Ideas & the Future. 450p. pap. text 20.00 (*0-7881-6949-1*) DIANE Pub.

Odyssey Project: Readings for Writing 105. Hahn et al. 204p. (C). 1997. per. 28.95 (*0-7872-4390-6*, 41439001) Kendall-Hunt.

"Odyssey" Re-Formed. Frederick Ahl & Hannah M. Roisman. 352p. 1996. text 52.50 (*0-8014-3221-9*); pap. text 19.95 (*0-8014-8335-2*) Cornell U Pr.

Odyssey Readalong. Homer. (Illustrated Classics Collection 5). 64p. 1994. pap. 14.95 incl. audio (*0-7854-0798-7*, 40567) Am Guidance.

Odyssey (Rendered into English Prose) see Shrewsbury Edition of the Works of Samuel Butler

Odyssey Singer. Michael Conway. 88p. (Orig.). 1985. pap. 6.00 (*0-912449-17-9*) Floating Island.

Odyssey Star Trek: The Ashes of Eden, the Return, Avenger. William Shatner. 1088p. 1998. pap. 14.00 (*0-671-02547-3*) S&S Trade.

Odyssey Student Book, Level 3. Kimbrough et al. (Illus.). 1988. text 19.95 (*0-8013-0329-X*, 78100) Longman.

Odyssey to Freedom: Four Themes in Colin Wilson's Novels. K. G. Bergstrom. 160p. (Orig.). 1983. pap. text 30.00 (*91-554-1405-2*) Coronet Bks.

Odyssey to Freedom: My Journey Eastern Europe to the Rocky Mountains of Montana. Ursula K. Moran. LC 98-90484. 1998. 19.95 (*0-533-12816-1*) Vantage.

Odyssey to Guadalajara. Griffith D. Lamdin. LC 86-64031. (Hindsight Saga Ser.). (Illus.). 120p. 1987. pap. 10.95 (*0-915433-14-1*) Packrat WA.

Odyssey to the North. Mario Bencastro. Tr. by Susan G. Rascon. LC 98-28339. 192p. 1998. pap. 12.95 (*1-55885-256-5*) Arte Publico.

Odyssey, XIII-XXIV see Opera

Odysseys: Personal Discoveries. Jerry D. Flack. (Journeys: an Individualized Reading, Writing, & Thinking Program Ser.). 96p. 1993. pap. text 12.95 (*0-944459-63-3*) ECS Lrn Systs.

***Odysseys in Psychotherapy.** Ed. by Joseph J. Shay & Joan Wheelis. (Illus.). 416p. 2000. text 44.95 (*0-8290-5215-1*) Ardent Media.

***Odysseys in West Africa: Commitments in Conservation.** Ted T. Cable. (Illus.). 256p. 2000. pap. write for info. (*1-57167-456-X*) Coaches Choice.

Oe & Beyond: Fiction in Contemporary Japan. Ed. by Stephen Snyder & Philip Gabriel. 317p. (C). 1998. 59.00 (*0-8248-2040-1*) UH Pr.

Oe & Beyond: Fiction in Contemporary Japan. Ed. by Stephen Snyder & Philip J. Gabriel. 392p. (C). 1999. pap. 29.95 (*0-8248-2136-X*) UH Pr.

101 Recognition Secrets: Tools for Motivating & Recognizing Today's Workforce. Rosalind Jeffries. (Illus.). 112p. (Orig.). 1996. pap. 6.95 (*0-9648444-2-7*) Perf Enhancemnt.

OEA y la Evolucion del Sistema Interamericano. OAS General Secretariat, Department of Scientific Research Staff. 50p. (C). 1982. pap. 5.00 (*0-685-05518-3*) OAS.

OECD Agricultural Outlook 1999-2004 (1999 Edition) OECD Staff. 152p. 1999. pap. 32.00 (*92-64-16964-4*, Pub. by Org for Econ) OECD.

***OECD Agricultural Outlook 2000/2005 (2000 Edition)** OECD Staff. 196p. 2000. pap. 31.00 (*92-64-17641-1*, 51 2000 03 1 P, Pub. by Org for Econ) OECD.

OECD & ASEAN Economies: The Challenge of Policy Coherence. OECD Staff. Ed. by K. Fukasaku et al. LC 96-117520. 236p. (Orig.). 1995. pap. 38.00 (*92-64-14482-X*, Pub. by Org for Econ) OECD.

OECD Benchmark Definition of Foreign Direct Investment. 3rd ed. OECD Staff. 58p. (Orig.). 1996. pap. 17.00 (*92-64-15283-0*, 21-96-08-1, Pub. by Org for Econ) OECD.

OECD Communications Outlook 1999. OECD Staff. 256p. 1999. pap. 71.00 (*92-64-17013-8*, 93 1999 02 1 P, Pub. by Org for Econ) OECD.

OECD Economic Outlook: OECD Wirtschaftsausblick, 1997. (GER.). 1997. pap. 35.00 (*92-64-55376-2*, Pub. by Org for Econ) OECD.

OECD Economic Outlook No. 62: December, 1997. OECD Staff. 224p. 1997. pap. 35.00 (*92-64-15377-2*, 12-97-62-1, Pub. by Org for Econ) OECD.

OECD Economic Studies, 1996, Vol. 2, No. 27. 200p. 1997. pap. 38.00 (*92-64-14717-9*, Pub. by Org for Econ) OECD.

OECD Economic Survey: Switzerland, 1995-1996. OECD Staff. 176p. (Orig.). 1996. pap. 26.00 (*92-64-14913-9*, 10-96-26-1, Pub. by Org for Econ) OECD.

***OECD Economic Survey: Turkey 1999.** OECD Staff. 184p. 1999. pap. 26.00 (*92-64-16986-5*, Pub. by Org for Econ) OECD.

OECD Economic Surveys: Australia, 1996-1997. 216p. (Orig.). 1996. pap. 25.00 (*92-64-15413-2*, 10-97-04-1, Pub. by Org for Econ) OECD.

OECD Economic Surveys: Australia, 1998. OECD Staff. (Economic Surveys Ser.). 188p. 1997. pap. 25.00 (*92-64-15984-3*, 10-98-04-1, Pub. by Org for Econ) OECD.

OECD Economic Surveys: Australia 1999. OECD Staff. (Economic Surveys Ser.). 184p. 1998. pap. 26.00 (*92-64-16971-7*, 10 1999 04 1 P, Pub. by Org for Econ) OECD.

***OECD Economic Surveys: Australia 2000.** OECD Staff. 180p. 2000. pap. 30.00 (*92-64-17504-0*, 10 2000 04 1 P, Pub. by Org for Econ) OECD.

OECD Economic Surveys: Austria, 1997. OECD Staff. 208p. (Orig.). 1997. pap. 25.00 (*92-64-15430-2*, 10-97-11-1, Pub. by Org for Econ) OECD.

OECD Economic Surveys: Austria 1997-1998. OECD Staff. (Economic Surveys Ser.). 144p. 1999. pap. 25.00 (*92-64-15989-4*, 10 98 11 1 P, Pub. by Org for Econ) OECD.

***OECD Economic Surveys: Austria 1999.** OECD Staff. 148p. (Orig.). 1999. pap. 26.00 (*92-64-16984-9*, 10-1999-11-1P, Pub. by Org for Econ) OECD.

OECD Economic Surveys: Belgium-Luxembourg, 1997. OECD Staff. (Economic Surveys Ser.). 232p. 1997. pap. 25.00 (*92-64-15440-X*, 10-97-29-1, Pub. by Org for Econ) OECD.

OECD Economic Surveys: Belgium/Luxembourg 1999. OECD Staff. (Economic Surveys Ser.). 204p. 1999. pap. 26.00 (*92-64-16970-9*, 10 1999 29 1 P) Org for Econ.

OECD Economic Surveys: Bulgaria, 1997. OECD Staff. 156p. (Orig.). 1997. pap. 25.00 (*92-64-15426-4*, 10-97-35-1, Pub. by Org for Econ) OECD.

OECD Economic Surveys: Bulgaria 1999. OECD Staff. 124p. 1999. pap. 26.00 (*92-64-17052-9*, 10 1999 35 1 P, Pub. by Org for Econ) OECD.

OECD Economic Surveys: Canada, 1995-1996. OECD Staff. 192p. (Orig.). 1996. pap. 26.00 (*92-64-15339-X*, 10-96-01-1, Pub. by Org for Econ) OECD.

OECD Economic Surveys: Canada, 1997. OECD Staff. (Economic Surveys Ser.). 148p. 1997. pap. 25.00 (*92-64-15427-2*, 10-97-01-1, Pub. by Org for Econ) OECD.

OECD Economic Surveys: Czech Republic, 1998. OECD Staff. 156p. 1998. pap. 25.00 (*92-64-15992-4*, 10 98 32 1 P, Pub. by European Conference Ministers Transp) OECD.

***OECD Economic Surveys: Czech Republic 2000.** OECD Staff. 232p. 2000. pap. 30.00 (*92-64-17532-6*, 10 2000 32 1 P, Pub. by Org for Econ) OECD.

OECD Economic Surveys: Denmark 1997. 164p. 1997. pap. 25.00 (*92-64-15431-0*, 10-97-13-1, Pub. by Org for Econ) OECD.

OECD Economic Surveys: Denmark 1999. OECD Staff. (Economic Surveys Ser.). 164p. 1999. pap. 26.00 (*92-64-16977-6*, 10 1999 13 1 P, Pub. by Org for Econ) OECD.

OECD Economic Surveys: Finland, 1995-1996. 72p. 1996. 26.00 (*92-64-15273-3*, Pub. by Org for Econ) OECD.

OECD Economic Surveys: Finland 1997. 128p. 1997. pap. 25.00 (*92-64-15590-2*, 10-97-31-1, Pub. by Org for Econ) OECD.

OECD Economic Surveys: Finland, 1998. OECD Staff. 156p. 1998. pap. 25.00 (*92-64-15996-7*, 10 98 31 1 P, Pub. by European Conference Ministers Transp) OECD.

***OECD Economic Surveys: Finland 1999.** OECD Staff. (Economic Surveys Ser.). 148p. (Orig.). 1999. pap. 26.00 (*92-64-16989-X*, 10 1999 31 1 P, Pub. by Org for Econ) OECD.

OECD Economic Surveys: France, 1997. (Economic Surveys Ser.). 176p. 1997. pap. 25.00 (*92-64-15432-9*, Pub. by Org for Econ) OECD.

***OECD Economic Surveys: France 1999.** OECD Staff. (Economic Surveys Ser.). 188p. 1999. pap. 26.00 (*92-64-16978-4*, 10 1999 14 1 P, Pub. by Org for Econ) OECD.

OECD Economic Surveys: Germany, 1995-1996. 194p. 1996. 26.00 (*92-64-15278-4*, Pub. by Org for Econ) OECD.

OECD Economic Surveys: Germany, 1998. OECD Staff. 180p. 1998. pap. 25.00 (*92-64-15993-2*, 10 98 15 1 P, Pub. by European Conference Ministers Transp) OECD.

OECD Economic Surveys: Greece, 1996-1997. 163p. 1997. pap. 25.00 (*92-64-15607-0*, Pub. by Org for Econ) OECD.

OECD Economic Surveys: Greece 1998. OECD Staff. (Economic Surveys Ser.). 200p. 1999. pap. 25.00 (*92-64-16002-7*, 10 98 16 1 P) Org for Econ.

OECD Economic Surveys: Hungary, 1996-1997. 156p. 1997. pap. 25.00 (*92-64-15441-8*, 10-97-30-1, Pub. by Org for Econ); pap. 25.00 (*92-64-55441-6*, Pub. by Org for Econ); pap. 25.00 (*963-593-223-5*, Pub. by Org for Econ) OECD.

OECD Economic Surveys: Hungary 1999. OECD Staff. (Economic Surveys Ser.). 164p. 1999. pap. 26.00 (*92-64-16979-2*, 10 1999 30 1, Pub. by Org for Econ) OECD.

OECD Economic Surveys: Iceland 1997. 176p. 1997. pap. 25.00 (*92-64-15434-5*, 10-97-17-1, Pub. by Org for Econ) OECD.

OECD Economic Surveys: Iceland, 1998. OECD Staff. 128p. 1998. pap. 25.00 (*92-64-15991-6*, 10 98 17 1 P, Pub. by Org for Econ) OECD.

OECD Economic Surveys: Ireland, 1996-1997. 128p. 1997. pap. 25.00 (*92-64-15435-3*, Pub. by Org for Econ) OECD.

***OECD Economic Surveys: Ireland 1999.** OECD Staff. 172p. 1999. pap. 26.00 (*92-64-16985-7*, Pub. by Org for Econ) OECD.

OECD Economic Surveys: Italy, 1996-1997. (ITA.). 186p. 1997. pap. 25.00 (*92-64-65436-4*, Pub. by Org for Econ) OECD.

OECD Economic Surveys: Italy, 1997. OECD Staff. 176p. (Orig.). 1997. pap. 25.00 (*92-64-15436-1*, 10-97-19-1, Pub. by Org for Econ) OECD.

OECD Economic Surveys: Italy 1999. OECD Staff. (Economic Surveys Ser.). 156p. 1999. pap. 26.00 (*92-64-16969-5*, 10 1999 19 1 P, Pub. by Org for Econ) OECD.

OECD Economic Surveys: Japan, 1995-1996. OECD Staff. 246p. (Orig.). 1997. pap. 26.00 (*92-64-15341-1*, 10-96-03-1, Pub. by Org for Econ) OECD.

OECD Economic Surveys: Japan, 1997. OECD Staff. (Economic Surveys Ser.). 198p. 1997. pap. 25.00 (*92-64-15429-9*, 10-97-03-1, Pub. by Org for Econ) OECD.

OECD Economic Surveys: Korea 1998. OECD Staff. 212p. 1998. pap. 25.00 (*92-64-15997-5*, 1098391P) OECD.

***OECD Economic Surveys: Korea 1999.** OECD Staff. (OECD Economic Surveys Ser.). 204p. 1999. pap. 26.00 (*92-64-16991-1*, 10 1999 39 1 P, Pub. by Org for Econ) OECD.

OECD Economic Surveys: Mexico, 1997. OECD Staff. 180p. (Orig.). 1997. pap. 25.00 (*92-64-15412-4*, 92-64-15412-4, Pub. by Org for Econ) OECD.

OECD Economic Surveys: Mexico, 1998. OECD Staff. (Economic Surveys Ser.). 156p. 1998. pap. 25.00 (*92-64-15983-5*, 10-98-40-4-P, Pub. by Org for Econ) OECD.

OECD Economic Surveys: Mexico 1999. OECD Staff. 188p. 1999. pap. 26.00 (*92-64-16981-4*, Pub. by Org for Econ) OECD.

OECD Economic Surveys: Netherlands, 1998. OECD Staff. 180p. 1998. pap. 25.00 (*92-64-15985-1*, 10 98 21 1 P, Pub. by Org for Econ) OECD.

OECD Economic Surveys: New Zealand, 1998. OECD Staff. (Economic Surveys Ser.). 196p. 1998. pap. 25.00 (*92-64-15990-8*, 10 98 05 1 P, Pub. by Org for Econ) OECD.

OECD Economic Surveys: New Zealand 1999. OECD Staff. 152p. 1999. pap. 26.00 (*92-64-16983-0*, 10-1999-05-1-P, Pub. by Org for Econ) OECD.

OECD Economic Surveys: Norway, 1997. OECD Staff. 172p. (Orig.). 1997. pap. 25.00 (*92-64-15437-X*, 10-97-22-1, Pub. by Org for Econ) OECD.

OECD Economic Surveys: Norway, 1998. OECD Staff. 140p. 1998. pap. 25.00 (*92-64-15987-8*, 10 98 22 1 P, Pub. by Org for Econ) OECD.

***OECD Economic Surveys: Norway 1999.** OECD Staff. 160p. 1999. pap. 26.00 (*92-64-16980-6*, 10 1999 22 1, Pub. by Org for Econ) OECD.

***OECD Economic Surveys: Norway 2000.** OECD Staff. 156p. 2000. pap. 30.00 (*92-64-17522-9*, 10 2000 22 1 P, Pub. by Org for Econ) OECD.

OECD Economic Surveys: Poland, 1996-1997. OECD Staff. 188p. (Orig.). 1996. pap. 25.00 (*92-64-15359-4*, 10-97-34-1, Pub. by Org for Econ) OECD.

OECD Economic Surveys: Poland, 1998. OECD Staff. 168p. 1998. pap. 25.00 (*92-64-15995-9*, 10 98 34 1 P, Pub. by European Conference Ministers Transp) OECD.

***OECD Economic Surveys: Poland 2000.** OECD Staff. 208p. 2000. pap. 30.00 (*92-64-17534-2*, 10 2000 34 1 P, Pub. by Org for Econ) OECD.

OECD Economic Surveys: Portugal, 1995-1996. 204p. 1996. 26.00 (*92-64-14927-9*, Pub. by Org for Econ) OECD.

OECD Economic Surveys: Portugal, 1998. OECD Staff. (Economic Surveys Ser.). 128p. 1998. pap. 25.00 (*92-64-15982-7*, 10-98-23-1-P, Pub. by Org for Econ) OECD.

***OECD Economic Surveys: Portugal 1999.** OECD Staff. (OECD Economic Surveys Ser.). 162p. 1999. pap. 26.00 (*92-64-16992-X*, 10 1999 23 1 P, Pub. by Org for Econ) OECD.

OECD Economic Surveys: Romania, 1998. OECD Staff. 179p. 1998. pap. 25.00 (*92-64-16006-X*, 10 98 38 1 P, Pub. by Org for Econ) OECD.

OECD Economic Surveys: Russian Federation, 1997. OECD Staff. (Economic Surveys Ser.). 282p. 1997. pap. 25.00 (*92-64-15981-9*, 10-97-37-1, Pub. by Org for Econ) OECD.

***OECD Economic Surveys: Russian Federation 2000.** 184p. 2000. pap. 30.00 (*92-64-17537-7*, 10-2000-37-1-P, Pub. by Org for Econ) OECD.

***OECD Economic Surveys: Slovak Republic 1999.** OECD Staff. 156p. 1999. pap. 26.00 (*92-64-17001-4*, 10 1999 33 1 P, Pub. by Org for Econ) OECD.

OECD Economic Surveys: Slovenia, 1996-1997. 135p. 1997. pap. 25.00 (*92-64-15493-0*, Pub. by Org for Econ) OECD.

OECD Economic Surveys: Spain, 1998. OECD Staff. 208p. 1998. pap. 25.00 (*92-64-15988-6*, 10 98 24 1 P, Pub. by Org for Econ) OECD.

***OECD Economic Surveys: Spain 2000.** OECD Staff. 184p. 2000. pap. 30.00 (*92-64-17524-5*, 10 2000 24 1 P, Pub. by Org for Econ) OECD.

OECD Economic Surveys: Sweden, 1996-1997. OECD Staff. 236p. (Orig.). 1997. pap. 25.00 (*92-64-15420-5*, 10-97-25-1, Pub. by Org for Econ) OECD.

OECD Economic Surveys: Sweden, 1998. OECD Staff. 196p. 1998. pap. 25.00 (*92-64-15986-X*, 10 98 25 1 P, Pub. by Org for Econ) OECD.

***OECD Economic Surveys: Sweden 1999.** OECD Staff. 186p. (Orig.). 1999. pap. 26.00 (*92-64-16988-1*, 10 99 25 1 P, Pub. by Org for Econ) OECD.

OECD Economic Surveys: Switzerland, 1997. OECD Staff. 172p. 1997. pap. 25.00 (*92-64-15438-8*, 10-97-26-1, Pub. by Org for Econ) OECD.

***OECD Economic Surveys: Switzerland 1999.** OECD Staff. 192p. (Orig.). 1999. pap. 26.00 (*92-64-16987-3*, 10 1999 26 1 P, Pub. by Org for Econ) OECD.

***OECD Economic Surveys: The Baltic States. A Regional Economic Assessment 2000.** OECD Staff. 280p. 2000. pap. 30.00 (*92-64-17541-5*, 10 2000 41 1 P, Pub. by Org for Econ) OECD.

OECD Economic Surveys: Turkey 1997. 120p. 1997. pap. 25.00 (*92-64-15439-6*, 10-97-27-1, Pub. by Org for Econ) OECD.

OECD Economic Surveys: United Kingdom, 1998. OECD Staff. 196p. 1998. pap. 25.00 (*92-64-15994-0*, 10 98 28 1 P, Pub. by European Conference Ministers Transp) OECD.

OECD Economic Surveys: United States, 1997. OECD Staff. (Economic Surveys Ser.). 224p. 1997. pap. 25.00 (*92-64-15428-0*, 10-97-02-1, Pub. by Org for Econ) OECD.

OECD Economic Surveys: United States 1999. OECD Staff. 220p. (Orig.). 1999. pap. 26.00 (*92-64-16982-2*, 10-1999-02-1P, Pub. by Org for Econ) OECD.

***OECD Economic Surveys: United States, 2000.** OECD Staff. 2000. pap. 30.00 (*92-64-17502-4*, Pub. by Org for Econ) OECD.

OECD Economics Surveys: Germany, 1997. OECD Staff. 184p. 1997. pap. 25.00 (*92-64-15433-7*, 10-97-15-1, Pub. by Org for Econ) OECD.

O

An Asterisk (*) at the beginning of an entry indicates that the title is appearing for the first time.

OECD Economies at a Glance: Structural Indicators. OECD Staff. LC 96-183235. 144p. (Orig.). 1996. pap. 39.00 (*92-64-14805-1*, Pub. by Org for Econ) OECD.
OECD Education Statistics, 1985-1992. (ENG & FRE.). 248p. (Orig.). 1995. pap. 40.00 (*92-64-04361-6*, Pub. by Org for Econ) OECD.
***OECD Employment Outlook, June 1999.** OECD Staff. 256p. 1999. pap. 55.00 (*92-64-17063-4*, Pub. by Org for Econ) OECD.
OECD Environmental Data Compendium, 1997. OECD Staff. 292p. 1997. pap. 50.00 (*92-64-05539-8*, 97-97-19-3, Pub. by Org for Econ) OECD.
OECD Environmental Performance Review: Australia, 1997. OECD Staff. (Environmental Performance Reviews Ser.). 212p. 1998. pap. 35.00 (*92-64-16044-2*, 97 98 02 1 P, Pub. by Org for Econ) OECD.
OECD Environmental Performance Review: Finland. OECD Staff. (Environmental Performance Reviews Ser.). 204p. 1997. pap. 35.00 (*92-64-15593-7*, 97-97-16-1, Pub. by Org for Econ) OECD.
OECD Environmental Performance Review: Mexico, 1997. OECD Staff. 220p. 1998. pap. 35.00 (*92-64-16045-0*, 97 98 01 1 P, Pub. by Org for Econ) OECD.
OECD Environmental Performance Review: New Zealand. 204p. (Orig.). 1996. pap. 35.00 (*92-64-15311-X*, 97-96-12-1, Pub. by Org for Econ) OECD.
OECD Environmental Performance Review: Sweden. OECD Staff. 150p. (Orig.). 1996. pap. 35.00 (*92-64-15280-6*, 97-96-11-1) OECD.
OECD Environmental Performance Reviews: Belgium. OECD Staff. 228p. 1998. pap. 35.00 (*92-64-16131-7*, 9798101P) OECD.
OECD Environmental Performance Reviews: France. OECD Staff. LC 97-181080. 175p. (Orig.). 1997. pap. 35.00 (*92-64-15443-4*, 97-97-03-1, Pub. by Org for Econ) OECD.
***OECD Environmental Performance Reviews: Greece.** OECD Staff. (OECD Environmental Performance Reviews Ser.). 208p. 2000. pap. 32.00 (*92-64-17189-4*, 97 2000 02 1 P, Pub. by Org for Econ) OECD.
OECD Environmental Performance Reviews: Korea. 153p. 1997. pap. 35.00 (*92-64-15558-9*, 97-97-12-1, Pub. by Org for Econ) OECD.
OECD Environmental Performance Reviews: Netherlands. 236p. (Orig.). 1995. pap. 35.00 (*92-64-14332-7*) OECD.
OECD Environmental Performance Reviews: Spain. 194p. 1997. pap. 35.00 (*92-64-15444-2*, 97-97-04-1, Pub. by Org for Econ) OECD.
OECD Environmental Performance Reviews: Switzerland. OECD Staff. 228p. 1998. pap. 35.00 (*92-64-16132-5*, 9798111P) OECD.
***OECD Globalisation & Education Policy.** Taylor et al. (Issues in Higher Education Ser.: Vol. 13). 2000. 50.00 (*0-08-043449-5*, Pergamon Pr) Elsevier.
OECD Guidelines for Multinational Enterprises & Labour Relations: Experience & Mid-Term Report, 1979-1982. Roger Blanpain. 244p. 1983. 75.50 (*90-312-0194-4*) Kluwer Law Intl.
OECD Guidelines for Multinational Enterprises & Labour Relations: 1976-1979 Experience & Review. Roger Blanpain. 366p. 1980. lib. bdg. 87.00 (*90-312-0108-1*) Kluwer Law Intl.
OECD Guidelines for Testing of Chemicals, 2 vols., Set. OECD Staff. 1994. ring bd. 323.00 (*92-64-14018-2*) OECD.
***OECD Historical Statistics: 1960/1997 (1999 Edition)** OECD Staff. 184p. 2000. pap. 40.00 (*92-64-05880-X*, 30 1999 08 3 P, Pub. by Org for Econ) OECD.
***OECD Information Technology Outlook 2000: ICTs, E-commerce & the Information Economy.** 260p. 2000. pap. 72.00 (*92-64-17185-1*, 93-2000-01-1-P, Pub. by Org for Econ) OECD.
OECD Input-Output Database. OECD Staff. LC 96-147474. (ENG & FRE.). 438p. (Orig.). 1996. pap. 67.00 (*92-64-04612-7*, Pub. by Org for Econ) OECD.
OECD International Education Indicators. OECD Staff. 118p. (Orig.). 1992. pap. 23.00 (*92-64-13726-2*) OECD.
OECD Jobs Strategy: Enhancing the Effectiveness of Active Labour Market Policies. OECD Staff. 52p. (Orig.). 1996. pap. 13.00 (*92-64-14908-2*, 81-96-07-1) OECD.
OECD Jobs Strategy: Technology, Productivity, & Job Creation. LC 96-183227. 260p. 1996. 50.00 (*92-64-14881-7*, 92-96-06-1, Pub. by Org for Econ) OECD.
OECD Jobs Strategy: Technology, Productivity & Job Creation - Best Policy Practices. OECD Staff. LC 98-204250. 328p. 1998. pap. 50.00 (*92-64-16096-5*, 92 98 05 1 P, Pub. by European Conference Ministers Transp) OECD.
OECD Jobs Study: Evidence & Explanations. OECD Staff. 400p. (Orig.). 1994. pap. 60.00 (*92-64-14241-X*) OECD.
OECD Jobs Study: Facts, Analysis, Strategies. LC 94-232791. 50p. 1994. pap. 11.00 (*92-64-14145-6*, Pub. by Org for Econ) OECD.
OECD Jobs Study: Implementing the Strategy. LC 96-117512. 32p. (Orig.). 1995. pap. 13.00 (*92-64-14469-2*, Pub. by Org for Econ) OECD.
OECD Jobs Study: Taxation, Employment & Unemployment. LC 96-125274. 192p. (Orig.). 1995. pap. 37.00 (*92-64-14400-5*, Pub. by Org for Econ) OECD.
OECD Model Convention, 1996 & Beyond: Proceedings of a Seminar Held in Geneva in 1996 During the 50th Congress of the International Fiscal Association. Ed. by International Fiscal Association Staff. LC 98-21733. (IFA Congress Seminar Ser.). 84p. 1998. pap. 48.00 (*90-411-1029-1*) Kluwer Law Intl.
OECD Model Convention-1997 & Beyond: Current Problems of the Permanent Establishment Definition : Proceedings Of A Seminar Held In New Delhi, In 1997 During The 51st Congress Of The International Fiscal Association. International Fiscal Association Staff. LC 99-13932. (IFA Congress Seminar Ser.). 1999. 39.00 (*90-411-1162-X*) Kluwer Law Intl.
OECD Model Income Tax Treaties & Commentaries, 1963 & 1977. 2nd rev. ed. Kees Van Raad. 404p. 1990. pap. 48.00 (*90-6544-457-2*) Kluwer Law Intl.
***OECD Principles of Corporate Governance.** OECD Staff. 48p. 1999. pap. 20.00 (*92-64-17126-6*, 21 1999 06 1 P, Pub. by Org for Econ) OECD.
OECD Report on Regulatory Reform: Synthesis Report. OECD Staff. LC 98-121690. 64p. 1997. pap. 7.00 (*92-64-15556-2*, 42-97-05-1, Pub. by Org for Econ) OECD.
OECD Report on Regulatory Reform Vols. I & II: Sectoral Studies & Thematic Studies. OECD Staff. LC 98-121318. 664p. 1997. pap. 47.00 (*92-64-15519-8*, 42-97-04-1, Pub. by Org for Econ) OECD.
OECD Review of Agricultural Policies: Slovak Republic. OECD Staff. 248p. 1997. pap. 46.00 (*92-64-15568-6*, 14-97-06-1, Pub. by Org for Econ) OECD.
OECD Reviews of Foreign Direct Investment: Argentina. (SPA.). 63p. 1997. pap. 15.00 (*92-64-45497-7*, Pub. by Org for Econ) OECD.
OECD Reviews of Foreign Direct Investment: Argentina. OECD Staff. 68p. 1997. pap. 15.00 (*92-64-15497-3*, 21-97-51-1, Pub. by Org for Econ) OECD.
OECD Reviews of Foreign Direct Investment: Brazil. OECD Staff. 84p. 1998. pap. 20.00 (*92-64-16097-3*, 21 98 51 1 P, Pub. by European Conference Ministers Transp) OECD.
OECD Reviews of National Policies for Education: Russian Federation. OECD Staff. (Reviews of National Policies for Education Ser.). 176p. 1998. pap. 30.00 (*92-64-16058-2*, 91 98 03 1 P, Pub. by Org for Econ) OECD.
***OECD Science, Technology & Industry Scoreboard 1999: Benchmarking Knowledge-Based Economics.** OECD Staff. 180p. 1999. pap. 43.00 (*92-64-17107-X*, 92 1999 07 1 P, Pub. by Org for Econ) OECD.
***OECD STAN Database for Industrial Analysis 1970/1997: 1998 Edition.** OECD Staff. 376p. 1999. pap. 79.00 (*92-64-05832-X*, 92 1999 01 3 P, Pub. by Org for Econ) OECD.
OECD STAN Database for Industrial Analysis 1976-1995. 366p. 1997. pap. 79.00 (*92-64-05265-8*, 92-97-04-3, Pub. by Org for Econ) OECD.
***OECD Steel Outlook 1999/2000: 1999 Edition.** Franco Mannato. 60p. 1999. pap. 32.00 (*92-64-17139-8*, 58 1999 03 1 P, Pub. by Org for Econ) OECD.
OECD Tourism Statistics: Design & Application for Policy. OECD Staff. 100p. (Orig.). 1996. pap. 24.00 (*92-64-15327-6*, 78-96-02-1) OECD.
***OECD/CSNI Specialist Meeting on Advanced Instrumentation & Measurement Techniques: Held at Fess Parker's Red Lion Resort, Santa Barbara, California, March 17-20, 1997.** John Lehner. 758p. 1998. per. 62.00 (*0-16-063028-2*) USGPO.
OECD/CSNI Specialists Meeting on Boron Dilution Reactivity Transients: Held in State College, Pennsylvania, US, October 18-20, 1995. 471p. 1997. per. 43.00 (*0-16-063019-3*) USGPO.
OECF Untied Credit Projects in Japan: A Strategic Entry Report, 1997. Compiled by Icon Group International Staff. (Illus.). 156p. 1999. ring bd. 1560.00 incl. audio compact disk (*0-7418-0947-8*) Icon Grp.
Oecology of Plants: An Introduction to the Study of Plant-Communities. Eugenius Warming & Martin Vahl. Ed. by Frank N. Egerton, 3rd. LC 77-74254. (History of Ecology Ser.). 1978. reprint ed. lib. bdg. 37.95 (*0-405-10423-5*) Ayer.
Oeconomia Hippocratis Alphabeti Serie Distincta. Anutius Foesius. 694p. reprint ed. write for info. (*0-318-72022-1*) G Olms Pubs.
Oeconomicus: A Social & Historical Commentary, with a New English Translation. Xenophon. Ed. & Tr. by Sarah B. Pomeroy. (Illus.). 400p. 1995. pap. text 32.00 (*0-19-815025-3*) OUP.
Oeconomy of Charity: 1801 Edition, 2 vols. Sarah Trimmer. (Classics in Education Ser.). 718p. 1996. reprint ed. 185.00 (*1-85506-312-3*) Bks Intl VA.
Oecophorine Genera of Australia Vol. II: The Chezala, Philobata, & Eulechria Groups (Lepidoptera: Oecophoridae) I. F. Common. LC 97-175121. (Monographs on Australian Lepidoptera: No. 5). (Illus.). 404p. 1996. 130.00 (*0-643-05934-2*, Pub. by CSIRO) Accents Pubns.
Oecophorine Genera of Australia I: The Wingia Group. I. F. Common. (Monographs on Australian Lepidoptera: Vol. 3). 390p. 1994. 100.00 (*0-643-05524-X*, Pub. by CSIRO) Accents Pubns.
OECS Law Reports: c. 1950-1990, 2 vols., Vol. 1. Ed. by Cecil E. Hewlett & N. J. Liverpool. 1991. pap. text 85.00 (*976-621-007-1*) Gaunt.
OECS Law Reports: c. 1950-1990, 2 vols., Vol. 2. Ed. by Cecil E. Hewlett & N. J. Liverpool. 1991. pap. text 85.00 (*976-621-008-X*) Gaunt.
Oedema in the Newborn see Molecular Aspects of Medicine
Oedipal Paradigms in Collision: A Centennial Emendation of a Piece of Freudian Canon (1897-1997) Howard Covitz. LC 97-31584. (Reshaping of Psychoanalysis: Vol. 9). XVI, 385p. (C). 1998. text 59.95 (*0-8204-3921-5*) P Lang Pubng.
Oedipus. Lucius Annaeus Seneca. Tr. by Moses Hadas. LC 55-13616. 1955. pap. 2.95 (*0-672-60210-5*, LLA44, Bobbs) Macmillan.
Oedipus. Sophocles. 190p. 1949. write for info. (*3-296-70700-X*) G Olms Pubs.
Oedipus. 3rd rev. ed. Menelaos Stefanidis. (Greek Mythology Pocket Ser.: Vol. 8). (Illus.). 256p. 1996. pap. 14.25 (*960-425-074-4*, Pub. by Sigma Publns) Cosmos.
Oedipus: A Folklore Casebook. Ed. by Lowell Edmunds & Alan Dundes. LC 95-31697. 284p. 1995. 45.00 (*0-299-14850-5*); pap. 18.95 (*0-299-14854-8*) U of Wis Pr.
Oedipus: The Ancient Legend & Its Later Analogues. Lowell Edmunds. LC 84-47948. 269p. reprint ed. pap. 83.40 (*0-7837-7058-8*, 204687000004) Bks Demand.
Oedipus: The Ancient Legend & Its Later Analogues. Lowell Edmunds. 272p. 1996. reprint ed. pap. text 16.95 (*0-8018-5490-3*) Johns Hopkins.
Oedipus: The Meaning of Masculine Life. Thomas Van Nortwick. LC 97-40655. (Oklahoma Series in Classical Culture: Vol. 22). 208p. 1998. 19.95 (*0-8061-3009-1*) U of Okla Pr.
Oedipus: The Tragedies see Greek Mythology
Oedipus & Beyond: A Clinical Theory. Jay Greenberg. 320p. (C). 1992. 41.00 (*0-674-63090-4*) HUP.
Oedipus & Beyond: A Clinical Theory. Jay Greenberg. 288p. 1993. pap. 18.50 (*0-674-63091-2*) HUP.
Oedipus & the Devil: Witchcraft, Sexuality, & Religion in Early Modern Europe. Lyndal Roper. LC 93-5903. 256p. (C). (gr. 13). 1994. pap. 24.99 (*0-415-10581-1*) Routledge.
Oedipus & the Fabrication of the Father: The Oedipus Tyrannus in Modern Criticism & Philosophy. Pietro Pucci. 240p. 1992. text 38.50 (*0-8018-4341-3*) Johns Hopkins.
Oedipus at Colonus see Sophocles One
Oedipus at Colonus see Theban Plays
Oedipus at Colonus. Sophocles. write for info. (*0-318-54900-X*) OUP.
Oedipus at Colonus. unabridged ed. Sophocles. LC 99-21444. 64p. 1999. pap. 1.00 (*0-486-40659-8*) Dover.
Oedipus at Colonus. unabridged ed. Sophocles. Ed. by William-Alan Landes. Tr. by R. C. Jebb. LC 98-13733. 55p. 1998. pap. 7.00 (*0-88734-778-9*) Players Pr.
Oedipus at Colonus & Electra. Sophocles. Ed. & Tr. by Peter D. Arnott. LC 74-76970. (Crofts Classics). 128p. (C). 1975. pap. text 4.95 (*0-88295-107-6*) Harlan Davidson.
Oedipus at Fenway Park: What Rights Are & Why There Are Any. Lloyd L. Weinreb. LC 94-3060. 240p. 1994. text 35.95 (*0-674-63092-0*, WEIOED) HUP.
Oedipus at Kolonos. Timberlake Wertenbaker. 1993. pap. 5.95 (*0-87129-204-1*, O50) Dramatic Pub.
Oedipus at Stalingrad. Gregor Von Rezzori. LC 94-9800. 304p. 1994. 25.00 (*0-374-22426-9*) FS&G.
Oedipus at Thebes. Akhter Ahsen. LC 83-70541. 80p. (Orig.). 1984. pap. 9.95 (*0-913412-35-X*) Brandon Hse.
Oedipus at Thebes: Sophocles' Tragic Hero & His Time. Bernard M. Knox. LC 97-18471. 304p. 1998. pap. 16.00 (*0-300-07423-9*) Yale U Pr.
Oedipus Cadet. Willie Smith. 185p. 1990. 18.95 (*0-930773-11-X*); pap. 8.95 (*0-930773-12-8*) Black Heron Pr.
Oedipus Complex Today: Clinical Implications. Ronald Britton et al. 160p. 1989. reprint ed. pap. text 25.00 (*0-946439-55-9*, Pub. by H Karnac Bks Ltd) Other Pr LLC.
Oedipus Cycle of Sophocles. Incl. Antigone. Oedipus Rex. Ed. by Dudley Fitts. Tr. by Robert Fitzgerald. 1955. pap. 264p. (C). 1955. Set pap. 11.00 (*0-15-683838-9*, Harvest Bks) Harcourt.
***Oedipus in Britain: Edward Glover & the Struggle over Klein.** Paul Roazen. LC 00-35661. 2000. write for info. (*1-892746-66-2*) Other Pr.
Oedipus in the Stone Age: A Psychoanalytic Study of Masculinization in Papua New Guinea. Theodore Lidz & Ruth W. Lidz. LC 88-25796. 215p. 1989. 35.00 (*0-8236-3727-1*) Intl Univs Pr.
Oedipus in the Trobriands. Melford E. Spiro. 204p. (C). 1992. pap. text 21.95 (*1-56000-627-7*) Transaction Pubs.
Oedipus in the Trobriands. Melford E. Spiro. LC 82-7032. 224p. (C). 1982. pap. text 8.00 (*0-226-76989-5*); lib. bdg. 26.00 (*0-226-76988-7*) U Ch Pr.
Oedipus, King of Thebes. Sophocles. LC 71-158290. (Augustan Translators Ser.). reprint ed. 49.50 (*0-404-54138-0*) AMS Pr.
Oedipus Lex: Psychoanalysis, History, Law. Peter Goodrich. LC 95-10026. (Philosophy, Social Theory & the Rule of Law Ser.: No. 3). (Illus.). 292p. 1995. 42.50 (*0-520-08990-1*, Pub. by U CA Pr) Cal Prin Full Svc.
Oedipus Meets the Press, & Other Tragi-Comedies of Our Time. Sanford Pinsker. LC 95-511. 64p. 1996. pap. 14.95 (*0-7734-2741-4*, Mellen Poetry Pr) E Mellen.
***Oedipus of Lucius Annaeus Seneca.** Tr. & Adapted by Michael Elliot Rutenberg. 1999. 20.00 (*0-86516-463-0*) Bolchazy-Carducci.
***Oedipus of Lucius Annaeus Seneca.** Lucius Annaeus Seneca. Tr. & Adapted by Michael Elliot Rutenberg. LC 99-41314. 1999. pap. 9.00 (*0-86516-459-2*) Bolchazy-Carducci.
Oedipus on the Road. Henry Bauchau. Tr. by Anne-Marie Glasheen. LC 97-72130. 1997. 24.45 (*1-55970-382-2*, Pub. by Arcade Pub Inc) Time Warner.
Oedipus, Philosopher. Jean-Joseph Goux. Tr. by Catherine Porter. LC 92-40387. (Meridian: Crossing Aesthetics Ser.). 240p. 1993. 39.50 (*0-8047-2169-6*); pap. 13.95 (*0-8047-2171-8*) Stanford U Pr.
Oedipus Plays of Sophocles. Tr. by Paul Roche. 1996. pap. 10.95 (*0-452-01167-1*, Plume) Dutton Plume.
Oedipus Rex see Oedipus Cycle of Sophocles
Oedipus Rex see Ten Greek Plays in Contemporary Translations
Oedipus Rex. Sophocles. Ed. by R. D. Dawe. (GRE.). 1996. pap. 18.95 (*3-8154-1813-5*, T1813, Pub. by B G Teubner) U of Mich Pr.
Oedipus Rex. Sophocles. Ed. by R. D. Dawe. LC 81-21626. (Cambridge Greek & Latin Classics Ser.). 282p. 1982. pap. text 22.95 (*0-521-28777-4*) Cambridge U Pr.
Oedipus Rex. Sophocles. Ed. by William-Alan Landes. Tr. by E. H. Plumptie from LAT. LC 92-53875. 70p. 1992. pap. 7.00 (*0-88734-251-5*) Players Pr.
Oedipus Rex. abr. ed. Sophocles. (Thrift Editions Ser.). 64p. 1993. pap. 1.00 (*0-486-26877-2*) Dover.
Oedipus Rex see Four Greek Plays
Oedipus Rex. Sophocles. 64p. 1999. reprint ed. pap. 6.95 (*1-57002-111-2*) Univ Publng Hse.
Oedipus Rex: Reproducible Teaching Unit. rev. ed. James Scott. 29p. (YA). (gr. 7-12). 1990. teacher ed., ring bd. 29.50 (*1-58049-071-9*, TU32/U) Prestwick Hse.
Oedipus Rex & The Rake's Progress. Igor Stravinsky. Ed. by Nicholas John. (English National Opera Guide Series: Bilingual Libretto, Articles: No. 43). (Illus.). (Orig.). 1991. pap. 9.95 (*0-7145-4193-1*) Riverrun NY.
Oedipus Road: Searching for a Father in a Mother's Fading Memory. Tom Dodge. LC 95-26697. 209p. (Orig.). 1996. pap. 15.95 (*0-87565-153-4*) Tex Christian.
Oedipus the Anti-Sociopath: or Autumn Angst. Jonathan Levant. 24p. (Orig.). 1992. pap. 5.00 (*0-926935-62-3*) Runaway Spoon.
Oedipus the King see Sophocles One
Oedipus the King. 32p. (YA). 1998. 9.95 (*1-56137-762-7*, NU7627) Novel Units.
***Oedipus the King.** (YA). 1999. 11.95 (*1-56137-763-5*) Novel Units.
***Oedipus the King.** Sophocles. Tr. by Nicholas Rudall. LC 00-25059. (Plays for Performance Ser.). 64p. 2000. 15.95 (*1-56663-307-9*, Pub. by I R Dee); pap. 7.95 (*1-56663-308-7*, Pub. by I R Dee) Natl Bk Netwk.
Oedipus the King. Sophocles. Tr. by Stephen Berg & Diskin Clay. (Greek Tragedy in New Translations Ser.). 128p. 1988. pap. text 8.95 (*0-19-505493-8*) OUP.
Oedipus the King. Sophocles. Tr. & Intro. by Bernard Knox. (Washington Square Press Enriched Classic Ser.). (Illus.). 176p. 1994. per. 5.50 (*0-671-88804-8*, WSP) PB.
Oedipus the King. Sophocles. Ed. by Whitney J. Oates & Eugene O'Neill, Jr. 1955. pap. write for info. (*0-318-55462-3*) Random.
Oedipus the King. Sophocles. (Washington Square Press Enriched Classic Ser.). 1994. 10.60 (*0-606-06630-6*, Pub. by Turtleback) Demco.
Oedipus the King. Sophocles. Tr. by Robert Bagg from GRE. LC 81-19735. 96p. 1982. pap. 13.95 (*0-87023-362-9*) U of Mass Pr.
Oedipus the King. Sophocles. Tr. & Intro. by Anthony Burgess. Intro. by Michael Langham. LC 72-85784. (Drama Editions Ser.: No. 8). 94p. 1972. pap. 8.95 (*0-8166-0667-6*) U of Minn Pr.
Oedipus the King & Antigone. Sophocles. Ed. & Tr. by Peter D. Arnott. LC 60-12550. (Crofts Classics). 128p. (C). 1960. pap. text 4.95 (*0-88295-094-0*) Harlan Davidson.
Oedipus the King by Sophocles: Curriculum Unit. Center for Learning Network Staff. (Drama Ser.). 116p. 1991. spiral bd. 18.95 (*1-56077-167-4*) Ctr Learning.
Oedipus the King, Oedipus at Colonus & Antigone Notes. Robert Milch. (Cliffs Notes Ser.). 64p. (Orig.). 1965. pap. 4.95 (*0-8220-0708-6*, Cliff) IDG Bks.
Oedipus Translation Booklet. Fitzpatrick. 1996. pap. text 2.00 (*0-312-14512-8*) St Martin.
***Oedipus Trilogy.** Ed. by Cliffs Notes Staff. (Cliffs Notes Ser.). 128p. 2000. pap. 4.99 (*0-7645-8581-9*) IDG Bks.
Oedipus Trilogy. Sophocles. Ed. by Gerald Lee Ratcliff. (Barron's Book Notes Ser.). (Orig.). (C). 1984. pap. 3.95 (*0-8120-3430-9*) Barron.
Oedipus Tryannos. Sophocles. Tr. by Timberlake Wertenbaker from GRE. 1993. pap. 5.95 (*0-87129-203-3*, O49) Dramatic Pub.
Oedipus Tyrannus. Ed. by Theodore F. Brunner. (Critical Editions Ser.). (Orig.). (C). 1970. pap. 12.50 (*0-393-09874-5*) Norton.
Oedipus Tyrannus. Sophocles. Ed. & Tr. by Peter Meineck & Paul Woodruff from GEC. LC 99-57521. 128p. (C). 2000. pap. 5.95 (*0-87220-492-8*) Hackett Pub.
***Oedipus Tyrannus.** Sophocles. Ed. & Tr. by Peter Meineck & Paul Woodruff from GEC. LC 99-57521. 128p. (C). 2000. lib. bdg. 19.95 (*0-87220-493-6*) Hackett Pub.
Oedipus Tyrannus. 2nd ed. Sophocles. Ed. by Luci Berkowitz. Tr. by Theodore F. Brunner. (Critical Editions Ser.). (C). 1998. pap. write for info. (*0-393-96788-3*, Norton Paperbks) Norton.
Oedipus Tyrannus: Tragic Heroism & the Limits of Knowledge. Charles Segal. LC 92-32279. (Masterwork Studies). 208p. 1993. 25.95 (*0-8057-7979-5*, Twyne) Mac Lib Ref.
***Oedipus Tyrannus: Tragic Heroism & the Limits of Knowledge.** 2nd ed. Ed. by Charles Segal. (Illus.). 240p. (C). 2000. pap. 14.95 (*0-19-513321-8*); text 39.00 (*0-19-513320-X*) OUP.
Oedipus Ubiquitous: The Family Complex in World Folk Literature. Allen W. Johnson & Douglass Price-Williams. LC 95-41368. 354p. 1996. 49.50 (*0-8047-2576-4*); pap. 16.95 (*0-8047-2577-2*) Stanford U Pr.
Oedipus Variations: Studies in Literature & Psychoanalysis. Karl Kerenyi & James Hillman. Tr. by Jon Solomon. LC 90-21611. (Dunquin Ser.: No. 19). 170p. (Orig.). 1990. pap. 14.50 (*0-88214-219-4*) Spring Pubns.
Oedogoniacees Africaines. L. Gauthier-Lievre. (Illus.). 1964. 64.00 (*3-7682-0216-X*) Lubrecht & Cramer.
***Oee for Operators: Overall Equipment Effectiveness.** Productivity Development Team (Productivity Press) Staff. LC 99-34532. 1999. 25.00 (*1-56327-221-0*) Productivity Inc.

O

Oeffentliche Finanzen & Finanzpolitik in Berlin, 1945-1961: Eine Vergleichende Untersuchung von Ost- & West-Berlin (Mit Datenanhang 1945-1989) Frank Zschaler. (Veroeffentlichungen der Historischen Kommission zu Berlin Ser.: Bd 88). (GER.). xix, 340p. (C). 1995. lib. bdg. 129.25 (*3-11-014409-3*) De Gruyter.

Oeflein. Fred Oeflein. (C). 1998. pap. text 67.00 (*0-321-04507-6*) Addson-Wesley Educ.

Oehlen Williams 95. Thomas Crow et al. Ed. by Cathy Gudis. LC 94-74635. (Illus.). 172p. 1995. pap. 29.95 (*1-881390-09-8*) OSU Wexner Ctr.

Oeil Clair see Oeuvres

Oeil Ecoute. Paul Claudel. (FRE., Illus.). 248p. 1990. pap. 13.95 (*0-7859-1148-0*, 2070325873) Fr & Eur.

Oeil Ecoute. Paul Claudel. (Folio Essais Ser.: No. 127). (FRE.). 1990. pap. 14.95 (*2-07-032587-3*) Schoenhof.

Oeil et l'Esprit. Maurice Merleau-Ponty. (Folio Essais Ser.: No. 13). (FRE.). 92p. 1985. pap. 9.95 (*2-07-032290-4*) Schoenhof.

Oeil Magique see Magic Eye

Oeil Magique III see Magic Eye III

Oeklogische Bedingungen Verschiedener Labuwaldgesellschaften Des Nordwestdeutschen Tieflandes. Thomas Gonnert. (Dissertationes Botanicae Ser.: Band 136). (GER., Illus.). iv, 224p. 1989. pap. 65.00 (*3-443-64048-6*, Pub. by Gebruder Borntraeger) Balogh.

Oekoaktiv - Buchlein. Patricia Colburn et al. (GER., Illus.). 40p. 1997. spiral bd. 17.00 incl. vdisk (*0-942017-48-X*, 04-64647) Amer Assn Teach German.

Oekologie der Diatomeen in Binnengewaessern. B. J. Cholnoky. (Illus.). 1968. 120.00 (*3-7682-5421-6*) Lubrecht & Cramer.

Oekologie der Halophytenvegetation in der Provinz Mendoza, Argentinien (Monte-Formation) Almut Therburg. (Dissertationes Botanicae Ser.: Band 273). (Illus.). 181p. 1997. pap. 53.00 (*3-443-64185-7*, Pub. by Gebruder Borntraeger) Balogh.

Oekologie der Keimung und Dormanz Von Koernerraps (Brassica Napus L.) und Ihre Bedeutung Fuer eine Uberdauerung der Samen Im Boden, Vol. 2. Susanne Schlink. (Dissertationes Botanicae Ser.: Band 222). (GER., Illus.). iv, 193p. 1994. pap. 53.00 (*3-443-64134-2*, Pub. by Gebruder Borntraeger) Balogh.

Oekologische Feuchtegrad Als Kriterium Zur Beurteilung Von Grunlandstandorten, ein Vergleich Bodenkundlicher und Vegetationskundlicher Standortmerkmale. Dieter Kunzmann. (Dissertationes Botanicae Ser.: Band 134). (GER., Illus.). ix, 278p. 1989. pap. 71.00 (*3-443-64046-X*, Pub. by Gebruder Borntraeger) Balogh.

Oekologische Untersuchungen Zum Nahrstoff- Und Wasserhaushalt in Niedermooren Des Westlichen Bodenseegebiets. Raimund Wamke-Gruttner. (Dissertationes Botanicae Ser.: Band 148). (GER., Illus.). viii, 214p. 1990. pap. 71.00 (*3-443-64060-5*, Pub. by Gebruder Borntraeger) Balogh.

Oekonomie Internationalen Umweltschutzes. Oliver Letzgus. (Illus.). 366p. 1998. 67.95 (*3-631-34265-9*) P Lang Pubng.

***Oekonomische Verfahren Im Naturschutz: Der Einsatz der Kontingenten Bewertung Im Entscheidungsprozess.** Ulrich Enneking. (Illus.). 245p. 1998. 45.95 (*3-631-34310-8*) P Lang Pubng.

Oekonomisches Woertebuch: German-Portuguese. Dora Von Helmut. (GER & POR.). 207p. 1986. 75.00 (*0-7859-8318-X*, 3349001106) Fr & Eur.

Oekonomisches Woertebuch: Portuguese-German. Wolker Wein. 208p. 1988. 75.00 (*0-7859-8472-0*, 3781920259) Fr & Eur.

Oekonomisches Woerterbuch: Spanish-German. Karl-Heinz Radde. (GER & SPA.). 640p. 1989. 105.00 (*0-7859-7034-7*) Fr & Eur.

Oekophysiologische Anpassungen im Gasstoffwechsel bei der Gattung Peperomia Ruiz y Pavon, Vol. 75. Gerhard Starnecker. (Dissertationes Botanicae Ser.). (GER., Illus.). 140p. 1984. pap. text 40.00 (*3-7682-1390-0*) Lubrecht & Cramer.

Oekophysiologische Untersuchungen Zur Salz- Und Cadmiumresistenz Von Tamarix Aphylla (L.) Karst. (Tamaricaceae) Jurgen Hagemeyer. (Dissertationes Botanicae Ser.: Band 155). (GER., Illus.). 194p. 1990. pap. 53.00 (*3-443-64067-2*, Pub. by Gebruder Borntraeger) Balogh.

Oelfeld-Fachwoerterbuch. deluxe ed. J. Moltzer. (DUT, ENG, FRE, GER & SPA.). 1965. 37.50 (*0-7859-0838-2*, M-7576) Fr & Eur.

***Oem Auto Parts in Saudi Arabia: A Strategic Entry Report, 1999.** Compiled by Icon Group International. (Illus.). 133p. 1999. ring bd. 1330.00 incl. audio compact disk (*0-7418-1787-X*) Icon Grp.

OEM Boards, Systems & Software. 525p. 1996. pap. 22.95 (*1-55512-253-1*) McGraw.

Oem Occupational Health & Safety Manual. 2nd ed. Deborah V. DiBenedetto et al. LC 98-180607. 1996. 495.00 (*1-883595-09-6*, OEM Pr) OEM Health.

Oenone in January. Kevin Crossley-Holland. 1993. 60.00 (*0-907664-17-2*, Pub. by Old Stiles) St Mut.

Oenothera: Contributions of a Plant to Biology. C. Harte. LC 93-29300. (Monographs on Theoretical & Applied Genetics: Vol. 20). 1994. 202.95 (*0-387-53114-9*) Spr-Verlag.

***O'er the Land of the Free.** Samuel Lombardo. 189p. 2000. pap. text 14.95 (*0-9677051-0-X*, Pub. by Lombardo Bks) White Mane Pub.

Oesterle, Leonard: Portfolio (Sculpture) (Illus.). 18p. 1994. 35.00 (*0-88962-534-4*) Mosaic.

Oesterreichische Gesellschaft fuer Gynaekologie & Geburtshilfe, Bayerische Gesellschaft fuer Geburtshilfe & Frauenheilkunde, Jahrestagung, Salzburg, June 1993. Ed. by E. Reinold. (Journal: Gynaekologische Geburtshilfliche Rundschau: Vol. 33, Suppl. 1, 1993). (Illus.). x, 354p. 1993. pap. 158.50 (*3-8055-5916-X*) S Karger.

Oesterreichische Gesellschaft fuer Gynaekologie und Geburtshilfe: Jahrestagung, Mayrofen, 1988. Eduard Gitsch & E. Reinold. (Journal: Gynaekologische Rundschau: Vol. 28, Suppl. 2, 1988). (Illus.). x, 278p. 1988. pap. 87.00 (*3-8055-4937-7*) S Karger.

Oesterreichische Gesellschaft fuer Gynaekologie und Geburtshilfe, Jahrestagung, Bregenz, June 1994: Journal: Gynaekologisch-geburtshilfliche Rundschau, 1994, Vol. 34, Supp. 1. Ed. by E. Reinold. (Illus.). viii, 214p. 1994. pap. 96.75 (*3-8055-6108-3*) S Karger.

Oesterreichische Gesellschaft fuer Gynaekologie und Geburtshilfe, Jahrestagung, Graz, Juni 1990: Journal: Gynaekologische Rundschau, Vol. 30, Suppl. 1, 1990. Ed. by Eduard Gitsch & E. Reinold. (Illus.). x, 260p. 1990. pap. 82.75 (*3-8055-5306-4*) S Karger.

Oestrogen Deficiency: Causes & Consequences. Robert W. Shaw. LC 96-16860. (Advances in Reproductive Endocrinology Ser.). 176p. 1996. 68.00 (*1-85070-719-7*) Prthnon Pub.

Oestrogens: Physiological & Clinical Aspects. F. Bidlingmaier & D. Knorr. (Pediatric & Adolescent Endocrinology Ser.: Vol. 4). (Illus.). 1978. 59.25 (*3-8055-2845-0*) S Karger.

Oetinger, Friedrich Ch. Vol. I: Lehrtafel der Prinzessin Antonia, 2 vols. Ed. by Friederich Haeussermann et al. (Texte zur Geschichte des Pietismus Ser.: Vol. 1, Sec. 7). (C). 1977. 242.30 (*3-11-004130-8*) De Gruyter.

Oetztaler und Stubaier Alpen. 2nd ed. F. Purtscheller. (Sammlung Geologischer Fuehrer Ser.: Band 53). (GER., Illus.). viii, 128p. 1978. spiral bd. 18.00 (*3-443-15022-5*, Pub. by Gebruder Borntraeger) Balogh.

Oeuf. Felicien Marceau. (FRE.). 160p. 1980. pap. 8.95 (*0-7859-4138-X*, 2070372383) Fr & Eur.

Oeufs de Porcelaine see China Eggs

Oeuvre. Emile Zola. (Coll. Diamant). 11.50 (*0-685-23953-5*) Fr & Eur.

Oeuvre. Emile Zola. 1975. write for info. (*0-318-63493-7*) Fr & Eur.

Oeuvre. Emile Zola. (FRE.). 1983. pap. 18.95 (*0-7859-2903-7*) Fr & Eur.

Oeuvre. Emile Zola. (FRE.). 440p. 1990. pap. 10.95 (*0-7859-1643-1*, 2080702785) Fr & Eur.

Oeuvre. Emile Zola. (Folio Ser.: No. 1437). (FRE.). 1975. pap. 14.95 (*2-07-037437-8*) Schoenhof.

Oeuvre Vol. 1: Satires; Le Lutrin. Nicolas Boileau. (FRE.). 1969. pap. 10.95 (*0-7859-3396-4*) Fr & Eur.

Oeuvre au Noir. Marguerite Yourcenar. (FRE.). 1976. pap. 13.95 (*0-8288-3807-0*, M5701) Fr & Eur.

Oeuvre au Noir. Marguerite Yourcenar. (Folio Ser.: No. 798). (FRE.). pap. 10.95 (*2-07-036798-3*) Schoenhof.

Oeuvre Complet de Eugene Delacroix: Peintures, Dessins, Gravures Lithographies. Alfred Robaut. LC 78-75310. (Graphic Arts, Painting & Sculpture Ser.). 1969. lib. bdg. 85.00 (*0-306-71628-3*) Da Capo.

Oeuvre de Francois Rabelais et la Culture Populaire au Moyen Age et sous Renaissance. Bakhtine. Tr. by Robel. (Bibliotheque des Idees Ser.). 26.95 (*0-685-34193-3*, F31460) Fr & Eur.

Oeuvre de Jean Prevost. Marc Bertrand. LC 68-64308. (U. C. Publ. in Modern Philology Ser.: Vol. 90). 133p. reprint ed. 41.30 (*0-8357-9634-5*, 201380500088) Bks Demand.

Oeuvre de Juste Aurele Meissonnier: The Complete Suite of Engravings of His Designs. Juste A. Meissonnier. LC 69-16909. (Illus.). 1978. reprint ed. 54.95 (*0-405-08785-3*, Pub. by Blom Pubns) Ayer.

Oeuvre de Pierre Loti et l'Esprit Fin de Siecle. C. M. Millward. 9.50 (*0-685-34266-2*) Fr & Eur.

Oeuvre d'Emil Zola. Brady. 29.95 (*0-685-37146-8*, F76750) Fr & Eur.

Oeuvre d'Henri de Saint-Simon & Saint Simon und die Okonomische Geschichtstehorie, 2 vols. Celestin Chalres et al. Ed. by J. P. Mayer. LC 78-67334. (European Political Thought Ser.). (FRE & GER.). 1979. reprint ed. lib. bdg. 28.95 (*0-405-11682-9*) Ayer.

Oeuvre Poetique. Leopold S. Senghor. (FRE.). 1980. pap. 19.95 (*0-7859-2717-4*) Fr & Eur.

Oeuvre Poetique. deluxe ed. Paul Claudel. Ed. by Jacques Petit. (FRE.). 1328p. 1957. 105.00 (*0-7859-3751-X*, 2070101436) Fr & Eur.

Oeuvre Poetique, 2 tomes, Tome I. Incl. Amers. Chronique. Eloges. Saint-John Perse, pseud. 1960. Vents. (Coll. Soleil Ser.). 1960. 11.95 (*0-685-35910-7*) Schoenhof.

Oeuvre Poetique, 2 tomes, Tome II. Saint-John Perse, pseud. (Coll. Soleil Ser.). 1960. 16.95 (*0-685-35911-5*) Schoenhof.

Oeuvre Romanesques, 5 tomes, Set. Jean-Paul Sartre. (FRE., Illus.). 350.00 (*0-685-36552-2*) Fr & Eur.

Oeuvre Romanesque, 8 vols., Set. Henry De Montherlant. 612.50 (*0-685-11433-3*) Fr & Eur.

Oeuvre Romanesque, 3 vols., Vol. 1: 1900-1919. Sidonie-Gabrielle Colette. (FRE.). 1989. pap. 60.00 (*0-7859-3027-2*) Fr & Eur.

Oeuvre Romanesque, 3 vols., Vol. 2: 1920-1940. Sidonie-Gabrielle Colette. (FRE.). 1989. pap. 60.00 (*0-7859-3028-0*) Fr & Eur.

Oeuvre Romanesque, 3 vols., Vol. 3: 1941-1949. Sidonie-Gabrielle Colette. (FRE.). 1989. pap. 60.00 (*0-7859-3029-9*) Fr & Eur.

Oeuvre Romanesque de Mark Aldanov: Revolution, Histoire, Hasard. Gervaise Tassis. (Slavica Helvetica Ser.: Vol. 48). (FRE.). 503p. 1995. 62.95 (*3-906753-75-1*, Pub. by P Lang) P Lang Pubng.

Oeuvres. Henri Bergson. 125.00 (*0-685-37204-9*) Fr & Eur.

Oeuvres. Rene Descartes. (FRE.). 1937. 99.50 (*0-8288-3425-3*, F36590) Fr & Eur.

Oeuvres. Denis Diderot. (FRE.). 1978. 95.00 (*0-8288-3434-2*, F46720) Fr & Eur.

Oeuvres. G. Fenelon. (FRE.). 1983. 120.00 (*0-8288-3445-8*, F1880) Fr & Eur.

Oeuvres. Julien Gracq. (POR.). 59.95 incl. audio (*0-685-21221-1*) Fr & Eur.

Oeuvres. Friedrich Holderlin. (FRE.). 1966. 95.00 (*0-8288-3504-7*, M5101) Fr & Eur.

Oeuvres. James Joyce. (FRE.). 1982. 125.00 (*0-8288-3510-1*, F11302) Fr & Eur.

Oeuvres. Rudyard Kipling. (FRE.). 1988. lib. bdg. 150.00 (*0-8288-3518-7*, F12807) Fr & Eur.

Oeuvres. V. Larbaud. (FRE.). 1957. lib. bdg. 110.00 (*0-8288-3519-5*, F10840) Fr & Eur.

Oeuvres. Saltykov-Chtchedrine Leskov. 1676p. 42.95 (*0-686-56534-7*) Fr & Eur.

Oeuvres. Saltykov-Chtchedrine Leskov & Chtchedri Leskov. Ed. by Andre Luneau. (FRE.). 1676p. 1967. lib. bdg. 110.00 (*0-7859-3764-1*, 2070103102) Fr & Eur.

Oeuvres. Malherbe. 1128p. 35.95 (*0-686-56536-3*) Fr & Eur.

Oeuvres. Marquis De Sade, pseud. (FRE.). 1990. lib. bdg. 125.00 (*0-8288-3533-0*) Fr & Eur.

Oeuvres. Pasternak. (FRE.). 1990. lib. bdg. 150.00 (*0-8288-3570-5*, F119390) Fr & Eur.

Oeuvres. Plato. (Vol. 1). (FRE.). 1940. lib. bdg. 95.00 (*0-8288-3572-1*, F17630) Fr & Eur.

Oeuvres. Plato. (Vol. 2). (FRE.). 1977. lib. bdg. 110.00 (*0-8288-3573-X*, F17180) Fr & Eur.

Oeuvres, 6 vols. Francois Rabelais. (FRE., Illus.). 400.00 (*0-686-54699-7*) Fr & Eur.

Oeuvres. Antoine de Saint-Exupery. (FRE.). 1987. lib. bdg. 85.00 (*0-8288-3534-9*, F123490) Fr & Eur.

Oeuvres. Saint Francois de Sales. Ed. by Roger Ravier. (FRE.). 2032p. 1969. lib. bdg. 140.00 (*0-7859-3758-7*, 2070102769) Fr & Eur.

Oeuvres. Jonathan Swift. (FRE.). 1988. lib. bdg. 120.00 (*0-8288-3540-3*, F49270) Fr & Eur.

Oeuvres. Jules Valles. (FRE.). 1975. lib. bdg. 105.00 (*0-8288-3581-0*, M2630) Fr & Eur.

Oeuvres. deluxe ed. Pierre De Beaumarchais. (FRE.). 1744p. 1988. 140.00 (*0-8288-3420-2*, F45970) Fr & Eur.

Oeuvres. deluxe ed. Pierre De Beaumarchais. (Pleiade Ser.). (FRE.). 1696p. 1988. 93.95 (*2-07-011137-7*) Schoenhof.

Oeuvres. deluxe ed. Jacques-Benigne Bossuet. Ed. by Velat & Champaailler. (FRE.). 1612p. 1971. 110.00 (*0-7859-4643-8*) Fr & Eur.

Oeuvres. deluxe ed. Theodore A. D'Aubigne. (Pleiade Ser.). (FRE.). 1664p. 1969. 110.00 (*0-8288-3418-0*, F28320) Fr & Eur.

Oeuvres. deluxe ed. Jean-Francois De Retz. Ed. by Marie-Therese Hipp & Michel Pernot. (FRE.). 1872p. 1984. 125.00 (*0-7859-3863-X*, 2070110281) Fr & Eur.

Oeuvres. deluxe ed. Denis Diderot. Ed. by Andre Billy. (Pleiade Ser.). (FRE.). 1989. 75.95 (*2-07-010173-8*) Schoenhof.

Oeuvres. deluxe ed. Antoine de Saint-Exupery. (Pleiade Ser.). (FRE.). 1044p. 1987. 63.95 (*2-07-010503-2*) Schoenhof.

Oeuvres. limited ed. Cydney Chadwick. 40p. (Orig.). 1995. pap. 10.00 (*0-9641837-4-9*) Texture Pr.

Oeuvres, 2 vols. Jean L. Balzac. lxviii, 1996p. reprint ed. write for info. (*0-318-71314-4*) G Olms Pubs.

Oeuvres. Joseph L. De Lagrange. xliii, 8063p. 1973. reprint ed. write for info. (*3-487-04710-1*) G Olms Pubs.

Oeuvres, 2 vols. in 1. Camille Desmoulins. LC 72-164282. reprint ed. 72.50 (*0-404-07124-4*) AMS Pr.

Oeuvres, 5 pts. in 1. Guillaume Du Vair. vi, 1241p. 1973. reprint ed. write for info. (*3-487-04589-3*) G Olms Pubs.

Oeuvres, 2 Vols. E. Laguerre. LC 70-125075. 1971. reprint ed. text 69.50 (*0-8284-0263-9*) Chelsea Pub.

Oeuvres. 3rd ed. Francois Villon. Ed. by Auguste Longon. (FRE.). 320p. 1977. pap. 28.95 (*0-7859-4575-X*) Fr & Eur.

Oeuvres, 14 vols., Set. Blaise Pascal & Leon Brunschvicg. (FRE.). 895.00 (*0-686-54849-3*) Fr & Eur.

Oeuvres, 3 vols., Set. Jean Racine. (FRE., Illus.). 450.00 (*0-686-54711-X*) Fr & Eur.

Oeuvres, 4 vols., Set. Jean Le Maire De Belges. 1790p. 1972. reprint ed. write for info. (*3-487-04348-3*) G Olms Pubs.

Oeuvres, 7 vols., Set. Gottfried Wilhelm Leibniz. ccliv, 3472p. 1969. reprint ed. write for info. (*0-318-71370-5*) G Olms Pubs.

Oeuvres, 4 vols., Set. Pierre L. Maupertius. liii, 1590p. 1974. reprint ed. write for info. (*3-487-01056-9*) G Olms Pubs.

Oeuvres, 8 vols., Set. Jean Racine. (FRE.). cxliv, 616p. 1973. reprint ed. write for info. (*3-487-05000-5*) G Olms Pubs.

Oeuvres, 50 vols., Set. Stendhal, pseud. (FRE.). 2581p. 1985. reprint ed. 3500.00 (*0-7859-1275-4*, 2051007292) Fr & Eur.

Oeuvres, Tome I. Incl. Bigote. Bigote. Bucoliques. Bucoliques. Cloportes. Coquecigrues. Jules Renard. Ed. by Leon Guichard. Coqueciqres. Cousin de Rose. Cousin de Rose. Crime de Village. Jules Renard. Ed. by Leon Guichard. Demande. Demande. Encornifleur. Histoires Naturelles. Histoires Naturelles. Huit Jours a la Campagne. Huit Jours a la Campagne. Lanterne Sourde. Jules Renard. Ed. by Leon Guichard. Lanterne Sourde. Maitresse. Maitresse. Monsieur Vernet. Monsieur Vernet. Nos Freres Farouches. Nos Freres Farouches. Oeil Clair. Oeil Clair. Pain de Menage. Pain de Menage. Plasir de Rompre. Plasir de Rompre. Poil de Carotte. Jules Renard. Ed. by Leon Guichard. Poil de Carotte. Jules Renard. Ed. by Leon Guichard. Poil de Carotte. Jules Renard. Ed. by Leon Guichard. Poil de Carotte. Jules Renard. Ed. by Leon Guichard. Ragotte. Ragotte. Roman Impromptu. Jules Renard. Ed. by Leon Guichard. Roman Impromptu. Jules Renard. Ed. by Leon Guichard. Sourires Pinces. Jules Renard. Ed. by Leon Guichard. Theatre. Vigneron dans Sa Vigne. Jules Renard. Ed. by Leon Guichard. Vigneron Dans Sa Vigne. X . . . Jules Renard. Ed. by Leon Guichard. X . . . write for info. (*0-318-63511-9*) Fr & Eur.

Oeuvres, Tome I. Incl. Bigote. Bigote. Bucoliques. Bucoliques. Cloportes. Coquecigrues. Jules Renard. Ed. by Leon Guichard. Coqueciqres. Cousin de Rose. Cousin de Rose. Crime de Village. Jules Renard. Ed. by Leon Guichard. Demande. Demande. Encornifleur. Histoires Naturelles. Histoires Naturelles. Huit Jours a la Campagne. Huit Jours a la Campagne. Lanterne Sourde. Jules Renard. Ed. by Leon Guichard. Lanterne Sourde. Maitresse. Maitresse. Monsieur Vernet. Monsieur Vernet. Nos Freres Farouches. Nos Freres Farouches. Oeil Clair. Oeil Clair. Pain de Menage. Pain de Menage. Plasir de Rompre. Plasir de Rompre. Poil de Carotte. Jules Renard. Ed. by Leon Guichard. Poil de Carotte. Jules Renard. Ed. by Leon Guichard. Poil de Carotte. Jules Renard. Ed. by Leon Guichard. Poil de Carotte. Jules Renard. Ed. by Leon Guichard. Ragotte. Ragotte. Roman Impromptu. Jules Renard. Ed. by Leon Guichard. Roman Impromptu. Jules Renard. Ed. by Leon Guichard. Sourires Pinces. Jules Renard. Ed. by Leon Guichard. Theatre. Vigneron dans Sa Vigne. Jules Renard. Ed. by Leon Guichard. Vigneron Dans Sa Vigne. X . . . Jules Renard. Ed. by Leon Guichard. X . . . (Pleiade Ser.). (FRE.). 68.95 (*2-07-010474-5*) Schoenhof.

Oeuvres, Tome I. Incl. Aurelia. Ed. by Dumesnil. Chimeres. Illumines. Nuits d'Octobre. Pandora. Petits Chateaux de Boheme. Promenades et Souvenirs. Ed. by Dumesnil. write for info. (*0-318-63502-X*) Fr & Eur.

Oeuvres, Tome I. deluxe ed. Incl. Ame et la Danse. Eupalinos. Histoires Brisees. Mauvaises Pensees et Autre. Mon Faust. Monsieur Teste. Pieces sur l'Art. Poesies, Melanges, Variete. Paul Valery. 1960. Tel quel. (Pleiade Ser.). (FRE.). 1960. 84.95 (*2-07-010576-8*) Schoenhof.

Oeuvres, Tome 1. deluxe ed. Sidonie-Gabrielle Colette. (Pleiade Ser.). (FRE.). 89.95 (*2-07-011079-6*) Schoenhof.

Oeuvres, Tome II. Jules Renard. Ed. by Guichard. (Pleiade Ser.). (FRE.). 61.95 (*2-07-010634-9*) Schoenhof.

Oeuvres, Tome 2. deluxe ed. Sidonie-Gabrielle Colette. (Pleiade Ser.). (FRE.). 1794p. 1986. 99.95 (*2-07-011101-6*) Schoenhof.

Oeuvres, Tome II. deluxe ed. Paul Valery. Ed. by Hytier. (Pleiade Ser.). (FRE.). 1960. 77.95 (*2-07-010577-6*) Schoenhof.

Oeuvres, Tome 3. deluxe ed. Sidonie-Gabrielle Colette. (Pleiade Ser.). (FRE.). 119.95 (*2-07-011215-2*) Schoenhof.

Oeuvres, Vol. 1. Hans Christian Andersen. (FRE.). 1648p. 1992. 185.00 (*0-7859-6512-2*) Fr & Eur.

Oeuvres, Vol. 1. Sidonie-Gabrielle Colette. Ed. by Claude Pichois. (FRE.). 1984. lib. bdg. 135.00 (*0-7859-3955-5*) Fr & Eur.

Oeuvres, Vol. 1. Joseph Conrad. (Pleiade Ser.). (FRE.). 1982. 110.00 (*0-8288-3465-2*, F60422) Fr & Eur.

Oeuvres, Vol. 1. Leon Daudet. (Pleiade Ser.). (FRE.). 1986. 120.00 (*0-8288-3471-7*, M10355) Fr & Eur.

Oeuvres, Vol. 1. Alexis De Tocqueville. Ed. by Jean Jardin. (FRE.). 1991. lib. bdg. 175.00 (*0-7859-3896-6*) Fr & Eur.

Oeuvres, Vol. 1. Gustave Flaubert. Ed. by Pierre Thibaudet. (FRE.). 1072p. 1988. lib. bdg. 105.00 (*0-7859-3754-4*, 2070102017) Fr & Eur.

Oeuvres, Vol. 1. Anatole France, pseud. (FRE.). 1984. 89.95 (*0-8288-3447-4*, F4020) Fr & Eur.

Oeuvres, Vol. 1. Arthur D. Gobineau. (FRE.). 1983. 120.00 (*0-8288-3487-3*, F15010) Fr & Eur.

Oeuvres, Vol. 1. Karl Marx. (FRE.). 1963. lib. bdg. 110.00 (*0-8288-3558-6*, F16290) Fr & Eur.

Oeuvres, Vol. 1. Jules Renard. Ed. by Leon Guichard. (FRE.). 1120p. 1970. lib. bdg. 105.00 (*0-7859-3784-6*, 2070104745) Fr & Eur.

Oeuvres, Vol. 1. Charles-Augustin Sainte-Beuve. Ed. by Jacques D. Leroy. (FRE.). 1300p. 1950. lib. bdg. 100.00 (*0-7859-3788-9*, 2070104931) Fr & Eur.

Oeuvres, Vol. 1. Paul Valery. Ed. by Marie-Therese Hytier. 1957. lib. bdg. 130.00 (*0-7859-3802-8*) Fr & Eur.

Oeuvres, 2 vols., Vol. 1. deluxe ed. Gustave Flaubert. Ed. by Dumesnil & Albert Thibaudet. (Pleiade Ser.). (FRE.). 64.95 (*2-07-010201-7*) Schoenhof.

Oeuvres, 2 vols., Vol. 1. deluxe ed. Gerard De Nerval. Ed. by Beguin & Richer. (Pleiade Ser.). (FRE.). 99.95 (*2-07-011067-2*) Schoenhof.

Oeuvres, Vol. 2. Sidonie-Gabrielle Colette. Ed. by Claude Pichois. (FRE.). 1986. lib. bdg. 140.00 (*0-7859-3872-9*) Fr & Eur.

Oeuvres, Vol. 2. Joseph Conrad. (Pleiade Ser.). (FRE.). 1985. 115.00 (*0-8288-3466-0*, F76970) Fr & Eur.

Oeuvres, Vol. 2. Leon Daudet. (Pleiade Ser.: No. 2). (FRE.). 1990. 120.00 (*0-8288-3472-5*, F98140) Fr & Eur.

Oeuvres, Vol. 2. Alexis De Tocqueville. Ed. by Andre Jardin. (FRE.). 1992. lib. bdg. 155.00 (*0-7859-3901-6*) Fr & Eur.

Oeuvres, Vol. 2. Gustave Flaubert. 1056p. 1988. 95.00 (*0-7859-5607-7*, 2070102025) Fr & Eur.

Oeuvres, Vol. 2. Anatole France, pseud. (FRE.). 1987. 89.95 (*0-8288-3448-2*, F29290) Fr & Eur.

Oeuvres, Vol. 2. Arthur D. Gobineau. (FRE.). 1983. 110.00 (*0-8288-3488-1*, F15030) Fr & Eur.

Oeuvres, Vol. 2. Rudyard Kipling. Ed. by Pierre Coustillas. (FRE.). 1992. lib. bdg. 175.00 (*0-7859-3902-4*) Fr & Eur.

Oeuvres, Vol. 2. Karl Marx. (FRE.). 1968. lib. bdg. 110.00 (*0-8288-3559-4*, F16300) Fr & Eur.

Oeuvres, 2 vols., Vol. 2. Gerard De Nerval. Ed. by Beguin & Richer. (Pleiade Ser.). (FRE.). 88.95 (*2-07-011029-X*) Schoenhof.

Oeuvres, Vol. 2. Jules Renard. Ed. by Leon Guichard. (FRE.). 1971. 100.00 (*0-7859-3809-5*) Fr & Eur.

Oeuvres, Vol. 2. Paul Valery. Ed. by Jean Hytier. 1988. lib. bdg. 125.00 (*0-7859-3803-6*) Fr & Eur.

An Asterisk (*) at the beginning of an entry indicates that the title is appearing for the first time.

Oeuvres, Vol. 2. Jules Valles. Ed. by Roger Bellet. (FRE.). 1989. lib. bdg. 185.00 (*0-7859-3889-3*) Fr & Eur.
Oeuvres, 2 vols., Vol. 2. deluxe ed. Gustave Flaubert. Ed. by Dumesnil & Albert Thibaudet. (Pleiade Ser.). (FRE.). 64.95 (*2-07-010202-5*) Schoenhof.
Oeuvres, Vol. 3. Sidonie-Gabrielle Colette. Ed. by Claude Pichois. (FRE.). 1986. lib. bdg. 195.00 (*0-7859-3898-2*) Fr & Eur.
Oeuvres, Vol. 3. J. Conrad. (Pleiade Ser.). (FRE.). 1987. 135.00 (*0-8288-3467-9*, F41030) Fr & Eur.
Oeuvres, Vol. 3. Anatole France, pseud. Ed. by Marie-Claire Bancquart. (FRE.). 1991. lib. bdg. 150.00 (*0-7859-3931-8*) Fr & Eur.
Oeuvres, Vol. 3. Arthur D. Gobineau. (FRE.). 1987. 135.00 (*0-8288-3489-X*, F63180) Fr & Eur.
Oeuvres, Vol. 3. Karl Marx. (FRE.). 1982. lib. bdg. 125.00 (*0-8288-3560-8*, F16380) Fr & Eur.
Oeuvres, Vol. 4. Joseph Conrad. (Pleiade Ser.). (FRE.). 1989. 135.00 (*0-8288-3468-7*, F41060) Fr & Eur.
Oeuvres, Vol. 5. Joseph Conrad. Ed. by Maurice Monod. (FRE.). 1992. lib. bdg. 165.00 (*0-7859-3956-3*) Fr & Eur.
Oeuvres: Avec: Le Cinquieme Livre, Vol. 5. Francois Rabelais. Ed. by Jean Plattard. (FRE.). 400p. 1948. pap. 12.95 (*0-7859-1459-5*, 2251360859) Fr & Eur.
Oeuvres: Avec: Le Quart-Livre, Vol. 4. Francois Rabelais. Ed. by Jean Plattard. (FRE.). 338p. 1959. pap. 17.95 (*0-7859-1458-7*, 2251360840) Fr & Eur.
Oeuvres: Avec: Le Tiers-Livre, Vol. 3. Francois Rabelais. Ed. by Jean Plattard. (FRE.). 78p. 1961. pap. 17.95 (*0-7859-1457-9*, 2251360832) Fr & Eur.
Oeuvres: Avec: Les Bijoux Indiscrets. Denis Diderot. (FRE.). 1480p. 1978. 105.00 (*0-7859-1097-2*, 2070101738) Fr & Eur.
Oeuvres: Collected Papers, 3 vols., Set. Jean-Pierre Serre. 2088p. 1986. 425.00 (*0-387-15621-6*) Spr-Verlag.
Oeuvres: De la Recherche de la Verite, Conversations Chretiennes, Vol. 1. Nicolas Malebranche. write for info. (*0-318-52179-2*) Fr & Eur.
Oeuvres: Economie: Economie et Philosophie, Salaire, Principes d'un Critique de l'Economie Politique, Le Capital (Livre deuxieme e Livre Troisieme), Vol. 2. Karl Marx. 2112p. 52.50 (*0-686-56539-8*) Fr & Eur.
Oeuvres: Economie: Le Capital, Livre Premier (1867), Le Manifeste Communiste, Misere de la Philosophie, etc., Vol. 1. Karl Marx. 2000p. 45.00 (*0-686-56538-X*) Fr & Eur.
Oeuvres: Gulliver, Conte du Tonneau, Journal a Stella. Jonathan Swift. (FRE.). 1984p. 46.95 (*0-686-56576-2*) Fr & Eur.
Oeuvres: Hyperion, Empedocle, Poemes, Essais, Lettres. Friedrich Holderlin. 1300p. 37.50 (*0-686-56528-2*) Fr & Eur.
Oeuvres: Introduction a la Vie Devote & Traite de l'Amour de Dieu, etc. Saint Francois de Sales. 2024p. 46.95 (*0-686-56512-6*) Fr & Eur.
Oeuvres: Le Lais, le Testament, Poesies Diverses, 2 vols. 2nd ed. Francois Villon. Ed. by Andre Lanly. (FRE.). 432p. 1969. pap. 36.95 (*0-7859-5508-9*) Fr & Eur.
Oeuvres: Le Malheur d'Avoir de l'Esprit un Heros de Notre Temps, Boris Godounov. Griboyedev et al. (FRE.). 1973. 99.50 (*0-8288-3501-2*, M3527) Fr & Eur.
Oeuvres: Pantagruel, Vol. 2. Francois Rabelais. Ed. by Jean Plattard. (FRE.). 220p. 1959. pap. 17.95 (*0-7859-1456-0*, 2251360824) Fr & Eur.
Oeuvres: Poesies - Lettres. Malherbe. (FRE.). 1971. lib. bdg. 89.95 (*0-8288-3551-9*, F39530) Fr & Eur.
Oeuvres: Portraits, Litteraires, Portraits de Femmes, Vol. 2. Charles-Augustin Saint-Beuve. 1690p. lib. bdg. 115.00 (*0-7859-3922-9*) Fr & Eur.
Oeuvres: Premiers Lundis, Portraits Literaires, Vol. 1. Charles-Augustin Saint-Beuve. 1300p. 37.50 (*0-686-56562-2*) Fr & Eur.
Oeuvres: Sade, Tome 1. deluxe ed. Marquis De Sade, pseud et al. (Pleiade Ser.). (FRE.). 99.95 (*2-07-011190-3*) Schoenhof.
Oeuvres: Theatre Complet-Recits (1882-1886), Vol. 1. Anton Chekhov. 1560p. 41.50 (*0-686-56579-7*) Fr & Eur.
Oeuvres Tome 1: Voyages, Ecrites Politiques et Academiques... deluxe ed. Alexis De Tocqueville. (Pleiade Ser.). (FRE.). 99.95 (*2-07-011213-6*) Schoenhof.
Oeuvres Tome 2: De la Democratie en Amerique I et II. deluxe ed. Alexis De Tocqueville. Ed. by Jean-Claude Lamberti. (Pleiade Ser.). (FRE.). 1191p. 1992. 99.95 (*2-07-011228-4*) Schoenhof.
Oeuvres Vol. 1: Poesies. Arthur Rimbaud. (FRE.). pap. 3.95 (*0-7859-2992-4*) Fr & Eur.
Oeuvres Vol. 1: Theatre. Anton Chekhov. (Pleiade Ser.). (FRE.). 1970. lib. bdg. 105.00 (*0-8288-3544-6*, M5194) Fr & Eur.
Oeuvres Vol. 2: Epitres; L'Art Poetique; Oeuvres Diverses. Nicolas Boileau. (FRE.). 1969. pap. 10.95 (*0-7859-2965-7*) Fr & Eur.
Oeuvres Vol. 2: Recits de 1887-1892. Anton Chekhov. (Pleiade Ser.). (FRE.). 1970. lib. bdg. 95.00 (*0-8288-3545-4*, M5195) Fr & Eur.
Oeuvres Vol. 2: Une Saison en Enfer; Verse Nouveaux. Arthur Rimbaud. (FRE.). 1989. pap. 10.95 (*0-7859-2993-2*) Fr & Eur.
Oeuvres Vol. 3: Illuminations - Correspondence, 1873-1891. Arthur Rimbaud. (FRE.). 1989. pap. 10.95 (*0-7859-2995-9*) Fr & Eur.
Oeuvres Vol. 3: Recits de 1892-1903. Anton Chekhov. (Pleiade Ser.). (FRE.). 1971. lib. bdg. 95.00 (*0-8288-3546-2*, F19130) Fr & Eur.
Oeuvres - Collected Papers, 3 vols. Armand Borel. 2240p. 1983. 350.00 (*0-387-12126-9*) Spr-Verlag.
***Oeuvres - Collected Papers, 1985-1998, Vol. 4.** J.-P. Serre. xiii, 660p. 1999. 159.00 (*3-540-65683-9*) Spr-Verlag.
Oeuvres Autobiographiques. L. Mauriac. (FRE.). 1990. lib. bdg. 125.00 (*0-8288-3561-6*, F89430) Fr & Eur.
Oeuvres Autobiographiques. George Sand. Ed. by Georges Lubin. Incl. Tome I. Histoire de Ma Vie. 40.95 Tome II. Histoire de Ma Vie (Fin) 35.95 (Pleiade Ser.). write for info. (*0-318-52141-5*) Fr & Eur.
Oeuvres Autobiographiques, Vol. 1. George Sand. (FRE.). 1978. lib. bdg. 99.50 (*0-8288-3535-7*, F72860) Fr & Eur.
Oeuvres Autobiographiques, Vol. 2. George Sand. (FRE.). 1978. lib. bdg. 110.00 (*0-8288-3536-5*, F72861) Fr & Eur.
Oeuvres Badines et Morales, Historiques et Philosophiques, 4 vols., Set. Jacques Cazotte. cxxix, 2118p. 1976. reprint ed. 400.00 (*3-487-06149-X*) G Olms Pubs.
Oeuvres Choisies, 2 vols. Marguerite de Navarre. Ed. by H. P. Clive. Incl. Vol. 1. Poemes. LC 68-12125. (FRE.). 1968. pap. text 6.95 Vol. 2. Theatre et Nouvelles. LC 68-12125. (FRE.). 1968. pap. text 6.95 (*0-89197-323-0*); LC 68-12125. (Medieval French Literature Ser.). (FRE.). 1968. pap. text. write for info. (*0-318-53720-6*) Irvington.
Oeuvres Choisies, 3 vols., Set. Claude-Henri Saint-Simon. xii, 1107p. 1973. reprint ed. write for info. (*3-487-04706-3*) G Olms Pubs.
Oeuvres Choisies du Prince de Ligne: Nouvelle Anthologie Critique. De Ligne. Ed. by Basil Guy. (Stanford French & Italian Studies: No. 13). (FRE.). xlvi, 282p. 1978. pap. 56.50 (*0-915838-28-1*) Anma Libri.
Oeuvres Choisies, Poemes et Prose. Walt Whitman. Tr. by Jules Laforgue et al. LC 77-11498. reprint ed. 37.50 (*0-404-16357-2*) AMS Pr.
Oeuvres Complete, Vol. 1. Andre Breton. Ed. by Marguerite Bonnet. (FRE.). 1988. lib. bdg. 155.00 (*0-7859-3883-4*) Fr & Eur.
Oeuvres Completes. Charles Baudelaire. (FRE.). 1980. pap. 48.95 (*0-7859-3034-5*) Fr & Eur.
Oeuvres Completes. Nicolas Boileau. Ed. by Marcelle Escal. (FRE.). 1360p. 1966. lib. bdg. 105.00 (*0-7859-3743-9*, 2070100693) Fr & Eur.
Oeuvres Completes. Rene Char. (Pleiade Ser.). (FRE.). 1983. 110.00 (*0-8288-3457-1*, F15070) Fr & Eur.
Oeuvres Completes. Andre Chenier. Ed. by Laurent Walter. (FRE.). 1120p. 1940. lib. bdg. 105.00 (*0-7859-3750-1*, 2070101320) Fr & Eur.
Oeuvres Completes. Tristan Corbiere-Cros. Ed. by Michel Forestier. (FRE.). 1970. lib. bdg. 105.00 (*0-7859-3919-9*) Fr & Eur.
Oeuvres Completes. Pierre Corneille. (FRE.). 1970. 59.95 (*0-8288-9169-9*, F35830) Fr & Eur.
Oeuvres Completes. Courier. (Pleiade Ser.). (FRE.). 1951. 85.00 (*0-8288-3469-5*, F59620) Fr & Eur.
Oeuvres Completes. Dante Alighieri. 1912p. 86.95 (*0-686-56492-8*) Fr & Eur.
Oeuvres Completes. Jean De La Bruyere. Ed. by Julien Benda. (FRE.). 768p. 1978. lib. bdg. 95.00 (*0-7859-3760-9*, 2070102947) Fr & Eur.
Oeuvres Completes. Jean De La Bruyere. Ed. by Benda. (Pleiade Ser.). (FRE.). 1935. 64.95 (*2-07-010294-7*) Schoenhof.
Oeuvres Completes. Pierre-Ambroise De Laclos. Ed. by Etienne Versini. (FRE.). 1979. lib. bdg. 125.00 (*0-7859-3841-9*) Fr & Eur.
Oeuvres Completes. Isidore De Lautreamont. Ed. by Germain Nouveau. (FRE.). 1460p. 1973. pap. 17.95 (*0-7859-4682-9*) Fr & Eur.
Oeuvres Completes. Alfred De Musset. 944p. 1963. 25.00 (*0-686-55553-8*) Fr & Eur.
Oeuvres Completes, 7 vols. in 8. Louis-Claude De Saint-Martin. 1975. write for info. (*0-318-71406-X*) G Olms Pubs.
Oeuvres Completes. Eugene Fromentin. (FRE.). 1984. 115.00 (*0-8288-3449-0*, F5090) Fr & Eur.
Oeuvres Completes. Nikolai Vasilevich Gogol. 2080p. 46.95 (*0-686-56516-9*) Fr & Eur.
Oeuvres Completes. Nikolai Vasilevich Gogol. (FRE.). 1966. 120.00 (*0-8288-3492-X*, F10159) Fr & Eur.
Oeuvres Completes. Graco. (FRE.). 1989. 150.00 (*0-8288-3494-6*, F20170) Fr & Eur.
Oeuvres Completes. Herodote-Thucydide. (FRE.). 1904p. 1973. lib. bdg. 120.00 (*0-7859-3759-5*, 2070102777) Fr & Eur.
Oeuvres Completes, 2 tomes. Jean de La Fontaine. Incl. Tome I. Fables, Contes et Nouvelles. 99.95 (*2-07-011202-0*); Tome II. Oeuvres Diverses. deluxe ed. 62.95 (*2-07-010297-1*); (Pleiade Ser.). write for info. (*0-318-52142-3*) Schoenhof.
Oeuvres Completes. Francois de La Rochefoucauld. Incl. Dernieres Oeuvres. 95.00 Tome Recapitulatif (1910-1965) 95.00: 1910-1929. 95.00: 1929-1934. 95.00: 1934-1938. 95.00: 1938-1946. 95.00: 1947-1951. 95.00: 1952-1957. 95.00: 1957-1965. 95.00 write for info. (*0-318-52163-6*) Fr & Eur.
Oeuvres Completes. Francois de La Rochefoucauld. Ed. by Robert Martin-Chauffier. (FRE.). 1056p. 1935. lib. bdg. 110.00 (*0-7859-3762-5*, 2070103013) Fr & Eur.
Oeuvres Completes. Isidore de Lautreamont. 428p. 1970. 19.95 (*0-686-54284-3*) Fr & Eur.
Oeuvres Completes. Lautreamont-Nouveau. Ed. by Gerard Walzer. (FRE.). 1488p. 1970. lib. bdg. 110.00 (*0-7859-3763-3*, 2070103048) Fr & Eur.
Oeuvres Completes. Niccolo Machiavelli. (FRE.). 1978. lib. bdg. 105.00 (*0-8288-3524-1*, F30070) Fr & Eur.
Oeuvres Completes. Nicolas Malebranche. (FRE.). 1978. lib. bdg. 105.00 (*0-8288-3550-0*, M5422) Fr & Eur.
Oeuvres Completes. Michel de Montaigne. Ed. by Albert Thibaudet. (FRE.). 1824p. 1962. lib. bdg. 125.00 (*0-7859-3767-6*, 2070103633) Fr & Eur.
Oeuvres Completes, 3 tomes. Alfred Musset. Ed. by Allem. Incl. Tome I. Poesies Completes. 54.95 (*2-07-010387-0*); Tome II. Theatre Complete. deluxe ed. 99.95 (*2-07-011180-6*); Tome III. Oeuvres Completes en Prose. 59.95 (*2-07-010389-7*); (Pleiade Ser.). (FRE.). write for info. (*0-318-52143-1*) Schoenhof.
Oeuvres Completes. Saint-John Perse, pseud. (FRE.). 1987. lib. bdg. 110.00 (*0-7859-3818-4*) Fr & Eur.
Oeuvres Completes. Plaute. (FRE.). 1971. lib. bdg. 95.00 (*0-8288-3574-8*, F40040) Fr & Eur.
Oeuvres Completes. Plaute & Terence. 1512p. 41.50 (*0-686-56550-9*) Fr & Eur.
Oeuvres Completes. Francois Rabelais. Ed. by Jacques Boulanger. (FRE.). 1072p. 1978. lib. bdg. 100.00 (*0-7859-3780-3*, 2070104702) Fr & Eur.
Oeuvres Completes. Raymond Radiguet. 1978. 75.00 (*0-686-54719-5*) Fr & Eur.
Oeuvres Completes. Arthur Rimbaud. Ed. by Antoine Adam. (FRE.). 1312p. 1972. lib. bdg. 105.00 (*0-7859-3785-4*, 2070104761) Fr & Eur.
Oeuvres Completes. Baruch Spinoza. 1636p. 42.95 (*0-686-56571-1*) Fr & Eur.
Oeuvres Completes. Baruch Spinoza. (FRE.). 1955. lib. bdg. 105.00 (*0-8288-3539-X*, F33534) Fr & Eur.
Oeuvres Completes, 2 vols. Stendhal, pseud. (Illus.). 22.50 (*0-685-73313-0*) Fr & Eur.
Oeuvres Completes. Tacitus. (FRE.). 1991. lib. bdg. 150.00 (*0-8288-3541-1*, F122980) Fr & Eur.
Oeuvres Completes, 11 vols. Auguste de Villiers De L'Isle-Adam. (FRE.). 3490p. 1970. 795.00 (*0-7859-5503-8*) Fr & Eur.
Oeuvres Completes, 2 tomes. deluxe ed. Adam Auguste de Villiers de l'Isle. (Pleiade Ser.). (FRE.). 179.95 (*2-07-011103-2*) Schoenhof.
Oeuvres Completes. deluxe ed. Andre Chenier. (Pleiade Ser.). (FRE.). 67.95 (*2-07-010132-0*) Schoenhof.
Oeuvres Completes. deluxe ed. Charles Cros & Tristan Corbiere. (Pleiade Ser.). (FRE.). 1512p. 63.95 (*2-07-010155-X*) Schoenhof.
Oeuvres Completes. deluxe ed. Dante Alighieri. (FRE.). 1920p. 1988. 125.00 (*0-8288-3470-9*, M5089) Fr & Eur.
Oeuvres Completes. deluxe ed. Choderlos De Laclos. Ed. by Allen. (Pleiade Ser.). 1943. 72.95 (*2-07-010937-2*) Schoenhof.
Oeuvres Completes. deluxe ed. Comte D. Lautreamont, pseud. (Pleiade Ser.). (FRE.). 77.95 (*2-07-010304-8*) Schoenhof.
Oeuvres Completes. deluxe ed. Stephane Mallarme. Ed. by Mondor & Georges Jean-Aubry. (Pleiade Ser.). (FRE.). 1945. 77.95 (*2-07-010326-9*) Schoenhof.
Oeuvres Completes. deluxe ed. Michel de Montaigne. Ed. by Albert Thibaudet & Rat. (Pleiade Ser.). (FRE.). 85.95 (*2-07-010363-3*) Schoenhof.
Oeuvres Completes. deluxe ed. Blaise Pascal. Ed. by Chevalier. (Pleiade Ser.). (FRE.). 1936. 73.95 (*2-07-010432-X*) Schoenhof.
Oeuvres Completes. deluxe ed. Saint-John Perse, pseud. (Pleiade Ser.). (FRE.). 1972p. 1982. 70.95 (*2-07-010736-1*) Schoenhof.
Oeuvres Completes. deluxe ed. Jacques Prevert. (FRE.). 1536p. 1993. 150.00 (*0-7859-0965-6*, 2070112306) Fr & Eur.
Oeuvres Completes. deluxe ed. Francois Rabelais. Ed. by Boulenger & Scheler. (Pleiade Ser.). (FRE.). 1934. 63.95 (*2-07-010470-2*) Schoenhof.
Oeuvres Completes. deluxe ed. Arthur Rimbaud. Ed. by Renneville & Moquet. (Pleiade Ser.). (FRE.). 1946. 68.95 (*2-07-010476-1*) Schoenhof.
Oeuvres Completes. fac. ed. Adam De la Halle. Ed. by Edmond De Coussemaker. (FRE., Illus.). 516p. 1970. lib. bdg. 85.00 (*0-8450-1003-4*) Broude.
Oeuvres Completes. Jacques C. Chambonnieres. Ed. by Paul Brunold & Andre Tessier. Tr. by Denise Restout. (Illus.). 170p. 1965. reprint ed. lib. bdg. 75.00 (*0-8450-1001-8*) Broude.
Oeuvres Completes, 14 vols. in 7. Claude A. Helvetius. xxviii, 3514p. 1969. reprint ed. write for info. (*0-318-71350-0*) G Olms Pubs.
Oeuvres Completes. Suger, pseud. xxiii, 486p. 1979. reprint ed. write for info. (*3-487-06862-1*) G Olms Pubs.
Oeuvres Completes. Francois Villon. LC 75-178562. reprint ed. 55.00 (*0-404-56681-2*) AMS Pr.
Oeuvres Completes, 3 vols. Francois Villon. 1045p. 1967. reprint ed. pap. 175.00 (*0-7859-5509-7*) Fr & Eur.
Oeuvres Completes, 1. Charles Baudelaire. Ed. by Le Dantec. (Pleiade Ser.). 72.95 (*2-07-010167-3*) Schoenhof.
Oeuvres Completes, 2 tomes, 1. deluxe ed. Charles-Louis De Montesquieu. Ed. by Roger Caillois. (Pleiade Ser.). (FRE.). 84.95 (*2-07-010365-X*) Schoenhof.
Oeuvres Completes, 2. Charles Baudelaire. Ed. by Le Dantec. (Pleiade Ser.). 65.95 (*2-07-010853-8*) Schoenhof.
Oeuvres Completes, 2 tomes, 2. deluxe ed. Charles-Louis De Montesquieu. Ed. by Roger Caillois. (Pleiade Ser.). (FRE.). 88.95 (*2-07-010366-8*) Schoenhof.
Oeuvres Completes, 2 tomes, Set. Incl. Tome I. Theatre - Poesies. deluxe ed. Jean Racine. Ed. by Picard. (FRE.). 64.95 (*2-07-010471-0*); Tome II. Prose. deluxe ed. (FRE.). 63.95 (*2-07-010472-9*); (Pleiade Ser.). (FRE.). write for info. (*0-685-34025-2*) Schoenhof.
Oeuvres Completes, 24 tomes, Set. Honore de Balzac. 2500.00 (*0-685-34067-8*) Fr & Eur.
Oeuvres Completes, 16 vols., Set. Sidonie-Gabrielle Colette. (FRE.). 1973. 995.00 (*0-7859-1164-2*, 2080606832) Fr & Eur.
Oeuvres Completes, 12 tomes, Set. Alfred De Musset. (Illus.). 850.00 (*0-685-34952-7*); 1487.50 (*0-685-34953-5*) Fr & Eur.
Oeuvres Completes, 2 tomes, Set. Gustave Flaubert. Ed. by Andre Masson. (Coll. L'Integrale). 75.00 (*0-685-34896-2*) Fr & Eur.
Oeuvres Completes, 30 tomes, Set. Marquis De Sade, pseud. 350.00 (*0-685-34060-0*) Fr & Eur.
Oeuvres Completes, 16 tomes, Set. Guy de Maupassant. Ed. by Pia. 2450.00 (*0-685-34942-X*) Fr & Eur.
Oeuvres Completes, 11 tomes, Set. Moliere. Ed. by Meyer. (Illus.). 850.00 (*0-685-34234-4*) Fr & Eur.
Oeuvres Completes, 12 vols., Set. Alfred Musset. (FRE., Illus.). 300p. 1969. 1995.00 (*0-8288-9648-8*, F69130) Fr & Eur.
Oeuvres Completes, 10 tomes, Set. Ernest Renan. Ed. by Henriette Psichari. 175.00 (*0-685-34960-8*) Fr & Eur.
Oeuvres Completes, 18 tomes, Set. Voltaire. 275.00 (*0-685-34062-7*) Fr & Eur.
Oeuvres Completes, 14 vols. in 7, Set. Joseph-Marie De Maistre. clx, 7056p. 1983. reprint ed. write for info. (*3-487-07361-7*) G Olms Pubs.
Oeuvres Completes, 4 vols., Set. Alfred Jarry. (FRE.). 2484p. 1992. reprint ed. 795.00 (*0-7859-5348-5*) Fr & Eur.
Oeuvres Completes, Tome I. Incl. Botanique. Confessions: Autre Textes Auto Biographiques. Jean-Jacques Rousseau. (FRE.). 1964. Contes et Apologues. Contes et Apologues. Education. Emile. Essais. (FRE.). Essais Litteraires. (FRE.). Essais Litteraires. (FRE.). Essais Politiques. (FRE.). Julie du la Nouvelle Heloise. Julie ou la Nouvelle Heloise. Morale. Poesies. Poesies. Theatre. (Pleiade Ser.). (FRE.). 1964. 92.95 (*2-07-010488-5*) Schoenhof.
Oeuvres Completes, Tome I. Jean Genet. (Gallimard Ser.). (FRE.). 1952. pap. 57.95 (*2-07-022723-5*) Schoenhof.
Oeuvres Completes, Tome 1. deluxe ed. Incl. Condition Humaine. Andre Malraux. 1989. Conquerants. Andre Malraux. 1989. Espoir. (FRE.). (Pleiade Ser.). (FRE.). 1989. 99.95 (*2-07-011142-3*) Schoenhof.
Oeuvres Completes, Tome 1. deluxe ed. Charles Baudelaire. (Pleiade Ser.). (FRE.). 1604p. 1975. 85.95 (*2-07-010829-5*) Schoenhof.
Oeuvres Completes, Tome 1. deluxe ed. Andre Breton. (Pleiade Ser.). (FRE.). 1798p. 1988. 99.95 (*2-07-011138-5*) Schoenhof.
Oeuvres Completes, Tome 1. deluxe ed. Pierre Corneille. (Pleiade Ser.). (FRE.). 1769p. 1980. 76.95 (*2-07-010946-1*) Schoenhof.
Oeuvres Completes, Tome 1. deluxe ed. Alfred Jarry. (Pleiade Ser.). (FRE.). 68.95 (*2-07-010746-9*) Schoenhof.
Oeuvres Completes, Tome 1. deluxe ed. Raymond Queneau. (Pleiade Ser.). (FRE.). 109.95 (*2-07-011168-7*) Schoenhof.
Oeuvres Completes, Tome II. Incl. Comment Jouer le Balcon. Saint Genet, Comedien et Martyr. Jean-Paul Sartre. (FRE.). (Gallimard Ser.). (FRE.). 1953. Set pap. 48.95 (*2-07-022724-3*) Schoenhof.
Oeuvres Completes, Tome II. Incl. Botanique. Confessions: Autre Textes Auto Biographiques. Jean-Jacques Rousseau. (FRE.). 1964. Contes et Apologues. Contes et Apologues. Education. Emile. Essais. (FRE.). Essais Litteraires. (FRE.). Essais Litteraires. (FRE.). Essais Politiques. (FRE.). Julie du la Nouvelle Heloise. Julie ou la Nouvelle Heloise. Morale. Poesies. Poesies. Theatre. 1964. write for info. (*0-318-63548-8*) Fr & Eur.
Oeuvres Completes, Tome II. Jean-Jacques Rousseau. Ed. by Andre Raymont. (FRE.). 1961. lib. bdg. 130.00 (*0-7859-3954-7*) Fr & Eur.
Oeuvres Completes, Tome II. Jean-Jacques Rousseau. Ed. by Gagnebin & Andre Raymont. (Pleiade Ser.). (FRE.). 1964. 88.95 (*2-07-010489-3*) Schoenhof.
Oeuvres Completes, Tome 2. deluxe ed. Pierre Corneille. (Pleiade Ser.). (FRE.). 82.95 (*2-07-011083-4*) Schoenhof.
Oeuvres Completes, Tome 2. deluxe ed. Alfred Jarry. (Pleiade Ser.). (FRE.). 1011p. 1987. 87.95 (*2-07-011127-X*) Schoenhof.
Oeuvres Completes, Tome III. Jean Genet. (Gallimard Ser.). (FRE.). 1953. pap. 44.95 (*2-07-022725-1*) Schoenhof.
Oeuvres Completes, Tome III. Marcel Pagnol. pap. 9.95 (*0-685-35902-6*) Fr & Eur.
Oeuvres Completes, Tome III. Jean-Jacques Rousseau. Ed. by Gagnebin & Andre Raymont. (Pleiade Ser.). (FRE.). 1964. 89.95 (*2-07-010490-7*) Schoenhof.
Oeuvres Completes, Tome 3. deluxe ed. Pierre Corneille. (Pleiade Ser.). (FRE.). 1749p. 1987. 88.95 (*2-07-011121-0*) Schoenhof.
Oeuvres Completes, Tome 3. deluxe ed. Alfred Jarry. (Pleiade Ser.). (FRE.). 1988. 89.95 (*2-07-011144-X*) Schoenhof.
Oeuvres Completes, Tome III. deluxe ed. Jean-Jacques Rousseau. (FRE.). 2224p. 1964. 125.00 (*0-7859-1622-9*, 2070104907) Fr & Eur.
Oeuvres Completes, 4 tomes, Tome IV. Incl. Cesar. Cinematurgie. Fabien. Marcel Pagnol. pap. Jofroi. Marcel Pagnol. pap. Judas. Marcel Pagnol. pap. Merlusse. Set pap. 9.95 (*0-685-35903-4*) Fr & Eur.
Oeuvres Completes, Tome IV. Incl. Balcon. Jean Gebet. 1953. Ce qui Est Reste d'un Rembrant Dechire en Petits Carres. Jean Gebet. (FRE.). 1953. Comment Jouer le Balcon. Comment Jouer les Bonnes. Etrange Mot D'... Jean Gebet. 1953. Haute Surveillance. Lettres a Roger Blin. 1953. write for info. (*0-318-63539-9*) Fr & Eur.
Oeuvres Completes, Tome IV. Jean Genet. (Gallimard Ser.). (FRE.). 1953. pap. 29.95 (*2-07-027030-0*) Schoenhof.
Oeuvres Completes, Tome IV. deluxe ed. Jean-Jacques Rousseau. (FRE.). 2184p. 1969. write for info. (*0-7859-1623-7*, 2070104915) Fr & Eur.
Oeuvres Completes, Tome V. Jean Genet. (Gallimard Ser.). (FRE.). 1979. pap. 29.95 (*2-07-028671-1*) Schoenhof.
Oeuvres Completes, Vol. 1. Adam Auguste de Villiers de l'Isle & Pierre-Georges Castex. (FRE.). 1986. lib. bdg. 140.00 (*0-7859-3866-4*) Fr & Eur.
Oeuvres Completes, Vol. 1. Charles Baudelaire. Ed. by Claude Pichois. (FRE.). 1664p. 1975. lib. bdg. 115.00 (*0-7859-3830-3*) Fr & Eur.
Oeuvres Completes, Vol. 1. Federico Garcia Lorca. (FRE.). 1981. 125.00 (*0-8288-3475-X*, F10120) Fr & Eur.

O

Oeuvres Completes, Vol. 1. J. Green. (FRE.). 1979. 99.50 (*0-8288-3495-4*, M3522) Fr & Eur.

Oeuvres Completes, Vol. 1. Franz Kafka. (FRE.). 1976. 110.00 (*0-8288-3511-X*, M5103) Fr & Eur.

Oeuvres Completes, Vol. 1. Roger Martin du Gard. (FRE.). 1955. lib. bdg. 105.00 (*0-8288-3556-X*, M5105) Fr & Eur.

Oeuvres Completes, Vol. 1. Alfred de Musset. Ed. by Maurice Allem. (FRE.). 972p. 1933. lib. bdg. 105.00 (*0-7859-3770-6*, 2070103870) Fr & Eur.

Oeuvres Completes, Vol. 1. Gerard De Nerval & Leon Guillaume. (FRE.). 1989. lib. bdg. 175.00 (*0-7859-3865-6*) Fr & Eur.

Oeuvres Completes, Vol. 1. Raymond Queneau. Ed. by Claude Debon. (FRE.). 1989. lib. bdg. 165.00 (*0-7859-3887-7*) Fr & Eur.

Oeuvres Completes, Vol. 1. Jean Racine. Ed. by Jacques Picard. (FRE.). 1216p. 1951. lib. bdg. 100.00 (*0-7859-3781-1*, 2070104710) Fr & Eur.

Oeuvres Completes, Vol. 1. Pierre De Ronsard. Ed. by Jean Cerard. (FRE.). 1184p. 1993. lib. bdg. 110.00 (*0-7859-3787-0*, 2070104850) Fr & Eur.

Oeuvres Completes, Vol. 1. William Shakespeare. (FRE.). 1959. lib. bdg. 110.00 (*0-8288-3537-3*, F109290) Fr & Eur.

Oeuvres Completes, Vol. 1. deluxe ed. Pierre Corneille. Ed. by Georges Couton. (FRE.). 1872p. 1980. 115.00 (*0-7859-3846-X*, 2070109461) Fr & Eur.

Oeuvres Completes, 2 tomes, Vol. 1. deluxe ed. Paul Eluard. Ed. by Alexandre Dumas & Scheler. (Pleiade Ser.). (FRE.). 1968. 82.95 (*2-07-010189-4*) Schoenhof.

Oeuvres Completes, Vol. 1. deluxe ed. Moliere. Ed. by Georges Couton. (FRE.). 1488p. 1972. 115.00 (*0-7859-3765-X*, 2070103609) Fr & Eur.

Oeuvres Completes, Vol. 2. Charles Baudelaire & Claude Pichois. (FRE.). 1712p. 1976. lib. bdg. 115.00 (*0-7859-3831-1*) Fr & Eur.

Oeuvres Completes, Vol. 2. Pierre Corneille & Georges Couton. (FRE.). 1984. lib. bdg. 125.00 (*0-7859-3868-0*) Fr & Eur.

Oeuvres Completes, Vol. 2. J. Green. (FRE.). 1973. 110.00 (*0-8288-3496-2*, M3523) Fr & Eur.

Oeuvres Completes, Vol. 2. Alfred Jarry. Ed. by Henri Bordillon. (FRE.). 1987. lib. bdg. 135.00 (*0-7859-3929-6*) Fr & Eur.

Oeuvres Completes, Vol. 2. Franz Kafka. (FRE.). 1980. 110.00 (*0-8288-3512-8*, F11330) Fr & Eur.

Oeuvres Completes, Vol. 2. Roger Martin du Gard. (FRE.). 1955. lib. bdg. 95.00 (*0-7859-0642-8*, M5106) Fr & Eur.

Oeuvres Completes, Vol. 2. Moliere. Ed. by Georges Couton. (FRE.). 1584p. 1988. lib. bdg. 110.00 (*0-7859-3766-8*, 2070103617) Fr & Eur.

Oeuvres Completes, Vol. 2. Gerard De Nerval. Ed. by Jean Guillaume. (FRE.). 1984. lib. bdg. 135.00 (*0-7859-3928-8*) Fr & Eur.

Oeuvres Completes, Vol. 2. William Shakespeare. (FRE.). 1959. lib. bdg. 110.00 (*0-7859-0643-6*, F117180) Fr & Eur.

Oeuvres Completes, Vol. 2. Auguste de Villiers de l'Isle-Adam. Ed. by Pierre-Georges Castex. (FRE.). 1986. lib. bdg. 140.00 (*0-7859-3871-0*) Fr & Eur.

Oeuvres Completes, 2 tomes, Vol. 2. deluxe ed. Paul Eluard. Ed. by Alexandre Dumas & Scheler. (Pleiade Ser.). (FRE.). 1968. 67.95 (*2-07-010190-8*) Schoenhof.

Oeuvres Completes, 2 tomes, Vol. 2. deluxe ed. Moliere. Ed. by Courton. (Pleiade Ser.). (FRE.). 1933. 72.95 (*2-07-010361-7*) Schoenhof.

Oeuvres Completes, Vol. 2. deluxe ed. Jean Racine. Ed. by Raymond Ricard. (FRE.). 1168p. 1952. 105.00 (*0-7859-3782-X*, 2070104729) Fr & Eur.

Oeuvres Completes, Vol. 3. Pierre Corneille. Ed. by Georges Couton. (FRE.). 1987. lib. bdg. 135.00 (*0-7859-3878-8*) Fr & Eur.

Oeuvres Completes, Vol. 3. J. Green. (FRE.). 1961. 110.00 (*0-8288-3497-0*, M3524) Fr & Eur.

Oeuvres Completes, Vol. 3. Franz Kafka. (FRE.). 1984. lib. bdg. 135.00 (*0-8288-3513-6*, F12150) Fr & Eur.

Oeuvres Completes, Vol. 3. Alfred de Musset. Ed. by Maurice Allem. (FRE.). 1344p. 1938. lib. bdg. 105.00 (*0-7859-3771-4*, 2070103897) Fr & Eur.

Oeuvres Completes, Vol. 3. deluxe ed. Alfred Jarry. Ed. by Henri Bordillon. (FRE.). 1136p. 1988. 140.00 (*0-7859-3930-X*, 207011144X) Fr & Eur.

Oeuvres Completes, Vol. 4. J. Green. (FRE.). 1976. 110.00 (*0-8288-3498-9*, M3525) Fr & Eur.

Oeuvres Completes, Vol. 4. Franz Kafka. (FRE.). 1989. lib. bdg. 150.00 (*0-8288-3514-4*, F12160) Fr & Eur.

Oeuvres Completes, Vol. 6. J. Green. (FRE.). 1990. 110.00 (*0-8288-3500-4*, F56610) Fr & Eur.

Oeuvres Completes, Vol. 11. Antonin Artaud. (FRE.). 368p. 1974. pap. 29.95 (*0-8288-9027-7*, 2070289672) Fr & Eur.

Oeuvres Completes: Avec: Minutes de Sable Memorial, Vol. 1. deluxe ed. Alfred Jarry. (FRE.). 1376p. 1988. reprint ed. 105.00 (*0-7859-4607-1*) Fr & Eur.

Oeuvres Completes: Avec: Philosophie et Mathematiques, Vol. 2. Denis Diderot & Jean-Pierre. (FRE.). 320p. 1984. 19.95 (*0-7859-1191-X*, 2705659838) Fr & Eur.

Oeuvres Completes: Belles Saisons, Nudite, le Fanal Bleu, Vol. 11. Sidonie-Gabrielle Colette. 1974. 150.00 (*0-686-54594-X*) Fr & Eur.

Oeuvres Completes: Cambara, la Recherche de l'Absolu, l'Enfant Maudit, Vol. 15. Honore de Balzac. (FRE., Illus.). 1970. 50.00 (*0-7859-5331-0*) Fr & Eur.

Oeuvres Completes: Carnets, Vol. 7. Antoine de Saint-Exupery. (FRE., Illus.). 436p. 1986. 225.00 (*0-7859-5487-2*) Fr & Eur.

Oeuvres Completes: Chambre d'Hotel, la Lune de Pluie, Julie de Carneilhan, Vol. 9. Sidonie-Gabrielle Colette. 1974. 150.00 (*0-686-54592-3*) Fr & Eur.

Oeuvres Completes: Cinq-Mars, Servitude et Grandeur Militaires, Etc., Vol. 2. Alfred De Vigny. 1404p. 79.95 (*0-686-56465-0*) Fr & Eur.

Oeuvres Completes: Citadelle 1, Vol. 5. Antoine de Saint-Exupery. (FRE., Illus.). 444p. 1986. 225.00 (*0-7859-5485-6*) Fr & Eur.

Oeuvres Completes: Citadelle 2, Vol. 6. Antoine de Saint-Exupery. (FRE., Illus.). 448p. 1986. 225.00 (*0-7859-5486-4*) Fr & Eur.

Oeuvres Completes: Claudine a l'Ecole, Claudine a Paris, Claudine en Menage, Vol. 1. Sidonie-Gabrielle Colette. (Illus.). 1973. 150.00 (*0-686-54584-2*) Fr & Eur.

Oeuvres Completes: Claudine s'en va, la Retraite Sentimentale, L'Ingenue Libertine, Vol. 2. Sidonie-Gabrielle Colette. 1973. 150.00 (*0-686-54585-0*) Fr & Eur.

Oeuvres Completes: Contes Drolatiques, Vol. 18. Honore de Balzac. (FRE., Illus.). 1970. 50.00 (*0-7859-5334-5*) Fr & Eur.

Oeuvres Completes: Courrier Sud, Terre des Hommes, Vol. 1. Antoine de Saint-Exupery. (FRE., Illus.). 372p. 1985. 225.00 (*0-7859-5481-3*) Fr & Eur.

Oeuvres Completes: De ma Fenetre, Trois, Six, Neuf, Gigi, Vol. 10. Sidonie-Gabrielle Colette. 1974. 150.00 (*0-686-54593-1*) Fr & Eur.

Oeuvres Completes: Deux Profonds Sclerats, un Mari qui Prende du Ventre, Espagnolas et Boyardinos, Vol. 4. Eugene Labiche & Gilbert Sigaux. (FRE., Illus.). 1967. 85.00 (*0-7859-5356-6*) Fr & Eur.

Oeuvres Completes: Duo, Le Toutounier, Mes Apprentissages, Vol. 8. Sidonie-Gabrielle Colette. 1974. 150.00 (*0-686-54591-5*) Fr & Eur.

Oeuvres Completes: Encyclopedie I (Lettre A), Vol. 5. Denis Diderot et al. 564p. 1977. 115.00 (*0-686-56014-0*) Fr & Eur.

Oeuvres Completes: Encyclopedie II (Lettres B-C), Vol. 6. Denis Diderot et al. (Illus.). 564p. 1977. 115.00 (*0-686-56015-9*) Fr & Eur.

Oeuvres Completes: Encyclopedie III (Lettres D-L), Vol. 7. Denis Diderot et al. 728p. 1977. 150.00 (*0-686-56016-7*) Fr & Eur.

Oeuvres Completes: Encyclopedie IV (Lettres M-Z), Vol. 8. Denis Diderot et al. 564p. 1977. 135.00 (*0-686-56017-5*) Fr & Eur.

Oeuvres Completes: Enquete sur la Politique des deux Ministeres, Ecrits et Articles Legitimistes, Enchantillon de Causerie Francaise, Vol. 23. Honore de Balzac. (FRE., Illus.). 1971. 50.00 (*0-7859-5338-8*) Fr & Eur.

Oeuvres Completes: Epaves, le Visionnaire, Minuit, Varouna, Si j'etais vous, etc., Vol. 2. J. Green. 1608p. 41.50 (*0-686-56519-3*) Fr & Eur.

Oeuvres Completes: Fables, Contes et Nouvelles, Vol. 1. Jean de La Fontaine. Ed. by Jean-Pierre Collinet. (FRE.). 1728p. 1991. lib. bdg. 195.00 (*0-7859-3761-7*, 2070102963) Fr & Eur.

Oeuvres Completes: Facino Cane, Sarrasine, Pierre Grassau, Vol. 9. Honore de Balzac. (FRE., Illus.). 1969. 150.00 (*0-7859-5328-0*) Fr & Eur.

Oeuvres Completes: Falthurne, Stenie, la Seconde Falthurne, Vol. 21. Honore de Balzac. (FRE., Illus.). 1970. 150.00 (*0-7859-5553-4*) Fr & Eur.

Oeuvres Completes: Ferragus, la Duchessa de Langeais, la Fille aux yeur d'Or, Vol. 8. Honore de Balzac. (FRE., Illus.). 1969. 150.00 (*0-7859-5327-2*) Fr & Eur.

Oeuvres Completes: Hippias, Protagoras, l'Apologie de Socrates, Criton, Le Banquet, Phedon, La Republique etc., Vol. 1. Plato. 1472p. 39.95 (*0-686-56548-7*) Fr & Eur.

Oeuvres Completes: Il Est de la Police, la Memoir d'Hortense, Doit-on le Dire?, Vol. 8. Eugene Labiche & Gilbert Sigaux. (FRE., Illus.). 1968. 85.00 (*0-7859-5359-0*) Fr & Eur.

Oeuvres Completes: J'ai Compromis ma Femme, le Vivacite du Capitaine Tic, L'Amour En Sabot, Vol. 6. Eugene Labiche & Gilbert Sigaux. (FRE., Illus.). 1968. 85.00 (*0-7859-5557-7*) Fr & Eur.

Oeuvres Completes: Je Croque ma Tante, le Clou aux Maris, L'Avare aux gants Jaunes, Vol. 5. Eugene Labiche & Gilbert Sigaux. (Illus.). 1968. 55.00 (*0-7859-5357-4*) Fr & Eur.

Oeuvres Completes: Journal (1926-1955), Vol. 4. J. Green. 1848p. 45.00 (*0-686-56521-5*) Fr & Eur.

Oeuvres Completes: Journal (1956-1972), Autobiographie, etc., Vol. 5. J. Green. 1808p. 47.95 (*0-686-56522-3*) Fr & Eur.

Oeuvres Completes: La Chambre Eclairee, Cheri, la Fin de Cheri, Vol. 5. Sidonie-Gabrielle Colette. 1974. 150.00 (*0-686-54588-5*) Fr & Eur.

Oeuvres Completes: La Femme Abandonee, Honorine, Beatrix, Vol. 3. Honore de Balzac. (FRE., Illus.). 1968. 150.00 (*0-7859-5323-X*) Fr & Eur.

Oeuvres Completes: La Jumelle Noire, Vol. 12. Sidonie-Gabrielle Colette. 1975. 150.00 (*0-686-54595-8*) Fr & Eur.

Oeuvres Completes: La Maison de Claudine, Sido Noces, Vol. 6. Sidonie-Gabrielle Colette. 1974. 150.00 (*0-686-54589-3*) Fr & Eur.

Oeuvres Completes: La Maison du Chat-Qui-Pelote, le Bal de Sceaux, Memoires de deux Jeunes Maries, Vol. 1. Honore de Balzac. (FRE., Illus.). 1712p. 1968. 150.00 (*0-7859-5322-1*) Fr & Eur.

Oeuvres Completes: La Mandragore, le Prince, Etc. Niccolo Machiavelli. 1664p. 42.95 (*0-686-56535-5*) Fr & Eur.

Oeuvres Completes: La Medicin de Capagne, le Cure de Village, Les Paysans, Vol. 13. Honore de Balzac. (FRE., Illus.). 1969. 150.00 (*0-7859-5332-9*) Fr & Eur.

Oeuvres Completes: La Peau de Chagrin, Jesus-Christ en Flanders, Melmoth Reconcile, Vol. 14. Honore de Balzac. (FRE., Illus.). 1969. 150.00 (*0-7859-5330-2*) Fr & Eur.

Oeuvres Completes: La Pere Goriot, le Colonel Chabert, la Messe de l'Athee, Vol. 4. Honore de Balzac. (FRE., Illus.). 1600p. 1968. 150.00 (*0-7859-5324-8*) Fr & Eur.

Oeuvres Completes: La Seconde, Prisons et Paradis, le Pur et l'Impur, Vol. 7. Sidonie-Gabrielle Colette. 1974. 150.00 (*0-686-54590-7*) Fr & Eur.

Oeuvres Completes: L'Amerique, le Proces, le Chateau, Vol. 1. Franz Kafka. 1408p. 45.00 (*0-686-56531-2*) Fr & Eur.

Oeuvres Completes: L'Auberge Rouge, sur Catherine de Medicis, L'Elexir de Longue Vie, Vol. 16. Honore de Balzac. (FRE., Illus.). 1970. 150.00 (*0-685-73314-9*) Fr & Eur.

Oeuvres Completes: Le Cabinet des Antiques, Illusions Perdues, Vol. 7. Honore de Balzac. (FRE., Illus.). 1968. 150.00 (*0-7859-5552-6*) Fr & Eur.

Oeuvres Completes: Le Cousin Pons, un Prince de la Boheme, Vol. 11. Honore de Balzac. (FRE., Illus.). 1969. 150.00 (*0-685-73315-7*) Fr & Eur.

Oeuvres Completes: Le Cure de Tours, la Rabouilleuse, l'Illustre Gaudissart, Vol. 6. Honore de Balzac. (FRE., Illus.). 1968. 150.00 (*0-7859-5326-4*) Fr & Eur.

Oeuvres Completes: Le Ministere de l'Homme-Esprit (1802), Bd. VI. Louis-Claude D. Saint-Martin. Ed. by Robert Amadou. (GER.). xvi, 472p. 1995. reprint ed. write for info. (*3-487-09977-2*) G Olms Pubs.

Oeuvres Completes: Le Modele Anglais, Vol. 1. Denis Diderot. 468p. 1975. 99.50 (*0-686-56012-4*) Fr & Eur.

Oeuvres Completes: Le Phenomene Humaine, Vol. 1. Pierre T. De Chardin. (FRE.). 1987. pap. 12.95 (*0-7859-2670-4*) Fr & Eur.

Oeuvres Completes: L'Entrave, l'Envers du Musichall, la Paix chez les Betes, Vol. 4. Sidonie-Gabrielle Colette. 1974. 150.00 (*0-686-54587-7*) Fr & Eur.

Oeuvres Completes: L'Epicier, la Femme comme Il Faut, le Notaire, Vol. 24. Honore de Balzac. (FRE., Illus.). 1971. 150.00 (*0-685-73316-5*) Fr & Eur.

Oeuvres Completes: Les Chants de Maldoror; Lettres; Poesies. Lautreamont. (Poesie Ser.). (FRE.). 512p. 1973. pap. 12.95 (*2-07-032000-6*) Schoenhof.

Oeuvres Completes: Les Vrilles de la Vigne, Douze Dialogues de Betes, Autres Betes, Vol. 3. Sidonie-Gabrielle Colette. 1973. 150.00 (*0-686-54586-9*) Fr & Eur.

Oeuvres Completes: Lettres a sa Mere, le Petit Prince, Vol. 4. Antoine de Saint-Exupery. (FRE., Illus.). 364p. 1985. 225.00 (*0-7859-5484-8*) Fr & Eur.

Oeuvres Completes: Lettres a un Otage. Un Sens a la Vie, Lettres de Jeunesse, Vol. 3. Antoine de Saint-Exupery. (FRE., Illus.). 396p. 1977. 225.00 (*0-7859-5483-X*) Fr & Eur.

Oeuvres Completes: Lettres au Petit Corsaire, Lettres a ses Pairs, Vol. 16. Sidonie-Gabrielle Colette. 1976. 150.00 (*0-686-54599-0*) Fr & Eur.

Oeuvres Completes: Lettres de Vagabonde, Lettres a Helene Picard, Vol. 15. Sidonie-Gabrielle Colette. 1976. 150.00 (*0-686-54598-2*) Fr & Eur.

Oeuvres Completes: Melanges, Derniers Ecrits, Discours de Reception, Vol. 14. Sidonie-Gabrielle Colette. 1975. 150.00 (*0-686-54597-4*) Fr & Eur.

Oeuvres Completes: Moira, le Malfaiteur, Chaque Homme dans sa Nuit, L'Autre, Theatre Complet, Vol. 3. J. Green. 1824p. 45.00 (*0-686-56520-7*) Fr & Eur.

Oeuvres Completes: Monsieur de Coylin, l'Avocat Loubet, L'Article, Vol. 1. Eugene Labiche & Gilbert Sigaux. (FRE., Illus.). 960p. 1966. 85.00 (*0-7859-5354-X*) Fr & Eur.

Oeuvres Completes: Mont-Cinere, Leviathan, Adrienne Mesurat, L'Autre Sommeil, etc., Vol. 1. J. Green. 1328p. 45.00 (*0-686-56518-5*) Fr & Eur.

Oeuvres Completes: Oeuvres en vers, Theatre en vers, la Defense Obstinee de la Poesie et des Poetes, Etc., Vol. 1. Alfred De Vigny. 1032p. 79.95 (*0-686-56464-2*) Fr & Eur.

Oeuvres Completes: Paris, 1877-1885, 52 vols., Set. Voltaire. Ed. by Louis Moland. 4000.00 (*0-686-55757-3*) Fr & Eur.

Oeuvres Completes: Paris, 1917-1955, 20 vols. Charles Peguy. 9827p. 1974. 1995.00 (*0-7859-5391-4*) Fr & Eur.

Oeuvres Completes: Paris, 1928-1934, 9 vols., Set. Joris-Karl Huysmans. (FRE.). 1972. 855.00 (*0-7859-0076-4*, M2398) Fr & Eur.

Oeuvres Completes: Physiologie du Mariage, Petites Miseres de la Vie Conjugale, Vol. 17. Honore de Balzac. (FRE., Illus.). 1970. 150.00 (*0-7859-5333-7*) Fr & Eur.

Oeuvres Completes: Poemes, Theatre. LaFontaine. (FRE.). 1196p. 1978. 125.00 (*0-7859-9748-2*) Fr & Eur.

Oeuvres Completes: Poemes-Theatre, Vol. 1. William Shakespeare. 1712p. 42.95 (*0-686-56567-3*) Fr & Eur.

Oeuvres Completes: Poesies, 2 vols., 3. Victor Hugo. 1985. pap. 48.95 (*0-7859-3024-8*) Fr & Eur.

Oeuvres Completes: Poesies, 2 vols., 4. Victor Hugo. 1985. pap. 48.95 (*0-7859-3025-6*) Fr & Eur.

Oeuvres Completes: Premier Prix de Piano, l'homme qui manque le Coche, le Bergere de la Rue Monthabar, Vol. 7. Eugene Labiche & Gilbert Sigaux. (FRE., Illus.). 1968. 85.00 (*0-7859-5358-2*) Fr & Eur.

Oeuvres Completes: Romeo et Juliette, Hamlet, Othello, Le Roi Lear, Macbeth, La Tempete, etc., Vol. 2. William Shakespeare. 1936p. 46.95 (*0-686-56568-1*) Fr & Eur.

Oeuvres Completes: Theatre: Cheri, la Vagabonde, l'Enfant et les Sortileges, Vol. 13. Sidonie-Gabrielle Colette. 1975. 150.00 (*0-686-54596-6*) Fr & Eur.

Oeuvres Completes: Theatre, la Moratre, le Faiseur, l'Ecole des Menages, Vol. 20. Honore de Balzac. (FRE., Illus.). 1970. 150.00 (*0-7859-5336-1*) Fr & Eur.

Oeuvres Completes: Theatre, Vautrin, les Ressources de Quinola, Pamela Giraud, Vol. 19. Honore de Balzac. (FRE., Illus.). 1970. 150.00 (*0-7859-5335-3*) Fr & Eur.

Oeuvres Completes: Theetete, Parmenide, Critias, les Lois, etc., Vol. 2. Plato. 1676p. 42.95 (*0-686-56549-5*) Fr & Eur.

Oeuvres Completes: Un Debut dans la Vie, Albert Savarus, La Vendetta, Vol. 2. Honore de Balzac. (FRE., Illus.). 1968. 150.00 (*0-7859-5551-8*) Fr & Eur.

Oeuvres Completes: Un Episode sous la Terrel, une Tenebreuse Affaire, le Depute d'Arcis, les Chouans, Vol. 12. Honore de Balzac. (FRE., Illus.). 1969. 150.00 (*0-685-73317-3*) Fr & Eur.

Oeuvres Completes: Un Homme d'Affaires, les Employes, la Cousine Bette, Vol. 10. Honore de Balzac. (FRE., Illus.). 1969. 150.00 (*0-7859-5329-9*) Fr & Eur.

Oeuvres Completes: Un Jeune Homme Presse, le Club Champen, Vol. 2. Eugene Labiche & Gilbert Sigaux. (FRE., Illus.). 1967. 85.00 (*0-7859-5355-8*) Fr & Eur.

Oeuvres Completes: Une Clarinette qui Passe, la Femme qui perd ses Jarretiers, on Demande Deux Culottieres, Vol. 3. Eugene Labiche & Gilbert Sigaux. (FRE., Illus.). 1967. 85.00 (*0-7859-5556-9*) Fr & Eur.

Oeuvres Completes: Ursule Mirouet, Eugenie Grandet, la Lys dans la Vallee, Vol. 5. Honore de Balzac. (FRE., Illus.). 1968. 150.00 (*0-7859-5535-6*) Fr & Eur.

Oeuvres Completes: Vie de Moliere, Vie de la Fontane, Souvenirs d'un Paria, Vol. 22. Honore de Balzac. (FRE., Illus.). 1971. 150.00 (*0-7859-5337-X*) Fr & Eur.

Oeuvres Completes: Vol de Nuit, Pilote de Guerre, Vol. 2. Antoine de Saint-Exupery. (FRE., Illus.). 352p. 1985. 225.00 (*0-7859-5482-1*) Fr & Eur.

Oeuvres Completes Tome IV: Emile Education, Morale, Botanique. deluxe ed. Incl. Botanique. (FRE.). 1969. Education. Morale. Jean-Jacques Rousseau. 1969. (Pleiade Ser.). (FRE.). 1958p. 1969. 89.95 (*2-07-010491-5*) Schoenhof.

Oeuvres Completes Vol. 1: Des Erreurs et de la Verite (1775) 667p. 1975. write for info. (*3-487-05850-2*) G Olms Pubs.

Oeuvres Completes Vol. 1: Poesie - Theatre. A. Vigny. (FRE.). 1986. lib. bdg. 135.00 (*0-8288-3585-3*, F75661) Fr & Eur.

Oeuvres Completes Vol. 2: Cinq-Mars, Etc. deluxe ed. A. Vigny. (FRE.). 1994. 105.00 (*0-7859-3720-X*, F75662) Fr & Eur.

Oeuvres Completes Vol. 2: Tableau Naturel Des Rapports Qui Existent Entre Dieu, l'Homme et l'Univers (1782) 584p. 1980. reprint ed. write for info. (*3-487-05851-0*) G Olms Pubs.

Oeuvres Completes Vol. 2: Theatre. Federico Garcia Lorca. (FRE.). 1990. 125.00 (*0-8288-3476-8*, F12815) Fr & Eur.

Oeuvres Completes Vol. 3: L'Homme de Desir (1790-1802) 548p. 1980. reprint ed. write for info. (*3-487-05852-9*) G Olms Pubs.

Oeuvres Completes Vol. 4: Ecce Homo (1792) & le Nouvel Homme (1792) 432p. 1987. reprint ed. write for info. (*3-487-07824-4*) G Olms Pubs.

Oeuvres Completes Vol. 5: Autobiographie. J. Green. (FRE.). 1977. 110.00 (*0-8288-3499-7*, M3526) Fr & Eur.

Oeuvres Completes Vol. 5: De l'Espret des Choses (1800) Controverse Avec Garat (1801), 2 vols., 1. Intro. by Robert Amadou. 856p. 1990. reprint ed. write for info. (*3-487-09345-6*) G Olms Pubs.

Oeuvres Completes Vol. 5: De l'Espret des Choses (1800) Controverse Avec Garat (1801), 2 vols., 2. Intro. by Robert Amadou. 856p. 1990. reprint ed. write for info. (*3-487-09346-4*) G Olms Pubs.

Oeuvres Completes Vol. 6: Le Ministere de l'Homme-Esprit (1802) write for info. (*0-318-71407-8*) G Olms Pubs.

Oeuvres Completes Vol. 7: Notes et Documents par Dr. Robert Amadou. write for info. (*0-318-71408-6*) G Olms Pubs.

Oeuvres Completes d'Alexandre Dumas, 48 vols., Set. Alexandre Dumas. 1000.00 (*0-686-55828-6*) Fr & Eur.

Oeuvres Completes d'Antoine de Fevin. Ed. by Edward Clinkscale. (Gesamtausgaben - Collected Works: Vol. XI, Pt. 1). (ENG & GER.). xvi, 134p. 1980. lib. bdg. 4.00 (*0-912024-68-2*) Inst Mediaeval Mus.

Oeuvres Completes d'Antoine de Fevin. Ed. by Edward Clinkscale. (Gesamtausgaben Collected Works: Vol. XI/2). (ENG & LAT.). xxvi, 179p. 1993. lib. bdg. 108.00 (*0-931902-82-7*) Inst Mediaeval Mus.

Oeuvres Completes de J. M. Charcot, 9 vols., Set. Jean M. Charcot. LC 70-169463. reprint ed. write for info. (*0-404-10000-7*) AMS Pr.

Oeuvres Completes de Jean-Baptiste Lully, 11 vols. Jean-Baptiste Lully. Ed. by Henry Prunieres et al. Incl. Ballets, I, 1654-1657: Ballet du Temps; Ballet des Plaisirs; Ballet de l'Amour malade. (Illus.). 1966. reprint ed. pap. 95.00 (*0-8450-1261-4*); Ballets, II, 1658-1660 Tome 2: Ballet d'Alcidiane; Ballet des Gardes; Ballet de Xerxes. (Illus.). 1966. reprint ed. pap. 95.00 (*0-8450-1262-2*); Comedies-Ballets, I 1664-1665 Tome 1: Le Mariage force; L'Amour medecin. (Illus.). 1966. reprint ed. pap. 95.00 (*0-8450-1263-0*); Comedies-Ballets, III 1669-1670 Tome 3: Monsieur de Pourceaugnac; Le Bourgeois Gentilhomme; Les Amants magnifiques. (Illus.). 1966. reprint ed. pap. 95.00 (*0-8450-1265-7*); Comedies-Ballets, II 1666-1668 Tome 2: Les Plaisirs de l'Ile enchantee; La Pastorale comique; Le Sicilien; Le Grand Di. (Illus.). 1966. reprint ed. pap. 95.00 (*0-8450-1264-9*); Motets, I ,1664 Tome 1: Miserere Mei Deus. (Illus.). 1966. reprint ed. pap. 95.00 (*0-8450-1266-5*); Motets, 1668-1677 Tome 2: Plaude, Laetare, Gallia; Te Deum Laudamus; Dies Irae; Dies Illa. (Illus.). 1966. reprint ed. pap. 95.00 (*0-8450-1267-3*); Operas Tome 1: Cadmus et Hermione. (Illus.). 1966. reprint ed. pap. 135.00 (*0-8450-1269-X*);

Operas II Tome 2: Alceste. (Illus.). 1966. reprint ed. pap. 135.00 (0-8450-1270-3); Operas, 1684 Tome 3: Amadis. (Illus.). 1966. reprint ed. pap. 135.00 (0-8450-1271-1); (Illus.). 1972. reprint ed. Set pap. 1165.00 (0-8450-1260-6) Broude.

Oeuvres Completes de Jean-Philippe Rameau, 18 vols. Incl. Cantates. Jean-Philippe Rameau. Ed. by Camille Saint-Saens. (Illus.). 1968. reprint ed. lib. bdg. 95.00 (0-8450-1803-5); Dardanus. Jean-Philippe Rameau. Ed. by Vincent D'Indy. (Illus.). 1968. reprint ed. lib. bdg. 200.00 (0-8450-1810-8); Fetes d'Hebe, ou les Talents Lyriques. Jean-Philippe Rameau. Ed. by Alexandre Guilmant. (Illus.). 1968. reprint ed. lib. bdg. 200.00 (0-8450-1809-4); Motets, (Premiere Serie) Jean-Philippe Rameau. Ed. by Camille Saint-Saens. (Illus.). 1968. reprint ed. lib. bdg. 95.00 (0-8450-1804-3); Motets, (Seconde Serie) Jean-Philippe Rameau. Ed. by Camille Saint-Saens. (Illus.). 1968. reprint ed. lib. bdg. 95.00 (0-8450-1805-1); Musique Instrumentale: Pieces de Clavecin en Concerts, Six Concerts en Sextour. Jean Philippe Rameau. Ed. by Hugues Imbert. (Illus.). 188p. 1968. reprint ed. lib. bdg. 95.00 (0-8450-1802-7); Nais. Ed. by Reynaldo Hahn. (Illus.). 1968. reprint ed. lib. bdg. 200.00 (0-8450-1818-3); Pieces de Clavecin. Jean-Philippe Rameau. Ed. by Camille Saint-Saens. (Illus.). 1968. reprint ed. lib. bdg. 95.00 (0-8450-1801-9); Zais. Jean-Philippe Rameau. Ed. by Vincent D'Indy. (Illus.). 1968. reprint ed. lib. bdg. 200.00 (0-8450-1816-7); Pt. 2. Anacreon; Les Sybarites. Jean-Philippe Rameau. Ed. by Henri Suesser. (Illus.). 1968. reprint ed. lib. bdg. 200.00 (0-8450-1820-5); Vol. 10. Dardanus, Appendice. Jean-Philippe Rameau. Ed. by Vincent D'Indy. (Illus.). 1968. reprint ed. lib. bdg. 95.00 (0-8450-1819-1); Vol. 17, Pt. 1. Pygmalion, les Surprises de l'Amour. Jean-Philippe Rameau. Ed. by Henri Suesser. (Illus.). 1968. reprint ed. lib. bdg. 200.00 (0-8450-1817-5); (Illus.). 1968. reprint ed. Set lib. bdg. 2500.00 (0-8450-1800-0) Broude.

Oeuvres Completes de Robert de Fevin. Ed. by Edward Clinkscale. (Gesamtausgaben - Collected Works: Vol. XIII). (ENG & LAT.). xx, 140p. 1993. lib. bdg. 140.00 (0-931902-77-0) Inst Mediaeval Mus.

Oeuvres Completes de Sally Mara. Raymond Queneau. (FRE.). 364p. 1979. pap. 17.95 (0-7859-1341-6, 2070287521) Fr & Eur.

Oeuvres Completes d'Hippocrates, 10 vols., Set. Hippocrates. 6435p. reprint ed. lib. bdg. 850.00 (0-317-66604-5) Coronet Bks.

Oeuvres Completes en Prose see Oeuvres Completes

Oeuvres Completes, 1952-1959, 15 vols., Vol. X. Jacques Maritain & Raissa Maritain. (FRE.). 1234p. 1985. 79.99 (2-8271-0302-8) I B C A.

Oeuvres Completes, 1945-1953, Vol. 2. Paul Eluard. Ed. by Marcelle Dumas. (FRE.). 1520p. 1976. lib. bdg. 120.00 (0-7859-3753-6, 2070101908) Fr & Eur.

Oeuvres Completes, 1906-1920, 15 vols., Vol. 1. Jacques Maritain & Raissa Maritain. 1175p. 1986. 79.00 (2-8271-0338-9) I B C A.

Oeuvres Completes, 1913-1945, Vol. 1. Paul Eluard. Ed. by M. C. Dumas. (FRE.). 1760p. 1971. lib. bdg. 120.00 (0-7859-3752-8, 2070101894) Fr & Eur.

Oeuvres Completes, 1935-1938, 15 vols., Vol. VI. Jacques Maritain & Raissa Maritain. (FRE.). 1317p. 1984. 72.99 (2-8271-0275-7, Pub. by Editions Univ) I B C A.

Oeuvres Completes, 1939-1943 Vol. 7. Jacques Maritain & Raissa Maritain. Ed. by J. Allion et al. (FRE.). 1402p. (C). 1988. 87.49 (2-8271-0388-5, Pub. by Editions Univ) I B C A.

Oeuvres Completes, 1932-1935, 15 vols., Vol. V. Jacques Maritain & Raissa Maritain. (FRE.). 1153p. 1982. 72.99 (2-8271-0224-2, Pub. by Editions Univ) I B C A.

Oeuvres Completes, 1924-1929, 15 vols., Vol. III. Jacques Maritain & Raissa Maritain. (FRE.). 1472p. 1985. 79.99 (2-8271-0287-0) I B C A.

Oeuvres Completes, 1929-1932, 15 vols., Vol. IV. Jacques Maritain & Raissa Maritain. (FRE.). 1259p. 1983. 72.99 (2-8271-0259-5, Pub. by Editions Univ) I B C A.

Oeuvres Completes, 1920 to 1923, 15 vols., Vol. 2. Jacques Maritan & Raissa Maritain. Ed. by J. Allion et al. 1331p. 1987. 79.99 (2-8271-0350-8) I B C A.

Oeuvres Completes, Poesies, Vol. 2. Victor Hugo. (FRE.). 1985. pap. 48.95 (0-7859-3023-X, 2221046927) Fr & Eur.

Oeuvres Completes Publiees sous la Direction de J. Derenbourg, Set, Vols. 1, 3, 5, 6 & 9. Saadia Ben Josef Al-Fayyoumi. clxiv, 1241p. 1979. reprint ed. write for info. (3-487-06838-9) G Olms Pubs.

Oeuvres Completes, Theatre. Paul Claudel. (FRE.). 160p. 1958. 10.95 (0-7859-1212-6, 207021530X) Fr & Eur.

Oeuvres Completes Theatre, Vol. 2. Victor Hugo. (FRE.). 1985. pap. 48.95 (0-7859-3405-7) Fr & Eur.

Oeuvres Completes Theatres, Vol. 1. Victor Hugo. 1985. pap. 48.95 (0-7859-3026-4) Fr & Eur.

Oeuvres de Arthur Rimbaud. Jean N. Rimbaud. Ed. by Paterne Berrichon. LC 77-11477. reprint ed. 41.50 (0-404-16338-6) AMS Pr.

Oeuvres de Guillaume de Machaut: Dits et Poemes Allegoriques, 3 tomes, Set. Ed. by Hoepffner. 150.00 (0-685-34020-1) Fr & Eur.

Oeuvres de Jeunesse. A. Marivaux. (FRE.). 1972. lib. bdg. 95.00 (0-8288-3552-7, F48070) Fr & Eur.

Oeuvres de Jeunesse. Pierre Carlet de Chamblain de Marivaux. 1972. 110.00 (0-8288-9606-2, F48070) Fr & Eur.

Oeuvres de Jeunesse (Alice) Lewis Carroll, pseud. (FRE.). 125.00 (0-8288-3455-5) Fr & Eur.

Oeuvres de Louis XIII a Charles X. Connaissance des Arts Editorial Staff.Tr. of French Master Goldsmiths & Silversmiths from the Seventeenth to the Nineteenth Century. (Illus.). 150.00 (0-685-11470-8) Fr & Eur.

Oeuvres de Louis XIII a Charles X. Connaissance des Arts Editorial Staff.Tr. of French Master Goldsmiths & Silversmiths from the Seventeenth to the Nineteenth Century. (FRE.). 1966. 150.00 (0-8288-7386-0) Fr & Eur.

Oeuvres de Mirabeau, 8 vols. Honore G. Mirabeau. LC 79-172736. reprint ed. 160.00 (0-404-07360-3) AMS Pr.

Oeuvres de Napoleon III, 5 vols., Set. Napoleon Third. LC 74-173015. reprint ed. 150.00 (0-404-07380-8) AMS Pr.

Oeuvres de Pierre Curie. Ed. by J. Revel et al. 624p. 1984. pap. text 73.00 (2-903928-07-X) Gordon & Breach.

Oeuvres Diverses. deluxe ed. Honore de Balzac. Ed. by Pierre-Georges Castex. (FRE.). 1904p. 1990. lib. bdg. 165.00 (0-7859-3811-7) Fr & Eur.

Oeuvres Diverses, 5 vols., Set. Pierre Bayle. 1990. reprint ed. 2225.00 (3-487-05456-6) G Olms Pubs.

Oeuvres Diverses see Oeuvres Completes

Oeuvres Diverses No. 3: Petri Poireti Cogitationum Rationalium De Deo Anima et Malo. Pierre Poiret. 1990. reprint ed. write for info. (3-487-09383-9) G Olms Pubs.

Oeuvres Diverses Nos. 1-4: DenHaag 1727-1731: Volumes Supplementaires aux Oeuvres Diverses: Choix d'Articles du Dictionnaire Historique et Critique. Pierre Bayle. cxxii, 5103p. 1982. reprint ed. 915.00 (3-487-07223-8) G Olms Pubs.

Oeuvres Dramatiques, 2 vols. in 1. Louis-Sebastien Mercier. 726p. 1984. reprint ed. write for info. (3-487-07477-X) G Olms Pubs.

Oeuvres en Prose. Edgar Allan Poe. (FRE.). 1932. lib. bdg. 89.95 (0-8288-3527-6, M5172) Fr & Eur.

Oeuvres en Prose. deluxe ed. Paul Claudel. Ed. by Jacques Petit & Charles Galperine. (Pleiade Ser.). (FRE.). 1680p. 1965. write for info. (0-7859-4540-7) Fr & Eur.

Oeuvres en Prose. deluxe ed. Rainer Maria Rilke. (FRE.). 1280p. 1992. 150.00 (0-7859-0966-4, 2070112551) Fr & Eur.

Oeuvres en Prose, Tome 1. deluxe ed. Guillaume Apollinaire. (Pleiade Ser.). (FRE.). 1988. 80.95 (2-07-010828-7) Schoenhof.

Oeuvres en Prose, Tome 2. deluxe ed. Guillaume Apollinaire. (Pleiade Ser.). (FRE.). 1991. 119.95 (2-07-011216-0) Schoenhof.

Oeuvres en Prose: Histoires Extraordinaires, Adventures d'Arthur Gordon Pym, Eureka, etc. Edgar Allan Poe. Tr. by Charles Baudelaire. 1184p. 41.50 (0-686-56551-7) Fr & Eur.

Oeuvres en Prose: 1909-1914, Vol. 2: 1905-1909. deluxe ed. Charles Peguy. Ed. by Marcel Peguy. (Pleiade Ser.). (FRE.). 1957. 99.95 (2-07-011134-2) Schoenhof.

Oeuvres en Prose: 1909-1914, Vol. 3. Charles Peguy. Ed. by Marcel Peguy. (Pleiade Ser.). (FRE.). 1957. 129.95 (2-07-011231-4) Schoenhof.

Oeuvres en Prose Complete, 1897-1899, 1900-1905, Vol. 1. Charles Peguy & Robert Burac. (FRE.). 1987. lib. bdg. 160.00 (0-7859-3876-1) Fr & Eur.

Oeuvres en Prose Completes. Paul M. Verlaine. (FRE.). 1972. lib. bdg. 95.00 (0-8288-3584-5, F75010) Fr & Eur.

Oeuvres en Prose Completes. Paul M. Verlaine & Jacques Borel. 1568p. 1972. 35.00 (0-686-55153-2) Fr & Eur.

Oeuvres en Prose Completes. deluxe ed. Paul Verlaine. (Pleiade Ser.). (FRE.). 1568p. 1972. 80.95 (2-07-010698-5) Schoenhof.

Oeuvres en Prose Completes, Vol. 1. deluxe ed. Guillaume Apollinaire. (Pleiade Ser.). (FRE.). 1584p. 1993. 110.00 (0-8288-3416-4, M4806) Fr & Eur.

Oeuvres en Prose Completes, Vol. 2. deluxe ed. Guillaume Apollinaire. Ed. by Michel Decaudin. (FRE.). 1872p. 1991. lib. bdg. 195.00 (0-7859-3899-0, 2070112160) Fr & Eur.

Oeuvres en Prose Completes, 1900-1914: Index. Charles Peguy. Ed. by Robert Burac. (FRE.). 1988. lib. bdg. 225.00 (0-7859-3881-8) Fr & Eur.

Oeuvres en Prose, 1898-1908, Vol. 1. deluxe ed. Charles Peguy. Ed. by M. Pebuy. (Pleiade Ser.). (FRE.). 1959. 98.95 (2-07-011114-8) Schoenhof.

Oeuvres en Proses Completes, Vol. 3. Guillaume Apollinaire. (FRE.). 1617p. 1993. 195.00 (0-7859-7573-X) Fr & Eur.

Oeuvres Esthetiques. Denis Diderot. Ed. by Paul Verniere. (FRE.). 896p. 1988. pap. 59.95 (0-7859-4653-5) Fr & Eur.

Oeuvres et Lettres. deluxe ed. Rene Descartes. (Pleiade Ser.). (FRE.). 1423p. 1983. 72.95 (2-07-010166-5) Schoenhof.

Oeuvres et Lettres: Avec: Discours de la Methode. Rene Descartes. 1424p. 1937. 99.50 (0-8288-9577-5, F36590) Fr & Eur.

Oeuvres Historiques. Voltaire. Ed. by Rene Pomeau. (Bibliotheque de la Pleiade Ser.). (FRE.). 1819p. 1978. 105.00 (0-7859-1278-9, 2070105849) Fr & Eur.

Oeuvres Historiques. deluxe ed. Voltaire. (Pleiade Ser.). (FRE.). 80.95 (2-07-010584-9) Schoenhof.

Oeuvres Inedites: Melanges Historiques, Vol. 1. Voltaire. Ed. by Fernand Caussy. (FRE.). 1914. 60.00 (0-7859-5515-1) Fr & Eur.

Oeuvres Intimes, 2 vols. deluxe ed. Stendhal, pseud. Ed. by Martineau. (Pleiade Ser.). (FRE.). 82.95 (2-07-010945-3) Schoenhof.

Oeuvres Intimes, 2 vols., 1. Stendhal, pseud & Vittorio Del Litto. (FRE.). 1982. lib. bdg. 120.00 (0-7859-3844-3) Fr & Eur.

Oeuvres Intimes, 2 vols., 2. Stendhal, pseud & Vittorio Del Litto. (FRE.). 1982. lib. bdg. 125.00 (0-7859-3845-1) Fr & Eur.

Oeuvres Intimes, 2 vols., Vol. 1. deluxe ed. Stendhal, pseud. Ed. by Martineau. (Pleiade Ser.). (FRE.). 78.95 (2-07-010944-5) Schoenhof.

Oeuvres, la Conjuration du Comte de Fiesque et Pamphlets. Cardinal De Retz. (Pleiade Ser.). (FRE.). 1256p. 81.95 (2-07-011028-1) Schoenhof.

Oeuvres-Lais, Testaments, Ballades. Francois Villon. 285p. 1968. 24.95 (0-8288-7438-7) Fr & Eur.

Oeuvres Litteraires Diverses: Prose Narrative: Critique. Jean Giraudoux. 85.00 (0-685-34177-1) Fr & Eur.

Oeuvres Mathematiques: Collected Papers, 1926-1978, 3 vols. Andre Weil. 1980. 417.95 (0-387-90330-5) Spr-Verlag.

Oeuvres Philosophiques, 3 vols. Rene Descartes. Ed. by Ferdinand Alquie. Incl. Vol. 1. 1618-1637. 1963. 18.50 Vol. 2. 1638-1642. 1975. 22.50 Vol. 3. 1643-1650. 1973. 37.50 write for info. (0-318-52181-4) Fr & Eur.

Oeuvres Philosophiques. Denis Diderot. Ed. by Paul Verniere. 1961. 37.95 (0-8288-9951-7, F46750) Fr & Eur.

Oeuvres Philosophiques, 2 vols. in 1. Julien O. De La Mettrie. vii, 623p. 1988. reprint ed. write for info. (3-487-02811-5) G Olms Pubs.

Oeuvres Philosophiques. Frans Hemsterhuis. viii, 698p. 1972. reprint ed. write for info. (3-487-04514-1) G Olms Pubs.

Oeuvres Philosophiques, Vol. 1. E. Kant. (FRE.). 1980. lib. bdg. 110.00 (0-8288-3515-2, F12806) Fr & Eur.

Oeuvres Philosophiques, Vol. 2. E. Kant. (FRE.). 1984. lib. bdg. 125.00 (0-8288-3516-0, F13310) Fr & Eur.

Oeuvres Philosophiques, Vol. 3. E. Kant. (FRE.). 1986. lib. bdg. 150.00 (0-8288-3517-9, F1400) Fr & Eur.

Oeuvres Philosophiques et Morales. Pierre Nicole. xxiii, 475p. 1970. reprint ed. write for info. (0-318-71383-7) G Olms Pubs.

Oeuvres Philosophiques et Scientifiques D'Al-Kindi, Vol. 2. Ed. by Jean Jolivet & Roshdi Rashed. (Islamic Philosophy, Theology & Science, Studies & Texts Ser.: Vol. 31). (Illus.). xiv, 246p. 1998. 111.25 (90-04-11073-9) Brill Academic Pubs.

Oeuvres Poetiques. Alfred De Vigny. (FRE.). 1978. 10.95 (0-8288-9670-4, F130070) Fr & Eur.

Oeuvres Poetiques. Paul M. Verlaine. Ed. by Robichez. (Coll. Prestige). 27.95 (0-685-37124-7); pap. 14.95 (0-685-37123-9) Fr & Eur.

Oeuvres Poetiques. Francois Villon. Ed. by Andre Mary. 3.95 (0-686-55738-7) Fr & Eur.

Oeuvres Poetiques. Francois Villon. 190p. 1965. 24.95 (0-8288-7424-7) Fr & Eur.

Oeuvres Poetiques. deluxe ed. Guillaume Apollinaire. Ed. by Adema & Decaudin. (Pleiade Ser.). (FRE.). 1957. 71.95 (2-07-010015-4) Schoenhof.

Oeuvres Poetiques. deluxe ed. Paul Claudel. Ed. by Fumet. (Pleiade Ser.). 1957. 69.95 (2-07-010143-6) Schoenhof.

Oeuvres Poetiques, 2 tomes, Set. Arthur Rimbaud. (FRE., Illus.). 87.50 (0-685-34968-3) Fr & Eur.

Oeuvres Poetiques Tome 1: Avant l'Exil (1802-1851) deluxe ed. Victor Hugo. (Pleiade Ser.). (FRE.). 1655p. 1964. 82.95 (2-07-010267-X) Schoenhof.

Oeuvres Poetiques Tome 2: Les Chatiments; Les Contemplations. deluxe ed. Victor Hugo. (Pleiade Ser.). (FRE.). 1792p. 1967. 81.95 (2-07-010268-8) Schoenhof.

Oeuvres Poetiques Tome 3: Les Chansons des Rues et des Bois; l'Annee Terrible; etc. deluxe ed. Victor Hugo. (Pleiade Ser.). (FRE.). 1410p. 1974. 74.95 (2-07-010675-6) Schoenhof.

Oeuvres Poetiques Vol. 1: Avant l'Exil, 1802-1951. deluxe ed. Victor Hugo. (FRE.). 1736p. 1987. 120.00 (0-7859-4675-6) Fr & Eur.

Oeuvres Poetiques Vol. 2: Avec: Les Chatiments, les Contemplations. deluxe ed. Victor Hugo. (FRE.). 1882p. 1987. 115.00 (0-7859-4676-4) Fr & Eur.

Oeuvres Poetiques Vol. 3: Avec: Les Chansons des Rues et des Bois, L'Anne Terrible, L'Art de d'Etre Grand-Pere. Victor Hugo. Ed. by Pierre Albouy. (FRE.). 1488p. 1974. 105.00 (0-7859-0073-X, M2370) Fr & Eur.

Oeuvres Poetiques Completes. Alphonse De Lamartine. Ed. by Jean Guyard. (FRE.). 1963. lib. bdg. 145.00 (0-7859-3920-2) Fr & Eur.

Oeuvres Poetiques Completes. Paul M. Verlaine. Ed. by Jacques Borel. (FRE.). 1938. lib. bdg. 125.00 (0-7859-3804-4) Fr & Eur.

Oeuvres Poetiques Completes. deluxe ed. Alphonse Lamartine. Ed. by Jean Guyard. (Pleiade Ser.). (FRE.). 1963. 93.95 (2-07-010298-X) Schoenhof.

Oeuvres Poetiques Completes. deluxe ed. Charles Peguy. Ed. by Marcel Peguy. (FRE.). 1664p. 1941. 130.00 (0-7859-3779-X, 2070104389) Fr & Eur.

Oeuvres Poetiques Completes. deluxe ed. Charles Peguy. Ed. by P. Peguy & Marcel Peguy. (Pleiade Ser.). (FRE.). 1939. 76.95 (2-07-010438-9) Schoenhof.

Oeuvres Poetiques Completes. deluxe ed. Paul Verlaine. Ed. by Le Dantec. (Pleiade Ser.). (FRE.). 1965. 80.95 (2-07-010579-2) Schoenhof.

Oeuvres Poetiques Completes, Vol. 1. deluxe ed. Guillaume Apollinaire. (Pleiade Ser.). (FRE.). 1344p. 1956. 110.00 (0-8288-3417-2, F82020) Fr & Eur.

Oeuvres Poetiques, Rymes de Pernette du Guille, Blasons du Corps Feminin. Louise Labe. (Poesie Ser.). (FRE.). 188p. 1983. pap. 11.95 (2-07-032238-6) Schoenhof.

Oeuvres Politiques. Denis Diderot. Ed. by Paul Verniere. 1963. 28.95 (0-8288-9952-5, F46760) Fr & Eur.

Oeuvres Postumes, 2 vols. in 1, Vol. 2. Louis-Claude De Saint-Martin. Ed. by Robert Amadou. xxxii, 892p. reprint ed. write for info. (0-318-71410-8) G Olms Pubs.

Oeuvres Romanesque Completes, 2 vols., Vol. 1. deluxe ed. Jules Barbey d'Aurevilly. Ed. by Marcel Petit. (FRE.). 1536p. 1964. lib. bdg. 115.00 (0-7859-3740-4, 2070100480) Fr & Eur.

Oeuvres Romanesques. Marcel Ayme. 1977. 150.00 (0-686-51920-5, F23830) Fr & Eur.

Oeuvres Romanesques. Denis Diderot. Ed. by Henri Benac. 1962. 39.95 (0-8288-9953-3, F46772) Fr & Eur.

Oeuvres Romanesques. Jean-Paul Sartre. Ed. by Michel Contat. (FRE.). 1982. lib. bdg. 155.00 (0-7859-3855-9) Fr & Eur.

Oeuvres Romanesques. deluxe ed. Jean-Paul Sartre. (Pleiade Ser.). (FRE.). 2288p. 1982. 98.95 (2-07-011002-8) Schoenhof.

Oeuvres Romanesques. deluxe ed. Marguerite Yourcenar. (FRE.). 1280p. 1982. 110.00 (0-7859-0447-6, 2070110184) Fr & Eur.

Oeuvres Romanesques. deluxe ed. Marguerite Yourcenar. (Pleiade Ser.). (FRE.). 1255p. 1988. 73.95 (2-07-011018-4) Schoenhof.

Oeuvres Romanesques, Tome I. Incl. Batailles dans la Montagne. Jean Giono. Chant de la Montagne. Jean Giono. Chant de la Montagne. Colline. de Beaumugnes. Grand Troupeau. Jean le Bleu. Jean Giono. Jean le Bleu. Jean Giono. Naissance de l'Odyssee. Que Ma Joie Demeure. Jean Giono. Que Ma Joie Demeure. Jean Giono. Regain. Solitude de la Pitie. write for info. (0-318-63562-3) Fr & Eur.

Oeuvres Romanesques, Tome II. Incl. Batailles dans la Montagne. Jean Giono. Chant de la Montagne. Jean Giono. Chant de la Montagne. Colline. de Beaumugnes. Grand Troupeau. Jean le Bleu. Jean Giono. Jean le Bleu. Jean Giono. Naissance de l'Odyssee. Que Ma Joie Demeure. Jean Giono. Que Ma Joie Demeure. Jean Giono. Regain. Solitude de la Pitie. (Bibliotheque de la Pleiade Ser.). 275.00 (0-685-34164-X) Schoenhof.

Oeuvres Romanesques, Vol. 1. Ernest Hemingway. (FRE.). 1966. 110.00 (0-8288-3502-0, F10330) Fr & Eur.

Oeuvres Romanesques, Vol. 2. Ernest Hemingway. (FRE.). 1969. 110.00 (0-8288-3503-9, F10380) Fr & Eur.

Oeuvres Romanesques: Les Vertes Collines d'Afrique, Chasses en Afrique, Depression en Amerique, etc., Vol. 2. Ernest Hemingway. 1560p. 42.95 (0-686-56524-X) Fr & Eur.

Oeuvres Romanesques: Sartoris, le Bruit et le Fureur, Sanctuaire, Tandis que J'Agonise, Vol. 1. Faulkner. 1760p. 75.00 (0-686-56509-6) Fr & Eur.

Oeuvres Romanesques: Torrents de Printemps, l'Adieu aux Armes, le Soleil se leve Aussi, Paris est une Fete, Mort dans l'apres-Midi, etc., Vol. 1. Ernest Hemingway. 1560p. 41.50 (0-686-56523-1) Fr & Eur.

Oeuvres Romanesques Completes. Georges Bernanos et al. Ed. by Picon et al. 1962. 75.00 (0-7859-0606-1, F87590) Fr & Eur.

Oeuvres Romanesques Completes. deluxe ed. Marcel Ayme. (Pleiade Ser.). (FRE.). 1648p. 1989. 150.00 (0-8288-3419-9, F23830) Fr & Eur.

Oeuvres Romanesques Completes, Vol. 1. Jean Giono. (FRE.). 1978. 99.50 (0-8288-3478-4, F103310) Fr & Eur.

Oeuvres Romanesques Completes, Vol. 1. Jean Giraudoux. (FRE.). 1990. 125.00 (0-8288-3486-5, F10157) Fr & Eur.

Oeuvres Romanesques Completes, 2 tomes, Vol. 1. deluxe ed. D'Aurevilly. Ed. by Petit. (Pleiade Ser.). (FRE.). 73.95 (2-07-010048-0) Schoenhof.

Oeuvres Romanesques Completes, Vol. 2. Jean Giono. (FRE.). 1972. 99.50 (0-8288-3479-2, F103311) Fr & Eur.

Oeuvres Romanesques Completes, 2 vols., Vol. 2. deluxe ed. Jules Barbey d'Aurevilly. Ed. by Jacques Petit. (FRE.). 1712p. 1966. lib. bdg. 120.00 (0-7859-3741-2, 2070100499) Fr & Eur.

Oeuvres Romanesques Completes, 2 tomes, Vol. 2. deluxe ed. D'Aurevilly. Ed. by Petit. (Pleiade Ser.). (FRE.). 73.95 (2-07-010049-9) Schoenhof.

Oeuvres Romanesques Completes, Vol. 3. Jean Giono. (FRE.). 1974. 99.50 (0-8288-3480-6, F10154) Fr & Eur.

Oeuvres Romanesques Completes, Vol. 4. Jean Giono. (FRE.). 1977. 110.00 (0-8288-3481-4, M5033) Fr & Eur.

Oeuvres Romanesques Completes, Vol. 5. Jean Giono. (FRE.). 1980. 110.00 (0-8288-3482-2, F10155) Fr & Eur.

Oeuvres Romanesques Completes, Vol. 6. Jean Giono. (FRE.). 1983. 110.00 (0-8288-3483-0, F10156) Fr & Eur.

Oeuvres Romanesques Completes: Angelo, Mort d'un Personnage, le Hussard sur le Toit, le Bonheur Fou, Vol. 4. Jean Giono. 1744p. 47.95 (0-686-56514-2) Fr & Eur.

Oeuvres Romanesques Completes: Pour Saluer Melville, l'Eau Vive, un Roi sans Divertissement, Noe, Fragments d'un Paradis, Vol. 3. Jean Giono. 1604p. 49.95 (0-686-56513-4) Fr & Eur.

Oeuvres Romanesques et Theatrales, Vol. 1. L. Mauriac. (FRE.). 1978. lib. bdg. 95.00 (0-8288-3562-4, M5109) Fr & Eur.

Oeuvres Romanesques et Theatrales, Vol. 2. L. Mauriac. (FRE.). 1987. lib. bdg. 95.00 (0-8288-3563-2, M5635) Fr & Eur.

Oeuvres Romanesques et Theatrales, Vol. 3. L. Mauriac. (FRE.). 1981. lib. bdg. 95.00 (0-8288-3564-0, F16630) Fr & Eur.

Oeuvres Romanesques et Theatrales, Vol. 4. L. Mauriac. (FRE.). 1985. lib. bdg. 140.00 (0-8288-3565-9, F16810) Fr & Eur.

Oeuvres Romanesques et Theatrales Completes, 2. deluxe ed. Francois Mauriac. Ed. by Jacques Petit. (Pleiade Ser.). 1978. 75.95 (2-07-010957-7) Schoenhof.

Oeuvres Romanesques et Theatrales Completes, 3. deluxe ed. Francois Mauriac. Ed. by Jacques Petit. (Pleiade Ser.). 1978. 74.95 (2-07-010990-9) Schoenhof.

Oeuvres Romanesques et Theatrales Completes, 4. deluxe ed. Francois Mauriac. Ed. by Jacques Petit. (Pleiade Ser.). 1978. 93.95 (2-07-011091-5) Schoenhof.

Oeuvres Romanesques et Theatrales Completes, I. deluxe ed. Francois Mauriac. Ed. by Jacques Petit. (Pleiade Ser.). 1978. 77.95 (2-07-010931-3) Schoenhof.

Oeuvres Romanesques et Voyages, 2 vols., 1. deluxe ed. Francois-Rene de Chateaubriand. Ed. by Maurice Regard. (Pleiade Ser.). 74.95 (2-07-010129-0) Schoenhof.

O

Oeuvres Romanesques et Voyages, 2 vols., 2. deluxe ed. Francois-Rene de Chateaubriand. Ed. by Maurice Regard. (Pleiade Ser.). 76.95 (2-07-010130-4) Schoenhof.

Oeuvres Romanesques et Voyages, Tome I. Incl. Atala. Rene De Chateaubriand & Maurice Regard. Natchez. Rene De Chateaubriand. Ed. by Maurice Regard. Rene. Vie de Rance. Rene De Chateaubriand. Ed. by Maurice Regard. Voyage en Amerique. Rene De Chateaubriand. Ed. by Maurice Regard. (Bibliotheque de la Pleiade Ser.). 77.50 (0-685-34883-0) Fr & Eur.

Oeuvres Romanesques et Voyages, Vol. 1. deluxe ed. Francois-Rene de Chateaubriand. Ed. by Maurice Regard. (FRE.). 1504p. 1969. 110.00 (0-7859-3748-X, 2070101290) Fr & Eur.

Oeuvres Romanesques et Voyages, Vol. 2. Francois-Rene de Chateaubriand. Ed. by Maurice Regard. (FRE.). 1824p. 1969. lib. bdg. 125.00 (0-7859-3749-8, 2070101304) Fr & Eur.

Oeuvres Romanesques Illustrees, 2 tomes, Set. Francois Mauriac. (FRE.). 1949. 59.95 (2-253-05511-5) Fr & Eur.

Oeuvres Romanesques, 1911-1951. Francois Mauriac. (FRE.). 1992. pap. 56.95 (0-7859-3160-0, 2253055115) Fr & Eur.

***Of.** Michael Lally. 106p. 1999. pap. 9.95 (1-882550-35-8, Pub. by Quiet Lion Pr) SPD-Small Pr Dist.

Of a Certain Age: A Guide to Contemporary Fiction Featuring Older Adults. Rhea J. Rubin. 308p. 1990. lib. bdg. 45.00 (0-87436-547-3) ABC-CLIO.

Of a Feather: Insights into Nature from Lake Merritt to the Feather River. Rex Burress. (Illus.). 145p. (Orig.). 1993. pap. 12.00 (0-9652079-1-9) Signs of the Seasons.

Of a Place & a Time: Remembering Lancaster. Richard D. Altick. LC 90-29296. (Illus.). 184p. (C). 1991. lib. bdg. 25.00 (0-208-02321-6, Archon Bks) Shoe String.

Of a Small & Modest Malignancy, Wicked & Bristling with Dots. deluxe limited ed. Norman Mailer. 120p. 1980. 200.00 (0-935716-05-X) Lord John.

Of All the Nerve: Deb Margolin Solo. Deb Margolin & Lynda Hart. LC 98-31201. 224p. 1999. 70.00 (0-304-70318-4); pap. 18.95 (0-304-70319-2) Continuum.

***Of All the Summers: A Novel.** Hellen Mclean. LC 99-185517. 1999. mass mkt. 14.95 (0-88961-235-8) Womens Pr.

Of All the Wide Torsos in All the Wild Glen. Paul Peddito. 46p. 1991. pap. 3.50 (0-87129-097-9, O47) Dramatic Pub.

Of All Things: Classic Quotations from Hugh Nibley. Hugh Nibley. LC 93-6508. xii, 292p. 1993. pap. 12.95 (0-87579-678-8) Deseret Bk.

Of Amorous Love: Elizabethan Erotic Verse. Ed. by Sandra C. Birkbeck. 300p. 1994. 8.50 (0-460-87530-2, Everyman's Classic Lib) Tuttle Pubng.

***Of Angels & Vipers: A Hawaiian Mystery.** Tom S. Adair. LC 99-91862. 2000. 25.00 (0-7388-1342-7); pap. 18.00 (0-7388-1343-5) Xlibris Corp.

Of Angels, Beasts, & Plagues: The Message of Revelation for a New Millennium. Kenneth H. Maahs. LC 98-32059. 1999. pap. 16.00 (0-8170-1299-0) Judson.

***Of Angels, Things & Death: Paul Klee's Last Painting in Context.** Mark Luprecht. LC 98-21962. (Hermeneutics of Art Ser.: Vol. 9). (Illus.). xii, 187p. (C). 1999. text 48.95 (0-8204-4115-5) P Lang Pubng.

Of Appalachia: Its Heart & Soul. Evelyn J. Seals. (Illus.). 65p. 1982. pap. 4.95 (0-9608268-0-7) E J Seals.

Of Apples & Oranges: Almost a Memoir. Sarah Winston. (Illus.). 182p. 1993. pap. 14.95 (0-9636587-0-0) S Winston.

Of Arms & Men: A History of War, Weapons, & Aggression. Robert L. O'Connell. (Illus.). 384p. 1990. reprint ed. pap. text 16.95 (0-19-505360-5) OUP.

Of Arms I Sing: A Novel. Joseph J. Bohnaker. Ed. by James C. Smith, Jr. LC 89-34611. (Illus.). 260p. (Orig.). 1989. pap. 10.95 (0-86534-136-2) Sunstone Pr.

Of Art & Artists: Selected Reviews of the Arts in Mississippi, 1955-1976. Louis D. Dollarhide. LC 80-52629. 176p. reprint ed. pap. 54.60 (0-7837-1402-5, 204158300021) Bks Demand.

Of Art & Wisdom: Plato's Understanding of Techne. David Roochnik. 1996. 45.00 (0-271-01563-2) Pa St U Pr.

Of Art & Wisdom: Plato's Understanding of Techne. David Roochnik. 312p. 1998. pap. 18.95 (0-271-01841-0) Pa St U Pr.

Of Arthour & of Merlin Vol. I: Text, Vol. I, Text. Ed. by O. D. Macrae-Gibson. (OS 268 Ser.: No. 26). 1973. 29.95 (0-19-722270-6) OUP.

Of Arthour & of Merlin Vol. II: Introduction, Notes & Glossary, Vol. II, Intro., Notes & Glossary. Ed. by O. D. Macrae-Gibson. (OS 279 Ser.: No. 279). 1979. 29.95 (0-19-722281-1) OUP.

Of Authors & Origins: Essays on Copyright Law. Ed. by Brad Sherman & Alain Strowell. 272p. 1994. text 55.00 (0-19-825792-9) OUP.

Of Babylon: A Musical. C. Michael Perry & Susan Lewis. 1997. pap. 4.00 (1-57514-302-X, 0100) Encore Perform Pub.

***Of Bats & Rainbows, Vol. 1.** Jay McCabe. 1999. pap. write for info. (1-58235-177-5) Watermrk Pr.

Of Battle & Beauty: Felice Beato's Photographs of China. David Harris & Felice Beato. LC 98-52794. 2000. pap. write for info. (0-89951-100-7, Pub. by Santa Barb Mus Art) U CA Pr.

***Of Battle & Beauty: Felice Beato's Photographs of China.** David Harris & Felice Beato. LC 98-52794. (Illus.). 2000. 60.00 (0-89951-101-5, Pub. by Santa Barb Mus Art) U CA Pr.

Of Being & Unity. Pico Della Mirandola. 1993. pap. 7.95 (1-55818-206-3, Sure Fire) Holmes Pub.

Of Being Expendable. Lucy Maroulleti. (Illus.). 120p. 1999. pap. 11.95 (1-888447-05-2) Vsns Two-Thousand.

Of Belly & Bone. Peter D. Zivkovic. 65p. 1997. pap. 10.00 (0-944048-10-2) Timberline Missouri.

Of Bench & Bear's: Alaska's Bear Hunting Judge. Richard C. Folta. (Illus.). 224p. 1986. 29.95 (0-937708-05-4) Great Northwest.

Of Bicycles, Bakelites, & Bulbs: Toward a Theory of Sociotechnical Change. Wiebe E. Bijker. (Inside Technology Ser.). 1995. 45.00 (0-262-02376-8) MIT Pr.

Of Bicycles, Bakelites, & Bulbs: Toward a Theory of Sociotechnical Change. Wiebe E. Bijker. (Inside Technology Ser.). (Illus.). 392p. 1997. reprint ed. pap. text 22.50 (0-262-52227-6) MIT Pr.

Of Birds & Beasties: Or Conversations with the Animals. Richard T. Ledger. (Illus.). 145p. 1999. pap. 10.95 (0-9668538-0-6, P03119) Siskiyou.

Of Bison & Man: From the Annals of a Bison Yesterday to a Refreshing Outcome from Human Involvement with America's Most Valiant of Beasts. Harold P. Danz. LC 97-15918. (Illus.). 232p. 1997. 32.50 (0-87081-454-0) Univ Pr Colo.

Of Body & Brush. Angela Zito. LC 97-12362. 244p. 1997. pap. text 17.95 (0-226-98729-9) U Ch Pr.

Of Body & Brush. Angela Zito. LC 97-12362. 244p. 1997. lib. bdg. 45.00 (0-226-98728-0) U Ch Pr.

Of Bookmen & Printers. Ward Ritchie. 189p. 1989. 50.00 (0-87093-275-6) Oak Knoll.

Of Books & Men. Joseph J. Reilly. LC 68-57336. (Essay Index Reprint Ser.). 1977. 23.95 (0-8369-0817-1) Ayer.

Of Books & Sloths - Chinese Edition. Moody Institute of Science Staff. Tr. by CRM Staff. (CHI.). 15p. 1982. pap. 0.50 (1-56582-057-6) Christ Renew Min.

Of Borders & Dreams: A Mexican-American Experience of Urban Education. Chris L. Carger. 176p. 1996. 40.00 (0-8077-3523-X); pap. 17.95 (0-8077-3522-1) Tchrs Coll.

Of Borders & Thresholds: Theatre History, Practice, & Theory. Ed. by Michal A. Kobialka. LC 98-34640. (Illus.). 248p. 1999. 54.95 (0-8166-3090-9); pap. 21.95 (0-8166-3091-7) U of Minn Pr.

Of Boundless Domains. Michael I. Sovern. (Illus.). 96p. (C). 1994. lib. bdg. 29.95 (0-8191-9627-4) U Pr of Amer.

Of Boys & Men. Stephen Keane. Ed. by Pamela Muzoleski. (Illus.). (Orig.). 1997. per. 22.95 (1-57532-031-2) Press-Tige Pub.

Of Breath & Earth: A Book of Days with Wisdom from Native America. John Netherton. (Illus.). 120p. 1999. 14.95 (0-87358-589-5) Northland AZ.

Of Brevity & Wit. Margaret C. Deming. 1997. pap. write for info. (1-57553-548-3) Watermrk Pr.

Of Bridles & Burnings: The Punishment of Women. E. J. Burford & Sandra Shulman. 1992. write for info. (0-318-69233-3) St Martin.

Of Brigands & Bravery: Kuniyoshi's Heroes of the Suikoden. Inge Klopmakers. LC 98-137975. (Illus.). 200p. 1998. 75.00 (90-74822-08-8) Weatherhill.

Of Building: Roger North's Writings on Architects. Roger North & John Henry Newman. Ed. by Howard Colvin. (Illus.). 1981. 59.00 (0-19-817325-3) OUP.

Of Bunsen Burners, Bones, & Belles Lettres: Classic Essays Across the Curriculum. James D. Lester. LC 95-11060. (Library of Classic Essays). 240p. 1995. pap. text, student ed. 14.95 (0-8442-5882-2) NTC Contemp Pub Co.

Of Bunsen Burners, Bones, & Belles Lettres: Classic Essays Across the Curriculum. James D. Lester. (Library of Classic Essays). 1998. pap., teacher ed. 23.99 (0-8442-5883-0) NTC Contemp Pub Co.

Of Butterflies & Unicorns: And Other Wonders of the Earth. Frances Cowden & Eve B. Hatchett. LC 94-75436. (Illus.). 68p. (J). (gr. 2-12). 1994. pap. 8.95 (1-884289-04-5) Grandmother Erth.

Of, by, & for the People: Dancing on the Left in the 1930s. rev. ed. Ed. by Lynn Garafola. (Studies in Dance History). (Illus.). 121p. 1994. reprint ed. pap. 21.95 (0-9653519-4-7, Wesleyan Univ Pr) U Pr of New Eng.

***Of Cabbages & Chemistry.** rev. ed. Jacqueline Barber. Ed. by Lincoln Bergman & Kay Fairwell. (Great Explorations in Math & Science (GEMS) Ser.). (Illus.). 88p. 1999. pap., teacher ed. 10.50 (0-924886-28-5, GEMS) Lawrence Science.

Of Cabbages & Kings: And Many Other Things. Marguerite H. Wolf. LC 84-61616. (Illus.). 134p. (Orig.). 1985. pap. 6.95 (0-933050-25-9) New Eng Pr VT.

Of Cabbages & Kings: Tales from Zinacantan. Robert M. Laughlin. LC 76-608180. (Smithsonian Contributions to Anthropology Ser.: No. 23). 437p. reprint ed. pap. 135.50 (0-608-13833-9, 202031100016) Bks Demand.

Of Cabbages & Kings County: Agriculture & the Formation of Modern Brooklyn. Marc Linder & Lawrence S. Zacharias. LC 98-51779. (Illus.). 512p. 1999. 32.95 (0-87745-670-4) U of Iowa Pr.

***Of Cabbages & Kings County: Agriculture & the Formation of Modern Brooklyn.** Marc Linder & Lawrence S. Zacharias. LC 98-51779. (Illus.). 484p. 2000. reprint ed. pap. text 21.95 (0-87745-714-X) U of Iowa Pr.

Of Camel Kings & Other Things: Rural Rebels Against Modernity in Late Imperial China. Roxann Prazniak. LC 98-23323. (State & Society in East Asia Ser.: Vol. 113). 334p. 1999. 69.00 (0-8476-9006-7); pap. 24.95 (0-8476-9007-5) Rowman.

Of Cannons & Caterpillars. Adela Turin & Syvie Selig. (Feminist Fables for Children Ser.). Orig. Title: Melaracconti. (Illus.). 32p. (J). (gr. 3-6). 1980. 4.95 (0-904613-62-3) Writers & Readers.

Of Caves & Shell Mounds. Ed. by Kenneth C. Carstens & Patty J. Watson. LC 95-20772. (Illus.). 232p. (Orig.). 1996. pap. text 29.95 (0-8173-0805-9) U of Ala Pr.

Of Centaurs & Doves: Guatemala's Peace Process. Susanne Jonas. 312p. 2000. text 65.00 (0-8133-3467-5); pap. text 22.00 (0-8133-3468-3) Westview.

Of Chameleons & Gods. Jack Mapanje. (African Writers Ser.). 80p. (Orig.). (C). 1991. pap. 8.95 (0-435-91194-5, 91194) Heinemann.

Of Chastity & Power: Elizabethan Literature & the Unmarried Queen. Philippa Berry. 240p. 1989. 35.00 (0-415-01507-3, A1584) Routledge.

Of Chastity & Power: Elizabethan Literature & the Unmarried Queen. Phillipa Berry. (Illus.). 192p. (C). 1995. pap. 29.99 (0-415-05672-1, B4776) Routledge.

Of Children. 2nd ed. Lefrancois. (Psychology Ser.). 1977. pap. 18.25 (0-534-00483-0) Brooks-Cole.

Of Children. 4th ed. Guy R. Lefrancois. 192p. (C). 1983. pap. write for info. (0-534-01308-2) Wadsworth Pub.

Of Children. 5th ed. LeFrancois. (Education Ser.). 1985. pap., teacher ed. write for info. (0-534-05504-4); pap., student ed. 8.50 (0-534-05503-6) Wadsworth Pub.

Of Children. 7th ed. Lefrancois. (Education Ser.). 1992. teacher ed. write for info. (0-534-16826-4) Wadsworth Pub.

Of Children. 8th ed. Lefrancois. (Education Ser.). 1994. student ed. 17.25 (0-534-21938-1) Wadsworth Pub.

Of Children: An Introduction to Child Development. 5th ed. Guy R. Lefrancois. 606p. (C). 1985. pap. write for info. (0-534-05502-8) Wadsworth Pub.

Of Children: An Introduction to Child Development. 6th ed. Guy R. Lefrancois. 698p. (C). 1988. pap. write for info. (0-534-09990-4) Wadsworth Pub.

Of Children: An Introduction to Child Development. 7th ed. Guy R. Lefrancois. 762p. (C). 1991. pap. 39.25 (0-534-16824-8) Wadsworth Pub.

Of Children: An Introduction to Child Development. 7th ed. Guy R. Lefrancois. 762p. (C). 1992. pap., student ed. 15.95 (0-534-16825-6) Wadsworth Pub.

Of Children: An Introduction to Child Development. 8th ed. Guy R. Lefrancois. LC 94-30151. 688p. 1994. pap. 83.95 (0-534-21936-5) Wadsworth Pub.

Of Children: An Introduction to Child Development. 8th ed. Guy R. LeFrancois. 1995. teacher ed. write for info. (0-534-21939-X) Brooks-Cole.

Of Chiles, Cacti, & Fighting Cocks: Notes on the American West. Frederick Turner. 88p. 1995. pap. 14.95 (0-8050-3066-2, Owl) H Holt & Co.

Of Christian Doctrine see Augustine De Doctrina Christiana

Of Cigarettes, High Heels & Other Interesting Things: An Introduction to Semiotics. Marcello Danesi. LC 99-17390. (Semaphores & Signs Ser.). 192p. 1999. pap. 17.95 (0-312-21450-2) St Martin.

Of Cities & Women: Letters to Fawwaz. Etel Adnan. LC 92-50342. 85p. 1993. pap. 11.00 (0-942996-21-6) Post Apollo Pr.

***Of Clowns & Gods, Brahmans & Babus: Humour in South Asian Literature.** Ed. by Christina Oesterheld & Claus P. Zoller. LC 99-932115. 181p. 1999. 28.50 (81-7304-260-8, Pub. by Manohar) St Mut.

Of Clowns & Kings. Mary Talken. (Illus.). 200p. (Orig.). 1992. pap. 4.95 (0-9619510-1-X) M Talken.

Of Codes & Crowns: The Development of Law. 96p. 1991. teacher ed. 16.95 (0-318-02222-2); student ed. 7.95 (0-318-02221-4) Constitutional Rights Found.

Of Colleges & Kings. Peter Sammartino. LC 84-14989. 152p. 1985. 13.95 (0-8453-4790-X, Cornwall Bks) Assoc Univ Prs.

Of Colors & Things. Tana Hoban. LC 92-43785. (Illus.). 24p. (J). (ps-k). 1989. 16.00 (0-688-07534-7, Grenwillow Bks) HarpC Child Bks.

Of Colors & Things. Tana Hoban. LC 92-43785. (Illus.). 24p. (J). (ps-k). 1989. 15.93 (0-688-07535-5, Grenwillow Bks) HarpC Child Bks.

Of Colors & Things. Tana Hoban. LC 88-11101. (Illus.). 40p. (J). 1996. mass mkt. 4.95 (0-688-04585-5, Wm Morrow) Morrow Avon.

Of Colors & Things. Tana Hoban. LC 98-229966. (Illus.). 14p. (J). 1998. bds. 6.95 (0-688-16389-0, Wm Morrow) Morrow Avon.

Of Colors & Things. Tana Hoban. 1996. 10.15 (0-606-11696-6, Pub. by Turtleback) Demco.

Of Cops & Priests: Uses of Social & Moral Authority in Contemporary Irish-American Literature. Dennis J. Carroll. LC 92-30422. (American University Studies: American Literature: Ser. XXIV, Vol. 40). IX, 131p. (C). 1993. text 39.95 (0-8204-1967-2) P Lang Pubng.

Of Councils & Counselors, 1570: An English Reworking by Thomas Blundeville of el Consejo I Consejeros Del Principe, 1559. Fadrique Furio Ceriol. LC 63-7083. 140p. 1963. 50.00 (0-8201-1018-3) Schol Facsimiles.

Of Counsel. 2nd ed. Harold G. Wren & Beverly J. Glascock. LC 98-11278. 1998. pap. 84.95 (1-57073-539-5) Amer Bar Assn.

***Of Courage Undaunted: Across the Continent with Lewis & Clark.** James Daugherty. (Illus.). 168p. (YA). (gr. 6-12). 1999. reprint ed. pap. 16.95 (1-893103-02-1) Beautiful Feet.

Of Course I Love You. Albert J. Nimeth. 126p. 1973. pap. 5.00 (0-8199-0951-3, Frncscn Herld) Franciscan Pr.

Of Course I'm for Monogamy. Marilyn Vos Savant. 224p. 1997. pap. 11.95 (0-312-16951-5) St Martin.

Of Course It Matters: Putting the National Commission Report into Action. Ed. by Mary E. Dilworth. 1998. 20.00 (0-89333-165-1) AACTE.

Of Course You Can Draw People. Sally Johnson. 14p. 1985. reprint ed. pap. 5.95 (1-56861-003-3) Swift Lrn Res.

***Of Course you Know That Chocolate is a Vegetable & Other Stories.** Barbara D'Amato. LC 00-24236. (Standard Print Mystery Ser.). 243p. 2000. 20.95 (0-7862-2539-4) Five Star.

Of Course, You're Angry. Gayle Rosellini. 1986. pap. 5.95 (0-86683-576-8) Harper SF.

Of Course You're Angry: A Family guide Dealing with the Emotions of Substance Abuse. Gayle Rossellini & Mark Worden. LC 96-37533. 120p. pap. 11.95 (1-56838-141-7) Hazelden.

Of Cradles & Careers: A Guide to Reshaping Your Job to Include a Baby in Your Life. Kaye Lowman. LC 84-80085. (Illus.). 300p. 1984. pap. 5.00 (0-912500-14-X) La Leche.

Of Crimes & Punishments. Cesare Beccaria. 200p. 1998. pap. text 11.95 (1-56886-054-4) Marsilio Pubs.

Of Critical Theory & Its Theorists. Stephen E. Bronner. 380p. 1994. pap. 28.95 (0-631-18738-3) Blackwell Pubs.

***Of Curious Workmanship: Musings on Things Mormon.** Edgar C. Snow, Jr. LC 99-41027. 132p. 1999. pap. 14.95 (1-56085-136-8) Signature Bks.

Of Customs & Excise: Short Fiction. Rachna Mara. 120p. pap. 14.95 (0-929005-25-2, Pub. by Sec Story Pr) LPC InBook.

***Of Days Gone By: Reflections of South Walton County, Florida.** SWTAA Staff. (Illus.). xii, 224p. 1999. pap. 21.00 (0-9666805-1-0) SWTAA.

Of DC. Robert Gibbons. (Illus.). 16p. (Orig.). 1992. pap. 125.00 (0-911623-10-8) I Klang.

Of Deadly Descent. G. G. Vandagriff. LC 96-17151. 1996. pap. 11.95 (1-57345-167-3) Deseret Bk.

Of Death & Black Rivers. Ann Woodward. (Mystery of Ancient Japan Ser.). 224p. 1998. mass mkt. 5.50 (0-380-79568-X, Avon Bks) Morrow Avon.

Of Derrida, Heidegger, & Spirit. Intro. by David Wood. (Studies in Phenomenology & Existential Philosophy). 160p. (Orig.). 1993. 42.95 (0-8101-1068-7); pap. 16.95 (0-8101-1093-8) Northwestern U Pr.

Of Desire & Disorder. Wayne Dodd. LC 93-73477. (Poetry Ser.). 72p. (Orig.). 1994. pap. 11.95 (0-88748-169-8) Carnegie-Mellon.

***Of Dishes & Discourse: Classical Arabic Literary Representations of Food.** Geert Jan Van Gelder. 250p. 1999. 75.00 (0-7007-1174-0, Pub. by Curzon Pr Ltd) Paul & Co Pubs.

Of Divers Arts. Naum Gabo. LC 62-9369. (Bollingen Ser.: No. 35). 222p. reprint ed. pap. 68.90 (0-8357-6929-1, 203798800009) Bks Demand.

Of Divorce for Adulterie & Marrying Againe: That There Is No Sufficient Warrant So to Do. Edmund Bunny. (English Experience Ser.: No. 781). 1977. reprint ed. lib. bdg. 20.00 (90-221-0781-7) Walter J Johnson.

Of Domesticall Duties. William Gouge. LC 76-57385. (English Experience Ser.: No. 803). 1977. reprint ed. lib. bdg. 75.00 (90-221-0803-1) Walter J Johnson.

***Of Dragons, Kings, Sages & Little Folk.** H. J. Adams. LC 99-63165. 120p. 1999. 22.50 (0-923687-52-1) Celo Valley Bks.

Of Dramatic Poesie: An Essay, 1668. John Dryden & T. S. Eliot. LC 72-1308. (Studies in Dryden: No. 10). 1972. reprint ed. lib. bdg. 75.00 (0-8383-1440-6) M S G Haskell Hse.

***Of Dreams & Assassins.** Malika Mokeddem. LC 99-43291. (Caraf Bks.). 2000. pap. 16.95 (0-8139-1994-0) U Pr of Va.

***Of Dreams & Assassins.** Malika Mokeddem. Tr. by K. Melissa Marcus from FRE. LC 99-43291. (Caraf Bks.). 128p. 2000. 45.00 (0-8139-1933-9) U Pr of Va.

Of Dreams & Demons: A Memoir of Modern India. Patwant Singh. Ed. by Philip Turner. 224p. 1995. pap. 14.00 (1-56836-086-X, Kodansha Globe) Kodansha.

Of Dreams & Fantasies. (Illus.). 16p. 1992. pap. text 52.50 (0-935493-56-5) Modern Learn Pr.

Of Dreams Deferred, Dead or Alive: African Perspectives on African-American Writers, 180. Ed. by Femi Ojo-Ade. LC 95-45960. (Contributions in Afro-American & African Studies: Vol. 180). 208p. 1996. 59.95 (0-313-26475-9, Greenwood Pr) Greenwood.

Of Dust. Don Schofield. Ed. by Robert Bixby. 27p. 1994. pap. text 6.00 (0-9624453-7-1) March Street Pr.

Of Earth & Elders: Visions & Voices from Native America. Serle Chapman. LC 98-73454. (Illus.). 218p. 1999. pap. 24.95 (0-9528607-4-0) Mountain Pr.

***Of Earth & Fire: The T. T. Tsui Collection of Chinese Art in the National Gallery of Australia.** Maud Girard-Geslan. (Illus.). 68p. 2000. pap. text 24.95 (0-642-54128-0, AusInfo) Aust Gov Pub.

Of Earth & Little Rain: The Papago Indians. Bernard L. Fontana. LC 89-5225. (Illus.). 170p. 1990. reprint ed. pap. 15.95 (0-8165-1146-2) U of Ariz Pr.

Of Earth & Timbers Made: New Mexico Architecture. Photos by Arthur LaZar. LC 73-91766. (Illus.). 93p. 1974. reprint ed. pap. 30.00 (0-608-04132-7, 206486500011) Bks Demand.

***Of Easter Eggs & Things.** large type ed. Nan Holcomb. LC 99-58702. (Illus.). 32p. (J). (ps-2). 2000. pap. 8.95 (0-944727-42-5) Jason & Nordic Pubs.

Of Ebony & Alabaster. Helen Arnold. LC 95-75751. 96p. (Orig.). (YA). (gr. 9 up). 1996. pap. 9.95 (1-884242-90-1) Multicult Pubns.

Of Englishe Dogges: The Diversities & the Properties. John Caius. Tr. by A. Fleming. LC 73-26240. (English Experience Ser.: No. 110). 44p. 1969. reprint ed. 15.00 (90-221-0110-X) Walter J Johnson.

Of Excellence & Equity: The 1990 Report of the Occidental College Strategic Planning Steering Committee. Occidental College Staff. (Illus.). 102p. 1991. pap. write for info. (0-940349-02-7) Occi Coll ERC.

Of Fairfield Plantation. Robert W. Hinson. 64p. (Orig.). (YA). (gr. 7-12). 1997. pap. 5.95 (1-890424-00-5) Dyn-Novel.

Of Faith, Miracles, Memories & Reflections. Rogier Donker. (Illus.). 160p. 1998. pap. 16.00 (0-9663775-0-8) Wabash River.

An Asterisk (*) at the beginning of an entry indicates that the title is appearing for the first time.

***Of Fears & Foes: Security & Insecurity in an Evolving Global Political Economy.** Jose V. Ciprut. LC 99-45990. 2000. write for info. (*0-275-96855-3*, Praeger Pubs) Greenwood.

Of Fiction & Faith: Twelve American Writers Talk about Their Vision & Work. W. Dale Brown. LC 97-17558. (Illus.). 278p. 1997. pap. 20.00 (*0-8028-4313-1*) Eerdmans.

***Of Fifty Summers.** Rose S. Melchers. LC 99-74745. (Illus.). 136p. 1999. pap. 12.95 (*0-9673493-1-1*) Les Cheneaux Hist.

***Of Fish, Fly, Worm & Man: Lessons from Developmental Biology for Human Gene Function & Disease.** Ed. by C. Nusslein-Vollhard & J. Kratzschmar. LC 99-56995. (Ernst Schering Research Foundation Workshop Ser.: Vol. 29). (Illus.). 260p. 2000. 76.95 (*3-540-66324-X*) Spr-Verlag.

Of Flame & Clay: Dialogues on Mind-Body Interaction, II. William James Seminar '82 D Members. Ed. by Jeffrey Saver. LC 86-80943. (Annals of the William James Seminars Ser.: Vol. II). 260p. (Orig.). 1986. pap. 25.00 (*0-938537-02-4*) W James Pr.

Of Flame & Clay: Dialogues on Mind-Body Interaction, Set. William James Seminar '82 D Members. Ed. by Jeffrey Saver. LC 86-80943. (Annals of the William James Seminars Ser.: Vol. II). 260p. (Orig.). 1986. pap. 25.00 (*0-938537-00-8*) W James Pr.

Of Flesh & Spirit. Wang Ping. LC 97-43199. 90p. 1998. pap. 12.95 (*1-56689-068-3*) Coffee Hse.

Of Flies, Mice, & Men: On the Revolution in Molecular Biology, by One of the Scientists Who Helped Make It. Francois Jacob. Tr. by Giselle Weiss from ENG. LC 98-7289. 192p. 1998. 24.00 (*0-674-63111-0*) HUP.

Of Force & Violence & Other Imponderables: Essays on War, Politics & Government. Reginald Bretnor. Ed. by Paul D. Seldis. LC 84-306. (Stokvis Studies in Historical Chronology & Thought: No. 6). 144p. (C). 1992. pap. 19.00 (*0-89370-421-0*, 10375498) Millefleurs.

Of Foxes & Hen Houses: Licensing & the Health Professions. Stanley J. Gross. LC 83-11218. (Illus.). 204p. 1984. 49.95 (*0-89930-059-6*, GFH/, Quorum Bks) Greenwood.

Of Foxfire & Phantom Soldiers. George B. Singleton. LC 91-62437. 236p. 1991. pap. write for info. (*1-880307-00-6*) SW AL Pub.

Of Free Trade & Native Interests: The Brookes & the Economic Development of Sarawak, 1841-1941. Ooi K. Gin. LC 96-49828. (South-East Asian Historical Monographs). (Illus.). 456p. 1998. text 45.00 (*983-56-0023-6*) OUP.

Of Friends & Angels. Claudia L. Boyfen. (God's Little Wonders Ser.). 120p. 1998. spiral bd. 4.50 (*1-879127-80-6*) Lighten Up Enter.

Of Frocks & Frogs & Clogs in Bogs: Short Vowel I Sequence. Ellis Richardson. (Read Aloud Ser.: Bk. 7). 32p. (Orig.). 1989. pap. text 4.00 (*1-56775-021-4*, SVIS7-6) ISM Teach Systs.

Of Frogs & Toads: Poems & Short Prose Featuring Amphibians. Ed. by Jill Carpenter. LC 98-93863. (Illus.). 131p. 1998. pap. 10.95 (*0-9666674-0-9*) Ione Pr.

Of Furnaces. Geber the Arabian. Tr. by Richard Russell. 1984. pap. 7.95 (*0-916411-38-9*) Holmes Pub.

Of Gardens & Grandchildren: Reflections on Love & Life. Brain K. Bauknight. LC 92-33158, 96p. 1993. 9.00 (*0-687-28423-6*) Dimen for Liv.

Of Gardens & Grandchildren: Reflections on Love & Life. large type ed. Brian K. Bauknight. 96p. 1993. pap. 1.88 (*0-687-28424-4*) Dimen for Liv.

Of Gary Owen & Glory: The History of the Seventh U. S. Calvary. Melbourne C. Chandler. 1976. 40.95 (*0-8488-0959-9*) Amereon Ltd.

Of Genes, Gods & Tyrants. Camilo Jose Cela & Penelope Lock. 208p. (C). 1987. pap. text 58.50 (*1-55608-036-0*, D Reidel); lib. bdg. 110.00 (*1-55608-024-7*, D Reidel) Kluwer Academic.

Of German Ways. Lavern Rippley. 320p. 1992. pap. 12.00 (*0-06-092380-6*) HarpC.

***Of Giants: Sex, Monsters & the Middle Ages.** Jeffrey J. Cohen. LC 98-53479. (Medieval Cultures Ser.). 1999. write for info. (*0-8166-3216-2*) U of Minn Pr.

***Of Giants: Sex, Monsters & the Middle Ages, 17.** Jeffery Jerome Cohen. LC 98-53479. Vol. 17. (Illus.). 240p. 1999. pap. text 18.95 (*0-8166-3217-0*) U of Minn Pr.

Of Glamor, Sex, & De Sade. Timo Airaksinen. LC 90-35686. 1990. 37.50 (*0-89341-591-X*, Longwood Academic) Hollowbrook.

Of God & Men. A. W. Tozer. 1995. pap. 9.99 (*0-87509-600-X*) Chr Pubns.

Of God Who Comes to Mind. Emmanuel Levinas. Tr. by Bettina Bergo from FRE. LC 97-49446. (Meridian Crossing Aesthetics Ser.). 274p. 1998. 45.00 (*0-8047-3093-8*); pap. 17.95 (*0-8047-3094-6*) Stanford U Pr.

Of Gods & Men. Jeffrey R. Konkol. (Illus.). 340p. (Orig.). 1996. per. 25.00 (*0-9652102-0-0*, NSQ1001) Non Sequitur.

Of Gods & Men: Studies in Lithuanian Mythology. Algirdas J. Greimas. Tr. by Milda Newman. LC 91-48034. (Folklore Studies in Translation). 252p. 1992. 19.95 (*0-253-32652-4*) Ind U Pr.

Of Gods & Men: Studies in Lithuanian Mythology. Algirdas J. Greimas. Tr. by Milda Newman. LC 91-48034. (Folklore Studies in Translation). 246p. Date not set. reprint ed. pap. 76.30 (*0-608-20547-8*, 205446100002) Bks Demand.

Of Gods & Monsters: A Critical Guide to Universal Studios' Science Fiction, Horror & Mystery Films, 1929-1939. John T. Soister. LC 98-38144. (Illus.). 405p. 1998. lib. bdg. 65.00 (*0-7864-0454-X*) McFarland & Co.

Of Gods, Kings, & Men: Bas-Reliefs of Angkor Wat & Bayon. Albert Le Bonheur. (Illus.). 112p. (Orig.). 1996. pap. 39.95 (*0-906026-37-7*, Pub. by Serindia) Weatherhill.

Of Good & Ill Repute: Gender & Social Control in Medieval England. Barbara A. Hanawalt. 224p. (C). 1998. text 47.95 (*0-19-510948-1*) OUP.

"Of Good & Ill Repute' Gender & Social Control in Medieval England. Barbara A. Hanawalt. LC 97-27325. 224p. (C). 1998. pap. 22.95 (*0-19-510949-X*) OUP.

Of "Good Laws" & "Good Men" A Law & Society in the Delaware Valley, 1680-1710. William M. Offutt, Jr. 352p. 1995. text 39.95 (*0-252-02152-5*) U of Ill Pr.

Of Goshen & Paradise: Selected Editorial Writings of Kenneth E. Postlethwaite. Kenneth E. Postlethwaite. LC 98-74319. 359p. 1998. pap. 16.95 (*1-893046-11-7*) Vernon Cty Hist Soc.

Of Grammatology. Jacques Derrida. Tr. by Gayatri Chakravorty Spivak. LC 76-17226. (Illus.). 446p. 1977. pap. 18.95 (*0-8018-1879-6*) Johns Hopkins.

Of Grammatology. Jacques Derrida. Tr. by Gayatri Chakravorty Spivak. LC 76-17226. 450p. 1998. pap. text 19.95 (*0-8018-5830-5*) Johns Hopkins.

Of Grammatology. Jacques Derrida. (C). 1994. text 28.50 (*81-208-1187-9*, Pub. by Motilal Bnarsidass) S Asia.

". . . Of Graves, of Worms & Epitaphs. . . ", Vol. 3. J. W. Kerr. 320p. 1998. 21.95 (*1-891668-02-1*) Lions Hd Pub.

Of Gravity & Angels. Jane Hirshfield. LC 87-21184. (Wesleyan Poetry Ser.). 80p. 1988. pap. 12.95 (*0-8195-1138-2*, Wesleyan Univ Pr) U Pr of New Eng.

Of Great Joy see De Pleno Gozo

Of Great Spaces. Les Galloway & Jerome Gold. (Illus.). 216p. (Orig.). 1987. pap. 9.95 (*0-930773-03-9*) Black Heron Pr.

Of Growing up in War. J. Wayne Beachy. 40p. 1988. 9.99 (*0-9608084-4-2*); pap. 3.99 (*0-685-17363-1*) B Hawkins Studio.

Of Gypsies & Horses & Things. Jacqueline A. Williams. 1998. pap. write for info. (*1-57553-555-6*) Watermrk Pr.

Of Happiness: An Essay. Volterra. LC 98-70640. iii, 350p. 1998. 19.95 (*0-9660806-0-2*) Andover Bks.

Of Heart & Mind: Social Policy Essays in Honor of Sar Levitan. Ed. by Garth L. Mangum & Stephen Mangum. 350p. 1996. 40.00 (*0-88099-172-0*); pap. 22.00 (*0-88099-171-2*) W E Upjohn.

***Of Heartache Humor & Hope: A Collection of Poetry & Song.** Jane M. Long. LC 98-91074. 2000. 14.95 (*0-533-13032-8*) Vantage.

***Of Heartbeats & Heroes.** G. R. Bradley. 58p. 2000. pap. 7.95 (*0-915153-38-6*) Gold Star Pr.

Of Hearts & Wheatfields. Richard M. Johnson. 134p. (Orig.). 1994. pap. 15.00 (*1-883957-04-4*) R Hood Little.

Of Heaven & Earth. Bo Crane. LC 92-36831. 232p. 1992. text 89.95 (*0-7734-9869-9*) E Mellen.

Of Heaven & Earth: Essays Presented at the First Sitchin Studies Day. Zecharia Sitchin et al. (Illus.). 164p. 1996. pap. 14.95 (*1-885395-17-5*) Book Tree.

Of Heaven & Earth: Reconciling Scientific Thought with LDS Theology. David Clark. LC 98-30966. 1998. 18.95 (*1-57345-394-3*) Deseret Bk.

Of Heaven & Hell: A Dialogue Between Junius, a Scholar & Theophorus, His Master. Jacob Boehme. 1986. pap. 4.95 (*0-916411-53-2*, Sure Fire) Holmes Pub.

Of Heroes & Villians. Mark Delaney. LC 98-36466. (Misfits, Inc. Ser.: No. 2). 207p. (YA). (gr. 7-11). 1999. pap. 5.95 (*1-56145-178-9*, 51789) Peachtree Pubs.

Of Heroes, Hooks & Heirlooms. Faye Silton. 1997. pap. 9.95 (*0-8276-0649-4*) JPS Phila.

Of Heroes, Hopes & Level Playing Fields: A Collection of Insights & Observations on Physical Activity & Women. Judy M. Lutter. LC 96-94034. (Illus.). 104p. (Orig.). 1996. pap. 10.00 (*0-9651137-0-1*) Melpomene Inst.

Of Holy Disobedience. A. J. Muste. 23p. (Orig.). 1964. pap. 1.50 (*0-934676-09-7*) Greenlf Bks.

Of Holy Disobedience. A. J. Muste. LC 52-1568. (Orig.). 1952. pap. 1.00 (*0-87574-064-2*) Pendle Hill.

***Of Home & Family: Art in Nineteenth Century Mississippi.** Patti C. Black et al. Ed. by Kathy L. Greenberg. LC 99-39646. (Illus.). 48p. 1999. pap. 20.00 (*1-887422-04-8*) Miss Mus Art.

Of Home & Heart: In a World of the Jewish Woman. S. Shapiro. (ArtScroll Judaiscope Ser.). 1993. 19.99 (*0-89906-890-1*); pap. 16.99 (*0-89906-891-X*) Mesorah Pubns.

***Of Honor & Treason.** C. J. Merle. 260p. 2000. pap. 11.50 (*0-9671979-3-7*) Speculation Pr.

Of Hoopoes & Hummingbirds. Marilyn Dorf. (Illus.). 30p. 1998. pap. 7.00 (*0-9616211-2-5*) Marilyn Dorf.

Of Hopes & Dreams: A Diary. Courtney Williams. Ed. by Margaret Garaway. (Illus.). 83p. (Orig.). (YA). (gr. 6-12). 1997. pap. 10.95 (*0-9638851-8-9*) Old Hogan Pubng.

Of Houses & Time: Personal Histories of America's National Trust Properties. William Seale. (Illus.). 240p. 1992. 49.50 (*0-8109-3671-2*, Pub. by Abrams) Time Warner.

Of Huck & Alice: Humorous Writing in American Literature. Neil Schmitz. LC 82-23895. 277p. 1983. reprint ed. pap. 85.90 (*0-7837-2919-7*, 205753500006) Bks Demand.

Of Human Bondage. W. Somerset Maugham. 1976. 31.95 (*0-8488-1095-3*) Amereon Ltd.

Of Human Bondage. W. Somerset Maugham. 656p. 1991. mass mkt. 5.95 (*0-553-21392-X*, Bantam Classics) Bantam.

Of Human Bondage. W. Somerset Maugham. 704p. 1991. mass mkt. 5.95 (*0-451-52556-6*, Sig Classics) NAL.

Of Human Bondage. W. Somerset Maugham. 1915. 17.05 (*0-606-01173-0*, Pub. by Turtleback) Demco.

Of Human Bondage. W. Somerset Maugham. LC 92-225714. (Twentieth-Century Classics Ser.). 608p. 1992. pap. 11.95 (*0-14-018522-4*, Penguin Classics) Viking Penguin.

***Of Human Bondage.** W. Somerset Maugham. 2000. pap. 14.00 (*0-375-72466-4*) Vin Bks.

Of Human Bondage. large type ed. W. Somerset Maugham. LC 98-49474. 375p. 1998. 27.95 (*1-56000-500-9*) Transaction Pubs.

Of Human Bondage. W. Somerset Maugham. 1981. reprint ed. lib. bdg. 41.95 (*0-89966-386-9*) Buccaneer Bks.

Of Human Bondage. W. Somerset Maugham. 774p. 1999. reprint ed. 39.95 (*0-7351-0121-3*) Replica Bks.

Of Human Bondage. W. Somerset Maugham. (Illus.). 684p. 1992. reprint ed. 33.95 (*1-877767-71-9*) Univ Publng Hse.

Of Human Bondage: Coming of Age in the Novel. Archie K. Loss. (Masterwork Studies: No. 40). 128p. 1989. 23.95 (*0-8057-8067-X*, Twyne); pap. 13.95 (*0-8057-8112-9*, Twyne) Mac Lib Ref.

Of Human Bondage: One of Modern Library's 100 Best Novels. W. Somerset Maugham. LC 98-46169. 1999. pap. 11.95 (*0-375-75315-X*) Modern Lib NY.

Of Human Bondage Notes. Frank B. Huggins. (Cliffs Notes Ser.). 88p. 1963. pap. 4.95 (*0-8220-0930-7*, Cliff) IDG Bks.

Of Human Bonding: Parent-Child Relations Across the Life-Course. Alice S. Rossi & Peter H. Rossi. (Social Institutions & Social Change Ser.). 560p. 1990. pap. text 43.95 (*0-202-30361-6*); lib. bdg. 69.95 (*0-202-30360-8*) Aldine de Gruyter.

Of Human Diversity. Rene Jules Dubos. LC 73-78352. (Heinz Werner Lectures: No. 7). 1974. 9.00 (*0-914206-24-9*) Clark U Pr.

Of Human Freedom. 2nd rev. ed. Jacques Barzun. LC 76-47651. 212p. 1977. reprint ed. lib. bdg. 38.50 (*0-8371-9321-4*, BAOH, Greenwood Pr) Greenwood.

Of Human Hands: A Reader in the Spirituality of Work. Ed. by Gregory F. Pierce. LC 90-44647. (Christian at Work in the World Ser.). 128p. 1991. pap. 8.95 (*0-87946-057-1*, 120) ACTA Pubns.

Of Human Kindness. Ruth C. Mitchell. LC 74-22798. (Labor Movement in Fiction & Non-Fiction Ser.). reprint ed. 45.00 (*0-404-58454-3*) AMS Pr.

Of Human Phenomena. Philip O'Souza. 136p. 1985. 13.95 (*0-318-37151-0*) Asia Bk Corp.

Of Ice & Engines: Twenty-Five Years of Eagle River World's Championship Snowmobile Derby Racing. C. J. Ramstad & Bob Satran. (Illus.). 146p. (Orig.). 1988. pap. text 19.95 (*0-9603786-2-6*) PPM Bks.

***Of Ice & Men: Steve Yzerman, Chris Chelios, Glen Sather, Dominik Hasek: The Craft of Hockey.** Bruce Dowbiggin. (Illus.), 288p. 2000. pap. text 13.95 (*1-55199-042-3*) MW&R.

Of Ice & Men: Steve Yzerman, Chris Chelios, Glen Sather, Dominik Hasek: The Craft of Hockey. Bruce Dowbiggin et al. LC 98-233031. (Illus.). 288p. (J). (gr. 3-6). 2000. text 24.95 (*1-55199-028-8*) MW&R.

Of Illustrious Men. Jean Rouaud. Tr. by Barbara Wright from FRE. LC 94-13979. 160p. 1994. 19.45 (*1-55970-265-6*, Pub. by Arcade Pub Inc) Time Warner.

Of Illustrious Men. Jean Rouaud. Tr. by Barbara Wright from FRE. 160p. 1995. pap. 10.45 (*1-55970-319-9*, Pub. by Arcade Pub Inc) Time Warner.

***Of Innocence & Bondage.** Florence B. Smith. 250p. 1999. pap. 8.00 (*1-893463-29-X*) F B Smith.

Of Inspiration see De Inspiracion

***Of Irish Ways.** Mary M. Delany. 368p. (J). (gr. k-3). 2005. pap. 14.00 (*0-06-092421-7*, Perennial) HarperTrade.

Of Islands & Men: Studies in Pacific History. H. E. Maude. 1969. 23.50 (*0-19-550177-2*) OUP.

Of Islands & Ships: Life & Times of Captain Harry G. Braun. abr. ed. Harry G. Braun. LC 90-93643. (Illus.). 575p. 1997. pap. 21.95 (*1-879393-01-8*) H G Braun P E.

Of Judges, Politics & Flounders: Perspectives on the Cleaning up of Boston Harbor. Ed. by Charles M. Haar. LC KF9921.. (Land Policy Roundtable Case Studies: No. 305). 365p. reprint ed. pap. 113.20 (*0-7837-5753-0*, 204541500006) Bks Demand.

Of Kennedys & Kings. Friend Stuart. 24p. 1971. pap. 2.95 (*0-912132-04-3*) Dominion Pr.

Of Kennedys & Kings: Making Sense of the Sixties. Harris Wofford. LC 92-12624. (Illus.). 544p. (C). 1992. reprint ed. pap. 16.95 (*0-8229-5808-2*) U of Pittsburgh Pr.

Of Kings & Fools: Stories from the French Tradition in North America. Michael Parent & Julien Olivier. LC 96-24379. 208p. 1996. pap. text 12.95 (*0-87483-481-3*) August Hse.

Of Kings & Poets: Cancionero Poetry of the Trastamara Courts. Ingrid Bahler & Katherine G. Gatto. LC 92-13266. (American University Studies: Romance Languages & Literature: Ser. II, Vol. 194). 130p. (C). 1994. text 35.95 (*0-8204-1974-5*) P Lang Pubng.

Of Knights & Fair Maidens: A Radical New Way to Develop Old-Fashioned Relationships. Jeff Myers & Danielle Myers. LC 95-95345. 104p. (Orig.). 1996. pap. 8.95 (*0-9650538-0-6*, B-002) Heartlnd Edu Consul.

Of Knights & Spires: Gothic Revival in France & Germany. Penelope Hunter-Stiebel. (Illus.). 62p. 1989. 25.00 (*0-614-14120-6*) Rosenberg & Stiebel.

Of Land & Labor: Gunston Hall Plantation Life in the 18th Century. M. Lauren Bisbee. (Illus.). 32p. 1994. pap. 4.95 (*1-884085-06-7*) Bd Regents.

Of Lands, Legends & Laughter: The Search for Adventure with National Geographic. Carolyn B. Patterson. LC 98-18616. (Illus.). 224p. 1998. 28.95 (*1-55591-332-6*) Fulcrum Pub.

***Of Landscape & Longing: Finding a Home at the Water's Edge.** Carolyn Servid. LC 99-46482. 198p. 2000. pap. 14.95 (*1-57131-238-2*) Milkweed Ed.

Of Law & Life & Other Things That Matter: Papers & Addresses of Felix Frankfurter, 1956-1963. Felix Frankfurter. Ed. by Philip B. Kurland. LC 65-13221. 269p. reprint ed. pap. 83.40 (*0-7837-2260-5*, 205734800004) Bks Demand.

Of Law & Nations: Between Power Politics & Human Hopes. Julius Stone. LC 73-93977. xvi, 484p. 1974. reprint ed. lib. bdg. 52.50 (*0-930342-03-8*, 301550) W S Hein.

Of Laws & Limitations: An Intellectual Portrait of Louis Dembitz Brandeis. Stephen W. Baskerville. LC 92-58957. 1994. 48.50 (*0-8386-3478-8*) Fairleigh Dickinson.

Of Laws in General. Herbert L. Hart. (Collected Works of Jeremy Bentham). (C). 1970. text 75.00 (*0-485-13210-9*, Pub. by Athlone Pr) Humanities.

Of Learning & Libraries: The Seminary Library at One Hundred. Herman Dicker. 1988. 22.50 (*0-87334-045-0*) Ktav.

Of Lena Geyer. Marcia Davenport. 1976. 30.95 (*0-8488-0795-2*) Amereon Ltd.

Of Lena Geyer. Marcia Davenport. 1998. lib. bdg. 30.95 (*1-56723-036-9*) Yestermorrow.

Of Liberty. Ed. by A. Phillips Griffiths. LC 83-1895. (Royal Institute of Philosophy Lectures: No. 15). 232p. 1983. pap. text 22.95 (*0-521-27415-X*) Cambridge U Pr.

Of Life & Love. Emil Ludwig. LC 72-128273. (Essay Index Reprint Ser.). 1977. 20.95 (*0-8369-1984-X*) Ayer.

Of Life & Salvation: Reflections on Living the Christian Faith. Stanley S. Harakas. 185p. 1997. pap. 12.95 (*1-880971-17-8*) Light&Life Pub Co MN.

Of Life Immense. Sarah Broadstreet. LC 91-42542. 507p. 1992. 25.00 (*0-933532-84-9*) BkMk.

Of Light & Silence. Marguerite G. Bouvard. LC 90-70708. 80p. 1990. pap. 8.95 (*0-944072-12-7*) Zoland Bks.

Of Like Mind Source Book II: For Spiritually-Minded Women. 2nd ed. Ed. by Lynnie Levy & Jade Levy. 122p. 1995. pap. 14.95 (*0-9626751-0-5*) Triple Crescent.

Of Lizards & Angels: A Saga of Siouxland. Frederick Manfred, pseud. LC 91-50865. 626p. (C). 1993. pap. 14.95 (*0-8061-2514-4*) U of Okla Pr.

Of Lobstering & Love: Trials & Triumphs. Roy P. Fairfield. LC 90-82742. (Orig.). 1990. pap. 7.95 (*0-9621921-2-0*) Bastille Bks.

Of Lodz & Love. Chava Rosenfarb. LC 98-52709. 362p. 1999. 29.95 (*0-8156-0577-3*) Syracuse U Pr.

Of Long Memory: Mississippi & the Murder of Medgar Evers. Adam Nossiter. LC 94-45. 303p. 1994. 22.00 (*0-201-60844-8*) Addison-Wesley.

Of Long Memory: Mississippi & the Murder of Medgar Evers. Adam Nossiter. 320p. 1995. pap. 12.00 (*0-201-48339-4*) Addison-Wesley.

Of Love & Asthma. Ferdinand Mount. 1995. pap. 7.99 (*0-7493-2188-1*) Buttrwrth-Heinemann.

***Of Love & Blood.** Henry Ben-Dov. LC 00-190432. 2000. pap. 18.00 (*0-7388-1704-X*) Xlibris Corp.

***Of Love & Blood: A Novel of Suspense.** Henry Ben-Dov. LC 00-190432. 2000. 25.00 (*0-7388-1703-1*) Xlibris Corp.

Of Love & Chivalry: An Anthology of Middle English Romance. Intro. by Jennifer Fellows. 288p. 1993. pap. 6.95 (*0-460-87237-0*, Everyman's Classic Lib) Tuttle Pubng.

Of Love & Death & Other Journeys. Isabelle Holland. LC 74-30012. (YA). (gr. 7 up). 1975. 12.95 (*0-397-31566-X*) HarpC Child Bks.

Of Love & Dust. Ernest J. Gaines. 282p. 1994. pap. 12.00 (*0-679-75248-X*) Vin Bks.

Of Love & Glory. Evelyn Kennedy. 192p. 1989. pap. 10.95 (*0-941483-32-0*) Naiad Pr.

Of Love & Hope - Selections from "Beauty & the Beast" Ed. by Milton Okun. pap. 12.95 (*0-89524-484-5*) Cherry Lane.

Of Love & Intrigue. Virginia Coffman. 1980. mass mkt. 1.95 (*0-451-09313-5*, J9313, Sig) NAL.

Of Love & Leland: A World War II Generation Memoir. Susanah Mayberry. 110p. 1997. 19.95 (*1-57860-003-0*) Guild Pr IN.

Of Love & Other Demons. Gabriel Garcia Marquez. Tr. by Edith Grossman. 160p. 1996. pap. 11.95 (*0-14-025636-9*, Penguin Bks) Viking Penguin.

***Of Love & Pain.** Robert Chamberlin. 2000. write for info. (*1-58235-512-6*) Watermrk Pr.

Of Love & Shadows. Isabel Allende. Tr. by Margaret Sayers Peden from SPA. Orig. Title: De amor y de sombra. 1987. 25.00 (*0-394-54962-7*) Knopf.

Of Love & Shadows. Isabel Allende. Tr. by Margaret Sayers Peden from SPA. LC 86-46164. Orig. Title: De amor y de sombra. 1988. 11.60 (*0-606-03879-5*, Pub. by Turtleback) Demco.

Of Love & Shadows. Isabel Allende & Margaret Sayers Peden. Orig. Title: De amor y de sombra. 304p. 1988. mass mkt. 7.99 (*0-553-27360-4*) Bantam.

Of Love & Shoes. Sarah Singer. (Orig.). 1987. pap. 7.95 (*0-87233-088-5*) Bauhan.

***Of Love & War.** Steve Brown. 260p. 1999. pap. 13.95 (*0-9670273-0-6*) Chick Springs.

***Of Love, Sex & Marriage.** Robert Stein. 190p. 2000. pap. 19.00 (*1-882670-20-5*, Pub. by Spring Jrnl) Continuum.

Of Love, Time & Places: Selected Poems. Charles Madge. 216p. 1994. 39.95 (*0-85646-231-4*, Pub. by Anvil Press) Dufour.

Of Lovers & Madmen. Anita Bush. Ed. by Carolyn S. Zagury. LC 95-60425. 240p. 1995. pap. 10.95 (*1-880254-26-3*) Vista.

Of Lucky Pebbles & Mermaids Tears. Mimi G. Carpenter. (Illus.). 32p. (J). (ps-5). 1994. pap. 9.95 (*0-9614628-2-5*) Beachcomber Pr.

O

Of Making Many Books: A Hundred Years of Reading, Writing, & Publishing. Roger Burlingame. LC 96-14230. (History of the Bk.). (Illus.). 386p. 1996. reprint ed. 55.00 (*0-271-01619-1*); reprint ed. pap. 19.95 (*0-271-01611-6*) Pa St U Pr.

Of Man: The Island & the Continent. 117p. 1997. 45.00 (*1-889954-54-3*); pap. 31.00 (*1-889954-55-1*) J Cassidy Prodns.

Of Man, Time & a River: The Skagit River, How Should It Be Used. De Lorme. (Occasional Papers: No. 10). 1986. pap. 4.00 (*0-318-23329-0*) WWU CPNS.

***Of Manatees & Man.** Douglas Faulkner. 2000. 25.00 (*0-7388-1558-6*); pap. 18.00 (*0-7388-1559-4*) Xlibris Corp.

Of Manners Gentle: Enforcement & Strategies of Australian Business Regulatory Agencies. Ed. by Peter N. Grabosky & John Braithwaite. (Australian Institute of Criminology Ser.). 308p. 1987. pap. 19.95 (*0-19-554690-3*); text 39.95 (*0-19-554691-1*) OUP.

Of Many Colors: Portraits of Multiracial Families. Gigi Kaeser & Peggy Gillespie. LC 97-6530. (Illus.). 160p. 1997. 40.00 (*1-55849-100-7*); pap. 19.95 (*1-55849-101-5*) U of Mass Pr.

"Of Many Heroes" An Indian Essay in Literary Historiography G. N. Devy. LC 98-905080. 213 p. 1998. write for info. (*81-250-1309-1*) Orient Longman Ltd.

Of Many Lands: Journal of a Traveling Childhood. Sara M. Taber. (Illus.). 104p. (Orig.). (YA). (gr. 8-12). 1997. pap. 10.50 (*0-9658538-0-2*) Foreign Serv Youth.

Of Manywhere-at-Once: Ruminations from the Site of a Poem's Construction. Bob Grumman. (Illus.). 214p. (Orig.). 1990. pap. 10.00 (*0-926935-38-0*) Runaway Spoon.

Of Manywhere-at-Once: Ruminations from the Site of a Poem's Construction. 3rd rev. ed. Bob Grumman. (Illus.). 190p. (Orig.). 1998. pap. 10.00 (*1-57141-045-7*) Runaway Spoon.

Of Manywhere-at-Once Vol. 1: Ruminations from the Site of a Poem's Construction. 2nd rev. ed. Bob Grumman. (Illus.). 222p. 1991. pap. 10.00 (*0-926935-58-5*) Runaway Spoon.

Of Marriage & Piracy: 25 Poems. Jim Benson. LC 99-25056. 72p. 1999. pap. text 14.95 (*0-7734-3115-2*) E Mellen.

Of Marriage & the Market: Women's Subordination Internationally & Its Lessons. Kate Young et al. 240p. (Orig.). 1984. pap. 13.95 (*0-415-03019-6*) Routledge.

Of Marshes & Maize: Preceramic Agricultural Settlements in the Cienega Valley. Bruce B. Huckell. 166p. 1995. pap. 14.95 (*0-8165-1582-4*) U of Ariz Pr.

Of Marxism & Indian Politics. Randhir Singh. (C). 1990. 14.00 (*81-202-0267-8*, Pub. by Ajanta) S Asia.

Of Mary, There Is Never Enough. William L. Biersach. 110p. (Orig.). (YA). (gr. 8 up). 1995. pap. 3.95 (*1-885692-01-3*) Cath Treas.

Of Masks & Minds. large type ed. Frederick E. Smith. 1990. 27.99 (*0-7089-2178-7*) Ulverscroft.

Of Masks & Mysteries. Ed. by S. B. Jones-Hendrickson. 70p. 1993. pap. 7.95 (*0-932831-11-7*) Eastern Caribbean Inst.

Of Masques & Martyrs. Christopher Golden. (Shadow Saga Ser.: Vol. 3). 1998. pap. 5.99 (*0-441-00584-5*) Ace Bks.

Of Me I Sing. Malcolm Bingay. (American Autobiography Ser.). 300p. 1995. reprint ed. lib. bdg. 79.00 (*0-7812-8459-7*) Rprt Serv.

Of Media & People. Everette Dennis. 160p. (C). 1992. 42.00 (*0-8039-4746-1*); pap. 19.95 (*0-8039-4747-X*) Sage.

Of Media & People. Everette E. Dennis. LC 92-28903. 195p. 1992. reprint ed. pap. 60.50 (*0-608-04306-0*, 206508500012) Bks Demand.

Of Memory & Desire: Stories. Gladys Swan. LC 88-38353. 184p. 1989. 16.95 (*0-8071-1480-4*) La State U Pr.

Of Memory, Reminiscence & Writing: On the Verge. David F. Krell. LC 89-46331. (Studies in Continental Thought). 352p. 1990. 39.95 (*0-253-33193-5*); pap. 19.95 (*0-253-20592-1*, MB-592) Ind U Pr.

Of Men & Angels. Paul Henri. 320p. 1988. 21.90 (*0-685-19930-4*) Clarion-Knight Pubns.

Of Men & Galaxies. Fred Hoyle. LC 64-25266. (Jessie & John Danz Lectures). 83p. 1964. 10.00 (*0-295-73859-6*) U of Wash Pr.

Of Men & Gods. Julius C. Bennett. LC 81-82234. 1982. 10.95 (*0-87212-149-6*) Libra.

Of Men & Gold. Stephen B. Shaffer. (Illus.). 216p. (Orig.). (YA). (gr. 7-12). 1994. pap. 19.95 (*0-9644378-0-5*) S B Shaffer.

Of Men & Marshes. Paul L. Errington. (Illus.). 160p. 1996. reprint ed. pap. 16.95 (*0-8138-2929-1*) Iowa St U Pr.

Of Men & Monsters. William Tenn. 256p. (Orig.). 1981. mass mkt. 2.50 (*0-345-29523-4*, Del Rey) Ballantine Pub Grp.

Of Men & Monsters: Jeffrey Dahmer & the Construction of the Serial Killer. Richard Tithecott. pap. 14.95 (*0-299-15684-2*) U of Wis Pr.

Of Men & Monsters: Jeffrey Dahmer & the Construction of the Serial Killer. Richard Tithecott. LC 97-15170. 208p. 1997. 24.95 (*0-299-15680-X*) U of Wis Pr.

Of Men & Mountains. William Douglas. 360p. 1990. pap. 10.95 (*0-87701-712-3*) Chronicle Bks.

Of Men & Music. Deems Taylor. LC 80-2305. reprint ed. 36.00 (*0-404-18873-7*) AMS Pr.

Of Men & Numbers: The Story of the Great Mathematicians. unabridged ed. Jane Muir. (Illus.). 256p. 1996. reprint ed. pap. text 7.95 (*0-486-28973-7*) Dover.

Of Men & of Angels. Bodie Thoene. (Galway Chronicles Ser.). 1999. pap. text 9.97 (*0-7852-6929-0*) Nelson.

Of Men & of Angels. Bodie Thoene & Brock Thoene. 324p. 1999. pap. 10.99 (*0-7852-6913-4*) Nelson.

Of Men & of Angels: A Novel. Bodie Thoene & Brock Thoene. LC 98-13533. (Galway Chronicles Ser.). 320p. 1998. 22.99 (*0-7852-8068-5*) Nelson.

Of Men & Stars: A History of Lockheed Aircraft Corporation. Lockheed Aircraft Corporation Staff. Ed. by James B. Gilbert. LC 79-7280. (Flight: Its First Seventy-Five Years Ser.). (Illus.). 1980. reprint ed. lib. bdg. 26.95 (*0-405-12189-X*) Ayer.

Of Men & Wings: The First 100 Missions of the 449th Bombardment Group. D. William Shepherd. LC 96-111738. (Illus.). 400p. 1996. 30.00 (*1-887715-00-2*) Norfield Pubng.

Of Men of Muskets Vol. XI: Stories of the Civil War. Robert P. Broadwater. LC 98-7161. (Civil War Heritage Ser.). 80p. 1998. pap. 7.95 (*1-57249-105-1*, Burd St Pr) White Mane Pub.

Of Men, Ropes & Remembrance: The Stories from Bound & Gagged Magazine. Larry Townsend. LC 98-219442. 160p. 1997. pap. 12.95 (*1-881684-15-6*) L T Pubns CA.

Of Messages & Media: Teaching & Learning by Public Television. Henry C. Alter. (Notes & Essays Ser.: No. 58). (C). 1968. pap. text 2.00 (*0-87060-022-2*, NES 58) Syracuse U Cont Ed.

Of Methods, Monarchs & Meanings: An Approach to Sociothetorical Exegesis. Gina Hens-Piazza. (Studies in Old Testament Interpretation: Vol. 3). 176p. 1996. text 30.00 (*0-86554-514-6*, MUP/H399) Mercer Univ Pr.

Of Mice. Susan Luca. (Illus.). 1970. pap. 12.50 (*0-912020-16-4*) Turtles Quill.

Of Mice & Magic: A History of American Animated Cartoons. Leonard Maltin. LC 87-20234. 1987. pap. 26.95 (*0-452-25993-2*, Plume) Dutton Plume.

Of Mice & Men. (Assessment Packs Ser.). 15p. 1998. pap. text 15.95 (*1-58303-055-7*) Pthways Pubng.

Of Mice & Men. Holt & Company Staff. 1989. pap., student ed. 11.00 (*0-03-023449-2*) Holt R&W.

Of Mice & Men. Emily Hutchinson. (Golden Leaf Classics). 48p. 1993. student ed. 9.95 (*1-56872-005-X*) Incent Lrning.

***Of Mice & Men.** Maureen Kirchhoefer & Mary Dennis. 32p. (YA). 1998. 11.95 (*1-56137-310-9*) Novel Units.

***Of Mice & Men.** Gloria Levine. 32p. 1998. 9.95 (*1-56137-187-4*) Novel Units.

Of Mice & Men. John Steinbeck. Ed. by Michael Goodman & Tessa Krailing. (Barron's Book Notes Ser.). (C). 1984. pap. 3.95 (*0-8120-3431-7*) Barron.

Of Mice & Men. John Steinbeck. 1950. pap. 5.25 (*0-8222-0838-5*) Dramatists Play.

Of Mice & Men. John Steinbeck. 1992. 11.05 (*0-606-00200-6*, Pub. by Turtleback) Demco.

Of Mice & Men. John Steinbeck. Ed. by Sarat Austin. 1997. pap. 19.95 (*0-14-018829-0*) Viking Penguin.

***Of Mice & Men.** John Steinbeck & Ruth Coleman. (Literature Made Easy Ser.). (Illus.). 96p. (YA). 1999. pap. 4.95 (*0-7641-0820-4*) Barron.

Of Mice & Men. large type ed. John Steinbeck. LC 95-12160. 126p. 1995. lib. bdg. 20.95 (*0-7838-1358-9*, G K Hall Lrg Type) Mac Lib Ref.

Of Mice & Men, Vol. 2. Linda Butler. (ESOL Companion Guide Ser.). 128p. (C). 1996. pap. 12.19 (*0-07-009427-6*) McGraw.

Of Mice & Men: A Kinship of Powerlessness. Charlotte Hadella. LC 94-49322. (Twayne's Masterwork Studies: No. 147). 1995. 25.95 (*0-8057-8589-2*, Twyne); pap. 18.00 (*0-8057-8590-6*, Twyne) Mac Lib Ref.

Of Mice & Men: A Study Guide. Selena Smith et al. (Novel-Ties Ser.). (YA). (gr. 9-12). 1983. pap. text, teacher ed. 15.95 (*0-88122-028-0*) Lrn Links.

Of Mice & Men: A Unit Plan. Mary B. Collins. 150p. 1994. teacher ed., ring bd. 26.95 (*1-58337-002-1*) Teachers Pet Pubns.

Of Mice & Men: Reproducible Teaching Unit. rev. ed. James Scott. 26p. (YA). (gr. 7-12). 1988. teacher ed., ring bd. 29.50 (*1-58049-072-7*, TU33/U) Prestwick Hse.

Of Mice & Men: The Play. John Steinbeck. 124p. (C). 1989. pap. 14.95 (*0-09-175758-4*) Dufour.

Of Mice & Men: The Play. John Steinbeck. 112p. 1993. pap. 6.95 (*0-14-017739-6*, Penguin Bks) Viking Penguin.

Of Mice & Men: The Play. John Steinbeck. LC 93-11712. 160p. 1994. pap. 13.99 (*0-14-018642-5*) Viking Penguin.

Of Mice & Men Notes. James L. Roberts. (Cliffs Notes Ser.). 56p. 1966. pap. 4.95 (*0-8220-0939-0*, Cliff) IDG Bks.

***Of Mice & Metaphors.** Brandell. 2000. 40.00 (*0-465-00712-0*, Pub. by Basic) HarpC.

Of Mice & Mice. deluxe ed. Jean G. Howard. LC 78-50486. (Illus.). (J). (gr. k-4). 1978. boxed set 35.00 (*0-930954-04-1*) Tidal Pr.

Of Mice & Mice. limited ed. Jean G. Howard. LC 78-50486. (Illus.). (J). (gr. k-4). 1978. 5.50 (*0-930954-03-3*) Tidal Pr.

Of Mice & Rats. Allan Fowler. LC 97-28658. (Rookie Read-About Science Ser.). (Illus.). 32p. (J). (gr. 1-2). 1998. 18.50 (*0-516-20800-4*) Childrens.

Of Mice & Rats. Allan Fowler. LC 97-28658. (Rookie Read-About Science Ser.). (Illus.). 32p. (YA). (gr. 1-2). 1999. pap. text 4.95 (*0-516-26418-4*) Childrens.

Of Mice & Women: Aspects of Female Aggression. Ed. by Kaj Bjorkqvist & Pirkko Niemela. (Illus.). 414p. 1992. text 55.00 (*0-12-102590-X*) Acad Pr.

Of Mice, Men & Microbes. David R. Harper & Andrea S. Meyer. LC 99-60590. (Illus.). 278p. 1999. 34.95 (*0-12-326460-X*) Acad Pr.

Of Mice, Models, & Men: A Critical Evaluation of Animal Research. Andrew N. Rowan. LC 83-4986. 323p. 1984. text 21.50 (*0-87395-776-8*) State U NY Pr.

***Of Microbes & Art: The Role of Microbial Communities in the Degradation & Protection of Cultural Heritage.** Orio Ciferri et al. LC 00-23508. 2000. write for info. (*0-306-46377-6*, Kluwer Plenum) Kluwer Academic.

Of Microbes & Molecules: Food Technology, Nutrition & Applied Biology at M. I. T., 1873-1988. Samuel A. Goldblith. LC 95-61147. 329p. 1995. 49.00 (*0-917678-35-4*, 3292) Food & Nut Pr.

***Of Midnight Born.** Lisa Cach. 368p. 2000. pap. 5.50 (*0-505-52399-X*, Love Spell) Dorchester Pub Co.

Of Midnight Tales Obsessed! George D. Kovach. (Illus.). 111p. 1999. pap. 19.95 (*0-7414-0078-2*) Buy Books.

Of Mikes & Men: From Ray Scott to Curt Gowdy: Broadcast Tales from the Pro Football Booth. Curt Smith. LC 97-35177. (Illus.). 1998. 24.95 (*1-888698-11-X*) Diamond Communications.

Of Milk & Honey: A Workbook on Israel & the Bible. Shoshana Rick. 56p. 1992. pap. 6.95 (*965-229-086-6*, Pub. by Gefen Pub Hse) Gefen Bks.

Of Mind & Music Laird Addis. LC 98-55442. 1999. 29.95 (*0-8014-3589-7*) Cornell U Pr.

Of Mind & Other Matters. Nelson Goodman. LC 83-12868. (Illus.). 224p. 1987. pap. 15.50 (*0-674-63126-9*) HUP.

***Of Minds & Molecules: New Philosophical Perspectives on Chemistry.** Nalini Bhushan & Stuart Rosenfeld. LC 99-40329. (Illus.). 320p. 2000. text. write for info. (*0-19-512834-6*) OUP.

***Of Minimal Things: Essays on The Notion of Relation.** Rodolphe Gasche. LC 99-38672. 1999. pap. text 19.95 (*0-8047-3677-4*) Stanford U Pr.

***Of Minimal Things: Studies on the Notion of Relation.** Rodolphe Gasche. LC 99-38672. (Cultural Memory in the Present Ser.). 380p. 1999. 55.00 (*0-8047-3676-6*) Stanford U Pr.

Of Mixed Blood: Kinship & History in Peruvian Amazonia. Peter Gow. (Oxford Studies in Social & Cultural Anthropology). (Illus.). 344p. 1991. text 85.00 (*0-19-827355-X*) OUP.

Of Mockingbirds & Other Irrelevancies. Edward T. Dell, Jr. LC 93-79273. 100p. 1993. 9.95 (*0-8338-0208-9*) Audio Amateur.

Of Moles & Molehunters: A Review of Counterintelligence Literature, 1977-92. (Illus.). 193p. (Orig.). (C). 1995. pap. text 50.00 (*0-7881-1642-8*) DIANE Pub.

Of Moment. Jonathan Greene. LC 98-70541. 64p. 1998. pap. 10.50 (*0-917788-68-0*) Gnomon Pr.

***Of Monkeys & Dragons: Freedom from the Tyranny of Disease.** Michele Longo O'Donnell. 224p. 2000. 21.95 (*0-9676861-0-5*, Pub. by LaVida); pap. 12.95 (*0-9676861-1-3*, Pub. by LaVida) Bk Marketing Plus.

Of Moonlight & Wishes. Ed. by Melissa Mitchell. Date not set. 69.95 (*1-57553-345-6*) Watermrk Pr.

Of Moons, Moods, Myths, & the Muse. Frederick C. Tillis. 70p. 1993. 14.95 (*0-9639417-0-4*) P & P Publns.

Of Moose & Men: Askewed Look at Life in Alaska. A. E. Poynor. LC 99-218014. xii, 208p. 1999. pap. 12.95 (*0-9667915-0-9*) O M M Bks.

Of Mosaics & Mosques: A Look at the Campaign to Preserve Cultural Heritage. David Wigg. LC 93-47286. (Development Essays Ser.: No. 3). 56p. 1994. pap. 22.00 (*0-8213-2732-1*, 12732) World Bank.

Of Moses & Marx: Folk Ideology & Folk History in the Jewish Labor Movement. Ed. by David P. Shuldiner. LC 98-31941. 264p. 1999. 65.00 (*0-89789-617-3*, Bergin & Garvey) Greenwood.

Of Mother Earth & Father Sky. Fred Bia & T. L. McCarthy. (Illus.). 69p. 1983. pap. 8.00 (*0-685-42612-2*) Rough Rock Pr.

Of Mozart, Parrots & Cherry Blossoms in the Wind: A Composer Explores Mysteries of the Musical Mind. Bruce Adolphe. LC 99-40618. 240p. 1999. pap. 13.95 (*0-87910-286-1*) Limelight Edns.

Of Mudlarkers & Measurers. Sarindar Dhaliwal et al. LC 98-171464. 23 p. 1997. pap. write for info. (*0-88911-742-X*) Queens U Inst Intergov.

Of Murder & Madness. Gerry Spence. LC KF224.E85S67. 1995. mass mkt. 6.99 (*0-312-95687-8*) St Martin.

Of Museums, Monsoon & Mausoleums: Poems. Richard E. Johnson. LC 98-33463. 68p. 1998. pap. 14.95 (*0-7734-2849-6*) E Mellen.

Of Music & Music-Making. Bruno Walter. 222p. reprint ed. lib. bdg. 39.00 (*0-685-14780-0*) Rprt Serv.

***Of My Flesh & This Wicked World.** Charles B. Lucier. LC 99-60692. 288p. 1999. 21.95 (*1-56167-491-5*) Noble Hse MD.

Of Mysticism & Mechanism. Ed. by Sarah Hutton. (C). 1989. lib. bdg. 163.00 (*0-7923-0095-5*) Kluwer Academic.

***Of Myths & Movements: Rewriting Chipko into Himalayan History.** Haripriya Rangan. 256p. 2000. 60.00 (*1-85984-783-8*, Pub. by Verso); pap. 20.00 (*1-85984-305-0*, Pub. by Verso) Norton.

Of Nature Seen & Heard & of Beauty Touched. Patti Weber. 1997. pap. 56.95 (*1-57553-559-9*) Watermrk Pr.

Of Nightingales That Weep. Katherine Paterson. LC 74-8294. (Illus.). (J). (gr. 5 up). 1974. 14.00 (*0-690-00485-0*) HarpC Child Bks.

Of Nightingales That Weep. Katherine Paterson. (J). 1974. 9.60 (*0-606-04039-0*, Pub. by Turtleback) Demco.

Of Nightingales That Weep. Katherine Paterson. LC 74-8294. (Trophy Bk.). (Illus.). 192p. (J). (gr. 4-7). 1989. reprint ed. pap. 4.95 (*0-06-440282-7*, HarpTrophy) HarpC Child Bks.

Of No Country I Know: New & Selected Poems & Translations. David Ferry. LC 99-20899. (Phoenix Poets Ser.). 224p. 1999. pap. 14.00 (*0-226-24487-3*) U Ch Pr.

Of No Country I Know: New & Selected Poems & Translations. David Ferry. LC 99-20899. (Phoenix Poets Ser.). 320p. 2000. lib. bdg. 30.00 (*0-226-24486-5*) U Ch Pr.

***Of Noble Birth.** Brenda Novak. 416p. 1999. mass mkt. 5.99 (*0-06-109859-0*) HarpC.

Of Noble Character. Joy Bray. 132p. (Orig.). 1988. pap. 5.95 (*0-89827-059-6*, BKD93) Wesleyan Pub Hse.

Of Nukes & Nose Cones: A Submarine Story. Arthur C. Bivens. LC 96-76395. (Illus.). iv, 125p. 1996. 12.00 (*0-9655171-0-1*) A C Bivens.

Of One Blood: Abolitionism & the Origins of Racial Equality. Paul Goodman. LC 97-45560. 426p. 1998. 35.00 (*0-520-20794-7*, Pub. by U CA Pr) Cal Prin Full Svc.

***Of One Blood: Abolitionism & the Origins of Racial Equality.** Paul Goodman. (Illus.). 426p. 2000. pap. 16.95 (*0-520-22679-8*) U CA Pr.

Of One Mind: Poems. Myrtle Stedman. LC 90-46382. (Illus.). 128p. (Orig.). 1990. pap. 10.95 (*0-86534-155-9*) Sunstone Pr.

Of One Mind: The Collectivization of Science. John M. Ziman. LC 94-34902. (Masters of Modern Physics Ser.: Vol. 13). 1994. write for info. (*1-56396-065-6*) Spr-Verlag.

***Of Orphans & Warriors: Inventing Chinese-American Culture & Identity.** Gloria H. Chun. LC 99-33563. 208p. 2000. text 50.00 (*0-8135-2708-2*); pap. text 19.00 (*0-8135-2709-0*) Rutgers U Pr.

Of Other Gods. Bryan Millar. 416p. mass mkt. 4.99 (*1-896329-27-6*) Picasso Publ.

Of Other Worlds. Timothy J. Reigler. 128p. 1992. pap. 4.95 (*0-9633459-0-7*) Top Shelf Pr.

Of Other Worlds: Essays & Stories. C. S. Lewis. Ed. by Walter Hooper. LC 75-6785. 168p. (C). 1975. pap. 10.00 (*0-15-667897-7*, Harvest Bks) Harcourt.

Of Oxygen, Fuels, & Living Matter, Pt. 1. Ed. by G. Semenza. LC 80-41420. (Evolving Life Sciences Ser.: Vol. 1). 361p. 1981. reprint ed. pap. 112.00 (*0-608-08445-X*, 202598300001) Bks Demand.

Of Oxygen, Fuels, & Living Matter, Pt. 2. Ed. by G. Semenza. LC 80-41420. (Evolving Life Sciences Ser.: Vol. 1). 520p. 1982. reprint ed. pap. 161.20 (*0-608-08446-8*, 202598300002) Bks Demand.

Of Pandas & People. 17.95 (*0-914513-40-0*) Fnd for Thought.

Of Pandas & People: The Central Question of Biological Origins. Percival Davis & Dean H. Kenyon. (Illus.). 166p. 1989. 17.95 (*0-685-58687-1*) Haughton.

Of Parks & People. John M. Doyle & Joanne M. Doyle. 50p. 1999. 10.00 (*0-9672703-0-8*) Wild Geese Ent.

Of Passionate Intensity: Right-Wing Populism & the Reform Party of Canada. Trevor Harrison. (Illus.). 360p. 1995. text 50.00 (*0-8020-0600-0*); pap. text 18.95 (*0-8020-7204-6*) U of Toronto Pr.

Of Peasants, Paupers & Migrants: Rural Labour Circulation & Capitalist Production in West India. Jan Breman. (Illus.). 500p. 1986. text 48.00 (*0-19-561649-9*) OUP.

Of Pen & Ink & Paper Scraps. Lucien Stryk. LC 89-4110. 72p. (C). 1989. pap. 11.95 (*0-8040-0919-8*); text 21.95 (*0-8040-0918-X*) Swallow.

Of People & Plants: The Autobiography of Europe's Most Celebrated Herbal Healer. Maurice Messegue. 336p. (Orig.). 1991. pap. 12.95 (*0-89281-437-3*) Inner Tradit.

Of People & Things. Stella M. Dickerson. Ed. by Janet Leih. (Illus.). 120p. 1990. pap. 8.00 (*1-877649-09-0*) Tesseract SD.

Of People, of Places: Sketches from an Economist's Diary. Kaushik Basu. LC 94-907468. (Oxford India Paperbacks Ser.). 180p. 1995. pap. text 6.95 (*0-19-563473-X*) OUP.

Of Permanent Value: The Story of Warren Buffett. Andrew Kilpatrick. (Illus.). 650p. 1994. 27.50 (*0-9641905-0-8*) A Kilpatrick.

***Of Permanent Value: The Story of Warren Buffett.** **Andrew Kilpatrick. (Illus.). 1162p. 2000. 30.00 (*0-9641905-3-2*) A Kilpatrick.**

Warren Buffett a Berkshire Hathaway was created by Buffett from a financial career he began while operating alone in his bedroom as a young man in Omaha. Even at the age of six Buffett paid a quarter for a six pack of Cokes & sold each Coke for a nickel .. a return of 20

. From then on he compounded his returns at slightly better than 20

. That's why he's a multi-billionaire - one of the richest people in the world. But not every year is a good one & 1999 was Buffett's worst. Still, despite a sharp drop in the stock price, the book value - or the accounting value - of Berkshire remained virtually unchanged. And the intrinsic value, the true value of the company in the real world as it would be set by rational buyers & sellers - not by the fearful & greedy at the edge of the market - remained well above the stock price. Today Berkshire is a huge insurance conglomerate which owns General Re Corp., one of the world's largest insurance companies, but which was hit by storm damages, movie flops & a $20 million home fire in 1999. Berkshire owns GEICO, the fast-growing auto insurer. Berkshire also is a significant shareholder in some of the greatest companies on hearth: Coca-Cola, Gillette, American Express & Dun &

An Asterisk (*) at the beginning of an entry indicates that the title is appearing for the first time.

Bradstreet ... a brand name extravaganza in addition to these & other stocks worth about $35 billion, Berkshire owns about $30 billion in bonds & holds about $3 billion in cash. ***Publisher Paid Annotation.***

Of Permanent Value: The Story of Warren Buffett. expanded rev. ed. Andrew Kilpatrick. 730p. 1996. 30.00 (*0-9641905-1-6*) A Kilpatrick.

***Of Permanent Value: The Story of Warren Buffett.** rev. ed. Andrew Kilpatrick. LC 99-45107. 890p. 1999. pap. 19.95 (*0-07-135773-4*) McGraw.

Of Permanent Value 1998 ed. The Story of Warren Buffett. 3rd rev. ed. Andrew Kilpatrick. (Illus.). 800p. 1998. 30.00 (*0-9641905-2-4*) A Kilpatrick.

Of Pigs & Spiders. Brett Savory et al. (Illus.). 63p. 1999. pap. 8.00 (*0-9665662-6-2*, Shadowlands Pr) Bereshith.

Of Pigs & Spiders. deluxe ed. Brett Savory et al. (Illus.). 63p. 1999. 30.00 (*0-9665662-9-7*, Shadowlands Pr) Bereshith.

Of Pines. Robert VanderMolen. 20p. (Orig.). 1989. pap. 4.00 (*0-945926-12-X*) Paradigm RI.

Of Piscator: Poems by Martin Corless-Smith. Martin Corless-Smith. LC 97-18690. (Contemporary Poetry Ser.). 1998. pap. 15.95 (*0-8203-1947-3*) U of Ga Pr.

Of Plants & People. Charles B. Heiser, Jr. LC 84-28126. (Illus.). 256p. (C). 1992. pap. 14.95 (*0-8061-2410-5*) U of Okla Pr.

Of Plymouth Plantation. William Bradford. 385p. (C). 1981. pap. 7.50 (*0-07-554281-1*) McGraw.

Of Plymouth Plantation, 1620 to 1647. William Bradford. Ed. by Samuel Eliot Morison. (American Past Ser.). (Illus.). 1952. 25.00 (*0-394-43895-7*) Knopf.

Of Poetry & Music's Power: Humanism & the Creation of Opera. Barbara R. Hanning. Ed. by George Buelow. LC 80-12637. (Studies in Musicology: No. 13). (Illus.). 388p. 1980. reprint ed. pap. 120.30 (*0-8357-1071-8*, 207004700063) Bks Demand.

Of Poetry & Poets. Richard Eberhart. LC 78-11597. 326p. 1979. text 29.95 (*0-252-00630-5*) U of Ill Pr.

Of Poetry & Politics: New Essays on Milton & His World. Ed. by P. G. Stanwood. LC 94-20124. (Medieval & Renaissance Texts & Studies: Vol. 126). 368p. 1997. reprint ed. 24.00 (*0-86698-131-4*, MR126) MRTS.

Of Poles & Zeros: Fundamentals of Digital Seismology. Frank Scherbaum. (Modern Approaches in Geophysics Ser.: Vol. 15). 1996. lib. bdg. 124.00 (*0-7923-4012-4*) Kluwer Academic.

Of Porcupines & Death. Ruth W. Schuler et al. (Illus.). 36p. 1986. pap. 4.00 (*0-910083-21-5*) Heritage Trails.

Of Power & Faith. Joseph S. Salzburg. 163p. 1967. 5.00 (*0-317-60912-2*, EP45678) Sovereign MD.

Of Power & Love & Sound Mind: Six Years with Undiagnosed Lyme Disease. Linda Hanner. 224p. 1989. 5.00 (*0-9622669-0-6*) Kashan Pub.

Of Preaching in America. Touma Al-Khouri. (Trilogy for Christ Ser.: Pt. 2). 300p. 1995. per. 10.95 (*1-879038-23-4*) Oakwood Pubns.

Of Predation & Life. Paul L. Errington. LC 67-20153. (Illus.). 291p. reprint ed. pap. 90.30 (*0-608-15493-8*, 202968000062) Bks Demand.

Of Presbyters & Kings: Church & State in the Law of Scotland. Francis Lyall. 220p. 1980. 27.00 (*0-08-025715-1*, Pergamon Pr) Elsevier.

Of Primary Importance: A Practical Guide for Directors of Younger Elementary Choristers. Helen Kemp. 90p. 1989. pap. text 15.95 (*1-929187-02-5*, CGBK50) Choristers.

Of Primary Importance: A Practical Guide for Directors of Your Choristers, 2 vols., Vol. II. Helen Kemp. 92p. 1991. reprint ed. pap. text 14.50 (*1-929187-03-3*, CGBK54) Choristers.

Of Primeval Steps & Future Leaps: An Essay on the Emergence of Human Beings, the Source of Women's Oppression, & the Road to Emancipation. Ardea Skybreak. LC 84-24448. 160p. (Orig.). 1985. pap. 8.95 (*0-916650-19-7*) Banner Pr Intl.

Of Princes & Beauties: Erotic Fairy Tales for Adults. Ed. & Intro. by Cecilia Tan. (Illus.). 96p. (Orig.). 1995. pap. 9.95 (*1-885865-03-1*) Circlet Pr.

Of Prisons & Ideas. Milovan Djilas. Tr. by Michael B. Petrovich from SER. 144p. 1986. 17.95 (*0-15-167979-7*) Harcourt.

Of Problematology: Philosophy, Science & Language. Michael Meyer. Tr. by David Jamison.Tr. of De la Problematologie. 318p. 1995. pap. text 18.95 (*0-226-52151-6*) U Ch Pr.

Of Problematology: Philosophy, Science & Language. Michel Meyer. Tr. by David Jamison from FRE. LC 94-46783.Tr. of De la Problematologie. 318p. 1995. lib. bdg. 49.95 (*0-226-52150-8*) U Ch Pr.

Of Prophets & Kings: A Late Ninth Century Document (1 Samuel 1-2 Kings 10 No. 17) Antony F. Campbell. Ed. by Robert J. Karris. LC 85-12791. (Catholic Biblical Quarterly Monographs: No. 17). vii, 240p. (Orig.). 1986. pap. 7.50 (*0-915170-16-7*) Catholic Bibl Assn.

Of Prophets' Visions & the Wisdom of Sages. Heather A. McKay & D. J. Clines. (JSOTS Ser.: Vol. 162). 335p. 1993. 60.00 (*1-85075-423-3*, Pub. by Sheffield Acad) CUP Services.

Of Pulleys & Ropes & Gear: The Gravity Railroads of the Delaware & Hudson Canal Company & the PA Coal Company. 2nd ed. Philip Ruth. LC 97-61456. (Illus.). 75p. 1997. reprint ed. pap. 15.00 (*0-9659540-0-5*) Wayne Cty Hist.

Of Quarks, Quasars, & Other Quirks: Quizzical Poems for the Supersonic Age. Ed. by Sara W. Brewton et al. LC 76-54747. (Illus.). 128p. (YA). (gr. 5 up). 1990. lib. bdg. 13.89 (*0-690-04885-8*) HarpC Child Bks.

Of Rainbows & Clouds: The Life of Yab Ugyen Dorji As Told to His Daughter. Queen Ashi D. Wangmo Wangchuck. LC 99-933530. (Illus.). 184p. 1999. 35.00 (*0-906026-49-0*, Pub. by Serindia) Weatherhill.

Of Rams & Sacks & Tramps in Shacks: Short Vowel I Sequence. Ellis Richardson. (Read Aloud Ser.: Bk. 4). 32p. (Orig.). 1988. pap. text 4.00 (*1-56775-018-4*, SVIS4-3) ISM Teach Systs.

Of Rare Design. William J. Barnum. Ed. by Doc Cote & Victoria Bonanni. 88p. 1999. pap. 10.00 (*0-9636942-6-X*) VB Document.

Of Rascals & Rainbows. large type ed. Marcella Thompson. (Magna Large Print Ser.). 271p. 1996. 27.99 (*0-7505-0988-0*, Pub. by Mgna Lrg Print) Ulverscroft.

Of Rats, Sparrows & Flies: A Lifetime in China. Arthur Chung. LC 94-77656. 256p. (C). 1994. text 23.95 (*0-9623048-8-3*) Heritage West.

Of Reason & Love: The Life & Works of Marie von Ebner-Eschenbach. Carl Steiner. (Studies in Austrian Literature, Culture, & Thought). 233p. 1994. 29.50 (*0-929497-77-5*) Ariadne CA.

Of Red Eagles & Royal Crowns. William E. Hamelman. (Illus.). 113p. 1978. reprint ed. 15.00 (*0-931065-00-3*) Matthaus Pubs.

Of Relations & the Dead: Four Societies Viewed from the Angle of Their Exchanges. Ed. by Cecile Barraud et al. Tr. by Stephen J. Suffern from FRE. (Explorations in Anthropology Ser.). 132p. 1994. 37.50 (*0-85496-953-5*, Pub. by Berg Pubs); pap. 16.50 (*1-85973-046-9*, Pub. by Berg Pubs) NYU Pr.

Of Responsible Command: A History of the U. S. Army War College. rev. ed. Harry P. Ball. LC 94-79283. (Illus.). 538p. 1994. 29.00 (*0-9613301-1-2*) Alumni Assn US.

Of Revelation & Revolution, Vol. 2. Comaroff. 560p. 1997. lib. bdg. 70.00 (*0-226-11443-0*) U Ch Pr.

Of Revelation & Revolution, Vol. 2. John L. Comaroff & Jean Comaroff. 560p. 1997. pap. text 24.95 (*0-226-11444-9*) U Ch Pr.

Of Revelation & Revolution Vol. 1: Christianity, Colonialism, & Consciousness in South Africa. Jean Comaroff & John L. Comaroff. LC 90-46753. (Illus.). 434p. 1991. pap. text 21.95 (*0-226-11442-2*) U Ch Pr.

Of Revelation & Revolution Vol. 1: Christianity, Colonialism, & Consciousness in South Africa. annuals Jean Comaroff & John L. Comaroff. LC 90-46753. Vol. 1. (Illus.). 434p. 1991. lib. bdg. 72.00 (*0-226-11441-4*) U Ch Pr.

Of Rhyme & Reason: My Lyrics & Other Loves. Bernard Spiro. (Illus.). 288p. (Orig.). 1990. pap. 9.95 (*0-89407-103-3*) Strawberry Hill.

Of Rule & Revenue. Margaret Levi. (California Series on Social Choice & Political Economy: Vol. 13). 1988. pap. 16.95 (*0-520-06750-9*, Pub. by U CA Pr) Cal Prin Full Svc.

Of Rural Proletarian Struggles: Mobilization & Organization of Rural Workers in South West India. K. P. Kannan. (Illus.). 412p. 1988. text 35.00 (*0-19-562116-6*) OUP.

Of Sagebrush & Slot Machines: This Curious Place. Scott E. Casper. 104p. (C). 1997. pap. 15.00 (*0-536-00089-1*, Macmillan Coll) P-H.

Of Saints & Shadows. Christopher Golden. (Shadow Saga Ser.: No. 1). 400p. 1998. pap. 5.99 (*0-441-00570-5*) Ace Bks.

Of Saints & Shadows. Christopher Golden. 400p. 1994. mass mkt. 5.99 (*0-515-11388-3*, Jove) Berkley Pub.

Of Saltimbanchi & Incendiari: Aldo Palazzeschi & Avant-Gardism in Italy. Anthony J. Tamburri. LC 88-46173. 232p. 1990. 37.50 (*0-8386-3375-7*) Fairleigh Dickinson.

Of Sapphire Dreams. Elizabeth A. Michaels. 320p. 1997. mass mkt. 4.99 (*0-8217-5540-4*, Zebra Kensgtn) Kensgtn Pub Corp.

Of Scribes & Scrolls: Studies on the Hebrew Bible, Intertestamental Judaism, & Christian Origins. Ed. by Harold W. Attridge et al. 298p. (C). 1990. pap. text 31.50 (*0-8191-7903-5*); lib. bdg. 50.00 (*0-8191-7902-7*) U Pr of Amer.

Of Seals & Jeeps & Steam That's Green: Introductory Sequence. Ellis Richardson. (Read Aloud Ser.: Bk. 1). 28p. (Orig.). 1988. pap. text 4.00 (*1-56775-012-5*, INS1-2) ISM Teach Systs.

***Of Self & Nation: Autobiography & the Representation of Modern Indonesia.** C. W. Watson. LC 99-41857. 272p. 2000. text 54.00 (*0-8248-2095-9*); pap. text 27.95 (*0-8248-2281-1*) UH Pr.

Of Sex & Sin. R. Thomas Dickman. LC 85-91068. 1986. 10.00 (*0-87212-195-X*) Libra.

Of Ships & Stars: Maritime Heritage & the Founding of the National Maritime Museum, Greenwich. Kevin Littlewood & Beverley Butler. LC 98-37234. 340p. 1999. 70.00 (*0-485-11537-9*, Pub. by Athlone Pr) Transaction Pubs.

***Of Ships & Stars: Maritime Heritage & the Founding of the National Maritime Museum, Greenwich.** Kevin Littlewood & Beverley Butler. 20p. 1999. pap. 33.95 (*0-485-12146-8*, Pub. by Athlone Pr) Transaction Pubs.

Of Ships & the Sea. TSR Inc. Staff. 1997. 19.95 (*0-7869-0706-1*, Pub. by TSR Inc) Random.

Of Shoes & Ships & Sealing Wax, Cabbages & Kings, & Aspirin As Needed. George W. Conklin. 1997. 9.95 (*0-533-12263-5*) Vantage.

Of Silver & Gold. Perry Tanksley. 4.50 (*0-686-15450-9*) Allgood Bks.

Of Simultaneous Orgasms & Other Popular Myths: A Realistic Look at Relationships. Haresh Shah. 240p. 1997. 20.00 (*0-9654429-0-X*, Azad Bks) Azad Publns.

Of Singles & Doubles. Rosalie Moore. LC 78-68474. 1979. 7.95 (*0-913506-06-0*) Woolmer-Brotherson.

Of Slaves & Ropes & Lovers. Victor Terry & Jeff Kincaid. Ed. & Pref. by Larry Townsend. (Illus.). 64p. (Orig.). 1995. student ed. 12.95 (*1-881684-07-5*) L T Pubns CA.

Of Sluts & Bastards: A Feminist Decodes the Child Welfare Debate. Louise Armstrong. 336p. (C). 1995. pap. 18.95 (*1-56751-066-3*); lib. bdg. 29.95 (*1-56751-067-1*) Common Courage.

Of Sneeches & Whos & the Good Dr. Seuss: Essays on the Writings & Life of Theodor Geisel. Ed. by Thomas Fensch. LC 97-36069. 231p. 1997. lib. bdg. 38.50 (*0-7864-0388-8*) McFarland & Co.

Of Social Prejudice. Juan Vargas-Sierra. LC 97-90082. 1998. pap. 14.95 (*0-533-12284-8*) Vantage.

Of Societies Perfect & Imperfect: Selected Readings from Eyn Ayah, Rav Kook's Commentary to Eyn Yaakov (Legends of the Talmud) Tr. & Intro. by Bezalel Naor. LC 95-37358. 1995. 17.50 (*0-87203-144-6*) Hermon.

Of Some Country. Robert D. Fitzgerald. (Illus.). 46p. 1963. 8.00 (*0-87959-053-X*) U of Tex H Ransom Ctr.

Of Soviet Bondage: Sequel to "Red Exodus" Mayme Sevander. LC 97-111906. (Illus.). 200p. (Orig.). 1996. pap. 13.20 (*1-887801-53-7*) Trident MN.

Of Special Interest Theme Set, 10 bks. 1991. 100.44 (*0-8123-7223-9*); pap. 10.52 (*0-8123-6950-5*); pap. 10.52 (*0-8123-6959-9*); pap. 10.52 (*0-8123-6973-4*); pap. 10.52 (*0-8123-6979-3*); pap. 10.52 (*0-8123-6992-0*); pap. 10.52 (*0-8123-6993-9*); pap. 10.52 (*0-8123-6994-7*) McDougal-Littell.

Of Special Interest Theme Set, 10 bks. (J). (gr. k-1). 1991. pap. 10.52 (*0-8123-6982-3*); pap. 10.52 (*0-8123-6989-0*); pap. 10.52 (*0-8123-6990-4*) McDougal-Littell.

Of Speech & Time: Temporal Speech Patterns in Interpersonal Contexts. Ed. by Aron W. Siegman & Stanley Feldstein. 240p. 1979. 49.95 (*0-89859-490-1*) L Erlbaum Assocs.

Of Spies & Spider Webs. Dandi Daley Mackall. (Cinnamon Lake Mysteries Ser.). (gr. 1-4). 1997. pap. text 4.99 (*0-570-04984-9*, 12-3334) Concordia.

Of Spirit: Heidegger & the Question. Jacques Derrida. Tr. by Geoffrey Bennington & Rachel Bowlby. LC 88-32212. 147p. 1989. 23.95 (*0-226-14317-1*) U Ch Pr.

Of Spirit: Heidegger & the Question. Jacques Derrida. LC 88-32212. 152p. 1991. pap. 12.00 (*0-226-14319-8*) U Ch Pr.

***Of Spirits: The Book of Rowan.** Ivo Dominguez, Jr. (Wheel of Trees Ser.: Vol. 2). (Illus.). 176p. 1998. pap. 14.95 (*0-9654198-1-9*) SapFire Prods.

Of Spirituality: A Feminist Perspective. Clare B. Fischer. LC 95-5660. (ATLA Bibliography Ser.: No. 35). (Illus.). 299p. 1996. 49.50 (*0-8108-3006-X*) Scarecrow.

Of Stars & Men: Human Response to an Expanding Universe. Harlow Shapley. LC 83-22528. 157p. 1984. reprint ed. lib. bdg. 55.00 (*0-313-24302-6*, SHST, Greenwood Pr) Greenwood.

Of Stars & Men: Reminiscences of an Astronomer. Zdenek Kopal. (Illus.). 496p. 1986. 130.00 (*0-85274-567-2*) IOP Pub.

Of Stone & Tears. Leonides Moreno. 1975. 2.00 (*0-912678-19-4*, Greenfld Rev Pr) Greenfld Rev Lit.

Of Stones & Strength. Steve Jeck & Peter Martin. LC 96-79461. 124p. (Orig.). 1996. pap. 17.95 (*0-926888-05-6*) IronMind Enterprises.

Of Stones, Steam & the Earth: The Pleasures & Meanings of a Sauna. Wendell Nelson. (Illus.). 88p. (Orig.). 1993. pap. 9.95 (*0-9632975-3-8*) Sampo Pub.

Of Stones, Steam & the Earth: The Pleasures & Meanings of a Sauna. Wendell Nelson. (Illus.). 88p. (Orig.). 1994. pap. 9.95 (*0-9632975-7-0*) Sampo Pub.

Of Strangers & Foreigners (Late Antiquity - Middle Ages) Claudia Storti-Storchi et al. Ed. by Laurent Mayali & Maria Mart. LC 93-84330. (Studies in Comparative Legal History). (ENG, FRE, GER, GRE & ITA.). 135p. (C). 1993. text 30.00 (*1-882239-03-2*) Robbins Collection.

Of Sunlight & Shadows. Charles J. Palmer & Jacqueline Palmer. LC 97-69556. (Illus.). 260p. 1997. 54.95 (*1-881808-35-1*) Creat Arts & Sci.

Of Sunrise, Stained Glass & Open Windows: Progress for a Troubled World. Bryce W. Yourd. LC 94-90507. 219p. (Orig.). 1994. pap. 9.95 (*0-9627285-1-9*) B W Yourd.

Of Swans, Sugarplums & Satin Slippers. Violette Verdy. LC 91-98. 1991. 12.19 (*0-606-11697-4*, Pub. by Turtleback) Demco.

Of Swans, Sugarplums & Satin Slippers: Ballet Stories for Children. Violette Verdy. (J). (ps-3). 1996. pap. text 6.99 (*0-590-43485-3*) Scholastic Inc.

Of Swords & Sorcerers: The Adventures of King Arthur & His Knights. Margaret Hodges & Margery Evernden. LC 91-40811. (Illus.). 112p. (J). (gr. 5-7). 1993. text 15.00 (*0-684-19437-6*) Scribner.

Of Tails & Teams: A Fable for Children & CEO's. H. James Harrington. LC 94-17990. (ASQ Briefing Ser.). 40p. 1994. 15.00 (*0-87389-270-4*, H0879) ASQ Qual Pr.

Of Tangible Ghosts. L. E. Modesitt, Jr. 384p. 1995. mass mkt. 5.99 (*0-8125-4822-1*, Pub. by Tor Bks) St Martin.

***Of Tears & Flowers.** Dadiva Lloyd-Jones. 1999. pap. write for info. (*1-58235-117-1*) Watermrk Pr.

Of Tears & Roses. Sarah Haines. 94p. 1999. pap. 10.95 (*0-7414-0017-0*) Buy Books.

***Of Tender Sin.** David Goodis. (Midnight Classics Ser.). 224p. 2001. pap. 12.00 (*1-85242-674-8*) Serpents Tail.

Of Texas Ladies, Cowboys . . . Jodi O'Donnell. (Special Edition Ser.). 1996. per. 3.99 (*0-373-24045-7*, 1-24045-6) Silhouette.

***Of the: Earth, Spheres & Consequences.** Michael S. Hamilton. LC 99-97533. 2000. 24.95 (*0-533-13414-5*) Vantage.

Of the Author & Substance of the Protestant Church & Religion Richard Smith. LC 76-370281. (English Recusant Literature, 1558-1640 Ser.). (ENG.). 334 p. 1975. write for info. (*0-85967-254-9*) Scolar Pr.

Of the Conduct of the Understanding. John Locke. Ed. by Francis W. Garforth. LC 66-20498. (Classics in Education Ser.: Vol. 31). 144p. 1966. reprint ed. pap. 44.70 (*0-7837-8878-9*, 204958900001) Bks Demand.

Of the Conduct of the Understanding: 1706 Edition. John Locke. (Key Texts Ser.). 160p. 1996. reprint ed. pap. 19.95 (*1-85506-225-9*) Bks Intl VA.

Of the Confusions & Revolutions of Governments. Anthony Ascham. LC 75-33731. 226p. 1975. lib. bdg. 50.00 (*0-8201-1161-9*) Schol Facsimiles.

Of the Crow Nation. Edwin T. Denig. Ed. by John C. Ewers. LC 76-43690. (BAE. Bulletin Ser.: 151). reprint ed. 27.50 (*0-404-15532-4*) AMS Pr.

Of the Dominion: or Ownership of the Sea. John Selden. Tr. by Marchamont Nedham from LAT. LC 76-38256. (Evolution of Capitalism Ser.). Orig. Title: Mare Clasum. 548p. 1979. reprint ed. 44.95 (*0-405-04137-3*) Ayer.

Of the Farm. John Updike. 176p. 1987. mass mkt. 5.99 (*0-449-21451-6*, Crest) Fawcett.

Of the Father's Love Begotten: Christmas Service Kit. Anita Schultz. 40p. (Orig.). 1996. pap. 49.99 (*0-8100-0597-2*, 18N0358) Northwest Pub.

Of the Festivity. William Dickey. LC 70-144759. (Yale Series of Younger Poets: No. 55). reprint ed. 18.00 (*0-404-53855-X*) AMS Pr.

Of the Fields, Lately. David French. (Illus.). 112p. (Orig.). 1991. reprint ed. pap. 8.95 (*0-88784-508-8*, Pub. by Hse of Anansi Pr) Genl Dist Srvs.

Of the Great House: A Book of Poems. Allen Grossman. LC 81-22453. 96p. (Orig.). (C). 1982. pap. 6.95 (*0-8112-0835-4*, NDP535, Pub. by New Directions) Norton.

Of the Hovrs: A Poem. Kevin T. Patrick di Camillo. LC 96-32116. 64p. 1996. pap. 14.95 (*0-7734-2679-5*, Mellen Poetry Pr) E Mellen.

Of the Imitation of Christ. A. Kempis Thomas & Thomas of Kempis. 256p. 1981. mass mkt. 5.99 (*0-88368-094-7*) Whitaker Hse.

Of the Investigation, or Search of Perfection. Geber. Tr. by Richard Russell. 1983. reprint ed. pap. 5.95 (*0-916411-08-7*) Holmes Pub.

Of the Just Shaping of Letters: From the Applied Geometry of Albrecht Durer, Book 3. Albrecht Durer. Tr. by R. T. Nichol. (Illus.). 43p. 1965. pap. 5.95 (*0-486-21306-4*) Dover.

Of the Knowledge & Conduct of Warres. Thomas Procter. LC 79-25921. (English Experience Ser.: No. 268). 96p. 1970. reprint ed. 20.00 (*90-221-0268-8*) Walter J Johnson.

Of the Knowledge of Good & Evil. George Bradley. LC 90-53417. 80p. 1992. pap. 12.00 (*0-679-74273-5*) Knopf.

Of the Law of Nature & Nations, 8 bks. Samuel Von Pufendorf. Tr. by W. A. Oldfather & C. H. Oldfather. LC 95-77182. (Classics in International Law Reprint Ser.: No. 17, Vol. 2). 64,xiii,1465p. 1995. reprint ed. 195.00 (*0-89941-960-7*) W S Hein.

Of the Law of Nature & Nations, Vol. 2, No. 17. LC 95-77182. (Classics in International Law Reprint Ser.: Vol. 17). 1995. reprint ed. 195.00 (*1-57588-261-2*, 310340) W S Hein.

Of the Laws of Ecclesiastical Polity, 3 vols., Set. Richard Hooker. (Hooker's Works). 2000p. (C). 1994. pap. text 49.00 (*0-9646362-0-4*) Via Media.

Of the Laws of Ecclesiastical Polity: Preface, Book I & Book VIII. Richard Hooker. Ed. by A. S. McGrade. (Cambridge Texts in the History of Political Thought Ser.). 288p. (C). 1989. pap. text 20.95 (*0-521-37908-3*) Cambridge U Pr.

Of the Laws of Ecclesiastical Polity Vol. 3: Books VI-VIII, Vol. 2. Richard Hooker. Ed. by P. G. Stanwood. LC 76-24883. (Folger Library Edition of the Works of Richard Hooker). (Illus.). 664p. 1981. 102.95 (*0-674-63210-9*) HUP.

Of the Laws of Ecclesiastical Polity Vol. 4: Attack & Response, Vol. 3. Richard Hooker. Ed. by John E. Booty. (Folger Library Edition of the Works of Richard Hooker). (Illus.). 320p. (C). 1983. 68.50 (*0-674-63216-8*) HUP.

Of the Making of Books: Medieval Manuscripts, Their Scribes & Readers. Pamela Robinson & Rivkah Zim. LC 96-51680. 344p. 1997. text 118.95 (*1-85928-079-X*, Pub. by Scolar Pr) Ashgate Pub Co.

***Of the Making of Nationalities: There Is No End, 2 vols.** Paul R. Magocsi. 2000. 140.00 (*0-88033-438-X*, 540, Pub. by East Eur Monographs) Col U Pr.

Of the Origin & Progress of Language, 6 vols. James B. Monboddo. LC 76-147982. reprint ed. 895.00 (*0-404-08260-2*) AMS Pr.

Of the Origin & Progress of Language, 6 vols., Set. James Burnet. (Anglistica & Americana Ser.: No. 108). 1974. reprint ed. 865.00 (*3-487-05432-9*) G Olms Pubs.

Of the People: U. S. History. Deborah Short et al. (Illus.). 178p. (YA). 1995. reprint ed. pap. text 12.50 (*0-937354-68-6*) Delta Systems.

***Of the People, by the People: Principles for Cooperative Civil Service Reform (in California)** Ed. by Carl D. Covitz. (Illus.). 103p. (C). 1999. pap. text 25.00 (*0-7881-8313-3*) DIANE Pub.

Of the People, by the People, for the People & Other Quotations from Abraham Lincoln. Ed. by Gabor S. Boritt. 224p. 1996. 21.00 (*0-231-10326-3*) Col U Pr.

Of the People, for the People. (Illus.). 1970. pap. 1.00 (*0-87898-050-4*) New Outlook.

Of the Raj, Maharajas & Me. M. A. Srenivasan. (C). 1991. 15.00 (*0-8364-2659-2*, Pub. by Ravi Dayal) S Asia.

An Asterisk (*) at the beginning of an entry indicates that the title is appearing for the first time.

Of the Rus Commonwealth. Giles Fletcher. Ed. by Albert J. Schmidt. (Documents Ser.). 1978. 28.50 (0-918016-44-4) Folger Bks.

Of the Sea & Skies: Historic Hampton & Its Times. Gene Williamson. (Illus.). 262p. (Orig.). 1993. pap. text 23.00 (1-55613-879-2) Heritage Bk.

***Of the Secret Earth.** Herbert Burke. LC 99-458652. 88p. 1998. pap. 9.75 (0-920635-12-1) Genl Dist Srvs.

Of the Sister Arts: An Essay. Jacob Hildebrand. LC 92-2398. (Augustan Reprints Ser.: No. 165). 1974. reprint ed. 14.50 (0-404-70165-5, PR3519) AMS Pr.

Of the Standard of Taste & Other Essays. David Hume. Ed. by John W. Lenz. LC 64-66070. 1965. pap. write for info. (0-672-60269-5) Macmillan.

Of the Sublime & Beautiful. Edmund Burke. 1986. reprint ed. pap. 28.95 (0-935005-28-5); reprint ed. lib. bdg. 45.95 (0-935005-27-7) Lincoln-Rembrandt.

Of the Sublime: Presence in Question: Essays by Jean-Francois Courtine, Michel Deguy, Eliane Escoubas, Philippe Lacoue-Labarthe, Jean-Francois Lyotard, Louis Marin, Jean-Luc Nancy, & Jacob Rogozinski. Tr. by Jeffrey S. Librett from FRE. LC 91-9447. (SUNY Series, Intersections: Philosophy & Critical Theory). 255p. (C). 1993. text 64.50 (0-7914-1379-9); pap. text 21.95 (0-7914-1380-2) State U NY Pr.

Of the Things Which Must Soon Come to Pass: Commentary on Revelation. Philip Mauro. 1984. reprint ed. 17.99 (0-87377-056-0) GAM Pubns.

Of Thee I Sing. Donald C. Kipfer. (Illus.). 299p. 1987. 18.00 (0-682-40350-4) Maedon.

Of Thee I Sing: Hardly Known Heroes & Happenings Revisited. George L. Jackson. Ed. & Illus. by Paul Chrastina. Illus. by Alyce Jackson. LC 92-97515. 75p. (Orig.). 1993. pap. text 14.95 (0-9635643-4-X) G L Jackson.

Of Thee I Sing: Vocal Score. Ed. by Carol Cuellar. 202p. (Orig.). (C). 1932. pap. text 50.00 (0-7692-0775-8, VP0012) Wrner Bros.

Of Thee I Sing: Vocal Selections. Ed. by Carol Cuellar. 36p. (Orig.). (C). 1984. pap. text 9.95 (0-7692-0765-0, SF0139) Wrner Bros.

Of Thee We Sing: Immigrants & American History. Dale R. Steiner. (Illus.). 259p. (C). 1987. pap. text 31.00 (0-15-567385-8, Pub. by Harcourt Coll Pubs) Harcourt.

Of Thee We Sing: Immigrants & American History. 2nd ed. Steiner. (C). 2001. pap. text 17.00 (0-15-503200-3) Harcourt.

Of These I Sing. Muriel R. Kulwin. 50p. 1996. pap. 10.00 (1-889080-07-1) Doublem Bks.

Of These Ye May Freely Eat: A Vegetarian Cookbook. rev. ed. JoAnn Rachor. 96p. 1999. pap. 2.95 (1-878726-02-1) Fam Hlth Pubns.

***Of Things: Poems from Hollywood.** Mark Dunster. 11p. 1999. pap. 5.00 (0-89642-884-2) Linden Pubs.

Of Things Natural, Wild, & Free: A Story about Aldo Leopold. Marybeth Lorbiecki. LC 92-44049. (Creative Minds Ser.). (Illus.). (J). (gr. 3-6). 1993. lib. bdg. 19.95 (0-87614-797-X, Carolrhoda) Lerner Pub.

Of Things Not Seen. unabridged ed. Don Aker. 176p. (YA). (gr. 7 up). 1997. mass mkt. 5.99 (0-7736-7435-7) STDK.

***Of Things of The Indies: Essays Old & New in Early Latin American History.** James Lockhart. LC 99-16980. 1999. pap. text 22.95 (0-8047-3810-6) Stanford U Pr.

Of Things Once Shared. Mary Bach-Lareaux. Ed. by Xavier O. Juaseaux. 32p. (Orig.). 1990. pap. text 4.50 (0-9623666-1-7) Green Rvr Writers.

Of Things to Come: Poems. Myrtle Stedman. LC 98-10978. 160p. 1998. pap. 14.95 (0-86534-274-1) Sunstone Pr.

Of This Time, of That Place & Other Stories. Lionel Trilling. LC 78-65748. 1979. 7.95 (0-15-168054-X) Harcourt.

Of This Time, of That Place & Other Stories. Lionel Trilling. LC 80-14022. 128p. 1980. pap. 3.95 (0-15-668062-9, Harvest Bks) Harcourt.

Of Those Who Died. Samuel B. Charters. 1980. pap. 3.00 (0-317-17645-5) Oyez.

Of Thoughts & Words: The Relation Between Language & Mind. Ed. by S. Allen. LC 96-130659. 308p. 1995. 78.00 (1-86094-005-6) World Scientific Pub.

Of Thoughts & Words: The Relation Between Language & Mind, Proceedings of Nobel Symposium 92, Stockholm, Sweden 8 - 12 August 1994. Ed. by S. Allen. 310p. 1996. text 78.00 (981-02-2446-X, GAIXnRa-P2918) World Scientific Pub.

Of Time & an Island. John Keats. (New York State Bks.). 256p. 1987. reprint ed. pap. 19.95 (0-8156-0211-1) Syracuse U Pr.

Of Time & Change. Frank Waters. LC 98-26707. (Illus.). 263p. 1998. 20.00 (1-878448-86-2) MacMurray & Beck.

***Of Time & Change.** Frank Waters. 2000. reprint ed. pap. 13.50 (1-878448-07-2) MacMurray & Beck.

Of Time & Eternity. James D. Freeman. LC 81-51069. 188p. 1981. 4.48 (0-87159-122-7) Unity Bks.

Of Time & Measurement. A. J. Turner. (Collected Studies: Vol. 407). 336p. 1993. 124.95 (0-86078-378-2, Pub. by Variorum) Ashgate Pub Co.

Of Time & Memory, A Mother's Story. Don J. Snyder. LC 99-28513. 1999. 25.00 (0-375-40408-2) Knopf.

Of Time & Place. Sigurd F. Olson. LC 98-21096. (Fesler-Lampert Minnesota Heritage Book Ser.). 192p. 1998. pap. 14.95 (0-8166-2995-1) U of Minn Pr.

Of Time & Place: American Figurative Art from the Corcoran Gallery. Edward J. Nygren & Peter C. Marzo. (Illus.). 208p. 1981. pap. 16.95 (0-86528-010-X) SITES.

Of Time & Place: Walker Evans & William Christenberry. Thomas W. Southall. Ed. by David Featherstone. LC 90-80082. (Untitled Ser.: No. 51). (Illus.). 88p. 1990. 29.95 (0-933286-57-0); pap. 19.95 (0-933286-56-2) Frnds Photography.

Of Time & Power: Leadership Duration in the Modern World. Henry S. Bienen & Nicolas Van De Walle. LC 90-42377. 232p. 1991. 32.50 (0-8047-1863-6) Stanford U Pr.

Of Time & the Artist: Thomas Wolfe, His Novels, & the Critics. Carol I. Johnston. (ENG Ser.). 225p. (C). 1996. 60.00 (1-57113-067-5) Camden Hse.

Of Time & the Prairie. Joseph Knue. LC 88-62899. (Illus.). 106p. (J). (gr. 7-12). 1988. 10.00 (0-9621367-1-9); pap. 3.00 (0-9621367-0-0) NDak Game & Fish.

Of Time & the Railroader. W. F. Cottrell. (Reprint Series in Social Sciences). (C). 1993. reprint ed. pap. text 5.00 (0-8290-2794-7, S-54) Irvington.

***Of Time & the River.** Thomas Wolfe & Pat Conroy. LC 99-32905. 864p. 1999. 45.00 (0-684-86785-0) S&S Trade.

Of Time & the River. Thomas Wolfe. (Hudson River Editions Ser.). 912p. 1976. reprint ed. 35.00 (0-684-14739-4, Scribners Ref) Mac Lib Ref.

Of Time, of Chance, of Circumstance. Henry W. Gurley. 1999. 14.95 (0-938645-54-4) In His Steps.

Of Tithes & Testimonies. Anita Holmes & Johnda M. Smith. 160p. (Orig.). 1996. pap. 12.98 (0-88290-572-4, 1020) Horizon Utah.

Of Toronto the Gay. Steven Maynard. 1997. 24.95 (0-226-51379-3) U Ch Pr.

Of Totems, Traps, Maps, & James Jesus Angleton: Richard Brothers, Yizhak Elyashiv, Harriet Pappas, Susannah Strong. JoAnn Conklinn. 12p. 1997. pap. 5.00 (0-933519-35-4) D W Bell Gallery.

Of Turkeys & Eagles. Spencer B. Pearson. LC 97-92850. (Illus.). 288p. 1998. 39.95 (0-9646325-3-5) Javelina AZ.

Of Two Minds. Carol Matas. 160p. (J). 1997. pap. text 7.95 (0-921368-44-5, Pub. by Bain & Cox) Genl Dist Srvs.

Of Two Minds. Carol Matas. 208p. (J). 1998. pap. text 4.50 (0-590-39468-1) Scholastic Inc.

Of Two Minds. Carol Matas. 1998. 9.60 (0-606-13672-X, Pub. by Turtleback) Demco.

Of Two Minds. Perry Nodelman & Carol Matas. 160p. (J). (gr. 5-9). 1995. mass mkt. 16.00 (0-689-80138-6) S&S Bks Yung.

Of Two Minds: Hypertext Pedagogy & Poetics. Michael Joyce. (Studies in Literature & Science). 288p. 1995. text 39.50 (0-472-09578-1, 09578) U of Mich Pr.

Of Two Minds: Hypertext Pedagogy & Poetics. Michael Joyce. (Studies in Literature & Science). 288p. (C). 1996. pap. 17.95 (0-472-06578-5, 06578) U of Mich Pr.

***Of Two Minds: The Growing Disorder in American Psychiatry.** T. M. Luhrmann. LC 99-40732. 400p. 2000. 26.95 (0-679-42191-2) Knopf.

Of Two Minds: The Nature of Inquiry. James Blachowicz. LC 97-13473. (SUNY Series in Philosophy). 448p. (C). 1998. text 73.50 (0-7914-3641-1); pap. text 24.95 (0-7914-3642-X) State U NY Pr.

Of Two Minds: The Revolutionary Science of Dual Brain Psychology. Frederic Schiffer. LC 98-23181. 288p. 1998. 24.50 (0-684-85424-4) Free Pr.

Of Una Jeffers: A Discovered Memoir. Edith Greenan. LC 98-36930. (Illus.). 160p. 1998. reprint ed. pap. 14.95 (1-885266-64-2) Story Line.

Of URFS & ORFS: A Primer on How to Analyze Derived Amino Acid Sequences. Russell F. Doolittle. (Illus.). 100p. (Orig.). (C). 1987. pap. text 14.00 (0-935702-54-7) Univ Sci Bks.

Of Virgins & Martyrs. Barbara A. Kathe. LC 98-30384. (Woman in History Ser.: No. 84). vi, 114p. 1998. pap. 10.00 (0-86663-223-9) Ide Hse.

Of Walls & Bridges: The United States & Eastern Europe. Bennett Kovrig. (Twentieth Century Fund Report). 352p. (C). 1991. text 50.00 (0-8147-4612-8); pap. text 20.00 (0-8147-4613-6) NYU Pr.

Of War & Love. Dorothee Solle. Tr. by Rita Kimber & Robert Kimber from GER. LC 83-8252. 186p. 1983. reprint ed. pap. 57.70 (0-7837-9821-0, 206055000005) Bks Demand.

Of War & Memory. Thomas Childers. 1998. write for info. (0-201-87044-4) Addison-Wesley.

Of War & Weddings: A Legacy of Two Fathers. Jerry Yellin. Ed. by Rodney Charles & Elizabeth Pasco. LC 94-64576. 275p. 1995. 17.95 (0-9638502-5-3) Sunstar Pubng.

Of Water & the Spirit: A Liturgical Study of Baptism. Alexander Schmemann. LC 74-30061. 1974. pap. 10.95 (0-913836-10-9) St Vladimirs.

Of Water & the Spirit: Ritual, Magic & Initiation in the Life of an African Shaman. Malidoma P. Some. 320p. 1995. pap. 13.95 (0-14-019496-7, Arkana) Viking Penguin.

Of Wee Sweetie Mice & Men. Colin Bateman. LC 96-29456. 1997. 23.45 (1-55970-376-8, Pub. by Arcade Pub Inc) Time Warner.

***Of Weeds & Views.** Frances Utterback Crain. 2000. pap. 9.75 (1-892343-10-X, Oak Tree Bk) Oak Tree Pub.

Of Whales & Men. Victor Perera. 1998. write for info. (0-375-40013-3) Random.

***Of When the Days Ended: A Tale of Epic Fantasy.** Matthew Allen Newland. LC 00-190634. 192p. 2000. 25.00 (0-7388-1876-3); pap. 18.00 (0-7388-1877-1) Xlibris Corp.

***Of White Sparks & Such.** Scott Salvage. 1999. pap. write for info. (1-58235-336-0) Watermrk Pr.

Of Whom the World Was Not Worthy. Intro. by Marie Chapian. LC 78-769. (Illus.). 256p. 1978. pap. 9.99 (0-87123-417-3) Bethany Hse.

Of Whom the World Was Not Worthy. Marie Chapian. LC 78-769. 1980. pap. text 9.99 (0-87123-250-2) Bethany Hse.

Of Wind, Water & Sand: The Natural Bridges Story. David Peterson. (Illus.). 21p. 1990. 3.50 (0-937407-02-X) Canyonlands.

Of Wine in the Jars - Wedding Homilies: Wedding Planning. William Hoffsummer. Tr. by James McGrath from GER. 136p. (Orig.). 1995. pap. 11.95 (0-8146-2259-3, Liturg Pr Bks) Liturgical Pr.

Of Winners, Losers, & Games: A Drama About Life. O. B. Rozell. (Illus.). 24p. 1976. pap. 3.25 (0-88680-145-1) I E Clark.

Of Wisdome, 3 bks. Pierre Charron. LC 79-171739. (English Experience Ser.: No. 315). 1971. reprint ed. 127.00 (90-221-0315-3) Walter J Johnson.

Of Witches: Celebrating the Goddess as a Solitary Pagan. Janet Thompson. LC 92-45542. (Illus.). 160p. (Orig.). 1993. reprint ed. pap. 9.95 (0-87728-762-7) Weiser.

Of Wolves & Men. Barry H. Lopez. LC 78-6070. (Illus.). 320p. 1979. pap. 18.00 (0-684-16322-5, Scribners Ref) Mac Lib Ref.

Of Wolves & Men. Barry H. Lopez. 1994. 27.00 (0-8446-6727-7) Peter Smith.

Of Woman Born: Motherhood As Experience & Institution. Adrienne Rich. 352p. 1995. pap. 14.95 (0-393-31284-4, Norton Paperbks) Norton.

Of Woman Caste: The Experience of Gender in Rural India. Anjani Bagwe. LC 95-31267. 192p. (C). 1995. text 65.00 (1-85649-321-0, Pub. by Zed Books); text 25.00 (1-85649-322-9, Pub. by Zed Books) St Martin.

***Of Women & Horses.** Comment by GaWaNi Pony Boy. LC 00-8922. (Illus.). 160p. 2000. 39.95 (1-889540-52-8) Bowtie Press.

Of Women, Outcastes, Peasants, & Rebels: A Selection of Bengali Short Stories. Ed. by Kalpana Bardhan. 1990. 55.00 (0-520-06713-4, Pub. by U CA Pr); pap. 18.95 (0-520-06714-2, Pub. by U CA Pr) Cal Prin Full Svc.

***Of Wonders & Wise Men: Religion & Popular Cultures in Southeast Mexico, 1800-1876.** Terry Rugeley. LC 00-29909. (Illus.). 384p. 2000. pap. 26.95 (0-292-77107-X) U of Tex Pr.

***Of Wonders & Wise Men: Religion & Popular Cultures in Southeast Mexico, 1800-1876.** Terry Rugeley. 2001. 55.00 (0-292-77106-1) U of Tex Pr.

Of Woods & Other Things. Emma B. Pitcher. Ed. by Monica A. Evans & Valerie A. Noble. (Illus.). 256p. (Orig.). 1996. pap. 10.95 (0-939294-18-4) Beech Leaf.

. . . Of Woodsmoke & Quiet Places. Jerry Wilber. LC 97-65477. (Illus.). 383p. 1997. 25.95 (0-9653381-1-8) Cabin Bkshelf.

Of Words & the World: Referential Anxiety in Contemporary French Fiction. David R. Ellison. 208p. 1993. text 39.50 (0-691-06964-6, Pub. by Princeton U Pr) Cal Prin Full Svc.

Of Work & Men: How Men Can Become More Than Their Careers. Harvey Deutschendorf. 224p. 1996. 19.95 (1-57749-013-4) Fairview Press.

Of Worlds Beyond. Ed. by Lloyd Eshbach. LC 64-57013. 104p. 1964. 15.00 (0-911682-05-8); pap. 8.00 (0-911682-14-7) Advent.

Of Yachts & Men. William Atkin. (Illus.). 160p. 1997. pap. 22.95 (1-888671-07-6) Tiller.

Of You & Other Paths: Third Collection of Poetry. Concetta Battaglia. LC 96-96886. 108p. (Orig.). 1996. pap. 11.95 (0-9654032-0-3) Arts in Media.

Of Your Seed. Janine Canan. 1977. 2.00 (0-685-80004-0) Oyez.

Of Youth & the River: The Mississippi Adventure of Raymond Kurtz Sr. Raymond Kurtz, Sr. & Mark Scheel. 80p. 1993. pap. 7.95 (0-9637680-0-X) Royal Pr KS.

O'Farrell's Law. Brian Freemantle. 352p. 1993. mass mkt. 3.99 (0-8125-8254-3) Tor Bks.

Ofay Watcher: Manuscript Edition. Frank Cucci. 1970. pap. 13.00 (0-8222-0836-9) Dramatists Play.

***OFC'98: Optical Fiber Communication Conference & Exhibit: Technical Digest: February 22-27, 1998, San Jose, California** Conference on Optical Fiber Communication Staff et al. LC 97-81329. (Technical Digest Ser.). vii, 541p. 1998. write for info. (1-55752-529-3) Optical Soc.

***OFDM for Wireless Multimedia Communications.** Richard D. Van Nee. LC 99-52312. 1999. 89.00 (0-89006-530-6) Artech Hse.

OFE & M: The Only Acronym You'll Ever Need. Mark A. Ousnamer. LC 97-11359. (Illus.). 118p. (Orig.). 1997. pap. 25.00 (0-89806-175-X, OUSNAM) Eng Mgmt Pr.

Oferta de Vida-Calif. (Offer of Life-Calif.) (SPA.). 1.50 (0-8423-6288-6, 490096) Editorial Unilit.

Oferta de Vida-Colombia (Offer of Life-Colombia) (SPA.). 1.50 (0-685-74967-3, 490092) Editorial Unilit.

Oferta de Vida-N. Y. (Offer of Life-N. Y.) (SPA.). 1.50 (0-318-72877-X, 490095) Editorial Unilit.

Off-Air Videotaping in Education: Copyright Issues, Decisions, Implications. Esther R. Sinofsky. 163p. 1984. 39.95 (0-8352-1755-8, Copy Info Svc) Assn Ed Comm Tech.

Off & on Rain. Gary Hotham. 16p. 1978. pap. 2.00 (0-913719-31-5, High Coo Pr) Brooks Books.

Off & Running. Gary Soto. (Illus.). 144p. (J). (gr. 3-7). 1997. pap. 4.50 (0-440-41432-6) BDD Bks Young Read.

Off & Running. Gary Soto. 1997. 9.60 (0-606-13673-8, Pub. by Turtleback) Demco.

Off & Running: Exploring Sports Careers. Girl Scouts of the U. S. A. Staff. LC 98-142981. (Illus.). 1997. write for info. Girl Scouts USA.

Off & Running: The Computer Offline Activities Book. Tim Erickson. (Equals Ser.). (Illus.). 145p. (J). (gr. 4-12). 1987. pap. 8.95 (0-912511-07-9, EQUALS) Lawrence Science.

Off-Balance Sheet Activities. Ed. by Joshua Ronen et al. LC 90-8909. 192p. 1990. 55.00 (0-89930-613-6, ROD/, Quorum Bks) Greenwood.

Off-Balance Sheet Financial Instruments: Maximizing Profitability & Managing Risk in Financial Services. Dimitris N. Chorafas & Heinrich Steinman. 475p. (C). 1994. text 75.00 (1-55738-398-7, Irwn Prfssnl) McGraw-Hill Prof.

Off Base: New Insights into an Old Game. Andrew Torrez. Ed. by C. David Burgin. 224p. 1999. 24.95 (0-942627-43-1) Woodford Pubng.

Off Broadway. Walter J. Kukkonen. 32p. (Orig.). (YA). 1990. pap. text 1.00 (0-685-49153-6) Polaris AZ.

Off Broadway: A Season with the Hartford Wolf Pack. Jack Lautier. (Illus.). 200p. 1999. pap. 19.95 (0-9650315-5-1) Glacier Publng.

Off Broadway: Essays about the Theatre. Maxwell Anderson. LC 75-77699. (Theatre, Film & the Performing Arts Ser.). 92p. 1971. reprint ed. lib. bdg. 21.50 (0-306-71337-3) Da Capo.

***Off-Broadway Daring.** John W. Pereira. 1999. text. write for info. (0-312-22624-1) St Martin.

***Off Camera: Private Thoughts Made Public.** Ted Koppel. 320p. 2000. 25.00 (0-375-41077-5) Knopf.

Off-Campus Library Services: Selected Readings from Central Michigan University's Conferences. Ed. by Barton M. Lessin. LC 91-38119. 256p. 1991. 31.50 (0-8108-2512-0) Scarecrow.

Off Center: Power & Culture Relations Between Japan & the United States. Masao Miyoshi. (Convergences Ser.). 289p. (C). 1991. 32.00 (0-674-63175-7) HUP.

Off Center: Power & Culture Relations Between Japan & the United States. Masao Miyoshi. (Convergences: Inventories of the Present Ser.). 304p. 1994. pap. text 17.50 (0-674-63176-5, MIYOFX) HUP.

Off Center: Standing Side by Side with Cancer & AIDS Is a Little Recognized 20th Century Disease That Today Is Affecting Millions. William T. Sette. LC 93-77694. 400p. 1993. pap. 14.95 (1-879560-19-4) Harpus Pr Intl.

Off Center Spliced Floor Joists, Vol. 4. NAHB Research Foundation Staff. (Research Report Ser.). 58p. 1982. pap. 9.00 (0-86718-143-5) Home Builder.

Off-Centered Riding: or Not So Swift. Ruth Perkins. (Illus.). 192p. 1993. pap. 9.95 (0-943955-81-5) Trafalgar.

Off-Course Golf Retail Store Directory. Ed. by National Golf Foundation Staff. 88p. 1998. pap. 99.00 (1-57701-081-7, 99GR114) Natl Golf.

Off-Flavors in Foods & Beverages. George Charalambous. (Developments in Food Science Ser.: Vol. 28). xiv,750p. 1992. 332.00 (0-444-88558-7) Elsevier.

Off-Flavours in Drinking Water & Aquatic Organisms. P. E. Persson et al. (Water Science & Technology Ser.: Vol. 25). 368p. 1992. 147.00 (0-08-041861-9, Pergamon Pr) Elsevier.

Off-Flavours in the Aquatic Environment. S. E. Hrudey et al. (Water Science & Technology Ser.: Vol. 31). 274p. 1994. 115.00 (0-08-042665-4, Pergamon Pr) Elsevier.

Off-Flavours in the Aquatic Environment: Proceedings of the 2nd IAWPRC International Symposium held in Kagoshima, Japan, 14-16 October, 1987. P. E. Persson et al. LC 82-645900. (Water Science & Technology Ser.: No. 20). (Illus.). 294p. 1988. pap. 112.00 (0-08-036887-5, Pergamon Pr) Elsevier.

Off for California: American Autobiography. William Dougal. 62p. 1995. lib. bdg. 69.00 (0-7812-8500-3) Rprt Serv.

Off for the Sweet Hereafter: A Novel. T. R. Pearson. 384p. 1995. pap. 12.00 (0-8050-3756-X, Owl) H Holt & Co.

Off-Gas & Air Cleaning Systems for Accident Conditions in Nuclear Power Plants. IAEA Staff. (Technical Reports: No. 358). 117p. 1993. pap. 40.00 (92-0-102993-4, STI/DOC/348, Pub. by IAEA) Bernan Associates.

Off-Hand Portraits of Prominent New Yorkers. Stephen Fiske. LC 75-1847. (Leisure Class in America Ser.). 1975. reprint ed. 25.95 (0-405-06914-6) Ayer.

Off-Highway Haulage in Surface Mines: Proceedings of the International Symposium, Edmonton, 15-17 May 1989. Ed. by Tad S. Golosinski & V. Srajer. 280p. (C). 1989. text 168.00 (90-6191-885-5, Pub. by A A Balkema) Ashgate Pub Co.

Off Hours. Jean Watts. LC 91-44156. (Illus.). 184p. (Orig.). 1992. pap. 12.00 (0-910707-20-6) Gifted Psych Pr.

Off in a Boat. Neil M. Gunn. (Illus.). 348p. (Orig.). (C). 1990. pap. 14.95 (0-941533-98-0, NAB) I R Dee.

Off in Zora. Alan Armstrong. 120p. (Orig.). 1997. pap. 12.95 (1-879923-13-0) Booksellers Pub.

***Off Keck Road.** Mona Simpson. 144p. 2000. 19.00 (0-375-41010-4) Knopf.

Off Limits. Katherine H. Brooks. LC 95-61179. 52p. (Orig.). 1995. pap. 4.00 (1-886467-05-6) WJM Press.

Off Limits. Lindsay McKenna. (Special Edition Ser.: No. 733). 1992. mass mkt. 3.39 (0-373-09733-6, 5-09733-2) Harlequin Bks.

Off Limits: Censorship & Corruptions. Ed. by Human Rights Watch Staff. 62p. (Orig.). 1991. pap. 7.00 (1-56432-026-X) Hum Rts Watch.

Off Limits: Rutgers University & the Avant-Garde, 1957-1963. Joan Marter. LC 98-37637. (Illus.). 256p. (C). 1999. 60.00 (0-8135-2610-8); pap. 30.00 (0-8135-2609-4) Rutgers U Pr.

Off Limits: Tales of Alien Sex. Ed. by Ellen Datlow. 304p. 1997. reprint ed. mass mkt. 5.99 (0-441-00436-9) Ace Bks.

Off Median Phenomena & International Reference Ionosphere. Karl Rawer et al. (Advances in Space Research Ser.: Vol. 15, No. 2). 216p. 1994. pap. 105.75 (0-08-042537-2, Pergamon Pr) Elsevier.

Off Minor. John Harvey. 288p. 1998. pap. 11.00 (0-8050-5498-7) H Holt & Co.

Off Minor. John Harvey. 288p. 1993. mass mkt. 4.99 (0-380-72009-4, Avon Bks) Morrow Avon.

Off Nevsky Prospekt: Life among Leningrad's Unofficial Artists. 1993. 16.95 (0-931416-09-4) Open Books.

O

An Asterisk (*) at the beginning of an entry indicates that the title is appearing for the first time.

Off Nevsky Prospekt: St. Petersburg's Theatre Studios in the 1980s & 1990s. Elena Markova. (Russian Theatre Archive Ser.). (Illus.). 125p. 1998. pap. text 22.00 (*90-5702-135-8*, Harwood Acad Pubs) Gordon & Breach.

***Off Nevsky Prospekt: St Petersburg's Theatre Studios in the 1980s & 1990s.** Elena Markova. (Russian Theatre Archive Ser.: Vol. 16). (Illus.). 125p. 1998. text 67.00 (*90-5702-134-X*, Harwood Acad Pubs) Gordon & Breach.

Off on a Comet: A Journey Through Planetary Space. Jules Verne. 520p. reprint ed. lib. bdg. 32.95 (*0-88411-902-5*) Amereon Ltd.

Off Our Rockers Hall Duncan. LC 98-70391. 145 p. 1998. write for info. (*0-9661367-1-3*) ICHH.

Off-Premise Catering Management. Bill Hansen. 368p. 1995. 39.95 (*0-471-04528-4*) Wiley.

Off-Premises Market. 150p. 1993. pap. 75.00 (*0-614-31121-7*, CS747) Natl Restaurant Assn.

Off Ramps. Don Taylor. (Illus.). 68p. 1995. pap. 3.95 (*0-9637314-3-2*) Quick Study.

Off-Road & 4-Wheel Drive Handbook. N. Fryatt. (Illus.). 184p. 1996. 19.95 (*0-947981-26-8*, Pub. by Motor Racing) Motorbooks Intl.

Off-Road Bikes. Charlie Webster & Mike Morris. LC 97-70521. (Pocket Gems Ser.). (J). (gr. 1). 1997. 3.95 (*0-7641-5036-7*) Barron.

Off-Road Biking. Jeremy Evans. LC 91-13629. (Adventurers Ser.). (Illus.). 48p. (J). (gr. 5-6). 1992. lib. bdg. 13.95 (*0-89686-687-4*, Crstwood Hse) Silver Burdett Pr.

Off-Road 4-Wheel Drive Book: Choosing, Using & Maintaining Go Anywhere Vehicles. Jack Jackson. (Illus.). 192p. 1999. 35.95 (*1-85960-606-7*) Haynes Manuals.

Off-Road Meditations. Becky G. Gibson. (Poetry Chapbook Ser.). 24p. (Orig.). 1989. pap. 5.00 (*0-9624274-4-6*) NC Writers Network.

Off Road Racing. A. T. McKenna. LC 97-51445. (Fast Tracks Ser.). (J). 1998. lib. bdg. 14.95 (*1-56239-833-4*) ABDO Pub Co.

***Off-Road Racing.** Sue Mead. (Race Car Legends Ser.). (Illus.). 2000. 16.95 (*0-7910-5851-4*) Chelsea Hse.

***Off-Road Racing.** Sue Mead. (Race Car Legends Ser.). (Illus.). 2001. pap. 5.95 (*0-7910-5852-2*) Chelsea Hse.

Off-Road Recovery Techniques: A Practical Handbook. Nick Cole. (Illus.). 72p. 1996. pap. 21.95 (*1-899870-13-X*, Pub. by Motor Racing) Motorbooks Intl.

Off-Road Transportation & Soil-Working: Means to Promote Development & Operations. Ed. by S. Areskoug et al. 120p. 1985. pap. 33.00 (*0-08-031652-2*, Pergamon Pr) Elsevier.

***Off-Road Truck Racing.** Bill McAuliffe. 1999. 19.93 (*0-516-21470-5*) Capstone Pr.

Off School, in Court: An Experimental & Psychiatric Investigation of Severe School Attendance Problems. Ian Berg et al. (Research in Criminology Ser.). (Illus.). 160p. 1988. 112.00 (*0-387-96744-3*) Spr-Verlag.

Off Screen: Women & Film in Italy. Ed. by Giuliana Bruno & Maria Nadotti. 160p. 1988. text 37.50 (*0-415-00856-5*); pap. text 16.95 (*0-415-00857-3*) Routledge.

Off Screen: Women & Film in Italy. Ed. by Giuliana Bruno & Maria Nadotti. LC 87-30778. (Illus.). 214p. reprint ed. pap. 66.40 (*0-608-20365-3*, 207161800002) Bks Demand.

***Off-Season.** Eliot Asinof. LC 99-32220. (Writing Baseball Ser.). 162p. 2000. 22.50 (*0-8093-2297-8*) S Ill U Pr.

Off-Season. Michael Covino. 224p. 1985. 14.95 (*0-89255-099-6*) Persea Bks.

Off-Season: A Guide to Visiting the Western National Parks Without the Crowds. Joseph E. Brown. 120p. 1988. pap. 14.95 (*0-15-667841-1*) Harcourt.

Off Season: A Martha's Vineyard Mystery. Philip R. Craig. 256p. 1994. 20.00 (*0-684-19617-4*, Scribners Ref) Mac Lib Ref.

Off Season: A Martha's Vineyard Mystery. Philip R. Craig. (Martha's Vineyard Ser.: No. 5). 224p. 1996. mass mkt. 5.99 (*0-380-72588-6*, Avon Bks) Morrow Avon.

***Off-Season: Living a Retirement Dream.** Susan White-Bowden & Jack Bowden. 216p. 2000. pap. 11.95 (*1-893116-14-X*) Baltimore Sun.

Off Season: The Unexpurgated Edition. unexpurgated limited ed. Jack Ketchum. 280p. 1999. 45.00 (*1-892950-10-3*) Overlook Connect.

Off Season: The Unexpurgated Edition - Lettered 1-52. unexpurgated num. ed. Jack Ketchum. 280p. 1999. lthr. 400.00 (*1-892950-08-1*) Overlook Connect.

Off Season: The Unexpurgated Edition - Sterling 1-100. unexpurgated limited ed. Jack Ketchum. 280p. 1999. 85.00 (*1-892950-09-X*) Overlook Connect.

Off-Season at the Edge of the World: Poems. Debora Greger. LC 93-30480. 104p. 1994. 12.95 (*0-252-06380-5*) U of Ill Pr.

Off-Season Training for Cyclists. Edmund Burke. LC 98-135336. (Illus.). 200p. 1997. pap. text 14.95 (*1-884737-40-4*) VeloPress.

***Off Side.** Vazquez Montalban. 278p. 2000. pap. 13.00 (*1-85242-742-6*) Serpents Tail.

***Off-Site Fabrication: Prefabrication, Pre-Assembly & Modularization.** Alistair G. Gibb. (Illus.). 288p. 1999. text 95.00 (*0-7881-8156-4*) DIANE Pub.

Off-Site Services: Results of a Survey. Urban Libraries Council Staff. LC 97-177457. (Frequent Fast Facts Ser.). (Orig.). 1995. pap. 45.00 (*1-885251-03-3*) Urban Libraries.

Off Soundings: Aspects of Rhode Island Maritime History. Alexander B. Hawes. LC 99-24813. (Illus.). 323p. 1999. 39.95 (*1-889274-05-4*) Posterity Press.

Off Stage. Ric Mandes. 144p. 1997. 12.95 (*0-9652800-2-0*) Mandes Pub.

Off Stage. Betty Comden. LC 96-2779. (Illus.). 216p. 1996. reprint ed. pap. 16.95 (*0-87910-084-2*) Limelight Edns.

Off Stage: My Non-Show Business Life. Betty Comden. LC 94-39115. 1995. 23.00 (*0-671-70579-2*) S&S Trade.

Off the Ancient Track: A Lovecraftian Guide to New England & Adjacent New York. Jason C. Eckhardt. (Illus.). (Orig.). 1987. pap. 3.50 (*0-940884-12-7*) Necronomicon.

***Off the Beadin' Path: Discovering Your Own Creative Trail of Bead Embellishment.** 2nd rev. ed. Nancy Eha. LC 96-93101. (Illus.). iii, 138p. 1999. 19.95 (*0-9656476-1-7*) Creative Visions.

Off the Beadin' Path Path: Discovering Your Own Creative Trail of Bead Embellishment. Nancy Eha. LC 96-93101. (Illus.). 138p. 1997. 19.95 (*0-9656476-0-9*) Creative Visions.

Off the Beat: A Book about Abnormal Heart Rhythms. Julia A. Purcell. Ed. by Nancy R. Hull. LC 91-33673. (Illus.). 24p. 1996. pap. text 6.25 (*0-939838-32-X*) Pritchett & Hull.

Off the Beaten Aisle: America's Quirky Spots to Tie the Knot. Lisa Primerano. LC 98-7804. (Illus.). 224p. 1998. pap. 12.95 (*0-8065-2003-5*, Citadel Pr) Carol Pub Group.

***Off the Beaten Path.** Michael Bogle. 2000. write for info. (*1-58235-535-5*) Watermrk Pr.

Off the Beaten Path: A Guide to More Than 1,000 Scenic & Interesting Places Still Uncrowded & Inviting. Reader's Digest Editors. LC 86-11372. (Illus.). 384p. 1987. 28.00 (*0-89577-253-1*, Pub. by RD Assn) Penguin Putnam.

Off the Beaten Path: Stories of Place. Ed. by Joseph Barbato & Lisa W. Horak. LC 98-66419. 224p. 1998. 24.00 (*0-86547-530-X*) N Point Pr.

***Off the Beaten Path: Stories of Place.** Ed. by Joseph Barbato & Lisa W. Horak. 272p. 1999. pap. 13.00 (*0-86547-538-5*) N Point Pr.

Off-the-Beaten-Path Job Book. Sandra Gurvis. 288p. 1995. pap. 11.95 (*0-8065-1644-5*, Citadel Pr) Carol Pub Group.

Off the Beaten Track: A Sampler of Oregon Poets. Ed. by Brian C. Hamilton. 135p. 1993. pap. 8.95 (*1-882550-00-5*) Quiet Lion Pr.

Off the Beaten Track: Irish Railway Walks. Kevin Cronin. (Illus.). 190p. 1997. 15.95 (*0-86281-563-0*, Pub. by Appletree Pr) Irish Bks Media.

Off the Beaten Track: Rethinking Gender Issues for Indian Women. Madhu Kishwar. 320p. 2000. text 29.95 (*0-19-564816-1*) OUP.

Off the Beaten Track Vol. II: A Guide to Mountain Biking in Western North Carolina - Pisgah. 2nd rev. ed. Jim Parham. (Off the Beaten Track Mountain Bike Guide Ser.). (Illus.). 88p. 1999. pap. 12.95 (*0-9631861-6-7*) Milestone NC.

***Off the Beaten Track Vol. III: A Guide to Mountain Biking in North Georgia.** 2nd rev. ed. Jim Parham. (Illus.). 144p. 1999. pap. 12.95 (*1-889596-07-8*) Milestone NC.

Off the Beaten Track Vol. IV: A Guide to Mountain Biking in East Tennessee. rev. ed. Jim Parham. (Illus.). 96p. (Orig.). 1998. pap. 12.95 (*1-889596-03-5*) Milestone NC.

Off the Beaten Track Vol. V: A Guide to Mountain Biking in Northern Virginia. Jim Parham. (Off the Beaten Track Mountain Bike Guide Ser.). (Illus.). 71p. (Orig.). 1995. pap. 12.95 (*0-9631861-7-5*) Milestone NC.

Off the Beaten Track Vol. VI: A Guide to Mountain Biking in West Virginia - Northern Highlands. Jim Parham. (Off the Beaten Track Mountain Bike Guide Ser.). (Illus.). 73p. (Orig.). 1995. pap. 12.95 (*0-9631861-8-3*) Milestone NC.

Off the Beaten Track in Israel. Ori Devir. LC 85-128603.Tr. of Nekudat-Chen. (Illus.). 200p. 1985. 24.95 (*0-915361-28-0*) Lambda Pubs.

***Off the Beaten Trade Vol. 1: A Guide to Mountain Biking in Western North Carolina - The Smokies.** 3rd rev. ed. Jim Parham. (Off the Beaten Track Mountain Bike Guide Ser.: Vol. I). (Illus.). 96p. 2000. pap. 12.95 (*1-889596-08-6*) Milestone NC.

Off the Beaten Trail. W. E. Syers. 493p. 1971. 10.95 (*0-87244-023-0*) Texian.

Off the Bench: A Perspective on Athletic Coaching. Curtis W. Tong. (Illus.). 155p. (Orig.). 1991. pap. 8.95 (*0-941736-04-0*) Arete Pr.

Off the Books: A Theory & Critique of the Underground Economy. Bruce Wiegand. LC 91-75937. 175p. 1992. pap. text 18.95 (*0-930390-12-1*); lib. bdg. 35.95 (*0-930390-13-X*) Gen Hall.

Off the Bridal Path. John L. Anderson. 1992. pap. 17.95 (*0-9616967-2-9*) Nordbook.

Off the Charts: Ruthless Days & Reckless Nights Inside the Music Industry. Bruce Haring. (Illus.). 256p. 1995. 19.95 (*1-55972-316-5*, Birch Ln Pr) Carol Pub Group.

Off the Church Wall. Rob Portlock. LC 87-2774. (Illus.). 108p. (Orig.). 1987. pap. 6.99 (*0-87784-753-3*, 753) InterVarsity.

Off the Clock. 1909. mass mkt. 14.95 (*0-385-47946-8*) Doubleday.

Off the Clock: A Lexicon of Time Words & Expressions. Kimberly O. Fakih. LC 94-2082. (Illus.). 128p. (J). (gr. 5 up). 1994. 16.00 (*0-395-66374-1*) Ticknor & Flds Bks Yng Read.

Off the Deckle Edge: A Papermaking Journey Through India. Neeta Premchand. (Illus.). 128p. 1995. 49.95 (*0-9525831-1-9*) Oak Knoll.

***Off the Eaten Path: Inspired Recipes for Adventurous Cooks.** Bob Blumer. LC 99-12488. (Illus.). 144p. 2000. pap. 20.00 (*0-345-42150-7*, Ballantine) Ballantine Pub Grp.

***Off the Edges & Outside the Lines: A Guide to Making Meaningful Personal Images.** Joy Vaughan. (Illus.). 108p. 1999. pap. 28.00 (*0-9672935-0-2*) Third Hse Pr.

Off the Face of the Earth. Aljean Harmetz. 1998. per. 6.99 (*0-671-00465-4*) PB.

Off the Face of the Earth. Aljean Harmetz. LC 96-40345. 288p. 1997. 21.50 (*0-684-83617-3*, Scribner Pap Fic) S&S Trade Pap.

Off the Floor & into Your Soup? An Expose of What Happens Behind the Closed Doors of Restaurant Kitchens. Charles E. Christmas, Jr. LC 91-67062. 128p. 1992. pap. 7.95 (*0-914984-38-1*) Starburst.

Off the Grid. Susan Phelps. (Orig.). 2000. pap. write for info. (*0-9651171-8-9*) Ashton Prods.

Off the Ground, Bks. 1[00ad]4. Ed. by William H. Kerr & Alexander Hadow. LC 76-75516. (Granger Index Reprint Ser.). 1977. 41.95 (*0-8369-6067-X*) Ayer.

Off the Ground: A Landmark Anthology of Student Writing. Landmark College Students. 144p. (Orig.). 1996. pap. 9.95 (*0-9655762-0-5*) Landmark College.

Off the Ground: First Steps to a Philosophical Consideration of the Dance. Francis E. Sparshott. LC 87-34699. 454p. 1988. reprint ed. pap. 140.80 (*0-608-07796-8*, 205986300010) Bks Demand.

Off the Interstates & Away from Tourist Traps: Wonderful Things to See & Do for Little or Nothing. Ray Cunningham. LC 96-96291. 110p. (Orig.). 1996. pap. 7.95 (*0-9631251-4-1*) R Cunningham.

Off the Job Living. G. Ott Romney. Date not set. write for info. (*0-8434-0439-6*, Pub. by McGrath NH) Ayer.

Off the Leash: Memoirs of a Royal Corgi. Matthew Sturgis. (Illus.). 98p. 1996. 19.95 (*0-340-65414-7*, Pub. by Hodder & Stought Ltd) Trafalgar.

Off the Leash: Subversive Journeys Around Vermont. Helen Husher. LC 99-28796. 192p. 1999. text 21.00 (*0-88150-427-0*, Pub. by Countryman) Norton.

Off the Main Road. George Venn. Ed. by Vi Gale. LC 77-95425. (First Bk.). (Illus.). 1978. pap. 5.00 (*0-915986-10-8*) Prescott St Pr.

Off the Main Road. limited ed. George Venn. Ed. by Vi Gale. LC 77-95425. (First Bk.). (Illus.). 1978. 20.00 (*0-915986-09-4*) Prescott St Pr.

Off the Main Road: San Vicente & Barona. 2nd ed. Charles R. LeMenager. (Illus.). 206p. (Orig.). 1997. reprint ed. pap., per. 10.95 (*0-9611102-3-6*) Eagle Peak Pub.

***Off the Mangrove Coast.** Louis L'Amour. LC 99-86061. 288p. 2000. 16.95 (*0-553-80160-0*, Spectra) Bantam.

***Off the Mangrove Coast: A Collection of Short Stories.** large type ed. Louis L'Amour. LC 00-21656. 448p. 2000. 16.95 (*0-375-43062-8*) Random Hse Lrg Prnt.

Off the Map. Joan Ackermann. LC 99-222949. 1998. pap. 5.25 (*0-8222-1591-8*) Dramatists Play.

Off the Map: An Expedition Deep into Imperialism, the Global Economy & Other Earthly Wherabouts. Chellis Glendinning. LC 99-22350. 288p. 1999. pap. 21.95 (*1-57062-360-0*, Pub. by Shambhala Pubns) Random.

Off the Map: Bicycling Across Siberia. Mark Jenkins. (Illus.). 256p. 1992. 22.00 (*0-688-09546-1*) H Leonard.

Off the Map: The Curious Histories of Place Names. Derek Nelson. LC 97-25499. 192p. 1997. 19.00 (*1-56836-174-2*) Kodansha.

***Off the Map: The Curious Histories of Place Names.** Derek Nelson. 208p. 1999. pap. 10.00 (*1-56836-298-6*) Kodansha.

Off the Map: The Journals of Lewis & Clark. Peter Roop & Connie Roop. LC 92-18340. (Illus.). 48p. (J). (gr. 3-7). 1993. 14.95 (*0-8027-8207-8*) Walker & Co.

Off the Map: The Journals of Lewis & Clark. rev. ed. Ed. by Peter Roop & Connie Roop. (Illus.). 48p. (J). (gr. 3-7). 1998. pap. 7.95 (*0-8027-7546-2*); lib. bdg. 15.85 (*0-8027-8208-6*) Walker & Co.

Off the Menu: Central Florida's Top Restaurants Recipes. Babette Anderson & Patti Kornberg. LC 97-94402. (Illus.). 1997. pap. 15.95 (*0-9660679-0-8*) II Diners.

***Off the Menu Cookbook: Four-Star Staff Meals from New York's Four-Star Restaurant. 200 Recipes for the Home Kitchen.** David Waltuck & Melicia Phillips. (Illus.). 256p. 1999. 23.95 (*0-7611-1698-2*) Workman Pub.

Off the Middle Way: Report from a Swedish Village. Sture Kallberg. Tr. by Angela Gibbs. LC 77-139709. 1972. 40.50 (*0-8290-1405-5*) Irvington.

Off the Pedestal: Transforming the Business of Medicine. Michael Greenberg. 167p. 1990. 14.95 (*0-942540-39-5*) Breakthru Pub.

Off the Pedestal: Transforming the Business of Medicine. Michael A. Greenberg. Ed. by Frank Reuter. 166p. 1992. pap. 9.95 (*0-9631700-0-7*) Making Med Wk.

Off the Planet: Surviving Five Perilous Months Aboard the Space Station Mir. Jerry M. Linenger. LC 99-31203. (Illus.). 256p. 1999. 22.50 (*1-55972-516-8*, Birch Ln Pr) Carol Pub Group.

***Off the Planet: Surviving Five Perilous Months Aboard the Space Station Mir.** Jerry M. Linenger. (Illus.). 256p. 1999. 24.95 (*0-07-136112-X*) McGraw.

Off the Post: Advanced Goaltending Techniques & Strategies. Vic LeMire. Ed. by Colleen Frizzell. (Illus.). 158p. 1998. pap. 19.95 (*1-892640-01-5*) Vics Hockey Schls.

Off the Rag: Lesbians Writing on Menopause. Ed. by Lee Lynch & Akia Woods. LC 96-19898. 250p. 1996. pap. 12.95 (*0-934678-77-4*) New Victoria Pubs.

***Off the Rails in Phnom Penh: Into the Dark Heart of Guns, Girls & Ganja.** Amit Gilboa. LC 97-946070. (Illus.), 189p. (Orig.). 1998. pap. 9.95 (*974-8303-34-9*, Pub. by Asia Bks) Amit Gilboa.

Off the Record. Mitch Spence. 464p. mass mkt. 4.99 (*1-55197-171-2*) Picasso Publ.

***Off the Record.** Sue Welfare. 1999. mass mkt. 11.00 (*0-00-651349-2*, Pub. by HarpC) Trafalgar.

Off the Record: A Life of Journalism. Harry Conroy. LC 96-212586. 239p. 1997. write for info. (*1-874640-67-X*) Argyll Pubng.

Off the Record: An Oral History of Popular Music. Joe Smith. LC 88-40090. 448p. 1989. mass mkt. 14.95 (*0-446-39090-9*, Pub. by Warner Bks) Little.

***Off the Record: Country Music's Top Label Executives Tell Their Stories.** Jennifer E. Pierce. LC 99-50264. 2000. 26.95 (*1-56833-148-7*) Madison Bks UPA.

Off the Record: Everything Related to Playing Recorded Dance Music in the Nightclub Industry. 2nd rev. ed. Doug Shannon. Ed. by Richard W. Kutnick. LC 84-20744. (Illus.). 412p. 1985. pap. 19.95 (*0-9603826-4-X*) Pacesetter Pub Hse OH.

Off the Record: Motown by Master Number, 1959-1989. Reginald J. Bartlette. LC 89-92326. (Rock & Roll Reference Ser.: No. 34). (Illus.). 544p. 1991. 60.00 (*1-56075-003-0*) Popular Culture.

Off the Record: The Life & Times of a Black Watch Officer. David Rose. (Illus.). 272p. 1997. 34.95 (*1-873376-76-6*, Pub. by Spellmnt Pubs) St Mut.

Off the Record: The Private Papers of Harry S. Truman. Ed. by Robert H. Ferrell. LC 96-37315. (Give 'Em Hell Harry Ser.). (Illus.). 488p. 1997. pap. 19.95 (*0-8262-1119-4*) U of Mo Pr.

Off the Record: The Technology & Culture of Sound Recording in America. David Morton. LC 99-27914. 180p. 2000. pap. 22.00 (*0-8135-2747-3*) Rutgers U Pr.

Off the Record: The Technology & Culture of Sound Recording in America. David L. Morton. LC 99-27914. (Illus.). 180p. 2000. text 50.00 (*0-8135-2746-5*) Rutgers U Pr.

Off the Reservation: Reflections on Boundary-Busting, Border-Crossing Loose Cannons. Paula Gunn Allen. Ed. by Tisha Hooks. LC 98-21247. 272p. 1998. 25.00 (*0-8070-4640-X*) Beacon Pr.

Off the Reservation: Reflections on Boundary-Busting, Border-Crossing Loose Canons. Paula Gunn Allen. LC 98-21247. 272p. 1999. pap. 17.00 (*0-8070-4641-8*) Beacon Pr.

Off the Rim. Fred Bowen. LC 98-20967. (Allstar SportStory Ser.). (Illus.). 112p. (J). (gr. 3-7). 1998. pap. 4.95 (*1-56145-161-4*, Peachtree) Peachtree Pubs.

Off the Rim: Thoughts & Observations of the Game. Sandy Slade. 88p. (Orig.). (YA). (gr. 5-12). 1995. pap. 5.95 (*0-9645906-0-3*) Spinsational Pub.

Off the Road. Nina Bawden. LC 97-42576. 192p. (J). (gr. 4 up). 1998. 16.00 (*0-395-91321-7*, Clarion Bks) HM.

Off the Road: My Years with Cassady, Kerouac, & Ginsberg. Carolyn Cassady. (Illus.). 448p. 1991. pap. 14.95 (*0-14-015390-X*, Penguin Bks) Viking Penguin.

Off-the-Road Mobility of Automobiles. IAkov Semenovich Ageikin. Tr. by V. S. Kothekar from RUS. 245p. (C). 1987. text 116.00 (*90-6191-495-7*, Pub. by A A Balkema) Ashgate Pub Co.

Off-the-Road Wheeled & Combined Traction Devices: Theory & Calculation. IAkov Semenovich Ageikin. Orig. Title: Vezdekhodnye kolesnye i kombinirovannye dvizhiteli. 219p. 1988. 168.00 (*90-6191-931-2*, Pub. by A A Balkema) Ashgate Pub Co.

Off-the-Road Wheeled & Combined Traction Devices: Theory & Calculation. IAkov Semenovich Ageikin. LC 87-904654. Orig. Title: Vezdekhodnye kolesnye i kombinirovannye dvizhiteli. xvii, 202 p. 1987. write for info. (*81-7087-013-5*) Oxonion Pr Pvt Ltd.

Off the Rocks. Wilfred T. Grenfell. LC 70-134963. (Short Story Index Reprint Ser.). 1977. 19.95 (*0-8369-3693-0*) Ayer.

Off the Shelf. Mary Shirey. 72p. 1998. pap. 8.00 (*0-8059-4386-2*) Dorrance.

Off the Shelf, Bk. 1. Ratcliffe & Richardson. 1993. pap. text. write for info. (*0-582-91281-4*, Pub. by Addison-Wesley) Longman.

Off the Shelf, Bk. 2. Ratcliffe & Richardson. 1993. pap. text. write for info. (*0-582-91282-2*, Pub. by Addison-Wesley) Longman.

Off the Shelf: A Marketing & Distribution Guide for Independent Literary & Artist Book Publishers. Ed. by Joan Murray. (Illus.). 160p. (Orig.). 1989. pap. 10.95 (*0-9618487-0-7*) Writers & Bks.

Off the Shelf & On-Line: Computers Move the Book Arts into Twenty-First Century Design. Margot Lovejoy et al. (Illus.). 56p. 1992. pap. 10.00 (*1-879832-04-6*) MN Ctr Book Arts.

***Off the Top of My Mind.** Karl A. Perkins. LC 00-190636. 121p. 2000. 25.00 (*0-7388-1874-7*); pap. 18.00 (*0-7388-1875-5*) Xlibris Corp.

Off the Track: The Decline of the Intercity Passenger Train in the United States, 62. Donald M. Itzkoff. LC 84-14050. (Contributions in Economics & Economic History Ser.: No. 62). (Illus.). 161p. 1985. 45.00 (*0-313-24339-5*, ITZ/) Greenwood.

Off the Village Mat. Love P. Maya. LC 97-91048. 1998. pap. 12.95 (*0-533-12548-0*) Vantage.

Off the Vine, Doin' Fine. Josephine A. Smith. LC 92-96865. (Hickle the Pickle Ser.). (Illus.). 48p. (Orig.). (J). (ps-3). 1992. pap. 2.99 (*1-881958-01-9*, TXU328879) Hickle Pickle.

Off the Wall. Frwd. by Tom Styron. (Illus.). 20p. 1978. pap. 2.50 (*0-940744-20-1*) Chrysler Museum.

***Off the Wall, Vol. 10.** unabridged ed. Michael Lizza. (Illus.). 120p. 2000. lib. bdg. 25.00 (*1-929326-63-7*) Hal Bar Pubg.

Off the Wall: Graffiti for the Soul. Ernie J. Zelinski. (Illus.). 280p. 1999. pap. 9.95 (*1-55209-311-5*) Firefly Bks Ltd.

Off the Wall: Interviews with Philip Whalen. Ed. by Philip Whalen & Donald Allen. 1978. pap. 3.50 (*0-87704-036-2*) Four Seasons Foun.

Off the Wall! School Year Bulletin Boards & Displays for the Library. Gayle Skaggs. LC 95-5693. (Illus.). 150p. (J). 1995. pap. 24.50 (*0-7864-0116-8*) McFarland & Co.

Off the Wall: The Best Graffiti off the Walls of America. Ken Frankel & Robert Wilson. LC 96-76033. (Illus.). 82p. 1996. pap. text 7.95 (*1-56352-323-X*) Longstreet.

O

An Asterisk (*) at the beginning of an entry indicates that the title is appearing for the first time.

Off the Wall: The Newspaper Columns of Ted Gardner. Ted Gardner. LC 93-77062. 288p. 1993. 17.95 (*0-9627297-7-9*) A A Knoll Pubs.

Off the Wall - Wall's Words of Wisdom. Patrick D. Wall. Ed. by M. J. VanDeventer. (Illus.). 68p. (Orig.). 1985. pap. 3.95 (*0-936523-01-8*) RF Prod.

Off the Wall & Still Bouncing. Anne M. Taylor. (Illus.). 91p. 1997. 14.95 (*0-9661806-0-7*) Beechtree OH.

Off the Wall at Callahan's. Spider Robinson. 160p. 1994. pap. 9.95 (*0-312-85661-X*, Pub. by Tor Bks) St Martin.

Off the Wall at Sardi's: The History of the Restaurant & Its People. Vincent Sardi, Jr. & Thomas E. West. LC 91-34476. (Illus.). 122p. 1991. 39.95 (*1-55783-051-7*) Applause Theatre Bk Pubs.

Off the Wall at Sardi's: The History of the Restaurant & Its People. Vincent Sardi, Jr. & Thomas E. West. (Illus.). 122p. 1993. pap. 19.95 (*1-55783-050-9*) Applause Theatre Bk Pubs.

***Off the Wall Marketing Ideas.** Nancy Michaels & Debbi J. Karpowicz. LC 99-27506. 224p. 1999. pap. 10.95 (*1-58062-205-4*) Adams Media.

Off the Wall Math: Focusing on the Concepts, Not on the Numbers. Carol M. Isaacs & Melissa L. Sergio. Ed. by Julie Fisher & Benno Isaacs. 144p. 1995. 24.99 (*1-888528-01-X*) Res Develop.

Off the Wall Science: A Poster Series Revisited. Harold Silvani. (J). (gr. 3-9). 1995. 16.95 (*1-881431-50-9*, 1710) AIMS Educ Fnd.

Off Their Rockers: Participation in Education by Retired Workers. Ivan Charner. 13p. 1990. 3.00 (*0-86510-065-9*) Natl Inst Work.

Off 13: The Eastern Shore of Virginia Guidebook. Kirk Mariner. LC 87-70771. (Illus.). 184p. 1994. reprint ed. pap. 14.95 (*0-9648393-1-8*) Miona Pubns.

Off to a Bad Start: Chicken Soup for the Sold. John Blesso. LC 96-92544. 170p. (Orig.). 1997. pap. 12.95 (*0-9654452-0-8*) Silk City Pr.

Off to a Good Start. Mary Thompson. LC 99-26460. 288p. 1999. pap. 10.95 (*1-58062-217-8*) Adams Media.

Off to a Good Start: Launching the School Year. Northeast Foundation for Children Staff. LC 97-68711. (Responsive Classroom Ser.: No. 1). (Illus.). 70p. (Orig.). 1997. pap. 8.50 (*0-9618636-6-8*) NE Found Child.

***Off to a Good Start: The First Year of Life.** UNICEF Jordan Staff. 79p. 1999. write for info. (*92-806-3420-8*) U N I C E.

Off to a Good Start: 464 Readiness Activities for Reading, Math, Social Studies & Science. Amy L. Toole & Ellen Boehm. LC 82-13474. 230p. 1984. reprint ed. pap. 7.95 (*0-8027-7238-2*) Walker & Co.

Off to a Great Start! Activities for Becoming Your Child's Best Teacher. Lilliann A. Noda et al. LC 95-24000. 1996. pap. 19.95 (*0-7802-4207-6*) Wright Group.

Off to America. Doreen Rappaport. 1924. write for info. (*0-688-17150-8*, Wm Morrow) Morrow Avon.

***Off to Bethlehem!** Dandi Daley Mackall. 24p. (ps-k). 1999. pap. 8.95 (*0-694-01505-9*) HarpC.

Off to Camp! Myra Pravda & Jeanne Weiland. LC 89-80301. (Illus.). 72p. (Orig.). (J). (gr. 2-7). 1989. pap., per. 8.95 (*0-9622328-0-7*) JSP Pub.

Off-to-College Cookbook. B. Layton. (Illus.). 176p. 1994. spiral bd. 5.95 (*1-57166-013-5*) Hearts N Tummies.

Off to College Journal: An Inspirational & Interactive Journal for First-Year College Students. Lisa Mullins. LC 98-30592. (Illus.). 170p. (Orig.). (C). 1999. pap. 9.95 (*1-56072-337-8*, Nova Kroshka Bks) Nova Sci Pubs.

Off to College, 1998: A Guide for College Bound Students. Jane L. Morse. 68p. 1998. pap. text 3.00 (*0-9654246-1-8*) Dees Comm.

Off to College, 1997: A Guide for College Bound Students. Ed. by Jane L. Dees-Morse. 68p. 1997. pap. text 3.00 (*0-9654246-0-X*) Dees Comm.

Off to Elephant School. James Preller. (Kratt's Creatures Ser.). (J). (ps-3). 1996. pap. text 3.50 (*0-590-53740-7*) Scholastic Inc.

Off to Grandma's House. 2nd ed. Illus. by Michelle Barnes. (Let Me Read Ser.). 16p. (J). (ps-1). 1995. bds. 2.95 (*0-673-36269-8*, GoodYrBooks) Addson-Wesley Educ.

Off to Grandpa's see Ver Al Abuelito

Off to Grandpa's. Bernice Myers. (Whole-Language Big Bks.). (Illus.). 16p. (Orig.). (J). (ps-2). 1994. pap. 16.95 (*1-56784-068-X*) Newbridge Educ.

Off to School. Gwendolyn Battle-Lavert. LC 94-43094. (Illus.). 32p. (J). (gr. k-3). 1995. lib. bdg. 15.95 (*0-8234-1185-0*) Holiday.

Off to School. Gill Davies & Stephanie Longfoot. (Not I Am Big Ser.). (Illus.). 24p. (J). (ps-1). 1996. 3.49 (*1-85854-368-1*) Brimax Bks.

Off to School see Take Along Stories

***Off to School: A Parent's-Eye View of the Kindergarten Year.** Irene L. Hannigan & National Association for the Education of Young Ch. LC 98-85536. viii, 136 p. 1998. 6.00 (*0-935989-86-2*) Natl Assn Child Ed.

Off to School, Baby Duck! Amy Hest. LC 98-51312. (Illus.). 32p. (J). 1999. 16.99 (*0-7636-0244-2*) Candlewick Pr.

Off to Sea: A Romance. Richard Stine. (Illus.). 64p. 1995. 14.95 (*1-55670-429-1*) Stewart Tabori & Chang.

Off to Sea: A Romance. Richard Stine. LC 95-90454. (Illus.). 1998. 14.95 (*0-941807-01-0*) Stewart Tabori & Chang.

***Off to Sea: An Inside Look at a Research Cruise.** Deborah Kovacs. (Turnstone Ocean Pilot Bks.). 48p. (J). (gr. 3-7). 1999. pap. 7.95 (*0-7398-1229-7*) Raintree Steck-V.

***Off to Sea: An Inside Look at a Research Cruise.** Deborah Kovacs. LC 99-24592. (Ocean Pilot Ser.). 48p. (J). (gr. 4-6). 2000. 25.69 (*0-7398-1228-9*) Raintree Steck-V.

***Off to the Fair!** Nancy I. Sanders. (Move Along Bead Bks.). (Illus.). 12p. (J). (gr. k-3). 2000. bds. 7.99 (*1-57584-368-4*, Pub. by Rdrs Digest) S&S Trade.

Off to the Library. Lynn Salem & Josie Stewart. (Illus.). 8p. (J). (gr. k-2). 1998. pap. 3.75 (*1-880612-73-9*) Seedling Pubns.

Off to the Revolution. Patrick Oliphant. (Illus.). 160p. 1995. pap. 9.95 (*0-8362-0429-8*) Andrews & McMeel.

***Off to the Sweet Shores of Africa & Other Talking Drum Rhymes.** Uzoamaka Chinyelu Unobagha & Julia Cairns. LC 00-8933. 2000. pap. write for info. (*0-8118-2378-4*) Chronicle Bks.

***Off to the War: An Original Farce for the Times.** Benjamin E. Woolf. (Americana Series). 22p. 2000. reprint ed. pap. 3.95 (*0-937657-55-7*) Feedbk Theabks & Prospero.

Off to the "Write" Start: A Young Astronaut's Journal. Marcy Wiinograd. (Illus.). 64p. (J). (gr. 3-6). 1994. 8.99 (*0-86653-781-3*, GA1475) Good Apple.

Off to War: Franklin Countians in World War II. Roscoe Barnes, III. LC 95-26626. (Illus.). 98p. (Orig.). 1996. pap. 9.95 (*1-57249-033-0*, Burd St Pr) White Mane Pub.

Off to War with 054. John Kemp. (C). 1989. 60.00 (*0-86303-459-4*) St Mut.

***Off to Work We Go.** (J). (gr. k-2). 1999. 6.99 (*0-8054-0823-1*) Broadman.

Off to Work with Access 97. Brian P. Favro. (Off to Work Ser.). (Illus.). 224p. 1997. pap. text 32.00 (*1-887281-43-6*) Labyrinth CA.

Off to Work with Access 97: Instructor's Guide. Brian P. Favro. (Off to Work Ser.). (Illus.). 50p. 1997. teacher ed. 24.00 (*1-887281-44-4*) Labyrinth CA.

Off to Work with Excel 97. Brian P. Favro. (Off to Work Ser.). (Illus.). 56p. 1997. teacher ed. 24.00 (*1-887281-35-5*); pap. text 32.00 (*1-887281-32-0*) Labyrinth CA.

Off to Work with Excel 97, Lessons 1-5. Brian P. Favro. (Off to Work Ser.). (Illus.). 140p. 1997. pap. text 14.00 (*1-887281-47-9*) Labyrinth CA.

Off to Work with Excel 97, Lessons 6-10. Brian P. Favro. (Off to Work Ser.). (Illus.). 150p. 1997. pap. text 14.00 (*1-887281-48-7*) Labyrinth CA.

Off to Work with Excel 97, Lessons 11-15. Brian P. Favro. (Off to Work Ser.). (Illus.). 120p. 1997. pap. text 14.00 (*1-887281-49-5*) Labyrinth CA.

Off to Work with Excel 97: Quick Course. Brian P. Favro. (Off to Work Ser.). (Illus.). 185p. 1997. pap. text 24.00 (*1-887281-37-1*) Labyrinth CA.

Off to Work with Office 97. Brian P. Favro. (Off to Work Ser.). (Illus.). 68p. 1997. teacher ed. 24.00 (*1-887281-40-1*); pap. text 36.00 (*1-887281-39-8*) Labyrinth CA.

Off to Work with Powerpoint 97. Brian P. Favro. (Off to Work Ser.). (Illus.). 40p. 1998. teacher ed. 24.00 (*1-887281-42-8*); pap. text 24.00 (*1-887281-41-X*) Labyrinth CA.

Off to Work with Word 97. Brian P. Favro. (Off to Work Ser.). (Illus.). 120p. 1997. teacher ed. 24.00 (*1-887281-34-7*); pap. text 32.00 (*1-887281-33-9*); pap. text 14.00 (*1-887281-46-0*) Labyrinth CA.

Off to Work with Word 97, Lessons 6-10. Brian P. Favro. (Off to Work Ser.). (Illus.). 120p. 1997. pap. text 14.00 (*1-887281-45-2*) Labyrinth CA.

Off to Work with Word 97: Lessons 1 to 5. Brian P. Favro. (Off to Work Ser.). (Illus.). 150p. 1997. pap. text 14.00 (*1-887281-64-9*) Labyrinth CA.

Off to Work with Word 97: Quick Course. Brian P. Favro. (Off to Work Ser.). (Illus.). 180p. 1997. pap. text 24.00 (*1-887281-38-X*) Labyrinth CA.

Off Track: When Poor Readers Become "Learning Disabled" Louise C. Spear-Swerling & robert J. Sternberg. LC 95-19900. (Renewing American Schools Ser.). (C). 1997. pap. 28.00 (*0-8133-8757-4*, Pub. by Westview) HarpC.

Off Vintage Guitar Price Guide. 6th ed. Alan Greenwood. pap. 19.95 (*1-884883-09-5*) Vintage Guitar.

Off Wall: Racquetball. Jessica Hedler. 64p. 1994. pap. text, per. 10.95 (*0-7872-0042-5*) Kendall-Hunt.

***Off We Go!** Jane Yolen. (J). 1999. 12.95 (*0-316-90111-3*, Pub. by Little) Time Warner.

Off We Go! Jane Yolen. LC 98-6893. (Illus.). 32p. (J). 2000. 12.95 (*0-316-90228-4*) Little.

Off We Go! large type ed. Beth Esh Smith. (HRL Little Bks.). (Illus.). 10p. (J). (ps-k). 1998. pap. text 10.95 (*1-57332-110-9*); pap. text 10.95 (*1-57332-111-7*) HighReach Lrning.

Off We Go Piano Book of Poetry Pieces. Diller & Quail. 48p. 1986. pap. 4.95 (*0-7935-5106-4*, 50326770) H Leonard.

Off White: Readings on Society, Race & Culture. Ed. by Michelle Fine et al. LC 96-25153. 448p. (C). 1996. pap. 25.99 (*0-415-91302-0*) Routledge.

Off White: Readings on Society, Race & Culture. Ed. by Michelle Fine et al. LC 96-25153. 448p. (C). 1996. 75.00 (*0-415-91301-2*) Routledge.

Off with Her Head! The Denial of Women's Identity in Myth, Religion, & Culture. Ed. by Howard Eilberg-Schwartz & Wendy Doniger. LC 95-13310. (Illus.). 242p. 1995. 48.00 (*0-520-08839-5*, Pub. by U CA Pr); pap. 17.95 (*0-520-08840-9*, Pub. by U CA Pr) Cal Prin Full Svc.

Off with the Old Love. Betty A. Neels. (Promo Ser.). 1999. per. 3.99 (*0-373-63103-0*, 1-63103-5) Harlequin Bks.

Offaly: History & Society. William Nolan & Timothy P. O'Neill. LC 99-165696. (County History & Society Ser.). (Illus.). xxxvi, 1000p. 1998. 85.00 (*0-906602-90-4*, Pub. by Geography Pubns) Irish Bks Media.

Offa's Dyke Path North: Knighton to Prestatyn. Mark Richards et al. (National Trail Guides Ser.). (Illus.). 168p. (Orig.). 1995. pap. 19.95 (*1-85410-016-5*, Pub. by Aurum Pr) London Brdge.

Offa's Dyke Path South. Ernie Kay et al. (National Trail Guides Ser.). (Orig.). 1994. pap. text 19.95 (*1-85410-295-8*, Pub. by Aurum Pr) London Brdge.

Offa's Dyke Path South. Mark Richards et al. (National Travel Guide Ser.). (Illus.). 168p. (Orig.). 1995. pap. 19.95 (*1-85410-017-3*, Pub. by Aurum Pr) London Brdge.

Offbeat Collection of Dutch & Flemish Paintings. Ivan Gaskell. (Illus.). 24p. 1995. pap. 6.00 (*0-916724-84-0*, 4840) Harvard Art Mus.

Offbeat Food: Adventures in an Omnivorous World. Alan Ridenour. LC 99-59930. (Illus.). 240p. 2000. pap. 19.95 (*1-891661-09-4*, 1094) Snta Monica.

Offbeat Golf: A Swingin' Guide to a Worldwide Obsession. Bob Loeffelbein. LC 98-11158. (Illus.). 192p. 1998. pap. 17.95 (*1-891661-02-7*, 1-02-7) Snta Monica.

Offbeat Marijuana: The Life & Times of the World's Grooviest Plant. Saul Rubin. LC 99-13285. (Illus.). 2p. 1999. pap. 19.95 (*1-891661-05-1*, 1051, Offbeat) Snta Monica.

Offbeat Museums: The Curators & Collections of America's Most Unusual Museums. Saul Rubin. LC 97-16766. (Illus.). 240p. 1997. pap. 19.95 (*0-9639946-4-6*, 46-4-6) Snta Monica.

Offbeat Overnights: A Guide to the Most Unusual Places to Stay in California. Lucy Poshek. LC 95-51139. 232p. 1996. pap. text 9.95 (*1-55853-390-7*) Rutledge Hill Pr.

Offbeat Prayers for the Modern Mystic: Making Life Easier Through Innovative Prayer. Anne Sermons Gillis. LC 98-72207. 1998. pap. 10.95 (*0-9662874-0-1*) Easy Times.

Offbeat Sicilian: Unorthodox Ways to Win with White! John Grefe. 51p. (Orig.). 1987. pap. 6.00 (*0-931462-70-3*) Chess Ent.

***Offbeat Uses for Everyday Things.** Joey Green. 400p. 2000. 8.98 (*1-56731-363-9*, MJF Bks) Fine Comms.

Offcuts from a Legal Literary Life. Nicholas Hasluck. (Orig.). pap. 9.95 (*1-875560-17-3*, Pub. by Univ of West Aust Pr) Intl Spec Bk.

Offenbach. Peter Gammond. (Illustrated Lives of the Great Composers Ser.). (Illus.). 166p. 1996. 17.95 (*0-7119-0257-7*, OP 42431) Omnibus NY.

Offenbach in America: Notes of a Travelling Musician. Jacques Offenbach. LC 74-24172. reprint ed. 37.50 (*0-404-13076-3*) AMS Pr.

Offenbach's Songs from the Great Operettas. Jacques Offenbach. 195p. 1976. pap. 12.95 (*0-486-23341-3*) Dover.

Offenbarung Als Kommunikation: Das Konzept Wahy in Nasr Hamid Abu Zayds Mafhum An-nass. Navid Kermani. (Europaische Hochschulschriften Ser.: Reihe 27, Bd. 58). (GER.). XVII, 138p. 1996. 35.95 (*3-631-30241-X*) P Lang Pubng.

Offenbarung Arabiens (Arabia Deserta) Charles M. Doughty. (Illus.). 613p. reprint ed. write for info. (*0-318-71501-5*) G Olms Pubs.

Offenbarung Nach Dem Lehrbegriffe der Synagoge, 4 band. Salomon L. Steinheim. (GER.). 352p. 1986. reprint ed. write for info. (*3-487-07752-3*) G Olms Pubs.

Offenbarung Nach dem Lehrbegriffe der Synagoge, 4 vols., Set. Salomon L. Steinheim. Ed. by Steven Katz. LC 79-7151. (Jewish Philosophy, Mysticism & History of Ideas Ser.). 1980. reprint ed. lib. bdg. 176.95 (*0-405-12286-1*) Ayer.

Offenbarung Nach dem Lehrbegriffe der Synagoge, 4 vols., Vol. 1. Salomon L. Steinheim. Ed. by Steven Katz. LC 79-7151. (Jewish Philosophy, Mysticism & History of Ideas Ser.). 1980. reprint ed. lib. bdg. 44.95 (*0-405-12288-8*) Ayer.

Offenbarung Nach dem Lehrbegriffe der Synagoge, 4 vols., Vol. 3. Salomon L. Steinheim. Ed. by Steven Katz. LC 79-7151. (Jewish Philosophy, Mysticism & History of Ideas Ser.). 1980. reprint ed. lib. bdg. 44.95 (*0-405-12220-9*) Ayer.

Offenbarung Nach dem Lehrbegriffe der Synagoge, 4 vols., Vol. 4. Salomon L. Steinheim. Ed. by Steven Katz. LC 79-7151. (Jewish Philosophy, Mysticism & History of Ideas Ser.). 1980. reprint ed. lib. bdg. 44.95 (*0-405-12221-7*) Ayer.

Offenbarung und Geschichte: Zur Hermeneutischen Bestimmung der Theologie Wolfhart Pannenbergs. Reginal Nnamdi. (Wurzburger Studien Zur Fundamentaltheologie Ser.: Bd. 13). (GER.). 473p. 1993. 68.80 (*3-631-44559-8*) P Lang Pubng.

Offences Against Property. J. H. Parry. (Criminal Law Library: Vol. 7). 464p. 1989. 100.00 (*0-08-033070-3*) Macmillan.

Offences Against the Person. P. F. Rook & P. B. Carter. (Criminal Law Library). 400p. 1991. 100.00 (*0-08-039202-4*, K130) Macmillan.

Offences Against the Person. Richard Stone. 251p. 1999. pap. 54.00 (*1-874241-13-9*, Pub. by Cavendish Pubng) Gaunt.

Offences of Violence. P. B. Carter & R. Harrison. (Waterlow Criminal Law Library). 320p. 1991. 100.00 (*0-08-040138-4*) Macmillan.

Offended. Bill Strayer. 1996. write for info. (*0-9636788-2-5*) Calvary Chapel.

***Offender in the Community.** Todd R. Clear & Harry R. Dammer. LC 99-39956. (Illus.). 428p. 1999. pap. 57.95 (*0-534-25374-1*) Brooks-Cole.

Offender Profiling: Theory, Research & Practice. Ed. by Janet L. Jackson & Debra A. Bekerian. LC 97-17402. (Wiley Series in Psychology of Crime, Policing, & Law). 254p. 1997. pap. 54.95 (*0-471-97565-6*) Wiley.

Offender Rehabilitation: Effective Correctional Intervention. Ed. by Francis T. Cullen & Brandon K. Applegate. LC 97-7873. (International Library of Criminology, Criminal Justice & Penology). 490p. 1997. text 179.95 (*1-85521-798-8*, Pub. by Ashgate Pub) Ashgate Pub Co.

Offender Rehabilitation in Practice. Betsy Bernfeld. 2000. pap. text. write for info. (*0-471-72026-7*) Wiley.

Offenders, Deviants or Patients? 2nd ed. Herschel A. Prins. LC 94-34150. (Illus.). 304p. (C). 1995. 80.00 (*0-415-10220-0*, C0116) Routledge.

Offending Behavior: Skills & Stratagems for Going Straight. James McGuire & Philip Priestley. LC 84-18395. 256p. 1985. text 32.50 (*0-312-58208-0*) St Martin.

Offending Girls: Sex, Youth & Justice. Kerry Carrington. 208p. 1994. pap. 21.95 (*1-86373-523-2*, Pub. by Allen & Unwin Pty) Paul & Co Pubs.

Offending Women: A Study in Social Control & Its Resistance - Female Lawbreakers & the Criminal Justice System. Anne Worrall. (Sociology of Law & Crime Ser.). 208p. (C). 1996. pap. 22.99 (*0-415-03725-5*, A4076) Routledge.

Offene Formen: Beitrage zur Literatur, Philosophie und Wissenschaft Im 18. Jahrhundert. Bernd Brautigam & Burghard Damerau. (Berliner Beitrage zur Neueren Deutschen Literaturgeschichte Ser.: Bd. 22). (GER.). 352p. 1997. 57.95 (*3-631-30163-4*) P Lang Pubng.

***Offene Lernsituationen Im Grundschulunterricht: Eine Empirische Studie zur Lernzeitnutzung Von Grundschulern Mit Unterschiedlicher Konzentrationsfahigkeit.** Frank Lipowsky. (Europaische Hochschulschriften: Reihe 11, Padagogik Ser.). X, 244p. 1999. 42.95 (*3-631-35075-9*) P Lang Pubng.

Offenhauser: The Legendary Racing Engine & the Men Who Built It. Gordon E. White. LC 96-9402. (Illus.). 200p. 1996. 39.95 (*0-87938-883-8*) MBI Pubg.

Offenheit und Interesse: Studien Zum 65. Gegurtstag von Gerhard Wirth. Rudiger Kinsky et al. (GER.). 291p. 1993. pap. 76.00 (*90-256-1029-3*, Pub. by AM Hakkert) BookLink Distributors.

Offense. Miriam Hellman. 19p. 1996. 2.00 (*1-891309-09-9*) Prophetic DC.

Offense & Defense in the International System. George H. Quester. 239p. 1987. 39.95 (*0-88738-156-1*) Transaction Pubs.

Offense to Others. Joel Feinberg. (Moral Limits of the Criminal Law Ser.: Vol. 2). 350p. 1988. pap. text 19.95 (*0-19-505215-3*) OUP.

Offense to Reason: A Theology of Sin. Bernard L. Ramm. 187p. 1992. reprint ed. ring bd. 12.95 (*1-57383-001-1*) Regent College.

Offenses: Keeping the Church from Stumbling. Randy Bunch. 47p. (Orig.). pap. 3.95 (*0-940487-10-1*) Jubilee CA.

Offensive Art: The Liberation of Poetic Imagination in Augustan Satirre. C. J. Purvis. 232p. (C). 1989. 100.00 (*0-907839-34-7*, Pub. by Brynmill Pr Ltd) St Mut.

Offensive Baseball Drills. Rod Delmonico. LC 95-42628. (Illus.). 184p. (Orig.). 1996. pap. 14.95 (*0-87322-865-0*, PDEL0865) Human Kinetics.

Offensive Drills see Women's Basketball Drills

Offensive Films: Toward an Anthropology of Cinema Vomitif, 72. Mikita Brottman. LC 96-49734. (Contributions to the Study of Science Fiction & Fantasy: Vol. 72). 224p. 1997. 55.00 (*0-313-30033-X*, Greenwood Pr) Greenwood.

***Offensive Football Strategies.** American Football Coaches Association. LC 99-47997. (Illus.). 336p. 1999. pap. 22.95 (*0-7360-0139-5*) Human Kinetics.

Offensive Literature: Decensorship in Britain, 1960-1982. John Sutherland. LC 82-22758. 216p. 1983. text 44.00 (*0-389-20354-8*, N7214) B&N Imports.

Offensive Operations, 1914-15 see Naval History of the World War

Offensive Strategy: Forging a New Competitiveness in the Fires of Head-to-Head Competition. Lee T. Perry. 1990. 24.95 (*0-88730-435-4*, HarpBusn) HarpInfo.

***Offensively Gross Jokes.** Julius Alvin. 2000. mass mkt. 4.99 (*0-8217-6644-9*, Zebra Kensgtn) Kensgtn Pub Corp.

Offentliche Nahverkehrspolitik in Berlin und Paris, 1890-1914. Elfi Bendikat. 672p. 1998. 186.00 (*3-11-015383-1*) De Gruyter.

Offentlichkeiten der Fruhen Neuzeit: Teilnehmer, Formen, Institutionen und Entscheidungen Offentlicher Kommunikation Im Herzogtum Preuben Von 1525 Bis 1618. Esther-Beate Korber. 496p. 1997. 174.00 (*3-11-015600-8*) De Gruyter.

Offer. Catherine Coulter. 1997. mass mkt. 7.50 (*0-451-40794-6*, Topaz) NAL.

***Offer in Compromise Process: Insights & Strategies.** Kip Dellinger & Royal Dellinger. 344p. 1999. pap. text 45.00 (*0-8080-0417-4*) CCH INC.

Offer Me a Flower. Savitri L. Bess. (Illus.). 1999. pap. 13.50 (*0-9668373-8-X*) Bharati Impress.

***Offer of Truth.** Taylor Daignault. (Another Great American First Novel Ser.: Vol. 9). 320p. 2000. 24.95 (*0-947993-89-4*, Pub. by Mlvrn Pubg Co) Brit Bk Co Inc.

Offer She Couldn't Refuse. Marie Ferrarella. (Yours Truly Ser.). 1998. per. 3.50 (*0-373-52061-1*, 1-52061-8) Silhouette.

Offer Them Christ. William M. Pickard. LC 98-65599. 128p. 1998. pap. 14.95 (*1-57736-090-7*) Providence Hse.

***Offer to Love.** large type ed. Gail Whitiker. 320p. 2000. 25.99 (*0-263-16327-X*, Pub. by Mills & Boon) Ulverscroft.

Offer Too Good to Refuse. 1998. write for info. (*0-201-33988-9*) Addison-Wesley.

Offering. Joe Duvernay. 64p. 1998. pap. 7.00 (*0-8059-4352-8*) Dorrance.
Offering: A Play in Two Acts. Gus Edwards. 1978. pap. 5.25 (*0-8222-0837-7*) Dramatists Play.
Offering: A Series of Meditations on the Meaning of Life. Jay Frankston. (Illus.). 112p. 1993. pap. 10.95 (*0-9629754-4-3*) Whole Loaf.
Offering: Aliscolidodi. Diane H. Glancy. (Illus.). 88p. (Orig.). 1988. pap. 6.95 (*0-930100-20-4*) Holy Cow.
Offering for the Dead. Hans E. Nossack. Tr. by Joachim Neugroschel from GER. LC 90-85935. 150p. 1992. 19.00 (*0-941419-29-0*, Eridanos Library) Marsilio Pubs.
Offering Meditations. Ray Miles. LC 97-43297. 1998. 5.99 (*0-8272-2709-4*) Chalice Pr.
Offering Meditations & Prayers. Laurence C. Keene. LC 84-266. 64p. (Orig.). 1984. pap. 5.99 (*0-8272-2706-X*) Chalice Pr.
Offering Smoke: The Sacred Pipe & Native American Religion. Jordan Paper. LC 88-28378. (Illus.). 181p. 1989. pap. 22.95 (*0-89301-126-6*) U of Idaho Pr.
Offering the Gospel to Children. Gretchen W. Pritchard. LC 92-23900. 219p. 1992. pap. 13.95 (*1-56101-065-0*) Cowley Pubns.
Offerings. Mark Dunster. 28p. (Orig.). (YA). (gr. 9-12). 1996. pap. 5.00 (*0-89642-325-5*) Linden Pubs.
***Offerings at the Wall: Artifacts from the Vietnam Veterans Memorial Collection.** Thomas B. Allen. (Illus.). 287p. 1999. reprint ed. pap. text 25.00 (*0-7881-6384-1*) DIANE Pub.
***Offerings at the Wall: Artifacts from the Vietnam Veterans Memorial Collection.** Thomas B. Allen. (Illus.). 288p. 2000. reprint ed. text 40.00 (*0-7881-9180-2*) DIANE Pub.
***Offerings for the Green Man: A Bardsong Press Celtic Voice Anthology.** Ed. by Kathleen Cunningham Guler. LC 99-85877. (Illus.). 64p. 2000. pap. 11.95 (*0-9660371-1-1*) Bardsong Pr.
Offerings from Nepal. Craig Potton. 1995. pap. 203.00 (*0-7855-7469-7*, Pub. by Ratna Pustak Bhandar) St Mut.
Offerings of Ambiance. Debra K. Markewicz. 1998. pap. write for info. (*1-57553-945-4*) Watermrk Pr.
Offerings, Sacrifices & Worship in the Old Testament. John H. Kurtz. Ed. by Patrick H. Alexander. 456p. 1998. reprint ed. 24.95 (*1-56563-395-4*) Hendrickson MA.
Offers in Compromise: Internal Revenue Manual 57(10)0. 54p. 1995. pap. 22.49 (*1-57402-318-7*) Athena Info Mgt.
***Offical Annual Statement Blanks of the NAIC: Hospital, Medical, Dental & Indemnity Corporations.** rev. ed. Ed. by Patti Carli. 106p. 1999. ring bd. 100.00 (*0-89382-616-2*) Nat Assn Insurance.
***Offical Annual Statement Blanks of the NIAC: Health Maintenance Organizations.** rev. ed. Ed. by Patti Carli. 100p. 1999. ring bd. 125.00 (*0-89382-609-X*, ASB-H499) Nat Assn Insurance.
***Offical Annual Statement Blanks of the NIAC: Limited Health Services Organizations.** rev. ed. Ed. by Patti Carli. 100p. 1999. ring bd. 100.00 (*0-89382-610-3*, ASB-S499) Nat Assn Insurance.
***Offical Annual Statement Blanks of the NIAC: Separate Accounts.** rev. ed. Ed. by Patti Carli. 75p. 1999. pap. 25.00 (*0-89382-617-0*) Nat Assn Insurance.
***Offical Annual Statement Blanks of the NIAC: Title.** rev. ed. Ed. by Patti Carli. 130p. 1999. ring bd. 100.00 (*0-89382-615-4*, ASB-T499) Nat Assn Insurance.
Offical Book of the Shih Tzu. Jo Ann White. LC 99-207039. 1998. 35.95 (*0-7938-0509-0*) TFH Pubns.
Offical Disability Guidelines, on CD-Rom, 1999. Ed. by Philip L. Denniston. 200p. 1999. pap. 165.00 (*1-880891-27-1*) Work-Loss Data.
Offical Disability Guidelines, Top 200 Conditions, 1999. rev. ed. Ed. by Philip L. Denniston. 200p. 1998. pap. 165.00 (*1-880891-26-3*) Work-Loss Data.
Offical GED Handbook. rev. ed. Chuck Herring & Judy Herring. (Offical GED Preparation Ser.). Orig. Title: The GED Handbook. (Illus.). 96p. 1982. write for info. (*0-937128-06-6*) GED Inst.
Offical Guide to American Historic Inns, Vol. 6. 6th ed. Deborah Sakach & American Historic Inns Incorporated Staff. Ed. by Tiffany Crosswy et al. (Illus.). 582p. 1998. pap. 15.95 (*1-888050-02-0*) American Hist.
Offical Guide to Role Playing Games. Timothy Brown & Tony Lee. 1998. pap. 17.00 (*0-676-60144-8*) Ballantine Pub Grp.
Offical Letters of Alexander Spotswood, 1710-'22, 2 vols. in 1. Alexander Spotswood. Ed. by R. A. Brock. LC 79-176002. (Virginia Historical Society: No. 3 & 4). 1885. 95.00 (*0-404-57652-4*) AMS Pr.
***Offical Museum Directory 2000, vols., 2, Set.** 30th ed. Ed. by National Register Publishing Editors. 1999. 245.00 (*0-87217-911-7*) Natl Register.
***Offical Nickellennium Scrapbook.** Karen Kuflick. (J). 1999. per. 9.95 (*0-671-04130-4*) S&S Trade.
***Offical Price Guide to Records: 2000 Edition.** 14th ed. Jerry Osborne. 2000. pap. 25.95 (*0-676-60186-3*) Hse Collectbls.
***Offical Rising Sun Strategy Guide.** 1999. pap. 19.99 (*0-9673565-3-9*) Illumination Pubns.
Offical Soviet AKM Manual. James F. Gebhardt. 120p. 1999. pap. 16.00 (*1-58160-010-0*) Paladin Pr.
Office. Jean-Paul Aron. Tr. by Matthew Ward & Irene Ilton from FRE. 144p. (Orig.). 1983. pap. text 8.95 (*0-913745-03-0*) Ubu Repertory.
Office. N. T. Morley. 1998. mass mkt. 6.95 (*1-56333-616-2*) Masquerade.
Office. Elisabeth Pelegrin-Grenel. (Illus.). 216p. 1996. 45.00 (*2-08-013589-9*, Pub. by Flammarion) Abbeville Pr.
Office: A Facility Based on Change. Robert Propst. 71p. 1986. 8.50 (*0-936658-01-0*) H Miller Res.
Office: Procedure & Technology. 3rd ed. Oliverio & White. (KF - Office Education Ser.). 1998. pap., teacher ed. 71.95 (*0-538-66739-7*); pap., teacher ed. 16.95 (*0-538-66740-0*) S-W Pub.
Office: Procedures & Technology. Oliverio. (KM - Office Procedures Ser.). 1987. mass mkt. 36.50 (*0-538-11353-7*) S-W Pub.
Office: Procedures & Technology. Oliverio. (KM - Office Procedures Ser.). 1991. mass mkt. 34.25 (*0-538-61747-0*) S-W Pub.
Office: Procedures & Technology. 2nd ed. Oliverio. (KM - Office Procedures Ser.). 1992. 3.00 (*0-538-60902-8*); mass mkt., wbk. ed. 16.25 (*0-538-60901-X*) S-W Pub.
Office: Procedures & Technology. 2nd ed. Mary E. Oliverio. (KM - Office Procedures Ser.). 1992. mass mkt. 34.25 (*0-538-60900-1*) S-W Pub.
Office: Procedures & Technology. 3rd ed. Oliverio & White. (KF - Office Education Ser.). 1997. pap. 15.50 (*0-538-66737-0*) S-W Pub.
Office Accounting. Rocco M. Santoro et al. LC 83-21891. 80p. (C). 1984. pap. text 6.95 (*0-471-80240-9*) P-H.
Office Accounting. Rocco M. Santoro et al. LC 83-21891. 80p. (C). 1984. pap. text 26.25 (*0-471-89305-6*) P-H.
Office Administrator for the Electrical Contractor. Michael Sammaritano. (Illus.). 120p. 1996. ring bd. 32.00 (*1-887720-21-9*) Contracting Pubns.
Office Aide. Jack Rudman. (Career Examination Ser.: C-1065). 1994. pap. 19.95 (*0-8373-1065-2*) Nat Learn.
Office & Bedside Procedures: Clinical Manual. Mary Chestnutt & Thomas Dewar. (Illus.). 483p. (C). 1996. pap. text 29.95 (*0-8385-1095-7*, A1095-7, Apple Lange Med) McGraw.
Office & Career Management for the Eyecare Paraprofessional. Bill Borover & Tammy Langley. LC 96-51005. (Basic Bookshelf for Eyecare Professionals Ser.). 144p. 1997. pap. text 30.00 (*1-55642-331-4*, 63314) SLACK Inc.
Office & Computer Careers, 6 vols., Set. 98.00 (*0-685-23036-8*, CG107S) Ready Ref Pr.
Office & Data Communication Dictionary: Fachwoerterbuch der Buero und Datenkommunikation. Johann J. Amkreutz. (ENG, FRE & GER.). 1985. write for info. (*0-8288-1369-8*, M8449) Fr & Eur.
Office & Data Communication French-German, German-French. Werner Barwald. (FRE & GER.). 197p. 1993. 125.00 (*0-8288-7384-4*, 3861170183) Fr & Eur.
Office & Industrial Cleaners. Ed. by ICC Information Group Staff. 1987. 695.00 (*1-85036-903-8*, Pub. by ICC Info Group Ltd) St Mut.
***Office & Ministry of - APOSTLE.** D. C. Mouzon. 69p. 2000. pap. write for info. (*1-929740-01-8*) Faith Love & Truth.
Office & Office Building Security. 2nd ed. Edward San Luis et al. LC 93-32389. 368p. 1994. 49.95 (*0-7506-9487-4*, BH Security) Buttrwrth-Heinemann.
Office & Science Assistant. Jack Rudman. (Career Examination Ser.: C-552). 1994. pap. 29.95 (*0-8373-0552-7*) Nat Learn.
Office & Secretarial Technology. (National Teacher Examination Ser.: NT-58). pap. 23.95 (*0-8373-8478-8*) Nat Learn.
***Office & Work Spaces: Portfolios of 40 Designers.** Vernon Mays. (Illus.). 192p. 1999. 50.00 (*1-56496-581-3*) Rockport Pubs.
Office Appliance Operator. Jack Rudman. (Career Examination Ser.: C-551). 1994. pap. 23.95 (*0-8373-0551-9*) Nat Learn.
Office Application Mini-Book. 1999. write for info. (*0-7897-1829-4*) Que.
Office Assistant. Jack Rudman. (Career Examination Ser.: C-1382). 1994. pap. 19.95 (*0-8373-1382-1*) Nat Learn.
Office Associate. Jack Rudman. (Career Examination Ser.). pap. 19.95 (*0-8373-2450-5*, C2450) Nat Learn.
Office Associate. 2nd ed. Hy Hammer. (Orig.). 1986. pap. 8.00 (*0-317-52493-3*) P-H.
Office at Home. Robert Scott. 320p. 1985. 16.95 (*0-684-18212-2*, Scribners Ref); write for info. (*0-684-18218-1*, Scribners Ref) Mac Lib Ref.
Office Automated Course, Perfect Office 3.0 for Windows. Wordperfect Corporation Staff. (DF - Computer Applications Ser.). 1995. mass mkt. 43.95 (*0-538-65200-4*) S-W Pub.
Office Automation. Ed. by J. Wix. (C). 1985. 140.00 (*0-86022-118-0*, Pub. by Build Servs Info Assn) St Mut.
Office Automation. Andrew Doswell. LC 82-6988. (Wiley Series in Information Processing). 293p. reprint ed. pap. 90.90 (*0-7837-6371-9*, 204608300010) Bks Demand.
Office Automation: A Glossary & Guide. Nancy M. Edwards & Carmine Shaw. Ed. by Patricia A. King. LC 82-4714. (Professional Librarian Ser.). 275p. 1986. 65.00 (*0-86729-012-9*, Hall Reference) Macmillan.
Office Automation: A Social & Organizational Perspective. Rudy A. Hirschheim. LC 85-22756. (John Wiley Information Systems Ser.). 345p. reprint ed. pap. 107.00 (*0-7837-6731-5*, 204635900011) Bks Demand.
Office Automation: A Survey of Tools & Technology. 2nd ed. David Barcomb. 350p. 1988. pap. text 28.00 (*0-13-631094-X*) P-H.
Office Automation: A System Approach. 3rd ed. Ray et al. 672p. boxed set 91.95 (*0-538-71048-9*); boxed set 91.95 (*0-538-71049-7*) S-W Pub.
Office Automation: A Systems Approach. 2nd ed. Palmer & Charles M. Ray. (KK - Legal Secretary Studies). (C). pap. 43.75 (*0-538-70036-X*) S-W Pub.
Office Automation: A User-Driven Method. Don Tapscott. LC 82-15133. (Applications of Modern Technology in Business Ser.). (Illus.). 264p. (C). 1982. pap. 35.00 (*0-306-41973-4*, Plenum Trade) Perseus Pubng.
Office Automation: Context, Experience & Future. 2nd ed. Andrew Doswell. LC 89-21516. 318p. 1991. 170.00 (*0-471-92553-5*) Wiley.
Office Automation: Jekyll or Hyde. Ed. by Judith Gregory & Daniel Marshall. LC 83-60764. 229p. (Orig.). 1983. pap. 12.95 (*0-912663-00-6*) Work Women Educ.
Office-Based Family Pharmacist. LC 78-58638. (Illus.). (Orig.). 1978. pap. text 10.95 (*0-9602034-1-9*) E V White.
Office-Based Surgery in Otolaryngology. Ed. by Andrew Blitzer et al. LC 97-42732. (Illus.). 700p. 1997. 98.00 (*0-86577-739-X*) Thieme Med Pubs.
Office-Based Surgery in Otolaryngology. Andrew Blitzer. LC 97-42732. 1998. 98.00 (*3-13-110511-9*) Thieme Med Pubs.
Office-Based Surgery in Otolaryngology. John H. Krouse et al. LC 98-26628. (Illus.). 300p. 1999. text. write for info. (*0-7216-7674-X*, W B Saunders Co) Harcrt Hlth Sci Grp.
Office-Based Surgery of the Head & Neck. Yosef P. Krespi. LC 97-20618. 304p. 1997. text 95.00 (*0-397-51590-1*) Lppncott W & W.
Office Basics Made Easy. Learning Express Staff. Ed. by Jim Gish. LC 97-11421. 160p. 1997. pap. 12.95 (*1-57685-118-4*) LrningExprss.
Office Builders. MacInnes. text. write for info. (*0-471-49148-9*) Wiley.
Office Building Acquisition Handbook: Checklists for Making Sure You Don't Overlook Anything Important When You Buy an Office Building. John T. Reed. LC 85-90317. 170p. 1985. ring bd. 39.95 (*0-939224-17-8*) John T Reed.
***Office Building Occupant's Guide to Indoor Air Quality.** Government Printing Office Staff. 19p. 1998. pap. 2.00 (*0-16-042729-0*) USGPO.
Office Buildings. Nippan Books Staff. LC 96-152249. (New Concepts in Architecture & Design Ser.). 1996. 85.00 (*4-938812-92-X*, Pub. by Puroto Gyarak) Bks Nippan.
Office Cashier see Gregg Office Job Training Program, Classroom Installation
Office Cashiering Practice Set. Fred C. Archer et al. 1969. text 12.96 (*0-07-002167-8*) McGraw.
Office Clutter Cure. Don A. Aslett. (Illus.). 192p. (Orig.). 1995. pap. 9.99 (*0-937750-08-5*) Marsh Creek Pr.
***Office Collectibles: One Hundred Years of Business Technology.** Tom Russo. (Illus.). 240p. 2000. 39.95 (*0-7643-1177-8*) Schiffer.
Office Communication. Christian Knoeller. (Illus.). 176p. (C). 1988. pap. text 23.60 (*0-13-631177-6*) P-H.
***Office Computing.** David Storey. LC 99-37537. (Self-Development for Success Ser.: Vol. 12). 96p. 1999. pap. 12.95 (*0-8144-7057-2*) AMACOM.
***Office D. A.** Oscar R. Ojeda. (Contemporary World Architects Ser.). (Illus.). 132p. 1999. pap. 25.00 (*1-56496-546-5*) Rockport Pubs.
Office Design Ideas. Ron Combs. 1995. 49.95 (*0-87814-451-X*) PennWell Bks.
Office Design That Really Works. Kathleen R. Allen. (Small Business Solutions Ser.). (Illus.). 128p. 1995. pap. 13.95 (*0-8442-2999-7*, NTC Business Bks) NTC Contemp Pub Co.
Office Design That Really Works! Design for the 90s. Kathleen R. Allen & Peter H. Engel. (Office Depot's Small Business Solutions Ser.). (Illus.). 128p. (Orig.). 1995. pap. 13.95 (*1-886111-21-9*) Affinity CA.
Office Designer. Stanley Tools Staff. (Stanley Project Planners Ser.). (Illus.). (Orig.). 1990. pap. 16.95 (*0-924648-06-6*) Stanley Tools.
Office Designer I. Stanley Tools Staff. (Plan-a-Flex Ser.). (Illus.). (Orig.). 1987. pap. 79.95 (*0-924648-00-7*) Stanley Tools.
Office Designer II. Stanley Tools Staff. (Plan-a-Flex Ser.). (Illus.). (Orig.). 1988. pap. 44.95 (*0-924648-01-5*) Stanley Tools.
Office Development & Capital Accumulation in the U. K. Lutz Luithlen. 320p. 1994. 72.95 (*1-85628-627-4*, Pub. by Avebry) Ashgate Pub Co.
Office Development Handbook. W. Paul O'Mara & John A. Casazza. LC 82-50078. (Community Builders Handbook Ser.). (Illus.). 272p. 1982. 64.95 (*0-87420-607-3*, OD1) Urban Land.
Office Development Handbook. 2nd ed. Urban Land Institute Staff. LC 98-85108. (ULI Development Handbook Ser.). 356p. 1998. 89.95 (*0-87420-822-X*, OD2) Urban Land.
Office Diagnosis & Management of Chronic Obstructive Pulmonary Disease. Geoffrey M. Davies. LC 81-8386. (Illus.). 142p. reprint ed. pap. 44.10 (*0-608-15989-1*, 205674000084) Bks Demand.
***Office Dirty Tricks: 50 Ways to Sabotage Your Coworkers & Bluff Your Way to the Top.** Hunter S. Fulghum. (Illus.). 112p. 2000. pap. 9.95 (*0-7407-0986-0*) Andrews & McMeel.
***Office E-Mails That Really Click.** Maureen Chase & Sandy Trupp. (Illus.). 150p. 2000. pap. 12.95 (*1-890154-18-0*) Aegis Pub Grp.
Office Emergencies. Scott. Date not set. pap. text. write for info. (*0-7216-7779-7*, W B Saunders Co) Harcrt Hlth Sci Grp.
Office Emergency Procedures. American Dental Hygienists' Association Staff & Block Drug Company. 1979. 20.00 (*0-318-19096-6*) Am Dental Hygienists.
Office Endoscopy. Bergin F. Overholt & Sarkis J. Chobanian. 216p. 1990. 49.00 (*0-683-06660-9*) Lppncott W & W.
Office Equipment Adviser. 3rd rev. ed. John Derrick. 500p. 1995. pap. text 24.95 (*1-882568-58-3*) What to Buy Busn.
Office Equipment in Egypt: A Strategic Entry Report, 1996. Compiled by Icon Group International Staff. (Illus.). 157p. 1999. ring bd. 1570.00 incl. audio compact disk (*0-7418-0726-2*) Icon Grp.
Office Ergonomics Tool Kit with Training Disk. Dan MacLeod. LC 98-28650. 272p. 1999. lib. bdg. 79.95 (*1-56670-318-2*) Lewis Pubs.
Office Etiquette & Protocol. Grace Fox. LC 98-27451. (Basics Made Easy...Ser.). 224p. 1998. pap. 13.95 (*1-57685-145-1*) LrningExprss.
***Office Finances Made Easy: A Get-Started Guide to Budgets, Purchasing & Financial Statements.** Robert G. Finney. LC 99-33974. (Get-Ahead Toolkit Ser.: Vol. 5). 144p. 1999. pap. 15.00 (*0-8144-7061-0*) AMACOM.
Office for Analysis & Evaluation of Operational Data: Annual Report, Technical Training. 49p. 1996. pap. 5.00 (*0-16-062674-9*) USGPO.
Office for Analysis & Evaluation of Operational Data: Annual Report, 1994-95, Nuclear Materials. 193p. 1996. per. 18.00 (*0-16-062675-7*) USGPO.
***Office for Analysis & Evaluation of Operational Data: 1996 Annual Report, Nuclear Materials.** 145p. 1998. per. 13.00 (*0-16-062731-1*) USGPO.
***Office for Analysis & Evaluation of Operational Data: 1996 Annual Report, Reactors.** 289p. 1998. per. 23.00 (*0-16-062730-3*) USGPO.
***Office for Analysis & Evaluation of Operational Data: 1996 Annual Report, Technical Training.** 46p. 1998. pap. 4.00 (*0-16-062732-X*) USGPO.
***Office for Analysis & Evaluation of Operational Data: 1997 Annual Report, Nuclear Materials.** 111p. 1999. per. 9.00 (*0-16-062986-1*) USGPO.
***Office for Analysis & Evaluation of Operational Data: 1997 Annual Report, Reactors.** 296p. 1999. per. 24.00 (*0-16-062985-3*) USGPO.
***Office for Analysis & Evaluation of Operational Data: 1997 Annual Report, Technical Training.** 47p. 1999. pap. 4.00 (*0-16-062987-X*) USGPO.
Office from Hell. Don Smith. Ed. by Cliff Carle. 64p. 1994. pap. 4.95 (*0-918259-73-8*) CCC Pubns.
Office Furnishings, UL 1286. 3rd ed. (C). 1993. pap. text 330.00 (*1-55989-271-4*) Underwrtrs Labs.
Office Furniture. Rotovision S. A. Staff. (Illus.). 160p. 1996. pap. text 39.95 (*0-8230-6559-6*) Watsn-Guptill.
***Office Furniture & Equipment in Vietnam: A Strategic Entry Report, 1998.** Compiled by Icon Group International Staff. (Country Industry Report). (Illus.). 160p. 1999. ring bd. 1600.00 incl. audio compact disk (*0-7418-0484-0*) Icon Grp.
Office Furniture in Canada: A Strategic Entry Report, 1997. Compiled by Icon Group International Staff. (Country Industry Report). (Illus.). 128p. 1999. ring bd. 1280.00 incl. audio compact disk (*0-7418-0210-4*) Icon Grp.
Office Furniture in Kuwait: A Strategic Entry Report, 1998. Compiled by Icon Group International Staff. (Country Industry Report). (Illus.). 115p. 1999. ring bd. 1150.00 incl. audio compact disk (*0-7418-0420-4*) Icon Grp.
***Office Furniture in Poland: A Strategic Entry Report, 1996.** Compiled by Icon Group International Staff. (Illus.). 183p. 1999. ring bd. 1830.00 incl. audio compact disk (*0-7418-1248-7*) Icon Grp.
Office Furniture Market. J. Wichert. 380p. 1997. 1195.00 (*0-317-55216-3*) Busn Trend.
***Office Furniture Product Standards in Europe & North America.** Stefan Wille et al. 2000. write for info. (*1-894330-16-1*) AKTRIN.
Office, Gift & Priesthood. A. J. Pollock. 51p. pap. 3.95 (*0-88172-174-3*) Believers Bkshelf.
Office Guide. Linda Mallinson. LC 97-23630. 155p. (C). 1997. spiral bd. 9.20 (*0-13-861402-4*) P-H.
Office Guide to Business English. 2nd ed. Margaret A. Haller. 288p. 1994. per. 5.95 (*0-671-89661-X*, Arc) IDG Bks.
Office Guide to Business Letters, Memos & Reports. 2nd ed. Leonard Rogoff. LC 94-25593. 256p. 1994. per. 5.95 (*0-671-89664-4*, Arc) IDG Bks.
Office Guide to Modern English Usage. 2nd ed. Jean Vermes. 246p. 1997. pap. 7.98 (*1-56731-224-1*, MJF Bks) Fine Comms.
Office Guide to Spelling & Word Division. 2nd ed. Margaret A. Haller. 288p. 1994. per. 5.95 (*0-671-89663-6*, Arc) IDG Bks.
Office Gynecology. 2nd ed. Ed. by Morton A. Stenchever. (Illus.). 640p. (C). (gr. 13). 1996. text 59.95 (*0-8151-8225-2*, 27459) Mosby Inc.
Office Gynecology. 4th ed. Robert H. Glass. (Illus.). 448p. 1992. 82.00 (*0-683-03546-0*) Lppncott W & W.
Office Gynecology: Advanced Management Concepts. Ed. by John V. Knaus & John H. Isaacs. LC 93-18079. 1993. write for info. (*0-383-94032-X*) Spr-Verlag.
Office Gynecology: Advanced Management Concepts. Ed. by John V. Knaus & John H. Isaacs. (Illus.). 384p. 1993. 75.00 (*0-387-94032-4*) Spr-Verlag.
***Office Hours.** M. Broughton Boone. LC 00-190827. (A Cape Winds Weekend Escape Ser.). 124p. 2000. pap. 10.95 (*0-9671203-4-9*) Cape Winds Pr.
Office Hours. Norm Foster. LC 98-183647. (Playwrights Canada Ser.). 180p. (Orig.). 1998. pap. 13.95 (*0-88754-541-6*) Theatre Comm.
Office Hours: A Guide to the Managerial Life. Walter Kiechel, III. 1988. 18.95 (*0-316-49174-8*) Little.
***Office Humor the Book, Vol. 1.** (Illus.). iv, 103p. 1999. 24.95 (*0-615-11631-0*) Basic Web.
Office Hysteroscopy. Ed. by Keith B. Isaacson. LC 96-2065. (Illus.). 192p. (C). (gr. 13). 1996. text 92.95 (*0-8151-4842-9*, 24690) Mosby Inc.
***Office Hysteroscopy & Operative Hysteroscopy on One Day Basis.** B. Blanc et al. (Illus.). 260p. 1999. 124.00 (*2-287-59652-6*, Pub. by Spl France Editions) Spr-Verlag.
Office Information Technology: A Decision-Maker's Guide to Systems Planning & Implementation. Randy J. Goldfield. LC 86-614. (Illus.). 240p. 1986. 62.95 (*0-89930-108-8*, GOI/, Quorum Bks) Greenwood.
Office Interior Design Guide: An Introduction for Facility & Design. Julie K. Rayfield. LC 93-21638. 264p. 1997. pap. 59.95 (*0-471-18138-2*) Wiley.
Office Laboratory. 2nd ed. Lois A. Addison & Paul M. Fischer. (Illus.). 433p. 1990. pap. text 75.00 (*0-8385-7244-8*, A7244-5) Appleton & Lange.

Office Ladies & Salaried Men: Power, Gender & Work in Japanese Companies. Yuko Ogasawara. LC 98-5332. 280p. 1998. pap. text 15.95 (*0-520-21044-1*, Pub. by U CA Pr) Cal Prin Full Svc.

Office Ladies & Salaried Men: Power, Gender, & Work in Japanese Companies. Yuko Ogasawara. LC 98-5332. 280p. 1998. 45.00 (*0-520-21043-3*, Pub. by U CA Pr) Cal Prin Full Svc.

Office Ladies/Factory Women: Life & Work at a Japanese Company. Jeannie Lo. LC 89-70365. 140p. (C). (gr. 13). 1990. text 44.95 (*0-87332-598-2*, East Gate Bk) M E Sharpe.

Office Ladies/Factory Women: Life & Work at a Japanese Company. Jeannie Lo. LC 89-70365. 140p. (C). (gr. 13). 1993. pap. text 22.95 (*0-87332-599-0*, East Gate Bk) M E Sharpe.

Office Leasing: Drafting & Negotiating the Lease, 2 vols. Margaret L. Adams et al. Ed. by Carolyn J. Stein. LC 96-83539. 1333p. 1996. ring bd. 179.00 (*0-88124-961-0*, RE-30890) Cont Ed Bar-CA.

Office Leasing: Drafting & Negotiating the Lease, 2 vols. rev. ed. Leslie M. Browne et al. Ed. by Dianne Millner. LC 96-83539. 626p. 1997. ring bd. 90.00 (*0-7626-0078-0*, RE-30891) Cont Ed Bar-CA.

***Office Leasing: Drafting & Negotiating the Lease - 1/98 Update.** Michael A. Dean et al. Ed. by Janis L. Blanchette. LC 96-83539. (California Commerical Leasing Ser.). 370p. 1998. ring bd. 88.00 (*0-7626-0178-7*, RE-30892) Cont Ed Bar-CA.

***Office Leasing: Drafting & Negotiating the Lease - 1/99 Update, 2 vols.** C. Gregg Ankenmen et al. Ed. by Janis L. Blanchette. LC 96-83539. (California Commercial Leasing Ser.). 604p. 1999. ring bd. 95.00 (*0-7626-0286-4*, RE-30893) Cont Ed Bar-CA.

***Office Leasing, 2000: Drafting & Negotiating the Lease.** C. Gregg Ankenmann et al. Ed. by Donald R. Briggs. LC 96-83539. 236p. 2000. 72.00 (*0-7626-0401-8*, RE-30894) Cont Ed Bar-CA.

Office Lighting: RP-1-93. (Illus.). 64p. 1993. pap. 28.00 (*0-87995-105-2*, RP-1-93) Illum Eng.

Office Linkages & Location see Progress in Planning

Office Location & Public Policy. Ian C. Alexander. LC 78-40206. (Topics in Applied Geography Ser.). 125p. reprint ed. pap. 38.80 (*0-608-12177-0*, 202527300043) Bks Demand.

Office Location in a Post-Industrial Urban Environment. Lyssa Jenkins. LC 96-85503. (Bruton Center for Development Studies). 106p. 1996. text 58.95 (*1-85972-452-3*, Pub. by Avebry) Ashgate Pub Co.

Office Machine Aide. Jack Rudman. (Career Examination Ser.: C-1579). 1994. pap. 19.95 (*0-8373-1579-4*) Nat Learn.

Office Machine Associate. Jack Rudman. (Career Examination Ser.: C-2451). 1994. pap. 23.95 (*0-8373-2451-3*) Nat Learn.

Office Machine Operating, Sr. H. S. Jack Rudman. (Teachers License Examination Ser.: T-45). 1994. pap. 27.95 (*0-8373-8045-6*) Nat Learn.

Office Machine Operator. Jack Rudman. (Career Examination Ser.: C-559). 1994. pap. 23.95 (*0-8373-0559-4*) Nat Learn.

Office Machines. 4th ed. Hughes. 1996. pap. text. write for info. (*0-13-312224-7*) Allyn.

***Office Machines.** 5th ed. Jimmy C. McKenzie. LC 99-13962. (Illus.). 313p. (C). 1999. spiral bd. 51.00 (*0-13-011643-2*) P-H.

Office Machines & Business Equipment Used Prices Guide Blue Book: Fall 1992. (Illus.). vii, 207p. (Orig.). 1992. pap. 33.00 (*1-58156-035-4*) Asay Pub.

Office Machines & Business Equipment Used Prices Guide Blue Book: Fall 1993. (Illus.). vii, 325p. (Orig.). 1993. pap. 33.00 (*1-58156-032-X*) Asay Pub.

Office Machines & Business Equipment Used Prices Guide Blue Book: Summer 1992. (Illus.). vii, 127p. (Orig.). 1992. pap. 33.00 (*1-58156-036-2*) Asay Pub.

Office Machines & Business Equipment Used Prices Guide Blue Book: Summer 1993. (Illus.). vii, 329p. (Orig.). 1993. pap. 33.00 (*1-58156-033-8*) Asay Pub.

Office Machines & Business Equipment Used Prices Guide Blue Book: Winter 1992-93. (Illus.). vii, 257p. (Orig.). 1992. pap. 33.00 (*1-58156-034-6*) Asay Pub.

Office Machines: Electronic Calculators. 6th ed. Richard R. McCready. LC 82-21337. (Math). 248p. 1983. mass mkt. 19.50 (*0-534-01285-X*) PWS Pubs.

Office Machines Market. 18p. 1994. 59.00 (*0-9632529-5-X*) Mktdata Ent.

Office Management. Didactic Systems Staff. (Simulation Game Ser.). 1970. pap. 26.25 (*0-89401-070-0*) Didactic Syst.

Office Management. Burton S. Kaliski. 1986. teacher ed. 2.50 (*0-12-394768-5*); text 21.00 (*0-12-394767-7*) Harcourt.

Office Management: A Productivity & Effectiveness Guide. Patricia Haddock & Marilyn Manning. LC 89-81242. (Fifty-Minute Ser.). 83p. 1990. pap. 10.95 (*1-56052-005-1*) Crisp Pubns.

Office Management Manual. rev. ed. Patricia M. Sweeney & Donna Gagnon. Ed. by Stephanie Legatos & A. E. Schwartz. 142p. 1992. reprint ed. pap. 35.00 (*0-9628564-0-1*) MA Halfway Hse.

Office Management Manual: A Guide for Secretaries, Administrative Assistants, & Other Office Professionals. 2nd ed. Anne Morton. (Reference Ser.). 336p. (Orig.). 1990. pap. 9.95 (*0-88908-537-4*) Self-Counsel Pr.

Office Management of Digestive Diseases. Joseph Danzi & Joseph Scopelliti. (Illus.). 200p. 1992. text 45.00 (*0-8121-1436-1*) Lppncott W & W.

Office Management of the Colon & Rectal Disease. Guy L. Kratzer & Robert J. Demarest. (Illus.). 251p. 1985. text 115.00 (*0-7216-1189-3*, W B Saunders Co) Harcrt Hlth Sci Grp.

Office Manager. Jack Rudman. (Career Examination Ser.: C-2398). 1994. pap. 29.95 (*0-8373-2398-3*) Nat Learn.

Office Max - Cig to Making Money on Wall Street. Christy Heady. 1994. 16.95 (*0-7897-0709-8*) Que.

Office Max - Easy Microsoft Office. Trudi Reisner. 1994. 24.99 (*0-7897-0697-0*) Que.

Office Max - Lotus Smartsuite 6-in-1. Sherry Kinkoph. 1994. 26.99 (*0-7897-0706-3*) Que.

Office Max - MS Office Quick Reference. Sue Plumley. 1994. 14.99 (*0-7897-0699-7*) Que.

Office Max - Organize Yourself PPR. Ronnie Eisenberg & Kate Ke. 1986. 8.95 (*0-02-861108-X*) Macmillan.

Office Max - Using Microsoft Office. Que Development Group Staff. 1994. student ed. 29.99 (*0-7897-0705-5*) Que.

Office Max - Using MS Works 3 for Windows. 1994. 24.95 (*0-7897-0715-2*) Que.

Office Max - Using the World Wide Web. William Eager. 1994. 27.99 (*0-7897-0696-2*) Que.

***Office 98: Learning the Suite.** Ed. by Ken Kozakis. (Illus.). 734p. (C). 1999. pap. write for info. (*0-7423-0363-2*) ComputerPREP.

***Office 95: Advanced Topics, 5 vols.** Ed. by Ken Kozakis. (Illus.). (C). 1999. pap. write for info. (*0-7423-0358-6*) ComputerPREP.

Office 95: Byte by Bite. Glenda Friesen. (Byte by Bite Ser.). (Illus.). ii, 168p. 1997. pap. 27.50 (*1-891412-07-8*) Training Solut.

***Office 95: Intermediate Topics, 5 vols.** Ed. by Ken Kozakis. (Illus.). 696p. (C). 1999. pap. write for info. (*0-7423-0357-8*) ComputerPREP.

***Office 95: Learning the Basics, 6 vols.** Ed. by Ken Kozakis. (Illus.). 846p. (C). 1999. pap. write for info. (*0-7423-0361-6*) ComputerPREP.

Office 95 - 97 with Windows, Word, Excel, Access, Powerpoint. Kenneth Laudon. 1997. pap. text. write for info. (*0-07-038456-8*) McGraw.

Office 95 - 97 with Windows, Word, Excel, Access. Kenneth Laudon. 1997. pap. text. write for info. (*0-07-038457-6*) McGraw.

***Office 95 to Office 2000 Transition.** (Illus.). 112p. (YA). 2000. pap. write for info. (*0-7423-0429-9*) ComputerPREP.

Office 97. Marangraphics Development Group. LC 97-7648. (Glencoe Visual Ser.). 1998. 34.95 (*0-02-803963-7*) Macmillan.

***Office 97: Advanced Topics.** Ed. by Ken Kozakis. (Illus.). 479p. (C). 1999. pap. write for info. (*0-7423-0360-8*) ComputerPREP.

Office 97: Byte by Bite. Glenda Friesen. (Byte by Bite Ser.). (Illus.). ii, 197p. 1997. pap. 27.50 (*1-891412-09-4*) Training Solut.

***Office 97: Intermediate Topics, 6 vols.** Ed. by Ken Kozakis. (Illus.). 1086p. (C). 1999. pap. write for info. (*0-7423-0362-4*) ComputerPREP.

***Office 97: Learning the Basics, 6 vols.** Ed. by Ken Kozakis. (Illus.). 871p. (C). 1999. pap. write for info. (*0-7423-0359-4*) ComputerPREP.

Office 97 Answers! Certified Tech Support. Martin S. Matthews & Carole B. Matthews. LC 97-209564. (Illus.). 448p. (Orig.). 1997. pap. text 24.99 (*0-07-882403-6*) Osborne-McGraw.

Office 97 Bible. Edward Jones & Derek Sutton. 1200p. 1997. pap. 39.99 (*0-7645-3037-2*) IDG Bks.

***Office 97 Computers: S-Cart.** 6th ed. Long Hughes. (C). 1998. pap. text 24.00 (*0-13-081752-X*) P-H.

Office 97 for Busy People. Stephen Nelson. LC 97-128635. 304p. 1997. pap. text 24.99 (*0-07-882280-7*) Osborne-McGraw.

Office 97 Guru. Bill Hartman. (Computer Guru Ser.). (Illus.). 20p. 1998. spiral bd. 5.99 (*1-58187-028-0*) Guru Books.

***Office 97 Intro with Windows 98 Essentials.** Shelly et al. (Shelly-Cashman Ser.). 1999. pap. 38.40 incl. disk (*0-7895-5795-9*) Course Tech.

Office 97 One Step at a Time. Nancy Stevenson. LC 96-79759. (New Tutorial Ser.). 460p. 1997. pap. 29.99 (*0-7645-3050-X*) IDG Bks.

Office 97 Secrets. Steve Cummings & Robert Cowart. LC 96-79757. 900p. 1997. pap. 49.99 (*0-7645-3015-1*) IDG Bks.

Office 97 Simplified. Maran Graphics Staff. LC 97-129182. 384p. 1997. pap. 29.99 (*0-7645-6009-3*) IDG Bks.

Office '97 Visual Learn. Elaine Marmel. LC 97-66154. 432p. 1997. per. 16.99 (*0-7615-1162-8*) Prima Pub.

Office of Christ & Its Expression in the Church: Prophet Priest King. David T. Williams. LC 97-952. (Biblical Press Ser.: Vol. 52). 348p. 1997. text 99.95 (*0-7734-2425-3*) E Mellen.

Office of Experiment Stations: Its History, Activities & Organization. Milton Conover. LC 72-3047. (Brookings Institution. Institute for Government Research. Service Monographs of the U. S. Government: No. 32). reprint ed. 25.00 (*0-404-57132-8*) AMS Pr.

Office of Fair Trading - Annual Report of the Director General of Fair Trading 1994. 86p. 1995. pap. 35.00 (*0-10-241995-7*, HM419957, Pub. by Statnry Office) Bernan Associates.

Office of Fair Trading - Annual Report of the Director General of Fair Trading, 1995. 86p. 1996. pap. 35.00 (*0-10-275896-4*, HM58964, Pub. by Statnry Office) Bernan Associates.

Office of Generall Remembrance-Kept in Cursitors Court. LC 74-80217. (English Experience Ser.: No. 681). 1974. reprint ed. 15.00 (*90-221-0681-0*) Walter J Johnson.

Office of Governor in the United States. Coleman B. Ransone, Jr. LC 78-130564. (Select Bibliographies Reprint Ser.). 1977. 26.95 (*0-8369-5537-4*) Ayer.

Office of Indian Affairs: Its History, Activities & Organizations. Laurence F. Schmeckebier. LC 74-175438. (Brookings Institution. Institute for Government Research. Service Monographs of the U. S. Government: No. 48). reprint ed. 37.50 (*0-404-07169-4*) AMS Pr.

***Office of Justice of the Peace in England: In Its Origin & Development.** Charles Austin Beard. LC 00-36237. 2000. write for info. (*1-58477-102-X*) Lawbk Exchange.

Office of Justice of the Peace in England Its Origin & Development. Charles Austin Beard. LC 74-18913. (Columbia University. Studies in the Social Sciences: No. 52). reprint ed. 31.50 (*0-404-51052-3*) AMS Pr.

Office of Management & Budget: Changes Resulting from the OMB 2000 Reorganization. (Illus.). 44p. (Orig.). (C). 1996. pap. text 20.00 (*0-7881-3111-7*) DIANE Pub.

Office of Peter. Hans U. Von Balthasar. Tr. by Andree Emery from GER. LC 86-80787.Tr. of Der Antiromische Affekt. 358p. 1986. pap. 17.95 (*0-89870-020-5*) Ignatius Pr.

Office of Prime Minister. Lord Blake. (Thank-Offering to Britain Fund Lectures). 1976. 7.98 (*0-19-725724-0*) David Brown.

Office of Prophet & the Prophetic Anointing: School of the Prophets, Vol. I. Tom Franks. 64p. (Orig.). 1997. pap., spiral bd. 10.00 (*0-926044-53-2*) Mercedes Ministries.

Office of Prophet & the Prophetic Anointing: School of the Prophets, Vol. II. Tom Franks. 64p. (Orig.). 1997. pap., spiral bd. 10.00 (*0-926044-54-0*) Mercedes Ministries.

Office of Telecommunications (OFTEL) Annual Report, 1994. Bryan Carsberg. 131p. 1995. pap. 30.00 (*0-10-234095-1*, HM40951, Pub. by Statnry Office) Bernan Associates.

Office of Telecommunications (OFTEL) Annual Report, 1997. Bryan Carsberg. 131p. 1998. pap. 45.00 (*0-10-293198-4*, HM31984, Pub. by Statnry Office) Bernan Associates.

Office of the Chief of Engineers of the Army: Its Non-Military History, Activities & Organization. William S. Holt. LC 72-3041. (Brookings Institution. Institute for Government Research. Service Monographs of the U. S. Government: No. 27). reprint ed. 25.00 (*0-404-57127-1*) AMS Pr.

Office of the Comptroller of the Currency: Its History, Activities & Organization. John G. Heinberg. LC 72-3053. (Brookings Institution. Institute for Government Research. Service Monographs of the U. S. Government: No. 38). reprint ed. 21.50 (*0-404-57138-7*) AMS Pr.

Office of the Comptroller of the Currency: Laws & Regulations. CCH Incorporated Staff. LC 94-213090. 339p. 1994. write for info. (*0-8080-0023-3*) CCH INC.

Office of the Comptroller of the Currency's Recent Regulatory Actions: Hearing Before the Subcommittee on Financial Institutions & Regulatory Relief of the Committee on Banking, Housing & Urban Affairs, United States Senate, 105th Congress, 1st Session... May 1, 1997. USGPO Staff. LC 98-211346. iii, 93 p. 1997. pap. write for info. (*0-16-057019-0*) USGPO.

***Office of the Dead.** Andrew Taylor. (Roth Trilogy Ser.: 3). 352p. 2000. text 24.95 (*0-312-20348-9*) St Martin.

Office of the Ministry in Nicholas Hunnius' Epitome Credendorum: A Voice from the Age of Lutheran Orthodoxy. James Heiser. 98p. 1996. 10.00 (*1-893118-07-X*) J Gerhard Inst.

Office of the Salt Merchant. Harry Clifton. 50p. 1979. pap. 11.95 (*0-902996-83-5*) Dufour.

Office of the Scarlet Letter. Sacvan Bercovitch. LC 90-25796. (Parallax). 200p. 1991. text 40.00 (*0-8018-4203-4*) Johns Hopkins.

Office of "The Scarlet Letter" Sacvan Bercovitch. (Parallax: Re-Visions of Culture & Society Ser.). 200p. 1993. reprint ed. pap. text 14.95 (*0-8018-4584-X*) Johns Hopkins.

Office of the Second Auditor Inventory. John S. Salmon & Emily J. Salmon. xv, 42p. 1981. pap. 7.95 (*0-88490-102-5*) Library of VA.

Office of the Secretary of the Air Force, 1947-1965. George M. Watson, Jr. LC 92-18308. (General Histories Ser.). 1992. text. write for info. (*0-912799-76-5*); per. write for info. (*0-912799-78-1*) AFH & MP.

Office of the Supervising Architect of Treasury: Its History, Activities & Organization. Darrell H. Smith. LC 72-3031. (Brookings Institution. Institute for Government Research. Service Monographs of the U. S. Government: No. 23). reprint ed. 37.50 (*0-404-57123-9*) AMS Pr.

Office Operative Arthroscopy. Neal C. Small. LC 93-40309. 96p. 1994. pap. text 45.00 (*0-7817-0140-6*) Lppncott W & W.

Office Oracle: Wisdom at Work. Patricia Monaghan. LC 98-53170. Orig. Title: Working Wisdom. (Illus.). 224p. 1999. 7.95 (*1-56718-464-2*) Llewellyn Pubns.

Office Organizer. Harper Collins UK. (Collins Gem Ser.). 336p. 1998. pap. text 12.00 (*0-00-472174-8*) Collins.

Office Orthopedics for Primary Care: Diagnosis & Treatment. Bruce C. Anderson. LC 94-25753. (Illus.). 208p. (C). 1994. pap. text 42.00 (*0-7216-4576-3*, W B Saunders Co) Harcrt Hlth Sci Grp.

Office Orthopedics for Primary Care: Diagnosis & Treatment. 2nd ed. Bruce C. Anderson. Ed. by Ray Kersey. LC 98-36303. (Illus.). 285p. (C). 1998. pap. text 42.00 (*0-7216-7089-X*, W B Saunders Co) Harcrt Hlth Sci Grp.

Office Planning & Design Desk Reference. Ed. by James Rappoport et al. LC 91-33863. 352p. 1991. 120.00 (*0-471-50820-9*) Wiley.

Office Politics. Mary Melfi. (Essential Poets Ser.: Vol. 88). 96p. 1999. pap. 10.00 (*1-55071-085-0*) Guernica Editions.

Office Politics: A Survival Guide. Jane Clarke. 144p. 1999. pap. 19.95 (*1-85835-532-X*, Indust Soc) Stylus Pub VA.

Office Politics: Computers & the Flight for Safety & Health in the Information Age. Vernon L. Mogensen. LC 95-46829. 325p. (C). 1996. text 48.00 (*0-8135-2286-2*); pap. text 17.95 (*0-8135-2287-0*) Rutgers U Pr.

Office Politics: Positive Results from Fair Practices. Rebecca L. Wolfe. LC 96-71269. (Fifty Minute Ser.). (Illus.). 108p. 1997. pap. 10.95 (*1-56052-445-6*) Crisp Pubns.

Office Politics: The Woman's Guide to Beat the System & Gain Financial Success. R. Don Steele. Ed. by Mary Thomas. 352p. (Orig.). 1994. 24.95 (*0-9620671-1-3*); pap. 18.95 (*0-9620671-2-1*) Steel Balls Pr.

Office Politics for the Utterly Confused. William A. Salmon. (Illus.). 210p. 1998. pap. 15.95 (*0-07-058046-4*) McGraw.

Office Politics, Seizing Power, Wielding Clout. Marilyn M. Kennedy. 1987. mass mkt. 4.95 (*0-446-35060-5*, Pub. by Warner Bks) Little.

Office Power with Personal Computers: Complete Highly Illustrated User's Guides & Smart Indexes for DOS BASICS, Windows 3.1, WordPerfect 5.1 (DOS), & Lotus 1-2-3 for Windows Plus Office Power Applications. Bernie Browne. LC 92-97506. (Illus.). 768p. (Orig.). 1993. pap. 19.95 (*0-9634182-0-3*) Byte Masters.

Office Practice Made Simple. G. Whitehad. 384p. (C). 1989. 60.00 (*0-7855-4624-3*, Pub. by Inst Pur & Supply) St Mut.

Office Practice Made Simple. G. Whitehead. 384p. (C). 1982. 70.00 (*0-7855-5685-0*, Pub. by Inst Pur & Supply) St Mut.

Office Practice of Medicine. 3rd ed. Ed. by William T. Branch. LC 93-20531. (Illus.). 1184p. 1994. text 115.00 (*0-7216-4338-8*, W B Saunders Co) Harcrt Hlth Sci Grp.

Office Practice of Medicine. 4th ed. Branch. 1999. text. write for info. (*0-7216-7672-3*, W B Saunders Co) Harcrt Hlth Sci Grp.

Office Practice of Neurology. Ed. by Martin A. Samuels et al. 1280p. 1995. text 199.00 (*0-443-08816-0*) Church.

Office Procedure Forms in the Academy Collection: Quick Reference Guides for Family Physicians. Thomas J. Zuber. LC 98-23693. (Academy Collection). 150p. 1998. pap., spiral bd. 29.95 (*0-683-30580-8*) Lppncott W & W.

Office Procedures. Harrison. 1996. pap. write for info. (*0-582-29341-3*, Pub. by Addison-Wesley) Longman.

Office Procedures. Jeffrey R. Stewart, Jr. et al. LC 79-9095. (Illus.). 1980. text 25.28 (*0-07-061440-7*) McGraw.

Office Procedures: Learning & Instructions. Anthony A. Olinzock. (KU - Office Procedures Ser.). 1983. mass mkt. 23.25 (*0-538-24140-3*) S-W Pub.

Office Procedures & Management. 5th ed. H. Moon. (KU - Office Procedures Ser.). 1986. pap. 32.75 (*0-87350-290-6*) Course Tech.

Office Procedures & Management. 5th ed. H. Moon. (KU - Office Procedures Ser.). 1986. 43.95 (*0-471-85029-2*) S-W Pub.

Office Procedures & Technology. Harry R. Moon. 1990p. 2.25 (*0-87350-339-2*) Milady Pub.

Office Procedures & Technology. 2nd ed. Harry R. Moon. 1990p. 1984. teacher ed. 19.95 (*0-87350-337-6*) Milady Pub.

Office Procedures & Technology. 2nd ed. Harry R. Moon. 1990p. 1988. 35.00 (*0-87350-289-2*) Milady Pub.

Office Procedures & Technology, Tests 1-15. Oliverio. (KM - Office Procedures Ser.). 1987. 3.00 (*0-538-11355-3*) S-W Pub.

Office Procedures & Technology for College. 11th ed. Fulton. LC 97-22052. (KF- Office Education Ser.). 1998. pap. 39.95 (*0-538-66981-0*) S-W Pub.

Office Procedures & Technology for Colleges. 10th ed. Patsy J. Fulton. LC 92-36568. (C). 1993. mass mkt. 33.25 (*0-538-61418-8*) S-W Pub.

Office Procedures for Primary Care. John L. Pfenninger & Grant C. Fowler. (Illus.). 1200p. (C). (gr. 13). 1994. pap. text 71.95 (*0-8016-6384-9*, 06384) Mosby Inc.

***Office Procedures in Managed Health Care with Data Disk for MediSoft for Windows.** Patricia M. Boyd & Brent D. Boyd. LC 98-39160. 400p. 1999. text 35.00 incl. disk (*0-02-801222-4*) Glencoe.

Office Procedures in Managed Health Care with Medisoft for Windows Data Disk. Patricia M. Boyd & Brent D. Boyd. 400p. write for info. (*0-02-801223-2*) McGraw-Hill HPD.

Office Procedures in the Academy Collection: Quick Reference Guides for Family Physicians. Thomas J. Zuber & American Academy of Family Physicians Staff. LC 98-22560. (Academy Collection). 214p. 1998. pap. 29.95 (*0-683-30424-0*) Lppncott W & W.

Office Procedures Manual. 92p. 1987. 12.50 (*0-685-30185-0*, 43,165) NCLS Inc.

***Office Professional 2000 & Frontpage Right Phlt.** 1999. 40.67 (*0-13-089157-6*) P-H.

***Office Professional's Desk Reference.** Ed. by Anthony S. Vlamis. LC 99-70262. (Webster's New World Ser.). 594p. 1999. pap. 16.95 incl. cd-rom (*0-02-862883-7*) Macmillan.

Office Professional's Quick Reference Handbook. 4th ed. Sheryl Lindsell-Roberts. 288p. 1995. 7.95 (*0-02-860027-4*, Arc) IDG Bks.

Office Professional's Quick Reference Handbook. 5th rev. ed. Sheryl Lindsell-Roberts. LC 94-32827. 1995. pap. 9.00 (*0-671-89919-8*, Arco) Macmillan Gen Ref.

Office Purchasing Guide: How to Buy Better, Easier & Save up to 50 per Cent on Office Supplies & Furniture, Business Forms & Printing, Office

O

Machines & Equipment. rev. ed. Tod J. Snodgrass. LC 85-5156. (Illus.). 256p. (Orig.). 1986. pap. 14.95 (*0-933051-15-8*) Lowen Pub.

Office Reading Exercises. 37p. 1991. 5.00 (*0-933964-33-1*) Natl Busn Ed Assoc.

Office Records Systems & Space Management: A Guide for Administrative Services Managers. Donald B. Tweedy. LC 85-19373. (Illus.). 213p. 1986. 59.95 (*0-89930-145-2*, TSM/, Quorum Bks) Greenwood.

Office Reference Guide. 120p. 1991. pap., spiral bd. 12.00 (*1-56243-053-X*, R-88) DDC Pub.

Office Relocating Planner. Karen E. Chessler & Christopher U. Carmen. (Illus.). 57p. 1998. 29.95 (*1-928742-00-9*) Vision Pubns IN.

Office Relocation Planner. 2nd ed. Karen E. Chessler & Christopher U. Carmen. 57p. 1999. 29.95 (*1-928742-01-7*) Vision Pubns IN.

***Official Rules of Ice Hockey 2000.** Hockey U. S. A. Association Staff. 1999. pap. 9.95 (*1-57243-375-2*) Triumph Bks.

Office Safety. (Illus.). 10p. Date not set. write for info. (*0-945100-76-0*) Parlay Intl.

Office Safety. Graham Roberts-Phelps. (Gower Health & Safety Workbook Ser.). 80p. 1998. pap., wbk. ed. 29.95 (*0-566-08068-0*, Pub. by Gower) Ashgate Pub Co.

Office Safety: The Guide to Tackling Today's Office Hazards. Bureau of Business Practice Staff. LC 98-178878. 110 p. 1997. write for info. (*0-87622-744-2*) Aspen Pub.

Office Safety Handbook. Roger Saunders. 300p. 1995. pap. 49.50 (*0-273-61246-8*, Pub. by Pitman Pub) Trans-Atl Phila.

Office Safety Pocket Guide. Richard M. Crossman. Ed. by Christine E. Gorman. (Illus.). 64p. 1993. pap. 41.80 (*0-931690-51-X*) Genium Pub.

Office Sector: A Review of Floorspace, Building Type, Market Potential & Construction Activity in Great Britain. G. Samuelsson-Brown & S. Whittome. 1991. 1280.00 (*0-86022-320-5*, Pub. by Build Servs Info Assn) St Mut.

Office Services Supervisor. Jack Rudman. (Career Examination Ser.: C-2196). 1994. pap. 29.95 (*0-8373-2196-4*) Nat Learn.

Office Setup & Operation for Construction Contracting see Advantage Contractor TM Business Success Series

Office Skills. Barrett. Date not set. text, teacher ed. 45.95 (*0-314-82302-6*) West Pub.

Office Skills. 2nd ed. Barrett. (Kf - Office Education Ser.). (C). 1997. mass mkt. 58.95 (*0-314-20550-0*) West Pub.

Office Skills. 4th ed. Thelma J. Foster. 506p. (C). 1998. pap. 34.50 (*0-7487-1796-X*, Pub. by S Thornes Pubs) Trans-Atl Phila.

Office Skills for the 90s: General Office Procedures. Barrett & Kimbrell. (Finishing Touches Ser.). 1992. pap., student ed. 18.00 (*0-314-86851-8*) Thomson Learn.

Office Skills, 1990. Charles Francis Barrett. 1991. mass mkt. 40.25 (*0-314-77273-1*) West Pub.

Office Skills Workbook: Office Procedures-Microcomputer. 2nd ed. Barrett & Kimbrell. (Finishing Touches Ser.). 1998. pap., student ed. 17.00 (*0-314-12988-X*) Thomson Learn.

Office Smart! Risk Management Techniques for Medical Office Professionals. Rosemary Gafner. 78p. 1993. student ed. 35.00 (*1-884269-01-X*) Med Risk Mgmt.

Office Smarts. Roy J. Blitzer. LC 94-15873. 160p. 1994. pap. 6.95 (*1-56440-386-6*) Globe Pequot.

Office Space: Tenants Guide to Profitable Leasing. Jack Saltman. Ed. by Nancy Justice. 220p. (C). 1996. 19.95 (*0-9623058-1-2*) Trinity Pub & Mktg.

Office Space Planning & Design. Marmot. (Time-Saver Standards Ser.). 320p. 2000. 44.95 (*0-07-134199-4*) McGraw-Hill Prof.

Office Space Planning & Management: A Manager's Guide to Techniques & Standards. Donald B. Tweedy. LC 85-13842. 158p. 1986. 45.00 (*0-89930-101-0*, TOS/, Quorum Bks) Greenwood.

Office Spaces. Rotovision S. A. Staff. (Commercial Spaces Ser.). (Illus.). 160p. 1995. pap. 35.00 (*0-8230-6474-3*, Whitney Lib) Watsn-Guptill.

Office Spanish for Secretaries & Receptionists, 4 cass. Sam L. Slick. (SPA.). 69p. 1998. ring bd. 49.50 incl. audio (*1-888467-11-8*) Command Spanish.

Office Sports Medicine. 2nd ed. Ed. by Morris B. Mellion. (Illus.). 400p. 1999. 54.00 (*1-56053-120-7*) Hanley & Belfus.

Office Staff Risk Management Resource: Audio Cassette & Handbook. RiskCare Staff. 38p. 1997. pap. text 29.00 incl. audio (*1-893929-09-4*) RiskCare.

Office Supplies in Russia: A Strategic Entry Report, 1996. Compiled by Icon Group International Staff. (Illus.). 145p. 1999. ring bd. 1450.00 incl. audio compact disk (*0-7418-0727-0*) Icon Grp.

Office Supplies Market. Ed. by Peter Allen. 200p. 1989. pap. 995.00 (*0-941285-53-7*) FIND-SVP.

Office Supply Buyer's Guide: The Smart Person's Guide to Buying the Right Items at the Right Price. Robert S. Rizzolo. (Illus.). 186p. (Orig.). 1996. pap. 14.95 (*0-9651874-0-3*); spiral bd. 14.95 (*0-9651874-1-1*) Oscan Pr.

Office Supply Buying Guide: How to Save 20 Percent to 60 Percent on the Cost of Office Supplies. Al Toth. LC 92-64339. 352p. 1992. 29.95 (*1-881624-06-4*) PBM Pub.

***Office Supply in Colombia: A Strategic Entry Report, 1999.** Compiled by Icon Group International. (Illus.). 194p. 1999. ring bd. 1940.00 incl. audio compact disk (*0-7418-1791-8*) Icon Grp.

Office Systems: People, Procedures & Technology. 2nd ed. Rosemary T. Fruehling et al. 168p. (C). 1992. teacher ed. 14.00 (*1-56118-404-7*); teacher ed. 8.00 (*1-56118-402-0*); student ed. 14.95 (*1-56118-405-5*); text 29.95 (*1-56118-403-9*) Paradigm MN.

Office Systems Analyst. Jack Rudman. (Career Examination Ser.: C-3100). 1994. pap. 34.95 (*0-8373-3100-5*) Nat Learn.

Office Systems & Careers: A Resource for Administrative Assistants. Olive D. Church & Anne E. Schatz. 780p. 1981. write for info. (*0-205-07135-X*) Allyn.

Office Systems Integration. Barbara S. Fischer. LC 87-2498. 236p. 1987. 59.95 (*0-89930-109-6*, CUI/, Quorum Bks) Greenwood.

Office Tales: Don't Push It. Ed. by Meg Bowman. (Illus.). 154p. 1996. spiral bd. 9.95 (*0-940483-12-2*) Hot Flash Pr.

Office Techniques for Diagnosing Skin Disease. William H. Eaglstein & David M. Pariser. LC 78-58240. (Illus.). 204p. 1978. reprint ed. pap. 63.30 (*0-8357-7590-9*, 205691100096) Bks Demand.

Office Trainer for Property & Casualty Insurance Agencies. Finn A. Sundheim. 224p. (Orig.). 1985. pap. 25.00 (*0-9612478-2-7*) Venture CA.

***Office 2000: Byte by Bite.** Glenda Friesen. (Byte by Bite Ser.). 275p. 1999. pap. 27.50 (*1-891412-17-5*) Training Solut.

***Office 2000 at a Glance Library II.** (At A Glance Ser.). 1999. pap. 79.96 (*0-7356-0770-2*) Microsoft.

Office 2000 Developer's Handbook. Michael Groh. 1999. pap. 49.99 (*0-7821-2474-7*) Sybex.

Office 2000 Fast & Easy. Richard Cravens & Diane Koers. LC 98-68147. (Fast & Easy Ser.). (Illus.). 435p. 1999. pap. 16.99 (*0-7615-1762-6*, Prima Tech) Prima Pub.

***Office 2000 New Features.** (Illus.). (YA). 1999. pap. write for info. (*0-7423-0406-X*, OFFC2KNF0LG) ComputerPREP.

***Office 2000 New Features: Instructor Guide.** (Illus.). 212p. 2000. pap., teacher ed. write for info. (*0-7423-0420-5*) ComputerPREP.

***Office 2000 Professional.** Tim Duffy. 448p. (C). 1999. pap. text, teacher ed. write for info. (*0-201-45907-8*) Addison-Wesley.

Office 2000 Professional Fast & Easy. Diane Koers et al. LC 98-68769. (Fast & Easy Ser.). 864p. 1999. pap. 29.99 (*0-7615-2032-5*) Prima Pub.

***Office 2000 Programmer's Reference Kit.** Dwayne Gifford et al. 2000p. 1999. pap. 59.99 (*1-86100-300-5*) Wrox Pr Inc.

***Office 2000 QuickPro.** Contexx, Inc. Staff. (QuickPro Ser.: Vol. 2). (Illus.). 36p. (C). 1999. pap. 14.99 (*1-929445-01-6*) Contexx.

Office 2000 Secrets. Steve Cummings. 1296p. 1999. 49.99 (*0-7645-3262-6*) IDG Bks.

Office Typist. Jack Rudman. (Career Examination Ser.: C-3373). 1994. pap. 19.95 (*0-8373-3373-3*) Nat Learn.

Office Urgencies & Emergencies: Quick Reference Guides for Family Physicians. Richard B. Birrer. (The Academy Collection Ser.). 208p. pap. text 29.95 (*0-7817-2055-9*) Lppncott W & W.

***Office Urology: The Clinician's Guide.** Ed. by Elroy D. Kursh & James C. Ulchaker. (Current Clinical Urology Ser.: Vol. 3). 550p. 2000. 99.50 (*0-89603-789-4*) Humana.

Office Virtual Tutor. Que Education & Training Staff. Date not set. pap. text 68.00 (*1-57576-095-9*) Que Educ & Trng.

Office Wife. large type ed. Faith Baldwin. LC 93-26416. 378p. 1993. pap. 17.95 (*1-56054-318-3*) Thorndike Pr.

Office Wife. Faith Baldwin. 1976. reprint ed. lib. bdg. 23.95 (*0-88411-603-4*) Amereon Ltd.

Office Worker's Game of up from Under. Dee Rosenfeld. (Illus.). 85p. 1999. pap. 8.95 (*0-9669335-1-6*, 001) MDR Pr.

Office Worker's Game of Up from Under. Dee Rosenfeld. LC 99-93026. 1999. pap. 8.95 (*0-9669335-0-8*) MDR Pr.

Office Workstations in the Home. National Research Council Staff. LC 85-3022. 168p. 1985. pap. text 19.95 (*0-309-03483-3*) Natl Acad Pr.

Office Writer: The Useable Portable Guide. Jon Haber & Herbert R. Haber. 32p. (C). 1989. pap. text 4.95 (*0-945765-14-2*) Useable Portable Pubns.

***Office Yoga: A Quickie Guide to Staying Balanced & Fit in the Work Environment.** large type ed. Diana Fairechild. LC 99-95178. (Illus.). 160p. 1999. pap. 9.95 (*1-892997-41-X*) Flyana.

***Office Yoga: Simple Stretches for Busy People.** Darrin Zeer. LC 99-38830. (Illus.). 96p. 2000. 9.95 (*0-8118-2685-6*) Chronicle Bks.

***Office Yoga: Tackling Tension with Simple Stretches You Can Do at Your Desk.** Ed. by Julie Friedeberger. 155p. 1999. pap. 42.50 (*81-208-1542-4*, Pub. by Motilal Bnarsidass) St Mut.

***Office 2000.** 1999. 32.00 (*0-13-019702-5*, Prentice Hall) P-H.

Office 2000: The Complete Reference. Stephen L. Nelson & Peter Weverka. LC 99-228522. (The Complete Reference Ser.). (Illus.). 1040p. 1999. pap. 39.99 incl. audio compact disk (*0-07-211859-8*) Osborne-McGraw.

***Office 2000 Introductory Concepts & Techniques.** Shelly & Cashman. (Shelly Cashman Ser.). (C). 1999. pap., wbk. ed. 14.95 (*0-7895-4690-6*) Course Tech.

Office 2000 & Advanced Excel 2000, Vol. 1. (C). 1999. text 58.67 (*0-13-017009-7*) S&S Trade.

Office 2000 Answers! Martin S. Matthews. 1999. pap. text 24.99 (*0-07-211888-1*) Osborne-McGraw.

***Office 2000 Essentials.** 1999. 21.33 (*0-13-017829-2*) P-H.

Office 2000 Essentials with CD-ROM. 632p. 1999. 49.99 (*1-58076-091-0*) Cisco Press.

Office 2000 for Busy People. Stephen Nelson & Peter Weverka. 305p. 1999. pap. 19.99 (*0-07-211857-1*) McGraw.

Office 2000 Made Easy: The Basics & Beyond. Alan Neibauer. (Made Easy Ser.). 608p. 1999. pap. text 24.99 (*0-07-882585-7*) Osborne-McGraw.

***Office 2000 Microsoft Certified Edition Brief.** 384p. (C). 1999. write for info. (*0-13-018686-4*) P-H.

***Office 2000 Spiral Bound.** (C). 2000. spiral bd. 0.00 (*0-201-69940-0*) HEPC Inc.

***Office 2000 Sprial Bound.** (C). 2000. spiral bd. 0.00 (*0-201-69939-7*) HEPC Inc.

Office 95 Made Simple. McBride. 160p. Date not set. pap. text 19.95 (*0-7506-2625-9*) Buttrwrth-Heinemann.

Office '97 Annoyances. Woody Leonhard et al. (Illus.). 396p. (Orig.). 1997. pap. 21.95 (*1-56592-310-3*) OReilly & Assocs.

Office 97 Common Elements. (Quick Study Computer Ser.). 4p. pap. 2.95 (*1-57222-239-5*) Barcharts.

Office 97 Complete. 414p. (C). 1998. pap. text 40.00 (*1-58076-015-5*) Que Educ & Trng.

Officepower, Inc. Formatting & Documenting. 4th ed. Hanks. (KU - Office Procedures Ser.). (C). 1990. 23.25 (*0-538-70237-0*) S-W Pub.

Office/Professional Building see Real Estate Taxpak USA: Residential

Officer & a Gentle Woman: Men in Blue. Doreen O. Malek. (Intimate Moments Ser.: No. 958). 1999. per. 4.25 (*0-373-07958-3*, 1-07958-1) Silhouette.

Officer & a Gentleman: The Military Career of Lieutenant Henry O. Flipper. Lowell D. Black & Sara H. Black. LC 89-183245. (Illus.). 202p. (Orig.). (C). 1985. 19.95 (*0-9624659-0-9*); pap. 12.95 (*0-685-29035-2*) Lora Co Ltd.

Officer & a Hero. Elizabeth Ashtree. (Superromance Ser.: No. 828). 1999. mass mkt. 4.25 (*0-373-70828-9*, 1-70828-8) Harlequin Bks.

***Officer & a Lady & Other Stories.** Rex Stout. 192p. 2000. mass mkt. 5.95 (*0-7867-0764-X*, Pub. by Carroll & Graf) Publishers Group.

Officer & the Renegade. Helen R. Myers. 1997. per. 3.50 (*0-373-76102-3*, 1-76102-2) Silhouette.

Officer Beetle: I'm a Book with Wheels. Rita Balducci & Reader's Digest Editors. (Pull-Back 'n Go Bks.: No. 4). (Illus.). 10p. (J). (gr. k-3). 1998. bds. 7.99 (*1-57584-214-9*, Pub. by Rdrs Digest) Random.

Officer Brown Keeps Neighborhoods Safe. Alice K. Flanagan. Ed. & Illus. by Christine Osinski. LC 97-49378. (Our Neighborhood Ser.). (J). 1998. 19.50 (*0-516-20780-6*) Childrens.

Officer Brown Keeps Neighborhoods Safe. Alice K. Flanagan. (Our Neighborhood Ser.). (Illus.). 32p. (J). (gr. k-3). 1999. pap. text 6.95 (*0-516-26407-9*) Childrens.

Officer Buckle & Gloria. Illus. by Peggy Rathmann. LC 93-43887. 37p. (J). (ps-3). 1995. 15.99 (*0-399-22616-8*, G P Putnam) Peng Put Young Read.

Officer-Cadet. Rick Shelley. 1998. mass mkt. 5.99 (*0-441-00526-8*) Ace Bks.

Officer Candidate School Admission Test (OCS) Jack Rudman. (Admission Test Ser.: Vol. 53). 43.95 (*0-8373-5153-7*) Nat Learn.

Officer Candidate School Admission Test (OCS) Jack Rudman. (Admission Test Ser.: ATS-53). 1994. pap. 23.95 (*0-8373-5053-0*) Nat Learn.

Officer Candidate Tests. LC 84-20437. 1985. 12.00 (*0-317-56572-9*, Arco) Macmillan Gen Ref.

Officer Candidate Tests. pap. 12.00 (*0-685-17146-9*) P-H.

Officer Candidate Tests. 3rd ed. Solomon Wiener. LC 93-4580. 384p. 1993. pap. 17.00 (*0-671-79973-8*, Arco) Macmillan Gen Ref.

Officer Candidate Tests. 4th ed. Solomon Weiner. 384p. 1997. pap. 21.95 (*0-02-862173-5*, Arc) IDG Bks.

Officer Candidate Tests. 5th ed. Solomon Wiener. 384p. 1999. pap. text 21.95 (*0-02-863543-4*, Arco) Macmillan Gen Ref.

***Officer Coffey Stories.** unabridged ed. Hugh B. Cave. 64p. 2000. 40.00 (*1-892284-72-3*); pap. 12.00 (*1-892284-71-5*) Subtrrnean Pr.

Officer Compensation Report. Farber. 134p. 395.00 (*1-56706-001-3*, 60013) Panel Pubs.

Officer Compensation Report, 1991-1992: Special Supplement: Executive Perquisites Report. 12th ed. Phillip Farber. Ed. by Mark D. Persons. (Illus.). 218p. 1991. pap. 96.00 (*1-878375-63-6*) Panel Pubs.

Officer Compensation Report, 1992-1993: The Executive Compensation Survey for Small & Medium Sized Businesses. 12th ed. Phillip Farber. Ed. by Mark D. Persons. (Illus.). 496p. 1991. pap. 385.00 (*1-878375-62-8*) Panel Pubs.

Officer down Code Three. Pierce R. Brooks. LC 75-23841. 1975. 9.95 (*0-916070-01-8*, MTI Film & Video) Coronet.

Officer in Trouble. James Viner & Brad Sagstetter. Ed. by Fred Zuber. 248p. 1982. pap. 5.95 (*0-89896-001-0*) Larksdale.

Officer in Trouble: The Detroit Cop Who Refused to Play the Game. James E. Crawford. 218p. (Orig.). 1992. pap. 8.95 (*0-9625423-5-0*) Four-G Pubs.

Officer Needs Assistance . . . Again! Don Parker. 256p. 1990. 15.95 (*0-9620073-2-3*) Caroldon Bks.

Officer of the Blue: Marc-Joseph Marion Dufresne, South Sea Explorer 1724-1772. Edward Duyker. LC 94-166017. (Miegunyah Press Ser.: No. 1:15). 256p. 1994. 39.95 (*0-522-84565-7*, Pub. by Melbourne Univ Pr) Paul & Co Pubs.

***Officer of the Deck: A Memoir of the Pacific War & the Sea.** Herbert Kriloff. LC 99-89382. (Illus.). 220p. 2000. 24.95 (*0-935553-44-4*, 130136AE) Pacifica Military.

Officer Safety: Tactics for Survival. 5th ed. Michel E. Amaral. (Illus.). 180p. 1996. 24.95 (*0-9645535-0-3*) IPAT.

Officer Safety Vol. 6: Tactics for Survival. 6th rev. ed. Michel Amaral. (Illus.). 248p. 1998. reprint ed. pap. text 29.95 (*0-9645535-1-1*) IPAT.

Officer Survival Manual. 2nd ed. Devallis Rutledge. (Illus.). 351p. (C). 1988. pap. 19.95 (*0-942728-36-X*) Copperhouse.

Officer's Alliance. Violet Hamilton. 448p. 1991. mass mkt. 4.50 (*0-8217-3520-9*, Zebra Kensgtn) Kensgtn Pub Corp.

Officers & Gentlemen. Evelyn Waugh. (Sword of Honor Ser.). 339p. 1979. pap. 12.95 (*0-316-92630-2*, Back Bay) Little.

Officers & Gentlemen: Historic West Point in Photographs. Jeffrey Simpson. LC 82-16820. (Illus.). 224p. 1982. 24.95 (*0-912882-53-0*) Sleepy Hollow.

Officers & Gentlemen: Historic West Point in Photographs. Jeffrey Simpson. (Illus.). 223p. 1999. reprint ed. pap. text 20.00 (*0-7881-6087-7*) DIANE Pub.

Officers & Gentlemen: Historic West Point in Photographs. Jeffrey Simpson. LC 82-16820. (Illus.). 224p. 1985. reprint ed. pap. 12.95 (*0-912882-55-7*) Sleepy Hollow.

***Officers & Soldiers of the American Civil War: Cavalry & Artillery, 2.** Andre Jouineau & Jean Marie Mongin. (Illus.). 2000. pap. 19.95 (*2-913903-00-2*, Pub. by Histoire) Combined Pub.

Officers at Risk: How to Identify & Cope with Stress. Dennis L. Conroy & Karen M. Hess. LC 91-73969. (Illus.). 271p. (C). 1991. pap. 19.95 (*0-942728-48-3*) Copperhouse.

Officer's Ball. Wong H. Yee. LC 96-13718. (Illus.). 32p. (J). 1997. 14.95 (*0-395-81182-1*) HM.

Officers' Camp. Giampiero Carocci. Tr. by George Hochfield from ITA. LC 97-10067. 1997. 49.95 (*0-8101-6025-0*, Marlboro); pap. text 15.95 (*0-8101-6026-9*) Northwestern U Pr.

Officers Candidates School. A. J. Sciarrino. 307p. 1993. pap. 15.00 (*0-9636504-0-8*) Gallaher Grp.

Officer's Companion (In Administration & Law) A. S. Misra. (C). 1988. 225.00 (*0-89771-783-X*, Pub. by Eastern Book) St Mut.

Officer's DUI Handbook. John Stephen et al. LC 98-87006. 105p. 1998. pap. 25.00 (*0-327-00309-X*, 3755310) LEXIS Pub.

***Officer's DUI Handbook, 1999 Edition.** John Kwasnoski et al. 200p. 1999. pap. 25.00 (*0-327-09778-7*, 3755311) LEXIS Pub.

***Officer's Guide to Fire Service EMS.** Gordon M. Sachs. LC 99-33298. 137p. 1999. write for info. (*0-912212-80-2*) Fire Eng.

Officers in Flight Suits: The Story of American Air Force Fighter Pilots in the Korean War. John D. Sherwood. (Illus.). 300p. (C). 1996. text 47.50 (*0-8147-8038-5*) NYU Pr.

Officers in Flight Suits: The Story of American Air Force Fighter Pilots in the Korean War. John D. Sherwood. 240p. 1998. pap. text 18.00 (*0-8147-8110-1*) NYU Pr.

Officer's Manual in the Field: Or, a Series of Military Plans Representing the Principle Operations of a Campaign. 2nd ed. LC 68-54780. (Illus.). 70p. 1969. reprint ed. lib. bdg. 49.50 (*0-8371-0599-4*, OFMF, Greenwood Pr) Greenwood.

Officers, Men & Women of the Australian Imperial Forces, Vol. 6. Roberts Staff. (C). 1989. 130.00 (*1-873058-66-7*, Pub. by Roberts) St Mut.

Officers, Men & Women of the Merchant Navy & Mercantile Fleet Auxiliary, Vol. 5. Roberts Staff. (C). 1989. 125.00 (*1-873058-41-1*, Pub. by Roberts) St Mut.

Officers, Men & Women of the New Zealand Expeditionary Forces, Vol. 8. Roberts Staff. (C). 1989. 125.00 (*1-873058-76-4*, Pub. by Roberts) St Mut.

Officers, Men & Women of the South African Forces, Vol. 7. Roberts Staff. (C). 1989. 125.00 (*1-873058-71-3*, Pub. by Roberts) St Mut.

Officers Mess: Life & Customs in the Regiments. R. J. Dickinson. 144p. (C). 1987. 125.00 (*81-7002-028-X*, Pub. by Himalayan Bks) St Mut.

Officers, Nobles, & Revolutionaries: Essays on Eighteenth-Century France. William Doyle. LC 95-38673. 238p. 1995. 55.00 (*1-85285-121-X*) Hambledon Press.

Officers of the War of 1812 with Portraits & Anecdotes: The United States Army Left Division Gallery of Honor. John C. Fredriksen. LC 89-9370. (Studies in Local & Institutional History: Vol. 1). (Illus.). 192p. 1989. lib. bdg. 79.95 (*0-88946-031-0*) E Mellen.

Officers Who Died in the Service of British, Indian & East African Regiments & Corps 1914-1919, Vol. 1. Roberts Staff. (C). 1989. 125.00 (*1-873058-26-8*, Pub. by Roberts) St Mut.

Officers Who Died in the Service of Commonwealth & Colonial Regiments & Corps, Vol. 3. Ed. by Roberts Staff. (C). 1989. 125.00 (*1-873058-36-5*, Pub. by Roberts) St Mut.

Officers Who Died in the Service of the Royal Navy, Royal Naval Reserve, Royal Naval Volunteer Reserve, Royal Marines, Royal Marines Reserve, Royal Navy Air Service & Royal Air Force, Vol. 2. Roberts Staff. (C). 1989. 125.00 (*1-873058-31-4*, Pub. by Roberts) St Mut.

Officers' Wives. 1986. mass mkt. 4.95 (*0-446-73351-2*, Pub. by Warner Bks) Little.

Officer's Woman. large type ed. Margot Arnold, pseud. 1982. 27.99 (*0-7089-8018-X*, Charnwood) Ulverscroft.

Offices. Stephen Bailey. LC 89-23944. (Briefing & Design Guide Ser.: No. 3). (Illus.). 200p. 1990. reprint ed. pap. 62.00 (*0-608-04411-3*, 206519200001) Bks Demand.

Offices from the Service Books of the Holy Eastern Church. Richard F. Littledale. LC 77-133819. 1970. reprint ed. 42.50 (*0-404-03996-0*) AMS Pr.

Offices of the Oriental Church. Orthodox Eastern Church Staff. LC 73-79805. reprint ed. 34.50 (*0-404-00874-7*) AMS Pr.

O

***Office2000 Essential Concepts & Techniques.** Shelly & Cashman. (Shelly Cashman Ser.). (C). 1999. pap. 33.95 (*0-7895-4652-3*) Course Tech.

Official A T & T Worldnet Web Discovery Guide. Adam C. Engst. LC 97-205624. 1997. pap., pap. text 24.99 incl. cd-rom (*0-07-882336-6*) Osborne-McGraw.

Official ABMS Directory of Board Certified Medical Specialists, 1998, 4 vols. 30th anniversary ed. Ed. by Marquis Who's Who Staff & American Board of Medical Specialities Staff. 1997. 485.00 (*0-8379-0551-6*) Marquis.

Official ABMS Directory of Board Certified Medical Specialists 2000, Set, 4 vols. 32nd ed. Ed. by Marquis Who's Who Staff. 1999. 510.00 (*0-8379-0565-6*) Marquis.

***Official ABMS Directory of Board Certified Medical Specialists 2001, Set, 4 vols.** 33rd ed. Ed. by Marquis Who's Who Staff. 2000. write for info. (*0-8379-0571-0*) Marquis.

Official Account of Military Operations in China 1900-1901. E. W. Norie. (Victorian War Ser.: No. 3). (Illus.). 510p. 1995. reprint ed. 59.95 (*0-89839-215-2*) Battery Pr.

Official Actor's Handbook: How to Become a Famous Actor & How to Deal with Stardom. Lee Dove. (Illus.). 96p. 1987. pap. 4.95 (*0-942435-03-6*) Collegiate Pub.

Official Adobe Electronic Publishing Guide. Andrew Faulkner & Adobe Creative Team Staff. 216p. 1999. pap. text 35.00 (*1-56830-469-2*, Pub. by Adobe Pr) Peachpit Pr.

Official Adobe Photoshop 5.0 Studio Techniques. Ben Willmore & Adobe Creative Team Staff. LC 98-86257. 456p. 1998. pap. text 39.99 (*1-56830-474-9*) Adobe Pr.

Official Adobe Print Publishing Guide. Andrew Faulkner & Adobe Creative Team Staff. 240p. 1998. 35.00 (*1-56830-468-4*) Adobe Pr.

Official African-American Museum & Cultural Galleries Directory. Willie E. Box, Jr. 276p. (Orig.). 1993. lib. bdg. write for info. (*1-882901-38-X*) W Box & Assocs.

Official Airport Hotel Guide Book. 750p. 1989. pap. write for info. (*0-945723-00-8*) AC-U-Kwik Inc.

Official All My Children Trivia Book. Gerard J. Waggett. LC 97-40011. (Illus.). 192p. (J). 1998. pap. 9.70 (*0-7868-8283-2*, Pub. by Hyperion) Time Warner.

***Official America Online Tour Guide.** 5th ed. Watson. 480p. 2000. pap. 39.99 (*0-7645-3419-X*) IDG Bks.

Official America Online Yellow Pages. John Kaufeld & Jennifer Kaufeld. LC 98-122135. (Illus.). 512p. 1997. pap. text 24.99 (*0-07-882416-8*, Oracle Press) Osborne-McGraw.

Official American Bar Association Guide to Approved Law Schools: 1999 Edition. American Bar Association Staff. 480p. 1998. pap. 21.95 (*0-02-862192-1*, Pub. by Macmillan) S&S Trade.

***Official American Bar Association Guide to Approved Law Schools: 2000 Edition.** American Bar Association Staff. Ed. by Kurt Snyder. (ABA Approved Law Schools Ser.). (Illus.). 480p. 1999. pap. 21.95 (*0-02-862824-1*, Arc) IDG Bks.

***Official American Bar Association Guide to Approved Law Schools 2001.** American Bar Association Staff. 400p. 2000. pap. 21.95 (*0-7645-6231-2*) IDG Bks.

Official American Board of Medical Specialties (ABMS) Directory of Board Certified Colon & Rectal Surgeons. 34p. 1992. 79.95 (*0-8379-2500-2*) Marquis.

Official American Board of Medical Specialties (ABMS) Directory of Board Certified Dermatologists. 209p. 1992. 79.95 (*0-8379-2501-0*) Marquis.

Official American Board of Medical Specialties (ABMS) Directory of Board Certified Emergency Medicine Physicians. 248p. 1992. 79.95 (*0-8379-2503-7*) Marquis.

Official American Board of Medical Specialties (ABMS) Directory of Board Certified Medical Geneticists. 32p. 1992. 99.95 (*0-8379-2504-5*) Marquis.

Official American Board of Medical Specialties (ABMS) Directory of Board Certified Neurological Surgeons. 100p. 1992. 99.95 (*0-8379-2505-3*) Marquis.

Official American Board of Medical Specialties (ABMS) Directory of Board Certified Nuclear Medicine Specialists. 103p. 1992. 99.95 (*0-8379-2506-1*) Marquis.

Official American Board of Medical Specialties (ABMS) Directory of Board Certified Ophthalmologists. 389p. 1992. 79.95 (*0-8379-2507-X*) Marquis.

Official American Board of Medical Specialties (ABMS) Directory of Board Certified Plastic Surgeons. 121p. 1992. 79.95 (*0-8379-2508-8*) Marquis.

Official American Board of Medical Specialties (ABMS) Directory of Board Certified Thoracic Surgeons. 147p. 1992. 79.95 (*0-8379-2509-6*) Marquis.

Official American Board of Medical Specialties (ABMS) Directory of Board Certified Urologists. 227p. 1992. 99.95 (*0-8379-2510-X*) Marquis.

Official & Confidential: The Secret Life of J. Edgar Hoover. Anthony Summers. Ed. by Julie Rubenstein. 672p. 1994. reprint ed. pap. 6.99 (*0-671-88087-X*, Pocket Star Bks) PB.

Official & Popular Religion. Ed. by Peter H. Vrijhof & Jacques Waardenburg. (Religion & Society Ser.). 1979. text 73.10 (*90-279-7998-7*) Mouton.

Official & Standardized Methods of Analysis. 3rd ed. Ed. by C. A. Watson. 802p. 1994. 205.00 (*0-85186-441-4*) CRC Pr.

Official & Standardized Methods of Analysis. 3rd ed. Ed. & Compiled by C. A. Watson. 802p. 1994. 195.00 (*0-85186-444-9*, R6444) CRC Pr.

Official & Statistical Register of the State of Mississippi. Dunbar Rowland. 1317p. 1995. reprint ed. lib. bdg. 125.00 (*0-8328-5050-0*) Higginson Bk Co.

Official Andy Griffith Show Scrapbook. Lee Pfeiffer. (Illus.). 224p. 1993. pap. 15.95 (*0-8065-1449-3*, Citadel Pr) Carol Pub Group.

Official Andy Griffith Show Scrapbook. Lee Pfeiffer. LC 97-31820. (Illus.). 256p. 1997. pap. text 18.95 (*0-8065-1934-7*, Citadel Pr) Carol Pub Group.

***Official Annual Statement Blanks of the NAIC: Franternal for 2001.** Ed. by Patti Carli. 130p. 2000. ring bd. 175.00 (*0-89382-996-X*, ASB-FU00) Nat Assn Insurance.

***Official Annual Statement Blanks of the NAIC: Fraternal.** rev. ed. Ed. by Patti Carli. 158p. 1998. ring bd. 175.00 (*0-89382-527-1*, ASB-FU98) Nat Assn Insurance.

***Official Annual Statement Blanks of the NAIC: Fraternal.** rev. ed. Ed. by Patti Carli. 160p. 1999. ring bd. 175.00 (*0-89382-613-8*, ASB-FU99) Nat Assn Insurance.

***Official Annual Statement Blanks of the NAIC: Health Maintenance Organizations.** Ed. by Patti Carli. 99p. 1998. ring bd. write for info. (*0-89382-523-9*, ASB-HU98) Nat Assn Insurance.

***Official Annual Statement Blanks of the NAIC: Hospital, Medical, Dental & Indemnity Corporations.** rev. ed. Patti Carli. 106p. 1999. ring bd. write for info. (*0-89382-529-8*, ASB-MU99) Nat Assn Insurance.

***Official Annual Statement Blanks of the NAIC: Life.** rev. ed. Ed. by Patti Carli. 182p. 1998. ring bd. 175.00 (*0-89382-525-5*, ASB-LU98) Nat Assn Insurance.

***Official Annual Statement Blanks of the NAIC: Life.** rev. ed. Ed. by Patti Carli. 184p. 1999. ring bd. 175.00 (*0-89382-612-X*, ASB-LU99) Nat Assn Insurance.

***Official Annual Statement Blanks of the NAIC: Life for 2001.** Ed. by Patti Carli. 130p. 2000. ring bd. 175.00 (*0-89382-995-1*, ASB-LU00) Nat Assn Insurance.

***Official Annual Statement Blanks of the NAIC: Property & Casualty.** rev. ed. Ed. by Patti Carli. 240p. 1998. ring bd. 175.00 (*0-89382-526-3*, ASB-PU98) Nat Assn Insurance.

***Official Annual Statement Blanks of the NAIC: Property & Casualty.** rev. ed. Ed. by Patti Carli. 242p. 1999. ring bd. 175.00 (*0-89382-611-1*, ASB-PU99) Nat Assn Insurance.

***Official Annual Statement Blanks of the NAIC: Property & Casualty for 2001.** Ed. by Patti Carli. 290p. 2000. ring bd. 175.00 (*0-89382-994-3*, ASB-PU00) Nat Assn Insurance.

***Official Annual Statement Blanks of the NAIC: Separate Accounts.** rev. ed. Ed. by Patti Carli. 51p. 1998. ring bd. 50.00 (*0-89382-524-7*, ASB-AS98) Nat Assn Insurance.

***Official Annual Statement Blanks of the NAIC: Title.** rev. ed. Ed. by Patti Carli. 128p. 1998. ring bd. 150.00 (*0-89382-528-X*, ASB-TU98) Nat Assn Insurance.

Official Anti Rush Limburger Handbook. Jon Michaels. 144p. (Orig.). 1995. pap. 14.95 (*0-9649839-0-7*) Gadfly Prodns.

Official Apple Computer Club Books: First Three Handbooks in a Series. Ed. by Richard Casabonne. 19.95 (*0-318-58189-2*); pap. 12.95 (*0-318-58190-6*) P-H.

Official Aptitude Maximized, Expense Minimized. Jeremy Bentham. Ed. by Philip Schofield. 556p. 1993. text 85.00 (*0-19-820403-5*) OUP.

***Official Armorines Project Swarm Strategy Guide.** Acclaim Entertainment Staff. (Illus.). 1999. pap. 12.99 (*1-57840-981-0*) Acclaim Bks.

Official Army Register of the Volunteer Force of the United States Army. Frwd. by John M. Carroll. reprint ed. 178.00 (*0-8488-0038-9*, J M C & Co) Amereon Ltd.

Official Arrow Street Map Atlas Metro Worcester, MA. Arrow Staff. 1999. 12.95 (*0-913450-97-9*) Arrow Map.

Official Arrow Street Map Atlas of Cape Cod. Arrow Staff. 1997. 13.95 (*1-55751-407-0*) Arrow Map.

***Official Arrow Street Map Atlas of Central/Eastern, CT.** Arrow Staff. 2000. 16.95 (*1-55751-445-3*) Arrow Map.

Official Arrow Street Map Atlas of Eastern, MA. Arrow Staff. 1999. 19.95 (*1-55751-401-1*) Arrow Map.

Official Arrow Street Map Atlas of Middlesex County, MA. Arrow Staff. 1999. 11.95 (*1-55751-403-8*) Arrow Map.

Official Arrow Street Map Atlas of Western, MA. Arrow Staff. LC 95-675710. 1998. 13.95 (*0-913450-83-9*) Arrow Map.

Official Assassin: Winston Churchill's SAS Hit Team. Peter Mason. Ed. by John Brunner & Jim Phillips. (Illus.). 425p. 1998. 29.95 (*0-932572-31-6*) Phillips Pubns.

Official Athletic College Guide: Baseball, 1997 Edition. 4th rev. ed. Ed. by Charlie Kadupski. (YA). (gr. 8-12). 1997. write for info. (*0-614-29655-2*) Spt Source TX.

Official Athletic College Guide: 1998 Baseball. Ed. by Charlie Kadupski. 696p. (YA). (gr. 9-12). 1998. pap. 24.95 (*0-9631148-2-4*) Spt Source TX.

Official Athletic College Guide: 1998 Soccer. Ed. by Charlie Kadupski. 752p. (YA). (gr. 9-12). 1998. pap. 24.95 (*0-9631148-1-6*) Spt Source TX.

Official Athletic College Guide: 1998 Softball. Ed. by Charlie Kadupski. (YA). (gr. 9-12). 1997. pap. 24.95 (*0-9631148-3-2*) Spt Source TX.

Official Athletic College Guide: 1999 Baseball. Ed. by Charlie Kadupski. (Illus.). 800p. (Orig.). (YA). (gr. 9-12). 1999. pap. 24.95 (*0-9631148-6-7*) Spt Source TX.

Official Athletic College Guide: 1999 Soccer. Ed. by Charlie Kadupski. (Illus.). 796p. (Orig.). 1998. pap. 24.95 (*0-9631148-5-9*) Spt Source TX.

Official Athletic College Guide: 1999 Softball. Ed. by Charlie Kadupski. (Illus.). 680p. (Orig.). (YA). (gr. 9-12). 1998. pap. 24.95 (*0-9631148-7-5*) Spt Source TX.

Official Athletic College Guide: 1999 Volleyball. Ed. by Charlie Kadupski. (Illus.). 800p. 1999. pap. 24.95 (*0-9631148-8-3*) Spt Source TX.

Official Athletic College Guide: 2000 Soccer. 11th rev. ed. Ed. by Charlie Kadupski. 864p. 1999. pap. 24.95 (*1-893588-00-9*) Spt Source TX.

Official Athletic College Guide: 2000 Volleyball. Ed. by Charlie Kadupski. 630p. (YA). 1999. pap. 24.95 (*0-9631148-9-1*) Spt Source TX.

***Official Athletic College Workbook: Baseball.** Ed. by Charlie Kadupski. (Illus.). 80p. (YA). (gr. 9). 2000. per., wbk. ed. 19.95 (*1-893588-51-3*) Spt Source TX.

***Official Athletic College Workbook: Soccer.** Ed. by Charlie Kadupski. (Illus.). 80p. (YA). (gr. 9). 2000. per., wbk. ed. 19.95 (*1-893588-50-5*) Spt Source TX.

***Official Athletic College Workbook: Softball.** Ed. by Charlie Kadupski. (Illus.). 80p. (YA). (gr. 9-12). 2000. per., wbk. ed. 19.95 (*1-893588-52-1*) Spt Source TX.

***Official Athletic College Workbook: Volleyball.** Ed. by Charlie Kadupski. (Illus.). 80p. (YA). (gr. 9-12). 2000. per., wbk. ed. 19.95 (*1-893588-53-X*) Spt Source TX.

***Official Autograph Collector Price Guide.** 2nd ed. Kevin Martin. (Illus.). 2000. pap. 24.95 (*0-9669710-3-5*) Odyssey Pubs.

Official Autograph Collector Price Guide, 1999 Kevin Martin. 1999. pap. text 24.95 (*0-9669710-0-0*) Odyssey Pubs.

Official Baby License Exam. David Rosenberg. LC 97-156042. (Illus.). 72p. (Orig.). 1996. pap. 9.95 (*0-9646603-0-X*) Hse of Toast.

Official Bad Golfers Test. Jim Carroll. (Illus.). 81p. 1999. pap. 8.95 (*0-9672841-0-4*) J Carroll.

Official Barbecue Cookbook. T. L. Bush. LC 95-45904. 70p. 1996. pap. 13.95 (*0-88415-593-5*, 5593) Gulf Pub.

Official Baseball Card Cross-Reference Guide, 1989-1990. 128p. 5.95 (*0-88128-367-3*) Martin-Smith.

Official Baseball Hall of Fame Book of Super Stars. Jim Kaplan. (J). (gr. 3 up). 1989. pap. 4.95 (*0-671-67379-3*) Litle Simon.

Official Baseball Register, 1995: A Who's Who of Baseball from A to Z. Sporting News Staff. 1995. pap. 13.95 (*0-89204-517-5*) Sporting News.

Official Baseball Register, 1996: Baseball Bios, from A to Z. 1996th ed. 600p. 1996. pap. 13.95 (*0-89204-545-0*) Sporting News.

Official Baseball Rules: 1998 Edition. Notes by Sporting News Staff. (Illus.). 104p. 1998. pap. 6.95 (*0-89204-595-7*) Sporting News.

Official Baseball Rules Annotated. Jim Evans. 400p. 1991. 69.50 (*0-9630626-0-3*) J Evans Acad.

***Official Baseball Rules Book.** Sporting News Staff. 104p. 2000. pap. 6.95 (*0-89204-631-7*, Contemporary Bks) NTC Contemp Pub Co.

Official Baseball Rules (1999 Edition) (Illus.). 104p. 1999. pap. 6.95 (*0-89204-607-4*) Sporting News.

Official Baseball Rules, 1996: The Book Used by the Men & Women in Blue. 1996th ed. (Illus.). 104p. 1996. pap. 4.95 (*0-89204-552-3*) Sporting News.

Official Baseball Rules 1995. 1995. pap. 4.95 (*0-89204-524-8*) Sporting News.

Official Battlezone Strategy Guide. Bradygames Staff. 1998. pap. text 19.99 (*1-56686-775-4*) Brady Pub.

Official BBEdit Book. Bob LeVitus & Natanya Pitts. 350p. 1997. 39.99 (*1-56276-505-1*, Ziff-Davis Pr) Que.

***Official Bbmak Scrapbook.** D. S. Cashion. (Illus.). 48p. (YA). (gr. 5 up). 2000. pap. 9.99 (*0-7868-1516-7*) Hyprn Ppbks.

Official Beanie Basher Handbook. B. Neebascher. LC 98-86600. 1998. pap. text 7.95 (*0-8362-8186-1*) Andrews & McMeel.

Official Bed & Breakfast Guide: For the U. S., Canada & Caribbean, No. VII. 7th ed. Phyllis Featherston & Barbara F. Ostler. (Illus.). 571p. 1995. pap. 17.95 (*0-9611298-6-7*) Natl Bed.

***Official Best of the Web Shopping Guide.** Alan Alper. 2000. 19.95 (*0-7615-2834-2*) Prima Pub.

Official Bewitched Cookbook. Kasey Rogers & Mark Wood. LC 97-112125. 256p. 1995. pap. 15.95 (*1-57566-095-4*, Knsington) Kensgtn Pub Corp.

Official Big Ten Football Fan's Guide, 1998-1999. Big Ten Conference Staff & Triumph Books Staff. (Illus.). 132p. 1998. pap. 9.95 (*1-57243-268-3*) Triumph Bks.

Official Big Ten Football Fan's Guide, 1997-1998. rev. ed. Big Ten Conference Staff. (Illus.). 128p. 1997. pap. 9.95 (*1-57243-203-9*) Triumph Bks.

Official Big 12 Football Guide, 1997-1998. Big 12 Conference Staff. (Illus.). 128p. (Orig.). 1997. pap. 9.95 (*1-57243-206-3*) Triumph Bks.

Official Big 12 Football Guide, 1998-1999. Big Twelve Conference Staff & Triumph Books Staff. (Illus.). 192p. 1998. pap. 9.95 (*1-57243-271-3*) Triumph Bks.

***Official Bilingualism & Linguistic Communication in Cameroon.** Ed. by George Echu & Allan W. Grundstrom. LC 98-26507. (Francophone Cultures & Literatures Ser.: Vol. 27). xx, 216p. (C). 1999. 32.95 (*0-8204-4092-2*) P Lang Pubng.

Official Bingo Manual. 4th rev. ed. Richard M. Greene, Jr. (Designed for Bingo Managers As Well As Bingo Players over 300 Bingo Game Diagrams Ser.). (Illus.). 200p. 1997. spiral bd. 29.95 (*0-934487-18-9*) R M Greene.

Official Blackbook Price Guide to World Coins. Marc Hudgeons. 480p. 1998. pap. 7.99 (*0-87637-067-9*) Hse Collectbls.

Official Book of Baseball Dreams & Memories. Anthony P. Tramontano. Ed. by Melissa A. Tramontano. (Illus.). v, 40p. (J). (gr. 6). 1998. 15.95 (*0-9663140-0-X*) SMC Pub.

Official Book of Excuses & Related Reasons. C. J. Phillips. Ed. by Philip Gurian. (Illus.). 64p. (Orig.). 1989. pap., per. 4.95 (*0-9621639-0-2*) Grand Natl Pr.

Official Book of Figure Skating. U. S. Figure Skating Association Staff. LC 98-27343. (Illus.). 266p. (YA). (gr. 4 up). 1998. 30.00 (*0-684-84673-X*, S&S Edns) Simon & Schuster.

Official Book of Super Bowl XXX: Showdown in the Desert. Laurence J. Hyman. LC 97-104411. (Illus.). 144p. 1996. pap. 19.95 (*0-942627-26-1*) Woodford Pubng.

Official Book of Super Bowl XXIX: The Golden State of Football. Ronnie Lott. Ed. by Laurence J. Hyman & Jon Rochmis. LC 95-60136. (Official Books of the Super Bowl: No. 1). (Illus.). 144p. (Orig.). 1995. pap. 19.95 (*0-942627-25-3*) Woodford Pubng.

Official Book of the Antique Automobile Club of America: A 60-Year History of Dedication to the Automobile. Bob Lichty. LC 98-84624. (Illus.). 496p. 1999. 59.95 (*0-87341-481-0*, AACA) Krause Pubns.

***Official Book of the Basset Hound.** Robert E. Booth. 1999. 79.95 (*0-7938-0508-2*) TFH Pubns.

Official Book of the Boston Terrier. Muriel P. Lee. 176p. 1998. 35.95 (*0-7938-0507-4*) TFH Pubns.

Official Book of the Dalmatian: AKC Rank #15. Dalmation Club of America Staff. (Illus.). 352p. Date not set. 79.95 (*0-7938-2081-2*, TS-254) TFH Pubns.

Official Book of the Labrador Retriever. B. Ziessow. (Illus.). 448p. 1995. 59.95 (*0-7938-0188-5*, TS241) TFH Pubns.

Official Book of the Neapolitan Mastiff, AKC Rank No. 48. Sherilyn Allen. (Illus.). 320p. 1996. 69.95 (*0-7938-2083-9*, TS255) TFH Pubns.

Official Book of the 1998 World Series: Great Moments. Ed. by Laurence J. Hyman. (Illus.). 144p. 1998. pap. 19.95 (*0-942627-42-3*) Woodford Pubng.

Official Book of the 1995 World Series: A Series for the Fans. Fimrite. (Illus.). 144p. 1995. pap. 19.95 (*0-942627-22-9*) Woodford Pubng.

Official Book of the 1997 World Series: A Series for the Americas. Jenkins. Ed. by Laurence J. Hyman. (Series for the Americas). (Illus.). 144p. 1997. pap. 19.95 (*0-942627-38-5*) Woodford Pubng.

Official Book of the 1996 World Series: A Series for New York. Jenkins. Ed. by Laurence J. Hyman. (Series for New York). (Illus.). 144p. 1996. pap. 19.95 (*0-942627-27-X*) Woodford Pubng.

Official Book of the 1993 World Series: A Series to Remember: Toronto & Philadelphia, 1993. Joe Morgan. Ed. by Laurence J. Hyman & Jon Rochmis. LC 93-61703. 144p. 1993. 29.95 (*0-942627-19-9*) Woodford Pubng.

Official Book of the Polish Lowland Sheepdog. E. Jane Brown et al. (Illus.). 160p. 1996. 39.95 (*0-7938-2084-7*, TS247) TFH Pubns.

Official Book of the 1999 World Series. Woodford Pub. Staff. 144p. 1999. 29.95 (*0-942627-60-1*); pap. text 19.95 (*0-942627-59-8*) Woodford Pubng.

Official Book of Thumb Wrestling. Andy Mayer & Jim Becker. LC 80-51513. (Illus.). 1983. bds. 5.95 (*0-89480-363-8*, 363) Workman Pub.

Official Book to Color. Robert J. Masters. 32p. (J). 1998. pap. 1.99 (*0-679-89168-4*, Pub. by Random Bks Yng Read) Random.

***Official Brave Fencer Musashi Strategy Guide.** BradyGames Inc. Staff. (Bradygames Strategy Guides Ser.). (Illus.). 1998. pap. 14.99 (*1-56686-832-7*, BradyGAMES) Brady Pub.

Official British Film Propaganda During the First World War. Nicholas Reeves. 304p. 1986. 49.95 (*0-7099-4225-7*, Pub. by C Helm) Routldge.

***Official Bus & Coach Driving Manual.** Driving Standards Agency Staff. (Illus.). vi, 253p. 1999. 26.00 (*0-11-552194-1*, Pub. by Statnry Office) Balogh.

Official California Handbook for School District Mapping: A Guide for Developing & Maintaining Current Maps for Administrative Planning, Transportation & Safety. John A. Johnson. LC 97-93674. 144p. (Orig.). 1997. pap. 99.00 (*1-57502-507-8*, P01508) Morris Pubng.

Official Cat Codependents Handbook: For People Who Love Their Cats Too Much! Ronnie Sellers. (Illus.). 128p. 1995. pap. text 9.95 (*1-56906-019-3*) R Sellers Prods.

Official Cat Lovers-Dog Lovers Joke Book. Larry Wilde. 1988. mass mkt. 2.95 (*1-55817-033-2*, Pinncle Kensgtn) Kensgtn Pub Corp.

Official Catalog of Canada Precancels. 14th ed. Ed. by H. G. Walburn. 56p. 1983. 3.50 (*0-685-53040-X*) G W Noble.

Official Catalog of U. S. Bureau Precancels. 64th ed. Ed. by Gilbert W. Noble. 1983. 6.00 (*0-685-53039-6*) G W Noble.

Official Catalogue of the Graphic Works of Salvador Dali. Albert Field. (Illus.). 280p. 285.00 (*0-9653611-0-1*) S Dali Archives.

Official Catalogue of the Graphic Works of Salvador Dali. deluxe ed. Albert Field. (Illus.). 280p. 1996. 360.00 (*0-9653611-4-4*) S Dali Archives.

Official Catholic College & University Guidebook, 98/99: Sponsored by the National Catholic College Admission Association. rev. ed. Ed. by Liz Schuetz. (Illus.). 130p. (YA). (gr. 9-12). 1998. pap. 8.95 (*0-9645495-2-2*) R H Bailey.

***Official Catholic Directory.** Ed. by National Register Publishing Editorial Staff. 1999. pap. 289.24 (*0-87217-987-7*) Natl Register.

Official Catholic Directory of Traditional Latin Masses & Resource Book, 1999. 4th rev. ed. Ed. by M. E. Morrison. 124p. 1999. pap. 10.00 (*1-883511-12-7*) Veritas Pr CA.

***Official Catholic Directory of Traditional Latin Masses & Resource Book, 2000.** Ed. by M.E. Morrison. 116p. 2000. pap. 10.00 (*1-883511-14-3*) Veritas Pr CA.

***Official Catholic Directory Supplement 2000.** Ed. by National Register Publishing Staff. 2000. write for info. (*0-87217-374-7*) Natl Register.

Official Catholic Directory 1998, Set, 2 vols. National Register Publishing Co. Staff. 1998. 225.00 (*0-87217-963-X*) Natl Register.

***Official Catholic Directory 2000, Set, 2 vols.** Ed. by National Register Publishing Staff. 2000. 259.00 (*0-87217-400-X*) Natl Register.

Official CB Crossword Puzzles for Big Dummy's. Aero Products Research, Inc., Industries Division. (Illus.). (J). (gr. 8 up). 1977. pap. 1.98 (*0-912682-18-3*) Aero Products.

Official CBS Viewers Guide to the 1992 Winter Olympics. Michael Rosenthal. 1991. pap. 3.95 (*0-918223-90-3*) Pindar Pr.

Official Chronology of the U.S. Navy in World War II. Robert J. Cressman. LC 99-39136. (Illus.). 400p. 1999. 49.95 (*1-55750-149-1*) Naval Inst Pr.

Official Client/Server Computing Guide to Data Warehousing. Harjinder Gill. LC 95-73284. 382p. 1996. pap. text 49.99 incl. cd-rom (*0-7897-0714-4*) Que.

Official Clinton Joke Book: The Complete Unadulterated Edition. 176p. 1998. pap. 7.99 (*0-7615-1982-3*) Prima Pub.

Official Code Book of America. 3rd rev. ed. Scott Morrison. Ed. by Rebecca Sutherland & Anastasia Terris. 96p. 1996. reprint ed. pap. 6.95 (*0-929150-56-2*) Castalia CA.

Official Code Book of America: Pocket Size. 3rd ed. Ed. by Scott Morrison. 96p. (Orig.). 1996. pap. 5.95 (*0-929150-57-0*) Castalia CA.

Official Code Book of America: Pocket Size, Pocket Size. 2nd rev. ed. Scott Morrison. Ed. by Rebecca Sutherland & Anastasia Terris. (Illus.). 96p. (Orig.). 1996. reprint ed. pap. 5.95 (*0-929150-51-1*) Castalia CA.

Official Code of Georgia. annot. ed. Sharyn McCrumb. write for info. (*0-614-05934-8*, MICHIE) LEXIS Pub.

Official Code of Georgia Annotated. 1982. write for info. (*0-87215-491-2*, MICHIE) LEXIS Pub.

Official Code of Georgia Annotated, 45 Vols. The Publisher's Editorial Staff. 400.00 (*0-327-11074-0*) LEXIS Pub.

Official Code of Georgia Annotated No. 3: 1998 Advance Legislative Service. 1196p. 1998. pap. 10.00 (*0-327-05105-1*, 41832-11) LEXIS Pub.

Official Code of Georgia Annotated No. 41: 1998 Edition Tables Volume. rev. ed. Ed. by Lexis Law Publishing Staff. 1998. write for info. (*0-327-05090-X*, 41741-11) LEXIS Pub.

Official Code of Georgia Annotated Vol. 2: 1998 Edition, Constitution of the State of Georgia. 922p. 1998. write for info. (*0-327-05438-7*, 41819-11, MICHIE) LEXIS Pub.

Official Code of Georgia Annotated Vol. 26: 1998 Edition, Title 34. 897p. 1998. write for info. (*0-327-05439-5*, 41916-11, MICHIE) LEXIS Pub.

Official Code of Georgia Annotated Vol. 38: 1998 Edition, Title 49 & 50. 1014p. 1998. write for info. (*0-327-05440-9*, 41964-12, MICHIE) LEXIS Pub.

***Official Code of Georgia Annotated - 2000 Advance Annotation Service - Pamphlet No. 1.** 100p. 1999. pap. Price not set. (*0-327-09625-X*, 4200816) LEXIS Pub.

Official Code of Georgia Annotated Index, 1998 Cumulative Supplement No. 42: Index to Local & Special Laws & General Laws of Local Application. 102p. 1998. write for info. (*0-327-05397-6*, 50162-15, MICHIE) LEXIS Pub.

Official Code of Georgia Annotated, 1998 Advance Legislative Service Pamphlet, No. 2. annot. ed. 1271p. 1998. pap. write for info. (*0-327-05049-7*, 41829-11) LEXIS Pub.

Official Code of Georgia Annotated, 1998 General Index: 1998 Edition, 2 vols. rev. ed. 2450p. 1998. write for info. (*0-327-05168-X*, 42057-14) LEXIS Pub.

Official Code of Georgia Annotated 1998 General Index: 1998 Edition, A to I, Vol. 43. rev. ed. 1281p. 1998. write for info. (*0-327-05235-X*, 42058-14) LEXIS Pub.

Official Code of Georgia Annotated 1998 General Index: 1998 Edition, J to Z, Vol. 44. rev. ed. 1169p. 1998. write for info. (*0-327-05236-8*, 42059-14) LEXIS Pub.

***Official Code of Georgia Annotation Citator.** Lexis Pub Editorial Staff. 1500p. 1999. pap. 39.95 (*0-327-09179-7*, 4135210) LEXIS Pub.

Official Code of Georgia, 1998 Cumulative Supplement, 38 vols. Incl. Vol. 1. 149p. 1998. pap., suppl. ed. (*0-327-05399-2*, 50121-15); Vol. 3. 219p. 1998. pap., suppl. ed. (*0-327-05400-X*, 50123-15); Vol. 4. 47p. 1998. pap., suppl. ed. (*0-327-05401-8*, 50124-15); Vol. 5. 72p. 1998. pap., suppl. ed. (*0-327-05402-6*, 50125-15); Vol. 6. 188p. 1998. pap., suppl. ed. (*0-327-05403-4*, 50126-15); Vol. 7. 108p. 1998. pap., suppl. ed. (*0-327-05404-2*, 50127-15); Vol. 8. 177p. 1998. pap., suppl. ed. (*0-327-05405-0*, 50128-15); Vol. 9. 176p. 1998. pap., suppl. ed. (*0-327-05406-9*, 50129-15); Vol. 10. 166p. 1998. pap., suppl. ed. (*0-327-05407-7*, 50130-15); Vol. 11. 171p. 1998. pap., suppl. ed. (*0-327-05408-5*, 50131-15); Vol. 12. 1998. pap., suppl. ed. (*0-327-05409-3*, 50132-15); Vol. 13. 320p. 1998. pap., suppl. ed. (*0-327-05410-7*, 50133-15); Vol. 14. 217p. 1998. pap., suppl. ed. (*0-327-05411-5*, 50134-15); Vol. 15. 25p. 1998. pap., suppl. ed. (*0-327-05412-3*, 50135-15); Vol. 16. 258p. 1998. pap., suppl. ed. (*0-327-05413-1*, 50136-15); Vol. 17. 142p. 1998. pap., suppl. ed. (*0-327-05414-X*, 50137-15); Vol. 18. 273p. 1998. pap., suppl. ed. (*0-327-05415-8*, 50138-15); Vol. 19. 83p. 1998. pap., suppl. ed. (*0-327-05416-6*, 50139-15); Vol. 20. 62p. 1998. pap., suppl. ed. (*0-327-05417-4*, 50140-15); Vol. 21. 240p. 1998. pap., suppl. ed. (*0-327-05418-2*, 50141-15); Vol. 22. 285p. 1998. pap., suppl. ed. (*0-327-05419-0*, 50142-15); Vol. 23. 120p. 1998. pap., suppl. ed. (*0-327-05420-4*, 50143-15); Vol. 24. 181p. 1998. pap., suppl. ed. (*0-327-05421-2*, 50144-15); Vol. 25. 93p. 1998. pap., suppl. ed. (*0-327-05422-0*, 50145-15); Vol. 27. 233p. 1998. pap., suppl. ed. (*0-327-05423-9*, 50147-15); Vol. 28. 57p. 1998. pap., suppl. ed. (*0-327-05424-7*, 50148-15); Vol. 29. 25p. 1998. pap., suppl. ed. (*0-327-05425-5*, 50149-15); Vol. 30. 257p. 1998. pap., suppl. ed. (*0-327-05426-3*, 50150-15); Vol. 31. 162p. 1998. pap., suppl. ed. (*0-327-05427-1*, 50151-15); Vol. 32. 235p. 1998. pap., suppl. ed. (*0-327-05428-X*, 50152-15); Vol. 33. 208p. 1998. pap., suppl. ed. (*0-327-05429-8*, 50153-15); Vol. 34. 164p. 1998. pap., suppl. ed. (*0-327-05430-1*, 50154-15); Vol. 35. 240p. 1998. pap., suppl. ed. (*0-327-05431-X*, 50155-15); Vol. 36. 262p. 1998. pap., suppl. ed. (*0-327-05432-8*, 50156-15); Vol. 37. 179p. 1998. pap., suppl. ed. (*0-327-05433-6*, 50157-15); Vol. 39. 230p. 1998. pap., suppl. ed. (*0-327-05434-4*, 50159-15); Vol. 40. 79p. 1998. pap., suppl. ed. (*0-327-05435-2*, 50160-15); Vol. 29a. 26p. 1998. pap., suppl. ed. (*0-327-05437-9*, 50120-15); write for info. (*0-327-05398-4*) LEXIS Pub.

Official Code of Georgia, 1999 Replacement, Vol. 13. 662p. 1999. write for info. (*0-327-08314-X*, 41864-12) LEXIS Pub.

Official Code of Georgia, 1999 Replacement, Vol. 14. 662p. 1999. write for info. (*0-327-08315-8*, 41869-12) LEXIS Pub.

Official Code of Georgia, 1999 Replacement, Vol. 16. 662p. 1999. write for info. (*0-327-08316-6*, 41875-11) LEXIS Pub.

Official Code of Georgia, 1999 Replacement, Vol. 30. 662p. 1999. write for info. (*0-327-08317-4*, 41933-12) LEXIS Pub.

Official Code of Georgia, 1999 Replacement, Vol. 36. 662p. 1999. write for info. (*0-327-08318-2*, 41955-11) LEXIS Pub.

Official Code of Georgia 1999 Advance Annotation Service, Vol. 3. 172p. 1999. pap. write for info. (*0-327-07712-3*, 4201015) LEXIS Pub.

Official Code of Georgia 1998 Replacement, Vol. 18. 662p. 1998. write for info. (*0-327-06816-7*, 4188411) LEXIS Pub.

Official Collector's Guide to Anheuser-Busch Steins, Vol. 1. Anheuser-Busch, Inc. Staff. 244p. 1993. pap. text. write for info. (*0-9637395-0-6*) Anheuser-Busch.

***Official College Guide for Baseball.** Charlie Kadupski. 2000. pap. 39.95 (*1-893588-02-5*) Spt Source TX.

Official College Quiz Book. Shoebox Greetings Staff. (Illus.). 72p. (Orig.). 1990. pap. 5.95 (*0-87529-634-3*) Hallmark.

Official Commentary on the International Standby Practice. James E. Byrne. Ed. by James G. Barnes. xx, 353p. Date not set. 129.00 (*1-888870-17-6*) Inst Intl Bnking.

***Official Communications & Speeches Relating to Peace Proposals, 1916-1917.** Carnegie Endowment for International Peace Staff. LC 99-48403. 1999. write for info. (*1-57588-583-2*) W S Hein.

Official Companion to the Olympic Games: Atlanta, 1996. (Illus.). 1996. pap. 18.95 (*1-85753-128-0*) Brasseys.

Official Compilation of Codes, Rules & Regulations of the State of New York & the State Register: Their History & Use. Robert A. Carter. 36p. 1984. 5.00 (*0-318-22975-7*) NYS Library.

***Official Compuserve 2000 Tour Guide** Charles Bowen. LC 99-38590. 1999. write for info. (*1-891556-55-X*) Amer Online.

***Official CompuServe 2000 Tour Guide.** Charles Bowen. (Illus.). 576p. 2000. pap. 24.99 (*0-7645-3492-0*) IDG Bks.

Official Concept of the Nation in the Former GDR: Theory, Pragmatism & the Search for Legitimacy. Joanna McKay. LC 97-78097. 176p. 1998. text 55.95 (*1-85972-622-4*, Pub. by Ashgate Pub) Ashgate Pub Co.

***Official Congressional Directory 1999-2000.** Claitors Publishing Staff. 1100p. 1999. pap. 32.00 (*1-57980-443-8*) Claitors.

Official Congressional Directory, 1995-1996. (Illus.). 1195p. 1995. pap., per. 23.00 (*0-16-047213-X*, 052-070-07003-0); text, boxed set 33.00 (*0-16-006312-4*, 052-070-07004-8) USGPO.

***Official Congressional Directory, 1999-2000.** 1217p. 1999. per. 32.00 (*0-16-058630-5*) USGPO.

***Official Congressional Directory, 1999-2000.** 1217p. 1999. boxed set 45.00 (*0-16-058631-3*, Congress) USGPO.

Official Congressional Directory, 1997-1998. Contrib. by Congress, Joint Committee on Printing. 1997. boxed set 43.00 (*0-16-055120-X*) USGPO.

Official Congressional Directory, 1997-1998. Congress, Joint Committee on Printing Staff. 1997. per. 30.00 (*0-16-055119-6*) USGPO.

***Official Congressional Directory 1999-2000.** Claitors Publishing Co. Staff. 1100p. 1999. 45.00 (*1-57980-444-6*) Claitors.

Official Consolidations: Acts Interpretation Act, 1901. 56p. 1995. reprint ed. 17.95 (*0-644-45419-9*, Pub. by Aust Gov Pub) Accents Pubns.

Official Consolidations: Bankruptcy Act, 1966. 396p. 1995. reprint ed. 32.95 (*0-644-42910-0*, Pub. by Aust Gov Pub) Accents Pubns.

Official Consolidations: Disability Discrimination Act, 1992. 84p. 1995. reprint ed. 19.95 (*0-644-36105-0*, Pub. by Aust Gov Pub) Accents Pubns.

Official Consolidations: Family Law Regulations. 64p. 1995. reprint ed. 20.50 (*0-644-35252-3*, Pub. by Aust Gov Pub) Accents Pubns.

Official Consolidations: Freedom of Information Act, 1982. 108p. 1995. reprint ed. 19.95 (*0-644-43019-2*, Pub. by Aust Gov Pub) Accents Pubns.

Official Consolidations: Migration Act, 1958. 256p. 1995. reprint ed. 38.95 (*0-644-46024-5*, Pub. by Aust Gov Pub) Accents Pubns.

Official Consolidations: Privacy Act, 1988. 126p. 1995. reprint ed. 21.95 (*0-644-43084-2*, Pub. by Aust Gov Pub) Accents Pubns.

Official Consolidations: Social Security Act, 1991, 4 vols. 3000p. 1995. reprint ed. 123.50 (*0-644-46524-7*, Pub. by Aust Gov Pub) Accents Pubns.

Official Consolidations: Superannuation Act, 1990. 432p. 1995. reprint ed. 45.50 (*0-644-45552-7*, Pub. by Aust Gov Pub) Accents Pubns.

Official Consolidations: Trade Practices Act, 1974. 260p. 1995. reprint ed. 17.95 (*0-644-42880-5*, Pub. by Aust Gov Pub) Accents Pubns.

Official Conversations & Meetings of Dean Acheson, 1949-1953. Dean Acheson et al. LC 86-892618. (Presidential Documents Ser.). 5 p. 1980. write for info. (*0-89093-354-5*) U Pubns Amer.

Official Cookbook Register. Suzie Stephens. (Illus.). 1988. pap. 4.95 (*0-913290-75-0*) Camaro Pub.

Official "Cooking Hot & Spicy Food with Beer" Cookbook. Robert Bennett. (Illus.). 82p. 1993. pap. 9.95 (*0-9638956-0-5*); disk 9.95 (*0-9638956-1-3*) R Bennett.

Official Couch Potato Cookbook. Mary B. Jung et al. 96p. (Orig.). 1988. mass mkt. 5.95 (*0-446-38927-7*, Pub. by Warner Bks) Little.

Official Couch Potato Handbook. Jack Munoo. 100p. 1987. pap. text 6.95 (*0-86719-358-1*) Last Gasp.

Official Country Music Directory, 1994. Steve Tolin. 1994. pap. text 90.00 (*1-882921-03-8*) Entertain Media.

Official Country Music Directory, 1993. Steve Tolin. 1993. pap. 80.00 (*1-882921-01-1*) Entertain Media.

Official Criticism Manual: Perfecting the Art of Giving & Receiving Criticism. Deborah Bright. 132p. 1991. 23.35 (*0-9635783-0-8*) Bright Ent.

Official CSPA Stylebook. 20th rev. ed. Ed. by Helen F. Smith. 80p. (Orig.). (YA). (gr. 9-12). 1996. pap. text 4.95 (*0-916084-26-4*) Columbia Scholastic.

Official Dark Reign Strategy Guide. Steve Schafer. 216p. 1997. 19.99 (*1-56686-703-7*) Brady Pub.

Official Deathtrap Dungeon: Strategy Guide. Glenn Broderick. LC 98-106489. 1997. pap. text 19.95 (*0-911295-44-5*) Air Age.

***Official Descent: Free Space II Strategy Guide.** Bart Farkas. 1999. pap. 19.99 (*0-9673565-4-7*) Illumination Pubns.

Official Descent: Freespace the Great War Strategy Guide. Bradygames Staff. 1999. pap. 19.99 (*1-56686-787-8*) Brady Pub.

***Official Desert Fighter Strategy Guide.** Bart Farkas. (Illus.). 1999. pap. 19.99 (*0-9673565-5-5*) Illumination Pubns.

***Official Dick Van Dyke Show Book.** Vince Waldron. (Illus.). 2000. 18.95 (*1-55783-453-9*) Applause Bks.

Official Dick Van Dyke Show Book: The Definitive History & Ultimate Viewer's Guide to Television's Most Enduring Comedy. Vince Waldron. LC 94-17317. (Illus.). 432p. 1994. pap. 14.45 (*0-7868-8008-2*, Pub. by Hyperion) Time Warner.

Official Directory of Connecticut, Rhode Island & Vermont Libraries & Media Centers 1998-99. Ed. by Andrew V. Ippolito. 250p. 1998. per. 89.95 (*0-935912-73-8*) LDA Pubs.

Official Directory of New Jersey Libraries & Media Centers 1998. Ed. by Andrew V. Ippolito. 300p. 1998. per. 89.95 (*0-935912-72-X*) LDA Pubs.

***Official Directory of New Jersey Libraries & Media Centers 1999.** Ed. by Andrew V. Ippolito. 300p. 1999. pap. 89.95 (*0-935912-74-6*) LDA Pubs.

Official Directory of New York State Business Permits. New York State of Business Permits Office. Ed. by Ruth S. Walters & OBPRA Staff. 1792p. 1992. pap. 35.00 (*0-942954-51-3*) NYS Bar.

Official Directory of New York State Business Permits. New York State of Business Permits Office. Ed. by Ruth S. Walters & OBPRA Staff. 1993. 25.00 (*0-942954-60-2*) NYS Bar.

***Official Directory to U. S. Flea Markets.** 7th ed. Ed. by Kitty Werner. 480p. 2000. pap. 10.00 (*0-676-60190-1*) Hse Collectbls.

Official Directory to United States Flea Markets. 6th ed. Kitty Werner. 432p. 1998. pap. 9.95 (*0-676-60139-1*) Random.

Official Disability Guidelines: Length of Disability Data by ICD-9-CM from CDC & OSHA Plus NHDS Hospital Length of Stay. Ed. by Philip L. Denniston. (Orig.). 1995. pap. 150.00 (*1-880891-21-2*) Work-Loss Data.

Official District of Columbia Book of Numbers. Nathaniel A. Dickens. Ed. by Brenda Lipkowitz. LC 83-90486. (Illus.). 90p. (Orig.). 1984. pap. 4.00 (*0-916191-00-1*) Dickens Pubns.

***Official Documents Bearing on the Armed Neutrality of 1780 & 1800.** LC 99-48342. 2000. write for info. (*1-57588-602-2*) W S Hein.

Official Documents of the European Community Telecommunications Policy. 338p. (Orig.). (C). 1994. pap. text 75.00 (*0-7881-0540-X*) DIANE Pub.

Official Dog Codependents Handbook: For People Who Love Their Dogs Too Much! Ronnie Sellers. (Illus.). 128p. 1996. pap. text 11.95 (*1-56906-047-9*) R Sellers Prods.

Official Dog I. Q. Test. Peter Mandel. (Illus.). 47p. 1995. pap. 6.95 (*1-56625-015-3*) Bonus Books.

Official Doll Record Book & Journal. Marlene Hochman. Ed. by Kenneth Hochman. 176p. (Orig.). 1995. ring bd. 49.50 (*0-9611774-2-X*) Ultimate Coll.

Official Drumbeat 3 Construction Kit. Cherly Kirk. 2000. text 39.99 (*0-672-31550-5*) Sams.

Official Dumper's Handbook. Tyrone Lawrence. 120p. 1996. pap. 9.95 (*0-9658676-1-7*) Dataway Inc.

Official E-Baying Guide to Buying, Selling & Collecting Just about Anything. Laura F. Kaiser & Michael Kaiser. 256p. 1999. per. 13.00 (*0-684-86954-3*, Fireside) S&S Trade Pap.

***Official Earth Day Guide to Planet Repair.** Denis Hayes. LC 99-50921. 192p. 2000. pap. 11.95 (*1-55963-809-5*) Island Pr.

***Official Easy-Bake Cookbook, Vol. 1.** Lucia Monfried. (Illus.). 48p. 1999. pap. 7.99 (*0-525-46256-2*, Dutton Child) Peng Put Young Read.

***Official Ebay Guide to Buying Selling & Collecting Just about Anything.** 1999. per. 26.00 (*0-684-87372-9*) S&S Trade.

Official Electronic Keyboard Blue Book, 1991-1992. 320p. (Orig.). 1991. pap. 50.00 (*0-7935-0708-1*, 00001585) H Leonard.

Official Electronic Keyboard Blue Book, 1994. rev. ed. 224p. per. 50.00 (*0-7935-3191-8*, 00330107) H Leonard.

Official Encouragement, Institutional Discouragement: Minorities in Academe - The Native American Experience. William G. Tierney. LC 92-10048. (Interpretive Perspectives on Education & Policy Ser.). 192p. 1992. text 73.25 (*0-89391-829-6*) Ablx Pub.

Official Encouragement, Institutional Discouragement: Minorities in Academe - The Native American Experience. William G. Tierney. LC 92-10048. (Interpretive Perspectives on Education & Policy Ser.). 192p. (C). 1992. pap. text 39.50 (*0-89391-946-2*) Ablx Pub.

Official Encyclopedia of Scotland Yard. Martin Fido & Keith Skinner. 1999. text 39.95 (*1-85227-712-2*, Pub. by Virgin Bks) London Brdge.

Official Exceptions to the Rules of Golf. Henry Beard. 1992. 15.00 (*0-679-40886-X*) Villard Books.

Official Exceptions to the Rules of Golf. Henry Beard & John Boswell. LC 97-6647. 160p. 1997. pap. 15.95 (*0-679-74123-2*) Villard Books.

Official Excite Yellow Pages. Cheri Robinson. 912p. 1998. pap. 34.99 (*0-7645-3145-X*) IDG Bks.

Official Export Guide, Supplement II, 1996. Ed. by Tery Moran-Lever. 336p. 1996. pap. text 95.00 (*0-9649630-0-0*) Primedia Directories.

Official Export Guide: 1997 Edition. Ed. by Tery Moran-Lever. (Illus.). 2492p. 1996. text 425.00 (*0-9649630-6-X*) Primedia Directories.

Official Export Guide: 1998 Edition. Ed. by Tery Moran-Lever. (ISSN Ser.: No. 0278-6389). (Illus.). 2612p. 1997. text 455.00 (*0-9649630-9-4*) Primedia Directories.

***Official Export Guide: 1999 Edition.** Tery Moran-Lever. 2612p. 1999. 575.00 (*1-891131-03-6*) Primedia Directories.

***Official Export Guide: 2000 Edition.** Ed. by Tery Moran-Lever. (Illus.). 2648p. 1999. 475.00 (*1-891131-06-0*) Primedia Directories.

***Official F/A 18e Super Hornet Strategy Guide.** Bart Farkas. 1999. pap. 19.99 (*0-9673565-6-3*) Illumination Pubns.

***Official Factory Guide to Building Ford Short Track Power.** Ford Racing Engineers Staff. (Do-it-Yourself Guides Ser.). (Illus.). 128p. 2000. pap. 18.95 (*1-884089-47-X*, Pub. by CarTech) Voyageur Pr.

Official Fair-Use Guidelines: Complete Texts of Four Official Documents Arranged for Use by Educators. 3rd ed. Intro. by J. K. Miller. 1987. pap. 5.95 (*0-914143-11-5*, Copy Info Svc) Assn Ed Comm Tech.

Official Fantasy Hockey Guide, 1998-1999: Definitive Hockey Pool Reference. 2nd ed. Stephen Cerutti. Ed. by Scott Morrison. (Illus.). 288p. 1998. pap. 14.95 (*1-57243-272-1*) Triumph Bks.

Official Financial for Developing Countries. International Monetary Fund Staff. LC 94-238681. (World Economic & Financial Surveys Ser.). 85p. 1994. pap. 20.00 (*1-55775-378-4*) Intl Monetary.

Official Financing for Developing Countries. (World Economic & Financial Surveys Ser.). 1995. pap. 20.00 (*1-55775-537-X*) Intl Monetary.

Official Financing for Developing Countries. Anthony R. Boote et al. LC 96-135458. 120 p. 1995. write for info. (*1-55775-527-2*) Intl Monetary.

Official Fitness Boot Camp Workout. Andrew Flach et al. (Official Fitness Ser.). (Illus.). 192p. 1999. pap. 14.95 (*1-57826-033-7*, Pub. by Hatherleigh) Norton.

Official Flashback: The Quest for Identity Strategy Guide. Corey Sandler. 96p. (Orig.). pap. text 7.95 (*0-9636392-0-X*) U S Gold.

Official Florida Coloring Book, Vol. 1. rev. ed. Carol Shore. (Illus.). 40p. (J). (ps-5). 1986. pap. 1.95 (*0-9612136-1-2*) C Shore Pr.

Official Florida Natives: A Friendly Introduction. Carol Shore. LC 84-91492. (Illus.). 56p. (J). (ps-7). 1985. pap. 2.95 (*0-9612136-2-0*) C Shore Pr.

Official Football Association Yearbook 1993-94. Football Association Staff. 1993. pap. write for info. (*0-09-177889-1*, Pub. by Random) Random House.

Official Foxtail Book. Klutz Press Editors. (Illus.). 80p. 1991. per. 11.95 (*1-878257-02-1*) Klutz.

Official Freebies for Teachers. 7th ed. Dianne J. Woo. Ed. by Freebies Magazine Staff. (Illus.). 128p. 1999. pap. 8.95 (*0-7373-0064-7*, 00647W) NTC Contemp Pub Co.

Official Frequent Flyer Guidebook. 3rd ed. Randy Petersen. 495p. (Orig.). 1994. pap. 14.99 (*1-882994-01-9*) AirPress.

Official Frequent Flyer Guidebook. 4th ed. Randy Petersen. 500p. (Orig.). 1995. pap. 14.99 (*1-882994-02-7*) AirPress.

Official Fundraising Almanac. Jerold Panas. LC 89-61428. 424p. 1989. pap. 50.00 (*0-944496-07-5*) Precept Pr.

Official G. I. Joe Collectors Guide to Completing & Collating Your G. I. Joes & Accessories. James DeSimone. (J). 1993. pap. 11.94 (*0-9635956-0-1*) GI Joe Collect.

Official Gamelan's Java Directory. Rebecca Tapley et al. 264p. 1996. pap. text 29.99 incl. audio compact disk (*1-56276-449-7*, Ziff-Davis Pr) Que.

O

Official Garlic Lover's Handbook. 116p. pap. 7.95 (*0-318-14782-3*) Lovers Stinking.

Official Garlic Lover's Handbook. Lloyd J. Harris & Rose Harris. (Illus.). 144p. (Orig.). 1986. pap. 7.95 (*0-943186-15-3*) Aris Bks.

Official Gazette of the United States Patent & Trademark Office: Patents. Government Printing Office Staff. per. 922.00 (*0-16-009624-3*) USGPO.

Official Gazette of the United States Patent & Trademark Office: Trademarks. Government Printing Office Staff. 1989. per. 666.00 (*0-16-009679-0*) USGPO.

Official Gd Wine Snb. Leonard S. Bernstein. LC 81-18707. 180p. 1982. pap. 10.95 (*0-688-01605-7*, Quil) HarperTrade.

Official General Hospital Trivia Book. Gerard J. Waggett. LC 97-20747. (Illus.). 208p. (J). 1997. pap. 8.70 (*0-7868-8275-1*, Pub. by Hyperion) Time Warner.

Official Generation 'n Pocket Guide to Bill Cruz's CubanAmericanisms. Bill Cruz. Ed. by Bill Teck. (ENG & SPA.). 22p. 1997. pap. 4.95 (*0-9661173-0-1*) O A Prodns.

Official Gift in Ancient Egypt. Edward Bleiberg. LC 96-20282. 192p. 1996. text 27.95 (*0-8061-2871-2*, 2871) U of Okla Pr.

Official Godzilla Compendium: A 40 Year Retrospective. J. D. Lees & M. Cerasini. LC 97-75898. 1998. pap. 16.00 (*0-679-88822-5*) Random.

Official Goldbuster Guidebook: Gold Games, Trivia Treasures & Double Takes. David Hage & Dennis Hage. (Illus.). 82p. (Orig.). 1989. 12.95 (*0-9622443-0-9*); lp. write for info. (*0-318-64883-0*) Doubletake Prodns.

***Official Goods Vehicle Driving Manual.** Driving Standards Agency Staff. (Illus.). vi, 224p. 1999. 30.00 (*0-11-552195-X*, Pub. by Statnry Office) Balogh.

Official GRE CGS Directory of Graduate Programs Vol. C: Social Sciences & Education. 16th ed. Ets Staff. 1997. pap. 20.00 (*0-446-39624-9*, Pub. by Warner Bks) Little.

Official GRE CGS Directory of Graduate Programs Vol. D: Arts, Humanities & Other Fields. 16th ed. Educational Testing Service Staff. 1997. pap. 20.00 (*0-446-39626-5*, Pub. by Warner Bks) Little.

Official GRE CGS Directory of Graduate Programs Vol. A: Natural Sciences. 16th ed. Ets Staff. 1997. pap. 20.00 (*0-446-39620-6*, Pub. by Warner Bks) Little.

Official GRE CGS Directory of Graduate Programs Vol. B: Engineering & Business. 16th ed. Ets Staff. 1997. pap. 20.00 (*0-446-39622-2*, Pub. by Warner Bks) Little.

Official Guide: Magic Gathering. Randy Buehler. 1999. pap. 16.99 (*0-7869-1375-4*, Pub. by TSR Inc) Random.

Official Guide: Outdoor Power Equipment. annuals 468p. 1997. write for info. (*0-318-17737-4*) NAEDA.

Official Guide for GMAT Review. Educational Testing Service Staff. 1988. pap. 9.95 (*0-446-35302-7*, Pub. by Warner Bks) Little.

Official Guide for GMAT Review. 9th ed. Ets Staff. (Illus.). 524p. 1997. pap. 19.95 (*0-446-39638-9*, Pub. by Warner Bks) Little.

***Official Guide for GMAT Review.** 10th ed. 2000. pap. write for info. (*0-446-39666-4*) Warner Bks.

Official Guide for GMAT Review, 1990-92. Educational Testing Service Staff. 465p. 1990. pap. 9.95 (*0-446-39207-3*, Pub. by Warner Bks) Little.

Official Guide Software for GMAT Review (IBM Edition), 1990-92. Educational Testing Service Staff. 1990. pap. 59.95 (*0-446-39211-1*, Pub. by Warner Bks) Little.

Official Guide to a Progressive Program for Raising Better Rabbits & Cavies. 240p. 6.50 (*0-318-32889-5*) Am Rabbit Breeders.

Official Guide to Adoptions in Eastern Europe, 1994-1995, 3 vols., Set. David Liviano. 2820p. 1994. pap. 200.00 incl. VHS (*0-9640536-0-8*) Melador Pubng.

Official Guide to Airline Careers. Alexander C. Morton. write for info. (*0-318-59582-6*) S&S Trade.

Official Guide to American Attitudes: Who Thinks What about the Issues That Shape Our Lives. Susan Mitchell. 415p. 1996. 89.95 (*1-885070-02-0*) New Strategist.

***Official Guide to American Historic Inns.** 7th ed. Deborah Edwards Sakach. (Illus.). 518p. 1999. pap. 15.95 (*1-888050-07-1*, Pub. by American Hist) Quality Bks IL.

Official Guide to Artifacts of Ancient Civilizations. Alex G. Malloy. 256p. 1997. pap. 19.95 (*0-676-60079-4*) Random.

Official Guide to Authorware 4. Nick Roberts. LC 97-204052. 704p. 1997. pap. 54.95 incl. cd-rom (*0-201-68899-9*) Addison-Wesley.

Official Guide to Blade Runner. Brady Games Staff. 192p. 1997. 19.99 (*1-56686-728-2*) Brady Pub.

Official Guide to Buying, Connecting & Using Consumer Electronics Products. (Illus.). 171p. (Orig.). 1995. pap. write for info. (*0-7908-0055-1*) Elec Ind Assn.

Official Guide to Caribbean Medical Schools. Salaish K. Sarin & Ravi K. Yalamanchi. (Illus.). 104p. 1997. pap. text 14.95 (*0-9663087-0-0*) CaribMed.

Official Guide to Chaos Island. Christine Cain. 192p. 1997. pap. 14.99 (*1-56686-740-1*) Brady Pub.

Official Guide to Coin Grading & Counterfeit Detection. David Hall. 400p. 1997. pap. 29.95 (*0-676-60040-9*) Random.

Official Guide to Collecting Applied Color Label Soda Bottles. Thomas E. Marsh. (Illus.). 104p. (Orig.). 1992. write for info. (*0-9633682-0-6*) T E Marsh.

Official Guide to Collecting Applied Color Soda Bottles, Vol. II. Thomas E. Marsh. 105p. (J). (ps up). pap., per. write for info. (*0-9633682-1-4*) T E Marsh.

Official Guide to Colonial Williamsburg. Michael Olmert et al. LC 98-17476. 176p. 1998. pap. 6.95 (*0-87935-184-5*) Colonial Williamsburg.

Official Guide to Command & Conquer. Mike Fay et al. 428p. 1995. 19.99 (*1-56686-247-7*) Brady Pub.

Official Guide to Communicator 4.5, Windows Edition. Phil James & Richard Cravens. 900p. 1998. 49.99 incl. cd-rom (*1-57610-325-0*) Coriolis Grp.

Official Guide to Corel VENTURA 7, Vol. 7. Ed Brown et al. LC 97-185331. 656p. (Orig.). 1997. pap. text 34.99 (*0-07-882169-X*) Osborne-McGraw.

Official Guide to Corel Wordperfect Suite 7 for Windows 95. Alan Neibauer. LC 96-219758. 656p. 1996. pap. text 34.99 (*0-07-882237-8*) Osborne-McGraw.

CorelDRAW 7: The Official Guide. Foster Coburn. LC 97-156031. 1997. pap. text 34.99 (*0-07-882278-5*) Osborne-McGraw.

Official Guide to CorelDRAW! 6 for Windows 95. Martin S. Matthews & Carole B. Matthews. (Illus.). 742p. 1995. pap. text 34.95 (*0-07-882168-1*) McGraw.

***Official Guide to DATACAD 9.** Michael Smith. (Architect's CAD Library). (Illus.). 800p. 2000. pap. text 49.95 (*0-07-136356-4*) McGraw.

Official Guide to Fallout. Bill Keith & Nina Keith. 216p. 1997. 19.99 (*1-56686-713-4*) Brady Pub.

Official Guide to Goldfish. Goldfish Society of America Staff. (Illus.). 128p. 1992. pap. 11.95 (*0-86622-607-9*, TS156) TFH Pubns.

Official Guide to Goosebumps: Attack of the Mutant. Brady Games Staff. (Illus.). 192p. (J). 1997. 14.99 (*1-56686-738-X*) Brady Pub.

Official Guide to Gunmarks. 3rd ed. Robert H. Balderson. (Illus.). 352p. 1996. pap. 15.00 (*0-676-60039-5*) Hse Collectbls.

Official Guide to Heavy Gear. Brady Games Staff. 192p. 1997. 19.99 (*1-56686-726-6*) Brady Pub.

Official Guide to Hiking the Grand Canyon. rev. ed. Scott Thybony. LC 94-75571. 68p. 1997. pap. 11.95 (*0-938216-48-1*) GCA.

Official Guide to Household Spending see Household Spending: Who Spends How Much on What

Official Guide to Janes Advanced Tactical Fighters. Origin Systems Inc. Staff. 1996. pap. text 19.95 (*0-7845-0739-2*) Elect Arts.

Official Guide to Junior Golf. (Illus.). 150p. 1998. pap. 4.95 (*1-891965-00-X*) Belmont Intl.

Official Guide to LGB Trains. Bob Roth & Decker Doggett. LC 98-178884. (Illus.). 193p. 1998. 59.95 (*0-89778-302-6*, 10-7815, Kalmbach Books) Kalmbach.

Official Guide to Living & Making Money in Costa Rica. LC 98-129824. (Illus.), 225p. 1997. pap. 15.00 (*9968-9779-3-4*) Off Gde Bks.

Official Guide to Mace: The Dark Ages. Brady Games Staff. (Illus.). 112p. (J). 1997. pap. 11.99 (*1-56686-739-8*) Brady Pub.

Official Guide to Marvel Cave. 2nd ed. Ronald L. Martin. (Illus.). 1987. pap. 3.95 (*0-685-18052-2*) Ozark Mtn Pubs.

Official Guide to MBA Programs. Educational Testing Service Staff. 1988. pap. 9.95 (*0-446-35300-0*, Pub. by Warner Bks) Little.

Official Guide to MBA Programs. 8th ed. 1996. pap. write for info. (*0-446-39610-9*) Warner Bks.

Official Guide to MBA Programs, 1992-94. Ed. by Jodi Z. Krasna. 465p. 1992. pap. 13.95 (*0-446-39441-6*) Warner Bks.

Official Guide to Millennium. Jane Goldman. 288p. 1998. pap. 16.00 (*0-06-105384-8*, HarperPrism) HarpC.

Official Guide to Mini SQL 2.0. Brian Jepson & David Hughes. LC 97-37927. 432p. 1998. pap., pap. text 49.99 incl. cd-rom, audio compact disk (*0-471-24535-6*) Wiley.

***Official Guide to October Expansion.** 1999. pap. 16.99 (*0-7869-1435-1*) TSR Inc.

***Official Guide to Pricing Your Crafts.** Sylvia Landman. 1999. pap. 16.99 (*0-7615-2123-2*) Prima Pub.

Official Guide to Programming with CGI.pm: The Standard for Building Web Scripts. Lincoln Stein. LC 98-10724. 320p. 1998. pap. 34.99 (*0-471-24744-8*) Wiley.

Official Guide to Skullmonkeys. Brady Games Staff. 112p. 1998. pap. 11.99 (*1-56686-741-X*) Brady Pub.

Official Guide to Success, Vol. I. rev. ed. Tom Hopkins. 153p. 1983. 19.95 (*0-938636-05-7*) T Hopkins Intl.

Official Guide to Texas State Parks. Laurence E. Parent. Ed. by George Zappler. LC 96-22956. (Illus.). 216p. 1997. pap. 19.95 (*0-292-76575-4*, Pub. by TX Prks & Wldlife) U of Tex Pr.

Official Guide to the Perkins Act of 1998. Ed. by Paul Plawin. 200p. (Orig.). 1998. pap. 34.95 (*0-89514-003-9*) ACTE.

Official Guide to the Smithsonian. LC 95-24972. (Illus.). 192p. 1996. pap. 7.95 (*1-56098-667-0*) Smithsonian.

Official Guide to Turok: Dinosaur Hunter. (Illus.). 1997. pap. 11.99 (*0-614-28466-X*) MCP SW Interactive.

Official Guide to Turok: Dinosaur Hunter. David Cassady. 128p. 1997. 11.99 (*1-56686-681-2*) Brady Pub.

Official Guide to U. S. Commemorative Coins: Current Information That All Collectors Want & Need. David L. Lpanz. (Illus.). 320p. 1999. pap. 12.95 (*1-56625-124-9*) Bonus Books.

Official Guide to U. S. Law School, 1999. Law School Admission Council Staff. LC 98-14303. 448p. 1998. pap. 20.00 (*0-7679-0078-2*) Broadway BDD.

Official Guide to U. S. Law Schools 2000. Law School Adimisson Council. (Illus.). 448p. 1999. pap. 20.00 (*0-8129-9046-3*, Times Bks) Crown Pub Group.

Official Guide to Urza's Destiny. Will Mcdermott. (Magic the Gathering Ser.). 1999. pap. 11.99 (*0-7869-1400-9*, Pub. by TSR Inc) Random.

***Official Guide to Urza's Legacy.** Will Mcdermott. (Magic the Gathering Ser.). 1999. pap. 11.99 (*0-7869-1353-3*, Pub. by TSR Inc) Random.

Official Guide to Urza's Saga. Will Mcdermott. 1998. pap. 16.99 (*0-7869-1302-9*, Pub. by TSR Inc) Random.

***Official Guide to U.S. Law Schools 2001.** Bonnie Gordon. 2000. pap. 19.50 (*0-942639-69-3*) Law Schl Admission.

Official Guide to Using OS-2 Warp. Karla Stagray. 552p. 1995. pap. 29.99 (*1-56884-466-2*) IDG Bks.

Official Guidebook to Baltimore & Beyond. James F. Waesche & Roland H. Read. (Illus.). 112p. (Orig.). 1988. pap. 4.25 (*0-9614299-2-5*) Read Pub Group.

Official Guidebook to Boston & Its Neighborhoods, 97-98. Parsons, Friedmann & Central, Inc. Staff. (ENG, FRE, GER, ITA & JPN., Illus.). 120p. (Orig.). 1997. pap. 4.95 (*1-887819-00-2*) P F & C Inc.

***Official Guitar Price Guide 2001.** Alan Greenwood. 336p. 2000. pap. 19.95 (*1-884883-11-7*) Vintage Guitar.

Official Handbook for Boys. Boy Scouts of America Staff. (Illus.). 416p. (J). (gr. 3 up). 1996. reprint ed. pap. 14.95 (*1-55709-441-1*) Applewood.

Official Handbook for New Home Salespeople. Bob Schultz. (Official New Home Sales Development System Ser.: Vol. 1). 148p. 1990. pap. 34.95 (*0-9678471-1-7*) New Home Spec.

Official Handbook of the American Quarter Horse Association. 37th ed. (Illus.). 168p. 1989. 1.00 (*0-318-41062-1*) Am Qtr Horse.

***Official Harvard Student Agencies Bartending Course.** 3rd ed. Harvard Student Agencies, Inc. Staff. (Illus.). 224p. 2000. pap. 12.95 (*0-312-25286-2*) St Martin.

Official Hayes Modem Companion. Caroline M. Halliday. LC 94-75047. (Illus.). 430p. 1994. pap. 29.95 (*1-56884-072-1*) IDG Bks.

Official Heavy Gear II Strategy Guide. Walker Mark H. LC 98-73573. (Brady Games Strategy Guides Ser.). (Illus.). 223p. 1999. pap. 19.99 (*1-56686-834-3*) Brady Pub.

Official Helicopter Specification Book. (Illus.). 1997. spiral bd. 50.00 (*0-943791-94-4*) HeliValues.

Official Herbs: Botanical Substances in the United States Pharmacopoeias: 1820-1990. Wade Boyle. (Illus.). 97p. (Orig.). 1991. pap. 12.95 (*0-9623518-3-0*) Eclectic Med.

Official Hiking Guide Book to Grand County. Susie Masterson. (Illus.). 44p. 1998. pap. 9.95 (*0-9665375-0-5*) GuestGuide.

Official Histories: Essays & Bibliographies from Around the World. Ed. by Robin Higham. 644p. 1970. 18.00 (*0-89126-087-0*) MA-AH Pub.

Official History & Manual of the Grand United Order of Odd Fellows in America. Charles H. Brooks. LC 74-157362. (Black Heritage Library Collection). 1977. 25.95 (*0-8369-8800-0*) Ayer.

Official History of Free Masonry among the Colored People in North America: Tracing the Growth of Masonry from 1717 Down to the Present Day, Bringing to Light Many Interesting Facts Unknown to the Great Body of the Craft. William H. Grimshaw. 415p. 1995. reprint ed. pap. 24.95 (*1-56459-487-4*) Kessinger Pub.

Official History of Freemasonry among the Colored People in North America. William H. Grimshaw. LC 74-157370. (Black Heritage Library Collection). 1977. 24.95 (*0-8369-8808-6*) Ayer.

Official History of Fulton County. Walter G. Cooper. LC 78-12918. 1978. reprint ed. 35.00 (*0-87152-280-2*) Reprint.

Official History of Karate in America: The Golden Age, 1968-1986. Al Weiss & David Weiss. Ed. by Stuart Sobel. LC 96-68764. (Illus.). 384p. 1997. text 29.95 (*0-9615126-8-7*) Pro Action Pub.

Official History of the Melrose Sevens. Walter Allan. (Illus.). 185p. 1995. 34.95 (*1-85158-660-1*, Pub. by Mainstream Pubng) Trafalgar.

Official Hogan's Heroes Companion. Nathan Shive. LC 95-19111. (Illus.). 304p. 1996. 12.95 (*0-02-860413-X*) Macmillan.

Official Honeymooners Treasury. Peter Crescenti. 1989. 8.98 (*0-88365-739-2*) Galahad Bks.

***Official ICAEW Directory of Firms.** Waterlow Staff. 850p. 1999. 524.00 (*0-333-67378-6*, Pub. by Waterlow Info Services) St Mut.

***Official ICAEW List of Members.** Waterlow Staff. 1000p. 1999. 352.00 (*0-333-67381-6*, Pub. by Waterlow Info Services) St Mut.

Official Icky-Poo Book. John Cassidy. (Illus.). 70p. (Orig.). 1990. pap. 10.95 (*0-932592-90-2*) Klutz.

***Official Illustrated History of the FA Cup.** B. Butler. 1998. text 55.00 (*0-7472-2276-2*, Pub. by Headline Bk Pub) Trafalgar.

***Official Illustrated NHL History: From the Original Six to a Global Game.** Arthur Pincus. 1999. pap. 36.95 (*1-57243-344-2*) Triumph Bks.

***Official Insignia of Native American Tribes: Study Pursuant to P. L. 105-330.** Ed. by Eleanor Meltzer. (Illus.). 47p. 2000. pap. write for info. (*0-9668180-3-2*) Work Grp Intell Rghts.

Official Integral Precancel Type List & Handbook. (Illus.). 1962. 1.50 (*0-685-46872-0*) G W Noble.

Official Internet Dictionary: A Comprehensive Reference for Professionals. Ed. by Russ Bahorsky. LC 98-10585. 227p. 1998. pap. text 49.00 (*0-86587-606-1*, 606) Gov Insts.

Official Internet Directory. 3rd ed. 900p. 1995. 29.99 (*1-56205-439-2*) New Riders Pub.

Official Internet World Guide to Internet Multimedia. Gary Welz. 250p. 1995. 19.99 (*0-614-10084-4*) Mecklermedia.

Official Internet World Internet Mall: A Shopper's Guide to the Internet. Dave Taylor. 150p. 1996. 19.95 (*0-88736-993-6*) Mecklermedia.

Official Internet World Internet Security Handbook. William Stallings. 320p. 1995. pap. 29.99 (*1-56884-700-9*) IDG Bks.

Official Internet World Internet Yellow Pages. Gregory B. Newby. 960p. 1995. pap. 39.99 (*1-56884-343-7*) IDG Bks.

Official Internet World Manual of Web Style. Patrick J. Lynch & Phillip I. Simon. 200p. 1995. 19.99 (*1-57207-016-1*) Mecklermedia.

Official Internet World 60 Minute Guide to VRML. Sebastian Hassinger. 218p. 1995. pap. 19.99 (*1-56884-710-6*) IDG Bks.

Official Internet World 60 Minute Guide to Internet. Andrew Kantor. 208p. 1995. pap. 19.99 (*1-56884-342-9*) IDG Bks.

Official Internet World 60 Minute Guide to JAVA. Ed Tittel. 288p. 1995. pap. 19.99 (*1-56884-711-4*) IDG Bks.

Official Internet World World-Wide Web Yellow Pages. Marshall Breeding. 912p. 1995. pap. 39.99 (*1-56884-344-5*) IDG Bks.

***Official Internet Yellow Pages 2001.** 1200p. 2000. 29.99 (*0-7897-2435-9*) Que.

Official Interpretations of Rural Under-Development: Mexico in the 1970s. Merilee S. Grindle. (Research Reports: No. 20). 49p. (Orig.). (C). 1981. pap. 5.00 (*0-935391-19-3*, RR-20) UCSD Ctr US-Mex.

Official IRS Answers to the One Thousand Most Frequently Asked Taxpayer Questions: 1995 Edition. Internal Revenue Service Staff. (Illus.). 300p. (Orig.). (C). 1995. pap. 7.95 (*1-56924-879-6*) Marlowe & Co.

Official ISRA Baseball Handbook: How to Beg, Borrow & Steal Your Way to a Pennant. Don Maddox. (International Sports Replay Association Handbooks Ser.). (Illus.). 243p. (Orig.). 1994. pap. 16.95 (*1-883358-18-3*) R&D Pub NJ.

***Official Jagged Alliance 2.** Bart Farkas. (Strategies & Secrets Ser.). (Illus.). 263p. 1999. pap. 19.99 (*0-7821-2441-0*) Sybex.

Official John Wayne Companion. Charles J. Kieskalt. LC 98-5057. (Illus.). 240p. 1998. pap. text 18.95 (*0-8065-1984-3*, Citadel Pr) Carol Pub Group.

Official John Wayne Reference Book. enl. rev. ed. Charles J. Kieskalt. (Illus.). 256p. 1993. pap. 17.95 (*0-8065-1443-4*, Citadel Pr) Carol Pub Group.

Official Journal Vol. 42/OJL278: Customs Tariff & Trade: Tariff & Statistical Nomenclature for the Year 1997. 701p. 2000. pap. 100.00 (*0-614-25694-1*, FXAL-96-152-ENC, Pub. by Comm Europ Commun) Bernan Associates.

Official Judging Handbook. Tom Stovall. (Illus.). 80p. 1975. pap. write for info. (*0-318-62037-5*) Intl Rodeo.

***Official Kick the Can Games Book.** Sharon E. McKay & David MacLeod. (Illus.). 64p. (Orig.). (ps-3). 1998. pap. 13.95 (*1-895897-22-X*) Somerville Hse.

***Official Kids' Book of Baseball.** Godfrey P. Jordan. (Illus.). 144p. (YA). (gr. 6-11). 1999. reprint ed. pap. text 10.00 (*0-7881-6571-2*) DIANE Pub.

***Official Kiss Magazine.** Ed. by Greig O'Brien. (Starlog Movie Ser.: No. 2). 1999. pap. 5.99 (*0-934551-93-6*, Pub. by Starlog Grp Inc) Kable News Co Inc.

***Official Know-It-All Guide to Coins.** Roderick P. Hughes. LC 99-34275. 328p. 1999. pap. 16.95 (*0-88391-006-3*) F Fell Pubs Inc.

***Official Know-It-All Guide to Magic for Beginners.** Walter Gibson. LC 99-16291. 224p. 1999. pap. 16.95 (*0-88391-005-5*) F Fell Pubs Inc.

***Official Know-It-All Guide to Palm Reading.** Litzka R. Gibson. LC 99-16292. 216p. 1999. pap. 16.95 (*0-88391-004-7*) F Fell Pubs Inc.

***Official Know-It-All Guide to Secrets of Mind Power.** Harry Lorayne. LC 99-16290. 224p. 1999. pap. 16.95 (*0-88391-008-X*) F Fell Pubs Inc.

***Official Know-It-All Wedding Planner.** Edith Gilbert. LC 99-16289. 288p. 1999. pap. 16.95 (*0-88391-007-1*) F Fell Pubs Inc.

Official Knowledge: Democratic Education in a Conservative Age. Michael W. Apple. LC 92-35829. 240p. (C). (gr. 13). 1993. pap. 19.99 (*0-415-90749-7*, B0262) Routledge.

Official Knoxville, Tennessee World's Fair Cookbook, 1982. Phila R. Hach. 1981. 7.50 (*0-9606192-0-8*) Hach.

***Official Koosh Book.** Klutz Editors. (Illus.). 88p. 2000. pap. 11.95 (*1-57054-480-8*) Klutz.

Official Kubotan Techniques. Takayuki Kubota & John G. Peters, Jr. (Illus.). 56p. 1981. pap. 5.95 (*0-923401-01-6*) Reliapon Police Prods.

Official Lab Research Notebook. (Chemistry Ser.). 50p. 1997. pap. 7.95 (*0-7637-0515-2*); pap. 9.95 (*0-7637-0516-0*) Jones & Bartlett.

***Official Laboratory Research Notebook.** Jones & Bartlett Publishers Staff. (Illus.). 75p. (C). 1998. pap. text 9.95 (*0-7637-0904-2*) JB Pubns.

Official Laws of Chess. FIDE Staff. 128p. 1990. pap. 14.95 (*0-02-028540-X*) Macmillan.

Official Laws of Chess. Bozidar Kazic et al. (Chess Library). (Illus.). 118p. 1986. pap. 10.95 (*0-02-029050-0*) Macmillan.

Official Leadership in the City: Patterns of Conflict & Cooperation. James H. Svara. (Illus.). 314p. 1990. text 65.00 (*0-19-505762-7*) OUP.

Official Letter Books, 1801 to 1816, 6 vols. William C. Claiborne. Ed. by Dunbar Rowland. LC 72-980. reprint ed. 575.00 (*0-404-01600-6*) AMS Pr.

Official Letters of the Military & Naval Officers of the United States, During the War with Great Britain in the Years 1812, 13, 14, & 15: With Some Additional Letters & Documents Elucidating the History of That Period. Ed. by John Brannan. LC 70-146378. (First American Frontier Ser.). 1971. reprint ed. 29.95 (*0-405-02829-6*) Ayer.

***Official License Plate Book: New Edition.** Thomson C. Murray. (Illus.). 128p. 2000. pap. 16.95 (*1-886777-03-9*, 130115AE, Pub. by Inter Directory) Motorbooks Intl.

Official License Plate Book, 1996. Thomson C. Murray. (Illus.). 128p. 1996. pap. 12.95 (*0-9629962-8-9*) Inter Directory.

Official License Plate Book, 1996: Current Plates of the United States & Canada. Thomson C. Murray. (Illus.). 128p. 1996. 16.95 (*0-9629962-9-7*) Inter Directory.

An Asterisk (*) at the beginning of an entry indicates that the title is appearing for the first time.

Official Lies: How Washington Misleads Us. James T. Bennett & Thomas J. DiLorenzo. 1992. 19.95 (*0-9632701-0-9*) Groom Bks.

***Official Lifeguard Workout.** Andrew Flach. (Illus.). 152p. 2001. pap. 14.95 (*1-57826-061-2*, Pub. by Hatherleigh) Norton.

Official Lite History & Cookbook of the Gulf War. Gordon Rottman et al. (Illus.). 160p. (Orig.). 1991. pap. 6.95 (*0-9623992-1-3*) Electric Strawberry.

Official Lite History & Cookbook of the Vietnam War. Alan Dawson. (Illus.). 160p. 1989. reprint ed. pap. 6.95 (*0-9623992-2-1*) Electric Strawberry.

Official Lite Unauthorized Biography of J. Danforth Quayle. Anne P. Burkett & Steve Sherman. (Illus.). 160p. (Orig.). 1992. pap. 6.95 (*0-9623992-4-8*) Electric Strawberry.

Official Little League Baseball Rules in Pictures. Phil Perez. (J). 1989. 14.15 (*0-606-04288-1*, Pub. by Turtleback) Demco.

Official Little League Baseball Rules in Pictures. rev. ed. Creighton J. Hale. (Illus.). 80p. 1989. pap. 8.95 (*0-399-51531-3*, Perigee Bks) Berkley Pub.

Official Lloyd Llewellyn Collection. Daniel Clowes. (Illus.). 96p. 1989. pap. 12.95 (*0-930193-90-3*) Fantagraph Bks.

***Official LSAT Prep Test with Explanations.** Bonnie Gordon. 2000. pap. 16.50 (*0-942639-68-5*) Law Schl Admission.

***Official LSAT Preptests; 10 Actual.** Law School Admission Staff. (LSAT Ser.). 1999. mass mkt. write for info. (*0-942639-63-4*) Law Schl Admission.

Official LSAT TriplePrep, Vo. 2. 1993. pap. 16.50 (*0-942639-39-1*) Law Schl Admission.

Official LSAT TriplePrep, Vol. 1. 1993. pap. 16.50 (*0-942639-38-3*) Law Schl Admission.

Official LSAT TriplePrep, Vol. 3. 1994. pap. 16.50 (*0-942639-42-1*) Law Schl Admission.

Official LSAT TriplePrep Plus. 1994. 18.50 (*0-942639-43-X*) Law Schl Admission.

Official M. A. X. 2 Strategy Guide. Bradygames Staff. 1998. pap. text 19.99 (*1-56686-789-4*) Brady Pub.

Official Magic: The Gathering Strategies & Secrets. Beth Moursund. 1997. pap. 19.99 (*0-614-28536-4*, Strategies & Secrets) Sybex.

Official Maine Scanner Guide. Ed. by Robert A. Coburn. 304p. (Orig.). 1987. pap. 17.95 (*0-943809-00-2*) Offical NH Scanner.

***Official Major League Baseball Fact Book.** Sporting News Staff. 488p. 2000. pap. text 19.95 (*0-89204-630-9*, 06309C, Contemporary Bks) NTC Contemp Pub Co.

Official Major League Baseball Fact Book: 1998 Edition. Sporting News Staff. (Illus.). 480p. 1998. pap. 19.95 (*0-89204-592-2*) Sporting News.

Official Major League Baseball Fact Book (1999 Edition) Major League Baseball's Official Fact Book. (Illus.). 488p. 1999. pap. 19.95 (*0-89204-606-6*) Sporting News.

Official Major League Baseball Stat Book, 1992. Major League Baseball Properties, Inc. Staff & Baseball Encyclopedia Editors. (Illus.). 480p. 1992. pap. 14.95 (*0-02-079646-3*) Macmillan.

***Official Major League Baseball Trivia.** Ken Shouler. 2000. pap. 10.95 (*0-06-107373-3*, HarpRes) HarpInfo.

Official Major League Fact Book (1997 Edition) Major League Baseball's Official Fact Book. annuals (Illus.). 480p. 1996. pap. 19.95 (*0-89204-570-1*) Sporting News.

Official "M&M's" Book of the Millennium. Larry D. Brimner. LC 99-19359. (Illus.). 32p. (YA). (ps up). 1999. 15.95 (*0-88106-071-2*); pap. 6.95 (*0-88106-072-0*) Charlesbridge Pub.

Official Manly Manual. Colom Keating. 288p. 1993. 15.00 (*1-880092-12-3*) Bright Bks TX.

***Official Manual of the Tennessee Real Estate Commission: 1998-99 Edition.** Lexis Pub Editorial Staff. 179p. 1999. pap. 15.00 (*0-327-09008-1*, 3318513) LEXIS Pub.

Official Map of The X-Files. Harper Collins Staff. 1996. pap. 10.00 (*0-06-105533-6*) HarpC.

Official Marimba Guide to Bongo. Danny Goodman. LC 96-71500. 511p. 1997. 39.99 (*1-57521-254-4*) Sams.

Official Marimba Guide to Castanet. Laura Lemay. LC 96-71499. 354p. 1997. 39.99 (*1-57521-255-2*) Sams.

***Official Mark Knopfler Guitar Styles, Vol. 1.** 152p. 1998. otabind 19.95 (*0-7935-7025-5*); otabind 19.95 (*0-7935-7026-3*) H Leonard.

Official Martian-English Handbook: Be an Expert in "Martian" Without Studying. Clark K. Himeda. 37p. (Orig.). (J). (gr. 1-6). 1991. pap. 3.50 (*0-9621721-0-3*) C K Himeda.

***Official MBA Handbook 1999/2000.** 15th ed. Godfrey Golzen. (Illus.). 340p. 1999. pap. 62.50 incl. cd-rom (*0-273-64247-2*, Pub. by F T P-H) Trans-Atl Phila.

***Official MBA Handbook 2000/2001.** Godfrey Golzen. (Illus.). 512p. 2000. pap. 57.50 (*0-273-64997-3*, Pub. by F T P-H) Trans-Atl Phila.

***Official Methods & Recommended Practices of the AOCS.** 5th ed. Ed. by David Firestone. 1200p. 1998. 600.00 (*0-935315-97-7*) Am Oil Chemists.

Official Methods of Analysis of AOAC International, 2 vols. 17th ed. Ed. by Williams Horwitz. (Illus.). 2000p. 2000. ring bd. 599.00 (*0-935584-54-4*) AOAC Intl.

Official Mickey Mouse Club Book. Lorraine Santoli. (Illus.). 256p. 1995. pap. 9.70 (*0-7868-8042-2*, Pub. by Hyperion) Time Warner.

Official Microsoft ActiveX Web Site Toolkit. Alan Simpson. LC 97-26385. 500p. 1997. pap. text 39.99 incl. cd-rom (*1-57231-572-5*) Microsoft.

Official Microsoft Frontpage 98 Book. Kerry Lehto. LC 97-33679. 416p. 1997. pap. text 24.99 (*1-57231-629-2*) Microsoft.

Official Microsoft FrontPage 2000 Book. W. Brett Polonsky. LC 98-52137. 1999. pap. text 24.99 (*1-57231-992-5*) Microsoft Pr.

Official Microsoft HTML Help Authoring Kit: Understanding, Creating & Migrating to Microsoft HTML Help for the Microsoft Windows 95 & Window. Steve Wexler. LC 97-29233. 300p. 1997. pap. 39.99 (*1-57231-603-9*) Microsoft.

Official Microsoft Image Composer Book. William Tait. LC 97-44406. 352p. 1997. pap. text 34.99 incl. cd-rom (*1-57231-593-8*) Microsoft.

Official Microsoft Internet Explorer Book. Bryan Pfaffenberger. LC 96-33397. 348p. 1996. pap. text 24.95 incl. cd-rom (*1-57231-309-9*) Microsoft.

Official Microsoft Internet Explorer 4.0 Book. Bryan Pfaffenberger. LC 97-41707. 350p. 1997. 24.99 (*1-57231-576-8*) Microsoft.

Official Microsoft Merchant Server Toolkit. Farhad Amirfaiz. LC 97-43124. 400p. 1997. pap. text 79.99 incl. cd-rom (*1-57231-622-5*) Microsoft.

Official Microsoft NetMeeting Book: The Comprehensive Guide to Internet Teleconferencing. Bob Summers. LC 97-39003. 400p. 34.99 incl. cd-rom (*1-57231-816-3*) Microsoft.

Official Microsoft NetMeeting 3.0 Book. Robert Summers. 1999. pap. text 34.99 (*0-7356-0582-3*) Microsoft.

Official Microsoft Site Server 3.0 Commerce Edition Toolkit. 2nd ed. Farhad Amirfaiz. LC 98-11187. 600p. 79.99 incl. cd-rom (*1-57231-813-9*) Microsoft.

Official Middleburg Life Cookbook. Vicky Moon. (Illus.). (Orig.). 1989. 10.00 (*0-9617683-0-4*) Pink Sheet.

Official Military Atlas of the Civil War: Atlas to Accompany the Official Records of the Union & Confederate Armies. C. N. Davis et al. 1979. 72.95 (*0-405-18842-0*, 19368) Ayer.

***Official Military Historical Offices & Sources.** Robin D. S. Higham. LC 99-49148. 416p. 2000. lib. bdg. write for info. (*0-313-28684-1*); lib. bdg. 79.50 (*0-313-30862-4*, Greenwood Pr) Greenwood.

Official Military History of Kansas Regiments During the War for the Suppression of the Great Rebellion. W. S. Burke. 464p. (C). 1995. text 40.00 (*1-878882-07-4*) KS Heritage Pr.

***Official Milky Book & Pen Kit.** Darice Bailer. (Illus.). 48p. (J). (gr. k-3). 2000. pap. 9.99 (*0-689-83806-9*) Litle Simon.

Official Miva Web-Scripting Book: Shopping Carts, Feedback Forms, Guestbooks & More. Kent Multer. LC 99-60719. (Illus.). 400p. 1999. pap. 34.95 (*0-9661032-1-1*, Pub. by Top Floor Pub) IPG Chicago.

Official Monogram U. S. Army Air Service & Air Corps Aircraft Color Guide, 1908-1941, Vol. 1. R. D. Archer. Ed. by T. H. Hitchcock. LC 94-76072. (Illus.). 241p. 1995. 54.95 (*0-914144-46-4*) Monogram Aviation.

Official Monogram U. S. Navy & Marine Corps Aircraft Color Guide 1940-1949, Vol. 2. 2nd ed. John M. Elliott. LC 86-62376. (Illus.). 194p. 1999. 74.95 (*0-914144-32-4*) Monogram Aviation.

Official Monogram U. S. Navy & Marine Corps Aircraft Color Guide 1960-1993, Vol. 4. (Illus.). 1994. 54.95 (*0-914144-34-0*) Monogram Aviation.

Official Mortal Kombat 4 Arcade Secrets. 1997. pap. 11.99 (*0-614-28467-8*) MCP SW Interactive.

Official Mortal Kombat 4 Arcade Secrets. Brady Publishing Staff. 112p. 1997. pap. text 11.99 (*1-56686-690-1*) Brady Pub.

Official Mortal Kombat 4 Fighter's Kompanion Strategy Guide. Bradygames Staff. 1998. pap. text 11.99 (*1-56686-795-9*) Brady Pub.

Official Mortal Kombat 4 Pocket Strategy Guide. Bradygames Staff. 1998. pap. 7.99 (*1-56686-796-7*) Brady Pub.

Official MP3.Com Guide to MP3. Michael Robertson & Ron Simpson. pap. 19.95 (*0-9670574-0-X*) MPThreecom.

Official Mr. Potatohead Cookbook. Ralph Roberts & Pat Roberts. (Illus.). 208p. (Orig.). Date not set. pap. 14.99 (*1-888295-04-X*) Elephant Books.

Official Museum Directory. 28th ed. American Association of Museums Staff. 1997. 219.00 (*0-87217-958-3*) Natl Register.

Official Museum Directory. 28th ed. American Association Of Museums Staff. 1998. pap. text 292.00 (*0-87217-960-5*) Natl Register.

Official Museum Directory 1999, Set, 2 vols. National Register Publishing Co. Staff. 1998. 229.00 (*0-87217-961-3*) Natl Register.

Official Mustang Price Guide. rev. ed. Jerry Heasley. (Illus.). 74p. 1993. reprint ed. pap. 4.95 (*0-9624908-5-7*) CA Mustang Sales.

Official NAIC Annual Statement Blanks: Fraternal. 3rd rev. ed. Ed. by Patti Carli. 160p. 1996. ring bd. 100.00 (*0-89382-392-9*) Nat Assn Insurance.

Official NAIC Annual Statement Blanks: Fraternal. 4th rev. ed. Ed. by Patti Carli. 162p. (C). 1997. ring bd. 100.00 (*0-89382-450-X*, ASB-FM) Nat Assn Insurance.

Official NAIC Annual Statement Blanks: Fraternal, 1994. 130p. (C). 1994. ring bd. 75.00 (*0-89382-272-8*) Nat Assn Insurance.

Official NAIC Annual Statement Blanks: Health Maintenance Organization. rev. ed. Ed. by Patti Carli. 68p. (C). 1997. ring bd. 75.00 (*0-89382-452-6*, ASB-HM) Nat Assn Insurance.

Official NAIC Annual Statement Blanks: Health Maintenance Organizations. 3rd rev. ed. Ed. by Patti Carli. 52p. 1996. ring bd. 75.00 (*0-89382-393-7*) Nat Assn Insurance.

Official NAIC Annual Statement Blanks: Health Maintenance Organizations, 1994. 48p. (C). 1994. ring bd. 50.00 (*0-89382-271-X*) Nat Assn Insurance.

Official NAIC Annual Statement Blanks: Health Maintenance Organizations, 1995. 64p. (C). 1995. ring bd. 50.00 (*0-89382-328-7*) Nat Assn Insurance.

Official NAIC Annual Statement Blanks: Hospital, Medical, & Dental Service or Indemnity Corporation. 3rd rev. ed. Ed. by Patti Carli. 114p. 1996. ring bd. 75.00 (*0-89382-394-5*) Nat Assn Insurance.

Official NAIC Annual Statement Blanks: Hospital, Medical & Dental Service or Indemnity Corporation, 1994. 78p. (C). 1994. ring bd. 50.00 (*0-89382-268-X*) Nat Assn Insurance.

Official NAIC Annual Statement Blanks: Hospital, Medical & Dental Service or Indemnity Corporation, 1995. 98p. (C). 1995. ring bd. 50.00 (*0-89382-326-0*) Nat Assn Insurance.

Official NAIC Annual Statement Blanks: Hospital, Medical, Dental or Indemnity. 6th rev. ed. Ed. by Patti Carli. 104p. (C). 1997. ring bd. 75.00 (*0-89382-453-4*, ASB-MM) Nat Assn Insurance.

Official NAIC Annual Statement Blanks: Life, Accident, & Health. 3rd rev. ed. Ed. by Patti Carli. 192p. 1996. ring bd. 100.00 (*0-89382-390-2*) Nat Assn Insurance.

Official NAIC Annual Statement Blanks: Life, Accident, & Health. 4th rev. ed. Ed. by Patti Carli. 190p. (C). 1997. ring bd. 100.00 (*0-89382-449-6*, ASB-LM) Nat Assn Insurance.

Official NAIC Annual Statement Blanks: Life & Accident & Health, 1994. 222p. (C). 1994. ring bd. 75.00 (*0-89382-230-2*) Nat Assn Insurance.

Official NAIC Annual Statement Blanks: Limited Health Service Organization. Ed. by Patti Carli. 46p. 1996. ring bd. 75.00 (*0-89382-395-3*) Nat Assn Insurance.

Official NAIC Annual Statement Blanks: Limited Health Service Organization. 6th rev. ed. Ed. by Patti Carli. 51p. (C). 1997. ring bd. 75.00 (*0-89382-451-8*, ASB-SM) Nat Assn Insurance.

Official NAIC Annual Statement Blanks: Limited Health Service Organization, 1995. 54p. (C). 1995. ring bd. 50.00 (*0-89382-327-9*) Nat Assn Insurance.

Official NAIC Annual Statement Blanks: Property & Casualty. 3rd rev. ed. Ed. by Patti Carli. 100.00p. 1996. ring bd. 100.00 (*0-89382-389-9*) Nat Assn Insurance.

Official NAIC Annual Statement Blanks: Property & Casualty. 4th rev. ed. Ed. by Patti Carli. 240p. (C). 1997. ring bd. 100.00 (*0-89382-448-8*, ASB-PM) Nat Assn Insurance.

Official NAIC Annual Statement Blanks: Property & Casualty, 1994. 222p. (C). 1994. ring bd. 75.00 (*0-89382-229-9*) Nat Assn Insurance.

Official NAIC Annual Statement Blanks: Separate Accounts. 2nd rev. ed. Ed. by Patti Carli. 57p. (C). 1997. ring bd. 25.00 (*0-89382-456-9*) Nat Assn Insurance.

Official NAIC Annual Statement Blanks: Separate Accounts. 3rd rev. ed. Ed. by Patti Carli. 52p. 1996. ring bd. 100.00 (*0-89382-391-0*) Nat Assn Insurance.

Official NAIC Annual Statement Blanks: Title. rev. ed. Ed. by Patti Carli. 132p. (C). 1997. ring bd. 75.00 (*0-89382-454-2*, ASB-TM) Nat Assn Insurance.

Official NAIC Annual Statement Blanks: Title Insurance Companies. 3rd rev. ed. Ed. by Patti Carli. 114p. 1996. ring bd. 75.00 (*0-89382-396-1*) Nat Assn Insurance.

Official NAIC Annual Statement Blanks - Fraternal. 132p. (C). 1995. ring bd. 75.00 (*0-89382-324-4*) Nat Assn Insurance.

Official NAIC Annual Statement Blanks - Life & Accident & Health. 224p. (C). 1995. ring bd. 75.00 (*0-89382-322-8*) Nat Assn Insurance.

Official NAIC Annual Statement Blanks - Limited Health Service Organization, 1994. 40p. (C). 1994. ring bd. 50.00 (*0-89382-270-1*) Nat Assn Insurance.

Official NAIC Annual Statement Blanks - Property-Casualty. 216p. (C). 1995. ring bd. 75.00 (*0-89382-323-6*) Nat Assn Insurance.

Official NAIC Annual Statement Blanks - Title. 90p. (C). 1995. ring bd. 50.00 (*0-89382-325-2*) Nat Assn Insurance.

Official NAIC Annual Statement Blanks - Title, 1994. Ed. by NAIC Staff. 86p. (C). 1994. ring bd. 50.00 (*0-89382-269-8*) Nat Assn Insurance.

Official NASCAR Busch Series Handbook. NASCAR Staff. LC 99-11063. (Illus.). 128p. 1999. pap. 19.95 (*0-06-107332-6*) HarpC.

***Official Nascar Craftsman Series Handbook.** Peter Pistone. 2000. pap. write for info. (*0-06-107331-8*, HarpEntertain) Morrow Avon.

Official NASCAR Handbook: Everything You Want to Know about the NASCAR Winston Cup Series. NASCAR Staff. LC 98-6580. (NASCAR/Winston Cup Stock Car Racing Ser.). (Illus.). 192p. 1998. pap. 19.95 (*0-06-107318-0*) HarpC.

Official NASCAR Trivia: The Ultimate Challenge for NASCAR Fans. Nascar Staff. LC 98-16564. 192p. 1998. pap. 9.95 (*0-06-107304-0*) HarpC.

Official NBA Finals Retrospective 1999, Vol. 1. National Basketball Association Staff. 1999. pap. 19.95 (*0-8129-3309-5*, Times Bks) Crown Pub Group.

Official National Football League Record & Fact Book, 1997: Record & Fact Book. 1997. pap. 15.95 (*0-614-27673-X*) Workman & Assoc.

Official National Table Hockey League Handbook, Vol. 1. Martin A. Phillips. Ed. by Zoe A. Phillips. LC 89-91696. (Illus.). 66p. (Orig.). (YA). (gr. 12). 1989. write for info. (*0-9623588-0-0*); pap. write for info. (*0-9623588-1-9*) Gnu Wine Pr.

***Official NBA Basketball Encyclopedia.** National Basketball Association Staff. (Illus.). 992p. 2000. 50.00 (*0-385-50130-7*) Doubleday.

Official NBA Guide: 1998-99 Edition. Ed. by Craig Carter & Mark Broussard. 684p. 1998. 15.95 (*0-89204-600-7*) Sporting News.

Official NBA Guide: 1999-2000 Edition. Sporting News Staff. (Illus.). 460p. 1999. pap. 15.95 (*0-89204-618-X*, 0618XC) NTC Contemp Pub Co.

Official NBA Guide, 1995-96. (Illus.). 640p. 1995. pap. 13.95 (*0-89204-531-0*) Sporting News.

Official NBA Guide, 1997-1998. annuals Sporting News Staff. (Illus.). 672p. 1997. pap. 15.95 (*0-89204-585-X*) Sporting News.

Official NBA Guide, 1996-97: The NBA from 1946 to Today. annuals Sporting News Staff. (Illus.). 696p. 1996. pap. 14.95 (*0-89204-559-0*) Sporting News.

***Official NBA Guide 2000-2001.** Sporting News Staff. (Sporting News Ser.). (Illus.). 2000. pap. 15.95 (*0-89204-639-2*) Sporting News.

***Official NBA Jam 2000 Play Book.** Acclaim Entertainment Staff. (Illus.). 1999. pap. text. write for info. (*1-57840-984-5*) Acclaim Bks.

***Official NBA Register: Every Player, Every Stat! 2000-2001.** Sporting News Staff. (Sporting News Ser.). (Illus.). 2000. pap. 15.95 (*0-89204-640-6*) Sporting News.

Official NBA Register: 1998-99 Edition. Ed. by Mark Bonavita & Brendan Roberts. 684p. 1998. 15.95 (*0-89204-601-5*) Sporting News.

Official NBA Register, 1995-96. (Illus.). 392p. 1995. pap. 13.95 (*0-89204-532-9*) Sporting News.

Official NBA Register, 1996-97: Complete Information about NBA Players, Past & Present. annuals Sporting News Staff. (Illus.). 400p. 1996. pap. 14.95 (*0-89204-560-4*) Sporting News.

Official NBA Register, 1996-1997: The Book Used by the Men in Stripes. annuals Sporting News Staff. (Illus.). 432p. 1997. pap. 15.95 (*0-89204-587-6*) Sporting News.

Official NBA Rules: 1998-99 Edition. Ed. by Craig Carter. 60p. 1998. 6.95 (*0-89204-602-3*) Sporting News.

Official NBA Rules, 1995-96. 1995. pap. 4.95 (*0-89204-538-8*) Sporting News.

Official NBA Rules, 1997-1998: The Book Used by the Men in Stripes. annuals Sporting News Staff. (Illus.). 60p. 1997. pap. 6.95 (*0-89204-586-8*) Sporting News.

Official NBA Rules, 1996-97: The Book Used by the Men in Stripes. annuals Sporting News Staff. (Illus.). 60p. 1996. pap. 5.95 (*0-89204-566-3*) Sporting News.

***Official NBA Rules 2000-2001.** Sporting News Staff. (Sporting News Ser.). 2000. pap. 6.95 (*0-89204-641-4*) Sporting News.

Official NBA Trivia: The Ultimate Team-by-Team Challenge for Hoop Fans. Clare Martin. 192p. 1999. pap. 10.95 (*0-06-107360-1*) HarpC.

Official NBA Workout Guide. Jan Hubbard. Date not set. write for info. (*0-06-107347-4*) HarpC.

Official NBC Viewers Guide to the 1992 Summer Olympics. Michael Rosenthal. 1992. pap. 14.95 (*0-918223-92-X*) Pindar Pr.

Official NBA Guide, 1994-95. (Illus.). 632p. 1994. pap. 12.95 (*0-89204-500-0*) Sporting News.

Official NCAA Football Records Book, 1998-1999. NCAA Staff. (Illus.). 568p. 1998. pap. 16.95 (*1-57243-269-1*) Triumph Bks.

***Official Negligence.** Cannon. 2000. pap. 18.00 (*0-8133-6818-9*, Pub. by Westview) HarpC.

Official Negligence: How Rodney King & the Riots Changed Los Angeles & the LAPD. Lou Cannon. 700p. 1999. pap. 19.00 (*0-8133-3725-9*, Pub. by Westview) HarpC.

Official Netscape Guide to the Navigator 5 Source Code. William B. McCarty. 500p. 1998. pap. 49.99 (*1-57610-292-0*) Coriolis Grp.

Official Netscape Navigator Gold 3.0 Book: Windows Edition: The Officie Guide to the Premiere Web Navigator & HTML Editor. Alan Simpson. (Illus.). . 934p. 1998. pap. 30.00 incl. disk (*0-7881-5717-5*) DIANE Pub.

Official Nevada Cat House Guide. rev. ed. J. R. Schwartz. (Illus.). 192p. (Orig.). 1995. pap. 14.95 (*0-9613653-1-5*) Straight Pubs.

Official Newborn Owner's Manual. 3rd rev. ed. Richard Herklots. (Illus.). 52p. 1998. pap. 5.95 (*0-9620760-1-5*) Birth to Success.

Official NFL 1998 Record & Fact Book. National Football League Staff. (Illus.). 480p. 1998. pap. 15.95 (*0-7611-1319-3*, 11319) Workman Pub.

***Official NFL Record & Fact Book, 1999.** Workman. 480p. 1999. pap. 15.95 (*0-7611-1700-8*) Workman Pub.

***Official NFL 2000 Record & Fact Book.** Ed. by Workman Publishing Staff. (Illus.). 480p. 2000. pap. 15.95 (*0-7611-1982-5*) Workman Pub.

Official NHL 1980s Quiz Book. Ed. by Dan Diamond. (Illus.). 128p. (Orig.). 1993. pap. 9.95 (*0-7710-0067-7*) McCland & Stewart.

Official NHL 1970s Quiz Book. Ed. by Dan Diamond. 128p. 1994. pap. 9.95 (*0-7710-2812-1*) McCland & Stewart.

Official NHL Philadelphia Flyers Quiz Book. Ed. by Dan Diamond. 112p. 1994. pap. 9.95 (*0-7710-2811-3*) McCland & Stewart.

Official NHL Rule Book, 1994-95. Dan Diamond. 1994. pap. 9.95 (*0-7710-2820-2*) McCland & Stewart.

Official NHL Stars Collector Coloring Album. 48p. 1993. pap. 10.95 (*1-883625-00-9*) Horus N Amer.

Official NHL Toronto Maple Leafs Quiz Book. Ed. by Dan Diamond. (Illus.). 128p. 1993. pap. 9.95 (*0-7710-0166-5*) McCland & Stewart.

Official 1948-1989-1990 Rookie Baseball Card Cross-Reference Guide. 158p. 1989. 6.95 (*0-88128-366-5*) Martin-Smith.

Official 1948-1989-1990 Baseball Card Alphabetical Cross-Reference Guide. 626p. 1989. 15.95 (*0-88128-368-1*) Martin-Smith.

Official 1999 Guide Book to Sarasota, Bradenton & Venice, Florida: Steve Rabow's Guide Book. 8th rev. ed. Steve Rabow. Tr. by Bill West. (Illus.). 1999. pap. 14.95 (*0-9639551-5-2*) Primitive Pr.

Official 1991 United States Golf Course Directory & Guide. (Illus.). 1990. pap. 19.95 (*1-885239-13-0*, Kayar Co) Success Retirement.

Official 1994 & 1995 Kentucky State Fair Blue Ribbon Recipes. 372p. 1996. pap. 11.95 (*0-9651999-0-8*) KY St Fair Bd.

***Official Nintendo Pokemon Stadium Player's Guide.** Nintendo of America Staff. (Illus.). 208p. 2000. pap. 14.95 (*1-930206-01-1*, NES B GD40) Nintendo.

***Official Nintendo Power Perfect Dark Player's Guide.** Nintendo of America Staff. (Illus.). 192p. 2000. pap. 14.95 (*1-930206-02-X*, NES B GD42) Nintendo.

***Official Nintendo Power Pokemon Trading Card Game Player's Guide.** Nintendo of America Staff. (Illus.). 112p. 2000. pap. 14.95 (*1-930206-00-3*, NES B GD44) Nintendo.

Official Notebook. Ted Cleanthes. 1987. pap. 5.95 (*0-9616172-2-5*) Official Shit Co.

Official NPA Certified Network: Professional Study Guide. J. Fitzgerald Stewart. (Illus.). 448p. 1997. pap., pap. text, student ed. 49.95 incl. cd-rom (*0-07-912988-9*) McGraw.

Official Number Sign, Asterisk, Percent Handbook. Ted Cleanthes. 1987. pap. 5.95 (*0-9616172-3-3*) Official Shit Co.

Official Old Geezer Humor Book. Rick Stromoski. (Illus.). 46p. 1994. write for info. (*1-886386-02-1*) Trisar.

Official Olympic Atlas & Guide. Ed. by Gousha, H. M. 1995. 17.50 (*0-671-55808-0*, H M Gousha) Prntice Hall Bks.

Official Overstreet Comic Book Price Guide. 18th ed. Robert M. Overstreet. (Illus.). 740p. pap. 12.95 (*0-685-07938-4*) Overstreet.

Official Overstreet Comic Book Price Guide. 22nd ed. Robert M. Overstreet. 1992. pap. write for info. (*0-87637-891-2*) Hse Collectbls.

Official Overstreet Guide to Indian Arrowheads. 2nd ed. Robert M. Overstreet. (Illus.). 768p. pap. 19.00 (*0-685-60183-8*) Overstreet.

Official Papers of Alfred Marshall. Peter Groenewegen. 371p. (C). 1996. text, suppl. ed. 74.95 (*0-521-55185-4*) Cambridge U Pr.

***Official Pendragon Forms (For Palm) Starter Kit.** Debra Sancho. 456p. 1999. pap. text 39.99 (*0-7645-4651-1*) IDG Bks.

Official PGP User's Guide. Philip R. Zimmermann. LC 95-13653. (Illus.). 216p. 1995. pap. text 16.00 (*0-262-74017-6*) MIT Pr.

Official Pictorial History of the AAF. Army Air Force Historical Office Staff. Ed. by James B. Gilbert. LC 79-7273. (Flight: Its First Seventy-Five Years Ser.). (Illus.). 1980. reprint ed. lib. bdg. 31.95 (*0-405-12384-1*) Ayer.

Official Pin Guide of the 1996 Olympic Games. Ed. by Harry Spector et al. (Illus.). 288p. (Orig.). 1996. pap. 19.95 (*0-9651795-0-8*) P G G.

Official Pocket Guide to Diabetic Exchanges. American Diabetes Association & American Dietetic Association Staff. LC 97-41452. (Illus.). 64p. 1997. pap. 5.95 (*1-58040-003-5*, 00035Q, Pub. by Am Diabetes) NTC Contemp Pub Co.

Official Pocket Player's Guide to Star Trek: The Next Generation Customizable Card Game. Bradygames Staff. (Illus.). 265p. (Orig.). 1995. 14.99 (*1-56686-248-5*) Brady Pub.

O

***Official Pokemon Collector's Sticker Book.** Maria S. Barbo. (Illus.). 48p. (J). (gr. 2-5). 1999. pap. 5.99 (*0-439-10659-1*) Scholastic Inc.

***Official Pokemon Handbook.** Scholastic, Inc. Staff & Maria S. Barbo. (J). (gr. 3-7). 1999. pap. text 9.99 (*0-439-10397-5*) Scholastic Inc.

***Official Pokemon Handbook.** deluxe ed. Scholastic, Inc. Staff & Maria S. Barbo. (Illus.). 159p. (gr. 2-7). 1999. pap. 12.99 (*0-439-15404-9*) Scholastic Inc.

***Official Pokemon Handbook, Nos. 151-250.** Maria S. Barbo. (Illus.). (J). 2000. pap. 10.99 (*0-439-15422-7*) Scholastic Inc.

Official Polish-Italian Joke Book. L. Wilde. 1988. pap. 3.50 (*1-55817-737-X*) Kensgtn Pub Corp.

Official Polish-Italian Joke Book. Larry Wilde. 1988. mass mkt. 2.95 (*1-55817-030-8*, Pinncle Kensgtn) Kensgtn Pub Corp.

Official Politically Correct Dictionary & Handbook. Henry Beard. 1993. pap. 10.00 (*0-679-74944-6*) Villard Books.

***Official Postcard Book.** Pocket Books Staff. (Illus.). 1998. pap. 8.00 (*0-671-02672-0*) PB.

Official Power J Enterprise Applications. Fish. (ITCP US Computer Science). 1998. pap. 44.99 (*1-85032-921-4*, VNR) Wiley.

Official Powerbuilder 6.0. 2nd ed. Derek Ball. LC 97-62045. (ITCP - US Computer Science Ser.). (C). 1998. mass mkt. 49.99 (*1-85032-918-4*) ITCP.

Official Powerbuilder 6.0 Desktop Reference. Kouros Gorgani. LC 98-11495. (ITCP - US Computer Science Ser.). 1998. pap. 49.99 (*1-85032-919-2*) ITCP.

Official Powerbuilder 6.0 Fundamentals 2. 2nd ed. Steve Erlank. LC 98-135915. (ITCP - US Computer Science Ser.). (C). 1998. mass mkt. 49.99 (*1-85032-917-6*) ITCP.

Official PPG Indycar Yearbook, 1994-1995. Alan Henry. (Illus.). 144p. 1994. 19.95 (*1-874557-85-3*, Pub. by Hazelton) Motorbooks Intl.

Official PPG/CART World Series Yearbook. Jeremy Shaw. (Illus.). 192p. 1997. 29.95 (*1-874557-62-4*, Pub. by Hazelton) Motorbooks Intl.

Official PPST Guide. 1988. 9.95 (*0-317-67893-0*) Educ Testing Serv.

Official Precancel Catalog, State Sections. Incl. Essential Florida. 1956. 1.50 Georgia. 1958. 1.50 Iowa. 1961. 3.00 Kentucky & Tennessee. 1952. 2.00 Louisiana. 1953. 1.00 Nebraska. 1963. 2.00 Pennsylvania. 1959. 5.00 South Carolina. 1957. 1.00 write for info. (*0-318-52350-7*) G W Noble.

Official Precancel Town & Type List, Pt. 1. 2nd ed. (Illus.). 1971. 2.00 (*0-685-46870-4*) G W Noble.

Official Presidents Cup TV Guide, 1998. Ed. by Robert Yehling & Charles Oldham. (Illus.). 1998. pap. 6.95 (*0-9644712-2-1*) Faircount Intl.

Official Presto Pressure Cooker Cookbook. (Illus.). 208p. 1992. 19.99 (*0-9654108-0-3*) Ntl Presto Ind.

Official Price Guide to Action Figures. 2nd ed. Wells Enterprises Staff. 1999. pap. 21.95 (*0-676-60179-0*) Hse Collectbls.

Official Price Guide to Antique & Modern Firearms. 9th ed. Robert H. Balderson. 672p. 1996. pap. 17.00 (*0-87637-907-2*) Hse Collectbls.

Official Price Guide to Antiques & Collectibles. 16th ed. Eric Alberta & Art Maier. 784p. 1998. pap. 15.95 (*0-87637-962-5*) Hse Collectbls.

***Official Price Guide to Antiques & Collectibles.** 18th ed. Rinker Enterprises Staff. (Illus.). 784p. 2000. pap. 16.00 (*0-676-60185-5*) Hse Collectbls.

Official Price Guide to Automobilia. David K. Bausch. (Illus.). 192p. 1996. pap. 19.95 (*0-676-60030-1*) Hse Collectbls.

***Official Price Guide to Baseball Cards: 2001 Edition.** 20th ed. James Beckett. (Illus.). 910p. 2000. pap. 6.99 (*0-676-60191-X*) Hse Collectbls.

***Official Price Guide to Basketball Cards.** 9th ed. James Beckett. 464p. 1999. pap. write for info. (*0-676-60182-0*) Hse Collectbls.

Official Price Guide to Bottles. 12th ed. Jim Megura. (Illus.). 480p. 1998. pap. 17.00 (*0-676-60009-3*) Random.

***Official Price Guide to Collectibles.** 4th ed. Harry L. Rinker. (Illus.). 480p. 2000. pap. 19.95 (*0-676-60159-6*) Hse Collectbls.

Official Price Guide to Collector Handguns. 5th ed. Robert H. Balderson. 560p. 1997. pap. 17.00 (*0-676-60038-7*) Random.

Official Price Guide to Country Antiques & Collectibles. 4th ed. Dana G. Morykan. 640p. (Orig.). 1999. pap. 15.95 (*0-676-60165-0*) Hse Collectbls.

Official Price Guide to Country Music Records. Jerry Osborne. (Illus.). 512p. 1996. pap. 15.00 (*0-676-60004-2*) Random.

Official Price Guide to Elvis. 2nd ed. Jerry Osborne. 432p. 1998. pap. 17.00 (*0-676-60141-3*) Hse Collectbls.

Official Price Guide to Elvis Presley Records & Memorabilia. Jerry Osborne. (Illus.). 384p. 1994. pap. 14.00 (*0-87637-939-0*) Hse Collectbls.

Official Price Guide to Fine Art. 2nd ed. Rosemary McKittrick & Michael McKittrick. 896p. 1993. pap. 20.00 (*0-87637-909-9*) Hse Collectbls.

***Official Price Guide to Football Cards.** 19th ed. James Beckett. (Illus.). 672p. 1999. pap. 6.99 (*0-676-60183-9*) Hse Collectbls.

***Official Price Guide to Glassware.** 3rd ed. Mark Pickvet. 800p. 2000. pap. 17.00 (*0-676-60188-X*) Ballantine Pub Grp.

Official Price Guide to Military Collectibles. 6th ed. Richard Austin. 1998. pap. 20.00 (*0-676-60052-2*) Random.

Official Price Guide to Movie, TV Soundtracks & Original Cast Albums. 2nd ed. Jerry Osborne. LC 97-210063. 1997. pap. 18.00 (*0-676-60044-1*) Random.

***Official Price Guide to Old Books.** 3rd ed. Marie Tedford & Pat Goudey. (Illus.). 480p. 1999. pap. 18.00 (*0-676-60157-X*) Hse Collectbls.

Official Price Guide to Pottery & Porcelain. 8th ed. Harvey Duke. (Illus.). 512p. 1995. pap. 18.00 (*0-87637-893-9*) Hse Collectbls.

Official Price Guide to The Money Records: 1000 Most Valuable. Jerry Osborne. LC 98-96064. 432p. 1998. pap. 17.95 (*0-676-60140-5*) Random.

Official Priests of Rome under the Julio-Claudians: A Study of the Nobility from 44 B. C. to 68 A. D. Martha W. Lewis. LC 56-2111. (American Academy in Rome. Papers & Monographs: Vol. 16). 192p. pap. 59.60 (*0-608-16481-X*, 202673000051) Bks Demand.

Official Printed Dated Control Precancel Catalog. 5th ed. (Illus.). 1981. 5.00 (*0-685-46873-9*) G W Noble.

***Official Printmaster Guide.** Michael Miller. (Illus.). 1999. pap. 17.99 (*0-7897-2081-7*) Que.

Official Pritikin Guide to Dining Out. Nathan Pritikin & Ilene Pritikin. LC 83-3853. 224p. 1984. write for info. (*0-672-52773-1*) Macmillan.

Official Privilege. Peter T. Deutermann. 1996. mass mkt. 6.50 (*0-312-95713-0*) St Martin.

Official Proceedings of the National Police Convention. National Police Convention Staff. LC 70-154579. (Police in America Ser.). 1971. reprint ed. 13.95 (*0-405-03379-6*) Ayer.

Official Proceedings of the 1996 AIUM Annual Convention. 1996. 22.00 (*1-930047-72-X*) Am Inst Ultrasound.

Official Proceedings of the Seventh International Symposium on the Transportation of Dangerous Goods by Sea & Inland Waterways. ICHCA Staff. (C). 1988. 315.00 (*0-7855-6154-4*, Pub. by ICHCA) St Mut.

Official Publication, 1990: Association of American Feed Control Official Incorporated. rev. ed. Association of American Feed Control Officials, In. Ed. by Earl M. Haas. 319p. 1990. 20.00 (*1-878341-00-6*) AAFCO.

Official Publication, 1991: Association of American Feed Control Official Incorporated. 1991. 15.00 (*1-878341-01-4*) AAFCO.

Official Publication of Associaton of American Feed Control Officials, Inc. rev. ed. AAFCO Staff. Ed. by Earl M. Haas. 336p. 1993. 20.00 (*1-878341-04-9*) AAFCO.

Official Publications of the Soviet Union & Eastern Europe, 1945-1980: A Select Annotated Bibliography. Ed. by G. Walker. 624p. 1982. text 140.00 (*0-7201-1641-4*) Continuum.

Official Record. 1999. text. write for info. (*0-312-01252-7*) St Martin.

Official Record of the Congress of Accountants: Proceedings. Congress of Accountants, World Fair, St Louis, Sep. Ed. by Richard P. Brief. LC 77-87266. (Development of Contemporary Accounting Thought Ser.). 1978. reprint ed. lib. bdg. 23.95 (*0-405-10895-8*) Ayer.

Official Record of the Old Settlers Society of Racine County: With Historical Address. Charles E. Dyer. (Illus.). 84p. 1997. reprint ed. pap. 16.00 (*0-8328-6983-X*) Higginson Bk Co.

Official Records. 13th ed. Jerry Osborne. 1999. 24.95 (*0-676-60090-5*) Hse Collectbls.

Official Records of Robert Dinwiddie, Set, Vols. 1 & 2. Robert Dinwiddie. LC 77-164836. (Illus.). reprint ed. 127.50 (*0-404-02135-2*) AMS Pr.

Official Records of the Conference on the Establishment of an International Compensation Fund for Oil Pollution Damage, 1971. International Maritime Organization Staff. 1978. text 75.00 (*0-89771-936-0*, Pub. by Intl Maritime Org) St Mut.

Official Records of the Diplomatic Conference of the Reaffirmation & Development of International Humanitarian Law Applicable in Armed Conflicts, 17 vols., Set: 1974-1977. 1981. reprint ed. 675.00 (*0-89941-149-5*, 301110) W S Hein.

Official Records of the Human Rights Committee, 1987-88, Vol. 2. (International Covenant on Civil & Political Rights Ser.). 470p. 70.00 (*92-1-154102-6*) UN.

Official Records of the Human Rights Committee, 1988-89, Vol. 1. 342p. 60.00 (*92-1-154103-4*) UN.

Official Records of the Human Rights Committee, 1988-89, Vol. 2. 504p. 70.00 (*92-1-154110-7*) UN.

Official Records of the Human Rights Committee, 1989-90, Vol. 1. (International Covenant on Civil & Political Rights Ser.). 340p. 60.00 (*92-1-154111-5*) UN.

Official Records of the Human Rights Committee, 1989-90, Vol. 2. 468p. 60.00 (*92-1-154108-5*) UN.

Official Records of the Human Rights Committee, 1990-91, Vol. 1. 420p. 60.00 (*92-1-154112-3*) UN.

Official Records of the Human Rights Committee, 1990-91, Vol. 2. 500p. 60.00 (*92-1-154113-1*, K3240) UN.

Official Records of the Human Rights Committee, 1991-92, Vol. I. 60.00 (*92-1-154116-6*) UN.

Official Records of the Human Rights Committee, 1991-92, Vol. II. 60.00 (*92-1-154117-4*) UN.

Official Records of the Human Rights Committee, 1992-93. International Covenant on Civil Political Rights Staff. 606p. 1997. pap. 60.00 (*92-1-154119-0*) UN.

Official Records of the Human Rights Committee, 1992-93, 1. 420p. 60.00 (*92-1-154118-2*) UN.

Official Records of the International Conference on Limitation of Liability for Maritime Claims, 1976. International Maritime Organization Staff. 1983. text 80.00 (*0-89771-940-9*, Pub. by Intl Maritime Org) St Mut.

Official Records of the International Legal Conference on Marine Pollution Damage, 1969. International Maritime Organization Staff. 1973. text 90.00 (*0-89771-890-9*, Pub. by Intl Maritime Org) St Mut.

Official Records of the Union & Confederate Navies in the War of the Rebellion, 31 vols. 1976. reprint ed. lib. bdg. 495.00 (*0-405-09847-2*) Ayer.

Official Records of the Union & Confederate Navies in the War of the Rebellion, 31 vols. 1987. reprint ed. 556.45 (*0-918678-30-7*) Natl Hist Soc.

Official Recycled Products Guide. 400p. 1998. ring bd. 315.00 (*1-880978-01-6*) RDMC.

Official Redneck Handbook. Jack S. Moore. Ed. by A. Lee Chichester. (Illus.). 146p. (Orig.). Date not set. pap. 14.95 (*0-89896-076-2*) Larksdale.

Official Redneck Handbook. Bo Whaley. LC 87-12708. (Illus.). 160p. (Orig.). 1987. pap. 6.95 (*0-934395-48-9*) Rutledge Hill Pr.

Official Register of the Officers & Men of New Jersey in the Revolutionary War. William S. Stryker. Ed. by James W. Campbell. LC 67-24883. 927p. 1997. reprint ed. pap. 65.00 (*0-8063-0324-7*) Clearfield Co.

Official Register of the Officers & Men of New Jersey in the Revolutionary War, 2 vols., Set. William S. Stryker. ii, 949p. 1993. reprint ed. pap. 52.00 (*1-55613-736-2*) Heritage Bk.

***Official Rent-A-Husband Guide.** Kaile R. Warren & Jane MacLean Craig. 2000. pap. 16.95 (*0-7679-0696-9*) Broadway BDD.

***Official Rent-a-Husband Guide.** 3rd ed. Craig J. Warren. LC 99-58567. 544p. 2000. pap. 16.95 (*0-7679-0545-8*) Broadway BDD.

Official Report of the Centennial Olympic Games. Atlanta Committee for the Olympic Games. LC 97-23578. 1997. 325.00 (*1-56145-150-9*) Peachtree Pubs.

Official Report of the Centennial Olympic Games, Vol. 2. Atlanta Committee for the Olympic Games. LC 97-23578. 1997. pap. 150.00 (*1-56145-151-7*) Peachtree Pubs.

***Official Report of the Lambeth Conference 1998.** Compiled by Anglican Consultative Council Staff. LC 99-12950. 544p. 1999. pap. 22.95 (*0-8192-1797-2*) Morehouse Pub.

***Official Report of the Trial of Sarah Jane Robinson for the Murder of Prince Arthur Freeman in the Supreme Judicial Court of Massachusetts from Notes of Mr. J. M. W. Yerrinton.** 469p. 2000. reprint ed. 118.00 (*1-56169-576-9*) Gaunt.

Official Report of the Trial of the Honorable Albert Jackson: Judge of the Fifteenth Judicial Circuit Before the Senate Composing the High Court of Impeachment of the State of Missouri. Thomas J. Henderson. iv, 492p. 1996. reprint ed. 98.00 (*1-56169-221-2*) Gaunt.

Official Reports on the Towns of Tequizistlan, Tepechpan, Acolman, & San Juan Teotihuacan, Sent to His Majesty Philip Second & the Council of the Indies in 1580. Zelia Nuttall. (HU PMP Ser.: Vol. 11, No. 2). 1926. pap. 25.00 (*0-527-01219-X*) Periodicals Srv.

Official Review Guide Book for National Registry of Environmental Manager's Examination. NREP Board Members Staff. 515p. 1989. 49.95 (*0-925760-29-3*) SciTech Pubs.

Official Review Guide Book for Registered Environmental Professionals (REP) Examination. SciTech Publishers Staff. (Illus.). 400p. 1989. 39.95 (*0-925760-04-8*) SciTech Pubs.

***Official Rising Sun Strategy Guide.** Bart Farkas. (Illus.). 1999. pap. 19.99 (*0-9673565-8-X*) Illumination Pubns.

Official Riven Hints & Solutions. Bill Keith & Nina Keith. 216p. 1997. 19.99 (*1-56686-691-X*) Brady Pub.

Official Riven Hints & Solutions. Ronald Wartow. 1997. pap. 19.99 (*0-614-28468-6*) MCP SW Interactive.

Official Riven Player's Guide: The Sequel to Myst. Brady Games Staff. (Brady Games Strategy Guides Ser.). 112p. 1997. pap. text 11.99 (*1-56686-762-2*) Brady Pub.

Official Riven Solutions: The Sequel to Myst. William H. Keith, Jr. & Nina Keith. 120p. 1997. pap. 9.99 (*1-56686-709-6*) Brady Pub.

Official Rocket Science Guide to Cadillacs & Dinosaurs. Jason R. Rich. (LAN Times Ser.). (Illus.). 208p. 1995. pap. text 16.95 (*0-07-882134-7*) McGraw.

Official Rocket Science Guide to Loadstar: The Legend of Tully Bodine. Jay Trimble. (LAN Times Ser.). (Illus.). 208p. 1995. pap. text 16.95 (*0-07-882135-5*) McGraw.

***Official Roster of the D&RGW&RGS (1923)** Colorado Rail Road Museum Staff. 160p. 1998. pap. 19.95 (*0-918654-56-4*) CO RR Mus.

***Official Rules & Explanations: The Original Guide to Surviving the Electronic Age with Wit, Wisdom & Laughter.** Paul Dickson. LC 99-62656. Orig. Title: The Official Rules, the Official Explanations. (Illus.). 512p. 1999. 9.98 (*1-892859-10-6*) Federal St Pr.

Official Rules at Home: The Laws That Determine What Can, & Probably Will, Go Awry in Your Daily Life. Paul Dickson. (Official Rules Ser.). 120p. 1996. 12.95 (*0-8027-1316-5*) Walker & Co.

Official Rules at Work: The Principles, Maxims, & Instructions That Define Your Life on the Job. Paul Dickson. (Official Rules Ser.). 120p. 1996. 12.95 (*0-8027-1317-3*) Walker & Co.

Official Rules for Golfers. Paul Dickson. LC 97-7816. 120p. 1997. 13.95 (*0-8027-1327-0*) Walker & Co.

Official Rules for Lawyers, Politicians . . . And Everyone They Torment. Paul Dickson. (Official Rules Ser.). (Illus.). 120p. 1996. 12.95 (*0-8027-1321-1*) Walker & Co.

Official Rules of Card Games. Albert Moorehead. 1996. pap. 12.95 (*0-449-91158-6*) Fawcett.

Official Rules of Card Games. 82nd rev. ed. Joli Q. Kansil. (Illus.). 400p. 1998. pap. 12.95 (*0-7611-0953-6*) Workman Pub.

***Official Rules of Chess.** Eric Schiller & Richard Peterson. LC 00-131806. (Illus.). 144p. 2000. 9.95 (*1-58042-025-7*, Pub. by Cardoza Pub) LPC Group.

***Official Rules of Golf: 2000.** United States Golf Association Staff. 1999. pap. 9.95 (*1-57243-331-0*) Triumph Bks.

Official Rules of Golf, 1999. United States Golf Association Staff. Ed. by Us Games Inc. Staff. 1998. pap. 9.95 (*1-57243-306-X*) Triumph Bks.

***Official Rules of Golf 2001.** United States Golf Association Staff. (Illus.). 2000. pap. 9.95 (*1-57243-400-7*) Triumph Bks.

Official Rules of In-Line Hockey: 2000. Triumph Books Staff. 1999. pap. text 9.95 (*1-57243-321-3*) Triumph Bks.

***Official Rules of Major League Baseball: 2000.** Major League Baseball Staff. LC 95-29374. 208p. 1999. pap. 9.95 (*1-57243-332-9*) Triumph Bks.

***Official Rules of NCAA Basketball: 2000.** National Collegiate Athletic Association Staff. (Illus.). 194p. 1999. pap. 9.95 (*1-57243-333-7*) Triumph Bks.

Official Rules of NCAA Basketball 1999. 1998. pap. 9.95 (*1-57243-307-8*) Triumph Bks.

Official Rules of Soccer. rev. ed. U. S. Soccer Staff. (Illus.). 192p. 1997. pap. 9.95 (*1-57243-184-9*) Triumph Bks.

Official Rules of Soccer: 2000. Triumph Book Staff. 1999. pap. text 9.95 (*1-57243-322-1*) Triumph Bks.

***Official Rules of Tennis: 2000.** USTA Education & Research Center et al. 192p. 1999. pap. 9.95 (*1-57243-341-8*) Triumph Bks.

Official Rules of the International Professional Rodeo Association. 100p. 1986. 1.00 (*0-318-14597-9*) Intl Rodeo.

Official Rules of the NFL. rev. ed. National Football League Staff. (Official Rules Ser.). (Illus.). 202p. 1996. pap. 8.95 (*1-57243-142-3*) Triumph Bks.

***Official Rules of the NFL: 2000.** National Football League Staff. 995p. 1999. pap. 9.95 (*1-57243-334-5*) Triumph Bks.

***Official Rules of the NFL 2001.** National Football League Staff. (Illus.). 2000. pap. 9.95 (*1-57243-401-5*) Triumph Bks.

Official Rules of the NHL. rev. ed. National Hockey League Staff. (Official Rules Ser.). (Illus.). 201p. (Orig.). 1996. pap. 8.95 (*1-57243-141-5*) Triumph Bks.

***Official Rules of the NHL: 2000.** National Hockey League Staff. LC 96-30000. 160p. 1999. pap. 9.95 (*1-57243-335-3*) Triumph Bks.

Official Rules of the NHL 1999. 1998. pap. 9.95 (*1-57243-309-4*) Triumph Bks.

***Official Rules of the NHL 2001.** National Football League Staff. (Illus.). 2000. pap. 9.95 (*1-57243-399-X*) Triumph Bks.

An Asterisk (*) at the beginning of an entry indicates that the title is appearing for the first time.

Official Rules, the Official Explanations see Official Rules & Explanations: The Official Guide to Surviving the Electronic Age with Wit, Wisdom & Laughter

Official San Francisco Visitor's Gay Escort. Brett Thomas & William Wolf. (Illus.). 154p. 1992. pap. text 7.17 (*0-9633794-0-2*) DELCOM.

*__Official Scrabble Brand Word Finder: The Ultimate Playing Companion to America's Favorite Word Game.__ rev. ed. Robert W. Schachner. 320p. 2000. pap. 10.98 (*1-57912-104-7*, 81104) Blck Dog & Leventhal.

Official Scrabble Players Dictionary. large type ed. Merriam-Webster Editors. LC 97-43212. 1998. pap. 29.95 (*0-87779-623-8*) Merriam-Webster Inc.

Official Scrabble Players Dictionary. 3rd ed. Merriam-Webster Editors. LC 95-20437. 704p. 1995. 19.95 (*0-87779-220-8*) Merriam-Webster Inc.

Official Scrabble Players Dictionary. 3rd ed. Merriam-Webster Editors. 672p. 1996. pap. 6.50 (*0-87779-915-6*) Merriam-Webster Inc.

Official Scrabble Puzzle Book. Joe Edley. LC 97-27761. 1997. per. 14.00 (*0-671-56900-7*, PB Trade Paper) PB.

Official Scrabble Quiz Game Book. Robert Allen. (Illus.). 128p. 1997. pap. text 9.95 (*0-8065-1945-2*, Citadel Pr) Carol Pub Group.

Official Scrabble Quiz Game Book, Vol. 2. Robert Allen. (Illus.). 128p. 1999. pap. 14.95 (*1-85868-522-2*, Pub. by Carlton Bks Ltd) Natl Bk Netwk.

Official Scrabble Word-Finder. Ed. by Robert W. Schachner. 304p. 1988. pap. 7.00 (*0-02-029802-1*) Macmillan.

Official Scrabble Word-Finder. Robert W. Schachner. LC 99-461858. 304p. 1998. pap. text 7.00 (*0-02-862132-8*, Pub. by Macmillan) S&S Trade.

Official SEC Football Guide, 1997-1998. rev. ed. Southeastern Conference Staff. (Illus.). 322p. 1997. pap. 9.95 (*1-57243-204-7*) Triumph Bks.

Official SEC Football Guide, 1998-1999. Southeastern Conference Staff & Triumph Books Staff. (Illus.). 350p. 1998. pap. 9.95 (*1-57243-270-5*) Triumph Bks.

Official Secrets. Lindsey Mitchell. 1990. mass mkt. 4.95 (*0-446-35329-9*, Pub. by Warner Bks) Little.

Official Secrets. Jim Moore. 214p. 1996. pap. 19.95 (*0-945980-58-2*) Nrth Country Pr.

Official Secrets. Jim Moore. LC 96-70108. 224p. 1997. 24.95 (*0-945980-64-7*) Nrth Country Pr.

Official Secrets: What the Nazis Planned, What the British & Americans Knew. Richard Breitman. LC 98-7997. 320p. 1998. 25.00 (*0-8090-3819-6*) Hill & Wang.

*__Official Secrets: What the Nazis Planned, What the British & Americans Knew.__ Richard Breitman. 336p. 1999. pap. 13.00 (*0-8090-0184-5*) Hill & Wang.

Official Sega Genesis Power Tips Book. Neil West. LC 92-33510. 1992. 14.99 (*1-55958-284-7*) Prima Pub.

Official Sega Genesis Power Tips Book. 2nd rev. ed. Neil West. (Illus.). 112p. 1993. pap. 14.95 (*1-55958-398-3*) Prima Pub.

Official Sega Genesis Power Tips Book, Vol. 2. Neil West. (Illus.). 112p. 1993. pap. 14.95 (*1-55958-399-1*) Prima Pub.

*__Official 7th Heaven Scrapbook.__ Scholastic Books Staff. (Illus.). 48p. (J). (gr. 3-9). 2000. mass mkt. 5.99 (*0-439-16008-1*) Scholastic Inc.

*__Official Shadow Man Strategy Guide.__ Acclaim Entertainment Staff. (Illus.). 1999. pap. text 12.99 (*1-57840-987-X*) Acclaim Bks.

Official Shit Notebook. Ted Cleanthes. Ed. by Pete Tortolini. (Illus.). 128p. 1987. pap. 5.95 (*0-9616172-1-7*) Official Shit Co.

Official Shit Notebook: The Book to Help You Get Your Shit Together. Pete Tortolini. 1982. pap. 5.95 (*0-9616172-0-9*) Official Shit Co.

Official SimCity Classic Planning Commission Handbook. 2nd ed. Johnny L. Wilson. 1993. pap. 19.95 (*0-07-881998-9*) Osborne-McGraw.

Official Simcity 2000 Handbook. 2nd ed. Johnny L. Wilson. 384p. 1994. pap. text 19.95 (*0-07-881950-4*) Osborne-McGraw.

Official Sin Strategy Guide. Bradygames Staff. 216p. 1998. pap. text 19.99 (*1-56686-776-2*) Brady Pub.

*__Official Slinky Book: Hundreds of Wild & Wacky Uses for the Greatest Toy on Earth.__ Joey Green. 1999. pap. 8.95 (*0-425-17155-8*) Berkley Pub.

Official Smart Kids - Dumb Parents Joke Book. Larry Wilde. 1988. mass mkt. 2.95 (*1-55817-034-0*, Pinncle Kensgtn) Kensgtn Pub Corp.

Official Smart Kids Joke Book. Larry Wilde. mass mkt. 2.25 (*0-318-23488-2*, Pinncle Kensgtn) Kensgtn Pub Corp.

Official Smokey Bear Book. Robin Bromley. (Illus.). (J). 1996. 15.99 (*0-614-19332-X*, Ladybrd) Penguin Putnam.

Official Soccer Book of the United States Soccer Federation. Walter Chyzowych. (Illus.). 256p. 13.00 (*0-318-16829-4*); pap. 7.00 (*0-318-16830-8*) US Soccer Fed.

Official Software for the GMAT Review: APPLE. Educational Testing Service Staff. 1986. 79.95 incl. disk (*0-446-38447-X*, Pub. by Warner Bks) Little.

Official Software for the GMAT Review: IBM. Educational Testing Service Staff. 1986. 79.95 incl. disk (*0-446-38449-6*, Pub. by Warner Bks) Little.

Official Soviet 7.62mm Handgun Manual: Instructions for Use & Maintenance of the Nagant 7.62mm Revolver Type 1895 & the Tokarev 7.62mm Semi-Automatic Pistol Type 1933. James F. Gebhardt. LC 97-117672. (Illus.). 89p. 1997. 20.00 (*0-87364-907-9*) Paladin Pr.

*__Official Soviet SVD Manual: Operating Instructions for the 7.62mm Dragunov.__ James F. Gebhardt. 112p. 1999. pap. 15.00 (*1-58160-032-1*) Paladin Pr.

Official Spanglish Dictionary: A User's Guide to More Than 300 Words & Phrases That Aren't Exactly Espanol or Ingles. Bill Teck & Bill Cruz. LC 98-33688. (ENG & SPA.). 176p. 1998. pap. 10.00 (*0-684-85412-0*, Fireside) S&S Trade Pap.

Official Special Olympics Celebrity Cook Book. Kathryn Buursma & Mary Stickney. 1980. 15.00 (*0-87832-046-6*) Piper.

*__Official Spinal Tap Companion.__ Ed. by Karl French. 240p. 2000. 19.95 (*1-58234-125-7*) Bloomsbury Pubg.

Official Spinrite II & Hard Disk Companion. John Goodman. LC 90-84497. 265p. 1994. 14.95 (*1-878058-08-8*) IDG Bks.

Official Splatter Movie Guide. John McCarty. 1989. pap. 10.95 (*0-312-02958-6*) St Martin.

Official Sports Guide of the Centennial Olympic Games: Atlanta, 1996. Pindar Press Staff. (Illus.). 128p. 1996. pap. 10.95 (*0-918223-93-8*) Pindar Pr.

Official Star Trek: First Contact Strategy Guide. Bradygames Staff. 1998. pap. text 19.99 (*1-56686-774-6*) Brady Pub.

Official Star Trek: Birth of the Federation Strategy Guide. Bradygames Staff. LC 98-70847. 1998. pap. 19.99 (*1-56686-794-0*) Brady Pub.

Official Starter Game Guide. Cory Herndon. (Magic the Gathering Ser.). 1999. pap. 11.99 (*0-7869-1425-4*, Pub. by TSR Inc) Random.

Official Statements for Offerings of Securities by Local Governments - Examples & Guidelines. Municipal Finance Officers Association Staff. 64p. 1981. 12.00 (*0-686-84334-7*); 10.00 (*0-686-84335-5*) Municipal.

*__Official Statements of War Aims & Peace Proposals: December 1916 to November 1918.__ James Brown Scott & Carnegie Endowment for International Peace Staff. LC 99-47542. 1999. write for info. (*1-57588-606-5*) W S Hein.

Official Statements of War Aims & Peace Proposals, December 1916 to November 1918. Ed. by James B. Scott. LC 83-22714. (Carnegie Endowment for International Peace, United Nations Studies: No. 31). 515p. 1984. reprint ed. lib. bdg. 82.50 (*0-313-24392-1*, SCOS) Greenwood.

Official Story of the 1996 Green Bay Packers see Titletown Again: The Super Bowl Season of the 1996 Green Bay Packers

Official Street Fighter Two Strategy Guide. Gamepro Magazine Staff. 164p. (YA). (gr. 7-12). 1992. 9.95 (*1-882455-00-2*) Gamepro Pub.

Official Strip Joint Guide, Vol. 1, Issue 2. Kinsley D. Jones & William A. Harland. 288p. 1993. pap. text 17.00 (*0-9636533-0-X*); 3.5 hd 12.95 (*0-9636533-1-8*) O S J G.

Official Stronghold Guide. Sameer Parketh. 800p. 1999. 59.99 (*1-56276-501-9*, Ziff-Davis Pr) Que.

*__Official Study Course for the National Counselor Examination for Licensure & Certification (NC), 1.__ Credentialing & E Center Staff. 1999. pap. text. write for info. (*1-56032-882-7*) Hemisp Pub.

*__Official Study Guide for the Certified Occupational Therapy Assistant Cota Certification Examination.__ (C). 1999. pap. 35.00 (*0-9677436-0-5*) Natl Board Cert Occp Ther.

Official Study Guide for the CGFNS Qualifying Examination. 3rd ed. Commission on Graduates of Foreign Nursing Schools. 200p. (C). 1995. write for info. (*0-9630592-2-X*) Grads of For Nursing.

*__Official Study Guide for the Occupational Therapist Registered OTR Certification Examination.__ (C). 1999. pap. 35.00 (*0-9677436-1-3*) Natl Board Cert Occp Ther.

Official Summary of Security Transactions & Holdings. Government Printing Office Staff. pap. 144.00 (*0-16-011680-5*) USGPO.

Official Sunday School Teacher's Handbook. Joanne Owens. LC 87-43102. (Illus.). 240p. 1987. pap., teacher ed. 12.95 (*0-916260-42-9*, B152) Meriwether Pub.

Official TASP Study Guide. 1989. pap. 12.00 (*0-89056-003-X*) Natl Eval Systs.

Official TASP Test Study Guide. National Evaluation Systems Inc. Staff. 1992. pap. 12.00 (*0-89056-007-2*) Natl Eval Systs.

Official Teacher's Guide to the Test of General Educational Development. GED Testing Service Staff. 1987. pap., teacher ed. 7.40 (*0-8092-4790-9*) NTC Contemp Pub Co.

Official Tech Support Yellow Pages. CyberMedia Staff. 1996. pap. text 19.95 incl. cd-rom (*1-887556-21-4*) Cybermedia.

Official Tekken 3 Totally Unauthorized Fighting Guide. Bradygames Staff. 1998. pap. 9.99 (*1-56686-793-2*) Brady Pub.

Official Telecommunications Dictionary: Legal & Regulatory Definitions. Ed. by Thomas F. Sullivan. LC 97-189728. 313p. 1997. pap. text 49.00 (*0-86587-564-2*) Gov Insts.

Official Tenchu Strategy Guide: Stealth Assassins. Bradygames. LC 98-73584. 1998. pap. text 11.99 (*1-56686-821-1*) Brady Pub.

Official Tex-Mex Cookbook. T. L. Bush. LC 96-29844. 74p. (Orig.). 1997. pap. 14.95 (*0-88415-592-7*, 5592) Gulf Pub.

*__Official Theory Test for Drivers Of Large Vehicles.__ Driving Standards Agency Staff. LC 99-488367. 350p. 1999. write for info. (*0-11-552168-2*, Pub. by Statnry Office) Balogh.

Official 30th Anniversary Salute to GI Joe. Vincent Santelmo. LC 94-75299. (Illus.). 192p. 1994. 34.95 (*0-87341-301-6*, JL01) Krause Pubns.

Official Three Stooges Cookbook. Robert Kurson. LC 98-25741. (Illus.). 224p. 1998. spiral bd. 14.95 (*0-8092-2929-3*, 292930, Contemporary Bks) NTC Contemp Pub Co.

Official Three Stooges Encyclopedia. Robert Kurson. LC 97-46511. (Illus.). 384p. 1998. 29.95 (*0-8092-2930-7*, 293070, Contemporary Bks) NTC Contemp Pub Co.

Official Three Stooges Encyclopedia: The Ultimate Knucklehead's Guide to Stoogedom - From Amalgamated Association of Morons to Ziller, Zeller, & Zoller. Robert Kurson. (Illus.). 384p. 1999. pap. 18.95 (*0-8092-2580-8*, 258080, Contemporary Bks) NTC Contemp Pub Co.

Official Toshinden 2 Fighters Guide. Bradygames Staff. 112p. 1996. 9.99 (*1-56686-557-3*) Brady Pub.

Official Tour Guide to Holusion Art. NVision Grafix Inc. Staff & Thomas Hripko. (Illus.). 40p. 1994. 24.95 (*0-9640923-1-X*) NVision Grafix.

Official Tournament Player's Handbook. Jeff Donais. 1999. pap. 9.99 (*0-7869-1517-X*, Pub. by TSR Inc) Random.

Official Travel Industry Directory, 1997: The Sourcebook for Travel Professionals. 528p. 1997. spiral bd. write for info. (*0-9644529-2-8*) Universal Media.

*__Official Trucking Safety Guide.__ rev. ed. Keller, J. J., & Associates, Inc. Staff. LC 74-31865. 1175p. 2000. ring bd. 199.00 (*0-934674-03-5*, 8-G) J J Keller.

*__Official 2001 Blackbook Price Guide to World Coins.__ 4th ed. Mark Hudgeons & Tom Hudgeons. (Illus.). 560p. 2000. pap. 7.99 (*0-676-60175-8*) Hse Collectbls.

*__Official 2001 Blackbook Guide to U. S. Postage Stamps.__ 23rd ed. Mark Hudgeons & Tom Hudgeons. (Illus.). 480p. 2000. pap. 7.99 (*0-676-60169-3*) Hse Collectbls.

*__Official 2001 Blackbook Price Guide to U. S. Paper Money.__ 33rd ed. Mark Hudgeons & Tom Hudgeons. (Illus.). 352p. 2000. pap. 6.99 (*0-676-60166-9*) Hse Collectbls.

*__Official 2001 Blackbook Price Guide to U. S. Coins.__ 39th ed. Mark Hudgeons & Tom Hudgeons. (Illus.). 608p. 2000. pap. 6.99 (*0-676-60172-3*) Hse Collectbls.

*__Official U. K. The Essential Guide to Government Websites.__ 2nd ed. Dan Jellinek. 306p. 2000. pap. 50.00 (*0-11-702446-5*, Pub. by Statnry Office) Balogh.

*__Official United States Air Force Elite Workout.__ Andrew Flach. LC 99-28830. (Official Fitness Guide Ser.). (Illus.). 180p. 1999. pap. 14.95 (*1-57826-029-9*, Pub. by Hatherleigh) Norton.

Official United States Army Ranger Workout. Andrew Flach. 120p. pap. 14.95 (*1-57826-045-0*, Pub. by Hatherleigh) Norton.

Official United States Naval Academy Workout. Andrew Flach. LC 98-18120. (Five Star Fitness Guides Ser.). (Illus.). 128p. 1998. pap. 14.95 (*1-57826-010-8*, Pub. by Hatherleigh) Norton.

Official United States Navy Seal Workout. Andrew Flach. LC 98-10159. (Five Star Fitness Guides Ser.). (Illus.). 152p. 1998. pap. 14.95 (*1-57826-009-4*, Pub. by Hatherleigh) Norton.

*__Official US Casino Chip Price Guide.__ James Campiglia & Steve Wells. (Illus.). 320p. 2000. pap. 29.95 (*0-7643-1157-3*) Schiffer.

Official Varieties & Synonyms of Surnames & Christian Names in Ireland for the Guidance of Registration Officers & the Public in Searching the Indexes of Births, Deaths, & Marriages. Robert E. Matheson. 94p. 1995. reprint ed. pap. 11.00 (*0-7884-0301-X*) Heritage Bk.

*__Official Vermont Maple Cookbook.__ 2nd ed. Betty Ann Lockhart et al. Ed. by Donald Lockhart. (Illus.). 65p. 1999. pap. write for info. (*1-880327-43-0*) Perceptions.

Official Video Directory & Buyer's Guide. Ed. by Steve Tolin. (Orig.). 1987. pap. 50.00 (*0-939271-00-1*) PS Media Inc.

Official Vietnam War Trivia Book. Alan Dawson. (Illus.). 130p. 1989. pap. 5.95 (*0-9623992-0-5*) Electric Strawberry.

Official Vintage Guitar Instrument Price Guide. 5th ed. Alan Greewood. (Illus.). 225p. pap. 19.95 (*0-7935-6712-2*) H Leonard.

Official Vintage Guitar Magazine Price Guide. 5th ed. Alan Greenwood. (Illus.). 228p. (Orig.). 1996. pap. 19.95 (*1-884883-05-2*) Vintage Guitar.

Official Vinyl Precancel Town & Type List. 1973. 1.50 (*0-685-46871-2*) G W Noble.

Official VisiBroker for Java Handbook. Michael McCaffery. LC 98-87216. 1998. pap. text 39.99 (*0-672-31451-7*) Sams.

Official Visitors Guide: Los Angeles. Camaro Editors. 1982. 4.95 (*0-913290-30-0*) Camaro Pub.

Official Visitors Guide: San Francisco. Camaro Editors. 1988. 4.95 (*0-913290-32-7*) Camaro Pub.

Official VR World: Cruisin' the VR World. Sandra K. Helsel. 400p. 24.99 (*0-614-10085-2*) Mecklermedia.

Official Warranty Guide. Joseph A. Grant. LC 98-208333. 88p. 1996. pap. 11.95 (*0-9637363-0-2*) J&L Srvs.

Official White House China: 1789 to the Present. 2nd ed. Margaret Brown Klapthor. LC 98-40696. (Illus.). 304p. 1999. 49.50 (*0-8109-3993-2*, Pub. by Abrams) Time Warner.

*__Official Whitman Statehood Quarters Collector's Handbook.__ Kenneth Bressett. 96p. 2000. mass mkt. 4.99 (*0-312-97804-9*) St Martin.

Official Wild 9 Strategy Guide. Bradygames Staff. 1998. pap. 11.99 (*1-56686-786-X*) Brady Pub.

Official Wilderness First-Aid Guide. Wayne Merry. (Illus.). 416p. 1994. pap. 14.95 (*0-7710-8253-3*) McCland & Stewart.

Official Wilderness First-Aid Guide. Wayne Merry. 390p. 1997. pap. 14.95 (*0-7710-8250-9*) McCland & Stewart.

*__Official Wimbledon Annual, 1999.__ John Parsons. (Illus.). 160p. 2000. 39.95 (*1-56554-714-4*) Pelican.

Official Wimbledon Championships 1998. John Parsons. (Illus.). 160p. 1998. 35.00 (*1-56554-411-0*) Pelican.

Official Wireless Application Protocol: The Complete Standard with Searchable CD-ROM. Wireless Application Protocol Forum, LTD. Staff. LC 98-53458. 768p. 1999. 64.99 incl. cd-rom (*0-471-32755-7*) Wiley.

*__Official WNBA Guide & Register: 2000 Edition.__ Ed. by Sporting News Staff. (Illus.). 416p. 2000. pap. 15.95 (*0-89204-634-1*, 06341C, Contemporary Bks) NTC Contemp Pub Co.

Official World Wide Web Directory & Internet Directory, 1 Vol. Marcia Layton. LC 98-86521. 1998. pap. text 19.99 (*0-7357-0015-X*) New Riders Pub.

Official World Wide Web Yellow Pages. 9th ed. Marcia Layton Turner. 1200p. 1999. pap. text 29.99 (*0-7897-2152-X*) Que.

Official World's Fair Pictorial Photography. Mitchel L. Osborne. 48p. 1984. 3.95 (*0-317-12231-2*) Picayune Pr.

Official World's Fair Preview & Vacation Planner. Ed. by Linda Delery. (Illus.). 112p. (C). 1983. pap. 3.75 (*0-685-07793-4*) Picayune Pr.

*__Official WWF Attitude Strategy Guide.__ Acclaim Entertainment Staff. (Illus.). 1999. pap. text. write for info. (*1-57840-982-9*) Acclaim Bks.

*__Official Xenogears Strategy Guide.__ Ron Wartow. LC 98-73574. 1998. pap. text 14.99 (*1-56686-825-4*) Brady Pub.

Official XTree Companion. 3rd ed. Beth Slick. 448p. 1992. pap. 19.95 (*1-878058-57-6*) IDG Bks.

Official XTree MS-DOS & Hard Disk Companion. 224p. 1990. 14.95 (*1-878058-07-X*) IDG Bks.

Official Xtree MS-DOS & Hard Disk Companion. 2nd ed. Beth Woods. LC 91-71239. 299p. 1991. pap. 15.95 (*1-878058-22-3*) IDG Bks.

Official 2000 Blackbook Price Guide to United States Coins. 38th ed. Marc Hudgeons & Tom Hudgeons. (Illus.). 596p. 1999. pap. 6.99 (*0-676-60069-7*) Hse Collectbls.

Officially Supported Export Credits: Developments & Prospects. K. Burke Dillon et al. LC 87-35493. (World Economic & Financial Surveys Ser.). vi, 47p. 1988. pap. 10.00 (*1-55775-006-8*) Intl Monetary.

Officially Supported Export Credits: Developments & Prospects. G. G. Johnson et al. (World Economic & Financial Surveys Ser.). 51p. 1990. pap. 20.00 (*1-55775-139-0*) Intl Monetary.

*__Official's Guide: Basketball 1999-2000.__ Bill Topp. 107p. 1999. pap. 9.95 (*1-58208-012-7*) Ref Enterps.

*__Official's Guide: Soccer 99-00.__ Carl P. Schwartz et al. 97p. 1999. pap. 9.95 (*1-58208-011-9*, Referee Books) Ref Enterps.

Officier Sans Nom. Guy Des Cars. (FRE.). 320p. 1985. pap. 7.95 (*0-7859-4787-6*) Fr & Eur.

Officine: The Pharmacy. 21st ed. F. Dorvault. (FRE.). 1958p. 1982. 250.00 (*0-8288-1800-2*, M15478) Fr & Eur.

Offizier der Cavallerie. Alexis F. L'Hotte. (GER., Illus.). 344p. 1979. write for info. (*3-487-08186-5*) G Olms Pubs.

Offizin Schriftenreihe 20 Tex und Metafont - Offizin I. Dante Alighieri. (GER.). (C). 1991. text. write for info. (*0-201-57863-8*) Addison-Wesley.

Offline. Lawrence Goldstone. LC 98-10202. 288p. 1998. text 22.95 (*0-312-18641-X*) St Martin.

*__Offramp 7: Detours & Dialogues.__ Alan Loomis et al. (Illus.). 120p. 2000. pap. 24.95 (*1-56898-222-4*) Princeton Arch.

Offrandes Vegetales dans l'Ancien Testament: Du Trigut d'Hommage au Repas Eschatologique. Alfred Marx. (FRE.). 186p. 1994. text 98.00 (*90-04-10136-5*) Brill Academic Pubs.

Offray's Glorious Weddings. Ellie Schneider. LC 99-19166. 1998. 27.50 (*1-56799-650-7*, Friedman-Fairfax) M Friedman Pub Grp Inc.

Offray's Splendor of Ribbon: More Than Fifty Glorious Ribbon Craft Projects. Ellie Schneider. LC 96-34089. 1997. 24.95 (*1-56799-397-4*, Friedman-Fairfax) M Friedman Pub Grp Inc.

Offroad Truck Racing. Bill McAuliffe. LC 98-7246. (Motorsports Ser.). (J). 1998. 19.00 (*0-7368-0026-3*) Capstone Pr.

Offseason: A Novel. Naomi Holech. LC 97-14164. 230p. 1997. 23.95 (*0-571-19922-4*) Faber & Faber.

*__Offset Berlin Post Office Stamps of 1920.__ David W. Barnette. Ed. by Jason H. Manchester. (15 G Handbook Ser.: Vol. 2). (Illus.). 26p. 1998. pap. 10.00 (*0-9624796-2-4*) D Manchester.

Offset-Dependent Reflectivity: Theory & Practice of AVO Analysis. Ed. by John P. Castagna & Milo M. Backus. LC 93-14279. (Investigations in Geophysics Ser.: No. 8). (Illus.). 345p. 1993. text 120.00 (*1-56080-059-3*, 108A) Soc Expl Geophys.

Offset Lithographic Technology. Kenneth F. Hird. LC 95-1914. (Illus.). 720p. (C). 1995. text 45.28 (*1-56637-191-0*) Goodheart.

Offset Lithography. Jack Rudman. (Occupational Competency Examination (OCE) Ser.: Vol. 27). 47.95 (*0-8373-5777-2*) Nat Learn.

Offset Lithography. Jack Rudman. (Occupational Competency Examination Ser.: OCE-27). 1994. pap. 27.95 (*0-8373-5727-6*) Nat Learn.

Offset Lithography - Visual Aid Kit. Pira Staff. 1998. 95.00 (*1-85802-056-5*, Pub. by Pira Pub) Bks Intl VA.

Offset Photographer. Jack Rudman. (Career Examination Ser.: C-560). 1994. pap. 27.95 (*0-8373-0560-8*) Nat Learn.

Offset Pressman. Jack Rudman. (Career Examination Ser.: C-561). 1994. pap. 27.95 (*0-8373-0561-6*) Nat Learn.

Offset Printing Machine Operator. Jack Rudman. (Career Examination Ser.: C-562). 1994. pap. 27.95 (*0-8373-0562-4*) Nat Learn.

Offsets. John Elsberg. Ed. by Ruth M. Kempher. LC 98-190515. (Illus.). 68p. (Orig.). 1994. pap. write for info. (*0-9637483-5-1*) Kings Estate.

Offsets. 2nd rev. ed. John Elsberg. LC 98-190515. (Orig.). 1998. pap. write for info. (*1-888832-14-2*) Kings Estate.

O

An Asterisk (*) at the beginning of an entry indicates that the title is appearing for the first time.

Offshore & Arctic Operations, 1994, Vol. 58. Ed. by N. M. Ismail et al. 164p. 1994. pap. 42.50 (*0-7918-1184-0*) ASME.

Offshore. Anne Atik. 80p. (Orig.). 1991. pap. 16.95 (*1-870612-02-7*, Pub. by Enitha Pr) Dufour.

Offshore. Penelope Fitzgerald. LC 97-50403. 141p. 1998. pap. 11.00 (*0-395-47804-9*) HM.

Offshore: Britain & the European Idea, March 1992. Giles Radice. 256p. 1992. text 22.95 (*1-85043-529-4*, Pub. by I B T) St Martin.

Offshore Advantage. Terry L. Neal. LC 98-40732. 272p. 1998. 29.95 (*1-57101-331-8*) MasterMedia Pub.

Offshore & Arctic Operations, 1993. Ed. by A. S. Tawfik & S. Khurana. (PD Ser.: Vol. 51). 159p. 1993. pap. 40.00 (*0-7918-0946-3*, H00778) ASME.

Offshore & Arctic Operations, 1995: Proceedings: The Energy & Environmental EXPO '95 - the Energy-Sources Technology Conference & Exhibition (1995: Houston, TX) Ed. by S. Khurana et al. LC 82-70515. (PD Ser.: Vol. 68). 261p. 1995. pap. 99.00 (*0-7918-1291-X*, H00923) ASME.

***Offshore & Nearshore Geotechnical Engineering: Proceedings of the International Conference, GEOShore, 2-3 December 1999.** Ed. by Sushil Kumar Singh & Suzanne Lacasse. (Illus.). 488p. (C). 2000. text 90.00 (*90-5809-211-9*, Pub. by A A Balkema) Ashgate Pub Co.

Offshore & Onshore Engineering. ICHEM Engineers Staff. (Institution of Chemical Engineers Symposium Ser.). 1996. 33.61 (*0-08-030284-X*, Pergamon Pr) Elsevier.

Offshore Asset Protection Workbook. unabridged ed. Alan Stang. (Illus.). 174p. 1997. spiral bd., wbk. ed. 49.00 (*0-9656313-3-8*) Catacombs Pr.

Offshore Bidding Agreements: Tailoring the Right One for Your Company. American Bar Association, Natural Resources Law St. LC 86-72950. 44p. 1986. pap. 39.95 (*0-89707-280-4*, 535-0010) Amer Bar Assn.

Offshore Blowouts: Causes & Control. Per Holand. LC 97-20910. 1997. 95.00 (*0-88415-514-5*, 5514) Gulf Pub.

Offshore Breakwaters & Shore Evolution Control. K. W. Pilarczyk & Ryszard B. Zeidler. LC 99-227568. (Illus.). 570p. (C). 1996. text 181.00 (*90-5410-627-1*, Pub. by A A Balkema) Ashgate Pub Co.

Offshore Conspiracy. large type ed. John N. Chance. 224p. 1996. pap. 18.99 (*1-85389-589-X*, Dales) Ulverscroft.

Offshore Cruising Encyclopedia, Version II. rev. ed. Steve Dashew & Linda Dashew. (Illus.). 1232p. 1997. 109.90 incl. audio compact disk (*0-9658028-6-8*) Beowulf.

Offshore Cruising Encyclopedia, Version II. 2nd rev. ed. Steve Dashew & Linda Dashew. LC 97-72568. (Illus.). 1232p. 1997. 89.95 (*0-9658028-1-7*) Beowulf.

Offshore Disposal - Results of the 106-Mile Dumpsite Study, Vol. 3. A. Robertson. 604p. 1997. pap. text 84.00 (*90-5699-059-4*) Gordon & Breach.

Offshore Disposal - Results of the 106-Mile Dumpsite Study: Biological Fates & Effects, Vol. 3. A. Robertson. 228p. 1996. pap. text 36.00 (*90-5699-034-9*) Gordon & Breach.

Offshore Disposal - Results of the 106-Mile Dumpsite Study: Transport Processes, Vol. 2. Ed. by A. Robertson. 180p. 1997. pap. text 26.00 (*2-919875-17-5*) Gordon & Breach.

Offshore Disposal - Results of the 106-Mile Dumpsite Study: Water Column & Sediment Fates, Vol. 2. Ed. by A. Robertson. 196p. 1997. pap. text 26.00 (*90-5699-033-0*) Gordon & Breach.

Offshore Disposal of Radioactive Waste by Drilled Emplacement: A Feasibility Study. M. R. Bury. 192p. 1985. lib. bdg. 112.00 (*0-86010-708-6*) G & T Inc.

Offshore Engineering. Ed. by F. L. Carneiro et al. LC 97-80093. 520p. 1997. 225.00 (*1-85312-537-7*, 5377) Computational Mech MA.

Offshore Engineering: An Introduction. Angus Mather. (Illus.). 290p. 1995. 135.00 (*1-85609-078-7*, Pub. by Witherby & Co) St Mut.

Offshore Engineering: Development of Small Oilfields. Goodfellow Associates Staff. (Illus.). 250p. 1986. lib. bdg. 145.00 (*0-86010-663-2*) G & T Inc.

Offshore Entrepreneur: Profit & Opportunity Have No Borders. Adam Starchild. LC 95-61681. 164p. (Orig.). 1995. pap. 12.95 (*0-9648115-0-2*) First Str Pr.

Offshore Field Development Atlas of North West Europe: 1998 Edition. 2nd ed. Oilfield Publications Limited Staff. (Illus.). 48p. 1997. pap. 162.00 (*1-870945-84-0*) Oilfield Publns.

Offshore Finance Centers & Tax Havens: The Rise of Global Capital. Mark Hampton & Jason Abbott. LC 98-56082. 1999. 45.95 (*1-55753-165-X*) Purdue U Pr.

Offshore Finance Handbook, 1998: A Guide to Offshore Centres for Asian Companies. Asia Law & Practice Staff. 268p. 1997. pap. 140.00 (*962-360-028-3*, Pub. by Asia Law & Practice) Am Educ Systs.

Offshore Finance Yearbook, 1999-2000. Euromoney Books Staff. (Euromoney Yearbks.). 273p. 1999. pap. 195.00 (*1-85564-715-X*, Pub. by Euromoney) Am Educ Systs.

***Offshore Financial Centers, Accounting Services & the Global Economy.** David L. McKee et al. LC 99-59832. 2000. write for info. (*1-56720-310-8*, Quorum Bks) Greenwood.

Offshore Financial Centres, Vol. 4. Ed. by Richard Roberts. (International Financial Centres Ser.). 640p. 1994. 200.00 (*1-85898-155-7*) E Elgar.

Offshore Financial Services Handbook. 2nd ed. W. Penman Brown. 304p. 1999. 155.00 (*1-85573-413-3*) Am Educ Systs.

Offshore Fire-Fighting Manual. Lorne & MacLean Marine & Offshore Publications Sta. (C). 1987. 400.00 (*0-7855-4373-2*, Pub. by Lorne & MacLean Marine) St Mut.

Offshore Fire Safety. A. Tony Paterson. LC 93-12103. 300p. 1993. 25.00 (*0-87814-381-5*, S4516) PennWell Bks.

***Offshore Funds.** 202p. 1999. pap. 145.00 (*962-7762-52-0*) ISI Publications.

Offshore Geologic Hazards: A Short Course Presented at Rice University, May 2-3, 1981 for the Offshore Technology Conference. Arnold H. Bouma. LC QE0026.2.A43. (Education Course Note Ser.: Vol. 18). 469p. reprint ed. pap. 145.40 (*0-608-08730-0*, 206936900004) Bks Demand.

Offshore Guide to Forty-Eight Fishing Waypoints: Loran C & Global Positioning System Coordinates. Enrico Monti. (Illus.). 9p. (Orig.). 1996. pap. text, spiral bd. 25.00 (*1-890322-01-6*) Monti & Assocs.

Offshore Haven Banks, Trusts & Companies: The Business of Crime in the Euromarket. Richard H. Blum. LC 83-27059. 310p. 1984. 55.00 (*0-275-91732-0*, C1732, Praeger Pubs) Greenwood.

Offshore Haven Banks, Trusts & Companies: The Business of Crime in the Euromarket. Richard H. Blum. LC 83-27059. 1984. 29.95 (*0-03-069629-1*) Holt R&W.

Offshore Havens. Arnold S. Goldstein. 256p. 1995. 20.95 (*1-880539-27-6*) Garrett FL.

Offshore Helicopter Operations. Geoffrey Russell. (Illus.). 360p. 1997. pap. 162.00 (*1-870945-87-5*) Oilfield Publns.

***Offshore Insurance Operations Conference.** 1999. ring bd. write for info. (*1-56423-074-0*) Ntl Ctr Tax Ed.

Offshore Insurance Operations Conference. Ed. by Bernard B. Goodman. 270p. 1992. text, ring bd. 125.00 (*1-56423-011-2*) Ntl Ctr Tax Ed.

Offshore Insurance Operations Conference Proceedings Book, 1994. Ed. by Bernard B. Goodman. 1994. ring bd. 125.00 (*1-56423-035-X*) Ntl Ctr Tax Ed.

***Offshore Investing Made E-Z.** Goldstein. 224p. 2000. pap. 17.95 (*1-56382-456-6*) E-Z Legal.

Offshore Investment Planning & Advice. Robin McGhee. 250p. 1996. pap. 120.00 (*0-85297-402-7*, Pub. by Chartered Bank) St Mut.

Offshore Lands: Oil & Gas Leasing & Conservation on the Outer Continental Shelf. Walter J. Mead et al. LC 85-63548. (Illus.). 172p. (Orig.). (C). 1985. 29.95 (*0-936488-10-7*); pap. 10.95 (*0-936488-01-8*) PRIPP.

Offshore Lending & Financing: A Practical & Legal Handbook for Lenders, Borrowers, Investors & Their Professional Advisers. Vaumini Amin. 192p. 1997. 210.00 (*1-85573-329-3*, Pub. by Woodhead Pubng) Am Educ Systs.

Offshore Log see Offshore Log: Your Essential GPS Companion

Offshore Log. rev. ed. Earl R. Hinz. (Illus.). 98p. 1994. pap. 15.95 (*1-878797-05-0*) Weems & Plath.

Offshore Log: Your Essential GPS Companion. rev. ed. Weems & Plath Staff. Orig. Title: The Offshore Log. (Illus.). 100p. 1997. pap. 19.99 (*1-878797-14-X*) Weems & Plath.

Offshore Mechanics & Arctic Engineering. Ed. by Mamdouh M. Salama. 569p. 1996. pap. text 170.00 (*0-7918-1492-0*, TN871) ASME Pr.

Offshore Mechanics & Arctic Engineering Vol. 1: Offshore Technology: Proceedings - International Conference (15th: 1996: Florence, Italy), 2 pts. Ed. by Subrata Chakrabarti et al. 991p. Date not set. pap. 270.00 (*0-7918-1490-4*, TN871) ASME.

Offshore Mechanics & Arctic Engineering, 1993 Vol. 1: Offshore Technology. Ed. by S. K. Chakrabarti et al. LC 82-70515. 550p. 1993. pap. 95.00 (*0-7918-0783-5*, G00677) ASME.

Offshore Mechanics & Arctic Engineering, 1993 Vol. 2: Safety & Reliability. Ed. by C. G. Soares et al. LC 82-70515. 426p. 1993. pap. 85.00 (*0-7918-0784-3*, G00678) ASME.

Offshore Mechanics & Arctic Engineering, 1993 Vol. 3, Pts. A & B: Materials Engineering. Ed. by M. M. Salama. LC 82-70515. 948p. 1993. pap. 125.00 (*0-7918-0785-1*, GX0679) ASME.

Offshore Mechanics & Arctic Engineering, 1993 Vol. 4: Arctic-Polar Technology. Ed. by W. A. Nixon et al. LC 82-70515. 219p. 1993. pap. 57.50 (*0-7918-0786-X*, G00680) ASME.

Offshore Mechanics & Arctic Engineering, 1993 Vol. 5: Pipeline Technology. Ed. by Mike Yoon et al. LC 82-70515. 464p. 1993. pap. 85.00 (*0-7918-0787-8*, G00681) ASME.

Offshore Medicine. 2nd ed. Ed. by R. A. Cox. (Illus.). 280p. 1986. 102.00 (*0-387-16201-1*) Spr-Verlag.

Offshore Money Book: How to Move Assets Offshore for Privacy, Protection, & Tax Advantage. Arnold Cornez. LC 98-7261. 288p. 1998. pap. 17.95 (*0-8092-2880-7*) NTC Contemp Pub Co.

***Offshore Money Book: How to Move Assets Offshore for Privacy, Protection & Tax Advantage.** Arnold Cornez. LC 99-36082. 288p. 2000. pap. 18.95 (*0-8092-2517-4*, 251740, Contemporary Bks) NTC Contemp Pub Co.

Offshore Moorings: Proceedings of a Conference Organized by the Institution of Civil Engineers. 168p. 1982. 50.00 (*0-7277-0158-4*, Pub. by T Telford) RCH.

Offshore Oil & Gas Exploration in United Kingdom: A Strategic Entry Report, 1998. Compiled by Icon Group International Staff. (Country Industry Report). (Illus.). 101p. 1999. ring bd. 1010.00 incl. audio compact disk (*0-7418-0518-9*) Icon Grp.

Offshore Oil & Gas Insurance. David W. Sharp. 500p. 1994. 495.00 (*1-85607-064-6*, Pub. by Witherby & Co) St Mut.

Offshore Oil & Gas Insurance. David W. Sharp. 500p. (C). 1994. 395.00 (*1-85609-064-7*, Pub. by Witherby & Co) St Mut.

Offshore Oil & Gas Resources: Interior Can Improve Its Management of Lease Abandonment. (Illus.). 46p. (Orig.). (C). 1995. pap. text 20.00 (*0-7881-1742-4*) DIANE Pub.

Offshore Oil Platforms (Rigs) & Offshore Oil Support Vessels Directory Owners, Operators & Managers Vol. 6: Foreign Companies Only. Compiled by James L. Pelletier. LC 97-93954. 220p. 1999. 85.00 (*0-9644915-7-5*) Marine Techn.

Offshore Oil Platforms (Rigs) & Offshore Oil Support Vessels, Owners, Operators & Managers Vol. 3: U. S. A. Companies Only. Compiled by James L. Pelletier. LC 97-93954. 215p. 1999. 85.00 (*0-9644915-4-0*) Marine Techn.

Offshore Pile Design: Design Guides for Offshore Structures. ARGEMA Staff. Ed. by Pierre Le Tirant. (Design Guides for Offshore Structures Ser.: Vol. 3). (Illus.). 324p. (C). 1992. 490.00 (*2-7108-0614-2*, Pub. by Edits Technip) Enfield Pubs NH.

Offshore Pioneers: Brown & Root Marine & History of Offshore Oil & Gas. LC 97-34516. 302p. 1997. 30.00 (*0-88415-138-7*, 5738) Gulf Pub.

Offshore Pipeline Design Elements. John B. Herbich. LC 81-15243. (Ocean Engineering, a Wiley Ser.: No. 2). (Illus.). 251p. reprint ed. pap. 77.90 (*0-7837-0954-4*, 204125900019) Bks Demand.

Offshore Platform Automation. M. A. Keyes & L. S. Rice. 222p. 1991. 39.95 (*0-9626691-0-5*) PC&OP Company.

Offshore Platforms & Pipelines: Selected Contributions. B. K. Mazurkiewicz. (Series on Rock & Soil Mechanics: Vol. 13). 390p. 1987. text 70.00 (*0-87849-058-2*, Pub. by Trans T Pub) Enfield Pubs NH.

Offshore Platforms in Brazil: A Strategic Entry Report, 1997. Compiled by Icon Group International Staff. (Country Industry Report). (Illus.). 157p. 1999. ring bd. 1570.00 incl. audio compact disk (*0-7418-0280-5*) Icon Grp.

***Offshore Platforms Update in Brazil: A Strategic Entry Report, 1999.** Compiled by Icon Group International. (Illus.). 156p. 1999. ring bd. 1560.00 incl. audio compact disk (*0-7418-1725-X*) Icon Grp.

Offshore Practice & Administration. Robin Mcghee. 300p. 1997. pap., wbk. ed. 120.00 (*0-85297-428-0*, Pub. by Chartered Bank) St Mut.

Offshore Production Concepts. 2nd ed. Oilfield Publications Limited Staff. (Illus.). 200p. 1993. pap. 155.00 (*1-870945-46-8*, P7496) Oilfield Publns.

Offshore Production in the Less Developed Countries: A Case Study of Multinationality in the Electronics Industry. Richard W. Moxon. LC HD0069.F6M68. (New York University, Institute of Finance, Bulletin Ser.: No. 98-99, July, 1974). 95p. reprint ed. pap. 30.00 (*0-608-17459-9*, 202993300066) Bks Demand.

Offshore Production Operations. (SPE Reprint Ser.). 384p. 1983. reprint ed. pap. 8.00 (*0-89520-320-0*, PRODRPT017) Soc Petrol Engineers.

***Offshore Risk Assessment Principles, Modelling & Applications of QRA Studies** Jan E. Vinnem. LC 99-38090. 1999. write for info. (*0-7923-5860-0*) Kluwer Academic.

Offshore Safety Procedures Manual. Ed. by Lorne & MacLean Marine & Offshore Publications Sta. 1987. 600.00 (*0-7855-1039-7*, Pub. by Lorne & MacLean Marine) St Mut.

Offshore Seismic Exploration: Data Acquisition, Processing, Interpretation. Rajni K. Verma. LC 86-292. 605p. 1986. reprint ed. pap. 187.60 (*0-608-01338-2*, 206208200001) Bks Demand.

Offshore Service Vessel Register, 1988. 10th ed. 1988. 275.00 (*0-8002-4221-1*) Taylor & Francis.

Offshore Site Investigation, Vol. 3. Society for Underwater Technology Staff. (Advances in Underwater Technology & Offshore Engineering Ser.). (Illus.). 316p. 1985. lib. bdg. 145.00 (*0-86010-668-3*) G & T Inc.

Offshore Site Investigation & Foundation Behaviour. Society for Underwater Technology Staff. LC 93-8336. (Advances in Underwater Technology, Ocean Science, & Offshore Engineering Ser.: Vol. 28). 788p. (C). 1993. text 442.00 (*0-7923-2363-7*) Kluwer Academic.

***Offshore Solutions: An Asset Protection Seminar.** David B. Mandell & Arnold Goldstein. 1999. 9.95 incl. audio (*1-890415-17-0*) Guardian Pub.

Offshore Structural Engineering. Thomas H. Dawson. (Illus.). 352p. 1983. text 74.00 (*0-13-633206-4*) P-H.

Offshore Structure Modeling. Subrata Chakrabarti. (Advanced Series in Ocean Engineering). 400p. 1994. text 78.00 (*981-02-1512-6*); pap. text 40.00 (*981-02-1513-4*) World Scientific Pub.

Offshore Structures, Vol. 2. 1995. text 192.95 (*3-540-19770-2*) Spr-Verlag.

Offshore Structures: Proceedings of a Conference Sponsored by the Institution of Civil Engineers, the Institution of Structural Engineers, & the Society for Underwater Technology. 216p. 1975. 82.00 (*0-7277-0008-1*, Pub. by T Telford) RCH.

Offshore Structures Vol. 1: Conceptual Design & Hydromechanics. G. Clauss et al. (Illus.). 352p. (C). 1992. 185.95 (*0-387-19709-5*) Spr-Verlag.

Offshore Structures Vol. 2: Strength & Safety for Structural Design. G. Clauss et al. (Illus.). 350p. 1995. 175.00 (*0-387-19770-2*) Spr-Verlag.

Offshore Structures Engineering: Proceedings of the International Conference...September, 1977. International Conference on Offshore Structures En. Ed. by F. L. Carneiro et al. LC 78-74102. (Illus.). 434p. reprint ed. pap. 134.60 (*0-608-17455-6*, 202992300066) Bks Demand.

Offshore Tax Planning. Giles Clarke. LC 99-187689. xxi, 225 p. 1997. write for info. (*0-406-89924-X*, Pub. by Butterworths) LEXIS Pub.

***Offshore Tax Planning.** 5th ed. Giles Clarke. LC 99-187603. xxii, 248 p. 1998. write for info. (*0-406-89923-1*, Pub. by Butterworths) LEXIS Pub.

Offshore Tax Planning for High Net Worth Individuals. 215.00 (*0-614-17019-2*, Pub. by IBC Finan Pubng) IBC Pubns.

Offshore Trust. Dennis Campbell et al. LC 96-23270. 1996. 200.00 (*90-411-0921-8*) Kluwer Law Intl.

Offside in Ecuatina. C. Rennie. Date not set. 4.99 (*1-871676-69-X*, Pub. by Christian Focus) Spring Arbor Dist.

Offsides: A Novel. Kerry Madden-Lunsford. LC 96-17164. 288p. 1996. 22.00 (*0-688-14935-9*, Wm Morrow) Morrow Avon.

Offsite Construction. Paul Dettenmaier & Bart Jahn. LC 96-40097. (Illus.). 452p. 1997. 49.95 (*0-07-016561-0*) McGraw.

Offspring. Jonathan Strong. LC 94-35508. 225p. 1995. pap. 14.95 (*0-944072-55-0*) Zoland Bks.

Offspring: A Dream in the Field. Nate Freeman. (Illus.). 40p. 1998. 16.96 (*0-9665016-0-8*) Manifest Poet.

***Offspring: Americana.** 80p. 1999. otabind 19.95 (*0-634-00632-0*) H Leonard.

Offspring: Smash. 56p. 1997. pap. 17.95 (*0-7935-8065-X*) H Leonard.

Offspring: The Generation the World Is Waiting For... Earl Paulk. 126p. (Orig.). 1996. pap. 8.99 (*1-56043-167-9*) Destiny Image.

Offspring Ixnay on 5 the Hombre. 64p. 1997. otabind 17.95 (*0-7935-8067-6*) H Leonard.

Offspring of Empire: The Koch'ang Kims & the Colonial Origins of Korean Capitalism, 1876-1945. Eckert. LC 90-47159. (Korean Studies of the Henry M. Jackson School of International). (Illus.). 406p. 1996. pap. 20.00 (*0-295-97533-4*) U of Wash Pr.

Offspring of Thought in Solitude. William C. Hazlitt. LC 79-37127. (Essay Index Reprint Ser.). 1977. reprint ed. 25.95 (*0-8369-2506-8*) Ayer.

Offspring Smash. 19.95 (*0-7935-3890-4*, 00690001) H Leonard.

Offtrack Betting Operations Analyst. Jack Rudman. (Career Examination Ser.: C-3302). 1994. pap. 29.95 (*0-8373-3302-4*) Nat Learn.

Offwatch. James Skellhorn. (Illus.). 210p. 1979. 39.95 (*0-8464-1431-7*) Beekman Pubs.

Ofice. Mark Dunster. LC 78-105243. 1978. pap. 4.00 (*0-89642-010-8*) Linden Pubs.

Oficio de Difuntos. Arturo Uslar Pietri. (Nueva Austral Ser.: Vol. 57). (SPA.). 1991. pap. text 24.95 (*84-239-1857-2*) Elliots Bks.

Oficio de la Mirada: Ensayos de Arte y Literatura Cubana. Carlos M. Luis. LC 98-87742. (Coleccion Arte). (SPA., Illus.). 231p. (Orig.). 1998. pap. 18.00 (*0-89729-884-5*) Ediciones.

Oficio de Tinieblas. Rosario Castellanos. 368p. 1998. pap. 13.95 (*0-14-026833-2*) Viking Penguin.

Oficios y Personas - Guia para Perplejos. Gladys M. Ilarregui. LC 96-61870. (Mujeres de Palabra Ser.: Vol. 1). (SPA.). 102p. (Orig.). 1996. pap. 10.50 (*0-9656050-0-0*) Los Signos.

Ofloxacin in Compromised Host: International Ofloxacin Symposium, July 12, 1990, Vancouver, Canada. Ed. by K. Shimizu. (Journal: Chemotherapy: Vol. 37, Suppl. 1, 1991). (Illus.). iv, 72p. 1991. pap. 50.50 (*3-8055-5423-0*) S Karger.

OFOTOne. John Wheatcroft. 5.95 (*0-8453-7680-2*, Cornwall Bks) Assoc Univ Prs.

Ofrendas del Templo Mayor de Tenochtitlan. Leonardo Lopez. 432p. 1993. pap. 30.00 (*968-29-4530-5*, IN001) UPLAAP.

Ofrendas Para los Dioses. Evon Vogt. (SPA.). pap. 12.99 (*968-16-0215-3*, Pub. by Fondo) Continental Bk.

OFSTED Inspections: The Early Experience. Ed. by Janet Ouston et al. 176p. 1996. pap. 27.95 (*1-85346-408-2*, Pub. by David Fulton) Taylor & Francis.

Oft Gestellte Fragen Uber den Groben Salzsee. J. Wallace Gwynn. Tr. by B. Long-Murdock. (Public Information Ser.: Vol. 55). (GER., Illus.). 22p. 1997. mass mkt. 1.75 (*1-55791-618-7*, PI-55) Utah Geological Survey.

Oft in the Stilly Night. John Rubel. (Illus.). 396p. Date not set. pap. write for info. (*0-7392-0336-3*, PO3506) Morris Pubng.

Often Asked Questions. Ed. by Joe Laird. 180p. (Orig.). 1995. pap. 5.00 (*1-56794-098-6*, C-2386) Star Bible.

Og & His Frogs. large type ed. Gabriel Simon. LC 98-19178. (Illus.). 32p. (J). (ps-3). 1998. pap., lib. bdg. 13.95 (*0-935343-72-5*) Peartree.

Og Mandino's Great Trilogy: The Greatest Salesman in the World, the Greatest Secret in the World, the Greatest Miracle in the World. Og Mandino. 419p. 1996. 14.98 (*0-8119-0852-5*) F Fell Pubs Inc.

OG Returns: OG's Further Adventures in Prayerbook Hebrew. Irene Resnikoff et al. Ed. by Jessica Goldstien. (OG the Terrible Ser.: Vol. 2). (HEB., Illus.). 24p. (J). (gr. 1-6). 1998. pap. 3.95 (*0-939144-27-1*) EKS Pub Co.

OG the Terrible: A Comic Book Introduction to Prayerbook Hebrew. Ethelyn Simon & Loren Kaplan. (HEB., Illus.). 24p. (Orig.). (J). (gr. 2-6). 1996. pap. text 3.95 (*0-939144-21-2*) EKS Pub Co.

Ogallala: A Century on the Trail, Vol. 1. Elaine Nielsen. (Illus.). 102p. 1984. 12.95 (*0-9614379-0-1*) Keith County Hist.

Ogallala: Water for a Dry Land. John Opie. LC 92-26718. (Our Sustainable Future Ser.: Vol. 1). (Illus.). xxi, 412p. 1993. text 50.00 (*0-8032-3557-7*) U of Nebr Pr.

Ogallala: Water for a Dry Land. 2nd ed. John Opie. LC 99-42161. (Our Sustainable Future Ser.). (Illus.). 536p. 2000. pap. text 25.00 (*0-8032-8614-7*) U of Nebr Pr.

Ogallala Aquifer (Of the Southern High Plains), Vol. 1. C. C. Reeves, Jr. & Judy A. Reeves. LC 96-84153. (Illus.). 360p. (Orig.). 1996. pap. 79.95 (*0-9652519-0-X*) Estacado Bks.

Ogallalah de Oro: My Life with Humans. Twintreess Staff. 139p. 1996. pap. 13.99 (*0-9645194-3-7*) TrHse Pr.

Ogam Consaine & Tifinag Alphabets - Ancient Uses. Warren W. Dexter. LC 84-70953. (Illus.). 72p. (Orig.). 1984. pap. text 8.50 (*0-914960-44-X*) Academy Bks.

An Asterisk (*) at the beginning of an entry indicates that the title is appearing for the first time.

Ogam Stones & Inscriptions. A. Gorham. (Orig.). 1993. pap. 6.95 (*1-55818-237-3*) Holmes Pub.
Ogbanje: Son of the Gods. Sam Chekwas. Ed. by Tracy Appia. (ENG & GRE.). 140p. 1994. 18.95 (*1-885778-01-5*); pap. 10.95 (*1-885778-00-7*) Seaburn.
Ogbe, the Odus of Ogbe: Including Their Interpretations, Sacrifices, Plants, Health, Taboos, Incense & Baths. Anthony C. Ferreira. 149p. 1997. pap. 21.96 (*1-890157-03-1*, Pub. by Athelia-Henrietta) BookWorld.
Ogbo: Sharing Life in an African Village. Ifeoma Onyefulu. LC 95-8882. (Illus.). 32p. (J). (gr. 2-6). 1996. 15.00 (*0-15-200498-X*, Gulliver Bks) Harcourt.
Ogden Codman & the Decoration of Houses. Ed. by Pauline C. Metcalf. LC 88-71607. (Illus.). 240p. 1988. reprint ed. 60.00 (*0-87923-777-5*) Godine.
Ogden Nash: A Descriptive Bibliography. George W. Crandell. LC 90-33726. 482p. 1990. 50.00 (*0-8108-2332-2*) Scarecrow.
Ogden Nash's Zoo. Ogden Nash. LC 86-23173. (Illus.). 84p. 1986. 10.95 (*0-941434-95-8*) Stewart Tabori & Chang.
***Ogden/Cache Entertainment, 2000.** (Illus.). 422p. 1999. pap. 20.00 (*1-880248-53-0*, 006E) Enter Pubns.
Ogden's Letters from the West, 1821-23, Bullock's Journey from New Orleans to New York, 1827, Gregg's Commerce of the Prairies, 1831-39 see Early Western Travels, 1748-1846
Oge ou le Prejuge de Couleur: Drame Historique, Suive de Poesies Fugitives et de Notes. Pierre Faubert. (B. E. Ser.: No. 2). (FRE.). 1856. 40.00 (*0-8115-2953-3*) Periodicals Srv.
Oggi in Italia, 5 vols. Ferdinando Merlonghi. (C). 1993. text 63.96 (*0-395-66859-X*) HM.
Oggi in Italia, 5 vols. Ferdinando Merlonghi. (C). 1993. pap., wbk. ed. 33.96 (*0-395-68534-6*) HM.
Oggi in Italia: A First Course in Italian. 2nd ed. Ferdinando Merlonghi et al. LC 81-85378. 1982. reel tape 270.00 (*0-685-42421-9*) HM.
Oggi in Italia: A First Course in Italian, 5 vols. 5th ed. Ferdinando Merlonghi et al. (ITA.). (C). 1994. text, teacher ed., wbk. ed. 7.56 (*0-395-68535-4*) HM.
Oggi in Italia: A First Course in Italian, 5 vols. 5th annot. ed. Ferdinando Merlonghi et al. (ITA.). (C). 1993. text, teacher ed. 65.16 (*0-395-66860-3*) HM.
Oggi in Italia: A First Course in Italian. 6th ed. Franca Merlonghi et al. (ITA.). 608p. (C). 1997. text 63.96 (*0-395-85900-X*) HM.
Oggi in Italia: A First Course in Italian. 6th ed. Franca Merlonghi et al. (ITA.). (C). 1998. pap. text, wbk. ed. 34.76 (*0-395-87970-1*) HM.
Oggi in Italia: A First Course in Italian. 6th annot. ed. Franca Merlonghi et al. (ITA.). (C). 1998. teacher ed. 65.16 (*0-395-85901-8*) HM.
Ogham: An Irish Alphabet. Cristoir M. Fhearaigh & Tim Stampton. 80p. 1998. reprint ed. pap. 7.95 (*0-7818-0665-8*) Hippocrene Bks.
OGI Pascal Development System Version 2: OGI Pascal2. Hal Clark. (Education Ser.). 1989. 65.00 (*0-918667-08-9*); student ed. 275.00 (*0-685-40820-5*) On-Going Ideas.
***Ogilvie at War.** Philip McCutchan. LC 00-28685. 2000. write for info. (*0-7862-2567-X*) Thorndike Pr.
Ogilvie at War. Philip D. McCutchan. 1999. 25.00 (*0-7278-5471-2*, Pub. by Severn Hse) Chivers N Amer.
Ogilvie Bird Collection. Enchanted Abiary Staff. 120p. (C). 1989. text 125.00 (*0-9512263-2-0*, Pub. by Enchanted Abiary) St Mut.
Ogilvie, Tallant & Moon. Chelsea Quinn Yarbro. LC 75-30658. (Red Mask Mystery Ser.). (Illus.). 214p. 1976. 6.95 (*0-399-11630-3*) Putnam Pub Group.
Ogilvy on Advertising. David Ogilvy. 1985. pap. 23.00 (*0-394-72903-X*) Vin Bks.
OGJ International Energy Statistics Sourcebook. 8th ed. Oil & Gas Journal Staff. 736p. 1996. 295.00 (*0-685-71331-8*, E1283) PennWell Bks.
Oglala Lakota Crazy Horse: A Preliminary Genealogical Study & an Annotated Listing of Primary Sources. Richard G. Hardorff. (Illus.). 22.95 (*0-8488-0019-2*, J M C & Co); pap. 16.95 (*0-8488-0020-6*, J M C & Co) Amereon Ltd.
Oglala People, 1841-1879: A Political History. Catherine Price. LC 95-23153. (Illus.). xiv, 244p. 1998. pap. text 16.00 (*0-8032-8758-5*) U of Nebr Pr.
Oglala Religion. William K. Powers. LC 76-30614. (Illus.). xxii, 237p. 1977. pap. 12.00 (*0-8032-8706-2*, Bison Books) U of Nebr Pr.
Oglala Women: Myth, Ritual, & Reality. Marla N. Powers. (Women in Culture & Society Ser.). (Illus.). xvi, 272p. 1988. pap. 15.95 (*0-226-67749-4*) U Ch Pr.
Oglasytel' Nija i Tajnovodstennija Pouchenija. St. Cyril of Jerusalem.Tr. of Prochatechisis & Mystagogical Catechesis. (RUS.). 376p. (Orig.). 1976. 18.00 (*0-88465-024-3*); pap. 13.00 (*0-88465-025-1*) Holy Trinity.
Oglasytel'nija I Tajnovdstvennija Pouchenija Svjatago Kirilma Jerusalimskago. Tr. of Prochatechisis & Mystagogical Catechesis of St. Cyril of Jerusalem. 366p. reprint ed. 18.00 (*0-317-28884-9*); reprint ed. pap. 13.00 (*0-317-28885-7*) Holy Trinity.
Ogle - Bertram, Ogle & Bothal: History of the Baronies of Ogle, Bothal & Hepple, & of the Families of Ogle & Bertram Who Held Possession of Those Baronies in Northumberland, to Which Is Added Accounts of Several Branches bearing the Name of Ogle. Henry Ogle. (Illus.). 496p. 1993. reprint ed. pap. 75.00 (*0-8328-3729-6*); reprint ed. lib. bdg. 85.00 (*0-8328-3728-8*) Higginson Bk Co.
Oglethorpe in Perspective: Georgia's Founder after Two Hundred Years. Phinizy Spalding. Ed. by Harvey H. Jackson. LC 87-19121. 256p. 1989. text 29.95 (*0-8173-0386-3*) U of Ala Pr.
Ogling Anchor. Christopher Reiner. 68p. 1998. pap. 10.00 (*1-880713-14-4*, Pub. by AVEC Bks) SPD-Small Pr Dist.
Ogljadivays Nazad: Stories Out of the Past. Eugenia Dimer. 1987. 8.00 (*0-685-22667-0*) RWCPH.
Ognennaia Pamiat' Vospominaniia o Aleksee Remizove. Natalie Reznikoff. (Modern Russian Literature & Culture, Studies & Texts: Vol. 4). (RUS., Illus.). 147p. 1980. pap. 8.50 (*0-933884-14-1*) Berkeley Slavic.
Ogoni's Agonies: Ken Saro-Wiwa & the Crisis in Nigeria. Abdul-Rasheed Naallah. LC 98-22493. 350p. 1998. 79.95 (*0-86543-646-0*); pap. 21.95 (*0-86543-647-9*) Africa World.
Ogonyok. Maria D. Lekic. (RUS., Illus.). 128p. 1995. pap. 49.95 incl. audio (*0-8442-4273-X*) NTC Contemp Pub Co.
Ogonyok: Advanced. Maria D. Lekic. (RUS.). 160p. (YA). 1994. teacher ed. 10.60 (*0-685-62844-2*, F4276-4, Natl Textbk Co) NTC Contemp Pub Co.
Ogonyok: Advanced. Maria D. Lekic. (RUS.). 144p. (YA). 1994. pap. 26.75 (*0-8442-4275-6*, F4275-6, Natl Textbk Co) NTC Contemp Pub Co.
Ogopogo: The Million Dollar Monster. Arlene Gaal. (Illus.). 128p. 1986. 6.95 (*0-88839-987-1*) Hancock House.
Ogopogo Affair. Mel D. Ames. 96p. 1993. pap. 12.95 (*0-88962-538-7*) Mosaic.
Ogranichennaia Zadacha Trekh Tel see Restricted Three-Body Problem: Plane Periodic Orbits
Ogre. Tournier. 1984. 10.95 (*0-07-544558-1*) McGraw.
Ogre. Michel Tournier. Tr. by Barbara Bray from FRE. LC 96-46778. 384p. 1997. reprint ed. pap. 15.95 (*0-8018-5590-X*) Johns Hopkins.
Ogre & the Angel: To Go & Tell Somebody. Micheal Hardgrove. Ed. by J. Franklin Hardgrove. (Illus.). 32p. (J). (ps-6). 1998. pap. 12.95 (*0-9660797-2-8*, OAA) Twinke Pub.
Ogre Battle: Official Secrets & Solutions. Prima Publishing Staff. LC 97-68840. 144p. 1997. per. 12.99 (*0-7615-1224-1*) Prima Pub.
***Ogre Battle 64.** Prima Temp Authors. (Official Strategy Guides Ser.). (Illus.). 144p. (YA). 2000. pap. 14.99 (*0-7615-2784-2*, Prima Tech) Prima Pub.
Ogre Battle the March of the Black Queen: Official Power Play Guide. Ed Dille. LC 95-70452. 1995. pap. 14.95 (*0-7615-0289-0*) Prima Pub.
***Ogre Battlefields.** Ed. by Steve Jackson. (Illus.). 2000. 14.95 (*1-55634-441-4*) S Jackson Games.
Ogre Fun. Loris Lesynski. (Illus.). 32p. (J). (ps-2). 1997. pap. 5.95 (*1-55037-446-X*, Pub. by Annick); lib. bdg. 15.95 (*1-55037-447-8*, Pub. by Annick) Firefly Bks Ltd.
Ogre Fun. Loris Lesynski. 1997. 11.15 (*0-606-12784-4*, Pub. by Turtleback) Demco.
Ogre Here, Ogre There - Musical. Jerry Kraft & Charles Kenfield. 60p. (J). 1996. pap. 5.50 (*0-87129-610-1*, O06) Dramatic Pub.
Ogre Miniatures. Steve Jackson. Ed. & Illus. by Steve Jackson Games Staff. 64p. 1992. pap., suppl. ed. 14.95 (*1-55634-219-5*, 7203, Pub. by S Jackson Games) BookWorld.
Ogre, Ogre. Piers Anthony. LC 82-6659. (Magic of Xanth Ser.). 320p. 1987. mass mkt. 5.95 (*0-345-35492-3*, Del Rey) Ballantine Pub Grp.
Ogre, Ogre. Piers Anthony. (Magic of Xanth Ser.). (J). 1982. 11.05 (*0-606-02599-5*, Pub. by Turtleback) Demco.
Ogre Slayer. Kei Kusunoki. (Illus.). 184p. 1997. pap. 15.95 (*1-56931-198-6*, Viz Comics) Viz Commns Inc.
Ogre Slayer: Loves Bitter Fruit. Kei Kusunoki. (Illus.). 184p. 1998. pap. text 15.95 (*1-56931-261-3*, Viz Comics) Viz Commns Inc.
O'Greenwich Village: A Primo Guide to Shopping, Eating, & Making Merry in True Bohemia. Robert Heide & John Gilman. LC 94-46638. 1995. pap. 13.95 (*0-312-11869-4*) St Martin.
***Ogre/Gev: Two Classic Games of Future Tank Warfare.** Steve Jackson. 2000. pap. 14.95 (*1-55634-426-0*, 925-118, Pub. by S Jackson Games) BookWorld.
Ogres see Ogros
***Ogres! Ogres! Ogres! A Feasting Frenzy from A to Z.** Nicholas Heller. LC 98-51919. (Illus.). 32p. (J). (gr. k-3). 1999. 15.89 (*0-688-16987-2*, Grenwillow Bks) HarpC Child Bks.
Ogres! Ogres! Ogres! A Feasting Frenzy from A to Z. Nicholas Heller. LC 98-51919. (Illus.). 32p. (YA). (gr. k-3). 1999. 16.00 (*0-688-16986-4*, Grenwillow Bks) HarpC Child Bks.
Ogre's Embrace. Rachid Mimouni. Tr. by Shirley Eber. 224p. 1993. 19.95 (*0-7043-7043-3*, Pub. by Quartet) Interlink Pub.
Ogres' Magic Clubs - The Tiger & the Dried Persimmons. Duance Vorhees & Mark Mueller. (Korean Folk Tales for Children Ser.: Vol. 5). (Illus.). 46p. (J). (gr. 2-5). 1998. lib. bdg. 10.95 (*0-930878-88-4*) Hollym Intl.
Ogri Collection, the Bumper Selection of Ogri Cartoons!, 3 vols. Paul Sample. 192p. 1999. pap. 29.95 (*1-85960-616-4*, Pub. by J H Haynes & Co) Motorbooks Intl.
Ogros. Illus. by Juan G. Herrera.Tr. of Ogres. (SPA.). 89p. (J). (gr. 4-6). 1994. 14.99 (*958-07-0314-0*, Pub. by Santillana) T R Bks.
Ogs Discover Fire. Felicity Everett. (Reading for Beginners Ser.). (Illus.). 24p. (J). (gr. k-4). 1995. text 4.95 (*0-7460-2016-3*, Usborne); lib. bdg. 12.95 (*0-88110-737-9*, Usborne) EDC.
Ogs Invent the Wheel. Felicity Everett. (Reading for Beginners Ser.). (Illus.). 24p. (J). (gr. k-4). 1995. pap. 4.95 (*0-7460-2018-X*, Usborne); lib. bdg. 12.95 (*0-88110-746-8*, Usborne) EDC.
Og's Learn to Float. Felicity Everett. (Illus.). (J). (gr. k-4). 1996. pap. 4.95 (*0-7460-2541-6*, Usborne); lib. bdg. 12.95 (*0-88110-785-9*, Usborne) EDC.
Og's Learn to Fly. Felicity Everett. (Reading for Beginners Ser.). (Illus.). 24p. (J). (gr. k-4). 1995. pap. 4.95 (*0-7460-2022-8*); lib. bdg. 12.95 (*0-88110-776-X*, Usborne) EDC.
Ogun: Ifa & the Spirit of Iron. Fa'lokum Fatuumbi. 32p. 1993. pap. 4.95 (*0-942272-28-5*) Original Pubns.
Ogunquit by-the-Sea. John D. Bardwell. LC 95-188693. (Images of America Ser.). 1994. pap. 14.99 (*0-7524-0080-0*) Arcadia Publng.
***Ogun's Children: The Literature & Politics of Wole Soyinka since the Nobel Prize** Onookome Okome. LC 99-22539. 1999. write for info. (*0-86543-667-3*) Africa World.
***Oh!** Kevin Henkes. LC 98-51890. (Illus.). 24p. (J). (ps-k). 1999. 14.89 (*0-688-17054-4*, Grenwillow Bks); 14.95 (*0-688-17053-6*, Grenwillow Bks) HarpC Child Bks.
Oh . . . Those Hot Lazy Days of Summer. Bernadine C. Taylor. 250p. 1998. pap. 18.95 (*1-890301-08-6*) M Bey.
Oh, A-Hunting We Will Go. John M. Langstaff. LC 91-1987. (Illus.). 32p. (J). (gr. k-3). 1991. reprint ed. mass mkt. 5.99 (*0-689-71503-X*) Aladdin.
Oh, A-Hunting We Will Go Big Book: Black & White Nellie Edge I Can Read & Sing Big Book. Illus. by Kathleen Brady. (J). (ps-2). 1988. pap. text 20.00 (*0-922053-14-6*) N Edge Res.
Oh Africa, My Africa: A Personal Encounter with the Ghanaian People & the Culture of Africa. Nancy H. Sweet. (Illus.). 95p. (Orig.). 1993. pap. 10.00 (*1-56411-030-3*) Untd Bros & Sis.
Oh Africa, My Africa: A Personal Encounter with the Ghanaian People & the Culture of Africa. 2nd rev. ed. Nancy H. Sweet. LC 93-91845. 120p. (Orig.). 1994. pap. text 14.95 (*0-9640134-0-1*) M H Sweet.
Oh, America. Cleve Miller. 93p. 1999. pap. 10.95 (*0-9669179-5-2*) Fifth Wrld.
Oh America & January 12, 1967. J. Chester Johnson. LC 75-12496. (Orig.). 1975. reprint ed. pap. 6.50 (*0-914426-01-X*) Juliet Pr.
Oh Angry Sea (a-ab-ba hu-luh-ha) The History of a Sumerian Congregational Lament. Raphael Kutscher. LC 74-77343. (Near Eastern Researches Ser.: No. 6). (Illus.). 208p. 1975. 35.00 (*0-300-01579-8*) Yale U Pr.
***Oh, Babies!** Susan Meier. (Romance Ser.: Vol. 144). 2000. per. 3.50 (*0-373-19433-1*) Silhouette.
Oh, Baby! Lauryn Chandler. (Silhouette Romance Ser.). 1994. per. 2.75 (*0-373-19033-6*, 1-19033-9) Harlequin Bks.
Oh Baby! Sara Stein. LC 93-12677. (J). 1993. 11.15 (*0-606-09703-1*, Pub. by Turtleback) Demco.
Oh Baby! Sara Stein. LC 93-12677. (Illus.). 32p. (J). (ps-3). 1995. pap. 5.95 (*0-8027-7464-4*) Walker & Co.
Oh, Baby! Sara Stein. (Illus.). 32p. (J). (ps-1). 1993. lib. bdg. 15.85 (*0-8027-8262-0*) Walker & Co.
Oh, Baby! Sara Stein. (Illus.). 32p. (J). (ps-1). 1993. 14.95 (*0-8027-8261-2*) Walker & Co.
Oh, Baby! A Touch-&-Feel Book, 1 vol. Elizabeth Hathon. (Touch & Feel Ser.). (Illus.). 12p. (J). (ps). 1999. 6.99 (*0-448-41897-5*, G & D) Peng Put Young Read.
***Oh, Baby! Bachelors & Babies.** Leandra Logan. (Temptation Ser.: No. 753). 1999. per. 3.75 (*0-373-25853-4*, 1-25853-2) Harlequin Bks.
Oh Baby! Cartoons for New Parents. Randy Glasbergen. Ed. by Cliff Carle. (Illus.). 96p. 1998. pap. 5.95 (*1-57644-064-8*) CCC Pubns.
Oh Baby, the Places You'll Go. Tish Rabe. 1997. 6.99 (*0-679-88975-2*) Random.
Oh, Baby, the Places You'll Go! A Book to Be Read in Utero. Dr. Seuss, pseud. LC 97-68651. (Life Favors Ser.). (Illus.). 32p. (J). 1997. 6.99 (*0-679-88572-2*, Pub. by Random Bks Yng Read) Random.
Oh, Be Careful. (Sing-Along Bible Songs Ser.). (Illus.). 10p. (J). (ps). 1998. 5.99 (*0-310-97558-1*) Zondervan.
Oh, Be Careful Little Ears: The Music We Choose - Is That the Bible? Kimberly A. Smith. LC 97-61414. 144p. 1997. pap. 9.99 (*1-57921-045-7*, Pub. by WinePress Pub) BookWorld.
Oh! Big Band. Date not set. 40.00 (*0-7935-4833-0*, 00000796) H Leonard.
Oh, Bother! No One's Listening. (Look-Look Bks.). (Illus.). 24p. (J). (ps-3). 1991. 3.29 (*0-307-12637-4*, 12637, Goldn Books) Gldn Bks Pub Co.
Oh, Bother! Someone Won't Share. Betty Birney. (Look-Look Bks.). (Illus.). 24p. (J). (ps-3). 1993. pap. 3.29 (*0-307-12766-4*, 12766) Gldn Bks Pub Co.
Oh, Bother! Someone's Afraid of the Dark! Betty Birney. LC 97-225449. (Look-Look Bks.). (Illus.). 24p. (J). (ps-3). 1994. 3.29 (*0-307-12843-1*, 12843) Gldn Bks Pub Co.
Oh, Bother! Someone's Baby-Sitting. Betty Birney & Mary J. Fulton. LC 98-102599. (Look-Look Bks.). (Illus.). (J). (ps-3). 1997. 3.29 (*0-307-12634-X*, 12634, Goldn Books) Gldn Bks Pub Co.
Oh Bother! Someone's Fibbing. Betty Birney & Mary J. Fulton. LC 98-102595. (Look-Look Bks.). (Illus.). 24p. (J). (ps-3). 1997. 3.29 (*0-307-12636-6*, 12636, Goldn Books) Gldn Bks Pub Co.
Oh, Bother! Someone's Fighting. Betty Birney & Mary J. Fulton. LC 98-102548. (Look-Look Bks.). (Illus.). (J). (ps-3). 1997. 3.29 (*0-307-12635-8*, 12635, Goldn Books) Gldn Bks Pub Co.
Oh, Bother! Someone's Grumpy. Betty Birney. LC 98-102593. (Look-Look Bks.). (Illus.). 24p. (J). (ps-3). 1997. 3.29 (*0-307-12667-6*, 12667, Goldn Books) Gldn Bks Pub Co.
Oh, Bother! Someone's Jealous. Betty Birney. LC PZ7.B52285Sog 1997. (Look-Look Bks.). (Illus.). 24p. (J). (ps-3). 1997. 3.29 (*0-307-12820-2*, 12820, Goldn Books) Gldn Bks Pub Co.
Oh, Bother! Someone's Messy. Betty Birney. LC 98-102581. (Look-Look Bks.). (Illus.). (J). (ps-3). 1997. 3.29 (*0-307-12690-0*, 12690, Goldn Books) Gldn Bks Pub Co.
Oh Bother! It's the Easter Bunny! A Honey Pot Book. Walter Elias Disney. LC 97-156040. (Pooh Ser.). 10p. (J). 1997. 4.98 (*1-57082-583-1*, Pub. by Mouse Works) Time Warner.
Oh Boy! Sex Comics by Brad Parker. Brad Parker. (Illus.). 96p. (Orig.). 1988. pap. 10.95 (*0-943595-11-8*) Leyland Pubns.
Oh Boy, Boston! Patricia Reilly Giff. (Polk Street Special Ser.). (Orig.). 1997. 9.09 (*0-606-12785-2*, Pub. by Turtleback) Demco.
Oh Boy, Boston! Patricia Reilly Giff. (Polk Street Special Ser.: No. 10). (Illus.). 128p. (Orig.). (J). (gr. 1-4). 1997. pap. 3.99 (*0-440-41365-6*) BDD Bks Young Read.
Oh Boy! Muskeg, Mosquitoes & Moose: It Just Doesn't Get Any Better Than This. Joyce A. Stone. LC 91-51232. (Illus.). 180p. (Orig.). 1992. pap. text 10.95 (*0-923568-25-5*) Wilderness Adventure Bks.
Oh Boy, Oh Boy, Oh Boy! Confronting Motherhood, Womanhood & Selfhood in a Household of Boys. Karin Kasdin. 194p. (Orig.). 1997. pap. 14.95 (*0-9638327-9-4*) Sibyl Pubns.
Oh Boy! What Is It? Story Cookbook, Vol. 1. Elaine A. Mueller. LC 85-61810. (Illus.). 128p. (Orig.). 1985. spiral bd. 14.95 (*0-934713-00-6*) Results Ent.
Oh Boyz! The New Boyzone Book. Kyran O'Brien & Aileen C. O'Reilly. (Illus.). 96p. 1997. pap. 12.95 (*0-86278-503-0*, Pub. by OBrien Pr) Irish Amer Bk.
Oh, Brother! Ariel Books Staff. LC 96-85926. 80p. 1997. 4.95 (*0-8362-2641-0*, Arie Bks) Andrews & McMeel.
***Oh, Brother!** Luke David. (Rugrats Ser.). (Illus.). (J). (ps-3). 1999. per. 3.50 (*0-671-02871-5*) S&S Trade.
Oh, Brother. Johnniece M. Wilson. 128p. (J). (gr. 4-6). 1989. pap. 3.99 (*0-590-41001-6*, Apple Paperbacks) Scholastic Inc.
Oh, Brother. Johnniece M. Wilson. 1989. 9.85 (*0-606-12457-8*) Turtleback.
Oh, Brother. Arthur Yorinks. (Illus.). 40p. (J). (gr. 2-4). 1989. 15.95 (*0-374-35599-1*) FS&G.
Oh, Brother. Arthur Yorinks. (Illus.). 40p. (J). (gr. 2 up). 1991. pap. 5.95 (*0-374-45598-8*, Sunburst Bks) FS&G.
Oh, Brother!, Vol. 1. Luke David. (Rugrats Ser.: Vol. 9). (Illus.). 24p. (J). (ps-2). 1999. pap. 3.50 (*0-689-82440-8*, 076714003507, Simon Spot) Litle Simon.
***Oh Brother: Hundred Acre Wood Book about Trying New Things.** Mary Hogan. (Illus.). 176p. (J). 2001. 14.99 (*0-7868-3279-7*, Pub. by Disney Pr) Time Warner.
Oh, Brother--Oh, Sister! A Sister's Guide to Getting Along. Illus. by Brooks Whitney & Laura Cornell. LC 99-14221. 1999. pap. text 7.95 (*1-56247-748-X*, Amer Girl Library) Pleasant Co.
Oh, Brother! It's the Easter Bunny! Mouse Works Staff. (Pooh Ser.). (J). (ps). 1998. 7.98 (*1-57082-773-7*, Pub. by Mouse Works) Time Warner.
Oh! Calcutta! Kenneth Tynan. (Illus.). 192p. 1986. pap. 5.95 (*0-936839-48-1*) Applause Theatre Bk Pubs.
Oh Canada! Oh Quebec! Mordecai Richler. 1992. 20.00 (*0-685-53593-2*) Knopf.
Oh, Cats! Nola Buck. (My First I Can Read Bks.). (Illus.). 32p. (J). (ps-k). 1997. 12.95 (*0-06-025373-8*); lib. bdg. 12.89 (*0-06-025374-6*) HarpC Child Bks.
Oh, Cats! Nola Buck. LC 95-10129. (My First I Can Read Bks.). (Illus.). 32p. (J). (ps-k). 1998. pap. 3.95 (*0-06-444240-3*, HarpTrophy) HarpC Child Bks.
Oh, Cats! Nola Buck. (My First I Can Read Bks.). (J). (ps-k). 1998. 8.95 (*0-606-13005-5*, Pub. by Turtleback) Demco.
Oh, China! Elementary Reader of Modern Chinese for Advanced Beginners. Chih-Ping Chou et al. LC 97-35876. 536p. 1998. pap. text 39.50 (*0-691-05878-4*, Pub. by Princeton U Pr) Cal Prin Full Svc.
Oh! Coloring Book. Josse Goffin. (Illus.). 34p. (J). (ps-2). 1994. pap. 9.95 (*0-8109-2599-0*, Pub. by Abrams) Time Warner.
Oh, Cuan Lejos Llegaras! (Oh, the Places You'll Go) Dr. Seuss, pseud. (SPA., Illus.). (J). (ps-3). 1993. 14.95 (*1-880507-05-6*) Lectorum Pubns.
Oh, Dad, Poor Dad, Mama's Hung You in the Closet & I'm Feelin So Sad see Best American Plays: Fifth Series, 1958-1963
Oh Deer! The Venison Cookbook for Beginners. Cheri Helregel. LC 98-87367. (Illus.). 150p. 1999. pap. 13.95 (*0-87341-693-7*, DRCB) Krause Pubns.
Oh, Didn't He Ramble: The Life Story of Lee Collins. Frank J. Gillis & John W. Miner. (Music in American Life Ser.). 200p. 1989. 12.95 (*0-252-06081-4*) U of Ill Pr.
"Oh, Divine Redeemer" & "Notwithstanding My Weakness" & a More Determined Discipleship Neal A. Maxwell. LC 98-72590. (Classic Talk Ser.). 69 p. 1998. write for info. (*0-87579-984-1*) Deseret Bk.
Oh, Doctor! Harry Leon Wilson. (Collected Works of Harry Leon Wilson). 384p. 1999. reprint ed. lib. bdg. 98.00 (*1-58201-881-2*) Classic Bks.
Oh, Doug! A Dragonfly's Day. Ann Leach. (Illus.). 26p. (J). (gr. k-3). 1999. pap. 10.95 (*1-929150-00-8*) Take Flight.
Oh, Downtrodden. David Zane. LC 75-42607. 1977. 19.50 (*0-87212-057-0*) Libra.
Oh! Flower, What Happened to Your Colors? Linda M. Mutz. LC 96-78876. 50p. (J). 1996. 29.95 (*1-888024-12-7*) Ahead Desktop.
Oh, Freedom! Classroom Guide. Casey King. (Illus.). (J). 1997. pap. 1.00 (*0-676-76111-9*) Random.
Oh, Freedom! Kids Talk about the Civil Rights Movement with the People Who Made It Happen. Casey King. (J). 1997. 16.09 (*0-606-13006-3*, Pub. by Turtleback) Demco.
Oh, Freedom! Kids Talk about the Civil Rights Movement with the People Who Made It Happen. Casey King & Linda B. Osborne. LC 96-13014. (Illus.). (J). 1997. lib. bdg. 19.99 (*0-679-95856-8*) Knopf.

O

An Asterisk (*) at the beginning of an entry indicates that the title is appearing for the first time.

Oh, Freedom! Kids Talk about the Civil Rights Movement with the People Who Made It Happen. Casey King & Linda B. Osborne. (J). 1997. pap. 10.99 (*0-679-89005-X*, Pub. by Random Bks Yng Read) Random.

Oh, Fudge! A Celebration of America's Favorite Candy. Lee E. Benning. 320p. 1995. pap. 12.95 (*0-8050-2546-4*) H Holt & Co.

Oh Fudge! A Celebration of America's Favorite Traditional Candy. Lee E. Benning. LC 89-27487. 256p. 1995. 19.95 (*0-8050-1196-X*) H Holt & Co.

Oh God: It's Grimm. Mike Peters. 1988. pap. 8.95 (*1-55824-064-0*) At-A-Glance Consumer.

Oh God, Help Me! A True Story of Faith in the Life of a Polio Survivor. John E. Lindell & Ethel B. Lindell. LC 88-91189. (Illus.). 209p. 1988. pap. 10.00 (*0-9620643-0-0*) J E Lindell.

Oh God, What Do You Want Me To Do Now? Judy Galloway. 64p. 1993. pap. 5.95 (*0-9632190-3-0*) Longwood.

Oh, God, Where Are You? Abie Abraham. LC 96-90313. (Illus.). 600p. 1996. 26.95 (*0-533-11987-1*) Vantage.

Oh Grandma, You're Kidding. Gladys Douglass. (Illus.). 110p. 1983. pap. 7.95 (*0-934904-00-6*) J & L Lee.

Oh, Grow Up! Poems to Help You Survive Parents, Chores, School, & Other Afflictions. Florence P. Heide & Roxanne H. Pierce. LC 95-23177. (Illus.). 32p. (J). (ps-3). 1996. 15.95 (*0-531-09471-5*); lib. bdg. 16.99 (*0-531-08771-9*) Orchard Bks Watts.

Oh Happy Venture: A Treatise on Carmelite Prayer. Peter Bourne. 55p. 1992. pap. 2.95 (*0-930887-14-X*) Wenzel Pr.

Oh Henry - Here Comes a U-Haul! Virginia Almy & Juanitta Baldwin. LC 97-13855. (Illus.). 112p. (Orig.). 1997. pap. 15.00 (*1-880308-08-8*) Suntop.

Oh, Holy Allen Ginsberg. Nicholas A. Patricca. 1995. 5.60 (*0-87129-510-5*, O52) Dramatic Pub.

Oh How Can I Keep Singing? Voices of Pioneer Women. Jana Harris. LC 93-15970. (Illus.). 102p. 1993. pap. 10.95 (*0-86538-079-1*) Ontario Rev NJ.

***Oh, How He Loves You.** adapted ed. Corrie Ten Boom. (Corrie Ten Boom Library Ser.). 144p. 2000. 11.99 (*0-8007-1776-7*) Revell.

Oh, How I Wished I Could Read! John Gile. (Illus.). 40p. (J). (gr. k-6). 1995. pap. 7.95 (*0-910941-11-4*); lib. bdg. 12.95 (*0-910941-10-6*) JGC.

Oh How My Piper Played. Lee Netzler. LC 95-94703. (Illus.). 72p. (Orig.). 1995. pap. 11.95 (*0-9647696-2-X*) Netzler Pubng.

Oh, How the Wheel Becomes It! A Novel. Anthony Powell. LC 84-105815. 143 p. 1983. 6.95 (*0-434-59925-5*) Buttrwrth-Heinemann.

Oh, How We Danced! Elizabeth Casciani. 152p. 1996. pap. 40.00 (*1-873644-29-9*, Pub. by Mercat Pr Bks) St Mut.

Oh I Can't She Says. Phyllis Koestenbaum. 1980. pap. 6.00 (*0-87922-110-0*) Christophers Bks.

Oh I Wish I Could Be a Mother-in-Law Like This. 142p. 8.95 (*0-9615622-6-9*) McElyea Pubns.

Oh, If I Only Knew I Was Saved! Over 50 Questions Most Asked about Being Saved. Ralph Sexton, Sr. (Illus.). 78p. (Orig.). 1997. pap. 78.00 (*1-57090-070-1*, Mountain Chrch) Alexander Dist.

Oh, Jackie: A Novel. Maudy Benz. LC 97-50370. 224p. 1998. 19.95 (*1-885266-59-6*) Story Line.

Oh, Jackie: A Novel. Maudy Benz. LC 99-461934. 208p. 1999. reprint ed. pap. 12.95 (*0-425-17044-6*) Berkley Pub.

Oh, Jerusalem. Jane Yolen. LC 95-6013. (Illus.). 32p. (J). (gr. 2 up). 1996. 15.95 (*0-590-48426-5*, Blue Sky Press) Scholastic Inc.

Oh, Kay! Vocal Selections. Ed. by Carol Cuellar. 56p. (Orig.). (C). 1984. pap. text 9.95 (*0-7692-0774-X*, SF0106) Wrner Bros.

Oh, Kojo! How Could You! Verna Aardema. 1993. pap. 5.99 (*0-14-054669-3*) NAL.

Oh, Kojo! How Could You! An Ashanti Tale. Verna Aardema. 1984. 10.19 (*0-606-03880-9*, Pub. by Turtleback) Demco.

Oh la La! Let's Go to France with Tigre. Barbara Huneke et al. 36p. (J). (gr. 1). 1988. pap. 12.00 (*1-884488-02-1*) Bonjour Tigre.

Oh La La! Level 1, Pt. 1: Sing Your Way to French. Susan M. Fenton. (ENG & FRE.). 32p. 1999. pap. 29.95 incl. lp (*0-9666606-1-7*) Sonic Creats.

***Oh La La Level 1, Pt. 2: Sing Your Way to French.** Susan M. Fenton. (FRE & ENG.). 1999. pap. write for info. incl. lp (*0-9666606-3-3*) Sonic Creats.

Oh les Beaux Jours. 2nd ed. Samuel Beckett. (FRE.). 92p. 1975. pap. 12.95 (*0-7859-0607-X*, F85980) Fr & Eur.

Oh Light Sleeper, Wild Dreamer. Ed. by Richard Solly. (Illus.). 135p. 1995. pap. 9.00 (*0-927663-26-0*) COMPAS.

Oh, Little Jack. Inga Moore. LC 91-71827. (Illus.). 32p. (J). (ps up). 1992. 14.95 (*1-56402-028-2*) Candlewick Pr.

***Oh Lonesome Me.** Weta Nichols. Ed. by Melinda Conrad. 1999. 7.99 (*1-893108-08-2*) Neighbrhd Pr Pubng.

Oh Look, It's a Nosserus. Kate Noble. (Africa Stories Ser.). (Illus.). 32p. (J). (ps-4). 1995. 14.95 (*0-9631798-2-9*) Silver Seahorse.

***Oh Lord! It's the Millennium.** Jim Martin. 2000. pap. 15.00 (*0-9663249-1-9*) Mustang Publ.

Oh Lord, I Sound Just Like Mama. Lynne Alpern & Esther Blumenfeld. (Illus.). 120p. 1986. pap. 6.95 (*0-931948-93-2*) Peachtree Pubs.

Oh, Lord, It's Monday Again. Esther Blumenfeld & Lynne Alpern. (Illus.). 128p. 1991. pap. 6.95 (*1-56145-026-X*) Peachtree Pubs.

***Oh Lord, You're Beautiful: Songs of Worship & Devotion.** 112p. 1999. otabind 14.95 (*0-634-00289-9*) H Leonard.

Oh Lucky Country. Rose Cappiello. Tr. by Gaetano Rando from ITA.Tr. of Paese Fortunato. 236p. 1985. pap. 16.95 (*0-7022-1935-5*, Pub. by Univ Queensland Pr) Intl Spec Bk.

Oh, Mama! No Papa! adapted ed. Alfonso Paso.Tr. of Cosas de Papa y Mama'. 1962. pap. 5.25 (*0-8222-0839-3*) Dramatists Play.

Oh Maria. (Easy Reader Ser.: Level 1). 32p. 1991. 5.25 (*3-468-49681-8*) Langenscheidt.

Oh Millersville! Fern Gravel, pseud. Tr. by Clarence A. Andrews. LC 41-3646. (Illus.). 128p. (J). (gr. 3 up). 1981. reprint ed. pap. 5.95 (*0-685-42267-4*); reprint ed. lib. bdg. 8.95 (*0-934582-01-7*) Midwest Heritage.

***"Oh Momma!" Secrets to Loving a Super Single Mom & Her Kids: A Single Man's Guide to Success.** 64p. 2000. pap. 9.95 (*0-9701291-0-6*) Danibooks.

Oh Money! Money! Eleanor H. Porter. 23.95 (*0-8488-0305-1*) Amereon Ltd.

Oh, Mr. President. Bill Majeski. (Orig.). 1985. pap. 6.00 (*0-88734-206-X*) Players Pr.

Oh Muh Darlin'! Joe Sharpnack. Ed. by Matt Pollard. (Illus.). 40p. 1998. pap. 3.95 (*1-893859-06-1*) Thumb Cinema.

Oh My Aching Back. Leon Roots. 1966. write for info. (*0-679-50384-6*) Random.

Oh My Baby Bear! Audrey Wood. LC 89-7564. (Illus.). 32p. (J). (ps-1). 1990. 13.95 (*0-15-257698-3*) Harcourt.

Oh My Baby Bear! Audrey Wood. LC 89-7564. (Illus.). 32p. (J). (ps-1). 1995. pap. 6.00 (*0-15-200774-1*, Voyager Bks) Harcourt.

Oh My Baby Bear! Audrey Wood. 1999. write for info. (*0-15-202169-8*) Harcourt.

Oh My Baby Bear! Audrey Wood. (J). 1995. 11.20 (*0-606-07964-5*) Turtleback.

Oh My Baby, Little One. Kathi Appelt. LC 99-6363. (Illus.). 32p. (J). (ps-k). 2000. 16.00 (*0-15-200041-0*) Harcourt.

Oh, My Darling Daughter. large type ed. Eric Malpass. 384p. 1982. 27.99 (*0-7089-0881-0*) Ulverscroft.

***Oh My Goddess!** 2000. pap. 13.95 (*1-56971-474-6*, Pub. by Dark Horse Comics) Penguin Putnam.

Oh My Goddess! Kosuke Fujishima. Vol. 1. (Illus.). 152p. (Orig.). 1996. pap. 12.95 (*1-56971-207-7*) Dark Horse Comics.

***Oh My Goddess! Terrible Master URD.** Tr. by Kosuke Fujishima et al. (Illus.). 176p. (J). 1999. pap. 14.95 (*1-56971-369-3*) Dark Horse Comics.

***Oh My Goddess! The Queen of Vengeance.** Kosuke Fujishimi. (Illus.). (J). 2000. pap. 13.95 (*1-56971-431-2*) Dark Horse Comics.

Oh My Godess! No. 9: Love Potion. 1997. 12.95 (*1-56971-252-2*) Dark Horse Comics.

Oh, My Gosh, We're Pregnant. unabridged ed. Paul Peebles. LC 97-92729. (Parent's Survival Kit Ser.: Bk. 1). (Illus.). v, 92p. 1998. pap. 16.95 (*0-9660853-0-2*) Pediatric Care.

***Oh My Goth!** Voltaire. (Illus.). 1999. pap. 13.00 (*1-57989-032-6*) Sirius Ent.

Oh My! Modula-2! Doug Cooper. (C). 1990. pap. 65.50 (*0-393-96009-9*) Norton.

Oh My! Modula-2! Doug Cooper. (Illus.). (C). 1991. pap. 73.75 incl. disk (*0-393-96115-X*) Norton.

Oh My! Modula-2! Stony Brook's QuickMod Complier for DOS. Doug Cooper. (Illus.). (C). 1991. write for info. (*0-393-96090-0*) Norton.

Oh My! Modula-2! With Macintosh Data Disk. Doug Cooper. (Illus.). (C). 1991. 65.50 incl. mac hd (*0-393-96107-9*) Norton.

Oh My! Modula-2! 5.25 Disks & Reference Manual. Doug Cooper. (Illus.). (C). 1991. write for info. incl. disk (*0-393-96091-9*) Norton.

Oh My! Modula-2! with Stony Brooks: QuickMod Compiler for DOS: Text, 3.5 Disks & Reference Manual. 1990. pap. 49.50 incl. 5.25 hd (*0-393-96088-9*) Norton.

Oh My Oh My Oh Dinosaurs! Sandra Boynton. LC 93-11287. (Illus.). 20p. (J). 1993. bds. 6.95 (*1-56305-441-8*, 3441) Workman Pub.

Oh, My Word! Frank Muir & Denis Norden. 128p. 1981. 7.95 (*0-416-00811-9*, NO. 0235) Routledge.

Oh No. Sheila Samton. 1999. pap. 3.95 (*0-14-054458-5*) NAL.

Oh No! Bronwen Scarffe. LC 94-30180. (Illus.). 16p. (Orig.). (J). (ps-2). 1994. pap. 3.95 (*1-879531-58-5*) Mondo Pubng.

Oh No! A Giant Flap Book. Keith Faulkner. (Illus.). 16p. (J). (ps-1). 1991. 14.95 (*0-671-74747-9*) S&S Bks Yung.

Oh No! How to Adjust to Hotel Room Surprises. Veronica Hartwell. 24p. 1994. pap. 5.95 (*1-878647-18-0*) APU Pub Grp.

Oh No . . . Jackie-O! January Jones. 400p. 1998. 24.00 (*0-9662951-0-2*) P J Pubng.

Oh No . . . Not Another Summer. Peggy Lehmann & Dania Pettus. 224p. (Orig.). 1984. pap. 4.95 (*0-9613376-0-5*) P & L Res.

Oh No, Anna! Vivian French. LC 97-5350. (Illus.). 24p. (J). (ps-3). 1997. 14.95 (*1-56145-125-8*) Peachtree Pubs.

Oh No It Isn't. Paul Cornell. (New Adventures Ser.). 256p. (Orig.). 1997. mass mkt. 5.95 (*0-426-20507-3*, Pub. by Virgin Bks) London Brdge.

Oh No, It's Robert. Barbara Seuling. LC 98-88523. (Illus.). 128p. (J). (gr. 4-7). 1999. 14.95 (*0-8126-2934-5*, Pub. by Front St-Cricket Bks) Publishers Group.

Oh No! Not Another Christmas Play! Becky Reilly. 24p. (Orig.). 1997. pap. 5.25 (*0-7880-1037-9*) CSS OH.

Oh No! Not Another 1,000 Jokes for Kids. Michael Kilgarriff. (J). 1983. 10.09 (*0-606-04289-X*, Pub. by Turtleback) Demco.

***Oh, No! Not Another Ruin: Wickedly Funny Travel Tales of an American Adventuress.** Mimi Bartel. LC 99-75764. (Illus.). 360p. 2000. pap. 16.95 (*0-9671636-1-7*, Pub. by Floating Gallery) ACCESS Pubs Network.

Oh No Not Another Sex Book. (C). 1984. write for info. (*0-8087-5600-1*) Pearson Custom.

***Oh No, Not My Baby.** Russell James. 240p. 2000. pap. 15.95 (*1-899344-53-5*, Pub. by Do-Not Pr) Dufour.

Oh No! Not My Electric Blanket, Too? A Guide to a Healthier Home. Janice M. Marchok. Ed. by Patricia DeSimone & Katherine Conway. LC 91-72193. (Illus.). 183p. (Orig.). 1991. pap. 14.95 (*0-9629215-0-5*) Jetmarc Grp.

Oh, No, Sherman! Betty Erickson. (Illus.). 12p. (J). (gr. k-1). 1996. pap. 3.75 (*1-880612-50-X*) Seedling Pubns.

Oh No, Steven! An Anthology of Steven Stories. Elizabeth Burton. Ed. by Adolph Caso. (Illus.). 60p. (J). (gr. 4-9). 1996. pap. 11.95 (*0-8283-2019-5*) Branden Bks.

Oh, No, Toto! Katrin H. Tchana & Louise T. Pami. LC 95-32075. (Illus.). 32p. (J). (ps-2). 1997. 15.95 (*0-590-46585-6*) Scholastic Inc.

Oh-Oh. unabridged ed. Madeline J. Kitt. (Illus.). 70p. 1998. spiral bd. 8.00 (*0-9663307-5-7*) M J Kitt.

Oh, Oh . . . Daddy's Cooking! Ted W. Parod. LC 91-75372. (Illus.). 128p. 1994. spiral bd. 9.95 (*0-9627432-4-0*) Echo Lake Pr.

Oh! Pascal! Doug Cooper. LC 92-31207. (C). 1993. pap. text. write for info. (*0-393-96400-0*) Norton.

Oh! Pascal! 3rd ed. Doug Cooper. LC 92-31207. (C). 1993. write for info. (*0-393-96397-7*) Norton.

Oh Pascal! 3rd ed. Clancy Johnson. pap. text 0.00 (*0-393-96074-9*) Norton.

Oh! Pascal! With DOS Program Disk. 3rd ed. Doug Cooper. LC 92-31207. (C). 1993. pap. text 62.50 incl. 3.5 hd (*0-393-96398-5*) Norton.

Oh! Pascal! With Macintosh Program Disk. 3rd ed. Doug Cooper. LC 92-31207. (C). 1993. pap. text 62.50 incl. mac hd (*0-393-96399-3*) Norton.

Oh! Pascal! (Turbo Pascal 6.0) With IBM 5.25 Program Disk. 3rd ed. Doug Cooper. 735p. (C). 1992. 61.25 incl. 5.25 hd (*0-393-96249-0*) Norton.

Oh! Pascal! (Turbo Pascal 6.0) 3rd ed. Doug Cooper. 735p. (C). 1992. pap. 61.25 (*0-393-96077-3*) Norton.

Oh Pioneers! see Pionniers

Oh Pray My Wings Are Gonna Fit Me Well. Maya Angelou. LC 75-10268. 80p. 1997. 15.00 (*0-679-45707-0*) Random.

Oh, Pretty Woman, Crying & 19 Country Classics. 80p. (Orig.). (YA). 1993. pap. 10.95 (*0-7692-1060-0*, VF1984) Wrner Bros.

Oh, Promised Land! Bynum Shaw. 276p. 1992. 19.95 (*0-9621194-3-1*) Stratford NC.

Oh, Ranger! 14th rev. ed. Horace M. Albright & Frank J. Taylor. Ed. by William R. Jones. (Illus.). 176p. 1981. reprint ed. pap. 6.95 (*0-89646-068-1*) Vistabooks.

Oh, Rick! Eve Bunting. (Author's Signature Collection). (Illus.). 40p. (J). (gr. 3-8). 1992. lib. bdg. 12.79 (*0-89565-774-0*) Childs World.

Oh, Rick! Eve Bunting. (FastBack Romance Ser.). 1984. 11.27 (*0-606-00364-9*, Pub. by Turtleback) Demco.

Oh, Sangre de Mi Jesus - Oh, Lagrimas de Maria! A Work of Charity & Faith, a Songbook to Provide Help in Prayer & Song in Spanish (with English Translation) Hermanos of the Morada of Our Lady of Guadalupe of. (ENG & SPA.). 218p. 1995. pap., spiral bd. 20.00 (*1-880047-35-7*) Creative Des.

Oh, Say Can You Di-No-Saur. Bonnie Worth. LC 97-52314. (J). 1999. lib. bdg. 11.99 (*0-679-99114-X*, Pub. by Random Bks Yng Read) Random.

Oh, Say Can You Rhyme. Linda Haywood & Dr. Seuss. (J). 1998. pap. write for info. (*0-679-87084-9*) Random Bks Yng Read.

Oh Say Can You Say? Dr. Seuss, pseud. LC 78-20716. (Illus.). (J). (gr. 1-4). 1979. lib. bdg. 11.99 (*0-394-94255-8*) Beginner.

Oh Say Can You Say? Dr. Seuss, pseud. LC 78-20716. (Illus.). 40p. (J). (ps-3). 1979. 7.99 (*0-394-84255-3*) Beginner.

Oh Say Can You Say? Dr. Seuss, pseud. (J). 1979. 7.99 (*0-606-02216-3*, Pub. by Turtleback) Demco.

Oh, Say Can You Say Di-No-Saur. Bonnie Worth. LC 97-52314. (J). 1999. 7.99 (*0-679-89114-5*, Pub. by Random Bks Yng Read) Random.

Oh, Say Can You See. John Whitcomb & Claire Whitcomb. LC 88-13708. 1988. pap. 12.95 (*0-688-08664-0*, Quil) HarperTrade.

Oh, Say, Can You See? The Semiotics of the Military in Hawai'i. Kathy E. Ferguson & Phyllis Turnbull. LC 98-26195. (Borderlines Ser.: Vol. 10). (Illus.). 240p. 1998. 49.95 (*0-8166-2978-1*); pap. 19.95 (*0-8166-2979-X*) U of Minn Pr.

***Oh Say Can You Seed.** Bonnie Worth. (J). 2001. mass mkt. 11.99 (*0-375-91095-6*, Pub. by Random Bks Yng Read); mass mkt. 7.99 (*0-375-81095-1*, Pub. by Random Bks Yng Read) Random.

Oh, Shenandoah. Dorothy Noble-Smith. (Illus.). 336p. 1995. pap. 15.95 (*1-57087-078-0*) Prof Pr NC.

Oh, Shoot! Confessions of an Agitated Sportsman. Rex Ellingwood Beach. (Collected Works of Rex Ellingwood Beach). 280p. 1998. reprint ed. lib. bdg. 88.00 (*1-58201-537-6*) Classic Bks.

***Oh! Sing No More That Gentle Song: The Musical Life & Times of William Cumming Peters, 1805-66.** Richard D. Wetzel. LC 00-38478. (Detroit Monographs in Musicology/Studies in Music). 2000. pap. write for info. (*0-89990-094-1*) Harmonie Park Pr.

Oh Snap Rap & Hip Hops Finest. Ricky Powell. LC 97-41181. 160p. 1998. pap. 22.95 (*0-312-18149-3*) St Martin.

Oh Snow. Monica Mayper. LC 90-42088. (Illus.). 32p. (J). (ps-1). 1991. 14.95 (*0-06-024203-5*); lib. bdg. 14.89 (*0-06-024204-3*) HarpC Child Bks.

Oh Soldier Soldier. Illus. by Pam Adams. (Books with Holes Ser.). (ITA.). (J). 1975. pap. 6.99 (*0-85953-594-0*) Childs Play.

Oh, Soldier! Soldier! Illus. by Pam Adams. LC 90-48946. (Books with Holes Ser.). 16p. (J). (ps-2). 1978. 13.99 (*0-85953-093-0*, Pub. by Childs Play) Random House.

Oh, Soldier! Soldier! Pam Adams. LC 90-48946. 16p. (J). (ps-3). 1990. pap. 6.99 (*0-85953-092-2*, Pub. by Childs Play) Random House.

Oh, Such Foolishness! Illus. by Tomie De Paola. LC 78-1622. 96p. (J). (gr. 3-6). 1978. 11.95 (*0-397-31807-3*) HarpC Child Bks.

Oh, Suzannah. Katharine E. Matchette. LC 97-94863. 158p. (YA). (gr. 6 up). 1998. pap. 8.75 (*0-9645045-2-9*) Deka Pr.

Oh Terrifying Mother: Sexuality, Violence & Worship of the Goddess Kali. S. Caldwell. (Illus.). 320p. 2000. text 24.95 (*0-19-564462-X*) OUP.

Oh, That Cat! Norma Simon. LC 85-15546. (Illus.). 32p. (J). (ps-4). 1986. lib. bdg. 13.95 (*0-8075-5919-9*) A Whitman.

Oh, That Nuzzle! David Johnson. LC 96-79105. (Puzzle Place Ser.). (Illus.). 32p. (Orig.). (J). (ps-2). 1997. pap. 5.95 (*0-448-41299-3*, G & D) Peng Put Young Read.

Oh! The Answer. Lewis Raphael. 200p. (Orig.). 1997. pap. text 20.00 (*0-9659190-0-5*) Telinet.

Oh, the Pain of It All. Paul W. Sparks. LC 96-48103. (Illus.). 74p. 1997. 15.00 (*1-883911-14-1*) Brandylane.

Oh, the Places He Went: A Story about Dr. Seuss - Theodore Seuss Geisel. Maryann N. Weidt. LC 93-41370. (Creative Minds Bks.). (Illus.). 56p. (J). (gr. 3-6). 1994. pap. 5.95 (*0-87614-627-2*, Carolrhoda); lib. bdg. 19.95 (*0-87614-823-2*, Carolrhoda) Lerner Pub.

***Oh, the Places He Went: A Story about Dr. Seuss - Theodore Seuss Geisel.** Maryann N. Weidt. (J). 2000. 9.95 (*1-56137-653-1*) Novel Units.

Oh, the Places You'll Go! Dr. Seuss, pseud. LC 89-36892. (Illus.). 48p. (J). (ps-3). 1990. 17.00 (*0-679-80527-3*, Pub. by Random Bks Yng Read); lib. bdg. 17.99 (*0-679-90527-8*, Pub. by Random Bks Yng Read) Random.

Oh, the Places You'll Go! Dr. Seuss, pseud. LC 89-36892. (Illus.). 48p. (J). (ps-3). 1993. 25.00 (*0-679-84736-7*, Pub. by Random Bks Yng Read) Random.

Oh, the Things You Can Count from 1-10: Learn about Counting. Adapted by Linda Hayward & Cathy Goldsmith. LC 96-119344. (Illus.). (ps-3). 1995. pap. 3.99 (*0-679-86753-8*) Random.

***Oh, the Things You Can Say from A-Z.** Random House Staff. (Dr. Seuss Beginner Fun Ser.). (J). 1998. pap. 2.99 (*0-679-89278-8*) Random.

Oh, the Things You Can Say from A-Z: Dr. Seuss Beginner Fun Book. Dr. Seuss, pseud. (Illus.). 1995. pap. 3.99 (*0-679-86840-2*) Random.

Oh! The Thinks You Can Think! Dr. Seuss, pseud. LC 75-1602. (Illus.). 48p. (J). (ps-1). 1975. lib. bdg. 11.99 (*0-394-93129-7*) Beginner.

Oh! The Thinks You Can Think! Dr. Seuss, pseud. (J). 1987. 7.99 (*0-606-02217-1*, Pub. by Turtleback) Demco.

Oh, The Thinks You Can Think! large type ed. Dr. Seuss, pseud. LC 75-1602. (Illus.). 41p. (J). (ps-3). 1975. 7.99 (*0-394-83129-2*) Random House.

***Oh, Those Gutsy Geezers! True Wild Adventures in Senior Land.** Ed Hibler & Jacklin Allen Hibler. LC 99-69462. 2000. 25.00 (*0-7388-1304-4*); pap. 18.00 (*0-7388-1305-2*) Xlibris Corp.

Oh, Those Harper Girls! Kathleen Karr. 176p. (YA). (gr. 7 up). 1992. 16.00 (*0-374-35609-2*) FS&G.

Oh, Those Harper Girls! Or, Young & Dangerous. Kathleen Karr. (J). 1995. 10.05 (*0-606-09704-X*, Pub. by Turtleback) Demco.

Oh Those Little Rascals. Diane Permenter. 100p. 1991. pap. text 10.50 (*1-56770-247-3*) S Scheewe Pubns.

Oh, to Be in Miss Collier's Class, Again! Austinville, Alabama, 1950. Christie S. Stephens & David Liverett. (Illus.). 192p. (Orig.). 1992. pap. 12.95 (*0-9632180-4-2*) Chinaberry.

Oh, to Be Twenty Again & Twins! Al Swalling. 29.95 (*0-9671230-0-3*) Todd Commns.

Oh, Tucker! Steven Kroll. LC 97-24612. (Illus.). 32p. (J). (ps-3). 1998. 15.99 (*0-7636-0429-1*) Candlewick Pr.

Oh Turbo 5 Pascal! James Folts et al. 1990. pap. 39.50 (*0-393-96029-3*) Norton.

***Oh, What a Beautiful Morning.** Hael Rodgers. 32p. (J). (ps-3). 2000. 24.95 (*0-06-027925-7*) HarpC Child Bks.

Oh What a Feeling: A Vital History of Canadian Music. Martin Melhuish. (Illus.). 208p. 1996. pap. 24.95 (*1-55082-177-6*, Pub. by Quarry Pr) LPC InBook.

Oh What a Feeling: A Vital History of Canadian Music. Martin Melhuish. LC 97-193174. (Illus.). 208p. 1996. 19.95 (*1-55082-164-4*, Pub. by Quarry Pr) LPC InBook.

Oh What a Lovely War. Charles Chilton. (Methuen Modern Plays Ser.). (Illus.). 109p. (C). 1988. pap. write for info. (*0-413-30210-5*, A0196, Methuen Drama) Methn.

Oh, What a Lovely War. John R. Nicholas. LC 91-75916. 400p. 1991. pap. 12.95 (*0-9630445-0-8*) Harper Hse.

Oh, What a Lovely War! A Soldier's Memoir. Stanley Swift. Ed. by Evelyn Luscher. LC 98-55130. (Illus.). 96p. 1999. pap. 10.95 (*1-55571-502-8*) PSI Resch.

Oh, What a Paradise It Seems. John Cheever. LC 91-55305. (Vintage International Ser.). 112p. 1992. pap. 10.00 (*0-679-73785-5*) Vin Bks.

Oh, What a Tangled Web. John R. Carroll. 1976. 3.50 (*0-87129-439-7*, O11) Dramatic Pub.

Oh, What a Thanksgiving! Steven Kroll. 1989. pap. 3.95 (*0-590-40616-7*) Scholastic Inc.

Oh, What a Web We Weave: Computer Technology in Secondary Schools. Ed. by Tim Hillman et al. 150p. 1997. pap. 14.95 (*0-9627671-5-8*) Avocus Pub.

An Asterisk (*) at the beginning of an entry indicates that the title is appearing for the first time.

Oh, What Joy Is This Journey. Ceceila Dziura & Jack Ellis. 50p. 1994. pap. 6.95 (*0-9643594-1-3*) Aljen Pubng.

Oh What Nonsense. William Cole. 80p. 1997. pap. 3.99 (*0-14-038554-1*) Penguin Putnam.

Oh! Where Are Bloody Mary's Earrings? A Mystery Story at the Court of Queen Victoria. Robert Player. LC 74-194032. (Illus.). 228 p. (J). 1972. write for info. (*0-575-01429-6*) V Gollancz.

Oh Where, Oh Where? John Prater. (Illus.). 24p. (J). 1998. bds. 6.95 (*0-7641-5109-6*) Barron.

Oh Where, Oh Where Has My Little Dog Gone? see Extended Nursery Rhymes

Oh Where, Oh Where Has My Little Dog Gone? Iza Trapani. (Illus.). 32p. (J). (ps-2). 1998. pap. 6.95 (*1-58089-005-9*, Whispering Coyote) Charlesbridge Pub.

Oh Where, Oh Where Has My Little Dog Gone? Iza Trapani. LC 98-229962. (Illus.). 30p. (J). (ps-k). 1998. bds. 6.95 (*1-58089-016-4*, Whispering Coyote) Charlesbridge Pub.

***Oh, Wow!** large type ed. Ed. by Marc Maurer. (Kernel Bk.: Vol. 18). (Illus.). 96p. 2000. pap. 3.00 (*1-885218-18-4*) Natl Fed Blind.

Oh Yeah? Edward Angly. LC 88-82234. 64p. 1988. reprint ed. pap. 10.00 (*0-87034-088-3*) Fraser Pub Co.

Oh Yes, I Still Will Write My Poem. Sally S. Levine. Ed. by Ann B. Edelman. 57p. (Orig.). 1993. pap. 10.00 (*0-9637922-2-9*) Cherry Stne Bks.

Oh, Yes, I Want to Go Home: A Novel about the American Civil War. John M. Wilson. LC 95-72322. (Civil War Ser.). (Illus.). 240p. (Orig.). 1995. pap. 12.95 (*0-9649394-0-1*, QBI96-20041) Paint Rock.

Oh, You Beautiful Doll. Judith Arnold. (American Romance Ser.). 1993. per. 3.50 (*0-373-16496-3*, 1-16496-1) Harlequin Bks.

***Oh, Yuck! The Encyclopedia of Everything Nasty.** Joy Masoff. LC 99-43603. (Illus.). 256p. (J). (gr. 3-7). 1999. pap. 15.95 (*0-7611-0771-1*) Workman Pub.

Oh, Zalmy! Or, the Tale of the Porcelain Pony, Bk. 1. Gitel Kleinbard. (Oh, Zalmy! Ser.). (Illus.). (J). (gr. k-3). 1976. 5.95 (*0-917274-04-0*); pap. 3.95 (*0-917274-01-6*) Mah-Tov Pubns.

Oh, Zalmy!: or Tales of Two Esthers, Bk. 3. Gitel Kleinbard. (Illus.). (J). (gr. 1-4). 1979. pap. 3.95 (*0-917274-05-9*) Mah-Tov Pubns.

Oh, Zalmy! or, the Tale of the Tooth, Bk. 2. Gitel Kleinbard. (Oh, Zalmy! Ser.). (Illus.). (J). (gr. k-3). 1977. 5.95 (*0-917274-02-4*); pap. 3.95 (*0-917274-03-2*) Mah-Tov Pubns.

OHA Law Journal. 60.00 (*1-57588-344-9*) W S Hein.

Ohacracy: The Undercurrent of Africa-Centered Nationalism. Chukwudi O. Maduno. (Illus.). 118p. (Orig.). 1995. pap. text 11.99 (*0-9644596-2-0*) Ekumeku Commun.

O'Hair on Prayer. Madalyn M. O'Hair. 12p. (Orig.). 1980. 1.00 (*0-910309-30-2*) Am Atheist.

Ohana-O Janet Stewart: Visual Songs of the Islands. Janet Stewart & Ray Charrom. (Illus.). 128p. 1998. 50.00 (*1-889741-12-4*) Internatl Graphics.

O'Hara Concern: A Biography of John O'Hara. Matthew J. Bruccoli. LC 95-10698. 488p. 1995. pap. 24.95 (*0-8229-5559-8*) U of Pittsburgh Pr.

Ohashi Bodywork Book: Beyond Shiatsu with the Ohashiatsu Method. Wataru Ohashi. Ed. by Paul DeAngelis. (Illus.). 208p. 1996. pap. 24.00 (*1-56836-096-7*) Kodansha.

Ohe Pit! Ohe! Marcus Pfister. (FRE., Illus.). 32p. (J). (gr. k-3). 1996. 15.95 (*3-314-20784-0*, Pub. by North-South Bks NYC) Chronicle Bks.

Ohiang Mai Chronicle. 2nd ed. David K. Wyatt. 261p. 1998. pap. text 24.50 (*974-7100-62-2*) U of Wash Pr.

O'Higgins of Chile. J. J. Mehegan. 1976. lib. bdg. 59.95 (*0-8490-2366-1*) Gordon Pr.

Ohio see From Sea to Shining Sea

Ohio see One Nation Series

***Ohio.** (Switched on Schoolhouse Ser.). (Illus.). (J). 2000. pap. 24.95 (*0-7403-0287-6*) Alpha AZ.

Ohio. Terry Allen et al. LC 86-25063. 24p. (Orig.). 1986. pap. 5.00 (*0-932706-11-8*) WSU Art Gallrs.

Ohio. Banta. text. write for info. (*0-8050-6110-X*) St Martin.

Ohio. Dottie Brown. Ed. by Lerner Geography Department Staff. (Hello U. S. A. Ser.). (Illus.). 72p. (J). (gr. 3-6). 1992. lib. bdg. 19.95 (*0-8225-2725-1*, Lerner Publctns) Lerner Pub.

Ohio. Dottie Brown. (Illus.). 72p. (J). 1995. pap. 5.95 (*0-8225-9708-X*) Lerner Pub.

Ohio. Capstone Press Geography Department Staff. (One Nation Ser.). (Illus.). 48p. (J). (gr. 3-7). 1996. lib. bdg. 19.00 (*0-516-20266-9*) Childrens.

Ohio. Craig Cooper. (Color My State Ser.). (J). 1994. pap. 6.95 (*0-89133-249-9*) Wiley.

***Ohio.** Jim Fizzell. (Midwest Fruit & Vegetables Ser.). 256p. 2000. pap. 19.95 (*1-930604-13-0*) Cool Springs Pr.

Ohio. Dennis B. Fradin. (From Sea to Shining Sea Ser.). (Illus.). 64p. (J). (gr. 3-5). 1993. pap. 7.95 (*0-516-43835-2*) Childrens.

Ohio. Ann Heinrichs. LC 98-50079. (America the Beautiful Ser.). 144p. (YA). (gr. 5-8). 1999. 32.00 (*0-516-20995-7*) Childrens.

Ohio. Paul Joseph. LC 97-18681. (United States Ser.). (Illus.). 32p. (J). 1998. lib. bdg. 19.93 (*1-56239-870-9*, Checkerboard Library) ABDO Pub Co.

Ohio. Emily McAuliffe. (States & Their Symbols Ser.). (ps-3). 1998. 14.00 (*0-531-11609-3*) Orchard Books.

Ohio. Helen L. Poole. (Whitewater Dynasty Ser.). (Orig.). 1981. mass mkt. 2.75 (*0-89083-733-3*, Zebra Kensgtn) Kensgtn Pub Corp.

Ohio. Kathleen Thompson. LC 95-44414. (Portrait of America Library). 48p. (J). (gr. 4-8). 1996. pap. 5.95 (*0-8114-7461-5*) Raintree Steck-V.

Ohio. Kathleen Thompson. LC 95-44414. (Portrait of America Library). (Illus.). 48p. (J). (gr. 3-6). 1996. lib. bdg. 22.83 (*0-8114-7380-5*) Raintree Steck-V.

Ohio. R. E. Banta. LC 98-30104. (Ohio River Valley Ser.). (Illus.). 608p. 1998. reprint ed. 39.95 (*0-8131-2098-5*); reprint ed. pap. 19.95 (*0-8131-0959-0*) U Pr of Ky.

Ohio see Celebrate the States - Group 5

Ohio: A Geography. Laurence Wolf. 1996. text 35.00 (*0-86531-117-X*) Westview.

Ohio: A Geography. Laurence Wolf. (C). 1996. pap. text 20.00 (*0-86531-494-2*) Westview.

***Ohio: A Guide to Unique Places.** 8th ed. George Zimmermann. (Off the Beaten Path Ser.). (Illus.). 2000. pap. 12.95 (*0-7627-0826-3*) Globe Pequot.

***Ohio: An Atlas of Ohio's Greatest Off-Road Bicycle Rides.** Adam Vincent. (Mountain Bike America Guidebks.). (Illus.). 240p. 2000. pap. 17.95 (*0-7627-0699-6*) Globe Pequot.

Ohio: First Fruits of the Ordinance of Seventeen Eighty-Seven. Rufus King. LC 72-3755. (American Commonwealths Ser.: No. 13). reprint ed. 47.50 (*0-404-57213-8*) AMS Pr.

Ohio: First Fruits of the Ordinance of 1787. Rufus King. 1993. reprint ed. lib. bdg. 89.00 (*0-7812-5384-5*) Rprt Serv.

Ohio: From Territory to Statehood - From Ordinance to Constitution. League of Women Voters of Cleveland Educational Fu. 99p. (J). (gr. 7-8). 1987. pap. text 10.00 (*1-880746-04-2*) LOWV Cleve Educ.

Ohio: From Wilderness to Territory - The Law of the Land. League of Women Voters of Cleveland Educational Fu. (J). (gr. 3-6). 1987. pap. text 10.00 (*1-880746-03-4*) LOWV Cleve Educ.

Ohio: Its Land & Its People. James Killoran et al. (Illus.). 220p. (YA). (gr. 4 up). 1994. pap. text 9.50 (*1-882422-11-2*) Jarrett Pub.

Ohio: Its Neighbors, Near & Far. James Killoran et al. (Illus.). 282p. (YA). (gr. 4 up). 1995. pap. text 10.95 (*1-882422-15-5*) Jarrett Pub.

Ohio: Off the Beaten Path: A Guide to Unique Places. 7th ed. George Zimmerman & Carol Zimmerman. LC 98-35828. (Off the Beaten Path Ser.). (Illus.). 288p. 1998. pap. 12.95 (*0-7627-0273-7*) Globe Pequot.

Ohio: Our State. 2nd ed. Robert T. Howe. (Illus.). 408p. (J). (gr. 6-8). 1997. text 35.00 (*0-9631313-3-8*) Roblen Pub.

Ohio: Our State. 2nd ed. Robert T. Howe. LC 97-92316. 260p. 1997. pap., teacher ed. 24.00 (*0-9631313-4-6*) Roblen Pub.

Ohio: The Ohio Guide. Federal Writers' Project Staff & Writers Program-WPA Staff. (American Guide Ser.). 1989. reprint ed. lib. bdg. 89.00 (*0-7812-1034-8*, 1034) Rprt Serv.

Ohio: The State & It's Educational System. Harold L. Hodgkinson. 10p. 1987. 7.00 (*0-937846-82-1*) Inst Educ Lead.

Ohio: Yesterday & Today. Robert T. Howe. LC 94-68683. (Illus.). 408p. (J). (gr. 4). 1995. text 35.00 (*0-9631313-7-0*) Roblen Pub.

Ohio: Yesterday & Today. Robert T. Howe. 175p. (J). (gr. 4). 1995. student ed., ring bd. 35.00 (*0-9631313-9-7*) Roblen Pub.

Ohio: Yesterday & Today. Robert T. Howe. 250p. (J). (gr. 4). 1995. pap., teacher ed. 24.00 (*0-9631313-8-9*) Roblen Pub.

Ohio - Collected Works of Federal Writers Project. Federal Writers' Project Staff. 1991. reprint ed. lib. bdg. 98.00 (*0-7812-5703-4*) Rprt Serv.

Ohio - Collected Works of Federal Writers Project, Vol. 3. Federal Writers' Project Staff. 1991. reprint ed. lib. bdg. 98.00 (*0-7812-5720-4*) Rprt Serv.

Ohio - Collected Works of Federal Writers Project Vol. 4: Cincinnati. Federal Writers' Project Staff. 1991. reprint ed. lib. bdg. 98.00 (*0-7812-5727-1*) Rprt Serv.

Ohio Administrative Code, 17 vols., Set. 10994p. 1994. write for info. (*0-8322-0018-2*) Banks-Baldwin.

Ohio Almanac, 1997-98: An Encyclopedia of Indispensable Information about the Buckeye Universe. rev. ed. Ed. by Michael O'Bryant. (Illus.). 744p. 1997. pap. text 29.95 (*1-882203-10-0*) Orange Frazer.

Ohio Amish Directory, 1997: Holmes County & Vicinity. 2nd rev. ed. Marvin Wengerd. (Illus.). 832p. 1997. text 25.00 (*1-890050-11-3*) Carlisle Press.

Ohio & Erie Canal: A Glossary of Terms. Compiled by Terry K. Woods. LC 94-32501. (Illus.). 48p. (Orig.). 1995. pap. 7.00 (*0-87338-522-5*) Kent St U Pr.

Ohio & Its People. George W. Knepper. LC 89-7993. (Illus.). 519p. 1989. 32.00 (*0-87338-377-X*) Kent St U Pr.

Ohio & Its People. 2nd ed. George W. Knepper. LC 97-5446. (Illus.). 519p. 1997. pap. 24.00 (*0-87338-595-0*) Kent St U Pr.

Ohio & Other State Greats (Biographies) Carole Marsh. (Carole Marsh Ohio Bks.). (Illus.). (J). 1994. pap. 19.95 (*1-55609-999-1*); lib. bdg. 29.95 (*1-55609-998-3*); disk 29.95 (*1-55609-854-5*) Gallopade Intl.

Ohio Angels. Harriet S. Chessman. LC 98-34208. 144p. 1999. 22.00 (*1-57962-020-5*); pap. 16.00 (*1-57962-071-X*) Permanent Pr.

Ohio Appellate Practice, 1996-97. Alba L. Whiteside. 805p. 1996. pap. 67.50 (*0-8322-0661-X*) Banks-Baldwin.

Ohio Arrest, Search & Seizure. Lewis R. Katz. LC 84-227425. (Baldwin's Ohio Handbook Ser.). 407 p. 1984. write for info. (*0-8322-0065-4*) Banks-Baldwin.

Ohio Arrest, Search & Seizure. Lewis R. Katz. LC 97-184709. (Baldwin's Ohio Handbook Ser.). xxvii, 507p. 1997. write for info. (*0-8322-0675-X*) Banks-Baldwin.

Ohio Arrest, Search & Seizure. 4th ed. Lewis R. Katz. 480p. 1995. 58.50 (*0-8322-0629-6*) Banks-Baldwin.

Ohio Arrest, Search & Seizure 1998. Lewis R. Katz. LC 98-169663. (Baldwin's Ohio Handbook Ser.). xxx, 550p. 1998. write for info. (*0-8322-0730-6*) West Group.

Ohio Art & Artists. Edna Clark. 1993. reprint ed. lib. bdg. 89.00 (*0-7812-5350-0*) Rprt Serv.

Ohio Art Book. Lisa Kerr et al. LC 97-48751. 160p. 1998. pap. 29.95 (*0-7643-0512-3*) Schiffer.

***Ohio Atlas & Gazetteer.** 5th ed. DeLorme Mapping Co. Staff. (Illus.). (Orig.). 2000. pap. 19.95 (*0-89933-281-1*) DeLorme Map.

***Ohio Atlas & Gazetteer: Detailed Maps of the Entire State: Back Roads, Outdoor Recreation.** 5th ed. DeLorme Mapping Co. Staff. (Illus.). 1999. pap. 16.95 (*0-89933-270-6*) DeLorme Map.

Ohio Attorney General Opinions: 1995 Annual Subscription. 1995. 137.50 (*0-8322-0607-5*) Banks-Baldwin.

Ohio Attorney General Opinions, 1964-1994, Set. 1995. 1100.00 (*0-8322-0134-0*) Banks-Baldwin.

Ohio Attorney's/Paralegal's/Secretary's Handbook, 1997. 9th ed. Ed. by Jean M. Walburg. (Attorney's/Paralegal's/Secretary's Handbooks Ser.). 730p. 1997. ring bd. 59.00 (*0-927573-51-2*) Mariposa Pub.

Ohio Attorney's/Paralegal's/Secretary's Handbook, 1997. 10th ed. Ed. by Jean M. Walburg. (Attorney's/Paralegal's/Secretary's Handbooks Ser.). 712p. 1997. ring bd. 59.00 (*0-927573-45-8*) Mariposa Pub.

Ohio Automotive Directory. Ed. by T. L. Spelman. 1985. 24.95 (*1-55527-025-5*) Auto Contact Inc.

Ohio Bandits, Bushwackers, Outlaws, Crooks, Devils, Ghosts, Desperadoes & Other Assorted & Sundry Characters! Carole Marsh. (Illus.). (J). 1994. pap. 19.95 (*0-7933-0888-7*); lib. bdg. 29.95 (*0-7933-0889-5*); disk 29.95 (*0-7933-0890-9*) Gallopade Intl.

***Ohio Bankruptcy Handbook.** rev. ed. Anderson Publishing Co. Staff. 1999. pap. 59.00 (*1-58360-085-X*) Anderson Pub Co.

Ohio Basic Building Code & Related Codes, 2 vols. 1059p. 1979. ring bd. 145.00 (*0-8322-0023-9*) Banks-Baldwin.

Ohio Before 1850. Robert E. Chaddock. LC 08-18567. (Columbia University. Studies in the Social Sciences: No. 82). reprint ed. 34.50 (*0-404-51082-5*) AMS Pr.

Ohio Before 1850. Robert E. Chaddock. 1993. reprint ed. lib. bdg. 89.00 (*0-7812-5349-7*) Rprt Serv.

Ohio "BIO" Bingo! 24 Must Know State People for Kids to Learn about While Having Fun! Carole Marsh. (Bingo! Ser.). (Illus.). (J). (gr. 2-8). 1998. pap. 14.95 (*0-7933-8627-6*) Gallopade Intl.

Ohio Birds. James Kavanagh. (Pocket Naturalist Ser.). (Illus.). (gr. 9). 1999. 5.95 (*1-889903-93-0*, Pub. by Waterford WA) Falcon Pub Inc.

Ohio Black History Guide. Sara Fuller. 221p. 1975. 5.00 (*0-318-03184-1*) Ohio Hist Soc.

Ohio Blue Tips. Jeanne E. Clark. LC 98-51955. (Akron Series in Poetry). 77p. 1999. 24.95 (*1-884836-43-7*); pap. 12.95 (*1-884836-44-5*) U Akron Pr.

Ohio Bookstore Book: A Surprising Guide to Our State's Bookstores & Their Specialties for Students, Teachers, Writers & Publishers. Carole Marsh. (Carole Marsh Ohio Bks.). (Illus.). 1994. pap. 19.95 (*0-7933-2961-2*); lib. bdg. 29.95 (*0-7933-2960-4*); disk 29.95 (*0-7933-2962-0*) Gallopade Intl.

Ohio Bottles. 5th rev. ed. Ed. by Don Dzuro. LC 99-220125. 557p. 1999. pap. write for info. (*0-9672032-0-1*) OH Bottle Club.

Ohio Boy: The Ceramic Sculpture of Jack Earl. Contrib. by Jack Earl & Robert T. Teske. (Illus.). 44p. 1987. pap. 12.95 (*0-932718-23-X*) Kohler Arts.

***Ohio Business Directory, 2000 Edition.** rev. ed. American Business Directories Staff. 4208p. 1999. boxed set 520.00 incl. cd-rom (*0-7687-0179-1*) Am Busn Direct.

***Ohio Business Directory 2001.** American Business Directories Staff. 2000. 495.00 (*0-7687-0266-6*) Am Busn Direct.

***Ohio Business Entities Handbook.** 1999. pap. 65.00 (*1-58360-145-7*) Anderson Pub Co.

Ohio Canals. Frank N. Wilcox. Ed. by William A. McGill. LC 70-99108. (Illus.). 150p. reprint ed. 46.50 (*0-8357-9371-0*, 205121300089) Bks Demand.

Ohio Cemeteries Addendum. Ed. by Teresa Klaiber. 1990. 10.00 (*0-935057-61-7*) OH Genealogical.

Ohio Cemetery Records Extracted from the "Old Northwest" Genealogical Quarterly. Old Northwest Genealogical Quarterly Staff. LC 84-80083. 495p. 1989. reprint ed. 30.00 (*0-8063-1071-5*) Genealog Pub.

Ohio Census Index, Cincinnati, 1798, 1799, 1817, Vol. 1. Ronald V. Jackson. (Illus.). lib. bdg. 45.00 (*0-89593-756-5*, Accel Indexing) Genealogical Srvcs.

Ohio Census Index, 1880, 3 vols., Set. Precision Indexing Staff. 3252p. 1991. lib. bdg. 395.00 (*1-877677-14-0*) Herit Quest.

Ohio Census Index, 1850 Mortality Schedule. (Illus.). 1979. lib. bdg. 54.00 (*0-89593-453-1*, Accel Indexing) Genealogical Srvcs.

Ohio Census Index, 1860 North West Federal. (Illus.). 1988. lib. bdg. 320.00 (*0-89593-455-8*, Accel Indexing) Genealogical Srvcs.

Ohio Census Index, 1860 North East Federal. (Illus.). 1988. lib. bdg. write for info. (*0-89593-454-X*, Accel Indexing) Genealogical Srvcs.

Ohio Census Index, 1860 South West Federal. (Illus.). 1988. lib. bdg. 330.00 (*0-89593-456-6*, Accel Indexing) Genealogical Srvcs.

Ohio Census Index, 1810. Ronald V. Jackson. (Illus.). lib. bdg. 45.00 (*0-89593-758-1*, Accel Indexing) Genealogical Srvcs.

Ohio Census Index, 1790, Vol. 1. Ronald V. Jackson. (Illus.). lib. bdg. 46.00 (*0-89593-757-3*, Accel Indexing) Genealogical Srvcs.

Ohio Census Index, 1790, Vol. 2. 1979. 46.00 (*0-89593-593-7*, Accel Indexing) Genealogical Srvcs.

Ohio Charles Galbreath's History of Ohio Index: Leaders of 1900's. Fay Maxwell. 7p. 1973. 10.00 (*1-885463-23-5*) Ohio Genealogy.

Ohio (City of Toledo & Lucas County) Federal Census, 1870. 1990. 125.00 (*0-89593-618-6*, Accel Indexing) Genealogical Srvcs.

Ohio Civil Justice Reform Act, 1987 House Bill. Comment by Stanton G. Darling, II. 302p. 1987. pap. 40.00 (*0-8322-0218-5*) Banks-Baldwin.

Ohio Civil Procedure Litigation Manual. pap. 55.00 (*1-58360-159-7*) Anderson Pub Co.

Ohio Civil Procedure Litigation Manual 1999. Glen Weissenberger & A. J. Stephani. 664p. 1998. pap. 55.00 (*0-87084-433-4*) Anderson Pub Co.

Ohio Civil Rules Handbook, 1992. Ed. by J. Patrick Browne. (Baldwin's Deskset Ser.). 699p. (Orig.). 1991. pap. 49.00 (*0-8322-0410-2*) Banks-Baldwin.

Ohio Civil Rules Practice with Electronic Forms. 2nd ed. John W. McCormac. 587p. 1992. 85.00 (*0-87084-596-9*) Anderson Pub Co.

Ohio Civil Service & Collective Bargaining Laws & Rules Annotated, 1996-97. Ed. by Jonathan J. Downes. 751p. 1997. 55.00 (*0-8322-0672-5*) Banks-Baldwin.

Ohio Civil War Genealogy Journal. Ed. by Amy Crow. 1997. 18.00 (*0-935057-87-0*) OH Genealogical.

Ohio Classic Christmas Trivia: Stories, Recipes, Activities, Legends, Lore & More! Carole Marsh. (Carole Marsh Ohio Bks.). (Illus.). (J). 1994. pap. 19.95 (*0-7933-0891-7*); lib. bdg. 29.95 (*0-7933-0892-5*); disk 29.95 (*0-7933-0893-3*) Gallopade Intl.

Ohio Close Corporation: Planning & Organization. 2nd ed. William R. Jacobs. LC 96-204006. (Manual Series Ohio Practice). 118p. 1996. pap. 37.00 (*0-87084-445-8*) Anderson Pub Co.

Ohio Coastales. Carole Marsh. (Carole Marsh Ohio Bks.). (Illus.). (J). 1994. pap. 19.95 (*1-55609-993-2*); lib. bdg. 29.95 (*1-55609-992-4*); disk 29.95 (*1-55609-994-0*) Gallopade Intl.

Ohio Coastales! Carole Marsh. (Carole Marsh Ohio Bks.). (J). 1994. lib. bdg. 29.95 (*0-7933-7300-X*) Gallopade Intl.

Ohio Comes of Age, 1873-1900 see History of the State of Ohio

***Ohio Commercial Law Handbook.** 2nd ed. 1999. pap. 59.50 (*1-58360-133-3*) Anderson Pub Co.

Ohio Consumer Law Handbook, 1997. Harold L. Williams. 757p. 1997. pap. 49.50 (*0-8322-0671-7*) Banks-Baldwin.

Ohio Cookin' B. Carlson. (Illus.). 160p. 1997. spiral bd. 5.95 (*1-57166-077-1*) Hearts N Tummies.

Ohio Corporation: Legal Aspects of Organization & Operation. Clifford A. Roe, Jr. (Corporate Practice Ser.: No. 55). 1989. 95.00 (*1-55871-102-3*) BNA.

***Ohio Corporation: Legal Aspects of Organization & Operation.** 2nd ed. Clifford A. Roe, Jr. (Corporate Practice Ser.: Vol. 55). 1999. pap. 95.00 (*1-55871-419-7*) BNA.

***Ohio Corporation Law, 2 vols. Set.** Brown et al. 1999. 220.00 (*0-87084-802-X*) Anderson Pub Co.

Ohio Corporation Law, 2 vols. rev. ed. Julie C. Shifman. 1988. 220.00 (*1-58360-176-7*) Anderson Pub Co.

Ohio Corporation Law, 2 vol., Set. Robert L. Seaver. 704p. 1988. text 220.00 (*0-87084-782-1*) Anderson Pub Co.

Ohio Corporation Law: 1996 Supplement. Robert L. Seaver. 1996. pap. 95.00 (*0-614-30943-3*) Anderson Pub Co.

Ohio Corporation Law & Practice. Robert E. Burton & Sandra L. Rich. (National Corporation Law Ser.). 1992. ring bd. 126.00 (*0-13-633371-0*) Aspen Law.

Ohio Corporation Law with Federal Tax Analysis, 2 vols. Zolman Cavitch. 1961. ring bd. 240.00 (*0-8205-1190-0*) Bender.

Ohio Corporations. Clifford A. Roe, Jr. Ed. by Christopher DeLuca. LC 98-15102. 670p. 1998. 250.00 (*0-8366-0038-X*) West Group.

Ohio Country Missionary: The Diary of David McClure, 1748-1820. Franklin B. Dexter. LC 96-69206. 245p. 1996. reprint ed. pap. 19.00 (*0-89725-272-1*, 1766) Picton Pr.

Ohio County Kentucky: 1850 Census. Rowena Lawson. iv, 87p. (Orig.). 1984. pap. 12.50 (*0-917890-40-X*) Heritage Bk.

Ohio County, Kentucky, in the Olden Days. Harrison D. Taylor. (Illus.). 204p. 1997. reprint ed. pap. 22.50 (*0-8063-4710-4*, Pub. by Clearfield Co) ACCESS Pubs Network.

Ohio County Maps & Recreational Guide. rev. ed. Ed. by C. J. Puetz. (Illus.). 136p. 1996. pap. 16.85 (*0-916514-12-9*) Cnty Maps.

Ohio County Profiles. 2nd ed. 69p. 1992. pap. 15.95 (*1-881951-00-6*) OH Pub Expend.

Ohio County Recorder Laws, 1998. Ohio Recorders' Association Staff. LC 98-228821. 557 p. 1998. write for info. (*0-8322-0737-3*) Banks-Baldwin.

***Ohio County (West Virginia) Index Vol. 4: Index to County Court Order Books 1777-1881.** Kenneth Fischer Craft, Jr. 401p. 1999. pap. 57.00 (*0-7884-1318-X*, C704) Heritage Bk.

Ohio County (WV) Index Vol. 1: Index to County Court Order Books, Pt. 1 - 1777. Kenneth F. Craft. LC 97-219683. 224p. 1998. pap. 39.00 (*0-7884-0797-X*, C603) Heritage Bk.

Ohio County (WV) Index Vol. 2: Index to County Court Order Books (Part 2) 1777-1881 Plus Gazetteer & Map Book. Kenneth F. Craft. (Illus.). 501p. 1998. pap. 69.00 (*0-7884-1023-7*, C702) Heritage Bk.

Ohio County (WV) Index Vol. 3, Pt. 3: Index to County Court Order Books, 1777-1881. Kenneth F. Craft, Jr. 396p. 1999. pap. 55.00 (*0-7884-1134-9*, C703) Heritage Bk.

O

***Ohio County (WV) Index Vol. 5: Index to County Court Order Books, 1777-1881.** Kenneth Fischer Craft, Jr. 387p. 2000. pap. 40.00 (0-7884-1469-0, C705) Heritage Bk.

Ohio Courtroom Evidence. John W. Palmer. 1994. ring bd., suppl. ed. 37.00 (0-614-03765-4, MICHIE) LEXIS Pub.

Ohio Courtroom Evidence. 2nd ed. John W. Palmer. 500p. 1988. spiral bd. 115.00 (1-55943-132-6, MICHIE) LEXIS Pub.

Ohio Courtroom Evidence. 3rd ed. John W. Palmer. 115.00 (0-327-12477-6) LEXIS Pub.

***Ohio Courtroom Evidence, Issue 3.** Palmer. 100p. 1999. ring bd. write for info. (0-327-01304-4, 8220215) LEXIS Pub.

Ohio Creditors' Rights. Botti. pap. 62.00 (0-87084-102-5) Anderson Pub Co.

***Ohio Crime in Perspective 2000.** Ed. by Kathleen O'Leary Morgan & Scott E. Morgan. 22p. 2000. spiral bd. 19.00 (0-7401-0334-2) Morgan Quitno Corp.

Ohio Crime, Ohio Justice. Keith N. Haley & James C. Todd. 400p. 1998. pap. 36.00 (0-07-228258-4) McGraw.

Ohio Crime Perspective, 1998. Ed. by Kathleen O'Leary Morgan & Scott E. Morgan. 20p. 1998. pap. 19.00 (1-56692-934-2) Morgan Quitno Corp.

Ohio Crime Perspectives,1999. Kathleen O'Leary Morgan. 22p. 1999. spiral bd. 19.00 (0-7401-0134-X) Morgan Quitno Corp.

Ohio Criminal Code: Annual Edition. Gould Editorial Staff. 6.00 (0-87526-273-2) Gould.

Ohio Criminal Code: Annual Edition. Gould Editorial Staff. 740p. (C). ring bd. 17.95 (0-87526-202-3) Gould.

Ohio Criminal Code Handbook. 17th ed. Anderson Publishing Company Staff. pap. 12.95 (1-58360-153-8) Anderson Pub Co.

Ohio Criminal Code Handbook for Law Enforcement Officers: For Use with All Crimes Committed Prior to July 1, 1996. annuals 16th ed. pap. 9.95 (0-87084-464-4) Anderson Pub Co.

Ohio Criminal Justice 1996. 1054p. (C). 1996. pap. text 42.00 (0-8322-0627-X) Banks-Baldwin.

Ohio Criminal Justice, 1997. Ed. by Lewis R. Katz & Paul C. Giannelli. LC 98-125319. 1054p. (C). 1997. pap. text 43.50 (0-8322-0669-5) Banks-Baldwin.

Ohio Criminal Law & Motor Vehicle Handbook: Annual Edition. annuals rev. ed. Ed. by Gould Editorial Staff. 1450p. (C). pap. text 23.00 (0-87526-386-0) Gould.

Ohio Criminal Law Handbook. 19th ed. pap. 34.95 (1-58360-155-4) Anderson Pub Co.

Ohio Criminal Law Handbook: For Use with All Crimes Committed Prior to July 1, 1996. 16th ed. 1996. pap. 31.95 (0-87084-726-0) Anderson Pub Co.

Ohio "Crinkum-Crankum" A Funny Word Book about Our State. Carole Marsh. (Carole Marsh Ohio Bks.). (Illus.). (J). (gr. 3-12). 1994. 29.95 (0-7933-4913-3); pap. 19.95 (0-7933-4914-1); disk 29.95 (0-7933-4915-X) Gallopade Intl.

Ohio Cum Laude: The Whole Ohio College Catalogue. James Baumann. LC 97-16302. (Illus.). 384p. 1997. pap. text 29.95 (1-882203-11-9) Orange Frazer.

Ohio Cuyahoga County Federal Census, 1870: Cleveland. 1990. 145.00 (0-89593-594-5, Accel Indexing) Genealogical Srvcs.

Ohio Dingbats! Bk. 1: A Fun Book of Games, Stories, Activities & More about Our State That's All in Code! for You to Decipher. Carole Marsh. (Carole Marsh Ohio Bks.). (Illus.). (J). (gr. 3-12). 1994. pap. 19.95 (0-7933-3879-4); lib. bdg. 29.95 (0-7933-3878-6); disk 29.95 (0-7933-3880-8) Gallopade Intl.

Ohio Dissolution of Marriage: Divorce in Ohio. D. C. Schultz. 260p. 1999. reprint ed. pap. 29.95 (1-879421-05-4) LawPak.

Ohio Doane Cancels. Bart Billings. (Illus.). 125p. (Orig.). (C). 1987. pap. 7.00 (0-685-24135-1) Machine Cancel Soc.

Ohio Domestic Violence Law. Ronald B. Adrine. LC 98-208667. (Baldwin's Ohio Handbook Ser.). 693p. 1998. write for info. (0-8322-0692-X) Banks-Baldwin.

Ohio Driving under the Influence Law, 1996-97. 3rd ed. Mark P. Painter & James M. Looker. 581p. 1996. pap. text 60.00 (0-8322-0665-2) Banks-Baldwin.

Ohio Early Census, Vol. 2. Ronald V. Jackson. (Illus.). 1980. lib. bdg. 40.00 (0-89593-741-7, Accel Indexing) Genealogical Srvcs.

Ohio Early Census Index, Vol. 1. Ronald V. Jackson. LC 77-86110. (Illus.). 1974. lib. bdg. 40.00 (0-89593-109-5, Accel Indexing) Genealogical Srvcs.

Ohio 1870 Census Index, 6 vols. lib. bdg. 695.00 (1-877677-80-9) Herit Quest.

Ohio 1820 Federal Population Index. lib. bdg. 105.00 (1-877677-71-X, Precision Index) Herit Quest.

***Ohio Employer's Guide: A Handbook of Employment Laws & Regulations.** 8th ed. Ed. by Summers Press, Inc. Staff. 664p. 2000. 92.50 (1-56759-058-6) Summers Pr.

Ohio Employment Laws & Regulations: How to Comply. Squire et al. 150p. 1995. pap. 75.00 (0-923606-02-5) Amer CC Pubs.

Ohio Employment Practices Law: A Practical Guide for Employers & Their Legal Counsel. Bradd N. Siegel & John M. Stephen. LC 97-188111. (Baldwin's Ohio Handbook Ser.). xxv, 791 p. 1997. write for info. (0-8322-0679-2) Banks-Baldwin.

Ohio Employment Practices Law: A Practical Guide for Employers & Their Legal Counsel. 2nd ed. Bradd N. Siegel & John M. Stephen. (Ohio Handbook Ser.). 694p. 1996. pap. 57.00 (0-8322-0508-7) Banks-Baldwin.

Ohio Endangered & Threatened Vascular Plants: Abstract of State-Listed Taxa. Barbara K. Andreas et al. Ed. by James F. Burns & Robert M. McCance, Jr. LC 84-620010. xii, 635p. (Orig.). 1984. pap. 10.00 (0-931079-00-4) Ohio Nat Res.

Ohio Environmental Law Handbook. 4th ed. Porter, Wright, Morris & Arthur Staff. LC 99-162550. 376p. 1997. pap. text 95.00 (0-86587-605-3, 605) Gov Insts.

Ohio EPA Laws & Regulations, 3 vols. Contrib. by Ohio Environmental Protection Agency Staff. 4090p. 1993. 185.00 (1-58360-091-4) Anderson Pub Co.

Ohio Estate Planning. Norman T. Musial & Mark N. Musial. (Illus.). x, 277p. (Orig.). 1995. pap. 29.95 (0-9618030-1-0) Pam Publishing Co.

Ohio Evidence: And Annual, 5 vols. Glen Weissenberger. 1996. pap. 275.00 (0-87084-940-9) Anderson Pub Co.

Ohio Evidence: And Annual, 4 vols., Set. Glen Weissenberger. 1432p. 1996. ring bd. 360.00 (0-87084-916-6) Anderson Pub Co.

Ohio Evidence: Objections & Responses with 1991 Cumulative Supplement. Louis A. Jacobs. 369p. 1989. 65.00 (0-87473-436-3, 63532-10, MICHIE) LEXIS Pub.

Ohio Evidence: 1990 Supplement. Louis A. Jacobs. 1990. write for info. (0-87473-711-7, 63533-10, MICHIE) LEXIS Pub.

Ohio Evidence Courtroom Manual. pap. 68.00 (1-58360-186-4) Anderson Pub Co.

Ohio Evidence Library. rev. ed. Glen Weissenberger. 720p. 1998. 360.00 (1-58360-008-6) Anderson Pub Co.

Ohio Evidence Treatise. Weissenberger. pap. 195.00 (1-58360-334-4) Anderson Pub Co.

***Ohio Experience Pocket Guide.** Carole Marsh. (Ohio Experience! Ser.). (Illus.). (J). 2000. pap. 6.95 (0-7933-9454-6) Gallopade Intl.

Ohio Facts & Factivities. Carole Marsh. (Carole Marsh State Bks.). (Illus.). (J). (gr. 4-7). 1996. pap., teacher ed. 19.95 (0-7933-7917-2, C Marsh) Gallopade Intl.

***Ohio Facts & Symbols.** Emily McAuliffe. LC 98-7359. (States & Their Symbols Ser.). 24p. (J). 1999. write for info. (0-7368-0085-9) Capstone Pr.

Ohio Families: A Bibliography of Books about Ohio Families. Donald M. Hehir. 403p. (Orig.). 1993. pap. text 30.00 (1-55613-895-4) Heritage Bk.

Ohio Family Law & Practice, 4 Vols. Ed. by Allen S. Spike. 400.00 (0-327-13439-9) LEXIS Pub.

***Ohio Family Law Handbook.** annuals 1262p. 2000. pap. 58.00 (1-58360-193-7) Anderson Pub Co.

Ohio Farm. Wheeler McMillen. LC 96-48321. 220p. 1997. pap. 18.00 (0-8142-0735-9) Ohio St U Pr.

Ohio Federal Census, 1870 Stark & Summit Counties (Cities of Akron, Canton) 1990. 160.00 (0-89593-620-8, Accel Indexing) Genealogical Srvcs.

Ohio Federal Census Index, 1850, 2 vols. Ronald V. Jackson. LC 77-86103. (Illus.). 1979. lib. bdg. 300.00 (0-89593-113-3, Accel Indexing) Genealogical Srvcs.

Ohio Federal Census Index, 1840. Ronald V. Jackson. LC 77-86102. (Illus.). lib. bdg. 150.00 (0-89593-112-5, Accel Indexing) Genealogical Srvcs.

Ohio Federal Census Index, 1830. Ronald V. Jackson. LC 77-86101. (Illus.). 1976. lib. bdg. 121.00 (0-89593-111-7, Accel Indexing) Genealogical Srvcs.

Ohio Federal Census Index, 1820. Ronald V. Jackson. LC 77-87432. (Illus.). 1977. lib. bdg. 76.00 (0-89593-110-9, Accel Indexing) Genealogical Srvcs.

Ohio Felony Sentencing Law, 1996-97 Edition. Burt W. Griffin & Lewis R. Katz. LC 98-128449. (Baldwin's Ohio Handbook Ser.). xxxviii, 754p. (Orig.). 1997. pap. write for info. (0-8322-0682-2) Banks-Baldwin.

Ohio Felony Sentencing Law, 1996-97 Edition. Lewis R. Katz & Burt W. Griffin. 595p. (Orig.). 1996. pap. 59.00 (0-8322-0653-9) Banks-Baldwin.

Ohio Festival Fun for Kids! Carole Marsh. (Carole Marsh Ohio Bks.). (Illus.). (J). (gr. 3-12). 1994. pap. 19.95 (0-7933-4032-2); lib. bdg. 29.95 (0-7933-4031-4) Gallopade Intl.

Ohio Festival Fun for Kids! Carole Marsh. (Carole Marsh Ohio Bks.). (Illus.). (YA). (gr. 3-12). 1994. disk 29.95 (0-7933-4033-0) Gallopade Intl.

Ohio First Settlers: The Indians - Native Americans, Vol. 3. 2nd rev. ed. Nicholas P. Georgiady & Louis G. Romano. (Illus.). (J). (gr. 4-8). 1995. pap. 4.50 (0-917961-05-6) Argee Pubs.

Ohio Fishing Guide. Jim Robey. (Illus.). 164p. (Orig.). 1991. pap. 5.50 (0-9616347-1-5) Dayton Newspapers.

Ohio Fishing Guide. Jim Robey & Jim Morris. LC 97-211563. (Illus.). 164p. (Orig.). 1997. pap. 9.95 (0-9656649-0-2) Cox Custom.

Ohio Forms & Transactions, 3 vols. Thomas R. Swisher. 992p. 1989. 291.50 (0-8322-0261-4) Banks-Baldwin.

Ohio Forms-Legal & Business, 11 vols. LC 72-134918. 1992. suppl. ed. 695.00 (0-318-57158-7) West Group.

Ohio Forms of Pleading & Practice, 18 vols. Bender's Editors & Paul W. Brown. 1970. ring bd. 2130.00 (0-8205-1502-7) Bender.

Ohio Franklin & Montgomery Counties Federal Census, 1870: Columbus & Dayton. 1990. 150.00 (0-89593-595-3, Accel Indexing) Genealogical Srvcs.

***Ohio Frontier: An Anthology of Early Writing.** Ed. by Emily Foster. (Ohio River Valley Ser.). (Illus.). 248p. 2000. pap. 18.00 (0-8131-0979-5) U Pr of Ky.

Ohio Frontier: An Anthology of Early Writings. Emily Foster. LC 95-45218. (Ohio River Valley Ser.). (Illus.). 248p. (C). 1996. 29.95 (0-8131-1957-X) U Pr of Ky.

Ohio Frontier: Crucible of the Old Northwest, 1720-1830. R. Douglas Hurt. LC 95-53278. (History of the Trans-Appalachian Frontier Ser.). (Illus.). 440p. 1998. 27.50 (0-253-33210-9); pap. 19.95 (0-253-21212-X) Ind U Pr.

Ohio Furniture Makers, 1790-1860, Vol. II. Jane S. Hageman. LC 85-113070. 1989. 45.00 (0-9620107-4-X); pap. 30.00 (0-9620107-5-8) OH Furniture Makers.

Ohio Gardening Guide. Jerry Minnich. (Illus.). 290p. (Orig.). 1995. pap. 18.95 (0-8214-1118-7) Ohio U Pr.

Ohio Genealogical Helper Covers Ohio Sources, Excellent for Out of State Searchers: Covering Available Record Locations. Fay Maxwell. 53p. 1975. 5.00 (1-885463-21-9) Ohio Genealogy.

Ohio Genealogical Research. George K. Schweitzer. LC 96-132769. 212p. 1999. pap. 15.00 (0-913857-16-5) Genealog Sources.

Ohio "GEO" Bingo! 38 Must Know State Geography Facts for Kids to Learn While Having Fun! Carole Marsh. (Bingo! Ser.). (Illus.). (J). (gr. 2-8). 1998. pap. 14.95 (0-7933-8628-4) Gallopade Intl.

Ohio Geological Society Anthology: Morrow Co., Ohio "Oil Boom", 1961-1967 & the Cambro-Ordovician Reservoir of Central Ohio. Ed. by William E. Shafer. (Illus.). xxix, 452p. 1994. pap. 65.00 (0-9660388-0-0, OG510) Ohio Geolog.

Ohio Geological Society Fifth Annual Technical Symposium Proceedings. Ed. by Arie Janssens. (Illus.). 117p. 1997. pap. 20.00 (0-9660388-1-9) Ohio Geolog.

Ohio Golfers Travel Guide. Ed. by Roy H. Rasmussen. 35p. (Orig.). 1992. pap. 6.95 (0-940703-02-5) RSG Pub MI.

Ohio Government! The Cornerstone of Everyday Life in Our State! Carole Marsh. (Carole Marsh Ohio Bks.). (Illus.). (J). (gr. 3-12). 1996. pap. 19.95 (0-7933-6287-3); lib. bdg. 29.95 (0-7933-6286-5); disk 29.95 (0-7933-6288-1) Gallopade Intl.

Ohio Governments Performance Standards, 1990. Ed. by Greg Michels. (Governments Performance Standards Ser.). (Illus.). 150p. 1990. text 125.00 (1-55507-497-9) Municipal Analysis.

Ohio Grants Guide, 1999-2001. 2nd ed. 1000p. 1999. pap. 199.00 (0-9658306-9-1) Grantseeker.

Ohio Grants Guide, 1997-1998. 900p. 1997. pap. 149.00 (0-9658306-0-8) Grantseeker.

Ohio Guide. Federal Writers' Project Staff. (American Guidebook Ser.). 634p. 1940. reprint ed. 95.00 (0-403-02184-7) Somerset Pub.

Ohio Guide to Genealogical Sources. Carol W. Bell. 372p. 1993. reprint ed. 30.00 (0-8063-1228-9, 397) Genealog Pub.

***Ohio Health Care in Perspective 1999.** Ed. by Kathleen O'Leary Morgan & Scott E. Morgan. 21p. 1999. spiral bd. 19.00 (0-7401-0084-X) Morgan Quitno Corp.

***Ohio Health Care in Perspective 2000.** Ed. by Kathleen O'Leary Morgan & Scott E. Morgan. 21p. 2000. spiral bd. 19.00 (0-7401-0234-6) Morgan Quitno Corp.

Ohio Health Care Perspective, 1998. Ed. by Kathleen O'Leary Morgan & Scott E. Morgan. 20p. 1998. pap. 19.00 (1-56692-834-6) Morgan Quitno Corp.

Ohio Health Care Provider Law. Susan O. Scheutzow. LC 94-234100. 388p. (Orig.). 1994. pap. 52.50 (0-8322-0381-5) Banks-Baldwin.

Ohio High School Map Directory. Dave Fletcher et al. 439p. 1993. pap. 14.95 (0-9639780-0-4) Pioneer Direct.

Ohio "HISTO" Bingo! 42 Must Know State History Facts for Kids to Learn While Having Fun! Carole Marsh. (Bingo! Ser.). (Illus.). (J). (gr. 2-8). 1998. pap. 14.95 (0-7933-8629-2) Gallopade Intl.

Ohio Historical & Biographical Index, Vol. 1. Ronald V. Jackson. LC 78-53712. (Illus.). 1984. lib. bdg. 50.00 (0-89593-195-8, Accel Indexing) Genealogical Srvcs.

Ohio Historical Sights, Vol. 4. 2nd rev. ed. Nicholas P. Georgiady & Louis G. Romano. (Illus.). 27p. (J). (gr. 4-8). 1995. pap. 4.50 (0-917961-06-4) Argee Pubs.

Ohio History! Surprising Secrets about Our State's Founding Mothers, Fathers & Kids! Carole Marsh. (Carole Marsh Ohio Bks.). (Illus.). (J). (gr. 3-12). 1996. pap. 19.95 (0-7933-6134-6); lib. bdg. 29.95 (0-7933-6133-8); disk 29.95 (0-7933-6135-4) Gallopade Intl.

Ohio History & Geography. Center for Learning Network Staff. 280p. (YA). (gr. 7). spiral bd. 34.95 (1-56077-435-5) Ctr Learning.

Ohio Hopewell Community Organization. Ed. by William S. Dancey & Paul J. Pacheco. LC 96-27659. 1997. 45.00 (0-87338-561-6) Kent St U Pr.

Ohio Hot Air Balloon Mystery. Carole Marsh. (Carole Marsh Ohio Bks.). (Illus.). (J). (gr. 2-9). 1994. 29.95 (0-7933-2633-8); pap. 19.95 (0-7933-2634-6); disk 29.95 (0-7933-2635-4) Gallopade Intl.

Ohio Hot Zones! Viruses, Diseases, & Epidemics in Our State's History. Carole Marsh. (Hot Zones! Ser.). (Illus.). (J). (gr. 3-12). 1998. pap. 19.95 (0-7933-8934-8); lib. bdg. 29.95 (0-7933-8933-X) Gallopade Intl.

Ohio Impromptu: Three Plays, Ohio Impromptu; Catastrophe; What Where. Samuel Beckett. LC 83-49372. 64p. (Orig.). 1984. pap. 6.95 (0-8021-5116-7, Grove) Grove-Atltic.

Ohio in Century Three: Quality of Life. Ed. by Ralph Pearson. (Illus.). 32p. 1977. pap. 1.00 (0-318-00841-6) Ohio Hist Soc.

Ohio in Historic Postcards: Self-Portrait of a State. H. Roger Grant. LC 96-27747. (Illus.). 268p. 1997. 20.00 (0-87338-569-1) Kent St U Pr.

Ohio in Perspective, 1998. Ed. by Kathleen O'Leary Morgan & Scott E. Morgan. 24p. 1998. pap. 19.00 (1-56692-884-2) Morgan Quitno Corp.

Ohio in Perspective, 1999. Ed. by Kathleen O'Leary Morgan. 26p. 1999. spiral bd. 19.00 (1-56692-984-9) Morgan Quitno Corp.

***Ohio in Perspective 2000.** Ed. by Kathleen O'Leary Morgan & Scott E. Morgan. 26p. 2000. spiral bd. 19.00 (0-7401-0284-2) Morgan Quitno Corp.

Ohio Indian Dictionary for Kids! Carole Marsh. (Carole Marsh State Bks.). (J). (gr. 2-9). 1996. 29.95 (0-7933-7749-8, C Marsh); pap. 19.95 (0-7933-7750-1, C Marsh) Gallopade Intl.

Ohio Indian, Revolutionary War & War of 1812 Trails. Fay Maxwell. 59p. 1974. 7.00 (1-885463-22-7) Ohio Genealogy.

Ohio Indian Trails. Frank N. Wilcox. 1993. reprint ed. lib. bdg. 89.00 (0-7812-5417-5) Rprt Serv.

Ohio Inscriptions Ashtabula County, Ohio: Winsdor, Windsor Mills Cemeteries. Glenn E. Griswold. 39p. (Orig.). 1994. pap. 10.00 (1-878545-03-5) ACETO Bookmen.

***Ohio Insurance Law Handbook.** 1999. pap. 68.00 (1-58360-132-5) Anderson Pub Co.

***Ohio Investment & Business Guide: Business, Investment, Export-Import Opportunities, 50, 35.** Global Investment Center, USA Staff. (U. S. Regional Investment & Business Library-99: Vol. 35). (Illus.). 350p. (Orig.). 1999. pap. 59.95 (0-7397-1134-2) Intl Business Pubns.

***Ohio Jeopardy.** Carole Marsh. (Ohio Experience! Ser.). (J). (gr. 2-6). 2000. pap. 7.95 (0-7933-9525-9) Gallopade Intl.

Ohio Jeopardy! Answers & Questions about Our State! Carole Marsh. (Carole Marsh Ohio Bks.). (Illus.). (J). (gr. 3-12). 1994. pap. 19.95 (0-7933-4185-X); lib. bdg. 29.95 (0-7933-4184-1); disk 29.95 (0-7933-4186-8) Gallopade Intl.

***Ohio JobBank.** 10th ed. Contrib. by Adams Media Corporation Staff. (Illus.). 400p. 1999. pap. 16.95 (1-58062-241-0) Adams Media.

***Ohio Jography.** Carole Marsh. (Ohio Experience! Ser.). (Illus.). (J). (gr. 2-6). 2000. pap. 7.95 (0-7933-9526-7) Gallopade Intl.

Ohio "Jography" A Fun Run Thru Our State! Carole Marsh. (Carole Marsh Ohio Bks.). (Illus.). (J). 1994. pap. 19.95 (1-55609-982-7); lib. bdg. 29.95 (1-55609-981-9); disk 29.95 (1-55609-983-5) Gallopade Intl.

Ohio Jurisprudence, 93 vols., Set. 3rd ed. LC 77-82021. 1992. suppl. ed. 2000.00 (0-318-57157-9) West Group.

Ohio Jury Instructions, 4 vols., Set. Ohio Judicial Conference, Jury Instruction Committ. 1997. pap. 220.00 (0-87084-675-2) Anderson Pub Co.

Ohio Juvenile Law, 1996-97. William A. Kurtz & Paul C. Giannelli. 642p. (C). 1996. pap. text 56.00 (0-8322-0660-1) Banks-Baldwin.

Ohio Kid's Cookbook: Recipes, How-To, History, Lore & More! Carole Marsh. (Carole Marsh Ohio Bks.). (Illus.). (J). 1994. pap. 19.95 (0-7933-0900-X); lib. bdg. 29.95 (0-7933-0901-8); disk 29.95 (0-7933-0902-6) Gallopade Intl.

Ohio Land Grants & Warrants, 1789-1801 Index. (Illus.). lib. bdg. 68.00 (0-89593-705-0, Accel Indexing) Genealogical Srvcs.

Ohio Land Surveying Law: Questions & Answers. John E. Keen. 39p. (C). 1995. pap. text 25.00 (1-56569-037-0) Land Survey.

Ohio Land Surveying Law Vol. II: Study Guide Answers. John E. Keen. 32p. 1995. pap. text 20.00 (1-56569-012-5) Land Survey.

Ohio Land Surveying Law with Study Guide Questions. 298p. (C). 1995. pap. text 49.00 (1-56569-011-7) Land Survey.

Ohio Landlord-Tenant Law, 1997. annuals Frederic White. (Ohio Handbook Ser.). 683p. (C). 1997. pap. text 51.50 (0-8322-0670-9) Banks-Baldwin.

Ohio Lands. Photos by Ian Adams. (Illus.). 144p. 1995. 39.95 (1-56313-739-9) BrownTrout Pubs Inc.

Ohio Lands. Photos by Ian Adams. (Illus.). 1996. 39.95 (0-7631-0739-5) BrownTrout Pubs Inc.

Ohio Lands - Hamilton County Deed Book A, 1787-1797: Territory Northwest of the River Ohio. Alma A. Smith. (Illus.). x, 88p. 1992. pap. 20.00 (0-9614863-5-X) Alma Smith.

Ohio Lands & Their History. 3rd ed. William E. Peters. Ed. by Stuart Bruchey. LC 78-53541. (Development of Public Land Law in the U. S. Ser.). (Illus.). 1979. reprint ed. lib. bdg. 30.95 (0-405-11383-8) Ayer.

Ohio Law for Everyone: With Legal Dictionary. Sherry A. Wells. (Law for Laypersons Ser.). (Illus.). 200p. (Orig.). Date not set. pap. 17.95 (0-934981-03-5) Lawells Pub.

Ohio Legal Research Guide. Melanie K. Putnam & Susan Schaefgen. LC 96-16186. xv, 371p. 1997. 65.00 (1-57588-087-3, 306700) W S Hein.

Ohio Library Book: A Surprising Guide to the Unusual Special Collections in Libraries Across Our State for Students, Teachers, Writers & Publishers - Includes Reproducible Mailing Labels Plus Activities for Young People! Carole Marsh. (Carole Marsh Ohio Bks.). (Illus.). 1994. pap. 19.95 (0-7933-3111-0); lib. bdg. 29.95 (0-7933-3110-2); disk 29.95 (0-7933-3112-9) Gallopade Intl.

Ohio Limited Liability Companies. Jeanne M. Rickert. LC 99-162663. (Baldwin's Ohio Handbook Ser.). 516p. 1999. write for info. (0-8322-0750-0) Banks-Baldwin.

Ohio Limited Liability Companies, 1996-97. Jeanne M. Rickert. 470p. 1996. pap. 43.50 (0-8322-0656-3) Banks-Baldwin.

Ohio Limited Liability Company Forms & Practice Manual. Harry L. Henning & Richard C. McQuown. LC 94-36227. 586p. 1994. ring bd. 219.90 (0-9637468-5-5) Data Trace Pubng.

Ohio Liquor Laws & Rules. pap. 22.50 (1-58360-305-0) Anderson Pub Co.

Ohio Living Will Act. Wayne A. Jenkins. 212p. 1991. pap. 42.50 (0-8322-0392-0) Banks-Baldwin.

Ohio Long-Range Program for the Improvement of Library Services, 1992-1995. 76p. (Orig.). (C). 1993. pap. text 25.00 (0-7881-0171-4) DIANE Pub.

Ohio Manual of Criminal Complaints & Indictments. 7th ed. pap. 48.00 (1-58360-154-6) Anderson Pub Co.

Ohio Manufacturers Directory. 17th rev. ed. Ed. by Frank Lambing. 1998. 157.00 (1-58202-063-9) Manufacturers.

Ohio Marriage Records in County Courts Through 1820: And Index. Ed. by Jean Nathan. 1996. 65.00 (0-935057-88-9) OH Genealogical.

Ohio Marriages: Extracted from the "Old Northwest" Genealogical Quarterly. Marjorie Smith. 350p. 1997. reprint ed. 25.00 (0-8063-0902-4, 5475) Genealog Pub.

An Asterisk (*) at the beginning of an entry indicates that the title is appearing for the first time.

Ohio Math! How It All Adds up in Our State. Carole Marsh. (Carole Marsh Ohio Bks.). (Illus.). (YA). (gr. 3-12). 1996. pap. 19.95 (*0-7933-6593-7*); lib. bdg. 29.95 (*0-7933-6592-9*) Gallopade Intl.

Ohio Media Book: A Surprising Guide to the Amazing Print, Broadcast & Online Media of Our State for Students, Teachers, Writers & Publishers - Includes Reproducible Mailing Labels Plus Activities for Young People! Carole Marsh. (Carole Marsh Ohio Bks.). (Illus.). 1994. pap. 19.95 (*0-7933-3267-2*); lib. bdg. 29.95 (*0-7933-3266-4*); disk 29.95 (*0-7933-3268-0*) Gallopade Intl.

***Ohio Memorials at Gettysburg: Report of the Gettyburg Memorial Commission.** (Army of the Potomac Ser.: Vol. 21). 142p. 1998. reprint ed. 25.00 (*0-935523-71-5*) Butternut & Blue.

Ohio Men, Vol. 2. 2nd rev. ed. Nicholas P. Georgiady et al. (Illus.). 44p. (J). (gr. 4-8). Date not set. pap. 4.50 (*0-917961-04-8*) Argee Pubs.

Ohio Mental Health Law. 2nd ed. Steven J. Eagle & Michael Kirkman. (Baldwin's Ohio Handbook Ser.). 419p. 1990. pap. 53.00 (*0-8322-0305-X*) Banks-Baldwin.

Ohio Metals: A Legacy. Pref. by JoAnn R. Stevens. LC 93-4972. (Illus.). 168p. (Orig.). 1993. pap. 19.00 (*0-9630969-2-3*) Interalia Des.

Ohio-Michigan Tax Handbook. Peter George & Mary A. Mead. 500p. 1988. 18.95 (*0-13-579772-1*, Busn) P-H.

Ohio Moravian Music. Lawrence W. Hartzell. LC 87-71082. 208p. 1988. 14.95 (*0-941642-02-X*) Morav Music Found.

Ohio Motor Vehicle Laws: Annual Edition. Gould Editorial Staff. 6.00 (*0-87526-283-X*) Gould.

Ohio Motor Vehicle Laws: Annual Edition. Gould Editorial Staff. 450p. (C). ring bd. 17.95 (*0-87526-257-0*) Gould.

Ohio Municipal Law, 3 vols. John E. Gotherman & Harold W. Babbit. (Baldwin's Ohio Practice Ser.). 3832p. 1975. 329.50 (*0-8322-0015-8*) Banks-Baldwin.

Ohio Mystery Van Takes Off! Handicapped Ohio Kids Sneak off on a Big Adventure, Bk. 1. Carole Marsh. (Carole Marsh Ohio Bks.). (Illus.). (J). (gr. 3-12). 1994. 29.95 (*0-7933-5066-2*); pap. 19.95 (*0-7933-5067-0*); disk 29.95 (*0-7933-5068-9*) Gallopade Intl.

Ohio Nature Reflections: Home-Grown Guidance from Mother Nature. Cassandra S. Clancy. LC 93-79004. (Illus.). 82p. (Orig.). 1994. pap. 9.95 (*0-9637114-0-7*) Inky Pr OH.

Ohio Nursing Law. Sue D. Calloway. 536p. 1991. pap. text 48.50 (*0-8322-0371-8*) Banks-Baldwin.

***Ohio on the Move: Transportation in the Buckeye State.** H. Roger Grant. LC 99-29728. (Ohio Bicentennial Ser.). (Illus.). 200p. 1999. pap. 17.95 (*0-8214-1284-1*); text 36.00 (*0-8214-1283-3*) Ohio U Pr.

Ohio One Hundred Years Ago. Kirke et al. (Historical Ser.). (Illus.). 1977. pap. 3.50 (*0-89540-050-2*, SB-050) Sun Pub.

Ohio Online: The Harvest of Ohio's Best Web Sites. Barbara Brattin. LC 97-40012. 288p. 1997. pap. 19.95 (*1-882203-18-6*) Orange Frazer.

Ohio Open Records Law & Genealogy: Researching Ohio Public Records. Ann Fenley. LC 88-92730. (Illus.). 115p. 1989. pap. 26.50 (*0-941331-14-8*); lib. bdg. 32.00 (*0-941331-15-6*) Ohio Connect.

Ohio Parks & Forest Guide. Barbara McCaig & Lynn D. Soli. (Illus.). 100p. (Orig.). 1986. pap. 7.95 (*0-935201-10-6*) Affordable Adven.

Ohio Passport. Ronald J. Reiser. (Illus.). 36p. (Orig.). (YA). (gr. 9-12). 1991. 3.95 (*0-9625515-6-2*) VJR Passports.

Ohio Personal Injury Practice 1998: Successful Trial Strategies. LC 98-218216. (Baldwin's Ohio Handbook Ser.). 1998. write for info. (*0-8322-0735-7*) West Group.

Ohio Personal Injury Practice, 1996: Successful Trial Strategies. Don C. Iler & Ronald E. Morgan. (Deskset Ser.). 444p. 1996. pap. 67.00 (*0-8322-0644-X*) Banks-Baldwin.

Ohio Perspectives: New Work in Clay, Glass, Textiles & Metals. Barbara Tannenbaum. (Illus.). 24p. (Orig.). 1988. pap. 5.00 (*0-940665-02-6*) Akron Art Mus.

Ohio Pioneer Artists: A Pictorial Review. Jane S. Hageman. (Illus.). 120p. 1994. 44.95 (*0-9620107-6-6*); pap. 34.95 (*0-9620107-7-4*) OH Furniture Makers.

Ohio Place-Names. Larry L. Miller. LC 95-14555. 320p. 1996. 25.95 (*0-253-32932-9*) Ind U Pr.

Ohio Planning & Zoning Law. Stuart Meck & Kenneth Pearlman. 730p. (Orig.). 1997. pap. 55.00 (*0-8322-0674-1*) Banks-Baldwin.

Ohio Players. Ed. by Dave Edwards. (Masters of Funk Ser.: Vol. 2). (Illus.). 72p. (Orig.). 1997. pap. 17.95 (*1-888885-04-1*, JPMC-1505) JPMC.

Ohio Politics. Ed. by Alexander P. Lamis. LC 94-7637. (Illus.). 417p. 1994. 24.00 (*0-87338-507-1*); pap. 17.00 (*0-87338-509-8*) Kent St U Pr.

Ohio Politics. Alexander P. Lamis & Mary A. Sharkey. LC 98-13737. 1998. pap. 24.00 (*0-87338-613-2*) Kent St U Pr.

Ohio Politics Almanac. Michael F. Curtin & Julia B. Bell. LC 95-37710. (Illus.). 216p. (C). 1996. pap. 16.00 (*0-87338-540-3*) Kent St U Pr.

Ohio Pretrial Litigation. 2nd ed. Michael L. Cioffi. 346p. 1998. pap. 62.00 (*0-87084-672-8*) Anderson Pub Co.

Ohio Probate. Daniel F. Carmack. LC 79-91159. (Practice Systems Library Manual). 120.00 (*0-317-00549-9*) West Group.

Ohio Probate. Daniel F. Carmack. LC 79-91159. (Practice Systems Library Manual). 1991. suppl. ed. 50.00 (*0-317-03201-1*) West Group.

Ohio Probate. 2nd ed. Rosemary Durkon. 135.00 (*0-327-11243-3*) LEXIS Pub.

Ohio Probate Code Annotated, 1996 Edition. 861p. (C). 1996. pap. text 45.00 (*0-8322-0652-0*) Banks-Baldwin.

Ohio Probate Law Handbook. annuals 1030p. 1998. pap. 55.50 (*0-87084-034-7*) Anderson Pub Co.

Ohio Probate, 1998 Cumulative Supplement. 2nd ed. Rosemary D. Durkin. 100p. 1998. suppl. ed. write for info. (*0-327-00517-3*, 6896011) LEXIS Pub.

Ohio Probate, 1999 Supplement. 2nd ed. Rosemary Durkon. 250p. 1999. ring bd. write for info. (*0-327-01498-9*, 6896012) LEXIS Pub.

Ohio Products Liability Manual. James T. O'Reilly & Nancy C. Cody. (Ohio Practice Manual Ser.). 299p. (Orig.). 1992. pap. 40.00 (*0-87084-670-1*) Anderson Pub Co.

Ohio Public Employee Collective Bargaining Law. 2nd ed. James T. O'Reilly. (Anderson's Ohio Practice Manual Ser.). 439p. 1992. pap. 50.00 (*0-87084-668-X*) Anderson Pub Co.

Ohio Public Employee Reporter. LRP Publications Staff. text 480.00 (*0-934753-03-2*) LRP Pubns.

Ohio Public Employee Reporter, Vol. 3. Ed. by LRP Publications Staff. 1987. text. write for info. (*0-934753-20-2*) LRP Pubns.

Ohio Purchasing Laws & Rules. Ohio, State Bar Association, Administrative Law Committee. LC 98-152104. iv, 36 p. 1997. 0.00 (*0-8322-0640-7*) Banks-Baldwin.

Ohio Quiz Crash Course! Carole Marsh. (Carole Marsh Ohio Bks.). (Illus.). (J). 1994. pap. 19.95 (*1-55609-996-7*); lib. bdg. 29.95 (*1-55609-995-9*); disk 29.95 (*1-55609-997-5*) Gallopade Intl.

Ohio Real Estate. 3rd ed. Charles J. Jacobus & Hemmeler. (C). 2001. text 46.67 (*0-13-206715-3*) P-H.

Ohio Real Estate Law. 6th ed. Irvin. 416p. 1996. pap. text 38.80 (*0-13-777095-2*) P-H.

Ohio Real Estate Law & Practice. 2nd ed. Robert L. Hausser. 1586p. 1993. 178.00 (*0-8322-0454-4*) Banks-Baldwin.

Ohio Real Estate Law Handbook. 3rd ed. pap. 52.50 (*1-58360-149-X*) Anderson Pub Co.

Ohio Real Estate Property: 1989 Supplement. 4th ed. Weiss & Magee. 1989. write for info. (*0-87473-527-0*, 62951-10, MICHIE) LEXIS Pub.

Ohio Real Estate Transactions. 2nd ed. Samuel Wilson & Thomas Sherman. (Ohio Practice Manual Ser.). 336p. 1997. pap. 68.00 (*0-87084-902-6*) Anderson Pub Co.

Ohio Real Property, Vol. 2. 5th ed. Durham & Curry. LC 96-79576. 834p. 1997. text 85.00 (*1-55834-436-5*, 62955-11, MICHIE) LEXIS Pub.

Ohio Real Property Law & Practice: 1998 Cumulative Supplement, Vol. 1. 5th ed. Robert M. Curry & James G. Durham. 1998. write for info. (*0-327-00804-0*) LEXIS Pub.

Ohio Real Property Law & Practice: 1998 Cumulative Supplement, Vol. 2. Robert M. Curry & James G. Durham. 1998. write for info. (*0-327-00805-9*) LEXIS Pub.

Ohio Real Property Law & Practice: 1998 Cumulative Supplement, Vol. 3. Robert M. Curry & James G. Durham. 1998. write for info. (*0-327-00806-7*) LEXIS Pub.

Ohio Records & Pioneer Families, Vol. 12. Ed. by Esther W. Powell. 1971. 5.00 (*0-935057-11-0*) OH Genealogical.

Ohio Records & Pioneer Families, Vol. 13. Ed. by Esther W. Powell. 1972. 2.50 (*0-935057-12-9*) OH Genealogical.

Ohio Records & Pioneer Families, Vol. 14. Ed. by Esther W. Powell. 1973. 5.00 (*0-935057-13-7*) OH Genealogical.

Ohio Records & Pioneer Families, Vol. 15. Ed. by Esther W. Powell. 1974. 5.00 (*0-935057-14-5*) OH Genealogical.

Ohio Records & Pioneer Families, Vol. 16. Ed. by Esther W. Powell. 1975. 5.00 (*0-935057-15-3*) OH Genealogical.

Ohio Records & Pioneer Families, Vol. 17. Ed. by Esther W. Powell. 1976. 5.00 (*0-935057-16-1*) OH Genealogical.

Ohio Records & Pioneer Families, Vol. 18. Ed. by Esther W. Powell. 1977. 5.00 (*0-935057-17-X*) OH Genealogical.

Ohio Records & Pioneer Families, Vol. 19. Ed. by Esther W. Powell. 1978. 5.00 (*0-935057-18-8*) OH Genealogical.

Ohio Records & Pioneer Families, Vol. 20. Ed. by William M. Houston. 1979. 5.00 (*0-935057-19-6*) OH Genealogical.

Ohio Records & Pioneer Families, Vol. 21. Ed. by William M. Houston. 1980. 5.00 (*0-935057-20-X*) OH Genealogical.

Ohio Records & Pioneer Families, Vol. 22. Ed. by William M. Houston. 1981. 5.00 (*0-935057-21-8*) OH Genealogical.

Ohio Records & Pioneer Families, Vol. 23. Ed. by William M. Houston. 1982. 5.00 (*0-935057-22-6*) OH Genealogical.

Ohio Records & Pioneer Families, Vol. 24. Ed. by William M. Houston. 1983. 5.00 (*0-935057-23-4*) OH Genealogical.

Ohio Records & Pioneer Families, Vol. 25. Ed. by William M. Houston. 1984. 5.00 (*0-935057-24-2*) OH Genealogical.

Ohio Records & Pioneer Families, Vol. 26. Ed. by William M. Houston. 1985. 5.00 (*0-935057-45-5*) OH Genealogical.

Ohio Records & Pioneer Families, Vol. 28. Ed. by William M. Houston. 1987. 9.00 (*0-935057-67-6*) OH Genealogical.

Ohio Records & Pioneer Families, Vol. 29. Ed. by William M. Houston. 1988. 9.00 (*0-935057-53-6*) OH Genealogical.

Ohio Records & Pioneer Families, Vol. 30. Ed. by William M. Houston. 1989. 9.00 (*0-935057-56-0*) OH Genealogical.

Ohio Records & Pioneer Families, Vol. 31. Ed. by William M. Houston. 1990. 9.00 (*0-935057-60-9*) OH Genealogical.

Ohio Records & Pioneer Families, Vol. 32. Ed. by William M. Houston. 1991. 9.00 (*0-935057-65-X*) OH Genealogical.

Ohio Records & Pioneer Families, Vol. 33. Ed. by Susan D. Lee. 1992. 9.00 (*0-935057-69-2*) OH Genealogical.

Ohio Records & Pioneer Families, Vol. 34. Ed. by Susan D. Lee. 1993. 18.00 (*0-935057-72-2*) OH Genealogical.

Ohio Records & Pioneer Families, Vol. 35. Ed. by Susan D. Lee. 1994. 18.00 (*0-935057-75-7*) OH Genealogical.

Ohio Records & Pioneer Families, Vol. 36. Ed. by Susan D. Lee. 1995. 18.00 (*0-935057-78-1*) OH Genealogical.

Ohio Records & Pioneer Families, Vol. 37. Ed. by Susan D. Lee. 1996. 18.00 (*0-935057-80-3*) OH Genealogical.

Ohio Records & Pioneer Families: Surname Index, Vol. 27. Ed. by Susan D. Lee. 1986. 15.00 (*0-935057-44-7*) OH Genealogical.

Ohio Records & Pioneer Families: Surname Index, 1985-1994. Compiled by Jana Broglin. 1996. per. 15.00 (*0-935057-83-8*) OH Genealogical.

Ohio Records & Pioneer Families: Topical Index, Vols. I-XXV. Ed. by Susan D. Lee. 1986. 1.00 (*0-935057-43-9*) OH Genealogical.

Ohio Related Laws to the Insurance Laws, 2 vols. NILS Publishing Company Staff. LC 98-67440. 1998. ring bd. write for info. (*0-89246-502-6*) NILS Pub.

Ohio Retirement & Relocation Guide. large type ed. (Retirement & Relocation Guides Ser.). (Illus.). 350p. Date not set. pap. 24.95 (*1-56559-133-X*) HGI-Over Fifty.

Ohio Review, No. 30. Ed. by Wayne D. Dodd. 280p. 1983. 13.95 (*0-942148-00-2*) Ohio Review.

Ohio Revolutionary War Soldiers, 1840 Census: Also Grave Locations. Fay Maxwell. 69p. 1985. 15.00 (*1-885463-24-3*) Ohio Genealogy.

Ohio River. John E. Pearce. LC 89-14830. (Illus.). 200p. 1989. 45.00 (*0-8131-1693-7*) U Pr of Ky.

Ohio River: A Course of Empire. Archer B. Hulbert. (Illus.). 378p. 1996. reprint ed. lib. bdg. 45.00 (*0-8328-5170-1*) Higginson Bk Co.

Ohio River, a Course of Empire. Archer B. Hulbert. 1993. reprint ed. lib. bdg. 89.00 (*0-7812-5380-2*) Rprt Serv.

Ohio Road Atlas. H. M. Gousha. 1995. 7.95 (*0-671-51956-5*) S&S Trade.

Ohio Rollercoasters! Carole Marsh. (Carole Marsh Ohio Bks.). (Illus.). (J). (gr. 3-12). 1994. pap. 19.95 (*0-7933-5330-0*); lib. bdg. 29.95 (*0-7933-5329-7*) Gallopade Intl.

Ohio Rollercoasters! Carole Marsh. (Carole Marsh Ohio Bks.). (Illus.). (YA). (gr. 3-12). 1994. disk 29.95 (*0-7933-5331-9*) Gallopade Intl.

Ohio Rules of Civil Procedure with Commentary, 2 vols., Set. Howard P. Fink et al. 1992. 150.00 (*0-87473-818-0*, 61930-10, MICHIE) LEXIS Pub.

Ohio Rules of Evidence Handbook, 1997 Edition. Ed. by Paul C. Gianelli & Barbara R. Snyder. (Baldwin's Ohio Practice Ser.). 464p. 1997. pap. 59.00 (*0-8322-0668-7*) Banks-Baldwin.

Ohio Rules of Evidence Trial Book. Janet R. Burnside et al. LC 99-61863. 500p. 1999. 75.00 (*0-327-01190-4*, 6353610) LEXIS Pub.

Ohio School Finance: A Practitioner's Guide. 2nd rev. ed. Richard E. Maxwell et al. LC 96-4100. 300p. 1996. pap. 35.00 (*0-87084-785-6*) Anderson Pub Co.

Ohio School Trivia: An Amazing & Fascinating Look at Our State's Teachers, Schools & Students! Carole Marsh. (Carole Marsh Ohio Bks.). (Illus.). (J). 1994. pap. 19.95 (*0-7933-0897-6*); lib. bdg. 29.95 (*0-7933-0898-4*); disk 29.95 (*0-7933-0899-2*) Gallopade Intl.

Ohio Search Warrant Manual. pap. 29.50 (*1-58360-130-9*) Anderson Pub Co.

Ohio Securities Law & Practice, 3 bks. 2nd ed. Howard M. Friedman. 1997. 385.00 (*1-58360-080-9*) Anderson Pub Co.

Ohio Securities Law & Practice: With Electronic Forms, 3 vols. 2nd ed. Howard M. Friedman. 1997. 385.00 (*0-87084-273-0*) Anderson Pub Co.

Ohio Securities Law & Practice Handbook. pap. 35.00 (*1-58360-081-7*) Anderson Pub Co.

Ohio Securities Law & Practice Handbook. annuals Howard M. Friedman. 514p. 1997. pap. 35.00 (*0-87084-272-2*) Anderson Pub Co.

Ohio Selections X. Jeffrey Grove et al. (Illus.). 36p. (Orig.). 1991. pap. text 12.00 (*1-880353-01-6*) Cleveland Ctr.

Ohio Silly Basketball Sportsmysteries, Vol. 1. Carole Marsh. (Carole Marsh Ohio Bks.). (Illus.). (J). 1994. pap. 19.95 (*0-7933-0894-1*); lib. bdg. 29.95 (*0-7933-0895-X*); disk 29.95 (*0-7933-0896-8*) Gallopade Intl.

Ohio Silly Basketball Sportsmysteries, Vol. 2. Carole Marsh. (Carole Marsh Ohio Bks.). (Illus.). (J). 1994. pap. 19.95 (*0-7933-1854-8*); disk 29.95 (*0-7933-1855-6*) Gallopade Intl.

Ohio Silly Basketball Sportsmysteries, Vol. 2. Carole Marsh. (Carole Marsh Ohio Bks.). (Illus.). (J). 1997. lib. bdg. 29.95 (*0-7933-1853-X*) Gallopade Intl.

Ohio Silly Football Sportsmysteries, Vol. 1. Carole Marsh. (Carole Marsh Ohio Bks.). (Illus.). (J). 1994. pap. 19.95 (*1-55609-987-8*); lib. bdg. 29.95 (*1-55609-986-X*); disk 29.95 (*1-55609-988-6*) Gallopade Intl.

Ohio Silly Football Sportsmysteries, Vol. 2. Carole Marsh. (Carole Marsh Ohio Bks.). (Illus.). (J). 1994. pap. 19.95 (*1-55609-990-8*); lib. bdg. 29.95 (*1-55609-989-4*); disk 29.95 (*1-55609-991-6*) Gallopade Intl.

Ohio Silly Trivia1. Carole Marsh. (Carole Marsh Ohio Bks.). (Illus.). (J). 1994. pap. 19.95 (*1-55609-112-5*); lib. bdg. 29.95 (*1-55609-979-7*); disk 29.95 (*1-55609-980-0*) Gallopade Intl.

Ohio Source Records from "The Ohio Genealogical Quarterly" Ohio Genealogical Society Staff. 666p. 1993. reprint ed. 29.95 (*0-8063-1137-1*, 4308) Genealog Pub.

Ohio Spelling Bee! Score Big by Correctly Spelling Our State's Unique Names. Carole Marsh. (Carole Marsh Ohio Bks.). (Illus.). (YA). (gr. 3-12). 1996. pap. 19.95 (*0-7933-6746-8*); lib. bdg. 29.95 (*0-7933-6745-X*) Gallopade Intl.

Ohio Sports Matters of Fact: Ohio Sporting Dictionary. Ed. by Damaine Vonada. LC 94-66497. (Illus.). 232p. 1994. pap. 14.95 (*1-882203-00-3*) Orange Frazer.

Ohio Sportsman's Atlas. Adapted by David D. Adams. (Illus.). 1995. spiral bd. 21.95 (*0-7625-0054-9*) Universal Map Enterprises Inc.

Ohio Star: New Quilts from an Old Favorite. Ed. by Victoria Faoro. 112p. 1996. pap. 16.95 (*0-89145-869-7*, 4627, Am Quilters Soc) Collector Bks.

Ohio State Atlas. 1996. pap. 9.95 (*0-7625-0312-2*, 760316Q) Universal Map Enterprises Inc.

Ohio State Atlas. H. M. Gousha. 1995. 7.95 (*0-671-53462-9*) S&S Trade.

***Ohio State Credit Directory, 2000 Edition.** rev. ed. American Business Directories Staff. 1040p. 1999. boxed set 175.00 incl. cd-rom (*0-7687-0316-6*) Am Busn Direct.

Ohio State Football . . . The Great Tradition. Jack L. Park. Ed. by Dave Stephenson. LC 92-90355. (Illus.). 248p. 1992. 19.95 (*1-881462-45-5*) Lexington OH.

Ohio State Football Encyclopedia. Jack L. Park. (Illus.). 1999. 39.95 (*1-58261-006-1*) Sprts Pubng.

Ohio State Football Trivia. Bill Borst. 1988. 7.95 (*0-685-44817-7*) Krank Pr.

Ohio State Grange Cookbook. Ohio State Grange Staff. LC 92-20292. 1992. spiral bd. write for info. (*0-87197-339-1*) Favorite Recipes.

Ohio State Institute of Accounting Conference Collected Papers, 1938 to 1963. Thomas J. Burns & Edward N. Coffman. Ed. by Richard P. Brief. LC 80-1455. (Dimensions of Accounting Theory & Practice Ser.). 1980. lib. bdg. 25.95 (*0-405-13477-0*) Ayer.

***Ohio State Man: Coach Esco Sarkkinen Remembers OSU Football.** Illus. by William Harper. 120p. 2000. pap. 9.99 (*0-89804-850-8*) Ariel GA.

Ohio State Parks: A Guide to Ohio State Parks. 2nd rev. ed. Art Weber & Bill Bailey. 385p. 1997. pap. 15.95 (*1-881139-16-6*) Glovebox Guidebks.

Ohio State Parks Guidebook. 2nd rev. ed. Art Weber & Bill Bailey. 384p. 1997. pap. 15.95 (*1-881139-04-2*) Glovebox Guidebks.

Ohio State Profile: A Year in the Life of America's Biggest Campus. Jane Ware. LC 91-9398. 236p. reprint ed. pap. 73.20 (*0-608-09895-7*, 206986100006) Bks Demand.

Ohio State '68: All the Way to the Top. Steve Greenberg & Larry Zelina. (Illus.). 143p. 1998. 29.95 (*1-57167-236-2*) Sports Pub.

Ohio State Tailgating. Illus. by Dorothy Well. 128p. 1995. pap. text 8.95 (*1-885623-13-5*) Owl Bay Pubs.

Ohio State University. Barth Falkenberg. (Illus.). 112p. 1987. 35.00 (*0-916509-08-7*) Harmony Hse Pub.

Ohio Studies Program: State Studies Program. Cathryn J. Long. (Illus.). 1996. teacher ed. 125.00 (*0-87746-577-0*) Graphic Learning.

Ohio Survival. rev. ed. Betty L. Hall. 160p. (YA). (gr. 10-12). 1986. pap. text 5.84 (*0-936159-00-6*) Westwood Pr.

Ohio Tax Handbook. Peter George. 384p. 1988. pap. 17.00 (*0-317-64612-5*) P-H.

Ohio Tax Handbook, 1985. Peter George. write for info. (*0-318-58211-2*) P-H.

Ohio Tax Lists, 1800-1810, Vol. 1. Ronald V. Jackson. (Illus.). lib. bdg. 83.00 (*0-89593-759-X*, Accel Indexing) Genealogical Srvcs.

Ohio Tax Lists, 1800-1810, Vol. 2. (Illus.). lib. bdg. 83.00 (*0-89593-457-4*, Accel Indexing) Genealogical Srvcs.

Ohio Tax Lists Index, 1800-1810. Ronald V. Jackson. LC 77-86051. lib. bdg. 80.00 (*0-89593-155-9*, Accel Indexing) Genealogical Srvcs.

Ohio Tea Trails: Tea Rooms & Other Treasures. unabridged ed. Rebecca K. Schroeder. Ed. by Charles J. Schroeder. (Illus.). xi, 100p. (Orig.). 1996. pap. 12.95 (*0-9655224-0-7*) Your Cup of Tea.

Ohio the Beautiful & Historic. Charles E. Hopkins. 1993. reprint ed. lib. bdg. 89.00 (*0-7812-5375-6*) Rprt Serv.

Ohio Timeline: A Chronology of Ohio History, Mystery, Trivia, Legend, Lore & More. Carole Marsh. (Carole Marsh Ohio Bks.). (Illus.). (J). (gr. 3-12). 1994. pap. 19.95 (*0-7933-5981-3*); lib. bdg. 29.95 (*0-7933-5980-5*); disk 29.95 (*0-7933-5982-1*) Gallopade Intl.

***Ohio Toolmakers & Their Tools.** Jack Devitt. 400p. 2000. 30.00 (*1-886855-39-0*) Tavenner Pub.

Ohio Tort Reform Guide. Anderson Publishing Company Staff. pap. 35.50 (*1-58360-269-0*) Anderson Pub Co.

Ohio Town. Helen Hooven Santmyer. LC 84-47558. (Illus.). 320p. 1984. 14.45i (*0-685-42728-5*) HarperTrade.

Ohio Town. Helen Hooven Santmyer. LC 97-51223. 1997. pap. 19.00 (*0-8142-0757-X*) Ohio St U Pr.

Ohio Traffic Code handbook. pap. 12.95 (*1-58360-156-2*) Anderson Pub Co.

Ohio Traffic Law Handbook. pap. 39.95 (*1-58360-157-0*) Anderson Pub Co.

Ohio Transaction Guide: Legal Forms, 16 vols. Zolman Cavitch & Thomas G. Belden. 1975. ring bd. 1340.00 (*0-8205-1538-8*) Bender.

Ohio Trivia. rev. ed. Ernie Couch & Jill Couch. LC 88-4979. 192p. 1992. pap. 6.95 (*1-55853-207-2*) Rutledge Hill Pr.

Ohio 2000! Coming Soon to a Calendar Near You - The 21st Century! - Complete Set of AL 2000 Items. Carole Marsh. (Two Thousand! Ser.). (Illus.). (J). (gr. 3-12). 1998. pap. 75.00 (*0-7933-9379-5*); lib. bdg. 85.00 (*0-7933-9380-9*) Gallopade Intl.

O

An Asterisk (*) at the beginning of an entry indicates that the title is appearing for the first time.

Ohio 2000! Coming Soon to a Calendar near You-The 21st Century! Carole Marsh. (Two Thousand! Ser.). (Illus.). (J). (gr. 3-12). 1998. pap. 19.95 (0-7933-8781-7); lib. bdg. 29.95 (0-7933-8780-9) Gallopade Intl.

Ohio UFO's & Extraterrestrials! A Look at the Sightings & Science in Our State. Carole Marsh. (Carole Marsh Ohio Bks.). (Illus.). (J). (gr. 3-12). 1997. pap. 19.95 (0-7933-6440-X); lib. bdg. 29.95 (0-7933-6439-6) Gallopade Intl.

Ohio UFO's & Others. Irena Scott. 217p. 1997. write for info. (1-57074-368-1) Greyden Pr.

Ohio University - Then & Now. Photos by Dan Dry. (First Edition Ser.). (Illus.). 112p. 1992. 39.95 (0-916509-87-7) Harmony Hse Pub.

Ohio University in Perspective II: The Annual Convocation Addresses of President Charles J. Ping, 1985-1993. Charles J. Ping. LC 94-9002. 285p. 1994. 24.95 (0-8214-1101-2) Ohio U Pr.

Ohio Valley. George Laycock & Ellen Laycock. LC 81-43579. 1983. pap. 10.95 (0-385-17591-4) Doubleday.

Ohio Valley Genealogies: Relating Chiefly to Families in Harrison, Belmont, & Jefferson Counties, Ohio, & Washington, Westmoreland, & Fayette Counties, Pennsylvania. Charles A. Hanna. 172p. 1998. reprint ed. 17.50 (0-8063-0167-8, 2517) Genealog Pub.

Ohio Valley German Biographical Index. Don H. Tolzmann. viii, 80p. (Orig.). 1992. pap. 17.00 (1-55613-587-4) Heritage Bk.

Ohio Valley in Colonial Days. Berthold Fernow. 299p. 1992. reprint ed. pap. text 22.00 (1-55613-667-6) Heritage Bk.

Ohio Valley in Colonial Days. Berthold Frenow. (Illus.). 299p. 1997. reprint ed. lib. bdg. 35.00 (0-8328-6288-6) Higginson Bk Co.

Ohio Valley Pioneer History: Being an Account of the First Examinations of the Ohio Valley & the Early Settlement of the Northwest Territory. S. P. Hildreth. (Illus.). 525p. 1997. reprint ed. lib. bdg. 55.00 (0-8328-6912-0) Higginson Bk Co.

Ohio Wildlife Viewing Guide. W. H. Gross. LC 96-16409. (Illus.). 96p. 1996. pap. 8.95 (1-56044-491-6) Falcon Pub Inc.

Ohio Women, Vol. 1. 2nd rev. ed. Nicholas P. Georgiady et al. (Illus.). 54p. (J). (gr. 6-8). 1995. pap. 4.50 (0-917961-03-X) Argee Pubs.

Ohio Worker's Compensation Act, 1993: House Bill 107. Jerald D. Harris. 192p. 1986. pap. 40.00 (0-8322-0490-0) Banks-Baldwin.

Ohio Worker's Compensation Claims. LC 82-82437. (Ohio Practice Systems Library). 1982. ring bd. 120.00 (0-318-11960-9) West Group.

Ohio Worker's Compensation Claims. (Ohio Practice Systems Library). 1992. suppl. ed. 67.50 (0-317-04341-2) West Group.

***Ohio Workers' Compensation Law.** 2nd ed. Fulton. 1999. 165.00 (0-87084-306-0) Anderson Pub Co.

***Ohio Workers' Compensation Law Handbook.** 5th ed. Fulton. 1999. pap. 62.50 (1-58360-136-8) Anderson Pub Co.

***Ohioepa Laws & Regulations, 1999, 3 vols. Set.** 1999. pap. 185.00 (0-87084-409-1) Anderson Pub Co.

Ohio's Best in Amateur Wrestling: A Thorough Look at Ohio Wrestling from 1938-1997. Mark Osgood. 328p. (Orig.). Date not set. pap. 24.95 (0-9659642-0-5) Mark Osgood.

***Ohio's Big Activity Book.** Carole Marsh. (Ohio Experience! Ser.). (Illus.). (J). (gr. k-5). 2000. pap. 9.95 (0-7933-9464-3) Gallopade Intl.

***Ohio's Biological Diversity.** Environmental Law Institute. LC 98-207087. (Illus.). 1998. write for info. (0-911937-74-9) Environ Law Inst.

Ohio's First Time Buyers & Investors Real Estate Guide. Ed Rothenberg. 1998. pap. 16.95 (0-9613865-2-5) E Rothenberg.

Ohio's Ghostly Greats: An Anthology of Ohio Ghost Stories. David J. Gerrick. 1973. pap. 4.95 (0-916750-40-X) Dayton Labs.

Ohio's Last Frontiersman: Connecticut Mariner Captain James Riley. Joyce L. Alig. (Illus.). viii, 432p. 1997. 39.95 (1-891095-09-9, 5362-9) Mercer Cty Hist.

Ohio's (Most Devastating!) Disasters & (Most Calamitous!) Catastrophies! Carole Marsh. (Carole Marsh Ohio Bks.). (Illus.). (J). 1994. pap. 19.95 (0-7933-0885-2); lib. bdg. 29.95 (0-7933-0886-0); disk 29.95 (0-7933-0887-9) Gallopade Intl.

Ohio's Railway Age in Postcards. H. Roger Grant. (Ohio History & Culture Ser.). (Illus.). 203p. 1996. 32.95 (1-884836-19-4) U Akron Pr.

Ohio's Statehouse Is Intriguing! Marilyn C. Davis. (Illus.). 132p. (Orig.). 1997. pap. 12.95 (0-9659338-0-6) M C Davis.

Ohio's Unsolved Mysteries (And Their "Solutions") Includes Scientific Information & Other Activities for Students. Carole Marsh. (Carole Marsh Ohio Bks.). (Illus.). (J). (gr. 3-12). 1994. pap. 19.95 (0-7933-5828-0); lib. bdg. 29.95 (0-7933-5827-2); disk 29.95 (0-7933-5829-9) Gallopade Intl.

Ohio's Virginia Military Tract Settlers: Also 1801 Tax List. Fay Maxwell. 25p. 1991. 15.00 (1-885463-25-1) Ohio Genealogy.

Ohio's Western Reserve: A Regional Reader. Ed. by Harry F. Lupold & Gladys Haddad. LC 88-691. 290p. 1988. pap. 15.00 (0-87338-372-9) Kent St U Pr.

Ohiotal - The Ohio Valley: The German Dimension. Ed. by Don H. Tolzmann. LC 92-34548. (New German-American Studies: Vol. 4). (Illus.). XIII, 203p. (C). 1993. text 49.95 (0-8204-1648-7) P Lang Pubng.

Ohitika Woman. B. Brave. LC 94-18040. 304p. 1994. pap. 13.50 (0-06-097583-0) HarpC.

Ohiyesa: Charles Eastman, Santee Sioux. Raymond Wilson. (Illus.). 242p. 1999. pap. text 24.50 (0-252-06851-3) U of Ill Pr.

Ohlbaum's Courtroom Guide to the Pennsylvania Rules of Evidence. Edward D. Ohlbaum. LC 98-10061. 1998. 80.00 (0-8205-2933-8) Bender.

Ohlone Past & Present: Native Americans of the San Francisco Bay Region. Ed. by Lowell J. Bean. (Anthropological Papers: No. 42). (Illus.). 408p. (C). 1994. 29.95 (0-87919-130-9) Ballena Pr.

Ohlone Past & Present: Native Americans of the San Francisco Bay Region. Ed. by Lowell J. Bean & Sylvia B. Vane. (Anthropological Papers: No. 42). (Illus.). 376p. (C). 1994. pap. 23.95 (0-87919-129-5) Ballena Pr.

Ohlone Way: Indian Life in the San Francisco-Monterey Bay Area. Malcolm Margolin. LC 78-56826. (Illus.). 182p. (Orig.). 1994. pap. 12.95 (0-930588-01-0) Heyday Bks.

OHM's Dictionary of Computers, English-Japanese-English. OHM Staff. (ENG & JPN.). 356p. 1985. 95.00 (0-8288-0252-1, F17250) Fr & Eur.

Ohm's Law, Electrical Math & Voltage Drop Calculations. rev. ed. Tom Henry. (Illus.). 189p. (C). 1992. reprint ed. pap. text 19.00 (0-945495-26-9) T Henrys CECB.

Ohne Muhe!, 001. Helmut Liedloff. LC 79-84596. (German Sequential Readers Ser.). (Illus.). (J). (gr. 9-10). 1980. pap. 12.52 (0-395-27931-3) HM.

***Ohr Hachayim: Commentary on the Tarah, 5 vols.** Tr. by Eliyahu Munki. 2066p. 2000. 100.00 (965-7108-12-8, Pub. by Urim Pubns) Shalom.

Ohr Hatfilla, Vol. 1. Yosef Y. Alperovits. (HEB.). 397p. 20.00 (0-8266-5226-3) Kehot Pubn Soc.

Ohr Hatfilla, Vol. 2. Yosef Y. Alperovits. (HEB.). 525p. 20.00 (0-8266-5227-1) Kehot Pubn Soc.

Ohr Hatfilla, Vol. 3. Yosef Y. Alperovits. (HEB.). 395p. 1992. 20.00 (0-8266-5228-X) Kehot Pubn Soc.

Ohr Hatfilla, Vol. 4. Yosef Y. Alperovits. (HEB.). 633p. 1994. 25.00 (0-8266-5229-8) Kehot Pubn Soc.

Ohr Hatorah: Vayikro, Vol. 2. Menachem M. Schneerson. (HEB.). 450p. 1992. 30.00 (0-8266-5372-3) Kehot Pubn Soc.

Ohr Hatorah Vol. 1: Vayikra. Menachem M. Schneerson. 496p. 1991. reprint ed. 30.00 (0-8266-5371-5) Kehot Pubn Soc.

Ohr Hatorah Bamidbar (The Light of Torah - Bamidbar) Menachem M. Schneerson. Ed. by Aharon Chitrik & Garriel Schapira. LC 98-42619. (HEB.). 464p. 1998. 30.00 (0-8266-5376-6) Kehot Pubn Soc.

Ohr Hatoran Bamidbar. Menahem Mendel Schneersohn.Tr. of Light of Torah - Bamidbar. (HEB.). 556p. 1995. 30.00 (0-8266-5374-X) Kehot Pubn Soc.

Ohr Somayach Haggadah. Comment by Uziel Mileusky. 180p. 1998. 16.95 (1-56871-137-9, Pub. by Targum Pr) Feldheim.

***Ohs & Ahs of Torah Reading: A Guide to the Kamatz Katan in the Torah, the Haftarot & the Megillot.** Rivka Sherman-Gold. LC 99-70828. 296p. 1999. pap. text 42.00 (0-9670474-0-4) Yodan Pub.

Oht - Biochemistry: An Extended Course. Garrett. (C). 1912. pap. text 201.00 (0-03-097376-7) Harcourt.

Oht - Biology: A Journey Into Life 3e. 3rd ed. Arms. (C). 1994. pap. text 288.00 (0-03-097834-3) Harcourt.

Oht Chem for English/Scientists+ Fine. (C). 1990. 441.50 (0-03-021549-8) Harcourt.

Oht-Intro College Acct:1-14 2E. 2nd ed. Bischof. 1992. 125.00 (0-15-541715-0, Pub. by Harcourt Coll Pubs) Harcourt.

Oht-oceanography:ocean Environments&proc. Moore. (C). 1997. pap. text 201.00 (0-03-097380-5) Harcourt.

Oht Physical Science W/Mod Appl 5e. 5th ed. Merken. (C). 1993. teacher ed. 246.00 (0-03-096041-X, Pub. by Harcourt Coll Pubs) Harcourt.

Oht Precalc w/ Applications. Grossman. 1990. 241.50 (0-03-033267-2, Pub. by Harcourt Coll Pubs) Harcourt.

Oht T/a Advanced Accounting, 6e. 6th ed. Arnold J. Pahler. (C). 1997. text 246.00 (0-03-018617-X) Harcourt Coll Pubs.

Oht T/a Earth Science & Environment 2e. 2nd ed. Thompson. (C). 1999. pap. text 441.50 (0-03-021477-7) Harcourt Coll Pubs.

Oht T/a Financial Accounting,alt.ed. Porter. (C). 1996. pap. text 246.00 (0-03-019689-2) Harcourt Coll Pubs.

Oht T/a Financial Acctng Alt Ed, 2e. 2nd ed. Porter. (C). 1998. pap. text 221.00 (0-03-021354-1) Harcourt Coll Pubs.

OHT T/A FUND OF ANALYT CHEM 6E. 6th ed. Skoog. (C). 1992. 441.50 (0-03-076018-6) Harcourt.

Oht T/A Human Geography. Nelson. 1995. 288.00 (0-03-044154-4, Pub. by Harcourt Coll Pubs) Harcourt.

Oht T/A International Business. 5th ed. Czinkota. (C). 1998. pap. text 515.00 (0-03-021593-5) Harcourt Coll Pubs.

Oht T/a Psychology New Millenium 7e. 7th ed. Rathus. (C). 1998. pap. text 441.50 (0-15-507172-6) Harcourt Coll Pubs.

Oht-teaching - International Business 4e. 4th ed. Czinkota. (C). 1995. pap. text 246.00 (0-03-016213-0) Harcourt Coll Pubs.

Oht's - In Search Of The Human Mind. Sternberg. (C). 1995. pap. text 287.00 (0-15-502925-8) Harcourt Coll Pubs.

Oht's - Invitation To Social Psychology. Philipchal. (C). 1994. pap. text 441.50 (0-15-502465-5) Harcourt Coll Pubs.

Ohts T/a Chemistry:sci Of Change 3/e. 3rd ed. Oxtoby. (C). 1997. pap. text 441.50 (0-03-020478-X) Harcourt Coll Pubs.

Oht's T/a Franknoil Voyages Thru Universe,1E. 6th ed. Fraknoi. (C). 1997. text 246.00 (0-03-016094-4) Harcourt Coll Pubs.

Oht's T/a Human Physiology 3/e Rv. 3rd ed. Rhoades. (C). 1996. pap. text 246.00 (0-03-019774-0) Harcourt Coll Pubs.

Oido. Chelsea House Publishing Staff & Andrew Llamas. (SPA., Illus.). 32p. (YA). (gr. 3 up). 1996. lib. bdg. 15.95 (0-7910-4001-1) Chelsea Hse.

Oido. 2nd ed. Maria Rius. (Cinco Sentidos Ser.). (SPA.). (J). 1986. 12.15 (0-606-01519-1, Pub. by Turtleback) Demco.

OIES Review of Long-Term Energy Demand. Philip Barnes. 76p. 1992. 165.95 (0-948061-69-3, P7490) PennWell Bks.

OIES Review of Long-Term Energy Supply. Philip Barnes. 75p. 1990. 137.95 (0-948061-45-6, P7494) PennWell Bks.

Oigan Ninos (Listen Children) Grace Barrington Hofer & Rachel Day. (ENG & SPA., Illus.). 96p. (J). 1997. 12.95 (1-57168-015-2, Eakin Pr) Sunbelt Media.

Oigan Ninos, Listen Children: A Book of Nursery Rhymes, Poems, Songs & Riddles in Spanish & in English. Grace Barrington Hofer & Rachel Day. (ENG & SPA., Illus.). 96p. (J). (ps-7). 1995. pap. 12.95 (0-89015-865-7, Eakin Pr) Sunbelt Media.

Oikumene. I. Hah. Ed. by L. Kakosy. 1976. pap. 75.00 (963-05-0760-9, Pub. by Akade Kiado) St Mut.

Oikumene, Vol. 2. I. Hahn. Ed. by L. Kakosy. 1978. pap. 115.00 (963-05-1590-3, Pub. by Akade Kiado) St Mut.

Oikumene, Vol. 4. I. Hahn. Ed. by L. Kakosy. 1987. pap. 115.00 (963-05-2961-0, Pub. by Akade Kiado) St Mut.

Oil. (Butterfly Bks.). (ARA., Illus.). 31p. 1989. 8.95 (0-86685-401-0, LDL254, Pub. by Librairie du Liban) Intl Bk Ctr.

Oil. Al Dempsey. 1996. write for info. (0-312-93167-0) Tor Bks.

Oil. Hartley. 1989. pap. write for info. (0-582-40400-2) Addison-Wesley.

Oil. Illus. by Pat Robson. (Butterfly Bks.). 32p. (J). (gr. 3-5). 1985. 9.95 (0-86685-449-5) Intl Bk Ctr.

Oil! Upton Sinclair. 533p. Date not set. 32.95 (0-8488-2391-5) Amereon Ltd.

Oil! Upton Sinclair. LC 96-34573. 528p. 1997. 15.95 (0-520-20727-0, Pub. by U CA Pr) Cal Prin Full Svc.

Oil. large type ed. Jonathan Black. 608p. 1983. 27.99 (0-7089-8102-X, Charnwood) Ulverscroft.

Oil. Thomas W. Gilkyson. LC 74-26108. (Labor Movement in Fiction & Non-Fiction Ser.). reprint ed. 49.50 (0-404-58432-2) AMS Pr.

Oil! Upton Sinclair. LC 79-24682. 1981. reprint ed. lib. bdg. 32.00 (0-8376-0444-3) Bentley Pubs.

Oil see **Political Economy of the Middle East**

Oil: The Buried Treasure. Roma Gans. LC 74-7375. (Let's-Read-&-Find-Out Science Bks.). (Illus.). (J). (gr. k-3). 1975. lib. bdg. 11.89 (0-690-00613-6) HarpC Child Bks.

Oil Additives Industry. Willinger. 214p. 1999. pap. 4500.00 (0-471-34440-0) Wiley.

Oil Age Eskimos. Joseph G. Jorgensen. 1990. 55.00 (0-520-06843-2, Pub. by U CA Pr) Cal Prin Full Svc.

Oil & America's Security. Ed. by Edward R. Fried & Nanette M. Blandin. LC 88-71646. (Dialogues on Public Policy Ser.). 148p. 1988. pap. 11.95 (0-8157-2975-8) Brookings.

Oil & Arab Regional Development. Ed. by Kamal S. Sayegh. LC 78-6838. (Praeger Studies in International Economics & Development). (Illus.). 357p. 1978. reprint ed. lib. bdg. 75.00 (0-313-20500-0, SAOA, Greenwood Pr) Greenwood.

Oil & Coffee: Latin American Merchant Shipping from the Imperial Era to the 1950s, 206. Rene De La Pedraja. LC 98-21665. (Contributions in Economics & Economic History: Vol. 206). 208p. 1998. 59.95 (0-313-30839-X, Greenwood Pr) Greenwood.

Oil & Development in the Middle East. David G. Edens. LC 79-848. 200p. 1979. 62.95 (0-275-90349-4, C0349, Praeger Pubs) Greenwood.

Oil & Development in Venezuela During the Twentieth Century. Jorge Salazar-Carrillo. LC 93-37882. 296p. 1994. 79.50 (0-275-92849-7, Praeger Pubs) Greenwood.

***Oil & Fat Derived Products.** Willinger. 1999. pap. 4250.00 (0-471-35375-2) Wiley.

Oil & Fiscal Federalism in Nigeria: The Political Economy of Resource Allocation in a Developing Country. Augustine Ikein & Comfort Briggs-Anigboh. LC 96-86363. (Making of Modern Africa Ser.). 390p. 1998. text 80.95 (1-85628-848-X, Pub. by Avebry) Ashgate Pub Co.

Oil & Gas. (Indian Law Ser.). 1980. 12.00 (0-944253-05-9) Inst Dev Indian Law.

Oil & Gas: Adaptable to Courses Utilizing Kuntz, Lowe, Anderson & Smith's Casebook on Oil & Gas Law. Casenotes Publishing Co., Inc. Staff. Ed. by Norman S. Goldenberg et al. (Legal Briefs Ser.). (Orig.). 1993. pap. text. write for info. (0-87457-155-3, 1541) Casenotes Pub.

Oil & Gas: Adaptable to Courses Utilizing Maxwell, Williams, Martin & Kramer's Casebook on Oil & Gas. Casenotes Publishing Co., Inc. Staff. Ed. by Norman S. Goldenberg & Peter Tenen. (Legal Briefs Ser.). 1992. pap. write for info. (0-87457-110-3, 1540) Casenotes Pub.

Oil & Gas: The Production Story. Ron Baker. (Illus.). 91p. (Orig.). 1983. pap. text 25.00 (0-88698-002-X, 3.90010) PETEX.

Oil & Gas: 1996 Case Supplement. 6th ed. Maxwell et al. 1998. 9.95 (1-56662-413-4) Foundation Pr.

Oil & Gas Acquisitions. (Mineral Law Ser.). 500p. 1995. student ed. 125.00 (0-929047-56-7) Rocky Mtn Mineral Law Found.

Oil & Gas Assessment: Methods & Applications. Ed. by Dudley D. Rice. LC 86-14158. (AAPG Studies in Geology: No. 21). (Illus.). 275p. reprint ed. pap. 85.30 (0-7837-2598-1, 204276200006) Bks Demand.

Oil & Gas Book. Anthony J. Welker. 259p. 1985. 15.00 (0-87814-279-7) PennWell Bks.

Oil & Gas, Cases & Materials On. 3rd ed. Owen L. Anderson et al. LC 98-16545. 1000p. 1998. 65.00 (0-314-22640-0) West Pub.

Oil & Gas Conservation Statutes: Annotated. Federal Oil Conservation Board Staff. Ed. by Northcutt Ely. 432p. 1982. reprint ed. lib. bdg. 47.50 (0-89941-226-2, 201520) W S Hein.

Oil & Gas Databook for Developing Countries: With Special Reference to the ACP Countries. 2nd ed. Derek A. Fee. (Illus.). 220p. (C). 1989. lib. bdg. 142.00 (1-85333-022-1, Pub. by Graham & Trotman) G & T Inc.

Oil & Gas Development in Latin America, 1. (Mineral Law Ser.). 716p. 1999. ring bd. 125.00 (0-929047-79-6) Rocky Mtn Mineral Law Found.

Oil & Gas Development on the Outer Continental Shelf, 2. (Mineral Law Ser.: Vol. 1998, No. 3). 1340p. 1998. ring bd. 165.00 (0-929047-78-8) Rocky Mtn Mineral Law Found.

Oil & Gas Developments in Pennsylvania in 1977. 2nd ed. Louis Heyman & Cheryl L. Cozart. (Progress Reports: No. 191). (Illus.). 39p. 1984. reprint ed. pap. 2.85 (0-8182-0039-1) Commonweal PA.

Oil & Gas Developments in Pennsylvania in 1978. R. G. Piotrowski et al. (Progress Reports: No. 192). (Illus.). 61p. 1984. reprint ed. pap. 3.45 (0-8182-0040-5) Commonweal PA.

Oil & Gas Developments in Pennsylvania in 1982. Compiled by John A. Harper. (Progress Reports: No. 196). (Illus.). 119p. (Orig.). 1983. pap. 2.65 (0-8182-0041-3) Commonweal PA.

Oil & Gas Developments in Pennsylvania in 1983. John A. Harper. (Progress Reports: No. 197). (Illus.). 86p. 1984. pap. 2.40 (0-8182-0056-1) Commonweal PA.

Oil & Gas Developments in Pennsylvania in 1985. John A. Harper. (Progress Reports: No. 199). (Illus.). 112p. 1986. pap. 3.25 (0-8182-0083-9) Commonweal PA.

Oil & Gas Developments in Pennsylvania in 1986. Commonwealth of Pennsylvania Staff. Ed. by Department of Environmental Resources Geological S. (Progress Reports: No. 200). (Illus.). 93p. 1987. pap. text 3.05 (0-8182-0098-7) Commonweal PA.

Oil & Gas Developments in Pennsylvania in 1988. John A. Harper & Cheryl L. Cozart. (Progress Reports: No. 202). (Illus.). 110p. (Orig.). 1989. pap. 3.60 (0-8182-0129-0) Commonweal PA.

Oil & Gas Developments in Pennsylvania in 1991. Cheryl A. Cozart & John A. Harper. (Progress Reports: No. 205). (Illus.). 96p. (Orig.). 1993. pap. 4.10 (0-8182-0178-9) Commonweal PA.

Oil & Gas Dictionary. Paul Stevens. 350p. 1988. 78.50 (0-89397-325-4) Nichols Pub.

Oil & Gas Drilling in Utah, 1990. Thomas C. Chidsey, Jr. et al. (Circular of the Utah Geological Survey Ser.: Vol. 86). (Illus.). 30p. (Orig.). 1994. pap. 5.00 (1-55791-291-2, C86) Utah Geological Survey.

Oil & Gas Equities: Evaluation & Trading. Robert Arnott & Nicholas Antill. (International Equities Ser.). 272p. 1994. 170.00 (1-85573-119-3, Pub. by Woodhead Pubng) Am Educ Systs.

Oil & Gas Exploration Services in Mexico: A Strategic Entry Report, 1997. Compiled by Icon Group International Staff. (Illus.). 140p. 1999. ring bd. 1400.00 incl. audio compact disk (0-7418-1061-1) Icon Grp.

Oil & Gas Federal Income Tax Manual. 13th ed. Ed. by J. Ray Jones. (Illus.). 1987. 50.00 (0-942319-01-X) A Andersen.

Oil & Gas Field Code Master List, 2 vols., Set. 1994. lib. bdg. 575.95 (0-8490-5824-4) Gordon Pr.

Oil & Gas Field Code Master List, 2 vols., Set. 1995. lib. bdg. 600.00 (0-8490-6498-8) Gordon Pr.

***Oil & Gas Field Code Master List, 1997.** 467p. 1998. per. 37.00 (0-16-063525-X) USGPO.

Oil & Gas Field Dictionary: English, French, Spanish, Italian, Dutch, German Arabic, Persian. Editions Technip Staff. 676p. 1992. 450.00 (0-7855-2698-6, Pub. by Edits Technip) Enfield Pubs NH.

Oil & Gas Field Dictionary in English, French, Spanish, Italian, German, Dutch, Arabic & Persian. Editions Technip Staff. (ARA, DUT, ENG, FRE & GER.). 676p. 1992. 195.00 (0-7859-0565-0, M2618) Fr & Eur.

***Oil & Gas Field Equipment in Denmark: A Strategic Entry Report, 1998.** Compiled by Icon Group International Staff. (Country Industry Report). (Illus.). 107p. 1999. ring bd. 1070.00 incl. audio compact disk (0-7418-0274-0) Icon Grp.

***Oil & Gas Field Equipment in Russia: A Strategic Entry Report, 1996.** Compiled by Icon Group International Staff. (Illus.). 146p. 1999. ring bd. 1460.00 incl. audio compact disk (0-7418-1345-9) Icon Grp.

***Oil & Gas Field Machinery & Services in Pakistan: A Strategic Entry Report, 1996.** Compiled by Icon Group International Staff. (Illus.). 169p. 1999. ring bd. 1690.00 incl. audio compact disk (0-7418-1346-7) Icon Grp.

***Oil & Gas Field Machinery in Colombia: A Strategic Entry Report, 1998.** Compiled by Icon Group International Staff. (Country Industry Report). (Illus.). 165p. 1999. ring bd. 1650.00 incl. audio compact disk (0-7418-0275-9) Icon Grp.

***Oil & Gas Field Machinery in Peru: A Strategic Entry Report, 1996.** Compiled by Icon Group International Staff. (Illus.). 139p. 1999. ring bd. 1390.00 incl. audio compact disk (0-7418-1344-0) Icon Grp.

***Oil & Gas Field Machinery in Thailand: A Strategic Entry Report, 1996.** Compiled by Icon Group International Staff. (Illus.). 147p. 1999. ring bd. 1470.00 incl. audio compact disk (0-7418-1347-5) Icon Grp.

***Oil & Gas Field Machinery in United Arab Emirates: A Strategic Entry Report, 1996.** Compiled by Icon Group International Staff. (Illus.). 102p. 1999. ring bd. 1020.00 incl. audio compact disk (0-7418-1349-1) Icon Grp.

O

An Asterisk (*) at the beginning of an entry indicates that the title is appearing for the first time.

Oil & Gas Field Waste Regulations Handbook. Michelle A. McFaddin. LC 95-45608. 1995. 99.95 (*0-87814-461-7*) PennWell Bks.

Oil & Gas Fields: Proceedings of the 27th International Geological Congress, Vol. 13. International Geological Congress Staff. 432p. 1984. lib. bdg. 125.00 (*90-6764-022-0*, Pub. by VSP) Coronet Bks.

Oil & Gas Finance Sourcebook, 1991. 2nd ed. Ed. by Ronald Schmela. 549p. 1991. ring bd. 420.00 (*0-912553-27-8*) Hart Pubns.

Oil & Gas Finance Sourcebook, 1992. 3rd ed. Ed. by Ronald Schmela. 549p. 1992. ring bd. 495.00 (*0-912553-34-0*) Hart Pubns.

Oil & Gas Forecasting: Reflections of a Petroleum Geologist. Lawrence J. Drew. (International Association for Mathematical Geology: Studies in Mathematical Geology: No. 2). (Illus.). 264p. 1990. text 65.00 (*0-19-506170-5*) OUP.

Oil & Gas Geology of the Amity & Claysville Quadrangles, Pennsylvania. William G. McGlade. (Mineral Resource Reports: No. 54). (Illus.). 131p. 1984. reprint ed. pap. 30.15 (*0-8182-0022-7*) Commonweal PA.

Oil & Gas in Alpidic Thrustbelts & Basins of Central & Eastern Europe. Ed. by G. Wessely & W. Liebl. (EAGE Special Publication Ser.: Vol. 5). (Illus.). 464p. 1996. 137.00 (*1-897799-73-X*, 242, Pub. by Geol Soc Pub Hse) AAPG.

***Oil & Gas in the Caucasus & Caspian: A History.** Charles Van Der Leeuw. 260p. 1999. 65.00 (*0-7007-1123-6*, Pub. by Curzon Pr Ltd) Paul & Co Pubs.

***Oil & Gas in the Caucasus & Caspian: A History.** Charles Van Der Leeuw. LC 00-27837. 224p. 2000. text 59.95 (*0-312-23254-3*) St Martin.

Oil & Gas in the Environment. Environment Agency Staff. (Environmental Issues Ser.). (Illus.). 104p. 1998. pap. 130.00 (*0-11-310152-X*, Pub. by Statnry Office) Balogh.

Oil & Gas in the Olympic Peninsula. Charles T. Lupton. (Shorey Prospecting Ser.). 60p. reprint ed. pap. 10.00 (*0-8466-0055-2*, S55) Shoreys Bkstore.

Oil & Gas Industry. 192p. 1996. pap. 18.00 (*0-16-062304-9*) USGPO.

Oil & Gas Industry: Market Segment Specialization Program - Audit Technique Guide. 1996. pap. 43.00 (*1-57402-154-0*) Athena Info Mgt.

Oil & Gas Industry in Vietnam: A Strategic Entry Report, 1998. Compiled by Icon Group International Staff. (Country Industry Report). (Illus.). 153p. 1999. ring bd. 1530.00 incl. audio compact disk (*0-7418-0517-0*) Icon Grp.

Oil & Gas Journal DataBook, 1996. 420p. 1996. 64.95 (*87-567-1649-4*, P4535) PennWell Bks.

Oil & Gas Law, 3 vols. 1954. 75.00 (*0-8377-0925-3*, Rothman) W S Hein.

Oil & Gas Law, 3 vols. 1959. 25.00 (*0-318-55551-4*) W S Hein.

Oil & Gas Law, 8 vols. H. R. Williams & Charles J. Meyers. 1959. ring bd. write for info. (*0-8205-1820-4*) Bender.

Oil & Gas Law. abr. ed. Howard R. Williams & Charles J. Meyers. 1973. ring bd. 155.00 (*0-8205-1822-0*); ring bd. 900.00 (*0-8205-2148-5*) Bender.

Oil & Gas Law in a Nutshell. 2nd ed. John S. Lowe. (Nutshell Ser.). 465p. (C). 1993. reprint ed. pap. text 18.50 (*0-314-39781-7*) West Pub.

Oil & Gas Law in a Nutshell. 3rd ed. John S. Lowe. LC 95-30469. (Nutshell Ser.). 474p. (C). 1995. pap. 22.95 (*0-314-06415-X*) West Pub.

Oil & Gas Lease Appeals in the Department of Interior. LC 92-74061. 160p. 1992. pap. 39.95 (*0-89707-832-2*, 535-0036, ABA Natl Res) Amer Bar Assn.

Oil & Gas Lease in Canada. John B. Ballem. LC 72-75734. 344p. reprint ed. pap. 106.70 (*0-608-16539-5*, 202635600049) Bks Demand.

Oil & Gas Lease in Canada. 2nd ed. John B. Ballem. LC 86-221667. 363p. 1985. text 75.00 (*0-8020-2550-1*) U of Toronto Pr.

Oil & Gas Machinery & Equipment in Egypt: A Strategic Entry Report, 1997. Compiled by Icon Group International Staff. (Country Industry Report). (Illus.). 162p. 1999. ring bd. 1620.00 incl. audio compact disk (*0-7418-0276-7*) Icon Grp.

Oil & Gas-Natural Resources. (Information Services Ser.). 1987. 447.00 (*0-685-07443-9*); 399.00 (*0-685-07444-7*) P-H.

Oil & Gas of the South Atlantic. Ed. by N. Cameron et al. (Geological Society Special Publication Ser.: No. 153). 400p. 1999. 149.00 (*1-86239-030-4*, Pub. by Geol Soc Pub Hse) AAPG.

Oil & Gas Pipeline Equipment in Canada: A Strategic Entry Report, 1997. Compiled by Icon Group International Staff. (Country Industry Report). (Illus.). 141p. 1999. ring bd. 1410.00 incl. audio compact disk (*0-7418-0277-5*) Icon Grp.

Oil & Gas Pipeline Fundamentals. 2nd ed. John L. Kennedy. LC 92-41879. 380p. 1993. 64.95 (*0-87814-390-4*) PennWell Bks.

***Oil & Gas Pollution Control Equipment in Indonesia: A Strategic Entry Report, 1998.** Compiled by Icon Group International Staff. (Country Industry Report). (Illus.). 170p. 1999. ring bd. 1700.00 incl. audio compact disk (*0-7418-0307-0*) Icon Grp.

***Oil & Gas Production Equipment in Mexico: A Strategic Entry Report, 1996.** Compiled by Icon Group International Staff. (Illus.). 157p. 1999. ring bd. 1570.00 incl. audio compact disk (*0-7418-1348-3*) Icon Grp.

Oil & Gas Production from Carbonate Rocks. George V. Chilingar et al. LC 70-153417. 108p. 1972. write for info. (*0-444-00099-2*) Elsevier.

Oil & Gas Projects Update in Saudi Arabia: A Strategic Entry Report, 1997. Compiled by Icon Group International Staff. (Illus.). 132p. 1999. ring bd. 1320.00 incl. audio compact disk (*0-7418-0873-0*) Icon Grp.

Oil & Gas Reporter. Ed. by Carol Holgren. text 1290.00 (*0-8205-2098-5*) Bender.

Oil & Gas Reserves of the Fergana Region, Uzbekistan, Tadzhikistan, & Kyrgystan. (Illus.). 147p. (Orig.). (C). 1994. pap. text 50.00 (*0-7881-0488-8*) DIANE Pub.

Oil & Gas Resources of the United Kingdom, 1997. Stationery Office. (Energy Report Ser.: Vol. 2). 184p. 1997. pap. 95.00 (*0-11-515429-9*, HM154299, Pub. by Statnry Office) Bernan Associates.

***Oil & Gas Resources of the West Siberian Basin, Russia.** 230p. 1998. per. 22.00 (*0-16-063499-7*) USGPO.

Oil & Gas Retail Equipment in Thailand: A Strategic Entry Report, 1998. Compiled by Icon Group International Staff. (Country Industry Report). (Illus.). 147p. 1999. ring bd. 1470.00 incl. audio compact disk (*0-7418-0281-3*) Icon Grp.

Oil & Gas Royalties on Non-Federal Lands. (Mineral Law Ser.). 1993. student ed. 125.00 (*0-929047-36-2*) Rocky Mtn Mineral Law Found.

***Oil & Gas Separation Plants in Argentina: A Strategic Entry Report, 1997.** Compiled by Icon Group International Staff. (Country Industry Report). (Illus.). 136p. 1999. ring bd. 1360.00 incl. audio compact disk (*0-7418-0278-3*) Icon Grp.

Oil & Gas Tax Quarterly, 1952-1995/96, 41 vols. 1951. mic. film 665.00 (*0-318-57452-7*) W S Hein.

Oil & Gas Tax Quarterly, 1952-1995/96, 45 vols., Set. 1951. 4050.00 (*0-8377-9127-8*, Rothman) W S Hein.

Oil & Gas Taxation in Nontechnical Language. Frank M. Burke, Jr. & Mark L. Starcher. LC 93-13053. 280p. 1993. 25.00 (*0-87814-397-1*) PennWell Bks.

Oil & Geopolitics in the Caspian Sea Region. Michael P. Croissont & Bulent Aras. LC 99-15398. 328p. 1999. 69.50 (*0-275-96395-0*, Praeger Pubs) Greenwood.

Oil & Grease in Stormwater Runoff. 241p. 1982. 20.00 (*0-317-05713-8*, P82004WAT) Assn Bay Area.

Oil & Hydrocarbon Spills: Modelling, Analysis & Control. Ed. by Reinaldo Garcia-Martinez & Carlos A. Brebbia. LC 99-159053. (Water Studies : Vol. 3). (Illus.). 384p. 1998. 198.00 (*1-85312-526-1*, 5261, Pub. by WIT Pr) Computational Mech MA.

Oil & Hydrocarbon Spills II: Modelling, Analysis & Control. Ed. by R. Garcia-Martinez et al. (Water Studies). 400p. 2000. 189.00 (*1-85312-828-7*, 8287, Pub. by WIT Pr) Computational Mech MA.

***Oil & Ideology: The Cultural Creation of the American Petroleum Industry.** Roger M. Olien. LC 99-29765. (Luther Hartwell Hodges Series on Business, Society & the State). 416p. 2000. lib. bdg. 49.95 (*0-8078-2523-9*) U of NC Pr.

***Oil & Ideology: The Cultural Creation of the American Petroleum Industry.** Roger M. Olien & Diana D. Olien. LC 99-29765. (Luther Hartwell Hodges Series on Business, Society & the State). 416p. 2000. pap. 18.95 (*0-8078-4835-2*) U of NC Pr.

Oil & International Relations: Energy, Trade, Technology & Politics. Michael Fulda. Ed. by Stuart Bruchey. LC 78-22681. (Energy in the American Economy Ser.). (Illus.). 1979. lib. bdg. 25.95 (*0-405-11984-4*) Ayer.

Oil & Islam. Farid A. Khavari. (Illus.). 288p. 1991. 19.95 (*0-915677-55-5*) Roundtable Pub.

Oil & Islam: Social & Economic Issues. Ystein Noreng. LC 97-16413. (Petro Research Series in Petroleum Economics & Politics). 352p. 1997. 135.00 (*0-471-97153-7*) Wiley.

Oil & Labor in the Middle East: Saudi Arabia & the Oil Boom. Peter N. Woodward. LC 88-2345. (Illus.). 204p. 1988. 57.95 (*0-275-92960-4*, C2960, Praeger Pubs) Greenwood.

Oil & Money. Andrew C. Hess. 280p. 1998. 55.00 (*0-8144-0466-9*) AMACOM.

Oil & Money: A Global Study of the Middle East in the Oil Era. Andrew C. Hess. (Glenlake Business Monographs). 300p. 1999. 55.00 (*1-57958-000-9*) Fitzroy Dearborn.

Oil & Natural Gas Pipelines: Wellhead to End User. Rocky Mountain Mineral Law Foundation Staff. (Mineral Law Ser.). 1995. student ed. 125.00 (*0-929047-51-6*) Rocky Mtn Mineral Law Found.

Oil & Revolution in Mexico. Jonathan C. Brown. LC 92-25649. 460p. 1993. 50.00 (*0-520-07934-5*, Pub. by U CA Pr) Cal Prin Full Svc.

Oil & Socioeconomic Crisis in Nigeria: A Regional Perspective to the Nigerian Disease & the Rural Sector. Emmanuel U. Nnadozie. LC 95-40212. 208p. 1996. text 49.95 (*0-7734-4240-5*) E Mellen.

Oil & State in the Middle East. George Lenczowski. LC 60-476. 399p. reprint ed. pap. 123.70 (*0-608-08538-3*, 206906100002) Bks Demand.

Oil & the Economic Geography of the Middle East & North Africa: Studies by Alexander Melamid. Ed. by C. Max Kortepeter. LC 90-25183. 288p. 1991. 24.95 (*0-87850-075-8*) Darwin Pr.

Oil & the International Economy. Geoffrey Heal & Graciela Chichilnisky. (Illus.). 160p. 1991. text 49.95 (*0-19-828517-5*) OUP.

Oil & the International Economy: Lessons from the Two Price Shocks. George Koopman et al. 431p. (C). 1989. pap. 24.95 (*0-88738-616-4*) Transaction Pubs.

Oil & the International System: The Case of France, 1918-1969. Eric D. Melby. Ed. by Stuart Bruchey. LC 80-2816. (Dissertations in European Economic History Ser.). (Illus.). 1981. lib. bdg. 42.95 (*0-405-14000-2*) Ayer.

Oil, Banks, & Politics: The United States & Postrevolutionary Mexico, 1917-1924. Linda B. Hall. LC 94-22408. (Illus.). 240p. (Orig.). 1995. pap. 40.00 (*0-292-73092-6*); pap. 17.95 (*0-292-73101-9*) U of Tex Pr.

Oil Baron of the Southwest: Edward L. Doheny & the Development of the Petroleum Industry in California & Mexico. Martin R. Ansell. LC 97-37567. 302p. 1998. text 62.50 (*0-8142-0749-9*) Ohio St U Pr.

Oil Birds of Venezuela: Ecology & Conservation. Roberto L. Roca. (Publications of the Nuttall OrinthＯlgical Club: No. 24). (Illus.). 83p. 1994. 11.00 (*1-877973-35-1*) Nuttall Ornith.

Oil Booms: Social Change in Five Texas Towns. Roger M. Olien & Diana D. Olien. LC 81-11686. (Illus.). 238p. reprint ed. pap. 73.80 (*0-7837-4668-7*, 204439500002) Bks Demand.

Oil Burners. 5th ed. Edwin M. Field. (Illus.). 387p. 1997. reprint ed. lib. bdg. 34.95 (*0-7351-0003-9*) Replica Bks.

Oil Burners, UL 296. 9th ed. (C). 1994. pap. text 195.00 (*1-55989-627-2*) Underwrtrs Labs.

Oil-Burning Stoves, UL 896, UL 896. 5th ed. (C). 1993. pap. text 330.00 (*1-55989-438-5*) Underwrtrs Labs.

Oil Cartel Case: A Documentary Study of Antitrust Activity in the Cold War Era, 72. Burton I. Kaufman. LC 77-87963. (Contributions in American History Ser.: No. 72). (Illus.). 217p. 1978. 57.95 (*0-313-20043-2*, KOC/, Greenwood Pr) Greenwood.

Oil Change: Perspectives on Corporate Transformation. Art Kleiner & George Roth. (The Learning History Library Ser.). (Illus.). 208p. (C). 2000. text 22.95 (*0-19-513487-7*) OUP.

Oil, Coal & Gas. William Russell. LC 94-2401. (From This Earth Discovery Library). 24p. (J). (gr. k-4). 1994. lib. bdg. 10.95 (*0-86593-357-X*) Rourke Corp.

Oil Company Divestiture & the Press: Economic vs. Journalistic Perceptions. Barbara Hobbie. LC 77-10627. (Praeger Special Studies). 167p. 1977. 55.00 (*0-275-90267-6*, C0267, Praeger Pubs) Greenwood.

Oil Company Financial Analysis in Nontechnical Language. Daniel Johnston. 362p. 1992. 64.95 (*0-87814-374-2*) PennWell Bks.

Oil Company Logos: Identification Guide. Scott Benjamin & Wayne Henderson. (Illus.). 128p. (Orig.). 1997. pap. 24.95 (*0-9655736-0-5*) PCM Bkshelf.

Oil Company Signs: A Collector's Guide. Scott Benjamin & Wayne Henderson. LC 95-24759. (Motorbooks International Ser.). (Illus.). 216p. 1995. pap. 14.98 (*0-7603-0073-9*) MBI Pubg.

Oil Conservation Through Interstate Agreement. Federal Oil Conservation Board Staff & Northcutt Ely. 393p. 1982. reprint ed. lib. bdg. 45.00 (*0-89941-225-4*, 201470) W S Hein.

Oil Crisis in Our Oceans: Coral: Roadkill on the Petrohighway. Barbara E. Ornitz. LC 97-107751. (Illus.). 320p. (Orig.). 1996. pap. 30.00 (*0-9638385-1-2*) Tageh Pr.

Oil Crisis Management: Strategic Stockpiling for International Security. Edward N. Krapels. LC 80-13358. (Illus.). 189p. reprint ed. pap. 58.60 (*0-608-06071-2*, 206640300008) Bks Demand.

Oil Dictionary: Dictionnaire du Petrole. Yves Barbier. (ENG & FRE.). 272p. 1980. pap. 175.00 (*0-8288-0696-9*, M15455) Fr & Eur.

Oil Diplomacy: The Atlantic Nations in Oil Crisis of 1978-79. Intro. by Foreign Policy Research Institute Staff & Alexander M. Haig, Jr. LC 80-11992. 151p. reprint ed. pap. 46.90 (*0-7837-1779-2*, 204197700001) Bks Demand.

***Oil Disasters.** Rob Alcraft. LC 99-27878. (World's Worst Ser.). 1999. lib. bdg. write for info. (*1-57572-990-3*) Heinemann Lib.

Oil Dispersants: New Ecological Approaches. Ed. by L. Michael Flaherty. LC 88-35988. (Special Technical Publication Ser.: No. STP 1018). (Illus.). 310p. 1989. text 62.00 (*0-8031-1194-0*, STP1018) ASTM.

Oil, Dollars & Politics. Burchard Brentjes. LC 98-68675. (Illus.). 314p. 1999. 28.00 (*0-9659623-3-4*) Rishi Pubns.

Oil, Economic Development, & Diversification of Brunei Darussalam. Mark Cleary & Chuang Yann Wong. LC 93-44270. (Studies in the Economies of East & Southeast Asia). 1994. text 75.00 (*0-312-12113-X*) St Martin.

Oil Exploration: Basin Analysis & Economics. Ian Lerche. (Illus.). 178p. 1992. text 77.00 (*0-12-444175-0*) Acad Pr.

Oil Exploration in Arctic - Sub-Arctic On-Shore Areas: Guidelines for Environmental Protection. 36p. (C). 1995. pap. text 16.00 (*2-8317-0188-0*, Pub. by IUCN) Island Pr.

Oil Exploration in Mangrove Areas: Guidelines for Environmental Protection. 36p. (C). 1993. pap. text 16.00 (*2-8317-0187-2*, Pub. by IUCN) Island Pr.

Oil Exploration in the Tropics: Guidelines for Environmental Protection. IUCN Environmental Impact Assessment Services Staf. 36p. (Orig.). 1991. pap. 16.00 (*2-8317-0018-3*, Pub. by IUCN) Island Pr.

Oil Exporters' Economic Development in an Interdependent World. Jahangir Amuzegar. (Occasional Paper Ser.: No. 18). 99p. 1983. pap. 5.00 (*1-55775-078-5*) Intl Monetary.

Oil-Field Chemistry: Enhanced Recovery & Production Stimulation. Ed. by John K. Borchardt & Teh Fu Yen. LC 89-6829. (Symposium Ser.: No. 396). (Illus.). xi, 616p. 1989. 129.95 (*0-8412-1630-4*) Am Chemical.

Oil Field Chemistry: Enhanced Recovery & Production Stimulation. Ed. by John K. Borchardt & Teh Fu Yen. LC 89-6829. (ACS Symposium Ser.: No. 396). (Illus.). 714p. 1989. reprint ed. pap. 200.00 (*0-608-03206-9*, 206372500007) Bks Demand.

Oil Field Child. Estha B. Stowe. LC 88-20141. (Chisholm Trail Ser.: No. 7). (Illus.). 178p. (Orig.). 1989. pap. 13.95 (*0-87565-033-3*) Tex Christian.

Oil Field Development Techniques: Proceedings of the Daqing International Meeting, 1982. Ed. by John F. Mason & Parke A. Dickey. LC 88-35723. (AAPG Studies in Geology: No. 28). (Illus.). 255p. reprint ed. pap. 79.10 (*0-8357-3071-9*, 203932800012) Bks Demand.

Oil Field Subsurface Injection of Water - STP 641. Ed. by C. C. Wright et al. 122p. 1984. pap. 10.75 (*0-8031-0530-4*, STP641) ASTM.

Oil Fields & Geology of the Pine Valley, Eureka County Area, Nevada. Ed. by Donna M. Flanigan et al. (NPS Fieldtrip Guidebooks Ser.). 74p. 1990. pap. text 15.00 (*1-881308-02-2*) NV Petroleum.

Oil Fields, Production Facilities & Reservoir Rocks of Northern Nye County, Nevada. Ed. by William J. Ehni & David M. Evans. (NPS Fieldtrip Guidebooks Ser.). 1989. pap. text 12.00 (*1-881308-00-6*) NV Petroleum.

Oil Finders: A Collection of Stories about Exploration. Ed. & Intro. by Allen G. Hatley. 1996. pap. 19.50 (*0-9649416-0-0*) Centex Pr.

Oil-Fired Air Heaters & Direct-Fired Heaters, UL 733. 4th ed. (C). 1993. pap. text 95.00 (*1-55989-457-1*) Underwrtrs Labs.

Oil-Fired Boiler Assemblies, UL 726. 7th ed. (C). 1995. pap. text 95.00 (*1-55989-858-5*) Underwrtrs Labs.

Oil-Fired Central Furnaces, UL 727. 8th ed. (C). 1994. pap. text 195.00 (*1-55989-577-2*) Underwrtrs Labs.

Oil-Fired Floor Furnaces, UL 729. 5th ed. (C). 1994. pap. text 330.00 (*1-55989-706-6*) Underwrtrs Labs.

Oil-Fired Storage Tank Water Heaters, UL 732. 5th ed. (C). 1995. pap. text 95.00 (*1-55989-818-6*) Underwrtrs Labs.

Oil-Fired Unit Heaters, UL 731. 5th ed. (C). 1995. pap. 135.00 (*1-55989-817-8*) Underwrtrs Labs.

Oil-Fired Wall Furnaces, UL 730. 4th ed. (C). 1994. pap. text 330.00 (*1-55989-569-1*) Underwrtrs Labs.

***Oil Flow Studies At Low Temperatures In Modern Engines.** Hal Staub & American Society for Testing & Materials Staff. LC 00-44157. (STP Ser.). 2000. write for info. (*0-8031-2857-6*) ASTM.

Oil from Shale: An Analysis of Technology, Economics, & Future. Brian M. Harney. LC 83-15011. (Series of Special Reports: No. 9). (Illus.). 211p. reprint ed. pap. 65.50 (*0-7837-0694-4*, 204102700019) Bks Demand.

Oil, Gas & Coal Supply Outlook. LC 96-101611. 250p. (Orig.). 1995. pap. 79.00 (*92-64-14392-0*, Pub. by Org for Econ) OECD.

Oil, Gas & Energy Quarterly, Vol. 46, No. 1. Ed. by D. Larry Crumbley & Linda M. Nichols. (Illus.). 1997. ring bd. 185.00 (*0-8205-1520-5*) Bender.

Oil, Gas, & Government: The U. S. Experience, 2 vols., Set, Vols. 1 & 2. Robert L. Bradley, Jr. 2000p. (C). 1996. lib. bdg. 195.00 (*0-8476-8110-6*) Rowman.

Oil, Gas, & Government: The U. S. Experience, Vol. I. Robert L. Bradley, Jr. 1000p. (C). 1996. lib. bdg. 125.00 (*0-8476-8108-4*) Rowman.

Oil, Gas, & Government: The U. S. Experience, Vol. II. Robert L. Bradley, Jr. 1000p. (C). 1996. lib. bdg. 125.00 (*0-8476-8109-2*) Rowman.

Oil, Gas, or . . . ? A Technical Support Document for a Consumer Decision Making Guide on Fuel Switching. 21p. 1994. 35.00 (*0-317-04968-2*) Consumer Energy Coun.

Oil, Gas, or? . . . Conservation Makes More Sense Than Switching Fuel: A Consumer Decision Making Guide on Conservation vs. Fuel Switching. 1991. 1.50 (*0-317-04970-4*) Consumer Energy Coun.

Oil, God, & Gold: The Story of Aramco & the Saudi Kings. Anthony Cave Brown. LC 98-39654. (Illus.). 480p. 1999. 30.00 (*0-395-59220-8*) HM.

Oil History: A Selected & Annotated Bibliography. E. Richard Neff. Ed. by George A. Williford. 373p. 1995. 35.00 (*0-9648314-0-6*) Intl Assn Drill.

Oil in Asia: Markets, Trading, Refining & Deregulation. Paul Horsnell. LC 97-221674. (Oxford Institute for Energy Studies). (Illus.). 446p. (C). 1997. text 75.00 (*0-19-730018-9*) OUP.

Oil in Freshwater: Chemistry, Biology, Countermeasure: Proceedings of the Symposium on Oil Pollution in Freshwater, Edmonton, Alberta, Canada, 15-19 October 1984. Ed. by J. H. Vandermeulen & S. E. Hrudey. 550p. 1987. 75.00 (*0-08-031861-4*, E140, G135, A12, Pergamon Pr) Elsevier.

Oil in Power Generation. John Paffenbarger. LC 99-172828. 96p. 1997. pap. 27.00 (*92-64-15451-5*, 61-97-04-1, Pub. by Org for Econ) OECD.

Oil in the California Monterey Formation. Ed. by MacKinnon. (IGC Field Trip Guidebooks Ser.). 64p. 1989. 21.00 (*0-87590-600-1*, T311) Am Geophysical.

Oil in the Deep South. Dudley J. Hughes. LC 92-37759. (History of the Oil Business in Mississippi, Alabama, & Florida, 1859-1945 Ser.). (Illus.). 272p. 1993. text 35.00 (*0-87805-615-7*) U Pr of Miss.

Oil in the New World Order. Ed. by Kate Gillespie & Clement M. Henry. LC 95-5517. (Illus.). 312p. 1995. 49.95 (*0-8130-1367-4*) U Press Fla.

Oil in the Sea: Inputs, Fates, & Effects. National Research Council (U. S.), Steering Commit. LC 85-60541. 621p. reprint ed. pap. 192.60 (*0-7837-0347-3*, 204066600018) Bks Demand.

Oil in Troubled Waters: Perceptions, Politics, & the Battle over Offshore Drilling. William R. Freudenburg & Robert Gramling. LC 93-24947. (SUNY Series in Environmental Public Policy). 179p. (C). 1994. text 59.50 (*0-7914-1881-2*); pap. text 19.95 (*0-7914-1882-0*) State U NY Pr.

Oil in Washington Waters: Boon or Bane? Scott et al. (Occasional Papers: No. 11). 1986. pap. 5.00 (*0-318-23330-4*) WWU CPNS.

Oil Industry & Government Strategy in the North Sea. Oystein Noreng. LC 80-81590. 1980. 22.00 (*0-918714-02-8*) Intl Res Ctr Energy.

O

An Asterisk (*) at the beginning of an entry indicates that the title is appearing for the first time.

Oil Industry & Microbial Ecosystems: Proceedings of a Meeting Organized by the Institute of Petroleum & Held at the University of Warwick, England, September, 1977. Ed. by K. W. A. Chater & H. J. Somerville. LC 80-462468. (Illus.). 260p. reprint ed. pap. 80.60 (*0-8357-3088-3*, 203934500012) Bks Demand.

Oil Industry & the Competitive System: A Study in Waste. George W. Stocking. LC 73-128075. (Library of Early American Business & Industry: No. 52). (Illus.). x, 323p. 1973. reprint ed. lib. bdg. 45.00 (*0-678-03555-5*) Kelley.

Oil Industry Experience: Technology Cooperation & Capacity Building: Contribution to Agenda 21. 65p. 1995. pap. text 19.00 (*92-807-1522-4*) UN.

Oil Industry in India. Biplab Dasgupta. 257p. 1971. 37.50 (*0-7146-2583-3*, Pub. by F Cass Pubs) Intl Spec Bk.

Oil Industry of the Former Soviet Union - Reserves, Extraction & Transportation. Ed. by N. A. Krylov et al. 277p. 1998. text 72.00 (*90-5699-062-4*) Gordon & Breach.

Oil Industry Outlook, 1997-2001. 13th ed. Robert J. Beck. 290p. 1993. 175.00 (*0-685-71333-4*) PennWell Bks.

***Oil Industry Restructurization in Poland: A Strategic Entry Report, 1996.** Compiled by Icon Group International Staff. (Illus.). 182p. 1999. ring bd. 1820.00 incl. audio compact disk (*0-7418-1350-5*) Icon Grp.

***Oil Information, 1998: (1999 Edition)** IEA Staff. 700p. 1999. pap. 150.00 (*92-64-05863-X*, 61 1999 14 3 P, Pub. by Org for Econ) OECD.

Oil Information, 1997 (1998 Edition) IEA Staff. 686p. 1998. pap. 150.00 (*92-64-05772-2*, 61 98 13 3 P, Pub. by European Conference Ministers Transp) OECD.

Oil Information 1996: 1997 Edition. IEA Staff. 616p. 1997. pap. 126.00 (*92-64-05533-9*, 61-97-21-3, Pub. by Org for Econ) OECD.

Oil Is First Found in the Mind: The Philosophy of Exploration. Compiled by Norman H. Foster & Edward A. Beaumont. LC 92-15418. (Treatise of Petroleum Geology Reprint Ser.: Vol. 20). (Illus.). 352p. reprint ed. pap. 109.20 (*0-608-20307-6*, 207156000002) Bks Demand.

Oil Jar & Other Stories. unabridged ed. Luigi Pirandello. Tr. by Stanley Appelbaum. (Thrift Editions Ser.). (Illus.). 96p. 1995. pap. text 1.00 (*0-486-28459-X*) Dover.

Oil Lamps, No. II. Catherine M. Thuro. (Illus.). 160p. 1994. 24.95 (*0-89145-226-5*, 2394) Collector Bks.

Oil Lamps: The Kerosene Era in North America. Catherine M. Thuro. LC 75-21331. (Illus.). 368p. 1992. 39.95 (*0-87069-653-X*) Krause Pubns.

Oil, Land, & Politics: The California Career of Thomas Robert Bard, 1. William H. Hutchinson. LC 65-10114. 287p. reprint ed. pap. 89.00 (*0-608-13522-4*, 201622500001) Bks Demand.

Oil, Land, & Politics: The California Career of Thomas Robert Bard, 2. William H. Hutchinson. LC 65-10114. 433p. reprint ed. pap. 134.30 (*0-608-13523-2*, 201622500002) Bks Demand.

Oil Legends of Fort Worth. Historical Committee. LC 93-73945. 320p. 1993. 50.00 (*0-9639414-0-2*) Petroleum Club.

Oil Locating. Verne L. Cameron. (Dowser's Hdbk. Ser.: No. 2). 40p. 1970. pap. 7.00 (*0-88234-004-2*) Life Understanding.

Oil Man: The Story of Frank Phillips & the Birth of Phillips Petroleum. Michael Wallis. LC 95-2131. 1995. pap. 16.95 (*0-312-13135-6*) St Martin.

Oil Market in the 1980s: A Decade of Decline. Ed. by Siamack Shojai & Bernard S. Katz. LC 91-37625. 280p. 1992. 65.00 (*0-275-93380-6*, C3380, Praeger Pubs) Greenwood.

Oil Markets in Turmoil: An Economic Analysis. Phillip K. Verleger, Jr. LC 81-22810. 328p. 1982. text 35.00 (*0-88410-867-8*, HarpBusn) HarpInfo.

Oil Markets Revisited. Kathryn M. Dominguez et al. LC 90-62427. (International Energy Studies: No. 6). 70p. 1990. pap. 16.50 (*0-942781-06-6*) Harvard EEPC.

Oil Mist Lubrication. Bloch & Shamim. 400p. 1998. 84.00 (*0-13-975210-2*) P-H.

Oil Mist Lubrication: Practical Applications. Heinz P. Bloch & Abdus Shamim. LC 97-53166. 280p. 1998. 84.00 (*0-88173-256-7*) Fairmont Pr.

Oil Notes. Rick Bass. LC 95-14871. (Illus.). 192p. 1995. pap. 10.95 (*0-87074-383-X*) SMU Press.

Oil of Gladness. Ed. by Martin Dudley & Geoffrey Rowell. 160p. (Orig.). 1993. pap. text 10.95 (*0-8146-2245-3*) Liturgical Pr.

Oil of Joy for Mourning. Jan Sheble. LC 97-28489. 366p. 1997. 16.95 (*1-56563-303-2*) Hendrickson MA.

Oil of Oregano: Nature's Premier Antiseptic. Charles A. Weisman. 40p. 1999. pap. text 4.00 (*0-9668921-6-X*) Weisman Pubns.

Oil of Sulphur. George Starkey. 1984. pap. 4.95 (*0-916411-20-6*) Holmes Pub.

Oil of Sweet Almond. Ed. by Carrie Newmann & Ginny Ballor. 40p. (C). 1997. pap. 3.00 (*1-882294-25-4*) Green Gate.

Oil, Oil, Oil! Carolee K. Michener. (Illus.). 128p. 1997. pap. 18.75 (*0-9662225-0-4*) Venango Co Hist Soc.

Oil on the Edge: Offshore Development, Conflict, Gridlock. Robert Gramling. LC 94-48605. 208p. (C). 1995. pap. text 12.95 (*0-7914-2694-7*) State U NY Pr.

Oil on the Edge: Offshore Development, Conflict, Gridlock. Robert Gramling. LC 94-48605. 208p. (C). 1995. text 39.50 (*0-7914-2693-9*) State U NY Pr.

Oil on Their Shoes: Petroleum Geology to 1918. Ellen S. Blakey. LC 85-20021. (Illus.). 204p. reprint ed. pap. 63.30 (*0-608-20301-7*, 207155600001) Bks Demand.

Oil on Troubled Waters: Gulf Wars 1980-91. John Creighton. 1992. text 70.00 (*1-873395-45-0*) St Martin.

Oil on Water: Oil Sketches by British Watercolorists. Malcolm Cormack. LC 86-50385. (Illus.). 64p. (Orig.). 1986. pap. 8.00 (*0-930606-52-3*) Yale Ctr Brit Art.

Oil Painter's Handbook. Patricia Monahan & Jenny Rodwell. (Illus.). 256p. 1996. 29.95 (*0-289-80137-0*, Pub. by SVista Bks) Sterling.

Oil Painter's Pocket Palette. Rosalind Cuthbert. (Pocket Palette Ser.). (Illus.). 64p. 1993. 16.99 (*0-89134-543-4*, 30521, North Lght Bks) F & W Pubns Inc.

***Oil Painter's Ultimate Flower & Portrait Companion.** Patricia Moran. (Illus.). 2000. pap. 24.99 (*1-929834-03-9*) Intl Artist Pubg.

Oil Painting. Koneman Staff. (Fine Arts for Beginners Ser.). (Illus.). 172p. 1999. pap. 9.95 (*3-8290-1933-5*, 521048) Konemann.

***Oil Painting.** Jose Maria Parramon. (Illus.). 96p. 2000. pap. 18.95 (*84-95323-31-1*) Lema Pubns.

Oil Painting: Art School. Lorenz Staff. 1998. 9.95 (*1-85967-824-6*) Anness Pub.

Oil Painting: Develop Your Natural Ability. Charles Sovek. (Illus.). 128p. 1996. pap. 23.99 (*0-89134-751-8*, North Lght Bks) F & W Pubns Inc.

Oil Painting: Impressionism. Keith Ward. (Artist's Library). (Illus.). 64p. (Orig.). 1989. pap. 7.95 (*0-929261-11-9*, AL11) W Foster Pub.

Oil Painting: Portraits-Royal Academy of Arts. Ray Smith. LC 93-34255. (DK Art School Ser.). 72p. 1999. pap. text 9.95 (*0-7894-4304-X*) DK Pub Inc.

Oil Painting: The Workshop Experience. Ted Goerschner & Lewis B. Lehrman. LC 95-8365. (Illus.). 144p. 1996. 28.99 (*0-89134-609-0*, North Lght Bks) F & W Pubns Inc.

Oil Painting Basics: An Artist's Guide to Mastering the Medium. Timothy Easton. 96p. 1998. pap. 14.95 (*0-8230-2712-0*) Watsn-Guptill.

Oil Painting Book: Materials & Techniques for Today's Artist. Bill Creevy. LC 94-26964. (Illus.). 176p. 1994. 35.00 (*0-8230-3273-6*) Watsn-Guptill.

Oil Painting Book: Materials & Techniques for Today's Artist. Bill Creevy. (Illus.). 176p. 1999. pap. text 19.95 (*0-8230-3274-4*) Watsn-Guptill.

Oil Painting for the Serious Beginner: Basic Lessons in Becoming a Good Painter. Steve Allrich. (Illus.). 144p. 1996. pap. text 19.95 (*0-8230-3269-8*) Watsn-Guptill.

Oil Painting Kit. William F. Powell. (Illus.). 32p. 1997. pap. text 19.95 (*1-56010-196-2*, K06) W Foster Pub.

Oil Painting Materials & Their Uses. William F. Powell. (Artist's Library). (Illus.). 64p. (Orig.). 1990. pap. 7.95 (*1-56010-056-7*, AL17) W Foster Pub.

Oil Painting Outdoors. Peter Gilman. (Leisure Arts Ser.: No. 16). (Illus.). 32p. pap. 4.95 (*0-85532-459-7*, 459-7, Pub. by Srch Pr) A Schwartz & Co.

Oil Painting Portraits. Ray Smith. LC 93-34255. (DK Art School Ser.). (Illus.). 72p. 1994. 16.95 (*1-56458-491-7*) DK Pub Inc.

Oil Painting Secrets from a Master. Linda Cateura. (Illus.). 144p. 1995. pap. 24.95 (*0-8230-3279-5*) Watsn-Guptill.

Oil Painting Step-by-Step. Ted Smuskiewicz. (Illus.). 144p. 1997. pap. 22.99 (*0-89134-741-0*, North Lght Bks) F & W Pubns Inc.

Oil Painting Techniques: Learn How to Master Oil Painting Working Techniques to Create Your Own Successful Paintings. Ed. by David Lewis. (Illus.). 144p. 1983. pap. 16.95 (*0-8230-3261-2*) Watsn-Guptill.

Oil Painting Techniques & Materials. 48th ed. Speed. (Illus.). 352p. reprint ed. pap. 8.95 (*0-486-25506-9*) Dover.

Oil Painting the Easy Way, Vol. 2. Bill Blackman. 71p. 1995. pap. 10.50 (*1-56770-337-2*) S Scheewe Pubns.

Oil Painting with a Basic Palette. Morgan Samuel Price. LC 98-31052. (Illus.). 128p. 1999. 27.99 (*0-89134-882-4*, 31366, North Lght Bks) F & W Pubns Inc.

Oil Painting Workbook: A Complete Course in Ten Lessons. Stan Smith. (Illus.). 128p. 1999. 24.95 (*0-7153-0936-6*, Pub. by D & C Pub) Sterling.

Oil Painting Workshop. Albert Handell & Leslie Trainor. (Illus.). 144p. 1991. pap. 18.95 (*0-8230-3293-0*) Watsn-Guptill.

Oil Palms & Other Oilseeds of the Amazon. 2nd ed. Celestino Pesce. Ed. & Tr. by Dennis V. Johnson from POR. LC 85-11958. (Studies in Economic Botany).Tr. of Oleaginosas da Amazonia. (Illus.). 200p. 1985. 29.00 (*0-917256-28-X*) Ref Pubns.

Oil Pipeline Construction & Maintenance. 2nd ed. (Illus.). 153p. 1973. pap. text 15.00 (*0-88698-078-X*, 4.22020) PETEX.

Oil Pollution & the Public Interest: A Study of the Santa Barbara Oil Spill. A. E. Keir et al. LC 72-5116. 171p. (Orig.). reprint ed. pap. 53.10 (*0-608-20116-2*, 207138800011) Bks Demand.

Oil Pollution at Sea: Civil Liability & Compensation for Damage. Gotthard Gauci. LC 97-20778. 1997. text 200.00 (*0-471-97066-2*) Wiley.

Oil Pollution Control. Sonia Z. Pritchard. 240p. 1987. 59.95 (*0-7099-2094-6*, Pub. by C Helm) Routldge.

Oil Pollution Deskbook. 601p. 1990. pap. 85.00 (*0-911937-39-0*) Environ Law Inst.

Oil Portraits Step by Step. rev. ed. Wendon Blake. LC 98-28210. (Illus.). 64p. 1998. pap. 8.95 (*0-486-40279-7*) Dover.

Oil, Power & Politics: Conflict in Arabia, the Red Sea & the Gulf. Mordechai Abir. 210p. 1974. 47.50 (*0-7146-2990-1*, BHA-02990, Pub. by F Cass Pubs) Intl Spec Bk.

Oil Price Revolution. Steven A. Schneider. LC 82-12639. 647p. reprint ed. pap. 200.00 (*0-608-06139-5*, 206647200008) Bks Demand.

Oil Prices & the Future of OPEC: The Political Economy of Tension & Stability in the Organization of Petroleum Exporting Countries. Theodore H. Moran. LC 78-2983. (Resources for the Future. Research Paper Ser.: No. R-8). 108p. reprint ed. pap. 33.50 (*0-608-18094-7*, 203216000078) Bks Demand.

Oil Prices & the Manufacturing Sector in Asia-Pacific Net Oil-Importing Developing Countries (with Special Reference to the Philippines) Dale Avery. LC HD9576.A689. (Working Papers: No. 81-18). 70p. reprint ed. pap. 30.00 (*0-608-14940-3*, 202597400047) Bks Demand.

Oil Prices & Trade Deficits: U. S. Conflicts with Japan & West Germany. David Gisselquist. LC 79-20632. (Praeger Special Studies). 144p. 1979. 59.95 (*0-275-90355-9*, C0355, Praeger Pubs) Greenwood.

Oil Prices, Energy Security, & Import Policy. Douglas R. Bohi & W. David Montgomery. LC 82-15083. 203p. 1982. 25.00 (*0-8018-2821-X*) Resources Future.

Oil Privatization, Public Choice & International Forces. Stephanie Hoopes. 256p. 1997. text 59.95 (*0-312-15975-7*) St Martin.

Oil Processing: Food Cycle Technology Source Book. UNIFEM Staff. 48p. (Orig.). 1993. pap. 15.00 (*1-85339-134-4*, Pub. by Intermed Tech) Stylus Pub VA.

Oil Refineries Upgrade in Saudi Arabia: A Strategic Entry Report, 1998. Compiled by Icon Group International Staff. (Country Industry Report). (Illus.). 133p. 1999. ring bd. 1330.00 incl. audio compact disk (*0-7418-0519-7*) Icon Grp.

Oil Refinery Terms in Oklahoma, Experiment in State-Wide Dialect Collecting, Problems Confronting the Investigator of Gullah. E. H. Criswell et al. (Publications of the American Dialect Society Ser.: No. 9). 89p. 1948. pap. text 8.90 (*0-8173-0609-9*) U of Ala Pr.

Oil Refining Equipment in Russia: A Strategic Entry Report, 1997. Compiled by Icon Group International Staff. (Illus.). 137p. 1999. ring bd. 1370.00 incl. audio compact disk (*0-7418-0874-9*) Icon Grp.

***Oil Refining Equipment in Russia: A Strategic Entry Report, 1999.** Compiled by Icon Group International. (Illus.). 163p. 1999. ring bd. 1630.00 incl. audio compact disk (*0-7418-1789-6*) Icon Grp.

Oil Resources: Who Gets What How? Kenneth W. Dam. LC 75-43239. 1993. pap. text 4.95 (*0-226-13498-9*, P 776) U Ch Pr.

Oil Resources: Who Gets What How? Kenneth W. Dam. LC 75-43239. 1995. lib. bdg. 24.00 (*0-226-13497-0*) U Ch Pr.

Oil Revenues, Absorptive Capacity & Prospects for Accelerated Growth. Kadhim A. Al-Eyd. LC 79-18596. 188p. 1979. 62.95 (*0-275-90328-1*, C0328, Praeger Pubs) Greenwood.

Oil Rig Moorings Handbook. 2nd ed. J. Vendrell. (C). 1987. 75.00 (*0-85174-495-8*) St Mut.

Oil Rigs: Law & Insurance. M. Summerskill. (C). 1979. 850.00 (*0-7855-4067-9*, Pub. by Witherby & Co) St Mut.

Oil Security: Retrospect & Prospect. Edward R. Fried & Philip H. Trezise. 80p. (C). 1993. 9.95 (*0-8157-2979-0*) Brookings.

Oil Shale: Proceedings of the 17th Symposium. Ed. by James H. Gary. (Illus.). 440p. 1984. pap. text 25.00 (*0-918062-58-6*) Colo Sch Mines.

Oil Shale: Proceedings of the 18th Symposium. Ed. by James H. Gary. (Illus.). 360p. 1985. pap. text 25.00 (*0-918062-62-4*) Colo Sch Mines.

Oil Shale: Proceedings of the 19th Symposium. Frwd. by James H. Gary. (Illus.). 268p. 1986. pap. text 25.00 (*0-918062-67-5*) Colo Sch Mines.

Oil Shale: The Environmental Challenges. Ed. by Kathy K. Peterson. LC 81-10118. (Proceedings of International Symposium Aug. 11-14, 1980, Vail, Colorado Ser.). (Illus.). 261p. 1981. text 10.00 (*0-918062-43-8*) Colo Sch Mines.

Oil Shale: The Environmental Challenges II. Ed. by Kathy K. Peterson. LC 82-14759. (Illus.). 392p. 1982. 11.00 (*0-918062-51-9*) Colo Sch Mines.

Oil Shale: The Environmental Challenges III. Ed. by Kathy Petersen. (Proceedings of an International Symposium Ser.: No III). (Illus.). 261p. 1983. text 11.00 (*0-918062-54-3*) Colo Sch Mines.

Oil Shale Processing Technology. V. Dean Allred. LC 81-65818. (Illus.). 240p. 1982. 60.00 (*0-86563-001-1*) Ctr Prof Adv.

Oil Shale Symposium Proceedings Index, 1964-82. Ed. by Jon W. Raese. LC 82-19839. 110p. 1982. pap. text 30.00 (*0-918062-52-7*) Colo Sch Mines.

Oil Shale, Tar Sands, & Related Materials. Ed. by H. C. Stauffer. LC 81-10948. (ACS Symposium Ser.: No. 163). 1981. 43.95 (*0-8412-0640-6*) Am Chemical.

Oil Shale, Tar Sands, & Related Materials. Ed. by H. C. Stauffer. LC 81-10948. (ACS Symposium Ser.: Vol. 163). 405p. 1981. reprint ed. pap. 125.60 (*0-608-03047-3*, 206350000007) Bks Demand.

Oil Shale, Tar Sands, & Related Materials: General Papers: Storch Award Symposium: Preprints of Papers Presented at San Francisco, California, August 24-29, 1980. American Chemical Society, Division of Fuel Chemis. LC TP0315.A4. (Preprints of Papers: Vol. 25, No. 3). 298p. reprint ed. pap. 92.40 (*0-608-13474-0*, 201327900094) Bks Demand.

Oil Shale Technology. Ed. by Sungyu Lee. 280p. 1990. lib. bdg. 225.00 (*0-8493-4615-0*, TP699) CRC Pr.

Oil Shales & Tar Sands: A Bibliography, Supplement 2. Ed. by M. Catherine Grissom. 590p. 1984. pap. 38.25 (*0-87079-526-0*, DOE/TIC-3367 SUPPLEMENT 2, DE83018001); fiche 9.00 (*0-87079-527-9*, DOE/TIC-3367 SUPPLEMEMT 2) DOE.

Oil Shales of the World: Their Origin, Occurrence & Exploitation. Paul L. Russell. LC 89-48957. (Illus.). 736p. 1990. 337.00 (*0-08-037240-6*, Pub. by Pergamon Repr) Franklin.

Oil Shock: Policy Response & Implementation. Ed. by Alvin L. Alm & Robert Weiner. LC 83-22459. 256p. 1984. text 32.00 (*0-88410-930-5*, HarpBusn) HarpInfo.

Oil Shocks & the Demand for Electricity. (Illus.). 30p. (Orig.). (C). 1993. pap. text 20.00 (*1-56806-728-3*) DIANE Pub.

Oil Sketches of Peter Paul Rubens: A Critical Catalogue. Julius S. Held. LC 77-2532. (Kress Foundation Studies in the History of European Art: Vol. 2). (Illus.). 522p. 1980. reprint ed. pap. 161.90 (*0-608-07573-6*, 206667100002) Bks Demand.

Oil Sketches of Peter Paul Rubens: A Critical Catalogue, Vol. 1. Julius S. Held. LC 77-2532. (Kress Foundation Studies in the History of European Art: No. 7). (Illus.). 770p. reprint ed. pap. 200.00 (*0-608-06309-6*, 206667100001) Bks Demand.

Oil Spill! Melvin Berger. LC 92-34779. (Illus.). 32p. (J). (gr. k-4). 1994. pap. 4.95 (*0-06-445121-6*, HarpTrophy) HarpC Child Bks.

Oil Spill! Melvin Berger. LC 92-34779. (Let's-Read-&-Find-Out Science Bks.: Stage 2). (Illus.). 32p. (J). (gr. k-4). 1994. 15.00 (*0-06-022909-8*) HarpC Child Bks.

Oil Spill! Melvin Berger. (Let's-Read-And-Find-Out Science. Stage 2 Ser.). 1994. 10.15 (*0-606-06631-4*, Pub. by Turtleback) Demco.

Oil Spill. Christopher Lampton. LC 91-43565. (Disaster! Ser.). (Illus.). 64p. (J). (gr. 4-6). 1992. pap. 5.95 (*1-56294-783-4*) Millbrook Pr.

Oil Spill! Russell Wright. Ed. by Katarina Stenstedt. (Event-Based Science Ser.). (Illus.). (Orig.). 1994. pap. text, teacher ed. 18.75 (*0-201-49415-9*) Addison-Wesley.

Oil Spill! Russell Wright. Ed. by Katarina Stenstedt. (Event-Based Science Ser.). (Illus.). (Orig.). (YA). (gr. 6-9). 1994. pap. text, wbk. ed. 7.95 (*0-201-49090-0*) Addison-Wesley.

Oil Spill!, Class Set. Russell Wright. Ed. by Katarina Stenstedt. (Event-Based Science Ser.). (Illus.). (Orig.). (J). (gr. 6-9). 1995. pap. text, teacher ed., wbk. ed. 115.00 incl. VHS (*0-201-49412-4*) Addison-Wesley.

Oil Spill Chemical Dispersants: Research, Experience, & Recommendations - STP 840. Ed. by T. E. Allen. 448p. 1984. 54.00 (*0-8031-0400-6*, STP840) ASTM.

Oil Spill Dispersants: Mechanisms of Action & Laboratory Tests. John R. Clayton, Jr. et al. 1993. lib. bdg. 59.95 (*0-87371-946-8*, TD427) Smoley.

Oil Spill Field Operations Guide, 1996, June. 150p. 1997. ring bd. 16.00 (*0-16-062472-X*) USGPO.

Oil Spill Prevention: Developing Alaska Demonstration Programs, & Use of Exxon Valdez Funds for Natural Resources. (Illus.). 67p. (Orig.). (C). 1994. pap. text 25.00 (*0-7881-0215-X*) DIANE Pub.

Oil Spill Prevention & Clean-Up. Richard K. Miller & Marcia E. Rupnow. LC 90-83867. (Survey on Technology & Markets Ser.: No. 162). 50p. 1991. pap. text 200.00 (*1-55865-187-X*) Future Tech Surveys.

Oil Spill Prevention & Response: How to Comply with OPA & OSPRA. Leslie Ray. LC 93-40393. 250p. 1994. 69.95 (*0-87814-389-0*) PennWell Bks.

Oil Spill Prevention Measures: Hearing Before the Subcommittee on Coast Guard & Maritime Transportation of the Committee on Transportation & Infrastructure, House of Representatives, 105th Congress, 1st Session, October 30, 1997. USGPO Staff. LC 98-143825. iii, 250p. 1997. pap. write for info. (*0-16-056162-0*) USGPO.

Oil Spill Response: Leader's Guide. Shirley Ayers. 64p. 1994. pap., teacher ed. 20.00 (*0-945790-08-2*) Detrick Lawrence.

***Oil Spill Response & Recovery Technology in Malaysia: A Strategic Entry Report, 1995.** Compiled by Icon Group International Staff. (Illus.). 108p. 1999. ring bd. 1080.00 incl. audio compact disk (*0-7418-1640-7*) Icon Grp.

Oil Spill Response in the Marine Environment. J. W. Doerffer. LC 92-580. 395p. 1992. 151.00 (*0-08-041000-6*, Pergamon Pr) Elsevier.

Oil Spill Response Performance Review of Skimmers. Robert Schultz. LC 98-40048. (Manual Ser.: Vol. MNL 34). (Illus.). x, 151p. 1998. pap. 110.00 (*0-8031-2078-8*, MNL34) ASTM.

***Oil Spill Risks from Tank Vessel Lightering** National Research Council (U. S.) Staff. LC 98-75577. xii, 125 p. 1998. write for info. (*0-309-06190-3*) Natl Acad Pr.

Oil Spills. Joanna Burger. LC 96-8340. (Illus.). 228p. (C). 1997. text 29.95 (*0-8135-2338-9*) Rutgers U Pr.

Oil Spills. Leslie A. DuTemple. LC 99-21614. (Overview Ser.). (Illus.). 128p. (YA). (gr. 4-12). 1999. lib. bdg. 23.70 (*1-56006-524-9*) Lucent Bks.

Oil Spills. Ed. by A. Alan Moghissi. 80p. 1980. pap. 15.50 (*0-08-026237-6*, Pergamon Pr) Elsevier.

Oil Spills. John M. Patten, Jr. LC 94-37162. (Read All about Eye on the Environment Ser.). 24p. (J). (gr. 1-4). 1995. lib. bdg. 18.60 (*1-55916-096-9*) Rourke Bk Co.

Oil Spills. Poynter. (J). 1995. 14.95 (*0-689-31849-9*) Atheneum Yung Read.

Oil Spills. Laurence Pringle. LC 92-30348. (Save-the-Earth Ser.). (Illus.). 64p. (J). (gr. 3 up). 1993. lib. bdg. 14.93 (*0-688-09861-4*, Wm Morrow) Morrow Avon.

Oil Spills: Management & Legislative Implications. Ed. by Malcolm L. Spaulding & Mark Reed. LC 90-49337. 584p. 1990. pap. text 7.00 (*0-87262-788-8*) Am Soc Civil Eng.

Oil Spills: Their Fate & Impact on the Marine Environment. OCIMF Staff & IPIECA Staff. 1980. 60.00 (*0-900886-49-8*, Pub. by Witherby & Co) St Mut.

Oil Substitution: World Outlook to 2020. World Energy Conference Staff. 415p. 1983. lib. bdg. 129.00 (*0-86010-476-1*) G & T Inc.

Oil Syndrome & Agricultural Development. Sara J. Scherr. LC 85-9509. 351p. 1985. 65.00 (*0-275-90224-2*, C0224, Praeger Pubs) Greenwood.

O

An Asterisk (*) at the beginning of an entry indicates that the title is appearing for the first time.

Oil Tankers. Lorne & MacLean Marine & Offshore Publications Sta. (C). 1987. 100.00 (*0-7855-4389-9*, Pub. by Lorne & MacLean Marine) St Mut.

Oil Taxation Acts (Great Britain Inland Revenue), 1997. HMSO Staff. 670p. 1998. pap. 100.00 (*0-11-641433-2*, HM14332, Pub. by Statnry Office) Bernan Associates.

Oil, Taxes, & the Cats: A History of the Devitt Family & the Mallet Ranch. David J. Murrah. LC 93-33654. (Illus.). 247p. 1994. 25.00 (*0-89672-332-1*) Tex Tech Univ Pr.

Oil That Heals: A Physician's Successes with Castor Oil. William A. McGarey. 248p. (Orig.). 1993. pap. 12.95 (*0-87604-308-2*, 381) ARE Pr.

Oil, the Arab-Israel Dispute & the Industrial World: Horizons of Crisis. Ed. by J. C. Hurewitz. 1976. pap. 12.95 (*0-89158-105-7*) Westview.

Oil, the Persian Gulf States, & the United States. Vo X. Han. LC 93-20300. 200p. 1993. 62.95 (*0-275-94505-7*, C4505, Praeger Pubs) Greenwood.

Oil Trade: Politics & Prospects. J. E. Hartshorn. LC 92-18233. (Studies in Energy & the Environment). (Illus.). 322p. (C). 1993. text 64.95 (*0-521-33143-9*) Cambridge U Pr.

Oil Trading Manual: Updated Semi-Annually. Ed. by David Long. (Illus.). 825p. 1999. 1250.00 (*1-85573-074-X*, Pub. by Woodhead Pubng) Am Educ Systs.

Oil, Turmoil, & Islam in the Middle East. Sheikh R. Ali. LC 85-31254. 238p. 1986. 55.00 (*0-275-92135-2*, C2135, Praeger Pubs) Greenwood.

***Oil, War, & Anglo-American Relations: American & British Reactions to Mexico's Expropriation of Foreign Oil Properties, 1937-1941.** Catherine E. Jayne. LC 00-23531. (Contributions in Latin American Studies: Vol. 19). 264p. 2000. 64.00 (*0-313-31276-1*, GM1276) Greenwood.

Oil Windfalls: Blessing or Curse? Alan H. Gelb. (World Bank Research Publications Ser.). (Illus.). 368p. 1988. text 49.95 (*0-19-520774-2*) OUP.

Oildrum Cookbook: Fifty-Five Back to Basic, Appropriate Technology Devices You Can Build from a Steel Oildrum. Steve Lafontaine. Ed. by Monique Lafontaine. (Illus.). 200p. (Orig.). 1990. pap. text 10.00 (*0-9625685-1-1*) Lafontaine Pr.

Oiled Birds: How to Search for & Capture Oiled Birds at Oregon Intertidal Areas. Range D. Bayer. (Studies in Oregon Ornithology: No. 5). (Illus.). 29p. 1988. pap. 7.00 (*0-939819-04-X*) Gahmken Pr.

Oiler. Jack Rudman. (Career Examination Ser.: C-553). 1994. pap. 27.95 (*0-8373-0553-5*) Nat Learn.

Oiler Blues: The Story of Pro Football's Most Frustrating Team. John Pirkle. LC 99-72809. (Illus.). 368p. 1999. 24.95 (*1-891422-00-6*); pap. 19.95 (*1-891422-01-4*) Sportline Pub.

Oilfield Processing Vol. 1: Natural Gas. Francis S. Manning & Richard Thompson. 420p. 1991. 99.95 (*0-87814-343-2*) PennWell Bks.

Oilfield Processing Vol. 2: Crude Oil. Francis S. Manning. Ed. by Richard E. Thompson. 400p. 1995. 99.95 (*0-87814-354-8*) PennWell Bks.

Oilfield Spanish Thousands of Words & Terms in Spanish & English from Company Man to Roughneck from Toolpusher to Roustabout: A Vocabulary of Walk-Around Rio-Spanish from Spud to Tank Battery from Reserve Pit to Crom Block. Special Section on Pumps. John T. Melzer. Tr. by Doris R. Ricci. LC TN865.M45.Tr. of Castellano para el Campo Petrolifero. (ENG & SPA., Illus.). 324p. 1997. pap. 56.95 (*0-9664440-0-0*) Oakbowery Bks.

Oilfield.Doc. Lee G. McWorkman. (Illus.). 184p. 1988. 9.95 (*0-933512-40-6*) McWorkman.

Oils. Barron's Educational Editors. LC 96-85325. (Art Handbooks). (Illus.). 96p. 1996. 9.95 (*0-8120-6615-4*) Barron.

Oils. Ann Creber. LC 94-4155. (Williams-Sonoma Essentials Ser.). (Illus.). 1994. 9.95 (*1-875137-21-1*) Weldon Owen.

***Oils.** Patricia Monahan & Patricia Seligman. (Step by Step Art School Ser.). (Illus.). 160p. 1999. pap. 16.95 (*0-600-59953-1*, Pub. by Hamlyn Publishing Group Ltd) Sterling.

Oils & Fats Manual. A. Karleskind & J. P. Wolff. 433.00 (*1-898298-08-4*) Spr-Verlag.

Oils & Perfumes of Ancient Egypt. Joann Fletcher. (Illus.). 64p. 1999. pap. text 29.95 (*0-8109-3697-6*, Pub. by Abrams) Time Warner.

Oils & Perfumes of Ancient Egypt Joann Fletcher. LC 98-223331. 64 p. 1998. write for info. (*0-7141-2703-5*) British Mus Pr.

***Oils & Vinegars.** Jean-Francois Plante. (Illus.). 224p. 2000. pap. 19.95 (*1-55209-437-5*) Firefly Bks Ltd.

***Oils & Vinegars: A Connoisseur's Guide.** Karen Farrington. (Illus.). 2000. pap. 16.95 (*1-85868-856-6*, Pub. by Carlton Bks Ltd) Natl Bk Netwk.

***Oils, Essences & Creams.** Joanne Rippin. (Illus.). 2000. pap. 9.95 (*0-7548-0141-1*, Lorenz Bks) Anness Pub.

Oils, Fats & Fatty Foods: Their Practical Examination. 4th ed. Edward R. Bolton. Ed. by K. A. Williams. LC 67-73132. 496p. reprint ed. pap. 153.80 (*0-608-10838-3*, 200459400044) Bks Demand.

Oils, Fatty-Pituitary Body, Vol. 9. Jocelyn F. Thorpe & M. A. Whiteley. LC 37-28650. 679p. 1949. reprint ed. pap. 200.00 (*0-608-08504-9*, 200454900089) Bks Demand.

***Oils for Beginners.** Alwyn Crawshaw. 1998. pap. 15.95 (*0-00-413344-7*, Pub. by HarpC) Trafalgar.

Oils for the Beginner. Alwyn Crawshaw. (Learn to Paint Ser.). (Illus.). 1999. pap. 15.95 (*0-00-413345-5*, Pub. by HarpC) Trafalgar.

Oils of Evening: Journeys in the Art Trade. G. E. Murray. Ed. by Carol Spelius. 156p. (Orig.). 1995. pap. 12.95 (*0-941363-36-8*) Lake Shore Pub.

Oils, Resins, Varnishes & Polymers see Organic Coating Technology

Oilseed Brassicas in Indian Agriculture. Ed. by V. L. Chopra & Shyam Prakash. (Series in Agricultural Sciences). 1991. text 35.00 (*0-7069-5605-2*, Pub. by Vikas) S Asia.

***Oilseed Crops.** 2nd ed. Edward Weiss. LC 99-38329. (Illus.). 608p. 2000. text 156.95 (*0-632-05259-7*, Pub. by Blckwell Science) Iowa St U Pr.

Oilseed in India. P. C. Agrawal. (C). 1990. 17.50 (*81-204-0553-6*, Pub. by Oxford IBH) S Asia.

Oilseeds & Edible Oil Economy of India. V. P. Gulati & S. J. Phansalkar. 1994. 32.00 (*0-7069-8169-3*, Pub. by Vikas) S Asia.

Oilseeds & Their Utilization. R. K. Suri. (C). 1988. text 210.00 (*0-89771-664-7*, Pub. by Intl Bk Distr) St Mut.

Oilseeds in Asia-Pacific Region. Food & Agriculture Organization Staff. 180p. 1995. text 45.00 (*1-886106-38-X*) Science Pubs.

OILSR Exemption Handbook. David G. Martin. 200p. 45.00 (*0-318-19278-0*) Land Dev Inst.

Oilwell Drilling Engineering: Principles & Practice. H. Rabia. 334p. 1986. pap. text 152.00 (*0-86010-661-6*) G & T Inc.

Oilwell Fishing Operations: Tools & Techniques. 2nd ed. Gore Kemp. (Illus.). 128p. 1990. 69.00 (*0-87201-627-7*, 1627) Gulf Pub.

Oily Grail: A Story of the Indy 500. Jack Albinson. LC 73-87667. 101p. 1974. write for info. (*0-513-01322-9*) Denison.

Oily-Water Separators & Monitoring Equipment. International Maritime Organization Staff. 1987. text 105.00 (*0-89771-968-9*, Pub. by Intl Maritime Org) St Mut.

Oime Bien, Satanas! Carlos Annacondia. (SPA.). 1997. 9.99 (*0-88113-438-4*, B106-4384) Caribe Betania.

Oink. Arthur Geisert. (SPA., Illus.). 32p. (J). (gr. 1-3). 1992. 12.99 (*968-16-3888-3*, Pub. by Fondo) Continental Bk.

Oink. Arthur Geisert. LC 90-46123. (Illus.). 32p. (J). 1991. 15.00 (*0-395-55329-6*) HM.

Oink. Arthur Geisert. (Illus.). 32p. (J). 1995. pap. 5.95 (*0-395-74516-0*, Sandpiper) HM.

***Oink!** David Wojtowycz. 10p. (J). 1999. 7.95 (*1-86233-084-0*) Levinson Bks.

Oink: Heaven's Butcher. John Mueller. LC 96-36760. (Illus.). 112p. 1996. pap. 19.95 (*0-87816-529-0*) Kitchen Sink.

Oink: Heaven's Butcher Collection. John Mueller. Ed. by Catherine Garnier. LC 96-36760. (Illus.). 112p. 1998. 27.95 (*0-87816-531-2*) Kitchen Sink.

Oink-Ha! Bernard Most. LC 96-10592. (Illus.). 20p. (J). 1997. pap. 5.95 (*0-15-201249-4*) Harcourt.

Oink! It's May! Beth H. Tubbs. (Illus.). 32p. (Orig.). (J). (ps). 1997. spiral bd. 9.95 (*0-9632993-8-7*) Storytime Pub.

Oink! Moo! How Do You Do? Grace Maccarone. LC 93-45962. (Illus.). 24p. (J). 1994. 6.95 (*0-590-48161-4*) Scholastic Inc.

Oink! Moo! How Do You Do? Grace Maccarone. (Illus.). 24p. (J). (ps). 1994. 6.95 (*0-590-20655-9*) Scholastic Inc.

Oink, Oink. Arthur Geisert. LC 92-31778. (Illus.). 32p. (J). (gr. k-3). 1993. 14.95 (*0-395-64048-2*) HM.

***Oink Oink Pig.** Tony Potter. 1998. 7.95 (*1-902553-09-8*) Grimond.

***Oink to Ointment.** Nitorig. (Illus.). 246p. 1999. pap. 17.95 (*0-9678955-0-2*) Antiok Onitar.

Oira Implementation of the Congressional Review Act: Hearing Before the Subcommittee on National Economic Growth, Natural Resources, & Regulatory Affairs of the Committee on Government Reform & Oversight, House of Representatives, One Hundred Fifth Congress, Second Session, March 10, 1998. United States. LC 98-208518. iii, 132p. 1998. write for info. (*0-16-057311-4*) USGPO.

Oirata: A Timorese Settlement on Kisar. Jan P. Josselin De Jong. LC 77-87501. reprint ed. 39.50 (*0-404-16733-0*) AMS Pr.

Oiseau Bleu: Feerie en Cinq Actes et Douze Tableaux. Maurice Maeterlinck. (FRE.). 186p. 1976. 34.95 (*0-8288-9898-7*, F118590) Fr & Eur.

Oiseau de Paradis. B. J. James. (Rouge Passion Ser.). (FRE.). 1994. pap. 3.50 (*0-373-37289-2*, 1-37289-5) Harlequin Bks.

Oiseau Noir dans le Soleil Levant. Paul Claudel. 248p. 1929. 8.95 (*0-686-54405-6*) Fr & Eur.

Oiseaux. Saint-John Perse, pseud. pap. 10.50 (*0-685-36544-1*) Fr & Eur.

Oiseaux de Senegambie (The Birds of Senegambia) Notices et Cartes de Distribution (Information & Distribution Maps) G. Morel & M. Y. Morel.Tr. of Birds of Senegambia - Information & Distribution Maps. (FRE.). 178p. 1990. pap. 22.00 (*2-7099-1012-8*, Pub. by LInstitut Francais) Balogh.

Oiseaux Vont Mourir au Perou. Romain Gary & Emile Ajar. (Folio Ser.: No. 668). (FRE.). pap. 8.95 (*2-07-036668-5*) Schoenhof.

Oiseaux Vont Mourir au Perou: Gloire a nos Illustres Pionniers. Romain Gary. (FRE.). 288p. 1982. pap. 11.95 (*0-7859-4772-8*) Fr & Eur.

OJ - 101 Theories, Conspiracies & Alibis: Guilty or Innocent? You Be the Judge. Peter Roberts. LC 95-163333. 160p. (Orig.). 1995. pap. 9.95 (*0-9641565-9-8*) Goldtree Pr.

Ojai: Land of Man's Sacred Nature. Glenn Emanuel. (Illus.). 80p. (Orig.). 1990. write for info. (*0-318-65719-8*) Now Edge Pr.

Ojai Festivals - The Maestros' Challenge: A 50th Commemorative Issue. Ellen M. James & John Henken. Ed. by Mary Embree. LC 95-71655. (Illus.). 66p. (Orig.). 1996. 25.00 (*0-9648970-0-8*); pap. 16.00 (*0-9648970-1-6*) Ojai Festivals.

***Ojai Valley: An Illustrated History.** 2nd rev. ed. Patricia L. Fry. (Illus.). 350p. 1999. pap. 19.95 (*0-9612642-4-1*) Matilija Pr.

Ojeada see Three New Mexico Chronicles

Ojebwewi-Ikodowinan see Concise Dictionary of Minnesota Ojibwe

OJI International Seminar on Organic Semiconductors: Forty Years. Ed. by H. Inokuchi. xii, 364p. 1989. pap. text 811.00 (*2-88124-369-X*) Gordon & Breach.

Ojibwa see Indians of North America

***Ojibwa.** Cathy McCarthy. LC 00-39026. (Indian Nations Ser.). (Illus.). (J). 2000. pap. 25.69 (*0-8172-5460-9*) Raintree Steck-V.

Ojibwa Chiefs, 1690-1890: An Annotated Listing. Compiled by John A. Ilko, Jr. LC 94-62093. (Illus.). vi, 79p. 1995. pap. 12.50 (*0-87875-462-8*) Whitston Pub.

Ojibwa Crafts. Carrie A. Lyford. (Illus.). 216p. 1982. reprint ed. pap. 8.95 (*0-936984-01-5*) Schneider Pubs.

Ojibwa Indians see Native Peoples Series

Ojibwa Indians. Bill Lund. (Native Peoples Ser.). (Illus.). (J). 1997. lib. bdg. 14.00 (*0-516-20524-2*) Childrens.

Ojibwa Narratives of Charles & Charlotte Kawbawgam & Jacques LePique, 1893-1895. Ed. by Arthur P. Bourgeois. LC 93-32783. (Illus.). 168p. 1994. text 29.95 (*0-8143-2514-9*, Great Lks Bks); pap. text 17.95 (*0-8143-2515-7*, Great Lks Bks) Wayne St U Pr.

Ojibwa of Berens River, Manitoba: Ethnography into History. Jennifer S. Brown & A. Irving Hallowell. (Illus.). 180p. (C). 1992. pap. text 18.50 (*0-03-055122-6*, Pub. by Harcourt Coll Pubs) Harcourt.

Ojibwa of Southern Ontario. Peter S. Schmalz. 448p. 1990. text 60.00 (*0-8020-2736-9*); pap. text 24.95 (*0-8020-6778-6*) U of Toronto Pr.

Ojibwa of Western Canada, 1780 to 1870. Laura Peers. LC 94-31544. (Manitoba Studies in Native History: 7). (Illus.). xviii, 288p. 1994. 32.95 (*0-87351-310-X*) Minn Hist.

Ojibwa of Western Canada, 1780 to 1870. Laura Peers. LC 94-31544. (Manitoba Studies in Native History: Vol. 7). (Illus.). xviii, 288p. 1994. pap. 15.95 (*0-87351-311-8*) Minn Hist.

Ojibwa Sociology. Ruth Landes. LC 79-84467. (Columbia Univ. Contributions to Anthropology Ser.: Vol. 29). reprint ed. 22.00 (*0-404-50579-1*) AMS Pr.

Ojibwa Texts, 2 vols. Ed. by Truman Michelson. LC 73-3542. (American Ethnological Society Publications: No. 7). reprint ed. 96.50 (*0-404-58157-9*) AMS Pr.

Ojibwa Woman. Ruth Landes. LC 97-24489. xxx, 247p. 1997. pap. 13.00 (*0-8032-7969-8*, Bison Books) U of Nebr Pr.

Ojibwa Woman. Ruth Landes. LC 70-82362. (Columbia Univ. Contributions to Anthropology Ser.: Vol. 31). reprint ed. 27.50 (*0-404-50581-3*) AMS Pr.

Ojibway Ceremonies. Basil H. Johnston. 1987. pap. 16.99 (*0-7710-4445-3*) McCland & Stewart.

Ojibway Ceremonies. Basil H. Johnston. LC 89-24972. (Illus.). vi, 188p. 1990. reprint ed. pap. 8.95 (*0-8032-7573-0*, Bison Books) U of Nebr Pr.

***Ojibway Chiefs: Portraits of Anishinaabe Leadership.** Mark Diedrich. LC 96-83324. (Illus.). 193p. (Orig.). 1999. pap. 29.95 (*0-9616901-8-6*) Coyote Bks MN.

***Ojibway Dream.** Arthur Shilling. (Illus.). 48p. 1999. reprint ed. pap. 17.95 (*0-88776-491-6*) Tundra Bks.

Ojibway Heritage. Basil Johnston. LC 89-24959. (Illus.). vi, 171p. 1990. reprint ed. pap. 10.95 (*0-8032-7572-2*, Bison Books) U of Nebr Pr.

Ojibway, Michigan, a Forgotten Village. (Copper Country Local History Ser.: Vol. 26). (Illus.). 92p. 1985. 2.50 (*0-942363-25-6*) C J Monette.

Ojibway Music from Minnesota: A Century of Song for Voice & Drum. Thomas Vennum, Jr. (Minnesota Musical Traditions). 56p. 1989. pap. 16.95 incl. audio compact disk (*0-87351-339-8*, 339-8) Minn Hist.

Ojibway on Walpole Island, Ontario: A Linguistic Study. Nils M. Holmer. LC 76-43748. reprint ed. 34.50 (*0-404-15587-1*) AMS Pr.

Ojibway Oratory. Illus. & Compiled by Mark Diedrich. LC 89-81116. 110p. (Orig.). 1990. pap. text 18.95 (*0-9616901-4-3*) Coyote Bks MN.

Ojibway Tales. Basil Johnston. LC 93-2380. Orig. Title: Moose Meat & Wild Rice. 188p. 1993. reprint ed. pap. 11.95 (*0-8032-7578-1*, Bison Books) U of Nebr Pr.

Ojibwe. Raymond Bial. LC 99-12202. (Lifeways Ser.). (Illus.). 128p. (YA). (gr. 4-7). 1999. lib. bdg. 32.79 (*0-7614-0863-0*) Marshall Cavendish.

Ojibwe. Susan Stan. (Native American People Ser.). (Illus.). 32p. (J). (gr. 5-8). 1989. 11.95 (*0-685-58581-6*) Rourke Corp.

Ojibwe. Susan Stan. (Native American People Ser.: Set I). (Illus.). 32p. (J). (gr. 4-8). 1989. lib. bdg. 22.60 (*0-86625-381-5*) Rourke Pubns.

Ojibwe, Basic, 2 bks., 4 cass., Set. (OJI.). 60p. pap. text 55.00 incl. audio (*1-57970-009-8*, AFOJ10) Audio-Forum.

***Ojibwe Singers: Hymns, Grief & a Native Culture in Motion.** Michael McNally. (Religion in America). (Illus.). 272p. 2000. text 45.00 (*0-19-513464-8*) OUP.

Ojime: Magical Jewels of Japan. Robert O. Kinsey. (Illus.). 60p. 1991. pap. 19.95 (*0-8109-2471-4*) Abrams.

Ojime, Magical Jewels of Japan. Robert O. Kinsey. (Illus.). 60p. 1994. pap. 19.95 (*0-8109-2600-8*, Pub. by Abrams) Time Warner.

Ojise: Messenger of the Yoruba Tradition. Baba I. Karade. LC 96-7803. (Illus.). 160p. (Orig.). 1996. pap. 9.95 (*0-87728-881-X*) Weiser.

Ojo de Dios. M.A.C.C. Team Staff. 6p. write for info. (*0-614-04896-6*) Mex Am Cult.

Ojo de Dios: Eye of God. Eileen B. Cummings. (ENG & SPA., Illus.). 14p. 1993. pap. 29.00 (*0-926272-02-0*) E C Pr.

Ojo de la Perdiz. Antonio Dal Masetto. (SPA.). 214p. 1980. pap. 9.00 (*0-910061-01-7*, 1102) Ediciones Norte.

Ojo de la Pitonisa. R. L. Stine, pseud. (Coleccion Fantasmas De Fear Street/Ghosts of Fear Street Ser.: No. 6).Tr. of Eye of the Fortuneteller. (SPA.). (J). (gr. 4-7). 1997. pap. 8.50 (*950-04-1660-3*) Emece.

***OJO Lympics.** (The Bear in the Big Blue House Ser.). (J). 2000. per. write for info. (*0-7434-0839-X*) PB.

***Ojo-Lympics.** Janelle Cherrington. (Bear in the Big Blue House Ser.: Vol. 3). (Illus.). 16p. (ps-3). 2000. pap. 3.99 (*0-689-83224-9*, Simon Spot) Litle Simon.

Ojos de Mama (Mama's Eyes) Lionel Koechlin. (SPA., Illus.). 32p. (J). (gr. k-2). 1999. pap. 6.95 (*980-257-213-6*, Pub. by Ediciones Ekare) Kane-Miller Bk.

Ojos de Perro Azul. Gabriel Garcia Marquez. 136p. 1987. pap. 17.95 (*0-7859-5176-8*) Fr & Eur.

Ojos de Perro Azul. Gabriel Garcia Marquez. (SPA.). 159p. 1997. pap. text 19.98 (*968-13-1731-9*) Libros Fronteras.

Ojos del Amarilis. Natalie Babbitt. (Via Libre Ser.). (SPA.). (J). 1988. 10.05 (*0-606-05915-6*, Pub. by Turtleback) Demco.

Ojos del Griego (Greek's Springs) Ranch. Kerson D. Diamos. 184p. (Orig.). 1985. pap. 7.95 (*0-9614985-0-1*) El Siglo Bks.

Ojos del Tejedor: Through the Eyes of the Weaver. Cristina Ortega. LC 96-11137. (Illus.). 64p. (YA). 1997. pap. 14.95 (*0-940666-81-2*) Clear Light.

Ojos para No Ver. Matias Montes-Huidobro. LC 79-52160. (Coleccion Teatro). (SPA., Illus.). 59p. 1980. pap. 6.00 (*0-89729-229-4*) Ediciones.

***Ojril: The Completely Incomplete Graham Chapman.** Graham Chapman. (Illus.). 2000. pap. 19.95 (*1-57488-270-8*) Brasseys.

***Ojril: The Completely Incomplete Graham Chapman.** Graham Chapman & Jim Yoakum. 2000. pap. write for info. (*0-7134-8605-8*, Pub. by B T B) Bks Intl VA.

OJT File Clerk Resource Materials. 2nd ed. Joyce A. Sherster. (Gregg Office Job Training Program Ser.). (Illus.). 104p. (gr. 11-12). 1981. text 9.88 (*0-07-056640-2*) McGraw.

OJT File Clerk Training Manual. 2nd ed. Joyce A. Sherster. (Gregg Office Job Training Program Ser.). (Illus.). 80p. (gr. 11-12). 1981. pap. text 7.56 (*0-07-056641-0*) McGraw.

OJT Mail Clerk Resource Materials. 2nd ed. Frances French. (Gregg Office Job Training Program Ser.). (Illus.). 112p. (gr. 11-12). 1981. text 9.88 (*0-07-022190-1*) McGraw.

OJT Module - Fundamentals of Classroom Instruction. (Instructor Training Ser.). 338p. 1983. ring bd. 90.00 (*0-87683-048-3*) GP Courseware.

OJT Module - Principles of Instructional Design. (Instructor Training Ser.). 116p. 1983. ring bd. 90.00 (*0-87683-049-1*) GP Courseware.

OJT Payroll Clerk Resource Materials. 2nd ed. Marcia S. Foster. (Gregg Office Job Training Program Ser.). (Illus.). 112p. (gr. 11-12). 1981. text 9.88 (*0-07-021641-X*) McGraw.

OJT Personnel Clerk Resource Materials. 2nd ed. Carol Norris. (Gregg Office Job Training Program Ser.). (Illus.). 112p. 1981. text 9.96 (*0-07-047225-4*) McGraw.

OJT Personnel Clerk Training Manual. 2nd ed. Carol Norris. (Gregg Office Job Training Program Ser.). (Illus.). 56p. (gr. 11-12). 1981. pap. text 7.56 (*0-07-047226-2*) McGraw.

OJT Traffic Clerk Resource Materials. 2nd ed. Joy Risser. (Gregg Office Job Training Program Ser.). (Illus.). 112p. (gr. 11-12). 1981. pap. text 9.88 (*0-07-052960-4*) McGraw.

***Ok: The Corral, the Earps & Doc Holliday.** Paul West. LC 99-89924. 320p. 2000. 23.50 (*0-684-84865-1*) Scribner.

OK - So You're Different: Making Differences Work for You. Dee Frances. Date not set. lib. bdg. 12.00 (*1-885519-65-6*) DDDD Pubns.

OK Best: A Collection of Short Stories. Contrib. by Shauna L. Struby et al. 129p. 1997. pap. 13.95 (*0-9661460-0-X*) Full Circle OK.

OK in My Backyard: Issues & Rights in Housing for the Mentally Ill. Marjorie Beggs. 34p. 1993. pap. 5.00 (*0-936434-64-3*, Pub. by Zellerbach Fam Fund) Intl Spec Bk.

Ok Tedi: Evolution of a Third World Mining Project. William S. Pintz. 206p. 1984. 34.00 (*0-685-50784-X*) EW Ctr HI.

***O.K. You Mugs: Writers on Movie Actors.** Luc Sante. 2000. pap. 13.00 (*0-375-70092-7*, Pub. by Knopf) Random House.

O.K. You Mugs: Writers on Movie Actors. Ed. by Luc Sante & Melissa Holbrook Pierson. LC 99-20669. 272p. 1999. 24.00 (*0-375-40101-6*) Pantheon.

Okagami, the Great Mirror: Fujiwara Michinaga, 966-1027 & His Time. Tr. & Intro. by Helen C. McCullough. LC 90-21410. (Michigan Classics in Japanese Studies: No. 4). x, 381p. 1991. reprint ed. pap. 12.95 (*0-939512-50-5*) U MI Japan.

***Okanagan Valley Entertainment, 2000.** (Illus.). 358p. 1999. pap. 35.00 (*1-58553-046-8*, 001U) Enter Pubns.

Okapi. Philippe Diole. (FRE.). 352p. 1985. pap. 12.95 (*0-7859-2010-2*, 2070376419) Fr & Eur.

Okapi: Mysterious Animal of Cong-Zaire. Susan Lyndaker Lindsey et al. LC 98-28740. 140p. 1999. pap. 17.95 (*0-292-74707-1*) U of Tex Pr.

Okapi: Mysterious Animal of Congo-Zaire. Susan Lyndaker Lindsey et al. LC 98-28740. 176p. 1999. 30.00 (*0-292-74706-3*) U of Tex Pr.

Okapi Passion. Ted Joans. 1994. pap. 4.95 (*0-918408-28-8*) Ishmael Reed.

Okavango: Africa's Last Eden. Frans Lanting. Ed. by Alexandra Arrowsmith. LC 93-10296. (Illus.). 168p. 1993. 45.00 (*0-8118-0527-1*) Chronicle Bks.

O

Okavango: Africa's Last Eden. Frans Lanting. (Illus.). 168p. 1995. pap. 24.95 (0-8118-1182-4) Chronicle Bks.

Okavango: Africa's Wetland Wilderness. Adrian Bailey. LC 98-172947. 1999. 49.95 (1-86872-041-1) Struik Pubs.

Okavango: Sea of Land. Photos by Peter Johnson & Anthony Bannister. (Illus.). 216p. 1984. 35.00 (0-312-58328-1) St Martin.

Okavango: Sea of Land, Land of Water. Ed. by Creina Bond. (Illus.). 192p. (C). 1988. 180.00 (0-685-32437-0, Pub. by New5 Holland) St Mut.

Okavango: Sea of Love, Land of Water. BHB International Staff & Robert T. Teske. 1997. pap. text 39.95 (1-86825-382-1, Pub. by New5 Holland) BHB Intl.

Okavango from the Air. Clive Walker. (Illus.). 156p. (C). 1989. 170.00 (1-85368-009-5, Pub. by New5 Holland) St Mut.

Okay Book. Todd Parr. LC 98-3283. (Illus.). 24p. (J). (gr. k-3). 1999. 5.95 (0-316-69220-4) Little.

Okay, Don't Quit: How to Stop Smoking Without Quitting Cold Turkey. James A. Davis. LC 91-61454. (Illus.). 130p. (Orig.). 1991. 19.95 (0-915377-03-9); pap. 11.95 (0-915377-02-0) Trad Pub.

***Okay, Let's Try It Again.** Willem Lange. LC 99-34966. 117p. 1999. pap. 12.95 (1-58465-004-4) U Pr of New Eng.

Okay Nelwyn . . . Hazel B. Mitchell. 1989. pap. 10.95 (0-938645-26-9) In His Steps.

Okay, So I Don't Have a Headache: What I Learned (And What All Women Need to Know) about Hormones, PMS, Stress, Diet, Menopause & Sex. 6th ed. Christina Ferrare. LC 99-25275. 192p. 1999. 21.95 (1-58238-029-5) St. Martin-in-the-Fields.

***Okay, So I Don't Have a Headache: What I Learned (And What You Need to Know) about PMS, Hormones, Stress, Diet, Menopause - And Sex.** Cristina Ferrare. 192p. 2000. pap. 12.95 (0-312-26366-X, St Martin Griffin) St Martin.

***Okay, So Now You're a Vegetarian: Advice & 100 Recipes from One Teenager to Another.** Lauren Butts. LC 99-86652. 240p. 2000. pap. 12.95 (0-7679-0527-X) Broadway BDD.

***OKB MiG: A History of the Design Bureau & Its Aircraft.** Piotr Butowski & Jay Miller. (Illus.). 250p. 2000. 39.95 (0-904597-80-6, Pub. by Midland Pubng) Specialty Pr.

OKB Sukhoi: A History of the Design Bureau & Its Aircraft. Vladimir Antonov et al. (Illus.). 300p. 1996. 59.95 (1-85780-012-5) Specialty Pr.

OKBomb! Conspiracy & Cover-Up. Jim Keith. LC 95-48365. (Illus.). 240p. 1996. pap. 14.95 (1-881532-08-9) IllumiNet Pr.

OKD's Cruise Ship Jobs Guide. Omar E. Dada. 100p. (Orig.). text. write for info. (0-9642899-0-3) O K D Mgmt.

Oke Family Cookbook: Favorite Recipes of Janette's Family. Barbara Oke & Deborah Oke. LC 94-37627. (Illus.). 224p. 1994. pap. 9.99 (1-55661-529-9) Bethany Hse.

Okeechobee: A Modern Frontier. Jim Janosky. (Illus.). 216p. 1997. 24.95 (0-8130-1467-0) U Press Fla.

O'Keefe: The Law of Weights & Measures. 2nd ed. Ed. by Anthony A. Painter & Brian W. Harvey. ring bd. write for info. (0-406-99896-5, OWMASET, MICHIE) LEXIS Pub.

O'Keefe: The Law of Weights & Measures, 2 vols., Set. 2nd ed. Ed. by Anthony A. Painter & Brian W. Harvey. ring bd. 390.00 (0-406-32645-2, U.K., MICHIE) LEXIS Pub.

***Okeefe Empire.** Coleman. LC 98-42373. Date not set. 19.95 (0-7862-1324-8) Thorndike Pr.

O'Keefe, Stieglitz & the Critics, 1916 to 1929. Barbara B. Lynes. LC 90-48860. (Illus.). 392p. 1998. pap. 17.95 (0-226-49824-7) U Ch Pr.

O'Keeffe. Britta Benke. 1994. pap. 9.99 (3-8228-8886-9) Taschen Amer.

O'Keeffe. Britta Benke. (SPA.). 1996. pap. 9.99 (3-8228-8825-7) Taschen Amer.

O'Keeffe: Days in a Life. C. S. Merrill. 140p. (Orig.). 1995. pap. 12.00 (0-9631909-8-9) La Alameda Pr.

O'Keeffe: The Life of an American Legend. Jeffrey Hogrefe. (Illus.). 448p. 1999. pap. 14.95 (0-553-38069-9) Bantam.

O'Keeffe & Me: A Treasured Friendship. Ralph Looney. (Illus.). 144p. 1995. 27.50 (0-87081-406-0) Univ Pr Colo.

O'Keeffe & Me: A Treasured Friendship. Ralph Looney. (Illus.). 134p. 1997. pap. 18.95 (0-87081-450-8) Univ Pr Colo.

O'Keeffe & Stieglitz: An American Romance. Benita Eisler. (Illus.). 560p. 1992. pap. 17.95 (0-14-017094-4, Penguin Bks) Viking Penguin.

O'Keeffe & Texas. Sharyn R. Udall & Marion Koogler McNay Art Museum Staff. LC 97-31801. (Illus.). 120p. 1998. 29.95 (0-8109-6356-6, Pub. by Abrams) Time Warner.

O'Keeffe & Texas. Sharyn R. Udall & Marion Koogler McNay Art Museum Staff. LC 97-31801. 1998. pap. write for info. (0-916677-39-7) M K McNay Art.

O'Keeffe at Abiquiu. Christine T. Patten. LC 94-39687. (Illus.). 120p. 1995. 39.95 (0-8109-3680-1, Pub. by Abrams) Time Warner.

Okeeffe Museum. 1997. pap. 11.25 (0-8109-2794-2) Viking Penguin.

***O'Keeffe on Paper.** Ruth E. Fine et al. LC 99-89039. (Illus.). 192p. 2000. 35.00 (0-8109-6698-0, Pub. by Abrams) Time Warner.

***O'Keeffe on Paper.** Ruth Fine et al. LC 99-89039. 2000. pap. write for info. (0-89468-275-X) Natl Gallery Art.

O'Keeffe's Cast. Herta Wittigenstein. Ed. by Margaret Duerkop. 494p. 1997. pap. 16.95 (0-932482-06-6) Blue Feather.

Okefenokee Album. Francis Harper & Delma E. Presley. LC 80-14220. (Brown Thrasher Bks.). (Illus.). 212p. 1990. reprint ed. pap. 17.95 (0-8203-1274-6) U of Ga Pr.

Oke's Magisterial Formulist. Ed. by Stuart Baker. ring bd. write for info. (0-406-99835-3, OMFASET, MICHIE) LEXIS Pub.

Oke's Magisterial Formulist, 2 vols., Set. Ed. by Stuart Baker. ring bd. 380.00 (0-406-32400-X, UK, MICHIE) LEXIS Pub.

Okhogiso: A Collection of Edo Folktales from Benin, Nigeria. Ademola Iyi-Eweka. LC 97-92629. 105p. 1998. pap. 10.00 (0-9656365-2-6) Ogiso Pubn-Commun.

Okhota K Peremene Mest: Rasskazy o Puteshestviiakh. Shtern Ludmila. LC 98-10776. (RUS., Illus.). 208p. 1998. pap. 12.00 (1-55779-106-6) Hermitage Pubs.

***Okhrana: The Paris Operations of the Russian Imperial Police.** Ben B. Fischer. 128p. 1999. per. 11.00 (0-16-058827-8) USGPO.

***Okhrana: The Paris Operations of the Russian Imperial Police.** Ben B. Fischer. 122p. (C). 1999. reprint ed. pap. text 30.00 (0-7881-8328-1) DIANE Pub.

Okie Dictionary. 2nd rev. ed. Stoney Hardcastle. 16p. 1995. mass mkt. 2.00 (0-9653874-1-0) Indian Nations.

Okie Joke Book. Otto K. Schwein. (Illus.). 96p. (Orig.). 1988. pap. write for info. (0-318-64811-3) Jaybird Pubns.

Okie Mafioso. Lee S. Cole. 231p. (Orig.). 1986. pap. 12.95 (0-939818-14-0) Lee Bks.

Okiek. Roderic H. Blackburn. (Kenya People Ser.). (Illus.). 42p. (YA). (gr. 6-9). 1991. pap. write for info. (0-237-50631-9) EVN1 UK.

Okies & the Dustbowl: Mini-Play. (California History Ser.). (J). (gr. 5 up). 1975. 6.50 (0-89550-335-2) Stevens & Shea.

***Okinawa: Cold War Island.** Chalmers Johnson. (Illus.). 312p. 1999. pap. 20.00 (0-9673642-0-5) Japan Pol Res.

***Okinawa: The History of an Island People.** rev. ed. George Kerr. (Illus.). 2000. pap. 24.95 (0-8048-2087-2) Tuttle Pubng.

Okinawa: The Last Battle of World War II. Robert Leckie. 256p. 1996. pap. 13.95 (0-14-017389-7, Penguin Bks) Viking Penguin.

Okinawa: Two Postwar Novellas. Oshiro Tatsuhiro & Higashi Mineo. Tr. & Contrib. by Steve Rabson. LC 89-85032. (Japan Research Monographs). xiv, 141p. pap. 15.00 (1-55729-015-6) IEAS.

Okinawa: Victory in the Pacific. Charles S. Nichols, Jr. & Henry I. Shaw, Jr. (Elite Unit Ser.: No. 19). (Illus.). 368p. 1989. reprint ed. 39.95 (0-89839-131-8) Battery Pr.

Okinawa Dreams OK. Tony Barrell & Rick Tanaka. 220p. Date not set. pap. 25.00 (3-931126-11-0, Pub. by Die Gestalten) Consort Bk Sales.

Okinawa Island of Karate. George W. Alexander. 127p. 1992. pap. 29.95 (0-9631775-0-8) Yamazato Pubns.

***Okinawa, 1945: Assault on the Empire.** Simon Foster. (Military Classics). (Illus.). 196p. 1999. pap. 9.95 (0-304-35172-5, Pub. by Cassell) Sterling.

Okinawan Goju-Ryu. Seikichi Toguchi. Ed. by Geraldine Adachi. Tr. by Toshio Tamano et al from JPN. LC 75-36054. (Japanese Arts Ser.). 1976. pap. text 16.95 (0-89750-018-0, 123) Ohara Pubns.

Okinawan Karate. Mark Bishop. pap. write for info. (0-7136-5666-2, Pub. by A & C Blk) Midpt Trade.

Okinawan Karate. rev. ed. Mark Bishop. 1999. pap. 16.95 (0-8048-3205-6) Tuttle Pubng.

Okinawan Weapons: Sai & Tonfa Fighting Techniques. Harold Long & Phil Little. (Illus.). 127p. 1997. pap. 17.95 (0-9658459-1-5) Isshin-Ryu.

Okinawan Weapons Bo Fighting Techniques. Harold Long & Phil Little. (Illus.). 112p. (Orig.). 1987. pap. 9.95 (0-89826-022-1) Natl Paperback.

Okino & the Whales. abr. ed. Arnica Esterl. LC 94-32676.Tr. of Okino und die Wale. (ENG., Illus.). 32p. (J). (gr. 1-5). 1995. 16.00 (0-15-200377-0) Harcourt.

Okino und die Wale see Okino & the Whales

Okla Hannali. R. A. Lafferty. LC 91-50692. 240p. 1991. pap. 12.95 (0-8061-2349-4) U of Okla Pr.

Oklahoma see From Sea to Shining Sea

Oklahoma see Atlas of Historical County Boundaries

Oklahoma. (Vocal Score Ser.). 216p. 1981. per. 45.00 (0-88188-039-6, 00312294) H Leonard.

***Oklahoma.** Guy Baldwin. (Celebrate the States Ser.). (Illus.). (J). 2000. 35.64 (0-7614-1067-8, Benchmark NY) Marshall Cavendish.

Oklahoma. Capstone Press Editors. LC 98-31227. (One Nation Ser.). (J). 1999. 19.00 (0-7368-0117-0, Cpstone High Low) Capstone Pr.

***Oklahoma.** Capstone Press Geography Department Staff. 1999. 19.93 (0-516-21795-X) Capstone Pr.

Oklahoma. Gousha, H. M., Editors. 1995. 2.95 (0-671-55112-4, H M Gousha) Prntice Hall Bks.

Oklahoma. Paul Joseph. LC 97-18682. (United States Ser.). (Illus.). 32p. (J). 1998. lib. bdg. 19.93 (1-56239-871-7, Checkerboard Library) ABDO Pub Co.

Oklahoma. Rita C. LaDoux. Ed. by Lerner Geography Department Staff. (Hello U. S. A. Ser.). (Illus.). 72p. (J). (gr. 3-6). 1992. lib. bdg. 19.95 (0-8225-2717-0, Lerner Publctns) Lerner Pub.

Oklahoma. Rita C. LaDoux. (Hello U. S. A. Ser.). (Illus.). 72p. (J). (gr. 3-6). 1997. pap. text 5.95 (0-8225-9783-7) Lerner Pub.

Oklahoma! Richard Rodgers & Oscar Hammerstein, II. 72p. 1981. pap. 5.95 (0-7935-3342-2, 00301805) H Leonard.

Oklahoma! Dana Fuller Ross. (Wagons West Ser.: No. 23). 1989. pap. 4.50 (0-685-25336-8) Bantam.

Oklahoma. Kathleen Thompson. LC 95-44436. (Portrait of America Library). 48p. (J). (gr. 4-8). 1996. pap. 5.95 (0-8114-7462-3) Raintree Steck-V.

Oklahoma. Kathleen Thompson. LC 95-44436. (Portrait of America Library). (Illus.). 48p. (J). (gr. 3-6). 1996. lib. bdg. 22.83 (0-8114-7381-3) Raintree Steck-V.

Oklahoma! Jay J. Wagoner. LC 89-90110. (Illus.). 229p. (YA). 1989. lib. bdg. 8.95 (0-9622361-0-1) Thunderbird Bks.

Oklahoma. 2nd ed. Jerry Reedy. LC 98-10772. (America the Beautiful Ser.). (J). 1998. lib. bdg. 32.00 (0-516-20639-7) Childrens.

Oklahoma: A Geography. Michael Roark. 1996. text 35.00 (0-86531-640-6) Westview.

Oklahoma: A Geography. Michael Roark. (C). 1996. pap. text 20.00 (0-86531-641-4) Westview.

Oklahoma: A Guide to the Sooner State. Federal Writers' Project Staff. (American Guidebook Ser.). 532p. reprint ed. 89.00 (0-403-02185-5) Somerset Pub.

Oklahoma: A Guide to the Sooner State. Federal Writers' Project Staff & Writers Program-WPA Staff. (American Guide Ser.). 1989. reprint ed. lib. bdg. 89.00 (0-7812-1035-6, 1035) Rprt Serv.

***Oklahoma: A Guide to Unique Places.** 3rd ed. Kendra Fox. (Off the Beaten Path Ser.). (Illus.). 2001. pap. 12.95 (0-7627-0832-8) Globe Pequot.

Oklahoma: A History. H. Wayne Morgan & Anne H. Morgan. (States & the Nation Ser.). (Illus.). 1984. pap. 7.95 (0-393-30181-8) Norton.

Oklahoma: A History of Five Centuries. Arrell M. Gibson. LC 81-40284. (Illus.). 316p. 1981. reprint ed. 29.95 (0-8061-1758-3) U of Okla Pr.

Oklahoma: Collected Works of Federal Writers Project. Federal Writers' Project Staff. 1991. reprint ed. lib. bdg. 98.00 (0-7812-5757-3) Rprt Serv.

Oklahoma! Easy Piano. (Easy Play Ser.: No. 13). 36p. 1984. pap. 6.95 (0-7935-0448-1, 00240622) H Leonard.

Oklahoma: Foot-Loose & Fancy Free. Angie Debo. LC 81-17865. (Illus.). 258p. 1982. reprint ed. lib. bdg. 65.00 (0-313-23085-4, DEOK, Greenwood Pr) Greenwood.

Oklahoma: History of the Sooner State. rev. ed. Edwin C. McReynolds. LC 54-10052. (Illus.). 477p. 1962. 24.95 (0-8061-0302-7) U of Okla Pr.

Oklahoma: New Views of the Forty-Sixth State. Anne H. Morgan & H. Wayne Morgan. LC 82-40327. (Illus.). 400p. 1982. 24.95 (0-8061-1651-X) U of Okla Pr.

Oklahoma: Off the Beaten Path: A Guide to Unique Places. 2nd ed. Barbara Palmer. LC 98-36932. (Off the Beaten Path Ser.). (Illus.). 288p. (Orig.). 1998. pap. 12.95 (0-7627-0274-5) Globe Pequot.

Oklahoma: The Land & Its People. Kenny A. Franks & Paul F. Lambert. LC 94-1554. (Illus.). 112p. (Orig.). 1994. pap. 15.95 (1-56037-044-0) Am Wrld Geog.

Oklahoma: The Land & Its People. Kenny A. Franks & Paul F. Lambert. LC 94-1554. (Illus.). 104p. (Orig.). 1997. pap. 15.95 (0-8061-9944-X) U of Okla Pr.

***Oklahoma: The Spirit of America, State by State.** Barbara Palmer. Ed. by Diana Landau. LC 98-43098. (Art of the State Ser.). (Illus.). 96p. 1999. 12.95 (0-8109-5563-6, Pub. by Abrams) Time Warner.

Oklahoma: The Story of Its Past & Present. Edwin C. McReynolds et al. LC 61-17309. (Illus.). 500p. 1961. 22.95 (0-8061-0509-7) U of Okla Pr.

Oklahoma - Sea to Shining Sea. Dennis B. Fradin. (From Sea to Shining Sea Ser.). (Illus.). 64p. (J). 1995. pap. 7.95 (0-516-43836-0) Childrens.

Oklahoma Almanac. 44th ed. Ed. by Oklahoma Department of Libraries Staff et al. 792p. 1993. pap. 12.00 (1-880438-01-1) OK Dept Lib.

Oklahoma Almanac. 45th ed. Ed. by Ann Hamilton. Orig. Title: Directory of Oklahoma. (Illus.). 922p. 1995. pap. 13.00 (1-880438-02-X) OK Dept Lib.

Oklahoma & Other State Greats (Biographies) Carole Marsh. (Carole Marsh Oklahoma Bks.). (Illus.). (J). 1994. pap. 19.95 (0-7933-1879-3); lib. bdg. 29.95 (0-7933-1878-5); disk 29.95 (0-7933-1880-7) Gallopade Intl.

Oklahoma Anthology for 1929. Ed. by Joseph F. Paxton. LC 78-116412. (Granger Index Reprint Ser.). 1977. 16.95 (0-8369-6153-6) Ayer.

Oklahoma Archeology: A 1981 Perspective. Don G. Wyckoff & Robert L. Brooks. (Archeological Resource Survey Report: Vol. 16). (Illus.). 365p. (C). 1988. reprint ed. pap. text 8.00 (1-881346-11-0) Univ OK Archeol.

Oklahoma at the Crossroads. Johnson et al. 154p. (C). 1998. per. 49.95 (0-7872-4639-5, 41463901) Kendall-Hunt.

***Oklahoma Atlas.** DeLorme Mapping Co. Staff. (Illus.). 2000. pap. 19.95 (0-89933-283-8) DeLorme Map.

Oklahoma Atlas & Gazetteer. Delorme Publishing Company Staff. (Illus.). 1998. pap. 19.95 (0-89933-234-X) DeLorme Map.

Oklahoma Automotive Directory. Ed. by T. L. Spelman. 1985. 24.95 (1-55527-026-3) Auto Contact Inc.

Oklahoma Bandits, Bushwackers, Outlaws, Crooks, Devils, Ghosts, Desperadoes & Other Assorted & Sundry Characters! Carole Marsh. (Carole Marsh Oklahoma Bks.). (Illus.). (J). 1994. pap. 19.95 (0-7933-0913-1); lib. bdg. 29.95 (0-7933-0914-X); disk 29.95 (0-7933-0915-8) Gallopade Intl.

Oklahoma Basic Intelligence Test. D. L. Birchfield. (Frank Waters Memorial Ser.). 182p. 1999. pap. 14.95 (0-912678-97-6) Greenfld Rev Lit.

Oklahoma "BIO" Bingo! 24 Must Know State People for Kids to Learn about While Having Fun! Carole Marsh. (Bingo! Ser.). (Illus.). (J). (gr. 2-8). 1998. pap. 14.95 (0-7933-8630-6) Gallopade Intl.

Oklahoma Bird Life. Frederick Baumgartner & Marguerite Baumgartner. (Illus.). 548p. (C). 1992. 49.95 (0-8061-1792-3) U of Okla Pr.

Oklahoma Birds. James Kavanagh. (Pocket Naturalist Ser.). (Illus.). 1999. 5.95 (1-58355-008-9, Pub. by Waterford WA) Falcon Pub Inc.

Oklahoma Bookstore Book: A Surprising Guide to Our State's Bookstores & Their Specialties for Students, Teachers, Writers & Publishers. Carole Marsh. (Carole Marsh Oklahoma Bks.). (Illus.). 1994. pap. 19.95 (0-7933-2964-7); lib. bdg. 29.95 (0-7933-2963-9); disk 29.95 (0-7933-2965-5) Gallopade Intl.

Oklahoma Botanical Literature. Forrest L. Johnson & T. H. Milby. LC 88-31247. (Oklahoma Museum of Natural History Publications). 160p. 1989. 27.95 (0-8061-2198-X) U of Okla Pr.

***Oklahoma Business Directory (2000)** American Business Directories Staff et al. 1,504p. 2000. boxed set 450.00 incl. cd-rom (0-7687-0214-3) Am Busn Direct.

Oklahoma Business Organizations, Issue 7. Faught. 151p. 1998. ring bd. write for info. (0-327-00587-4, 8221214) LEXIS Pub.

Oklahoma Business Organizations: Formation & Representation. Irving L. Faught. 1000p. 1994. spiral bd. 115.00 (0-8342-0164-X, MICHIE); ring bd., suppl. ed. 69.00 (0-685-74601-1, MICHIE) LEXIS Pub.

Oklahoma Celebrity Cookbook. Chuck Allen. Ed. by Stacey Wyett. 160p. 1991. 14.95 (0-9631825-0-1) Exec Coffee Srv.

Oklahoma Census Index: 1890 Union Veterans. Ronald V. Jackson. (Illus.). 1989. lib. bdg. 49.00 (0-89593-761-1, Accel Indexing) Genealogical Srvcs.

Oklahoma City: A Better Living, a Better Life. Susan Wallace & Tamara Hermen. LC 97-34342. 431p. 1997. 45.00 (1-885352-68-9) Community Comm.

Oklahoma City: A Detailed Account of the Bombing of the Alfred P. Murrah Federal Building, Oklahoma City, OK, April 19, 1995, 3 vols. Michele M. Moore. Incl. Vol. 1. Oklahoma City Day One: A Detailed Account of the Bombing of the Alfred P. Murrah Federal Building, Oklahoma City, OK, April 19, 1995. unabridged ed. (Illus.). 640p. 1996. pap. 29.95 (0-9653307-1-0); 75.00 (0-9653307-0-2) Harvest Trust.

***Oklahoma City: Land Run to Statehood.** Terry L. Griffith. (Images of America Ser.). (Illus.). 128p. 1999. pap. 18.99 (0-7385-0209-X) Arcadia Publng.

***Oklahoma City: Statehood to 1930.** Terry L. Griffith. (Images of America Ser.). (Illus.). 128p. 1999. pap. 18.99 (0-7385-0314-2) Arcadia Publng.

Oklahoma City Bombing: Terror in the Heartland. Victoria Sherrow. LC 97-45750. (American Disasters Ser.). 48p. (YA). (gr. 4-10). 1998. 18.95 (0-7660-1061-9) Enslow Pubs.

Oklahoma City Bombing: The Suppressed Truth. 2nd ed. Henry B. Stein & Jon Rappoport. 112p. 1997. reprint ed. pap. 12.95 (1-885395-22-1) Book Tree.

Oklahoma City Day One: A Detailed Account of the Bombing of the Alfred P. Murrah Federal Building, Oklahoma City, OK, April 19, 1995, Vol. 1. limited num. unabridged ed. Michelle M. Moore. 640p. 1996. 60.00 (0-9653307-9-6) Harvest Trust.

Oklahoma City Day One: A Detailed Account of the Bombing of the Alfred P. Murrah Federal Building, Oklahoma City, OK, April 19, 1995 see Oklahoma City: A Detailed Account of the Bombing of the Alfred P. Murrah Federal Building, Oklahoma City, OK, April 19, 1995

***Oklahoma City Entertainment, 2000.** (Illus.). 486p. 1999. pap. 25.00 (1-880248-54-9, 00R6) Enter Pubns.

Oklahoma City National Memorial: Hearing Before the Subcommittee on National Parks & Public Lands of the Committee on Resources, House of Representatives, 105th Congress, 1st Session, on H. R. 1849... September 9, 1997, Washington, D. C. USGPO Staff. LC 98-160870. iii, 118 p. 1998. pap. write for info. (0-16-056156-6) USGPO.

Oklahoma City, OK. (Streetfinder Ser.). (Illus.). 1995. pap. 14.95 (0-528-91122-8) Rand McNally.

Oklahoma City Secrets: A Resource Guide for the Home & Garden. Virginia McCubbin. (Illus.). 224p. (Orig.). 1993. pap. 12.95 (1-883554-02-0) City Secrets.

Oklahoma Civil Procedure Forms, 2 vols. Clyde A. Muchmore & Harvey Ellis. 1993. suppl. ed. 89.00 (0-685-74633-X, MICHIE) LEXIS Pub.

Oklahoma Civil Procedure Forms. Clyde Muchmore & Harvey Ellis. LC 98-67078. 1998. ring bd. 250.00 (0-327-00197-6, 82218-20) LEXIS Pub.

Oklahoma Civil Procedure Forms, 2 vols., Set. Clyde A. Muchmore & Harvey Ellis. 1000p. 1994. spiral bd. 250.00 (0-87189-074-7, 82216-10, MICHIE) LEXIS Pub.

Oklahoma Classic Christmas Trivia: Stories, Recipes, Activities, Legends, Lore & More! Carole Marsh. (Carole Marsh Oklahoma Bks.). (Illus.). (J). 1994. pap. 19.95 (0-7933-0916-6); lib. bdg. 29.95 (0-7933-0917-4); disk 29.95 (0-7933-0918-2) Gallopade Intl.

Oklahoma Coastales. Carole Marsh. (Oklahoma Bks.). (J). 1994. lib. bdg. 29.95 (0-7933-7301-8) Gallopade Intl.

Oklahoma Coastales. Carole Marsh. (Carole Marsh Oklahoma Bks.). (Illus.). (J). 1994. pap. 19.95 (0-7933-1873-4); lib. bdg. 29.95 (0-7933-1872-6); disk 29.95 (0-7933-1874-2) Gallopade Intl.

***Oklahoma Cook Book.** Mary Beth Lilley. (Cooking Across America Ser.). (Illus.). 2000. pap. 6.95 (1-885590-49-0) Golden West Pub.

Oklahoma Corporate Forms. Randall D. Mock. 1120p. 1993. spiral bd. 250.00 (0-87189-975-2, 82225-10, MICHIE) LEXIS Pub.

Oklahoma Corporate Forms, 2 vols., Issue 9. Mock & Holloman. 301p. 1998. ring bd. write for info. (0-327-00526-2, 8222914) LEXIS Pub.

***Oklahoma Corporate Forms, Issue 10.** Randall D. Mock & James H. Holloman, Jr. 200p. 1999. ring bd. write for info. (0-327-01582-9, 8222915) LEXIS Pub.

Oklahoma Cowboy Cartoons. Daryl Talbot. (Illus.). 64p. 1999. pap. 7.95 (1-58107-014-4) New Forums.

O

An Asterisk (*) at the beginning of an entry indicates that the title is appearing for the first time.

***Oklahoma Crime in Perspective 2000.** Ed. by Kathleen O'Leary Morgan & Scott E. Morgan. 22p. 2000. spiral bd. 19.00 (*0-7401-0335-0*) Morgan Quitno Corp.

Oklahoma Crime Perspective, 1998. Ed. by Kathleen O'Leary Morgan & Scott E. Morgan. 20p. 1998. pap. 19.00 (*1-56692-935-0*) Morgan Quitno Corp.

Oklahoma Crime Perspectives, 1999. Kathleen O'Leary Morgan. 22p. 1999. spiral bd. 19.00 (*0-7401-0135-8*) Morgan Quitno Corp.

Oklahoma Criminal Law: Statutes & Rules Annotated Charles L. Cantrell. LC 98-214959. 850 p. 1997. write for info. (*0-9648201-6-1*) Grail & Tucker.

Oklahoma "Crinkum-Crankum" A Funny Word Book about Our State. Carole Marsh. (Oklahoma Bks.). (Illus.). (J). (gr. 3-12). 1994. 29.95 (*0-7933-4916-8*); pap. 19.95 (*0-7933-4917-6*); disk 29.95 (*0-7933-4918-4*) Gallopade Intl.

Oklahoma Crossroads. Michael Wallis. LC 97-52759. 1998. 27.00 (*1-55868-311-9*) Gr Arts Ctr Pub.

Oklahoma Delaware Ceremonies, Feasts & Dances. Frank G. Speck. LC 76-43845. (Memoirs of the American Philosophical Society Ser.: Vol. 7). reprint ed. 45.00 (*0-404-15696-7*) AMS Pr.

Oklahoma Dingbats! Bk. 1: A Fun Book of Games, Stories, Activities & More about Our State That's All in Code! for You to Decipher. Carole Marsh. (Carole Marsh Oklahoma Bks.). (Illus.). (J). (gr. 3-12). 1994. pap. 19.95 (*0-7933-3882-4*); lib. bdg. 29.95 (*0-7933-3881-6*); disk 29.95 (*0-7933-3883-2*) Gallopade Intl.

Oklahoma Discovery Practice Manual. Charles Adams. 590p. 1987. ring bd. 120.00 (*0-327-01040-1*, 82233, MICHIE) LEXIS Pub.

Oklahoma Discovery Practice Manual. Charles W. Adams. 590p. 1993. ring bd. 120.00 (*0-614-05936-4*, MICHIE) LEXIS Pub.

Oklahoma Discovery Practice Manual, 1987-1993. Charles W. Adams. 590p. 1993. ring bd. 120.00 (*0-409-25104-6*, 82233-10, MICHIE) LEXIS Pub.

Oklahoma Elementary School Injury Prevention Eduation: The Subject-Integrated Safety Curriculum for Teachers - Grade Four. Ruth Azeredo. Ed. by Sue Mallonee & Shelli S. Stidham. (Illus.). 130p. (Orig.). 1995. pap. 7.50 (*1-889728-05-5*) OK St Dept Hlth Injury.

Oklahoma Elementary School Injury Prevention Education: The Subject-Integrated Safety Curriculum for Teachers - Grade Five. Ruth Azeredo. Ed. by Sue Mallonee & Shelli S. Stidham. (Illus.). 130p. (Orig.). 1995. pap. 7.50 (*1-889728-06-3*) OK St Dept Hlth Injury.

Oklahoma Elementary School Injury Prevention Education: The Subject-Integrated Safety Curriculum for Teachers - Grade One. Ruth Azeredo. Ed. by Sue Mallonee & Shelli S. Stidham. (Illus.). 130p. (Orig.). 1995. pap. 7.50 (*1-889728-02-0*) OK St Dept Hlth Injury.

Oklahoma Elementary School Injury Prevention Education: The Subject-Integrated Safety Curriculum for Teachers - Grade Three. Ruth Azeredo. Ed. by Sue Mallonee & Shelli S. Stidham. (Illus.). 130p. (Orig.). 1995. pap. 7.50 (*1-889728-04-7*) OK St Dept Hlth Injury.

Oklahoma Elementary School Injury Prevention Education: The Subject-Integrated Safety Curriculum for Teachers - Grade Two. Ruth Azeredo. Ed. by Sue Mallonee & Shelli S. Stidham. (Illus.). 130p. (Orig.). 1995. pap. 7.50 (*1-889728-03-9*) OK St Dept Hlth Injury.

Oklahoma Elementary School Injury Prevention Education: The Subject-Integrated Safety Curriculum for Teachers - Kindergarten. Ruth Azeredo. Ed. by Sue Mallonee & Shelli S. Stidham. (Illus.). 130p. (Orig.). 1995. pap. 7.50 (*1-889728-01-2*) OK St Dept Hlth Injury.

Oklahoma Elementary School Injury Prevention Education: The Subject-Integrated Safety Curriculum for Teachers - Kindergarten Through Grade Five. Ruth Azeredo. Ed. by Sue Mallonee & Shelli S. Stidham. (Illus.). 130p. (Orig.). 1995. pap. 40.50 (*1-889728-00-4*) OK St Dept Hlth Injury.

Oklahoma Estate Planning, Will Drafting & Estate Administration Forms. W. Thomas Coffman. 970p. 1993. spiral bd. 240.00 (*0-87189-977-9*, 82238-10, MICHIE) LEXIS Pub.

***Oklahoma Estate Planning, Will Drafting & Estate Administration Forms, 2 vols., Issue 9.** Incl. Vol. 1. 1998. ring bd., suppl. ed. (*0-327-00906-3*, 8224213); Vol. 2. 1998. ring bd., suppl. ed. (*0-327-00907-1*, 8224213); 410p. 1998. write for info. (*0-327-00908-X*, 8224213) LEXIS Pub.

***Oklahoma Experience Pocket Guide.** Carole Marsh. (Oklahoma Experience! Ser.). (Illus.). (J). 2000. pap. 6.95 (*0-7933-9594-1*) Gallopade Intl.

Oklahoma Facts & Factivities. Carole Marsh. (Carole Marsh State Bks.). (Illus.). (J). (gr. 4-7). 1996. pap., teacher ed. 19.95 (*0-7933-7919-9*, C Marsh) Gallopade Intl.

***Oklahoma Facts & Symbols.** Karen Bush Gibson. LC 00-22775. (States & Their Symbols Ser.). (Illus.). 24p. (J). (ps-3). 2000. lib. bdg. 15.93 (*0-7368-0643-1*, Hilltop Bks) Capstone Pr.

Oklahoma Federal Census Index, 1860: Arkansas Edition. Ronald V. Jackson. (Illus.). 1989. lib. bdg. 49.00 (*0-89593-760-3*, Accel Indexing) Genealogical Srvcs.

Oklahoma Festival Fun for Kids! Carole Marsh. (Carole Marsh Oklahoma Bks.). (Illus.). (J). (gr. 3-12). 1994. pap. 19.95 (*0-7933-4035-7*); lib. bdg. 29.95 (*0-7933-4034-9*) Gallopade Intl.

Oklahoma Festival Fun for Kids! Carole Marsh. (Carole Marsh Oklahoma Bks.). (Illus.). (YA). (gr. 3-12). 1994. disk 29.95 (*0-7933-4036-5*) Gallopade Intl.

Oklahoma Football see Sooners: A Story of Oklahoma Football

Oklahoma Gardener's Guide: The What, Where, When, How & Why of Gardening in Oklahoma. Steve Dobbs. LC 99-39389. (Illus.). 424p. 1999. pap. 19.95 (*1-888608-56-0*) Cool Springs Pr.

Oklahoma "GEO" Bingo! 38 Must Know State Geography Facts for Kids to Learn While Having Fun! Carole Marsh. (Bingo! Ser.). (Illus.). (J). (gr. 2-8). 1998. pap. 14.95 (*0-7933-8631-4*) Gallopade Intl.

Oklahoma Goverment & Politics: An Introduction. 2nd ed. Chris Markwood. 262p. (C). per. write for info. (*0-7872-6724-4*) Kendall-Hunt.

Oklahoma Government! The Cornerstone of Everyday Life in Our State! Carole Marsh. (Carole Marsh Oklahoma Bks.). (Illus.). (J). (gr. 3-12). 1996. pap. 19.95 (*0-7933-6290-3*); lib. bdg. 29.95 (*0-7933-6289-X*); disk 29.95 (*0-7933-6291-1*) Gallopade Intl.

Oklahoma Government & Politics. Chris Markwood. LC 98-134673. 272p. (C). 1998. per. 40.95 (*0-7872-4397-3*, 41439701) Kendall-Hunt.

Oklahoma Governments Performance Standards, 1990. Ed. by Greg Michels. (Governments Performance Standards Ser.). (Illus.). 150p. 1990. text 125.00 (*1-55507-498-7*) Municipal Analysis.

***Oklahoma Health Care in Perspective 2000.** Ed. by Kathleen O'Leary Morgan & Scott E. Morgan. 21p. 2000. spiral bd. 19.00 (*0-7401-0235-4*) Morgan Quitno Corp.

Oklahoma Health Care Perspective, 1998. Ed. by Kathleen O'Leary Morgan & Scott E. Morgan. 20p. 1998. pap. 19.00 (*1-56692-835-4*) Morgan Quitno Corp.

Oklahoma Health Care Perspective, 1999. Kathleen O'Leary Morgan. 21p. 1999. spiral bd. 19.00 (*0-7401-0085-8*) Morgan Quitno Corp.

Oklahoma Heritage. rev. ed. Billie J. English & Sharon C. Calhoun. (Illus.). 433p. 1989. 25.00 (*0-9619496-0-0*) Holt Calhoun Clark & Quaid Pubs.

Oklahoma Herpetology: An Annotated Bibliography. Charles C. Carpenter & James J. Krupa. LC 88-38318. (Oklahoma Museum of Natural History Publication Ser.). 272p. 1989. 26.95 (*0-8061-2210-2*) U of Okla Pr.

Oklahoma "HISTO" Bingo! 42 Must Know State History Facts for Kids to Learn While Having Fun! Carole Marsh. (Bingo! Ser.). (Illus.). (J). (gr. 2-8). 1998. pap. 14.95 (*0-7933-8632-2*) Gallopade Intl.

Oklahoma Historical Tour Guide. Burnis Argo & Kent Ruth. Ed. by D. Ray Wilson. LC 91-70305. (Illus.). 355p. 1991. 19.95 (*0-916445-34-8*); pap. 15.00 (*0-916445-31-3*) Crossroads Comm.

Oklahoma History! Surprising Secrets about Our State's Founding Mothers, Fathers & Kids! Carole Marsh. (Carole Marsh Oklahoma Bks.). (Illus.). (J). (gr. 3-12). 1996. pap. 19.95 (*0-7933-6137-0*); lib. bdg. 29.95 (*0-7933-6136-2*); disk 29.95 (*0-7933-6138-9*) Gallopade Intl.

Oklahoma Hot Air Balloon Mystery. Carole Marsh. (Carole Marsh Oklahoma Bks.). (Illus.). (J). (gr. 2-9). 1994. 29.95 (*0-7933-2642-7*); pap. 19.95 (*0-7933-2643-5*); disk 29.95 (*0-7933-2644-3*) Gallopade Intl.

Oklahoma Hot Zones! Viruses, Diseases, & Epidemics in Our State's History. Carole Marsh. (Hot Zones! Ser.). (Illus.). (J). (gr. 3-12). 1998. pap. 19.95 (*0-7933-8937-2*); lib. bdg. 29.95 (*0-7933-8936-4*) Gallopade Intl.

Oklahoma I Had Never Seen Before: Alternative Views of Oklahoma History. Davis Joyce. LC 93-27247. (Illus.). 384p. 1998. pap. 14.95 (*0-8061-2945-X*) U of Okla Pr.

Oklahoma I Had Never Seen Before: Alternative Views of Oklahoma History. Ed. by David D. Joyce. LC 93-27247. 384p. 1994. 29.95 (*0-8061-2599-3*) U of Okla Pr.

Oklahoma in Perspective, 1998. Ed. by Kathleen O'Leary Morgan & Scott E. Morgan. 24p. 1998. pap. 19.00 (*1-56692-885-0*) Morgan Quitno Corp.

Oklahoma in Perspective, 1999. Ed. by Kathleen O'Leary Morgan. 26p. 1999. spiral bd. 19.00 (*1-56692-985-7*) Morgan Quitno Corp.

***Oklahoma in Perspective 2000.** Ed. by Kathleen O'Leary Morgan & Scott E. Morgan. 26p. 2000. spiral bd. 19.00 (*0-7401-0285-0*) Morgan Quitno Corp.

Oklahoma Indian Artifacts. Robert E. Bell. Ed. by J. K. Greer et al. (Contributions from the Stovall Museum, University of Oklahoma Ser.: No. 4). (Illus.). 114p. (C). 1980. pap. text 6.00 (*1-881346-02-1*) Univ OK Archeol.

Oklahoma Indian Dictionary for Kids! Carole Marsh. (Carole Marsh State Bks.). (J). (gr. 2-9). 1996. 29.95 (*0-7933-7752-8*, C Marsh); pap. 19.95 (*0-7933-7753-6*, C Marsh) Gallopade Intl.

Oklahoma Indian Markings. Ed. by Francine Ringold. 160p. 1989. 6.95 (*0-685-45300-6*) Art & Human Council Tulsa.

***Oklahoma Investment & Business Guide: Business, Investment, Export-Import Opportunities, 50, 36.** Global Investment Center, USA Staff. (U. S. Regional Investment & Business Library-99: Vol. 36). (Illus.). 350p. (Orig.). 1999. pap. 59.95 (*0-7397-1135-0*) Intl Business Pubns.

***Oklahoma Jeopardy.** Carole Marsh. (Oklahoma Experience! Ser.). (Illus.). (J). (gr. 2-6). 2000. pap. 7.95 (*0-7933-9596-8*) Gallopade Intl.

Oklahoma Jeopardy! Answers & Questions about Our State! Carole Marsh. (Carole Marsh Oklahoma Bks.). (Illus.). (J). (gr. 3-12). 1994. pap. 19.95 (*0-7933-4188-4*); lib. bdg. 29.95 (*0-7933-4187-6*); disk 29.95 (*0-7933-4189-2*) Gallopade Intl.

***Oklahoma Jography.** Carole Marsh. (Oklahoma Experience! Ser.). (Illus.). (J). (gr. 2-6). 2000. pap. 7.95 (*0-7933-9597-6*) Gallopade Intl.

Oklahoma "Jography" A Fun Run Thru Our State! Carole Marsh. (Carole Marsh Oklahoma Bks.). (Illus.). (J). 1994. pap. 19.95 (*1-55609-086-2*); lib. bdg. 29.95 (*0-7933-1858-0*); disk 29.95 (*0-7933-1859-9*) Gallopade Intl.

Oklahoma Justice: A Century of Gunfighters, Gangsters & Terrorists. Ron Owens. LC 95-62081. 336p. 1995. 29.95 (*1-56311-280-9*) Turner Pub KY.

Oklahoma Kid. Boen Hallum. (Illus.). 114p. 1982. pap. 5.50 (*0-685-07912-0*) B Hallum.

Oklahoma Kid's Cookbook: Recipes, How-To, History, Lore & More! Carole Marsh. (Carole Marsh Oklahoma Bks.). (Illus.). (J). 1994. pap. 19.95 (*0-7933-0925-5*); lib. bdg. 29.95 (*0-7933-0926-3*); disk 29.95 (*0-7933-0927-1*) Gallopade Intl.

Oklahoma Land Rush. Compiled by Sidney Theil. 39.00 (*1-56696-046-0*) Jackdaw.

Oklahoma Land Surveying Law: Questions & Answers. John E. Keen. 87p. (C). 1995. pap. text 25.00 (*1-56569-038-9*) Land Survey.

***Oklahoma Legislative Directory, 2001-02, Vol. 48.** Ed. by Jennifer Gilliland. 2000. spiral bd. 75.00 (*1-929876-02-5*) Oklahoma Pr.

Oklahoma Library Book: A Surprising Guide to the Unusual Special Collections in Libraries Across Our State for Students, Teachers, Writers & Publishers - Includes Reproducible Mailing Labels Plus Activities for Young People! Carole Marsh. (Carole Marsh Oklahoma Bks.). (Illus.). 1994. pap. 19.95 (*0-7933-3114-5*); lib. bdg. 29.95 (*0-7933-3113-7*); disk 29.95 (*0-7933-3115-3*) Gallopade Intl.

Oklahoma Limited Liability Company Forms & Practice Manual. Richard D. Craig et al. LC 99-42622. 440p. 1999. ring bd. 219.90 (*1-57400-027-6*) Data Trace Pubng.

Oklahoma Mammalogy: An Annotated Bibliography & Checklist. Robert D. Owen & Gary D. Schnell. LC 88-27959. (Oklahoma Museum of Natural History Publications). 240p. 1989. 28.95 (*0-8061-2185-8*) U of Okla Pr.

Oklahoma Manufacturers Register. 8th rev. ed. Ed. by Frank Lambing. 1998. 75.00 (*1-58202-064-7*) Manufacturers.

Oklahoma Math! How It All Adds up in Our State. Carole Marsh. (Carole Marsh Oklahoma Bks.). (Illus.). (YA). (gr. 3-12). 1996. pap. 19.95 (*0-7933-6596-1*); lib. bdg. 29.95 (*0-7933-6595-3*) Gallopade Intl.

Oklahoma Media Book: A Surprising Guide to the Amazing Print, Broadcast & Online Media of Our State for Students, Teachers, Writers & Publishers - Includes Reproducible Mailing Labels Plus Activities for Young People! Carole Marsh. (Carole Marsh Oklahoma Bks.). (Illus.). 1994. pap. 19.95 (*0-7933-3270-2*); lib. bdg. 29.95 (*0-7933-3269-9*); disk 29.95 (*0-7933-3271-0*) Gallopade Intl.

***Oklahoma Media Guide, 2000.** Ed. by Jennifer Gilliland. 124p. 2000. spiral bd. 25.00 (*1-929876-00-9*) Oklahoma Pr.

Oklahoma Memorial, Clair Engle Lake, & Marjory Stoneman Douglas Wilderness: Hearing Before the Subcommittee on National Parks, Historic Preservation, & Recreation of the Committee on Energy & Natural Resources, United States Senate, One Hundred Fifth Congress, First Session on S. 871 ... S. 895 ... S. 931 ... July 17, 1997. United States Staff. LC 98-114854. (S. Hrg. Ser.). iii, 15 p. 1997. write for info. (*0-16-055738-0*) USGPO.

Oklahoma Mystery Van Takes Off! Bk. 1: Handicapped Oklahoma Kids Sneak off on a Big Adventure. Carole Marsh. (Oklahoma Bks.). (Illus.). (J). (gr. 3-12). 1994. 29.95 (*0-7933-5069-7*); pap. 19.95 (*0-7933-5070-0*); disk 29.95 (*0-7933-5071-9*) Gallopade Intl.

Oklahoma Notes: Internal Medicine. Dala R. Jarolim. LC 92-48925. 241p. 1993. 16.95 (*0-387-97960-3*) Spr-Verlag.

Oklahoma Notes: Pediatrics. A. E. Osburn. LC 92-49140. 280p. 1993. write for info. (*3-540-97955-7*) Spr-Verlag.

Oklahoma Notes: Pediatrics. A. E. Osburn. LC 92-49140. 280p. 1993. 16.95 (*0-387-97955-7*) Spr-Verlag.

Oklahoma Notes: Study Skills & Test-Taking Strategies for Medical Students. 2nd ed. Deborah D. Shain. LC 95-18354. (Oklahoma Notes Ser.). (Illus.). 204p. 1995. 17.95 (*0-387-94396-X*) Spr-Verlag.

***Oklahoma Open Meeting & Open Records Book.** 10th rev. ed. Ed. by Jennifer Gilliland. 76p. 1999. spiral bd. 10.00 (*1-929876-01-7*) Oklahoma Pr.

Oklahoma Ornithology: An Annotated Bibliography. Joseph A. Grzybowski & Gary D. Schnell. LC 83-40327. (Stovall Museum Publications: Vol. 5). 176p. 1984. 24.95 (*0-8061-1812-1*) U of Okla Pr.

***Oklahoma Outlaw Tales.** David A. Farris. (Illus.). 118p. 1999. pap. 12.95 (*0-9646922-1-X*, Pub. by D A Farris) Herveys Bklink.

Oklahoma Place Names. George H. Shirk. LC 65-14803. (Illus.). 288p. 1987. reprint ed. pap. 14.95 (*0-8061-2028-2*) U of Okla Pr.

Oklahoma Politics & Policies: Governing the Sooner State. David R. Morgan et al. LC 90-13044. (Politics & Governments of the American States Ser.). xxviii, 264p. 1991. pap. text 25.00 (*0-8032-8136-6*) U of Nebr Pr.

Oklahoma Politics & Policies: Governing the Sooner State. David R. Morgan et al. LC 90-13044. (Politics & Governments of the American States Ser.). xxviii, 264p. 1991. text 45.00 (*0-8032-3106-7*) U of Nebr Pr.

Oklahoma Populism: A History of the People's Party in the Oklahoma Territory. Worth R. Miller. LC 87-40214. (Illus.). 304p. 1987. 29.95 (*0-8061-2072-X*) U of Okla Pr.

Oklahoma Pride. large type ed. Dana Fuller Ross. (General Ser.). 1991. lib. bdg. 20.95 (*0-8161-5101-6*, G K Hall Lrg Type) Mac Lib Ref.

Oklahoma Quiz Bowl Crash Course! Carole Marsh. (Carole Marsh Oklahoma Bks.). (Illus.). (J). 1994. pap. 19.95 (*0-7933-1882-3*); lib. bdg. 29.95 (*0-7933-1881-5*); disk 29.95 (*0-7933-1883-1*) Gallopade Intl.

Oklahoma Real Estate Forms, 3 vols. C. Temple Bixler & Alan C. Durbin. 1994. ring bd., suppl. ed. 89.00 (*0-685-74602-X*, MICHIE) LEXIS Pub.

Oklahoma Real Estate Forms, 3 vols., Issue 11. Bixler & Durbin. 151p. 1998. ring bd. write for info. (*0-327-00588-2*, 8225214) LEXIS Pub.

Oklahoma Real Estate Forms, 3 vols., Set. C. Temple Bixler & Alan C. Durbin. 1390p. 1994. spiral bd. 309.00 (*0-87189-978-7*, 82247-10, MICHIE) LEXIS Pub.

Oklahoma Recipe Roundup. Oklahoma Future Homemakers of America Staff. LC 92-20293. 1992. pap. write for info. (*0-87197-340-5*) Favorite Recipes.

***Oklahoma Related Regulations.** NILS Publishing Company. LC 97-76152. 1999. write for info. (*0-89246-492-5*) NILS Pub.

Oklahoma Renegades: Their Deeds & Misdeeds. Ken Butler. LC 96-44302. (Illus.). 160p. 1997. pap. 10.95 (*1-56554-231-2*) Pelican.

Oklahoma Rollercoasters! Carole Marsh. (Oklahoma Bks.). (Illus.). (YA). (gr. 3-12). 1994. pap. 19.95 (*0-7933-5333-5*); lib. bdg. 29.95 (*0-7933-5332-7*); disk 29.95 (*0-7933-5334-3*) Gallopade Intl.

Oklahoma School Trivia: An Amazing & Fascinating Look at Our State's Teachers, Schools & Students! Carole Marsh. (Carole Marsh Oklahoma Bks.). (Illus.). (J). 1994. pap. 19.95 (*0-7933-0922-0*); lib. bdg. 29.95 (*0-7933-0923-9*); disk 29.95 (*0-7933-0924-7*) Gallopade Intl.

Oklahoma Seminoles: Medicines, Magic & Religion. James H. Howard & Willie Lena. LC 83-40328. (Civilization of the American Indian Ser.: Vol. 166). (Illus.). 300p. 1990. pap. 12.95 (*0-8061-2238-2*) U of Okla Pr.

Oklahoma Silly Basketball Sportsmysteries, Vol. 1. Carole Marsh. (Carole Marsh Oklahoma Bks.). (Illus.). (J). 1994. pap. 19.95 (*0-7933-0919-0*); lib. bdg. 29.95 (*0-7933-0920-4*); disk 29.95 (*0-7933-0921-2*) Gallopade Intl.

Oklahoma Silly Basketball Sportsmysteries, Vol. 2. Carole Marsh. (Carole Marsh Oklahoma Bks.). (Illus.). (J). 1994. pap. 19.95 (*0-7933-1885-8*); lib. bdg. 29.95 (*0-7933-1884-X*); disk 29.95 (*0-7933-1886-6*) Gallopade Intl.

Oklahoma Silly Football Sportsmysteries, Vol. 1. Carole Marsh. (Carole Marsh Oklahoma Bks.). (Illus.). (J). 1994. pap. 19.95 (*0-7933-1864-5*); lib. bdg. 29.95 (*0-7933-1863-7*); disk 29.95 (*0-7933-1865-3*) Gallopade Intl.

Oklahoma Silly Football Sportsmysteries, Vol. 2. Carole Marsh. (Carole Marsh Oklahoma Bks.). (Illus.). (J). 1994. pap. 19.95 (*0-7933-1867-X*); lib. bdg. 29.95 (*0-7933-1866-1*); disk 29.95 (*0-7933-1868-8*) Gallopade Intl.

Oklahoma Silly Trivia! Carole Marsh. (Carole Marsh Oklahoma Bks.). (Illus.). (J). 1994. pap. 19.95 (*1-55609-082-X*); disk 29.95 (*0-7933-1857-2*) Gallopade Intl.

Oklahoma Silly Trivia! Carole Marsh. (Carole Marsh Oklahoma Bks.). (J). 1997. lib. bdg. 29.95 (*0-7933-1856-4*) Gallopade Intl.

Oklahoma Spelling Bee! Score Big by Correctly Spelling Our State's Unique Names. Carole Marsh. (Carole Marsh Oklahoma Bks.). (Illus.). (YA). (gr. 3-12). 1996. pap. 19.95 (*0-7933-6749-2*); lib. bdg. 29.95 (*0-7933-6748-4*) Gallopade Intl.

***Oklahoma State Constitution: A Reference Guide.** Danny M. Adkison & Lisa McNair Palmer. (Reference Guides to the State Constitutions of the United States Ser.: Vol. 32). 494p. 2000. lib. bdg. 138.00 (*0-313-27507-6*, AOS) Greenwood.

***Oklahoma State Credit Directory, 2000 Edition.** rev. ed. American Business Directories Staff. 1999. boxed set 145.00 incl. cd-rom (*0-7687-0317-4*) Am Busn Direct.

Oklahoma State Plan for the Prevention of Child Abuse: 1990 Review. (Illus.). 100p. (Orig.). (C). 1993. pap. text 25.00 (*0-7881-0173-0*) DIANE Pub.

Oklahoma State University: History-Making Basketball. Mike McKenzie. Ed. by Missouri Editing Group Staff & Kelly Anderson. (Illus.). 1992. write for info. (*1-56166-049-3*) Walsworth Pub.

Oklahoma Statutes Annotated. write for info. (*0-318-57500-0*) West Pub.

Oklahoma Story. Arrell M. Gibson. LC 77-18608. (Illus.). 262p. 1978. 24.95 (*0-8061-1461-4*) U of Okla Pr.

Oklahoma Story. Barbara Schindler. vi, 70p. 1982. pap., teacher ed. 3.95 (*0-8061-1772-9*) U of Okla Pr.

Oklahoma Supplement see American Slave: A Composite Autobiography, Supplement Series 1

Oklahoma Survival. Betty L. Hall & Mary L. Brown. 160p. (Orig.). (gr. 10-12). 1979. pap. text 5.84 (*0-03-051191-7*) Westwood Pr.

Oklahoma Symbols Coloring Book. Illus. by Phillip R. Buntin. 16p. (J). (ps up). 1997. pap. 2.95 (*1-882404-10-6*) KS Herit Ctr.

Oklahoma Timeline: A Chronology of Oklahoma History, Mystery, Trivia, Legend, Lore & More. Carole Marsh. (Oklahoma Bks.). (Illus.). (J). (gr. 3-12). 1994. pap. 19.95 (*0-7933-5984-8*); lib. bdg. 29.95 (*0-7933-5983-X*); disk 29.95 (*0-7933-5985-6*) Gallopade Intl.

Oklahoma Town. George Milburn. LC 72-134969. (Short Story Index Reprint Ser.). 1977. 15.95 (*0-8369-3700-7*) Ayer.

Oklahoma Travel Handbook. Kent Ruth. LC 76-62517. (Illus.). 1979. pap. 14.95 (*0-8061-1539-4*) U of Okla Pr.

Oklahoma Treasure Trails: Adventure Fun Pack. Thurman Hardin et al. (J). (gr. 3 up). 1993. 14.95 incl. audio (*0-9638173-0-2*) MythicMedia.

O

An Asterisk (*) at the beginning of an entry indicates that the title is appearing for the first time.

Oklahoma Treasures & Treasure Tales. Steve Wilson. LC 74-15912. (Illus.). 344p. 1989. pap. 22.95 (*0-8061-2174-2*) U of Okla Pr.

Oklahoma Tribal Court Reports, Vol. 1. Ed. by Dennis W. Arrow. 612p. 1994. 75.00 (*0-9641790-0-8*) OCU Native Amer.

Oklahoma Tribal Court Reports, Vol. 2. Ed. & Pref. by Dennis W. Arrow. 584p. 1995. 75.00 (*0-9641790-1-6*) OCU Native Amer.

Oklahoma Tribal Court Reports, Vol. 3. Dennis W. Arrow. 1996. 75.00 (*0-9641790-2-4*) OCU Native Amer.

Oklahoma Trivia. Ernie Couch. LC 99-13904. 192p. 1999. pap. 6.95 (*1-55853-732-5*) Rutledge Hill Pr.

Oklahoma II. Photos by David Fitzgerald. LC 94-77262. (Illus.). 144p. 1994. 39.95 (*1-55868-198-1*) Gr Arts Ctr Pub.

Oklahoma 2000! Coming Soon to a Calendar Near You - The 21st Century! - Complete Set of AL 2000 Items. Carole Marsh. (Two Thousand! Ser.). (Illus.). (J). (gr. 3-12). 1998. pap. 75.00 (*0-7933-9381-7*); lib. bdg. 85.00 (*0-7933-9382-5*) Gallopade Intl.

Oklahoma 2000! Coming Soon to a Calendar near You-The 21st Century! Carole Marsh. (Two Thousand! Ser.). (Illus.). (J). (gr. 3-12). 1998. pap. 19.95 (*0-7933-8784-1*); lib. bdg. 29.95 (*0-7933-8783-3*) Gallopade Intl.

Oklahoma UFO's & Extraterrestrials! A Look at the Sightings & Science in Our State. Carole Marsh. (Carole Marsh Oklahoma Bks.). (Illus.). (J). (gr. 3-12). 1997. pap. 19.95 (*0-7933-6443-4*); lib. bdg. 29.95 (*0-7933-6442-6*) Gallopade Intl.

Oklahoma Voter: Politics, Elections, & Political Parties in the Sooner State. Samuel A. Kirkpatrick et al. (Illus.). 1978. pap. 12.95 (*0-8061-1498-3*) U of Okla Pr.

Oklahoma vs. Texas: When Football Becomes War. Robert Heard. LC 80-82909. (Illus.). 544p. 1980. 25.00 (*0-937642-00-2*) Honey Hill.

Oklahoma Watchable Wildlife Viewing Guide, 2 vols. Oklahoma Department of Wildlife Conservation Staff. 84p. 1993. pap. 7.95 (*0-614-06141-5*) Falcon Pub Inc.

Oklahoma Wildflowers. Doyle McCoy. (Illus.). 206p. 1987. 19.95 (*0-9619985-0-4*); pap. 16.95 (*0-9619985-1-2*) McCoy Pub Co.

Oklahoma Wills & Interstate Succession. Nancy Kenderdine. 270p. 1987. ring bd. 105.00 (*0-327-00950-0*, 82257, MICHIE) LEXIS Pub.

Oklahoma Wills & Interstate Succession, 1987-1989. Nancy I. Kenderdine. 270p. Date not set. ring bd. 105.00 (*0-409-25173-9*, 82257, MICHIE) LEXIS Pub.

Oklahoma Wills & Interstate Succession, 1987-1989. Nancy I. Kenderdine. 270p. 1993. suppl. ed. 45.00 (*0-250-42971-3*, MICHIE) LEXIS Pub.

***Oklahoma's Big Activity Book.** Carole Marsh. (Oklahoma Experience! Ser.). (Illus.). (J). (gr. k-5). 2000. pap. 9.95 (*0-7933-9598-4*) Gallopade Intl.

Oklahoma's Depression Radicals: Ira M. Finley & the Veterans of Industry of America. Patrick E. McGinnis. LC 90-19401. (Recent American History Ser.: Vol. 3). VI, 196p. (C). 1991. text 36.95 (*0-8204-1295-3*) P Lang Pubng.

Oklahoma's First Ladies. Lu C. Wise. LC 83-82947. (Illus.). 88p. (J). (gr. 5-12). 1984. 14.95 (*0-934188-10-6*) Evans Pubns.

Oklahoma's Forest Products Industry: Performance & Contribution to the State's Economy, 1970 to 1980. Wilbur R. Maki et al. (Illus.). 30p. 1988. reprint ed. pap. 4.00 (*0-89904-933-8*, Ecosytems Resrch) Crumb Elbow Pub.

Oklahoma's (Most Devastating!) Disasters & (Most Calamitous!) Catastrophies! Carole Marsh. (Oklahoma Bks.). (Illus.). (J). 1994. pap. 19.95 (*0-7933-0910-7*); lib. bdg. 29.95 (*0-7933-0911-5*); disk 29.95 (*0-7933-0912-3*) Gallopade Intl.

Oklahoma's Unsolved Mysteries (And Their "Solutions") Includes Scientific Information & Other Activities for Students. Carole Marsh. (Oklahoma Bks.). (Illus.). (J). (gr. 3-12). 1994. pap. 19.95 (*0-7933-5831-0*); lib. bdg. 29.95 (*0-7933-5830-2*); disk 29.95 (*0-7933-5832-9*) Gallopade Intl.

Oklahombres. Robert Kammen. 1991. mass mkt. 3.50 (*0-8217-3594-2*, Zebra Kensgtn) Kensgtn Pub Corp.

Oklahombres, Particularly the Wilder Ones. Evett D. Nix. LC 92-37966. xxxiv, 316p. 1993. pap. 12.95 (*0-8032-8366-0*, Bison Books) U of Nebr Pr.

Oklahombres Revisited: The Gunpowder Meredian. Thomas R. Holland. 256p. 1993. pap. 14.50 (*0-9638622-0-0*) T R Holland.

Okno V Ianvare: Stikhi, 1984-1994. Denis G. Novikov. LC 95-1982. (RUS.). 102p. 1995. pap. 8.50 (*1-55779-082-5*) Hermitage Pubs.

***Oko-Audit: Drei Europaische Produktionsstandorte Der Daimler-Benz Ag Im Vergleich.** Erika Voigt. (Illus.). 358p. 1999. 56.95 (*3-631-34303-5*) P Lang Pubng.

Okoboji Wetlands: A Lesson in Natural History. Michael J. Lannoo. LC 95-43617. (Bur Oak Original Ser.). (Illus.). 190p. 1996. pap. 14.95 (*0-87745-533-3*); text 29.95 (*0-87745-532-5*) U of Iowa Pr.

O'kohome: The Coyote Dog. Hap Gilliland. (Beginning Reading for All Ages Ser.). (Illus.). 47p. (Orig.). (J). (gr. 4-10). 1989. pap. 5.95 (*0-89992-102-7*) Coun India Ed.

***Okologie der Gewasserbegleitenden Agriophyten Angelica Archangelica Ssp. Litoralis, Bidens Frondosa und Rorippa Austriaca im Ruhrgebiet, Band 321.** Peter Keil. (Illus.). 186p. 1999. 65.00 (*3-443-64233-0*, Pub. by Gebruder Borntraeger) Balogh.

Okologie in Zahlen (Ecology by Numbers) Dietmar Kalusche. (Illus.). 415p. 1996. pap. 49.00 (*3-437-20521-8*) Gustav Fischer.

***Okologie und Literatur.** Ed. by Peter Morris-Keitel & Michael Niedermeier. (German Life & Civilization Ser.: Vol. 33). (GER.). 224p. (C). 2000. 49.95 (*0-8204-4872-9*) P Lang Pubng.

Okologiegerichtete Wertschopfung in Industrieunternehmungen: Industrielle Produktion im Spannungsfeld Zwischen Markterfolg & Naturbewahrung. Uwe Schmid. (GER., Illus.). 292p. 1996. 54.95 (*3-631-30857-4*) P Lang Pubng.

Okologieorientierte Profilierung im Vertikalen Marketing: Dargestellt am Beispiel der Elektrobranche. Michael H. Ceyp. (GER., Illus.). XXII, 284p. 1996. 57.95 (*3-631-30996-1*) P Lang Pubng.

Okologieorientiertes Handelsmarketing: Grundlegungen, Konzeptuale Ausformungen und Empirische Einsichten. Stephan Kull. Ed. by Ursula Hansen. (Markt und Konsum Ser.: Vol. 6). 479p. 1998. pap. 73.95 (*3-631-33067-7*) P Lang Pubng.

***Okologisch-Orientierte Unternehmensberichterstattung: Ein Instrument Zur Unterstutzung des Umweltschutzmanagements Und Zur Publizitat Betrieblicher Umweltauswirentriungen.** Norbert Hoffmann. (Illus.). XX, 236p. 1999. 48.95 (*3-631-34669-7*) P Lang Pubng.

***Okologische und Okonomische Bewertung von Agrarumweltprogrammen: Delphi-Studie, Kosten-Wirksamkeits-Analyse und Nutzen-Kosten-Betrachtung.** Jurgen Wilhelm. (Europaische Hochschulschriften Ser.: Bd. 2542). 284p. 1999. 48.95 (*3-631-35593-9*) P Lang Pubng.

Okonometrische Bestimmung der Lebensmittel- und Nahrstoffzufuhr von Personen Anhand des Lebensmittelverbrauchs von Haushalten. Kurt Gedrich. (Studien zur Haushaltsokonomie: Bd. 13). (GER., Illus.). 226p. 1996. pap. 44.95 (*3-631-31031-5*) P Lang Pubng.

Okonomie der Wehrpflicht: Eine Analyse unter Besonderer Berucksichtigung der Grundsatze der Besteuerung. Michael Schleicher. (GER., Illus.). 155p. 1996. 35.95 (*3-631-30951-1*) P Lang Pubng.

Okonomie M(m)acht Angst: Zum Verhaltnis von Okonomie und Religion. Ed. by Ursula M. Ernst et al. (Frauen, Forschung und Wirtschaft Ser.: Bd. 7). (GER., Illus.). 261p. 1997. 51.95 (*3-631-31945-2*) P Lang Pubng.

Okonomische Theorie der Nebenhaushalte: Am Beispiel des Fonds "Deutsche Einheit" In-Suk Kim. (GER., Illus.). XVI, 105p. 1996. 32.95 (*3-631-30998-8*) P Lang Pubng.

Okonomische Weltbild: Beitrage zu einer Neuen Politischen Okonomie. Ed. by Peter Bernholz & Gerard Radnitzky. (International Carl Menger Library). (GER.). 350p. (C). 1991. 59.00 (*3-88405-072-9*) Philosophia Pr.

Okophysiologie der Pflanzen see Physiological Plant Ecology: Ecophysiology & Stress Physiology of Function Groups

***Okotrophologie - Wissenschaft Fur die Menschen.** Georg Karg & Gunter Wolfram. (Illus.). 323p. 1999. 56.95 (*3-631-33626-8*) P Lang Pubng.

***Okra Soup: A Soulful Dish of Reasoning & Poetry.** Gwendolyn Bobo. vii, 166p. 1999. pap. 9.95 (*0-9675627-0-8*, 010991) Bobo.

Oksana: My Own Story. Oksana Baiul & Heather Alexander. LC 96-69537. 1997. 16.99 (*0-679-88382-7*) Random.

Oksana Baiul. Lonnie H. DuPont. LC 98-21901. (Female Figure Skating Legends Ser.). (Illus.). 64p. (J). (gr. 2 up). 1998. lib. bdg. 16.95 (*0-7910-4201-4*) Chelsea Hse.

Oksana Baiul: Rhapsody on Ice. Linda Shaughnessy. LC 96-25083. (Figure Skaters Ser.). 1997. pap. 6.95 (*0-382-39449-6*, Crstwood Hse); lib. bdg. 18.95 (*0-382-39448-8*, Crstwood Hse) Silver Burdett Pr.

Oksana's Dream, 3 vols. Mem. of Oksana Baiul. (J). 1997. write for info. (*0-614-29289-1*) Random Bks Yng Read.

Oksforder Yidish: A Yearbook of Yiddish Studies II, Vol. 2. Ed. by David Katz. 313p. 1991. text 107.00 (*3-7186-5206-4*, Harwood Acad Pubs) Gordon & Breach.

Oktoberfest. (Easy Reader Ser.: Level 1). 32p. 1995. 5.25 (*3-468-49691-5*) Langenscheidt.

Oktoberfest. Patrick Jaros et al. (Evergreen Ser.). 1998. spiral bd. 14.99 (*3-8228-7631-3*) Taschen Amer.

Oktoberfest, Vienna, Marzen. George Fix & Laurie Fix. (Classic Beer Style Ser.). (Illus.). 117p. 1992. pap. 11.95 (*0-937381-27-6*) Brewers Pubns.

Oktojikh see Tserkovno-Pjevcheskiji Sbornik

Oku-no-Hosomichi see Back Roads to Far Towns: Basho's Oku-no-Hosomichi

Okubo Diary: Portrait of a Japanese Valley. Brian Moeran. 272p. 1985. pap. 12.95 (*0-8047-1521-1*) Stanford U Pr.

OKW (Oberkommando der Wehrmacht) War Diary Series see World War II German Military Studies

Okyo Book. Ed. by Abbot D. Hosokawa. 38p. 1988. pap. 3.00 (*1-877982-01-6*) Daihonzan Chozen-ji.

Ol' Blue Eyes: A Frank Sinatra Encyclopedia. Leonard Mustazza. LC 97-33017. 480p. 1998. lib. bdg. 59.95 (*0-313-30486-6*, Greenwood Pr) Greenwood.

***Ol' Bug Eye Fly.** Debbie McPherson. 60p. (J). (gr. 1-4). 2000. pap. 8.99 (*1-57532-268-4*) Press-Tige Pub.

Ol' Chef's Favorite Recipes. George G. Atcheson. (Illus.). 130p. (Orig.). 1989. spiral bd. 9.75 (*0-9624683-0-4*) Tillamook Pub.

Ol' Coach on the Banquet Circuit. Ray Franks. (Illus.). 80p. 1984. pap. 7.95 (*0-943976-01-4*) R Franks Ranch.

Ol' Cookbook. Dott McGill. (Illus.). 240p. (Orig.). 1992. pap. 13.95 (*0-935069-13-5*) White Oak Pr.

Ol' Hook & Eye: A History of the Kishacoquillas Valley Railroad. John G. Hartzler. (Illus.). 176p. 1988. pap. 16.50 (*0-317-89902-3*) J G Hartzler.

Ol' Lady Grizelda. Justin Matott. LC 99-159840. (Illus.). 36p. (J). (gr. 2-6). 1998. 16.95 (*1-889191-09-4*) Clove Publns.

Ol' Mikes Philosophy & Foolishness. Mike Oatman. (Illus.). 160p. (Orig.). 1993. pap. 14.95 (*0-9638429-0-0*) Hearth KS.

Ol' Mizzou: A Century of Tiger Football. Bob Broeg. Ed. by Missouri Editing Group Staff & Kelly Anderson. (Illus.). 1992. write for info. (*1-56166-028-0*) Walsworth Pub.

Ol or a Machine Called SKEETS. 2nd limited ed. Artemis Smith, pseud. Ed. by Alana Collos et al. 310p. 1991. reprint ed. pap. 200.00 (*1-878998-11-0*) Savant Garde.

Ol or a Machine Called SKEETS, 2 vols., Set. limited ed. Artemis Smith, pseud. Ed. by Alana Collos & Judith Hebert. 330p. 1991. boxed set 1000.00 (*1-878998-16-1*) Savant Garde.

Ol or a Machine Called SKEETS: Gallery Edition. deluxe limited ed. Artemis Smith, pseud. Ed. by Alana Collos & Judith Hebert. 330p. 1991. 2000.00 (*1-878998-10-2*) Savant Garde.

Ol' Paul, the Mighty Logger. Glen Rounds. LC 75-22163. (Illus.). 96p. (J). (gr. 4-6). 1988. pap. 5.95 (*0-8234-0713-6*) Holiday.

Ol' Pete: The Grover Cleveland Alexander Story. Jack Kavanagh. (Illus.). 1996. 22.95 (*1-888698-03-9*) Diamond Communications.

Ol' S. O. B. Sez: Cowboy Limericks. S. Omar Barker. LC 98-23260. (Illus.). 96p. 1998. pap. 9.95 (*1-56044-641-2*) Falcon Pub Inc.

Ol' Sam Payton. Larry Incollingo. 1992. pap. 9.50 (*0-9619795-4-2*) Reunion Bks.

Ol' Strom: An Unauthorized Biography of Strom Thurmond. Jack Bass & Marilyn W. Thompson. LC 98-66360. (Illus.). 272p. 1998. 24.00 (*1-56352-523-2*) Longstreet.

Ola. Albert Wendt. LC 95-7329. 352p. 1995. pap. 16.95 (*0-8248-1585-8*) UH Pr.

Ola Anfenson: Pioneer Photographer. Natasha Boyd. Ed. by Neva N. Harden. LC 97-75055. (Illus.). 84p. 1997. pap. 14.95 (*0-913945-59-5*) Horizon Comms.

Ola Shakes It Up. Joanne Hyppolite. (Illus.). 176p. (J). (gr. 4-7). 1999. pap. 4.50 (*0-440-41204-8*) BDD Bks Young Read.

Ola Shakes It Up. Joanne Hyppolite. LC 97-17718. (Illus.). 176p. (J). (gr. 2-6). 1998. 14.95 (*0-385-32235-6*) Delacorte.

Olacaceae. H. O. Sleumer. LC 84-4831. (Flora Neotropica Monographs: No. 38). (Illus.). 160p. 1984. pap. 26.00 (*0-89327-254-X*) NY Botanical.

Olaf Martens: The Recent Work. Olaf Martens. LC 97-149268. (Illus.). 176p. 1996. 49.95 (*3-908162-40-8*, Pub. by Edit Stemmle) Dist Art Pubs.

Olaf Marten's Photographs. Olaf Martens. (Illus.). 128p. 1994. 45.00 (*3-905514-11-7*, Pub. by Edit Stemmle) Dist Art Pubs.

Olaf Reads Independent Reader 5-Pack, 5 bks., Set. (Networks Ser.). (J). (gr. 1). 1991. pap. 15.00 (*0-88106-734-2*, N148) Charlesbridge Pub.

Olaf Stapledon. John Kinnaird. Ed. by Roger C. Schlobin. LC 84-2656. (Starmont Reader's Guide Ser.: Vol. 21). 107p. 1986. pap. 17.00 (*0-916732-54-1*) Millefleurs.

Olaf Stapledon: A Bibliography, 2. Compiled by Harvery J. Satty & Curtis C. Smith. LC 84-6549. (Bibliographies & Indexes in World Literature Ser.: No. 2). (Illus.). 167p. 1984. lib. bdg. 49.95 (*0-313-24099-X*, SOS/, Greenwood Pr) Greenwood.

Olaf Stapledon: Speaking for the Future. Robert Crossley. (Illus.). 480p. 1994. 45.00 (*0-8156-0281-2*) Syracuse U Pr.

Olaf Stapledon Reader. Ed. by Robert Crossley. LC 96-31975. 352p. 1996. 45.00 (*0-8156-2724-6*, CRPP); pap. 19.95 (*0-8156-0430-0*, CRPPP) Syracuse U Pr.

Olaf the Ship's Cat. Bengt Martin. (Illus.). 32p. (J). (ps-3). 1992. 7.95 (*1-56288-266-X*) Checkerboard.

Olam Gadol Bet - Reader. Abraham Shumsky & Adaia Shumsky. (Olam Gadol Ser.). (Illus.). 1973. pap. 6.00 (*0-8074-0185-4*, 405252) UAHC.

Olam Gadol Bet - Reader. Abraham Shumsky & Adaia Shumsky. (Olam Gadol Ser.). (Illus.). 1973. pap., teacher ed. 5.00 (*0-8074-0187-0*, 205254); pap., wbk. ed. 6.00 (*0-8074-0186-2*, 405253) UAHC.

Olami Sefer Rishon, Bk. 1. rev. ed. Kalman Bachrach. (HEB., Illus.). 59p. (J). (gr. 2). 1943. pap. text 2.00 (*1-878530-14-3*) K Bachrach Co.

Olami Sefer Sheini, Bk. 2. rev. ed. Kalman Bachrach. (HEB., Illus.). 71p. (J). (gr. 3-4). 1950. pap. text 2.00 (*1-878530-15-1*) K Bachrach Co.

Olami Sefer Shlishi, Bk. 3. Kalman Bachrach. (HEB., Illus.). 92p. (J). (gr. 4-6). 1936. pap. text 2.00 (*1-878530-16-X*) K Bachrach Co.

Olancha Remembered. unabridged ed. Wilma R. Olson. Ed. by Mark Olson. LC 97-92709. (Illus.). 180p. 1997. pap. 7.95 (*0-9659709-3-0*) W R Olson.

OLAP Database Design: Delivering on the Promise of the Data Warehouse. Dan Bulos & Sarah Forsman. 400p. 1999. pap. text 49.95 (*1-55860-525-8*, Pub. by Morgan Kaufmann) Harcourt.

***Olap Services Fundamentals.** Train Olap. LC 99-86771. 1999. pap. text 39.99 (*0-7356-0904-7*) Microsoft.

OLAP Solutions: Building Multidimensional Information Systems. Erik Thomsen. LC 96-46688. 608p. 1997. pap., pap. text 54.99 incl. cd-rom (*0-471-14931-4*) Wiley.

Olas. John W. Rudolph. LC 87-80761. (Illus.). 101p. (Orig.). (YA). 1987. pap. 9.00 (*0-941611-09-4*) Shasta San Rafael.

***Olas Wake.** B. J. Stone. LC 99-48325. (Illus.). 96p. (gr. 3-7). 2000. text 15.95 (*0-8050-6157-6*) St Martin.

Olaudah Equiano the Interesting Narrative. abr. ed. Ed. by Wilfred D. Samuels & Crit R. Kilens. 200p. 1998. pap. write for info. incl. audio (*0-9656532-2-6*) University Pub.

O'Laughlin Book. Michael C. O'Laughlin. (Irish Family Histories Ser.). 50p. 1981. 15.00 (*0-940134-17-9*) Irish Genealog.

Olavus Petri & the Ecclesiastical Transformation in Sweden (1521-1552) A Study in the Swedish Reformation. Conrad J. Bergendoff. LC 83-45600. reprint ed. 32.50 (*0-404-19868-6*) AMS Pr.

Olbers Studies: With Three Unpublished Manuscripts by Olbers. Stanley L. Jaki. (History of Astronomy Ser.: Vol. 8). 1990. pap. 28.00 (*0-88126-221-8*) Pachart Pub Hse.

Olbia. J. G. Vinogradov & S. D. Kryzicky. 304p. 1995. 101.50 (*90-04-09677-9*, MNS, 149) Brill Academic Pubs.

***Ol'blue Eyes: A Frank Sinatra Encyclopedia.** Leonard Mustazza. 480p. 1999. pap. 35.00 (*0-275-96758-1*, Praeger Pubs) Greenwood.

***OLC Student Version Living World.** 3rd ed. Johnson. 2002. 12.00 (*0-07-239432-3*, McGrw-H College) McGrw-H Hghr Educ.

Olcott: Descendants of Thomas Olcott, One of the First Settlers of Hartford, Ct. Nathaniel Goodwin. 63p. 1995. reprint ed. pap. 13.00 (*0-8328-4810-7*); reprint ed. lib. bdg. 23.00 (*0-8328-4809-3*) Higginson Bk Co.

Olcu Ve Yoldaki Isiklar see Criteria or Lights of the Way

Old Abbeville: Scenes of the Past of a Town Where Old Time Things Are Not Forgotten. Lowry Ware. LC 92-60197. 260p. 1992. 25.00 (*0-913363-11-1*) SCMAR.

Old Abe the War Eagle: A True Story of the Civil War & Reconstruction. Richard H. Zeitlin. LC 85-26126. (Illus.). 120p. (Orig.). 1986. pap. 9.95 (*0-87020-239-1*, OLAB) State Hist Soc Wis.

Old Aberdeen: An Historical Guide. John Smith. (Illus.). 94p. 1991. pap. 10.25 (*0-08-041406-0*, Pub. by Aberdeen U Pr) Macmillan.

Old Abe's Jokes: Humorous Stories Told of & by Abraham Lincoln. Walbrook D. Swank. LC 96-25806. (Civil War Heritage Ser.: Vol. IX). (Illus.). 100p. 1996. pap. 12.00 (*1-57249-030-6*, Burd St Pr) White Mane Pub.

Old Abe's Jokes, Fresh from Abraham's Bosom. LC 79-91089. (American Humorists Ser.). 1979. reprint ed. lib. bdg. 27.00 (*0-8398-1450-X*) Irvington.

Old Academy on the Hill: A Bicentennial History, 1791-1991. Marie Donahue. LC 92-64437. 224p. 1992. 35.00 (*0-89725-093-1*, 1393) Picton Pr.

***Old Acquaintances.** Frances Anne Bond. 288p. 2000. 26.00 (*0-7278-2289-6*, Pub. by Severn Hse) Chivers N Amer.

Old Adam. Arnold Bennett. LC 74-17296. (Collected Works of Arnold Bennett: Vol. 60). 1977. reprint ed. 33.95 (*0-518-19141-9*) Ayer.

***Old Adam.** unabridged ed. Charles Barron. 32p. 2000. pap. 5.00 (*0-88734-844-0*) Players Pr.

Old Advertising Spirits Glasses. LC 88-91095. (Illus.). 307p. 1988. pap. text 18.50 (*0-9620504-3-1*) B Edmonson.

Old Aeroplanes. David Ogilvy. 1989. pap. 25.00 (*0-7478-0107-X*, Pub. by Shire Pubns) St Mut.

Old Age see Selected Works

Old Age: A Guide for Professional & Lay Careers. W. J. MacLennan. 141p. (C). 1989. pap. 40.00 (*0-7855-6815-8*, Pub. by St Andrew) St Mut.

Old Age: A Guide for Professional & Lay Careers. Tr. by W. J. MacLennan. 141p. (C). 1991. pap. text 50.00 (*86-15-30640-0*, Pub. by St Andrew) St Mut.

Old Age: A Guide for Professional & Lay Careers. W. J. MacLennan. 141p. 1993. pap. 24.00 (*0-7152-0640-0*) St Mut.

***Old Age: Continuity or Change in English Culture.** Pat Thane. LC 99-54442. 544p. 2000. 55.00 (*0-19-820382-9*) OUP.

Old Age: From Antiquity to Postmodernity. Ed. by Paul Johnson & Pat Thane. LC 98-20561. 320p. (C). 1998. 85.00 (*0-415-16464-8*) Routledge.

Old Age: Its Cause & Prevention. Sanford Bennett. 394p. 1996. reprint ed. spiral bd. 26.00 (*0-7873-0092-6*) Hlth Research.

Old Age: Its Compensations & Rewards. A. L. Vischer. LC 79-8698. (Growing Old Ser.). (Illus.). 1980. reprint ed. lib. bdg. 21.95 (*0-405-12809-6*) Ayer.

Old Age: Journey into Simplicity. 4th ed. Helen M. Luke. (Illus.). 112p. 1987. pap. 9.95 (*0-930407-05-9*) Parabola Bks.

Old Age: The Major Involution. Aldred S. Warthin. Ed. by Robert J. Kastenbaum. LC 78-22224. (Aging & Old Age Ser.). (Illus.). 1979. reprint ed. lib. bdg. 19.95 (*0-405-11837-6*) Ayer.

Old Age - A Balance Sheet. Hope L. Cahill. LC 80-54452. (Illus.). 102p. 1981. pap. 3.95 (*0-933174-13-6*) Wide World-Tetra.

Old Age Abuse. Ed. by Mervyn Eastman. (C). 1989. 35.00 (*0-86242-030-X*, Pub. by Age Concern Eng) St Mut.

Old Age Abuse: A New Perspective. 2nd ed. M. Eastman. 272p. 1994. 39.95 (*1-56593-291-9*, 0615) Singular Publishing.

Old Age among Slum Dwellers. Shabeen Ara. (C). 1994. 16.00 (*81-7003-179-6*, Pub. by S Asia Pubs) S Asia.

Old Age among the Ancient Greeks. Bessie E. Richardson. LC 74-93775. (Illus.). reprint ed. 42.50 (*0-404-05289-4*) AMS Pr.

Old Age & Finitude: A Contribution to Psychogerontology. Joep M. Munnichs. Ed. by Leon Stein. LC 79-8676. (Growing Old Ser.). 1980. reprint ed. lib. bdg. 18.95 (*0-405-12792-8*) Ayer.

Old Age & Political Behavior: A Case Study. Frank A. Pinner et al. Ed. by Leon Stein. LC 79-8678. (Growing Old Ser.). (Illus.). 1980. reprint ed. lib. bdg. 35.95 (*0-405-12796-0*) Ayer.

Old Age & the Search for Security: An American Social History. Carole Haber & Brian Gratton. LC 93-12258. (Interdisciplinary Studies in History). 256p. 1994. pap. 15.95 (*0-253-20836-X*) Ind U Pr.

Old Age & Treachery. W. C. Green. 198p. 1995. 18.00 (*0-9645082-0-6*) New Vent Pr.

An Asterisk (*) at the beginning of an entry indicates that the title is appearing for the first time.

Old Age Assistance Reports for Business, Consumers & Health Sciences: Index of New Information. Justin A. Kimberly. 160p. 1997. 47.50 (*0-7883-1694-X*); pap. 44.50 (*0-7883-1695-8*) ABBE Pubs Assn.

Old Age Challenge to the Biomedical Model: Paradigm Strain & Health Policy. Charles Longino & John Murphy. LC 94-30642. (Society & Aging Ser.). 169p. (C). 1995. 28.95 (*0-89503-165-5*) Baywood Pub.

Old Age Comes at a Bad Time: Wit & Wisdom for the Young at Heart. Eliakim Katz. LC 98-226177. 160p. 1998. 11.95 (*0-7737-5929-8*) Stoddart Publ.

Old-Age Crisis: Actuarial Opportunities: The 1996 Bowles Symposium. James C. Hickman et al. (SOA Monograph Ser.: No. M-RS98-1). 1999. pap. text 35.00 (*0-938959-51-4*) Soc Actuaries.

Old Age, Handicapped & Vietnam-Era Antidiscrimination. rev. ed. James P. Northrup. LC 80-53990. (Labor Relations & Public Policy Ser.: No. 14). 280p. reprint ed. pap. 86.80 (*0-608-14865-2*, 202591400047) Bks Demand.

Old Age Homes. Roger Clough. 1981. 60.00 (*0-7855-0583-0*, Pub. by Natl Inst Soc Work) St Mut.

Old Age in Bureaucratic Society: The Elderly, the Experts & the State in American Society, 4. Ed. by David D. Van Tassel & Peter N. Stearns. LC 85-14662. (Contributions to the Study of Aging Ser.: No. 4). (Illus.). 279p. 1986. 57.95 (*0-313-25000-6*, VOA/) Greenwood.

Old Age in Global Perspective. Albert Cattell & Maria Cattell. LC 93-18773. (Reference Ser.). 304p. 1993. 26.95 (*0-8161-7393-1*, Hall Reference); 15.95 (*0-8161-1604-0*, Hall Reference) Macmillan.

Old Age in Greek & Latin Literature. Ed. by Thomas M. Falkner & Judith DeLuce. LC 88-29358. (SUNY Series in Classical Studies). 260p. (C). 1989. pap. text 21.95 (*0-7914-0031-X*) State U NY Pr.

Old Age in Late Medieval England. Joel Thomas Rosenthal. LC 96-14736. (Middle Ages Ser.). 288p. 1996. text 39.95 (*0-8122-3355-7*) U of Pa Pr.

Old Age in Modern Society: A Textbook of Social Gerontology. C. Victor. 288p. 1994. 49.99 (*1-56593-233-1*, 0565) Singular Publishing.

Old Age in Myth & Symbol: A Cultural Dictionary. Jennifer McLerran & Patrick McKee. LC 91-9163. 208p. 1991. lib. bdg. 55.00 (*0-313-27845-8*, MGM, Greenwood Pr) Greenwood.

Old Age in Preindustrial Society. Peter N. Stearns. LC 81-6874. 250p. (C). 1983. 39.95 (*0-8419-0645-9*) Holmes & Meier.

Old Age in Sparta. Ephraim David. ii, 178p. 1991. pap. 42.00 (*90-256-1013-7*, Pub. by AM Hakkert) BookLink Distributors.

Old Age in the Modern World: Report of the Third Congress of the International Association of Gerontology, London. International Association of Gerontology Staff. Ed. by Leon Stein. LC 79-8671. (Growing Old Ser.). 1980. reprint ed. lib. bdg. 63.95 (*0-405-12786-3*) Ayer.

Old Age in the New Age: Irreverent Reflections on Millennial Madness. Arlene Stone. 157p. 1999. pap. 14.95 (*0-9640771-1-6*) Optimist Pr.

Old Age in the New Land: The American Experience since 1790. W. Andrew Achenbaum. LC 77-28666. (Illus.). 251p. reprint ed. pap. 77.90 (*0-8357-4333-0*, 203713300007) Bks Demand.

Old Age in the Old Regime: Image & Experience in Eighteenth-Century France. David Troyansky. LC 88-43286. 288p. 1989. text 42.50 (*0-8014-2299-X*) Cornell U Pr.

Old Age in the Welfare State: The Political Economy of Public Pensions John Myles. LC 83-24923. (Little Brown Series on Gerontology Ser.). xii, 140 p. 1984. write for info. (*0-316-59367-2*) Little.

Old Age in Transition: The Geriatric Ward. Peter Woolfson. LC 96-19120. 152p. 1997. 52.95 (*0-89789-497-9*, Bergin & Garvey) Greenwood.

Old Age Insurance As a Socioethical Responsibility: Nigeria in Transition. Cyprian I. Aginah. Ed. by Richard Friedli et al. (European University Studies, Series 23: Vol. 593). (Illus.). 395p. 1997. pap. 63.95 (*3-631-31382-9*) P Lang Pubng.

Old Age Insurance As a Socioethical Responsibility: Nigeria in Transition. Cyprian I. Aginah. (European University Studies, Series 23: Vol. 593). (Illus.). 395p. 1997. pap. 63.95 (*0-8204-3247-4*) P Lang Pubng.

Old Age Is Another Country: A Traveler's Guide. Page Smith. (Illus.). 226p. 1995. pap. 12.95 (*0-89594-776-5*) Crossing Pr.

Old Age Is Contagious but You Don't Have to Catch It. Eve Blake. 119p. (Orig.). 1986. pap. 8.95 (*0-939171-00-7*) Lee Pub NV.

Old Age Is Not for Sissies. Contrib. by Lois L. Kaufman & Lyn P. Rice. (Pocket Gift Editions Ser.). (Illus.). 64p. 1998. 4.95 (*0-88088-096-1*) Peter Pauper.

Old Age Pensions & Policy Making in Canada. Kenneth Bryden. (Canadian Public Administration Ser.). 288p. 1974. 49.95 (*0-7735-0206-8*, Pub. by McG-Queens Univ Pr); pap. 24.95 (*0-7735-0221-1*, Pub. by McG-Queens Univ Pr) CUP Services.

Old Age Pensions & Policy-Making in Canada. Kenneth Bryden. LC 74-75972. (Canadian Public Administration Ser.). 274p. reprint ed. pap. 85.00 (*0-7837-6931-8*, 204676000003) Bks Demand.

Old Age Poverty in Greenwich Village: A Neighborhood Study. Mabel L. Nassau. Ed. by Leon Stein. LC 79-8696. (Growing Old Ser.). 1980. reprint ed. lib. bdg. 17.95 (*0-405-12793-6*) Ayer.

Old Age Security: Pension Reform in China see China 2020

Old-Age Security in Comparative Perspective. John B. Williamson & Fred C. Pampel. LC 92-17455. 320p. 1993. text 65.00 (*0-19-506859-9*) OUP.

Old Akkadian Inscriptions in Chicago Natural History Museum: Texts of Legal & Business Interest. Ignace J. Gelb. LC 55-3660. (Chicago Natural History Museum, Publication 748, Anthropology Ser.: Vol. 44, No. 2). 181p. 1955. reprint ed. pap. 56.20 (*0-608-03766-4*, 206458900009) Bks Demand.

Old, Alone, & Neglected: Care of the Aged in Scotland & in the United States. Jeanie S. Kayser-Jones. LC 80-19711. (Comparative Studies of Health Systems & Medical Care: Vol. 4). 160p. 1981. pap. 14.95 (*0-520-06961-7*, Pub. by U CA Pr) Cal Prin Full Svc.

Old, Alone, & Neglected: Care of the Aged in Scotland & the United States. Jeanie S. Kayser-Jones. LC 80-19711. (Comparative Studies of Health Systems & Medical Care). 171p. reprint ed. pap. 53.10 (*0-7837-4827-2*, 204447400003) Bks Demand.

***Old American: A Novel.** Ernest Hebert. LC 00-8467. (Hardscrabble Book Ser.). 2000. 24.95 (*1-58465-073-7*) U Pr of New Eng.

Old Americans: A Physiological Profile. Ales Hrdlicka. LC 75-129402. (American Immigration Collection. Series 2). (Illus.). 1970. reprint ed. 26.95 (*0-405-00555-5*) Ayer.

Old & Growing: Conversations, Letters, Observations, & Reflections on Growing Old. Florence E. Vickery. (Illus.). 176p. 1978. pap. 22.95 (*0-398-06473-3*) C C Thomas.

Old & Growing: Conversations, Letters, Observations, & Reflections on Growing Old. fac. ed. Florence E. Vickery. (Illus.). 176p. 1978. 34.95 (*0-398-03804-X*) C C Thomas.

Old & Historic Churches of New Jersey, Vol. 2. Ellis L. Derry. 372p. 1994. 29.95 (*0-937548-25-1*); pap. 19.95 (*0-937548-26-X*) Plexus Pub.

Old & Ill. Ed. by Linda Challis & Helen Bartlett. (C). 1989. 40.00 (*0-86242-059-8*, Pub. by Age Concern Eng) St Mut.

Old & Middle English: An Anthology. Ed. by Elaine Treharne. LC 99-34413. (Anthologies Ser.). 900p. 2000. text 74.95 (*0-631-20465-2*); pap. text 39.95 (*0-631-20466-0*) Blackwell Pubs.

Old & Middle English Literature. 8th ed. Ed. by Jeffrey Helterman & Jerome Mitchell. LC 94-22381. (Dictionary of Literary Biography Ser.: Vol. 146). 549p. 1994. text 155.00 (*0-8103-5707-0*) Gale.

Old & Middle English Texts with Accompanying Textual & Linguistic Apparatus Vol. 12. Ed. by William Vantuono. LC 93-23524. (Berkeley Insights in Linguistics & Semiotics Ser.: Vol. 12). X, 177p. (Orig.). (C). 1995. text 28.95 (*0-8204-2346-7*) P Lang Pubng.

Old & New. Charles H. Grandgent. LC 79-121472. (Essay Index Reprint Ser.). 1977. 19.95 (*0-8369-1809-6*) Ayer.

***Old & New.** Steck-Vaughn Company Staff. (Read All about It Ser.). (Illus.). (J). 2000. pap. 4.95 (*0-8114-3719-1*) Raintree Steck-V.

Old & New Dopamine Agonists in Parkinson's Disease. Ed. by U. Bonuccelli & J. M. Rabey. LC 95-37404. (Journal of Neural Transmission: No. 45). 1995. write for info. (*0-387-82717-X*) Spr-Verlag.

Old & New Dopamine Agonists in Parkinson's Disease. Ed. by U. Bonuccelli & J. M. Rabey. LC 95-37404. (Journal of Neural Transmission: No. 45). 300p. 1996. pap. 105.00 (*3-211-82717-X*) Spr-Verlag.

Old & New Evidence on the Meaning of Life: The Mystical World-View & Inner Contest. J. H. Whiteman. 268p. 1986. 30.00 (*0-86140-241-3*) Dufour.

Old & New Forces of Nature. Ed. by Antonio L. Zichichi. (Subnuclear Ser.: Vol. 23). (Illus.). 390p. 1985. 95.00 (*0-306-43235-8*, Plenum Trade) Perseus Pubng.

***Old & New Frontiers.** Norma Francis. 1999. pap. write for info. (*1-58235-269-0*) Watermrk Pr.

Old & New in Southern Shona, Independent Churches Vol. 1: Background & Rise of the Major Movements. M. L. Daneel. (Change & Continuity in Africa Ser.). 1971. text 56.95 (*90-279-6940-X*) Mouton.

Old & New Masters. Robert Lynd. LC 79-111845. (Essay Index Reprint Ser.). 1977. 20.95 (*0-8369-1616-6*) Ayer.

Old & New Methods in Historical Demography. Ed. by David S. Reher & Roger S. Schofield. LC 93-6635. (Illus.). 440p. (C). 1994. text 75.00 (*0-19-828793-3*, Clarendon Pr) OUP.

Old & New Methods of Initiation. Rudolf Steiner. pap. 24.95 (*0-85440-446-5*, 1454, Pub. by R Steiner Pr) Anthroposophic.

Old & New Monongahela. John S. Van Voorhis. 504p. 1997. reprint ed. pap. 38.50 (*0-8063-0625-4*, 6010, Pub. by Clearfield Co) ACCESS Pubs Network.

Old & New Nobility in Aix-en-Provence, 1600-1695: Portrait of an Urban Elite. Donna Bohanan. LC 92-6707. 200p. (C). 1992. text 30.00 (*0-8071-1624-6*) La State U Pr.

Old & New Poems. Donald Hall. 256p. 1990. pap. 16.00 (*0-89919-954-2*, Pub. by Ticknor & Fields) HM.

***Old & New Prayers for the High Holidays, Shabbat & Festive Occasions.** Illus. by Dov Peretz Elkins. LC 99-91832. 100p. 2000. pap. 15.00 (*0-918834-21-X*) Growth Assoc.

Old & New Problems & Results in Combinatorial Number Theory. P. Erdos et al. 250p. 1998. 39.95 (*0-387-98460-7*) Spr-Verlag.

Old & New Questions in Physics, Cosmology, Philosophy, & Theoretical Biology: Essays in Honor of Wolfgang Yourgrau. Ed. by Alwyn Van Der Merwe. 936p. 1983. 135.00 (*0-306-40962-3*, Plenum Trade) Perseus Pubng.

Old & New Quilt Patterns in the Southern Tradition. Bets Ramsey. LC 87-25182. 132p. 1987. 19.95 (*0-934395-92-6*); pap. 9.95 (*0-934395-63-2*) Rutledge Hill Pr.

Old & New Testaments. Lynn Powell. LC 95-16361. (Brittingham Prize in Poetry Ser.). 82p. 1995. 18.95 (*0-299-14900-5*); pap. 11.95 (*0-299-14904-8*) U of Wis Pr.

Old & New Testaments: Their Relationship & the Intertestamental Literature. James H. Charlesworth & Walter P. Weaver. LC 93-31235. (Faith & Scholarship Colloquies Ser.). 160p. 1993. pap. 14.00 (*1-56338-062-5*) TPI PA.

Old & New Testaments Concluded: Word in the Hellenistic World, Year 4. Denver Catholic Biblical School Staff. (Denver Catholic Biblical School Program Ser.). 224p. (Orig.). 1997. pap., teacher ed. 29.95 (*0-8091-9426-0*, 9426-0); pap., student ed., wbk. ed. 19.95 (*0-8091-9425-2*, 9425-2) Paulist Pr.

Old & New Testaments in Muslim Religious Art. T. W. Arnold. (British Academy, London, Schweich Lectures on Biblical Archaeology Series, 1930). 1974. reprint ed. pap. 25.00 (*0-8115-1270-3*) Periodicals Srv.

Old & New Unsolved Problems in Plane Geometry & Number Theory. Victor Klee & Stan Wagon. LC 91-61591. (Dolciani Mathematical Expositions Ser.). 352p. 1991. pap. text 29.95 (*0-88385-315-9*, DOL-11) Math Assn.

***Old & New Views of Protein Folding.** Kunihiro Kuwajima & Munehito Arai. LC 99-48244. (Excerpta Medica International Congress Ser.). 1999. write for info. (*0-444-50291-2*) Elsevier.

Old & New Westmoreland (County), 4 vols. John N. Boucher. Ed. by Fenwick Y. Hedley. (Illus.). 2617p. 1997. reprint ed. lib. bdg. 236.00 (*0-8328-6461-7*) Higginson Bk Co.

Old & New World Romanticism of Washington Irving. Ed. by Stanley Brodwin. LC 86-3168. 201p. 1986. 52.95 (*0-313-25441-9*, BWG/, Greenwood Pr) Greenwood.

***Old & New Worlds: Historical & Post Medieval Archaeology Papers.** Ed. by Geoff Egan & Ronald L. Michael. (Illus.). 404p. 2000. 60.00 (*1-900188-92-9*, Pub. by Oxbow Bks) David Brown.

Old & Obsolete: Age Discrimination & the American Worker, 1860-1920. Judith C. Hushbeck. (Studies in Historical Demography). 225p. 1989. text 15.00 (*0-8240-3399-X*) Garland.

Old & On Their Own. Coles. (Illus.). 192p. 1999. pap. 19.95 (*0-393-31912-1*) Norton.

Old & on Their Own. Robert Coles. LC 97-36922. (Illus.). 192p. 1998. 27.50 (*0-393-04606-0*) Norton.

Old & Rare: Forty Years in the Book Business. rev. ed. Leona Rostenberg & Madeleine B. Stern. (Illus.). 272p. 1988. reprint ed. pap. 18.00 (*0-929246-00-4*) Modoc Pr.

Old & Rare: Thirty Years in the Book Business. Leona Rostenberg. (American Autobiography Ser.). 234p. 1995. reprint ed. lib. bdg. 79.00 (*0-7812-8632-8*) Rprt Serv.

Old & the New: History of the Post Offices of Wallowa County. Irene Barklow. (Illus.). 184p. (Orig.). (YA). (gr. 8 up). 1987. reprint ed. pap. 14.95 (*0-9618185-1-4*) Enchant Pub Oregon.

Old & the Young. Margiad Evans. LC 99-195827. (Illus.). 160p. 1998. pap. 17.95 (*1-85411-221-X*, Pub. by Seren Bks) Dufour.

Old Angel Midnight. Jack Kerouac. Ed. by Donald Allen. LC 93-14684. xxi, 67p. 1993. pap. 10.00 (*0-912516-97-6*) Grey Fox.

Old Arlington: The Story of the Lee Mansion National Memorial. Murray H. Nelligan. LC F234.A7N45. (Illus.). 480p. 1996. pap. 29.95 (*1-57420-051-8*) Chatelaine.

Old Army: A Portrait of the American Army in Peacetime, 1784-1898. Edward M. Coffman. 536p. (C). 1988. reprint ed. pap. text 27.95 (*0-19-504555-6*) OUP.

Old Army Game. George P. Garrett. LC 94-27048. 344p. (Orig.). 1994. pap. 10.95 (*0-87074-381-3*) SMU Press.

Old Army Game: A Novel & Stories. George P. Garrett. LC 94-27048. 344p. 1994. 22.50 (*0-87074-380-5*) SMU Press.

Old Army in Texas: A Research Guide to the U. S. Army in Nineteenth-Century Texas. Thomas T. Smith. LC 99-49712. (Illus.). 300p. 2000. 29.95 (*0-87611-170-3*) Tex St Hist Assn.

Old Art of Clarino Playing on Trumpets. Hermann L. Eichborn. Tr. by Bryan R. Simms from GER. (Illus.). 1976. pap. text 6.00 (*0-914282-53-0*) Brass Pr.

Old Assyrian Copper Trade in Anatolia. J. G. Dercksen. LC 96-140142. x, 280p. (Orig.). 1996. pap. text 59.50 (*90-6258-076-9*, Pub. by Netherlands Inst) Eisenbrauns.

Old Assyrian Letters & Business Documents. Ferris J. Stephens. LC 78-63525. (Babylonian Inscriptions in the Collection of James B. Nies Ser.: No. 6). reprint ed. 30.00 (*0-404-60136-7*) AMS Pr.

Old Babe. Rick Stromoski. (Illus.). 46p. 1994. write for info. (*1-886386-00-5*) Trisar.

Old Babylonian Account Texts in the Horn Archaeology Museum, Vol. 4. Marcel Sigrist. LC 89-82597. (Assyriological Ser.: AS Vol. 7; AUCT Vol. 4). (Illus.). 144p. (C). 1990. text 39.99 (*0-943872-53-7*) Andrews Univ Pr.

Old Babylonian Archival Texts in the Nies Babylonian Collection. Gary M. Beckman. Ed. by Ulla Kasten. (Catalogue of the Babylonian Collection at Yale: No. 2). viii, 173p. (C). 1995. 48.00 (*1-883053-11-0*) CDL Pr.

Old Babylonian Contracts from Nippur I. Elizabeth C. Stone. 6p. 1976. lib. bdg. 4.50 (*0-226-77551-8*) U Ch Pr.

Old Babylonian Extispicy: Omen Texts in the British Museum. Ulla Jeyes. xii, 219p. 1989. pap. text 42.00 (*90-6258-064-5*, Pub. by Netherlands Inst) Eisenbrauns.

Old Babylonian Legal & Adm. Texts. E. Peters. 1998. 42.95 (*90-6831-063-1*, Pub. by Peeters Pub) Bks Intl VA.

Old Babylonian Letters from Tell Asmar. Robert M. Whiting, Jr. LC 86-61412. (Assyriological Studies: No. 22). (Illus.). xiii, 177p. 1987. pap. 30.00 (*0-918986-47-8*) Orient Inst.

Old Babylonian Omen Texts. Albrecht Goetze. LC 79-3537. (Yale Oriental Series: Babylonian Texts: No. 10). (Illus.). 176p. reprint ed. 42.50 (*0-404-60265-7*) AMS Pr.

Old Babylonian Period (2003-1595 B.C.) Douglas Frayne. (Royal Inscriptions of Mesopotamia Ser.). 888p. 1990. text 195.00 (*0-8020-5873-6*) U of Toronto Pr.

Old Babylonian Public Buildings in the Diyala Region: Pt. 1: Excavations at Ishchali, Pt. 2: Khafajah Mounds B, C, & D. H. D. Hill et al. LC 89-64443. (Oriental Institute Publications: No. 98). (Illus.). xxxvi, 261p. 1990. lib. bdg. 50.00 (*0-918986-62-1*) Orientl Inst Pr.

Old Babylonian Real Estate Documents from Sippar in the British Museum: Documents from the Reign of Hammurabi. L. Dekiere. (Texts Ser.: Series 3, Vol. 2). ix, 343p. 1995. pap. 65.00 (*0-614-96328-1*, Pub. by Recherches et Pubns) Eisenbrauns.

Old Babylonian Real Estate Documents from Sippar in the British Museum: Documents from the Reign of Hammurabi. L. Dekiere. (Texts Ser.: Series 3, Vol. 2, Bk. 2). ix, 343p. 1995. 90.00 (*0-614-96327-3*, Pub. by Recherches et Pubns) Eisenbrauns.

Old Babylonian Real Estate Documents from Sippar in the British Museum: Documents from the Reign of Samsu-Iluna. L. Dekiere. (Texts Ser.: Series 3, Vol. 2, Bk. 3). x, 224p. 1995. 90.00 (*0-614-96329-X*, Pub. by Recherches et Pubns) Eisenbrauns.

Old Babylonian Real Estate Documents from Sippar in the British Museum: Documents from the Reign of Samsu-Iluna. L. Dekiere. (Texts Ser.: Series 3, Vol. 3). x, 224p. 1995. pap. 65.00 (*0-614-96330-3*, Pub. by Recherches et Pubns) Eisenbrauns.

Old Babylonian Real Estate Documents from Sippar in the British Museum: Post-Samsu-Iluna Documents. L. Dekiere. (Texts Ser.: Series 3, Vol. 2, Bk. 4). x, 153p. 1995. 90.00 (*0-614-96331-1*, Pub. by Recherches et Pubns) Eisenbrauns.

Old Babylonian Real Estate Documents from Sippar in the British Museum: Post-Samsu-Iluna Documents. L. Dekiere. (Texts Ser.: Series 3, Vol. 4). x, 153p. 1995. pap. 65.00 (*0-614-96332-X*, Pub. by Recherches et Pubns) Eisenbrauns.

Old Babylonian Real Estate Documents from Sippar in the British Museum: Pre-Hammurabi Documents. L. Dekiere. (Texts Ser.: Series 3, Vol. 1). ix, 293p. 1995. pap. 65.00 (*0-614-96326-5*, Pub. by Recherches et Pubns) Eisenbrauns.

Old Babylonian Real Estate Documents from Sippar in the British Museum: Pre-Hammurabi Documents. L. Dekiere. (Texts Ser.: Series 3, Vol. 2, Bk. 1). ix, 293p. 1995. 90.00 (*0-614-96325-7*, Pub. by Recherches et Pubns) Eisenbrauns.

Old Babylonian Tablets from Ischali & Vicinity. Samuel Greengus. x, 100p. 1979. pap. text 56.00 (*90-6258-044-0*, Pub. by Netherlands Inst) Eisenbrauns.

Old Babylonian Tablets from Tell Al Rimah. Stephanie Dalley et al. (Illus.). 271p. 1976. 42.00 (*0-903472-03-1*, Pub. by Brit Sch Archaeol Iraq) David Brown.

Old Babylonian Temple Records. Robert J. Lau. (Columbia University. Oriental Studies: No. 3). reprint ed. 39.50 (*0-404-50493-0*) AMS Pr.

Old Babylonian Texts in the Ashmolean Museum: Texts from Kish & Elsewhere. Ed. by Stephanie Dalley & Norman Yoffee. (Oxford Editions of Cuneiform Texts Ser.: Vol. XIII). (Illus.). 154p. 1991. pap. text 110.00 (*0-19-814479-2*) OUP.

Old Bachelor. William Wirt. LC 85-18476. 248p. 1985. reprint ed. 50.00 (*0-8201-1407-3*) Schol Facsimiles.

Old Bag of Bones. Janet Stevens. (Illus.). 32p. (J). (gr. k-3). 1996. reprint ed. pap. 6.95 (*0-8234-1337-3*) Holiday.

Old Bag of Bones: A Coyote Tale. Illus. & Retold by Janet Stevens. 32p. (J). (gr. k-3). 1996. lib. bdg. 16.95 (*0-8234-1215-6*) Holiday.

***Old Bailey: Eight Hundred Years of Crime, Cruelty & Corruption.** Theresa Murphy. 224p. 1999. 35.00 (*1-84018-234-2*, Pub. by Mainstream Pubng) Trafalgar.

Old Bailey & Its Trials. Bernard O'Donnell. LC 78-2732. (Illus.). 226p. 1978. reprint ed. lib. bdg. 69.50 (*0-313-20362-8*, ODOB, Greenwood Pr) Greenwood.

Old Ball Yard: McCormick Field: Home of Memories. Bob Terrell. LC 96-23818. (Illus.). 100p. (Orig.). 1997. pap. 9.95 (*1-56664-099-7*) WorldComm.

Old Ballerina. Ellen Cooney. LC 99-35462. 208p. 1999. 23.95 (*1-56689-086-1*, Pub. by Coffee Hse) Consort Bk Sales.

Old Bank - New Bank: The First National Bank, Houston, 1866-1956. William A. Kirkland. LC 74-27681. (Illus.). 125p. reprint ed. pap. 38.80 (*0-608-15982-4*, 205226300082) Bks Demand.

Old Bank House. Angela M. Thirkell. LC 97-3797. 400p. 1997. pap. 12.95 (*1-55921-205-5*) Moyer Bell.

***Old Banyan & Other Stories.** Ahmad Nadeem Qasimi. Ed. by Muhammad Umar Memon. Tr. by Faruq Hasan. (Pakistan Writers Ser.). 260p. 2000. pap. 9.95 (*0-19-579328-5*) OUP.

Old Barn. Rose Miller. LC 92-35283. (Publish-a-Book Contest Ser.). (Illus.). 32p. (J). (gr. 1-6). 1992. lib. bdg. 22.83 (*0-8114-3581-4*) Raintree Steck-V.

***Old Barn: Springtime.** Joe Maniscalco. 32p. (J). (gr. 2-4). 1988. pap. 3.99 (*0-8280-0423-4*) Review & Herald.

Old Barn Book: A Field Guide to North American Barns & Other Farm Structures. Allen G. Noble & Richard K. Cleek. (Illus.). 222p. 1996. 32.95 (*0-8135-2172-6*) Rutgers U Pr.

Old Barn Book: A Field Guide to North American Barns & Other Farm Structures. Allen G. Noble & Richard K. Cleek. LC 94-41300. (Illus.). xii, 222p. (C). 1996. pap. 17.95 (*0-8135-2173-4*) Rutgers U Pr.

Old Barn Puppet Plays: Eight Plans for 10-Minute Puppetry Experiences for Children 5-8. Taffy Jones. LC 97-11198. 165p. 1997. 25.00 (*0-7864-0327-6*) McFarland & Co.

Old Barns in the New World: Reconstructing History. Richard W. Babcock & Lauren R. Stevens. LC 96-21932. (Illus.). 256p. 1996. reprint ed. pap. 21.95 (*0-936399-79-1*, Pub. by Berkshire Hse) Natl Bk Netwk.

O

***Old Beaded Bag.** Robert W. Dixon. 36p. 1999. pap. 8.95 (*1-58535-000-1*) In His Steps.

Old Bear. Jane Hissey. LC 86-12227. (Illus.). 32p. (J). (ps-2). 1986. 15.95 (*0-399-21401-1*, Philomel) Peng Put Young Read.

Old Bear Board Book. Jane Hissey. LC 98-143940. (Illus.). 28p. (J). (ps-1). 1998. bds. 6.95 (*0-399-23205-2*, Philomel) Peng Put Young Read.

Old Believers & the World of Antichrist: The Vyg Community & the Russian State, 1694-1855. Robert O. Crummey. LC 79-98121. (Illus.). 286p. reprint ed. pap. 88.70 (*0-8357-4743-3*, 203766400009) Bks Demand.

Old Believers in Modern Russia. Roy R. Robson. LC 95-22663. (Illus.). 250p. 1996. lib. bdg. 30.00 (*0-87580-205-2*) N Ill U Pr.

***Old Bell Falls: A Xmas Story.** Evangelin Evers. LC 98-44845. 1998. write for info. (*1-882723-35-X*) Gold Leaf.

Old Beloved Path: Daily Life among the Indians of the Lower Chattahoochee River Valley. William W. Winn. 279p. 1992. 19.95 (*0-945477-10-4*) Hist Chattahoochee.

Old Ben. rev. ed. Jesse H. Stuart. Ed. by James M. Gifford & Chuck D. Charles. LC 91-35578. (Jesse Stuart Foundation Juvenile Ser.). (Illus.). 64p. (YA). (gr. 3-6). 1992. reprint ed. 10.00 (*0-945084-22-6*); reprint ed. pap. 4.00 (*0-945084-23-4*) J Stuart Found.

Old Bergen History & Reminiscences. Daniel Van Winkle. (Illus.). 319p. 1993. reprint ed. lib. bdg. 35.00 (*0-8328-3510-2*) Higginson Bk Co.

Old Bergen (N. J.) History & Reminiscences. Daniel Van Winkle. (Illus.). xii, 325p. 1997. reprint ed. pap. 25.50 (*0-7884-0694-9*, V059) Heritage Bk.

***Old Best Friend.** Korman. 24p. (J). 1999. pap. text 3.29 (*0-307-13147-5*, Goldn Books) Gldn Bks Pub Co.

Old Bethpage Village Restoration. Ed. by Art Beltrone. (Illus.). 48p. 1990. pap. 3.25 (*0-911357-03-3*) Friends Long Island.

Old Betsey: The Life & Times of a Famous Dakota Woman & Her Family. Mark Diedrich. LC 94-71724. (Illus.). 170p. (Orig.). 1995. pap. 24.95 (*0-9616901-9-4*) Coyote Bks MN.

***Old Bibles: An Account of the Various Versions of the English Bible.** J. R. Dore. 1999. pap. 15.00 (*1-58329-008-7*) Lazarus Minist.

Old Bill, the Whooping Crane. Joseph W. Lippincott. (Illus.). (YA). (gr. 7-9). 1958. 10.95 (*0-397-30429-3*) HarpC Child Bks.

Old Bill Williams: Mountain Man. Alpheus H. Favour. LC 62-10767. 234p. 1981. pap. 14.95 (*0-8061-1698-6*) U of Okla Pr.

Old Bird, A Love Story. limited ed. J. F. Powers. (Winter Bks.: No. 4). (Illus.). 32p. 1991. pap. 65.00 (*1-879832-26-7*) MN Ctr Book Arts.

Old Birmingham, New Architecture: Student Projects for an Historic Downtown Context. Ed. by Birmingham Historical Society Staff & Auburn University, Department of Architecture Staf. (Illus.). 48p. (Orig.). 1984. pap. 4.00 (*0-943994-10-1*) Birmingham Hist Soc.

Old Black. limited ed. Doug Briggs. LC 97-72767. (Illus.). 387p. 1997. 24.95 (*1-881287-12-2*) Beverly Bk.

Old Black Fly. Jim Aylesworth. LC 91-26825. (Illus.). 32p. (J). (ps-2). 1995. 15.95 (*0-8050-1401-2*, Bks Young Read); pap. 5.95 (*0-8050-3924-4*) H Holt & Co.

Old Black Fly. Jim Aylesworth. 1995. 11.15 (*0-606-12458-6*, Pub. by Turtleback) Demco.

Old Black Fly. Jim Aylesworth & Stephen Gammell. LC 91-26825. (Illus.). 32p. (J). (ps-2). 1995. pap. 19.95 (*0-8050-3925-2*) H Holt & Co.

Old Black Fly. Jim Aylesowth. (Illus.). 32p. (J). 1998. bds. 6.95 (*0-8050-5840-0*) H Holt & Co.

Old Black Magic: A Robin Miller Mystery. Jaye Maiman. LC 97-10004. Vol. 6. 288p. (Orig.). 1997. pap. 11.95 (*1-56280-175-9*) Naiad Pr.

Old Black Witch. Wende Devlin & Harry Devlin. LC 91-42133. (Illus.). 32p. (J). (gr. k-3). 1992. reprint ed. mass mkt. 3.95 (*0-689-71636-2*) Aladdin.

Old Black Witch. 2nd ed. Wende Devlin & Harry Devlin. LC 92-19897. (Illus.). 32p. (J). (gr. k-3). 1992. text 13.95 (*0-02-729185-5*, Four Winds Pr) S&S Childrens.

***Old Bloomington Cemetery: Hennepin County, Minnesota.** Kermit Frye. LC 99-46748. (Illus.). 46p. 1999. pap. 15.00 (*0-915709-71-6*, M - 354) Pk Geneal Bk.

Old Bob's Gift. Jeff Muise. LC 96-4929. (Illus.). 158p. (J). (gr. 4-12). 1996. pap. 12.95 (*1-885482-04-3*) Shawangunk Pr.

Old Bohemian & Moravian Jewish Cemeteries. Jiri Fiedler. (Illus.). 172p. 1997. reprint ed. text 20.00 (*0-7881-5070-7*) DIANE Pub.

Old Bones. 1990. mass mkt. 3.95 (*0-445-77318-9*, Pub. by Warner Bks) Little.

Old Bones: A Gideon Oliver Mystery. Aaron J. Elkins. 243p. 1988. mass mkt. 6.50 (*0-445-40687-9*, Pub. by Warner Bks) Little.

Old Bones & Northern Memories. 2nd ed. Cully Gage. LC 91-76053. (Northwoods Reader Ser.). 1991. pap. 10.95 (*0-932212-70-0*) Avery Color.

Old Bones & Serpent Stones: A Guide to Interpreted Fossil Localities in Canada & the United States, Vol. 2: Western Sites. T. Skwara. (Guides to the American Landscape Ser.). (Illus.). vii, 302p. 1992. pap. 16.95 (*0-939923-09-2*) M & W Pub Co.

Old Bones Are Scattered: The Cawnpore Massacre & the Indian Mutiny of 1857. Andrew Ward. LC 95-23298. 1995. 30.00 (*0-8050-2437-9*) H Holt & Co.

Old Book Value Guide. 11th ed. Sharon Huxford & Bob Huxford. 432p. 1999. 19.95 (*1-57432-119-6*) Collector Bks.

Old Books & Grotesque Design. F. W. Fairholt. (Illus.). 70p. 1996. reprint ed. pap. 25.00 (*0-87556-955-2*) Saifer.

Old Books in the Old World: Reminiscences of Book Buying Abroad. Leona Rostenberg & Madeleine B. Stern. (Illus.). 160p. 1996. 22.95 (*1-884718-18-3*) Oak Knoll.

Old Books in the Old World: Reminiscences of Book Buying Abroad. deluxe ed. Leona Rostenberg & Madeleine B. Stern. 1996. 45.00 (*1-884718-21-3*) Oak Knoll.

Old Books, Rare Friends. large type ed. Leona Rostenberg. LC 98-11524. 1998. 25.95 (*0-7862-1414-7*) Thorndike Pr.

Old Books, Rare Friends: Two Literary Sleuths & Their Shared Passion. Leona Rostenberg & Madeleine B. Stern. (Illus.). 288p. 1998. pap. 11.95 (*0-385-48515-8*) Doubleday.

Old Booksellers of New York. W. L. Andrews. 1972. 59.95 (*0-8490-0753-4*) Gordon Pr.

Old Boot. Chris Baines. LC 89-77747. (Ecology Story Book Ser.). (Illus.). 24p. 1990. 7.95 (*0-940793-52-0*, Crocodile Bks) Interlink Pub.

Old Boston Fare in Food & Pictures. Jerome Rubin. (Illus.). 128p. (Orig.). 1997. pap. 13.50 (*0-88278-047-6*) Yankee Products.

Old Boston in Early Photograph. 18th ed. Philip Bergen. (Illus.). 128p. 1990. pap. 11.95 (*0-486-26184-0*) Dover.

Old Boston Museum Days. Kate Ryan. LC 77-131822. (Illus.). 1971. reprint ed. 49.00 (*0-403-00709-7*) Scholarly.

Old Boy. A. R. Gurney. 1992. pap. 5.25 (*0-8222-0840-7*) Dramatists Play.

Old Boys. Kirk Winkler. 1991. 19.95 (*0-8027-4114-2*) Walker & Co.

Old Bread, New Wine: A Portrait of the Italian-Americans. Patrick J. Gallo. LC 80-20401. 360p. 1981. 32.95 (*0-88229-146-7*) Burnham Inc.

Old Breed: A History of the First Marine Division in World War II. George McMillan. LC 79-16880. 1980. reprint ed. 49.95 (*0-89201-052-5*) Zenger Pub.

Old Brethren. James H. Lehman. LC 76-20274. (Illus.). 384p. 1976. pap. 2.45 (*0-87178-650-8*, 8011) Brethren.

Old-Breton Glosses. Ed. by Whitley Stokes. 1996. pap. 10.00 (*0-89979-090-9*) British Am Bks.

Old Brewery & the New Mission House at the Five Points. Ladies of the Mission Staff. LC 72-112563. (Rise of Urban America Ser.). (Illus.). 1976. reprint ed. 29.95 (*0-405-02461-4*) Ayer.

Old Bridge: The Third Balkan War & the Age of the Refugee. Christopher Merrill. LC 95-20061. 100p. 1995. pap. 6.95 (*1-57131-208-0*) Milkweed Ed.

Old Brooklyn Heights. Clay Lancaster. (Illus.). 1980. pap. 8.95 (*0-486-23872-5*) Dover.

Old Brooklyn in Early Photographs, 1865-1929. William L. Younger. LC 77-77028. (New York City Ser.). (Illus.). 165p. 1978. pap. 13.95 (*0-486-23587-4*) Dover.

Old Brown Dog: Women, Workers, & Vivisection in Edwardian England. Coral Lansbury. LC 85-40369. 227p. 1985. reprint ed. pap. 70.40 (*0-608-07453-5*, 206768000009) Bks Demand.

Old Brown Suitcase: A Teenager's Story of War & Peace. Lillian Boraks-Nemetz. LC 94-76876. 148p. (Orig.). (YA). (gr. 8-12). 1994. pap. 9.50 (*0-914539-10-8*) Ben-Simon.

Old Buckingham by the Sea on the Eastern Shore of Maryland. I. Marshall Price. (Illus.). 252p. 1997. reprint ed. lib. bdg. 32.50 (*0-8328-7112-5*) Higginson Bk Co.

Old Buddy, Old Pal. Michael Laser. LC 98-34209. 173p. 1999. 22.00 (*1-57962-021-3*) Permanent Pr.

Old Building Owner's Manual. Ohio Historical Society Staff & Judith L. Kitchen. 86p. 1983. spiral bd. 9.95 (*0-87758-016-2*) Ohio Hist Soc.

Old Buildings, Gardens, & Furniture in Tidewater Maryland. Henry C. Forman. LC 67-17538. (Illus.). 342p. 1967. reprint ed. pap. 106.10 (*0-7837-9083-X*, 204983300003) Bks Demand.

Old Bunch. Meyer Levin. 976p. 1985. reprint ed. 19.95 (*0-8065-0974-0*, Citadel Pr); reprint ed. pap. 14.95 (*0-8065-0967-8*, Citadel Pr) Carol Pub Group.

Old Burial Grounds of New Jersey: A Guide. Janice K. Sarapin. LC 94-14635. (Illus.). 230p. (C). 1994. pap. 14.95 (*0-8135-2111-4*); text 35.00 (*0-8135-2110-6*) Rutgers U Pr.

Old Burma, Early Pagan, 3 Vols., Set. Gordon H. Luce. 1969. 380.00 (*0-686-92654-4*) J J Augustin.

Old Burnside. Harriet S. Arnow. (Illus.). 148p. 1996. pap. 12.50 (*0-8131-0860-8*) U Pr of Ky.

***Old Burying Ground: Colonial Park Cemetery, Savannah Georgia, 1750-1853.** Elizabeth C. Piechocinski. (Illus.). 1999. pap. 18.00 (*1-891495-09-7*) Oglethorpe Pr.

Old Burying Ground: Colonial Park Cemetery, Savannah Georgia, 1750-1853. unabridged ed. Elizabeth C. Piechocinski. (Illus.). 23.50 (*1-891495-08-9*) Oglethorpe Pr.

Old Burying Ground of Ancient Westbury & Present Watertown. (Illus.). 145p. 1997. reprint ed. pap. 19.00 (*0-8328-5695-9*) Higginson Bk Co.

Old Buses. David Kaye. (Album Ser.: No. 94). (Illus.). 32p. 1989. pap. 5.25 (*0-85263-613-X*, Pub. by Shire Pubns) Parkwest Pubns.

Old Cahaba Land Office Records & Military Warrants, 1817-1853. (Illus.). xxvii, 260p. 1986. 24.00 (*0-89308-384-4*) Southern Hist Pr.

Old Cahier of the 33 Degree. Albert Pike. 50p. 1996. reprint ed. pap. 12.95 (*1-56459-995-7*) Kessinger Pub.

Old Calabor, 1600 to 1891: The Impact of the International Economy Upon a Traditional Society. A. J. Latham. 1973. 36.00 (*0-19-821687-4*) OUP.

Old Calabria. Norman Douglas. LC 96-38229. 325p. 1996. pap. 15.95 (*0-8101-6022-6*, Marlboro) Northwestern U Pr.

Old California: Almanac of Fairs & Festivals. Camaro Editors. (Old California Ser.: No. 1). (Illus.). 1988. pap. 4.95 (*0-913290-43-2*) Camaro Pub.

Old California: Art, Theater, & Museums. Camaro Editors. (Old California Ser.: No. 10). (Illus.). 1983. pap. 3.95 (*0-913290-51-3*) Camaro Pub.

Old California: Camping Sites & Campgrounds. Camaro Editors. (Old California Ser.: No. 7). (Illus.). 1985. pap. 3.95 (*0-913290-48-3*) Camaro Pub.

Old California: Christmas Time & Mountain Recreation. Camaro Editors. (Old California Ser.: No. 12). (Illus.). 1984. pap. 3.95 (*0-913290-53-X*) Camaro Pub.

Old California: Cooking, Recipes, & Menus. Camaro Editors. (Old California Ser.: No. 11). (Illus.). 1983. pap. 3.95 (*0-913290-52-1*) Camaro Pub.

Old California: Country Inns & Historic Hotels. Camaro Editors. (Old California Ser.: No. 4). (Illus.). 1983. pap. 3.95 (*0-913290-45-9*) Camaro Pub.

Old California: Gold Mines & Gold Mining Towns. Camaro Editors. (Old California Ser.: No. 8). (Illus.). 1985. pap. 3.95 (*0-913290-49-1*) Camaro Pub.

Old California: Historical Landmarks & Scenic Backroads. Camaro Editors. (Old California Ser.: No. 9). (Illus.). 1984. pap. 4.95 (*0-913290-50-5*) Camaro Pub.

Old California: Historical Restaurants, Wineries, & Wine Tasting. Camaro Editors. (Old California Ser.: No. 3). (Illus.). 1983. pap. 3.95 (*0-913290-44-0*) Camaro Pub.

Old California: The Missions, Ranchos & Romantic Adobes. Bret Shipman. LC 80-36856. (Old California Ser.: No. 2). (Illus.). 1987. 4.95 (*0-913290-17-3*) Camaro Pub.

Old California: Visitors Guide. Camaro Editors. (Old California Ser.: No. 5). (Illus.). 1983. pap. 3.95 (*0-913290-46-7*) Camaro Pub.

Old California for Children: Picnic Spots, Haunted Houses, & Ghost Towns. Camaro Editors. (Old California Ser.: No. 6). (Illus.). 1983. pap. 3.95 (*0-913290-47-5*) Camaro Pub.

Old Calvary Cemetery - New Yorkers Carved in Stone. Rosemary M. Ardolina. (Illus.). 549p. (Orig.). 1996. pap. 76.00 (*0-7884-0453-9*, A615) Heritage Bk.

Old Camera Value Guide. 1989. 4.95 (*0-89816-036-7*) Embee Pr.

Old Campbell County, Georgia Land Records, 1828-1854: Deed Books A, C, D & E. Joan T. Westmoreland. Ed. by Freda R. Turner & Willis O. Westmoreland. (Illus.). 508p. 1993. 30.00 (*0-9628557-7-4*) Genlgcl Socs Henry & Clayton.

Old Cape Cod Fare in Food & Pictures. Jerome Rubin. (Illus.). 128p. (Orig.). 1997. pap. 13.50 (*0-88278-046-8*) Yankee Products.

Old Capital. Yasunari Kawabata. Tr. by J. Martin Holman from JPN. LC 86-62836. Orig. Title: Koto. 176p. 1989. pap. 8.95 (*0-86547-411-7*) N Point Pr.

Old Capitol: Portrait of an Iowa Landmark. Margaret N. Keyes. LC 88-22689. (Bur Oak Original Ser.). (Illus.). 187p. 1988. 24.95 (*0-87745-210-5*) U of Iowa Pr.

Old Captivity. Nevil Shute. 25.95 (*0-88411-321-3*) Amereon Ltd.

Old Car. Val Marshall & Bronwyn Tester. LC 92-27264. (Voyages Ser.). (Illus.). (J). 1993. 3.75 (*0-383-03644-5*) SRA McGraw.

Old Car Wrecks. Ron Kowalke. LC 97-169635. (Illus.). 224p. 1997. pap. 14.95 (*0-87341-510-8*) Krause Pubns.

Old Carmarthen. Alan H. Davies. 96p. 1985. 30.00 (*0-86383-171-0*, Pub. by Gomer Pr) St Mut.

Old Cars. Harry Knill. (Illus.). (J). (gr. 1-9). 1994. pap. 3.95 (*0-88388-145-4*) Bellerophon Bks.

Old Castle, & Other Essays. Caleb T. Winchester. LC 75-152220. (Essay Index Reprint Ser.). 1977. reprint ed. 23.95 (*0-8369-2261-1*) Ayer.

Old Cathedral. 2nd ed. Gregory M. Franzwa. LC 80-15885. (Illus.). 1980. 14.95 (*0-935284-18-4*) Patrice Pr.

Old Catholic Church: A History & Chronology. expanded rev. ed. Karl Pruter. LC 95-3866. (Autocephalous Orthodox Churches Ser.: No. 3). (Illus.). 96p. 1996. pap. 17.00 (*0-912134-19-4*) Millefleurs.

Old Catholic Missal & Ritual. Tr. by Arnold H. Mathew. LC 73-84708. reprint ed. 37.50 (*0-404-01949-8*) AMS Pr.

***Old Catholic Missal & Ritual.** Arnold Harris Mathew. Ed. by Elijah. LC 73-84708. 652p. 2000. reprint ed. 34.95 (*1-883938-65-1*) Dry Bones Pr.

Old Catholic Prayer Book. Ed. & Tr. by Aidan Keller from ANG. (Old Catholic Missal & Ritual Sarum Rite Ser.: Vol. 2). (Illus.). 336p. 1991. 29.95 (*0-923864-01-6*) St Hilarion Pr.

Old Catholic Sourcebook. Karl Pruter & J. Gordon Melton. LC 83-47610. 254p. 1983. text 30.00 (*0-8240-9111-6*) Garland.

Old Cedar Bar. Margaret Randall. (Fine Art Ser.). (Illus.). 100p. 1992. 350.00 (*0-89556-092-5*) Gateways Bks & Tapes.

Old Cemeteries of Southeastern Massachusetts. (Illus.). 220p. 1995. 50.00 (*0-9647693-0-1*) Middleborough Pub Lib.

Old Cemetery Burials of Milwaukee Co. Wisconsin. Elizabeth D. Herzfeld. xii, 217p. (Orig.). 1997. pap. 20.00 (*0-7884-0646-9*, H170) Heritage Bk.

Old Cemetery Burials of Milwaukee County, WI. Elizabeth D. Herzfeld. 331p. (Orig.). 1995. pap. 24.00 (*0-7884-0268-4*) Heritage Bk.

Old Cemetery Findings, Spencer, N. Y. & Surrounding Areas, Vol. 1. Laura C. Uhl. 1983. 3.00 (*0-943240-06-9*) UHLs Pub.

Old Century, a New Testament. Jennie Hair. 24p. pap. text 6.00 (*1-878173-10-3*) Birnham Wood.

Old Century & the New. Ed. by Alfred F. Rosa. LC 76-2853. 287p. 1978. 38.50 (*0-8386-1954-1*) Fairleigh Dickinson.

Old Charlie & the Gold Smell'n Burro. Jacqueline Joyce. LC 96-84847. (Illus.). 36p. (Orig.). (J). (ps-4). 1997. pap. 7.95 (*0-9652211-1-3*, 1125) Bear Path.

Old Charlie & the Gold Smell'n Burro. Jacqueline Joyce. Tr. by DelMar Communications Int'l. Staff. (SPA., Illus.). 36p. (Orig.). (J). (ps-4). 1997. pap. 7.95 (*0-9652211-3-X*, 11126) Bear Path.

Old Chatham & Neighboring Dwellings South of the Berkshires, Vol. 5, No. 5. A. T. Covell. 1993. reprint ed. lib. bdg. 89.00 (*0-7812-5322-5*) Rprt Serv.

Old Cheque-Book: or Book of Rememberance of the Chapel Royal from 1561 to 1744. Ed. by Edward F. Rimbault. LC 65-23407. (Music Ser.). 1966. reprint ed. lib. bdg. 35.00 (*0-306-70911-2*) Da Capo.

Old Chest. Agnes Adam. Ed. by William-Alan Landes. LC 98-52429. (Illus.). 28p. 1998. pap. 5.00 (*0-88734-822-X*) Players Pr.

Old Chester Days. Margaret W. Deland. LC 79-113657. (Short Story Index Reprint Ser.). 1977. 23.95 (*0-8369-3386-9*) Ayer.

Old Chester Tales. Margaret W. Deland. LC 70-97884. (BCL Ser. I). reprint ed. 32.50 (*0-404-02075-5*) AMS Pr.

Old Chester Tales. Margaret W. Deland. 1972. reprint ed. lib. bdg. 20.00 (*0-8422-8037-5*) Irvington.

Old Chester Tales. Margaret W. Deland. (C). 1986. reprint ed. pap. text 7.95 (*0-8290-1940-5*) Irvington.

Old Chestnuts Warmed Up: And Other Favourites. John Murray. (Illus.). 128p. 1998. 19.95 (*0-7195-5839-5*, Pub. by John Murray) Trafalgar.

Old Chick-a-Biddy. Sadie H. Hawthorne. (True Tales from Hootin' Hollow Ser.). (Illus.). 40p. (J). (gr. k-1). 1994. 10.00 (*0-931647-04-5*) S & B Pubs.

Old Children of God. Catharine S. Roache. (Illus.). 16p. 1973. 2.00 (*0-913478-00-8*) Hermosa.

Old China Hands. Charles G. Finney. LC 73-429. (Illus.). 258p. 1973. reprint ed. lib. bdg. 38.50 (*0-8371-6772-8*, FIOC, Greenwood Pr) Greenwood.

Old China Trade. Foster R. Dulles. LC 70-111470. reprint ed. 32.50 (*0-404-02216-2*) AMS Pr.

Old Chore. John Hildebidle. LC 80-70828. 72p. (C). 1981. pap. 3.95 (*0-914086-34-0*) Alice James Bks.

Old Christmas. Washington Irving. Ed. by John Langstaff. (Illus.). 140p. 1996. 19.95 (*0-939218-15-1*) Chapman Billies.

Old Church Slavonic Grammar. rev. ed. Horace G. Lunt. (Slavistic Printings & Reprintings Ser.: No. 3). 1974. text 66.15 (*90-279-3362-6*) Mouton.

Old Church Slavonic Grammar: Handbook of Old Church Slavonic, Pt. 1. Grigore Nandris. LC 88-3481. (London East European Ser.). (C). 1965. pap. 39.95 (*0-485-17520-7*, Pub. by Athlone Pr) Humanities.

Old Church Slavonic Kiev Fragment. G. L. Trager. (LM Ser.: No. 13). 1933. pap. 25.00 (*0-527-00817-6*) Periodicals Srv.

Old Church Slavonic Translation of the Andron Hagion Biblos in the Edition of Nikolas Van Wijk. D. Armstrong et al. Ed. by C. H. Van Schooneveld. (Slavistic Printings & Reprintings Ser.: No. 1). 310p. 1975. text 172.35 (*90-279-3196-8*) Mouton.

Old Churches, Ministers & Families of Virginia, 2 vols. William Meade. (Illus.). 985p. 1997. reprint ed. lib. bdg. 99.00 (*0-8328-7178-8*) Higginson Bk Co.

Old Churches, Ministers, & Families of Virginia, 2 vols., Set. Bishop Meade. (Illus.). 1067p. (Orig.). 1993. reprint ed. pap. text 58.00 (*1-55613-691-9*) Heritage Bk.

Old Churches, Ministers, & Families of Virginia: Digested Index & Genealogical Guide, 2 vols. William Meade. 1100p. 1995. reprint ed. 70.00 (*0-8063-0238-0*) Genealog Pub.

Old Churches of the Province of Quebec, 1647-1800. Historic Monuments Commission. (Illus.). 334p. 1998. reprint ed. pap. 29.95 (*1-58211-046-8*, 098300) Quintin Pub RI.

***Old Cities, New Assets: Preserving Latin America's Urban Heritage.** Eduardo Rojas. 2000. pap. text 26.95 (*1-886938-62-8*) IADB.

Old Cities, New Predicaments: A Study of Hyderabad. Ratna Naidu. 178p. 1991. text 27.50 (*0-8039-9658-6*) Sage.

***Old Civilizations of the New World.** Alpheus H. Verrill. (LC History-America-E). 393p. 1999. reprint ed. lib. bdg. 89.00 (*0-7812-4275-4*) Rprt Serv.

Old Clocks & Watches & Their Makers. 3rd ed. Antique Collectors Club Staff. (Illus.). 520p. 1978. reprint ed. 69.50 (*0-902028-69-3*) Antique Collect.

Old Coach Road. Wilma Alexander. 128p. (Orig.). (J). (gr. 3-6). 1990. pap. 5.95 (*0-7736-7305-9*) Stoddart Publ.

Old Coast Guard Stations Vol. I: Virginia: Popes Island to False Cape. Richard Chenery. LC 98-184652. (Illus.). viii, 94p. 1998. pap. 19.95 (*0-9665204-0-8*) Station Bks.

Old College Reflections: A Family Story. Louise L. Dick. 148p. 1999. 21.95 (*0-9668657-3-1*) Ark Pubg.

Old College Try: Balancing Academics & Athletics in Higher Education. John R. Thelin & Lawrence L. Wiseman. Ed. by Jonathan D. Fife. LC 89-63440. (ASHE-ERIC Higher Education Reports: No. 89-4). 141p. (Orig.). (C). 1989. pap. text 24.00 (*0-9623882-3-8*) GWU Grad Schl E&HD.

Old Colony Mennonites: Dilemmas of Ethnic Minority Life. Calvin W. Redekop. LC 69-13192. 322p. reprint ed. pap. 99.90 (*0-608-30354-2*, 202173700022) Bks Demand.

Old Comedy & the Iambographic Tradition. Ralph Rosen. LC 88-33324. (American Philological Association, American Classical Studies). 103p. 1988. pap. 12.95 (*1-55540-305-0*, 40 04 19) OUP.

Old Contemptibles. Martha Grimes. 1992. mass mkt. 5.99 (*0-345-37456-8*) Ballantine Pub Grp.

Old Contemptibles: BEF, 1914. Michael Barthorp. (Elite Ser.: No. 24). (Illus.). 64p. pap. 12.95 (*0-85045-898-6*, 9424, Pub. by Ospry) Stackpole.

O

An Asterisk (*) at the beginning of an entry indicates that the title is appearing for the first time.

Old Continental: or The Price of Liberty. James K. Paulding. (Notable American Authors Ser.). 1999. reprint ed. lib. bdg. 125.00 (*0-7812-8707-3*) Rprt Serv.

Old Continental Seasonal & Holiday Recipes. Compiled by Cornelia Schrader-Muggenthaler. (Illus.). 72p. 1990. spiral bd. 7.00 (*1-55856-076-9*, 370) Closson Pr.

Old Cookery Books & Ancient Cuisine. W. Carew Hazlitt. 1972. 59.95 (*0-8490-0755-0*) Gordon Pr.

Old Cooking Utensils. David J. Eveleigh. (Illus.). 32p. 1989. pap. 6.25 (*0-85263-812-4*, Pub. by Shire Pubns) Parkwest Pubns.

Old Copper Collar. Dan Cushman. 17.50 (*0-7540-8017-X*, Gunsmoke) Chivers N Amer.

Old Copper Mines of Snowdonia. Pound House Staff. 128p. (C). 1985. pap. text 40.00 (*0-906885-03-5*, Pub. by Pound Hse) St Mut.

Old Core. John A. Gunn. (Illus.). 208p. 1992. 19.95 (*0-9631034-0-7*) J&J Pub.

Old Cornish Crosses. Arthur G. Langdon. 1977. lib. bdg. 134.95 (*0-8490-2367-X*) Gordon Pr.

Old Cotton Blues. Linda England. LC 96-28535. (Illus.). 32p. (J). (ps-2). 1998. 16.00 (*0-689-81074-1*) S&S Bks Yung.

Old Country & Farming Words: Gleaned from Agricultural Books. James Britten. (English Dialect Society Publications: No. 30). 1974. reprint ed. pap. 25.00 (*0-8115-0457-3*) Periodicals Srv.

Old Country Cookin' Elam Lapp & Naomi Lapp. (Illus.). 148p. (Orig.). 1996. spiral bd. 7.95 (*0-9642548-9-1*) Carlisle Press.

Old Country School: The Story of Rural Education in the Middle West. Wayne E. Fuller. LC 81-16069. (Illus.). x, 302p. (C). 1994. 25.00 (*0-226-26882-9*) U Ch Pr.

Old Country School: The Story of Rural Education in the Middle West. Wayne E. Fuller. LC 81-16069. (Illus.). x, 302p. (C). 1995. pap. text 14.50 (*0-226-26883-7*) U Ch Pr.

Old Country School: The Story of Rural Education in the Middle West. Wayne E. Fuller. LC 81-16069. (Illus.). 312p. reprint ed. pap. 96.80 (*0-608-08812-9*, 206945100004) Bks Demand.

Old Country Store Cookbook. rev. ed. Ed. by Joyce Jones et al. LC 86-50882. 167p. 12.95 (*0-9637980-0-6*) Old Cntry Store.

Old Country Store on the Miracle Mile: A True Story. Mel Spahr. 1999. pap. 8.95 (*0-533-12837-4*) Vantage.

Old County Court House & Other Northampton County History: Papers on the Court House, the Easton Flag, & the Early Easton Settlers. A. D. Chidsey, Jr. et al. 24p. (Orig.). 1964. pap. text 5.00 (*1-877701-03-3*) NCH&GS.

Old Courthouse: Americans Build a Forum on the Frontier. Donald F. Dosch. Ed. by Dan Murphy. LC 79-66506. (Gateway Ser.). (Illus.). 129p. (Orig.). (C). 1979. pap. 9.95 (*0-931056-02-0*) Jefferson Natl.

Old Covenant & the New. Daniel G. Samuels. 1989. pap. 0.50 (*1-887621-14-8*) Found Ch Divine Truth.

Old Coyote of Big Sur: The Life of Jaime de Angulo. Gui De Angulo. (Illus.). 472p. (Orig.). 1995. pap. 26.00 (*1-879042-03-7*) Stonegarden Pr.

Old Crackfoot. Gordon Allred. (Illus.). (J). (gr. 5 up). 1965. 8.95 (*0-8392-3051-6*) Astor-Honor.

Old Creed for the New Smith: Proslavery Ideology & Historiography, 1865-1918, 89. John D. Smith. LC 84-27935. (Contributions in Afro-American & African Studies: No. 89). 314p. 1985. 55.00 (*0-313-23648-8*, SOC/, Greenwood Pr) Greenwood.

Old Creole Days see Collected Works of George W. Cable

Old Creole Days. George W. Cable. LC 89-25567. 312p. 1990. reprint ed. pap. 4.95 (*0-88289-780-2*) Pelican.

Old Creole Days. George W. Cable. (Works of George Washington Cable). 1990. reprint ed. lib. bdg. 79.00 (*0-7812-1132-8*) Rprt Serv.

Old Creole Days, Set, Pts. 1 & 2. George W. Cable. LC 79-83932. (Black Heritage Library Collection). 1977. 25.95 (*0-8369-8530-3*) Ayer.

Old Crook County, the Heart of Oregon. Frances Juris. (Illus.). 46p. 1975. pap. 5.95 (*1-930405-00-6*) Crook County Hist.

Old Cross & the New. A. W. Tozer. (Heritage Ser.). 1995. pap. 1.59 (*0-87509-597-6*) Chr Pubns.

Old Croton Aqueduct: Rural Resources Meet Urban Needs. Jeffrey Kroessler et al. LC 92-62429. (Illus.). 64p. (Orig.). 1992. pap. 12.00 (*0-943651-25-5*) Hudson Riv.

Old Crumlin to Pontymister in Photographs, Vol. 2. Brian Collins & Terry Powell. (C). 1989. 59.00 (*0-900807-53-9*, Pub. by D Brown & Sons Ltd) St Mut.

Old Cryes of London. Frederick Bridge. LC 74-24050. 1976. reprint ed. 36.50 (*0-404-12872-6*) AMS Pr.

Old Curiosity Shop see Oxford Illustrated Dickens

***Old Curiosity Shop.** James P. Blaylock. 54p. 1999. 50.00 (*1-892011-10-7*) ASAP Pub.

Old Curiosity Shop. Charles Dickens. 1995. 23.00 (*0-679-44373-8*) Knopf.

Old Curiosity Shop. Charles Dickens. Ed. by Elizabeth M. Brennan. LC 97-6474. (Clarendon Dickens Ser.). (Illus.). 742p. 1998. 175.00 incl. cd-rom (*0-19-812493-7*) OUP.

Old Curiosity Shop. Charles Dickens. Ed. & Intro. by Elizabeth M. Brennan. (Oxford World's Classics Ser.). (Illus.). 658p. 1998. pap. 7.95 (*0-19-282924-6*) OUP.

Old Curiosity Shop. Charles Dickens. Ed. by Paul Schlicke. 512p. 1995. pap. 6.95 (*0-460-87600-7*, Everyman's Classic Lib) Tuttle Pubng.

Old Curiosity Shop. Charles Dickens. Ed. by Angus Easson. (English Library). 720p. 1972. pap. 8.95 (*0-14-043075-X*, Penguin Classics) Viking Penguin.

Old Curiosity Shop. Charles Dickens. (Classics Library). 350p. pap. 3.95 (*1-85326-244-7*, 2447WW, Pub. by Wrdsworth Edits) NTC Contemp Pub Co.

***Old Curiosity Shop.** deluxe ed. James P. Blaylock. 1999. 125.00 (*1-892011-11-5*) ASAP Pub.

Old Curiosity Shop. Charles Dickens. 1990. reprint ed. lib. bdg. 21.95 (*0-89966-682-5*) Buccaneer Bks.

Old Czech Legends. Alois Jirasek. Tr. by M. Holecek from CZE. LC 91-72160. 208p. (Orig.). (YA). 1992. pap. 25.00 (*1-85610-020-0*, Pub. by Forest Bks) Dufour.

Old Dad Chiro: A Biography of D. D. Palmer Founder of Chiropractic. Vern Gielow. 142p. 1995. pap. 16.95 (*1-885048-07-6*) Barge Chiropract.

Old Dance: Love Stories of One Kind or Another. Ed. by Bonnie Burnard. 368p. 1986. mass mkt. 5.95 (*0-919926-56-8*, Pub. by Coteau) Genl Dist Srvs.

Old Days in Nashville & Historical Sketch of 1854. Jane H. Thomas & J. G. Ramsey. (Illus.). 190p. 1980. reprint ed. 15.00 (*0-918450-15-2*) C Elder.

Old Days Old Ways: An Illustrated Folk History of Ireland. Olive Sharkey. 1997. pap. text 14.95 (*0-86278-258-9*, Pub. by OBrien Pr) Irish Amer Bk.

Old Days Old Ways: An Illustrated Folk History of Ireland. Olive Sharkey. (Irish Studies). 175p. 1987. pap. 16.95 (*0-8156-0218-9*) Syracuse U Pr.

***Old Dead White Men's Philosophy.** Laura Lyn Inglis & Peter K. Steinfeld. 300p. 2000. 59.95 (*1-57392-823-2*, Humanity Bks) Prometheus Bks.

Old Dead White Men's Philosphy. Laura L. Inglis & Peter K. Steinfeld. LC 97-23238. (Society/Religion - Religion/Society Ser.). 184p. 1998. 55.00 (*0-391-04060-X*); pap. 17.50 (*0-391-04061-8*) Humanities.

Old Deadwood Days. Estelline Bennett. LC 81-14737. (Illus.). xiii, 314p. 1982. reprint ed. pap. 12.95 (*0-8032-6065-2*, Bison Books) U of Nebr Pr.

Old Debauchees: A Comedy. Henry Fielding. LC 92-2369. (Augustan Reprints Ser.: No. 258). 1989. reprint ed. 14.50 (*0-404-70258-9*, PR3454) AMS Pr.

Old Delaware Clockmakers. Henry C. Conrad. (Illus.). 34p. 1998. reprint ed. pap. 7.00 (*0-8328-9589-X*) Higginson Bk Co.

Old Delaware County: A Memoir. Gertrude F. Horton. (Illus.). 222p. (Orig.). 1993. pap. 14.50 (*0-935796-45-2*) Purple Mnt Pr.

Old Delivery Vans. Nick Baldwin. 1989. pap. 30.00 (*0-85263-845-0*, Pub. by Shire Pubns) St Mut.

Old Demopolis Land Office Records & Military Warrants, 1818-1860, & Records of the Vine & Olive Colony. Marilyn D. Barefield. (Illus.). 172p. 1988. 20.00 (*0-89308-637-1*, BH 16) Southern Hist Pr.

Old Devil Wind. Bill Martin, Jr. LC 92-37908. (Illus.). 32p. (J). (ps-3). 1993. 13.95 (*0-15-257768-8*) Harcourt.

Old Devil Wind. Bill Martin, Jr. LC 92-37908. (Illus.). 32p. (J). 1996. pap. 5.00 (*0-15-201384-9*) Harcourt.

Old Devil Wind. Bill Martin, Jr. LC 92-37908. (J). 1996. 10.20 (*0-606-11698-2*, Pub. by Turtleback) Demco.

Old Diary Leaves. Henry S. Olcott. 1974. 9.50 (*0-8356-7106-2*) Theos Pub Hse.

Old Diary Leaves, II. Henry S. Olcott. 1973. 9.50 (*0-8356-7123-2*) Theos Pub Hse.

Old Diary Leaves, III. Henry S. Olcott. 1973. 9.50 (*0-8356-7480-0*) Theos Pub Hse.

Old Diary Leaves, IV. Henry S. Olcott. 1973. 9.50 (*0-8356-7484-3*) Theos Pub Hse.

Old Diary Leaves, V. Henry S. Olcott. 1973. 9.50 (*0-8356-7487-8*) Theos Pub Hse.

Old Diary Leaves, VI. Henry S. Olcott. 1973. 9.50 (*0-8356-7491-6*) Theos Pub Hse.

Old Direction of Heaven: Poems. Jennifer Rose. LC 99-53745. 64p. 2000. pap. 15.00 (*0-943549-23-X*) Truman St Univ.

Old Dispensation: Loyalty in Business. John J. Clancy. LC 98-7073. 344p. 1998. 48.50 (*0-8386-3793-0*) Fairleigh Dickinson.

Old Doc. Elizabeth Seifert. 244p. 1973. reprint ed. lib. bdg. 22.95 (*0-88411-014-1*) Amereon Ltd.

Old Docks. Nancy Ritchie-Noakes. 1989. pap. 25.00 (*0-85263-893-0*, Pub. by Shire Pubns) St Mut.

Old Dog. rev. ed. Charlotte Zolotow. LC 93-41081. (Illus.). 32p. (J). (ps-3). 1995. 15.95 (*0-06-024409-7*); lib. bdg. 15.89 (*0-06-024412-7*) HarpC Child Bks.

Old Dog Cora & the Christmas Tree. Consie Powell. LC 98-53797. (Illus.). 32p. (J). (gr. 2-5). 1999. text 15.95 (*0-8075-5968-7*) A Whitman.

Old Dogs. Melissa Cleary. 224p. 1997. mass mkt. 5.99 (*0-425-15858-6*, Prime Crime) Berkley Pub.

***Old Dogs & Children.** Robert Inman. 1998. pap. 12.95 (*0-316-18998-7*, Back Bay) Little.

Old Dogs & Children: A Novel. Robert Inman. 456p. 1994. pap. 12.95 (*0-316-41914-1*) Little.

Old Dogs & New Tricks. large type ed. Ed. & Intro. by Kenneth Jernigan. (Kernel Bk.: No. 11). (Illus.). 96p. 1996. pap. 3.00 (*1-885218-05-2*) Natl Fed Blind.

Old Dogs Can (And Must) Learn New Tricks: More Warren Bennis on Leadership & Change. Warren G. Bennis. 1999. write for info. (*1-890009-34-2*) Exec Excell.

Old Dogs, Old Friends: Enjoying Your Older Dog. Bonnie Wilcox & Chris Walkowicz. (Illus.). 256p. 1991. 22.95 (*0-87605-750-4*) Howell Bks.

Old Dogs Remembered. Ed. & Intro. by Bud Johns. 232p. 1999. reprint ed. pap. 12.95 (*0-912184-12-4*) Synergistic Pr.

Old Dominion - Her Making & Her Manners. Thomas N. Page. (Notable American Authors Ser.). 1999. reprint ed. lib. bdg. 125.00 (*0-7812-4711-X*) Rprt Serv.

Old Dominion in the Seventeenth Century: A Documentary History of Virginia, 1606-1689. Ed. by Warren M. Billings. LC 74-8302. (Institute of Early American History & Culture Ser.). xxiv, 324p. 1975. pap. 22.95 (*0-8078-1237-4*) U of NC Pr.

Old Dorset. Robert C. Rogers. LC 76-140338. (Short Story Index Reprint Ser.). 1977. 17.95 (*0-8369-3730-9*) Ayer.

Old Drama & the New: An Essay in Re-Valuation. William Archer. 1972. 26.95 (*0-405-18113-2*, 1320) Ayer.

Old Drama & the New: An Essay in Re-Valuation. William Archer. (BCL1-PR English Literature Ser.). 396p. 1992. reprint ed. lib. bdg. 89.00 (*0-7812-7075-8*) Rprt Serv.

Old Drugstore: A Commentary on the Independent Drugstore in America. large type unabridged ed. James G. Higgs. Ed. by Barbara Hope. LC 98-83198. (Illus.). 256p. 1999. 24.95 (*1-892697-01-7*) QLP CA.

Old Drury of Philadelphia: A History of the Philadelphia Stage, 1800-1835. William C. Wood. LC 69-10108. (Illus.). 694p. 1968. reprint ed. lib. bdg. 89.50 (*0-8371-0115-8*, JAHP, Greenwood Pr) Greenwood.

Old Dry Frye: A Deliciously Funny Tall Tale. Paul Brett Johnson. LC 98-31787. (Illus.). 40p. (J). (gr. k-3). 1999. 15.95 (*0-590-37658-6*, Pub. by Scholastic Inc) Penguin Putnam.

Old Dualities: Deconstructing Robert Kroetsch & His Critics. Dianne Tiefensee. 240p. 1994. 60.00 (*0-7735-1191-1*, Pub. by McG-Queens Univ Pr) CUP Services.

Old Dude. Rick Stromoski. (Illus.). 46p. 1994. write for info. (*1-886386-01-3*) Trisar.

***Old Durner Pipe Organs Continue to Speak: Durner Organs & Music Personnel from 10 Selected Bucks County Churches; Home of the Durner Organ Factory - Quakertown, PA.** Henrietta Moyer Landis Jahnsen. 224p. 1999. pap. write for info. (*0-9676181-0-X*) Saint John Pubng.

Old Eagle-Nester: The Lost Legends of the Catskills. Doris W. Brooks. LC 92-73745. (Illus.). 128p. 1992. pap. 13.95 (*0-9628523-5-X*) Blk Dome Pr.

Old Earl Died Pulling Traps: A Story. deluxe limited ed. George V. Higgins. (Illus.). 33p. 1984. 75.00 (*0-89723-044-2*) Bruccoli.

Old Ebbw Vale in Photographs, 2. Keith Thomas. (C). 1989. 69.00 (*0-900807-41-5*, Pub. by D Brown & Sons Ltd) St Mut.

Old Ebbw Vale in Photographs, 3. Keith Thomas. (C). 1989. 69.00 (*0-900807-54-7*, Pub. by D Brown & Sons Ltd) St Mut.

Old Ebbw Vale in Photographs, 4. Keith Thomas. (C). 1989. 69.00 (*0-900807-66-0*, Pub. by D Brown & Sons Ltd) St Mut.

Old Egyptian Medical Papyri: The Hearst Papyrus. Chauncey D. Leake. 108p. (C). 1994. pap. text 15.00 (*0-89005-271-9*) Ares.

"Old" El Toro Reader: A Guide to the Past. Joe Osterman. Ed. by Doris Walker & Tim Osterman. LC 92-96902. (Illus.). 112p. (J). (gr. 3-6). 1992. pap. 9.95 (*1-881129-02-0*) Old El Toro Pr.

Old Electrical Wiring. David E. Shapiro. LC 97-48869. (Illus.). 400p. 1998. pap. 39.95 (*0-07-057879-6*) McGraw.

Old Eliot, Bk. 1. Ed. by John L. Wills. (Illus.). 720p. 1985. reprint ed. 45.00 (*0-89725-053-2*, 1204) Picton Pr.

Old Eliot, Bk. 2. John L. Wills. (Illus.). 720p. 1985. reprint ed. 50.00 (*0-89725-056-7*, 1205) Picton Pr.

Old Eliot, Bk. 3. Ed. by John L. Wills. (Illus.). 720p. 1985. reprint ed. 45.00 (*0-89725-057-5*, 1206) Picton Pr.

Old Elm Speaks: Tree Poems. Kristine O'Connel George. LC 97-49333. (Illus.). 48p. (J). (gr. k-4). 1998. 15.00 (*0-395-87611-7*, Clarion Bks) HM.

Old Emigrant Trail: Story of the Lost Trail to Oregon, the Oregon Trail. Ezra Meeker. LC 93-43227. 64p. 1994. pap. 7.50 (*0-936738-78-2*) Webb Research.

Old Empires, New Nations. Mason. 1994. pap. text. write for info. (*0-582-22666-X*, Pub. by Addison-Wesley) Longman.

Old Enchantment. Amanda Browning. (Presents Ser.). 1994. per. 2.99 (*0-373-11677-2*, 1-11677-1) Harlequin Bks.

Old Enemies. Janet Lapierre. 256p. 1993. text 20.00 (*0-684-19614-X*, Scribners Ref) Mac Lib Ref.

Old Enemy: Satan & the Combat Myth. Neil Forsyth. 480p. (C). 1989. pap. text 29.50 (*0-691-01474-4*, Pub. by Princeton U Pr) Cal Prin Full Svc.

Old Enemy Juice. Phil Hall. 80p. 1988. pap. 12.95 (*0-919627-92-7*, Pub. by Quarry Pr) LPC InBook.

Old England & New England, in a Series of Views Taken on the Spot, 2 vols., 1 bk. Alfred Bunn. LC 68-20213. (Illus.). 1972. reprint ed. 26.95 (*0-405-08330-0*, Pub. by Blom Pubns) Ayer.

Old English: A Historical Linguistic Companion. Roger Lass. LC 93-18182. 320p. (C). 1994. pap. text 34.95 (*0-521-45848-X*) Cambridge U Pr.

Old English: A Historical Linguistic Companion. Roger Lass. LC 93-18182. 320p. (C). 1994. text 95.00 (*0-521-43087-9*) Cambridge U Pr.

Old English: Grammar & Reader. Robert E. Diamond. LC 89-5763. (Waynebooks Ser.: No. 38). 304p. (C). 1970. pap. text 17.95 (*0-8143-1510-0*) Wayne St U Pr.

Old English & Its Closest Relatives: A Survey of the Earliest Germanic Languages. LC 93-25183. 1993. pap. write for info. (*0-415-10406-8*) Routledge.

Old English & Its Closest Relatives: A Survey of the Earliest Germanic Languages. Orrin W. Robinson. (Illus.). 304p. (C). 1992. 47.50 (*0-8047-1454-1*) Stanford U Pr.

Old English & Its Closest Relatives: A Survey of the Earliest Germanic Languages. Orrin W. Robinson. 304p. (C). 1993. pap. 16.95 (*0-8047-2221-8*) Stanford U Pr.

Old English & Medieval Literature. Ed. by Gordon H. Gerould. LC 70-114913. (Select Bibliographies Reprint Ser.). 1977. 23.95 (*0-8369-5312-6*) Ayer.

Old English & Medieval Literature. Gordon H. Gerould. 1988. reprint ed. lib. bdg. 49.00 (*0-7812-0479-8*) Rprt Serv.

Old English & Medieval Literature. Ed. by Gordon H. Gerould. LC 74-145040. 404p. 1972. reprint ed. 65.00 (*0-403-00989-8*) Scholarly.

Old English & New: Studies in Language & Linguistics in Honor of Frederick G. Cassidy. Ed. by Joan H. Hall et al. LC 92-20823. 504p. 1992. text 75.00 (*0-8153-1086-2*, H1652) Garland.

Old English Andreas & Bishop Acca of Hexham. Albert S. Cook. (Connecticut Academy of Arts & Sciences Ser., Trans.: Vol. 26). 1924. pap. 49.50 (*0-685-22820-7*) Elliots Bks.

Old English Apocrypha & Their Manuscript Source: "The Gospel of Nichodemus" & "The Avenging of the Saviour" Ed. by J. E. Cross. (Studies in Anglo-Saxon England: No. 19). (Illus.). 318p. (C). 1997. text 74.95 (*0-521-56194-9*) Cambridge U Pr.

Old English Biblical Verse: Studies in Genesis, Exodus & Daniel. Paul G. Remley. LC 96-176696. (Studies in Anglo-Saxon England: No. 16). 493p. (C). 1996. text 80.00 (*0-521-47454-X*) Cambridge U Pr.

Old English Dramatists. James Russell Lowell. 1977. text 12.95 (*0-8369-8166-9*, 8306) Ayer.

Old English Dramatists. James Russell Lowell. (Notable American Authors Ser.). 1999. reprint ed. lib. bdg. 125.00 (*0-7812-3899-4*) Rprt Serv.

Old English Edition, 25 vols., Set. Incl. Anthems & Motets. Robert White. 1968. reprint ed. pap. 37.50 (*0-8450-1621-0*); First Book of Songs: or Ayres of Four Parts: Part One 1605. Francis Pilkington. Ed. by G. E. Arkwright. (Illus.). 1968. reprint ed. pap. 37.50 (*0-8450-1618-0*); First Book of Songs: or Ayres of Four Parts: Part Threes 1605. Francis Pilkington. Ed. by G. E. Arkwright. (Illus.). 1968. reprint ed. pap. 37.50 (*0-8450-1620-2*); First Book of Songs: or Ayres of Four Parts: Part Two 1605. Francis Pilkington. Ed. by G. E. Arkwright. (Illus.). 1968. reprint ed. pap. 37.50 (*0-8450-1619-9*); Five Madrigals to Six Voices from Musica Transalpina, 1588. Alfonso Ferrabosco. Ed. by G. E. Arkwright. 1968. reprint ed. pap. 37.50 (*0-8450-1612-1*); Masque in Honor of the Marriage of Lord Hayes, 1607. Thomas Campion. Ed. by G. E. Arkwright. 1968. reprint ed. pap. 37.50 (*0-8450-1601-6*); Nine Madrigals to Five Voices from Musica Transalpina, 1588. Alfonso Ferrabosco. 1968. reprint ed. pap. 37.50 (*0-8450-1611-3*); Six Anthems. John Milton. Ed. by G. E. Arkwright. 1968. reprint ed. pap. 37.50 (*0-8450-1622-9*); Six Madrigals to Four Voices, 1597. George Kirbye. Ed. by G. E. Arkwright. 1968. reprint ed. pap. 37.50 (*0-8450-1603-2*); Six Madrigals to Six Voices, 1597. George Kirbye. Ed. by G. E. Arkwright. 1968. reprint ed. pap. 37.50 (*0-8450-1605-9*); Six Songs. Thomas A. Arne. Ed. by G. E. Arkwright. 1968. reprint ed. pap. 37.50 (*0-8450-1602-4*); Six Songs from Amphion Anglicus, 1700. John Blow. 1968. reprint ed. pap. 37.50 (*0-8450-1623-7*); Six Songs from the "Orpheus Britannicus" Henry Purcell. Ed. by G. E. Arkwright. (Illus.). 1968. reprint ed. pap. 37.50 (*0-8450-1624-5*); Twelve Madrigals to Five Voices, 1597. George Kirbye. Ed. by G. E. Arkwright. 1968. reprint ed. pap. 37.50 (*0-8450-1604-0*); 1968. reprint ed. Set pap. 675.00 (*0-8450-1600-8*) Broude.

Old English Elegies: A Critical Edition & Genre Study. Anne L. Klinck. (Illus.). 520p. 1992. 95.00 (*0-7735-0836-8*, Pub. by McG-Queens Univ Pr) CUP Services.

Old English Elegies: New Essays in Criticism & Research. Ed. by Martin Green. LC 82-48525. 240p. 1983. 38.50 (*0-8386-3141-X*) Fairleigh Dickinson.

Old English Exodus. Ed. by Joan Turville-Petre. Tr. & Text by J. R. R. Tolkien. (C). 1982. 48.00 (*0-19-811177-0*) OUP.

Old English Farmhouses. Bill Laws. (Illus.). 160p. 1992. 29.95 (*1-55859-407-8*) Abbeville Pr.

Old English Finding of the True Cross. Ed. & Tr. by Mary-Catherine Bodden from ANG. (Illus.). 144p. 1987. 75.00 (*0-85991-198-5*) Boydell & Brewer.

Old English Glosses, Chiefly Unpublished. Ed. by Arthur S. Napier. (Anecdota Oxoniensia Ser.: No. 11). 1988. reprint ed. 76.50 (*0-404-63961-5*) AMS Pr.

Old English Glosses, Chiefly Unpublished. Ed. by Arthur S. Napier. (Anecdota Oxoniensia Ser.: Vol. IV, Pt. XI). xxxix, 302p. 1969. reprint ed. 50.70 (*0-685-66495-3*, 05102254) G Olms Pubs.

Old English Grammar. Randolph Quirk & C. L. Wren. LC 93-39877. 186p. (C). 1994. reprint ed. pap. text 15.00 (*0-87580-560-4*) N Ill U Pr.

Old English Grammar. 3rd ed. Alistair Campbell. 440p. (C). 1983. pap. text 24.95 (*0-19-811943-7*) OUP.

Old English Grammar. 3rd ed. Eduard Sievers. Tr. by Albert S. Cook. LC 73-120775. reprint ed. 37.50 (*0-404-05998-8*) AMS Pr.

Old English Grammar. 3rd ed. Eduard Sievers. Tr. by Albert S. Cook. LC 68-9713. (Illus.). 442p. 1969. reprint ed. lib. bdg. 38.50 (*0-8371-0228-6*, SIOE, Greenwood Pr) Greenwood.

Old English Heptateuch, Ms Cott. S. J. Crawford. (EETS, OS Ser.: Vol. 160). 1974. reprint ed. 65.00 (*0-8115-3417-0*) Periodicals Srv.

Old English Herbals. Eleanor S. Rohde. 1989. pap. 8.95 (*0-486-26193-X*) Dover.

Old English Herbarium & Medicina de Quadrupedibus. Ed. by H. J. De Vriend. (Early English Text Society Original Ser.: No. 286). 1984. 59.00 (*0-19-722288-9*) OUP.

Old English Hexateuch: Aspects & Approaches. Ed. by Rebecca Barnhouse & Benjamin C. Withers. (Publications of the Richard Rawlinson Center). (C). 40.00 (*1-58044-024-X*); pap. 20.00 (*1-58044-050-9*) Medieval Inst.

Old English Homilies & Homiletic Treatises, Pts. I & II. Ed. by Richard Morris. (EETS, OS Ser.: No. 29 & 34). 1974. reprint ed. 55.00 (*0-527-00029-9*) Periodicals Srv.

O

An Asterisk (*) at the beginning of an entry indicates that the title is appearing for the first time.

Old English Homilies from MS. Bodley 343. Ed. by Susan Irvine. (Early English Text Society Original Ser.: No. 302). (Illus.). 328p. (C). 1993. text 45.00 (*0-19-722304-4*) OUP.

Old English Homilies of the 13th Century. Ed. by Richard Morris. (EETS, OS Series II: No. 53). 1974. reprint ed. 50.00 (*0-527-00048-5*) Periodicals Srv.

Old English Homily & Its Background. Ed. by Paul E. Szarmach & Bernard F. Huppe. LC 77-21447. 267p. (C). 1978. text 24.50 (*0-87395-376-2*) State U NY Pr.

Old English Illustrated Hexateuch see Early English Manuscripts in Facsimile

***Old English in Ireland, 1625-42.** Aidan Clarke. 288p. 2000. pap. 29.95 (*1-85182-552-5*, Pub. by Four Cts Pr) Intl Spec Bk.

Old English Instruments of Music: Their History & Character. Francis W. Galpin. 1988. reprint ed. lib. bdg. 89.00 (*0-7812-0213-2*) Rprt Serv.

Old English Instruments of Music: Their History & Character. 3rd rev. ed. Francis W. Galpin. LC 74-181161. 327p. 1932. reprint ed. 69.00 (*0-403-01562-6*) Scholarly.

Old English Life of Machutus. Ed. by David Yerkes. (Old English Ser.: No. 9). 288p. 1984. text 50.00 (*0-8020-5626-1*) U of Toronto Pr.

Old English Literature. Edith E. Wardale. 1988. reprint ed. lib. bdg. 75.00 (*0-7812-0693-6*) Rprt Serv.

Old English Literature: A Select Bibliography. Fred C. Robinson. LC 76-464039. (Toronto Medieval Bibliographies Ser.: No. 2). 86p. reprint ed. pap. 30.00 (*0-608-16237-X*, 202647000049) Bks Demand.

Old English Literature: Twenty-Two Analytical Essays. Ed. by Martin Stevens & Jerome Mandel. LC 68-11565. 347p. reprint ed. pap. 107.60 (*0-7837-1902-7*, 204210600001) Bks Demand.

Old English Manor: A Study in English Economic History. Charles M. Andrews. LC 78-64257. (Johns Hopkins University. Studies in the Social Sciences. Thirtieth Ser. 1912: 12). reprint ed. 41.50 (*0-404-61360-8*) AMS Pr.

Old English Miscellany Containing a Bestiary, Etc. Ed. by Richard Morris. (EETS, OS Ser.: No. 49). 1974. reprint ed. 55.00 (*0-527-00045-0*) Periodicals Srv.

Old English Orosius. Ed. by Janet Bately. (SS 6 Ser.). (Illus.). 1981. text 69.00 (*0-19-722406-7*) OUP.

Old English Paperweights. Robert Hall. LC 98-16917. 1998. 39.95 (*0-7643-0539-5*) Schiffer.

Old English Personal Names in Bede's History. H. Strom. (Lund Studies in English: Vol. 8). 1974. reprint ed. pap. 30.00 (*0-8115-0551-0*) Periodicals Srv.

***Old English Poem "Judgement Day II" A Critical Edition with Editions of Bede's "De Die Iudich" & the Hatton 113 "Be Domes Daege"** Ed. by Graham D. Caie. LC 99-52815. (Anglo-Saxon Texts Ser.). 192p. 2000. 75.00 (*0-85991-570-0*, DS Brewer) Boydell & Brewer.

Old English Poetic Metre. B. R. Hutcheson. 367p. 1995. 99.00 (*0-85991-435-6*) Boydell & Brewer.

Old English Poetry: Alliterative Verse. Tr. by J. Duncan Spaeth. LC 67-30879. 200p. 1967. reprint ed. 50.00 (*0-87752-103-4*) Gordian.

Old English Poetry & the Genealogy of Events. Richard J. Schrader. (Medieval Texts & Studies: No. 12). 206p. 1993. 24.95 (*0-937191-52-3*) Mich St U Pr.

Old English Poetry in Medieval Christian Perspective: A Doctrinal Approach. Judith N. Garde. 240p. 1991. 75.00 (*0-85991-307-4*) Boydell & Brewer.

Old English Prepositional Compounds in Relationship to Their Latin Originals. J. R. Hendrickson. (LD Ser.: No. 43). 1948. pap. 25.00 (*0-527-00789-7*) Periodicals Srv.

Old English Prose. Ed. by Carl Berkhout et al. (Basic Readings on Anglo-Saxon England Ser.). 300p. Date not set. text 40.00 (*0-8153-0305-X*) Garland.

Old English Prose of Secular Learning. Stephanie Hollis & Michael Wright. (Annotated Bibliographies Ser.: Vol. IV). 416p. (C). 1993. 75.00 (*0-85991-343-0*, DS Brewer) Boydell & Brewer.

***Old English Prose Translations of King Alfred's Reign.** Gregory Waite. (Annotated Bibliographies of Old & Middle English Literature Ser.: Vol. 1353-8675). 352p. 2000. 75.00 (*0-85991-591-3*) Boydell & Brewer.

Old English Recipes. Michael Barry. (Illus.). 144p. 1996. pap. 16.95 (*0-7117-0811-8*, Pub. by JARR UK) Seven Hills Bk.

Old English Riddles: From the Exeter Book. Michael Alexander. 72p. 1984. pap. 14.95 (*0-85646-070-2*, Pub. by Anvil Press) Dufour.

Old English Riddles of the "Exeter Book" Craig Williamson. LC 76-46278. (Illus.). xx, 484p. 1977. text 55.00 (*0-8078-1272-2*) U of NC Pr.

Old English Riddles of the "Exeter Book" Ed. by Craig Williamson. LC 76-46278. (Illus.). 504p. 1977. reprint ed. pap. 156.30 (*0-7837-9024-4*, 204977500003) Bks Demand.

Old English Roses in Embroidery: Cross Stitch, Freestyle, Embroidery, Quilting, Cutwork, Canvaswork. Jane Iles. (Illus.). 96p. 1994. 24.95 (*0-7153-0201-9*, Pub. by D & C Pub) Sterling.

Old English Rune Poem: A Critical Edition. Maureen Halsall. LC 82-114659. (McMaster Old English Studies & Texts: No. 2). 208p. reprint ed. pap. 64.50 (*0-8357-4727-1*, 203764300009) Bks Demand.

Old English Semantic-Field Studies. Vic Strite. (American University Studies: English Language & Literature: Ser. IV, Vol. 100). XII, 239p. (C). 1989. text 37.95 (*0-8204-1067-5*) P Lang Pubng.

Old English Sheepdog. Joan M. Brearley. (Illus.). 356p. 1989. 24.95 (*0-86622-710-5*, PS-817) TFH Pubns.

Old English Sheepdog Champions, 1952-1987. Camino E. E. & Bk. Co. Staff. 175p. 1989. pap. 36.95 (*0-940808-88-9*) Camino E E & Bk.

Old English Sheepdogs. Stuart A. Kallen. LC 97-14830. (Dogs Ser.). (J). 1998. lib. bdg. 13.95 (*1-56239-575-0*) ABDO Pub Co.

Old English Sheepdogs. Beverly Pisano. (Illus.). 1996. pap. 9.95 (*0-7938-2367-6*, KW-093S) TFH Pubns.

***Old English Sheepdogs.** Joan H. Walker. LC 99-14172. (Complete Pet Owner's Manual Ser.). (Illus.). 104p. 1999. pap. 6.95 (*0-7641-0735-6*) Barron.

Old English Shorter Poems: Basic Readings. Katherine O. O'Keefe. LC 94-10194. (Basic Readings on Anglo-Saxon England Ser.: Vol. 3). 456p. 1994. text 77.00 (*0-8153-0097-2*, H1432) Garland.

Old English Songs. Ed. by Austin Dobson. LC 70-116398. (Granger Index Reprint Ser.). 1977. 18.95 (*0-8369-6139-0*) Ayer.

Old English "Soul & Body" Ed. & Tr. by Douglas Moffat. (Illus.). 111p. (C). 1990. 75.00 (*0-85991-232-9*) Boydell & Brewer.

Old English Syntax: Concord, the Parts of Speech & the Sentence, 2 vols., Vol. 1. Bruce Mitchell. 884p. 1985. text 165.00 (*0-19-811935-6*) OUP.

Old English Syntax: Subordination, Indedpendent Element & Element Order, 2 vols., II. Bruce Mitchell. 1,124p. 1985. text 200.00 (*0-19-811944-5*) OUP.

Old English Tile Designs for Artists & Craftspeople. Carol B. Grafton. (Pictorial Archive Ser.). 128p. 1985. reprint ed. pap. 7.95 (*0-486-24777-5*) Dover.

Old English Verse Saints Lives: A Study in Direct Discourse & the Iconography of Style. Robert E. Bjork. 192p. 1985. text 32.50 (*0-8020-2569-2*) U of Toronto Pr.

Old English Version of Bede's Ecclesiastical History, Pt. II, No. 1. Ed. by T. Miller. (EETS, OS Ser.: Vol. 110). 1974. reprint ed. 50.00 (*0-8115-3368-9*) Periodicals Srv.

Old English Version of the Enlarged Rule of Chrodegang. Chrodegang. (EETS, OS Ser.: No. 150). 1974. reprint ed. 36.00 (*0-527-00146-5*) Periodicals Srv.

***Old English Version of the Gospels, Vol. 2.** Ed. by R. M. Liuzza. (Early English Text Society Original Ser.: Vol. 314). 381p. 2000. text 74.00 (*0-19-722313-3*) OUP.

Old English Versions of the Gospels Vol. I: Text & Introduction. Ed. by Roy M. Liuzza. (Early English Text Society-Original Ser.: No. 304). (Illus.). 280p. 1994. text 55.00 (*0-19-722306-0*) OUP.

Old English Villages. Clay Perry et al. (Country Ser.). (Illus.). 160p. 1997. pap. 17.95 (*0-7538-0263-5*, Pub. by Weidenfeld & Nicolson) Trafalgar.

Old English Vision of St. Paul. Ed. by Antonette DiPaolo-Healey. LC 77-89928. 1978. 20.00 (*0-910956-76-6*, SAM 2); pap. 12.00 (*0-910956-62-6*) Medieval Acad.

Old English Wisdom Poetry, Vol. 5. Russell Poole. LC 98-27022. (Annotated Bibliographies of Old & Middle English Ser.). 432p. 1998. 99.00 (*0-85991-530-1*) Boydell & Brewer.

Old English Word Studies: A Preliminary Author & Word Index. Ed. by Angus Cameron et al. (McMaster Old English Studies & Texts). 208p. 1983. text 65.00 (*0-8020-5526-5*) U of Toronto Pr.

Old Enough & Other Stories. Ed. by Christine Evans. (YA). (gr. 6-12). 1997. pap. 13.95 (*0-8464-4601-4*) Beekman Pubs.

Old Enough & Other Stories. Christine Evans. 1997. pap. 23.00 (*1-85902-418-1*, Pub. by Gomer Pr) St Mut.

Old Enough for Magic. Anola Pickett. LC 88-30320. (I Can Read Bks.). (Illus.). 64p. (J). (ps-3). 1989. 13.00 (*0-06-024731-2*) HarpC Child Bks.

Old Enough to Die. Ridley Wills, II. LC 95-81701. (Illus.). 192p. 1996. 24.95 (*1-881576-81-7*, Hillsboro Pr) Providence Hse.

Old Enough to Feel Better: A Medical Guide for Seniors. rev. ed. Michael Gordon. LC 89-1682. (Illus.). 416p. reprint ed. pap. 129.00 (*0-608-06119-0*, 206645200008) Bks Demand.

Old Enough to Know see Edad para Saber

***Old Enough to Know.** Michael W. Smith. 160p. (J). (gr. 5-9). 2000. pap. 9.99 (*0-8499-7587-5*) Tommy Nelson.

Old Enough to Know: What Teenagers Must Know about Life & Relationships. Michael W. Smith & Fritz Ridenour. 146p. (YA). (gr. 7 up). 1989. pap. 9.99 (*0-8499-3162-2*) Tommy Nelson.

Old Estonian Folk Religion. Ivar Paulson. LC 76-63029. (Uralic & Altaic Ser.: Vol. 108). (Orig.). 1971. pap. text. write for info. (*0-87750-154-8*) Curzon Pr Ltd.

Old European Jewries. David Philipson. LC 74-178586. reprint ed. 41.50 (*0-404-56663-4*) AMS Pr.

Old European Order 1660-1800. 2nd ed. William Doyle. (Short Oxford History of the Modern World Ser.). (Illus.). 438p. (C). 1993. pap. text 29.95 (*0-19-820387-X*) OUP.

Old Europe's Suicide, or the Building of a Pyramid of Errors see Three Generals on War

Old Faith: Poems. William Miller. LC 92-15312. 64p. 1992. pap. 14.95 (*0-7734-0042-7*, Mellen Poetry Pr) E Mellen.

Old Faith & the New, 2 vols. in 1. David F. Strauss. Tr. by Mathilde Blind from GER. LC 96-37772. 405p. 1997. pap. 32.95 (*1-57392-118-1*) Prometheus Bks.

Old Faith, Hope & Charityy: A Two-Act Comedy with Lots of Heart. Pat Cook. 1998. pap. 8.99 (*0-8341-9087-7*) Lillenas.

Old Faithful. Bob Reese. (Yellowstone Ser.). (Illus.). (J). (gr. k-6). 1986. 9.95 (*0-89868-167-7*); pap. 3.95 (*0-89868-168-5*) ARO Pub.

Old Faithful: Eighteen Writers Present Their Favorite Writing Assignments. Ed. by Christopher Edgar & Ron Padgett. (Illus.). 160p. (Orig.). 1995. pap. 14.95 (*0-915924-45-5*) Tchrs & Writers Coll.

Old Faithful Murder. Valerie Wolzien. 1992. mass mkt. 5.99 (*0-449-14744-4*, GM) Fawcett.

Old Familiar Faces. Theodore Watts-Dunton. LC 76-105048. (Essay Index Reprint Ser.). 1977. 23.95 (*0-8369-1585-2*) Ayer.

Old Familiar Places. Robert Funderburk. LC 96-4505. (Innocent Years Ser.: No. 4). 288p. 1996. pap. 8.99 (*1-55661-463-2*) Bethany Hse.

***Old Families of Louisiana.** Stanley C. Arthur & George C. de Kernion. 432p. 1999. reprint ed. pap. 36.50 (*0-8063-4688-4*, Pub. by Clearfield Co) ACCESS Pubs Network.

***Old Families of Newry & District from Gravestone Inscriptions, Wills & Biographical Notes.** Brian Traynor. LC 99-175803. xx, 249p. 1998. 17.00 (*0-901905-76-3*, Pub. by Ulster Hist Fnd) Irish Bks Media.

Old Families of Salisbury & Amesbury, Massachusetts. David W. Hoyt. LC 81-83877. 1097p. 1979. reprint ed. 65.00 (*0-89725-026-5*, 1236) Picton Pr.

***Old Families of Staten Island.** J. J. Clute. 103p. 2000. reprint ed. pap. 16.00 (*0-8063-4768-6*, Pub. by Clearfield Co) ACCESS Pubs Network.

Old Family Movies: A Book of Poems. Robert Kirschten. LC 99-32223. 84p. 1999. pap. text 14.95 (*0-7734-3127-6*) E Mellen.

Old Family Recipes: Now You Can Cook Like Grandma. Ed. by Dana S. Cutts & Gretchen S. Cutts. (Illus.). 120p. 1996. spiral bd. 10.95 (*0-9658705-0-2*) Old Fmly Recipes.

Old Farm Buildings. Nigel Harvey. (Album Ser.: No. 10). (Illus.). 32p. 5.25 (*0-85263-865-5*, Pub. by Shire Pubns) Parkwest Pubns.

***Old Farm Dogs.** David Hancock. 1999. pap. 25.00 (*0-7478-0429-X*, Pub. by Shire Pubns) St Mut.

Old Farm Machinery in Australia: A Fieldguide & Sourcebook. Margaret Simpson & Phillip Simpson. 1993. reprint ed. pap. 21.95 (*0-86417-158-7*, Pub. by Kangaroo Pr) Seven Hills Bk.

Old Farmer & His Almanack. George L. Kittredge. (Illus.). 403p. 1974. reprint ed. 32.95 (*0-87928-049-2*) Corner Hse.

Old Farmer's Almanac. 1992. 14.95 (*0-89909-250-0*) Random.

Old Farmer's Almanac. Old Farmer's Almanac Staff. 1997. pap. 4.95 (*0-375-75037-1*) Villard Books.

Old Farmer's Almanac: Book of Everyday Advice. Ed. by Judson D. Hale, Sr. (Illus.). 212p. 1998. text 22.00 (*0-7881-5957-7*) DIANE Pub.

Old Farmer's Almanac 2000. Judson Hale. (Illus.). 320p. 1999. pap. 5.95 (*1-57198-146-2*, Pub. by Yankee NH) Random.

Old Farmer's Almanac 2000. Ed. by Judson Hale. (Illus.). 320p. 1999. 15.95 (*1-57198-151-9*, Pub. by Yankee NH) Random.

Old Farmer's Almanac Garden, 1992. Yankee Books Staff. Date not set. 4.95 (*0-89909-234-9*) St Martin.

Old Farmer's Almanac, 1997. Ed. by Judson D. Hale. 1996. 15.95 (*1-57198-027-X*) Random.

Old Farmer's Almanac 1999. Ed. by Judson D. Hale. 288p. 1998. pap. 4.95 (*1-57198-086-5*) Yankee NH.

Old Farmer's Almanac 1999. Ed. by Yankee Publishing Staff. 1998. 15.90 (*1-57198-090-3*) Yankee NH.

***Old Farmer's Almanac 2001.** Judson D. Hale. (Illus.). 2000. 15.95 (*1-57198-166-7*); pap. 5.95 (*1-57198-155-1*) Villard Books.

Old Farmers Almanac, '99. Old Farmers Almanac Staff. 1998. write for info. (*0-676-57785-7*) Villard Books.

***Old Farmer's Encyclopedia: A Practical Compendium of Traditional American Wisdom & Know-How.** Sheila Buff. 2000. pap. 19.95 (*1-58574-155-8*) Lyon Press.

***Old Fart.** John Halvorsen. LC 99-96680. 2000. 15.95 (*0-533-13315-7*) Vantage.

Old Fart Book. Bruce Cochran. (Illus.). 10p. 1994. write for info. (*1-886386-26-9*) Trisar.

Old Fashinoed Roses (London) James Whitcomb Riley. (Notable American Authors Ser.). 1999. reprint ed. lib. bdg. 125.00 (*0-7812-8784-7*) Rprt Serv.

Old-Fashioned Afghans to Knit & Crochet. Rita Weiss. 48p. (Orig.). 1986. pap. 3.50 (*0-486-25054-7*) Dover.

Old-Fashioned All-Occasion Postcards. Gabriella Oldham. 1990. pap. text 4.95 (*0-486-26265-0*) Dover.

Old Fashioned Amish Cooking. Victor Eicher et al. (Illus.). Date not set. spiral bd. 8.95 (*0-917925-00-9*) Pike Printing Publishing.

Old Fashioned Amish-Mennonite Cookin' A Collection of Sugarless Favorites. Susie Christner. (Illus.). 240p. 1995. spiral bd. 12.95 (*0-9647852-0-X*) Favorite Cookbks.

Old-Fashioned Applique Quilt Designs. Susan Johnston. (Design Library). 48p. 1985. pap. 3.95 (*0-486-24845-3*) Dover.

Old Fashioned Baki. Jim Fobel. 1996. pap. write for info. (*0-517-88629-4*) C Potter.

Old-Fashioned Birds. Carol Belanger Grafton. 1998. 3.95 (*0-486-40071-9*) Dover.

Old Fashioned, Bygone, Yesteryear & Way Back When Products Catalogs: A Report. rev. ed. Data Notes Research Staff. LC 83-90728. 100p. 1996. ring bd. 32.95 (*0-911569-62-6*) Prosperity & Profits.

Old-Fashioned Cats Stickers & Seals. Maggie Kate. (Illus.). (J). 1995. pap. 3.95 (*0-486-28649-5*) Dover.

Old Fashioned Children's Games: Over 200 Outdoors, Car Trip, Song, Card & Party Activities. Sharon O'Bryan. (Illus.). 143p. 1998. pap. 23.50 (*0-7864-0558-9*) McFarland & Co.

Old-Fashioned Christmas. Colleen L. Reece et al. LC 98-101317. (Christmas Fiction Collection). 352p. 1997. pap. 4.97 (*1-57748-083-X*) Barbour Pub.

Old-Fashioned Christmas: A One-Act Comedy. Sally Bowman. (Illus.). 12p. 1996. pap. 3.25 (*0-88680-424-8*) I E Clark.

Old Fashioned Christmas: Piano/Vocal Folio. 60p. (Orig.). 1988. pap. 8.95 (*0-7692-1107-0*, VF1468) Wrner Bros.

Old-Fashioned Christmas Charted Designs. Barbara Christopher. LC 92-5583. (Needlework Ser.). 48p. 1992. pap. 3.50 (*0-486-27153-6*) Dover.

Old-Fashioned Christmas Gift Labels: An Unabridged Reprint of the 1901-2 Edition, Vol. 275. Carol B. Grafton. 1989. pap. 2.95 (*0-486-26046-1*) Dover.

Old-Fashioned Christmas in Illustration & Decoration. Clarence P. Hornung. (Illus.). 158p. (Orig.). 1975. pap. 7.95 (*0-486-22367-1*) Dover.

Old-Fashioned Country Christmas: A Celebration of the Holiday Season. LC 97-28366. (Illus.). 256p. (gr. 7). 1999. 19.95 (*0-7835-5283-1*) Time-Life.

Old-Fashioned Country Christmas: A Holiday Keepsake of Recipes, Traditions, Homemade Gifts, Decorating Ideas & Favorite Childhood Memories. 7th ed. Ed. by Gooseberry Patch Staff. (Illus.). 224p. 1992. spiral bd. 14.95 (*0-9632978-0-5*) Gooseberry Patch.

Old Fashioned Country Cookies: Yummy Recipes, Tips, Traditions, How-to's & Sweet Memories...Everything Cookies! Ed. by Gooseberry Patch Staff. LC 95-229450. (Illus.). 224p. 1994. spiral bd. 14.95 (*0-9632978-2-1*) Gooseberry Patch.

Old-Fashioned Courtship & How It Works Today. Jeff Barth. Ed. by Marge Barth. LC 98-220727. Orig. Title: Guidelines for Courtship & Preparation for Marriage. 96p. 1998. pap. 8.00 (*1-891484-00-1*) Parable Pub.

Old-Fashioned Dogs. Maggie Kate. 1998. 3.95 (*0-486-40184-7*) Dover.

Old-Fashioned Doilies to Crochet. Ed. by Rita Weiss. (Illus.). 48p. (Orig.). 1987. pap. 3.95 (*0-486-25402-X*) Dover.

Old-Fashioned Dutch Oven Cookbook. Don Holm. LC 70-84782. (Illus.). (Orig.). 1969. pap. 14.95 (*0-87004-133-9*) Caxton.

Old Fashioned Festivals & Community Celebrations in Washington see Wonderful Washington Events Guide, 1998

Old Fashioned Festivals & Community Celebrations in Washington see Wonderful Washington Events Guide, 1997

Old-Fashioned Floral Charted Designs. Barbara Christopher. (Illus.). 48p. 1990. pap. 3.95 (*0-486-26302-9*) Dover.

***Old-Fashioned Floral Designs.** (Electronic Clip Art Ser.). (Illus.). 64p. 1999. text 9.95 (*0-486-99963-7*) Dover.

Old-Fashioned Floral Iron-On Transfer Patterns. Waldrep. (Illus.). pap. 3.95 (*0-486-27392-X*) Dover.

***Old-Fashioned Flowers: Classic Blossoms to Grow in Your Garden.** Tovah Martin. (Illus.). 112p. 2000. pap. text 9.95 (*1-889538-15-9*) Bklyn Botanic.

Old-Fashioned Frames. Dover Staff. (Illus.). 64p. 1998. pap. 9.95 incl. cd-rom (*0-486-99950-5*) Dover.

***Old-Fashioned Fruit & Vegetable Stickers: 62 Full-Color Pressure-Sensitive Stickers.** Carol Belanger Grafton. (Illus.). (J). 1998. pap. 4.95 (*0-486-40388-2*) Dover.

Old Fashioned Gardens. Trevor Nottle. (Illus.). 192p. 1993. 29.95 (*0-86417-436-5*, Pub. by Kangaroo Pr) Seven Hills Bk.

Old-Fashioned Girl. Louisa May Alcott. LC 96-29254. 352p. (J). (gr. 4-6). 1997. pap. 9.95 (*0-316-03775-3*) Little.

Old-Fashioned Girl. Louisa May Alcott. LC 96-29254. (J). 1999. 25.01 (*0-316-03809-1*) Little.

Old-Fashioned Girl. Louisa May Alcott. (J). 1997. pap. 2.95 (*0-8167-1462-2*) Troll Communs.

Old-Fashioned Girl. Louisa May Alcott. (Puffin Classics). (J). 1996. 10.09 (*0-606-11700-8*, Pub. by Turtleback) Demco.

Old-Fashioned Girl. Louisa May Alcott. (Illus.). 368p. (YA). (gr. 5-9). 1996. pap. 5.99 (*0-14-037449-3*) Viking Penguin.

Old-Fashioned Girl. Everett A. Blackman. 96p. (C). 1999. lib. bdg. 10.95 (*0-9622469-5-6*) Norcor Enterprises.

Old-Fashioned Girl. Betty A. Neels. 1993. per. 2.99 (*0-373-15533-6*) Harlequin Bks.

Old-Fashioned Girl. Louisa May Alcott. (Works of Louisa May Alcott). 1989. reprint ed. lib. bdg. 79.00 (*0-7812-1628-1*) Rprt Serv.

***Old-Fashioned Girl, Vol. 1.** Louisa May Alcott. LC 98-36885. (Chapter Book Charmers Ser.). 80p. (J). (gr. 2-5). 1999. 2.99 (*0-694-01287-4*, HarpFestival) HarpC Child Bks.

Old Fashioned Home. 92p. 9.95 (*0-930061-06-3*) Interspace Bks.

Old-Fashioned Homemade Ice Cream: With 58 Original Recipes. Thomas R. Quinn. (Illus.). 48p. (Orig.). 1983. pap. 2.95 (*0-486-24495-4*) Dover.

Old-Fashioned Love. Arlene James. 1997. per. 4.50 (*0-373-87010-8*, 1-87010-4, Steeple Hill) Harlequin Bks.

Old-Fashioned Love: This Side of Heaven. Arlene James. (Romance Ser.). 1993. per. 2.75 (*0-373-08968-6*, 5-08968-5) Silhouette.

***Old Fashioned Love Songs.** (E-Z Play Today Ser.: Vol. #294). 112p. 1998. otabind 9.95 (*0-7935-9314-X*) H Leonard.

Old-Fashioned Love Story. Mildred E. Reeves. 209p. 1974. 7.50 (*0-318-04130-8*) Prairie Pub.

Old Fashioned Norman Rockwell Christmas. Norman Rockwell. 96p. 1997. 14.99 (*1-57866-010-6*) Galahad Bks.

Old-Fashioned Ribbon Art: Ideas & Designs for Accessories & Decorations. Ribbon Art Publishing Company Staff. (Illus.). 32p. 1986. pap. 2.95 (*0-486-25174-8*) Dover.

Old-Fashioned Ribbon Trimmings & Flowers. abr. ed. Mary B. Picken. LC 93-2506. Orig. Title: Ribbon Trimmings & Flowers: Instruction Paper with Examination Questions. (Illus.). 48p. 1993. reprint ed. pap. 3.50 (*0-486-27521-3*) Dover.

Old-Fashioned Roses: Address Book. Barbara Worl. (Illus.). 72p. 1990. 19.50 (*0-317-99996-6*) Sweetbrier.

Old-Fashioned Roses: Address Book. Barbara Worl. (Illus.). 72p. 1992. 24.50 (*0-936736-08-9*) Sweetbrier.

An Asterisk (*) at the beginning of an entry indicates that the title is appearing for the first time.

Old-Fashioned Silhouettes: Nine Hundred Forty-Two Copyright-Free Illustrations. Selected by Carol B. Grafton. LC 92-36762. (Pictorial Archive Ser.). (Illus.). 96p. 1993. pap. 7.95 (*0-486-27444-6*) Dover.

***Old-Fashioned Southern Christmas.** Leigh Greenwood et al. 448p. 1999. reprint ed. pap. 5.99 (*0-8439-4659-8*, Leisure Bks) Dorchester Pub Co.

Old-Fashioned Storybook. Ed. by Betty Schwartz. (Illus.). 144p. (J). (gr. k-6). 1985. 12.95 (*0-685-10340-4*) S&S Trade.

Old-Fashioned Thanksgiving. Louisa May Alcott. LC 93-36951. 62p. 1990. pap. 5.95 (*1-55709-135-8*) Applewood.

Old-Fashioned Thanksgiving. Louisa May Alcott. LC 93-20352. (Illus.). 40p. (J). (gr. k-3). 1993. 13.95 (*0-8249-8620-2*, Ideals Child) Hambleton-Hill.

Old-Fashioned Thanksgiving. Louisa May Alcott. LC 73-15698. (Illus.). 72p. (J). (gr. 4-6). 1974. 12.95 (*0-397-31515-5*) HarpC Child Bks.

Old-Fashioned Thanksgiving. Louisa May Alcott. LC 89-1908. (Illus.). 32p. (J). (gr. 4-6). 1989. lib. bdg. 14.95 (*0-8234-0772-1*) Holiday.

Old-Fashioned Thanksgiving. Louisa May Alcott. LC 93-20352. (Illus.). 40p. (J). (gr. k-3). 1995. reprint ed. pap., per. 5.95 (*1-57102-053-5*, Ideals Child) Hambleton-Hill.

Old-Fashioned Vignettes in Full Color: 397 Designs from Victorian Chromolithographs, Printed One Side. Ed. by Carol B. Grafton. (Pictorial Archive Ser.). (Illus.). 48p. (Orig.). 1988. pap. 7.95 (*0-486-25625-1*) Dover.

***Old-Fashioned Wild Animals Stickers: 84 Full-Color Pressure-Sensitive Designs.** Carol Belanger Grafton. (Illus.). (J). 1998. pap. 4.95 (*0-486-40389-0*) Dover.

Old-Fashioned Woman: Primitive Fancies about the Sex. Elsie C. Parsons. LC 72-2618. (American Women Ser.: Images & Realities). 378p. 1974. reprint ed. 26.95 (*0-405-04471-2*) Ayer.

Old Fashioned X-Mas. 60p. (YA). 1988. pap. 6.95 (*0-7692-0661-1*, PF0557); pap. 7.95 (*0-7692-0662-X*, PF0556) Wrner Bros.

Old, Fat, White Guys Guide to Ebonics. I. B. White. Ed. by Cliff Carle. 136p. 1997. pap. 5.95 (*1-57644-060-5*) CCC Pubns.

Old Father Storyteller: Grandfather Stories of the Pueblo Native American Indians. Pablita Velarde. LC 92-21175. (Illus.). 56p. 1993. reprint ed. pap. 14.95 (*0-940666-24-3*) Clear Light.

Old Father, the Story Teller: Grandfather Stories of the Pueblo Native American Indians. Pablita Velarde. LC 89-86056. 56p. 1994. 24.95 (*0-940666-10-3*) Clear Light.

Old Favorite Honey Recipes & Honey Recipes Book, 2 bks. in 1. American Honey Institute Staff & Iowa Honey Producers Association Staff. (Illus.). 96p. (Orig.). 1988. pap. 5.95 (*0-916638-17-0*) Meyerbooks.

Old Favorites in Miniature. Tina Gravatt. LC 93-15891. 103p. 1993. pap. 15.95 (*0-89145-808-5*, 3469, Am Quilters Soc) Collector Bks.

***Old Fears.** John Wooley & Ron Wolfe. 286p. 1999. pap. 14.95 (*0-9673131-1-2*) HAWK Pubng Grp.

Old, Female, & Rural: What Is the Reality? Ed. by B. Jan McCulloch. 97p. 1998. pap. 14.95 (*0-7890-0671-5*) Haworth Pr.

Old, Female & Rural: What Is the Reality? Ed. by B. Jan McCulloch. LC 98-44956. 97p. 1998. 39.95 (*0-7890-0664-2*) Haworth Pr.

Old Fences, New Neighbors. Peter R. Decker. LC 98-8925. 175p. 1998. 40.00 (*0-8165-1771-1*); pap. 19.95 (*0-8165-1905-6*) U of Ariz Pr.

Old Fires & Profitable Ghosts: A Book of Stories. Arthur T. Quiller-Couch. LC 72-10813. (Short Story Index Reprint Ser.). 1977. reprint ed. 24.95 (*0-8369-4224-8*) Ayer.

Old Firm: Sectarianism, Sport & Society in Scotland. 3rd ed. W. Murray. (Illus.). 304p. (C). 1996. pap. 50.00 (*0-85976-121-5*, Pub. by J Donald) St Mut.

Old Firm Guide. Picton Publishing Staff. (C). 1987. 25.00 (*0-7855-2202-6*, Pub. by Picton) St Mut.

Old Firm in the New Age: Rangers & Celtic since the Souness Revolution. Bill Murray. (Illus.). 192p. 1998. 35.00 (*1-85158-984-8*, Pub. by Mainstream Pubng) Trafalgar.

Old Fisherman of Lamu. Shenaaz Nanji & Shahd Shaker. 1996. pap. 6.95 (*0-920661-53-X*, Pub. by TSAR Pubns) LPC InBook.

Old Fishing Lures & Tackle. 5th ed. Carl F. Luckey. LC 98-87368. (Illus.). 672p. 1999. per. 29.95 (*0-87341-728-3*) Krause Pubns.

Old Fishing Tackle. Nigel Dowden. (Illus.). 32p. 1995. pap. 25.00 (*0-7478-0278-5*, Pub. by Shire Pubns) Parkwest Pubns.

***Old Flame.** Liz Thompson. LC 99-91308. 192p. 2000. 18.95 (*0-8034-9395-9*, Avalon Bks) Bouregy.

Old Flames. Sandra Dark. (Shadows Ser.). 1996. per. 3.50 (*0-373-27063-1*, 1-27063-6) Silhouette.

Old Floating Cloud: Two Novellas. Can Xue. Tr. by Ronald J. Janssen & Jian Zhang from CHI. 269p. 1991. 32.95 (*0-8101-0974-3*); pap. 13.95 (*0-8101-0988-3*) Northwestern U Pr.

Old Florida. Nichols & Woolson. (Historical Ser.). (Illus.). 1977. pap. 3.50 (*0-89540-054-5*, SB-054) Sun Pub.

Old Flying Days. C. C. Turner. LC 74-169440. (Literature & History of Aviation Ser.). 1972. reprint ed. 33.95 (*0-405-03783-X*) Ayer.

Old Forest & Other Stories. Peter Taylor. 368p. 1986. mass mkt. 5.99 (*0-345-90172-X*) Ballantine Pub Grp.

Old Forest & Other Stories. Peter Taylor. LC 95-15821. 322p. 1995. 15.50 (*0-679-60177-5*) Random.

Old Forest & Other Stories. 2nd ed. Peter Taylor. LC 96-8468. 368p. 1996. pap. 15.00 (*0-312-14695-7*) St Martin.

***Old Formalism: Character in Contemporary American Poetry.** Jonathan Holden. LC 99-38397. 144p. 1999. 26.00 (*1-55728-568-3*); pap. 16.00 (*1-55728-569-1*) U of Ark Pr.

Old Fort Benton, Montana. 32p. 1997. pap. 5.95 (*0-87770-144-X*) Ye Galleon.

Old Fort Edward, Before 1800: An Account of the Historic Ground Now Occupied by the Village of Ft. Edward. William H. Hill. (Illus.). 383p. 1997. reprint ed. lib. bdg. 44.00 (*0-8328-6141-3*) Higginson Bk Co.

Old Fort Klamath: An Oregon Frontier Post, 1863-1890. Buena C. Stone. Ed. by Bert Webber. LC 90-12410. (Illus.). 112p. 1990. pap. 10.95 (*0-936738-50-2*) Webb Research.

Old Fort Niagara: An Illustrated History. rev. ed. Frederic Ray. (Illus.). 16p. (J). 1988. reprint ed. pap. 1.75 (*0-941967-06-9*) Old Fort Niagara Assn.

Old Fort Niagara in Four Centuries: A History of Its Development. Brian L. Dunnigan & Patricia K. Scott. (Illus.). 64p. (Orig.). 1991. pap. 4.50 (*0-941967-12-3*) Old Fort Niagara Assn.

Old Fort Snelling Instruction Book for Fife, with Music of Early America. 2nd ed. Donald E. Mattson et al. LC 74-7298. (Minnesota Historic Sites Pamphlet Ser: No. 11). 112p. 1976. pap. 11.95 (*0-87351-090-9*) Minn Hist.

***Old Forts of the Apache Wars: A Travel Guide.** Ron Swartley. (Illus.). 84p. 1999. pap. 7.95 (*1-888571-03-9*) Frontier Image.

Old Forts of the Great Lakes: Sentinels of the Wilderness. James P. Barry. LC 95-109263. (Illus.). (Orig.). 1994. pap. 19.95 (*1-882376-05-6*) Thunder Bay Pr.

Old Forunatus: The Pleasant Comedy of Old Fortunatus by Thomas Dekker, London 1600. Suzanne Blow. LC 86-72942. 160p. (C). 1987. pap. text 20.00 (*0-938991-05-1*) Colonial Pr AL.

Old Fox Deceived. Martha Grimes. 1999. pap. 9.98 (*0-671-04430-3*) PB.

Old Foxcroft Maine: Traditions & Memories, with Family Records. Mary C. Lowell. (Illus.). 262p. 1997. reprint ed. lib. bdg. 32.00 (*0-8328-7104-4*) Higginson Bk Co.

***Old Fox's Sack.** Jim Aylesworth. LC 00-35773. (Illus.). (J). 2001. pap. write for info. (*0-439-09544-1*) Scholastic Inc.

Old France & Revolution, Vol. 6. Intro. by Albert Feuillerat. Date not set. 30.95 (*0-8369-4797-5*) Ayer.

Old Free State: A Contribution to the History of Lunenburg County & Southside Virginia, 2 vols. Landon C. Bell. LC 74-5469. (Illus.). 1267p. 1995. reprint ed. pap. 95.00 (*0-8063-0623-8*, 415) Clearfield Co.

Old Freight Train Coloring Book. James E. Brown. (ENG & SPA.). 24p. (Orig.). (J). 1992. pap. 0.50 (*0-9632358-0-X*) J E Brown.

Old French: A Concise Handbook. E. C. Einhorn. 209p. 1975. pap. text 28.95 (*0-521-09838-6*) Cambridge U Pr.

***Old French-English Dictionary.** Alan Hindley et al. 590p. 2000. write for info. (*0-521-34564-2*) Cambridge U Pr.

Old French Epic. Jessie Crosland. LC 73-117589. (Studies in French Literature: No. 45). 1970. reprint ed. lib. bdg. 79.95 (*0-8383-1022-2*) M S G Haskell Hse.

Old French Evangile de L'Enfance: An Edition with Introduction & Notes. Maureen B. Boulton. (ENG & FRO.). x, 117p. pap. text 18.29 (*0-88844-070-7*) Brill Academic Pubs.

Old French Narrative Lay: An Analytical Bibliography. Glyn S. Burgess. 148p. (C). 1997. reprint ed. 60.00 (*0-85991-478-X*) Boydell & Brewer.

Old French Romances, Done into English. William Morris. LC 75-113680. (Short Story Index Reprint Ser.). 1977. 19.95 (*0-8369-3409-1*) Ayer.

Old-French Titles of Respect in Direct Address. William A. Stowell. LC 79-8373. reprint ed. 37.50 (*0-404-18355-7*) AMS Pr.

Old Friend of the Family. Fred Saberhagen. 1992. mass mkt. 4.99 (*0-8125-2385-7*, Pub. by Tor Bks) St Martin.

Old Friends. Lynne Barasch. LC 97-4987. (Illus.). 32p. (J). (gr. k-3). 1998. 16.00 (*0-374-35611-4*) FS&G.

Old Friends. Tracy Kidder. 384p. 1994. pap. 12.00 (*0-395-71088-X*) HM.

Old Friends. large type ed. Tracy Kidder. 385 p. 1993. 24.95 (*1-56895-043-8*) Wheeler Pub.

Old Friends. Andrew Lang. LC 70-101914. reprint ed. 37.50 (*0-404-03838-7*) AMS Pr.

Old Friends: Being Literary Recollections of Other Days. William Winter. LC 74-156732. (Essay Index Reprint Ser.). 1977. reprint ed. 30.95 (*0-8369-2339-1*) Ayer.

Old Friends: Being Recollections of Other Days. William Winter. (Notable American Authors Ser.). 1999. reprint ed. lib. bdg. 125.00 (*0-7812-7756-6*) Rprt Serv.

Old Friends: Best of Bob Hill. Bob Hill. 1991. pap. 13.95 (*0-9621352-8-3*) Green Thumb Pub.

Old Friends: Great Texas Courthouses. Bill Morgan. (Illus.). 160p. 1999. 55.00 (*0-9667999-4-1*) Landmark Publ.

Old Friends & Married People. Phillip Cargile. LC 96-94730. 184p. 1998. pap. 13.95 (*0-9653711-0-7*, Pub. by IP Books) Barnes & Noble Inc.

Old Friends & New. Sarah Orne Jewett. LC 79-90584. (Short Story Index Reprint Ser.). 269p. 1977. 17.95 (*0-8369-3067-3*) Ayer.

Old Friends & New. Sarah Orne Jewett. (Collected Works of Sarah Orne Jewett). 1988. reprint ed. lib. bdg. 59.00 (*0-7812-1303-7*) Rprt Serv.

Old Friends & New Fancies: An Imaginary Sequel to the Novels of Jane Austen. Sybil G. Brinton. Ed. by Ted Bader. 320p. 1998. reprint ed. 26.95 (*0-9654299-1-1*) Revive.

Old Frontier of France Vols. 1 & 2: The Niagara Region & Adjacent Lakes under French Control. Frank H. Severance. LC 98-188000. (Illus.). 1024p. 1998. pap. 64.00 (*0-7884-0951-4*, S182) Heritage Bk.

Old Frontier of France, the Niagara Region & Adjacent Lakes under French Control, 2 vols. Frank H. Severance. LC 77-146421. (First American Frontier Ser.). (Illus.). 1971. reprint ed. 62.95 (*0-405-02885-7*) Ayer.

Old Frontiers: The Story of the Cherokee Indians from the Earliest Times to the Date of Their Removal to the West, 1838. John P. Brown. LC 74-146379. (First American Frontier Ser.). (Illus.). 1975. reprint ed. 74.95 (*0-405-02830-X*) Ayer.

Old Furniture. 2nd rev. ed. Nancy A. Smith. (Illus.). 224p. 1991. pap. 13.95 (*0-486-26339-8*) Dover.

Old Fuss & Feathers: The Life & Exploits of Lt. General Winfield Scott. Arthur D. Smith. 1977. 22.95 (*0-8369-6990-1*, 7867) Ayer.

Old Gaffer's Tale. Martin Eve. (Illus.). 200p. 1991. pap. 16.50 (*0-85036-424-8*, Pub. by Seafarer Bks) Sheridan.

Old Gang & the New Gang. Wyndham Lewis. LC 72-3159. (English Literature Ser.: No. 33). 1972. reprint ed. lib. bdg. 75.00 (*0-8383-1525-9*) M S G Haskell Hse.

Old Gang of Mine. Richard F. West. 224p. 1997. mass mkt. 5.99 (*0-425-15964-7*, Prime Crime) Berkley Pub.

Old Garden Flowers. Brian Halliwell. (Illus.). 168p. 1987. 19.95 (*0-900873-80-9*, Pub. by Bishopsgte Pr) Intl Spec Bk.

Old Garden, New Gardener. Gay Search & Geoff Hamilton. LC 95-83722. (Illus.). 192p. 1996. pap. 16.95 (*0-563-37126-9*, BBC-Parkwest) Parkwest Pubns.

Old Garden Tools. Kay N. Sanecki. (Album Ser.: No. 41). (Illus.). 32p. 1989. pap. 5.25 (*0-85263-869-8*, Pub. by Shire Pubns) Parkwest Pubns.

Old Gardener. Otto U. Adams. 13p. 1985. pap. 2.00 (*0-87770-372-8*) Ye Galleon.

Old Geezer. Bruce Cochran. (Illus.). 10p. 1994. write for info. (*1-886386-25-0*) Trisar.

Old Gent. Jose Yglesias. LC 96-13274. 176p. 1996. 15.95 (*1-55885-161-5*) Arte Publico.

Old Gentleman of the Black Stock. Thomas N. Page. (Notable American Authors Ser.). 1999. reprint ed. lib. bdg. 125.00 (*0-7812-4695-4*) Rprt Serv.

Old Georgia Privies. 7th ed. Mary Frazier-Long. (Illus.). 50p. (Orig.). 1998. reprint ed. pap. 6.00 (*0-9614192-5-3*) Frazier-Long.

Old German Love Songs. Frank C. Nicholson. 1973. 59.95 (*0-8490-0759-3*) Gordon Pr.

Old Gimlet Eye: Adventures of Smedley D. Butler. Lowell Thomas. 310p. 1981. reprint ed. 8.95 (*0-940328-01-1*) Marine Corps.

Old Gipsy's Dream Book & Fortune Teller & Napolean's Book of Fate. J. R. Vial & A. M. Vial. 65p. 1998. reprint ed. pap. 7.95 (*0-7661-0678-0*) Kessinger Pub.

Old Girls' Network. Averback. pap. 11.00 (*0-06-251057-6*) HarperTrade.

Old Glade Road see Historic Highways of America...with Maps & Illustrations

Old Glass Paperweights of Southern New Jersey: An American Folk Art. Clarence A. Newell. LC 87-62586. (Illus.). 96p. 1989. pap. 20.00 (*0-9619547-0-1*) Papier Presse.

Old Glory. Jonathan Raban. LC 98-11006. 544p. 1998. pap. 14.00 (*0-375-70100-1*) Vin Bks.

***Old Glory: Endecott & the Red Cross; My Kinsman, Major Molineux; & Benito Cereno.** Robert Lowell. 208p. 2000. pap. 13.00 (*0-374-52704-0*) FS&G.

Old Glory: The American Flag in Contemporary Art. David Rubin & Gary Sangster. (Illus.). 64p. 1994. pap. text. write for info. (*1-880353-07-5*) Cleveland Ctr.

Old Glory & the Stars & Bars: Stories of the Civil War. Ed. by George W. Koon. LC 95-15222. 233p. 1995. pap. 14.95 (*1-57003-057-X*); text 34.95 (*1-57003-056-1*) U of SC Pr.

Old Goat. Ralph F. Parkison. Ed. by Marion O. Withrow. (Illus.). 112p. (Orig.). (J). (gr. 2-8). 1988. pap. write for info. (*0-318-64004-X*) Little Wood Bks.

Old Goat Song. Jules Tasca. 1994. 3.50 (*0-87129-487-7*, O53) Dramatic Pub.

Old Gods Falling. Malcolm Elwin. LC 73-142622. (Essay Index Reprint Ser.). 1977. 23.95 (*0-8369-2045-7*) Ayer.

Old Goriot. Honore de Balzac. Tr. by Marion A. Crawford. (Classics Ser.). 304p. 1951. pap. 10.95 (*0-14-044017-8*, Penguin Classics) Viking Penguin.

Old Gotham Theatricals: Selections from a Series, "Reminiscences of a Man about Town" Tom Picton. Ed. by William L. Slout. LC 95-20579. (Clipper Studies in the Theater: No. 12). x, 170p. 1995. pap. 21.00 (*0-89370-462-8*) Millefleurs.

Old Grammar Schools. Foster Watson. (Illus.). 150p. 1968. reprint ed. 35.00 (*0-7146-1449-1*, BHA-01449, Pub. by F Cass Pubs) Intl Spec Bk.

Old Gramophones & Other Talking Machines. Benet Bergonzi. 1989. pap. 4.75 (*0-7478-0104-5*, Pub. by Shire Pubns) St Mut.

Old Granny Fox. Thornton W. Burgess. (J). 18.95 (*0-8488-0392-2*) Amereon Ltd.

Old Gravestones of Columbia County, New York. Ed. by Arthur C. Kelly. LC F127.C8K45 1996. 139p. 1996. lib. bdg. 29.00 (*1-56012-144-0*, 145) Kinship Rhinebeck.

Old Gravestones of Ulster County: 22,000 Inscriptions. With Index. Ed. by J. Wilson Poucher et al. (Illus.). 434p. 1998. reprint ed. lib. bdg. 45.00 (*0-8328-9616-0*) Higginson Bk Co.

Old Graveyards of Northampton & Adjacent Counties, Vol. I, Pts. I-VI; Vol. II, Pts. I & III. John Eyerman. (Illus.). 328p. 1997. reprint ed. pap. 32.50 (*0-8328-6438-2*) Higginson Bk Co.

Old Greek Translation of Daniel 7-12. Jeansonne S. Pace. Ed. by Robert J. Karris. LC 87-15865. (Catholic Biblical Quarterly Monographs: No. 19). x, 147p. 1988. pap. 5.00 (*0-915170-18-3*) Catholic Bibl Assn.

Old Greenbottom Inn & Other Stories. George M. McClellan. LC 74-144654. reprint ed. 35.00 (*0-404-00199-8*) AMS Pr.

Old Greenwich Village: An Architectural Portrait. Steve Gross et al. LC 93-3234. (Illus.). 128p. 1995. 39.95 (*0-471-14405-3*) Wiley.

Old Gringo. Carlos Fuentes. Orig. Title: El Gringo Viejo. 208p. 1997. pap. text 11.00 (*0-374-52522-6*) FS&G.

Old Growler's Last Match. John Richardson. (Illus.). 32p. (J). (gr. 1-3). 1997. 18.95 (*0-09-176675-3*, Pub. by Hutchinson) Trafalgar.

Old Growth: Selected Poems & Notebooks, 1986-1994. Andrew Schelling. 142p. (Orig.). 1995. pap. 10.00 (*1-887289-01-1*) Rodent Pr.

Old Growth in the East: A Survey. Mary B. Davis. Ed. by John Davis. (Illus.). 150p. (Orig.). 1993. spiral bd. 20.00 (*0-9638402-0-7*) Cenozoic Soc.

Old Guard. Grace Livingston Hill. 17.95 (*0-89190-401-8*) Amereon Ltd.

Old Guard & the Avant-Garde: Modernism in Chicago, 1910-1940. Ed. by Sue A. Prince. LC 90-35236. (Illus.). 312p. 1990. 42.00 (*0-226-68284-6*) U Ch Pr.

Old Guard Rest Home. Illus. by George Fisher. 64p. 1984. pap. 6.95 (*0-914546-57-0*) Rose Pub.

Old Guitar Mania: A Guide to Guitar Collecting, Vol. 1. Bill Blackburn. (Illus.). 108p. 1992. pap. 10.95 (*0-931759-60-9*, 00000141) Centerstream Pub.

Old Gunsights: A Collector's Guide, 1850 to 1965. Nicholas Stroebel. LC 98-84099. (Illus.). 320p. 1999. pap. 29.95 (*0-87341-559-0*, OLGU) Krause Pubns.

Old Guy Poems. Utah Phillips. 31p. (Orig.). 1988. pap. 6.00 (*0-9621041-0-8*) Brownell Library Pr.

Old Hallowell on the Kennebec, Maine. Emma H. Nason. (Illus.). 359p. 1997. reprint ed. lib. bdg. 42.00 (*0-8328-5849-8*) Higginson Bk Co.

Old Hancock County Families: Containing Genealogies of Families Resident in Hancock County in 1933, Whose Ancestors of Their Surnames Settled in the Town in or Before 1790. W. MacBeth Pierce. (Illus.). 133p. 1997. reprint ed. pap. 18.50 (*0-8328-5852-8*) Higginson Bk Co.

Old Handmade Lace: With a Dictionary of Lace. F. Nevill Jackson. (Illus.). 288p. 1987. reprint ed. pap. 10.95 (*0-486-25309-0*) Dover.

Old Hanoi. Mark Sidel. (Illus.). 96p. 1999. 19.95 (*983-56-0051-1*) OUP.

Old Hat, New Hat. Stan Berenstain & Jan Berenstain. (Bright & Early Bks.). (Illus.). (J). (ps-3). 1970. 7.99 (*0-394-80669-7*, Pub. by Random Bks Yng Read) Random.

Old Hat, New Hat. Stan Berenstain & Jan Berenstain. LC 96-70730. (Bright & Early Bks.). (J). (ps-3). 1997. 4.99 (*0-679-88630-3*, Pub. by Random Bks Yng Read) Random.

Old Hatreds & Young Hopes: The French Carbonari Against the Bourbon Restoration. Alan B. Spitzer. LC 76-139722. (Historical Monographs: No. 63). 446p. 1971. 30.00 (*0-674-63220-6*) HUP.

Old Havana Cookbook: Cuban Recipes in Spanish & English. Tr. by Rafael Marcos. (Bi-Lingual Cookbks.). (ENG & SPA., Illus.). 128p. 1999. 11.95 (*0-7818-0767-0*) Hippocrene Bks.

Old Havana, Cuba. Nicolas Sapieha. (Travel to Landmarks Ser.). (Illus.). 128p. 1992. 24.95 (*1-85043-503-0*, Pub. by I B T) St Martin.

Old Heart of Nevada: Ghost Towns & Mining Camps of Elko County. Shawn Hall. LC 96-49497. (Illus.). 280p. (Orig.). 1998. pap. 21.95 (*0-87417-295-0*) U of Nev Pr.

Old Henderson Mine. Jana Nolan. LC 97-61443. 1997. pap. 11.95 (*0-944851-11-8*) Earth Star.

Old Henry. Joan W. Blos. LC 86-21745. (Illus.). 32p. (J). (ps-4). 1987. lib. bdg. 15.93 (*0-688-06400-0*, Wm Morrow) Morrow Avon.

Old Henry. Joan W. Blos. LC 86-21745. (Illus.). 32p. (J). (ps-3). 1990. mass mkt. 6.95 (*0-688-09935-1*, Wm Morrow) Morrow Avon.

Old Henry. Joan W. Blos. (J). 1990. 11.15 (*0-606-04761-1*, Pub. by Turtleback) Demco.

Old Herb Doctor. 2nd rev. ed. Joseph E. Meyer. (Illus.). 176p. 1984. pap. 8.95 (*0-916638-08-1*) Meyerbooks.

Old Herb Doctor: Rare Herbal Formulas Which Have Healed Thousands Where Others Have Failed. 1991. lib. bdg. 79.95 (*0-8490-4995-4*) Gordon Pr.

Old Herb Doctor, His Secrets & Treatments. Ed. by Health Research Staff. 200p. 1996. reprint ed. spiral bd. 17.00 (*0-7873-0396-8*) Hlth Research.

Old Hermit & the Boy Who Couldn't Stop Laughing: An African Fable. Kimani C. Toussaint. Ed. by Alice I. Toussaint & Princess E. Toussaint. (Illus.). vi, 32p. (YA). (gr. 6-12). 1999. 10.00 (*1-893811-00-X*) UAES Fndt.

Old Hermit's Almanac: Daily Meditations for the Journey of Life. Edward Hays. LC 97-35596. 400p. 1997. pap. 15.95 (*0-939516-37-3*) Forest Peace.

Old Hickory: 30th Infantry Division. Thirtieth Infantry Association Staff. LC 90-70160. (Illus.). 136p. 1990. 39.95 (*0-938021-86-9*) Turner Pub KY.

Old Hickory & the Elusive PUC. Richard L. Jepsen. (Illus.). 90p. Date not set. write for info. (*0-9656324-1-5*) R L Jepsen.

Old Hickory's War: Andrew Jackson & the Quest for Empire. David S. Heidler & Jeanne T. Heidler. (Illus.). 320p. 1996. 24.95 (*0-8117-0113-1*) Stackpole.

Old Hicks, the Guide: or Adventures in the Comanche Country in Search of a Gold Mine. Charles W. Webber. LC 77-104591. (C). 1987. reprint ed. pap. text 7.95 (*0-8290-2135-3*); reprint ed. lib. bdg. 22.00 (*0-8398-2158-1*) Irvington.

Old Hieratic Paleography. Hans Goedicke. 162p. (Orig.). 1988. pap. text 72.00 (*0-9613805-4-3*) Halgo Inc.

Old High German Biteilen & Biskerien. Luise Haessler. (LD Ser.: Vol. 19). 1935. pap. 25.00 (*0-527-00765-X*) Periodicals Srv.

O

Old High German Preposition Compounds in Relation to Their Latin Originals. Harold Rosen. (LD Ser.: No. 16). 1934. pap. 25.00 (*0-527-00762-5*) Periodicals Srv.

Old High German Reader. John Newman. 158p. (Orig.). (C). 1981. pap. text 8.65 (*0-89894-012-5*) Advocate Pub Group.

Old Hiram: And Other Memories from the Hills of West Virginia. Vivian B. Smith. LC 94-72151. 120p. 1990. reprint ed. pap. 9.00 (*0-9642276-0-6*) V S Boston. OLD HIRAM... recites poetry of our Appalachian heritage. Numerous photos enhance many of the poems which depict yesteryear in the hills of the mountain state. ***Publisher Paid Annotation.***

Old Historic Churches in America. Edward Rines. 373p. 1993. reprint ed. lib. bdg. 89.00 (*0-7812-5225-3*) Rprt Serv.

Old Historic Homes of Cheshire, with an Account of the Early Settlement of the Town, Etc. Compiled by Edwin R. Brown. (Illus.). 138p. 1997. reprint ed. lib. bdg. 25.00 (*0-8328-5627-4*) Higginson Bk Co.

Old Hogan. rev. ed. Margaret K. Garaway. (Illus.). 32p. (Orig.). (J). (gr. k-6). 1995. pap. 4.95 (*0-9638851-0-3*) Old Hogan Pubng.

Old Hollywood - New Hollywood: Ritual, Art, & Industry. Thomas G. Schatz. Ed. by Diane Kirkpatrick. LC 82-1910. (Studies in Cinema: No. 15). 326p. reprint ed. 101.10 (*0-8357-1308-3*, 207033400082) Bks Demand.

Old Home Day. Donald Hall. LC 93-3658. (Illus.). 48p. 1996. 16.00 (*0-15-276896-3*, Harcourt Child Bks) Harcourt.

Old Home Place. Susan Dart. (Illus.). 96p. 1997. pap. 12.00 (*1-886094-72-1*) Chicago Spectrum.

Old Home Town. Rose W. Lane. LC 85-8645. vii, 309p. 1985. reprint ed. pap. 12.00 (*0-8032-7917-5*, Bison Books) U of Nebr Pr.

Old Homes & Families in Nottoway. W. R. Turner. (Illus.). 105p. 1998. reprint ed. pap. 18.00 (*0-8063-4789-9*, 9449) Clearfield Co.

Old Homes & History of Montgomery County, Maryland. Roger B. Farquhar. (Illus.). 1981. 35.00 (*0-910086-06-0*) Am Hist Res.

Old Homes, New Families: Innovating Living Arrangements for Older Persons. Gordon Streib. Ed. by Abraham Monk. LC 84-1772. (New Columbia Studies of Social Gerontology & Aging). 256p. 1984. text 76.00 (*0-231-05652-4*, King's Crown Paperbacks) Col U Pr.

Old Homes of Houston County. 35.00 (*0-317-39616-1*) Pubns Devl Co.

Old Homes of South Carolina. Joy S. Rust. LC 92-15746. (Illus.). 272p. 1992. 22.50 (*0-88289-874-4*) Pelican.

Old Homes That Made New Friends. Bette Williams. (Illus.). 88p. 1999. pap. write for info. (*0-9654497-7-7*) Transit Pub.

Old Homestead. (On Stage, America! Ser.). 59p. 1996. spiral bd. 4.95 (*0-937657-31-X*) Feedbk Theabks & Prospero.

Old Homestead. George L. Aiken. (Works of George Aiken (1830-1876)). 1989. reprint ed. lib. bdg. 79.00 (*0-7812-1591-9*) Rprt Serv.

Old Homestead. Denman Thompson. (Notable American Authors). 1999. reprint ed. lib. bdg. 125.00 (*0-7812-9768-0*) Rprt Serv.

Old Homestead: A Play in Four Acts. Denman Thompson. (BCL1-PS American Literature Ser.). 93p. 1992. reprint ed. lib. bdg. 59.00 (*0-7812-6878-8*) Rprt Serv.

Old Homestead Tales, Set 4. Neil W. Northey. (Illus.). 1998. pap. 27.80 (*1-881545-89-X*) Angelas Bkshelf.

Old Hong Kong, 3 vols. Trea Wiltshire. (Illus.). 1998. boxed set 51.00 (*962-7283-23-1*, Pub. by FormAsia) Weatherhill.

Old Hong Kong, Vol. 1. Trea Wiltshire. (Illus.). 150p. 1997. write for info. (*962-7283-01-0*, Pub. by FormAsia) Weatherhill.

Old Hong Kong, Vol. 2. (Illus.). 150p. 1997. write for info. (*962-7283-13-4*, Pub. by FormAsia) Weatherhill.

Old Horse That Would Not Go Out to Pasture. Carol A. Vercz. (Illus.). 36p. (J). (gr. k-5). 1998. pap. write for info. (*0-910119-51-1*) SOCO Pubns.

Old Horsefly. Karl Jay Shapiro. 64p. 1992. 12.95 (*1-880811-05-7*) North Lights.

Old Horseshoes. Ivan G. Sparkes. (Album Ser.: No. 19). (Illus.). 32p. 1998. pap. 6.25 (*0-85263-348-3*, Pub. by Shire Pubns) Parkwest Pubns.

Old House. (Fix-It-Yourself Ser.). (Illus.). 144p. 1990. 17.27 (*0-8094-6288-5*); lib. bdg. 23.27 (*0-8094-6289-3*) Time-Life.

Old House. Time-Life Books Editors. LC 95-39668. (Home Repair & Improvement Ser.). (Illus.). 128p. (gr. 11). 1999. spiral bd. 14.95 (*0-7835-3898-7*) Time-Life.

Old House. rev. ed. Time-Life Books Editors. (Home Repair & Improvement Ser.). (Illus.). 128p. 1989. 14.60 (*0-8094-7383-6*); pap. write for info. (*0-8094-7386-0*); lib. bdg. 20.00 (*0-8094-7384-4*) Time-Life.

Old House at Coate. Richard Jefferies. LC 70-111840. (Essay Index Reprint Ser.). 1977. 20.95 (*0-8369-1664-6*) Ayer.

Old House at Railes. large type ed. Mary E. Pearce. LC 94-8760. 595p. 1994. lib. bdg. 24.95 (*0-8161-5989-0*, G K Hall Lrg Type) Mac Lib Ref.

Old-House Dictionary: An Illustrated Guide to American Domestic Architecture (1600-1940) Steven J. Phillips. LC 96-23062. (Illus.). 240p. 1995. reprint ed. pap. 16.95 (*0-471-14407-X*) Wiley.

Old House Doctor. Kit Evers. LC 83-4353. (Illus.). 192p. 1988. pap. 14.95 (*0-87951-239-3*, Pub. by Overlook Pr) Penguin Putnam.

Old House in Greenville, Virginia: A Study of Human Intention in Vernacular Architecture. Michael S. Shutty, Jr. LC 96-41855. (Illus.). 204p. (Orig.). 1997. pap. 15.95 (*0-939923-66-1*) M & W Pub Co.

Old-House Journal. Patricia Poore. 1999. pap. 19.95 (*0-452-26850-8*, Plume) Dutton Plume.

Old-House Journal Compendium. Ed. by Clem Labine & Carolyn Flaherty. LC 78-4360. (Illus.). 400p. 1983. pap. 22.95 (*0-87951-186-9*, Pub. by Overlook Pr) Penguin Putnam.

Old House Measured & Scaled Drawings for Builders & Carpenters: An Early 20th Century Pictorial Sourcebook, with 183 Detailed Plates. 2nd ed. William A. Radford. (Illus.). 200p. 1983. reprint ed. pap. 12.95 (*0-486-24438-5*) Dover.

Old House, New House: A Child's Exploration of American Architectural Styles. Michael Gaughenbaugh & Herbert Camburn. (Illus.). 56p. (YA). (gr. 5 up). 1995. 16.95 (*0-471-14408-8*) Wiley.

***Old House Repair & Renovation** Editors Of Time Life Books. (gr. 11). 1999. pap. 14.95 (*0-7370-1139-4*) T-L Custom Pub.

Old Houses. Photos by Steve Gross & Susan Daley. (Illus.). 256p. 1995. pap. 27.50 (*1-55670-404-6*) Stewart Tabori & Chang.

Old Houses: A Rebuilder's Manual. George Nash. (Illus.). 1979. pap. 12.95 (*0-686-96841-7*) P-H.

Old Houses, Good Neighbors: Reflections & Celebrations of Everyday Life in a Small Town. Cynthia G. La Ferle. 112p. (Orig.). 1994. pap. 10.00 (*0-9642404-0-8*) Self Rel Pubng.

Old Houses of Connecticut. Ed. by Berta C. Trowbridge. (Illus.). 1923. 250.00 (*0-685-89768-0*) Elliots Bks.

***Old Houses of Jordan.** Frwd. by Noor Al Hussein. (Illus.). 115p. 1999. 93.50 (*0-7103-0636-9*, Pub. by Kegan Paul Intl) Col U Pr.

Old Houses of King & Queen County Virginia. Virginia D. Cox & Willie Weathers. LC 73-89225. (Illus.). 404p. 1998. 22.00 (*0-9664788-0-0*) King & Queen.

Old Houses of King & Queen County Virginia. Virginia D. Cox & Willie Weathers. LC 73-89225. (Illus.). 404p. 1998. reprint ed. 25.00 (*0-9664788-2-7*) King & Queen.

***Old Houses of the Ancient Town of Norwich, 1660-1800.** Mary E. Perkins. (Illus.). 621p. 2000. reprint ed. pap. 38.50 (*0-7884-1515-8*, 1515) Heritage Bk.

Old Houses of the Ancient Town of Norwich, 1660-1800. Mary E. Perkins. (Illus.). 621p. 1992. reprint ed. lib. bdg. 65.00 (*0-8328-2268-X*) Higginson Bk Co.

Old Houses on Nantucket. Kenneth Duprey. (Illus.). 1986. pap. 14.95 (*0-8038-5399-8*) Archit CT.

Old Hungarian Painted Woodwork, 15th-19th Centuries. Ilona Tombor. 62p. 1967. 40.00 (*0-7855-1601-8*) St Mut.

Old Huntsville Book of Recipes & Timeless Tips. Cathey Carney. 1995. 15.95 (*0-9650939-0-5*) Old Huntsville.

Old Huntsville Land Office Records & Military Warrants, 1810-1854. Marilyn D. Hahn. (Illus.). 240p. 1985. 22.50 (*0-89308-574-X*) Southern Hist Pr.

***Old Icelandic Literature & Society.** Ed. by Margaret Clunies Ross. (Cambridge Studies in Medieval Literature: Vol. 42). 340p. 2000. write for info. (*0-521-63112-2*) Cambridge U Pr.

Old Icelandic Medical Miscellany. Henning Larsen. LC 75-23736. reprint ed. 40.00 (*0-404-13293-6*) AMS Pr.

Old Icelandic Poetry: Eddic Lay & Skaldic Verse. Peter Hallberg. Tr. by Paul Schach & Sonja Lindgrenson. LC 74-27186. 232p. reprint ed. pap. 72.00 (*0-608-10680-1*, 2013387); reprint ed. pap. 72.00 (*0-608-30605-3*, 201338700086) Bks Demand.

Old in New Atlanta. Hugh Sawyer. LC 96-83985. 1976. 14.95 (*0-9652573-0-4*) JEMS Publns.

Old Indian Chronicle. Ed. by Samuel G. Drake. LC 74-7963. reprint ed. 47.50 (*0-404-11850-X*) AMS Pr.

Old Indian Days. Charles A. Eastman. LC 90-25561. (Illus.). xxiv, 279p. 1991. reprint ed. pap. 9.95 (*0-8032-6718-5*, Bison Books) U of Nebr Pr.

Old Indian Legends. Zitkala-Sa. LC 85-8639. (Illus.). xviii, 165p. 1985. reprint ed. pap. 8.95 (*0-8032-9903-6*, Bison Books) U of Nebr Pr.

Old Indian Recipes (Not Really) A Father's Method of Feeding His "Tribe" Ted W. Parod. (Illus.). 118p. 1990. spiral bd. 9.95 (*0-9627432-3-2*) Echo Lake Pr.

Old Indian Trails. Walter McClintock. 416p. 1992. pap. 15.00 (*0-395-61155-5*) HM.

Old Industries of Dean. Pound House Staff. (C). 1985. pap. text 45.00 (*0-7855-6572-8*, Pub. by Pound Hse) St Mut.

Old Inns of England. Albert E. Richardson. LC 72-80704. (Illus.). 128p. 1972. reprint ed. lib. bdg. 18.95 (*0-405-08886-8*, Pub. by Blom Pubns) Ayer.

Old Inverness in Pictures. Loraine MacLean. 1978. 24.95 (*0-8464-0682-9*) Beekman Pubs.

Old Iowa Houses: New Loves. Bruce Carlson. (Illus.). 173p. (Orig.). 1991. pap. 9.95 (*1-878488-37-6*) Quixote Pr IA.

Old Iowegian Legends. David L. Rosheim. (Illus.). 196p. (Orig.). 1991. pap. 12.95 (*0-9602996-2-9*) Andromeda.

Old Iowegian Sagas. David L. Rosheim. (Illus.). 181p. (Orig.). 1989. pap. 12.95 (*0-9602996-1-0*) Andromeda.

Old Ireland. Ed. by Robert McNally. LC 65-20468. 264p. reprint ed. pap. 81.90 (*0-7837-5583-X*, 204537400005) Bks Demand.

Old Irish Glosses at Wurzburg & Carlsruhe. Ed. by Whitley Stokes. LC 78-72645. (Celtic Language & Literature Ser.: Goidelic & Brythonic). reprint ed. 29.00 (*0-404-17587-2*) AMS Pr.

Old Irish Monastic Prayer-Poetry. Ed. & Tr. by Malachi McCormick. (Irish Poetry Ser.). 32p. 1986. 9.00 (*0-943984-23-8*) Stone St Pr.

Old Irish of New England. Robert E. Cahill. (Collectible Classics Ser.: No. 10). (Illus.). 50p. (Orig.). 1985. pap. 3.95 (*0-916787-09-5*) Chandler-Smith.

Old Irish Reader. R. Thurneysen. 1981. reprint ed. 30.00 (*0-901282-32-4*) Colton Bk.

Old Irish Verbs & Vocabulary. Antony Green. LC 95-25857. 1995. pap. 15.00 (*1-57473-003-7*); lib. bdg. 65.00 (*1-57473-103-3*) Cascadilla Pr.

Old-Irish Village: Six Full Color Buildings in H-O Scale. Edmund V. Gillon, Jr. 1991. pap. 6.95 (*0-486-26337-1*) Dover.

Old Irish Wisdom Attributed to Aldfrith of Northumbria: An Edition of Briathra Flainn Fhina Maic Ossu. Aldfrith et al. LC 99-34089. (Medieval & Renaissance Texts & Studies: Vol. 205). 1999. 28.00 (*0-86698-247-7*) MRTS.

Old Ironsides. David Weitzman. LC 95-52485. (Illus.). 32p. (J). 1997. 15.95 (*0-395-74678-7*) HM.

Old Ironsides: The Rise, Decline, & Resurrection of the USS Constitution. Thomas C. Gillmer. (Illus.). 256p. 1997. pap. 19.95 (*0-07-024564-9*) Intl Marine.

Old Is . . . Jerry Cooper. 24p. (Orig.). 1996. pap. 3.95 (*1-889419-05-2*) J Cooper.

Old Is New. Evan Skolnick. (Disney's Action Club Ser.). 1997. pap. text 4.50 (*1-57840-079-1*, Pub. by Acclaim Bks) Penguin Putnam.

Old Is Not A Dirty Word: Aging Observed...aging Experienced, 1. Wallace C Matsen. 1998. pap. text 12.50 (*1-881907-27-9*) Two Bytes Pub.

Old Is Not a Four-Letter Word: A Midlife Guide. Ann E. Gerike. LC 97-494. (Illus.). 144p. (Orig.). 1997. pap. 10.95 (*1-57601-002-3*) Gerike.

Old Is Older Than Me: And Other Devotionals for the Best Years of Your Life. Maxine D. Jensen. LC 90-21257. 156 P. ;p. (Orig.). 1991. write for info. (*0-89840-316-2*) WCLC.

Old is...great. Marcella Markham. 1998. 9.00 (*1-86187-105-8*) Exley Giftbooks.

Old Issues & New Strategies in Arms Control & Verification. Ed. by James Brown. 410p. 1996. 50.00 (*90-5383-421-4*, Pub. by VUB Univ Pr) Paul & Co Pubs.

Old Italian Patterns for Linen Embroidery. rev. ed. Frieda Lipperheide. Ed. & Tr. by Kathleen A. Epstein from GER. (Illus.). 60p. 1996. 45.00 (*0-9633331-7-8*) Curious Works.

Old Jack: Life of Stonewall Jackson. Marta Kastner. (Illus.). 162p. (Orig.). 1994. pap. 12.95 (*0-9637343-0-X*) Cedar Hill Pr.

Old Jail Remembers Tuscaloosa. Sandra S. Townsend. (Illus.). 44p. (Orig.). (J). (gr. 5-12). 1987. pap. 4.50 (*0-943487-03-X*) Sevgo Pr.

Old Jake's Skirts. Cynthia A. Scott. LC 97-42328. (Illus.). 36p. (J). (ps-4). 1998. lib. bdg. 15.95 (*0-87358-615-8*, Rising Moon Bks) Northland AZ.

Old Japan. Andrew Haslam & Claire Doran. (Make It Work! Ser.). (Illus.). 64p. (YA). (gr. 4-9). 2000. 13.95 (*0-7166-4607-2*) World Bk.

Old Jewish Dishes. Zorica Herbst-Krausz. 75p. (C). 1988. 60.00 (*0-569-09169-1*, Pub. by Collets) St Mut.

***Old Jewish Folk Music: The Collections & Writings of Moshe Beregovski.** Ed. by Mark Slobin. (Illus.). 592p. 2000. pap. 29.95 (*0-8156-2868-4*) Syracuse U Pr.

Old John see Viejo John

Old John Neptune & Other Maine Indian Shamans. Fannie H. Eckstorm. LC 45-9452. 209p. 1980. reprint ed. pap. 10.95 (*0-89101-044-0*) U Maine Pr.

Old Jonah's Book of Tales. Jerry W. Vencill. Ed. & Illus. by Ken W. Henderson. 72p. 1997. 14.95 (*1-891029-00-2*) Henderson Pub.

Old Jonah's Book of Tall Tales. large type unabridged ed. Jerry W. Vencill. Ed. & Illus. by Ken W. Henderson. 144p. 1998. 16.95 (*1-891029-01-0*) Henderson Pub.

Old Judge Poems. Carol Sherman. (Illus.). 30p. (Orig.). (C). 1993. pap. text 5.00 (*1-878173-32-4*) Birnham Wood.

Old Judge Priest. Irvin S. Cobb. (Collected Works of Irvin S. Cobb). 401p. 1998. reprint ed. lib. bdg. 108.00 (*1-58201-603-8*) Classic Bks.

Old Jules. Mari Sandoz. 448p. 1997. 8.98 (*1-56731-175-X*, MJF Bks) Fine Comms.

Old Jules: 50th Anniversary Edition. Mari Sandoz. LC 85-1114. (Illus.). xi, 438p. 1985. pap. 13.95 (*0-8032-5173-4*, Bison Books); text 40.00 (*0-8032-4164-X*) U of Nebr Pr.

Old Junk. Henry M. Tomlinson. LC 74-156724. (Essay Index Reprint Ser.). 1977. reprint ed. 19.95 (*0-8369-2574-2*) Ayer.

Old Kalevala, & Certain Antecedents. Francis P. Magoun & Elias Lhonnrot. LC 74-78520. 331p. reprint ed. pap. 102.70 (*0-7837-4119-7*, 205794200011) Bks Demand.

Old Kanawha Baptist Church Minutes--Indexed, Plus Unpublished County Court Records of West Virginia. Eugene L. Peck & Regina P. Andrus. x, 87p. 1997. pap. 13.00 (*0-7884-0735-X*, P115) Heritage Bk.

Old Kensington & the Story of Elizabeth: 1873/1876 Editions. Anne I. Thackeray. Ed. by Marie M. Roberts. (Her Write His Name Ser.). 496p. 1996. reprint ed. pap. 34.95 (*1-85506-388-3*) Bks Intl VA.

Old Kensington Palace, & Other Papers. Austin Dobson. LC 68-54344. (Essay Index Reprint Ser.). 1977. 20.95 (*0-8369-0110-X*) Ayer.

Old Kentucky Entries & Deeds: A Complete Index of All of the Earliest Land Entries, Military Warrants, Deeds & Wills of the Commonwealth of Kentucky. Willard R. Jillson. LC 73-86808. (Filson Club Publications Ser.: No. 34). (Illus.). 571p. 1999. reprint ed. 37.50 (*0-8063-0193-7*) Genealog Pub.

***Old Kentucky Talk: A Collection of Words, Expressions & Folklore from the Old Days of the Commonwealth.** unabridged ed. E. Clayton Gooden & David Gooden. (Illus.). iv, 136p. 1999. 19.95 (*0-9674028-2-4*); spiral bd. 9.95 (*0-9674028-0-8*) Victoria Publishing.

***Old Kentucky Talk: A Collection of Words, Expressions & Folklore from the Old Days of the Commonwealth, No.1.** unabridged ed. E. Clayton Gooden & David Gooden. (Illus.). iv, 136p. 1999. per. 9.95 (*0-9674028-1-6*) Victoria Publishing.

Old Key West in Three-D. Joan Langley & Wright Langley. LC 85-82420. (Illus.). 64p. 1986. pap. 14.95 (*0-911607-04-8*) Langley Pr Inc.

Old King Cole. Ken Campell. (Oberon Bks.). 96p. 1997. pap. 12.95 (*1-870259-12-2*) Theatre Comm.

Old King Cole & Friends. Michelle Marriott. (Soap Opera Ser.). (Illus.). 8p. (J). (gr. 4 up). 1990. 6.99 (*0-85953-446-4*) Childs Play.

Old King William Holmes & Families: Families of King William County VA. Peyton N. Clarke. LC 98-117888. (Illus.). 211p. 1998. pap. 18.00 (*0-7884-0772-4*, C406) Heritage Bk.

Old King William Homes & Families: An Account of Some of the Old Homesteads & Families of King William County, Virginia, from Its Earliest Settlement. Peyton N. Clarke. (Illus.). 211p. 1995. reprint ed. pap. 21.50 (*0-8063-7956-1*, 1010) Clearfield Co.

Old Kingdom Cemetery at Hamra Dom: El-Qasr Wa Es-Saiyad. Torgny Save-Soderbergh. (Illus.). 152p. 1994. 53.50 (*91-7402-248-2*) Coronet Bks.

Old Kingdom Tombs at el-Hammaniya: ACE Report, No. 2. Khouli & Kanawati. (Mascquarie University to Egypt Ser.). 1990. pap. 75.00 (*0-85668-567-4*, Pub. by Aris & Phillips) David Brown.

Old Kittery. John D. Bardwell. (Images of America Ser.). 1995. pap. 16.99 (*0-7524-0088-6*) Arcadia Publng.

Old Kittery & Her Families. E. S. Stackpole. (Illus.). 822p. 1989. reprint ed. lib. bdg. 82.00 (*0-8328-0560-2*) Higginson Bk Co.

Old Kuala Lumpur. J. M. Gullick. (Images of Asia Ser.). (Illus.). 90p. 1995. text 19.95 (*967-65-3073-5*) OUP.

***Old Kuching.** Alice Yen Ho. LC 98-4302. (Images of Asia Ser.). (Illus.). 112p. 1999. text 19.95 (*983-56-0050-3*) OUP.

***Old Kyoto.** John Lowe. (Images of Asia Ser.). (Illus.). 96p. 2000. 16.95 (*0-19-590940-2*) OUP.

Old Kyoto: A Guide to Traditional Shops, Restaurants, & Inns. Diane Durston. LC 85-45709. (Illus.). 240p. (Orig.). 1987. pap. 17.00 (*0-87011-757-2*) Kodansha.

Old Labor & New Immigrants in American Political Development: Union, Party, & State, 1875-1920. Gwendolyn Mink. LC 85-30963. 304p. 1986. 42.50 (*0-8014-1863-1*) Cornell U Pr.

Old Labor & New Immigrants in American Political Development: Union, Party, & State, 1875-1920. Gwendolyn Mink. LC 85-30963. 304p. 1990. reprint ed. pap. text 17.95 (*0-8014-9680-2*) Cornell U Pr.

Old Lace: A Handbook for Collectors; an Account of the Different Styles of Lace, Their History, Characteristics & Manufacture. M. Jourdain. (Illus.). 1981. reprint ed. 35.00 (*1-55888-202-2*) Omnigraphics Inc.

Old Lace & Linens: Identification & Value Guide. Maryanne Dolan. 160p. 1989. pap. 10.95 (*0-89689-072-4*, Bks Amrcana) Krause Pubns.

Old Ladies with Brooms Aren't Always Witches. Paula Woolf. 154p. (J). (gr. 3-6). 1998. pap. 9.99 (*0-88092-395-4*, 3954) Royal Fireworks.

Old Lady & the Birds. abr. ed. Tony Johnston. LC 91-45124. (Illus.). 32p. (J). (ps-3). 1994. 14.95 (*0-15-257769-6*, Harcourt Child Bks) Harcourt.

Old Lady in Dubuque & Her Neighbors. Albert Kwasky. LC 96-90918. 1997. 21.95 (*0-533-12215-5*) Vantage.

Old Lady in Dubuque's Town. Albert Kwasky. 1991. 18.95 (*0-533-08926-3*) Vantage.

Old Lady in Dubuque's Town: A Memory Diary. Albert Kwasky. 1991. 18.95 (*0-533-05706-X*) Vantage.

Old Lady on Harrison Street: Cook County Hospital, 1833-1995. Ed. by John Raffensperger. LC 96-36391. (International Healthcare Ethics Ser.: Vol. 3). X, 455p. (C). 1997. text 65.95 (*0-8204-3461-2*) P Lang Pubng.

Old Lady Says "No" Denis Johnston. LC 91-22324. (Irish Dramatic Texts Ser.). 142p. 1992. text 24.95 (*0-8132-0751-7*) Cath U Pr.

Old Lady Who . . . 10p. (J). 1996. 34.99 (*1-888074-28-0*) Pckts Lrning.

Old Lady's Guide to Survival. Mayo Simon. LC 95-146528. 1994. pap. 5.95 (*0-87129-193-2*, O48) Dramatic Pub.

Old Lamps & New: Restoring & Decorating. Ruth Little. LC 64-17394. (Illus.). 1964. 15.00 (*0-9624294-2-2*) R Little.

Old Lamps for the New: The Ancient Wisdom in the Modern World. Claude Bragdon. 201p. 1998. reprint ed. pap. 16.95 (*0-7661-0139-8*) Kessinger Pub.

Old Land & the New: Journals of Two Swiss Families in America in the 1820s. Ed. by Robert H. Billigmeier & Fred A. Picard. LC 65-15544. (Illus.). 291p. reprint ed. pap. 90.30 (*0-608-14093-7*, 205584400039) Bks Demand.

Old Land, Dark Land, Strange Land: Stories by John F. Suter. John F. Suter. LC 96-60068. 260p. 1996. 21.95 (*0-9651108-0-X*) U of Charleston.

Old Landmarkism & the Baptists. Bob L. Ross. 1979. mass mkt. 4.00 (*1-56186-504-4*) Pilgrim Pubns.

Old Landmarks of Conton & Stark County, Ohio, 2 vols., Set. John Danner. (Illus.). 1511p. 1994. reprint ed. lib. bdg. 150.00 (*0-8328-4363-6*) Higginson Bk Co.

***Old Latin Gospels: A Study of Their Texts & Language.** Philip Burton. (Oxford Early Christian Studies). 250p. 2000. text 70.00 (*0-19-826988-9*) OUP.

Old Law & the New Law: The Ten Commandments & the Sermon on the Mount. Ed. by William Barclay. 128p. (C). 1992. pap. 35.00 (*0-7855-6827-1*, Pub. by St Andrew) St Mut.

Old Law & the New Law: The Ten Commandments & the Sermon on the Mount. William Barclay. 128p. 1993. pap. 30.00 (*0-7152-0197-2*, Pub. by St Andrew) St Mut.

An Asterisk (*) at the beginning of an entry indicates that the title is appearing for the first time.

Old Law for a New World? The Applicability of International Law to Information Warfare. Lawrence T. Greenberg et al. 38p. 1997. pap. 10.00 (0-935371-44-3) CFISAC.

Old Law, New Medicine Medical Ethics & Human Rights. Sheila McLean. 1999. pap. text 19.50 (0-86358-402-0) Harper SF.

Old Law, New Medicine: Medical Ethics & Human Rights. Sheila McLean. 224p. 1999. 50.00 (0-86358-403-9, Pub. by Rivers Oram) NYU Pr.

Old Lawn Mowers. David G. Halford. (Album Ser.: No. 91). (Illus.). 32p. 1989. pap. 25.00 (0-85263-607-5, Pub. by Shire Pubns) Parkwest Pubns.

Old Left. Julia Dietrich. LC 95-6126. (Literature & Society Ser.: No. 8). 1995. 33.00 (0-8057-8861-1, Twyne) Mac Lib Ref.

Old Left in History & Literature. Julia Dietrich. 1995. pap. 20.00 (0-8057-7819-5, Twyne) Mac Lib Ref.

Old Letivia & the Mountain of Sorrows see Vieja Letivia y el Monte de los Pesares

Old Letter Boxes. Martin Robinson. 1989. pap. 25.00 (0-85263-846-9, Pub. by Shire Pubns) St Mut.

Old Liberators: New & Selected Poems & Translations. Robert Hedin. LC 98-2601. 116p. 1998. 18.95 (0-930100-81-6); pap. text 12.95 (0-930100-80-8) Holy Cow.

Old Liberty. Marshall Terry. vi, 186p. 1991. reprint ed. 18.00 (0-89672-256-2) Tex Tech Univ Pr.

Old Lies Revisited: The Young Readers & the Literature of War & Violence. Whitehead. 1995. pap. 19.50 (0-7453-0429-X, Pub. by Pluto GBR) Stylus Pub VA.

Old Lies Revisited: Young Readers & the Literature of War & Violence. Winifred Whitehead. 302p. (C). 48.50 (0-7453-0428-1, Pub. by Pluto GBR) Stylus Pub VA.

Old Life. Donald Hall. 144p. 1997. pap. 13.00 (0-395-85600-0) HM.

Old Light Cord. Helen F. Poissons. (Illus.). 68p. (Orig.). 1991. pap. text 9.00 (0-9621498-7-X, Robin Hood) R Hood Little.

Old Light on Seperate Ways: The Narragansett Diary of Joseph Fish, 1765-1776. Joseph Fish. Ed. by William S. Simmons & Cheryl L. Simmons. LC 81-71906. (Illus.). 187p. Date not set. reprint ed. pap. 58.00 (0-608-20676-8, 207178300002) Bks Demand.

Old Line State: Her Heritage. Thomas E. Jones & Charles W. Titus. LC 79-180858. (Illus.). 96p. 1971. reprint ed. pap. 30.00 (0-7837-9084-8, 204983400003) Bks Demand.

Old Lines, New Forces: Essays on the Contemporary British Novel, 1960-1970. Ed. by Robert K. Morris. LC 75-18243. 211p. 1976. 32.50 (0-8386-1771-9) Fairleigh Dickinson.

Old Llanelli. Roger W. Davies. (Illus.). 97p. (C). 1985. text 39.00 (0-86383-139-7, Pub. by Gomer Pr) St Mut.

Old London: Belgravia, Chelsea & Kensington. Village Press Editorial Board Staff. (C). 1989. pap. 50.00 (0-7855-6530-2, Pub. by Village Pr) St Mut.

Old London: Charterhouse to Holborn. Village Press Editorial Board Staff. (C). 1989. pap. 45.00 (0-946619-29-8, Pub. by Village Pr) St Mut.

Old London: Covent Garden to Whitehall. Village Press Editorial Board Staff. (C). 1989. pap. 39.95 (0-946619-30-1, Pub. by Village Pr) St Mut.

Old London: Haymarket to Mayfair. Village Press Editorial Board Staff. (C). 1989. pap. 39.95 (0-946619-37-9, Pub. by Village Pr) St Mut.

Old London: Highgate & Hampstead to the Lea. Village Press Editorial Board Staff. (C). 1989. pap. 39.95 (0-7855-5969-8, Pub. by Village Pr) St Mut.

Old London: Hyde Park to Bloomsbury. Village Press Editorial Board Staff. (C). 1989. pap. 39.95 (0-946619-38-7, Pub. by Village Pr) St Mut.

Old London: Shoreditch to Smithfield. Village Press Editorial Board Staff. (C). 1989. pap. 45.00 (0-946619-28-X, Pub. by Village Pr) St Mut.

Old London: Strand to Soho. Village Press Editorial Board Staff. (C). 1989. pap. 45.95 (0-946619-31-X, Pub. by Village Pr) St Mut.

Old London: Westminster to St. James's. Village Press Editorial Board Staff. (C). 1989. pap. 39.95 (0-946619-36-0, Pub. by Village Pr) St Mut.

Old Lop-Ear Wolf. Royce Q. Holland. Ed. by Hap Gilliland. (Illus.). 56p. 1991. pap. 6.95 (0-89992-129-9) Coun India Ed.

Old-Lore Miscellany, 10 vols., Set. Ed. by Alfred W. Johnston & Amy Johnston. (Viking Society for Northern Research: Old Lore Ser.). reprint ed. 275.00 (0-404-60220-7) AMS Pr.

Old Love see Viejo Amor

Old Love: A Novel. Margaret Erhart. LC 95-48320. 246p. 1996. 24.00 (1-883642-07-8) Steerforth Pr.

Old Love: A Novel. Margaret Erhart. LC 95-48320. 246p. 1998. reprint ed. pap. 13.00 (1-883642-73-6) Steerforth Pr.

***Old Love: Lessons Learned along the Way.** Mary Jo Blackwood. 72p. 1999. pap. 7.95 (0-9671840-0-2, Hepp U Pr) Healthsite Assocs.

Old Love Spells & Charms. Tarostar & Maya Britan. (Spells Ser.). (Illus.). 24p. 1998. 5.95 (0-943832-26-8) Intl Imports.

Old Lovers see Antiguos Amantes: The Rancher's Spittin' Image

Old Lover's Ghost. Joan Smith. 1994. mass mkt. 3.99 (0-449-22220-9) Fawcett.

Old Loves Die Hard. Joe C. Faust. LC 87-61307. 1986. pap. 6.00 (0-88734-217-5) Players Pr.

Old Low Franconian Psalms & Glosses. Ed. by Robert L. Kyes. LC 69-15843. 170p. reprint ed. pap. 52.70 (0-608-30036-5, 205104800074) Bks Demand.

Old Loyalties, New Ties: Therapeutic Strategies with Stepfamilies. Emily B. Visher & John S. Visher. LC 87-23899. 272p. 1989. text 31.95 (0-87630-489-7) Brunner-Mazel.

Old Luang Prabang. Betty Gosling. (Images of Asia Ser.). (Illus.). 100p. 1996. text 21.00 (983-56-0006-6) OUP.

***Old Macdonald.** (J). (gr. k-3). 2000. bds. 6.99 (0-689-83411-X) Litle Simon.

Old MacDonald. Pam Adams. LC 99-57504. 1999. pap. text 19.99 (0-85953-637-8) Childs Play.

Old Macdonald. Cathy Beylon. (Window Book Ser.). (J). (ps). 1992. 4.95 (1-56288-281-3) Checkerboard.

Old MacDonald. Amy Schwartz. LC 97-10111. 32p. (J). (ps-1). 1997. 15.95 (0-590-46189-3) Scholastic Inc.

Old MacDonald. Jessica Souhami. LC 95-18797. (Illus.). 24p. (J). (ps-1). 1996. 11.95 (0-531-09493-6) Orchard Bks Watts.

Old MacDonald. Rosemary Wells. (Bunny Reads Back Ser.). (Illus.). 16p. (J). (ps-k). 1998. bds. 4.99 (0-590-76985-5) Scholastic Inc.

Old MacDonald Had a Farm. (Play - a - Sound Ser.). (Illus.). 24p. (J). 1993. 12.98 (1-56173-751-8) Pubns Intl Ltd.

Old MacDonald Had a Farm. Illus. by Pam Adams. (Books with Holes Ser.). (FRE.). 16p. (J). 1975. pap. 6.99 (0-85953-461-8); pap. 6.99 (0-85953-592-4) Childs Play.

Old MacDonald Had a Farm. Illus. by Pam Adams. LC 90-46923. (Books with Holes Ser.). 16p. (J). (ps-2). 1975. pap. 6.99 (0-85953-053-1, Pub. by Childs Play) Random House.

Old MacDonald Had a Farm. Illus. by R. W. Alley. (Pudgy Pal Board Bks.). 18p. (J). (ps up). 1991. bds. 3.99 (0-448-40106-1, G & D) Peng Put Young Read.

Old MacDonald Had a Farm. Illus. by Holly Berry. LC 93-41328. 32p. (J). (ps-2). 1994. lib. bdg. 14.88 (1-55858-282-7, Pub. by North-South Bks NYC) Chronicle Bks.

Old MacDonald Had a Farm. Illus. by Holly Berry. LC 93-41328. 32p. (J). (ps-2). 1997. pap. 6.95 (1-55858-703-9, Pub. by North-South Bks NYC) Chronicle Bks.

Old MacDonald Had a Farm. Frances Cony et al. LC 98-67008. (Illus.). 12p. (J). (ps-k). 1999. 9.95 (0-531-30129-X) Orchard Bks Watts.

Old MacDonald Had a Farm. Penny Dann. (Toddler Bks.). 20p. (J). 1999. pap. text 4.95 (0-7641-0869-7) Barron.

Old MacDonald Had a Farm. Illus. by Kathi Ember. LC 94-73369. (Little Golden Bks.). 24p. (J). (ps-k). 1997. 2.29 (0-307-98806-6, 98806, Goldn Books) Gldn Bks Pub Co.

Old MacDonald Had a Farm. Bernie Fass et al. 32p. (J). (gr. k-4). 1981. pap. 14.95 (0-86704-007-6) Clarus Music.

Old MacDonald Had a Farm. Illus. by Carol Jones. (J). (ps-3). 1989. 15.00 (0-395-49212-2) HM.

Old Macdonald had A Farm. Illus. by Carol Jones. (J). (ps-3). 1998. pap. 5.95 (0-395-90125-1) HM.

Old MacDonald Had a Farm. Pat Paris. (Illus.). 12p. (J). (ps-1). 1989. text 11.95 (0-8120-6107-1) Barron.

***Old MacDonald Had a Farm: Flip-Flap.** Siobhan Dodds. LC 98-73052. (Illus.). 32p. (J). 1999. pap. 3.99 (0-7636-0761-4) Candlewick Pr.

Old MacDonald Had a Farm: Level Two, Yellow. Illus. by Jane Chapman. LC 98-88076. (Reading Together Ser.). (J). 1999. pap. write for info. (0-7636-0854-8) Candlewick Pr.

Old MacDonald Had an Apartment House. Judi Barrett. LC 97-17349. (Illus.). 32p. (J). (ps-2). 1998. 16.00 (0-689-81757-6) Atheneum Yung Read.

Old MacDonald's Barn. Peter Lippman. (Mini House Bks.). (Illus.). 20p. (J). (ps). 1993. bds. 9.95 (1-56305-500-7, 3500) Workman Pub.

Old MacDonald's Farm. Cathy Beylon. (Little Activity Bks.). (Illus.). (J). 1997. pap. 1.00 (0-486-29409-9) Dover.

Old MacDonald's Farm. Illus. by Angela Kamstra. 16p. (Orig.). (J). (ps-3). 1994. pap. 7.95 (0-8249-8658-X, Ideals Child) Hambleton-Hill.

Old Macdonald's Farm. Michelle Knudsen. LC 97-21254. (J). 1998. 4.99 (0-679-88912-4, Pub. by Random Bks Yng Read) Random.

Old MacDonald's Farm. McClanahan Staff. (I Can Learn Ser.). (Illus.). 24p. (J). (ps-2). 1994. 1.95 (1-56293-512-7, McClanahan Book) Learn Horizon.

Old MacDonald's Musical Farm. Illus. by Judith Stuchly & Janice Castiglione. 6p. (J). 1997. vinyl bd. 5.00 (1-883043-01-8) Straight Edge.

Old MacDonald's Pop-Up Farm. Katy Rhodes. (Illus.). 12p. (J). 1997. 13.95 (0-7641-5055-3) Barron.

Old MacDonald's Tub. Anne Shufflebotham. (Soap Opera Ser.). 8p. (J). (gr. 3 up). 1990. 4.99 (0-85953-444-8) Childs Play.

Old Madam Yin: A Memoir of Peking Life. Ida Pruitt. LC 78-68782. xii, 129p. 1979. 24.50 (0-8047-1038-4) Stanford U Pr.

Old Magazines: Price & Identification Guide. 5th rev. ed. Denis C. Jackson. (Illus.). 56p. 2000. pap. 7.95 (1-888687-09-6) Illust Collectors.

Old Magazines Price Guide, One. rev. ed. Ed. by L-W Books Staff & Neil L. Wood. (Illus.). 112p. 1994. pap. 9.95 (0-89538-064-1) L-W Inc.

Old Magic Meets Today's Science: A Look at Scientific Recreations from the 1890's. Robert A. Friedhoffer. LC 98-42074. (Fun with Science Ser.). (Illus.). 2001. write for info. (0-531-11365-5) Watts.

Old Mahony & the Bear Family. Wolfram Hanel. Tr. by Rosemary Lanning. LC 96-44518. (Illus.). 48p. (J). (gr. 2-4). 1997. 13.95 (1-55858-713-6, Pub. by North-South Bks NYC); lib. bdg. 13.88 (1-55858-714-4, Pub. by North-South Bks NYC) Chronicle Bks.

***Old Mahony & the Bear Family.** Wolfram Hanel. Tr. by Rosemary Lanning. LC 95-52219. (Illus.). 48p. (J). (gr. 2-4). 1999. pap. 5.95 (0-7358-1102-4, Pub. by North-South Bks NYC) Chronicle Bks.

Old Maids to Radical Spinsters: Unmarried Women in the Twentieth-Century Novel. Ed. by Laura L. Doan. 304p. 1991. text 39.95 (0-252-01731-5); pap. text 15.95 (0-252-06134-9) U of Ill Pr.

Old Main Images of a Legend. Roy V. Scott & Charles D. Lowery. Ed. by Allen Snow. (Illus.). 152p. 1995. 29.95 (1-56469-028-8) Harmony Hse Pub.

Old Malacca. Sarnia H. Hoyt. LC 93-14633. (Images of Asia Ser.). (Illus.). 114p. (C). 1993. text 18.95 (0-19-588619-4) OUP.

Old Mammoth: A First Hand Account. Adele Reed. Ed. by Genny Smith. LC 82-60130. (Illus.). 200p. 1994. reprint ed. pap. 17.95 (0-931378-04-4) Live Oak.

Old Man see Three Famous Short Novels

Old Man. 229p. 1995. pap. 8.00 (0-9633479-3-4) Dummer Pub.

Old Man. Gary Cook. 1988. 17.50 (0-913150-58-4) Pioneer Pr.

***Old Man.** Yury V. Trifonov. Tr. by Jacqueline Edwards & Mitchell Schneider from RUS. LC 99-44289. 272p. 1999. pap. 17.95 (0-8101-1571-9) Northwestern U Pr.

Old Man. E. G. Marsh. 1990. reprint ed. pap. 4.99 (0-88019-265-8) Schmul Pub Co.

***Old Man: The Biography of Walter J. Travis.** Bob Labbance. (Illus.). 300p. 2000. 29.95 (1-886947-91-0) Sleepng Bear.

Old Man & His Door. Gary Soto. LC 94-27085. (Illus.). 32p. (J). (ps-3). 1996. 15.95 (0-399-22700-8, G P Putnam) Peng Put Young Read.

Old Man & His Door. Gary Soto. (Illus.). 32p. (J). (ps-3). 1998. pap. 5.99 (0-698-11654-2, PapStar) Peng Put Young Read.

Old Man & His Sons. Hedin Bru. Tr. by John F. West. (Illus.). 1970. 15.95 (0-8397-8412-0) Eriksson.

***Old Man & Other Colonel Weatherford Stories.** Gordon Grand. (Illus.). 239p. 2000. pap. 16.95 (1-56833-143-6, Pub. by Derrydale Pr) Natl Bk Netwk.

Old Man & the Bear. Wolfram Hanel. LC 93-39757. (Illus.). (J). (gr. 2-4). 1995. pap. 4.95 (1-55858-411-0, Pub. by North-South Bks NYC) Chronicle Bks.

Old Man & the Bear. Wolfram Hanel. 1995. 10.15 (0-606-08836-9, Pub. by Turtleback) Demco.

Old Man & the Boy. Robert Ruark. LC 57-10425. 320p. 1995. 24.95 (0-8050-0239-1); pap. 12.95 (0-8050-2669-X) H Holt & Co.

Old Man & the Boy. large type ed. Robert Ruark. LC 94-5764. 417p. 1994. reprint ed. lib. bdg. 21.95 (0-8161-5966-1, G K Hall Lrg Type) Mac Lib Ref.

Old Man & the Bureaucrats. Mircea Eliade. Tr. by Mary P. Stevenson. (Phoenix Fiction Ser.). vi, 130p. 1995. pap. 7.95 (0-226-20410-3) U Ch Pr.

Old Man & the Bureaucrats. Mircea Eliade. Tr. by Mary P. Stevenson. 1980. text 15.00 (0-268-01497-3) U of Notre Dame Pr.

Old Man & the Dog. Carroll S. Leatherman. 1991. 16.95 (1-879034-01-8) MS River Pub.

Old Man & the Medal. Ferdinand Oyono. Tr. by John Reed from FRE. (African Writers Ser.).Tr. of Le Vieux Negre et la Medaille. 167p. (Orig.). (C). 1969. reprint ed. pap. 8.95 (0-435-90039-0, 90039) Heinemann.

***Old Man & the Mice.** large type ed. Tr. by Donna Tamaki.Tr. of Nezumi Choja. (ENG & JPN., Illus.). 12p. (J). (ps-2). 1999. 35.00 (1-893533-13-1, 19) Kamish for Kids.

Old Man & the Moat. Kelli C. Foster & Gina C. Erickson. LC 94-36090. (Get Ready...Get Set...Read! Ser.). (Illus.). 26p. (gr. k-3). 1995. pap. 3.50 (0-8120-1097-3) Barron.

Old Man & the Rabbit. Tracey Lloyd. (Junior African Writers Ser.). (Illus.). 80p. (J). (gr. 3 up). 1992. pap. 4.95 (0-7910-2917-4) Chelsea Hse.

***Old Man & the Road: Reflections While Completing a Crossing of All 50 States on Foot at Age 80.** Paul Reese. Ed. by Joe Henderson. 304p. (Orig.). 2000. pap. 14.95 (1-879628-20-1) Keokee ID.

Old Man & the Sea. 36p. (YA). 1998. 11.95 (1-56137-404-0, NU4040SP) Novel Units.

Old Man & the Sea. Harold Bloom. (Bloom's Notes Ser.). 1998. pap. 4.95 (0-7910-4144-1) Chelsea Hse.

Old Man & the Sea. Stanley Cooperman. (C). 3.95 (0-671-00673-8, Arco) Macmillan Gen Ref.

Old Man & the Sea. Ernest Hemingway. Ed. by Harold Bloom. LC 98-24047. (Modern Critical Interpretations Ser.). 176p. (YA). 1999. 34.95 (0-7910-4778-4) Chelsea Hse.

Old Man & the Sea. Ernest Hemingway. 1990. 10.92 (0-02-635123-4) Glencoe.

Old Man & the Sea. Ernest Hemingway. 1989. pap., student ed. 11.00 (0-03-023452-2) Holt R&W.

Old Man & the Sea. Ernest Hemingway. 128p. 1950. 14.00 (0-684-10245-5, Scribners Ref) Mac Lib Ref.

Old Man & the Sea. Ernest Hemingway. 128p. 1977. 30.00 (0-684-15363-7, Scribners Ref); lib. bdg. 20.00 (0-685-04566-8, Scribners Ref) Mac Lib Ref.

Old Man & the Sea. Ernest Hemingway. (Illus.). 128p. 1984. 18.00 (0-684-18227-0, Scribners Ref) Mac Lib Ref.

Old Man & the Sea. Ernest Hemingway. 128p. 1995. per. 9.00 (0-684-80122-1) S&S Trade.

Old Man & the Sea. Ernest Hemingway. 96p. 1996. pap. 19.50 (0-684-83049-3) S&S Trade.

Old Man & the Sea. Ernest Hemingway. 1995. 14.10 (0-606-00201-4, Pub. by Turtleback) Demco.

***Old Man & the Sea.** Kathleen Millin. 28p. 1999. 9.95 (1-56137-403-2) Novel Units.

Old Man & the Sea. large type ed. Ernest Hemingway. LC 94-14262. 113p. 1994. lib. bdg. 20.95 (0-8161-5970-X, G K Hall Lrg Type) Mac Lib Ref.

Old Man & the Sea. large type ed. Ernest Hemingway. reprint ed. 10.00 (0-89064-252-4) NAVH.

Old Man & the Sea: A Study Guide. Joyce Friedland & Rikki Kessler. (Novel-Ties Ser.). (J). (gr. 6-8). 1983. pap. text, student ed. 15.95 (0-88122-029-9) Lrn Links.

Old Man & the Sea: A Unit Plan. Mary B. Collins. 146p. 1994. teacher ed., ring bd. 26.95 (1-58337-009-9) Teachers Pet Pubns.

***Old Man & The Sea: Heston,&Charlton, Set.** unabridged ed. Ernest Hemingway. LC 76-740411. 1998. audio 18.00 (0-89845-952-4, CPN 2084, Caedmon) HarperAudio.

Old Man & the Sea: Story of a Common Man. Gerry Brenner. (Twayne's Masterwork Studies: No. 80). 136p. 1991. 29.00 (0-8057-7991-4, Twyne) Mac Lib Ref.

***Old Man & the Sea: Study Guide.** Calvin Roso. (YA). 2000. pap. 14.99 (1-58609-172-7) Progeny Pr WI.

Old Man & the Sea by Ernest Hemingway - Ethan Frome by Edith Wharton: Curriculum Unit. Center for Learning Network Staff. (Novel Ser.). 83p. (YA). (gr. 9-12). 1993. teacher ed., spiral bd. 18.95 (1-56077-279-4) Ctr Learning.

Old Man & the Sea Notes. Gary K. Carey. (Cliffs Notes Ser.). 64p. (Orig.). (C). 1973. pap. 4.95 (0-8220-0935-8, Cliff) IDG Bks.

***Old Man & the Tree.** Vicki Wisenfeld. (Illus.). (J). 2000. 14.99 (0-7459-4231-8) Lion USA.

Old Man & the Wolves. Julia Kristeva. Tr. by Barbara Bray. LC 94-11795. 192p. 1994. 29.50 (0-231-08020-4) Col U Pr.

Old Man at the Moat: A Bring It All Together Book. Kelli C. Foster & Gina C. Erickson. (Get Ready...Get Set...Read! Ser.: Set 4). (Illus.). 24p. (J). (gr. k-2). 1996. lib. bdg. 11.95 (1-56674-141-6) Forest Hse.

Old Man at the Railroad Crossing: And Other Tales. William Maxwell. LC 86-46248. 192p. (Orig.). 1987. pap. 10.95 (0-87923-676-0) Godine.

***Old Man Brown & His Magic Bike.** Preston McClear. (Illus.). 30p. (J). (gr. k-5). 1999. 16.95 (1-929084-06-4); pap. 12.95 (1-929084-07-2) Malibu Bks Chldn.

Old Man Brunner Country. Leo Dangel. 60p. 1987. pap. 4.95 (0-933180-94-2) Spoon Riv Poetry.

Old Man Coyote. Frank B. Linderman. LC 96-32438. (Illus.). v, 254p. 1996. pap. 11.95 (0-8032-7964-7, Bison Books) U of Nebr Pr.

Old Man Does As He Pleases. Burton Watson. 1973. text 41.00 (0-231-03766-X) Col U Pr.

Old Man Fog & the Last Aborigines of Barrow Point. John B. Haviland & Roger Hart. Ed. by William L. Merrill & Iv Merrill. LC 98-38563. (Series in Ethnographic Inquiry). (Illus.). 256p. 1999. 29.95 (1-56098-913-0) Smithsonian.

Old Man Fog & the Last Aborigines of Barrow Point. John B. Haviland & Roger Hart. LC 98-38563. (Ethnographic Inquiry Ser.). 1998. pap. write for info. (1-56098-803-7) Smithsonian Institution Office of Museum.

Old Man Gilbert. Elizabeth W. Bellamy. (Works of Elizabeth Whitfield Bellamy). 1989. reprint ed. lib. bdg. 79.00 (0-7812-1948-5) Rprt Serv.

Old Man Hoover's Dead Rabbit. Pam Conrad. LC 94-45773. (Laura Geringer Bks.). (Illus.). 48p. (J). lib. bdg. 14.89 (0-06-021515-1) HarpC Child Bks.

Old Man in a Baseball Cap: A Memoir of World War II. Fred Rochlin. LC 99-21421. 160p. 1999. 20.00 (0-06-019426-X) HarpC.

Old Man in a Baseball Cap: A Memoir of World War II. Fred Rochlin. 160p. 2000. pap. 12.00 (0-06-093227-9, Perennial) HarperTrade.

***Old Man in a Baseball Cap: A Memoir of World War II.** large type ed. Fred Rochlin. LC 99-57453. (Americana Series). 2000. 28.95 (0-7862-2371-5) Thorndike Pr.

***Old Man in the Corner.** Emmuska Orczy. 1998. lib. bdg. 16.95 (1-56723-080-6) Yestermorrow.

Old Man in the Corner. Emmuska Orczy. 340p. 1980. reprint ed. lib. bdg. 15.95 (0-89968-196-4, Lghtyr Pr) Buccaneer Bks.

Old Man Joseph & His Family. Romulus Linney. 1978. pap. 5.25 (0-8222-0841-5) Dramatists Play.

Old Man, New Man. (ENG & IND.). 1996. write for info. (0-934920-73-7) Derek Prince.

***Old Man, New Man: Closing the Gap Between the Life You Should Live & the Life You Are Living.** Stephen Strang. 224p. 2000. 19.99 (0-88419-697-6) Creation House.

Old Man of Gilfach. 2nd ed. Eirlys Trefor. 108p. (J). (gr. 4). 1997. reprint ed. pap. 11.95 (0-8464-4845-9) Beekman Pubs.

Old Man on 52nd Street. Stanley-Pierre Ngeyi. 115p. (Orig.). 1998. pap. 8.50 (0-9636079-3-6) Mt Zion Pub.

Old Man Ontario: Leslie M. Frost. Roger Graham. (Ontario Historical Studies). 608p. 1990. text 35.00 (0-8020-3459-4) U of Toronto Pr.

Old Man Out. Gail Radley. LC 94-10858. 144p. (J). (gr. 3-7). 1995. mass mkt. 14.00 (0-02-775792-7, Mac Bks Young Read) S&S Childrens.

***Old Man River & Me: One Man's Journey down the Mighty Mississippi.** Mark A. Knudsen & Shawn Plank. LC 98-49762. (Illus.). 240p. 1999. pap. 12.95 (1-55853-738-4) Rutledge Hill Pr.

***Old Man River & Me: One Man's Journey Down the Mighty Mississippi.** large type unabridged ed. Mark Knudsen & Shawn Plank. 2000. 26.95 (0-7531-5209-6, 152096, Pub. by ISIS Lrg Prnt) ISIS Pub.

Old Man Savarin Stories: Tales of Canada & Canadians. Edward W. Thomson. LC 70-37567. (Short Story Index Reprint Ser.). 1977. reprint ed. 23.95 (0-8369-4126-8) Ayer.

Old Man Thunder: Father of the Bullet Train. Bill Hosokawa. LC 97-69044. (Illus.). 270p. 1997. 30.00 (0-9659580-0-0) Sogo Way.

O

An Asterisk (*) at the beginning of an entry indicates that the title is appearing for the first time.

Old Man Told Us: Excerpts from Micmac History, 1500-1950. Ruth H. Whitehead. (Illus.). 304p. 1991. pap. 17.95 (*0-921054-83-1*) Nimbus Publ.

Old Man Who Does As He Pleases. Burton Watson. 1994. pap. 14.00 (*0-231-10155-4*) Col U Pr.

Old Man Who Loved Cheese. Garrison Keillor. (Illus.). 32p. (J). (gr. k-3). 1998. pap. 5.95 (*0-316-48610-8*) Little.

Old Man Who Loved Cheese. Garrison Keillor. (Illus.). 1998. 11.15 (*0-606-13674-6*, Pub. by Turtleback) Demco.

Old Man Who Loved to Sing. John Winch. LC 95-5307. (Illus.). 40p. (J). (ps-2). 1996. 14.95 (*0-590-22640-1*) Scholastic Inc.

Old Man Who Loved to Sing. John Winch. 1998. pap. 4.99 (*0-590-22641-X*) Scholastic Inc.

Old Man Who Read Love Stories. Luis Sepulveda. Tr. by Peter Bush from SPA. LC 93-29103. 1994. 14.95 (*0-15-168550-9*) Harcourt.

Old Man Who Read Love Stories. Luis Sepulveda. Tr. by Peter Bush. 144p. (C). 1995. pap. 9.00 (*0-15-600272-8*) Harcourt.

Old Man Who Swam Away & Left Only His Wet Feet. Gene Frumkin. 120p. 1998. pap. 14.00 (*1-888809-08-6*) La Alameda Pr.

Old Manchester, Virginia & Its Environs, 1769-1910. Benjamin B. Weisiger, III. 190p. 1993. 22.50 (*0-9638320-0-X*) Rocky Ridge.

Old Manor House. Barbara Holliday. (Illus.). 184p. (J). (gr. 6-8). 1994. pap. 9.99 (*0-88092-056-4*) Royal Fireworks.

Old Man's Boy Grows Older. Robert Ruark. 300p. 1995. 22.00 (*0-8050-2980-X*); pap. 12.95 (*0-8050-2974-5*) H Holt & Co.

Old Man's Diary Forty Years Ago, 1823-33, 4 vols. in 1. J. Payne Collier. reprint ed. 49.50 (*0-404-07289-5*) AMS Pr.

Old Man's Gold, & Other Stories. Ovid W. Pierce. LC 75-19101. 80p. reprint ed. pap. 30.00 (*0-8357-3876-0*, 203660800004) Bks Demand.

***Old Man's Letters.** Michael Reisig. 110p. 1999. pap. 5.99 (*0-9651240-4-5*) Clear Creek Pr.

Old Man's Love, 2 vols. Anthony Trollope. Ed. by N. John Hall. LC 80-1905. (Selected Works of Anthony Trollop). 1981. reprint ed. lib. bdg. 55.95 (*0-405-14202-1*) Ayer.

Old Man's Mitten. Yevonne Pollock. LC 94-30195. (Illus.). 24p. (Orig.). (J). (ps-3). 1994. pap. 4.95 (*1-879531-60-7*) Mondo Pubng.

Old Man's Money. Charles B. Brooks. vii, 277p. 1998. pap. 17.50 (*0-9667578-3-1*) Brooks Hse.

Old Man's New. Dave Cochran. 55p. (Orig.). 1996. pap. 5.00 (*0-88734-360-0*) Players Pr.

Old Man's Reader: History & Legends of Franconia Notch. Ed. & Compiled by John T. Mudge. (Illus.). 231p. (Orig.). 1995. pap. 13.95 (*0-9633560-3-8*) Durand Pr.

Old Man's Trail: A Novel about Vietcong. Tom Campbell. LC 95-18660. 256p. 1995. 25.95 (*1-55750-117-3*) Naval Inst Pr.

Old Manse. Nathaniel Hawthorne. 96p. 1997. pap. 9.95 (*0-939218-00-3*) Chapman Billies.

Old Marine Engines: The World of the One-Lunger. 3rd ed. Stan Grayson. Ed. by Kathy Brandes & Jackie Pellaton. (Illus.). 272p. 1998. pap. 34.95 (*0-9640070-2-9*) Devereux Bks.

Old Marlborough Road: "A Journey into Wonder" Ken Wolgemuth. LC 91-65384. 160p. (Orig.). 1991. pap. 9.95 (*0-944072-16-X*) Zoland Bks.

Old Marsden. Frank Roderus. 272p. 1999. mass mkt. 4.50 (*0-8439-4506-0*) Dorchester Pub Co.

Old Maryland. Mayer et al. (Historical Ser.). (Illus.). 1976. pap. 3.50 (*0-89540-022-7*, SB-022) Sun Pub.

Old Masks, New Faces: Religion & Latino Identities, 4 vols., Set. Ed. by Anthony M. Stevens & Gilbert R. Cadena. (Paral Studies: Vol. 2). 250p. 1995. 29.95 (*0-929972-09-0*); pap. write for info. (*0-929972-10-4*) Bildner Ctr.

Old Master: And Other Political Essays. Woodrow Wilson. LC 73-1227. (Essay Index Reprint Ser.). 1977. reprint ed. 18.95 (*0-518-10071-5*) Ayer.

Old Master Drawings at Bowdoin College. David P. Becker. LC 84-72390. (Illus.). 260p. (Orig.). 1985. 30.00 (*0-916606-08-2*); pap. 14.95 (*0-685-73717-9*) Bowdoin Coll.

Old Master Drawings at Holkham Hall. A. E. Popham. Ed. by Christopher Lloyd. (Illus.). 152p. 1987. lib. bdg. 150.00 incl. fiche (*0-226-69273-6*) U Ch Pr.

Old Master Drawings from Area Collections. Barry Wind. Ed. by Sheila Schwartz. LC 97-71384. (Illus.). 72p. (Orig.). 1997. pap. 19.95 (*0-944110-79-7*) Milwauk Art Mus.

Old Master Drawings from the Ashmolean Museum. Christopher White et al. (Illus.). 232p. 1992. text 165.00 (*1-85444-027-6*, 0003) OUP.

Old Master Drawings from the Museum of Art, Rhode Island School of Design. Deborah Johnson. (Illus.). 263p. 1983. pap. 18.00 (*0-911517-03-0*) Mus of Art RI.

Old Master Landscape Drawings: Forty-Five Works. Ed. by James Spero. (Illus.). 48p. (Orig.). 1992. pap. 3.95 (*0-486-26947-7*) Dover.

Old Master Life Drawings: Forty-Four Plates. Ed. by James Spero. (Art Library). (Illus.). 43p. 1987. pap. 4.95 (*0-486-25233-7*) Dover.

Old Master Paintings in Britain: An Index of Old Master Paintings in U. K. Public Collections. Christopher Wright. (Illus.). 288p. 1976. 65.00 (*0-85667-024-3*) Wittenborn Art.

Old Master Paintings in North America. John D. Morse. (Illus.). 256p. 1996. pap. 19.95 (*0-89659-050-X*) Abbeville Pr.

Old Master Paintings in Soviet Museums. I. V. Linnik. (Illus.). 211p. (C). 1989. text 235.00 (*0-569-09217-5*, Pub. by Collets) St Mut.

Old Master Portrait Drawings. James Spero. (Illus.). 48p. 1990. pap. 4.95 (*0-486-26364-9*) Dover.

Old Master Prints & Drawings: A Guide to Preservation & Conservation. Carlo James et al. LC 97-223088. (C). 1997. 110.00 (*90-5356-243-5*, Pub. by Amsterdam U Pr) U of Mich Pr.

Old Masters: A Comedy. Thomas Bernhard. Tr. by Ewald Osers. LC 92-18986. (Phoenix Fiction Ser.). iv, 160p. 1992. pap. 12.95 (*0-226-04391-6*) U Ch Pr.

Old Masters & New. Kenyon Cox. LC 74-90627. (Essay Index Reprint Ser.). 1977. 23.95 (*0-8369-1403-1*) Ayer.

Old Masters Brought to Light: European Paintings from the National Museum of Art of Romania. Muzeul National De Art et al. LC 96-54293. 1997. pap. 19.95 (*0-88397-122-4*) Art Srvc Intl.

Old Masters, New Subjects: Early Modern & Poststructuralist Theories of Will. Dolora A. Wojciehowski. LC 94-28354. xviii, 260p. 1995. 35.00 (*0-8047-2386-9*) Stanford U Pr.

Old Masters Repainted: A Detailed Investigation into the Authenticity of Paintings Attributed to Wu Zhen (1280-1354) Joan Stanley-Baker. (Illus.). 562p. (C). 1995. pap. 97.50 (*962-209-302-7*, Pub. by HK Univ Pr) Coronet Bks.

Old Masters Signatures & Monograms, 1400-Born 1800. John Castagno. 396p. 1996. 110.00 (*0-8108-3082-5*) Scarecrow.

Old Maud: The Story of the Palatine, Lake Zurich & Wauconda Railroad. Richard Whitney. LC 92-18326. (Illus.). 184p. 1992. text 52.00 (*0-933449-14-3*) Transport Trails.

Old McDonald's Farm. Nina Filipek. (Illus.). 16p. (J). 1995. 2.95 (*0-689-80259-5*, Mac Bks Young Read) S&S Childrens.

Old McLean County Courthouse. Greg Koos. (Illus.). 28p. 1997. pap. 5.00 (*0-943788-14-5*) McLean County.

Old Meadow. George Selden. (Chester Cricket Ser.). (Illus.). 192p. (J). (gr. 3-6). 1987. 15.00 (*0-374-35616-5*) FS&G.

***Old Meadow.** George Selden. (Chester Cricket Ser.). (Illus.). 208p. (YA). (gr. 4-7). 2000. pap. 5.95 (*0-374-45605-4*, Sunburst Bks) FS&G.

Old Media, New Media: Mass Communication in Inforamtion Age. 2nd ed. 272p. (C). 1996. text. write for info. (*0-8013-1947-1*) Longman.

Old Media/New Media. 3rd ed. Wilson Dizard. LC 99-29688. 233p. (C). 1999. pap. text 41.40 (*0-8013-3277-X*) Longman.

Old Mercersburg (Historical & Genealogical Sketches) Mercersburg Woman's Club Staff. (Illus.). 215p. 1997. reprint ed. lib. bdg. 29.50 (*0-8328-6429-3*) Higginson Bk Co.

Old Meshikee & the Little Crabs. Spooner. (Illus.). (J). 1995. 15.95 (*0-8050-4357-8*) H Holt & Co.

Old Meshikee & the Little Crabs: An Ojibwe Story. Illus. by John Hart. LC 95-23498. 88p. (J). (gr. k-5). 1995. 15.95 (*0-8050-3487-0*) H Holt & Co.

Old Middlesex Canal. Mary S. Clark. LC 87-29957. 191p. 1987. reprint ed. 14.00 (*0-930973-05-4*); reprint ed. pap. 6.00 (*0-930973-06-2*) H M Historical.

Old Mills in the Midwest. Leslie C. Swanson. (Illus.). 1985. pap. 4.00 (*0-911466-15-0*) Swanson.

Old Milwaukee: A Historic Tour in Picture Postcards. Gregory Filardo. LC 88-26170. (Illus.). 128p. (Orig.). 1988. pap. 11.95 (*0-911572-73-2*, Vestal Pr) Madison Bks UPA.

Old Mine Road. Charles G. Hine. (Illus.). 171p. 1963. pap. 12.95 (*0-8135-0426-0*) Rutgers U Pr.

Old Miner & the Spider. Laura J. Cochran. LC 96-90708. (J). (gr. 6-8). 1998. 8.95 (*0-533-12151-5*) Vantage.

Old Mr. Bennet's Carrots. Pierre Coran. (Child's World Library). (Illus.). 32p. (J). (gr. k-5). 1992. lib. bdg. 18.50 (*0-89565-749-X*) Childs World.

Old Mistresses: Women, Art & Ideology. Rozsika Parker & Griselda Pollock. 1981. pap. 19.50 (*0-86358-185-4*, Pub. by Rivers Oram) NYU Pr.

Old Mistresses' Apologue. Benjamin Franklin. Ed. by Whitfield Bell. LC 57-37785. 10p. 1956. pap. 5.00 (*0-939084-05-8*) R Mus & Lib.

Old Mobile: Fort Louis de la Louisiane, 1702-1711. Jay Higginbotham. LC 90-22776. (Library of Alabama Classics). 592p. 1991. pap. text 24.95 (*0-8173-0528-9*) U of Ala Pr.

***Old Mobile Archaeology.** Gregory A. Waselkov. (Archaeology Booklet Ser.). (Illus.). ii, 62p. 1999. pap. 12.00 (*1-893955-04-4*) Univ S AL Ctr Archa.

Old Modes of Production & Capitalist Encroachment. Ed. by Peter Geschiere & Wim M. Binsbergen. (Monographs from the African Studies Centre, Leiden). 400p. 67.50 (*0-7103-0089-1*) Routledge.

Old Mok: The Story of a Gold Camp. Richard K. Epstein. (Illus.). 150p. (Orig.). 1995. pap. 21.95 (*1-883938-18-X*) Dry Bones Pr.

Old Money. Thomas J. Martin. mass mkt. 5.99 (*1-55197-289-1*) Picasso Publ.

Old Money. Thomas J. Martin. 546p. 1998. 5.95 (*1-893627-01-2*) T J Martin.

***Old Money.** Elizabeth Palmer. 1999. per. 5.99 (*1-55166-547-6*, 1-66547-0, Mira Bks) Harlequin Bks.

Old Money. rev. ed. Thomas J. Martin. 546p. 1998. pap. 6.95 (*1-893627-00-4*) T J Martin.

Old Money: The Mythology of Wealth in America. 2nd expanded ed. Nelson W. Aldrich, Jr. LC 96-84663. 352p. 1996. pap. 16.95 (*1-880559-64-1*) Allworth Pr.

Old Mongolian Newpapers. (Mongolia Society Special Papers: Issue V). 3.00 (*0-910980-25-X*) Mongolia.

Old Mongoose & Other Poems. Gerald Locklin. 35p. (Orig.). 1993. pap. 6.00 (*0-9628094-6-2*) Pearl Edit.

Old Montgomery Land Office Records. Marilyn D. Barefield. 1991. write for info. (*0-87651-945-1*) Southern U Pr.

Old Moore's Almanack, 1995. Foulsham Editors. 1995. pap. 1.95 (*0-572-02033-3*, Pub. by Foulsham UK); pap. 39.00 (*0-572-02034-1*, Pub. by Foulsham UK) Assoc Pubs Grp.

Old Moore's Almanack, 1994. Francis Moore. 79p. 1993. pap. 1.95 (*0-572-01879-7*, Pub. by Foulsham UK) Assoc Pubs Grp.

Old Moore's Dream Book. Gilbert Oakley. 96p. 1995. pap. 9.95 (*0-572-01345-0*, Pub. by Foulsham UK) Assoc Pubs Grp.

Old Morality see Works of Sir Walter Scott

Old Morals, Small Continents, Darker Times. Philip F. O'Connor. LC 70-158043. (Iowa Short Fiction Award Ser.). 198p. 1971. pap. 3.25 (*0-87745-023-4*) U of Iowa Pr.

Old Morristown Postcard Album. Timothy G. Cutler. (Illus.). 32p. 1995. pap. 7.99 (*1-58057-057-7*, PA001) Digital Antiq.

Old Mortality. Sir Walter Scott. (Cloth Bound Pocket Ser.). 1998. 7.95 (*3-8290-0900-3*, 520663) Konemann.

Old Mortality. Sir Walter Scott. Ed. by Jane Stevenson & Peter Davidson. LC 92-43878. (World's Classics Ser.). 612p. 1993. pap. 11.95 (*0-19-282630-1*) OUP.

Old Mortality. Sir Walter Scott. (Oxford World Classics Ser.). 612p. 1999. pap. 11.95 (*0-19-283763-X*) OUP.

Old Motel Mystery. Created by Gertrude Chandler Warner. (Boxcar Children Ser.: No. 23). (Illus.). (J). (gr. 2-5). 1991. pap. 5.95 (*0-8075-5966-0*); lib. bdg. 19.95 (*0-8075-5967-9*) A Whitman.

Old Motel Mystery. Created by Gertrude Chandler Warner. (Boxcar Children Ser.: No. 23). (J). (gr. 2-5). 1992. 9.05 (*0-606-00661-3*, Pub. by Turtleback) Demco.

Old Mother Bear's Book of Hug Rhymes. Le Landgren. LC 88-38973. (Illus.). 40p. (Orig.). (J). (ps-9). 1989. pap. 6.95 (*0-943367-02-6*) Princess Pub.

***Old Mother Hubbard.** (Illus.). 12p. (J). 2001. bds. 2.99 (*0-307-30154-0*, 30154, Goldn Books) Gldn Bks Pub Co.

***Old Mother Hubbard.** David Johnson & Sarah C. Martin. LC 97-719. (Illus.). 32p. (J). (ps-2). 1998. pap. 16.00 (*0-689-81485-2*) McElderry Bks.

Old Mother Hubbard. Sarah C. Martin. LC 94-210510. 1994. write for info. (*0-7853-0562-9*) Pubns Intl Ltd.

Old Mother Hubbard, Incl. 2 puppets. Illus. by Rebecca Archer. LC 97-71901. (Hand Puppet Bks.). 16p. (J). (ps). 1998. 12.95 (*0-448-41743-X*, G & D) Peng Put Young Read.

Old Mother Hubbard: Mother Goose. Illus. by Carl Morton. (J). (gr. k-1). 1992. 10.00 (*1-57842-095-4*) Delmas Creat.

Old Mother Hubbard & Her Wonderful Dog. James Marshall. 32p. (J). (ps-3). 1991. 13.95 (*0-374-35621-1*) FS&G.

Old Mother Hubbard & Her Wonderful Dog. James Marshall. 32p. (J). (ps-3). 1993. pap. 4.95 (*0-374-45611-9*) FS&G.

Old Mother Hubbard & Her Wonderful Dog. Sarah Catherine Martin. 1991. 10.15 (*0-606-05958-X*, Pub. by Turtleback) Demco.

Old Mother West Wind. Thornton W. Burgess. (J). 16.95 (*0-8488-0385-X*) Amereon Ltd.

Old Mother West Wind. Thornton W. Burgess. LC 89-20088. (Illus.). 90p. (J). (gr. 2-4). 1995. 18.95 (*0-8050-1005-X*, Bks Young Read) H Holt & Co.

Old Mother West Wind. Thornton W. Burgess. (Old Mother West Wind Bks.: Vol. 1). (Illus.). 152p. (J). 1996. 9.95 (*1-883684-11-0*) Peninsula MA.

Old Mother West Wind. Thornton W. Burgess. (J). 1985. 16.05 (*0-606-03992-9*, Pub. by Turtleback) Demco.

Old Mother West Wind. anniversary ed. Thornton W. Burgess. (Nature-Story Bks.). (Illus.). 140p. (J). (gr. k-3). 1985. pap. 12.95 (*0-316-11655-6*) Little.

Old Mother West Wind. Thornton W. Burgess. (Illus.). 160p. (J). 1992. reprint ed. lib. bdg. 14.95 (*0-89966-900-X*) Buccaneer Bks.

Old Mother West Wind. unabridged ed. Thornton W. Burgess. LC 95-36751. (Children's Thrift Classics Ser.). (Illus.). 112p. (J). 1995. reprint ed. pap. text 1.00 (*0-486-28849-8*) Dover.

Old Mother West Wind & 6 Other Stories. Thornton W. Burgess. (J). 1996. pap., boxed set 7.00 (*0-486-29455-2*) Dover.

Old Mother West Wind's Animal Friends. Thornton W. Burgess. Date not set. lib. bdg. 19.95 (*0-88411-779-0*, Aeonian Pr) Amereon Ltd.

Old Mother West Wind's Children. Thornton W. Burgess. (J). 18.95 (*0-8488-0386-8*) Amereon Ltd.

Old Mother West Wind's Children. Thornton W. Burgess. (Old Mother West Wind Bks.: Vol. 2). (Illus.). 152p. (J). 1996. 9.95 (*1-883684-12-9*) Peninsula MA.

Old Mother West Wind's "How" Stories. Thornton W. Burgess. 19.95 (*0-88411-780-4*) Amereon Ltd.

Old Mother West Wind's Neighbors. Thornton W. Burgess. (J). (gr. 5-6). 19.95 (*0-88411-786-3*) Amereon Ltd.

Old Mother West Wind's "When" Stories. Thornton W. Burgess. (J). 21.95 (*0-8488-0387-6*) Amereon Ltd.

Old Mother West Wind's "Where" Stories. Thornton W. Burgess. (J). 18.95 (*0-8488-0388-4*) Amereon Ltd.

Old Mother West Wind's "Why" Stories. Thornton W. Burgess. 19.95 (*0-88411-778-2*) Amereon Ltd.

Old Mother Witch. Prod. by Mark Chodzko. (Literature to Go Ser.). (YA). (gr. 4-9). 1989. pap., student ed. 99.00 incl. vdisk (*0-7919-2686-9*) Phoenix Films.

Old Mr. Boston's Bartender's Guide. Leo Cotton. 1974. 7.95 (*0-685-22064-8*) Wehman.

Old Mrs. Ommanney Is Dead. large type ed. Margaret Erskine. 1991. 11.50 (*0-7089-2389-5*) Ulverscroft.

Old Mules, New Ground & Cotton Blooms. Samuel Cowart. 1991. pap. 9.95 (*0-938645-52-8*) In His Steps.

Old Myers Place. Kelly O'Rourke. (Halloween Ser.: No. 2). 1997. mass mkt. 4.50 (*1-57297-341-2*) Blvd Books.

Old Myths & New Realities in United States-Soviet Relations. Ed. by Donald R. Kelley & Hoyt Purvis. LC 90-34368. 192p. 1990. 52.95 (*0-275-93498-5*, C3498, Praeger Pubs) Greenwood.

Old Names & Golden Splendors: A Handbook of Colorado Names & Their Origins. Lou Walther. (Illus.). 106p. (Orig.). 1984. pap. 6.50 (*0-9612672-2-4*) Walther.

***Old Napa Valley: The History to 1900** Lin Weber. LC 98-96606. 277p. 1998. write for info. (*0-9667014-0-2*) Wine Ventures Pubg.

Old National Road: A Chapter of American Expansion. Archer B. Hulbert. (Ohio History, Travel in Ohio Ser.). 182p. (C). 1991. reprint ed. lib. bdg. 37.55 (*1-56651-016-3*) A W McGraw.

Old National Road: The Historic Highway of America. Archer B. Hulbert. (Ohio History, Travel in Ohio Ser.). 118p. (C). 1994. reprint ed. pap. 10.40 (*1-56651-112-7*) A W McGraw.

Old Naumkeag: An Historical Sketch of the City of Salem. C. H. Webber & W. S. Nevins. LC 98-143991. (Illus.). 812p. 1998. reprint ed. pap. 24.50 (*0-7884-0798-8*, W101) Heritage Bk.

Old Navajo Rugs see One Hundred Years of Navajo Rugs

Old Nazis, the New Right & the Reagan Administration: The Role of Domestic Fascist Networks in the Republican Party & Their Effect on U. S. Cold War Politics. 2nd ed. Russ Bellant. (Illus.). 100p. (Orig.). 1989. spiral bd. 6.50 (*0-915987-05-8*) Political Rsch Assocs.

Old Nazis, the New Right, & the Republican Party: Domestic Fascist Networks & Their Effect on U. S. Cold War Politics. Russ Bellant. (Political Research Associates Bk.). 144p. 1991. 25.00 (*0-89608-419-1*); pap. 11.00 (*0-89608-418-3*) South End Pr.

Old Neighborhood. David Mamet. LC 97-32224. 96p. 1998. pap. 10.00 (*0-679-74652-8*) Vin Bks.

Old Neighborhood: What We Lost in the Great Suburban Migration, 1966-1999. Ray Suarez. LC 98-53349. 272p. 1999. 24.50 (*0-684-83402-2*) Free Pr.

Old Neutriment. Glendolin D. Wagner. (Illus.). 1924. 22.00 (*0-914074-01-6*, J M C & Co) Amereon Ltd.

Old Neutriment: Memories of the Custers. Glendolin D. Wagner. LC 88-31145. (Illus.). xx, 268p. 1989. reprint ed. pap. 7.95 (*0-8032-9725-4*, Bison Books) U of Nebr Pr.

Old New England. Lynn M. Stone. LC 93-22881. (Back Roads Ser.). 48p. (J). (gr. 3-6). 1993. lib. bdg. 15.95 (*0-86593-303-0*) Rourke Corp.

Old New England Homes. Stanley Schuler. LC 84-52713. (Illus.). 224p. 1985. 35.00 (*0-88740-034-5*) Schiffer.

***Old New England Homes.** 2nd rev. ed. Stanley Schuler. (Illus.). 224p. 2000. 35.00 (*0-7643-0995-1*) Schiffer.

Old New England Splint Baskets & How to Make Them. John E. McGuire. LC 85-61526. (Illus.). 100p. (Orig.). 1985. pap. 14.95 (*0-88740-045-0*) Schiffer.

Old New England Town, Sketches of Life, Scenery, Character (Fairfield, Connecticut) Frank S. Child. (Illus.). 230p. 1994. reprint ed. lib. bdg. 29.50 (*0-8328-4263-X*) Higginson Bk Co.

Old New England's Curious Customs & Cures, Vol. 1. Robert E. Cahill. (Illus.). 48p. 1990. per. 4.95 (*0-9626162-0-6*) Old Salt Box.

Old New Land. Theodor Herzl. Ed. by Jacques Kornberg. Tr. by Lotta Levensohn from GER. LC 96-40568. Orig. Title: Altneuland. (Illus.). 325p. (C). 1997. reprint ed. pap. text 18.95 (*1-55876-160-8*) Wiener Pubs Inc.

Old New Orleans: Walking Tours of the French Quarter. rev. ed. Stanley C. Arthur. Ed. by Susan C. Dore. LC 89-31668. (Illus.). 160p. 1990. pap. 8.95 (*0-88289-740-3*) Pelican.

Old New York. Edith Wharton. 320p. 1995. per. 11.00 (*0-02-038314-2*, Pub. by Macmillan) S&S Trade.

Old New York. Edith Wharton. (Enriched Classics Edition Ser.). 336p. (YA). 1998. per. 5.99 (*0-671-02336-5*, Pocket Books) PB.

Old New York, 4 vols. Edith Wharton. (Collected Works of Edith Wharton). 1998. reprint ed. lib. bdg. 480.00 (*1-58201-990-8*) Classic Bks.

Old New York Frontier: Its Wars with Indians & Tories, Its Missionary Schools. Francis W. Halsey. (Illus.). 432p. 1996. pap. 35.00 (*0-7884-0409-1*, H049) Heritage Bk.

Old New York Frontier, 1614-1800. Francis W. Halsey. 432p. 1993. reprint ed. lib. bdg. 99.00 (*0-7812-5181-8*) Rprt Serv.

Old New York in Early Photographs, 1853-1901. Mary Black. (Illus.). 288p. (Orig.). 1973. pap. 13.95 (*0-486-22907-6*) Dover.

***Old New York in Picture Postcards, 1900-1945.** Jack H. Smith. LC 99-21467. (Illus.). 224p. 1999. pap. 17.95 (*1-879511-43-6*, Pub. by Madison Bks UPA) Natl Bk Netwk.

Old Newmarket: Historical Sketches. Nellie P. George. 133p. 1995. reprint ed. pap. 18.00 (*0-8328-5060-8*); reprint ed. lib. bdg. 25.00 (*0-8328-5059-4*) Higginson Bk Co.

Old Newquay. S. Teague Husband. (C). 1989. 70.00 (*0-907566-86-3*, Pub. by Dyllansow Truran) St Mut.

Old Nooks of Stirling. Picton Publishing Staff. (Illus.). (C). 1987. 25.00 (*0-7855-2207-7*, Pub. by Picton) St Mut.

Old Norse - Icelandic Studies: A Select Bibliography. Hans Bekker-Nielsen. LC Z 2556.. 95p. reprint ed. pap. 30.00 (*0-608-11160-0*, 201915700011) Bks Demand.

Old Norse & Finnish Religious & Cultic Place-Names. Ed. by Tore Ahlback. (Illus.). 507p. (Orig.). 1990. pap. 59.50 (*951-649-695-4*) Coronet Bks.

Old Norse Biblical Compilation: Studies in Stjorn. Reider Astas. LC 91-17596. (American University Studies: Theology & Religion: Ser. VII, Vol. 109). 251p. 1992. 40.95 (*0-8204-1585-5*) P Lang Pubng.

An Asterisk (*) at the beginning of an entry indicates that the title is appearing for the first time.

Old Norse Elucidarius: Original Text & English Translation. Ed. & Tr. by Evelyn S. Firchow. LC 92-17547. (Medvl Ser.). 114p. 1992. 50.00 (*1-879751-18-6*) Camden Hse.

Old Norse Images of Women. Jenny Jochens. (Middle Ages Ser.). 320p. 1996. text 39.95 (*0-8122-3358-1*) U of Pa Pr.

Old North Davis: Guide to Walking a Traditional Neighborhood. John Lofland & Yolo County Historical Society Staff. LC 98-38074. (Illus.). 192p. 1998. pap. 10.95 (*1-892626-05-5*) Yolo County.

Old North Esk on the Miramichi W. D. Hamilton. LC 80-465084. 479p. 1979. write for info. (*0-920332-06-4*) W Hamilton.

Old North ESK Revised W. D. Hamilton. LC 89-142866. x, 570p. 1988. write for info. (*0-920114-88-1*) UNBGS.

Old North Road. W. J. De Burgh. 188p. pap. 18.95 (*0-85564-243-2*, Pub. by Univ of West Aust Pr) Intl Spec Bk.

Old North State Fact Book. 4th rev. ed. (Illus.). vi, 59p. 1999. pap. 8.00 (*0-86526-248-9*) NC Archives.

Old North Trail: Life, Legends & Religion of the Blackfeet Indians. Walter McClintock. LC 99-31857. (Illus.). 539p. 1999. pap. 16.95 (*0-8032-8258-3*, Bison Books) U of Nebr Pr.

Old North Trail: Life, Legends & Religion of the Blackfeet Indians. Walter McClintock. LC 92-16001. (Illus.). xxiv, 539p. (C). 1992. reprint ed. pap. 14.95 (*0-8032-8188-9*, Bison Books) U of Nebr Pr.

Old Northampton County. David B. Skillman. (Orig.). 1952. pap. text 3.00 (*1-877701-10-6*) NCH&GS.

Old Northwest: A Chronicle of the Ohio Valley & Beyond. Frederic A. Ogg. (BCL1 - United States Local History Ser.). 220p. 1991. reprint ed. lib. bdg. 79.00 (*0-7812-6563-0*) Rprt Serv.

Old Northwest: Studies in Regional History, 1787-1910. Ed. by Harry N. Scheiber. LC 68-11564. 422p. reprint ed. 130.90 (*0-8357-9711-2*, 201114900075) Bks Demand.

Old Northwest: The Beginnings of Our Colonial System (Revised Edition) Burke A. Hinsdale. LC 75-104. (Mid-American Frontier Ser.). 1975. reprint ed. 36.95 (*0-405-06872-7*) Ayer.

Old Northwest Indian Removal, Eighteen Twenty-Five to Eighteen Fifty-Five: A Bibliography. James A. Clifton. LC 86-115302. 125p. 1988. reprint ed. pap. 38.80 (*0-608-08447-6*, AU00365000081) Bks Demand.

Old Nova Scotian Quilts. Scott Robson. LC 96-119200. (Illus.). 128p. 1998. pap. text 24.95 (*1-55109-118-6*) Nimbus Publ.

Old Nubian Dict. Appendic, No. SUBS 92. E. Peters. LC 97-179785. 1998. 43.95 (*90-6831-925-6*, Pub. by Peeters Pub) Bks Intl VA.

Old Nubian Dictionary, No. SUBS90. E. Peters. LC 97-103160. 1998. 93.95 (*90-6831-787-3*, Pub. by Peeters Pub) Bks Intl VA.

***Old Ocean City: The Journal & Photography of Robert Craighead Walker, 1904-1916.** Robert C. Walker & C. John Sullivan. LC 00-9629. (Illus.). 2001. write for info. (*0-8018-6585-9*) Johns Hopkins.

Old, Old Man & the Very Little Boy. Kristine L. Franklin. LC 91-2611. (Illus.). 32p. (J). (ps-1). 1992. 14.95 (*0-689-31735-2*) Atheneum Yung Read.

Old Oman. W. D. Peyton. 1983. 30.00 (*0-86685-530-0*) Intl Bk Ctr.

Old Oman. 2nd ed. W. D. Peyton. (Illus.). 128p. 1983. boxed set 29.95 (*0-905743-34-2*, Pub. by Stacey Intl) Intl Bk Ctr.

Old One-Room Country School. Herbert A. Ellison. LC 96-67236. (Illus.). 56p. (Orig.). 1996. pap. 12.00 (*0-88100-090-6*) Natl Writ Pr.

Old Ones. Manny Sievert. 80p. (Orig.). 1996. pap. write for info. (*1-57502-368-7*, PO1177) Morris Pubng.

Old Ones: Old Ones. 2nd rev. ed. Kevin Siembieda. Ed. by Alex Marciniszyn et al. (RPG Sourcebook Ser.: Vol. 2). (Illus.). 224p. (Orig.). 1996. pap. 19.95 (*0-916211-09-6*, 453) Palladium Bks.

Old Ones of San Ildefonso. large type ed. Lauran Paine. LC 98-24416. 1999. 18.95 (*0-7862-0767-1*) Thorndike Pr.

Old Ones Told Me: American Indian Stories for Children. 3rd ed. Berry Keeper. (Illus.). 36p. (J). (gr. 4-7). 1988. reprint ed. pap. 7.95 (*0-8323-0473-5*) Binford Mort.

***Old Ontario Houses: Traditions in Local Architecture.** Photos by John De Visser. (Illus.). 224p. 2000. 50.00 (*1-55209-499-5*) Firefly Bks Ltd.

Old Oraibi: A Study of the Hopi Indians of Third Mesa. Mischa Titiev. LC 92-3702. (Illus.). 300p. 1992. reprint ed. pap. 93.00 (*0-608-07870-0*, 205405300011) Bks Demand.

Old Orchard Beach. Jeffrey A. Scully. (Images of America Ser.). 1995. pap. 16.99 (*0-7524-0087-8*) Arcadia Publng.

Old Orchard Farm. Hugh Orchard. Ed. by Paul Sharp. LC 87-34488. (Iowa Heritage Collection). (Illus.). 252p. 1988. reprint ed. pap. 9.95 (*0-8138-0084-6*) Iowa St U Pr.

Old Order: Stories of the South from Flowering Judas, Pale Horse, Pale Rider & The Leaning Tower. Katherine Anne Porter. LC 66-380. 180p. (Orig.). 1955. pap. 9.00 (*0-15-668519-1*, Harvest Bks) Harcourt.

Old Order Amish: In Plain Words & Pictures. T. J. Redcay. (Illus.). 32p. 1996. pap. 4.00 (*1-890541-30-3*) Americana Souvenirs & Gifts.

Old Order Amish: Their Enduring Way of Life. Donald B. Kraybill. (Illus.). 208p. (C). 1996. reprint ed. pap. 24.95 (*0-8018-5417-2*) Johns Hopkins.

Old Order & a New: The Split World of Liam O'Flaherty's Novels. Hedda Friberg. (Studia Anglistica Upsaliensia Ser.: Vol. 95). 266p. (Orig.). 1996. pap. 48.50 (*91-554-3694-3*) Coronet Bks.

***Old Order Mennonites in New York State: Rituals, Beliefs & Community.** Daniel B. Lee. LC 00-33739. (Illus.). 2000. pap. write for info. (*0-8304-1573-4*) Burnham Inc.

Old Organs of Princeton: Being an Historical Chronology & Description of All the Known Pipe Organs Installed in the Town of Princeton, New Jersey, from 1760 to 1925, Including Photographs & Stoplists When Available, as Well as Accounts from Newspapers, Church Records, Histories, & Diaries. Stephen L. Pinel. LC 89-62170. 146p. 1989. 29.95 (*0-9610092-2-5*) Boston Organ Club.

Old Original Bookbinder's Restaurant Cookbook. Judith Frazin. 200p. 1991. pap. 12.95 (*0-9631189-0-0*) Old Orig Bkbind Rest.

Old Orkney Trades. Sheila Spence. (C). 1986. 55.00 (*0-907618-19-7*, Pub. by Orkney Pr) St Mut.

Old Orthodox Prayer Book. Ed. by Pimen Simon & Theodore Jurewicz. (Illus.). 406p. 1986. 22.00 (*0-9617062-0-1*) Russian Orthodox Church of Nativity.

Old Outboard Book. 2nd rev. ed. Peter Hunn. LC 94-18675. (Illus.). 278p. 1994. pap. 19.95 (*0-07-031281-8*) Intl Marine.

Old Outboard Motor Service Manual, Vol. 1. 264p. 1983. pap. 26.95 (*0-87288-186-5*, OOS-1) Intertec Pub.

Old Outboard Motor Service Manual, Vol. 2. 264p. 1985. pap. 26.95 (*0-87288-187-3*, OOS-2) Intertec Pub.

Old Paint New: The Image of the Horse in Contemporary Art. Francine Marcel & Gussie Fauntleroy. Ed. by Peter Held. (Illus.). 1999. pap. 5.00 (*1-891695-02-9*) Holter Museum.

Old Palace: The Catholic Chaplaincy at Oxford. Walter Drumm. 272p. 1989. pap. 40.00 (*1-85390-192-X*, Pub. by Veritas Pubns) St Mut.

Old Parish. Doran Hurley. LC 75-122724. (Short Story Index Reprint Ser.). 1977. 19.95 (*0-8369-3557-8*) Ayer.

Old Pasadena Then & Now: A Pictorial History & Guide of Its Significant Commercial Buildings. Fred Hartley. (Illus.). 60p. (Orig.). 1997. pap. 19.95 (*0-9656187-0-6*) F Hartley.

Old Passion. large type ed. Robyn Donald. LC 94-13993. 220p. 1994. lib. bdg. 17.95 (*0-8161-5995-5*, G K Hall Lrg Type) Mac Lib Ref.

Old Past Master (1924) Carl H. Claudy. 112p. 1998. reprint ed. pap. 16.95 (*0-7661-0203-3*) Kessinger Pub.

Old Patagonian Express: By Train Through the Americas. Paul Theroux. LC 98-162535. 416p. 1989. reprint ed. pap. 14.00 (*0-395-52105-X*) HM.

Old Patchwork Quilts & the Women Who Made Them. Ruth E. Finley. LC 92-28745. 204p. 1992. pap. 19.95 (*0-939009-68-4*, EPM) Howell Pr VA.

Old Path Tarot, Vol. 1. Howard Rodway. 1990. pap. 20.00 (*0-88079-490-9*, OP78) US Games Syst.

Old Path Tarot Set: Includes Tarot of the Old Path. Howard Rodway. 160p. 1990. pap. 39.95 (*0-88079-492-5*, OPT99) US Games Syst.

Old Path White Clouds: Walking in the Footsteps of the Buddha. Thich Nhat Hanh. LC 90-21483. (Illus.). 599p. 1990. 40.00 (*0-938077-40-6*) Parallax Pr.

Old Path White Clouds: Walking in the Footsteps of the Buddha. Thich Nhat Hanh & Nguyen T. Hop. LC 90-21483. (Illus.). 599p. 1990. pap., per. 25.00 (*0-938077-26-0*) Parallax Pr.

Old Paths see Foundations of Faith

Old Paths. J. C. Ryle. 521p. 1999. reprint ed. pap. text 11.99 (*0-85151-760-9*) Banner of Truth.

Old Peabody Pew. Kate Douglas Wiggin. 157p. Date not set. 18.95 (*0-8488-2603-5*) Amereon Ltd.

Old Peking: City of the Ruler of the World. Ed. by Chris Elder. LC 97-18602. (Illus.). 312p. (Orig.). 1997. pap. text 32.00 (*0-19-590304-8*) OUP.

Old Pembrokeshire. Roger W. Davies. (Illus.). 100p. (C). 1989. text 55.00 (*0-86383-506-6*, Pub. by Gomer Pr) St Mut.

Old Pembrokeshire & Carmarthenshire. Roger W. Davies. 132p. 1991. 22.95 (*0-8464-4688-X*) Beekman Pubs.

Old Pembrokeshire & Carmarthenshire. Roger W. Davies. 132p. (C). 1991. 45.00 (*0-86383-726-3*, Pub. by Gomer Pr) St Mut.

Old Peninsula Days: Tales & Sketches of the Door County Peninsula. Hjalmar R. Holand. LC 90-2129. (Illus.). viii, 246p. 1990. reprint ed. pap. 9.95 (*0-940473-21-6*) Wm Caxton.

Old People: Report of a Survey Committee on the Problems of Aging & the Care of Old People. B. Seebohm Rowntree. Ed. by Leon Stein. LC 79-8682. (Growing Old Ser.). (Illus.). 1980. reprint ed. lib. bdg. 23.95 (*0-405-12799-5*) Ayer.

Old People, Frogs, & Albert. Nancy Hope Wilson. LC 97-4986. (Illus.). 64p. (J). (gr. 2-4). 1997. 14.00 (*0-374-35625-4*) FS&G.

***Old People, Frogs, & Albert.** Nancy Hope Wilson. (Illus.). 64p. (J). (gr. 2-4). 1999. pap. 4.95 (*0-374-45615-1*, Sunburst Bks) FS&G.

Old People in Three Industrial Societies. Ethel Shanas et al. Ed. by Leon Stein. LC 79-8686. (Growing Old Ser.). 1980. reprint ed. lib. bdg. 48.95 (*0-405-12803-7*) Ayer.

Old People, New Lives: Community Creation in a Retirement Residence. Jennie-Keith Ross. LC 76-8103. (Illus.). 1995. lib. bdg. 22.00 (*0-226-72825-0*) U Ch Pr.

Old People Pet Doves: Poems by Elders. Ed. by Christine Tarantino. 86p. 1988. spiral bd. 5.95 (*1-887480-46-3*) Wrds Lght Intl.

Old People Say! The Wisdom of the Forefathers in Setswana Proverbs. Letshama. (Illus.). 87p. 1999. pap. 9.00 (*0-627-02247-2*, Pub. by J L Van Schaik) BHB Intl.

Old Peoples, New Lives: Community Creation in a Retirement Residence. Jennie-Keith Ross. LC 76-8103. (Illus.). 240p. 1982. pap. text 10.00 (*0-226-42965-2*) U Ch Pr.

Old Persian: Grammar, Texts, Lexicon. 2nd rev. ed. Roland G. Kent. (American Oriental Ser.: Vol. 33). (PER.). 219p. 1953. 35.00 (*0-940490-33-1*) Am Orient Soc.

Old Person in Your Home. W. Poe. 1986. pap. 2.45 (*0-684-71871-5*, Scribners Ref) Mac Lib Ref.

Old Phantoms. Gus Edwards. 1979. pap. 5.25 (*0-8222-0842-3*) Dramatists Play.

Old Philadelphia Houses on Society Hill, 1750-1840. Elizabeth B. McCall. (Illus.). 17p. 1966. 22.50 (*0-8038-0194-7*) Archit CT.

Old Philadelphia in Early Photographs, 1839-1914: 215 Prints from the Collection of the Free Library of Philadelphia. Robert F. Looney. LC 75-41688. (Illus.). 230p. 1976. pap. 14.95 (*0-486-23345-6*) Dover.

Old Picture Postcards: A Historic Journey along California's Central Coast. Loren Nicholson. (California Heritage Ser.: No. 1). (Illus.). 144p. (Orig.). (YA). (gr. 9-12). 1989. pap. 12.95 (*0-9623233-1-4*) CA HPA.

Old Pictures. M. Edward Burtt. (Illus.). 50p. (Orig.). 1995. pap. write for info. (*1-888913-15-0*) M E Burtt.

Old Pig. Margaret Wild. 40p. (J). (ps-3). 1999. pap. 5.99 (*0-14-056211-7*, PuffinBks) Peng Put Young Read.

Old Pine Church Baptisms, 1783-1828, Mill Creek, Virginia. Ed. by Klaus Wust et al. Tr. by Ilse Martin & George M. Smith. 64p. 1987. pap. 10.00 (*0-917968-14-X*) Shenandoah Hist.

Old Pine Tree, & Other Noh Plays. Makoto Ueda. LC 62-9881. 91p. reprint ed. pap. 30.00 (*0-608-16138-1*, 200288400015) Bks Demand.

Old Pipes & the Dryad see Creative Short Stories

***Old Pirate of Central Park.** Robert Priest. LC 98-11913. 32p. (J). (ps-3). 1999. 15.00 (*0-395-90505-2*) HM.

Old Planes, Young Men & Red Wooden Shoes. Sherman F. Morgan. 227p. (Orig.). 1993. pap. 10.00 (*0-944792-26-X*) Pendragon TX.

Old Plantation Hymns. William E. Barton. LC 72-38499. reprint ed. 27.50 (*0-404-09918-1*) AMS Pr.

Old Planters of Beverly in Massachusetts, & the Thousand Acre Grant of 1635. Alice G. Lapham. (Illus.). 133p. 1995. reprint ed. pap. 19.50 (*0-8328-4703-8*); reprint ed. lib. bdg. 29.50 (*0-8328-4695-3*) Higginson Bk Co.

Old Poetries & the New. Richard Kostelanetz. LC 80-16318. (Poets on Poetry Ser.). 336p. 1981. pap. 13.95 (*0-472-06319-7*, 06319) U of Mich Pr.

***Old Poet's Tale: Collected Works of Carl Rakosi, Vol. 1.** Carl Rakosi. 261p. 1999. 49.95 (*1-901538-21-4*, Pub. by etruscan bks); pap. 27.95 (*1-901538-14-1*, Pub. by etruscan bks) SPD-Small Pr Dist.

Old Point Loma Lighthouse. rev. ed. F. Ross Holland. 51p. (Orig.). pap. 4.95 (*0-941032-01-9*) Cabrillo Natl Monumnt.

Old Polish Legends (Gift Edition) Ed. by F. C. Anstrother. (Illus.). 66p. 1997. 11.95 (*0-7818-0521-X*) Hippocrene Bks.

Old Polish Traditions in the Kitchen & at the Table. Davidovic Mladen. 304p. 1997. reprint ed. pap. 11.95 (*0-7818-0488-4*) Hippocrene Bks.

***Old Poor Law in Scotland: The Experience of Poverty, 1574-1845.** Rosalind Mitchison. 352p. 2000. pap. text 28.00 (*0-7486-1344-7*) Col U Pr.

Old Portraits & Modern Sketches. John Greenleaf Whittier. (Notable American Authors Ser.). 1999. reprint ed. lib. bdg. 125.00 (*0-7812-9973-X*) Rprt Serv.

Old Portuguese Vocalic Finals, Phonology & Orthography of Accented -Ou, -Eu, Iu, & -Ao, Eo, -Io. E. Learned. (LD Ser.: No. 44). 1950. pap. 25.00 (*0-527-00790-0*) Periodicals Srv.

Old Possums' Book of Practical Cats. T. S. Eliot. 1995. 9.00 (*0-15-600277-9*) Harcourt.

Old Possum's Book of Practical Cats. T. S. Eliot. (C). 1939. 15.00 (*0-15-168657-2*) Harcourt.

Old Possum's Book of Practical Cats. T. S. Eliot. LC 39-33125. 64p. (C). 1968. pap. 7.00 (*0-15-668570-1*, Harvest Bks) Harcourt.

Old Possum's Book of Practical Cats. T. S. Eliot. LC 39-33125. (Illus.). 486p. 1982. 15.00 (*0-15-168656-4*); pap. 7.00 (*0-15-668568-X*, Harvest Bks) Harcourt.

Old Possum's Book of Practical Cats. T. S. Eliot. 1982. 11.20 (*0-606-01525-6*, Pub. by Turtleback) Demco.

Old Possums Book of Practical Cats. T. S. Eliot. 64p. Date not set. 16.95 (*0-8488-2257-9*) Amereon Ltd.

***Old Possum's Book of Practical Cats: Gielgud,&Sir John.** abr. ed. T. S. Eliot. 1999. audio 12.00 (*0-89845-885-4*, CPN 1713) HarperAudio.

Old Possum's Book of Practical Cats Calendar-Diary, 1989. T. S. Eliot. (Illus.). 96p. 1988. pap. 8.95 (*0-15-668571-X*) Harcourt.

***Old Poultry Breeds.** Fred Hams. (Illus.). 40p. 1999. pap. 30.00 (*0-7478-0396-X*, Pub. by Shire Pubns) Parkwest Pubns.

Old Powder Line. Richard Parker. (J). (gr. 4-7). 1990. 20.25 (*0-8446-6432-4*) Peter Smith.

Old Prater Mill. Albert Duncan. LC 90-92905. (Illus.). 70p. (Orig.). 1990. pap. text 6.95 (*0-9626306-0-8*) Duncan-Everden.

Old Printer & the Modern Press. Charles Knight. LC 71-148340. reprint ed. 39.50 (*0-404-08838-4*) AMS Pr.

Old Probability, Perhaps Rain-Perhaps Not. Henry W. Shaw. LC 72-104563. (Illus.). reprint ed. lib. bdg. 22.50 (*0-8398-1856-4*) Irvington.

Old Problems. 2.00 (*0-944253-08-3*) Inst Dev Indian Law.

Old Problems in New Times: Urban Strategies for the 1990s. Oliver Byrum. LC 92-73811. (Illus.). 140p. 1993. reprint ed. 36.00 (*0-918286-80-8*, Planners Press); reprint ed. pap. 27.95 (*0-918286-79-4*, Planners Press) Am Plan Assn.

Old Protestantism & the New: Essays on the Reformation Heritage. B. A. Gerrish. LC 82-2730. 432p. (C). 1982. 45.95 (*0-226-28869-2*) U Ch Pr.

Old Protestantism & the New: Essays on the Reformation Heritage. Brain A. Gerrish. 448p. 69.95 (*0-567-09340-9*) T&T Clark Pubs.

Old Protestantism & the New: Essays on the Reformation Heritage. Brian A. Gerrish. LC 82-2730. 432p. reprint ed. pap. 134.00 (*0-608-09308-4*, 205418200004) Bks Demand.

Old Prouts Neck. Augustus F. Moulton. (Illus.). 119p. 1997. reprint ed. pap. 15.00 (*0-8328-5901-X*) Higginson Bk Co.

***Old Provence.** Theodore Andrea Cook. (Illus.). 2000. pap. 16.00 (*1-56656-372-0*) Interlink Pub.

Old Provincetown in Early Photographs. Irma Ruckstuhl. (Illus.). 96p. (Orig.). 1987. pap. 11.95 (*0-486-25410-0*) Dover.

Old Prussian Church & the Weimar Republic: A Study in Political Adjustment, 1917-1927. Daniel R. Borg. LC 83-40559. 387p. reprint ed. pap. 120.00 (*0-8357-6508-3*, 203587900097) Bks Demand.

Old Prussian Grammar: The Phonology & Morphology of the Three Catechisms. William R. Schmalstieg. LC 74-8736. 368p. 1974. 35.00 (*0-271-01170-X*) Pa St U Pr.

Old Pub Near the Angel. 2nd ed. James Kelman. 90p. 1991. pap. 8.95 (*0-913006-48-3*) Puckerbrush.

Old Quebec, the Fortress of New France. Gilbert Parker & Claude G. Bryan. (Illus.). 486p. 1992. reprint ed. pap. 30.00 (*1-55613-594-7*) Heritage Bk.

Old Queens N. Y. in Early Photos. Vincent F. Seyfried & William Asadorian. (Illus.). 1991. pap. 12.95 (*0-486-26358-4*) Dover.

Old Radical & His Brood: A Portrait of Sir John Bowring & His Family. George Bartle. (Illus.). 148p. 1995. pap. 12.95 (*1-85756-132-5*, Pub. by Janus Pubng) Paul & Co Pubs.

Old Radicalism: John R. Rogers & the Populist Movement in Washington. Thomas W. Riddle. LC 91-15137. (Modern American History Ser.). 336p. 1991. text 25.00 (*0-8240-1896-6*) Garland.

Old Radio Sets. Jonathan Hill. (Album Ser.: No. 295). (Illus.). 32p. 1989. pap. 6.25 (*0-7478-0219-X*, Pub. by Shire Pubns) Parkwest Pubns.

Old Raging Erie . . . There Have Been Several Changes: A Postcard History of the Erie & Other New York State Canals, 1895-1915. Harry L. Rinker. (Illus.). 20.00p. (Orig.). 1984. pap. 20.00 (*0-9613675-0-4*) Canal Captains.

Old Rail Fence Corners: Frontier Tales Told by Minnesota Pioneers. Ed. by Lucy W. Morris. xxi, 344p. 1976. reprint ed. pap. 14.95 (*0-87351-109-3*, Borealis Book) Minn Hist.

Old Ramon. Jack Schaefer. (Newbery Honor Roll Ser.). 1993. 12.05 (*0-606-05959-8*, Pub. by Turtleback) Demco.

Old Ramon. Jack Schaeffer. (Newbery Honor Roll Ser.). (Illus.). 112p. (J). (gr. 3-7). 1993. reprint ed. pap. 6.95 (*0-8027-7403-2*) Walker & Co.

Old Rangoon: City of Shwedagon. Noel F. Singer. (Illus.). 224p. 1995. 50.00 (*1-870838-47-5*, Pub. by Kiscadale) Weatherhill.

Old Reading Room: An Installation by Ilya & Emilia Kabakov in Amsterdam. Ilya Kabakov. (Film Culture in Transition Ser.). (Illus.). 64p. (C). text 19.95 (*90-5629-069-X*, Pub. by Amsterdam U Pr) U of Mich Pr.

Old Red Rocking Chair. Phyllis Root. (Illus.). 32p. (J). (ps-3). 1992. 14.45 (*1-55970-063-7*, Pub. by Arcade Pub Inc) Time Warner.

Old Red Sandstone: or New Walks in an Old Field. Hugh G. Miller. Ed. by Claude C. Albritton, Jr. LC 77-6531. (History of Geology Ser.). (Illus.). 1978. reprint ed. lib. bdg. 37.95 (*0-405-10451-0*) Ayer.

Old Reddy Drum: A Tale of Redfish. Suzanne Tate. LC 93-83435. (Suzanne Tate's Nature Ser.: No. 14). (Illus.). 28p. (J). (gr. k-4). 1993. pap. 4.95 (*1-878405-08-X*) Nags Head Art.

Old Reddy Drum, a Tale of Redfish. Suzanne Tate. LC 93-83435. 1993. 9.15 (*0-606-10315-5*, Pub. by Turtleback) Demco.

***Old Regime & Revolution, Vol. 2.** Alexis De Tocqueville. 1998. pap. text 9.95 (*0-226-80534-4*); lib. bdg. 40.00 (*0-226-80533-6*) U Ch Pr.

Old Regime & the French Revolution. Alexis De Tocqueville. Ed. by J. P. Mayer & A. P. Kerr. LC 55-10160. 320p. 1955. pap. 12.95 (*0-385-09260-1*, A60, Anchor NY) Doubleday.

Old Regime & the French Revolution. Alexis De Tocqueville. Tr. by Stuart Gilbert. 1990. 22.25 (*0-8446-1973-6*) Peter Smith.

Old Regime & the Revolution. Alexis De Tocqueville. Tr. by Alaln S. Kahan. LC 97-43814. 451p. 1998. 32.50 (*0-226-80529-8*) U Ch Pr.

Old Regime & the Revolution. Alexis De Tocqueville et al. Tr. by Alan S. Kahan from FRE. LC 97-43814. 1998. pap. 32.50 (*0-226-80530-1*) U Ch Pr.

Old Regime Colleges, 1789-1795: Local Initiatives in Recasting French Secondary Education, Vol. 147. Charles R. Bailey. LC 93-2277. (American University Studies: History: Ser. IX, Vol. 147). X, 292p. (C). 1994. text 47.95 (*0-8204-2247-9*) P Lang Pubng.

***Old Regime in Canada.** Francis Parkman. (Notable American Authors Ser.). 1999. reprint ed. lib. bdg. 125.00 (*0-7812-4734-9*) Rprt Serv.

Old Regime, 1713-1763 see New Cambridge Modern History

Old Regular Baptists of Central Appalachia: Brothers & Sisters in Hope. Howard Dorgan. LC 89-4832. (Illus.). 296p. 1989. 31.00 (*0-87049-616-6*) U of Tenn Pr.

Old Reliable. P. G. Wodehouse. 17.95 (*0-8488-0678-6*) Amereon Ltd.

Old Reliable: A History of Bingham Canyon, Utah. Lynn R. Bailey. (Illus.). 220p. 1988. 29.95 (*0-87026-068-5*) Westernlore.

O

An Asterisk (*) at the beginning of an entry indicates that the title is appearing for the first time.

Old Religion: A Novel. David Mamet. LC 97-17854. 288p. 1997. 23.50 (*0-684-84119-3*) Free Pr.

Old Retold: Archetypal Patterns in German Literature of the 19th & 20th Centuries. H. J. Schueler. LC 94-31071. (American University Studies I: Vol. 106). 144p. (C). 1996. text 35.95 (*0-8204-2600-8*) P Lang Pubng.

Old Rhodesian Days. Hugh M. Hole. 140p. 1968. reprint ed. 35.00 (*0-7146-1680-X*, BHA-01680, Pub. by F Cass Pubs) Intl Spec Bk.

Old Richland Families, Including Descendants of Edward Roberts, Thomas Roberts, Thomas Lancaster, Peter Lester (et al) Historical & Genealogical Data Being Derived from the Records of Friends & Other Original Sources. Ellwood Roberts. (Illus.). 246p. 1997. reprint ed. lib. bdg. 34.00 (*0-8328-6444-7*) Higginson Bk Co.

Old Richmond Today. John G. Zehmer. (Illus.). 128p. 1988. 19.95 (*1-889569-00-3*) Historic Richmond.

Old Ridge Runner. Herman Hebb. 196p. 1995. pap. 10.00 (*0-87012-540-0*) McClain.
Reminisce with THE OLD RIDGE RUNNER himself, Herman Hebb, as you read his ever-popular articles first printed in the PARSONS ADVOCATE, Parsons, West Virginia. This is the first time the entire collection of the Old Ridge Runner's childhood experiences & memories have been incorporated into one volume for his faithful readers. Anyone who has ever lived in the beautiful hills of Tucker County will want a copy of Herman's tales. *Publisher Paid Annotation.*

*__Old Rifle Scopes.__ Nick Stroebel. LC 99-68111. (Illus.). 400p. 2000. pap. 31.95 (*0-87341-830-1*) Krause Pubns.

Old Rights & New. Robert A. Licht. 213p. 1993. 19.95 (*0-8447-3775-5*, AEI Pr) Am Enterprise.

Old Roads, New Highways: Fifty Years of Pakistan. Ed. by Victoria Schofield. LC DS379.O45 1997. (The Jubilee Ser.). (Illus.). 362p. (C). 1998. text 25.00 (*0-19-577845-6*) OUP.

Old Roads of the Midwest. George Cantor. LC 96-45829. 248p. (Orig.). 1997. pap. 17.95 (*0-472-08288-4*, 08288) U of Mich Pr.

Old Rockaway, New York, in Early Photographs. Vincent Seyfried & William Asadorian. (Illus.). Date not set. pap. 14.95 (*0-486-40668-7*) Dover.

Old Romania. Juliet Thompson. 1977. lib. bdg. 59.95 (*0-8490-2370-X*) Gordon Pr.

Old Rome & the New. William J. Stillman. LC 72-8538. (Essay Index Reprint Ser.). 1977. reprint ed. 23.95 (*0-8369-7329-1*) Ayer.

Old Roots in New Lands: Historical & Anthropological Perspectives on Black Experiences in the Americas, 31. Ed. by Ann M. Pescatello. LC 76-50409. (Contributions in Afro-American & African Studies: No. 31). (Illus.). 301p. 1977. 55.00 (*0-8371-9476-8*, PEA/) Greenwood.

Old Roper. John R. Rose. 224p. 1992. pap. write for info. (*1-881170-01-2*) Rose Pub OR.

Old Rosa & the Brightest Star. Reinaldo Arenas. LC 88-21421. 106p. 1995. pap. 10.00 (*0-8021-3406-8*, Grove) Grove-Atltic.

Old Rose Adventurer: The Once-Blooming Old European Roses & More. Brent C. Dickerson. LC 98-19092. (Illus.). 680p. 1999. 69.95 (*0-88192-466-0*) Timber.

Old Roses: At-a-Glance Guide to Varieties, Cultivation & Care. Andrew Mikolajski. Ed. by Lin Hawthorne. (The New Plant Library). (Illus.). 64p. 1997. 9.95 (*1-85967-389-9*, Lorenz Bks) Anness Pub.

Old Roses & English Roses. David Austin. (Illus.). 224p. (Orig.). 1993. 25.00 (*1-85149-150-3*) Antique Collect.

Old Routes of Western Iran: Narrative of an Archaeological Journey. Mark A. Stein. LC 75-88946. (Illus.). 432p. 1969. reprint ed. lib. bdg. 79.50 (*0-8371-2256-2*, STOR, Greenwood Pr) Greenwood.

Old Ruff & Life on the Farm. Vesta Webster-Seek. LC 92-12956. (On My Own Book). 32p. (J). (gr. 1-4). 1993. pap. 4.99 (*0-7814-0966-7*, Chariot Bks) Chariot Victor.

Old Ruff & the Mother Bird. Vesta Seek. LC 89-25264. (On My Own Bks.). (Illus.). 32p. (J). (ps-2). 1991. pap. 4.99 (*1-55513-361-4*, 33613, Chariot Bks) Chariot Victor.

Old Russia in Modern America: A Case from Russian Old Believers in Alaska. 3rd unabridged ed. Alexander B. Dolitsky. (Alaska-Siberia Research Center Ser.: Vol. 10). (Illus.). 60p. 1988. pap. 12.00 (*0-9653891-2-X*, 94-3121266) Alaska-Siberia.

Old Russian Decorative & Applied Art. I. Pleshanova & Ludmila Likhachova. (Illus.). 224p. (C). 1985. text 330.00 (*0-7855-5873-X*, Pub. by Collets) St Mut.

Old Russian Ways: Cultural Variations among Three Russian Groups in Oregon. Richard A. Morris. LC 91-8067. (Immigrant Communities & Ethnic Minorities in the U. S. & Canada Ser.: No. 74). 1991. 64.50 (*0-404-19484-2*) AMS Pr.

Old Sadie & the Christmas Bear. Phyllis Reynolds Naylor. LC 84-2995. (Illus.). 32p. (J). (ps-2). 1984. 15.00 (*0-689-31052-8*) Atheneum Yung Read.

Old Sage of Atlantis. Willigis. 208p. 1994. pap. 10.25 (*1-885394-01-2*) Bluestar Communs.

Old Saint Augustine, a Story of Three Centuries. Charles B. Reynold. (Illus.). 144p. 1997. reprint ed. pap. 21.00 (*0-8328-6616-4*) Higginson Bk Co.

*__Old St. Paul's.__ W. H. Ainsworth. 252p. 2000. pap. 9.95 (*0-594-00171-4*) Eightn Hundrd.

Old Salem Mystery. Carole Marsh. (History Mystery Ser.). (Orig.). (J). (gr. 3-12). 1994. 29.95 (*1-55609-184-2*); pap. 19.95 (*0-935326-59-6*) Gallopade Intl.

*__Old Salem Official Guidebook.__ 3rd rev. ed. Penelope E. Niven. Ed. by Cornelia B. Wright. LC 99-39890. (Illus.). 128p. 1999. pap. 8.00 (*1-879704-07-2*) Old Salem NC.

Old Salt, Young Salt. Jonathan London. LC 94-14593. (Illus.). 32p. (J). (gr. 1 up). 1996. 16.00 (*0-688-12975-7*) Lothrop.

Old Sam's Thunder. unabridged ed. Jack Noon. LC 98-6203. (Illus.). 328p. (YA). 1998. pap. 16.00 (*0-9642213-6-5*) Moose Cntry.

Old San Juan, El Morro, San Cristobal. Patricia L. Wilson. (Illus.). (Orig.). 1994. pap. 12.95 (*1-56037-077-7*) Am Wrld Geog.

Old Santa Clara Valley: A Guide to Historic Buildings from Palo Alto to Gilroy. rev. ed. Phyllis F. Butler. LC 91-23254. (Illus.). 192p. 1991. pap. 9.95 (*0-933174-81-0*) Wide World-Tetra.

Old Santa Fe Trail. Stanley Vestal. LC 96-2238. (Illus.). xix, 304p. (C). 1996. pap. 14.00 (*0-8032-9615-0*, Bison Books) U of Nebr Pr.

Old Santa Fe Trail North Branch: A History. Ronald E. Kessler. LC 97-50404. (Illus.). 512p. (Orig.). 1998. pap. 24.95 (*0-86534-270-9*) Sunstone Pr.

Old Saundersfoot: From Monkstone to Marros. Roscoe Howells. (Illus.). 133p. (C). 1977. text 45.00 (*0-85088-423-3*, Pub. by Gomer Pr) St Mut.

Old Saws & Modern Instances. William L. Courtney. LC 69-18924. (Essay Index Reprint Ser.). 1977. 20.95 (*0-8369-0039-1*) Ayer.

Old Saxon Language: Grammar, Epic Narrative, Linguistic Formation. Irmengard Rauch. LC 92-20320. (Berkeley Models of Grammar Ser.: Vol. 1). XLIII, 416p. (C). 1992. text 60.95 (*0-8204-1893-5*) P Lang Pubng.

Old Scapes, New Maps: A Training Program for Psychotherapy Supervisors. Ludmila W. Hoffman. LC 90-61678. iii, 223p. (Orig.). 1990. pap. text 10.95 (*0-9628475-0-X*) Milusik Pr.

Old Scapes, New Maps: A Training Program for Psychotherapy Supervisors. Ludmila W. Hoffman. LC 90-61678. iii, 223p. (Orig.). (C). 1991. reprint ed. 19.95 (*0-9628475-1-8*) Milusik Pr.

Old Schenectady. George S. Roberts. (Illus.). 296p. 1997. reprint ed. lib. bdg. 37.00 (*0-8328-6228-2*) Higginson Bk Co.

Old School. Ed. by Jim Villani. (Mahoning Valley Writer Ser.). 94p. 1993. spiral bd. 9.95 (*0-917530-42-X*) Pig Iron Pr.

Old School Dies. Kate Morgan. 240p. (Orig.). 1996. mass mkt. 5.99 (*0-425-15552-8*, Prime Crime) Berkley Pub.

Old School Ties. Leigh Michaels. (Romance Ser.: No. 184). 1992. per. 2.89 (*0-373-03184-X*, 1-03184-8) Harlequin Bks.

Old School Ties: The Public School in British Literature. John R. Reed. LC 64-23341. 344p. reprint ed. pap. 106.70 (*0-8357-3980-5*, 203667800005) Bks Demand.

*__Old Scofield Reader Edition Study Bible.__ SCF RDR STDY OLD. 1616p. 1998. 44.99 (*0-19-527415-6*) OUP.

*__Old Scofield Readers Edition Study Bible.__ 1616p. 1998. 44.99 (*0-19-527417-2*) OUP.

*__Old Scofield Readers Edition Study Bible.__ 1998. 81.00 (*0-19-527445-8*) OUP.

Old Scofield Readers Edition Study Bible. Old Scofield Readers Staff. 1616p. 1998. 75.00 (*0-19-527446-6*) OUP.

*__Old Scofield Readers Study Bible.__ 1616p. 1998. 54.99 (*0-19-527435-0*) OUP.

*__Old Scofield Readers Study Bible.__ Old Scofield Staff. 1616p. 1998. 44.99 (*0-19-527419-9*) OUP.

*__Old Scofield Readers Study Bible.__ Oxford University Press Staff. 1616p. 1998. 39.99 (*0-19-527414-8*) OUP.

*__Old Scofield Readers Study Bible: 274RRL.__ Old Scofield Staff. 1616p. 1998. 54.99 (*0-19-527437-7*) OUP.

Old Scofield Study Bible. 1616p. 1997. 49.99 (*0-19-527315-X*) OUP.

Old Scofield Study Bible. 1616p. 1997. 89.99 (*0-19-527319-2*); 89.99 (*0-19-527318-4*); 79.99 (*0-19-527317-6*); 79.99 (*0-19-527316-8*) OUP.

Old Scofield Study Bible. 1616p. 1997. 56.99 (*0-19-527320-6*); 86.99 (*0-19-527321-4*); 86.99 (*0-19-527322-2*); 96.99 (*0-19-527324-9*) OUP.

Old Scofield Study Bible. 1616p. 1998. 76.99 (*0-19-527431-8*); 69.99 (*0-19-527430-X*); 79.99 (*0-19-527440-7*); 76.99 (*0-19-527427-X*); 69.99 (*0-19-527426-1*) OUP.

*__Old Scofield Study Bible.__ 1616p. 1998. 76.99 (*0-19-527403-2*); bond lthr. 39.99 (*0-19-527416-4*) OUP.

Old Scofield Study Bible. 1616p. 1998. 76.99 (*0-19-527429-6*); 86.99 (*0-19-527441-5*) OUP.

*__Old Scofield Study Bible.__ 1616p. 1998. 86.99 (*0-19-527409-1*) OUP.

*__Old Scofield Study Bible.__ 1998. 79.99 (*0-19-527408-3*) OUP.

Old Scofield Study Bible. 1616p. 1998. 107.00 (*0-19-527449-0*); 100.00 (*0-19-527450-4*) OUP.

*__Old Scofield Study Bible.__ 1616p. 1998. 107.00 (*0-19-527451-2*); 100.00 (*0-19-527448-2*) OUP.

*__Old Scofield Study Bible.__ 1616p. 1999. 34.99 (*0-19-527468-7*) OUP.

*__Old Scofield Study Bible.__ SCF STDY OLD. 1616p. 1998. 54.99 (*0-19-527433-4*) OUP.

*__Old Scofield Study Bible.__ Old Scofield Readers Staff. 1616p. 1998. 86.99 (*0-19-527439-3*) OUP.

Old Scofield Study Bible. Oxford University Press Staff. 1632p. 1998. 39.99 (*0-19-527452-0*); 39.99 (*0-19-527453-9*); 39.99 (*0-19-527454-7*); 39.99 (*0-19-527455-5*); 39.99 (*0-19-527456-3*); 39.99 (*0-19-527457-1*) OUP.

*__Old Scores.__ Nicholas Delbanco. 2000. reprint ed. pap. 13.95 (*0-446-67450-8*) Warner Bks.

Old Scores: A Chris Norgren Mystery. Aaron J. Elkins. (Northwest Mysteries Ser.). 1994. mass mkt. 5.99 (*0-449-14899-8*, GM) Fawcett.

Old Scores, New Goals. Joan Finnigan. (Illus.). 240p. 1992. 24.95 (*1-55082-054-0*, Pub. by Quarry Pr) LPC InBook.

Old Scores, New Goals: The Story of the Ottawa Senators. Joan Finnigan. (Illus.). 240p. 1992. pap. 11.95 (*1-55082-041-9*, Pub. by Quarry Pr) LPC InBook.

*__Old Scotland, New Scotland.__ Jef Fall. 1999. pap. 11.95 (*0-946487-40-5*) Luath Pr Ltd.

Old Script Mongolian Language & Its Development in Khalkla. (Mongolia Society Occasional Papers: No. 13). 1988. pap. 12.00 (*0-910980-53-5*) Mongolia.

Old Sebec Lake. Dorothy A. Blanchard. LC 97-183784. (Images of America Ser.). 128p. 1999. pap. 16.99 (*0-7524-0273-0*) Arcadia Publng.

Old Self, New Self. (ENG & IND.). 1995. pap. write for info. (*0-934920-66-4*) Derek Prince.

Old Sergeant's Story: Or Fighting Indians & Badmen in Texas. Robert G. Carter. (Illus.). 1976. 32.95 (*0-8488-0000-1*, J M C & Co) Amereon Ltd.

Old Series see Southern Literary Journal & Monthly Magazine

Old Service: Royalist Regimental Colonels & the Civil War, 1642-46. P. R. Newman. LC 93-14678. (C). 1993. text 59.95 (*0-7190-3752-2*, Pub. by Manchester Univ Pr) St Martin.

Old Settler. John H. Redwood. 1998. pap. 5.25 (*0-8222-1642-6*) Dramatists Play.

Old Settlers' History of York County & Individual Biographies. Compiled by John Lett et al. (Illus.). 175p. 1997. reprint ed. lib. bdg. 25.00 (*0-8328-6872-8*) Higginson Bk Co.

Old Settlers of the Grand Traverse Region. S. E. Wait. 1978. reprint ed. pap. 9.00 (*0-912382-25-2*) Black Letter.

Old Settlers' Tales, Pottawatamie & Nemaha Counties: Historical & Biographical Sketches of the Early Settlement & Settlers of Northeastern Pottawatomie & Southwestern Nemaha Counties, from Earliest Settlement to the Year 1877. E. E. Crevecoeur. (Illus.). 162p. 1995. reprint ed. pap. 17.00 (*0-8328-5031-4*); reprint ed. lib. bdg. 25.00 (*0-8328-5030-6*) Higginson Bk Co.

Old Sewing Machines. Carol Head. (Shire Album Ser.: No. 84). (Illus.). 32p. 1989. pap. 25.00 (*0-85263-591-5*, Pub. by Shire Pubns) Lubrecht & Cramer.

Old Shanghai. Betty P. Wei. LC 92-39412. (Images of Asia Ser.). (Illus.). 80p. (C). 1993. text 17.95 (*0-19-585747-X*) OUP.

Old Sheffield Plate. Annecke Bambery. 1989. pap. 50.00 (*0-85263-965-1*, Pub. by Shire Pubns) St Mut.

Old Shell: Poems of the Galapagos. Tony Johnston. LC 98-3212. (Illus.). 64p. (YA). (gr. 2-7). 1999. 15.00 (*0-374-35648-3*) FS&G.

*__Old Ship Figureheads & Sterns.__ Leonard Laughton. 329p. 2000. reprint ed. lib. bdg. 79.00 (*0-7812-0011-3*) Rprt Serv.

Old Ship of Zion: The Afro-Baptist Ritual in the African Diaspora. Walter F. Pitts. (Religion in America Ser.). 216p. 1996. reprint ed. pap. 19.95 (*0-19-511145-1*) OUP.

Old Shipmasters of Salem, Massachusetts, with Mention of Eminent Merchants. Chas E. Trow. (Illus.). 337p. 1998. reprint ed. lib. bdg. 42.50 (*0-8328-7128-1*) Higginson Bk Co.

Old Shipmasters of Salem with Mention of Eminent Merchants. Charles E. Trow. (Illus.). 337p. 1989. reprint ed. lib. bdg. 39.00 (*0-8328-1398-2*) Higginson Bk Co.

Old Shirts & New Skins. Sherman Alexie. LC 93-53282. (Native American Literature Ser.: No. 9). (Illus.). 100p. (Orig.). pap. 12.00 (*0-935626-36-0*) U Cal AISC.

Old Shrines & Ivy. William Winter. (Notable American Authors Ser.). 1999. reprint ed. lib. bdg. 125.00 (*0-7812-7753-1*) Rprt Serv.

Old Silent. Martha Grimes. 448p. 1990. mass mkt. 6.99 (*0-440-20492-5*) Dell.

Old Silent. large type ed. Martha Grimes. LC 90-10807. 623p. 1990. lib. bdg. 20.95 (*0-89621-990-9*) Thorndike Pr.

Old Silent, Set. abr. ed. Martha Grimes. 1992. audio 16.00 (*0-671-73617-5*) S&S Audio.

Old Silver of American Churches, 2 vols. E. Alfred Jones. (Illus.). 400p. 2000. reprint ed. 295.00 (*0-8150-0002-2*) Wittenborn Art.

Old Singapore. Maya Jayapal. (Images of Asia Ser.). (Illus.). 96p. (C). 1994. text 17.95 (*0-19-588552-X*) OUP.

Old Sinners Never Die. large type ed. Dorothy S. Davis. (Nightingale Series Large Print Bks.). 262p. 1991. pap. 14.95 (*0-8161-5167-9*, G K Hall Lrg Type) Mac Lib Ref.

Old Sister Moon: The Very Best of Anita Speer Smith. Anita S. Smith. 32p. (Orig.). 1992. pap. 5.00 (*1-880649-30-6*) Writ Ctr Pr.

Old Skye Tales: Traditions, Reflections & Memories. William Mackenzie & Alasdair MacLean. (Illus.). 94p. pap. 19.95 (*1-899272-01-1*, Pub. by Maclean Pr) Dufour.

Old Sleuth's Freaky Female Detectives. Ed. by Garyn G. Roberts et al. LC 89-85966. (Dime Novels Ser.). 118p. 1986. 31.95 (*0-87972-475-7*) Bowling Green Univ Popular Press.

Old Smoky Mountain Days: Selected Writings by Harvey Broome, Horace Kephart, & Charles Hall. Horace Kephart et al. Ed. by Arthur McDade. (Illus.). 134p. (Orig.). 1996. pap. 8.95 (*1-887205-08-X*) Panther TN.

Old Smyrna Excavations: The Temples of Athena. R. M. Cook & R. V. Nicholls. (BSA Supplementary Volumes Ser.: Vol. 30). (Illus.). 246p. 1999. lib. bdg. 90.00 (*0-904887-28-6*, Pub. by Brit Sch Athens) David Brown.

Old Snow. Bei Dao. Tr. by Bonnie S. McDougall from CHI. LC 91-16507. 96p. 1991. 16.95 (*0-8112-1182-7*, Pub. by New Directions); pap. 8.95 (*0-8112-1183-5*, NDP727, Pub. by New Directions) Norton.

Old Social Classes & the Revolutionary Movements of Iraq: A Study of Iraq's Old Landed & Commercial Classes & of Its Communists, Bathists, & Free Officers. Hanna Batatu. LC 78-51157. (Princeton Studies on the Near East). (Illus.). 1310p. reprint ed. pap. 200.00 (*0-608-06413-0*, 206662600008) Bks Demand.

Old Soggy No. 1: The Uninhibited Story of Slats Rodgers. Hart Stilwell & Slats Rodgers. LC 72-169437. (Literature & History of Aviation Ser.). 1972. reprint ed. 27.95 (*0-405-03779-1*) Ayer.

Old Soldiers. Richard Nason. LC 88-90815. (Illus.). 68p. 1988. pap. 10.00 (*0-912292-80-6*) Smith.

*__Old Soldiers Never Die.__ Margaret Mayhew. 224p. 2000. 25.00 (*0-7278-5441-0*, Pub. by Severn Hse) Chivers N Amer.

Old Soldiers Never Die: The Life of Douglas MacArthur. Geoffrey Perret. LC 97-8759. 1997. pap. text 14.95 (*1-55850-723-X*) Adams Media.

*__Old Somerset Railroad: A Lifeline for Northern Maine 1874-1929.__ Walter M. Macdougall. LC 99-87562. 176p. 2000. 24.95 (*0-89272-492-7*) Down East.

Old Song: And Edifying Letters of the Rutherford Family. Robert Louis Stevenson. Ed. & Intro. by Roger G. Swearingen. LC 82-1627. 102p. (C). 1982. lib. bdg. 27.50 (*0-208-01973-1*, Archon Bks) Shoe String.

Old Songs & New Songs: Piano. 160p. (Orig.). Date not set. pap. 12.95 (*0-7692-1143-7*, PF0668) Wrner Bros.

Old Songs & Singing Games. Ed. by Richard Chase. LC 72-85499. (Illus.). 64p. 1972. reprint ed. pap. 2.95 (*0-486-22879-7*) Dover.

Old Songs, Fellowships & a Few Skits for Younger Senior Adults. Jane Montgomery. Ed. by Charles Montgomery. 1985. write for info. (*0-916043-03-7*) Light Hearted Pub Co.

Old Songs in a New Cafe' Selected Essays by Robert James Waller. Robert James Waller. 192p. 1999. reprint ed. 29.95 (*0-7351-0065-9*) Replica Bks.

Old Songs Made New. Kerry Hart. (Illus.). viii, 119p. (J). (gr. 1-6). 1997. pap. text 29.95 (*0-9659687-0-7*) Hartline Pr.

Old Soul with a Young Spirit: Poetry in the Era of Desegregation Recovery. Antronette K. Yancey. Ed. by Octavia Miles. (Illus.). 32p. 1997. mass mkt. write for info. (*0-9666488-0-3*) Imhotep Pub Inc.

*__Old Souls: Aged Women, Poverty & the Experience of God.__ Helen K. Black & Robert L. Rubinstein. LC 99-54971. 216p. 2000. lib. bdg. 47.95 (*0-202-30633-X*) Aldine de Gruyter.

*__Old Souls: Aged Women, Poverty & the Experience of God.__ Helen K. Black & Robert L. Rubinstein. LC 99-54971. 216p. 2000. reprint ed. pap. text 23.95 (*0-202-30634-8*) Aldine de Gruyter.

*__Old Souls: The Scientific Evidence for Past Lives.__ Tom Shroder. LC 99-12705. (Illus.). 256p. 1999. 23.50 (*0-684-85192-X*) Simon & Schuster.

Old South. Fletcher M. Green. LC 79-55730. (Goldentree Bibliographies Series in American History). (C). 1980. pap. text 14.95 (*0-88295-580-2*) Harlan Davidson.

Old South. Insight Guides Staff. (Insight Guides). 1998. pap. text 22.95 (*0-88729-733-1*) Langenscheidt.

*__Old South.__ Ed. by Mark M. Smith. 2000. 62.95 (*0-631-21926-9*); pap. 27.95 (*0-631-21927-7*) Blackwell Pubs.

Old South: A Monograph. Howard M. Hamill. 1977. text 12.95 (*0-8369-9223-7*, 9077) Ayer.

Old South: A Psychohistory. Earl E. Thorpe. LC 78-15165. 313p. 1979. reprint ed. lib. bdg. 35.00 (*0-313-21113-2*, THOL, Greenwood Pr) Greenwood.

Old South: Essays Social & Historical. Thomas N. Page. (Notable American Authors Ser.). 1999. reprint ed. lib. bdg. 125.00 (*0-7812-4706-3*) Rprt Serv.

Old South: Essays Social & Political. Thomas N. Page. LC 69-14026. (Illus.). 269p. 1970. reprint ed. lib. bdg. 38.50 (*0-8371-1977-4*, PAO&) Greenwood.

Old South: Essays Social & Political. Thomas N. Page. LC 68-24992. (American History & Americana Ser.: No. 47). 1969. reprint ed. lib. bdg. 75.00 (*0-8383-0226-2*) M S G Haskell Hse.

Old South: Essays Social & Political. Thomas N. Page. (BCL1 - United States Local History Ser.). 344p. 1991. reprint ed. text 89.00 (*0-7812-6284-4*) Rprt Serv.

Old South, New South: Revolutions in the Southern Economy since the Civil War. Gavin Wright. LC 97-197547. 336p. 1996. pap. text 18.95 (*0-8071-2098-7*) La State U Pr.

Old Southampton: Politics & Society in a Virginia County, 1824-1869. Daniel W. Crofts. LC 92-6778. (Illus.). 424p. 1992. text 39.50 (*0-8139-1385-3*) U Pr of Va.

Old Southern Apples. Creighton L. Calhoun, Jr. (Illus.). 336p. 1995. 49.95 (*0-939923-37-8*); pap. 39.95 (*0-939923-59-9*) M & W Pub Co.

Old Southwest Humor from the St. Louis Reveille, 1844-1850. Ed. & Tr. by Fritz Oehlschlaeger. 304p. 1990. text 34.95 (*0-8262-0741-3*) U of Mo Pr.

Old Southwest, 1795-1830: Frontiers in Conflict. Thomas D. Clark & John D. Guice. LC 95-42772. (Illus.). 335p. (Orig.). (C). 1996. pap. 18.95 (*0-8061-2836-4*, 2836) U of Okla Pr.

Old Spanish Readings. Jeremiah D. Ford. LC 67-21713. 355p. 1967. reprint ed. 40.00 (*0-87752-037-2*) Gordian.

Old Spanish Readings Selected on the Basis of Critically Edited Texts. Ed. by J. D. Ford. 1977. lib. bdg. 59.95 (*0-8490-2371-8*) Gordon Pr.

Old Spanish Santa Barbara. Walker A. Tompkins. pap. 4.00 (*0-87461-030-3*) McNally & Loftin.

Old Spanish Trail, Vol. 1. Ralph Compton. 1998. mass mkt. 5.99 (*0-312-96408-0*) St Martin.

 An Asterisk (*) at the beginning of an entry indicates that the title is appearing for the first time.

Old Spanish Trail: Santa Fe to Los Angeles: With Extracts from Contemporary Records & Including Diaries of Antonio Armijo & Orville Pratt. LeRoy R. Hafen & Ann W. Hafen. LC 92-38604. (Illus.). 375p. reprint ed. pap. 116.30 (*0-608-08692-4*, 206921500003) Bks Demand.

***Old Spanish Trail Across the Mojave Desert.** Harold A. Steiner. LC 96-94106. (Illus.). 258p. 1999. pap. 24.95 (*0-9614517-1-8*) Haldor Co.

Old Sparky. Willard Gellis. 39p. 1987. pap. 7.00 (*0-917455-06-1*) Big Foot NY.

Old Sparta & Elba Land Office Records & Military Warrants, 1822-1860. Marilyn D. Hahn. 172p. 1983. 20.00 (*0-89308-339-9*) Southern Hist Pr.

Old Speedwell Families. enl. rev. ed. Lawrence Edwards & Joy E. Davis. 760p. 1983. reprint ed. 25.00 (*0-89308-176-0*) Southern Hist Pr.

Old Springfield: Race & Religion in Augusta, Georgia. Edward J. Cashin. LC 95-72536. (Illus.). 134p. 1996. 20.00 (*0-9649511-5-0*) Sprngfield Village.

Old St. Andrews Music Book. James H. Baxter. LC 70-178515. (Medieval Studies). reprint ed. 52.50 (*0-404-56525-5*) AMS Pr.

Old St. Charles. Sue Schneider. LC 93-2747. 102p. 1993. pap. 5.95 (*1-880397-01-3*) Patrice Pr.

Old St. Nick Carving: Classic Santas from Wood. David Sabol. (Illus.). 64p. 1996. pap. 12.95 (*0-7643-0039-3*) Schiffer.

Old St. Patrick's: New York's First Cathedral. Mary P. Carthy. (Monographs: No. 23). (Illus.). 1947. 10.00 (*0-930060-05-9*) US Cath Hist.

Old St. Stephens Land Office Records & American State Papers, Public Lands, 1768-1888, Vol. 1. Marilyn D. Hahn. 168p. 1983. 20.00 (*0-89308-332-1*) Southern Hist Pr.

Old St. Thomas' at Poplar Neck, Bardstown, Kentucky. William J. Howlett. (Illus.). 200p. 1971. reprint ed. pap. 3.25 (*0-913228-02-8*) R J Liederbach.

Old Stationery Engines. David Edgington. (Album Ser.: No. 49). (Illus.). 32p. 1989. pap. 4.75 (*0-85263-500-1*, Pub. by Shire Pubns) Parkwest Pubns.

Old Steam Navy Vol. 1: Frigates, Sloops, & Gunboats, 1815-1885. Donald L. Canney. LC 89-13675. (Illus.). 288p. 1990. 49.95 (*0-87021-004-1*) Naval Inst Pr.

Old Steam Train. Heather Amery. (Farmyard Tales Readers Ser.). (Illus.). 16p. 1999. pap. text 4.95 (*0-7460-3336-2*, Usborne) EDC.

Old Steamboat Days on the Hudson River. David L. Buckman. (Illus.). 136p. 1990. pap. 18.50 (*0-941567-05-2*) J C & A L Fawcett.

Old Stone Age in European Russia. Eugenii A. Golomshtok. LC 76-44723. (Illus.). 368p. 1983. reprint ed. 82.50 (*0-404-15927-3*) AMS Pr.

Old Stone Church: In the Heart of the City since 1830. Jeanette E. Tuve. LC 94-18810. 1994. write for info. (*0-89865-899-3*) Donning Co.

Old Stone Fort. Archie P. McDonald. v, 41p. 1981. pap. 7.95 (*0-87611-057-X*) Tex St Hist Assn.

Old Stone Fort: Exploring an Archaeological Mystery. Charles H. Faulkner. LC 68-17145. (University of Tennessee Study in Anthropology Ser.). (Illus.). 84p. reprint ed. pap. 30.00 (*0-8357-6540-7*, 203590300097) Bks Demand.

Old Stone House, & Other Stories. Anna K. Green. LC 71-132117. (Short Story Index Reprint Ser.). 1977. 16.95 (*0-8369-3674-4*) Ayer.

Old Stone House Museum: Brownington, Vermont. Photos by John Miller. (Illus.). 26p. (Orig.). 1996. pap. 5.00 (*0-614-30163-7*) Orleans.

Old Stones of Kingston: Its Buildings Before 1867. Margaret Angus. LC 66-6913. (Illus.). 1980. pap. 17.95 (*0-8020-6419-1*) U of Toronto Pr.

Old Stories: Folk Tales from East Anglia & the Fen Country Kevin Crossley-Holland. LC 98-165781. 215 p. 1997. write for info. (*0-905899-51-2*) Colt Bks Ltd.

Old Stuff. Carol J. Peterson. (Illus.). 148p. (Orig.). 1995. pap. write for info. (*1-57579-001-7*) Pine Hill Pr.

Old Stuff I Never Thought Would See the Light of Day. Brendan Tripp. 28p. 1982. pap. 5.00 (*1-57353-006-9*) Eschaton Prods.

Old Sturbridge Village. Kent McCallum. Ed. by Jack Larkin. LC 96-6909. (Illus.). 224p. 1996. 45.00 (*0-8109-3686-0*, Pub. by Abrams) Time Warner.

Old Sturbridge Village Cookbook: Authentic Early American Recipes for the Modern Kitchen. 2nd ed. Ed. by Caroline Sloat. LC 96-197546. (Illus.). 254p. 1995. pap. 14.95 (*1-56440-728-4*) Globe Pequot.

Old Suitcase. Monty M. Stanley. 378p. 1989. 18.95 (*0-9622667-0-1*) Illini Pubns.

Old Sumerian & Old Akkadian Texts in Philadelphia, Chiefly from Nippur, Part 1: Literary & Lexical Texts, & the Earliest Administrative Documents from Nippur. Aage Westenholz. LC 74-21135. (Bibliotheca Mesopotamica Ser.: Vol. 1). (Illus.). xii, 213p. 1975. 35.00 (*0-89003-008-1*) Undena Pubns.

Old Survey Bk. 1: 1746-1782, Pittsylvania County, Virginia. Marian D. Chiarito. 400p. 1988. 35.00 (*0-945503-15-6*) Clarkton Pr.

Old Survey Book 2, 1797-1829, Pittsylvania County, Virginia. Marian D. Chiarito. 102p. 1988. 12.00 (*0-945503-16-4*) Clarkton Pr.

Old Swedish Quilts. Asa Wettre. Tr. by Kristine Fredricksson from SWE. (Illus.). 192p. 1995. 24.95 (*1-883010-15-2*) Interweave.

Old Swimmin' Hole. James Whitcomb Riley. (Notable American Authors Ser.). 1999. reprint ed. lib. bdg. 125.00 (*0-7812-8781-2*) Rprt Serv.

Old Syriac Inscriptions of Edessa & Osrhoene: Texts, Translations & Commentary. H. J. Drijvers & John F. Healey. LC 98-43667. (Handbuch der Orientalistik). xvi, 358p. 1998. 105.00 (*90-04-11284-7*) Brill Academic Pubs.

Old Tales - New Tails. Joseph Keenan. LC 98-67464. vi, 106p. 1998. pap. 10.14 (*0-9665921-0-7*, 98-1) Pinnacle Pr.

Old Tales & New Truths: Charting the Bright-Shadow World. James R. King. LC 90-26345. 267p. (C). 1992. pap. text 21.95 (*0-7914-0854-X*) State U NY Pr.

Old Tales for a New Day. 2nd ed. Sophia L. Fahs & Alice Cobb. LC 92-21050. (Young Readers Ser.). (Illus.). 219p. (J). (gr. 4-9). 1992. reprint ed. pap. 15.95 (*0-87975-730-2*) Prometheus Bks.

Old Tales of China. Nian P. Li. (Illus.). 206p. 1983. reprint ed. pap. 4.95 (*9971-947-34-X*) Heian Intl.

Old Tales of San Francisco. 2nd ed. Arthur B. Chandler. 304p. (C). 1996. pap. text, per. 28.95 (*0-8403-4385-X*) Kendall-Hunt.

Old Tales Retold from Grecian Mythology in Talks Around the Fire (1876) Augusta Larned. 498p. 1998. reprint ed. pap. 36.00 (*0-7661-0250-5*) Kessinger Pub.

***Old Taoist: The Life, Art & Poetry of Kodojin.** Stephen Addiss. Tr. & Comment by Jonathan Chaves. (Illus.). 2000. 27.50 (*0-231-11656-X*) Col U Pr.

Old Taverns of New York. W. H. Bayles. 1977. lib. bdg. 59.95 (*0-8490-2373-4*) Gordon Pr.

Old Teddy Bear Postcards, Vol. II. Patricia Shoonmaker. Vol. II. (Illus.). 12p. 1987. pap. text 4.95 (*0-87588-316-8*) Hobby Hse.

Old Telephones. Andrew Emmerson. (Album Ser.: No. 161). (Illus.). 32p. 1989. pap. 4.75 (*0-85263-781-0*, Pub. by Shire Pubns) Parkwest Pubns.

Old Television. Andrew Emmerson. LC 99-492013. (Album Ser.: No. 337). (Illus.). 32p. 1998. pap. 6.25 (*0-7478-0367-6*, Pub. by Shire Pubns) Parkwest Pubns.

Old Tennant. Margot Miles. 127p. (C). 1988. 49.00 (*0-7316-4200-7*) St Mut.

Old Testament. (Praying with...Ser.). (Orig.). 1989. 1.79 (*0-687-86038-5*) Abingdon.

Old Testament. Bellerophon Books Staff. (J). (gr. 1-9). 1992. pap. 4.95 (*0-88388-003-2*) Bellerophon Bks.

***Old Testament.** Broadman & Holman Publishing Staff. LC 99-53654. (Shepherd's Notes Bible Summary Ser.). 1999. pap. 5.95 (*0-8054-9377-8*) Broadman.

Old Testament. Everyman's Library Staff. LC 96-22789. 1996. 35.00 (*0-679-45102-1*) McKay.

Old Testament. Frank Schaffer Publications Staff. 1997. pap. text 5.95 (*0-7647-0097-9*) Schaffer Pubns.

Old Testament. Ed. by E. Galbiati-Mimep. (Illus.). (C). 1988. 39.00 (*0-7855-3226-9*, Pub. by St Paul Pubns) St Mut.

Old Testament. Geoffrey M. Horn. (Barron's Book Notes Ser.). (C). 1986. pap. 2.50 (*0-8120-3531-3*) Barron.

Old Testament. J. G. Horton. (Bible At-a-Glance Study & Teaching Tools Ser.). (Illus.). 1992. pap. 4.95 (*1-880426-01-3*) Bible At A Glance.

Old Testament, 36 cass.. Narrated by Stephen Johnston. 1996. audio 59.99 (*0-529-10640-X*, World Audio) World Publng.

Old Testament. Sherry Nedreberg & Glorianne Muggli. (Classroom Activity Book Ser.). (Illus.). 100p. 1997. pap. 7.95 (*1-57665-036-7*) Muggli Graphics.

Old Testament. Nan Pollard. 1998. pap. text 1.49 (*0-7847-0755-3*) Standard Pub.

***Old Testament.** Warner Press Staff. (Illus.). (J). 1999. pap. 3.95 (*0-87162-861-9*) Warner Pr.

Old Testament see Zondervan NIV Bible Commentary

Old Testament: A Byzantine Perspective. John Custer. 247p. (Orig.). 1995. pap. 10.00 (*1-887158-08-1*) God With Us.

Old Testament: A Collection of Bible Stories. Heather Amery. (Children's Bible Ser.). (Illus.). 72p. 1999. text 15.95 (*0-7460-3457-1*, Usborne) EDC.

Old Testament: An Introduction. Rolf Rendtorff. Tr. by John Bowden. LC 85-47728. (GER.). 320p. 1991. pap. 21.00 (*0-8006-2544-7*, 1-2544, Fortress Pr) Augsburg Fortress.

Old Testament: An Overview of Sacred History & Truth. rev. ed. Wilbur Fields. LC 96-36168. (Illus.). 688p. (Orig.). 1998. text 26.99 (*0-89900-646-9*) College Pr Pub.

Old Testament: Classic Bible Stories. Lise Caldwell. LC 97-50564. (Illus.). 24p. (J). (ps-1). 1998. pap. 1.99 (*0-7847-0827-4*, 24-04257) Standard Pub.

***Old Testament: God's Unfolding Promise.** Phil Campbell & Bryson Smith. (Faith Walk Bible Studies). 80p. 2000. 4.99 (*1-58134-145-8*) Crossway Bks.

Old Testament: KJV Bible Bed Books for Seniors. large type unabridged ed. Ed. by A. L. Wilson. 1200p. 2000. pap. write for info. (*1-892113-02-3*) Lightside.

Old Testament: Ten Plays for Readers' Theater. Josephine Davidson. LC 92-90957. (Illus.). 189p. (Orig.). (J). (gr. 6-8). 1992. pap. text. write for info. (*0-9628252-1-2*) Right Bk.

Old Testament: Text & Context. Victor H. Matthews & James C. Moyer. LC 97-2428. 308p. (C). 1997. 29.95 (*1-56563-168-4*) Hendrickson MA.

***Old Testament Bk. 1: The Maker's Instructions.** David Pawson & Andy Peck. (Unlocking the Bible Ser.). 2000. pap. 13.00 (*0-551-03186-7*, Pub. by M Pickering) Trafalgar.

***Old Testament Bk. 2: A Land & a Kingdom.** David Pawson & Andy Peck. (Unlocking the Bible Ser.). 2000. pap. 13.00 (*0-551-03188-3*, Pub. by M Pickering) Trafalgar.

***Old Testament Bk. 3: Poems of Worship & Wisdom.** David Pawson & Andy Peck. (Unlocking the Bible Ser.). 2000. pap. 13.00 (*0-551-03189-1*, Pub. by M Pickering) Trafalgar.

***Old Testament Activity Bible.** Chariot Victor Publishing Staff. 2000. pap. text 12.99 (*0-7814-3317-7*) Chariot Victor.

Old Testament Activity Book. Susan Taylor Brown. (Activity Book Ser.). (Illus.). 100p. 1997. pap. 7.95 (*1-57665-035-9*) Muggli Graphics.

Old Testament Activity Book. Linda Giampa. (Illus.). 32p. (J). (gr. k-3). 1992. pap. 3.99 (*0-570-04724-2*, 56-1683) Concordia.

Old Testament & After. C. G. Montefiore. 601p. 1977. 26.95 (*0-8369-6862-X*) Ayer.

Old Testament & Criticism. Carl E. Amerding. (Biblical & Theological Classics Library: Vol. 20). vii, 134p. 1997. reprint ed. pap. 9.99 (*0-85364-812-3*, Pub. by Paternoster Pub) OM Literature.

Old Testament & Folklore Study. Patricia G. Kirkpatrick. (JSOTS Ser.: Vol. 62). 152p. 1988. pap. 17.50 (*1-85075-113-7*, Pub. by Sheffield Acad) CUP Services.

***Old Testament & Process Theology.** Robert Gnuse. 2000. pap. 29.99 (*0-8272-2713-2*) Chalice Pr.

Old Testament & Related Studies. Hugh Nibley. LC 85-27544. (Collected Works of Hugh Nibley: Vol. 1). xiv, 290p. 1986. 24.95 (*0-87579-032-1*) Deseret Bk.

Old Testament & the Archaeologist. H. Darrell Lance. Ed. by Gene M. Tucker. LC 80-2387. (Guides to Biblical Scholarship: Old Testament Ser.). 112p. (Orig.). 1981. pap. 12.00 (*0-8006-0467-9*, 1-467, Fortress Pr) Augsburg Fortress.

***Old Testament & the Significance of Jesus: Embracing Change - Maintaining Christian Identity.** Frederick C. Holmgren. LC 98-50025. 213p. 1999. pap. 16.00 (*0-8028-4453-7*) Eerdmans.

Old Testament Art Vol. I: Eighteenth Century Biblical Etchings in Postcards - Genesis. (Old Testament Art in Postcards Ser.). (Illus.). 30p. 1999. pap. 8.95 (*1-893262-00-6*) Robern Pubg.

Old Testament Art Vol. II: Eighteenth Century Biblical Etchings in Postcards - Genesis, Exodus, Leviticus, Numbers, Deuteronomy, Joshua & Judges. (Old Testament Art in Postcards Ser.). (Illus.). 30p. 1999. pap. 8.95 (*1-893262-01-4*) Robern Pubg.

Old Testament Art Vol. III: Eighteenth Century Biblical Etchings in Postcards - Prophets & Writings. (Old Testament Art in Postcards Ser.). (Illus.). 30p. 1999. pap. 8.95 (*1-893262-02-2*) Robern Pubg.

Old Testament As Living Literature. Ruth H. Blackburn. 1976. 4.95 (*0-671-00964-8*, Arco) Macmillan Gen Ref.

***Old Testament As Sacred Literature.** Marion Gordon. LC 00-190901. 2000. 25.00 (*0-7388-2080-6*); pap. 18.00 (*0-7388-2081-4*) Xlibris Corp.

Old Testament Bible Adventure Kit: Bible Storyboard Adventures for Kids. Dawn Reagan. Ed. by Toon Takes. (Illus.). 16p. 1999. pap. 29.95 (*1-929456-00-X*) Myrtle Seal Pubg.

Old Testament Bible Sketches for Children: 24 Interactive Scripts for Youth & Adults to Perform for Kids. Gillette Elvgren. 1998. 9.99 (*0-8341-9743-X*) Nazarene.

Old Testament Bible Stories. (Magic Pad Ser.). (J). 1993. pap. 1.75 (*1-895877-08-3*) Novar Cottage.

Old Testament Canon in the Old Testament Church: The Internal Rationale for Old Testament Canonicity. Robert I. Vasholz. LC 90-35598. (Ancient Near Eastern Texts & Studies: Vol. 7). 116p. 1990. lib. bdg. 69.95 (*0-88946-084-1*) E Mellen.

Old Testament Canon of the New Testament Church & Its Background in Early Judaism. fac. ed. Roger T. Beckwith. LC 85-6850. 572p. 1986. reprint ed. pap. 177.40 (*0-7837-7944-5*, 204770000008) Bks Demand.

***Old Testament Characters.** 2nd rev. ed. Peter Scazzero. 64p. 2000. pap. 4.99 (*0-8308-3059-6*) InterVarsity.

Old Testament Characters: Learning to Walk with God. Peter L. Scazzero. (LifeGuide Bible Studies). (Orig.). 1988. pap., wbk. ed. 4.99 (*0-8308-1059-5*, 1059) InterVarsity.

Old Testament, Christianity & Pluralism. Cristina Grenholm. LC 96-227016. (Beitrage Zur Geschichte der Biblischen Exegese Ser.: No. 33). 303p. 1996. 127.50 (*3-16-146587-3*, Pub. by JCB Mohr) Coronet Bks.

Old Testament Commentaries, 10 vols. Incl. Vol. 2. Joshua - Second Samuel. Carl F. Keil & Franz Delitzsch. 1971. 25.00 (*0-8028-8036-3*); Vol. 6. Proverbs - Song of Solomon. 25.00 (*0-8028-8040-1*); Vol. 7. Isaiah. 25.00 (*0-8028-8041-X*); Vol. 8. Jeremiah-Lamentations. Carl F. Keil & Franz Delitzsch. 1971. 25.00 (*0-8028-8042-8*); Vol. 9. Ezekiel-Daniel. Carl F. Keil & Franz Delitzsch. 1971. 25.00 (*0-8028-8043-6*); Vol. 10. Minor Prophets. 25.00 (*0-8028-8044-4*); 1971. reprint ed. 249.99 (*0-8028-8034-7*) Eerdmans.

Old Testament Commentary: Daniel 1-6. John Calvin. LC 93-206. 1993. 35.00 (*0-8028-2451-X*); pap. 25.00 (*0-8028-0750-X*) Eerdmans.

Old Testament Commentary on Its History & Literature see Antiguo Testamento: Un Comentario Sobre Su Historia y Literatura

Old Testament Commentary Survey. 2nd ed. Tremper Longman, III. LC 95-12250. 192p. 1995. pap. 12.99 (*0-8010-2024-7*) Baker Bks.

Old Testament Condensed: From the Authorized King James Version. Eileen Bayless. LC 96-79928. 288p. (Orig.). 1997. pap. 11.95 (*1-56167-345-5*) Am Literary Pr.

Old Testament Criticism in the Nineteenth Century. John W. Rogerson. 320p. 1984. 85.00 (*0-281-04094-X*, Pub. by Society Prom Christ Know) Intl Pubs Mktg.

***Old Testament Days: An Activity Guide.** Nancy I. Sanders. LC 99-12454. (Illus.). 166p. (J). (gr. 2-5). 1999. pap. 14.95 (*1-55652-354-8*) Chicago Review.

Old Testament Digest: Gen-Deut., Vol. 1. William MacDonald & Mike Hamel. 1981. pap. 7.95 (*0-937396-59-1*) Walterick Pubs.

Old Testament Digest Vol. 2: Joshua-Esther. William MacDonald & Mike Hamel. 1982. pap. 7.95 (*0-937396-61-3*) Walterick Pubs.

Old Testament Digest Vol. 3: Job-Malachi. William MacDonald. 1981. pap. 7.95 (*0-937396-29-X*) Walterick Pubs.

Old Testament Dramas. Hersey E. Spence. LC 74-175994. 1976. reprint ed. 34.50 (*0-404-06176-1*) AMS Pr.

Old Testament Ethics: A Paradigmatic Approach. Waldemar Janzen. LC 93-32885. 240p. (Orig.). 1994. pap. 22.95 (*0-664-25410-1*) Westminster John Knox.

Old Testament Evangelistic Sermons. D. Martyn Lloyd-Jones. 268p. 1995. 27.99 (*0-85151-683-1*) Banner of Truth.

Old Testament Exegesis: A Primer for Students & Pastors. 2nd enl. rev. ed. Douglas Stuart. LC 84-10431. 142p. (C). 1984. pap. 14.95 (*0-664-24559-5*) Westminster John Knox.

***Old Testament Explorer: Discovering the Essence, Background & Meaning of Every Book in the Old Testament.** Charles Dyer. 700p. 2000. 29.99 (*0-8499-1447-7*) Word Pub.

Old Testament for Children. Regina Press Staff. (J). (ps-3). 1.95 (*0-88271-044-3*) Regina Pr.

Old Testament Form Criticism. Ed. by John H. Hayes. LC 72-97351. (Trinity University Monograph Series in Religion: Vol. 2). 310p. reprint ed. pap. 96.10 (*0-608-13440-6*, 202256600028) Bks Demand.

Old Testament Fun Activities - First & Second Grade. Cindy Jackson. (Illus.). 16p. (J). (gr. 1-2). 1998. 3.95 (*1-878669-69-9*, CRE 3541) Crea Tea Assocs.

Old Testament Fun Activities - Pre-School & Kindergarten. Cindy Jackson. (Illus.). 16p. (J). (ps-k). 1998. 3.95 (*1-878669-68-0*, CRE 3540) Crea Tea Assocs.

Old Testament Fun Activities - Third & Fourth Grade. Cindy Jackson. (Illus.). 16p. (J). (gr. 3-4). 1998. 3.95 (*1-878669-70-2*, CRE 3542) Crea Tea Assocs.

Old Testament Healings, Vol. 1 of 7. Gordon Lindsay. (Miracles in the Bible Ser.: Vol. 1). 1976. 2.95 (*0-89985-179-7*) Christ for the Nations.

***Old Testament Hidden Pictures: Bible Story Puzzle.** 1998. pap. 6.95 (*0-7647-0437-0*) Schaffer Pubns.

Old Testament History. John H. Sailhamer. LC 97-45989. 96p. 1998. pap. 6.99 (*0-310-20394-5*) Zondervan.

Old Testament in Fiction & Film. Larry J. Kreitzer. LC 95-176928. (Biblical Seminar Ser.: Vol. 24). 243p. 1994. pap. 28.50 (*1-85075-487-X*, Pub. by Sheffield Acad) CUP Services.

Old Testament in Scots. Jamie Stuart. 112p. 1993. pap. 30.00 (*0-7152-0691-5*, Pub. by St Andrew) St Mut.

Old Testament in Syriac According to the Peshitta Version Pt. II, Fasc. 1a: Job. L. G. Rignell. LC 78-339247. xix, 55p. 1993. reprint ed. 56.00 (*90-04-06342-0*) Brill Academic Pubs.

Old Testament in Syriac According to the Peshitta Version Pt. III, Fasc. 1: Isaiah. S. P. Brock. LC 78-339247. xxxix, 121p. 1993. reprint ed. 86.00 (*90-04-07766-9*) Brill Academic Pubs.

Old Testament in Syriac According to the Peshitta Version Pt. III, Fasc. 3: Ezekiel. M. J. Mulder. LC 78-339247. xxxvi, 113p. 1993. reprint ed. 79.00 (*90-04-07314-0*) Brill Academic Pubs.

Old Testament in the Book of Revelation. Steve P. Moyise. (JSNT Supplement Ser.: Vol. 115). 173p. 1995. 52.50 (*1-85075-554-X*, Pub. by Sheffield Acad) CUP Services.

Old Testament in the Gospel Passion Narratives. D. J. Moo. (Almond Press Individual Titles Ser.). 464p. 1975. pap. 18.95 (*0-907459-29-3*, Pub. by Sheffield Acad) CUP Services.

Old Testament in the New: An Argument for Biblical Inspiration. S. Lewis Johnson. (Contemporary Evangelical Perspective Ser.). 128p. (Orig.). 1980. pap. 7.95 (*0-310-41851-8*, 18244P) Zondervan.

***Old Testament in the New Testament: Essays in Honour of J. L. North.** Ed. by Steve Moyise. (Journal for the Study of the New Testament, Supplement Ser.: No. 189). 304p. 2000. 82.00 (*1-84127-061-X*, Pub. by Sheffield Acad) CUP Services.

Old Testament in the New Testament Church. Michael Pomazansky. 40p. (Orig.). 1994. pap. 2.00 (*0-317-30281-7*) Holy Trinity.

Old Testament in the Old Princeton School (1812-1929) Marion A. Taylor. LC 92-6907. 596p. 1992. lib. bdg. 119.95 (*0-7734-9824-9*) E Mellen.

Old Testament Interpretation: Past, Present & Future Essays in Honor of Gene M. Tucker. James L. Mays et al. 400p. (Orig.). 1995. pap. 20.00 (*0-687-13871-X*) Dimen for Liv.

Old Testament Introduction. Edwin C. Hostetter. LC 95-8768. (IBR Bibliographies Ser.). 112p. (C). 1995. pap. 7.99 (*0-8010-2017-4*) Baker Bks.

Old Testament Introduction, 3 vols. Paul N. Tarazi. Incl. Vol. 1. Historical Traditions. 173p. (Orig.). 1990. pap. 9.95 (*0-88141-105-1*); Vol. 3. Psalms & Wisdom. LC 91-26542. 251p. (Orig.). 1996. pap. 9.95 (*0-88141-107-8*); Vol. 2. Prophetic Traditions. LC 91-26542. 240p. (Orig.). 1994. pap. 10.95 (*0-88141-106-X*); 26.95 (*0-88141-108-6*) St Vladimirs.

Old Testament Introduction. Werner H. Schmidt. 384p. 1990. reprint ed. pap. 16.95 (*0-8245-1051-8*) Crossroad NY.

***Old Testament Introduction.** 2nd ed. Werner H. Schmidt. LC 99-32845. 475p. 2000. pap. 44.95 (*0-664-22195-5*, Pub. by Westminster John Knox) Presbyterian Pub.

Old Testament Kings. Carolyn Nystrom. (LifeGuide Bible Studies). 64p. (Orig.). 1993. pap., wbk. ed. 4.99 (*0-8308-1070-6*, 1070) InterVarsity.

Old Testament Life & Literature. James A. Borland. (Illus.). 194p. (C). 1989. pap. text 15.95 (*0-936461-02-0*) Univ Book Hse.

Old Testament Made Simple. Melton Short. 112p. 1994. pap. text 10.00 (*0-9643096-0-2*) Wrld Impact.

Old Testament Men of Faith. F. B. Meyer. (World Classic Reference Library). 575p. 1995. reprint ed. 19.99 (*0-529-10423-7*, OTMF) World Publng.

O

Old Testament Miniatures: A Medieval Picture Book with 283 Paintings from the Creation to the Story of David. Sydney C. Cockerell & John Plummer. LC 75-82000. (Illus.). 210p. 1969. boxed set 125.00 (*0-8076-0513-1*, Pub. by Braziller) Norton.

***Old Testament Names of God.** W. H. Lockyear. 499p. 1999. pap. 38.00 (*1-57910-281-6*) Wipf & Stock.

Old Testament Notes. Charles H. Patterson. (Cliffs Notes Ser.). 96p. 1965. pap. 4.95 (*0-8220-0949-8*, Cliff) IDG Bks.

Old Testament Parallels: Laws & Stories from the Ancient Near East. 2nd expanded rev. ed. Victor H. Matthews & Don C. Benjamin. LC 97-15575. 384p. 1997. pap. 19.95 (*0-8091-3731-3*, 3731-3) Paulist Pr.

Old Testament Parsing Guide. rev. ed. Todd S. Beall et al. 688p. 2000. 32.99 (*0-8054-2032-0*) Broadman.

Old Testament Pictures of God. Rex Mason. LC 93-28067. 216p. 1993. pap. 16.00 (*1-880837-33-1*) Smyth & Helwys.

Old Testament Priests & the New Priest. Albert Vanhoye. Tr. by Bernard Orchard from FRE. LC 85-2171. (Studies in Scripture: Vol. II).Tr. of Pretres anciens, pretre nouveau selon le nouveau testament. 333p. 1986. pap. 24.95 (*0-932506-38-0*) St Bedes Pubns.

Old Testament Prophecy: From Oracle to Canon. Ronald E. Clements. 288p. 1996. 32.95 (*0-664-22082-7*) Westminster John Knox.

Old Testament Prophets see Portavoces del Eterno

Old Testament Pseudepigrapha, 2 vols., Set. Ed. by James H. Charlesworth. 1056p. 1986. boxed set 80.00 (*0-385-19491-9*) Doubleday.

Old Testament Pseudepigrapha Vol. I: Apocalyptic Literature & Testaments, Vol. 1. Ed. by James H. Charlesworth. LC 80-2443. 1056p. 1983. 49.95 (*0-385-09630-5*) Doubleday.

Old Testament Pseudepigrapha Vol. II: Expansions of the Old Testament & Legends, Wisdom & Philosophical Literature, Prayers, Psalms & Odes, Fragments of Lost Judeo-Hellenistic Words, Vol. 2. Ed. by James H. Charlesworth. 1056p. 1985. 49.95 (*0-385-18813-7*) Doubleday.

***Old Testament Pseudepigrapha & the New Testament: Prolegomena for the Study of Christian Origins.** James H. Charlesworth. LC 98-39834. 192p. 1998. pap. 17.00 (*1-56338-257-1*) TPI PA.

Old Testament Puzzle Books: The Beautiful - Rebecca. Ros Woodman. (Illus.). 1996. 2.50 (*1-85792-139-9*, Pub. by Christian Focus) Spring Arbor Dist.

Old Testament Puzzle Books: The Great Celebration - Hezekiah. Ros Woodman. (Illus.). 1996. 2.50 (*1-85792-138-0*, Pub. by Christian Focus) Spring Arbor Dist.

Old Testament Quotations in the New Testament. 3rd ed. Ed. by Robert G. Bratcher. LC 87-18632. xii, 88p. 1987. pap. 6.99 (*0-8267-0031-4*, 102739) Untd Bible Soc.

Old Testament Read-Along Video. Little Mooring Staff. 1995. 9.99 incl. VHS (*0-679-87639-1*) Random.

Old Testament Role Models for the Bride of Jesus Christ. 3rd rev. ed. B. R. Hicks. (Illus.). 59p. 1993. pap. 3.50 (*1-58363-065-1*, B-1301) Christ Gospel.

Old Testament Roots for New Testament Faith see Teologia del Antiguo Testamento, Raices para la Fe Neotestamentaria

Old Testament Roots of Our Faith. 8th rev. ed. Paul J. Achtemeier & Elizabeth Achtemeier. 142p. 1994. pap. 9.95 (*1-56563-144-7*) Hendrickson MA.

***Old Testament Sampler.** 2000. pap. 16.00 (*1-891833-10-3*) Davidson Pr.

Old Testament Scriptures. Michael Castoro, Sr. Date not set. 3.99 (*0-9660781-5-2*) St Michael Archangel Soc.

Old Testament Scrolls of Obadiah, Jonah & Micah. Comment by J. J. Hurtak. 108p. 1984. 7.00 (*0-9603450-9-4*) Acad Future Sci.

Old Testament Set. 70.00 (*0-687-09621-9*) Abingdon.

***Old Testament Speaks: A Complete Survey of Old Testament Histo.** 5th ed. Samuel J. Schultz. 464p. 2000. 29.00 (*0-06-251674-4*) HarpC.

Old Testament Speaks: A Complete Survey of Old Testament History & Literature. 4th ed. Samuel J. Schultz. LC 89-46250. (Illus.). 448p. 1990. 26.00 (*0-06-250767-2*, Pub. by Harper SF) HarpC.

Old Testament Sticker Book. Kathy B. Smith. (Illus.). 32p. (Orig.). (J). (gr. k-6). 1993. pap. 3.95 (*1-879424-63-0*) Nickel Pr.

Old Testament Stories: For Church & Home. Elaine M. Ward. 70p. (Orig.). (J). (gr. 1-8). 1984. pap. 7.95 (*0-940754-19-3*) Ed Ministries.

Old Testament Stories: The Kid's Translation. Mark Lawrence. (Orig.). 1997. pap. 5.75 (*0-7880-0768-8*) CSS OH.

Old Testament Stories from the Back Side. J. Ellsworth Kalas. (Orig.). 10.00 (*0-687-08186-6*) Abingdon.

Old Testament Story. Benjamin. (Religion Ser.). 1919. mass mkt. 33.95 (*0-534-19188-6*) Wadsworth Pub.

Old Testament Story. 5th ed. (C). 2000. write for info. (*0-13-016286-8*) P-H.

Old Testament Story. 5th ed. Ed. by Prentice-Hall Staff. LC 99-19378. (Illus.). 397p. (C). 1999. 57.00 (*0-13-011293-3*) P-H.

Old Testament Studies. Rudolf Frieling. 160p. 1990. 29.50 (*0-86315-057-8*, 1246, Pub. by Floris Bks) Anthroposophic.

Old Testament Survey. Paul R. House. 224p. 1992. 26.99 (*0-8054-1015-5*, 4210-15) Broadman.

Old Testament Survey. Ken Malmin & Kevin Conner. 47p. 1974. pap. 5.99 (*0-914936-21-2*) City Bible Pub.

***Old Testament Survey.** Samuel J. Schultz & Clarence H. Benson. (Discovery Ser.). Orig. Title: Broadening Your Biblical Horizons - Old Testament Survey Pts. 1 & 2. (Illus.). 212p. 1999. pap. text. write for info. (*1-891110-08-X*, ATTS Pubns) Africa Theolog Trng.

Old Testament Survey: The Message, Form & Background of the Old Testament. 2nd ed. William S. La Sor et al. (Illus.). 877p. (C). 1996. text 45.00 (*0-8028-3788-3*) Eerdmans.

Old Testament Survey, Genesis-Esther Pt. 1: Broadening Your Biblical Horizons. LC 64-10037. 90p. 1985. teacher ed., ring bd. 24.95 (*0-910566-20-8*) Evang Trg Assn.

Old Testament Survey, Genesis-Esther Pt. 1: Broadening Your Biblical Horizons. rev. ed. Samuel J. Schultz. LC 64-10037. 96p. 1968. pap. text 9.95 (*0-910566-01-1*) Evang Trg Assn.

Old Testament Survey, Job-Malachi Pt. 2: Broadening Your Biblical Horizons. 90p. 1991. teacher ed., ring bd. 24.95 (*0-910566-49-6*) Evang Trg Assn.

Old Testament Survey, Job-Malachi Pt. 2: Broadening Your Biblical Horizons. Gary V. Smith. 96p. 1991. pap. text 9.95 (*0-910566-47-X*) Evang Trg Assn.

Old Testament Survey I: Genesis-Esther. Bob Utley. (Illus.). 117p. 1997. ring bd. 20.00 (*0-9661098-7-2*) Bible Lessons.

Old Testament Survey II: Job-Malachi. Bob Utley. (Illus.). 143p. 1997. ring bd. 20.00 (*0-9661098-8-0*) Bible Lessons.

Old Testament Textual Criticism: A Practical Introduction. Ellis R. Brotzman. LC 93-42726. (Illus.). 208p. 1993. pap. 10.99 (*0-8010-1065-9*) Baker Bks.

***Old Testament Themes.** Victor H. Matthews. 2000. pap. 15.99 (*0-8272-2712-4*) Chalice Pr.

Old Testament Theology. Paul R. House. LC 98-8087. 600p. 1998. 34.99 (*0-8308-1523-6*, 1523) InterVarsity.

Old Testament Theology. Elmer A. Martens. LC 97-34326. (IBR Bibliographies Ser.). 144p. (C). 1997. pap. 11.99 (*0-8010-2146-4*) Baker Bks.

Old Testament Theology. Horst D. Preuss. Tr. by Leo G. Perdue. (Old Testament Library: Vol. 1). 384p. 1995. 34.00 (*0-664-21844-X*) Westminster John Knox.

Old Testament Theology. Horts D. Preuss. Tr. by Leo G. Purdue from GER. (Old Testament Library: Vol. 2). 432p. 1996. 34.00 (*0-664-21843-1*) Westminster John Knox.

Old Testament Theology: Basic Issues in the Current Debate. 4th rev. ed. Gerhard F. Hasel. 304p. (C). 1991. pap. text 16.00 (*0-8028-0537-X*) Eerdmans.

Old Testament Theology: Essays on Structure, Theme, & Text. Walter Brueggemann. Ed. by Patrick D. Miller. LC 91-37202. 336p. 1992. pap. 24.00 (*0-8006-2537-4*, 1-2537) Augsburg Fortress.

Old Testament Theology in a Canonical Context. Brevard S. Childs. LC 85-45503. 272p. 1986. pap. 21.00 (*0-8006-2772-5*, 1-2772, Fortress Pr) Augsburg Fortress.

Old Testament Theology in Outline. Walther Zimmerli. Tr. by David Green. 258p. 1978. pap. 24.95 (*0-567-22353-1*, Pub. by T & T Clark) Bks Intl VA.

Old Testament Theology of the Spirit of God. Wilf Hildebrandt. LC 95-2442. 238p. 1995. pap. 14.95 (*1-56563-051-3*) Hendrickson MA.

Old Testament VALUable Bible Plays. Darlene E. Resling. (VALUable Bible Plays Ser.: Bk. 1). 48p. 1998. 6.95 (*1-878669-78-8*) Crea Tea Assocs.

Old Testament Wisdom. Manly P. Hall. pap. 15.95 (*0-89314-827-X*) Philos Res.

Old Testament Wisdom: An Introduction. James L. Crenshaw. LC 80-82183. 262p. (C). 1981. pap. 18.95 (*0-8042-0142-0*) Westminster John Knox.

Old Testament Wisdom: An Introduction. enl. rev. ed. James L. Crenshaw. LC 98-7520. xv, 255p. 1998. pap. 20.00 (*0-664-25462-4*) Westminster John Knox.

Old Testament Word Search Puzzles. Gertrude Knabbe. 68p. (Orig.). (YA). (gr. 3 up). 1995. pap. 1.99 (*0-87813-560-X*) Christian Light.

Old Testament Yahweh Texts in Paul's Christology. David B. Capes. (Wissenschaftliche Untersuchungen Zum Neuen Testament Ser.: No. 2, Pt. 47). 220p. (Orig.). 1992. pap. 62.50 (*3-16-145819-2*, Pub. by JCB Mohr) Coronet Bks.

***Old Texts, New Sermons: The Quiet Revolution in Biblical Preaching.** Joseph M. Webb. LC 99-50558. 190p. 2000. pap. 21.99 (*0-8272-2711-6*) Chalice Pr.

Old Theatre Days & Ways. William J. Lawrence. LC 68-20236. 255p. 1972. reprint ed. 20.95 (*0-405-08737-3*, Pub. by Blom Pubns) Ayer.

Old Three Waters. Robert Glover. LC 96-1504. (Illus.). (J). 1996. 12.95 (*1-56763-176-2*); pap. 5.95 (*1-56763-177-0*) Ozark Pub.

***Old Thunder & Miss Raney.** Sharon Darrow. LC 99-462361. (Illus.). 32p. (J). (ps-3). 2000. 15.95 (*0-7894-2619-6*, D K Ink) DK Pub Inc.

Old Ties. Saxon Bennett. LC 96-39471. 208p. (Orig.). 1997. pap. 11.95 (*1-56280-159-7*) Naiad Pr.

Old Tiger Inn, Beverley. John Markham. (C). 1989. text 40.00 (*0-948929-15-4*) St Mut.

Old-Time Advertising Cuts. Stephen O. Saxe. (Illus.). 192p. 1989. pap. 6.95 (*0-486-26023-2*) Dover.

Old-Time Angels Stickers: 26 Pressure-Sensitive Designs. Carol Belanger Grafton. (Illus.). (J). 1993. pap. 1.00 (*0-486-27466-7*) Dover.

Old-Time Animal Vignettes in Full Color. Ed. by Carol B. Grafton. (Illus.). 48p. 1995. pap. 6.95 (*0-486-28510-3*) Dover.

Old-Time Art of Thrift. Ed. by Ken Tate. LC 97-70768. (Good Old Days Ser.). (Illus.). 160p. 1997. 14.97 (*1-882138-27-9*) Hse White Birches.

Old-Time Autos in the Ads. Robert F. Karolevitz. LC 73-86937. 120p. (Orig.). 1973. pap. 7.95 (*0-914161-03-6*) Dakota Homestead Pub.

***Old-Time Babies.** Carol Belanger Grafton. (Illus.). 2000. pap. 1.00 (*0-486-41085-4*) Dover.

Old-Time Baseball Trivia The Stormy Years 1969-89. Kerry Banks. 1999. pap. text 5.95 (*1-55054-675-9*) DGL.

Old-Time Bird Vignettes in Full Color. Ed. by Carol B. Grafton. (Illus.). 48p. 1998. pap. 9.95 (*0-486-40267-3*) Dover.

Old-Time Birds. Carol Belanger Grafton. 1997. 2.50 (*0-486-29832-9*) Dover.

***Old-Time Brand-Name Desserts.** Bunny Crumpacker. (Illus.). 96p. 2000. 12.98 (*0-7651-1653-7*) Smithmark.

***Old-Time Brand-Name Recipe Cookbook.** Bunny Crumpacker. LC 97-62144. (Illus.). 160p. 1998. 12.98 (*0-7651-9077-X*) Smithmark.

Old-Time Bunny Rabbit Stickers. Maggie Kate. (Illus.). (J). 1996. pap. 1.00 (*0-486-28874-9*) Dover.

Old-Time Butterfly Vignettes in Full Color. Ed. by Carol B. Grafton. LC 98-116310. (Illus.). 48p. pap. 7.95 (*0-486-29860-4*) Dover.

Old Time Cattlemen: And Other Pioneers of the Anza-Borrego Area. 3rd ed. Lester Reed. 146p. 1986. reprint ed. pap. 7.95 (*0-910805-02-4*) Anza-Borrego.

Old-Time Children Vignettes in Full Color. Ed. by Carol B. Grafton. (Illus.). 48p. pap. 7.95 (*0-486-29581-8*) Dover.

***Old-Time Children with Dolls Stickers.** Carol Belanger Grafton. (J). 1999. pap. text 1.00 (*0-486-40833-7*) Dover.

Old-Time Children's Stickers. Carol Belanger Grafton. (Illus.). (J). 1991. pap. text 1.00 (*0-486-26790-3*) Dover.

Old-Time Christmas. Helen Steiner Rice & Virginia J. Ruehlmann. LC 97-15594. (Illus.). 96p. 1997. 19.99 (*0-8007-1744-9*) Revell.

Old Time Christmas Angels Stickers. Maggie Kate. (Illus.). (J). 1997. pap. text 1.00 (*0-486-29726-8*) Dover.

Old-Time Christmas Stickers. Ed. by Dover Publications Staff. (Illus.). (J). 1997. pap. 1.00 (*0-486-27146-3*) Dover.

Old-Time Christmas Vignettes in Full Color. Ed. by Carol B. Grafton. LC 99-207050. (Illus.). 48p. 1998. pap. 8.95 (*0-486-40255-X*) Dover.

Old-Time Cigar Labels in Full Color. Ed. by Carol B. Grafton. (Illus.). 1996. pap. 8.95 (*0-486-29052-2*) Dover.

Old Time Circus Cuts: A Pictorial Archive of Two Hundred & Two Illustrations. Ed. by Charles P. Fox. LC 79-50262. (Pictorial Archive Ser.). (Illus.). 128p. 1979. pap. 8.95 (*0-486-23653-6*) Dover.

***Old-Time Circus Stickers.** Maggie Kate. (Illus.). (J). 1999. pap. 1.00 (*0-486-40602-4*) Dover.

Old Time College President. George P. Schmidt. LC 75-127432. (Columbia University. Studies in the Social Sciences: No. 317). reprint ed. 31.50 (*0-404-51317-4*) AMS Pr.

Old-Time Country Guitar. Fly Bredenberg & Stephen Cichetti. (Illus.). 96p. 1976. pap. 17.95 (*0-8256-0167-3*, OK63172, Oak) Music Sales.

Old-Time Country Wisdom: A Celebration of Good Old-Fashioned Common Sense. Criswell Freeman. 1997. pap. text 6.95 (*1-887655-26-3*) Walnut Gr Pr.

Old-Time Cowboy Songbook. Will M. Clauson. 160p. 1996. pap. 17.95 (*0-7866-0200-7*, MB95350) Mel Bay.

***Old-Time Crochet Made Easy.** Ed. by Laura Scott. (Illus.). 176p. 2000. write for info. (*1-882138-65-1*) Hse White Birches.

Old Time Cures-Farmers Folklore. David J. Gerrick & Doreen Dietsche. 104p. (Orig.). 1980. pap. 3.95 (*0-916750-41-8*) Dayton Labs.

Old-Time Easter Animal Stickers. Carol B. Grafton. (Illus.). (J). (gr. 4-7). 1994. pap. 1.00 (*0-486-27843-3*) Dover.

Old-Time Fans Stickers. Carol Belanger Grafton. (Illus.). (J). 1995. pap. 1.00 (*0-486-28429-8*) Dover.

Old-Time Favorites. American Diabetes Association. (Month of Meals Ser.). 64p. 1998. pap. 14.95 (*1-58040-017-5*, 00175Q, Pub. by Am Diabetes) NTC Contemp Pub Co.

Old Time Fiddle Solos. Bay, Mel, Publications, Inc. Staff. 24p. 1977. pap. 6.95 (*0-87166-880-7*, 93449) Mel Bay.

Old-Time Fiddler's Repertory: Two Hundred Forty-Five Traditional Tunes, Vol. 2. R. P. Christeson. 188p. 1984. 27.50 (*0-8262-0440-6*) U of Mo Pr.

Old-Time Fiddling Across America. David Reiner & Peter Anick. 184p. 1989. pap. 17.95 (*0-87166-766-5*, 94205); audio 9.98 (*1-56222-641-X*, 94205C) Mel Bay.

Old-Time Fiddling Across America. David Reiner & Peter Anick. 1993. pap., spiral bd. 23.95 incl. audio (*0-7866-0975-3*, 94205P) Mel Bay.

***Old-Time Frames & Borders in Full Color.** Carol Belanger Grafton. (Illus.). 2000. pap. 9.95 (*0-486-41079-X*) Dover.

Old-Time Fruit Crate Labels in Full Color. Ed. by Carol B. Grafton. LC 99-182234. (Illus.). 48p. 1998. pap. 8.95 (*0-486-40006-9*) Dover.

***Old Time Fruits & Flowers Vignettes in Full Color: Made with Acid-Free Paper & Inks.** Carol Belanger Grafton. 48p. 1999. text 9.95 (*0-486-40704-7*) Dover.

***Old-Time Gospel Banjo Solos.** Jack Hatfield. 112p. 1998. pap. 17.95 (*0-7866-3082-5*, 96755) Mel Bay.

***Old-Time Gospel Banjo Solos.** Jack Hatfield. 112p. 1998. 32.95 incl. audio compact disk (*0-7866-3826-5*, 96775CDP) Mel Bay.

Old Time Gospel Piano. Tr. by Linda Cummings. 96p. 1996. 15.98 incl. audio compact disk (*0-7866-2502-3*, 96320) Mel Bay.

Old Time Gospel Piano CD Package. Stan Whitmire. 64p. 1996. 25.95 (*0-7866-2816-2*, 96320COP) Mel Bay.

Old Time Gospel Songbook. Wayne Erbsen. 80p. 1997. pap. 24.95 incl. audio compact disk (*0-7866-3233-X*, 95033CDP) Mel Bay.

Old Time Gospel Songs for EZ Play Guitar. (E-Z Guitar Ser.). 1996. pap. 9.95 (*0-7935-6006-3*) H Leonard.

Old Time Herbs for Northern Gardens. Minnie W. Kamm. (Illus.). 1971. reprint ed. pap. 6.95 (*0-486-22695-6*) Dover.

Old-Time Home Remedies. Ed. by Ken Tate. LC 97-72868. (Illus.). 160p. 1998. 14.97 (*1-882138-30-9*) Hse White Birches.

***Old-Time Horses Notebook.** Maggie Kate. (Illus.). (J). 1999. pap. 1.00 (*0-486-40609-1*) Dover.

Old-Time Horses-Stickers. Carol Belanger Grafton. (Illus.). (J). 1993. pap. 1.00 (*0-486-27467-5*) Dover.

Old-Time Makers of Medicine. James J. Walsh. LC 75-23767. reprint ed. 36.00 (*0-404-13394-0*) AMS Pr.

Old Time Masquerading in the U. S. Virgin Islands. Robert W. Nicholls. (Illus.). 256p. 1998. pap. 15.00 (*1-886007-09-8*) VI Human Coun.

Old-Time Minature Animal Stickers. Maggie Kate. (Illus.). (J). 1995. pap. 1.00 (*0-486-28430-1*) Dover.

Old Time Mountain Banjo. Art Rosenbaum. (Illus.). 88p. 1968. pap. 15.95 (*0-8256-0116-9*, OK62034, Oak) Music Sales.

Old Time Music Makers of New York State. Simon J. Bronner. (New York State Bks.). (Illus.). 304p. 1987. 42.95 (*0-8156-0216-2*) Syracuse U Pr.

Old-Time New England Cookbook. Duncan MacDonald & Robb Sagendorph. LC 92-47279. Orig. Title: Rain, Hail, & Baked Beans: A New England Seasonal Cookbook. (Illus.). 224p. 1993. reprint ed. pap. 6.95 (*0-486-27630-9*) Dover.

Old Time Power. rev. ed. Vinson Synan. LC 98-75221. 1998. pap. 18.95 (*0-911866-67-1*) LifeSprings Res.

Old-Time Preacher Men. Compiled by Mary Wallace. LC 92-11302. (Illus.). 288p. (Orig.). 1992. pap. 8.99 (*1-56722-000-2*) Word Aflame.

Old Time Products: A Catalogue. 1992. lib. bdg. 79.95 (*0-8490-5344-7*) Gordon Pr.

Old-Time Radios: Restoration & Repair. Joseph J. Carr. (Illus.). 256p. 1990. pap. 16.95 (*0-8306-3342-1*) McGraw-Hill Prof.

Old-Time Radios! Restoration & Repair. Joseph J. Carr. 264p. 1992. pap. 19.95 (*0-07-155735-0*) McGraw.

Old-Time Remedies for Modern Ailments. Hanna Kroeger. 105p. (Orig.). 1971. pap. 5.00 (*1-883713-05-6*) Hanna Kroeger.

Old Time Rock 'n Roll. 176p. 1995. per. 14.95 (*0-7935-4432-7*, 00310038) H Leonard.

Old Time Rock 'n Roll. 176p. 1995. per. 14.95 (*0-7935-4433-5*, 00222502) H Leonard.

Old Time Rock 'n Roll: Big Note for Piano. 64p. 1995. pap. 9.95 (*0-7935-4434-3*, 00221830) H Leonard.

Old-Time Romantic Vignettes in Full Color. Ed. by Carol B. Grafton. (Illus.). 48p. pap. 7.95 (*0-486-29221-5*) Dover.

Old Time Roses Notebook. Grafton. 1998. pap. 1.00 (*0-486-40232-0*, 884105Q) Dover.

Old-Time Schools & School-Books. Clifton Johnson. LC 99-42784. (Illus.). 381p. 1999. reprint ed. lib. bdg. 44.00 (*1-55888-205-7*) Omnigraphics Inc.

Old-Time Silhouettes. Compiled by Judy M. Johnson. LC 93-45545. (Pictorial Archive Ser.). (Illus.). 80p. 1994. pap. 7.95 (*0-486-27940-5*) Dover.

Old-Time Southern Cooking. Laurie Stickland & Elizabeth Dunn. LC 93-43037. (Illus.). 144p. 1994. pap. 11.95 (*1-56554-020-4*) Pelican.

Old-Time String Band Songbook. Ed. by John Cohen & Mike Seger. (Illus.). 240p. 1976. pap. 17.95 (*0-8256-0179-7*, OK63255, Oak) Music Sales.

Old-Time Tools & Toys of Needlework. Gertrude Whiting. (Illus.). 357p. 1970. pap. 11.95 (*0-486-22517-8*) Dover.

Old-Time Toys see Historic Communities Series

Old-Time Toys. Bobbie Kalman. (Historic Communities Ser.). 1995. 13.40 (*0-606-07965-3*) Turtleback.

Old Time Violin Melodies, Bk. 1. W. H. Morris. 25p. 1992. pap. 10.00 (*0-9637812-1-9*) MO St Old Time.

Old Time Whittling: An Introductory Text by Keith Randich. Keith Randich. LC 94-92208. (Illus.). 60p. (Orig.). 1994. pap. 9.95 (*0-9642327-2-3*) K Randich Pubng.

Old Timers The One That Got Away. Noa Schwartz. 1998. pap. text 5.95 (*0-9683303-1-2*) Tumbleweed Pr.

Old Timers Childhood Memories. Donald P. Schulz. Ed. by Sandi S. Frank. LC 95-79010. 100p. (Orig.). pap. write for info. (*0-9645945-3-6*) Sheraton Pub.

***Old Timer's Motorcycle Tall Tales.** Ed Robinson. (Illus.). 182p. 1999. pap. write for info. (*0-9673116-0-8*) WordPro Pr.

Old Timers' Reunion: Reflecting on Early Days in Arlington Heights. Margery Frisbie. (Illus.). vi, 54p. (Orig.). 1997. pap. 6.95 (*0-9658085-0-5*) Frisbie Comns.

Old Times. Bill Brooks. 1995. mass mkt. 4.50 (*0-8217-5109-3*, Zebra Kensgtn) Kensgtn Pub Corp.

Old Times. Harold Pinter. LC 72-182581. 80p. 1989. pap. 7.95 (*0-8021-5029-2*, Grove) Grove-Atltic.

Old Times: San Luis Obispo CA Memoirs. Charles A. Maino. Ed. by Jeannette G. Maino. 50p. (Orig.). 1990. write for info. (*0-318-66925-0*) Dry Creeks Bks.

Old Times in Contra Costa: A Journey to the Past. Robert D. Tatam. 208p. 1993. pap. 14.99 (*0-9637954-0-6*) Highlnd Pubs.

***Old Times in Old Monmouth: Historical Reminiscences of Old Monmouth County, New Jersey Being a Series of Historical Sketches Relating to Old Monmouth County (Now Monmouth & Ocean)** Edwin Salter. 487p. 1999. reprint ed. (*0-7884-1228-0*, S049) Heritage Bk.

Old Times in Stanislaus County: A Journey to the Past. Robert D. Tatam & Loicy Myers. (Illus.). 182p. (Orig.). pap. 14.99 (*0-9637954-2-2*) Highlnd Pubs.

***Old Times in the Colonies.** Charles Coffin. (Illus.). 460p. 2000. write for info. (*1-889128-68-6*) Mantle Ministries.

Old Times on the Mississippi. Mark Twain, pseud. LC 97-60838. (Public Library Ser.). 192p. 1997. pap. 4.95 (*0-87243-233-5*) Templegate.

O

An Asterisk (*) at the beginning of an entry indicates that the title is appearing for the first time.

Old Times There Are Not Forgotten, Bk. 1 of 3. Michael R. Bradley. 62p. (Orig.). 1992. pap. 8.95 (*0-9624100-7-1*) Bell Buckle.

Old Times There Are Not Forgotten: Tales from Sowega. Ross Malone. 136p. 1995. text 14.95 (*0-941072-16-9*) Southern Herit.

Old Timey Southern Talk. Ray E. Cunningham. 1986. 6.95 (*0-8187-0069-6*) Harlo Press.

Old Tioga & Ninety Years of Existence: A Descriptive, Statistical & Chronological History of Tioga County from Its Earliest Settlement to (1877) Maro O. Rolfe. (Illus.). 116p. 1997. reprint ed. pap. 15.00 (*0-8328-6455-2*) Higginson Bk Co.

Old Tippecanoe: William Henry Harrison & His Times. Freeman Cleaves. Ed. by Katherine E. Speirs. LC 90-80486. (Signature Ser.). (Illus.). 420p. 1990. reprint ed. 30.00 (*0-945707-01-0*) Amer Political.

Old Tired Giving Tree. Janie S. Gill. (Illus.). 23p. 1999. 5.95 (*0-89868-445-5*); lib. bdg. 10.95 (*0-89868-443-9*) ARO Pub.

Old Tokyo: Walks in the City of the Shogun. Sumiko Enbutsu. (Illus.). 216p. 1993. pap. 16.95 (*0-8048-1874-6*) Tuttle Pubng.

Old Tom & Young Tom: A Commentary on the Monographs. George Wing. LC 72-180834. (Monographs on the Life, Times & Works of Thomas Hardy). 509-539 P.p. 1971. write for info. (*0-900749-60-1*) Toucan Pr OH.

Old Tom, Young Tom. Thomas B. Adams. 376p. 1988. 19.95 (*0-933905-11-4*); pap. 12.95 (*0-933905-12-2*) Claycomb Pr.

Old Tombstones & Unusual Cemeteries in Columbia County, New York Vol. 1: Eastern Columbia County. Gerda E. Divine. 148p. 1988. reprint ed. pap. 12.00 (*1-56012-088-6*, 88) Kinship Rhinebeck.

***Old Tools - New Eyes: A Primal Primer of Flintknapping.** Bob Patten. (Illus.). 160p. 1999. pap. 13.95 (*0-9668701-0-7*) Stone Dagger.

Old Tools, Town & Country: Locks, Keys, & Closures. 3rd rev. ed. Jack P. Wood. Ed. by L-W Book Publishing Staff. (Illus.). 290p. 1996. pap. 12.95 (*0-89145-417-9*) L-W Inc.

Old Torquay Potteries. D. Lloyd Thomas & E. Lloyd Thomas. 319p. (C). 1989. 75.00 (*0-7223-1103-6*, Pub. by A H S Ltd) St Mut.

Old Town. Matthew Brady. 96p. 1992. pap. text 5.95 (*0-9631643-2-5*) SF Ind Newspaper.

Old Town Albuquerque: The Story of a Famous New Mexico Town. rev. ed. Peter Hertzog. Ed. by James C. Smith, Jr. LC 94-42799. (Illus.). 16p. (Orig.). 1994. pap. 4.95 (*0-86534-000-5*) Sunstone Pr.

Old Town-Albuquerque in the 1940's & a Little Beyond. Bette D. Casteel et al. (Illus.). 52p. 1996. per. 8.00 (*0-9654431-9-1*) Chaparral Press.

Old Town Art Fair: 50 Years & Counting. Ed. by Diane Gonzalez. LC 99-90585. (Illus.). 64p. 1999. pap. 20.00 (*0-9672296-0-X*) Old Town Tri.

Old Town by the Sea. Thomas Bailey Aldrich. (Works of Thomas Bailey Aldrich). 1989. reprint ed. lib. bdg. 79.00 (*0-7812-1680-X*) Rprt Serv.

Old Town Canoe Company: Our First Hundred Years. Susan T. Audette & David E. Baker. LC 98-41658. (Illus.). 1998. 50.00 (*0-88448-202-2*); pap. 30.00 (*0-88448-203-0*) Tilbury Hse.

Old Town II: More Tales of Real Life in Early Frisco. Matthew Brady. LC 98-61865. 117 p. 1998. write for info. (*0-9665020-3-5*) Pan Asia.

Old Town San Diego Retailers Reference. 2nd ed. Mary Helmich. (Illus.). (C). pap. text 20.00 (*0-941925-18-8*) Cal Parks Rec.

Old Towpaths. Alvin F. Harlow. 403p. 1993. reprint ed. lib. bdg. 99.00 (*0-7812-5212-1*) Rprt Serv.

Old Toys. Pauline Flick. (Album Ser.). (Illus.). 32p. 1989. pap. 25.00 (*0-85263-754-3*, Pub. by Shire Pubns) Lubrecht & Cramer.

Old Tractors & the Men Who Love Them: How to Keep Your Tractors Happy & Your Family Running. Roger Welsch. LC 95-389. (Illus.). 160p. 1995. pap. 14.95 (*0-7603-0129-8*) MBI Pubg.

Old Traditional Way of Life: Essays in Honor of Warren E. Roberts. Ed. by Robert E. Walls et al. LC 89-50952. (Illus.). 400p. (Orig.). (C). 1989. pap. 14.95 (*0-915305-02-X*) Trickster Pr.

Old Trail to Love. Florence B. Smith. 164p. 1999. pap. 6.00 (*1-893463-22-2*) F B Smith.

Old Trail to Santa Fe: Collected Essays. Marc Simmons. LC 96-26016. 200p. 1996. pap. 16.95 (*0-8263-1737-5*) U of NM Pr.

Old Train see Viejo Tren

Old Train. Rich Latta. (Books for Young Learners). (Illus.). 12p. (J). (gr. k-2). 1998. pap. text 5.00 (*1-57274-133-3*, A2487) R Owen Pubs.

Old Trams. Keith Turner. (Album Ser.: No. 148). (Illus.). 32p. pap. 6.25 (*0-7478-0409-5*, Pub. by Shire Pubns) Parkwest Pubns.

Old Travois Trails. Gressley. 1976. 37.00 (*0-914074-11-3*, J M C & Co) Amereon Ltd.

Old Trolley Buses. David Kaye. (Album Ser.: No. 215). (Illus.). 32p. 1989. pap. 5.25 (*0-85263-922-8*, Pub. by Shire Pubns) Parkwest Pubns.

Old Trolley Postcards. K. P. Fletcher. 1987. pap. text 3.95 (*0-486-25320-1*) Dover.

***Old Turkic Grammar.** Marcel Erdal. (Handbook of Oriental Studies). 384p. 2000. 122.00 (*90-04-10294-9*) Brill Academic Pubs.

Old Turtle. Douglas Wood. LC 91-73527. (Illus.). 48p. (J). (ps-2). 1991. 17.95 (*0-938586-48-3*) Pfeifer-Hamilton.

Old Turtle Peace Journal. Ed. by Nancy L. Tubesing. 109p. 1994. pap. 12.95 (*1-57025-044-8*) Pfeifer-Hamilton.

Old Turtle's 90 Knock-Knocks, Jokes, & Riddles: Jokes & Riddles. Leonard Kessler. LC 89-77505. (Illus.). 48p. (J). (ps-3). 1991. 15.00 (*0-688-09585-2*, Greenwillow Bks) HarpC Child Bks.

Old Turtle's Ninety Knock-Knocks, Jokes, & Riddles. Leonard Kessler. LC 92-43782. (Illus.). 48p. (J). (gr. 1-4). 1993. pap. 5.95 (*0-688-04586-3*, Wm Morrow) Morrow Avon.

Old Tuskaloosa Land Office Records & Military Warrants, 1821-1855. Marilyn D. Hahn. (Illus.). 240p. 1984. 22.50 (*0-89308-530-8*) Southern Hist Pr.

Old Tyme Christmas in New Brunswick. David Goss. (Images of America Ser.). 1997. pap. 16.99 (*0-7524-0523-3*) Arcadia Publng.

Old Typewriters. Duncan James. (Album Ser.: No. 293). (Illus.). 32p. 1989. pap. 4.75 (*0-7478-0193-2*, Pub. by Shire Pubns) Parkwest Pubns.

Old U. S. 80 Highway Traveler's Guide: Phoenix - San Diego. Eric J. Finley. Ed. by Jon Gabriel. LC 96-92219. (Illus.). 156p. 1997. pap. 10.95 (*0-9652358-0-7*) Narrow Road.

Old Ugly Hill: A G. I.'s Fourteen Months in the Korean Trenches, 1952-1953. Rudolph W. Stephens. LC 94-24527. (Illus.). 176p. 1995. pap. 26.50 (*0-7864-0059-5*) McFarland & Co.

Old Utah Trails. William B. Smart. LC 87-51172. (Illus.). 136p. 1988. 28.95 (*0-936331-09-7*); pap. 17.95 (*0-936331-08-9*) Utah Geo Series.

Old Values in a New Town: The Politics of Race & Class in Columbia, Maryland. Lynne C. Burkhart. LC 80-26556. 165p. 1981. 45.00 (*0-275-90588-8*, C0588, Praeger Pubs) Greenwood.

Old Vengeful. Anthony Price. 224p. 1989. mass mkt. 4.95 (*0-445-40257-1*, Pub. by Warner Bks) Little.

Old Verona. Robert E. Williams. (Images of America Ser.). (Illus.). 128p. 1998. pap. 16.99 (*0-7524-0992-1*) Arcadia Publng.

Old Vic Theatre: A History. George Rowell. (Illus.). 219p. (C). 1993. text 69.95 (*0-521-34625-8*) Cambridge U Pr.

Old Village & the Great House: An Archaeological & Historical Examination of Drax Hall Plantation, St. Ann's Bay, Jamaica. Douglas V. Armstrong. (Blacks in the New World Ser.). (Illus.). 424p. 1990. text 44.95 (*0-252-01617-3*) U of Ill Pr.

Old Villita. Texas Writer's Project Staff. 1993. reprint ed. lib. bdg. 75.00 (*0-7812-5978-9*) Rprt Serv.

Old Vines, a History of Wine Growing in Amador County (CA) Eric J. Costa. Ed. by Costa & Gold Country Enterprises Staff. (Illus.). 86p. (Orig.). 1994. pap. 9.95 (*0-938121-08-1*) Cenotto Pubns.

Old Virginia & Her Neighbors. John Fiske. (Notable American Authors Ser.). 1992. reprint ed. lib. bdg. 75.00 (*0-7812-2855-7*) Rprt Serv.

Old Virginia & Her Neighbours, Vols. 1 & 2. John Fiske. 1997. reprint ed. pap. 49.50 (*0-7884-0719-8*, F376) Heritage Bk.

Old Voices, New Faces: (Soviet) Jewish Artists from the 1920's - 1990's. Ori Z. Soltes & Sonia Melnikova-Levigne. 20p. (Orig.). 1992. pap. 5.00 (*1-881456-03-X*) B B K Natl Jew Mus.

Old Warrior. Jerry Evans. LC 95-77109. 132p. (Orig.). 1995. pap. 7.95 (*0-9623698-6-1*) Magnum Pr.

Old Warsaw Cookbook. Irena Lorentowicz. 300p. pap. 12.95 (*0-87052-932-3*) Hippocrene Bks.

Old Washington, D. C. in Early Photographs. Robert Reed. LC 79-52841. (Illus.). 240p. (Orig.). 1980. pap. 12.95 (*0-486-23869-5*) Dover.

Old Waterfront Walls: Management, Maintenance & Rehabilitation. R. N. Bray & P. J. B. Tatham. (Illus.). 296p. (C). 1992. 125.00 (*0-419-17640-3*, E & FN Spon) Routledge.

Old Way of Seeing: How Architecture Lost Its Magic (& How to Get It Back) Jonathan Hale. (Illus.). 256p. 1995. pap. 18.00 (*0-395-74010-X*) HM.

Old Waybills: The Romance of the Express Companies. Alvin F. Harlow. LC 75-22820. (America in Two Centuries Ser.). (Illus.). 1976. reprint ed. 35.95 (*0-405-07692-4*) Ayer.

Old Ways. Kathleen R. Leo. Ed. by Allen Berlinski. 12p. (Orig.). 1990. pap. 4.95 (*0-941543-01-3*) Sun Dog Pr.

Old Ways New Ways. West Golden. 1992. pap. text 3.95 (*0-929526-14-7*) Double B Pubns.

Old Ways of Working Wood. Alex W. Bealer. 256p. 1996. 9.98 (*0-7858-0710-1*) Bk Sales Inc.

Old Ways Rediscovered. Clarence Meyer. Ed. by David C. Meyer. (Illus.). 156p. (Orig.). 1988. pap. 8.95 (*0-916638-18-9*) Meyerbooks.

Old Ways to Fold - New Paper. Leza Lowitz. 98p. (Orig.). 1996. pap. 10.00 (*0-9653304-1-9*) Wandering Mind.

Old Well. Yi Zheng. Tr. by David Kwan from CHI. LC 89-60882. 176p. (Orig.). 1989. 16.95 (*0-8351-2275-1*); pap. 8.95 (*0-8351-2276-X*) China Bks.

Old Welsh Airs. 30p. 1995. pap. 15.00 (*1-882712-41-2*) Dragonflower.

Old West: A Salute to Black Inventors. rev. ed. Ann C. Howell. Ed. by Evelyn L. Ivery. (Black Inventors Activity Bks.). (Illus.). 24p. (J). (gr. 3-7). 1992. reprint ed. pap. text 1.50 (*1-877804-03-7*) Chandler White.

Old West: Day by Day. Mike Flanagan. LC 94-4663. (Illus.). 512p. 1995. 60.00 (*0-8160-2689-0*) Facts on File.

Old West - New West: Centennial Essays. Ed. by Barbara H. Meldrum. LC 92-29828. 352p. (C). 1993. pap. 29.95 (*0-89301-163-0*); lib. bdg. 36.00 (*0-89301-166-5*) U of Idaho Pr.

Old West Adventures in Arizona. Charles D. Lauer. LC 88-24676. 176p. (Orig.). 1989. pap. 6.95 (*0-914846-39-6*) Golden West Pub.

Old West Baking Book. Lon Walters. LC 95-23399. (Illus.). 184p. (Orig.). 1996. spiral bd. 14.95 (*0-87358-637-9*) Northland AZ.

Old West Cookbook. Barbara Blackburn. LC 86-81884. (Illus.). 150p. 1987. pap. 14.95 (*0-934188-23-8*) Evans Pubns.

Old West Frisian - Skeltana Riucht. Sidney Fairbanks. (FRI.). xii, 176p. 1983. 27.50 (*1-57588-345-7*, 502030) W S Hein.

***Old West Hurley Revisited: A Nostalgic Tour.** Allen M. Rowe. (Illus.). 210p. 1999. pap. write for info. (*0-910746-31-1*) Hope Farm.

Old West in Fact. Ed. by Irwin R. Blacker. 1962. 27.95 (*0-8392-1081-7*) Astor-Honor.

Old West in Fiction. Ed. by Irwin R. Blacker. 1961. 27.95 (*0-8392-1082-5*) Astor-Honor.

Old West in Grant County Country. Monty Hormel. LC 92-91270. (Illus.). 75p. (Orig.). 1993. pap. 6.95 (*0-9635583-0-7*) Tamanawahs.

Old West in Miniature: Sculptures by Don Polland. Norton, R. W., Art Gallery Staff. LC 74-24491. 1974. pap. 2.50 (*0-913060-06-2*) Norton Art.

Old West, New West. Ed. by Gene M. Gressley. LC 97-9215. (Illus.). 208p. 1997. pap. 13.95 (*0-8061-2962-X*) U of Okla Pr.

Old West Pictorialized by Joe Ruiz Grandee. Norton, R. W., Art Gallery Staff. LC 79-171014. (Contemporary Realists Ser.). (Illus.). 1971. pap. 1.50 (*0-9600182-5-5*) Norton Art.

Old West Quiz & Fact Book. Rod Gragg. 1993. 6.98 (*0-88394-085-X*) Promntory Pr.

Old West Trail Cookbook: Time-Honored Recipes & New Favorites. 32p. Date not set. pap. text. write for info. (*1-56944-140-5*) Terrell Missouri.

Old West Trivia Book. Don Bullis. Ed. by Robin Shepherd. LC 92-75447. (Illus.). 160p. (Orig.). 1992. pap. 10.95 (*0-935182-62-4*) Gem Guides Bk.

***Old Westmoreland: A History of Pennsylvania During the Revolution.** Edgar W. Hassler. 200p. 1999. reprint ed. pap. 22.50 (*0-8063-4941-7*, Pub. by Clearfield Co) ACCESS Pubs Network.

Old Westmoreland: A History of Pennsylvania During the Revolution. Edgar W. Hassler. 200p. 1999. reprint ed. lib. bdg. 22.50 (*0-7812-5466-3*) Rprt Serv.

Old West/New West: Quo Vadis? Intro. by Gene M. Gressley. LC 93-80785. 196p. 1994. 27.50 (*1-881019-07-1*) High Plns WY.

Old Whaling Days. William Barron. LC 97-106459. (Conway Classics Ser.). 1998. 19.95 (*0-85177-695-7*) Brasseys.

Old Wicked Songs. Jon Marans. LC 98-178033. 1996. pap. 5.25 (*0-8222-1544-6*) Dramatists Play.

Old Wife's Tales. 2nd ed. Ed. by Charles Whitworth. (New Mermaids Ser.). pap. 7.00 (*0-393-90080-0*) Norton.

Old Windmill of Brisbane Town. Grenfell Heap. (C). 1990. pap. 30.00 (*0-908175-61-2*, Pub. by Boolarong Pubns) St Mut.

Old Wine. Phyllis Bottome. LC 98-227923. 360p. 1998. pap. text 18.95 (*0-8101-1472-0*) Northwestern U Pr.

Old Wine in a New Bottle. Murray Schisgal. 1987. pap. 5.25 (*0-8222-0844-X*) Dramatists Play.

Old Wine in New Skins: Calls to Worship & Other Worship Resources. George A. Nye. LC 93-38001. 168p. 1994. pap. 9.75 (*1-55673-824-2*, 9422) CSS OH.

***Old Wine in New Skins: Centering Prayer & Systems Theory - Congregational Leadership for the Next Millennium.** Paul D. Lawson. 2000. pap. 20.00 (*1-930051-29-8*) Lantern Books.

Old Wine in New Wineskins: Doctrinal Preaching in a Changing World. Millard J. Erickson & James L. Heflin. LC 96-53603. 272p. (YA). (gr. 12). 1997. pap. 19.99 (*0-8010-2113-8*) Baker Bks.

Old Wine, New Flasks: Reflections on Science & Jewish Tradition. Roald Hoffmann & Shira L. Schmidt. LC 97-2706. 1997. pap. text 28.95 (*0-7167-2899-0*) W H Freeman.

Old Wines--New Wineskins: Three Wise Men Enlighten Azad. Loyal E. Fields. LC 95-92277. (Illus.). 176p. (Orig.). 1995. pap. 12.95 (*0-9646662-3-5*) Candlelight IN.

Old Winter. Judith B. Richardson. LC 96-85. (Illus.). 32p. (J). (ps-2). 1996. lib. bdg. 16.99 (*0-531-08883-9*) Orchard Bks Watts.

Old Winter. Judith B. Richardson. LC 96-85. (Illus.). 32p. (J). (ps-3). 1996. 15.95 (*0-531-09533-9*) Orchard Bks Watts.

Old Wires & New Waves. Alvin F. Harlow. LC 70-161145. (History of Broadcasting: Radio to Television Ser.). 1976. reprint ed. 39.95 (*0-405-03566-7*) Ayer.

***Old Wisdom in the New World: Americanization in Two Immigrant Theravada Buddhist Temples.** Paul D. Numrich. (Illus.). 208p. 1999. pap. text 14.00 (*1-57233-063-5*) U of Tenn Pr.

Old Wives for New see Collected Works of David G. Phillips

Old Wives for New. David C. Phillips. (Collected Works of David G. Phillips). 1988. reprint ed. lib. bdg. 59.00 (*0-7812-1335-5*) Rprt Serv.

***Old Wives' Lore for Gardeners.** Maureen Boland & Bridget Boland. (Illus.). 64p. 2000. 9.95 (*1-85479-409-4*, Pub. by M OMara) Trafalgar.

***Old Wives' Tale.** Arnold Bennett. LC 99-41699. 640p. 1999. pap. 9.95 (*0-375-75490-3*) Modern Lib NY.

Old Wives' Tale. Arnold Bennett. 624p. 1991. pap. 11.95 (*0-14-018255-1*, Penguin Classics) Viking Penguin.

Old Wives Tale. Harold Bennett. 1998. pap. 3.95 (*1-85326-272-2*, Pub. by Wrdsworth Edits) NTC Contemp Pub Co.

Old Wives' Tale. Arnold Bennett. 622p. 1980. reprint ed. pap. 10.00 (*0-915864-77-0*) Academy Chi Pubs.

Old Wives' Tale. Arnold Bennett. LC 74-17060. (Collected Works of Arnold Bennett: Vol. 61). 1977. reprint ed. 47.95 (*0-518-19142-7*) Ayer.

Old Wives Tale. George Peele. Ed. by Patricia Binnie. LC 79-48011. (Revels Plays Ser.). 107p. reprint ed. pap. 33.20 (*0-608-06036-4*, 206636700008) Bks Demand.

Old Wives' Tales. Susan M. Dodd. LC 84-8879. (Iowa Short Fiction Award Ser.). 192p. (Orig.). (C). 1984. pap. 3.25 (*0-87745-133-8*) U of Iowa Pr.

Old Wives Tales, Bk. II. Peter Engel. LC 96-27926. 144p. 1996. pap. 8.95 (*0-312-14696-5*) St Martin.

Old Wives' Tales: And Other Women's Stories. Tania Modleski. (Illus.). 264p. 1998. pap. 17.95 (*0-8147-5594-1*) NYU Pr.

Old Wives' Tales: And Other Women's Stories. Tania Modlesli. LC 98-25366. (Illus.). 264p. 1998. text 55.00 (*0-8147-5593-3*) NYU Pr.

Old Wives' Tales: The Truth Behind Common Notions. Sue Castle. (Illus.). 144p. 1992. pap. 7.95 (*0-8065-1378-0*, Citadel Pr) Carol Pub Group.

Old Wolfville: Chapters from the Fiction of Alfred Henry Lewis. Ed. by Alfred H. Lewis. LC 68-13363. (Illus.). 274p. reprint ed. pap. 85.00 (*0-608-14200-X*, 202171500023) Bks Demand.

Old Woman: Of Irish Blood. Pat Andrus. 80p. (Orig.). 1996. pap. 9.95 (*0-940880-59-8*) Open Hand.

Old Woman & Her Pig. Illus. by Giora Carmi. 32p. (J). (ps-3). 1992. pap. 6.95 (*0-8234-1234-2*) Holiday.

Old Woman & Her Pig. Illus. by Giora Carmi. LC 91-44185. 32p. (J). (gr. k-3). 1992. lib. bdg. 16.95 (*0-8234-0970-8*) Holiday.

Old Woman & Her Pig. Rosanne Litzinger. LC 91-38227. (Illus.). 32p. 1997. pap. 5.00 (*0-15-201490-X*) Harcourt.

***Old Woman & Her Pig.** Margaret MacDonald. (J). (ps-1). 2001. lib. bdg. 15.89 (*0-06-028090-5*) HarpC Child Bks.

***Old Woman & Her Pig.** Margaret MacDonald. 32p. (J). (ps-1). 2001. 15.95 (*0-06-028089-1*) HarpC Child Bks.

Old Woman & Her Pig: An Old English Tale. Rosanne Litzinger. LC 91-38227. (Illus.). 32p. (J). (ps-1). 1993. 13.95 (*0-15-257802-1*) Harcourt.

Old Woman & Her Pig, an Old English Tale. Rosanne Litzinger. 1997. 10.20 (*0-606-11699-0*, Pub. by Turtleback) Demco.

Old Woman & Her Pig & Ten Other Stories. Anne Rockwell. LC 78-13901. (Illus.). (J). (gr. 1 up). 1979. 13.95 (*0-690-03927-1*); lib. bdg. 13.89 (*0-690-03928-X*) HarpC Child Bks.

Old Woman & the Ghost. Evelyne Reberg. (I Love to Read Collection). (Illus.). 46p. (J). (ps-3). 1992. lib. bdg. 12.79 (*0-89565-814-3*) Childs World.

Old Woman & the Red Pumpkin: Level 4, Green. Betsy Bang. LC 98-88095. (Reading Together Ser.). (Illus.). 32p. (J). 1999. pap. write for info. (*0-7636-0857-2*) Candlewick Pr.

Old Woman & the Wave. Shelley Jackson. LC 97-34114. (Illus.). 32p. (J). (ps-2). 1998. 15.95 (*0-7894-2484-3*) DK Pub Inc.

Old Woman Remembers: The Recollected History of West Indians in Panama 1855-1955. Carlos E. Russell. (Illus.). 50p. (Orig.). 1995. pap. text 10.00 (*1-878433-20-2*) Caribbean Diaspora Pr.

Old Woman Who Lived in a Vinegar Bottle. Margaret R. MacDonald. LC 94-46967. (Illus.). (J). (ps-3). 1995. 15.95 (*0-87483-415-5*) August Hse.

Old Woman Who Lived in a Vinegar Bottle. Rumer Godden. (Illus.). 50p. (J). 1995. reprint ed. lib. bdg. 18.95 (*1-56849-600-1*) Buccaneer Bks.

Old Woman Who Loved to Read. John Winch. LC 96-19665. (Illus.). 32p. (J). (gr. k-3). 1997. 16.95 (*0-8234-1281-4*) Holiday.

Old Woman Who Loved to Read. John Winch. (Illus.). (J). (ps-3). 1997. pap. 6.95 (*0-8234-1348-9*) Holiday.

Old Woman Who Named Things. Cynthia Rylant. LC 93-40537. (Illus.). 32p. (C). (ps-3). 1996. 16.00 (*0-15-257809-9*) Harcourt.

Old Woman Who Named Things. Cynthia Rylant. (Illus.). 32p. (ps-3). 2000. pap. 6.00 (*0-15-202102-7*, Harcourt Child Bks) Harcourt.

Old Woman Who Swallowed a Fly. (Play - a - Sound Ser.). (Illus.). 24p. (J). 1993. 12.98 (*0-7853-0041-4*) Pubns Intl Ltd.

Old Women of Magione. Ciaran O'Driscoll. LC 98-106067. 72p. 1998. 19.95 (*1-901233-09-X*); pap. 13.95 (*1-901233-08-1*) Dufour.

***Old Wood - New Home.** G. Lawson Drinkard, III. (Illus.). 135p. 2000. 39.95 (*0-87905-953-2*) Gibbs Smith Pub.

Old Wood Burning Cook Stove: Heart of My Farmhouse Kitchen. Alana Craven. Ed. by Heather A. Wightman. (Illus.). 40p. (Orig.). 1997. pap. 5.50 (*1-888911-02-6*) Benson Smythe.

Old Woodcutter. Janis J. Kinens. LC 88-81904. (Illus.). 32p. (J). (gr. k-12). 1988. lib. bdg. 12.95 (*0-9620999-0-2*); 12.95 (*0-9620999-1-0*) Guzzy Pr.

Old Wooden Buildings. Donovan Clemson. (Illus.). 96p. pap. 4.95 (*0-919654-90-8*) Hancock House.

Old Working Dogs. David Hancock. (Illus.). 123p. 1998. pap. 6.25 (*0-7478-0376-5*, Pub. by Shire Pubns) Parkwest Pubns.

Old World. Philip Sauvain. (Illus.). 192p. (Orig.). 1991. pap. 27.00 (*0-7487-1184-8*) Dufour.

Old World. Jonathan Strong. LC 97-3166. 176p. (Orig.). 1997. pap. 13.95 (*0-944072-81-X*) Zoland Bks.

Old World: Early Man to the Development of Agriculture Robert Stigler. LC 75-320467. 164 p. 1974. 4.00 (*0-500-05021-X*) Thames Hudson.

Old World & America. Philip J. Furlong. LC 82-51247. (Illus.). 384p. (J). (gr. 6). 1984. reprint ed. pap. text 18.00 (*0-89555-202-7*) TAN Bks Pubs.

Old World & America - Answer Key. Maureen K. McDevitt. LC 98-90276. 71p. 1998. pap. 10.00 (*0-89555-620-0*, 1550) TAN Bks Pubs.

Old World & the New. John H. Elliott. (Canto Book Ser.). (Illus.). 134p. (C). 1992. pap. 10.95 (*0-521-42709-6*) Cambridge U Pr.

O

Old World & the New: Literary Perspectives of German-Speaking Canadians. Ed. by Walter E. Riedel. LC 85-135731. 199p. reprint ed. pap. 61.70 (0-8357-6388-9, 203574300096) Bks Demand.

Old World Archaeology: Foundations of Civilization: Readings from Scientific American. C. C. Lamberg-Karlovsky. LC 72-1961. 260p. 1972. write for info. (0-7167-0860-4) W H Freeman.

Old World Breads. Charel Scheele. LC 97-24526. (Specialty Cookbook Ser.). (Illus.). 176p. 1997. pap. 6.95 (0-89594-902-4) Crossing Pr.

*__Old World Charm.__ Connie Parkinson. (Illus.). 52p. 1999. 10.95 (1-57377-068-X, 19884-2282) Easl Pubns.

Old World Cooking: Your Complete Guide to Greek Cooking. Mary Genkos & Joan Mejia. LC 94-76195. (Illus.). 200p. (Orig.). 1994. pap. text 15.00 (0-9641316-0-9) Ladies Guild.

Old World Encounters: Cross-Cultural Contacts & Exchanges in Pre-Modern Times. Jerry H. Bentley. (Illus.). 240p. (C). 1993. pap. text 21.95 (0-19-507640-0) OUP.

Old World History in Verse. John V. Southworth. LC 77-77321. (Illus.). 120p. 1978. 20.00 (0-912760-42-7) Valkyrie Pub Hse.

*__Old World Kitchen: The Rich Tradition of European Peasant Cooking.__ Elisabeth Luard. (Common Reader Edition Ser.). 2000. reprint ed. pap. 24.95 (1-888173-50-5, Pub. by Akadine Pr) Trafalgar.

Old World Monkeys see Zoobooks

Old World Monkeys. Ed. by Paul F. Whitehead & Clifford J. Jolly. LC 99-20192. (Illus.). 528p. (C). 2000. 115.00 (0-521-57124-3) Cambridge U Pr.

Old World Monkeys. Wildlife Education, Ltd. Staff. (Zoobooks Ser.). (Illus.). 24p. (J). 1993. 13.95 (0-937934-92-5) Wildlife Educ.

Old World Monkeys. Wildlife Education, Ltd. Staff. (Zoobooks Ser.). (Illus.). 24p. (J). 1995. pap. 2.75 (0-937934-69-0) Wildlife Educ.

Old World, New Horizons: Britain, Europe, & the Atlantic Alliance. Edward M. Heath. LC 71-106959. (Godkin Lectures). 95p. 1970. 17.00 (0-674-63260-5) HUP.

Old World Origins, 10 vols., Set. Johni Cerny. 1995. write for info. (0-9617478-6-2) Lineages Inc.

Old World Recollections: Writings & Pastels of a Denver Painter. Roland Detre. LC 94-16300. (Documents of Colorado Art Ser.: Vol. 3). (Illus.). 1994. pap. 34.95 (0-938075-44-6) Ocean View Bks.

Old World Tales: Stories. Stephan Lackner. LC 98-34548. 192p. 1999. pap. 12.00 (1-56474-291-1) Fithian Pr.

Old World Traits Transplanted see Americanization Studies: The Acculturation of Immigrant Groups into American Society

Old World Traits Transplanted. Robert Ezra Park & Herbert A. Miller. LC 69-18788. (American Immigration Collection. Series 1). (Illus.). 1969. reprint ed. 16.95 (0-405-00536-9) Ayer.

Old World Traits Transplanted: With Intro. & Index Added. William I. Thomas. (Criminology, Law Enforcement, & Social Problems Ser.). (C). 1975. pap. 15.00 (0-87585-905-4) Patterson Smith.

Old World's New World. C. Vann Woodward. 176p. 1992. 27.50 (0-19-506451-8) OUP.

Old Worlds to New: The Age of Exploration & Discovery. Steven Anzovin & Janet Podell. LC 92-19264. 296p. 1993. 44.00 (0-8242-0838-2) Wilson.

*__Old Wounds.__ Nora Kelly. LC 99-66273. 300p. 1999. pap. 12.95 (1-890208-25-6) Poisoned Pen.

Old Wounds: Jews, Ukrainians, & the Hunt for Nazi War Criminals in Canada. Harold M. Troper & Morton Weinfeld. LC 88-40535. 473p. 1989. pap. 146.70 (0-608-05216-7, 206575300001) Bks Demand.

Old Wounds, New Words: An Anthology of Recent Appalachian Poetry. Ed. by Bob H. Baber et al. LC 94-7994. 224p. 1994. pap. 9.95 (0-945084-44-7) J Stuart Found.

*__Old Wrecks' Jokes.__ Stuart Macfarlane & Linda MacFarlane. Ed. by Helen Exley. (Joke Bks.). (Illus.). 64p. 1999. 8.50 (1-86187-124-4) Exley Giftbooks.

Old Yamhill: The Early History of Its Town & Cities. Compiled by Ruth Stoller. LC 89-61195. (Illus.). 112p. 1989. reprint ed. pap. 15.00 (0-8323-0470-0) Binford Mort.

*__Old Yeller.__ (J). 1999. 9.95 (1-56137-081-9) Novel Units.

Old Yeller. Fred Gipson. 192p. (J). Date not set. 20.95 (0-8488-2273-0) Amereon Ltd.

Old Yeller. Fred Gipson. (J). (gr. 5). 1995. 9.32 (0-395-73259-X) HM.

Old Yeller. Fred Gipson. LC 56-8780. (Trophy Bk.). 208p. (J). (gr. 5-7). 1990. mass mkt. 4.95 (0-06-440382-3, HarpTrophy) HarpC Child Bks.

Old Yeller. Fred Gipson. LC 56-8780. (Illus.). 176p. (YA). (gr. 7-9). 1956. 23.00 (0-06-011545-9) HarperTrade.

Old Yeller. Fred Gipson. (J). 1989. 10.60 (0-606-01189-7, Pub. by Turtleback) Demco.

Old Yeller. Fred Gipson. (J). 1999. lib. bdg. 21.95 (1-56723-204-3) Yestermorrow.

Old Yeller. Fred Gipson. 192p. (YA). 1992. reprint ed. 25.95 (0-89966-906-9) Buccaneer Bks.

Old Yeller: A Literature Unit. Michael Levin. (Literature Units Ser.). (Illus.). 48p. (Orig.). 1993. pap., student ed. 7.95 (1-55734-427-2) Tchr Create Mat.

Old Yeller: A Study Guide. Brenda H. McGee. Ed. by Joyce Friedland & Rikki Kessler. (Novel-Ties Ser.). 21p. (J). (gr. 5-7). 1990. pap. text 15.95 (0-88122-415-4) Lrn Links.

Old Yeller Reissue. Fred Gipson. LC 88-45960. 192p. (J). (gr. 4-7). 1989. reprint ed. mass mkt. 5.50 (0-06-080971-X, P 971, Perennial) HarperTrade.

Old Yellow Book: Source of Robert Browning's "The Ring & the Book" (BCL1-PR English Literature Ser.). 289p. 1992. reprint ed. lib. bdg. 79.00 (0-7812-7464-8) Rprt Serv.

Old Yellow Book Source of Robert Browning's the Ring & the Book. John M. Gest. LC 78-92953. (Studies in Browning: No. 4). 1924. lib. bdg. 75.00 (0-8383-1058-3) M S G Haskell Hse.

Old Yellowstone Days. Ed. by Paul D. Schullery. LC 78-6732. (Illus.). 1979. pap. 19.95 (0-87081-121-5) Univ Pr Colo.

Old Yiddish to Haskalah, Vol. 7. Israel Zinberg. 25.00 (0-87068-465-5) Ktav.

Old York. John D. Bardwell. LC 95-188151. (Images of America Ser.). 1994. pap. 14.99 (0-7524-0064-9) Arcadia Publng.

Old York Beach. John D. Bardwell. LC 95-180892. (Images of America Ser.). 1994. pap. 16.99 (0-7524-0004-5) Arcadia Publng.

Old York Beach, Vol. II. John D. Bardwell. LC 95-180892. (Images of America Ser.). 128p. 1996. pap. 16.99 (0-7524-0267-6) Arcadia Publng.

Old Yuma: An Archaeological Testing Program of Twelve Downtown Parcels. Matthew A. Sterner. (Statistical Research Technical Ser.: No. 23). (Illus.). 76p. 1990. spiral bd. 10.00 (1-879442-21-3) Stats Res.

Oldcat & Ms. Puss: A Book of Days for You & Me. Joe Taylor. LC 97-438. 176p. 1997. 23.00 (1-881320-72-3, Black Belt) Black Belt Communs.

Olde Bead Monger's Trade Bead Sketchbook. James E. Byrd. LC 92-81662. (Illus.). 68p. (Orig.). 1992. pap. 7.95 (1-880655-02-0) Scurlock Pub.

Olde Boston Soup Bowl Cookery. Merilyn Devos. Ed. by Vincent F. Zarrilli. 84p. 1998. pap. 11.95 (1-891827-03-0) Pot Shop.

Olde Cape Cod, No. 26. Noel W. Beyle. (Illus.). 48p. 1986. pap. write for info. (0-912609-09-5) First Encounter.

Olde Daunce: Love, Friendship, Sex, & Marriage in the Medieval World. Ed. by Robert R. Edwards & Stephen Spector. LC 89-26349. (SUNY Series in Medieval Studies). 311p. (C). 1991. text 67.50 (0-7914-0439-0); pap. text 24.95 (0-7914-0440-4) State U NY Pr.

Olde English Traditional Country Style Recipes. Norma Latimer et al. (Traditional Cooking of Great Britain Ser.). (Illus.). 105p. (Orig.). 1984. pap. 8.95 (0-941869-00-8) Latimers.

Olde Mother Goose. Perf. by Hubbards. (Little Star Collection). (Illus.). 32p. (J). (ps up). 1993. 12.95 incl. audio (0-87483-213-6) August Hse.

Olde New England's Sugar & Spice & Everything... America's First Cookbook & Food History. Robert E. Cahill. Ed. by Keri M. Cahill. (Olde New England Ser.). (Illus.). 63p. (YA). 1991. pap. 6.50 (0-9626162-2-2) Old Salt Box.

Olde Thyme Folk Art, Vol. 1. Teresa Gregory. (Illus.). 70p. 1997. pap. 10.50 (1-56770-390-9) S Scheewe Pubns.

Olde Traditional New England & Yankee Cooking. Elizabeth H. Warner. (Illus.). 327p. 1985. 12.95 (0-9615972-0-8) E H Warner.

Olde Tyme Family Reunion Cookbook. Ray D. Thrower. Ed. by Kathy White. (Illus.). 440p. 1997. spiral bd. 19.95 (0-9660082-0-0) Thor Pub TX.

Olde Ulster, 1905, Vol. I. Benjamin M. Brink. 384p. 1988. 29.95 (0-941567-00-1) J C & A L Fawcett.

Olde Women. Ann Dunn. 60p. 1995. 12.00 (0-9648305-1-5) Urthona Pr.

Olden Days Coat. Margaret Laurence. (Illus.). 40p. (J). (gr. k-5). pap. 14.95 (0-7710-4743-6) McCland & Stewart.

Olden Days Coat. rev. ed. Margaret Laurence. LC 98-60285. (Illus.). 32p. 1998. 14.95 (0-88776-455-X) Tundra Bks.

Olden-Time Music. Henry M. Brooks. LC 70-39537. reprint ed. 42.50 (0-404-09919-X) AMS Pr.

Oldenburger Sachsenspiegel. (Codex Picturatus Oldenburgenesis, Hannover, Niedersaechsiches Sparkassenstiftung), 2 vols. fac. limited ed. (Codices Selecti A Ser.: Vol. CI). (GER.). 400p. 1336. reprint ed. lthr. 2157.00 (3-201-01623-3, Pub. by Akademische Druck-und) Balogh.

Older Adult Education: A Guide to Research, Programs, & Policies. Ronald J. Manheimer et al. LC 95-10277. 264p. 1995. lib. bdg. 69.50 (0-313-28878-X, Greenwood Pr) Greenwood.

Older Adult Friendship: Structure & Process. Ed. by Rebecca Adams & Rosemary H. Blieszner. (Focus Editions Ser.: Vol. 103). 320p. 1989. text 59.95 (0-8039-3143-3) Sage.

Older Adult Friendship: Structure & Process. Ed. by Rebecca Adams & Rosemary H. Blieszner. (Focus Editions Ser.: Vol. 103). 320p. (C). 1989. pap. text 26.00 (0-8039-3144-1) Sage.

Older Adult Friendship: Structure & Process. Ed. by Rebecca G. Adams & Rosemary Blieszner. LC 88-28287. (Sage Focus Editions Ser.: No. 103). 268p. 1989. reprint ed. pap. 83.10 (0-608-04295-1, 206507400012) Bks Demand.

*__Older Adult Issues Series Set.__ 1999. pap. 44.95 (0-664-50104-4) Geneva Press.

Older Adult Psychotherapy Treatment Planner. Deborah Frazer & Arthur E. Jongsma, Jr. LC 98-42397. (Practice Planners Ser.). 274p. 1998. pap. 39.95 (0-471-29574-4); pap. 175.00 incl. cd-rom (0-471-29581-7) Wiley.

Older Adult Resource Guide. SRG Publishing Staff. 216p. 1997. pap. text 5.95 (0-8151-2208-X) Mosby Inc.

Older Adults: Nutritional Interventions... For Major Chronic Conditions. Jonathan Silver. 75p. (C). 1999. spiral bd. 15.00 (1-892870-07-X) Best Years Inc.

Older Adults Coping with Cancer: Integrating Cancer into a Life Mostly Lived. rev. ed. Sarah H. Kagan. LC 96-30015. (Studies on the Elderly in America). (Illus.). 137p. 1997. text 44.00 (0-8153-2859-1) Garland.

Older Adults Decision-Making & the Law. Ed. by K. Warner Schaie et al. (Illus.). 312p. 1996. 46.95 (0-8261-8990-3) Springer Pub.

Older Adults in Psychotherapy: Case Histories. Bob G. Knight. (Illus.). 240p. 1992. 48.00 (0-8039-3628-1); pap. 21.00 (0-8039-3629-X) Sage.

Older Adults' Misuse of Alcohol, Medicines & Other Drugs: Research & Practice Issues. Ed. by Anne M. Gurnack. LC 96-35208. (Illus.). 296p. 1997. 39.95 (0-8261-9500-8) Springer Pub.

Older Adults with Developmental Disabilities. Claire Lavin & Kenneth Doka. LC 97-44006. (Society & Aging Ser.). 151p. 1999. 32.00 (0-89503-188-4) Baywood Pub.

Older Adults with Developmental Disabilities: Optimizing Choice & Change. Ed. by Evelyn C. Sutton et al. LC 92-47442. 416p. 1993. pap. 37.00 (1-55766-120-0) P H Brookes.

Older Adults with Developmental Disabilities & Leisure: Issues, Policy, & Practice. Ed. by Ted Tedrick. LC 96-46303. (Activities, Adaptation & Aging Ser.: Vol. 21, No. 3). 116p. (C). 1997. 29.95 (0-7890-0023-7) Haworth Pr.

Older Americans Act: Funding Formula Could Better Reflect State Needs. (Illus.). 84p. (Orig.). (C). 1995. pap. text 20.00 (0-7881-2211-8) DIANE Pub.

*__Older Americans & the Worldwide Web: The New Wave of Internet Users: Congressional Hearing.__ Ed. by Charles E. Grassley. 112p. (C). 2000. reprint ed. pap. text 25.00 (0-7881-8759-7) DIANE Pub.

*__Older American's Information Directory.__ 2nd ed. Ed. by Laura Mars. 900p. 2000. 190.00 (1-891482-27-0) Grey Hse Pub.

*__Older Americans Information Directory, 1999-2000.__ Ed. by Laura Mars. 956p. 1998. pap. 165.00 (1-891482-36-X) Grey Hse Pub.

Older Americans Information Directory 1999. Ed. by Laura Mars. 956p. 1998. 190.00 (1-891482-37-8) Grey Hse Pub.

Older American's Medications Guide. Jonathan Silver. 45p. 1998. 20.00 (1-892870-06-1) Best Years Inc.

Older & Growing: Your Eternal Life Beginning Now. Leslie E. Moser. 1990. 14.95 (1-878938-01-0) Mlti-Media Prodns.

Older & Wiser. Richard Restack. LC 97-14232. 304p. 1997. 23.50 (0-684-82976-2) S&S Trade.

*__Older & Wiser: How to Maintain Peak Mental Ability for As Long As You Live.__ Richard M. Restak. 272p. 1999. reprint ed. pap. 12.95 (0-425-16586-8) Berkley Pub.

Older & Wiser: Public Policy Issues for an Aging America. Ed. by Robert N. Butler. 240p. 1998. 24.95 (0-87078-424-2) Century Foundation.

Older & Wiser: The Economics of Public Pensions. Lawrence Thompson. LC 98-10300. 192p. 1998. pap. 23.95 (0-87766-679-2); lib. bdg. 59.50 (0-87766-678-4) Urban Inst.

Older & Wiser: Wit, Wisdom, & Spirited Advice from the Older Generation. Eric W. Johnson. 256p. 1986. 18.95 (0-8027-0903-6) Walker & Co.

Older Bank Customers: An Expanding Market, Set. 1989. student ed. 535.00 incl. VHS (0-89982-297-5, 629302); student ed. 395.00 incl. VHS (0-685-63175-3, 629302) Am Bankers.

Older Bereaved Spouses. Ed. by Dale A. Lund. 196p. 1989. pap. 30.95 (1-56032-240-3) Hemisp Pub.

Older Boy. Created by Francine Pascal. (Sweet Valley Twins Ser.: No. 15). (J). (gr. 3-7). 1987. pap. 4.95 (0-553-16788-X) BDD Bks Young Read.

Older Brother Returns: Finding a Renewed Sense of God's Love & Mercy. Neal Lozano. LC 95-41024. 152p. (Orig.). 1995. pap. 10.00 (1-883551-51-X) Attic Studio Pub.

Older Brother, Younger Brother, a Koren Folktale. Nina Jaffe. (Picture Puffin Ser.). (J). 1997. 11.19 (0-606-11701-6, Pub. by Turtleback) Demco.

*__Older but Wilder: More Notes from the Pasture.__ Effie Leland Wilder. LC 99-89392. (Paperback Ser.). 2000. 23.95 (0-7838-8959-3, G K Hall Lrg Type) Mac Lib Ref.

Older but Wilder: More Notes from the Pasture. Effie Leland Wilder. LC 98-19371. (Illus.). 179p. (J). 1998. 14.95 (1-56145-182-7, Peachtree) Peachtree Pubs.

Older Child Adoption. Grace Robinson. LC 97-37545. 229p. 1998. pap. 17.95 (0-8245-1707-5, Crsrd) Crossroad NY.

Older Deaf Child. P. Hoiberg et al. (Modern Approaches to the Diagnosis & Instruction of Multi-Handicapped Children Ser.: Vol. 12). viii, 64p. 1973. 17.75 (90-237-4112-9) Taylor & Francis.

Older Graces. D. Manicom. LC 97-203868. 80p. 1997. pap. text 12.95 (0-88982-164-X, Pub. by Oolichan Bks) Genl Dist Srvs.

Older Hispanics in Nebraska: Their Characteristics, Attitudes & Needs. David R. DiMartino & Carole M. Davis. 148p. (Orig.). 1980. pap. 8.50 (1-55719-084-4) U NE CPAR.

Older Horse see Keeping the Older Horse Young

Older Horse: A Complete Guide to Care & Conditioning. Eleanor M. Kellon. LC 85-73734. (Illus.). 240p. 1986. 34.00 (0-914327-50-X) Breakthrgh NY.

Older Hospitalized Patient. Charlotte K. Eliopoulos. 78p. 1991. pap. text 25.00 (1-882515-05-6) Hlth Educ Netwk.

Older Love. Warren Hanson. LC 99-19826. 36p. 1999. 15.95 (0-931674-40-9) Waldman Hse Pr.

Older Male Mortality & Cigarette Smoking, Vol. 6. Samuel H. Preston. LC 76-4875. (Population Monograph: No. 7). (Illus.). 150p. 1976. reprint ed. lib. bdg. 24.75 (0-8371-8830-X, PROM, Greenwood Pr) Greenwood.

Older Man. Barbara McMahon. (Desire Ser.). 1998. per. 3.75 (0-373-76161-9, 1-76161-8) Silhouette.

Older Men's Lives. Ed. by Edward H. Thompson, Jr. (Research on Men & Masculinities Ser.: Vol. 6). 272p. 1994. 58.00 (0-8039-5080-2); pap. 26.00 (0-8039-5081-0) Sage.

Older Mothers: Conception, Pregnancy & Birth After 35. Julia C. Berryman. LC 99-215731. 1998. pap. text 17.00 (0-86358-410-1) Harper SF.

Older Mothers: Conception, Pregnancy & Birth after 35. Julia C. Berryman et al. 276p. 1998. pap. 17.00 (0-04-440906-0, Pub. by Rivers Oram) NYU Pr.

Older Offenders: Current Trends. Sol Chaneles. LC 88-13805. (Journal of Offender Counseling, Services & Rehabilitation: Vol. 13, No. 2). (Illus.). 248p. 1989. text 49.95 (0-86656-806-9) Haworth Pr.

Older Offenders: Perspectives in Criminology & Criminal Justice. Ed. by Belinda R. McCarthy & Robert J. Langworthy. LC 87-7147. 253p. 1988. 67.95 (0-275-92734-2, C2734, Praeger Pubs) Greenwood.

Older People. Robert J. Havighurst & Ruth Albrecht. Ed. by Leon Stein. LC 79-8670. (Growing Old Ser.). (Illus.). 1980. reprint ed. lib. bdg. 41.95 (0-405-12785-5) Ayer.

*__Older People: Law & Finance.__ John Costello & Joe Christle. 150p. 1999. pap. 15.00 (1-901657-80-9, 18427, Pub. by Blackhall Pub) Gaunt.

Older People & Community Care: Critical Theory & Practice. Beverley Hughes. LC 95-14731. (Rethinking Aging Ser.). 176p. 1995. 98.95 (0-335-19157-6); pap. 30.95 (0-335-19156-8) OpUniv Pr.

*__Older People & Their Needs, 1.__ Gianetta Corley. 1999. pap. text 39.95 (1-86156-083-4) Whurr Pub.

Older People Giving Care: Helping Family & Community. Sally K. Gallagher. LC 93-9017. 200p. 1994. 57.95 (0-86569-233-5, Auburn Hse) Greenwood.

Older People in Florida: A Statistical Abstract 1978. 2nd ed. Ed. by Carter C. Osterbind & Angela M. O'Rand. LC HQ1064.46. 277p. reprint ed. pap. 85.90 (0-7837-0597-2, 204094500019) Bks Demand.

Older People in Florida, 1980-1981: A Statistical Abstract. 3rd ed. Ed. by John Kraft & Carter C. Osterbind. LC HQ1064.U6F6O. 272p. (Orig.). reprint ed. pap. 84.40 (0-7837-5072-2, 204477000004) Bks Demand.

Older People in Modern Society. 4th ed. Anthea Tinker. LC 96-37684. (Longman Social Policy in Britain Ser.). 1997. pap. text. write for info. (0-582-29488-6) Addison-Wesley.

Older People, Nursing & Mental Health. Ed. by Stuart Darby et al. LC 98-29335. (Illus.). 192p. 1998. pap. text 32.50 (0-7506-2440-X) Buttrwrth-Heinemann.

Older Persons & Service Providers: An Instructor's Training Guide. Ed. by Glorian Sorensen. LC 80-22868. 366p. 1981. text 45.95 (0-89885-020-7, Kluwer Acad Hman Sci) Kluwer Academic.

Older Refugees in the U. S. From Dignity to Despair. Elizabeth Gozdziak. 56p. (Orig.). (C). 1995. pap. text 25.00 (0-7881-2337-8) DIANE Pub.

Older Residents' Legal Rights: Supported Accommodation in New South Wales. Ed. by Sandra McCullough. 546p. 1992. pap. 64.00 (1-86287-090-X, Pub. by Federation Pr) Gaunt.

Older Than Dirt: 365 Ways to Show You're over the Hill! Patrick Caton. 365p. 1998. 6.50 (1-56245-350-5) Great Quotations.

Older Than My Mother: A Nurse's Life & Triumph over Breast Cancer. Augusta H. Gale. LC 96-18873. (Illus.). 144p. 1996. 18.00 (0-9605670-8-9) Ananse Pr.

Older Than Rain. Fred Ferraris. 126p. 1997. pap. 8.00 (1-882775-08-2) Selva Edit.

Older Than Ravens. Doug Reimer. 1997. pap. 10.95 (0-88801-137-7, Pub. by Turnstone Pr) Genl Dist Srvs.

Older Than the Dinosaurs: The Origin & Rise of the Mammals. Edward R. Ricciuti. LC 77-26606. (Illus.). 96p. (J). (gr. 5-12). 1980. 8.20 (0-690-01328-0); lib. bdg. 12.89 (0-690-03879-8) HarpC Child Bks.

Older Than Time: A Woman Travels Around the World in Search of the Wisdom That Comes with Age. Allegra Taylor. 1994. pap. 13.00 (1-85538-152-4, Pub. by Aqrn Pr) HarpC.

Older Veterans: Linking VA & Community Resources. Ed. by Terrie Wetle & John Rowe. (Division of Health Policy Research & Education Ser.). 464p. 1985. 26.00 (0-674-63275-3) HUP.

Older Volunteer: An Annotated Bibliography, 21. Ed. by Nancy D. Levine. LC 92-41898. (Bibliographies & Indexes in Gerontology Ser.: No. 21). 136p. 1993. lib. bdg. 49.95 (0-313-28125-4, BOV, Greenwood Pr) Greenwood.

Older Volunteer Leaders in the Rural Community. Nancy H. Reynolds. LC 91-32211. (Studies on the Elderly in America). 152p. 1992. text 25.00 (0-8153-0528-1) Garland.

Older Volunteers: A Guide to Research & Practice. Lucy R. Fischer & Kay B. Schaffer. (Illus.). 208p. (C). 1993. text 49.95 (0-8039-5008-X); pap. text 22.95 (0-8039-5009-8) Sage.

Older Wards & Their Guardians. Pat M. Keith. LC 94-6375. 248p. 1994. 65.00 (0-275-94424-7, Praeger Pubs) Greenwood.

Older, Wiser . . . Pregnant. Marilyn Pappano. (Special Edition Ser.). 1998. per. 4.25 (0-373-24200-X, 1-24200-7) Silhouette.

Older, Wiser, Stronger: Southern Elders. Ed. by Mary Eldridge. (Southern Exposure Ser.). (Illus.). 152p. 1985. pap. 6.00 (0-943810-19-1) Inst Southern Studies.

Older Woman: The Able Self. rev. ed. Kathleen D. Ahern. LC 95-51444. (Studies on the Elderly in America). 118p. 1996. text 15.00 (0-8153-2333-6) Garland.

Older Woman in Industry. Johanna Lobsenz. LC 74-3961. (Women in America Ser.). (Illus.). 298p. 1974. reprint ed. 24.95 (0-405-06110-2) Ayer.

An Asterisk (*) at the beginning of an entry indicates that the title is appearing for the first time.

Older Women: Surviving & Thriving (A Manual for Group Leaders) Ruth H. Jacobs. LC 86-32900. 130p. (Orig.). 1987. pap. 18.95 (*0-87304-221-2*) Manticore Pubs.

Older Women in Poverty: Private Lives & Public Policies. Amanda S. Barusch. LC 94-12588. (Illus.). 272p. (C). 1994. 34.95 (*0-8261-7960-6*) Springer Pub.

Older Women in the City. Department for the Aging, City of New York. Ed. by Robert J. Kastenbaum. LC 78-73649. (Aging & Old Age Ser.). 1979. lib. bdg. 19.95 (*0-405-11839-2*) Ayer.

Older Women with Chronic Pain. Ed. & Intro. by Karen A. Roberto. LC 94-27471. (Journal of Women & Aging). (Illus.). 128p. 1994. lib. bdg. 39.95 (*1-56024-706-1*) Haworth Pr.

Older Women with Chronic Pain. Ed. & Intro. by Karen A. Roberto. LC 94-27471. (Journal of Women & Aging Ser.). (Illus.). 119p. 1994. pap. 9.95 (*1-56023-061-4*, Harrington Park) Haworth Pr.

***Older Women, Younger Men: New Options for Love & Romance.** Felicia Brings & Susan Winter. LC 00-132571. 208p. 2000. pap. 14.95 (*0-88282-200-4*, Pub. by New Horizon NJ) Natl Bk Netwk.

Older Worker: Effective Strategies for Management & Human Resource Development. Noreen Hale. LC 90-4583. (Management Ser.). 197p. 1990. text 30.95 (*1-55542-284-5*) Jossey-Bass.

Older Worker in Industry. Guy Crook & Martin Heinstein. Ed. by Leon Stein. LC 79-8664. (Growing Old Ser.). (Illus.). 1980. reprint ed. lib. bdg. 17.95 (*0-405-12782-0*) Ayer.

Older Workers. Sara E. Rix. LC 90-46349. (Choices & Challenges: An Older Adult Reference Ser.). 243p. 1990. lib. bdg. 45.00 (*0-87436-259-8*) ABC-CLIO.

Older Workers: What Voc Ed Can Do. Denie Denniston. 48p. 1983. 4.95 (*0-318-22162-4*, IN256) Ctr Educ Trng Employ.

Olderr's Fiction Index, 1987. 87th ed. Ed. by Steven Olderr. 350p. 1988. 65.00 (*0-912289-85-6*) St James Pr.

Olderr's Fiction Index, 1988. 88th ed. Ed. by Steven Olderr. 1989. 65.00 (*1-55862-028-1*) St James Pr.

Olderr's Fiction Index, 1989. 89th ed. Ed. by Steven Olderr. 450p. 1990. 65.00 (*1-55862-057-5*) St James Pr.

Olderr's Fiction Index, 1990. 90th ed. Ed. by Steven Olderr. 557p. 1991. 65.00 (*1-55862-090-7*, 200143) St James Pr.

Olderr's Fiction Subject Headings: A Supplement & Guide to the LC Thesaurus. Steven Olderr. LC 91-8679. 160p. (C). 1991. pap. text 35.00 (*0-8389-0562-5*) ALA.

Olderr's Young Adult Fiction Index, 1990. 90th ed. Ed. by Steven Olderr. 310p. 1991. 65.00 (*1-55862-091-5*, 200144) St James Pr.

Olderr's Young Adult Fiction Index, 1988. 88th ed. Ed. by Steven Olderr. 1989. 65.00 (*1-55862-020-6*) St James Pr.

Olderr's Young Adult Fiction Index, 1989. 89th ed. Ed. by Steven Olderr. 250p. 1990. 65.00 (*1-55862-058-3*) St James Pr.

Oldest Allies, Guarded Friends: The United States & France since 1940. Charles G. Cogan. LC 94-1150. 256p. 1994. 69.50 (*0-275-94868-4*, Praeger Pubs); pap. 21.95 (*0-275-95116-2*, Praeger Pubs) Greenwood.

Oldest Ally: A Portrait of Salazar's Portugal. Peter Fryer & Patricia M. Pinheiro. LC 81-7020. (Illus.). 280p. 1982. reprint ed. lib. bdg. 65.00 (*0-313-23146-X*, FROA, Greenwood Pr) Greenwood.

Oldest Ally: Britain & the Portuguese Connection, 1936-1941. Glyn Stone. LC 94-7840. (Royal Historical Society Studies in History: Vol. 69). 240p. (C). 1994. 75.00 (*0-86193-227-7*, Royal Historical Soc) Boydell & Brewer.

Oldest Biography of Spinoza: 1927 Edition. A. Wolf. 208p. 1996. reprint ed. 58.00 (*1-85506-173-2*) Bks Intl VA.

Oldest Books in the World: An Account of the Religion, Wisdom, Philosophy, Ethics, Psychology, Manners, Proverbs, Sayings, Refinement, etc., of the Ancient Egyptians (1900) Isaac Meyer. 540p. 1995. reprint ed. pap. 33.00 (*1-56459-486-6*) Kessinger Pub.

***Oldest Brother's Story: Tales of the Pwo Karen.** Elizabeth Hinton. (Illus.). 96p. 2000. pap. 14.95 (*974-7100-91-6*) U of Wash Pr.

Oldest Christian People. William C. Emhardt & G. M. Lamsa. LC 71-126651. reprint ed. 31.50 (*0-404-02339-8*) AMS Pr.

Oldest City: St. Augustine, Saga of Survival. George E. Buker et al. Ed. by Jean P. Waterbury. LC 83-50479. (Illus.). 274p. (Orig.). 1983. 25.00 (*0-9612744-1-7*); pap. 14.95 (*0-9612744-0-9*) St Augustine Hist.

***Oldest Code of Laws in the World: The Code of Laws Promulgated by Hammurabi, King of Babylon, B.C. 2285-2242.** fac. ed. Hammurabi & C. H. W. Johns. LC 99-53070. 2000. write for info. (*1-58477-061-9*) Lawbk Exchange.

Oldest Dead White European Males: And Other Reflections on the Classics. Bernard Knox. 144p. 1994. pap. 9.95 (*0-393-31233-X*) Norton.

Oldest Dead White European Males & Other Reflections on the Classics. Bernard M. Knox. LC 92-32689. 144p. 1993. 15.95 (*0-393-03492-5*) Norton.

Oldest Elf. James Stevenson. LC 94-25355. (Illus.). 32p. (J). 1996. 15.00 (*0-688-13755-5*, Grenwillow Bks); lib. bdg. 14.93 (*0-688-13756-3*, Grenwillow Bks) HarpC Child Bks.

Oldest Elf. James Stevenson. (J). 1998. mass mkt. 4.95 (*0-688-16154-5*, Wm Morrow) Morrow Avon.

Oldest English Texts. Ed. by H. Sweet. (EETS Original Ser.: No. 83). 676p. 1963. reprint ed. 40.00 (*0-19-722083-5*, Pub. by EETS) Boydell & Brewer.

Oldest English Texts, Charters, Etc. Ed. by H. Sweet. (EETS, OS Ser.: Vol. 83). 1974. reprint ed. 40.00 (*0-8115-3363-8*) Periodicals Srv.

Oldest Gay Couple in America: A Seventy-Year Journey Through Same-Sex America. Gean Harwood. LC 97-16955. 320p. 1997. write for info. (*1-55972-426-9*) Carol Pub Group.

Oldest Living Confederate Widow Tells All. Allan Gurganus. 1996. pap. 15.00 (*0-449-91169-1*) Fawcett.

Oldest Living Confederate Widow Tells All. Allan Gurganus. 912p. 1990. mass mkt. 6.99 (*0-8041-0643-6*) Ivy Books.

Oldest Living Graduate. Preston Jones. 1976. pap. 5.25 (*0-8222-0845-8*) Dramatists Play.

Oldest Living Married Virgin: The Bachelor Battalion. Maureen Child. 1998. per. 3.75 (*0-373-76180-5*, 1-76180-8) Silhouette.

Oldest Magic: The History & Early Influence of Music. Lew P. Price. (Illus.). 200p. 1995. pap. 26.00 (*0-917578-10-4*) L Paxton Price.

Oldest Map with the Name America: New & Selected Poems. Lucia Perillo. LC 98-34561. 160p. 1999. 19.95 (*0-375-50160-6*) Random.

Oldest Mommy in the Park. Barbara Grancell-Frank. (Illus.). 64p. (Orig.). (YA). (gr. 6-12). 1993. pap. 8.95 (*1-56883-022-X*) Colonial Pr AL.

Oldest Old. Ed. by Richard M. Suzman et al. (Illus.). 456p. 1995. pap. text 47.50 (*0-19-509757-2*) OUP.

Oldest Precursor of the Automobile - Ferdinand Verbiest's Steam Turbine-Powered Vehicle Model: 1995 International Congress & Exposition Meeting. LC 94-74754. 36p. 1995. pap. 24.00 (*1-56091-652-4*, SP1102) Soc Auto Engineers.

***Oldest Ranch in Texas.** Joe Wreford Hipp. LC 00-24610. 2000. write for info. (*1-57168-322-4*, Eakin Pr) Sunbelt Media.

***Oldest Religion in Mesopotamia.** Jean Bottero. 1998. 25.00 (*0-226-06717-3*) U Ch Pr.

Oldest Revolutionary: Essays on Benjamin Franklin. J. Leo Lemay. LC 75-41618. x, 165p. 1976. write for info. (*0-8122-7707-4*) U of Pa Pr.

Oldest Revolutionary: Essays on Benjamin Franklin. Ed. by J. Leo Lemay. 165p. (C). 1999. reprint ed. 25.00 (*0-7881-6093-1*) DIANE Pub.

Oldest Social Science: Configuration of Law & Modernity. Timothy Murphy. LC 97-4164. (Oxford Socio-Legal Studies). 282p. 1997. text 65.00 (*0-19-826559-X*) OUP.

Oldest Story Ever Told. David F. Eliet. (J). 2000. pap. 7.00 (*0-87602-377-4*) Anchorage.

Oldest Vocation: Christian Motherhood in the Middle Ages. Clarissa Atkinson. (Illus.). 288p. 1994. pap. text 16.95 (*0-8014-8204-6*) Cornell U Pr.

Oldies but Goodies: Country Western Line Dancer's Reference Handbook, No. 1. Jean Y. Woolman. 94p. (Orig.). 1994. pap. text 9.95 (*0-9638125-1-3*) Wild & Wooly.

Oldies on CD: A Guide to Oldies on Compact Disc. 2nd ed. Mike Callahan. LC 94-71069. 480p. 1994. pap. 29.95 (*0-9641180-0-9*) Both Sides.

Oldies on CD: A Guide to Oldies on Compact Disc. 2nd limited ed. Mike Callahan. LC 94-71069. 480p. 1994. 59.95 (*0-9641180-1-7*) Both Sides.

***Oldman's Ordeal.** Kirtley R. Cook. 159p. 1999. pap. 13.95 (*0-7414-0127-4*) Buy Books.

Oldport Days. Thomas W. Higginson. (Notable American Authors Ser.). 1992. reprint ed. lib. bdg. 75.00 (*0-7812-3112-4*) Rprt Serv.

Olds Calais, Pontiac Grand Am, Buick Skylark, Buick Somerset, 1985-92: Total Car Care. 784p. 1992. pap. 21.95 (*0-8019-8257-X*) Nichols Pub.

Gm Cutlass Rwd 1970-87. Chilton Automotive Editorial Staff. LC 94-69442. (Illus.). 472p. (C). 1996. pap. 22.95 (*0-8019-8668-0*) Thomson Learn.

Oldsmobile 4-4-2 & W-Machine: Restoration Guide. T. Patrick Sullivan. (Illus.). 192p. 1992. pap. 29.95 (*0-87938-577-4*) MBI Pubg.

Oldsmobile Muscle Cars. Bill Holder & Phil Kunz. LC 94-23274. (Illus.). 128p. 1994. pap. 19.95 (*0-87938-957-5*) MBI Pubg.

Oldster's Poetic Perceptions. Abraham J. Heller. 1997. pap. write for info. (*1-57553-552-1*) Watermrk Pr.

Oldtimer Sewing Machine. Otto Landgraf. Tr. by Graham Forsdyke from GER. (Illus.). 192p. 1992. reprint ed. 29.00 (*3-926879-06-8*, Pub. by Weppert GmbH) A Stitch Back.

Oldtimers: Stories of Our Pioneers in the Cass & Crow Wing Lake Region. Carl A. Zapffe. Ed. by Louis Hoglund. LC 87-81243. (Illus.). 175p. (Orig.). 1987. pap. 9.95 (*0-910623-03-1*) Hist Heart Assn Inc.

Oldtimers: Their Own Stories. Florence Fenley. LC 91-24996. (Illus.). 282p. 1991. reprint ed. 24.95 (*0-938349-78-3*) State House Pr.

Oldtimers & Alzheimer's Vol. 1: The Descriptive Organization of Senility. Ed. by Jaber F. Gubrium. LC 86-10404. (Contemporary Ethnographic Studies). 219p. 1986. 73.25 (*0-89232-697-2*) Jai Pr.

Oldtimers Game. Lee Blessing. 1988. pap. 5.25 (*0-8222-0843-1*) Dramatists Play.

Oldtimers III, Stories of Our Pioneers see Indian Days in Minnesota's Lake Region

Oldtown Folks. Harriet Beecher Stowe. Ed. by Dorothy Berkson. (American Women Writers Ser.). 519p. (C). 1987. text 45.00 (*0-8135-1219-0*); pap. text 17.00 (*0-8135-1220-4*) Rutgers U Pr.

Oldtown Folks. Harriet Beecher Stowe. LC 70-127455. reprint ed. 35.00 (*0-404-06293-8*) AMS Pr.

Oldtown Folks. Harriet Beecher Stowe. (BCL1-PS American Literature Ser.). 608p. 1992. reprint ed. lib. bdg. 109.00 (*0-7812-6873-7*) Rprt Serv.

Oldtown Folks. Harriet Beecher Stowe. LC 08-16119. 1969. reprint ed. 13.00 (*0-403-00053-X*) Scholarly.

Olduvai. unabridged ed. Larry E. Henry. 135p. 1998. pap. 11.95 (*1-892896-31-1*) Buy Books.

Olduvai Gorge Vol. 5: Excavations in Beds III, IV & the Masek Beds. Mary Leakey. (Illus.). 341p. (C). 1995. text 199.95 (*0-521-33403-9*) Cambridge U Pr.

Ole & Lena Jokes. Red Stangland. (Illus.). 1986. pap. 2.50 (*0-9613274-2-1*) Norse Pr.

Ole & Lena Jokes Book 5. Red Stangland. (Illus.). 488p. 1990. pap. 2.50 (*0-9613274-9-9*) Norse Pr.

Ole & Lena Jokes Book 7. Red Stangland. 1993. pap. 2.50 (*1-880104-03-2*) Norse Pr.

Ole & Lena Jokes Book 6. Red Strangland. 1992. pap. 2.50 (*1-880104-02-4*) Norse Pr.

Ole & Lena Jokes Book 3. E. C. Stangland. (Illus.). 48p. 1988. pap. 2.50 (*0-9613274-5-6*) Norse Pr.

Ole & Lena Jokes Four. Red Stangland. (Illus.). 48p. 1989. pap. 2.50 (*0-9613274-8-0*) Norse Pr.

Ole Blue. Dave Sargent. Ed. by Debbie Bowen. (Illus.). 43p. (J). (gr. k-6). pap. text 2.95 (*1-56763-111-8*) Ozark Pub.

Ole Bull: A Memoir. Sara C. Bull. LC 81-1508. (Music Ser.). (Illus.). iv, 417p. 1981. reprint ed. lib. bdg. 39.50 (*0-306-76120-3*) Da Capo.

Ole Bull: Norway's Romantic Musician & Cosmopolitan Patriot. Einar Haugen & Camilla Cai. LC 91-50989. (Illus.). 384p. (C). 1993. 21.95 (*0-299-13250-1*) U of Wis Pr.

Ole! Cantina Cookery: Hot Stuff from Corpus Christi, Texas. large type ed. Maxine S. Sommers. (Illus.). 28p. 1996. spiral bd. 6.00 (*0-943991-42-0*) Pound Sterling Pub.

***Ole Db & Ado Developer's Guide.** Peter Hipson. 1999. pap. text 49.99 (*0-07-135065-9*) McGraw.

Ole Dewey: A Brown Shephard Dog That Belonged to the Martins & Was Claimed by the Author from 1935 to 1952, That Was Written up by "Ripley Believe It or Not" Twice. Norman R. Martin. Ed. by Judy C. Mullins. (Illus.). 78p. (YA). 1997. lib. bdg. 8.95 (*0-9646489-6-2*) Martain Pub.

Ole Doc Methuselah. L. Ron Hubbard. 288p. 1991. 9.48 (*0-88404-653-2*) Bridge Pubns Inc.

Ole Doc Methuselah. large type ed. L. Ron Hubbard. 1993. 65.95 (*0-7862-9994-0*, G K Hall Lrg Type) Mac Lib Ref.

Ole Doc Methuselah. L. Ron Hubbard. 1976. reprint ed. lib. bdg. 20.95 (*0-88411-899-1*) Amereon Ltd.

Ole Doc Methuselah: Soldier of Light. L. Ron Hubbard. 288p. pap. 11.95 (*0-88404-824-1*) Bridge Pubns Inc.

Ole Edvart Rolvaag. Ann Moseley. LC 87-70033. (Western Writers Ser.: No. 80). (Illus.). 52p. (Orig.). 1987. pap. 4.95 (*0-88430-079-X*) Boise St U W Writ Ser.

OLE for Dummies. Wallace Wang. 360p. 1995. pap. 19.99 (*1-56884-338-0*) IDG Bks.

Ole Man River & Me. Fred P. Newton. write for info. (*0-318-54680-9*) Newton.

Ole Mars An' Ole Miss. Edmund K. Goldsborough. LC 74-37592. (Black Heritage Library Collection). 1977. reprint ed. 22.95 (*0-8369-8968-6*) Ayer.

Ole Miss. 2nd ed. Nash Buckingham. (Fifty Greatest Bks.). (Illus.). 243p. 1992. reprint ed. 50.00 (*1-56416-034-3*) Derrydale Pr.

***Ole Roy, Mother & Me.** Robert Gentry. Ed. by Patricia Martinez. 94p. 1999. 9.95 (*1-893693-06-6*) Sweet Dreams.

Ole Rynning's True Account of America. Ole Rynning. Ed. & Tr. by Theodore C. Blegen. LC 70-160992. (Select Bibliographies Reprint Ser.). 1977. reprint ed. 16.95 (*0-8369-5827-6*) Ayer.

Ole 2.0 & Dde Distilled: A Programmer's Crash Course/Book & Disk. Al Williams. 320p. 1994. pap. 36.95 incl. disk (*0-201-40639-X*) Addison-Wesley.

OLE 2 Programmer's Reference Library, 2 vols., Set. 2nd ed. Microsoft Corporation Staff. (Professional Editions Ser.). 1499p. 1995. pap. 50.00 (*1-55615-749-5*) Microsoft.

OLE 2 Programmer's Reference Library: Working with 32-Bit Windows Objects, 1. 2nd ed. Microsoft Corporation Staff. 1100p. 1995. pap. 29.95 (*1-55615-850-5*) Microsoft.

OLE Wizardry: Programming OLE Applications & Custom Controls Using Wizards. William H. Murray, III & Chris H. Pappas. 448p. 1995. pap. text 39.95 (*0-07-882102-9*) Osborne-McGraw.

Oleaginosas da Amazonia see Oil Palms & Other Oilseeds of the Amazon

Oleander, Jacaranda: A Childhood Perceived. Penelope Lively. LC 93-39760. 160p. 1995. pap. 12.00 (*0-06-092622-8*, Perennial) HarperTrade.

Oleander Odyssey: The Kempners of Galveston, Texas 1854-1980s. Harold M. Hyman. LC 89-20622. (Montague Series in Oil & Business History: No. 6). (Illus.). 512p. 1990. 44.50 (*0-89096-438-6*) Tex A&M Univ Pr.

Oleander's Guide to Kansas: Guide to Kansas. Thomas F. Averill. (Illus.). 160p. 1996. pap. 12.95 (*1-880652-88-9*) Wichita Eagle.

Oleanna. David Mamet. 1993. pap. 5.25 (*0-8222-1343-5*) Dramatists Play.

Oleanna. David Mamet. LC 92-50638. 1993. pap. 11.00 (*0-679-74536-X*) Vin Bks.

Olef in Metathesis & Ring-Opening Polymerization of Cyclo-Olefins. 2nd rev. ed. Valerian Dragutan et al. LC 83-10189. (Illus.). 544p. reprint ed. pap. 168.70 (*0-8357-5596-7*, 203523500093) Bks Demand.

Olefin Metathesis & Metathesis Polymerization. 2nd ed. K. J. Ivin & J. C. Mol. (Illus.). 496p. 1997. text 105.00 (*0-12-377045-9*) Morgan Kaufmann.

Olefin Metathesis & Polymerization Catalysts: Synthesis, Mechanism & Utilization. Ed. by Yavuz Imamoglu et al. (NATO Advanced Science Institutes Series C: Mathematical & Physical Sciences). 592p. 1990. text 294.00 (*0-7923-1040-3*) Kluwer Academic.

Olefinic Paint Technology. 65p. 1998. 35.00 (*0-7680-0154-4*) Soc Auto Engineers.

Olefins, Diolefins & Acetylene see Petrochemical Manufacturing & Marketing Guide

Olelo No'eau: Proverbs & Poetical Sayings, No. 71. Mary Kawena Pukui. (Special Publication Ser.). (Illus.). 368p. 1983. pap. 24.95 (*0-910240-93-0*) Bishop Mus.

Olelo O'iwi ke Kahua: He Puke A'o 'Olelo Hawai'i. Hokulani Cleeland. (ENG & HAW.). xi, 439p. (YA). (gr. 10 up). 1994. text 26.95 (*1-58191-012-6*) Aha Punana Leo.

Olelo O'iwi ke Kahua: He Puke A'o 'Olelo Hawai'i. Hokulani Creeland. (ENG & HAW.). xi, 439p. (YA). (gr. 10 up). 1994. pap. 16.95 (*1-58191-013-4*) Aha Punana Leo.

Oleomargarine. U. S. House of Representatives Committee on Bankin. LC 75-26318. (World Food Supply Ser.). (Illus.). 1976. reprint ed. 34.95 (*0-405-07794-7*) Ayer.

Olephia Leafy King: Dust & Desire, Laughter & Tears: Recollections of a Nevada Pioneer Cowgirl & Poet. Intro. by Carol Colip. 281p. 1980. lib. bdg. 46.50 (*1-56475-197-X*); fiche. write for info. (*1-56475-198-8*) U NV Oral Hist.

Olesha's Envy: A Critical Companion. Rimgaila Salys. LC 99-37099. 1999. pap. text 17.95 (*0-8101-1312-0*) Northwestern U Pr.

Oleum Magistrale. George Baker. LC 72-171. (English Experience Ser.: No. 123). 104p. 1969. reprint ed. 16.00 (*90-221-0123-1*) Walter J Johnson.

Oley Valley Heritage: The Colonial Years, 1700-1775, Vol. 28. Phillip E. Pendleton. Ed. by Don Yoder. (Illus.). 232p. 1995. write for info. (*0-911122-59-1*) Penn German Soc.

Oley's Journal. Ed. by Edwin T. Greninger. 171p. pap. 9.95 (*1-57072-009-6*) Univ South Pr.

Olfaction: A Model System for Computational Neuroscience. Ed. by Joel L. Davis & Howard Eichenbaum. (Illus.). 320p. 1991. 55.00 (*0-262-04124-3*) MIT Pr.

Olfaction & Taste: Proceedings of the 2nd International Symposium, Tokyo, Sept. 1965. T. Hayashi. LC 63-1222. (Wenner Gren Center International Symposium Ser.: Vol. 8). 1967. 366.00 (*0-08-011695-7*, Pub. by Pergamon Repr) Franklin.

Olfaction & Taste XI: Proceedings of the 11th International Symposium on Olfaction & Taste & of the 27th Japanese Symposium on Taste & Smell - Joint Meeting Held at Kosei-Nenkin Kaikan, Sapporo, Japan, July 12-16, 1993. Eleventh International Symposium on Olfaction & Ta & Twenty-Seventh Japanese Symposium on Taste & Smell. Ed. by L. Kurihara et al. LC 94-28107. 1994. write for info. (*4-431-70142-7*) Spr-Verlag.

Olfaction & Taste XII: An International Symposium. Ed. by Claire Murphy. LC 98-39456. (Annals of the New York Academy of Sciences Ser.: Vol. 855). 872p. 1999. 160.00 (*1-57331-139-1*); pap. write for info. (*1-57331-140-5*) NY Acad Sci.

Olfaction & Taste XI: Proceeding of the 11th International Symposium on Olfaction & Taste & of the 27th Japanese Symposium on Taste & Smell. Joint Meeting Held at Kosei-nenkin Kaikan, Sapporo, Japan, July 12-16, 1993. Ed. by K. Kurihara & N. Suzuki. 900p. 1994. 308.00 (*0-387-70142-7*) Spr-Verlag.

Olfaction in Mosquito-Host Interactions - Symposium No. 200. Ed. by Gregory R. Bock & Gail Cardew. LC 96-15908. (Ciba Foundation Symposium Ser.: Vol. 200). 342p. 1996. 128.00 (*0-471-96362-3*) Wiley.

Olfactory Imprinting & Homing in Salmon: Investigations into the Mechanism of the Imprinting Process. A. D. Hasler. (Zoophysiology Ser.: Vol. 14). (Illus.). 150p. 1983. 59.00 (*0-387-12519-1*) Spr-Verlag.

Olfato. Chelsea House Publishing Staff & Andrew Llamas. (SPA., Illus.). 32p. (YA). (gr. 3 up). 1996. 15.95 (*0-7910-4005-4*) Chelsea Hse.

Olfato. Parramont Puig Staff. 1986. 12.15 (*0-606-13365-8*, Pub. by Turtleback) Demco.

Olfert Dapper's Description of Benin. Olfert Dapper & Adam Jones. LC 98-29219. (DUT & ENG.). 1998. write for info. (*0-942615-34-4*) African Studies Assn.

***Olga Broumas: A Listener's Guide.** Olga Broumas. (Listener's Guides for Poetry Ser.). 32p. 2000. 12.00 incl. cd-rom (*1-55659-997-8*) Copper Canyon.

Olga De Amaral: Nine Stelae & Other Landscapes. Ana M. Escallon & Ricardo Pau-Llosa. Ed. by Doris Hall. (Illus.). 24p. (Orig.). 1996. pap. 7.50 (*0-932325-33-5*) Fresno Arts Mus.

Olga De Amaral: Tapestries from the Moonbasket. Louise Allrich. (Illus.). 12p. 1989. write for info. (*0-318-66602-2*) Allrich Gallery.

Olga Masters: A Lot of Living. Julie Lewis. 1991. pap. 16.95 (*0-7022-2387-5*, Pub. by Univ Queensland Pr) Intl Spec Bk.

Olga Preobrazhenskaya: A Portrait. Fernau Hall. LC 77-27883. (Dance Program Ser.: No. 9). (Illus.). 192p. reprint ed. pap. 59.60 (*0-7837-0812-2*, 204112700019) Bks Demand.

Olga Rozanova. Nina Gurianova. (Illus.). 220p. 1999. pap. text 28.00 (*90-5701-202-2*) Gordon & Breach.

Olga Rozanova & the Culture of Avant-Garde Russia. Nina Gurianova. (Illus.). 220p. 1999. text 58.00 (*90-5701-192-1*) Gordon & Breach.

Olga Sur, Kust Sireni (Olga Sur, the Lilac Bush) Alexander Kuprin. (Voices from Russia Ser.). (RUS.). 52p. pap. text 9.50 (*1-58085-011-1*) Interlingua VA.

Olga Taussky Todd, in Memoriam. Ed. by Michael Ashbacher et al. (Illus.). 357p. 1998. 20.00 (*1-57146-051-9*) Intl Pr Boston.

Olga's Cup & Saucer: A Picture Book with Recipes. Olga Bravo. (Illus.). 88p. (J). 1995. 15.95 (*0-8050-3301-7*) H Holt & Co.

O

***Olibanum & Myrrh: Poems from Hollywood.** Mark Dunster. 11p. 1999. pap. 5.00 (*0-89642-948-2*) Linden Pubs.

Olice: The Adventure of Olive Oil. Paolo Villoreni. (Illus.). 96p. (YA). 1997. pap. 14.95 (*0-9663135-0-X*) Italian Culinary.

Oligocene Bridge Creek Flora of the John Day Formation, Oregon. Herbert W. Meyer & Steven R. Manchester. LC 97-31080. (University of California Publications in Geological Sciences). 364p. 1998. 50.00 (*0-520-09816-1*) Univ of California Angeles Ctr.

Oligocene Haynes Creek Flora of Eastern Idaho. Daniel I. Axelrod. LC 98-6394. (Publications in Geological Sciences). 160p. 1998. pap. 22.00 (*0-520-09824-2*, Pub. by U CA Pr) Cal Prin Full Svc.

Oligocene Reef-Tract Development, Southwestern Puerto Rico: Part 1 Text; Part 2, Holocene Analog, Modern Reef & Reef-Associated Sediements, Southern Insular Shelf of Puerto Rico; Part 3 , Field Guide to Representative Exposures & Modern Analog. S. H. Frost et al. (Sedimenta Ser.: Vol. IX). (Illus.). 144p. 1983. 16.00 (*0-932981-08-9*) Univ Miami CSL.

Oligochaeta. J. Stephenson. (Illus.). 1930. 160.00 (*3-7682-0750-1*) Lubrecht & Cramer.

Oligochaeta. J. Stephenson. (Fauna of British India Ser.). xxiv, 518p. 1983. 50.00 (*1-55528-040-4*, Pub. by Today Tomorrow) Scholarly Pubns.

Oligodendroglia. Ed. by William T. Norton. (Advances in Neurochemistry Ser.: Vol. 5). 338p. 1984. 95.00 (*0-306-41547-X*, Plenum Trade) Perseus Pubng.

Oligomer Technology & Applications. Uglea. LC 97-43495. (Illus.). 1025p. 1998. text 225.00 (*0-8247-9978-X*) Dekker.

Oligomorphic Permutation Groups. P. J. Cameron. (London Mathematical Society Lecture Note Ser.: No. 152). 168p. (C). 1990. pap. text 38.95 (*0-521-38836-8*) Cambridge U Pr.

Oligonucleotide & Gene Therapy-Base Antisense Therapeutics. Ed. by Wendy Mori. (IBC Library Ser.). (Illus.). (Orig.). 1997. pap. write for info. (*1-57936-039-4*) IBC USA.

***Oligonucleotide Array: Methods & Protocols.** Ed. by Jang B. Rampal. (Methods in Molecular Biology Ser.). 350p. 2000. 99.50 (*0-89603-822-X*) Humana.

Oligonucleotides & Analogues: A Practical Approach. Ed. by Fritz Echstein. (Practical Approach Ser.). (Illus.). 340p. 1992. pap. 55.00 (*0-19-963279-0*) OUP.

Oligonucleotides As Inhibitors of Gene Expression. Cohen. 1990. 104.00 (*0-8493-7118-X*, QH) CRC Pr.

Oligonucleotides As Therapeutic Agents, Vol. 209. Derek J. Chadwick & Gail Cardew. LC 97-24989. (CIBA Foundation Symposium Ser.). 260p. 1997. 128.00 (*0-471-97279-7*) Wiley.

Oligopoly & Technical Progress. rev. ed. Paolo Sylos-Labini. Tr. by Elizabeth Henderson. (Reprints of Economic Classics Ser.). xvi, 265p. 1993. reprint ed. lib. bdg. 39.50 (*0-678-01468-X*) Kelley.

***Oligopoly Pricing: Old Ideas & New Tools.** Xavier Vives. LC 99-32864. (Illus.). 350p. 1999. 35.00 (*0-262-22060-1*) MIT Pr.

Oligosaccharides: Production, Properties & Applications, Vol. 3. Ed. by Teruo Nakakuki. (Japanese Technology Reviews Ser.). 235p. 1993. pap. text 101.00 (*2-88124-890-X*) Gordon & Breach.

***Oligosaccharides: Their Synthesis & Biological Role.** Helen M. I. Osborn & Tariq H. Khan. (Illus.). 208p. 2000. text 65.00 (*0-19-850265-6*); pap. text 34.95 (*0-19-850260-5*) OUP.

Olinda's Adventures: or The Amours of a Young Lady: From the Second Volume of Familiar Letters of Love, Gallantry & Several Occasions, by the Wits of the Last & Present Age with the Best of Voiture's Letters. Catherine Trotter. Tr. by Dryden & T. Brown. LC 92-24285. (Augustan Reprints Ser.: No. 138). 1996. reprint ed. 14.50 (*0-404-70138-8*, PR3349) AMS Pr.

Olinghouse Mining District Guidebook. Jamison Station Press Staff. (Powder Box Mining Ser.: No. 1). (Illus.). 26p. 1985. 1.95 (*0-317-01483-8*) Jamison Stn.

Olio: Poems from Hollywood. Mark Dunster. 12p. 1998. pap. 5.00 (*0-89642-440-5*) Linden Pubs.

Olio Large Print Crossword Puzzle Book. Avery P. Bromfield. 64p. 1984. spiral bd. 4.00 (*0-934381-00-3*) Olio Pubs.

Oliphant: The New World Order in Drawing & Sculpture, 1983-1993. Patrick Oliphant. LC 94-2147. (Illus.). 96p. 1994. pap. 12.95 (*0-8362-1755-1*) Andrews & McMeel.

Oliphant's Anthem: Pat Oliphant at the Library of Congress. Pat Oliphant & Harry Katz. Ed. by Sara Day. LC 97-51785. (Illus.). 130p. 1998. pap. 24.95 (*0-8362-5898-3*) Andrews & McMeel.

Oliphants of the Civil War (1861-1865) Dale Oliphant. (Illus.). 120p. 1998. 30.00 (*0-8059-4273-4*) Dorrance.

Oliphant's Presidents: Twenty-Five Years of Caricature. Patrick Oliphant. (Illus.). 96p. (Orig.). 1990. pap. 12.95 (*0-8362-1813-2*) Andrews & McMeel.

Olive. Darlene Boll. (Illus.). 201p. (J). (ps-2). 1983. pap. 6.90 (*0-7399-0073-0*, 2338) Rod & Staff.

Olive. Joachim Du Bellay & E. Caldarini. (FRE.). 180p. 1975. 49.95 (*0-7859-0060-8*, M11796) Fr & Eur.

Olive & the Caper. Hoffman. 1992. 25.00 (*0-13-633298-6*) P-H.

Olive & the Half-Caste. Dinah Craik. Ed. & Intro. by Cora Kaplan. LC 95-25866. (Oxford Popular Fiction Ser.). 398p. 1996. pap. 10.95 (*0-19-289262-2*) OUP.

***Olive Book.** Gareth Renowden. (Illus.). 114p. (Orig.). 1999. pap. 39.95 (*0-908812-80-9*, Pub. by Canterbury Univ) Accents Pubns.

Olive Branch: An Evangelical Anglican Doctrine of the Church. Timothy Bradshaw. xiv, 306p. (Orig.). 1990. pap. text 25.00 (*0-85364-512-4*) Paternoster Pub.

Olive Branch: Or, Faults on Both Sides, Federal & Democratic. Mathew Carey. LC 69-16848. (Select Bibliographies Reprint Ser.). 1977. 29.95 (*0-8369-5002-X*) Ayer.

Olive Branch: Photographs & Texts by Cedric Chatterley, 1987-1993. Contrib. by Debra Risberg. (Illus.). 32p. 1994. 10.00 (*0-945558-22-8*) ISU Univ Galls.

Olive Branch & Sword: The Compromise of 1833. Merrill D. Peterson. LC 81-13739. (Walter Lynwood Fleming Lectures in Southern History Ser.). 144p. 1982. reprint ed. pap. 44.70 (*0-608-00868-0*, 206166000010) Bks Demand.

Olive Branch & Sword: The United States & Mexico, 1845-1848. Dean B. Mahin. LC 96-29655. (Illus.). 239p. 1997. lib. bdg. 39.95 (*0-7864-0258-X*) McFarland & Co.

Olive Branch for the Conquered. Charles Roberts. 64p. 1990. pap. 6.95 (*0-932616-31-3*) Brick Hse Bks.

Olive By-Products for Animal Feed. 49p. 1985. 12.00 (*92-5-101488-4*, F2795, Pub. by FAO) Bernan Associates.

Olive Drab in an Eight-Cornered Hat. Jeffrey Granberry. 102p. 1998. write for info. (*0-7541-0091-X*, Pub. by Minerva Pr) Unity Dist.

Olive Fairy Book. Ed. by Andrew Lang. 24.95 (*0-89190-086-1*) Amereon Ltd.

Olive Fairy Book. Ed. by Andrew Lang. (Illus.). 335p. (J). (gr. 4-6). 1968. pap. 7.95 (*0-486-21908-9*) Dover.

Olive Fairy Book. Ed. by Andrew Lang. (Illus.). (J). (gr. 2 up). 1990. 22.75 (*0-8446-0754-1*) Peter Smith.

***Olive Grove.** Evelyn Hood. 272p. 2000. 31.99 (*0-7505-1504-X*) Ulverscroft.

Olive Grove: Travels in Greece. Katherine Kizilos. (Illus.). 260p. (Orig.). 1997. pap. 12.95 (*0-86442-459-0*) Lonely Planet.

***Olive in California: History of an Immigrant Tree.** Judith M. Taylor. LC SB367.T29 2000. (Illus.). 256p. 2000. pap. 24.95 (*1-58008-131-2*) Ten Speed Pr.

Olive Leaf Extract. Morton Walker. 100p. 1997. mass mkt. 5.99 (*1-57566-226-4*, Knsington) Kensgtn Pub Corp.

Olive Leaf Extract: A New/Old Healing Bonanza for Mankind. James R. Privitera. (Orig.). 1996. pap. write for info. (*0-9655872-0-7*) J Privitera.

***Olive Octopus's Deep Sea Ditties.** Giles Andreae & David Wojtowycz. (Illus.). (J). (ps-1). 2000. bds. 6.95 (*1-888444-69-X*) Little Tiger.

Olive Oil. Apostolos K. Kiritsakis. 348p. 1998. 100.00 (*0-917678-42-7*, 3313) Food & Nut Pr.

Olive Oil: Basic Flavorings. Clare Gordon-Smith. (Illus.). 64p. 1999. reprint ed. text 20.00 (*0-7881-6411-2*) DIANE Pub.

Olive Oil: Chemistry & Technology. Ed. by Dimitrios Boskou. LC 96-14787. 1996. 75.00 (*0-935315-73-X*) Am Oil Chemists.

***Olive Oil: Fresh Recipes With Olive Oil From Leading Chefs.** Sian Irvine. LC 99-59797. (Illus.). 160p. 2000. 24.95 (*962-593-530-4*) Periplus.

Olive Oil: From Tree to Table. Peggy Knickerbocker. LC 96-48843. 168p. 1997. pap. 19.95 (*0-8118-1350-9*) Chronicle Bks.

Olive Oil: Source of Life. George Monemuastis. (ENG & FRE.). 144p. 1998. 17.95 (*960-7436-44-X*) Grco Crd GR.

Olive Oil: The Good Heart Protector. Rita Greer & Cyril Blau. (Illus.). 128p. 1996. pap. text 9.95 (*0-285-63237-X*, Pub. by Souvenir Pr Ltd) IPG Chicago.

Olive Oil Cookery: The Mediterranean Diet. Maher A. Abbas & Marilyn J. Spiegl. 164p. (Orig.). 1995. pap. 12.95 (*0-913990-11-6*) Book Pub Co.

Olive Oil Miracle. Jean Barilla. (Good Health Guides Ser.). 48p. 1997. pap. 3.95 (*0-87983-763-2*, 37632K, Keats Publng) NTC Contemp Pub Co.

Olive Oil Processing in Cyprus: From the Bronze Age to the Byzantine Period. Sophocles Hadjisavvas. (Studies in Mediterranean Archaeology: Vol. XCIX). (Illus.). 150p. 1992. pap. 59.50 (*91-7081-033-8*, Pub. by P Astroms) Coronet Bks.

Olive Orchard & Other Stories. Guy de Maupassant. Ed. by Ernest A. Boyd. Tr. by Storm Jameson from FRE. LC 75-157791. (Collected Novels & Stories Ser.: Vol. 14). 1977. reprint ed. 18.95 (*0-8369-3903-4*) Ayer.

Olive Production Manual. Ed. by George C. Martin et al. LC 94-60033. (Illus.). 160p. 1994. pap. 32.00 (*1-879906-15-5*, 3353) ANR Pubns CA.

Olive Rush: A Hoosier Artist in New Mexico. Stanley L. Cuba. (Illus.). vii, 91p. (Orig.). 1992. pap. write for info. (*0-9623291-4-2*) Minnetrista.

Olive Schreiner. Cherry Clayton. LC 96-36020. 1997. 32.00 (*0-8057-8287-7*, Twyne) Mac Lib Ref.

Olive Schreiner. Ruth First & Ann Scott. 385p. (C). 1990. reprint ed. pap. 15.95 (*0-8135-1622-6*); reprint ed. text 40.00 (*0-8135-1621-8*) Rutgers U Pr.

***Olive Schreiner & the Progress of Feminism: Evolution, Gender, Empire.** Carolyn Burdett. LC 00-33304. 2000. write for info. (*0-312-23763-4*) St Martin.

Olive Schreiner Reader: Writings on Women & South Africa. Carol Barash. 1987. pap. 12.95 (*0-86358-118-8*, Pub. by Pandora) Routldge.

Olive Schreiner's Fiction: Landscape & Power. Gerald Monsman. LC 91-9431. 220p. (C). 1991. text 45.00 (*0-8135-1724-9*) Rutgers U Pr.

Olive Shoots Around Your Table: Raising Functional Kids in a Dysfunctional World. 2nd ed. John Visser. (Illus.). 325p. 1997. reprint ed. pap. 13.95 (*1-896400-14-0*) Essence Pr.

Olive Street Transfer. Pat Schneider. 80p. 1999. pap. 14.00 (*0-941895-17-3*) Amherst Wri Art.

***Olive the Orphan Reindeer.** Michael G. Christie. LC 99-88346. 1999. pap. 9.95 (*1-889658-16-2*) New Canaan Pub.

***Olive, the Other Reindeer.** J. Otto Seibold. (Illus.). 40p. 1999. boxed set 19.95 (*0-8118-2574-4*) Chronicle Bks.

Olive, the Other Reindeer. Vivian Walsh. LC 97-9876. (Illus.). 40p. (J). 1998. 13.95 (*0-8118-1807-1*) Chronicle Bks.

Olive Tree. Aldous Huxley. LC 72-167361. (Essay Index Reprint Ser.). 1977. reprint ed. 20.95 (*0-8369-2456-8*) Ayer.

Olive Tree: Growing up in Utica. Arlene C. Stein. LC 92-64465. 1992. 28.00 (*0-9634085-2-6*); pap. 18.00 (*0-9634085-1-8*) S I M A Pubs.

Olive-Tree Bed & Other Quests. M. Owen Lee. (Robson Classical Lectures). 175p. 1997. text 50.00 (*0-8020-4138-8*) U of Toronto Pr.

Olive-Tree Bed & Other Quests, Vol. 4. M. Owen Lee. (Robson Classical Lectures). 186p. 1997. pap. text 16.95 (*0-8020-7984-9*) U of Toronto Pr.

Olive White Garvey: Uncommon Citizen. Billy Jones. (Illus.). 244p. 1985. 10.00 (*0-86546-066-3*) Wichita Ctr Entrep SBM.

***Olive You! And Other Valentine Knock-Knock Jokes You'll A-Door.** Katy Hall. (Illus.). 16p. (J). (gr. k-3). 2000. 6.95 (*0-694-01355-2*) HarpC Child Bks.

Oliver. Syd Hoff. (I Can Read Bks.). (Illus.). 64p. (J). (ps-1). 1960. lib. bdg. 14.89 (*0-06-022516-5*) HarpC Child Bks.

Oliver. Syd Hoff. (I Can Read Bks.). (Illus.). 64p. (J). (ps-1). 2000. pap. 3.95 (*0-06-444272-1*, HarpTrophy) HarpC Child Bks.

Oliver. Syd Hoff. LC 99-25591. (I Can Read Bks.). (Illus.). 64p. (J). (ps-2). 2000. 14.95 (*0-06-028708-X*) HarpC Child Bks.

***Oliver.** Syd Hoff. LC 99-25591. (I Can Read Bks.). (Illus.). 64p. (J). (ps-2). 2000. lib. bdg. 14.89 (*0-06-028709-8*) HarpC Child Bks.

Oliver: A Story about Adoption. Lois Wickstrom. (Illus.). 32p. (J). 1991. 14.95 (*0-9611872-5-5*) Our Child Pr.

Oliver, Amanda, & Grandmother Pig. Jean Van Leeuwen & Ann Schweninger. (Easy-to-Read Bks.: Level 2, Red). (Illus.). (J). (ps-3). 1995. pap. 3.99 (*0-14-037386-1*, PuffinBks) Peng Put Young Read.

***Oliver & Albert, Friends Forever.** Jean Van Leeuwen. LC 99-27593. (Illus.). 48p. (J). (ps-3). 2000. 13.99 (*0-8037-2517-5*, Dial Yng Read) Peng Put Young Read.

Oliver & Amanda & the Big Snow. Jean Van Leeuwen. (Puffin Easy-to-Read Program Ser.). 48p. (J). (gr. k-3). 1998. pap. 3.99 (*0-14-038250-X*, PuffinBks) Peng Put Young Read.

Oliver & Amanda & the Big Snow. Jean Van Leeuwen. LC 93-48598. (Illus.). 48p. (J). (ps-2). 1995. 12.99 (*0-8037-1762-8*, Dial Yng Read) Peng Put Young Read.

Oliver & Amanda's Christmas. Jean Van Leeuwen. (Illus.). (J). 9.95 (*0-685-29542-7*, Dial Yng Read) Peng Put Young Read.

Oliver & Amanda's Christmas. Jean Van Leeuwen. (Puffin Easy-to-Read Ser.). (J). 1996. 8.70 (*0-606-11702-4*, Pub. by Turtleback) Demco.

Oliver & Amanda's Christmas. Jean Van Leeuwen. (Illus.). 56p. (J). (gr. k-3). 1996. pap. 3.99 (*0-14-037717-4*) Viking Penguin.

Oliver & Amanda's Christmas. Jean Van Leeuwen & Ann Schweninger. (Illus.). (J). 1989. 10.95 (*0-8037-0636-7*, Dial Yng Read) Peng Put Young Read.

Oliver & Amanda's Halloween. Jean Van Leeuwen. LC 91-30941. (Easy-to-Read Bks.). (Illus.). 48p. (J). (ps-3). 1992. 13.99 (*0-8037-1237-5*, Dial Yng Read) Peng Put Young Read.

***Oliver & Audrey's Big Sand Box.** Maureen A. Bennett. (Oliver & Audrey Otter's Adventures Presents Ser.: Vol. 2). (Illus.). 46p. (J). (ps-6). 1998. pap. 14.95 (*1-929914-02-4*, Ruf-Fur Pubns) Megaverse.

***Oliver & Audrey's First Adventure.** Maureen A. Bennett. (Oliver & Audrey Otter's Adventures Presents Ser.: Vol. 1). (Illus.). 58p. (J). (ps-6). 1998. pap. 14.95 (*1-929914-01-6*, Ruf-Fur Pubns) Megaverse.

Oliver & Cockshutt: I&T Shop Manual - Oliver & Cockshutt Collection Models Also Includes Minneapolis-Moline Models. (Illus.). 440p. Date not set. reprint ed. pap. 29.95 (*0-87288-372-8*, O-202) Intertec Pub.

Oliver & Cockshutt: I&T Shop Manual - Oliver Cockshutt Collection Models 99(6 Cyl.)4-Speed, Super 99(6 Cyl.)6-Speed, Super 99G(3 Cyl.)6-Speed, Super & Non-Super Models 66, 77, 88, 660, 770, 880 - Series 99 GMTC, 950, 990, 995, - Series Super 55, 550. (Illus.). 280p. Date not set. reprint ed. pap. 29.95 (*0-87288-363-9*, O-201) Intertec Pub.

Oliver & Company. (Classics Ser.). (Illus.). 96p. (J). (ps-4). 1994. 7.98 (*1-57082-044-9*, Pub. by Mouse Works) Time Warner.

Oliver & Company. (Disney Read-Alongs Ser.). (J). 7.99 incl. audio (*1-55723-024-2*) W Disney Records.

Oliver & Company. Mouseworks Staff. (Classics Ser.). (Illus.). (J). 1997. write for info. (*1-57082-800-8*) Mouse Works.

Oliver & the Oil Spill. Aruna Chandrasekhar. Ed. by Nancy R. Thatch. LC 91-3340. (Books for Students by Students). (Illus.). 26p. (J). (gr. k-4). 1991. lib. bdg. 15.95 (*0-933849-33-8*) Landmark Edns.

Oliver Bean Can't Get Clean. Joy Bacon. LC 93-60480. (Illus.). 48p. (Orig.). (J). (ps-3). 1996. pap. 8.95 (*1-883650-31-3*) Windswept Hse.

Oliver Bean Visits the Queen. Joy Bacon. LC 97-62543. (Illus.). 48p. (J). (gr. k-5). 1998. pap. 8.95 (*1-883650-45-3*) Windswept Hse.

Oliver Bean's Halloween. Joy Bacon. Ed. by Jane Weinberger. LC 90-70907. (Illus.). 68p. (J). (ps-3). 1991. pap. 8.95 (*0-932433-73-1*) Windswept Hse.

Oliver Bean's Thanksgiving. Joy Bacon. Ed. by Jane Weinberger. LC 93-61630. (Illus.). 40p. (Orig.). (J). (ps-3). 1994. pap. 8.95 (*1-883650-13-5*) Windswept Hse.

Oliver Button Is a Sissy. Tomie De Paola. LC 78-12624. (Illus.). 43p. (J). (ps-3). 1979. 13.00 (*0-15-257852-8*, Harcourt Child Bks); pap. 6.00 (*0-15-668140-4*, Voyager Bks) Harcourt.

Oliver Button Is a Sissy. Tomie De Paola. (J). 1979. 11.20 (*0-606-04494-9*, Pub. by Turtleback) Demco.

Oliver Cromwell. Peter Gaunt. LC 95-20324. (Historical Association Studies). (Illus.). 272p. 1997. pap. 16.95 (*0-631-20480-6*) Blackwell Pubs.

Oliver Cromwell. Frederic Harrison. LC 78-39196. (Select Bibliographies Reprint Ser.). 1977. reprint ed. 20.95 (*0-8369-6798-4*) Ayer.

***Oliver Cromwell: A Biographical Companion.** Martyn Bennett. 2002. lib. bdg. 45.00 (*1-57607-145-6*) ABC-CLIO.

Oliver Cromwell: Politics & Religion in the English Revolution, 1640-1658. David L. Smith. (Topics in History Ser.). 128p. (C). 1992. pap. 17.95 (*0-521-38896-1*) Cambridge U Pr.

Oliver Cromwell: Pretender, Puritan, Statesman, Paradox? Ed. by John F. New. LC 76-23190. (European Problem Studies). 128p. 1977. reprint ed. pap. text 10.50 (*0-03-085178-5*) Krieger.

Oliver Cromwell & the Battle of Gainsborough. John West. (C). 1989. text 21.00 (*0-902662-43-0*, Pub. by R K Pubns) St Mut.

Oliver Cromwell & the English People. Ernest Barker. LC 72-37329. (Select Bibliographies Reprint Ser.). 1977. reprint ed. 15.95 (*0-8369-6674-0*) Ayer.

Oliver Cromwell & the English Revolution. John Morrill. 300p. (C). 1990. pap. 48.00 (*0-582-01675-4*, 78528) Addison-Wesley.

Oliver Cromwell's Letters & Speeches with Elucidations see Works of Thomas Carlyle

Oliver Dibbs & the Dinosaur Cause. Barbara Steiner. 160p. (J). 1988. pap. 2.95 (*0-380-70466-8*, Avon Bks) Morrow Avon.

Oliver Dibbs to the Rescue! Barbara Steiner. (Illus.). 128p. (J). 1988. pap. 2.50 (*0-380-70465-X*, Avon Bks) Morrow Avon.

Oliver Ellsworth & the Creation of the Federal Republic. William R. Casto. LC 97-27882. (Illus.). 145p. (Orig.). 1997. pap. write for info. (*0-9618400-2-1*) Second Circuit Committee on Bicentennial.

Oliver Evans: A Chronicle of Early American Engineering. Greville Bathe & Dorothy Bathe. LC 72-5031. (Technology & Society Ser.). (Illus.). 380p. 1978. reprint ed. 46.95 (*0-405-04684-7*) Ayer.

Oliver Evans: Inventive Genius of the American Industrial Revolution. Eugene S. Ferguson. (Illus.). 72p. 1980. pap. 4.95 (*0-914650-18-1*) Hagley Museum.

Oliver Franks: Founding Father. Alex Danchev. LC 92-40948. (Illus.). 250p. (C). 1993. text 45.00 (*0-19-821577-0*, Clarendon Pr) OUP.

Oliver Goldsmith see 18th Century Literature

Oliver Goldsmith. Ed. by Gordon Campbell. (Everyman's Poetry Ser.). 1997. pap. 3.50 (*0-460-87827-1*, Everyman's Classic Lib) Tuttle Pubng.

Oliver Goldsmith. Stephen L. Gwynn. LC 74-30338. (English Literature Ser.: No. 33). 1974. lib. bdg. 75.00 (*0-8383-1843-6*) M S G Haskell Hse.

Oliver Goldsmith. Washington Irving. LC 72-1507. (English Literature Ser.: No. 33). 1972. reprint ed. lib. bdg. 75.00 (*0-8383-1446-5*) M S G Haskell Hse.

Oliver Goldsmith: Essays Towards an Interpretation. Robert W. Jackson. (Biography Index Reprint Ser.). 1977. reprint ed. 11.95 (*0-8369-8199-5*) Ayer.

Oliver Goldsmith Revisited. Peter Dixon. (Twayne's English Authors Ser.: TEAS No. 487). 200p. 1991. 24.95 (*0-8057-7008-9*, Twyne) Mac Lib Ref.

Oliver Goldsmith, (1730-1774) Selected Poems. Oliver Goldsmith. Ed. by John Lucas. pap. write for info. (*0-85635-623-9*, Pub. by Carcanet Pr) Paul & Co Pubs.

Oliver Hart-Parr. Chuck Wendel. (Crestline Ser.). (Illus.). 296p. 1993. 44.95 (*0-87938-742-4*, Crestline Pub) MBI Pubg.

Oliver Hazard Perry & the Battle of Lake Erie. Gerard T. Altoff. (Illus.). 38p. 1990. pap. 2.50 (*1-887794-00-X*) Perry Grp.

Oliver Heaviside: Sage in Solitude. Paul J. Nahin. LC 87-26044. 344p. 1988. 39.95 (*0-87942-238-6*, PCO2279) Inst Electrical.

Oliver Holden (1765-1844) Selected Works. David W. Music. (Music of the New American Nation Ser.: Vol. 13). 258p. 1997. text 94.00 (*0-8153-2428-6*) Garland.

Oliver in the City. Harry Bornstein & Lillian B. Hamilton. (Signed English Ser.). (Illus.). 56p. (J). (ps-3). 1975. pap. 6.50 (*0-913580-49-X*, Pub. by K Green Pubns) Gallaudet Univ Pr.

Oliver Jackson. Thomas Albright & Jan Butterfield. LC 82-61511. (Illus.). 32p. 1982. pap. 7.95 (*0-932216-10-2*) Seattle Art.

Oliver La Farge & the American Indian: A Biography. Robert A. Hecht. LC 91-3430. (Native American Resources Ser.: No. 2). (Illus.). 400p. 1991. 45.00 (*0-8108-2408-6*); pap. 26.50 (*0-8108-2461-2*) Scarecrow.

Oliver Madox Brown. John H. Ingram. LC 70-148798. reprint ed. 36.00 (*0-404-03503-5*) AMS Pr.

Oliver Newberry Chaffee (1881-1944) Solveiga Rush. LC 91-65383. (Illus.). 44p. (Orig.). 1991. pap. 10.00 (*0-915577-22-4*) Taft Museum.

Oliver O & the Olives. DeeAnn Champlin. (Little Lyrics Short Vowel Collection: Vol. 4). (Illus.). (J). (gr. k-2). 1998. pap. 12.00 (*1-893429-28-8*) Little Lyrics.

"Oliver Optic" Checklist: An Annotated Catalog-Index to the Series, Nonseries Stories & Magazine Publications of William Taylor Adams, 4. Compiled by Dolores B. Jones. LC 85-745. (Bibliographies & Indexes in American Literature Ser.: No. 4). 181p. 1985. lib. bdg. 55.00 (*0-313-24415-4*, JOL/) Greenwood.

Oliver Photographic History. April Halberstadt. LC 97-48364. (Illus.). 128p. 1997. pap. 19.95 (*0-7603-0158-1*) MBI Pubg.

Oliver Pig at School. Jean Van Leeuwen. 1999. pap. 3.25 (*0-14-054928-5*) NAL.

Oliver Pollock: The Life & Times of an Unknown Patriot. James A. James. LC 70-130554. (Select Bibliographies Reprint Ser.). 1977. reprint ed. 23.95 (*0-8369-5527-7*) Ayer.

***Oliver Reed: Ten Top Movies.** Andy Black. (Illus.). 2000. pap. 14.95 (*1-902588-06-1*) Glitter Bks.

Oliver Smith: A Bio-Bibliography, 43. Tom Mikotowicz. LC 93-21635. (Bio-Bibliographies in the Performing Arts Ser.: No. 43). 264p. 1993. lib. bdg. 69.50 (*0-313-28709-0*, Greenwood Pr) Greenwood.

Oliver St. John Gogarty. J. B. Lyons. (Irish Writers Ser.). 89p. 1976. 8.50 (*0-8387-1359-9*); pap. 1.95 (*0-8387-1397-1*) Bucknell U Pr.

***Oliver Stone: Interviews.** Ed. by Charles L. P. Silet. (Conversations with Filmmakers Ser.). (Illus.). 192p. 2001. pap. 18.00 (*1-57806-303-5*); lib. bdg. 45.00 (*1-57806-302-7*) U Pr of Miss.

Oliver Stone: Maverick Filmmaker. Frank Beaver. (Twayne's Filmmakers Ser.). (Illus.). 175p. 1994. 26.95 (*0-8057-9326-7*, Twyne) Mac Lib Ref.

Oliver Stone: Maverick Filmmaker. Frank E. Beaver. (Twayne's Filmmakers Ser.). (Illus.). 175p. 1994. pap. 20.00 (*0-8057-9332-1*, Twyne) Mac Lib Ref.

Oliver Stone - Close Up: The Making of His Movies. Chris Salewicz. (Close Up Ser.). (Illus.). 144p. 1998. pap. text 13.95 (*1-56025-162-X*, Thunders Mouth) Avalon NY.

Oliver Stone's "Heaven & Earth" Adaptation of the Screenplay by Michael Singer. Intro. by Oliver Stone. (Illus.). 160p. 1993. 30.00 (*0-8048-1991-2*) Tuttle Pubng.

***Oliver Stone's U. S. A. Film, History & Controversy.** Ed. by Robert Brent Toplin. LC 00-21665. (Illus.). 320p. 2000. text 34.95 (*0-7006-1035-9*) U Pr of KS.

Oliver System--Using the Factor Ranking-Benchmark-Guidechart Evaluation Plan, 2 vols. Philip M. Oliver. LC 84-90567. (Illus.). 267p. 1984. 90.00 (*0-9617464-2-4*) P M Oliver.

Oliver System--Using the Factor Ranking-Benchmark-Guidechart Evaluation Plan, 2 vols., Set. Philip M. Oliver. LC 84-90567. (Illus.). 267p. 1984. 90.00 (*0-9617464-0-8*) P M Oliver.

Oliver Township Cemetery, Kalkaska County, Michigan. Betty Dunham. (Illus.). 34p. 1990. pap. 6.00 (*0-940133-26-1*) Kinseeker Pubns.

Oliver Tractors. Herbert Morrell & Jeff Hackett. LC 97-13151. (Illus.). 160p. 1997. 29.95 (*0-7603-0356-8*) MBI Pubg.

Oliver Tractors: Oliver, Hart-Parr & Cockshutt. Robert A. Pripps & Andrew Morlands. (Tractor Color Histories Ser.). (Illus.). 128p. 1994. pap. text 21.95 (*0-87938-853-6*) MBI Pubg.

Oliver Tractors Photo Archive. Ed. by P. A. Letourneau. LC 93-61074. (Photo Archive Ser.). (Illus.). 144p. 1993. pap. 29.95 (*1-882256-09-3*) Iconografix.

Oliver Twist. (Nelson Readers Ser.). (J). Date not set. pap. text. write for info. (*0-17-557020-5*) Addison-Wesley.

Oliver Twist. (J). 2.98 (*1-56156-372-2*) Kidsbks.

Oliver Twist. (Spanish Children's Classics Ser.: No. 800-4). (SPA.). (J). 1990. boxed set 3.50 (*0-7214-1398-6*, Ladybrd) Penguin Putnam.

Oliver Twist. Arco Editorial Staff. (C). 3.95 (*0-671-00824-2*, Arco) Macmillan Gen Ref.

Oliver Twist. Intro. by Steven Connor. 432p. 1994. 3.95 (*0-460-87490-X*, Everyman's Classic Lib) Tuttle Pubng.

Oliver Twist. Charles Dickens. 478p. Date not set. 30.95 (*0-8488-2536-5*) Amereon Ltd.

Oliver Twist. Charles Dickens. 448p. (YA). (gr. 7-12). 1982. mass mkt. 4.95 (*0-553-21102-1*, Bantam Classics) Bantam.

Oliver Twist. Charles Dickens. (Barron's Book Notes Ser.). 1985. pap. 2.95 (*0-8120-3532-1*) Barron.

Oliver Twist. Charles Dickens. LC 98-44179. (Eyewitness Classics Ser.). (J). 1999. 14.95 (*0-7894-3959-X*) DK Pub Inc.

***Oliver Twist.** Charles Dickens. LC 99-50014. (Read & Listen Ser.). (Illus.). 64p. (J). (gr. 4-7). 2000. pap. text 7.95 (*0-7894-5463-7*, D K Ink) DK Pub Inc.

Oliver Twist. Charles Dickens. LC 92-52899. 1992. 20.00 (*0-679-41724-9*) Everymns Lib.

***Oliver Twist.** Charles Dickens. (Illus.). 1999. 7.95 (*3-8290-3004-5*) Konemann.

Oliver Twist. Charles Dickens. Ed. by Richard Adams. (Study Texts Ser.). 1988. pap. text 5.95 (*0-582-33150-1*, 72056) Longman.

Oliver Twist. Charles Dickens. (English As a Second Language Bk.). 1988. pap. text 4.46 (*0-582-53496-8*) Longman.

Oliver Twist. Charles Dickens. LC 93-36278. (Books of Wonder). (Illus.). 464p. (gr. 4-7). 1994. 20.00 (*0-688-12911-0*, Wm Morrow) Morrow Avon.

Oliver Twist. Charles Dickens. 496p. (J). (gr. 7). 1961. mass mkt. 4.95 (*0-451-52351-2*, Sig Classics) NAL.

Oliver Twist. Charles Dickens. Ed. by Fred Kaplan. LC 92-34792. (Critical Editions Ser.). 611p. (C). 1992. pap. text 20.25 (*0-393-96292-X*) Norton.

Oliver Twist. Charles Dickens. (Now Age Illustrated V Ser.). (Illus.). 64p. (gr. 4-12). 1979. student ed. 1.25 (*0-88301-418-1*); pap. text 2.95 (*0-88301-394-0*) Pendulum Pr.

Oliver Twist. Charles Dickens. Ed. by Malvina Vogel. (Great Illustrated Classics Ser.: Vol. 5). (Illus.). 240p. (J). (gr. 3-6). 1989. 9.95 (*0-86611-956-6*) Playmore Inc.

Oliver Twist. Charles Dickens. 1998. mass mkt. 3.99 (*0-8125-8003-6*, Pub. by Tor Bks) St Martin.

Oliver Twist. Charles Dickens. 1993. pap. 2.95 (*0-89375-784-5*) Troll Communs.

Oliver Twist. Charles Dickens. (Signet Classics). 1961. 10.05 (*0-606-00928-0*, Pub. by Turtleback) Demco.

Oliver Twist. Charles Dickens. Ed. by Peter Fairclough. (English Library). 496p. 1966. pap. 6.95 (*0-14-043017-2*, Penguin Classics) Viking Penguin.

Oliver Twist. Charles Dickens. (Classics Library). 355p. 1997. pap. 3.95 (*1-85326-012-6*, 0126WW, Pub. by Wrdsworth Edits) NTC Contemp Pub Co.

Oliver Twist. Charles Dickens. LC 89-24279. (Step into Classics Ser.). (Illus.). 96p. (J). (gr. 2-6). 1990. pap. 3.99 (*0-679-80391-2*, Pub. by Random Bks Yng Read) Random.

Oliver Twist. Charles Dickens & S. N. Rizvi. 122p. 1997. pap. 20.00 (*81-209-0071-5*, Pub. by Pitambar Pub) St Mut.

Oliver Twist. Ed. by Tricia Hedge. (Illus.). 110p. 1992. pap. text 5.95 (*0-19-422683-2*) OUP.

Oliver Twist. Michael Lancy & Chuck Lakin. 80p. 1981. pap. 5.00 (*1-890298-27-1*) Centerstage Pr.

Oliver Twist. Les Martin. LC 89-24279. (Bullseye Step into Classics Ser.). (J). 1994. 9.09 (*0-606-09705-8*, Pub. by Turtleback) Demco.

Oliver Twist. Joanne Mattern. (Wishbone Classics Ser.). 1996. 9.09 (*0-606-10368-6*, Pub. by Turtleback) Demco.

Oliver Twist. Adapted by Robert Thomas Noll. 85p. Date not set. pap. 5.60 (*0-87129-990-9*, O61) Dramatic Pub.

***Oliver Twist.** David Paroissien. LC 99-24649. 1999. write for info. (*0-404-62471-5*) AMS Pr.

Oliver Twist. Ed. by D. K. Swan. (English As a Second Language Bk.). 1981. pap. write for info. (*0-318-54127-0*) Longman.

Oliver Twist. abr. ed. Charles Dickens. (Classics for Young Readers Ser.). (Illus.). 448p. (YA). (gr. 5 up). 1994. pap. 4.99 (*0-14-036814-0*, PuffinBks) Peng Put Young Read.

***Oliver Twist.** deluxe ed. Charles Dickens. (Signature Classics Ser.). 464p. 1999. 29.95 (*1-58279-049-3*) Trident Pr Intl.

Oliver Twist. large type ed. Charles Dickens. 560p. 1998. lib. bdg. 24.00 (*0-939495-52-X*) North Bks.

Oliver Twist. large type ed. Charles Dickens. (Classics Ser.). 13.95 (*0-7089-8019-8*, Charnwood) Ulverscroft.

Oliver Twist. Charles Dickens. 1982. reprint ed. lib. bdg. 28.95 (*0-89966-372-9*) Buccaneer Bks.

***Oliver Twist.** Charles Dickens. 482p. 1998. reprint ed. lib. bdg. 24.00 (*1-58287-054-3*) North Bks.

Oliver Twist. unabridged ed. Charles Dickens. (Classics Ser.). (YA). (gr. 9 up). 1963. mass mkt. 3.50 (*0-8049-0009-4*, CL-9) Airmont.

***Oliver Twist.** 2nd ed. Charles Dickens. Ed. by Kathleen Tillotson. (Oxford World's Classics Ser.). (Illus.). 538p. 1999. pap. 5.95 (*0-19-283339-1*) OUP.

Oliver Twist. 2nd ed. Ed. by D. H. Howe. (Illus.). 78p. 1993. pap. text 5.95 (*0-19-585260-5*) OUP.

Oliver Twist: In Arabic. Charles Dickens. 1982. pap. 14.95 (*0-86685-138-0*) Intl Bk Ctr.

***Oliver Twist: The Adventures of Oliver Twist.** Charles Dickens. (Signature Classics Ser.). 464p. 1999. 24.95 (*1-58279-037-X*) Trident Pr Intl.

***Oliver Twist: The Official Companion.** Tom McGregor. (Illus.). 160p. 2000. 19.95 (*1-85227-837-4*) Virgin Pubng.

Oliver Twist: Whole Heart & Soul. Richard J. Dunn. (Masterwork Studies). 180p. 1993. 23.95 (*0-8057-9426-3*, Twyne); pap. 13.95 (*0-8057-8579-5*, Twyne) Mac Lib Ref.

Oliver Twist Notes. Harry Kaste. (Cliffs Notes Ser.). 104p. 1965. pap. 4.95 (*0-8220-0958-7*, Cliff) IDG Bks.

Oliver Untwisted. Muriel A. Payne. 1972. 34.95 (*0-8490-0761-5*) Gordon Pr.

Oliver Wendell Holmes. G. Edward White. LC 99-34529. (Oxford Portraits Ser.). (Illus.). 160p. (YA). 2000. lib. bdg. 22.00 (*0-19-511667-4*) OUP.

Oliver Wendell Holmes: An Appreciation. William L. Schroeder. (BCL1-PS American Literature Ser.). 120p. 1992. reprint ed. lib. bdg. 69.00 (*0-7812-6742-0*) Rprt Serv.

Oliver Wendell Holmes: Representative Selections. Oliver W. Holmes. LC 75-41138. reprint ed. 64.50 (*0-404-14764-X*) AMS Pr.

Oliver Wendell Holmes: Representative Selections. Oliver W. Holmes. Ed. & Notes by Howard M. Jones. LC PS1953.H4. 502p. reprint ed. pap. 155.70 (*0-608-17399-1*, 205223000066) Bks Demand.

Oliver Wendell Holmes: Soldier, Lawyer, Supreme Court Justice. Helen S. Peterson. LC 78-71848. (Illus.). 91p. 1979. 7.95 (*0-914932-03-9*) Fox Hills Pr.

Oliver Wendell Holmes, Jr. What Manner of Liberal? Ed. by David H. Burton. LC 78-23645. (American Problem Studies). 168p. 1979. pap. 11.50 (*0-88275-793-8*) Krieger.

Oliver Wendell Holmes, Jr., Papers. Oliver W. Holmes & University Publications of America Inc. LC 88-893905. (American Legal Manuscripts from the Harvard). 72p. 1985. write for info. (*0-89093-803-2*) U Pubns Amer.

Oliver Wendell Holmes, the Autocrat & His Fellow-Boarders. Samuel M. Crothers. LC 72-124231. (Select Bibliographies Reprint Ser.). 1977. 12.95 (*0-8369-5420-3*) Ayer.

Oliver Wight ABCD Checklist for Operational Excellence. Oliver Wight. 128p. 1995. pap. 24.95 (*0-471-13267-5*) Wiley.

Oliver Wight ABCD Checklist for Operational Excellence. 4th ed. Oliver W. Wight. LC 92-62444. 115p. 1992. pap. 54.00 (*0-939246-30-9*) Wiley.

***Oliver Wight ABCD Checklist for Operational Excellence.** 5th ed. Oliver Wight. 116p. 2000. pap. 27.95 (*0-471-38819-X*) Wiley.

Oliver Wiswell. Kenneth Roberts. LC 99-17851. 836p. 1999. reprint ed. pap. 24.95 (*0-89272-468-4*) Down East.

Oliver's Alphabets. Lisa Bruce. LC 92-39471. (Illus.). 24p. (J). (ps-1). 1993. text 13.95 (*0-02-735996-4*, Bradbury S&S) S&S Childrens.

Oliver's Birthday. Marilee R. Burton. LC 85-45682. (Illus.). 32p. (J). (ps). 1986. 11.95 (*0-06-020879-1*) HarpC Child Bks.

Oliver's Fruit Salad. Vivien French. LC 97-32704. (Illus.). 32p. (J). (ps-1). 1998. 14.95 (*0-531-30087-0*) Orchard Bks Watts.

Oliver's Guide to the City of London, 1998 Edition. AP Professional Staff. 1999. pap. 125.00 (*0-906247-93-4*) Kogan Page Ltd.

Oliver's High Five. Beverly S. Brown. LC 97-35089. (Illus.). 32p. (J). (gr. k-3). 1997. pap. 8.95 (*0-929173-26-0*) Health Press.

***Oliver's Milk Shake.** Vivian French. LC 99-44069. (Illus.). (J). 2000. pap. write for info. (*0-531-30304-7*) Orchard Bks Watts.

Oliver's Numbers. Bruce. (J). 1997. 14.95 (*0-689-80544-6*) S&S Childrens.

Oliver's Secretary. Dora N. Raymond. LC 71-174302. reprint ed. 32.50 (*0-404-05229-0*) AMS Pr.

Oliver's Story. Erich Segal. 208p. 1988. mass mkt. 7.50 (*0-553-27529-1*) Bantam.

***Oliver's Towns: More Columns by Oliver Towne.** Gareth Hiebert. (Illus.). 285p. 2000. pap. 15.95 (*1-880654-19-9*, Pub. by Pogo Pr) SCB Distributors.

Oliver's Vegetables. Vivian French. LC 94-45475. (Illus.). 32p. (J). (ps-1). 1996. 14.95 (*0-531-09462-6*) Orchard Bks Watts.

Oliver's Vegetables. Vivian French. LC 94-45475. (Illus.). 32p. (J). (ps-1). 1998. pap. 6.95 (*0-531-07104-9*) Orchard Bks Watts.

Oliver's Wars. unabridged ed. Budge Wilson. 128p. (Orig.). (J). (gr. 3-6). 1996. pap. 5.99 (*0-7736-7416-0*) STDK.

Oliver's Wood. Sue Hendra. LC 95-40986. (Illus.). 32p. (J). (ps). 1996. 15.99 (*1-56402-932-8*) Candlewick Pr.

Olives: Cooking with Olives & Its Oil. Marlena Spieler. 1998. 12.99 (*0-7858-0895-7*) Bk Sales Inc.

Olives: The Life & Lore of a Noble Fruit. Mort Rosenblum. (Illus.). 250p. 1996. 25.00 (*0-86547-503-2*) N Point Pr.

Olives: The Life & Lore of a Noble Fruit. Mort Rosenblum. (Illus.). 336p. 1998. pap. 15.00 (*0-86547-526-1*) N Point Pr.

Olives & Olive Oil for the Gourmet: 100 Recipes of Foods Made with Olives & Olive Oil. George F. Steffanides. (Illus.). v, 50p. 1980. pap. 2.50 (*0-9600114-6-3*, TX-389-182) Steffanides.

***Olives Dessert Table: Extraordinary Restaurant Desserts You Can Make in Your Home Kitchen.** Todd English et al. (Illus.). 256p. 2000. 35.00 (*0-684-82335-7*) S&S Trade.

Olives on the Apple Tree. Guido D'Agostino. LC 74-17924. (Italian American Experience Ser.). 1975. reprint ed. 21.95 (*0-405-06397-0*) Ayer.

Olives Table. Todd English. LC 96-44532. 368p. 1997. 31.50 (*0-684-81572-9*) S&S Trade.

Olivetti English-Spanish Computer Dictionary (Diccionario de Informatica Olivetti Ingles-Espanol) 10th ed. Olivetti. (ENG & SPA.). 271p. 1991. pap. 39.95 (*0-7859-4873-2*) Fr & Eur.

Olivi & Franciscan Poverty: The Origins of the Usus Pauper Controversy. David Burr. LC 88-39056. (Middle Ages Ser.). 224p. (C). 1989. text 39.95 (*0-8122-8151-9*) U of Pa Pr.

***Olivia.** (gr. k-3). 2000. per. 17.00 (*0-689-83495-0*) S&S Childrens.

Olivia. V. C. Andrews. 400p. 1999. 24.00 (*0-671-00760-2*) S&S Trade.

Olivia. V. C. Andrews. (YA). 1999. per. 7.99 (*0-671-00761-0*) S&S Trade.

Olivia. Olivia De Berardinis. 1996. 100.00 (*0-9622646-3-6*) R Bane Ltd.

***Olivia.** Ian Falconer. LC 99-24003. (J). (gr. k-3). 2000. 16.00 (*0-689-82953-1*) Atheneum Yung Read.

Olivia. Gladys T. Newman & William Kroll. (Illus.). 212p. 1996. text 18.95 (*0-9649532-0-X*, OL 112696-1) G T Newman.

Olivia. Rosie Rushton. 224p. (gr. 5-9). 2000. mass mkt. 3.99 (*0-7868-1392-X*, Pub. by Hyprn Ppbks) Little.

Olivia. large type ed. V. C. Andrews. LC 99-18825. 1999. 27.95 (*0-7838-8592-X*) Mac Lib Ref.

Olivia. Olivia. LC 75-12342. (Homosexuality Ser.). 1975. reprint ed. 22.55 (*0-405-07382-8*) Ayer.

Olivia. 2nd ed. Marie Hanson. LC 84-71812. 175p. 1985. pap. 7.95 (*0-933753-03-9*) Canterbury.

Olivia: My Life of Exile in Kalaupapa. Olivia R. Breitha. (Illus.). 104p. 1991. reprint ed. pap. 4.95 (*0-9631388-3-9*) AZ Mem Mus.

Olivia Cosmos Montevideo. Warloe. 1994. 22.00 (*0-671-79702-6*, Pocket Books) PB.

Olivia Cosmos Montevideo. Warloe. 1995. per. 12.00 (*0-671-79703-4*, Pocket Books) PB.

Olivia, More Than Physical: A Collector's Guide. Gregory Branson-Trent. LC 97-5238. (Illus.). 149p. 1995. 12.95 (*0-9695736-6-9*) CN06.

Olivia: or The Weight of the Past. large type ed. Judith Rossner. LC 94-42583. (Large Print Bks.). 1995. 23.95 (*1-56895-166-3*) Wheeler Pub.

Olivia Pride Burtt's Nova Scotian Ancestry: The Story of the Prides, Abbotts & Coles. M. Edward Burtt et al. (Illus.). iii, 55p. 1993. pap. write for info. (*1-888913-07-X*) M E Burtt.

Olivia/Lucy. Charles Graham. 1998. pap. text 10.95 (*1-897809-44-1*) Silver Moon.

Olivia's Story. Kate William. (Sweet Valley High Super Star Ser.: No. 4). (YA). (gr. 7 up). 1991. 8.60 (*0-606-00667-2*, Pub. by Turtleback) Demco.

***Olivia's Touch.** Peggy Stoks. LC 99-89359. (Abounding Love Ser.). 300p. 2000. pap. 8.99 (*0-8423-1942-5*) Tyndale Hse.

Olivier. Mark Dunster. 12p. (Orig.). 1993. pap. 4.00 (*0-89642-222-4*) Linden Pubs.

Olivier de Clisson & Political Society in France under Charles V & Charles VI. John B. Henneman. LC 96-11190. (Middle Ages Ser.). (Illus.). 360p. 1996. text 54.95 (*0-8122-3353-0*) U of Pa Pr.

Olivier de la Marche, Le Chevalier Delibere (The Resolute Knight) Olivier de LaMarche. Ed. by Carleton W. Carroll. Tr. by Lois Hawley Wilson. (Medieval & Renaissance Texts & Studies: Vol. 199). (Illus.). 368p. 1999. 30.00 (*0-86698-241-8*, MR 199) MRTS.

***Olivier Messiaen: Eclairs Sur L'Au-Dela: Die Christlich-Eschatologische Dimension Des Opus Ultimum.** Julian Christopher Tolle. (GER., Illus.). 341p. 1999. 52.00 (*3-631-34846-0*) P Lang Pubng.

Olivier Messiaen: Music & Color - Conversations with Claude Samuel. Claude Samuel. Tr. by E. Thomas Glasow. LC 93-28281. (Illus.). 296p. 1994. 29.95 (*0-931340-67-5*, Amadeus Pr) Timber.

Olivier Messiaen, the Musical Mediator: A Study of the Influence of Liszt, Debussy, & Bartok. Madeleine Hsu. LC 95-9598. 1995. write for info. (*0-614-07996-9*) Fairleigh Dickinson.

Olivier Messiaen, the Musical Mediator: A Study of the Influence of Liszt, Debussy, & Bartok. Madeleine Hsu. (Illus.). 184p. 1996. 34.50 (*0-8386-3595-4*) Fairleigh Dickinson.

Olivier Mosset. (Illus.). 24p. 1990. pap. 20.00 (*3-906700-27-5*, Pub. by Lars Muller) Dist Art Pubs.

Olivier Mosset: Monograph. (Illus.). 120p. 1990. 45.00 (*3-906700-20-8*, Pub. by Lars Muller) Dist Art Pubs.

Olivier Ne Sait Pas. Ardyth Brott. (Droles D'Histories Ser.). (FRE., Illus.). 24p. (J). (ps up). 1995. pap. 6.95 (*2-89021-230-0*, Pub. by La Courte Ech) Firefly Bks Ltd.

Olivier, Olivier. Leon Steinmetz et al. Ed. by Inga Karetnikova. LC 96-26989. 86p. 1996. pap. 12.95 (*0-435-07003-7*, 07003) Heinemann.

Olivi's Peaceable Kingdom: A Reading of the Apocalypse Commentary. David Burr. LC 93-25557. (Middle Ages Ser.). 320p. (C). 1993. text 42.50 (*0-8122-3227-5*) U of Pa Pr.

Olivopontocerebellar Atrophies. fac. ed. Ed. by Roger C. Duvoisin & Andreas Plaitakis. LC 84-9861. (Advances in Neurology Ser.: No. 41). (Illus.). 304p. pap. 94.30 (*0-7837-7268-8*, 204703700005) Bks Demand.

OL/Last Gift: A Christmas Story about Family Forgiveness. Gary Parker. LC 99-27375. 1999. 12.99 (*1-56476-779-5*) SP Pubns.

Ollie All Over. Denis Roche. LC 96-21359. (Illus.). 14p. (J). 1997. 4.95 (*0-395-81124-4*) HM.

Ollie Goes to School. Elizabeth Rodgers. (Illus.). 32p. (J). (ps-2). 1992. pap. 2.50 (*0-590-44785-8*, Cartwheel) Scholastic Inc.

Ollie in Orbit. Derek A. Kelly. (Illus.). 140p. (Orig.). 1988. 16.95 (*0-89433-323-2*); pap. 11.95 (*0-89433-324-0*) Petrocelli.

Ollie Knows Everything. Abby Levine. LC 93-29600. (J). 1994. 12.15 (*0-606-09706-6*, Pub. by Turtleback) Demco.

Ollie Knows Everything. Abby Levine. (Illus.). 32p. (J). (ps-2). 1996. reprint ed. pap. 6.95 (*0-8075-6021-9*) A Whitman.

Ollie Miss. George W. Henderson. 276p. 1973. reprint ed. 15.95 (*0-911860-41-X*) Chatham Bkseller.

Ollie Owl. Suzanne Burke. Ed. by Alton Jordan. (I Can Eat an Elephant Ser.). (Illus.). (J). (gr. k-3). 1984. 7.95 (*0-89868-015-8*, Read Res); pap. 3.95 (*0-89868-048-4*, Read Res) ARO Pub.

Ollie the Elephant. Burny Bos. LC 89-42608. (Illus.). 32p. (J). (gr. k-3). 1995. pap. 6.95 (*1-55858-485-4*, Pub. by North-South Bks NYC) Chronicle Bks.

Ollie the Elephant. Burny Bos. 1995. 12.15 (*0-606-08837-7*, Pub. by Turtleback) Demco.

Ollie the Elephant: A Pop-Up Book. Burny Bos. (Illus.). 12p. (J). (ps-2). 1997. bds. 15.95 (*1-55858-709-8*, Pub. by North-South Bks NYC) Chronicle Bks.

Ollie the Owl Talks about Alpine Skiing. William T. Valentine. (Illus.). 24p. (Orig.). (J). (ps-7). 1995. 2.99 (*1-887693-10-6*) Who Pubng.

Ollie the Owl Talks about Ambulances. William T. Valentine. (Illus.). (Orig.). (J). (ps-7). 1995. 1.99 (*1-887693-01-7*) Who Pubng.

Ollie the Owl Talks about Bicycling. William T. Valentine. (Illus.). 24p. (Orig.). (J). (ps-7). 1995. 2.99 (*1-887693-06-8*) Who Pubng.

Ollie the Owl Talks about Camping. William T. Valentine. (Illus.). 24p. (Orig.). (J). (ps-7). 1995. pap. 2.99 (*1-887693-05-X*) Who Pubng.

Ollie the Owl Talks about Canoeing. William T. Valentine. (Illus.). 24p. (Orig.). (J). (ps-7). 1995. 2.99 (*1-887693-07-6*) Who Pubng.

Ollie the Owl Talks about Cross-Country Skiing. William T. Valentine. (Illus.). 24p. (Orig.). (J). (ps-7). 1995. 2.99 (*1-887693-09-2*) Who Pubng.

Ollie the Owl Talks about Fire Safety at Your House. William T. Valentine. (Illus.). 8p. (Orig.). (J). (ps-7). 1995. 1.99 (*1-887693-03-3*) Who Pubng.

Ollie the Owl Talks about Hiking. William T. Valentine. (Illus.). 21p. (Orig.). (J). (ps-7). 1995. 2.99 (*1-887693-04-1*) Who Pubng.

Ollie the Owl Talks about Your New Pet Dog. William T. Valentine. (Illus.). 24p. (Orig.). (J). (ps-7). 1995. 2.99 (*1-887693-08-4*) Who Pubng.

Ollie the Owl Talks about Your New Pet Fish. William T. Valentine. (Illus.). 24p. (Orig.). (J). (ps-7). 1995. 2.99 (*1-887693-11-4*) Who Pubng.

Ollie the Owl Visits the Emergency Room. William T. Valentine. (Illus.). 10p. (Orig.). (J). (ps-7). 1995. 1.99 (*1-887693-02-5*) Who Pubng.

Ollie the Robot... Talks about Robots. Derek A. Kelly. (Illus.). 128p. 1987. text 14.95 (*0-89433-303-8*); pap. text 9.95 (*0-89433-279-1*, NO. 8228) Petrocelli.

***Ollie's Cabin in the Woods.** Robert F. Hessong & Katheryn Hessong. LC 99-73486. (Illus.). 70p. (J). 1999. 14.95 (*1-57860-045-6*); pap. 9.95 (*1-57860-031-6*) Guild Pr IN.

Ollie's Ski Trip. Elsa Beskow. Tr. by Ernest Benn Ltd. Staff. (Illus.). (J). (ps-2). 15.95 (*0-86315-091-8*, Pub. by Floris Bks) Gryphon Hse.

Ollie's Song. Rob Lewis. 1999. pap. 10.99 (*0-8037-1102-6*, NewStar Pr); pap. 10.89 (*0-8037-1103-4*, NewStar Pr) NewStar Media.

Olliff Family History: Descendants of John Shears Olliff & Johannah (Jackson) Olliff of Bulloch County, Georgia. Robert B. Casey & Bernice B. Casey. (Illus.). 384p. (C). text 25.00 (*0-9619051-3-1*) Brooks TX.

Olly's Prison. Edward Bond. 88p. (C). 1993. pap. 10.95 (*0-413-67610-2*, A0671, Methuen Drama) Methn.

Olmans' Guide to Golf Antiques: And Other Treasures of the Game. John M. Olman & Morton W. Olman. (Illus.). 280p. 1992. 24.95 (*0-942117-02-6*) Market St Pr.

Olmec & Their Neighbors: Essays in Memory of Matthew W. Stirling. Ed. by Elizabeth P. Benson. LC 79-49262. (Illus.). 346p. 1981. 30.00 (*0-88402-098-3*) Dumbarton Oaks.

***Olmec Art & Archaeology in Meso-America.** Ed. by John E. Clark & Mary E. Pye. (Illus.). 344p. 2000. 50.00 (*0-300-08522-2*) Yale U Pr.

Olmec Art of Ancient Mexico. Ed. by Elizabeth P. Benson & Beatriz de la Fuente. (Illus.). 400p. 1996. 80.00 (*0-8109-6328-0*, Pub. by Abrams) Time Warner.

Olmec Figure at Dumbarton Oaks. Elizabeth P. Benson. LC 70-184640. (Studies in Pre-Columbian Art & Archaeology: No. 8). (Illus.). 95p. 1971. pap. 6.00 (*0-88402-035-5*) Dumbarton Oaks.

Olmec World: Ritual & Rulership. Michael D. Coe et al. Ed. by Jill Guthrie. LC 95-78295. (Illus.). 325p. (Orig.). 1996. 75.00 (*0-8109-6311-6*, Pub. by Abrams) Time Warner.

Olmec World: Ritual & Rulership. Michael D. Coe et al. Ed. by Jill Guthrie. LC 95-78295. (Illus.). (Orig.). 1995. pap. 45.00 (*0-943012-19-8*) Prince U Art.

Olmecas (The Olmecs) Jacques Soustelle. (SPA., Illus.). 192p. 1992. reprint ed. 14.99 (*968-16-1541-7*, Pub. by Fondo) Continental Bk.

Olmo & the Dragon. unabridged ed. Vivi Escriva. LC 95-4722. (SPA., Illus.). 24p. (Orig.). (J). (gr. 3-6). 1997. pap. 9.95 (*1-56492-219-7*) Laredo.

Olmo y la Mariposa Azul. Ed. by Alma F. Ada. (Laredo Children's Bilingual Library). (Illus.). 24p. (J). (gr. k-3). 1992. lib. bdg. 7.50 (*1-56492-095-X*) Laredo.

Olms - Festschrift 100 Jahre Olms. Ed. by W. Joachim Freyburg. 138p. 1987. write for info. (*3-487-07920-8*) G Olms Pubs.

***Olmstead Window.** 1999. write for info. (*0-684-00897-1*) S&S Trade.

Olmsted Family in America. Henry K. Olmsted & George K. Ward. LC 93-79946. (Illus.). 550p. 1994. reprint ed. 60.00 (*1-55787-046-2*) Hrt of the Lakes.

Olmsted South: Old South Critic - New South Planner, 43. Ed. by Dana F. White & Victor A. Kramer. LC 78-20019. (Contributions in American Studies: No. 43). 259p. 1979. 65.00 (*0-313-20724-0*, WOS/, Greenwood Pr) Greenwood.

Olmsted's Sudbrook - The Making of a Community. Melanie D. Anson. Ed. by Barry Kessler. LC 97-61916. (Illus.). 1998. pap. 24.95 (*0-9661031-0-6*) Sudbrook Park.

Olney Street Anthology. Olney Street Group Staff. LC 88-92293. 120p. (Orig.). 1988. pap. 5.00 (*0-9621084-0-5*) Olney St Pr.

Olodumare. E. Bqlaji Idowu. Ed. by Al I. Obaba. (Illus.). 248p. 1990. pap. text 17.00 (*0-916157-82-2*) African Islam Miss Pubns.

Olodumare: God in Yoruba Belief. E. Bolasi Idowu. (Illus.). 256p. 1995. pap. 14.95 (*0-942272-41-2*) Original Pubns.

Olof Christian Telemak Andren, Ambassador of Good Will. Oscar N. Olson. LC 55-2674. (Augustana Historical Society Publications: Vol. 14). 103p. 1954. pap. 3.00 (*0-910184-14-3*) Augustana.

Olof Palme Memorial Lecture on Disarmament & Development. Oliver Tambo et al. Ed. by Cora Weiss. (Illus.). 86p. (Orig.). 1987. pap. 7.95 (*0-9618304-0-9*) Rvrside Disarmament.

Ology: The Study Of . . . C. D. Whitfield. (Illus.). 148p. 1998. pap. 5.95 (*1-892084-14-7*) Vineyard Pub.

Olomeinu: Our World Alphabetical Index of Themes & Personalities. (J). 1987. 3.00 (*0-914131-72-9*, D050) Torah Umesorah.

Olompali, in the Beginning. June E. Gardner. 1995. pap. text 7.50 (*1-882897-02-1*) Lost Coast.

Olookun: Owner of Rivers & Seas. John Mason. LC 96-60309. (Illus.). 180p. (Orig.). (C). 1996. pap. 20.00 (*1-881244-05-9*) Yoruba Theol Arch.

Olor de la Guayaba. Gabriel Garcia Marquez. (SPA., Illus.). 166p. 1997. pap. 14.98 (*968-13-2546-X*) Libros Fronteras.

Olor del Popcorn. Jose L. Ramos Escobar. 1996. pap. text. write for info. (*1-56758-043-2*) Edit Cultl.

Olorgesailie: Archeological Studies of a Middle Pleistocene Lake Basin in Kenya. Glynn L. Isaac & Barbara Isaac. LC 76-22962. (Prehistoric Archeology & Ecology Ser.). (Illus.). 288p. 1996. lib. bdg. 20.50 (*0-226-38483-7*) U Ch Pr.

Olowe of Ise: A Yoruba Sculptor to Kings. Roslyn A. Walker. LC 98-23973. (Illus.). 150p. 1998. pap. 49.95 (*0-9656001-1-4*) Mus African Art.

Olsen Endomyocardial Biopsy. 1989. lib. bdg. write for info. (*0-85200-674-8*) Kluwer Academic.

***Olsen Twins.** Paul Joseph. LC 99-27235. 1999. pap. 5.95 (*1-57765-353-X*, ABDO & Dghtrs) ABDO Pub Co.

Olson-Den Boer: A Letter. Charles Olson & James Den Boer. 1977. pap. 6.00 (*0-87922-051-1*) Christophers Bks.

Olson Family Recipe Book. Ed. by Virginia Lees & Edith Einspahr. (Illus.). 1997. spiral bd. 45.00 (*0-9625714-6-6*) Spruce Gulch Pr.

***Olson Sundberg Kundig Allen Architects: Architecture, Art & Craft.** Compiled by Oscar Riera Ojeda. (Illus.). 256p. 2000. 65.00 (*1-58093-078-6*, Pub. by Monacelli Pr) Penguin Putnam.

Olson's Book of Library Clip Art Vol. 1: 204 Original Library Graphics for All Types of Libraries. Ed. by Christine A. Olson. (Olson's Library Clip Art Ser.). (Illus.). 30p. (Orig.). 1992. pap. text 45.00 (*0-9632754-0-2*) C Olson & Assocs.

Olson's Gloucester. fac. ed. Lynn Swigart. LC 80-15124. (Illus.). 86p. 1980. reprint ed. pap. 30.00 (*0-7837-7746-9*, 204750200007) Bks Demand.

Olson's New Deal for California. Robert E. Burke. LC 82-984. (Illus.). 279p. 1982. reprint ed. lib. bdg. 65.00 (*0-313-23414-0*, BUON, Greenwood Pr) Greenwood.

Olson's Penny Arcade. Elder Olson. LC 75-5080. 1993. reprint ed. pap. 2.95 (*0-226-62894-9*, PP16) U Ch Pr.

Olti'Daga'at Dik Haa (Olti' & His Wife Dik) K. Peter. 11p. 1975. pap. 2.00 (*1-55500-003-7*) Alaska Native.

OLTP Systems 1. Riverside Reading Staff. (J). 1989. pap., teacher ed. 57.32 (*0-8292-8526-1*) HM.

OLTP Systems 2, Vol. 2. Riverside Reading Staff. (J). 1989. pap., teacher ed. 57.32 (*0-8292-8527-X*) HM.

Olvidados. large type ed. Peter McCurtin. (Linford Western Library). 1989. pap. 16.99 (*0-7089-6763-9*, Linford) Ulverscroft.

Olvidar el Pasado. Emma Darcy. (Bianca Ser.: No. 33402).Tr. of Fatherhood Affair. (SPA.). 1997. per. 3.50 (*0-373-33402-8*, 1-33402-8) Harlequin Bks.

Olya's Story: A Survivor's Dramatic Account of the Persecution of Baha in Revolutionary Iran. Olya Roohizadegan. 238p. 1994. pap. 12.95 (*1-85168-073-X*, Pub. by Onewrld Pubns) Penguin Putnam.

Olympia see Greek Museums

Olympia. Dennis Bock. 272p. 1999. 22.95 (*1-58234-023-4*) Bloomsbury Pubg.

Olympia. Dennis Bock. 256p. 1998. mass mkt. write for info. (*0-385-25698-1*) Doubleday.

Olympia. Taylor Downing. (BFI Film Classics Ser.). (Illus.). 96p. 1993. pap. 10.95 (*0-85170-341-0*, Pub. by British Film Inst) Ind U Pr.

Olympia. Johann H. Krause. xliv, 440p. 1972. reprint ed. write for info. (*3-487-04381-5*) G Olms Pubs.

Olympia: Paris in the Age of Manet. Otto Friedrich. (Illus.). 352p. 1993. pap. 14.00 (*0-671-86411-4*, Touchstone) S&S Trade Pap.

***Olympia: Sport, Cult & Ancient Festival.** Ulrich Sinn. Tr. by Thomas Thornton from GER. 1600p. 2000. text 39.95 (*1-55876-239-6*); pap. text 16.95 (*1-55876-240-X*) Wiener Pubs Inc.

Olympia Brown: The Battle for Equality. Charlotte Cote. LC 88-60777. 200p. 1989. pap. 9.95 (*0-941300-09-9*); text 16.95 (*0-941300-11-0*) Mother Courage.

Olympia Reader. 3rd ed. Ed. by Maurice Girodias. 725p. 1991. pap. 16.95 (*1-56201-005-0*) FoxRock.

Olympiad. Albert I. Mayer, Jr. LC 61-12875. (Illus.). (YA). (gr. 7 up). 1938. 22.00 (*0-8196-0115-2*) Biblo.

Olympian. Peter Dixon. LC 83-63198. 274p. 1984. 13.95 (*0-915677-00-8*) Roundtable Pub.

Olympian. Brian Glanville. 182p. 1991. reprint ed. pap. 12.95 (*0-915297-08-6*, OLY) Cedarwinds.

Olympian & Pythian Odes. Peter Pindar. Ed. by W. R. Connor. LC 78-18577. (Greek Texts & Commentaries Ser.). (Illus.). 1979. reprint ed. lib. bdg. 41.95 (*0-405-11420-6*) Ayer.

Olympian & the Leprechaun: W. B. Yeats & James Stephens. Richard J. Finneran. (Illus.). 40p. 1978. pap. 12.95 (*0-85105-338-6*, Pub. by Smyth) Dufour.

Olympian Cars: The Great American Luxury Automobiles of the Twenties & Thirties. 2nd rev. ed. Richard B. Carson. (Illus.). 304p. 1998. 99.95 (*1-890676-02-0*) Beavers Pond.

Olympian Dreams & Youthful Rebellion of Rene Descartes. John R. Cole. 312p. 1992. text 34.95 (*0-252-01870-2*) U of Ill Pr.

Olympian Games. Burton Holmes. Ed. by Arthur Meier Schlesinger, Jr. & Fred L. Isreal. LC 98-23503. (World 100 Years Ago Ser.). (Illus.). 144p. (YA). (gr. 5 up). 1999. lib. bdg. 29.95 (*0-7910-5056-4*) Chelsea Hse.

Olympian Plays: A Comprehensive Introduction to Greek Mythology Written in Television Script Form. Viola M. Raguso. LC 87-91373. (Illus.). 646p. (YA). (gr. 9-12). 1987. reprint ed. text 11.95 (*0-9619674-0-4*) Olympian Plays.

Olympians. Annie Leibovitz. LC 96-85445. (gr. 8). 1996. 29.95 (*0-8212-2366-6*) Little.

***Olympian's Against the Wind: The Black American Female Difference.** A. D. Emerson. (Illus.). 2000. pap. 19.95 (*0-9676348-0-6*) Darmonte.

Olympiastat: Spreadsheet Based Statistical Analysis Demo Version with Doing Statistics wth Olympiastat - Workbook & Documentation Set. Goldstein. 1994. 21.95 (*0-471-57967-X*) Wiley.

Olympiastat Spreadsheet Based Statistical Analysis for Students & Doing Statistics with Olympiastat: Workbook & Documentation Set. L. G. Goldstein. 355p. 1994. pap. text. write for info. (*0-471-01642-X*) Wiley.

Olympic: A Visitor's Companion. George Wuerthner & Douglas W. Moore. LC 98-32146. 1999. 19.95 (*0-8117-2869-2*) Stackpole.

Olympic: Ecosystems of the Peninsula. Michael Smithson & Pat O'Hara. LC 93-10420. (Illus.). 104p. (Orig.). 1993. pap. 9.95 (*1-56037-042-4*) Am Wrld Geog.

Olympic: The Story Behind the Scenery. Henry C. Warren. LC 82-82580. (Illus.). 64p. (Orig.). 1982. pap. 7.95 (*0-916122-77-8*) KC Pubns.

Olympic & Titanic, Ocean Liners of the Past. Shipbuilder Magazine Staff. Date not set. lib. bdg. 49.95 (*0-8488-1751-6*) Amereon Ltd.

***Olympic Architecture 2000: Building Sydney.** Patrick Bingham-Hall. (Illus.). 280p. 2000. 60.00 (*0-949284-39-4*, Pub. by Watermark) Antique Collect.

***Olympic Battleground: The Power Politics of Timber Preservation.** 2nd ed. Carsten Lien. (Illus.). 464p. 2000. pap. 18.95 (*0-89886-736-3*) Mountaineers.

Olympic Black Women. Martha W. Plowden. LC 95-32067. (Illus.). 160p. (J). (gr. 4-7). 1995. pap. 16.95 (*1-56554-080-8*) Pelican.

Olympic Century: The Official 1st Century History of the Modern Olympic Movement 1896-1996, 15 vols., Set. LC 97-1144. (Illus.). 184p. 1997. text. write for info. (*1-888383-00-3*) Warwick Publ.

Olympic Crisis: Sport, Politics & the Moral Order. John M. Hoberman. 220p. (C). 1986. lib. bdg. 30.00 (*0-89241-224-0*) Caratzas.

Olympic Cyclery Simulation. 8th ed. Burton S. Kaliski & Robert A. Schultheis. (BB - Record Keeping I Ser.). 1995. 20.95 (*0-538-63324-7*) S-W Pub.

***Olympic Death.** Vazquez Montalban. (Mask Noir Ser.). 207p. 2000. pap. 11.99 (*1-85242-257-2*) Serpents Tail.

Olympic Development Program (ODP) U. S. A. Gymnastics Staff. 41p. 1993. pap. 7.50 (*1-885250-21-5*); VHS 29.95 (*1-885250-22-3*) USA Gymnastics.

Olympic Dream. (Official United States Olympic Committee Sports Ser.). 80p. (J). (gr. k-3). 1998. pap. 9.95 (*1-58000-014-2*) Griffin CA.

Olympic Dream. Matt Christopher. LC 95-45653. (Illus.). 160p. (J). (gr. 3-7). 1996. 15.95 (*0-316-14048-1*); pap. 3.95 (*0-316-14163-1*) Little.

Olympic Dream. Matt Christopher. LC 95-45653. (J). 1996. 9.05 (*0-606-09707-4*, Pub. by Turtleback) Demco.

Olympic Dream. Teacher Created Materials Staff. 80p. (J). (gr. 1-3). 1997. pap. 9.95 (*1-57690-200-5*) Tchr Create Mat.

***Olympic Dream & Spirit No. 1: Stories of Courage, Perseverance & Dedication.** Bob Schaller. 224p. 1999. pap. 8.99 (*1-929478-06-2*) Cross Trng.

***Olympic Dream & Spirit No. 2: Life Lessons from Olympic Journeys.** Bob Schaller. 224p. 1999. pap. 8.99 (*1-929478-07-0*) Cross Trng.

***Olympic Dream & Spirit No. 3: Growing Through Commitment, Challenge & Goal-Setting.** Bob Schaller. 224p. 1999. pap. 8.99 (*1-929478-08-9*) Cross Trng.

Olympic Dreams. Lauraine Snelling. LC 95-483. (High Hurdles Ser.: No. 1). 160p. (YA). (gr. 6-9). 1995. pap. 5.99 (*1-55661-505-1*) Bethany Hse.

Olympic Dreams: 100 Years of Excellence. Douglas Collins. (Illus.). 272p. 1996. pap. 25.00 (*0-7893-0030-3*, Pub. by Universe) St Martin.

***Olympic Equestrian: The Sport & the Stories from Stockholm to Sydney.** Jennifer O. Bryant. 2000. pap. 29.95 (*1-58150-044-0*) Blood-Horse.

Olympic Eventing Masterclass: Behind the Scenes with the World's Top Competitors. Debby Sly. (Illus.). 192p. 1996. 27.95 (*0-7153-0375-9*, Pub. by D & C Pub) Sterling.

Olympic Factbook: A Spectator's Guide to the Winter Games 1998. 2nd rev. ed. Anne J. Johnson & George Cantor. Ed. by Bradley Morgan. LC 97-29271. 392p. 1997. pap. 14.95 (*1-57859-016-7*, 111063) Visible Ink Pr.

Olympic Factbook Summer Games: 2000. Date not set. 24.95 (*1-57859-077-9*); 19.95 (*1-57859-100-7*) Visible Ink Pr.

Olympic Facts & Fables: The Best Stories from the First Century of the Modern Olympics. Tom Ecker. LC 97-133611. (Illus.). 160p. 1996. 17.50 (*0-911521-45-3*) Tafnews.

***Olympic Facts & Fun.** Kathleen Fieffe & Brad Herzog. Ed. by Sherie Holder. 16p. (J). (gr. 2-8). 2000. pap. text. write for info. (*1-886749-92-2*) SI For Kids.

Olympic Fun. (U. S. Olympic Committee's Activity Book). (Illus.). 16p. (J). (gr. k-3). 1996. pap. 2.95 (*1-882180-60-7*) Griffin CA.

Olympic Games. Stephen Currie. LC 98-50360. (Overview Ser.). (Illus.). 128p. (YA). (gr. 4-12). 1999. lib. bdg. 23.70 (*1-56006-395-5*) Lucent Bks.

Olympic Games. Eaton. 1992. pap. text. write for info. (*0-17-556279-2*) Addison-Wesley.

***Olympic Games.** Chris Oxlade. (Eyewitness Books). (Illus.). (J). (gr. 4-7). 2000. 19.99 (*0-7894-6628-7*) DK Pub Inc.

***Olympic Games.** Chris Oxlade. (Eyewitness Books). (J). (gr. 4-7). 2000. 15.95 (*0-7894-6292-3*) DK Pub Inc.

***Olympic Games: A Social Science Approach.** K. Toohey & Anthony J. Veal. LC 99-37882. 224p. 2000. 70.00 (*0-85199-342-7*) OUP.

***Olympic Games: Athens 1896-Sydney 2000.** Kindersley Dorling. (Illus.). 352p. 2000. 29.95 (*0-7894-5975-2*) DK Pub Inc.

Olympic Games: Complete Track & Field Results 1896-1988. Barry J. Hugman & Peter Arnold. 384p. 1989. 40.00 (*0-8160-2120-1*) Facts on File.

***Olympic Games As Performance & Public Event: The Case of the XVII Winter Olympic Games in Norway.** Arne M. Klausen. LC 98-49638. (Illus.). 272p. 1999. 59.95 (*1-57181-706-9*) Berghahn Bks.

***Olympic Games as Performance & Public Event: The Case of the XVII Winter Olympic Games in Norway.** Arne M. Klausen. (Illus.). 240p. 1999. pap. 19.95 (*1-57181-203-2*) Berghahn Bks.

Olympic Games in Ancient Greece. Shirley Glubok & Alfred Tamarin. LC 75-25408. (Illus.). 128p. (J). (gr. 5-9). 1976. lib. bdg. 16.89 (*0-06-022048-1*) HarpC Child Bks.

Olympic Games Quilts: America's Welcome to the World. Quiltmakers of Georgia Staff. 144p. 1996. pap. 19.95 (*0-8487-1505-5*) Oxmoor Hse.

Olympic Glory Denied: A Final Opportunity for Glory Restored. Frank Zarnowski. 1996. pap. text 18.95 (*1-882180-70-4*) Griffin CA.

Olympic Glow. Barbara Birenbaum. LC 93-34122. (Historical Adventure Ser.: No. 9). (Illus.). 56p. (YA). 1994. pap. 5.95 (*0-935343-46-6*) Peartree.

Olympic Glow. Barbara Birenbaum. LC 93-34122. (Historical Adventure Ser.: No. 9). (Illus.). 56p. (J). (gr. 3-6). 1994. lib. bdg. 12.95 (*0-935343-45-8*) Peartree.

Olympic Heroes. Kristi Sb Newcombe. LC 97-42696. 32p. (J). (gr. 3-7). 1997. 10.99 (*0-7814-3021-6*, Chariot Bks) Chariot Victor.

Olympic Ideal of Commitment Vol. 6: Personal Leadership Through the Olympic Ideals. Ed. by Nancy Moore. (U. S. Olympic Committee's Curriculum Guide Ser.). (Illus.). 16p. (YA). 1997. pap., wbk. ed. 3.95 (*1-58000-005-3*) Griffin CA.

Olympic Ideal of Discipline Vol. 5: Personal Leadership Through the Olympic Ideals. Ed. by Nancy Moore. (U. S. Olympic Committee's Curriculum Guide Ser.). (Illus.). 16p. (YA). 1997. pap., wbk. ed. 3.95 (*1-58000-004-5*) Griffin CA.

Olympic Ideal of Focus Vol. 3: Personal Leadership Through the Olympic Ideals. Ed. by Nancy Moore. (U. S. Olympic Committee's Curriculum Guide Ser.). (Illus.). 16p. (YA). 1997. pap., wbk. ed. 3.95 (*1-58000-002-9*) Griffin CA.

Olympic Ideal of Persistence Vol. 4: Personal Leadership Through the Olympic Ideals. Nancy Moore. (U. S. Olympic Committee's Curriculum Guide Ser.). (Illus.). 16p. (YA). 1997. pap., wbk. ed. 3.95 (*1-58000-003-7*) Griffin CA.

Olympic Ideal of Vision Vol. 2: Personal Leadership Through the Olympic Ideals. Mary L. Retton. Ed. by Nancy Moore. (U. S. Olympic Committee's Curriculum Guide Ser.). (Illus.). 16p. (YA). 1997. pap., wbk. ed. 3.95 (*1-58000-001-0*) Griffin CA.

Olympic Jokes. Jim Rothaus. (Funny Side Up Ser.). (Illus.). 24p. (J). (gr. 1-4). 1996. lib. bdg. 19.93 (*1-56766-270-6*) Childs World.

Olympic Journey: The Saga of an American Hero: Leroy T. Walker. Charles Gaddy. (Illus.). 288p. 1998. 24.95 (*1-882180-92-5*) Griffin CA.

***Olympic Marathon.** David E. Martin & Roger W. H. Gynn. LC 99-57645. (Illus.). 528p. 2000. pap. 27.95 (*0-88011-969-1*) Human Kinetics.

Olympic Marathon: A Centennial History of the Games' Most Storied Race. Charles Lovett. LC 96-47618. 192p. 1997. 37.95 (*0-275-95771-3*, Praeger Pubs) Greenwood.

Olympic Moose Salami. George Hesselberg. 1996. pap. 12.95 (*1-878569-40-6*) Badger Bks Inc.

Olympic Mountains Trail Guide. 2nd ed. Robert L. Wood. LC 91-18909. 320p. 1991. pap. 14.95 (*0-89886-320-1*) Mountaineers.

***Olympic Mountains Trail Guide: National Park & National Forest.** 3rd ed. Robert Wood. LC 00-8289. (Illus.). 320p. (Orig.). 2000. pap. 16.95 (*0-89886-618-9*) Mountaineers.

Olympic Myth of Greek Amateur Athletics. D. C. Young. xii, 203p. 1984. pap. 15.00 (*0-89005-523-8*, YOU01) Ares.

Olympic National Park. Sharlene Nelson. (True Bks.). (J). 1998. pap. text 6.95 (*0-516-26271-8*) Childrens.

Olympic National Park. Sharlene P. Nelson & Ted W. Nelson. LC 96-39888. (True Bk.). (J). 1997. lib. bdg. 21.00 (*0-516-20446-7*) Childrens.

Olympic National Park: A Natural History. Tim McNulty. 272p. 1999. pap. 16.95 (*1-57061-168-8*) Sasquatch Bks.

Olympic National Park, WA. rev. ed. Ed. by Trails Illustrated Staff. 1996. 8.99 (*0-925873-16-0*) Trails Illustrated.

***Olympic Peninsula: Best Places Destinations.** 2nd ed. Ed. by Rachel Bard. (Best Places Destinations Ser.). (Illus.). 208p. 2000. pap. 12.95 (*1-57061-235-8*) Sasquatch Bks.

Olympic Peninsula Best Places: A Destination Guide. Ed. by Rachel Bard. 128p. (Orig.). 1996. pap. 9.95 (*1-57061-059-2*) Sasquatch Bks.

Olympic Peninsula Rivers Guide: Floating & Fishing the Peninsula's Best Streams. Steve Probasco. LC 99-43817. 1999. pap. 15.95 (*0-963705-5-0*) Ecopress.

Olympic Politics. 2nd ed. Hill. LC 95-36982. 336p. 1997. pap. 24.95 (*0-7190-4451-0*, Pub. by Manchester Univ Pr) St Martin.

Olympic Politics: Athens to Atlanta, 1896-1996. 2nd rev. ed. Christopher R. Hill. LC 95-36982. 336p. 1996. 35.00 (*0-7190-4450-2*, Pub. by Manchester Univ Pr) St Martin.

Olympic Rain Forest: An Ecological Web. Ruth Kirk & Jerry N. Franklin. LC 92-7883. (Illus.). 128p. 1992. pap. 22.50 (*0-295-97187-8*) U of Wash Pr.

Olympic Results, Barcelona 1992: A Complete Compilation of Results from the Games of the XXV Olympiad. Brad Lewis & Gabriella Goldstein. LC 93-15813. 648p. 1993. text 30.00 (*0-8153-0333-5*, H1752) Garland.

Olympic Spirit: 100 Years of the Games. Tehabi Books Staff. LC 96-32258. 180p. 1996. lthr. 195.00 (*1-887656-04-9*) Tehabi Bks.

Olympic Spirit: 100 Years of the Games (Corporate Edition) Tehabi Books Staff. LC 96-32258. 180p. 1996. 50.00 (*1-887656-03-0*) Tehabi Bks.

Olympic Spirit: 100 Years of the Games (Post Atlanta Edition) 2nd ed. Tehabi Books Staff. LC 96-43243. 192p. 1996. 50.00 (*1-887656-09-X*) Tehabi Bks.

O

An Asterisk (*) at the beginning of an entry indicates that the title is appearing for the first time.

Olympic Sports, 8 bks. Robert Sandelson et al. (Illus.). (J). (gr. 6). 1991. lib. bdg. 81.46 (*0-89686-754-4*, Crstwood Hse) Silver Burdett Pr.

Olympic Sports & Propaganda Games: Moscow, 1980. Baruch A. Hazan. LC 81-7447. 250p. 1982. text 39.95 (*0-87855-436-X*) Transaction Pubs.

***Olympic Summer Games 2000.** Meredith Costain. Ed. by Puffin Books Staff. (Illus.). 64p. (J). (gr. 3-7). 2000. pap. 3.99 (*0-14-130903-2*, PuffinBks) Peng Put Young Read.

Olympic Winners: Reading Activities for Schools & Libraries. Marcia Lund. LC 96-15624. 1996. pap. 14.95 (*0-917846-81-8*, Alleyside) Highsmith Pr.

Olympicmath: Gold Medal Activities & Projects. Sharon Vogt. 116p. (Orig.). (YA). (gr. 4-8). 1995. pap. 9.95 (*0-673-36306-6*, GoodYrBooks) Addson-Wesley Educ.

***Olympics.** Barbara Hennessy. (Picture Puffin Ser.). (Illus.). 32p. (J). (ps-3). 2000. pap. 5.99 (*0-14-038487-1*, PuffinBks) Peng Put Young Read.

***Olympics.** 2nd rev. ed. Christine Dillon. (My First Report Ser.). (Illus.). 50p. (J). (gr. 1-3). 1999. ring bd. 5.95 (*1-57896-049-5*, Hewitt Homeschl Res) Hewitt Res Fnd.

Olympics, No. 79. Chris Oxlade. LC 99-22807. 1999. lib. bdg. 20.99 (*0-375-90222-8*) Random.

Olympics, No. 79. Chris Oxlade. LC 99-22807. 60p. (J). (gr. 4-8). 1999. 19.00 (*0-375-80222-3*) Random.

Olympics: A History of the Modern Games. Allen Guttmann. (Illinois History of Sports Ser.). (Illus.). 224p. 1992. 14.95 (*0-252-06396-1*) U of Ill Pr.

Olympics: History, Geography, & Sports. Amanda Bennett. (Unit Study Adventures Ser.). 136p. 1996. pap. text 13.99 (*1-888306-03-3*, Home School Pr) Holly Hall.

Olympics & Other Ancient Games. E. Knill. (Illus.). 48p. (Orig.). 1984. pap. 4.95 (*0-88388-104-7*) Bellerophon Bks.

Olympics at 100: A Celebration in Pictures. Associated Press Staff. (Illus.). 224p. 1995. 19.95 (*0-02-860346-X*, Arco) Macmillan Gen Ref.

***Olympics at the Millennium: Power, Politics, & the Games.** Ed. by Kay Schaffer & Sidonie Smith. LC 99-56801. (Illus.). 304p. 2000. text 55.00 (*0-8135-2819-4*) Rutgers U Pr.

***Olympics at the Millennium: Power, Politics, & the Games.** Ed. by Kay Schaffer & Sidonie Smith. LC 99-56801. (Illus.). 304p. (C). 2000. pap. 23.00 (*0-8135-2820-8*) Rutgers U Pr.

Olympics Factbook: A Spectator's Guide to the Winter & Summer Games. 400p. 1991. 16.95 (*0-8103-9417-0*) Visible Ink Pr.

Olympics of 1972: A Munich Diary. Richard D. Mandell. LC 90-23544. 223p. reprint ed. pap. 69.20 (*0-7837-5239-3*, 204497300005) Bks Demand.

Olympics Out of Cobb: Spiked! Jon-Ivan Weaver & Pat Hussain. (Illus.). 212p. (C). 1996. text. write for info. (*1-883793-18-1*) Wolfe Pubng.

***Olympics 2000: Stars & Stats.** Brad Herzog. Ed. by Amy Goehner. (Illus.). 32p. (J). (gr. 3-8). 2000. pap. 3.99 (*1-886749-97-3*) SI For Kids.

Olympics, 2004? Ask Yia Yia & Pa Pou. large type ed. Eunice D. Mosher. Ed. by Adolph Caso. LC 97-53260. (Illus.). 32p. (J). (ps-3). 1998. pap. 9.95 (*0-8283-2033-0*) Branden Bks.

Olympio Ou la Vie de Victor Hugo. Andre Maurois. 28.50 (*0-685-36951-X*) Fr & Eur.

Olympiodori. Ed. by Westerink. (GRE.). 1970. 49.50 (*3-322-00234-9*, Pub. by B G Teubner) U of Mich Pr.

Olympiodorus: Commentary on Platos "Gorgias" Olympiodorus. Tr. by Harold Tarrant et al. LC 98-16149. (Philosophia Antiqua Ser.: No. 78). (ENG & GRE.). 336p. 1998. 118.00 (*90-04-10972-2*) Brill Academic Pubs.

Olympiodorus of Thebes & the Sack of Rome: A Study of the Historikoi Logoi, with Translated Fragments, Commentary & Additional Material. Christopher Chaffin. LC 93-11697. 392p. 1993. text 99.95 (*0-7734-9321-2*) E Mellen.

Olympiodorus Philosophus, In Platonis Gorgiam Commentaria. Ed. by W. Norvin. 250p. 1966. reprint ed. write for info. (*0-318-70988-0*) G Olms Pubs.

Olympiodorus Philosophus, In Platonis Phaedonem Commentaria. Ed. by W. Norwin. xi, 272p. 1987. reprint ed. write for info. (*0-318-70989-9*) G Olms Pubs.

Olympiques. Henry De Montherlant. (FRE.). 1973. pap. 10.95 (*0-8288-3750-3*, M3791) Fr & Eur.

Olympism: A Guide to the Histories, Ideals & Sports of the Olympic Games. Richard Burns. 1996. pap. text 8.95 (*1-882180-55-0*) Griffin CA.

Olympism: Lighting the Way to a Legacy of Peace. (U. S. Olympic Curriculum Guide Ser.: Vol. 6). 192p. (J). (gr. 3-12). 1996. pap. 16.95 (*1-882180-59-3*) Griffin CA.

Olympus. Ed. by Martin H. Greenberg. 320p. 1998. mass mkt. 5.99 (*0-88677-775-5*, Pub. by DAW Bks) Penguin Putnam.

Olympus IS 1000/2000/3000. Hove Foto Books Staff. (Illus.). 220p. 1993. pap. text 19.95 (*1-874031-11-8*, Pub. by Hove Foto) Watsn-Guptill.

Olympus IS-2, IS-3, IS-10. Bob Shell & Richard Hunecke. Tr. by Phyllis M. Rieffler-Bonham from GER. LC 95-161467. (Magic Lantern Guides Ser.). (Illus.). 176p. (Orig.). (C). 1998. pap. 19.95 (*1-883403-05-7*, H 160, Silver Pixel Pr) Saunders Photo.

Olympus Modern Classics OM-1, OM-2, OM-10, OM-3/OM-4, OM-2sp, OM-40. (Modern Classics Ser.). (Illus.). 196p. pap. 19.95 (*0-906447-90-9*, Pub. by Hove Foto) Watsn-Guptill.

Olympus on Main Street: A Process for Planning a Community Arts Facility. Joseph Golden. LC 80-16479. (Illus.). 248p. reprint ed. pap. 76.90 (*0-608-18104-8*, 203223600078) Bks Demand.

Olympus World Report . . . the Year Three Thousand. Torkom Saraydarian. LC 92-85571. 216p. 1993. 18.00 (*0-929874-46-3*) TSG Pub Found.

Olynthiacs 1-3, Vol. I. Tr. by J. H. Vince. (Loeb Classical Library: No. 238). (ENG & GRE.). 15.50 (*0-674-99263-6*) HUP.

Om: Creative Meditations. Alan Watts. LC 79-54101. 160p. 1995. pap. 8.95 (*0-89087-793-9*) Celestial Arts.

***Om: One God Universal: A Garland of Offerings, Vol. 3.** (Illus.). 300p. 1999. pap. 35.00 (*0-943913-31-4*) Intl Lib Ctr.

***Om: The Secret of Ahbor Valley.** Talbot Mundy. LC 00-132771. 334p. 2000. reprint ed. write for info. (*1-893766-19-5*) Aeon Pub Co.

Om - Secret of Ahbor Valley. Talbot Mundy. 1976. reprint ed. 27.95 (*0-8488-1110-0*, Rivercity Pr) Amereon Ltd.

Om - The Magical Mystical Sound. Arun A. Amin. 24p. 1997. pap. 4.95 (*1-891253-03-4*) Aurovision Bks.

Om Egerien. Die Egerer, Pouzdraner, Puchkirchener Schichtengruppe und die Bretkaer Formation, Band V. T. Baldi & Jan Senes. (Chronostratigraphie und Neostratotypen Ser.). (DUT.). 580p. 1975. 38.00 (*3-510-60005-3*, Pub. by E Schweizerbartsche) Balogh.

Om, Gayatri, & Sandhya. 3.95 (*81-7120-166-0*) Vedanta Pr.

Om-Kas-Toe: Blackfeet Twin Captures an Elkdog. Kenneth Thomasma. LC 89-14879. (Amazing Indian Children Ser.). (Illus.). 224p. (YA). (gr. 7-10). 1989. pap. 5.99 (*0-8010-8884-4*) Baker Bks.

Om-Kas-Toe: Blackfeet Twin Captures an Elkdog. Kenneth Thomasma. LC 89-14879. (Amazing Indian Children Ser.). (Illus.). 216p. (YA). (gr. 7-10). 1992. 9.99 (*0-8010-8883-6*) Baker Bks.

Om-Kas-Toe: Blackfeet Twin Captures an Elkdog. Kenneth Thomasma. LC 89-14879. (Amazing Indian Children Ser.). 1986. 12.05 (*0-606-10272-8*, Pub. by Turtleback) Demco.

Om Mani Padme Hum: The Sound of Silence: The Diamond in the Lotus. Osho. Ed. by Deva Sarito. LC 97-220030. (Mantra Ser.). (Illus.). 242p. 1990. 21.95 (*3-89338-050-7*, Pub. by Rebel Hse) Oshos.

***Om Revient Toujours Chez Soi - Cocagne.** Germaine Breau-Major. Tr. by Flora Cormier & Edna Geoguen from ENG.Tr. of We Will Always Return - Cocagne. (FRE., Illus.). 7p. 2000. pap. 10.00 (*0-9701316-0-7*) Les Editions Bleuts.

Om Shantih Shantih Shantih: The Soundless Sound Peace, Peace, Peace. Osho. Ed. by Dhyan Sagar & Deva Nirvesha. LC 97-219998. (Mantra Ser.). (Illus.). 290p. 1990. 19.95 (*3-89338-048-5*, Pub. by Rebel Hse) Oshos.

Om, the Secret of Ahbor Valley. Talbot Mundy. 400p. 1984. pap. 3.95 (*0-88184-045-9*) Carroll & Graf.

Om, the Secret of Ahbor Valley. Talbot Mundy. 392p. 1980. pap. 15.95 (*0-913004-39-1*) Point Loma Pub.

Oma. Georgia Smelser & Oma Ellis. LC 85-31579. (Illus.). 254p. 1981. pap. 8.99 (*0-912315-16-4*) Word Aflame.

Oma & Angels. Oma Ellis & Rita Dawson. LC 88-31557. (Illus.). 192p. (Orig.). 1989. pap. 8.99 (*0-932581-44-7*) Word Aflame.

Oma & Bobo. Amy Schwartz. 32p. (J). (ps-2). 1998. pap. 5.99 (*0-689-82115-8*) S&S Childrens.

***Oma & Bobo.** Amy Schwartz. 1998. 11.19 (*0-606-13675-4*, Pub. by Turtleback) Demco.

Oma Ellis Talks about Prayer & Faith. Oma Ellis & Georgia Smelser. Ed. by David K. Bernard. LC 87-13306. (Illus.). 160p. (Orig.). 1987. pap. 8.99 (*0-932581-16-1*) Word Aflame.

Oma Rem Koolhaas: Living, Vivre, Leben. Rem Koolhaas & Arc en reve centre d'architecture. Tr. by Gila Walker et al from FRE. LC 99-10764. (ENG & GER.). 1999. write for info. (*0-8176-5638-3*) Birkhauser.

***Oma the Faithful Daughter.** Ogo Okoye-Johnson. 32p. (J). (gr. k-8). 1999. 15.00 (*0-9670024-9-4*) Noon Prodns.

***Omaha.** Madelyn K. Anderson. LC 99-29816. (Watts Library). 2000. 24.00 (*0-531-20404-9*) Watts.

***Omaha.** Madelyn K. Anderson. (Indians of the Americas Library). (Illus.). (YA). 2000. pap. 8.95 (*0-531-16481-0*) Watts.

Omaha & Ponka Letters. James O. Dorsey. (Bureau of American Ethnology Bulletins Ser.). 127p. 1995. lib. bdg. 79.00 (*0-7812-4011-5*) Rprt Serv.

Omaha & Ponka Letters. James O. Dorsey. 1988. reprint ed. lib. bdg. 49.00 (*0-7812-0232-9*) Rprt Serv.

Omaha & Ponka Letters. James O. Dorsey. reprint ed. 45.00 (*0-403-03675-5*) Scholarly.

Omaha Awareness Tours: The Near South Side. Center for Applied Urban Research Staff. (Illus.). 16p. (Orig.). 1979. pap. 2.00 (*1-55719-104-2*) U NE CPAR.

Omaha Beachhead. (Military History Ser.). 1995. lib. bdg. 250.75 (*0-8490-7419-3*) Gordon Pr.

Omaha Beachhead: June 6-13, 1944. 175p. 1999. per. 19.00 (*0-16-001935-4*) USGPO.

***Omaha Entertainment, 2000.** (Illus.). 630p. 1999. pap. 20.00 (*1-880248-55-7*, 008A) Enter Pubns.

Omaha Holdem Poker. Bob Ciaffone. 106p. 1999. reprint ed. pap. 20.00 (*0-9661007-2-7*) B Ciaffone.

Omaha Housing Market: An Appraisal of the Occupancy Potential for Subsidized Rental Units, 1971-1973. Ralph H. Todd & David W. Hinton. 33p. (Orig.). 1972. pap. 2.50 (*1-55719-099-2*) U NE CPAR.

***Omaha-Lincoln Area Business Directory, 1999.** American Business Directories Staff. 1824p. 1999. boxed set 495.00 (*0-7687-0192-9*) Am Busn Direct.

Omaha Metropolitan Statistical Area Input-Output Tables & Multipliers: A User's Manual: A Guide for Identifying & Assessing the Effects of Business Changes on the Omaha Economy. William J. Corcoran. (Illus.). 63p. (C). 1988. ring bd. 29.95 (*1-55719-179-4*) U NE CPAR.

Omaha Orange: History of EMS in America. Carl J. Post. 1992. pap. 26.25 (*0-86720-187-8*) Jones & Bartlett.

Omaha Public Schools: Opinion Surveys of a Parent & Taxpayer Group. Center for Applied Urban Research Staff. 56p. (Orig.). 1987. pap. 3.50 (*1-55719-112-3*) U NE CPAR.

Omaha Secret Societies. Reo F. Fortune. LC 70-82351. (Columbia Univ. Contributions to Anthropology Ser.: Vol. 14). reprint ed. 32.50 (*0-404-50564-3*) AMS Pr.

***Omaha Steaks: Let's Grill.** John Harrisson & Frederick J. Simon. LC 00-39958. 2001. write for info. (*0-609-60776-6*) C Potter.

Omaha System: Applications for Community Health Nursing. Ed. by Karen S. Martin & Nancy J. Scheet. (Illus.). 423p. 1991. pap. text 81.00 (*0-7216-6126-2*, W B Saunders Co); pap. text 30.50 (*0-7216-6123-8*, W B Saunders Co) Harcrt Hlth Sci Grp.

Omaha the Cat Dancer, Vol. 1. Reed Waller & Kate Worley. 128p. 1995. pap. 14.95 (*1-56097-161-4*) Fantagraph Bks.

Omaha the Cat Dancer, Vol. 3. Reed Waller & Kate Worley. 136p. 1995. pap. 15.95 (*1-56097-166-5*) Fantagraph Bks.

Omaha the Cat Dancer, Vol. 6. Reed Waller & Kate Worley. (Illus.). 168p. 1998. pap. 18.95 (*1-56097-179-7*) Fantagraph Bks.

Omaha, the Gate City, & Douglas County: Record of Settlement, Organization, Progress & Achievement, 2 vols. Ed. by Arthur C. Wakeley. (Illus.). 997p. 1997. reprint ed. lib. bdg. 99.50 (*0-8328-6870-1*) Higginson Bk Co.

***Omaha, Times Remembered.** Omaha World-Herald Staff. Ed. by Kristine Gerber. (Illus.). 176p. 1999. 39.95 (*0-9674995-0-X*) Kids Prodns.

Omaha Tribal Myths & Trickster Tales. Roger Welsch. 285p. 1994. pap. 14.95 (*0-934904-11-1*) J & L Lee.

Omaha Tribe, 2 vols., Vol. 1. Alice C. Fletcher & Francis La Flesche. LC 91-42657. (Illus.). vi, 395p. 1992. reprint ed. pap. 12.95 (*0-8032-6876-9*, Bison Books) U of Nebr Pr.

Omaha Tribe, 2 vols., Vol. 2. Alice C. Fletcher & Francis La Flesche. LC 91-42657. (Illus.). vii, 384p. 1992. reprint ed. pap. 12.95 (*0-8032-6877-7*, Bison Books) U of Nebr Pr.

***Omaha/Council Bluffs, New England, 1.** Rand McNally Staff. 1999. 3.95 (*0-528-98005-X*) Rand McNally.

***Omaha/Lincoln Business Directory 2000.** American Business Directories Staff. 2000. 495.00 (*0-7687-0279-8*) Am Busn Direct.

Omaha's Bell. Penny Hayes. LC 98-44751. 256p. 1999. pap. 11.95 (*1-56280-232-1*) Naiad Pr.

Omaha's Neighborhood Housing Services Area: A Physical Conditions Inventory. Jack J. Ruff & R. K. Piper. 80p. (Orig.). 1982. pap. 6.50 (*1-55719-032-1*) U NE CPAR.

Omaha's Traditional Business Districts: Their Impact & Proposals for Revitalization. Center for Applied Urban Research Staff. 267p. (Orig.). 1976. pap. 16.00 (*1-55719-003-8*) U NE CPAR.

O'Malley of Notre Dame. John W. Meaney. LC 90-50968. (Orig.). 1991. pap. text 13.00 (*0-268-01505-8*) U of Notre Dame Pr.

O'Malley Picture Book. Kevin O'Malley. (Illus.). 14.89 (*0-06-027627-4*) HarpC Child Bks.

O'Malley Saga Bk. 1: The Blood Oath. LC 96-96757. 192p. 1996. 18.95 (*0-8034-9175-1*, Avalon Bks) Bouregy.

O'Malley Saga Bk. 2: Thunder Mountain. Tom Austin. LC 98-96233. 192p. 1998. 18.95 (*0-8034-9311-8*, Avalon Bks) Bouregy.

Oman see Commercial Laws of the Middle East

Oman. Leila M. Foster. LC 98-19572. (Enchantment of the World Ser.). 144p. (YA). (gr. 5-9). 1999. 32.00 (*0-516-20964-7*) Childrens.

Oman. 2nd rev. ed. Frank A. Clements. LC 96-192673. (World Bibiographical Ser.: Vol. 29). 372p. 1994. lib. bdg. 79.00 (*1-85109-197-1*) ABC-CLIO.

***Oman: A Country Study Guide.** Global Investment & Business Center, Inc. Staff. (World Country Study Guides Library: Vol. 129). (Illus.). 350p. 2000. pap. 59.00 (*0-7397-2427-4*) Intl Business Pubns.

Oman: Economic, Social & Strategic Developments. Ed. by Brian R. Pridham. 59.95 (*0-7099-4056-4*, Pub. by C Helm) Routldge.

Oman: Political Development in a Changing World. Carol J. Riphenburg. LC 97-33208. 264p. 1998. 59.95 (*0-275-96144-3*, Praeger Pubs) Greenwood.

Oman: Politics & Development. Ian Skeet. LC 91-26079. 216p. 1992. text 49.95 (*0-312-06886-7*) St Martin.

Oman - A Country Study Guide: Basic Information for Research & Pleasure. Global Investment Center, USA Staff. (World Country Study Guide Library: Vol. 129). (Illus.). 350p. 1999. pap. 59.00 (*0-7397-1526-7*) Intl Business Pubns.

Oman a History. Wendel Phillips. 246p. 1971. 16.00 (*0-86685-024-4*, LDL0244, Pub. by Librairie du Liban) Intl Bk Ctr.

Oman Adorned: A Portrait in Silver. Miranda Norris & Pauline Shelton. (Illus.). 368p. 1997. 200.00 (*1-898888-04-3*, Pub. by Art Bks Intl) Partners Pubs Grp.

Oman & Its Renaissance. 6th ed. Donald Hawley. (Illus.). 256p. 1990. 59.95 (*0-86685-519-X*, Pub. by Stacey Intl) Intl Bk Ctr.

Oman & the South-Eastern Shore of Arabia. Ed. by Rahbih El-Solh. (Archive Documents on the History of the Arab World Ser.). 336p. 1997. 50.00 (*0-86372-199-0*, Pub. by Garnet-Ithaca) LPC InBook.

Oman & the Uae. Insight Guides Staff. (Insight Guides Ser.). 1998. pap. text 22.95 (*0-88729-287-9*) Langenscheidt.

Oman & the World: The Emergence of an Independent Foreign Policy. Joseph A. Kechichian. LC 96-131215. 434p. 1995. pap. 30.00 (*0-8330-2332-2*); text 40.00 (*0-8330-2334-9*, MR-680-RC) Rand Corp.

***Oman Beyond the Oil Horizon: Policies Toward Sustainable Growth.** Ahsan S. Mansur & Volker Treichel. LC 99-52694. (Occasional Paper Ser.). 1999. write for info. (*1-55775-833-6*) Intl Monetary.

Oman Business & Investment Opportunities Yearbook, 1998: Business, Investment, Export-Import. Russian Information & Business Center, Inc. Staff. (Business & Investment Opportunities Library, '98). (Illus.). 1998. pap. 99.00 (*1-57751-995-7*) Intl Business Pubns.

***Oman Business Intelligence Report, 190 vols.** Global Investment & Business Center, Inc. Staff. (World Business Intelligence Library: Vol. 129). (Illus.). 350p. 2000. pap. 99.95 (*0-7397-2627-7*) Intl Business Pubns.

***Oman Business Law Handbook.** Global Investment & Business Center, Inc. Staff. (Global Business Law Handbooks Library: Vol. 129). (Illus.). 2000. pap. 99.95 (*0-7397-2027-9*) Intl Business Pubns.

***Oman Business Opportunity Yearbook.** Global Investment & Business Center, Inc. Staff. (Global Business Opportunity Yearbooks Library: Vol. 129). (Illus.). 2000. pap. 99.95 (*0-7397-2227-1*) Intl Business Pubns.

***Oman Business Opportunity Yearbook: Export-Import, Investment & Business Opportunities.** International Business Publications, U. S. A. Staff & Global Investment Center, U. S. A. Staff. (Global Business Opportunity Yearbooks Library: Vol. 129). (Illus.). 350p. 1999. pap. 99.95 (*0-7397-1327-2*) Intl Business Pubns.

***Oman Country Review 2000.** Robert C. Kelly et al. (Illus.). 60p. 1999. pap. 39.95 (*1-58310-553-0*) CountryWatch.

***Oman Foreign Policy & Government Guide.** Contrib. by Global Investment & Business Center, Inc. Staff. (World Foreign Policy & Government Library: Vol. 124). (Illus.). 350p. 1999. pap. 99.00 (*0-7397-3622-1*) Intl Business Pubns.

***Oman Foreign Policy & Government Guide.** Global Investment & Business Center, Inc. Staff. (World Foreign Policy & Government Library: Vol. 124). (Illus.). 350p. 2000. 99.95 (*0-7397-3827-5*) Intl Business Pubns.

Oman in Early Islamic History. Ali Ahmed Al-Rawas. 275p. 2000. 62.00 (*0-86372-238-5*, Pub. by Garnet-Ithaca) LPC InBook.

***Oman Investment & Business Guide.** Global Investment & Business Center, Inc. Staff. (Global Investment & Business Guide Library: Vol. 129). (Illus.). 2000. pap. 99.95 (*0-7397-1827-4*) Intl Business Pubns.

Oman Investment & Business Guide: Economy, Export-Import, Business & Investment Climate, Business Contacts. Contrib. by Russian Information & Business Center, Inc. Staff. (Russia, NIS & Emerging Markets Investment & Business Library-98). (Illus.). 350p. 1998. pap. 99.00 (*1-57751-917-5*) Intl Business Pubns.

***Oman Investment & Business Guide: Export-Import, Investment & Business Opportunities.** International Business Publications, USA Staff & Global Investment Center, USA Staff. (World Investment & Business Guide Library-99: Vol. 129). (Illus.). 350p. 1999. pap. 99.95 (*0-7397-0324-2*) Intl Business Pubns.

Oman to Zimbabwe, Vol. III. (Abortion Policies Ser.). 247p. 25.00 (*92-1-151296-4*) UN.

***Oman under Qaboos: From Coup to Constitution, 1970-1996.** Calvin H. Allen & W. Lynn Rigsbee, II. 272p. 2000. 57.50 (*0-7146-5001-3*, Pub. by F Cass Pubs) Intl Spec Bk.

Omani Proverbs. A. S. Jayakar. (Arabia Past & Present Ser.: Vol. 20). 80p. 1986. 16.95 (*0-906672-12-0*) Oleander Pr.

Omano Oracle. Jack Joseph. 137p. 1997. pap. 13.95 (*0-9651546-8-8*) Med Bear.

OMAR. Craig O. Thompson. LC 98-89467. 375p. 1998. text 25.00 (*0-7388-0293-X*) Xlibris Corp.

Omar. Craig O. Thompson. LC 98-89467. 375p. 1998. pap. text 15.00 (*0-7388-0294-8*) Xlibris Corp.

Omar: The Second Caliph of Islam. Fazl Ahmad. (Heroes of Islam Ser.: Bk. 3). 100p. (Orig.). (YA). (gr. 7-12). 1984. pap. 3.50 (*1-56744-241-2*) Kazi Pubns.

Omar Al-Makhtar. Santarelli et al. 240p. 1990. 95.00 (*1-85077-095-6*, Pub. by Darf Pubs Ltd); pap. 75.00 (*1-85077-135-9*, Pub. by Darf Pubs Ltd) St Mut.

***Omar Khayyam.** (Everyman Paperback Classics). 1998. pap. 4.95 (*0-460-87954-5*, Everyman's Classic Lib) Tuttle Pubng.

Omar Nelson Bradley: The Centennial. Charles E. Kirkpatrick. 28p. 1993. pap. 1.25 (*0-16-061305-1*) USGPO.

***Omar on Ice.** Maryann Kovalski. (J). 1999. pap. write for info. (*1-55041-407-0*) Fitzhenry & W Ltd.

Omar on Ice. Maryann Kovalski. (First Flight Ser.). (Illus.). 32p. (J). (ps-1). 1999. 13.95 (*1-55041-507-7*, Pub. by Fitzhenry & W Ltd) Genl Dist Srvs.

Omar Vizquel: The Man with the Golden Glove. Dennis Manoloff. Ed. by Rob Rains. (Super Star Ser.). (Illus.). 96p. (J). (gr. 4-7). 1999. pap. 4.95 (*1-58261-045-2*) Sprts Pubng.

Oma's Character-Building Stories. Oma Ellis & Rita Dawson. LC 91-36230. (Illus.). 200p. (Orig.). 1992. pap. 8.99 (*0-932581-89-7*) Word Aflame.

***OMB Circular A-133, Compliance Supplement, March 2000.** 840p. 2000. ring bd. 64.00 (*0-16-050330-2*) USGPO.

Ombibulous Mister Mencken. Bud Johns. LC 68-8421. (Illus.). 64p. 1968. bds. 3.95 (*0-912184-09-4*) Synergistic Pr.

Ombilic de Limbes & Correspondance Avec Jacques Riviere, le Pese-Nerfs, Fragments d'un Journal d'Enfer, l'Art et la Mot, Etc. Antonin Artaud. (Poesie Ser.). (FRE.). 256p. 1968. pap. 9.95 (*2-07-030019-6*) Schoenhof.

Ombras Completas. Miguel De Cervantes Saavedra. write for info. (*0-318-63624-7*) Fr & Eur.

O

Ombre des Jeunes Filles en Fleurs. unabridged ed. Marcel Proust. (FRE.). pap. 7.95 (*2-87714-142-X*, Pub. by Bookking Intl) Distribks Inc.

Ombre e Luci. Vincenzo Tripodi. (ITA.). 125p. 1995. 62.50 (*1-882528-14-X*) Scripta.

Ombre sur un Mariage. Emma Darcy. (Azur Ser.: Bk. 741). 1999. mass mkt. 3.50 (*0-373-34741-3*, 1-34741-8) Harlequin Bks.

Ombu & Other South American Stories. William Henry Hudson. reprint ed. 64.50 (*0-404-03400-4*) AMS Pr.

Ombu Tree. Elise Dallemagne. LC 98-6672. 288p. 1998. pap. 14.95 (*1-56474-261-X*) Fithian Pr.

Ombudsman: A Classroom Community. 2nd ed. Ed. by Helen Harrill. (Illus.). 218p. (C). 1991. teacher ed. 40.00 (*0-934337-03-9*) Drug Ed Ctr.

Ombudsman: Citizen's Defender. Ed. by Donald C. Rowat. LC K 3416.R. 401p. reprint ed. pap. 124.40 (*0-608-12869-4*, 202366400033) Bks Demand.

Ombudsman: Twenty Five Years On. Ed. by Neil Hawke. (Series on Conference Papers Presented at Leicester Polytechnic March 1992)). 67p. 1993. 40.00 (*1-874241-17-1*, Pub. by Cavendish Pubng) Gaunt.

Ombudsman for American Government? Ed. by Stanley V. Anderson. LC 68-14460. 1968. 4.95 (*0-317-02958-4*, 63420) Am Assembly.

Ombudsman Plan: The Worldwide Spread of an Idea. rev. ed. Donald C. Rowat. 208p. (Orig.). (C). 1986. pap. text 22.00 (*0-8191-5040-1*) U Pr of Amer.

Ombudsmen & Others: Citizen's Protectors in Nine Countries. Walter Gellhorn. LC 66-23465. 464p. reprint ed. 143.90 (*0-8357-9171-8*, 201701200006) Bks Demand.

Ombudsmen Compared. Frank Stacey. 1978. 49.95 (*0-19-827420-3*) OUP.

OMC Cobalt Rhoduym Iridium. 1985. ring bd. write for info. (*0-412-26800-0*) Chapman & Hall.

OMC Cobra Stern Drive, 1985-95. Joan Coles & Clarence W. Coles. LC 91-201997. (Marine Tune-Up & Repair Manuals). (Illus.). 660p. (C). 1998. pap. 34.95 (*0-89330-025-X*, Pub. by Seloc) Natl Bk Netwk.

OMC Cobra Stern Drive Shop Manual, 1986-1993 (Includes 1988 & 1989 King Cobra Models) 4th rev. ed. LC 93-79777. (Illus.). 560p. 1993. pap. 36.95 (*0-89287-610-7*, B738) Intertec Pub.

OMC Stern Drive, 1964-1986. Clarence W. Coles & Howard U. Young. (Marine Tune-Up & Repair Manuals). (Illus.). 580p. (C). 1998. pap. 34.95 (*0-89330-004-7*, Pub. by Seloc) Natl Bk Netwk.

OMC Stern Drive Shop Manual, 1964-1986. 4th rev. ed. Kalton C. Lahue. (Illus.). 456p. (Orig.). 1988. pap. 34.95 (*0-89287-398-1*, B730) Clymer Pub.

Omdurman Diaries, 1898: Eye-Witness Accounts of the Legendary Campaign. John Meredith. 1998. 39.95 (*0-85052-607-8*, Pub. by Leo Cooper) Trans-Atl Phila.

Omdurman, 1898. Don Featherstone. (Campaign Ser.). (Illus.). 96p. 1994. pap. 14.95 (*1-85532-368-0*, 9528, Pub. by Osprey) Stackpole.

Omdurman, 1898: The Eyewitnesses Speak: The British Conquest of the Sudan As Described by Participants in Letters, Diaries, Photos, & Drawings. Peter Harrington & Frederic A. Sharf. LC 98-17752. (Illus.). 144p. 1998. 29.95 (*1-85367-333-1*, Pub. by Greenhill Bks) Stackpole.

Omega. Patrick Lynch. 1998. mass mkt. 6.99 (*0-451-19323-7*, Sig) NAL.

Omega. Lewis R. Walton. LC 81-5943. 96p. reprint ed. pap. 30.00 (*0-7837-6432-4*, 204643000012) Bks Demand.

Omega: The Last Days of the World. Camille Flammarion. LC 98-51566. (Illus.). 287p. 1999. pap. 14.95 (*0-8032-6898-X*, Bison Books) U of Nebr Pr.

Omega: The Last Days of the World. Camille Flammarion. LC 74-15971. (Science Fiction Ser.). (Illus.). 287p. 1975. reprint ed. 24.95 (*0-405-06291-5*) Ayer.

Omega-Bibliography of Mathematical Logic, 6 vols., Set. (Perspectives in Mathematical Logic Ser.). cclviii, 3456p. 1987. 1455.00 (*0-387-17457-5*) Spr-Verlag.

Omega-Bibliography of Mathematical Logic, Vol. I. Ed. by W. Rautenberg. (Perspectives in Mathematical Logic Ser.). xxxix, 483p. 1987. 275.00 (*0-387-17321-8*) Spr-Verlag.

Omega-Bibliography of Mathematical Logic, Vol. II. Ed. by W. Rautenberg. (Perspectives in Mathematical Logic Ser.). xxxvii, 468p. 1987. 245.00 (*0-387-15521-X*) Spr-Verlag.

Omega-Bibliography of Mathematical Logic, Vol. III. Heinz-Dieter Ebbinghaus. (Perspectives in Mathematical Logic Ser.). xlv, 615p. 1987. 280.00 (*0-387-15522-8*) Spr-Verlag.

Omega-Bibliography of Mathematical Logic, Vol. IV. Ed. by P. G. Hinman. (Perspectives in Mathematical Logic Ser.). xlv, 696p. 1987. 325.00 (*0-387-15523-6*) Spr-Verlag.

Omega-Bibliography of Mathematical Logic, Vol. V. Ed. by A. R. Blass. (Perspectives in Mathematical Logic Ser.). li, 790p. 1987. 355.00 (*0-387-15525-2*) Spr-Verlag.

Omega-Bibliography of Mathematical Logic, Vol. VI. Ed. by J. E. Kister et al. (Perspectives in Mathematical Logic Ser.). xli, 404p. 1987. 255.00 (*0-387-15524-4*) Spr-Verlag.

Omega Code: Another Has Risen from The Dead. Paul F. Crouch. 1999. 19.99 (*1-888848-35-9*) Western Front.

Omega Conspiracy: Satan's Last Assault on God's Kingdom. I. D. Thomas & Noah W. Hutchings. 254p. (Orig.). 1986. pap. 11.95 (*0-9624517-4-6*) Hearthstone OK.

Omega Conspiracy: Satan's Last Assault on God's Kingdom. rev. ed. I. D. Thomas. 250p. (Orig.). (C). 1990. reprint ed. pap. 8.95 (*0-685-37691-5*) Hearthstone OK.

***Omega Deception.** John F. Bayer. LC 99-46480. 320p. 2000. pap. 12.99 (*0-8054-1966-7*) Broadman.

Omega Desktop, Inc. - A Desktop Publishing. Boyce & Auvil. (DF - Computer Applications Ser.). 1990. mass mkt. 18.95 (*0-538-60535-9*) S-W Pub.

Omega Diet: The Life-Saving Nutritional Program Based on the Diet of the Island of Crete. Artemis P. Simopoulos. LC 98-33990. 400p. 1999. pap. 14.00 (*0-06-093023-3*) HarpC.

***Omega Files: Secret Nazi UFO Bases Revealed!** Ed. by Branton. (Illus.). 140p. 2000. pap. 25.00 (*1-892062-09-7*) Inner Light.

***Omega Game.** Stephen Krane. 2000. mass mkt. 6.99 (*0-88677-907-3*, Pub. by DAW Bks) Penguin Putnam.

Omega Game. Don Pendleton. LC 95-22346. (Superbolan Ser.). 346p. 1995. per. 4.99 (*0-373-61443-8*, 1-61443-7) Harlequin Bks.

Omega Government Travel & Hotel Directory. Ed. by Maria Whelan. LC 86-90545. 668p. (Orig.). 1987. pap. 75.00 (*0-939769-01-8*) Omega Travel Pubns.

Omega Missile, Vol. 1. McGuire & Joe Dalton. 304p. 1998. pap. 6.99 (*0-312-96660-1*, Pub. by Tor Bks) St Martin.

Omega Network. Thomas Locke. (Thomas Locke Mystery Ser.: Bk. 2). 256p. 1995. pap. 8.99 (*1-55661-502-7*) Bethany Hse.

***Omega Odyssey: A Business Metaphor.** Bill Gage. LC 00-190665. 96p. 2000. pap. 8.95 (*0-9679964-0-6*) Exec Trans.

Omega One Thousand Best Values for Government Travelers. Ed. by Zarguna Saleh. 150p. 1992. pap. write for info. (*0-939769-02-6*) Omega Travel Pubns.

Omega Path. James Axler. (Outlanders Ser.: No. 4). 1998. per. 5.99 (*0-373-63817-5*, 1-63817-0, Wrldwide Lib) Harlequin Bks.

Omega Point: An Apocalyptic Parable of Spiritual Transcendence for the New Millennium. Angela Browne-Miller & Charles Klotsche. (Illus.). 400p. (Orig.). 1995. pap. 18.50 (*0-9645472-0-1*) Metaterra Pubns.

Omega Prophecy. David Anderson. LC 98-86291. 325p. 1998. 25.00 (*0-7388-0053-8*); pap. 15.00 (*0-7388-0054-6*) Xlibris Corp.

Omega Reunion. Frank D. Carmical. 110p. (Orig.). 1986. pap. 3.95 (*0-9607576-5-1*) Redencion Viva.

Omega Sanction. Joe Dalton. 320p. 1999. pap. 6.99 (*0-312-97188-5*, St Martins Paperbacks) St Martin.

Omega Seed. Paolo Soleri. 1981. pap. 9.95 (*0-385-15889-0*) Doubleday.

Omega Station. Alfred Slote. LC 82-48461. (Illus.). 160p. (J). (gr. 2-5). 1983. 12.95 (*0-397-32035-3*); lib. bdg. 11.89 (*0-397-32036-1*) HarpC Child Bks.

Omega Station. Alfred Slote. LC 85-45395. (Trophy Bk.). (Illus.). 160p. (J). (gr. 2-5). 1986. pap. 3.95 (*0-06-440167-7*, HarpTrophy) HarpC Child Bks.

Omega Sub, No. 1. J. D. Cameron. 256p. 1991. pap. 2.95 (*0-380-76049-5*, Avon Bks) Morrow Avon.

Omega Sub No. 2: Command Decision. J. D. Cameron. 240p. 1991. pap. 2.95 (*0-380-76206-4*, Avon Bks) Morrow Avon.

Omega Sub No. 3: City of Fear. J. D. Cameron. 192p. (Orig.). 1991. pap. 2.95 (*0-380-76050-9*, Avon Bks) Morrow Avon.

Omega Sub No. 4: Blood Tide. J. D. Cameron. 224p. (Orig.). 1991. pap. 3.50 (*0-380-76321-4*, Avon Bks) Morrow Avon.

Omega Sub No. 5: Death Dive. J. D. Cameron. 224p. (Orig.). 1992. pap. 3.50 (*0-380-76492-X*, Avon Bks) Morrow Avon.

Omega Sub No. 6: Raven Rising. J. D. Cameron. 224p. (Orig.). 1992. pap. 3.50 (*0-380-76493-8*, Avon Bks) Morrow Avon.

Omega Syndrome. Sylvia Fleener. 388p. 1997. 22.95 (*1-57854-001-1*); pap. 10.95 (*1-57854-002-X*) Hope Manor.

***Omega-3 Connection: How You Can Restore Your Body's Natural Balance & Treat Depression.** Andrew Stoll. 2000. 22.00 (*0-684-87138-6*) Simon & Schuster.

Omega-3 Fatty Acids: Metabolism & Biological Effcts. Ed. by Christian A. Drevon et al. LC 93-17079. (Advances in Life Sciences Ser.). ix, 389p. 1993. 93.50 (*0-8176-2884-3*) Birkhauser.

Omega-Three Fatty Acids in Health & Disease. Lees & Karel. (Food Science & Technology Ser.: Vol. 37). (Illus.). 328p. 1990. text 165.00 (*0-8247-8292-5*) Dekker.

Omega-3 Oils: Why You Can't Afford to Live Without Essential Oils. Donald O. Rudin & Clara Felix. 224p. 1996. pap. 11.95 (*0-89529-721-3*, Avery) Penguin Putnam.

Omega Transmissions. Nancy Parker. LC 94-94606. 404p. 1994. pap. 12.95 (*0-9642272-0-7*) Ashland Hills.

Omega Workshops. Frwd. by Judith Collins & Quentin Bell. LC 83-18285. (Illus.). x, 310p. (C). 1984. 25.00 (*0-226-11374-4*) U Ch Pr.

Omega Workshops. Frwd. by Judith Collins & Quentin Bell. LC 83-18285. (Illus.). x, 320p. (C). 1985. pap. 21.00 (*0-226-11375-2*) U Ch Pr.

Omega Wristwatches: Feast for the Eyes. Anton Kreuzer. (Illus.). 224p. 1996. 59.95 (*0-7643-0058-X*) Schiffer.

***Omei I Ching: Mechanics of the I Ching.** large type ed. Monica Salyer & Gilbert Leal. 1999. pap. 15.00 (*0-934955-39-5*) Watercress Pr.

Omelet Murder Case. Tim Kelly. 1984. pap. 3.25 (*0-8222-0846-6*) Dramatists Play.

Omelets see Mahrajan Alijja

Omelette a la Follembuche. Eugene Labiche. Ed. by Michel Marc. (FRE.). 50p. 1947. pap. 9.95 (*0-7859-5360-4*) Fr & Eur.

Omelette & a Glass of Wine. Elizabeth David. 1989. pap. 14.95 (*0-14-046846-3*) Viking Penguin.

Omelette & a Glass of Wine. Elizabeth David. LC 96-37821. (Cook's Classic Library). 320p. 1997. reprint ed. pap. 14.95 (*1-55821-571-9*) Lyons Pr.

Omelettes: Eggs at Their Best. Laurence Sombke. (Illus.). 128p. (Orig.). 1992. pap. 7.95 (*0-312-08275-4*) St Martin.

***Omelettes, Pancakes & Fritters.** (Mini Cook Bks.). (Illus.). 64p. 1999. pap. 1.95 (*3-8290-1614-X*) Konemann.

Omelettes, Souffles & Frittatas. Lou Seibert Pappas. LC 98-30315. (Illus.). 96p. 1999. pap. 14.95 (*0-8118-2120-X*) Chronicle Bks.

O'Melveny & Myers Guide to Acquisition & Management of a U. S. Business. 160.00 (*1-85271-142-6*, Pub. by IBC Finan Pubng) IBC Pubns.

Omen. John Galt. LC 79-8265. reprint ed. 44.50 (*0-404-61854-5*) AMS Pr.

Omen of the Hawks. Virginia C. Trenholm. LC 89-63585. (Illus.). 312p. (YA). (gr. 9-12). 1989. 18.95 (*0-943255-26-0*); pap. 9.95 (*0-943255-35-X*) Portfolio Pub.

Omens & Elegies; Descent; Visions & Ruins; Agamemnon in Hades. Peter Russell. 102p. 1997. pap. 15.95 (*3-7052-0112-3*, Pub. by Poetry Salzburg) Intl Spec Bk.

Omens & Oracles: Collective Psychology in the Nuclear Age. Jerry Kroth. LC 90-27792. 240p. 1992. 55.00 (*0-275-93889-1*, C3889, Praeger Pubs) Greenwood.

Omens, Curses & Superstitions: How to Remove & Reverse Them. Suzanne Miller. 1998. pap. 12.00 (*1-892062-02-X*) Inner Light.

Omens from Your Dreams. Philippa Waring. 1993. 6.98 (*1-55521-818-0*) Bk Sales Inc.

Omens of Death. large type ed. Nicholas Rhea. (Magna Large Print Ser.), 416p. 1998. 29.99 (*0-7505-1219-9*, Pub. by Mgna Lrg Print) Ulverscroft.

Omens of the Millennium: The Gnosis of Angels, Dreams & Resurrection. Harold Bloom. 272p. 1997. reprint ed. pap. 13.00 (*1-57322-629-7*, Riverhd Trade) Berkley Pub.

Omens, Oghams & Oracles: Divination in the Druidic Tradition. Richard Webster. LC 95-1559. (Illus.). 224p. 1999. pap. 12.95 (*1-56718-800-1*) Llewellyn Pubns.

Omensetter's Luck. William H. Gass. LC 97-150733. 320p. 1997. pap. 12.95 (*0-14-118010-2*) Viking Penguin.

Omentum: Proceedings of the First International Conference on the Omentum Held in Research Triangle Park, North Carolina, October 28-31, 1988. Ed. by H. S. Goldsmith. (Illus.). x, 252p. 1990. 108.00 (*0-387-97337-0*) Spr-Verlag.

***Omentum Application to the Brain & Spinal Cord.** Ed. by Harry S. Goldsmith. (Illus.). 250p. 2000. pap. text 59.95 (*0-9674933-0-7*) Forefront Pub.

Omeprazole & Acid Inhibition: The Essential Issues - Journal: Digestion, Vol. 47, Suppl. 1, 1990. Ed. by R. H. Hunt. (Illus.). iv, 84p. 1991. pap. 26.25 (*3-8055-5386-2*) S Karger.

Omeros. Derek Walcott. 325p. 1992. pap. 14.00 (*0-374-52350-9*, Noonday) FS&G.

***Omerta: A Novel.** Mario Puzo. LC 00-28082. 316p. 2000. 25.95 (*0-375-50254-8*) Random.

***Omerta: A Novel.** large type ed. Mario Puzo. LC 00-21660. 512p. 2000. 25.95 (*0-375-43058-X*) Random Hse Lrg Prnt.

Omi-Tutu-Kekere. Alma Burnette. Ed. by Lafe Miller. (Illus.). 28p. (Orig.). (J). (gr. 1-8). 1994. 2.95 (*1-886452-02-4*) Amer Recycling.

Omicron. R. K. Hughes. Ed. by Judy Hilvosky. LC 90-32436. (YA). 1990. pap. 18.95 (*0-87949-286-4*) Ashley Bks.

***Omikron.** Prima Publishing Staff. LC 99-67120. (Illus.). 175p. 1999. pap. 19.99 (*0-7615-2605-6*) Prima Pub.

***Omikron: The Nomad Soul.** Greg Kramer. (Prima's Official Strategy Guides). (Illus.). 184p. 2000. pap. 14.99 (*0-7615-2941-1*) Prima Pub.

Ominous Evenings: Modern Reflections of Madness by Satya Palani. Satya Palani. LC 94-67019. 72p. 1994. pap. 7.00 (*0-9641928-0-2*) Ominous Whispers.

Ominous Parallels. Ed. by Leonard Peikoff. 1983. pap. 13.95 (*0-452-01117-5*, Mer) NAL.

Ominous Star. large type ed. Rae Foley. 1978. 27.99 (*0-7089-0107-7*) Ulverscroft.

Ominous Transition: Commerce & Colonial Expansion in the Senegambia & Guinea, 1857-1919. Joye Bowman. LC 96-86716. (Making of Modern Africa Ser.). (Illus.). 224p. 1997. text 69.95 (*1-85972-154-0*, Pub. by Avebry) Ashgate Pub Co.

Omissions Are Not Accidents: Gender in the Art of Marianne Moore. Jeanne Heuving. 196p. (C). 1992. 34.95 (*0-8143-2335-9*) Wayne St U Pr.

Omitted Chapters of History. Moncure D. Conway. (Works of Moncure Daniel Conway). 1990. reprint ed. lib. bdg. 79.00 (*0-7812-2339-3*) Rprt Serv.

***Omitted Genocide.** unabridged ed. Mulat Gebi. 137p. 1999. pap. 16.50 (*0-9674096-0-8*) M Gebi.

***Omitted Variable Tests & Dynamic Specification: An Application to Demand Homogeneity.** Bjhorn Schmolck. LC 00-38753. (Lecture Notes in Economics & Mathematical Systems Ser.). (Illus.). 2000. pap. write for info. (*3-540-67358-X*) Spr-Verlag.

Omiyage, Set. rev. ed. Marilyn Turkovich et al. LC 90-42183. (Illus.). 220p. (YA). (gr. 6-12). 1990. ring bd. 54.95 incl. audio (*0-930141-37-7*) World Eagle.

***Omiyage: Handmade Gifts from Fabric in the Japanese Tradition.** Kumiko Sudo. LC 00-31412. (Illus.). 160p. 2000. pap. 21.95 (*0-8092-2909-9*, Contemporary Bks) NTC Contemp Pub Co.

Omkring Faedrearven see Concerning Our Heritage

Omne Bonum: A Fourteenth-Century Encyclopedia of Universal Knowledge, Set, 2 vols. Lucy F. Sandler. (Illus.). 288p. 1997. text 185.00 (*1-872501-75-3*, Pub. by Harvey Miller) Gordon & Breach.

Omne Ens Est Aliquid. E. Peters. 1998. 18.95 (*90-6831-814-4*, Pub. by Peeters Pub) Bks Intl VA.

Omneagens Agit Sibi Simili: A "Repetition" of Scholastic Metaphysics. Philipp W. Rosemann. LC 98-126078. (Louvain Philosophical Studies: No. 12). (Illus.). 368p. 1998. pap. 67.50 (*90-6186-777-0*, Pub. by Leuven Univ) Coronet Bks.

Omneros. Mohammed Dib. Tr. by Carol Lettieri & Paul Vangelisti. 1978. pap. 3.00 (*0-88031-050-2*) Invisible-Red Hill.

Omni-Americans: Black Experience & American Culture. Albert Murray. (Quality Paperbacks Ser.). 227p. 1990. reprint ed. pap. 13.95 (*0-306-80395-X*) Da Capo.

Omni Best Science Fiction One. Ed. by Ellen Datlow. 1992. 8.95 (*0-87455-277-X*) Omni Bks.

Omni Best Science Fiction Three. Ed. by Ellen Datlow. 256p. 1993. pap. 10.00 (*0-87455-284-2*) Omni Bks.

Omni Best Science Fiction Two. Ed. by Ellen Datlow. 1992. 8.95 (*0-87455-278-8*) Omni Bks.

Omni Book of Medicine. Ed. by Owen Davies. 1984. mass mkt. 3.95 (*0-8217-1364-7*, Zebra Kensgtn) Kensgtn Pub Corp.

Omni Book of Science Quotations. Keith Ferrell. LC 93-21991. 1993. write for info. (*0-87455-290-7*) Omni Bks.

Omni Book of Scientific Quotations. Keith Ferrell. LC 93-21991. 360p. 1994. pap. 15.00 (*0-87455-285-0*) Omni Bks.

Omni Future Almanac. Ed. by Robert Weil. 320p. 1983. pap. 8.95 (*0-345-31034-9*, World Almanac) Newspaper Ent.

Omni Gazetteer of the United States of America: National Edition, 11 vols., Set. Ed. by Frank R. Abate. (Illus.). 9400p. 1991. lib. bdg. 1400.00 (*1-55888-336-3*) Omnigraphics Inc.

Omni Gazetteer of the United States of America Vol. 1: New England. Ed. by Frank R. Abate. (Illus.). 396p. 1991. lib. bdg. 150.00 (*1-55888-325-8*) Omnigraphics Inc.

Omni Gazetteer of the United States of America Vol. 2: Northeastern States. Ed. by Frank R. Abate. (Illus.). 720p. 1991. lib. bdg. 150.00 (*1-55888-326-6*) Omnigraphics Inc.

Omni Gazetteer of the United States of America Vol. 3: Southeast. Ed. by Frank R. Abate. (Illus.). 786p. 1991. lib. bdg. 150.00 (*1-55888-327-4*) Omnigraphics Inc.

Omni Gazetteer of the United States of America Vol. 4: South Central States. Ed. by Frank R. Abate. (Illus.). 1156p. 1991. lib. bdg. 150.00 (*1-55888-328-2*) Omnigraphics Inc.

Omni Gazetteer of the United States of America Vol. 5: Southwestern States. Ed. by Frank R. Abate. (Illus.). 651p. 1991. lib. bdg. 150.00 (*1-55888-329-0*) Omnigraphics Inc.

Omni Gazetteer of the United States of America Vol. 6: Great Lakes States. Ed. by Frank R. Abate. (Illus.). 757p. 1991. lib. bdg. 150.00 (*1-55888-330-4*) Omnigraphics Inc.

Omni Gazetteer of the United States of America Vol. 7: Plains States. Ed. by Frank R. Abate. (Illus.). 495p. 1991. lib. bdg. 150.00 (*1-55888-331-2*) Omnigraphics Inc.

Omni Gazetteer of the United States of America Vol. 8: Mountain States. Ed. by Frank R. Abate. (Illus.). 744p. 1991. lib. bdg. 150.00 (*1-55888-332-0*) Omnigraphics Inc.

Omni Gazetteer of the United States of America Vol. 9: Pacific. Ed. by Frank R. Abate. (Illus.). 902p. 1991. lib. bdg. 150.00 (*1-55888-333-9*) Omnigraphics Inc.

Omni Gazetteer of the United States of America Vol. 10: National Index. Ed. by Frank R. Abate. 1582p. 1991. lib. bdg. 150.00 (*1-55888-334-7*) Omnigraphics Inc.

Omni Gazetteer of the United States of America Vol. 11: Appendices: U. S. Data Sourcebook. Ed. by Frank R. Abate. 570p. 1991. lib. bdg. 150.00 (*1-55888-335-5*) Omnigraphics Inc.

Omni-Horizon-Rampage, 1978-89: Repair & Tune-Up Guide. Chilton Automotive Editorial Staff. LC 88-43176. (Illus.). 352p. (C). 1989. pap. 16.95 (*0-8019-7934-X*) Thomson Learn.

***Omni Lite Millennium Calendar of Champions.** (Illus.). 14p. 1999. pap. 16.00 (*0-9673595-0-3*) Next Up.

Omnibus. Katherine Paterson. 1999. pap. 12.95 (*0-452-27486-9*, Plume) Dutton Plume.

Omnibus. Jules Verne. 822p. Date not set. 38.95 (*0-8488-2601-9*) Amereon Ltd.

Omnibus Anti-Crime Act: A Legislative History of the Violent Crime Control & Law Enforcement Act of 1994 Public Law 103-322, 20 vols. Ed. by Bernard D. Reams, Jr. LC 97-80048. 1997. 1995.00 (*1-57588-346-5*, 308970) W S Hein.

Omnibus Budget Reconciliation Act of 1990. 118p. 1991. pap. 75.00 (*0-614-25936-3*, OBA-LB) Nat Assn Insurance.

Omnibus Copyright Revision: Legislative History, 18 bks. Ed. by George S. Grossman. LC 76-54496. 1981. fiche 445.00 (*0-89941-146-0*, 300460) W S Hein.

Omnibus Hearing: An Experiment in Relieving Inefficiency, Unfairness & Judicial Delay. Raymond T. Nimmer. (American Bar Foundation Publications). ix, 125p. 1971. 22.50 (*1-57588-347-3*, 304990) W S Hein.

Omnibus Idea. Victor F. Yellin. LC 97-45589. (Detroit Monographs in Musicology/Studies in Music: Vol. 22). 1997. 40.00 (*0-89990-081-X*) Harmonie Park Pr.

Omnibus of Prayer: A Simple Guide for Communicating with Our Heavenly Father. Don Edwards. Ed. by Kas Winters. 48p. 1998. pap. 6.95 (*1-892225-10-7*, OP-1) Winmark Comm.

Omnibus of Twentieth Century Ghost Stories. Ed. by Robert Phillips. 384p. 1991. pap. 11.95 (*0-88184-780-1*) Carroll & Graf.

Omnibus Press Presents the Story of Bewitched. Vincent Vincent. (Illus.). 30p. 1999. pap. text 9.95 (*0-7119-7635-X*, OZ100144) Music Sales.

An Asterisk (*) at the beginning of an entry indicates that the title is appearing for the first time.

Omnibus Press Presents the Story of Britney Spears. Ashley Adams. (Illus.). 31p. (J). (gr. 4-7). 1999. pap. 9.95 (0-8256-1744-8, OP48149) Omnibus NY.

Omnibus Press Presents the Story of Korn. Doug Small. (Illus.). 60p. 1998. pap. 14.95 (0-8256-1688-3, OP48122) Music Sales.

Omnibus Series: E. S. Byrd Library. Compiled by Alexander N. Charters. 1976. 4.65 (0-686-50190-X, MSS 24) Syracuse U Cont Ed.

Omnicide: The Nuclear Dilemma. Lisl M. Goodman & Lee A. Hoff. LC 90-31363. 176p. 1990. 47.95 (0-275-93298-2, C3298, Praeger Pubs) Greenwood.

Omnidirectional Gravitational Radiation Observatory. Ed. by O. D. Aguiar et al. 300p. 1997. text 54.00 (981-02-3209-8) World Scientific Pub.

OmniMark at Work Vol. 1: Getting Started. Brian E. Travis. Ed. by Denielle C. Travis. (Illus.). 400p. 1997. pap. 65.00 (0-9649602-1-4) Architag Pr.

***OmniMark at Work Vol. 2: Building.** 350p. 2000. pap. 65.00 (0-9649602-2-2) Architag Pr.

Omniphobia: Stories. R. H. Dillard. LC 94-27047. 208p. 1995. 22.95 (0-8071-1839-7) La State U Pr.

Omnipotence & Other Theological Mistakes. Charles Hartshorne. LC 83-6588. 144p. 1984. pap. text 18.95 (0-87395-771-7) State U NY Pr.

Omnipotence & the Wheelbarrow Man. Alan Haehnel. 24p. (Orig.). (YA). (gr. 7-12). 1995. pap. 3.00 (1-57514-226-0, 3018) Encore Perform Pub.

Omnipotence, Covenant & Order: An Excursion in the History of Ideas from Abelard to Leibniz. Francis Oakley. LC 83-45945. 166p. 1984. text 32.50 (0-8014-1631-0) Cornell U Pr.

Omnipotent Fantasies & the Vulnerable Self. Ed. by Carolyn S. Ellman & Joseph Reppen. LC 96-38978. 1997. 50.00 (0-7657-0046-8) Aronson.

Omnipotent Government: The Rise of the Total State & Total War. Ludwig Von Mises. 291p. (C). 1985. reprint ed. pap. text 10.95 (0-910884-15-3) Libertarian Press.

Omnipowerful Brand. Frank Delano. LC 98-20739. xvi, 256p. 1999. 35.95 (0-8144-0459-6) AMACOM.

Omnipresent Debate: Empiricism & Transcendentalism in Nineteenth-Century English Prose. Wendell V. Harris. LC 80-8663. 378p. 1981. 32.00 (0-87580-076-9) N Ill U Pr.

Omni's Future Medical Almanac. Dick Teresi & Patrice Adcroft. (Paperbacks Ser.). 372p. 1988. mass mkt. 7.95 (0-07-063506-4) McGraw.

Omniscience: The Basic Game of Knowledge in Book Form. rev. ed. John P. Campbell. 392p. 2000. pap. 16.95 (0-944322-12-3) Patricks Pr.

Omnivore. Piers Anthony. 1978. pap. 3.95 (0-380-00262-0, Avon Bks) Morrow Avon.

Omo Micromammals: Systematics & Paleoecology of Early Man Sites from Ethiopia. H. B. Wesselman. (Contributions to Vertebrate Evolution Ser.: Vol. 7). (Illus.). x, 222p. 1984. 85.25 (3-8055-3935-5) S Karger.

Omohundro Genealogical Record: The Omohundro & Allied Families in America . . . From the First Omohundro in Westmoreland County, Va., 1670 . . . To 1950. Malvern H. Omohundro. (Illus.). 1287p. 1998. reprint ed. pap. 159.00 (0-8328-9483-4); reprint ed. lib. bdg. 169.00 (0-8328-9482-6) Higginson Bk Co.

Omon Ra. Victor Pelevin. LC 95-47618. 154p. 1996. 21.00 (0-374-22592-3) FS&G.

Omon Ra. Victor Pelevin. Tr. by Andrew Bromfield from RUS. LC 97-34302. 160p. 1998. pap. 9.95 (0-8112-1364-1, NDP851, Pub. by New Directions) Norton.

Omoo. Herman Melville. 1976. 23.95 (0-8488-1098-8) Amereon Ltd.

***Omoo.** Herman Melville. LC 99-43708. 320p. 2000. text 8.95 (0-486-40873-6) Dover.

Omoo. Herman Melville. Ed. by Harrison Hayford et al. LC 67-11991. (Northwestern-Newberry Edition of the Writings of Herman Melville: Vol. 2). 380p. 1968. 59.95 (0-8101-0162-9); pap. text 19.95 (0-8101-0160-2) Northwestern U Pr.

Omoo. Herman Melville. (BCL1-PS American Literature Ser.). 299p. 1992. reprint ed. lib. bdg. 79.00 (0-7812-6796-X) Rprt Serv.

Omoo: A Narrative of Adventures in the South Seas. Herman Melville. LC 99-41391. 336p. 1999. pap. 16.95 (0-8101-1765-7) Northwestern U Pr.

Omoo: Adventures in the South Seas. Herman Melville. (Pacific Basin Bks.). 220p. (Orig.). 1985. pap. 14.95 (0-7103-0133-2) Routledge.

Omori Sogen: The Art of a Zen Master. Hosokawa Dogen. LC 97-25743. (Illus.). 180p. 1997. 93.50 (0-7103-0588-5, Pub. by Kegan Paul Intl) Col U Pr.

Omphale see Chefs-d'Oeuvre Classiques de l'Opera Francais

***Omphale Musings.** T. K. Splake. Ed. by Joyce Metzger. 48p. 1999. pap. 6.95 (1-878116-93-2) JVC Bks.

Omphalinae (Clitocybeae-Tricholomataceae, Basidiomycetes), Phaeocollybia (Cortinariaceae, Basidiomycetes), Strobilomycetaceae (Basidiomycetes) Rolf Singer. LC 79-136205. (Flora Neotropica Monographs: Nos. 3-5). (Illus.). 84p. 1986. reprint ed. pap. text 13.00 (0-89327-304-X) NY Botanical.

Omphalos, Vol. I. Wilhelm H. Roscher. (Abhandlungen der Kgl. Sachsischen Gesellschaft der Wissenschaften. Philologisch-Historische Klasse, 29 Ser.: Bd., Nr. 9). (GER.). 142p. 1974. reprint ed. write for info. (3-487-05279-2) G Olms Pubs.

Omphalos: An Attempt to Untie the Geological Knot. Philip H. Gosse. LC 97-45526. (Illus.). xiv, 376p. 1998. reprint ed. pap. 34.95 (1-881987-10-8) Ox Bow.

Omraam Mikhael Aivanhov: Master of the Great Universal White Brotherhood. Agnes Lejbowicz. (Testimonials Ser.). 115p. (Orig.). 1982. pap. 6.95 (2-85566-191-9, Pub. by Prosveta) Prosveta USA.

OMRI Annual Survey of Eastern Europe & the Former Soviet: 1996: Forging Ahead, Falling Behind. Open Media Research Institute Staff, Prague. (Illus.). 344p. (C). (gr. 13). 1997. text 94.95 (1-56324-925-1) M E Sharpe.

OMRI Annual Survey of Eastern Europe & the Former Soviet Republic: 1995: Buidling Democracy. Open Media Research Institute Staff. LC 96-19263. (Illus.). 344p. (C). (gr. 13). 1996. text 94.95 (1-56324-924-3) M E Sharpe.

Omsi Cookbook. Leslie J. Whipple. 184p. 1993. pap. 14.95 (0-89288-244-1) Maverick.

Omsk Oblast: Economy, Industry, Government, Business. 2nd rev. ed. Russian Information & Business Center, Inc. Staff. (Russian Regional Business Directories Ser.). (Illus.). 200p. 1997. pap. 99.00 (1-57751-403-3) Intl Business Pubns.

***Omsk Oblast Regional Investment & Business Guide.** Global Investment & Business Center, Inc. Staff. (Russian Regional Investment & Business Guides Ser.: Vol. 55). (Illus.). 350p. 1999. pap. 99.00 (0-7397-0854-6) Intl Business Pubns.

***Omsk Oblast Regional Investment & Business Guide.** Contrib. by Global Investment & Business Center, Inc. Staff. (Russian Regional Investment & Business Guides Ser.: Vol. 13). (Illus.). 350p. 2000. pap. 99.95 (0-7397-3003-7) Intl Business Pubns.

OMT Insights: Perspectives on Modeling from the Journal of Object-Oriented Programming. James Rumbaugh. LC 96-18006. (SIGS Reference Library: No. 6). 412p. (C). 1996. pap. 44.95 (0-13-846965-2) Cambridge U Pr.

Omuluabi: Ulli Beier, Yoruba Society & Culture. Wole Ogundele. LC 98-37142. 304p. 1998. 79.95 (0-86543-720-3); pap. 21.95 (0-86543-721-1) Africa World.

On. Hilaire Belloc. LC 68-28742. (Essay Index Reprint Ser.). 1977. 19.95 (0-8369-0190-8) Ayer.

On Vol. 1: A Book of Poetry. deluxe limited large type ed. Ronald W. Mealing. LC 96-984788. 314p. 1996. 49.95 (0-9654293-3-4) R Mealing Ent.

On Vol. 1: A Book of Poetry. limited large type ed. Ronald W. Mealing. LC 96-984788. 314p. 1996. 34.95 (0-9654293-0-X) R Mealing Ent.

On a Bed of Rice: An Asian American Erotic Feast. Ed. by Geraldine Kudaka. LC 95-15723. 528p. (Orig.). 1995. pap. 15.95 (0-385-47640-X, Anchor NY) Doubleday.

On a Bike. Nikki Bundey. LC 97-25359. (First Sports Science Ser.). 32p. (J). (gr. 1-2). 1997. 21.27 (1-57505-278-4, Carolrhoda) Lerner Pub.

On a Blood Stained Sea. Daniel L. Houston. LC 99-179129. 224p. 1998. pap. 11.95 (0-9663540-0-1) Counterbattery Pr.

On a Building Site. Henry Arthur Pluckrose. LC 98-17934. (Machines at Work Ser.). (Illus.). (J). 1998. 18.00 (0-531-14495-X) Watts.

On a Building Site. Henry Arthur Pluckrose. (Machines at Work Ser.). (Illus.). 32p. (J). (gr. k-2). 1999. pap. text 6.95 (0-531-15355-X) Watts.

On a Clear Day You Can See Forever. Alan J. Lerner & Lane. 120p. 1994. per. 35.00 (0-7935-3408-9, 00312501) H Leonard.

On a Clear Day You Can See Forever: Vocal Selections. (Illus.). 48p. 1981. pap. 8.95 (0-88188-100-7, 00312297) H Leonard.

On a Clear Day You Can See Forever: Vocal Selections. Ed. by Carol Cuellar. 40p. (Orig.). (C). 1994. pap. text 10.95 (0-89724-287-4, VF2132) Wrner Bros.

On a Clear Day You Can See General Motors. J. Patrick Wright. 304p. 1980. mass mkt. 5.95 (0-380-51722-1, Avon Bks) Morrow Avon.

On a Clear Day You Can See Yourself. Sonya Friedman. 1994. mass mkt. 5.50 (0-8041-1228-2) Ivy Books.

On a Cold & Frosty Morning. Pam Adams. (Soap Opera Ser.). 8p. (J). (gr. 4 up). 1990. 6.99 (0-85953-442-1) Childs Play.

On a Complex Theory of a Simple God: An Investigation in Aquinas' Philosophical Theology. Christopher Hughes. LC 89-42877. (Cornell Studies in the Philosophy of Religion). 336p. 1989. text 45.00 (0-8014-1759-7) Cornell U Pr.

On a Country Road: 20 Bicycle Rides in Beautiful & Historic Southeastern Pennsylvania. Barry Johnston & Lois Johnston. 120p. 1998. pap. 10.95 (1-57502-712-7, PO2003) Morris Pubng.

***On a Dark Night I Left My Silent House.** Peter Handke. Tr. by Krishna Winston from GER.Tr. of In Einer Nacht Ging Ich Aus Meinem Stillen Haus. 160p. 2000. 23.00 (0-374-17547-0) FS&G.

On a Far Wild Shore. MacDonald. mass mkt. write for info. (0-312-90295-6) Tor Bks.

***On a Farm.** Susan Canizares & Betsey Waugh. LC 99-462012. (Illus.). (J). 2000. pap. write for info. (0-439-15371-9) Scholastic Inc.

On a Golden Chain. Ruth Benjamin. 300p. (C). 1919. pap. 16.95 (1-56062-081-1) CIS Comm.

On a Good Day. Gay Rubin. (Orig.). Date not set. pap. 14.95 (0-911051-96-1) Plain View.

On a Healthy Wok: Quick & Easy. Sue E. Willett. (Health Ser.). 160p. (Orig.). 1991. pap. text 3.00 (1-56383-002-7, 9030) G & R Pub.

On a High Horse: Views Mostly of Latin American & Texan Poetry. Dave Oliphant. 1983. pap. 9.95 (0-933384-11-4) Prickly Pear.

On a Hill Far Away: Journal of a Missionary Doctor in Rwanda. 2nd ed. C. Albert Snyder. (Illus.). 310p. 1995. pap. 13.95 (0-89367-202-5) Light & Life Comm.

On a Hinge of History: The Mutual Vulnerability of South & North. Ivan L. Head. 256p. 1992. text 35.00 (0-8020-2766-0); pap. text 17.95 (0-8020-7364-6) U of Toronto Pr.

On a Journey, Vol. 4, No. 2. Tom Ehrich. 95p. (Orig.). 1997. pap. 6.00 (0-9653442-1-5) Jrny Pub Co.

On a Journey, Vol. IV No. 3. Tom Ehrich. 96p. (Orig.). 1997. pap. 6.00 (0-9653442-2-3) Jrny Pub Co.

***On a Late Spring Day.** Rennie Saville. 2000. pap. 5.95 (0-533-13449-8) Vantage.

On a Ledge: New & Selected Poems. Bryan Guinness. 1996. 24.95 (0-946640-76-9, Pub. by Lilliput Pr) Irish Bks Media.

On a Lonely Island: Without the Heretic Paul. John M. Schofield. 112p. (Orig.). 1992. pap. 9.95 (0-9631882-0-8) Cresset Pr.

***On a Long Ago Night.** Susan Sizemore. 384p. 2000. mass mkt. 5.99 (0-380-80419-0, Avon Bks) Morrow Avon.

On a Marche Sur la Lune see Explorers on the Moon

On a Marche sur la Lune. Herge.Tr. of Explorers on the Moon. (FRE., Illus.). (J). (gr. 7-9). ring bd. 19.95 (0-8288-5053-4) Fr & Eur.

On a Method of Multiprogramming. W. H. Feijen & A. J. Van Gasteren. LC 99-15370. (Monographs in Computer Science). 392p. 1999. 59.95 (0-387-98870-X) Spr-Verlag.

On a Mexican Mustang, Through Texas. Alex Sweet. 1993. reprint ed. lib. bdg. 75.00 (0-7812-5906-1) Rprt Serv.

On a Mission: Selected Poems & a History of the Last Poets. Abiodun Oyewole et al. 1996. pap. 12.95 (0-614-20811-4, Owl) H Holt & Co.

On a Moon-Struck Gravel Road. Rodney Torreson. 58p. 1994. pap. 8.00 (1-55780-139-8) Juniper Pr ME.

On a Note of Triumph: Norman Corwin & the Golden Years of Radio. R. LeRoy Bannerman & Erik Barnouw. (Illus.). 275p. reprint ed. pap. 8.95 (0-8184-0512-0) Carol Pub Group.

On a Painted Ocean: Art of the Seven Seas. Peter Neill et al. Ed. by Gareth L. Steen. LC 95-32496. 188p. (C). 1995. text 45.00 (0-8147-5787-1) NYU Pr.

On a Pale Horse. Piers Anthony. (Incarnations of Immortality Ser.: Bk. 1). 336p. 1986. mass mkt. 5.95 (0-345-33858-8, Del Rey) Ballantine Pub Grp.

On a Pale Horse. Piers Anthony. (Incarnations of Immortality Ser.: Bk. 1). 1983. 11.05 (0-606-02598-7, Pub. by Turtleback) Demco.

On a Par with Murder. John Logue. (Morris & Sullivan Mystery Ser.: Vol. 5). 288p. 1999. mass mkt. 5.99 (0-440-22400-4) Dell.

On a Positive Note. CeCe Winans & Renita Weems. (Illus.). 288p. 1999. 24.00 (0-671-02000-5, PB Hardcover) PB.

On A Positive Note. CeCe Winans. 256p. 2000. reprint ed. pap. 12.95 (0-671-02001-3, PB Trade Paper) PB.

On a Rainy Day: A Playtime Pop-Up. Pat Paris. (Illus.). 10p. (J). (ps). 1992. pap., boxed set 4.95 (0-671-74175-6) Litle Simon.

On a Riverboat Journey: A Handscroll by Ito Jakuchu, with Poems by Daiten. Hiroshi Onishi. LC 89-62484. (Illus.). 180p. 1990. boxed set 45.00 (0-8076-1229-4) Braziller.

On a Roll: A Conversation & Listening Text. Sharon Peters. 160p. (C). 1990. pap. text 26.93 (0-13-155326-7) P-H.

On a Roll: A History of Gambling & Lotteries in New Zealand David Grant. LC 94-230480. 336 p. 1994. write for info. (0-86473-266-X) Lubrecht & Cramer.

On a Roll: How to Play Craps & Win. Damon M. Farris. (Illus.). (Orig.). 1989. pap., per. 14.95 (0-685-29117-0) MU-TECH.

On a Safari. Roma Bishop. 1994. pap. 3.95 (0-671-88309-7) Litle Simon.

On a Scaffold High. 254p. (YA). (gr. 6). 1993. pap. 26.95 (0-8464-4814-9) Beekman Pubs.

On a Scale That Competes with the World: The Art of Edward & Nancy Reddin Kienholz. Robert L. Pincus. (Illus.). 135p. 1990. 60.00 (0-520-06730-4, Pub. by U CA Pr) Cal Prin Full Svc.

On a Scale That Competes with the World: The Art of Edward & Nancy Reddin Kienholz. Robert L. Pincus. (Illus.). 135p. (C). 1994. pap. 34.95 (0-520-08446-2, Pub. by U CA Pr) Cal Prin Full Svc.

On a Scotch Bard: An Illustrated Life of Robert Burns. Keith Mitchell. (Illus.). 96p. 1996. pap. 9.95 (1-897784-22-8, Pub. by N Wilson Pubng) Interlink Pub.

***On a Shoestring.** Samela Harris. (Illus.). 256p. 2000. pap. 12.95 (1-86254-388-7, Pub. by Wakefield Pr) BHB Intl.

On a Shoestring to Coorg: A Travel Memoir of India. Dervla Murphy. LC 89-8830. 272p. 1989. 22.95 (0-87951-372-1, Pub. by Overlook Pr) Penguin Putnam.

On a Shoestring to Coorg: A Travel Memoir of India. Dervla Murphy. LC 89-8830. 272p. 1990. pap. 13.95 (0-87951-381-0, Pub. by Overlook Pr) Penguin Putnam.

On a Silver Diamond: The Story of Rochester Community Baseball from 1956-1996. Brian A. Bennett. viii, 358p. (Orig.). 1997. pap. 19.95 (0-9651863-1-8, 0297-01) Triphammer Pubng.

On a Silver Platter: CD-ROMs & the Promises of a New Technology. Ed. by Greg M. Smith. LC 98-25494. (Illus.). 256p. 1999. text 55.00 (0-8147-8080-6) NYU Pr.

***On a Silver Platter: CD-ROMs & the Promises of a New Technology.** Ed. by Greg M. Smith. LC 98-25494. (Illus.). 256p. 1999. pap. 17.95 (0-8147-8081-4) NYU Pr.

On a Spaceship with Beelzebub: By a Grandson of Gurdjieff. David Kherdian. LC 97-47237. 288p. 1998. pap. 14.95 (0-89281-673-2, Inner Trad) Inner Tradit.

On a Stair. Ann Lauterbach. 1997. pap. 16.95 (0-614-29442-8) Penguin Putnam.

On a Stair. Anne Lauterbach. LC 97-3564. 89p. 1997. pap. 14.95 (0-14-058793-4) Viking Penguin.

On a Starry Night. Natalie Kinsey-Warnock. LC 93-4878. (Illus.). 32p. (J). (ps-2). 1994. 15.95 (0-531-06820-X); lib. bdg. 16.99 (0-531-08670-4) Orchard Bks Watts.

On a Street Called Easy, in a Cottage Called Joye. Gregory W. Smith & Steven W. Naifeh. LC 95-35880. 1996. 23.95 (0-614-08320-6) Little.

***On a Street Called Easy, in a Cottage Called Joye.** Gregory White Smith. 321p. 2000. 23.95 (0-913391-21-2) Woodward-White.

On a Variety of Subjects. Paul M. Angle. 1974. 10.00 (0-940550-05-9) Caxton Club.

On a Voiceless Shore. Stephen Minta. LC 97-11474. 1998. text 25.00 (0-8050-3778-0) St Martin.

On a Walk. Bob Komives. 128p. 1996. spiral bd. 6.00 (0-9629281-4-3) RPK Pr.

On a White Horse: A Case Study. Neil Steiger. Ed. by Judith Kleinfeld. (Teaching Cases in Cross-Cultural Education Ser.: No. 8). 35p. (Orig.). (C). 1991. pap. text 7.50 (1-877962-17-1, LB2157A35741991) Univ AK Ctr CCS.

***On a Wicked Wind.** Linda Jones. 400p. 1998. mass mkt. 5.99 (0-505-52251-9, Love Spell) Dorchester Pub Co.

On a Windy Day: A Playtime Pop-Up. Pat Paris. (Illus.). 10p. (J). (ps). 1992. pap., boxed set 4.95 (0-671-74174-8) Litle Simon.

On a Wing & a Prayer. Helen Carey. 416p. 1998. 27.00 (1-85797-642-8, Pub. by Orion Pubng Grp) Trafalgar.

On a Wing & a Prayer: Devotions for Busy Christians. Brian K. Bauknight. LC 97-44055. 208p. 1998. pap. 10.00 (0-687-05211-4) Dimen for Liv.

***On a Wintry Morning.** Doris J. Chaconas. LC 99-89535. (Illus.). 32p. (J). (ps-k). 2000. 15.99 (0-670-89245-9, PuffinBks) Peng Put Young Read.

On Abstinence from Animal Food. Porphyry. 250p. 1989. pap. 25.00 (0-87556-238-8) Saifer.

***On Abstinence from Killing Animals.** Porphyry & Gillian Clark. LC 00-22675. (Ancient Commentators on Aristotle Ser.). 2000. write for info. (0-8014-3692-3) Cornell U Pr.

On Abstract Art. Briony Fer. LC 96-41297. (Illus.). 208p. 1997. 40.00 (0-300-06975-8) Yale U Pr.

***On Abstract Art.** Briony Fer. (Illus.). 208p. 2000. pap. 22.50 (0-300-08735-7) Yale U Pr.

On Account Of: Selected Poems. Karl Krolow. Tr. by Stuart Friebert from GER. LC 84-62769. (Field Translation Ser.: No. 10). 117p. 1985. 11.50 (0-932440-18-5); pap. 6.50 (0-932440-19-3) Oberlin Coll Pr.

On Account of Sex: An Annotated Bibliography on the Status of Women in Librarianship, 1987-1992. Ed. by Lori A. Goetsch et al. LC 93-8164. (Illus.). 272p. 1993. 38.00 (0-8108-2701-8) Scarecrow.

***On Account of Sex: An Annotated Bibliography on the Status of Women in Librarianship, 1993-1997.** Ed. by Betsy Kruger & Catherine A. Larson. LC 99-43957. 344p. 1999. 65.00 (0-8108-3725-0) Scarecrow.

On Account of Sex: Annotated Bibliography on the Status of Women in Librarianship, 1982-1986. Katharine Phenix et al. 152p. 1990. pap. text 10.00 (0-8389-3375-0) ALA.

On Account of Sex: The Politics of Women's Issues, 1945-1968. Cynthia Harrison. 370p. 1988. pap. 16.95 (0-520-06663-4, Pub. by U CA Pr) Cal Prin Full Svc.

On Acheve Bien les Chevaux. Horace McCoy. (FRE.). 1977. pap. 10.95 (0-7859-4086-3) Fr & Eur.

On Acting. David Mamet. 1999. pap. write for info. (0-14-010104-7, Viking) Viking Penguin.

On Action. Carl Ginet. (Cambridge Studies in Philosophy). 171p. (C). 1990. text 69.95 (0-521-38124-X); pap. text 19.95 (0-521-38818-X) Cambridge U Pr.

On Actors & Acting: Essays by Alexander Knox. Anthony Slide. LC 98-18806. (Filmmakers Ser.: No. 63). (Illus.). 120p. 1998. 32.50 (0-8108-3499-5) Scarecrow.

On Actors & the Art of Acting. George Henry Lewes. LC 68-56038. (Illus.). 237p. 1970. reprint ed. lib. bdg. 59.50 (0-8371-0533-1, LEAA, Greenwood Pr) Greenwood.

***On Adam Smith & Confucius.** Wei B. Zhang. LC 99-55098. 152p. 1999. 34.00 (1-56072-765-9) Nova Sci Pubs.

On Adam's House in Paradise: The Idea of the Primitive Hut in Architectural History. 2nd ed. Joseph Rykwert. (Illus.). 240p. (C). 1981. reprint ed. pap. text 17.50 (0-262-68036-X) MIT Pr.

***On Addams.** Fischer. 2000. pap. 8.25 (0-534-58358-X) Wadsworth Pub.

On Adolescence: A Psychoanalytic Interpretation. Peter Blos. LC 61-14110. 1966. pap. 14.95 (0-02-904330-1) Free Pr.

On Aesthetics in Science. Ed. by Judith Wechsler. (Design Science Collections). 194p. 1987. 32.50 (0-8176-3379-0) Birkhauser.

On Afrocentricity, Intercultural Communication, & Racism. E. Lama Wonkeryor. LC 98-14642. (Black Studies: Vol. 2). 132p. 1998. text 69.95 (0-7734-8505-8) E Mellen.

On Aggression. Konrad Lorenz. 306p. 1996. 7.98 (1-56731-107-5, MJF Bks) Fine Comms.

On Aggression. Konrad Lorenz. Tr. by Marjorie K. Wilson from GER. LC 74-5306. (Helen & Kurt Wolff Bk.). (Illus.). 320p. 1974. reprint ed. pap. 13.00 (0-15-668741-0, Harvest Bks) Harcourt.

On Aging: Revolt & Resignation. Jean Amery. Tr. by John D. Barlow. LC 93-41804. 160p. 1994. 19.95 (0-253-30675-2) Ind U Pr.

On Agriculture. Tr. by H. B. Ash. (Loeb Classical Library: No. 283). 570p. 1972. 18.95 (0-674-99313-6) HUP.

On Ahavas Yisrael. 2nd ed. Shalom D. Schneersohn. Ed. by Shalom B. Wineberg. Tr. by Uri Kaploun from HEB. LC 96-194102. 126p. 1996. reprint ed. 14.00 (0-8266-0435-8) Kehot Pubn Soc.

***On Air.** Maniza Naqvi. 164p. 2000. pap. 10.95 (0-19-579397-8) OUP.

O

An Asterisk (*) at the beginning of an entry indicates that the title is appearing for the first time.

On Air: Methods & Meanings of Radio. Martin Shingler & Cindy Wieringa. LC 98-18248. (An Arnold Publication). (Illus.). 192p. 1998. text 65.00 (*0-340-65232-2*, Pub. by E A); pap. text 19.95 (*0-340-65231-4*, Pub. by E A) OUP.

On Air: Radio in Saskatchewan. Wayne Schmalz. (Illus.). 224p. 1990. pap. 12.95 (*1-55050-009-0*, Pub. by Coteau); text 21.95 (*1-55050-010-4*, Pub. by Coteau) Genl Dist Srvs.

On Air: The Best of Tavis Smiley on the Tom Joyner Morning Show. Tavis Smiley. 170p. 1998. pap. 12.00 (*1-890194-33-6*) Pines One.

On Air Defense. James Crabtree. LC 94-8639. (Military Profession Ser.). 256p. 1994. pap. 21.95 (*0-275-94939-7*, Praeger Pubs) Greenwood.

On Air Defense. James D. Crabtree. LC 94-8639. (Military Profession Ser.). 256p. 1994. 69.50 (*0-275-94792-0*, Praeger Pubs) Greenwood.

On Alberti & the Art of Building. Robert Tavernor. LC 98-15258. (Illus.). 292p. 1998. 60.00 (*0-300-07615-0*) Yale U Pr.

On Alert! Gang Prevention: School In-Service Guidelines. California Department of Education Staff. 96p. 1994. pap. 7.50 (*0-8011-1113-7*) Calif Education.

On Alexander's Track in the Indus: Personal Narrative of the Explorations on the North-West Frontier of India. Marc A. Stein. LC 72-79947. (Illus.). 1972. reprint ed. 30.95 (*0-405-08995-3*) Ayer.

On Alexander's Track to the Indus. Aurel Stein. (Illus.). 198p. 1974. pap. 25.00 (*0-89005-036-8*) Ares.

On Alexander's Track to the Indus. Aurel Stein. 1996. 62.00 (*81-206-0978-6*, Pub. by Asian Educ Servs) S Asia.

On All Fronts. Jay R. Nash. LC 74-81911. (Illus.). 147p. 1974. pap. 15.00 (*0-913204-03-X*) December Pr.

On All Fronts: Australian Stories of World War II. Ed. by J. T. Laird. 250p. (Orig.). 1989. pap. 16.95 (*0-7022-2160-0*, Pub. by Univ Queensland Pr) Intl Spec Bk.

On All Fronts: Czechoslovaks & Slovaks in World War II. Lewis M. White. 360p. 1992. text 66.50 (*0-88033-216-6*, Pub. by East Eur Monographs) Col U Pr.

***On All Fronts: Czechoslovaks in World War II.** Ed. by Lewis M. White. 340p. 2000. text 40.00 (*0-88033-456-8*) Col U Pr.

On All Fronts Pt. II: Czechoslovaks in World War II. Ed. by Lewis M. White. 303p. 1995. 47.50 (*0-88033-319-7*, 422, Pub. by East Eur Monographs) Col U Pr.

***On All Hallows' Eve.** Grace Chetwin. (Illus.). 127p. (J). (ps-3). 1999. pap. 20.00 (*0-9649349-9-X*, Rivet Bks) Feral Press.

On Alternate Days: The Paintings of Nancy Witt. Nancy Witt. LC 95-71875. (Illus.). 88p. (Orig.). 1995. 55.00 (*0-9649214-0-5*); pap. 30.00 (*0-9649214-1-3*) Cross Mill Gallery.

On Alternate Days: The Paintings of Nancy Witt. Nancy Witt. LC 95-71875. (Illus.). 88p. (Orig.). 1995. 60.00 (*0-614-14741-7*); pap. 35.00 (*0-614-14742-5*) Cross Mill Gallery.

On Alternatives to Industrial Flight: The Moral Issues. Judith Lichtenberg. Ed. by Gertrude Ezorsky. 1987. 2.50 (*0-318-33306-6*) IPPP.

On America: Performance Research 31. Ed. by Richard Gough & Claire MacDonald. (Performance Research Ser.). (Illus.). 128p. (C). (gr. 13). 1998. pap. 18.00 (*0-415-18201-8*) Routledge.

On Amethyst Glass: Two Voices, One Song. Rita Bregman & Barbara Michelman. 112p. 2000. pap. 11.95 (*0-9664856-2-9*) Manto Pr.

On an All Time High: A New Wave Collection for Corporate Seminars. Richard E. Petitti. (Self Realization Bks.: Bk. XI). (Illus.). 100p. 1988. write for info. (*0-938582-15-1*) Sensitive Man.

On an Average Day in Japan. Tom Heymann. 228p. 1998. pap. text 8.00 (*0-7881-5584-9*) DIANE Pub.

On Analogy: An Essay Historical & Systematic. Ralf M. Stammberger. (European University Studies: Series 23, Vol. 540). 97p. 1995. pap. 29.95 (*3-631-48909-9*) P Lang Pubng.

On Analogy: An Essay Historical & Systematic. Ralf M. Stammberger. LC 95-37268. (European University Studies, Series XXIII, Theology: Vol. 540). 97p. 1995. 29.95 (*0-8204-2903-1*) P Lang Pubng.

On Analyzing Crime. Edwin H. Sutherland. Ed. by Karl Schuessler. LC 72-94733. xxxvi, 284p. 1974. pap. text 2.95 (*0-226-78056-2*, P545) U Ch Pr.

On Anarchy & Schizoanalysis. Rolando Perez. (Illus.). 160p. (Orig.). (C). 1990. pap. text 8.00 (*0-936756-39-X*) Autonomedia.

On Ancient Central - Asian Tracks. A. Stein. (C). 1984. text 600.00 (*81-85046-13-1*, Pub. by Scientific Pubs) St Mut.

On Ancient Central - Asian Tracks: Brief Narrative of Three Expeditions in Innermost Asia & North Western China. Aurel Stein. (Illus.). xxiv, 342p. 1982. reprint ed. 45.00 (*957-638-128-2*) Oriental Bk Store.

On & About the Postmodern Crisis: Working Papers, No. 6: Writing - Rewriting. Text by R. S. Khare. LC 93-44729. 96p. (Orig.). (C). pap. text 17.00 (*0-8191-9428-X*); lib. bdg. 41.00 (*0-8191-9427-1*) U Pr of Amer.

On & Beyond the Georgetown Divide: Two Senators, the Ralston Inheritance, the Georgetown Gazette 1880-1900. Phyllis Gernes. Ed. by Kenneth Deibert & Jeffrey Gernes. LC 99-231792. (Illus.). ix, 403p. 1999. pap. 16.00 (*0-9670717-0-4*, P L Gernes) Gernes Ent.

***On & Off: Brief Guide to Research.** Harnack & Andrea Lunsford. 2001. pap. text. write for info. (*0-312-25851-8*) St Martin.

On & off Broadway: A Theater/Dining/Lodging Guide to New York City. Sharon Watson. LC 97-93212. (Illus.). 420p. 1997. 17.95 (*1-882310-03-9*) Britain Bks.

On & off the Beaten Path: The Central & Southern Bahamas Guide. Stephen V. Pavlidis. LC 97-36533. (Illus.). 332p. 1997. pap. 34.95 (*0-9639566-9-8*) Seaworthy WI.

On & off the Campus: With a Biographical Introduction by George E. Vincent. Guy Ford. LC 38-28216. 520p. reprint ed. pap. 161.20 (*0-608-14622-6*, 205586700039) Bks Demand.

On & off the Record: Colosi on Negotiation. Thomas R. Colosi. 1993. write for info. (*0-943001-27-7*) Am Arbitration.

On & off the Record: Colosi on Negotiations. AAA Staff. 144p. 1996. pap. text, per. 19.95 (*0-8403-8585-4*) Kendall-Hunt.

***On & On: Poems from Hollywood.** Mark Dunster. 11p. 1999. pap. 5.00 (*0-89642-903-2*) Linden Pubs.

On Angels. Lazar Puhalo. 32p. Date not set. pap. 3.50 (*1-879038-60-9*, 9030) Synaxis Pr.

***On Angels & Devils & Stages Between: Contemporary Lives in Contemporary Dance.** David Wood. (Choreography & Dance Studies: Vol. 19). (Illus.). 253p. 1999. text 44.00 (*90-5755-077-6*, Harwood Acad Pubs); pap. text 30.00 (*90-5755-078-4*, Harwood Acad Pubs) Gordon & Breach.

On Angel's Wings. Mary J. Calhoun. 58p. (Orig.). 1995. pap. write for info. (*1-57502-019-X*, P00406) Morris Pubng.

On Angiotensin - Degrading Aminopeptidases in the Rat Kidney. P. N. Kugler. Tr. by Terry C. Telger. (Advances in Anatomy, Embryology & Cell Biology Ser.: Vol. 76). (Illus.). 86p. 1982. 34.95 (*0-387-11452-1*) Spr-Verlag.

On Another Man's Wound. Ernie O'Malley. 343p. 1979. reprint ed. pap. 17.95 (*0-947962-31-X*, Pub. by Anvil Books Ltd) Irish Bks Media.

On Another Man's Wound: A Personal History of Ireland's War of Independence. Ernie O'Malley. 336p. 1999. reprint ed. pap. 14.95 (*1-57098-277-5*) Roberts Rinehart.

***On Any Given Day.** Joe Martin & Ross Yockey. 160p. 2000. 21.95 (*0-89587-233-1*) Blair.

On Anything. Hilaire Belloc. LC 79-76893. (Essay Index Reprint Ser.). 1977. 20.95 (*0-8369-0003-0*) Mnemosyne Pub.

On Appeal: Courts, Lawyering & Judging. Frank Coffin. (C). 1995. pap. text 12.50 (*0-393-96731-X*, Norton Paperbks) Norton.

***On Aquinas.** Inglis. 2000. pap. 8.25 (*0-534-58360-1*) Wadsworth Pub.

On Architecture, 2 vols., 1. Pollio Vitruvius. (Loeb Classical Library: No. 251, 280). 358p. 1931. 19.95 (*0-674-99277-6*) HUP.

On Architecture, 2 vols., 2. Pollio Vitruvius. (Loeb Classical Library: No. 251, 280). 430p. 1934. 19.95 (*0-674-99309-8*) HUP.

On Architecture: A Journal. (Illus.). 128p. 1994. 17.95 (*0-87654-085-X*) Pomegranate Calif.

***On Arendt.** Johnson. 2000. pap. 8.25 (*0-534-58361-X*) Wadsworth Pub.

On Aristotle. Peterman. (Philosophy Ser.). 1999. pap. text 13.95 (*0-534-57607-9*) Brooks-Cole.

On Aristotle on the Intellect (De Anima 3, 408) John Philoponus. Tr. by William Charlton from GRE. LC 91-8806. (Ancient Commentators on Aristotle Ser.). 180p. 1991. text 55.00 (*0-8014-2681-2*) Cornell U Pr.

On Aristotle's "Categories" Ammonius. Tr. by S. Marc Cohen & Gareth B. Matthews. LC 91-55258. (Ancient Commentators on Aristotle Ser.). 176p. 1992. text 52.50 (*0-8014-2688-X*) Cornell U Pr.

On Aristotle's Categories. Dexippus. Tr. by John Dillon. (Ancient Commentators on Aristotle Ser.). 1988. text 47.50 (*0-8014-2266-3*) Cornell U Pr.

On Aristotle's Categories. Porphyry. Tr. by Steven K. Strange. LC 92-14908. (Ancient Commentators on Aristotle Ser.). 1992. text 49.95 (*0-8014-2816-5*) Cornell U Pr.

***On Aristotle's "Categories 9-15"** Simplicius & Richard Gaskin. LC 00-37680. 2000. write for info. (*0-8014-3691-5*) Cornell U Pr.

On Aristotle's Metaphysics, No. 1. Alexander of Aphrodisias. Tr. by W. E. Dooley. LC 88-47752. (Ancient Commentators on Aristotle Ser.). 192p. 1988. text 47.50 (*0-8014-2235-3*) Cornell U Pr.

On Aristotle's "Metaphysics 5" Alexander of Aphrodisias. Tr. by William E. Dooley. (Ancient Commentators on Aristotle Ser.). 232p. 1994. text 47.50 (*0-8014-2969-2*) Cornell U Pr.

On Aristotle's "Metaphysics 4" Alexander of Aphrodisias. Tr. by Arthur Madigan. (Ancient Commentators on Aristotle Ser.). 208p. 1994. text 47.50 (*0-8014-2977-3*) Cornell U Pr.

On Aristotle's Metaphysics 2&3. Alexander of Aphrodisias. Tr. by William E. Dooley & Arthur Madigan. LC 91-41606. (Ancient Commentators on Aristotle Ser.). 224p. 1992. text 52.50 (*0-8014-2740-1*) Cornell U Pr.

On Aristotle's "Meteorology 4" Alexander of Aphrodisias. Tr. by Eric Lewis. LC 95-37120. (Ancient Commentators on Aristotle Ser.). 1995. text 47.50 (*0-8014-3225-1*) Cornell U Pr.

On Aristotle's "On Interpretation 1-8" Hermiae Ammonius. Tr. by David Blank. (Ancient Commentators on Aristotle Ser.). 1995. text 47.50 (*0-8014-3223-5*) Cornell U Pr.

On Aristotle's "On Interpretation 9" Ammonius. Tr. by David Blank from GEC. LC 98-16299. (Ancient Commentators on Aristotle Ser.). 1996. text 49.95 (*0-8014-3335-5*) Cornell U Pr.

On Aristotle's "On Physics 5" Simplicius. Tr. by J. O. Urmson. LC 97-6546. (Ancient Commentators on Aristotle Ser.). 1996. 45.00 (*0-8014-3407-6*) Cornell U Pr.

***On Aristotle's "On Sense Perception"** Alexander. LC 00-31558. 2000. write for info. (*0-8014-3690-7*) Cornell U Pr.

On Aristotle's "On the Soul 1 & 2.1-4" Simplicius. Tr. by Peter Lautner & J. O. Urmson. (Ancient Commentators on Aristotle Ser.). 1995. text 45.00 (*0-8014-3160-3*) Cornell U Pr.

On Aristotle's "On the Soul 1-2.5" Themistius. Tr. by Robert B. Todd. LC 96-448. (Ancient Commentators on Aristotle Ser.). 1996. text 55.00 (*0-8014-3281-2*) Cornell U Pr.

***On Aristotle's "On the Soul 3.9-13"** John Philoponus et al. LC 99-88450. (Ancient Commentators on Aristotle Ser.). 2000. write for info. (*0-8014-3795-4*) Cornell U Pr.

On Aristotle's "On the Soul 2.5-2.12" with On Theophrastus' "On Sensation" Simplicius & Priscian. Tr. by J. O. Umson et al. LC 97-29518. (Ancient Commentators on Aristotle Ser.). 1996. text 49.95 (*0-8014-3282-0*) Cornell U Pr.

On Aristotle's "Physics 5-8", with On Aristotle on the Void. Philoponus & Simplicius. Tr. by Paul Lettinck & J. O. Urmson. LC 93-31609. (Ancient Commentators on Aristotle Ser.). 288p. 1994. text 49.95 (*0-8014-3005-4*) Cornell U Pr.

On Aristotle's "Physics 4, 1-5 & 10-14" Simplicius. Tr. by J. O. Urmson. (Ancient Commentators on Aristotle Ser.). 1993. 45.00 (*0-8014-2817-3*) Cornell U Pr.

On Aristotle's "Physics 7" Simplicius. Tr. by Charles Hagen. LC 93-26377. (Ancient Commentators on Aristotle Ser.). 216p. 1994. 42.50 (*0-8014-2992-7*) Cornell U Pr.

On Aristotle's "Physics 6" Simplicius. Tr. by David Konstan. LC 88-47747. (Ancient Commentators on Aristotle Ser.). (ENG & GRE.). 206p. 1988. 45.00 (*0-8014-2238-8*) Cornell U Pr.

On Aristotle's "Physics 3" John Philoponus. Tr. by M. J. Edwards. (Ancient Commentators on Aristotle Ser.). 1994. text 47.50 (*0-8014-3089-5*) Cornell U Pr.

On Aristotle's "Physics 2" John Philoponus. Tr. by A. R. Lacey. (Ancient Commentators on Aristotle Ser.). 1993. text 45.00 (*0-8014-2815-7*) Cornell U Pr.

On Aristotle's "Physics 2" Simplicius. Tr. by D. B. Fleet. LC 96-50076. (Ancient Commentators on Aristotle Ser.). 1997. 45.00 (*0-8014-3283-9*) Cornell U Pr.

On Aristotle's "Prior Analytics", Vol. 1. Alexander of Aphrodisias. Ed. by Richard Sorabji. Tr. by Ian Mueller & Josiah Gould. LC 98-42203. (Ancient Commentators on Aristotle Ser.). 224p. 1998. 49.95 (*0-8014-3618-4*) Cornell U Pr.

On Aristotle's "Prior Analytics", Vol. 2. Alexander of Aphrodisias. Ed. by Richard Sorabji. Tr. by Ian Mueller & Josiah Gould. (Ancient Commentators on Aristotle Ser.). 256p. 1998. 49.95 (*0-8014-3617-6*) Cornell U Pr.

On Aristotle's "Prior Analytics 1. 1-7" Alexander of Aphrodisias. Tr. by Jonathan Barnes et al from GRE. LC 91-55257. (Ancient Commentators on Aristotle Ser.). 272p. 1992. 49.95 (*0-8014-2689-8*) Cornell U Pr.

On Aristotle's "Topics 1" Alexander of Aphrodisias. Ed. by Richard Sorabji. Tr. by Johannes M. Van Ophuijsen. (Ancient Commentators on Aristotle Ser.). 240p. 1998. 49.95 (*0-8014-3616-8*) Cornell U Pr.

***On Aristotles's "Physics 8.6-10"** Aristotle. (Ancient Commentators on Aristotle Ser.). 2000. 55.00 (*0-8014-3787-3*) Cornell U Pr.

On Art. Glenn Thompson. Ed. by Rudolph Baranik. 1988. 19.95 (*0-86316-121-9*); pap. 9.95 (*0-86316-120-0*) Writers & Readers.

On Art & Literature: Critical Writings. Jose Marti. Ed. by Philip S. Foner. Tr. by Elinor Randall. LC 81-81697. 416p. 1982. 23.00 (*0-85345-589-9*, Pub. by Monthly Rev); pap. 15.00 (*0-85345-590-2*, Pub. by Monthly Rev) NYU Pr.

On Art & the Mind. Richard Wollheim. Date not set. 32.00 (*0-674-63405-5*) HUP.

On Art & the Mind. Richard Wollheim. 352p. 1983. pap. 15.95 (*0-674-63406-3*) HUP.

On Art & Therapy: An Exploration. Martina Thomson. LC 98-112203. 1997. 45.00 (*1-85343-366-7*, Pub. by Free Assoc Bks); pap. 18.50 (*1-85343-368-3*, Pub. by Free Assoc Bks) NYU Pr.

On Art, Religion, & the History of Philosophy: Introductory Lectures. Georg Wilhelm Friedrich Hegel. Ed. by J. Glenn Gray. LC 97-26470. 342p. (C). 1997. pap. text 12.95 (*0-87220-370-0*); lib. bdg. 34.95 (*0-87220-371-9*) Hackett Pub.

On Artillery. Bruce I. Gudmundsson. LC 93-17105. 192p. 1993. 59.95 (*0-275-94047-0*, Praeger Pubs); pap. 22.95 (*0-275-94673-8*, Praeger Pubs) Greenwood.

On Artin's Conjecture for Odd 2-Dimensional Representations. Jacques Basmaji et al. Ed. by Gerhard Frey. LC 94-23241. (Lecture Notes in Mathematics Ser.: Vol. 1585). 1994. text. write for info. (*0-387-58387-4*) Spr-Verlag.

On Artin's Conjecture for Odd 2-Dimensional Representations. Jacques Basmaji et al. Ed. by Gerhard Frey. LC 94-23241. (Lecture Notes in Mathematics Ser.: Vol. 1585). 1994. 35.95 (*3-540-58387-4*) Spr-Verlag.

On Ascetical Life. St. Isaac of Nineveh. LC 89-38492. (Popular Patristics Ser.). 116p. (Orig.). 1991. pap. 7.95 (*0-88141-077-2*) St Vladimirs.

On Asking God Why: And Other Reflections on Trusting God in a Twisted World. Elisabeth Elliot. 168p. (gr. 11). 1990. pap. 8.99 (*0-8007-5303-8*) Revell.

On Assignment. Marilyn Kok. 266p. 1998. pap. 9.99 (*1-57673-279-7*, Palisades OR) Multnomah Pubs.

On Assignment, Vol. 1. Marilyn R. Kok. LC 99-21867. 1999. 23.95 (*0-7862-1966-1*) Thorndike Pr.

On Assignment: Photographs by Jay Maisel. Ed. by Constance Sullivan. (Photographers at Work Ser.). (Illus.). 1990. pap. 16.95 (*1-56098-002-8*) Smithsonian.

On Assignment: The Stories Behind the Stories: Inspiring Experiences of an LDS Broadcast Journalist. Art Rascon. LC 98-28168. 1998. 15.95 (*1-57734-294-1*, 01113526) Covenant Comms.

On Assuming a College or University Presidency: Lessons & Advice from the Field. Estela M. Bensimon et al. 80p. 1989. pap. 10.00 (*1-56377-001-6*, NO8901) Am Assn Higher Ed.

***On Asthma.** Moses Maimonides. Ed. by Gerrit Bos & Machael McVaugh. (Graeco-Arabic Sciences Ser.). (ARA & ENG.). 350p. 2000. 29.95 (*0-8425-2475-4*) Brigham.

On Astrocytes & Glutamate Neurotransmission: New Waves in Brain Information Processing. Elisabeth Hansson & Torsten Olsson. LC 97-13739. (Neuroscience Intelligence Unit Ser.). 209p. 1997. text 99.00 (*1-57059-446-5*) Landes Bioscience.

On Atmospheric Pollution: A Group of Contributions. J. H. Carter et al. (Meteorological Monograph: Vol. 1, No. 4). (Illus.). 55p. (Orig.). 1951. pap. 17.00 (*0-933876-00-9*) Am Meteorological.

***On Augustine.** Kaye & Thomson. 2000. pap. 8.25 (*0-534-58362-8*) Wadsworth Pub.

On Autobiography. Philippe Lejeune. Ed. by Paul J. Eakin. Tr. by Katherine Leary. (Theory & History of Literature Ser.: Vol. 52). 1989. pap. 19.95 (*0-8166-1632-9*) U of Minn Pr.

On Axiom A Diffeomorphisms. R. Bowen. LC 78-6745. (CBMS Regional Conference Series in Mathematics: Vol. 35). 45p. 1978. reprint ed. pap. 19.00 (*0-8218-1685-3*, CBMS/35C) Am Math.

On Axiomatic Approaches to Vertex Operator Algebras & Modules. Igor B. Frenkel et al. LC 93-17169. (Memoirs of the American Mathematical Society Ser.: No. 494). 64p. 1993. pap. 26.00 (*0-8218-2555-0*, MEMO/104/494) Am Math.

***On Ayer.** Martin. 2000. pap. 8.25 (*0-534-58370-9*) Wadsworth Pub.

On Baby Patrol: Bundles of Joy/Lullabies & Love. Sharon De Vita. (Romance Ser.: No. 1276). 1998. per. 3.50 (*0-373-19276-2*, 1-19276-4) Silhouette.

On Baile's Strand see Eleven Plays of William Butler Yeats

On Baking. Sarah R. Labensky & Eddy Van Damme. (C). 2002. 48.00 (*0-13-533647-3*, Macmillan Coll) P-H.

On Balanchine. Suki Schorer. LC 98-16012. 448p. 1999. 40.00 (*0-679-45060-2*) McKay.

On Ballycastle Beach. Medbh McGuckian. LC 87-40624. 59p. 1988. pap. 6.95 (*0-916390-30-6*) Wake Forest.

On Baseball. Stephen Jay Gould. 2001. 24.00 (*0-609-60140-7*) Harmony Bks.

On Basilisk Station. David Weber. (Honor Harrington Ser.: No. 1). 416p. 1993. per. 5.99 (*0-671-72163-1*) Baen Bks.

On Basilisk Station. limited ed. David Weber. 1998. mass mkt. 1.99 (*0-671-57772-7*) Baen Bks.

On Basilisk Station: Collectors Edition. deluxe ed. David Weber. LC 98-32222. 336p. 1999. 18.00 (*0-671-57793-X*) Baen Bks.

On Bataille: Critical Essays. Ed. by Leslie A. Boldt-Irons. LC 94-22405. (SUNY Series, Intersections). 338p. (C). 1995. text 59.50 (*0-7914-2455-3*); pap. text 21.95 (*0-7914-2456-1*) State U NY Pr.

On Bataille No. 78: Yale French Studies. Allan Stoekl. (C). 1990. pap. 18.00 (*0-300-04843-2*) Yale U Pr.

On Bear Mountain: A Novel. Deborah Smith. 352p. 2001. 24.95 (*0-316-80077-5*) Little.

***On Beauty & Being Just.** Elaine Scarry. LC 99-35075. 1999. 15.95 (*0-691-04875-4*, Pub. by Princeton U Pr) Cal Prin Full Svc.

On Becoming a Biologist. John Janovy, Jr. LC 95-25798. xiv, 162p. 1996. pap. 10.00 (*0-8032-7586-2*, Bison Books) U of Nebr Pr.

On Becoming a Cosmetology Teacher. James K. Nighswander. 1992. pap. 35.75 (*1-56253-086-0*) Thomson Learn.

On Becoming a Counselor: A Basic Guide for Non-Professional Counselors. enl. ed. Eugene Kennedy & Sara C. Charles. 337p. 1989. pap. 19.95 (*0-8245-1333-9*) Crossroad NY.

On Becoming a God. Areeb Malik Shabazz. (Illus.). 340p. 1999. reprint ed. pap. 18.00 (*1-56411-213-6*, Kitabu Pub) Untd Bros & Sis.

On Becoming a Grandparent: A Diary of Family Discovery. Alma H. Bond. LC 94-9051. 176p. 1994. 19.95 (*1-882593-08-1*) Bridge Wrks.

On Becoming a Language Educator: Personal Essays on Professional Development. Ed. by Christine P. Casanave & Sandra R. Schecter. LC 96-39504. 232p. 1997. 55.00 (*0-8058-2263-1*); pap. 24.95 (*0-8058-2264-X*) L Erlbaum Assocs.

On Becoming a Lawyer: The Insider'S Guide to a Legal Career in Canada. Cochrane. 288p. 2000. pap. write for info. (*0-471-64196-0*) Wiley.

On Becoming a Leader. Warren G. Bennis. 1990. pap. 12.95 (*0-201-55087-3*) Addison-Wesley.

On Becoming a Leader. 2nd ed. Bennis Warren. LC 97-121102. 226p. 1994. pap. 16.00 (*0-201-40929-1*) Addison-Wesley.

On Becoming a Musical Mystical Bear: Spirituality American Style. Matthew Fox. LC 75-34842. 156p. 1976. pap. 9.95 (*0-8091-1913-7*) Paulist Pr.

On Becoming a Novelist. John Gardner. 172p. 1999. pap. 12.00 (*0-393-32003-0*, Norton Paperbks) Norton.

***On Becoming a Novelist.** John Gardner. 2000. 24.50 (*0-8446-7120-7*) Peter Smith.

On Becoming a Person: A Therapist's View of Psychotherapy. Carl Ransom Rogers. 416p. 1995. pap. 16.00 (*0-395-75531-X*) HM.

On Becoming a Psychotherapist. Ed. by Wendy Dryden & Laurence Spurling. 272p. 1989. 52.50 (*0-415-01933-8*, A3639) Routledge.

On Becoming a Psychotherapist. Ed. by Wendy Dryden & Laurence Spurling. 272p. (C). 1989. pap. 25.99 (*0-415-03611-9*, A3643) Routledge.

An Asterisk (*) at the beginning of an entry indicates that the title is appearing for the first time.

On Becoming a School Leader: A Person-Centered Challenge. Arthur W. Combs et al. LC 98-58054. 231p. 1999. pap. 22.95 (0-87120-336-7, 199024) ASCD.

On Becoming a Servant-Leader: The Private Writings of Robert K. Greenleaf. Robert K. Greenleaf. Ed. by Don T. Frick & Larry C. Spears. (Nonprofit Sector Ser.). 380p. 1996. 29.95 (0-7879-0230-6) Jossey-Bass.

On Becoming a Social Scientist. Shulamit Reinharz. 466p. (C). 1991. pap. 24.95 (0-87855-968-X) Transaction Pubs.

On Becoming a Social Scientist. Shulamit Reinharz. LC 79-83577. (Jossey-Bass Social & Behavioral Science Ser.). 442p. reprint ed. pap. 137.10 (0-8357-6886-4, 203793800009) Bks Demand.

On Becoming a Special Parent: A Mini-Support Group in a Book. Marcia Routburg. (Illus.). 130p. (Orig.). 1987. pap. 9.00 (0-9619347-0-0) Parent Prof Pubns.

On Becoming a Teacher. 2nd ed. Frank Paoni. 272p. (C). 1997. per. 40.62 (0-7872-4196-2) Kendall-Hunt.

On Becoming a Teacher: Some Important Things You'll Need to Know & Use. 2nd ed. Frank Paoni. 238p. (C). per. 50.95 (0-7872-6434-2) Kendall-Hunt.

On Becoming a 21st Century Mystic: Pathways to Intuitive Living. Alan Seale. (Illus.). 336p. 1997. pap. 19.95 (0-9657736-1-2) Skytop Pub.

On Becoming an Angel. Jeff Conant. (Illus.). 20p. 1993. pap. 125.00 (0-945303-14-9) Evanescent Pr.

On Becoming an Artist see How to Start & Succeed as an Artist

On Becoming an Educated Person: A Practical Handbook for Developing Your Basic Thinking, Problem Solving & Communicating Skills. W. A. Mambert. LC 80-81014. 1982. pap. text 18.95 (0-941822-00-1) C E R I Pr.

On Becoming an Innovative University Teacher: Reflection in Action. John Cowan. LC 98-9787. 173p. 1998. 85.00 (0-335-19994-1); pap. 29.95 (0-335-19993-3) OpUniv Pr.

On Becoming Babywise: More Than a Survival Guide. Gary Ezzo & Robert Buckham. 160p. (Orig.). 1993. pap. text 6.95 (1-883035-99-6) Grow Families.

On Becoming Babywise Vol. 1: Learn How over 500,000 Babies Were Trained to Sleep Through the Night the Natural Way. rev. ed. Gary Ezzo. 198p. 1998. pap. 11.99 (1-57673-458-7) Multnomah Pubs.

On Becoming Babywise II Vol. 11: Parenting Your Pretoddler Five to Fifteen Months. Gary Ezzo & Robert Buckman. 134p. 1995. pap. 9.99 (0-88070-807-7, Multnomah Bks) Multnomah Pubs.

On Becoming Childwise: Parenting Your Child from Three to Seven Years. Gary Ezzo & Robert Buckham. LC 99-51371. 300p. 1999. pap. 10.99 (1-57673-421-8) Multnomah Pubs.

On Becoming Christian. Henri Bourgeois. (C). 1988. 45.00 (0-85439-230-0, Pub. by St Paul Pubns) St Mut.

On Becoming Cuban: Identity, Nationality & Culture. Louis A. Perez, Jr. LC 98-42664. (Illus.). 608p. 1999. 39.95 (0-8078-2487-9) U of NC Pr.

On Becoming Filipino: Selected Writings of Carlos Bulosan. E. San Juan, Jr. (Asian American History & Culture Ser.). 240p. (Orig.). (C). 1995. text 69.95 (1-56639-309-4); pap. text 22.95 (1-56639-310-8) Temple U Pr.

On Becoming Homeless: The Shelterization Process for Homeless Families. Ione Y. DeOllos. LC 97-13285. 272p. (C). 1997. 56.00 (0-7618-0839-6); pap. 34.50 (0-7618-0838-8) U Pr of Amer.

On Becoming Human: A Journey of 5,000,000 Years. Arthur Niehoff. LC 94-92303. 420p. (Orig.). 1996. pap. 14.95 (0-9643072-3-5, GN281) Hominid Pr.

On Becoming Powerful. John Volkmar. LC 88-20582. 193p. (Orig.). 1988. pap. 8.95 (0-87728-676-0) Weiser.

***On Becoming Preteen Wise: Parenting Your Child from Eight to Twelve Years.** Gary Ezzo & Anne Marie Ezzo. LC 00-8191. 200p. 2000. pap. 10.99 (1-57673-668-7, Pub. by Multnomah Pubs) GL Services.

On Becoming Responsible. Michael S. Pritchard. LC 90-41613. x, 278p. 1991. 29.95 (0-7006-0444-8) U Pr of KS.

***On Becoming Teenwise.** Gary Ezzo. (Illus.). (YA). 2000. pap. 10.99 (1-57673-711-X) Multnomah Pubs.

On Becoming the Person You Want to Be Henry E. Roberts. LC 97-73790. 152 p. 1997. write for info. (1-888676-04-3) Ardara Hse.

On Beginning an Analysis. Ed. by Theodore J. Jacobs & Arnold Rothstein. 309p. 1998. pap. 25.95 (0-8236-8168-8) Intl Univs Pr.

On Behalf of God: A Christian Ethic for Biology. Bruce R. Reichenbach & V. Elving Anderson. (Studies in a Christian World View). 368p. (Orig.). 1995. pap. 23.00 (0-8028-0727-5) Eerdmans.

On Behalf of the Creatures. John T. Ferrier. 132p. 1926. pap. text 6.75 (0-900235-51-9) Order Of The Cross.

On Behalf of the Insane Poor: Selected Reports, 1843-1852. Dorothea L. Dix. LC 78-137163. (Poverty U. S. A. Historical Record Ser.). 1975. reprint ed. 30.95 (0-405-03101-7) Ayer.

On Behalf of the Wolf & the First Peoples. Joseph Marshall, 3rd. LC 95-41844. (Illus.). 256p. 1995. pap. 13.95 (1-878610-45-7) Red Crane Bks.

On Behavior: Essays & Research. Karen Pryor. (Illus.). 280p. (Orig.). 1995. pap. 14.95 (0-9624017-1-4) Sunshine MA.

On Being a Bishop: Papers on Episcopacy from the Moscow Consultation 1992. Ed. by J. Robert Wright. LC 98-203036. 230p. 1993. pap. 16.95 (0-89869-235-0) Church Pub Inc.

On Being a Christian. Henry P. Hamann. (Orig.). 1996. pap. 8.99 (0-8100-0578-6, 12N1763) Northwest Pub.

On Being a Christian. Hans Kung. LC 83-16431. 720p. 1984. reprint ed. pap. 24.95 (0-385-19286-X, Image Bks) Doubleday.

On Being a Client: Understanding the Process of Counselling & Psychotherapy. David Howe. (Illus.). 224p. (C). 1993. text 49.95 (0-8039-8888-5); pap. text 18.95 (0-8039-8889-3) Sage.

On Being a Clinical Supervisor: Psychodynamic Psychotherapy Teaching & Learning. Rosemary M. Balsam. 250p. 2000. 40.00 (0-8236-5642-X, 05642) Intl Univs Pr.

On Being a Conceptual Animal. Arthur H. Niehoff. LC 97-76969. xv, 313p. 1998. pap. 13.95 (0-9643072-4-3) Hominid Pr.

On Being a Department Head, a Personal View. John B. Conway. LC 96-22067. 107p. 1996. pap. 24.00 (0-8218-0615-7, AHEAD) Am Math.

On Being a Doctor. Ed. & Intro. by Michael A. LaCombe. 192p. 1995. reprint ed. pap. 18.00 (0-943126-65-7) Amer Coll Phys.

***On Being a Doctor II: Voices of Physicians & Patients.** Michael A. LaCombe. LC 99-40565. 363p. 1999. 26.00 (0-943126-82-7) Amer Coll Phys.

On Being a Jewish Christian. Anthea Parsons. 1998. 10.99 (0-340-71377-1, Pub. by Hodder & Stought Ltd) Trafalgar.

On Being a Jewish Feminist: A Reader. Ed. & Intro. by Susannah Heschel. 352p. 1995. pap. 16.00 (0-8052-1036-9) Schocken.

On Being a Leader. Ed. by Roger Neugebauer. (Best of Exchange Ser.). (Illus.). 48p. (Orig.). (C). 1990. pap. 10.00 (0-942702-06-9) Child Care.

On Being a Machine: Formal Aspects of Artificial Intelligence, Vol. 1. Ajit Narayanan. 192p. 1988. text 41.95 (0-470-21235-7) P-H.

On Being a Missionary. Thomas Hale. LC 94-31473. 422p. 1997. pap. 16.95 (0-87808-255-7, WCL255-7) William Carey Lib.

On Being a Muslim: Finding a Religious Path in the World Today. Farid Esack. LC 99-488318. 224p. 1997. pap. 13.95 (1-85168-146-9, Pub. by Onewrld Pubns) Penguin Putnam.

On Being a Parent: The Crash Course in Character Development. Beppie Harrison. 1995. 12.95 (0-88494-970-2) Bookcraft Inc.

On Being a Photographer: A Practical Guide. David Hurn & Bill Jay. LC 97-75635. 96p. 1997. pap. 12.95 (1-888803-06-1) Lenswrk.

On Being a Psychotherapist. Carl Goldberg. LC 90-14498. 424p. 1991. reprint ed. 55.00 (0-87668-885-7) Aronson.

On Being a Psychotherapist. Carl Goldberg. LC 90-14498. 424p. 1994. reprint ed. pap. 50.00 (1-56821-163-5) Aronson.

On Being a Scientist: Responsible Conduct in Research. 2nd rev. ed. National Academy of Sciences Staff et al. 40p. (C). 1995. pap. text 5.00 (0-309-05196-7) Natl Acad Pr.

On Being a Servant of God. Warren W. Wiersbe. LC 98-33932. 168p. 1999. reprint ed. pap. 9.99 (0-8010-9086-5) Baker Bks.

***On Being a Superpower: Scenarios for Security in the New Century & Not Knowing What to Do About It.** Seymour J. Deitchman. LC 99-39624. 1999. 32.00 (0-8133-6775-1, Pub. by Westview) HarpC.

On Being a Teacher. Nathalie J. Gehrke. LC 87-26141. 128p. 1987. pap. 15.00 (0-912099-03-8, 103) Kappa Delta Pi.

On Being a Teacher. Jonathan Kozol. 192p. 1994. pap. 14.95 (1-85168-065-9, Pub. by Onewrld Pubns) Penguin Putnam.

On Being a Teacher. Ed. by Amrik Singh. 276p. 1991. text 30.00 (81-220-0203-X, Pub. by Konark Pubs Pvt Ltd) Advent Bks Div.

On Being a Teacher: The Human Dimension. Stanley J. Zehm & Jeffrey A. Kottler. LC 92-35968. 152p. 1993. pap. 21.95 (0-8039-6041-7) Corwin Pr.

***On Being a Teacher: The Human Dimension.** 2nd ed. Stanley J. Zehm & Jeffrey A. Kottler. LC 00-8489. 2000. pap. write for info. (0-7619-7696-5) Corwin Pr.

***On Being a Theologian.** John MacQuarrie. 1998. pap. 23.00 (0-334-02771-3) TPI PA.

On Being a Theologian of the Cross: Reflections on Luther's Heidelberg Disputation, 1518. Gerhard O. Forde. LC 97-8591. (Theology Ser.). 1997. pap. text 20.00 (0-8028-4345-X) Eerdmans.

On Being a Therapist. fac. ed. Jeffrey A. Kottler. LC 86-10267. (Jossey-Bass Social & Behavioral Science Ser.). 187p. 1986. reprint ed. pap. 58.00 (0-7837-8049-4, 204780200008) Bks Demand.

On Being a Therapist. 2nd rev. ed. Jeffrey A. Kottler. LC 93-15864. (Social & Behavioral Science Ser.). 320p. 1993. mass mkt. 20.00 (1-55542-555-0) Jossey-Bass.

On Being a Woman: Psychopoetic Notes from a Sister Traveler. Peola B. Dews. (Illus.). 115p. (Orig.). 1993. pap. 13.95 (0-9639674-0-1) DEWS HRD Assocs.

On Being & Essence see Selected Writings of St. Thomas Aquinas

On Being & Saying: Essays for Richard Cartwright. Ed. by Judith J. Thomson. 1987. 37.50 (0-262-20063-5) MIT Pr.

On Being & What There Is: Classical Vaisesika & the History of Indian Ontology. Wilhelm Halbfass. LC 91-43295. 303p. (C). 1992. pap. text 21.95 (0-7914-1178-8) State U NY Pr.

On Being Black, Vol. 2. 1991. 8.00 (0-940248-40-9) Guild Pr.

On Being Black - An In-Group Analysis: Essays in Honor of W. E. B. Du Bois. Ed. by David Pilgrim. LC 85-52309. 187p. 1986. 30.00 (0-932269-75-3) Wyndham Hall.

On Being Black in San Diego - Anytown U. S. A. Carrol W. Waymon. 110p. 1997. pap. 14.95 (0-9661488-0-0) WW Pubns.

On Being Blue: A Philosophical Inquiry. William H. Gass. LC 75-43103. 96p. 1978. pap. 11.95 (0-87923-237-4) Godine.

***On Being Brown: What It Means to Be a Cleveland Browns Fan.** Scott Huler. (Illus.). 184p. 1999. 18.95 (1-886228-36-1) Gray & Co Pubs.

***On Being Brown: What It Means to Be a Cleveland Browns Fan.** Scott Huler. LC 99-6760. 184p. 1999. pap. 10.95 (1-886228-31-0) Gray & Co Pubs.

On Being Buddha: The Classical Doctrine of Buddhahood. Paul J. Griffiths. LC 93-45500. (SUNY Series, Toward a Comparative Philosophy of Religions). 261p. (C). 1994. text 59.50 (0-7914-2127-9); pap. text 19.95 (0-7914-2128-7) State U NY Pr.

On Being Butterfly Friendly: The Step Beyond Butterfly Gardening. 3rd ed. David W. Bouton. (Illus.). 62p. 1999. pap. 18.95 (1-881494-14-4) Continuum Pubs.

On Being Catholic. Thomas Howard. LC 96-75716. 1997. pap. text 12.95 (0-89870-608-4) Ignatius Pr.

On Being Catholic: Reflections Addressed to Youth. Ed. by John Cardinal O'Connor. LC 94-30653. 176p. (Orig.). (J). 1994. pap. 8.95 (0-8189-0718-5) Alba.

On Being Christian. Ariel Books Staff. (Illus.). 374p. 1995. pap. 4.95 (0-8362-0720-3, Arie Bks) Andrews & McMeel.

On Being Different. C. Kottak. 1998. teacher ed. 20.93 (0-07-035974-1) McGraw.

On Being Different: Diversity & Multiculturalism in the North American Mainstream. Conrad P. Kottak & Kathryn A. Kozaitis. LC 98-8621. 360p. 1998. 24.69 (0-07-035973-3) McGraw.

On Being Evil. Sachinja Hiro. 190p. 1987. pap. 9.95 (0-912624-08-6) Nembutsu Pr.

***On Being Expendable.** Benjamin Braginsky. 74p. 1998. pap. 8.00 (0-8059-4258-0) Dorrance.

On Being Family: A Social Theology of the Family. Ray S. Anderson & Dennis B. Guensey. 168p. 1992. reprint ed. pap. 20.00 (0-9602638-9-6) Fuller Seminary.

On Being Female, Black & Free: Essays by Margaret Walker, 1932-1992. Margaret Walker. Ed. by Maryemma Graham. LC 96-51235. 272p. 1997. pap. 16.00 (0-87049-981-5) U of Tenn Pr.

On Being Foreign: Culture Shock in Short Fiction: An International Anthology. Ed. by Tom J. Lewis & Robert E. Jungman. LC 86-81109. 308p. (Orig.). (C). 1986. pap. text 17.95 (0-933662-62-9) Intercult Pr.

On Being Free. Frithjof Bergmann. LC 77-89760. 1988. pap. text 15.00 (0-268-01493-0) U of Notre Dame Pr.

On Being Free. Adin Steinsaltz. LC 94-31951. 264p. 1995. 25.00 (1-56821-327-1) Aronson.

On Being Free. Adin Steinsaltz. LC 94-31951. 264p. 1997. reprint ed. pap. 30.00 (0-7657-9985-5) Aronson.

On Being Freer. rev. ed. Caleb Gattegno. 1988. pap. 12.95 (0-87825-070-0) Ed Solutions.

On Being Gay. Brian Mcnaught. (Stonewall Inn Editions Ser.). 1989. pap. 10.95 (0-312-02959-4) St Martin.

On Being Happy. Patrick Yee. (Illus.). 48p. 1995. 6.95 (0-8118-0496-8) Chronicle Bks.

On Being Hawaiian. John D. Holt. 1973. reprint ed. pap. 3.50 (0-914916-23-8) Ku Paa.

On Being Homeless. David Rothman et al. Ed. by Rick Beard. (Illus.). 176p. (Orig.). 1987. 29.95 (0-317-67769-1) Mus City NY.

On Being Homeless: Historical Perspectives. Ed. by Rick Beard. (Illus.). 176p. (C). 1989. pap. 19.00 (0-8135-1508-4); text 35.00 (0-8135-1507-6) Rutgers U Pr.

On Being Human. Erich Fromm. 180p. 1997. pap. 15.95 (0-8264-1005-7) Continuum.

On Being Human. Paul E. More. LC 68-57334. (Essay Index Reprint Ser.). 1977. 19.95 (0-8369-0717-5) Ayer.

On Being Human. Woodrow Wilson. LC 96-24916. 32p. 1996. reprint ed. 9.95 (1-55709-440-3) Applewood.

On Being Human: Essays in Theological Anthropology. Ray S. Anderson. 234p. (Orig.). (C). 1991. reprint ed. pap. 20.00 (0-9602638-4-5) Fuller Seminary.

On Being Human: Interpretations of Humanism from the Renaissance to the Present. Salvatore Puledda. Tr. by Andrew Hurley from SPA. LC 96-3253. (New Humanism Ser.). Orig. Title: Interpretaciones del Humanismo. 224p. (Orig.). 1997. pap. 11.95 (1-878977-18-0, 18-0) Latitude Pr.

On Being Human: The Folklore of Mormon Missionaries. William A. Wilson. 28p. 1981. pap. text 4.95 (0-87421-114-X) Utah St U Pr.

On Being Human: The Life of Truth & Its Realization. Fritz Medicus. LC 72-178170. 324p. 1973. 9.75 (0-8044-5673-9) Green.

On Being Human & Pleasure & Pain: Two Humanistic Works. G. Marian Kinget. LC 99-15087. 344p. 1999. pap. 27.50 (0-7618-1410-8) U Pr of Amer.

On Being in Charge: A Guide to Management in Primary Health Care. 2nd ed. R. McMahon et al. (ENG & FRE.). vii, 472p. 1992. pap. text 30.00 (92-4-154426-0, 1152125) World Health.

On Being Intelligent. Ashley Montagu. LC 72-11742. 236p. 1973. reprint ed. lib. bdg. 59.50 (0-8371-6704-3, MOOB, Greenwood Pr) Greenwood.

On Being L. D. Perspectives & Strategies of Young Adults. Stephen T. Murphy. (Special Education Ser.). 200p. (C). 1992. text 41.00 (0-8077-3170-6); pap. text 17.95 (0-8077-3169-2) Tchrs Coll.

On Being Literate. Margaret Meek. LC 92-24785. 266p. (C). 1992. pap. 16.95 (0-435-08726-6, 08726) Heinemann.

On Being Mad or Merely Angry: John W. Hinckley, Jr. & Other Dangerous People. James W. Clarke. 160p. 1990. text 26.95 (0-691-07852-1, Pub. by Princeton U Pr) Cal Prin Full Svc.

On Being Old: The Psychology of Later Life. Graham Stokes. (Contemporary Psychology Ser.). 224p. 1992. 85.00 (1-85000-839-6, Falmer Pr); pap. 29.95 (1-85000-840-X, Falmer Pr) Taylor & Francis.

***On Being 100.** Liane Enkelis. 2000. 29.95 (0-7615-2828-8) Prima Pub.

On Being Poor in Utah. Garth L. Mangum et al. LC 97-40575. 384p. 1998. 24.95 (0-87480-554-6) U of Utah Pr.

On Being Present Where You Are. Douglas V. Steere. LC 67-12913. (Orig.). 1967. pap. 4.00 (0-87574-151-7) Pendle Hill.

On Being Real. Scott Crom. LC 67-29811. (Orig.). 1967. pap. 4.00 (0-87574-155-X) Pendle Hill.

On Being Reformed: Distinctive Characteristics & Common Misunderstandings. 2nd ed. Illus. by I. John Hesselink. 1988. reprint ed. pap. 6.95 (0-916466-01-9) Reformed Church.

On Being Salt & Light. Raymond Foiles. 60p. 1997. reprint ed. pap. write for info. (1-57579-063-7) Pine Hill Pr.

On Being Sarah. Elizabeth Helfman. Ed. by Judith Mathews. (Illus.). 144p. (J). (gr. 5-9). 1992. lib. bdg. 13.95 (0-8075-6068-5) A Whitman.

On Being Single. Joanne Tangedahl. 150p. 1982. pap. 7.95 (0-942494-15-6) Coleman Pub.

On Being the Boss. Barbara McEwan et al. LC 94-68539. (Quick Read Ser.). (Illus.). 98p. (Orig.). 1995. pap. 13.95 (1-56052-309-3) Crisp Pubns.

On Being the Church: Essays on the Christian Community. Ed. by Colin E. Gunton & Daniel W. Hardy. 268p. 1993. pap. text 29.95 (0-567-29501-X, Pub. by T & T Clark) Bks Intl VA.

On Being the Church in the United States: Contemporary Theological Critiques of Liberalism. Barry P. Hollar. LC 93-29225. (American University Studies, VII: Vol. 170). XII, 343p. (C). 1994. text 55.95 (0-8204-2350-5) P Lang Pubng.

On Being Told That Her Second Husband Has Taken His First Lover, & Other Stories. Tess Slesinger. 408p. 1990. reprint ed. pap. 12.95 (0-929587-32-4, Elephant Paperbacks) I R Dee.

On Being with Others: Heidegger, Wittgenstein, Derrida. Simon Glendinning. LC 97-24111. 184p. (C). 1998. 65.00 (0-415-17123-7); pap. 19.99 (0-415-17124-5) Routledge.

On Being Wounded. Edward W. Wood, Jr. LC 91-71368. 200p. 1991. 12.95 (1-55591-076-9) Fulcrum Pub.

On Belay! The Life of Legendary Mountaineer Paul Petzoldt. Raye C. Ringholz. LC 97-41247. (Illus.). 272p. 1998. 24.95 (0-89886-558-1) Mountaineers.

***On Belay! The Life of Legendary Mountaineer Paul Petzoldt.** Raye C. Ringholz. (Illus.). 272p. 2000. pap. 16.95 (0-89886-725-8) Mountaineers.

On Believing - De La Croyance: Epistemological & Semetic Approaches. Ed. by Herman H. Parret. LC 83-15232. (Foundations of Communication & Cognition Ser.).Tr. of Approches Epistemologiques et Semiotiques. viii, 359p. 1983. 113.10 (3-11-008884-3) De Gruyter.

On Bended Knee. Tanya A. Crosby. 384p. 1999. mass mkt. 5.99 (0-380-78573-0, Avon Bks) Morrow Avon.

On Bended Knee: The Ring of Love. Sandy Greer. Ed. by Bill Greer. LC 95-79875. (Illus.). 160p. (Orig.). 1995. pap. 8.95 (0-9641332-1-0) Jormax Pubng.

On Bended Knee & Other Hot Pop Singles. Ed. by Carol Cuellar. 72p. (Orig.). (YA). 1995. pap. text 9.95 (0-89724-610-1, MF9519) Wrner Bros.

On Bended Knees: The Night Rider Story. Bill Cunningham. 224p. 1996. 18.95 (0-913383-43-0) McClanahan Pub.

***On Bereavement: The Culture of Grief.** Tony Walter. LC 99-13298. (Facing Death Ser.). 256p. 1999. pap. 29.95 (0-335-20080-X) OpUniv Pr.

On Best Behavior: The Clinton Administration & Ethics in Government. Gregory S. Walden. 637p. (Orig.). 1996. pap. text 19.95 (1-55813-056-X) Hudson Instit IN.

On Bethel Ridge: A Christmas Fable. Phil Austin. LC 98-34797. 128p. 1998. 15.00 (1-890932-03-5) Sherman Asher Pub.

On Beulah Height. Reginald Hill. 560p. 1999. mass mkt. 6.50 (0-440-22590-6) Dell.

On Beyond a Million: An Amazing Math Journey. David M. Schwartz. LC 98-52990. 32p. 1999. 15.95 (0-385-32217-8) Bantam.

On Beyond Bugs: All about Insects. Lucille R. Penner. (J). 1999. lib. bdg. 11.99 (0-679-97303-6, Pub. by Random Bks Yng Read) Random.

On Beyond Bugs: All about Insects. Dr. Seuss, pseud & Tish Rabe. LC 98-51746. (Cat in the Hat's Learning Library Ser.). (Illus.). 45p. (J). 1999. 7.99 (0-679-87303-1) Random.

On Beyond Living: Rhetorical Transformations of the Life Sciences. Richard Doyle. LC 96-38493. (Writing Science Ser.). 1997. write for info. (0-8047-2764-3); pap. 18.95 (0-8047-2765-1) Stanford U Pr.

On Beyond Zebra! Dr. Seuss, pseud. (Illus.). (J). (ps-3). 1966. lib. bdg. 15.99 (0-394-90084-7, Pub. by Random Bks Yng Read) Random.

O

On Beyond Zebra! Dr. Seuss, pseud. (Illus.). (J). (ps-3). 1966. 14.00 (*0-394-80084-2*, Pub. by Random Bks Yng Read) Random.

On Bicycles. Kyle Carter. LC 94-20174. (J). 1994. lib. bdg. 14.60 (*1-57103-078-6*) Rourke Pr.

On Biomineralization. Heinz A. Lowenstam & Stephen Weiner. (Illus.). 336p. 1989. text 75.00 (*0-19-504977-2*) OUP.

*__On Black Men.__ David Marriott. LC 00-38342. 2000. pap. 16.50 (*0-231-12227-6*); text 49.50 (*0-231-12226-8*) Col U Pr.

On Blindness: Letters Between Bryan Magee & Martin Milligan. Bryan Magee & Martin Milligan. 200p. (C). 1996. 22.00 (*0-19-823543-7*) OUP.

On Blood Turf. J. Terrell Wynne. 184p. (Orig.). 1989. pap. 10.00 (*0-925854-00-X*) Defiant Pr.

*__On Blue Felix Paper.__ Casey L. Kwang. (Illus.). 91p. 1999. pap. 13.00 (*0-9647066-4-4*) Wellstone Pr.

On Blue Water: A Limited Edition in Recognition of the Ernest Hemingway Centennial. limited ed. Art Lee. LC 99-94721. (Illus.). 60p. 1999. 50.00 (*0-9670639-0-6*) Beaverkill Prods.

On Blueberry Hill. Thompson. 1994. per. 2.99 (*0-373-15572-7*) Harlequin Bks.

*__On Blue's Waters.__ Gene Wolfe. 384p. 2000. pap. 15.95 (*0-312-87257-7*) St Martin.

*__On Blue's Waters, 3 vols., Vol. 1.__ Gene Wolfe. LC 99-26659. 381p. 1999. 24.95 (*0-312-86614-3*, Pub. by Tor Bks) St Martin.

On Board: Guiding Principles for Trustees of Not-for-Profit Organizations. Robert W. Crawford. LC 90-50992. (Illus.). (Orig.). 1991. pap. 7.50 (*0-9611710-5-7*) Western States.

On Board the Titanic. Shelley Tanaka. (Illus.). 1997. 16.45 (*0-7868-1269-9*) Hyperion.

On Board the Titanic. Shelley Tanaka. LC 95-49035. (I Was There Book Ser.). (Illus.). 48p. (J). (gr. 4-8). 1996. 16.95 (*0-7868-0283-9*, Pub. by Hyprn Child) Time Warner.

On Board the Titanic: What It Was Like When the Great Liner Sank. Shelley Tanaka. LC 95-49035. (I Was There Ser.). (Illus.). 48p. (J). (gr. 4-8). 1998. pap. 8.95 (*0-7868-1318-0*, Pub. by Hyperion) Time Warner.

*__On Board the Titanic: What It Was Like When the Great Liner Sank.__ Shelly Tanaka. (Illus.). (J). 1999. 12.40 (*0-606-15659-3*, Pub. by Turtleback) Demco.

On Board the U. S. S. Mason: The World War II Diary of James A. Dunn. Ed. by Mansel G. Blackford. LC 95-48969. (Illus.). 130p. (C). 1996. text 18.95 (*0-8142-0698-0*) Ohio St U Pr.

On Board with the Duke: John Wayne & the Wild Goose. Bert Minshall. LC 92-27938. 168p. 1992. text 39.95 (*0-929765-13-3*) Seven Locks Pr.

*__On Bobwhites.__ Fred S. Guthery. LC 99-41820. (W. L. Moody, Jr., Natural History Ser.). 224p. 2000. 24.95 (*0-89096-915-9*) Tex A&M Univ Pr.

On Bohemia: The Code of the Self-Exiled. Ed. by Cesar Grana & Marigay Grana. 565p. 1989. pap. 34.95 (*0-88738-292-4*) Transaction Pubs.

On Book Design. Richard Hendel. LC 98-17186. (Illus.). 224p. 1998. 30.00 (*0-300-07570-7*) Yale U Pr.

*__On Borders: Perspectives on International Migration in Southern Africa.__ David A. McDonald. 2000. text 45.00 (*0-312-23268-3*) St Martin.

On Borrowed Land: Public Policies for Floodplains. Scott Faber. 32p. 1996. pap. 14.00 (*1-55844-127-1*, GB656) Lincoln Inst Land.

On Borrowed Time. adapted ed. L. E. Watkins. 1945. pap. 5.25 (*0-8222-0847-4*) Dramatists Play.

On Both Banks of the Jordan: A Political Biography of Wasfial-Tall. Asher Susser. (Illus.). 208p. 1994. 49.50 (*0-7146-4542-7*, Pub. by F Cass Pubs) Intl Spec Bk.

On Both Sides of Al-Mandab: Ethiopian, South-Arabic & Islamic Studies. Ed. by Swedish Research Institute Staff. (Transactions Ser.: No. 2). (Illus.). 168p. (Orig.). 1989. pap. 59.50 (*91-22-01289-3*) Coronet Bks.

On Both Sides of the Ocean: The Memoirs of Per Hagen. Harald S. Naess & Kate Stafford. Ed. by Odd Sverre Lovoll. (Travel & Description Ser.). (Illus.). 70p. 1984. 12.00 (*0-87732-069-1*) Norwegian-Am Hist Assn.

On Both Sides of the River. Alberto Ramon. 1998. pap. 16.95 (*1-878208-84-5*) Guild Pr IN.

On Both Sides of the Wall. Vladka Meed. Tr. by Steven Meed. LC 78-71300. (Illus.). 304p. 1979. pap. 13.95 (*0-89604-013-5*, Holocaust Library) US Holocaust.

On Boundaries of American Evangelicalism: The Postwar Evangelical Coalition. Jon R. Stone. LC 97-10593. 230p. 1997. text 45.00 (*0-312-17342-3*) St Martin.

On Boxing. Joyce Carol Oates. LC 94-17428. (Illus.). 1995. reprint ed. pap. 14.00 (*0-88001-385-0*) HarpC.

On Brentano. Velarde. (Philosophy Ser.). 1999. pap. text 13.95 (*0-534-57611-7*) Brooks-Cole.

On Britain. Ralf Dahrendorf. LC 82-60102. 198p. 1996. pap. text 8.50 (*0-226-13410-5*) U Ch Pr.

On Broadway. Cherry Lane Music Company Staff. 1998. pap. 14.95 (*1-57560-090-0*, Pub. by Cherry Lane) H Leonard.

*__On Broken Glass: Loving & Losing John Gardner.__ Susan Thornton. 320p. 2000. 25.00 (*0-7867-0774-7*, Pub. by Carroll & Graf) Publishers Group.

On Building-Related Causes of Sick Building Syndrome. Lena Lundin. (Illus.). 314p. (Orig.). 1992. pap. 52.50 (*91-22-01466-7*) Coronet Bks.

On Buildings: General Index see History of the Wars. Secret History

On Burke's Reflections on the French Revolution, 1790. Catharine Macaulay. LC 96-34848. (Revolution & Romanticism Ser.). 1997. 55.00 (*1-85477-204-X*) Continuum.

On Burning Ground: A Son's Memoir. Michael Skakun. LC 99-21744. 256p. 1999. text 23.95 (*0-312-20566-X*) St Martin.

*__On Burning Ground: A Son's Memoir.__ Michael Skakun. 256p. 2000. pap. 13.95 (*0-312-26367-8*) St Martin.

On Calculating the Factor of Chance in Language Comparison. Donald A. Ringe, Jr. LC 92-70402. (Transactions Ser.: Vol. 82, Pt. 1). 110p. (C). 1992. pap. 16.00 (*0-87169-821-8*, T821-RID) Am Philos.

On Call. Grace Cutts. (Junior Jaffray Collection: Bk. 3). 30p. (J). (ps-2). 1991. pap. 3.99 (*0-87509-452-X*) Chr Pubns.

On Call. Eric Nelson. (Moonsquilt Chadbook Ser.). 28p. (Orig.). 1983. pap. 3.50 (*0-943216-04-4*) MoonsQuilt Pr.

On Call. David C. Thompson. LC 90-86213. (Jaffray Collection of Missionary Portraits: Bk. 3). 220p. 1991. pap. 9.99 (*0-87509-443-0*) Chr Pubns.

On Call. large type ed. Elizabeth Harrison. 288p. 1984. 27.99 (*0-7089-1112-9*) Ulverscroft.

On Call: A Devotional for Nurses. Lois Rowe. LC 58-7316. 230p. 1988. pap. 9.99 (*0-8010-7749-4*) Baker Bks.

On Call: Cardiology. Gabriel Khan. Ed. by William Schmitt. LC 96-14137. 336p. 1997. pap. text 21.95 (*0-7216-6848-8*, W B Saunders Co) Harcrt Hlth Sci Grp.

On Call: High Adventure in Medical Missions. David C. Thompson. LC 90-862113. 220p. 1991. mass mkt. 5.99 (*0-87509-579-8*) Chr Pubns.

On Call: Neurology. Marshall. (C). 1998. text. write for info. (*0-8089-2099-5*, Grune & Strat) Harcrt Hlth Sci Grp.

On Call: Obstetrics & Gynecology. Chin. (C). 1998. text. write for info. (*0-8089-2076-6*, Grune & Strat) Harcrt Hlth Sci Grp.

On Call: Obstetrics & Gynecology. Homer G. Chin. Ed. by Williams Schmitt. LC 96-16716. 416p. 1997. pap. text 21.95 (*0-7216-1316-0*, W B Saunders Co) Harcrt Hlth Sci Grp.

On Call: Out-of-Hours Telephone Calls & Home Visits. James D. Knox. (Practical Guides for General Practice Ser.: No. 9). (Illus.). 80p. 1989. pap. 14.95 (*0-19-261777-X*) OUP.

On Call: Pediatrics. Lewis. (C). 1998. text. write for info. (*0-8089-2096-0*, Grune & Strat) Harcrt Hlth Sci Grp.

On Call: Political Essays. June Jordan. 157p. (Orig.). 1985. 25.00 (*0-89608-268-7*); pap. 10.00 (*0-89608-269-5*) South End Pr.

On Call: Surgery. Adams. (C). 1998. text. write for info. (*0-8089-2070-7*, Grune & Strat) Harcrt Hlth Sci Grp.

On Call: Surgery. Gregg A. Adams. (C). 1998. text. write for info. (*0-8089-2136-3*, Grune & Strat) Harcrt Hlth Sci Grp.

On Call: Surgery. Gregg A. Adams & Stephen D. Bresnick. Ed. by William Schmitt. LC 96-29954. (Illus.). 320p. 1997. pap. text 21.95 (*0-7216-6432-6*, W B Saunders Co) Harcrt Hlth Sci Grp.

On Call: The Work of Telephone Helplines for Child Abusers. W. Colman. 104p. 1989. pap. text 18.00 (*0-08-037958-3*, Pergamon Pr) Elsevier.

On Call Back Mountain. Eve Bunting. LC 96-19983. (Illus.). 32p. (J). 1997. 15.95 (*0-590-25929-6*) Scholastic Inc.

On Call in Anesthesia & Surgery. Ronald A. Malt. (Illus.). 248p. 1994. pap. text 40.00 (*0-7216-3884-8*, W B Saunders Co) Harcrt Hlth Sci Grp.

On Call Laboratory Medicine & Pathology. John H. Henry & Sharad C. Mathur. 415p. Date not set. pap. text. write for info. (*0-7216-9004-1*, W B Saunders Co) Harcrt Hlth Sci Grp.

On Call Neurology: Neurology. Randolph S. Marshall & Stephan A. Mayer. Ed. by William Schmitt. LC 96-36902. 352p. 1997. pap. text 21.95 (*0-7216-6523-3*, W B Saunders Co) Harcrt Hlth Sci Grp.

On Call Orthopedics. Douglas R. Dirschi & C. Michael LeCroy. Ed. by Bill Schmitt. LC 98-3606. (On Call Ser.). (Illus.). 384p. (C). 1998. pap. text 21.95 (*0-7216-7990-0*, W B Saunders Co) Harcrt Hlth Sci Grp.

On Call Pediatrics. David Lewis & James J. Norton. Ed. by Bill Schmitt. LC 96-49867. (Illus.). 336p. 1997. pap. text 21.95 (*0-7216-6757-0*, W B Saunders Co) Harcrt Hlth Sci Grp.

On Call Principles & Protocols. 2nd ed. Shane A. Marshall & John Ruedy. (Illus.). 416p. 1993. pap. text 29.95 (*0-7216-3982-8*, W B Saunders Co) Harcrt Hlth Sci Grp.

On Call Principles & Protocols. 3rd ed. Shane A. Marshall & John Ruedy. Ed. by Ray Kersey. LC 98-32244. (On Call Ser.). (Illus.). 415p. 1999. pap. text. write for info. (*0-7216-5079-1*, W B Saunders Co) Harcrt Hlth Sci Grp.

On Call Procedures. Stephen D. Bresnick & Gregg A. Adams. Ed. by William Schmitt. LC 98-19200. (On Call Ser.). (Illus.). 220p. 1999. pap. write for info. (*0-7216-7304-X*, W B Saunders Co) Harcrt Hlth Sci Grp.

On Call Psychiatry. Carol Bernstein et al. Ed. by William Schmitt. LC 96-42344. (Illus.). 272p. 1997. pap. text 21.95 (*0-7216-6526-8*, W B Saunders Co) Harcrt Hlth Sci Grp.

On-Call Radiology. Mark Mittelman & Marc R. Hamet. (Illus.). 225p. 1997. pap. text 39.00 (*0-397-58444-X*) Lppncott W & W.

On Camera: Essential Know-How for Program-Makers. 2nd ed. Harris Watts. 334p. 1998. pap. text 26.95 (*0-9507582-3-X*, Focal) Buttrwrth-Heinemann.

On Campaign. K. Rocco. (Illus.). 1995. 25.00 (*1-883476-01-1*, Pub. by Emperors Pr) Combined Pub.

On Campus. Simon & Schuster Staff. 1995. pap. 35.22 (*0-671-05323-X*) S&S Trade.

On Campus & Off: Reminiscences & Reflections of the First Professor of Modern History at the University of Western Australia 1916-1986. Fred Alexander. 29.95 (*0-85564-264-5*, Pub. by Univ of West Aust Pr) Intl Spec Bk.

On Campus Cookbook. Mollie Fitzgerald. LC 84-40319. (Illus.). 128p. (Orig.). 1984. pap. 7.95 (*0-89480-775-7*, 775) Workman Pub.

On Canadian Literature: A Checklist of Articles, Books, & Theses on English-Canadian Literature, Its Authors, & Language. Reginald E. Watters. LC 66-1582. 177p. reprint ed. pap. 54.90 (*0-608-11472-3*, 201445200093) Bks Demand.

On Cancer & Hormones: Essays in Experimental Biology. Alexander Haddow et al. LC 62-13921. 358p. reprint ed. pap. 111.00 (*0-608-13442-2*, 202019100016) Bks Demand.

On Cannibals see Famous Utopias of the Renaissance

On Capital Punishment. John H. Redekop & Elmer A. Martens. 32p. 1987. pap. 1.50 (*0-919797-69-5*) Kindred Prods.

On Caring Ri. Milton Mayeroff. LC 90-55052. 144p. 1990. reprint ed. pap. 11.00 (*0-06-092024-6*, Perennial) HarperTrade.

On Casanova: Essays by Tom Vitelli. Tom Vitelli. LC 97-94808. 220p. 1998. 30.00 (*1-883696-05-4*) EveryWare Bks.

On Catechesis in Our Time: Catechesi Tradendae. John Paul, II, pseud. 67p. pap. 2.95 (*0-8198-1486-5*) Pauline Bks.

On Catechesis in Our Time: Catechesis Tradendae. 100p. 1979. pap. 6.95 (*1-55586-654-9*) US Catholic.

On Celestial Wings. Ed Whitcomb. (Illus.). 227p. 1995. pap. 14.00 (*1-58566-003-5*) Air Univ.

*__On Celtic Tides: One Man's Journey Around Ireland by Sea Kayak.__ Chris Duff. (Illus.). 288p. 2000. pap. 13.95 (*0-312-26368-6*) St Martin.

On Celtic Tides: One Man's Journey Around Ireland by Sea Kayak. 2nd ed. Chris Duff. LC 99-21989. 288p. 1999. text 23.95 (*0-312-20508-2*) St Martin.

*__On Central Asian Tracks: Brief Narrative of Three Expeditions in Innermost Asia & Northwestern China.__ Aurel Stein. 1998. pap. 19.50 (*81-7303-108-8*) Book Faith.

On Certain Priority Queues. Sreekantan S. Nair. LC 78-132638. 171p. 1969. 22.00 (*0-403-04521-5*) Scholarly.

On Certainty. Ludwig Josef Johann Wittgenstein. 192p. (C). 1972. pap. 14.00 (*0-06-131686-5*, TB1686, Torch) HarpC.

On Cervantes: Essays for L. A. Murillo. James A. Parr. (Documentacion Cervantina Ser.: Vol. 11). 305p. 1991. 22.00 (*0-936388-49-8*) Juan de la Cuesta.

On Character: Essays. expanded ed. James Q. Wilson. (Landmarks of Contemporary Political Thought Ser.). 248p. 1995. pap. text 12.95 (*0-8447-3787-9*) Am Enterprise.

On Character: Essays. expanded ed. James Q. Wilson. (Landmarks of Contemporary Political Thought Ser.). 248p. (C). 1995. 24.95 (*0-8447-3786-0*, AEI Pr) Am Enterprise.

On Charity. Aquinas, Thomas, Saint. Tr. by Lottie H. Kendzierski. (Medieval Philosophical Texts in Translation Ser.: No. 10). 1960. pap. 15.00 (*0-87462-210-7*) Marquette.

On Children & Death. Elisabeth Kubler-Ross. 1997. per. 11.00 (*0-684-83939-3*, Touchstone) S&S Trade Pap.

On Chinese Body Thinking: A Cultural Hermeneutic Kuang-ming Wu. LC 97-183418. (Philosophy of History & Culture Ser.). xvi, 492p. 1997. write for info. (*90-04-10150-0*) Brill Academic Pubs.

On Chinese Poetry. Chih Wei Luh. 1972. lib. bdg. 79.95 (*0-87968-540-9*) Krishna Pr.

*__On Choice.__ Sugarman. 2000. 40.00 (*0-465-09590-9*, Pub. by Basic); 28.00 (*0-465-09591-7*, Pub. by Basic) HarpC.

On Choosing Social Policy Instruments: The Case of Non-Profit Housing, Housing Allowances or Income Assistance. G. Fallis. (Progress in Planning Ser.: Vol. 40). 88p. 1993. 70.00 (*0-08-042341-8*, Pergamon Pr) Elsevier.

On Christian Dogma: An Interview with Josefina Chacin Ducharne. Celso R. Balboa. Tr. by Bertha Gonzales from SPA. LC 87-71301.Tr. of Sobre el Dogma Cristiano. 42p. 1987. pap. 4.00 (*0-9607590-6-9*) Action Life Pubns.

On Christian Marriage: Casti Connubii. Pius XI, pseud. 72p. pap. 3.75 (*0-8198-1488-1*) Pauline Bks.

On Christian Teaching. Augustine, Saint. Ed. by Green. LC 96-40146. 194p. 1999. pap. 9.95 (*0-19-283928-4*) OUP.

*__On Christian Theology.__ Rowan Williams. LC 99-36585. (Challenges in Contemporary Theology Ser.). 256p. 1999. 64.95 (*0-631-21439-9*); pap. 26.95 (*0-631-21440-2*) Blackwell Pubs.

On Christianity. Edward Gibbon. LC 90-63887. (Great Minds Ser.). 143p. (C). 1991. reprint ed. pap. 9.95 (*0-87975-674-8*) Prometheus Bks.

On Christmas Day. Pat Paris. (Illus.). 10p. (J). (ps). 1991. pap., boxed set 4.95 (*0-671-74173-X*) Little Simon.

*__On Christmas Day in the Morning.__ John Langstaff. LC 98-51122. (Illus.). 32p. (J). 1999. 15.99 (*0-7636-0375-9*) Candlewick Pr.

*__On Christmas Day in the Morning: A Traditional Carol.__ Melissa Sweet & John M. Langstaff. LC 98-51122. (J). 1999. write for info. (*0-7636-0634-0*) Candlewick Pr.

On Christmas Eve. Margaret Wise Brown. (Illus.). (J). 1985. lib. bdg. 12.89 (*0-06-020764-7*) HarpC Child Bks.

On Christmas Eve. Margaret Wise Brown. LC 93-43636. (Illus.). 32p. (J). (ps-3). 1996. 14.95 (*0-06-023648-5*) HarpC Child Bks.

*__On Christmas Eve.__ Margaret Wise Brown. LC 93-43636. (Illus.). 32p. (J). (ps-3). 2000. pap. 5.95 (*0-06-443670-5*, HarpTrophy) HarpC Child Bks.

*__On Christmas Eve.__ Liz Rosenberg. LC 99-462310. (Illus.). (J). 2000. write for info. (*0-7894-2620-X*) DK Pub Inc.

On Circuit, 1924-1937. Frank D. MacKinnon. 313p. 1997. reprint ed. 80.00 (*1-56169-342-1*) Gaunt.

*__On Civil Liberty & Self-Government, 1859.__ fac. ed. Francis Lieber. LC 99-56928. 2000. write for info. (*1-58477-070-8*) Lawbk Exchange.

*__On Civil Procedure.__ J. A. Jolowicz. (Cambridge Studies in International & Comparative Law: No. 13). 450p. (C). 2000. 95.00 (*0-521-58419-1*) Cambridge U Pr.

On Civilization Power & Knowledge. Elias. LC 97-20799. 272p. 1997. lib. bdg. 46.00 (*0-226-20431-6*) U Ch Pr.

On Civilization Power & Knowledge. Norbert Elias. Ed. by Stephen Mennell & Johan Goudsblom. LC 97-20799. 272p. 1997. pap. text 17.95 (*0-226-20432-4*) U Ch Pr.

On Clarifying Objectives of Arms Control. Bernard Brodie. (CISA Working Papers: No. 1). 33p. (Orig.). 1976. pap. 15.00 (*0-86682-000-0*) Ctr Intl Relations.

On Classic Ground: Picasso, Leger, De Chirico & the New Classicism, 1910-1930. Elizabeth Cowling. 1991. pap. text 39.95 (*1-85437-043-X*) Tate Gallery.

On Clausewitz & the History of War: Essays. Peter Paret. 224p. 1992. text 39.50 (*0-691-03199-1*, Pub. by Princeton U Pr) Cal Prin Full Svc.

*__On Clear & Confused Ideas: An Essay about Substance Concepts.__ Ruth Garrett Millikan. LC 99-58059. 2000. write for info. (*0-521-62386-3*); write for info. (*0-521-62553-X*) Cambridge U Pr.

On Closed Three-Braids. Kunio Murasugi. LC 74-17176. (Memoirs Ser.: No. 1/151). 114p. 1974. pap. 18.00 (*0-8218-1851-1*, MEMO/1/151) Am Math.

On Cloud Nine: Visualizing & Verbalizing for Math. Kimberly Turley & Nanci Bell. LC 98-204445. 328 p. 1997. 39.95 (*0-945856-07-5*) Gander Educ.

On Clowns: The Dictator & the Artist - Essays. Norman Manea. LC 91-23866. 192p. 1993. pap. 12.00 (*0-8021-3375-4*, Grove) Grove-Atltic.

On Clusters & Clustering: From Atoms to Fractals. Ed. by Peter J. Reynolds. LC 93-9513. (Random Materials & Processes Ser.). 422p. 1993. pap. 93.25 (*0-444-89022-X*, North Holland) Elsevier.

On Coalition Course. Arun Kumar & Press Trust of India Staff. LC 98-908771. 200 p. 1998. write for info. (*81-212-0609-X*) Gian Publng Hse.

On Coasts of Eternity: Jack Hodgins' Fictional Universe. Ed. by J. R. Struthers. 246p. 1996. text 18.95 (*0-88982-156-9*, Pub. by Oolichan Bks) Genl Dist Srvs.

On Cogenic Herpesviruses, Vol. 1. Ed. by Fred Rapp. 208p. 1980. 120.00 (*0-8493-5619-9*, QR400, CRC Reprint) Franklin.

On Cogenic Herpesviruses, Vol. 2. Ed. by Fred Rapp. 152p. 1980. 89.00 (*0-8493-5620-2*, CRC Reprint) Franklin.

On Collecting: An Investigation into Collecting in the European Tradition. Susan M. Pearce. LC 94-35151. 1995. pap. write for info. (*0-415-07561-0*) Routledge.

On Collecting: An Investigation into Collecting in the European Tradition. Susan M. Pearce. LC 94-35151. (Collecting Cultures Ser.). (Illus.). 304p. (C). (gr. 13). 1995. 75.00 (*0-415-07560-2*, C0035) Routledge.

*__On Collecting, Collector & Collections.__ 2000. pap. 19.95 (*0-9653701-1-9*) Brimfield Publns.

On Collecting, Collectors & Collections: The Collector's Paradise. Robert E. Brown. (Illus.). 175p. (Orig.). 1999. pap. 19.95 (*0-9653701-0-0*) Brimfield Publns.

On Collective Memory. Maurice Halbwachs. LC 91-47551. (Heritage of Sociology Ser.). 254p. (C). 1992. pap. text 16.95 (*0-226-11596-8*); lib. bdg. 47.50 (*0-226-11594-1*) U Ch Pr.

*__On Colonial Grounds: A Comparative Study of Colonialism & Rural Settlement in First Millenium BC West Central Sardinia.__ P. van Dommelen. (Archaeological Studies : No. 2). 296p. 1998. pap. 55.00 (*90-76368-02-3*, Pub. by Leiden Univ Pr) David Brown.

On Colonialism. Karl Marx. (C). text 15.00 (*0-85315-129-6*, Pub. by Lawrence & Wishart) NYU Pr.

On Colour. Georg C. Behnisch. 100p. 1994. pap. 35.00 (*3-7757-0474-4*, Pub. by Gerd Hatje) Dist Art Pubs.

On-Column Injection in Capillary Gas Chromatography: Basic Technique, Retention Gaps, Solvent Effects. 2nd ed. Konrad Grob. 1998. 145.00 (*3-527-29701-4*) Wiley.

On-Column Injection in Capillary Gas Chromatography: Basic Technique, Retention Gaps, Solvent Effects 2nd ed. Konrad Grob. LC 99-184518. (Chromatographic Methods Ser.). xx, 591 p. 1991. write for info. (*3-7785-2055-5*, Pub. by Huethig BRD) U Pr of Amer.

On Coming-to-Be & Passing-Away (De Generatione et Corruptione) rev. ed. Aristotle. (GER.). xxxviii, 303p. 1982. reprint ed. lib. bdg. 70.00 (*3-487-02901-4*) G Olms Pubs.

On Coming-to-Be & Perishing 1.1-5: Philoponus. Ed. by Richard Sorabji. Tr. by C. J. Williams. LC 98-55360. (Ancient Commentators on Aristotle Ser.). 240p. 1998. 49.95 (*0-8014-3615-X*) Cornell U Pr.

On Coming-to-Be & Perishing 1.6-2.4: Philoponus. Ed. by Richard Sorabji. Tr. by C. J. Williams from GEC. LC 99-15554. (Ancient Commentators on Aristotle Ser.). 240p. 1998. 49.95 (*0-8014-3614-1*) Cornell U Pr.

On Commemoration of the Dead. Lazar Puhalo. 40p. Date not set. pap. 5.00 (*1-879038-95-1*, 9061) Synaxis Pr.

On Common Ground: Caring for Shared Land from Town Common to Urban Park. Ronald L. Fleming & Lauri A. Halderman. LC 81-20215. 1982. pap. text 12.95 (*0-916782-25-5*) Harvard Common Pr.

On Common Ground: Photographs from the Crossroads of the New South. Chip Simone. 112p. (C). 1996. 39.95 (*0-86554-486-7*, MUP/H381) Mercer Univ Pr.

On Communicating. Mark H. McCormack. 224p. 1999. pap. 14.00 (*0-7871-1838-9*, NewStar Pr) NewStar Media.

On Communication: Essays in Understanding. Lee Thayer. LC 87-11384. (Communication: The Human Context Ser.). 272p. 1988. pap. 39.50 (*0-89391-457-6*); text 73.25 (*0-89391-409-6*) Ablx Pub.

On Communion in the Hand & Similar Frauds. Michael Davies. Ed. by Matto Michael. 52p. 1998. 5.50 (*1-890740-03-9*) Remnant Pr.

On Communitarian Divinity: An African Interpretation of the Trinity. A. Ogbonnaya. LC 94-12161. 144p. 1995. 29.95 (*1-55778-704-2*) Paragon Hse.

An Asterisk (*) at the beginning of an entry indicates that the title is appearing for the first time.

On Communitarian Divinity: An African Interpretation of the Trinity. A. Okechukwu Ogbonnaya. 144p. 1999. pap. 14.95 (*1-55778-770-0*) Paragon Hse.

On Community. Ed. by Leroy S. Rouner. LC 91-50573. (Boston University Studies in Philosophy & Religion: Vol. 12). (C). 1991. text 34.50 (*0-268-01507-4*) U of Notre Dame Pr.

***On Community & Environment.** Ed. by RSA Staff. 160p. 1999. 61.95 (*0-566-08106-7*, Pub. by Gower) Ashgate Pub Co.

On Competence: A Critical Analysis of Competence-Based Reforms in Higher Education. Gerald Grant et al. LC 79-83572. (Jossey-Bass Series in Higher Education). 614p. reprint ed. pap. 190.40 (*0-8357-4941-X*, 203787100009) Bks Demand.

On Competition. Michael E. Porter. LC 98-7643. 485p. 1998. 35.95 (*0-87584-795-1*) Harvard Busn.

On Competition in Economic Theory. Philip W. Andrews. LC 81-6246. 141p. 1981. reprint ed. lib. bdg. 55.00 (*0-313-23053-6*, ANOC, Greenwood Pr) Greenwood.

On Compiling an Annotated Bibliography. rev. ed. James L. Harner. LC 85-3009. 42p. 1991. pap. text 10.00 (*0-87352-138-2*, S325P) Modern Lang.

***On Compiling an Annotated Bibliography.** 2nd ed. James L. Harner. LC 00-38663. 2000. pap. write for info. (*0-87352-979-0*) Modern Lang.

On Composition & Computers. Deborah H. Holdstein. LC 87-22917. (Technology & the Humanities Ser.: No. 3). xi, 104p. 1987. pap. 19.75 (*0-87352-555-8*, S803P); lib. bdg. 37.50 (*0-87352-554-X*, S803C) Modern Lang.

On Concepts & Classifications of Musical Instruments. Margaret J. Kartomi. LC 90-31361. (Chicago Studies in Ethnomusicology). (Illus.). 350p. 1990. pap. text 27.00 (*0-226-42549-5*) U Ch Pr.

On Concepts of Multifactor Productivity in Canada. Alexandra Cas & Thomas K. Rymes. (Illus.). 270p. (C). 1991. text 89.95 (*0-521-36536-8*) Cambridge U Pr.

On Concurrent Programming. Fred B. Schneider. LC 97-1017. (Graduate Texts in Computer Science Ser.). 500p. 1997. 49.95 (*0-387-94942-9*) Spr-Verlag.

On Conditionals Again. Ed. by Angeliki Athanasiadou & Rene Dirven. LC 96-50283. (Current Issues in Linguistic Theory Ser.: Vol. 143). viii, 418p. 1997. lib. bdg. 94.00 (*1-55619-598-2*) J Benjamins Pubng Co.

On Conducting: A Treatise on Style in the Execution of Classical Music. Richard Wagner. 1988. reprint ed. lib. bdg. 49.00 (*0-7812-0113-6*) Rprt Serv.

On Conducting: A Treatise on Style in the Execution of Classical Music. 4th ed. Richard Wagner. LC 74-181291. 127p. 1940. reprint ed. 17.00 (*0-403-01714-9*) Scholarly.

On Confession & Power to Reimit Sins. George Gabriel. 5.00 (*1-879038-83-8*) Oakwood Pubns.

On Constitutional Ground. John H. Ely. 510p. 1996. text 69.50 (*0-691-08644-3*, Pub. by Princeton U Pr); pap. text 24.95 (*0-691-02553-3*, Pub. by Princeton U Pr) Cal Prin Full Svc.

On Consulting the Faithful in Matters of Doctrine. John Henry Newman. Ed. by John Coulson. LC 62-9877. 128p. 1985. reprint ed. pap. 7.95 (*0-934134-51-0*) Sheed & Ward WI.

On Contemporary Bibliography: With Particular Reference to Ezra Pound. Donald Gallup. LC 73-630258. (Bibliographical Monograph: No. 4). (Illus.). 1974. reprint ed. 12.00 (*0-87959-047-5*) U of Tex H Ransom Ctr.

On Contemporary History. John L. Gaddis. 28p. 1995. pap. text 8.95 (*0-19-951365-1*) OUP.

On Contemporary Literature. Stuart P. Sherman. LC 75-105037. (Essay Index Reprint Ser.). 1977. 23.95 (*0-8369-1480-5*) Ayer.

On Contemporary Literature. Stuart P. Sherman. LC 75-127905. 1975. reprint ed. 27.50 (*0-404-05958-9*) AMS Pr.

On Contemporary Literature. Stuart P. Sherman. (BCL1-PR English Literature Ser.). 312p. 1992. reprint ed. lib. bdg. 89.00 (*0-7812-7056-1*) Rprt Serv.

On Contemporary Literature. 2nd ed. Ed. by Richard Kostelanetz. LC 72-156674. 699p. (C). 1969. 200.00 (*0-932360-02-5*); pap. 50.00 (*0-932360-00-9*) Archae Edns.

On Contemporary Literature: An Anthology of Critical Essays on the Major Movements & Writings of Contemporary Literature. Ed. by Richard Kostelanetz. LC 72-156674. (Essay Index Reprint Ser.). 1977. reprint ed. 44.95 (*0-8369-2406-1*) Ayer.

On Contract, the Indian Contract Act, 1872. D. C. Dutta. (C). 1990. 210.00 (*0-89771-231-5*) St Mut.

On Cooking, Pt. 1. 75p. 1998. pap. text 2.04 (*0-536-01228-8*) Pearson Custom.

On Cooking, Pt. 2. 185p. 1998. pap. text 4.30 (*0-536-01229-6*) Pearson Custom.

On Cooking, Pt. 3. 197p. 1998. pap. text 7.10 (*0-536-01230-X*) Pearson Custom.

On Cooking, Pt. 4. 123p. 1998. pap. text 7.21 (*0-536-01231-8*) Pearson Custom.

***On Cooking, Pt. 5.** 290p. 1998. pap. text 6.43 (*0-536-01232-6*) Pearson Custom.

On Cooking, Pt. 7. 27p. 1998. pap. text 3.70 (*0-536-01234-2*) Pearson Custom.

On Cooking, Vol. 4. Richard Gough. (Performance Research Ser.). 1999. pap. 18.00 (*0-415-19802-X*) Routledge.

On Cooking: A Textbook of Culinary Fundamentals. Sarah R. Labensky & Alan M. Hause. LC 94-12053. 896p. 1994. text 77.00 (*0-13-194515-7*) P-H.

On Cooking: A Textbook of Culinary Fundamentals. 2nd ed. Sarah R. Labensky & Alan M. Hause. LC 98-17965. 1157p. (C). 1998. 80.00 (*0-13-862640-5*) P-H.

On Cooking: Appendix & Index. 50p. 1998. pap. text 1.70 (*0-536-01235-0*) Pearson Custom.

On Cooking: Techniques from Expert Chefs. 2nd ed. Sarah R. Labensky & Alan M. Hause. LC 98-17966. (Illus.). 1125p. 1998. 49.95 (*0-13-924101-9*) P-H.

On Cooking Part 6. 220p. 1998. pap. text 7.21 (*0-536-01233-4*) Pearson Custom.

***On Cooking (trade Version) Techniques from Expert Chefs, 2.** 2nd ed. Sarah R. Labensky & Alan M. Hause. 327p. 1999. 10.00 (*0-13-018785-2*) P-H.

***On Cooking (trade Version) Techniques from Expert Chefs, 3.** 2nd ed. Sarah R. Labensky & Alan M. Hause. 1999. 22.00 (*0-13-018786-0*) P-H.

On Coon Mountain: Scenes from a Childhood in the Oklahoma Hills. Glen Ross. LC 91-29392. 192p. (C). 1992. 21.95 (*0-8061-2405-9*) U of Okla Pr.

On Coping & Change. Lois B. Murphy. 17p. (Orig.). pap. 2.50 (*0-918374-19-7*) City Coll Wk.

On Copra Ships & Coral Isles. large type ed. Rosaline Redwood. 352p. 1992. 27.99 (*0-7089-2614-2*) Ulverscroft.

On Corinthian Iconography: The Bridled Winged Horse & the Helmeted Female Head in the Sixth Century B. C. Peter E. Blomberg. LC 97-156619. (Uppsala Studies in Ancient Mediterranean & Near Eastern Civilizations: No. 25). (Illus.). 109p. (Orig.). 1996. pap. 37.50 (*91-554-3702-8*, Pub. by Uppsala Univ Acta Univ Uppsaliensis) Coronet Bks.

On Corporate Governance. Michael Novak. LC 97-174722. (Pfizer Lecture Ser.). 51p. 1997. pap. 9.95 (*0-8447-7082-5*) Am Enterprise.

On Correspondence among Christians. Lisa Kuenning. 1986. pap. 1.25 (*0-930682-01-7*) Friends Truth.

On Count. David Appelbaum. Ed. by Patricia Schultz. LC 89-33518. (Poetry Ser.: Vol. 5). 88p. 1989. pap. 14.95 (*0-88946-889-3*) E Mellen.

On Country Roads & Fields: The Depiction of the 18th & 19th Century Landscape. Wiepke Loos. LC 98-182980. 1998. pap. 50.00 (*90-6611-921-7*, Pub. by Lund Humphries) Antique Collect.

***On Course.** 2nd ed. Skip Downing. LC 98-72017. xviii, 219 p. 1999. write for info. (*0-395-93422-2*) HM.

On Course: A Guide to the Region's Public Golf Courses. Gerry Dulac & Marino Parascenzo. Ed. by Debra Alward. 1998. pap. 9.75 (*0-9657325-1-7*) Pittsbrgh Post-Gazette.

On Course: Chevron's Century at Sea. Robert Spector. LC 95-83176. (Illus.). 80p. 1995. pap. 19.95 (*0-935503-17-X*) Document Bk.

On Course: Strategies for Creating Success in College in Life: A Guided Journal Appproach. Michael A. Palmer. (Contributions to Naval History Ser.: No. 5). (Illus.). 201p. (Orig.). (C). 1992. pap. 11.00 (*0-945274-08-4*) Naval Hist Ctr.

On Course: Student Book 1. Carol Cellman. (Illus.). 96p. 1989. pap. text, student ed. 9.95 (*0-19-434285-9*) OUP.

On Course: Student Book 2. Jacqueline Flamm. (Illus.). 96p. 1990. pap. text, student ed. 9.95 (*0-19-434289-1*) OUP.

On Course: Teacher's Book 1. Carol Cellman. (Illus.). 108p. 1989. pap. text, teacher ed. 15.95 (*0-19-434286-7*) OUP.

On Course: Teacher's Book 2. Jacqueline Flamm. (Illus.). 202p. 1990. pap. text, teacher ed. 15.95 (*0-19-434290-5*) OUP.

On Course: The U. S. Ski & Snowboard Teams' Cookbook. LC 97-60651. (Illus.). 128p. 1997. 14.95 (*0-9656950-0-X*) US Ski Snowboard.

On Course - The Revolutionary Process. Gus Hall. 1969. pap. 0.50 (*0-87898-038-5*) New Outlook.

***On Course for GCSE Maths Foundation & Intermediate Tiers.** Paul Metcalf. (Illus.). 208p. (YA). (gr. 9-11). 2000. pap. 19.95 (*0-7487-4511-4*, Pub. by S Thornes Pubs) Trans-Atl Phila.

***On Course for GCSE Maths Foundation & Intermediate Tiers with Answers.** Paul Metcalf et al. (Illus.). 208p. (YA). (gr. 9-11). 2000. pap. 19.95 (*0-7487-4512-2*, Pub. by S Thornes Pubs) Trans-Atl Phila.

***On Course for GCSE Maths Intermediate & Higher Tiers.** Paul Metcalf et al. (Illus.). 208p. (YA). (gr. 9-11). 2000. pap. 19.95 (*0-7487-4454-1*, Pub. by S Thornes Pubs) Trans-Atl Phila.

***On Course for GCSE Maths Intermediate & Higher Tiers with Answers.** Paul Metcalf et al. (Illus.). 208p. (YA). (gr. 9-11). 2000. pap. 19.95 (*0-7487-4455-X*, Pub. by S Thornes Pubs) Trans-Atl Phila.

On Course for Murder. large type ed. P. A. Foxall. (Linford Mystery Library). 320p. 1995. pap. 16.99 (*0-7089-7713-8*, Linford) Ulverscroft.

On Course: Strategies for Creating Success in College in Life: A Guided Journal Approach. Skip Downing. (C). 1995. pap. text, teacher ed. 11.96 (*0-395-73879-2*) HM.

On Course to Desert Storm: The U. S. Navy & the Persian Gulf. Michael A. Palmer. (Illus.). 201p. (Orig.). (C). 1993. pap. text 35.00 (*1-56806-556-6*) DIANE Pub.

On Course to Desert Storm: The U. S. Navy & the Persian Gulf. Michael A. Palmer. 213p. (Orig.). 1992. per. 14.00 (*0-16-035946-5*) USGPO.

On Course to Oblivion: An Analogy of the Kriegsmarine & the Battleship Bismarck. Robert C. Gramberg. 163p. 1998. 34.95 (*1-883228-24-7*) Invictus MI.

On Courts & Democracy: Selected Nonjudicial Writings of J. Skelly Wright, 75. Ed. by Arthur S. Miller. LC 83-22810. (Contributions in American Studies: No. 75). 291p. 1984. 55.00 (*0-313-23938-X*, MDE/, Greenwood Pr) Greenwood.

On Creating a Community: A Guide for Organizations, Personal Productivity & International Peace. William Polowniak. 296p. 1994. 23.95 (*0-9639142-1-9*) Quantum Publications CA.

On Creating a Community: A Guide for Organizations, Personal Productivity & International Peace. William Polowniak. LC 93-87084. 296p. (C). 1994. pap. 14.95 (*0-9639142-0-0*) Quantum Publications CA.

***On Creation, Conservation, & Concurrence: Metaphysical Disputations 20, 21, & 22.** Francisco Suarez. Tr. & Intro. by A. J. Freddoso. 464p. 2000. 40.00 (*1-890318-76-0*, Pub. by St Augustines Pr) Chicago Distribution Ctr.

On Creativity. David Bohm & Lee Nichol. LC 97-29460. 160p. (C). 1998. 60.00 (*0-415-17395-7*); pap. 17.99 (*0-415-17396-5*) Routledge.

On Crime, Punishment & Psychiatric Care: An Introduction to Swedish Philosophy of Criminal Law & Forensic Psychiatry. Lennart Nordenfelt. 87p. (Orig.). 1992. pap. 36.00 (*91-22-01487-X*) Coronet Bks.

On Crimes & Punishments. Cesare Beccaria. (International Pocket Library). 1992. pap. 5.95 (*0-8283-1800-X*) Branden Bks.

On Crimes & Punishments. Cesare Beccaria. Ed. & Tr. by David Young from ITA. LC 85-17578. (HPC Classics Ser.). 129p. (C). 1986. pap. 6.95 (*0-915145-97-9*); lib. bdg. 27.95 (*0-915144-99-9*) Hackett Pub.

On Crimes & Punishments. Cesare Beccaria. Tr. by Henry Paolucci. LC 61-18589. 128p. (C). 1963. pap. text 5.80 (*0-02-391360-6*, LLA107, Macmillan Coll) P-H.

On Crimes & Punishments: Beccaria. 10th ed. Cesare Beccaria. Tr. by Henry Paolucci. 99p. 1963. pap. 15.00 (*0-672-60302-0*, Bobbs) Macmillan.

On Crimes & Punishments & Other Writings. Cesare Beccaria. Ed. by Richard Bellamy. (Cambridge Texts in the History of Political Thought Ser.). (Illus.). 229p. (C). 1995. pap. text 19.95 (*0-521-47982-7*) Cambridge U Pr.

On Criminalization: An Essay in the Philosophy of the Criminal Law. abr. ed. Jonathan Schonsheck. LC 93-44434. (Law & Philosophy Library: Vol. 19). 324p. (C). 1994. lib. bdg. 127.00 (*0-7923-2663-6*, Pub. by Kluwer Academic) Kluwer Academic.

On Critical Theory. Ed. by John O'Neill. 270p. (C). 1989. reprint ed. pap. text 25.00 (*0-8191-7514-5*) U Pr of Amer.

On Criticizing Music: Five Philosophical Perspectives. Ed. by Kingsley Price. LC 81-47597. 127p. reprint ed. pap. 39.40 (*0-608-15319-2*, 202924100059) Bks Demand.

On Crown Service: A History of the Colonial Service. Anthony Kirk-Greene. 256p. 1999. text 45.00 (*1-86064-260-8*) St Martin.

On Crusade: More Tales of the Knight's Templar. Ed. by Katherine Kurtz. LC 97-34461. 256p. (Orig.). 1998. mass mkt. 11.99 (*0-446-67339-0*, Pub. by Warner Bks) Little.

***On Cukor.** Gavin Lambert. Ed. by Robert Trachtenberg. (Illus.). 208p. 2000. 50.00 (*0-8478-2297-4*) Rizzoli Intl.

On Cultivating Liberty: Reflections on Moral Ecology. Michael Novak. Ed. by Brian C. Anderson. 256p. 1999. 24.95 (*0-8476-9405-4*, Pub. by Rowman) Natl Bk Netwk.

On Cultivating Liberty: Writings on Moral Ecology. Michael Novak. 1999. 63.00 (*0-8476-8689-2*) Rowman.

On Cultural Freedom: An Exploration of Public Life in Poland & America. Jeffrey C. Goldfarb. LC 82-8325. (Chicago Original Paperback Ser.). 184p. (C). 1983. pap. text 14.95 (*0-226-30100-1*) U Ch Pr.

On Cultural Freedom: An Exploration of Public Life in Poland & America. Jeffrey C. Goldfarb. LC 82-8325. (Chicago Original Paperback Ser.). 216p. (C). 1993. lib. bdg. 25.00 (*0-226-30099-4*) U Ch Pr.

On Cultural Ground: Essays in International History. Ed. by Robert David Johnson. LC 94-79738. (Imprint Studies in International Relations: Vol. 1). 1994. pap. 19.95 (*1-879176-21-1*) Imprint Pubns.

***On Cultural Values & Human Progress.** Huntington. 2000. pap. 18.00 (*0-465-03176-5*, Pub. by Basic) HarpC.

On Culture Contact & Its Working in Modern Palestine. Raphael Patai. LC 48-4054. (American Anthropological Association Memoirs Ser.: No. 67). 1974. reprint ed. pap. 25.00 (*0-527-00566-5*) Periodicals Srv.

On Current Problems & the Fourth Alternative. L. C. Fabre. (Illus.). 212p. (Orig.). 1986. pap. 9.95 (*0-89729-471-8*) Ediciones.

On Custom in the Economy. Ekkehart Schlicht. LC HB74.P8S357 1998. (Illus.). 342p. 1998. text 76.00 (*0-19-829224-4*) OUP.

On Cutting off a Ratio. Apollonius. Tr. by Edward Macierowski from ARA. (Illus.). 160p. 1987. lib. bdg. 30.00 (*0-931267-00-5*) Golden Hind Pr.

On Damascus Steel. Leo S. Figiel. (Illus.). 145p. (C). 1991. text 40.00 (*0-9628711-1-7*) Atlantis Arts.

On Dangerous Ground. Jack Higgins. 336p. 1995. mass mkt. 6.50 (*0-425-14828-9*) Berkley Pub.

***On Dangerous Ground.** Maggie Price. (Intimate Moments Ser.: Vol. 989). 2000. mass mkt. 4.50 (*0-373-07989-3*) Silhouette.

On Dangerous Ground. large type ed. Jack Higgins. LC 94-10354. 408p. 1994. lib. bdg. 25.95 (*0-7862-0231-9*) Thorndike Pr.

On Dangerous Ground. Jack Higgins. 1995. reprint ed. lib. bdg. 26.95 (*1-56849-595-1*) Buccaneer Bks.

On Days Like This: Poems. Dan Quisenberry. LC 98-12832. 90p. 1998. pap. 12.95 (*1-884235-24-7*) Helicon Nine Eds.

On Deadline: Labor Relations in Newspaper Publishing. Stephen R. Sleigh. LC 97-61728. 150p. 1997. pap. 17.95 (*0-9644437-1-6*) Social Change Pr.

***On Deadline: Managing Media Relations.** 3rd ed. Carole M. Howard. 346p. 1999. pap. 22.95 (*1-57766-086-2*) Waveland Pr.

On Dearborn Street. Miles Franklin. LC 81-11570. 219p. 1989. pap. 14.95 (*0-7022-1954-1*, Pub. by Univ Queensland Pr) Intl Spec Bk.

On Death. Caleb Gattegno. 1978. pap. 8.00 (*0-87825-145-6*) Ed Solutions.

On Death: Helping Children Understand & Cope. Sara Smilansky. 247p. 1988. text 34.00 (*0-8204-0525-6*) P Lang Pubng.

On Death: Wisdom & Consolation from the World's Great Writers. Compiled by Barry Ulanov. LC 96-26515. 256p. 1996. pap. 16.00 (*0-89243-926-2*, Liguori Triumph) Liguori Pubns.

On Death & Dying. Elisabeth Kubler-Ross. (Hudson River Editions Ser.). 272p. 1991. 50.00 (*0-02-567111-1*) Macmillan.

On Death & Dying. Elisabeth Kubler-Ross. LC 97-177294. 288p. 1997. 22.50 (*0-684-84223-8*) S&S Trade.

On Death & Dying. Elisabeth Kubler-Ross. 1997. 16.10 (*0-606-04230-X*, Pub. by Turtleback) Demco.

On Death & Dying. Elisabeth K[0081]bler-Ross. 272p. 1997. per. 11.00 (*0-684-83938-5*) S&S Trade Pap.

On Death Mountain. Tabor Evans. (Longarm Ser.: No. 100). 192p. 1987. mass mkt. 2.95 (*0-515-08934-6*, Jove) Berkley Pub.

On Death Without Dignity: The Human Impact of Technological Dying. David W. Moller. (Perspectives on Death & Dying Ser.). 134p. 1990. text 45.95 (*0-89503-067-5*) Baywood Pub.

On Deconstructing Life-Worlds: Buddhism, Christianity, Culture. Robert R. Magliola. LC 96-27889. (American Academy of Religion Cultural Criticism Ser.). 202p. 1997. 29.95 (*0-7885-0295-6*, 010703) OUP.

On Deconstruction: Theory & Criticism after Structuralism. Jonathan Culler. LC 82-7414. 312p. 1982. text 42.50 (*0-8014-1322-2*); pap. text 14.95 (*0-8014-9201-7*) Cornell U Pr.

On Decoration. David Bret. LC 91-191539. 1997. 49.95 (*0-7188-2801-1*, Lutterworth-Parkwest) Parkwest Pubns.

On Defining Death: An Analytic Study of the Concept of Death in Philosophy & Medical Ethics. Douglas N. Walton. 1979. 27.95 (*0-7735-0331-5*, Pub. by McG-Queens Univ Pr) CUP Services.

On Defining Death: An Analytic Study of the Concept of Death in Philosophy & Medical Ethics. Douglas N. Walton. LC 80-453967. (Illus.). 200p. reprint ed. pap. 62.00 (*0-7837-6920-2*, 204674900003) Bks Demand.

On Defining the Phoneme. William F. Twaddell. (LM Ser.: No. 16). 1935. pap. 25.00 (*0-527-00820-6*) Periodicals Srv.

On Defining the Proper Name. John Algeo. LC 73-9849. (University of Florida Humanities Monographs: No. 41). 102p. reprint ed. pap. 31.70 (*0-7837-0593-X*, 204094100019) Bks Demand.

On Definiteness: A Study with Special Reference to English & Finnish. Andrew Chesterman. (Cambridge Studies in Linguistics: No. 56). (Illus.). 228p. (C). 1991. text 69.95 (*0-521-39194-6*) Cambridge U Pr.

On Degenerations of Algebraic Surfaces. U. Persson. LC 77-8972. (Memoirs Ser.: No. 11/189). 144p. 1977. pap. 22.00 (*0-8218-2189-X*, MEMO/11/189) Am Math.

***On-Demand & Digital Printing Primer.** Howard M. Fenton. LC 98-74334. (Illus.). 23p. (C). 1998. pap. text 25.00 (*0-88362-219-X*, 1328) GATFPress.

On-Demand Printing: The Revolution in Digital & Customized Printing. 2nd ed. Howard M. Fenton. LC 98-8328. 320p. 1998. 64.99 (*0-13-096424-7*) P-H.

On-Demand Printing: The Revolution in Digital & Customized Printing. 2nd ed. Howard M. Fenton & Frank J. Romano. LC 96-78324. (Illus.). 320p. (C). 1997. text 75.00 (*0-88362-194-0*, 1341) GATFPress.

***On Democracy.** Robert A. Dahl. LC 98-21375. 224p. 1998. 25.00 (*0-300-07627-4*) Yale U Pr.

***On Democracy.** Robert A. Dahl. 224p. 2000. pap. 10.95 (*0-300-08455-2*) Yale U Pr.

On Demonology & Witchcraft in Ceylon. Dandris de Silva Gooneratne. LC 98-905009. 120 p. 1998. write for info. (*81-206-1309-0*) Asian Educ Servs.

On Deployment of Health Resources in Rural Valle del Cauca, Colombia. David Eaton. (Working Paper Ser.: No. 11). 50p. 1979. pap. 2.50 (*0-89940-507-X*) LBJ Sch Pub Aff.

On Descartes. Thomson. (Philosophy Ser.). 1999. pap. text 13.95 (*0-534-57593-5*) Brooks-Cole.

On Desert Trails with Everett Ruess: Commemorative Edition. Everett Ruess. Ed. by Gary J. Bergera. (Illus.). 144p. 2000. 17.95 (*0-87905-825-0*) Gibbs Smith Pub.

***On Design & Innovation: A Selection of Lecturers Organized by the Royal Society for the Encouragement of Arts, Manufactures & Commerce.** RSA Staff. (RSA Lecture Ser.). 144p. 1999. 61.95 (*0-566-08107-5*, Pub. by Ashgate Pub) Ashgate Pub Co.

On Desperate Seas: A Biography of Gilbert Stuart. James T. Flexner. LC 95-10188. (Illus.). xii, 195p. 1995. text 20.00 (*0-8232-1612-8*) Fordham.

On Development: The Biology of Form. John T. Bonner. LC 73-88053. (Commonwealth Fund Publications). 224p. 1977. pap. 15.50 (*0-674-63412-8*) HUP.

On Dewey. Robert Talisse. (Wadsworth Notes Ser.). 2000. pap. text 13.95 (*0-534-57617-6*) Thomson Learn.

On Dialogue. David Bohm & Lee Nichol. LC 96-20527. xviii, 101p. 1996. pap. 17.99 (*0-415-14912-6*) Routledge.

On Dialogue. David Bohm & Lee Nichol. LC 96-20527. 128p. (C). 1996. 60.00 (*0-415-14911-8*) Routledge.

On Dialogue. Robert Grudin. 240p. 1997. pap. 13.00 (*0-395-86495-X*) HM.

***On Dialogue: Contempory Australian Art.** Ed. by Bernice Murphy et al. (Illus.). 216p. 1999. pap. 39.95 (*3-931321-61-4*, Pub. by Jovis Verlags) Dist Art Pubs.

On Dickinson. Ed. by Edwin H. Cady & Louis J. Budd. LC 89-17004. (Best from American Literature Ser.). 240p. (C). 1990. text 49.95 (*0-8223-1014-7*) Duke.

On Different Planes: An Organizational Analysis of Cooperation & Conflict among Airline Unions. David J. Walsh. LC 93-48443. 224p. 1994. text 37.50 (*0-87546-323-1*, ILR Press); pap. text 17.95 (*0-87546-329-0*, ILR Press) Cornell U Pr.

On Different Shores. Jen McVeity. LC 98-4481. 167p. (YA). (gr. 5 up). 1998. lib. bdg. 17.99 (*0-531-33115-6*) Orchard Bks Watts.

O

On Different Shores. Jen McVeity. LC 98-4481. (Illus.). 167p. (YA). (gr. 5-9). 1998. 16.95 (*0-531-30115-X*) Orchard Bks Watts.

On Dinosaur Days. Ed. by Martha A. Hayes. (Creative Concept Ser.). (Illus.). 48p. 1990. pap. 6.95 (*1-878727-00-1*) First Teacher.

On Directing. Harold Clurman. LC 96-46762. 1997. per. 15.00 (*0-684-82622-4*, Fireside) S&S Trade Pap.

On Directing. Elia Kazan. 1998. write for info. (*0-679-45473-X*) Random.

On Directing: Interviews with Directors. Ed. by Gabriella Giannachi & Mary Luckhurst. LC 99-25274. 142p. 1999. pap. 16.95 (*0-312-22483-4*) St Martin.

On Directing Film. David Mamet. 128p. 1992. pap. 12.95 (*0-14-012722-4*, Penguin Bks) Viking Penguin.

On Dis Corner: A Collection of Ruffneck Short Stories. Henry Hardee. 49p. 1995. pap. text 6.00 (*1-884978-00-2*, PA686-909) Black Boys Dream.

On Disarmament: The Role of Conventional Arms Control in National Security Strategy. David E. Shaver & Ralph A. Hallenbeck. LC 90-44146. 256p. 1991. pap. 22.95 (*0-275-93726-7*, B3726, Praeger Pubs) Greenwood.

On Disarmament: The Role of Conventional Arms Control in National Security Strategy. David E. Shaver & Ralph A. Hallenbeck. LC 90-44146. 248p. 1991. 65.00 (*0-275-93717-8*, C3717, Praeger Pubs) Greenwood.

***On Display: 25 Themes to Promote Reading.** Gayle Skaggs. LC 98-54964. (Illus.). 168p. 1999. pap. 27.50 (*0-7864-0657-7*) McFarland & Co.

On Distant Ground. Robert Olen Butler. 1995. 25.00 (*0-8050-3198-7*); pap. 11.00 (*0-8050-3140-5*, Owl) H Holt & Co.

On Distant Shores. Barbara Novak. LC 94-71401. 40p. (Orig.). 1994. pap. text. write for info. (*1-885206-01-1*, Iliad Pr) Cader Pubng.

On Distant Shores: Colonial Houses Around the World. Ovidio Guaita. LC 99-39552. (Illus.). 368p. 1999. text 60.00 (*1-58093-051-4*, Pub. by Monacelli Pr) Penguin Putnam.

On Distribution & Continuity of Water Substance in Atmospheric Circulation. Edwin Kessler. (Meteorological Monograph Ser.: Vol. 10, No. 32). (Illus.). 84p. 1969. 23.00 (*0-933876-30-0*) Am Meteorological.

On Divers Arts: The Foremost Medieval Treatise on Painting, Glassmaking, & Metalwork. Theophilus of Antioch. Tr. by Cyril S. Smith & John G. Hawthorne from LAT. (Illus.). 216p. 1979. pap. text 9.95 (*0-486-23784-2*) Dover.

On Divination & Synchronicity. Marie-Louise Von Franz. (Illus.). 128p. 1980. pap. 16.00 (*0-919123-02-3*, Pub. by Inner City Bks) BookWorld.

On Divine Foreknowledge: "Concordia", Pt. IV. Luis De Molina. LC 88-3887. 320p. 1988. text 45.00 (*0-8014-2131-4*) Cornell U Pr.

On Divine Predicates. A. R. Zayd. 1994. 12.50 (*1-56744-172-6*) Kazi Pubns.

On Divorce. Louis De Bonald. Tr. by Nicholas Davidson. 120p. (C). 1991. text 34.95 (*0-88738-439-0*) Transaction Pubs.

On Divorce. Sara B. Stein. (Open Family Ser.). (Illus.). 48p. (J). 1979. 10.95 (*0-8027-6344-8*) Walker & Co.

On Divorce. Sara B. Stein. LC 78-15687. (Open Family Ser.). (Illus.). 48p. (J). (ps-8). 1984. pap. 4.95 (*0-8027-7226-9*) Walker & Co.

On Divorce: A Guide to Illinois Matrimonial Law, 2 Vols. 2nd ed. H. Joseph Gitlin. 185.00 (*0-327-12424-5*) LEXIS Pub.

***On Dobrushin's Way: From Probability Theory to Statistical Physics.** Ed. by R. A. Minlos et al. LC 91-640741. (TRANS2 Ser.: Vol. 198). 243p. 2000. 99.00 (*0-8218-2150-4*) Am Math.

On Doctoral Education in Nursing: The Voice of the Student. Dona R. Carpenter & Sharon Hudacek. 1996. 27.95 (*0-88737-670-3*) Natl League Nurse.

On Doctoring: Stories, Poems, Essays. rev. expanded ed. Richard Reynolds. 448p. 1995. 29.50 (*0-684-80255-4*) S&S Trade.

On Doing Local History: Reflections on What Local Historians Do, Why & What It Means. Carol Kammen. LC 95-46414. (American Association for State & Local History Book Ser.). 192p. 1986. reprint ed. pap. 21.95 (*0-7619-9137-9*) AltaMira Pr.

On Doing the Right Thing & Other Essays. Albert J. Nock. LC 76-128282. (Essay Index Reprint Ser.). 1977. 23.95 (*0-8369-2006-6*) Ayer.

On down the Trail. Tina Knight. LC 96-104781. 217p. (Orig.). 1995. pap. 9.95 (*1-883893-14-3*) WinePress Pub.

***On Drag Hunting.** Strawson. 2000. 50.00 (*0-85131-757-X*, Pub. by J A Allen) Trafalgar.

On Drawing. Roger Winter. (Illus.). 142p. (C). 1997. pap. text 24.75 (*0-939693-42-9*) Collegiate Pr.

On Drawing & Painting. D. W. Ross. LC 78-137285. (Illus.). reprint ed. 44.50 (*0-404-05406-4*) AMS Pr.

On Dreams. Sigmund Freud. 1976. 29.95 (*0-8488-1330-8*) Amereon Ltd.

On Dreams. Sigmund Freud. Ed. by James Strachey. 1990. pap. 8.95 (*0-393-00144-X*) Norton.

On Dreams. Sigmund Freud. 1989. reprint ed. lib. bdg. 28.95 (*0-89966-633-7*) Buccaneer Bks.

On Dreams & Death. Marie Louise Von Franz. 1986. 17.95 (*0-394-55249-0*) Random.

On Dreams & Death: A Jungian Interpretation. 2nd rev. ed. Marie-Louise Von Franz. Tr. by Emmanuel Kennedy-Xypolitas & Vernon Brooks. LC 97-37852. 216p. (C). 1997. pap. 18.95 (*0-8126-9367-1*) Open Court.

On Drugs. David Lenson. 256p. 1995. 29.95 (*0-8166-2710-X*) U of Minn Pr.

On Dryden's Relation to Germany. M. Baumgartner. (Studies in Dryden: No. 10). 1979. pap. 29.95 (*0-8383-0084-7*) M S G Haskell Hse.

On Durkheim's Elementary Forms of Religious Life. N. J. Allen et al. LC 97-29595. (Studies in Social & Political Thought). 240p. (C). 1998. 85.00 (*0-415-16286-6*) Routledge.

On Durkheim's Rules of Sociological Method. Mike Gane. 224p. 1989. 52.50 (*0-415-00251-6*, A1941) Routledge.

On Duties see Selected Works

On Duty: A Canadian at the Making of the United Nations, 1945 to 1946. Escott Reid. LC 83-12021. 203p. reprint ed. pap. 63.00 (*0-7837-1342-8*, 204149000020) Bks Demand.

On Duty: A Nurse's Notes on Life & Death. Carolyn P. Fink. 1996. mass mkt. 5.99 (*0-449-14965-X*) Fawcett.

On Duty Vol. 2: Interviews with Military Veterans from North of Quabbin. Alan W. Bowers. LC 94-78652. (Illus.). 120p. (Orig.). 1995. pap. 9.95 (*1-884540-10-4*) Haleys.

On Duty Vol. 3: Interviews with Military Veterans from North of Quabbin. Alan W. Bowers. LC 95-78652. (Illus.). 220p. (Orig.). 1995. pap. 19.95 (*1-884540-14-7*) Haleys.

On Duty in Bangladesh: The Story the Newspapers Didn't Publish... 2nd ed. Jeannie Lockerbie. LC 72-95513. (Illus.). 191p. (Orig.). 1980. reprint ed. pap. text 6.95 (*1-888796-01-4*) ABWE Pubng.

On Duty, Multi-Volume: Interviews with Military Veterans from North of Quabbin. Alan W. Bowers. LC 94-78649. (Illus.). 112p. (Orig.). 1994. pap. 9.95 (*1-884540-08-2*) Haleys.

***On 'E' Ecstasy.** Push & Mireille Silcott. 200p. 1999. 19.95 (*0-7119-7519-1*) Omnibus NY.

On Eagle's Wings see Con Alas de Aquila

On Eagle's Wings. E. Charlotte Baker. 154p. 1990. 9.99 (*1-56043-853-3*) Destiny Image.

On Eagles' Wings. Marsha Driscoll. LC 97-94014. 192p. 1997. 18.95 (*0-8034-9252-9*, Avalon Bks) Bouregy.

On Eagle's Wings. Lord Exeter. 186p. (Orig.). 1987. pap. 4.95 (*0-8467-0324-6*, B9) Foundation Hse.

On Eagle's Wings. Tina Scarpitti. 1998. pap. write for info. (*1-57553-767-2*) Watermrk Pr.

On Eagle's Wings. David R. Veerman. LC 95-7998. 128p. 1995. 12.99 (*0-8423-4589-2*) Tyndale Hse.

On Eagle's Wings: A Practical Guide for the Care of Terminally Ill Loved Ones. Connie C. Bobo. LC 98-93065. (Illus.). 136p. 1998. pap. 19.95 (*0-9665418-0-4*) Freefall Fact.

On Eagles' Wings: How to Let Jesus Bear Your Burdens. Randy Maxwell. Ed. by Ken McFarland. LC 85-17036. (Illus.). 64p. 1986. pap. 4.99 (*0-8163-1345-8*) Pacific Pr Pub Assn.

On Early English Pronounciation of the Thirteenth & Previous Centuries of Anglosaxon, Icelandic, Old Norse & Gothic, Pt. 2. Alexander J. Ellis. (EETS, ES Ser.: No. 7). 1974. reprint ed. 36.00 (*0-527-00214-3*) Periodicals Srv.

On Early English Pronunciation, with Especial Reference to Shakespeare & Chaucer, 6 vols., Set. Alexander J. Ellis. LC 68-24964. (Studies in Language: No. 41). 1969. reprint ed. lib. bdg. 250.00 (*0-8383-0158-4*) M S G Haskell Hse.

On Early Female Novelists. Alexander M. Williams. LC 76-152408. (English Literature Ser.: No. 33). 1971. reprint ed. lib. bdg. 75.00 (*0-8383-1231-4*) M S G Haskell Hse.

***On Earth & in the Cosmos.** 2nd ed. Geoffrey L. Zubay. (ORIGINS OF LIFE SER). 544p. 1999. 59.95 (*0-12-781910-X*) Morgan Kaufmann.

On Earth As in Heaven: A Liberation Spirituality of Sharing. Dorothee Soelle. Tr. by Marc Batko. LC 93-1314. 96p. (Orig.). 1993. pap. 12.95 (*0-664-25494-2*) Westminster John Knox.

On Earth As in Heaven: Justice Rooted in Spirituality. Arthur P. Boers. LC 90-85237. 216p. (Orig.). 1991. pap. 10.99 (*0-8361-3545-8*) Herald Pr.

On Earth As It Is. Steven Heighton. LC 95-190465. 240p. 1995. pap. write for info. (*0-88984-151-9*) Porcup Quill.

On Earth As It Is in Heaven. Gregg Finley & Lynn Wigginton. (Illus.). 240p. 1995. pap. 34.95 (*0-86492-175-6*, Pub. by Goose Ln Edits) Genl Dist Srvs.

On Earth As It Is in Heaven. Stephen Hill. 136p. (Orig.). 1993. pap. 8.99 (*1-56043-797-9*, Treasure Hse) Destiny Image.

On Earth As It Is in Heaven. Jeffrey R. Holland & Patricia T. Holland. LC 89-17092. xi, 221p. 1989. 10.95 (*0-87579-186-7*) Deseret Bk.

On Earth As It Is in Heaven. Jeffrey R. Holland & Patricia T. Holland. LC 89-17092. xi, 221p. 1994. pap. 7.95 (*0-87579-839-X*) Deseret Bk.

On Earth... As It Is in Heaven. Daniel Neusom. Ed. by Bob Cecilio. 190p. 1999. pap. 15.00 (*0-9664226-1-9*) Oneness Pr.

On Earth as It Is in Heaven. N. A. Noel & John W. Sisson. (Illus.). 32p. (J). (gr. k-8). 1999. 19.95 (*0-9652531-3-9*) Noel Studio.

On Earth As It Is in Heaven: A Classic Bible Reading Guide. Stephen L. Hill. 125p. 1993. pap. 4.99 (*0-9637090-0-3*) Togthr Hrvest.

On Earth As It Is in Heaven: Jews, Christians, & Liberation Theology. Dan Cohn-Sherbok. LC 86-23509. 144p. (Orig.). reprint ed. pap. 44.70 (*0-7837-5507-4*, 204527700005) Bks Demand.

On Earth As It Is in Heaven: Temple Symbolism in the New Testament. Margaret Barker. 112p. 1996. pap. 19.95 (*0-567-29278-9*, Pub. by T & T Clark) Bks Intl VA.

***On Earth As It Is in Heaven: The Church in Modern Latin America** Virginia Garrard-Burnett. LC 99-32335. (Jaguar Bks. on Latin America). 1999. write for info. (*0-8420-2585-5*) Scholarly Res Inc.

On Earth Peace. Ed. by Donald F. Durnbaugh. 412p. 1978. pap. 9.95 (*0-87178-660-5*, 8605) Brethren.

On Ecclesiastical Power: De Ecclesiastica Potestate. Aegidius. Tr. by Arthur Monahan from LAT. LC 89-35825. (Texts & Studies in Religion: Vol. 41). 340p. 1990. lib. bdg. 99.95 (*0-88946-830-3*) E Mellen.

On Ecology. While H. Whyte. 1995. 19.95 (*0-8050-3303-3*) H Holt & Co.

***On Economic Inequality.** Amartya Kumar Sen & James E. Foster. LC 98-907628. 1998. write for info. (*0-19-564734-3*) OUP.

On Economic Inequality. 2nd ed. Amartya Sen. LC 97-150339. (Illus.). 280p. 1997. pap. text 18.95 (*0-19-828193-5*) OUP.

On Economic Inequality. 2nd ed. Amartya Sen. LC 97-150339. (Illus.). 274p. 1997. text 60.00 (*0-19-829297-X*) OUP.

On Economic Institutions: Theory & Applications. Ed. by John Groenewegen et al. LC 94-43573. 256p. 1995. 90.00 (*1-85898-142-5*) E Elgar.

On Economic Knowledge: Toward a Science of Political Economics. enl. ed. Adolph Lowe. LC 83-649. 365p. 1983. reprint ed. pap. 113.20 (*0-7837-9947-0*, 206067400006) Bks Demand.

On Economics & Society: Selected Essays. Harry G. Johnson. LC 74-11625. (Phoenix Ser.). xii, 368p. 1982. pap. text 14.50 (*0-226-40163-4*) U Ch Pr.

On Economizing the Theory of A-Bar Dependencies. Wei-Tien D. Tsai. LC 98-51530. (Outstanding Dissertations in Linguistics Ser.). 222p. 1999. 53.00 (*0-8153-3299-8*) Garland.

On Edge. Ermellia Williams-Kelly. 316p. (Orig.). 1997. pap. 12.95 (*1-57502-405-5*, PO1262) Morris Pubng.

***On Edge.** 2nd rev. ed. Meme Kelly. 312p. 1998. pap. 12.95 (*0-9673602-0-X*, 602-0, Pub. by Mount Top) Cultre Plus Bks.

On Edge: Breaking the Boundaries of Graphic Design. Karen D. Fishler. (Illus.). 192p. 1998. pap. 40.00 (*1-56496-454-X*) Rockport Pubs.

On Edge: International Banking & Country Risk. Ellen S. Goldberg & Dan Haendel. LC 86-25324. 126p. 1987. 49.95 (*0-275-92604-4*, C2604, Praeger Pubs) Greenwood.

On Edge: Performance at the End of the Twentieth Century. C. Carr. LC 93-8182. (Illus.). 357p. 1993. pap. 24.95 (*0-8195-6269-6*, Wesleyan Univ Pr) U Pr of New Eng.

On Edge: The Crisis of Contemporary Latin American Culture. Ed. by George Yudice et al. (Cultural Politics Ser.: Vol. 4). 280p. (C). 1992. pap. 18.95 (*0-8166-1939-5*) U of Minn Pr.

On Edge of Dreams. Jennifer Heath. LC 98-207365. 144p. 1998. pap. 11.95 (*0-452-27938-0*, Plume) Dutton Plume.

On Education. Jane Addams. LC 93-47022. 250p. (C). 1994. pap. 24.95 (*1-56000-734-6*) Transaction Pubs.

On Education. Sri Aurobindo & Mother. 168p. 1986. pap. 4.95 (*81-7058-028-5*, Pub. by SAA) E-W Cultural Ctr.

On Education. Rhodes Boyson. 224p. 1996. pap. write for info. (*0-7206-1016-8*, Pub. by P Owen Ltd) Dufour.

On Education. Rhodes Boyson. 128p. 1996. pap. 27.95 (*0-7206-1019-2*, Pub. by P Owen Ltd) Dufour.

On Education: Articles on Educational Theory & Pedagogy, & Writings for Children from the Age of Gold. Jose Marti. Ed. by Philip Foner. Tr. by Elinor Randall. LC 79-2326. 320p. 1979. pap. 12.00 (*0-85345-565-1*, Pub. by Monthly Rev) NYU Pr.

On Educational Testing. Ed. by Scarvia B. Anderson & John S. Helmick. LC 83-48155. (Jossey-Bass Social & Behavioral Science Ser.). 311p. reprint ed. pap. 96.50 (*0-7837-0161-6*, 204045800017) Bks Demand.

On Efficient Causality: Metaphysical Disputations 17-19. Francisco Suarez. Tr. by Alfred J. Freddoso. LC 94-12480. (Yale Library of Medieval Philosophy). 416p. 1995. 50.00 (*0-300-06007-6*) Yale U Pr.

On Einstein's Path: Essays in Honor of Engelbert Schucking. Ed. by A. Harvey. (Illus.). 528p. 1998. 79.95 (*0-387-98564-6*) Spr-Verlag.

On Emerson. Ed. by Edwin H. Cady & Louis J. Budd. LC 88-3750. (Best from American Literature Ser.). 296p. 1988. text 49.95 (*0-8223-0861-4*) Duke.

On Emerson & Other Essays. Maurice Maeterlinck. Tr. by Montrose J. Moses from FRE. LC 78-58262. (Essay Index in Reprint Ser.). 1978. reprint ed. 25.00 (*0-8486-3024-6*) Roth Pub Inc.

On Empathy. Bornstein & Silver. (Psychoanalytic Inquiry Book Ser.: Vol. 1, No. 3). 1994. 20.00 (*0-88163-989-3*) Analytic Pr.

On Emphasis & Word Order in Hungarian. Ferenc Kiefer. LC 66-64930. (Uralic & Altaic Ser.: Vol. 76). 243p. 1967. pap. text. write for info. (*0-87750-027-4*) Curzon Pr Ltd.

***On Empire, Liberty & Reform.** Edmund Burke & David Bromwich. LC 99-45105. (Lewis Walpole Series in 18th Century Culture & History). 416p. 2000. 40.00 (*0-300-08146-4*) Yale U Pr.

***On Empire, Liberty & Reform: Speeches & Letters.** Edmund Burke. 416p. 2000. pap. 15.00 (*0-300-08147-2*) Yale U Pr.

On England, & Other Addresses. Stanley Baldwin. LC 70-156609. (Essay Index Reprint Ser.). 1977. reprint ed. 23.95 (*0-8369-2305-7*) Ayer.

On English Costume. Mary Kelly. LC 98-44797. (Illus.). 64p. (Orig.). 1994. pap. 6.00 (*0-88734-910-2*) Empire Pub Srvs.

On English Homophones see Preliminary Announcement

On English Poetry: Being an Irregular Approach to the Psychology of This Art from Evidence Mainly Subjective. Robert Graves. LC 78-185878. (English Literature Ser.: No. 33). 159p. (C). 1972. reprint ed. lib. bdg. 75.00 (*0-8383-1386-8*) M S G Haskell Hse.

On English Poetry: Being an Irregular Approach to the Psychology of This Art from Evidence Mainly Subjective. Robert Graves. (BCL1-PR English Literature Ser.). 149p. 1992. reprint ed. lib. bdg. 69.00 (*0-7812-7064-2*) Rprt Serv.

On English Prose. James R. Sutherland. LC 85-30565. 131p. 1986. reprint ed. lib. bdg. 59.50 (*0-313-25095-2*, SUEN, Greenwood Pr) Greenwood.

On Entering the Sea: The Erotic & Other Poetry of Nizar Qabbani. Nizar Qabbani. Tr. by Lena Jayyusi et al from ARA. 208p. 1996. 22.95 (*1-56656-186-8*) Interlink Pub.

On Entering the Sea: The Erotic & Other Poetry of Nizar Qabbani. Nizar Qabbani. Tr. by Lena Jayyusi et al from ARA. 184p. 1996. pap. 15.00 (*1-56656-193-0*) Interlink Pub.

On Equal Terms. Catherine O'Connor. (Presents Ser.: No. 94). 1998. pap. 3.75 (*0-373-18694-0*, 1-18694-9) Harlequin Bks.

On Equal Terms: A Thesaurus for Nonsexist Indexing & Cataloging. Joan K. Marshall. LC 77-8987. 152p. 1977. 35.00 (*0-918212-02-2*) Neal-Schuman.

On Equal Terms: The Social Integration of Handicapped Persons in Canada: A Challenge for Everyone. Ed. by Denis Lazure. (Illus.). 328p. 1999. reprint ed. pap. text 40.00 (*0-7881-8017-7*) DIANE Pub.

On Equal Terms: Working with Disabled People. Sally French. LC 94-3718. 280p. 1996. pap. text 32.00 (*0-7506-0751-3*) Buttrwrth-Heinemann.

On Equality. Meghnad Desai & London School of Economics & Political Science Dep. LC 97-3858. 308p. 1997. pap. text 24.95 (*1-56000-979-9*) Transaction Pubs.

On Errors in Surveys. W. Edwards Deming. (Reprint Series in Social Sciences). (C). 1993. reprint ed. pap. text 5.00 (*0-8290-3430-7*, S-373) Irvington.

On Escalation: Metaphors & Scenarios. Herman Kahn. LC 86-336. 326p. 1986. reprint ed. lib. bdg. 75.00 (*0-313-25163-0*, KAES, Greenwood Pr) Greenwood.

On Essence. Xavier Zubiri. LC 78-68067. 529p. reprint ed. pap. 164.00 (*0-608-18731-3*, 202951400061) Bks Demand.

On Est Toujours Trop Bon avec les Femmes. Raymond Queneau. (FRE.). 1981. pap. 10.95 (*0-8288-3773-2*) Fr & Eur.

On Est Toujours Trop Bon avec les Femmes: Un Roman Irlandais De Sally Mara. Raymond Queneau. (Folio Ser.: No. 1312). (FRE.). 200p. 1971. pap. 8.95 (*2-07-037312-6*) Schoenhof.

On Ethics & Economics. Amartya K. Sen. 128p. 1989. pap. text 28.95 (*0-631-16401-4*) Blackwell Pubs.

On Evangelization in the Modern World. Paul, VI, pseud. 62p. 1976. pap. text 2.50 (*0-8198-2325-2*) Pauline Bks.

On Evangelization in the Modern World. Paul, VI, pseud. 70p. 1975. pap. 4.95 (*1-55586-129-6*) US Catholic.

On Every Front: The Making & Unmaking of the Cold War. 2nd ed. Thomas G. Paterson. (C). 1993. pap. text 11.00 (*0-393-96435-3*, Norton Paperbks) Norton.

On Every Front: The Making & Unmaking of the Cold War. 2nd rev. ed. Thomas G. Paterson. 256p. 1992. 24.95 (*0-393-03060-1*) Norton.

On Everything. Hilaire Belloc. LC 70-128208. (Essay Index Reprint Ser.). 1977. 21.95 (*0-8369-1865-7*) Ayer.

On Evil. Aquinas, Thomas, Saint. Tr. by John A. Oesterle from LAT. LC 94-44961. (C). 1995. text 49.95 (*0-268-03700-0*) U of Notre Dame Pr.

On Evil Spirits. Lazar Puhalo. 28p. Date not set. pap. 4.00 (*1-879038-61-7*, 9031) Synaxis Pr.

On Evolution: The Development of the Theory of Natural Selection. Charles Darwin. Ed. by Thomas F. Glick & David Kohn. LC 96-9388. (HPC Classics Ser.). 416p. 1996. pap. text 12.95 (*0-87220-285-2*) Hackett Pub.

On Evolution: The Development of the Theory of Natural Selection. Charles Darwin. Ed. by Thomas F. Glick et al. LC 96-9388. (HPC Classics Ser.). 416p. 1996. lib. bdg. 37.95 (*0-87220-286-0*) Hackett Pub.

On Evolution & Fossil Mammals. Bjorn Kurten. LC 86-32630. 304p. 1988. text 68.50 (*0-231-05868-3*) Col U Pr.

On Evolutionary Anthropology: In Honor of Harry Hoijer 1983. L. L. Cavalli-Sforza et al. LC 85-51127. (Other Realities Ser.: Vol 7). 104p. 1986. 26.00 (*0-89003-170-3*); pap. 16.00 (*0-89003-171-1*) Undena Pubns.

On Exchange Rates. Jeffrey A. Frankel. LC 92-40156. (Illus.). 350p. 1993. 55.00 (*0-262-06154-6*) MIT Pr.

***On Exhibit: Victorians & Their Museums.** Barbara J. Black. LC 99-16415. (Victorian Literature & Culture Ser.). 256p. 2000. 37.50 (*0-8139-1897-9*) U Pr of Va.

On Exhibit, 1999: Art Lover's Travel Guide to American Museums. Patti Sowalsky & Judith Swirsky. (Illus.). 448p. 1998. pap. 24.95 (*0-7892-0454-1*) Abbeville Pr.

On Exhibit, 1997: The Art Lover's Travel Guide to American Museums. 5th rev. ed. Patti L. Sowalsky & Judith Swirsky. 512p. (Orig.). 1997. pap. 19.95 (*0-9633650-5-3*) On Exhib Fine Art.

On Exhibit 2000: Art Lover's Travel Guide to American Museums. Judith Swirsky. 448p. 1999. pap. 17.95 (*0-7892-0532-7*) Abbeville Pr.

***On Exhibition.** Dale Forbes. LC 00-190406. 243p. 2000. 25.00 (*0-7388-1653-1*); pap. 18.00 (*0-7388-1654-X*) Xlibris Corp.

On Existential Psychotherapy. Norton Staff. 0.00 (*0-393-01725-7*) Norton.

On Explaining Language Change. Roger Lass. LC 79-51825. (Cambridge Studies in Linguistics: No. 27). 200p. reprint ed. pap. 57.00 (*0-608-12082-0*, 2024580) Bks Demand.

An Asterisk (*) at the beginning of an entry indicates that the title is appearing for the first time.

***On Exponential Functionals of Brownian Motion & Related Processes.** M. Yor. (Finance Ser.). 160p. 2000. pap. 49.95 (*3-540-65943-9*) Spr-Verlag.

On Expressive Language. Ed. by Heinz Werner. LC 55-4041. (Monographs in Psychology & Related Disciplines: No. 1). 81p. 1955. pap. 6.00 (*0-914206-02-8*) Clark U Pr.

On Extended Wings: Wallace Stevens' Longer Poems. Helen H. Vendler. LC 70-82299. 334p. (C). 1969. pap. 17.50 (*0-674-63436-5*) HUP.

On Extraction & Extraposition in German. Ed. by Uli Lutz & Jurgen Pafel. LC 95-51022. (Linquistik Aktuell/Linguistics Today Ser.: No. 11). xii, 315p. 1996. lib. bdg. 74.00 (*1-55619-229-0*) J Benjamins Pubng Co.

On F. R. Scott: Essays on His Contributions to Law, Literature, & Politics. Ed. by Sandra Djwa & R. St. J. Macdonald. 256p. 1983. pap. 24.95 (*0-7735-0398-6*, Pub. by McG-Queens Univ Pr) CUP Services.

On F. R. Scott: Essays on His Contributions to Law, Literature, & Politics. Ed. by Sandra Djwa & R. S. Macdonald. LC 84-171017. 225p. reprint ed. pap. 69.80 (*0-7837-1155-7*, 204168400022) Bks Demand.

***On Fairness.** 148p. 2000. 59.95 (*0-7546-1298-8*, Pub. by Ashgate Pub) Ashgate Pub Co.

On Faith. Philip Berman. 1999. write for info. (*0-671-00161-2*) S&S Trade.

On Faith. Philip Berman. 1999. pap. write for info. (*0-671-00162-0*) S&S Trade.

On Faith. Rotenstreich. LC 97-40092. 192p. 1998. lib. bdg. 35.00 (*0-226-72875-7*) U Ch Pr.

On Faith. Nathan Rotenstreich & Paul R. Mendes-Flohr. LC 97-40092. 192p. 1998. pap. text 15.00 (*0-226-72876-5*) U Ch Pr.

On Faith & Free Government. Ed. by Daniel C. Palm. LC 97-18641. 215p. 1997. 60.50 (*0-8476-8602-7*); pap. 24.95 (*0-8476-8603-5*) Rowman.

On Faith & Reason. Aquinas, Thomas, Saint. Ed. & Intro. by Stephen F. Brown. LC 98-50833. 320p. (C). 1999. pap. 10.95 (*0-87220-456-1*); lib. bdg. 34.95 (*0-87220-457-X*) Hackett Pub.

On Faith & Works. Augustine, Saint. Tr. by Gregory J. Lombardo. (Ancient Christian Writers Ser.: No. 48). 128p. 1988. 14.95 (*0-8091-0406-7*) Paulist Pr.

On Familiar Terms: A Journey Across Cultures. Donald Keene. Ed. by John Urda. LC 93-28224. 296p. 1994. 23.00 (*1-56836-006-1*) Kodansha.

***On Familiar Terms: A Journey Across Cultures.** Donald Keene. 292p. 1999. reprint ed. 23.00 (*0-7881-6415-5*) DIANE Pub.

On Familiar Terms: To Japan & Back, a Lifetime Across Cultures. Donald Keene. Ed. by Joshua Sitzer. (Illus.). 304p. 1996. pap. 14.00 (*1-56836-129-7*, Kodansha Globe) Kodansha.

On Families & the Re-Valuing of Childhood. Warren Umamsky. 8p. 1983. pap. 1.50 (*0-87173-103-7*) ACEI.

On-Farm Composting Handbook. Robert Rynk et al. (Illus.). 186p. 1992. pap. text 20.00 (*0-935817-19-0*, NRAES-54) NRAES.

On-Farm Drying & Storage Systems. Otto Loewer et al. LC 94-72087. 576p. 1994. 68.00 (*0-929355-53-9*) Am Soc Ag Eng.

On-Farm Research: An Annotated Bibliography. N. Clinch. 127p. 1994. pap. 45.00 (*0-85954-371-4*, Pub. by Nat Res Inst) St Mut.

On-Farm Research Techniques: Report on a Workshop, St. Paul, Minnesota, November 15-16, 1990. unabridged ed. Molly D. Anderson & William Lockeretz. (Occasional Paper Ser.: No. 1). 18p. 1991. pap. 7.00 (*1-893182-11-8*) H A Wallace Inst.

On Farming. Cato. LC 99-177125. (Illus.). 243p. 1998. pap. 24.00 (*0-907325-80-7*) Food Words.

On Farts. Cannum. (Illus.). 8p. 1979. pap. 0.95 (*0-89708-002-5*) And Bks.

On Fashion. Ed. by Shari Benstock & Suzanne Ferriss. LC 93-13886. (Illus.). 320p. (C). 1994. text 45.00 (*0-8135-2032-0*); pap. text 19.00 (*0-8135-2033-9*) Rutgers U Pr.

On Fasting. Lazar Puhalo. 36p. Date not set. pap. 5.00 (*1-879038-59-5*, 9029) Synaxis Pr.

On Faulkner: The Best from American Literature. Ed. by Louis J. Budd & Edwin H. Cady. LC 89-30913. 288p. (C). 1989. text 49.95 (*0-8223-0960-2*) Duke.

On Fear. Jiddu Krishnamurti. LC 94-19322. 144p. 1994. pap. 12.00 (*0-06-251014-2*, Pub. by Harper SF) HarpC.

On Feeling, Knowing, & Valuing: Selected Writings. Max Ferdinand Scheler. LC 92-2976. (Heritage of Sociology Ser.). 278p. 1992. pap. text 17.95 (*0-226-73671-7*) U Ch Pr.

On Feeling, Knowing, & Valuing: Selected Writings. Max Ferdinand Scheler. LC 92-2976. (Heritage of Sociology Ser.). 278p. 1992. lib. bdg. 47.50 (*0-226-73670-9*) U Ch Pr.

On Feet of Gold. Ira Cohen. (Illus.). 148p. 1986. pap. 7.95 (*0-907791-10-7*) Synerg CA.

On Feminine Sexuality, the Limits of Love & Knowledge. Jacques Lacan. 160p. 1999. pap. 15.95 (*0-393-31916-4*) Norton.

On Feminine Sexuality, the Limits of Love & Knowledge, Vol. 20. Ed. by Jacques-Alain Miller. Tr. by Bruce Fink. LC 97-43225. (The Seminar of Jacques Lacan Ser.). 192p. 1998. 30.00 (*0-393-04573-0*) Norton.

On Feminist Ethics & Politics. Claudia Card. LC 99-11259. (Feminist Ethics Ser.). 368p. 1999. pap. 19.95 (*0-7006-0968-7*) U Pr of KS.

***On Feminist Ethics & Politics.** Ed. by Claudia Card. LC 99-11259. (Feminist Ethics Ser.). 368p. 1999. 45.00 (*0-7006-0967-9*) U Pr of KS.

On Fencing. Aldo Nadi. LC 93-80473. (Illus.). 300p. 1994. reprint ed. pap. 19.95 (*1-884528-04-X*) Laureate Pr.

On Feuerstein's Instrumental Enrichment: A Collection. Ed. by Meir Ben-Hur. LC 94-78544. 284p. 1994. pap. 24.95 (*0-932935-76-1*) SkyLght.

On Field Evaluation & Treatment of Sport Injuries. James R. Andrews. Ed. by William G. Clancy. LC 96-49798. (Illus.). 288p. (C). (gr. 13). 1997. pap. text 32.95 (*0-8151-0218-6*, 24095) Mosby Inc.

On Fifth Avenue: Then & Now. Ronda Wist. (Illus.). 256p. 1992. 25.00 (*1-55972-155-3*, Birch Ln Pr) Carol Pub Group.

On Fighting a Nuclear War. Michael E. Howard. (CISA Working Papers: No. 31). 45p. (Orig.). 1981. pap. 15.00 (*0-86682-030-2*) Ctr Intl Relations.

On Film Editing. Edward Dmytryk. 148p. (C). 1984. pap. 27.95 (*0-240-51738-5*, Focal) Buttrwrth-Heinemann.

On Final Approach: The Women Airforce Service Pilots of World War II. Claudia M. Oakes. LC 90-82246. (Illus.). 710p. 1991. 39.95 (*0-9626267-0-8*) Falconer Pub.

On Financial Reform. 3rd ed. Henry B. Congleton. LC 68-56560. (Library of Money & Banking History). viii, 383p. 1968. reprint ed. 49.50 (*0-678-00452-8*) Kelley.

On Finite Groups & Homotopy Theory. Ran Levi. LC 95-34452. (Memoirs of the American Mathematical Society Ser.: No. 567). 100p. 1995. pap. 35.00 (*0-8218-0401-4*, MEMO/118/567) Am Math.

On Finite Rank Operators & Preannihilators. Edward A. Azoff. LC 86-22274. (Memoirs of the American Mathematical Society Ser.: No. 64/357). 85p. 1986. pap. 18.00 (*0-8218-2419-8*, MEMO/64/357) Am Math.

On Fire. Larry Brown. 192p. 1995. mass mkt. 12.99 (*0-446-67114-2*, Pub. by Warner Bks) Little.

On Fire. Carla Neggers. 384p. 1999. per. 5.99 (*1-55166-541-7*, 1-66541-3, Mira Bks) Harlequin Bks.

On Fire. Ouida Sebestyen. 208p. (J). (gr. 6 up). 1985. 12.95 (*0-87113-010-6*, Joy St Bks) Little.

***On Fire, Vol. 1.** (Encanto Ser.). 1999. mass mkt. 5.99 (*0-7860-1029-0*) Kensgtn Pub Corp.

On Fire for Christ: Stories of Anabaptist Martyrs Retold from Martyrs Mirror. Dave Jackson & Neta Jackson. LC 89-32711. (Illus.). 184p. 1989. pap. 10.99 (*0-8361-3503-2*) Herald Pr.

On Fire for God: Great Missionary Pioneers. John Pollock. 173p. (Orig.). 1995. reprint ed. mass mkt. 5.99 (*1-884543-01-4*) O M Lit.

On Fire with Selling: A Rich Analysis of Sales Experiences Mixed with Amazing Real-Life Stories. Kenneth D. MacDonald. LC 94-30534. (Illus.). 80p. 1995. pap. 9.95 (*0-942963-54-7*) Distinctive Pub.

On Firm Foundation Grounded: The First Century of Concordia College, 1891-1991. Carroll Engelhardt. (Illus.). 416p. 1991. 24.95 (*0-9630111-0-3*) Concordia Coll.

On First Looking into Arden's Goethe: Adaptations & Translations of German Plays for the Modern English Stage. Ewald Mengel. (GERM Ser.). x, 198p. 1994. 60.00 (*1-879751-84-4*) Camden Hse.

On First Principles: Being Koetschau's Text of the De Principiis. Origen. Tr. by G. W. Butterworth. 1990. 27.00 (*0-8446-2685-6*) Peter Smith.

On First Reading: Ideas for Developing Reading Skills with Children from Four to Seven. Frances James & Ann Kerr. 1995. pap. 15.95 (*0-947882-24-3*) Incentive Pubns.

On Flatwillow Creek: The Story of Montana's N Bar Ranch. 2nd ed. Linda A. Grosskopf & Rick Newby. (Illus.). 392p. (Orig.). 1995. pap. 18.95 (*0-944882-21-X*) Except Bks NM.

On Flirtation. Adam Phillips. LC 94-18821. 256p. 1994. text 19.95 (*0-674-63437-3*, PHIFLI) HUP.

On Flirtation. Adam Phillips. 256p. 1996. pap. 14.00 (*0-674-63440-3*) HUP.

***On Fodor.** Preti & Velarde. 2000. pap. 8.25 (*0-534-58365-2*) Wadsworth Pub.

On Food & Cooking. Harold McGee. 1997. per. 21.00 (*0-684-84328-5*) S&S Trade.

On Food & Cooking: The Science & Lore of the Kitchen. Harold J. McGee. (Illus.). 672p. 1984. 45.00 (*0-684-18132-0*, Scribners Ref) Mac Lib Ref.

On Foot: A Journal for Walkers, Hikers & Trekkers. Illus. by Kurt Holloman. 128p. 1999. pap. 14.95 (*0-8118-2221-4*) Chronicle Bks.

On Foot & Finger. Jim Watson. (Illus.). 96p. 1989. pap. 3.95 (*0-938567-12-8*) Mountaineers.

On Foot in Arizona's Red Rock Country: Seven Spectacular Hikes with Interpretive Guide. 2nd rev. ed. Stephan M. Block. 24p. 1994. pap. text 3.95 (*0-9641888-0-5*) Kokopelli Pr.

On Foot in Joshua Tree National Park: A Comprehensive Hiking Guide. 4th ed. Patricia Furbush. Ed. by Jim Schlinkman. LC 95-69043. (Illus.). 164p. 1995. pap. text 10.95 (*0-9616395-7-1*) MI Adventure Pubns.

On Foot to the Golden Horn: A Walk to Istanbul. Jason Goodwin. LC 95-33659. 88p. 1995. pap. 16.95 (*0-8050-4082-X*, Owl) H Holt & Co.

***On Foot to the Golden Horn: A Walk to Istanbul.** Jason Goodwin. 2000. pap. 14.00 (*0-8050-6409-5*, Owl) H Holt & Co.

On Footings from the Past. Donna S. Packer. 1988. 19.95 (*0-88494-681-9*) Bookcraft Inc.

On Foreign Assignment: The Inside Story of Journalism's Elite Corps. Ab Douglas. (Illus.). 191p. (Orig.). 1993. pap. 17.95 (*1-55059-057-X*) Temeron Bks.

On Foreign Soil: Government Programs in U. S.-Mexico Relations. Beth Sims. LC 94-121498. 84p. 1994. pap. 9.95 (*0-911213-44-9*) Interhemisp Res Ctr.

On Formally Undecidable Propositions of Principia Mathematica & Related Systems. Kurt Godel. 80p. 1992. reprint ed. pap. 5.95 (*0-486-66980-7*) Dover.

On Fortune's Wheel. Cynthia Voigt. (Illus.). 304p. (J). (gr. 7). 1999. per. 5.50 (*0-689-82957-4*) Aladdin.

On Fortune's Wheel. Cynthia Voigt. LC 89-39010. 288p. (YA). (gr. 6 up). 1990. 17.00 (*0-689-31636-4*) Atheneum Yung Read.

On Fortune's Wheel. Cynthia Voigt. 304p. (YA). 1991. mass mkt. 4.50 (*0-449-70391-6*, Juniper) Fawcett.

On Fortune's Wheel. Cynthia Voigt. 1991. 9.60 (*0-606-01218-4*, Pub. by Turtleback) Demco.

***On Foster... Foster On.** Ed. by David Jenkins. (Illus.). 800p. 2000. 75.00 incl. cd-rom (*3-7913-2405-5*) Prestel Pub NY.

On Foucault. Alison Brown. (Wadsworth Notes Ser.). 1999. pap. text 13.95 (*0-534-57614-1*) Thomson Learn.

On Four Modern Humanists: Hofmannsthal, Gundolf, Curtius, Kantorowicz. Ed. by Arthur R. Evans, Jr. LC 76-90945. (Princeton Essays in European & Comparative Literature Ser.). 234p. 1970. reprint ed. pap. 72.60 (*0-608-03354-5*, 206406600008) Bks Demand.

On Fragile Wings: Stories of Hope from the Inner City. Doug Forsberg. (Illus.). 72p. 1995. pap. 6.99 (*0-8341-1553-0*) Beacon Hill.

On Free Choice see Selected Writings of St. Thomas Aquinas

On Free Choice of the Will. Augustine, Saint. Tr. & Intro. by Thomas Williams. LC 93-22170. (Hackett Classics Ser.).Tr. of De Libero Arbitrio. (ENG.). 192p. (C). 1993. pap. text 6.95 (*0-87220-188-0*); lib. bdg. 27.95 (*0-87220-189-9*) Hackett Pub.

On Free Choice of the Will: Augustine. A. Benjamin & L. H. Hackstaff. 208p. (C). 1964. pap. text 8.00 (*0-02-308030-2*, Macmillan Coll) P-H.

On Freedom. Eileen Barker. LC 97-3860. 357p. 1997. pap. text 24.95 (*1-56000-976-4*) Transaction Pubs.

On Freedom. Ed. by Leroy S. Rouner. LC 89-33164. (Boston University Studies in Philosophy & Religion: Vol. 10). (C). 1989. text 34.50 (*0-268-01502-3*) U of Notre Dame Pr.

On Freedom. Friedrich Daniel Ernst Schleiermacher. Tr. by Albert L. Blackwell. LC 92-24108. (Schleiermacher Studies & Translations: Vol. 9). 216p. 1992. text 89.95 (*0-7734-9583-5*) E Mellen.

On Freedom: Essays from the Frankfurt Economic Conference, 1982. Ed. by John A. Howard. 160p. 1984. 12.95 (*0-8159-5520-0*) Devin.

On Freedom & Free Enterprise: Essays in Honor of Ludwig von Mises. Ed. by Mary Sennholz. 346p. 1994. reprint ed. pap. 15.95 (*1-57246-025-3*) Foun Econ Ed.

On Freedom Street. Yesim Atil. 1991. 18.95 (*0-89924-076-3*); pap. 10.95 (*0-89924-075-5*) Lynx Hse.

On Freemasonry - Humanum Genus. Leo XIII, pseud. 32p. 1992. reprint ed. pap. 1.50 (*0-89555-171-3*) TAN Bks Pubs.

***On Frege.** Salerno. 2000. pap. 8.25 (*0-534-58367-9*) Wadsworth Pub.

***On Freud.** Michael S. Trupp. (Philosophers Ser.). 83p. 2000. 12.95 (*0-534-57618-4*) Wadsworth Pub.

On Freud's "A Child Is Being Beaten" Ethel S. Person et al. LC 97-8960. (Contemporary Freud). 1997. pap. write for info. (*0-300-07162-0*) Yale U Pr.

On Freud's "A Child Is Being Beaten" Ethel S. Person et al. LC 97-8960. (Contemporary Freud Turning Points & Critical Issues Ser.: Vol. 5). 256p. 1997. 25.00 (*0-300-07161-2*) Yale U Pr.

On Freud's "Analysis Terminable & Interminable" Ed. by Joseph Sandler. (Contemporary Freud: Turning Points & Critical Issues Ser.). 176p. (C). 1991. 32.00 (*0-300-04452-6*) Yale U Pr.

On Freud's Couch: Seven New Interpretations of Freud's Case Histories. Ed. by Irene Matthis & Imre Szecsody. LC 97-29931. (Illus.). 288p. 1998. 50.00 (*0-7657-0115-4*) Aronson.

On Freud's "Creative Writers & Day-Dreaming" Ed. by Ethel S. Person et al. LC 94-48270. (Contemporary Freud Ser.). 1995. 25.00 (*0-300-06266-4*) Yale U Pr.

On Freud's "Observations on Transference-Love" Ed. by Ethel S. Person et al. LC 92-41560. (Contemporary Freud Turning Points & Critical Issues Ser.). 202p. 1993. reprint ed. pap. 62.70 (*0-608-07844-1*, 205402000011) Bks Demand.

***On Friendship.** Ray Pahl. 2000. 56.95 (*0-7456-2280-1*, Pub. by Polity Pr); pap. 21.95 (*0-7456-2281-X*, Pub. by Polity Pr) Blackwell Pubs.

***On Friendship: A Book for Teenagers.** Kimberly Kirberger. (Teen Love Ser.). (Illus.). (J). 2000. pap. 12.95 (*1-55874-815-6*) Health Comm.

On Frost: The Best from American Literature. Ed. by Edwin H. Cady & Louis J. Budd. LC 91-7885. 271p. 1991. text 49.95 (*0-8223-1159-3*) Duke.

On Functions & Functional Equations. J. Smital. (Illus.). 164p. 1988. 62.00 (*0-85274-418-8*) IOP Pub.

On Fundamental Rights. Carol. (C). Date not set. write for info. (*0-8147-7994-8*) NYU Pr.

On Gadamer. Johnson. (Philosophy Ser.). 1999. pap. text 13.95 (*0-534-57598-6*) Brooks-Cole.

On Garden Style. Bunny Williams & Nancy Drew. LC 97-41699. 288p. 1998. 34.50 (*0-684-82605-4*) S&S Trade.

On Gardening. Storey. 1997. 40.00 (*0-676-57136-0*) Random.

On Gaza Beach. Ari Shavit. 1999. pap. 24.95 (*0-670-84965-0*) Viking Penguin.

On Gendering Texts: Female & Male Voices in the Hebrew Bible. Fokkelien Van Dijk-Hemmes & Athalya Brenner. LC 92-38412. (Biblical Interpretation Ser.: Vol. 1). xiii, 211p. 1993. 87.50 (*90-04-09642-6*) Brill Academic Pubs.

On Gendering Texts: Female & Male Voices in the Hebrew Bible. Athalya Brenner & Fokkelien Van Dijk-Hemmes. (Biblical Interpretation Ser.: Vol. I). xiv, 211p. 1996. reprint ed. pap. 39.50 (*90-04-10644-8*) Brill Academic Pubs.

On Generalized Surfaces of Finite Topological Types. L. C. Young. LC 52-42839. (Memoirs Ser.: No. 1/17). 63p. 1987. reprint ed. pap. 16.00 (*0-8218-1217-3*, MEMO/1/17) Am Math.

On Genesis: Two Books on Genesis Against the Manichees & on the Literal Interpretation of Genesis: An Unfinished Book. Augustine, Saint. Tr. by Roland J. Teske from LAT. LC 90-39711. (Fathers of the Church Ser.: Vol. 84). 198p. 1991. text 29.95 (*0-8132-0084-9*) Cath U Pr.

On Genius: Affirmation & Denial from Schopenhauer to Wittgenstein. Jerry S. Clegg. LC 93-48244. (American University Studies, V, Philosophy: Vol. 158). IX, 211p. (C). 1994. text 37.95 (*0-8204-2370-X*) P Lang Pubng.

On Geopolitics: Classical & Nuclear. Ed. by Ciro E. Zoppo & Charles Zorgbibe. 1984. lib. bdg. 160.50 (*90-247-3119-4*) Kluwer Academic.

On Germanic Linguistics: Issues & Methods. Ed. by Irmengard Rauch et al. LC 92-21566. (Trends in Linguistics, Studies & Monographs: No. 68). viii, 416p. (C). 1992. lib. bdg. 152.35 (*3-11-013000-9*) Mouton.

***On Getting a Moral Education.** Robert Lawrence Smith. 2001. write for info. (*0-688-17682-8*, Wm Morrow) Morrow Avon.

On Getting Old for the First Time. Peg Bracken. LC 96-85316. (Illus.). 192p. 1996. 14.95 (*1-885221-53-3*) BookPartners.

***On Giants' Shoulders: Great Scientists & Their Discoveries -- From Archimedes to DNA.** Melvyn Bragg. 2000. pap. 16.95 (*0-471-39684-2*) Wiley.

On Giant's Shoulders: Great Scientists & Their Discovers--From Architect. Bragg. LC 99-29005. 368p. 1999. 22.95 (*0-471-35732-4*) Wiley.

On Giving the Spiritual Exercises: The Early Jesuit Manuscript Directories & the Official Directory of 1599. Tr. by Martin E. Palmer from LAT. LC 95-81839. (Jesuit Primary Sources in English Translation Ser.: Series I, Vol. 14). viii, 363p. (Orig.). 1996. 42.95 (*1-880810-17-4*); pap. 34.95 (*1-880810-18-2*) Inst Jesuit.

On Glassy Wings. Anne Szumigalski. LC 98-111488. 264p. 1997. pap. 17.95 (*1-55050-114-3*, Pub. by Coteau) Genl Dist Srvs.

On Goaltending: Fundamentals of Netminding by the Master of the Game. 2nd ed. Jacques Plante. (Illus.). 144p. 1997. pap. 15.99 (*1-55207-003-4*, Pub. by R Davies Pub) Genl Dist Srvs.

On God. Jiddu Krishnamurti. LC 91-55329. 176p. 1992. pap. 13.00 (*0-06-250607-2*, Pub. by Harper SF) HarpC.

On God & Dogs: A Christian Theology of Compassion for Animals. Stephen H. Webb. LC 97-23342. 240p. (C). 1998. 32.00 (*0-19-511650-X*) OUP.

On God, Space, & Time. Akiva J. Vroman. LC 98-40493. 243p. 1998. 39.95 (*1-56000-397-9*) Transaction Pubs.

On Godel. Jaakko Hintikka. (Philosophy Ser.). 2000. pap. text 13.95 (*0-534-57595-1*) Brooks-Cole.

On God's Side: A Life of George Tyrrell. Nicholas Sagovsky. (Illus.). 288p. 1990. text 62.00 (*0-19-826728-2*) OUP.

On Going to Church see Modern Essays

On Going to Church. George Bernard Shaw. 24p. 1973. pap. 1.75 (*0-934676-13-5*) Greenlf Bks.

On Gold Mountain. Lisa See. 1996. pap. 14.00 (*0-679-76852-1*) Vin Bks.

On Golden Ground: Our Journey to the Eldorado. Lynette Clark & Dexter Clark. LC 97-70712. (Illus.). 160p. (Orig.). (J). 1997. pap. 13.95 (*0-9657676-0-4*) Larson & Larrigan.

O

On Golden Pond. Ernest Thompson. 1979. pap. 5.25 (*0-8222-0848-2*) Dramatists Play.

On Golf: Lessons from a Master Teacher. Jim Flick & Glen Waggoner. LC 96-29587. 256p. 1997. 24.00 (*0-679-44995-7*) Villard Books.

On Good Land: The Autobiography of an Urban Farm. Michael Ableman. LC 97-30801. 144p. 1998. 18.95 (*0-8118-1921-3*) Chronicle Bks.

On Government. Marcus Tullius Cicero. Tr. & Intro. by Michael Grant. 432p. 1994. pap. 13.95 (*0-14-044595-1*, Penguin Classics) Viking Penguin.

On Government. rev. ed. John Fortescue. Ed. by Simona Draghici. LC 97-8434. Orig. Title: The Governance of England. 136p. (C). 1997. pap. text 8.95 (*0-943045-08-8*) Plutarch Pr OR.

On Grafting in Animals: The Degli Innesti Animali. Giuseppe Baronio. Tr. by Joan B. Sax. (Illus.). 87p. 1985. bds. 100.00 (*0-318-04638-5*) F A Countway.

On Grammatical Inversion see Preliminary Announcement

On Grandpa's Farm. Vivian Sathre. LC 96-2995. (Illus.). 32p. (J). (ps-3). 1997. 16.00 (*0-395-76506-4*) HM.

On Great Service: A Framework for Action. Leonard L. Berry. 1995. 30.00 (*0-02-918555-6*) Free Pr.

On Great Writing on the Sublime. Longinus. Tr. by G. M. Grube. LC 57-14628. 1957. pap. 2.40 (*0-672-60261-X*, LLA79, Bobbs) Macmillan.

On Great Writing (On the Sublime) Longinus. Tr. & Intro. by G. M. Grube. LC 90-49700. 88p. (C). 1991. reprint ed. pap. text 6.95 (*0-87220-080-9*); reprint ed. lib. bdg. 24.95 (*0-87220-081-7*) Hackett Pub.

On Grief & Reason: Essays. Joseph Brodsky. LC 94-10872. 458p. 1996. 24.00 (*0-374-23415-9*) FS&G.

On Grief & Reason: Essays. Joseph Brodsky. 496p. 1997. pap. text 16.00 (*0-374-52509-9*) FS&G.

On Grieving the Death of a Father. Harold I. Smith. LC 94-24890. 144p. 1994. pap. 12.99 (*0-8066-2714-X*, 9-2714, Augsburg) Augsburg Fortress.

On Group-Theoretic Decision Problems & Their Classification. Charles F. Miller, III. LC 70-146647. (Annals of Mathematics Studies: No. 68). 116p. 1971. reprint ed. pap. 36.00 (*0-608-06492-0*, 206678900009) Bks Demand.

On Growing up Tough. Taylor Caldwell. 160p. Date not set. reprint ed. lib. bdg. 20.95 (*0-88411-170-9*, Aeonian Pr) Amereon Ltd.

***On Growth & Form.** M. Chaplain. LC 99-35919. 436p. 1999. 170.00 (*0-471-98451-5*) Wiley.

An Asterisk (*) at the beginning of an entry indicates that the title is appearing for the first time.

On Growth & Form. D'Arcy W. Thompson. Ed. by John T. Bonner. (Canto Book Ser.). (Illus.). 368p. (C). 1992. pap. 13.95 (*0-521-43776-8*) Cambridge U Pr.

On Growth & Form: Fractal & Non-Fractal Patterns in Physics. Ed. by H. Eugene Stanley & Nicole Ostrowsky. 1985. lib. bdg. 116.50 (*90-247-3234-4*) Kluwer Academic.

On Growth & Form: Fractal & Non-Fractal Patterns in Physics. Ed. by H. Eugene Stanley & Nicole Ostrowsky. 1985. pap. text 54.00 (*0-89838-850-3*) Kluwer Academic.

On Growth & Form: The Complete Revised Edition. rev. ed. D'Arcy W. Thompson. (Illus.). viii, 1116p. 1992. reprint ed. pap. 24.95 (*0-486-67135-6*) Dover.

On Guard. Donna Jo Napoli. 128p. (YA). (gr. 3-7). 1999. pap. 4.99 (*0-14-130118-X*, PuffinBks) Peng Put Young Read.

On Guard: Bella Fleace Gave a Party. Martin Amis et al. 22p. 3.95 (*1-86092-000-4*, Pub. by Travelman Pub) IPG Chicago.

On Guard! How You Can Win the War Against the Bad Guys. Laura E. Quarantiello. LC 93-48851. 128p. 1994. 17.95 (*0-936653-50-7*, Limelight Bks) Tiare Pubns.

On Guard, a History of the Detroit Free Press. Frank Angelo. LC 81-1719. vi, 279 p. 1981. write for info. (*0-9605692-0-0*) Detroit Pr.

On Guard for Religious Liberty: Six Decades of the Baptist Joint Committee. Pam Parry. LC 96-31881. (Illus.). 96p. 1996. pap. 9.00 (*1-57312-090-1*) Smyth & Helwys.

***On Guerrilla Warfare.** 2nd ed. Mao Tse-Tung. Tr. by Samuel B. Griffith, II from CHI. 176p. 2000. reprint ed. pap. 12.00 (*0-252-06892-0*) U of Ill Pr.

On Gwendolyn Brooks: Reliant Contemplation. Ed. by Stephen C. Wright. LC 95-40036. 288p. (C). 1996. text 44.50 (*0-472-10423-3*, 10423) U of Mich Pr.

On Hallowed Ground. Colin McComb. 1996. 25.00 (*0-7869-0430-5*, Pub. by TSR Inc) Random.

***On Hallowed Ground: Abraham Lincoln & the Foundations of American History.** John P. Diggins. LC 00-35915. 352p. 2000. 27.95 (*0-300-08237-1*) Yale U Pr.

On Halloween. Carrier. LC 98-74411. (Illus.). 40p. (YA). (ps-k). 1999. 7.95 (*0-694-01292-0*) HarpC Child Bks.

On Halloween Night. Ferida Wolff. 1997. 10.15 (*0-606-11703-2*, Pub. by Turtleback) Demco.

On Halloween Night. Ferida Wolff et al. LC 93-26859. (Illus.). 32p. (J). 1997. mass mkt. 4.95 (*0-688-15482-4*, Wm Morrow) Morrow Avon.

On Hallowing One's Diminshments. John R. Yungblut. LC 90-61735. 32p. (Orig.). 1990. pap. 4.00 (*0-87574-292-0*) Pendle Hill.

On Hallucination, Intuition, & the Becoming of "O" Eric Rhode. (Illus.). 230p. 1998. pap. text 29.95 (*1-883881-26-9*, 26-9) S Freud RT&PF.

On Hamlet. 2nd ed. De Salvador Madariaga. 145p. 1964. 35.00 (*0-7146-2068-8*, Pub. by F Cass Pubs) Intl Spec Bk.

On Hanukkah. Cathy G. Fishman. LC 96-44696. (Illus.). 40p. (J). (gr. 1-3). 1998. 16.00 (*0-689-80643-4*) S&S Childrens.

On Hawthorne. Ed. by Edwin H. Cady & Louis J. Budd. LC 89-25696. (Best from American Literature Ser.). 282p. (C). 1990. text 49.95 (*0-8223-1032-5*) Duke.

***On Hegel.** Brown. 2000. pap. 8.25 (*0-534-58357-1*) Wadsworth Pub.

On Hegel's Critique of Kant. Josef Maier. LC 39-31564. reprint ed. 20.00 (*0-404-04168-X*) AMS Pr.

On Hegel's Epistemology & Contemporary Philosophy. Tom Rockmore. LC 95-32854. 320p. (C). 1996. text 60.00 (*0-391-03918-0*) Humanities.

On Hegel's Logic: Fragments of a Commentary. John W. Burbidge. 292p. (C). 1995. pap. 17.50 (*0-391-03902-4*) Humanities.

On Heidegger. Johnson. (Philosophy Ser.). 1999. pap. text 13.95 (*0-534-57597-8*) Brooks-Cole.

On Heidegger & Language. Ed. by Joseph J. Kockelmans. LC 77-162929. (Studies in Phenomenology & Existential Philosophy). 380p. 1972. pap. 22.95 (*0-8101-0612-4*) Northwestern U Pr.

On Heidegger's Nazism & Philosophy. Tom Rockmore. LC 91-22072. (C). 1992. 55.00 (*0-520-07711-3*, Pub. by U CA Pr) Cal Prin Full Svc.

On Heidegger's Nazism & Philosophy. Tom Rockmore. 1997. pap. text 19.95 (*0-520-20898-6*, Pub. by U CA Pr) Cal Prin Full Svc.

On Henry James: The Best from American Literature. Ed. by Louis J. Budd & Edwin H. Cady. LC 90-37352. 328p. (C). 1990. text 49.95 (*0-8223-1064-3*) Duke.

On Her Doorstep. Kay Hooper. 192p. 1994. mass mkt. 4.50 (*0-515-11423-5*, Jove) Berkley Pub.

On Her Doorstep. Kay Hooper. 192p. 25.00 (*0-7278-5526-3*) Severn Hse.

On Her Face the Light of la Luna. Mairym Cruz-Bernal. LC 96-71163. 1997. pap. 10.00 (*0-944854-22-2*) Provincetown Arts.

On Her Face the Light of la Luna. Mairym Cruz-Bernal. LC 96-71163. 1998. 35.00 (*0-944854-23-0*) Provincetown Arts.

On Her Majesty's Secret Service. Ian Fleming. (James Bond Ser.). 288p. 1995. 9.98 (*1-56731-079-6*, MJF Bks) Fine Comms.

On Her Majesty's Secret Service. Ian Fleming. pap. 9.95 (*0-685-11468-6*) Fr & Eur.

On Her Own. Carolyn Keene. (Nancy Drew on Campus Ser.: No. 2). (YA). (gr. 8 up). 1995. mass mkt. 3.99 (*0-671-52741-X*, Archway) PB.

***On Her Own.** Donna Jo Napoli. LC 99-27370. (Aladdin Angelwings Ser.: No. 3). Orig. Title: Room to Grow. 96p. (J). (gr. 2-5). 1999. per. 3.99 (*0-689-82985-X*) Aladdin.

***On Her Own.** Donna Jo Napoli. Orig. Title: Room to Grow. (Illus.). (J). 1999. 9.34 (*0-606-17906-2*) Turtleback.

On Her Own: Growing Up in the Shadow of the American Dream. Ruth Sidel. 288p. 1991. pap. 12.95 (*0-14-014670-9*) Viking Penguin.

On Her Own: Journalistic Adventures from San Francisco to the Chinese Revolution, 1917-1927. Milly Bennett. Ed. by A. Tom Grunfeld. LC 92-39241. 384p. (gr. 13). 1993. text 66.95 (*0-87332-523-0*, East Gate Bk); pap. text 26.95 (*1-56324-182-X*, East Gate Bk) M E Sharpe.

On Her Own: That Special Woman! Pat Warren. (Special Edition Ser.). 1993. per. 3.50 (*0-373-09841-3*, 5-09841-3) Silhouette.

On Her Own Ground. A'Lelia Bundles. 2001. write for info. (*0-684-82582-1*) Simon & Schuster.

On Her Their Lives Depend: Munitions Workers in the Great War. Angela Woollacott. LC 93-20667. 1994. 48.00 (*0-520-08397-0*, Pub. by U CA Pr); pap. 16.95 (*0-520-08502-7*, Pub. by U CA Pr) Cal Prin Full Svc.

On Her Way: The Life & Music of Shania Twain. Barbara Hager & Meet S. Twain. LC 99-167184. (Illus.). 208p. 1998. pap. 12.00 (*0-425-16451-9*) Blvd Books.

On Her Way: The Shania Twain Story. Scott Gray. LC ML420.T953G73 1998. 1998. mass mkt. 5.99 (*0-345-42936-2*) Ballantine Pub Grp.

On Her Way Rejoicing: The Fiction of Muriel Spark. Jennifer L. Randisi. LC 90-32628. (Contexts & Literature Ser.: Vol. 3). 129p. 1991. text 29.95 (*0-8132-0730-4*) Cath U Pr.

On Heroes & the Heroic: In Search of Good Deeds. Ed. by Patra McSharry & Roger Rosen. (Icarus World Issues Ser.). (Illus.). (YA). (gr. 7-12). 1993. pap. 8.95 (*0-8239-1385-6*); lib. bdg. 16.95 (*0-8239-1384-8*) Rosen Group.

On Heroes, Hero-Worship & the Heroic in History. Thomas Carlyle. LC 91-33937. (Charlotte & Norman Strouse Edition of the Writings of Thomas Carlyle: Vol. 1). 622p. (C). 1992. 55.00 (*0-520-07515-3*, Pub. by U CA Pr) Cal Prin Full Svc.

On Heroes, Hero-Worship & the Heroic in History. Thomas Carlyle. Ed. & Intro. by Carl Niemeyer. LC 66-12130. (Illus.). xxv, 257p. 1966. pap. text 12.00 (*0-8032-5030-4*, Bison Books) U of Nebr Pr.

On Higher Education: The Academic Enterprise in an Era of Rising Student Consumerism. David Riesman. LC 98-9622. (Foundations of Higher Education Ser.). 421p. 1998. pap. text 27.95 (*0-7658-0438-7*) Transaction Pubs.

On Higher Education: The Academic Enterprise in an Era of Rising Student Consumerism. David Riesman. LC 80-8007. (Carnegie Council Ser.). 459p. reprint ed. pap. 142.30 (*0-8357-4690-9*, 205234500008) Bks Demand.

***On Higher Ground: A Postmodern Romance.** Ed. by Tim Holt & Sandra Hood. (Illus.). 288p. 2000. pap. 12.95 (*0-914485-19-9*, Pub. by Trill Pr) Suttertown Pub.

On Higher Ground: Education & the Case for Affirmative Action. Walter Feinberg. LC 97-26160. 1997. 36.00 (*0-8077-3699-6*); pap. 16.95 (*0-8077-3698-8*) Tchrs Coll.

On Higher Ground: Reclaiming a Civil Society. William D. Gairdner. 240p. 1996. 19.95 (*0-7737-2939-9*) Stoddart Publ.

On Higher Ground: Understanding Others Through Diversity. Gamma Vision, Inc. Staff. 303p. 1993. ring bd. 375.00 (*1-884031-07-2*) Gamma Vision.

***On Highest Ground: Surveying Your Resources in Christ.** Derick Bingham. 360p. 1999. 9.99 (*1-84030-068-X*) Emerald House Group Inc.

On-Highway Trucks: Power Trains & Suspension Systems. Robert N. Brady. 1982. text 78.80 (*0-8359-5232-0*) P-H.

On Hindu Philosophies of Experience: Cults, Mysticism & Meditations. Ashok K. Malhotra. 59p. 1993. 3.00 (*1-883058-03-1*, Oneonta Philosophy) Global Pubns.

On Hinduism: From Darkness to Light. Pandit Bhopaul Maraj. (Illus.). 250p. (Orig.). 1994. pap. write for info. (*0-614-32026-7*) K Maraj.

On His Deafness & Other Melodies Unheard. Robert F. Panara. LC 97-33126. 90p. 1997. pap. 12.95 (*0-9634016-5-3*, Deaf Life Pr) MSM Prods.

***On His Heart: Our High Priest's Loving Care.** Madge Beckon. 167p. 1999. pap. 8.99 (*1-882701-59-3*, Gospel Folio Pr) Uplook Min.

On His Majesty's Service: Observations of the British Home Fleet from the Diary, Reports, & Letters of Joseph H. Wellings, Assistant U. S. Naval Attache, London, 1940-41. Ed. by John B. Hattendorf. LC 82-6416. (Historical Monographs: No. 5). (Illus.). 249p. (C). 1983. reprint ed. pap. 6.00 (*0-9637973-6-0*) Naval War Coll.

On Historians: Reappraisals of Some of the Masters of Modern History. J. H. Hexter. 317p. 1986. pap. 16.00 (*0-674-63427-6*) HUP.

***On Historical Astrology: The Book of Religions & Dynasties (On the Great Conjunctions)** Abeu Ma0shar et al. LC 99-35114. (Islamic Philosophy, Theology & Science Ser.). 1999. write for info. (*90-04-11074-7*) Brill Academic Pubs.

On Historical Materialism. Karl Marx & Friedrich Engels. (C). text 17.50 (*0-85315-270-5*, Pub. by Lawrence & Wishart) NYU Pr.

On Historical Materialism. Friedrich Engels. LC 76-42699. (BCL Ser.: II). reprint ed. 27.50 (*0-404-15370-4*) AMS Pr.

On History. Fernand Braudel. Tr. by Sarah Matthews from FRE. LC 80-11201. 236p. 1982. pap. text 13.00 (*0-226-07151-0*) U Ch Pr.

On History. Eric J. Hobsbawm. 1997. 25.00 (*1-56584-393-2*, Pub. by New Press NY) Norton.

On History. Eric J. Hobsbawm. 320p. 1998. pap. 15.95 (*1-56584-468-8*, Pub. by New Press NY) Norton.

***On History.** Eric J. Hobsbawm. 1999. 25.50 (*0-8446-7019-7*) Peter Smith.

On History & Other Essays. Michael Oakeshott. LC 99-32045. 1999. pap. 12.00 (*0-86597-267-2*) Liberty Fund.

***On History & Other Essays.** Michael Oakeshott. LC 99-32045. 1999. 20.00 (*0-86597-266-4*) Liberty Fund.

On History & Philosophers of History. William H. Dray. LC 89-15793. (Philosophy of History & Culture Ser.). viii, 237p. 1989. 107.00 (*90-04-09000-2*) Brill Academic Pubs.

On History Kant. Lewis W. Beck et al. 192p. (C). 1963. pap. text 8.00 (*0-02-307860-X*, Macmillan Coll) P-H.

On History's Coattails: Commentaries by an English Journalist. Michael Henderson. 204p. (Orig.). 1988. pap. 8.75 (*1-85239-503-6*) Grosvenor USA.

On Hobbes. Missner. (Philosophy Ser.). 1999. pap. text 13.95 (*0-534-57592-7*) Brooks-Cole.

On Hobos & Homelessness. Nels Anderson. LC 98-19274. 299p. 1999. pap. text 18.00 (*0-226-01967-5*); lib. bdg. 50.00 (*0-226-01966-7*) U Ch Pr.

On Hogback Mountain. Elaine Magarrell. LC 84-52606. (Series Nine). 54p. 1985. pap. 7.00 (*0-931846-27-7*) Wash Writers Pub.

***On Holiday: A History of Vacationing.** Orvar Lvfgren. LC 99-31304. 347p. 1999. 29.95 (*0-520-21767-5*, Pub. by U CA Pr) Cal Prin Full Svc.

On Holiday Again. Derek Prime. (Sarah & Paul Ser.). 3.99 (*1-871676-37-1*, Pub. by Christian Focus) Spring Arbor Dist.

On Holiday Again, Doctor? large type ed. Robert Clifford. 1991. 27.99 (*0-7089-2496-4*) Ulverscroft.

On Hollywood. Kathleen Tynan. 1992. write for info. (*0-679-41243-3*) McKay.

On Holography. Richard Kostelanetz. (Illus.). 1979. 1500.00 (*0-932360-31-9*) Archae Edns.

On Holy Ground: A Daily Devotional. Charles Stanley. LC 99-15321. 384p. 1999. 19.99 (*0-7852-7662-9*) Nelson.

On Holy Ground: Reflections in a New England Town. Beverley F. Edwards. 200p. 1991. 20.00 (*0-9630591-0-6*) Awashonks.

On Holy Ground: The Impact of Psychotherapists' Spirituality on Their Practice. John P. Sullivan. LC 98-23788. 144p. (C). 1998. 44.00 (*0-7618-1176-1*); pap. 24.50 (*0-7618-1177-X*) U Pr of Amer.

On Holy Images. Damascenus Joannes. Tr. by Mary H. Allies from GRE. 1977. pap. 3.95 (*0-89981-063-2*) Eastern Orthodox.

On Home Ground. Alan Lelchuk. LC 87-8496. (Illus.). 80p. (YA). (gr. 5 up). 1987. 9.95 (*0-15-200560-9*, Gulliver Bks) Harcourt.

On Home Meetings. Witness Lee. 64p. 1986. per. 4.75 (*0-87083-257-3*, 12-014-001) Living Stream Ministry.

On Homosexuality: Lysis, Phaedrus & Symposium. Plato. Tr. by Benjamin Jowett & Eugene O'Connor. LC 90-63048. (Great Books in Philosophy). 157p. (Orig.). (C). 1991. pap. 6.95 (*0-87975-632-2*) Prometheus Bks.

On Hope's Wings. Melody Carlson. LC 97-33854. (Allison Chronicles Ser.). 192p. (J). 1998. pap. 5.99 (*1-55661-957-X*) Bethany Hse.

On Horseback. Charles D. Warner. (Notable American Authors Ser.). 1999. reprint ed. lib. bdg. 125.00 (*0-7812-9891-1*) Rprt Serv.

On Howells. Ed. by Edwin H. Cady & Louis J. Budd. LC 92-23839. (Best from American Literature Ser.). 288p. 1993. text 49.95 (*0-8223-1300-6*) Duke.

On Human Attitudes: Root Metaphors in Theoretical Conceptions. Valentin E. Gonzalez. (Goteborg Studies in Educational Sciences: No. 85). 238p. (Orig.). 1992. pap. 58.00 (*91-7346-249-7*) Coronet Bks.

***On Human Being: A Spiritual Anthropology.** Olivier Clement. 176p. 2000. pap. 14.95 (*1-56548-143-7*) New City.

On Human Conduct. Michael Oakeshott. 340p. 1991. reprint ed. pap. text 29.95 (*0-19-827758-X*) OUP.

On Human Diversity: Nationalism, Racism, & Exoticism in French Thought. Tzvetan Todorov. Tr. by Catherine Porter from FRE. LC 92-24568. (Convergences: Inventories of the Present Ser.).Tr. of Nous et les Autres. 442p. 1993. 62.50 (*0-674-63438-1*) HUP.

On Human Diversity: Nationalism, Racism, & Exoticism in French Thought. Tzvetan Todorov.Tr. of Nous et les Autres. 440p. 1994. pap. text 19.95 (*0-674-63439-X*, TODHUX) HUP.

On Human Memory: Evolution, Progress, & Reflections on the 30th Anniversary of the Atkinson-Shiffrin Model. Ed. by Chizuko Izawa. LC 99-21291. 304p. 1999. 59.95 (*0-8058-2952-0*) L Erlbaum Assocs.

On Human Nature. Aquinas, Thomas, Saint. Ed. & Intro. by Thomas S. Hibbs. LC 98-50832. Orig. Title: Sentencia Libri De Anima/Summa Theologica. 224p. (C). 1999. pap. 9.95 (*0-87220-454-5*); lib. bdg. 34.95 (*0-87220-455-3*) Hackett Pub.

On Human Nature. Edward O. Wilson. LC 78-17675. 260p. 1978. 32.50 (*0-674-63441-1*) HUP.

On Human Nature. Edward O. Wilson. 260p. 1978. reprint ed. pap. text 13.95 (*0-674-63442-X*) HUP.

On Human Nature, Bk. VI. unabridged ed. Arthur Schopenhauer. (Classic Reprint Ser.). 106p. 1997. reprint ed. 15.00 (*0-936128-72-0*) De Young Pr.

On Human Symbiosis & the Vicissitudes of Individuation Vol. 1: Infantile Psychoses. Margaret S. Mahler & Manuel Furer. LC 68-24453. 271p. 1968. 45.00 (*0-8236-3780-8*) Intl Univs Pr.

On Human Work: Encyclical Laborem Exercens. John Paul, II, pseud. 66p. pap. 3.95 (*0-8198-3348-7*) Pauline Bks.

On Human Work: Laborem Exercens. John Paul, II, pseud. LC 81-214589. 62p. 1981. pap. 3.95 (*1-55586-825-8*) US Catholic.

On Humane Governance: Toward a New Global Politics. Richard A. Falk. 280p. 1995. 50.00 (*0-271-01511-X*); pap. 18.95 (*0-271-01512-8*) Pa St U Pr.

On Humanistic Education: Six Inaugural Orations, 1699-1707. Giambattista Vico. Tr. by Giorgio A. Pinton & Arthur W. Shippee from LAT. LC 92-56787. 172p. 1993. text 32.50 (*0-8014-2838-6*); pap. text 12.95 (*0-8014-8087-6*) Cornell U Pr.

On Hume. Radcliffe. (Philosophy Ser.). 1999. pap. text 13.95 (*0-534-57605-2*) Brooks-Cole.

On Hume & Eighteenth-Century Aesthetics: The Philosopher on a Swing. Tr. by Giancarlo Carabelli from ITA. LC 94-27991. Vol. 22.Tr. of Intorno a Hume. (Illus.). XI, 222p. (C). 1995. text 48.95 (*0-8204-2528-1*) P Lang Pubng.

On Humor. Luigi Pirandello. LC 74-4281. (University of North Carolina Studies in Comparative Literature: No. 58). 166p. 1974. reprint ed. pap. 51.50 (*0-7837-9034-1*, 204978500003) Bks Demand.

On Humor: The Best from American Literature. Ed. by Louis J. Budd & Edwin H. Cady. LC 91-4113. 288p. 1992. text 49.95 (*0-8223-1173-9*) Duke.

On Husserl. Velarde. (Philosophy Ser.). 1999. pap. text 13.95 (*0-534-57610-9*) Brooks-Cole.

On Hyphens & Shall & Will, Should & Would see Preliminary Announcement

On Ibsen. James Joyce. Ed. by Dennis Phillips. (Green Integer Ser.: No. 12). 96p. 1999. pap. 8.95 (*1-55713-372-7*, Pub. by Green Integer) Consort Bk Sales.

***On Ice: A Thriller.** David Ramus. LC 99-89929. 321p. 2000. 24.95 (*0-671-04184-3*, Pocket Books) PB.

On Ideas: Aristotle's Criticism of Plato's Theory of Forms. Gail Fine. 416p. 1995. reprint ed. pap. text 28.00 (*0-19-823549-6*) OUP.

On Identity: A Study in Genetic Phenomenology. Giuseppina Moneta. (Phaenomenologica Ser.: No. 71). 108p. 1977. pap. text 71.50 (*90-247-1860-0*, Pub. by M Nijhoff) Kluwer Academic.

***On Illustrious Men.** JEROME ST. LC 99-30556. 1999. 34.95 (*0-8132-0100-4*) Cath U Pr.

On Implementing a National Graduate Medical Education Trust Fund. Institute of Medicine (U.S.). LC 97-184448. xii, 74 p. 1997. write for info. (*0-309-05779-5*) Natl Acad Pr.

On Improving the Status of Women. Theodor G. Hippel. Ed. & Tr. by Timothy F. Sellner. LC 78-23302. (Illus.). 231p. reprint ed. pap. 71.70 (*0-608-10622-4*, 207124400009) Bks Demand.

On Infancy & Toddlerhood: An Elementary Textbook. David A. Freedman. LC 96-37168. 200p. 1997. 35.00 (*0-8236-3785-9*, BN 03785) Intl Univs Pr.

On Infancy & Toddlerhood: An Elementary Textbook. David A. Freedman. 247p. 1999. pap. 27.95 (*0-8236-8171-8*, 23785) Intl Univs Pr.

On Infantry. rev. ed. John A. English & Bruce I. Gudmundsson. LC 94-12071. (Military Profession Ser.). 216p. 1994. 65.00 (*0-275-94588-X*, Praeger Pubs); pap. 22.95 (*0-275-94972-9*, Praeger Pubs) Greenwood.

On Inhibition. B. B. Breese. (Psychology Monographs General & Applied: Vol. 3). reprint ed. 55.00 (*0-8115-1402-1*) Periodicals Srv.

On Innovative Music(ian)s. Richard Kostelanetz. LC 89-2813. 310p. (Orig.). 1989. pap. 12.95 (*0-87910-121-0*) Limelight Edns.

On Innovative Performance(s) Three Decades of Recollections on Alternative Theater. Richard Kostelanetz. LC 93-42505. 288p. 1994. lib. bdg. 49.95 (*0-89950-473-6*) McFarland & Co.

***On Inoculating Moral Philosophy Against God.** John M. Rist. LC 99-50978. (Aquinas Lecture Ser.). 2000. write for info. (*0-87462-167-4*) Marquette.

On Insanity & Its Classification. Vincenzo Chiarugi. Ed. & Tr. by George Mora. LC 86-17746. 1987. 35.00 (*0-88135-084-2*) Watson Pub Intl.

On Insects. Ed. by Applewood Books Staff. (Wonderlings Ser.). (Illus.). 32p. (Orig.). (J). (ps up). 1996. pap. 1.50 (*1-55709-380-6*) Applewood.

On Insoluble Sentences. William Heytesbury. Tr. by Paul V. Spade. pap. text 8.00 (*0-88844-270-X*) Brill Academic Pubs.

On Integral Functionals with Variable Domain of Integration, Vol. 4. Ed. by I. I. Daniljuk. LC 76-12567. (Proceedings of the Steklov Institute of Mathematics Ser.: Vol. 118). 144p. 1976. pap. 55.00 (*0-8218-3018-X*, STEKLO/118) Am Math.

On Integration in Plants. Rudolf Dostal. Ed. by Kenneth V. Thimann. Tr. by Jana M. Kiely. LC 67-27083. (Illus.). 239p. 1967. 31.50 (*0-674-63450-0*) HUP.

On Intelligence. Hippolyte A. Taine. 588p. 120.00 (*1-85506-660-2*) Thoemmes Pr.

On Intelligence, 3. Hippolyte A. Taine. LC 77-72191. (Contributions to the History of Psychology Ser.: Vol. III, Pt. A). 320p. 1977. lib. bdg. 89.50 (*0-313-26927-0*, U6927, Greenwood Pr) Greenwood.

On Intelligence: A Bio-Ecological Treatise on Intellectual Development. Stephen J. Ceci. (Illus.). 288p. 1996. pap. 19.50 (*0-674-63456-X*) HUP.

***On Intelligence: Spies & Secrecy in an Open World.** Robert David Steele. LC 00-29284. 2000. write for info. (*0-916159-28-0*) AFCEA Intl Pr.

On Interest Rates & Asset Prices in Europe: The Selected Essays of Martin M.G. Fase. Martin M. G. Fase. LC 98-31694. 299p. 1999. 90.00 (*1-84064-020-0*) E Elgar.

On Internal War: American & Soviet Approaches to Third World Clients & Insurgents. William E. Odom. LC 91-18572. 280p. 1991. text 37.95 (*0-8223-1182-8*) Duke.

On Internet, 1994: An International Guide to Electronic Journals, Newsletters, Books, & Discussion Lists on the Internet. 480p. 1994. pap. 45.00 (*0-88736-929-4*) Mecklermedia.

An Asterisk (*) at the beginning of an entry indicates that the title is appearing for the first time.

On Interpretation. Aristotle. (Loeb Classical Library). (ENG & GRE.). (C). write for info. (*0-318-53020-1*) HUP.

On Interpretation: Sociology for Interpreters of Natural & Cultural History. rev. ed. Ed. by Gary E. Machlis & Donald R. Field. LC 92-3386. (Illus.). 320p. (C). 1992. pap. text 21.95 (*0-87071-365-5*) Oreg St U Pr.

On Interpreting Morphological Change: The Greek Reflexive Pronoun. Roger D. Woodard. 144p. 1990. pap. 40.00 (*90-5063-049-9*, Pub. by Gieben) J Benjamins Pubng Co.

On Intersubjectivity & Cultural Creativity. Martin Buber. LC 91-47187. (Heritage of Sociology Ser.). 272p. 1992. lib. bdg. 44.00 (*0-226-07805-1*) U Ch Pr.

On Intersubjectivity & Cultural Creativity. Martin Buber. LC 91-47187. (Heritage of Sociology Ser.). 272p. 1992. pap. text 25.00 (*0-226-07807-8*) U Ch Pr.

On Intimate Ground: A Gestalt Approach to Working with Couples. Ed. by Gordon Wheeler & Stephanie Backman. (Gestalt Institute of Cleveland Press Book Ser.). 448p. 1994. 42.50 (*0-88163-264-3*) Analytic Pr.

On Intimate Terms: The Psychology of Difference in Lesbian Relationships. Beverly Burch. 192p. (C). 1993. text 21.50 (*0-252-01801-X*) U of Ill Pr.

On Intuition & Discursive Reasoning in Aristotle. V. Kal. 196p. 1988. pap. 57.00 (*90-04-08308-1*, PHA, 46) Brill Academic Pubs.

On Iowa. Irving Weber. Ed. by Gregory M. Johnson & Eileen Bartos. (Illus.). 115p. (Orig.). 1996. pap. 12.95 (*0-87414-104-4*) U IA Pubns Dept.

On Ireland & the Irish Question. Marx. (C). text 19.95 (*0-85315-247-0*, Pub. by Lawrence & Wishart) NYU Pr.

On Islam Shi'ism, Bk. 1. Ahmad Kasravi. Ed. by Mohammad A. Jazayery. Tr. by Mohammad R. Ghanoonparvar from PER. LC 94-8737. 180p. 1990. pap. 14.95 (*0-939214-42-3*) Mazda Pubs.

***On Island Time.** Hilary Stewart. LC 98-13060. (Illus.). 184p. 1998. 30.00 (*0-295-97710-8*) U of Wash Pr.

***On Island Time.** Hilary Stewart. (Illus.). 192p. 1999. pap. text 17.95 (*0-295-97830-9*) U of Wash Pr.

On Issues: Strategies of Argument in Later Greek Rhetoric. Hermogenes. Tr. & Comment by Malcolm F. Heath. (Illus.). 284p. 1995. text 85.00 (*0-19-814982-4*) OUP.

***On Its Own Ground: Celebrating the Permanent Collection of the Whitney Museum of American Art.** Whitney Museum of American Art Staff et al. LC 00-21903. (Illus.). 2000. write for info. (*0-87427-119-3*) Whitney Mus.

***On Jean-Jacques Rousseau: Considered as One of the 1st Authors of the Revolution.** James Swenson. LC 99-39445. (Atopia Ser.). 1999. pap. text 19.95 (*0-8047-3864-5*) Stanford U Pr.

On Jean-Luc Nancy: The Sense of Philosophy. Simon Sparks et al. LC 96-46363. (Warwick Studies in European Philosophy Ser.). 232p. (C). 1997. 80.00 (*0-415-14793-X*); pap. 22.99 (*0-415-14794-8*) Routledge.

On Jewelry & Gems: Contemporary Jewelry & Gem Design at the Department of Gem & Jewelry Design of the Fachhochschule Idar-Oberstein, Germany. Arnoldsche. (ENG & GER., Illus.). 168p. 1997. 75.00 (*3-925369-62-7*, Pub. by Arnoldsche Art Pubs) Antique Collect.

On Jewish Folklore. Raphael Patai. LC 82-11034. (Illus.). 512p. reprint ed. pap. 158.80 (*0-608-10593-7*, 207121400009) Bks Demand.

On Jewish Identity. Emily Benedek. 1998. write for info. (*0-8052-4138-8*) Schocken.

On Job: God-Talk & the Suffering of the Innocent. Gustavo Gutierrez. Tr. by Matthew O'Connell from SPA. LC 87-5661.Tr. of Hablar de Dios desde el Sufrimento del Inocente. 160p. (Orig.). 1987. pap. 15.00 (*0-88344-552-2*) Orbis Bks.

***On John Muir's Trail.** Gary Thompson. LC 99-61601. 1999. write for info. (*0-9657177-3-9*) Bear Star.

On Jordan's Stormy Banks: Evangelicalism in Mississippi, 1773-1876. Randy J. Sparks. LC 93-43020. 288p. 1994. 45.00 (*0-8203-1627-X*) U of Ga Pr.

***On Jordan's Stormy Banks: Personal Accounts of Slavery in Georgia.** Ed. by Andrew Waters. 103p. 2000. pap. 7.95 (*0-89587-228-5*) Blair.

On Jordan's Stormy Banks: Religion in the South (A Southern Exposure Profile) Ed. by Samuel S. Hill, Jr. LC 82-14524. vi, 160p. 1982. pap. 11.95 (*0-86554-035-7*, MUP-P010) Mercer Univ Pr.

On Judaism. Ed. by Martin Buber. 272p. 1996. pap. 13.00 (*0-8052-1050-4*) Schocken.

On Judaism. Emanuel Feldman. 24.99 (*0-89906-034-X*, JUDH); pap. 17.99 (*0-89906-035-8*, JUDP) Mesorah Pubns.

On Judging Books: In General & in Particular. Francis Hackett. LC 79-156657. (Essay Index Reprint Ser.). 1977. reprint ed. 20.95 (*0-8369-2400-2*) Ayer.

On Judicial Opinions. Irving Younger. write for info. (*0-943380-69-3*); audio. write for info. (*0-943380-56-1*) PEG MN.

***On Jung.** Anthony Stevens. LC 99-32343. 312p. 1999. pap. 14.95 (*0-691-01048-X*, Pub. by Princeton U Pr) Cal Prin Full Svc.

On Jurisprudence & the Conflict of Laws. Frederic Harrison. LC 94-77535. 179p. 1994. reprint ed. 45.00 (*0-89941-898-8*, 308400) W S Hein.

On Justice: An Essay in Jewish Philosophy. L. E. Goodman. 296p. (C). 1991. 50.00 (*0-300-04943-9*) Yale U Pr.

On Justice & Law. Stig Jorgensen. 168p. 1996. 19.95 (*87-7288-614-5*, Pub. by Aarhus Univ Pr) David Brown.

On Justice, Power, & Human Nature: Selections from "History of the Peloponnesian War" Thucydides. Tr. & Intro. by Paul Woodruff. LC 93-29617. 216p. (Orig.). (C). 1993. pap. text 7.95 (*0-87220-168-6*); lib. bdg. 29.95 (*0-87220-169-4*) Hackett Pub.

On (K-Z-n) & K-Fq(t)-(t2) Janet E. Aisbett et al. LC 85-15802. (Memoirs of the American Mathematical Society Ser.: No. 329). 200p. 1985. pap. 24.00 (*0-8218-2330-2*, MEMO/57/329C) Am Math.

On Kafka's Castle: A Study. Richard Sheppard. LC 73-175901. 234p. reprint ed. pap. 72.60 (*0-608-10225-3*, 201400200088) Bks Demand.

On Kant. Thomson. 1999. pap. text 13.95 (*0-534-57591-9*) Brooks-Cole.

On Karel Capek: A Michigan Slavic Colloquium. Ed. by Michael Makin & Jindrich Toman. LC 92-20812. (Materials Ser.: No. 34). 1992. pap. 15.00 (*0-930042-71-9*) Mich Slavic Pubns.

On Key Economic Issues. Paul W. McCracken et al. LC 84-70039. (AEI Studies: No. 399). 56p. reprint ed. pap. 30.00 (*0-8357-4518-X*, 203737700008) Bks Demand.

***On Kierkegaard.** Anderson. (Philosophy Ser.). 1999. pap. text 13.95 (*0-534-57601-X*) Brooks-Cole.

On Killing: The Psychological Cost of Learning to Kill in War & Society. Dave Grossman. 400p. 1996. pap. 15.95 (*0-316-33011-6*) Little.

***On Killing: The Psychological Cost of Learning to Kill in War & Society.** Dave Grossman. 1998. mass mkt. 16.00 (*0-316-19144-2*, Back Bay) Little.

On Kilroy's Trail: A World of Travel. Joe E. Robertson. LC 99-206945. (Illus.). 344p. 1998. pap. 22.95 (*0-89745-226-7*) Sunflower U Pr.

On King Lear. Lawrence Danson. LC 81-47120. 194p. reprint ed. pap. 60.20 (*0-8357-3700-4*, 203642400003) Bks Demand.

On Kissing: Travels in an Intimate Landscape. Adrianne Blue. LC 97-2763. 208p. 1997. 22.00 (*1-56836-173-4*) Kodansha.

On Kissing: Travels in an Intimate Landscape. Adrianne Blue. 224p. 1999. pap. 15.00 (*1-56836-261-7*, Kodansha Globe) Kodansha.

On Kissing, Tickling, & Being Bored: Psychoanalytic Essays on the Unexamined Life. Adam Phillips. 152p. 1994. pap. text 12.95 (*0-674-63463-2*, PHIKAX) HUP.

On Kissing, Tickling & Being Bored: Psychoanalytic Essays on the Unexamined Life. Adam Phillips. LC 92-20662. 152p. 1993. text 19.95 (*0-674-63462-4*) HUP.

On Klauder's Path: A Field Trip. G. G. Emch et al. 284p. 1994. text 78.00 (*981-02-1687-4*) World Scientific Pub.

On Knots. Louis H. Kauffman. (Annals of Mathematics Studies: No. 115). (Illus.). 425p. 1987. pap. text 35.00 (*0-691-08435-1*, Pub. by Princeton U Pr) Cal Prin Full Svc.

On Knowing: Essays for the Left Hand. Jerome S. Bruner. LC 62-13264. (Illus.). 201p. 1979. 27.50 (*0-674-63475-6*); pap. text 10.95 (*0-674-63525-6*) Belknap Pr.

On Knowing: The Natural Sciences. Richard McKeon. Ed. by Zahava K. McKeon. LC 94-8953. (Illus.). 420p. 1994. pap. text 17.95 (*0-226-56027-9*) U Ch Pr.

On Knowing: The Natural Sciences. Richard McKeon. Ed. by Zahava K. McKeon. LC 94-8953. (Illus.). 420p. 1994. lib. bdg. 65.00 (*0-226-56026-0*) U Ch Pr.

On Knowing & the Known: Introductory Readings in Epistemology. Ed. by Kenneth G. Lucey. LC 96-12549. 437p. 1998. pap. 23.95 (*1-57392-050-9*) Prometheus Bks.

On Knowing Reality: The Tattvartha Chapter of Asanga's Bodhisattvabhumi. Asanga. Tr. & Comment by Janice D. Willis. LC 79-16047. 216p. reprint ed. pap. 67.00 (*0-608-17356-8*, 202982500065) Bks Demand.

On Knowing Reality: The Tattvartha Chapter of Asanga's Bodhisattvabhumi. Janice D. Willis. 1982. reprint ed. 16.00 (*0-8364-2520-0*, Pub. by Motilal Bnarsidass) S Asia.

On Knowing That One Knows: The Logic of Skepticism & Theory. Richard Bosley. LC 92-41287. (Revisioning Philosophy Ser.: Vol. 13). XI, 310p. (Orig.). (C). 1993. pap. text 31.95 (*0-8204-1985-0*) P Lang Pubng.

On Knowing The Bible. Witness Lee. 64p. 1990. pap. 4.00 (*0-87083-561-0*, 10-059-001) Living Stream Ministry.

On Knowledge Base Management Systems. Ed. by M. L. Brodie & John Mylopoulos. (Topics in Information Systems Ser.). (Illus.). 690p. 1986. 87.95 (*0-387-96382-0*) Spr-Verlag.

***On Kripke.** Pregi. 2000. pap. 8.25 (*0-534-58366-0*) Wadsworth Pub.

***On Kuhn.** Andersen. 2000. pap. 8.25 (*0-534-58356-3*) Wadsworth Pub.

***On Lake Worth.** Beverly A. Mustaine. (Images of America Ser.). (Illus.). 128p. 1999. pap. 18.99 (*0-7385-0055-0*) Arcadia Publng.

On Lambda Nuclearity. Ed Dubinsky & M. S. Ramanujan. LC 72-4515. (Memoirs Ser.: No. 1/128). 101p. 1972. pap. 17.00 (*0-8218-1828-7*, MEMO/1/128) Am Math.

On Lampreys & Fishes: A Memorial Anthology in Honor of Vadim D. Vladykov. Ed. by D. E. McAllister. (Developments in Environmental Biology of Fishes Ser.). (C). 1988. text 177.50 (*90-6193-661-6*) Kluwer Academic.

On Land & Sea: or California in the Years 1843, '44 & '45. William H. Thomas. 1992. reprint ed. lib. bdg. 75.00 (*0-7812-5099-4*) Rprt Serv.

On Land & Sea with Caesar. Reuben F. Wells. LC 61-28142. (Illus.). (YA). (gr. 7-11). 1926. pap. 20.00 (*0-8196-0107-1*) Biblo.

On Language. Roman Jakobson. Ed. by Linda R. Waugh & Monique Monville-Burston. (Illus.). 640p. 1990. text 58.50 (*0-674-63535-3*) HUP.

On Language. Roman Jakobson & Monique Monville-Burston. Ed. by Linda R. Waugh. 672p. (C). 1995. pap. text 24.95 (*0-674-63536-1*) HUP.

On Language: Chomsky's Classic Works "Reflections on Language" & "Language & Responsibility", 2 vols. in 1. Noam Chomsky. 512p. 1998. reprint ed. pap. 16.95 (*1-56584-475-0*, Pub. by New Press NY) Norton.

On Language: Selected Writings of Joseph H. Greenberg. Ed. by Keith Denning & Suzanne Kemmer. LC 89-26199. 761p. 1990. 79.50 (*0-8047-1613-7*) Stanford U Pr.

On Language Change: The Invisible Hand in Language. Rudi Keller. Tr. by Brigitte Nerlich from GER. LC 93-42376. 208p. (C). 1995. pap. 25.99 (*0-415-07672-2*, C0286) Routledge.

On Language Development & Planning: A Pluralistic Paridigm. Udaya N. Singh. 1992. text 20.00 (*81-215-0556-9*, Pub. by M Manoharial) Coronet Bks.

On Language Rhetorica, Phonologica, Syntactica: A Festschrift for Robert P. Stockwell from His Friends & Colleagues. Ed. by Caroline Duncan-Rose et al. 520p. 1988. lib. bdg. 89.95 (*0-415-00312-1*) Routledge.

On Languages & Language: The Presidential Address of the 1991 Meeting of the Societas Linguistica Europaeca. Ed. by Werner Winter. LC 94-32192. (Trends in Linguistics, Studies & Monographs: No. 78). 304p. (C). 1994. lib. bdg. 121.55 (*3-11-013257-5*) Mouton.

On Lao Tzu. Cheng. (Philosophy Ser.). 1999. pap. text 13.95 (*0-534-57609-5*) Brooks-Cole.

On Largemouth Bass. Bill Dance & Tim Tucker. 1996. pap. text 12.95 (*0-937866-53-9*) Atlantic Pub Co.

On Latin: Linguistic & Literary Studies in Honour of Harm Pinkster. Ed. by Rodie Risselada et al. 216p. 1996. lib. bdg. 54.00 (*90-5063-137-1*, Pub. by Gieben) J Benjamins Pubng Co.

On Law & Country: The Biography & Speeches of Russell Archibald Ramsey. Russell W. Ramsey. (Illus.). 200p. 1993. pap. 12.95 (*0-8283-1970-7*) Branden Bks.

On Law & Justice. Paul A. Freund. LC 67-29626. 265p. 1968. 23.50 (*0-674-63550-7*) Belknap Pr.

On Law & Policy in the European Court of Justice. H. Rasmussen. 1986. lib. bdg. 245.50 (*90-247-3217-4*) Kluwer Academic.

On Law & Reason. abr. ed. Aleksander Peczenik. (Law & Philosophy Library: No. 8). 456p. 1989. lib. bdg. 166.00 (*0-7923-0444-6*, Pub. by Kluwer Academic) Kluwer Academic.

On Law, Morality, & Politics. Aquinas, Thomas, Saint. Ed. by Richard J. Regan & William P. Baumgarth. LC 87-28272. (HPC Classics Ser.). 316p. (C). 1988. 32.95 (*0-87220-032-9*); pap. 8.95 (*0-87220-031-0*) Hackett Pub.

On Laws in Courts. Morris & Frederic S. Mishkin. 1965. text 27.00 (*0-88277-360-7*) Foundation Pr.

On Leadership. John W. Gardner. 1989. 27.95 (*0-02-911311-3*) Free Pr.

On Leadership. John W. Gardner. 220p. 1993. per. 17.95 (*0-02-911312-1*) Free Pr.

On Leading a Clinical Department: A Guide for Physicians. Harry W. Fritts, Jr. LC 97-15181. 224p. 1997. text 45.00 (*0-8018-5647-7*); pap. text 16.95 (*0-8018-5781-3*) Johns Hopkins.

On Learning from the Patient. Patrick J. Casement. 232p. (Orig.). (C). 1985. pap. text 15.95 (*0-318-58396-8*, NO. 9235) Routledge.

On Learning Golf. Percy Boomer. (Illus.). 1946. 20.00 (*0-394-41008-4*) Knopf.

On Learning Golf. rev. ed. Percy Boomer. (Illus.). 220p. 1989. reprint ed. 28.00 (*0-940889-22-6*) Classics Golf.

On Learning to Plan & Planning to Learn. Donald N. Michael. LC 73-7153. (Jossey-Bass Behavioral Science Ser.). 359p. reprint ed. pap. 111.30 (*0-8357-4701-8*, 205235600008) Bks Demand.

On Leave with Norgood. Howard Bernstein. Ed. by Kathleen Iddings. LC 86-63864. 72p. (Orig.). 1989. pap. text, per. 9.95 (*0-931289-00-9*) San Diego Poet Pr.

On Leaving Charleston. Alexandra Ripley. 576p. 1991. mass mkt. 6.50 (*0-446-36001-5*, Pub. by Warner Bks) Little.

On Leiris. Ed. by Marc Blanchard. (French Studies: No. 81). (Illus.). 164p. (C). 1992. pap. 18.00 (*0-300-05707-5*) Yale U Pr.

On Leon Baptista Alberti: His Literary & Aesthetic Theories. Mark Jarzombek. (Illus.). 300p. 1990. 37.50 (*0-262-10042-8*) MIT Pr.

On Liberal Peace: Democracy, War, & the International Order. John MacMillan. 256p. 1998. text 59.50 (*1-86064-010-9*, Pub. by I B T) St Martin.

On Liberal Peace: Democracy, War & the International Order John MacMillan. LC 95-61532. (Library of International Relations). 306p. 1998. write for info. (*1-86064-080-X*) I B T.

***On Liberal Revolution.** Piero Gobetti. Ed. by Nadia Urbinati. Tr. by William McCuaig. LC 00-25022. (Illus.). 304p. 2000. 35.00 (*0-300-08117-0*) Yale U Pr.

***On Liberal Revolution.** Piero Gobetti et al. LC 00-25022. (Italian Literature & Thought Ser.). (Illus.). 304p. 2000. pap. 16.95 (*0-300-08118-9*) Yale U Pr.

***On Liberty.** John Stuart Mill. Ed. & Intro. by Gertrude Himmelfarb. 192p. (C). 1998. pap. 5.33 (*0-14-043207-8*) Addson-Wesley Educ.

***On Liberty.** John Stuart Mill. Ed. by Edward Alexander. (Literary Texts Ser.). 294p. 1999. pap. 5.95 (*1-55111-199-3*) Broadview Pr.

On Liberty. John Stuart Mill. Ed. & Intro. by Elizabeth Rapaport. LC 77-26848. (HPC Classics Ser.). 139p. (C). 1978. pap. text 4.95 (*0-915144-43-3*); lib. bdg. 24.95 (*0-915144-44-1*) Hackett Pub.

On Liberty. John Stuart Mill. Ed. by Alburey Castell. LC 47-3494. (Crofts Classics). 128p. (C). 1947. pap. text 4.95 (*0-88295-056-8*) Harlan Davidson.

On Liberty. John Stuart Mill. Ed. & Intro. by Currin V. Shields. LC 96-209150. 176p. (C). 1956. pap. text 5.80 (*0-02-409690-3*, Pub. by P-H) S&S Trade.

On Liberty. John Stuart Mill. LC 85-63408. (Great Books in Philosophy). 129p. 1986. pap. 5.95 (*0-87975-336-6*) Prometheus Bks.

***On Liberty: Jewish Philosophical Perspectives.** Daniel H. Frank. 288p. 1999. 75.00 (*0-7007-1144-9*, Pub. by Curzon Pr Ltd) Paul & Co Pubs.

***On Liberty: Jewish Philosophical Perspectives.** Ed. by Daniel H. Frank. LC 99-33848. 219p. 1999. text 59.95 (*0-312-22729-9*) St Martin.

On Liberty: With the Subjection of Women & Chapters on Socialism. John Stuart Mill. Ed. by Stefan Collini. (Cambridge Texts in the History of Political Thought Ser.). 328p. (C). 1989. pap. text 9.95 (*0-521-37917-2*) Cambridge U Pr.

On Liberty: With the Subjection of Women & Chapters on Socialism. John Stuart Mill. Ed. by Stefan Collini. (Cambridge Texts in the History of Political Thought Ser.). 260p. (C). 1989. 21.95 (*0-521-37015-9*) Cambridge U Pr.

On Liberty & Liberalism: The Case of John Stuart Mill. Gertrude Himmelfarb. LC 90-4570. 325p. 1990. reprint ed. pap. 19.95 (*1-55815-059-5*) ICS Pr.

On Liberty & Other Essays. John Stuart Mill. Ed. & Intro. by John Gray. (Oxford World's Classics Ser.). 628p. 1998. pap. 8.95 (*0-19-283384-7*) OUP.

On Liberty & Utilitaranism. John Stuart Mill. 1992. 15.00 (*0-679-41329-4*) Everymns Lib.

On Liberty & Utilitarianism. John Stuart Mill. 240p. 1993. mass mkt. 5.95 (*0-553-21414-4*) Bantam.

On Liberty Mill. 1974. write for info. (*0-201-43893-3*) Addison-Wesley.

On Liberty, Society, & Politics: The Essential Essays of William Graham Sumner. William G. Sumner. Ed. by Robert C. Bannister. LC 91-36630. (Liberty Classics Ser.). (Illus.). xlii, 424p. (Orig.). (C). 1992. 18.00 (*0-86597-100-5*) Liberty Fund.

On Liberty, Society, & Politics: The Essential Essays of William Graham Sumner. William G. Sumner. Ed. by Robert C. Bannister. LC 91-36630. (Liberty Classics Ser.). 448p. (Orig.). (C). 1992. pap. 7.50 (*0-86597-101-3*) Liberty Fund.

On Lie Algebras & Some Special Functions of Mathematical Physics. W. B. Miller, Jr. LC 52-42839. (Memoirs of the American Mathematical Society Ser.: No. 50). 43p. 1987. reprint ed. pap. 16.00 (*0-8218-1250-5*, MEMO/1/50C) Am Math.

On Lie Algebras & Some Special Functions of Mathematical Physics. Willard Miller. LC 52-42839. (American Mathematical Society Ser.: No. 50). 49p. reprint ed. pap. 30.00 (*0-608-09175-8*, 205267900002) Bks Demand.

On Lie Algebras of Prime Characteristic. George B. Seligman. LC 52-42839. (Memoirs Ser.: No. 1/19). 85p. 1970. reprint ed. pap. 17.00 (*0-8218-1219-X*, MEMO/1/19) Am Math.

On Lies, Secrets & Silence: Selected Prose, 1966-1978. Adrienne Rich. 320p. 1995. pap. 13.95 (*0-393-31285-2*, Norton Paperbks) Norton.

On Life after Death. Elisabeth Kubler-Ross. 96p. (Orig.). 1995. pap. 7.95 (*0-89087-653-3*) Celestial Arts.

On Life & Death: The Edgar Cayce Readings. Compiled by Association for Research & Enlightenment, Readings. (Library: Vol. 1). 188p. 1973. lib. bdg. 19.95 (*0-87604-065-2*, 1101) ARE Pr.

On Life & Letters, First Series. Anatole France, pseud. Ed. by F. Chapman & James Lewis May. Tr. by A. W. Evans. LC 77-156643. (Essay Index Reprint Ser.). 1977. reprint ed. 23.95 (*0-8369-2357-X*) Ayer.

On Life & Letters, Fourth Series. Anatole France, pseud. Ed. by F. Chapman. LC 77-156643. (Essay Index Reprint Ser.). 1977. reprint ed. 24.95 (*0-8369-2360-X*) Ayer.

On Life & Letters, Second Series. Anatole France, pseud. Ed. by F. Chapman. LC 77-156643. (Essay Index Reprint Ser.). 1977. reprint ed. 23.95 (*0-8369-2358-8*) Ayer.

On Life & Letters, Third Series. Anatole France, pseud. Ed. by F. Chapman. LC 77-156643. (Essay Index Reprint Ser.). 1977. reprint ed. 24.95 (*0-8369-2359-6*) Ayer.

On Life & Love: A Guide to Catholic Teaching on Marriage & Family. rev. ed. William Urbine & William Seifert. LC 96-60699. 216p. (Orig.). 1996. pap. 14.95 (*0-89622-705-7*) Twenty-Third.

On Life, Faith & the Church see O Zhizni o Vjere o Tzerkvje

On Life Letters, vols. 4, Set. France Anatole. Date not set. 86.95 (*0-8369-4977-3*) Ayer.

On Light Alone: A Guru Meditation on the Good Death of Helen Nearing. Ellen LaConte. (Illus.). 125p. 2000. pap. 13.00 (*0-9656077-0-4*, Pub. by Loose Leaf) Chelsea Green Pub.

On Line. 4th ed. Kennedy. (Bedford Guide Ser.). 1996. pap. text 4.00 (*0-312-11978-X*) St Martin.

On-Line Algorithms. Ed. by Lyle A. McGeoch & Daniel D. Sleator. LC 91-43417. (DIMACS Series in Doscrete Mathematics & Theoretical Computer Science: Vol. 7). 179p. 1992. text 32.00 (*0-8218-6596-X*, DIMACS/7C) Am Math.

On-Line Analysers, Pt. 1. EEMUA Staff. 1974. 100.00 (*0-85931-068-X*, Pub. by EEMUA) St Mut.

On-Line Analytical Processing Systems for Business. Robert J. Thierauf. LC 96-54260. 352p. 1997. 72.95 (*1-56720-099-0*, Quorum Bks) Greenwood.

On Line & on Paper: Visual Representations, Visual Culture, & Computer Graphics in Design Engineering. Kathryn Henderson. LC 98-5211. (Inside Technology Ser.). (Illus.). 256p. 1998. 30.00 (*0-262-08269-1*) MIT Pr.

On-Line Business Computer Applications. 3rd ed. Alan L. Eliason. 544p. (C). 1991. pap. text 23.00 (*0-02-332481-3*, Macmillan Coll) P-H.

***On-line Business Survival Guide: Featuring The Wall Street Journal Interactive Edition.** 96p. 1999. pap. 21.95 (*0-471-32738-7*) Wiley.

O

An Asterisk (*) at the beginning of an entry indicates that the title is appearing for the first time.

***On-Line Business Survival Guide in Finance: Featuring the Wall Street Journal Interactive Edition.** Wiley Staff. 65p. 1998. pap. 23.95 (*0-471-25232-8*) Wiley.

***On-Line Business Survival Guide in Information Systems & Decision Sciences.** Wiley Staff. 64p. 1998. pap. 23.95 (*0-471-25503-3*) Wiley.

On-Line Cognition in Person Perception. Ed. by John N. Bassili. 240p. (C). 1989. 49.95 (*0-8058-0423-4*) L Erlbaum Assocs.

On Line Criminal Activity: An Investigative Primer for Law. Alfred O. Olsen & Franklin Clark. (Practical Aspects Of Criminal & Forensic Investigation Ser.). 1998. 69.95 (*0-8493-8161-4*) CRC Pr.

On-Line Database of Literature, Arts, & Medicine: An Annotated Bibliography. annot. ed. Ed. by Felice Aull. 445p. (Orig.). (C). 1996. pap. 35.00 (*0-9651593-1-0*) NY Univ Med Ctr.

***On-line Education: Learning & Teaching In Cyberspace.** Kearsley. LC 99-52303. (Education Ser.). 2000. pap. text 54.95 (*0-534-50689-5*) Wadsworth Pub.

On-Line Electrical Troubleshooting. Lynn Lundquist. 240p. 1989. text 47.00 (*0-07-039110-6*) McGraw.

On-Line Estimation & Adaptive Control of Bioreactors: Process Measurement & Control. Ed. by G. Bastin & D. Dochain. 394p. 1990. 231.00 (*0-444-88430-0*) Elsevier.

On-Line Evaluation of Meat. Howard J. Swatland. LC 95-61607. 360p. 1995. pap. 149.95 (*1-56676-333-9*) Technomic.

On-Line Expert: How to Get the Best Results with On-Line Searching. Ralph D. Thomas. 62p. (C). 1995. pap. text 19.95 (*0-918487-81-1*) Thomas Investigative.

On-Line Fault Detection & Supervision in the Chemical Process. Morris & Martin. LC 96-41804. (IPPV IFAC Postprint Ser.). 246p. 1996. pap. 71.00 (*0-08-042607-7*, Pergamon Pr) Elsevier.

On-Line Fault Detection & Supervision in the Chemical Process Industries: Selected Papers from the IFAC Symposium, Newark, Delaware, U. S. A., 22-24 April 1992. Ed. by P. S. Dhurjati & George Stephanopoulos. LC 92-44353. (IFAC Symposia Ser.: 9301). 328p. 1993. 167.00 (*0-08-041896-1*, Pergamon Pr) Elsevier.

On-Line Fault Detection & Supervision in the Chemical Process Industries, 1998: Proceedings of the 3rd IFAC Workshop, IFP, Solaize (Lyon), France, 4-5 June 1998. Ed. by P. S. Dhurjati & Sylvie Cauvin. LC 98-31476. 416p. 1998. pap. 96.50 (*0-08-043233-6*, Pergamon Pr) Elsevier.

On-Line Friendship, Chat-Room Romance & Cybersex: Your Guide to Affairs of the Net. Michael Adamse & Sheree Motta. 250p. (Orig.). 1996. pap. 11.95 (*1-55874-418-5*, 4185) Health Comm.

On-Line Games: In-Depth Strategies & Secrets. Bill Mann. 1995. pap. text 19.95 (*0-7615-0076-6*) Prima Pub.

On-Line Investor: Busing Your Personal Computer to Find & Invest in the Most Profitable Stocks. 2nd ed. Ted Allrich. LC 99-462634. 256p. 1999. pap. 15.95 (*0-312-20808-1*, St Martins Paperbacks) St Martin.

On-Line Journ@list: Using the Internet & Other Electronic Resources. 2nd ed. Randy Reddick & Elliot King. LC 96-80011. 288p. (C). 1997. pap. text 31.00 (*0-15-505222-5*, Pub. by Harcourt Coll Pubs) Harcourt.

***On-Line Learning Handbook: Developing Web-Based Learning Materials & Systems.** Ed. by Alan Jolliffe et al. 320p. 2000. pap. 35.00 (*0-7494-3208-X*, Pub. by Kogan Page Ltd) Stylus Pub VA.

***On-Line Learning in Neural Networks.** Ed. by David Saad. LC 98-31983. (Publications of the Newton Institute: No. 17). (Illus.). 408p. (C). 1999. text 69.95 (*0-521-65263-4*) CSLI.

On Line Marketing Handbook. 2nd ed. Daniel S. Janal. LC 97-135687. (Communications Ser.). 436p. 1997. text 30.95 (*0-442-02482-7*, VNR) Wiley.

On-Line Materials Property Base. (MDC Ser.: Vol. 20). 1983. pap. text 30.00 (*0-317-02638-0*, H00284) ASME.

On-Line Monitoring of Continuous Process Plant. D. W. Butcher. 326p. 1983. text 107.00 (*0-470-27504-9*) P-H.

On-Line Optimization Techniques in Industrial Control: Proceedings of the 5th Annual Advanced Control Conference. Ed. by Edward J. Kompass & Theodore J. Williams. 204p. 1983. reprint ed. 18.00 (*0-914331-04-3*, Control Engrng) Cahners Busn Des Plaines.

On-Line Particle Size & Shape Characterization by Narrow Angle Light Scattering. Camiel Heffels. (Illus.). 167p. (Orig.). 1995. pap. 59.50 (*90-407-1181-X*, Pub. by Delft U Pr) Coronet Bks.

On-Line Process Analyzers. Gary D. Nichols. LC 87-30538. 320p. 1988. 149.00 (*0-471-86608-3*) Wiley.

On-Line Process Simulation Techniques in Industrial Control: Proceedings of the 11th Annual Advanced Control Conference. Ed. by Edward J. Kompass & Theodore J. Williams. 200p. 1985. 30.00 (*0-914331-11-6*, Control Engrng) Cahners Busn Des Plaines.

On-Line Production Scheduling & Plant-Wide Control: Proceedings of the 8th Annual Advanced Control Conference. Ed. by Edward J. Kompass & Theodore J. Williams. 149p. 1982. 27.50 (*0-914331-07-8*, Control Engrng) Cahners Busn Des Plaines.

On-line Profits: A Manager's Guide to Electronic Commerce. Harvard Business School Press Staff. 287p. 1997. 34.95 (*0-07-105060-4*) McGraw.

On-Line Profits: A Manager's Guide to Electronic Commerce. Peter G.W. Keen & Craigg Ballance. LC 97-11882. 304p. 1997. pap. 18.95 (*0-87584-821-4*, HBS Pr) Harvard Busn.

On-Line Revolution in Libraries: Proceedings of the 1977 Conference in Pittsburgh, PA. Ed. by Allen Kent & Thomas J. Galvin. LC 78-15800. (Books in Library & Information Science: No. 23). 323p. reprint ed. pap. 100.20 (*0-8357-6241-6*, 203454400090) Bks Demand.

On-Line Search: Papers from the 1997 AAAI Workshop. Ed. by Sven Koenig. (AAAI Technical Reports). (Illus.). 133p. 1997. spiral bd. 25.00 (*1-57735-041-3*) AAAI Pr.

On-Line Sensors for Food Processing, Vol. 4, No. 2. Ed. by Isao Karube. (Japanese Technology Reviews Ser.: Section E). 180p. 1994. pap. text 73.00 (*2-88124-962-0*) Gordon & Breach.

On-Line Spaceman & Other Cases. Seymour Simon. LC 96-34416. (Einstein Anderson, Science Detective Ser.). (Illus.). 96p. (J). (gr. 3-6). 1997. 15.00 (*0-688-14433-0*, Wm Morrow) Morrow Avon.

***On-Line Spaceman & Other Cases.** Seymour Simon. (Einstein Anderson, Science Detective Ser.). (J). (gr. 3-6). 1998. 9.09 (*0-606-13352-6*, Pub. by Turtleback) Demco.

***On-Line Spaceman & Other Cases.** Seymour Simon. (Einstein Anderson, Science Detective Ser.). 96p. (J). (gr. 3-6). 1998. reprint ed. mass mkt. 3.99 (*0-380-72662-9*, Avon Bks) Morrow Avon.

On-Line Student: Making the Grade on the Internet. Randy Reddick & Elliot King. LC 95-81842. 337p. (C). 1995. pap. text 22.00 (*0-15-503189-9*, Pub. by Harcourt Coll Pubs) Harcourt.

On-Line Testing. Michael Nicolaidis & Yervant Zorian. LC 98-2694. 1998. 125.00 (*0-7923-8132-7*) Kluwer Academic.

***On-line Testing Certificate Level 2.** Barksdale & Rutter. 2000. pap. 6.00 (*0-538-69169-7*) S-W Pub.

On-Line Testing of Calibration of Process Instrumentation Channel in Nuclear Power Plants. H. M. Hashemian. (Illus.). (Orig.). 1995. pap. write for info. (*1-882148-04-5*) Analysis & Measurement.

On-Line with Accu-Weather: Instructional Modules in Meteorology. Accu-Weather, Inc. Staff. 80p. 1996. spiral bd. 9.75 (*0-8403-7132-2*) Kendall-Hunt.

On Linguistic Anthropology: Essays in Honor of Harry Hoijer, 1979. J. Greenberg et al. Ed. by Jacques P. Maquet. LC 80-50214. (Other Realities Ser.: Vol. 2). 140p. (C). 1980. pap. text 13.00 (*0-89003-062-6*) Undena Pubns.

On Linguistic Method: Selected Papers. Paul L. Garvin. LC 75-182468. (Janua Linguarum, Ser. Minor: No. 30). (Illus.). 199p. (Orig.). 1972. pap. text 36.95 (*90-279-2005-2*) Mouton.

On Lisp: Advanced Techniques for Common Lisp. Paul Graham. LC 93-9047. 413p. (C). 1993. pap. 52.00 (*0-13-030552-9*) P-H.

On Listening. Carl A. Faber. LC 80-4512. 1976. 5.95 (*0-918026-02-4*) Perseus Pr.

On Listening. Carl A. Faber. 1987. 7.95 (*0-685-17665-7*) Perseus Pr.

On Listening to Holocaust Survivors: Recounting & Life History. Henry Greenspan. LC 98-4944. 224p. 1998. 24.95 (*0-275-95718-7*, Pub. by Greenwood) Natl Bk Netwk.

On Literacy & Its Teaching: Issues in English Education. Ed. by Gail E. Hawisher et al. LC 89-35802. (SUNY Series, Literacy, Culture, & Learning). 259p. (C). 1990. text 74.50 (*0-7914-0265-7*); pap. text 24.95 (*0-7914-0266-5*) State U NY Pr.

***On Literary Biography.** John Updike. 1999. 75.00 (*1-57003-345-5*) U of SC Pr.

On Literary Farces see Popeiana

On Literary Theory & Philosophy: A Cross-Disciplinary Encounter. Ed. by Richard Freadman & Lloyd Reinhardt. LC 91-12463. 292p. 1991. text 49.95 (*0-312-06508-6*) St Martin.

On Literature & Society. Antonio Candido. Ed. & Tr. by Howard S. Becker. LC 94-32403. 248p. 1995. text 49.50 (*0-691-03629-2*, Pub. by Princeton U Pr); pap. text 17.95 (*0-691-03630-6*, Pub. by Princeton U Pr) Cal Prin Full Svc.

On Literature Today. Van Wyck Brooks. (BCL1-PS American Literature Ser.). 290p. 1993. reprint ed. lib. bdg. 59.00 (*0-7812-6578-9*) Rprt Serv.

On Liturgical Theology. Aidan Kavanagh. 205p. 1992. pap. 14.95 (*0-8146-6067-3*, Pueblo Bks) Liturgical Pr.

On Living in a Revolution. Julian S. Huxley. LC 70-167363. (Essay Index Reprint Ser.). 1977. reprint ed. 16.95 (*0-8369-2510-6*) Ayer.

On Living in a Revolution & Other Essays. Mysore N. Srinivas. 224p. 1993. 19.95 (*0-19-563050-5*) OUP.

On Living Simply: The Golden Voice of Saint John Chrysostom. John Chrysostom. LC 96-39148. 96p. 1997. pap. 7.00 (*0-7648-0056-6*, Liguori Triumph) Liguori Pubns.

On Loan from the Angels. Dale W. Emme & R. Darlene Emme. (Illus.). 177p. (Orig.). 1998. pap. 17.95 (*1-889529-12-5*) Two Feathers.

On Location: Settings from Famous Children's Books, No. 1. Joanne Kelly. (Illus.). xv, 129p. (Orig.). 1992. pap. text 18.00 (*1-56308-023-0*) Teacher Ideas Pr.

On Location: The Film Fan's Guide to Britain & Ireland. Brian Pendreigh. (Illus.). 208p. 1996. 29.95 (*1-85158-729-2*, Pub. by Mainstream Pubng) Trafalgar.

On Location! at "Got Milk?" 4th ed. (C). 1998. write for info. (*0-13-081470-9*) P-H.

***On Location in Malibu: Paintings by Contemporary Members of the California Art Club.** Michael Zakian. 72p. 1999. pap. 25.00 (*0-9672257-1-X*) CA Art Acad.

On-Location Recording Techniques. Bruce Bartlett & Jenny Bartlett. LC 99-10574. 304p. 1999. pap. text 29.95 (*0-240-80379-5*, Focal) Buttrwrth-Heinemann.

On Location III. Lynn Davis. (Aperture Ser.: Vol. 146). 1997. pap. text 27.95 (*0-89381-697-3*) Aperture.

On Location with Love & Brandy. Hewitt. (J). 1998. 7.99 (*0-671-02852-9*) PB.

On L1-Approximation. Allan M. Pinkus. (Cambridge Tracts in Mathematics Ser.: No. 92). 256p. (C). 1989. text 64.95 (*0-521-36650-X*) Cambridge U Pr.

On Long Mountain: Poems. Elizabeth S. Morgan. LC 97-41958. 64p. 1998. pap. 11.95 (*0-8071-2253-X*) La State U Pr.

On Longing: Narratives of the Miniature, the Gigantic, the Souvenir, the Collection. Susan Stewart. LC 92-40004. 232p. (C). 1993. pap. text 16.95 (*0-8223-1366-9*) Duke.

***On Looking Inward & Being Scientific: A Tribute to G.L. Engel, MD.** Ed. by G. A. Fava. (Psychotherapy & Psychosomatics Ser.: Vol. 69). (Illus.). 64p. 2000. pap. 25.25 (*3-8055-7107-0*) S Karger.

On-loom Cardweaving: A Modern Extension of an Ancient Craft. Herbi Gray. (Illus.). 60p. (Orig.). 1982. pap. 8.95 (*0-9608406-0-5*) H Gray.

On Losing the Soul: Essays in the Social Psychology of Religion. Ed. by Richard K. Fenn & Donald Capps. LC 94-31494. 249p. (C). 1995. text 59.50 (*0-7914-2493-6*); pap. text 19.95 (*0-7914-2494-4*) State U NY Pr.

On Lough Derg. Deidre Purcell. (Illus.). 122p. 1989. 39.00 (*1-85390-095-8*, Pub. by Veritas Pubns) St Mut.

On Louis Simpson: Depths Beyond Happiness. Ed. by Hank Lazer. (Under Discussion Ser.). 408p. (Orig.). 1988. pap. text 17.95 (*0-472-06382-0*, 06382) U of Mich Pr.

On Love. Alain De Botton. LC 92-24888. 240p. 1993. pap. 10.00 (*0-8021-3409-2*, Grove) Grove-Atltic.

On Love. Caleb Gattegno. 1977. pap. 8.00 (*0-87825-074-3*) Ed Solutions.

On Love. Edward Hirsch. LC 97-49460. 96p. 1998. 22.00 (*0-375-40253-5*) Knopf.

On Love. Ishwar C. Puri. Ed. by Edward D. Scott. 28p. (Orig.). 1984. pap. 2.00 (*0-937067-03-2*) Insti Study Aware.

On Love. 3rd ed. Sri Aurobindo & Mother. Ed. by Pavitra. 49p. 1988. pap. 2.95 (*81-7058-104-4*, Pub. by SAA) E-W Cultural Ctr.

***On Love: Poems.** Edward Hirsch. 2000. pap. 15.00 (*0-375-70260-1*) Knopf.

On Love & Barley: Haiku of Basho. Matsu Basho. Tr. & Intro. by Lucien Stryk. (Classics Ser.). 96p. 1986. pap. 9.95 (*0-14-044459-9*, Penguin Classics) Viking Penguin.

On Love & Loneliness. Jiddu Krishnamurti. LC 93-6068. 176p. 1994. pap. 12.00 (*0-06-251013-4*, Pub. by Harper SF) HarpC.

On Love & Loving: Psychological Perspectives on the Nature & Experience of Romantic Love. Kenneth S. Pope et al. LC 80-8012. (Jossey-Bass Social & Behavioral Science Ser.). 397p. reprint ed. pap. 123.10 (*0-7837-2548-5*, 204270700006) Bks Demand.

On Love & Psychological Exercises, 2 vols. in 1. A. R. Orage. LC 97-43968. 200p. 1998. reprint ed. pap. 14.95 (*1-57863-100-9*) Weiser.

On Loving God: Selections from Sermons by St. Bernard of Clairvaux. Bernard of Clairvaux. Ed. by Hugh Martin. LC 79-8706. (Treasury of Christian Bks.). 125p. 1981. reprint ed. lib. bdg. 49.50 (*0-313-20787-9*, BEOL, Greenwood Pr) Greenwood.

On Loving, Hating, & Living Well: The Public Psychoanalytic Lectures of Ralph R. Greenson, M.D. Ed. by Robert A. Nemiroff et al. LC 92-1438. (Monograph Series of the Ralph R. Greenson Memorial Library of the San Diego Psychoanalytic Institute & Society). 382p. 1992. 55.00 (*0-8236-3790-5*) Intl Univs Pr.

On Loving Neighbors & Aliens. Organizers Against Deportation & Refugees in Oakda. (Common Ground Ser.: Vol. II). (Illus.). 24p. (Orig.). 1986. pap. 5.00 (*1-884478-01-8*) Common Grnd.

On Lynchings: Southern Horrors, a Red Record, & Mob Rule in New Orleans. Ida B. Wells-Barnett. LC 72-75854. 188p. 1990. pap. 18.95 (*0-88143-118-4*) Ayer.

On Lynchings: Southern Horrors, a Red Record, Mob Rule in New Orleans. Ida B. Wells-Barnett. Date not set. 37.96 (*0-405-01849-5*) Arno Press.

On Machine Translation. Paul L. Garvin. LC 79-182469. (Janua Linguarum, Series Minor: No. 128). 142p. (Orig.). 1972. pap. text 47.70 (*90-279-2004-4*) Mouton.

On Macintosh Programming: Advanced Techniques. Daniel K. Allen. 512p. 1989. pap. text 24.95 (*0-201-51737-X*) Addison-Wesley.

On Maeterlinck. Henry Rose. LC 73-21891. (Studies in French Literature: No. 45). 1974. lib. bdg. 75.00 (*0-8383-1829-0*) M S G Haskell Hse.

On Mahler & Britten Vol. 3: Essays in Honour of Donald Mitchell on His Seventieth Birthday. Ed. by Philip Reed. (Aldeburgh Studies in Music). (Illus.). 374p. 1998. pap. 35.00 (*0-85115-614-2*, Boydell Pr) Boydell & Brewer.

On Man in His Environment: Social Scientific Foundations for Research & Policy. Samuel Z. Klausner. LC 77-146736. (Jossey-Bass Behavioral Science Ser.). 240p. reprint ed. pap. 74.40 (*0-608-14922-5*, 202567600045) Bks Demand.

On Managing, Set. abr. ed. Mark H. McCormack. 1996. audio. write for info. (*0-7871-1004-3*, Dove Audio) NewStar Media.

On Mankind Their Origin & Destiny. Arthur D. Thomson. 800p. 1993. reprint ed. pap. 50.00 (*1-56459-392-4*) Kessinger Pub.

On Manly Courage: A Study of Plato's "Laches" Walter T. Schmid. LC 91-30776. (Philosophical Explorations Ser.). 256p. (C). 1992. 36.95 (*0-8093-1745-1*) S Ill U Pr.

On Many a Bloody Field: Four Years in the Iron Brigade. Alan D. Gaff. LC 96-1728. (Illus.). 520p. 1997. text 29.95 (*0-253-33063-7*) Ind U Pr.

On Many a Bloody Field: Four Years in the Iron Brigade. Alan D. Gaff. LC 96-1728. (Illus.). 520p. 1999. pap. 17.95 (*0-253-21294-4*) Ind U Pr.

On Mardi Gras Day. Fatima Shaik. Ed. by Cindy Kane. LC 97-10588. (Illus.). 32p. (J). (ps-3). 1999. 16.99 (*0-8037-1442-4*, Dial Yng Read) Peng Put Young Read.

On Mark Twain: The Best from American Literature. Ed. by Edwin H. Cady & Louis J. Budd. LC 87-9020. x, 303p. 1987. text 49.95 (*0-8223-0759-6*) Duke.

On Market Street. Arnold Lobel. LC 80-21418. (Illus.). 40p. (J). (ps-3). 1981. 16.89 (*0-688-84309-3*, Grenwillow Bks) HarpC Child Bks.

On Market Street. Anita Lobel. (J). 1981. 10.15 (*0-606-04290-3*, Pub. by Turtleback) Demco.

On Market Street. Arnold Lobel. LC 80-21418. (Illus.). 40p. (J). (ps-2). 1981. 17.00 (*0-688-80309-1*, Grenwillow Bks) HarpC Child Bks.

On Market Street. Arnold Lobel. LC 80-21418. (Illus.). 40p. (J). (ps-3). 1989. mass mkt. 6.95 (*0-688-08745-0*, Wm Morrow) Morrow Avon.

On Market Street. large type ed. Arnold Lobel. (J). (ps-2). 1993. 19.95 (*0-590-71697-2*) Scholastic Inc.

On Marriage. Theodor G. Von Hippel. Tr. & Intro. by Timothy F. Sellner. (Illus.). 324p. 1994. text 29.95 (*0-8143-2495-9*) Wayne St U Pr.

On Marriage & Family Life: St. John Chrysostom. St. John Chrysostom. Tr. by Catharine P. Roth & David Anderson. LC 86-6756. 114p. (Orig.). 1986. pap. 8.95 (*0-913836-86-9*) St Vladimirs.

On Marx. Lee-Lampshire. (Philosophy Ser.). 2000. pap. text 13.95 (*0-534-57602-8*) Brooks-Cole.

On Marxian Perspectives in Anthropology: Essays in Honor of H. Hoijer, 1981. S. Mintz et al. Ed. by Jaques P. Maquet & N. C. Daniels. LC 84-52206. (Other Realities Ser.: Vol. 5). vi, 98p. 1985. 26.00 (*0-89003-178-9*); pap. 16.00 (*0-89003-179-7*) Undena Pubns.

On Materialism. Sebastiano Timpanaro. Tr. by Lawrence Garner from ITA. 268p. (C). 1985. pap. 19.00 (*0-86091-721-5*, Pub. by Verso) Norton.

On Max Horkheimer: New Perspectives. Ed. by Seyla Benhabib et al. (Studies in Contemporary German Social Thought). (Illus.). 533p. 1993. 44.00 (*0-262-02355-5*) MIT Pr.

On Max Horkheimer: New Perspectives. Ed. by Seyla Benhabib et al. (Studies in Contemporary German Social Thought). 1995. pap. text 22.00 (*0-262-52207-1*) MIT Pr.

On Mean Values of the Riemann Zeta Function. A. Ivic. Ed. by S. Raghavan & V. Singh. (Tata Institute Lectures on Mathematics & Physics Ser.). 365p. 1993. 32.95 (*0-387-54748-7*) Spr-Verlag.

On Meaning-Making: Essays in Semiotics. Mieke Bal. 320p. (C). 1994. pap. 29.95 (*0-944344-39-9*) Polebridge Pr.

On Measure for Measure: An Essay in Criticism of Shakespeare's Drama. Lawrence J. Ross. LC 96-48852. (Illus.). 184p. 1997. 34.50 (*0-87413-593-1*) U Delaware Pr.

On Measuring Democracy. Ed. by Alex Inkeles. 196p. (C). 1991. pap. 24.95 (*0-88738-881-7*) Transaction Pubs.

On Medieval & Renaissance Slavic Writings. Henrik Birnbaum. LC 73-85243. (Slavistic Printings & Reprintings Ser.: No. 266). 381p. 1974. text 100.00 (*90-279-2680-8*) Mouton.

On Meditation & Discipline. 3rd ed. Pavitra. 14p. 1996. pap. 0.50 (*81-7058-282-2*, Pub. by SAA) E-W Cultural Ctr.

On Melville. Ed. by Louis J. Budd & Edwin H. Cady. LC 88-18897. (Best from American Literature Ser.). x, 300p. (C). 1988. text 49.95 (*0-8223-0867-3*) Duke.

On Meritocracy. Nicholas Lemann. 1999. write for info. (*0-679-42176-9*) Knopf.

On Mermaid Avenue. Binnie Kirshenbaum. LC 92-23224. 166p. 1993. 15.00 (*0-88064-139-8*) Fromm Intl Pub.

On Mermaid Avenue. Binnie Kirshenbaum. LC 94-5458. 166p. 1994. pap. 8.95 (*0-88064-156-8*) Fromm Intl Pub.

On Message Structure: A Framework for the Study of Language & Communication. Ragnar Rommetveit. LC 74-174. 151p. reprint ed. pap. 46.90 (*0-608-14620-X*, 202428400035) Bks Demand.

On Metaphor. Ed. by Sheldon Sacks. LC 79-5080. 204p. 1979. pap. text 11.95 (*0-226-73334-3*, P856) U Ch Pr.

On Metascrotum & Infradeaths. Doru Chirodea. (Illus.). 36p. (Orig.). 1990. pap. 3.00 (*0-926935-41-0*) Runaway Spoon.

On Method: Toward a Reconstruction of Psychological Investigation. David Bakan. LC 67-28628. (Jossey-Bass Behavioral Science Ser.). 205p. reprint ed. pap. 63.60 (*0-608-16880-7*, 202774500056) Bks Demand.

On Method Acting. Edward Dwight. LC 97-90691. 1997. pap. 11.00 (*0-449-00138-5*) Fawcett.

On Method Acting. Edward D. Easty. 246p. 1989. mass mkt. 5.99 (*0-8041-0522-7*) Ivy Books.

On Method in Ecology. Mark Sagoff. (Working Papers on Forensic Ecology). 1988. 2.50 (*0-318-33313-9*, FE1) IPPP.

On Methuselah's Trail: Living Fossils & the Great Extinctions. Peter D. Ward. LC 91-17071. 1993. pap. text 14.95 (*0-7167-2488-X*) W H Freeman.

***On Mexican Time.** Tony Cohan. 2000. reprint ed. pap. 13.00 (*0-7679-0319-6*) Broadway BDD.

On Mexican Time: A New Life in San Miguel. Tony Cohan. LC 99-29296. 288p. 2000. 25.00 (*0-7679-0318-8*) Broadway BDD.

On Military Intervention. 1985. 88.95 (*0-566-05045-5*) Ashgate Pub Co.

***On Mill.** Anderson. 1999. pap. text 13.95 (*0-534-57600-1*) Brooks-Cole.

On Minds & Symbols: The Relevance of Cognitive Science for Semiotics, 117. Thomas C. Daddesio. (Approaches to Semiotics Ser.: No. 117). 271p. (C). 1994. lib. bdg. 118.70 (*3-11-013866-2*) Mouton.

On Minerals & Mineral Products. Eucharius Roesslin. (Ars Medica Ser.: Section 1V, Vol. 1). (C). 1978. 300.00 (*3-11-006907-5*) De Gruyter.

An Asterisk (*) at the beginning of an entry indicates that the title is appearing for the first time.

On Miracle Ground: Essays on the Fiction of Lawrence Durrell. Ed. by Michael H. Begnal. LC 89-43051. 216p. 1990. 38.50 (*0-8387-5158-X*) Bucknell U Pr.

On Misperception. Auther Stein. (CISA Working Papers: No. 23). 47p. (Orig.). 1980. pap. 15.00 (*0-86682-022-1*) Ctr Intl Relations.

***On Missing Link Road.** Bruce Dale. LC 99-90824. 1999. 25.00 (*0-7388-0528-9*); pap. 18.00 (*0-7388-0529-7*) Xlibris Corp.

On Model Uncertainty & Its Statistical Implications. Ed. by T. K. Dijkstra. (Lecture Notes in Economics & Mathematical Systems Ser.: Vol. 307). 138p. 1988. 28.40 (*0-387-19367-7*) Spr-Verlag.

On Modern American Art: Selected Essays. Robert Rosenblum. LC 99-22015. 384p. 1999. 39.95 (*0-8109-3683-6*, Pub. by Abrams) Time Warner.

On Modern Jewish Politics. Ezra Mendelsohn. (Studies in Jewish History). (Illus.). 184p. 1993. text 60.00 (*0-19-503864-9*); pap. text 19.95 (*0-19-508319-9*) OUP.

On Modern Literature: Lectures & Addresses. William Ker. (Collected Works of Sarah Orne Jewett). 281p. 2000. reprint ed. lib. bdg. 59.00 (*0-7812-0295-7*) Rprt Serv.

On Modern Literature: Lectures & Addresses. William P. Ker. Ed. by Terence Spencer & James Sutherland. LC 70-158500. 1971. reprint ed. 13.00 (*0-403-01299-6*) Scholarly.

On Modern Marriage & Other Observations. Isak Dinesen. Tr. by Anne Born. 144p. 1987. pap. 7.95 (*0-312-01074-5*) St Martin.

On Mole & Amount of Substance: A Study of the Dynamics of Concept Formation & Concept Attainment. Helge Stromdahl. (Goteburg Studies in Educational Science: No. 106). (Illus.). 276p. (Orig.). 1996. pap. 62.50 (*91-7346-293-4*) Coronet Bks.

On Moment Theory & Controllability of One-Dimensional Vibrating Systems & Heating Processes. W. Krabs. Ed. by M. Thoma & A. Wyner. (Lecture Notes in Control & Information Sciences: Vol. 173). v, 174p. 1992. 53.95 (*0-387-55102-6*) Spr-Verlag.

On Monasticism see O Monashestvje

On Monday When It Rained. Cherryl Kachenmeister. (Illus.). 40p. (J). (gr. k-3). 1989. 14.00 (*0-395-51940-3*) HM.

On Monetary Causes of Real Exchange Rate Changes. Reinhard Furstenberg. 115p. 1985. lib. bdg. 39.00 (*3-16-345000-8*, Pub. by JCB Mohr) Coronet Bks.

On Monetary Policy & Interest Rate Determination in an Open Economy. Lars Horngren. 274p. (Orig.). 1986. pap. text 70.00 (*91-7258-222-7*) Coronet Bks.

On Money & Credit in Europe: The Selected Essays of Martin M. G. Fase. Martin M. Fase. LC 98-13922. 416p. 1998. 100.00 (*1-85898-885-3*) E Elgar.

***On Money & Markets: A Wall Street Memoir.** Henry Kaufman. LC 99-86024. 356p. 2000. 24.95 (*0-07-136049-2*) McGraw.

On Monosemy: A Study in Linguistic Semantics. Charles Ruhl. LC 88-17494. (SUNY Series in Linguistics). 299p. (C). 1989. text 89.50 (*0-88706-946-0*); pap. text 29.95 (*0-88706-947-9*) State U NY Pr.

On Monsters & Marvels. Ambroise Pare. Tr. by Janis L. Pallister from FRE. LC 81-16297. (Illus.). xxxii, 224p. (C). 1983. pap. text 23.00 (*0-226-64563-0*) U Ch Pr.

On Moods. Kay R. Jamison. 1999. pap. write for info. (*0-375-70148-6*) Vin Bks.

On Moral Business: Classical Contemporary Resources for Ethics in Economic Life. Ed. by Dennis P. McCann et al. LC 94-21941. 991p. (Orig.). 1995. pap. text 39.00 (*0-8028-0626-0*) Eerdmans.

On Moral Considerability: An Essay on who Morally Matters. Mark H. Bernstein. 208p. 1998. text 35.00 (*0-19-512391-3*) OUP.

On Moral Fiction. John Gardner. LC 77-20409. 224p. 2000. pap. 15.00 (*0-465-05226-6*, TB-5069, Pub. by Basic) HarpC.

***On Moral Grounds: President Harry S. Truman & the Birth of the State of Israel.** Robert Kirschner et al. Ed. by Grace Cohen Grossman. LC 98-65335. (Illus.). 40p. 1998. pap. 9.95 (*0-9651640-7-1*) Skirball Cultural.

On Moral Medicine: Theological Perspectives in Medical Ethics. Ed. by Stephen E. Lammers & Allen Verhey. 667p. 1987. pap. 20.00 (*0-8028-0293-1*) Eerdmans.

On Moral Medicine: Theological Perspectives in Medical Ethics. 2nd expanded rev. ed. Ed. by Stephen E. Lammers & Allen Verhey. LC 97-35605. 1000p. 1998. pap. 49.00 (*0-8028-4249-6*) Eerdmans.

On Moral Personhood: Philosophy, Literature, Criticism, & Self-Understanding. Richard Eldridge. 224p. 1989. 33.95 (*0-226-20316-6*) U Ch Pr.

On Moral Sentiments: Contemporary Responses to Adam Smith. John Reeder. (Key Issues Ser.: No. 18). 256p. 1998. 72.00 (*1-85506-549-5*); pap. 22.00 (*1-85506-550-9*) Thoemmes Pr.

On More Feet & Fingers. Jim Watson. (Illus.). 96p. 1989. pap. 3.95 (*0-938567-13-6*) Mountaineers.

On Mortality. St. Cyprian of Carthage. 1986. pap. 1.50 (*0-89981-064-0*) Eastern Orthodox.

***On Mother Brown's Doorstep.** Mary Jane Staples. (J). 2000. pap. 6.95 (*0-552-13975-0*, Pub. by Transworld Publishers Ltd) Trafalgar.

On Mother's Day. Andrea Edwards. (Great Expectations Ser.). 1996. per. 3.99 (*0-373-24029-5*, 1-24029-0) Silhouette.

On Mother's Lap. Ann H. Scott. LC 91-17765. (Illus.). 32p. (J). (ps-k). 1992. 15.00 (*0-395-58920-7*, Clarion Bks); pap. 6.95 (*0-395-62976-4*, Clarion Bks) HM.

On Mother's Lap. Ann H. Scott. 1994. pap. 9.95 incl. audio (*0-395-69173-7*, 111692, Clarion Bks) Ticknor & Flds Bks Yng Read.

***On Mother's Lap.** Ann Herbert Scott. (Illus.). 28p. (J). (ps-k). 2000. 4.95 (*0-618-05159-7*, Clarion Bks) HM.

On Mother's Lap. Ann Herbert Scott. LC 91-17765. 1992. 11.15 (*0-606-06633-0*, Pub. by Turtleback) Demco.

On Mountains & Mountaineers. Mikel Vause. LC 93-5216. (Illus.). 112p. (Orig.). 1993. pap. 12.95 (*1-879415-06-2*) Mtn n Air Bks.

On Mountains' Breath. Harold Littlebird. (Illus.). 72p. 1982. pap. 6.00 (*0-940510-03-0*) Tooth of Time.

On Movies. Oliver Stone. 1998. write for info. (*0-8129-2864-4*, Times Bks) Crown Pub Group.

On Mozart. Ed. by James M. Morris. (Woodrow Wilson Center Press Ser.). (Illus.). 260p. (C). 1994. text 54.95 (*0-521-47065-X*); pap. text 18.95 (*0-521-47661-5*) Cambridge U Pr.

On Multimedia Vol. 1: Technologies for the 21st Century. Ed. by Martin Greenberger. 263p. (Orig.). 1990. pap. 24.95 (*1-55940-141-9*) Coun For Tech.

On Music. Friedrich Daniel Ernst Schleiermacher. Tr. & Intro. by Albert Blackwell. (Schleiermacher Studies & Translations: Vol. 4). 1995. write for info. (*0-88946-363-8*) E Mellen.

On My Beach There Are Many Pebbles. Leo Lionni. (Illus.). (J). (gr. k-1). 1961. 15.95 (*0-8392-3024-9*) Astor-Honor.

On My Beach There Are Many Pebbles. Leo Lionni. (J). 1995. 10.15 (*0-606-07966-1*, Pub. by Turtleback) Demco.

On My Beach There Are Many Pebbles. Leo Lionni. LC 94-6484. (Illus.). 32p. (J). (ps up). 1995. reprint ed. mass mkt. 6.95 (*0-688-13284-7*, Wm Morrow) Morrow Avon.

On My Being Dead & Other Stories. L. W. Michaelson. LC 83-81251. (Orig.). 1984. pap. 4.00 (*0-913123-02-1*) Galileo.

***On My Boat: The Sound of Long O.** Cynthia Klingel. LC 99-15887. (Wonder Books Ser.). (Illus.). 24p. (J). (ps-2). 1999. lib. bdg. 21.41 (*1-56766-733-3*) Childs World.

***On My Brother's Shoulders.** Ty Andre. LC 97-205475. 1998. 16.95 (*1-86254-378-X*) Wakefield Pr.

On My Honor. Marion Dane Bauer. 96p. (J). (gr. k-6). 1987. pap. 4.99 (*0-440-46633-4*, YB BDD) BDD Bks Young Read.

On My Honor. Marion Dane Bauer. LC 86-2679. 96p. (J). (gr. 4-7). 1986. 15.00 (*0-89919-439-7*, Clarion Bks) HM.

On My Honor. Marion Dane Bauer. 90p. (J). (gr. 5-6). pap. 4.50 (*0-8072-1455-8*) Listening Lib.

On My Honor. Marion Dane Bauer. (J). 1986. 9.60 (*0-606-03630-X*, Pub. by Turtleback) Demco.

***On My Honor.** Phyllis A. Green. 32p. 1999. 9.95 (*1-56137-335-4*) Novel Units.

On My Honor. Thane Packer. LC 98-72460. 1998. pap. 9.95 (*1-57008-439-4*) Bookcraft Inc.

On My Honor. unabridged ed. Marion D. Bauer. (J). (gr. 5-6). 1992. pap. 21.98 incl. audio (*0-8072-7370-8*, YA 839 SP) Listening Lib.

On My Honor: A Literature Unit. Gail D. Hanna. (Literature Units Ser.). (Illus.). 48p. (Orig.). 1993. student ed. 7.95 (*1-55734-426-4*) Tehr Create Mat.

On My Honor: A Paper Doll History of the Girl Scout Uniform, Vol. 1. Kathryn M. Hunt. (Illus.). 40p. (J). (gr. 2-6). 1994. pap. 8.95 (*0-89672-333-X*) Tex Tech Univ Pr.

On My Honor: A Study Guide. Kathy Danielson. Ed. by Joyce Friedland & Rikki Kessler. (Novel-Ties Ser.). (J). (gr. 4-6). 1991. pap. text 15.95 (*0-88122-576-2*) Lrn Links.

On My Honor, I Will. rev. ed. Randy Pennington & Marc Bockman. 210p. (Orig.). 1995. pap. 10.99 (*1-56043-846-0*, Treasure Hse) Destiny Image.

On My Mind. Manfred Lehmann. LC 96-70932. (Illus.). 334p. 1997. 29.95 (*0-88400-194-6*, Shengold Bks) Schreiber Pub.

On My Own. Roger Emerson & Richard Derwingson. (J). (gr. 5-8). 1989. 2.95 (*0-931205-50-6*); 2.95 (*0-931205-49-2*); teacher ed. 12.95 (*0-931205-48-4*) Jenson Pubns.

***On My Own.** Created by Francine Pascal. (Sweet Valley High Senior Year Ser.: No. 15). (YA). (gr. 7 up). 2000. pap. 4.50 (*0-553-49314-0*, SweetDreams) BDD Bks Young Read.

On My Own. Alan Seaburg. (Illus.). 52p. 1992. pap. text 10.00 (*0-9625794-3-2*) A Miniver Pr.

On My Own: Fix-It! Clean-It! large type ed. Carol Loeb. (Illus.). 63p. (Orig.). (YA). (gr. 9 up). 1996. pap. text 9.95 (*1-890524-02-6*) On My Own.

On My Own: Getting (& Keeping) a Job. large type ed. Carol Loeb. (Illus.). (Orig.). (YA). (gr. 9 up). 1996. pap. text 9.95 (*1-890524-01-8*) On My Own.

On My Own: Helping Kids Help Themselves. Tova Navarra. (Illus.). 128p. (J). (gr. 2-8). 1993. pap. 9.95 (*0-8120-1563-0*) Barron.

On My Own: Helping Kids Help Themselves. Tova Navarra. 1993. 14.15 (*0-606-05521-5*, Pub. by Turtleback) Demco.

On My Own: How-To Moving Out - Moving On. large type ed. Carol Loeb. (Illus.). (Orig.). (YA). (gr. 9 up). 1996. pap. text 9.95 (*1-890524-03-4*) On My Own.

On My Own: In the Kitchen. large type ed. Carol Loeb. (Illus.). 70p. (Orig.). (YA). (gr. 9 up). 1996. pap. text 9.95 (*1-890524-04-2*) On My Own.

On My Own: Korean Businesses & Race Relations in America. In-Jin Yoon. LC 96-39395. 1997. pap. text 17.95 (*0-226-95928-7*); lib. bdg. 45.00 (*0-226-95927-9*) U Ch Pr.

On My Own: Living Well on Not Much Money. large type ed. Carol Loeb. (Illus.). 69p. (Orig.). (YA). (gr. 9 up). 1996. pap. text 9.95 (*1-890524-00-X*) On My Own.

On My Own: Setting up a Small Business. large type ed. Carol Loeb. (Illus.). 83p. (Orig.). (YA). (gr. 9 up). 1996. pap. text 9.95 (*1-890524-05-0*) On My Own.

***On My Own & Clueless.** Clark Kidd & Kathy H. Kidd. LC 00-25337. 2000. write for info. (*1-57345-650-0*) Deseret Bk.

On My Own at 107: Reflections on Life Without Bessie. large type ed. Sarah L. Delany & Amy H. Hearth. 176p. 1998. pap. 14.00 (*0-06-251486-5*) HarpC.

On My Own Board Book. Miela Ford. LC 98-24130. (Illus.). 16p. (J). (ps-k). 1999. bds. 5.95 (*0-688-16452-8*, Grenwillow Bks) HarpC Child Bks.

On My Own Handbook: 100 Secrets of Success. Bobb Biehl. 320p. (Orig.). 1991. pap. 10.99 (*1-55513-338-X*) Chariot Victor.

On My Painting. 2nd ed. Max Beckmann. Tr. by George Scrivani from GER. 125p. (Orig.). 1994. reprint ed. pap. 5.95 (*0-937815-19-5*) Hanuman Bks.

On My Street. Eve Merriam & Melanie Greenberg. LC 98-74004. (Growing Tree Ser.). (Illus.). 24p. (YA). (ps up). 2000. 9.95 (*0-694-01258-0*, HarpFestival) HarpC Child Bks.

On My Terms: Against the Current. Larry L. Martin. 450p. 1999. pap. 12.99 (*1-892732-03-3*) J E Ferguson Publ.

***On My Way.** Tomie De Paola. LC 00-38229. (26 Fairmount Avenue Bk.). 2001. write for info. (*0-399-23583-3*) Putnam Pub Group.

On My Way: Dealing with a Move. Bonnie S. Linder. LC 94-92235. (Children in the Military Ser.). 20p. (J). (ps-4). 1994. pap. 4.95 (*0-9643966-0-2*) Sylvan Crest.

On My Way: Fragments of My Life As an Artist. Bob Nash. (Illus.). 64p. (Orig.). 1996. pap. 10.00 (*0-931104-42-4*) SunInk Pubn.

***On My Way: The Arts of Sarah Albritton.** Susan Roach. LC 98-67413. (Illus.). 96p. 1998. pap. 15.00 (*1-57806-114-8*) U Pr of Miss.

On My Way Home: An Autobiography of a Priest in Today's World. Jay Samonie. (Illus.). 290p. 1998. pap. 14.95 (*1-57502-788-7*, PO2177) Morris Pubng.

On My Way to Basic Skills. (Fisher-Price Preschool Learning Pads Ser.). (Illus.). 48p. (J). (ps). 1998. pap., wbk. ed. write for info. (*0-7666-0116-1*, Honey Bear Bks) Modern Pub NYC.

On My Way to Math. (Fisher-Price Preschool Learning Pads Ser.). (Illus.). 48p. (J). (ps). 1998. pap., wbk. ed. write for info. (*0-7666-0117-X*, Honey Bear Bks) Modern Pub NYC.

On My Way to Planned Giving: Inspiring Anecdotes & Advice for Gift-Planning Professionals. G. Roger Schoenhals. LC 96-104115. 128p. (Orig.). 1995. pap. 29.00 (*0-9645517-1-3*) Planned Giving.

On My Way to Reading. (Fisher-Price Preschool Learning Pads Ser.). (Illus.). 48p. (J). (ps). 1998. pap., wbk. ed. write for info. (*0-7666-0118-8*, Honey Bear Bks) Modern Pub NYC.

On My Way to Writing. (Fisher-Price Preschool Learning Pads Ser.). (Illus.). 48p. (J). (ps). 1998. pap., wbk. ed. write for info. (*0-7666-0119-6*, Honey Bear Bks) Modern Pub NYC.

On Myself & Other Princeton Lectures. 2nd rev. ed. Thomas Mann. LC 98-12586. (European University Studies: Vol. 36). 201p. (C). 1998. pap. text 37.95 (*0-8204-3522-8*) P Lang Pubng.

On Myself & Other Princeton Lectures: An Annotated Edition by James N. Bade Based on Mann's Lecture Typescripts. 2nd ed. Thomas Mann. Ed. by Herbert Kraft. (Historisch-kritische Arbeiten zur Deutschen Literatur Ser.: Bd. 18). 166p. 1997. 35.95 (*3-631-32403-0*) P Lang Pubng.

On Mystic Lake. Kristin Hannah. LC 00-190013. 404p. 2000. mass mkt. 6.99 (*0-449-14967-6*, Ballantine) Ballantine Pub Grp.

On Mystic Lake. Kristin Hannah. LC 98-26448. 323p. 1999. 1.11 (*0-609-60249-7*, Crown) Crown Pub Group.

On Mystic Lake. Kristin Hannah. LC 98-48376. (Large Print Book Ser.). 1999. 26.95 (*1-56895-631-2*) Wheeler Pub.

On Naming the Present: God, Hermeneutics & Church. David Tracy. LC 94-36878. 180p. (Orig.). 1994. pap. 17.00 (*0-88344-972-2*) Orbis Bks.

On Narrative. W. J. Mitchell. LC 80-53137. 280p. (C). 1981. pap. text 14.95 (*0-226-53217-8*) U Ch Pr.

***On Narrow Ground: Urban Policy & Conflict in Jerusalem & Belfast.** Scott A. Bollens. LC 99-39693. (SUNY Series in Urban Public Policy). (Illus.). 448p. (C). 2000. text 73.50 (*0-7914-4413-9*); pap. text 24.95 (*0-7914-4414-7*) State U NY Pr.

On Nationality. David Miller. (Oxford Political Theory Ser.). 220p. 1997. reprint ed. pap. text 19.95 (*0-19-829356-9*) OUP.

On Native Ground: Memoirs & Impressions. Jim Barnes. LC 96-36292. (American Indian Literature & Critical Studies Ser.: Vol. 23). 296p. 1997. 27.95 (*0-8061-2898-4*) U of Okla Pr.

On Native Grounds: An Interpretation of Modern American Prose Literature. 3rd ed. Alfred Kazin. LC 94-45100. (Harvest Bks.). 1995. pap. 16.00 (*0-15-600271-X*) Harcourt.

On Nature. Ed. by Leroy S. Rouner. LC 84-7502. (Boston University Studies in Philosophy & Religion: Vol. 6). 224p. (C). 1984. text 33.50 (*0-268-01499-X*) U of Notre Dame Pr.

On Nature: Essays on Nature, Landscape, & Natural History. Ed. by Daniel Halpern. LC 86-62839. 320p. 1987. pap. 10.95 (*0-86547-284-X*) N Point Pr.

On Nature, Contemplation & the One. Plotinus. Ed. & Tr. by Thomas Taylor from GRE. 1989. pap. 5.95 (*1-55818-160-1*) Holmes Pub.

On Nature's Terms: Contemporary Voices. Rick Bass et al. Ed. by Peter Stine & Thomas J. Lyon. LC 92-5239. (Louise Lindsey Merrick Natural Environment Ser.: No. 13). 224p. 1992. 35.00 (*0-89096-511-0*); pap. 15.95 (*0-89096-522-6*) Tex A&M Univ Pr.

***On Nature's Terms: Contemporary Voices.** Christopher Hallowell. 2001. 25.00 (*0-06-019446-4*) HarpC.

***On Nature's Terms: Contemporary Voices.** Christopher Hallowell. 2002. pap. 14.00 (*0-06-093243-0*, Perennial) HarperTrade.

On ne Badine Pas avec l'Amour. Alfred Musset. (FRE.). 159p. 1992. 49.95 incl. audio (*0-7859-0582-0*); pap. 10.95 (*0-7859-1258-4*, 2038713448) Fr & Eur.

On ne Saurait Penser a Tout. Alfred De Musset. pap. 5.95 (*0-686-55555-4*) Fr & Eur.

On Ne Se Marie Qu'une Fois. Kristine Rolofson. (Rouge Passion Ser.). 1999. mass mkt. 3.50 (*0-373-37513-1*, 1-37513-8) Harlequin Bks.

On Neuroses. Paul Schilder. Ed. by Lauretta Bender. LC 78-61181. 387p. 1979. 57.50 (*0-8236-3810-3*) Intl Univs Pr.

On New Economic Citizenship, Also Called on Free Enterprise Socialism, That Is, Charismatic, or Green Socialism, "An Open Letter to the Presidents of the U. S. A. & the U. S. S. R. on the Historic Synthesis of Their Economic Systems. Thomas J. Kuna-Jacob. 21p. 1991. reprint ed. ring bd. 8.85 (*1-878030-16-7*) Assn World Peace.

On New Ground: Contemporary Hispanic-American Plays. Ed. by M. Elizabeth Osborn. LC 87-26734. 288p. (Orig.). 1987. reprint ed. pap. 13.95 (*0-930452-68-2*) Theatre Comm.

On New York Police Case. David Kocieniewski. Date not set. pap. 14.00 (*0-8050-6534-2*); text 26.00 (*0-8050-6533-4*) St Martin.

On Newfound River. Thomas N. Page. LC 78-110427. reprint ed. 39.50 (*0-404-04858-7*) AMS Pr.

On Newfound River. Thomas N. Page. (BCL1-PS American Literature Ser.). 240p. 1992. reprint ed. lib. bdg. 79.00 (*0-7812-6823-0*) Rprt Serv.

On Newfound River. Thomas N. Page. (Notable American Authors Ser.). 1999. reprint ed. lib. bdg. 125.00 (*0-7812-4691-1*) Rprt Serv.

***On Niebuhr.** Langdon Gilkey. 2000. 29.00 (*0-226-29341-6*) U Ch Pr.

On Nietzsche. Georges Bataille. 1993. pap. 14.95 (*1-55778-644-5*) Paragon Hse.

On Nietzsche. Steinhart. (Philosophy Ser.). 1999. pap. text 13.95 (*0-534-57606-0*) Brooks-Cole.

On Nights Like This. Marianne Bluger. 40p. 1984. pap. 6.95 (*0-919626-25-4*, Pub. by Brick Bks) Genl Dist Srvs.

On, No! Miss Dent Is Coming to Dinner: A Story of Manners. 2nd ed. Raymond S. Moore & Dorothy N. Moore. (Illus.). 32p. (J). (gr. 3-5). 1985. 5.95 (*0-8407-6654-8*) Moore Fnd.

On Not Being Able to Paint. rev. ed. Marion Milner. (Illus.). 184p. (Orig.). 1990. pap. 24.95 (*0-8236-8202-1*, BN23820) Intl Univs Pr.

On Not Being Able to Paint. 2nd ed. Joanna Field. (Illus.). 228p. 1983. pap. 9.95 (*0-87477-263-X*, Tarcher Putnam) Putnam Pub Group.

On Not Knowing How to Live. Allen Wheelis. LC 75-4294. 128p. (C). 1976. 24.50 (*0-8290-0572-2*); pap. text 12.95 (*0-8290-1607-4*) Irvington.

On Not Speaking Chinese: Diaspora & Identity. Ed. by Judith Squires. (New Formations Ser.: No. 24). 192p. (C). 1994. pap. 19.95 (*0-85315-765-0*, Pub. by Lawrence & Wishart) NYU Pr.

On Not Understanding God. Martin Henry. 320p. 1997. 79.95 (*1-85607-217-7*, Pub. by Columba Press); pap. 54.95 (*1-85607-196-0*, Pub. by Columba Press) Intl Scholars.

On Nothing & Kindred Subjects. Hilaire Belloc. LC 70-104994. (Essay Index Reprint Ser.). 1977. 21.95 (*0-8369-1448-1*) Ayer.

On Nuclear Energy: Its Potential for Peacetime Use. Donald J. Hughes. LC 57-12848. 272p. reprint ed. pap. 84.40 (*0-608-30383-6*, 200601500055) Bks Demand.

On Nuclear Energy & the Occult Atom. Georg Unger. Tr. by Lisa Davisson & Charles Davisson from GER. 42p. (Orig.). 1982. pap. 3.95 (*0-88010-010-9*) Anthroposophic.

On Numerical Approximation: Proceedings of a Symposium Conducted by the Mathematics Research Center, United States Army, at the University of Wisconsin, Madison, April 21-23 1958. Ed. by Rudolph E. Langer. LC 59-9018. (Army Mathematics Research Center Ser.: No. 1). 474p. reprint ed. pap. 147.00 (*0-608-10287-3*, 202113600021) Bks Demand.

On Numerical Approximation in Bifurcation Theory. M. Crouzeix & J. Rappaz. Ed. by P. G. Ciarlet & J. L. Lions. (Recherches en Mathematiques Appliquees Ser.: Vol. 13). (Illus.). ix, 165p. 1990. 41.95 (*0-387-51552-6*) Spr-Verlag.

On Nursing: A Literary Celebration. Ed. by Margretta M. Styles & Patricia Moccia. 288p. (C). 1993. pap. text 22.95 (*0-88737-574-X*, 323) Natl League Nurse.

On Nursing: A Literary Celebration. limited ed. Ed. by Margretta M. Styles & Patricia Moccia. 288p. (C). 1993. 41.95 (*0-88737-577-4*) Natl League Nurse.

On Object-Oriented Database Systems. Ed. by K. R. Dittrich et al. (Topics in Information Systems Ser.). (Illus.). x, 422p. 1991. 71.95 (*0-387-53496-2*) Spr-Verlag.

***On Obligations.** Marcus Tullius Cicero & P. G. Walsh. LC 99-56114. 240p. 2000. text 70.00 (*0-19-924018-3*) OUP.

On Obscure Diseases of the Brain & Disorders of the Mind: Their Incipient Symptoms, Pathology, Diagnosis, Treatment & Prophylaxis. Forbes Winslow. LC 75-16739. (Classics in Psychiatry Ser.). 1976. reprint ed. 47.95 (*0-405-07463-8*) Ayer.

On Occasion: Selected Poems, 1968-92. Mary Pryor. 1992. per. 5.00 (*0-941127-12-5*) Dacotah Terr Pr.

On Occupational Clusters: Early Thoughts on the Work of the National Skills Standards. Date not set. 12.00 (*0-9627063-7-X*) Natl Ctr & Econ.

***On Ockham.** Kaye & Martin. 2000. pap. 8.25 (*0-534-58363-6*) Wadsworth Pub.

On Operational Art: Origins & Evolution. Michael D. Krause. LC 93-22093. (Operational Level of War Ser.). 1993. write for info. (*0-415-05044-8*) Routledge.

O

An Asterisk (*) at the beginning of an entry indicates that the title is appearing for the first time.

On Optimal Interconnections for VLSI. Andrew B. Kahng. (International Series in Engineering & Computer Science, Natural Language Processing & Machine Translation). 304p. (C). 1994. text 126.50 (*0-7923-9483-6*) Kluwer Academic.

On Optimal Population Paths. J. S. Lane. LC 77-704. (Lecture Notes in Economics & Mathematical Systems Ser.: Vol. 142). 1977. pap. 26.00 (*0-387-08070-8*) Spr-Verlag.

On or about December, 1910: Early Bloomsbury & Its Intimate World. Peter Stansky. LC 96-17588. (Studies in Cultural History). (Illus.). 296p. 1996. 27.95 (*0-674-63605-8*) HUP.

On or about December, 1910: Early Bloomsbury & Its Intimate World. Peter Stansky. (Studies in Cultural History: No. 8). (Illus.). 304p. 1997. pap. 14.95 (*0-674-63606-6*) HUP.

On Orbit: The First Space Shuttle Era. Dixon P. Otto. (Illus.). 112p. (Orig.). pap. text 9.95 (*0-936447-00-1*) Main Stage.

On-Orbit Servicing of Space Systems. Donald M. Waltz. LC 89-31729. (Orbit Ser.). 294p. 1993. 74.50 (*0-89464-002-X*) Krieger.

On Order: Two Addresses Newly Translated into English. Juan D. Cortes. Ed. & Tr. by S. Draghici from SPA. LC 89-3711. 90p. (C). 1989. pap. text 3.95 (*0-943045-03-7*) Plutarch Pr OR.

On Organizational Learning. Chris Argyris. 480p. 1995. pap. text 30.95 (*1-55786-663-5*) Blackwell Pubs.

On Organizational Learning. Chris Argyris. LC 98-54396. 560p. 1999. 72.95 (*0-631-21308-2*) Blackwell Pubs.

***On Organizational Learning.** 2nd ed. Chris Argyris. LC 98-54396. 1999. pap. text 39.95 (*0-631-21309-0*) Blackwell Pubs.

On Original Sin & A Disputation with the Jew, Leo, Concerning the Advent of Christ, the Son of God: Two Theological Treatises. Odo of Tournai. Tr. by Irven M. Resnick from LAT. LC 94-16217. (Middle Ages Ser.). 168p. (Orig.). (C). 1994. text 32.50 (*0-8122-3288-7*) U of Pa Pr.

On Original Sin & A Disputation with the Jew, Leo, Concerning the Advent of Christ, the Son of God: Two Theological Treatises. Intro. by Irven M. Resnick. LC 94-16217. (Middle Ages Ser.). 168p. (Orig.). (C). 1994. pap. text 13.95 (*0-8122-1540-0*) U of Pa Pr.

***On Other Grounds: Landscape Gardening & Nationalism in Eighteenth-Century England & France.** Brigitte Weltman-Aron. (C). 2000. pap. text 16.95 (*0-7914-4806-1*) State U NY Pr.

***On Other Grounds: Landscape Gardening & Nationalism in Eighteenth-Century England & France.** Brigitte Weltman-Aron. (C). 2001. text 49.50 (*0-7914-4805-3*) State U NY Pr.

On Our Knees & in His Arms. Peter Lewis. LC 98-192706. (Foundations of the Faith). 1998. pap. 8.99 (*0-8024-3051-1*) Moody.

On Our Own. unabridged ed. Judy Resnick. LC 97-25527. 224p. 1998. text 22.00 (*0-307-44005-2*, Whitman Coin) St Martin.

On Our Own: Americans in the Sixties. Douglas Miller. 366p. (C). 1996. pap. text 24.76 (*0-669-24777-4*) HM Trade Div.

On Our Own: Independent Living for Older Persons. Ursula Falk. (Golden Age Books - Perspectives on Aging Ser.). 159p. 1988. pap. 17.95 (*0-87975-449-4*) Prometheus Bks.

On Our Own: Unmarried Motherhood in America. Melissa Ludtke. LC 96-52233. 496p. 1997. 25.95 (*0-679-42414-8*) Random.

On Our Own: Unmarried Motherhood in America. Melissa Ludtke. LC 98-38033. 465p. 1999. pap. 16.95 (*0-520-21830-2*, Pub. by U CA Pr) Cal Prin Full Svc.

On Our Own Behalf: Women's Tales from Catalonia. Ed. by Kathleen McNerney. LC 87-12465. (European Women Writers Ser.). viii, 234p. 1988. text 45.00 (*0-8032-3122-9*) U of Nebr Pr.

On Our Own Ground: The Complete Writings of William Apess, a Pequot. William Apess. LC 91-27750. (Native Americans of the Northeast Ser.). 432p. (C). 1992. pap. 20.95 (*0-87023-770-5*); lib. bdg. 50.00 (*0-87023-766-7*) U of Mass Pr.

On Our Own Terms: Portraits of Women Business Leaders. Liane Enkelis et al. LC 95-34421. (Illus.). 168p. (Orig.). 1995. pap. 19.95 (*1-881052-69-9*) Berrett-Koehler.

On Our Own Terms: Portraits of Women Business Leaders. Liane Enkelis et al. (Illus.). 154p. (Orig.). 1998. pap. text 20.00 (*0-7881-5546-6*) DIANE Pub.

On Our Own Terms: Race, Class & Gender in the Lives of African-American Women. Leith Mullings. LC 96-28853. 224p. (C). 1996. 75.00 (*0-415-91285-7*) Routledge.

On Our Own Terms: Race, Class, & Gender in the Lives of African-American Women. Leith Mullings. LC 96-28853. 224p. (C). 1996. pap. 19.99 (*0-415-91286-5*) Routledge.

On Our Own Terms: Redefining Competence & Femininity. Maggie Mulqueen. LC 91-12245. 221p. (C). 1992. pap. text 21.95 (*0-7914-0952-X*) State U NY Pr.

On Our Selection: The Original Dad & Dave Stories. Steele Rudd. 1995. pap. 16.95 (*0-7022-2844-3*, Pub. by Univ Queensland Pr) Intl Spec Bk.

On Our Selection: The Screenplay. George Whaley. 1995. pap. 19.95 (*0-7022-2819-2*, Pub. by Univ Queensland Pr) Intl Spec Bk.

On Our Spiritual Journey: A Creative Shabbat Service. Ed. by Jackie Tolley. (Illus.). 74p. (Orig.). 1984. pap. 7.95 (*0-9608054-3-5*) Womans Inst-Cont Jewish Ed.

On Our Way. Franklin D. Roosevelt. LC 72-2383. (FDR & the Era of the New Deal Ser.). 216p. 1973. reprint ed. lib. bdg. 39.50 (*0-306-70476-5*) Da Capo.

***On Our Way Rejoicing.** rev. ed. Ingrid Trobisch. LC 85-52332. (Illus.). 208p. 2000. pap. 16.00 (*0-9663966-2-6*) Quiet Waters.

***On Our Way Rejoicing: Recollections from the Concordia College Christmas Concerts.** David J. Hetland. 128p. 1999. 39.95 (*0-9630111-3-8*) Concordia Coll.

On Our Way to Market. Dayle A. Dodds. LC 91-6436. (Illus.). 40p. (J). (ps). 1991. pap. 13.95 (*0-671-73567-5*) S&S Bks Yung.

On Our Way to the Barn. Harriet Ziefert. LC 85-42627. (Illus.). 10p. (J). (ps). 1985. 3.95 (*0-694-00051-5*) HarpC Child Bks.

On Our Way to the Forest! Harriet Ziefert. LC 85-42628. (Illus.). 10p. (J). (ps). 1985. 3.95 (*0-694-00052-3*) HarpC Child Bks.

On Our Way to the Water! Harriet Ziefert. LC 85-42629. (Illus.). 10p. (J). (ps). 1985. 3.95 (*0-694-00053-1*) HarpC Child Bks.

On Our Way to the Zoo. Harriet Ziefert. LC 85-42630. (Illus.). 10p. (J). (ps). 1985. 3.95 (*0-694-00054-X*) HarpC Child Bks.

On Overgrown Paths. Knut Hamsun. Tr. by Sverre Lyngstad. (Green Integer Bks.: No. 22). 248p. 1999. pap. 12.95 (*1-892295-10-5*, Pub. by Green Integer) Consort Bk Sales.

On Overlapping Generations Models with Productive Capital. Gunther Lang. LC 96-38441. (Lecture Notes in Economics & Mathematical Systems Ser.: Vol. 443). (Illus.). 98p. 1996. 46.00 (*3-540-61603-9*) Spr-Verlag.

On Paganism/Afterglow. Arthur Machen & Mitchell S. Buck. 58p. 1998. reprint ed. 25.95 (*1-872621-30-9*, Pub. by Tartarus Pr) Firebird Dist.

On Pagans, Jews & Christians. Arnaldo D. Momigliano. LC 87-24264. 357p. 1989. pap. 22.95 (*0-8195-6218-1*, Wesleyan Univ Pr) U Pr of New Eng.

On Painting. Leon Battista Alberti. Ed. by Martin Kemp. Tr. by Cecil Grayson. (Illus.). 112p. 1991. pap. 12.95 (*0-14-043331-7*, Penguin Classics) Viking Penguin.

On Painting. Leon Battista Alberti. Tr. by John R. Spencer from ITA. LC 76-22485. (Illus.). 141p. 1976. reprint ed. lib. bdg. 38.50 (*0-8371-8974-8*, ALOP, Greenwood Pr) Greenwood.

On Painting: De Pictura Praestantissima, 1540. Leon Battista Alberti. (Printed Sources of Western Art Ser.). (LAT.). 128p. 1981. reprint ed. pap. 35.00 (*0-915346-55-9*) A Wofsy Fine Arts.

On Parchment, Paper & Palm Leaves: Treasures of the Royal Library, Denmark. Harald Ilsoe. (Illus.). 364p. 1994. 128.00 (*87-7023-621-6*, Pub. by Mus Tusculanum) Paul & Co Pubs.

***On Parole.** Akira Yoshimura. Tr. by Stephen Snyder from JPN. LC 99-25991. 256p. (C). 2000. 23.00 (*0-15-100270-3*, Harvest Bks) Harcourt.

***On Parole.** Akira Yoshimura. 256p. 2000. pap. 13.00 (*0-15-601147-6*) Harcourt.

On Parties: Essays Honoring Austin Ranney. Nelson W. Polsby & Raymond E. Wolfinger. LC 99-22656. 13p. 1999. 21.95 (*0-87772-388-5*) UCB IGS.

On Partisan War. Wojciech Chrzanowski. Tr. by Arthur T. Orawski & Nancy Tabb from GOH. LC 95-61880. Orig. Title: O Wojnie Partyzanckiej (1835 Polish); Ueber den Partheiganger-Krieg (1839 Old German Translation). 129p. 1996. lib. bdg. 38.00 (*0-9633995-3-5*) TIPRAC.

On Pascha & Fragments. Melito of Sardis. Ed. by Stuart G. Hall. (Oxford Early Christian Texts Ser.). 1979. text 49.95 (*0-19-826811-4*) OUP.

On Passover. Cathy Fishman. LC 91-43110. (Illus.). 32p. (J). 1995. text 14.95 (*0-02-735320-6*, Mac Bks Young Read) S&S Childrens.

On Passover. Cathy Goldberg Fishman. (Illus.). 40p. (J). (gr. k-3). 2000. mass mkt. 5.99 (*0-689-83264-8*) Aladdin.

On Passover. Cathy Goldberg Fishman. LC 91-43110. (Illus.). 40p. (J). (gr. k up). 1997. 16.00 (*0-689-80528-4*) S&S Childrens.

On Peace, War, & Gender: A Challenge to Genetic Explanations. Ed. by Anne E. Hunter. LC 90-14107. (Genes & Gender Ser.). 192p. 1991. 35.00 (*1-55861-037-5*); pap. 12.95 (*1-55861-025-1*) Feminist Pr.

On Perception & Event Structure, & the Psychological Environment: Selected Papers. Fritz Heider. (Psychological Issues Monographs: Vol. 1, No. 3). 123p. (Orig.). 1959. 27.50 (*0-8236-3840-5*) Intl Univs Pr.

On Persephone's Island: A Sicilian Journal. Mary T. Simeti. 352p. 1995. pap. 14.00 (*0-679-76414-3*) Random.

On Persian Roads: Glimpses of Revolutionary Iran, 1985-1998. Laurence Deonna. Tr. by Christopher Snow from FRE. LC 98-52712. Orig. Title: Persianeries: Rapportage dans l'Iran des Mollahs, 1995-1998. (Illus.). 180p. 1998. pap. 16.00 (*1-57889-088-8*) Passeggiata.

On Perspective. Russel D. Light. (Illus.). 160p. 1998. pap. 28.95 (*0-7506-1694-6*) Buttrwrth-Heinemann.

On Philology. Ed. by Jan Ziolkowski. LC 90-7579. 104p. 1990. pap. text 15.95 (*0-271-00716-8*) Pa St U Pr.

***On Philosophical Style.** Brand Blanshard. LC 99-49474. (Key Texts Ser.). 2000. pap. text 14.00 (*1-890318-53-1*) St Augustines Pr.

On Philosophical Style. Brand Blanshard. LC 69-13830. 69p. 1969. reprint ed. lib. bdg. 55.00 (*0-8371-1975-8*, BLPS, Greenwood Pr) Greenwood.

On Photography. Susan Sontag. 224p. 1990. pap. 13.95 (*0-385-26706-1*, Anchor NY) Doubleday.

On Physical Education. 2nd ed. Sri Aurobindo & Mother. 248p. 1996. pap. 15.95 (*81-7058-441-8*, Pub. by SAA) E-W Cultural Ctr.

On Piano Playing: Motion, Sound, & Expression. Gyorgy Sandor. (Illus.). 240p. (C). 1981. 35.00 (*0-02-872280-9*, Schirmer Books) Mac Lib Ref.

On Piano Teaching & Performing. F. Waterman. 1986. 8.95 (*0-7935-2857-7*, 50440610) H Leonard.

On Picket Duty & Other Tales. Louisa May Alcott. 1988. reprint ed. lib. bdg. 49.00 (*0-7812-0078-4*) Rprt Serv.

On Pictures & the Words That Fail Them. James Elkins. LC 97-27900. (Illus.). 352p. (C). 1998. 65.00 (*0-521-57108-1*) Cambridge U Pr.

On Pilgrimage. Dorothy Day. LC 99-23525. 266p. 1999. pap. 16.00 (*0-8028-4629-7*) Eerdmans.

On Pilgrimage. Jennifer Lash. 224p. 1999. 23.95 (*1-58234-012-9*) Bloomsbury Pubg.

***On Pilgrimage.** Jennifer Lash. 224p. 2000. pap. 14.95 (*1-58234-090-0*) Bloomsbury Pubg.

On Pilgrimage. Douglas C. Vest. LC 97-47374. 160p. 1998. 10.95 (*1-56101-150-9*) Cowley Pubns.

On Pilgrimage: The Best of Ten Years of Vox Benedictina. Ed. by Margot H. King. 607p. 1994. pap. 25.00 (*0-920669-62-X*, Pub. by Peregrina Pubng) Cistercian Pubns.

On Pilots & UFOs. Willy Smith. (Illus.). 137p. 1997. pap. 12.95 (*0-9660232-9-3*) Pharaoh.

On PL DeRham Theory & Rational Homotopy Type. A. K. Bousfield & V. M. Gugenheim. LC 76-44398. 94p. 1976. pap. 21.00 (*0-8218-2179-2*, MEMO/8/179) Am Math.

On Planet Earth: Travels in an Unfamiliar Land. Luc Sante. (Illus.). 96p. 1997. 60.00 (*0-89381-730-9*) Aperture.

On Plato. Peterman. (Philosophy Ser.). 1999. pap. text 13.95 (*0-534-57608-7*) Brooks-Cole.

On Playing a Poor Hand Well: Insights from the Lives of Those Who Have Overcome Childhood Risks & Adversities. Mark Katz. LC 96-38185. 224p. 1997. 29.00 (*0-393-70232-4*) Norton.

On Playing Oboe Recorder & Flageolet. J. P. Poncein. LC 91-33938. (Publications of the Early Music Institute). 128p. 1992. pap. text 15.95 (*0-253-28881-9*) Ind U Pr.

On Playing Oboe, Recorder & Flageolet. Jean-Pierre Freillon-Poncein. Tr. & Intro. by Catherine P. Smith. LC 91-33938. (Publications of the Early Music Institute Ser.). (Illus.). 122p. Date not set. reprint ed. pap. 37.90 (*0-608-20542-7*, 205445600002) Bks Demand.

On Playing Shakespeare: Advice & Commentary from Actors & Actresses of the Past, 37. Leigh Woods. LC 90-22817. (Contributions in Drama & Theatre Studies: No. 37). 256p. 1991. 55.00 (*0-313-27823-7*, WPJ, Greenwood Pr) Greenwood.

On Plays, Playwrights & Playgoers: Selections from the Letters of Booth Tarkington. Booth Tarkington. Ed. by Alan S. Downer. LC 59-15575. (Illus.). 110p. 1959. 15.00 (*0-87811-005-4*) Princeton Lib.

On Pleasing the Heavenly Bridegroom. unabridged ed. Dale M. Yocum. 96p. (Orig.). 1995. pap. 5.99 (*0-88019-332-8*) Schmul Pub Co.

On Pleasure see De Voluptate

On Poe. Ed. by Louis J. Budd & Edwin H. Cady. LC 92-28839. (Best from American Literature Ser.). 288p. 1993. text 49.95 (*0-8223-1311-1*) Duke.

On Poetic Imagination & Reverie: Selections from Gaston Bachelard. rev. ed. Gaston Bachelard. Tr. & Intro. by Colette Gaudin. LC 87-23314. lviii, 112p. 1987. pap. 14.00 (*0-88214-331-X*) Spring Pubns.

On Poetic Language. Jan Mukarovsky. Tr. by Peter Steiner & John Burbank from CZE. 88p. 1976. pap. 21.00 (*90-316-0080-6*) J Benjamins Pubng Co.

On Poetry. Giovanni Boccaccio. Tr. by Charles G. Osgood. 1956. pap. 5.80 (*0-672-60265-2*, LLA82, Bobbs) Macmillan.

On Poetry. Giovanni A. Viperano. Tr. by Philip Rollinson from LAT. (Library of Renaissance Humanism: Vol. 1). 208p. 1987. text 65.00 (*0-87921-077-X*, Koberger) Attic Pr.

On Poetry & Poets. T. S. Eliot. LC 84-26862. 262p. 1985. reprint ed. pap. 14.95 (*0-571-08983-6*) Faber & Faber.

On Poetry & Prayer: The Eighth Morning. John Fandel. 136p. (Orig.). 1995. pap. 5.95 (*0-88028-159-6*, 1304) Forward Movement.

On Poetry & Style. Aristotle. Tr. & Intro. by G. M. A. Grube. LC 58-13827. (HPC Classics Ser.). 144p. (C). 1989. reprint ed. 21.95 (*0-87220-073-6*); reprint ed. pap. 6.95 (*0-87220-072-8*) Hackett Pub.

On Poetry, Painting, & Politics: The Letters of May Morris & John Quinn. Janis Londraville. LC 96-20004. (Illus.). 232p. 1997. 38.50 (*0-945636-96-2*) Susquehanna U Pr.

On Poets & Others. Octavio Paz. Tr. by Michael Schmidt. 1991. pap. 9.70 (*1-55970-139-0*, Pub. by Arcade Pub Inc) Time Warner.

On Poets & Others. Octavio Paz. Tr. by Michael Schmidt from SPA. LC 86-11904. 1986. text 18.95 (*0-8050-0003-8*) Seaver Bks.

***On Point: A Rifleman's Year in the Boonies: Vietnam 1967-1968.** Roger Hayes. (Illus.). 256p. 2000. 27.95 (*0-89141-709-5*) Presidio Pr.

On Political Economy: In Connection with the Moral State & Moral Aspects of Society. Thomas Chalmers. LC 67-19707. (Reprints of Economic Classics Ser.). viii, 566p. 1968. reprint ed. 57.50 (*0-678-00370-X*) Kelley.

On Political Obligation. Paul Harris. 224p. 1989. 59.50 (*0-415-03027-7*) Routledge.

On Political Socialization & Education: Investigations into an Argumentation for a Good Political Belief System. Ola Westin. 170p. (Orig.). 1981. pap. text 31.00 (*91-554-1180-0*) Coronet Bks.

On Politics. Karl Von Clausewitz. reprint ed. lib. bdg. 25.95 (*0-89190-375-5*, Rivercity Pr) Amereon Ltd.

On Politics. Karl Von Clausewitz. 1990. reprint ed. lib. bdg. 21.95 (*0-89968-496-3*) Buccaneer Bks.

On Politics: A Carnival of Buncombe. H. L. Mencken. Ed. by Malcolm Moos. LC 96-10531. (Maryland Paperback Bookshelf Ser.). 377p. 1996. reprint ed. pap. 15.95 (*0-8018-5342-7*) Johns Hopkins.

On Pornography. Harold Jantz. 1987. pap. 1.50 (*0-919797-66-0*) Kindred Prods.

On Poultry & Game. Ian McAndrew. (gr. 13). 1990. mass mkt. 24.95 (*0-442-30274-6*) Chapman & Hall.

On Power. Bornstein. (Psychoanalytic Inquiry Book Ser.: Vol. 6, No. 1). 1995. 20.00 (*0-88163-971-0*) Analytic Pr.

On Power. Robert L. Dilenschneider. LC 93-5277. 256p. 1994. 25.00 (*0-88730-652-7*, HarpBusn) HarpInfo.

On Power: Its Nature & the History of Its Growth. Bertrand De Jouvenel. Tr. by J. F. Huntington from FRE. LC 80-24721. 421p. 1981. reprint ed. lib. bdg. 45.50 (*0-313-22515-X*, JOOP, Greenwood Pr) Greenwood.

On Power: The Natural History of Its Growth. Bertrand De Jouvenel. Tr. by J. F. Huntington. LC 93-1656. 466p. 1993. 25.00 (*0-86597-112-9*); pap. 8.50 (*0-86597-113-7*) Liberty Fund.

On Power & Ideology. Noam Chomsky. 146p. write for info. (*0-921689-05-5*); pap. write for info. (*0-921689-04-7*) Black Rose.

On Power & Ideology: The Managua Lectures. Noam Chomsky. LC 87-4569. 140p. (Orig.). 1987. 25.00 (*0-89608-290-3*); pap. 13.00 (*0-89608-289-X*) South End Pr.

On Practice of Sociology. Sorokin. LC 97-32778. 280p. 1998. lib. bdg. 55.00 (*0-226-76828-7*) U Ch Pr.

On Practice of Sociology. Pitirim A. Sorokin. Ed. by Barry V. Johnston. LC 97-32778. (Illus.). 280p. 1998. pap. text 21.00 (*0-226-76829-5*) U Ch Pr.

On Praxis: Performance Research 32. Richard Gough. (Illus.). 128p. (C). (gr. 13). 1998. pap. 18.00 (*0-415-18202-6*) Routledge.

On Prayer. I. Sofroni. LC 98-40508. 1998. write for info. (*0-88141-194-9*) St Vladimirs.

On Prayer. St. John of Kronstadt. (Orig.). 1985. pap. 3.00 (*0-317-30263-9*) Holy Trinity.

On Prayer. Phyllis Zagano. LC 94-10782. 72p. 1994. pap. 3.95 (*0-8091-3492-6*) Paulist Pr.

On Prayer: From the Alphabetalphabetos. St. Meletios. Tr. by Hieromonk Ioannkios from GRE. 32p. (Orig.). 1991. pap. 3.00 (*0-912927-44-5*, X044) St John Kronstadt.

On Prayer: The Lord's Prayer in Today's World. Gerhard Ebeling. Tr. by James W. Leitch. LC 78-5079. 111p. reprint ed. pap. 34.50 (*0-608-16835-1*, 202685300052) Bks Demand.

On Prayer, from the Letters of Bp. Theophan the Recluse. Theophan the Recluse. Tr. by Stefan Pavlenko from RUS. 12p. (Orig.). 1984. pap. 1.00 (*0-912927-09-7*, X009) St John Kronstadt.

On Predestined Terms of Life. Germanos. Ed. by Charles Garton & Leendert G. Westerink. (Arethusa Monographs: No. 7). xxix, 82p. (C). 1979. pap. 7.00 (*0-930881-04-4*) Dept Classics.

On Predestined Terms of Life. Theophylactus Simocates. Ed. by Charles Garton & Leendert G. Westerink. (Arethusa Monographs: No. 6). xv, 42p. (C). 1978. pap. 5.00 (*0-930881-03-6*) Dept Classics.

***On-Premise Catering.** Patti J. Shock & John M. Stefanelli. LC 00-36820. 2001. write for info. (*0-471-38908-0*) Wiley.

On Premise Digital Communications Upgrades with Emphasis on Fiber Optics. (Fiber Optics User's Manual & Design Ser.: Vol. XIV). 1986. 75.00 (*0-614-18470-3*, 152U14) Info Gatekeepers.

On-Premises Wireless Telecommunications Equipment - World Markets & Opportunities: 1997-2002 Analysis & Forecasts. Ely Lurin. 93p. 1997. pap. text 2400.00 (*1-878218-81-6*) World Info Tech.

On Presence: Variations & Reflections. Ralph Harper. LC 90-24283. 144p. (Orig.). (C). 1991. pap. 15.00 (*1-56338-005-6*) TPI PA.

On Preserving Shared Values. British-North American Committee Staff. 16p. (Orig.). 1989. pap. text 2.00 (*0-902594-49-4*, BN 37 (NPA 240)) Natl Planning.

On Printing in the Tradition. Lillian S. Marks. 24p. 1989. 8.00 (*0-929722-31-0*) CA State Library Fndtn.

On Private Madness. Andre Green. LC 86-27641. 390p. 1987. 57.50 (*0-8236-3853-7*) Intl Univs Pr.

On Problem-Solving. Karl Duncker. Tr. by Lynne S. Lees. LC 73-138621. (Illus.). 113p. 1972. reprint ed. lib. bdg. 35.00 (*0-8371-5733-1*, DUPS, Greenwood Pr) Greenwood.

On Proclus & His Influence in Medieval Philosophy. Ed. by E. P. Bos & P. A. Meijer. (Philosophia Antiqua Ser.: No. 53). viii, 206p. 1991. 74.50 (*90-04-09429-6*) Brill Academic Pubs.

On Producing Shakespeare. Ronald Watkins. LC 64-14718. (Illus.). 1972. reprint ed. 24.95 (*0-405-09054-4*, Pub. by Blom Pubns) Ayer.

On Production Budget Book. Robert Koster. LC 97-19981. 288p. 1997. pap. 29.95 incl. cd-rom (*0-240-80298-5*, Focal) Buttrwrth-Heinemann.

On Professionalism. R. M. Hoot. (Current Topics of Contemporary Thought Ser.: Vol. 8). 123p. 1990. text 90.00 (*2-88124-441-6*) Gordon & Breach.

On Promoting Successful Adjustment: Some Lessons from Ghana; Economic Restructuring in New Zealand since 1984. J. L. Abbey & David Caygill. LC HC0517.G6A33. (Per Jacobsson Lecture Ser.: Vol. 1989). 47p. reprint ed. pap. 30.00 (*0-608-08774-2*, 206941300004) Bks Demand.

On Proof for the Existence of God, & Other Reflective Inquiries. Paul Vjecsner. LC 87-62964. (Illus.). 264p. (C). 1988. text 24.00 (*0-9619519-0-7*) Penden.

On Prophecy: Man's Fascination with the Future. J. Vernon McGee. LC 93-38942. 1993. 15.99 (*0-8407-6798-6*) Nelson.

***On Providence & Other Essays.** Ulrich Zwingli. 314p. 1999. pap. 25.00 (*1-57910-296-4*) Wipf & Stock.

On Psychological Prose. Lydia Ginzburg. 408p. 1991. text 60.00 (*0-691-06849-6*, Pub. by Princeton U Pr); pap. text 21.95 (*0-691-01513-9*, Pub. by Princeton U Pr) Cal Prin Full Svc.

O

On Psychoses. Paul Schilder. Ed. by Lauretta Bender. LC 75-33517. 594p. 1975. 90.00 (0-8236-4055-8) Intl Univs Pr.

On Psychotherapy. Clarkson. 266p. 1993. pap. 48.00 (1-56593-247-1, 0313) Singular Publishing.

On Psychotherapy. Petruska Clarkson. LC 94-71773. 266p. 1994. pap. 45.00 (1-56821-310-7) Aronson.

***On Purpose: A Writer's Guide to Rhetorical Situation.** 2nd ed. Martha Dolly. 116p. (C). 1999. pap. text 23.95 (0-7872-6508-X, 41650801) Kendall-Hunt.

On Purpose: Collected Papers. Harold H. Mosak. LC 76-42942. 1977. pap. 14.95 (0-918560-19-5) Adler Sch Prof Psy.

On-Purpose Person: How to Discover, Clarify, & Achieve Your Life Purpose. Kevin W. McCarthy. LC 92-61234. 143p. 1992. 16.00 (0-89109-705-8) NavPress.

On Purposeful Systems. Russell L. Ackoff & Fred Emery. (Systems Inquiry Ser.). 296p. (C). 1982. reprint ed. pap. text 15.95 (0-914105-00-0) Intersystems Pubns.

On Q: Causing Quality in Higher Education. Daniel T. Seymour. 1992. lib. bdg. 27.95 (0-02-897375-5) Macmillan.

On Q: Causing Quality in Higher Education. Daniel T. Seymour. LC 92-38216. (Illus.). 208p. 1992. pap. 24.95 (0-89774-994-4) Oryx Pr.

***On Quakers, Medicine & Property: The Autobiography of Mray Pennington, 1624-1682.** Mary A. Pennington. 61p. 2000. reprint ed. pap. 10.50 (1-889298-14-X) Rhwymbooks.

On Quanta, Mind & Matter: Hans Primas in Context. Hans Primas et al. LC 99-20457. (Fundamental Theories of Physics Ser.). 1999. write for info. (0-7923-5696-9) Kluwer Academic.

On Questions of Public Law, 2 bks., Vol. 2. Cornelius Von Bynkershoek. LC 95-77094. (Classics in International Law Reprint Ser.: No. 14). 1995. reprint ed. 100.00 (1-57588-258-2, 310280) W S Hein.

On Quine: New Essays. Ed. by Paolo Leonardi & Marco Santambrogio. (Illus.). 371p. (C). 1995. text 80.00 (0-521-47091-9) Cambridge U Pr.

On Race & Philosophy. Lucius Outlaw. LC 96-25170. 256p. (C). 1996. pap. 20.99 (0-415-91535-X) Routledge.

On Race & Philosophy. Lucius Outlaw. LC 96-25170. 264p. (C). 1996. 65.00 (0-415-91534-1) Routledge.

On Racial Frontiers: The New Culture of Frederick Douglass, Ralph Ellison & Bob Marley. Gregory Stephens. LC 98-38597. (Illus.). 320p. (C). 1999. text 59.95 (0-521-64352-X); pap. text 19.95 (0-521-64393-7) Cambridge U Pr.

On Racine. Roland Barthes. Tr. by Richard Howard. 1992. pap. 13.95 (0-520-07824-1, Pub. by U CA Pr) Cal Prin Full Svc.

On Raising Children: Lessons on Love & Limits. Compiled by Mary Hollingsworth. LC 93-7689. 1993. 4.99 (0-8499-5030-9) Word Pub.

On Ramon's Farm: Five Tales of Mexico. Campbell Geeslin. LC 96-20034. (Illus.). 48p. (J). (ps-3). 1998. 16.00 (0-689-81134-9) S&S Childrens.

On Rand. Allan Gotthelf. (Philosophy Ser.). 1999. pap. 13.95 (0-534-57625-7) Wadsworth Pub.

On Rapture's Wing. Caroline Bourne. 1988. mass mkt. 3.75 (0-8217-1352-3, Zebra Kensgtn) Kensgtn Pub Corp.

***On Rawls.** Robert Talisse. 2000. pap. 8.25 (0-534-58369-5) Wadsworth Pub.

On Reading. Dorothy S. Strickland. 8p. 1979. 1.50 (0-87173-092-8) ACEI.

On Reading: A Commons-Sense Look at the Nature of Language & the Science of Reading. Kenneth S. Goodman. LC 96-215414. 152p. 1996. pap. text 21.00 (0-435-07200-5) Heinemann.

On Reading French Verse: A Study of Poetic Form. Roy Lewis. 1982. 29.95 (0-19-815775-4) OUP.

On Reading Karl Barth in South Africa. Ed. by Charles Villa-Vicencio. LC 88-7153. 182p. reprint ed. pap. 56.50 (0-7837-3171-X, 204280700006) Bks Demand.

On Reading Nietzsche. E. Faguet. 1976. 250.00 (0-87968-278-7) Gordon Pr.

On Reading Paradise Lost. Kerry Cardell. 91p. (C). 1980. 25.00 (0-86828-050-X, Pub. by Deakin Univ) St Mut.

On Reading Prophetic Texts: Gender-Specific & Related Studies in Memory of Fokkelien van Dijk-Hemmes. Ed. by Bob Becking & Meindert Dijkstra. LC 95-46889. (Biblical Interpretation Ser.: Vol. 18). 1996. 98.00 (90-04-10274-4) Brill Academic Pubs.

On Reading Ruskin. Marcel Proust. Ed. & Tr. by William Burford. LC 86-22467. (Illus.). 192p. 1987. 15.00 (0-300-03513-6) Yale U Pr.

On Reading Shakespeare. Logan P. Smith. 1988. reprint ed. lib. bdg. 75.00 (0-7812-0185-3) Rprt Serv.

On Reading Shakespeare. Logan P. Smith. reprint ed. 39.00 (0-403-08600-0) Somerset Pub.

On Reading the Constitution. Laurence H. Tribe & Michael C. Dorf. (Illus.). 144p. 1992. pap. text 14.50 (0-674-63626-0) HUP.

***On Reason & Belief.** Louis Jacobs. LC 99-10682. 272p. 1999. 39.50 (1-874774-58-7) Intl Spec Bk.

On Reasonable Liability. J. A. Diening. 452p. pap. 32.00 (90-6000-250-4) Kluwer Academic.

On Rebellion. John Knox. Ed. by Roger A. Mason. LC 93-19944. (Cambridge Texts in the History of Political Thought Ser.). 290p. (C). 1994. text 59.95 (0-521-39089-3); pap. text 19.95 (0-521-39988-2) Cambridge U Pr.

On Reconciliation & Penance in the Mission of the Church Today: Reconciliatio et Paenitentia. John Paul, II, pseud. 136p. pap. 4.95 (0-8198-6430-7) Pauline Bks.

On Reconstructing Grammar: Comparative Cariban Morphosyntax. Spike Gildea. LC 98-24621. (Oxford Studies in Anthropological Linguistics). (Illus.). 304p. 1998. text 85.00 (0-19-510952-X) OUP.

On Record: Files & Dossiers in American Life. Ed. by Stanton Wheeler. LC 73-98421. 450p. 1970. 45.00 (0-87154-919-0) Russell Sage.

On Record: Files & Dossiers in American Life. Ed. by Stanton Wheeler. LC 75-43359. (Law & Society Ser.). 450p. 1976. pap. text 24.95 (0-87855-607-9) Transaction Pubs.

***On Record: Rock, Pop & the Written Word.** Simon Frith. 2000. pap. 22.99 (0-415-05306-4) Routledge.

On Reduplication: Logical Theories of Qualification. Allan T. Back. LC 95-53247. (Studien und Texte zur Geistesgeschichte des Mittelalters Ser.: Bd. 49). 1996. 185.50 (90-04-10539-5) Brill Academic Pubs.

On Reduplication: Logical Theories of Qualification. Allan T. Back. (Analytica Ser.). 768p. (C). 1991. 188.50 (3-88405-045-1) Philosophia Pr.

On Referring in Literature. Ed. by Anna Whiteside & Michael Issacharoff. LC 86-45748. (Illus.). 224p. 1987. 29.95 (0-253-34262-7) Ind U Pr.

***On Reflection.** Jonathan Miller. LC 98-66560. (Illus.). 224p. 1998. pap. 40.00 (1-85709-236-8) Nat Gallery Pubns.

On Reflection. Jonathan Miller. (Illus.). 224p. 1998. 40.00 (0-300-07713-0) Yale U Pr.

On Reflection. J. Rawson. (C). 1990. 39.00 (0-7223-2568-1, Pub. by A H S Ltd) St Mut.

On Reflection: A Workable Relief. Macmillan & Gilleasbuig. 90p. 1993. pap. 21.00 (0-7152-0683-4, Pub. by St Andrew) St Mut.

On Reflection: Laughter & Tears. James A. Whyte. 106p. 1993. pap. 21.00 (0-7152-0682-6, Pub. by St Andrew) St Mut.

On Reflection: Wrestle & Fight & Pray. John L. Bell. 116p. 1993. pap. 22.00 (0-7152-0681-8, Pub. by St Andrew) St Mut.

On Refuge. Richard Gough & Claire MacDonald. (Performance Research Ser.: No. 23). (Illus.). 128p. (C). 1998. pap. 17.99 (0-415-16180-0) Routledge.

On Relationship. Jiddu Krishnamurti. LC 91-55330. 176p. 1992. pap. 13.00 (0-06-250608-0, Pub. by Harper SF) HarpC.

On Relativity Theory: Sir Arthur Eddington Century Symposium Vol. 2, India, 1984. Ed. by Y. Choquet & T. M. Karade. 284p. 1985. 66.00 (9971-978-21-0) World Scientific Pub.

On Religion. Karl Marx & Friedrich Engels. LC 82-17032. (American Academy of Religion, Classics in Religious Studies). 384p. 1982. reprint ed. 25.95 (0-89130-599-8, 01 05 03) OUP.

On Religion: Speeches to Its Cultured Despisers. John C. Oman & Friedrich Daniel Ernst Schleiermacher. 312p. 1994. pap. 18.95 (0-664-25556-6) Westminster John Knox.

On Remembrance. David Hafer. (Illus.). 59p. (Orig.). 1997. pap. 5.00 (1-884257-13-5) AGEE Keyboard.

***On Repentance.** Ed. by Pinchas Peli. LC 96-22665. 336p. 2000. pap. 30.00 (0-7657-6140-8) Aronson.

On Repentance & Almsgiving. St. John Chrysostom. Tr. by Gus G. Christo. LC 97-31542. (Fathers of the Church Ser.: Vol. 96). xviii, 159 p. (C). 1998. text 27.95 (0-8132-0096-2) Cath U Pr.

On Revolt: Strategies of National Liberation. J. Bowyer Bell. LC 75-44026. 300p. 1976. reprint ed. pap. 93.00 (0-7837-2223-0, 205731300004) Bks Demand.

On Revolution. Hannah Arendt. 352p. 1991. pap. 13.95 (0-14-018421-X, Penguin Classics) Viking Penguin.

On Revolution. Hannah Arendt. LC 82-6266. 343p. 1982. reprint ed. lib. bdg. 69.50 (0-313-23493-0, AROR, Greenwood Pr) Greenwood.

On Revolutions & Progress in Economic Knowledge. T. W. Hutchinson. (Modern Revivals in Economics Ser.). 350p. 1992. 63.95 (0-7512-0093-X, Pub. by Gregg Pub) Ashgate Pub Co.

On Rhetoric: A Theory of Civil Discourse. Aristotle. Tr. & Intro. by George A. Kennedy. 368p. (C). 1992. pap. text 19.95 (0-19-506487-9) OUP.

On Rice: 60 Fast & Easy Toppings That Make the Meal. Rick Rodgers. LC 96-7069. (Illus.). 144p. 1997. pap. 16.95 (0-8118-1352-5) Chronicle Bks.

***On Right Pleasure & Good Health, Vol. 37.** Ed. & Tr. by Mary E. Milham from LAT. LC 98-55450. 200p. 1999. pap. text 12.95 (1-889818-12-7) Pegasus Pr.

On Rims & Ridges: The Los Alamos Area since 1880. Hal K. Rothman. LC 91-24418. (Illus.). xvi, 364p. 1992. text 50.00 (0-8032-3901-7) U of Nebr Pr.

On Rims & Ridges: The Los Alamos Area since 1880. Hal K. Rothman. LC 91-24418. (Illus.). xvi, 398p. 1997. pap. text 18.95 (0-8032-8966-9) U of Nebr Pr.

On Rims of Empty Moons. John P. McAfee. LC 97-33405. 267p. 1997. 25.95 (0-89672-386-0) Tex Tech Univ Pr.

On Ritual: Performance Research 33. Ed. by Richard Gough. (Illus.). 304p. (C). (gr. 13). 1999. pap. 18.00 (0-415-18203-4) Routledge.

On Roman Time: The Codex-Calendar of 354 & the Rhythms of Urban Life in Late Antiquity. Michele R. Salzman. LC 89-5116. (Transformation of the Classical Heritage Ser.: Vol. 17). (Illus.). 335p. 1990. 75.00 (0-520-06566-2, Pub. by U CA Pr) Cal Prin Full Svc.

On Romans: And Other New Testament Essays. C. E. Cranfield. 192p. 1998. 44.95 (0-567-08624-0, Pub. by T & T Clark) Bks Intl VA.

On Rope. 2nd ed. Allen Padgett & Bruce Smith. (Illus.). 382p. 1996. 32.00 (1-879961-05-9, 07-0010) Natl Speleological.

***On Rosh Hashanah & Yom Kippur.** 2000. 6.99 (0-689-83892-1) Aladdin.

On Rosh Hashanah & Yom Kippur. Cathy G. Fishman. (Illus.). 40p. (J). (gr. k-3). 1997. 16.00 (0-689-80526-8) S&S Childrens.

***On Rousseau.** Scholz. 2000. pap. 8.25 (0-534-58368-7) Wadsworth Pub.

On Ruins of Empire: Ethnicity & Nationalism in the Former Soviet Union, 375. Georgiy I. Mirsky. LC 96-5789. (Contributions in Political Science Ser.: No. 375). 192p. 1997. 57.95 (0-313-30044-5, Greenwood Pr) Greenwood.

On Russell. Scott O'Dell. 1999. pap. text 13.95 (0-534-57616-8) Thomson Learn.

On Russian Music. Gerald E. Abraham. LC 73-134046. (Essay Index Reprint Ser.). 1977. 18.95 (0-8369-1900-9) Ayer.

On Russian Music. Gerald E. Abraham. 1976. lib. bdg. 59.00 (0-403-03757-3) Scholarly.

On Russian Music. Gerald E. Abraham. 1988. reprint ed. lib. bdg. 49.00 (0-7812-0272-8) Rprt Serv.

On Russian Music: Critical & Historical Studies of Glinka's Operas. Gerald Abraham. LC 73-134046. (Essay Index Reprint Ser.). 280p. 1982. reprint ed. lib. bdg. 14.00 (0-8290-0786-5) Irvington.

On Sacred Mountain. Edward Tick. 24p. 1984. pap. 2.00 (0-913719-74-9, High Coo Pr) Brooks Books.

On Safari. (Fisher-Price Little People Coloring & Activity Ser.). (Illus.). 48p. (J). (gr. k-2). 1997. pap. write for info. (1-56144-956-3, Honey Bear Bks) Modern Pub NYC.

On Safari. Tessa Paul. LC 98-10862. (Animal Trackers Ser.). (Illus.). 32p. (J). (gr. 1-7). 1998. pap. 7.95 (0-86505-597-1) Crabtree Pub Co.

***On Safari.** Tessa Paul. LC 98-10862. (Animal Trackers Ser.). (Illus.). 32p. (J). (gr. 2-3). 1998. lib. bdg. 20.60 (0-86505-589-0) Crabtree Pub Co.

***On Safari.** rev. ed. Claire Watts. (First Look at Animals Ser.). (Illus.). (J). 2000. pap. 3.95 (1-58728-863-X) Two Can Pub.

***On Salads: Sensation on a Plate.** Sue Lawrence. (Illus.). 160p. 2000. 29.95 (1-85626-323-1, Pub. by Cathie Kyle) Trafalgar.

***On Sandy Shores.** Craig Strang et al. Ed. by Lincoln Bergman et al. (Great Explorations in Math & Science (GEMS) Ser.). (Illus.). 212p. (J). (gr. 2-4). 1999. pap., teacher ed. 18.00 (0-924886-33-1, GEMS) Lawrence Science.

On Santa Cruz Island. Clifford McElrath. 128p. (Orig.). 1993. pap. 12.95 (0-9634635-3-5) Caractacus.

On Saying Tehillim. 6th ed. Yosef Y. Schneersohn. Tr. by Zalman I. Posner. 60p. (Orig.). 1975. reprint ed. pap. 3.00 (0-8266-0426-9) Kehot Pubn Soc.

On-Scene Guide for Crisis Negotiators. Frederick J. Lanceley. LC 99-28068. 232p. (C). 1999. per. 39.95 (0-8493-0784-8) CRC Pr.

On-Scene Traffic Accident Investigator's Manual see Traffic Accident Investigator's Manual: A Levels 1 & 2 Reference, Training & Investigation Manual

On "Schacht's Origins of Muhammadan Jurisprudence" Muhammad M. Al-Azami. 1996. pap. 24.95 (0-946621-46-2, Pub. by Islamic Texts) Intl Spec Bk.

On "Schacht's Origins of Muhammadan Jurisprudence" Muhammad M. Al-Azami. LC 84-2270. 500p. 1986. text 26.00 (0-471-89145-2) Wiley.

On "Schacht's Origins of Muhammadan Jurisprudence" Muhammad M. Al-Azami. 237p. 1995. reprint ed. pap. 14.95 (0-946621-49-7, Pub. by Islamic Texts) Intl Spec Bk.

On Schleiermacher & Gender Politics. Patricia E. Guenther-Gleason. LC 97-40279. (Harvard Theological Studies: Vol. 43). 384p. (Orig.). 1997. pap. 23.00 (1-56338-220-2) TPI PA.

On Schopenhauer's Fourfold Root of the Principle of Sufficient Reason. F. C. White. LC 91-31538. (Philosophy of History & Culture Ser.: Vol. 8). xii, 184p. 1991. 75.00 (90-04-09543-8) Brill Academic Pubs.

On Science, Inference, Information & Decision Making: Selected Essays in the Philosophy of Science. Klemens Szaniawski et al. LC 97-49838. (Synthese Library). 1998. 130.00 (0-7923-4922-9) Kluwer Academic.

On Scientific Discovery: The Erice Lectures, 1977. Ed. by Mirko D. Grmek et al. (Boston Studies in the Philosophy of Science Ser.: No. 34). 342p. 1980. lib. bdg. 117.50 (90-277-1122-4) Kluwer Academic.

On Scotland & the Scotch Intellect. Henry T. Buckle. Ed. by Henry J. Hanham. 414p. (C). 1986. 45.00 (0-7855-2152-6) St Mut.

On Scotland & the Scotch Intellect. Henry T. Buckle. Ed. by Henry J. Hanham. LC 78-114958. (Classics of British Historical Literature Ser.). 1972. pap. text 3.45 (0-226-07977-5, P383) U Ch Pr.

On Scotland & the Scotch Intellect. Henry T. Buckle. LC 78-114958. (Classics of British Historical Literature Ser.). 452p. Date not set. reprint ed. pap. 140.20 (0-608-20670-9, 207210700003) Bks Demand.

On Scottish Ground: Selected Essays of Kenneth White. Kenneth White. LC 99-237286. 288p. 1998. pap. 17.95 (0-7486-6237-5, Pub. by Polygon) Subterranean Co.

***On Screen Rivals: Cinema & Television in the United States & Britain.** Jane C. Stokes. LC 99-33682. 256p. 1999. pap. 17.95 (0-312-22768-X) St Martin.

***On Screen Rivals: Cinema & Television in the United States & Britian.** Jane C. Stokes. LC 99-33682. 256p. 1999. text 55.00 (0-312-22767-1) St Martin.

On Screen Writing. Edward Dmytryk. 180p. 1985. pap. 24.95 (0-240-51753-9, Focal) Buttrwrth-Heinemann.

On Second Glance: Midwest Photographs by Larry Kanfer. Larry Kanfer. LC 92-9651. (Visions of Illinois Ser.). (Illus.). 96p. (C). 1992. 29.95 (0-252-01968-7) U of Ill Pr.

***On Second Language Writing.** Ed. by Tony Silva & Paul Matsuda. 248p. 2000. pap. write for info. (0-8058-3516-4) L Erlbaum Assocs.

***On Second Language Writing.** Ed. by Tony Silva & Paul Matsudaira. 248p. 2000. write for info. (0-8058-3515-6) L Erlbaum Assocs.

On Second Thought: A Compilation. Maurice Kenny. LC 95-5891. (American Indian Literature & Critical Studies: Vol. 18). 288p. 1995. 18.95 (0-8061-2766-X) U of Okla Pr.

On Second Thought: Poems. Daniel Green. LC 91-1352. (Illus.). 160p. (Orig.). 1992. pap. 8.95 (1-56474-024-2) Fithian Pr.

***On Secret Service.** John Jakes. LC 99-47951. 464p. 2000. 25.95 (0-525-94544-X, Dutt) Dutton Plume.

***On Secret Service.** large type ed. John Jakes. LC 00-39923. 2000. write for info. (1-56895-905-2) Wheeler Pub.

On Security. Ed. by Ronnie D. Lipschutz. LC 95-16627. (New Directions in World Politics Ser.). 1995. 57.50 (0-231-10270-4) Col U Pr.

On Security. Ed. by Ronnie D. Lipschutz. LC 95-16627. (New Directions in World Politics Ser.). 240p. 1995. pap. 19.50 (0-231-10271-2) Col U Pr.

On Seeing Forms. William R. Uttal. 352p. 1988. 59.95 (0-89859-994-6) L Erlbaum Assocs.

On Seeing Forms. William R. Uttal. LC 88-421. (Illus.). 361p. reprint ed. pap. 112.00 (0-608-20011-5, 207128700010) Bks Demand.

On Self & Social Organization. Cooley. LC 98-13172. 259p. 1998. pap. text 19.00 (0-226-11509-7) U Ch Pr.

On Self & Social Organization. Cooley. LC 98-13172. 1998. lib. bdg. 48.00 (0-226-11508-9) U Ch Pr.

On Self-Esteem. Gloria Steinem. 143p. 1995. 16.95 incl. audio (1-879323-15-X) Sound Horizons AV.

On Self-Organization: An Interdisciplinary Search for a Unifying Principle. R. K. Mishra et al. LC 93-38258. 1994. 73.95 (0-387-56485-3) Spr-Verlag.

On Semiotic Modeling. Ed. by Myrdene Anderson & Floyd Merrell. (Approaches to Semiotics Ser.: No. 97). (Illus.). vii, 619p. (C). 1991. lib. bdg. 206.15 (3-11-012314-2) Mouton.

On Sensations from Pressure & Impact. Arnold Griffing. (Psychology Monographs General & Applied: Vol. 1). 1974. reprint ed. 55.00 (0-8115-1400-5) Periodicals Srv.

***On Sentence Interpretation** Lyn Frazier. LC 98-49685. (Studies in Theoretical Psycholinguistics). 11p. 1999. write for info. (0-7923-5508-3) Kluwer Academic.

On Set: The British Television Location Guide. Steve Clark. (Illus.). 256p. 1999. pap. 14.95 (1-85782-391-5, Pub. by Blake Publng) Seven Hills Bk.

On Sets Not Belonging to Algebras of Subsets. L. S. Grinblat. LC 92-28572. (Memoirs Ser.: No. 480). 111p. 1992. pap. 26.00 (0-8218-2541-0, MEMO/100/480) Am Math.

On Sex & Gender: Thoughts of Dr. Schenk. Roy U. Schenk. (Illus.). vii, 134p. (Orig.). 1991. pap. 6.00 (0-9613177-2-8) MPC Pr.

On Sexuality: Psychoanalytic Observations. Toksoz B. Karasu & Charles W. Socarides. LC 78-67478. 412p. 1979. 60.00 (0-8236-3857-X) Intl Univs Pr.

***On Shabbat.** Cathy Fishman & Melanie W. Hall. LC 00-22584. (Illus.). (YA). 2001. write for info. (0-689-83894-8) Atheneum Yung Read.

On Shakespeare. Anthony Lane. 1999. pap. write for info. (0-375-70062-5) Vin Bks.

On Shaky Ground. John J. Nance. 448p. 1989. mass mkt. 4.95 (0-380-70743-8, Avon Bks) Morrow Avon.

On Shaky Ground: The New Madrid Earthquakes of 1811-1812. Norma H. Bagnall. Ed. by Rebecca B. Schroeder. (Missouri Heritage Readers Ser.). (Illus.). 128p. (C). 1996. pap. 9.95 (0-8262-1054-6) U of Mo Pr.

***On Shantaraksita.** Marie-Louise Friquegnon. 2000. pap. 8.25 (0-534-58359-8) Wadsworth Pub.

On Shel na Svijaz: A Novel. Yevgeny Lubin. 1980. 5.00 (0-685-44306-X) RWCPH.

On Shifting Ground: The Story of Continental Drift. J. S. Kidd & Renee A. Kidd. LC 96-54299. (Science & Society Ser.). (Illus.). (YA). (gr. 7-12). 1997. 19.95 (0-8160-3582-2) Facts on File.

On Shifting Sands: And Other Poems of Transition. Chas Ridley. (Illus.). 92p. 1992. pap. 15.00 (1-890894-01-X, 97002) Chas HotBooks.

On Shifting Sands: New Art & Literature from South Africa. Ed. by Kirsten H. Peterson & Anna Rutherford. 180p. (C). 1992. pap. 16.95 (0-435-08070-9, 08070) Heinemann.

On-Side: Version Two. Bill Willis. 80p. 1992. 19.95 (0-614-04242-9) Expressware.

On Sidesaddles to Heaven: The Women of the Rocky Mountain Mission. Laurie W. Carlson. Ed. by Wayne Cornell. LC 98-10199. (Illus.). 256p. 1998. 19.95 (0-87004-384-6) Caxton.

On Sight & Insight: A Journey into the World of Blindness. John M. Hull. 176p. 1997. pap. 11.95 (1-85168-141-8, Pub. by Onewrld Pubns) Penguin Putnam.

On Signs. Ed. by Marshall Blonsky. LC 84-47952. (Illus.). 576p. 1985. pap. 21.95 (0-8018-3007-9) Johns Hopkins.

On Silent Wings. Don Conroy. (Illus.). 240p. 1997. pap. 7.95 (0-86278-369-0, Pub. by OBrien Pr) Irish Amer Bk.

***On Silent Wings II.** Hiroaki Samura. (Blade of the Immortal Ser.). (Illus.). (YA). 2000. pap. 14.95 (1-56971-444-4) Dark Horse Comics.

On Simplicity: Dialogue Between an Orthodox & a Barlaamite. St. Gregory Palamas. Tr. by Rein Ferwerda from GRE. (Episteme Ser.). 140p. (Orig.). 1998. pap. 17.00 (1-883058-21-X, Episteme) Global Pubns.

On Singers & Singing. Reynaldo Hahn. Tr. by Leopold Simoneau from FRE. LC 89-14987. (Illus.). 244p. 1990. 22.95 (0-931340-22-5, Amadeus Pr) Timber.

On Singing Onstage. 2nd rev. ed. David Craig. (Acting Ser.). 296p. 1990. pap. 12.95 (1-55783-043-6) Applause Theatre Bk Pubs.

***On Site: Contemporary Photography of Place.** Ed. by Laurie Dahlberg. (Illus.). 28p. 1999. pap. write for info. (0-941276-81-3) Bard Coll Pubns.

O

An Asterisk (*) at the beginning of an entry indicates that the title is appearing for the first time.

On Site: Preparing Middle Level Teachers Through Field Experiences. Deborah A. Butler et al. 76p. 1991. 9.00 (1-56090-059-8) Natl Middle Schl.

On Site: The Construction of a High-Rise. Richard Younker. LC 79-7889. (Illus.). (J). (gr. 5-12). 1980. lib. bdg. 10.89 (0-690-04004-0) HarpC Child Bks.

On-Site Bioreclamation: Processes for Xenobiotic & Hydercarbon Treatment 1(1) Ed. by Robert E. Hinchee & Robert F. Olfenbuttel. (International in Situ & On-Site Bioremediation Symposium Ser.). 624p. 1991. text 75.00 (0-935470-80-8) Battelle.

On-Site Contractors. Neville Williams. (Safety Instruction Booklet Ser.). (Illus.). 28p. 1994. pap. 45.00 (1-85573-166-5, Pub. by Woodhead Pubng) Am Educ Systs.

***On-Site Emergency Response Planning Guide for Office, Manufacturing & Industrial Operations.** Richard T. Vulpitta. LC 99-23017. 1999. pap. text 41.95 (0-87912-218-8) Natl Safety Coun.

On-Site Inspection in Theory & Practice: A Primer on Modern Arms Control Regimes. George L. Rueckert. LC 97-23346. 296p. 1998. 69.50 (0-275-96047-1, Praeger Pubs) Greenwood.

On-Site Inspection under the INF Treaty. 1996. lib. bdg. 251.75 (0-8490-6020-6) Gordon Pr.

On-Site Power Generation: A Reference Book. 2nd ed. Ed. by Gordon S. Johnson. (Illus.). 360p. 1993. 95.00 (0-9625949-1-1) Electrical Gen.

On-Site Waste Ink Recycling. (Illus.). 58p. (Orig.). (C). 1994. pap. text 55.00 (0-7881-0422-5) DIANE Pub.

On-Site Wastewater Treatment. Ed. by Dennis M. Sievers. LC 97-78438. (Illus.). 544p. 1998. pap. 62.00 (0-929355-91-1, 701P0398) Am Soc Ag Eng.

On-Site Wastewater Treatment, Vol. 4. LC 85-70629. 383p. 1985. pap. 41.25 (0-916150-71-2, P0785) Am Soc Ag Eng.

On-Site Wastewater Treatment Vol. 5: The Proceedings of the Fifth National Symposium on Individual & Small Community Sewage Systems. LC 88-71467. 415p. 1988. pap. 53.00 (0-916150-91-7, P1087) Am Soc Ag Eng.

On-Site Wastewater Treatment Vol. 6: Proceedings Sixth National Symposium on Individual & Small Community Sewage Systems, December 1991, Vol. 6. LC 91-76822. 375p. 1991. pap. 53.25 (0-929355-22-9, P1091) Am Soc Ag Eng.

On Size & Life. Thomas McMahon & James Bonner. (Scientific American Library). (Illus.). 255p. 1983. pap. text 32.95 (0-7167-5000-7) W H Freeman.

On Skin Care. Barney Kenet. 1998. write for info. (0-375-50019-7) Villard Books.

On Skis to the North Pole. Vladimir Snegiryev. Tr. by George Watts from RUS. LC 84-10666. (Illus.). vi, 240p. 1985. 29.95 (0-943071-05-4) Sphinx Pr.

On Small Press As Class Struggle. Merritt Clifton. 1976. pap. 1.00 (0-686-20630-4) Samisdat.

On Smart Dither by Absolute One-Bit Coding for Noise-Shaped PCM. Antonius J. Coenen. (Illus.). 192p. (Orig.). 1996. pap. 57.50 (90-407-1377-4, Pub. by Delft U Pr) Coronet Bks.

***On Snooker: A Brilliant Exploration of the Game & the Characters.** Mordecai Richler. 112p. 2000. 20.00 (1-58574-179-5) Lyons Pr.

O

On Social Concern: Solicitudo Rei Socialis. John Paul, II, pseud. 112p. pap. 4.50 (0-8198-6923-6) Pauline Bks.

On Social Concern: Sollicitudo Rei Socialis. John Paul, II, pseud. 104p. 1987. pap. 5.95 (1-55586-205-5) US Catholic.

On Social Facts. Margaret Gilbert. 536p. (C). 1992. text 80.00 (0-691-07401-1, Pub. by Princeton U Pr); pap. text 24.95 (0-691-02080-9, Pub. by Princeton U Pr) Cal Prin Full Svc.

On Social Facts. Margaret Gilbert. 512p. 1989. 95.00 (0-415-02444-7) Routledge.

On Social Organization & Social Control. Morris Janowitz. Ed. by James Burk. (Heritage of Sociology Ser.). 332p. 1991. pap. text 21.00 (0-226-39303-8) U Ch Pr.

On Social Organization & Social Control. Morris Janowitz. Ed. by James Burk. (Heritage of Sociology Ser.). 332p. 1991. lib. bdg. 42.00 (0-226-39301-1) U Ch Pr.

On Social Reconstruction: Quadragesimo Anno. Pius XI, pseud. 75p. pap. 1.25 (0-8198-6926-0) Pauline Bks.

On Social Research & Its Language. Paul F. Lazarsfeld. LC 93-12748. (Heritage of Sociology Ser.). (Illus.). 344p. 1993. pap. text 19.95 (0-226-46963-8); lib. bdg. 49.95 (0-226-46961-1) U Ch Pr.

On Social Science. Helen Sasson & D. R. Diamond. LC 97-3859. 258p. 1997. pap. text 24.95 (1-56000-977-2) Transaction Pubs.

On Social Structure & Science. Robert K. Merton. Ed. by Piotr Sztompka. 400p. 1996. pap. text 19.95 (0-226-52071-4) U Ch Pr.

On Social Structure & Science. Robert K. Merton. Ed. by Piotr Sztompka. 400p. 1996. lib. bdg. 55.00 (0-226-52070-6) U Ch Pr.

On Social Welfare. Henry Aaron. LC 80-80680. (Illus.). 143p. 1980. 25.00 (0-89011-549-4) Abt Bks.

On Social Welfare. Henry Aaron. (Illus.). 144p. 1984. lib. bdg. 58.50 (0-8191-4102-X) U Pr of Amer.

On Socialism. Oscar A. Echevarria Salvat. (SPA.). 1975. pap. 9.95 (0-89729-149-2) Ediciones.

On Socialism. John Stuart Mill. LC 87-61246. (Great Books in Philosophy). 146p. (Orig.). 1976. pap. 7.95 (0-87975-404-4) Prometheus Bks.

On Socialists & "The Jewish Question" after Marx. Jack Jacobs. (Reappraisals in Jewish Social & Intellectual History Ser.). 288p. (C). 1993. pap. text 19.50 (0-8147-4213-0) NYU Pr.

On Socialization in Hamadryas Baboons: A Field Study. Jean-Jacques Abegglen. LC 80-70316. (Illus.). 208p. 1984. 45.00 (0-8387-5017-6) Bucknell U Pr.

On Society. Frederic Harrison. LC 70-142640. (Essay Index Reprint Ser.). 1977. 23.95 (0-8369-2052-X) Ayer.

On Society & Social Change. Karl Marx. Ed. by Neil J. Smelser. LC 73-78669. (Heritage of Sociology Ser.). xlii, 248p. 1975. reprint ed. pap. text 18.00 (0-226-50918-4, P567) U Ch Pr.

***On Sociology: Numbers, Narratives, & the Integration of Research & Theory.** John H. Goldthorpe. 320p. 2000. pap. 24.95 (0-19-829572-3); text 65.00 (0-19-829571-5) OUP.

On Solid Ground. Tom Osborne. 266p. 1996. 26.95 (0-9648992-1-3) Neb Bk Co.

***On Solid Ground: Strategies for Teaching Reading, K-3.** Sharon Taberski. LC 00-20275. 304p. 2000. pap. text 22.00 (0-325-00227-4) Heinemann.

On Solid Ground: The Christian Basics. Tim Alspach. LC 97-61854. 128p. 1997. pap. 9.99 (1-57921-052-X) WinePress Pub.

On Solid Ground: The Christian Basics. Timothy Alspach. (Illus.). 86p. (Orig.). 1996. pap. 5.00 (1-57502-361-X) Morris Pubng.

On Solitude. Francis Petrarch. Tr. by Jay Livernois. (Dunquin Ser.: Vol. 26). 316p. 2000. pap. 18.00 (0-88214-228-3, Pub. by Spring Pubns) Continuum.

On Some Disputed Points in English Grammar see Society's Work

On Some of Shakespeare's Female Characters. 5th ed. Helena F. Martin. LC 75-111773. reprint ed. 49.50 (0-404-04194-9) AMS Pr.

***On Some of the Smarandache's Problems, 1.** Krassimir T. Atanasson. Ed. by M. L. Perez. (Illus.). 88p. 2000. pap. text 16.95 (1-879585-72-3) American Res Pr.

On Something. Hilaire Belloc. LC 68-8437. (Essay Index Reprint Ser.). 1977. reprint ed. 18.95 (0-8369-0191-6) Ayer.

On Something Un Personal Inside All Us. Mark Sonnenfeld. 24p. 1998. pap. 3.00 (1-887379-16-9) M Sonnenfeld.

On Sonic Art. rev. ed. Trevor Wishart. Ed. by Simon Emmerson. (Contemporary Music Studies: Vol. 12). 368p. 1996. pap., pap. text 20.00 incl. cd-rom (3-7186-5847-X, ECU25, Harwood Acad Pubs); text 60.00 incl. cd-rom (3-7186-5846-1, ECU77, Harwood Acad Pubs) Gordon & Breach.

On Sophistical Refutations, on Coming-To-Be & Passing-Away, on the Cosmos. Tr. by J. D. Furley & E. S. Forster. (Loeb Classical Library: No. 400). 442p. 1955. 18.95 (0-674-99441-8) HUP.

On Soul & Conscience: Forensic Medicine in Glasgow, 1839-1989. M. A. Crowther & B. White. (Illus.). 248p. 1988. text 29.95 (0-08-036406-3, Pub. by Aberdeen U Pr); pap. text 16.00 (0-08-036407-1, Pub. by Aberdeen U Pr) Macmillan.

On South Africa. Mike Nicol. 1999. pap. 13.00 (0-679-78095-5) Vin Bks.

On Sovereignty. Jean Bodin. Ed. by Julian H. Franklin. (Cambridge Texts in the History of Political Thought Ser.). 188p. (C). 1992. text 54.95 (0-521-34206-6); pap. text 17.95 (0-521-34992-3) Cambridge U Pr.

On Soviet Dissent: Interviews with Piero Ostellino. Roy A. Medvedev. Tr. by William A. Packer from ITA. LC 79-27877. 158p. 1980. text 44.00 (0-231-04812-2) Col U Pr.

On Soviet Dissent: Interviews with Piero Ostellino. Roy A. Medvedev. Tr. by William A. Packer from ITA. LC 79-27877. 158p. 1985. pap. text 17.50 (0-231-04813-0) Col U Pr.

On Space Warfare: A Space Power Doctrine. 1991. lib. bdg. 75.00 (0-8490-4388-3) Gordon Pr.

On Spanish, Portuguese, & Catalan Linguistics. fac. ed. Colloquium on Spanish, Portuguese, & Catalan Lingu. Ed. by John J. Staczek. LC 88-4282. (Romance Languages & Linguistics Ser.). (Illus.). 245p. 1988. reprint ed. pap. 76.00 (0-7837-7785-X, 204754000007) Bks Demand.

On Speaking Out of the Silence: Vocal Ministry. Douglas V. Steere. LC 72-182983. 24p. (Orig.). 1972. pap. 4.00 (0-87574-182-7) Pendle Hill.

On Speaking Terms with Earth. Jean Pearson. 32p. 1988. pap. 4.50 (0-945251-42-4) Great Elm.

On Speaking Terms with Earth. Jean Pearson. 32p. 1992. reprint ed. pap. 5.00 (0-9627741-5-4) Green World Pr.

***On Speaking Well.** Peggy Noonan. LC 97-32537. 224p. 1999. pap. 13.00 (0-06-098740-5, ReganBks) HarperTrade.

***On Spec: Novel of Young Hollywood.** Richard Rushfield. LC 99-54821. 192p. 2000. text 21.95 (0-312-24226-3) St Martin.

On Specialness: Essays in Anglo-American Relations. Alex Danchev. LC 97-16439. 202p. 1998. text 59.95 (0-312-17647-3) St Martin.

On Spectral Theory of Elliptic Operators. Y. Egorov & V. Kondratiev. 344p. 1996. 151.50 (3-7643-5390-2) Birkhauser.

On Speech Act Verbs. Jef Verschueren. (Pragmatics & Beyond Ser.: Vol. I:4). viii, 83p. 1980. pap. 29.00 (90-272-2508-7) J Benjamins Pubng Co.

On Spelling. Caleb Gattegno. 28p. 1977. pap. text 3.00 (0-87825-138-3) Ed Solutions.

On Spinoza. Steinberg. (Philosophy Ser.). 2000. pap. text 13.95 (0-534-57612-5) Brooks-Cole.

On Spiritual Creatures. Aquinas, Thomas, Saint. Tr. by Mary C. Fitzpatrick. (Medieval Philosophical Texts in Translation Ser.: No. 5). 1949. pap. 15.00 (0-87462-205-0) Marquette.

On Spiritual Unity: A Slavophile Reader. Aleksey Khomiakov & Ivan Kieerevsky. Ed. by Robert Bird & Boris Jakim. LC 98-38587. (Esalen-Lindisfarne Library of Russian Philosophy). 1998. pap. 24.95 (0-940262-91-6, 2076, Lindisfarne) Anthroposophic.

On Spiritualism, Pt. 2. Ahmad Nawaz. LC 98-71083. xiv, 66p. 1998. pap. 10.00 (1-58225-024-3) Ananta Prakashani.

***On Spiritualism Part 1.** Ahmad Nawaz. LC 00-131827. 89p. 2000. pap. 10.00 (1-58225-229-7) Ananta Prakashani.

***On Spiritualism Part 2.** Ahmad Nawaz. LC 00-131822. 66p. 2000. pap. 10.00 (1-58225-224-6) Ananta Prakashani.

On Stability & Endoscopic Transfer of Unipotent Orbital Integrals on P-Adic Symplectic Groups. Magdy Assem. LC 98-18262. (Memoirs of the American Mathematical Society Ser.: Vol. 134, No. 635). 101p. 1998. pap. 40.00 (0-8218-0765-X, MEMO/134/635) Am Math.

On Stage! Bringing Out the Better Performer in You. Samuel P. Smith. (Illus.). 64p. (Orig.). 1992. pap. 10.00 (1-881099-01-6) SPS Pubns.

On Stage! Short Plays for Acting Students. Robert Mauro. Ed. by Arthur L. Zapel. LC 90-52982. 240p. (Orig.). (YA). (gr. 9-12). 1990. pap. text 15.95 (0-916260-67-4, B165) Meriwether Pub.

On Stage! Theater Games & Activities for Kids. Lisa Bany-Winters. LC 97-14018. (Illus.). 160p. (J). (gr. 1-7). 1997. pap. 14.95 (1-55652-324-6) Chicago Review.

On Stage America! A Selection of Distinctly American Plays. Ed. by Walter J. Meserve. LC 96-85294. (Illus.). 576p. (Orig.). 1996. pap. 24.95 (0-937657-20-4) Feedbk Theabks & Prospero.

On Stage, Gypsies: A Memoir of a Dancer in the 30s. Shyrle S. Hacker. (Illus.). 370p. (Orig.). 1994. pap. 15.95 (0-9613901-4-X) Ankh Pr CA.

On Stage, off Stage: A Memoir. Regine Crespin. Tr. by G. S. Bourdain. LC 97-19907. (Illus.). 256p. 1997. text 29.95 (1-55553-328-0) NE U Pr.

On Stage, off Stage: Memories of a Lifetime in the Yiddish Theatre. Luba Kadison et al. (Illus.). 161p. (C). 1993. pap. text 29.95 (0-674-63726-7) HUP.

On Stage with English: Spotlighting Two-Word Verb Idioms. Charlotte Perkins Gilman. (Illus.). 136p. 1998. 16.95 (1-882483-58-8); pap. text 16.95 (1-882483-54-5) Alta Bk Ctr.

***On Stage with the Igor System: Is This Our Future?** Harvey Arcel. (Illus.). 435p. 2000. pap. 39.95 (1-930002-04-1) I&L Pubs.

On Station. George R. Dasher. (Illus.). 242p. 1994. 17.00 (1-879961-03-2, 07-0008) Natl Speleological.

On Stepfathers & Stepfathering. Ed. by Stanley H. Cath et al. Date not set. write for info. (0-88163-176-0) Analytic Pr.

On Stepwise Procedures for Some Multiple Inference Problems. Tommy Johnsson. 156p. (Orig.). 1990. pap. 33.00 (91-22-01322-9) Coronet Bks.

On Stochastic Differential Equations. Kiyoshi Ito. LC 52-42839. (Memoirs Ser.: No. 1/4). 51p. 1982. reprint ed. pap. 17.00 (0-8218-1204-1, MEMO/1/4) Am Math.

On Stochastic Differential Equations. Kiyosi Ito. LC 52-42839. (American Mathematical Society Ser.: No. 4). 55p. reprint ed. pap. 30.00 (0-608-09209-6, 205271300005) Bks Demand.

On Stone: A Builder's Notebook. Bob Arnold. Ed. by Cid Corman. (Illus.). 96p. (Orig.). 1988. pap. text 15.00 (0-9620575-0-9) Origin Pr.

On Stone: The Art & Use of Typography on the Personal Computer. Sumner Stone. (Illus.). 112p. 1998. pap. text 25.00 (0-7881-5806-6) DIANE Pub.

On Stone or Sand: The Ethics of Christianity, Capitalism, & Socialism. Michael Kelley. Ed. by Larry Woiwode. 2410p. (Orig.). 1993. pap. 10.95 (0-9636834-0-3) Pleroma Pr.

On Stories: And Other Essays on Literature. C. S. Lewis. Ed. by Walter Hooper. LC 81-48014. 180p. 1982. pap. 8.00 (0-15-668788-7, Harvest Bks) Harcourt.

On Story-Telling: Essays in Narratology. Mieke Bal. LC 90-26587. (Illus.). 288p. (C). 1991. pap. 29.95 (0-944344-17-8) Polebridge Pr.

On Strategy: A Critical Analysis of the Vietnam War. Harry G. Summers. LC 82-7498. 288p. 1995. pap. 14.95 (0-89141-563-7) Presidio Pr.

On Strategy Surprise. Klaus Knorr. (Research Note Ser.: No. 10). 1982. 10.00 (0-86682-042-6) Ctr Intl Relations.

On-Stream Characterization & Control of Particulate Processes. Ed. by John A. Herbst & K. V. Sastry. 308p. 1981. pap. 30.00 (0-939204-02-9, 78-19) Eng Found.

On Streets. Ed. by Stanford Anderson. (Illus.). 424p. 1986. pap. text 27.50 (0-262-51039-1) MIT Pr.

On Strike: Capital Cities & the Willies-Barre Newspaper Unions. Thomas J. Keil. LC 86-30881. (Illus.). 268p. 1988. pap. 76.40 (0-608-05130-6, 2065691) Bks Demand.

On Strike: Six Key Labour Struggles in Canada. Ed. by Irving Abella. 196p. 1975. pap. 16.95 (0-88862-057-8, Pub. by J Lorimer) Formac Dist Ltd.

On Strike: Six Key Labour Struggles in Canada, 1919-1949. Irving Abella. 196p. 1975. 24.95 (0-88862-058-6, Pub. by J Lorimer) Formac Dist Ltd.

On Strike at Hormel: The Struggle for a Democratic Labor Movement. Hardy Green. (Labor & Social Change Ser.). 336p. (C). 1990. 29.95 (0-87722-635-0) Temple U Pr.

On Strike at Hormel: The Struggle for a Democratic Labor Movement. Harvey Green. (Labor & Social Change Ser.). 336p. 1991. pap. 22.95 (0-87722-832-9) Temple U Pr.

On Strike for Respect: The Clerical & Technical Workers' Strike at Yale University, 1984-85. Toni Gilpin. LC 94-22669. 96p. 1995. pap. text 6.95 (0-252-06454-2) U of Ill Pr.

On Striving to Be a Muslim. Abdul Qayyum. 1992. pap. 14.50 (0-935782-10-9) Kazi Pubns.

On Studying Organizational Cultures: Diagnosis & Understanding. Majken Schultz. (De Gruyter Studies in Organization: No. 58). 180p. (C). 1994. pap. text 24.95 (3-11-014649-5); lib. bdg. 52.95 (3-11-014137-X) De Gruyter.

On Studying Singing. Sergius Kagen. 119p. 1960. pap. 4.95 (0-486-20622-X) Dover.

On Style. Demetrius. (Loeb Classical Library). write for info. (0-318-53146-1) HUP.

On Subject & Theme: A Discourse Functional Perspective. Ed. by Ruqaiya Hasan & Peter H. Fries. (Current Issues in Linguistic Theory Ser.: Vol. 118). xii, 414p. 1995. 29.95 (1-55619-868-X) J Benjamins Pubng Co.

On Suicide: A Discourse on Voluntary Death. Jean Ambery. Tr. by John D. Barlow from GER. LC 98-53904. 160p. 1999. 19.95 (0-253-33563-9) Ind U Pr.

On Suicide: Great Writers on the Ultimate Question. Ed. by John Miller. 224p. 1993. pap. 10.95 (0-8118-0231-0) Chronicle Bks.

On Suicide: With Particular Reference to Suicide among Young Students. Ed. by Paul Friedman. LC 67-26190. 142p. 1967. 27.50 (0-8236-3860-X) Intl Univs Pr.

On Suicide in European Countries: Some Theoretical, Legal & Historical Views on Suicide Mortality & Its Concomitants. Ilkka H. Makinen. LC 97-165184. (Stockholm Studies in Sociology: Vol. 5). 140p. 1997. pap. 47.50 (91-22-01753-4, Pub. by Almqvist Wiksell) Coronet Bks.

On Summability Methods for Conjugate Fourier-Stieltjes Integrals in Several Variables & Generalizations. Thomas Walsh. LC 73-2729. (Memoirs Ser.: No. 1/131). 103p. 1973. pap. 19.00 (0-8218-1831-7, MEMO/1/131) Am Math.

On Sundays We Wore White. large type ed. Eileen Elias. (Non-Fiction Ser.). 512p. 1992. 27.99 (0-7089-2692-4) Ulverscroft.

On Sunset Boulevard: The Life & Times of Billy Wilder. Ed Sikov. LC 98-23504. (Illus.). 416p. (J). 1998. 29.95 (0-7868-6194-0, Pub. by Hyperion) Time Warner.

On Sunset Boulevard: The Life & Times of Billy Wilder. Ed Sikov. (Illus.). 416p. 1999. reprint ed. pap. 17.95 (0-7868-8503-3, Pub. by Hyperion) Time Warner.

On Surfing. William Finnegan. 1998. write for info. (0-679-44871-3) Random.

On Surgery & Instruments. Al-Zahrawi. 288p. (C). 1997. text 40.00 (0-934905-81-9, Library of Islam) Kazi Pubns.

On Swift's Poetry. John I. Fischer. LC 77-12705. 215p. reprint ed. pap. 66.70 (0-7837-4894-9, 204455900004) Bks Demand.

On Symbols & Society. Kenneth Burke. (Heritage of Sociology Ser.). 342p. 1989. pap. text 17.00 (0-226-08078-1) U Ch Pr.

On Symbols & Society. Kenneth Burke. (Heritage of Sociology Ser.). 352p. 1989. lib. bdg. 39.95 (0-226-08077-3) U Ch Pr.

On Symbols in Anthropology, Essays in Honor of Harry Hoijer, 1980. Milton B. Singer et al. LC 81-52797. (Other Realities Ser.: Vol. 3). vi, 134p. 1982. pap. 16.00 (0-89003-090-1) Undena Pubns.

On Syntax of Negation. Itzial Laka. LC 94-598. (Outstanding Dissertations in Linguistics Ser.). 1994. write for info. (0-8153-0696-2) Garland.

On Systemic Balance: Flexibility & Stability in Social, Economic & Environmental Systems. Michael K. Goldberg. LC 89-3917. 196p. 1989. 55.00 (0-275-93249-4, C3249, Praeger Pubs) Greenwood.

On Systems Analysis & Simulation of Ecological Processes. 2nd ed. P. A. Leffelaar. LC 98-49744. (Current Issues in Production Ecology Ser.). 16p. 1999. write for info. (0-7923-5525-3) Kluwer Academic.

On Systems Analysis & Simulation of Ecological Processes with Examples in CSMP & FORTRAN. Ed. by P. A. Leffelaar. (Current Issues in Production Ecology Ser.). 308p. (C). 1993. pap. text 67.00 (0-7923-2435-8); lib. bdg. 137.00 (0-7923-2434-X) Kluwer Academic.

On Tablets of Human Hearts: Christian Education with Children. Mary E. Drushal. 224p. 1990. 17.99 (0-310-36840-5) Zondervan.

On Tai Chi Chuan. T. Y. Pang. (Illus.). 325p. (Orig.). 1988. pap. 25.00 (0-9612070-1-9) Tai Chi Schl Philos.

On Tap: A Cavalcade of Trivia & Tall Stories Celebrating 200 Years of the Australian Pub. Mark McKay. (Illus.). 160p. 1999. pap. 14.95 (1-86254-473-5, Pub. by Wakefield Pr) BHB Intl.

On Tap: A Field Guide to North American Brewpubs & Craft Breweries, Including Restaurants. Steve Johnson. 266p. 1994. pap. 12.95 (0-9629368-6-3) On Tap Pubns.

On Tap: Guide to North American Brewpubs & Craft Breweries, 2 vols., Set. 2nd ed. Steve Johnson. (Illus.). 1993. pap. 29.00 (0-9629368-2-0) On Tap Pubns.

On Tap: Guide to North American Brewpubs & Craft Breweries, 2 vols., Vol. 1: U. S. East of the Mississippi & Canada. 2nd ed. Steve Johnson. (Illus.). 1993. pap. 14.50 (0-9629368-3-9) On Tap Pubns.

On Tap: Guide to North American Brewpubs & Craft Breweries, 2 vols., Vol. 2: U. S. West of the Mississippi. 2nd ed. Steve Johnson. (Illus.). 1993. pap. 14.50 (0-9629368-4-7) On Tap Pubns.

On Tap: The Guide to U. S. Brewpubs. Steve Johnson. 314p. 1991. pap. 15.95 (0-9629368-0-4) On Tap Pubns.

On Tap Companion: New Brewpubs & Microbreweries since the Spring of 1991. Steve Johnson. (Illus.). 108p. (Orig.). 1992. pap. 8.00 (0-9629368-1-2) On Tap Pubns.

On Tap Dancing. Paul Draper. Ed. by Fran Avallone. LC 77-17886. (Dance Program Ser.: Vol. 8). 175p. reprint ed. pap. 54.30 (0-608-16751-7, 202782400054) Bks Demand.

An Asterisk (*) at the beginning of an entry indicates that the title is appearing for the first time.

On Tap Midwest: The Beer Connoisseur's Guide to Brewpubs, Restaurant Breweries & Craft Breweries in the Midwest. Steve Johnson & Marty Nachel. (Illus.). 220p. 1995. 18.95 (*0-9629368-7-1*) Login Pubs Consort.

On Tap New England: The Beer Connoisseurs Guide to Brewpubs Restaurant Breweries Craft. Steve Johnson. (Illus.). 212p. 1994. pap. 18.95 (*0-9629368-5-5*) On Tap Pubns.

***On Target.** Tim Scully. 2000. pap. 11.95 (*1-902644-32-8*) Prowler Pr.

***On Target: Achieving the Best Business Performance.** David Irwin. (ITBP Textbooks Ser.). 1999. 19.99 (*1-86152-527-3*, Pub. by ITBP) Thomson Learn.

***On Target: History & Hunting in Central Africa.** limited ed. Christian Le Noel. LC 99-66167. (Illus.). 263p. 1999. 85.00 (*1-882458-24-9*) Trophy Rm Bks.

***On Target: The German Tiger Tanks.** (On Target; Vol. I). (Illus.). 44p. 1998. 11.95 (*1-930607-39-3*, VPI 1330) Verlinden Prod.

On Target for the Toeic. Lin Lougheed. (C). 1994. pap. text. write for info. (*0-201-59496-X*) Addison-Wesley.

On Target for Tuning Your Compound Bow: Including Fast Flight Cable System & Carbon Arrows. 3rd ed. Larry Wise. LC 98-25661. (On Target Series of Outdoor Sports: No. 6). 1998. pap. write for info. (*0-913305-15-4*) Target Comm.

On Target in Children's Church. Ruth Gibson. 128p. 1984. pap. 7.99 (*0-8341-0921-2*) Beacon Hill.

On-Target Marketing: Promotion Strategies for Child Care Centers. Ed. by Roger Neugebauer. (Best of Exchange Ser.). 48p. (Orig.). 1996. pap. 10.00 (*0-942702-18-2*) Child Care.

***On Target 1: Intermediate.** 2nd ed. James E. Purpura & Diane Pinkley. LC 99-36749. 1999. 15.67 (*0-201-57978-2*) Addison-Wesley.

On Target with Mark Duncan: An Illustrated Pocket Guide to Handgun Accuracy. Mark Duncan. (Illus.). 52p. (Orig.). 1984. pap. 4.95 (*0-9613502-0-2*) Duncan Gun.

On Taste, 1732 to 1735 see Popeiana

On Teaching & Learning in College. Paul L. Dressel & Dora Marcus. LC 82-48077. (Jossey-Bass Series in Higher Education). 271p. reprint ed. pap. 84.10 (*0-8357-4879-0*, 203781200009) Bks Demand.

On Teaching Genealogy. Fran Carter. (Illus.). 53p. 1989. pap. 9.95 (*0-945433-05-0*) Herit Quest.

On Teaching Physics. Ed. by Melba Phillips. 192p. 1980. per. 24.00 (*0-917853-77-6*, OP-17) Am Assn Physics.

On Teaching Speech in Elementary & Junior High Schools. Ed. by J. Jeffery Auer & Edward B. Jenkinson. LC 73-138412. (Indiana University English Curriculum Studies). 192p. reprint ed. 59.60 (*0-8357-9228-5*, 201546400094) Bks Demand.

On Teaching Swimming. Charles F. Cicciarella. (Orig.). 1987. pap. text 11.95 (*0-926152-56-4*) Persimmon Soft.

On Teams. Ron Archer. 156p. 1996. text 19.95 (*0-7863-0498-7*, Irwn Prfssnl) McGraw-Hill Prof.

On Tears. Ignatius Brianchaninov. 1993. pap. 0.75 (*0-89981-121-3*) Eastern Orthodox.

On Television. Pierre Bourdieu. Tr. by Priscilla P. Ferguson from FRE. LC 97-40535. 112p. 1998. 18.95 (*1-56584-407-6*, Pub. by New Press NY) Norton.

***On Television.** Pierre Bourdieu. Tr. by Priscilla Parkhurst Ferguson from FRE. 104p. 1999. pap. 12.95 (*1-56584-512-9*, Pub. by New Press NY) Norton.

On Television. 4th ed. Hood. LC 98-179806. 1997. 49.95 (*0-7453-1110-5*, Pub. by Pluto GBR); pap. 15.95 (*0-7453-1111-3*, Pub. by Pluto GBR) Stylus Pub VA.

On Ten Plays of Shakespeare. Stopford A. Brooke. LC 72-149655. reprint ed. 32.50 (*0-404-01109-8*) AMS Pr.

On Tender Feet & Eagles' Wings. Kevin R. Murray. 128p. 1996. pap. 11.98 (*0-88290-587-2*) Horizon Utah.

***On Tenderness Express.** Maxim Jakubowski. 2000. 31.00 (*1-899344-55-1*, Pub. by Do-Not Pr); pap. 15.95 (*1-899344-54-3*, Pub. by Do-Not Pr) Dufour.

***On Tendrils of Fire Bk. 1: The Privateer.** Nicole Margot Spencer. LC 00-190674. 293p. 2000. 25.00 (*0-7388-1562-4*); pap. 18.00 (*0-7388-1563-2*) Xlibris Corp.

On Terrorism & Combating Terrorism. Ed. by Ariel Merari. LC 84-22037. 188p. 1985. pap. 19.95 (*0-313-27061-9*, P7061); lib. bdg. 49.95 (*0-313-27047-3*, U7047) Greenwood.

On TESOL '79: The Learner in Focus: Selected Papers from the 13th Annual Convention of TESOL, Boston, MA, February 27-March 4, 1979. Teachers of English to Speakers of Other Languages. Ed. by Carlos A. Yorio & Kyle Perkins. LC 80-50151. 370p. reprint ed. pap. 114.70 (*0-608-14977-2*, 202596200047) Bks Demand.

On Text & Context: Methodological Approaches to the Context of Literature. Eduardo Forastieri-Braschi et al. LC 79-18001. 159p. 1980. pap. 10.00 (*0-8477-3194-4*) U of PR Pr.

On Textual Understanding. Peter Szondi. Tr. by Harvey Mendelsohn from GER. (Theory & History of Literature Ser.: Vol. 15). 245p. (Orig.). 1986. pap. 17.95 (*0-8166-1288-9*) U of Minn Pr.

On That Day. Carroll F. Terrell. 1983. pap. 2.00 (*0-915032-15-5*) Natl Poet Foun.

On the Academy. Friedrich Daniel Ernst Schleiermacher. Tr. by Terrence Tice & Edwina Lawler. (Schleiermacher Studies & Translations: Vol. 2). 1995. write for info. (*0-88946-361-1*) E Mellen.

On the Adirondack Survey with Verlanck Colvin: The Diaries of Percy Reese Morgan. Norman J. Van Valkenburgh. LC 91-23671. (Illus.). 96p. (Orig.). 1991. pap. 10.00 (*0-935796-21-5*) Purple Mnt Pr.

On the Administrative Frontier of Medicine: The First Ten Years of the American Hospital Association, 1899-1908. Ed. by Charles E. Rosenberg. (Medical Care in the United States Ser.). 440p. 1989. text 25.00 (*0-8240-8330-X*) Garland.

On the Advantage & Disadvantage of History for Life. Friedrich Wilhelm Nietzsche. Tr. & Intro. by Peter Preuss. LC 80-16686. (HPC Classics Ser.). 70p. (C). 1980. pap. text 5.95 (*0-915144-94-8*); lib. bdg. 19.95 (*0-915144-95-6*) Hackett Pub.

On the Advantages & Disadvantages of Ethics & Politics. Charles E. Scott. LC 95-53713. (Studies in Continental Thought). 240p. 1996. pap. 15.95 (*0-253-21076-3*) Ind U Pr.

On the Aesthetic Education of Man, in a Series of Letters. Friedrich Schiller. Ed. by Elizabeth M. Wilkinson & L. A. Willoughby. 572p. 1983. reprint ed. pap. 28.00 (*0-19-815786-X*) OUP.

On the Aesthetics of Architecture: A Psychological Approach to the Structure & the Order Perceived Architectural Spaces & Forms. Ralf Weber. 304p. 1995. text 82.95 (*1-85628-977-X*, Pub. by Avebury) Ashgate Pub Co.

On the Aesthetics of Roman Ingarden: Interpretations & Assessments. Ed. by Bohdan Dziemidok & Peter McCormick. 312p. (C). 1988. lib. bdg. 147.00 (*0-7923-0071-8*, Pub. by Kluwer Academic) Kluwer Academic.

On the Agenda: Current Issues & Conflicts in U. S. Foreign Policy. Howard J. Wiarda. (C). 1990. pap. text 36.46 (*0-673-39763-7*) Addson-Wesley Educ.

***On the Air.** Melanie Stewart. (Generation Girl Ser.: Vol. 15). (Illus.). (J). 2000. pap. 3.99 (*0-307-23464-9*, Goldn Books) Gldn Bks Pub Co.

On the Air: Behind the Scenes at a TV Newscast. Esther Hautzig. LC 91-6407. (Illus.). 48p. (J). (gr. 1-4). 1991. text 15.95 (*0-02-743361-7*, Mac Bks Young Read) S&S Childrens.

On the Air: Listening to Radio Talk. Catherine Sadow & Edgar Sather. 224p. (C). 1998. pap. text 17.95 (*0-521-65747-4*) Cambridge U Pr.

On the Air: Listening to Radio Talk: Instructor's Manual. Catherine Sadow & Edgar Sather. 60p. (C). 1998. pap. text, teacher ed. 6.00 (*0-521-65746-6*) Cambridge U Pr.

***On the Air: Russian Television & Politics.** 1999. pap. text 55.00 (*0-7872-5387-1*) Kendall-Hunt.

On the Air: The Encyclopedia of Old-Time Radio. John Dunning. LC 96-41959. 840p. 1998. 55.00 (*0-19-507678-8*) OUP.

On the Air: The King Broadcasting Story. Daniel J. Chasan. (Illus.). 256p. Date not set. 22.95 (*0-9615580-6-7*); pap. 14.95 (*0-9615580-7-5*) Island Pubs WA.

On the Air with Dylan Thomas: The Broadcasts. Dylan Thomas. LC 91-39495. 320p. 1992. 22.95 (*0-8112-1209-2*, Pub. by New Directions) Norton.

On the Altar of Freedom: A Black Soldier's Civil War Letters from the Front. James H. Gooding. Ed. by Virginia M. Adams. (Illus.). 200p. 1999. pap. 14.95 (*1-55849-202-X*) U of Mass Pr.

On the Altar of Freedom: A Black Soldier's Civil War Letters from the Front. James H. Gooding. Ed. by Virginia M. Adams. (Illus.). 192p. 1992. reprint ed. mass mkt. 9.99 (*0-446-39414-9*) Warner Bks.

On the Analysis of Ground Combat: Study Appendix. Roland Tiede. 297p. (Orig.). 1979. pap. text 43.95 (*0-89126-067-6*) MA-AH Pub.

On the Anatomy of Vertebrates, 3 vols. Richard Owen. LC 72-1701. (Illus.). reprint ed. 225.00 (*0-404-08300-5*) AMS Pr.

On the Ancient British, Roman & Saxon Antiquities & Folk-Lore of Worcestershire. 2nd ed. Jabez Allies. Ed. by Richard M. Dorson. LC 77-70577. (International Folklore Ser.). (Illus.). 1977. reprint ed. lib. bdg. 42.95 (*0-405-10078-7*) Ayer.

On the Ancient Coins & Measures of Ceylon. T. W. Rhys Davis. (Illus.). 1975. pap. 10.00 (*0-916710-24-6*) Obol Intl.

On the Anvil see Sobre el Yunque

On the Anvil. Ed. by Francisco De Quevedo. (C). 1989. 30.00 (*0-948268-48-4*, Pub. by Dedalus); pap. 15.00 (*0-948268-47-6*, Pub. by Dedalus) St Mut.

On the Anvil. Max Lucado. 140p. 1994. 14.99 (*0-8423-4568-X*) Tyndale Hse.

On the Anvil: Stories on Being Shaped into God's Image. large type ed. Max Lucado. 180p. 1996. pap. 13.95 (*0-8027-2704-2*) Walker & Co.

On the Apocalypse of St. John: An Interview with Josefina Chacin Ducharne. Tr. by Bertha Gonzales from SPA. LC 88-71428. 48p. (Orig.). 1988. pap. 4.00 (*0-936707-00-3*) Action Life Pubns.

On the Apostolic Preaching. Irenaeus. Tr. by John Behr from ARM. LC 97-42422. 1997. 8.95 (*0-88141-174-4*) St Vladimirs.

On the Application of Data Assimilation in Regional Coastal Models. Rafael Canizares. (IHE Thesis Ser.: Vol. 18). (Illus.). 144p. (C). 1999. pap. text 40.00 (*90-5410-416-3*) A A Balkema.

On the Appropriate Size of a Development Program. Edward S. Mason. LC 76-25007. (Harvard University. Center for International Affairs. Occasional Papers in International Affairs: No. 8). reprint ed. 24.50 (*0-404-54608-0*) AMS Pr.

On the Arizona Trail: A Guide for Hiker's, Cyclists & Equestrians. Karen Tighe & Susan Moran. LC 97-42170. (Illus.). 301p. 1998. pap. 19.95 (*0-87108-884-3*) Pruett.

On the Art of Building in Ten Books. Leon Battista Alberti. Tr. by Joseph Rykwert et al. (Illus.). 470p. 1991. pap. text 29.50 (*0-262-51060-X*) MIT Pr.

On the Art of Cutting Metals: Seventy Five Years Later. Ed. by L. Kops & R. Ramalingham. (PED Ser.: Vol. 7). 1982. 40.00 (*0-685-06283-X*, H00251) ASME.

***On the Art of Doing Field Studies: An Experience-Based Research Methodology.** Ib Andersen. LC 98-106335. 1999. 48.00 (*87-16-13269-6*) Mksgaard.

On the Art of Poetry. Aristotle. Tr. by Ingram Bywater & Gilbert Murray. 96p. 1920. pap. text 16.95 (*0-19-814110-6*) OUP.

On the Art of Singing. Richard Miller. (Illus.). 336p. 1996. 30.00 (*0-19-509825-0*) OUP.

On the Art of Teaching. Horace Mann. 31p. 1990. 9.95 (*1-55709-129-3*) Applewood.

On the Art of Teaching from the Initiatic Point of View. 3rd ed. Omraam M. Aivanhov. (Complete Works: Vol. 29). (Illus.). 242p. 1989. pap. 14.95 (*2-85566-274-5*, Pub. by Prosveta) Prosveta USA.

On the Art of the Kabbalah. Johann Reuchlin. Tr. by Martin Goodman & Sarah Goodman. LC 93-13872. (ENG & LAT.). xxix, 376p. 1993. pap. 15.00 (*0-8032-8946-4*, Bison Books) U of Nebr Pr.

***On the Art of Writing Copy.** 2nd ed. Herschell G. Lewis. LC 99-43415. 424p. 1999. pap. 29.95 (*0-8144-7031-9*) AMACOM.

On the Automorphisms of the Classical Groups. Jean A. Dieudonne. LC 52-42839. (American Mathematical Society Ser.: No. 2). 129p. 1951. reprint ed. pap. 40.00 (*0-608-07822-0*, 205266700010) Bks Demand.

On the Automorphisms of the Classical Groups. Jean Dieudonne & L. K. Hua. LC 52-42839. (Memoirs Ser.: No. 1/2). 123p. 1989. reprint ed. pap. 21.00 (*0-8218-1202-5*, MEMO/1/2) Am Math.

On the Autonomy of the Democratic State. Eric A. Nordlinger. LC 81-1683. (Center for International Affairs Ser.). (Illus.). 247p. 1981. 37.95 (*0-674-63407-1*) HUP.

On the Autonomy of the Democratic State. Eric A. Nordlinger. (Center for International Affairs Ser.). (Illus.). 247p. 1981. pap. 13.95 (*0-674-63409-8*) HUP.

On the Back of the Swallow. Danny Morrison. 256p. (Orig.). 1996. pap. 14.95 (*1-57098-101-9*) Roberts Rinehart.

On the Back Porch with Barry & Holly Tashian. Ed. by Milton Okun. 32p. (YA). 1995. pap. 12.95 (*0-89524-974-X*) Cherry Lane.

On the Back Roads: Discovering Samll Towns of America. Bill Graves. 312p. 1999. pap. 16.95 (*1-886039-36-4*) Addicus Bks.

On the Bajada: Archaeological Studies at Davis-Monthan Air Force Base, Tucson, Arizona. Ed. by Jeffrey H. Altschul & Sylvia Lindsay. (Statistical Research Technical Ser.: No. 41). (Illus.). 249p. (Orig.). (C). 1993. pap. text, per. 22.50 (*1-879442-03-5*) Stats Res.

On the Ball. Dina Rosenfeld. LC 97-75102. (Yossi & Laibel Ser.). (Illus.). (J). 1998. 9.95 (*0-922613-83-4*) Hachai Pubng.

On the Banks . . . Poems about Indiana & Hoosiers. L. D. Gilley. 30p. 1994. pap. 5.00 (*0-9643707-0-0*) L D Gilley.

On the Banks of Big Elk Creek: The Life of Martha Finley - Beloved Author of the Elsie Books. Barbara Zahn & Nancy Drazga. (Orig.). (J). (gr. 5-9). 1997. pap. 5.99 (*1-888306-19-X*, Full Quart Pr) Holly Hall.

On the Banks of Plum Creek. Laura Ingalls Wilder. (Little House). (Illus.). 352p. (J). (gr. 3-6). 1953. pap. 4.95 (*0-06-440004-2*, HarpTrophy) HarpC Child Bks.

On the Banks of Plum Creek. Laura Ingalls Wilder. (Little House). (J). (gr. 3-6). 1971. 10.05 (*0-606-04233-4*, Pub. by Turtleback) Demco.

On the Banks of Plum Creek. rev. ed. Laura Ingalls Wilder. (Little House). (Illus.). 352p. (J). (gr. 3-6). 1953. 16.95 (*0-06-026470-5*) HarpC Child Bks.

On the Banks of Plum Creek. rev. ed. Laura Ingalls Wilder. LC 52-7528. (Little House). (Illus.). 352p. (J). (gr. 4-7). 1953. lib. bdg. 16.89 (*0-06-026471-3*) HarpC Child Bks.

On the Banks of the Bayou. Roger L. MacBride. LC 98-5573. (Little House: Vol. 1). (Illus.). 240p. (J). (gr. 3-7). 1998. pap. 4.95 (*0-06-440582-6*) HarpC.

On the Banks of the Bayou. Roger L. MacBride. LC 98-5573. (Little House: Vol. 1). (Illus.). 240p. (J). (gr. 3-7). 1998. 15.95 (*0-06-024973-0*) HarpC Child Bks.

On the Banks of the Cimarron. Daniel Mundy. (Illus.). 407p. 1998. pap. write for info. (*0-7541-0487-7*, Pub. by Minerva Pr) Unity Dist.

On the Banks of the Grasshopper: Oral Traditions of the Kansas Kickapoo. Ed. by Donald D. Stull. (Illus.). 82p. (Orig.). (J). (gr. 7-12). 1984. pap. text 7.95 (*0-317-13553-8*) Kickapoo Tribal.

On the Banks of the Ole St. Joe: A Selected History of the Twin Cities of St. Joseph & Benton Harbor, Michigan. Kathryn S. Zerler. Ed. by Peggy L. Farrington & James Pomeroy. (Illus.). 172p. 1990. 15.95 (*0-9627532-0-3*) Sleeping Cat.

On the Banks of the Pharaoh's Nile. Corinne Courtalon. LC 87-37195. (Illus.). 38p. (J). (gr. k-5). 1988. 5.95 (*0-944589-07-3*, 073) Young Discovery Lib.

On the Banks of the River: A History of Hardin County, Tennessee. Tony Hays. (Illus.). 236p. 1996. 20.00 (*0-9654267-0-X*) Tennessee River.

On the Barricades: Religion & Free Inquiry in Conflict. Ed. by Robert Basil et al. LC 89-63454. 384p. (Orig.). 1989. pap. 23.95 (*0-87975-563-6*) Prometheus Bks.

On the Barricades, & Off. Melvin J. Lasky. 256p. (Orig.). 1989. pap. 24.95 (*0-88738-726-8*) Transaction Pubs.

On the Basis of Morality. 2nd ed. Arthur Schopenhauer. Tr. by E. F. Payne. LC 94-41038. (Classics Ser.). (ENG & GER.). 226p. (C). 1998. reprint ed. lib. bdg. 39.95 (*0-87220-399-9*) Hackett Pub.

***On the Basis of Morality.** 2nd ed. Arthur Schopenhauer. Tr. by E. F. Payne. LC 94-41038. (ENG & GER.). 226p. (C). 1998. reprint ed. pap. 10.95 (*0-87220-442-1*) Hackett Pub.

On the Battle-Lines, 1919-1939. Art Shields. LC 86-20966. (Art Shields' Autobiography Ser.: Vol. 2). (Illus.). 292p. 1986. 14.00 (*0-7178-0646-4*); pap. 6.95 (*0-7178-0644-8*) Intl Pubs Co.

On the Bay - on the Hill: The Story of the First Baptist Church of Pensacola, Florida. Toni M. Clevenger. Ed. by Martha P. Trotter. LC 86-82174. (Illus.). xiv, 338p. 1986. 19.95 (*0-9617503-0-8*) FBC Pensacola.

***On the Beach.** (Rock & Pop Classics: Vol. 8). (Illus.). 30p. 1999. write for info. (*1-892207-37-0*) Intl Masters Pub.

On the Beach. Deni Bown. (What Can You Find? Ser.). 10p. (J). (ps). 1993. 4.95 (*1-56458-270-1*) DK Pub Inc.

On the Beach. Photos by Elliott Erwitt. (Illus.). 128p. 1991. 39.95 (*0-393-03028-8*) Norton.

On the Beach. W. Murray. (Sunstart Ser.: No. 747-2). (Illus.). 50p. (J). (ps-5). 3.50 (*0-7214-8001-2*, Ladybrd) Penguin Putnam.

On the Beach. Nevil Shute. 1972. pap. text. write for info. (*0-582-53775-4*, Pub. by Addison-Wesley) Longman.

On the Beach. Nevil Shute. 22.95 (*0-88411-349-3*) Amereon Ltd.

On the Beach. Nevil Shute. 288p. 1983. mass mkt. 5.99 (*0-345-31148-5*, Ballantine) Ballantine Pub Grp.

On the Beach. Nevil Shute. 1966. 23.95 (*0-434-69919-5*) Buttrwrth-Heinemann.

On the Beach. Nevil Shute. 1974. 11.09 (*0-606-01699-6*, Pub. by Turtleback) Demco.

***On the Beach.** Photos by Linda Yore & Sean Yore. (Illus.). 6p. 2000. 19.95 (*1-891791-06-0*, 1004) Dont Know Pub.

On the Beach. Nevil Shute. 256p. 1993. reprint ed. lib. bdg. 32.95 (*0-89968-365-7*, Lghtyr Pr) Buccaneer Bks.

On the Beach, No. A. (Sunstart Ser.: Series S50). (Illus.). (J). (ps-5). student ed. 1.95 (*0-317-04022-7*, Ladybrd) Penguin Putnam.

On the Beat. Wesley G. Skogan et al. LC 99-462604. 264p. 1999. 65.00 (*0-8133-6673-9*, Pub. by Westview) HarpC.

On the Beat & Offbeat. Nixon Smiley. LC 83-70681. 157p. (Orig.). 1983. pap. 7.95 (*0-916224-90-2*) Banyan Bks.

***On the Beaten Path: An Appalachian Pilgrimage.** Robert Alden Rubin. LC 99-56989. 256p. 2000. 24.95 (*1-58574-023-3*) Lyons Pr.

On the Beaten Track: Tourism, Art, & Place. Contrib. by Lucy R. Lippard. (Illus.). 192p. 1999. 25.00 (*1-56584-454-8*, Pub. by New Press NY) Norton.

***On the Beaten Track: Tourism, Art & Place.** Lucy R. Lippard. (Illus.). 2000. reprint ed. pap. 17.95 (*1-56584-639-7*, Pub. by New Press NY) Norton.

On the Beauty of Women. Agnolo Firenzuola. Ed. & Tr. by Konrad Eisenbichler & Jacqueline Murray from ITA. LC 92-21836. (Illus.). 136p. (Orig.). (C). 1992. text 29.95 (*0-8122-3158-9*); pap. text 12.95 (*0-8122-1404-8*) U of Pa Pr.

On the Beginnings of the Order of Preachers. 1991. write for info. (*0-318-68823-9*, Pub. by Dominican Sources) Parable.

***On the Bible: Eighteen Studies.** Martin Buber. (Martin Buber Library). 224p. 2000. pap. 22.95 (*0-8156-2840-4*) Syracuse U Pr.

On the Bifurcation & Repression Theories of Germanic & German. Christopher M. Stevens. LC 98-229267. (Journal of Indo-European Monograph Ser.: No. 29). 108p. (C). 1998. pap. text 26.00 (*0-941694-67-4*) Inst Study Man.

On the Bilingual Person. Ed. by Leonard G. Sbrocchi. (Biblioteca di Quaderni d'Italianistica Ser.). 142p. (Orig.). (C). 1989. pap. 15.00 (*0-9691979-6-9*, Pub. by Can Soc Ital Stu) Speedimpex.

On the Birth of a Child see Nacimiento de un Nino

On the Birth of Your Child. Appel. LC 99-36065. 1999. text 11.95 (*0-312-20690-9*) St Martin.

On the Black Hill. Bruce Chatwin. LC 83-7575. 256p. 1984. pap. 12.95 (*0-14-006896-1*, Penguin Bks) Viking Penguin.

On the Blanket: The Inside Story of the IRA Prisoners "Dirty" Protest. Tim P. Coogan. 264p. 1997. pap. 14.95 (*1-57098-133-7*) Roberts Rinehart.

On the Blockade. Oliver Optic. LC 98-88130. (Blue & the Gray Ser.). (Illus.). 354p. (YA). (gr. 4 up). 1999. reprint ed. pap. 14.95 (*1-890623-10-5*) Lost Classics.

On the Bloodstained Field: 130 Fascinating Human Interest Stories of the Battle of Gettysburg. Gregory A. Coco. (Illus.). 56p. (C). 1989. reprint ed. pap. text 4.95 (*0-939631-12-1*) Thomas Publications.

On the Bloodstained Field II: 132 More Human Interest Stories of the Battle of Gettysburg. Gregory A. Coco. LC 88-90643. (Illus.). 128p. (C). 1989. pap. text 5.95 (*0-939631-13-X*) Thomas Publications.

On the Blossoming. Leah Goldberg. Tr. & Afterword by Miriam B. Sivan. LC 92-10598. (World Literature in Translation Ser.: Vol. 22). (ENG & HEB.). 84p. 1992. text 15.00 (*0-8240-0034-X*) Garland.

On the Board. 2nd ed. Geoffrey Mills. 256p. 1985. text 24.95 (*0-04-658250-9*) Routledge.

On the Bone. Edna O'Brien. (C). 1990. 35.00 (*0-906887-38-0*, Pub. by Greville Pr) St Mut.

On the Bones of the Serpent: Person, Memory & Mortality in Sabarl Island Society. Debbora Battaglia. (Illus.). 264p. 1990. pap. text 17.95 (*0-226-03889-0*) U Ch Pr.

On the Bones of the Serpent: Person, Memory & Mortality in Sabarl Island Society. Debbora Battaglia. (Illus.). 264p. 1996. lib. bdg. 49.50 (*0-226-03888-2*) U Ch Pr.

On the Book of Psalms: Exploring the Prayers of Ancient Israel. Nahum M. Sarna. LC 94-30375. 1995. pap. 14.00 (*0-8052-1023-7*) Schocken.

On the Border. Annemarie Austin. 64p. 1994. pap. 12.95 (*1-85224-214-0*, Pub. by Bloodaxe Bks) Dufour.

On the Border: An Anthology. Ed. by Hildi Hawkins & Soila Lehtonen. 220p. 1996. pap. 18.95 (*1-85754-242-8*, Pub. by Carcanet Pr) Paul & Co Pubs.

O

An Asterisk (*) at the beginning of an entry indicates that the title is appearing for the first time.

On the Border: Analysis of Materials Recovered from the 1964 & 1991-1992 Excavations at the Garden Canyon Site. Ed. by Steven D. Shelley & Jeffrey H. Altschul. (Statistical Research Technical Ser.: Vol. 61). (Illus.). 186p. (Orig.). 1996. pap., per. 17.50 (*1-879442-58-2*) Stats Res.

On the Border - The Otherness of God & the Multiplicity of the Religions: The Intercultural Dialogue from an Anthropological Perspective As an Inquiry into the Theology of Religions. Thomas Mooren. Tr. by Peter G. Pandimakil from GER. LC 94-145215. (European University Studies: Series 23, Vol. 500). (Illus.). 210p. 1994. pap. 37.95 (*3-631-47000-2*) P Lang Pubng.

*__On the Border of Economic Theory & History.__ Amit Bhaduri. (Illus.). 204p. 2000. text 27.50 (*0-19-564901-X*) OUP.

On the Border of Opportunity. Marleen Pugach. LC 98-22068. 256p. 1998. write for info. (*0-8058-2463-4*); pap. write for info. (*0-8058-2464-2*) L Erlbaum Assocs.

On the Border with Crook. John G. Bourke. (American Biography Ser.). 491p. 1991. reprint ed. lib. bdg. 89.00 (*0-7812-8031-1*) Rprt Serv.

On the Border with Crook. John G. Bourke. LC 74-155699. vii, 491p. 1971. reprint ed. pap. 17.95 (*0-8032-5741-4*, Bison Books) U of Nebr Pr.

On the Border with Mackenzie: Winning West Texas from the Comanches. 1935th ed. Robert G. Carter. 39.95 (*0-8488-0023-0*, J M C & Co) Amereon Ltd.

On the Borders of Crime: Conflict Management & Criminology. Leslie W. Kennedy. 192p. (Orig.). (C). 1990. pap. text 13.56 (*0-8013-0151-3*, 75814) Longman.

On the Borders of Hiroshima: I Heard a Rumor of War. Cranston Knight. LC 98-93244. 78p. 1998. pap. 12.99 (*0-9651768-1-9*) Hunan Pr.

On the Boulevard: The Best of John L. Smith. John L. Smith. 315p. (Orig.). 1999. pap. 12.95 (*0-929712-69-2*) Huntington Pr.

On the Boulevard of the Galleons. Wallace B. Farrell & Sandra Burns. LC 94-73976. (Illus.). 256p. (Orig.). 1994. pap. 14.95 (*0-939837-10-2*) Paradise Cay Pubns.

*__On The Boundaries of American Evangelicalism: The Postwar Evangelical Coalition.__ Jon R. Stone. 1999. pap. 18.95 (*0-312-22462-1*) St Martin.

On the Boundaries of Conversation. J. Wilson. LC 88-17808. (Language & Communication Library). (Illus.). 134p. 1988. text 51.00 (*0-08-036569-8*, Pergamon Pr) Elsevier.

On the Bowery: Confronting Homelessness in American Society. Benedict Giamo. LC 89-32099. (Illus.). 288p. 1989. 33.95 (*0-87745-243-1*) U of Iowa Pr.

On the Breath of the Gods. 3rd ed. Ariel Tomioka. 265p. 1988. reprint ed. pap. 12.95 (*0-923490-09-4*) Helios Hse.

On the Bridge. David Cope. LC 86-21074. (Vox Humana Ser.). 90p. 1986. 14.95 (*0-89603-113-6*); pap. 12.95 (*0-89603-114-4*) Humana.

On The Bright Road. Paddy Figgis. LC 99-31978. 256p. 2000. 14.95 (*0-7145-3057-3*) Mari.

On the Bright Winter Hills. Mary R. Birkelbach. LC 90-86059. (Illus.). 53p. (Orig.). 1991. pap. 10.95 (*0-9628619-0-1*) Bun Pubns.

On the Brink. (Illus.). 218p. 1999. pap. 14.99 (*1-56530-301-6*, Pub. by Summit TX) BookWorld.

On the Brink: Australia's Universities Confronting Their Future. Peter Coaldrake. LC 98-199972. 234p. 1998. pap. 29.95 (*0-7022-3050-2*, Pub. by Univ Queensland Pr) Intl Spec Bk.

*__On the Brink: Breaking Through Every Obstacle into the Glory of God.__ Rod Parsley. 192p. 2000. 16.99 (*0-7852-6808-1*) Nelson.

On the Brink: Defense, Deficits & Welfare Spending. James L. Clayton. LC 83-23052. (Orig.). 1984. 8.95 (*0-915071-01-0*) Ramapo Pr.

On the Brink: Easy-to-Understand End-Time Bible Prophecy. Daymond R. Duck. LC 93-85140. 256p. 1995. pap. 11.95 (*0-914984-58-6*) Starburst.

On the Brink: English Novels of 1866. Monica C. Fryckstedt. (Studia Anglistica Upsaliensia Ser.: No. 69). 157p. (Orig.). 1989. pap. 42.50 (*91-554-2354-X*) Coronet Bks.

On the Brink: How to Survive the Coming Great Depression 1993-2000. Michael W. Haga. LC 92-73187. (Illus.). 363p. (Orig.). 1992. pap. 19.95 (*1-881872-09-2*) Acclaim Pub.

On the Brink: Negotiating Literature & Life with Adolescents. Susan Hynds. (Language & Literacy Ser.). 320p. 1997. 42.00 (*0-8077-3688-0*) Tchrs Coll.

On the Brink: Negotiating Literature & Life with Adolescents. Susan Hynds. LC 97-34284. (Language & Literacy Ser.). 302p. 1997. pap. 20.95 (*0-8077-3687-2*) Tchrs Coll.

On the Brink: The Life & Leadership of Norman Brinker. Norman Brinker & Donald T. Phillips. (Illus.). 234p. 1996. 24.95 (*1-56530-212-5*) Summit TX.

*__On the Brink: Travels in the Wilds of India.__ Vivek Menon. LC 99-936253. (Illus.). 1999. write for info. (*0-14-027826-5*) Penguin Books.

On the Brink of a Bloody Racial War. Ben Klassen. Ed. by Rudy Stanko. 1993. 8.00 (*0-9636094-9-1*, K8) Creativity Bk Pub.

*__On the Brink of Annihilation: How the Feminine Principle Can Save Us.__ Gertrude Morin & Dr. Harold J. Breen. LC 99-61667. 176p. 1999. pap. 9.99 (*1-56384-167-3*, Pub. by Huntington Hse) BookWorld.

On the Brink of Competition: RCG's Guide to the Northeast Power Market. Reed Consulting Group, Inc. Staff. LC 98-138599. (Illus.). 202p. 1997. pap. write for info. (*0-9654813-0-1*) Reed Cnslting.

On the Brink of Extinction: Conserving the Diversity of Life. Edward C. Wolf. LC 87-50615. (Worldwatch Papers). 52p. (Orig.). 1987. pap. 5.00 (*0-916468-79-8*) Worldwatch Inst.

On the Brink of Extinction: The California Condor. Caroline Arnold. 1993. 14.20 (*0-606-12461-6*) Turtleback.

On the Brink of Extinction: The California Condor. abr. ed. Caroline Arnold. LC 92-14914. (Illus.). 48p. (J). (gr. 3-7). 1993. 17.95 (*0-15-257990-7*, Gulliver Bks) Harcourt.

On the Brink of Ministry. unabridged ed. Katherine Duke. 1998. pap. 9.99 (*0-9666158-0-8*, 100) Marimae Publ.

*__On the Brink of Paradise: From Tetons to Tropics.__ Kim McMahill. 115p. 1999. pap. 12.95 (*0-7414-0140-1*) Buy Books.

On the Brink of Tomorrow: Frontiers of Science. Ed. by Donald J. Crump. LC 81-48075. (Special Publications Series 17: No. 3). 200p. (YA). (gr. 7 up). 1982. 12.95 (*0-87044-414-X*) Natl Geog.

On the Brink of War: India, Pakistan, & the 1990 Kashmir Crisis. Tinaz Pavri. (Pew Case Studies in International Affairs). 50p. (C). 1996. text 3.50 (*1-56927-373-1*) Geo U Inst Dplmcy.

On the Buddha. Bart Gruzalski. (Philosophy Ser.). 1999. pap. text 13.95 (*0-534-57596-X*) Brooks-Cole.

On the Bum: or The Next Train Through. Neal Bell. 1994. pap. 5.25 (*0-8222-1344-3*) Dramatists Play.

On the Bus: The Complete Guide to the Legendary Trip of Ken Kesey & the Merry Pranksters & the Birth of the Counterculture. 2nd ed. Paul Perry & Ken Babbs. 205p. 1997. pap. text 22.95 (*1-56025-114-X*, Thunders Mouth) Avalon NY.

On the Bus: The Legendary Trip of Ken Kesey & the Merry Pranksters. Paul Perry & Ken Babbs. (Non-Fiction - Photo Ser.). (Illus.). 224p. 1990. pap. 22.95 (*0-685-37673-7*, Thunders Mouth) Avalon NY.

On the Bus No. 14: A Literary Anthology, Vol. VI, No. 2. Ed. by Jack Grapes. 320p. 1997. pap. 11.00 (*0-941017-46-X*) Bombshelter Pr.

On the Bus, 12: A Literary Anthology. Ed. by Jack Grapes. 240p. 1993. pap. 10.00 (*0-941017-29-X*) Bombshelter Pr.

On the Bus with Joanna Cole. Joanna Cole & Wendy Saul. LC 95-40133. (Creative Sparks Ser.). 36p. (J). 1996. 16.95 (*0-435-08131-4*, 08131) Heinemann.

*__On the Bus with Rosa Parks.__ Rita Dove. (Illus.). 96p. 2000. pap. text 11.00 (*0-393-32026-X*) Norton.

On the Buses with Dostoyevsky. Geoff Hattersley. LC 99-216101. 64p. 1998. pap. 15.95 (*1-85224-439-9*, Pub. by Bloodaxe Bks) Dufour.

On the Button: Practical Advice for the Nature Photographer. Mark Warner. LC 97-91293. 95p. 1997. pap. 14.95 (*0-9661382-1-X*) M Warner.

On the C-Algebras of Foliations in the Plane. X. Wang. (Lecture Notes in Mathematics Ser.: Vol. 1257). v, 165p. 1987. 34.95 (*0-387-17903-8*) Spr-Verlag.

On the Case: Explorations in Social History. Ed. by Franca Iacovetta & Wendy Mitchinson. LC 98-229696. (Illus.). 432p. 1998. pap. text 29.95 (*0-8020-8129-0*) U of Toronto Pr.

*__On the Case: Explorations in Social History.__ Ed. by Franca Iacovetta & Wendy Mitchinson. LC 98-229696. (Illus.). 432p. 1998. text 60.00 (*0-8020-4302-X*) U of Toronto Pr.

On the Causes of Idiocy. Samuel G. Howe. LC 79-180578. (Medicine & Society in America Ser.). 100p. 1979. reprint ed. 23.95 (*0-405-03955-7*) Ayer.

On the Causes of War. Emile L. Laveleye. 1972. 59.95 (*0-8490-0763-1*) Gordon Pr.

On the Causes of War. Hidemi Suganami. 244p. 1996. text 62.00 (*0-19-827338-X*) OUP.

*__On the Ceiling.__ Eric Chevillard. Tr. by Jordan Stump. 96p. 2000. 45.00 (*0-8032-1504-5*); pap. 15.00 (*0-8032-6396-1*, Bison Books) U of Nebr Pr.

On the Celebrated & Neglected Poems of Andrew Marvell. Ed. by Claude J. Summers & Ted-Larry Pebworth. (Illus.). 272p. (C). 1992. text 42.50 (*0-8262-0795-2*) U of Mo Pr.

On the Centre of Gravity of the Human Body. W. Braune & Fischer. Tr. by P. G. Maquet et al from GER. (Illus.). 115p. 1984. 72.39 (*0-387-13216-3*) Spr-Verlag.

On the Cessation of the Charismata: A Critique of the Protestant Polemic on Postbiblical Miracles. Jon Ruthven. (JPT Supplement Ser.: No. 3). 271p. 1993. pap. 21.95 (*1-85075-405-5*, Pub. by Sheffield Acad) CUP Services.

*__On the Chalkboard Reading & Writing Grade 1.__ Lori Mammen. 2000. write for info. (*1-57022-230-4*) ECS Lrn Systs.

*__On the Chalkboard Reading & Writing Grade 2.__ Lori Mammen. 2000. write for info. (*1-57022-231-2*) ECS Lrn Systs.

*__On the Chalkboard Reading & Writing Grade 3.__ Lori Mammen. 2000. write for info. (*1-57022-232-0*) ECS Lrn Systs.

*__On the Chalkboard Reading & Writing Grade 4.__ Lori Mammen. 2000. write for info. (*1-57022-233-9*) ECS Lrn Systs.

*__On the Chalkboard Reading & Writing Grade 5.__ Lori Mammen. 2000. write for info. (*1-57022-234-7*) ECS Lrn Systs.

*__On the Chalkboard Reading & Writing Grade 6.__ Lori Mammen. 2000. write for info. (*1-57022-235-5*) ECS Lrn Systs.

On the Challenges of Unemployment in a Regional Europe. C. H. Verhaar. 352p. 1996. 77.95 (*1-85972-217-2*, Pub. by Avebry) Ashgate Pub Co.

On the Changing Role of the U. S. Military in Space. Daniel Gonzales. LC 98-43375. (Illus.). 70p. 1998. pap. text 12.00 (*0-8330-2661-5*, MR-895-AF) Rand Corp.

On the Character of a True Theologian. Herman Witsius. Ed. by J. Ligon Duncan, III. 60p. (C). 1995. pap. text 6.95 (*1-884416-09-8*) A Press.

On the Character of Sir John Falstaff. James O. Halliwell-Phillipps. LC 21-15513. reprint ed. 27.50 (*0-404-03083-1*) AMS Pr.

On the Characteristics of Animals, 3 vols., 1. Claudius Aelian. (Loeb Classical Library: No. 446, 448, 449). 390p. 1958. 19.95 (*0-674-99491-4*) HUP.

On the Characteristics of Animals, 3 vols., 2. Claudius Aelian. (Loeb Classical Library: No. 446, 448, 449). 1958. 19.95 (*0-674-99493-0*) HUP.

On the Characteristics of Animals, 3 vols., Vol. 3. Claudius Aelian. (Loeb Classical Library: No. 449). 452p. 1959. 19.95 (*0-674-99494-9*) HUP.

*__On the Christian Eduction of Youth: Divini Illius Magistri.__ Pius XII, pseud. 58p. 2000. pap. 4.25 (*1-892331-03-9*) Angelus Pr.

On the Christian Meaning of Human Suffering. 48p. 1984. pap. 3.95 (*1-55586-919-X*) US Catholic.

On the Christian Meaning of Human Suffering: Salvifici Doloris. John Paul, II, pseud. 58p. pap. 2.95 (*0-8198-1484-9*) Pauline Bks.

On the Christian Sacraments. Cyril of Jerusalem. Ed. by F. L. Cross. 83p. 1977. pap. 7.95 (*0-913836-39-7*) St Vladimirs.

On the Chronological Sequence of the Coins of Ephesus. Barclay V. Head. (Illus.). 1979. 20.00 (*0-916710-40-8*) Obol Intl.

On the Chronology of Sound Changes in Tocharian Vol. 1: From Proto-Indo-European to Proto-Tocharian. Don Ringe. LC 96-171340. (Monographs: No. 80). xxv, 203p. 1996. 45.00 (*0-940490-80-3*) Am Orient Soc.

On the Circulation of the Blood: Latin Text of His Sixty-Fifth Letter to the Royal Society, 1688. Antoni Van Leeuwenhoek. (Illus.). 33p. 1962. reprint ed. text 47.50 (*90-6004-098-8*, Pub. by B De Graaf) Coronet Bks.

On the Classification of C*-Algebras of Real Rank Zero: Inductive Limits of Matrix Algebras over Non-Hausdorff Graphs. Hongbing Su. LC 94-43209. (Memoirs Ser.: Vol. 547). 83p. 1995. pap. 33.00 (*0-8218-2607-7*, MEMO/114/547) Am Math.

On the Classification of Economic Fluctuations. John R. Meyer & Daniel H. Weinberg. (Explorations in Economic Research Two Ser.: No. 2). 36p. 1975. reprint ed. 35.00 (*0-685-66195-4*) Natl Bur Econ Res.

On the Client's Path: A Manual for the Practice of Solution-Focused Therapy. A. J. Chevalier. LC 95-69483. 176p. 1995. 49.95 (*1-57224-021-0*) New Harbinger.

On the Cliffs of Acoma: A Story for Children. John Dressman. Tr. by Pedro R. Ortega from SPA. LC 83-20177. (Illus.). 32p. (J). (gr. 2-4). 1984. pap. 5.95 (*0-86534-021-8*) Sunstone Pr.

On the Clipper Ship Kathay. 1990. 11.95 (*0-9607530-4-4*) Seacoast CA.

On the Coefficients of Cyclotomic Polynomials. Gennady Bachman. LC 93-31295. (Memoirs of the American Mathematical Society Ser.: No. 510). 80p. 1993. pap. 28.00 (*0-8218-2572-0*, MEMO/106/510) Am Math.

On the Collectible Trail. Dorothy Dean & Rilla Simmons. Ed. by Kenneth C. Weyand. (Illus.). 92p. (Orig.). 1990. pap. 9.95 (*1-878496-00-X*) Discovery MO.

On the Commonwealth Cicero. George H. Sabine & Stanley B. Smith. 288p. (C). 1996. pap. text 13.51 (*0-02-404980-8*, Macmillan Coll) P-H.

On the Compactification of Moduli Spaces for Algebraic K3 Surfaces. F. Scattone. LC 87-19555. (Memoirs Ser.: No. 70/374). 86p. 1987. pap. 18.00 (*0-8218-2437-6*, MEMO/70/374) Am Math.

On the Comparative Accuracy of RPC Estimating Techniques. Benjamin H. Stevens et al. (Discussion Papers: No. 131). 20p. (C). 1988. pap. 10.00 (*1-55869-137-5*) Regional Sci Res Inst.

On the Compatibility of Flexible Instruments. C. J. Jepma & Wytze van der Gaast. LC 99-22953. (Environment & Policy Ser.). 169p. 1999. write for info. (*0-7923-5728-0*) Kluwer Academic.

On the Complete System Approach to Demand Analysis. A. Klevmarken. (Industrial Institute for Social & Economic Research Ser.). 92p. (Orig.). 1981. pap. 37.50 (*91-7204-140-4*, Pub. by Industriens) Coronet Bks.

On the Compositional Nature of the Aspects. H. J. Verkuyl. LC 77-188006. (Foundations of Language Supplementary Ser.: No. 15). 185p. 1972. text 142.00 (*90-277-0227-6*) Kluwer Academic.

On the Computational Geometry of Pocket Machining. M. Held. Ed. by G. Goos & J. Hartmanis. (Lecture Notes in Computer Science Ser.: Vol. 500). x, 179p. 1991. 25.95 (*0-387-54103-9*) Spr-Verlag.

On the Concept of Function in Social Science. A. R. Radcliffe-Brown. (Reprint Series in Sociology). (C). 1993. reprint ed. pap. text 5.00 (*0-8290-3815-9*, S-227) Irvington.

On the Condition of Labor & the Social Question One Hundred Years Later: Commemorating the One Hundredth Anniversary of Rerum Novarum, & the Fiftieth Anniversary of the Association for Social Economics. Ed. by Thomas O. Nitsch. LC 94-17918. (Toronto Studies in Theology: Vol. 69). 626p. 1994. text 129.95 (*0-7734-9069-8*) E Mellen.

On the Condition of the Working Classes: Rerum Novarum. Leo XIII, pseud. 56p. pap. 3.50 (*0-8198-1492-X*) Pauline Bks.

On the Congruence of Sets see Congruence of Sets, & Other Monographs

On the Connexion of the Physical Sciences. 7th ed. Mary Somerville. LC 74-26296. (History, Philosophy & Sociology of Science Ser.). 1975. reprint ed. 42.95 (*0-405-06621-X*) Ayer.

On the Constitution of Athens. 2nd ed. Aristotle. Tr. & Anno. by E. Poste. xiv, 172p. 1993. reprint ed. 36.00 (*0-8377-2520-8*, Rothman) W S Hein.

On the Construction, Organization, & General Arrangements of Hospitals for the Insane. 2nd ed. Thomas S. Kirkbride. LC 73-2405. (Mental Illness & Social Policy; the American Experience Ser.). 1973. reprint ed. 25.95 (*0-405-05215-4*) Ayer.

On the Content & Object of Presentations: A Psychological Investigation. Twardowski. (Melbourne International Philosophy Ser.: No. 4). 140p. 1977. pap. text 78.50 (*90-247-1926-7*) Kluwer Academic.

On the Continuity of Development. Ira J. Gordon. 8p. 1976. 1.50 (*0-87173-071-5*) ACEI.

On the Continuity of English Prose. R. W. Chambers. (EETS, OS Ser.: Vol. 191A). 1974. reprint ed. 20.00 (*0-8115-3379-4*) Periodicals Srv.

On the Continuity of English Prose from Alfred to More & His School: (An Extract from the Introduction to OS 186) Ed. by R. W. Chambers. (EETS Original Ser.: No. 191). 1963. reprint ed. 20.00 (*0-19-722556-X*, Pub. by EETS) Boydell & Brewer.

On the Contoocook. Eleanor Vinton. 1974. pap. 8.95 (*0-87233-034-6*) Bauhan.

On the Contrary. Miroslav Holub. 128p. 1984. 21.00 (*0-906427-75-4*, Pub. by Bloodaxe Bks) Dufour.

On the Contrary: Critical Essays, 1987-1997. Paul M. Churchland & Patricia S. Churchland. LC 97-40386. (Illus.). 320p. 1998. 30.00 (*0-262-03254-6*, Bradford Bks) MIT Pr.

On the Contrary: Critical Essays, 1987-1997. Paul M. Churchland & Patricia S. Churchland. (Illus.). 368p. 1999. pap. 16.00 (*0-262-53165-8*, Bradford Bks) MIT Pr.

On the Contrary: Essays by Men & Women. Ed. by Martha Rainbolt & Janet Fleetwood. LC 82-19421. 340p. (C). 1984. pap. text 14.95 (*0-87395-720-2*) State U NY Pr.

On the Contrary: The Protocol of Traditional Rhetoric. Thomas O. Sloane. LC 96-26257. 336p. (C). 1997. text 79.95 (*0-8132-0879-3*) Cath U Pr.

On the Contrary: What Every Revolutionary-in-Reverse Should Know by Now. Solange S. Hertz. LC 98-101732. 264p. (Orig.). 1997. pap. 12.50 (*1-883511-09-7*) Veritas Pr CA.

On the Contributions of Hugh Owen Thomas of Liverpool, Sir Robert Jones of Liverpool & London, John Ridlon, M. D. of New York & Chicago to Modern Orthopedic Surgery. H. Winnett Orr. Ed. by William R. Phillips & Janet Rosenberg. LC 79-6920. (Physically Handicapped in Society Ser.). 1980. reprint ed. lib. bdg. 26.95 (*0-405-13129-1*) Ayer.

On the Corner: Male Social Life in a Paramaribo Creole Neighborhood. Gary Brana-Shute. (Illus.). 123p. 1989. reprint ed. pap. text 10.50 (*0-88133-468-5*) Waveland Pr.

On the Corner to off the Corner. Tina Darrach. (Contemporary Literature Ser.: No. 10). 30p. 1981. pap. 5.95 (*0-940650-10-X*) Sun & Moon CA.

On the Correlation of Multiplicative & the Sum of Additive Arithmetic Functions. Peter D. Elliott. LC 94-26458. (Memoirs of the American Mathematical Society Ser.: Vol. 538). 88p. 1994. pap. 31.00 (*0-8218-2598-4*, MEMO/112/538) Am Math.

On the Cosmic Relations, Vols. 1 & 2. Henry Holt. 951p. 1998. reprint ed. pap. 75.00 (*0-7661-0358-7*) Kessinger Pub.

On the Couch: Great American Stories about Therapy. Ed. by Erica Kates. 400p. 1999. reprint ed. pap. 14.00 (*0-87113-740-2*) Grove-Atltic.

On the Counselor's Path: A Guide to Teaching Brief Solution-Focused Therapy. A. J. Chevalier. 92p. (Orig.). 1996. pap. 24.95 (*1-57224-048-2*) New Harbinger.

On the Counterscarp: Limerick Writing, 1961-1991. Ciaran O'Driscoll & Anthony P. O'Brien. 240p. 1991. pap. 14.95 (*0-948339-85-3*, Pub. by Poolbeg Pr) Dufour.

*__On the Course with--Tiger Woods.__ Matt Christopher. LC 97-36990. (Illus.). 128p. (J). (gr. 3-7). 1998. pap. 4.95 (*0-316-13445-7*) Little.

On the Course With...Tiger Woods. Matt Christopher. 1998. 9.60 (*0-606-13676-2*, Pub. by Turtleback) Demco.

On the Court with - Andre Agassi. Matt Christopher. (Matt Christopher Sports Biographies Ser.). 1997. 9.60 (*0-606-11704-0*, Pub. by Turtleback) Demco.

On the Court with - Grant Hill. Matt Christopher. LC 96-22360. (Illus.). 128p. (J). (gr. 3-7). 1996. pap. 4.95 (*0-316-13790-1*) Little.

On the Court with - Grant Hill. Matt Christopher. LC 96-22360. 1996. 9.60 (*0-606-10273-6*, Pub. by Turtleback) Demco.

On the Court with - Hakeem Olajuwon. Matt Christopher. LC 97-21551. 144p. (J). 1997. pap. 4.50 (*0-316-13721-9*) Little.

On the Court with - Michael Jordan. Matt Christopher. LC 96-971. 1996. 9.60 (*0-606-10274-4*, Pub. by Turtleback) Demco.

*__On the Court with... Lisa Leslie, Vol. 1.__ Matt Christopher. LC 98-21711. 128p. (J). (gr. 3-7). 1998. pap. 4.50 (*0-316-14216-6*) Little.

On the Court With...Hakeem Olajuwon. Matt Christopher. 1997. 9.60 (*0-606-13677-0*, Pub. by Turtleback) Demco.

On the Court with....Michael Jordan. Matt Christopher. LC 96-971. (Matt Christopher Sports Biographies Ser.). (Illus.). 128p. (J). (gr. 3-7). 1996. pap. 4.95 (*0-316-13792-8*) Little.

On the Crest: Growing Through Effective Choices. Richard C. Nelson. LC 92-70821. (Illus.). 192p. (Orig.). (C). 1992. pap. text 9.95 (*0-932796-39-7*) Ed Media Corp.

On the Crest of Time: Andre Optic Meets Sara Berlin - A Historical Novel, Circa 1990. X. Y. Zebra. LC 96-83139. (Pseudonymous Ser.). (Illus.). 192p. 1998. 21.00 (*0-915090-14-7*) Firefall.

O

An Asterisk (*) at the beginning of an entry indicates that the title is appearing for the first time.

On the Cross Road: A Daily Devotional for Lent. Joan Trustly Moore. LC 98-50657. 1999. pap. 12.00 (*0-8170-1316-4*) Judson.

On the Crossroads of Asia & Europe. Daniel Bourne & Tomasz Jastrun. 104p. 1998. pap. 10.00 (*1-887573-05-4*) Salmon Run.

On the Crown. Demosthenes. 377p. 1973. reprint ed. lib. bdg. 77.50 (*3-487-05013-7*) G Olms Pubs.

On the Cultural Achievements of Negroes. Henri Gregoire. Tr. by Thomas Cassirer & Jean-Francois Briere from FRE. LC 95-47293. 192p. 1996. 40.00 (*1-55849-031-0*); pap. 15.95 (*1-55849-032-9*) U of Mass Pr.

On the Current Situation in the Ukraine. Serhifi Mazlakh & Vasyl Shakhrai. Ed. by Peter J. Potichnyj. LC 76-107976. 254p. reprint ed. pap. 78.80 (*0-608-13966-1*, 205563100029) Bks Demand.

On the Cutting Edge. Ed. by Michael Skjei. 16p. 1999. pap. 20.00 (*1-884788-03-3*) S S H & S Pubs.

On the Cutting Edge: Selected Poems. Justo J. Padron. Tr. & Intro. by Louis Bourne. LC 87-82774. 156p. (Orig.). 1988. pap. 19.95 (*0-948259-42-6*, Pub. by Forest Bks) Dufour.

On the Cutting Edge: Textile Collectors, Collections, & Traditions. Ed. by Jeannette Lasansky et al. LC 93-46431. (Illus.). 120p. 1994. pap. 24.00 (*0-8122-1518-4*) U of Pa Pr.

On the Cutting Edge: Textile Collectors, Collections, & Traditions. Jeannette Lasansky et al. LC 93-46431. 1994. 24.95 (*0-917127-08-0*) Oral Traditions.

On the Cutting Edge: The Story of a Surgeon & His Family who Served Country Folk to Kings in Four Nations. E. Anna Nixon. LC 87-72972. (Illus.). 325p. 1987. pap. 11.95 (*0-913342-61-0*) Barclay Pr.

On the Cutting Edge - A Great American Surgeon: Richard B. Cattell, M.D. Mary V. Dunmore. LC 91-60402. (Illus.). 256p. 1991. 29.95 (*0-9628738-0-2*) Jones Riv Pr.

On the Cyclonic Distribution of Rainfall. Johan A. Udden. LC 06-19923. (Augustana College Library Publications: No. 4). 21p. 1905. pap. 1.00 (*0-910182-02-7*) Augustana Coll.

On the Dalai Lama. Martin Scorsese. 1998. write for info. (*0-375-50029-4*) Random.

***On the Day His Daddy Left.** Eric J. Adams & Kathleen Adams. LC 00-8290. (Illus.). 24p. (J). (gr. k-4). 2000. lib. bdg. 14.95 (*0-8075-6072-3*) A Whitman.

On the Day I Was Born. Debbi Chocolate. LC 94-40994. (Illus.). 32p. (J). (gr. k-4). 1995. 12.95 (*0-590-47609-2*, Cartwheel) Scholastic Inc.

On the Day the Tall Ships Sailed. Betty Paraskevas. LC 99-22600. Orig. Title: Did You See That Eagle?. (Illus.). 32p. (J). (ps-3). 2000. pap. 16.00 (*0-689-82864-0*) S&S Bks Yung.

On the Day You Were Born. Debra Fraser. (J). (ps). 1992. pap. 20.00 incl. audio (*0-15-257996-6*) HarBrace.

On the Day You Were Born. abr. ed. Debra Frasier. LC 90-36816. (Illus.). 32p. (J). (ps up). 1991. 16.00 (*0-15-257995-8*) Harcourt.

On the Day You Were Born. large type ed. Debra Frasier. 1993. 9.50 (*0-614-09849-1*, L-34089-00) Am Printing Hse.

On the Day You Were Born. large type ed. Debra Frasier. LC 90-36816. (Illus.). 32p. (J). (ps up). 1995. pap. 23.95 (*0-15-200234-0*, Red Wagon Bks) Harcourt.

On the Day You Were Born: Book Rattle Gift Set. Debra Frasier. (J). 1997. 24.95 (*0-15-201639-2*) Harcourt.

On the Death of My Father: A Psychoanalyst's Memoir. Martin Silberberg. LC 94-28483. 164p. 1995. text 79.95 (*0-7734-9052-3*) E Mellen.

On the Death of My Son. Jasper Swain. (Illus.). 112p. 1988. pap. 7.95 (*0-85030-788-0*, Pub. by Aqrn Pr) Harper SF.

On the Defense of the Comedy of Dante, Introduction & Summary. Jacopo Mazzoni & Giacopo Mazzoni. Tr. & Pref. by Robert L. Montgomery. LC 83-3579. 157p. 1983. reprint ed. pap. 48.70 (*0-608-04509-8*, 206525400001) Bks Demand.

On the Defensive? The Future of SDI. Ed. by Joseph S. Nye, Jr. & James A. Schear. LC 88-17342. (Aspen Strategy Group Reports). 222p. (Orig.). (C). 1989. pap. text 20.00 (*0-8191-7021-6*) U Pr of Amer.

On the Definition of Binding Domains in Spanish: Evidence from Child Language. Jose A. Padilla. (C). 1990. text 118.00 (*0-7923-0744-5*) Kluwer Academic.

On the Desert. David Eppele. 100p. 1990. 5.00 (*0-9622635-1-6*) Tortilla Pr.

On the Design of Shakespearian Tragedy. LC 79-362489. (University of Toronto, Department of English Studies & Texts: No. 5). 262p. reprint ed. pap. 81.30 (*0-608-14619-6*, 205582800038) Bks Demand.

On the Determinants of Brazil's Exports: An Empirical Analysis. Ugo Fassano-Filho et al. 137p. 1987. lib. bdg. 52.00 (*3-16-345290-6*, Pub. by JCB Mohr) Coronet Bks.

On the Determination of Advertising Effectiveness: An Empirical Study of the German Cigarette Market. Jan C. Reuijl. 1982. lib. bdg. 126.00 (*0-89838-125-8*) Kluwer Academic.

***On the Determination of Sediment Accumulation Rates.** Ed. by P. Bruns & H. C. Hass. (GeoResearch Forum Ser.: Vol. 5). (Illus.). 256p. (C). 1999. pap. 96.00 (*0-87849-837-0*, Pub. by Trans T Pub) Enfield Pubs NH.

On the Deutie of Kings. Lauder. Ed. by F. Hall. (EETS, OS Ser.: Nos. 3, 41). 1974. reprint ed. 20.00 (*0-8115-3957-1*) Periodicals Srv.

On the Development of Developmental Psychology. Ed. by J. A. Meacham & Deanna Kuhn. (Contributions to Human Development Ser.: Vol. 8). (Illus.). xii, 160p. 1982. pap. 42.75 (*3-8055-3568-6*) S Karger.

On the Development of Peoples: Populorum Progressio. Paul, VI, pseud. 53p. 1967. pap. 1.95 (*0-8198-1824-0*) Pauline Bks.

On the Development of Peoples: Populorum Progressio. Paul, VI, pseud. 50p. 1987. 2.95 (*1-55586-260-8*) US Catholic.

On the Devil's Court. Carl Deuker. 256p. (YA). 1991. mass mkt. 4.99 (*0-380-70879-5*, Avon Bks) Morrow Avon.

On the Devil's Court. Carl Deuker. (YA). 1998. 19.25 (*0-8446-6969-5*) Peter Smith.

On the Devil's Court. Carl Deuker. 1991. 9.60 (*0-606-04995-9*, Pub. by Turtleback) Demco.

On the Dialects of Monmouthshire, Herefordshire... with a New Classification of the English Dialects see English Dialect Society Publications: Miscellanies

On the Diamond: Treasury of Baseball Stories. 1986. 8.98 (*0-685-16823-9*, 625423) Random Hse Value.

On the Difficulties Encountered by the Deaf & Dumb in Learning Language. Collins Stone. 1972. 250.00 (*0-8490-0764-X*) Gordon Pr.

On the Dignity & Vocation of Women: Mulieris Dignitatem. John Paul, II, pseud. 120p. 1988. pap. 4.50 (*0-8198-1845-3*) Pauline Bks.

On the Dignity & Vocation of Women: Mulieris Dignitatem. John Paul, II, pseud. 120p. 1988. pap. 4.95 (*1-55586-244-6*) US Catholic.

On the Dignity of Man. Giovanni Pico Della Mirandola. Tr. by Charles G. Wallis et al. LC 65-26540. 1965. pap. 7.00 (*0-672-60483-3*, LLA227) Macmillan.

On the Dignity of Man. Pico Della Mirandola. Tr. by Paul J. Miller et al. LC 97-51631. (Classics Ser.). 208p. (C). 1998. reprint ed. pap. text 8.95 (*0-87220-396-4*); reprint ed. lib. bdg. 29.95 (*0-87220-397-2*) Hackett Pub.

On the Dignity of Man: Oriental & Classical Studies in Honour of Frithiof Rundgren. Ed. by Tryggve Kronholm & Eva Riad. 524p. (Orig.). 1986. pap. text 109.00 (*91-22-00839-X*) Coronet Bks.

On the Discrimination of Gothicisms. rev. ed. William E. Coleman. Ed. by Devendra P. Varma. LC 79-8447. (Gothic Studies & Dissertations). 1980. lib. bdg. 31.95 (*0-405-12651-4*) Ayer.

On the Distances between Sun, Moon & Earth According to Ptolemy, Copernicus & Reinhold. Janice A. Henderson. LC 91-11833. (Studia Copernicana: No. 1). (Illus.). xvi, 220p. 1991. 99.00 (*90-04-09378-8*) Brill Academic Pubs.

On the Divide. Ronald T. Anderson. (Illus.). 96p. (Orig.). 1986. pap. 5.95 (*0-9616710-0-9*) Buck Mntn Pr.

On the Divine Images: St. John of Damascus. Tr. by David Anderson from GRE. LC 80-13409. 106p. 1980. pap. 7.95 (*0-913836-62-1*) St Vladimirs.

On the Divine Liturgy. St. Germanus of Constantinople. Tr. by Paul Meyendorff from GRE. LC 84-27615. 107p. 1984. pap. text 8.95 (*0-88141-038-1*) St Vladimirs.

On the Divine Liturgy: Orthodox Homilies, 2 vols., Set. Augoustinos N. Kantiotes. (Illus.). 1986. 34.00 (*0-914744-71-2*) Inst Byzantine.

On the Divine Liturgy: Orthodox Homilies, Vol. 1. Augoustinos N. Kantiotes. LC 85-81949. (Illus.). 274p. 1997. pap. 17.50 (*0-914744-72-0*) Inst Byzantine.

On the Divine Liturgy: Orthodox Homilies, Vol. 2. Augoustinos N. Kantiotes. Tr. by Asterios Gerostergios. (Illus.). 292p. 1986. 17.50 (*0-914744-73-9*) Inst Byzantine.

On the DMZ. Paul Ahuja. 26p. 1994. pap. 2.50 (*0-89567-124-7*) World View Forum.

On the Doctrine of the Modernists: Pascendi Dominici: Syllabus Condemning the Errors of the Modernists: Lamentabili Sane. Pius, X, pseud. 77p. pap. 2.50 (*0-8198-0248-4*) Pauline Bks.

On the Door: The Continuing Adventures of a Nightclub Bouncer. Geoff Thompson. 1998. 21.95 (*1-873475-72-1*, Pub. by Summers) Howell Pr VA.

***On the Door Pt. 3: The Geoff Thompson Story.** Geoff Thompson. 191p. 1999. 22.95 (*1-84024-082-2*) Summers.

On the Doorposts of Your House: A Mezuzot Beitecha - Prayers & Ceremonies for the Jewish Home, Hebrew Opening. Ed. by Chaim Stern. LC 93-24005. (Illus.). 384p. 1994. 22.00 (*0-88123-043-X*) Central Conf.

On the Dormition: Early Patristic Homilies. Tr. by Brian J. Daley from GRE. LC 97-36467. 1997. pap. 9.95 (*0-88141-177-9*) St Vladimirs.

On the Dotted Line: Police Executive Contracts. Sheldon F. Greenberg. LC 92-60472. 180p. (Orig.). 1992. pap. 16.50 (*1-878734-27-X*) Police Exec Res.

On the Duties of Brotherhood. Al-Ghazali. 1991. 8.95 (*1-56744-173-4*) Kazi Pubns.

On the Duties of Brotherhood in Islam. Al-Ghazali. Tr. by Muhtar Holland from ARA. 95p. (Orig.). 1980. pap. 4.95 (*0-86037-068-2*, Pub. by Islamic Fnd) New Era Publns MI.

On the Duty of Civil Disobedience. Henry David Thoreau. 26p. 1980. pap. 6.00 (*0-88286-130-1*) C H Kerr.

On the Duty of Civil Disobedience. Henry David Thoreau. 61p. 1992. 85.00 (*1-886015-01-5*) Sandlins Bks.

On the Duty of Civil Disobedience. deluxe ed. Henry David Thoreau. 61p. 1992. 195.00 (*1-886015-00-7*) Sandlins Bks.

On the Duty of Civil Disobedience. Henry David Thoreau. (BCL1-PS American Literature Ser.). 37p. 1992. reprint ed. lib. bdg. 59.00 (*0-7812-6880-X*) Rprt Serv.

On the Duty of Females to Promote the Cause of Peace. William Ladd. 1972. lib. bdg. 59.95 (*0-8490-0765-8*) Gordon Pr.

On the Duty of Man & Citizen According to Natural Law. Samuel Pufendorf. Ed. by James Tully. Tr. by Michael Silverthorne. (Cambridge Texts in the History of Political Thought Ser.). 248p. (C). 1991. text 59.95 (*0-521-35195-2*); pap. text 19.95 (*0-521-35980-5*) Cambridge U Pr.

On the Dynamics of Cables with Application to Marine Use. Michail Aleksandrov. LC VM0791.A434. (University of Michigan, Dept. of Naval Architecture & Marine Engineering, Report Ser.: No. 76). 32p. reprint ed. pap. 30.00 (*0-608-13482-1*, 202263000028) Bks Demand.

On the Dynamics of Exploited Fish Populations. R. J. Beverton & S. J. Holt. 533p. (C). 1993. text 97.00 (*0-412-54960-3*, 530.17C) Chapman & Hall.

On the Dynamics of Growth & Debt. Caser Van Ewijk. (Illus.). 232p. 1992. text 65.00 (*0-19-828346-6*) OUP.

On the Early Development of Mind: Selected Papers on Psychoanalysis, Vol. 1. Edward Glover. 483p. 1956. pap. 24.95 (*0-8236-8169-6*, 023760) Intl Univs Pr.

On the Early History of Radio Guidance. B. F. Miessner. (Illus.). 1964. 15.00 (*0-911302-00-X*) San Francisco Pr.

On the Early Story of Red Boiling Springs, Tennessee, with Selected Supporting Materials. Vernon Roddy & Joan C. Reddy. (Illus.). 438p. 1991. 28.00 (*0-614-29710-9*) Upper Country.

On the Easter Proclamation: And Other Declarations. Liam De Paor. 128p. 1997. boxed set 30.00 (*1-85182-322-0*, Pub. by Four Cts Pr) Intl Spec Bk.

On the Eaves of the World, 2 vols. Reginald Farrer. LC 79-136386. (BCL Ser.: I). (Illus.). reprint ed. 125.00 (*0-404-02368-1*) AMS Pr.

On the Eaves of the World, 2 vols. Reginald Farrer. LC 75-46508. (Illus.). 1977. reprint ed. write for info. (*0-685-78306-5*) Theophrastus.

On the Ebb. Mike Peyton. (Illus.). 96p. 1998. pap. 15.95 (*1-898660-53-0*) Motorbooks Intl.

On the Economics of Integrated Rural Development. Robert E. Klitgaard. LC HD0111.L5. (Lincoln Institute Monograph: No. 81-6). 66p. reprint ed. pap. 30.00 (*0-7837-3871-4*, 204370700010) Bks Demand.

On the Economics of Intra-Industry Trade. Ed. by Herbert Giersch. 283p. 1979. lib. bdg. 57.50 (*0-685-43624-1*) Coronet Bks.

On the Economy of Machinery & Manufactures. 4th ed. Charles Babbage. LC 86-10645. (Reprints of Economic Classics Ser.). xxiv, 408p. 1986. reprint ed. 49.50 (*0-678-00001-8*) Kelley.

On the Economy of Plant Form & Function: Evolutionary Constraints on Primary Productivity: Adaptive Patterns of Energy Capture in Plants. Ed. by Thomas J. Givnish. (Illus.). 736p. 1986. text 125.00 (*0-521-26296-8*) Cambridge U Pr.

On the Edge. Sebastian Beaumont. 213p. (Orig.). 1992. pap. 13.95 (*1-873741-00-6*, Pub. by Millvres Bks) LPC InBook.

On the Edge. Cherie Bennett. (Wild Hearts Ser.). (J). (gr. 3-6). 1994. pap. 3.50 (*0-671-88781-5*, Archway) PB.

On the Edge. Marilyn Cunningham. (Intimate Moments Ser.). 1993. per. 3.50 (*0-373-07527-8*, 5-07527-0) Silhouette.

On the Edge. Marvin Heiferman & Carole Kismaric. 1989. pap. 10.95 (*0-685-26535-8*) Vin Bks.

On the Edge. Guy Hibbert. 1987. pap. 5.25 (*0-8222-0849-0*) Dramatists Play.

***On the Edge.** F. Parker Hudson & Liptak. LC 98-93439. 397p. 1998. pap. write for info. (*0-9666614-0-0*) Parker Hudson.

On the Edge. Peter Lovesey. 1990. mass mkt. 4.50 (*0-445-40863-4*, Pub. by Warner Bks) Little.

On the Edge. C. E. Poverman. LC 96-35491. 311p. 1997. 22.95 (*0-86538-087-2*) Ontario Rev NJ.

On the Edge. C. E. Poverman. 1999. mass mkt. 6.99 (*0-312-97089-7*, St Martins Paperbacks) St Martin.

On the Edge. Sports Illustrated for Kids Staff. (J). 1996. pap. 4.99 (*0-553-54247-8*) BDD Bks Young Read.

On the Edge. Kate William. (Sweet Valley High Ser.: No. 40). (YA). (gr. 7 up). 1987. 8.35 (*0-606-03136-7*, Pub. by Turtleback) Demco.

On the Edge: A New History of America in the Twentieth Century. David Horowitz et al. Ed. by Baxter. 604p. (C). 1990. pap. 37.75 (*0-314-58086-7*) West Pub.

On the Edge: A New History of the 20th Century America since World War II. 2nd ed. David A. Horowitz & Peter N. Carroll. LC 97-48577. (History Ser.). (C). 1998. 51.95 (*0-314-12713-5*) Wadsworth Pub.

On the Edge: A New History of 20th Century America. 2nd ed. David Horowitz & Peter N. Carroll. LC 97-47266. (History Ser.). (C). 1998. 61.95 (*0-314-12882-4*) Wadsworth Pub.

On the Edge: Artistic Visions of a Shrinking Landscape. Ed. by Catherine Gibbon. LC 96-157886. (Illus.). 112p. 1996. 24.00 (*1-55046-153-2*, Pub. by Boston Mills) Genl Dist Srvs.

On the Edge: Contemporary Art from the Werner & Elaine Dannheisser Collection. Robert Storr. LC 97-72613. (Illus.). 160p. 1997. 29.95 (*0-8109-6178-4*, Pub. by Abrams) Time Warner.

On the Edge: Contemporary Art from the Werner & Elaine Dannheisser Collection. Robert Storr. LC 97-72613. (Illus.). 160p. 1997. pap. 29.95 (*0-87070-054-5*, 0-8109-6178-4, Pub. by Mus of Modern Art) Abrams.

***On the Edge: Extreme Travel.** Jeff Greenwald et al. Ed. by Cecil Kuhne. 2000. pap. 12.99 (*1-86450-222-3*) Lonely Planet.

On the Edge: Four True Stories of Extreme Outdoor Sports Adventures. Martin Dugard. (Sports Illustrated for Kids Ser.). 1995. 9.09 (*0-606-07967-X*) Turtleback.

On the Edge: How South African Companies Cope with Change. Piet Human & Frank Horwitz. 177p. 1992. text 41.50 (*0-7021-2874-0*, Pub. by Juta & Co) Intl Spec Bk.

***On the Edge: Political Cults Right & Left.** Ed. by Dennis Tourish & Tim Wohlforth. LC 00-24818. (Illus.). 256p. 2000. text 34.95 (*0-7656-0639-9*) M E Sharpe.

***On the Edge: Stories at the Brink.** Ed. by Lois Duncan. LC 99-54262. (Illus.). 224p. (J). (gr. 7-12). 2000. per. 17.00 (*0-689-82251-0*) S&S Bks Yung.

***On the Edge: Striptease in a Small-Town Setting.** 4th rev. ed. John W. Prehn. (Illus.). viii, 150p. 1999. pap. 25.00 (*0-9652983-1-0*) J W Prehn.

On the Edge: The Clinton Presidency. Elizabeth Drew. 512p. 1995. per. 14.00 (*0-684-81309-2*, Touchstone) S&S Trade Pap.

On the Edge: The U. S. in the Twentieth Century. 3rd ed. Horowitz. (History Ser.). 2001. 37.75 (*0-534-57186-7*) Wadsworth Pub.

On the Edge: The U. S. since 1941. 3rd ed. Horowitz. (History Ser.). 2000. 31.75 (*0-534-57187-5*) Wadsworth Pub.

On the Edge: True Tales of High Adventures from Outdoor Life's Best Storytellers. Creative Publishing International Staff. LC 99-32155. (Times Mirror - Outdoor Life Ser.). (Illus.). 224p. 1999. pap. write for info. (*0-86573-105-5*) Creat Pub Intl.

***On the Edge: Ukrainian-Central European-Russian Security Triangle.** Ed. by Margarita Balmaceda. 300p. (C). 2000. 49.95 (*963-9116-80-7*) Ctrl Europ Univ.

On the Edge: Women Making Hockey History. Elizabeth Etue & Megan K. Williams. (Illus.). 225p. 1996. pap. 16.95 (*0-929005-79-1*, Pub. by Sec Story Pr) LPC InBook.

On the Edge & in Control: A Proven 8-Step Program for Getting the Most Out of Life. Deborah Bright. 288p. 1998. pap. 15.95 (*0-07-007916-1*) McGraw.

***On the Edge & Keeping on the Edge: The University of Georgia Annual Lectures on Creativity.** E. Paul Torrance & University of Georgia Staff. LC 99-55003. (Publications in Creativity Research). 2000. pap. write for info. (*1-56750-499-X*) Ablx Pub.

***On the Edge Between Two Worlds: Ireland & the Ways of Healing.** Kathleen Milner. (Healing Arts Ser.). 2000. pap. write for info. (*1-886903-21-2*) K Milner.

On-the-Edge Games for Youth Ministry. Karl Rohnke. Ed. by Amy Simpson. LC 98-15310. (Illus.). 112p. (YA). 1998. per. 14.99 (*0-7644-2058-5*, Vital Ministry) Group Pub.

On the Edge of a Dream: Magic & Madness in Bali. Michael Wiese. LC 94-35198. (Illus.). 326p. 1994. pap. 16.95 (*0-941188-19-1*, BALI) M Wiese.

On the Edge of a Truth: A Small Anthology of Poetry by Northwest Quakers. Ed. & Intro. by Nancy Thomas. 112p. 1980. pap. 4.50 (*0-913342-25-4*) Barclay Pr.

On the Edge of America: California Modernist Art, 1900-1950. Ed. by Paul J. Karlstrom. LC 95-25237. (Illus.). 328p. 1996. 49.95 (*0-520-08850-6*, Pub. by U CA Pr) Cal Prin Full Svc.

On the Edge of an Island. Jean Breeze. LC 97-208847. 96p. 1997. pap. 17.95 (*1-85224-405-4*, Pub. by Bloodaxe Bks) Dufour.

On the Edge of Anarchy: Locke, Consent, & the Limits of Society. A. John Simmons. 312p. (C). 1993. pap. text 19.95 (*0-691-04483-X*, Pub. by Princeton U Pr) Cal Prin Full Svc.

On the Edge of Anarchy: Locke, Consent, & the Limits of Society. A. John Simmons. LC 92-44658. (Studies in Moral, Political, & Legal Philosophy). 328p. (C). 1993. text 45.00 (*0-691-03303-X*, Pub. by Princeton U Pr) Cal Prin Full Svc.

On the Edge of Certainity. Tallis. LC 99-22107. 236p. 1999. text 45.00 (*0-312-22416-8*) St Martin.

On the Edge of Darkness: Conversations about Conquering Depression. Kathy Cronkite. 368p. 1995. pap. 13.95 (*0-385-31426-4*, Delta Trade) Dell.

On the Edge of Destruction: Jews of Poland Between the Two World Wars. Celia S. Heller. (Illus.). 400p. 1994. reprint ed. pap. 19.95 (*0-8143-2494-0*) Wayne St U Pr.

On the Edge of Dream: Celtic Tales for Grown Women. Jennifer Heath. 150p. (Orig.). 1995. pap. 22.00 (*1-887997-02-4*) Baksun Bks.

On the Edge of Empire: The Taos Hacienda of Los Martinez. David Weber. (Illus.). 132p. 1996. 24.95 (*0-89013-299-2*); pap. 17.50 (*0-89013-301-8*) Museum NM Pr.

On the Edge of Europe: Mountaineering in the Caucasus. Audrey Salkeld. 256p. 1994. 24.95 (*0-89886-388-0*) Mountaineers.

On the Edge of Forest, On the Edge of Roads: People Dependent on Forest Resources in Kim Kong Province, 6 vols., Vol. 3. Rebecca Catalla et al. 55p. 2000. pap. 4.00 (*0-910082-39-1*) Am Fr Serv Comm.

On the Edge of Greatness: The Diaries of John Humphrey, First Director of the United Nations Division of Human Rights: 1948-1949. Ed. by A. J. Hobbins. LC 95-153662. (Fontanus Monograph Ser.: No. 4). 286p. 1995. 45.00 (*0-7717-0440-2*, Pub. by McG-Queens Univ Pr) CUP Services.

On the Edge of Greatness: The Diaries of John Humphrey, First Director of the United Nations Human Rights Division, Vol. I. Ed. by A. J. Hobbins. (Illus.). 304p. 1995. 49.95 (*0-7735-1383-3*, Pub. by McG-Queens Univ Pr) CUP Services.

On the Edge of Greatness: The Diaries of John Humphrey, First Director of the United Nations Human Rights Division, 1952-1957, Vol. II. Ed. by A. J. Hobbins. (Illus.). 308p. 1996. 49.95 (*0-7735-1454-6*, Pub. by McG-Queens Univ Pr) CUP Services.

On the Edge of Greatness, 1952-1957: The Diaries of John Humphrey, First Director of the United Nations Human Rights Division, Vol. III. Ed. by A. J. Hobbins. (Fontanus Monograph Ser.). (Illus.). 250p. 1997. 49.95 (*0-7735-1456-2*, Pub. by McG-Queens Univ Pr) CUP Services.

***On the Edge of Life: Diary of a Medical Intensive Care Unit.** Ed. by Mikkael A. Sekeres & Theodore A. Stern. 200p. 2000. 19.95 (*0-07-135881-1*) McGraw.

On the Edge of Nowhere. James Huntington. 192p. 1992. reprint ed. pap. 12.95 (*0-938271-03-2*) Press N Amer.

O

An Asterisk (*) at the beginning of an entry indicates that the title is appearing for the first time.

On the Edge of Paradise: A. C. Benson; the Diarist. David Newsome. LC 80-12747. (Illus.). 416p. 1996. 30.00 (*0-226-57742-2*) U Ch Pr.

On the Edge of Paradise: A. C. Benson, the Diarist. David Newsome. LC 80-12747. (Illus.). 426p. reprint ed. pap. 132.10 (*0-608-09488-9*, 205428900005) Bks Demand.

On the Edge of Politics: The Roots of Jewish Political Thought in America, 14. William S. Berlin. LC 78-4018. (Contributions in Political Science Ser.: No. 14). 206p. 1979. 55.00 (*0-313-20422-5*, BEP/, Greenwood Pr) Greenwood.

On the Edge of Reason. Miroslav Krleza. Tr. by Zora Depolo from CRO. LC 95-37589. (New Directions Classics Ser.). 192p. 1995. pap. 10.95 (*0-8112-1306-4*, NDP810, Pub. by New Directions) Norton.

On the Edge of Splendor: Exploring Grand Canyon's Human Past. Douglas W. Schwartz. (Illus.). 80p. 1989. pap. 12.95 (*0-933452-30-6*) Schol Am Res.

On the Edge of the Auspicious: Gender & Caste in Nepal. Mary M. Cameron. LC 97-45408. 376p. 1998. text 49.95 (*0-252-02412-5*); text 24.95 (*0-252-06716-9*) U of Ill Pr.

On the Edge of the Bush: Anthropology As Experience. Victor W. Turner. Ed. by Edith L. Turner. LC 85-20885. (Anthropology of Form & Meaning Ser.). 328p. 1985. 40.95 (*0-8165-0949-2*) U of Ariz Pr.

On the Edge of the Cliff: History, Language, & Practices. Roger Chartier. Tr. by Lydia G. Cochrane. LC 96-18980. (Parallax). 288p. 1996. text 45.00 (*0-8018-5435-0*); pap. text 16.95 (*0-8018-5436-9*) Johns Hopkins.

On the Edge of the Desert: Stories. fac. ed. Gladys Swan. LC 79-15858. (Illinois Short Fiction Ser.). 133p. 1979. reprint ed. pap. 41.30 (*0-7837-8063-X*, 204781600008) Bks Demand.

On the Edge of the Desert. Stories. Gladys Swan. LC 79-15858. (Illinois Short Fiction Ser.). 140p. 1979. 9.95 (*0-252-00781-6*) U of Ill Pr.

On the Edge of the Great Rift. Paul Theroux. 656p. 1996. pap. 14.95 (*0-14-024835-8*, Viking) Viking Penguin.

On the Edge of the Hudson. Laura Boss. Tr. by Ana Esapova.Tr. of Na Bregovite na Xadson. (ENG & MAC.). 96p. 1989. 15.00 (*0-89304-064-9*); pap. 7.50 (*86-373-0302-1*) Cross-Cultrl NY.

On the Edge of the Hudson. Laura Boss. Ed. by Stanley H. Barkan. (Review Women Writers Chapbook Ser.: No. 4).Tr. of Na Bregovite na Xadson. 48p. 1989. reprint ed. audio 10.00 (*0-89304-419-9*) Cross-Cultrl NY.

On the Edge of the Hudson. Laura Boss. Ed. by Stanley H. Barkan. (Review Women Writers Chapbook Ser.: No. 4).Tr. of Na Bregovite na Xadson. 48p. 1989. reprint ed. 15.00 (*0-89304-417-2*); reprint ed. 15.00 (*0-89304-415-6*, CCC163); reprint ed. pap. 5.00 (*0-89304-416-4*); reprint ed. pap. 5.00 (*0-89304-418-0*); reprint ed. boxed set 50.00 (*0-89304-909-3*); reprint ed. boxed set 25.00 (*0-89304-908-5*) Cross-Cultrl NY.

***On the Edge of the New Century: In Conversation with Antonio Polito.** Eric J. Hobsbawm. LC 99-54525. 176p. 2000. 21.00 (*1-56584-603-6*, Pub. by New Press NY) Norton.

On the Edge of the Organization: The Role of the Outside Director. Anne Spencer. LC 82-11135. 149p. reprint ed. pap. 46.20 (*0-8357-4605-4*, 203753800008) Bks Demand.

On the Edge of the Primeval Forest & More from the Primeval Forest: Experiences & Observations of a Doctor in Equatorial Africa. Albert Schweitzer. LC 75-41244. (Illus.). 1976. reprint ed. 37.50 (*0-404-14598-1*) AMS Pr.

On the Edge of the Sea. Betty Paraskevas. LC 91-31489. (Illus.). 32p. (ps-3). 1999. pap. 5.99 (*0-689-82533-1*, 076714005990) S&S Childrens.

On the Edge of the Sea: Mural Painting at Tancah-Tulum, Quintana Roo, Mexico. Arthur G. Miller. LC 81-15278. (Illus.). 164p. 1982. 35.00 (*0-88402-105-X*) Dumbarton Oaks.

On the Edge of the War Zone, From the Battle of the Marne to the Entrance of the Stars & Stripes. Mildred Aldrich. (American Biography Ser.). 311p. 1991. reprint ed. lib. bdg. 69.00 (*0-7812-8011-7*) Rprt Serv.

On the Edge of the Wild: Passions & Pleasures of a Naturalist. Stephen Bodio. LC 97-28147. 208p. 1998. 25.00 (*1-55821-648-0*) Lyons Pr.

On the Edge of the World. Nikolai Leskov. Tr. by Michael Prokurat from RUS. LC 92-31940.Tr. of Na Kraiu Sveta. 136p. 1993. pap. 8.95 (*0-88141-118-3*) St Vladimirs.

On the Edge of the World: Four Architects in San Francisco at the Turn of the Century. Richard W. Longstreth. LC 97-36898. 455p. 1998. 24.95 (*0-520-21415-3*, Pub. by U CA Pr) Cal Prin Full Svc.

On the Edge Standard Version. Jonathan Tweet & John Nephew. (On the Edge Ser.). 1995. 7.95 (*1-887801-18-9*, Atlas Games); 1.95 (*1-887801-20-0*, Atlas Games) Trident MN.

On the Edges of the Time. Rabindranath Tagore. LC 78-10671. 191p. 1978. reprint ed. lib. bdg. 35.00 (*0-313-20760-7*, TAET, Greenwood Pr) Greenwood.

On the Eighteenth Century As a Category of Asian History: Van Leur in Retrospect. Ed. by Leonard Blusse & Femme S. Gaastra. LC 98-17321. (Illus.). 313p. 1998. text 83.95 (*1-84014-610-9*, Pub. by Ashgate Pub) Ashgate Pub Co.

On the Eighth Day: Reflections on Spirit & Creativity. Dianne Valla. Ed. by David Rioux. LC 97-90277. x, 234p. 1997. 20.00 (*0-9667471-3-5*) Word Maker.

***On the Eighth Day Adam Slept Alone: New Poems.** Nancy Boutilier. LC 00-29742. 200p. 2000. 30.00 (*1-57423-133-2*); pap. 16.00 (*1-57423-132-4*) Black Sparrow.

***On the Eighth Day Adam Slept Alone: New Poems.** aut. ed. Nancy Boutilier. LC 00-29742. 200p. 2000. 40.00 (*1-57423-134-0*) Black Sparrow.

On the Eighth Day Entered Satan. Michael Dennis. 60p. 1997. pap. text 10.00 (*1-887778-02-0*) Free Mind Free Spirit.

***On the 8th Day God Laughed.** Bob Darden. LC 00-8483. 2000. write for info. (*0-941037-84-3*, BIBAL Press) D & F Scott.

On the 8th Day God Laughed. Perret. 1995. mass mkt. 5.95 (*0-929292-81-2*) Hannibal Bks.

On the Election of Grace & Theosophic Questions. Jacob Boehme. 327p. 1992. reprint ed. pap. 27.00 (*1-56459-146-8*) Kessinger Pub.

On the Elevation of the Poor: A Selection from His Reports As Minister at Large in Boston. Joseph Tuckerman. LC 79-137190. (Poverty U. S. A. Historical Record Ser.). 1977. reprint ed. 18.95 (*0-405-03128-9*) Ayer.

***On the Emotions.** Richard Wollheim. (Illus.). 264p. 1999. 25.00 (*0-300-07974-5*) Yale U Pr.

On the Employment of Children in Factories & Other Works in the United Kingdom & in Some Foreign Countries. Leonard Horner. LC 72-180445. (The Development of Industrial Society Ser.). vi, 135p. 1971. write for info. (*0-7165-1596-2*) Intl Spec Bk.

On the Enforcement of Law in Cities. Brand Whitlock. LC 69-14952. (Criminology, Law Enforcement, & Social Problems Ser.: No. 74). 1969. reprint ed. 16.00 (*0-87585-074-X*) Patterson Smith.

On the Enumeration of Non-Planar Maps. W. G. Brown. LC 52-42839. (Memoirs of the American Mathematical Society Ser.: No. 65). 42p. 1966. pap. 16.00 (*0-8218-1265-3*, MEMO/1/65C) Am Math.

On the Enumeration of Non-Planar Maps. William G. Brown. LC 52-42839. (American Mathematical Society Ser.: No. 65). (Illus.). 44p. pap. 30.00 (*0-608-05168-3*, 205258900001) Bks Demand.

***On the Erudition of the Historical St. Patrick.** Raymond M. Herbenick. LC 00-24723. (Celtic Studies: 2). 164p. 2000. 79.95 (*0-7734-7738-1*) E Mellen.

On the Essence of Chassidus. Menachem M. Schneerson. Tr. by Y. H. Greenber & S. S. Handleman. 160p. 1978. reprint ed. 7.00 (*0-8266-0470-6*) Kehot Pubn Soc.

On the Estimation of Regional Purchase Coefficients, Export Employment, & Elasticities of Response for Regional Economic Models. B. H. Stevens et al. (Discussion Papers: No. 114). 1979. pap. 10.00 (*1-55869-081-6*) Regional Sci Res Inst.

On the Ethnography of Communication: The Legacy of Sapir: Essays in Honor of Harry Hoijer, 1984. Ed. by Paul V. Kroskrity. LC 87-51717. (Other Realities Ser.: Vol. 8). 146p. (Orig.). 1988. pap. 12.50 (*0-945453-01-9*) UCLA Dept Anthropology.

On the Eucharist: A Divine Appeal. rev. ed. Ed. by Jude O. Mbukanma. 215p. 1994. reprint ed. pap. 11.95 (*1-885417-00-4*) MET Pubng.

On the Evaluation of Global Bearing Capacities of Structures. Ed. by G. Sacchi-Landriani & J. Salencon. (CISM International Centre for Mechanical Sciences Ser.: No. 332). vii, 280p. 1994. 65.95 (*0-387-82493-6*) Spr-Verlag.

On the Evaluation of Verbal Material in Parapsychology. J. G. Pratt. LC 70-94866. (Parapsychological Monographs: No. 10). 1969. pap. 5.00 (*0-912328-14-2*) Parapsych Foun.

On the Eve of Colonialism: North Africa Before the French Conquest 1790-1830. Lucette Valensi. Tr. by Kenneth Perkins from FRE. LC 77-9589. 154p. (C). 1978. 35.00 (*0-8419-0322-0*, Africana); pap. text 18.95 (*0-8419-0360-3*, Africana) Holmes & Meier.

On the Eve of Conquest: The Chevalier De Raymond's Critique of New France in 1754. Charles D. Raymond & Joseph L. Peyser. LC 97-34837. xii, 181 p. 1998. 39.95 (*0-87013-433-7*) Mich St U Pr.

***On the Eve of Contact.** Darling. 2000. 27.00 (*0-465-01563-8*, Pub. by Basic); pap. 14.00 (*0-465-01564-6*, Pub. by Basic) HarpC.

On the Eve of the Atonement. 1995. pap. 10.99 (*0-85234-321-3*, Pub. by Evangelical Pr) P & R Pubng.

On the Eve of the Millennium: The Future of Democracy Through an Age of Unreason. Conor C. O'Brien. LC 95-35636. 1995. 25.00 (*0-02-874098-X*); per. 12.00 (*0-02-874094-7*, M Kessler Bks) Free Pr.

***On the Eve of the 21st Century: Challenges & Responses.** Ed. by Erzsebet Gidai. LC 99-163096. 268p. 1999. pap. 48.00 (*963-05-7509-4*, Pub. by Akade Kiado) Intl Spec Bk.

On the Eve of the Twenty-First Century: Perspectives of Russian & American Philosophers. Ed. by William C. Gay & T. A. Alekseeva. (Studies in Social & Political Philosophy). 288p. (Orig.). (C). 1994. pap. text 27.95 (*0-8476-7830-X*); lib. bdg. 75.00 (*0-8476-7829-6*) Rowman.

On the Evening Road. Dannie Abse. 64p. 1995. 15.95 (*0-09-178941-9*, Pub. by Hutchnson) Trafalgar.

On the Evidences of the Occupation of Certain Regions by the Miwok Indians. fac. ed. A. L. Kroeber. (University of California Publications in American Archaeology & Ethnology: Vol. 6: 3). 12p. (C). 1908. reprint ed. pap. text 1.56 (*1-55567-176-4*) Coyote Press.

On the Evolution of Complex Societies: Essays in Honor of Harry Hoijer. W. Sanders et al. Ed. by Timothy Earle. (Other Realities Ser.: Vol. 6). viii, 128p. 1984. pap. 19.00 (*0-89003-139-8*) Undena Pubns.

On the Evolution of Phase Boundaries. Ed. by A. Friedman et al. (IMA Volumes in Mathematics & Its Applications Ser.: Vol. 43). (Illus.). xiii, 136p. 1992. 63.95 (*0-387-97803-8*) Spr-Verlag.

On the Existence of Feller Semigroups with Boundary Conditions. Kazuaki Taira. LC 92-18061. (Memoirs Ser.: No. 475). 65p. 1992. pap. 23.00 (*0-8218-2535-6*, MEMO/99/475) Am Math.

On the Existence of God: Lectures Given at the Universities of Wurzburg & Vienna (1868-1891) F. C. Brentano. Ed. & Tr. by S. F. Krantz. (Nijhoff International Philosophy Ser.: No. 29). 370p. 1987. lib. bdg. 201.00 (*90-247-3538-6*) Kluwer Academic.

On the Existence of Most Preferred Alternatives. Tony E. Smith. (Discussion Papers: No. 60). 1972. pap. 10.00 (*1-55869-082-4*) Regional Sci Res Inst.

On the Fabric of the Human Body Bk. 1: The Bones & Cartilages. Andreas Vesalius. Tr. by William F. Richardson & John B. Carman from LAT. LC 96-34817. (Norman Anatomy Ser.: No. 1). Orig. Title: De Humani Corporis Fabrica Libri Septem. (Illus.). lxiv, 416p. 1998. 225.00 (*0-930405-73-0*, NP32874) Norman SF.

On the Fabric of the Human Body Bk. II: The Ligaments & Muscles. Andreas Vesalius. Tr. by William F. Richardson from LAT. LC 98-34677. (Anatomy Ser.: No. 2). Orig. Title: De Humani Corporis Fabrica Libri Septem. (Illus.). 600p. 1999. text 250.00 (*0-930405-75-7*, NP35688) Norman SF.

***On the False Embassy (Oration 19) Edited with Introduction & Commentary.** Demosthenes. Ed. by Douglas M. MacDowell. 600p. 2000. text 130.00 (*0-19-815303-1*) OUP.

On the Family: Familiaris Consortio. 93p. 1981. pap. 5.95 (*1-55586-833-9*) US Catholic.

On the Far Side of the Mountain. Jean Craighead George. (Illus.). (J). (gr. 4-7). 1990. 15.99 (*0-525-46348-8*, Dutton Child) Peng Put Young Read.

On the Far Side of the Mountain. Jean Craighead George. LC 91-52562. (Illus.). 170p. (J). (gr. 3-7). 1991. pap. 4.99 (*0-14-034248-6*, PuffinBks) Peng Put Young Read.

On the Far Side of the Mountain. Jean Craighead George. (J). 1991. 10.09 (*0-606-04996-7*, Pub. by Turtleback) Demco.

On the Farm see Critter Sitters Cloth Books

On the Farm see En la Granja

On the Farm. (Interactive Turn & Learn Ser.: No. 8401). (Illus.). 12p. (J). (ps). 1999. bds. write for info. (*1-85854-768-7*) Brimax Bks.

On the Farm. (Illus.). 32p. (J). (ps-3). 1994. pap. 4.95 (*1-56458-734-7*) DK Pub Inc.

On the Farm. Heather Amery. (What's Happening? Ser.). (Illus.). 20p. (J). (ps-3). 1984. pap. text 4.50 (*0-7460-1538-0*, Usborne) EDC.

On the Farm. Deni Bown. (What Can You Find? Ser.). 12p. (J). (ps). 1993. 4.95 (*1-56458-269-8*) DK Pub Inc.

On the Farm. Karen Bryant-Mole. LC 99-10866. (Picture This Ser.). (Illus.). (J). 1999. write for info. (*1-57572-901-6*) Heinemann Lib.

On the Farm. Frantisek Chochola. (J). (ps). 1988. bds. 5.50 (*0-86315-051-9*, 20235, Pub. by Floris Bks) Gryphon Hse.

On the Farm. Kathleen Cubley. (Illus.). 32p. (J). (ps-k). 1999. pap. 3.95 (*1-57029-257-4*, 01109) Totline Pubns.

On the Farm. DK Publishing Staff. 1996. 4.99 (*0-7894-1372-8*) DK Pub Inc.

***On the Farm.** George Fryer. (Find & Fit Ser.). (Illus.). 10p. (J). (ps-k). 2000. 14.95 (*1-57145-432-2*, Silver Dolph) Advantage Pubs.

On the Farm. Illus. by Polly Jordan. (What's Missing? Ser.). 24p. (J). (ps-2). 1994. 2.95 (*1-56293-452-X*, McClanahan Book) Learn Horizon.

On the Farm. Tessa Krailing. (Little Bitty Ser.). (Illus.). 20p. (J). (ps). 1991. bds. 2.50 (*0-8120-6262-0*) Barron.

On the Farm. Illus. by Moira Maclean. (Magic Lanterns Ser.). (J). 7.98 (*1-57717-114-4*) Todtri Prods.

***On the Farm.** Christopher Nicholas. (Storyshapes Ser.). 24p. 1999. pap. text 2.25 (*0-7681-0134-4*, McClanahan Book) Learn Horizon.

On the Farm. Henry Arthur Pluckrose. LC 97-51398. (Machines at Work Ser.). (Illus.). (J). 1998. 18.00 (*0-531-14496-8*) Watts.

On the Farm. Henry Arthur Pluckrose. (Machines at Work Ser.). (Illus.). 32p. (J). (gr. k-2). 1999. pap. text 6.95 (*0-531-15352-5*) Watts.

On the Farm. Richard Powell. (Illus.). 20p. (J). 1994. pap. 4.99 (*1-881445-27-5*) Sandvik Pub.

***On the Farm.** Random House Staff. (J). 2000. pap. 2.99 (*0-375-80501-X*, Pub. by Random Bks Yng Read) Random.

On the Farm. Sterling Publishing Company, Inc. Staff. LC 97-208044. (Balloon Bks.). (Illus.). 20p. (J). (ps). 1997. 3.95 (*0-8069-0501-8*) Sterling.

***On the Farm.** J. Tatchell. (Lift-the-Flap Learners Ser.). (Illus.). 16p. (J). (ps-3). 2000. pap. 8.95 (*0-7460-2775-3*, Pub. by Usbrne Pbng UK) EDC.

On the Farm. Photos by Bill Thomas et al. LC 97-23461. (Baby's Big Board Bks.). (Illus.). 12p. (J). (ps). 1997. bds. 6.95 (*1-887734-23-6*) Star Brght Bks.

On the Farm. Illus. by Thompson Bros. Staff. LC 99-172554. (Little People Ser.). 1998. write for info. (*0-7853-2745-2*) Pubns Intl Ltd.

On the Farm. Weinstein. 48p. 1997. pap. 7.81 (*0-07-292791-7*) McGraw.

On the Farm. Ed. & Illus. by Better Homes & Gardens. (Max the Dragon Project Book Ser.). 32p. (J). (gr. k-3). 1991. reprint ed. lib. bdg. 12.95 (*1-878363-33-6*) Forest Hse.

***On the Farm.** rev. ed. Diana James. (First Look at Animals Ser.). (Illus.). (J). 2000. pap. 3.95 (*1-58728-862-1*) Two Can Pub.

On the Farm: A Sticker Book. Anna Nilsen. (Illus.). 16p. (J). 1998. pap. 3.99 (*0-7636-0499-2*) Candlewick Pr.

***On the Farm: Flip-Flap Facts.** Sally Hobson. LC 99-43675. (Illus.). 32p. (J). 2000. pap. write for info. (*0-7636-0915-3*) Candlewick Pr.

On the Feasibility of a Labor Market Information System, 3 vols., Set. Malcolm S. Cohen. 1974. pap. 10.95 (*0-87736-331-5*) U of Mich Inst Labor.

On the Feminine. Ed. by Mireille Calle. Tr. by Catherine McGann. LC 95-49878. 200p. 1996. 49.95 (*0-391-03968-7*); pap. 15.00 (*0-391-03969-5*) Humanities.

On the Field. Nikki Bundey. LC 98-24379. (First Sports Science Ser.). (Illus.). 32p. (J). (gr. 2-4). 1999. 21.27 (*1-57505-357-8*, Carolrhoda) Lerner Pub.

On the Field & by the Campfire. Bonnie Holmes. (Illus.). 150p. (Orig.). 1996. pap. 19.00 (*1-883228-09-3*) Invictus MI.

On the Field of Glory. Henryk Sienkiewicz. Tr. by Miroslav Lipinski from POL. LC 99-55811. 278p. 1999. 24.95 (*0-7818-0762-X*) Hippocrene Bks.

***On the Field With . . . Mia Hamm.** Matt Christopher. LC 98-14937. 128p. (J). (gr. 3-7). 1998. pap. 4.95 (*0-316-14217-4*) Little.

On the Field With . . . Mia Hamm. Matt Christopher. (Matt Christopher Sports Biographies Ser.). 1998. 9.60 (*0-606-13678-9*, Pub. by Turtleback) Demco.

On the Field with - Emmitt Smith. Matt Christopher. LC 97-12530. 144p. (J). (gr. 3-7). 1997. pap. 4.50 (*0-316-13722-7*) Little.

On the Field with - Emmitt Smith. Matt Christopher. (Matt Christopher Sports Biographies Ser.). (J). 1997. 9.60 (*0-606-12786-0*, Pub. by Turtleback) Demco.

***On the Field with Briana Scurry.** Matt Christopher. (On the Field with... Ser.). (Illus.). 144p. (J). (gr. 3-7). 2000. pap. 4.95 (*0-316-13507-0*) Little.

***On the Field with Derek Jeter.** Matt Christopher. (On the Field with... Ser.). 144p. (J). (gr. 3-7). 2000. pap. 4.95 (*0-316-13508-9*) Little.

***On the Field with Julie Foudy.** Matt Christopher. LC 99-47174. (Illus.). 128p. (J). (gr. 3-7). 2000. pap. 4.95 (*0-316-13577-1*) Little.

***On the Field with Mia Hamm.** Matt Christopher. (J). 1999. pap. 4.95 (*0-316-13484-8*, Pub. by Little) Time Warner.

***On the Field with Terrell Davis.** Matt Christopher. LC 99-41273. (Illus.). 128p. (J). (gr. 3-7). 2000. pap. 4.95 (*0-316-13552-6*) Little.

On the Fields of Glory: The Battlefields of the 1815 Campaign. Andrew Uffindell & Michael Corum. (Illus.). 360p. 1996. 44.95 (*1-85367-232-7*, Pub. by Greenhill Bks) Stackpole.

***On the Finland Watch: An American Diplomat in Finland During the Cold War.** rev. ed. James Ford Cooper. LC 99-51717. Orig. Title: Asemamaana Suomi. (Illus.). 416p. 1999. 39.50 (*0-941690-94-6*) Regina Bks.

***On the Finland Watch: An American Diplomat in Finland During the Cold War.** rev. ed. James Ford Cooper. LC 99-51717. Orig. Title: Asemamaana Suomi. (Illus.). 416p. 1999. pap. 19.50 (*0-941690-95-4*) Regina Bks.

On the Firing Line: My 500 Days at Apple. Gil F. Amelio & William L. Simon. 298p. 1999. pap. 15.00 (*0-88730-919-4*, HarpBusn) HarpInfo.

***On the First Day of Christmas.** Cindy Holbrook. (Regency Romance Ser.). 1999. mass mkt. 4.99 (*0-8217-6304-0*, Zebra Kensgtn) Kensgtn Pub Corp.

On the First Day of School. Michael Walker, Jr. (Amazing English Ser.: Little Bks., Level A). (J). 1995. pap. text 17.64 (*0-201-85337-X*) Addison-Wesley.

***On the Formal Cause of Substance: Metaphysical Disputation XV.** Francisco Suarez & John Kronen. LC 99-50569. (Medieval Philosophical Texts in Translation Ser.). 2000. write for info. (*0-87462-239-5*) Marquette.

On the Formal Description of Pl-1 see Annual Review in Automatic Programming

On the Formal Syntax of the Westgermania: Papers from the "Third Groningen Grammar Talks", Groningen, January 1981. Werner Abraham. (Linguistik Aktuell/Linguistics Today Ser.: No. 3). vi, 242p. 1983. 59.00 (*90-272-2723-3*) J Benjamins Pubng Co.

On the Formation of Vegetable Mould, Through the Action of Worms with Observation of Their Habits. Charles Darwin. (Illus.). xxx, 326p. 1985. pap. 12.95 (*0-226-13663-9*) U Ch Pr.

On the Formulation of Gradient Adaptive Transfinite Elements (GATE) Family. Nesrin Sarigul-Klijn. 1996. 20.00 (*0-9643757-1-0*) N Sarigul-Klijn.

On the Foundations of Crystal Optics. Paul P. Ewald. Tr. by L. M. Hollingsworth & H. J. Juretschke from GER. (Monographs of the American Crystallographic Association: Vol. 10). 300p. (Orig.). (C). 1991. pap. text 25.00 (*0-937140-33-3*) Am Crystallographic.

On the Fringe: Gays & Lesbians Politics. David Rayside. LC 97-35245. (Illus.). 384p. 1998. pap. 19.95 (*0-8014-8374-3*, Comstock Pub); text 49.95 (*0-8014-3321-5*) Cornell U Pr.

On the Front Line: Guerrilla Poems of El Salvador. Ed. by Claribel Alegria & Darwin J. Flakoll. LC 89-62126. 90p. (Orig.). 1989. pap. 7.95 (*0-915306-86-7*) Curbstone.

***On the Front Line: Organization of Work in the Information Economy, 35.** Stephen Frenkel et al. LC 98-36539. (Cornell International Industrial & Lab Ser.: Vol. 35). (Illus.). 318p. 1999. pap. 19.95 (*0-8014-8567-3*) Cornell U Pr.

On the Front Line in the Cold War: An Ambassador Reports. George C. McGhee. LC 96-21321. 240p. 1997. 57.95 (*0-275-95649-0*, Praeger Pubs) Greenwood.

On the Front Line of the Culture War: Recent Attacks on the Boy Scouts of America. William A. Donohue. LC 99-229406. 32p. (Orig.). (C). 1993. pap. 5.00 (*0-930783-20-4*) Claremont Inst.

On the Front Lines: Following America's Foreign Correspondents Across the Twentieth Century. Michael Emery. 364p. (C). 1995. 24.95 (*1-879383-36-5*) Am Univ Pr.

On the Front Lines: The Experience of War Through the Eyes of the Allied Soldiers in WW II. John A. Ellis. 384p. 1991. pap. 15.95 (*0-471-55148-1*) Wiley.

An Asterisk (*) at the beginning of an entry indicates that the title is appearing for the first time.

***On the Front Lines of the Cold War: Documents on the Intelligence War in Berlin, 1946-1961.** Donald P. Steury. 646p. 1999. 55.00 (*0-16-059036-1*) USGPO.

On the Frontier. Bret Harte. LC 72-3290. (Short Story Index Reprint Ser.). 1977. reprint ed. 18.95 (*0-8369-4147-0*) Ayer.

On the Frontier: A Melodrama in Three Acts. W. H. Auden & Christopher Isherwood. LC 75-41011. (BCL Ser.: No. 2). reprint ed. 27.50 (*0-404-14638-4*) AMS Pr.

On the Frontier: A Trincheras-Hohokam Farmstead, Arivaca, Arizona. Stephanie M. Whittlesey & Richard S. Ciolek-Torrello. (Statistical Research Technical Ser.: No. 30). (Illus.). 159p. 1993. pap. text, per. 15.00 (*1-879442-28-0*) Stats Res.

On the Frontier: My Life in Science. Frederick Seitz. LC 94-17625. (Illus.). 400p. 1994. 39.95 (*1-56396-197-0*) Spr-Verlag.

On the Frontier of Virgina & North Carolina: A Gazetteer of the First "Old West" Carrie Eldridge. (Illus.). 17p. 1999. ring bd. 15.00 (*1-928979-28-9*) C Eldridge.

On the Frontier with Mr. Audubon. Barbara Brenner. LC 97-70578. (Illus.). 96p. (J). (gr. 4 up). 1997. pap. 7.95 (*1-56397-679-X*) Boyds Mills Pr.

On the Frontiers of Science: How Scientists See Our Future. Nigel Calder & John Newell. (Illus.). 256p. (J). 1989. 35.00 (*0-8160-2205-4*) Facts on File.

On the Function of the Cerebrum. Shepherd I. Franz. (Psychology Monographs General & Applied: Vol. 19). 1974. reprint ed. 55.00 (*0-8115-1418-8*) Periodicals Srv.

On the Future of Our Educational Institutions & Homer & Classical Philology. Friedrich Wilhelm Nietzsche. 1974. lib. bdg. 300.00 (*0-87968-200-0*) Gordon Pr.

On the Genealogy of Morality. Friedrich Wilhelm Nietzsche. Tr. by Maudemarie Clark & Alan Swenson. LC 98-37868. (HPC Classics Ser.). (GER.). 192p. (C). 1998. pap. text 9.95 (*0-87220-283-6*) Hackett Pub.

On the Genealogy of Morality. Friedrich Wilhelm Nietzsche. Tr. by Maudmarie Clark & Alan Swenson. LC 98-37868. (HPC Classics Ser.). (GER.). 192p. (C). 1998. lib. bdg. 34.95 (*0-87220-284-4*) Hackett Pub.

On the Genealogy of Morality & Other Writings. Friedrich Wilhelm Nietzsche. Ed. by Keith Ansell-Pearson & Carol Diethe. LC 93-41334. (Cambridge Texts in the History of Political Thought Ser.). 243p. (C). 1994. text 44.95 (*0-521-40459-2*); pap. text 12.95 (*0-521-40610-2*) Cambridge U Pr.

On the Genealogy of Morals. Friedrich Wilhelm Nietzsche. Tr. by Walter Kaufman. 1967. 5.95 (*0-394-70401-0*) Vin Bks.

On the Genealogy of Morals. Friedrich Wilhelm Nietzsche. Tr. by Walter Kaufmann. 1989. pap. 12.00 (*0-679-72462-1*) Vin Bks.

On the Genealogy of Morals: A Polemic, by Way of Clarification & Supplement to My Last Book Beyond Good & Evil. Friedrich Wilhelm Nietzsche. Tr. & Intro. by Douglas Smith. (Oxford World's Classics Ser.). 208p. 1999. pap. 10.95 (*0-19-283617-X*) OUP.

On the General Rogers-Ramanujan Theorem. George E. Andrews. LC 74-18067. (Memoirs Ser.: No. 1/152). 86p. 1974. pap. 17.00 (*0-8218-1852-X, MEMO/1/152*) Am Math.

On the General Rogers-Ramanujan Theorem. George E. Andrews. LC 52-42839. (American Mathematical Society Ser.: No. 152). (Illus.). 88p. reprint ed. pap. 30.00 (*0-608-09179-0*, 205268300002) Bks Demand.

On the Genre & Message of Revelation: Star Visions & Sky Journeys. Bruce J. Malina. 350p. 1995. 24.95 (*1-56563-040-8*) Hendrickson MA.

***On the Geometry of Diffusion Operators & Stochastic Flows.** K. D. Elworthy et al. LC 99-56079. (Lecture Notes in Mathematics Ser.: Vol. 1720). iv, 118p. 1999. pap. 29.80 (*3-540-66708-3*) Spr-Verlag.

On the Geometry of External Involute Spur Gears. T. W. Khiralla. LC 76-49243. (Illus.). 1976. 25.00 (*0-9601752-1-0*) T W Khiralla.

On the Glassy Sea: An Astronomer's Journey. Tom Gehrels. (Illus.). 250p. 1988. 35.00 (*0-88318-565-2*) Spr-Verlag.

On the Glassy Sea: An Astronomer's Journey. Tom Gehrels. (Illus.). 300p. 1989. 44.95 (*0-88318-598-9*) Spr-Verlag.

On the Glaubenslehre: Two Letters to Dr. Lhucke. Friedrich Daniel Ernst Schleiermacher & Friedrich Lhucke. LC 80-20717. (Texts & Translations Ser.). lx, 136p. 1981. write for info. (*0-89130-419-3*) OUP.

On the Glaubenslehre: Two Letters to Dr. Lucke. Friedrich Daniel Ernst Schleiermacher. Tr. by James Duke & Francis S. Fiorenza from GER. LC 80-20717. (American Academy of Religion, Texts & Translation Ser.: No. 3). Orig. Title: Sendschreiben Uber Seine Glaubenslehre an Lucke. 136p. 1991. pap. 19.95 (*0-89130-420-7*, 01-02-03) OUP.

On the Go. Joe Mathiu & George Siede. LC 97-196617. (Illus.). 1997. write for info. (*0-7853-2225-6*) Pubns Intl Ltd.

On the Go. Ann Morris. LC 90-33842. 1994. 10.15 (*0-606-06635-7*, Pub. by Turtleback) Demco.

On the Go! Mouse Works Staff. (Illus.). 10p. (J). 1997. 7.98 (*1-57082-637-4*, Pub. by Mouse Works) Time Warner.

On the Go. Ann Norris. LC 90-33842. (Illus.). 32p. (J). 1990. 16.00 (*0-688-06336-5*) Lothrop.

On the Go! John Pace & John Erickson. (Illus.). 116p. (Orig.). 1995. pap. 15.00 (*0-9649297-0-8*) J Erickson.

On the Go. Roger Pare. (Illus.). 24p. (J). 1996. pap. 4.95 (*1-55037-476-1*, Pub. by Annick); text 15.95 (*1-55037-409-5*, Pub. by Annick); lib. bdg. 15.95 (*1-55037-477-X*, Pub. by Annick) Firefly Bks Ltd.

On The Go. Roger Pare. (FRE & ENG., Illus.). 24p. (J). 1996. pap. 4.95 (*1-55037-408-7*, Pub. by Annick) Firefly Bks Ltd.

***On the Go.** Random House Staff. (J). 2000. pap. 2.99 (*0-375-80502-8*, Pub. by Random Bks Yng Read) Random.

***On the Go.** Lisa Trumbauer. LC 00-36480. (Illus.). (J). 2000. write for info. (*0-7368-0735-7*) Capstone Pr.

On the Go! deluxe ed. Margaret Snyder. (Talking Pages Ser.). 1999. 7.95 (*1-58224-002-7*) Futech Interactive.

On the Go. Ann Morris. Ed. by Amy Cohn. LC 90-33842. (Illus.). 32p. (J). (gr. k up). 1994. reprint ed. mass mkt. 5.95 (*0-688-13637-0*, Wm Morrow) Morrow Avon.

On the Go, Vol. 3511. Rozanne L. Williams. (Emergent Reader Science Ser.). 8p. 1994. pap. 1.75 (*0-916119-34-3*, 3511) Creat Teach Pr.

On the Go, Vol. 3569. Rozanne L. Williams. (Emergent Reader Big Bks.). 8p. (J). (gr. k-2). 1995. pap. 8.98 (*0-916119-77-7*) Creat Teach Pr.

On the Go in New Jersey. John T. Cunningham. 1996. pap., teacher ed. write for info. (*0-89359-116-5*) Afton Pub.

On the Go in New Jersey. John T. Cunningham. 1998. pap. 5.50 (*0-89359-115-7*) Afton Pub.

On the Go in New York. 1990. pap., teacher ed. write for info. (*0-89359-071-1*) Afton Pub.

On the Go in New York. (J). (gr. 4). 1990. pap. text, student ed. write for info. (*0-89359-070-3*) Afton Pub.

On the Go in Pennsylvania. 1991. pap., teacher ed. write for info. (*0-89359-028-2*) Afton Pub.

On the Go in Pennsylvania. (J). (gr. 4). 1991. pap. text, student ed. write for info. (*0-89359-027-4*) Afton Pub.

On the Go Songs Illus. by DiCicco Digital Arts Staff. LC 98-162776. (Disney Babies Ser.). 6p. (J). 1998. write for info. (*0-7853-2339-2*) Pubns Intl Ltd.

***On the Go Travel Pack.** 2000. pap. 7.95 (*1-55254-123-1*) Brighter Vision.

On the Gods: And Other Essays. Robert G. Ingersoll. LC 90-40283. 177p. 1990. 24.95 (*0-87975-629-2*) Prometheus Bks.

On the Golden Porch. Tatyana Tolstaya. LC 89-40514. (Vintage International Ser.). 208p. 1990. pap. 13.00 (*0-679-72843-0*) Vin Bks.

On the Good Life. Marcus Tullius Cicero. Tr. by Michael Grant. LC 77-30399. (Classics Ser.). 384p. 1971. pap. 16.99 (*0-14-044244-8*, Penguin Classics) Viking Penguin.

On the Government of Rulers: De Regimine Principum. Bartholomew of Lucca. Tr. by James M. Blythe from LAT. LC 97-2015. (Middle Ages Ser.). 320p. 1997. text 55.00 (*0-8122-3370-0*) U of Pa Pr.

On the Grammar & Semantics of Sentence Accents. C. Gussenhoven. (Publications in Language Sciences). viii, 352p. 1984. pap. 80.80 (*90-6765-022-6*) Mouton.

On the Grapevine. Linda Burgess. LC 96-223431. 200p. 1996. pap. 24.95 (*1-877133-12-4*) Intl Spec Bk.

On the Great Atlantic Railway. Kenneth Koch. LC 94-28070. 352p. 1994. 25.00 (*0-679-43418-6*) Knopf.

On the Great Atlantic Rainway. Kenneth Koch. 1996. pap. 17.00 (*0-679-76582-4*) Knopf.

On the Greater View: Collected Thoughts & Ideas on Macrobiotics & Humanity. Michio Kushi. LC 85-22828. 144p. pap. 7.95 (*0-89529-269-6*, Avery) Penguin Putnam.

On the Greek of the Code of Justinian: A Supplement of Liddell-Scott-James Together with Observations on the Influence of Latin on Legal Greek. Ivars Avotins. (Altertumswissenschaftliche Texte und Studien: Vol. 17). (GER.). x, 178p. 1989. pap. 30.00 (*3-487-09196-8*) G Olms Pubs.

***On the Grill.** A. D. Livingston. LC 99-20143. Orig. Title: Grilling, Smoking & Barbecuing. (Illus.). 208p. 1999. pap. 14.95 (*1-55821-806-8*) Lyons Pr.

On the Grill: The Backyard Bungler's Barbecue Cookbook. Steven Tyler. (Illus.). 240p. 1993. spiral bd. 19.95 (*0-9636903-0-2*) Culinary Concoctions.

On the Grotesque: Strategies of Contradiction in Art & Literature. Geoffrey G. Harpham. LC 82-47597. (Illus.). 291p. 1982. reprint ed. pap. 90.30 (*0-7837-8590-9*, 204940500011) Bks Demand.

On the Groups JO(G) Chung-Nim Lee & Arthur G. Wasserman. (Memoirs Ser.: No. 2/159). 62p. 1975. pap. 17.00 (*0-8218-1859-7*, MEMO/2/159) Am Math.

On the Growing Edge. Philip Rusten. (Illus.). 96p. 1981. 23.00 (*0-686-29722-9*) Way of Seeing.

On the Guard II. 3rd rev. ed. YMCA of the U. S. A. Staff. LC 97-14580. (Illus.). 272p. 1997. pap. 19.00 (*0-88011-815-6*, LYMC5334, YMCA USA) Human Kinetics.

On the Gulf. Elizabeth Spencer. LC 90-29012. (Author & Artist Ser.). (Illus.). 1991. 25.00 (*0-87805-507-X*) U Pr of Miss.

On the Gulf. deluxe limited ed. Elizabeth Spencer. LC 90-29012. (Author & Artist Ser.). (Illus.). 1991. boxed set 90.00 (*0-87805-508-8*) U Pr of Miss.

On the Head of the Macropetalichthyids, with Certain Remarks on the Head of the Other Arthrodires. Erik A. Stensio. LC 26-7108. (Field Museum of Natural History, Publication 184, Anthropological Ser.: Vol. 4, No. 4). 165p. 1925. reprint ed. pap. 51.20 (*0-608-02116-4*, 206276500004) Bks Demand.

On the Heavens. Aristotle. Tr. by W. K. Guthrie. (Loeb Classical Library: No. 338). 420p. 1939. 18.95 (*0-674-99372-1*) HUP.

On the Heights of Despair. E. M. Cioran. Tr. by Ilinca Zarifopol-Johnston. LC 91-35173. 150p. 1992. 18.95 (*0-226-10670-5*) U Ch Pr.

On the Heights of Despair. E. M. Cioran. Tr. by Ilinca Zaripofol-Johnston. xxii, 128p. 1996. pap. 10.95 (*0-226-10671-3*) U Ch Pr.

On the Heights (1908) Christian D. Larson. 75p. 1998. reprint ed. pap. 16.95 (*0-7661-0312-9*) Kessinger Pub.

On the High Seas: Ships Then & Now see Here We Go! - Group 2

On the Highest Good. Friedrich Daniel Ernst Schleiermacher. Tr. by H. Victor Froese from GER. LC 92-23476. (Schleiermacher Studies & Translations: Vol. 10). 168p. 1992. text 69.95 (*0-7734-9585-1*) E Mellen.

On the Highest Hill. Roderick L. Haig-Brown. (Northwest Reprints Ser.). 336p. 1994. reprint ed. 27.95 (*0-87071-518-6*); reprint ed. pap. 15.95 (*0-87071-519-4*) Oreg St U Pr.

On the Highroad of Surrender. Frances J. Roberts. 1973. pap. 8.50 (*0-932814-15-8*) Kings Farspan.

On the Highroad of Surrender. Frances J. Roberts. 1973. 11.99 (*0-932814-14-X*) Kings Farspan.

On the Hill. Bessie M. Mason. 42p. 1984. 5.00 (*0-916768-07-4*) Sycamore Pr.

On the Hill: A Photographic History of the University of Kansas. 2nd rev. ed. Compiled by Virginia Adams et al. LC 93-1258. 1993. 25.00 (*0-7006-0611-4*) U Pr of KS.

On the Hill, Reflections of a Miner. Brian R. Woolfe. (Illus.). 1994. 19.95 (*0-87026-084-7*) Westernlore.

On the Hills of God. Ibrahim Fawal. LC 98-23925. 1998. 27.95 (*1-57966-002-9*, Black Belt) Black Belt Communs.

On the Historical Novel. Alessandro Manzoni. Tr. by Sandra Bermann. LC 83-10583. x, 134p. 1984. pap. text 12.00 (*0-8032-8226-5*, Bison Books) U of Nebr Pr.

On the History & Development of Guilds & the Origin of Trade Unions. Lujo Brentano. 1972. 59.95 (*0-8490-0766-6*) Gordon Pr.

On the History & Method of Economics: Selected Essays. Frank Hyneman Knight. LC 56-6632. 1963. pap. text 2.45 (*0-226-44689-1*, P122) U Ch Pr.

On the History of Economic Thought: British & American Economic Essays, Vol. 1. A. W. Coats. LC 91-47898. (British & American Economic Essays Ser.). 512p. (C). (gr. 13). 1992. 90.00 (*0-415-06715-4*, A7548) Routledge.

On the History of Film Style. David Bordwell. LC 97-4016. (Illus.). 352p. 1998. 60.00 (*0-674-63428-4*); pap. 24.95 (*0-674-63429-2*) HUP.

On the History of Grammar among the Arabs. Ignaz Goldziher. Ed. & Tr. by Kinga Devenyi & Tamas Ivanyi. LC 94-1394. (Amsterdam Studies in the Theory & History of Linguistic Science, Series Four, Current Issues in Linguistic Theory: Vol. 73). xx, 153p. 1994. lib. bdg. 45.00 (*1-55619-609-1*) J Benjamins Pubng Co.

On the History of Modern Philosophy. Friedrich Wilhelm Joseph Schelling. Ed. & Tr. by Andrew Bowie. (Texts in German Philosophy Ser.). 207p. (C). 1994. text 59.95 (*0-521-40299-9*); pap. text 21.95 (*0-521-40861-X*) Cambridge U Pr.

On the History of the Process by Which the Aristotelian Writings Arrived at Their Present Form. Richard Shute. LC 75-13294. (History of Ideas in Ancient Greece Ser.). 1976. reprint ed. 18.95 (*0-405-07338-0*) Ayer.

On the History of Vpered see Vpered, 1873-1877

On the History of Word-Final Vowels in the Permian Languages. Ferenc A. Molnar. (Studia Uralo-altaica Ser.: No. 5). 87p. 1974. pap. 26.00 (*0-686-31504-9*) J Benjamins Pubng Co.

On the Holy Icons. Tr. by Catharine P. Roth. LC 81-18319. 115p. (Orig.). 1981. pap. 8.95 (*0-913836-76-1*) St Vladimirs.

On the Holy Spirit. Photos by David Anderson. LC 80-25502. 118p. (Orig.). (C). 1980. pap. 8.95 (*0-913836-74-5*) St Vladimirs.

On the Holy Spirit in the Life of the Church & the World: Dominum et Vivificantem. John Paul, II, pseud. 144p. pap. 3.95 (*0-8198-3349-5*) Pauline Bks.

On the Home Front: Growing up in Wartime England. Ann Stalcup. LC 97-32673. (Illus.). xiv, 91p. (J). (gr. 5 up). 1998. lib. bdg. 19.50 (*0-208-02482-4*, Linnet Bks) Shoe String.

On the Home Front: The Cold War Legacy of the Hanford Nuclear Site. Michele S. Gerber. LC 92-8746. (Illus.). x, 324p. 1992. text 50.00 (*0-8032-2145-2*) U of Nebr Pr.

On the Home Front: The Cold War Legacy of the Hanford Nuclear Site. Michele S. Gerber. LC 92-18511. (Illus.). x, 364p. 1992. pap. 20.00 (*0-8032-7068-2*, Bison Books) U of Nebr Pr.

***On the Home Front: Western Australia During World War II.** Ed. by Jenny Gregory. LC 97-194467. 274p. 2000. pap. 45.00 (*1-875560-90-4*, Pub. by Univ of West Aust Pr) Intl Spec Bk.

***On the Homefront: A Family Survival Guide.** Katrina L. Cassel. LC 99-47327. (Illus.). 128p. (gr. 7-12). 2000. 6.99 (*0-570-07000-7*) Concordia.

On the Homefront: A Woman's Reflections on Hearth & Heart. Tamera S. Allred. (Illus.). 206p. 1992. pap. text 12.95 (*0-9635429-0-7*) Homefront Prods.

On the Homefront: Western Australia & World War II. Jenny Gregory. LC 97-194467. 364p. 1996. write for info. (*1-875560-95-5*) Intl Spec Bk.

On the Horn of Africa: Let's Travel to Somalia Together see Windows on the World Series

***On the Horns of a Dilemma: The Story of the Ukrainian Division Halychyna.** Taras Hunczak. 256p. 2000. 44.50 (*0-7618-1661-5*) U Pr of Amer.

On the Horns of the Beast: The Federal Reserve & the New World Order. Bill Still. (Illus.). (Orig.). 1996. pap. 19.95 (*0-9640485-3-1*) Reinhardt & Still.

On the Horse's Foot, Shoes & Shoeing: The Bibliographic Record; & a Brief Timeline History of Horseshoeing. Henry Heymering. LC 90-63744. xii, 366p. (C). 1990. lib. bdg. 65.00 (*0-9627965-0-6*) St Eloy.

On the House, with Love. Sheila Horder. LC 94-27089. (Illus.). 216p. (Orig.). 1996. pap. 12.95 (*0-89407-110-6*) Strawberry Hill.

On the Hundredth Anniversary of Rerum Novarum: Centissimus Annus. John Paul, II, pseud. 96p. pap. 4.95 (*0-8198-5418-2*) Pauline Bks.

On the Hunt. Ace Reid. (Illus.). 64p. (Orig.). 1992. pap. 6.00 (*1-879894-02-5*) Saratoga Pub.

On the Ice, Vol. 1. Mouse Works Staff. (J). 1996. 8.98 (*1-57082-405-3*) Little.

On the Ice: Kids' Views & Interviews with Famous (& Not So Famous) Skaters. Alexis Burakoff. Ed. by Pamela Econoply & Suzanne Burakoff. LC 95-125140. (Kids' Views & Interviews Ser.: Vol. 1). (Illus.). 100p. (Orig.). (J). (gr. 2-9). 1994. pap. 11.95 (*0-9640792-0-8*) Hare & Hatter.

On the Ice with . . . Wayne Gretzky. Matt Christopher. LC 96-3042. (Illus.). 128p. (J). (gr. 3-7). 1997. pap. 4.50 (*0-316-13789-8*) Little.

On the Ice with . . . Wayne Gretzky. Matt Christopher. LC 96-3042. 1997. 9.60 (*0-606-10275-2*, Pub. by Turtleback) Demco.

On the Idea of a University. James M. Cameron. LC 78-318149. 106p. reprint ed. pap. 32.90 (*0-8357-4135-4*, 203690700006) Bks Demand.

On the Ideal Structure of Operator Algebras. Reese T. Prosser. LC 52-42839. (Memoirs of the American Mathematical Society Ser.: No. 45). 28p. 1974. reprint ed. pap. 17.00 (*0-8218-1245-9*, MEMO/1/45C) Am Math.

On the Impact of Morality in Our Times. Bernard M. Bane. 113p. 1985. pap. 5.00 (*0-930924-22-3*) BMB Pub Co.

On the Improvement of the Understanding. Baruch Spinoza. 420p. 1955. pap. text 8.95 (*0-486-20250-X*) Dover.

On the Incarnation. St. Anthanasius. 120p. 1977. pap. 8.95 (*0-913836-40-0*) St Vladimirs.

On the Incarnation of the Word. Athanasius. 1990. pap. 2.95 (*0-89981-065-9*) Eastern Orthodox.

On the Inclination of Developers to Help the Poor: Designing Affirmative Measures to Induce the Construction of Lower Income Housing after Mt. Laurel II. Robert A. Williams. LC HD0111.L36. (Land Policy Roundtable Policy Analysis Ser.: No. 211). 44p. reprint ed. pap. 30.00 (*0-7837-5752-2*, 204541400006) Bks Demand.

On the Inevitability of War: An Explanation & Theory & Proposed Game. (Analysis Ser.: No. 13). 1983. pap. 12.50 (*0-686-42846-3*) Inst Analysis.

On the Influence Attributed to Philosophers, Free-Masons, & to the Illuminati, on the Revolution of France. Jean J. Mounier. LC 74-13148. 280p. 1974. reprint ed. 50.00 (*0-8201-1135-X*) Schol Facsimiles.

On the Influence of Germanic Languages on Finnish & Lapp. Vilhelm Thomsen. LC 67-63427. (Uralic & Altaic Ser.: Vol. 87). (GER.). 1967. reprint ed. pap. text. write for info. (*0-87750-035-5*) Curzon Pr Ltd.

On the Influence of Trades, Professions & Occupations in the United States in the Production of Disease. Benjamin W. McCready. LC 78-180583. (Medicine & Society in America Ser.). 144p. 1980. reprint ed. 19.95 (*0-405-03960-3*) Ayer.

On the Inherent Danger of Undervaluing Species. Bryan G. Norton. (Working Papers on the Preservation of Species). 1988. 2.50 (*0-318-33312-0*, PS3) IPPP.

On the Inner Life of the Mind. Augustine, Saint. Ed. by Robert E. Meagher. LC 98-34867. 340p. 1998. pap. 12.95 (*0-87220-444-8*); lib. bdg. 37.95 (*0-87220-445-6*) Hackett Pub.

On the Inside. Lesline Amedee-Jones. 32p. (Orig.). 1994. pap. 10.00 (*1-886094-00-4*) Chicago Spectrum.

On the Inside. Clive Matson. LC 82-14621. (Illus.). 70p. (Orig.). 1982. pap. 4.00 (*0-916156-65-6*) Cherry Valley.

On the Inside: A Reid Bennett Mystery. Ted Wood. 224p. 1991. reprint ed. pap. 3.95 (*0-373-26076-8*) Harlequin Bks.

On the Integration of Agebraic Function. J. H. Davenport. (Lecture Notes in Computer Science Ser.: Vol. 102). 197p. 1981. pap. 23.00 (*0-387-10290-6*) Spr-Verlag.

On the Intelligibility of Political Philosophy: Essays of Charles N. R. McCoy. Charles N. McCoy. Ed. by James V. Schall & John J. Schrems. LC 88-31601. 318p. 1989. reprint ed. pap. 98.60 (*0-7837-9109-7*, 204991100004) Bks Demand.

On the International Use of Currencies: The Case of the Deutsche Mark. George S. Tavlas. Ed. by Margaret B. Riccardi. LC 90-10869. (Essays in International Finance Ser.: No. 181). 46p. 1991. pap. text 10.00 (*0-685-49343-1*) Princeton U Int Finan Econ.

***On the Interpretation & Use of the Bible: With Reflection on Experience.** Ronald S. Wallace. x, 137p. 1999. pap. 12.00 (*0-8028-4719-6*) Eerdmans.

On the Interpretation of Nature. Francis Bacon. 50p. 1996. reprint ed. pap. 9.95 (*1-56459-645-1*) Kessinger Pub.

On the Interpretation of Plato's Timaeus. John C. Wilson. Ed. by Leonardo Taran. LC 78-66577. (Ancient Philosophy Ser.). 160p. 1982. lib. bdg. 20.00 (*0-8240-9571-5*) Garland.

On the Interpretation of Statutes. Peter B. Maxwell. xxxii, 458p. 1991. reprint ed. 48.50 (*0-8377-2440-6*, Rothman) W S Hein.

On the Interpretation of the Melodies of Claude Debussy: Bathori or Debussy. Linda Laurent. LC 98-19192. (Vox Musicae Ser.: No. 2). (Illus.). 101p. 1998. pap. text 27.00 (*1-57647-008-3*) Pendragon NY.

On the Invocation of the Name of Jesus. Lev Gillet. 96p. 1985. pap. 6.95 (*0-87243-133-9*) Templegate.

On the Irish Freedom Struggle. Bernadette D. McAliskey. 16p. 1983. reprint ed. pap. 2.00 (*0-87348-478-9*) Pathfinder NY.

On the Irregular Motion of the Moon. Richard Petersen. 32p. 1999. 3.95 (*0-9662134-2-4*) Engwald & Co.

On the Issue of the Continental. 1986. 32.00 (*0-387-81932-0*) Spr-Verlag.

On the Jewish Question. Leon Trotsky. 31p. 1970. pap. 4.50 (*0-87348-157-7*) Pathfinder NY.

O

On the Job. David Fennario. 112p. 1976. reprint ed. pap. 11.95 (*0-88922-102-2*, Pub. by Talonbks) Genl Dist Srvs.

On the Job, Bk. 1. Larry Mikulecky & Rad A. Drew. (On the Job Ser.). 144p. (Orig.). 1988. pap. text 6.00 (*0-8428-0160-X*) Cambridge Bk.

On the Job, Bk. 3. Larry Mikulecky & Rad A. Drew. (On the Job Ser.). 144p. (Orig.). 1988. pap. text 6.00 (*0-8428-0162-6*) Cambridge Bk.

On the Job, Vol. 1. McCauley. (C). 1984. pap. text. write for info. (*0-7730-4322-5*) Addison-Wes.

On the Job: A Work Skills Development Program from Finney Company. Finney Company Staff. LC 75-20074. 1993. 45.00 (*0-912486-66-X*) Finney Co.

On the Job: Activity Book II. Larry Mikulecky & Rad A. Drew. (On the Job Ser.). 80p. (Orig.). 1988. pap. text 4.00 (*0-8428-0164-2*) Cambridge Bk.

On the Job: Confronting the Labour Process in Canada. Ed. by Craig Heron & Robert Storey. 376p. 1986. pap. 27.95 (*0-7735-0599-7*, Pub. by McG-Queens Univ Pr) CUP Services.

***On the Job: Design & the American Office.** Ed. by Donald Albrecht & Chrysanthe B. Broikos. (Illus.). 128p. 2000. pap. 24.95 (*1-56898-241-0*) Princeton Arch.

***On the Job: Is Long-Term Employment a Thing of the Past?** Ed. by David Neumark. 608p. 2000. 59.95 (*0-87154-618-3*) Russell Sage.

On the Job: Safeguarding Workers' Rights. Michael R. Bradley. LC 92-9015. (Human Rights Ser.). 112p. (J). 1992. lib. bdg. 18.95 (*0-86593-175-5*) Rourke Corp.

On-the-Job Communications for Business, the Professions, Govern. Ernst Jacobi & G. Jay Christensen. 400p. (C). 1990. pap. text 28.00 (*0-13-636101-3*) P-H.

***On the Job English Student Book.** Newman. 1999. pap. 11.50 (*1-56420-147-3*) New Readers.

On the Job in Illinois, Then & Now. Ed. by Leslie F. Orear. (Illus.). 1976. 8.00 (*0-916884-04-X*); pap. 7.50 (*0-916884-02-3*) Ill Labor Hist Soc.

On the Job Learning in the Software Industry: Corporate Culture & the Acquisition of Knowledge. Marc Sacks. LC 93-37026. 224p. 1994. 62.95 (*0-89930-865-1*, Quorum Bks) Greenwood.

On-the-Job Orientation & Training: A Practical Guide to Enhanced Performance. Larry R. Smalley. LC 93-74766. (Management Skills Ser.). (Illus.). 112p. 1994. pap. 14.95 (*0-7879-5112-9*) R Chang Assocs.

***On-the-Job Skills.** (Overcoming Obstacles). 34p. (YA). (gr. 9-12). 1999. pap. text 9.38 (*1-929393-25-3*) Community for Ed.

On-the-Job Sourcebook for School Librarians. Anthony Tilke. 192p. 1998. pap. 45.00 (*1-85604-270-7*, LAP2707, Pub. by Library Association) Bernan Associates.

On the Job Student Book, Connections: School & Work Transitions - Employer's Choice. National Center for Research in Vocational Educati. 1987. 7.25 (*0-317-04614-4*, SP100BB02) Ctr Educ Trng Employ.

On the Job Survival. Michael H. Cohen. 94p. (Orig.). (C). 1984. pap. 6.95 (*0-9613768-0-5*) Canoe Press.

On the Job Training. John M. Barron et al. LC 97-10295. 210p. (C). 1997. text 35.00 (*0-88099-178-X*) W E Upjohn.

On the Job Training. John M. Barron et al. LC 97-10295. 210p. (C). 1997. pap. text 17.00 (*0-88099-175-5*) W E Upjohn.

On the Job Training. Barbara L. McCombs & Linda Brannan. (Skills for Job Success Ser.). (Illus.). (Orig.). 1990. pap. 49.95 (*1-56119-057-8*) Educ Pr MD.

On-the-Job Training: The Key to Staff Success. Ida M. Halasz. (Illus.). 110p. 1999. pap. 17.95 (*1-56991-104-5*) Am Correctional.

On the Kabbalah & Its Symbolism. Gershom Scholem. Tr. by Ralph Manheim. 240p. 1996. pap. 12.00 (*0-8052-1051-2*) Schocken.

On the Lake Poets. Francis Jeffrey. LC 97-28637. (Revolution & Romanticism Ser.). 128p. 1998. 55.00 (*1-85477-206-6*) Continuum.

On the Landing. M. W. Simpson. 49p. 1986. pap. text 2.00 (*0-940392-19-4*) Indian U Pr OK.

On the Law of Nations. Daniel P. Moynihan. 224p. 1990. text 33.95 (*0-674-63575-2*) HUP.

On the Law of Nations. Daniel P. Moynihan. 224p. 1992. pap. text 10.95 (*0-674-63576-0*) HUP.

On the Law of War & on the Duties, Connected with War & on Military Discipline, Vol. 2. LC 95-77190. (Classics in International Law Reprint Ser.: No. 2). 1995. reprint ed. 100.00 (*1-57588-251-5*, 310050) W S Hein.

On the Law of War & Peace: Washington, D. C. - Carnegie Institution 1913, Vol. 2. LC 95-77193. (Classics in International Law Reprint Ser.: No.3, Vol.1). 618 (45)p. 1995. reprint ed. 135.00 (*0-89941-942-9*, 310070) W S Hein.

On the Laws of the Poetic Art. Anthony Hecht. LC 94-32716. (A. W. Mellon Lectures in the Fine Arts: Vol. XXXV, 41). (Illus.). 216p. 1995. text 31.95 (*0-691-04363-9*, Pub. by Princeton U Pr) Cal Prin Full Svc.

On the Left in America: Memoirs of the Scandinavian-American Labor Movement. Henry Bengston. Ed. by Michael Brook. Tr. by Kermit B. Westerberg. LC 96-20709. 237p. 1997. pap. 19.95 (*0-8093-2104-1*) S Ill U Pr.

On the Left in America: Memoirs of the Scandinavian-American Labor Movement. Henry Bengston. Ed. by Michael Brook. Tr. by Kermit B. Westerberg. LC 96-20709. 272p. 1999. 39.95 (*0-8093-2079-7*) S Ill U Pr.

On the Level: Foundations for Violence-Free Living Participant's Workbook. David J. Mathews. Ed. by Vincent Hyman. LC 95-36815. 160p. (Orig.). 1995. pap. text, student ed. 15.00 (*0-940069-06-7*) A H Wilder.

On-the-Level: Performance Communication That Works. 2nd rev. ed. Patricia A. McLagan & Peter Krembs. LC 95-18624. (Illus.). 140p. 1995. pap. 19.95 (*1-881052-76-1*) Berrett-Koehler.

On the Level Everyday: Selected Talks on Poetry & the Art of Living. Ed. by Joel Lewis. LC 97-6862. 128p. 1997. 32.95 (*1-883689-56-2*); pap. 12.95 (*1-883689-55-4*) Talisman Hse.

On the Life of Christ. St. Romanos. 1995. 39.95 (*0-7619-8987-0*) Sage.

On the Life of Christ: Chanted Sermons by the Great Sixth Century Poet & Singer. Saint Romanos. (Sacred Literature Ser.). 304p. 1995. pap. 27.95 (*0-7619-8988-9*) AltaMira Pr.

On the Life of the Soul. Rudolf Steiner. Ed. by Gisela O'Neil & Alan Howard. Tr. by Samuel L. Borton. 18p. (Orig.). 1985. pap. 3.95 (*0-88010-076-1*) Anthroposophic.

On the Limits of Poetry: Nineteen Twenty-Eight to Nineteen Forty-Eight. Allen Tate. LC 74-105042. (Essay Index Reprint Ser.). 1977. 25.95 (*0-8369-1484-8*) Ayer.

On the Limits of the Law: The Ironic Legacy of Title VI of the 1964 Civil Rights Act. Stephen C. Halpern. LC 94-28375. 384p. (Orig.). 1995. text 55.00 (*0-8018-4896-2*); pap. text 18.95 (*0-8018-4897-0*) Johns Hopkins.

On the Line. Fred Bowen. LC 99-22977. (Allstar SportStory Ser.). (Illus.). 112p. (J). (gr. 3-7). 1999. pap. 4.95 (*1-56145-199-1*) Peachtree Pubs.

On the Line. Gilles Deleuze & Felix Guattari. 114p. Date not set. 7.00 (*0-936756-01-2*) Autonomedia.

On the Line. Frank Hughes. 320p. 1989. write for info. (*0-942407-10-5*) Father & Son.

On the Line. Harvey Swados. 260p. 1989. reprint ed. text 29.95 (*0-252-01674-2*); reprint ed. pap. text 9.95 (*0-252-06055-5*) U of Ill Pr.

On the Line: Back to the Ranch. Anne M. Duquette. (Romance Ser.). 1993. per. 2.99 (*0-373-03289-7*, 1-03289-5) Harlequin Bks.

On the Line: Essays in the History of Auto Work. Ed. by Nelson Lichtenstein & Stephen Meyer. (Working Class in American History Ser.). (Illus.). 280p. 1989. pap. 12.95 (*0-252-06015-6*) U of Ill Pr.

On the Line: Life on the U. S. - Mexican Border. Augusta Dwyer. 200p. (Orig.). (C). 1994. pap. text 16.00 (*0-85345-897-9*, Pub. by Monthly Rev) NYU Pr.

On the Line: New Road to the White House. Larry King. 1993. 21.95 (*0-15-177877-9*) Harcourt.

On the Line: Readings in the Short Fiction of Clark Blaise, John Metcalf & Hugh Hood. Robert Lecker. 130p. (C). 1982. pap. 8.95 (*0-920802-31-1*, Pub. by ECW) Genl Dist Srvs.

On the Line: Women's Career Advancement. 64p. 1992. 60.00 (*0-89584-177-0*) Catalyst.

On the Line at Subaru-Isuzu: The Japanese Model & the American Worker. Laurie Graham. 176p. 1995. pap. 13.95 (*0-87546-346-0*, ILR Press) Cornell U Pr.

On the Local Structure of Morita & Rickard Equivalences Between Brauer Blocks. L. Puig. LC 99-15831. (Progress in Mathematics Ser.: Vol. 178). 268p. 1999. 98.00 (*3-7643-6156-5*) Birkhauser.

On the Location of the Tooth Critical Section for the Determination of the AGMA J-Factor. Jose I. Pedrero et al. (Technical Papers: Vol. 97FTM6). (Illus.). 7p. 1997. pap. text 30.00 (*1-55589-700-2*) AGMA.

On the Logic of Ordinary Conditionals. Robert N. McLaughlin. LC 89-21611. (SUNY Series in Logic & Language). 202p. 1990. pap. text 21.95 (*0-7914-0294-0*) State U NY Pr.

On the Logic of the Social Sciences. Jurgen Habermas. Tr. by Shierry W. Nicholsen from GER. 240p. 1990. reprint ed. pap. text 17.00 (*0-262-58104-3*) MIT Pr.

On the "Logic" of Togetherness: A Cultural Hermeneutic. Kuang-Ming Wu. LC 98-9775. (Philosophy of History & Culture Ser.). xii, 470p. 1998. 154.50 (*90-04-11000-3*) Brill Academic Pubs.

On the Long Trail Home. Elisabeth J. Stewart. LC 93-34666. (Illus.). 96p. (J). 1994. 15.00 (*0-395-68361-0*, Clarion Bks) HM.

On the Loose: Big-City Days & Nights of Three Single Women. Melissa Roth. LC 98-49942. 256p. 1999. 23.00 (*0-688-15801-3*, Wm Morrow) Morrow Avon.

On the Loose . . . the Cafeteria Lady. Martha Bolton. LC 94-16857. (J). 1994. pap. 6.99 (*1-56179-280-2*) Focus Family.

On the Loose with Dr. Seuss: Using the Works of Theodor Geisel to Develop Reading, Writing, & Thinking Skills. Shirley Cook. Ed. by Leslie Britt. (Illus.). 96p. (J). (gr. k-6). 1994. pap. text 10.95 (*0-86530-233-2*) Incentive Pubns.

On the Lord's Appearing: An Essay on Prayer & Tradition. Jonathan Robinson. LC 96-36924. 280p. 1997. pap. text 19.95 (*0-8132-0887-4*) Cath U Pr.

On the Lord's Appearing: An Essay on Prayer & Tradition. Jonathan Robinson. LC 96-36924. 280p. 1997. text 39.95 (*0-8132-0886-6*) Cath U Pr.

On the Lord's Prayer. Simone W. St. Teresa. 71p. (Orig.). 1990. pap. 5.95 (*0-937815-34-9*) Hanuman Bks.

On the Loschian Spatial Demand Curve. Colin A. Gannon. (Discussion Papers: No. 32). 1969. pap. 10.00 (*1-55869-083-2*) Regional Sci Res Inst.

On the Love of God. rev. ed. Thomas, a Kempis. Ed. by S. Abhayananda. (Classics of Mystical Literature Ser.). 160p. (Orig.). 1992. pap. 7.95 (*0-914557-00-9*) Atma Bks.

On the Love of God & Other Writings. St. Bernard of Clairvaux Staff. Ed. by Charles Dollen. LC 95-46997. (Orig.). 1996. pap. 8.95 (*0-8189-0731-2*) Alba.

On the Mahabharata. Sri Aurobindo. 187p. 1997. pap. 4.95 (*81-7058-256-3*, Pub. by SAA) Lotus Pr.

***On the Makaloa Mat.** Jack London. (Collected Works of Jack London). 229p. 1998. reprint ed. lib. bdg. 88.00 (*1-58201-731-X*) Classic Bks.

On the Make: The Rise of Bill Clinton. Meredith L. Oakley. LC 94-10787. (Illus.). 368p. 1994. 24.95 (*0-89526-493-5*) Regnery Pub.

On the Make: The Rise of Bill Clinton. Meredith L. Oakley. (Illus.). 591p. 1996. pap. 16.95 (*0-89526-719-5*) Regnery Pub.

On the Make Again: Otra Vez en la Movida. Jim Sagel. 93p. (Orig.). 1991. pap. 8.95 (*0-931122-54-6*) West End.

On the Mall: Presenting Maroon Tradition-Bearers at the 1992 Festival of American Folklife. Richard Price & Sally Price. (Special Publications: No. 4). (Illus.). 123p. (C). 1995. text 25.00 (*1-879407-07-8*) IN Univ Folk Inst.

On the Mall: Presenting Maroon Tradition-Bearers at the 1992 Festival of American Folklore. Richard Price & Sally Price. (Illus.). 122p. 1995. pap. 12.00 (*0-87940-706-9*); text 25.00 (*0-87940-707-7*) Ind U Pr.

On the Man Question: Gender & Civic Virtue in America. Mark E. Kann. 352p. 1991. 49.95 (*0-87722-807-8*) Temple U Pr.

On the Manipulation of Money & Credit. Ludwig Von Mises. Ed. by Percy L. Greaves, Jr. Tr. by Bettina B. Greaves from GER. LC 77-90572. 350p. 1978. 30.00 (*0-930902-01-7*) Free Market.

***On the Manner of Negotiating with Princes.** Francois De Callieres. LC 99-87273. 128p. 2000. 16.00 (*0-618-05512-6*) HM.

On the Map. Ed. by Steck-Vaughn Staff. 1998. 191.76 (*0-8114-3423-0*) Raintree Steck-V.

On the Map to Your Life. Bill O'Connell. 27p. 1992. pap. 5.00 (*0-933292-20-1*, Dytiscid Pr) Arts End.

On the Margin of Capitalism: People & Development in Mukim Plentong, Johor, Malaysia. Patrick Guinness. (South-East Asian Social Science Monographs). (Illus.). 238p. 1992. text 48.00 (*0-19-588556-2*) OUP.

On the Margin the Feminist Impact on Economics & Feminism. Ra Albelda. LC 97-12263. 1997. 33.00 (*0-8057-9759-9*, Twyne) Mac Lib Ref.

On the Margins: Men Who Have Sex with Men in the Developing World. Neil McKenna. 112p. 1997. pap. 19.95 (*1-870670-37-X*, Pub. by Panos Bks) Paul & Co Pubs.

On the Margins: The Art of Exile in V. S. Naipaul. Timothy F. Weiss. LC 92-5719. 288p. 1993. 30.00 (*0-87023-820-5*) U of Mass Pr.

On the Margins of Discourse: The Relation of Literature to Language. Barbara H. Smith. LC 78-18274. 1979. lib. bdg. 20.00 (*0-226-76452-4*) U Ch Pr.

On the Margins of Discourse: The Relation of Literature to Language. Barbara H. Smith. LC 78-18274. xviii, 226p. 1983. pap. text 7.50 (*0-226-76453-2*) U Ch Pr.

On the Margins of Japanese Society: Volunteer Work With the Urban Underclass. Carolyn S. Stevens. LC 96-43246. (Nissan Institute/Routledge Japanese Studies Ser.). 296p. (C). 1997. 90.00 (*0-415-14648-8*) Routledge.

On the Margins of Modernism: Decentering Literary Dynamics. Chana Kronfeld. (Contraversions: Critical Studies in Jewish Literature, Culture, & Society Ser.: Vol. 2). 275p. 1995. 48.00 (*0-520-08346-6*, Pub. by U CA Pr); pap. 18.95 (*0-520-08347-4*, Pub. by U CA Pr) Cal Prin Full Svc.

On the Margins of Old Books. Jules Lemaitre. Tr. by Clarence Stratton. LC 70-163041. (Short Story Index Reprint Ser.). 1977. reprint ed. 23.95 (*0-8369-3955-7*) Ayer.

On the Margins of Reality: The Paradoxes of Representation in Bruno Schulz's Fiction. Krzysztof Stala. (Stockholm Slavic Studies: No. 23). vii, 131p. (Orig.). 1993. pap. 43.00 (*91-22-01584-1*) Coronet Bks.

On the Margins of the Good Earth. Donald W. Meinig. 246p. (C). 1989. pap. text 40.00 (*0-89771-022-3*, Pub. by Bob Mossel) St Mut.

On the Mark: A Manual on Proofreading Marks. Maria E. den Boer. (Author's Assistant Ser.: Vol. 4). (Illus.). 24p. 1999. 3.95 (*1-928929-03-6*) Blue Thunder.

On the Market: Surviving the Academic Job Search. Ed. by Christina Boufis & Victoria C. Olsen. LC 97-8549. 368p. 1997. pap. 12.95 (*1-57322-626-2*, Riverhd Trade) Berkley Pub.

On the Martingale Problem for Interactive Measure-Valued Branching Diffusions. Edwin Perkins. LC 95-3279. (Memoirs Ser.: Vol. 549). 89p. 1995. pap. 33.00 (*0-8218-0358-1*, MEMO/115/549) Am Math.

On the Mass Bombing of Kuwait, Commonly Known As the "Gulf War" Tom Leonard. 24p. (Orig.). 1992. pap. 4.00 (*1-873176-25-2*, AK Pr San Fran) AK Pr Dist.

On the Mayflower: The Voyage of the Ship's Apprentice & a Passenger Girl. Kate Waters. LC 95-43980. (Illus.). 40p. (J). (gr. 1-4). 1996. 16.95 (*0-590-67308-4*) Scholastic Inc.

On the Mayflower: Voyage of the Ship's Apprentice & a Passenger Girl, 1 vol. Kate Waters. (Illus.). 40p. (J). (gr. 1-4). 1999. pap. text 5.99 (*0-439-09941-2*) Scholastic Inc.

On the Meaning of Alienation. Melvin Seeman. (Reprint Series in Social Sciences). (C). 1993. reprint ed. pap. text 5.00 (*0-8290-2730-0*, S-254) Irvington.

On the Meaning of Restructuring. H. Dickson Corbett. 15p. 1990. pap. 5.95 (*1-56602-035-2*) Research Better.

***On the Meaning of the Mahabharata.** V. S. Sukthankar. 1998. 14.00 (*81-208-1503-3*, Pub. by Motilal Bnarsidass) S Asia.

On the Meaning of the University. Eric Ashby et al. Ed. by Sterling M. McMurrin. LC 74-22637. 133p. reprint ed. pap. 41.30 (*0-8357-4378-0*, 203720900007) Bks Demand.

On the Means Which Conduce to True Philosophy & on the True Philosopher. Emanuel Swedenborg. Tr. by Augustus Clissold from LAT. 42p. 1968. reprint ed. pap. 1.00 (*0-915221-15-2*) Swedenborg Sci Assn.

On the Measurement of Cosmological Variations of the Gravitational Constant: Proceedings of the Workshop Meetings Held Nov. 12-14, 1975, at the Dept. of Physics, Florida State University, Tallahassee. Leopold Halpern. LC 78-8350. (Monograph Publishing on Demand: Imprint Ser.). 126p. reprint ed. pap. 39.10 (*0-608-14333-2*, 201649400004) Bks Demand.

On the Media: Your World. Andrew Gitlin. 5.95 (*0-8050-4898-7*) H Holt & Co.

On the Medieval Origins of the Modern State. Joseph R. Strayer. 120p. 1970. pap. text 10.95 (*0-691-00769-1*, Pub. by Princeton U Pr) Cal Prin Full Svc.

On the Medieval Origins of the Modern State. Joseph R. Strayer. LC 79-113011. 120p. 1970. reprint ed. pap. 37.20 (*0-7837-9455-X*, 206019700004) Bks Demand.

On the Medieval Theory of Signs. Ed. by Umberto Eco & Costantino Marmo. Tr. by Shona Kelly. LC 89-232. (Foundations of Semiotics Ser.: Vol. 21). ix, 224p. 1989. 59.00 (*90-272-3293-8*) J Benjamins Pubng Co.

On the Melodic Relativity of Tones. Otto Ortmann. (Psychology Monographs General & Applied: Vol. 35). 1974. reprint ed. pap. 55.00 (*0-8115-1434-X*) Periodicals Srv.

On the Mersey Beat: Policing Liverpool Between the Wars. Michael Brogden. 192p. 1991. 32.00 (*0-19-825430-X*) OUP.

On the Mesa. Photos & Text by John Nichols. LC 95-15130. (Illus.). 208p. 1995. pap. 12.95 (*0-941270-87-4*) Ancient City Pr.

On the Mesa. deluxe ed. Photos & Text by John Nichols. (Illus.). 208p. 1995. 24.95 (*0-941270-86-6*) Ancient City Pr.

On the Methodology of Architectural History. Prophyrius. 1982. pap. 14.95 (*0-312-53149-4*) St Martin.

***On the Methodology of Economics & the Formalist Revolution.** Terence Hutchison. LC 99-87151. 392p. 2000. 120.00 (*1-84064-040-5*) E Elgar.

On the Methodology of the Social Sciences. Max M. Weber. 1949. 24.95 (*0-02-934360-7*) Free Pr.

On the Mexican Border. Paul Hutchens. LC 98-155771. (Sugar Creek Gang Ser.: Vol. 18). 128p. (J). (gr. 4-7). 1998. mass mkt. 4.99 (*0-8024-7022-X*) Moody.

On the Ministry & the Role of the Laity: Selected Sections of Locus XXIII, on the Ecclesiastical Ministry. Johann Gerhard. Tr. by Martin Jackson. (LAT.). 28p. 1998. pap. 4.00 (*1-891469-16-9*) Repristination.

On the Minor Prophecies of William Blake. Emily S. Hamblen. 408p. 1996. reprint ed. pap. 39.95 (*1-56459-543-9*) Kessinger Pub.

On the Minor Prophecies of William Blake. Emily S. Hamblen. LC 68-24120. (Studies in Blake: No. 3). 1969. reprint ed. lib. bdg. 75.00 (*0-8383-0786-8*) M S G Haskell Hse.

On the Mission in Missouri, 1857-1868. John J. Hogan. (American Biography Ser.). 211p. 1991. reprint ed. lib. bdg. 69.00 (*0-7812-8187-3*) Rprt Serv.

***On the Missionary Trail: An Adventure Around the World with the London Mission Society.** Tom Hiney. (Illus.). 2000. 25.00 (*0-87113-823-9*, Atlntc Mnthly) Grove-Atltic.

On the Mixed Problem for a Hyperbolic Equation. T. Balaban. LC 52-42839. (Memoirs Ser.: No. 1/112). 117p. 1971. pap. 16.00 (*0-8218-1812-0*, MEMO/1/112) Am Math.

On the Modernist Long Poem. Margaret Dickie. LC 85-20958. 190p. 1986. pap. text 24.95 (*0-87745-140-0*) U of Iowa Pr.

On the Mommy Track. Bill Holbrook. (Illus.). 128p. (Orig.). 1991. mass mkt. 5.95 (*0-380-76433-4*, Avon Bks) Morrow Avon.

On the Monday Side of the Street: A Text on Alcoholism for Professional & Lay People. Corey A. Bohling. Tr. by Virginia Fieser. (Illus.). 100p. (Orig.). (C). 1989. pap. 5.95 (*0-9625478-3-2*, TXU-368-156) C Bohling Pub.

On the Moral Nature of the Universe: Theology, Cosmology & Ethics. George Ellis & Nancy Murphy. LC 96-38384. (Theology & the Sciences Ser.). 272p. 1996. pap. 22.00 (*0-8006-2983-3*, 1-2983, Fortress Pr) Augsburg Fortress.

On the Mormon Frontier: The Diary of Hosea Stout, 1844-1861, Vol. 1. Hosea Stout. Ed. by Juanita Brooks. LC 64-24537. 347p. reprint ed. pap. 107.60 (*0-7837-5705-0*, 204531100001) Bks Demand.

On the Mormon Frontier: The Diary of Hosea Stout, 1844-1861, Vol. 2. Hosea Stout. Ed. by Juanita Brooks. LC 64-24537. 391p. reprint ed. pap. 121.30 (*0-7837-5706-9*, 204531100002) Bks Demand.

On the Morn of Mayfest. Erica Silverman. LC 96-9828. 32p. (J). (gr. k-2). 1998. 16.00 (*0-689-80674-4*) S&S Bks Yung.

On the Most Ancient Wisdom of the Italians: Unearthed from the Origins of the Latin Language: Including the Disputation with the Giornale de'letterati d'Italia. Giambattista Vico. Tr. & Intro. by L. M. Palmer. LC 87-47865. xi, 198p. 1988. text 39.95 (*0-8014-1280-3*); pap. text 14.95 (*0-8014-9511-3*) Cornell U Pr.

On the Mother: The Chronicle of a Manifestation & Ministry. K. R. Iyengar. 1979. pap. 30.00 (*0-89744-947-9*) Auromere.

On the Mother: The Chronicle of a Manifestation & Ministry. 3rd ed. K. R. Srinivasa Iyengar. 924p. 1995. pap. 29.95 (*81-7058-036-6*, Pub. by SAA) E-W Cultural Ctr.

On the Mother of God. Jacob. LC 98-31363. 1998. 8.95 (*0-88141-184-1*) St Vladimirs.

An Asterisk (*) at the beginning of an entry indicates that the title is appearing for the first time.

On the Motion of the Heart & Blood in Animals. William Harvey. LC 92-25948. (Great Minds Ser.). 91p. 1993. pap. 9.95 (*0-87975-854-6*) Prometheus Bks.

On the Motives Which Led Husserl to Transcendental Idealism. R. S. Ingarden. (Phaenomenologica Ser.: No. 64). 80p. 1975. pap. text 66.50 (*90-247-1751-5*, Pub. by M Nijhoff) Kluwer Academic.

On the Mound With - Randy Johnson. Matt Christopher. LC 97-32500. 128p. (J). (gr. 3-7). 1998. pap. 4.50 (*0-316-14221-2*) Little.

On the Mound with--Greg Maddux. Matt Christopher. LC 96-40973. (Illus.). 144p. (J). 1997. pap. 4.95 (*0-316-14191-7*) Little.

On the Mound with--Greg Maddux. Matt Christopher. (Matt Christopher Sports Biographies Ser.). 1997. 9.60 (*0-606-11705-9*, Pub. by Turtleback) Demco.

On the Mountain. Thomas Bernhard. Tr. by Russell Stockman from GER. LC 91-61533. 128p. 1993. pap. 10.95 (*0-910395-76-4*) Marlboro Pr.

On the Mountain: A Touch-&-Feel Adventure. Maurice Pledger. (Nature Trails Ser.: Vol. 3). (Illus.). 16p. (J). (ps-1). 1999. 12.95 (*1-57145-353-9*, Silver Dolph) Advantage Pubs.

***On the Move.** 2000. student ed. write for info. (*0-13-019755-6*) P-H.

On the Move. Sarah Fecher et al. LC 97-32802. (Ladders Ser.). (Illus.). 32p. (J). (gr. k-3). 1999. write for info. (*0-7166-7711-3*) World Bk.

On the Move. S. Freeman. (Easy Readers Ser.). 16p. (J). (gr. k-1). 1997. pap. 2.49 (*1-57690-043-6*) Tchr Create Mat.

On the Move. Sharon Goodman et al. 1985. pap. text 3.50 (*0-935369-02-3*) In Tradition Pub.

On the Move. Deborah Heiligman. LC 95-6738. (Let's-Read-&-Find-Out Science Bks.). (Illus.). 32p. (J). (ps-1). 1996. lib. bdg. 14.89 (*0-06-024742-8*) HarpC Child Bks.

On the Move. Deborah Heiligman. LC 95-6738. (Let's-Read-And-Find-Out Science. Stage 2 Ser.). (J). 1996. 10.15 (*0-606-09708-2*, Pub. by Turtleback) Demco.

***On the Move!** Jane Jarrell & Deborah Saathoff. (One-Stop Thematic Units Ser.). 64p. 1999. pap., teacher ed. 9.50 (*0-570-05239-4*, 12-4046) Concordia.

***On the Move.** Wendy Madgwick. LC 98-30064. (Science Starters Ser.). 32 p. 1999. 5.95 (*0-8172-5884-1*) Raintree Steck-V.

On the Move. Wendy Madgwick. 1999. 22.83 (*0-8172-5333-5*) Raintree Steck-V.

On the Move. Henry Arthur Pluckrose. LC 98-17951. (Machines at Work Ser.). (Illus.). (J). 1998. 18.00 (*0-531-14497-6*) Watts.

On the Move. Henry Arthur Pluckrose. (Machines at Work Ser.). (Illus.). 32p. (J). (gr. k-2). 1999. pap. text 6.95 (*0-531-15354-1*) Watts.

On the Move. Joyce Pope. (Curious Creatures Ser.). (Illus.). 48p. (J). 1992. lib. bdg. 5.00 (*0-8114-3156-8*) Raintree Steck-V.

On the Move, 4 bks. Paul Stickland. Incl. Boats. LC 98-14525. (Illus.). 16p. (J). (ps up). 1998. lib. bdg. 17.27 (*0-8368-2151-3*); Cars. LC 98-3350. (Illus.). 16p. (J). (ps up). 1998. lib. bdg. 17.27 (*0-8368-2152-1*); Planes. LC 98-3351. (Illus.). 16p. (J). (ps up). 1998. lib. bdg. 17.27 (*0-8368-2153-X*); Trains. LC 98-3349. (Illus.). 16p. (J). (ps up). 1998. lib. bdg. 17.27 (*0-8368-2154-8*); (J). Set lib. bdg. 69.08 (*0-8368-2150-5*) Gareth Stevens Inc.

***On the Move.** rev. ed. (Ladders Ser.). (J). 2000. 9.95 (*1-58728-620-3*); pap. 4.95 (*1-58728-605-X*) Two Can Pub.

On the Move: A Chronology of Advances in Transportation. Ed. by Leonard C. Bruno. (Illus.). 423p. 1998. text 30.00 (*0-7881-5615-2*) DIANE Pub.

On the Move: A Handbook for Exploring Creative Movement with Young Children. Ginger Zukowski & Ardie Dickson. LC 88-37032. (Illus.). 100p. (C). 1990. pap. 15.95 (*0-8093-1542-4*) S Ill U Pr.

On the Move: A Study of Migration & Ethnic Persistence among Mennonites from East Freeman, South Dakota. Marilyn P. Rose. LC 87-45793. (Immigrant Communities & Ethnic Minorities in the U. S. & Canada Ser.: No. 28). 1988. 45.00 (*0-404-19438-9*, F659) AMS Pr.

On the Move: American Women in the 1970's. Winifred D. Wandersee. LC 87-29050. (Twayne's American Women in the Twentieth Century Ser.). 288p. 1988. 24.95 (*0-8057-9909-5*, Twyne); pap. 14.95 (*0-8057-9910-9*, Twyne) Mac Lib Ref.

On the Move: Essays in Labour & Transport History Presented to Philip Bagwell. Ed. by Chris Wrigley & John Shepherd. 288p. 1991. 55.00 (*1-85285-060-4*) Hambledon Press.

***On the Move: Great Transportation Photographs from LIFE.** Ed. by Maryann Kornely & Jennie Hirschfeld. LC 99-35351. (Illus.). 144p. 2000. 35.00 (*0-8212-2622-3*, Pub. by Bulfinch Pr) Little.

On the Move: How & Why Animals Travel in Groups. Sue Boinski & Paul A. Garber. LC 99-13382. 2000. pap. text 35.00 (*0-226-06340-2*) U Ch Pr.

***On the Move: How & Why Animals Travel in Groups.** Sue Boinski & Paul Alan Garber. LC 99-13382. 2000. lib. bdg. 95.00 (*0-226-06339-9*) U Ch Pr.

On the Move: How to Succeed & Survive As an Entrepreneur. Tim Moore & Carol Davis. LC 99-191505. (Illus.). 288p. 1997. pap. 16.50 (*0-919292-01-1*, Pub. by McLeod Pub) Genl Dist Srvs.

On the Move: Lesson Plans to Accompany Children Moving. 4th ed. Shirley A. Holt. 1998. pap. text 21.95 (*1-55934-923-9*, 1923) Mayfield Pub.

On the Move: Patterns of Change. Sharon Franklin. (Explore! Science Ser.). (Illus.). 48p. (J). (gr. 3-6). 1995. 12.95 (*0-673-36219-1*, GoodYrBooks); pap. 4.95 (*0-673-36214-0*, GoodYrBooks) Addson-Wesley Educ.

On the Move: Teaching the Learner's Way in Grades 4-7. Anne Forester & Margaret Reinhard. (Illus.). 360p. 1991. pap., teacher ed. 19.00 (*1-895411-35-1*) Peguis Pubs Ltd.

On the Move: The Status of Women in Policing. Susan E. Martin. LC 90-62667. 197p. (Orig.). 1990. pap. text 20.95 (*1-884614-06-X*) Police Found.

On the Move in Japan: Useful Phrases & Common Sense for the Traveler. Scott Rutherford. (JPN.). 176p. 1995. pap. text 8.95 (*4-900737-14-3*, Pub. by Yen Bks) Tuttle Pubng.

On the Move-to-the-Left in Uganda, 1969-1971. Tertit Aasland. (Research Report Ser.: No. 26). 71p. 1974. write for info. (*91-7106-083-9*, Pub. by Nordic Africa) Transaction Pubs.

On the Move with Moses. Phyllis Vos Wezeman & Colleen A. Wiessner. (Celebrate: A Creative Approach to Bible Studies). 33p. (Orig.). (J). (gr. 1-6). 1988. pap. 5.95 (*0-940754-60-6*) Ed Ministries.

On the Move with the Master: A Daily Devotional Guide on World Mission. Duain W. Vierow. LC 76-57679. 166p. 1977. 5.95 (*0-87808-155-0*) William Carey Lib.

On the Movement & Progression of Animals: Aristotle & Michael of Ephesus. Aristotle & Michael of Ephesus. Tr. & Intro. by Anthony Preus. (Studien und Materialien Zur Geschichte der Philosophie Ser.: Vol. XXII). 209p. 1981. 50.70 (*3-487-07073-1*) G Olms Pubs.

On the Movement of Animals. G. A. Borelli. (Illus.). 480p. 1989. 216.00 (*0-387-19419-3*) Spr-Verlag.

On the Museum's Ruins. Douglas Crimp. (Illus.). 368p. 1995. pap. text 21.00 (*0-262-53126-7*) MIT Pr.

On the Music of the North American Indians. Theodore Baker. Tr. by Ann Buckley from GER. (Music Reprint Ser.: 1977). 1978. lib. bdg. 25.00 (*0-306-70888-4*) Da Capo.

On the Musically Beautiful. Edward Hanslick. Ed. & Tr. by Geoffrey Payzant from GER. LC 85-27249. (HPC Classics Ser.). 151p. (C). 1986. pap. 8.95 (*0-87220-014-0*); lib. bdg. 27.95 (*0-87220-015-9*) Hackett Pub.

On the Mystagogy of the Holy Spirit Patriarcha C. Photius. LC 83-60028. 213p. 1983. write for info. (*0-943670-00-4*) Studion Pubs Inc.

On the Mysteries. Andokides. 236p. 1989. pap. text 40.00 (*0-19-814692-2*) OUP.

On the Mysteries. 3rd ed. Iamblichus & Thomas Taylor. Ed. by R. I. Robb. LC 81-50200. (Secret Doctrine Reference Ser.). 400p. 1997. reprint ed. 25.00 (*0-913510-70-X*) Wizards.

On the Mysteries of Eleusis. Albert Steffen. Tr. by Daisy Aldan. 1986. pap. 3.50 (*0-913152-13-7*) Folder Edns.

On the Mysteries of Unemployment: Causes, Consequences, & Policies. Ed. by C. H. Verhaar et al. LC 92-31352. (Studies in Operational Regional Science: Vol. 10). 1992. lib. bdg. 189.00 (*0-7923-1976-1*) Kluwer Academic.

On the Mysterious Leap from the Mind to the Body: A Workshop Study on the Theory of Conversion. Ed. by Felix Deutsch. LC 59-8411. 1969. reprint ed. pap. 24.95 (*0-8236-8174-2*, 023800) Intl Univs Pr.

On the Mystical Body of Christ & Our Union in It with Christ: Mystici Corporis. Pius XII, pseud. 73p. pap. 2.50 (*0-8198-4739-9*) Pauline Bks.

On the Mystical Life: The Ethical Discourses: On Virtue & the Christian Life, Vol. 2. St. Symeon. Tr. by Alexander Golitzin from GRE. LC 95-36925. 178p. (Orig.). 1996. pap. 9.95 (*0-88141-143-4*) St Vladimirs.

On the Mystical Shape of the Godhead. Gershom Scholem. 1997. pap. 15.00 (*0-8052-1081-4*) Schocken.

On the Na Pali Coast: A Guide for Hikers & Boaters. Kathy Valier. LC 88-1166. (Illus.). 112p. 1988. pap. 12.95 (*0-8248-1154-2*, Kolowalu Bk) UH Pr.

On the Name. Jacques Derrida. Ed. by Thomas Dutoit. Tr. by David Wood et al from FRE. LC 94-42209. (Meridian: Crossing Aesthetics Ser.). 168p. 1995. 37.50 (*0-8047-2554-3*); pap. 14.95 (*0-8047-2555-1*) Stanford U Pr.

***On the Nameways.** Clark Coolidge. 128p. 2000. pap. 13.95 (*1-930589-02-6*, Pub. by Figures) SPD-Small Pr Dist.

On the Napoleonic Wars. David Chandler. LC 98-49191. (Greenhill Military Paperbacks Ser.). 1999. pap. text 19.95 (*1-85367-349-8*) Greenhill Bks.

On the Napoleonic Wars: Collected Essays. David G. Chandler. LC 93-32339. 240p. 1994. 34.95 (*1-85367-158-4*) Stackpole.

On the Natural Faculties. Galen. (Loeb Classical Library: No. 71). 396p. 1916. 18.95 (*0-674-99078-1*) HUP.

On the Natural State of Men. Samuel Pufendorf. Tr. by Michael Seidler. LC 89-77198. (Studies in History of Philosophy: Vol. 13). (ENG & LAT.). 152p. 1990. lib. bdg. 69.95 (*0-88946-299-2*) E Mellen.

On the Nature of Consciousness: Cognitive, Phenomenological, & Transpersonal Perspectives. Harry T. Hunt. LC 94-48759. (Illus.). xvi, 358p. 1995. 42.00 (*0-300-06230-3*) Yale U Pr.

On the Nature of Grammatical Relations. Alec P. Marantz. 351p. (Orig.). 1984. 37.50 (*0-262-13193-5*); pap. text 18.50 (*0-262-63090-7*) MIT Pr.

On the Nature of Health. Lennart Nordenfelt. (C). 1987. text 127.50 (*1-55608-032-8*) Kluwer Academic.

On the Nature of Health: An Action-Theoretic Approach. Lennart Nordenfelt. 244p. 1995. pap. text 50.50 (*0-7923-3470-1*, Pub. by Kluwer Academic) Kluwer Academic.

On the Nature of Love. unabridged ed. J. Krishnamurti. 1990. 10.95 incl. audio (*1-56176-150-8*) Mystic Fire.

On the Nature of Music. Hewitt Pantaleoni. LC 85-50599. (Illus.). 464p. (C). 1985. 36.00 (*0-9614873-0-5*) Welkin Bks.

On the Nature of Musical Experience. Ed. by Bennett Reimer & Jeffrey E. Wright. 327p. (C). 1992. text 39.95 (*0-87081-248-3*) Univ Pr Colo.

On the Nature of Persons. A. R. Duncan. LC 89-28145. (John MacMurray Studies: Vol. 1). X, 148p. (C). 1990. text 47.95 (*0-8204-1241-4*) P Lang Pubng.

On the Nature of Rivers: With Case Stories of the Nile, Zaire, & Amazon. Julian Rzoska. 1978. text 44.00 (*90-6193-589-X*) Kluwer Academic.

On the Nature of Suicide. Ed. by Edwin S. Shneidman. LC 78-92890. (Jossey-Bass Behavioral Science Ser.). 160p. reprint ed. pap. 49.60 (*0-608-30951-6*, 201385700088) Bks Demand.

On the Nature of the Bilirubin Pigments in the Newborn Infant. Sina Aziz. (Acta Biomedica Lovaniensia Ser.). 194p. (Orig.). 1995. pap. 36.50 (*90-6186-696-0*, Pub. by Leuven Univ) Coronet Bks.

On the Nature of the Psyche. C. G. Jung. Ed. by G. Adler. Tr. by R. F. C. Hull. (Bollingen Ser.: Vol. 20). 184p. 1969. pap. 12.95 (*0-691-01751-4*, Pub. by Princeton U Pr) Cal Prin Full Svc.

On the Nature of the Puerto Rican Universe: De Rerum Natura Puertorriquena. Ivan Diaz. 286p. (Orig.). 1997. pap. 12.00 (*0-9655929-0-1*) Domino Pr.

On the Nature of the Universe. Tr. by R. E. Latham. 320p. 1994. pap. 13.95 (*0-14-044610-9*, Penguin Classics) Viking Penguin.

On the Nature of the Universe. Lucretius. Ed. by Don Fowler. Tr. by Ronald Melville. LC 97-40071. 310p. 1998. text 86.00 (*0-19-815097-0*) OUP.

On the Nature of the Universe. Lucretius. LC 98-35967. 314p. 1999. pap. 11.95 (*0-19-281761-2*) OUP.

***On the Nature of Things.** Gavin Keeney. (Illus.). 176p. 2000. 70.00 (*3-7643-6192-1*, Pub. by Birkhauser) Princeton Arch.

On the Nature of Things. Lucretius. 1976. 20.95 (*0-8488-0824-X*) Amereon Ltd.

On the Nature of Things. Lucretius. Tr. by John S. Watson from LAT. LC 97-34295. (Great Books in Philosophy). 310p. 1997. pap. text 7.95 (*1-57392-179-3*) Prometheus Bks.

On the Nature of Things. rev. ed. Lucretius. (Loeb Classical Library: No. 181). 664p. 1975. text 18.95 (*0-674-99200-8*) HUP.

On the Nature of Things: The Scientific Photography of Fritz Goro. Intro. by Stephen Jay Gould. 128p. 1993. 60.00 (*0-89381-542-X*) Aperture.

On the Nature of Things-De Rerum Natura. Lucretius. Ed. by Anthony M. Esolen. LC 94-25165. 336p. 1995. text 38.00 (*0-8018-5054-1*) Johns Hopkins.

On the Nature of Things Erotic. Frank Gonzalez-Crussi. 208p. 1988. 16.95 (*0-15-169966-6*) Harcourt.

On the Nature of Things Erotic. Frank Gonzalez-Crussi. 1989. pap. 8.95 (*0-679-72199-1*) Vin Bks.

On the Nature of Threat: A Social Psychological Analysis. Ed. by Thomas W. Milburn & Kenneth H. Watman. LC 80-20814. 148p. 1981. 45.00 (*0-275-90683-3*, C0683, Praeger Pubs) Greenwood.

On the Nature of War. Julian Lider. 420p. 1978. text 109.95 (*0-566-00178-0*) Ashgate Pub Co.

On the Need for, & Derivation of a Comprehensive Behavioral Theory, & a Subset, Organization Theory. Steven Davidian. (Illus.). viii, 300p. (C). 1998. pap. text 24.95 (*0-9664417-0-2*, CBT001) Zebra Skim.

On the New World Chalcididae (Hymenoptera) G. Delvare & Z. Boucek. (Memoirs of the American Entomological Institute Ser.: No. 53). (Illus.). iv, 470p. 1992. 60.00 (*1-56665-053-4*) Assoc Pubs FL.

***On the Next Tide: Portraits & Anecdotes of New Zealand Fishermen & Women.** Kirk Hargreaves. (Illus.). 112p. (Orig.). 1998. pap. 39.95 (*0-908812-71-X*, Pub. by Canterbury Univ) Accents Pubns.

On the Night Before Christmas: When Every Creature Is Stirring. (Look & Find Ser.). (Illus.). 24p. (J). 1993. 7.98 (*1-56173-521-3*) Pubns Intl Ltd.

On the Night He Was Betrayed: Peter Tosh, the Man, the Prophet, the Legend. Ricardo Scott. (Ras Cardo Speaks of Unknown Truths Ser.). (Illus.). 100p. 1999. pap. 35.00 (*1-883427-89-4*, RAS1999) Crnerstone GA.

On the Night of the Seventh Moon. Victoria Holt, pseud. 384p. 1986. mass mkt. 3.50 (*0-449-21228-9*, Crest) Fawcett.

On the Night the Hogs Ate Willie: And Other Quotations on All Things Southern. Barbara Binswanger & Jim Charlton. 1996. pap. 9.95 (*0-614-97891-2*, Plume) Dutton Plume.

***On the Night They Were Betrayed: The Tragic Deaths of Junior, Bob, & Peter.** Ricardo Scott. (Ras Cardo Speaks Reggae Ser.). 85p. 2000. pap. write for info. (*1-58470-043-2*, RCR9949, RAS Cardo Prodn) Crnerstone GA.

On the Nile. Mindy Aloff & Marty Cohen. 4p. 1978. pap. 1.00 (*0-932264-23-9*) Trask Hse Bks.

On the North Atlantic Circulation. L. V. Worthington. LC 76-17244. (Johns Hopkins Oceanographic Studies: No. 6). 110p. reprint ed. pap. 34.10 (*0-608-13743-X*, 202073500018) Bks Demand.

On the Northweest: Commercial Whaling in the Pacific Northwest, 1790-1967. Robert L. Webb. (Illus.). 452p. 1988. 39.95 (*0-7748-0292-8*) U of Wash Pr.

On the Nose: Fostering Creativity, Problem Solving & Social Reasoning. George G. Bear & Carolyn M. Callahan. (Orig.). 1984. pap. 14.95 (*0-936386-23-1*) Creative Learning.

On the Notion of Mental Illness: Problematizing the Medical Model Conception of Abnormal Behavior & Mental Afflictions. Tommy Svensson. (Avebury Series in Philosophy). 160p. 1995. 61.95 (*1-85972-160-5*, Pub. by Avebury) Ashgate Pub Co.

On the Number of Simply Connected Minimal Surfaces Spanning a Curve. Anthony J. Tromba. LC 77-12180. (Memoirs Ser.: No. 12/194). 121p. 1977. pap. 21.00 (*0-8218-2194-6*, MEMO/12/194) Am Math.

On the Objective Necessity to Indict, Arrest & Try Saddam Hussein for Crimes Against the Humanity of One or More Peoples. Thomas J. Kuna-Jacob. 19p. 1992. ring bd. 2.64 (*1-878030-07-8*) Assn World Peace.

On the Observance of Foods. Anthimus. Ed. by Mark Grant. Orig. Title: De Observatione Ciborum. 142p. 1996. pap. 20.00 (*0-907325-75-0*, Pub. by Prospect) Food Words.

On the Observance of Sunday. Ed. & Tr. by J. G. O'Keefe. (IRI.). 1996. pap. 1.50 (*0-89979-083-6*) British Am Bks.

***On the Occasion of My Last Afternoon.** Kaye Gibbons. LC 98-12947. 288p. (YA). 1998. 22.95 (*0-399-14299-1*, G P Putnam) Peng Put Young Read.

On the Occasion of My Last Afternoon. large type ed. Kaye Gibbons. LC 98-29238. (Large Print Book Ser.). 1998. 25.95 (*1-56895-624-X*) Wheeler Pub.

On the Occasion of My Last Afternoon. Kaye Gibbons. LC 98-12947. 288p. 1999. reprint ed. pap. 12.50 (*0-380-73214-9*, Avon Bks) Morrow Avon.

On the Occult Path. John P. Scott. 22p. 1999. reprint ed. pap. 5.00 (*0-7661-0826-0*) Kessinger Pub.

***On the Oceans of Eternity.** S. M. Stirling. 630p. 2000. mass mkt. 6.99 (*0-451-45780-3*, ROC) NAL.

On the Offensive: Wall Street's Socially Incorrect Humor--A Treasury of the Unprintable 100. T. H. Pincus. LC 98-90312. 1999. 16.95 (*0-533-12763-7*) Vantage.

On the Old Plantation Reminiscences of His Childhood. John G. Clinkscales. LC 77-91255. 142p. 1969. reprint ed. lib. bdg. 35.00 (*0-8371-2063-2*, CLO&) Greenwood.

On the Old West Coast. Major H. Bell. 1992. reprint ed. lib. bdg. 75.00 (*0-7812-5007-2*) Rprt Serv.

On the Old West Coast: Being Further Reminiscences of a Ranger. Horace Bell. Ed. by Lanier Bartlett. LC 76-1242. (Chicano Heritage Ser.). (Illus.). 1977. reprint ed. lib. bdg. 34.95 (*0-405-09485-X*) Ayer.

***On the Old Western Frontier.** R. Conrad Stein. LC 98-23100. (How We Lived Ser.). (J). (gr. 4-7). 1999. lib. bdg. 27.07 (*0-7614-0909-2*, Benchmark NY) Marshall Cavendish.

On the Open Road: A New Play. Steve Tesich. LC 92-9141. 96p. 1992. pap. 7.95 (*1-55783-134-3*) Applause Theatre Bk Pubs.

On the Open Road: Being Some Thoughts & a Little Creed of Wholesome Living. Ralph W. Trine. 65p. 1993. pap. 5.50 (*0-89540-252-1*, SB-252) Sun Pub.

On the Oregon Trail: With the Ira Hooker Family - 1848. Marguariete Overholder. LC 96-79729. (Illus.). 96p. 1993. pap. 6.95 (*0-8323-0519-7*) Binford Mort.

On the Origin & Early History of the Runic Script: Typology & Graphic Variation in the Older Futbark. Bengt Odenstedt. (Acta Academiae Regiae Gustavi Adolphi Ser.: No. 59). 181p. (Orig.). 1990. pap. 48.50 (*91-85352-20-9*) Coronet Bks.

On the Origin & Nature of Management. B. G. Schumacher. LC 86-7066. (Illus.). 261p. 1986. lib. bdg. 34.50 (*0-940013-00-2*) Eugnosis Pr.

On the Origin of Language. Jean-Jacques Rousseau & Johann G. Herder. Tr. by John H. Moran & Alexander Gode from FRE. LC 85-20945. x, 186p. 1986. pap. text 9.95 (*0-226-73012-3*) U Ch Pr.

On the Origin of Languages. Merritt Ruhlen. 1996. pap. text 18.95 (*0-8047-2805-4*) Stanford U Pr.

On the Origin of Languages: Studies in Linguistic Taxonomy. Merritt Ruhlen. LC 93-39188. xiv, 342p. 1994. 45.00 (*0-8047-2321-4*) Stanford U Pr.

On the Origin of Objects. Brian C. Smith. (Illus.). 424p. 1996. 40.00 (*0-262-19363-9*, Bradford Bks) MIT Pr.

On the Origin of Objects. Brian C. Smith. (Illus.). 440p. 1998. reprint ed. pap. text 19.50 (*0-262-69209-0*, Bradford Bks) MIT Pr.

On the Origin of Species: A Facsimile of the First Edition. Charles Darwin. LC 63-17196. 528p. 1964. pap. text 13.50 (*0-674-63752-6*) HUP.

***On the Origin of the Native Races of America. A Dissertation by Hugo Grotius. To Which Is Added a Treatise on Foreign Languages & Unknown Islands.** Hugo Grotius. (LC History-America-E). 63p. 1999. reprint ed. lib. bdg. 69.00 (*0-7812-4326-2*) Rprt Serv.

On the Origin of the Solar System. Hannes Alfven. LC 72-9604. (International Series of Monographs on Physics). (Illus.). 194p. 1982. reprint ed. lib. bdg. 115.00 (*0-8371-6595-4*, AEALOS, Greenwood Pr) Greenwood.

On the Original Inhabitants of Bharatavarsa or India. Gustav Oppert. Ed. by Kees W. Bolle. (Mythology Ser.). 1978. reprint ed. lib. bdg. 60.95 (*0-405-10557-6*) Ayer.

On the Origins & Treatment of Homosexuality: A Psychoanalytic Reinterpretation. Gerald J. M. Van Den Aardweg. LC 85-9266. 320p. 1985. 42.95 (*0-275-90233-1*, C0233, Praeger Pubs) Greenwood.

***On the Origins of Human Emotions: A Sociological Inquiry into the Evolution of Human Affect.** Jonathan H. Turner. 2000. pap. 17.95 (*0-8047-3720-7*) Stanford U Pr.

***On the Origins of Human Emotions: A Sociologicalinquiry into the Evolution of Human Affect.** Jonathan H. Turner. (Illus.). 2000. 49.50 (*0-8047-3719-3*) Stanford U Pr.

***On the Origins of Norms in International Politics: A Conference at UCLA.** (New Ser.: Vol. 25). 32p. 1999. pap. 15.00 (*0-86682-111-2*) Ctr Intl Relations.

On the Origins of the Ottoman Emperors. Theodore Spandounes. Ed. & Tr. by Donald M. Nicol. 192p. (C). 1997. text 49.95 (*0-521-58510-4*) Cambridge U Pr.

On the Origins of the Pahari Painting. Vishwa C. Ohri. (C). 1991. 25.00 (*81-85182-53-1*, Pub. by Motilal Bnarsidass) S Asia.

On the Origins of War & the Preservation of Peace. Donald Kagan. 624p. 1996. pap. 17.50 (*0-385-42375-6*, Anchor NY) Doubleday.

O

An Asterisk (*) at the beginning of an entry indicates that the title is appearing for the first time.

On the Osteology of Nyctosaurus (Nyctodactylus) With Notes on American Pterosaurs. Samuel W. Williston. LC 04-5197. (Field Columbian Museum, Publication 78 Ser.: Vol. 2, No. 3). 61p. 1903. reprint ed. pap. 30.00 (0-608-03773-7, 206460000009) Bks Demand.

On the Other: Dialogue & - or Dialectics. Ed. by Robert P. Scharlemann. 84p. (C). 1991. pap. text 12.00 (0-8191-8447-0); lib. bdg. 28.50 (0-8191-8382-2) U Pr of Amer.

On the Other Hand... Essays on Economics, Economists & Politics. Herbert Stein. LC 94-24823. 150p. 1995. pap. 16.95 (0-8447-3877-8) Am Enterprise.

On the Other Hand... Essays on Economics, Economists & Politics. Herbert Stein. LC 94-24823. 275p. 1995. 25.95 (0-8447-3876-X, AEI Pr) Am Enterprise.

On the Other Hand, Death. Richard Stevenson. 1995. text 8.95 (0-312-11871-6, Stonewall Inn) St Martin.

On the Other Shore Poems. T. K. Ravindran. 104p. 1991. text 10.00 (81-220-0214-5, Pub. by Konark Pubs Pvt Ltd) Advent Bks Div.

On the Other Side. Paul Borgese. (J). (gr. k up). 1986. pap. 6.95 (1-878347-06-3) NL Assocs.

On the Other Side. Gerald Szyszkowitz. Tr. by Todd C. Hanlin. (Studies in Austrian Literature, Culture, & Thought. Translation Ser.). 156p. 1991. pap. 12.50 (0-929497-42-2) Ariadne CA.

On the Other Side of Life: Exploring the Phenomenon of the Near-Death Experience. Evelyn E. Valarino. Tr. by Michelle H. Escobar. LC 96-49353. (Illus.). 366p. (C). 1997. 29.95 (0-306-45561-7, Plen Insight) Perseus Pubng.

On the Other Side of Sorrow: Nature & People in the Scottish Highlands. James Hunter. (Illus.). 224p. 1996. 35.00 (1-85158-765-9, Pub. by Mainstream Pubng) Trafalgar.

On the Other Side of That Window. Ed. by California Poets in the Schools Staff. 1993. pap. 10.95 (0-939927-10-1) Calif Poets Schls.

On the Other Side of the Camera. Arnold Crane. (ENG, FRE & GER., Illus.). 240p. 1997. 39.95 (3-89508-093-4, 810045) Konemann.

On the Other Side of the Garden. Virginia Fugate. 1992. pap. text 9.95 (0-86717-008-5) Alpha AZ.

On the Other Side of the Hill. Roger L. MacBride. LC 95-14263. (Little House). (Illus.). 352p. (J). (gr. 4-7). 1995. pap. 4.95 (0-06-440575-3, HarpTrophy) HarpC Child Bks.

On the Other Side of the Hill. Roger Lea Macbride. LC 95-14263. (Little House). (Illus.). 356p. (J). (gr. 4-7). 1995. 15.95 (0-06-024967-6) HarpC Child Bks.

On the Other Side of the Hill. Roger Lea Macbride. (Little House). (Illus.). (J). (gr. 3-6). 1995. 10.05 (0-606-08450-9, Pub. by Turtleback) Demco.

On the Other Side of the Rainbow. Dinker Dawg. (Illus.). 128p. 1997. 14.00 (1-887750-66-5) Rutledge Bks.

On the Other Side of the River. John E. Sorrell. LC 91-37276. (First Poetry Ser.). 160p. 1992. pap. 9.95 (0-922811-15-6) Mid-List.

On the Other Side of the Sea. Yan Ge Lin. (CHI.). pap. 12.95 (7-5387-0918-5, Pub. by China Intl Bk) Distribks Inc.

On the Other Side the Garden. Fugate. 1994. pap. text, wbk. ed. 9.95 (0-86717-010-7) Alpha AZ.

On the Outside. Emma W. Mereday. 80p. (Orig.). 1995. pap. 25.00 (0-9647131-0-1) Emmae.

On the Outside: Extraordinary People in Search of Ordinary Lives. Ed. by Julie Pratt. (Illus.). 97p. 1998. pap. 6.95 (0-9662522-0-9) WV Dev Disabilities.

On the Outside Looking In. Michael Reagan & Joe Hyams. 1988. 17.95 (0-8217-2392-8, Zebra Kensgtn) Kensgtn Pub Corp.

On the Outside Looking In. Vacirca Vaughn. (Illus.). 100p. 2000. pap. 10.00 (1-886383-95-2) Pride & Imprints.

On the Outside Looking In: A Year in an Inner-City High School. Cristina Rathbone. 400p. 1999. reprint ed. pap. 14.00 (0-87113-736-4, Atlntc Mnthly) Grove-Atltic.

On the Outside Looking Out. John Shoptaw. LC 94-25956. 432p. 1995. text 56.00 (0-674-63612-0); pap. text 25.95 (0-674-63613-9, SHOOUX) HUP.

On the Padre's Trail. Christopher Vecsey. LC 96-9754. (American Indian Catholics Ser.: Vol. 1). xvii, 440p. (C). 1996. text 50.00 (0-268-03702-7) U of Notre Dame Pr.

On the Pampas. Maria C. Brusca. LC 90-40938. (Illus.). 40p. (J). (ps-2). 1995. pap. 5.95 (0-8050-2919-2, Bks Young Read) H Holt & Co.

On the Pampas. Maria Cristina Brusca. (Owlet Bks.). 1993. 11.15 (0-606-05960-1, Pub. by Turtleback) Demco.

On the Parish. Raymond K. Grant. 108p. (C). 1989. 59.00 (0-905243-13-7, Pub. by D Brown & Sons Ltd) St Mut.

On the Parts of the Animals. Aristotle. Tr. & Intro. by William Ogle. LC 86-29613. 263p. 1987. reprint ed. 40.00 (0-8240-6925-0) Garland.

On the Path to Void: Buddhist Art of the Tibetan Realm. Ed. by Pratapaditya Pal. LC 96-900302. (C). 1996. 95.00 (81-85026-33-5, Pub. by Marg Publns) Art Media Resources.

On the Peace: Second Philippic on Chersonesus & Third Philippic. Demosthenes. Ed. by W. R. Connor. LC 78-18602. (Greek Texts & Commentaries Ser.). 1979. reprint ed. lib. bdg. 36.95 (0-405-11443-5) Ayer.

On the People's Democratic Dictatorship. Mao Tse-Tung. 1951. 6.95 (0-88710-052-X) Yale Far Eastern Pubns.

On the Perfect State. Abu N. Al-Farabi. 500p. (C). 1997. 59.95 (1-871031-71-0) Kazi Pubns.

On the Periphery of Nineteenth-Century Mexico: Sonora & Sinaloa, 1810-1877. Stuart Voss. LC 81-21983. 318p. 1982. 41.95 (0-8165-0768-6) U of Ariz Pr.

On the Permanent Validity of the Church's Missionary Mandate: Redemptoris Missio. John Paul, II, pseud. 160p. (Orig.). (C). 1990. pap. 6.95 (1-55586-424-4) US Catholic.

On the Person of Christ: The Christology of Emperor Justinian. Tr. by Kenneth P. Wesche from GRE. 203p. (Orig.). 1991. pap. 12.95 (0-88141-089-6) St Vladimirs.

On the Phenomenology of the Consciousness of Internal Time (1883-1913) Edmund Husserl. Tr. by John B. Brough from GER. (Husserliana Collected Works). 464p. 1991. lib. bdg. 210.00 (0-7923-0891-3, Pub. by Kluwer Academic) Kluwer Academic.

On the Philosophical Stone: The Little Book of Lambsprinck. Patrick Smith. (Alchemical Studies: Vol. 19). (Illus.). 1999. pap. 9.95 (1-55818-456-2, Alchemical) Holmes Pub.

On the Philosophy of Aristotle: Fragments of the First Five Books. Nicolaus Damascenus. 1969. pap. 34.00 (90-04-01725-9, PHA, 13) Brill Academic Pubs.

On the Philosophy of History. Jacques Maritain. LC 73-128059. 180p. 1973. reprint ed. 29.50 (0-678-02760-9) Kelley.

***On the Phone, Incl. bandages.** Patricia Quinlan. (Life Skills for Little Ones Ser.). (Illus.). 24p. (J). (ps-k). 1998. pap. 12.95 (1-895897-24-6) Somerville Hse.

On the Pig's Back: An Autobiographical Excursion. Bill Naughton. 266p. 1991. 21.95 (1-85089-530-9, Pub. by ISIS Lrg Prnt) Transaction Pubs.

On the Pilgrim's Way: Christian Stewardship & the Tithe. John Brackett. LC 96-23112. 144p. 1996. pap. 10.95 (0-8192-1663-1) Morehouse Pub.

On the Pilgrims' Way: Conversations on Christian Discipleship. J. Nelson Kraybill. LC 98-40632. 240p. 1999. pap. 15.99 (0-8361-9097-1) Herald Pr.

On the Pill: A Social History of Oral Contraceptives, 1950-1970. Elizabeth S. Watkins. LC 98-5003. (Illus.). 208p. 1998. 25.95 (0-8018-5876-3) Johns Hopkins.

On the Placement & Morphology of Clitics. Aaron L. Halpern. 1995. text 49.95 (1-881526-61-5) CSLI.

On the Placement & Morphology of Clitics. Aaron L. Halpern. (Dissertations in Linguistics Ser.). 1995. pap. 22.95 (1-881526-60-7) CSLI.

On the Placement & Morphology of Clitics. Aaron L. Halpern. (CSLI Lecture Notes Ser.). 1995. 49.95 (0-521-52661-2) Cambridge U Pr.

***On the Plains.** Peter Brown. LC 98-46999. (Illus.). 128p. 1999. 39.95 (0-393-04730-X) Norton.

On the Plains with Custer & Hancock: The Journal of Isaac Coates, Army Surgeon. W. J. Kennedy. LC 96-32360. (Illus.). 208p. 1997. 24.95 (1-55566-183-1); pap. 16.95 (1-55566-184-X) Johnson Bks.

On the Plantation: A Story of a Georgia Boy's Adventures During the War. Joel Chandler Harris & William C. McDonald. Ed. by Pia S. Seagrave. LC 97-30540. (Illus.). 280p. 1997. pap. 19.95 (1-887901-16-7) Sergeant Kirk.

On the Plantation: A Story of a Georgia Boy's Adventures During the War. Joel Chandler Harris. LC 79-5189. (Brown Thrasher Bks.). (Illus.). 248p. 1980. reprint ed. pap. 12.95 (0-8203-0495-6) U of Ga Pr.

On the Playground. Playskool Staff. (J). 1999. 5.99 (0-525-45623-6) NAL.

***On the Plaza: The Politics of Public Space & Culture.** Setha M. Low. LC 99-50899. (Illus.). 288p. 2000. 40.00 (0-292-74713-6); pap. 18.95 (0-292-74714-4) U of Tex Pr.

On the Plurality of Actual Worlds. Andrew L. Blais. LC 96-51454. 240p. (C). 1997. text 35.00 (1-55849-072-8) U of Mass Pr.

On the Poems of Henry Vaughan: Characteristics & Intimations. Edmund C. Blunden. (BCL1-PR English Literature Ser.). 64p. 1992. reprint ed. lib. bdg. 59.00 (0-7812-7416-8) Rprt Serv.

On the Poems of Tennyson. Ward Hellstrom. LC 72-150654. 172p. 1972. 18.95 (0-8130-0322-9) U Press Fla.

On the Poetry of Allen Ginsberg. Ed. by Lewis Hyde. (Under Discussion Ser.). 480p. 1984. pap. text 19.95 (0-472-06353-7, 06353) U of Mich Pr.

On the Poetry of Galway Kinnell: The Wages of Dying. Ed. by Howard Nelson. 304p. 1988. text 42.50 (0-472-09376-2, 09376); pap. text 18.95 (0-472-06376-6, 06376) U of Mich Pr.

On the Poetry of Keats. E. C. Pettet. LC 83-45459. reprint ed. 34.50 (0-404-20200-4) AMS Pr.

On the Poetry of Philip Levine: Stranger to Nothing. Ed. by Christopher Buckley. 376p. 1990. pap. 18.95 (0-472-06392-8, 06392); text 44.50 (0-472-09392-4, 09392) U of Mich Pr.

On the Poetry of Spenser & the Form of Romances. John Arthos. LC 77-119951. (Select Bibliographies Reprint Ser.). 1977. 19.95 (0-8369-5394-0) Ayer.

On the Political Economy of Social Democracy: Selected Papers of J.C. Weldon. J. C. Weldon. Ed. by Allen Fenichel & Sidney H. Ingerman. 240p. (C). 1991. text 65.00 (0-7735-0812-0, Pub. by McG-Queens Univ Pr) CUP Services.

On the Political System of the Islamic State. Muhammad S. El-Awa. 1980. pap. 4.50 (0-89259-107-2) Am Trust Pubns.

On the Political System of the Islamic State. Muhammad S. El-Awa. 132p. 1996. pap. 5.50 (0-614-21496-3, 919) Kazi Pubns.

On the Possibility & Desirability of Peace. abr. ed. Leonard Lewin. LC 67-27553. 43p. 1987. reprint ed. pap. 5.00 (0-942153-18-9) Entropy Conserv.

On the Possibility of a Vortex Theory of Matter. Valerii Chalidze. 20p. 1992. pap. 7.00 (1-56541-179-X) Chalidze.

On the Possibility of Jewish Mysticism in Our Time: And Other Essays. Gershom Scholem. Ed. by Avraham Shapira. Tr. by Jonathan Chipman from GER. LC 96-48613. 1997. 24.95 (0-8276-0579-X) JPS Phila.

***On the Postcolony.** Achille Mbembe. (Studies on the History of Society & Culture: Vol. 41). (Illus.). 292p. 2001. 45.00 (0-520-20434-4, Pub. by U CA Pr); pap. 16.95 (0-520-20435-2, Pub. by U CA Pr) Cal Prin Full Svc.

On the Practice of Safety. 2nd ed. Fred A. Manuele. 304p. 1997. 74.95 (0-471-29213-3, VNR) Wiley.

On the Practice of Safety. 2nd ed. Fred A. Manuele. LC 97-26554. (Occupational Health & Safety Ser.). (Illus.). 268p. 1997. 54.95 (0-442-02423-1, VNR) Wiley.

***On the Pragmatics of Communication.** Jurgen Habermas. LC 98-18171. (Studies in Contemporary German Social Thought). (Illus.). 416p. 1998. 35.00 (0-262-08265-9) MIT Pr.

***On the Pragmatics of Communication.** Jurgen Habermas. LC 98-18171. (Illus.). 464p. 2000. reprint ed. pap. 18.50 (0-262-58187-6) MIT Pr.

***On the Pragmatics of Social Interaction: Preliminary Studies in the Theory of Communicative Action.** Jurgen Habermas. (Studies in Contemporary German Social Thought). (Illus.). 322p. 2000. 30.00 (0-262-08288-8) MIT Pr.

On the Prairie of Palo Alto: Historical Archaeology of the U. S.-Mexican War Battlefield. Charles M. Haecker & Jeffrey G. Mauck. LC 97-12335. (Texas A&M University Military History Ser.: Vol. 55). (Illus.). 248p. 1997. 39.95 (0-89096-758-X) Tex A&M Univ Pr.

On the Prayer of Jesus: With Introduction & "The Prayer Rope" by an Exiled Athonite Monk. Ignatius Brianchaninov. Ed. by Gregory Williams. Tr. by Lazarus Moore from RUS. 112p. 1995. 15.00 (0-912927-61-5, X047) St John Kronstadt.

On the Prejudices, Predilections & Firm Beliefs of William Faulkner. Cleanth Brooks. LC 87-2968. (Southern Literary Studies). 168p. 1987. 16.95 (0-8071-1391-3) La State U Pr.

On the Preparation & Delivery of Sermons: Fourth Edition. 4th ed. John A. Broadus. LC 78-20602. 368p. 1979. 25.00 (0-06-061112-X, Pub. by Harper SF) HarpC.

On the Present Unsettled Condition of the Law & Its Administration. John Miller. iv, 172p. 1995. reprint ed. 30.00 (0-8377-2478-3, Rothman) W S Hein.

***On the Press.** Wicker. 2001. pap. text. write for info. (0-312-25844-5) St Martin.

On the Priesthood. John Chrysostom. 160p. 1977. pap. 8.95 (0-913836-38-9) St Vladimirs.

On the Principles of Political Economy & Taxation. David Ricardo. 597p. 1977. reprint ed. 96.20 (3-487-06311-5) G Olms Pubs.

On the Probable Fall in the Value of Gold: The Commercial & Social Consequences Which May Ensue, & the Measures Which It Invites. Michel Chevalier. 211p. 1968. reprint ed. lib. bdg. 69.50 (0-8371-0045-3, CHPF, Greenwood Pr) Greenwood.

On the Problem of Empathy. Edith Stein. (Collected Works of Edith Stern). 160p. (C). 1989. text 101.50 (0-7923-0485-3) Kluwer Academic.

On the Problem of Surrogate Parenthood: Analyzing the Baby in Case. Ed. by Herbert W. Richardson. LC 87-24752. (Symposium Ser.: Vol. 25). 144p. 1987. lib. bdg. 69.95 (0-88946-717-X) E Mellen.

On the Production of Knowledge. Hein Streefkerk. 75p. 1993. pap. text 15.00 (90-5383-188-6, Pub. by VU Univ Pr) Paul & Co Pubs.

On the Properties of Things: John Trevisa's Translation of Bartholomaeus Anglicus, De Proprietatibus Rerum: A Critical Text, Vol. III. John De Trevisa. 338p. 1988. text 125.00 (0-19-818530-8) OUP.

On the Pulse of Morning. Maya Angelou. LC 93-83496. 32p. 1993. pap. 6.00 (0-679-74838-5) Random.

***On the Purity of the Art of Logic: The Shorter & the Longer Treatises.** Walter Burley. Tr. by Paul V. Spade. 384p. 2000. 60.00 (0-300-08200-2) Yale U Pr.

***On the Race History & Facial Characteristics of the Aboriginal Americans.** William H. Holmes. (LC History-America-E). 432p. 1999. reprint ed. lib. bdg. 99.00 (0-7812-4259-2) Rprt Serv.

On the Rack. Gerald Locklin. 24p. (Orig.). 1988. pap. 4.00 (0-916155-09-9) Trout Creek.

On the Radio: Music Radio in Britain. Stephen Barnard. 176p. 1989. 113.00 (0-335-15284-8); pap. 41.95 (0-335-15130-2) OpUniv Pr.

On the Rails: A Woman's Journey. 2nd ed. Linda Niemann. LC 96-45546. Orig. Title: Boomer: Railroad Memoirs. 250p. 1997. reprint ed. pap. 14.95 (1-57344-064-7) Cleis Pr.

On the Rails Around Britain & Ireland. Neil Wenborn. (Illus.). 352p. (Orig.). 1995. pap. 14.95 (0-8442-9020-3, Passprt Bks) NTC Contemp Pub Co.

On the Rails Around Britain & Ireland: Day Trips & Holidays by Train. 2nd ed. Neil Wenborn. (On the Rails Around . . . Ser.). (Illus.). 352p. 1998. pap. 16.95 (0-8442-4955-6, 49556, Passprt Bks) NTC Contemp Pub Co.

On the Rails Around Eastern Europe: A Comprehensive Guide to Travel by Train. Anthony J. Lambert. (On the Rails Around . . . Ser.). (Illus.). 352p. (Orig.). 1996. pap. 16.95 (0-8442-9992-8, 99982, Passprt Bks) NTC Contemp Pub Co.

On the Rails Around Europe. Thomas Cook. 416p. 1995. pap. 14.95 (0-8442-9037-8, Passprt Bks) NTC Contemp Pub Co.

On the Rails Around Europe: A Comprehensive Guide to Europe by Train. 2nd ed. Ed. by Melissa Shales. LC 95-71676. (Illus.). 424p. 1996. pap. text 15.95 (0-8442-9034-3, Passprt Bks) NTC Contemp Pub Co.

On the Rails Around Europe: The Practical Guide to Holidays by Train. 3rd ed. Melissa Shales. (On Rails Around . . . Ser.). (Illus.). 544p. 1998. pap. 18.95 (0-8442-4958-0, 49580, Passprt Bks) NTC Contemp Pub Co.

On the Real Side. Shirley E. Riley. (Illus.). 56p. 1989. pap. 6.50 (0-936073-05-5) Gumbs & Thomas.

On the Real Side: A History of African American Comedy. Mel Watkins. LC 98-52336. 654p. 1999. pap. 16.95 (1-55652-351-3, Pub. by Chicago Review) IPG Chicago.

On the Real Side: Laughing, Lying & Signifying - the Underground Tradition of African-American Humor that Transformed American Culture, from Slavery to Richard Pryor. Mel Watkins. (Illus.). 656p. 1995. 27.50 (0-671-68982-7) S&S Trade.

On the Real Side: Laughing, Lying & Signifying - the Underground Tradition of African-American Humor that Transformed American Culture, from Slavery to Richard Pryor. Mel Watkins. (Illus.). 656p. 1995. pap. 15.00 (0-671-51103-3, Touchstone) S&S Trade Pap.

On the Rebound: Helping Workers Cope with Plant Closings. Terry F. Buss & Roger J. Vaughn. LC 88-38398. 1989. 14.95 (0-934842-57-4) CSPA.

On the Receiving End: A Collection of Works for Realizing the Potential Within Ourselves. Monica Davis. LC 97-71575. 144p. (Orig.). 1997. pap. 11.95 (1-56167-357-9) Am Literary Pr.

***On the Recent Advances of the Ultrasonic Nondestructive Evaluation & Composite Material Characterization: Proceedings International Mechanical Engineering Congress & Exposition.** Ed. by Tribikram Kundu & Vikram K. Kinra. (AMD-NDE Ser.: Vol. 234, Vol. 17). 133p. 1999. 100.00 (0-7918-1651-6) ASME Pr.

On the Record. John Gaffney. 188p. 1997. pap. 11.00 (1-879418-87-8) Audenreed Pr.

On the Reduction of Continental Armies. a Proposel see Arms Limitation: Plans for Europe Before 1914

On the Refinement Calculus. Ed. by Carroll Morgan & Trevor Vickers. LC 92-40591. (Formal Applications of Computing & Information Technology Ser.). 1994. 49.95 (0-387-19809-1) Spr-Verlag.

On the Refinement Calculus. Ed. by C. Morgan et al. (Formal Approaches to Computing & Information Technology Ser.). 176p. 1994. reprint ed. 46.95 (3-540-19931-4) Spr-Verlag.

On the Regulation of Currencies. 2nd ed. John Fullarton. LC 68-55714. (Library of Money & Banking History). xii, 253p. 1969. reprint ed. 45.00 (0-678-00571-0) Kelley.

On the Relations Between the Physical & Moral Aspects of Man, Vol. 1. Pierre J. Cabanis. Tr. by Margaret D. Saidi. LC 80-21694. 448p. reprint ed. pap. 138.90 (0-608-30801-3, 201994900001) Bks Demand.

On the Relations Between the Physical & Moral Aspects of Man, Vol. 2. George Mora. Tr. by Margaret D. Saidi. LC 80-21694. 438p. reprint ed. pap. 135.80 (0-608-30804-8, 201994900002) Bks Demand.

On the Relative-Frequence Interpretation of Finite Maximum-Entropy Distributions. Tony E. Smith. (Discussion Papers: No. 54). 1972. pap. 10.00 (1-55869-084-0) Regional Sci Res Inst.

On the Relative Stabilities of Conjugated Heterocycles Containing Divalent Sulfur (SR) M. Randic & Nenad Trinajstic. 48p. 1986. pap. text 53.00 (3-7186-0372-1) Gordon & Breach.

On the Reliability of Economic Models: Essays in the Philosophy of Economics. Ed. by Daniel Little. (Recent Economic Thought Ser.). 304p. (C). 1995. lib. bdg. 127.00 (0-7923-9494-1, Pub. by Kluwer Academic) Kluwer Academic.

On the Representation of Markovian Systems by Network Models. Victor L. Wallace. LC 70-137674. 121p. 1969. 19.00 (0-403-04544-4) Scholarly.

On the Revolutions. Nicolaus Copernicus. LC 92-16304. (Foundations of Natural History Ser.). (Illus.). 475p. reprint ed. pap. 147.30 (0-608-06276-6, 206660500008) Bks Demand.

On the Revolutions of Heavenly Spheres. Nicolaus Copernicus. Tr. by Charles G. Wallis. LC 95-35654. (Great Minds Ser.). 444p. 1995. pap. 8.95 (1-57392-035-5) Prometheus Bks.

***On the Rez.** Ian Frazier. LC 99-28353. (Illus.). 311p. 2000. text 25.00 (0-374-22638-5) FS&G.

On the Rheology of Blood & Synovial Fluids. Horst Chmiel & Eckehard Walitze. LC 80-40948. (Chemical Engineering Aspects of Biomedicine Research Studies: No. 1). (Illus.). 178p. reprint ed. pap. 55.20 (0-608-18492-6, 203149400075) Bks Demand.

On the Right Course. Irene Leland. (Illus.). 26p. (J). 1993. pap. text 11.95 (0-9646386-0-6) Uplifting Pr.

On the Right Track: A Spectator's Guide to the Olympic Running Events. Eric Olsen. xiv, 225 p. 1984. pap. write for info. (0-672-52807-X) Macmillan.

***On the Rim: Looking for the Grand Canyon.** Mark Neumann. LC 99-35133. 320p. 1999. 29.95 (0-8166-2784-3, Pub. by U of Minn Pr) Chicago Distribution Ctr.

***On the Rim: Looking for the Grand Canyon** Mark Neumann. LC 99-35133. 1999. pap. write for info. (0-8166-2785-1) U of Minn Pr.

On the Rim of Kilauea: Excerpts from the Volcano House Register, 1865-1955. Ed. by Darcy Bevens. LC 92-85122. (Illus.). 168p. (Orig.). 1992. pap. text 9.95 (0-940295-11-3) HI Natural Hist.

***On the Rim of Mexico: Encounters of the Rich & Poor.** Ramon E. Ruiz. LC 98-23319. 272p. 1998. 27.00 (0-8133-3499-3, Pub. by Westview) HarpC.

***On the Rim of Mexico: Encounters of the Rich & Poor.** Ramon Eduardo Ruiz. 1999. pap. 16.00 (0-8133-3734-8, Pub. by Westview) HarpC.

On the Rise & Growth of the Law of Nations: As Established by General Usage & by Treaties, from the Earliest Time to the Treaty of Utrecht. John Hosack. xii, 394p. 1982. reprint ed. 45.00 (0-8377-0647-5, Rothman) W S Hein.

O

An Asterisk (*) at the beginning of an entry indicates that the title is appearing for the first time.

On the Rise, New Traditions Cooking with Russell Siu. Russell Siu. Ed. by Arnold Hiura. LC 96-77949. (Illus.). 176p. 1996. 31.00 (*0-9654443-0-9*) L A K Ent.

On the Rite of Election. Rite. LC 94-10735. (Forum Essays Ser.: Vol. 3). 108p. 1994. pap. 6.00 (*1-56854-025-6*, ELECT) Liturgy Tr Pubns.

On the River ABC. Caroline Stutson. (Illus.). 32p. (J). (ps-2). 1997. pap. 7.95 (*1-57098-142-6*) Roberts Rinehart.

***On the River of Grace: A Spiritual Journey in the Alaskan Wilderness.** Liller Burk Cotter. LC 99-57087. 157p. 2000. pap. 12.95 (*1-887400-21-4*, EVB-1022) Earthen Vessel Prodns.

On the River Styx & Other Stories. Peter Matthiessen. LC 89-40508. 224p. 1990. pap. 8.95 (*0-685-29463-3*) Vin Bks.

On the River Styx & Other Stories. Peter Matthiessen. LC 89-40508. 224p. 1991. pap. 12.00 (*0-679-72852-X*) Vin Bks.

On the Road. (Hot Wheels Coloring & Activity Book Ser.). (Illus.). 96p. (J). (ps-1). 1998. pap. write for info. (*0-7666-0104-8*, Honey Bear Bks) Modern Pub NYC.

On the Road. (Illus.). 44p. 1998. 29.95 (*0-87633-121-5*) Phila Mus Art.

On the Road. Michael Burgan & Linda Jean Lally. (Illus.). 48p. 21.26 (*0-7368-0458-7*) Capstone Pr.

***On the Road.** Capstone Press Staff. 1999. 80.00 (*0-531-19418-3*) Capstone Pr.

On the Road. Joe Harris. 1999. pap. text 24.95 (*0-7851-0734-7*) Marvel Entrprs.

On the Road. Jack Kerouac. 1976. 24.95 (*0-8488-1401-0*) Amereon Ltd.

On the Road. Jack Kerouac. LC 91-178943. 310p. 1976. 35.95 (*0-89966-134-3*) Buccaneer Bks.

On the Road. Jack Kerouac. 1976. 18.05 (*0-606-03881-7*, Pub. by Turtleback) Demco.

On the Road. Jack Kerouac. 316p. 1976. pap. 12.95 (*0-14-004259-8*, Penguin Bks) Viking Penguin.

On the Road. Jack Kerouac. LC 91-13204. (Twentieth-Century Classics Ser.). xxxiii, 310p. (C). 1991. pap. 18.99 (*0-14-018521-6*) Viking Penguin.

On the Road. Jack Kerouac. 1999. pap. 13.95 (*0-14-028329-3*) Viking Penguin.

On the Road. abr. ed. Jack Kerouac. 1993. Price not set. incl. audio (*0-453-00830-5*, 391308, Pub. by Penguin-HghBrdg) Penguin Putnam.

On the Road: An Inside View of Life with a NHL Team. Howard Berger. (Illus.). 256p. 1995. pap. 14.95 (*1-895629-51-9*) Warwick Publ.

On the Road: Fun Travel Games & Activities. rev. ed. George Shea. (Illus.). 48p. (J). (gr. 3-10). 1998. pap. 4.95 (*0-8069-0316-3*) Sterling.

***On the Road: Kerouac's Ragged American Journey.** Robert Holton. LC 99-33122. Vol. 172. 1999. 29.00 (*0-8057-1692-0*, Twyne) Mac Lib Ref.

On the Road: The Quest for Stamps. Stephen R. Datz. 168p. (Orig.). 1991. pap. 9.95 (*0-88219-025-3*) General Trade.

On the Road: Trucks Then & Now see Here We Go! - Group 2

On the Road: 40th Anniversary Edition. anniversary ed. Jack Kerouac. LC 97-12899. 352p. 1997. 24.95 (*0-670-87478-7*) Viking Penguin.

On the Road - Again. Howard Berger. (Illus.). 256p. 1999. pap. 15.95 (*1-894020-62-6*, Pub. by Warwick Publ) Firefly Bks Ltd.

On the Road Again. Wayne Rostad. (Illus.). 320p. 1997. 24.95 (*0-7710-7582-0*) McCland & Stewart.

On the Road Again. Wayne Rostad. (Illus.). 352p. 1997. pap. text 19.99 (*0-7710-7583-9*) McCland & Stewart.

On the Road Again: Travel, Love & Marriage. William Hendricks & Jim Cote. LC 97-38083. 208p. 1998. pap. 9.99 (*0-8007-5649-5*) Revell.

***On the Road Again! Vol. 30: The Complete Rivers' Log.** Bob T. Epstein & Barbara Epstein. 2000. 13.95 (*0-9657854-9-1*) Wild Water.

***On the Road Again; The Best Years of Our Lives: Three Plays.** Laurence Allen. 180p. 2000. pap. 19.95 (*1-85411-265-1*, Pub. by Seren Bks) Dufour.

On the Road Again to the Far East - Fabulous Food - Fascinating Travel Adventures: Indonesia, Malaysia & Thailand-Via Plane, Ship, Bus, Pickup Truck & Elephant What a Way to Go! Maxine S. Sommers. Ed. by Thomas Tagliabue. (Illus.). 228p. 1992. spiral bd. 14.95 (*0-943991-17-X*) Pound Sterling Pub.

On the Road Again with Man's Best Friend: A Selective Guide to the Mid Atlantic Bed & Breakfast. Dawn Habgood. 1999. pap. text 17.95 (*0-933603-08-8*) Dawbert Pr.

On the Road Again with Man's Best Friend: An Insider's Guide to New England's B & Bs, Inns, & Hotels That Welcome You & Your Dog. 4th rev. ed. Dawn Habgood & Robert Habgood. Ed. by Pamela Gerloff. (Illus.). 395p. 1997. pap. 17.95 (*0-933603-03-7*) Dawbert Pr.

***On the Road Again with Man's Best Friend: An Insider's Guide to the B&B's, Inns, & Hotels Throughout the U. S. That Welcome You & Your Dog.** Dawn Habgood & Robert Habgood. Ed. by Jean Dooley. LC 99-173210. (Illus.). 898p. (Orig.). 1999. pap. 24.95 (*0-933603-09-6*) Dawbert Pr.

On the Road Again with Man's Best Friend: An Insider's Guide to the Southeast's B&Bs, Inns, & Hotels That Welcome You & Your Dog. 2nd ed. Dawn Habgood & Robert Habgood. Ed. by Pamela Gerloff. (Illus.). 288p. 1999. pap. 15.95 (*0-933603-06-1*) Dawbert Pr.

On the Road Again with Man's Best Friend: An Insider's Guide to the Southwest's B&Bs, Inns, & Hotels That Welcome You & Your Dog. 2nd rev. ed. Dawn Habgood & Robert Habgood. Ed. by Pamela Gerloff. (Illus.). 245p. 1997. pap. 15.95 (*0-933603-05-3*) Dawbert Pr.

On the Road Again with Man's Best Friend: An Insider's Guide to the West Coast's B & B, Inns, & Hotels That Welcome You & Your Dog. 5th rev. ed. Dawn Habgood & Robert Habgood. Ed. by Pamela Gerloff. (Illus.). 598p. 1997. pap. 19.95 (*0-933603-04-5*) Dawbert Pr.

On the Road Again with Man's Best Friend: California. Dawn Habgood & Robert Habgood. (On the Road Again with Man's Best Friends Ser.). (Illus.). 288p. (Orig.). 1996. 14.95 (*0-87605-716-4*) Howell Bks.

On the Road Again with Man's Best Friend: Mid Atlantic. Robert Habgood & Dawn Habgood. (Illus.). 272p. 1995. 14.95 (*0-87605-706-7*) Howell Bks.

On the Road Again with Man's Best Friend: New England. rev. ed. Robert Habgood & Dawn Habgood. (Illus.). 272p. 1995. 14.95 (*0-87605-705-9*) Howell Bks.

On the Road Again with Man's Best Friend: Northwest Washington, Oregon, British Columbia. Dawn Habgood & Robert Habgood. (On the Road Again with Man's Best Friend Ser.). (Illus.). 288p. (Orig.). 1996. 14.95 (*0-87605-714-8*) Howell Bks.

On the Road Again with Man's Best Friend: Southeast. Robert Habgood & Dawn Habgood. (Illus.). 272p. 1995. 14.95 (*0-87605-708-3*) Howell Bks.

On the Road Again with Man's Best Friend: Southwest. Dawn Habgood. LC 96-225113. 288p. 1996. pap. text 14.95 (*0-87605-710-5*) Howell Bks.

On the Road Again with Man's Best Friend (Eastern U. S.) A Selective Guide to the Best Places to Stay with Your Dog in the Eastern United States. Robert P. Habgood & Dawn W. Habgood. Ed. by Jean Dooley. (Illus.). 750p. 2000. pap. 19.95 (*0-933603-32-0*, Pub. by Dawbert Pr) IPG Chicago.

***On the Road Again with Man's Best Friend (United States) A Detailed Guide to 18,000 Accommodations that Welcome Pets.** Dawn Habgood & Robert Habgood. (Illus.). 888p. 2000. pap. 19.95 (*0-933603-11-8*, Pub. by Dawbert Pr) IPG Chicago.

***On the Road Again with Man's Best Friend (Western U. S.) A Selective Guide to Bed & Breakfasts, Inn, Hotels & Resorts that Welcome You & Your Pet.** Dawn Habgood & Robert Habgood. (Illus.). 640p. 2000. pap. 19.95 (*0-933603-31-2*, Pub. by Dawbert Pr) IPG Chicago.

On the Road Around California. Maxine Cass & Fred Gebhardt. 352p. 1994. pap. 14.95 (*0-8442-9015-7*, Passprt Bks) NTC Contemp Pub Co.

On the Road Around Capital Region U. S. A. Eric Bailey et al. (On the Road Around... Ser.). (Illus.). 372p. 1997. pap. 15.95 (*0-8442-4950-5*, 49505, Passprt Bks) NTC Contemp Pub Co.

On the Road around England & Wales: Driving Holidays, Short Breaks & Day Trips Across England & Wales. Ed. by Eric Bailey & Ruth Bailey. (On the Road Around...Ser.). (Illus.). 372p. 1998. pap. 17.95 (*0-8442-9995-2*, 99952, Passprt Bks) NTC Contemp Pub Co.

On the Road Around Florida: The Complete Fly - Drive Guide. Maxine Cass et al. LC 96-233497. (Illus.). 352p. 1995. pap. 14.95 (*0-8442-9014-9*, Passprt Bks) NTC Contemp Pub Co.

On the Road Around Normandy, Brittany, & the Loire Valley: Driving Holidays in Northern France. Ed. by Roger Thomas. (On the Road Around . . . Ser.). (Illus.). 352p. 1996. pap. text 14.95 (*0-8442-9011-4*, 90114, Passprt Bks) NTC Contemp Pub Co.

On the Road around Northern Italy: Driving Holidays & Tours in Tuscany, Umbria, the Italian Lakes & Rivieria, Veneto & the South Tyrol. Ed. by Christopher Catling. LC DG416.O5 1998. (On the Road Around...Ser.). (Illus.). 372p. 1998. pap. 17.95 (*0-8442-9994-4*, 99944, Passprt Bks) NTC Contemp Pub Co.

On the Road Back. Ruth Soderstrom. 120p. 1990. 12.95 (*0-945027-04-4*) Sparrow Hawk Pr.

On the Road for Work: Migratory Workers on the East Coast of the United States. G. Thomas-Lycklama Niejolt. (Ser. on the Development of Societies: Vol. VII). 224p. 1980. lib. bdg. 73.50 (*0-89838-043-X*) Kluwer Academic.

On the Road from Start to Story: Writing Creatively & All That Fun Stuff. Betty Grimshaw. 100p. 1999. wbk. ed. 13.99 (*0-9668240-0-8*) Janroy West.

On the Road in Egypt: A Motorist's Guide. Mary D. Megalli. (Illus.). 78p. 1990. pap. 14.95 (*977-424-202-5*, Pub. by Am Univ Cairo Pr) Col U Pr.

On the Road North of Boston: New Hampshire Taverns & Turnpikes, 1700-1900. Donna-Belle Garvin & James L. Garvin. (Illus.). 250p. (Orig.). 1988. pap. 19.95 (*0-915916-19-3*) NH Hist Soc.

On the Road of Stars: Native American Night Poems & Sleep Charms. Illus. by Judy Pedersen. LC 92-20001. 40p. (J). (gr. 1 up). 1994. mass mkt. 15.95 (*0-02-709735-8*, Mac Bks Young Read) S&S Childrens.

***On the Road of the Winds.** Patrick V. Kirch. LC 99-36664. 416p. 2000. 45.00 (*0-520-22347-0*, Pub. by U CA Pr) Cal Prin Full Svc.

On the Road Review. Heidi Matthews & Eric Walser. 156p. 1999. 29.95 (*1-889366-10-2*) Cramer Prods.

***On the Road to Alaska (Fiction by Ray Miller)** Ray Miller. 33p. 2000. pap. 6.00 (*1-882983-48-3*) March Street Pr.

On the Road to Autonomy: Promoting Self-Competence in Children & Youth with Disabilities. Ed. by Laurie E. Powers et al. LC 96-10802. 432p. 1996. pap. text 48.00 (*1-55766-235-5*, 2355) P H Brookes.

On the Road to Bethlehem. unabridged ed. Judy McGorray. Ed. by Del Meyers & David McGorray. 43p. 1997. spiral bd. 10.00 (*1-888200-16-2*) JayMac Commun.

***On the Road to Coronation.** Harold N. Wendt. (Illus.). 56p. 2000. pap. text. write for info. (*1-891245-04-X*) Crossways Intl.

***On the Road to Damascus.** Gerren Liles. vi, 96p. 2000. pap. 10.95 (*0-9671082-2-5*, Division of Wrds) Black Alchemist.

On the Road to Detour. Thomas E. Grothus. (Illus.). 20p. (Orig.). 1982. pap. 3.00 (*0-930257-00-6*) Function Ind Pr.

On the Road to Economic Development: A Guide for Continuing Education Programs at Historically Black Colleges & Universities. Peggy A. Richmond & Sheilah Maramark. (Illus.). 89p. (Orig.). (C). 1997. pap. text 30.00 (*0-7881-3996-7*) DIANE Pub.

On the Road to Economic Development: Continuing Education Programs at Historically Black Colleges & Universities. Peggy A. Richmond. 95p. 1997. pap. 13.00 (*0-16-063605-1*) USGPO.

On the Road to Economic Freedom: An Agenda for Black Progress. Ed. by Robert L. Woodson. LC 87-9823. 140p. 1987. 16.95 (*0-89526-578-8*) Regnery Pub.

On the Road to Emmaus: Eucharist Renewal Today. Donal Murray. 1989. pap. 25.00 (*1-85390-111-3*, Pub. by Veritas Pubns) St Mut.

On the Road to EU Accession: Financial Sector Development in Central Europe. Michael S. Borish et al. (Discussion Paper Ser.: No. 345). 176p. 1996. pap. 22.00 (*0-8213-3800-5*, 13800) World Bank.

On the Road to Freedom: A Pilgrimage in India. Neal Rosner. 282p. (Orig.). 1987. 13.00 (*0-9615875-4-7*) M A Ctr.

***On the Road to Freedom Vol. 2: A Pilgrimage to India.** Swami Paramatmananda. (Illus.). 242p. 2000. pap. 13.00 (*1-879410-68-0*, Pub. by M A Ctr) New Leaf Dist.

On the Road to Higher Ground: The Poetry of God's Word. David E. Welch. (Illus.). 72p. (Orig.). 1996. pap. 5.95 (*0-9654391-0-0*) CJ Scott Pubng.

On the Road to Learning. (Fisher-Price Preschool Workbook Series II). (Illus.). 72p. (J). (ps). 1997. pap. write for info. (*1-56144-921-0*, Honey Bear Bks) Modern Pub NYC.

***On the Road to Love.** Leta N. Childers. 1999. 6.50 incl. audio (*1-58495-026-9*) DiskUs Publishing.

On the Road to Mandalay: Portraits of Ordinary People. Mya T. Tint. 284p. 1999. pap. 23.00 (*974-8299-25-2*, Pub. by Weatherhill) Weatherhill.

On the Road to Michigan's Past. Larry B. Massie. (Illus.). 288p. 1995. 18.95 (*1-886167-04-4*); pap. 12.50 (*1-886167-03-6*) Priscilla Pr.

On the Road to Motherhood. M. J. Bovo. 1997. pap. text 19.95 (*1-889972-33-9*) Newpt Media.

On the Road to Nirvana. Gina Arnold. (Illus.). 224p. (Orig.). 1993. pap. 13.95 (*0-312-09376-4*) St Martin.

On the Road to Nowhere: A History of Greer, Arizona, 1879-1979. 2nd ed. Karen M. Applewhite. (Illus.). 122p. reprint ed. pap. text 7.95 (*0-9603472-0-8*) Applewhite.

On the Road! to Oz. V. Glasgow Koste. 52p. 1983. reprint ed. pap. 3.50 (*0-87129-032-4*, O43) Dramatic Pub.

On the Road to Perfection: Christian Humility in Modern Society. George A. Maloney. 144p. 1995. pap. 9.95 (*1-56548-035-X*) New City.

On the Road to Rebellion: The United Irishmen & Hamburg, 1796-1803. Paul Weber. 205 p. 1997. boxed set 45.00 (*1-85182-311-5*, Pub. by Four Cts Pr) Intl Spec Bk.

On the Road to Same Sex Marriage: A Supportive Guide to Psychological, Political & Legal Issues. Ed. by Robert P. Cabaj & David W. Purcell. LC 97-24507. 256p. 1997. mass mkt. 23.00 (*0-7879-0962-9*) Jossey-Bass.

On the Road to Tara: The Making of Gone with the Wind. Aljean Harmetz. (Illus.). 224p. 1996. 39.95 (*0-8109-3684-4*, Pub. by Abrams) Time Warner.

On the Road to Tara: The Making of Gone with the Wind. Aljean Harmetz. 1996. pap. 39.95 (*0-8109-2678-4*) Abrams.

On the Road to Tetlama: Mexican Adventures of a Wandering Naturalist. Jim Conrad. (Illus.). 196p. 1991. 21.95 (*0-8027-1152-9*) Walker & Co.

On the Road to the Healing Place Vol. I: "Life Extension - The Ultimate Revolutionary Act" A. S. Sharif. 140p. 1993. 24.95 (*0-9637036-0-9*) Sharif Ent.

On the Road to the Wolf's Lair: German Resistance to Hitler. Theodore S. Hamerow. LC 96-44364. (Illus.). 464p. 1997. 29.95 (*0-674-63680-5*) Belknap Pr.

On the Road to the Wolf's Lair: German Resistance to Hitler. Theodore S. Hamerow. 1999. pap. 18.95 (*0-674-63681-3*) HUP.

On the Road to the World Championship, Nineteen Twenty-Three to Twenty-Seven. A. Alekhine. Ed. by Kenneth P. Neat. Tr. by C. J. Feather. LC 84-3051. (Chess Ser.). (Illus.). 250p. 1984. 29.95 (*0-08-029731-5*, Pergamon Pr) Elsevier.

On the Road to Total War: The American Civil War & the German Wars of Unification, 1861-1871. Ed. by Stig Forster & Jorg Nagler. (Publications of the German Historical Institute, Washington, D.C.). (Illus.). 717p. (C). 1997. text 95.00 (*0-521-56071-3*) Cambridge U Pr.

On the Road to Tribal Extinction: Depopulation, Deculturation, & Adaptive Well-Being among the Batak of the Philippines. James F. Eder. (C). 1992. pap. 16.95 (*0-520-07882-9*, Pub. by U CA Pr) Cal Prin Full Svc.

On the Road to Tribal Extinction: Depopulation, Deculturation, & Maladaptation among the Batak of the Philippines. James F. Eder. LC 87-1861. (Illus.). 292p. 1987. 55.00 (*0-520-06046-6*, Pub. by U CA Pr) Cal Prin Full Svc.

On the Road to Unification for the Law of Sales. John Honnold. 1984. pap. text 24.00 (*90-6544-166-2*) Kluwer Law Intl.

On the Road to Vegetarian Cooking: Easy Meals for Everyone. Anne Lukin. (Illus.). 255p. 1991. pap. 14.95 (*0-929005-28-7*, Pub. by Sec Story Pr) LPC InBook.

On the Road to Worldwide Science. Ed. by M. Moravscik. 576p. (C). 1989. text 114.00 (*9971-5-0617-3*); pap. text 44.00 (*9971-5-0620-3*) World Scientific Pub.

On the Road, Too. E. D. Santos. LC 88-83628. (Illus.). 263p. (Orig.). 1989. pap. 6.95 (*0-9621831-0-5*) La Sombra Pub.

On The Road With Archangel. Frederick Buechner. LC 97-4099. 160p. 1997. 17.00 (*0-06-061125-1*, Pub. by Harper SF) HarpC.

On the Road with Bob Hatch: 100 Injection Molding Problems Solved by IMM's Troubleshooter. Bob Hatch. LC 99-166172. (IMM Book Club Injection Molding Management Ser.). (Illus.). 185p. 1997. pap. 49.00 (*0-9642570-8-4*) Abby Communs.

On the Road With Charles Kuralt. Charles Kuralt. 364p. 1986. mass mkt. 5.95 (*0-449-13067-3*) Fawcett.

On the Road with Mark Twain in California & Nevada. George J. Williams, III. LC 93-31. (Mark Twain in the West Ser.). 136p. 1993. 29.95 (*0-935174-26-5*); pap. 16.95 (*0-935174-25-7*) Tree by River.

On the Road with NAFTA. James B. Reed & Janet Goehring. 16p. 1995. 15.00 (*1-55516-399-8*, 7302-2014) Natl Conf State Legis.

On the Road with Patsy Cline: Poems. John Reinhard. Ed. by John Minczeski. LC 96-67818. (Minnesota Voices Project Ser.: No. 77). 88p. 1996. pap. 11.95 (*0-89823-171-X*) New Rivers Pr.

On the Road with Poppa Whopper. Marianne Busser & Ron Schroder. LC 94-40590. (Illus.). 64p. (J). (gr. 1-4). 1997. pap. 5.95 (*1-55858-776-4*, Pub. by North-South Bks NYC) Chronicle Bks.

On the Road with the Archangel. large type ed. Frederick Buechner. LC 98-12005. (Inspirational Ser.). 152p. 1998. 22.95 (*0-7838-0129-7*, G K Hall & Co) Mac Lib Ref.

***On the Road with the Host of Public Radio's "Marketplace"** Brancaccio. 2000. write for info. (*0-684-86499-1*) S&S Trade.

On the Road with the Jimmy Dorsey Aggravation: 1947-1949. Eugene D. Bockemuehl. Ed. by Don Kader. LC 96-77334. (Illus.). v, 135p. (Orig.). 1996. pap. 14.95 (*0-9653272-0-5*) Gray Castle.

On the Road with Thibadeau Ya Ya: In North & South Carolina. Donna Gilbert. (Illus.). 48p. (Orig.). (J). (gr. 1-3). 1997. pap. 10.00 (*1-884570-74-7*) Research Triangle.

On the Road with Wellington: The Diary of a War Commissary. August Ludol Schaumann. LC 98-49193. 1999. 39.95 (*1-85367-353-6*) Kitch Keepsakes.

On the Road with Will Rogers. Lance Brown. LC 97-70649. (Illus.). 312p. (Orig.). 1997. pap. 14.00 (*1-879418-25-8*) Biddle Pub.

On the Roads to Modernity - Conscience, Science, & Civilizations: Selected Writings. Benjamin Nelson. Ed. by Toby E. Huff. LC 79-21321. 340p. 1981. 41.00 (*0-8476-6209-8*) Rowman.

On the Rock: The History of Madeline Island Told Through Its Families. Ed. by Michael J. Goc. (Illus.). 404p. 1997. 40.00 (*0-938627-37-6*); pap. 35.00 (*0-938627-36-8*) New Past Pr.

On the Rocks. Sandra Chick. (Livewire Ser.). 148p. (YA). (gr. 7-11). 1997. pap. 7.95 (*0-7043-4938-8*, Pub. by Womens Press) Trafalgar.

On the Rocks: Earth Science for Everyone. John S. Dickey. LC 95-46167. (Illus.). 280p. 1996. pap. 16.95 (*0-471-13234-9*) Wiley.

On the Rocks: Tales of Shipping & Insurance. C. Hewer & M. Grey. (C). 1982. 55.00 (*0-7855-4066-0*, Pub. by Witherby & Co) St Mut.

On the Rocks with Richard. R. M. Schneider. 64p. 1984. text 3.22 (*0-07-055476-5*) McGraw.

On the Rocks with Richard: Answer Key. R. M. Schneider. 1986. pap. text 1.53 (*0-07-055508-7*) McGraw.

On the Role of Division, Jordan & Related Algebras in Particle Physics. 480p. 1996. lib. bdg. 70.00 (*981-02-2863-5*) World Scientific Pub.

On the Roof. Ilya Kabakov. 1997. 95.00 (*3-928762-66-4*, Pub. by Richter Verlag) Dist Art Pubs.

On the Run. Philip Agee. 480p. 1987. 19.95 (*0-8184-0419-1*) Carol Pub Group.

On the Run. Christie Golden. (Invasion America Ser.). 1998. mass mkt. 5.99 (*0-451-45693-9*, ROC) NAL.

On the Run. John MacDonald. 1999. lib. bdg. 19.95 (*1-56723-165-9*) Yestermorrow.

On the Run. Jack Weyland. LC 95-2956. 188p. (YA). (gr. 9-12). 1995. 13.95 (*0-87579-891-8*) Deseret Bk.

On the Run. Kate William. (Sweet Valley High Super Thriller Ser.). (YA). (gr. 7 up). 1988. 9.60 (*0-606-03882-5*, Pub. by Turtleback) Demco.

***On the Run: Exercise & Fitness for Busy People.** Grete Waitz. (Illus.). 240p. 2000. pap. 14.95 (*1-57954-253-0*) Rodale Pr Inc.

On the Run: Exercise & Fitness for Busy People. Grete Waitz & Gloria Averbuch. LC 97-26320. (Illus.). 256p. 1997. text 19.95 (*0-87596-456-7*) Rodale Pr Inc.

On the Run: The Distraught Runner's Companion. Ron Yezzi. (Illus.). 92p. (Orig.). 1987. pap. 5.95 (*0-9619368-0-0*) G Bruno.

***On the Run: The Kids Are on the Run.** Jerry B. Jenkins & Tim LaHaye. (Left Behind: Bk. 10). (YA). (gr. 5 up). 2000. mass mkt. 5.99 (*0-8423-4330-X*) Tyndale Hse.

On the Run from Dogs & People. 3rd ed. Hal Higdon. LC 95-78899. (Illus.). 225p. 1995. pap. 14.95 (*0-9636346-2-3*) Rdrunner Pr.

On the Russian Front in World War I: Memoirs of an American War Correspondent. Stanley Washburn. 1982. 12.95 (*0-8315-0139-1*) Speller.

On the Rycroft Painter & Other Athenian Black-Figure Vase-Painters with a Feeling for Nature. Erik J. Holmberg. (Studies in Mediterranean Archaeology & Literature: No. 115). (Illus.). 41p. (Orig.). 1992. pap. 22.50 (*91-7081-027-3*, Pub. by P Astroms) Coronet Bks.

O

An Asterisk (*) at the beginning of an entry indicates that the title is appearing for the first time.

On the Safe Side: How to Teach Your Child to Be Safe, Strong, & Street Smart, Set. Paula Statman. (Illus.). 50p. 1992. student ed. 17.95 incl. audio (*0-9640042-0-8*) Picollo Pr CA.

On the Safe Side: Your Complete Reference to Childproofing for Infants & Toddlers. Cindy Wolf. LC 97-92701. 128p. 1998. pap. 12.95 (*0-9662569-5-6*) Whirlwind Pub.

On the Saints of Ireland. Cuimmin. Ed. & Tr. by Whitley Stokes from IRI. 1996. pap. 3.00 (*0-89979-081-X*) British Am Bks.

On the Salt March: The Historiography of Gandhi's March to Dandi. Thomas Weber. LC 97-913709. xxii, 594p. 1997. write for info. (*81-7223-263-2*) CE25.

On the Same Day in March. Marilyn Singer. LC 98-52797. (Illus.). 40p. (J). (ps-3). 2000. pap. 5.95 (*0-06-443528-8*) HarpC.

On the Same Day in March: A Tour of the World's Weather. Marilyn Singer. LC 98-52797. (Illus.). 40p. (J). (ps-3). 2000. 15.95 (*0-06-028187-1*); lib. bdg. 15.89 (*0-06-028188-X*) HarpC.

On the Santa Fe Trail. Ed. by Marc Simmons. LC 86-19001. (Illus.). x, 150p. 1986. 19.95 (*0-7006-0315-8*); pap. 9.95 (*0-7006-0316-6*) U Pr of KS.

On the Sawdust Trail: A Collection of Poems & Ballads. Donald R. Derk. 60p. 1998. pap. 10.95 (*1-57502-992-8*, PO2704) Morris Pubng.

On the Scene: Guide Roadside (Fifty Pack) AAA Foundation Staff. (Emergency Care Ser.). 16p. 1995. pap. 25.00 (*0-86720-525-3*) Jones & Bartlett.

On the Scent of Danger. large type ed. Phyllis Rossiter. LC 93-30109. 205p. 1993. lib. bdg. 13.95 (*0-7862-0045-6*) Thorndike Pr.

On the Scent with Sherlock Holmes. Walter Shepherd. (Illus.). 85p. Date not set. 15.95 (*0-934468-18-4*) Gaslight.

On the Score of Hospitality: Selected Receipts of a Van Rensselaer Family, Albany, New York 1785-1835. rev. ed. Ed. by Jane C. Kellar et al. LC 86-81677. (Illus.). 112p. 1986. reprint ed. pap. 7.95 (*0-943366-06-2*) Hist Cherry Hill.

On the Scriptural Call to Legalize & Regulate the Drug Trade & to Protect the Sanctity of Life. Thomas J. Kuna-Jacob. 20p. 1992. ring bd. 2.70 (*1-878030-10-8*) Assn World Peace.

On the Search for Well-Being. Henry J. Bruton. LC 96-40106. 240p. (C). 1997. text 49.50 (*0-472-10791-7*, 10791) U of Mich Pr.

On the Selection of Gear Dynamic Factor & Application Factor Applying the Law of Mechanics to Judge the Truth of Empirical Data. C. C. Wang. (Nineteen Eighty-Nine Fall Technical Meeting Ser.: Vol. 89FTM5). (Illus.). 14p. 1989. pap. text 30.00 (*1-55589-544-1*) AGMA.

On the Self-Regulation of Behavior. Charles S. Carver & Michael F. Scheier. LC 98-15204. (Illus.). 300p. (C). 1998. 49.95 (*0-521-57204-5*) Cambridge U Pr.

On the Semantics of Wh-Clauses. Stephen Berman. LC 93-46330. 200p. 1994. text 15.00 (*0-8153-1742-5*) Garland.

On the Senescence of Human Vision. Robert A. Weale. LC 92-13162. (Oxford Medical Publications). (Illus.). 288p. (C). 1992. 75.00 (*0-19-262034-7*) OUP.

On the Sensations of Tone. Hermann Helmholtz. 576p. 1954. pap. 15.95 (*0-486-60753-4*) Dover.

On the Sensations of Tone. Hermann Helmholtz. 852p. 190.00 (*1-85506-664-5*) Thoemmes Pr.

On the Serendipity Road: Exploring the Unexpected. James R. Hine & Wayne F. Peate. 156p. 1998. pap. text 17.95 (*0-913951-05-6*) Develop Pubns.

On the Seventh Day: Portrait of the Artist As a Creative Writer. John Mitchell. LC 96-53995. (Plover Nivola Ser.). 90p. 1997. 15.95 (*0-917635-22-1*); pap. 7.95 (*0-917635-25-6*) Plover Pr.

***On the Seventh Day, He Rested: An Exploration of the Nature of Rest on Shabbat.** David Snyder. xi, 86p. 2000. pap. 19.95 (*0-9653689-4-7*) Tailor Pr.

On the Shape of Mathematical Arguments. A. J. Van Gasteren. Ed. by G. Goos & J. Hartmanis. (Lecture Notes in Computer Science Ser.: Vol. 445). viii, 181p. 1990. 28.00 (*0-387-52849-0*) Spr-Verlag.

On the Shore of That Beautiful Shore. Jack Matthews. 1991. pap. 3.50 (*0-87129-082-0*, O46) Dramatic Pub.

On the Shore of the Sundown Sea. T. H. Watkins. LC 90-42194. (American Land Classics). (Illus.). 131p. reprint ed. pap. 40.70 (*0-608-06087-9*, 206641900008) Bks Demand.

***On the Shores of Eternity: Poems from Tagore on Death & Immortality.** Deepak Chopra. Tr. by Rabindranath Tagore from BEN. LC 99-20930. 96p. 1999. 14.00 (*0-609-60564-X*) Harmony Bks.

On the Shores of Politics. Jacques Ranciere. Tr. by Liz Heron. (Phronesis Ser.). 256p. (C). 1995. pap. 18.00 (*0-86091-637-5*, B3632, Pub. by Verso) Norton.

On the Shores of Politics. Jacques Ranciere. Tr. by Liz Heron. (Phronesis Ser.). 256p. (C). (gr. 13). 1995. 60.00 (*0-86091-467-4*, B3628, Pub. by Verso) Norton.

On the Shores of the Mediterranean. Eric Newby. 1998. pap. 14.95 (*0-86442-621-6*) Lonely Planet.

On the Short Waves, 1923-1945: Broadcast Listening in the Pioneer Days of Radio. Jerome S. Berg. (Illus.). 280p. 1999. boxed set 42.50 (*0-7864-0506-6*) McFarland & Co.

On the Shoulder of Marti: Cuban Literature of the Angolan War. Donald Burness. (Illus.). 203p. (Orig.). 1996. pap. 16.00 (*0-89410-768-2*, Three Contnts) L Rienner.

On the Shoulders of a Giant. Marion R. Cody & Doris I. Walker. (Illus.). 180p. 1995. pap. text 9.95 (*1-57166-021-6*) Quixote Pr IA.

On the Shoulders of Freud: Freud, Lacan, & the Psychoanalysis of Phallic Ideology. Roberto Speziale-Bagliacca. 110p. (C). 1991. 34.95 (*0-88738-409-9*) Transaction Pubs.

On the Shoulders of Giants. Malcom E. Lines. (Illus.). 296p. 1994. 110.00 (*0-7503-0104-X*); pap. 34.00 (*0-7503-0103-1*) IOP Pub.

On the Shoulders of Giants. Craig Loehle. 201p. (Orig.). 1994. pap. 9.95 (*0-85398-362-3*) G Ronald Pub.

On the Shoulders of Giants: A Shandean Postscript. Robert K. Merton. LC 65-12859. (Illus.). 302p. 1985. 14.95 (*0-15-169962-3*) Harcourt.

On the Shoulders of Giants: A Shandean Postscript. Robert K. . Merton. LC 65-12859. (Illus.). 290p. 1967. pap. 4.95 (*0-15-668781-X*, Harvest Bks) Harcourt.

On the Shoulders of Giants: New Approaches to Numeracy. National Research Council Staff. Ed. by Lynn A. Steen. 144p. 1990. 17.95 (*0-309-04234-8*) Natl Acad Pr.

On the Shoulders of Giants: The Post-Italianate Edition. Robert K. Merton. LC 92-43871. (Illus.). xxxii, 348p. (C). 1993. pap. text 18.00 (*0-226-52086-2*) U Ch Pr.

On the Shoulders of Merchants: Exchange & the Mathematical Conception of Nature in Early Europe. Richard W. Hadden. LC 93-37849. (SUNY Series in Science, Technology, & Society). 191p. (C). 1994. pap. text 16.95 (*0-7914-2012-4*) State U NY Pr.

On the Shoulders of Merchants: Exchange & the Mathematical Conception of Nature in Early Modern Europe. Richard W. Hadden. LC 93-37849. (SUNY Series in Science, Technology, & Society). 191p. (C). 1994. text 49.50 (*0-7914-2011-6*) State U NY Pr.

On the Shoulders of Women: The Feminization of Psychotherapy. Ilene J. Philipson. LC 93-25404. 177p. 1993. lib. bdg. 24.95 (*0-89862-017-1*) Guilford Pubns.

On the Shuttle: Eight Days in Space. Barbara Bondar. 1993. 15.15 (*0-606-05961-X*, Pub. by Turtleback) Demco.

On the Shuttle: Eight Days in Space. Barbara Bondar & Roberta Bondar. (Illus.). 64p. (YA). (gr. 4 up). 1995. 16.95 (*1-895688-12-4*, Pub. by Owl Bks); pap. 8.95 (*1-895688-10-8*, Pub. by Owl Bks) Firefly Bks Ltd.

On the Side. Joyce Goldstein. LC 98-9542. (Williams-Sonoma Kitchen Library: Vol. 40). (Illus.). 108p. (gr. 11). 1999. 18.95 (*0-7370-2001-6*) T-L Custom Pub.

On the Side of My People. Louis A. Decaro. 1997. pap. text 19.00 (*0-8147-1891-4*) NYU Pr.

On the Side of My People: A Religious Life of Malcolm X. Louis A. Decaro, Jr. (Illus.). 328p. (C). 1995. text 45.00 (*0-8147-1864-7*) NYU Pr.

On the Sidelines. Emily Costello. (Soccer Stars Ser.: No. 2). 128p. (J). (gr. 3-7). 1998. pap. 3.99 (*0-553-48645-4*, Skylark BDD) BDD Bks Young Read.

On the Sidelines. Emily Costello. (Soccer Stars Ser.: No. 2). (J). (gr. 3-7). 1998. 9.09 (*0-606-13786-6*, Pub. by Turtleback) Demco.

On the Silence of the Declaration of Independence. Paul Eidelberg. LC 76-8759. 148p. (C). 1980. 22.50 (*0-87023-216-9*) U of Mass Pr.

On the Situation of the Orthodox Christian in the Contemporary World. Archbishop Averky. 12p. (Orig.). 1984. pap. 2.00 (*0-912927-12-7*, X012) St John Kronstadt.

On the Sky's Clayey Bottom: Sketches & Happenings from the Years of Silence. Zdenek Urbanek. Tr. by William Harkins. LC 91-39511. 232p. 1992. 17.95 (*0-941423-76-X*) FWEW.

On the Slates. limited ed. Clark Coolidge. 62p. 1992. 65.00 (*1-880392-05-4*) Flockophobic Pr.

On the Small Screen. Harold Himmelstein. LC 80-25141. 206p. 1981. 45.00 (*0-275-90646-9*, C0646, Praeger Pubs) Greenwood.

On the Smell of an Oily Rag. John Cherrington. (Illus.). 256p. pap. 12.95 (*0-85236-256-0*, Pub. by Farming Pr) Diamond Farm Bk.

On the Social Analysis of Science. David W. Chambers. 102p. (C). 1979. 33.00 (*0-86828-065-8*, Pub. by Deakin Univ) St Mut.

On the Social Contract. Jean-Jacques Rousseau. Ed. by Roger D. Masters. Tr. by Judith R. Masters. LC 77-86291. 245p. 1978. pap. text 11.95 (*0-312-69446-6*) St Martin.

On the Social Contract. rev. ed. Jean-Jacques Rousseau. Ed. & Tr. by Donald A. Cress. LC 88-28260. 112p. (C). 1988. pap. 5.95 (*0-87220-068-X*); lib. bdg. 24.95 (*0-87220-069-8*) Hackett Pub.

On the Social Origins of Medieval Institutions: Essays in Honor of Joseph F. O'Callaghan. Joseph F. O'Callaghan et al. LC 98-35744. (Medieval Mediterranean Ser.). xxiv, 348p. 1998. 128.00 (*90-04-11096-8*) Brill Academic Pubs.

On the Social Psychology of the Psychological Experiment: With Particular Reference to Demand Characteristics & Their Implications. Martin T. Orne. (Irvington Reprint Series in Psychology). (C). 1991. reprint ed. pap. text 1.30 (*0-8290-2624-X*, Y-678) Irvington.

On the Social Utility of Psychopathology: A Deviant Majority & Its Keepers. Nathaniel J. Pallone. 110p. 1985. 34.95 (*0-88738-048-4*) Transaction Pubs.

On the Sociology of Islam. 3rd ed. Ali Shariati. Tr. by Hamid Algar from PER. LC 79-83552. 1980. 19.95 (*0-933782-01-2*); pap. 9.95 (*0-933782-00-4*) Mizan Pr.

***On the Socratic Education: An Introduction to the Shorter Platonic Dialogues.** Christopher Bruell. LC 99-13993. 240p. 1999. 35.00 (*0-8476-9401-1*) Rowman.

On the Solution of the Differential Equations of Motion of a Double Pendulum. William E. Cederberg. LC 24-3604. (Augustana College Library Publications: No. 9). 62p. 1923. pap. 1.00 (*0-910182-06-X*) Augustana Coll.

On the Sonnets of Robert Frost: A Critical Examination of the 37 Poems. H. A. Maxson. LC 97-34951. 157p. 1997. lib. bdg. 32.50 (*0-7864-0389-6*) McFarland & Co.

On the Soul. Aristotle. Tr. & Comment by Hippocrates G. Apostle. LC 81-86481. (Apostle Translations of Aristotle's Works: Vol. 5). Orig. Title: De Anima. 225p. (C). 1981. pap. 15.00 (*0-9602870-9-4*); text 30.00 (*0-9602870-8-6*) Peripatetic.

On the Soul & Resurrection. St. Gregory of Nyssa. Tr. & Intro. by Catharine P. Roth. LC 92-36384. 1993. pap. 8.95 (*0-88141-120-5*) St Vladimirs.

On the Soul, Parva Naturalia, on Breath. Tr. by W. S. Hett. (Loeb Classical Library: No. 288). 546p. 1936. 18.95 (*0-674-99318-7*) HUP.

On the Sources of Patriarchal Rage: The Commonplace Books of William Byrd II & Thomas Jefferson & the Gendering of Power in the Eighteenth Century. Kenneth A. Lockridge. (Illus.). 133p. (C). 1993. text 42.50 (*0-8147-5069-9*) NYU Pr.

On the Sources of Patriarchal Rage: The Commonplace Books of William Byrd II & Thomas Jefferson & the Gendering of Power in the Eighteenth Century. Kenneth A. Lockridge. (Illus.). 133p. (C). 1994. pap. text 15.50 (*0-8147-5089-3*) NYU Pr.

On the Sources of the Nonne Prestes Tale. Kate O. Petersen. 144p. (C). 1966. lib. bdg. 75.00 (*0-8383-0673-X*) M S G Haskell Hse.

***On the South China Track: Perspectives on Anthropological Research & Teaching.** Ed. by Sidney C. H. Cheung. 279p. 1998. pap. 27.00 (*962-441-540-4*, Pub. by Chinese Univ of Hong Kong) St Mut.

On the Spanish-Moroccan Frontier: A Study in Ritual, Power & Ethnicity. Henk Driessen. 249p. 1992. 30.00 (*0-85496-702-8*) Berg Pubs.

On the Specification of Autocorrelated Errors. Tony E. Smith. (Discussion Papers: No. 67). 1973. pap. 10.00 (*1-55869-085-9*) Regional Sci Res Inst.

On the Spine of Time: A FlyFisher's Journey among Mountain People, Streams & Trout. Harry Middleton. LC 97-36183. 179p. 1997. pap. 18.00 (*0-87108-892-4*) Pruett.

***On the Spot Discovery Books (Package-Slipcase)** Angela Royston et al. (Illus.). 48p. (J). (gr. 1-2). 2000. write for info. (*1-57584-703-5*, Pub. by Rdrs Digest) S&S Trade.

On the Spot Geographies. Greta James & Rex Walford. LC 70-488617. 1968. write for info. (*0-582-18309-X*) Addison-Wesley.

On the Spring Tide: A Special Kind of Courage. William Rowan. LC 98-72212. x, 201p. 1998. pap. 12.95 (*0-9662860-4-9*) Cenografix.

On the Stairs. Julie Hofstrand Larios. LC 99-25625. (Illus.). 32p. (J). (ps-1). 1999. 15.95 (*1-886910-34-0*, Pub. by Front Str) Publishers Group.

On the Stairs. Henry B. Fuller. (Collected Works of Henry B. Fuller). 1988. reprint ed. lib. bdg. 59.00 (*0-7812-1209-X*) Rprt Serv.

On the State of Europe Before & after the French Revolution. Friedrich Von Gentz. Tr. by John C. Herries. LC 73-118630. reprint ed. 69.50 (*0-404-02711-3*) AMS Pr.

On the State of the Public Health, 1995. 222p. 1996. pap. 35.00 (*0-11-321989-X*, HM1989X, Pub. by Statnry Office) Bernan Associates.

On the State of the Public Health, 1996. annuals HMSO Staff. 222p. 1997. pap. 40.00 (*0-11-322097-9*, HM20979, Pub. by Statnry Office) Bernan Associates.

On the State of the Public Health, 1997 Edition. HMSO Books Staff. (1997 Ser.). 1998. pap. text 40.00 (*0-11-322113-4*) Statnry Office.

On the Steppes of Central Asia. Matt Stone. Ed. by Richard D. Fuerle. 148p. (Orig.). 1992. pap. 10.95 (*0-9635918-0-0*) Spooner Pr.

On the Stoop. Macklyn W. Hubbell. LC 93-20924. 1994. 10.00 (*0-914520-30-X*) Insight Pr.

On the Storied Ohio. Reuben G. Thwaites. LC 75-127. (Mid-American Frontier Ser.). (Illus.). 1977. reprint ed. 29.95 (*0-405-06892-1*) Ayer.

***On the Streets.** Rupert Thomas. 224p. 1999. pap. 10.95 (*0-352-33374-X*) Virgin Bks.

On the Strength of a Planet Gear with an Integral Bearing (A Re-evaluation) Raymond J. Drago & Ravi N. Margasahayam. (Nineteen Eighty-Six Fall Technical Meeting Ser.: Vol. 86FTM9). (Illus.). 13p. 1986. pap. 30.00 (*1-55589-473-9*, 86FTM9) AGMA.

On the Stroll. Alix K. Shulman. (Cassandra Edition Ser.). 301p. 1987. reprint ed. pap. 10.00 (*0-89733-243-1*) Academy Chi Pubs.

***On the Structure of Physical Vacuum & a New Interaction in Nature Vol. 235: Theory, Experiment, Applications.** A. Baurov. LC 00-25277. (Horizons in World Physics Ser.). 217p. 2000. lib. bdg. 89.00 (*1-56072-805-1*) Nova Sci Pubs.

On the Study Methods of Our Time. Giambattista Vico. Tr. by Elio Gianturco & Donald Phillip Verene. LC 90-55226. xlix, 90p. 1990. reprint ed. text 29.95 (*0-8014-2543-3*); reprint ed. pap. text 10.95 (*0-8014-9778-7*) Cornell U Pr.

***On the Study of Celtic Literature & on Translating Homer.** Matthew Arnold. 320p. 1998. reprint ed. pap. 24.95 (*0-7661-0436-2*) Kessinger Pub.

On the Study of Chasidus: A Trilogy of Chasidic Essays. unabridged ed. Yosef Y. Schneerschn. 204p. 1997. 18.00 (*0-8266-0438-2*) Kehot Pubn Soc.

***On the Study of Greek Poetry.** Friedrich von Schlegel. (C). 2000. pap. text 18.95 (*0-7914-4830-4*) State U NY Pr.

***On the Study of Greek Poetry.** Friedrich von Schlegel. (C). 2001. text 57.50 (*0-7914-4829-0*) State U NY Pr.

On the Study of Indian Art. Pramod Chandra. (Illus.). 152p. (C). 1983. 31.50 (*0-674-63762-3*) HUP.

On the Subject of Drama. Ed. by David Hornbrook. LC 97-44628. 216p. (C). 1998. 75.00 (*0-415-16882-1*); pap. 24.99 (*0-415-16883-X*) Routledge.

On the Subject of "Java" John Pemberton. (Illus.). 320p. 1994. text 45.00 (*0-8014-2672-3*); pap. text 18.95 (*0-8014-9963-1*) Cornell U Pr.

On the Sublime see Classical Literary Criticism

On the Sublime. Longinus. (Loeb Classical Library). write for info. (*0-318-53145-3*) HUP.

On the Success of Failure: A Reassessment of the Effects of Retention in the Primary Grades. Karl L. Alexander et al. (Illus.). 284p. (C). 1995. text 54.95 (*0-521-41504-7*) Cambridge U Pr.

***On the Supposed Change in the Temperature of Winter.** Noah Webster. (Facsimile Edition Series of Historic Papers Published by the Academy: Vol. 2). Orig. Title: Memoirs of the Connecticut Academy of Arts & Sciences, Vol. 1, Pt. 1. 68p. 1999. pap. 12.50 (*1-878508-16-4*) CT Acad Arts & Sciences.

***On the Suppression of the Society of Jesus: A Contemporary Account (1704-1785)** Giulio Cesare Cordara. Tr. by John P. Murphy from LAT. LC 99-24712. (Illus.). 200p. 1999. pap. 21.95 (*0-8294-1295-6*, Jesuit Way) Loyola Pr.

On the Surface: Catalhoyuk, 1993-95. Ed. by Ian Hodder. (Monographs Ser.). (Illus.). xvi, 366p. 1996. 70.00 (*0-9519420-3-4*, Pub. by McDonald Inst) David Brown.

On the Surface: Thread Embellishment & Fabric Manipulation. Wendy Hill. Ed. by Liz Aneloski. LC 97-12599. (Illus.). 144p. 1997. 25.95 (*1-57120-032-0*, 10156) C & T Pub.

On the Surface of Things: Images of the Extraordinary in Science. Felice Frankel & G. M. Whitesides. LC 97-852. 1997. 35.00 (*0-8118-1371-1*); pap. 22.95 (*0-8118-1394-0*) Chronicle Bks.

On the Survival of Early English Words in Our Present Dialects see English Dialect Society Publications: Miscellanies

On the Syncope of the Old English Present Endings. M. T. Lofvenberg. (Essays & Studies on English Language & Literature: Vol. 1). 1974. reprint ed. pap. 25.00 (*0-8115-0199-X*) Periodicals Srv.

On the Syntax of Negation. Itziar Laka. LC 94-598. (Outstanding Dissertations in Linguistics Ser.). 200p. 1994. text 20.00 (*0-8153-1728-X*) Garland.

On the Systems Formed by Points Regularly Distributed on a Plane or in Space. A. Bravais. (American Crystallographic Association Monograph Ser.: Vol. 4). 113p. 1969. pap. 15.00 (*0-686-60370-2*) Polycrystal Bk Serv.

On the Tail of a Comet: The Life of Frank Buchman. Garth Lean. LC 87-32740. (Illus.). 632p. 1988. 39.95 (*0-939443-06-6*); pap. 22.95 (*0-939443-07-4*) Helmers Howard Pub.

On the Take. Stevie Cameron. LC 96-110133. 592p. 1995. pap. 8.99 (*0-7704-2708-1*) Bantam.

On the Take: Crime, Corruption & Greed in the Mulroney Years. Stevie Cameron. (Illus.). 528p. 1995. 29.95 (*0-921912-73-0*) MW&R.

On the Take: From Petty Crooks to Presidents. 2nd ed. William J. Chambliss. LC 77-15213. 320p. 1988. 31.95 (*0-253-34244-9*); pap. 14.95 (*0-253-20298-1*, MB-298) Ind U Pr.

***On the Tall of Mystery & Suspense.** John Hemminger. 169p. 2000. 21.95 (*0-7541-1248-9*, Pub. by Minerva Pr) Unity Dist.

On the Teaching & Writing of History: Responses to a Series of Questions. Ed. by Edward C. Lathem. LC 95-62168. 97p. 1994. pap. 9.95 (*0-87451-720-6*) U Pr of New Eng.

On the Teaching of Creative Writing: Responses to a Series of Questions. Wallace Stegner. Ed. by Edward C. Lathem. LC 89-117864. 72p. (Orig.). 1989. pap. 9.95 (*0-87451-843-1*) U Pr of New Eng.

On the Technique of Acting: The First Complete Edition of Chekhov's Classic to the Actor. Nor Simpson. LC 90-55493. 240p. 1991. pap. 15.00 (*0-06-273037-1*, Perennial) HarperTrade.

On the Temporal Interpretation of Noun Phrases. rev. ed. Renate Musan. LC 97-12397. (Outstanding Dissertations in Linguistics Ser.). 224p. 1997. text 56.00 (*0-8153-2886-9*) Garland.

On the Terrible Art & Vision of Hunter S. Thompson. Ed. by Todd B. Fahey. LC 96-83733. (Orig.). Date not set. pap. 15.95 (*0-9651839-1-2*) Far Gone.

On the Texas Frontier. 2nd ed. Henry H. Beck. LC 98-51155. (Illus.). 308p. 1999. reprint ed. 24.95 (*1-56474-303-9*) Fithian Pr.

On the Texture of Brains: An Introduction to Neuroanatomy for the Cybernetically Minded. Tr. by E. H. Braitenbach from GER. LC 77-21851. (Illus.). 1977. 23.95 (*0-387-08391-X*) Spr-Verlag.

On the Theory & Applications of Differential Torsion Products. V. M. Gugenheim & J. Peter May. LC 74-2164. (Memoirs Ser.: No. 1/142). 93p. 1974. pap. 17.00 (*0-8218-1842-2*, MEMO/1/142) Am Math.

O

An Asterisk (*) at the beginning of an entry indicates that the title is appearing for the first time.

On the Theory & Policy of Systemic Change. Ed. by H. J. Wagener et al. (Studies in Contemporary Economics). (Illus.). viii, 234p. 1992. 64.95 (*0-387-91438-2*) Spr-Verlag.

On the Theory of Achievement Test Items. John R. Bormuth. LC 70-102071. 1970. lib. bdg. 10.50 (*0-226-06630-4*) U Ch Pr.

On the Theory of Achievement Test Items With an Appendix by Peter Menzel: On the Linguistic Bases of the Theory of Writing Items. John R. Bormuth. LC 70-102071. 173p. Date not set. reprint ed. pap. 53.70 (*0-608-20599-0*, 205456400003) Bks Demand.

On the Theory of Modulation: Music Book Index. Max Reger. 50p. 1993. reprint ed. lib. bdg. 69.00 (*0-7812-9663-3*) Rprt Serv.

On the Theory of Vector Measures. William H. Graves. LC 77-12182. (Memoirs Ser.: No. 12/195). 72p. 1990. reprint ed. pap. 21.00 (*0-8218-2195-4*, MEMO/12/195) Am Math.

On the Therapeutic Method, Set. Galen. Tr. & Comment by R. J. Hankinson. (Clarendon Later Ancient Philosophers Ser.). 312p. 1991. 90.00 (*0-19-824494-0*) OUP.

On the Third Hand: Humor in the Dismal Science, an Anthology. Ed. by Caroline P. Clotfelter. LC 96-41214. 352p. (Orig.). 1996. pap. 20.95 (*0-472-06529-7*, 06529); text 52.50 (*0-472-09529-3*, 09529) U of Mich Pr.

On the Thirty Nine Articles: A Conversation with Tudor Christianity. Oliver O'Donovan. 160p. 1993. reprint ed. pap. text 16.99 (*0-85364-435-7*) Paternoster Pub.

On the Threshold of Adolescence: The Struggle for Independence in the Twelfth Year. Hermann Koepke. Tr. by Catherine E. Creeger from GER. LC 91-26276. Orig. Title: Das Zwolfte Lebensjahr. (Illus.). 160p. (Orig.). 1992. pap. 14.95 (*0-88010-357-4*) Anthroposophic.

On the Threshold of Central Africa: Record of Twenty Years Pioneering among the Barotsi of the Upper Zambesi. Francois Coillard. (Illus.). 664p. 1971. reprint ed. 47.50 (*0-7146-1865-9*, Pub. by F Cass Pubs) Intl Spec Bk.

On the Threshold of Hope: Opening the Door to Hope & Healing for Survivors of Sexual Abuse. Diane Mandt Langberg. LC 98-48043. (AACC Counseling Library). 217p. 1999. pap. 10.99 (*0-8423-4362-8*) Tyndale Hse.

On the Threshold of Independence: Progress on Legislative Recommendations Toward Independence. National Council on the Handicapped Staff. 100p. (Orig.). 1988. write for info. (*0-936825-01-4*) Nat Coun Handicapped.

On the Threshold of Modernity: Relativism in the French Renaissance. Zachary S. Schiffman. LC 91-2938. (Studies in Historical & Political Science: 109th Series, No. 3 (1991)). 232p. 1991. 35.00 (*0-8018-4209-3*) Johns Hopkins.

On the Threshold of the Closed Empire: Mid-Nineteenth Century Missionaries in Okinawa. Edward E. Bollinger. LC 91-73083. 249p. (Orig.). (C). 1991. pap. text 14.95 (*0-87808-230-1*, WCL230-1) William Carey Lib.

On the Threshold of the New Ukraine: Articles & Source Materials: Na Porozi Novoi Ukrainy: Statti i Dzerelni Materialy. Mykhailo Hrushevs'kyi. (Illus.). 280p. (C). 1991. text. write for info. (*1-879070-01-4*) Ukrainian Hist.

On the Threshold of the People's Home of Sweden. Lars Olsson. LC 97-14995. 176p. (Orig.). 1997. pap. 19.95 (*1-57703-002-8*) CMS.

On the Threshold of the Unseen (1917) William F. Barrett. 354p. 1998. reprint ed. pap. 27.95 (*0-7661-0561-X*) Kessinger Pub.

On the Throne Reading. George E. Mascioli. LC 94-96034. 1994. pap. text 12.95 (*0-9644336-0-5*) GEM Pub NY.

On the Throne with the King. Chuck Oliver. 224p. 1998. pap. 5.99 (*0-7860-0543-2*, Pinncle Kensgtn) Kensgtn Pub Corp.

On the Throne with the King: The Ultimate Elvis Bathroom Book. Chuck Oliver. 300p. 1999. pap. 14.95 (*1-891847-06-6*, Pub. by Dowling Pr) Midpt Trade.

On the Tiger's Back. Bernard E. Grady, Jr. LC 94-70938. 240p. (Orig.). 1994. pap. 12.95 (*1-879418-13-4*) Biddle Pub.

On the Tightrope. Ruth Belchetz. 32p. (Orig.). 1993. pap. 7.50 (*0-9636459-0-0*) Harpswell Rd.

On the Tongue of a Bird. West Glamorgan Youth Theatre Staff. 1998. pap. 13.50 (*0-8464-4916-1*) Beekman Pubs.

***On the Tongue of a Bird: West Glamorgan Youth Theatre & Dance Company.** Ed. by Derek Cobley. (Illus.). 14p. 1998. pap., teacher ed. 4.95 (*0-8464-4937-4*) Beekman Pubs.

On the Top of Pisgah - A Bird's Eye View of the Bible: A Glimpse into the Old Testament. Christian Chen & K. H. Wong. (CHI.). 440p. 1998. pap. 30.00 (*0-9661121-4-8*) Liv Word.

On the Top of Pisgah - A Bird's Eye View of the Bible Vol. 2: A Glimpse into the New Testament. Christian Chen & K. H. Wong. (CHI.). 336p. 1998. pap. 28.00 (*0-9661121-5-6*) Liv Word.

On the Town: A Marketing Preview. Maria E. den Boer. (Author's Assistant Ser.: Vol. 10). (Illus.). 10p. 1999. 3.95 (*1-928929-09-5*) Blue Thunder.

On the Town: Vocal Selections. Ed. by Carol Cuellar. 24p. (Orig.). (C). 1989. pap. text 9.95 (*0-89724-397-8*, VF1568) Wrner Bros.

On the Town in New York. 2nd anniversary ed. Michael Batterberry & Ariane Batterberry. LC 98-23443. (Illus.). 354p. (Orig.). (C). (gr. 13). 1998. 30.00 (*0-415-92020-5*) Routledge.

On the Track of a Prehistoric Economy. Maglemosian Subsistence in Early Postglacial South Scandinavia. Hans P. Blankholm. (Illus.). 320p. 1996. 40.00 (*87-7288-439-8*, Pub. by Aarhus Univ Pr) David Brown.

On the Track of the Dixie Limited. Petersen. (Illus.). 64p. 10.00 (*0-936610-00-X*) Colophon Bk Shop.

On the Track of the Exodus. C. C. Robertson. LC 89-82327. (Illus.). 120p. 1990. reprint ed. pap. 8.00 (*0-934666-40-7*) Artisan Pubs.

On the Track of the Poltergeist. D. Scott Rogo. 1985. 16.95 (*0-13-634445-3*) P-H.

On the Track of the Sasquatch. John Green. 64p. 1994. pap. 7.95 (*0-88839-341-5*) Hancock House.

On the Track of Tyranny. Beloff. Date not set. pap. 12.50 (*0-85303-075-8*, Pub. by M Vallentine & Co) Intl Spec Bk.

On the Track of Tyranny. Wiener Library Staff. Ed. by Max Beloff. LC 70-134159. (Essay Index Reprint Ser.). 1977. 20.95 (*0-8369-2090-2*) Ayer.

On the Track of Water's Secret: From Viktor Schauberg to Johann Grander. 2nd ed. Hans Kronberger & Siegbert Lattacher. Tr. by Ann Dubsky from GER. (Illus.). 175p. 1998. reprint ed. pap. 14.95 (*0-9632091-6-7*, Pub. by Wishland Inc) IPG Chicago.

On the Tracks of Unknown Animals. Bernard Heuvelmans. Tr. by Richard Garnett from FRE. LC 94-34307.Tr. of Sur la Piste de Betes Ignorees. (Illus.). 570p. 1995. 42.50 (*0-7103-0498-6*) Routledge.

On the Trail! A Practical Guide to the Working Bloodhound & Other Search & Rescue Dogs. Jan Tweedie. LC 97-40170. (Illus.). 240p. 1998. pap. 19.95 (*1-57779-005-7*) Alpine Pubns.

On the Trail: Malibu to Santa Barbara. Cathy Philipp. LC 97-91534. (Illus.). 250p. (Orig.). 1997. pap. 17.95 (*0-9655848-0-1*) C Philipp.

On the Trail: The Adventures of a Middle-Aged Tenderfoot. Helen R. Nieberl. (Illus.). 104p. 1994. pap. 11.95 (*0-9636921-1-9*) Pack & Paddle.

***On the Trail Made of Dawn: American Indian Creation Myths.** M. L. Webster. (Illus.). 96p. (YA). (gr. 4 up). 2000. 19.50 (*0-208-02497-2*, Linnet Bks) Shoe String.

On the Trail March. L. C. Harnsberger. 4p. Date not set. pap. 2.50 (*0-7390-0720-3*, 19702) Alfred Pub.

On the Trail of a Spy. G. Lehmann. (J). (gr. 3-6). 1987. mass mkt. 4.95 (*0-87508-437-0*) Chr Lit.

On the Trail of Actuaries in Texas, 1844-1964. Annie N. Friedman & Lloyd K. Friedman. LC 88-50717. (Illus.). xii, 218p. 1988. 15.00 (*0-934955-11-5*) Watercress Pr.

On the Trail of an Uncertain Dream: Indian Immigrant Experience in America. Sathi Dasgupta. LC 88-46198. (Immigrant Communities & Ethnic Minorities in the U. S. & Canada Ser.: No. 38). 1989. 47.00 (*0-404-19448-6*) AMS Pr.

On the Trail of Bears. Remy Marion. LC 98-5829. (Nature Travel Guides Ser.). (Illus.). 128p. 1998. pap. 11.95 (*0-7641-0596-5*) Barron.

On the Trail of Big Cats. Geraldine Veron. LC 98-4548. (Nature Travel Guides Ser.). (Illus.). 128p. 1998. pap. 11.95 (*0-7641-0597-3*) Barron.

***On the Trail of Colorado Critters.** Mary Taylor Young. LC 99-86255. (Illus.). 96p. (J). (gr. 4-7). 2000. pap. 14.95 (*1-56579-350-1*) Westcliffe Pubs.

On the Trail of Eklutna. Ann Chandonnet. 76p. 1979. pap. text 10.00 (*1-878100-87-4*) Todd Commns.

***On the Trail of Elder Brother: Glous'gap Stories of the Micmac Indians.** Michael B. RunningWolf & Patricia Clark Smith. LC 99-87597. (Illus.). 160p. 2000. 17.95 (*0-89255-248-4*, Pub. by Persea Bks) Norton.

On the Trail of Flicka's Friend: The Biography of a Biography. Sharon Whitehill. (Illus.). 160p. (Orig.). 1995. pap. 11.95 (*1-56474-144-3*) Fithian Pr.

On the Trail of Forgotten People: A Personal Account of the Life & Career of Mark Raymond Harrington. Marie Harrington. (Illus.). 346p. (Orig.). 1985. pap. 12.50 (*0-930830-11-3*) Great Basin.

On the Trail of Heart Attacks in Seven Countries. Henry Blackburn. 180p. 1995. write for info. (*1-887268-00-6*) H Blackburn.

On the Trail of Homo Economics: Essays by Gordon Tullock. Gordon Tullock. Ed. by Gordon L. Brady & Robert D. Tollison. 256p. (C). 1994. lib. bdg. 49.50 (*0-913969-73-7*) Univ Pub Assocs.

On the Trail of Incredible Dinosaurs. Ed. by William Lindsay. LC 98-26396. 96p. (J). (gr. k-3). 1998. pap. 14.95 (*0-7894-3628-0*) DK Pub Inc.

***On the Trail of John Muir.** Cherry Good. 192p. 2000. pap. 14.95 (*0-946487-62-6*, Pub. by Luath Pr Ltd) Midpt Trade.

***On the Trail of Mary Queen of Scots.** J. Keith Cheetham. (On the Trail of... Ser.). (Illus.). 224p. 1999. pap. 14.95 (*0-946487-50-2*, Pub. by Luath Pr Ltd) Midpt Trade.

On the Trail of Merlin: A Guidebook to the Western Mystery Tradition. Ean Begg & Deike Rich. 1991. 30.00 (*0-85030-939-5*, Pub. by Aqrn Pr) Harper SF.

***On the Trail of Monkeys.** Barron's Educational Editors. (On the Trail Ser.). 128p. 1999. pap. text 11.95 (*0-7641-1163-9*) Barron.

***On the Trail of Queen Victoria in the Highlands.** Ian Mitchell. 2000. pap. 14.95 (*0-946487-79-0*) Luath Pr Ltd.

***On the Trail of Rob Roy McGregor.** John Barrington. (Illus.). 192p. 2000. pap. 14.95 (*0-946487-59-6*) Luath Pr Ltd.

***On the Trail of Robert Burns.** John Cairney. 2000. pap. 14.95 (*0-946487-51-0*) Luath Pr Ltd.

***On the Trail of Robert Service.** G. W. Lockhart. (On the Trail of... Ser.). (Illus.). 160p. 1999. pap. 14.95 (*0-946487-24-3*, Pub. by Luath Pr Ltd) Midpt Trade.

***On the Trail of Robert the Bruce.** David R. Ross. (On the Trail of... Ser.). (Illus.). 192p. 1999. pap. 14.95 (*0-946487-52-9*, Pub. by Luath Pr Ltd) Midpt Trade.

On the Trail of Scotland's Past. Louise Chessmen. LC 99-189859. (Illus.). 64p. 1998. pap. 6.95 (*1-901663-05-1*, Pub. by Natl Mus Scotland) A Schwartz & Co.

***On the Trail of Sea Turtles.** Barron's Educational Editors. (On the Trail Ser.). 128p. 1999. pap. text 11.95 (*0-7641-1162-0*) Barron.

On the Trail of Spider Woman: Petroglyphs, Pictographs, & Myths of the Southwest. unabridged ed. Carol Patterson-Rudolph. LC 97-72062. (Illus.). 160p. 1997. 29.95 (*0-941270-97-1*); pap. 16.95 (*0-941270-98-X*) Ancient City Pr.

On the Trail of Stoddard Glass: New Hampshire Glassworks. Anne E. Field. (Illus.). 1975. pap. 15.00 (*0-87233-021-4*) Bauhan.

On the Trail of the Ancient Opium Poppy. Mark D. Merlin. LC 80-70994. (Illus.). 320p. 1984. 50.00 (*0-8386-3097-9*) Fairleigh Dickinson.

On the Trail of the Assassins: My Investigation & Prosecution of the Murder of President Kennedy. Jim Garrison. (Illus.). 336p. 1988. 19.95 (*0-941781-02-X*) IMA NYC.

On the Trail of the Buffalo Soldier: Bibliographies of African-Americans in the U. S. Army, 1866-1917. Compiled by Frank N. Schubert. LC 93-46408. 1994. 125.00 (*0-8420-2482-4*) Scholarly Res Inc.

On the Trail of the Feathered Serpent. Gene Savoy. LC 72-89709. (Illus.). xi, 216p. 1974. text 25.00 (*0-672-51668-3*) Intl Comm Christ.

On the Trail of the Grizzly. Carol A. Amato. LC 96-19930. (Young Readers' Ser.). (Illus.). 48p. (J). (gr. 2-4). 1997. pap. 4.95 (*0-8120-9312-7*) Barron.

On the Trail of the Grizzly. Carol A. Amato. (Young Readers' Series). 1997. 10.15 (*0-606-11706-7*, Pub. by Turtleback) Demco.

On the Trail of the Grizzly, Vol. 9. Carol A. Amato. (Young Reader Ser.: No. 9). (Illus.). 48p. (J). (gr. 3-6). 1998. lib. bdg. 13.45 (*1-56674-240-4*) Forest Hse.

On the Trail of the Immigrant. Edward A. Steiner. LC 69-18789. (American Immigration Collection. Series 1). (Illus.). 1969. reprint ed. 20.95 (*0-405-00538-5*) Ayer.

On the Trail of the Komodo Dragon: And Other Explorations of Science in Action. Jack Myers. LC 98-73073. (Illus.). 64p. (J). (gr. 4-7). 1999. 17.95 (*1-56397-761-3*) Boyds Mills Pr.

On the Trail of the Phoenix: An Adventure & a Meditation. Sheila Taylor. LC 98-65791. 192p. 1999. 21.95 (*1-887750-94-0*) Rutledge Bks.

***On the Trail of the Pilgrim Fathers.** J. Keith Cheetham. 192p. 2000. pap. 14.95 (*0-946487-83-9*, Pub. by Luath Pr Ltd) Midpt Trade.

***On the Trail of the Poets of the Great War: Edmund Blunden.** Helen McPhail. (Battleground Europe Ser.). 1999. pap. text. write for info. (*0-85052-678-7*) Pen & Sword Bks Ltd.

On the Trail of the Presidents: An Historical Guide to Burial Sites & Monuments. Jack B. Jones & Joy E. Jones. (Illus.). 96p. (Orig.). 1994. pap. 19.95 (*0-9645499-0-5*) J B Jones.

On the Trail of the Shroud. Gian M. Zaccone. 1996. pap. 39.95 (*0-85439-534-2*, Pub. by St Paul Pubns) St Mut.

On the Trail of the Truth. large type ed. Michael Phillips. 450p. 1995. 21.95 (*0-7838-1490-9*, G K Hall Lrg Type) Mac Lib Ref.

On the Trail of the Tumbling T. Clarence E. Mulford. 1976. 24.95 (*0-88411-209-8*) Amereon Ltd.

On the Trail of the Tumbling T see Hopalong Cassidy Series

***On the Trail of the Women Warriors.** Lyn W. Wilde. (Illus.). 240p. 2000. text 24.95 (*0-312-26213-2*) St Martin.

***On the Trail of Trouble.** Carolyn Keene. (Nancy Drew Mystery Stories Ser.: No. 148). (J). (gr. 3-6). 1999. pap. 3.99 (*0-671-02664-X*) PB.

On the Trail of Truth No. 3: The Journal of Corrie Belle Hollister. Michael Phillips. 32p. (Orig.). 1991. pap. 9.99 (*1-55661-106-4*) Bethany Hse.

On the Trail of Whales. Jean-Michael Dumont & Remy Marion. LC 98-4550. (Nature Travel Guides Ser.). (Illus.). 128p. 1998. pap. 11.95 (*0-7641-0598-1*) Barron.

***On the Trail of William Wallace.** David R. Ross. (On the Trail of... Ser.). (Illus.). 192p. 1999. pap. 14.95 (*0-946487-47-2*, Pub. by Luath Pr Ltd) Midpt Trade.

On the Trail to Avikwaame: Results of a Noncollection Class II Cultural Resources Survey of Quien Sabe - Big Maria Terrace, Riverside County, California. Joseph A. Ezzo. (Statistical Research Technical Ser.: No. 49). (Illus.). 322p. (Orig.). (C). 1994. pap. text 32.50 (*1-879442-40-X*) Stats Res.

On the Trail with Miss Pace. Sharon P. Denslow. LC 94-38206. (Illus.). 40p. (J). (ps-3). 1995. pap. 15.00 (*0-02-728688-6*, Four Winds Pr) S&S Childrens.

On the Trail with Your Canine Companion: Getting the Most of Hiking & Camping with Your Dog. Cheryl S. Smith. (Illus.). 224p. 1996. 14.95 (*0-87605-442-4*) Howell Bks.

On the Transformational Invariance of Maximum-Likelihood Estimators. Tony E. Smith. (Discussion Papers: No. 56). 1972. pap. 10.00 (*1-55869-086-7*) Regional Sci Res Inst.

On the Transition to Socialism. Paul M. Sweezy & Charles Bettelheim. LC 72-158924. 128p. 1972. pap. 10.00 (*0-85345-191-5*, Pub. by Monthly Rev) NYU Pr.

On the Transmigration of Souls in El Paso: Poems. Bobby Byrd. LC 92-54826. 96p. (Orig.). 1992. pap. 9.95 (*0-938317-19-9*) Cinco Puntos.

On the Trial of Jesus. 2nd ed. Paul Winter. Ed. by T. A. Burkill & Geza Vermes. (Studia Judaica: Vol. 1). (C). 1973. 62.35 (*3-11-002283-4*) De Gruyter.

***On the Trip & Around the Bend.** Greg Dew. Ed. by Haggard Burns. 212p. 1999. pap. write for info. (*0-7392-0393-2*, PO3618) Morris Pubng.

On the Tropic of Time: Poems. Anthony Robbins. LC 95-8286. 1995. write for info. (*0-89924-092-5*); pap. write for info. (*0-89924-091-7*) Lynx Hse.

On the Trout Stream with Joe Humphreys. Joseph B. Humphreys. LC 89-33191. (Illus.). 240p. 1989. 37.95 (*0-8117-1156-0*) Stackpole.

On the True Doctrine. Photos by R. Joseph Hoffmann. (Illus.). 160p. 1987. pap. text 19.95 (*0-19-504151-8*) OUP.

On the Truth of Being: Reflections on Heidegger's Later Philosophy. Joseph J. Kockelmans. LC 83-49191. (Studies in Phenomenology & Existential Philosophy). 352p. reprint ed. pap. 109.20 (*0-608-09345-9*, 205409100002) Bks Demand.

On the Twentieth Century: Vocal Selections. Ed. by Carol Cuellar. 100p. (Orig.). (C). 1992. pap. text 12.95 (*0-7692-0540-2*, VF1841) Wrner Bros.

On the Typology of Wh-Questions. rev. ed. Lisa L. Cheng. LC 97-12243. (Outstanding Dissertations in Linguistics Ser.). 220p. 1997. text 51.00 (*0-8153-2887-7*) Garland.

On the Unity of Christ. St. Cyril of Alexandria. Tr. by John A. McGuckin from GRE. LC 95-18709. 151p. (Orig.). 1995. pap. 8.95 (*0-88141-133-7*) St Vladimirs.

On the Unity of the Intellect Against the Averroists. Aquinas, Thomas, Saint. Ed. by Beatrice H. Zedler. LC 68-28029. (Medieval Philosophical Texts in Translation Ser.: No. 19). 1968. pap. 10.00 (*0-87462-219-0*) Marquette.

On the Upbringing of Children. Bishop Irenaius. Tr. by Xenia Skete from GRE. (Illus.). 64p. (Orig.). 1991. pap. 4.00 (*0-938635-45-X*) St Herman Pr.

On the Upward Road. Richard V. Clearwaters. 176p. (Orig.). 1991. pap. write for info. (*0-9631570-0-0*) R V Clearwater.

On the Use & Abuse of Alcoholic Liquors, in Health & Disease. William B. Carpenter. Ed. by Gerald N. Grob. LC 80-1216. (Addiction in America Ser.). 1981. reprint ed. lib. bdg. 18.95 (*0-405-13572-6*) Ayer.

On the Use of Input-Output Models for Regional Planning. W. A. Schaffer. (Studies in Applied Regional Science: No. 1). 1976. pap. text 78.50 (*90-207-0626-8*) Kluwer Academic.

On the Use of Philosophy: Three Essays. Jacques Maritain. LC 81-13338. 71p. 1982. reprint ed. lib. bdg. 42.50 (*0-313-23199-0*, MAUP, Greenwood Pr) Greenwood.

On the Use of Stochastic Processes in Modeling Reliability Problems. A. Birolini. (Lecture Notes in Economics & Mathematical Systems Ser.: Vol. 252). (Illus.). vi, 105p. 1985. 29.50 (*0-387-15699-2*) Spr-Verlag.

On the Use of the Perfect & the Pluperfect in Modern Greek. Eva Hedin. (Studia Graeca Stockholmiensia: No. 6). 126p. (Orig.). 1987. pap. text 32.50 (*91-7146-369-0*, Pub. by Stockholms Universitet) Coronet Bks.

On the Use of Two-Phase Sampling in Estimation of Parameters in Domains Where Data Contain Misclassification & Measurement Errors. Claes Andersson. LC 95-109317. (Studia Statistica Upsaliensia: No. 3). 120p. (Orig.). 1994. pap. 34.50 (*91-554-3305-7*) Coronet Bks.

On the Uses of the Humanities: Vision & Application. Hastings Center Staff. LC 84-22445. 1984. 8.00 (*0-916558-20-7*) Hastings Ctr.

On the USS Colorado. Wilbur Parker & Ruby P. Goodwin. (Illus.). 345p. pap. 12.95 (*0-934482-03-9*) Hathor House Bks.

On the Verb in Modern Greek. Irene P. Warburton. LC 68-65316. (Language Science Monographs: Vol. 4). (Illus.). (Orig.). 1970. pap. text 18.00 (*0-87750-151-3*) Res Inst Inner Asian Studies.

On the Verge. Alexandra Burack. 32p. 1997. pap. 8.00 (*1-887628-03-7*) Plinth Bks.

On the Verge. Roland Green. 320p. 1998. pap. 5.99 (*0-7869-1191-3*, Pub. by TSR Inc) Random.

On the Verge. Eric Overmyer. 76p. (Orig.). 1986. pap. 6.95 (*0-88145-046-4*) Broadway Play.

On the Verge: The Gypsies of England. Donald Kendrick & Siam Bakewell. (Illus.). 86p. 1990. pap. 15.95 (*0-900458-57-7*, Pub. by Univ of Herfordshire) Bold Strummer Ltd.

***On the Verge of Convergence: Social Stratification in Eastern Europe.** Henryk Domanski. LC 00-31472. 200p. (C). 2000. 44.95 (*963-9116-81-5*); pap. 21.95 (*963-9116-82-3*) Ctrl Europ Univ.

***On the Verge of War: International Relations & the Jhulich-Kleve Succession Crises, 1609-1614.** Alison D. Anderson. LC 99-25332. (Studies In Central European Histories). 1999. write for info. (*0-391-04092-8*) Humanities.

On the Vineyard: A Year in the Life of an Island. Jane Carpineto. LC 98-5546. 272p. 1998. 24.95 (*0-312-15584-0*, Thomas Dunne) St Martin.

On the Vineyard: A Year in the Life of an Island. Jane Carpineto. 1999. pap. 13.95 (*0-312-20666-6*) St Martin.

On the Vineyard, II. Peter Simon. 1990. pap. 24.95 (*0-9626285-0-6*) Simon Pr.

On the Virtues in General see Selected Writings of St. Thomas Aquinas

On the Vocation & the Mission of the Lay Faithful in the Church & in the World: Christifideles Laici. John Paul, II, pseud. 196p. 1989. pap. 8.95 (*1-55586-274-8*) US Catholic.

On the Vocation of Our Age for Legislation & Jurisprudence. Carl F. Von Savigny. Tr. by Abraham Hayward. LC 74-25795. (European Sociology Ser.). 192p. 1979. reprint ed. 25.95 (*0-405-06546-9*) Ayer.

On the Void of to Be: Incoherence & Trope in Finnegans Wake. Susan S. Sailer. LC 93-9632. 232p. (C). 1993. text 44.50 (*0-472-10414-4*, 10414) U of Mich Pr.

On the Wallaby. Ashton Murphy. (C). 1990. pap. 30.00 (*0-86439-108-0*, Pub. by Boolarong Pubns) St Mut.

On the Walls & in the Streets: American Poetry Broadsides from the 1960s. James D. Sullivan. LC 96-45885. 224p. 1997. pap. text 14.95 (*0-252-06624-3*) U of Ill Pr.

O

An Asterisk (*) at the beginning of an entry indicates that the title is appearing for the first time.

On the Water. Gail Stewart. (Living Spaces Ser.). (Illus.). 32p. (J). (gr. 3-8). 1989. 11.95 (*0-685-58597-2*) Rourke Corp.

On the Water. Gail Stewart. (Living Spaces Ser.). (Illus.). 32p. (J). (gr. 3-8). 1989. lib. bdg. 21.27 (*0-86592-109-1*) Rourke Enter.

***On the Water: Rowing, Yachting, Canoeing & Lots, Lots More.** Jason Page. (Zeke's Olympic Pocket Guide Ser.). (Illus.). 32p. (YA). 2000. pap. 3.95 (*0-8225-5051-2*, LernerSports) Lerner Pub.

On the Water, Michigan: Your Comprehensive Guide to Water Recreation in the Great Lake State. Eric Freedman. 1992. pap. 19.95 (*0-9631741-1-8*) H-S-M Pr.

***On the Waterbed They Sank to Their Own Levels.** Sarah Rosenblatt. LC 99-74770. (Poetry Ser.). (Illus.). 88p. 2000. pap. 12.95 (*0-88748-331-3*, Pub. by Carnegie-Mellon) CUP Services.

On the Waterfront. Gareth Mills. 130p. 1994. pap. 30.00 (*1-85902-037-2*, Pub. by Gomer Pr) St Mut.

On the Waterfront: The Original Screenplay. Budd Schulberg. (Illus.). 153p. 1988. pap. 12.95 (*0-573-60696-X*) S French Trade.

On the Way. Thalia Blundell. 1999. pap. text 10.99 (*1-85792-407-X*) Christian Focus.

On The Way, 11. TNT Resource Material Staff. 1999. pap. text 10.99 (*1-85792-406-1*) Christian Focus.

On The Way, 14. TNT Resource Material Staff. 1999. pap. text 10.99 (*1-85792-409-6*) Christian Focus.

On the Way, Bk. 6. Ed. by Christian Focus Staff. 1998. pap. 6.99 (*1-85792-326-X*, Pub. by Christian Focus) Spring Arbor Dist.

***On the Way, Vol. 7.** Christian Focus Publishing Staff. (J). 2000. pap. 10.99 (*1-85792-327-8*) Christian Focus.

On the Way, Vol.13. TNT Resource Material Staff. 1999. pap. text 10.99 (*1-85792-408-8*) Christian Focus.

On the Way: General Patton's Eyes & Ears on the Enemy. Edward A. Marinello. LC 98-35928. 1998. 27.95 (*1-56072-605-9*, Nova Kroshka Bks) Nova Sci Pubs.

***On the Way: Poems from Hollywood.** Mark Dunster. 11p. 1999. pap. 5.00 (*0-89642-810-9*) Linden Pubs.

On the Way: The Journey of the Idaho Benedictine Sisters. Mary L. Nachtsheim. LC 97-98877. 344p. 1998. pap. 14.95 (*0-9658209-0-4*) Idaho Corp of Benedctne.

On the Way Back. Myrna L. Etheridge. (Illus.). 70p. (Orig.). 1996. student ed. 10.00 (*0-937417-05-X*) Etheridge Minist.

On the Way Here. 100p. 1997. pap. 12.00 (*1-887997-09-1*) Baksun Bks.

On the Way Home. Marion Barnwell et al. Ed. by Elizabeth Sarcone & Leila Wynn. 200p. (Orig.). 1996. pap. 12.95 (*0-9655383-0-3*) Ruby Shoes Pr.

***On the Way Home.** Robert Bausch. (Voices of the South Ser.). 240p. 2000. pap. 15.95 (*0-8071-2638-1*) La State U Pr.

On the Way Home. Robert Bausch. 240p. 1983. pap. 3.50 (*0-380-63131-8*, 63131-8, Avon Bks) Morrow Avon.

***On the Way Home.** Jill Murphy. (Illus.). (J). 2000. pap. 3.99 (*0-333-37572-6*) Mcm Child Bks.

On the Way Home: The Diary of a Trip from South Dakota to Mansfield, Missouri, in 1894. Laura Ingalls Wilder. Ed. by Rose W. Lane. LC 62-17966. (Trophy Bk.). (Illus.). 112p. (J). (gr. 4-7). 1976. pap. 4.95 (*0-06-440080-8*) HarpC Child Bks.

On the Way Home: The Diary of a Trip from South Dakota to Mansfield, Missouri, in 1894. Laura Ingalls Wilder. 1990. 10.05 (*0-606-00738-5*, Pub. by Turtleback) Demco.

On the Way Home: The Diary of a Trip from South Dakota to Mansfield, Missouri, in 1894. 60th ed. Laura Ingalls Wilder. Ed. by Rose W. Lane. LC 62-17966. 128p. (J). (gr. 4-7). 1962. 16.95 (*0-06-026489-6*) Zondervan.

On the Way of Faith: Faith, Freedom & Love. Roman Braga. Ed. by Gabriella & Ruxandra Shelden. Tr. by Veloff Nektaria from RUM. LC 96-77520. (RUM., Illus.). 225p. (Orig.). 1997. pap. text 15.00 (*0-9643478-1-4*) HDM Pr.

On the Way of the Cross with the Disabled. Elizabeth Greeley. (Illus.). 62p. (C). 1996. pap. 39.95 (*0-85439-312-9*, Pub. by St Paul Pubns) St Mut.

On the Way to a Wedding. Ingrid Weaver. 1997. per. 3.99 (*0-373-07761-0*, 1-07761-9) Silhouette.

On the Way to Bethlehem. C. M. De Vries. Tr. by Frederic Vilain from DUT. LC 90-43765. (Illus.). 14p. (Orig.). (J). (ps-1). 1990. pap. 2.95 (*0-8198-5415-8*) Pauline Bks.

On the Way to Bethlehem: Advent Dialogues. Richard H. Goodlin. 24p. 1998. pap. 4.25 (*0-7880-1285-1*) CSS OH.

***On the Way to Bethlehem: Reflections on Christmas for Every Day in Advent.** Hilary McDowell. Ed. by Holly Halverson. 160p. 2000. pap. 13.00 (*0-8358-0920-X*) Upper Room Bks.

On the Way to Canon: Creative Tradition History in the Old Testament. Magne Saebo. (JSOTS Ser.: Vol. 191). 408p. 1998. 57.50 (*1-85075-927-8*, Pub. by Sheffield Acad) CUP Services.

On the Way to Death: Essays Toward a Comic Vision. A. Roy Eckardt. 180p. (C). 1996. text 39.95 (*1-56000-234-4*) Transaction Pubs.

On the Way to Diplomacy. Costas M. Constantinou. LC 96-6310. (Borderlines Ser.: Vol. 7). 208p. (C). 1996. pap. 19.95 (*0-8166-2685-5*); text 49.95 (*0-8166-2684-7*) U of Minn Pr.

On the Way to Feed the Swans. Hannelore Hahn. LC 82-99824. 80p. 1982. pap. 15.00 (*0-9603310-3-4*) Tenth Hse Ent.

On the Way to Finding Your Soulmate, Vol. 1. Terri Nelson. Ed. by Victorya Stone. LC 97-73855. 226p. 1997. pap. 19.95 (*0-9659600-3-X*) Above The Din.

On the Way to God: An Exploration into the Theology of Wolfhart Pannenberg. David P. Polk. LC 88-27871. 350p. (C). 1989. lib. bdg. 46.00 (*0-8191-7229-4*) U Pr of Amer.

On the Way to Gretna Green. large type ed. Marian Devon. LC 98-41392. 1998. 30.00 (*0-7838-0381-8*, G K Hall Lrg Type) Mac Lib Ref.

On the Way to Heaven. Tina Wainscott. 1995. mass mkt. 5.50 (*0-312-95417-4*) St Martin.

On the Way to Individuality: Current Methodological Issues in Behavioral Genetics. Ed. by Michele C. LaBuda & Elena L. Grigorenko. 14p. (C). 1998. lib. bdg. 85.00 (*1-56072-427-7*) Nova Sci Pubs.

On the Way to Knowledge: Man, the Earth, Outer Space, Acceleration. V. Lysenko. 266p. (C). 1988. 40.00 (*0-7855-4996-X*, Pub. by Collets) St Mut.

On the Way to Krsna. 79p. 1991. pap. 1.95 (*0-912776-39-0*, OTW) Bhaktivedanta.

On the Way to Language. Martin Heidegger. LC 77-124708. 208p. 1982. pap. 16.00 (*0-06-063859-1*, CN 4023) HarperTrade.

***On the Way to Nineveh: Studies in Honor of George M. Landes.** George M. Landes. Ed. by Stephen L. Cook & S. C. Winter. LC 99-43279. (ASOR Bks.: Vol. 4). 368p. 1999. pap. 49.95 (*0-7885-0585-8*, 855004, Pub. by Am Sch Orient Res) David Brown.

On the Way to over the Hill: A Guide for Aging Gracefully. Grace Lee. Ed. by Kieran O'Mahony. 150p. (Orig.). 1997. pap. 12.95 (*0-944638-11-2*) EduCare Pr.

On the Way to Satori: A Woman's Experience to Enlightenment. Gerta Ital. 1993. pap. 17.95 (*1-85230-155-4*, Pub. by Element MA) Penguin Putnam.

On the Way to Self: Ego & Early Oedipal Development. Johanna K. Tabin. LC 84-15558. 392p. 1985. text 57.50 (*0-231-05944-2*) Col U Pr.

On the Way to Supermanhood. Satprem Staff. Tr. by Luc Venet from FRE. LC 85-23187. Orig. Title: La Genese du Surhomme. 200p. (Orig.). 1985. pap. text 8.95 (*0-938710-11-7*) Inst Evolutionary.

***On the Way to the Beach.** Henry Cole. (J). 2001. 15.95 (*0-688-17515-5*, Grenwillow Bks) HarpC Child Bks.

On the Way to the Melting Pot: A Novel. Waldemar Ager. Tr. by Harry T. Cleven from NOR. LC 94-33998. (Prairie Classics Ser.: No. 4).Tr. of Paa Veien til Smeltepotten. 224p. 1995. pap. 14.95 (*1-879483-23-8*) Prairie Oak Pr.

On the Way to the Postmodern: Old Testament Essays, 1967-1998, Vol. 1. David J. Clines. LC 99-158696. (JSOTS Ser.: No. 292). 443p. 1998. 85.00 (*1-85075-901-4*, Pub. by Sheffield Acad) CUP Services.

On the Way to the Postmodern Vol. 2: Old Testament Essays 1967-1998. David J. A. Clines. LC 99-158696. (JSOT Supplement Ser.: No. 293). 450p. 1998. 85.00 (*1-85075-983-9*, Pub. by Sheffield Acad) CUP Services.

On the Way to the Venus de Milo. Pearson Marx. LC 94-25976. 1995. 21.00 (*0-671-88335-6*) S&S Trade.

On the Way to Understanding the Time Phenomenon: The Constructions of Time in Natural Science. A. P. Levich. (Series on Advances in Mathematics for Applied Sciences). 216p. 1995. text 48.00 (*981-02-1360-3*) World Scientific Pub.

On the Way to Understanding the Time Phenomenon: The Constructions of Time in Natural Science, Pt. 2. A. P. Levich. (Series on Advances in Mathematics for Applied Sciences). 500p. 1996. text 109.00 (*981-02-1606-8*) World Scientific Pub.

On the Way Up. Shirley Williams. 50p. 1993. 6.00 (*0-9636408-0-1*) S D Williams.

On the Way with Jesus in the Gospel of Mark. Elaine M. Ward. 84p. 1997. pap. 8.95 (*1-57438-017-6*) Ed Ministries.

On the Wealth of Nations: Contemporary Responses to Adam Smith. Ed. by Ian S. Ross. (Key Issues Ser.: No. 19). 250p. 1998. 72.00 (*1-85506-566-5*); pap. 23.00 (*1-85506-567-3*) Thoemmes Pr.

On the Web or Off: Hypermedia Design Basics. Irene Smith & Sharon Yoder. (Instant Success Ser.). 151p. 1998. spiral bd. 18.95 (*1-56484-118-9*) Intl Society Tech Educ.

On the Western Front. Robert Cowley. 1999. write for info. (*0-201-62639-X*) Addison-Wesley.

On the Whispering Wind. Nikki Benjamin. (Family Continuity Program Ser.: No. 23). 1999. per. 4.50 (*0-373-82171-9*, 1-82171-9) Harlequin Bks.

On the Wild Side. Tony Reed. 200p. (Orig.). 1995. pap. write for info. (*1-885591-67-5*) Morris Pubng.

On the Wild Side: Reflections of a Kansas Naturalist. Kerry Knudsen. (Illus.). 196p. 1987. 16.95 (*0-941974-08-1*) Baranski Pub Co.

On the Wild Side: The Big Bang, ESP, the Beast 666, Levitation, Rain Making, Trance-Channeling, Seances & Ghosts, & More. Martin Gardner. LC 91-43151. (Illus.). 255p. (C). 1992. 26.95 (*0-87975-713-2*) Prometheus Bks.

On the Wild Side: West Moloka'i. Faith M. Roelofs. (Exploring the Islands: Islands of Maui & Moloka'i Ser.). 28p. 1994. pap. write for info. (*1-882163-26-5*) Moanalua Grdns Fnd.

On the Wind: Scent Work for Hunting Dogs. Susan Bulanda. Ed. by Mark Anderson. (Illus.). 104p. Date not set. pap. write for info. (*0-944875-52-1*) Doral Pub.

On the Window Licks the Night: A Nivola. John Mitchell. LC 93-48949. (Plover Nivola Ser.). 104p. 1994. pap. 8.95 (*0-917635-18-3*) Plover Pr.

On the Wing. Douglas Florian. LC 95-9976. (Illus.). 47p. (J). (ps-3). 1996. 16.00 (*0-15-200497-1*) Harcourt.

On the Wing. Douglas Florian. 48p. (J). 2000. pap. 6.00 (*0-15-202366-6*) Harcourt.

On the Wing. Carol Lerner. (J). 1924. 15.95 (*0-688-16649-0*, Wm Morrow); lib. bdg. 15.89 (*0-688-16650-4*, Wm Morrow) Morrow Avon.

On the Wing. Joseph Milosch. Ed. by Erikheath A. Thomas. (Illus.). 35p. (Orig.). 1995. pap. 5.00 (*0-9638412-1-1*) Drury Ln.

***On the Wing.** Marilyn Singer. LC 00-35078. (Illus.). (J). 2001. write for info. (*0-8234-1547-3*) Holiday.

On the Wing: Jessie Woods & the Flying Aces Air Circus. Ann Cooper. (Illus.). 159p. 1993. 23.95 (*1-879630-17-6*) Black Hawk Pub.

On the Wing of Occasions. Joel Chandler Harris. LC 71-90582. (Short Story Index Reprint Ser.). 1977. 27.95 (*0-8369-3065-7*) Ayer.

On the Wing of Occasions. Joel Chandler Harris. LC 75-96883. (Illus.). 317p. reprint ed. lib. bdg. 20.50 (*0-8398-0765-1*) Irvington.

On the Wing of Occasions. Joel Chandler Harris. (Illus.). 317p. (C). 1986. reprint ed. pap. text 7.95 (*0-8290-2385-2*) Irvington.

On the Wing of Occasions. Joel Chandler Harris. (Notable American Authors Ser.). 1992. reprint ed. lib. bdg. 75.00 (*0-7812-3022-5*) Rprt Serv.

On the Wings of a Butterfly: A Guide to Total Christian Education. fac. ed. Shirley J. Heckman. LC 80-26406. (Illus.). 166p. 1981. pap. 51.50 (*0-7837-7344-7*, 204729700007) Bks Demand.

On the Wings of a Butterfly: A Story about Life & Death. Marilyn Maple. LC 91-50854. (Illus.). 32p. (Orig.). (J). (gr. 1-6). 1992. 15.95 (*0-943990-69-6*) Parenting Pr.

***On the Wings of a North Wind: Following the Migration of Waterfowl.** Michael Furtman. 161p. 1999. pap. 14.95 (*1-885061-72-2*) Adventure Pubns.

On the Wings of a Prayer. Clyde D. Blevins. 159p. 1998. pap. 8.00 (*1-55630-880-9*) Brentwood Comm.

On the Wings of a Unicorn: It Is the Strength of Seven Women That Forms the Framework of Her Story But When Life Whirled Out of Control It Was the Unicorn That Saved Her. Mary Lou Fuller. 115p. 1999. pap. 14.95 (*0-9657894-2-X*) Kalm Pub.

On the Wings of an Ant. Arthur Hoffman. (Illus.). 32p. (Orig.). 1986. pap. 3.95 (*0-936953-00-4*) Elenchus Ent.

On the Wings of Angels. 1993. 8.99 (*0-685-66668-9*) Random Hse Value.

On the Wings of Angels. Ariel Books Staff. LC 95-197054. (Illus.). 48p. 1995. 6.95 (*0-8362-4730-2*, Arie Bks) Andrews & McMeel.

On the Wings of Awe: A Machzor for Rosh Hashanah & Yom Kippur. Ed. by Richard N. Levy. 1985. 13.95 (*0-685-31415-4*) Bnai Brith-Hillel.

On the Wings of Books: A Guide for Enriching Young Minds with Fine Literature . . . Barbara A. Kohli & Carolyn N. Troutwine. LC 89-700194. 1989. 85.00 (*0-685-29124-3*); VHS 39.95 (*0-685-29123-5*) Cleary Connection.

On the Wings of Eagles. Jeffrey Schrier. LC 97-24562. (Illus.). 32p. (J). (gr. 2 up). 1998. lib. bdg. 20.90 (*0-7613-0004-X*) Millbrook Pr.

***On the Wings of Heaven: A True Story from a Messenger of Love.** G. W. Hardin. LC 99-90170. 1999. pap. 17.95 (*1-893641-00-7*) Dreamspeak.

On the Wings of Love. large type ed. Cynthia Harrod-Eagles. 283p. 1996. pap. 18.99 (*1-85389-443-5*, Dales) Ulverscroft.

On the Wings of Love: Michael's Story. Donna R. Collins. LC 96-80498. (Illus.). 171p. 1997. 24.95 (*1-878044-52-4*) Mayhaven Pub.

On the Wings of Magic: Witch World. Andre Norton et al. (Turning Ser.: Bk. 3). 416p. 1995. mass mkt. 5.99 (*0-8125-0828-9*, Pub. by Tor Bks) St Martin.

On the Wings of Peace: Writers & Illustrators Speak Out for Peace, In Memory of Hiroshima & Nagasaki. Intro. by Sheila Hamanaka. LC 95-17241. (Illus.). 112p. (YA). (gr. 6 up). 1995. 21.95 (*0-395-72619-0*, Clarion Bks) HM.

On the Wings of Pegasus. Charlotte Schlender. LC 98-90632. 199 p. 1998. write for info. (*0-9666038-0-X*) C Schlender.

On the Wings of Self Esteem. Louise Hart. 136p. (Orig.). 1995. pap. 8.95 (*0-89087-731-9*) Celestial Arts.

On the Wings of Song. Wanda Weiskopf. 240p. 1994. 22.95 (*0-9627735-2-2*) Excllnc Entrps.

On the Wings of the Storm. large type ed. Connie Monk. (Charnwood Large Print Ser.). 512p. 1998. 29.99 (*0-7089-8997-7*, Charnwood) Ulverscroft.

On the Wings of the Wild Wind. Schultz. (Occasional Papes: No. 21). 1986. pap. 9.95 (*0-317-89455-2*) WWU CPNS.

On the Wings of the Wind. Mary R. Stott. 1990. 9.95 (*0-89697-418-9*) Intl Univ Pr.

On the Wings of the Zephyr. M. Reutter. 352p. 2000. 27.50 (*0-06-018233-4*) HarperTrade.

On the Winning Side: A Southern Story of Ante-Bellum Times. Jeanette H. Walworth. LC 72-2927. (Black Heritage Library Collection). 1977. reprint ed. 28.95 (*0-8369-9088-9*) Ayer.

On the Wires of Our Nerves: The Art of Electroacoustic Music. Ed. by Robin J. Heitetz. LC 87-46435. (Illus.). 208p. 1989. 36.50 (*0-8387-5155-5*) Bucknell U Pr.

On the Witness Stand: Controversies in the Courtroom. Ed. by Lawrence S. Wrightsman et al. 300p. (C). 1987. text 46.00 (*0-8039-3168-9*); pap. text 22.50 (*0-8039-2793-2*) Sage.

On the Witness Stand: Controversies in the Courtroom. Ed. by Lawrence S. Wrightsman et al. LC 87-23373. (Illus.). 312p. reprint ed. pap. 96.80 (*0-608-09789-6*, 206996300007) Bks Demand.

On the Witness Stand: Essays on Psychology & Crime. Hugo Muensterberg. Ed. by Richard Moss. LC 70-156030. reprint ed. 35.00 (*0-404-09180-6*) AMS Pr.

On the Witness Stand: Essays on Psychology & Crime. Hugo Munsterberg. 269p. 1981. reprint ed. 38.00 (*0-8377-0840-0*, Rothman) W S Hein.

On the Word of Command: A Pictorial History of the Regimental Sergeant Major. Ed. by Richard Alford. 208p. (C). 1991. 135.00 (*0-946771-65-0*, Pub. by Spellmnt Pubs) St Mut.

On the Work of Leonhard Euler: Berlin Colloquium - May 1983. Ed. by E. Kuobloch et al. (ENG, FRE & GER.). 252p. 1984. 67.50 (*0-8176-1609-8*) Birkhauser.

On the Write Track: Beginning Literacy for Secondary Students. Deborah Becker Cotto. (Illus.). 178p. (YA). (gr. 6-12). 1997. pap. text 16.95 (*1-882483-38-3*) Alta Bk Ctr.

On the Write Track Teacher's Guide: Beginning Literacy for Secondary Students. Deborah B. Cotto. (Illus.). 122p. (YA). (gr. 6-12). 1997. teacher ed. 14.50 (*1-882483-39-1*) Alta Bk Ctr.

On the Writing of History in Kievan Rus' Omeljan Pritsak. 40p. 1994. write for info. (*0-9609822-9-9*) Ukrainian Studies Fund.

On the Wrong Track: Fragments of an Autobiography. Milo Dor. Tr. by Jerry Glenn & Jennifer Kelley. LC 92-45251. (Studies in Austrian Literature, Culture, & Thought. Translation Ser.). 241p. 1993. pap. 23.50 (*0-929497-66-X*) Ariadne CA.

On the Yankee Station. William Boyd. 1999. pap. write for info. (*0-375-70511-2*) Vin Bks.

On the Yaquina & Big Elk. Evelyn P. Parry. (Illus.). (Orig.). 1985. pap. text 9.95 (*0-911443-07-X*) Lincoln Coun Hist.

On the Yeti Trail: The Search for the Elusive Snowman. Tribhuvan Nath & Madan M. Gupta. (C). 1995. 7.00 (*81-86112-29-4*, Pub. by UBS Pubs Dist) S Asia.

On the 14th Century Punctuation of Mongolian in the Yan-ch'ao Pi-Shih. John C. Street. (Mongolia Society Occasional Papers: No. 12). 12.00 (*0-910980-52-7*) Mongolia.

On Their Own: Adventure Athletes in Solo Sports, 3 bks. Steve Boga. Ed. by Betty Lou Kratoville. (Illus.). (J). (gr. 3-9). 1992. student ed. 14.00 (*0-87879-929-X*) High Noon Bks.

On Their Own: Adventure Athletes in Solo Sports, 3 bks., Set. Steve Boga. Ed. by Betty Lou Kratoville. (Illus.). (J). (gr. 3-9). 1992. pap. text 12.00 (*0-87879-928-1*) High Noon Bks.

On Their Own: Making the Transition from School to Work in the Information Age. Stewart Crysdale et al. 222p. 55.00 (*0-7735-1785-5*); pap. 19.95 (*0-7735-1805-3*) McG-Queens Univ Pr.

***On Their Own: Three New Hampshire Scholars Chronicle Their Adventures Abroad.** Alvah W. Sulloway. (Illus.). 544p. 2000. 35.00 (*0-914659-89-8*) Phoenix Pub.

On Their Own: Widows & Widowhood in the American Southwest, 1848-1939. Ed. by Arlene Scadron. LC 86-30850. 344p. 1988. text 29.95 (*0-252-01439-1*) U of Ill Pr.

On Their Own Power: The Story of Michigan Electric Cooperatives. unabridged ed. Raymond G. Kuhl. Ed. by Michael Buda. (Illus.). 200p. 1997. 9.95 (*0-9660251-0-5*); pap. 6.95 (*0-9660251-1-3*) MI Elect Cooper.

On Their Side: Helping Children Take Charge of Their Learning. Bob Strachota. LC 95-71980. (Illus.). 141p. (Orig.). 1996. pap. 12.95 (*0-9618636-3-3*) NE Found Child.

On Their Way: Celebrating Second Graders As They Read & Write. Jane Fraser & Donna Skolnick. LC 94-3695. 200p. 1994. pap. text 22.00 (*0-435-08830-0*, 08830) Heinemann.

On Their Way Rejoicing: The History & Role of the Bible in Africa. Ype Schaaf. Tr. by Paul Ellingworth. LC 97-983298. xi, 254p. 1994. reprint ed. pap. 16.99 (*0-85364-561-2*, Pub. by Paternoster Pub) OM Literature.

On Theology. Schubert M. Ogden. LC 91-52782. 176p. 1992. reprint ed. pap. text 12.95 (*0-87074-330-9*) SMU Press.

On Theoretical Sociology: Five Essays, Old & New. Robert K. Merton. 1967. pap. 16.95 (*0-02-921150-6*) Free Pr.

On Theory & Practice of Robots & Manipulators: Proceedings of CISM, IFTOMM Symposium, 1st, 1972. CISM (International Center for Mechanical Sciences. (CISM International Centre for Mechanical Sciences Ser.: No. 201). (Illus.). 668p. 1974. 85.95 (*0-387-81252-0*) Spr-Verlag.

On Thermonuclear War. Herman Kahn. LC 77-25930. (Illus.). 668p. 1978. reprint ed. lib. bdg. 95.00 (*0-313-20060-2*, KAOT, Greenwood Pr) Greenwood.

On These Walls: Inscriptions & Quotations in the Buildings of the Library of Congress. 1996. lib. bdg. 251.95 (*0-8490-6875-4*) Gordon Pr.

On These Walls: Inscriptions & Quotations in the Buildings of the Library of Congress. John Y. Cole. (Illus.). 106p. 1995. pap. 8.50 (*0-8444-0845-X*) Lib Congress.

On Thin Ice. Susan Anderson. 320p. 1995. mass mkt. 4.99 (*0-8217-5046-1*, Zebra Kensgtn) Kensgtn Pub Corp.

***On Thin Ice: How Advocates & Opponents Could Misread the Public's Views on Vouchers & Charter Schools.** Steve Farkas et al. 45p. 1999. pap. 10.00 (*1-889483-62-1*) Public Agenda.

On This Christmas Night. 32p. 1985. pap. 4.95 (*0-7935-2730-9*, 00123568) H Leonard.

On This Crust of Earth. Ed. by Lynda Sorensen & Ralph Nazareth. LC 86-90461. 100p. (Orig.). 1986. pap. 5.95 (*0-938999-00-1*) Yuganta Pr.

On This Day. (C). write for info. (*0-09-178657-6*) OUP.

On This Day. Thomas Nelson Incorporated Staff. 1998. 12.97 (*0-7852-1400-3*) Nelson.

On This Day: A Brief History of Nashville & Middle Tennessee. James A. Crutchfield. (Illus.). 152p. 1995. pap. 9.95 (*0-9640392-1-4*) Cool Springs Pr.

An Asterisk (*) at the beginning of an entry indicates that the title is appearing for the first time.

On This Day: 365 Inspiring Stories about Saints, Martyrs & Heroes. Robert J. Morgan. LC 97-8956. 384p. 1997. 14.99 (*0-7852-1162-4*) Nelson.

On This Day in History. Leonard Spinrad & Thelma Spinrad. Ed. by Jared Brown & Anistatia Miller. LC 99-176060. (Illus.). 352p. 1999. pap. 16.00 (*0-7352-0064-5*) PH Pr.

*On This Day in Kentucky. Robert A. Powell. (Illus.). 96p. 1999. pap. 7.90 (*0-9651406-2-8*) Silverhawke.

On This Day in North Carolina. Lew Powell. LC 95-41603. (Illus.). (Orig.). 1996. pap. 16.95 (*0-89587-139-4*) Blair.

*On This Day in Television History... David Blevins. 60p. 1999. pap. 15.00 (*0-9672731-3-7*) David Blevins.

*On This Day in Television History... 2nd ed. Dave Blevins. 48p. 2000. pap. 15.00 (*0-9672731-5-3*) David Blevins.

*On This Day in the Church: An Illustrated Almanac of the Latter-Day Saints Richard N. Holzapfel. LC 99-17001. 1999. write for info. (*1-57345-579-2*) Deseret Bk.

*On This Day in UFO History... 2nd rev. ed. David Blevins. 89p. 1999. pap. 15.00 (*0-9672731-0-2*) David Blevins.

*On This Day in UFO History... 3rd ed. Dave Blevins. 77p. 2000. spiral bd. 20.00 (*0-9672731-9-6*) David Blevins.

On This High Hill. Grim Reaper Books-Cherry Valley Editions Staff & Barbara Holland. 1974. write for info. (*0-318-64126-7*) Poets Pr.

On This Hill: A Narrative History of Hampden-Sydney College, 1774-1994. John L. Brinkley. (Illus.). 896p. 1995. 39.95 (*1-886356-06-8*) Hampden-Sydney.

On this Island: Photographs of Long Island. Photos by Larry Kanfer. (Illus.). 40.00 (*0-685-39064-0*) Viking Penguin.

On This Rock: A Commentary on First Peter. Donald G. Miller. LC 93-30951. (Princeton Theological Monographs: No. 34). 1993. pap. 25.00 (*1-55635-020-1*) Pickwick.

On This Rock: A Study of Peter's Life & Ministry. Joseph Wang & Anne B. Crumpler. 80p. 1999. pap. 7.95 (*0-687-08558-6*) Abingdon.

On This Rockne: A Notre Dame Mystery. Ralph McInerny. LC 97-15341. 224p. 1997. text 20.95 (*0-312-17054-8*, 749186) St Martin.

On This Rockne: A Notre Dame Mystery, Vol. 1. Ralph McInerny. 320p. 1998. pap. 5.99 (*0-312-96738-1*, Pub. by Tor Bks) St Martin.

On This Site: Landscape in Memoriam. Photos by Joel Sternfeld. LC 96-12574. (Illus.). 112p. 1996. 45.00 (*0-8118-1448-3*); pap. 27.50 (*0-8118-1437-8*) Chronicle Bks.

*On This Spot: Pinpointing the Past in Washington D. C. Douglas E. Evelyn & Paul Dickson. LC 99-36102. 266p. 1999. per. 16.95 (*0-7922-7499-7*) Natl Geog.

On This Spot: Pinpointing the Past in Washington D. C. Douglas E. Evelyn & Paul Dickson. Date not set. reprint ed. pap. 14.95 (*0-9650998-0-6*) On This Spot.

On Thom Spectra, Orientability & Cobordism. Yu. B. Rudyak. LC 97-32730. (Monographs in Mathematics). xii, 583p. (C). 1998. 129.00 (*3-540-62043-5*) Spr-Verlag.

On Thomas Hardy: Late Essays & Earlier. Peter Widdowson. LC 97-26677. 176p. 1998. text 49.95 (*0-312-21078-7*) St Martin.

On Thoreau. Stephen Hahn. (Wadsworth Notes Ser.). 1999. pap. text 13.95 (*0-534-57613-3*) Thomson Learn.

On Thought & Life: Conversations with Karel Capek. Thomas G. Masaryk. Tr. by Miles Weatherall & R. Weatherall from CZE. LC 78-156689. (Essay Index Reprint Ser.). 1971. reprint ed. 18.95 (*0-405-02782-6*) Ayer.

*On Thoughts & Aphorisms. 2nd ed. Mother. 362p. 1998. pap. 15.95 (*81-7058-528-7*, Pub. by SAA) E-W Cultural Ctr.

On Three Levels: Micro-, Meso- & Macro-Approaches in Physics. M. Fannes et al. (NATO ASI Ser.: Vol. 324). (Illus.). 496p. (C). 1994. 145.00 (*0-306-44704-5*, Kluwer Plenum) Kluwer Academic.

*On Three Pillars: The History of Chizuk Amuno Congregation. Jan Bernhardt Schein. (Illus.). 375p. 2000. write for info. (*0-9673940-1-5*) Chizuk Amuno.

On Thrones of Gold: Three Japanese Shadow Plays. Ed. by James R. Brandon. LC 73-88802. 429p. reprint ed. pap. 133.00 (*0-7837-2226-5*, 205731600004) Bks Demand.

On Thrones of Gold: Three Javanese Shadow Plays. Ed. by James R. Brandon. LC 93-14879. (Illus.). 426p. (C). 1993. reprint ed. pap. text 28.00 (*0-8248-1425-8*) UH Pr.

On Time. Peter Diamond. (Churchill Lectures in Economics). (Illus.). 134p. (C). 1994. text 30.95 (*0-521-46289-4*) Cambridge U Pr.

On Time. Ed. by Mark Frankel & Victoria Tillotson. (Theory@Buffalo Ser.: No. 3). (C). 1997. pap. 8.00 (*0-922668-18-3*) SUNYB Poetry Rare Bks.

On Time. Dianne Tucker-La Plount. (Phonetic Fiction Ser.). 58p. (Orig.). 1994. pap. 5.00 (*1-884896-02-2*) Red Van Pubs.

*On Time: From Seasons to Split Seconds. Gloria Skurzynski. LC 99-33927. (Illus.). 48p. (J). (gr. 4-6). 2000. 17.95 (*0-7922-7503-9*, Pub. by Natl Geog) S&S Trade.

On Time - Musical. Joy Chaitin & Sarah Stevens-Estabrook. 1994. 5.50 (*0-87129-468-0*, O05) Dramatic Pub.

On Time - On Budget: A Step-by-Step Guide for Managing Any Project. Sunny Baker & Kim Baker. LC 92-12298. 320p. (C). 1992. text 39.95 (*0-13-633447-4*) P-H.

On Time - On Budget: A Step-by-Step Guide for Managing Any Project. Sunny Baker & Kim Baker. (Illus.). 304p. 1997. reprint ed. text 20.00 (*0-7881-5087-1*) DIANE Pub.

On Time & Method. Janice R. Kelly & Joseph E. McGrath. (Applied Social Research Methods Ser.: Vol. 13). 160p. (C). 1988. text 42.00 (*0-8039-3046-1*); pap. text 18.95 (*0-8039-3047-X*) Sage.

On Time & on Budget: A Home Renovation Survival Guide. John Rusk. 320p. 1997. pap. 11.95 (*0-385-47511-X*) Doubleday.

On Time On Budget: Planning & Building the Office Environment, Vol. II. B. Alan Whitson. (Corporate Real Estate Ser.). (Illus.). 225p. 1992. 119.95 incl. disk (*0-9627392-6-X*); lib. bdg. 119.95 (*0-9627392-7-8*) B A Whitson.

*On Time, On Target: The World War II Memoir of a Field Artillery Paratrooper in the 82d Airborne. John McKenzie. LC 99-58260. (Illus.). 304p. 2000. 27.95 (*0-89141-714-1*) Presidio Pr.

*On Time on Target on Budget: Get (a Whole Lot More Than) Your Money's Worth from the Next Consultant You Hire. (Management Excellence Library: Vol. 1). 125p. 1999. ring bd. write for info. (*1-891019-14-7*) Morris Communs.

On-Time Services to Preserve Families: A Guide for Child Protection Agency Administrators & Policy Makers. G. Diane Dodson et al. LC 97-14571. 1997. write for info. (*1-57073-447-X*) Amer Bar Assn.

On Time Technology Implementation: How to Achieve Implementation Success with Limited Time. Bennet P. Lientz. 285p. 1999. pap. text 44.95 (*0-12-449975-9*) Acad Pr.

On Time to the Doctorate: A Study of the Lengthening Time to Completion for Doctorates in Science & Engineering. National Research Council Staff. 163p. 1990. pap. text 19.00 (*0-309-04085-X*) Natl Acad Pr.

On Time, Within Budget: Software Project Management Practices & Techniques. 2nd ed. E. M. Bennatan. 256p. 1995. pap. 54.99 (*0-471-12811-2*) Wiley.

*On Time, Within Budget: Software Project Management Practices & Techniques. 3rd ed. E. M. Bennatan. LC 00-27330. 400p. 2000. pap. 54.99 (*0-471-37644-2*) Wiley.

On to C. Patrick H. Winston. 290p. (C). 1994. pap. 25.00 (*0-201-58042-X*) Addison-Wesley.

On to C Plus Plus. Patrick H. Winston. 305p. (C). 1994. pap. 25.00 (*0-201-58043-8*) Addison-Wesley.

On to Java. 2nd ed. Patrick Henry Winston. 379p. (C). 1998. pap. 25.00 (*0-201-38598-8*) Addison-Wesley.

On to Maturity: A Sequel to Living God's Way. Arthur Wallis. 144p. (Orig.). 1988. reprint ed. pap. 5.95 (*0-939159-06-6*) Cityhill Pub.

On to Oregon. Adrietta A. Applegate & Hixon Applegate. 117p. 1973. 16.95 (*0-87770-117-2*) Ye Galleon.

On to Oregon! Honore Morrow. (Illus.). (J). (gr. 4-7). 1946. reprint ed. 16.00 (*0-688-21639-0*, Wm Morrow) Morrow Avon.

On to Oregon! Honore Morrow. LC 90-19554. (Illus.). 240p. (J). (gr. 5-9). 1991. reprint ed. pap. 4.95 (*0-688-10494-0*, Wm Morrow) Morrow Avon.

On to Oregon: The Diaries of Mary Walker & Myra Eells. Ed. & Intro. by Clifford M. Drury. LC 97-50202. (Illus.). iv, 382p. 1998. pap. 16.00 (*0-8032-6613-8*, Bison Books) U of Nebr Pr.

On to Smalltalk. Patrick H. Winston. LC 97-15969. 320p. (C). 1997. pap. 25.00 (*0-201-49827-8*) Addison-Wesley.

On to Square Two. Marsha R. McCloskey. (Illus.). 80p. 1996. pap. text 8.95 (*0-486-29476-5*) Dover.

On to the Summit: The Len Moules Story. Pat Wraight. 189p. 1998. reprint ed. mass mkt. 5.99 (*1-884543-20-0*) O M Lit.

On to Victory: Propaganda Plays of the Woman Suffrage Movement. Bettina Friedl. (Illus.). 378p. 1987. pap. text 18.95 (*1-55553-073-7*) NE U Pr.

On Tobacco Wars. David Kessler. 1999. write for info. (*0-375-50135-5*) Random.

On Toleration. Ed. by Susan Mendus & David Edwards. 152p. 1988. text 49.95 (*0-19-827529-3*) OUP.

On Toleration. Michael Walzer. LC 96-47779. (Castle Lectures in Ethics, Politics, & Economics). 126p. 1997. 27.50 (*0-300-07019-5*) Yale U Pr.

On Toleration. Michael Walzer. 144p. 1999. pap. text 9.95 (*0-300-07600-2*) Yale U Pr.

*On Top of Concord Hill. Maria D. Wilkes. (Little House). (Illus.). 192p. (J). (gr. 3-7). 2000. 15.95 (*0-06-026999-5*); pap. 4.95 (*0-06-440689-X*, HarpTrophy); lib. bdg. 15.89 (*0-06-027003-9*) HarpC Child Bks.

On Top of Old Smoky: A Collection of Songs & Stories from Appalachia. Illus. by Linda Anderson. LC 92-14437. 40p. (J). 1992. 13.95 (*0-8249-8569-9*, Ideals Child) Hambleton-Hill.

On Top of Old Smoky: A Collection of Songs & Stories from Appalachia, Set. Ronald Kidd. LC 92-14437. (Illus.). 40p. (J). 1992. 17.95 incl. audio (*0-8249-7513-8*, Ideals Child) Hambleton-Hill.

On Top of Spaghetti. Tom Glazer. 32p. 14.95 (*0-06-028272-X*); pap. 4.95 (*0-06-443547-4*); lib. bdg. 14.89 (*0-06-028273-8*) HarpC.

On Top of Spaghetti: A Lift-the-Flap Poetry Book. Time-Life Books Editors. (Early Learning Program Ser.). (Illus.). 20p. (J). (ps-2). 1992. write for info. (*0-8094-9291-1*); lib. bdg. write for info. (*0-8094-9292-X*) Time-Life.

On Top of Strawberry Hill. LC 92-34165. (Voyages Ser.). (J). 1993. 14.00 (*0-383-03645-3*) SRA McGraw.

On Top of the Chess World: The 1995 World Chess Championships. Larry Christiansen et al. (Competitive Chess Ser.). (Illus.). 100p. (Orig.). Date not set. pap. 14.95 (*1-886040-20-6*) Hypermodern Pr.

On Top of the World. John Prater. LC 98-16344. (J). (ps-2). 1998. 15.95 (*1-57255-649-8*) Mondo Pubng.

On Top of the World: Five Women Explorers in Tibet. Luree Miller. LC 84-16619. (Illus.). 224p. 1984. reprint ed. pap. 12.95 (*0-89886-097-0*) Mountaineers.

On Top of the World: Women's Political Leadership in Scandinavia & Beyond, 177. Bruce O. Solheim. LC 99-15393. 144p. 2000. 52.95 (*0-313-31000-9*, Greenwood Pr) Greenwood.

On Toplecote Bayou. Catherine Postell. LC 72-1518. (Black Heritage Library Collection). 1977. reprint ed. 15.95 (*0-8369-9048-X*) Ayer.

On Tour: Passport 3. R. A. Montgomery. (YA). 1992. mass mkt. 3.95 (*0-553-54090-4*) BDD Bks Young Read.

On Tourism: Performance Research. Ed. by Richard Gough & Claire MacDonald. (Illus.). 128p. (C). 1998. pap. 17.99 (*0-415-16179-7*) Routledge.

On Tracing the Line of Syntactic Dependence: A Computer-Assisted Study of the Old Testament Hebrew Participial Constructions. J. W. Dyk. LC 95-101514. 1994. pap. 33.00 (*90-5383-278-5*, Pub. by VU Univ Pr) Paul & Co Pubs.

On Track: A Comprehensive System for Early Childhood Intervention. Shelley Neilsen et al. 426p. 1994. pap. text, teacher ed. 47.50 (*1-57035-034-5*, C66MAN) Sopris.

On Track: Activity Book. S. Parks et al. (Illus.). 62p. 1990. pap. text 8.95 (*0-19-458496-8*) OUP.

On Track: The Railway Mail Service in Canada. Susan M. O'Reilly. (Illus.). 152p. 1993. pap. 14.95 (*0-660-14005-5*, Pub. by CN Mus Civilization) U of Wash Pr.

On Track - Antonio. Cameron. (J). 1992. mass mkt., teacher ed. 7.95 (*0-8384-2935-1*) Heinle & Heinle.

On Track in Math: Decimals. Chris Rohde. 95p. 1998. pap. text 13.49 (*1-891559-06-0*) R & R.

On Track in Math: Whole Numbers. Chris Rohde. 103p. 1998. pap. text 13.49 (*1-891559-05-2*) R & R.

On Track Investing: A Guide to Simulation Trading. David R. Hebert. LC 98-27600. 240p. 1999. 19.95 (*0-910019-79-7*) Lghthse Pub Gp.

On Track Julio-intructors Manual. Cameron. (Adult ESL). (J). 1992. teacher ed. 5.95 (*0-8384-2929-7*) Heinle & Heinle.

On Track with the Japanese: A Case-by-Case Approach to Building Successful Relationships. Patricia Gercik. Ed. by Maya Rao. 288p. 1996. pap. 14.00 (*1-56836-130-0*) Kodansha.

On Track/Off Track: Playing the Horses in Troubled Times. James Quinn. LC 96-33872. 320p. 1996. 25.00 (*0-688-07512-6*, Wm Morrow) Morrow Avon.

On Tradition: Essays on the Use & Valuation of the Past. Clifford Davidson. LC 91-57959. (Studies in the Middle Ages: No. 20). (Illus.). 250p. 1992. 45.00 (*0-404-64160-1*) AMS Pr.

On Training Associates. Theodore Voorhees. 278p. 1989. text 29.00 (*0-8318-0535-8*, B535) Am Law Inst.

On Transforming Africa: Discourse with Africa's Leaders. Kofi B. Hadjor. LC 86-73049. 175p. 1987. 25.95 (*0-86543-044-6*) Africa World.

On Transforming Philosophy: A Metaphilosophical Inquiry. Kai Nielsen. 304p. (C). 1995. text 75.00 (*0-8133-0666-3*, Pub. by Westview) HarpC.

On Translating Homer. Matthew Arnold. LC 78-136411. (BCL Ser.: No. 2). reprint ed. 27.50 (*0-404-00388-5*) AMS Pr.

*On Translation: Reflections & Conversations. Edmund Keeley. (Greek Poetry Archive Ser.). 117p. 1999. pap. text 23.00 (*90-5755-072-5*, Harwood Acad Pubs) Gordon & Breach.

*On Translation: Reflections & Conversations. Edmund Keeley. (Greek Poetry Archive Ser.). 117p. 2000. text 28.00 (*90-5755-071-7*, Harwood Acad Pubs) Gordon & Breach.

*On Translation: The Audience. Muntadas. 2000. pap. 15.00 (*90-73362-43-1*) Witte De With CFCA.

On Trek in Kordofan: The Diaries of a British District Officer in the Sudan, 1931-1933. C. A. Lea. Ed. by Martin W. Daly. (Oriental & African Archives Ser.: No. 2). (Illus.). 314p. 1994. text 49.95 (*0-19-726128-0*) OUP.

*On Trial. John Roman. 1999. pap. 18.95 (*1-58374-006-6*) Chicago Spectrum.

On Trial: America's Courts & Their Treatment of Sexually Abused Children. rev. ed. Billie W. Dziech & Charles B. Schudson. LC 90-23545. 240p. 1991. reprint ed. pap. 17.00 (*0-8070-0415-4*) Beacon Pr.

On Trial: The Soviet State vs. "Abram Tertz" & "Nikolai Arzhak" Andrei D. Siniavskii. Ed. by Max Hayward. LC 80-16756. vi, 310p. 1980. reprint ed. lib. bdg. 69.50 (*0-313-22457-9*, HAOT, Greenwood Pr) Greenwood.

On Trial Vol. I: American History Through Court Proceedings & Hearings. Ed. by Robert D. Marcus & Anthony Marcus. 222p. (C). 1998. pap. text 16.50 (*1-881089-24-X*) Brandywine Press.

On Trial Vol. II: American History Through Court Proceedings & Hearings. Ed. by Robert D. Marcus & Anthony Marcus. 230p. (C). 1997. pap. text 16.50 (*1-881089-26-6*) Brandywine Press.

On Trial for My Country. Stanlake Samkange. (African Writers Ser.). 160p. (C). 1967. pap. 8.95 (*0-435-90033-1*, 90033) Heinemann.

On Trout Streams & Salmon Rivers. Dana S. Lamb. (Illus.). 97p. 1996. reprint ed. 50.00 (*1-886967-03-2*) Meadow Run Pr.

On True & False Ideas with Arnauld's New Objections to Descartes' Meditations & Descartes' Replies. Antoine Arnauld. Tr. by Elmar J. Kremer. LC 89-77476. (Studies in the History of Philosophy: Vol. 16). 232p. 1990. lib. bdg. 89.95 (*0-88946-287-9*) E Mellen.

*On Trust: Art & the Temptations of Suspicion. Gabriel Josipovici. LC 99-16233. 289p. 1999. 27.50 (*0-300-07991-5*) Yale U Pr.

*On Trusting the Heart: A Commentary on An Early Ch'an (Zen) Poem by Seng Ts'an. Jim Wilson. 120p. 2000. 15.00 (*0-9677158-2-2*) Hse of Ho Tei.

On Truth: Original Manuscript Materials from the Ramsey Collection at the University of Pittsburgh (1927-1929) Frank P. Ramsey. (Episteme Ser.). 160p. (C). 1991. lib. bdg. 107.50 (*0-7923-0857-3*, Pub. by Kluwer Academic) Kluwer Academic.

On Trying to Teach: The Mind in Correspondence. Robert Gardner. LC 94-28731. 1997. reprint ed. pap. text 24.95 (*0-88163-281-3*) Analytic Pr.

On Tumbledown Hill. Tim Wynne-Jones. (Northern Lights Books for Children Ser.). (Illus.). 32p. 1998. text 15.95 (*0-88995-186-1*, Pub. by Red Deer) Genl Dist Srvs.

*On Turing. Prager. 2000. pap. 8.25 (*0-534-58364-4*) Wadsworth Pub.

On Turner's Trail: 100 Years of Writing Western History. Wilbur R. Jacobs. LC 93-38244. (Illus.). 368p. 1994. 35.00 (*0-7006-0616-5*) U Pr of KS.

On Turning Fifty. Joe Illing. (Illus.). 38p. 1997. pap. text 24.95 incl. audio (*1-57637-005-4*) Blck Hills.

On Turning Sixty-Five: Notes from the Field. John Jerome. LC 99-42761. 272p. 2000. 24.95 (*0-375-50056-1*) Random.

On Two Fronts. Yirmiyahu Bindman. LC 90-82062. (C). 1990. 14.95 (*1-56062-028-5*) CIS Comm.

*On Two Wheels. Anness Publishing Staff. 2000. pap. 19.95 (*1-84215-203-3*) Anness Pub.

*On Tycho's Island: Tycho Brahe & His Assistants, 1570-1601. John Robert Christianson. (Illus.). 464p. 2000. 34.95 (*0-521-65081-X*) Cambridge U Pr.

On Tyranny by Leo Strauss. Ed. by Victor Gourevitch & Michael S. Roth. 1991. pap. 16.95 (*0-02-912735-1*) Free Pr.

On Unbelievable Tales: Palaephatus Peri Apiston. Palaephatus. Ed. & Intro. by Jacob Stern. LC 96-17173. (ENG & GEC.). 1996. 40.00 (*0-86516-310-3*); pap. 20.00 (*0-86516-320-0*) Bolchazy-Carducci.

On Understanding Art Museums. Ed. by Sherman E. Lee. 1975. pap. 2.95 (*0-13-936278-9*) Am Assembly.

On Understanding Art Museums. American Assembly Staff. LC 74-34015. 224p. reprint ed. pap. 69.50 (*0-608-18816-6*, 202986300066) Bks Demand.

On Understanding Buddhists: Essays on the Theravada Tradition in Sri Lanka. John R. Carter. LC 92-10830. (SUNY Series in Buddhist Studies). 251p. 1993. text 19.50 (*0-7914-1413-2*) State U NY Pr.

On Understanding Emotion. Norman K. Denzin. LC 83-23853. (Jossey-Bass Social & Behavioral Science Ser.). 335p. reprint ed. pap. 103.90 (*0-7837-2518-3*, 204267700006) Bks Demand.

On Understanding Intervention in Psychology & Education. Howard S. Adelman & Linda Taylor. LC 94-2986. 296p. 1994. 55.00 (*0-275-94888-9*, Praeger Pubs) Greenwood.

On Understanding Islam. Wilfred C. Smith. (Religion & Reason Ser.: No. 19). 352p. 1984. 80.80 (*90-279-3448-7*); pap. 32.95 (*3-11-010020-7*) Mouton.

On Understanding the Supreme Court: A Series of Lectures Delivered under the Auspices of the Julius Rosenthal Foundation at Northwestern University, School of Law. Paul A. Freund. LC 77-23550. (Illus.). 130p. 1977. reprint ed. lib. bdg. 55.00 (*0-8371-9699-X*, FROU) Greenwood.

On Understanding Understanding: A Philosophy of Knowledge. 2nd rev. ed. Vincent Potter. LC 93-7931. 179p. (C). 1993. pap. 17.00 (*0-8232-1486-9*) Fordham.

On Understanding Variables & Hypotheses in Scientific Research. W. W. Charters, Jr. LC 91-77518. viii, 44p. 1992. pap. 5.95 (*0-86552-115-8*) U of Oreg ERIC.

On Understanding Women. Mary R. Beard. LC 68-54773. (Illus.). 541p. 1969. reprint ed. lib. bdg. 59.75 (*0-8371-0302-9*, BEUW, Greenwood Pr) Greenwood.

On Understanding Works of Art: An Essay in Philosophical Aesthetics. Petra Von Morstein. LC 86-3043. (Problems in Contemporary Philosophy Ser.: Vol. 1). 275p. 1986. lib. bdg. 89.95 (*0-88946-326-3*) E Mellen.

*On Union with God. Albertus Magnus. 96p. 2000. 14.95 (*0-8264-4998-0*) Continuum.

On Unique & Non-Unique Reference & Asymmetric Quantification. Nirit Kadmon. LC 92-13240. (Outstanding Dissertations in Linguistics Ser.). 392p. 1992. text 30.00 (*0-8153-0699-7*) Garland.

On Universals: An Essay in Ontology. Nicholas Wolterstorff. LC 73-121819. 1970. lib. bdg. 20.00 (*0-226-90565-9*) U Ch Pr.

On Universals (De Universalibus), 2 vols. John Wycliffe. Ed. by Ivan J. Mueller. Tr. by Anthony Kenny from LAT. (Illus.). 500p. 1985. text 85.00 (*0-19-824680-3*) OUP.

On Universals (De Universalibus), 2 vols. John Wycliffe. Ed. by Ivan J. Mueller. Tr. by Anthony Kenny from LAT. (Illus.). 240p. 1985. text 75.00 (*0-19-824681-1*) OUP.

On unto Perfection . . . the Choice of the Last Generation! Jim R. Gloyd. LC 97-75244. viii, 100p. (Orig.). 1996. pap. 9.99 (*0-9652067-2-6*) Glory Publng.

On Us. Douglas Woolf. LC 76-52385. 120p. (Orig.). 1977. pap. 10.00 (*0-87685-284-3*) Black Sparrow.

On Valor's Side: Tom Green & the Battles for Early Texas. unabridged ed. Brian Sayers. (Illus.). 189p. 1999. pap. 15.00 (*1-887745-11-4*) Dogwood TX.

On Value in Education. Patricia F. Carini. (Occasional Papers). 33p. (C). 1987. pap. 5.00 (*0-918374-23-5*) City Coll Wk.

On Value in the Arts & Other Essays. Elder Olson. LC 75-9057. 380p. 1992. lib. bdg. 24.00 (*0-226-62895-7*) U Ch Pr.

*On Various Supposed Relations Between the American & Asian Races. Daniel G. Brinton. (LC History-America-E). 151p. 1999. reprint ed. lib. bdg. 69.00 (*0-7812-4312-2*) Rprt Serv.

O

On Verbal Accentuation in the Rigveda. Jared S. Klein. (American Oriental Ser.: Vol. 11). iv, 118p. 1992. pap. 18.50 (*0-940490-90-0*) Am Orient Soc.

On Verse, Its Masters & Explorers see Selected Writings

On Villamayor & Zelinsky's Long Exact Sequence. Mitsuhiro Takeuchi. LC 81-12835. (Memoirs of the American Mathematical Society Ser.: No. 33/249). 178p. 1981. pap. 19.00 (*0-8218-2249-7*, MEMO/33/249) Am Math.

On Violence. Hannah Arendt. LC 74-95867. 114p. (C). 1970. reprint ed. pap. 8.00 (*0-15-669500-6*, Harvest Bks) Harcourt.

On Virginity. Ambrose of Milan. Tr. by Daniel Callam. (Translation Ser.). 65p. 1996. pap. 8.00 (*0-920669-06-9*, Pub. by Peregrina Pubng) Cistercian Pubns.

On Virtue & Vice: Metaphysical Foundations of the Doctrine of the Mean. Richard Bosley. LC 90-25971. (Revisioning Philosophy Ser.: Vol. 6). (Illus.). 303p. (C). 1991. text 46.95 (*0-8204-1442-5*) P Lang Pubng.

***On Virtue Ethics.** Rosalind Hursthouse. LC 99-33141. 288p. 2000. write for info. (*0-19-823818-5*) OUP.

On Visual Media Racism. Franklin E. Wong. Ed. by Roger Daniels. LC 78-3221. (Asian Experience in North America Ser.). 1979. lib. bdg. 31.95 (*0-405-11303-X*) Ayer.

On Vit une Epoque Formidable. Jean-Marc Reiser. (FRE.). 1978. pap. 10.95 (*0-7859-4092-8*) Fr & Eur.

On Vital Reserves: The Energies of Men, How to Push Ourselves to the Utmost. William James. 1991. lib. bdg. 79.95 (*0-8490-4378-6*) Gordon Pr.

On Vivian's Terms. S. Lee Garner. 240p. 1998. pap. 11.95 (*1-891929-04-6*) Four Seasons.

On Voidness: A Study on Buddhist Nihilism. Fernando Tola & Carmen Dragonetti. LC 95-904375. (C). 1995. 16.00 (*81-208-1061-9*, Pub. by Motilal Bnarsidass) S Asia.

On Voluntary Servitude: False Consciousness & the Theory of Ideology. Michael Rosen. LC 95-51510. 304p. (C). 1996. 95.00 (*0-674-63779-8*) HUP.

On Voting: A Public Choice Approach. Gordon Tullock. LC 97-30636. (John Locke Ser.). 208p. (C). 1998. 80.00 (*1-85898-666-4*) E Elgar.

On Wages & Combinations. Robert Torrens. LC 73-95604. (Reprints of Economic Classics Ser.). xi, 133p. 1969. reprint ed. 35.00 (*0-678-00577-X*) Kelley.

On Walter Benjamin: Critical Essays & Recollections. Ed. by Gary Smith. (Studies in Contemporary German Social Thought). 412p. 1991. reprint ed. pap. text 20.00 (*0-262-69143-4*) MIT Pr.

On War. Carl Von Clausewitz. LC 92-55054. 1993. 23.00 (*0-679-42043-6*) Everymns Lib.

On War. Carl Von Clausewitz. Ed. by Michael C. Howard & Peter Paret. LC 75-30190. 752p. 1984. text 75.00 (*0-691-05657-9*, Pub. by Princeton U Pr) Cal Prin Full Svc.

On War. Carl Von Clausewitz. Ed. & Tr. by Michael C. Howard & Peter Paret. 752p. (C). 1984. pap. text 19.95 (*0-691-01854-5*, Pub. by Princeton U Pr) Cal Prin Full Svc.

On War. Carl Von Clausewitz. Ed. & Intro. by Anatol Rapoport. 464p. 1982. pap. 12.95 (*0-14-044427-0*, Penguin Classics) Viking Penguin.

O

On War. Raymond Aron. Tr. by Terence Kilmartin. 164p. 1985. reprint ed. pap. text 19.50 (*0-8191-4565-3*) U Pr of Amer.

On War. Karl Von Clausewitz. reprint ed. lib. bdg. 29.95 (*0-89190-376-3*, Rivercity Pr) Amereon Ltd.

On War. Karl Von Clausewitz. 1990. reprint ed. lib. bdg. 25.95 (*0-89968-497-1*) Buccaneer Bks.

On War Against Japan: Franklin D. Roosevelt's "Day of Infamy" Address of 1941. Raymond Geselbracht. LC 88-600065. (Milestone Documents in the National Archives Ser.). (Illus.). 16p. 1988. pap. text 3.50 (*0-911333-70-3*, 200114) National Archives & Recs.

On War & Morality. Robert L. Holmes. 320p. 1989. pap. text 18.95 (*0-691-02300-X*, Pub. by Princeton U Pr) Cal Prin Full Svc.

On Watching Birds. Lawrence Kilham. LC 97-2883. (Illus.). 208p. (C). 1997. pap. 13.95 (*0-89096-763-6*) Tex A&M Univ Pr.

On Watching Birds. Lawrence Kilham. LC 88-2060. (Illus.). 206p. reprint ed. pap. 63.90 (*0-608-08583-9*, 206910600002) Bks Demand.

On Water. Thomas Farber. (Illus.). 20p. 1991. pap. 15.00 (*0-942067-03-7*) Okeanos Pr.

On Water. Lee Sullivan Hill. LC 99-24228. (Get Around Book Ser.). 32p. (J). (gr. k-3). 1999. 21.27 (*1-57505-309-8*, Carolrhoda) Lerner Pub.

On Waterloo. Christopher Bassford. 260p. 1999. 24.95 (*0-8133-1737-1*) Westview.

On Wave Propagation in Elastic Solids with Cracks. C. Zhang & D. Gross. LC 97-67342. (Advances in Fracture Mechanics Ser.: Vol. 2). 272p. 1997. text 125.00 (*1-85312-535-0*, 5350) Computational Mech MA.

On Way to Wedding. Linda S. Leonard. 1986. 15.95 (*0-394-55250-4*) Random.

On Wealth & Poverty. St. John Chrysostom. Tr. & Intro. by Catharine P. Roth. LC 84-22920. 140p. 1984. pap. text 8.95 (*0-88141-039-X*) St Vladimirs.

On Weathering: The Life of Buildings in Time. Mohsen Mostafavi & David Leatherbarrow. (Illus.). 139p. 1993. 31.50 (*0-262-13291-5*); pap. text 16.95 (*0-262-63144-X*) MIT Pr.

On Wednesday I Cleaned out My Wallet. David Ray. 32p. 1985. 11.00 (*0-942908-15-5*) Pancake Pr.

On Wednesday I Cleaned out My Wallet. David Ray. 32p. (C). 1985. pap. 5.95 (*0-942908-07-4*) Pancake Pr.

On Wellington: The Duke & His Art of War. Jac Weller & Andrew Uffindell. LC 98-17737. (Illus.). 224p. 1998. 34.95 (*1-85367-334-X*, Pub. by Greenhill Bks) Stackpole.

On What Day Did Christ Die? The Last Week of Christ. 2nd rev. ed. Ruth Lascelle. LC 96-80198. 162p. 1997. pap. text 10.00 (*0-9654519-9-2*) Bedrock Pub.

On What Gives Value to Life. Friedrich Daniel Ernst Schleiermacher. Tr. by Edwina Lawler & Terrence N. Tice from GER. LC 94-34621. (Schocken Classics Ser.: Vol. 14). 144p. 1995. text 69.95 (*0-7734-9041-8*) E Mellen.

On "What Is History?" From Carr & Elton to Rorty & White. Keith Jenkins. LC 95-3801. 208p. (C). 1995. pap. 20.99 (*0-415-09725-8*) Routledge.

On "What Is History?" From Carr & Elton to Rorty & White. 208th ed. Keith Jenkins. LC 95-3801. 208p. (C). (gr. 13). 1995. 65.00 (*0-415-09724-X*) Routledge.

On What the Constitution Means. Sotirios A. Barber. LC 83-48049. 256p. 1983. 38.00 (*0-8018-3020-6*) Johns Hopkins.

On What the Constitution Means. Sotirios A. Barber. LC 83-48049. 240p. 1986. reprint ed. pap. text 14.95 (*0-8018-3344-2*) Johns Hopkins.

On What We Don't Know: Explanation, Theory, Linguistics, & How Questions Shape Them. Sylvain Bromberger. LC 92-10906. viii, 240p. (C). 1992. pap. text 18.95 (*0-226-07540-0*) U Ch Pr.

On What We Don't Know: Explanation, Theory, Linguistics, & How Questions Shape Them. Sylvain Bromberger. LC 92-10906. viii, 240p. (C). 1992. lib. bdg. 47.50 (*0-226-07539-7*) U Ch Pr.

On What We Know We Don't Know: Explanation, Theory, Linguistics, & How Questions Shape Them. Sylvain Bromberger. LC 92-10906. 1992. 39.95 (*0-937073-89-X*); pap. 16.95 (*0-937073-88-1*) CSLI.

On Whether or Not to Believe in Your Mind. Norman Fischer. 1987. pap. 7.50 (*0-935724-26-5*) Figures.

On Whitman: The Best from American Literature. Ed. by Louis J. Budd & Edwin Cady. LC 87-8997. x, 298p. 1987. text 49.95 (*0-8223-0752-9*) Duke.

On Whom I Have Mercy. Veronica F. Frame. LC 92-63008. (Illus.). 271p. 1993. 19.00 (*0-9635160-0-0*); pap. 10.00 (*0-9635160-1-9*) Riverview Pub.

On Why the Quiltmaker Became a Dragon: A Visionary Poem. Sheila Nickerson. (Illus.). 59p. 1985. pap. 7.95 (*0-914221-04-3*) Vanessapress.

On Wilhelm Reich & Orgonomy. Wilhelm Reich et al. Ed. by James DeMeo. (Illus.). 176p. (Orig.). (C). 1994. pap. text 20.00 (*0-9621855-3-1*) Natural Energy.

On William Stafford: The Worth of Local Things. Tom Andrews. 296p. 1995. pap. text 18.95 (*0-472-08321-X*, 08321) U of Mich Pr.

On Wing & Wild Water. large type ed. Mike Tomkies. (Illus.). 500p. 1989. 27.99 (*0-7089-2035-7*) Ulverscroft.

On Wings Like Eagles. Lamar Dodson. LC 97-72253. 128p. (Orig.). 1997. pap. 12.95 (*1-882897-16-1*) Lost Coast.

***On Wings Like Eagles Quote Book: Inspiration from Scripture for the Golf Enthusiast.** Ed. by Barbour Publishing Staff. 1998. pap. 3.97 (*1-57748-297-2*) Barbour Pub.

On Wings of Change: Self-Portrait of a Developing Country, Trinidad-Tobago. Clement B. London. 201p. (Orig.). 1991. pap. 13.95 (*0-685-59146-8*) Calaloux Pubns.

On Wings of Eagles. Ken Follett. 432p. 1984. mass mkt. 7.99 (*0-451-16353-2*, Sig) NAL.

On Wings of Eagles: A Collection of Contemporary Prayers. Jerry D. Johnson. 119p. (Orig.). 1994. pap. 8.95 (*1-885473-04-4*) Wood N Barnes.

On Wings of Faith. Frederick Babbel. pap. 13.98 (*1-55517-354-3*) CFI Dist.

On Wings of Faith. Verna Hall Bishop. LC 98-93794. (Illus.). 112p. 1998. pap. 12.95 (*1-57579-092-0*) Pine Hill Pr.

On Wings of Freedom: The Hillel Haggadah. Richard N. Levy. 15.00 (*0-88125-319-7*) Ktav.

On Wings of Healing. Vernelle B. Allen. 90p. 1995. pap. write for info. (*1-885984-06-5*) Wings of Healing.

On Wings of Healing. Ronald Crabtree. 80p. 1986. 40.00 (*0-7223-2002-7*, Pub. by A H S Ltd) St Mut.

***On Wings of Inspiration.** Clara Gerl et al. (Illus.). 68p. 1999. spiral bd. 5.00 (*0-9663820-3-X*) Gerl Publishing.

***On Wings of Light: A Shabat Siddur.** Levy. 2000. write for info. (*0-88125-638-2*) Ktav.

On Wings of Light: The Teachings of Archangel Michael. Ronna Herman. Ed. by Rodney Charles. LC 97-65713. 240p. 1997. pap. 19.95 (*1-887472-19-3*) Sunstar Pubng.

On Wings of Love. Cynthia Harrod-Eagles. 192p. 1999. 24.00 (*0-7278-5422-4*, Pub. by Severn Hse) Chivers N Amer.

On Wings of Love. Elaine L. Schulte. (Serenade Serenata Ser.: No. 1). 192p. (Orig.). 1983. pap. 1.49 (*0-310-46412-9*, 15501P) Zondervan.

On Wings of Love. Ashley Summers. 1997. per. 3.50 (*0-373-76050-7*, 1-76050-3) Silhouette.

On Wings of Magic. Kay Hooper. 224p. 1994. mass mkt. 5.50 (*0-553-56965-1*) Bantam.

On Wings of Power. Lucile M. Campbell. 35p. (Orig.). 1986. pap. 1.95 (*0-9607114-2-2*) L M Campbell.

On Wings of Praise: How I Found Real Joy in a Personal Friendship with God. Kay D. Rizzo. LC 95-49789. 176p. 1996. pap. 12.99 (*0-8280-1050-1*) Review & Herald.

On Wings of Prayer. Mendel Weinbach. 224p. 1973. 8.50 (*0-87559-223-6*) Shalom.

On Wings of Progress: The Story of the Kent County International Airport. James VanVulpen. (Illus.). 96p. (Orig.). (C). 1989. pap. 9.95 (*0-9617708-2-1*) GRMI Hist Comm.

On Wings of Silver Dreams. Sri Chinmoy. 102p. 1997. pap. 6.95 (*0-88497-991-1*) Aum Pubns.

On Wings of Song. Thomas M. Disch. 359p. 1988. mass mkt. 3.95 (*0-88184-443-8*) Carroll & Graf.

***On Wings of Song: Poems about Birds.** J. D. McClatchy. 2000. 12.50 (*0-375-40749-9*) Knopf.

On Wings of Thought. Sarah M. Fountain. (Illus.). 158p. 1982. 6.50 (*0-942078-02-0*) R Tanner Assocs Inc.

On Wings of Truth: A Channeled Book. Janith. Ed. by Teri Griswold & Carol Gino. LC 87-62688. (Illus.). 224p. (Orig.). 1987. pap. 12.95 (*0-944672-00-0*) Star Water Pr.

On Wings to War: Teresa James, Aviator. 2nd ed. Jan Churchill. (Illus.). 184p. (Orig.). 1997. reprint ed. pap. 14.95 (*0-89745-130-9*) Sunflower U Pr.

On Winning the Lottery. Maureen Baldwin. LC 98-90490. (Illus.). 120p. 1998. pap. 12.95 (*0-9664676-0-4*) Winners Pr.

On Wisconsin: The History of Badger Athletics. Don Kopriva & Jim Mott. (Illus.). 221p. 1998. 34.95 (*1-57167-038-6*) Sports Pub.

On Wisconsin Women: Working for Their Rights from Settlement to Suffrage. Genevieve G. McBride. LC 93-846. (History of American Thought & Culture Ser.). (Illus.). 304p. (Orig.). (C). 1993. lib. bdg. 45.00 (*0-299-14000-8*) U of Wis Pr.

On Witchcraft: An Abridged Translation of Johann Weyer's "De Praestigiis Daemonum" abr. ed. Johann Weyer. Ed. by Benjamin G. Kohl & H. Erik Midelfort. Tr. by John Shea. LC 97-36160. 350p. 1998. pap. text 19.95 (*1-889818-02-X*, P34) Pegasus Pr.

On with the Race!, No. 2. Kathryn D. Grace. LC 97-91128. (Carita & Her Friends Ser.). (Illus.). 96p. (J). (gr. 2-6). 1998. pap. 5.95 (*0-9653414-1-0*) Your Books.

On with the Show! Gare Thompson. LC 97-221078. 33 p. 1998. write for info. (*0-8172-7291-7*) Raintree Steck-V.

On with the Show! Cecilia Venn. LC 97-31369. (Real Kids Readers Ser.). (Illus.). 48p. (J). (gr. 1-3). 1998. pap. 3.99 (*0-7613-2036-9*); lib. bdg. 17.90 (*0-7613-2011-3*) Millbrook Pr.

On with the Show! Featuring Brenda Dubrowski. Barbara Aiello & Jeffrey Shulman. (Kids on the Block Bks.). (Illus.). 56p. (J). (gr. 5-8). 1995. 13.95 (*0-941477-06-1*) TFC Bks NY.

On with the Shrew! William Shakespeare. 1983. 3.50 (*0-87129-515-6*, O36) Dramatic Pub.

On with the Story: Adolescents Learning Through Narrative. Susan Wanner. LC 94-5587. (Illus.). 175p. (YA). 1994. pap. text 21.50 (*0-86709-337-4*, 0337, Pub. by Boynton Cook Pubs) Heinemann.

On with the Story: Stories. John Barth. 272p. 1997. pap. 13.95 (*0-316-08359-3*) Little.

***On with the Story: Stories.** John Barth. 1998. pap. 13.95 (*0-316-19094-2*, Back Bay) Little.

On with Torchy. Sewell Ford. LC 75-125210. (Short Story Index Reprint Ser.). (Illus.). 1977. 21.95 (*0-8369-3577-2*) Ayer.

On Wittgenstein. Jaakko Hintikka. (Philosophy Ser.). 1999. pap. text 13.95 (*0-534-57594-3*) Brooks-Cole.

On Wollstonecraft. Johnson. (Philosophy Ser.). 1999. pap. text 13.95 (*0-534-57599-4*) Brooks-Cole.

On Women. Sri Aurobindo & Mother. Ed. by Vijay. 126p. 1985. pap. 5.95 (*81-7060-014-6*, Pub. by SAA) E-W Cultural Ctr.

On Women. Sri Aurobindo Ashram Publications Department Staff & Sri Aurobindo. 126p. (Orig.). pap. 5.95 (*0-89744-236-9*, Pub. by Sri Aurob Ashram Trust) Acrpls Bks CO.

On Women. Clara M. Thompson. Ed. by Maurice R. Green. 7.95 (*0-317-53377-0*, Mer) NAL.

On Women & Friendship: A Collection of Victorian Keepsakes & Traditions. Starr Ockenga. LC 92-27152. (Illus.). 208p. 1993. 17.50 (*1-55670-242-6*) Stewart Tabori & Chang.

On Women & Judaism: A View from Tradition. Blu Greenberg. LC 81-11779. 192p. 1983. pap. 12.95 (*0-8276-0226-X*) JPS Phila.

On Women Healthsharing. Ed. by Enakshi Dua et al. 369p. pap. 17.95 (*0-88961-201-3*, Pub. by Womens Pr) LPC InBook.

On Women Turning Fifty: Celebrating Mid-Life Discoveries. Cathleen Rountree. LC 92-54617. 224p. 1994. reprint ed. pap. 17.00 (*0-06-250731-1*, Pub. by Harper SF) HarpC.

On Women Turning Forty: Coming Into Our Fullness. Cathleen Rountree. (Illus.). 214p. 1991. pap. 16.00 (*0-89594-517-7*) Crossing Pr.

On Women Turning 70: Honoring the Voices of Wisdom. Cathleen Rountree. LC 98-40145. (Illus.). 243p. 1999. 25.00 (*0-7879-4512-9*) Jossey-Bass.

***On Women Turning 70: Honoring the Voices of Wisdom.** large type ed. Cathleen Rountree. LC 00-30290. 2000. write for info. (*0-7862-2563-7*) Thorndike Pr.

On Women Turning Sixty: Embracing the Age of Fulfillment. Cathleen Roundtree. LC 97-5889. 1997. 25.00 (*0-517-70757-8*) Harmony Bks.

On Women Turning 60: Embracing the Age of Fulfillment. Cathleen Rountree. (Illus.). 288p. 1998. pap. 15.00 (*0-609-80228-3*) Harmony Bks.

***On Women Turning 30: Making Choices, Finding Meaning.** Cathleen Rountree. LC 99-50520. 2000. 26.00 (*0-7879-5036-X*) Jossey-Bass.

On-Words: The Game of Word Structures. Layman E. Allen et al. 1978. 25.00 (*0-911624-40-6*) Wffn Proof.

On Wordsworth's Prelude. Herbert S. Lindenberger. LC 75-25493. 316p. 1976. reprint ed. lib. bdg. 60.50 (*0-8371-8417-7*, LIOW, Greenwood Pr) Greenwood.

***On Work & Leadership: A Selection of Lecturers Organized by the Royal Society for the Encouragement of Arts, Manufactures & Commerce.** RSA Staff. (RSA Lecture Ser.). 90p. 1999. 61.95 (*0-566-08108-3*, Pub. by Ashgate Pub) Ashgate Pub Co.

On Work, Race, & the Sociological Imagination. Everett C. Hughes. Ed. by Lewis A. Coser. LC 93-40057. 218p. 1994. pap. text 15.95 (*0-226-35972-7*); lib. bdg. 37.50 (*0-226-35971-9*) U Ch Pr.

On Works & Alms. St. Cyprian of Carthage. 1992. pap. 1.95 (*0-89981-127-2*) Eastern Orthodox.

On World History: An Anthology. Johann G. Herder. Ed. by Hans Adler. Ed. & Tr. by Ernest A. Menze. Tr. by Michael Palma. LC 96-19973. (Sources & Studies in World History). 360p. (gr. 13). 1996. pap. text 36.95 (*1-56324-541-8*) M E Sharpe.

On World History: An Anthology. Johann G. Herder. Ed. by Hans Adler. Ed. & Tr. by Ernest A. Menze. Tr. by Michael Palma. LC 96-19973. (Sources & Studies in World History). 360p. (YA). (gr. 13). 1996. text 76.95 (*1-56324-540-X*) M E Sharpe.

On World Peace. Benito F. Reyes. 24p. 1977. pap. text 1.50 (*0-939375-10-9*) World Univ Amer.

On Wounds in the Head. in the Surgery. on Fractures, on Joints, Mochlikon see Medical Works

On Writers & Writing. John Gardner. Ed. by Stewart O'Nan. LC 94-50798. 1994. 25.00 (*0-201-62672-1*) Addison-Wesley.

On Writers & Writing. John Gardner & Stewart O'Nan. 320p. 1995. pap. 12.00 (*0-201-48338-6*) Addison-Wesley.

On Writer's Block: Removing the Barriers to Creativity. Victoria Nelson. LC 92-38147. 192p. 1993. pap. 14.00 (*0-395-64727-4*) HM.

***On Writing: A Memoir of the Craft.** Stephen King. 304p. 2000. 25.00 (*0-684-85352-3*) Scribner.

***On Writing: A Memoir of the Craft.** large type ed. Stephen King. 2000. 25.00 (*0-7432-0436-0*) S&S Trade.

On Writing: Advice for Those Who Write to Publish (Or Would Like To) George V. Higgins. 240p. 1995. pap. 9.95 (*0-8050-1687-2*, Owl) H Holt & Co.

On Writing & Politics, 1967-1983. Gunter Grass. Tr. by Ralph Manheim from GER. LC 85-786. (Helen & Kurt Wolff Bk.). xv, 157p. 1985. 13.95 (*0-15-169969-0*) Harcourt.

On Writing & Politics, 1967-1983. Gunter Grass. Tr. by Ralph Manheim from GER. 180p. 1986. pap. 11.00 (*0-15-668793-3*, Harvest Bks) Harcourt.

On Writing & Writers: Being Extracts from His Notebooks. Walter Raleigh. Ed. by G. Gordon. LC 68-22939. (Essay Index Reprint Ser.). 1977. 19.95 (*0-8369-0806-6*) Ayer.

On Writing, Editing, & Publishing: Essays Explicative & Hortatory. Jacques Barzun. LC 85-16562. (Chicago Guides to Writing, Editing & Publishing Ser.). 160p. (C). 1986. pap. 8.95 (*0-226-03858-0*) U Ch Pr.

On Writing Qualitative Research: Living by Words. Margot Ely. LC 97-158531. 1997. pap. 27.95 (*0-7507-0603-1*, Falmer Pr) Taylor & Francis.

On Writing Research: The Braddock Essays, 1975-1998. Ed. by Lisa S. Ede & Conference on College Composition and Communication (U.S.). LC 98-89302. 496 p. 1999. pap. 26.95 (*0-312-20264-4*) St Martin.

On Writing Science Fiction: (The Editors Strike Back) George H. Scithers et al. 240p. 1981. 19.50 (*0-913896-19-5*) Owlswick Pr.

On Writing Short Stories. Thomas Bailey. LC 99-35471. 352p. (C). 1999. pap. text 31.95 (*0-19-512272-0*) OUP.

On Writing the College Application Essay: The Key to Acceptance at the College of Your Choice. Harry Bauld. LC 86-46043. 160p. 1987. pap. 12.00 (*0-06-463722-0*, EH 722) HarpC.

***On Writing Well.** 6th rev. ed. William K. Zinsser. LC 97-46201. 320p. 1998. pap. 14.00 (*0-06-273523-3*) HarpC.

On Writing Well: Zinsser,&William K., Set. abr. ed. William Zinsser. 1994. audio 12.00 (*1-55994-349-1*, CPN 1879) HarperAudio.

On Y Va! 2nd ed. Bragger. (Secondary French Ser.). (FRE.). 1994. mass mkt. 37.95 (*0-8384-5535-2*); mass mkt. 37.95 (*0-8384-5536-0*); mass mkt., wbk. ed. 7.95 (*0-8384-5537-9*); mass mkt., wbk. ed. 7.95 (*0-8384-5538-7*) Heinle & Heinle.

On Y Va! 2nd ed. Bragger. (Secondary French Ser.). (FRE.). 1994. mass mkt., teacher ed. 36.95 (*0-8384-5491-7*) Heinle & Heinle.

On y Va, Level 1. Donald Rice & Bragger. 1989. VHS. write for info. (*0-685-30549-X*) Heinle & Heinle.

On Y Va!, Level 1. 2nd ed. Bragger. (Secondary French Ser.). (FRE.). 1993. mass mkt. 47.95 (*0-8384-4142-4*) Heinle & Heinle.

On y Va!, Level 1, 2, 3. 2nd ed. Bragger. (Secondary French Ser.). (FRE.). 1993. audio 18.95 (*0-8384-4182-3*) Heinle & Heinle.

On y Va, Level 2. Donald Rice & Bragger. (YA). (gr. 7-12). 1989. pap. 44.95 (*0-8384-1682-9*) Heinle & Heinle.

On y Va!, Level 2. 2nd ed. Bragger & Rice. (SPA.). 1993. text, teacher ed., wbk. ed. 16.50 (*0-8384-4161-0*) Heinle & Heinle.

On y Va!, Level 3. Bragger. (Secondary French Ser.). 1990. teacher ed. 18.95 (*0-8384-1936-4*) Heinle & Heinle.

On y Va, Level 3. Donald Rice & Bragger. (YA). (gr. 7-12). 1990. mass mkt. 48.95 (*0-8384-1925-9*); mass mkt. 49.95 (*0-8384-1926-7*) Heinle & Heinle.

On y Va!, Level 3. 2nd ed. Bragger & Rice. (SPA.). 1993. pap. text, teacher ed., wbk. ed. 16.75 (*0-8384-4178-5*) Heinle & Heinle.

On Y Va! Level 1, Level 1. 2nd ed. Bragger. (Secondary French Ser.). 1993. mass mkt., suppl. ed. 182.95 (*0-8384-4153-X*); suppl. ed. 196.95 incl. trans. (*0-8384-4156-4*) Heinle & Heinle.

On Y Va! Level 1, Level 1. 2nd ed. Bragger. (Secondary French Ser.). (FRE.). 1993. pap., wbk. ed., lab manual ed. 15.95 (*0-8384-4144-0*) Heinle & Heinle.

On Y Va! Level 1, Level 1. 2nd ed. Bragger. (Secondary French Ser.). 1993. mass mkt., teacher ed., wbk. ed. 18.95 (*0-8384-4145-9*); teacher ed., student ed. 19.95 incl. audio (*0-8384-4154-8*) Heinle & Heinle.

On Y Va! Level 1, Level 1. 2nd ed. Bragger. (Secondary French Ser.). 1993. suppl. ed. 62.95 incl. audio (*0-8384-4319-2*) Heinle & Heinle.

An Asterisk (*) at the beginning of an entry indicates that the title is appearing for the first time.

On Y Va! Level 1, Level 1. 2nd ed. Donald Rice & Bragger. (Secondary French Ser.). 1994. pap., suppl. ed. 17.95 (*0-8384-4152-1*) Heinle & Heinle.

On Y Va! Level 1, Level 1. 2nd annot. ed. Bragger. (Secondary French Ser.). 1993. mass mkt., teacher ed. 56.95 (*0-8384-4143-2*) Heinle & Heinle.

On Y Va! Level 1 Text, Level 1. Donald Rice & Bragger. (Secondary French). 1989. pap. 31.75 (*0-8384-1614-4*) Heinle & Heinle.

On Y Va! Level 2, Level 2. 2nd ed. Bragger. (Secondary French Ser.). 1993. mass mkt., suppl. ed. 21.95 (*0-8384-4163-7*) Heinle & Heinle.

On Y Va! Level 2, Level 2. 2nd ed. Bragger. (Secondary French Ser.). (SPA.). 1993. mass mkt., wbk. ed., lab manual ed. 15.95 (*0-8384-4160-2*); suppl. ed. 196.95 incl. trans. (*0-8384-4171-8*) Heinle & Heinle.

On Y Va! Level 2, Level 2. 2nd ed. Bragger. (Secondary French Ser.). (FRE.). 1993. mass mkt. 49.95 (*0-8384-4158-0*) Heinle & Heinle.

On Y Va! Level 2, Level 2. 2nd ed. Bragger. (Secondary French Ser.). 1993. teacher ed., suppl. ed. 18.95 incl. audio (*0-8384-4170-X*); suppl. ed. 303.95 incl. audio (*0-8384-4162-9*) Heinle & Heinle.

On Y Va! Level 2, Level 2. 2nd ed. Bragger. (Secondary French Ser.). 1994. suppl. ed. 60.95 incl. audio (*0-8384-4191-2*) Heinle & Heinle.

On Y Va! Level 2, Level 2. 2nd ed. Donald Rice & Bragger. (Secondary French Ser.). 1993. mass mkt., suppl. ed. 182.95 (*0-8384-4183-1*) Heinle & Heinle.

On Y Va! Level 2, Level 2. 2nd ed. Donald Rice & Bragger. (Secondary French Ser.). 1994. mass mkt., suppl. ed. 13.95 (*0-8384-4169-6*) Heinle & Heinle.

On Y Va! Level 2, Level 2. 2nd annot. ed. Bragger. (Secondary French Ser.). (FRE.). 1993. mass mkt., teacher ed. 57.95 (*0-8384-4159-9*) Heinle & Heinle.

On Y Va! Level 3, Level 3. 2nd ed. Bragger. (Secondary French Ser.). (SPA.). 1993. mass mkt., wbk. ed., lab manual ed. 15.95 (*0-8384-4177-7*) Heinle & Heinle.

On Y Va! Level 3, Level 3. 2nd ed. Bragger. (Secondary French Ser.). (FRE.). 1993. mass mkt. 50.95 (*0-8384-4172-6*) Heinle & Heinle.

On Y Va! Level 3, Level 3. 2nd ed. Bragger. (Secondary French Ser.). 1993. suppl. ed. 196.95 incl. trans. (*0-8384-4180-7*) Heinle & Heinle.

On Y Va! Level 3, Level 3. 2nd ed. Bragger. (Secondary French Ser.). 1993. mass mkt., suppl. ed. 21.95 (*0-8384-4174-2*) Heinle & Heinle.

On Y Va! Level 3, Level 3. 2nd ed. Bragger. (Secondary French Ser.). 1993. teacher ed., suppl. ed. 18.95 incl. audio (*0-8384-4181-5*); suppl. ed. 62.95 incl. audio (*0-8384-4192-0*) Heinle & Heinle.

On Y Va! Level 3, Level 3. 2nd ed. Bragger. (Secondary French Ser.). 1994. suppl. ed. 303.95 incl. audio (*0-8384-4179-3*) Heinle & Heinle.

On Y Va! Level 3, Level 3. 2nd ed. Donald Rice et al. (Secondary French Ser.). 1993. mass mkt., suppl. ed. 182.95 (*0-8384-4176-9*) Heinle & Heinle.

On Y Va! Level 3, Level 3. 2nd annot. ed. Bragger. (Secondary French Ser.). (FRE.). 1993. mass mkt., teacher ed. 59.95 (*0-8384-4173-4*) Heinle & Heinle.

On Y Va! Level 3 Transparencies. Gutierrez. (Secondary French). 1991. pap., suppl. ed. 95.95 (*0-8384-2382-5*) Heinle & Heinle.

On Y Va! Level 3 Laboratory Tape Program, Level 3. Donald Rice & Bragger. (Secondary French). (YA). (gr. 7-12). 1990. 347.95 (*0-8384-1928-3*) Heinle & Heinle.

On Yankee Station: The Naval Air War over Vietnam. Barrett Tillman & John B. Nichols. (Illus.). 179p. 1987. 22.95 (*0-87021-559-0*) Naval Inst Pr.

On Yonder Mountain. Milly Howard. (Illus.). 120p. (J). (gr. 2-4). 1989. pap. 6.49 (*0-89084-462-3*, 037358) Bob Jones Univ.

On Your Anniversary, Vol. 5. Upper Room Books Staff. (In Your Time of Ser.). 1997. pap. text 20.00 (*0-8358-0790-8*) Upper Room Bks.

On Your Birthday, Vol. 5. Upper Room Books Staff. (In Your Time of Ser.). 1997. pap. text 19.75 (*0-8358-0792-4*) Upper Room Bks.

On Your Feet! Karin L. Badt. LC 94-11651. (World of Difference Ser.). (Illus.). 32p. (J). (gr. 4-6). 1994. pap. 6.95 (*0-516-48189-4*); lib. bdg. 21.00 (*0-516-08189-6*) Childrens.

On Your Knees. Michael Green. 160p. 1992. pap. 6.99 (*0-86347-085-8*, Pub. by Eagle Bks) Shaw Pubs.

On Your Knees, Citizen: A Collection of "Prayers" for the "Public" (Schools) Ed. by Rod Smith et al. 50p. (Orig.). 1996. pap. 6.00 (*0-9619097-8-1*) Edge Bks.

On Your Left: The New Historical Materialism. Ann Kibbey. Ed. by Thomas Foster et al. (Illus.). 340p. (C). 1996. text 55.00 (*0-8147-4681-0*); pap. text 19.50 (*0-8147-4682-9*) NYU Pr.

On Your Mark. (C). 1997. pap. text, teacher ed. 28.07 (*0-673-43787-6*) Addson-Wesley Educ.

***On Your Mark.** 2nd ed. Karen Davy. LC 99-33870. 2000. write for info. (*0-201-47174-4*) Addison-Wesley.

***On Your Mark.** 2nd ed. Karen Davy. LC 99-33871. 2000. 15.67 (*0-201-66394-5*) Addison-Wesley.

On Your Mark, Bk. 2. 2nd ed. (C). 1997. text, teacher ed. 42.14 (*0-673-19594-5*) Addson-Wesley Educ.

ON YOUR MARK BK 2, Bk. 2. 136p. 1997. text 15.23 (*0-673-19593-7*) Addison-Wesley.

On Your Mark, Get Set, Go! Marathon Training. Hatherleigh Press Staff. LC 99-87621. 120p. 2000. pap. 14.95 (*1-57826-050-7*, Pub. by Hatherleigh) Norton.

On Your Mark, Get Set, Ready, Go! Simple Steps to Successful Job-Hunting. George Acquaah. (Illus.). 64p. (Orig.). (C). 1994. pap. text 8.00 (*0-9639370-0-6*) G Acquaah.

On Your Marks: Ready, Set - Learn How to Get a Good Education. Ed. by Kathleen O'Gorman. (Illus.). 208p. 1994. pap. 9.95 (*0-937247-63-4*) Detroit Pr.

***On Your Marks, Get Set, Laugh.** Brendon M. Marks. LC 99-91261. 1999. 25.00 (*0-7388-0708-7*); pap. 18.00 (*0-7388-0709-5*) Xlibris Corp.

***On Your Own.** (Overcoming Obstacles). 28p. (YA). (gr. 9-12). 1999. pap. text 9.38 (*1-929393-26-1*) Community for Ed.

***On Your Own: A Resource Manual for Starting a Successful Private Practice as a Solo Practitioner in Speech-Language Pathology.** Ann M. Coleman. LC 00-27971. 2000. write for info. (*0-89079-853-2*) PRO-ED.

On Your Own: A Widow's Passage to Emotional & Financial Well-Being. Alexandra Armstrong & Mary R. Donahue. 377p. 1999. reprint ed. text 25.00 (*0-7881-6190-3*) DIANE Pub.

***On Your Own: A Widow's Passage to Emotional & Financial Well-Being.** 3rd ed. Alexandra Armstrong & Mary R. Donahue. 392p. 2000. pap. 17.95 (*0-7931-3727-6*, 56087503) Dearborn.

On Your Own: Adult Independence for Ages 18-100. James Stallone & Linda Stallone. LC 91-32157. 212p. (Orig.). 1992. pap. 11.95 (*0-912975-11-3*) Upshur Pr.

On Your Own: Discovering Your New Life & Career Beyond the Corporation. C. D. Peterson. LC 96-35572. 303p. 1997. pap. 16.95 (*0-471-14845-8*) Wiley.

On Your Own: Grammar. Beverly Ann Chin. (C). 1991. pap. text 9.15 (*0-13-634106-3*) P-H.

On Your Own: Professional Growth Through Independent Nursing Practice. Mary L. Lynch. LC 81-19702. 250p. 1983. 33.75 (*0-8185-0507-9*) Jones & Bartlett.

On Your Own: Reading (Text) Donna Stelluto. 336p. (C). 1990. pap. text 9.15 (*0-13-634064-4*) P-H.

On Your Own: Scrumptious, Fail-Safe Recipes & Kitchen Advice. Alice Stern. (Illus.). 201p. (Orig.). 1996. pap. 14.95 (*0-9651489-0-4*, 001) Strght Arrow.

On Your Own, A Personal Budgeting Simulaltion. Donnelly. 1995. 1525.00 (*0-538-62328-4*) Thomson Learn.

On Your Own Again: The Down-to-Earth Guide to Getting Through a Divorce Or Separation & Getting on with Your LIfe. Keith Anderson. 1998. pap. 12.95 (*0-7710-0750-7*) McCland & Stewart.

On Your Own As a Computer Professional: How to Get Started & Succeed As an Independent. 2nd ed. Richard H. Rachals. LC 94-90130. 180p. (Orig.). 1997. pap. 19.95 (*0-9641054-1-1*) Turner Hse Pubns.

On Your Own (But Not Alone) In & Around Phila. rev. ed. Elizabeth Glaze. 160p. 1995. pap. 9.95 (*0-9642482-3-9*) Radnor-Hill Pub.

On Your Own (But Not Alone) In & Around Philadelphia. rev. ed. Elizabeth Glaze. 160p. (Orig.). 1995. pap. 9.95 (*0-9642482-2-0*) Radnor-Hill Pub.

On Your Own but Not Alone: Life after College. William H. Willimon. LC 94-19608. 80p. 1995. 3.88 (*0-687-15526-6*) Dimen for Liv.

On Your Own in El Salvador. Jeff Brauer et al. (Illus.). 1995. pap. 14.95 (*0-9643789-0-6*) On Your Own.

On Your Own in San Francisco: An Entry Plan with Shops, Cafes, Public Transit & Restrooms. rev. ed. Carolyn Caine. Ed. by Ann Gardiner. (Illus.). 160p. 1995. pap. 16.00 (*0-9621246-1-3*) Blue Pearl Pr.

On Your Own Terms: The Seniors' Guide to an Independent Life. large type ed. Linda D. Cirino. 470p. 1996. pap. 23.95 (*0-7838-1594-8*, G K Hall Lrg Type) Mac Lib Ref.

On Your Own Time: The Fortune Guide to Executive Leisure. Marilyn Wellemeyer. 192p. 1988. 24.95 (*0-316-92949-2*) Little.

On Your Potty! Virginia Miller. LC 98-4895. (Illus.). 32p. (J). (ps-k). 1998. pap. 5.99 (*0-7636-0694-4*) Candlewick Pr.

***On Your Potty!** Virginia Miller. LC 98-4895. (Illus.). 22p. (J). 2000. 5.99 (*0-7636-1268-5*) Candlewick Pr.

On Your Retirement: Tax & Benefit Considerations. 192p. 1995. pap. 15.00 (*0-8080-0051-9*, BLS-3413) CCH INC.

On Your Toes. (Vocal Score Ser.). 184p. 1985. per. 45.00 (*0-88188-590-8*, 00312302) H Leonard.

On Your Toes: Vocal Selections. (Illus.). 40p. 1983. pap. 8.95 (*0-88188-265-8*, 00312299) H Leonard.

On Your Way. Anger et al. 1987. pap. text, teacher ed. 18.95 (*0-582-99875-1*, 75299) Longman.

On Your Way (Level One) Building Basic Skills in English. Anger et al. (Illus.). 1987. teacher ed. 18.95 (*0-8013-0126-2*, 75790) Longman.

On Your Way (Level Three) Building Basic Skills in English. Anger et al. 1987. audio 46.95 (*0-582-99878-6*, 75302) Longman.

On Your Way (Level Two) Building Basic Skills in English. Anger et al. 1987. audio 46.95 (*0-582-99876-X*, 75300) Longman.

On Your Way WB 2. Anger et al. 1987. pap. text, student ed. 4.87 (*0-582-90758-6*, 75262) Longman.

On Yuan Chwang's Travels in India, 629-645 A. D., 2 vols., Set. Thomas Watters. LC 74-158213. reprint ed. 67.50 (*0-404-06878-2*) AMS Pr.

On Yuan Chwang's Travels in India, 629-645 A.D. Thomas Watters. 1988. 50.00 (*81-206-0296-X*, Pub. by Asian Educ Servs) S Asia.

On Zarathustra's Language. F. B. J. Kuiper. (Mededelingen der Koninklijke Nederlandse Akademie van Wetenschappen, Afd. Letterkunde Ser.: No. 41(4)). 1978. pap. text 18.75 (*0-7204-8462-6*) Elsevier.

On Zen Practice: Foundations of Practice. Ed. by Hakuyu T. Maezumi & Bernard T. Glassman. LC 76-9463. (Zen Writings Ser.: Vol. 1). (Illus.). 1976. pap. 5.00 (*0-916820-02-5*) Center Pubns.

On Zion. Martin Buber. 194p. 1993. pap. 19.95 (*0-567-29129-4*, Pub. by T & T Clark) Bks Intl VA.

On Zion: The History of an Idea. Martin Buber. Tr. by Stanley Godman. LC 97-15823. xxii, 165p. 1997. pap. 16.95 (*0-8156-0482-3*) Syracuse U Pr.

Ona Dokalskaite: The Art of Ona Dokalskaite-Paskeviciene. Ona Dokalskaite. LC 92-72672. (Illus.). 170p. 1993. 35.00 (*0-9617756-5-3*) Galerija.

Onager. Catran. 1998. pap. 6.95 (*0-7322-5700-X*) HarpC.

***Onarigami.** Monika Wacker. 2000. 42.95 (*3-631-36061-4*) P Lang Pubng.

***Onassis Women: An Eyewitness Account.** Kiki F. Moutsatsos & Phyllis Karas. LC 98-17129. (Illus.). 304p. 1998. 25.95 (*0-399-14443-9*, G P Putnam) Peng Put Young Read.

***Onassis Women: Kaye,&Judy, Set.** Kiki F. Moutsatsos. 1998. audio 18.00 (*0-694-52117-5*) HarperAudio.

Onate & the Nightbirds: A Journey along the Camino Real. Gene Keller. (Illus.). 56p. 1998. 20.00 (*0-944551-29-7*) Sundance Pr TX.

Onawa Bestiary: An Opinionated Survey with Digressions. Henry D. Sherrerd, Jr. LC 87-17984. (Illus.). 154p. (Orig.). 1988. pap. 9.95 (*0-945432-01-1*) Nrth Country Pr.

Onboard Medical Handbook: First Aid & Emergency Medicine Afloat. Paul G. Gill. LC 96-22063. (Illus.). 230p. 1996. pap. 17.95 (*0-07-024274-7*) McGraw.

Once. Hugh Fox. 1995. pap. 5.95 (*1-882633-03-2*) Permeable.

Once: A Lullaby. B. P. Nichol. (Illus.). 24p. (J). (ps-1). 1996. pap. write for info. (*0-88753-105-9*) Black Moss.

Once: Poems. Alice Walker. LC 75-29307. 81p. (C). 1976. reprint ed. pap. 11.00 (*0-15-668745-3*, Harvest Bks) Harcourt.

Once - upon - a - Time Tales: Snow White; The Three Little Pigs; Hansel & Gretel; The Sleeping Beauty; Puss in Boots; Little Red Riding Hood; Jack & the Beanstalk; Rumpelstiltskin; The Ugly Duckling; Beauty & the Beast; Goldilocks & the Three Bears; Cinderella, 12 bks., Set. (Illus.). (J). 1993. pap. 15.48 (*1-56173-499-3*) Pubns Intl Ltd.

***Once a Bride.** Jen Holling. 2000. mass mkt. 6.50 (*0-06-101437-0*) HarpC.

Once a Catholic. Tony Coffey. LC 92-45212. 166p. 1993. pap. 8.99 (*1-56507-045-3*) Harvest Hse.

***Once a Cavalier.** Linda Johnston. 304p. 2000. mass mkt. 5.99 (*0-515-12847-3*, Jove) Berkley Pub.

Once a Cigar Maker: Men, Women, & Work Culture in American Cigar Factories, 1900-1919. Patricia A. Cooper. LC 86-11207. (Working Class in American History Ser.). (Illus.). 376p. 1987. text 23.95 (*0-252-01333-6*) U of Ill Pr.

Once a Cowboy . . . Back to the Ranch. Day Leclaire. (Romance Ser.). 1994. mass mkt. 2.99 (*0-373-03301-X*, 1-03301-8) Harlequin Bks.

***Once a Customer, Always a Customer: How to Deliver Customer Service That Creates Customers for Life.** 3rd ed. Chris Daffy. 320p. 2000. pap. 16.95 (*1-86076-164-X*, Pub. by Oak Tr) Midpt Trade.

Once a Dancer: An Autobiography. Allegra Kent. (Illus.). 340p. Date not set. 26.95 (*0-614-26586-X*) St Martin.

Once a Dancer: An Autobiography. Allegra Kent. 352p. 1998. pap. 16.95 (*0-312-18750-5*) St Martin.

Once a Dewdrop: Essays on the Poetry of Parvin E'Tesami. Intro. by Heshmat Moayyad. LC 94-13077. (Bibliotheca Iranica Ser.: No. 2). (Illus.). 282p. 1994. lib. bdg. 19.95 (*1-56859-016-4*) Mazda Pubs.

Once a Doctor, Always a Doctor: The Memoirs of a German-Jewish Immigrant Physician. Heinz Hartmann. LC 86-42573. 189p. 1986. 27.95 (*0-87975-342-0*) Prometheus Bks.

Once a Fighter Pilot. Jerry W. Cook. (Illus.). 223p. 1996. 22.95 (*0-07-012549-X*) McGraw.

Once a Hermit Kingdom: Ethnicity & Education & National Integration in Nepal. Tod A. Ragsdale. 1989. 75.00 (*0-7855-0232-7*, Pub. by Ratna Pustak Bhandar) St Mut.

Once a Hermit Kingdom: Ethnicity & Education & National Integration in Nepal. Tod A. Ragsdale. 252p. (C). 1989. 300.00 (*0-89771-043-6*, Pub. by Ratna Pustak Bhandar) St Mut.

Once a Hermit Kingdom: Ethnicity, Education & National Integration in Nepal. Tod A. Ragsdale. (C). 1989. 34.00 (*81-85054-75-4*, Pub. by Manohar) S Asia.

***Once a Hero.** Kate Hoffmann. (Harlequin Temptation Ser.). 1999. mass mkt. 3.75 (*0-373-25858-5*, Harlequin) Harlequin Bks.

***Once a Hero.** Theresa Michaels. (Historical Ser.: Vol. 505). 2000. per. 4.99 (*0-373-29105-1*) Harlequin Bks.

Once a Hero. Elizabeth Moon. LC 96-48176. 416p. 1997. 21.00 (*0-671-87769-0*) Baen Bks.

Once a Hero. Elizabeth Moon. 1998. per. 6.99 (*0-671-87871-9*) Baen Bks.

***Once a Hero.** Elizabeth Moon. 1999. per. 1.99 (*0-671-57842-1*) S&S Trade.

Once a Hero. Michael A. Stackpole. 528p. 1994. mass mkt. 5.99 (*0-553-56112-X*) Bantam.

Once a Hero. Katherine Sutcliffe. 352p. 1994. mass mkt. 5.99 (*0-515-11387-5*, Jove) Berkley Pub.

***Once a Hobo: The Autobiography of Monte Holm.** Monte Holm & Dennis L. Clay. LC 99-74413. (Illus.). 353p. 1999. 25.00 (*1-882792-76-9*) Proctor Pubns.

Once a Jolly Bagman. Alistair McAlpine. (Illus.). 256p. 1997. 45.00 (*0-297-81737-X*) Weidenfeld & Nicolson.

Once a Knight. Christina Dodd. 416p. 1999. mass mkt. 3.99 (*0-06-109899-X*) HarpC.

Once a Lawman. Theresa Michaels. (Historical Ser.). 1996. per. 4.99 (*0-373-28916-2*, 1-28916-4) Harlequin Bks.

Once a Legend. Jack Cummings. 1988. 16.95 (*0-8027-4075-8*) Walker & Co.

Once a Legend. large type ed. Jack Cummings. LC 92-25936. 275p. 1992. reprint ed. lib. bdg. 15.95 (*1-56054-436-8*) Thorndike Pr.

Once a Legend. Jack Cummings. 224p. 1992. reprint ed. mass mkt. 3.50 (*1-55817-650-0*, Pinncle Kensgtn) Kensgtn Pub Corp.

Once a Londoner. unabridged ed. James Dowie. Ed. by Frank Szivos. (Illus.). 157p. 1989. pap. 15.95 (*0-9637705-4-3*) Benchmark UT.

***Once a Man Twice a Boy: No. 9 Mine (Open-Closed & Rebirth)** David Kuchta. Ed. by Joy E. Kovalycsik. LC 99-96344. (Illus.). 60p. 2000. pap. 9.95 (*0-9649861-8-3*) Kiwis R Us.

Once a Man, Twice a Child: Driven into Poverty. Ricardo A. Scott. (For Crying Out Loud Ser.). (Illus.). 55p. 1995. pap. 19.95 (*1-883427-44-4*) Crnerstone GA.

Once a Marine: The Memoirs of General A. A. Vandegrift, U.S.M.C. Told to Robert B. Asprey. 348p. 1982. reprint ed. lib. bdg. 9.95 (*0-940328-03-8*) Marine Corps.

Once a Marshal. Peter Brandvold. 288p. 1998. pap. 5.99 (*0-425-16622-8*) Berkley Pub.

Once a Maverick. Theresa Michaels. LC 95-19046. (Historical Ser.). 296p. 1995. per. 4.50 (*0-373-28876-X*, 1-28876-0) Harlequin Bks.

Once a Mistress. Debra Mullins. 384p. 1999. mass mkt. 5.99 (*0-380-80444-1*, Avon Bks) Morrow Avon.

Once a Month: Understanding & Treating PMS. 6th ed. Katharina Dalton. LC 99-10080. (Illus.). 320p. 1999. 25.95 (*0-89793-256-0*); pap. 15.95 (*0-89793-255-2*) Hunter Hse.

Once-a-Month Cooking. Mimi Wilson & Mary B. Lagerborg. (Illus.). 104p. 1986. pap. 11.95 (*0-312-58478-4*) St Martin.

Once-a-Month Cooking. rev. ed. Marilyn S. Wilson & Mary E. Lagerborg. LC 98-40917. 112p. 1999. pap. 11.99 (*0-8054-1835-0*) Broadman.

Once a Month Cooking. rev. ed. Mimi Wilson & Mary Beth Lagerborg. LC 99-30057. 128p. 1999. pap. 12.95 (*0-312-24318-9*) St Martin.

Once a Mouse... Marcia Brown. LC 61-14769. (Illus.). 32p. (J). (ps-3). 1972. lib. bdg. 16.00 (*0-684-12662-1*) Atheneum Yung Read.

Once a Mouse: A Fable Cut in Wood. Marsha Brown. (J). 1989. 9.15 (*0-606-00546-3*, Pub. by Turtleback) Demco.

Once a Nurse, Always a Nurse? Exploring Your Career Alternatives. Betty Hafner. 200p. 1999. pap. 14.95 (*0-87576-223-9*) Pilot Bks.

Once a Parent, Always a Parent. 238p. 1999. mass mkt. 5.99 (*1-56179-674-3*) Focus Family.

Once a Perfect Woman. Paul Wilson. LC 93-206164. 296p. 1992. write for info. (*0-340-56687-6*, Pub. by Hodder & Stought Ltd) Trafalgar.

***Once a Pirate.** Susan Grant. (Timeswept Ser.). 320p. 2000. mass mkt. 4.99 (*0-505-52364-7*, Love Spell) Dorchester Pub Co.

***Once a Pirate.** Tammy Hilz. (Jewels of the Sea Ser.). 2000. mass mkt. 5.50 (*0-8217-6697-X*, Zebra Kensgtn) Kensgtn Pub Corp.

Once a Pony Time at Chincoteague. Barbara Lockhart & Lynne N. Lockhart. (Illus.). 30p. (J). (gr. k-5). 1992. 8.95 (*0-87033-436-0*, Tidewtr Pubs) Cornell Maritime.

Once a Princess. Johanna Lindsey. 432p. 1991. mass mkt. 6.99 (*0-380-75625-0*, Avon Bks) Morrow Avon.

Once a Princess. large type ed. Johanna Lindsey. (General Ser.). 403p. 1992. 18.95 (*0-8161-5313-2*, G K Hall Lrg Type) Mac Lib Ref.

Once a River: Bird Life & Habitat Changes on the Middle Gila. Amadeo M. Rea. LC 82-23815. (Illus.). 285p. 1983. 41.00 (*0-8165-0799-6*) U of Ariz Pr.

***Once a Rogue.** Megan Gray. (Zebra Bks.). 352p. 1999. mass mkt. 5.99 (*0-8217-6406-3*, Zebra Kensgtn) Kensgtn Pub Corp.

Once a Runner. rev. ed. John L. Parker, Jr. LC 78-59993. 194p. (Orig.). 1990. pap. 12.95 (*0-915297-01-9*, OAR) Cedarwinds.

Once a Thief... Evan Skolnick. (Disney's Action Club Ser.). (J). 1998. pap. text 4.50 (*1-57840-219-0*, Pub. by Acclaim Bks) Penguin Putnam.

Once a Thousand Times. Christopher V. Hollister. (Lewiston Poetry Ser.: Vol. 6). (Illus.). 64p. 1989. lib. bdg. 24.95 (*0-88946-895-8*) E Mellen.

Once a Warrior. Fran Baker. LC 98-92659. 344p. 1998. pap. 12.95 (*0-9663397-0-3*, 16579330) Delphi Bks.

Once a Warrior. Karyn Monk. 384p. 1997. mass mkt. 5.99 (*0-553-57422-1*, Fanfare) Bantam.

Once a Warrior King: Memories of an Officer in Vietnam. David Donovan. 352p. 1986. mass mkt. 5.99 (*0-345-33316-0*) Ballantine Pub Grp.

Once-A-Week Cookbook. Joni Hilton. LC 98-32311. 256p. 1999. pap. 15.95 (*0-7615-1773-1*) Prima Pub.

Once a Wicked Lady: A Biography of Margaret Lockwood. large type ed. Hilton Tims. 416p. 1993. 23.95 (*1-85695-110-3*, Pub. by ISIS Lrg Prnt) Transaction Pubs.

Once a Wife (Women Who Dare) Patricia Keelyn. (Superromance Ser.). 1996. per. 3.99 (*0-373-70682-0*, 1-70682-9) Harlequin Bks.

***Once a Wolf.** Susan Krinard. 2000. mass mkt. 5.99 (*0-553-58021-3*) Bantam.

Once a Wolf: How Wildlife Biologists Brought Back the Gray Wolf. Stephen R. Swinburne. LC 98-16865. (The Scientists in the Field Ser.). (Illus.). 48p. (YA). (gr. 5 up). 1999. 16.00 (*0-395-89827-7*) HM.

Once Again for Thucydides. Peter Handke. Tr. by Tess Lewis. LC 98-17509. 96p. 1998. 18.95 (*0-8112-1388-9*, Pub. by New Directions) Norton.

Once an Angel. Teresa Medeiros. 432p. 1993. mass mkt. 5.99 (*0-553-29409-1*) Bantam.

Once an Austalian: Journeys with Barry Humphries, Clive James, Germaine Greer & Robert Hughes. Ian Britain. LC DU121.B75 1997. (Illus.). 304p. 1998. text 29.95 (*0-19-553742-4*) OUP.

Once an Eagle. Anton Myrer. 1976. 49.95 (*0-8488-1438-X*) Amereon Ltd.

***Once an Eagle.** Anton Myrer. 960p. 2000. 25.00 (*0-06-019696-3*) HarpC.

An Asterisk (*) at the beginning of an entry indicates that the title is appearing for the first time.

Once an Outlaw. Theresa Michaels. LC 96-709. 296p. 1995. per. 4.50 (*0-373-28896-4*, 1-28896-8) Harlequin Bks.

***Once & Always.** Alyssa Deane. 352p. 2000. mass mkt. 5.99 (*0-8217-6615-5*, Zebra Kensgtn) Kensgtn Pub Corp.

Once & Always. Judith McNaught. Ed. by Linda Marrow. 1990. per. 7.99 (*0-671-73762-7*) PB.

Once-&-Coming Spirit at Pentecost: Essays on the Liturgical Readings between Easter & Pentecost, Taken from the Acts of the Apostles & from the Gospel According to John. Raymond E. Brown. LC 93-28726. 104p. (Orig.). 1994. pap. 4.95 (*0-8146-2154-6*) Liturgical Pr.

Once & for All. Beatrice Abernathy. LC 93-74790. 1994. pap. 12.95 (*1-55673-891-9*, Express Pr) CSS OH.

Once & for All. Kane Hartman & Art Duerr. (Illus.). 200p. 1990. 18.95 (*0-9627266-0-5*) K Hartman.

Once & for All Cooking: Instructions & Recipes for Preparing a Month's Worth of Meals. 3rd ed. Stephanie Stephens. Ed. by Tara Aronson. (Illus.). 120p. 1994. 19.95 (*0-9675966-0-2*) Family Cookery.

Once & for Always. Stella Cameron. 2000. per. 5.99 (*1-55166-580-8*) Harlequin Bks.

Once & for Always. large type ed. Leigh Michaels. 1995. 11.50 (*0-7505-0827-2*, Pub. by Mgna Lrg Print) Ulverscroft.

***Once & Forever.** Constance O Day Flannery. LC 99-94448. 384p. 1999. mass mkt. 6.50 (*0-380-80170-1*, Avon Bks) Morrow Avon.

Once & Forever. Kenji Miyazawa. 1998. pap. text 12.00 (*4-7700-2184-4*, Pub. by Kodansha Intl) Kodansha.

Once & Forever: The Tales of Kenji Miyazawa. Kenji Miyazawa. Ed. by Shaw. Tr. by John Bester. (Illus.). 304p. 1994. 25.00 (*4-7700-1780-4*) Kodansha.

Once & Future Church: Reinventing the Congregation for a New Mission Frontier. Loren B. Mead. LC 91-72968. (Once & Future Church Ser.). 100p. (Orig.). 1992. pap. 10.95 (*1-56699-050-5*, AL129) Alban Inst.

***Once & Future Con.** Peter Guttridge. 2000. pap. 11.00 (*0-7472-6252-7*, Pub. by Headline Bk Pub) Trafalgar.

***Once & Future Father.** Marie Ferrarella. (Intimate Moments Ser.: Bk. 1017). 2000. mass mkt. 4.50 (*0-373-27087-9*, 1-27087-5) Silhouette.

Once & Future Forest: A Guide to Forest Restoration Strategies. Leslie J. Sauer. LC 97-14843. 350p. 1998. text. write for info. (*1-55963-552-5*); pap. text 30.00 (*1-55963-553-3*) Island Pr.

***Once & Future Gardener: Garden Writing from the Golden Age of Magazines, 1900-1940.** Ed. by Virginia T. Clayton. LC 99-25661. (Illus.). 352p. 1999. 45.00 (*1-56792-102-7*) Godine.

Once & Future Goddess: A Symbol of Our Time. Elinor Gadon. LC 89-45399. (Illus.). 432p. 1989. pap. 29.00 (*0-06-250354-5*, Pub. by Harper SF) HarpC.

Once & Future Goddess British. Elinor Gadon. 1995. pap. write for info. (*0-85030-962-X*, Pub. by Aqrn Pr) Harper SF.

***Once & Future Jesus.** LC 00-42768. 2000. pap. write for info. (*0-944344-80-1*) Polebridge Pr.

***Once & Future King.** Cliffs Notes Staff. (Cliffs Notes Ser.). 112p. 2000. pap. 4.99 (*0-7645-8550-9*) IDG Bks.

Once & Future King. T. H. White. LC 00-722. 639p. 1987. mass mkt. 6.99 (*0-441-62740-4*) Ace Bks.

Once & Future King. T. H. White. 688p. 1996. pap. 16.95 (*0-441-00383-4*) Ace Bks.

Once & Future King. T. H. White. 1958. 25.95 (*0-399-10597-2*, G P Putnam) Peng Put Young Read.

Once & Future King. T. H. White. (Berkley Medallion Book Ser.). 1966. 12.09 (*0-606-01195-1*, Pub. by Turtleback) Demco.

Once & Future King: Curriculum Unit. Center for Learning Network Staff. (Novel Ser.). 122p. (YA). (gr. 9-12). 1994. spiral bd. 18.95 (*1-56077-287-5*) Ctr Learning.

Once & Future Liturgy. J. D. Crichton. 143p. 1989. pap. 22.00 (*0-905092-40-6*, Pub. by Veritas Pubns) St Mut.

Once & Future Love. Anne Kelleher. (Time Passages Ser.). 1998. mass mkt. 5.99 (*0-515-12409-5*, Jove) Berkley Pub.

Once & Future Moon. Paul D. Spudis. LC 95-51343. (Smithsonian Library of the Solar System). (Illus.). 320p. 1996. 34.95 (*1-56098-634-4*) Smithsonian.

Once & Future Moon. Paul D. Spudis. 320p. 1998. pap. 17.95 (*1-56098-847-9*) Smithsonian.

Once & Future Nerd. David C. Morrow. 20p. (Orig.). 1994. pap. 5.00 (*0-9641836-0-9*) Textar Media.

Once & Future Park. Herbert Muschamp et al. Ed. by Deborah Karasov & Stephen Waryan. LC 92-40464. (Illus.). 64p. (Orig.). 1993. pap. 19.95 (*1-878271-76-8*) Princeton Arch.

Once & Future Pastor: The Changing Role of Religious Leaders. William C. Hobgood. LC 97-78130. (Once & Future Church Ser.). 1998. pap. 14.25 (*1-56699-200-1*, AL191) Alban Inst.

Once & Future Resource: A History of Solar Energy. Michael Silverstein. 1977. pap. text 8.00 (*0-915250-32-2*) Environ Design.

Once & Future School: Three Hundred & Fifty Years of American Secondary Education. Jurgen Herbst. LC 96-24908. (Illus.). 280p. (C). 1996. pap. 19.99 (*0-415-91194-X*) Routledge.

Once & Future Wife. Laurie Paige. 1994. per. 3.99 (*0-373-50168-4*, 1-50168-3) Harlequin Bks.

***Once Around.** Barbara Bretton. 338p. 1998. mass mkt. 6.99 (*0-425-16412-8*) Berkley Pub.

Once Around. Ed. by Barbara Bretton. 352p. 1998. mass mkt. 6.99 (*0-425-16555-8*) Berkley Pub.

Once Around. Ward M. LeHardy & Judy N. LeHardy. LC 96-92919. (Illus.). 292p. (Orig.). 1997. pap. 11.95 (*0-9656111-0-8*, A794-133) Once Around.

Once around Bloch. Bloch. 1995. mass mkt. 4.99 (*0-8125-2089-0*) Tor Bks.

Once Around Bullough's Pond. Douglas Worth. (Orig.). 1987. pap. 8.95 (*0-87233-092-3*) Bauhan.

Once Around San Diego: The Essential Sights. F. Robert Richards & Richards. (Illus.). 50p. 1997. pap. 12.95 incl. audio (*0-9661311-0-X*, 100) Comp Cir Tours.

Once Around the Bases: Bittersweet Memories of Only One Game in the Majors. Richard Tellis. LC 98-15934. (Illus.). 308p. 1998. 24.95 (*1-57243-277-2*) Triumph Bks.

Once Around the Realms. Brian Thomsen. 320p. (Orig.). 1995. pap. 4.95 (*0-7869-0119-5*, Pub. by TSR Inc) Random.

***Once Around the Table: Recipes for the Body & Soul.** Riverwood Roundtable Writers Staff. 2000. 9.50 (*1-891609-06-8*) Home Brew Pr.

Once Around the Track. Chikuyo Alimayo, pseud. (Illus.). (YA). (gr. 9-12). 1974. 7.95 (*0-9606692-2-1*) Eko Pubns.

Once around the Track. Chikuyo Alimayo, pseud. (Illus.). (YA). (gr. 9-12). 1974. pap. 3.95 (*0-9606692-3-X*) Eko Pubns.

Once Around the Wheel: Want to Go Again? Lynne Rich. LC 95-81030. 90p. (Orig.). 1995. pap. 12.99 (*1-888207-00-0*) LghtHeart Bks.

Once Before I Go. Wayne Newton & Dick Maurice. 320p. 1991. mass mkt. 4.95 (*0-380-71405-1*, Avon Bks) Morrow Avon.

***Once Below a Time: The Genesis of a Speaking Subject in the Poetry of Dylan Thomas.** Eynel Wardi. LC 99-89097. (C). 2000. text 59.50 (*0-7914-4559-3*); pap. text 19.95 (*0-7914-4560-7*) State U NY Pr.

Once Bitten Twice Shy. Robyn Donald. (Presents Ser.). 1993. per. 2.99 (*0-373-11565-2*, 1-11565-8) Harlequin Bks.

Once-Born, Twice-Born Zen: The Soto & Rinzai Schools of Japanese Zen. Conrad Hyers. LC 88-13789. 118p. 1989. pap. 15.95 (*0-89341-524-3*, Longwood Academic) Hollowbrook.

Once Burned. Margaret Way. LC 96-478. 188p. 1995. mass mkt. 2.99 (*0-373-03381-8*, 1-03381-0) Harlequin Bks.

Once Burned. large type ed. Margaret Way. (Harlequin Romance Ser.). 1997. 20.95 (*0-263-14973-0*) Mac Lib Ref.

Once Charitable Enterprise: Hospitals & Health Care in Brooklyn & New York, 1855-1915. David Rosner. LC 81-21725. (Interdisciplinary Perspectives on Modern History Ser.). 288p. 1982. text 59.95 (*0-521-24217-7*) Cambridge U Pr.

Once Charitable Enterprise: Hospitals & Health Care in Brooklyn & New York, 1855-1915. David Rosner. LC 81-21725. (Illus.). 248p. 1986. pap. text 16.95 (*0-691-02835-4*, Pub. by Princeton U Pr) Cal Prin Full Svc.

Once Daily Ceftriaxone vs. Multiple Comparative Drugs. Ed. by F. Fraschini. (Journal: Chemotherapy: Vol. 34, Suppl. 1). (Illus.). iv, 60p. 1989. pap. 19.25 (*3-8055-4961-X*) S Karger.

Once Drunk - Opening. Vicky Edmonds. 33p. 1995. pap. 8.00 (*0-9639918-2-5*) E All Above.

Once Five Years Pass: And Other Dramatic Works. Federico Garcia Lorca. Ed. & Tr. by William B. Logan & Angel G. Orrios from SPA. (Illus.). 248p. 1989. 24.95 (*0-88268-070-6*) Station Hill Pr.

Once for the Asking: Manuscript Edition. Owen G. Arno. 1964. pap. 13.00 (*0-8222-0850-4*) Dramatists Play.

Once I Gazed at You in Wonder. Jan H. Levi. LC 98-50182. 96p. 1999. 19.95 (*0-8071-2364-1*); pap. 12.95 (*0-8071-2365-X*) La State U Pr.

Once I Loved Him Madly. Mariann Ritzer. (Orig.). 1996. pap. 6.00 (*0-9644333-5-4*) CrossplusRds.

***Once I Saw a Butterfly.** Sharon Shi. (Illus.). 15p. (J). (ps-2). 2000. pap. 4.99 (*0-9678636-0-0*, B001, Tattootles Bks) Tattoo Manuf.

Once I Was.... Niki Leopold. LC 98-15461. (Illus.). 32p. (J). (gr. k up). 1999. 15.99 (*0-399-23105-6*, G P Putnam) Peng Put Young Read.

Once I Was a Child & There Was Much Pain . . . A Glimpse into the Soul of an Incest Survivor. E. Nancy. LC 88-28281. (Illus.). 104p. (Orig.). 1989. pap. 6.95 (*0-9603628-7-8*) Frog in Well.

Once I Was a Plum Tree. Johanna Hurwitz. Ed. by ALC Staff. LC 79-23518. (Illus.). 160p. (J). (gr. 4-7). 1992. mass mkt. 3.95 (*0-688-11848-8*, Wm Morrow) Morrow Avon.

Once I Was a Plum Tree. Johanna Hurwitz. (J). 1992. 9.05 (*0-606-01384-9*, Pub. by Turtleback) Demco.

Once I Was Very Small. Elizabeth Ferber. (Illus.). 24p. (J). (ps up). 1995. pap. 4.95 (*1-55037-321-8*, Pub. by Annick); lib. bdg. 14.95 (*1-55037-318-8*, Pub. by Annick) Firefly Bks Ltd.

***Once I Was Very Young.** Mary Coolidge Perkins. LC 99-56335. (Illus.). 2000. write for info. (*0-914339-88-5*) P E Randall Pub.

Once in a Blue Moon. Kristin James. 1995. per. 3.25 (*0-373-05962-0*, 1-05962-5) Silhouette.

***Once in a Blue Moon Boot Bus.** Rebecca Ondov Blasing. LC 00-24226. (Illus.). (J). 2000. 10.99 (*0-7814-3439-4*) Cook Communs Minist.

Once in a House on Fire. Andrea Ashworth. LC 97-46680. 327p. 1998. 23.00 (*0-8050-5762-5*, Metropol Bks) H Holt & Co.

Once in a House on Fire: A Memoir. Andrea Ashworth. 336p. 1999. pap. 14.00 (*0-8050-5763-3*, Owl) H Holt & Co.

***Once in a Lifetime.** Hurley B. Miller. LC 99-74704. 128p. 2000. pap. 11.95 (*1-57197-195-5*, Pub. by Pentland Pr) Assoc Pubs Grp.

Once in a Lifetime. Constance Oday-Flannery. 1994. mass mkt. 5.99 (*0-8217-5918-3*, Zebra Kensgtn) Kensgtn Pub Corp.

Once in a Lifetime. Danielle Steel. 480p. (Orig.). 1983. mass mkt. 6.99 (*0-440-16649-7*) Dell.

***Once in a Lifetime: A World War II Memoir.** Robert A. Nusbaum. (World War II Memoir Ser.: Vol. 54). (Illus.). 116p. 1999. 34.95 (*1-57638-171-4*, 54-H); pap. 24.95 (*1-57638-170-6*, 54-S) Merriam Pr.

Once in a Long While: The Romancing of a Contemporary Cowboy. Sandra Mansfield & Judy Groover. 192p. 1996. 24.95 (*0-9630463-8-1*) S & D.

Once in a Very Blue Moon: A Pat Alger Songbook. Pat Alger. Ed. by Milton Okun. 1994. pap. 16.95 (*0-89524-779-8*) Cherry Lane.

Once in a While the Odd Thing Happens: A Play from the Life of Benjamin Britten. Paul Godfrey. LC 95-221516. (Methuen New Theatrescripts Ser.). 86p. (Orig.). (C). 1990. pap. 10.95 (*0-413-64480-4*, A0492, Methuen Drama) Methn.

Once in a Wood. Houghton Mifflin Company Staff. (Literature Experience 1991 Ser.). (J). (gr. 2). 1990. pap. 9.48 (*0-395-55149-8*) HM.

Once in a Wood. Houghton Mifflin Company Staff. (Literature Experience 1993 Ser.). (J). (gr. 2). 1992. pap. 9.48 (*0-395-61779-0*) HM.

Once in a Wood: Ten Tales from Aesop. Eve Rice. 1993. 10.15 (*0-606-05522-3*, Pub. by Turtleback) Demco.

Once in a Wood: Ten Tales from Aesop. Aesop. LC 92-24605. (Illus.). 64p. (J). (gr. 1 up). 1993. reprint ed. pap. 4.95 (*0-688-12268-X*, Wm Morrow) Morrow Avon.

Once in Blueberry Dell. Dawn L. Watkins. (Illus.). 32p. (J). 1995. pap. 5.49 (*0-89084-828-9*, 088377) Bob Jones Univ.

Once in Christ in Christ Forever: More Than 100 Biblical Reasons Why a True Believer Cannot Be Lost. William MacDonald. 1997. pap. 10.95 (*1-882701-43-7*) Uplook Min.

***Once in Europa.** John Berger. (Illus.). 2000. 27.50 (*1-58234-070-6*) Bloomsbury Pubg.

Once in Europa. John Berger. LC 92-50075. 1992. pap. 14.00 (*0-679-73716-2*) Vin Bks.

Once in Every Life. Kristin Hannah. 1993. mass mkt. 4.99 (*0-449-14838-6*, GM) Fawcett.

Once in Every Life. large type ed. Kristin Hannah. LC 93-22680. 501p. 1993. lib. bdg. 21.95 (*0-8161-5827-4*, G K Hall Lrg Type) Mac Lib Ref.

***Once in Golconda: A True Drama of Wall Street, 1920-1938.** LC 99-33868. 307p. 1999. pap. 19.95 (*0-471-35752-9*) Wiley.

***Once in Golconda: A True Drama of Wall Street, 1920-1938.** John Brooks. LC 99-33868. (Wiley Investment Classics Ser.). 320p. 1999. 34.95 (*0-471-35753-7*) Wiley.

Once in Love with a Puppy. Lee Netzler. 38p. 1984. reprint ed. pap. 6.95 (*0-9647696-0-3*) Netzler Pubng.

Once in, Never Out. Dan Mahoney. LC 97-40422. 352p. 1998. text 24.95 (*0-312-18228-7*) St Martin.

Once in, Never Out. Dan Mahoney. 480p. Date not set. pap. 6.99 (*0-312-96676-8*, Pub. by Tor Bks) St Martin.

Once in Old Frederica Town. unabridged ed. Bill Westhead. LC 93-94674. (Illus.). 348p. (Orig.). 1994. pap. 9.95 (*1-56883-001-7*) Colonial Pr AL.

Once in Paris. Diana Palmer. 377p. 1998. mass mkt. 5.99 (*1-55166-470-4*, 1-66470-5, Mira Bks) Harlequin Bks.

Once in the Country: Poems of a Farm. Tony Johnston. LC 94-40899. (Illus.). 32p. (J). (ps-3). 1996. 15.95 (*0-399-22644-3*, G P Putnam) Peng Put Young Read.

Once in the Saddle: The Cowboy's Frontier 1866-1896. Laurence I. Seidman. (Illus.). 160p. (YA). (gr. 7-12). 1991. 19.95 (*0-8160-2373-5*) Facts on File.

***Once in the Saddle: The Cowboy's Frontier 1866-1896.** Laurence I. Seidman. 158p. 1999. 21.95 (*0-7351-0221-X*) Replica Bks.

Once, in the Time of Trolls. Sandra F. Asher. 1995. 5.50 (*0-87129-594-6*, O28) Dramatic Pub.

Once in the Wind of Morning. H. J. Adams. LC 95-74948. (Illus.). 208p. 1996. lib. bdg. 15.95 (*0-923687-37-8*) Celo Valley Bks.

***Once in Vermont.** Bob Arnold. LC 99-73467. 128p. 1999. pap. 13.50 (*0-917788-74-5*, Pub. by Gnomon Pr) SPD-Small Pr Dist.

Once Is Enough. Miles Smeeton. 207p. 1984. 18.95 (*0-916025-03-9*) Armchair Sail Pub.

Once Is for Always. Tisziji Munoz. (Orig.). 1991. pap. 10.00 (*0-945174-24-1*) Illum Soc Pubns.

Once Is Not Enough. Jacqueline Susann. 480p. 1998. pap. 14.00 (*0-8021-3545-5*, Grove) Grove-Atltic.

Once More. Colleen Faulkner. 352p. 1998. pap. 5.99 (*0-8217-5984-1*, Zebra Kensgtn) Kensgtn Pub Corp.

Once More . . . from the Beginning: Reminiscences of a Virtuoso & Teacher of the Double Bass. Oscar G. Zimmerman & George Murphy. 400p. 1993. pap. write for info. (*1-883568-00-5*) A J Zimmerman.

Once More a Family. Paula D. Riggs. (Intimate Moments Ser.: No. 933). 1999. per. 4.25 (*0-373-07933-8*, 1-07933-4) Silhouette.

Once More Around the Block: Familiar Essays. Joseph Epstein. 256p. 1990. pap. 8.95 (*0-393-30633-X*) Norton.

Once More from Emmaus. Carlo M. Martini. Tr. by Matthew J. O'Connell. 120p. (Orig.). 1995. pap. 8.95 (*0-8146-2158-9*) Liturgical Pr.

Once More Out of Darkness. Alicia S. Ostriker. 32p. 1974. pap. 9.95 (*0-917658-00-0*) BPW & P.

***Once More with a .44.** Peter Brandvold. 2000. mass mkt. 5.99 (*0-425-17556-1*) Berkley Pub.

Once More with Feeling. Peggy J. Herring. 240p. 1995. pap. 11.95 (*1-56280-089-2*) Naiad Pr.

Once More with Feeling. Emilie Richards. 384p. (Orig.). 1996. mass mkt. 5.99 (*0-380-78363-0*, Avon Bks) Morrow Avon.

Once More with Feeling. Nora Roberts. LC 95-21497. 251p. 1995. mass mkt. 5.99 (*0-373-15311-2*, 1-15311-3) Harlequin Bks.

Once More, with Feeling. large type ed. Caroline Anderson. 288p. 1995. 23.99 (*0-263-14329-5*, Pub. by Mills & Boon) Ulverscroft.

Once More, with Feeling: Manuscript Edition. Harr Kurnitz. 1961. pap. 13.00 (*0-8222-0851-2*) Dramatists Play.

Once More with Feeling: You'll Never Make Love in This Town Again, Again, 2 cass. abr. ed. Joanne Parrent. 1996. audio. write for info. (*0-7871-1036-1*, Dove Audio) NewStar Media.

Once More with Joy: Perspectives of Cranbrook School for Boys. Ben M. Snyder, III. Ed. by Charles T. Shaw & Jeffrey Welch. (Illus.). 320p. 1997. 29.95 (*0-9636492-2-1*) Cranbrook Educ.

Once More with Love: A Guide to Marrying Again. Bobbi Coyle-Hennessey. LC 92-74312. 192p. 1993. pap. 11.95 (*0-87793-498-3*) Ave Maria.

Once My Name Was Sara. I. Betty Grebenschikoff. (Illus.). 200p. 1999. reprint ed. pap. text 14.95 (*0-9639344-0-6*) Orig Seven.

Once on a Quiet Night. Sandra T. Ford. 1.00 (*0-687-08124-6*) Abingdon.

Once on This Island. Gloria Whelan. LC 94-48228. 192p. (J). (gr. 3-7). 1995. lib. bdg. 14.89 (*0-06-026249-4*) HarpC Child Bks.

Once on This Island. Gloria Whelan. LC 94-48228. 192p. (J). (gr. 4-7). 1995. 15.95 (*0-06-026248-6*) HarpC Child Bks.

Once on This Island. Gloria Whelan. LC 94-48228. (Trophy Bk.). 192p. (J). (gr. 4-7). 1996. pap. 4.95 (*0-06-440619-9*, HarpTrophy) HarpC Child Bks.

Once on This Island. Gloria Whelan. LC 94-48228. (J). 1996. 10.05 (*0-606-09709-0*, Pub. by Turtleback) Demco.

Once on This Island: Vocal Selections. 68p. (Orig.). 1994. pap. 18.95 (*0-89724-333-1*, VF1680) Wrner Bros.

Once on This River. Sharon D. Wyeth. LC 97-28779. 150p. (J). (gr. 5-8). 1997. lib. bdg. 17.99 (*0-679-98350-3*, Pub. by Knopf Bks Yng Read) Random.

Once on This River. Sharon D. Wyeth. (J). 1999. pap. 4.99 (*0-679-89446-2*, Pub. by Random Bks Yng Read) Random.

Once Out of Nature. Jim Simmerman. LC 88-18062. 67p. (Orig.). 1989. pap. 9.95 (*0-913123-21-8*) Galileo.

Once over & Lightly. 2nd ed. Howard E. Crouch & Sister Mary Augustine. LC 94-84819. 239p. 1996. reprint ed. 12.00 (*0-9606330-3-0*) Damien-Dutton Soc.

Once Remembered, Twice Lived. Roser Caminals-Heath. LC 92-31509. (Catalan Studies: Translations & Criticism: Vol. 4). 258p. (Orig.). (C). 1993. pap. text 32.95 (*0-8204-1969-9*) P Lang Pubng.

Once Removed. David Applefield. LC 96-931076. 1997. pap. 15.95 (*0-88962-622-7*) Mosaic.

Once Round the Sun. Elsa-Brita Titchenell. LC 81-52615. (Illus.). iv, 57p. (J). (gr. 1 up). 1981. reprint ed. 12.95 (*0-911500-61-8*) Theos U Pr.

Once Saved, Always Saved. J. E. Elliott. 74p. (Orig.). 1986. pap. 2.25 (*0-934942-62-5*, 4115) White Wing Pub.

Once Saved, Always Saved. R. T. Kendall. (Biblical Classics Library: Vol. 28). 238p. (Orig.). 1997. reprint ed. mass mkt. 5.99 (*0-85364-796-8*, Pub. by Paternoster Pub) OM Literature.

Once Saved, Always Saved: Truth or Delusion? Paul Landis. (Cornerstone Ser.). 143p. 1991. pap. 4.75 (*0-7399-0198-2*, 2332) Rod & Staff.

***Once So Bright.** Louis Gamba. LC 99-65233. 192p. 2000. pap. 12.95 (*1-58501-022-7*, Pub. by CeShore Pubg) Natl Bk Netwk.

Once the Buddha Was a Monkey: Arya Sura's Jatakamala. Arya Sura. Tr. by Peter Khoroche from SAN. (Illus.). 294p. 1989. 29.95 (*0-226-78003-1*) U Ch Pr.

Once the Dust. Carol Hamilton. 24p. 1995. reprint ed. 5.00 (*0-936908-03-3*) Broncho Pr.

Once There Was a Bull . . . Frog. Rick Walton. (Illus.). 32p. (J). 1998. pap. 5.99 (*0-698-11607-0*, PapStar) Peng Put Young Read.

Once There Was a Bull--Frog. Rick Walton. LC 94-32513. (Illus.). 32p. (J). (ps-3). 1995. 15.95 (*0-87905-652-5*) Gibbs Smith Pub.

Once There Was a Bull...(Frog) Rick Walton. 1998. 11.19 (*0-606-13679-7*, Pub. by Turtleback) Demco.

***Once There Was a Central Europe.** Mikios Meszoly. 196p. 1999. pap. 21.00 (*963-13-3738-3*, Pub. by Corvina Bks) St Mut.

Once There Was a Farm . . . large type ed. Virginia Bell Dabney. 1990. lib. bdg. 18.95 (*1-56054-030-3*) Thorndike Pr.

Once There Was a Farm: A Country Childhood Remembered. Virginia B. Dabney. LC 98-4241. (Virginia Bookshelf Ser.). 283p. 1998. reprint ed. pap. 14.95 (*0-8139-1847-2*) U Pr of Va.

Once There Was a Hassid. Devorah Omer. (Illus.). 28p. (J). (gr. 4 up). 1987. 9.95 (*0-915361-73-6*) Lambda Pubs.

***Once There Was a Hoodie.** Sam McBratney. LC 00-23137. (Illus.). (J). 2001. write for info. (*0-399-23581-7*, G P Putnam) Peng Put Young Read.

Once There Was a Man. Cille Fletcher. viii, 321p. 1999. pap. 15.99 (*0-9672556-0-0*) L Streun.

Once There Was a President. rev. ed. S. J. Frolick. LC 80-69972. (Once There Was ... Ser.). 64p. (J). (gr. 3-7). 1980. reprint ed. pap. 6.95 (*0-9605426-0-4*) Black Star Pub.

Once There Was a Stream. Joel Rothman. LC 72-90692. (Illus.). 32p. (J). (gr. k-4). 1973. 12.95 (*0-87592-038-1*) Scroll Pr.

Once There Was a Tree. Natalia Romanova. 1989. 11.19 (*0-606-05056-6*, Pub. by Turtleback) Demco.

Once There Was a Tree. Natalie Romanova. 1992. pap. 5.99 (*0-14-054677-4*) NAL.

An Asterisk (*) at the beginning of an entry indicates that the title is appearing for the first time.

Once There Was a Village: A Russian Artist's Memoirs from the Fast Village in the Late Sixties. Yuri Kapralov. Ed. by Gabrielle Danchick. LC 98-70718. (Illus.). 164p. 1998. reprint ed. pap. 12.00 (*1-888451-05-X*, AKB 02) Akashic Bks.

Once There Was a War. John Steinbeck. LC 94-167754. (Penguin Twentieth-Century Classics Ser.). 256p. 1994. pap. 12.95 (*0-14-018747-2*, Penguin Classics) Viking Penguin.

Once There Was a Way Back Home. Louise M. Gouge. LC 94-12226. (Homeward Journey Ser.: Bk. 1). 1994. pap. 8.99 (*0-89107-804-5*) Crossway Bks.

Once There Were Giants. Martin Waddell. LC 94-40021. (Illus.). 32p. (J). (ps-3). 1997. reprint ed. pap. 5.99 (*0-7636-0286-8*) Candlewick Pr.

Once There Were Giants. 2nd ed. Martin Waddell. LC 94-40021. (Illus.). 32p. (J). (ps up). 1995. 15.99 (*1-56402-612-4*) Candlewick Pr.

Once There Were Greenfields: How Urban Sprawl Is Undermining America's Environment, Economy, Social Fabric. Kaid Benfield et al. LC 99-19928. 1999. pap. 20.00 (*1-893340-17-1*) Natl Resources Defense Coun.

Once They Moved Like the Wind: Cochise, Geronimo, & the Apache Wars. David Roberts. LC 93-7112. (Illus.). 320p. 1993. 24.00 (*0-671-70221-1*) S&S Trade.

Once They Moved Like the Wind: Cochise, Geronimo, & the Apache Wars. David Roberts. LC 93-7112. 386p. 1994. per. 14.00 (*0-671-88556-1*, Touchstone) S&S Trade Pap.

Once They Were Eagles: The Men of the Black Sheep Squadron. Frank E. Walton. (Illus.). 240p. 1996. pap. 18.00 (*0-8131-0875-6*) U Pr of Ky.

Once to Every Man & Nation: Stories about Becoming a Baha'i. Randie Gotlieb & Steven Gotlieb. 160p. 1985. pap. 8.95 (*0-85398-211-2*) G Ronald Pub.

Once Told Tales of Worcester County. Albert B. Southwick. LC 94-71907. (Illus.). 170p. 1994. reprint ed. pap. 14.99 (*0-9636277-4-0*) Chandler Hse.

Once Told, They're Gold: Stories to Enliven & Enrich the Workplace. David M. Armstrong. (Illus.). 320p. 1998. pap. 16.00 (*0-9648027-2-4*) D M Armstrong.

Once Too Often: An Inspector Luke Thanet Novel. Dorothy Simpson. LC 97-32513. 224p. 1998. 20.50 (*0-684-84578-4*) S&S Trade.

Once Too Often: An Inspector Luke Thanet Novel. aut. ed. Dorothy Simpson. LC 97-32513. 1998. 21.00 (*0-684-84912-7*) S&S Trade.

Once Unknown Familiar: Shamanic Paths to Unleash Your Animal Powers. Timothy Roderick. LC 94-5748. (Illus.). 240p. 1994. pap., wbk. ed. 10.00 (*0-87542-439-2*) Llewellyn Pubns.

Once upon a Bagel. Jay Harlow. LC 94-34557. (Illus.). 120p. 1994. pap. 10.95 (*1-883791-01-4*, Astolat Bks) Harlow & Ratner.

Once upon a Bedtime Story: Classic Tales. Illus. by Ruth T. Councell. LC 96-80397. 96p. (J). (ps-1). 1997. 17.95 (*1-56397-484-3*) Boyds Mills Pr.

Once Upon a Breath: The Story of a Wolf, 3 Pigs & Asthma. Aaron Zevy. 1998. pap. text 6.99 (*0-9680678-1-6*) Tumbleweed Pr.

Once upon a Broomstick: A Halloween Happening in One Act. Sylvia Ashby. (Illus.). 28p. (Orig.). (J). (gr. 1-8). 1990. pap. 3.25 (*0-88680-329-2*) I E Clark.

Once upon a Campus: Lessons for Improving Quality & Productivity in Higher Education. Daniel T. Seymour. LC 94-47394. 208p. 1995. pap. 24.95 (*0-89774-965-0*) Oryx Pr.

***Once upon a Carpet.** Kathleen Ryniker Bashian. LC 99-90654. (Illus.). 96p. 1999. 34.95 (*0-9672698-0-6*) Cultl Conn VA.

Once upon a Castle. Nora Roberts et al. 1998. mass mkt. 6.99 (*0-515-12241-6*, Jove) Berkley Pub.

Once Upon a Castle. large type ed. Nora Roberts et al. LC 98-22097. 1998. 20.00 (*0-7862-1507-0*) Thorndike Pr.

Once upon a Chassid. Yanki Tauber. 284p. 1995. 17.00 (*0-8266-0384-X*) Kehot Pubn Soc.

Once upon a Child: Writing Your Child's Special Story. Debbie McChesney. (Illus.). 1995. 19.95 (*1-56145-100-2*) Peachtree Pubs.

Once upon a Childhood. Kathy Nickerson. (Fresh Perspective Ser.). 30p. 1998. pap. 3.50 (*0-9660886-2-X*) Scribbles & Scribes.

Once upon a Childhood: Fingerplays, Action Rhymes, & Fun Times for the Very Young. Dolores C. Chupela. LC 98-3301. (School Library Media Ser.: No. 16). 144p. 1998. pap. 24.00 (*0-8108-3485-5*) Scarecrow.

Once upon a Christmas. Chrysostom Society Staff. (Illus.). 1993. 9.50 (*0-8378-5922-0*) Gibson.

***Once upon a Christmas.** Diane Farr. (Regency Romance Ser.). 2000. mass mkt. 4.99 (*0-451-20162-0*, Sig) NAL.

Once upon a Christmas. James D. Freeman. LC 78-53345. (Illus.). 173p. 1995. 16.95 (*0-87159-119-7*) Unity Bks.

Once upon a Christmas. William R. Goetz. LC 99-181078. (Illus.). 70p. (J). 1998. pap. 6.99 (*0-88965-153-1*, Pub. by Horizon Books) Chr Pubns.

Once upon a Christmas. Nancy Lawrence. 1997. pap. 4.99 (*0-8217-5791-1*) Kensgtn Pub Corp.

Once upon a Christmas. Thomas O'Malley. 19p. (J). (gr. k-5). 1997. mass mkt. 7.00 (*1-58193-168-9*) Brown Bag Prods.

***Once upon a Christmas: I Believe in Jesus Read Aloud Stories.** William R. Goetz. 40p. 1999. 12.99 (*0-88965-178-7*, Pub. by Horizon Books) Chr Pubns.

Once upon a Christmas Time. Leisure Arts Staff. (Christmas Remembered Ser.: No. 12). (Illus.). 96p. 1996. 24.95 (*1-57486-010-0*) Leisure AR.

Once upon a Christmastime. LC 97-26741. vii, 278p. 1997. 16.95 (*1-57345-287-4*) Deseret Bk.

Once upon a Company. Wendy Anderson Halperin. LC 98-13735. (Illus.). 40p. (J). (gr. k-4). 1998. lib. bdg. 17.99 (*0-531-33089-3*) Orchard Bks Watts.

Once upon a Company. Wendy Anderson Halperin. LC 98-13735. (Illus.). 40p. (J). (gr. 2-6). 1998. 16.95 (*0-531-30089-7*) Orchard Bks Watts.

Once upon a Country Doctor. Dick Turner. (Illus.). 268p. 1995. 39.50 (*0-9644379-0-2*) Sonrise.

Once upon a Cricket Jump see Short Story Longs

Once upon a Crime. M. D. Lake. 275p. (Orig.). 1995. mass mkt. 5.50 (*0-380-77520-4*, Avon Bks) Morrow Avon.

Once upon a Crime: Fairy Tales for Mystery Lovers. Ed. by Edward Gorman & Martin H. Greenberg. LC 97-31612. 432p. 1998. 21.95 (*0-425-16301-6*) Berkley Pub.

***Once upon a Crime: Fairy Tales for Mystery Lovers.** Ed. by Edward Gorman & Martin H. Greenberg. 1999. reprint ed. pap. 13.95 (*0-425-17128-0*, Prime Crime) Berkley Pub.

Once upon a Cross: A Group of Short Christian Stories to Manifest God's Presence in You. Frank Britto. LC 95-3990. 1995. 10.00 (*1-877633-27-5*) Luthers.

Once upon a Death. LC 84-19421. 142p. 1984. pap. 7.50 (*0-918323-00-2*) Lynx Hse.

***Once upon a December & 50 Christmas Favorites.** Ed. by Warner Brothers Publications Staff. (Illus.). 1999. pap. 14.95 (*0-7692-8450-7*) Wrner Bros.

Once upon a Desert: A Bicentennial Project. Ed. by Patricia J. Keeling. (Illus.). 296p. (C). 1994. text 35.95 (*0-918614-07-4*); pap. text 25.95 (*0-918614-06-6*) Mojave Riv Val.

Once upon a Dime: A Math Adventure. Nancy K. Allen. LC 99-11928. (Illus.). (J). 1999. 6.95 (*1-57091-161-4*) Charlesbridge Pub.

Once upon a Distant Star: David Halberstam, Neil Sheehan, Peter Arnett--Young War Correspondents & Their Early Vietnam Battles. William Prochnau. 576p. 1996. pap. 15.00 (*0-679-77265-0*) McKay.

Once upon a Distant War: Young War Correspondents & the Early Vietnam Battles. William Prochnau. 1996. pap. 15.00 (*0-614-20772-X*) Vin Bks.

Once upon a Dream. Katherine Kingsley. 432p. 1997. mass mkt. 6.50 (*0-440-22076-9*) Dell.

Once upon a Dream. large type ed. Paula Lindsay. (Linford Romance Library). 240p. 1997. pap. 16.99 (*0-7089-5083-3*, Linford) Ulverscroft.

Once upon a Dream: The Vietnamese-American Experience. Ed. by De Tran et al. LC 95-20603. (Illus.). 160p. 1995. pap. 14.95 (*0-8362-0584-7*) Andrews & McMeel.

Once upon a Family. Elizabeth E. Kennedy. LC 90-33505. (Illus.). 80p. (Orig.). 1990. pap. 7.95 (*0-931832-56-X*) Fithian Pr.

Once upon a Family. Les Parrott, III. 36p. 1996. pap., teacher ed. 4.99 (*0-8341-1593-X*) Nazarene.

Once upon a Family: Building a Healthy Home When Your Family Isn't a Fairy Tale. Les Parrott, III. LC 96-44598. 112p. (Orig.). 1997. pap. 9.99 (*0-8341-1597-2*) Beacon Hill.

Once upon a Family Reunion. Gloria J. Smith. 64p. 1994. 14.95 (*0-9644018-1-9*) G&L Pubns.

***Once upon a Farm.** Bob Artley. LC 00-26270. (Illus.). 2000. 21.95 (*1-56554-753-5*) Pelican.

Once upon a Farm. Fern Stearns et al. (Illus.). 196p. (Orig.). 1993. pap. 14.95 (*0-9639247-0-2*) Fiddlehead Follies.

Once upon a Farm: How to Look, Listen, Laugh, & Survive. Bill Johnson & Karen Johnson. LC 93-84973. (Illus.). 280p. 1993. 17.95 (*0-9635812-1-X*) Sigler Print.

Once upon a Felt Board. Roxane Chadwick. (Illus.). 128p. (J). (gr. k-4). 1986. student ed. 12.99 (*0-86653-338-9*, GA 798) Good Apple.

Once upon a Folktale: Capturing the Folktale Process with Children. Ed. by Gloria T. Blatt. LC 92-36897. 208p. (C). 1993. pap. text 18.95 (*0-8077-3232-X*) Tchrs Coll.

Once upon a Folktale: Eight Classic Stories with Easy Songs & Stick Puppet Drawings. Linda R. High & Carol L. Kindt. Ed. by Michael D. Bennett. (Illus.). 60p. (Orig.). (J). (gr. 1-4). 1994. pap. text 11.95 (*0-934017-20-4*) Memphis Musicraft.

***Once upon a Frame.** Tom J. Ulrich. (Illus.). 170p. 2000. 29.95 (*0-87842-412-1*); pap. 23.95 (*0-87842-411-3*) Mountain Pr.

Once upon a Future Time: Studies in a Buddhist Prophecy of Decline. Jan Nattier. LC 91-42549. (Nanzan Studies in Asian Religions: Vol. 1). 352p. (C). 1992. text 50.00 (*0-89581-925-2*); pap. text 25.00 (*0-89581-926-0*) Asian Humanities.

Once upon a Galaxy. Josepha Sherman. 256p. 1994. pap. 11.95 (*0-87483-387-6*) August Hse.

Once upon a Garage Sale: From Fairy Tale to Reality: How to Make More Money, Get Rid of More Stuff, & Otherwise Succeed at Your Garage Sale. Lisa R. Payne. LC 97-66241. (Illus.). 168p. (Orig.). 1997. pap. 14.95 (*0-9657137-2-5*) Clover Creat.

Once upon a GEMS Guide: Connecting Young People's Literature to Great Explorations in Math & Science. rev. ed. Jacqueline Barber et al. Ed. by Carl Babcock & Florence Stone. (Great Explorations in Math & Science (GEMS) Ser.). (Illus.). 412p. 1994. reprint ed. pap., teacher ed. 31.50 (*0-912511-78-8*, GEMS) Lawrence Science.

***Once upon a Guide: Connecting Young People'a Literature to Great Explorations in Math & Science.** Jacqueline Barber. (Illus.). (J). 2000. pap. 13.50 (*0-924886-53-6*, GEMS) Lawrence Science.

Once upon a Heroine. Alison Cooper-Mullin & Jennifer Marmaduke Coye. LC 97-32121. 320p. 1998. pap. 16.95 (*0-8092-3020-8*, 302080, Contemporary Bks) NTC Contemp Pub Co.

Once upon a Holy Night. Ed. by Ellen Wood-Bryce. (J). (gr. 2-5). 8.00 (*0-687-07254-9*) Abingdon.

Once Upon a Holy Night: A Musical Christmas Story Based on Luke 2:1-20 & Matthew 2:1-2. Ellen Bryce. 72p. pap. 17.95 (*0-687-09850-5*) Abingdon.

Once upon a Holy Night: Listening Tape. Ellen Bryce. (J). (gr. 2-5). 12.00 (*0-687-09870-X*) Abingdon.

Once upon a Holy Night: Singer's Edition. Ellen Bryce. (J). (gr. 2-5). 4.00 (*0-687-09860-2*) Abingdon.

Once upon a Holy Night: Value Pak. Ellen Bryce. (J). (gr. 2-5). 25.00 (*0-687-09900-5*) Abingdon.

Once upon a Hopeful Night. Risa Sacks Yaffe. LC 98-68238. (Illus.). 32p. (J). (gr. k-3). 1998. pap. 7.00 (*1-890504-10-6*) Oncology Nursing.

Once upon a Kingdom: Myth, Hegemony, & Identity. Isidore Okpewho. LC 98-19792. (Illus.). 288p. 1998. 39.95 (*0-253-33396-2*) Ind U Pr.

Once upon a Kingdom: Myth, Hegemony & Identity. Isidore Okpewho. LC 98-19792. (Illus.). 288p. 1998. pap. 19.95 (*0-253-21189-1*) Ind U Pr.

Once upon a Kiss. Tanya A. Crosby. 416p. (Orig.). 1995. mass mkt. 4.99 (*0-380-77680-4*, Avon Bks) Morrow Avon.

Once upon a Kiss. Claire Cross. (Magical Love Ser.). 1998. mass mkt. 5.99 (*0-515-12300-5*, Jove) Berkley Pub.

Once Upon a Kiss. Carola Dunn et al. (Zebra Regency Romance Ser.). 255p. 1999. mass mkt. 4.99 (*0-8217-6210-9*) Kensgtn Pub Corp.

Once upon a (Life) Time: Stories from Western Montana, 1908-1960. Illus. by A. S. Morkert. 96p. (Orig.). 1990. pap. text. write for info. (*0-9620902-6-3*) Vernon Print & Pub.

Once upon a Lifetime. C. I. Greenwood. (Illus.). 214p. (Orig.). (C). 1989. pap. 4.95 (*0-9624605-0-8*) Tomahawk Pub.

Once upon a Lifetime. 2nd ed. Lou Sharon. (Illus.). (C). 1992. reprint ed. pap. 10.00 (*0-9628801-6-7*) Coyote Pub.

Once upon a Lily Pad: Froggy Love in Monet's Garden. Joan Sweeney. LC 94-46655. (Illus.). 32p. (J). 1995. 9.95 (*0-8118-0868-8*) Chronicle Bks.

Once upon a Little Town. Mac Coleman. 228p. mass mkt. 4.99 (*1-55197-065-1*) Picasso Publ.

Once upon a Mat. Shirley Aliverti & Ed Aliverti. 32p. 1993. pap. text 6.95 (*1-882336-03-8*) OK Bylines.

Once upon a Mattress: Vocal Score. Ed. by Michael Lefferts. (Vocal Score Ser.). 160p. (Orig.). (C). 1981. per. 45.00 (*0-88188-041-8*, 00312301) H Leonard.

Once upon a Mattress: Vocal Selections. Ed. by Michael Lefferts. (Illus.). 32p. (Orig.). (C). 1981. pap. 8.95 (*0-88188-101-5*, 00312300) H Leonard.

Once upon a Midlife: Classic Stories & Mythic Tales to Illuminate the Middle Years. Allan B. Chinen. 256p. 1993. pap. 13.95 (*0-87477-725-9*, Tarcher Putnam) Putnam Pub Group.

Once upon a Midnight... New Dark Verse. Ed. by James A. Riley et al. (Unnameable Poetry Works Ser.). (Illus.). 87p. 1995. pap. 10.95 (*0-934227-16-0*) Unnameable Pr.

Once upon a Midnight Moon. Carol Finch, pseud. 352p. 1997. mass mkt. 5.99 (*0-8217-5747-4*, Zebra Kensgtn) Kensgtn Pub Corp.

Once upon a Miracle: Drama for Worship & Religious Education. Michael E Moynahan. LC 92-41325. 224p. 1993. pap. 12.95 (*0-8091-3361-X*) Paulist Pr.

Once upon a More Enlightened Time: More Politically Correct Bedtime Stories. James Finn Garner. (Illus.). 96p. 1995. 9.95 (*0-02-860419-9*) Macmillan.

Once upon a Murder. S. I. Gudger. Ed. by Wendy Allyson. 352p. (Orig.). 1995. pap. 6.95 (*0-9650224-7-1*) Ampersand CA.

Once upon a Mystery: What Happens Next? Michael E. Moynahan. LC 98-23004. 208p. 1998. pap. 14.95 (*0-8091-3791-7*) Paulist Pr.

Once upon a Number: A Mathematical Bridges Stories & Statistics. John A. Paulos. LC 98-39252. 224p. 1998. 23.00 (*0-465-05158-8*, Pub. by Basic) HarpC.

Once upon a Number: The Hidden Mathematical Logic of Stories. John A. Paulos. Date not set. pap. 12.00 (*0-465-05159-6*, Pub. by Basic) HarpC.

Once upon a Parable. Mack Thomas. (Illus.). 64p. (J). 1995. 14.99 (*0-88070-746-1*, Gold n Honey) Zondervan.

Once upon a Parable. Elaine M. Ward. 135p. 1994. pap. 14.95 (*1-877871-70-2*, 8159) Ed Ministries.

Once upon a Pew: More Fun Than Having the Preacher Over! Ken Alley. LC 95-69412. 209p. (Orig.). 1995. pap. 10.95 (*0-9645085-0-8*) Prtnrshp Bk Servs.

Once upon a Picnic. Illus. by John Prater. LC 95-19912. (J). (ps-3). 1996. 14.99 (*1-56402-810-0*) Candlewick Pr.

Once upon a Picnic. Vivian French. LC 95-19912. (Illus.). (J). (ps up). 1997. reprint ed. pap. 5.99 (*0-7636-0142-X*) Candlewick Pr.

***Once upon a Place.** Robert Ingpen. (Illus.). 48p. (J). 2000. 14.95 (*0-85091-909-6*, Pub. by Lothian Pub) Star Brght Bks.

Once upon a Pony: A Mountain Christmas. Nancy W. Balderose. LC 92-13814. (Illus.). 32p. (J). (ps up). 1994. pap. 9.95 (*0-8192-7001-6*) Morehouse Pub.

Once upon a Potty: Boy & Doll. Alona Frankel. (Illus.). (J). (ps up). 2000. 16.95 (*0-694-01376-5*) HarpC Child Bks.

Once upon a Potty: Girl & Doll. Alona Frankel. (Illus.). (J). (ps up). 1999. 16.95 (*0-694-01375-7*) HarpC Child Bks.

Once Upon a Potty--boy. Alona Frankel. LC 79-53769. (Illus.). 48p. (J). (ps up). 1999. 5.95 (*0-694-01387-0*) HarpC Child Bks.

***Once Upon a Potty--girl.** Alona Frankel. LC 83-45965. (Illus.). 48p. (J). (ps-k). 1999. 5.95 (*0-694-01388-9*) HarpC Child Bks.

Once Upon a Potty (boy) Book & Tape. Alona Frankel. (Illus.). 48p. (J). (ps up). 1999. 9.95 incl. audio (*0-694-70103-3*) HarpC Child Bks.

Once Upon a Potty (girl) Book & Tape. Alona Frankel. (Illus.). 48p. (J). (ps up). 1999. 9.95 incl. audio (*0-694-70104-1*) HarpC Child Bks.

Once upon a Princess & a Pea. Ann Campbell. LC 92-30526. (Illus.). 32p. (J). (gr. 1 up). 1993. 14.95 (*1-55670-289-2*) Stewart Tabori & Chang.

Once upon a Quilt: Fairy Tales in Fabric. Bonnie Kaster & Virginia Athey. Ed. by Janet White. LC 96-49187. (Illus.). 64p. (Orig.). 1997. pap. 21.95 (*1-56477-165-2*, B276) Martingale & Co.

Once upon a Rainbow. Nancy Richard. (Illus.). 31p. (Orig.). 1992. pap. 4.95 (*0-9631685-0-9*) N&R Enter.

Once Upon a Reptar. Kitty Richards. (Rugrats Ser.). (Illus.). 16p. (ps-3). 1999. pap. 3.99 (*0-689-82389-4*, 076714003996) S&S Childrens.

***Once upon a Rhyme.** Matt Mitter. (Talking Pages Deluxe Ser.). 2000. 12.95 (*1-58224-131-7*) Futech Interactive.

Once upon a Rhyme. Marge Rogers. (Illus.). 100p. (C). 1997. pap. text. write for info. (*1-886352-14-3*) Natl Poets Assn.

Once upon a Rhyme: A Wizard's Wacky Story Time. Pam Records. (Shuffle-a-Book Ser.). (Illus.). 21p. (J). (ps). 1993. pap. 8.00 (*0-9639839-0-3*) MP Records.

Once upon a River: His, Pineville, Louisiana. Elaine H. Brister. 1968. 17.50 (*0-87511-578-0*) Claitors.

Once upon a Rose. Judith O'Brien. 352p. 1996. mass mkt. 5.99 (*0-671-50225-5*) S&S Trade.

Once upon a Rose. Judy O'Brien. 1996. pap. 5.99 (*0-614-98084-4*, Pocket Books) PB.

Once upon a Rose. large type ed. Judith O'Brien. LC 97-9698. (Large Print Book Ser.). 1997. pap. 22.95 (*1-56895-444-1*) Wheeler Pub.

Once upon a Santa Claus: A Musical Play. Adapted by Sylvia Ashby. (Illus.). 44p. (J). (ps up). 1988. pap. 4.00 (*0-88680-296-2*) I E Clark.

Once upon a Saturday Morning. Rockwell. (J). 1996. 13.00 (*0-689-80525-X*) S&S Childrens.

Once upon a Scandal, Vol. 1. Barbara Dawson Smith. 336p. 1997. reprint ed. mass mkt. 5.99 (*0-312-96277-0*) St Martin.

Once upon a Schooner. Silver D. Cameron. (Illus.). 146p. 1995. 24.95 (*0-88780-226-5*, Pub. by Formac Publ Co); pap. 14.95 (*0-88780-225-7*, Pub. by Formac Publ Co) Formac Dist Ltd.

***Once upon a Secret.** Catherine Andorka. 216p. 1999. pap. 7.99 (*1-893108-17-1*) Neighbrhd Pr Pubng.

Once upon a Shabbos. Jacqueline Jules. LC 98-24828. (Illus.). 32p. (J). (ps-2). 1998. 15.95 (*1-58013-020-8*); pap. 6.95 (*1-58013-021-6*) Kar-Ben.

Once upon a Shoe - Straight. Joseph Robinette. 1979. 3.50 (*0-87129-491-5*, O29) Dramatic Pub.

Once upon a Shoe: Or The Rhymes & Mimes of Mother Goose & Her Traveling Troubadours - The Musical. Joseph Robinette. 1988. pap. 4.95 (*0-87129-322-6*, O04) Dramatic Pub.

Once upon a Soul. 2nd ed. Hanoch Teller. (Soul Ser.). 224p. (YA). (gr. 12). 1984. reprint ed. 12.95 (*0-9614772-3-7*) NYC Pub Co.

Once upon a Soul: The Story Continues . . . Joyce A. Kovelman. Ed. by Susan Remkus. LC 97-25570. 240p. 1998. 24.95 (*1-880396-52-1*, JP9652-1) Jalmar Pr.

Once upon a Sound: Literature-Based Phonological Activities. Linda Smith-Kiewel & Tracy Claeys. LC 98-30856. 1998. 42.00 (*1-888222-31-X*) Thinking Pubns.

Once upon a Springtime. Jean Marzollo. LC 96-10586. (Hello Reader! Ser.). (Illus.). (J). 1997. 3.50 (*0-590-46017-X*) Scholastic Inc.

Once upon a Stage: Story-Based Creative Dramatics with Young Children. Dina Strong & Randi Goldstein. (Illus.). 80p. (J). (ps-3). 1998. pap. 14.95 (*1-889108-40-5*) Liv Good News.

O

***Once upon a Star.** Nora Roberts et al. 1999. mass mkt. 5.99 (*0-515-12700-0*, Jove) Berkley Pub.

Once upon a Stove. Birmingham Children's Theatre Staff. LC 86-47955. (Cookbook Ser.). 400p. (Orig.). 1986. pap. 12.95 (*0-9617659-0-9*) Birmingham Child.

Once upon a Suicide. Judy Hollar. LC 89-64101. 1990. 13.95 (*0-87212-236-0*) Libra.

Once Upon a Summer. Janette Oke. LC 81-10183. 28p. 1981. pap. 8.99 (*0-87123-413-0*) Bethany Hse.

Once Upon a Summer. Janette Oke. 1981. 14.09 (*0-606-03051-4*, Pub. by Turtleback) Demco.

Once Upon a Summer. large type ed. Janette Oke. LC 81-10183. 28p. 1987. pap. 10.99 (*0-87123-981-7*) Bethany Hse.

Once Upon a Summer, Vol. 1. Janette Oke. LC 99-21866. 1999. 23.95 (*0-7862-1970-X*) Thorndike Pr.

Once upon a Summertime: A Personal Memoir of Summer Cottage Days in Door County, Wisconsin During the Mid-Twentieth Century. Janet H. McCray. (Illus.). 120p. 1998. pap. 12.95 (*0-9666023-0-7*) Hough House.

Once upon a Table: A Cookbook. Women's Auxiliary of the American Cancer Society S. Ed. by Anita Zebrovious. LC 81-69959. (Illus.). 1981. pap. 8.95 (*0-9607282-0-1*) Womens Auxiliary Cancer.

Once upon a Telephone. Stern. 1996. pap. 14.00 (*0-15-600233-7*) Harcourt.

Once upon a Telephone: An Illustrated Social History. Ed. by Ellen Stern & Emily Gwathmey. LC 93-50854. (Illus.). 144p. 1994. 27.95 (*0-15-100086-7*) Harcourt.

Once upon a Texas: With Pecos Bill & the Texas Stars. I. E. Clark. (Illus.). 44p. 1985. pap. 4.25 (*0-88680-238-5*) I E Clark.

Once upon a Thyme. Young Women's Auxiliary of the Women's Club of Eva & Cindi Schuneman. Ed. by Lynn Hoos. (Illus.). 254p. 1982. 11.95 (*0-685-08506-6*) Y W A W C E.

***Once upon a Tide: Tales from a Foxhole in the South Pacific.** LeRoy B. Bronemann. 208p. 2000. pap. 14.99 (*1-57921-281-6*) WinePress Pub.

Once Upon a Time. Date not set. write for info. (*0-517-80128-0*) Random Hse Value.

Once Upon a Time. Eve Bunting. LC 94-47220. (Illus.). 32p. (J). (gr. 2-5). 1995. 14.95 (*1-878450-59-X*, 711) R Owen Pubs.

An Asterisk (*) at the beginning of an entry indicates that the title is appearing for the first time.

Once upon a Time, 10 vols. Arlene Capriola & Rigmor Swensen. Ed. by Cherisse Mastry. (Illus.). 320p. (J). (gr. k-2). 1998. pap., wbk. ed. 69.50 (*1-57022-144-8*, ECS1448) ECS Lrn Systs.

Once upon a Time. Christina Dodd. 416p. 1996. mass mkt. 5.99 (*0-06-108398-4*) HarpC.

Once upon a Time. Carola Dunn et al. 288p. 1998. pap. 4.99 (*0-8217-5995-7*) Kensgtn Pub Corp.

Once upon a Time. Fred L. Fifer & Cynthia E. Ledbetter. (Do It Now Ser.). 30p. (J). 1991. student ed. 19.95 (*1-885568-12-6*) SCE Assocs.

Once upon a Time. Alan Garner. LC 93-9686. (Illus.). 32p. (J). (gr. k-4). 1993. 12.95 (*1-56458-381-3*) DK Pub Inc.

Once upon a Time . . . Grampa Gray. 48p. (Orig.). 1996. pap. 7.50 (*1-885631-25-1*, 25-1) G F Hutchison.

Once upon a Time. Illus. by Gill Guile. 96p. (J). (ps-3). 1997. 5.98 (*1-85854-282-0*) Brimax Bks.

Once upon a Time . . . Charlotte Hansen. (Illus.). 115p. (J). 1994. text 15.00 (*0-9644402-0-2*) A Cappella Pubng.

Once upon a Time. Mohammad A. Jamalzada. Tr. by Heshmat Moayyad & Paul Sprachman from PER. (Modern Persian Literature Ser.: Vol. 6). x, 112p. 1985. text 18.00 (*0-933273-00-2*) Bibliotheca Persica.

Once upon a Time. Created by Francine Pascal. (Sweet Valley High Ser.: No. 132). 208p. (YA). (gr. 7 up). 1997. mass mkt. 3.99 (*0-553-57066-8*, Sweet Valley) BDD Bks Young Read.

Once upon a Time. Cathie Pelletier. 1999. pap. write for info. (*0-14-012087-4*) Viking Penguin.

Once upon a Time. Illus. & Concept by John Prater. LC 92-53139. 32p. (J). (ps up). 1993. 14.99 (*1-56402-177-7*) Candlewick Pr.

Once upon a Time. Illus. & Concept by John Prater. LC 92-53139. (J). (ps-3). 1995. pap. 5.99 (*1-56402-456-3*) Candlewick Pr.

Once Upon a Time. John Prater. (J). 1995. 11.44 (*0-606-07969-6*) Turtleback.

Once upon a Time. Marylyle Rogers. 1996. mass mkt. 5.99 (*0-312-95758-0*, Pub. by Tor Bks) St Martin.

Once upon a Time: A Coloring Book. Mark Schaufler. (Illus.). 25p. (J). (ps-2). 1995. spiral bd. 2.00 (*1-886904-26-X*) MST Minist.

Once upon a Time: A Floating Opera. John Barth. 408p. 1995. pap. 13.95 (*0-316-08258-9*) Little.

Once upon a Time: A Humorous Retelling of the Genesis Story. WJA Power Staff. 1992. pap. 5.95 (*0-687-28849-5*) Abingdon.

Once upon a Time: A Storytelling Handbook. Lucille N. Breneman & Bren Breneman. LC 83-10990. (Illus.). 208p. 1983. text 27.95 (*0-8304-1007-4*) Burnham Inc.

Once upon a Time: Chicken Licken. Arlene Capriola & Rigmor Swensen. Ed. by Cherisse Mastry. (Illus.). 32p. (J). (gr. k-2). 1998. pap., wbk. ed. 6.95 (*1-57022-139-1*, ECS1391) ECS Lrn Systs.

Once upon a Time: Erotic Fairy Tales for Queer Women. Ed. by Mike Ford. 1996. pap. 12.95 (*1-56333-449-6*, R Kasak Bks) Masquerade.

Once upon a Time: Jack & the Beanstalk. Arlene Capriola & Rigmor Swensen. Ed. by Cherisse Mastry. (Illus.). 32p. (J). (gr. k-2). 1998. pap., wbk. ed. 6.95 (*1-57022-142-1*, ECS1421) ECS Lrn Systs.

Once upon a Time: Level Three, Blue. Vivan French. LC 98-53139. (Reading Together Ser.). (Illus.). 32p. (J). 1999. pap. write for info. (*0-7636-0858-0*) Candlewick Pr.

Once upon a Time: Little Red Riding Hood. Arlene Capriola & Rigmor Swensen. Ed. by Cherisse Mastry. (Illus.). 32p. (J). (gr. k-2). 1998. pap., wbk. ed. 6.95 (*1-57022-136-7*, ECS1367) ECS Lrn Systs.

Once upon a Time: Night Watch, A Wish... & a Kiss, the Missing Heir, 3 bks. in 1. rev. ed. Carla Neggers et al. (By Request Ser.). 1999. per. 6.99 (*0-373-20159-1*, 1-20159-9) Harlequin Bks.

Once upon a Time: On the Nature of Fairy Tales. Max Luthi. Tr. by Lee Chadeayne & Paul Gottwald. LC 76-6992. 192p. 1976. reprint ed. pap. 13.95 (*0-253-20203-5*, MB-203) Ind U Pr.

Once upon a Time: The Billy Goats Gruff. Arlene Capriola & Rigmor Swensen. Ed. by Cherisse Mastry. (Illus.). 32p. (J). (gr. k-2). 1998. pap., wbk. ed. 6.95 (*1-57022-135-9*, ECS1359) ECS Lrn Systs.

Once upon a Time: The Boy Who Cried Wolf. Arlene Capriola & Rigmor Swensen. Ed. by Cherisse Mastry. (Illus.). 32p. (J). (gr. k-2). 1998. pap., wbk. ed. 6.95 (*1-57022-143-X*, ECS143X) ECS Lrn Systs.

Once upon a Time: The Elves & the Shoemaker. Arlene Capriola & Rigmor Swensen. Ed. by Cherisse Mastry. (Illus.). 32p. (J). (gr. k-2). 1998. pap., wbk. ed. 6.95 (*1-57022-141-3*, ECS1413) ECS Lrn Systs.

Once upon a Time: The Films of Sergio Leone. Robert C. Cumbow. LC 86-22065. (Illus.). 278p. 1987. 41.50 (*0-8108-1947-3*) Scarecrow.

Once upon a Time: The Gingerbread Man. Arlene Capriola & Rigmor Swensen. Ed. by Cherisse Mastry. (Illus.). 32p. (J). (gr. k-2). 1998. pap., wbk. ed. 6.95 (*1-57022-138-3*, ECS1383) ECS Lrn Systs.

Once upon a Time: The Little Red Hen. Arlene Capriola & Rigmor Swensen. Ed. by Cherisse Mastry. (Illus.). 32p. (J). (gr. k-2). 1998. pap., wbk. ed. 6.95 (*1-57022-140-5*, ECS1405) ECS Lrn Systs.

Once upon a Time: The Storytelling Card Game. Richard Lambert et al. 1995. 18.95 (*1-887801-00-6*, Atlas Games) Trident MN.

Once upon a Time: The Three Bears. Arlene Capriola & Rigmor Swensen. Ed. by Cherisse Mastry. (Illus.). 32p. (J). (gr. k-2). 1998. pap., wbk. ed. 6.95 (*1-57022-134-0*, ECS1340) ECS Lrn Systs.

Once upon a Time: The Three Little Pigs. Arlene Capriola & Rigmor Swensen. Ed. by Cherisse Mastry. (Illus.). 32p. (J). (gr. k-2). 1998. pap., wbk. ed. 6.95 (*1-57022-137-5*, ECS1375) ECS Lrn Systs.

Once upon a Time: Using Stories in the Language Classroom. John Morgan & Mario Rinvolucri. (Cambridge Handbooks for Language Teachers Ser.). 128p. 1984. pap. text 17.95 (*0-521-27262-9*) Cambridge U Pr.

Once upon a Time & Grandma. Lenore Blegvad. LC 92-7407. (Illus.). 32p. (J). (ps-3). 1993. 14.95 (*0-689-50548-5*) McElderry Bks.

Once upon a Time & Today. Maud Nathan. LC 74-3964. (Women in America Ser.). (Illus.). 360p. 1974. reprint ed. 31.95 (*0-405-06113-7*) Ayer.

Once upon a Time & Today. Maud Nathan. (American Biography Ser.). 327p. 1991. reprint ed. lib. bdg. 79.00 (*0-7812-8294-2*) Rprt Serv.

***Once Upon a Time as a Child.** Maria S. Fiedler. 2000. write for info. (*1-58235-441-3*) Watermrk Pr.

Once upon a Time at La Napoule: The Memoirs of Marie Clews. Maire Clews. LC 98-5230. 1998. pap. 17.95 (*1-889833-03-7*) Memoirs Unltd.

Once upon a Time Big Book. Illus. & Concept by John Prater. LC 92-53139. 32p. (J). (ps-2). 1996. pap. 19.99 (*1-56402-806-2*) Candlewick Pr.

Once upon a Time for Young People & Their Books: An Annotated Resource Guide. Rita Kohn. LC 86-14628. 219p. 1987. 24.00 (*0-8108-1922-8*) Scarecrow.

Once upon a Time in a Pigpen & Three Other Stories. Margaret Wise Brown. LC 84-43130. (Illus.). (J). 1980. 12.95 (*0-201-00343-0*) HarpC Child Bks.

Once upon a Time in America. Adrian Martin. LC 98-229713. (Modern Classics Ser.). (Illus.). 96p. 1998. pap. 10.95 (*0-85170-544-8*) Ind U Pr.

***Once upon a Time in America: The Mottahedan Collection.** Tom Godfrey. 2000. 45.00 (*0-903432-63-3*) CMW Ltd.

Once upon a Time in Chicago. Winter. (J). 2000. mass mkt. 15.00 (*0-689-80342-7*) S&S Bks Yung.

Once Upon a Time in Chicago. Jonah Winter. LC 99-59954. 32p. (J). (ps-3). 2000. 14.99 (*0-7868-0462-9*, Pub. by Hyprn Child) Time Warner.

Once upon a Time in Chicago. Jonah Winter. LC 99-59954. 32p. (J). (ps-3). 2000. lib. bdg. 15.49 (*0-7868-2404-2*, Pub. by Hyprn Child) Time Warner.

Once upon a Time in Italy: The Vita Italiana of an American Journalist. Jack Casserly. (Illus.). 284p. 1995. pap. 12.95 (*1-57098-019-5*) Roberts Rinehart.

Once upon a Time in Jamaica: Storytelling in Our Jamaican Culture. Ricardo Scott. (Preserving Our Jamaican Culture - Pass It On Ser.). (Illus.). 150p. 1999. pap. write for info. (*1-58470-015-7*, RAS1949) Crnerstone GA.

Once upon a Time in Junior High. Lisa Norment. 128p. (J). (gr. 4-6). 1994. pap. 2.95 (*0-590-45287-8*) Scholastic Inc.

***Once Upon a Time in New York: Jimmy Walker, Franklin Roosevelt & the Last Great Battle of the Jazz Age.** Herbert Mitgang. LC 99-16631. (Illus.). 272p. 2000. 25.00 (*0-684-85579-8*) Free Pr.

Once upon a Time in Rhyme: 28 Folk Tale Poems & Song Activities. Meish Goldish. (Illus.). (J). 1994. pap. text 10.95 (*0-590-48801-5*) Scholastic Inc.

Once upon a Time in the East. Lionel Fenn. 1993. pap. 4.50 (*0-441-62782-X*) Ace Bks.

Once upon a Time in the Motherland: An African Storybook for Children. A. C. Osunwa-Oguamanam. LC 97-91446. (Illus.). 80p. (J). (ps-12). 1997. pap. 8.00 (*0-9656642-0-1*) PalmTree Pubs.

Once upon a Time Map Book. B. G. Hennessy. LC 98-72608. (Illus.). 18p. (J). (gr. 1-5). 1999. 14.99 (*0-7636-0076-8*) Candlewick Pr.

Once upon a Time on a Plantation. Nancy Rhyne. LC 88-9896. (Illus.). 160p. 1988. 13.95 (*0-88289-702-0*) Pelican.

Once upon a Time on the Banks. Cathie Pelletier. Ed. by Jane Rosenman. 384p. 1991. reprint ed. pap. 14.00 (*0-671-72447-9*, WSP) PB.

Once upon a Time Saints. rev. ed. Ethel Pochocki. LC 96-83473. (Golden Key Bks.). (Illus.). 96p. (J). (gr. 1 up). 1996. pap. 9.95 (*1-883937-15-9*, 15-9) Bethlehem ND.

Once upon a Time This Morning. Anne Rockwell. LC 96-6349. (Illus.). 24p. (J). (ps up). 1997. 15.00 (*0-688-14706-2*, Grenwillow Bks); lib. bdg. 14.93 (*0-688-14707-0*, Grenwillow Bks) HarpC Child Bks.

Once upon a Time When the Princess Beat the Dragon. Rosemary Lake. (Once upon a Time When the Princess...Ser.). (Illus.). 100p. (Orig.). (J). (gr. 4-10). 2001. pap. 10.00 (*0-940918-51-X*) Dragon Tree.

Once upon a Time When the Princess Cast the Spell. Rosemary Lake. (Once upon a Time When the Princess...Ser.). (Illus.). 100p. (Orig.). (J). (gr. 4-10). 2000. pap. 10.00 (*0-940918-52-8*) Dragon Tree.

Once upon a Time When the Princess Got the Treasure. Rosemary Lake. (Once upon a Time When the Princess...Ser.). (Illus.). 100p. (Orig.). (J). (gr. 4-10). 2002. pap. 10.00 (*0-940918-53-6*) Dragon Tree.

Once upon a Time When the Princess Rescued the Prince. Rosemary Lake. (Once upon a Time When the Princess...Ser.). (Illus.). 100p. (Orig.). (J). (gr. 4-10). 2000. pap. 10.00 (*0-940918-50-1*) Dragon Tree.

Once upon a Time When We Were Colored. Clifton L. Taulbert. 160p. 1997. 11.99 (*1-57778-028-0*, AP-028, Pub. by Albury Pub) Appalach Bk Dist.

Once upon a Time with Mary-Kate & Ashley: A Disney Princess Story & Activity Collection. Gabrielle Charbonnet. LC 97-80386. (Illus.). 96p. (J). (gr. k-4). 1998. 16.95 (*0-7868-3189-8*, Pub. by Disney Pr) Time Warner.

Once upon a Time with Mary-Kate & Ashley: A Disney Princess Story & Activity Collection. Gabrielle Charbonnet et al. LC 97-80386. 96p. (J). (gr. k-4). 1999. pap. 9.99 (*0-7868-4343-8*, Pub. by Hyperion) Time Warner.

***Once upon a Time with Winnie the Pooh.** Kathleen Zoehfeld. 192p. (J). 2001. 19.99 (*0-7868-3254-1*, Pub. by Disney Pr) Time Warner.

***Once upon a Tourniquet: September in Europe.** Joyce Metzger. 88p. 1998. pap. 8.95 (*1-878116-85-1*) JVC Bks.

***Once upon a Town: The Gorazde Safe Area in the Bosnian War.** Joe Sacco. 2000. 28.95 (*1-56097-392-7*, Pub. by Fantagraph Bks) Seven Hills Bk.

Once upon a Tradition: Using Traditional Literature to Develop Reading, Writing, Thinking, & Research Skills. Jan G. Philpot. Ed. by Jan Keeling. (Illus.). 80p. (Orig.). (J). (gr. k-4). 1993. pap. text 9.95 (*0-86530-286-3*, 270-5) Incentive Pubns.

Once upon a Vine. Arnold Somers & Judith Weinstein. 58p. Date not set. pap. 5.95 (*1-58342-014-2*, O62) Dramatic Pub.

Once upon a Wedding: Romantic Traditions. Paula D. Riggs. (Intimate Moments Ser.). 1993. per. 3.50 (*0-373-07524-3*, 5-07524-7) Silhouette.

Once upon a Whoopee: A Town, a Team, a Song, a Dream. Bill Buckley & Ed Grisamore. LC 98-38041. 1998. 22.95 (*0-86554-625-8*, H468) Mercer Univ Pr.

Once upon a Wilderness. Fred Van Dyke. 40p. 1993. pap. text 6.95 (*1-883449-00-6*) Stone House.

Once upon a Wishing Tree. Jamie M. Bays. 318p. (Orig.). 1988. pap. 4.95 (*0-9620341-0-X*) J M Bays.

Once upon a Wolf: Steph DeFerie. Steph DeFerie. 48p. (Orig.). (J). 1997. pap. 4.00 (*0-87440-037-6*) Bakers Plays.

Once upon a Wonder. Kenneth L. Gibble. 1992. pap. 8.95 (*0-687-60827-9*) Abingdon.

Once upon Ago. Adrian Gwin. 133p. 1993. pap. 4.95 (*0-87012-508-7*) McClain.
ONCE UPON AGO is a fascinating collection of "Looking Back" columns from his features in the Charleston DAILY MAIL with which Gwin has rounded out more than fifty years of exceptional feature writing. This book contains adventure stories which will perhaps, strum a chord of similar experiences in your own memory. *Publisher Paid Annotation.*

Once upon an Advent. Elaine M. Ward. 85p. 1995. pap. 8.45 (*1-877871-89-3*, 2585) Ed Ministries.

Once upon an American Dream: The Story of Euro Disneyland. Andrew Lainsbury. LC 99-37813. (CultureAmerica Ser.). 280p. 2000. 35.00 (*0-7006-0989-X*) U Pr of KS.

Once upon an Avalanche. (Adventures in Odyssey Ser.: No. 6). (YA). (gr. 1 up). 1995. 14.99 incl. VHS (*0-8499-8460-2*, 7005) Tommy Nelson.

Once upon an Earth. 2nd ed. Denton Cantwell. LC 98-89362. 200p. (Orig.). 1998. pap. 6.99 (*1-893181-11-1*) Le Gesse Stevens.

***Once upon an Easter: I Believe in Jesus Read Aloud Stories.** William R. Goetz. LC 99-80160. (Illus.). 40p. 2000. 12.99 (*0-88965-181-7*, Pub. by Horizon Books) Chr Pubns.

Once upon an Elephant. Ashok Mathur. LC 99-166689. 1999. pap. 13.95 (*1-55152-058-3*) Arsenal Pulp.

Once upon an Eskimo Time: A Year of Eskimo Life Before the White Man Came As Told to Me by My Wonderful Mother Whose Eskimo Name Was Nedercook. Edna Wilder. LC 85-7417. (Illus.). 202p. (Orig.). 1987. pap. 12.95 (*0-88240-274-9*, Alaska NW Bks) Gr Arts Ctr Pub.

Once upon an Eternity. Jean M. Warner. 176p. (C). 1996. pap. 39.95 (*0-85439-401-X*, Pub. by St Paul Pubns) St Mut.

Once Upon an Island. Lila Linzer. LC 98-12935. (Illus.). 76p. (J). (gr. 3-7). 1999. 15.95 (*1-886910-10-3*) Front Str.

Once upon an Island: A Collection of New Key West Authors. Allen Meece et al. LC 97-68162. 150p. 1997. pap. 9.95 (*1-57502-515-9*, PO1529) Morris Pubng.

Once upon an Island: The History of Chincoteague. Kirk Mariner. LC 96-77369. 224p. 1996. pap. 14.95 (*0-9648393-3-4*) Miona Pubns.

***Once upon an Oldman: Special Interest Politics & the Oldman River Dam.** Jack Glenn. (Illus.). 320p. 2000. pap. 19.95 (*0-7748-0713-X*, Pub. by UBC Pr) U of Wash Pr.

Once upon Forever. Becky L. Weyrich. 352p. 1994. mass mkt. 4.99 (*1-55817-883-X*, Pinncle Kensgtn) Kensgtn Pub Corp.

Once upon Ice: And Other Frozen Poems. Jane Yolen. LC 96-84165. (Illus.). 40p. (J). (gr. 5-7). 1997. 17.95 (*1-56397-408-8*) Boyds Mills Pr.

Once upon MacDonald's Farm. Stephen Gammell. LC 89-17792. (Illus.). 32p. (J). (gr. k-3). 1990. pap. 4.95 (*0-689-71379-7*) Aladdin.

Once upon MacDonald's Farm. Stephen Gammell. LC 99-30691. (Illus.). 32p. (J). (ps-3). 2000. reprint ed. per. 15.00 (*0-689-82885-3*) S&S Bks Yung.

Once upon Our Lifetimes: Something to Believe in Like: A Good God & Yourself. 3rd ed. Arthur Trice. (Once upon Our Lifetime's Children Bk.: No. 3). 250p. (J). (gr. 3-12). 1997. pap. 13.50 (*1-886217-02-5*) W O A Pubng.

Once upon Sinatra's Moon. Terry Stellias. 1999. pap. 9.95 (*0-9649272-4-1*) Cielo Pubng.

***Once upon Springtime.** Jean Marzollo. 1998. 9.44 (*0-606-13680-0*) Turtleback.

***Once upon the Earth: An African Folktale.** Michael C. Mbabuike. (Illus.). 50p. (YA). (gr. 3-12). 2000. 15.50 (*0-9678460-4-8*) Timbuktu.

Once upon the Eighth Day. D. V. Randall. 325p. 1993. write for info. (*0-9636838-0-2*) D V Randall.

Once upon the Lagan: The Story of the Lagan Canal. May Blair. LC 95-101891. (Illus.). 139p. 1995. reprint ed. pap. 19.95 (*0-85640-245-1*, Pub. by Blackstaff Pr) Dufour.

Once upon the River Love. Andrei Makine. Tr. by Geoffrey Strachan from FRE. LC 98-22706. 224p. 1998. 23.95 (*1-55970-438-1*, Pub. by Arcade Pub Inc) Time Warner.

Once upon the River Love. Andrei Makine. 224p. 1999. pap. 12.95 (*0-14-028362-5*) Viking Penguin.

Once upon the 1950s. Ernesto E. Cervantez. LC 97-66795. 128p. 1997. 14.95 (*1-887750-65-7*) Rutledge Bks.

Once Was Enough: Celebrities (& Others) Who Appeared a Single Time on the Screen. Douglas Brode. (Illus.). 256p. 1996. pap. 16.95 (*0-8065-1735-2*, Citadel Pr) Carol Pub Group.

Once Water. Nancy Frye. 45p. (Orig.). 1992. pap. 5.00 (*0-926935-61-5*) Runaway Spoon.

Once We Had a Horse. rev. ed. Glen Rounds. (Illus.). 32p. (J). (ps-3). 1996. 15.95 (*0-8234-1241-5*); pap. 6.95 (*0-8234-1243-1*) Holiday.

Once Were Warriors. Alan Duff. 208p. 1995. 19.95 (*0-8248-1762-1*) UH Pr.

Once Were Warriors. Alan Duff. LC 93-43507. 1995. pap. 11.00 (*0-679-76181-0*) Vin Bks.

Once When the World Was Green. Jan Wahl. LC 94-49534. (Illus.). 32p. (J). (gr. 2 up). 1996. 14.95 (*1-883672-12-0*) Tricycle Pr.

***Once Wicked.** Sherri Browning. 2000. mass mkt. 5.99 (*0-440-23528-6*) Bantam Dell.

Once y Sereno: Tipo Mexicanos Del Siglo XIX. Cristina Barros. (SPA., Illus.). 130p. 1994. 23.99 (*968-16-4531-6*, Pub. by Fondo) Continental Bk.

Once You're Over the Hill: (You Begin to Pick Up Speed) Charles M. Schulz. (Peanuts Wisdom Ser.). (Illus.). 32p. 1997. 7.95 (*0-06-757450-5*) HarpC.

Once You're over the Hill (You Begin to Pick up Speed) Selma Jacobs. LC 92-23145. (Illus.). 186p. (Orig.). 1993. pap. 8.95 (*0-929173-12-0*) Health Press.

Onced Removed: Portraits by J. John Priola. Photos by J. John Priola. (Illus.). 128p. 1998. text 65.00 (*0-9657280-3-X*, 810311) Arena Editions.

Onceupona. Gerald Kaminski. LC 93-26242. (Circumstantial Evidence Ser.: Vol. 3). 43p. 1993. pap. 50.00 (*0-931896-10-X*) Cove View.

Onchi & Singing Development: A Cross-Cultural Perspective. Graham Welch & Tadahiro Murao. LC 94-234027. (Advanced Studies in Music Education). 112p. 1994. pap. 29.00 (*1-85346-331-0*, Pub. by David Fulton) Taylor & Francis.

Onchocerciasis: Symptomatology, Pathology, Diagnosis. Ed. by A. A. Buck. 1974. pap. text 12.00 (*92-4-156041-X*, 1150123) World Health.

Onchocerciasis & Its Control: Report of a WHO Expert Committee on Onchocerciasis Control. (Technical Reports: No. 852). (ENG, FRE & SPA.). viii, 103p. (C). 1995. pap. text 15.00 (*92-4-120852-X*, 1100852) World Health.

Onchocerciasis & Mectizan: Training Activities for Community Health Workers. Helen Keller Internatinal Staff. LC 95-9921. 1995. 10.00 (*0-915173-33-6*) Helen Keller Intl.

Onchocerciasis & Mectizan: Training Activities for Community Health Workers. Helen Keller International Staff. LC 95-9921. 1995. 10.00 (*0-915173-34-4*) Helen Keller Intl.

Onchocerciasis Control Programme in West Africa: An Example of Effective Public Health Management. E. M. Samba. LC 95-129803. (Public Health in Action Ser.). (ENG & FRE.). vii, 107p. 1994. pap. text 23.00 (*92-4-156168-8*, 1390001) World Health.

Oncle Anghel (Les Recits d'Adrien Zograffi) Panait Istrati. (FRE.). 215p. 1981. pap. 10.95 (*0-7859-2440-X*, 2070372669) Fr & Eur.

Oncle Charles s'Est Enferme, la Veuve Couderc, Cecile Est Morte. Georges Simenon. (FRE.). 1018p. 1992. 49.95 (*0-7859-0495-6*, 2258035287) Fr & Eur.

Oncles de Sicile. Leonardo Sciascia. (FRE.). 1985. pap. 15.95 (*0-7859-4220-3*) Fr & Eur.

Oncogene & Transgenics Correlates of Cancer Risk Assessments. C. Zervos. LC 92-21812. (NATO ASI Ser.: Vol. 232). (Illus.). 364p. (C). 1992. text 125.00 (*0-306-44242-6*, Kluwer Plenum) Kluwer Academic.

Oncogene & Tumour Supressor Gene Factsbook. 2nd ed. Robin Hesketh. (Factsbooks Ser.). (Illus.). 608p. 1997. pap. text 49.95 (*0-12-344548-5*) Morgan Kaufmann.

Oncogene-Directed Therapies. Ed. by Scott M. Freeman & Aizen J. Marrogi. (Cancer Drug Discovery & Development Ser.). 1999. 125.00 (*0-89603-712-6*) Humana.

Oncogene Factsbook. Robin T. Hesketh. (Factsbook Ser.). (Illus.). 370p. 1995. pap. text 45.00 (*0-12-344550-7*) Acad Pr.

Oncogene Handbook. Robin T. Hesketh. (Illus.). 640p. 1994. text 115.00 (*0-12-344555-8*) Acad Pr.

Oncogene Studies. Ed. by George Klein. LC 82-10167. (Advances in Viral Oncology Ser.: No. 1). (Illus.). 272p. 1982. reprint ed. pap. 84.40 (*0-608-00659-9*, 206124700001) Bks Demand.

Oncogene Techniques. Melvin I. Simon. Ed. by John N. Abelson et al. (Methods in Enzymology Ser.: Vol. 254). (Illus.). 703p. 1995. text 104.00 (*0-12-182155-2*) Acad Pr.

Oncogenes. (Current Topics in Microbiology & Immunology Ser.: Vol. 147). (Illus.). 168p. 1989. 102.00 (*0-387-51050-8*) Spr-Verlag.

Oncogenes. Ed. by Christopher C. Benz. (Cancer Treatment & Research Ser.). (C). 1989. text 217.50 (*0-7923-0237-0*) Kluwer Academic.

Oncogenes. Ed. by David M. Glover & B. David Hames. (Frontiers in Molecular Biology Ser.). (Illus.). 232p. 1990. 60.00 (*0-19-963034-8*) OUP.

An Asterisk (*) at the beginning of an entry indicates that the title is appearing for the first time.

Oncogenes. Enrique Pimentel. LC 85-28085. 224p. 1986. 125.00 (*0-8493-6566-X*, RC268, CRC Reprint) Franklin.
Oncogenes. 2nd ed. Geoffrey M. Cooper. LC 94-42582. (Biology Ser.). (Illus.). 400p. 1995. 58.75 (*0-86720-937-2*) Jones & Bartlett.
Oncogenes, Vol. 1. 2nd ed. Enrique Pimentel. LC 85-28085. 528p. 1989. 206.00 (*0-8493-6505-8*, RC268) Franklin.
Oncogenes, Vol. II. 2nd ed. Ed. by Enrique Pimentel. 448p. 1989. 234.00 (*0-8493-6506-6*, RC268, CRC Reprint) Franklin.
Oncogenes: An Introduction to the Concept of Cancer Genes. K. B. Burck et al. xv, 300p. 1989. reprint ed. 75.00 (*0-387-96423-1*) Spr-Verlag.
Oncogenes & Cancer: Proceedings of the Seventeenth International Symposium of the Princess Takamatsu Cancer Research Fund, June 1986. Ed. by Stuart A. Aaronson et al. 320p. 1987. lib. bdg. 140.00 (*90-6764-101-4*, Pub. by VSP) Coronet Bks.
Oncogenes & Growth Control. Ed. by P. Kahn & T. Graf. (Illus.). 370p. 1986. 96.00 (*0-387-16839-7*) Spr-Verlag.
Oncogenes & the Molecular Origins of Cancer. Ed. by Robert A. Weinberg. LC 89-23927. (Monographs: No. 18). 366p. 1990. 39.00 (*0-87969-336-3*) Cold Spring Harbor.
Oncogenes & Tumor Suppressor Genes. F. MacDonald & C. H. Ford. (Medical Perspectives Ser.). 112p. (Orig.). 1991. pap. 46.50 (*1-872748-55-4*, Pub. by Bios Sci) Coronet Bks.
Oncogenes & Tumour Suppressors. Ed. by Gordon Peters & Karen H. Vousden. (Frontiers in Molecular Biology Ser.: No. 19). (Illus.). 352p. 1997. text 120.00 (*0-19-963595-1*); pap. text 55.00 (*0-19-963594-3*) OUP.
Oncogenes & Viral Genes. Ed. by George F. Vande Woude et al. LC 83-26336. (Cancer Cells Ser.: No. 2). 582p. reprint ed. pap. 180.50 (*0-7837-2006-8*, 204228000002) Bks Demand.
Oncogenes As Transcriptional Regulators, 2 vols. Ed. by M. Yaniv et al. Incl. Vol. 1: Retroviral Oncogenes. (Illus.). 300p. 1997. text 138.00 (*3-7643-5486-0*); Vol. 2: Cell Cycle Regulators & Chromosomal Translocation Products. (Illus.). 200p. 1997. 245.00 (*3-7643-5709-6*); (Progress in Gene Expression Ser.). (Illus.). 1997. Set text 245.00 (*3-7643-5710-X*) Spr-Verlag.
Oncogenes As Transcriptional Regulators. Moshe Yaniv & J. Ghysdael. LC 97-8142. (Progress in Gene Expression Ser.). 1997. write for info. (*0-8176-5486-0*); write for info. (*0-8176-5710-X*) Birkhauser.
Oncogenes As Transcriptional Regulators. Moshe Yaniv & J. Ghysdael. LC 97-8142. (Progress in Gene Expression Ser.). 1997. text. write for info. (*0-8176-5709-6*) Birkhauser.
Oncogenes in Cancer Diagnostics. Ed. by K. Munk et al. (Beitraege Zur Onkologie, Contributions to Oncology Ser.: Vol. 39). (Illus.). viii, 198p. 1990. 68.75 (*3-8055-5231-9*) S Karger.
Oncogenes in Pediatric Tumors. Ed. by L. Massimo et al. (Ettore Majorana International Life Sciences Ser.). xvii, 269p. 1988. text 195.00 (*3-7186-0469-8*) Gordon & Breach.
Oncogenes in the Development of Leukemia. Ed. by O. N. Witte. (Cancer Surveys Ser.: Vol. 15). (Illus.). 191p. (C). 1992. text 66.00 (*0-87969-406-8*) Cold Spring Harbor.
Oncogenesis & Herpesviruses II: Proceedings of a Symposium Held in Nuremberg, Federal Republic of Germany, 14-16 October, 1974, Pt. 1. International Symposium on Oncogenesis & Herpesvir. Ed. by G. De-The et al. LC 76-372380. (IARC Scientific Publications: No. 11). 538p. reprint ed. pap. 166.80 (*0-7837-3994-X*, 204382500001) Bks Demand.
Oncogenesis & Herpesviruses II: Proceedings of a Symposium Held in Nuremberg, Federal Republic of Germany, 14-16 October, 1974, Pt. 2. International Symposium on Oncogenesis & Herpesvir. Ed. by G. De-The et al. LC 76-372380. (IARC Scientific Publications: No. 11). 416p. reprint ed. pap. 129.00 (*0-7837-3995-8*, 204382500002) Bks Demand.
Oncogenesis & Herpesviruses III: Proceedings of the Third International Symposium on Oncogenesis & Herpesviruses Held in Cambridge, MA, U. S. A. 25-29 July 1977. International Symposium on Oncogenesis & Herpesvir. Ed. by G. De-The et al. LC 79-317591. (IARC Scientific Publications: No. 24). 639p. reprint ed. pap. 198.10 (*0-7837-4045-X*, 204387500011); reprint ed. pap. 150.40 (*0-7837-4046-8*, 204387500002) Bks Demand.
Oncogenesis & Herpesviruses I. Ed. by P. M. Biggs et al. (IARC Scientific Publications: No. 2). (Illus.). 515p. 1986. 65.00 (*0-19-723001-6*) OUP.
Oncogenesis & Molecular Biology of Pituitary Tumors. Shlomo Melmed. (Frontiers of Hormone Research Ser.: Vol. 20). (Illus.). vi, 198p. 1996. 198.25 (*3-8055-6254-3*) S Karger.
Oncogenesis & Natural Immunity in Syrian Hamsters. Ed. by F. Homburger & J. J. Trentin. (Progress in Experimental Tumor Research Ser.: Vol. 23). (Illus.). 1979. 85.25 (*3-8055-2824-8*) S Karger.
Oncogenic Adenoviruses. Ed. by L. P. Merkow & M. Slifkin. (Progress in Experimental Tumor Research Ser.: Vol. 18). 1973. 85.25 (*3-8055-1348-8*) S Karger.
Oncogenic Virus, 2 vols. 3rd ed. Gross. 1985. 120.00 (*0-08-032003-1*, Pergamon Pr) Elsevier.
Oncologic Imaging. 2nd ed. Rubin. 1999. text. write for info. (*0-7216-7494-1*, W B Saunders Co) Harcrt Hlth Sci Grp.
Oncologic Imaging: A Clinical Perspective. Claudia G. Berman et al. LC 96-32622. (Illus.). 700p. 1997. text 95.00 (*0-07-005114-3*) McGraw-Hill HPD.
***Oncologic Therapeutics.** E. E. Vokes. LC 98-37566. 1999. pap. text 49.00 (*3-540-64052-5*) Spr-Verlag.
Oncological Nursing. 2nd ed. JoAnn H. Eriksson. LC 93-21898. (Notes Ser.). 240p. 1993. pap. 18.95 (*0-87434-613-4*) Springhouse Corp.
Oncologists Managed Care Manual. Ed. by David B. Nash. (Illus.). 250p. (Orig.). 1997. spiral bd. 54.95 (*1-890045-02-0*) T L C Med Pub.
Oncology. Hilmar M. Warenius. (Medico-Legal Practitioner Ser.). 208p. 1998. 72.00 (*1-85941-219-X*) Gaunt.
Oncology. fac. ed. Ed. by Neil T. Gorman. LC 87-55436. (Contemporary Issues in Small Animal Practice Ser.: No. 6). (Illus.). 314p. 1986. reprint ed. pap. 97.40 (*0-7837-7881-3*, 204763800007) Bks Demand.
Oncology: A Case-Based Manual. Paul R. Harnett et al. LC 99-20413. (Illus.). 216p. 1999. pap. text 28.50 (*0-19-262978-6*) OUP.
***Oncology & Hematology, 2000: An Internet Resource Guide.** Ed. by Martin D. Abeloff. (Physician Ser.). xvi, 500p. 2000. pap. 24.95 (*0-9676811-0-3*) eMedguides.
***Oncology Diet & Nutrition Patient Education Resource Manual.** Simon B. Weavers et al. LC 00-38956. 2000. pap. write for info. (*0-8342-1715-5*) Aspen Pub.
Oncology Fact Finder: The Johns Hopkins Manual of Oncology Nursing. Constance R. Ziegfeld. LC 98-11143. 384p. 1998. spiral bd. 29.95 (*0-7817-1480-X*) Lppncott W & W.
Oncology for Health-Care Professionals. V. Pervan. 1995. pap. 63.50 (*0-7021-2669-1*, Pub. by Juta & Co) Gaunt.
Oncology for Palliative Medicine. Peter Hoskin & Wendy Makin. LC 97-41041. (Illus.). 250p. 1998. text 48.50 (*0-19-262812-7*) OUP.
Oncology for the House Officer. Joseph F. O'Donnell et al. (Illus.). 352p. 1992. 21.95 (*0-683-06626-9*) Lppncott W & W.
Oncology Intern Pocket Survival Guide. Scott M. Tenner et al. 78p. (Orig.). (C). 1993. pap. text 7.50 (*0-9634063-9-6*) Intl Med Pub.
Oncology Nursing. Ed. by Christine Miaskowski. LC 94-32089. (Plans of Care for Specialty Practice Ser.). 260p. (C). 1995. pap. 45.95 (*0-8273-6118-1*) Delmar.
Oncology Nursing. Cynthia C. Snyder. (Illus.). 464p. (C). 1986. text 26.50 (*0-673-39406-9*) Lppncott W & W.
Oncology Nursing. 3rd ed. Shirley E. Otto. (Illus.). 928p. (C). (gr. 13). 1996. pap. text 54.95 (*0-8151-8955-9*, 29032) Mosby Inc.
***Oncology Nursing.** 4th ed. Otto. 2001. pap. text. write for info. (*0-323-01217-5*) Mosby Inc.
Oncology Nursing: Advances, Treatments, & Trends into the Twenty-First Century. Ashwanden & Belcher Staff. LC 90-648. 414p. 1990. 70.00 (*0-8342-0168-2*, 20168) Aspen Pub.
Oncology Nursing: An Essential for Patient Care. Christine Miaskowski. Ed. by Barbara N. Cullen. (Illus.). 329p. 1996. pap. text 32.00 (*0-7216-6041-X*, W B Saunders Co) Harcrt Hlth Sci Grp.
Oncology Nursing: Assessment & Clinical Care. Christine Miaskowski & Patricia Buschsel. (Illus.). 1700p. 1999. text 95.00 (*0-8151-6990-6*, 27463) Mosby Inc.
Oncology Nursing Ambulatory Setting. Patricia C. Buchsel & Connie H. Yarbro. 275p. 1993. 64.95 (*0-86720-637-3*) Jones & Bartlett.
Oncology Nursing Care. Theresa W. Gillespie et al. Ed. by Gloria York. (Illus.). 300p. (Orig.). (C). 1995. pap. text 49.95 (*1-878025-76-7*) Western Schls.
Oncology Nursing Care Plans. Danielle Gale & Jane Charette. 400p. (Orig.). (C). 1995. pap. text 38.95 (*1-56930-004-6*) Skidmore Roth Pub.
Oncology Nursing Homecare Handbook. Margaret Barton Burke. 285p. 1993. pap. text 39.95 (*0-86720-643-8*) Jones & Bartlett.
Oncology Nursing Review Connie H. Yarbro. LC 99-11078. 1999. write for info. (*0-7637-1040-7*) Jones & Bartlett.
***Oncology Nursing Review.** Connie Henke Yarbro et al. (Illus.). 272p. (C). 1999. pap. text. write for info. (*0-7637-1127-6*) JB Pubns.
Oncology Nursing Secrets. Rose A. Gates & Regina M. Fink. LC 97-3107. (Secrets Ser.). 1997. 35.00 (*1-56053-210-6*) Hanley & Belfus.
Oncology of the Eye & Adnexa: Atlas of Clinical Pathology. A. Brini et al. (Monographs in Ophthalmology). (C). 1990. text 304.50 (*0-7923-0409-8*) Kluwer Academic.
Oncology of the Nervous System. Michael D. Walker. 1983. text 187.00 (*0-89838-567-9*) Kluwer Academic.
Oncology Patient Education Manual. Aspen Reference Group Staff. Ed. by Kenneth E. Lawrence & Sara N. Di Lima. LC 94-1144. ring bd. 210.00 (*0-8342-0543-2*, S125) Aspen Pub.
Oncology Policy & Procedures. Texas M. D. Anderson Cancer Center Staff. 1993. 140.00 (*1-879575-38-8*) Acad Med Sys.
Oncology Reviews, Vol. 3. Z. V. Pavlova & M. E. Isakova. (Soviet Scientific Reviews Ser.: Vol. 3, Pt. 3). 72, ivp. 1989. pap. text 61.00 (*3-7186-4913-6*) Gordon & Breach.
Oncology Reviews Vol. 3, Pt. 5: Poly-Radiomodification in the Radiotherapy of Tumors - Termoradio-Therapy in the U. S. S. R. - Oxybaro- & Hypoxyradiotherapy, Vol. 3. S. P. Yarmonenko. (Soviet Medical Reviews Ser.: Section F). 146p. 1991. pap. text 190.00 (*3-7186-5228-5*, Harwood Acad Pubs) Gordon & Breach.
Oncology Reviews Vol. 4, Pt. 2: Oropharyngeal Region Cancer - Modern Problems of Diagnosis, Treatment & Prognosis - the Oncological Service in the U. S. S. R., Vol. 4. E. G. Matyakin. (Soviet Medical Reviews Ser.: Section F). 108p. 1991. pap. text 130.00 (*3-7186-5230-7*, Harwood Acad Pubs) Gordon & Breach.
Oncology Reviews Vol. 4, Pt. 4.3: Review of Soviet Literature on the Problem of Esophageal Cancer for 1980-1990, Vol. 4. M. Davydov. (Soviet Medical Reviews Ser.: Section F). 89p. 1992. pap. text 96.00 (*3-7186-5360-5*, Harwood Acad Pubs) Gordon & Breach.
Oncology Reviews Vol. 4, Pt. 5: Hormonocytostatics - Antitumor Drugs with a Target Effect, Vol. 4. Z. Sof'ina. (Soviet Medical Reviews Ser.: Setion F). 55p. 1992. pap. text 68.00 (*3-7186-5385-0*, Harwood Acad Pubs) Gordon & Breach.
Oncology Services Administration Forms: Forms, Checklists & Guidelines. Aspen Staff. LC 97-44161. 1998. 189.00 (*0-8342-0906-3*, S468) Aspen Pub.
Oncology Services Policy & Procedure Guideline Manual. Diane Johnson. 198p. 1998. spiral bd. 110.00 (*1-879575-98-1*) Acad Med Sys.
***Oncology, Stupology . . . I Want to Go Home!** Marilyn K. Hershey. (Illus.). 32p. (J). (ps-6). 1999. pap. 5.00 (*0-9673550-0-1*) Butterfly Pr PA.
Oncology Therapeutics: A Quick Reference Guide. Mark J. Ratain et al. (Illus.). 350p. pap. text. write for info. (*0-7216-8123-9*, W B Saunders Co) Harcrt Hlth Sci Grp.
Oncotips. James Metz. 256p. pap. text 19.95 (*0-7817-2564-X*) Lppncott W & W.
Onda Latina en Poesia: Latin Sounds in Poetry, Vol. 1. Ed. by Casa de Unidad Staff.Tr. of Detroit la Onda Latina en Poesia. (ENG & SPA., Illus.). 100p. (Orig.). 1985. pap. 6.00 (*0-9615977-0-4*) Casa Unidad.
Ondansetron - a New Concept in Anti-Emetic Therapy. Ed. by J. Smyth & K. Cunningham. (Journal: Oncology: Vol. 49, Vol. 4, 1992). (Illus.). 64p. 1992. pap. 88.75 (*3-8055-5656-X*) S Karger.
Ondansetron - Global Experience & Future Potential. Ed. by M. Soukop & K. Cunningham. (Journal: Oncology: Vol. 50, No. 3, 1993). (Illus.). 48p. 1993. pap. 88.75 (*3-8055-5783-3*) S Karger.
Ondansetron & Chemotherapy Induced Emesis: 3rd International Congress on Neo-Adjuvant Chemotherapy. Ed. by M. Marty & M. Pappo. viii, 77p. 1992. 49.95 (*0-387-54599-9*) Spr-Verlag.
Onde Existe Luz (Where There Is Light) (POR.). 11.00 (*0-87612-277-2*) Self Realization.
Ondelettes en, 1989: Seminaire d'Analyse Harmonique Universite de Paris-Sud, Orsay. P. G. Lemaire. Ed. by A. Dold et al. (Lecture Notes in Mathematics Ser.: Vol. 1438). v, 212p. 1990. 41.95 (*0-387-52932-2*) Spr-Verlag.
Ondernemingsreg. H. S. Cilliers et al. (AFR.). 459p. 1993. pap. write for info. (*0-409-01979-8*, MICHIE) LEXIS Pub.
Onderwysaangeleenthede Seventy van 1988, Wet Op: Education Affairs Act 70 of 1988. ring bd. write for info. (*0-7021-2577-6*, Pub. by Juta & Co) Gaunt.
Ondes de Gradients Multidimensionnelles. Monique Sable-Tougeron. LC 93-31686. (Memoirs of the American Mathematical Society Ser.: Vol. 106, No. 511). 93p. 1993. 29.00 (*0-8218-2573-9*, MEMO/106/511C) Am Math.
Ondina: A Narrative Poem. John Roberts. (Illus.). 136p. 1986. 18.00 (*0-9615617-0-X*); pap. 12.00 (*0-9615617-1-8*) Cloud Ridge Pr.
***Ondine.** Drake. LC 98-44599. 1999. 30.00 (*0-7862-1715-4*) Thorndike Pr.
Ondine. Shannon Drake. 480p. 1996. mass mkt. 6.50 (*0-8217-5414-9*, Zebra Kensgtn) Kensgtn Pub Corp.
Ondine. Jean Giraudoux. pap. 9.50 (*0-685-33921-1*) Fr & Eur.
Ondine. Jean Giraudoux. (FRE.). 288p. 1953. pap. 10.95 (*0-8288-9744-1*, 2253009776); pap. 3.95 (*0-686-54008-5*) Fr & Eur.
One. Richard Bach. 400p. 1989. mass mkt. 7.50 (*0-440-20562-X*) Dell.
One. David R. Furford. 43p. 1994. pap. write for info. (*0-9641207-1-2*) D R Furford.
One. Ken Ohara. 496p. 1997. 29.99 (*3-8228-7866-9*, Pub. by Benedikt Taschen) Bks Nippan.
One. Brian Porzak. (Illus.). 395p. (Orig.). 1987. pap. 12.95 (*0-937983-00-4*) Copy Concepts.
One: A Study of the Absolute. Lillian De Waters. 222p. 1998. reprint ed. pap. 18.95 (*0-7661-0222-X*) Kessinger Pub.
One: East & West. Troy W. Organ. 464p. (Orig.). (C). 1991. lib. bdg. 52.00 (*0-8191-7877-2*) U Pr of Amer.
One: The Last Word in Superheroes. Rich Veitch. (Illus.). 216p. (Orig.). 1989. pap. 14.95 (*0-685-29813-2*) King Hell Pr.
One: The Official Strategy Guide. Ted Chapman. LC 97-75577. 96p. 1998. per. 12.99 (*0-7615-1365-5*) Prima Pub.
***1 - 4 Motion Offenses: For Men's & Women's Basketball.** Harry L. Harkins & Jerry Krause. LC 98-88111. (Art & Science of Coaching Ser.). (Illus.). 180p. 1998. pap. 16.95 (*1-57167-273-7*) Coaches Choice.
I-75 & The 401: A Traveller's Guide Between Toronto & Miami. Christine Marks. (Illus.). 240p. 1999. pap. 13.95 (*1-55046-255-5*, Pub. by Boston Mills) Genl Dist Srvs.
***1 - 2 - 3 Draw Dinosaurs & Other Prehistoric Animals.** Freddie Levin. (Illus.). 64p. (J). (gr. 1-7). 2000. pap. 8.95 (*0-939217-41-4*) Peel Prod.
***1 - 2 - 3 Draw Pets & Farm Animals.** Freddie Levin. (Illus.). 64p. (J). (gr. 1-7). 2000. pap. 8.95 (*0-939217-40-6*) Peel Prod.
***One * Liners.** aut. ed. Roberta Mendel. (Jots & Gists Ser.). 42p. 1999. pap. 10.00 (*0-936424-26-5*, 021) Pin Prick.
1a. Gail Sher. 80p. (Orig.). 1996. pap. 10.00 (*1-887289-26-7*) Rodent Pr.
One a Day: An Anthology of Jewish Historical Anniversaries for Every Day of the Year. Abraham P. Bloch. 29.50 (*0-88125-108-9*) Ktav.
One-a-Day Web Page Wake-Ups! Richard Raucci. 464p. 1996. 29.99 (*1-56276-490-X*, Ziff-Davis Pr) Que.
One-a-Day Writeamins. Bernetta Gresko. (Illus.). 34p. (J). 1987. spiral bd. 4.95 (*0-939755-15-7*) Sunset Prods.
***One Above & One Below: New Poems.** Erin Belieu. 85p. 2000. pap. 14.00 (*1-55659-144-6*) Copper Canyon.
***One Acre & Security: How to Live off the Earth Without Destroying It.** Bradford Angier. (Illus.). 320p. 2000. reprint ed. pap. 15.95 (*1-57223-394-X*) Willow Creek Pr.
One Across, Two Down. Ruth Rendell. 1999. lib. bdg. 21.95 (*1-56723-149-7*, 158) Yestermorrow.
One Act - Eleven Short Plays of the Modern Theatre: Miss Julie, August Strindberg; Purgatory, William Butler Yeats; The Man with the Flower in His Mouth, Luigi Pirandello; Pullman Car Hiawatha, Thornton Wilder; Hello Out There, William Saroyan. Ed. by Samuel Moon. 384p. 1961. reprint ed. pap. 14.00 (*0-8021-3053-4*, Grove) Grove-Atltic.
One-Act Comedies of Moliere: Seven Plays, Vol. 4. Moliere. Tr. & Intro. by Albert Bermel. 192p. 1991. reprint ed. pap. 9.95 (*1-55783-109-2*) Applause Theatre Bk Pubs.
One-Act Play Today. Ed. by William Kozlenko. LC 70-105022. (Essay Index Reprint Ser.). 1977. 21.95 (*0-8369-1473-2*) Ayer.
One-Act Plays for Acting Students: An Anthology of Short One-Act Plays for One, Two or Three Actors. Norman A. Bert. Ed. by Arthur L. Zapel. LC 87-42871. 288p. (YA). (gr. 9 up). 1987. pap. 16.95 (*0-916260-47-X*, B159) Meriwether Pub.
One-Act Plays for Children: 5 Short Plays. Kathleen Schurman-O'Connor. 52p. (J). 1993. pap. 4.00 (*0-88680-384-5*) I E Clark.
***One Acts: A Collection of One Act Plays.** Richard LaMonte Pierce. 199p. 1999. pap. text 12.95 (*1-889534-36-6*) Jay St Pubs.
One Acts & Monologues for Women. Ludmillow Bollow. (Illus.). 96p. 1983. pap. 6.95 (*0-88145-008-1*) Broadway Play.
One Afternoon. Yumi Heo. LC 93-49394. (Illus.). 32p. (J). (ps-1). 1994. 15.95 (*0-531-06845-5*); lib. bdg. 16.99 (*0-531-08695-X*) Orchard Bks Watts.
One Afternoon. Yumi Heo. LC 93-49394. (Illus.). 32p. (J). (ps-1). 1998. pap. 6.95 (*0-531-07103-0*) Orchard Bks Watts.
One Against the Wilderness. Tom Roulstone. 1996. pap. 12.98 (*1-55517-267-9*) CFI Dist.
One Age in a Dream: Poems. Diane H. Glancy. LC 86-62394. (Illus.). 104p. (Orig.). 1986. pap. 6.95 (*0-915943-20-4*) Milkweed Ed.
One Alaskan's Potpourri Vol. 2: A Collection of Frontier Stories: The Homestead Years. H. P. Moss. LC 97-60982. (Illus.). 240p. (Orig.). 1997. pap. 14.95 (*0-9653074-1-7*) Eagle Riv.
One America in the 21st Century: Forging a New Future, the President's Initiatvce on Race, the Advisory Board's Report to the President. (Illus.). 266p. 1998. pap. 21.00 (*0-16-049813-9*) USGPO.
***One America Indivisible: A National Conversation on American Pluralism & Identity.** Sheldon Hackney. 236p. (C). 1999. text 25.00 (*0-7881-7659-5*) DIANE Pub.
One American Reality: A Photographic Essay. Photos by Dong Lin. (Illus.). 90p. 1996. 35.00 (*0-8351-2577-7*) China Bks.
One & a Half-Eyed Archer. Benedikt Livshits. Ed. by John E. Bowlt. (Illus.). 1977. 35.00 (*0-89250-102-2*) Orient Res Partners.
One & All: A Schizophrenic Comedy. Alan Haehnel. 33p. (J). (gr. 7-12). 1994. pap. 3.00 (*1-57514-155-8*, 3028) Encore Perform Pub.
One & Indivisible French Republic. Jack Hayward. (Comparative Modern Government Ser.). 306p. (C). 1974. 12.50 (*0-393-05506-X*) Norton.
One & Inseparable: Daniel Webster & the Union. Maurice G. Baxter. LC 83-26597. (Illus.). 664p. 1984. 42.50 (*0-674-63821-2*) HUP.
One & Its Relation to Intellect in Plotinus. J. Bussanich. vii, 258p. 1988. pap. 71.00 (*90-04-08996-9*, PHA, 49) Brill Academic Pubs.
One & Many in Aristotle's Metaphysics: The Central Books. Edward C. Halper. LC 88-22496. 351p. reprint ed. pap. 108.90 (*0-608-09679-2*, 206979400006) Bks Demand.
One & One-Half & Two Story Home Plans. National Plan Service Inc. Staff. (Illus.). 32p. reprint ed. pap. 3.95 (*0-934039-05-4*, A55) Hme Dsgn Altntves.
One & One Half Missions. Leland A. Dowden. LC 89-50089. (Illus.). 248p. 1989. 19.95 (*0-936029-41-2*) Western Bk Journ.
One & One Makes Three. Muriel Jensen. (American Romance Ser.). 1993. mass mkt. 3.39 (*0-373-16478-5*, 1-16478-9) Harlequin Bks.
One & One Makes Three. Muriel Jensen. (Bestselling Authors Ser.). 1998. mass mkt. 1.99 (*0-373-83362-8*, 1-83362-3) Harlequin Bks.
One & Only. Barbara Bretton. 320p. (Orig.). 1994. pap. text 4.99 (*0-425-14358-9*) Berkley Pub.
One & Only. Carole Mortimer. LC 95-23063. (Presents Ser.). 186p. 1996. per. 3.50 (*0-373-11793-0*, 1-11793-6) Harlequin Bks.
One & Only: Peter Berrett - Homme Fatale. Nina Antonia. 1999. pap. 17.95 (*0-946719-16-0*) Interlink Pub.
One & Only: The Ballet Russe de Monte Carlo. Jack Anderson. (Illus.). 333p. 1981. 29.95 (*0-903102-65-X*, Pub. by Dance Bks) Princeton Bk Co.
One & Only Autobiography of Ralph Miller: The Dog Who Knew He Was a Boy. David Melton. LC 86-27551. (Illus.). 104p. (J). (gr. 2-6). 1986. reprint ed. pap. 5.95 (*0-933849-05-2*); reprint ed. lib. bdg. 14.95 (*0-933849-30-3*) Landmark Edns.
One & Only Delgado Cheese: A Tale of Talent, Fame, & Friendship. Bob Hartman. LC 92-29059. (Illus.). 40p. (J). (gr. k-3). 1993. 13.95 (*0-7459-2405-0*) Lion USA.
One & Only Looks Back. Dyne Steel. 205p. (C). 1989. text 60.00 (*1-872795-30-7*, Pub. by Pentland Pr) St Mut.

O

An Asterisk (*) at the beginning of an entry indicates that the title is appearing for the first time.

One & Only Me. Marilyn Singer. LC 98-75696. (Growing Tree Ser.). (Illus.). 24p. (J). (ps up). 2000. 9.95 (*0-694-01279-3*, HarpFestival) HarpC Child Bks.

One & Only Original Sanibel-Captiva Alphabet Coloring Book. Monty Montgomery. (Illus.). 32p. (Orig.). (YA). (gr. 7 up). 1988. pap. 6.95 (*0-945026-00-5*) S-ME Pr.

One & Only Robin Hood. Nigel Gray. LC 87-2680. (Illus.). 32p. (J). (ps-3). 1987. 12.95 (*0-316-32578-3*, Joy St Bks) Little.

One & Only Second Autobiography of Ralph Miller: The Dog Who Knew He Was a Boy. David Melton. LC 86-27556. (Illus.). 128p. (J). (gr. 2-6). 1986. reprint ed. pap. 5.95 (*0-933849-06-0*); reprint ed. lib. bdg. 14.95 (*0-933849-31-1*) Landmark Edns.

One & Only Special Me, Vol. 3937. Rozanne L. Williams. (Social Studies Learn to Read Ser.). (Illus.). 16p. (J). (ps-2). 1996. pap. 2.49 (*1-57471-142-3*, 3937) Creat Teach Pr.

One & Only Special Me, Vol. 3980. Rozanne L. Williams. (Social Studies Big Bks.). (Illus.). 16p. (J). (ps-2). 1997. pap. 12.98 (*1-57471-188-1*, 3980) Creat Teach Pr.

One & Other Poems. Thomas Kinsella. 72p. 1979. pap. 8.95 (*0-85105-341-6*, Pub. by Smyth) Dufour.

***1 & 2 Corinthians.** Richard L. Pratt, Jr. (Holman New Testament Commentary Ser.: Vol. 7). 2000. 16.99 (*0-8054-0206-3*) Broadman.

***One & the Many: A Contemporary Thomistic Metaphysics.** W. Norris Clarke. 2001. pap. 24.00 (*0-268-03707-8*, Pub. by U of Notre Dame Pr); lib. bdg. 45.00 (*0-268-03706-X*, Pub. by U of Notre Dame Pr) Chicago Distribution Ctr.

One & the Many: America's Struggle for the Common Good. Martin E. Marty. LC 96-48411. (Joanna Jackson Goldman Memorial Lecture on American Civilization & Government Ser.). 288p. 1997. 24.95 (*0-674-63827-1*) HUP.

One & the Many: America's Struggle for the Common Good. Martin E. Marty. 256p. 1998. pap. 15.95 (*0-674-63828-X*) HUP.

One & the Many: Reflections on the American Identity. Arthur Mann. LC 78-27849. 1993. 12.95 (*0-226-50337-2*) U Ch Pr.

One & the Many: Universalism & the Vision of Unity. Nicholas Hagger. 176p. 1999. pap. 16.95 (*1-86204-532-1*, Pub. by Element MA) Penguin Putnam.

One & the Many in the Canterbury Tales. Traugott Lawler. 209p. 1980. 69.50 (*0-208-01842-5*) Elliots Bks.

One & Two Color Graphics. Tomoe Nakazawa. LC 98-127380. (Illus.). 224p. 1997. 59.95 (*4-89444-040-7*, Pub. by PIE Bks) Bks Nippan.

One & Two Color Graphics, Vol. 2. Ed. by Pie Editorial Staff. 1998. 69.95 (*4-89444-093-8*, Pub. by Pie Bks) Bks Nippan.

1 y 2 Pedro. Eugenio Green. (Serie Comentario Biblico Hispanoamericano). (SPA.). 461p. 18.99 (*0-89922-373-7*, C850-3737) Caribe Betania.

1 y 2 Pedro - Judas. Simon J. Kistemaker. (Comentario al Nuevo Testamento Ser.). (SPA.). 479p. 20.00 (*1-55883-052-9*, 6703-4585C) Libros Desafio.

***1 & 2 Peter & Jude, Chapters. 1-2.** Comment by Tyndale House Publishers Staff. (Life Application Bible Studies). 80p. 1999. pap. 5.99 (*0-8423-3419-X*) Tyndale Hse.

***1 & 2 Samuel.** Mary J. Evans. LC 00-23014. (New International Biblical Commentary Ser.: Vol. 6). 300p. 2000. pap. 11.95 (*1-56563-215-X*) Hendrickson MA.

***1 & 2 Samuel.** James E. Smith. LC 00-22696. (NIV Commentary Ser.). 2000. write for info. (*0-89900-881-X*) College Pr Pub.

1 y 2 Tesalonicenses. William Hendriksen. (Comentario al Nuevo Testamento Ser.). (SPA.). 248p. 12.00 (*1-55883-040-5*, 6703-4560C) Libros Desafio.

1 y 2 Timoteo - Tito. William Hendriksen. (Comentario al Nuevo Testamento Ser.). (SPA.). 460p. 16.00 (*1-55883-039-1*, 6703-4570C) Libros Desafio.

One Animal among Many: Gaia, Goats & Garlic. David Waltner-Toews. 128p. (Orig.). 1991. pap. 14.95 (*1-55021-067-X*, Pub. by NC Ltd) U of Toronto Pr.

One-Anothering. Simon Schrock. 142p. (Orig.). 1986. pap. 4.95 (*0-940883-00-7*) Calvary Pubns.

One Anothering. Simon Schrock. LC 91-61712. 160p. 1991. reprint ed. pap. 7.95 (*0-89221-212-8*) New Leaf.

One Anothering Vol. 1: Biblical Building Blocks for Small Groups. Richard C. Meyer. LC 90-46181. 160p. (Orig.). 1998. pap. 12.95 (*0-931055-73-3*) Innisfree Pr.

One Anothering Vol. 2: Building Spiritual Community in Small Groups. Richard C. Meyer. LC 90-46181. 160p. 1999. pap. 12.95 (*1-880913-35-6*) Innisfree Pr.

One Answer to Cancer. William D. Kelley. 38p. 1997. reprint ed. pap. 10.00 (*0-7873-1262-2*) Hlth Research.

***One Answer to Cancer 1999 with Cancer Cure Suppressed.** William D. Kelley. (Illus.). 200p. 1999. pap. 47.77 (*0-9669422-0-5*) Metabolic Medicine.

One April Morning: Children Remember The Oklahoma City Bombing. Nancy Lamb et al. LC 95-39210. (Illus.). 48p. (YA). (gr. 5 up). 1996. 16.00 (*0-688-14666-X*) Lothrop.

***One Arabian Morning.** Pete Marlowe. (Illus.). 32p. (J). (gr. k-3). 2000. lib. bdg. 19.95 (*1-55037-659-4*, Pub. by Annick Pr); per. 6.95 (*1-55037-658-6*, Pub. by Annick Pr) Firefly Bks Ltd.

One Arm & Other Stories. Tennessee Williams. LC 57-31974. 1967. pap. 11.95 (*0-8112-0223-2*, NDP237, Pub. by New Directions) Norton.

One-Armed Bandits & Other Stories of Iowa's Past & Present. George Mills. 281p. 1997. pap. 14.00 (*0-931209-66-8*) Focus Bks.

One-Armed Flyer. Annette Hayn. 1976. 4.00 (*0-318-64161-5*) Poets Pr.

One-Armed Queen. Jane Yolen. LC 98-23525. 352p. 1998. 23.95 (*0-312-85243-6*, Pub. by Tor Bks) St Martin.

One Armed Queen. Jane Yolen. 1999. mass mkt. 6.99 (*0-8125-6479-0*, Pub. by Tor Bks) St Martin.

One-Armed Wonder: Pete Gray, Wartime Baseball & the American Dream. William C. Kashatus. LC 95-5143. (Illus.). 171p. 1995. pap. 24.95 (*0-7864-0094-3*) McFarland & Co.

***One Arrow, One Life: Zen, Archery, Enlightenment.** Kenneth Kushner. (Illus.). 2000. pap. 16.95 (*0-8048-3246-3*, Periplus Eds) Tuttle Pubng.

One Art: Letters. Elizabeth Bishop. Ed. & Selected by Robert Giroux. 725p. 1994. 35.00 (*0-374-22640-7*) FS&G.

One Art: Letters. Elizabeth Bishop. Ed. & Selected by Robert Giroux. 668p. 1995. pap. 16.00 (*0-374-52445-9*) FS&G.

One Aryan Nation under God: Exposing the New Racial Extremists. Jerome Walters. 160p. 1999. pap. 16.95 (*0-8298-1363-2*) Pilgrim OH.

One at a Time. Gary Lenhart. 1983. pap. 4.00 (*0-935992-06-5*) United Art Bks.

One at a Time. David McCord. (Illus.). (J). (gr. 4 up). 1986. 18.95 (*0-316-55516-9*) Little.

One at the Table: The Reception of Baptized Christians. Ed. by Ronald Oakham. 159p. (Orig.). 1996. pap. text 11.00 (*1-56854-070-1*, ONETBL) Liturgy Tr Pubns.

One Atom to Another. Brian F. McCabe. LC 87-63148. 76p. (Orig.). 1988. pap. 10.95 (*0-948275-22-7*) Dufour.

One August Day. Charlotte Morgan. LC 97-23020. 196p. 1998. 24.00 (*0-9657639-1-9*) Van Neste.

One August Day. 2nd rev. ed. Charlotte Morgan. 198p. 1998. pap. 16.00 (*0-9657639-5-1*) Van Neste.

One Average Day: Oregon Project Dayshoot Photographs - 15 July 1983. Oregon Historical Society Staff. (Illus.). 152p. (Orig.). 1984. 21.95 (*0-87595-132-5*); pap. 14.95 (*0-87595-133-3*) Oregon Hist.

One Baby, Two Baby, Three Baby, Four! Christi Robert. (Illus.). 16p. (J). (ps). 1998. pap. 5.95 (*1-891846-00-0*) Busn Word.

***One Bad Thing.** Bill Eidson. 384p. 2000. text 24.95 (*0-312-87646-7*) St Martin.

One Ballerina Two. Vivian French. LC 90-45969. (Illus.). 32p. (J). (ps up). 1991. 13.95 (*0-688-10333-2*) Lothrop.

One Bar Fill-Ins for the Rock Drummer. Rod Sims. 36p. 1995. pap. text 14.95 incl. audio (*1-57424-011-0*, Centerbrook Publishing) Centerstream Pub.

One Barber's Story: From Sicily to America. Pasquale Spanguolo. 1995. 18.95 (*0-312-11872-4*) St Martin.

One Battle too Many. Richard P. Galloway. 348p. 1987. 28.00 (*0-942211-00-6*) Olde Soldier Bks.

One Bean. Anne Rockwell. LC 97-36249. (Illus.). 32p. (J). (gr. k-1). 1999. 14.95 (*0-8027-8648-0*); lib. bdg. 15.85 (*0-8027-8649-9*) Walker & Co.

One Bean. Walker & Company & Anne Rockwell. (Illus.). 32p. (J). (gr. k-1). 1999. reprint ed. pap. 5.95 (*0-8027-7572-1*) Walker & Co.

One Belfast Boy. Patricia McMahon. LC 98-28568. (Illus.). 64p. (J). (gr. 2-7). 1999. 16.00 (*0-395-68620-2*) HM.

One Best System: A History of American Urban Education. David B. Tyack. LC 74-77184. (Illus.). 368p. (C). 1974. pap. 18.95 (*0-674-63782-8*) HUP.

One Best Way: Frederick Winslow Taylor & the Enigma of Efficiency. Robert Kanigel. 432p. 1999. pap. 17.95 (*0-14-026080-3*) Viking Penguin.

One Best Way? Trajectories & Industrial Models of the World's Automobile Producers. Ed. by Michel Freyssenet et al. (Illus.). 496p. 1999. text 100.00 (*0-19-829089-6*) OUP.

One Better. Rosalyn McMillan. 400p. 1998. mass mkt. 7.50 (*0-446-60599-9*, Pub. by Warner Bks) Little.

One Bible, Many Voices: Different Approaches to Biblical Studies. Ed. by Sue Gillingham. 304p. 1998. pap. text 24.95 (*0-281-04886-X*) Intl Pubs Mktg.

One Bible, Many Voices: Different Approaches to Biblical Studies. Susan E. Gillingham. LC 99-17094. (Illus.). 280p. 1999. pap. 19.00 (*0-8028-4661-0*) Eerdmans.

One Big Bed. John Krich. 1987. pap. 5.95 (*0-07-035493-6*) McGraw.

One Big Happy: Should I Spit on Him? Rick Detorie. (Illus.). 128p. 1997. pap. 9.95 (*1-56163-172-8*) NBM.

***One Big Happy Vol. 3: Nice Costs Extra!** Rick Detorie. (Illus.). 128p. 1999. pap. 9.95 (*1-56163-239-2*) NBM.

One Big Happy Family. Andrea Edwards. 1996. per. 3.99 (*0-373-24064-3*, 1-24064-7) Silhouette.

One Big Happy Family. Irene Tiersten. 366p. 1999. pap. 18.95 (*1-58444-056-2*, Looking Glass Pr) DiscUs Bks.

One Big Union: A History of the Australian Workers Union 1886-1994. Mark Hearn & Harry Knowles. (Illus.). 395p. (C). 1996. text 69.95 (*0-521-55138-2*) Cambridge U Pr.

One Big Union: Founding the Transport & General Workers Union. Ed. by Ken Coastes & Tony Topham. (Birth of the Modern Labour Movement Ser.). (C). 1992. 25.00 (*1-85041-063-1*, Pub. by Univ Nottingham) St Mut.

One Big Union: Industrial Workers of the World. 7th rev. ed. 1984. reprint ed. pap. 3.00 (*0-917124-09-X*) Indus Workers World.

***One Bike, One Dream.** Barbara Lambrecht. LC 00-100106. (Illus.). 256p. 2000. pap. 14.00 (*0-9678578-4-8*) E Bks.

One Billion Shoppers: Accessing Asia's Consuming Passions, Fast Moving Trends & Future Markets - After the Meltdown. Paul French & Matthew Crabbe. LC 98-27034. (Illus.). 288p. 1998. 29.95 (*1-85788-210-5*) Nicholas Brealey.

One Bird. Kyoko Mori. (YA). (gr. 7 up). 1996. mass mkt. 4.50 (*0-449-70453-X*) Fawcett.

One Bird, One Cage, One Flight, Homage to Emily Dickinson: A Poetry Collection. Roger White. LC 83-22119. 144p. 1983. pap. 7.95 (*0-87961-141-3*) Naturegraph.

***One Bite Won't Kill You: More Than 200 Recipes to Tempt Even the Pickiest Kids on Earth & the Rest of the Family Too.** Ann Hodgman. LC 99-32151. (Illus.). 300p. 1999. pap. 15.00 (*0-395-90146-4*) HM.

One Blanket & Ten Days Rations. Charles Meketa & Jacqueline D. Meketa. Ed. by Carolyn Dodson & Earl Jackson. LC 79-67811. (Illus.). 112p. (Orig.). 1980. pap. 5.00 (*0-911408-54-1*) SW Pks Mnmts.

One Block Equals Many Quilts. Kay Agnete. LC 98-51824. (Illus.). 112p. 1998. per. 18.95 (*1-57432-719-4*, Am Quilters Soc) Collector Bks.

One Blood. Pauline Hopkins. 1997. pap. 9.95 (*1-874509-38-7*, Pub. by X Pr) LPC InBook.

One Blood. Earl Paulk. 152p. 1996. 12.99 (*1-56043-175-X*) Destiny Image.

***One Blood: The Biblical Answer to Racism.** Ken Ham. LC 99-67331. 2000. pap. 10.99 (*0-89051-276-0*) Master Bks.

One Blood: The Death & Resurrection of Charles R. Drew. Spencie Love. 400p. 1997. pap. 17.95 (*0-8078-4682-1*) U of NC Pr.

One Blood: The Jamaican Body. Elisa J. Sobo. LC 92-22887. (SUNY Series, The Body in Culture, History, & Religion). 329p. (C). 1993. text 64.50 (*0-7914-1429-9*); pap. text 21.95 (*0-7914-1430-2*) State U NY Pr.

One Blood: Under Cover of Darkness. Ricardo Scott & Inez Scott. (Ras Cardo Speaks Ser.). (Illus.). 110p. 1995. pap. 30.00 (*1-883427-90-8*, RAS9949-G) Crnerstone GA.

One Bloody Sunday. Sam Gronning & Robert Kammen. 350p. (Orig.). 1995. pap. 7.95 (*0-932482-50-3*) Blue Feather.

One Blue Moon. large type ed. Catrin Collier. 584p. 1995. 27.99 (*0-7505-0712-8*, Pub. by Mgna Lrg Print) Ulverscroft.

***One Boat One Destiny: A Study in the Book of Jonah.** Samson Gitau. LC 98-91036. 1999. pap. 14.95 (*0-533-13024-7*) Vantage.

One Body . . . Many Members. Philip J. Anderson. 35p. 1983. pap. 2.95 (*0-910452-53-9*) Covenant.

One Body - Different Gifts, Many Roles: Reflections on the American Catholic Laity. Intro. by Dolores R. Leckey. 64p. (Orig.). 1987. pap. 4.95 (*1-55586-162-8*) US Catholic.

One Body & One Spirit. Witness Lee. 30p. 1992. pap. 3.50 (*0-87083-816-4*, 15-046-001) Living Stream Ministry.

One Body, One Spirit: Building Relationships in the Church. Dale Larsen & Sandy Larsen. (Fisherman Bible Studyguide Ser.). 64p. (Orig.). 1988. pap. text 4.99 (*0-87788-619-9*, H Shaw Pubs) Waterbrook Pr.

One Body, One Spirit, One Lord. Gordon Lindsay. 1982. per. 3.95 (*0-89985-991-7*) Christ for the Nations.

One Book - Five Ways: The Publishing Procedures of Five University Presses. Ed. by Association of American University Presses Staff. (Illus.). xiv, 344p. 1994. pap. text 18.95 (*0-226-03024-5*) U Ch Pr.

One Book at a Time: The History of the Library in New Mexico. Linda G. Harris. LC 98-5624. 1998. 75.00 (*1-887045-03-1*); 75.00 (*1-887045-04-X*) Arroyo Pr.

***One Book Rightly Divided: The Key to Understanding the Bible.** Douglas D. Stauffer. (Illus.). 272p. 1999. 24.99 (*0-9677016-1-9*) McCowen Mills.

One Boss Too Many. Devra Newberger Speregen. (Full House Sisters Ser.). 153p. (J). (gr. 4-6). 1998. per. 3.99 (*0-671-02150-8*, Minstrel Bks) PB.

One Bowl: One-Pot Meals from Around the World. Kelly McCune. LC 96-33956. (Illus.). 108p. 1996. pap. 14.95 (*0-8118-1111-5*) Chronicle Bks.

***One Boy from Kosovo.** Trish Marx. LC 99-51793. (Illus.). 32p. (YA). (gr. 2-5). 2000. 15.95 (*0-688-17732-8*, Wm Morrow); lib. bdg. 15.89 (*0-688-17733-6*, Wm Morrow) Morrow Avon.

One Bride Delivered. Jeanne Allan. (Larger Print Ser.). 1999. per. 3.50 (*0-373-15814-9*, 1-15814-6) Harlequin Bks.

One Bride Delivered. Jeanne Allan. (Romance Ser.). 1999. per. 3.50 (*0-373-03568-3*, 1-03568-2) Harlequin Bks.

One Bride Required! Emma Richmond. (Romance Ser.). 1998. per. 3.50 (*0-373-03505-5*, 0-03505-5) Harlequin Bks.

One Bride Required! large type ed. Emma Richmond. (Large Print Ser.). 1998. per. 3.50 (*0-373-15751-7*, Harlequin) Harlequin Bks.

One Bridegroom Required. Sharon Kendrick. 1999. per. 3.75 (*0-373-12011-7*, Harlequin) Harlequin Bks.

***One Bridegroom Required.** large type ed. Sharon Kendrick. (Harlequin Ser.). 1999. 21.95 (*0-263-16078-5*) Mills & Boon.

One Brief Moment. Frank R. Nichols. LC 97-65341. (Illus.). 160p. 1997. pap. 14.95 (*0-923687-41-6*) Celo Valley Bks.

One Brief Shining Moment: Remembering Kennedy. William Manchester. (Illus.). 280p. 1988. pap. 16.95 (*0-316-54511-2*) Little.

One Bright & Shining Path see Qyacucho Para Cristo

***One Bright Child.** large type ed. Patricia Cumper. 288p. 1999. 31.99 (*0-7089-4086-2*) Ulverscroft.

One Bright Day. Sigmund Miller. 1952. pap. 5.25 (*0-8222-0852-0*) Dramatists Play.

One Bright Star. Suzanne Goodwin. 160p. 1998. 24.00 (*0-7278-5387-2*) Severn Hse.

One Bright Star. Mickee Madden. 352p. 1997. mass mkt. 5.99 (*0-7860-0273-5*, Pinncle Kensgtn) Kensgtn Pub Corp.

***One Bright Star.** large type ed. Suzanne Goodwin. 320p. 2000. 31.99 (*0-7089-4192-3*) Ulverscroft.

One Broken Dream. large type ed. Ivy Preston. (Dales Large Print Ser.). 257p. 1997. pap. 18.99 (*1-85389-718-3*) Ulverscroft.

One Bugle, No Drums: The Marines at Chosin Reservoir. William B. Hopkins. 288p. 1988. mass mkt. 4.95 (*0-380-70455-2*, Avon Bks) Morrow Avon.

One Bullet for Me: A Woman's Journey Through the Horror of WW II. Magdalene K. Klinksiek & Janet M. Hixon. LC 96-85144. 1996. pap. 11.99 (*0-87509-678-6*) Chr Pubns.

One-Burner Gourmet. rev. ed. Harriett Barker. (Illus.). 288p. 1981. reprint ed. pap. 14.95 (*0-8092-5883-8*, 58838) NTC Contemp Pub Co.

1 Business, 2 Approaches: How to Succeed in Internet Business by Employing Real-World Strategies. Ron Gielgun. (Illus.). 202p. (YA). (gr. 11 up). 1998. 19.95 (*0-9657617-6-2*) Actium Pub.

One by One. Judy Hindley. LC 95-9499. (Illus.). (J). 1996. pap. 4.99 (*1-56402-678-7*) Candlewick Pr.

***One by One.** Gilbert Morris. (A Dani Ross Mystery Ser.). Orig. Title: Guilt by Association. 288p. 2000. reprint ed. pap. 11.99 (*1-58134-192-X*) Crossway Bks.

***One by One: A Teacher Considers His Years in the Classroom.** Stuart Deane. (Illus.). 180p. 2000. 15.95 (*1-884540-49-X*) Haleys.

***One by One: A Teacher Considers His Years inthe Classroom.** Stuart Deane. (Illus.). 180p. 2000. 25.95 (*1-884540-53-8*) Haleys.

One by One from the Inside Out: Essays & Reviews on Race & Responsibility in America. Glenn C. Loury. LC 94-46593. 332p. 1995. 25.00 (*0-02-919441-5*) Free Pr.

One Call System Manual. (Illus.). 1978. pap. text 5.00 (*0-917084-28-4*) Am Public Works.

One Calling, Many Vocations: I'll Be a Friend to Jesus. Gilbert N. Hulme & Mary A. Bruening. LC 96-70899. 64p. (Orig.). 1996. pap. 8.95 (*1-57736-027-3*) Providence Hse.

One Came Back: A Civil War Adventure. Margaret Langford.Tr. of UnRevenant. (Illus.). 256p. 2000. 30.00 (*1-884592-22-8*, Pub. by Images from the Past) Koen Bk Distributors.

One Can Make a Difference: The Challenges & Opportunities of Dealing with World Poverty - The Role of Rural Development Facilitators (RDFs) in the Process of Rural Development. James B. Mayfield. LC 97-5519. 514p. 1997. 69.50 (*0-7618-0714-4*); pap. 46.50 (*0-7618-0715-2*) U Pr of Amer.

One Candle. Eve Bunting. 32p. (ps). 14.89 (*0-06-028116-2*) HarpC.

One Candle. Eve Bunting. (Illus.). 32p. (ps-3). 14.95 (*0-06-028115-4*) HarpC.

One Career Guide. 400p. 1996. pap. text 29.99 (*0-7821-1757-0*) Sybex.

One Carton of Oops! Judy Bradbury. LC 96-37547. (Illus.). 46p. (J). (ps-2). 1997. 10.95 (*0-07-007039-3*) McGraw.

One Case at a Time: Judicial Minimalism on the Supreme Court. Cass R. Sunstein. LC 98-36954. 304p. 1999. 29.95 (*0-674-63790-9*) HUP.

One Catholic to Another see IVP Booklets

One Cause One Cure: The Health & Life Philosophy of Chiropractic, Vol. VI. Fredrick H. Barge. LC 94-79233. 177p. 1996. reprint ed. text 37.95 (*1-885048-05-X*) Barge Chiropract.

***One Centimeter.** 2nd ed. Cheryl C. Burguieres. (Illus.). 1999. 21.95 (*0-87719-368-1*) Gulf Pub.

One Championship Season: The Story of the 1944 St. Louis Browns. Carson Van Lindt. (Illus.). 220p. 1994. pap. 10.95 (*0-9632595-6-3*) Marabou Pub.

***One Child.** Christopher C. Cheng. LC 99-38380. (Illus.). 32p. (J). (gr. 3-6). 1999. 14.95 (*1-56656-330-5*) Interlink Pub.

One Child. Torey L. Hayden. 1995. 10.84 (*0-606-02242-2*, Pub. by Turtleback) Demco.

One Child. Torey L. Hayden. 224p. 1981. reprint ed. mass mkt. 5.99 (*0-380-54262-5*, Avon Bks) Morrow Avon.

One Child at a Time: A Parent's Guide to Rebuilding American Mindpower. Patricia H. Logue. (Illus.). 96p. (Orig.). 1992. pap. 10.00 (*0-9630488-0-5*) Mindbuilder.

One Child Dreaming. Elaine Greenstein. LC 99-25125. (Illus.). (J). 2000. write for info. (*0-439-06303-5*) Itsy.

One Child, Many Worlds: Early Learning in Multicultural Communities. Ed. by Eve Gregory. (Primary Curriculum Ser.). 192p. 1997. pap. 25.95 (*1-85346-460-0*, Pub. by David Fulton) Taylor & Francis.

One Child, Many Worlds: Early Learning in Multicultural Communities. Eve Gregory. LC 97-38011. (Language & Literacy Ser.). 182p. 1997. 20.95 (*0-8077-3715-1*) Tchrs Coll.

One Child, Two Languages: A Guide for Preschool Educators of Children Learning English as a Second Language. Palton Tabors. LC 96-36565. 1997. pap. text 24.95 (*1-55766-272-X*) P H Brookes.

One Chinese Dragon in New York City. Hoong Y. Krakauer. LC 95-22102. (J). 1996. write for info. (*0-316-50323-1*) Little.

One Christ - Many Religions: Toward a Revised Christology. Stanley J. Samartha. LC 90-46863. (Faith Meets Faith Ser.). 1991. pap. 20.00 (*0-88344-733-9*) Orbis Bks.

One Christmas. Canna Funakoshi. LC 90-7445. (Illus.). 40p. (J). (gr. k up). 1991. pap. 12.95 (*0-88708-140-1*, Picture Book Studio) S&S Childrens.

One Christmas Dawn. Candice F. Ransom. LC 93-39751. (Illus.). 32p. (J). (ps-3). 1996. 15.95 (*0-8167-3384-8*) BrdgeWater.

One Christmas Dawn. Candice F. Ransom. LC 93-39751. (Illus.). 32p. (J). (gr. k-3). 1997. pap. 4.95 (*0-8167-3385-6*) Troll Communs.

One Christmas I Met an Angel. J. Grant Swank, Jr. 70p. (Orig.). 1996. pap. 6.99 (*0-8341-1578-6*) Beacon Hill.

One Christmas Knight. Kathleen Creighton. (Intimate Moments Ser.: No. 825). 1997. per. 3.99 (*0-373-07825-0*, 1-07825-2) Harlequin Bks.

O

An Asterisk (*) at the beginning of an entry indicates that the title is appearing for the first time.

One Christmas Night. Rhona Pipe. Ed. by Julie Smith. (Illus.). 24p. (J). (ps-3). 1994. 4.99 (*0-7814-1511-X*, Chariot Bks); 4.99 (*0-7814-1510-1*, Chariot Bks) Chariot Victor.

***One Christmas Night: Highland Christmas; A Wife for Christmas; Ian's Gift.** Ruth Langan et al. (Historical Ser.). 304p. 1999. mass mkt. 4.99 (*0-373-29087-X*, Harlequin) Harlequin Bks.

***One Christmas Star.** Kaye Jacobs Volk. 1999. pap. 3.95 (*1-57734-523-1*, 01114212) Covenant Comms.

***One Christmas Wish: Wish upon a Star; Christmas Wishes; More Than a Miracle.** Carolyn Davidson et al. (Historical Ser.: Bk. 531). 2000. mass mkt. 4.99 (*0-373-29131-0*, 1-29131-9) Harlequin Bks.

One Church, Many Congregations: The Key Church Strategy. J. V. Thomas & J. Timothy Ahlen. LC 99-21484. (Ministry for the Third Millennium Ser.). 1999. 15.00 (*0-687-08599-3*) Abingdon.

One Church, Many Cultures: The Challenge of Diversity. Joseph P. Fitzpatrick. LC 86-61359. 210p. (Orig.). 1987. pap. 11.95 (*0-934134-63-4*) Sheed & Ward WI.

One Circle: How to Grow a Complete Diet in Less Than 1000 Square Feet. David Duhon. (Illus.). 199p. 1985. pap. 12.50 (*0-614-11404-7*) Ecology Action.

One City's Wilderness: Portland's Forest Park. rev. ed. Marcy C. Houle. (Illus.). 120p. (Orig.). 1995. pap. 14.95 (*0-87595-284-4*) Oregon Hist.

One Classroom, Many Cultures: Teaching Strategies for Culturally Different Children. Anne-Katrin Eckermann. 224p. 1994. pap. 22.95 (*1-86373-622-0*, Pub. by Allen & Unwin Pty) Paul & Co Pubs.

One Coffee With. Margaret Maron. 192p. 1995. mass mkt. 5.99 (*0-446-40415-2*, Pub. by Warner Bks) Little.

One Coffee With. large type ed. Margaret Maron. 1991. 27.99 (*0-7089-2433-6*) Ulverscroft.

1, Conker... Tom Davies. 308p. 1994. pap. 60.00 (*1-85902-100-X*) St Mut.

One Continuous Mistake. Gail Sher. LC 98-36537. 224p. 1999. pap. 12.95 (*0-14-019587-4*, Arkana) Viking Penguin.

One Cool Cat. John Laing. (Methuen Young Drama Ser.). 43p. (J). (gr. 1). 1988. pap. 5.95 (*0-413-54220-3*, A0197) Heinemann.

One Cop's Story: A Life Remembered. John H. Briant. LC 95-71016. (Illus.). 182p. 1995. 21.95 (*0-9648327-1-2*); pap. 14.95 (*0-9648327-0-4*) Chalet Pubng.

I Corinthians 12 & 13. Ed. by David Meyer & Alice Meyer. 32p. 1999. pap. 12.95 (*1-879099-29-2*) Thy Word.

One Corpse Too Many. Ellis Peters. 224p. 1994. mass mkt. 6.50 (*0-446-40051-3*, Pub. by Warner Bks) Little.

One Country or Two? Ronald M. Burns. LC 76-174566. 297p. reprint ed. pap. 92.10 (*0-608-16143-8*, 202383600034) Bks Demand.

One Country, Two International Legal Personalities: The Case of Hong Kong. Roda Mushkat. LC 97-160891. 232p. (Orig.). 1997. pap. 42.50 (*962-209-427-9*, Pub. by HK Univ Pr) Coronet Bks.

One Country, Two Systems, Three Languages: A Survey of Changing Language Use in Hong Kong. Ed. by Sue Wright & Helen Kelly-Holmes. LC 97-2543. 96p. 1997. 49.00 (*1-85359-396-6*, Pub. by Multilingual Matters) Taylor & Francis.

One Couple, Four Realities: Multiple Perspectives on Couple Therapy. Ed. by Richard Chasin et al. LC 90-3037. 420p. 1990. lib. bdg. 45.00 (*0-89862-437-1*) Guilford Pubns.

One Couple, Four Realities: Multiple Perspectives on Couple Therapy. Ed. by Richard Chasin et al. LC 90-3037. 420p. 1992. reprint ed. pap. text 25.00 (*0-89862-029-5*) Guilford Pubns.

One Cow Coughs: A Counting Book for the Sick & Miserable. Christine Loomis. LC 93-1836. (Illus.). 32p. (J). (ps-2). 1994. 14.95 (*0-395-67899-4*) Ticknor & Flds Bks Yng Read.

One Cow Moo Moo. David Bennett. LC 90-32065. (Illus.). 32p. (J). (ps-2). 1995. 15.95 (*0-8050-1416-0*, Bks Young Read) H Holt & Co.

One Cowboy's Roundup. Ham Hamilton. LC 94-61537. (Illus.). 144p. 1995. pap. 12.95 (*0-9643426-1-8*) A Wide Line.

One Crazy Christmas. Janet Quin-Harkin. (Sister, Sister Ser.: No. 5). 144p. (J). (gr. 5-7). 1996. pap. 3.99 (*0-671-00283-X*) PB.

One Crossed Out. Fanny Howe. LC 97-70217. 64p. 1997. pap. 12.95 (*1-55597-259-4*) Graywolf.

1 Crow. Jim Aylesworth. LC 85-45856. (Trophy Picture Bk.). (Illus.). 32p. (J). (ps-1). 1990. pap. 5.95 (*0-06-443242-4*, HarpTrophy) HarpC Child Bks.

One Cubit of Stature. Myron E. Gruenwald. (Illus.). 82p. 1985. pap. 6.00 (*0-9601536-2-4*) G J OConnell.

One Culture: Essays in Science & Literature. Ed. by George Levine. LC 87-40143. (Science & Literature Ser.). 368p. 1987. pap. text 14.95 (*0-299-11304-3*) U of Wis Pr.

One Culture: Essays in Science & Literature. Ed. by George L. Levine. LC 87-40143. (Science & Literature Ser.). 368p. (C). 1988. text 45.00 (*0-299-11300-0*) U of Wis Pr.

One Culture, Many Systems: Politics in the Reunification of China. Donald H. McMillen & Michael E. DeGolyer. 334p. (Orig.). 1997. pap. text 26.95 (*962-201-577-8*, Pub. by Chinese Univ) U of Mich Pr.

One Cup Faith. Victor Knowles. 194p. pap. 5.99 (*0-89900-380-X*) College Pr Pub.

One Cup of Water. Ed. by Janice K. Brauer. (Illus.). 160p. (Orig.). 1997. pap. 6.00 (*0-9614955-6-1*, 23000) Lutheran Womens.

One Dad, Two Dads, Brown Dad, Blue Dads. Johnny Valentine. (Illus.). 32p. (J). (ps-1). 1994. 10.95 (*1-55583-253-9*, Alyson Wonderland) Alyson Pubns.

One Damned Island after Another. Clive Howard & Joe Whitley. LC 47-30014. 481p. reprint ed. pap. 149.20 (*0-7837-2080-7*, 204235400004) Bks Demand.

One Damned Island after Another: The Saga of the Seventh Air Force in World War II. Clive Howard & Joe Whitley. LC 79-16254. 1979. reprint ed. 35.00 (*0-89201-049-5*) Zenger Pub.

***One Dare Too Many.** Shelagh Noden. 212p. 2000. 19.95 (*1-929085-42-7*); pap. 4.95 (*1-929085-41-9*) Rgncy Pr.

***One Dare Too Many.** large type ed. Shelagh Noden. 2000. pap. 19.95 (*1-929085-45-1*) Rgncy Pr.

One Dark & Scary Night. Bill Cosby. LC 98-8813. (Little Bill Books for Beginning Readers Ser.). (Illus.). (J). (gr. k-3). 1999. 15.95 (*0-590-51475-X*); pap. 3.99 (*0-590-51476-8*) Scholastic Inc.

***One Dark & Scary Night.** Bill Cosby. (Little Bill Books for Beginning Readers Ser.). (J). (gr. k-3). 1999. pap. text 47.88 (*0-439-04655-6*, Cartwheel) Scholastic Inc.

One Dark Mile: A Widower's Story. Eric Robinson. LC 89-32046. 200p. 1990. 30.00 (*0-87023-684-9*) U of Mass Pr.

***One Dark Night.** Pamela Bennetts. 232p. 2000. 31.99 (*0-7089-4213-X*) Ulverscroft.

***One Dark Night: 13 Masterpieces of the Macabre.** Kathleen Blease. (Illus.). 144p. 2000. pap. 10.00 (*0-345-44044-7*, Ballantine) Ballantine Pub Grp.

One Dark Night C. Wheeler. 2001. Price not set. (*0-15-202318-6*) Harcourt Coll Pubs.

One Day: A Poem in Three Parts. Donald Hall. 72p. 1988. pap. 14.00 (*0-89919-816-3*, Pub. by Ticknor & Fields) HM.

One Day a Stranger Came. Naomi Wakan. Tr. by Tatjana K. Volz. (Illus.). 32p. (J). (gr. k-2). 1994. 14.95 (*1-55037-354-4*, Pub. by Annick); pap. 4.95 (*1-55037-353-6*, Pub. by Annick) Firefly Bks Ltd.

One Day & Forever: A Novel. Sarah Birnhack. 1993. 16.99 (*0-89906-133-8*); 13.99 (*0-89906-143-5*) Mesorah Pubns.

***One Day as a Private Eye.** Louise Longo. LC 99-97059. 2000. 18.75 (*0-533-13382-3*) Vantage.

***One Day As A Tiger.** Anne Haverty. LC 97-3140. 264p. 1999. pap. 15.00 (*0-88001-667-1*) HarpC.

One Day As A Tiger. Anne M. Haverty. LC 97-3140. 224p. 1998. 22.00 (*0-88001-558-6*) HarpC.

***One Day at a Time.** Jim Gallery & Criswell Freeman. 128p. 2000. pap. 4.95 (*1-58334-079-3*, Pub. by Walnut Gr Pr) Midpt Trade.

One Day at a Time. Marshall Kline. 1998. pap. write for info. (*1-58235-031-0*) Watermrk Pr.

One Day at a Time. 2nd ed. William MacDonald. 1998. reprint ed. 24.99 (*1-882701-48-8*) Uplook Min.

One Day at a Time: A Personal Guide to Coping with a Terminal Diagnosis. Lon G. Nungesser. 1988. write for info. (*0-318-61942-3*) St Martin.

One Day at a Time: A Vietnam Diary. D. J. Dennis. (Orig.). 1992. pap. 16.95 (*0-7022-2442-1*, Pub. by Univ Queensland Pr) Intl Spec Bk.

One Day at a Time: Biography of Cristy Lane. Lee Stoller & Pete Chaney. 1984. 16.95 (*0-9614370-8-1*); pap. 10.99 (*0-9614370-0-6*); pap. text 9.99 incl. digital audio (*0-9614370-7-3*) L S Records.

One Day at a Time: Children Living with Leukemia see **Don't Turn Away**

One Day At a Time: Christy Lane, Her Life Story. Lee Stoller & Pete Chaney. 1984. audio, VHS 25.00 (*0-9614370-1-4*) L S Records.

One Day at a Time: How Families Manage the Experience of Dementia. Carole-Lynne Le Navenec. LC 95-24263. 240p. 1996. 57.95 (*0-86569-257-2*, Auburn Hse) Greenwood.

***One Day at a Time: The Devotional for Overcomers.** Neil T. Anderson et al. 2000. pap. 14.99 (*0-8307-2400-1*, Regal Bks) Gospel Lght.

***One Day at a Time, Box Set.** Mark Allen. 1152p. 1999. boxed set 19.95 (*2-921556-92-8*, Pub. by Modus Viv) ACCESS Pubs Network.

One Day at a Time in Al-Anon. Al-Anon Family Group Headquarters, Inc. Staff. LC 72-85153. 1989. 8.00 (*0-910034-21-4*) Al-Anon.

One Day at a Time in Al-Anon. large type ed. Al-Anon Family Group Headquarters, Inc. Staff. LC 72-85153. 1989. 10.00 (*0-910034-63-X*) Al-Anon.

One Day at a Time in Phobics Victorious. Rosemary. LC 94-71004. 1995. pap. 9.95 (*0-8158-0500-4*) Chris Mass.

One-Day-at-a-Time Therapy. Christine A. Adams. LC 90-80719. (Illus.). 72p. (Orig.). 1990. pap. 4.95 (*0-87029-228-5*, 20204-4) Abbey.

***One Day at Disney.** (Illus.). 2000. 40.00 (*0-7868-6592-X*, Pub. by Disney Pr) Time Warner.

One Day at Horrorland see **Dia en Horrorland**

One Day at Horrorland. R. L. Stine, pseud. LC 96-208097. (Goosebumps Ser.: No. 16). 160p. (J). (gr. 3-7). 1994. pap. 3.99 (*0-590-47738-2*) Scholastic Inc.

One Day at Horrorland. R. L. Stine, pseud. (Goosebumps Ser.: No. 16). (J). 1994. 9.09 (*0-606-05963-6*, Pub. by Turtleback) Demco.

One Day at Shirley's . . . Ruth Forman et al. 86p. 1986. pap. 5.00 (*0-9610038-1-2*) Heatherdown Pr.

One Day at the Zoo. G. M. Thompson. 57p. 1996. pap. 3.50 (*0-87129-741-8*, O58) Dramatic Pub.

One Day at Time: A Journal of Inspiration. Illus. by Kari Albery. 160p. 1996. spiral bd. 15.95 (*1-55670-520-4*) Stewart Tabori & Chang.

One Day Celestial Navigation. Otis S. Brown. LC 79-67243. (Illus.). 133p. 1988. pap. 9.95 (*0-89709-132-9*) Liberty Pub.

One Day Celestial Navigation for Offshore Sailing. 2nd ed. Otis Brown. 218p. 1994. pap. 12.95 (*1-56790-021-6*) C & O Research.

One-Day Christmas Crafts. (Illus.). 64p. 1993. 5.98 (*0-7853-0281-6*, 3617200) Pubns Intl Ltd.

One Day Closer to Death: Eight Stabs at Immortality. Bradley Denton. LC 97-38440. 352p. 1997. text 23.95 (*0-312-18150-7*) St Martin.

One Day Course for Create a Web Page with Word 97. D D C Publishing Staff. (One-Day Course Ser.). 1997. pap. text 22.00 (*1-56243-568-X*, DC23) DDC Pub.

One Day Course for Frontpage. D D C Publishing Staff. (One-Day Course Ser.). 1997. pap. text 22.00 (*1-56243-448-9*, DC22) DDC Pub.

One Day Course for Windows NT 4.0. D D C Publishing Staff. (One-Day Course Ser.). 1997. pap. text 22.00 (*1-56243-297-4*, DC24) DDC Pub.

***One Day, Daddy: Picture Book.** Frances Thomas. (Illus.). 32p. (J). 2001. 15.99 (*0-7868-0732-6*, Pub. by Disney Pr) Time Warner.

One Day Everything... (Illus.). (J). (ps-2). 1991. pap. 5.10 (*0-8136-5962-0*) Modern Curr.

One Day Everything . . . Elizabeth Vreeken. (Illus.). (J). (ps-2). 1991. lib. bdg. 7.95 (*0-8136-5204-9*) Modern Curr.

One Day in Alabama Vol. II: Statehood to Civil War. Clarke Stallworth. (Illus.). 144p. (Orig.). (J). (gr. 4-5). 1994. pap. text 8.95 (*1-878561-37-5*) Seacoast AL.

One Day in Alabama Vol. III: The Civil War Years. Clarke Stallworth. (Illus.). 144p. (J). (gr. 4-5). 1997. pap. 8.95 (*1-878561-55-3*) Seacoast AL.

***One Day in April: Part One (A Novel) 1998.** David Wilde. 1999. pap. 16.00 (*1-882204-17-4*) Wilde Pub.

One Day in Crinkle Canyon. Arnosky. 1999. per. 5.99 (*0-689-81599-9*) S&S Childrens.

One Day in Crinkle Canyon. Arnosky. (J). 1999. per. 14.00 (*0-689-81598-0*) S&S Childrens.

One Day in Dallas: The Only Eyewitness Who Saw Lee Harvey Oswald Shoot John F. Kennedy. Howard Brennan & J. Edward Cherryholmes. (Illus.). 224p. 1998. 28.95 (*0-89896-331-1*) Larksdale.

One Day in Ithica see **May 17, 1988: One Day in an American Community**

One Day in My Life. Bobby Sands. LC 85-11251. 118p. (Orig.). 1985. pap. 5.95 (*0-916650-20-0*) Banner Pr Intl.

***One Day in September: The Story of the 1972 Munich Olympics Massacre.** Simon Reeve. 2000. 25.95 (*1-55970-547-7*, Pub. by Arcade Pub Inc) Time Warner.

One Day in the Alpine Tundra. Jean Craighead George. LC 82-45590. (Illus.). 48p. (J). (gr. 5-7). 1984. lib. bdg. 15.89 (*0-690-04326-0*) HarpC Child Bks.

One Day in the Alpine Tundra. Jean Craighead George. LC 82-45590. (Trophy Chapter Bk.). (Illus.). 64p. (J). (gr. 2-5). 1996. pap. 4.25 (*0-06-442027-2*, HarpTrophy) HarpC Child Bks.

One Day in the Alpine Tundra. Jean Craighead George. LC 82-45590. (J). 1996. 9.70 (*0-606-09711-2*, Pub. by Turtleback) Demco.

One Day in the Desert. Jean Craighead George. LC 82-45924. (Illus.). 48p. (J). (gr. 5-7). 1983. lib. bdg. 15.89 (*0-690-04341-4*) HarpC Child Bks.

One Day in the Desert. Jean Craighead George. LC 82-45924. (Trophy Chapter Bk.). (Illus.). 64p. (J). (gr. 2-5). 1996. pap. 4.25 (*0-06-442038-8*, HarpTrophy) HarpC Child Bks.

One Day in the Desert. Jean Craighead George. LC 82-45924. (J). 1996. 9.15 (*0-606-09712-0*, Pub. by Turtleback) Demco.

One Day in the Jungle. Colin West. LC 95-7888. (Illus.). 24p. (J). (ps up). 1995. 9.95 (*1-56402-646-9*) Candlewick Pr.

One Day in the Jungle. Colin West. LC 95-7888. (Illus.). 24p. (J). (ps-1). 1997. reprint ed. pap. 3.29 (*1-56402-987-5*) Candlewick Pr.

***One Day in the Life of a Born Again Loser & Other Stories.** Helen Norris. LC 99-6957. 224p. 2000. 24.95 (*0-8173-1029-0*) U of Ala Pr.

One Day in the Life of Ivan Denisocvich: Reproducible Teaching Unit. James Scott. 46p. (YA). (gr. 7-12). 1999. teacher ed., ring bd. 29.50 (*1-58049-098-0*, TU78) Prestwick Hse.

One Day in the Life of Ivan Denisovich. Aleksandr Solzhenitsyn. 160p. 1998. pap. text 2.67 (*0-451-52310-5*) Addson-Wesley Educ.

One Day in the Life of Ivan Denisovich. Aleksandr Solzhenitsyn. 224p. 1984. mass mkt. 4.99 (*0-553-24777-8*, Noonday) FS&G.

One Day in the Life of Ivan Denisovich. Aleksandr Solzhenitsyn. Tr. by H. T. Willetts. LC 91-29970. 188p. 1992. pap. 13.00 (*0-374-52195-6*) FS&G.

One Day in the Life of Ivan Denisovich. Aleksandr Solzhenitsyn. Tr. by H. T. Willetts. 159p. 1995. 15.00 (*0-679-44464-5*) Knopf.

One Day in the Life of Ivan Denisovich. Aleksandr Solzhenitsyn. write for info. (*0-614-22113-7*, Sig Classics) NAL.

One Day in the Life of Ivan Denisovich. Aleksandr Solzhenitsyn. Tr. by Ralph Parker from RUS. LC 97-62429. (Signet Classics Ser.). 1998. mass mkt. 4.95 (*0-451-52709-7*, Sig Classics) NAL.

One Day in the Life of Ivan Denisovich. Aleksandr Solzhenitsyn. (Signet Bks.). (J). 1963. 10.05 (*0-606-04237-7*, Pub. by Turtleback) Demco.

***One Day in the Life of Ivan Denisovich.** 8th ed. Aleksandr Solzhenitsyn. 1999. pap. 5.00 (*5-7684-0706-5*) Distribks Inc.

One Day in the Life of Ivan Denisovich: A Critical Companion. Aleksandr Solzhenitsyn. Ed. by Alexis Klimoff. LC 97-21430. (Northwestern/Aatseel Critical Companions To Russian Literature Ser.). 180p. (C). 1996. pap. text 16.95 (*0-8101-1214-0*) Northwestern U Pr.

One Day in the Life of Ivan Denisovich: A Unit Plan. Mary B. Collins. 144p. 1994. teacher ed., ring bd. 26.95 (*1-58337-121-4*) Teachers Pet Pubns.

One Day in the Life of Ivan Denisovich (Monarch Notes) Albert L. Weeks. 1976. 4.25 (*0-671-00976-1*, Arco) Macmillan Gen Ref.

One Day in the Life of Ivan Denisovich Notes. Franz G. Blaha. (Cliffs Notes Ser.). 64p. (Orig.). (C). 1986. pap. text 4.95 (*0-8220-0960-9*, Cliff) IDG Bks.

One Day in the Life of Zechariah. Shadrach Linscomb. (Illus.). 1998. pap. 9.95 (*0-9663420-3-8*) View Hse Pubg.

One Day in the Prairie. Jean Craighead George. LC 85-48254. (Illus.). 64p. (J). (gr. 2-5). 1996. pap. 4.25 (*0-06-442039-6*, HarpTrophy) HarpC Child Bks.

One Day in the Prairie. Jean Craighead George. LC 85-48254. (J). 1996. 9.15 (*0-606-09713-9*, Pub. by Turtleback) Demco.

One Day in the Tropical Rain Forest. Jean Craighead George. LC 89-36583. (Illus.). 64p. (J). (gr. 4-7). 1990. 15.95 (*0-690-04767-3*); lib. bdg. 15.89 (*0-690-04769-X*) HarpC Child Bks.

One Day in the Tropical Rain Forest. Jean Craighead George. LC 89-36583. (Trophy Chapter Bk.). (Illus.). 80p. (J). (gr. 2-5). 1995. pap. 4.25 (*0-06-442016-7*, HarpTrophy) HarpC Child Bks.

One Day in the Tropical Rain Forest. Jean Craighead George. (J). 1995. 9.15 (*0-606-08444-4*, Pub. by Turtleback) Demco.

One Day in the Woods. Jean Craighead George. LC 87-21712. (Illus.). 48p. (J). (gr. 4-7). 1988. lib. bdg. 15.89 (*0-690-04724-X*) HarpC Child Bks.

One Day in the Woods. Jean Craighead George. LC 87-21712. (Trophy Chapter Bk.). (Illus.). 64p. (J). (gr. 4-7). 1995. pap. 4.25 (*0-06-442017-5*, HarpTrophy) HarpC Child Bks.

One Day in the Woods. Jean Craighead George. 1995. 9.15 (*0-606-08445-2*, Pub. by Turtleback) Demco.

One Day into Twenty Three. Ernest T. Moriarty. 164p. (Orig.). 1987. pap. text 14.50 (*0-9620139-0-0*) E T Moriarty.

One-Day Marketing Plan. 2nd ed. Roman G. Hiebing & Scott W. Cooper. LC 99-38658. 256p. 1999. pap. 24.95 (*0-8442-1283-0*, 12830, NTC Business Bks) NTC Contemp Pub Co.

One-Day Marketing Plan: Organizing & Completing the Best Plan for Your Company. 2nd ed. Roman G. Hiebing, Jr. LC 99-38658. 1999. 49.95 (*0-8442-0247-9*) NTC Contemp Pub Co.

***One-day Mba in Finance & Accounting.** Muckian. 2000. 49.95 (*0-13-028459-9*) P-H.

***One-day Mba in Marketing.** Muckian. 2000. 49.95 (*0-13-028156-5*) P-H.

***One-Day Millionaires.** large type ed. Hazel Townson. (Illus.). (J). 1998. pap. 16.95 (*0-7540-6017-9*, Galaxy Child Lrg Print) Chivers N Amer.

***One Day Millionaires: An Arthur Venger Story.** Hazel Townson. (Illus.). 80p. (J). 1998. pap. 8.95 (*0-86264-835-1*, Pub. by Random) Trafalgar.

One Day, Mother / Un Dia, Madre. Dorothy T. Johnson. (ENG & SPA.). (Orig.). (J). (gr. 1-6). 1996. pap. 6.95 (*0-533-11716-X*) Vantage.

***One Day, My Prince.** Linda Jones. 400p. 2000. pap. 5.99 (*0-505-52388-4*, Love Spell) Dorchester Pub Co.

One Day My Soul Just Opened Up: 40 Days & 40 Nights Toward Spiritual Strength & Personal Growth. Iyanla Vanzant. LC 97-31113. 320p. 1998. per. 13.00 (*0-684-84134-7*, Fireside) S&S Trade Pap.

One Day My Soul Just Opened Up: 40 Days & 40 Nights Toward Spiritual Strength & Personal Growth. large type ed. Iyanla Vanzant. LC 98-51853. (G.K. Hall Large Print Inspirational Ser.). 405p. 1999. 26.95 (*0-7838-8513-X*) Macmillan Gen Ref.

One Day of Life. Manlio Argueta. LC 90-50213. (Vintage International Ser.). 224p. 1991. pap. 13.00 (*0-679-73243-8*) Vin Bks.

One Day of the Civil War: America in Conflict, April 10, 1863. Robert L. Willett, Jr. (Illus.). 352p. 1997. 24.95 (*1-57488-082-9*) Brasseys.

One Day of the Civil War: America in Conflict, April 10, 1863. Robert L. Willett, Jr. LC 98-6226. 320p. 1998. pap. 14.95 (*0-452-27977-1*, Plume) Dutton Plume.

One Day on Earth: A Third Eye View. Catherine Lazers Bauer. LC 99-27397. 318p. 1999. 15.95 (*0-9620507-8-4*, Pub. by Cosmic Concepts Pr) New Leaf Dist.

One Day-One Lifetime: An Illustrated Guide to the Spirit, Practice, & Philosophy of Seido Karate Meditation. Kaicho T. Nakamura. (Illus.). 210p. 1995. 25.00 (*0-8048-3064-9*) Tuttle Pubng.

One Day, One Long Day, a Child Looked over All That Was, & Was Not Pleased at All. rev. ed. Jim Sorcic. 30p. 1994. pap. 12.00 (*1-880723-03-4*) Morgan Pr WI.

One Day Plan for Jobhunters. Katherine Kurtz & Judith Segalini. LC 88-61398. 100p. 1988. pap. 11.95 (*0-911168-72-9*) Prakken.

One-Day Quick Course in Microsoft Windows 98: Education - Training Edition. Joyce Cox. Ed. by Christina Dudley. LC 98-66726. (One-Day Quick Course). (Illus.). 128p. 1998. pap. text 10.95 (*1-879399-90-3*) Online Training.

One-Day Retreats for Junior High Youth. Geri Braden-Whartenby & Joan Finn Connelly. 124p. (J). 1997. pap. 27.95 (*0-88489-436-3*) St Marys.

One Day Retreats for Senior High Youth. Geri Braden-Whartenby & Joan Finn Connelly. Ed. by Robert Stamschror. 144p. (J). 1997. pap. 27.95 (*0-88489-369-3*) St Marys.

One Day Self-Guided Tours of Southern California. Beverly Gillett & Laurey Venn. 1998. pap. 9.95 (*0-9662639-0-1*) B B L T.

One Day There Was Nothing to Do. Jill Creighton. (Illus.). 24p. (J). (ps-3). 1990. pap. 4.95 (*1-55037-090-1*, Pub. by Annick); lib. bdg. 14.95 (*1-55037-091-X*, Pub. by Annick) Firefly Bks Ltd.

O

One Day, They Won't Laugh No More: Inspirational Black History - An Autobiography of the Author's Teen-Age Life, from Years. 15-19 Years. Sue Thompson. 204p. 1980. pap. 6.95 (0-9603672-0-9) Crossrds CA.

One Day Too Long: Top Secret Site 85 & the Bombing of North Vietnam. Timothy N. Castle. LC 98-43117. (Illus.). 352p. 1999. 24.95 (0-231-10316-6) Col U Pr.

***One Day Too Long: Top Secret Site 85 & the Bombing of North Vietnam.** Timothy N. Castle. 368p. 2000. pap. text 15.95 (0-231-10317-4) Col U Pr.

***One-Day Trips Through History.** Jane Ockershausen. (Illus.). 336p. 2000. pap. 14.95 (1-57427-090-7) Howell Pr VA.

One Day We Had to Run! Refugee Children Tell Their Stories in Words & Paintings. Sybella Wilkes. (Illus.). 64p. (J). (gr. 4-8). 1995. pap. 8.95 (1-56294-844-X); lib. bdg. 20.90 (1-56294-557-2) Millbrook Pr.

One Day We Had to Run! Refugee Children Tell Their Stories in Words & Paintings. Sybella Wilkes. LC 94-3743. (J). 1994. 14.15 (0-606-09714-7, Pub. by Turtleback) Demco.

One Day We Met the Lions. J. Mackenzie. 1995. 2.99 (1-871676-79-7, Pub. by Christian Focus) Spring Arbor Dist.

One Day When I Was Lost: A Scenario Based on Alex Haley's "The Autobiography of Malcolm X" James Baldwin. 272p. 1990. mass mkt. 6.50 (0-440-20660-X, LE) Dell.

One Day with a Goat Herd. C. J. Stevens. LC 91-67945. (Illus.). 100p. 1992. pap. 8.95 (0-9623934-6-0); text 15.00 (0-9623934-7-9) J Wade.

One Day with God: A Guide to Retreats & the Contemplative Life. rev. ed. Karl Pruter. LC 91-35733. (St. Willibrord Studies in Philosophy & Religion: No. 1). 56p. 1991. pap. 13.00 (0-912134-11-9); lib. bdg. 23.00 (0-912134-10-0) Millefleurs.

One Day's Perfect Weather: More Twice-Told Tales. Daniel Stern. LC 99-36813. 224p. 1999. 19.95 (0-87074-445-3, Pub. by SMU Press) Tex A&M Univ. Pr.

One Dead Dean. Bill Crider. 208p. 1988. 17.95 (0-8027-5711-1) Walker & Co.

One Dead Diva. Phillip Scott. 230p. 1996. pap. text 12.95 (1-875243-21-6, Pub. by Blackwattle) LPC InBook.

***One Dead Drag Queen: A Tom & Scott Mystery.** Mark R. Zubro. LC 00-29674. 256p. 2000. text 22.95 (0-312-20937-1) St Martin.

One Deadly Summer. Sebastian Japisot. Tr. by Alan Sheridan. LC 97-14302. 288p. 1997. pap. 11.95 (0-452-27780-9, Plume) Dutton Plume.

One Deadly Summer. Sidney D. Kirkpatrick. 1999. pap. 4.95 (0-14-011044-5, Viking) Viking Penguin.

One Death to Die: A Kayankaya Mystery. Jakob Arjouni. Tr. by Anselm Hollo from GER. LC 96-18593. (Kayankaya Mysteries Ser.). 192p. 1997. reprint ed. pap. 21.95 (0-88064-170-3) Fromm Intl Pub.

One Deathless Hour. large type ed. Roger Ormerod. (Mystery Library). 336p. 1995. pap. 16.99 (0-7089-7650-6, Linford) Ulverscroft.

One Degree Beyond: A Reiki Journey into Energy Medicine: Your 21-Day Step-by-Step Guide to Relax, Open & Celebrate. 2nd rev. ed. JaneAnne Narrin. (Illus.). 320p. (Orig.). 1998. pap. 18.95 (0-9658545-4-X) Little Whte Buffalo.

Winner, National book award. Coalition of Visionary Retailer's Visionary Award, 1st runner up, Best Alternative Health Book of 1999. Widely acclaimed book by JaneAnne Narrin, celebrated seminar leader & popular speaker about owning your own power. Details ways to touch in with the energy medicine "available at your very fingertips" through Reiki (simple hands-on technique.) Looks at the practical relationship between Reiki & modern scientific theory. Uses tools of self-inquiry, stories & a great workbook section to engage readers. Excellent reference section for research in energy medicine, Reiki teachers, success stories & more. The "Put Reiki to Work in Your Life" book perfect for anyone interested in learning about Reiki for the first time or for advanced practitioners. Says Whole Life Times: "Interested in learning more about Reiki, stress management, relaxation, alternative medicine? This book will teach you these things & more ...." Awareness Magazine says: "What a pleasure to find a book on Reiki that brings healing, even by reading it. ...." Available through Ingram, Baker & Taylor, Bookpeople & online at Amazon.com, barnesandnoble.com, or through Little White Buffalo Publishing Cottage, Inc.PMB204, 12345 Lake City Way, NE, Seattle, WA 98125, 425-771-2744
Publisher Paid Annotation.

One Degree West: Reflections of a Plainsdaughter. Julene Bair. (First Series). 192p. 2000. pap. 16.00 (0-922811-45-8) Mid-List.

***One Deluxe Order of Healthy Self-Esteem to Go: An Easy to Follow Recipe for Positive Self-Esteem.** Billie Bacon. (Illus.). 99p. 1999. pap. 11.95 (0-9672971-0-9) P Result SC.

One Dialogue or Colloquy Entitled Diversoria. Desiderius Erasmus. LC 71-26509. (English Experience Ser.: No. 244). 20p. 1970. reprint ed. 15.00 (90-221-0244-0) Walter J Johnson.

One-Dichloroethene. (BUA Report Ser.: Vol. 33). 60p. 1992. pap. 32.00 (3-527-28452-4, Wiley-VCH) Wiley.

One Dies, Get Another: Convict Leasing in the American South, 1866-1928. Matthew J. Mancini. LC 95-50208. (Illus.). 290p. 1996. text 34.95 (1-57003-083-9) U of SC Pr.

One-Digit Addition & Subtraction with Cuisenaire Rods. Cuisenaire. 1995. pap. write for info. (0-201-48223-1) Addison-Wesley.

One Digital Day: How the Microchip is Changing Our World. Rick Smolan. LC 97-48434. 223p. 1998. 40.00 (0-8129-3031-2, Times Bks) Crown Pub Group.

One Dimensional & Two Dimensional NMR Spectra by Modern Pulse Techniques. Koji Nakanishi. (Illus.). 336p. 1990. pap. text 38.50 (0-935702-63-6) Univ Sci Bks.

One-Dimensional Conductors. Hiroshi Nagasawa et al. (Solid-State Sciences Ser.: Vol. 72). (Illus.). 270p. 1988. 79.95 (0-387-18154-7) Spr-Verlag.

One-Dimensional Digital Signal Processing. Chen. (Electrical Engineering & Electronics Ser.: Vol. 9). (Illus.). 464p. 1979. text 69.75 (0-8247-6877-9) Dekker.

One-Dimensional Dynamics. Welington De Melo & Sebastian Van Strien. LC 93-7846. (Ergebnisse der Mathematik und Ihrer Grenzgebiete Ser.: Vol. 3). 1996. 119.00 (0-387-56412-8) Spr-Verlag.

One-Dimensional Heat Equation. J. R. Cannon. 1984. 68.00 (0-201-13522-1) Cambridge U Pr.

One-Dimensional Heat Equation. John R. Cannon. (Encyclopedia of Mathematics & Its Applications Ser.: No. 23). 576p. 1984. text 100.00 (0-521-30243-9, 30243-9) Cambridge U Pr.

One-Dimensional Introduction to Continuum Mechanics. A. J. Roberts. LC 94-30315. 172p. 1994. text 28.00 (981-02-1913-X) World Scientific Pub.

One-Dimensional Inverse Problems of Mathematical Physics. M. A. Lavrent'ev et al. LC 86-7917. (AMS Translations Ser.: Series 2, Vol. 130). 70p. 1986. text 47.00 (0-8218-3099-6, TRANS2/130) Am Math.

One-Dimensional Linear Singular Integral Equations Vol. I: Introduction. Ed. by I. Gohberg & N. Y. Krupnik. (Operator Theory: Advances & Applications Ser.: Vol. 53). 272p. 1991. 137.00 (0-8176-2584-4) Birkhauser.

One-Dimensional Linear Singular Integral Equations Vol. II: General Theory & Applications. I. Gohberg & N. Y. Krupnik. (Operator Theory Ser.: Vol. 54). ix, 223p. 1992. 114.00 (0-8176-2796-0) Birkhauser.

One-Dimensional Man: Studies in the Ideology of Advanced Industrial Society. Herbert Marcuse. LC 91-18246. 320p. 1992. pap. 16.00 (0-8070-1417-6) Beacon Pr.

One-Dimensional Metals: Physics & Materials Science. Siegmar Roth. 247p. 1995. 135.00 (3-527-26875-8, Wiley-VCH) Wiley.

One-Dimensional Organometallic Materials. M. C. Bohm. (Lecture Notes in Chemistry Ser.: Vol. 45). v, 180p. 1987. 32.95 (0-387-17216-5) Spr-Verlag.

One Dimensional Spline Interpolation Algorithms. Helmuth Spath. LC 93-40858. (Illus.). 416p. (C). 1995. text 65.00 (1-56881-016-4) AK Peters.

One-Dimensional Stable Distributions. V. M. Zolotarev. LC 86-10943. (Translations of Mathematical Monographs: Vol. 65). 284p. 1986. pap. 49.00 (0-8218-4519-5, MMONO/65) Am Math.

One-Dimensional Variational Problems Vol. 15: An Introduction. Giuseppe Buttazzo et al. LC 99-214744. (Oxford Lecture Series in Mathematics & Its Applications: 15). (Illus.). 270p. 1999. text 65.00 (0-19-850465-9) OUP.

***One Dish Meals.** Jean Pare. 1999. pap. 10.99 (1-895455-54-5) Companys Coming.

One-Dish Meals from Around the World. Kay S. Nelson. 1993. pap. 14.95 (0-8128-8551-1, Scrbrough Hse) Madison Bks UPA.

One Dish Meals from Popular Cuisines. rev. ed. Jia-Tzu Yeh et al. Ed. by Huang Su Huei. Tr. by Innie Chang et al. (Chinese One Dish Meals Ser.). (CHI, ENG & SPA., Illus.). 96p. (Orig.). 1995. pap. 15.95 (0-941676-56-0) Wei-Chuan Pub.

One-Dish Stovetop Meals. Jane M. Dieckmann. LC 98-26028. (Specialty Cookbook Ser.). (Illus.). 96p. 1998. pap. 6.95 (0-89594-968-7) Crossing Pr.

One Dish Vegetarian. Maria Robbins. LC 98-29938. 182p. 1998. text 24.95 (0-312-18151-5) St Martin.

***One-dish Vegetarian.** Maria Robbins. (Illus.). 192p. 2000. pap. 14.95 (0-312-25403-2) St Martin.

One Doctor Learns to Be a Patient. Kenneth B. Olson. Ed. by Susan E. Wills. LC 93-83044. (Illus.). 320p. 1993. 29.00 (1-883122-00-7) Pearce Pub.

One Does Not Spell Mozart with a "T" John R. Shannon. (Illus.). 115p. 1983. pap. 5.95 (0-937276-05-7) Hinshaw Mus.

One Dog Canoe. Mary Casanova. LC 98-47172. 1999. write for info. (0-7894-2582-3) DK Pub Inc.

One Dog Day. J. Patrick Lewis. LC 92-24573. (Illus.). 64p. (J). (gr. 2-5). 1993. 12.95 (0-689-31808-1) Atheneum Yung Read.

One Dog, His Man & His Trials. Marjorie Quarton. (Illus.). 176p. 1993. pap. 12.95 (0-85236-253-6, Pub. by Farming Pr) Diamond Farm Bk.

One Dog, His Man & His Trials. large type ed. Marjorie Quarton. 166p. 1995. 19.95 (1-85695-337-8, Pub. by ISIS Lrg Prnt) Transaction Pubs.

One Dog Twenty Stars. Carolyn B. Otto. (J). 1995. 14.95 (0-8050-2369-0) H Holt & Co.

One Dollar: My First Book About Money. Lynette Long. LC 97-42946. (Illus.). 32p. (J). (ps-2). 1998. bds. 8.95 (0-7641-0319-9); bds. 13.95 (0-7641-7132-1) Barron.

One Dollar a Day: Poverty in Indonesia. Yong H. Bang. 240p. 1998. pap. 16.00 (0-8059-4443-5) Dorrance.

One Dollar Empowerment. LC TX4197365. 97p. 1995. pap. 12.95 (0-9677907-0-0) D Spader.

$1.00 Word Riddle Book. Marilyn Burns. (Illus.). 48p. (J). (gr. 3-8). 1990. pap. 7.50 (0-938587-29-3) Cuisenaire.

$1.00 Word Riddle Book. Marilyn Burns. 48p. (J). (gr. k-5). 1990. pap. text 8.95 (0-941355-02-0) Math Solns Pubns.

One Dollar Word Riddle Book. Marilyn Burns. (J). (gr. 4-7). 1995. pap. 7.50 (0-201-48025-5) Addison-Wesley.

One Dough, Fifty Cookies: Baking Favorite & Festive Cookies in a Snap. Leslie Pendleton. LC 98-17818. (Illus.). 112p. 1998. 13.00 (0-688-15443-3, Wm Morrow) Morrow Avon.

One Dozen & One. Gladys Taber. 22.95 (0-8488-1196-8) Amereon Ltd.

One Dozen Pre-Revolutionary Families of Eastern North Carolina & Some of Their Descendants. P. W. Fisher. (Illus.). 629p. 1995. reprint ed. pap. 57.50 (0-8328-5088-8); reprint ed. lib. bdg. 67.50 (0-8328-5087-X) Higginson Bk Co.

One Dreaded Christmas Eve. John Kincaid. 188p. 1998. pap. 9.95 (0-9651707-3-X) Kincaid Kountry.

***One Drop of Blood: The American Misadventure of Race.** Scott L. Malcomson. LC 00-24487. 544p. 2000. 30.00 (0-374-24079-5) FS&G.

One-Drous Light. Ruth M. Bublitz. 128p. (Orig.). 1985. pap. 5.95 (0-87516-556-7) DeVorss.

One Dry Season: In the Footsteps of Mary Kingsley. Caroline Alexander. LC 90-50188. (Vintage Departures Ser.). 304p. 1990. pap. 10.95 (0-679-73189-X) Vin Bks.

One Duck. Hazel J. Hutchins. (Illus.). 32p. (J). (ps-2). 1999. text 18.95 (1-55037-561-X, Pub. by Annick Pr) Firefly Bks Ltd.

One Duck. Hazel J. Hutchins. (Illus.). 32p. (J). (ps-2). 1999. pap. 6.95 (1-55037-560-1, Pub. by Annick Pr) Firefly Bks Ltd.

One Duck, Another Duck. Charlotte Pomerantz. LC 83-20767. (Illus.). 24p. (J). (ps-3). 1984. 15.93 (0-688-03745-3, Grenwillow Bks) HarpC Child Bks.

***One Duck, Another Duck.** Charlotte Pomerantz. 2000. pap. write for info. (0-688-17719-0, Wm Morrow) Morrow Avon.

One Duck, Another Duck. 93rd ed. Ed. by Harcourt Brace Staff. 1993. pap. text 10.80 (0-15-300310-3, Harcourt Child Bks) Harcourt.

One Duck Stuck. Phyllis Root. LC 97-34103. (Illus.). 40p. (J). (ps-k). 1998. 15.99 (0-7636-0334-1) Candlewick Pr.

One Earth, Four or Five Worlds: Reflections on Contemporary History. Octavio Paz. 228p. 1986. pap. 5.95 (0-15-668746-1) Harcourt.

One Earth, One Future: Our Changing Global Environment. Cheryl S. Silver et al. 208p. (C). 1992. pap. 17.95 (0-309-04632-7) Natl Acad Pr.

One Earth One Mind. Michael W. Fox. LC 84-3929. 264p. (C). 1984. reprint ed. lib. bdg. 24.50 (0-89874-752-X) Krieger.

One Earth, One Spirit: A Child's Book of Prayers from Many Faiths & Cultures. Compiled by Tessa Strickland. LC 96-40387. (Illus.). 40p. (J). (gr. k-3). 1997. 14.95 (0-87156-978-7, Pub. by Sierra Club Childrens) Little.

One Earth, Two Worlds: Environment. Dave Dalton. (Environment). 32p. (C). 1995. pap. 6.95 (0-85598-276-4, Pub. by Oxfam Pub) Stylus Pub VA.

One Edge Then the Other. Ave Jeanne. 1984. 1.00 (0-932593-00-3) Black Bear.

1-888-Cecilia: An Inside Line, Vol. 1. Cecilia Peterson & Writers of Saint Louis Staff. 300p. 1996. 24.95 (0-9651865-2-0) Writers St Louis.

1-800-AWAY-IRS: The Answer to a Nations Plea. 2nd ed. Robert Bennington & Cort W. Christie. 192p. 1998. reprint ed. pap. 12.95 (1-882180-99-2) Griffin CA.

One-Eight Hundred-Call-Jerry. Peter Stein & Tom Nadeau. (Illus.). (Orig.). 1992. 7.95 (0-9633180-0-4) Stein Frowick Pubs.

1-800-Courtesy: Connecting with a Winning Telephone Image. Terry Wildemann. LC 98-33554. (Illus.). 144p. 1998. pap. 9.95 (1-890154-07-5, TC23) Aegis Pub Grp.

1-800-Deadbeat: How to Collect Your Child Support. Simone Spence. LC 99-90151. 182p. 1999. pap. 19.95 (0-9670647-0-8) EggShell Pr.

One-Eight Hundred God: The Spiritual Basis of Self-Esteem. Jacqueline Fortunata. 75p. (Orig.). 1991. pap. 6.95 (0-9628394-0-X) Aha Pub.

1-800-God-Help-Me: A Love Story. Michael Farkas. 122p. 1998. pap. 15.95 (1-891824-08-2) Light Tech Pubng.

1-800-Hero: Hero for the Bride. Joann Ross. (Temptation Ser.: Vol. 693). 1998. per. 3.75 (0-373-25793-7, 1-25793-0) Harlequin Bks.

1-800-911. Barbara Anderson. LC 96-48231. (Illus.). 104p. (Orig.). 1996. 25.00 (0-933313-30-6); pap. 14.95 (0-933313-31-4) SUN Gemini Pr.

1-800-911. deluxe ed. Barbara Anderson. (Illus.). 104p. (Orig.). 1996. 35.00 (0-933313-29-2) SUN Gemini Pr.

1-800-President: The Report of the Twentieth Century Fund Task Force on Television Coverage of Presidential Elections. Contrib. by Ken Auletta et al. LC 93-9722. (Orig.). 1993. pap. 9.95 (0-87078-349-1) Century Foundation.

One-Eight Hundred-Ziggy. Tom Wilson. (Illus.). 104p. 1994. pap. 6.95 (0-8362-1749-7) Andrews & McMeel.

One Elephant Went Out to Play Big Book: Black & White Nellie Edge I Can Read & Sing Big Book. Illus. by Bryce Kimberling. (J). (ps-2). 1988. pap. text 20.00 (0-922053-16-2) N Edge Res.

One Enchanted Night. Debra Carroll. (It Happened One Night...Ser.). 1997. per. 3.50 (0-373-25730-9, 1-25730-2) Harlequin Bks.

One Enchanted Summer. large type ed. Anne T. Brooks. 1990. 27.99 (0-7089-2277-5) Ulverscroft.

***One Encounter, One Chance: The Essence of Karate.** Terrence Webster-Doyle. (Illus.). 2000. pap. 14.95 (0-8348-0477-8) Weatherhill.

One Encounter, One Chance: The Essence of the Art of Karate. Terrence Webster-Doyle. LC 87-23246. (Illus.). 202p. (Orig.). 1996. pap. 14.95 (0-942941-02-0) Atrium Soc Educ.

One Enobled Engineer: Pierre-Joseph Laurent 1713-1773: from the Anzin Coal Mining Company to the Saint-Quentin Underground Canal see Mecanicien Anobli Pierre-Joseph Laurent 1713-1773: Des Mines d'Anzin au Canal de Saint Quentin

One Equals Zero: And Other Mathematical Surprises. Nitsa Movshovitz-Hadar & John Webb. LC 98-232540. (Illus.). xvi, 168p. (YA). (gr. 9-12). 1998. pap. text 13.95 (1-55953-309-9) Key Curr Pr.

One Europe. Nancy Dunnan. (YA). 1992. pap. 4.80 (0-395-62470-3) HM.

One Europe. Nancy Dunnan. LC 91-30083. (Headliners Ser.). 64p. (J). (gr. 5-8). 1992. pap. 6.95 (1-878841-96-3) Millbrook Pr.

One Europe - One Hundred Nations. Roy N. Pedersen. 150p. 1992. 39.00 (1-85359-123-8, Pub. by Multilingual Matters) Taylor & Francis.

***One Europe, Many Nations: A Historical Dictionary of European National Groups.** James Minahan. LC 99-46040. 800p. 2000. lib. bdg. 99.50 (0-313-30984-1) Greenwood.

One Evening. Canna Funakoshi. LC 87-29243. (Illus.). (J). (ps up). 1991. pap. 11.95 (0-88708-063-4, Picture Book Studio) S&S Childrens.

One Evil Summer. R. L. Stine, pseud. Ed. by Pat MacDonald. (Fear Street Ser.: No. 26). 176p. (YA). (gr. 7 up). 1994. mass mkt. 3.99 (0-671-78596-6, Archway) PB.

One Evil Summer. R. L. Stine, pseud. (Fear Street Ser.: No. 26). (YA). (gr. 7 up). 1996. pap. 9.99 (0-671-00384-4, Archway) PB.

One Evil Summer. R. L. Stine, pseud. (Fear Street Ser.: No. 26). (YA). (gr. 7 up). 1994. 9.09 (0-606-06636-5, Pub. by Turtleback) Demco.

One Evil Summer: With Watch. R. L. Stine, pseud. (Fear Street Ser.: No. 26). (YA). (gr. 7 up). 1997. pap. text 3.99 (0-671-01903-1, Archway) PB.

One Ewe over the Cuckoo's Nest. Kathryn Lamb. (Illus.). 96p. 1991. pap. 8.95 (0-85236-227-7, Pub. by Farming Pr) Diamond Farm Bk.

One Explorer's Glossary of Quaker Terms. rev. ed. Warren S. Smith. Ed. by Mae S. Bixby. (Illus.). 52p. 1992. reprint ed. pap. 6.00 (0-9620912-4-3) Friends Genl Conf.

***One Eye Closed, the Other Red: The California Bootlegging Years.** Clifford James Walker. (Illus.). 579p. 1999. 25.00 (0-9673141-0-0); pap. 18.00 (0-9673141-1-9) Back Door Pubg.

***One Eye Laughing, the Other Weeping: The Diary of Julie Weiss.** Barry Denenberg. LC 00-21920. (Dear America Ser.). (Illus.). 256p. (YA). (gr. 4-9). 2000. 12.95 (0-439-09518-2) Scholastic Inc.

One Eye, Two Eyes, Three Eyes: A Hutzul Tale. Illus. by Dirk Zimmer. LC 94-42362. 32p. (J). (gr. k-3). 1996. lib. bdg. 15.95 (0-8234-1183-4) Holiday.

***One-Eyed: A View of Australian Sport.** Douglas Booth & Colin Tatz. (Illus.). 280p. 2000. pap. 24.95 (1-86508-055-1, Pub. by Allen & Unwin Pty) Paul & Co Pubs.

One Eyed Cat. 224p. (J). 1986. pap. 3.99 (0-440-76641-9) Dell.

***One-Eyed Cat.** (J). 1999. 9.95 (1-56137-107-6) Novel Units.

One-Eyed Cat. Paula Fox. 224p. (J). (gr. k-6). 1985. pap. 5.50 (0-440-46641-5, YB BDD) BDD Bks Young Read.

One-Eyed Cat. Paula Fox. LC 84-10964. (Illus.). 192p. (J). (gr. 6-8). 1984. text 14.95 (0-02-735540-3, Bradbury S&S) S&S Childrens.

One-Eyed Cat. Paula Fox. 1984. 10.09 (0-606-00363-0, Pub. by Turtleback) Demco.

One-Eyed Cat. Manuel Media. 1985. 14.60 (0-676-31284-5) Random.

One-Eyed Cat. Paula Fox. 224p. (J). (gr. 5-9). 1998. reprint ed. mass mkt. 4.99 (0-440-22776-3, LLL BDD) BDD Bks Young Read.

One-Eyed Cat. 93rd ed. Paula Fox. 1993. pap. text 15.40 (0-15-300376-6, Harcourt Child Bks) Harcourt.

One-Eyed Cat: A Study Guide. Karen Hanus. Ed. by Joyce Friedland & Rikki Kessler. (Novel-Ties Ser.). (J). (gr. 5-7). 1991. pap. text 15.95 (0-88122-580-0) Lrn Links.

One-Eyed Charley: The California Whip. Randall A. Reinstedt. Ed. by John Bergez. LC 90-81382. (History & Happenings of California Ser.). (Illus.). 84p. (J). (gr. 3-6). 1990. 13.95 (0-933818-23-8); pap. 9.95 (0-933818-77-7) Ghost Town.

One-Eyed Cowboy Wild. John D. Nesbitt. LC 93-37741. 180p. 1994. 19.95 (0-8027-4135-5) Walker & Co.

One-Eyed Cowboy Wild. large type ed. John D. Nesbitt. LC 94-26349. 221p. 1994. pap. 18.95 (0-8161-7477-6, G K Hall Lrg Type) Mac Lib Ref.

One-Eyed Doctor: Sigmund Freud. Ed. by Jay Harris & Jean Harris. LC 81-65787. 260p. 1984. 50.00 (0-87668-453-3) Aronson.

One-Eyed Dream. Terry C. Johnston. LC 85-37842. (Frontier Library). 450p. 1988. 19.95 (0-915463-38-5, Frontier Libr) Jameson Bks.

One Eyed Dream. Terry C. Johnston. 592p. 1994. mass mkt. 6.99 (0-553-28139-9) Bantam.

One-Eyed Giant. Anne Rockwell. LC 95-12326. (Illus.). 32p. (J). (ps-3). 1996. 16.00 (0-688-13809-8, Grenwillow Bks) HarpC Child Bks.

One-Eyed Giant & Other Monsters from the Greek Myths. Anne Rockwell. LC 95-12326. (Illus.). 32p. (J). (ps up). 1996. lib. bdg. 15.93 (0-688-13810-1, Grenwillow Bks) HarpC Child Bks.

***One-Eyed Jacks.** Brad Smith. 272p. 2000. 21.50 (0-385-25920-4) Doubleday.

An Asterisk (*) at the beginning of an entry indicates that the title is appearing for the first time.

One-Eyed Jake. Pat Hutchins. LC 93-26296. 1994. 10.15 (*0-606-06638-1*, Pub. by Turtleback) Demco.

One-Eyed Jake. Pat Hutchins. (Illus.). 32p. (J). (ps up). 1994. reprint ed. pap. 4.95 (*0-688-13113-1*, Wm Morrow) Morrow Avon.

One-Eyed Man Is King. Gordon Graham. 221p. reprint ed. pap. 8.95 (*0-9616353-0-4*) G Graham.

One Eyed Man Is King: A Story of Breaking Barriers. rev. ed. Ed. by Pat Jusich. LC 98-96484. (Illus.). 268p. 1998. pap. 12.00 (*0-9616353-1-2*, OEMIK#2) G Graham.

One-Eyed Science: Occupational Health & Women Workers. karen Messing. LC 97-26885. 264p. 1998. 59.95 (*1-56639-597-6*) Temple U Pr.

One-Eyed Science: Occupational Health & Women Workers. Karen Messing. LC 97-26885. 264p. 1998. pap. 22.95 (*1-56639-598-4*) Temple U Pr.

One Facet of an Autobiography. O. S. Nock. 141p. (C). 1989. text 59.00 (*1-872795-73-0*, Pub. by Pentland Pr) St Mut.

One Facing Us. Ronit Matalon. Tr. by Marsha Weinstein. LC 97-32303. 296p. 1998. 25.00 (*0-8050-4880-4*) H Holt & Co.

One Facing Us: A Novel. Ronit Matalon. Tr. by Marsha Weinstein. (Illus.). 304p. 1999. pap. 14.00 (*0-8050-6185-1*, Pub. by H Holt & Co) VHPS.

One-Factorizations. W. D. Wallis. LC 96-48829. (Mathematics & Its Applications Ser.: Vol. 390). 242p. (C). 1997. text 161.50 (*0-7923-4323-9*) Kluwer Academic.

One Fairy Story Too Many: The Brothers Grimm & Their Tales. John M. Ellis. LC 83-1193. 219p. 1983. lib. bdg. 17.50 (*0-226-20546-0*) U Ch Pr.

One Fairy Story Too Many: The Brothers Grimm & Their Tales. John M. Ellis. LC 83-1193. x, 224p. 1985. pap. 8.95 (*0-226-20547-9*) U Ch Pr.

One Faith: Biblical & Patristic Contributions Toward Understanding Unity in Faith. William Henn. 352p. (Orig.). 1995. pap. 22.95 (*0-8091-3577-9*) Paulist Pr.

One Faith, One Church, Man, Many Moralities, Vol. 150. Ed. by Jacques Pohier & Dietmar Mieth. (Concilium Ser.). 128p. 1981. 6.95 (*0-8164-2350-4*) Harper SF.

One Faith, One Lord: A Study of Basic Catholic Belief. John F. Barry. 128p. 1994. text. write for info. (*0-8215-2197-7*) Sadlier.

One Faith, One Lord: A Study of Basic Catholic Belief. Gloria Hutchinson. 128p. 1994. teacher ed. 15.60 (*0-8215-2198-5*) Sadlier.

One Faith, One Lord Journal. Gloria Hutchinson. 40p. 1994. 4.95 (*0-8215-2199-3*) Sadlier.

One Fall Day. Molly Bang. LC 93-36490. (Illus.). 24p. (J). (ps up). 1994. 15.00 (*0-688-07015-9*, Grenwillow Bks) HarpC Child Bks.

One False Move. T. Davis Bunn. LC 96-38695. 400p. (Orig.). 1997. pap. 12.99 (*0-7852-7368-9*) Nelson.

***One False Move.** Stacey Sauter. 2000. mass mkt. 6.99 (*0-451-19136-6*, Sig) NAL.

***One False Move: A Myron Bolitar Novel.** Harlan Coben. 400p. 1999. mass mkt. 6.50 (*0-440-22544-2*) Dell.

***One Family.** Vaughn Sills & Tina Toole Truelove. LC 99-53096. 192p. 2000. 29.95 (*0-8203-2199-0*) U of Ga Pr.

***One Family: Before & During the Holocaust.** Andrew Kolin. 2000. 42.50 (*0-7618-1678-X*) U Pr of Amer.

One Family, Many Animals. Edwin R. Ling. LC 88-18580. 166p. 1988. 13.75 (*0-930950-21-6*); pap. 8.75 (*0-930950-22-4*) Nopoly Pr.

One Family, One Meal: Two-Tiered Meals to Please Both Parents & Kids. Kristene Fortier. LC 98-27269. 160p. 1998. 14.95 (*1-55972-481-1*, Birch Ln Pr) Carol Pub Group.

One Family, Two Worlds: An Italian Family's Correspondence Across the Atlantic, 1901-1922. Ed. by Samuel L. Baily & Franco Ramella. Tr. by John Lenaghan. (Illus.). 224p. (C). 1988. text 45.00 (*0-8135-1331-6*); pap. text 16.00 (*0-8135-1354-5*) Rutgers U Pr.

One Family under God. U. S. Bishops' Committee on Migration Staff. 24p. (Orig.). 1995. pap. 1.95 (*1-57455-042-X*) US Catholic.

One Family under the Same Sky. Laura A. Cohen et al. (Illus.). 88p. (J). 1997. pap. 13.95 (*1-882801-04-0*) Feelings Factory.

***One Family's Journey Through Alzheimer's.** Mary Kunkel Walsh. 2000. pap. 9.99 (*0-8423-4095-5*) Tyndale Hse.

One Family's Story. McKissack. (J). 1995. 19.95 (*0-8050-1671-6*) H Holt & Co.

One Family's War: Wartime Letters from Many Fronts 1939-1945. Ed. by Patrick Mayhew. (Illus.). 264p. (Orig.). 1997. pap. 15.95 (*1-873376-47-2*, Pub. by Spellmnt Pubs) St Mut.

***One Family's War: Where's Your Medal Mother?** Muriel Gane Pushman. (Illus.). 128p. 2000. pap. 19.99 (*0-7524-2002-X*, Pub. by Tempus Pubng) Arcadia Publng.

One Fat Summer. Robert Lipsyte. LC 76-49746. (Trophy Bk.). 240p. (YA). (gr. 7-12). 1991. pap. 4.95 (*0-06-447073-3*, HarpTrophy) HarpC Child Bks.

One Fat Summer. Robert Lipsyte. 1991. 10.05 (*0-606-01085-8*, Pub. by Turtleback) Demco.

One Fateful Summer. Way. 1994. per. 2.99 (*0-373-15541-7*) Harlequin Bks.

One Fateful Summer. Margaret Way. (Romance Ser.). 1994. per. 2.99 (*0-373-03295-1*, 1-03295-2) Harlequin Bks.

One Father, One Family: A Biblical Study on Unity. Alger Fitch. (C). 1990. text 12.99 (*0-89900-269-2*) College Pr Pub.

One Father One Mother One Race. Patricia A. Daniel. Ed. by Rosella Mackey. (Illus.). 200p. (Orig.). pap. text 15.00 (*0-9628081-0-5*) Daw Enter.

One Fearful Yellow Eye. John D. MacDonald. 1996. mass mkt. 5.99 (*0-449-22458-9*) Fawcett.

One Fearful Yellow Eye. John D. MacDonald. 1997. mass mkt. 5.99 (*0-449-45639-0*) Fawcett.

***One Fiancee to Go, Please.** Jackie Braun. (Romance Ser.: Bk. 1479). 2000. mass mkt. 3.50 (*0-373-19479-X*, 1-19479-4) Silhouette.

1/5, the Trellis: Poems Lana Wolkonsky. LC 97-90778. 61p. 1997. write for info. (*0-9653306-4-8*) L E Wolkonsky.

One Final Pass. Art Lindsay & Jan Berringer. 160p. 1996. 19.95 (*1-887002-36-7*) Cross Trng.

***One Fine Day.** (J). 1999. 9.95 (*1-56137-249-8*) Novel Units.

One Fine Day. H. B. Gilmour. 1997. mass mkt. 5.99 (*0-312-96115-4*) St Martin.

One Fine Day. Illus. by Nonny Hogrogian. 32p. (J). (gr. k-3). 1997. mass mkt. 5.99 (*0-689-81414-3*) Aladdin.

One Fine Day. Nonny Hogrogian. LC 75-119834. (Illus.). 32p. (J). (gr. k-3). 1974. mass mkt. 5.99 (*0-02-043620-3*) Macmillan.

One Fine Day. Nonny Hogrogian. LC 75-119834. (Illus.). 32p. (J). (gr. k-3). 1971. text 16.00 (*0-02-744000-1*, Mac Bks Young Read) S&S Childrens.

One Fine Day. Nonny Hogrogian. 1974. 11.19 (*0-606-01196-X*, Pub. by Turtleback) Demco.

***One Fine Day.** James Marshall. (Carry-Along Book & Cassette Favorites Ser.). (Illus.). 32p. (J). 2000. pap. 9.95 incl. audio (*0-618-04936-3*) HM.

One Finger Too Many. Alfred Brendel. LC 98-44869. 80p. 1999. 16.00 (*0-375-50293-9*) Random.

One Fish, Two Fish, Red Fish, Blue Fish. Dr. Seuss, pseud. LC 60-7180. (Illus.). 72p. (J). (gr. 1-2). 1966. lib. bdg. 11.99 (*0-394-90013-8*, Pub. by Random Bks Yng Read) Random.

One Fish, Two Fish, Red Fish, Blue Fish. Dr. Seuss, pseud. LC 60-7180. (Illus.). 72p. (J). (gr. 1-2). 1966. 7.99 (*0-394-80013-3*, Pub. by Random Bks Yng Read) Random.

One Fish, Two Fish, Red Fish, Blue Fish. Dr. Seuss, pseud. (J). 1960. 7.99 (*0-606-04238-5*, Pub. by Turtleback) Demco.

One Fish, Two Fish, Red Fish, Blue Fish, Set. Dr. Seuss, pseud. (Beginner Book & Cassette Library). (Illus.). 64p. (J). (ps-1). 1987. 8.95 incl. audio (*0-394-89224-0*, Pub. by Random Bks Yng Read) Random.

One Five Many. Kveta Pacovska. (J). (ps-3). 1990. 16.95 (*0-685-54064-2*, Clarion Bks) HM.

One Flesh: Body, Mind, Spirit. Gerald E. Poesnecker. (Illus.). 284p. 1996. pap. 12.00 (*0-916285-41-3*) Humanitarian.

One Flesh: God's Gift of Passion, Love, Sex & Romance in Marriage. Bob Yandian. 237p. 1994. pap. 10.99 (*0-88419-380-2*) Creation House.

One Flesh: Paradisal Marriage & Sexual Relations in the Age of Milton. James G. Turner. (Illus.). 338p. 1994. reprint ed. pap. text 24.00 (*0-19-818249-X*) OUP.

One Flew over the Cuckoo's Nest. Ken Kesey. 272p. 1963. mass mkt. 6.99 (*0-451-16396-6*, Sig) NAL.

One Flew over the Cuckoo's Nest. Ken Kesey. 1962. 12.09 (*0-606-04239-3*, Pub. by Turtleback) Demco.

One Flew over the Cuckoo's Nest. Ken Kesey. Ed. by John C. Pratt. LC 95-31069. (Critical Studies). (Illus.). xxv, 652p. 1996. pap. 15.95 (*0-14-023601-5*, Penguin Bks) Viking Penguin.

One Flew over the Cuckoo's Nest. Ken Kesey. (Great Books of the 20th Century Ser.). 288p. 1999. pap. 13.95 (*0-14-028334-X*, Penguin Bks) Viking Penguin.

One Flew over the Cuckoo's Nest. Crystal Norris. Ed. by Joyce Friedland & Rikki Kessler. (Novel-Ties Ser.). (YA). (gr. 9-12). 1993. pap. text, student ed. 15.95 (*0-88122-121-X*) Lrn Links.

One Flew over the Cuckoo's Nest. M. Gilbert Porter. (Twayne's Masterwork Studies: No. 22). 136p. 1988. 29.00 (*0-8057-7988-4*, Twyne) Mac Lib Ref.

One Flew over the Cuckoo's Nest. large type ed. Ken Kesey. LC 93-47340. 528p. 1994. lib. bdg. 22.95 (*0-7862-0111-8*) Thorndike Pr.

One Flew Over the Cuckoo's Nest: A Novel. Ken Kesey. LC 76-28166. 311p. (C). 1999. reprint ed. pap. 12.95 (*0-14-004312-8*) Viking Penguin.

***One Flew Over the Cuckoo's Nest: Reproducible Teaching Unit.** James Scott. 66p. (YA). (gr. 7-12). 2000. pap. 29.50i (*1-58049-199-5*, TU137) Prestwick Hse.

One Flew over the Cuckoo's Nest (Kesey) Peter Fish. (Barron's Book Notes Ser.). (C). 1984. pap. 2.50 (*0-8120-3433-3*) Barron.

One Flew over the Cuckoos Nest Notes. Thomas R. Holland. (Cliffs Notes Ser.). 72p. 1974. pap. 4.95 (*0-8220-0962-5*, Cliff) IDG Bks.

One Flower While I Live: Elvis As I Remember Him. Nash L. Pritchett. LC 87-32391. (Illus.). 154p. 1987. pap. 10.95 (*0-942179-05-6*) Shelby Hse.

One Foggy Night. Brenda Parkes. LC 92-32514. (Voyages Ser.). (Illus.). (J). 1993. 4.25 (*0-383-03588-0*) SRA McGraw.

One Followed by Eternity of Zeros. Ali Shariati. Tr. by Ali Asghar Ghasemy. 23p. 1980. pap. 2.00 (*0-941722-15-5*) Book Dist Ctr.

One Foot Ashore. Jacqueline Greene. LC 93-22961. 144p. (J). (gr. 4-6). 1994. 16.95 (*0-8027-8281-7*) Walker & Co.

***One Foot Ashore.** Jacqueline Dembar Greene. 208p. (J). (gr. 3-6). 2000. pap. write for info. (*0-8027-7601-9*) Walker & Co.

***One Foot in Atlantis: The Sevret Occult History of World War II & It's Impact on New Age Politics.** William Henry. 248p. 1998. pap. 16.95 (*1-890693-49-9*) Earthpulse Pr.

One Foot in Eden. M. J. Bloor et al. (Sociological Study of the Range of Therapeutic Community Practice). 256p. (C). 1988. lib. bdg. 55.00 (*0-415-00254-0*) Routledge.

One Foot in Eden: A Celtic View of the Stages of Life. J. Philip Newell. LC 98-53159. 112p. 1999. pap. 8.95 (*0-8091-3869-7*) Paulist Pr.

One Foot in Heaven. Loraine McDaniel. (American Romance Ser.). 1993. per. 3.50 (*0-373-16499-8*, 1-16499-5) Harlequin Bks.

One Foot in Heaven. Hartzell Spence. Ed. by Anne C. Martens. 1976. pap. 5.50 (*0-87129-224-6*, O14) Dramatic Pub.

One Foot in the Future: A Woman's Spiritual Journey. Nina Graboi. 360p. 1991. 12.95 (*0-942344-10-3*) Dakota Bks.

One Foot in the Grave. William Mark Simmons. 352p. 2000. mass mkt. 5.99 (*0-671-87721-6*) PB.

One Foot in the Grave: The Basis of a British Comedy. large type ed. David Renwick. 21.95 (*1-85695-361-0*, Pub. by ISIS Lrg Prnt) Transaction Pubs.

One Foot in the Sea. Robert Smith. 140p. (C). 1996. pap. 50.00 (*0-85976-342-0*, Pub. by J Donald) St Mut.

***One Foot in the Stars: Story of the World's Most Extraordinary Healer.** Matthew Manning. 2000. 29.95 (*1-86204-591-7*, Pub. by Element MA) Penguin Putnam.

One Foot in the Stirrup: Western Stories. John D. Nesbitt. 126p. 1998. reprint ed. pap. 7.95 (*0-9651856-3-X*) R R Prodns.

One Foot off the Gutter. Peter Plate. 200p. (Orig.). 1995. pap. 13.00 (*1-884615-11-2*) Incommcdo San Diego.

***One Foot on the Floor: The Curious Evolution of Sex on Television from "I Love Lucy" to "South Park"** Louis Chunovic. (Illus.). 256p. 2000. 25.00 (*1-57500-186-1*, Pub. by TV Bks) HarpC.

One Foot on the Rockies: Women & Creativity in the Modern American West. Joan M. Jensen. LC 94-18695. (Calvin P. Horn Lectures in Wester History & Culture). 178p. (C). 1995. pap. 18.95 (*0-8263-1539-9*) U of NM Pr.

One Foot on the Stage: The Biography of Richard Wilson. James Roose-Evans. (Illus.). 256p. 1997. 40.00 (*0-297-81662-4*, Pub. by Weidenfeld & Nicolson) Trafalgar.

One for All: NATO Strategy & Logistics Through the Formative Period, 1949-1969. James A. Huston. LC 82-49305. 336p. 1984. 50.00 (*0-87413-231-2*) U Delaware Pr.

One for All: The Logic of Group Conflict. Russell Hardin. 276p. 1995. text 35.00 (*0-691-04350-7*, Pub. by Princeton U Pr); pap. text 16.95 (*0-691-04825-8*, Pub. by Princeton U Pr) Cal Prin Full Svc.

One for All: The United States & International Logistics Through the Formative Period of NATO (1949-1969) James A. Huston. LC 82-49305. 420p. 1984. 42.50 (*0-686-89522-3*) U Delaware Pr.

One for All & All for Illinois: Representing the Land of Lincoln in Congress. Jack R. Van Der Slik. LC 95-7799. 151p. 1995. pap. 7.50 (*0-938943-08-1*) U IL Spgfld Pub Affrs.

One for My Lady EZ Play, Vol. 174. 144p. 1995. otabind 14.95 (*0-7935-4656-7*, 00100018) H Leonard.

One for New York. John A. Williams. 184p. 1975. reprint ed. 15.95 (*0-911860-52-5*) Chatham Bkseller.

***One for Sorrow.** Mary Reed. 288p. 2000. pap. 12.95 (*1-890208-42-6*) Poisoned Pen.

***One for Sorrow.** Mary Reed & Eric Mayer. LC 99-61907. 302p. 1999. 23.95 (*1-890208-19-1*) Poisoned Pen.

One for the Books: Confessions of a Small-Press Publisher. John M. Daniel. 128p. (Orig.). 1997. pap. 10.00 (*1-56474-224-5*) Fithian Pr.

One for the Fans: Celebratory Commentary on the Championship of the Century - a Salute to America's Best Football Team. Glen Smith. (Illus.). 144p. (Orig.). 1993. pap. 9.95 (*0-9639019-0-7*) Fanview.

One for the Gipper. rev. ed. Patrick Chelland. Ed. by Tony DiMarco. (Illus.). 256p. 1996. pap. 16.95 (*1-886571-01-5*) Arrowhead Classics.

One for the Gods, Vol. 2. Gordon Merrick. 312p. 1996. reprint ed. pap. text 11.95 (*1-55583-291-1*) Alyson Pubns.

One for the Lord: Insights for Singles. Earl G. Creps, III. LC 97-122117. 112p. 1997. pap., student ed. 4.95 (*0-88243-117-X*, 02-217) Gospel Pub.

One for the Lord: Insights for Singles. Earl G. Creps, 3rd. LC 97-122117. (Spiritual Discovery Ser.). 128p. 1996. pap., teacher ed. 9.95 (*0-88243-217-6*, 02-0217) Gospel Pub.

One for the Master, Two for the Fool: A Bruce MacLeod Mystery. Larry Townsend. 214p. 1992. pap. 9.95 (*1-55583-209-1*) Alyson Pubns.

One for the Money. Dick Belsky. (Academy First Mystery Ser.). 191p. 1985. pap. 5.95 (*0-89733-221-0*) Academy Chi Pubs.

One for the Money. D. B. Borton. 208p. 1993. pap. 4.99 (*0-425-15328-2*) Berkley Pub.

One for the Money. Janet Evanovich. 304p. 1998. mass mkt. 6.99 (*0-06-100905-9*, Harp PBks) HarpC.

One for the Money. Janet Evanovich. 256p. 1994. 20.00 (*0-684-19639-5*) Scribner.

One for the Money. large type ed. Janet Evanovich. LC 94-42304. 333p. 1995. 23.95 (*0-7838-1186-1*, G K Hall Lrg Type) Mac Lib Ref.

One for the Money: A Financial Guide for Direct Sales. Sharon M. Tahaney. 1998. pap. text 10.95 (*1-56052-472-3*) Crisp Pubns.

One for the Morning Glory. John Barnes. 320p. 1996. 22.95 (*0-312-86106-0*) Tor Bks.

One for the Morning Glory. John Barnes. 1996. 22.95 (*0-614-32238-3*) Tor Bks.

One for the Morning Glory. John Barnes. 1997. mass mkt. 5.99 (*0-8125-5160-5*, Pub. by Tor Bks) St Martin.

One for the Morning Glory. John Barnes. 1997. 11.05 (*0-606-11707-5*, Pub. by Turtleback) Demco.

One for the Road. Kid Stoker. 112p. 1996. pap. 10.95 (*1-898928-15-0*, Pub. by S T Pubng) AK Pr Dist.

***One for the Road.** rev. ed. Tony Horwitz. 1999. pap. 12.00 (*0-375-70613-5*) Vin Bks.

One for the Road: A Play. Harold Pinter. LC 86-4662. (Illus.). 80p. 1986. pap. 7.95 (*0-8021-5188-4*, Grove) Grove-Atltic.

One for the Rose. Philip Levine. LC 98-74552. (Classic Contemporaries Ser.). 80p. 1999. reprint ed. pap. 12.95 (*0-88748-307-0*, Pub. by Carnegie-Mellon) Cornell U Pr.

One for the Seasons: Poems of Love. Jay Frank. 30p. 1993. pap. 7.95 (*1-883699-20-7*) Candlelght Pub.

One for You & One for Me. Margie Burton et al. Ed. by Alison Adams. (Early Connections Ser.). 16p. (gr. k-2). 1999. pap. text 4.50 (*1-58344-075-5*) Benchmark Educ.

One Forever Promise. Lori Wick. 464p. 1999. 12.99 (*0-88486-247-X*) Galahad Bks.

One Forgotten Night. Suzanne Sanders. 1995. per. 3.75 (*0-373-07672-X*, 1-07672-8) Silhouette.

One Fortunate Fellow. Robert D. McKee. LC 95-94340. (Illus.). 150p. 1995. pap., per. 14.50 (*0-9647019-0-1*) R D McKee.

1-4-3 Means I Love You. Jon Ballard. LC 98-94377. 188p. 1999. pap. text 14.95 (*0-9668850-0-7*) CNC Pubg.

1 4:1-113,16 Temptations of Jesus. E. Peters. 1998. 56.95 (*90-6831-880-2*, Pub. by Peeters Pub) Bks Intl VA.

One Frog Too Many. Mercer Mayer. 1992. pap. 4.99 (*0-14-054679-0*) NAL.

One Frog Too Many. Mercer Mayer. (J). 1977. 9.19 (*0-606-03306-8*, Pub. by Turtleback) Demco.

One from the Heart. large type ed. Cinda Richards. (Linford Romance Library). 320p. 1994. pap. 16.99 (*0-7089-7521-6*, Linford) Ulverscroft.

One Furrow at a Time: The Autobiography of Dave Low. Ed. by Tom A. Low. (Illus.). 160p. 1995. 25.00 (*1-887301-00-3*) Palmetto Bookworks.

One Game Season: 92 Games of College Football's Greatest Rivalry. 2nd ed. Steve White. 400p. 1996. 39.95 (*0-9643228-0-3*) Steve White.

One Gaping Wide-Mouthed Hopping Frog. Leslie Tryon. LC 92-11368. (Illus.). 32p. (J). (ps-1). 1993. 14.95 (*0-689-31785-9*) Atheneum Yung Read.

One Giant Leap. Mary A. Fraser. LC 92-41044. (Illus.). 88p. (J). (gr. 3-7). 1995. 15.95 (*0-8050-2295-3*) H Holt & Co.

One Giant Leap. Mary Ann Fraser. (Illus.). (YA). (gr. 3-7). 1998. pap. 6.95 (*0-8050-5773-0*) H Holt & Co.

One Giant Leap. Tim Furniss. 1999. 14.95 (*1-85868-605-9*, Pub. by Carlton Bks Ltd) Natl Bk Netwk.

One Giant Leap: The First Moon Landing. Dana M. Rau. LC 96-15035. (Smithsonian Odyssey Ser.). (Illus.). 32p. (J). (gr. 2-5). 1996. 14.95 (*1-56899-343-9*); pap. 5.95 (*1-56899-344-7*) Soundprints.

One Giant Leap: The First Moon Landing. Dana M. Rau. (Odyssey Ser.). (Illus.). 32p. (J). (gr. 2-5). 1996. 19.95 incl. audio (*1-56899-360-9*, BC6001) Soundprints.

One Giant Leap: The First Moon Landing, Incl. toy. Dana M. Rau. (Smithsonian Odyssey Ser.). (Illus.). 32p. (J). (gr. 2-5). 1996. 29.95 (*1-56899-345-5*); 35.95 incl. audio (*1-56899-347-1*); pap. 17.95 (*1-56899-346-3*) Soundprints.

One Giant Leap: The Story of Neil Armstrong. Don Brown. LC 97-42152. 32p. (J). (gr. k-3). 1998. 16.00 (*0-395-88401-2*) HM.

One Giant Leap for Mankind. rev. ed. Carter Smith, III. (Turning Points in American History Ser.). (Illus.). 64p. (YA). (gr. 5 up). 1989. pap. 7.95 (*0-382-09910-9*) Silver Burdett Pr.

One Giant Leap, the First Moon Landing. Dana Meachen Rau. LC 96-15035. (Smithsonian Institution Odyssey Ser.). 1996. 11.15 (*0-606-10276-0*, Pub. by Turtleback) Demco.

***One Girl: A Novel in Stories.** Sheila Kohler. LC 99-37346. 160p. 1999. pap. 12.95 (*1-884235-29-8*) Helicon Nine Eds.

One Girl in Ten: A Self Portrait of the Teen-Age Mother. Sallie Foster. 160p. 1988. pap. 13.95 (*0-87868-343-7*, 3437) Child Welfare.

One Girl's War. Joan Miller. 156p. 1989. 15.95 (*0-312-03410-5*) St Martin.

One Glad Man. Lynea Bowdish. LC 98-53086. (Rookie Readers Ser.). 32p. (J). (gr. 1-2). 1999. write for info. (*0-516-21595-7*) Childrens.

***One Glad Man.** Lynea Bowdish. (Rookie Readers Ser.). (J). 2000. pap. text 4.95 (*0-516-26545-8*) Childrens.

One Glorious Summer: A Photographic History of the 1996 Centennial Olympic Games. Glenn Hannigan. 192p. 1996. 29.95 (*1-56352-410-4*) Longstreet.

One God: Peoples of the Book. Ed. by Edith S. Engel & Henry W. Engel. 146p. 1996. pap. 12.95 (*0-614-21678-8*, 921) Kazi Pubns.

One God: The Everlasting Refuge: Commentary & Vocabulary Reference of Surat Al-Ikhlas. Ahmad Z. Hammad. (Quran Ser.). 264p. 1998. 69.99 (*0-9650746-6-8*) QLI.

One God Clapping: The Spiritual Path of a Zen Rabbi. Alan Lew & Sherril Jaffe. LC 99-29401. 1999. 24.00 (*1-56836-287-0*) Kodansha.

One God, Many Gods: Bible Studies for Postmodern Times. Ed. by Concordia Publishing House Staff. 96p. (YA). 1998. pap. 16.00 (*0-570-06834-7*, 20-2427GJ) Concordia.

One God, Many Names: Inspirational Songs & Hymns. 3rd rev. ed. Ed. by Genia P. Haddon. (Christian-Feminist Resources Ser.). 56p. 1994. pap. 9.95 (*1-881311-24-4*) Plus Pubns CT.

One God, One Lord: Early Christian Devotion & Ancient Jewish Monotheism. 2nd ed. Larry W. Hurtado. 208p. pap. 29.95 (*0-567-08657-7*) T&T Clark Pubs.

One God, One Voice. 136p. 1989. 6.99 (*0-8341-9317-5*) Lillenas.

***One God or Many? Concepts of Divinity in the Ancient World.** Barbara Nevling Porter et al. (Transactions of the Casco Bay Assyriological Institute Ser.). 320p. 2000. pap. 25.00 (*0-9674250-0-X*, Pub. by Casco Bay) Univ Pr MD.

O

An Asterisk (*) at the beginning of an entry indicates that the title is appearing for the first time.

One God, Sixteen Houses: An Illustrated Introduction to the Churches & Synagogues of the Old York Road Corridor. Simeon J. Maslin et al. (Illus.). 197p. (Orig.). 1990. pap. 25.00 (*0-9627062-0-5*) Cong Ken Israel.

One God, Two Faiths: When Christians & Muslims Meet, Study Guide to "the World of Islam" Sarah Klos. 48p. (Orig.). 1989. pap. 4.95 (*0-377-00197-X*) Friendship Pr.

*__One Golden Christmas.__ Lenora Worth. (Love Inspired Ser.). 2000. mass mkt. 4.50 (*0-373-87128-7*, 1871284) Harlequin Bks.

*__One Golden Year.__ Coleen Hubbard. 128p. (J). (gr. 3-7). 1999. pap. 4.50 (*0-590-18975-1*) Scholastic Inc.

One Good Apple: Growing Our Food for the Sake of the Earth. Catherine Paladino. LC 97-45866. (Illus.). 32p. (YA). (gr. 4 up). 1999. 15.00 (*0-395-85009-6*) HM.

One Good Friend. 2nd ed. Michael Sage. LC 68-22454. iv, 126p. (YA). (gr. 7-12). 1999. reprint ed. pap. 10.00 (*0-9669813-0-8*) J Sage.

One Good Man. Rui Alfonso. write for info. (*965-229-129-3*, Pub. by Gefen Pub Hse) Gefen Bks.

One Good Man. Kathleen Creighton. (Intimate Moments Ser.). 1995. per. 3.75 (*0-373-07639-8*, 1-07639-7) Silhouette.

*__One Good Man.__ Julie Miller. (Intrigue Ser.: Bk. 588). 2000. mass mkt. 4.25 (*0-373-22588-1*, 1-22588-7) Harlequin Bks.

One Good Turn. Judith Arnold. (American Romance Ser.: No. 378). 1991. per. 2.95 (*0-373-16378-9*) Harlequin Bks.

One Good Turn. large type ed. Judith Arnold. 327p. 1991. reprint ed. lib. bdg. 18.95 (*1-56054-219-5*) Thorndike Pr.

*__One Good Turn: A Natural History of the Screwdriver & the Screw.__ Witold Rybczynski. (Illus.). 176p. 2000. 22.00 (*0-684-86729-X*) Scribner.

One Good Turn Deserves Another: Heinsian Down Hill Skiing. Gary Heins. LC 97-91089. (Illus.). 148p. 1997. pap. 10.00 (*1-882369-21-1*) Swingin G Bks.

One Good Woman Come & Gone. Robert Gamble. LC 98-131378. 1998. pap. 12.00 (*1-886094-82-9*) Chicago Spectrum.

*__One Good Woman Come & Gone: A Love Story.__ rev. ed. Robert Gamble. 272p. 2000. pap. 14.95 (*1-58374-014-7*) Chicago Spectrum.

One Gorilla. Atsuko Morozumi. 32p. 1993. pap. 7.50 (*0-385-25410-5*) Doubleday.

One Gorilla. Atsuko Morozumi. LC 89-46577. (Illus.). 32p. (J). (ps). 1993. pap. 4.95 (*0-374-45646-1*, Sunburst Bks) FS&G.

One Gorilla: A Counting Book. Atsuko Morozumi. LC 89-46577. (Illus.). 26p. (J). (ps-1). 1990. 15.00 (*0-374-35644-0*) FS&G.

One Gorilla, A Counting Book. Atsuko Morozumi. 1993. 10.15 (*0-606-05524-X*, Pub. by Turtleback) Demco.

One Gospel - Many Clothes: Anglicans & the Decade of Evangelism. Ed. by Chris Wright & Chris Sugden. 190p. 1990. reprint ed. pap. 14.99 (*1-870345-08-8*, Pub. by Regnum Bks) OM Literature.

One Grain of Rice: A Mathematical Folktale. Demi. LC 96-7002. (J). 1997. pap. write for info. (*0-614-13399-8*) Scholastic Inc.

One Grain of Rice: A Mathematical Folktale. Demi. LC 96-7002. (Illus.). 40p. (YA). (gr. 1-4). 1997. 19.95 (*0-590-93998-X*) Scholastic Inc.

One Grain of Sand. Helen C. Doerfel. 620p. 1991. lib. bdg. 73.50 (*1-880487-00-4*) Eldredge Hse.

One Grain of Sand. Illus. by Megan Noller. 20p. 1995. pap. 3.95 (*1-883869-16-1*) Gldn Gate Natl Parks Assoc.

One Grand Pursuit: A Brief History of the American Philosophical Society's First 250 Years, 1743-1993. Edward C. Carter, II. LC 93-71157. (APS Ser.: No. 9). (Illus.). 118p. (C). 1993. pap. 15.00 (*0-87169-938-9*, APS9-CAE) Am Philos.

One Gray Mouse. unabridged ed. Katherine Burton & Eugenie Fernandes. (Illus.). 24p. (J). (ps-k). 1997. 12.95 (*1-55074-225-6*, Pub. by Kids Can Pr) Genl Dist Srvs.

One Great Cloud of Witnesses: You & Your Congregation in the Evangelical Lutheran Church in America. Lowell G. Almen. LC 97-19707. 1997. 8.99 (*0-8066-3622-X*, 10-362210) Augsburg Fortress.

One Green Frog. Yvonne Hooker. (Poke & Look Bks.). (Illus.). 16p. (J). (ps-1). 1989. spiral bd. 9.99 (*0-448-21031-2*, G & D) Peng Put Young Read.

One Green Island. Charlotte Hard. LC 94-25698. (Illus.). 32p. (J). (ps-1). 1995. 12.95 (*1-56402-578-0*) Candlewick Pr.

One Green Island: An Animal Counting Gamebook. Charlotte Hard. LC 94-25698. (Candlewick Gamebks.). (Illus.). 32p. (J). (ps-k). 1996. reprint ed. pap. 7.99 (*1-56402-863-1*) Candlewick Pr.

One Green Mesquite Tree. 2nd ed. Gisela Jernigan. LC 90-5205. (Illus.). 32p. (J). (ps-1). 1990. 10.95 (*0-943173-35-3*) Roberts Rinehart.

One Grey Mouse. Katherine Burton.Tr. of Une Souris Grise. (Illus.). 24p. (J). 1995. pap. 5.95 (*1-55074-324-4*) Kids Can Pr.

One Guinea Pig Is Not Enough. Kate Duke. LC 97-21367. (Illus.). 48p. (J). 1998. 15.99 (*0-525-45918-9*, Dutton Child) Peng Put Young Read.

One Half of a Shell. Yeoh S. Kee. (Illus.). 198p. 1995. 60.00 (*983-9808-00-1*, Pub. by Delta Edits) Weatherhill.

One-Half of a Telephone Conversation. D. Dan Nedelkoff. 1976. 4.00 (*0-685-67938-1*) Windless Orchard.

One Half the People: The Fight for Woman Suffrage. Anne F. Scott & Andrew M. Scott. LC 82-8563. 92p. 1982. reprint ed. pap. text 13.95 (*0-252-01005-1*) U of Ill Pr.

One Halloween Night. Mark Teague. LC 98-47719. (Illus.). 32p. (J). (ps-2). 1999. 14.95 (*0-590-84625-6*, Pub. by Scholastic Inc) Penguin Putnam.

*__One Hand Alone Cannot Clap: An Arab-Israeli Universe, Vol. 1.__ Greville Janner. 162p. 1999. 25.95 (*1-86105-217-0*) Robson.

One Hand at a Time. Patricia E. Smith. 1997. pap. text 10.95 (*0-86651-347-7*) Seymour Pubns.

One Hand Clapping. Anthony Burgess. 1999. pap. 11.95 (*0-7867-0631-7*) Carroll & Graf.

One Hand Clapping: Zen Stories for All Ages. Rafe Martin & Junko Morimoto. LC 94-35257. (Illus.). 46p. 1995. 16.95 (*0-8478-1853-5*, Pub. by Rizzoli Intl) St Martin.

One Hand for Yourself, One for the Ship: The Essentials of Single-Handed Sailing. Tristan Jones. (Illus.). 226p. 1990. pap. 16.50 (*0-924486-03-1*) Sheridan.

*__One Hand Is No Applauder.__ Paul Heinberg & Terry A. Welden. 2000. pap. 14.95 (*0-533-13442-0*) Vantage.

*__One Hand on the Wheel.__ Dan Bellm. (California Poetry Ser.: Vol. 1). 65p. 1999. pap. 12.50 (*0-9666691-0-X*, Pub. by Heyday Bks) SPD-Small Pr Dist.

One Hand One Heart: From West Side Story Piano & Violin. Leonard Bernstein. 6p. 1986. pap. 3.95 (*0-7935-5319-9*, 50287990) H Leonard.

One Hand Tied Behind Us: The Rise of the Women's Suffrage Movement. Jill Liddington & Jill Norris. 304p. 1999. 55.00 (*1-85489-110-3*) Rivers Oram.

One Hand Tied Behind Us: The Rise of the Women's Suffrage Movement, Revised Ed. Jill Liddington. 1999. pap. text 19.50 (*1-85489-111-1*, Pub. by Rivers Oram) NYU Pr.

*__One Handed: A Guide to Piano Music for One Hand, 80.__ Donald L. Patterson. LC 99-36260. (Music Reference Collection). 336p. 1999. lib. bdg. 75.00 (*0-313-31179-X*, Greenwood Pr) Greenwood.

One-Handed Basket Weaving: Poems on the Theme of Work from the Mathnawi. Jalal Al-Din Rumi. Tr. & Intro. by Coleman Barks. 136p. (C). 1992. pap. 9.00 (*0-9618916-3-7*) Maypop.

One-Handed Histories: The Eroto-Politics of Gay Male Video Pornography. John R. Burger. LC 93-15575. 143p. 1994. pap. 14.95 (*1-56023-852-6*) Haworth Pr.

One-Handed Histories: The Eroto-Politics of Gay Male Video Pornography. John R. Burger. LC 93-15575. 143p. 1995. lib. bdg. 39.95 (*1-56024-860-2*) Haworth Pr.

One-Handed in a Two-Handed World. Tommye K. Mayer. (Illus.). 229p. 1999. reprint ed. pap. 16.95 (*0-9652805-0-0*) Prince-Gallison.

*__One-Handed in a Two-Handed World.__ 2nd ed. Tommye-Karen Mayer. LC 99-90859. (Illus.). 2000. 20.00 (*0-9652805-1-9*) Prince-Gallison.

One-Handed Pianist: And Other Stories. Ilan Stavans. LC 95-4354. 196p. 1996. pap. 22.50 (*0-8263-1645-X*) U of NM Pr.

One Happy Classroom. Charnan Simon. LC 96-21172. (Rookie Readers Ser.). (Illus.). 32p. (J). (gr. k-2). 1997. lib. bdg. 17.00 (*0-516-20318-5*) Childrens.

One Happy Classroom. Charnan Simon. (Rookie Readers Ser.). (J). (ps-2). 1997. pap. 4.95 (*0-516-26154-1*) Childrens.

One Harmonic Whole Vol. 1: The Song of the Universe. unabridged ed. Jackie L. Hofer. LC 98-96005. 176p. 1998. pap. 12.00 (*0-9615743-9-9*) SunShine CO.

One Heart. Rosalyn Alsobrook. 384p. 1997. mass mkt. 5.50 (*0-8217-5599-4*, Zebra Kensgtn) Kensgtn Pub Corp.

One Heart: A Novel. Jane McCafferty. LC 98-49469. 304p. 1999. 24.00 (*0-06-019263-1*) HarpC.

*__One Heart: A Novel.__ Jane McCafferty. 304p. 2000. pap. 13.00 (*0-06-109757-8*) HarpC.

One Heart & One Soul. Micha Haykin. 1995. pap. 16.99 (*0-85234-326-4*, Pub. by Evangelical Pr) P & R Pubng.

*__One Heart at a Time: Renewing the Church in the New Millennium.__ J. Ronald Knott & Becky J. Hollingsworth. LC 99-94071. vii, 215p. 1999. write for info. (*0-9668969-0-4*) Sophronismos.

One Heart Full of Love. Mother Teresa of Calcutta. Ed. by Jose L. Gonzalez-Balado. 170p. 1988. pap. 6.99 (*0-89283-393-9*) Servant.

One Heart, One Mind: The Rebirth of Virgil's Hero in Medieval French Romance. Raymond J. Cormier. LC 73-81571. (Romance Monographs: No. 3). 1973. pap. 28.00 (*84-399-1292-7*) Romance.

One Heartbeat Away: Presidential Disability & Succession. Birch Bayh. LC 68-28241. 1968. pap. 5.80 (*0-672-51385-4*, Bobbs) Macmillan.

One Heartbeat from Heaven: O'Keeffe Hunting Camp, 1914-1965. Daniel O'Keeffe, 2nd. Ed. by Gerald Cashion. (Illus.). 85p. 1997. pap. 11.95 (*0-9654280-1-X*) Sunset Ent.

One "Heil" of a Family: Some Ancestors & Other Relatives of Louis Heil & Elizabeth Susan (Steves) Heil. Robert A. Heil. 612p. 1993. write for info. (*0-9638621-0-3*) R A Heil.

"One Hell of a Gamble" Khruschev, Castro & Kennedy, 1958-1964. Aleksandr Fursenko & Timothy Naftali. (Illus.). 448p. 1998. pap. 14.95 (*0-393-31790-0*) Norton.

One Heroic Hour at King's Mountain. Pat Alderman. (Illus.). 94p. 1968. pap. 7.95 (*0-932807-40-2*) Overmountain Pr.

One Hole in the Road. W. Nikola-Lisa. LC 95-41321. (Illus.). 32p. (J). (ps-2). 1995. 15.95 (*0-8050-4285-7*, B Martin BYR) H Holt & Co.

One Holy & Happy Society: The Public Theology of Jonathan Edwards. Gerald R. McDermott. 256p. 1992. 35.00 (*0-271-00850-4*) Pa St U Pr.

*__One, Holy, Catholic & Apostolic: The Early Church was the Catholic Church.__ Kenneth D. Whitehead. 144p. 2000. pap. 14.95 (*0-89870-802-8*, Pub. by Ignatius Pr) Midpt Trade.

*__One Holy Hunger: When God Is All You Want.__ Mike Cope. 200p. 2000. pap. 11.95 (*0-89112-443-8*, Hill Crest Pubg) Abilene Christ U.

One Holy Passion *see* **Pasion Santa**

One Holy Passion: Growing Deeper in Your Walk with God. Compiled by Judith Couchman. LC 98-229071. 256p. 1998. 16.95 (*1-57856-038-1*) Waterbrook Pr.

One Home at a Time: Restoring the Soul of America Through God's Plan for Your Marriage & Family, 1. 1999. pap. 11.99 (*1-56179-715-4*) Focus Family.

One Home at a Time: Restoring the Soul of America Through God's Plan for Your Marriage & Family. Dennis Rainey. LC 97-10893. 267p. 1997. 16.99 (*1-56179-545-3*) Focus Family.

*__One Horse Waiting for Me.__ Illus. by Patricia Mullins. LC 97-68018. 32p. (J). (ps-2). 1998. per. 16.00 (*0-689-81381-3*, 878849) S&S Bks Yung.

One Hot Cowboy. Cathy G. Thacker. (How to Marry...Ser.). 1997. per. 3.75 (*0-373-16673-7*, 1-16673-5) Harlequin Bks.

One Hot Daddy-to-Be? 4 Tots for 4 Texans. Judy Christenberry. (American Romance Ser.: No. 773). 1999. per. 3.99 (*0-373-16773-3*, 1-16773-3) Harlequin Bks.

One Hot Minute. Composed by Red Hot Chili Peppers. 80p. 1996. per. 18.95 (*0-7935-5825-5*); otabind 22.95 (*0-7935-5824-7*) H Leonard.

One Hot Minute. Composed by Red Hot Chili Peppers. 224p. 1997. per. 27.95 (*0-7935-6672-X*) H Leonard.

One Hot Summer. Suzanne Scott. 1997. per. 3.50 (*0-373-25747-3*, 1-25747-6) Harlequin Bks.

One Hot Summer Day. Nina Crews. LC 94-6268. (Illus.). 32p. (J). (ps-3). 1995. 15.00 (*0-688-13393-2*, Grenwillow Bks) HarpC Child Bks.

One Hot Summer Day. Nina Crews. LC 94-6268. (Illus.). 32p. (J). (ps-3). 1995. 14.89 (*0-688-13394-0*, Grenwillow Bks) HarpC Child Bks.

One Hot Summer in Kyoto. John Haylock. LC 93-85075. 176p. (Orig.). 1993. reprint ed. pap. 10.95 (*1-880656-08-6*) Stone Bridge Pr.

One Hot Winter in Estes. Raymond R. St. John. 200p. (Orig.). Date not set. pap. 11.95 (*0-9650328-0-9*) Pigiron Prods.

One Hour. Robert Frank. (Illus.). 82p. (Orig.). 1992. pap. 5.95 (*0-937815-50-0*) Hanuman Bks.

One Hour. Lillian Smith. (Chapel Hill Bks.). 460p. 1994. pap. 18.95 (*0-8078-4489-6*); text 32.50 (*0-8078-2178-0*) U of NC Pr.

One-Hour BASIC. Thomas Wnorowski. LC 84-9449. (Illus.). 220p. (Orig.). 1984. pap. text 9.95 (*0-931543-00-2*) IM-Pr.

One Hour Bible. Larry D. Perry. Ed. by Eloise Boughner. 120p. 1996. 10.00 (*0-942442-01-6*) Perry Publns.

One-Hour Christmas Crafts. Leisure Arts Staff. LC 98-65189. (Illus.). 128p. 1998. 19.95 (*0-8487-6118-9*) Oxmoor Hse.

One-Hour Christmas Crafts for Kids. (Illus.). 64p. 1993. 5.98 (*0-7853-0280-8*, 3617300) Pubns Intl Ltd.

One-Hour Crafts for Kids. Cindy G. Harry. (Arts-Crafts-Cooking-Drawing Books for Children Ser.). (Illus.). 64p. (J). (gr. 2-6). 1995. lib. bdg. 17.95 (*1-56674-099-1*) Forest Hse.

One-Hour Cross Stitch. Symbol of Excellence Staff. LC 92-60991. 144p. 1992. 24.99 (*0-8487-1097-5*) Oxmoor Hse.

*__One Hour from "Always Broke" Easy Money Solutions for the Perpetually Overdrawn.__ abr. ed. Sally Atman. 1999. 10.95 incl. audio (*1-928843-07-7*) Ad Lib Res.

One-Hour Holiday Crafts for Kids. Cindy G. Harry. (Art-Crafts-Cooking-Drawing Books for Children Ser.). (Illus.). 64p. (J). (ps up). 1995. lib. bdg. 17.95 (*1-56674-108-4*, HTS Bks) Forest Hse.

One Hour Kites. Jim Rowlands. 1989. pap. 14.95 (*0-312-03218-8*) St Martin.

One Hour Management Check-Up. Dave Ray. (Illus.). 61p. (Orig.). 1996. pap., wbk. ed. 6.95 (*1-57326-020-7*, 311) Core Ministries.

One-Hour Nature Crafts. Janelle Hayes & Kim Solga. (Craft & Project Books for Children). (Illus.). 64p. (J). (gr. 2-6). 1996. lib. bdg. 17.95 (*1-56674-174-2*, HTS Bks) Forest Hse.

One Hour Orgasm: A New Approach to Achieving Maximum Sexual Pleasure. Bob Schwartz. 179p. 1992. pap. 10.95 (*0-942540-07-7*) Breakthru Pub.

*__One Hour Orgasm: How to Learn the Amazing Venus Butterfly Technique.__ 3rd ed. Bob Schwartz & Leah Schwartz. (Illus.). 208p. 1999. pap. 12.95 (*0-942540-14-X*) Breakthru Pub.

One Hour Orgasm: The Ultimate Guide to Totally Satisfying Any Woman or Man...Every Time! 2nd rev. ed. Bob Schwartz & Leah Schwartz. Ed. by Frank Reuter & Jack Mayer. (Illus.). 208p. 1995. pap. 12.95 (*0-942540-22-0*) Breakthru Pub.

One Hour Purim Primer: Everything a Family Needs to Understand, Celebrate & Enjoy Purim. Shimon Apisdorf. pap. 7.95 (*1-881927-04-0*) Leviathan OH.

One Hour Telecomputing. Roger C. Alford et al. LC 84-9450. (C). 1985. pap. text 9.95 (*0-931543-01-0*) IM-Pr.

*__One-Hour Watercolorist.__ Patrick Seslar. LC 00-42717. (Illus.). 2001. pap. write for info. (*1-58180-035-5*, North Lght Bks) F & W Pubns Inc.

One House: The Battle of Aowa 1896 - 100 Years. Ed. by Pamela S. Brown & Fassil Yirgu. 1996. 37.00 (*0-9642068-1-1*) Nyala Pubng.

One Human Minute. Stanislaw Lem. Tr. by Catherine S. Leach. 112p. 1986. pap. 5.00 (*0-15-668795-X*, Harvest Bks) Harcourt.

One-Humped Camel in Eastern Africa: A Pictorial Guide to Diseases, Health Care & Management. Ed. by H. J. Schwartz & M. Dioli. (Illus.). 282p. 1992. 89.00 (*3-8236-1218-2*, Pub. by Backhuys Pubs) Balogh.

One Hundred. Tom Gilmore. 128p. 1995. pap. text 6.95 (*1-879352-17-6*) Mini-Novel Pub.

One Hundred: A Ranking of the Most Influential Persons in History. rev. ed. Michael H. Hart. (Illus.). 576p. 1992. 25.00 (*0-8065-1343-8*, Citadel Pr) Carol Pub Group.

100: A Ranking of the Most Influential Persons in History. rev. ed. Michael H. Hart. (Illus.). 576p. Date not set. pap. 21.95 (*0-8065-1350-0*, Citadel Pr) Carol Pub Group.

101 Dives from the Mainland of Washington & B. C. Betty Pratt-Johnson. LC 94-910292. (Illus.). 1997. pap. 24.95 (*1-895811-20-1*) Heritage Hse.

*__101 Key Stat Words.__ Rachel Kranz. LC 99-180771. 96 p. 1998. write for info. (*0-8167-4938-8*) Troll Communs.

101 Mutual Fund FAQs: Straight Answers That Help You Make Good Investment Decisions. Dian Vujovich. LC 98-74423. 156p. 1999. pap. 12.95 (*1-886284-23-7*, Pub. by Chandler Hse) Natl Bk Netwk.

*__101 Questions Your Cat Would Ask.__ Honor Head. (Illus.). 112p. 1999. pap. 12.95 (*0-7641-0887-5*) Barron.

*__100-Pound Problem.__ Jennifer Dussling. LC 99-42679. (Math Matters Ser.). (Illus.). (J). (gr. k-2). 2000. pap. 4.95 (*1-57565-095-9*) Kane Pr.

*__100 Absolutely Unbreakable Laws of Business Success.__ Brian Tracy. LC 00-26693. 300p. 2000. pap. 24.95 (*1-57675-107-4*, Pub. by Berrett-Koehler) Publishers Group.

One Hundred Acres-More or Less: History of Bow, New Hampshire. David Bundy. LC 75-38922. (Illus.). 576p. 1975. 20.00 (*0-914016-24-5*) Phoenix Pub.

100 Action Principles of the Shaolin. Bill Fitzpatrick. 128p. 1997. pap. 6.00 (*1-884864-09-0*) Am Success Inst.

100 Action Principles of the Shaolin. rev. ed. Bill FitzPatrick. (Illus.). 128p. reprint ed. pap. 6.00 (*1-884864-13-9*) Am Success Inst.

100 Action Principles of the Shaolin. 2nd ed. Bill Fitzpatrick. 224p. 1998. pap. 12.95 (*1-884864-10-4*) Am Success Inst.

100 Activities: Based on the Catechism of the Catholic Church. Ellen Rossini. 125p. 1996. pap. text 11.95 (*0-89870-615-7*) Ignatius Pr.

One Hundred Activities for Gifted Children. Leslie Landin & Paul Meredith. 1957. pap. 5.99 (*0-8224-5050-X*) Fearon Teacher Aids.

100 Affirmations for Creative People. Jo Ann Lordahl. LC 99-174899. 100 p. 1998. pap. write for info. (*0-9664528-0-1*) Target Pubng.

100 African-Americans Who Shaped American History. Chrisanne Beckner. 1995. pap. text 7.95 (*0-912517-18-2*) Bluewood Bks.

*__100 Historic Airplanes in Full Color.__ John H. Batchelor. LC 00-31775. (Pictorial Archive Ser.). (Illus.). 2000. write for info. (*0-486-41246-6*) Dover.

One-Hundred Albums of the Sixties. John Tobler. LC 94-25581. (Illus.). 112p. 1995. 15.95 (*0-87951-569-4*, Pub. by Overlook Pr) Penguin Putnam.

One Hundred Alchemical Aphorisms & the Summary of Philosophy. Baro Urbigerus & Flamel Nicholas. 1986. pap. 5.95 (*0-916411-55-9*) Holmes Pub.

One Hundred Alive & Stay Alive! Double Your Life Expectancy. Ed. by E. Masterdy. 162p. 1984. 12.95 (*0-8159-6415-3*) Devin.

One-Hundred All-Time Popular Hits. 1992. pap. 16.95 (*0-943748-45-3*) Ekay Music.

One Hundred All-Time Standards for All Organs, EFS165. Ed. by Edward J. Burns & Joseph H. Greener. (Illus.). 128p. 1962. pap. 14.95 (*0-8256-2165-8*, AM40783) Music Sales.

100 Allegories to Represent the World. Peter Greenaway. (Illus.). 272p. 1998. pap. 39.95 (*1-85894-060-5*, Pub. by Merrell Holberton) U of Wash Pr.

One Hundred Amazing Facts about the Negro. rev. ed. J. A. Rogers & Helga Rogers. (Illus.). (Orig.). 1995. reprint ed. pap. 4.95 (*0-9602294-7-7*) H M Rogers.

One Hundred Amazing Facts about the Nubian Man & Woman. African Islamic Mission Staff. Ed. by Al I. Obaba. (Illus.). 124p. (Orig.). (YA). 1991. pap. text 8.95 (*0-916157-87-3*) African Islam Miss Pubns.

100 Amazing Make-It-Yourself Science Fair Projects. Glen Vecchione. (Illus.). 224p. (J). 1995. pap. 12.95 (*0-8069-0367-8*) Sterling.

100 Amazing Make-It-Yourself Science Fair Projects. Glen Vecchione. LC 93-41681. 1995. 18.05 (*0-606-10116-0*, Pub. by Turtleback) Demco.

One Hundred American Festivals & Their Foods. Helen Naismith. 232p. 1990. write for info. (*0-87651-989-3*) Southern U Pr.

100 Americans Who Shaped American History. Samuel W. Crompton. 1998. pap. text 7.95 (*0-912517-32-8*) Bluewood Bks.

One Hundred & Fifty Folk Tales of India. Kanwarjit Singh & Kang Singh. 300p. (C). 1987. 26.00 (*81-202-0180-9*, Pub. by Ajanta) S Asia.

One Hundred & Fifty-Four Steps to Revitalize Your Sunday School: And Keep Your Church Growing, Set. Elmer L. Towns. Ed. by Larry A. Gilbert & Wayne Cook. (C). 1987. student ed., ring bd. 99.95 incl. VHS (*0-941005-25-9*) Chrch Grwth VA.

One Hundred & Fifty Years of American Painting, 1794-1944: From the Collections of the Museum of Art, Brigham Young University. Compiled by Linda Jones Gibbs. LC 94-21018. 1998. 49.95 (*0-8425-2318-9*, Pub. by Brigham) U Ch Pr.

One Hundred & Fifty Years of Collecting, 1824-1974. Nicholas B. Wainwright. 105p. 1974. 10.00 (*0-910732-09-4*) Pa Hist Soc.

One Hundred & Fifty Years of Music Publishing in the U. S., 1783-1933. William A. Fisher. 1988. reprint ed. lib. bdg. 49.00 (*0-7812-0757-6*) Rprt Serv.

One Hundred & Fifty Years of Music Publishing in the U. S., 1783-1933. William A. Fisher. 1981. reprint ed. lib. bdg. 59.00 (*0-686-71937-9*) Scholarly.

An Asterisk (*) at the beginning of an entry indicates that the title is appearing for the first time.

One Hundred & Fifty Years of Music Publishing in the United States: An Historical Sketch with Special Reference to the Pioneer Publisher, Oliver Ditson Company, Inc., 1783-1933 William A. Fisher. LC 70-181152. xvi, 146 p. 1977. write for info. (*0-403-01554-5*) Scholarly.

One Hundred & Forty-Four Doors of the Zodiac. Thyrza Escobar. LC 85-73312. 120p. 1986. 13.00 (*0-86690-314-3*, F2345-014) Am Fed Astrologers.

One-Hundred-&-One African-American Read-Aloud Stories. Susan Kantor. 416p. 1998. 12.98 (*1-57912-039-3*) Blck Dog & Leventhal.

One Hundred & One Aggie Jokes: Or, Is It True What They Say about Aggies? Illus. by Bob Taylor. (One Hundred & One Aggie Jokes Ser.). 50p. (Orig.). 1965. 3.00 (*0-945430-01-9*) Gigem Pr.

One Hundred & One Apple Recipes. Carole Eberly. (Illus.). 96p. (Orig.). 1978. pap. 4.95 (*0-932296-02-5*) Eberly Pr.

One Hundred & One Best Businesses to Start. rev. ed. Sharon Kahn. 544p. 1992. pap. 17.50 (*0-385-42623-2*) Doubleday.

***101 Best Websites for Kids.** Consumer Guide Editors. 2000. mass mkt. 5.99 (*0-7853-4047-5*) Pubns Intl Ltd.

One Hundred & One Botanists. Duane Isely. LC 94-28380. (Illus.). 358p. 1994. text 44.95 (*0-8138-2498-2*) Iowa St U Pr.

One Hundred & One Careers: A Guide to the Fastest-Growing Opportunities. Michael Harkavy. 368p. 1990. pap. 18.95 (*0-471-52195-7*) Wiley.

One Hundred & One Chinese Poems. Tr. by Shun-Liu Shih. LC PL3277.E3L5. (Unesco Collection of Representative Works, Series of Translations from the Literature of the Union of Soviet Socialist Republics). 211p. reprint ed. pap. 65.50 (*0-608-11040-X*, 201769900007) Bks Demand.

101 Classic Jewish Jokes: Jewish Humor from Groucho Marx to Jerry Seinfeld. Robert Menchin. LC 97-36233. (Illus.). 96p. 1997. pap. 9.95 (*0-914457-88-8*) Mustang Pub.

One Hundred & One Classic Love Poems. 144p. 1988. 12.00 (*0-8092-4475-6*, 447560, Contemporary Bks) NTC Contemp Pub Co.

One Hundred & One Crocheted Doilies, 3 bks., Set. Rita Weiss & Linda Macho. 144p. 1985. pap. 10.50 (*0-486-25013-X*) Dover.

101 Dalmatians: Illustrated Classic. Disney Staff. (J). 1997. pap. 5.95 (*0-7868-4199-0*, Pub. by Disney Pr) Time Warner.

101 Dalmatians Counting Book & Puppy, Set. Fran Manushkin. (Illus.). 32p. (J). (ps-1). 1993. pap. 16.95 (*1-56282-572-0*, Pub. by Disney Pr) Little.

101 Dalmatians Junior Novelization. Anne Mazer. (Illus.). 96p. (J). (gr. 2-6). 1996. pap. 3.95 (*0-7868-4101-X*, Pub. by Disney Pr) Little.

101 Dalmatians. Walter Elias Disney. LC 99-160962. (J). 1997. 9.98 (*1-57082-537-8*, Pub. by Mouse Works) Time Warner.

One Hundred & One Dalmations Sing-A-Long. Prod. by Walt Disney Productions Staff. (J). 1996. pap. 22.50 incl. audio (*0-7634-0109-9*) W Disney Records.

***101 Easy Home Accents in Plastic Canvas.** Ed. by Laura Scott. (Illus.). 176p. 2000. 19.95 (*1-882138-54-6*) Hse White Birches.

One Hundred & One Facts about Snakes & Reptiles. Walter Retan. 96p. (J). (gr. 4-6). 1992. pap. 1.95 (*0-590-44891-9*) Scholastic Inc.

One Hundred & One Famous Poems. Roy J. Cook. 202p. Date not set. 20.95 (*0-8488-2238-2*) Amereon Ltd.

One Hundred & One Famous Poems. Ed. by Roy J. Cook. (Illus.). 186p. (YA). (gr. 9-12). 1990. reprint ed. lib. bdg. 21.95 (*0-89966-667-1*) Buccaneer Bks.

One Hundred & One Favorite Wild Rice Recipes. Duane R. Lund. 76p. 1983. pap. 8.95 (*0-934860-24-6*) Adventure Pubns.

One Hundred & One Fruit Recipes. Carole Eberly. (Illus.). 96p. (Orig.). 1983. pap. 4.95 (*0-932296-09-2*) Eberly Pr.

One Hundred & One Ideas for Volunteer Programs. Steve McCurley & Sue Vineyard. (Brainstorm Ser.). (Illus.). 72p. (Orig.). 1986. pap. text 11.95 (*0-911029-04-4*) Heritage Arts.

***101 Must-know Blues Licks: A Quick, Easy Reference for All Guitarists.** 48p. 1999. pap. 14.95 incl. audio compact disk (*0-7935-9587-8*) H Leonard.

One Hundred & One Openings for Church Schools. Carolyn Short. 64p. 1994. pap. 11.99 (*0-8066-2720-4*, 10-27204, Augsburg) Augsburg Fortress.

One Hundred & One Other Uses for a Condom. Glenn Haumann et al. (Illus.). 48p. (Orig.). 1991. pap. 4.95 (*0-927203-05-7*) Apple Pr PA.

One Hundred & One Patchwork Patterns. rev. ed. Ruby S. McKim. (Illus.). 124p. 1962. pap. 5.95 (*0-486-20773-0*) Dover.

101 Perfect. Jeff Hadfield & Allen Biehl. LC 94-30481. 1994. 24.95 (*0-201-40892-9*) Addison-Wesley.

One Hundred & One Photographs: Selections from the Arthur & Yolanda Steinman Collection. Richard Ross. LC 84-71041. (Illus.). (Orig.). 1984. pap. 3.50 (*0-89951-052-3*) Santa Barb Mus Art.

One Hundred & One Poems: A Bilingual Edition. Tr. by Norman R. Shapiro. LC 98-29016. 1999. 25.00 (*0-226-85344-6*) U Ch Pr.

One Hundred & One Poems of Romance. Compiled by Christine Benton. LC 92-15046. (Illus.). 144p. 1992. 12.00 (*0-8092-3929-9*, 392990, Contemporary Bks) NTC Contemp Pub Co.

One Hundred & One Puzzles in Thought & Logic. Clarence R. Wylie, Jr. 1957. pap. 3.95 (*0-486-20367-0*) Dover.

One Hundred & One Questions about dBASE III: Software Application Guide. write for info. (*0-318-58222-8*) P-H.

One Hundred & One Questions about Framework: Software Application Guide. write for info. (*0-318-58223-6*) P-H.

One Hundred & One Questions & Answers about Pets & People. Ann Squire. LC 87-36457. (Illus.). 96p. (J). (gr. 3-7). 1988. text 13.95 (*0-02-786580-0*, Mac Bks Young Read) S&S Childrens.

One Hundred & One Questions Your Cat Would Ask Its Vet, If Your Cat Could Talk. Bruce Fogle. 144p. 1995. 5.98 (*0-7858-0439-0*) Bk Sales Inc.

One Hundred & One Questions Your Dog Would Ask Its Vet, If Your Dog Could Talk. Bruce Fogle. 144p. 1995. 5.98 (*0-7858-0438-2*) Bk Sales Inc.

One Hundred & One Reasons Why a Cat Is Better Than a Man. Allia Zobel. (Illus.). 80p. 1994. pap. 6.95 (*1-55850-436-2*) Adams Media.

One Hundred & One Secretos de Costura - 101 Sewing Secrets. Singer. (Singer Biblioteca de Costura Ser.). (SPA., Illus.). 128p. 1993. 17.95 (*0-86573-282-5*) Creat Pub Intl.

One Hundred & One Silly Monster Jokes. Jovial Bob Stine, pseud. (One Hundred One Jokes Ser.). (Illus.). 96p. (Orig.). (J). (gr. 4-6). 1986. pap. 1.95 (*0-590-33889-7*) Scholastic Inc.

One Hundred & One Spooky Halloween Jokes. Melvin Berger. 96p. (J). (gr. 4-6). 1993. pap. 1.95 (*0-590-47143-0*) Scholastic Inc.

One Hundred & One Spreadsheet Exercises. Lloyd D. Brooks. 144p. 1986. pap. text 15.56 (*0-07-008135-2*) McGraw.

One Hundred & One Therapeutic Successes: Overcoming Transference & Resistance in Psychotherapy. Gerald Schoenewolf. LC 88-7612. 304p. 1989. 50.00 (*0-87668-869-5*) Aronson.

One Hundred & One Things to Do to Develop Your Child's Gifts & Talents, Vol. 1. Susan Amerikaner. 1989. mass mkt. 5.95 (*0-8125-9497-5*, Pub. by Tor Bks) St Martin.

One Hundred & One Things to Do with Your Private License. LeRoy Cook. (Illus.). 224p. (Orig.). 1985. pap. 13.95 (*0-8306-2359-0*, 2359) McGraw-Hill Prof.

101 Uses for a Dead Angel. Marty Norman. LC 95-8867. 1995. pap. 6.99 (*0-312-13227-1*) St Martin.

One Hundred & One Uses for a Dead Cat. Simon Bond. 96p. 1988. pap. 6.00 (*0-517-54516-0*) C Potter.

One Hundred & One Uses for an Ex-Wife. Slug Sherman. LC 89-92174. (Illus.). 104p. (Orig.). 1990. pap. 8.95 (*0-945609-85-X*) Keel Pubns.

One Hundred & One Valentine Jokes. Pat Brigandi. 96p. (J). (gr. 4-6). 1994. pap. 1.95 (*0-590-47141-4*) Scholastic Inc.

One Hundred & One Wacky Kid Jokes. Jovial Bob Stine, pseud. (Illus.). 96p. (J). (gr. 4-6). 1988. pap. 2.99 (*0-590-41399-6*) Scholastic Inc.

One Hundred & One Wacky State Jokes. Melvin Berger. 96p. (J). (gr. 4-6). 1991. pap. 1.95 (*0-590-44487-5*) Scholastic Inc.

One Hundred & One Ways. Mako Yoshikawa. LC 98-45483. 288p. 1999. 21.95 (*0-553-11099-3*) Bantam.

***One Hundred & One Ways.** Mako Yoshikawa. 288p. 2000. pap. 12.95 (*0-553-37969-0*, Spectra) Bantam.

101 Ways to Flirt. Sue Rabin. LC 96-43265. 1997. pap. 9.95 (*0-452-27685-3*, Plume) Dutton Plume.

One Hundred & One Ways to Raise Resources. Sue Vineyard & Steve McCurley. (Brainstorm Ser.). (Illus.). 63p. 1987. pap. 11.95 (*0-911029-05-2*) Heritage Arts.

101 Ways to See the Light: How You Can Have a Near-Death Experience. Jerry Biederman & Lorin Michelle. 1996. mass mkt. 6.99 (*0-312-95665-7*, Pub. by Tor Bks) St Martin.

One Hundred & One Ways to Start an Argument. Edward Kimball. 1994. pap. 6.95 (*0-936184-14-0*) Boston Common Pr.

One Hundred & One Ways to Transform Your Life. Wayne W. Dyer. 1995. pap. text 5.95 (*1-56170-169-6*) Hay House.

One Hundred & One Word Games. George P. McCallum. 176p. 1980. pap. text 12.50 (*0-19-502742-6*) OUP.

One Hundred & Seventy Chinese Poems. Arthur Waley. 224p. 1997. pap. 14.95 (*0-939218-17-8*) Chapman Billies.

One Hundred & Seventy Foundation Studies for Violoncello, Vol. III. Alvin Schroeder. 104p. 1916. pap. 15.95 (*0-8258-0177-X*, 02471) Fischer Inc NY.

One Hundred & Seventy-Six Woodworking Projects. Workbench Magazine Staff. LC 86-30139. (Illus.). 256p. 1987. pap. 14.95 (*0-8069-6528-2*) Sterling.

One Hundred & Sixteen Modern Classroom Combinations. Ray Cook. (Illus.). 40p. (Orig.). (C). 1979. pap. text 7.00 (*0-9602002-2-3*) Ray Cook.

***160.** Aperture Books Staff. (Illus.). 80p. 2000. pap. 18.50 (*0-89381-925-5*) Aperture.

One Hundred & Twentieth Regiment N. Y. Volunteers. C. Jan Santvoord. (Illus.). 328p. 1997. reprint ed. pap. 28.00 (*0-910746-55-9*) Hope Farm.

One Hundred & Twenty Year Diet. Roy L. Walford. 1991. per. 6.50 (*0-671-74474-7*) PB.

One Hundred & Two Steps. Donna Guthrie. 1995. 11.19 (*0-606-08838-5*, Pub. by Turtleback) Demco.

100 Answers to the Most Uncommon 100 Questions. Elijah Muhammad. 64p. 1995. pap. text 6.95 (*1-884855-09-1*) Secretarius.

100 Answers to Your Questions on Annullments. Edward N. Peters. 250p. 1997. 24.99 (*0-9642610-7-3*) Basilica Pr.

100 Answers to Your Questions on Annulments. Edward N. Peters. LC 97-224547. 240p. (C). 1997. text 8.00 (*0-536-00172-3*) Pearson Custom.

One Hundred Aphorisms of Sandilya: With the Commentary of Svapnesvara. Sandilya. Tr. by Manmathanath Paul. LC 73-3793. (Sacred Books of the Hindus: Vol. 7 Pt. 2). reprint ed. 17.50 (*0-404-57834-9*) AMS Pr.

100 Artists Who Shaped World History. Barbara Krystal. 1997. pap. 7.95 (*0-912517-26-3*) Bluewood Bks.

100 Athletes Who Shaped Sports History. Timothy Jacobs. (Illus.). 112p. (J). 1994. pap. 7.95 (*0-912517-13-1*) Bluewood Bks.

100 Authors Who Shaped World History. Bill Yenne. (One Hundred Ser.). (Illus.). 112p. (Orig.). 1996. pap. 7.95 (*0-912517-21-2*) Bluewood Bks.

100 Award-winning Country Hits. 2nd ed. 320p. 1985. otabind 17.95 (*0-634-00877-3*) H Leonard.

100 Awesome Chess Moves. Eric Schiller. LC 99-72542. 288p. 2000. pap. 18.95 (*1-58042-021-4*) Cardoza Pub.

Banned Books, 4 vols. Nicholas J. Karolides et al. Ed. by Ken Wachsberger. (Banned Bks.). 1998. pap. 140.00 (*0-8160-3302-1*, Checkmark) Facts on File.

100 Battles That Shaped World History. Samuel Crompton. 1997. pap. 7.95 (*0-912517-27-1*) Bluewood Bks.

100 Beautiful Himalayan Orchids & How to Grow Them. S. Pradhan. 1996. pap. write for info. (*0-7855-7524-3*) St Mut.

100 Beef Production-Health Sheets. 1995. 8.95 (*0-944079-09-1*) Lessiter Pubns.

100 Best Album Covers: The Stories Behind the Sleeves. Storm Thorgerson. LC 99-24280. 160p. 1999. pap. 19.95 (*0-7894-4951-X*) DK Pub Inc.

100 Best All-Inclusive Resorts in the World. Jay Paris & Carmi Z. Paris. LC 99-33143. (Illus.). 320p. 1999. pap. text 16.95 (*0-7627-0415-2*) Globe Pequot.

100 Best Annuities You Can Buy. Gordon K. Williamson. LC 94-38102. 288p. 1995. pap. 19.95 (*0-471-01025-1*) Wiley.

One Hundred Best Books by American Women, 1833-1933. Anita Browne. 1985. 250.00 (*0-8490-0767-4*) Gordon Pr.

100 Best Brain-Boosters: Puzzles & Games to Stimulate Students' Thinking. Helen H. Moore. (Illus.). 1994. pap. text 9.95 (*0-590-49795-2*) Scholastic Inc.

100 Best Businesses for the 21st Century. Gregg Ramsay & Lisa Rogak. 224p. 1999. pap. 15.95 (*0-9652502-3-7*) Williams Hill.

100 Best Careers for Writers & Artists: Writers & Artists. Shelly Field. LC 97-71489. 288p. 1997. 15.95 (*0-02-861926-9*, Arc) IDG Bks.

One Hundred Best Careers for the Year 2000. Shelly Field. 288p. 1992. per. 15.00 (*0-13-117342-1*, Arco) Macmillan Gen Ref.

100 Best Careers for the 21st Century. 2nd ed. Shelly Field. 320p. 1999. pap. text 15.95 (*0-02-863539-6*, Arco) Macmillan Gen Ref.

100 Best Careers in Allied Health. Lois A. Mark. 304p. 1999. 15.95 (*0-02-862520-X*) Macmillan.

100 Best Careers in Crime Fighting. Mary P. Lee et al. LC 97-80221. (Illus.). 200p. 1997. pap. 15.95 (*0-02-861397-X*, Arc) IDG Bks.

100 Best Careers in Entertainment. Shelly Field. 352p. 1995. 14.95 (*0-02-860017-7*) Macmillan.

100 Best Careers in Entertainment. Shelly Field. LC 94-36715. 1994. pap. 15.00 (*0-671-88355-0*, Arco) Macmillan Gen Ref.

100 Best Careers in Fashion & Modeling. Jeanne Rejaner. 304p. 1999. pap. 15.95 (*0-02-862177-8*) Macmillan.

***100 Best Careers in Media & Communications.** Robert Bly. 304p. 1999. pap. 15.95 (*0-02-862178-6*) Macmillan.

***100 Best Chess Games of the 20th Century.** Andrew Soltis. (Illus.). 280p. 2000. lib. bdg. 45.00 (*0-7864-0926-6*) McFarland & Co.

100 Best Colleges for African-American Students. rev. ed. Erlene B. Wilson. LC 97-46387. 352p. 1998. pap. 14.95 (*0-452-27954-2*, Plume) Dutton Plume.

One Hundred Best Colleges for African-American Students. Erlene B. Wilson. LC 93-2941. 352p. 1993. pap. 12.95 (*0-452-27020-0*, Plume) Dutton Plume.

100 Best Comics of the Century: The Funniest Cartoons of All Time. Ed. by Ray Schwartz. (Illus.). 204p. 1998. text 30.00 (*0-7881-5586-5*) DIANE Pub.

100 Best Comics of the Century: The Funniest Cartoons of All Time. Ed. by Ray Schwartz. (Illus.). 204p. 1995. 24.95 (*0-9645057-0-3*) Metrop Pub.

One Hundred Best Companies for Gay Men & Lesbians. Ed Mickens. Ed. by Dana Isaacson. 288p. (Orig.). 1994. per. 12.00 (*0-671-87479-9*) PB.

One Hundred Best Companies to Work for in America. Robert Levering & Milton Moskowitz. LC 93-6406. 528p. 1994. pap. 15.95 (*0-452-27123-1*, Plume) Dutton Plume.

100 Best Cruise Vacations of the World: The Top Cruises Throughout the World for All Interests & Budgets. Theodore W. Scull. LC 99-43819. (Illus.). 320p. 1999. pap. text 18.95 (*0-7627-0495-0*) Globe Pequot.

***100 Best Family Resorts in North America: 100 Quality Resorts with Leisure Activities for Children & Adults.** 5th ed. Jane Wilford & Janet Tice. LC 99-87632. (Illus.). 304p. 1999. pap. text 17.95 (*0-7627-0504-3*) Globe Pequot.

One Hundred Best Films of the Century. Barry Norman. LC 93-2520. (Illus.). 280p. 1993. pap. 16.95 (*0-8065-1426-4*, Citadel Pr) Carol Pub Group.

***100 Best Films of the Century.** Barry Norman. (Illus.). 276p. 1999. 29.95 (*0-7528-1777-9*, Pub. by Orion Media) Trafalgar.

100 Best Films to Rent. Meyer. 1999. text. write for info. (*0-312-18031-4*) St Martin.

100 Best Films to Rent You've Never Heard Of: Neglected Classics, Hits from By-Gone Eras & Hidden Treasures. 3rd ed. David N. Meyer. LC 96-32865. (Illus.). 224p. 1996. pap. 11.95 (*0-312-15042-3*) St Martin.

One Hundred Best Folk Songs. 1990. 7.95 (*0-685-32152-5*, K600) Hansen Ed Mus.

***100 Best Games.** Barron's Educational Editors & Eulalia Perez. 136p. (J). 2000. pap. 12.95 (*0-7641-1343-7*) Barron.

100 Best Hikes in the Northeast: Classic Hikes from the Catskills, the Adirondacks & New England. Jared Gange. (Illus.). 256p. Date not set. pap. write for info. (*1-886064-14-8*) Huntington Graphics.

One-hundred Best IBM Utilities. Mark R. Sawusch. 230p. 1988. 24.95 (*0-8306-9606-7*, 3006); pap. 29.95 (*0-8306-9306-8*) McGraw-Hill Prof.

100 Best Ideas for Primary Language Arts. Carole MacKenthun & Kathy Thoresen. (One Hundred Best Ideas Ser.). (Illus.). 112p. (J). (gr. k-3). 1994. pap., teacher ed. 9.95 (*1-57310-001-3*) Teachng & Lrning Co.

100 Best Ideas for Primary Math. Holly S. Dye. (One Hundred Best Ideas Ser.). (Illus.). 112p. (J). (gr. k-3). 1994. pap., teacher ed. 9.95 (*1-57310-003-X*) Teachng & Lrning Co.

100 Best Ideas for Primary Science. Beverly Hartman. (One Hundred Best Ideas Ser.). (Illus.). 112p. (J). (gr. k-3). 1994. pap., teacher ed. 9.95 (*1-57310-002-1*) Teachng & Lrning Co.

***100 Best Internet Stocks to Own.** Greg Kyle. (Illus.). 256p. 2000. pap. 19.95 (*0-07-135725-4*) McGraw.

***100 Best Internet Stocks to Own for the Long Run.** Gene Wilder & Tom Shaughnessy. 2000. 28.43 (*0-7931-3941-4*) Dearborn.

***100 Best Internet Stocks to Own for the Long Run: Investing in the Internet Economy & the Companies That Make It Click.** Gene Walden & Tom Shaughnessy. LC 00-29433. (Illus.). 371p. 2000. pap. 18.95 (*0-7931-3850-7*) Dearborn.

One Hundred Best Jobs for the 1990's & Beyond. Carol Kleiman. 320p. (Orig.). 1994. mass mkt. 5.99 (*0-425-14149-7*) Berkley Pub.

100 Best Loved Piano Solos. 252p. (YA). 1995. pap. 16.95 (*0-89724-894-5*, AF9533) Wrner Bros.

One-Hundred Best Loved Piano Solos, Vol. 2. Ed. by Robert Schultz. 160p. (Orig.). (YA). (gr. 9-12). 1993. pap. text 16.95 (*0-89898-976-0*, F3423PFX) Wrner Bros.

100 Best Loved Piano Solos BN: Piano Arrangements. 212p. 1991. pap. 16.95 (*0-7692-0338-8*, F3181P3X) Wrner Bros.

100 Best Loved Piano Solos Composer PCS. Warner. 256p. (YA). 1995. pap. 16.95 (*0-89724-520-2*, AF9503) Wrner Bros.

100 Best-Loved Poems. unabridged ed. Ed. by Philip Smith. (Thrift Editions Ser.). 96p. (Orig.). 1995. pap. text 1.00 (*0-486-28553-7*) Dover.

100 Best Managed Companies in North America. Kinni. 288p. write for info. (*0-471-15999-9*) Wiley.

***100 Best Mutual Funds You Can Buy, 2000.** Gordon K. Williamson. 304p. 1999. pap. 12.95 (*1-58062-170-8*) Adams Media.

100 Best Mutual Funds to Own in America. 3rd ed. Gene Walden. LC 98-12372. 371p. 1998. pap. 19.95 (*0-7931-2859-5*) Dearborn.

***100 Best Mutual Funds to Own in America.** 4th ed. Gene Walden. 432p. 2000. pap. 19.95 (*0-7931-3816-7*, 56801104) Dearborn.

***100 Best Mutual Funds You Can Buy 2001.** Gordon K. Williamson. 320p. 2000. pap. 12.95 (*1-58062-424-3*) Adams Media.

O

100 Best Nonfiction Books. Modern Library Staff. pap. 14.95 (*0-375-75504-7*) Random.

100 Best Nonprofits to Work For. Leslie Hamilton & Robert Tragert. LC 97-70018. 352p. 1998. pap. text 16.95 (*0-02-861840-8*, Arc) IDG Bks.

***100 Best Nonprofits to Work For.** 2nd ed. Leslie Hamilton & Robert Tragert. 288p. 2000. pap. 15.95 (*0-7645-6096-4*) IDG Bks.

One Hundred Best Opening Lines. Eric Weber. 1977. reprint ed. pap. 6.95 (*0-914094-02-5*) Symphony Pr.

100 Best Perennials. Elvin McDonald. 1997. pap. 14.00 (*0-679-76028-8*) Random.

100 Best Plants for the Coastal Garden: The Botanical Bones of Great Gardening. Steve Whysall. (Illus.). 256p. 1998. pap. 16.95 (*1-55110-704-X*) Whitecap Bks.

100 Best Pre-Independence Speeches, 1870-1947. H. D. Sharma. LC 98-908214. xiii, 480 p. 1998. 30.00 (*81-7223-324-8*) HarpC.

***100 Best Products of the Century.** B. Martin Pedersen. 240p. 1999. 40.00 (*1-888001-81-X*) Graphis US.

***100 Best Resorts of the Caribbean.** 4th ed. Kay Showker. (Illus.). 2000. pap. 19.95 (*0-7627-0824-7*) Globe Pequot.

***100 Best Restaurants in Ireland 2000.** John McKenna & Sally McKenna. (Illus.). 128p. 2000. pap. 14.95 (*1-874076-34-0*, Pub. by Estragon Pr Ltd) Irish Bks Media.

One Hundred Best Restaurants of Los Angeles & Southern California. 21st ed. Paul Wallach. (Illus.). 600p. 1996. pap. text 14.95 (*0-9619156-9-2*) P Wallach.

One Hundred Best Restaurants of New York City: A Guide to Good Eating at Good Prices for the Budget-Minded. Raoul Gordon. 1981. lib. bdg. 59.95 (*0-8490-3219-9*) Gordon Pr.

100 Best Resumes for Today's Hottest Jobs. Ray Potter. 240p. 1998. pap. 12.95 (*0-02-862187-5*, Arc) IDG Bks.

One Hundred Best Retirement Businesses. Lisa A. Rogak & David H. Bangs, Jr. 393p. 1994. pap. 15.95 (*0-936894-54-7*) Dearborn.

100 Best Romantic Resorts of the Caribbean. 3rd ed. Kay Showker. LC 98-39217. (One Hundred Best Resorts Ser.). (Illus.). 250p. 1998. pap. 18.95 (*0-7627-0323-7*) Globe Pequot.

***100 Best Romantic Resorts of the World: Perfect Places in All Price Ranges for Honeymooners & Others.** 3rd ed. Katharine D. Dyson. (One Hundred Best Resorts Ser.). (Illus.). 352p. 2000. pap. 19.95 (*0-7627-0624-4*) Globe Pequot.

100 Best Safety Savers. 1995. write for info. (*0-9645093-1-8*) Ransom & Benjamin.

100 Best Small Art Towns in America: Where to Discover Creative Communities, Fresh Air, & Affordable Living. 3rd rev. ed. John Villani. LC 98-16900. (Illus.). 256p. 1998. 16.95 (*1-56261-405-3*) Avalon Travel.

100 Best Small Towns. Barbara Lowenstein Association Staff. 1995. pap. 12.00 (*0-671-89300-9*) Prntice Hall Bks.

100 Best Small Towns in America. 2nd ed. Norman Crampton. LC 95-42820. 400p. 1995. 13.95 (*0-02-860577-2*, Arco) Macmillan Gen Ref.

***100 Best Spas of the World.** Bernard I. Burt. (Illus.). 2001. pap. 19.95 (*0-7627-0807-7*) Globe Pequot.

***100 Best Stocks You Can Buy, 2000.** John Slatter. 304p. 1999. pap. 12.95 (*1-58062-169-4*) Adams Media.

***100 Best Stocks to Own for under $20.** Gene Walden. LC 99-29670. (Illus.). 318p. 1999. pap. 19.95 (*0-7931-3230-4*) Dearborn.

***100 Best Stocks to Own for under $25.** 2nd ed. Gene Walden. 2000. pap. 19.95 (*0-7931-3826-4*) Dearborn.

100 Best Stocks to Own in America. 5th ed. Gene Walden. LC 97-28266. 416p. 1997. pap. 22.95 (*0-7931-2574-X*, 5608-1305) Dearborn.

***100 Best Stocks to Own in America.** 6th ed. Gene Walden. 1999. 34.42 (*0-7931-3533-8*) Dearborn.

***100 Best Stocks to Own in America.** 6th ed. Gene Walden. LC 99-43476. 416p. 1999. pap. 22.95 (*0-7931-3169-3*) Dearborn.

***100 Best Stocks You Can Buy 2001.** John Slatter. 352p. 2000. pap. 12.95 (*1-58062-425-1*) Adams Media.

One Hundred Best Treatment Centers for Alcoholism & Drug Abuse. John W. Wright & Linda Sunshine. (Orig.). 1988. pap. 10.95 (*0-380-75489-4*, Avon Bks) Morrow Avon.

100 Best TV Commercials: And Why They Worked. Bernice Kanner. LC 98-47855. (Illus.). 252p. 1999. 29.95 (*0-8129-2995-0*, Times Bks) Crown Pub Group.

100 Bible Games. Edith B. Allen. (Game & Party Bks.). 90p. (YA). (gr. 10 up). 1967. pap. 5.99 (*0-8010-0033-5*) Baker Bks.

One Hundred Bible Lessons see Cien Lecciones Biblicas

One Hundred Bible Stories. Concordia Publishing House Staff. (Illus.). 224p. (J). (gr. k-4). 1998. pap. 9.99 (*0-570-05465-6*, 56-1928) Concordia.

One Hundred Bible Stories Activity Book. Concordia Publishing House Staff. 1998. pap. text 5.50 (*0-570-00663-5*) Concordia.

100 Bible Studies You Need: A Layperson's Guide for Growth. Elmer C. Brown. LC 97-78180. 399p. 1998. 24.95 (*0-9661986-1-1*) Avalon Valley.

$100 Billion Allowance: Getting Your Share of the Global Teen Market. Elissa Moses. LC 00-36494. 256p. 2000. 29.95 (*0-471-29848-4*) Wiley.

One Hundred Billion Suns: The Birth, Life, & Death of the Stars. Rudolf Kippenhahn. Tr. by Jean Steinberg. LC 92-15753. (Science Library). (Illus.). 282p. (C). 1993. pap. 16.95 (*0-691-08781-4*, Pub. by Princeton U Pr) Cal Prin Full Svc.

100 Blackboard Games. rev. ed. Leslie Landin & Linda Hagelin. 48p. (J). (gr. 1-6). 6.99 (*0-86653-919-0*, FE0919) Fearon Teacher Aids.

100 Blackboard Games Series, 4 bks., Set. Les Landin & Linda Hagelin. 26.99 (*1-56417-772-6*, FE0060) Fearon Teacher Aids.

100 Blackboard Math Activities. Les Landin & Linda Hagelin. (100 Blackboard Games Ser.). 48p. 6.99 (*0-86653-921-2*, FE0921) Fearon Teacher Aids.

100 Blackboard Problem-Solving Activities. Les Landin & Linda Hagelin. (100 Blackboard Games Ser.). 48p. 6.99 (*0-86653-922-0*, FE0922) Fearon Teacher Aids.

100 Blackboard Science Activities. Les Landin & Linda Hagelin. (100 Blackboard Games Ser.). 48p. 6.99 (*0-86653-920-4*, FE0920) Fearon Teacher Aids.

One Hundred Blessings Every Day: Daily Twelve Step Recovery Affirmations, Exercises for Personal Growth & Renewal Reflecting Seasons of the Jewish Year. Kerry M. Olitzky. LC 93-9090. 432p. (Orig.). 1993. pap. 14.95 (*1-879045-30-3*) Jewish Lights.

100 Boat Designs Reviewed: Design Commentaries by the Experts. Woodenboat Publications Staff. (Illus.). 260p. 1997. pap. text 24.95 (*0-937822-44-2*) WoodenBoat Pubns.

One Hundred Books about Bookmaking. Hellmut Lehmann-Haupt. LC 75-34148. 87p. 1976. reprint ed. lib. bdg. 55.00 (*0-8371-8546-7*, LEOB, Greenwood Pr) Greenwood.

***100 Books for Girls to Grow on.** Shireen Dodson. LC 98-27606. 352p. 1998. pap. 14.00 (*0-06-095718-2*, Perennial) HarperTrade.

One Hundred Booming Years. George B. Anderson. Ed. by H. J. Row & D. Stupek. LC 80-65338. (Illus.). 305p. 1980. 55.00 (*0-9604136-0-X*) Bucyrus-Erie Co.

100 Briefe Deutsch fur Export & Import: Langenscheidts Musterbriefe. Von B. Abegg. (GER.). 160p. 1997. pap. 15.95 (*3-468-41112-X*) Langenscheidt.

***100 Bullets: First Shot, Last Call.** Brian Azzarello. (Illus.). 128p. 2000. pap. text 9.95 (*1-56389-645-1*, Pub. by DC Comics) Time Warner.

100 Calligraphic Alphabets. Dan X. Solo. LC 97-22680. (Dover Pictorial Archives Ser.). 1997. pap. 8.95 (*0-486-29798-5*) Dover.

One Hundred Carols for Choirs. Ed. by David Willcocks & John Rutter. 384p. 1988. pap. 17.95 (*0-19-353227-1*) OUP.

***100 Cars 100 Years: The First Century of the Automobile.** Fred Winkowski & Frank Sullivan. LC 99-47737. (100 Years Ser.). (Illus.). 160p. 2000. 19.98 (*0-7651-1016-4*) Smithmark.

One Hundred Case Histories for the MRCP. 3rd ed. Peter S. Sever et al. LC 93-10622. 1993. pap. text 19.95 (*0-443-04701-4*) Church.

One Hundred Case Histories in Obstetrics & Gynaecology. Michael D. Gillmer et al. 264p. (Orig.). 1991. pap. text 35.95 (*0-443-02465-0*) Church.

100 Case Histories MRCP. 2nd ed. Spalaton. 1989. pap. text 19.00 (*0-443-02140-6*, W B Saunders Co) Harcrt Hlth Sci Grp.

100 Celebrated Chinese Women. Illus. by Lu Yanguang. 227p. 1994. 19.95 (*981-3029-81-1*, Pub. by Asiapac) China Bks.

100 Center Guide to Commercial Property, 1975-1976. 1976. 40.00 (*0-8464-4431-3*) Beekman Pubs.

One Hundred Centuries of Solitude: Redirecting America's High-Level Nuclear Waste Policy. James Flynn. 129p. (C). 1995. pap. 65.00 (*0-8133-8915-1*, Pub. by Westview) HarpC.

100 Challenging Go Problems for 100 Days of Study. Hihon Kiin Staff. Tr. by Robert J. Terry. LC 96-163981. (Illus.). 212p. 1995. pap. text 14.95 (*0-9641847-4-5*) Yutopian Ent.

100 Chess Gems. P. Wenman. (Illus.). 150p. 1999. reprint ed. text 15.00 (*0-7881-6272-1*) DIANE Pub.

One Hundred Children's Classics. Brimhall. (Children's Classics Ser.). 1990. 12.95 (*0-685-32041-3*, O109) Hansen Ed Mus.

100 Chinese Emperors. Tr. by Wang Xuewen & Wang Yanxi. (Illus.). 218p. 1996. 19.95 (*981-3029-96-X*, Pub. by Asiapac) China Bks.

One Hundred Choice Selections, No. 8. Ed. by Phineas Garrett. 1977. 19.95 (*0-8369-6342-3*) Ayer.

One Hundred Choice Selections, No. 9. Ed. by Phineas Garrett. 1977. 19.95 (*0-8369-6343-1*) Ayer.

One Hundred Choice Selections, No. 10. Ed. by Phineas Garrett. 1977. 19.95 (*0-8369-6344-X*) Ayer.

One Hundred Choice Selections, No. 15. 3rd ed. Ed. by Phineas Garrett. 1977. 19.95 (*0-8369-6361-X*) Ayer.

One Hundred Choice Selections, No. 19. Ed. by Phineas Garrett. 1977. 20.95 (*0-8369-6362-8*) Ayer.

One Hundred Choice Selections, No. 20. Ed. by Phineas Garrett. 1977. 19.95 (*0-8369-6363-6*) Ayer.

One Hundred Choice Selections, Vols. 1,2,4,5,7,18 & Ed. by Phineas Garrett. Incl. Vol. 2. LC 78-133069. 1977. 18.95 (*0-8369-6198-6*); Vol. 4. LC 78-133069. 1977. 18.95 (*0-8369-6199-4*); Vol. 5. LC 78-133069. 1977. 18.95 (*0-8369-6254-0*); Vol. 7. LC 78-133069. 1977. 19.95 (*0-8369-6255-9*); Vol. 18. LC 78-133069. 1977. 18.95 (*0-8369-6256-7*); Vol. 31. LC 78-133069. 1977. 19.95 (*0-8369-6269-9*); LC 78-133069. (Granger Index Reprint Ser.). 18.95 (*0-8369-6197-8*) Ayer.

***100 Christian Books That Changed the Century.** William J. Petersen & Randy Petersen. 224p. 2000. pap. 12.99 (*0-8007-5735-1*) Chosen Bks.

100 Classic Backcountry Ski & Snowboard Routes in Washington. Rainer Burgdorfer. LC 99-6535. 1999. pap. 17.95 (*0-89886-661-8*) Mountaineers.

100 Classic Cocktails. Barry Shelby. LC 97-38699. (Tiny Folio Ser.). (Illus.). 288p. 1998. 11.95 (*0-7892-0426-6*) Abbeville Pr.

100 Classic Folk & Bluegrass Songs: Words to Your Favorite Old Time Mountain Music. large type ed. J. R. Miller & Nita Q. Miller. (Illus.). 128p. (Orig.). 1997. pap., spiral bd. 15.00 (*0-9636500-3-3*) Flying M Grp.

***100 Classic Hikes in Arizona.** 2nd ed. Scott S. Warren. (100 Hikes in Ser.). (Illus.). 208p. 2000. pap. 19.95 (*0-89886-651-0*) Mountaineers.

***100 Classic Hikes in Northern California.** 2nd ed. John R. Soares & Marc J. Soares. (100 Hikes in Ser.). (Illus.). 208p. 2000. pap. 19.95 (*0-89886-702-9*) Mountaineers.

100 Classic Hikes in Washington: North Cascades, Olympics, Mount Rainier & South Cascades, Alpine Lakes, Glacier Peak. Ira Spring & Harvey Manning. LC 98-13632. (One Hundred Hikes Ser.). (Illus.). 256p. 1998. pap. 19.95 (*0-89886-586-7*) Mountaineers.

One Hundred Classical Themes for Clarinet. Martin Firth. (Illus.). 64p. 1991. pap. 12.95 (*0-7119-2588-7*, AM84161) Music Sales.

One Hundred Classical Themes for Flute. Martin Frith. (Illus.). 64p. 1991. pap. 12.95 (*0-7119-2589-5*, AM84179) Music Sales.

One Hundred Classical Themes for Saxophone. Martin Frith. (Illus.). 64p. 1991. pap. 12.95 (*0-7119-2586-0*, AM84146) Music Sales.

One Hundred Classical Themes for Violin. Martin Frith. (Illus.). 64p. 1991. pap. 12.95 (*0-7119-2587-9*, AM84153) Music Sales.

100 Classics of the Chessboard. A. S. Dickens & H. Ebert. (Illus.). 217p. 1998. pap. text 17.00 (*0-7881-5651-9*) DIANE Pub.

One Hundred Classics of the Chessboard. Anthony S. Dickins & Hilmar Ebert. (Chess Ser.). 208p. 1983. 25.90 (*0-08-026921-4*, Pergamon Pr); pap. 13.90 (*0-08-026920-6*, Pergamon Pr) Elsevier.

***100 Clear Grammar Tests: Reproducible Grammar Tests for Beginning to Intermediate ESL/Self Classes.** Keith S. Folse et al. (Illus.). 216p. (C). 2000. pap. text 29.95 (*0-472-08654-5*, 08654) U of Mich Pr.

100 Clever Crosswords. Thomas Joseph. (Illus.). 128p. 1998. pap. 5.95 (*0-8069-1757-1*) Sterling.

100 Colleges Where Average Students Can Excel. Joanne Adler. LC 96-78703. 1997. 14.95 (*0-02-861044-X*, Arc) IDG Bks.

One Hundred Color & Activity Book: Tom & Jerry. 56p. (J). (ps-3). pap. write for info. (*1-57041-000-3*) Rose Art Indust.

100 Common Clubmaking Questions. Jeff Jackson. (Illus.). 295p. 1995. pap. text 29.95 (*0-614-04191-0*) Dyna Golf Prods.

***One Hundred Companies Receiving the Largest Dollar Volume of Prime Contract Awards, Fiscal Year 1997.** 36p. 1998. pap. 3.50 (*0-16-061135-0*) USGPO.

Illegal Withholding Tax. Max. (Illus.). 45p. (Orig.). 1997. pap. 35.00 (*0-922070-30-X*) M Tecton Pub.

One Hundred Contractors Receiving The Largest Dollar Volume of Prime Contract Awards for Research, Development, Test & Evaluation, Fiscal Year 1996. 21p. 1997. pap. 2.50 (*0-16-061124-5*) USGPO.

***One Hundred Contractors Receiving the Largest Dollar Volume of Prime Contract Awards for Research, Development, Test & Evaluation, Fiscal Year 1997.** 21p. 1998. pap. 3.75 (*0-16-061140-7*) USGPO.

100 Crafts for Preschoolers. (One Hundred Ser.). (J). 1990. 6.99 (*1-55513-140-9*, 70821) Cook.

One Hundred Cranes: Praying with the Chorus of Creation. William J. Fitzgerald. LC 96-11900. (Illus.). 143p. 1996. pap. 9.95 (*0-939516-31-4*) Forest Peace.

100 Dairy Production-Health Sheets. 1995. 8.95 (*0-944079-10-5*) Lessiter Pubns.

100 Days. Anne Rockwell. 40p. (ps). pap. 14.95 (*0-06-029144-3*) HarpC.

100 Days. Anne Rockwell. 40p. (ps-1). pap. 5.95 (*0-06-443727-2*); lib. bdg. 14.89 (*0-06-029145-1*) HarpC.

***One Hundred Days: My Unexpected Journey from Doctor to Patient.** David Biro. LC 99-34956. 304p. 2000. 23.00 (*0-375-40715-4*) Pantheon.

One Hundred Days: Napoleon's Road to Waterloo. Alan Schom. (Illus.). 320p. 1992. text 28.00 (*0-689-12097-4*) Atheneum Yung Read.

One Hundred Days: Napoleon's Road to Waterloo. Alan Schom. (Illus.). 432p. 1993. reprint ed. pap. 12.95 (*0-19-508177-3*) OUP.

One Hundred Days: The Memoirs of the Falklands Battle Group Commander. Sandy Woodward & Patrick Robinson. LC 91-66210. (Bluejacket Books Ser.). (Illus.). 408p. 1997. pap. 16.95 (*1-55750-652-3*) Naval Inst Pr.

100 Days in the Life of a Superboss: Motivating People to Achieve Phenomenal Results. David Freemantle. 216p. 1998. pap. 16.95 (*0-07-022154-5*, BusinessWeek Bks) McGraw.

100 Days in the Life of a Superboss: Stimulating People to Achieve Phenomenal Results. LC 96-6713. 1997. pap. text write for info. (*0-07-709344-5*) McGraw.

***100 Days of Fun at School.** Janet Craig. LC 98-208163. (First Start Easy Reader Ser.). 1998. pap. text 2.95 (*0-8167-4541-2*) Troll Communs.

***100 Days of School.** Trudy Harris. LC 98-18952. (Illus.). (J). (gr. k-3). 1999. lib. bdg. 21.90 (*0-7613-1271-4*) Millbrook Pr.

***100 Days of School.** Trudy Harris. (Illus.). (J). 2000. pap. 7.95 (*0-7613-1431-8*) Millbrook Pr.

100 Days to Better Health, Good Sex & Long Life: A Guide to Taoist Yoga & Chi Kung. Eric S. Yupelove. LC 97-33493. (Illus.). 320p. (Orig.). 1999. pap. 17.95 (*1-56718-833-8*) Llewellyn Pubns.

One Hundred Deadliest Karate Moves. Ted Gambordella. (Illus.). 88p. 1981. pap. 18.00 (*0-87364-245-7*) Paladin Pr.

100 Decisive Battles. Paul K. Davis. LC 99-47618. (Illus.). 468p. 1999. lib. bdg. 75.00 (*1-57607-075-1*) ABC-CLIO.

One Hundred Decorative Condensed Alphabets. Selected by Dan X. Solo. LC 93-21478. (Pictorial Archive Ser.). 112p. 1993. 6.95 (*0-486-27849-2*) Dover.

One Hundred Desert Wildflowers of the Southwest. Janice E. Bowers. Ed. by T. J. Priehs. LC 88-63877. (Illus.). 64p. (Orig.). 1987. pap. 7.95 (*0-911408-72-X*) SW Pks Mnmts.

100 Designers' Favorite Rooms: Selected Projects of the World's Finest Designers & Architects. John L. Pellam. (Illus.). 236p. 1993. 30.00 (*1-882292-00-6*) Barons Whos Who.

100 Designers' Favorite Rooms: Selected Projects of the World's Finest Designers & Architects. 2nd ed. John L. Pellam. (Illus.). 236p. 1994. 45.00 (*1-882292-03-0*) Barons Whos Who.

100 Designers' Favorite Rooms: Selected Projects of the World's Finest Designers & Architects. 3rd ed. John L. Pellam. (Illus.). 236p. 1996. 45.00 (*1-882292-06-5*) Barons Whos Who.

100 Desserts Kids. Robin Zinberg. 1993. pap. 3.99 (*0-425-13817-8*) Berkley Pub.

One Hundred Details. Kenneth Clark. (Illus.). 120p. 1991. write for info. (*0-318-68195-1*) HUP.

One Hundred Details. Kenneth Clark. (Illus.). 120p. 1991. pap. text 22.00 (*0-674-63863-8*, CLAONX) HUP.

$100 Hamburger: A Guide to Pilots' Favorite Fly-In Restaurants. John F. Purner. LC 98-16271. (Illus.). 352p. 1998. pap. 24.95 (*0-07-083714-7*) McGraw.

One Hundred Dollar Misunderstanding. Robert Gover. LC 80-19795. 256p. 1989. pap. 10.95 (*0-8021-3181-6*, Grove) Grove-Atltic.

One Hundred Drawings. Gustav Klimt. 99p. (Orig.). 1972. pap. 8.95 (*0-486-22446-5*) Dover.

One Hundred Drawings in the Chrysler Museum at Norfolk. Eric M. Zafran. LC 79-83564. (Illus.). 145p. 1979. pap. 4.95 (*0-940744-22-8*) Chrysler Museum.

One Hundred Drugs That Work: A Guide to Prescription & Non-Prescription Drugs. Mike Oppenheim. 348p. 1994. 22.95 (*1-56565-115-4*) Lowell Hse.

100 Early American Residential Details: Collection A28. Mike Tecton. (Illus.). 64p. 1998. reprint ed. pap. 32.00 (*1-58203-013-8*, A28) M Tecton Pub.

100 Easy Listening. Ed. by Carol Cuellar. 228p. (Orig.). 1995. pap. text 17.95 (*0-89724-801-5*, PF0540A) Wrner Bros.

***100 Easy Talk Thoughts for LDS Youth.** Sandra N. Harper & Joseph Harper. 1999. pap. 10.95 (*1-55517-417-5*) CFI Dist.

***100 Easy Talk Thoughts for LDS Youth, Vol. II.** Sandra N. Harper & Joseph Harper. 1999. pap. 10.95 (*1-55517-445-0*) CFI Dist.

100 Easy-to-Grow Native Plants: For American Gardens in Temperate Zones. Lorraine Johnson. (Illus.). 160p. 1999. pap. 19.95 (*1-55209-327-1*) Firefly Bks Ltd.

100 ECG Problems. John R. Hampton. LC 97-7204. 1997. pap. text 18.95 (*0-443-05678-1*) Church.

One Hundred Eight Animal Patterns. Tom James Wolfe. (Illus.). 64p. (YA). (gr. 10-13). 1996. pap. 9.95 (*0-88740-962-8*) Schiffer.

108 Insights into Tai Chi Chuan: A String of Pearls. 2nd ed. Michael Gilman. LC 97-62400. (Tai Chi Treasures Ser.). (Illus.). 128p. 1998. pap. 10.95 (*1-886969-58-2*, B031/582) YMAA Pubn.

108 Names of Ganesha. Vijaya Kumar. LC 97-914116. 108p. 1997. write for info. (*81-207-2012-1*) Sterling Pubs.

108 Portraits. limited ed. Gus Van Sant. (Illus.). 116p. 1992. 200.00 (*0-944092-23-3*) Twin Palms Pub.

***108 Questions Children Ask about Friends & School.** Dave Veerman. LC 99-12588. (Questions Children Ask Ser.). (Illus.). 108p. 1999. pap. 10.99 (*0-8423-5182-5*) Tyndale Hse.

108 Recipes: Gourmet Vegetarian Cooking from Nyingma Institute. 177p. pap. 15.00 (*0-9639130-0-X*) Dharma Pub.

108 Twentieth Century Spanish Poets. 400p. 1991. text 155.00 (*0-8103-4588-9*) Gale.

118 Tips for Creating the Perfect Customer. Terry L. Mayfield. Ed. by Stacey E. Mayfield. 16p. 1997. 5.00 (*1-890805-15-7*) Motivat Discov.

180 Days Around the World: Learning about Countries & Cultures Through Research & Thinking-Skills Activities. Shirley Cook. Ed. by Jan Keeling. (Illus.). 240p. (J). (gr. 4-8). 1993. pap. text 16.95 (*0-86530-253-7*, 253-7) Incentive Pubns.

180 Days of Character. Donna B. Forrest. (Illus.). (J). (gr. k-12). 1998. pap. 8.95 (*1-889636-10-X*) Youtlight.

One Hundred Eighty Degree Theory: How to Become Mentally Self-Sufficient. Robert O. Nara & Steven A. Mariner. LC 79-90866. 194p. 1979. pap. write for info. (*0-933420-02-1*) Oramedics Intl.

185 Sales Tips for Sure-Fire Success. Robert F. Taylor. 234p. 1995. pap. 24.50 (*0-85013-233-9*) Dartnell Corp.

180 Hidden Pictures for Articulation Practice. Sharon G. Webber. (Illus.). 180p. (J). 1991. spiral bd. 26.95 (*1-58650-025-2*, BK-216) Super Duper.

180 Icebreakers to Strengthen Critical Thinking & Problem-Solving Skills. Imogene Forte & Sandra Schurr. Ed. by Anna Quinn. LC 96-205230. 96p. (Orig.). (J). (gr. 5-8). 1996. pap. text 10.95 (*0-86530-345-2*, IP 345-2) Incentive Pubns.

189 Ways to Contact God. Marlene Halpin. LC 99-26830. 190p. 1999. pap. 10.95 (*0-8294-1365-0*) Loyola Pr.

180 Seconds at Willow Park. Rick Lynch. 1998. 21.95 (*0-7871-1601-7*, NewStar Pr) NewStar Media.

187 Men to Avoid. Danielle Brown. LC 95-190728. 96p. (Orig.). 1995. pap. 7.95 (*0-425-14783-5*) Berkley Pub.

187 Things Teenagers Should Know Before Leaving Home'--Love, Mom. Lisa Zawodny-Obergfell. LC 98-90537. 1999. pap. 8.95 (*0-533-12836-6*) Vantage.

187th Airborne. 2nd ed. William Webber. (Illus.). 352p. Date not set. 49.95 (*1-56311-290-6*) Turner Pub KY.

182 Bible Questions Answered: Scriptural Solutions to Practical & Perplexing Questions. R. A. Torrey. LC 90-35988. 128p. 1990. 4.99 (*0-8254-3844-6*) Kregel.

100 Elegies for Modernity. John Leonard. LC 97-152974. (Illus.). 1997. write for info. (*0-86806-617-6*) Hale & Iremnger.

111 American Literary Biographers. 2nd ed. 400p. 1991. text 155.00 (*0-8103-4591-9*) Gale.

111 Days to Zion: The Day by Day Trek of the Mormon Pioneers. Hal Knight & Stanley B. Kimball. (Illus.). 256p. 1997. reprint ed. pap. 14.95 (*0-9656694-0-8*) Big Moon Traders.

111 Viennese Dishes. Gertrude A. Ulrich. pap. 11.95 (*0-87557-103-4*) Saphrograph.

111 Dynamite Ways to Ace Your Interview. Richard Fein. LC 96-44481. 176p. 1997. pap. 13.95 (*1-57023-065-X*) Impact VA.

One Hundred Eleven Yard & Garden Projects. 1991. 25.95 (*0-8306-5302-3*) McGraw-Hill Prof.

One Hundred Eleventh Annual Exhibition - "9" Text by Patricia Davidson. (Illus.). 29p. (Orig.). 1992. pap. 5.00 (*0-930495-18-7*) San Fran Art Inst.

One Hundred English Folksongs for Medium Voice. Ed. by Cecil J. Sharp. LC 75-12133. 235p. 1975. reprint ed. pap. 13.95 (*0-486-23192-5*) Dover.

One Hundred English Gardens: The Best of the English Heritage Parks & Gardens. Patrick Taylor. LC 95-31992. (Illus.). 208p. 1996. 40.00 (*0-8478-1935-3*, Pub. by Rizzoli Intl) St Martin.

One Hundred Epic Events of Wold War II in Stamps. Fleetwood Publications Staff. 63p. 1995. 150.00 (*0-913376-50-7*) Fleetwood Pubns.

One Hundred Epigrams: From the Greek Anthology. Tr. by Richard O'Connell. 1977. pap. 10.00 (*0-685-63924-X*) Atlantis Edns.

100 Essay Plans for Economics. Ernie Jowsey. LC 97-36678. (Illus.). 272p. 1998. pap. text (*0-19-877592-X*) OUP.

100 Essential Books for Irish-American Readers. Morgan Llywelyn. (Illus.). 256p. 1998. 24.95 (*0-8065-1957-6*, Citadel Pr) Carol Pub Group.

***100 Essential Books for Jewish Readers.** Daniel B. Syme & Cindy F. Kanter. 315p. 1999. reprint ed. text 27.00 (*0-7881-6680-8*) DIANE Pub.

One Hundred Essential Books for Jewish Readers. Daniel B. Syme & Cindy F. Kanter. LC 97-34613. 288p. 1997. 27.50 (*0-8065-1906-1*, Citadel Pr) Carol Pub Group.

One Hundred Essential Guitar Chords. 32p. pap. 14.95 (*0-7119-3197-6*, AM90135) Omnibus NY.

100 Events that Shaped World History. Bill Yenne. (Illus.). 112p. (Orig.). 1993. pap. 7.95 (*0-912517-03-4*) Bluewood Bks.

O

100 Everyday Words to Read, Write, & Understand: A Guide for Teaching the Instant Usage of High Frequency Words. Darlene Mannix. (C). 1996. pap. text 29.00 (*0-89079-645-9*) PRO-ED.

100 Excuses for Kids. Mike Joyer & Zack Robert. Ed. by Cynthia Black. (Kids' Books by Kids Ser.). (Illus.). 96p. (Orig.). (YA). 1990. pap. 5.95 (*0-941831-48-5*) Beyond Words Pub.

100 Explorers Who Shaped World History. Bill Yenne. (One Hundred Ser.). (Illus.). 112p. (Orig.). 1996. pap. 7.95 (*0-912517-22-0*) Bluewood Bks.

100 Faces of Health Care. American Hospital Pub Staff. 1999. pap. text 60.00 (*1-55648-276-0*) AHPI.

100 Families Who Shaped World History. Samuel W. Crompton. 1998. pap. 7.95 (*0-912517-34-4*) Bluewood Bks.

One Hundred Famous American Festivals & Their Foods. Compiled by Helen Naismith. LC 75-30398. (Illus.). 1979. pap. 12.95 (*0-933718-30-6*) Browning Pubns.

One Hundred Famous Americans. Helen A. Smith. LC 72-5677. (Essay Index Reprint Ser.). 1977. reprint ed. 41.95 (*0-8369-7286-4*) Ayer.

***100 Famous Sieges in History.** Paul K. Davis. 2001. lib. bdg. 65.00 (*1-57607-195-2*) ABC-CLIO.

One Hundred Favorite Fiddle Tunes. Bill Guest. 68p. 1980. pap. 9.95 (*0-87166-922-6*, 93730) Mel Bay.

100 Favorite Flowering Shrubs. Pat Kite. LC 99-18984. (One Hundred Favorite Ser.). (Illus.). 120p. 1999. 15.98 (*1-56799-699-X*, MetroBooks) M Friedman Pub Grp Inc.

One Hundred Favorite Folktales. Ed. by Stith Thompson. LC 68-27355. (Illus.). 456p. (J). 1968. 39.95 (*0-253-15940-7*); pap. 18.95 (*0-253-20172-1*, MB-172) Ind U Pr.

100 Favorite Garden Wildflowers. Teri Dunn. LC 99-18983. (One Hundred Favorite Ser.). (Illus.). 120p. 1999. 15.98 (*1-56799-641-8*, MetroBooks) M Friedman Pub Grp Inc.

100 Favorite Herbs. Teri Dunn. LC 98-152307. (Illus.). 120p. 1998. 15.98 (*1-56799-526-8*, MetroBooks) M Friedman Pub Grp Inc.

100 Favorite Perennials. Teri Dunn. LC 96-34520. (Illus.). 120p. 1998. 15.98 (*1-56799-527-6*, MetroBooks) M Friedman Pub Grp Inc.

100 Favorite Plants for Shade. Teri Dunn. LC 99-18982. (One Hundred Favorite Ser.). (Illus.). 120p. 1999. 15.98 (*1-56799-653-1*, MetroBooks) M Friedman Pub Grp Inc.

100 Favorite Roses. Teri Dunn. LC 96-34521. (Illus.). 120p. 1997. 15.98 (*1-56799-435-0*, Friedman-Fairfax) M Friedman Pub Grp Inc.

Easy Way to Play. Reader's Digest Editors. LC 97-701256. 224p. 1996. 30.00 (*0-89577-833-5*, Pub. by RD Assn) Penguin Putnam.

100 Favourite Nursery Rhymes. Ladybird Staff. 1999. text 4.99 (*0-7214-2020-6*, Ladybrd) Penguin Putnam.

153 "Fold & Say" Artic Stories: S, R, L, D, CH, SH, TH, F, G, K, T, V, S, R, L Blends. Illus. by Chris Parker et al. 185p. (J). (gr. k-5). 1997. spiral bd., wbk. ed. 34.95 (*1-58650-062-7*, BK-259) Super Duper.

One Hundred-Fifteen Saintly Fun Facts. Bernadette M. Snyder. LC 93-78618. (Illus.). 144p. (J). 1993. pap. 8.95 (*0-89243-562-3*) Liguori Pubns.

105th Congress Guide. (Illus.). Date not set. pap. 17.00 (*0-939900-55-6*) Soc Human Resc Mgmt.

One Hundred Fiftieth Anniversary Cookbook. June Towers. Ed. by Richard Brown. (Illus.). 162p. (Orig.). 1993. pap. write for info. (*0-9637402-0-2*) Brown Comm.

150th Anniversary of St. Peter's Episcopal Church: 1844-1944 Cazenovia, New York. Ed. by William Strode & Marion Bickford. (Illus.). 124p. (C). 1995. pap. 30.00 (*1-56469-026-1*) Harmony Hse Pub.

150th Anniversary of the Settlement of Boscowen & Webster, Merrimack Co. Also Births Recorded on the Town Records from 1733 to 1850 & Biographical Sketches. (Illus.). 211p. 1998. reprint ed. pap. 24.50 (*0-8328-9713-2*); reprint ed. lib. bdg. 34.50 (*0-8328-9712-4*) Higginson Bk Co.

150 Most-Asked Questions about Midlife Sex, Love & Intimacy: What Women & Their Partners Really Want to Know. Ruth S. Jacobowitz. 1996. pap. 10.00 (*0-614-97847-5*, Quil) HarperTrade.

***One Hundred Fifty & Beyond: Healthy, Happy & Prosperous Lifestyle to Any Age...** Doug White. 70p. 1999. 89.95 (*1-888369-05-1*) Searchlight.

150 & More Basic NMR Experiments. 2nd ed. Siegmar Braun. 610p. 1998. pap. 69.95 (*3-527-29512-7*, Wiley-VCH) Wiley.

One-Hundred Fifty Best Companies for Liberal Arts Graduates: How to Get a Winning Job in Tough Times. Cheryl Woodruff & Greg Ptacek. LC 93-13998. 304p. 1992. pap. 15.95 (*0-471-54793-X*) Wiley.

One Hundred Fifty Careers in Health Care. rev. ed. 555p. 1993. 59.95 (*0-87228-054-3*) US Direct Serv.

150 Delicious Squares. Jean Pare. 160p. 1989. pap. 10.99 (*0-9690695-0-2*) Companys Coming.

One Hundred Fifty-Eight Pound Marriage. John Irving. 256p. 1990. mass mkt. 5.99 (*0-345-36743-X*) Ballantine Pub Grp.

One Hundred Fifty-Eight Pound Marriage. John Irving. 1997. pap. 11.00 (*0-345-41796-8*) Ballantine Pub Grp.

One Hundred Fifty Eight Saxophone Exercises. S. M. Rascher. 68p. 1986. pap. 10.95 (*0-7935-5431-4*, 50332850) H Leonard.

150 Extra-Easy Ornaments in Plastic Canvas, Bk. 9. Leisure Arts Staff. 96p. 1997. pap. 15.95 (*1-57486-044-5*) Oxmoor Hse.

One Hundred Fifty Facts about Grieving Children. Erin Linn. 96p. (Orig.). 1990. pap. 6.00 (*0-9614636-3-5*) Pub Mark.

***151st Pennsylvania Volunteers in Gettysburg: Ripe Apples in a Storm.** Michael A. Dreese. LC 99-89289. (Illus.). 200p. 2000. 45.00 (*0-7864-0804-9*) McFarland & Co.

155 Awesome Ideas to Energize Any VBS! John Cutshall. LC 98-21731. 112p. 1998. per. 14.99 (*0-7644-2118-2*, Vital Ministry) Group Pub.

155 Legal Do's (And Dont's) for the Small Business. Paul Adams. LC 96-17961. 256p. 1996. pap. 18.95 (*0-471-13161-X*) Wiley.

One Hundred Fifty-Five Mile per Gallon California Commuter. Douglas J. Malewicki. 8p. 1984. 3.00 (*0-912468-30-0*) CA Rocketry.

One Hundred Fifty Fun Facts Found in the Bible: For Kids of All Ages. Bernadette M. Snyder. LC 90-70802. (Illus.). 144p. (J). (gr. 1-6). 1990. pap. 8.95 (*0-89243-330-2*) Liguori Pubns.

150 Fun-to-Stitch Projects. Ed. by Laura Scott. LC 97-76986. (Illus.). 176p. 1998. 19.95 (*1-882138-33-3*) Hse White Birches.

One-Hundred Fifty International Favorites - C Book. 80p. (Orig.). 1993. pap. 12.95 (*0-89724-068-5*, IF0514) Wrner Bros.

One-Hundred Fifty International Favorites - E Flat Book. 80p. (Orig.). 1993. pap. 12.95 (*0-89724-069-3*, IF0515) Wrner Bros.

One Hundred Fifty Jahre Archaeologische Gesellschaft zu Berlin. Ed. by Ursula Kaestner & Adolf Borbein. (Winckelmannsprogramm der Archaologischen Gesellschaft zu Berlin Ser.: No. 134). (GER., Illus.). viii, 43p. (Orig.). (C). 1993. pap. text 32.35 (*3-11-014054-3*) De Gruyter.

150 Japanese Polearm Terms. rev. ed. W. M. Hawley. Ed. by Panchita Seyssel-Hawley. (Illus.). 27p. 1997. pap. 9.95 (*0-910704-37-6*) Hawley.

One Hundred Fifty Masterpieces of Drawing. Anthony Toney. (Illus.). 150p. (Orig.). 1963. pap. 9.95 (*0-486-21032-4*) Dover.

One Hundred-Fifty More Stories for Preachers & Teachers. Jack McArdle. LC 92-82675. 96p. (Orig.). 1993. pap. 7.95 (*0-89622-540-2*) Twenty-Third.

150 Most Asked Questions about Midlife Sex, Love & Intimacy: What Women & Their Partners Really Want to Know. Ruth S. Jacobowitz. 336p. 1996. pap. 10.00 (*0-688-14767-4*, Quil) HarperTrade.

150 Most-Asked Questions about Menopause: What Women Really Want to Know. Ruth S. Jacobowitz. LC 96-17715. 1996. pap. 10.00 (*0-688-14768-2*, Quil) HarperTrade.

150 Most Asked Questions about Osteoporosis: What Women Really Want to Know. Ruth S. Jacobowitz. LC 96-17714. 224p. 1996. pap. 10.00 (*0-688-14769-0*, Quil) HarperTrade.

***150 Most Profitable Home Businesses for Women.** Katina Z. Jones. LC 99-58541. 224p. 2000. pap. 9.95 (*1-58062-299-2*) Adams Media.

***150 Nifty Super Crafts.** Cambria Cohen. (Illus.). (J). 2000. pap. 9.95 (*0-7373-0514-2*) Lowell Hse Juvenile.

One Hundred Fifty-One Brand New Old Time Fiddle Tunes: By Pacific Northwest Fiddle Champions. Ed. by Vivian T. Williams. (Brand New Old Time Fiddle Tunes Ser.: Vol. 1). 50p. (Orig.). 1983. 6.95 (*0-9631484-0-0*) Voyager Rec.

One Hundred Fifty-One Fun Activities to Increase Your Child's IQ: Will Your Children Be Successful? This Program Is for People Who Care! unabridged ed. Simone Bibeau. 16p. (J). (ps-6). 1986. pap. text 25.00 incl. audio (*0-940406-15-2*, 015) Perception Pubns.

One Hundred Fifty-One Secrets of Insurance Direct Marketing Practices Revealed. Donald R. Jackson. LC 88-32365. 394p. 1989. 44.75 (*0-930950-38-0*) Nopoly Pr.

151 Sermon Outlines. Jabez Burns. LC 86-27520. (Sermon Outline Ser.). 224p. 1987. pap. 11.99 (*0-8254-2266-3*) Kregel.

One Hundred Fifty-One Ways to Raise Your Self-Esteem: A Book of Activities That Will Enhance Your Life. Libby Rosenauer. (Aware Person Ser.). (Illus.). 96p. (Orig.). 1993. pap. 9.95 (*1-881762-00-9*) Aware Pr.

150 Opening & Closing Prayers. Carl Koch. 72p. 1990. pap. 4.95 (*0-88489-241-7*) St Marys.

150 Plus! Games & Activities for Early Childhood. Zane A. Spencer. LC 75-32842. (J). (ps-k). 1976. 8.99 (*0-8224-5068-2*, FE5068) Fearon Teacher Aids.

***150 + Easy Science Experiements.** (Illus.). 128p. (YA). (gr. 5). 1999. pap. text 11.95 (*1-58037-107-8*, Pub. by M Twain Media) Carson-Dellos.

150 Practice ECGs. George J. Taylor. (Illus.). 224p. 1997. pap. 29.95 (*0-86542-511-6*) Blackwell Sci.

One Hundred Fifty Questions for a Guerrilla. Alberto Bayo. Ed. by Robert K. Brown. Tr. by Hugo Hartenstein & Dennis Harber from SPA. LC 63-2215. (Illus.). 96p. 1963. pap. 15.00 (*0-87364-022-5*) Paladin Pr.

150 Reasons Why I Can't Serve on Jury Duty, 2 vols., Vol. 1. large type ed. Minnie Dix. LC 96-94614. (Illus.). 70p. 1999. pap. 7.95 (*0-7392-0092-5*, PO2968) Morris Pubng.

157 of America's Favorite Hot Dog Recipes. Illus. by James Knake & Laurie McDonald. 212p. 1998. pap. 14.95 (*0-9670403-0-2*) H & H Prodns.

One Hundred Fifty-Seventh New York Volunteer (Infantry) Reigment, 1862-1865: Madison & Cortland Counties. Isabel Bracy. LC 91-14111. 126p. (Orig.). 1991. pap. 12.00 (*1-55787-080-2*, NY27032) Hrt of the Lakes.

156 Best of Rodgers & Hart. (E-Z Play Today Ser.). 48p. 1996. pap. 6.95 (*0-7935-6942-7*) H Leonard.

150 Skill-Building Reference Lists: Language Remediation & Expansion. Catharine S. Bush. (Illus.). 268p. 1989. pap. text 29.00 (*0-7616-7559-0*) Commun Skill.

150 Solitaire Games. D. Brown. 144p. 1991. pap. 10.00 (*0-06-092315-6*) HarpC.

150 Songs with Just 3 Chords. Julia Pena. 184p. (YA). pap. 16.95 (*0-943748-47-X*, PF0723) Ekay Music.

***150 Nifty Super Rainy-Day Activities.** Eric Ladizinsky. (Illus.). (J). 2000. pap. 9.95 (*0-7373-0515-0*) Lowell Hse Juvenile.

One Hundred Fifty Thematic Writings. UK. 128p. (gr. 3-7). 1993. pap. 14.95 (*0-590-49244-6*) Scholastic Inc.

150 Things You Should Know about Security. Louis A. Tyska & Lawrence J. Fennelly. LC 97-23801. 224p. 1997. pap. 34.95 (*0-7506-9833-0*) Buttrwrth-Heinemann.

153 Fun Things to Do in Austin & the Texas Hill Country. Karen Foulk. (Illus.). 232p. 1999. pap. 12.95 (*0-9652464-7-7*) Into Fun.

153-92 EEMUA Supplement to ASME B31.3-1990 & B31.3B 1991 Addenda Chemical Plant & Petroleum: Refinery Piping. EEMUA Staff. 1990. 125.00 (*0-85931-139-2*, Pub. by EEMUA) St Mut.

153/96 EEMUA Supplement to ASME B 31.3 Edition: Process Piping. EEMUA Staff. 1996. pap. 125.00 (*0-85931-051-5*, Pub. by EEMUA) St Mut.

150 Totally Terrific Writing Prompts: Lively, Fun Prompts to Motivate Every Writer in Your Class. Justin Martin. 32p. 1999. pap. text 7.95 (*0-439-04086-8*) Scholastic Inc.

150 Vegan Favorites: Fresh, Easy & Incredibly Delicious Recipes You Can Enjoy Everyday. Jay Solomon. LC 98-4849. 224p. 1998. per. 14.00 (*0-7615-1243-8*) Prima Pub.

One Hundred Fifty Ways for Teens to Make a Difference. Marian Salzman & Teresa Reisgies. LC 91-2965. 207p. (Orig.). (YA). 1991. pap. 7.95 (*1-56079-093-8*) Petersons.

One Hundred Fifty Ways to Be a Savvy Medical Consumer. Charles B. Inlander. (Illus.). 96p. 1992. pap. 5.95 (*0-9627334-5-8*) Peoples Med Soc.

***150 Ways to Enjoy Potatoes.** Duane Lund. (Illus.). 100p. 2000. 9.95 (*1-885061-85-4*) Adventure Pubns.

150 Ways to Help Your Child Succeed: Simple, Fun Tips to Help Your Children Live, Learn, & Grow. Karin Ireland. LC 98-222970. 176p. 1998. pap. 12.00 (*0-425-16550-7*) Berkley Pub.

150 Ways to Increase Intrinsic Motivation in the Classroom. James P. Raffini. LC 95-18933. 304p. (C). 1995. pap. text 47.50 (*0-205-16566-4*); pap. text 34.00 (*0-205-16567-2*) Allyn.

150 Ways to Tell If You're Ghetto. Shawn Wayans. LC 96-54857. 80p. 1997. pap. 8.95 (*0-440-50793-6*, Delta Trade) Dell.

150 "What's Wrong with This Picture?" Scenes. M. Thomas Webber, Jr. & Sharon G. Webber. (Illus.). 157p. (J). (ps-3). 1993. spiral bd., wbk. ed. 26.95 (*1-58650-035-X*, BK-226) Super Duper.

150 Years of Amalgam. Fredrik Berglund. 66p. 1995. 20.00 (*0-941011-14-3*, B54) Bio-Probe.

150 Years of American Art: The Amon Carter Museum Collection. Compiled by Carter J. Martin. LC 96-83425. (Illus.). 40p. (Orig.). 1996. pap. 8.00 (*0-88360-087-0*) Amon Carter.

150 Years of British Psychiatry Vol. II: The Aftermath. Ed. by German E. Berrios & Hugh Freeman. LC 96-209910. 650p. 1996. 90.00 (*0-485-11506-9*, Pub. by Athlone Pr) Humanities.

One Hundred Fifty Years of British Psychiatry, 1841-1991. Ed. by German E. Berrios & Hugh Freeman. LC RC0450.G7A15. 480p. 1991. reprint ed. pap. 148.80 (*0-608-01822-8*, 206247100003) Bks Demand.

One Hundred Fifty Years of Builders Hardware: Forms, Use, & Lore. Maud L. Eastwood. Ed. & Illus. by Stephen Holloway. Illus. by Gordon Tomson et al. 135p. (Orig.). 1993. pap. 22.50 (*0-9610800-6-X*); pap., ring bd. 27.50 (*0-9610800-8-6*) Ant Doorknob Pub.

150 Years of Denton County Sheriffs. Nita Thurman & Weldon Lucas. (Illus.). 150p. Date not set. 29.95 (*0-9670020-0-1*) Old Alton.

One Hundred Fifty Years of Excellence: A Pictorial View of Ohio Wesleyan University. Barbara Tull. 184p. 1991. 38.95 (*0-9630909-0-9*) OH Wesleyan U.

150 Years of International Harvester. Charles H. Wendel. LC 92-46461. (Agricultural Ser.). 416p. 1993. reprint ed. 44.95 (*0-87938-683-5*) MBI Pubg.

***150 Years of Landform Evolution Studies in Hungary.** Ed. by Marton Pecsi. (Illus.). 210p. 1999. 48.00 (*963-05-7670-8*, Pub. by Akade Kiado) Intl Spec Bk.

One Hundred Fifty Years of Ministry, 1838-1988: The First Presbyterian Church of Freehold, New Jersey. William L. Griffin. (Illus.). 148p. 1989. 10.00 (*0-9623047-1-9*) W L Griffin.

One Hundred Fifty Years of Music for Saxophone: Bibliographical Index of Music & Educational Literature for the Saxophone: 1844-1994. Jean-Marie Londeix. Ed. by Bruce Ronkin. LC 94-67611. (ENG & FRE.). 448p. 1994. 54.95 (*0-939103-04-4*) Roncorp.

***150 Years of Photo Journalism.** Konemann Inc. Staff. (Illus.). 900p. 2000. pap. 29.95 (*3-8290-5031-3*) Konemann.

***150 Years of Popular Musical Theatre.** Andrew Lamb. LC 00-25281. 2000. write for info. (*0-300-07538-3*) Yale U Pr.

One Hundred Fifty Years of the General Catalogue of Printed Books in the British Museum. A. H. Chaplin. Orig. Title: A Hundred Years of Cataloguing at the British Museum. 300p. 1985. text 74.95 (*0-85967-728-1*, Pub. by Scolar Pr) Ashgate Pub Co.

***150 Years of Train Models.** Harold H. Carstens. (Illus.). 150p. 1999. 30.95 (*0-911868-95-X*, C95) Carstens Pubns.

150 Years of Wisconsin Printmaking. Andrew Stevens. LC 98-44236. 88p. 1998. pap. 19.95 (*0-932900-44-5*) Elvejhem Mus.

150 Years of Worcester: 1848-1998. Albert B. Southwick. LC 97-78120. 96p. 1998. pap. 12.00 (*1-886284-16-4*) Chandler Hse.

101st Airborne Division: Screaming Eagles. Robert Jones. (Illus.). 328p. Date not set. 54.95 (*1-56311-144-6*) Turner Pub KY.

101st Airborne Division: 3rd Brigade, Desert Shield/Desert Storm. Turner Publishing Company Staff. LC 91-67164. (Illus.). 96p. 1992. 29.95 (*1-56311-075-X*) Turner Pub KY.

One Hundred First Communions. Veronica Kelly & Wendy Goody. (Illus.). (J). (gr. k-5). 1998. 14.95 (*0-9657218-2-5*) WhipperSnapper.

One Hundred First Congress in Review: The Omnibus Crime Control Act of 1990 P. L. No. 101-647, Vol. 4, No. 2. Deneen Snow. Ed. by Jon Felde & Karen Hansen. 10p. 1991. pap. text 6.50 (*1-55516-891-4*, 8500-0402) Natl Conf State Legis.

100 First Prize Make It Yourself Science Fair Projects. Glen Vecchione. LC 98-16662. (Illus.). 192p. (J). 1998. 19.95 (*0-8069-0703-7*) Sterling.

***100 First Prize Make It Yourself Science Fair Projects.** Glen Vecchione. (J). 1999. pap. text 12.95 (*0-8069-2483-7*) Sterling.

One Hundred First Words. Edwina Riddell. (Illus.). 32p. (J). (ps). 1991. pap. 4.95 (*0-8120-4888-1*) Barron.

105 American Poets since W. W. II. 2nd ed. 400p. 1991. text 155.00 (*0-8103-4585-4*) Gale.

105 Best of Todays Movie Hits. 72p. 1997. pap. 7.95 (*0-7935-7924-4*) H Leonard.

One-Hundred Five Ev Tamasiban: 105 Years in Tamasi. Laszlo L. Konnyu. LC 80-65905. (Illus.). 124p. 1980. 6.00 (*0-911862-09-9*) Hungarian Rev.

***105 Preguntas Que Los Ninos Hacen Acerca Del Dinero.** (SPA., Illus.). 256p. (J). 1999. pap. 9.99 (*0-311-38654-7*, Edit Mundo) Casa Bautista.

105 Questions Children Ask about Money Matters. Daryl Lucas & David Veerman. LC 97-951. 249p. 1997. pap. 9.99 (*0-8423-4526-4*) Tyndale Hse.

One Hundred Flowered Postcards. Georgia O'keefe. 1990. pap. write for info. (*0-316-88849-4*) Little.

***One Hundred Flowers.** Photos by Harold Feinstein. (Illus.). 160p. 2000. 50.00 (*0-8212-2665-7*, Pub. by Bulfinch Pr) Little.

One Hundred Flowers. Florence Poor. (Illus.). 115p. 1997. pap. 12.00 (*0-9658710-0-2*) F Poor.

One Hundred Flowers: Address Book. Georgia O'Keefe. 1990. pap. write for info. (*0-316-88850-8*) Little.

100 Flowers & How They Got Their Names. Diana Wells. LC 96-22296. (Illus.). 256p. 1997. 16.95 (*1-56512-138-4*) Algonquin Bks.

100 Folk Heros Who Shaped World History. Sarah Krall. 1995. pap. text 7.95 (*0-912517-17-4*) Bluewood Bks.

One Hundred Folk Songs. 1990. 12.95 (*0-685-32148-7*, HH52) Hansen Ed Mus.

Neoclassical. Young Mi Kim. LC 96-34520. (Architecture & Design Library Ser.). (Illus.). 96p. 1997. 17.95 (*1-56799-434-2*, MetroBooks) M Friedman Pub Grp Inc.

140. (Puzzlers Detect-a-Word Ser.). (J). 1998. pap. write for info. (*1-56144-796-X*, Honey Bear Bks) Modern Pub NYC.

140 Don'ts to Do Before You Die. Mary C. Bradley. 8p. 1999. pap. 2.95 (*0-9663931-1-2*) M C Bradley.

***145th Street Stories.** Walter Dean Myers. LC 99-36097. 176p. (gr. 7-12). 2000. 15.95 (*0-385-32137-6*) Delacorte.

145 Wonderful Writing Prompts: From Favorite Literature. Susan Ohanian. 1998. pap. text 10.95 (*0-590-01973-2*) Scholastic Inc.

144,000 on Mt. Zion. Gordon Lindsay. (Revelation Ser.: Vol. 11). 1962. 1.95 (*0-89985-044-8*) Christ for the Nations.

144 Ways to Walk the Talk. Eric Harvey & Alexander Lucia. 56p. (Orig.). 1995. pap. 6.95 (*1-885228-26-0*) Performce Pub.

140 Moldings of the Tudor Period: Collection A182. Mike Tecton. (Illus.). 64p. 1998. reprint ed. pap. 45.00 (*1-58203-083-9*, A182) M Tecton Pub.

149th Pennsylvania Volunteer Infantry Unit in the Civil War. Richard E. Matthews. LC 94-21041. (Illus.). 346p. 1994. lib. bdg. 42.00 (*0-89950-993-2*) McFarland & Co.

141. (Puzzlers Detect-a-Word Ser.). (J). 1998. pap. write for info. (*1-56144-797-8*, Honey Bear Bks) Modern Pub NYC.

One Hundred Forty-One Brand New Old Time Fiddle Tunes: By Pacific Northwest Composers. Ed. by Vivian T. Williams. (Brand New Old Time Fiddle Tunes Ser.: Vol. 2). 68p. (Orig.). 1986. pap. 10.00 (*0-9631484-1-9*) Voyager Rec.

141 West Jackson: A Journey Through Trading Discoveries. J. Peter Steidlmayer. LC 96-72352. (Illus.). xli, 137p. 1997. 40.00 (*0-9656134-0-2*) Steidlmayer Sftware.

147 Fun Things to Do in Houston. 2nd ed. Karen Foulk. (Illus.). 189p. (Orig.). 1996. pap. 12.95 (*0-9652464-1-8*) Into Fun.

***147 Fun Things to Do in Houston.** 3rd ed. Karen Foulk. (Illus.). 208p. (Orig.). 1999. pap. 12.95 (*0-9652464-5-0*) Into Fun.

147 Practical Tips for Teaching Professors. Ed. by Robert Magnan. 63p. 1990. reprint ed. pap. text 12.50 (*1-891859-01-3*) Atwood Pub LLC.

One Hundred Forty-Seven Practical Tips for Teaching Professors. Ed. by Robert Magnan. LC 92-9593. 45p. 1990. pap. 12.50 (*0-912150-09-2*) Atwood Pub LLC.

142. (Puzzlers Detect-a-Word Ser.). (J). 1998. pap. write for info. (*1-56144-798-6*, Honey Bear Bks) Modern Pub NYC.

***142 Fun Things to Do in New Orleans.** Karen Foulk. (Illus.). 216p. 1999. pap. 12.95 (*0-9652464-4-2*) Into Fun.

104 British Prose Writers 1660-1800. 2nd ed. 400p. 1991. text 155.00 (*0-8103-4584-6*) Gale.

***104 Preguntas Que los Ninos Haven Acerca del Cielo y los Angeles: Con Respuestas Biblicas Para Padre, Vol. 1.** Daryl J. Lucas & David R. Veerman.Tr. of 104 Questions Children Ask about Heaven & Angles. (SPA., Illus.). 240p. 1998. pap. text 9.99 (0-311-38653-9, Edit Mundo) Casa Bautista.

104 Questions Children Ask about Heaven & Angels. David R. Veerman et al. Ed. by Daryl J. Lucas. (Illus.). 256p. (J). 1996. pap. 9.99 (0-8423-4529-9) Tyndale Hse.

One Hundred Fourth Congress. Novak. 1997. 25.00 (0-02-874082-3) Macmillan.

One Hundred Frogs: From Matsu (i.e. Matsuo) Basho to Allen Ginsberg. Hiroaki Sato. LC 94-48328. (Illus.). 128p. 1995. pap. 7.95 (0-8348-0335-6) Weatherhill.

100 Full-Color Graphics, 2 vols. Erte. pap. 17.90 (0-486-25292-2) Dover.

***100 Fun & Fabulous Ways to Flirt with Your Spouse.** gif. ed. Doug Fields. (Illus.). 64p. 2000. pap. 6.99 (0-7369-0390-9) Harvest Hse.

100 Fun Ways to Livelier Lessons. Maxine Inkel. LC 95-60421. 128p. 1995. pap., teacher ed. 14.95 (0-89622-654-9) Twenty-Third.

One Hundred Funniest Golf Limericks: A Golf Classic. Joe James. 112p. 1992. pap. 7.95 (0-9631584-0-6) Rocking J Pr.

One Hundred Garden Designs. 2nd rev. ed. Andrew R. Addkison & Jack Kramer. LC 93-23824.Tr. of One Hundred Garden Plans. (Illus.). 288p. 1993. 22.95 (1-55821-255-8) Lyons Pr.

One Hundred Garden Plans see One Hundred Garden Designs

One Hundred Girls' Mother. Lenore Carroll. LC 98-23497. (Women of the West Ser.). 348p. 1998. 24.95 (0-312-85994-5, Pub. by Forge NYC) St Martin.

One Hundred Glimpses of Christ. M. Nassan. 1990. pap. 24.00 (0-7220-6345-8) St Mut.

One Hundred Glimpses of Our Lady. Ed. by M. Nassan. 1990. pap. 24.00 (0-7220-6346-6) St Mut.

100 Good Tunes for the Descant Recorder. 48p. 1995. pap. text 14.95 (0-521-56994-X) Cambridge U Pr.

One Hundred Gospel Favorites for Gt. William Bay. 112p. 1983. pap. 11.95 (0-87166-694-4, 93977) Mel Bay.

One Hundred Graces: Mealtime Blessings. Marcia Kelly & Jack Kelly. 112p. 1997. pap. 8.00 (0-609-80093-0) Bell T.

One Hundred Graded Classical Guitar Studies. Ed. & Selected by Frederick M. Noad. (Illus.). 176p. 1985. pap. 21.95 (0-7119-0612-2, AM38597) Music Sales.

One Hundred Great Africans. Alan Rake. LC 94-25934. (Illus.). 441p. 1994. text 62.50 (0-8108-2929-0) Scarecrow.

One Hundred Great Antique Automobiles in Full-Color Prints. Clarence P. Hornung. Orig. Title: Gallery of the American Automobile. (Illus.). 128p. 1991. reprint ed. pap. 19.95 (0-486-26841-1) Dover.

100 Great Chinese Posters. Stewart E. Fraser. 112p. Date not set. 30.00 (0-9664202-4-1) Posters Please.

100 Great Christmas Songs. Ed. by Carol Cuellar. 212p. (Orig.). 1995. pap. text 19.95 (0-89724-873-2, MF9549) Wrner Bros.

100 Great Cities of World History. Chrisanne Beckner. (One Hundred Ser.). (Illus.). 112p. 1995. pap. 7.95 (0-912517-14-X) Bluewood Bks.

100 Great Country Songs. Ed. by Carol Cuellar. 392p. (Orig.). 1995. pap. text 19.95 (0-89724-871-6, MF9550) Wrner Bros.

One Hundred Great Detectives. Ed. by Maxim Jakubowski. 256p. 1993. pap. 9.95 (0-88184-920-0) Carroll & Graf.

100 Great Fantasy Short Short Stories. Ed. by Isaac Asimov et al. 336p. 1985. pap. 3.95 (0-380-69917-6, Avon Bks) Morrow Avon.

100 Great Freelance Careers. Kelly Reno. 256p. 1997. 14.95 (0-02-861938-2) Macmillan.

***100 Great Hikes in & Near Palm Springs.** 2nd rev. ed. Phillip Ferranti. (Illus.). 216p. 2000. pap. 17.95 (1-56579-349-8) Westcliffe Pubs.

***100 Great Homeopaths.** Jay Yasgur. LC 99-95147. (ENG, SPA, FRE, GER & CHI., Illus.). 220p. 2000. pap. text 16.00 (1-886149-07-0) Van Hoy Pubs.

One Hundred Great Indians Through the Ages. rev. ed. H. N. Verma & Amrit Verma. LC 92-70354. 288p. 1992. pap., per. 17.95 (1-881155-00-5) GIP Bks.

100 Great Jobs & How to Get Them. Richard Fein. LC 99-24356. 225p. 1999. pap. 17.95 (1-57023-116-8) Impact VA.

100 Great Love Songs. Warner Brothers Staff. Ed. by Carol Cueller. 420p. 1995. pap. text 19.95 (0-89724-969-0, MF9565) Wrner Bros.

One Hundred Great Modern Lives. Ed. by John Canning. 36.95 (0-88411-286-1) Amereon Ltd.

100 Great Moments in Hockey. Brian Kendall. (Illus.). 208p. 1994. 26.95 (1-57243-021-4) Triumph Bks.

100 Great Monologues from the Neo-Classical Theatre. Ed. by Jocelyn A. Beard. LC 94-33114. (Monologue Audition Ser.). 172p. 1994. pap. 9.95 (1-880399-60-1) Smith & Kraus.

100 Great Monologues from the 19th Century Romantic & Realistic Theatres. Ed. by Jocelyn A. Beard. LC 94-33110. (Monologue Audition Ser.). 186p. 1994. pap. 9.95 (1-880399-61-X) Smith & Kraus.

100 Great Monologues from the Renaissance Theatre. Ed. by Jocelyn A. Beard. LC 94-19393. (Monologue Audition Ser.). 186p. 1994. pap. 9.95 (1-880399-59-8) Smith & Kraus.

One Hundred Great Operas & Their Stories. rev. ed. Henry W. Simon. LC 68-27816. (Reference Bk.). 560p. 1989. pap. 14.00 (0-385-05448-3) Doubleday.

One Hundred Great Paintings: Duccio to Picasso. Dillian Gordon. (Illus.). 1989. pap. 25.00 (0-300-06149-8) Yale U Pr.

***100 Great Poems by Women.** Ed. by Carolyn Kizer. LC 95-9762. (Golden Ser.). 1998. 25.00 (0-88001-422-9) HarpC.

One Hundred Great Poems By Women. Ed. by Carolyn Kizer. 200p. 1998. pap. 15.00 (0-88001-581-0) HarpC.

One Hundred Great Problems of Elementary Mathematics: Their History & Solution. Heinrich Dorrie. Tr. by David Antin from GER. 393p. 1965. pap. 9.95 (0-486-61348-8) Dover.

One Hundred Great Religious Poems. Ed. by Randolph Ray. LC 78-80378. (Granger Index Reprint Ser.). 1977. 18.95 (0-8369-6060-2) Ayer.

100 Great Rock Songs: Guitar. 4th rev. ed. pap. 14.95 (0-7692-0420-1, GF0309) Wrner Bros.

One Hundred Great Salad Dressings. Sally Griffiths. 64p. 1994. 9.98 (0-7858-0189-8) Bk Sales Inc.

One Hundred Great Scottish Songs. Pat Conway. 112p. 1986. pap. 17.95 (0-7866-1590-7, 95175WW) Mel Bay.

***100 Great Songs from Hollywood.** Warner Brothers Staff. 1999. 22.95 (0-7692-6663-0) Wrner Bros.

One Hundred Greatest Advertisements, Who Wrote Them & What They Did. 2nd ed. Julian L. Watkins. (Illus.). 233p. 1959. pap. 10.95 (0-486-20540-1) Dover.

100 Greatest Athletes of All Time: A Sports Editor's Personal Ranking. Bert R. Sugar. (Illus.). 352p. Date not set. 24.95 (0-8065-1614-3, Citadel Pr) Carol Pub Group.

***100 Greatest Baby Boomer Toys.** Mark Rich. LC 99-68134. (Illus.). 208p. 2000. pap. 24.95 (0-87341-880-8, BOOM) Krause Pubns.

***100 Greatest Baseball Games of the 20th Century Ranked.** Joseph J. Dittmar. (Illus.). 263p. 2000. per. 30.00 (0-7864-0915-0) McFarland & Co.

***100 Greatest Baseball Players Not in the Hall of Fame.** Mike Shalin & Neil Shalin. (Illus.). 2000. 22.95 (1-58261-217-X) Sprts Pubng.

100 Greatest Baseball Players of All Time. Blatt. 1998. 10.00 (0-671-01177-4, Pocket Books) PB.

***100 Greatest Baseball Players of the 20th Century Ranked.** Mark McGuire & Michael Sean Gormley. (Illus.). 215p. 2000. pap. 30.00 (0-7864-0914-2) McFarland & Co.

100 Greatest Basketball Players of All Time. Alex Sachare. LC 99-196370. 1997. per. 9.99 (0-671-01168-5) PB.

100 Greatest Basketball Moments of All Time. Alex Sachare. 1997. per. 10.00 (0-671-01178-2, PB Trade Paper) PB.

100 Greatest Basketball Moments of All Time. Alex Sachare. 1997. 15.10 (0-606-12611-2, Pub. by Turtleback) Demco.

100 Greatest Beach Vacations: A Guide for Families, Singles, & Couples. Irene Korn. LC 97-52289. (Illus.). 224p. 1998. pap. text 14.95 (0-8065-1975-4, Citadel Pr) Carol Pub Group.

100 Greatest Inventions see 100 Greatest Series

100 Greatest Man-made Wonders see 100 Greatest Series

100 Greatest Medical Discoveries see 100 Greatest Series

100 Greatest Men see 100 Greatest Series

***One Hundred Greatest Moments in St. Louis Sports.** Bob Broeg. (Illus.). 240p. 2000. write for info. (1-883982-31-6, Pub. by MO Hist Soc) Booksource.

100 Greatest Movies Ever Made. Time-Life Books Editors. LC 99-71058. 144p. (gr. 7). 1999. 24.95 (1-883013-68-2) Little.

100 Greatest Series, 12 vols. Incl. 100 Greatest Inventions. LC 96-38069. (J). 1997. lib. bdg. Not sold separately (0-7172-7683-X); 100 Greatest Man-made Wonders. Patricia Sechi-Johnson. LC 96-38050. (J). 1997. lib. bdg. Not sold separately (0-7172-7689-9); 100 Greatest Medical Discoveries. LC 96-40233. (J). 1997. lib. bdg. Not sold separately (0-7172-7681-3); 100 Greatest Men. LC 96-29663. (J). 1997. lib. bdg. Not sold separately (0-7172-7679-1); 100 Greatest Sports Champions. LC 96-50104. (J). 1997. lib. bdg. Not sold separately (0-7172-7686-4); 100 Greatest Women. LC 96-29662. (J). 1997. lib. bdg. Not sold separately (0-7172-7680-5); 1997. Set lib. bdg. 265.00 (0-7172-7691-0) Grolier Educ.

100 Greatest Sports Champions see 100 Greatest Series

100 Greatest Women see 100 Greatest Series

***100 Guitar Tips You Should Have Been Told: Including Hints from 20 of the World's Greatest Guitarists.** David Mead. (Illus.). 200p. 2000. pap. 20.00 (1-86074-295-5) Sanctuary Pub.

***100-Gun Ship Victory.** John McKay. (Anatomy of the Ship Ser.). (Illus.). 120p. 2000. 39.95 (1-55750-418-0) Naval Inst Pr.

One Hundred Haiku. Howard S. Levy. (East Asian Poetry in Translation Ser.: No. 5). 1976. pap. 8.00 (0-89986-300-0) Oriental Bk Store.

100 Haiku Selected from a Decade (1982-1991) limited ed. Guy R. Beining. (Codex Edition Ser.). (Illus.). 30p. 1993. 6.50 (1-884185-00-2) O Zone.

100 Harleys: Tod Rafferty's 100 Hottest Harleys. Tod Rafferty. (Style Ser.). 1999. pap. text 9.99 (1-84100-136-8) Quadrillion Media.

One Hundred Healthy Desserts Your Kids Will Love. Robin Zinberg. 176p. (Orig.). 1993. mass mkt. 3.99 (0-425-13816-X) Berkley Pub.

***100 Heirloom Roses for the American Garden.** Clair G. Martin. LC 99-51652. (Illus.). 288p. 2000. pap. 17.95 (0-7611-1341-X) Workman Pub.

***100 Heirloom Tomatoes for the American Garden.** Carolyn Male. LC 99-17665. (Smith & Hawken Ser.). (Illus.). 246p. 1999. pap. 17.95 (0-7611-1400-9) Workman Pub.

One Hundred Hikes in California's Central Sierra & Coastal Range. Vicky Spring. (Illus.). 240p. 1995. pap. 14.95 (0-89886-418-6) Mountaineers.

One Hundred Hikes in Colorado. Scott S. Warren. (Illus.). 240p. 1995. pap. 14.95 (0-89886-429-1) Mountaineers.

One Hundred Hikes in Northern California: Northern Sierra Nevada, Lake Tahoe Region, Lassen National Park, Trinity Alps Wilderness, San Francisco Bay Area, North Coast. John R. Soares & Marc J. Soares. LC 93-44838. (Illus.). 240p. 1994. pap. 14.95 (0-89886-385-6) Mountaineers.

100 Hikes in Northwest Oregon. William L. Sullivan. (Illus.). 240p. 1993. pap. 14.95 (0-9618152-2-1) Navillus Pr.

***100 Hikes in Northwest Oregon.** William L. Sullivan. 240p. 2000. pap. 14.95 (0-9618152-8-0) Navillus Pr.

***100 Hikes in Oregon.** 2nd ed. George Ostertag & Rhonda Ostertag. LC 99-50629. (100 Hikes in Ser.). (Illus.). 352p. 2000. pap. 14.95 (0-89886-619-7) Mountaineers.

100 Hikes in Southern Oregon. William L. Sullivan. (Illus.). 240p. (Orig.). 1997. pap. 14.95 (0-9618152-5-6) Navillus Pr.

One Hundred Hikes in the Alps: Switzerland, France, Italy, Austria, Germany, Lichtenstein. 2nd ed. Vicky Spring & Harvey Edwards. LC 92-18752. (Illus.). 224p. (Orig.). 1992. pap. 14.95 (0-89886-333-3) Mountaineers.

100 Hikes in the Central Oregon Cascades. 2nd ed. William L. Sullivan. (Illus.). 240p. 1998. pap. 14.95 (0-9618152-6-4) Navillus Pr.

100 Hikes in the Great Smoky Mountains National Park. 2nd ed. Russ Manning. LC 99-6456. 1999. pap. 14.95 (0-89886-636-7) Mountaineers.

One Hundred Hikes in the Inland Northwest. Spokane Mountaineers et al. LC 87-24635. (Illus.). 240p. (Orig.). 1987. pap. 14.95 (0-89886-130-6) Mountaineers.

***100 Hikes in Washington's Alpine Lakes.** 3rd ed. Vicky Spring et al. (100 Hikes in Ser.). (Illus.). 256p. 2000. pap. 16.95 (0-89886-707-X) Mountaineers.

One Hundred Hikes in Washington's Alpine Lakes. 2nd ed. Ira Spring et al. LC 92-41915. (One Hundred Hikes Ser.). (Illus.). 240p. 1993. pap. 14.95 (0-89886-306-6) Mountaineers.

One Hundred Hikes in Washington's Glacier Peak Region: The North Cascades. 3rd ed. Ira Spring & Harvey Manning. (Illus.). 240p. 1996. pap. 14.95 (0-89886-433-X) Mountaineers.

***100 Hikes in Washington's North Cascades National Park Region.** 3rd ed. Ira Spring & Harvey Manning. LC 99-50912. (100 Hikes in Ser.). (Illus.). 256p. 2000. pap. 16.95 (0-89886-694-4) Mountaineers.

One Hundred Hikes in Washington's North Cascades National Park Region. 2nd ed. Ira Spring & Harvey Manning. (Illus.). 240p. 1994. pap. 14.95 (0-89886-401-1) Mountaineers.

100 Hikes in Washington's South Cascades & Olympics: Chinook Pass, White Pass, Goat Rocks, Mou. 3rd ed. Ira Spring & Harvey Manning. LC 98-20117. 240p. 1998. pap. 14.95 (0-89886-594-8) Mountaineers.

100 Hikes/Travel Guide - Oregon Coast & Coast Range. William L. Sullivan. (Illus.). 240p. (Orig.). 1995. pap. 14.9^{e} (0-9618152-3-X) Navillus Pr.

One Hundred Hill Walks Around Birmingham. Richard Shurey. (Illus.). 224p. 1994. pap. 17.95 (1-85158-618-0, Pub. by Mainstream Pubng) Trafalgar.

100 Hill Walks Around Edinburgh. Chalmers. pap. 15.95 (1-85158-537-0, Pub. by Mainstream Pubng) Trafalgar.

100 Hill Walks Around Glasgow. J. Chalmers. pap. 15.95 (1-85158-536-2, Pub. by Mainstream Pubng) Trafalgar.

100 Hill Walks in the Lake District. Grindle. pap. 17.95 (1-85158-609-1, Pub. by Mainstream Pubng) Trafalgar.

100 Hill Walks in the Peak District. pap. 15.95 (1-85158-525-7, Pub. by Mainstream Pubng) Trafalgar.

***One Hundred Historic Tulsa Homes.** John Brooks Walton. Ed. by Alice Lindsay Price. (Illus.). 250p. 2000. 29.95 (0-9641148-1-X, Pub. by HCE Pubns) Tulsa Foundation.

One-Hundred Hour War. Howard H. Diamond. (Pew Case Studies in International Affairs). 50p. (C). 1996. pap. text 3.50 (1-56927-469-X, GU Schl Foreign) Geo U Inst Dplmcy.

One Hundred Hungry Ants. Houghton Mifflin Company Staff. (Mathematics Big Book Ser.). (J). 1994. pap. 44.32 (0-395-70378-6) HM.

One Hundred Hungry Ants. Elinor J. Pinczes. (Illus.). 32p. (J). (gr. k-3). 1993. 16.00 (0-395-63116-5) HM.

***One Hundred Hungry Ants.** Elinor J. Pinczes. LC 91-45415. (Illus.). 32p. (J). (ps-3). 1999. pap. 5.95 (0-395-97123-3, Sandpiper) HM.

100 Hymn Preludes. (Kevin Mayhew Ser.). 240p. 1993. pap. 34.95 (0-7866-2220-2, MB96089) Mel Bay.

One Hundred Hymns of Hope. Frwd. by George H. Shorney. 126p. 1992. pap. 9.95 (0-916642-47-X, 923) Hope Pub.

100 Ideas for Better Patient Relations in Registration, Billing, & Collections. Chenyl Soburn. 1996. 29.00 (0-8342-0909-8, 20909) Aspen Pub.

100 Ideas That Work! Discipline in the Classroom. Sharon R. Berry. 24p. 1998. reprint ed. pap. text 6.15 (1-58331-006-1) Assn Christ Sch.

One Hundred Improvements Guaranteed to Sell Your House Faster. R. Dodge Woodson. LC 93-6487. 240p. 1993. pap. 19.95 (0-471-59253-6) Wiley.

One Hundred Indian Feature Films: An Annotated Filmography. Srivastava Banerjee. LC 88-22716. 214p. 1988. text 10.00 (0-8240-9483-2, H728) Garland.

One Hundred Indoor Plants. A. C. Muller-Idzerda. (Illus.). 1959. 10.95 (0-87523-114-4) Emerson.

***100 Inspiring Stories: Finding Love & Laughter, Hope & Healing, Forgiveness & Faith.** Teresa Pirola. LC 98-61013. 128p. 1999. pap. 9.95 (0-89622-942-4) Twenty-Third.

100 Inventions That Shaped World History. Bill Yenne. Ed. by Morton Grosser. LC 94-71776. (Illus.). 112p. 1993. pap. 7.95 (0-912517-02-6) Bluewood Bks.

One Hundred Irish Ballads, Vol. 1. 112p. 1981. pap. 16.95 incl. audio (0-7866-1588-5, 95173WW) Mel Bay.

One Hundred Irish Ballads, Vol. 2. 112p. 1987. pap. 16.95 incl. audio (0-7866-1589-3, 95174WW) Mel Bay.

***100 Irish Tunes for Piano Accordion.** David DiGiuseppe. 120p. 1999. pap. 24.95 incl. audio compact disk (0-7866-3604-1, 97211BCD) Mel Bay.

One Hundred Is a Family. Pam Munoz Ryan. LC 93-30914. (Illus.). 32p. (J). (ps-3). 1994. lib. bdg. 13.89 (1-56282-673-5, Pub. by Hyprn Child) Little.

One Hundred Is a Family. Pam Munoz Ryan. (Illus.). 24p. (J). 1998. 5.95 (0-7868-0405-X, Pub. by Hyperion) Time Warner.

One Hundred Is a Family. Pam Munoz Ryan. LC 93-30914. (Illus.). 32p. (J). (ps-3). 1996. pap. 4.95 (0-7868-1120-X, Pub. by Hyprn Ppbks) Little.

One Hundred Is a Family. Pam Munoz Ryan. LC 93-30914. (J). 1996. 10.15 (0-606-09715-5, Pub. by Turtleback) Demco.

100+ Jewish Art Projects for Children. Nina S. Sher & Margaret A. Feldman. LC 96-84136. (Illus.). 144p. (J). (ps-6). 1996. pap. 25.00 (0-86705-039-X) A R E Pub.

One Hundred Jobs: A Panorama of Work in the American City. Ronald H. Howell. LC 99-23756. 240p. 2000. pap. 15.95 (1-56584-430-0) Norton.

100 Jobs for Kids & Young Adults Vol. 1: A Self-Empowerment Tool. Eva Marques. LC 97-90664. (Illus.). 224p. (Orig.). (YA). (gr. 7-12). 1997. pap. 13.95 (0-9658934-0-5, 100-44) WiseChild Pr.

100 Jobs in Social Change. Harley Jebens. (100 Jobs Ser.). 1996. 14.95 (0-02-861430-5) Macmillan.

100 Jobs in Technology. Lori Hawkins. (100 Jobs Ser.). 1996. 14.95 (0-02-861431-3) Macmillan.

100 Jobs in the Environment. Debra Quintana. (100 Jobs Ser.). 1996. 14.95 (0-02-861429-1) Macmillan.

100 Jobs in Words. Scott Meyer. (100 Jobs Ser.). 1996. 14.95 (0-02-861432-1) Macmillan.

100 Key Documents in American Democracy. Ed. by Peter B. Levy. LC 93-1137. 536p. 1993. 59.95 (0-313-28424-5, LVK/, Greenwood Pr) Greenwood.

100 Key Documents in American Democracy. Ed. by Peter B. Levy. LC 93-1137. 528p. 1999. pap. 27.50 (0-275-96525-2, Praeger Pubs) Greenwood.

100 Keys to Great Acrylic Painting. Judy Martin. (One Hundred Keys Ser.). (Illus.). 64p. 1995. 16.99 (0-89134-694-5, North Lght Bks) F & W Pubns Inc.

100 Keys to Great Calligraphy. Judy Kastin. (One Hundred Keys Ser.). (Illus.). 64p. 1996. 17.99 (0-89134-752-6, North Lght Bks) F & W Pubns Inc.

100 Keys to Great Fabric Painting. Julia Richardson. (One Hundred Keys Ser.). (Illus.). 64p. 1996. 17.99 (0-89134-754-2, North Lght Bks) F & W Pubns Inc.

100 Keys to Great Oil Painting. Helen Douglas-Cooper. (One Hundred Keys Ser.). (Illus.). 64p. 1995. 16.99 (0-89134-693-7, North Lght Bks) F & W Pubns Inc.

100 Keys to Great Pastel Painting. Miranda Fellow. (One Hundred Keys Ser.). (Illus.). 64p. 1994. 16.99 (0-89134-564-7, North Lght Bks) F & W Pubns Inc.

100 Keys to Preventing & Fixing Woodworking Mistakes. Alan Bridgewater & Gill Bridgewater. (Illus.). 64p. 1996. 17.99 (1-55870-429-9, Betrwy Bks) F & W Pubns Inc.

100 Keys to Woodshop Safety. Alan Bridgewater & Gill Bridgewater. (Illus.). 64p. 1996. 17.99 (1-55870-430-2, Betrwy Bks) F & W Pubns Inc.

***100 Kids' Songs.** Hal Leonard Publishing Company Staff. 184p. (J). 2000. otabind 14.95 (0-634-01494-3) H Leonard.

***100 Language Arts Activities.** Anne Schraff & Debra Edwards. 1999. ring bd. 27.95 (1-58659-181-9) Artesian.

One Hundred Lead Licks for Guitar. Alan Warner. (Illus.). 1993. pap. 19.95 (0-7119-2787-1, AM78098) Music Sales.

100 Leaders Who Shaped Colonial North America. Samuel W. Crompton. 1998. pap. 7.95 (0-912517-35-2) Bluewood Bks.

100 Leos: Wit & Wisdom from Leo Burnett. Leo Burnett. (Illus.). 128p. 1995. pap. 6.95 (0-8442-3420-6, NTC Business Bks) NTC Contemp Pub Co.

One Hundred Lessons in Classical Ballet. Vera S. Kostrovitskaya. Tr. & Intro. by Oleg Briansky. LC 86-27743. (Illus.). 400p. 1987. reprint ed. pap. 18.95 (0-87910-068-0) Limelight Edns.

***100 Library Lifesavers: A Survival Guide for School Library Media Specialists.** Pamela S. Bacon. LC 99-38136. 270p. 1999. pap. 37.50 (1-56308-750-2) Libs Unl.

One Hundred Love Sonnets: Cien Sonetos de Amor. Pablo Neruda. Tr. by Stephen Tapscott from SPA. (Texas Pan American Ser.). 232p. 1986. pap. 12.95 (0-292-76028-0) U of Tex Pr.

100 Low Fat Small Meals & Salads, 100 Low Fat Pasta & Grain Recipes, 100 Low Fat Vegetable & Legume Recipes, 100 Low Fat Soup & Stew Recipes, 100 Low Fat Fish & Shellfish Recipes & 100 Low Fat Chicken & Turkey Recipes. Corinne T. Netzer. 1997. mass mkt. 5.99 (0-614-27732-9) Dell.

100 Lustre Color Effects. D. M. Campana. Date not set. 4.50 (0-939608-04-9) Campana Art.

One-Hundred Magic Tricks. Ian Adair. 1991. 12.98 (1-55521-729-X) Bk Sales Inc.

One Hundred Major Modern Writers: Essays for Composition. Ed. by Robert Atwan & William Vesterman. 704p. (C). 1984. pap. text. write for info. (0-672-61602-5) Macmillan.

100 Male Nudes. Taschen, Benedikt Staff. (Illus.). 64p. 1996. pap. 3.99 (3-8228-8162-7) Taschen Amer.

One Hundred Management Charts. 2nd ed. Soichiro Nagashima. 344p. 1987. reprint ed. text 38.00 (92-833-1043-8); reprint ed. pap. text 32.75 (92-833-1044-6) Productivity Inc.

One Hundred Master Drawings. Ed. by Agnes Mongan. LC 75-95129. (Illus.). 208p. 1971. reprint ed. lib. bdg. 59.50 (0-8371-3989-9, MOMD, Greenwood Pr) Greenwood.

An Asterisk (*) at the beginning of an entry indicates that the title is appearing for the first time.

One Hundred Masterpieces from the Collection of Dr. Walter A. Compton: Japanese Swords, Sword Fittings & Other Accoutrements. Ed. by Sebastian Izzard. LC 91-77749. (Illus.). 330p. 1992. 60.00 (*1-880907-00-3*) Christies.

One Hundred Masterpieces from the Courtauld Collections: Bernardo Daddi to Ben Nicholson. Dennis Farr. (Illus.). 216p. (C). 1987. 60.00 (*0-85331-535-3*, Pub. by Lund Humphries); pap. 29.95 (*0-85331-534-5*, Pub. by Lund Humphries) Antique Collect.

One Hundred Masterpieces of Painting. John La Farge. (Notable American Authors Ser.). 1999. reprint ed. lib. bdg. 125.00 (*0-7812-3686-X*) Rprt Serv.

One Hundred Maxims in Neurology: Behavioral Neurology. Porter. 384p. (gr. 13). 1993. 43.95 (*0-340-57720-7*) Mosby Inc.

100 Maxims in Neurology: Parkinson Disease. Porter. 169p. 1992. 42.95 (*0-340-58947-7*) Mosby Inc.

One Hundred Maxims in Neurology: Stroke, 3. Frank M. Yatsu et al. (Illus.). 178p. (C). (gr. 13). 1995. 47.95 (*0-8016-7281-3*, 07281) Mosby Inc.

100 Maxims of Guidance. Bahram Elahi. (Illus.). 154p. 1995. 15.00 (*2-911331-00-1*, Pub. by Comite de Comm) Baker & Taylor.

100 Medical Milestones of World History. Ruth Dejauregui. 1997. pap. text 7.95 (*0-912517-31-X*) Bluewood Bks.

***100 Meditations: Selections from Unitarian Universalist Meditation Manuals.** Kathleen Montgomery. LC 00-28536. 2000. write for info. (*1-55896-403-7*, Skinner Hse Bks) Unitarian Univ.

100 Meditations - Advent - Christmas. 1940. 19.25 (*0-687-60833-3*) Abingdon.

100 Meditations on Hope. Marilyn B. Oden. 128p. 1995. 13.00 (*0-8358-0741-X*) Upper Room Bks.

100 Men Who Shaped World History. Bill Yenne. (One Hundred Ser.). (Illus.). 112p. (Orig.). 1994. pap. 7.95 (*0-912517-05-0*) Bluewood Bks.

100 Men's Stage Monologues from the 1980s. Ed. by Jocelyn A. Beard. (Monologue Audition Ser.). 170p. 1991. pap. 11.95 (*0-9622722-4-8*) Smith & Kraus.

100 Methods for Total Quality Management. Gopal K. Kanji. 256p. 1996. 75.00 (*0-8039-7746-8*); pap. 27.50 (*0-8039-7747-6*) Sage.

One Hundred Middle English Lyrics. Ed. by Robert D. Stevick. LC 93-31813. (Illus.). 248p. 1994. pap. text 14.95 (*0-252-06379-1*) U of Ill Pr.

One Hundred Mile City. Detab Sudjic. 320p. 1993. pap. 18.95 (*0-15-642357-X*) Harcourt.

One Hundred Miles from Bagdad: With the French in Desert Storm. James J. Cooke. LC 92-39282. 256p. 1993. 47.95 (*0-275-94528-6*, C4528, Praeger Pubs) Greenwood.

One Hundred Miles in Mammoth Cave Eighteen Eighty. H. C. Hovey. Ed. by William R. Jones. (Illus.). 1982. reprint ed. pap. 3.95 (*0-89646-015-3*) Vistabooks.

100 Military Leaders Who Shaped World History. Samuel W. Crompton. 1998. pap. text 7.95 (*0-912517-33-6*) Bluewood Bks.

One Hundred Million Dollar Game. Ed Linn & Mel Durslag. 320p. 1985. 16.95 (*0-671-47054-X*) S&S Trade.

One Hundred Million Dollars in Profits: An Anatomy of a Market Killing & a Realistic Trading. Kelly Angle. 1990. 50.00 (*0-930233-38-7*) Windsor.

One Hundred Million Guinea Pigs: Dangers in Everyday Foods, Drugs, & Cosmetics. Arthur Kallet & F. J. Schlink. LC 75-39252. (Getting & Spending: The Consumer's Dilemma Ser.). 1976. reprint ed. 26.95 (*0-405-08025-5*) Ayer.

100 Minds That Made the Market. Kenneth L. Fisher. (Illus.). 470p. 1995. 24.95 (*0-931133-01-7*, Busn Class) Pac Pub Grp.

100 Modern Reagents. Simpkins. 1989. 66.00 (*0-85186-893-2*) CRC Pr.

One Hundred Monkeys. Daniel S. Cutler. LC 90-22446. (Illus.). 40p. (J). 1991. pap. 13.95 (*0-671-73564-0*) Litle Simon.

One Hundred Monologues: An Audition Sourcebook from New Dramatists. Ed. by Laura Harrington. 1989. mass mkt. 6.99 (*0-451-62688-5*, Ment) NAL.

One Hundred More Poems from the Chinese: Love & the Turning Year. Kenneth Rexroth. LC 71-114845. 1970. 12.00 (*0-8112-0369-7*, Pub. by New Directions); pap. 9.95 (*0-8112-0179-1*, NDP308, Pub. by New Directions) Norton.

One Hundred More Poems from the Japanese. Tr. by Kenneth Rexroth from JPN. LC 76-7486. (Illus.). 120p. 1976. pap. 9.95 (*0-8112-0619-X*, NDP420, Pub. by New Directions) Norton.

100 More Profits, Plus Ideas for Power Promoting. Tom Shay. 110p. 1998. pap. 8.00 (*1-891964-05-4*) Profits Plus.

100 More Research Topic Guides for Students. Dana McDougald. LC 99-17855. (Professional Guides in School Librarianship Ser.). 240p. 1999. 39.95 (*0-313-30852-7*) Greenwood.

One Hundred More Story Poems. Ed. by Elinor Parker. LC 60-11543. (Illus.). (J). (gr. 5 up). 1960. 15.95 (*0-690-59690-1*) HarpC Child Bks.

100 More Ways To Keep Your Soul Alive. Frederic Brussat & Mary A. Brussat. LC 97-2617. 128p. 1997. pap. 10.00 (*0-06-251521-7*, Pub. by Harper SF) HarpC.

100 More Ways to Live to Be 100. Charles B. Inlander & Christine Kuehn Kelly. LC 99-17896. (People's Medical Society Book Ser.). 128p. 1999. pap. 10.95 (*0-8027-7557-8*) Walker & Co.

100 Most Asked Questions about Your Social Security Benefits. Robert J. Myers. Ed. by Victor Todd. LC 94-67720. 136p. 1994. pap. 2.95 (*0-9648635-1-0*) Srs Coalition.

One Hundred Most Difficult Business Letters You'll Ever Have to Write, Fax, or E-Mail. Bernard Heller. LC 94-5696. 256p. (Orig.). 1994. 16.00 (*0-88730-683-7*, HarpBusn) HarpInfo.

One Hundred Most Frequently Cited OSHA Construction Standards: A Guide for the Abatement of the Top 25 Associated Physical Hazards. 1994. lib. bdg. 250.95 (*0-8490-8510-1*) Gordon Pr.

One Hundred Most Frequently Cited OSHA Construction Standards in 1991: A Guide for the Abatement of the Top 25 Associated Physical Hazards. (Illus.). 87p. (Orig.). (C). 1993. pap. text 25.00 (*0-7881-0130-7*) DIANE Pub.

100 Most Important Events in Christian History. A. Kenneth Curtis et al. LC 97-35333. 208p. 1998. pap. 11.99 (*0-8007-5644-4*, Dates With Dest) Revell.

***100 Most Important Women of the 20th Century.** Ladies' Home Journal Staff. LC 98-66257. (Illus.). 192p. 1998. 34.95 (*0-696-20823-7*) Meredith Bks.

100 Most Influential Books Ever Written: The History of Thought from Ancient Times to Today. Martin Seymour-Smith. (Illus.). 500p. 1997. 29.95 (*0-8065-1865-0*, Citadel Pr) Carol Pub Group.

100 Most Influential Books Ever Written: The History of Thought from Ancient Times to Today. Martin Seymour-Smith. LC 98-10027. (Illus.). 498p. 1998. 34.95 (*0-8065-2000-0*, Citadel Pr) Carol Pub Group.

100 Most Influential Women of All Time: A Ranking Past & Present. Deborah G. Felder. LC 95-21240. 400p. Date not set. 24.95 (*0-8065-1726-3*, Citadel Pr) Carol Pub Group.

100 Most Influential Women of All Time: A Ranking Past & Present. Deborah G. Felder. (Illus.). 384p. 1998. pap. text 19.95 (*0-8065-1976-2*, Citadel Pr) Carol Pub Group.

***100 Most Popular Children's Authors: Biographical Sketches & Bibliographies.** Sharron L. McElmeel. LC 98-41942. (Popular Authors Ser.). 495p. (YA). (gr. 6-9). 1999. 48.00 (*1-56308-646-8*) Teacher Ideas Pr.

100 Most Popular Picture Book Authors & Illustrators: Biographical Sketches & Bibliographies. Sharron L. McElmeel. (Popular Authors Ser.). 575p. 2000. 49.00 (*1-56308-647-6*) Libs Unl.

100 Most Popular Scientists for Young Adults: Biological Sketches & Professional Paths. Kendall Haven & Donna Clark. LC 99-13755. (Profiles & Pathways Ser.). 526p. (YA). (gr. 6). 1999. 56.00 (*1-56308-674-3*) Teacher Ideas Pr.

100 Most Popular Young Adult Authors: Biographical Sketches & Bibliographies. rev. ed. Bernard A. Drew. LC 97-25882. 531p. 1997. 55.00 (*1-56308-615-8*) Libs Unl.

100 Motivators for Educators: Affirmations for Good Health & Good Living. Jo A. Lordahl. LC 97-4903. 112p. 1997. 39.95 (*0-8039-6625-3*); pap. 16.95 (*0-8039-6626-1*) Sage.

100 Motorcycles 100 Years: The First Century of the Motorcycle. Fredric Winkowski et al. LC 98-48210. (100 Years Ser.). (Illus.). 168p. 1999. 19.98 (*0-7651-1015-6*) Smithmark.

100 Must Reads for African-Americans: From the African Past to Today. Columbus Salley. LC 96-30215. 320p. 1997. 24.95 (*0-8065-1729-8*, Citadel Pr) Carol Pub Group.

One Hundred Names of God. Torkom Saraydarian. 264p. 1995. pap. 13.95 (*0-929874-49-8*) TSG Pub Found.

100 Napa County Roadside Wildflowers, Vol. 1. unabridged ed. Richards Lyon & Jake Ruyet. LC 96-92461. 1996. pap., per. 14.95 (*0-9616004-7-0*) Stonecrest Pr.

100 Natural Wonders of the World. Bill Yenne. (One Hundred Ser.). (Illus.). 112p. 1995. pap. 7.95 (*0-912517-15-8*) Bluewood Bks.

One Hundred Nature Walks in the Missouri Ozarks. Alan McPherson. (Illus.). 352p. (Orig.). 1997. pap. 17.95 (*1-889899-00-3*) Cache River Pr.

100 New Bobbin Lace Patterns. Yusai Fukuyama. LC 98-9803. (Illus.). 144p. 1998. pap. 16.95 (*0-486-40070-0*) Dover.

100 New Profits+Plus ideas for Power Managing. Tom Shay. 108p. 1998. pap. 8.00 (*1-891964-03-8*) Profits Plus.

One Hundred New Tales: Les Cents Nouvelles Nouvelles. Ed. & Tr. by Judith B. Diner from FRE. LC 89-23570. (Library of Medieval Literature). 394p. 1990. text 25.00 (*0-8240-8510-8*) Garland.

109 18th Century British Poets. 2nd ed. 400p. 1991. text 155.00 (*0-8103-4589-7*) Gale.

One Hundred Ninety-Eight Easy Wood Projects. Floyd Morris. 96p. 1989. pap. 13.28 (*0-87006-629-3*) Goodheart.

195 Lakes of the Fraser Valley, Vol. 1. Ed A. Rychkun. 500p. 1995. pap. 17.95 (*0-88839-339-3*) Hancock House.

One Hundred Ninety Great Old-Time Baseball Cards, 2 bks. 81st ed. Ed. by Bert R. Sugar. 32p. (Orig.). 1986. pap. 8.90 (*0-486-25149-7*) Dover.

199 Days: The Battle for Stalingrad. Edwin P. Hoyt. LC 98-51313. 2000. pap. 15.95 (*0-312-86853-7*, Pub. by Tor Bks) St Martin.

199 Great Home Businesses You Can Start & Succeed In!: How to Choose the Best Home Business for You Based on Your Personality Type. Tyler Gregory Hicks. 288p. 1992. pap. 12.95 (*1-55958-224-3*) Prima Pub.

***199 Great Home Businesses You Can Start (And Succeed in) for under $1,000: How to Choose the Best Home Businesses for You Based on Your Personality.** 2nd rev. ed. Tyler Gregory Hicks. LC 98-50841. 274p. 2000. pap. 14.95 (*0-7615-1743-X*) Prima Pub.

199 Ideas & Suggestions to Honor & Love Your Wife. Robert J. Vickers et al. LC 97-60626. 94p. 1997. pap. 7.95 (*1-57921-021-X*, Pub. by WinePress Pub) BookWorld.

199 Things to Do with a Politician. Purj. Ed. by Mike Jackson et al. (Illus.). 168p. (Orig.). 1994. pap. 5.95 (*1-56245-088-3*) Great Quotations.

197th Regiment Pennsylvania Infantry: One Hundred-Day Troops. unabridged ed. 15p. (Orig.). 1995. pap. 7.00 (*0-9654312-1-5*) J Williamson.

1996 National Storytelling Directory & Guidebook. 152p. pap. 11.95 (*1-879991-19-5*, Natl Storytell) Natl Storytlng Network.

191 Jazz Love Songs. 80p. 1997. pap. 7.95 (*0-7935-8235-0*) H Leonard.

197 Acoustic Classics. 112p. 1997. otabind 9.95 (*0-7935-8238-5*) H Leonard.

100 Nudes. Taschen, Benedikt Staff. (Illus.). 64p. 1996. pap. 3.99 (*3-8228-8166-X*) Taschen Amer.

100 of America's Best Pick-Up Lines. Maxwell Trano. (Illus.). 112p. 1998. mass mkt. 9.95 (*0-9667774-0-9*, 01/PW/98) Trano Grp.

One Hundred of the Best Real Estate Agents Northern Virginia: 1988 Guide. C & M Associates Staff. 111p. (Orig.). 1988. pap. 2.25 (*0-945927-00-2*) C & M Associates.

***100 of the World's Greatest Mysteries: Strange Secrets of the Past Revealed.** E. Randall Floyd. 275p. 2000. pap. 16.95 (*1-891799-05-3*, Pub. by Harbor Hse) BookWorld.

100 of the World's Tallest Buildings. Dolores Rice et al. (Illus.). 220p. 1998. 59.95 (*3-927258-60-1*) Gingko Press.

101 Ways to Improve Your Self-Esteem: A Fast & Easy Guide for Very Busy People. Sheena Ashdown. 84p. (Orig.). 1995. pap. text 9.95 (*0-9641975-2-9*) Gibsons Pubng.

101 Activities for Creating Effective Technology Staff Development Programs: A Sourcebook of Games, Stories, Role Playing & Learning Exercises for Administrators. Gerald D. Bailey & Gwen L. Baily. LC 93-43260. 1995. 21.95 (*0-590-49748-0*, 1028.3.b35 1994) Scholastic Inc.

One-Hundred One Activities for Kids in Tight Spaces. Carol S. Kranowitz. (Illus.). 160p. 1995. pap. 9.95 (*0-312-13420-7*) St Martin.

One Hundred One Activities for Students Affected by Someone Else's Alcohol - Drug Use. Martin Fleming. LC 92-9405. 184p. 1992. pap. 54.95 (*1-56246-038-2*, 3095, HazeldenJohnson Inst) Hazelden.

One Hundred One Advanced Spreadsheet Exercises (Using Lotus 1-2-3, VP-Planner, or Twin) Lloyd D. Brooks. 1990. pap., wbk. ed. 18.64 (*0-07-008186-7*) McGraw.

***101 Advent Activities for Kids.** Ellyn Sanna. (Christmas at Home Ser.). (Illus.). (J). 2000. pap. text 2.97 (*1-57748-942-X*) Barbour Pub.

One Hundred One Adventures in Saudi Arabia & Passage to Jerusalem. Claire W. Schumacher. LC 94-90015. (Illus.). 170p. (Orig.). 1994. pap. 10.00 (*0-917378-08-3*, 04-090015) Zenith City.

101 Affirmations for Teenagers: Esteem-Building Activities for Yourth Ministry. Ed. by Michael Warden. LC 92-44531. 1993. 14.99 (*1-55945-176-9*) Group Pub.

101 All Time Best Loved Songs: For Piano & Guitar. Al Cimino. 256p. 1997. pap. text 16.95 (*1-878427-54-7*, XC7700) Cimino Pub Grp.

One Hundred One Amazing Card Tricks. Bob Longe. LC 93-23861. (Illus.). 128p. 1993. pap. 4.95 (*0-8069-0342-2*) Sterling.

***101 Amazing Jazz Bass Patterns.** Larry McCabe. 48p. 2000. pap. 17.95 incl. audio compact disk (*0-7866-3631-9*, 97336BCD) Mel Bay.

101 Amazing Optical Illusions: Fantastic Visual Tricks. Terry Jennings. LC 96-37628. (Illus.). 88p. (J). 1997. 17.95 (*0-8069-9462-2*) Sterling.

***101 American English Customs: Understanding Language & Culture Through Common Practices.** Harry Collis. LC 99-29186. 128p. 1999. pap. 7.95 (*0-8442-2407-3*, 24073) NTC Contemp Pub Co.

101 American English Idioms. Harry Collis. (Illus.). 128p. 1995. pap. 7.95 (*0-8442-5446-0*, 54460, Passprt Bks) NTC Contemp Pub Co.

101 American English Idioms. Harry Collis & Mario Risso. (Illus.). 128p. 1995. pap. 29.95 incl. audio (*0-8442-5424-X*, 5424X, Passprt Bks) NTC Contemp Pub Co.

101 American English Idioms: Teacher's Manual & Resource Book. teacher ed. 21.13 (*0-8442-5457-6*) NTC Contemp Pub Co.

101 American English Idioms: 101 Learning Cards, Teacher's Manual & Resource Book. 66.60 (*0-8442-5455-X*) NTC Contemp Pub Co.

101 American English Proverbs. Harry Collis. (Illus.). 144p. pap. 29.95 incl. audio (*0-8442-0594-X*, 0594X, Passprt Bks) NTC Contemp Pub Co.

101 American English Proverbs. Harry Collis. LC 91-60823. (Illus.). 144p. 1994. pap. 6.95 (*0-8442-5412-6*, 54126, Passprt Bks) NTC Contemp Pub Co.

101 American English Proverbs: Teacher's Manual & Resource Book. Harry Collins. 1992. teacher ed. 21.15 (*0-8442-0595-8*) NTC Contemp Pub Co.

101 American English Proverbs: 101 Learning Cards, Teacher's Manual & Resource Book. 70.58 (*0-8442-5438-X*) NTC Contemp Pub Co.

101 American English Riddles. Harry Collis. Ed. by John Nolan. (Illus.). 128p. (Orig.). 1995. pap. 6.95 (*0-8442-5606-4*, 56064, Natl Textbk Co) NTC Contemp Pub Co.

101 American English Superstitions. Harry Collis. LC 98-140548. (Illus.). 144p. 1997. pap. 7.95 (*0-8442-5599-8*, 55998, Natl Textbk Co) NTC Contemp Pub Co.

One Hundred One Amusing Ways to Develop Your Child's Thinking Skills & Creativity. Sarina Simon. Ed. by Janice Gallagher. (Illus.). 132p. (Orig.). 1989. pap. 8.95 (*0-929923-03-0*, Legcy) Lowell Hse.

101 Annoying Noises, Vol. 1. Michael Winslow et al. (Illus.). (Orig.). Date not set. mass mkt. write for info. (*0-9651973-1-X*) Vocal Vision.

101 Answers to Dilbert People Problems. Craig S. Rice. LC 97-41229. 169p. 2000. pap. 18.95 (*1-56072-460-9*, Nova Kroshka Bks) Nova Sci Pubs.

***101+ Answers to the Most Frequently Asked Questions from Entrepreneurs.** Courtney Price. LC 98-40649. 320p. 1999. pap. 16.95 (*0-471-31572-9*) Wiley.

One Hundred One Apple Computer Programming Tips & Tricks. Fred White. 128p. (Orig.). 1982. pap. 8.95 (*0-86668-015-2*) ARCsoft.

101 Arena Exercises: A Ringside Guide for Horse & Rider. Cherry Hill. LC 95-12930. (Illus.). 224p. 1995. pap. 29.95 (*0-88266-316-X*, Garden Way Pub) Storey Bks.

One Hundred One Atari Computer Programming Tips & Tricks. Alan North. 128p. (Orig.). 1982. pap. 8.95 (*0-86668-022-5*) ARCsoft.

101 Attacking Ideas in Chess. Joe Gallagher. 128p. 1999. pap. 17.95 (*1-901983-20-X*, Pub. by Gambit) BHB Intl.

One Hundred One Back-to-School Jokes. Lisa Eisenberg. 96p. (J). (gr. 4-6). 1994. pap. 1.95 (*0-590-48574-1*) Scholastic Inc.

***101 Bad to the Bone Blues Guitar Rhythm Patterns.** Larry McCabe. 48p. 1999. pap. 17.95 incl. audio compact disk (*0-7866-4044-8*, 97760BCD) Mel Bay.

101 Baking Recipes for Children on Restricted Diets. Susan Swann. LC 98-43148. 1998. write for info. (*0-86025-489-5*) Empire Pub.

***101 Basic: Blue Scales for Guitar.** Yoichi Arakawa. (Illus.). 29p. 1999. pap. 6.95 (*1-891370-05-7*, SSM00765, Pub. by Six Strings) Music Sales.

***101 Basic: Guitar Chords.** Yoichi Arakawa. (Illus.). 29p. 1999. pap. 6.95 (*1-891370-02-2*, SSM00762, Pub. by Six Strings) Music Sales.

101 Basic: Major Pentatonic Scales for Guitar. Yoichi Arakawa. (Illus.). 29p. 1999. pap. 6.95 (*1-891370-04-9*, SSM00764, Pub. by Six Strings) Music Sales.

***101 Basic: Minor Pentatonic Scales for Guitars.** Yoichi Arakawa. (Illus.). 32p. 1999. pap. 6.95 (*1-891370-03-0*, SSM00763, Pub. by Six Strings) Music Sales.

***101 Basic Reading for Guitar.** Yoichi Arakawa. (Illus.). 37p. 1999. pap. 6.95 (*1-891370-06-5*, SSM00766, Pub. by Six Strings) Music Sales.

101 Basketball Out-of Bounds Drills. George Karl et al. LC 97-205617. 1997. pap. 16.95 (*1-57167-099-8*) Coaches Choice.

101 Basketball Rebounding Drills. George Karl et al. 1997. pap. 16.95 (*1-57167-080-7*) Coaches Choice.

***101 Bazaar Best-Sellers.** Ed. by Laura Scott. (Illus.). 176p. 2001. 19.96 (*1-882138-63-5*) Hse White Birches.

***101 Best Businesses to Start.** 3rd ed. Russell D. Roberts. 2000. pap. 19.95 (*0-7679-0659-4*) Broadway BDD.

101 Best Cover Letters. Block. LC 99-19053. 1999. 11.95 (*0-07-134257-5*) McGraw.

***101 Best Dot.coms to Start: The Essential Sourcebook of Startup Wisdom, Financial Tips & Inside Secrets for Building a Business on the Internet.** Lynie Arden et al. LC 00-39774. 544p. 2000. 17.95 (*0-7679-0604-7*) Broadway BDD.

O

101 Best Extra-Income Opportunities for Women. Jennifer Basye. LC 97-23634. 192p. 1997. per. 14.00 (*0-7615-0916-X*) Prima Pub.

One Hundred One Best Family Card Games. Alfred Sheinwold. LC 92-33759. (Illus.). 128p. 1992. pap. 4.95 (*0-8069-8635-2*) Sterling.

***101 Best Freelance Careers.** Kelly Reno. LC 99-217722. 224p. (Orig.). 1999. pap. 12.00 (*0-425-16865-4*) Berkley Pub.

101 Best Home-Based Businesses. Priscilla Huff. LC 98-30181. 389p. 1998. 14.95 (*0-7615-1651-4*) Prima Pub.

101 Best Home-Based Success Secrets for Women: Proven Ideas & Strategies to Help You Start, Manage & Profit from Whatever Business You Choose. Priscilla Y. Huff. LC 99-27989. (Illus.). 409p. 1999. pap. 16.00 (*0-7615-1974-2*) Prima Pub.

101 Best Home Businesses. Dan Ramsey. LC 96-37685. 192p. (Orig.). 1997. pap. 14.99 (*1-56414-263-9*) Career Pr Inc.

***101 Best Plants for the Prairies.** Liesbeth Leatherbarrow & Lesley Reynolds. (Illus.). 264p. 1999. pap. 14.95 (*1-894004-30-2*) Fifth Hse Publ.

101 Best Resumes: Endorsed by the Professional Association of Resume Writers. Jay A. Block & Michael Betrus. LC 96-49936. 197p. 1997. pap. 11.95 (*0-07-032893-5*) McGraw.

101 Best Small Businesses for Women: Everything You Need to Know about Success. Priscilla Y. Huff. LC 96-28166. 432p. 1996. pap. 14.00 (*0-7615-0580-6*) Prima Pub.

101 Best Web Sites for Kids. Trevor Meers. 160p. 1999. mass mkt. 5.99 (*0-7853-3931-0*) Pubns Intl Ltd.

101 Best Weekend Businesses. Dan Ramsey. 192p. (Orig.). 1996. pap. 14.99 (*1-56414-257-4*) Career Pr Inc.

One Hundred One Bible Reasons Why I Am a Baptist. 10th ed. R. H. Faulkner. 1985. reprint ed. pap. 1.25 (*0-945906-00-5*) R H Faulkner.

One Hundred One Bible Riddles for All Ages. Benjamin Macias. (Illus.). 112p. (Orig.). (J). (gr. 1 up). 1993. pap. 7.95 (*0-9638277-1-5*) Fam of God.

101 Bible Secrets That Christians Do Not Know. unabridged ed. Ernest L. Martin. (Illus.). 228p. (Orig.). (C). 1993. pap. 14.95 (*0-945657-94-3*) Acad Scriptural Knowledge.

One Hundred One Big Ideas for Promoting a Business on a Small Budget. Barbara Lambesis. LC 89-91071. 112p. (Orig.). 1989. pap. 12.95 (*0-9624798-0-2*) Mktg Methods Pr.

101 Bike Routes in Scotland. Harry Henniker. (Illus.). 240p. 1996. pap. 22.95 (*1-85158-785-3*, Pub. by Mainstream Pubng) Trafalgar.

101 Blues Guitar Turnaround Licks. Larry McCabe. 48p. 1997. pap. 17.95 incl. audio compact disk (*0-7866-2778-6*, 95860BCD) Mel Bay.

101 Blues Patterns for Bass Guitar. Larry McCabe. 40p. 1996. pap. 17.95 incl. cd-rom (*0-7866-2559-7*, 95330BCD) Mel Bay.

***101 Bodice Designs: Dress Ideas for Women, Children & Dolls.** Julie Mueller. (Illus.). 53p. 1998. pap. 20.00 (*1-929867-00-X*) Acorn IL.

***101 Bouncy Bible Rhyme-Time Games for Childrens Ministry: 101 Bible Games That Can Be Used Indoors.** Dawn M. Benegar. 2000. pap. text 16.99 (*0-7644-2217-0*) Group Pub.

***101 Brain-Boosting Math Problems: An Awesome Assortment of Fun-to-Solve Reproducible Puzzles That Build Essential Math Skills.** Lorraine H. Egan. (Illus.). 96p. (J). 1999. pap. 12.95 (*0-590-37869-4*) Scholastic Inc.

One Hundred One Bright Bulletin Board Ideas. Glenda Lee. 1991. pap. 8.00 (*0-89137-626-7*) Quality Pubns.

101 Bright Ideas: ESL Activities for All Ages. Claire M. Ford. 146p. 1996. pap. 21.33 (*0-201-89529-3*) Longman.

***101 Brilliant Chess Miniatures.** John Nunn. (Illus.). 176p. 2000. pap. 19.95 (*1-901983-16-1*, Pub. by Gambit) BHB Intl.

101 British Prose Writers 1660-1800. 400p. 1990. text 155.00 (*0-8103-4581-1*) Gale.

101 Bulletin Boards for the Music Classroom Book. 144p. 1990. per. 24.95 (*0-7935-2885-2*) H Leonard.

101 Business Opportunity Scams: How to Recognize & Avoid Rip-Offs. Charles J. Phelan. LC 96-75923. 130p. (Orig.). 1996. pap. 19.95 (*0-9652288-1-9*) Manchstr Pub.

101 Businesses You Can Start on the Internet. Daniel S. Janal. 1996. 24.95 (*0-614-14505-8*, VNR) Wiley.

101 Businesses You Can Start on the Internet. Daniel S. Janal. (Communications Ser.). 506p. 1996. pap. 25.95 (*0-442-02202-6*, VNR) Wiley.

101 CAD/CAM Traps. John K. Krouse. Ed. by Michael Abrams. 145p. 1995. 79.95 (*0-934869-19-7*) Cad-Cam Pub.

***101 Card Games.** David Galt. (Illus.). 2000. mass mkt. 6.99 (*0-7853-3959-0*) Pubns Intl Ltd.

101 Careers: A Guide to the Fastest Growing Opportunities. 2nd ed. Michael Harkavy. LC 98-21896. 360p. 1998. pap. 16.95 (*0-471-24189-X*) Wiley.

101 Careers in Mathematics. unabridged ed. Ed. by Andrew Sterrett. LC 96-75575. (Classroom Resource Materials Ser.). (Illus.). 250p. (Orig.). 1996. pap. 23.00 (*0-88385-704-9*, 101) Math Assn.

101 Casino Gambling Tips: Affordable Strategies & Techniques for Maximizing Profits & Reducing Loses. John Marchel. Ed. by T. Laine Cunningham. LC 98-96353. (Illus.). 160p. 1998. pap. 14.95 (*0-9665167-0-2*) Four Suits.

O

One Hundred One Cat & Dog Jokes. Kathy Hall. (J). 1990. pap. 1.95 (*0-590-43336-9*) Scholastic Inc.

101 Cat & Dog Jokes. Katy Hall. (J). 1990. 7.05 (*0-606-04495-7*, Pub. by Turtleback) Demco.

One Hundred One Categories. Marilyn M. Toomey. (Illus.). 106p. 1985. spiral bd. 21.95 (*0-923573-01-1*) Circuit Pubns.

101 Championship Baseball Drills. Glenn Cecchine. (101 Drills Ser.). 1999. pap. text. write for info. (*1-57167-361-X*) Coaches Choice.

***101 Checker Puzzles.** Robert W. Pike. LC 00-28503. (Illus.). 2000. 7.95 (*0-8069-6080-9*) Sterling.

One Hundred One Cherry Recipes. Carole Eberly. (Illus.). 96p. (Orig.). 1984. pap. 4.95 (*0-932296-11-4*) Eberly Pr.

101 Chess Opening Traps. Steve Giddins. 1998. pap. text 14.95 (*1-901983-13-7*) Gambit.

***101 Winning Chess Strategies.** Angus Dunnington. (Illus.). 128p. 2000. pap. 17.95 (*1-901983-22-6*, Pub. by Gambit) BHB Intl.

101 Christmas Crafts: Ornaments, Decorations & Gifts. Pat Richards. LC 96-28405. (Pat Richards Craft Collection). (Illus.). 160p. 1996. 27.95 (*1-56799-340-0*, Friedman-Fairfax) M Friedman Pub Grp Inc.

One Hundred One Christmas Melodies. 1990. 9.95 (*0-685-32147-9*, M301) Hansen Ed Mus.

***101 Christmas Ornaments.** Leisure Arts Inc. Staff. (Clever Crafter Series). (Illus.). 128p. 2000. 19.95 (*1-57486-173-5*) Leisure AR.

***101 Classic Chinese Fables.** Howard Zhai et al. 1998. pap. 19.95 (*0-9682995-0-4*) Dragon.

101 Classic Homes of the Twenties: Floor Plans & Photographs. McHenry & Baker Harris Staff. LC 99-15551. 107p. 1999. text 9.95 (*0-486-40731-4*) Dover.

101 Great Collectibles for Kids. Diane L. Oswald. (Illus.). 192p. (Orig.). (J). 1997. pap. 16.95 (*0-930625-75-7*) Krause Pubns.

One Hundred One Color Computer Programming Tips & Tricks. Ron Clark. 128p. (Orig.). 1982. pap. 7.95 (*0-86668-007-1*) ARCsoft.

101 Comforting Things to Do While You're Getting Better. Erica L. Klein. LC 98-231830. 176p. (Orig.). 1998. pap. 8.95 (*1-56561-132-2*) Wiley.

101 Comforting Things to Do While You're Getting Better at Home or in the Hospital. Erica L. Klein. 128p. 1998. pap. 8.95 (*1-56561-139-X*) Wiley.

101 Common Sense Ways to Let God Lead You to Total Stress Eliminating Riches, Health & Contentment! Richard Starr. 225p. (Orig.). 1995. pap. text 70.00 (*1-888221-17-8*) Results Now.

101 Common Sense Ways to Let God Lead You to Stress Free Riches, Health & Contentment! Richard Starr. 225p. (Orig.). 1995. pap. text 70.00 (*1-888221-26-7*) Results Now.

One Hundred One Common Therapeutic Blunders: Countertransference & Counterresistance in Psychotherapy. Richard C. Robertiello & Gerald Schoenewolf. LC 87-1406. 294p. 1987. 50.00 (*0-87668-960-8*) Aronson.

101 Commonsense Rules for the Office: How to Get along & Get Ahead. John R. Brinkerhoff. LC 91-27344. (Illus.). 176p. 1992. pap. 9.95 (*0-8117-2418-2*) Stackpole.

101 Commonsense Rules for Making Things Happen: How to Make Plans & Implement Projects. John R. Brinkerhoff. LC 93-1215. (Illus.). 256p. 1993. pap. 9.95 (*0-8117-2419-0*) Stackpole.

101 Communicative Games for the English Classroom. 128p. 1995. pap. 21.12 (*0-8442-0796-9*) NTC Contemp Pub Co.

***101 Computer Projects for Libraries.** Patrick R. Dewey. LC 99-38371. 224p. 1999. pap. 42.00 (*0-8389-0772-5*) ALA.

101 Computer Related Businesses: For All Those Who Thought That There Must Be a Way to Make Money with Their PC. Michael A. Tims. 250p. 1996. pap. 29.95 (*0-9650692-1-4*); 3.5 ld 29.95 (*0-9650692-0-6*) Matco Electronic.

101 Cookie Recipes: A Collection of Your Favorites. Publications International, Ltd. Editorial Staff. LC 98-66091. 192p. 1998. write for info. (*0-7853-2810-6*) Pubns Intl Ltd.

One Hundred One Corporate Haiku. William Warriner. LC 94-18234. 112p. 1994. pap. 9.00 (*0-201-40942-9*) Addison-Wesley.

One Hundred One Costumes for All Ages, All Occasions. rev. ed. Richard Cummings, Jr. LC 87-20298. (Illus.). 200p. 1987. pap. 12.95 (*0-8238-0286-8*) Kalmbach.

***101 Craft Projects under $10.** LC 99-52546. (Illus.). 2000. write for info. (*1-57389-017-0*) Butterick Co.

***101 Crafts under L6: Easy to Make Ideas for Gifts & Home.** Butterick Editors. (Illus.). 160p. 2000. write for info. (*1-57389-025-1*) Butterick Co.

***101 Crafts under $10: Easy-to-Make Ideas for Gifts & Home.** Ed. by Butterick Patterns Staff. (Illus.). 160p. 2000. pap. 14.95 (*1-57389-024-3*) Butterick Co.

101 Crafty Cats (& How to Make Them) Melinda Coss. (Illus.). 96p. (Orig.). 1995. 14.95 (*1-85410-340-7*, Pub. by Aurum Pr) London Brdge.

One Hundred One Creative Problem Solving Techniques: A Handbook of New Ideas for Business. James M. Higgins. Ed. by Carolyn Smith. LC 93-87802. (Illus.). 250p. (Orig.). 1994. pap. 17.95 (*1-883629-00-4*) New Mgmt Pub.

101 Creative Ways to Ask & Answer That Date. Lisa Crawford. (Illus.). (Orig.). pap. 8.95 (*0-9651163-4-4*) Harkness Pubng.

101 Crossword Puzzles, Vol. 2. Michelle Arnot. (For Dummies Ser.). 192p. 1998. pap. 9.99 (*0-7645-5110-8*) IDG Bks.

101 Crossword Puzzles, Vol. 3. Michelle Arnot. (For Dummies Ser.). 192p. 1998. pap. 9.99 (*0-7645-5111-6*) IDG Bks.

101 Crossword Puzzles for Dummies, Vol. 1. Michelle Arnot. (For Dummies Ser.). 192p. 1998. pap. 9.99 (*0-7645-5068-3*) IDG Bks.

101 Fabulous Dairy-Free Desserts Everyone Will Love: For the Lactose-Intolerant, the Dairy-Allergic, & their Friends & Families. Annette Pia-Hall. (Illus.). 256p. 1998. pap. 14.95 (*1-58177-018-9*) Barrytown Ltd.

101 Dalmatians. (Tell-a-Story Sticker Bks.). (J). pap. text 3.29 (*0-307-07610-5*, 07610) Gldn Bks Pub Co.

101 Dalmatians. LC 97-226317. (Classics Ser.). (Illus.). 96p. (J). 1995. 7.98 (*1-57082-045-7*, Pub. by Mouse Works) Little.

One Hundred One Dalmatians. (Disney Read-Alongs Ser.). (J). 7.99 incl. audio (*1-55723-020-X*) W Disney Records.

101 Dalmatians. Mary J. Fulton. (Look-Look Bks.). (Illus.). 24p. (J). (ps-3). 1994. pap. 3.29 (*0-307-12819-9*, 12819, Goldn Books) Gldn Bks Pub Co.

101 Dalmatians. Ann Mazer. (J). 1996. pap. 3.95 (*0-7868-4140-0*, Pub. by Disney Pr) Little.

101 Dalmatians: Escape from De Vil Mansion. Gabrielle Varela. LC PZ7.C37355Di 1996. (Disney Chapters Ser.). (Illus.). 64p. (J). (gr. 2-4). 1996. pap. 3.50 (*0-7868-4109-5*, Pub. by Disney Pr) Little.

101 Dalmatians: Escape from De Ville Mansion. Gabrielle Charbonnet. (J). 1996. pap. write for info. (*0-7868-4148-6*) Disney Pr.

101 Dalmatians: Giant Coloring Book. (Super Coloring Book Ser.). (J). 2.29 (*0-307-03413-5*, 03413, Goldn Books) Gldn Bks Pub Co.

101 Dalmatians: Proud to Be a Pup. Disney Enterprises, Inc. Staff. (Disney's "Storytime Treasures" Library: Vol. 2). (Illus.). 44p. (J). (gr. 1-6). 1997. 3.49 (*1-885222-98-X*) Advance Pubs.

101 Dalmatians: Special Collectors' Edition. Anne Mazer. LC 96-85929. 96p. (J). 1996. lib. bdg. 14.89 (*0-7868-5045-0*, Pub. by Disney Pr) Little.

101 Dalmatians: The Movie Storybook. Walt Disney Staff. LC 96-231439. 24p. (J). 1996. 6.98 (*1-57082-430-4*, Pub. by Mouse Works) Time Warner.

101 Dalmatians & Parents Guide: Proud to Be a Pup. Disney Enterprises, Inc. Staff. (Disney's "Storytime Treasures" Library: Vols. 2 & 19). (Illus.). 44p. (J). (gr. 1-6). 1997. 3.49 (*1-57973-016-7*) Advance Pubs.

101 Dalmatians Christmas. (Super Coloring Book Ser.). (J). 2.29 (*0-307-08540-6*, 08540) Gldn Bks Pub Co.

101 Dalmatian's Cruise Caper. Marilyn Bollinger. LC 97-162941. (Magic Touch Talking Bks.). (Illus.). 22p. (J). (ps-2). 1996. 19.99 (*1-888208-14-7*) Hasbro.

101 Dalmatians Flip-Book. 40p. (J). 1996. 2.98 (*1-57082-413-4*, Pub. by Mouse Works) Time Warner.

101 Dalmatians Movie Scrapbook: Behind the Scenes of the Live-Action Movie. Lucy Dahl. LC 97-65446. (Illus.). 32p. (J). (gr. 2-5). 1997. pap. 7.95 (*0-7868-4173-7*, Pub. by Disney Pr) Time Warner.

101 Dalmatians. Mouse Works Staff. (Illus.). 96p. (J). 1995. 7.98 (*1-57082-365-0*, Pub. by Mouse Works) Time Warner.

101 Dalmatians. Mouse Works Staff. 5p. (J). 1996. 5.98 (*1-57082-079-1*, Pub. by Mouse Works) Little.

101 Dalmatians. Mouse Works Staff. (Disney's Read-Aloud Storybooks Ser.). 64p. 1999. 6.99 (*0-7364-0112-1*, Pub. by Mouse Works) Time Warner.

101 Dalmatians. Dodie Smith. (Illus.). 192p. (J). (gr. 5-9). 1989. pap. 4.99 (*0-14-034034-3*, PuffinBks) Peng Put Young Read.

101 Dalmatians. Walt Disney Company Staff. (FRE.). 96p. (J). (gr. k-5). pap. 9.95 (*0-7859-8847-5*) Fr & Eur.

***101 Dalmatians/The Lion King, 2 vols.** 75th anniversary ed. Mouse Works Staff. (Illus.). (J). (ps-3). 1998. 9.99 (*0-7364-0085-0*) Mouse Works.

101 Dalmatians: Cruella Returns. Justine Korman. LC PZ7.K83692Dic 1997. (Disney Chapters Ser.). (Illus.). 64p. (J). (gr. 2-4). 1997. pap. 3.50 (*0-7868-4134-6*, Pub. by Disney Pr) Time Warner.

101 Dalmations: Escape from De Ville Mansion. Gabrielle Varela. (J). 1996. pap. write for info. (*0-7868-5794-3*) Disney Pr.

101 Dalmations: Escape from De Ville Mansion. Gabrielle Varella. (J). 1996. pap. write for info. (*0-7868-4143-5*) Disney Pr.

101 Dance Games for Children: Fun & Creativity with Movement. Paul Rooyackers. LC 95-13201. (Smart Fun Bks.). (Illus.). 160p. 1996. pap. 11.95 (*0-89793-171-8*); spiral bd. 14.95 (*0-89793-172-6*) Hunter Hse.

101 Database Exercises. 2nd ed. Jeffrey R. Stewart, Jr. et al. 150p. 1992. text, wbk. ed. 20.20 incl. disk (*0-02-800750-6*) Glencoe.

One Hundred One Days in the Epistles with Oswald Chambers. Harry Verploegh & James Adair. 380p. 1994. 16.99 (*1-56476-292-0*, 6-3292, Victor Bks) Chariot Victor.

101 Defensive Back Drills. Ron Dickerson & James Peterson. 1997. pap. 16.95 (*1-57167-089-0*) Coaches Choice.

101 Defensive Basketball Drills. George Karl et al. LC 97-67163. 1997. pap. 16.95 (*1-57167-079-3*) Coaches Choice.

101 Defensive Line Drills. Mark Snyder. (Illus.). 120p. 1999. pap. 16.95 (*1-57167-372-5*) Coaches Choice.

101 Delaware Wing-T Drills. Harold R. Raymond & Ted Kempshi. LC 97-80944. (Illus.). 120p. 1997. pap. 16.95 (*1-57167-162-5*) Coaches Choice.

101 Delaware Wing-T Plays. Harold R. Raymond & Ted Kempshi. LC 97-80943. (Illus.). 116p. 1997. pap. 16.95 (*1-57167-163-3*) Coaches Choice.

101 Delicious Soul Food Dessert Recipes. rev. ed. Wilbert Jones. 136p. 1999. pap. 10.95 (*0-8065-2104-X*, Citadel Pr) Carol Pub Group.

One Hundred One Desktop Publishing & Graphics Programs. Patrick R. Dewey. LC 93-13642. (One Hundred One Micro Ser.). 225p. 1993. pap. text 30.00 (*0-8389-0606-0*) ALA.

***101 Devotions for Homeschool Moms.** Jackie Wellwood. LC 99-42493. 208p. 1999. pap. 12.99 (*1-58134-139-3*) Crossway Bks.

101 Devotions with Children. LC 99-30151. 176p. 1999. pap. 9.99 (*0-8361-9117-X*) Herald Pr.

***101 Differences between Men & Women: From Closets Full of Shoes to Never Asking Directions.** Peter Laufer. 1999. pap. text 12.95 (*0-8065-2158-9*) Carol Pub Group.

101 Drama Games for Children: Fun & Learning with Acting & Make-Believe. Paul Rooyackers. LC 97-20957. (Smart Fun Bks.). (Illus.). 160p. 1996. spiral bd. 14.95 (*0-89793-212-9*) Hunter Hse.

101 Drama Games for Children: Fun & Learning with Acting & Make-Believe. Paul Rooyackers. LC 97-20957. (Smart Fun Ser.). (Illus.). 160p. (J). (ps-6). 1998. pap. 11.95 (*0-89793-211-0*) Hunter Hse.

***101 Drills & Games for Youth Basketball.** Bruce E. Brown. (Illus.). 150p. 2000. pap. 16.95 (*1-57167-441-1*) Coaches Choice.

101 Drills to Improve Your Golf Game. Alan Moyer & Glen Berggoetz. (Illus.). 224p. 1999. pap. 16.95 (*1-58382-035-3*) Sports Masters.

101 Dynamite Answers to Interview Questions: Sell Your Strengths! 4th ed. Caryl Rae Krannich & Ron Krannich. LC 99-27994. 210p. 1999. pap. 12.95 (*1-57023-113-3*, Pub. by Impact VA) Natl Bk Netwk.

***101 Dynamite Blues Guitar Fill-In Licks.** Larry McCabe. 56p. 1998. pap. 17.95 incl. audio compact disk (*0-7866-0855-2*, 97014BCD) Mel Bay.

101 Dynamite Latin Bass Patterns. Larry McCabe. (SPA & ENG., Illus.). 32p. 1997. pap. 17.95 incl. audio compact disk (*0-7866-2387-X*, 9622813CD) Mel Bay.

101 Dynamite Questions to Ask at Your Job Interview. Richard Fein. 144p. 1996. pap. 14.95 (*1-57023-053-6*) Impact VA.

***101 Dynamite Questions to Ask at Your Job Interview.** 2nd ed. Richard Fein. 156p. 2000. pap. 13.95 (*1-57023-144-3*) Impact VA.

101 Dynamite Rock Bass Patterns. Larry McCabe. (SPA & ENG.). 48p. 1997. pap. 17.95 incl. audio compact disk (*0-7866-2388-8*, 9622913CD) Mel Bay.

101 Dynamite Rock Guitar Rhythm Patterns. Larry McCabe. 40p. 1997. pap. 17.95 incl. audio compact disk (*0-7866-2732-8*, 96591BCD) Mel Bay.

***101 Dynamite Rock Guitar Riffs.** Larry McCabe. 56p. 1998. pap. 17.95 incl. audio compact disk (*0-7866-3268-2*, 97049BCD) Mel Bay.

***101 Dynamite Slide Guitar Licks in Open E Tuning.** Larry McCabe. 56p. 1999. 17.95 (*0-7866-3502-9*, 97223BCD) Mel Bay.

One Hundred One Easy Saxophone Solos or Duets. M. Edging. 1990. 9.95 (*0-685-32224-6*, M012) Hansen Ed Mus.

101 Easy Scrap Crochet Projects. Ed. by Laura Scott. (Illus.). 192p. 1999. 19.95 (*1-882138-42-2*) Hse White Birches.

One Hundred One Easy Standard Trumpet Solos. 1990. 9.95 (*0-685-32174-6*, M026) Hansen Ed Mus.

One Hundred One Easy-to-Do Magic Tricks. unabridged ed. Bill Tarr. LC 92-22895. Orig. Title: One Hundred One Easy-to-Learn Classic Magic Tricks. (Illus.). 224p. (J). 1992. pap. text 8.95 (*0-486-27367-9*) Dover.

One Hundred One Easy-to-Learn Classic Magic Tricks see One Hundred One Easy-to-Do Magic Tricks

***101 Easy, Wacky, Crazy Activities for Young Children.** Carole H. Dibble & Kathy Lee. LC 00-24516. (Illus.). 144p. 2000. pap. 12.95 (*0-87659-207-8*) Gryphon Hse.

101 Educational Conversations You Should Have with Your Child, 6 vols. Vito Perrone. (Illus.). 112p. 1993. lib. bdg. 95.70 (*0-7910-1917-9*) Chelsea Hse.

101 Educational Conversations You Should Have with Your Fourth Grader. Vito Perrone. (101 Educational Conversations You Should Have with Your Child Ser.). (Illus.). 96p. 1993. lib. bdg. 15.95 (*0-7910-1920-9*) Chelsea Hse.

101 Educational Conversations You Should Have with Your Sixth Grader. Vito Perrone. (101 Educational Conversations You Should Have with Your Child Ser.). (Illus.). 96p. 1993. pap. 5.95 (*0-7910-1989-6*) Chelsea Hse.

101 Educational Conversations You Should Have with Your Sixth Grader. Vito Perrone. (101 Educational Conversations You Should Have with Your Child Ser.). (Illus.). 96p. 1994. lib. bdg. 15.95 (*0-7910-1922-5*) Chelsea Hse.

101 Educational Conversations You Should Have with Your Kindergarten-First Grader. Vito Perrone. (101 Educational Conversations You Should Have with Your Child Ser.). (Illus.). 96p. 1992. pap. 5.95 (*0-7910-1981-0*) Chelsea Hse.

101 Educational Conversations You Should Have with Your Kindergartner-First Grader. Vito Perrone. (101 Educational Conversations You Should Have with Your Child Ser.). (Illus.). 96p. 1993. lib. bdg. 15.95 (*0-7910-1918-7*) Chelsea Hse.

101 Educational Conversations You Should Have with Your Second Grader. Vito Perrone. (101 Educational Conversations You Should Have with Your Child Ser.). (Illus.). 96p. 1992. pap. 5.95 (*0-7910-1982-9*) Chelsea Hse.

101 Educational Conversations You Should Have with Your Second Grader. Vito Perrone. (101 Educational Conversations You Should Have with Your Child Ser.). (Illus.). 96p. 1992. lib. bdg. 15.95 (*0-7910-1937-3*) Chelsea Hse.

101 Educational Conversations You Should Have with Your Third Grader. Vito Perrone. (101 Educational Conversations You Should Have with Your Child Ser.). (Illus.). 96p. 1993. lib. bdg. 15.95 (*0-7910-1919-5*) Chelsea Hse.

101 Educational Conversations You Should Have with Your Third Grader. Vito Perrone. LC 92-28529. (101 Educational Conversations You Should Have with Your Child Ser.). (Illus.). 96p. 1993. pap. 5.95 (*0-7910-1984-5*) Chelsea Hse.

101 Educational Conversations You Should Have with Your Fifth Grader. Vito Perrone. (101 Educational Conversations You Should Have with Your Child Ser.). (Illus.). 96p. 1993. lib. bdg. 15.95 (*0-7910-1921-7*) Chelsea Hse.

101 Educational Conversations You Should Have with Your Fifth Grader. Vito Perrone. (101 Educational Conversations You Should Have with Your Child Ser.). (Illus.). 96p. 1993. pap. 5.95 (*0-7910-1987-X*) Chelsea Hse.

101 Erotic Cocktails & Shooters. Glenn Gallacher. Ed. & Illus. by Christopher Tepas. 74p. (Orig.). 1997. spiral bd. 7.95 (*0-9655518-8-1*) Pimento Pubns.

***101 Essays from Across America: The Happy Marriage Book.** Ed. by Patricia M. Lytle. (Illus.). 134p. 2000. pap. 19.95 (*0-9679830-0-2*) Lytle Research.

Video: Video. Deni Bown. (101 Essential Tips Ser.). (Illus.). 72p. 1995. pap. 4.95 (*0-7894-0183-5*, 6-70497) DK Pub Inc.

101 Event Ideas: (I Wish I'd Thought Of) International Festivals & Events Assoc. Staff. Ed. by Bruce Storey. (Illus.). 43p. 1993. pap. 44.95 (*1-891202-08-1*) Intl Festivals.

101 Exciting New Uses for Condoms: A Handy Pocket Guide to Fun & Practical Uses for Condoms. Lori Katz & Barbara Meyer. LC 94-78293. (Illus.). 128p. (Orig.). 1997. pap. 9.95 (*0-9641907-1-0*) High Stress.

101 Exciting New Ways to Energize Your Cheerleaders! Gwen Holtsclaw. 76p. 1998. pap. text 10.00 (*1-884778-49-6*) Old Mountain.

101 Fabulous Rotary-Cut Quilts. Nancy J. Martin & Judy Hopkins. LC 98-28906. (Illus.). 272p. 1998. pap. 29.95 (*1-56477-240-3*, B352, Pub. by Martingale & Co) F & W Pubns Inc.

101 Family Activities for the Holidays. Ellyn Sanna. (Christmas at Home Ser.). 160p. 1999. pap. 2.97 (*1-57748-592-0*) Barbour Pub.

101 Famous Poems. Roy J. Cook. 186p. 1985. 12.95 (*0-8092-5096-9*, 509690, Contemporary Bks) NTC Contemp Pub Co.

One Hundred One Famous Poems. Compiled by Roy J. Cook. 186p. 1919. reprint ed. 14.95 (*0-8092-8833-8*, 883380); reprint ed. pap. 11.00 (*0-8092-8834-6*, 883460) NTC Contemp Pub Co.

An Asterisk (*) at the beginning of an entry indicates that the title is appearing for the first time.

One Hundred One Famous Poems. Compiled by Roy J. Cook. LC 97-514. 186p. 1984. reprint ed. 12.95 (*0-8092-8831-1*, 883110) NTC Contemp Pub Co.

101 Favorite Cat Poems. 160p. 1991. 12.95 (*0-8092-4078-5*, 407850, Contemporary Bks) NTC Contemp Pub Co.

One Hundred One Favorite Freshwater Fish Recipes. Duane R. Lund. 88p. 1979. pap. 8.95 (*0-934860-11-4*) Adventure Pubns.

101 Favorite Play Therapy Techniques. 1997. pap. 40.00 (*0-7657-0282-7*) Aronson.

101 Favorite Quotations. Tom Letourneau. 101p. 1998. pap. 15.00 (*1-885074-20-4*) Kito Enter.

101 Feng Shui Tips for the Home. Richard Webster. LC 98-9695. (Illus.). 166p. 1998. pap. 9.95 (*1-56718-809-5*) Llewellyn Pubns.

***101 Fingerplays, Stories & Songs to Use with Finger Puppets.** Diane Briggs. LC 98-42136. 144p. 1999. 25.00 (*0-8389-0749-0*) ALA.

***101 Fingerstyle Guitar Accompaniment Patterns.** Larry McCabe. (SPA & ENG.). 56p. 1998. 17.95 (*0-7866-2383-7*, 96224BCD) Mel Bay.

***101 Fly Fishing Tips.** Lefty Kreh. LC 99-58499. (Illus.). 96p. 2000. pap. 12.95 (*1-58574-035-7*) Lyons Pr.

One Hundred One Folk Art Designs for Counted Cross-Stitch & Other Needlecrafts. Carter Houck. (Crafts Ser.). (Illus.). 48p. (Orig.). 1982. pap. 3.50 (*0-486-24369-9*) Dover.

***101 Foot Care Tips for People with Diabetes.** Jessie Ahroni. LC 99-55685. 128p. 2000. pap. 12.95 (*1-58040-040-X*, 0040XQ, Pub. by Am Diabetes) NTC Contemp Pub Co.

One Hundred One Fragments of a Prayer. Stanley Nelson. Ed. by Guy Gauthier. (Midnight Sun Ser.). (Illus.). 1979. 2.00 (*0-935292-00-4*) Midnight Sun.

101 Frantic Fears of the Golfing Class: Golf's Phunniest Phobias from the Founder of Fake Fears. Bob Garrison. LC 97-91970. (Illus.). 72p. 1997. pap. 6.95 (*0-9659061-5-9*) Plaid Elephant.

101 French Idioms. Jean-Marie Cassagne & Lucques Nisset-Raidon. (101...Idioms Ser.). (Illus.). 128p. 1995. pap. 6.95 (*0-8442-1290-3*, 12903, Passprt Bks) NTC Contemp Pub Co.

101 French Proverbs: Understanding French Language & Culture Through Common Savings. J. M. Cassagne. (ENG & FRE., Illus.). 160p. 1998. pap. 6.95 (*0-8442-1291-1*, 12911, Passprt Bks) NTC Contemp Pub Co.

***101 Frequently Asked Art Marketing Questions... And Their Answers.** Barbara L. Dougherty. Ed. by Drew Steis. (Art Calendar Guide Ser.). 43p. 1999. pap. 9.95 (*0-945388-23-3*) Art Calendar.

***101 Frequently Asked Questions about "Health & Wellness" & "Nutrition"** Cedric X. Bryant et al. (Illus.). 160p. 2000. pap. 16.95 (*1-57167-452-7*) Coaches Choice.

***101 Fresh & Fun Critical Thinking Activities: Engaging Activities & Reproducibles to Develop Kids' Higher-Level Thinking Skills.** Laurie E. Rozakis. 128p. 1998. pap. 12.95 (*0-590-37523-7*) Scholastic Inc.

101 Full-Size Quilt Blocks & Borders. Ed. by Carol F. Dahlstrom. LC 97-75842. (Illus.). 216p. 1998. 34.95 (*0-696-20739-7*, Better Homes) Meredith Bks.

101 Fun Bible Crosswords. F. Carroll. 256p. 1989. mass mkt. 4.99 (*0-8423-0976-4*) Tyndale Hse.

***101 Fun Facts about Kurt Warner.** Sports Publishing Inc. Staff. (Illus.). 101p. 2000. pap. 4.95 (*1-58261-281-1*, Pub. by Sprts Pubng) Partners-West.

101 Fun Hugs. Ed Fischer. 66p. 1995. pap. 5.95 (*0-9624482-3-0*) E Fischer.

***101 Fun Skill Builders for Kids.** Joe Dinoffer. 144p. 1999. pap. 16.95 (*1-57167-431-4*) Coaches Choice.

101 Fun Things to Do on the Texas Coast. Karen Foulk. LC 98-72721. (Illus.). 216p. 1998. pap. 13.95 (*0-9652464-2-6*) Into Fun.

101 Fun to Crochet Projects. Ed. by Laura Scott. LC 98-75146. (Illus.). 176p. 1996. 19.95 (*1-882138-17-1*) Hse White Birches.

101 Further Uses for a John Major. Patrick Wright. (Illus.). 96p. 1995. pap. 9.95 (*0-233-98897-1*, Pub. by Andre Deutsch) Trafalgar.

101 Games for Groups. Ashton. (Illus.). 145p. 1998. pap. text 34.50 (*0-12-784550-X*) Acad Pr.

101 Games for Trainers. Bob Pike. 1998. pap. text 21.95 (*0-943210-41-0*) Lakewood Pubns.

***101 Games for Trainers: A Collection of the best Activities from Creative Training Techniques, 1 Vol.** Bob Pike & Chris Busse. (Illus.). 108p. 1998. pap. 21.95 (*0-943210-38-0*) Lakewood Pubns.

One Hundred One Ghost Jokes. Lisa Eisenberg & Katy Hall. (Illus.). 96p. (J). (gr. 4-6). 1988. pap. 1.95 (*0-590-41811-4*) Scholastic Inc.

101 Good Ideas: How to Improve Just about Any Process. Ed. by Karen Bemowski & Brad Stratton. LC 98-8553. (Illus.). xiv, 284p. 1998. pap. 21.00 (*0-87389-391-3*, H0986) ASQ Qual Pr.

101 Grade A Resumes for Teachers. 2nd ed. Rebecca Anthony & Gerald Roe. LC 97-29628. 184p. 1998. pap. 10.95 (*0-7641-0129-3*) Barron.

101 Great American Poems: An Anthology. American Poetry & Literacy Project Staff. LC 97-51163. (Thrift Editions Ser.). 96p. 1998. pap. 1.00 (*0-486-40158-8*) Dover.

***101 Great Answers to the Toughest Interview Questions.** 4th ed. Ron Fry. LC 99-88155. 224p. 2000. pap. 12.99 (*1-56414-464-X*) Career Pr Inc.

101 Great Choices: Chicago. Sharon L. Spence. Ed. by Dan Spinella. (101 Great Choices Ser.). (Illus.). 128p. (Orig.). 1995. pap. 7.95 (*0-8442-8986-8*, 89868, Passprt Bks) NTC Contemp Pub Co.

101 Great Choices: New Orleans. Martin Hintz. (Illus.). 128p. (Orig.). 1996. pap. 7.95 (*0-8442-8988-4*, 89884, Passprt Bks) NTC Contemp Pub Co.

101 Great Choices: New York City. Jan Aaron. LC 97-17560. (Illus.). 128p. 1996. pap. 7.95 (*0-8442-8987-6*, 89876, Passprt Bks) NTC Contemp Pub Co.

101 Great Choices: San Francisco. Anne Bianchi. LC 97-18693. (101 Great Choices Ser.). (Illus.). 128p. 1997. pap. text 8.95 (*0-8442-8989-2*, 89892) NTC Contemp Pub Co.

101 Great Choices: Washington, D.C. Jan Aaron. (Illus.). 128p. (Orig.). 1995. pap. 7.95 (*0-8442-8992-2*, 89922, Passprt Bks) NTC Contemp Pub Co.

101 Great Drinking Games. Andrew Studdard. (Illus.). 64p. 1997. pap. 5.95 (*1-889647-30-6*) Boston Am.

101 Great Games & Activities. Arthur B. Vangundy. LC 97-76316. 368p. 1998. ring bd. 89.95 (*0-7879-4138-7*, Pfffr & Co) Jossey-Bass.

101 Great Games & Activities. Arthur B. VanGundy. LC 97-76316. 348 p. 1998. 89.95 (*0-7879-4416-5*) Jossey-Bass.

***101 Great Games for Kids: Active, Bible-Based Fun for Christian Education.** (Illus.). 128p. (J). 2000. pap. 14.00 (*0-687-08795-3*) Abingdon.

101 Best Home-Based Businesses for Women: Everything You Need to Know about Getting Started on the Road to Success. Priscilla Y. Huff. LC 94-34095. 368p. 1995. pap. 14.95 (*1-55958-703-2*) Prima Pub.

101 Great Ideas for Managing People: From America's Most Innovative Small Companies. 2nd ed. Ed. by Martha Mangelsdorf. 192p. 1999. pap. 14.95 (*1-880394-93-6*) Thomson Learn.

***101 Great Ideas for Secondary School Mathematics.** Alfred S. Posamentier & Herbert A. Hauptman. LC 00-34558. 2000. write for info. (*0-7619-7513-6*) Corwin Pr.

101 Great Ideas to Create a Caring Group. Thom Corrigan. LC 98-126700. (Pilgrimage Ser.). 84p. 1997. pap. 8.00 (*1-57683-072-1*) NavPress.

101 Great Lowfat Desserts: No Butter, No Cream, No Kidding! Donna Rodnitzky. LC 94-33548. 304p. 1995. pap. 12.95 (*1-55958-666-4*) Prima Pub.

101 Great Lowfat Mexican Dishes: Hot, Spicy & Healthful! Margaret Martinez. LC 95-5282. (Illus.). 288p. 1995. pap. 12.95 (*0-7615-0009-X*) Prima Pub.

101 Great Lowfat Pasta Dishes: Fresh, Zesty & Healthful! Margaret Martinez. LC 96-221. (Illus.). 240p. 1996. per. 12.95 (*0-7615-0414-1*) Prima Pub.

***101 Great Mail-Order Businesses.** Tyler Hicks. LC 99-57703. 2000. pap. 14.95 (*0-7615-2130-5*) Prima Pub.

101 Great Mail Order Businesses: The Very Best (& Most Profitable!) Mail Order Businesses You Can Start with Little or No Money. Tyler Gregory Hicks. 256p. 1996. pap. 12.95 (*0-7615-0337-4*) Prima Pub.

101 Great Resumes: Unique Resumes, Creative Resumes, but Most Important, Resumes that Work! Career Press Editors. LC 95-50099. 210p. 1996. pap. 9.99 (*1-56414-201-9*) Career Pr Inc.

101 Great Sauces - No Butter, No Cream, No Kidding: Easy & Delicious Good-for-You Sauces for Every Occasion. John Ettinger. LC 93-49715. 128p. 1994. pap. 9.95 (*1-55958-498-X*) Prima Pub.

One Hundred One Great Ways to Keep Your Child Entertained: While You Get Something Else Done. Danelle Hickman & Valerie Teurlay. (Illus.). 96p. 1992. pap. 8.95 (*0-312-07618-5*) St Martin.

***101 Greatest Magic Secrets: A Tell-All Guide to the Most Amazing Tricks & Illusions of All Time.** Herbert L. Becker. 1999. pap. text 14.00 (*0-8065-2154-6*, Birch Ln Pr) Carol Pub Group.

***101 Greatest Mystery Films.** Otto Penzler. 2000. per. 14.00 (*0-7434-0717-2*, Pub. by ibooks) S&S Trade.

101 Greatest Rock 'n' Roll Classics Vol. 1: Piano/Vocal Mixed Folio. 3rd rev. ed. Ed. by Carol Cuellar. 272p. (Orig.). 1994. pap. 18.95 (*0-89898-816-0*, TMF0219C) Wrner Bros.

101 Grrreat Quickies. Laura Corn. 1997. pap. text 25.95 (*0-9629628-5-6*) Park Ave Pubs.

101 Guitar Tips & Tricks. Andy Jones & Arthur Dick. 1997. 14.95 incl. audio (*0-7119-3755-9*, AM 91533) Omnibus NY.

101 Harley-Davidson Evolution Weekend Projects. Kenna Love & Kip Woodring. LC 98-37893. (Illus.). 256p. 1998. pap. 24.95 (*0-7603-0370-3*) Motorbooks Intl.

One Hundred-One Hechos Acerca del Satanismo en America. John Hagee. (SPA.). 31p. (Orig.). 1991. pap., per. 3.00 (*1-56908-007-0*) Global Evang.

***101 Hikes in Northern California.** Matt Heid. (Illus.). 2000. pap. text 15.95 (*0-89997-257-8*) Wilderness Pr.

101 Hikes in Southern California: Exploring Mountains, Seashore, & Desert. Jerry Schad. LC 96-25593. (Illus.). 288p. (Orig.). 1996. pap. 15.95 (*0-89997-193-8*) Wilderness Pr.

***101 Hiring Mistakes Employers Make... & How to Avoid Them.** Richard Fein. LC 99-88886. (Savvy CareerBuilder Ser.). 2000. pap. 14.95 (*1-57023-129-X*) Impact VA.

101 Holiday Gift Ideas. Ellyn Sanna. (Christmas at Home Ser.). 160p. 1999. pap. 2.97 (*1-57748-591-2*) Barbour Pub.

***101 Home Office Success Secrets.** 2nd ed. Lisa Kanarek. LC 00-36003. 192p. 2000. pap. 12.99 (*1-56414-455-0*) Career Pr Inc.

One Hundred One Homeschool Teaching Tips from the Sycamore Tree. Sandra L. Gogel. (Illus.). (Orig.). 1989. pap. 3.95 (*0-9627906-0-5*) Sycamore Tree.

101 Hopelessly Hilarious Jokes. Lisa Eisenberg. (J). 1990. 7.05 (*0-606-04497-3*, Pub. by Turtleback) Demco.

One Hundred One Hopelessly Hilarious Jokes. Lisa Eisenberg. 96p. (J). (gr. 4-6). 1990. pap. 1.95 (*0-590-43636-8*) Scholastic Inc.

101 Horsemanship & Equitation Patterns: A Western & English Ringside Guide for Practice & Show. Cherry Hill. LC 98-55399. 224p. 1999. spiral bd. 29.95 (*1-58017-159-1*) Storey Bks.

One Hundred One Hot Licks Fingerstyle Guitar. Tommy Flint. 32p. 1982. 15.95 incl. audio compact disk (*0-7866-2371-3*, 93804BCD) Mel Bay.

101 Hot Sex Tips. James Massey. 160p. (Orig.). 1997. pap. 9.95 (*0-9650574-0-2*) Tristan Pr.

One Hundred One Hurry-Up Pasta Recipes. (Favorite All Time Recipes Ser.). (Illus.). 96p. 1993. spiral bd. 3.50 (*1-56173-700-3*, 2014100) Pubns Intl Ltd.

101 Hymn Stories. Kenneth W. Osbeck. LC 81-17165. 288p. (C). 1982. pap. 12.99 (*0-8254-3416-5*) Kregel.

101 Ideas for Homebrew Fun. Ray Daniels. LC 97-47350. (Illus.). 144p. 1998. pap. 14.95 (*0-937381-57-8*) Brewers Pubns.

***101 Ideas for Making Family Memories.** Ruthann Winans & Linda Lee. LC 99-43333. (Mom's Little Helpers Ser.). 64p. 2000. pap. 6.99 (*0-7369-0223-6*) Harvest Hse.

101 Ideas for Serving the Impaired Elderly. Library Service to Impaired Elderly Forum Publicat. 1990. 8.00 (*0-8389-7356-6*) ASCLA.

101 Ideas for the Best-Ever Christmas. Caryl W. Krueger. LC 94-4445. 224p. (Orig.). 1992. 4.50 (*0-687-29069-4*) Dimen for Liv.

One Hundred One Ideas to Help Your Child Learn to Read & Write. Mary Behm & Richard Behm. Ed. by Michael Shermis. LC 89-49266. (Illus.). 39p. 1989. pap. 6.50 (*0-927516-13-6*) ERIC-REC.

One Hundred One Inexpensive Ways to Entertain Children. Juanita Matheson-Ferrey. LC 88-72476. 125p. (Orig.). 1987. pap. write for info. (*0-317-59719-1*, 662-4685) AFCOM Pub.

***101 Innovative Ideas for Creative Kids.** Claudia Dodson. LC 00-8085. (Illus.). (J). 2000. pap. write for info. (*0-7619-7645-0*) Corwin Pr.

101 Inspirational Stories. Gordon R. Wren. 224p. (Orig.). 1995. pap. 12.00 (*0-9650496-9-8*) Phun From Phoenix.

One Hundred One Instant Essays. Edward Kimball. 115p. pap. write for info. (*0-9634021-0-2*) Pennington CA.

101 Interventions in Family Therapy. Ed. by Thorana S. Nelson & Terry S. Trepper. 428p. 1993. pap. 24.95 (*1-56024-193-4*); lib. bdg. 54.95 (*0-86656-902-2*) Haworth Pr.

101 Tough Interview Questions: . . . And Answers that Win the Job! Daniel Porot & Frances Bolles Haynes. LC 99-186720. (Illus.). 206p. 1999. pap. 12.95 (*1-58008-068-5*) Ten Speed Pr.

101 Investment Lessons from the Wizards of Wall Street: The Pros' Secrets for Running with the Bulls Without Losing Your Shirt. Michael Sincere. LC 98-45106. 256p. 1999. pap. 14.99 (*1-56414-382-1*) Career Pr Inc.

***101 Investment Tips: How To Maximize Returns & Reduce Risk.** Vos & Christina Heliker. 2000. pap. 22.95 (*0-13-031107-3*) P-H.

***101 Investment Tools for Buying Low & Selling High.** Jae K. Shim. 1999. 39.95 (*0-910944-13-X*) St Lucie Pr.

One Hundred-One Japanese Idioms. Senko K. Maynard & Michael L. Maynard. (JPN & ENG., Illus.). 224p. 1993. pap. 7.95 (*0-8442-8496-3*, 84963, Natl Textbk Co) NTC Contemp Pub Co.

One Hundred One Jazz Guitar Licks. Alan De Mause. 44p. 1996. 17.95 incl. audio compact disk (*0-7866-2300-4*, 93863BCD) Mel Bay.

***101 Keys for Life: Powerful Thoughts on Christian Living.** Vickie Phelps. 40p. 2000. 1.99 (*1-57748-941-1*) Barbour Pub.

One Hundred One Kitchen Projects. Percy W. Blandford. 1991. 23.95 (*0-8306-5324-4*) McGraw-Hill Prof.

One Hundred One Kitchen Projects, Fall-Winter. 1991. 23.95 (*0-8306-5306-6*) McGraw-Hill Prof.

One Hundred One Kitchen Projects for the Woodworker. Percy W. Blandford. (Illus.). 270p. 1987. 23.95 (*0-8306-7884-0*, 2884); pap. 14.95 (*0-8306-2884-3*) McGraw-Hill Prof.

101 Law Forms for Personal Use. Robin Leonard & Marcia Stewart. LC 98-5035. (Quick & Legal Ser.). (Illus.). 272p. (Orig.). 1997. pap. 24.95 (*0-87337-412-6*) Nolo com.

One Hundred One Legal Ways to Stay in the U. S. A.: or How to Get a Green Card According to the Immigration Act of 1990, Bk. 1. Loida N. Lewis. Ed. by Elliott Wiley et al. LC 91-71185. 222p. (Orig.). 1994. 29.95 (*1-880808-01-3*) Bookmark NY.

One Hundred One Legal Ways to Stay in the U. S. A.: or How to Get a Green Card According to the Immigration Act of 1990, Bk. 1. Loida N. Lewis. Ed. by Sybil Eakin et al. LC 91-71185. 308p. (Orig.). 1992. pap. 19.95 (*1-880808-00-5*) Bookmark NY.

101 Lessons of Tao. Luke Chan. (Illus.). 150p. (Orig.). 1995. pap. 12.95 (*0-9637341-2-1*) Benefactor.

One Hundred One Licks & Exercises for Electric Bass. Dan Gutt. 40p. 1996. 17.95 incl. audio compact disk (*0-7866-2717-4*, 93991BCD) Mel Bay.

101 Lies Men Tell Women -- And Why Women Believe Them. Dory Hollander. 384p. 1997. pap. 13.50 (*0-06-092812-3*, Perennial) HarperTrade.

101 Lies Men Tell Women: And Why Women Believe Them. abr. ed. Dory Hollander. 1995. audio 12.00 (*0-694-51597-3*, CPN 10064) HarperAudio.

101 Lies Men Tell Women & Why Women Believe Them. Dory Hollander. (Illus.). 343p. 1997. reprint ed. text 20.00 (*0-7881-5086-3*) DIANE Pub.

101 Linebacker Drills. Jerry Sandusky et al. 1997. pap. 16.95 (*1-57167-087-4*) Coaches Choice.

***101 Little Instructions for Surviving Your Divorce: A No-Nonsense Guide to the Challenges at Hand.** Barbara J. Walton. 128p. 1999. pap. 12.95 (*1-886230-24-2*) Impact Pubs CA.

101 Little Known Facts about Karl Malone. Dale Ratermann. (One Hundred One Little Known Facts Ser.). (Illus.). 101p. 1997. pap. 6.95 (*1-57167-150-1*) Sports Pub.

101 Little Known Facts about Tiger Woods. Sports Publishing Inc. Staff. (One Hundred One Little Known Facts Ser.). (Illus.). 101p. 1997. pap. 6.95 (*1-57167-151-X*) Sports Pub.

101 Little Known Facts about Troy Aikman. Sports Publishing Inc. Staff. (One Hundred One Little Known Facts Ser.). (Illus.). 101p. 1997. pap. 6.95 (*1-57167-152-8*) Sports Pub.

101 Little Known Facts about Ken Griffey Jr. Sports Publishing Inc. Staff. (One Hundred One Little Known Facts Ser.). (Illus.). 101p. 1997. pap. 6.95 (*1-57167-173-0*) Sports Pub.

101 Longing & Long Lining Exercises: English & Western. Cherry Hill. LC 98-35577. 224p. 1998. pap. 29.95 (*0-87605-046-1*) Howell Bks.

101 Low Cost Marketing Methods That Attract Customers. write for info. (*0-614-04307-7*) Busn Toolbox.

Six Silent Men: 101st LRP, Rangers, Book 2, Bk. 2. Kenn Miller. 1997. mass mkt. 5.99 (*0-8041-1564-8*) Ivy Books.

***101 Made-to-Fit Quilts for Your Home.** Ed. by Jeanne Stauffer & Sandra L. Hatch. (Illus.). 176p. 2000. 19.96 (*1-882138-62-7*) Hse White Birches.

One Hundred One Marketing Ideas, Vol. IV. Bank Marketing Association Staff. 212p. (Orig.). 1990. 45.00 (*1-55695-001-2*) Bank Mktg Assn.

101 Marvelous Money-Making Ideas for Kids. Heather Wood. 128p. (Orig.). (YA). 1995. 3.99 (*0-8125-2060-2*, Pub. by Tor Bks) St Martin.

101 Mathematical Projects. Brian Bolt & David Hobbs. 168p. 1991. pap. 20.95 (*0-521-34759-9*) Cambridge U Pr.

101 Meatless Family Dishes: Delicious & Satisfying Recipes the Whole Family Will Love (Even the Kids!) John Ettinger. LC 95-3365. 192p. 1995. pap. 14.95 (*0-7615-0019-7*) Prima Pub.

101 Media & Marketing Tips for the Sole Proprietor. Nanette J. Miner. 100p. 1998. pap. 7.95 (*0-9650666-2-2*) BVC Pubng.

***101 Medication Tips for People with Diabetes.** Betsy A. Carlisle et al. LC 99-23163. (Illus.). 128p. 1999. pap. 14.95 (*1-58040-032-9*, 00329Q, Pub. by Am Diabetes) NTC Contemp Pub Co.

101 Medicinal Herbs: An Illustrated Guide. Steven Foster. LC 98-28056. (Illus.). 1998. pap. 19.95 (*1-883010-51-9*) Interweave.

One Hundred One Microcomputer Projects to Do in Your Library: Putting Your Micro to Work. Patrick Dewey. 176p. 1990. pap. text 6.00 (*0-8389-0518-8*) ALA.

One Hundred One Microwave Favorites Plus Four. rev. ed. Arlene Hamernik. (Illus.). 82p. 1984. reprint ed. spiral bd. 3.50 (*0-9602930-4-3*) Microwave Helps.

***101 Miracle Foods That Heal Your Heart.** Liz Applegate. (Illus.). 2000. pap. 12.00 (*0-7352-0169-2*) PH Pr.

101 Miracles of Natural Healing. Luke Chan. 144p. (Orig.). 1995. pap. 14.95 (*0-9637341-4-8*) Benefactor.

101 Mississippi Delta Blues Fingerpicking Licks. Larry McCabe. 48p. 1997. pap. 17.95 incl. audio compact disk (*0-7866-2400-0*, 96241BCD) Mel Bay.

101 Money-Saving Household Repairs. Time-Life Books Editors. Ed. by Brian Parsons. LC 94-42181. (Illus.). 96p. 1995. write for info. (*0-8094-9177-X*) Time-Life.

101 Montunos. Rebecca Mauleon. (Illus.). 250p. 1999. text 28.00 (*1-883217-07-5*) Sher Music.

101 More Best Resumes. Jay A. Block et al. LC 99-18630. 208p. 1999. pap. 11.95 (*0-07-032969-9*) McGraw.

101 More Favorite Play Therapy Techniques. Ed. by Heidi Gerard Kaduson & Charles E. Schaefer. 50.00 (*0-7657-0299-1*) Aronson.

101 More Hymn Stories. Kenneth W. Osbeck. LC 84-27847. 328p. (C). 1985. pap. 12.99 (*0-8254-3420-3*) Kregel.

101 More Ideas for Increasing Your Profit Plus Building Your Business for the Future. Tom Shay. 109p. 1998. pap. 8.00 (*1-891964-04-6*) Profits Plus.

101 More Ideas for Volunteer programs. Sue Vineyard & Steve McCurley. 1995. pap. 11.95 (*0-911029-46-X*) Heritage Arts.

101 More Interventions in Family Therapy. Ed. by Thorana S. Nelson & Terry S. Trepper. LC 97-51448. (Illus.). 511p. (C). 1998. 69.96 (*0-7890-0058-X*); pap. 39.95 (*0-7890-0570-0*) Haworth Pr.

One Hundred One More Monster Jokes. Jovial Bob Stine, pseud. (One Hundred One Jokes Ser.). 96p. (Orig.). (J). (gr. 4-6). 1990. pap. 1.99 (*0-590-43171-4*) Scholastic Inc.

***101 More Music Games for Children: More Fun & Learning with Rhythm & Song.** Jerry B. Storms. (Illus.). 160p. (ps up). 2000. pap. 12.95 (*0-89793-298-6*) Hunter Hse.

***101 More Music Games for Children: More Fun & Learning with Rhythm & Song.** Jerry B. Storms. (Illus.). 160p. (J). (ps up). 2000. 17.95 (*0-89793-299-4*) Hunter Hse.

101 More Read-Aloud Classics. Ed. by Pamela Horn. LC 96-30679. (Illus.). 400p. (J). (gr. k-4). 1996. 12.98 (*1-884822-78-9*) Blck Dog & Leventhal.

101 More Reasons Why a Cat Is Better Than a Man. Allia Zobel & Nicole Hollander. LC 97-20868. (Illus.). 80p. 1997. pap. 6.95 (*1-55850-794-9*) Adams Media.

One Hundred One More Talks for Children. Marianne J. Shampton. 1990. 9.95 (*0-88494-729-7*) Bookcraft Inc.

101 Most Asked Questions about Las Vegas & Casino Gambling. George Joseph. (Illus.). 186p. 1996. pap., mass mkt. 14.95 (*0-9660017-0-2*) G & E Ent.

O

An Asterisk (*) at the beginning of an entry indicates that the title is appearing for the first time.

One Hundred One Most Asked Questions about the Mac. Fred Fuld, III. 80p. 1992. pap. text 12.95 (*0-9634816-0-6*); disk 15.00 (*0-9634816-1-4*) Invest Res Inst.

101 Most Asked Questions by Women. George G. Bloomer. 1997. pap. text 8.99 (*1-56229-118-1*) Pneuma Life Pub.

101 Most Common Mistakes. Clay Carr. LC 97-199204. (C). 1997. pap. text 16.95 (*0-13-234170-0*) P-H.

101 Most Popular Songs of the Rock Era. Ed. by Carol Cuellar. 392p. (Orig.). 1995. pap. text 22.95 (*0-89724-795-7*, VF1959A) Wrner Bros.

101 Mountain Bike Routes in Scotland. Harry Henniker. (Illus.). 224p. 1998. 29.95 (*1-85158-936-8*, Pub. by Mainstream Pubng) Trafalgar.

101 Music Games for Children: Fun & Learning with Rhythm & Songs. Jerry B. Storms. LC 94-11810. (Smart Fun Bks.). (Illus.). 160p. 1994. pap. 11.95 (*0-89793-164-5*); spiral bd. 14.95 (*0-89793-165-3*) Hunter Hse.

*__101 Myths of the Bible.__ Gary Greenberg. 2000. 24.95 (*1-57071-586-6*) Sourcebks.

101 Myths of the Bible: How Ancient Scribes Invented Biblical History. Gary Greenberg. LC 99-20316. 368p. 1999. 24.95 (*1-55972-510-9*, Birch Ln Pr) Carol Pub Group.

101 Nashville-Style Guitar Licks Book. Larry McCabe. 48p. 1996. pap. 15.95 incl. audio compact disk (*0-7866-0408-5*, 95447BCD) Mel Bay.

One Hundred One Needlepoint Stitches & How to Use Them. Hope Hanley. (Illus.). 112p. 1986. reprint ed. pap. 6.95 (*0-486-25031-8*) Dover.

101 Nights of Grrreat Sex: Secret Sealed Seductions for Fun Loving Couples. Laura Corn. (Illus.). 210p. 1995. pap. 29.95 (*0-9629628-1-3*) Park Ave Pubs.

101 Nights of Grrreat Romance: How to Make Love with Your Clothes On. Laura Corn. (Illus.). 420p. 1996. pap. 29.95 (*0-9629628-2-1*) Park Ave Pubs.

101 Solved Nuclear Engineering Problems. J. A. Camara. 168p. 1999. pap. 52.95 (*1-888577-30-4*, NESP) Prof Pubns CA.

101 Nutrition Tips for People with Diabetes. Patti Geil & Lee Ann Holzmeister. LC 99-14515. 128p. 1999. pap. 14.95 (*1-58040-028-0*, 00280Q, Pub. by Am Diabetes) NTC Contemp Pub Co.

*__101 of the Best Corporate Team Building Activities We Know.__ Simon Priest & Karl Rohnke. 114p. 1999. per. 39.95 (*0-7872-6601-9*) Kendall-Hunt.

101 of the World's Most Effective Pick-Up Lines. Keith Allen & Anthony M. Ferrari. Ed. by Matthew Huijgen. (Illus.). 128p. (Orig.). 1997. pap. 9.95 (*0-9634641-2-4*) Ace Co & Assocs.

101 Offensive Basketball Drills. George Karl et al. LC 97-67164. 1997. pap. 16.95 (*1-57167-078-5*) Coaches Choice.

101 Offensive Line Drills. Steve Loney. (Illus.). 120p. 1999. pap. 16.95 (*1-57167-391-1*) Coaches Choice.

101 Opera Librettos: Complete Texts with English Translations of the World's Best Loved Operas. Ed. by Jessica M. MacMurray. 1482p. 1996. 29.98 (*1-884822-79-7*) Blck Dog & Leventhal.

101 Amazing Optical Illusions. Terry Jennings. (Illus.). 88p. (J). 1998. 9.95 (*0-8069-9463-0*) Sterling.

One Hundred One Optoelectronic Projects. Delton T. Horn. (Illus.). 250p. (Orig.). 1989. 24.95 (*0-8306-9205-3*); pap. 16.95 (*0-8306-3205-0*) McGraw-Hill Prof.

101 Outrageous Things to Do on Birthday. Herb Kavet. (Illus.). 64p. 1998. pap. 5.95 (*1-889647-39-X*) Boston Am.

101 Pasta Recipes: A Collection of Your Favorites. Publications International, Ltd. Editorial Staff. LC 97-75998. 192p. 1998. write for info. (*0-7853-2801-7*) Pubns Intl Ltd.

*__101 Pearls in Refractive, Cataract & Corneal Surgery.__ Dimitri T. Azar & Samir A. Melki. 150p. (C). 2001. pap. text 45.00 (*1-55642-489-2*) SLACK Inc.

101 Pensamientos de Liderazgo Efectivo: 131 Thoughts for Effective Leadership. Jorge Espinoza. (ENG & SPA.). 1996. pap. 11.95 (*0-9628722-4-5*) NUVO Ltd.

101 Perfectly Good Reasons to Hate Young Skinny Women. Kathy Shaskan. LC 97-65432. (Illus.). 108p. 1998. pap. 11.95 (*0-9665425-0-9*) MotherBee Prod.

*__101 Philosophy Problems.__ Martin Cohen. LC 98-31117. 1999. 60.00 (*0-415-19126-2*); pap. 14.99 (*0-415-19127-0*) Routledge.

*__101 Picture Prompts to Spark Super Writing: Reproducible Photographs, Cartoons & Art Masterpiece.__ Karen Kellaher. (Illus.). 64p. (J). 1999. pap. 9.95 (*0-590-63229-9*) Scholastic Inc.

101 Pitching Drills. Bob Bennett. (Illus.). 164p. 2000. pap. 16.95 (*1-57167-318-0*) Coaches Choice.

101 Plus Great Gift-Giving Ideas: For Special Friends, Secret Pals...To Show You Care. Sherry Brooks. (Giftables Ser.). 1998. pap. 5.99 (*0-932081-61-4*) Victory Hse.

One Hundred One Plus Hurry-Up Chicken Recipes. (Favorite All Time Recipes Ser.). (Illus.). 96p. 1993. spiral bd. 3.50 (*1-56173-661-9*, 2011700) Pubns Intl Ltd.

One Hundred One Plus Hurry-Up Hamburger Recipes. (Favorite All Time Recipes Ser.). (Illus.). 96p. 1993. spiral bd. 3.50 (*1-56173-771-2*, 2002800) Pubns Intl Ltd.

101 Plus Practical Solutions for the Family Lawyer. Ed. by Gregg M. Herman. LC 96-14882. 1996. pap. 64.95 (*1-57073-328-7*) Amer Bar Assn.

*__101 Plus Reasons to Read to Your Child.__ Brenda Star. 66p. 2001. pap. 12.95 (*1-884886-11-6*) Star Group.

101+ Uses for Kudzu. Diane Hoots & Matthew Hoots. (Illus.). 56p. 1999. pap. 6.50 (*1-880308-14-2*) Suntop.

101+ Ways God Speaks (& How to Hear Him) Sandy Warner. Ed. by Jocy Voorhies. (Illus.). 331p. (Orig.). 1997. pap. 13.95 (*0-9656768-0-3*) SOS Pubns OR.

One Hundred One Plus Ways to Get Out of a Traffic Ticket: Honk If You See a Cop, Vol. 2. Jeff Hodge. Ed. by Paulette Hodge. (Illus.). 120p. (Orig.). 1997. pap. 5.95 (*0-9633347-2-7*) Talent Wrld Pubns.

*__101+ Ways to Steal by a Clerk: How to Analyze, Entrap & Eject a Thief.__ Barry Bryant. 110p. 2000. pap. 12.95 (*0-9676916-0-5*) W Davis Corp.

One Hundred One Pocket Computer Programming Tips & Tricks. Jim Cole. (Illus.). 128p. (Orig.). 1982. pap. 7.95 (*0-86668-004-7*) ARCsoft.

One Hundred One Power Thoughts. Louise L. Hay. 1994. 7.95 (*1-56170-103-3*, 513) Hay House.

101 Practical Exercises for Sexual Addiction Recovery. Douglas Weiss. 140p. 1996. pap. text 39.95 (*1-881292-19-3*) Discov TX.

101 Preguntas Que los Ninos Hacen Acerca de Dios, Vol. 1. David R. Veerman et al.Tr. of 101 Questions Children Ask about God. (SPA., Illus.). 216p. 1996. pap. text 9.99 (*0-311-38650-4*, Edit Mundo) Casa Bautista.

One Hundred One President Jokes. Melvin Berger. 96p. (J). (gr. 4-6). 1990. pap. 1.95 (*0-590-43166-8*) Scholastic Inc.

One Hundred One Problematic Phrases in Translating from English to French: Clearing up Misleading Meanings. J. L. Cova & Charles Maingon. LC 90-25039. 124p. 1991. lib. bdg. 59.95 (*0-88946-496-0*) E Mellen.

*__101 Professional Tips to Make Your Photos Sing.__ Billy E. Barnes. 56p. 1999. pap. 12.95 (*0-9676198-9-0*, 101T99) Robuck Pr.

One Hundred One Program Surprises & Tricks. David L. Heiserman. 1984. pap. text 19.95 (*0-8306-6610-9*) McGraw-Hill Prof.

One Hundred One Programming Surprises & Tricks for Your ATARI Computer. David L. Heiserman. (Illus.). 208p. (Orig.). 1984. pap. 11.50 (*0-8306-1731-0*, 1731) McGraw-Hill Prof.

One Hundred One Programming Tips & Tricks for the Texas Instruments TI 99-4A Home Computer. Len Turner. 128p. 1983. 8.95 (*0-86668-025-X*) ARCsoft.

One Hundred One Programming Tips & Tricks for the VIC-20 & Commodore 64. Howard Adler. 128p. 1983. 8.95 (*0-86668-030-6*) ARCsoft.

One Hundred One Projects for the Z80. Frank P. Tedeschi & Robert Colon. (Illus.). 368p. 1983. 23.95 (*0-8306-0491-X*, 1491H) McGraw-Hill Prof.

101 Promises Worth Keeping. gif. ed. Neil Eskelin. LC 95-68304. 222p. 1999. pap. 10.99 (*0-88419-405-1*) Dake Pub.

One Hundred-One Proof Pure Old Jess: Jesse Helms Quoted. Ed. by Seth A. Effron. (Illus.). 90p. (Orig.). 1993. pap. 5.00 (*0-935400-18-4*) News & Observer.

101 Proven Ways to Make Your School Studies Easier. Laura Miller. (Illus.). x, 70p. 1998. pap. 6.95 (*0-9665522-0-2*) EduSource.

101 Quarterback Drills. Steve Axman. LC 97-69612. (Art & Science of Coaching Ser.). (Illus.). 128p. 1998. pap. 16.95 (*1-57167-195-1*) Coaches Choice.

101 Questions about Ancient Indians of the Southwest. David G. Noble. LC 98-25115. (Illus.). 32p. (J). (gr. 1-6). 1998. pap. 9.95 (*1-877856-87-8*) SW Pks Mnmts.

101 Questions about Copyright Law. Andrew Alpern. LC 98-41538. 80p. 1998. pap. 2.95 (*0-486-40448-X*) Dover.

One Hundred One Questions about dBASE III. Adam B. Green et al. 1984. 19.95 (*0-13-634890-4*) S&S Trade.

One Hundred One Questions about Desert Life. Alice Jablonsky. Ed. by Ronald J. Foreman. LC 93-84874. (Illus.). 32p. (Orig.). (YA). 1994. pap. 6.95 (*1-877856-32-0*) SW Pks Mnmts.

101 Questions about Santa Claus. Bob Litak. Ed. by Christine Hilt Muehlenberg. LC 99-189814. (Illus.). 128p. (gr. 4-7). 1998. 12.95 (*0-911493-23-9*) Blue Sky.

101 Questions about the Seashore. Sy Barlowe. LC 97-20552. 1998. pap. 2.00 (*0-486-29914-7*) Dover.

One Hundred One Questions about Volcanoes. John Calderazzo. Ed. by Randolph Jorgen. LC 93-84875. (Illus.). 32p. (Orig.). (J). 1994. pap. 6.95 (*1-877856-33-9*) SW Pks Mnmts.

*__101 Questions about Your Immune System You Felt Defenseless to Answer... until Now.__ Faith H. Brynie. LC 99-33368. 176p. (J). (gr. 7). 2000. lib. bdg. 25.90 (*0-7613-1569-1*) TFC Bks NY.

*__101 Questions Adventists Ask.__ Bert Beverly Beach et al. Ed. by Tim Lale. LC 00-23565. 138p. 2000. 14.99 (*0-8163-1790-9*) Pacific Pr Pub Assn.

101 Questions & Answers about Backyard Wildlife. Ann Squire. LC 96-25408. (Illus.). 128p. (J). (gr. 5 up). 1996. 16.95 (*0-8027-8457-7*) Walker & Co.

101 Questions & Answers about Backyard Wildlife. Ann Squire. LC 96-25408. (Illus.). (J). 1996. lib. bdg. 16.85 (*0-8027-8458-5*) Walker & Co.

*__101 Questions & Answers on Demon Powers.__ Lester Sumrall. 1999. pap. text 6.95 (*1-58568-202-0*) Sumrall Pubng.

101 Questions & Answers on Small Business. Bill FitzPatrick. 120p. (Orig.). 1996. pap. 6.00 (*1-884864-05-8*) Am Success Inst.

101 Questions Answered about Dinosaurs. Philip J. Currie & Eva B. Koppelhus. (Illus.). 64p. (Orig.). 1996. pap. text 2.00 (*0-486-29172-3*) Dover.

101 Questions Children Ask about God. David R. Veerman. 202p. 1992. pap. 9.99 (*0-8423-5102-7*) Tyndale Hse.

101 Questions Every African-American Man Asks. Dermot D. Givens. LC 94-92382. (Illus.). 128p. (Orig.). 1995. pap. 9.95 (*0-9643384-0-8*) Say It Loud.

101 Questions on How to Play Chess. Fred Wilson. LC 94-34799. (Illus.). 64p. 1994. pap. 1.00 (*0-486-28273-2*) Dover.

One Hundred One Questions to Ask Your Heart Doctor: An Insider's View. Joy Hannah. LC 88-51511. 150p. (Orig.). 1988. pap. 9.95 (*0-9621546-3-6*) Tamarack Hse.

101 Questions Your Brain Has Asked about Itself. Faith H. Brynie. LC 98-9797. 176p. (J). (gr. 7 up). 1998. 23.90 (*0-7613-0400-2*, Copper Beech Bks) Millbrook Pr.

*__101 Questions Your Dog Would Ask: What's Bothering Your Dog & How to Solve It's Problems.__ Helen T. Dennis. (Illus.). 112p. 1999. pap. 12.95 (*0-7641-0886-7*) Barron.

One Hundred One Questions Your Pastor Hopes You Never Ask. Earl Paulk & Don Paulk. 128p. 1990. 12.95 (*0-917595-36-X*) Kingdom Pubs.

101 Questions Your Skin Has Always Wanted to Ask Itself. Faith H. Brynie. LC 98-50695. 128p. (YA). (gr. 7 up). 1999. 23.90 (*0-7613-1259-5*, Copper Beech Bks) Millbrook Pr.

One Hundred One Ranch. Ellsworth Collings & Alma M. England. LC 73-167774. (Illus.). 286p. 1986. pap. 15.95 (*0-8061-1047-3*) U of Okla Pr.

101 Read-Aloud Bible Stories: Best-Loved Stories from the Old & New Testament. Joan C. Verniero. LC 98-5112. 368p. 1998. 12.98 (*1-57912-024-5*) Blck Dog & Leventhal.

*__101 Read-Aloud Celtic Myths & Legends.__ Ed. by Joan C. Verniero. (Read-Aloud Ser.). (Illus.). 320p. (J). 2000. 12.98 (*1-57912-098-9*, 81098) Blck Dog & Leventhal.

101 Read Aloud Classics. Pamela Horn. (Read-Aloud Ser.). (Illus.). 416p. (J). 1999. 12.98 (*1-884822-24-X*) Blck Dog & Leventhal.

101 Read-Aloud Myths & Legends. Joan Verniero. LC 98-54655. 352p. 1999. 12.98 (*1-57912-057-1*) Blck Dog & Leventhal.

*__101 Reasons Children Love to Read by Sam's Club Kids.__ Brenda Star. 66p. 2001. pap. 12.95 (*1-884886-13-2*) Star Group.

*__101 Reasons Children Love to Read by Sam's Club Kids.__ Brenda Star. 66p. 2001. pap. 12.95 (*1-884886-12-4*) Star Group.

*__101 Reasons Children Love to Read by Pizza Hut Kids.__ Brenda Star. 66p. 2001. pap. 12.95 (*1-884886-14-0*) Star Group.

101 Reasons I'm Glad I Quit. Joab J. Dick & Lee H. Monk. 136p. 1999. 8.95 (*0-9669802-0-4*, 1996-1) Dick & Monk.

101 Reasons It's Great to Be a Woman. Mitzi Pinkerton. 128p. 1999. pap. 6.95 (*1-84024-097-0*, Pub. by Summers) Seven Hills Bk.

101 Reasons Not to Be a Liberal. Errol Smith & Matt Embers. Ed. by Michael Toth. 120p. 1995. 15.95 (*0-9625578-5-4*) St Clair Rene Pub.

101 Reasons Not to Do Anything: A Collection of Cynical & Defeatist Quotations, 1. Robert Bircher. 1998. pap. text 6.95 (*1-84024-043-1*, Pub. by Summers) Seven Hills Bk.

*__101 Reasons Not to Get Married.__ Terri Tardy. (Illus.). 113p. 2000. pap. 8.95 (*0-9679484-0-1*, TXU 850-985) Perform Bulder Pub.

101 Reasons to Hate George Steinbrenner. Brandon Toropov. LC 97-11409. (Illus.). 160p. 1997. 14.95 (*0-8065-1854-5*, Citadel Pr) Carol Pub Group.

*__101 Reasons to Read to Your Child.__ Brenda Star. 120p. 2000. pap. 10.00 (*1-884886-10-8*) Star Group.

*__101 Reasons Why You're the Greatest Mom.__ Virginia Reynolds. (Charming Petites Ser.). (Illus.). 80p. 2000. 4.95 (*0-88088-514-9*) Peter Pauper.

101 Reasons Why Cats Make Great Kids. Allia Zobel & Nicole Hollander. LC 96-204873. 80p. 1996. pap. text 6.95 (*1-55850-639-X*) Adams Media.

101 Reasons Why He Didn't Call You Back. Audrey Thompson & Hillary Jacobs. LC 97-3772. (Illus.). 96p. 1997. pap. 8.95 (*0-7867-0416-0*) Carroll & Graf.

One Hundred One Reasons Why We're Doomed: A Cynic's Guide to What's Left of the Future. Meredith Anthony et al. 128p. (Orig.). 1993. pap. 7.50 (*0-380-77188-8*, Avon Bks) Morrow Avon.

101 Reasons Why You Should Be Proud to Be a Black Man: Meditations & Quotations Aimed to Make You the Best You Can Be. Areeb Malik Shabazz. (Illus.). 76p. 1999. reprint ed. pap. 8.00 (*1-56411-177-6*, Kitabu Pub) Untd Bros & Sis.

101 Reasons Why You Should Be a Proud Black Woman: Plus 101 Meditations & Quotations to Help You to Be All You Can Be. Areeb Malik Shabazz. 76p. 1999. reprint ed. pap. 8.00 (*1-56411-183-0*, Kitabu Pub) Untd Bros & Sis.

101 Receiver Drills. Stan Zweifel. (Illus.). 128p. 1998. pap. 16.95 (*1-57167-191-9*) Coaches Choice.

*__101 Red-Hot Swing Guitar Licks.__ Larry McCabe. 48p. 1999. pap. 17.95 incl. audio compact disk (*0-7866-3630-0*) Mel Bay.

*__101 Reflections on Tai Chi Chuan.__ Michael Gilman. (Tai Chi Treasures Ser.). (Illus.). 128p. 2000. pap. 10.95 (*1-886969-86-8*, Pub. by YMAA Pubn) Natl Bk Netwk.

101 Resumes for Sure-Hire Results. Robbie M. Kaplan. 150p. 1994. pap. 12.95 (*0-8144-7857-3*) AMACOM.

101 Rhythmic Rest Pat Alto Sax. 24p. (YA). 1985. pap. 5.95 (*0-7692-1454-1*, EL00552) Wrner Bros.

101 Rhythmic Rest Patterns: Bb Tenor Saxophone. Grover C. Yaus. Ed. by Thom Proctor. 24p. (C). 1953. pap. text 5.95 (*0-7692-1749-4*, EL00553) Wrner Bros.

101 Rhythmic Rest Patterns: Trombone. Prod. by Zobeida Perez. 24p. (Orig.). (YA). 1985. pap. 5.95 (*0-7692-1486-X*, EL00557) Wrner Bros.

101 Salon Promotions. Robert Oppenheim. LC 98-4064. (Milady - Cosmetology). 256p. 1999. pap. text 31.95 (*1-56253-358-4*) Thomson Learn.

101 Sample Write-Ups for Documenting Employee Performance Problems: A Guide to Progressive Discipline & Termination. Paul Falcone. LC 98-27584. 336p. 1998. pap. 42.95 (*0-8144-7977-4*) AMACOM.

One Hundred One School Cafeteria Jokes. Jovial Bob Stine, pseud. (One Hundred One Jokes Ser.). 96p. (Orig.). (J). (gr. 4-6). 1990. pap. 1.95 (*0-590-43759-3*) Scholastic Inc.

101 School Cafeteria Jokes. Jovial Bob Stine, pseud. (J). 1990. 7.05 (*0-606-04597-X*, Pub. by Turtleback) Demco.

101 School Jokes. Lisa Eisenberg. (J). 1987. 7.05 (*0-606-03701-2*, Pub. by Turtleback) Demco.

One Hundred One School Jokes. Katy Hall & Lisa Eisenberg. (Illus.). 96p. (J). (gr. 4-6). 1987. pap. 1.95 (*0-590-41182-9*) Scholastic Inc.

101 Science Poems & Songs for Young Learners: Includes Hands-On Activities! Scholastic, Inc. Staff. LC 97-148440. 1997. pap. 12.95 (*0-590-96369-4*) Scholastic Inc.

One Hundred One Science Surprises: Exciting Experiments with Everyday Materials. Roy Richards. LC 92-32491. (Illus.). 104p. (J). 1993. 17.95 (*0-8069-8822-3*) Sterling.

One Hundred One Science Surprises: Exciting Experiments with Everyday Materials. Roy Richards. (Illus.). 104p. (J). 1994. pap. 10.95 (*0-8069-8823-1*) Sterling.

One Hundred One Science Tricks: Fun Experiments with Everyday Materials. Roy Richards. LC 91-13263. (Illus.). 104p. (J). (gr. 4-10). 1995. 16.95 (*0-8069-8388-4*) Sterling.

101 Secrets a Good Dad Knows. Sue Ellin Browder & Walter Browder. LC 99-44983. (Illus.). 224p. 1999. text 14.95 (*1-55853-719-8*) Rutledge Hill Pr.

*__101 Secrets for a Great Retirement: Practical, Inspirational, & Fun Ideas for the Best Years of Your Life.__ Mary Helen Smith & Shuford Smith. 160p. 2000. pap. 12.95 (*0-7373-0420-0*, 04200W, Pub. by Lowell Hse) NTC Contemp Pub Co.

101 Secrets of a High-Performance Veterinary Practice. Bob Levoy. LC 96-60137. (Illus.). 101p. 1996. pap. 29.95 (*0-935078-60-6*) Veterinary Med.

101 Secrets of a High-Performance Dental Practice: From the Success Files of Bob Levoy. Robert P. Levoy. LC 96-51693. 1996. 44.95 (*0-87814-593-1*) PennWell Bks.

101 Secrets of Highly Effective Speakers: Controlling Fear, Commanding Attention. Caryl R. Krannich. LC 98-10594. 176p. 1998. pap. 14.95 (*1-57023-090-0*) Impact VA.

101 Secrets to Negotiating Success. Elaine F. Rbe. LC 98-73721. ix, 203p. 1998. write for info. (*0-9666933-0-2*) Canyon Crest Pubg.

101 Secrets to Winning Beauty Pageants. Ann-Marie Bivans. (Illus.). 240p. 1995. pap. 12.95 (*0-8065-1643-7*, Citadel Pr) Carol Pub Group.

One Hundred One Self-Defense Techniques of Kung-Fu: Basic to Advanced. Scott Davis. (Illus.). 92p. (Orig.). 1993. pap. 16.00 (*0-939427-02-8*) Alpha Pubns OH.

One Hundred One Sermon Outlines. Frank L. Cox. 1971. 4.95 (*0-88027-028-4*) Firm Foun Pub.

101 Sewing Secrets, Vol. 12. Cy DeCosse Incorporated Staff. LC 89-1416. (Singer Sewing Reference Library). (SPA.). 128p. 1989. 18.95 (*0-86573-249-3*) Creat Pub Intl.

101 Sherlock Holmes Crossword Puzzles. Franklin B. Saksena. Date not set. 25.00 (*1-55246-192-0*) Battered Silicon.

*__101 Sherlock Holmes Crossword Puzzles.__ Franklin B. Saksena. 1999. pap. 16.00 (*1-55246-193-9*) Battered Silicon.

101 Short & Sweet Cookie Recipes. (Illus.). xxi, 143p. Date not set. pap. 16.95 (*0-9656199-0-7*) K V McGrath.

101 Short Problems (101 Problemas Cortos) A Collection of Short, Open Mathematics Problems. Ed. by Jean Stenmark. Tr. by Grace Coates & Jose Franco. (Equals Ser.). (ENG & SPA., Illus.). 250p. (J). (gr. 2-9). 1997. pap. 19.95 (*0-912511-26-5*, EQUALS) Lawrence Science.

101 Signs You're Spending Too Much Time with Your Cat. John Baynham. Ed. by Cliff Carle. (Illus.). 96p. 1999. pap. 6.95 (*1-57644-097-4*) CCC Pubns.

One Hundred One Silly Summertime Jokes. Stephanie Calmenson. 96p. (J). (gr. 4-6). 1989. pap. 1.95 (*0-590-42556-0*) Scholastic Inc.

*__101 Simple Holiday Craft Ideas.__ Ellyn Sanna. (Christmas at Home Ser.). (Illus.). 2000. pap. text 2.97 (*1-57748-943-8*) Barbour Pub.

*__101 Simple Service Projects Kids Can Do.__ Susan L. Lingo. (Illus.). 128p. 2000. pap. text 14.99 (*0-7847-1154-2*, 02270) Standard Pub.

101 Simple Things to Grow Your Business. Dottie Walters & Lilly Walters. Ed. by Colleen Wilder. LC 94-68300. (Illus.). 200p. (Orig.). 1995. pap. 12.95 (*1-56052-316-6*) Crisp Pubns.

One Hundred One Simple Things You Can Do to Stay on a Diet & Lose Weight! Douglas Kirkpatrick. Ed. by Vikki Richards. LC 91-76748. 128p. (Orig.). 1992. pap. 4.95 (*0-913193-04-6*) Baker Pub.

101 Simple Ways to Be Good to Yourself: How to Discover Joy & Peace in Your Life. Donna Watson. 1992. pap. 7.95 (*0-9631195-0-8*) Energy Pr.

101 Simple Ways to Be Good to Yourself: How to Discover Joy & Peace in Your Life. Donna Watson. 1992. 12.95 (*0-9631195-2-4*) Energy Pr.

101 Sins of Golf. Mike L. McColgan. (Illus.). 101p. 1998. write for info. (*0-9666893-0-5*) Ultra Clb Clean.

One Hundred One Solderless Breadboarding Projects. Delton T. Horn. (Illus.). 220p. 1988. 24.95 (*0-8306-0385-9*); pap. 15.95 (*0-8306-2985-8*) McGraw-Hill Prof.

101 Solved Civil Engineering Problems. 3rd ed. Michael R. Lindeburg. LC 96-24168. 185p. 1999. pap. 39.95 (*1-888577-32-0*) Prof Pubns CA.

*__101 Solved Environmental Engineering Problems.__ R. Wane Schneiter. 160p. 2000. pap. 49.95 (*1-888577-61-4*) Prof Pubns CA.

101 Solved Mechanical Engineering Problems. Michael R. Lindeburg. LC 98-113908. 130p. 1994. pap. 39.95 (*0-912045-77-9*) Prof Pubns CA.

An Asterisk (*) at the beginning of an entry indicates that the title is appearing for the first time.

101 Songs You Love to Sing: Piano/Vocal Mixed Folio. 140p. (Orig.). 1994. pap. 12.95 (*0-7692-1211-5*, SF0017) Wrner Bros.

101 Songs You Love to Sing: Piano/Vocal Mixed Folio. 24p. (Orig.). 1996. pap. 105.00 (*0-7692-1213-1*, CN0026A); pap. 75.00 (*0-7692-1214-X*, CN0026) Wrner Bros.

101 Songs You Love to Sing: Piano/Vocal Mixed Folio. 10p. (Orig.). 1997. pap. 20.00 (*0-7692-1212-3*, CN0026C) Wrner Bros.

One Hundred One Songwriting & Composing Techniques. Jack Weaton. (C). 1987. pap. 9.98 (*0-939067-13-7*) Alexander Pub.

101 Spanish Idioms. Jean-Marie Cassagne. (ENG & SPA.). 128p. 1995. pap. 6.95 (*0-8442-7217-5*, 72175) NTC Contemp Pub Co.

101 Spanish Proverbs: Understanding Spanish Language & Culture Through Common Sayings. Eduardo Aparicio. LC 97-69973. (ENG & SPA., Illus.). 160p. 1998. pap. 6.95 (*0-8442-7227-2*, 72272) NTC Contemp Pub Co.

101 Sportscard Investments: Best Buys From 5 Dollars to 500 Dollars. SCD Staff. LC 93-77546. (Illus.). 224p. 1993. pap. 6.95 (*0-87341-259-1*) Krause Pubns.

101 Spreadsheet Exercises. Brooks. (One Hundred One Ser.). Date not set. teacher ed. write for info. (*0-02-800759-X*) Glencoe.

101 Stocking Stuffers. Symbol of Excellence Staff. LC 93-87578. 144p. 1994. pap. 14.95 (*0-8487-1420-2*) Oxmoor Hse.

101 Favorite Stories from the Bible. Miller. 1996. 12.99 (*1-885270-00-3*) Christian Aid.

One Hundred One Stories of the Great Ballets. George Balanchine & Francis Mason. LC 73-9140. 560p. 1975. pap. 14.00 (*0-385-03398-2*) Doubleday.

One Hundred One Strawberry Recipes. Carole Eberly. (Illus.). 96p. (Orig.). 1987. pap. 4.95 (*0-932296-13-0*) Eberly Pr.

101 Stupid Things Business Travelers Do to Sabotage Success. Harry Knitter. LC 97-69477. (One Hundred One Stupid Things . . . Ser.). (Illus.). 126p. 1998. pap. 9.95 (*1-883553-98-9*, KGS-105) R Chang Assocs.

101 Stupid Things Collection, 5 vols. (Illus.). 1998. pap. 44.95 (*1-883553-99-7*, KGS-151) R Chang Assocs.

101 Stupid Things Employees Do to Sabotage Success. Richard Baisner. LC 97-69478. (One Hundred One Stupid Things . . . Ser.). (Illus.). 128p. 1998. pap. 9.95 (*1-883553-97-0*) R Chang Assocs.

101 Stupid Things Salespeople Do to Sabotage Success. Mark S. Loper. LC 97-66240. (One Hundred One Stupid Things . . . Ser.). (Illus.). 130p. 1998. pap. 9.95 (*1-883553-95-4*, KGS-103) R Chang Assocs.

101 Stupid Things Supervisors Do to Sabotage Success. Mark S. Loper & Peter R. Garber. LC 97-65523. (Illus.). (Orig.). 1997. pap. 9.95 (*1-883553-94-6*, KGS-102) R Chang Assocs.

101 Stupid Things Trainers Do to Sabotage Success. Nancy B. Stern & Maggie Payment. (Illus.). 126p. 1995. pap. 9.95 (*1-883553-93-8*) R Chang Assocs.

One Hundred One Success Stories of Information Technology in Higher Education: The Joe Wyatt Challenge. Ed. by Judith V. Boettcher. LC 92-38940. 1992. write for info. (*0-390-59763-5*) McGraw.

101 Successful Businesses You Can Start on the Internet. 2nd ed. Daniel Janal. 496p. (Orig.). 1997. pap. 29.95 (*0-471-28843-8*, VNR) Wiley.

101 Successful Businesses You Can Start on the Internet. 2nd rev. expanded ed. Daniel Janal. LC 97-30693. 500p. (Orig.). 1997. pap. 29.95 (*0-442-02608-0*, VNR) Wiley.

101 Summer Job Ideas for Teenagers. Bruce Kienapfel. 112p. (YA). (gr. 7 up). 1999. 20.40 (*0-7613-0363-4*, Copper Beech Bks) Millbrook Pr.

101 Super Oldies from the Early 60s. Ed. by John L. Haag. (Illus.). 272p. (Orig.). 1994. pap. 24.95 (*1-56922-056-5*, 07-1100) Creat Cncpts.

101 Super Uses for Tampon Applicators: Helpful Guide for the Environmentally Conscious Consumer of Feminine Hygiene Products. 3rd ed. Lori Katz & Barbara Meyer. LC 94-78293. (Illus.). 128p. (Orig.). 1995. reprint ed. pap. 9.95 (*0-9641907-0-2*) High Stress.

***101 Superstitions of Golf.** M. L. McColgan. (Illus.). 103p. 2000. write for info. (*0-9666893-1-3*) Ultra Clb Clean.

One Hundred One Support Group Activities for Teenagers at Risk for Chemical Dependence or Related Problems: A Leader's Manual for Secondary Educators & Other Professionals. Martin Fleming. LC 92-18786. 232p. 1992. pap. 54.95 (*1-56246-042-0*, 3097, HazeldenJohnson Inst) Hazelden.

One Hundred One Support Group Activities for Teenagers Recovering from Chemical Dependence: A Leader's Manual for Secondary Educators & Other Professionals. Martin Fleming. LC 92-15221. 184p. 1992. pap. 54.95 (*1-56246-041-2*, 3096, HazeldenJohnson Inst) Hazelden.

One Hundred One Survival Tactics for New & Used Parents. Ruth D. Lambert. (Illus.). (Orig.). 1991. pap. 11.95 (*0-927054-15-9*) H Sq Co.

101 Survival Tips for Missionary Moms, Vol. 1. Mary Yoachum. (Illus.). 64p. 1995. reprint ed. pap. 4.95 (*0-9651086-0-0*) Yoachum Pub.

One Hundred One Talks for Children. Marianne J. Shampton. 1987. 9.95 (*0-88494-580-4*) Bookcraft Inc.

101 Tax Saving Ideas. 2nd ed. Randy Gardner & Julie Welch. LC 93-61739. 256p. 1995. pap. 14.95 (*0-9639734-1-X*) Wealth Builders.

101 Tax Saving Ideas. 3rd ed. Randy Gardner & Julie Welch. 1997. pap. write for info. (*0-9639734-2-8*) Wealth Builders.

101 Tax Saving Ideas. 4th ed. Randy Gardner & Julie Welch. 1999. pap. 18.95 (*0-9639734-3-6*) Wealth Builders.

***101 Team Games for Kids.** Joe Dinoffer. 144p. 1999. pap. 16.95 (*1-57167-430-6*) Coaches Choice.

101 Telephone Jokes. Katy Hall & Lisa Eisenberg. 96p. (J). (gr. 4-6). 1994. pap. 1.99 (*0-590-48575-X*) Scholastic Inc.

One Hundred One Tennis Tips: Very Simple Hints for a Truly Excellent Game. Seth Geeslin. Ed. by Mary Horne. ii, 101p. 1998. pap. 16.95 (*0-9660375-0-2*) Booner Pubns.

101 Theatre Games: For Drama Teachers, Classroom Teachers & Directors. Mila Johansen. (Illus.). 154p. (Orig.). 1994. pap. 20.00 (*0-88734-911-0*) Players Pr.

***101 Thematic Poems for Emergent Readers: Playful Rhymes & Easy Activities that Build Early Rea.** Mary Sullivan. 16p. 1999. pap. text 12.95 (*0-590-96733-9*) Scholastic Inc.

101 Therapeutic Successes: Overcoming Transference & Resistance in Psychotherapy. Gerald Schoenewolf. LC 88-7612. 304p. 1996. pap. 45.00 (*1-56821-841-9*, AR1) Aronson.

101 Things a College Girl Should Know from a Big Sister Who's Been There. Stephanie Edwards. 64p. (Orig.). (C). 1996. pap. 5.95 (*0-8362-1090-5*) Andrews & McMeel.

101 Things a College Guy Should Know. Stephen Edwards. LC 97-39235. 1998. pap. 5.95 (*0-8362-5293-4*) Andrews & McMeel.

101 Things Children Can Do to Annoy Their Parents. Ray Comfort. LC 98-73143. (Illus.). 184p. 1998. pap. 7.99 (*0-88270-759-0*, Bridge) Bridge-Logos.

101 Things Every Kid Should Know About Science. Samantha Beres. LC 97-49847. (Illus.). 96p. (J). (gr. 2-5). 1998. 14.95 (*1-56565-956-2*) Lowell Hse Juvenile.

101 Things Every Kid Should Know About Science. Samantha Beres. LC 97-49847. (Illus.). 96p. (J). (gr. 3-7). 1998. pap. 9.95 (*1-56565-916-3*, 09163W, Pub. by Lowell Hse Juvenile) NTC Contemp Pub Co.

101 Things Every Kid Should Know about the Human Body. Samantha Beres. LC 99-30621. (Illus.). 112p. (J). (gr. 3-6). 2000. 14.95 (*0-7373-0329-8*, 03298W, Pub. by Lowell Hse) NTC Contemp Pub Co.

101 Things Every Kid Should Know about the Human Body. Samantha Beres. LC 99-30621. (Illus.). 112p. (J). (gr. 3-7). 2000. pap. 9.95 (*0-7373-0222-4*, 02224W) NTC Contemp Pub Co.

101 Things for Kids in Atlanta: A Complete Family Directory. Carol A. Stout. (101 Things for Kids Ser.). 150p. Date not set. pap. 14.95 (*1-886161-04-6*) One-Hndred One Things.

101 Things for Kids in Indianapolis: A Complete Family Directory. Carol A. Stout. (101 Things for Kids Ser.). 150p. Date not set. pap. 14.95 (*1-886161-01-1*) One-Hndred One Things.

101 Things for Kids in Las Vegas: A Complete Family Directory. Carol A. Stout. (101 Things for Kids Ser.). 150p. 1997. pap. 14.95 (*1-886161-03-8*) One-Hndred One Things.

101 Things for Kids in Las Vegas: A Complete Family Guide. Carol A. Stout. LC 99-90069. (Kids Ser.). (Illus.). 224p. 1999. pap. 12.95 (*1-886161-20-8*) One-Hndred One Things.

101 Things for Kids in New Orleans Vol. II: A Complete Family Guide. 2nd rev. ed. Carol A. Stout. (101 Things for Kids Ser.). 164p. 1997. 12.95 (*1-886161-05-4*) One-Hndred One Things.

101 Things for Kids in New Orleans: A Complete Family Guide. Carol A. Stout. 160p. 1995. pap. 14.95 (*1-886161-00-3*) One-Hndred One Things.

101 Things for Kids in New Orleans: A Complete Family Guide. 2nd rev. ed. Carol A. Stout. LC 98-96678. (Kids Ser.). (Illus.). 184p. 1998. pap. 12.95 (*1-886161-19-4*) One-Hndred One Things.

101 Things for Kids in Phoenix: A Complete Family Directory. Carol A. Stout. (101 Things for Kids Ser.). 150p. Date not set. pap. 14.95 (*1-886161-02-X*) One-Hndred One Things.

101 Things God Can't Do. Maisie Sparks. 112p. 1997. pap. 4.99 (*0-7852-7462-6*) Nelson.

***101 Things God Can't Do.** Maisie Sparks. LC 99-52877. 2000. pap. write for info. (*0-7852-6863-4*) Tommy Nelson.

101 Things God Can't Do, Vol. 1. 2nd rev. ed. Maisie C. Sparks. 108p. (Orig.). 1996. pap. 6.95 (*0-9651003-8-3*) Sparks Grp.

101 Things Husbands Do to Annoy Their Wives. Ray Comfort. (Illus.). 260p. 1998. pap. 5.00 (*1-878859-20-X*) Living Wat CA.

***101 Things Parents Should Know Before Volunteering to Coach Their Kids' Sports Teams.** Gary S. Goodman. LC 99-53839. 2000. 14.95 (*0-8092-9871-6*, Contemporary Bks) NTC Contemp Pub Co.

***101 Things That Worked So Well I Had to Stop Doing Them.** David J. Kats. 170p. 2000. pap. write for info. (*0-9701782-0-4*) Levi Pubng.

***101 Things the Enemy Can't Do.** Maisie Sparks. LC 99-47569. 112p. 2000. pap. 5.99 (*0-7852-6862-6*) Nelson.

***101 Things to Cook.** large type ed. Jane Scoggins Bauld & Kim Hefner. 125p. (J). (ps-3). 1999. pap. 8.95 (*1-929701-01-2*) Under Green.

101 Things to Do in the Year 2000. Dan Penwell. 224p. 1999. pap. 9.99 (*1-56292-802-3*) Honor Bks OK.

101 Things to Do During a Dull Sermon. Tim Sims & Dan Pegoda. 88p. 1989. mass mkt. 7.99 (*0-310-51691-9*) Zondervan.

101 Things to Do for Christmas. Debbie T. O'Neal. LC 94-46532. (Illus.). 64p. (J). (gr. 1). 1995. pap. 10.99 (*0-8066-2792-1*, 9-2792) Augsburg Fortress.

101 Things to Do in Door County. Richard Rusnack. 2nd. 1996. pap. 6.95 (*0-932212-91-3*) Avery Color.

101 Things to Do in Traverse City. Richard Rusnack. 1997. pap. 6.95 (*0-932212-95-6*) Avery Color.

101 Things to Do on the Internet. Ed. by Mark Wallace. (Computer Guides Ser.). (Illus.). 64p. (YA). (gr. 5 up). 1999. pap. 10.95 (*0-7460-3294-3*, Usborne); lib. bdg. 17.95 (*1-58086-166-0*, Usborne) EDC.

101 Things to Do with a Baby. Jan Ormerod. (Illus.). 32p. (J). (ps up). 1994. pap. 4.95 (*0-688-12770-3*, Wm Morrow) Morrow Avon.

101 Things to Do with a Baby. Jan Ormerod. 1993. 10.15 (*0-606-06153-3*, Pub. by Turtleback) Demco.

101 Things to Do with a Dull Church. Martin Wroe & Adrian Reith. LC 94-1059. (Illus.). 104p. (Orig.). 1994. pap. 6.99 (*0-8308-1824-3*, 1824) InterVarsity.

One Hundred One Things to Do with Lutefisk, Vol. 1. Edward Fischer. (Illus.). 76p. (Orig.). 1989. pap., per. 4.95 (*0-685-29342-4*) E Fischer.

101 Things to Do with Your Computer. Gillian Doherty. (Computer Guides Ser.). (Illus.). 64p. (YA). (gr. 5-9). 1998. lib. bdg. 18.95 (*1-58086-123-7*, Usborne) EDC.

***101 Things to Do with Your Computer.** Gillian Doherty. (Computer Guides Ser.). (Illus.). 64p. (YA). (gr. 5-9). 2000. pap. 10.95 (*0-7460-2935-7*, Usborne) EDC.

One Hundred One Things to Do with Your Private License. 2nd ed. LeRoy Cook. 256p. 1990. pap. 24.95 (*0-07-155914-0*) McGraw.

101 Things You Can Teach Your Kids about Baseball: Actually There's at Least 367 of Them. Don Marsh. (Illus.). 120p. (Orig.). 1995. pap. text 9.95 (*0-9647420-9-8*) Campbell Marsh Commun.

101 Things You Can Teach Your Kids about Baseball: Actually There's at Least 427 of Them. 2nd ed. Don Marsh. (Illus.). 136p. (Orig.). (J). (gr. 1-12). 1998. pap. 9.95 (*0-9647420-4-7*, Pub. by Campbell Marsh Commun) IPG Chicago.

101 Things You Don't Know about Science & No One Else Does Either. James S. Trefil. LC 97-36902. 368p. 1997. pap. 11.00 (*0-395-87740-7*) HM.

***101 Things You Need to Know about Wine.** Andrew Jefford. (Evening Standard Ser.). (Illus.). 2000. pap. 15.00 (*0-7432-0509-X*) Simon & Schuster.

101 Things You Need to Know, 1. Donald H. Mayo. LC 98-201698. 1999. 10.00 (*1-56243-675-9*) DDC Pub.

101 Things You Should Never Ask a Marine to Do. Edward A. Temple, Jr. (Illus.). 104p. (Orig.). 1989. pap. 7.95 (*0-9655781-0-0*) P Temple.

***101 Things You Need to Know about Internet Law.** Jonathan Bick. LC 00-37726. (Illus.). 224p. 2000. pap. 12.95 (*0-609-80633-5*, Three Riv Pr) Crown Pub Group.

One Hundred One Timex-Sinclair 1000 ZX-81 Programming Tips & Tricks. Edward Page. 128p. (Orig.). (gr. 7-12). 1982. pap. 7.95 (*0-86668-020-9*) ARCsoft.

101 Quick Tips for a Dynamite Resume: Great Examples for Producing Powerful Results. Richard Fein. LC 98-33533. 208p. 1999. pap. 13.95 (*1-57023-082-X*) Impact VA.

101 Tips for Child Development Training: 101 Quick Tips for Managing a Preschool or Daycare. Silvana Clark. Ed. by Gayle Bittinger et al. (101 Tips for Directors Ser.). (Illus.). 24p. (Orig.). 1996. pap. text 3.95 (*1-57029-078-4*, WPH 4006) Totline Pubns.

***101 Tips for College Bound Students.** Linda Jacobs & Pauline Reiter. 60p. (YA). (gr. 9 up). 1999. pap. 6.95 (*0-9676237-0-7*) U Pathways.

101 Tips for Resources for You & Your Center: 101 Quick Tips for Managing a Preschool or Daycare. Silvana Clark. Ed. by Gayle Bittinger et al. (101 Tips for Directors Ser.). (Illus.). 24p. (Orig.). 1996. pap. text 3.95 (*1-57029-079-2*, WPH 4005) Totline Pubns.

101 Tips for Improving Your Blood Sugar. 2nd ed. University of New Mexico Staff. LC 99-22929. 128p. 1999. pap. 14.95 (*1-58040-026-4*, 00264Q, Pub. by Am Diabetes) NTC Contemp Pub Co.

101 Tips for Health & Safety: 101 Quick Tips for Managing a Preschool or Daycare. Silvana Clark. Ed. by Gayle Bittinger et al. (101 Tips for Directors Ser.). (Illus.). 24p. (Orig.). 1996. pap. text 3.95 (*1-57029-076-8*, WPH 4003) Totline Pubns.

101 Tips for Improving Your Blood Sugar: Feel Better Now & Avoid Complications Later. David S. Schade et al. (Illus.). 128p. 1996. pap. 12.50 (*0-945448-47-3*, 4805-01) Am Diabetes.

101 Tips for Marketing Your Center: 101 Quick Tips for Managing a Preschool or Daycare. Silvana Clark. Ed. by Gayle Bittinger et al. (101 Tips for Directors Ser.). (Illus.). 24p. (Orig.). 1996. pap. text 3.95 (*1-57029-080-6*, WPH 4004) Totline Pubns.

101 Tips for More Profitable Catalogs. Maxwell Sroge. (Illus.). 320p. 1995. pap. 29.95 (*0-8442-3660-8*) NTC Contemp Pub Co.

101 Tips for Parent Communication: 101 Quick Tips for Managing a Preschool or Daycare. Silvana Clark. Ed. by Gayle Bittinger et al. (101 Tips for Directors Ser.). (Illus.). 24p. (Orig.). 1996. pap. text 3.95 (*1-57029-077-6*, WPH 4002) Totline Pubns.

101 Tips for Preschool Teachers - Encouraging Creativity. Barbara Backer. Ed. by Susan Hodges. (Illus.). 24p. (Orig.). 1996. mass mkt. 3.95 (*1-57029-093-8*, 4008) Totline Pubns.

101 Tips for Preschool Teachers - Developing Language Skills. Barbara Backer. Ed. by Susan Hodges. (Illus.). 24p. (Orig.). 1996. mass mkt. 3.95 (*1-57029-097-0*, 4010) Totline Pubns.

101 Tips for Preschool Teachers - Developing Motor Skills. Barbara Backer. Ed. by Susan Hodges. (Illus.). 24p. (Orig.). 1996. mass mkt. 3.95 (*1-57029-096-2*, 4009) Totline Pubns.

101 Tips for Preschool Teachers - Creating Theme Environments. Barbara Backer. Ed. by Susan Hodges. (Illus.). 24p. (Orig.). 1996. mass mkt. 3.95 (*1-57029-092-X*, 4007) Totline Pubns.

101 Tips for Preschool Teachers - Spicing up Learning Centers. Barbara Backer. Ed. by Susan Hodges. (Illus.). 24p. (Orig.). 1996. 3.95 (*1-57029-099-7*, 4012) Totline Pubns.

101 Tips for PS Teachers - Teaching Basic Concepts. Barbara Backer. Ed. by Susan Hodges. (Illus.). 24p. (Orig.). 1996. mass mkt. 3.95 (*1-57029-098-9*, 4011) Totline Pubns.

101 Tips for Staff & Parent Self-Esteem: 101 Quick Tips for Managing a Preschool or Daycare. Silvana Clark. Ed. by Gayle Bittinger et al. (101 Tips for Directors Ser.). (Illus.). 24p. (Orig.). 1996. pap. text 3.95 (*1-57029-075-X*, WPH 4001) Totline Pubns.

101 Tips for Staying Healthy with Diabetes: And Avoiding Complications. University of New Mexico Diabetes Care Group Staff. LC 96-18928. 112p. 1996. pap. 12.50 (*0-945448-71-6*, 4810-01) Am Diabetes.

101 Tips for Staying Healthy with Diabetes: (& Avoiding Complications) 2nd ed. University of New Mexico Staff. LC 99-22930. 112p. 1999. pap. 14.95 (*1-58040-007-8*, 00078Q, Pub. by Am Diabetes) NTC Contemp Pub Co.

101 Tips for Telecommuters: Successfully Manage Your Work, Team, Technology & Family. Debra A. Dinnocenzo. LC 99-35779. 250p. 1999. pap. 15.95 (*1-57675-069-8*) Berrett-Koehler.

101 Tips for Trainers. T. Miller & S. Brelade. (Financial Times Management Briefings Ser.). 1997. pap. 94.50 (*0-273-63225-8*, Pub. by F T P-H) Trans-Atl Phila.

101 Tips for Youth Sports Officials. 2nd rev. ed. Ed. by Jeffrey Stern & Bob Still. (Illus.). 80p. 1998. pap. 9.95 (*1-58208-005-4*) Ref Enterps.

***101 Tips on How to Survive the Summer with Your Kids.** Marty W. Stewart. 1999. write for info. (*0-9671588-1-8*) M Stewart PA.

101 Tips, Traps & To-Dos for Creating Teams: A Guidebook for School Leaders. Gerald D. Bailey et al. 394p. 1998. ring bd. 89.00 (*1-879639-61-0*) Natl Educ Serv.

***101 Tools for Thriving in the Classroom.** Groeber Joan & Hansell T. Steve. 226p. 1999. 24.95 (*1-57517-160-0*) SkyLght.

101 Top Secret Techniques Used by Successful Part-Time Video Producers! David Valin. (Illus.). 128p. 1998. 24.95 (*1-884939-68-6*); pap. 19.95 (*1-884939-57-0*) Antoine Versailles.

101 Top Secret Techniques Used by Successful Part-Time Party Caterers! David Valin. (Illus.). 128p. 1998. 24.95 (*1-884939-65-1*); pap. 19.95 (*1-884939-54-6*) Antoine Versailles.

101 Top Secret Techniques Used by Successful Part-Time Stock Traders! David Valin. (Illus.). 128p. 1998. 24.95 (*1-884939-61-9*); pap. 19.95 (*1-884939-51-1*) Antoine Versailles.

101 Top Secret Techniques Used by Successful Part-Time Software Developers! David Valin. (Illus.). 128p. 1998. 24.95 (*1-884939-70-8*); pap. 19.95 (*1-884939-58-9*) Antoine Versailles.

101 Top Secret Techniques Used by Successful Part-Time Publishers! David Valin. (Illus.). 128p. 1998. 24.95 (*1-884939-67-8*); pap. 19.95 (*1-884939-56-2*) Antoine Versailles.

101 Top Secret Techniques Used by Successful Part-Time Musician Managers! David Valin. (Illus.). 128p. 1998. 24.95 (*1-884939-66-X*); pap. 19.95 (*1-884939-55-4*) Antoine Versailles.

101 Top Secret Techniques Used by Successful Part-Time Mail Order Businesses! David Valin. (Illus.). 128p. 1998. 24.95 (*1-884939-64-3*); pap. 19.95 (*1-884939-53-8*) Antoine Versailles.

101 Top Secret Techniques Used by Successful Part-Time Inventors! David Valin. (Illus.). 128p. 1998. 24.95 (*1-884939-71-6*); pap. 19.95 (*1-884939-59-7*) Antoine Versailles.

101 Top Secret Techniques Used by Successful Part-Time Internet Businesses! David Valin. (Illus.). 128p. 1998. 24.95 (*1-884939-62-7*); pap. 19.95 (*1-884939-52-X*) Antoine Versailles.

101 Top Secret Techniques Used by Successful Part-Time Fine Art Dealers! David Valin. (Illus.). 128p. 1998. 24.95 (*1-884939-60-0*); pap. 19.95 (*1-884939-50-3*) Antoine Versailles.

One Hundred One Torchon Patterns. rev. ed. Robin Lewis-Wild. (Illus.). 132p. 1992. reprint ed. pap. 19.95 (*0-9633892-0-3*) Robins Bobbins.

***101 More Training Games.** Gary Kroehnert. 1999. 29.95 (*0-07-470749-3*, McGrw-H College) McGrw-H Hghr Educ.

One Hundred One Training Tips for Dogs. Kate D. Condax. LC 94-6387. 256p. 1994. pap. 9.95 (*0-440-50568-2*) Dell.

101 Trends Every Investor Should Know about the Global Economy. Joseph P. Quinlan & Kathryn L. Stevens. LC 97-46461. 240p. 1998. pap. 17.95 (*0-8092-2976-5*, 297650, Contemporary Bks) NTC Contemp Pub Co.

101 Unuseless Japanese Inventions: The Art of Chindogu. Kenji Kawakami. Ed. by Hugh Fearnley-Whittingstall. Tr. by Dan Papia. (Illus.). 160p. 1995. pap. 12.95 (*0-393-31369-7*, Norton Paperbks) Norton.

***101 Upward Glances.** Sandra P. Aldrich. 2000. pap. 10.99 (*0-8423-3604-4*) Tyndale Hse.

101 Uses of a Dead Cat. Simon Bond. 1997. mass mkt. write for info. (*0-7493-0834-6*) Random House.

101 Useful Notary Tips. National Notary Association Editors. 46p. 1997. pap. 14.00 (*0-933134-98-3*) Natl Notary.

101 Uses for a Bridesmaid Dress. Cindy Walker & Mehalko Donna. LC 98-27955. (Illus.). 128p. 1999. 19.95 (*0-688-16608-3*, Wm Morrow) Morrow Avon.

One Hundred One Uses for a Crooked Politician. Gene Machamer. LC 92-90220. (Illus.). 104p. (Orig.). 1992. pap. 6.95 (*0-9627369-1-0*) Carlisle Pr.

O

One Hundred One Uses for a Dead Spotted Owl (Strix Occidentalis Caurina) David B. Jaques. (Illus.). 128p. (Orig.). 1989. pap. write for info. (*0-318-65368-0*) D B Jaques.

101 Uses for a Golden. Photos by Denver Bryan. LC 99-10839. ("Just Pets" Ser.). (Illus.). 112p. 1999. 14.95 (*1-57223-211-0*, 2110) Willow Creek Pr.

101 Uses for a John Major. Patrick Wright & Peter Richardson. (Illus.). 96p. 1995. pap. 9.95 (*0-233-98862-9*, Pub. by Andre Deutsch) Trafalgar.

101 Uses for a Lab. Dale C. Spartas. LC 98-10114. (Illus.). 112p. 1998. 14.95 (*1-57223-131-9*) Willow Creek Pr.

101 Uses for a Losing Lottery Ticket. Martin Shovel. 1998. pap. text 6.95 (*1-873475-84-5*, Pub. by Summers) Howell Pr VA.

101 Uses for an Ex-Husband. Richard Smith. LC 97-60617. (Illus.). 144p. (Orig.). 1997. mass mkt. 6.99 (*0-446-67372-2*, Pub. by Warner Bks) Little.

***101 Uses for an Old Farm Tractor.** Ed. by Michael Dregni. (Illus.). 108p. 2000. 14.95 (*0-89658-496-8*) Voyageur Pr.

One Hundred One Uses for Really Old Fruitcake. P. B. Smith. 132p. 1992. pap. 7.00 (*0-9635530-0-3*) Hawthorne Hse.

101 Uses for the Royal Family: New Uses for Old Royals. Jennifer Basye et al. LC 93-32302. (Illus.). 96p. 1993. pap. 5.95 (*1-55958-475-0*) Prima Pub.

101 Uses for This Book: The Astonishing Uses & Everyday Abuses of the Humble Book. Paul Glescoe. (Illus.). 160p. (Orig.). 1996. pap. 8.50 (*1-55192-009-3*) Raincoast Bk.

101 Vacations to Change Your Life: A Guide to Wellness Centers, Spiritual Retreats & Spas. Karin Baji-Holms. LC 99-36059. (Illus.). 208p. 1999. pap. 12.95 (*0-8065-2082-5*, Citadel Pr) Carol Pub Group.

One Hundred One Vegetable Recipes. Carole Eberly. (Illus.). 96p. (Orig.). 1981. pap. 4.95 (*0-932296-08-4*) Eberly Pr.

One Hundred One Vegetarian Delights. Lily Chuang. LC 91-41184. 176p. 1992. pap. 12.95 (*0-937064-52-1*) SevenStar Comm.

101 Visions: Centurions. Cynda L. Benson. Ed. by Betsey Brairton. (Illus.). 40p. 1997. pap. write for info. (*0-9654682-1-6*) Savannah Coll.

101 Volleyball Drills. Peggy Martin. LC 98-87714. (Illus.). 128p. 1998. pap. 16.95 (*1-57167-316-4*) Coaches Choice.

One Hundred One Wacky Camping Jokes. Melvin Berger. 96p. (gr. 4-6). 1992. pap. 2.99 (*0-590-45773-X*) Scholastic Inc.

101 Wacky Camping Jokes. Melvin Berger. (J). 1992. 8.09 (*0-606-01768-2*, Pub. by Turtleback) Demco.

101 Wacky Computer Jokes. Judith Stamper. (J). (gr. 2-5). 1998. pap. 2.99 (*0-590-13004-8*) Scholastic Inc.

***101 Wacky Computer Jokes.** Judith Bauer Stamper. 1998. 8.09 (*0-606-13105-1*, Pub. by Turtleback) Demco.

101 Wacky Facts about Bugs & Spiders. Jean Waricha. (J). 1991. 7.05 (*0-606-01769-0*, Pub. by Turtleback) Demco.

One Hundred One Wacky Facts about Bugs & Spiders. Illus. by Brian Hendryx. 96p. (J). (gr. 4-6). 1992. pap. 1.95 (*0-590-44892-7*) Scholastic Inc.

One Hundred One Wacky Facts about Mummies. Harris. 96p. (J). (gr. 4-6). 1992. pap. 1.95 (*0-590-44889-7*) Scholastic Inc.

101 Wacky Facts about Snakes & Reptiles. Walter Retan. (J). 1991. 7.05 (*0-606-01771-2*, Pub. by Turtleback) Demco.

101 Wacky Kid Jokes. Jovial Bob Stine, pseud. (J). 1988. 8.09 (*0-606-04024-2*, Pub. by Turtleback) Demco.

101 Wacky State Jokes. Melvin Berger. (J). 1991. 7.05 (*0-606-01772-0*, Pub. by Turtleback) Demco.

101 Ways to Make Money at Home. Gwen Ellis. 222p. (Orig.). 1996. pap. 10.99 (*0-89283-898-1*, Vine Bks) Servant.

***101 Ways for Running a Successful Home Business: Proven Strategies & Sage Advice for the At-Home Entrepreneur.** Maxye Henry & Lou Henry. 224p. 2000. pap. 12.95 (*0-7373-0421-9*, 04219W, Pub. by Lowell Hse) NTC Contemp Pub Co.

101 Ways Kids Can Spoil Their Parents . . . Gift Book: And Increase Their Allowance. Roman Brown & Ramsey Brown. (Illus.). 128p. (J). (gr. k-10). 1998. 5.99 (*1-881830-92-6*) Garborgs.

***101 Ways to Add Joy to Your Life.** Ashley Kohly. 1999. pap. 7.95 (*0-9628733-5-7*, Pub. by Legacy Pub FL) BookWorld.

One Hundred One Ways to Add to Your Income. Duane R. Lund. 100p. 1994. pap. 8.95 (*0-934860-10-6*) Adventure Pubns.

One Hundred One Ways to Avoid a Drunk Driving Conviction. William C. Head & Reese I. Joye, Jr. 320p. 1991. pap. text 19.95 (*0-9631218-0-4*); pap. text 19.95 (*0-9631218-1-2*) Maximar Pub.

One Hundred One Ways to Avoid Reincarnation: Or Getting It Right the First Time. Hester Mundis. LC 88-40606. (Illus.). 160p. 1989. pap. 6.95 (*0-89480-383-2*, 1383) Workman Pub.

101 Ways to Be a Long-Distance Super-Dad... or Mom, Too! rev. ed. George Newman. LC 99-94689. (Illus.). 123p. (Orig.). 1999. pap. 9.95 (*0-939894-02-5*) Blossom Valley.

101 Ways to Be a Special Dad. Vicki Lansky. LC 92-41271. 120p. 1993. 6.95 (*0-8092-3820-9*, 382090, Contemporary Bks) NTC Contemp Pub Co.

101 Ways to Be a Special Mom. Vicki Lansky. (Illus.). 120p. 1995. 6.95 (*0-8092-3530-7*, 353070, Contemporary Bks) NTC Contemp Pub Co.

101 Ways to Be an Earth Angel. Barb Nugent et al. 112p. 1995. text 18.00 (*1-885499-20-5*) Angelight.

101 Ways to Be Family Friendly. Tom Lytle et al. 112p. (Orig.). 1996. pap. 7.99 (*0-8341-1659-6*) Beacon Hill.

101 Ways to Transform Your Love Life. Barbara De Angelis. Ed. by Jill Kramer. 101p. (Orig.). 1996. pap. 5.95 (*1-56170-277-3*, 178) Hay House.

101 Ways to Boost Your Math Skills. 1996. pap. 2.95 (*0-8167-3836-X*) Troll Communs.

101 Ways to Boost Your Web Traffic: Internet Promotion Made Easier. deluxe ed. Thomas Wong. LC 99-94427. (Illus.). 320p. 2000. pap. 24.95 (*0-9638349-5-9*) Intesync.

101 Ways to Boost Your Writing Skills. 1996. pap. 2.95 (*0-8167-3835-1*) Troll Communs.

101 Ways to Bug Your Parents. Lee Wardlaw. LC 95-18845. 208p. (YA). (gr. 4-7). 1996. 14.99 (*0-8037-1901-9*, Dial Yng Read) Peng Put Young Read.

101 Ways to Bug Your Parents. Lee Wardlaw. LC 95-18845. (J). (gr. 4-7). 1999. pap. 14.89 (*0-8037-1902-7*, Dial Yng Read) Peng Put Young Read.

101 Ways to Bug Your Parents. Lee Wardlaw. 1998. 9.09 (*0-606-13076-4*, Pub. by Turtleback) Demco.

101 Ways to Bug Your Parents. Lee Wardlaw. 208p. (J). (gr. 4-7). 1998. reprint ed. pap. 4.50 (*0-440-41423-7*, YB BDD) BDD Bks Young Read.

One Hundred One Ways to Build Enrollment in Your Early Childhood Program. Ellen Orton-Montanari. 135p. 1992. pap. text 12.95 (*1-882149-39-4*) CPG Pub.

101 Ways to Buy Real Estate Without Cash. 2nd ed. Wade Cook. LC 98-37362. 320p. 1996. pap. 16.95 (*0-910019-74-6*) Lghthse Pub Gp.

101 Ways to Captivate a Business Audience. Sue Gaulke. LC 96-32669. 144p. (Orig.). 1996. pap. 15.95 (*0-8144-7920-0*) AMACOM.

101 Ways to Count Sheep: Holy Cow Not Another Sheep! Stuart R. Kaplan. LC 94-72583. (Illus.). 104p. (Orig.). 1994. pap. 5.95 (*1-57281-000-9*, CBK900) US Games Syst.

101 Ways to Cut Your Business Insurance Costs Without Sacrificing Protection. 2nd ed. William S. McIntyre, IV et al. 199p. (C). 1996. 24.95 (*1-886813-10-8*) Intl Risk Mgt.

101 Ways to Date Your Mate: Hundreds of Fun Dating Ideas. 2nd ed. Rose Smith & Earl Smith. 160p. (Orig.). 1997. reprint ed. pap. 7.95 (*1-882401-57-3*) W Havens Pub.

101 Ways to Date Your Mate: Hundreds of Fun Dating Ideas. 3rd ed. Rose Smith. 176p. (Orig.). 1997. reprint ed. pap. 7.95 (*1-882401-75-1*) W Havens Pub.

101 Ways to Defeat the Devil. Marilyn Hickey. 1998. pap. 1.00 (*1-56441-178-8*) M Hickey Min.

One Hundred One Ways to Develop Student Self-Esteem & Responsibility. Jack Canfield & Frank Siccone. LC 94-21227. 526p. 1994. pap. text 36.00 (*0-205-16884-1*, Longwood Div) Allyn.

One Hundred One Ways to Develop Student Self-Esteem & Responsibility, Vol. I: The Teachers Coach. Jack Canfield & Frank Siccone. 288p. (C). 1992. pap. text 34.50 (*0-205-13368-1*) Allyn.

One Hundred One Ways to Develop Student Self-Esteem & Responsibility, Vol. I: The Teachers Coach. Jack Canfield & Frank Siccone. 256p. (C). 1993. pap. text 63.95 (*0-205-13370-3*) Allyn.

One Hundred One Ways to Develop Student Self-Esteem & Responsibility, Vol. II: The Power to Succeed in School & Beyond. Frank Siccone. 256p. (C). 1993. pap. text 34.50 (*0-205-14068-8*) Allyn.

One Hundred One Ways to Do Better in School. Penny Colman. LC 93-30872. (Illus.). (J). 1996. pap. 2.95 (*0-8167-3285-X*) Troll Communs.

One Hundred One Ways to Dump on Your Ex! The All-Purpose Get Even! Book. Oaky Miller. (Illus.). 108p. (Orig.). 1986. pap. 5.95 (*0-930753-01-1*) Spect Ln Pr.

101 Ways to Enjoy Baseball. Steve Cameron. LC 99-21239. (Illus.). 144p. 1999. 9.95 (*1-886110-73-5*, Pub. by Addax Pubng) Midpt Trade.

101 Ways to Enjoy Life's Simple Pleasures. Donna Watson. (Illus.). 116p. 1994. 12.95 (*1-885167-01-6*); pap. 7.95 (*1-885167-00-8*) Bard Press.

101 Ways to Enrich Your Life: Clear Mindsets & Simple Tools That Help You See Everyday Experiences in a Different Way, & Handle them with Confidence. Robert J. Lemke & Karen K. Diedrich. LC 98-89943. 232p. 1998. pap. 12.95 (*0-9669686-0-3*) Living Rich.

***101 Ways to Feel & Look Great! A Plastic Surgeon's Guide to Improve Your Life from the Inside Out.** Stanley P. Maximovich. LC 99-93136. 280p. 1999. 29.95 (*0-9671054-2-0*) Biddle Hse Pubng.

***101 Ways to Get a Life: How to Be Happy... No Matter What's Happening.** LC 99-96258. 160p. 2000. pap. 14.95 (*0-9670348-0-9*) New Day.

101 Ways to Get at Your Ex. Samantha Charles. LC 97-180654. 96p. 1996. 5.99 (*0-7860-0286-7*, Pinncle Kensgtn) Kensgtn Pub Corp.

101 Ways to Get 100+Financing for Real Estate & Business. 10th ed. Tyler Gregory Hicks. 282p. 1999. pap. 24.50 (*1-56150-278-2*) Intl Wealth.

***101 Ways to Get 100+Financing for Real Estate & Business.** 11th ed. Tyler G. Hicks. 282p. 2000. pap. 24.50 (*1-56150-338-X*) Intl Wealth.

One Hundred One Ways to Get Out of a Traffic Ticket. Jeffrey Hodge. Ed. by Carolyn Cooper. (Illus.). 80p. (Orig.). (C). 1992. pap. 4.50 (*0-9633347-0-0*) Talent Wrld Pubns.

One-Hundred One Ways to Get Straight A's. Robin Dellabough. LC 94-28851. (Illus.). 96p. (J). (gr. 3-8). 1997. pap. 2.95 (*0-8167-3565-4*) Troll Communs.

101 Ways to Get Your Adult Children to Move Out: (And Make Them think it Was Their Idea) Rich Melheim. LC 95-32761. 64p. 1996. pap. 6.95 (*0-385-48006-7*, Main St Bks) Doubleday.

One Hundred One Ways to Get Your Adult Children to Move Out (& Make Them Think It Was Their Idea) Rich Melheim. (Illus.). 76p. (Orig.). 1994. pap. 9.95 (*0-9635106-6-5*) Creat Outlet.

101 Ways to Get 100 Plus Percent Financing for Real Estate & Business. 8th ed. Tyler Gregory Hicks. 282p. 1996. pap. 24.50 (*1-56150-177-8*) Intl Wealth.

101 Ways to Get 100 Plus Percent Financing for Real Estate & Business. 9th ed. Tyler Gregory Hicks. 282p. 1998. pap. 24.50 (*1-56150-227-8*) Intl Wealth.

101 Ways to Give Children Business Cents: At Home, Work & Play. Cindy Iannarelli. (Illus.). 115p. 1998. pap. 16.95 (*1-889107-01-8*) Busn Cents.

101 Ways to Grow a Healthy Sunday School. Stan Toler. 108p. 1995. pap. text 7.99 (*0-8341-1620-0*) Beacon Hill.

101 Ways to Grow Your Business with Barter. 2nd rev. ed. Kirk Whisler & Jim Sullivan. (Stepping Stones to Success Ser.). 1998. pap. 16.95 (*1-889379-12-3*) WPR Pubng.

101 Ways to Grow Your Business with Barter: A Guide to Thriving in the 90'S & Beyond. Kirk Whisler. 1997. pap. 16.95 (*1-889379-01-8*) WPR Pubng.

101 Ways to Hang Out with a Teen: Building Relationships That Make a Difference. Greg Kenerly et al. 56p. (Orig.). 1996. pap. 5.99 (*0-8341-1591-3*) Beacon Hill.

101 Ways to Happiness. Louise L. Hay. 112p. 1998. pap. 9.95 (*1-56170-495-4*) Hay House.

101 Ways to Have a Great Day at Work. Stephanie G. Davidson. LC 99-216192. 112p. 1998. pap. 7.95 (*1-887166-41-6*) Sourcebks.

101 Ways to Health & Happiness. Louise L. Hay. 112p. 1998. pap. 9.95 (*1-56170-496-2*) Hay House.

101 Ways to Help Your Child Learn to Read & Write. Mary Behm & Richard Behm. LC 95-18220. (Illus.). 58p. (Orig.). 1995. pap. 5.99 (*1-883790-16-6*, EDINFO Pr) Grayson Bernard Pubs.

101 Ways To Improve Business Performance. Donald Waters. 1999. pap. text 17.95 (*0-7494-2981-X*, Kogan Pg Educ) Stylus Pub VA.

101 Ways to Improve Your Communication Skills Instantly. Jo Condrill & Bennie Bough. LC 97-97110. (Illus.). xii, 116p. 1998. pap. 14.95 (*0-9661414-7-4*) GoalMinds.

101 Ways to Improve Your Communication Skills Instantly. rev. ed. Jo Condrill & Bennie Bough. LC 99-90350. (Illus.). xii, 116p. 1999. reprint ed. pap. 14.95 (*0-9661414-9-0*) GoalMinds.

***101 Ways to Improve Your Pharmacy Worklife.** Mark R. Jacobs. 150p. 2000. pap. 29.00 (*1-58212-014-5*) Am Pharm Assn.

***101 Ways to Improve Your Salary.** Daniel Porot & Frances Haynes. 240p. 2001. pap. 12.95 (*1-58008-230-0*) Ten Speed Pr.

101 Ways to Increase Class Enrollment & Bottom Line Profit. Rik Feeney. (Illus.). 76p. 1996. spiral bd. 29.95 (*0-9637991-1-8*) Richardson Pub.

101 Ways to Increase Your Sales. Patrick Forsyth. (101 Ways Ser.). 1996. pap. 15.95 (*0-7494-1985-7*) Kogan Page Ltd.

101 Ways to Influence People on the Job. Communication Briefings Editors. 48p. 1998. pap. 25.00 (*1-878604-26-0*) Briefings Pub Grp.

***101 Ways to Integrate Personal Development into Core Curriculum: Lessons in Character Education for Grades K-12.** Mary Ann Conroy. LC 99-462072. 320p. 1999. pap. 29.50 (*0-7618-1642-9*) U Pr of Amer.

101 Ways to Know If You're a Teacher. David C. Barnette. (Illus.). 103p. (Orig.). 1995. pap. 8.95 (*1-888769-10-6*) Pub One Hund One.

101 Ways to Know You're "Black" in Corporate America: You Know You're Black in Corporate America When... Deborah A. Watts. LC 98-90708. 143p. 1998. pap. 11.95 (*0-9666276-0-1*) Watts-Five Prodns.

***101 Ways to Lift Your Spirits.** gif. ed. Emilie Barnes. (Illus.). 64p. 2000. pap. 6.99 (*0-7369-0388-7*) Harvest Hse.

101 Ways to Live 150 Years Young & Healthy. Betty J. Y. Ho. Ed. by Amanda Elkan. (System of Government in the Living Body Ser.). 62p. 1992. pap. 15.00 (*0-9600148-6-1*) Juvenescent.

One Hundred One Ways to Love a Black Man! Karen Haley. LC 93-86782. 72p. (Orig.). 1994. pap. 7.95 (*1-882368-03-7*) Quantum Christ.

One Hundred-One Ways to Love a Black Woman! Karen Haley. (Illus.). 72p. (Orig.). 1994. pap. 9.95 (*1-882368-04-5*) Quantum Christ.

***101 Ways to Make Every Second Count: Time Management Tips & Techniques for More Success with Less Stress.** Robert W. Bly. LC 99-25026. 224p. 1999. pap. 14.99 (*1-56414-406-2*) Career Pr Inc.

101 Ways to Make Meetings Active: Surefire Ways to Engage Your Group. Mel Silberman & Kathy Clark. LC 99-6095. 336p. 1999. pap. 29.95 (*0-7879-4607-9*, Pfffr & Co) Jossey-Bass.

One Hundred One Ways to Make Money in the Trading-Card Market. Paul Green & Kit Kiefer. LC 93-74135. (Illus.). 236p. 1994. pap. 8.95 (*1-56625-002-1*) Bonus Books.

One-Hundred One Ways to Make Money Right Now in the Music Business: The A-Z Guide to Cashing in on Your Talents. Bob Baker. Ed. by Gary Hustwit. LC 92-82622. 140p. (Orig.). (C). 1993. pap. 14.95 (*0-9627013-4-3*) Rockpress Pub.

***101 Ways To Make More Effective Presentations.** Elizabeth P. Tierney. 1999. pap. text 15.95 (*0-7494-2968-2*, Kogan Pg Educ) Stylus Pub VA.

One Hundred One Ways to Make Ramen Noodles: Creative Cooking When You Can Only Afford Ten-for-One-Dollar Pasta. Toni Patrick. (Illus.). 96p. (Orig.). 1993. spiral bd. 9.95 (*0-9626335-2-6*) C&G Pub CO.

***101 Ways to Make Things Worse: And Even More Ways to Make Them Better.** Drew Cangelosi. LC 00-190191. 2000. 25.00 (*0-7388-1540-3*); pap. 18.00 (*0-7388-1541-1*) Xlibris Corp.

101 Ways to Make Training Active. Melvin L. Silberman & Karen Lawson. LC 95-7738. (Illus.). 304p. 1995. pap. 39.95 (*0-88390-475-6*) Jossey-Bass.

101 Ways to Make Your Child Feel Special. Vicki Lansky. (Illus.). 120p. 1991. 6.95 (*0-8092-3997-3*, 399730, Contemporary Bks) NTC Contemp Pub Co.

***101 Ways to Make Your Classroom Special: Creating a Place Where Significance, Teamwork & Spontaneity Can Sprout & Flourish.** James D. Sutton. LC 99-17478. (Illus.). 170p. 1999. pap. 11.95 (*1-878878-57-3*) Friendly Oaks Pubns.

One Hundred One Ways to Make Your Home Toddler-Friendly. Joy M. Johnson. (Illus.). 100p. (Orig.). 1993. pap. 6.95 (*1-880782-24-3*) Spirit Dance.

AR Made EZ: A Basic Guide to Using the Accelerated Reader Teacher Progr. School Renaissance Institute Staff. 14p. 1998. spiral bd. 19.95 (*0-9646404-0-6*) Schl Ren Inst.

101 Ways to Nourish Your Soul. Mitch Finley. 168p. 1996. pap. text 13.95 (*0-8245-1589-7*) Crossroad NY.

101 Ways to Overcome Insecurity. Marilyn Hickey. 1998. pap. 1.00 (*1-56441-175-3*) M Hickey Min.

101 Ways to "Piss-Off" Dad. Karen S. Hyer. (Illus.). (Orig.). 1995. pap. 5.95 (*0-9648660-0-5*) CharToons Pub.

101 Ways to "Piss off" Dad. Karen S. Hyer. LC 97-69279. (Illus.). 104p. 1997. pap. 9.95 (*0-9649394-3-6*) Paint Rock.

101 Ways to Pop the Question: The Most Ingenious Ways to Say "Will You Marry Me?" - From Newlyweds Nationwide, Vol. 2. Cynthia C. Muchnick. LC 97-116814. 176p. 1997. pap. 8.95 (*0-02-861513-1*, Arco) Macmillan Gen Ref.

101 Ways to Power up Your Job Search. Tom Buck et al. LC 96-51986. (Illus.). 222p. 1997. pap. 12.95 (*0-07-041043-7*) McGraw.

101 Ways to Power up Your Job Search. William R. Matthews & Robert N. Leetch. 1997. pap. 12.95 (*0-614-20466-6*) McGraw.

***101 Ways to Promote Your Web Site: Filled with Proven Internet Marketing Tips, Tools, Techniques, & Resources to Increase Your Web Site Traffic.** 2nd rev. ed. Susan Sweeney. LC 00-8349. 287p. 2000. pap. write for info. (*1-885068-45-X*, Pub. by Maximum Pr) IPG Chicago.

One Hundred One Ways to Promote Yourself: A Fast & Easy Guide for Real Estate Agents. Sheena Ashdown. 76p. (Orig.). 1994. pap. 9.95 (*0-9641975-0-2*) Gibsons Pubng.

101 Ways to Promote Yourself: Tricks Of The Trade For Taking Charge Of Your Own Success. Raleigh Pinskey. LC 96-95160. 352p. 1997. mass mkt. 6.99 (*0-380-78508-0*, Avon Bks) Morrow Avon.

***101 Ways to Promote Yourself: Tricks Of The Trade For Taking Charge Of Your Own Success.** Raleigh Pinskey. LC 99-96994. 416p. 1999. pap. 12.50 (*0-380-81054-9*, Avon Bks) Morrow Avon.

101 Ways to Protect Your Children: Simple Precautions to Keep Your Children Safe from Crime. Chris Harris. 220p. 1998. pap. 9.95 (*0-9653837-1-7*, C Harris Publns) Harris Personal Safety.

***101 Ways to Raise a Happy Baby.** Lisa McCourt. LC 99-23464. (Illus.). 160p. 1999. pap. 13.95 (*0-7373-0270-4*, 02704W) NTC Contemp Pub Co.

***101 Ways to Raise a Happy Toddler.** Lisa McCourt. 2000. pap. 13.95 (*0-7373-0473-1*, Pub. by Lowell Hse) NTC Contemp Pub Co.

101 Ways to Recycle a Hockey Stick: The Definitive Guide. David More. (Illus.). 128p. 1992. pap. 7.95 (*0-88995-089-X*, Pub. by Red Deer) Genl Dist Srvs.

101 Ways to Romance. Barbara De Angelis. 1998. pap. 9.95 (*1-56170-494-6*) Hay House.

101 Ways to Run the Option. Tony DeMeo. LC 98-89621. 138p. 1999. 16.95 (*1-57167-368-7*) Sagamore Pub.

***101 Ways to Save on Home Office Expenses.** Writers at Work Editors. 48p. 1999. pap. 4.95 (*1-929369-05-0*) Free State Pr.

101 Ways to Save Your Life. Chris Harris. 213p. (Orig.). 1996. pap. 8.95 (*0-9653837-0-9*) Harris Personal Safety.

One Hundred One Ways to Say "I Love You" Vicki Lansky. (Illus.). 128p. 1991. per. 7.95 (*0-671-72350-2*) S&S Trade.

***101 Ways to Say Merry Christmas.** Virginia Unser. (Charming Petites Ser.). (Illus.). 80p. 1999. 4.95 (*0-88088-395-2*) Peter Pauper.

One Hundred One Ways to Simplify Your Life. Paul Borthwick. 144p. (Orig.). 1992. pap. 1.80 (*0-89693-058-0*, 6-1058, Victor Bks) Chariot Victor.

101 Ways to Sneak a Crafty Smoke. Shovel & Nadler. 1997. pap. text 8.95 (*0-575-60174-4*, Pub. by V Gollancz) Trafalgar.

***101 Ways to Soothe a Crying Baby.** Jim Peinkofer. LC 99-88337. (Illus.). 112p. 2000. pap. 8.95 (*0-8092-9842-2*, Contemporary Bks) NTC Contemp Pub Co.

101 Ways to Spoil Your Grandchild. Vicki Lansky. (Illus.). 120p. 1996. 6.95 (*0-8092-3231-6*, 323160, Contemporary Bks) NTC Contemp Pub Co.

***101 Surefire Ways to Start the School Year Right, 1.** Susanne M. Shafer. 64p. 1999. pap. text 8.95 (*0-590-36515-0*) Scholastic Inc.

One Hundred One Ways to Stay Awake When on the Road. Jeff Hodge. Ed. by Paulette Hodge. LC 93-61600. (Illus.). 100p. (Orig.). 1994. pap. 5.95 (*0-9633347-1-9*) Talent Wrld Pubns.

***101 Ways to Stop School Violence.** Jason Dorsey. 1999. pap. 9.99 (*1-890900-18-4*) Insight Intl.

An Asterisk (*) at the beginning of an entry indicates that the title is appearing for the first time.

*101 Ways to Stretch Your Dollars. gif. ed. Ann F. Chodakowski & Susan Wood. (Illus.). 64p. 2000. pap. 6.99 (0-7369-0285-6) Harvest Hse.

101 Ways to Succeed As an Independent Consultant. 2nd ed. Timothy R. V. Foster. 82p. 1999. pap. 15.95 (0-7494-2962-3, Kogan Pg Educ) Stylus Pub VA.

101 Ways to Survive the Y2K Crisis. Steve F. Tomajczyk. LC 99-30087. 240p. 1999. pap. 8.99 (0-312-24591-2, St Martins Paperbacks) St Martin.

101 Ways to Tell Your Child "I Love You" Vicki Lansky. (Illus.). 120p. 1988. 6.95 (0-8092-4527-2, 452720, Contemporary Bks) NTC Contemp Pub Co.

101 Ways to Transform Your Life. Wayne W. Dyer. 112p. 1998. pap. 9.95 (1-56170-493-8) Hay House.

One Hundred One Ways to Use a Dead Riverfly. Bruce Carlson. (Illus.). 106p. (Orig.). 1991. pap. 7.95 (1-878488-60-0) Quixote Pr IA.

101 Ways to Your Wife's/Husband's Heart. Nick Allen & Rosie Allen. 128p. 1995. pap. 5.99 (0-7852-7788-9) Nelson.

One Hundred One Weapons for Women: Implement Weaponry. Rodney R. Rice. Ed. by Lynn Jones. (Illus.). 128p. 1992. pap. 10.95 (0-9632402-1-8) RiJo Prods.

*101 Weekend Crochet Projects. Ed. by Laura Scott. (Illus.). 176p. 2000. 19.95 (1-882138-53-8) Hse White Birches.

*101 Welding Projects. Jeffus. 2001. pap. 13.50 (0-7668-1894-2) Delmar.

*101 Winning Drills from the AVCA. Ed. by Kinda Lenberg. (Illus.). 160p. 1999. pap. 16.95 (1-58382-039-6) Coaches Choice.

101 Winning Ways. Nick Baker. 1995. pap., per. write for info. (0-9643367-4-X) Peak Performance.

*101 Wisconsin Unsolved Mysteries. Marv Balousek. (Illus.). 224p. 2000. pap. 12.95 (1-878569-70-8) Badger Bks Inc.

101 Women's Basketball Drills. Theresa Grentz & Gary Miller. 1997. pap. 16.95 (1-57167-083-1) Coaches Choice.

101 Word Games: A Wide Variety of Games for Puzzlers Who Love a Challenge. Mayme Allen & Janine Kelsch. LC 90-19740. (Illus.). 128p. 1991. pap. 5.95 (0-8069-8234-9) Sterling.

101 Word Processing Exercises. Brooks. (One Hundred One Ser.). 1992. teacher ed. write for info. (0-02-800755-7) Glencoe.

One Hundred One Word Processing Exercises. Lloyd D. Brooks. 128p. 1986. pap. text 15.56 (0-07-008118-2) McGraw.

101 Wraps & More: A Collection of your Favorites. Publications International, Ltd. Editorial Staff. LC 98-65616. 192 p. 1998. write for info. (0-7853-2475-5) Pubns Intl Ltd.

*One Hundred One Years of Living & Learning. Mary Freeman. 1999. pap. 6.95 (1-58334-031-9) Walnut Gr Pr.

*101 Youth Soccer Drills. Malcolm Cook. (Illus.). 128p. (J). (gr. 2-5). 1999. pap. 14.95 (1-890946-22-2) Reedswain.

*101 Youth Soccer Drills. Malcolm Cook. (Illus.). 128p. (YA). (gr. 7-11). 1999. pap. 14.95 (1-890946-23-0) Reedswain.

*One Hundred or So: North Dakota Centenarians at the End of the 20th Century. Illus. by Everett C. Albers & Rebecca J. Weisgerber. 128p. 2000. pap. 19.95 (0-9654579-3-1) N Dakota Hum.

One Hundred Ornamental Alphabets. Ed. & Selected by Dan X. Solo. LC 95-6215. (Pictorial Archive Ser.). (Illus.). 112p. 1995. pap. 7.95 (0-486-28696-7) Dover.

100 Orthopaedic Conditions Every Doctor Should Understand. Roy A. Meals. (Illus.). 328p. 1992. pap. 36.00 (0-942219-37-6) Quality Med Pub.

One Hundred Outlines from the Old Testament. John Phillips. LC 94-16340. 100p. 1994. pap., student ed. 7.99 (0-87213-575-6) Loizeaux.

One Hundred Paediatrics Picture Tests. A. P. Winrow et al. LC 93-29088. 1994. pap. text 32.00 (0-443-04942-4) Church.

One Hundred P&S Desktop Publishing Exercises. 2nd ed. Helen Youth. LC 94-32552. 288p. 1995. pap. text 48.00 (0-13-124843-X) P-H.

100 Parables of Zen. Tr. by Joyce Lim. (Illus.). 201p. 1995. 14.95 (981-3029-49-8, Pub. by Asiapac) China Bks.

100 Peaceful Easy Feeling Songs: Piano/Vocal Mixed Folio. 326p. (Orig.). 1978. pap. 18.95 (0-7692-1210-7, VF1259) Wrner Bros.

One Hundred Percent Chance of Frogs. James C. Schaap. LC 92-24941. (Devotions for Today Ser.). (J). 1992. pap. text 5.00 (1-56212-025-5, 1701-0550) CRC Pubns.

One Hundred Percent Christian. C. S. Lovett. 1970. pap. 6.95 (0-938148-07-9) Prsnl Christianity.

100Dead. Elizabeth Zipern. 1996. mass mkt. 9.99 (0-312-95800-5) St Martin.

100Deductible: Retirement Plans for Small Business. D. Kirk Buchanan. Ed. by Lon L. Davis. 239p. (C). 1997. 14.95 (0-9654078-3-7) Intl Legal Pubng.

100Deductible: Tax Advantaged Pension & Retirement Plans for Small Business. D. Kirk Buchanan. (Illus.). 225p. 1996. 19.95 (0-9630879-2-4) Buchanan Res.

100Healthy in 100 Days. Ranjit Chandra. 2000. 25.00 (0-06-019245-3) HarpC.

100Laugh Riot. Paul Zindel. (J). 1994. pap. 4.50 (0-553-54184-6) BDD Bks Young Read.

100Mathematical Proof. Rowan Garnier & John Taylor. 326p. 1996. 149.95 (0-471-96198-1); pap. 49.95 (0-471-96199-X) Wiley.

100Money. Irving Fisher. LC 96-12211. (Works of Irving Fisher). 1996. write for info. (1-85196-236-0, Pub. by Pickering & Chatto) Ashgate Pub Co.

100Pleasure: From Appetizers to Desserts, the Low-Fat Cookbook for People Who Love to Eat. Nancy Baggett & Ruth Glick. 384p. 1996. pap. 15.95 (0-87596-368-4) Rodale Pr Inc.

100Pure Cowboy. Cathleen Galitz. (Romance Ser.: No. 1279). 1998. per. 3.50 (0-373-19279-7, 1-19279-8) Silhouette.

*100Pure Florida Fiction: An Anthology. Susan Hubbard & Robley Wilson. LC 99-39571. 232p. 2000. pap. 16.95 (0-8130-1753-X) U Press Fla.

*100Pure Florida Fiction: An Anthology. Ed. by Susan Hubbard & Robley Wilson. 232p. 2000. 49.95 (0-8130-1752-1) U Press Fla.

100Return Options Trading Strategy. Jon Schiller. 224p. 1999. 59.95 (0-930233-67-0) Windsor.

One Hundred Percent Solution: Solve Every Problem, Positively! Colleen Patrick. 1992. pap. 11.95 (0-9634281-0-1) Meadow Brook.

One Hundred Percent Vegetarian: Eating Naturally from Your Grocery Store. Julianne M. Pickle. LC 90-92224. 120p. (Orig.). 1990. pap., spiral bd. 6.95 (0-9627645-0-7) Pickle Pub Co.

One Hundred Personal Effectiveness Traps & Their Solutions. Bob Miller. Ed. by Jane Morgan. (Illus.). 206p. (Orig.). 1987. pap. 15.00 (0-942227-01-8) Universal Lrn Ctr.

100 Photographs from the Collection of the Stedelijk Museum Amsterdam. Hripsime Visser. (Illus.). 100p. 1997. pap. 35.00 (90-6868-147-8, Pub. by Thoth Pubs) Bks Nippan.

One Hundred Pieced Patterns for Eight Inch Quilt Blocks. Marsha R. McCloskey. 64p. 1993. pap. 11.95 (0-9635422-0-6) Feathered Star.

100 Places in Washington: From the Center for Land Use Interpretation Archives. Center for Land Use Interpretation Staff. (Illus.). 112p. 1999. pap. write for info. (0-9650962-2-X) Ctr Land Use Interpret.

100 Planes 100 Years: The First Century of Aviation. Fredric Winkowski & Frank D. Sullivan. LC 98-7450. (100 Years Ser.). (Illus.). 168p. 1998. 19.98 (0-7651-0821-6) Smithmark.

100 Platinum Hits. (Guitar Supertab Ser.). 400p. (Orig.). 1994. pap. 22.95 (0-89724-341-2, GF0654) Wrner Bros.

100+ B. A. S. S. Tips: Tricks, Techniques & Tactics to Better Bassin. B. A. S. S. Inc. Staff. (Illus.). 162p. (Orig.). 1992. pap. 4.95 (1-890280-02-X) B A S S.

One Hundred Plus Craft & Gift Ideas: Fun & Easy Ideas for Any Occasion. Sally E. Stuart & Woody C. Young. (Illus.). 96p. (Orig.). (J). (gr. 1 up). 1990. pap. 9.95 (0-939513-62-5) Joy Pub SJC.

One Hundred Plus Desserts & Appetizers. Shirley Lundgren & Woody Young. (Illus.). 96p. 1992. pap. 9.95 (0-939513-63-3) Joy Pub SJC.

100+ Essential Guitar Chords. Contrib. by John Mories. 1996. 9.95 (0-7119-3935-7, AM 91816) Omnibus NY.

100 Plus Innovative Lessons in Literature: Integrating Substance Abuse Prevention in World, America & British Literature. Ed. by Helen S. Harrill. (C). 1995. teacher ed. 45.00 (0-934337-05-5) Drug Ed Ctr.

One Hundred Plus Motivational Moments for Writers & Speakers: Anthology by 109 Authors. 256p. 1991. pap. 9.95 (0-939513-45-5) Joy Pub SJC.

One-Hundred Plus Party Games. Sally E. Stuart & Woody Young. Ed. by Kathryn Dongarra. (Illus.). 96p. (Orig.). (J). 1988. pap. text 7.95 (0-939513-61-7) Joy Pub SJC.

100+ Ways to Better Deer Hunting. 2nd ed. B. A. S. S. Inc. Staff. (Illus.). 128p. 1990. pap. 4.95 (1-890280-03-8) B A S S.

One Hundred Poems. Ed. by A. J. Smith. LC 73-133073. (Granger Index Reprint Ser.). 1977. 23.95 (0-8369-6203-6) Ayer.

One Hundred Poems by One Hundred Poets. Selected by Harold Pinter et al. LC 87-206. 192p. 1995. pap. 12.00 (0-8021-3279-0, Grove) Grove-Atltic.

One Hundred Poems from One Hundred Poets (Ogura Hyaku-nin Isshu) Heihachiro Honda. (Illus.). 104p. 1956. pap. 12.95 (4-590-00086-5, Pub. by Hokuseido Pr) Book East.

One Hundred Poems from the Chinese. Tr. by Kenneth Rexroth. LC 56-13351. 1965. pap. 9.95 (0-8112-0180-5, NDP192, Pub. by New Directions) Norton.

One Hundred Poems from the Japanese. Tr. by Kenneth Rexroth. LC 56-2557. (ENG & JPN.). 140p. 1964. pap. 9.95 (0-8112-0181-3, NDP147, Pub. by New Directions) Norton.

One Hundred Poems of Peace: An Anthology. Ed. by Thomas C. Clark & Winfred E. Garrison. LC 75-160902. (Granger Index Reprint Ser.). 1977. reprint ed. 15.95 (0-8369-6265-6) Ayer.

100 Poems Without a Country. Erich Fried. Tr. by Stuart Hood from GER. LC 80-50150. 1980. 8.95 (0-87376-035-2) Red Dust.

One Hundred Popular Harmonica Solos & How to Play Them. 1990. 9.95 (0-685-32195-9, M384) Hansen Ed Mus.

One Hundred Popular Songs for Trumpet & Clarinet. 1990. 9.95 (0-685-32203-3, 9.95) Hansen Ed Mus.

100 Portraits of Christ. Henry Gariepy. 240p. 1993. 11.99 (1-56476-121-5, 6-3121, Victor Bks) Chariot Victor.

100 Posters of Paul Colin. Jack Rennert. (Illus.). 112p. Date not set. 30.00 (0-9664202-2-5) Posters Please.

100 Posters of Tadanori Yokoo. Koichi Tanikawa. (Illus.). 112p. Date not set. 30.00 (0-9664202-3-3) Posters Please.

One Hundred Pounds of Tomatoes Out of an Inexpensive Foam Box. Leopold Klein. LC 87-92082. 1988. pap. 14.95 (0-9619778-0-9) Leopold Klein.

One Hundred Practical Exercises for Piano, Op. 139. Carl Czerny. (Carl Fischer Music Library: No. 371). 76p. (J). 1905. pap. 9.95 (0-8258-0134-6) Fischer Inc NY.

*100 Practically Perfect Places in the North Carolina Mountains. Robert L. Williams. (Illus.). 324p. 1998. pap. 15.00 (1-893330-00-1) SW Pubg Co.

*100 Prayers for making Faith Connections. John Van Bemmel. 216p. 1999. pap. text 14.95 (0-88347-428-X, Pub. by T More) BookWorld.

One Hundred Predictions for the Baby Boom: The Next 50 Years. C. Russell. (Illus.). 250p. (C). 1987. 17.95 (0-306-42527-0, Plenum Trade) Perseus Pubng.

One Hundred Prison Meditations. Richard Wurmbrand. 1986. pap. 5.00 (0-88264-180-8) Living Sacrifice Bks.

*One Hundred Problems in Celestial Navigation. 2nd ed. Leonard Gray. (Illus.). 168p. 1999. pap., student ed. 19.95 (0-939837-33-1) Paradise Cay Pubns.

One Hundred Problems in Elementary Mathematics. Hugo Steinhaus. 174p. 1979. reprint ed. pap. 5.95 (0-486-23875-X) Dover.

100 Processional & Recessionals. (Kevin Mayhew Ser.). 288p. 1995. pap. 34.95 (0-7866-2153-2, MB96023) Mel Bay.

100 Profits+Plus Ideas for Power Promoting. Tom Shay. 105p. 1997. pap. 8.00 (1-891964-01-1) Profits Plus.

100 Profits+Plus ideas for Power Managing. Tom Shay. 107p. 1997. pap. 8.00 (1-891964-02-X) Profits Plus.

One Hundred Programs for the BBC Microcomputer. John Gordon. (Illus.). 1984. pap. 11.95 (0-13-634741-X); audio 9.95 (0-13-634733-9) P-H.

*100 Proof: Tips & Tales for Spirited Drinkers Everywhere. P. T. Elliot. 2000. pap. 10.95 (0-452-28179-2, Plume) Dutton Plume.

100 Publicity Ideas for Local Churches. Elizabeth W. Crisci. Ed. by Cindy G. Spear. 113p. 1997. ring bd. 38.95 (1-57052-076-3) Chrch Grwth VA.

100 Questions & Personal Finance. Ilyce R. Glink. 1999. 114.00 (0-676-58259-1, Times Bks) Crown Pub Group.

One Hundred Questions & Answers: Religion in America. George H. Gallup, Jr. & Sara Jones. 269p. (Orig.). 1989. pap. 25.00 (0-940303-01-9) Princeton Rlgn Res Ctr.

100 Questions & Answers about AIDS: What You Need to Know. Michael T. Ford. LC 92-46187. 208p. (YA). (gr. 7 up). 1993. mass mkt. 4.95 (0-688-12697-9, Wm Morrow) Morrow Avon.

100 Questions & Answers about AIDS: What You Need to Know Now. Michael T. Ford. 1993. 10.05 (0-606-05722-6, Pub. by Turtleback) Demco.

One Hundred Questions & Answers about AIDS: A Guide for Young People. Michael T. Ford. LC 92-15072. (Illus.). 208p. (J). (gr. 6 up). 1992. lib. bdg. 14.95 (0-02-735424-5, New Dscvry Bks) Silver Burdett Pr.

*100 Questions & Answers about Hypertension. William M. Manger & Ray W. Gifford, Jr. (Illus.). 191p. 2000. pap. 14.95 (0-632-04481-0) Blackwell Sci.

*100 Questions Every First-Time Home Buyer Should Ask. 2nd ed. Ilyce R. Glink. LC 99-41015. 464p. 1999. pap. 17.00 (0-8129-3235-8, Times Bks) Crown Pub Group.

One Hundred Questions Every First-Time Homebuyer Should Ask: Answered by Top Brokers from Around the Country. Ilyce R. Glink. 1994. pap. 15.00 (0-8129-2283-2, Times Bks) Crown Pub Group.

One Hundred Questions for Citizenship: English-Spanish. Thomas Esparza, Jr. (Illus.). 40p. (Orig.). 1990. reprint ed. pap. text 6.95 (1-879817-02-0) Star Light Pr.

100 Questions for the Home Seller: With Answers from Top Brokers from Around the Country. Ilyce R. Glink. 1995. pap. 15.00 (0-8129-2406-1, Times Bks) Crown Pub Group.

100 Questions That Non-Members Ask Unitarian Universalists. 2nd rev. ed. John Sias. 50p. 1994. pap. 5.95 (0-9654497-3-4) Transit Pub.

100 Questions You Should Ask about Your Personal Finances: And the Answers You Need to Help You Save, Invest & Grow Your Money. Ilyce R. Glink. LC 98-41101. 512p. 1998. pap. 19.00 (0-8129-2741-9, Times Business) Random.

100 Quick Fashion Tips. Andrea Rose. Ed. by Amber Michelle. 26p. 1998. pap. 9.00 (1-890469-04-1) A R Prod.

One Hundred Quick Tips for Business Success. John W. Myrna. Ed. by Don Taylor. 112p. (Orig.). 1994. pap. 3.95 (0-9637314-1-6) Quick Study.

100 Quick Tips for Time Management: A Values Approach, It's Not Just the Time, It's the Stress. Vicki Harding & Doug MacFarlane. (Short Attention Span Library: Vol. 3). 1997. pap. 4.95 (0-9637314-5-9) Quick Study.

One Hundred Ready-to-Run Programs. John C. Craig & Jeff Bretz. 1991. 29.95 (0-8306-1049-9) McGraw-Hill Prof.

*100 Reasons to Keep Dumb. Sharon Naylor. 2000. pap. 6.99 (0-517-20965-9) Random Hse Value.

One Hundred Recipes for the Chafing Dish. Herbert Kinsley. LC 72-9795. (Cookery Americana Ser.). reprint ed. 7.00 (0-405-05048-8) Ayer.

One Hundred Renaissance Jokes: A Critical Anthology. Barbara C. Bowen. LC 88-61672. 128p. 1988. lib. bdg. 21.95 (0-917786-65-3) Summa Pubns.

100 Rides in New South Wales. 2nd rev. ed. Sven Klinge. (Cycling the Bush Ser.). (Illus.). 382p. (Orig.). 1995. pap. 15.95 (0-85572-250-9, Pub. by Hill Content Pubng) Seven Hills Bk.

One Hundred Roadside Wildflowers of the Southwest Woodlands. Janice E. Bowers. Ed. by T. J. Priehs. LC 87-60531. (Illus.). 64p. (Orig.). 1989. pap. 7.95 (0-911408-73-8) SW Pks Mnmts.

One Hundred Rules on How to Trade Profitably. George Seamans. 1973. pap. 5.00 (0-685-40600-8) Windsor.

One Hundred Saints: Their Lives & Likenesses Drawn from Butler's "Lives of the Saints" & Great Works of Western Art. Bulfinch Press Staff. LC 93-4416. (Illus.). 288p. 1994. 40.00 (0-8212-2009-8, Pub. by Bulfinch Pr) Little.

100 SAT Math Tips, & How to Master Them Now! Charles Gulotta. (Illus.). 120p. (Orig.). (YA). (gr. 10-12). 1996. pap. 14.95 (0-9653263-1-4) Mostly Bright.

100 Sauces for Today's Healthy Gourmet. Carl Jerome. 1996. 22.50 (0-8050-4798-0) H Holt & Co.

100 Sauces for Today's Healthy Gourmet. Carl Jerome. LC 96-44779. 1997. pap. 12.95 (0-8050-4799-9) H Holt & Co.

One Hundred Saxophone Solos. (Illus.). 96p. 1987. pap. 14.95 (0-8256-1099-0, AM33705) Music Sales.

*100 Science Experiments with Paper. Steven W. Moje. (J). 1999. pap. text 5.95 (0-8069-6353-0) Sterling.

*100 Secrets of the Carolina Coast. Duckett. LC 99-86588. 288p. 2000. pap. write for info. (1-55853-813-5) Rutledge Hill Pr.

One Hundred Secrets for a Six-Figure Private Practice Income. Ryan Elliott. Ed. by Beth Billstrom. (Your Six-Figure Private Practice Success Course Ser.). 120p. (Orig.). 1994. pap. text. write for info. (0-9615140-1-9) Relaxed Bks.

100 Secrets of the Smokies. Randall Duckett & Maryellen Duckett. LC 98-5214. (Illus.). 224p. 1998. pap. 12.95 (1-55853-586-1) Rutledge Hill Pr.

One Hundred Selected Games. Mikhail M. Botvinnik. (Illus.). 272p. 1960. pap. 8.95 (0-486-20620-3) Dover.

One Hundred Selected Poems. E. E. Cummings. LC 59-15193. 128p. (Orig.). 1988. pap. 10.00 (0-8021-3072-0, Grove) Grove-Atltic.

100 Selected Stories. O. Henry. (Classics Library). 400p. 1997. pap. 3.95 (1-85326-241-2, 2412WW, Pub. by Wrdsworth Edits) NTC Contemp Pub Co.

100 Selected Stories. unabridged ed. O. Henry. (Wordsworth Classics). (YA). (gr. 6-12). 1998. 5.27 (0-89061-241-2, R2412WW, Jamestwn Pub) NTC Contemp Pub Co.

One Hundred Sermon Outlines from the New Testament. John Phillips. LC 94-16339. 112p. 1994. pap. 7.99 (0-87213-576-4) Loizeaux.

107 British Romanic Prose Writers 1789-32. 400p. 1991. text 155.00 (0-8103-4587-0) Gale.

107 Favorite Level I Ideas for Drama. Karen L. Erickson. 64p. (J). (gr. k up). 1995. teacher ed. 20.00 (1-884771-03-3) Creative Dir.

One Hundred-Seven Great Chess Battles, 1938-1945, Vol. 945. Alexander Alekhine. 256p. 1992. reprint ed. pap. 7.95 (0-486-27104-8) Dover.

107 Questions Children Ask about Prayer. Daryl Lucas & David Veerman. LC 98-23034. 1998. pap. 10.99 (0-8423-4542-6) Tyndale Hse.

One Hundred Seventeen Days. Ruth First. (Voices of Resistance Ser.). 192p. (YA). (gr. 11-12). 1989. reprint ed. pap. 13.00 (0-85345-790-5, Pub. by Monthly Rev) NYU Pr.

One Hundred Seventeen Days Adrift. Maurice Bailey & Maralyn Bailey. (Illus.). 192p. 1992. pap. 14.95 (0-924486-31-7) Sheridan.

One Hundred-Seventeen House Designs of the Twenties. Gordon-Van Tine Co. Staff. (Illus.). 144p. 1992. reprint ed. pap. 10.95 (0-486-26959-0) Dover.

One Hundred Seventeenth Illinois Infantry Volunteers, 1862-1865. Edwin G. Gerling. LC 93-206327. (Illus.). 222p. 1994. 26.95 (0-9640542-1-3) One Hund Seventeenth.

One Hundred Seventieth Power of Ten. Connie Fox, pseud. 36p. (Orig.). 1986. pap. 4.00 (0-916155-02-1) Trout Creek.

One Hundred Seventy-Five Amazing Nature Experiments. Rosie Harlow & Gareth Morgan. LC 91-21113. (Illus.). 176p. (Orig.). (J). (gr. 4-7). 1992. pap. 14.00 (0-679-82043-4, Pub. by Random Bks Yng Read) Random.

175 Easy-to-Do Christmas Crafts. Ed. by Sharon D. Umnik. LC 94-79156. (Illus.). 64p. (J). (ps-5). 1996. pap., student ed. 6.95 (1-56397-373-1) Boyds Mills Pr.

175 Easy-to-Do Easter Crafts. Ed. by Sharon D. Umnik. LC 93-20871. (Illus.). 64p. (J). (gr. k-5). 1994. pap. 6.95 (1-56397-316-2) Boyds Mills Pr.

175 Easy-to-Do Everyday Crafts. Sharon D. Umnik. LC 94-72626. (Illus.). 64p. (J). (gr. 1-5). 1995. 6.95 (1-56397-441-X) Boyds Mills Pr.

175 Easy-to-Do Halloween Crafts. Sharon D. Umnik. LC 94-79157. (Illus.). 64p. (J). (gr. 1-5). 1995. 6.95 (1-56397-372-3) Boyds Mills Pr.

175 Easy-to-Do Thanksgiving Crafts. Ed. by Sharon D. Umnik. LC 95-80773. (Illus.). 64p. (J). (ps-5). 1996. pap., student ed. 6.95 (1-56397-374-X) Boyds Mills Pr.

175 High-Impact Cover Letters. 2nd ed. Richard H. Beatty. LC 95-52821. 240p. 1996. pap. 10.95 (0-471-12385-4) Wiley.

175 High-Impact Resumes. 2nd ed. Richard H. Beatty. LC 98-24356. 288p. 1998. pap. 10.95 (0-471-31476-5) Wiley.

175 More Science Experiments to Amuse & Amaze Your Friends: Experiments! Tricks! Things to Mak. Terry Cash. 1991. 20.09 (0-606-04852-9, Pub. by Turtleback) Demco.

One Hundred Seventy-Five More Science Experiments to Amuse & Amaze Your Friends. Terry Cash & Barbara Taylor. LC 90-39250. (Illus.). 176p. (Orig.). (J). (gr. 4-7). 1991. pap. 14.99 (0-679-80390-4, Pub. by Random Bks Yng Read) Random.

175+ Uses for the Dremel Multipro & Cordless Multipro. Eric G. McAtlee. (Illus.). 96p. (Orig.). 1989. pap. 5.15 (0-9606512-1-7) Dremel.

One Hundred Seventy-Five Science Experiments to Amuse & Amaze Your Friends. Brenda Walpole. LC 88-4526. (Illus.). 176p. (Orig.). (J). (gr. 4-7). 1988. pap. 13.99 (0-394-89991-1, Pub. by Random Bks Yng Read) Random.

175 Sermon Outlines. John L. Mayshack. (Sermon Outline Ser.). 60p. 1979. pap. 4.99 (0-8010-6085-0) Baker Bks.

One Hundred Seventy-Five SW PA Marriages: Performed by Rev. Abraham Boyd 1802-1849. Ed. by Mary Closson. 7p. 1994. reprint ed. pap. 2.50 (1-55856-164-1, 480) Closson Pr.

One Hundred Seventy-Five Thousand-Mile-Car. Joseph Grieco. Ed. by Marye Myers. (Illus.). 40p. (Orig.). 1984. pap. 7.95 (0-931843-00-6) Grieco.

O

175 Ways to Advance Your Career. Don Kennedy. 112p. (Orig.). 1996. pap. 5.95 (*0-9640380-6-4*) SuccessBooks.
175 Ways to Fund Your Youth Ministry. Larry A. Maxwell. Ed. by Cindy G. Spear. 26p. 1995. ring bd. 54.95 (*1-57052-048-8*) Chrch Grwth VA.
176 Stupidest Things Ever Done. Ross Petras & Kathryn Petras. 208p. 1996. pap. 10.95 (*0-385-48341-4*) Doubleday.
***176 Ways to Involve Parents.** Betty Boult. LC 98-61832. 117 p. 1999. write for info. (*1-57517-153-8*) SkyLght.
173rd Airborne Brigagde (Sep) Turner Publishing Company Staff. LC 91-67153. (Illus.). 168p. 1992. 49.95 (*1-56311-071-7*) Turner Pub KY.
173rd Airborne Brigade. 2nd ed. Turner Publishing Company Staff. 240p. Date not set. 52.50 (*1-56311-326-0*) Turner Pub KY.
One Hundred Sheep: Songbook. Roger Nichols. 12p. (J). (gr. 1-3). 1995. pap. 10.00 (*1-880892-69-3*) Com Sense FL.
100 Sheep Production-Health Sheets. 1995. 8.95 (*0-944079-11-3*) Lessiter Pubns.
100 Ships & Planes That Shaped World History. William Caper. 1999. pap. text 7.95 (*0-912517-38-7*) Bluewood Bks.
100 Short Cases for the MRCP. 2nd ed. Ed. by K. Gupta et al. (An Arnold Publication). 304p. 1994. pap. text 14.95 (*0-412-54860-7*, Pub. by E A) OUP.
One Hundred Short Prayers. May S. Hilburn. 100p. 1995. reprint ed. pap. 5.95 (*0-88053-313-7*, S-250) Macoy Pub.
One-Hundred Show: The Seventeenth Annual of the American Center for Design. Ed. by Rob Dewey. (Illus.). 160p. 1995. pap. 30.00 (*0-941447-05-7*) Amer Ctr Design.
100 Show 19: The Nineteenth Annual of the American Center for Design. American Center for Design Staff. (Illus.). 176p. 1997. 35.00 (*2-88046-337-8*, Rotovision) Watsn-Guptill.
100 Simple Chinese Recipes. Lenli Jackson. pap. 11.95 (*0-87557-104-2*) Saphrograph.
100 Simple Sauces for Today's Healthy Home Cooking. Carl Jerome. (Orig.). 1997. pap. 12.95 (*0-614-28093-1*, Owl) H Holt & Co.
100 Simple Science Experiments in Paper. Moje. LC 98-34948. (Illus.). 128p. 1999. pap. 14.95 (*0-8069-6391-3*) Sterling.
***100 Simple Secrets of Happy People: What Scientists Have Learned & How You Can Use It.** David Niven. LC 99-87647. 224p. 2000. pap. 9.95 (*0-06-251650-7*, Pub. by Harper SF) HarpC.
106 Common Mistakes Homebuyers Make: And How to Avoid Them. 2nd ed. Gary W. Eldred. LC 97-36016. 320p. 1998. pap. 14.95 (*0-471-19999-0*) Wiley.
***106 Preguntas Que los Ninos Hacen Acerca.** David J. Lucas & David R. Veerman. Tr. by Sandra Adkison. (SPA., Illus.). 256p. 2000. pap. text 9.99 (*0-311-38655-5*, Edit Mundo) Casa Bautista.
106 Questions Children Ask about Our World. Daryl Lucas & David Veerman. LC 97-41761. (J). 1998. 8.99 (*0-8423-4527-2*) Tyndale Hse.
One Hundred Sixth NARUC Annual Convention Proceedings, November 14-17, 1995, 2 vols., Set. 1995. 45.00 (*0-317-05553-4*) NARUC.
160 Colonial Details: Collection A174. Mike Tecton. (Illus.). 64p. 1998. reprint ed. pap. 45.00 (*1-58203-078-2*, A174) M Tecton Pub.
160 Details of French Provincial Architecture: Collection A180. Mike Tecton. (Illus.). 64p. 1998. reprint ed. pap. 45.00 (*1-58203-081-2*, A180) M Tecton Pub.
***160 Essential Chinese Herbal Patent Medicines.** Bob Flaws. LC 99-73748. 220p. 1999. pap. 29.95 (*1-891845-12-8*) Blue Poppy Pr.
165 Million Years of Dinosaurs: All about Theropods, Sauropods, Duck-Billed Dinosaurs & A. T. Rex or Two. Francois Gohier. LC 94-30912. (Close Up Ser.). (Illus.). 48p. (J). (gr. 1 up). 1995. pap. 7.95 (*0-382-24904-6*); lib. bdg. 14.95 (*0-382-24903-8*) Silver Burdett Pr.
One Hundred Sixty-Nine Brand New Old Time Fiddle Tunes: By Western American & Canadian Composers. Ed. by Vivian T. Williams. (Brand New Old Time Fiddle Tunes Ser.: Vol. 3). 76p. (Orig.). 1990. pap. 10.00 (*0-9631484-2-7*) Voyager Rec.
169 Ways to Score Points with Your Boss. Alan R. Schonberg et al. LC 97-46456. 1998. write for info. (*0-8092-2998-6*) NTC Contemp Pub Co.
169 Ways to Score Points with Your Boss. Alan R. Schonberg et al. LC 97-46456. 192p. 1998. pap. 14.95 (*0-8092-2999-4*, 299940, Contemporary Bks) NTC Contemp Pub Co.
161 Waterfowling Secrets: Time Honored, Field Tested Waterfowling Tips & Advice from DU Members. Ducks Staff. Ed. by Matt Young. (Illus.). 76p. 1995. pap. 10.95 (*0-9617279-2-6*, Pub. by Ducks Unltd) Willow Creek Pr.
One Hundred Sixty-Seven New Art Lessons for a Single Class Period. Alice Escobar. (Illus.). 1978. text 21.95 (*0-13-634873-4*, Parker Publishing Co) P-H.
167 Vermont Reports. 800p. 1999. write for info. (*0-327-08507-X*, 48837-10) LEXIS Pub.
One Hundred Sixty-Two Traditional & Contemporary Designs for Stained Glass Projects. Ed. by Joel Wallach. (Illus.). 64p. (Orig.). 1991. pap. 6.95 (*0-486-26928-0*) Dover.
160 Ways to Help the World: Community Service Projects for Young People. Linda L. Duper. 192p. (J). (gr. 5-12). 1996. pap. 9.95 (*0-8160-3503-2*) Facts on File.
160 Ways to Help the World: Community Service Projects for Young People. Linda L. Duper. LC 95-34223. 192p. (YA). 1996. 19.95 (*0-8160-3324-2*) Facts on File.
100 Small Boat Rigs. Czeslaw A. Marchaj. 1996. pap. text 19.95 (*0-07-156806-9*) McGraw.
100 Small-Group Experiences: The Teacher's Idea Book 3. Michelle Graves. (Illus.). 220p. 1997. pap. 25.95 (*1-57379-029-X*, P1115) High-Scope.
***100 Social Studies Activities.** Anne Schraff & Candyce Norvell. 1999. ring bd. 27.95 (*1-58659-182-7*) Artesian.
100 Solos: Trumpet. (Illus.). 96p. 1987. pap. 15.95 (*0-8256-1096-6*, AM33697) Music Sales.
One Hundred Solos for Clarinet. (Illus.). 96p. 1987. pap. 14.95 (*0-8256-1097-4*, AM33689) Music Sales.
One Hundred Solos for Flute. (Illus.). 96p. 1987. pap. 14.95 (*0-8256-1098-2*, AM38365) Music Sales.
100 Solos for Violin. (Illus.). 96p. 1987. pap. 14.95 (*0-8256-1095-8*, AM33671) Music Sales.
***100 Solos Saxophone.** Wise Publications Staff. 1999. pap. text 14.95 (*0-7119-0358-1*) Wise Publns.
One Hundred Sonnets for St. Augustine. Richard Ball. 100p. 1986. pap. 8.00 (*0-940066-04-1*) Dalmas & Ricour.
100 Soviet Chess Miniatures. P. H. Clarke. LC 99-51927. 192p. 2000. pap. text 8.95 (*0-486-40844-2*) Dover.
100 Sow-Litter Production-Health Sheets. 1995. 8.95 (*0-944079-12-1*) Lessiter Pubns.
100 Spectacular Science Fair Projects. Glen Vecchione. (J). Date not set. write for info. (*0-8069-4261-4*) Sterling.
***100 Spring Wildflowers of Henry W. Coe State Park, California.** Lee Dittmann. (Illus.). 48p. 2000. pap. 4.75 (*0-9675548-1-0*) budda-nature.
One Hundred Statistical Tests. Gopal K. Kanji. (Illus.). 240p. 1993. 75.00 (*0-8039-8704-8*); pap. 22.95 (*0-8039-8705-6*) Sage.
***100 Statistical Tests.** 2nd ed. Gopal K. Kanji. LC 98-61738. 224p. 1999. 56.00 (*0-7619-6152-6*); pap. 25.95 (*0-7619-6151-8*) Sage.
How to Kill Your Loved Ones with Food & Get Away with It. E. Stanford. (SPA.). 230p. 1997. pap. 11.00 (*1-885778-25-2*) Seaburn.
100 Steps Necessary for Survival on the Earth. R. M. Soccolich. (One Hundred Steps Necessary Ser.). 196p. (Orig.). 1995. pap. 4.95 (*1-885778-05-8*) Seaburn.
100 Steps Necessary for Survival in the Global Village. R. M. Soccolich. (Survival Ser.). 112p. (Orig.). 1997. mass mkt. 4.95 (*1-885778-20-1*) Seaburn.
100 Steps Necessary for Survival in a Stressful Environment. Clive Williams. Ed. by R. Soccolich. (Survival Ser.). 112p. 1997. mass mkt. 4.95 (*1-885778-34-1*) Seaburn.
100 Steps Necessary for Survival in America: (For People of Color) Sam Chekwas. (Survival Ser.). 112p. 1998. pap. 4.95 (*1-885778-46-5*) Seaburn.
100 Steps Necessary for Survival in America: (For the Immigrant) Sam Chekwas. (Survival Ser.). 112p. 1998. pap. 4.95 (*1-885778-47-3*) Seaburn.
***100 Steps to Better Health.** Claude R. Rothe. LC 99-96681. 2000. pap. 11.95 (*0-533-13318-1*) Vantage.
100 Stories in Black: A Collection of Bright, Breezy, Humorous Stories of the Colored Race As Seen in the Sunny South. Bridges Smith. (Illus.). 318p. 1977. 20.95 (*0-8369-9126-5*) Ayer.
One Hundred Stories to Change Your Life: Small Tales in Answer to Large Questions. Ed. by Pierre Lefevre. 150p. (C). 1996. pap. 39.95 (*0-85439-382-X*, Pub. by St Paul Pubns) St Mut.
100 Strategies of War. Wang Xuanming. Tr. by Yeo Ai Hoon. (Illus.). 216p. 1993. pap. 14.95 (*981-3029-16-1*, Pub. by Asiapac) China Bks.
One Hundred Successful College Application Essays. Ed. by Gigi Georges & Harvard Independent Staff. 304p. 1991. mass mkt. 6.99 (*0-451-62835-7*, Ment) NAL.
100 Super Hits of Country. 430p. 1994. pap. 19.95 (*0-89724-215-7*, VF2115) Wrner Bros.
***100 Super Supplements for a Longer Life.** Frank Murray. 2000. pap. 24.95 (*0-658-00973-7*, Keats Publng) NTC Contemp Pub Co.
One Hundred Sure Ways to Sharpen Your Game. Golf Magazine Editors. (Illus.). 23p. 1990. pap. 4.95 (*1-878728-02-4*) Golf Gifts.
110 Best Job Search Sites on the Internet. Katherine K. Yonge. (Illus.). 80p. 1998. pap., per. 10.95 (*1-891818-00-7*) Linx Educ Pubg.
110 Biggest Mistakes Job Hunters Make: (And How to Avoid Them) 2nd ed. Richard L. Hermann & Linda P. Sutherland. Ed. by Jeanette J. Sobajian. 214p. 1994. 19.95 (*0-929728-23-8*) Federal Reports Inc.
110 British Romantic Prose Writers 1789-32. 400p. 1991. text 155.00 (*0-8103-4590-0*) Gale.
110 Classics of Christmas. 1990. pap. 12.95 (*0-7935-0161-X*, 00001316) H Leonard.
110 Great Room Fireplaces: Collection A104. Mike Tecton. (Illus.). 1995. pap. 35.00 (*0-922070-13-X*, COLLECTION A104) M Tecton Pub.
One Hundred Ten in the Shade: Vocal Selections. (Illus.). 32p. 1981. pap. 8.95 (*0-88188-102-3*, 00312303) H Leonard.
One Hundred Ten Livingston Street Revisited: Decentralization in Action. David Rogers & Norman H. Chung. LC 83-3937. 264p. (C). 1984. pap. text 18.50 (*0-8147-7392-3*) NYU Pr.
110 Succes Musette No. 3: Piano/Vocal Mixed Folio. 1p. (Orig.). 1997. pap. 34.95 (*0-7692-1215-8*, 01020103) Wrner Bros.
110 Succes Musette No. 4: Piano/Vocal Mixed Folio. 1p. (Orig.). 1997. pap. 34.95 (*0-7692-1216-6*, 01020105) Wrner Bros.
110 Succes Musette No. 5: Piano/Vocal Mixed Folio. 1p. (Orig.). 1997. pap. 34.95 (*0-7692-1217-4*, 01020108) Wrner Bros.
One Hundred Tennessee Tall Tales. Reed Scarbrough. 100p. (Orig.). 1988. pap. 4.98 (*1-881878-00-7*) Gift Bks Am.
One Hundred Texas Wildflowers. Dorothy B. Mattiza. Ed. by Ronald J. Foreman. LC 93-84561. (Illus.). 72p. (Orig.). 1993. pap. 7.95 (*1-877856-35-5*) SW Pks Mnmts.
***100 Things Every Adult College Student Ought to Know.** abr. ed. Carlette J. Hardin. (Illus.). 225p. (C). 2000. pap. text 9.95 (*0-935637-27-3*) Cambridge Strat.
100 Things Every College Freshman Ought to Know. William Disbro. (Illus.). 226p. 1995. pap. text 9.95 (*0-935637-22-2*) Cambridge Strat.
100 Things Every Writer Needs to know. Scott Edelstein. LC 99-20096. 245p. 1999. pap. 11.95 (*0-399-52508-4*, Perigee Bks) Berkley Pub.
100 Things I Am Not Going to Do Now That I'm over 50. Wendy Reid Crisp. LC 94-24657. 224p. 1995. pap. 14.00 (*0-399-51936-X*, Perigee Bks) Berkley Pub.
100 Hundred Things to Always Remember. . . And One Thing to Never Forget. Alin Austin. LC 93-25766. (Illus.). 64p. 1993. pap. 8.95 (*0-88396-373-6*) Blue Mtn Art.
***100 Things to Do Before You Die: Travel Events You Can't Miss.** Neil Teplica & Dave Freeman. LC 99-37504. 264p. 1999. pap. 15.95 (*0-87833-243-X*) Taylor Pub.
100 Things to Write About. Koertge. 100p. (C). 1997. pap. 13.00 (*0-673-98239-4*) Addson-Wesley Educ.
One Hundred Things We Can Do about Anger & Violence. Betty Doty. 212p. (Orig.). 1994. pap. 9.95 (*0-930822-18-8*) Bookery.
One Hundred Things You Can Do for Our Children's Future. Richard Louv. LC 93-3774. 384p. 1993. pap. 10.00 (*0-385-46878-4*, Anchor NY) Doubleday.
103rd Infantry Division: The Trail of the Cactus. Turner Publishing Company Staff. (Illus.). 208p. Date not set. 49.95 (*1-56311-288-4*) Turner Pub KY.
One Hundred Thirteen Galician-Portuguese Troubadour Poems. Richard Zenith. LC 96-146120. (ENG & POR.). 144p. 1996. pap. 18.95 (*1-85754-207-X*, Pub. by Carcanet Pr) Paul & Co Pubs.
113 Modern Latin-American Fiction Writers. 400p. 1992. text 155.00 (*0-8103-7590-7*) Gale.
130 Bush Street: An Illustrated Story about Four Buildings & a Monument in San Francisco. Larry G. Segedin. LC 96-92664. (Illus.). 75p. (Orig.). 1996. pap. 19.95 (*0-9654381-0-4*) Stackwell Bks.
One Hundred Thirty-Eight Quick Ideas to Get More Clients. Howard L. Shenson & Jerry Wilson. 176p. 1993. 69.95 (*0-471-58952-7*); pap. 19.95 (*0-471-58951-9*) Wiley.
***130 Evident Miracles in the Qur'an.** Mazhar U. Kazi. 146p. 1998. pap. 6.95 (*0-9638962-1-0*) Crescent NY.
139. (Puzzlers Detect-a-Word Ser.). (J). 1998. pap. write for info. (*1-56144-795-1*, Honey Bear Bks) Modern Pub NYC.
***131 Christians Everyone Should Know.** Christian History Magazine Staff. 2000. pap. 14.99 (*0-8054-9040-X*) Broadman.
131 Stress Reducin' Recession Bustin' Profit Proven Furniture Ads. Clyde B. Bedell & J. A. Alexander. LC 82-71190. 288p. 1982. 129.00 (*0-916014-01-0*) BASIC Bedell.
133 Fun Things to Do in Dallas. Karen Foulk. (Illus.). 216p. 1999. pap. 12.95 (*0-9652464-6-9*) Into Fun.
132 New England Georgian Architecture: Collection A172. Mike Tecton. (Illus.). 64p. 1998. reprint ed. pap. 45.00 (*1-58203-076-6*, A172) M Tecton Pub.
One Hundred Thirty Winemaking Recipes. C. J. Berry. 128p. (Orig.). 1993. reprint ed. pap. 10.95 (*0-9619072-5-8*) G W Kent.
***130 Years of Catching up with the West: A Comparative Perspective of Hungarian Science & Technology Policy-Making since Industrialization.** Peter S. Biegelbauer. LC 99-75542. 250p. 2000. text 74.95 (*1-84014-930-2*, Pub. by Ashgate Pub) Ashgate Pub Co.
100,000 Brainteasers. Date not set. 22.00 (*1-56997-217-6*) Knowldge Adv.
$100,000 Club: How to Make a Six-Figure Income. D. A. Benton. 304p. pap. write for info. (*0-446-67514-8*) Warner Bks.
$100,000 Club: How to Make a Six-Figure Income. D. A. Benton. LC 97-29934. 304p. 1998. 25.00 (*0-446-52083-7*, Pub. by Warner Bks) Little.
***$100,000 Club: How to Make a Six-Figure Income.** D. A. Benton. 320p. 2000. mass mkt. 7.50 (*0-446-60825-4*) Warner Bks.
$100,000 Resume. Craig Rice. LC 98-23199. 256p. 1998. pap. 16.95 (*0-07-052586-2*, BusinessWeek Bks) McGraw.
***$100,000 Writer.** Nancy Flynn. LC 99-88708. 224p. 2000. pap. 12.95 (*1-58062-265-8*) Adams Media.
$100,000 & Above: The New Realities of Executive Job Hunting. Bob Gerberg. LC 95-92429. 112p. 1996. 15.00 (*1-882885-07-4*) Prince-Mstrs.
$100,000 & Above: The New Realities of the Executive Job Market. Bob Gerberg. Ed. by Princeton/Masters Press Staff. (Easier Way Ser.). 182p. 1995. 20.00 (*1-882885-04-X*) Prince-Mstrs.
One Hundred Thousand Miles...Two Hundred Thousand Miles...or More: Practical Car Care. James Wesner & Joseph Ettwein. (Illus.). 192p. 1988. 17.95 (*0-8306-9067-0*, 3067); pap. 10.95 (*0-8306-9367-X*, 3067) McGraw-Hill Prof.
100,000 Plus Power Phrases. Robert B. Johnson, Jr. 1996. pap. 19.95 (*0-7880-0661-4*, Express Pr); spiral bd. 21.95 (*0-7880-0668-1*, Express Pr) CSS OH.
One Hundred Thousand Tractors: The MTS & the Development of Controls in Soviet Agriculture. Robert F. Miller. LC 70-95929. (Russian Research Center Studies: No. 60). (Illus.). 439p. 1970. 37.00 (*0-674-63875-1*) HUP.
103 American Literary Biographers 1st. 400p. 1991. text 155.00 (*0-8103-4583-8*) Gale.
***103 Great Poems (103 Meistergedichte) A Dual-Language Book.** Johann Wolfgang Von Goethe. LC 98-49292. (ENG & GER.). 1999. pap. text 9.95 (*0-486-40667-9*) Dover.
103 Hikes in Southwestern British Columbia. 4th ed. Mary MacAree & David Macaree. 224p. 1994. pap. 14.95 (*0-89886-395-3*) Mountaineers.
***103 Preguntas Que los Ninos Haven Acerca de lo Quees Bueno O Es Malo, Vol. 3.** 2nd ed. David R. Veerman et al. (Right from Wrong Ser.).Tr. of 103 Questions Children Ask about Right & Wrong. (SPA., Illus.). 256p. (J). (gr. 1 up). 1998. pap. text 9.99 (*0-311-38652-0*, Edit Mundo) Casa Bautista.
***103 Purfect Pet Names.** Pleasant Publishers Staff. (American Girl Backpack Bks.: Vol. 26). (Illus.). 32p. (J). (ps-3). 2000. 1.95 (*1-58485-063-9*) Pleasant Co.
103 Questions Children Ask about Right from Wrong. David R. Veerman et al. LC 95-24130. 240p. 1995. pap. 10.99 (*0-8423-4595-7*) Tyndale Hse.
103 Vignettes of Life & the Alphabet, with Other Thoughts & Opinions. (Vignettes Ser.: Vol. I). (Illus.). 96p. 1998. pap. 16.95 (*0-9667149-0-3*) D Mabray.
100 Tips for Better Bridge: The Macallan the Malt. Paul Mendelson. 128p. 1995. pap. 19.95 (*0-09-180767-0*, Pub. by Random) Trafalgar.
100 Top Hits of the 90's. Dan Coates. 1998. pap. text 18.95 (*0-7692-1513-0*) Wrner Bros.
100 Top Hospitals. 1996. write for info. (*1-57372-066-6*) HCIA.
100 Top Hospitals: Benchmarks for Success, 1997. 1997. 80.00 (*1-57372-103-4*) HCIA.
***100 Top Internet Job Sites: Get Wired, Get Hired in Today's New Job Market.** Kristina M. Ackley. LC 99-89877. (Savvy CareerBuilder Ser.). 2000. pap. 12.95 (*1-57023-128-1*) Impact VA.
100 Top Psychics in America: Their Stories, Specialties & How to Contact Them. Paulette Cooper & Paul Noble. 186p. 1996. mass mkt. 6.99 (*0-671-53401-7*) PB.
100 Research Topic Guides for Students. Barbara W. Borne. LC 95-42446. (Greenwood Professional Guides in School Librarianship Ser.). 256p. 1996. 39.95 (*0-313-29552-2*, Greenwood Pr) Greenwood.
One-Hundred Topographic Maps. Richard Debruin. 128p. (Orig.). (C). 1970. pap. text 13.35 (*0-8331-1704-1*, 534) Hubbard Sci.
One Hundred Towers: An Italian Odyssey of Cultural Survival. Lola E. Romanucci-Ross. LC 90-1123. 240p. 1991. 59.95 (*0-89789-250-X*, H250, Bergin & Garvey) Greenwood.
One Hundred Traditional Bobbin Lace Patterns. Geraldine Stott & Bridget M. Cook. LC 93-30184. 144p. 1994. pap. 12.95 (*0-486-27908-1*) Dover.
100 Traditional Garden Layouts & Features: Collection A179. Mike Tecton. (Illus.). 64p. 1997. pap. 35.00 (*1-58203-080-4*, A179) M Tecton Pub.
***100 Trails of the Big South Fork: Tennessee & Kentucky Hiking, Mountain Biking, Horseback Riding.** 4th ed. Russ Manning. LC 99-50715. (100 Hikes in Ser.). (Illus.). 208p. 2000. pap. 14.95 (*0-89886-638-3*) Mountaineers.
One Hundred Training Games. Gary Kroehnert. 176p. 1992. pap. 24.95 (*0-07-452770-3*) McGraw.
***100 Trains 100 Years: A Century of Locomotives & Trains.** Fredric Winkowski et al. (100 Years Ser.). (Illus.). 160p. 2000. 19.98 (*0-7651-1017-2*) Smithmark.
One Hundred Treasures from the British Library. Harry N. Abrams Inc., Staff. 1998. 29.95 (*0-8109-5156-8*) Abrams.
One Hundred Tree Myths. Alex L. Shigo. (Dr. Shigo's Tree Ser.). (Illus.). 80p. (Orig.). 1993. pap. 13.00 (*0-943563-11-9*) Shigo & Trees Assocs.
One Hundred Trivia Quizzes for Stamp Collectors. Bill Olcheski. 130p. 1982. pap. 4.95 (*0-933580-09-6*) Am Philatelic Society.
100 Tudor Wood Paneling Details: Collection A49. Mike Tecton. (Illus.). 64p. 1998. reprint ed. pap. 35.00 (*1-58203-028-6*, A49) M Tecton Pub.
One Hundred Turn-of-the-Century Brick Bungalows with Floor Plans. Rogers & Manson Staff. LC 94-6540. (Illus.). 128p. 1994. reprint ed. pap. 8.95 (*0-486-28119-1*) Dover.
***112 Things Kids Should Be Taught Before the Age of 18.** Colin P. Byrnes. 1999. pap. 5.95 (*1-929342-03-9*) Olde Ridge Bk.
One Hundred Twentieth-Century Philosophers. Stuart C. Brown et al. LC 97-30846. 256p. (C). 1998. pap. 19.99 (*0-415-17996-3*) Routledge.
One Hundred Twentieth Report on Manpower Planning in Judiciary: A Blue Print. (C). 1988. 35.00 (*0-7855-3692-2*) St Mut.
120 Best Known Christmas Songs: Piano/Vocal Mixed Folio. 196p. (Orig.). 1996. pap. 16.95 (*1-57623-539-4*, VF1854A) Wrner Bros.
***120 Competitive Games & Exercises.** Nicola Pica. (Illus.). 245p. 1999. pap. 14.95 (*1-890946-29-X*) Reedswain.
120 Days of Sodom & Other Writings. Tr. by Richard Seaver & Austryn Wainhouse from FRE. LC 87-7394. 800p. 1987. pap. 17.95 (*0-8021-3012-7*, Grove) Grove-Atltic.
120 Days of Sodom: Adapted for the Stage by Nick Hedges from the Novel by the Marquis De Sade. Adapted by Nick Hedges. (Illus.). 112p. 1991. pap. 12.95 (*1-897767-00-5*, Pub. by Delectus Bks) Xclusiv Distrib.
125 African Parables & Wise Sayings. Josiah Nwaogwugwu. LC 99-173641. (Illus.). 1998. pap. 20.00 (*1-886094-78-0*) Chicago Spectrum.
125 Brain Games for Babies. Jackie Silberg. LC 99-17317. (Illus.). 160p. (J). (ps). 1999. pap. 14.95 (*0-87659-199-3*, Pub. by Gryphon Hse) Consort Bk Sales.
***125 Brain Games for Toddlers & Twos: Simple Games to Promote Early Brain Development.** Jackie Silberg. 2000. pap. 14.95 (*0-87659-205-1*) Gryphon Hse.

An Asterisk (*) at the beginning of an entry indicates that the title is appearing for the first time.

125 Christmas Ornament Patterns for the Scroll Saw. Arthur L. Grover. LC 97-80074. (Schiffer Book for Woodworkers Ser.). (Illus.). 64p. 1997. pap. 14.95 (*0-7643-0323-6*) Schiffer.

125 Cookies to Bake, Nibble & Savor. Elinor Klivans. LC 98-10234. (Illus.). 240p. 1998. 25.00 (*0-7679-0154-1*) Broadway BDD.

One Hundred Twenty-Five Ideas for Successful Events. Ken Cicora. 171p. 24.95 (*0-914951-74-2*) LERN.

125 Jahre Sueskanal - Lauchhammers Eisenguss am Nil. Ed. by Wolfgang Schwanitz. (Historische Texte und Studien). 1997. write for info. (*3-487-10315-X*) G Olms Pubs.

One Hundred Twenty-Five Masterpieces from the Collection of the Albright-Knox Art Gallery. LC 86-14092. (Illus.). 264p. 1987. 50.00 (*0-8478-0786-X*) Buffalo Fine-Albrght-Knox.

***125 Most Asked Questions about Cats: (And the Answers)** John Malone. 160p. 1999. 5.98 (*1-56731-338-8*, MJF Bks) Fine Comms.

125 Promotions for Your Restaurant & Bar: Complete Reference Including Guides. Lisa H. Murphy. LC 93-85256. 182p. 1994. wbk. ed. 20.00 (*1-881908-10-0*) PanPress.

125 Super Songs/Superstars: Guitar. pap. 19.95 (*0-7692-0422-8*, GF0655A) Wrner Bros.

125 Super Songs of Superstars: Guitar. pap. 16.95 (*0-7692-0421-X*, GF0321) Wrner Bros.

125 Supersongs/Superstars: Guitar. pap. 19.95 (*0-7692-0423-6*, GF0655) Wrner Bros.

125 Things You Must Know about Being Pregnant. Nina Landi. LC 98-2644. (Illus.). 48p. 1998. pap. 9.95 (*0-8050-5860-5*, Owl) H Holt & Co.

One Hundred Twenty-Five Ways to Be a Better Listener: A Program for Listening Success. Stutzman Eller. 123p. 1992. spiral bd. 34.95 (*1-55999-232-8*) LinguiSystems.

One Hundred Twenty-Five Ways to Be a Better Student: A Program for Study Skills Success. Paula S. Currie et al. 136p. (YA). 1987. spiral bd. 34.95 (*1-55999-063-5*) LinguiSystems.

125 Ways to Improve Your Life. Dee Frances. Date not set. pap. 6.00 (*1-885519-49-4*) DDDD Pubns.

125 Ways to Meet the Love of Your Life. Jan Yager. 150p. 2001. 26.95 (*1-889262-52-8*); pap. 19.95 (*1-889262-50-1*) Hannacroix.

125 Years: The Physical Society & the Institute of Physics. J. L. Lewis. LC 99-10834. 256p. 1999. 25.00 (*0-7503-0609-2*) IOP Pub.

125 Years of American Watercolor Painting. Ira Spanierman Gallery Staff. LC 98-156705. (Illus.). 120p. 1998. pap. text 30.00 (*0-945936-16-8*) Spanierman Gallery.

125 Years of Service: St. Lukes Hospital, 1873-1998. Richard A. Martin. (Illus.). 350p. text 31.95 (*1-889668-16-8*) S & D.

One Hundred Twenty-Five Years of State Public Works, 1895-1984. Ian Cameron. 324p. (C). 1990. 90.00 (*0-86439-083-1*, Pub. by Boolarong Pubns) St Mut.

***124 High-Impact Letters for Busy Principals.** Marilyn L. Grady. LC 00-8357. (Illus.). 2000. pap. write for info. (*0-7619-7664-7*) Corwin Pr.

124 Prayers for Caregivers. Joan Guntzelman. (Illus.). 144p. 1995. pap. 5.95 (*0-88489-340-5*) St Marys.

120 Hikes on the Oregon Coast. 2nd ed. Bonnie Henderson. LC 98-53385. 240p. 1999. pap. 14.95 (*0-89886-576-X*) Mountaineers.

One-Hundred Twenty Million. Michael Gold. LC 77-178438. (Short Story Index Reprint Ser.). 1977. reprint ed. 18.95 (*0-8369-4039-3*) Ayer.

120 Modern Crossword Puzzles. Ken Russell. 1997. pap. text 9.95 (*0-572-02289-1*, Pub. by W Foulsham) Trans-Atl Phila.

120 MPH That Way! In Search of: the Market Test. Linzo South. 160p. 1995. pap. 10.00 (*0-9644964-9-6*) AX-S.

129 Tips for Building a Fantastic Future. Gladys Hotchkiss. 24p. 1998. pap. 5.00 (*0-88100-098-1*) Natl Writ Pr.

121 Internet Businesses You Can Start from Home: Plus: A Beginner's Guide to Starting a Business Online. Ron Gielgun. LC 97-72020. (Illus.). 306p. 1997. pap. 19.95 (*0-9657617-3-8*) Actium Pub.

One Hundred Twenty-One Real Estate T. I. P. S. Techniques & Ideas on Purchasing & Selling. Paul M. Palmer. Ed. by Sherman Lipstein & Pat B. Cockhill. (Illus.). 272p. (Orig.). 1985. pap. 12.95 (*0-935679-01-4*) Commercial Choice.

121 Timed Writings with Selected Drills. 5th ed. Clayton. (TA - Typing/Keyboarding Ser.). 1991. mass mkt. 14.25 (*0-538-60169-8*) S-W Pub.

Endorphin Dancing! Tricks & Techniques to Tickle Your Endorphins & Entice Them to Dance. Valla D. Fotiades et al. 2000. pap. write for info. (*0-926565-03-6*) Edgeworth & North.

One Hundred Twenty Seven Authentic Art Deco Patterns in Full Color. Aug H. Thomas & G. Darcy. LC 94-18583. (Pictorial Archive Ser.). 48p. 1994. 8.95 (*0-486-28249-X*) Dover.

One Hundred Twenty-Seven Insights into Megillas Esther. Mendel Weinbach. 193p. 1990. 16.95 (*0-944070-50-7*, Pub. by Targum Pr) Feldheim.

120 Singing Games & Dances for Elementary Schools. Lois Choksy & David Brummitt. (Illus.). 208p. (C). 1996. pap. 61.00 (*0-13-635038-0*) P-H.

One Hundred Twenty-Six Strategies to Build Language Art Abilities: A Month-by-Month Resource. Cathy Collins. LC 91-6672. 320p. (C). 1991. pap. text 57.00 (*0-205-13025-9*) Allyn.

120 Studies for Right Hand Development. Mauro Giuliani. Ed. by Paul Brelinsky. 1983. pap. 7.50 (*0-89898-190-5*, F1887GCX) Wrner Bros.

123. (Mira Bebe Ser.). (SPA.). 1995. bds. 2.98 (*1-85854-307-X*) Brimax Bks.

123 Engineering Math Handbook. Edward F. Blick. 1991. pap. text 11.75 (*0-201-50607-6*) Addison-Wesley.

123 Puzzlers. Ann R. Fisher. Ed. by Judy Mitchell. (Illus.). 144p. (Orig.). (J). (ps-2). 1996. pap., teacher ed. 13.95 (*1-57310-031-5*) Teachng & Lrning Co.

***123 Sticker Book.** (First Steps Ser.). 16p. (J). 1999. pap. 2.99 (*0-7214-2994-7*, Ladybrd) Penguin Putnam.

123 Super Sales Tips. Gerhard Gschwandtner & Jennifer Linch. LC 97-76459. 139p. 1997. 19.95 (*0-939613-14-X*) Personal Selling.

123 Yippie. Lisa Jahn-Clough. LC 97-1568. 32p. (J). (ps-4). 1998. 5.95 (*0-395-87003-8*) HM.

One Hundred Twenty-Two Clues for Jews Whose Children Intermarry. Sidney J. Jacobs & Betty J. Jacobs. LC 87-83147. 144p. (Orig.). 1988. pap. 9.95 (*0-933647-01-8*) Jacobs Ladder Pubns.

***122 Fun Things to Do in San Antonio.** Karen Foulk. (Illus.). 232p. 1999. pap. 12.95 (*0-9652464-3-4*) Into Fun.

120 Walks in Victoria. 6th rev. ed. Tyrone Thomas. (Illus.). 402p. (Orig.). 1995. pap. 15.95 (*0-85572-251-7*, Pub. by Hill Content Pubng) Seven Hills Bk.

***120 Year Diet: How to Double Your Vital Years.** 2nd rev. ed. Roy Walford. (Illus.). 432p. 2000. pap. 16.00 (*1-56858-157-2*, Pub. by FWEW) Publishers Group.

One Hundred Twenty Years of American Education: A Statistical Portrait. 1994. lib. bdg. 259.75 (*0-8490-5690-X*) Gordon Pr.

120 Years of Jeanne Calmunt. Michel Allard et al. Tr. by Beth Coupland. LC 98-31252. 175p. 1998. text 22.95 (*0-7167-3251-3*) W H Freeman.

One Hundred Twenty Years of Medicine in Los Angeles County, 1871-1991. Barbara B. Gray. 144p. 1991. 32.50 (*1-881547-11-6*) Pioneer Pubns.

102 American Short Story Writers 1910-45, Vol. 2. 400p. 1991. text 155.00 (*0-8103-4582-X*) Gale.

One Hundred Two Bright Bulletin Board Ideas. Glenda Lee. 1992. pap. 8.00 (*0-89137-627-5*) Quality Pubns.

One Hundred Two Cat & Dog Jokes. Michael J. Pellowski. LC 91-42769. (Illus.). 64p. (J). (gr. 2-6). 1997. pap. 2.95 (*0-8167-2790-2*) Troll Communs.

One Hundred Two Creepy, Crawly Bug Jokes. Ski Michaels. LC 91-42737. (Illus.). 64p. (J). (gr. 2-6). 1996. pap. 2.95 (*0-8167-2745-7*) Troll Communs.

***102 Dalmatians.** Charles Bazaldua. (Illus.). (J). 2000. pap. 3.99 (*0-307-20006-X*, Goldn Books) Gldn Bks Pub Co.

***102 Dalmatians.** Golden Books Staff. (Illus.). (J). 2000. pap. 3.99 (*0-307-25253-1*, Goldn Books) Gldn Bks Pub Co.

***102 Dalmatians: Mutts in a Mess.** Golden Books Staff. (Illus.). (J). 2000. pap. 3.99 (*0-307-29901-5*, Goldn Books) Gldn Bks Pub Co.

***102 Dalmatians: Numbers.** Douglas Love. 64p. (J). 2000. 14.99 (*0-7364-0192-X*, Pub. by Mouse Works) Time Warner.

***102 Dalmations.** Tk. 32p. (J). 2000. pap. 3.99 (*0-7868-1479-9*, Pub. by Disney Pr) Time Warner.

***102 Dalmations.** abr. ed. Mouseworks Staff. (Read-Aloud Storybook Ser.). 64p. (J). (ps-2). 2000. 6.99 (*0-7364-0195-4*) Mouse Works.

***102 Dalmatians: Colorful Pups.** Mouseworks Staff. (Lift the Flaps Bks.). 10p. (J). (ps). 2000. 4.99 (*0-7364-0228-4*, Pub. by Mouse Works) Time Warner.

***102 Dalmatians: Junior Novel.** (Illus.). 96p. (J). (gr. 3-7). 2000. pap. 4.99 (*0-7868-4440-X*, Pub. by Disney Pr) Time Warner.

***102 Dalmatians: Pull-Out Posters & Trading Cards Book.** (Illus.). 32p. (J). (ps-2). 2000. lib. bdg. 7.99 (*0-7364-1066-X*) Mouse Works.

***102 Dalmatians: Take Me Home.** 10p. (J). (ps-k). 2000. bds. 7.99 (*0-7364-0208-X*, Pub. by Mouse Works) Time Warner.

One Hundred Two Haunted House Jokes. Ski Michaels. LC 91-21891. (Illus.). 64p. (J). (gr. 2-6). 1997. pap. 2.95 (*0-8167-2578-0*) Troll Communs.

102 Preguntas Que los Ninos Hacen Acerca de la Biblia, Vol. 2. 2nd ed. David R. Veerman et al.Tr. of 102 Questions Children Ask about the Bible. (SPA., Illus.). 222p. 1996. reprint ed. pap. text 9.99 (*0-311-38651-2*, Edit Mundo) Casa Bautista.

102 Questions Children Ask about the Bible. David R. Beerman. LC 93-41888. 208p. 1994. pap. 9.99 (*0-8423-4570-1*) Tyndale Hse.

102 Tools for Teachers & Counselors Too. 2nd ed. Mary J. Hannaford. (Illus.). 159p. (J). (gr. k-12). 1991. pap. 21.95 (*1-57543-006-1*) Mar Co Prods.

102 Ways to Market Your Choir: A Public Relations Workbook. T. Janssen. 262p. 1984. spiral bd. 30.00 (*0-7935-1071-6*) H Leonard.

100 Ultimate Blues Riffs. Andrew D. Gordon. 1995. 22.95 incl. cd-rom (*1-882146-41-7*) A D G Prods.

100 Ultimate Jazz Riffs. Andrew D. Gordon. 60p. 1999. 22.95 incl. audio compact disk (*1-882146-70-0*) A D G Prods.

100 Unforgettable Moments in Tennis. Robert Italia. LC 96-22379. (100 Unforgettable Moments in Sports Ser.). (Illus.). 64p. (gr. 3-7). 1996. lib. bdg. 16.98 (*1-56239-693-5*) ABDO Pub Co.

100 Unforgettable Moments in Pro Football. Robert Italia. LC 96-7008. (100 Unforgettable Moments in Sports Ser.). (Illus.). 64p. (J). (gr. 3-7). 1996. lib. bdg. 16.98 (*1-56239-690-0*) ABDO Pub Co.

100 Unforgettable Moments in Pro Baseball. Robert Italia. LC 96-10649. (100 Unforgettable Moments in Sports Ser.). (Illus.). 64p. (J). (gr. 3-7). 1996. lib. bdg. 16.98 (*1-56239-689-7*) ABDO Pub Co.

100 Unforgettable Moments in Pro Hockey. Robert Italia. LC 96-33874. (100 Unforgettable Moments in Sports Ser.). (Illus.). 64p. (J). (gr. 3-7). 1996. lib. bdg. 16.98 (*1-56239-691-9*) ABDO Pub Co.

100 Unforgettable Moments in Pro Golf. Robert Italia. LC 96-8142. (One Hundred Unforgettable Moments in Sports Ser.). (Illus.). 64p. (J). (gr. 3-7). 1996. lib. bdg. 16.98 (*1-56239-694-3*) ABDO Pub Co.

100 Unforgettable Moments in Pro Basketball. Robert Italia. LC 96-15014. (One Hundred Unforgettable Moments in Sports Ser.). (Illus.). 64p. (J). (gr. 3-7). 1996. lib. bdg. 16.98 (*1-56239-692-7*) ABDO Pub Co.

100 Unforgettable Moments in the Summer Olympics. Robert Italia. LC 96-7597. (One Hundred Unforgettable Moments in Sports Ser.). (J). 1996. pap. 7.95 (*1-56239-687-0*) ABDO Pub Co.

100 Unforgettable Moments in the Summer Olympics. Robert Italia. LC 96-7597. (100 Unforgettable Moments in Sports Ser.). (Illus.). 64p. (J). (gr. 3-7). 1996. lib. bdg. 16.98 (*1-56239-695-1*) ABDO Pub Co.

100 Unforgettable Moments in the Winter Olympics. Robert Italia. LC 96-23093. (100 Unforgettable Moments in Sports Ser.). (Illus.). 64p. (gr. 3-7). 1996. lib. bdg. 16.98 (*1-56239-696-X*) ABDO Pub Co.

One Hundred Unorthodox Strategies: Battle & Tactics of Chinese Warfare. Ralph Sawyer et al. LC 96-22134. (C). 1998. pap. text 19.00 (*0-8133-2861-6*, Pub. by Westview) HarpC.

100 Utah Waterfalls. Dick Wunder. (Illus.). 144p. 1999. mass mkt. 12.95 (*1-891858-08-4*, 4012) Arch Hunter Bks.

100 Vagar Till Afrika: En Introduktion Till Modern Afrikansk Skonlitteratur. Barbro Norstrom Ridaeus. 168p. 1995. write for info. (*91-7106-368-4*, Pub. by Nordic Africa) Transaction Pubs.

***100 Vegetables & Where They Came From.** William Woys Weaver. 288p. 2000. 18.95 (*1-56512-238-0*) Algonquin Bks.

***100 Voices: Words That Shaped Our Souls & Wisdom to Guide Our Future.** Anne Buchanan & Debra K. Klingsporn. 176p. 1999. 12.99 (*1-58375-478-4*) Garborgs.

One Hundred Walks Around Bristol. Peter Brock. (Illus.). 256p. 1994. pap. 22.95 (*1-85158-606-7*, Pub. by Mainstream Pubng) Trafalgar.

100 Walks Around Manchester. David Frith. (Illus.). 224p. 1996. pap. 17.95 (*1-85158-717-9*, Pub. by Mainstream Pubng) Trafalgar.

100 Walks in Buchinghamshire & Hertfordshire. Ed. by Crowood Press Staff. (Illus.). 192p. 1998. pap. 19.95 (*1-86126-102-0*, Pub. by Cro1wood) Trafalgar.

100 Walks in Cambridgeshire & Bedfordshire. Ed. by Crowood Press Staff. (Illus.). 192p. 1998. pap. 19.95 (*1-86126-103-9*, Pub. by Cro1wood) Trafalgar.

100 Walks in Cheshire. (Illus.). 192p. 1995. pap. 19.95 (*1-85223-814-3*, Pub. by Cro1wood) Trafalgar.

One Hundred Walks in County Durham. (Illus.). 208p. 1992. pap. 19.95 (*1-85223-521-7*, Pub. by Cro1wood) Trafalgar.

100 Walks in Derbyshire. Ed. by Richard Sale. (Illus.). 208p. 1997. pap. 19.95 (*1-86126-077-6*, Pub. by Cro1wood) Trafalgar.

100 Walks in Devon & Cornwall. Richard Sale. (Illus.). 192p. 1996. pap. 19.95 (*1-85223-952-2*, Pub. by Cro1wood) Trafalgar.

100 Walks in Dorset. (Illus.). 192p. 1995. pap. 19.95 (*1-85223-848-8*, Pub. by Cro1wood) Trafalgar.

One Hundred Walks in East Sussex. (Illus.). 192p. 1994. pap. 19.95 (*1-85223-807-0*, Pub. by Cro1wood) Trafalgar.

100 Walks in Essex. (Illus.). 192p. 1995. pap. 19.95 (*1-85223-873-9*, Pub. by Cro1wood) Trafalgar.

One Hundred Walks in Gloucestershire. (Illus.). 192p. 1994. pap. 17.95 (*1-85223-827-5*, Pub. by Cro1wood) Trafalgar.

100 Walks in Great London. Richard Sale. (Illus.). 192p. 1996. pap. 19.95 (*1-85223-951-4*, Pub. by Cro1wood) Trafalgar.

One Hundred Walks in Hampshire & Isle of Wight. (Illus.). 192p. 1994. pap. 17.95 (*1-85223-805-4*, Pub. by Cro1wood) Trafalgar.

100 Walks in Hereford & Worcester. 1994. pap. 17.95 (*1-85223-785-6*, Pub. by Cro1wood) Trafalgar.

100 Walks in Kent. (Illus.). 192p. 1995. pap. 19.95 (*1-85223-872-0*, Pub. by Cro1wood) Trafalgar.

100 Walks in Lancashire. (Illus.). 192p. 1995. pap. 19.95 (*1-85223-892-5*, Pub. by Cro1wood) Trafalgar.

100 Walks in Lincolnshire & Humberside. Ed. by Richard Sale. (Illus.). 192p. 1997. pap. 19.95 (*1-86126-015-6*, Pub. by Cro1wood) Trafalgar.

One Hundred Walks in New South Wales. 4th ed. Tyrone Thomas. (Hill of Content Walking Guides Ser.). (Illus.). 307p. 1994. pap. 15.95 (*0-85572-230-4*, Pub. by Hill Content Pubng) Seven Hills Bk.

100 Walks in Norfolk. Ed. by Richard Sale. (Illus.). 192p. 1997. pap. 19.95 (*1-86126-016-4*, Pub. by Cro1wood) Trafalgar.

One Hundred Walks in Northumberland. (Illus.). 208p. 1993. pap. 19.95 (*1-85223-676-0*, Pub. by Cro1wood) Trafalgar.

100 Walks in Nottinghamshire. Ed. by Richard Sale. (Illus.). 208p. 1997. pap. 19.95 (*1-86126-025-3*, Pub. by Cro1wood) Trafalgar.

100 Walks in Oxfordshire & Berkshire. Ed. by Richard Sale. (Illus.). 208p. 1997. pap. 19.95 (*1-86126-026-1*, Pub. by Cro1wood) Trafalgar.

One Hundred Walks in Somerset & Avon. (Illus.). 192p. 1993. pap. 17.95 (*1-85223-766-X*, Pub. by Cro1wood) Trafalgar.

One Hundred Walks in Staffordshire. (Illus.). 207p. 1993. pap. 19.95 (*1-85223-522-5*, Pub. by Cro1wood) Trafalgar.

100 Walks in Suffolk. Richard Sale. (Illus.). 192p. 1996. pap. 19.95 (*1-85223-949-2*, Pub. by Cro1wood) Trafalgar.

One Hundred Walks in Surrey. (Illus.). 192p. 1994. pap. 19.95 (*1-85223-806-2*, Pub. by Cro1wood) Trafalgar.

100 Walks in the French Alps. Terry Marsh. (Illus.). 221p. 1995. pap. text 34.95 (*0-340-57478-X*, Pub. by Hodder & Stought Ltd) Trafalgar.

100 Walks in Warwickshire & West Midlands. Richard Sale. (Illus.). 192p. 1996. pap. 19.95 (*1-85223-950-6*, Pub. by Cro1wood) Trafalgar.

100 Walks in West Sussex. (Illus.). 192p. 1995. pap. 17.95 (*1-85223-847-X*, Pub. by Cro1wood) Trafalgar.

100 Walks in Wiltshire. Ed. by Richard Sale. (Illus.). 208p. 1997. pap. 19.95 (*1-86126-060-1*, Pub. by Cro1wood) Trafalgar.

One Hundred Walks in Yorkshire, Vol. I. Glen Hood. (Illus.). 207p. 1991. pap. 17.95 (*1-85223-417-2*, Pub. by Cro1wood) Trafalgar.

100 Walks in Yorkshire (East) Ed. by Richard Sale. (Illus.). 208p. 1997. pap. 19.95 (*1-86126-061-X*, Pub. by Cro1wood) Trafalgar.

100 Walks in Yorkshire (Western) Richard Sale. (Illus.). 192p. 1996. pap. 19.95 (*1-85223-967-0*, Pub. by Cro1wood) Trafalgar.

100 Wars That Shaped World History. Samuel Crompton. 1997. pap. 7.95 (*0-912517-28-X*) Bluewood Bks.

One Hundred Washington Square: Structural Design & Construction, Pt. 2. (PCI Journal Reprints Ser.). 28p. 1984. pap. 18.00 (*0-318-19803-7*, JR294) P-PCI.

100 Ways to Attract Angels. Sally Sharp. LC 94-60742. (Illus.). 108p. 1994. 18.00 (*0-9634910-2-4*) Samara Anjelae.

One Hundred Ways to Avoid Common Legal Pitfalls Without a Lawyer. Stephen G. Christianson. (Illus.). 288p. 1992. pap. 12.95 (*0-8065-1330-6*, Citadel Pr) Carol Pub Group.

100 Ways to Beat the Market. Gene Walden. LC 98-19369. 176p. 1998. 20.00 (*0-7931-2854-4*) Dearborn.

100 Ways to Become a Successful Student: Motivational Book for Students. large type ed. Yvonne Bowes-Brooks. 90p. (YA). (gr. 5-12). Date not set. pap. 10.98 (*0-9682530-1-6*) Brooks & Brooks.

100 Ways to Build Teams. Carol Scearce. LC 92-62450. (Illus.). 205p. 1999. pap. 24.95 (*0-932935-47-8*) SkyLght.

100 Ways to Cheer Yourself Up. 2nd rev. ed. L. Seper & W. Seper. (Illus.). 54p. 1998. pap. 5.00 (*0-9636426-3-4*) Windham Pr.

One Hundred Ways to Defeat Satan. Vernon Howard. 1982. pap. 2.00 (*0-911203-14-1*) New Life.

One Hundred Ways to Enhance Self-Concept in the Classroom. 2nd ed. Jack Caufield & Harold C. Wells. 250p. 1993. pap. text 34.99 (*0-205-15415-8*, Longwood Div) Allyn.

One Hundred Ways to Enhance Values & Morality in Schools & Youth Settings. Howard Kirschenbaum. 320p. (C). 1994. pap. text 59.95 (*0-205-16411-0*, Longwood Div) Allyn.

One Hundred Ways to Enhance Values & Morality in Schools & Youth Settings. Howard Kirschenbaum. 320p. (C). 1994. pap. text 25.00 (*0-205-15489-1*) Allyn.

100 Ways to Improve Teaching Using Your Voice & Music: Pathways to Accelerate Learning. Don G. Campbell. 112p. 1992. pap. 27.00 incl. audio (*0-913705-74-8*) Zephyr Pr AZ.

One Hundred Ways to Improve Your Writing. Gary Provost. 1985. mass mkt. 5.99 (*0-451-62721-0*, Ment) NAL.

100 Ways to Increase Your Sales with Checks by Phone & Checks by Web. 8th rev. ed. Larry Schwartz & Pearl Sax. 70p. 2000. ring bd. 59.95 (*0-914801-24-4*) Fraud & Theft Info.

100 Ways to Keep Your Soul Alive: Living Deeply & Fully Every Day. Frederic Brussat & Mary Ann Brussat. LC 93-46210. 128p. 1994. pap. 10.00 (*0-06-251050-9*, Pub. by Harper SF) HarpC.

One Hundred Ways to Love America. Bill Adler, Jr. 1991. pap. 2.95 (*0-380-76746-5*, Avon Bks) Morrow Avon.

100 Ways to Meet People. Ben White. 1998. mass mkt. 4.99 (*0-440-50790-1*) Dell.

100 Ways to Motivate Yourself. Steve Chandler. 192p. 1996. 16.99 (*1-56414-249-3*) Career Pr Inc.

100 Ways to Obtain Peace: Overcoming Anxiety. Richard Flournoy et al. 128p. (gr. 10). 1993. mass mkt. 4.99 (*0-8007-8614-9*, Spire) Revell.

100 Ways to Overcome Depression. Frank Minirth et al. 128p. (gr. 11). 1993. reprint ed. mass mkt. 4.99 (*0-8007-8613-0*, Spire) Revell.

100 Ways to Please a Foreign Man. Joanne Thomas. 114p. 1996. 6.95 (*0-9674144-0-7*) Jo Thomas.

One Hundred Ways to Praise. 16p. (C). 1998. text. write for info. (*0-13-010809-X*) P-H.

***100 Ways to Profit in Today's Economy: Battle-Tested Business Strategies That Work Now.** Barry R. Schimel. LC 99-45134. 1999. write for info. (*1-892123-06-1*) Capital VA.

One Hundred Ways to Prosper in Today's Economy: Battle-Tested Business Strategies That Work Now. fac. ed. Barry R. Schimel. LC 91-29862. (Illus.). 239p. 1991. pap. 74.10 (*0-7837-8232-2*, 204799600009) Bks Demand.

100 Ways to Say I Love You: Handmade Gifts & Heartfelt Expressions. Jane Laferla. LC 98-18892. 128p. 1998. pap. 18.95 (*1-57990-064-X*, Pub. by Lark Books) Random.

***One Hundred Ways to Serenity.** Celia Haddon. (Illus.). 95p. 1998. pap. 5.95 (*0-340-71417-4*, Pub. by Hodder & Stought Ltd) Lubrecht & Cramer.

100 Ways to Stay Together. Ben White. 1998. mass mkt. 4.99 (*0-440-50787-1*) Dell.

***100 Ways to Teach Your Child about God.** Karyn Henley. LC 00-22190. 2000. pap. 6.99 (*0-8423-3784-9*) Tyndale Hse.

O

One Hundred Ways to Use Wheat. Laura M. Hawkes. (Orig.). 1978. pap. 4.95 (*0-89036-116-9*) Liahona Pub Trust.

***100 Who Made a Difference: Greater Cincinnatians Who Changed the Tri-State - & the World.** Barry M. Horstman. Ed. by Lisa Warren. (Illus.). 256p. 1999. pap. text. write for info. (*0-933002-07-6*) Cin Post.

One Hundred Winning Bridge Tips. Ron Klinger. (Master Bridge Ser.). 128p. 1992. pap. 12.00 (*0-395-62887-3*) HM.

100 Winning Resumes for $100,000+ Jobs: Resumes That Can Change Your Life. Wendy S. Enelow. LC 97-7914. 224p. 1997. pap. 24.95 (*1-57023-070-6*) Impact VA.

One Hundred Wisconsin Fishing Trips. (Illus.). 440p. 1984. pap. 15.00 (*0-685-09633-5*) Wisconsin Sptmn.

One Hundred Wives. Gilbert A. Pierce. (Notable American Authors Ser.). 1999. reprint ed. lib. bdg. 125.00 (*0-7812-8746-4*) Rprt Serv.

100 Women Who Shaped World History. Gail M. Rolka. (One Hundred Ser.). (Illus.). 112p. (Orig.). 1994. pap. 7.95 (*0-912517-06-9*) Bluewood Bks.

100 Women's Stage Monologues from the 1980s. Ed. by Jocelyn A. Beard. (Monologue Audition Ser.). 196p. 1991. pap. 11.95 (*0-9622722-9-9*) Smith & Kraus.

***100 Woods: A Guide to the Popular Timbers of the World.** Peter Bishop. (Illus.). 224p. 1999. 40.00 (*1-86126-167-5*, Pub. by Crolwood) Trafalgar.

100 Words about Animals. Richard Brown. LC 86-22774. (Illus.). 32p. (J). (ps). 1987. 5.95 (*0-15-200550-1*, Gulliver Bks) Harcourt.

100 Words about Animals. Illus. by Richard Brown. LC 86-22744. (One Hundred Words about Ser.). 32p. (J). (ps-1). 1989. pap. 4.95 (*0-15-200554-4*, Gulliver Bks) Harcourt.

100 Words about My House. Illus. by Richard Brown. LC 87-7574. (One Hundred Words about Ser.). 32p. (J). (ps-1). 1989. pap. 3.95 (*0-15-200556-0*, Gulliver Bks) Harcourt.

100 Words about My House. Richard Brown. (Illus.). (J). (gr. k-2). 1990. 22.95 incl. audio (*0-87499-153-6*) Live Oak Media.

One Hundred Words about My House, 4 bks., Set. Richard Brown. (Illus.). (J). (gr. k-2). 1990. pap. 29.95 incl. audio (*0-87499-154-4*) Live Oak Media.

100 Words about Transportation. Richard Brown. LC 86-22781. (Illus.). 32p. (J). (ps). 1987. 5.95 (*0-15-200551-X*, Gulliver Bks) Harcourt.

100 Words about Transportation. Illus. by Richard Brown. LC 86-22781. (One Hundred Words about Ser.). 32p. (J). (ps-3). 1989. pap. 3.95 (*0-15-200555-2*) Harcourt.

100 Words about Transportation. Richard Brown. (Illus.). (J). (gr. k-2). 1990. 22.95 incl. audio (*0-87499-186-2*) Live Oak Media.

100 Words about Working. Illus. by Richard Brown. LC 87-8363. (One Hundred Words about Ser.). 32p. (J). (ps-1). 1989. pap. 3.95 (*0-15-200557-9*, Gulliver Bks) Harcourt.

One Hundred World-Class Thin Books: or What to Read When Your Book Report Is Due Tomorrow. Joni R. Bodart. xviii, 206p. (YA). (gr. 6-12). 1993. lib. bdg. 27.50 (*0-87287-986-0*) Libs Unl.

One Hundred World's Greatest Big Band Hits. 288p. (Orig.). 1994. pap. 19.95 (*0-89724-161-4*, SF0089) Wrner Bros.

100 World's Greatest Soft Rock Classics. 448p. (Orig.). 1994. pap. 19.95 (*0-89724-202-5*, VF1678) Wrner Bros.

One Hundred Writing Remedies: Practical Exercises for Technical Writing. Edmond H. Weiss. LC 90-7047. 192p. 1990. pap. 16.95 (*0-89774-638-4*) Oryx Pr.

One Hundred Year History of the Pilots' Association Bay & River Delaware. LC 96-84243. (Illus.). 133p. 1996. pap. 10.00 (*0-924117-07-9*) Delaware HP.

100 Years of Landscape Architecture. Melanie Simo. 364p. 1999. text 49.95 (*1-888931-20-5*) Spacemkr Pr.

One Hundred Years after Tomorrow: Brazilian Women's Fiction in the Twentieth Century. Ed. & Tr. by Darlene J. Sadlier. LC 91-22132. (Illus.). 260p. 1992. text 36.95 (*0-253-35045-X*); pap. text 6.95 (*0-253-20699-5*, MB-699) Ind U Pr.

One Hundred Years Ago. Frank Davis. 1980. pap. 4.95 (*0-910286-79-5*) Boxwood.

100 Years Ago, Vol. 4416. Donna Marriott. Ed. by Joel Kupperstein. (Learn to Read Social Studies). (Illus.). 16p. (J). (ps-2). 1998. pap. 2.75 (*1-57471-339-6*, 4416) Creat Teach Pr.

One Hundred Years Ago in Burrillville (RI) Selected Stories from the Local Newspapers. Patricia A. Mehrtens. viii, 231p. (Orig.). 1993. pap. 21.00 (*1-55613-716-8*) Heritage Bk.

One Hundred Years Ago in Nevada. Jock Taylor. 364p. 1964. pap. 9.95 (*0-913814-67-9*) Nevada Pubns.

One Hundred Years at Hull-House. Ed. by Mary L. Bryan & Allen F. Davis. LC 88-46032. (Illus.). 351p. 1991. 20.95 (*0-253-31621-9*); pap. 10.95 (*0-253-20579-4*, MB 579) Ind U Pr.

100 Years at Mackinac: A Centennial History of the Mackinac Island State Park Commission 1895-1995. David A. Armour. LC 96-622027. (Illus.). 138p. 1995. 29.95 (*0-911872-63-9*) Mackinac St Hist Pks.

One Hundred Years Exploring Life, 1888-1988, the Marine Biological Laboratory at Woods Hole. Jane Maienschein. 208p. 1989. pap. 24.95 (*0-86720-120-7*) Jones & Bartlett.

One Hundred Years from Today. Jack Hartman. 90p. 1985. pap. 4.00 (*0-915445-03-4*) Lamplight FL.

One Hundred Years' History of the Chinese in Singapore. Song Ong Siang. (Illus.). 1984. reprint ed. 59.00 (*0-19-582603-5*) OUP.

100 Years in Idaho. Charles Potts. LC 96-61673. 76p. 1996. pap. 10.00 (*0-9644440-1-1*) Tsunami.

100 Years in Photographs. George A. Sullivan. (Illus.). 96p. (J). (gr. 3-7). 1999. pap. text 8.99 (*0-590-22858-7*) Scholastic Inc.

***100 Years of American Film.** Frank E. Beaver. LC 99-48482. 1999. write for info. (*0-02-865380-7*) Macmillan Gen Ref.

100 Years of American Nursing: Celebrating a Century of Caring. Thelma M. Schorr & Maureen Shawn Kennedy. LC 99-10472. 240p. 1999. text 34.95 (*0-7817-1865-1*) Lppncott W & W.

One Hundred Years of American Women Writing, 1848-1948: An Annotated Bio-Bibliography. Jane M. Barstow. LC 97-4001. (Magill Bibliographies Ser.). 1997. 42.00 (*0-8108-3314-X*) Scarecrow.

One Hundred Years of Appalachian Visions. deluxe ed. Bill Best. 216p. 1997. pap. write for info. (*0-935680-67-5*) Kentucke Imprints.

100 Years of Archaeological Research in Lumbini, Kapilvastu & Devacana. B. K. Rijal. 1996. pap. 187.00 (*0-7855-7509-X*, Pub. by Ratna Pustak Bhandar) St Mut.

100 Years of Architecture at Notre Dame: A History of the School of Architecture, 1898-1998. Ed. by Jane A. Devine. (Illus.). 120p. 1999. pap. 23.95 (*0-9670548-0-X*, Pub. by U Notre Dame Sch Arch) Hammes Notre Dame.

One Hundred Years of Art in Israel. Gideon Ofrat. Tr. by Peretz Kidron. LC 97-49058. (Illus.). 400p. 1998. text 50.00 (*0-8133-3377-6*, Pub. by Westview) HarpC.

One Hundred Years of Art in San Diego: Selections from the Collection of the San Diego Historical Society. Bruce A. Kamerling. (Illus.). 112p. 1991. pap. 34.95 (*0-918740-12-6*) San Diego Hist.

100 Years of Bell Telephone. Richard D. Mountjoy. LC 95-31133. (Illus.). 176p. (Orig.). 1995. pap. 29.95 (*0-88740-872-9*) Schiffer.

One Hundred Years of BGA Football, 1894-1994. Cris Perkins. (Illus.). 128p. 1994. 29.95 (*1-881576-38-8*) Providence Hse.

***100 Years of Bicycle Component & Accessory Design: The Data Book.** Van Der Plas Publications Staff. 1999. 39.95 (*1-892495-01-5*) Van der Plas.

One Hundred Years of Bicycle Posters. Jack Rennert. (Illus.). 1977. pap. 30.00 (*0-601-35336-6*) Darien Hse.

***100 Years of Big Trucks.** Ronald Adams. (Crestline Ser.). (Illus.). 320p. 2000. 44.95 (*0-7603-0769-5*, 130098AP, Pub. by MBI Pubg) Motorbooks Intl.

One Hundred Years of Bread: Classic Breads from Your Bread Machine. Sidney B. Carlisle. LC 96-207995. 128p. 1995. pap. 11.95 (*0-9643380-1-7*) Riviera Publng.

One Hundred Years of British Colonial Policy. Edgar L. Erickson. LC 58-4393. (Augustana College Library Occasional Papers, Wallin Lecture: No. 2). 19p. 1958. pap. 1.00 (*0-910182-23-X*) Augustana Coll.

One Hundred Years of Brown's Park & Diamond Mountain. Richard F. DeJournette & Daun T. DeJournette. Ed. by Ray L. Huber & Dana M. Colovich. LC 96-92971. (Illus.). 450p. (Orig.). 1996. pap. 37.50 (*0-9651933-0-6*) DeJournette.

One Hundred Years of Chemical Engineering: From Lewis M. Norton (M.I.T. 1888) to Present. (C). 1989. text 207.50 (*0-7923-0145-5*) Kluwer Academic.

100 Years of Children's Books in America: Decade by Decade. Marjorie N. Allen. LC 95-34104. 352p. 1996. 35.00 (*0-8160-3044-8*) Facts on File.

***One Hundred Years of Children's Poetry.** Ed. by Michael Harrison & Christopher Stuart-Clark. (Illus.). 176p. (YA). 2000. pap. 12.95 (*0-19-276258-3*) OUP.

One Hundred Years of Citrus: A Glimpse of Citrus. Barry M. Nord. (Illus.). 64p. (Orig.). 1993. VHS 29.95 (*0-935656-08-1*) Nords Studio.

One Hundred Years of Citrus: A Glimpse of Citrus, Set. Barry M. Nord. (Illus.). 64p. (Orig.). 1993. pap. 29.95 incl. VHS (*0-935656-04-9*) Nords Studio.

100 Years of Classic Steam. Colin Garratt. (Illus.). 304p. 1997. 22.99 (*1-85833-661-9*, Pub. by CLib Bks) Whitecap Bks.

One Hundred Years of Collectible Jewelry. Lillian Baker. (Illus.). 169p. 1997. pap. 9.95 (*0-89145-066-1*, 1181) Collector Bks.

100 Years of Cowboy Stories. Ed. by Ted Stone. 1994. pap. 12.95 (*1-55105-054-4*) Lone Pine.

One Hundred Years of Critical Solitudes. Ed. by Caroline Bayard. 356p. (C). 1992. text 25.00 (*1-55022-117-5*, Pub. by ECW) Genl Dist Srvs.

One Hundred Years of Dance Posters. Jack Rennert & Walter Terry. (Illus.). 1977. pap. 30.00 (*0-88201-010-7*) Darien Hse.

***100 Years of Derry.** Roy W. Hamilton. (Illus.). 174p. 2000. pap. 22.95 (*0-85640-661-9*, Pub. by Blackstaff Pr) Dufour.

100 Years of Development Through Science. G. Marter. 1995. pap. 135.00 (*0-85954-394-3*, Pub. by Nat Res Inst) St Mut.

***One Hundred Years of Difference: The Hampton Project.** Carrie Mae Weems. (Illus.). 112p. 2000. 35.00 (*0-89381-913-1*) Aperture.

One Hundred Years of Dominican Aposolate Informosa, 1859-1958. Ed. by Pablo Fernandez. Tr. by Felix B. Bautisa & Lourdes Syquia-Bautista. 315p. 1994. reprint ed. 35.00 (*957-638-191-6*) Oriental Bk Store.

One Hundred Years of Educating at Savannah State College, 1890-1990. Clyde W. Hall. LC 91-90585. (Illus.). 162p. 1991. pap. 14.15 (*0-9630967-0-2*) C W Hall.

100 Years of Eichendorff Songs. Fanny Hensel et al. Ed. by Jurgen Thym. (Recent Researches in Music of the 19th & Early 20th Centuries Ser.: Vol. RRN5). (Illus.). xxvi, 70p. 1983. pap. 35.00 (*0-89579-173-0*) A-R Eds.

One Hundred Years of Engineering at Colorado State University: Fulfilling the Land-Grant Mission. Ann Hilfinger. 74p. 1989. 55.00 (*0-9624477-0-6*) CSU Coll Eng.

100 Years of Erotica: A Photographic Portfolio of Mainstream American Culture from 1845 to 1945. Paul Aratow. LC 99-30837. 128p. 1999. pap. text 24.95 (*1-58008-087-1*) Ten Speed Pr.

***One Hundred Years of Fiat Products, Faces, Images.** Umberto/Allemandi Company Staff. (Illus.). 2000. pap. text 19.95 (*88-422-0888-4*) U Allemandi.

100 Years of Filmmaking in New Mexico. New Mexico Magazine Staff. Ed. by Jon Bowman. LC 98-66406. (Illus.). 140p. 1999. 38.95 (*0-937206-54-7*) New Mexico Mag.

100 Years of Fishing: The Ultimate Tribute to Our Hunting Heritage. Voyageur Press Editors. LC 99-27420. (Illus.). 223p. 1999. 39.95 (*0-89658-430-5*) Voyageur Pr.

100 Years of Football. Jerry Brondfield. Date not set. lib. bdg. 17.95 (*0-8488-1856-3*) Amereon Ltd.

One Hundred Years of French Song: Cent Ans de Chanson Francaise. C. Brunschwig et al. (FRE.). 447p. 1981. pap. 14.95 (*0-8288-4427-5*, M12411) Fr & Eur.

100 Years of Front Page News: From the 1st Century of the Daily Press. Jerry Micco. LC 95-38670. 1995. pap. write for info. (*0-8092-3199-9*) NTC Contemp Pub Co.

One Hundred Years of Frontier Living. 2nd ed. Ed. by Jacky Barrington. 184p. (Orig.). 1994. pap. 10.00 (*0-9617036-2-8*) Bandar Log.

100 Years of Glasgow's Amazing Cinemas. Bruce Peter. 256p. 1996. 24.00 (*0-7486-6210-3*, Pub. by Polygon) Subterranean Co.

100 Years of Golf in San Diego County. Norrie West. LC 97-193964. (Illus.). 333p. 1997. pap. 19.95 (*0-9659597-0-8*) N West.

One Hundred Years of Good Cooking: The Minnesota Centennial Cookbook. 7th ed. Jacobsen. Ed. by Virginia Huck & Ann H. Andersen. LC 58-12061. 190p. 1958. pap. 7.95 (*0-87351-014-3*) Minn Hist.

***One Hundred Years of Gynaecology.** James Ricci. 651p. 2000. reprint ed. 85.00 (*1-57898-218-9*) Martino Pubng.

One Hundred Years of Gypsy Studies. Ed. by Matt T. Salo et al. LC 90-3098. (Publications: No. 5). vi, 286p. (Orig.). 1990. pap. 20.00 (*0-9617107-4-8*) Gypsy Lore Soc.

***100 Years of Headline News.** Phil Brigandi. Ed. by David Whiting. (Illus.). 256p. 2000. pap. 19.95 (*0-9635868-7-4*, Pub. by OC Register) Sunbelt Pubns.

One Hundred Years of History in the California Desert No. 13: An Overview of Historical Resources at Joshua Tree National Monument. Patricia Parker. (National Park Service Ser.). (Illus.). 160p. 1980. reprint ed. pap. text 17.50 (*1-55567-422-4*) Coyote Press.

***One Hundred Years of Hockey: Chronicle of a Century on Ice.** Al Strachan & Eric Duhatschek. LC 99-39986. 1999. 50.00 (*1-57145-225-7*, Thunder Bay) Advantage Pubs.

***100 Years of Hollywood.** Time-Life Books Editors. LC 99-38437. (Our American Century Ser.). 192p. 1999. 29.95 (*0-7835-5515-6*) Time-Life.

100 Years of Hollywood: A Century of Movie Magic. Caroline Krentz. 176p. (Orig.). 1999. text 27.98 (*1-56799-645-0*, MetroBooks) M Friedman Pub Grp Inc.

100 Years of Hollywood Westerns: Gunslingers, Sheriffs, Train Robbers, Cowboys & Indians. William K. Everson. (Illus.). 288p. 1996. pap. 21.95 (*0-8065-1766-2*, Citadel Pr) Carol Pub Group.

One Hundred Years of Homosexuality: And Other Essays on Greek Love. David M. Halperin. 320p. (C). 1989. pap. 21.99 (*0-415-90097-2*, A2753) Routledge.

One Hundred Years of Homosexuality: And Other Essays on Greek Love. David M. Halperin. 320p. 1989. 39.95 (*0-415-90096-4*, A2749) Routledge.

One Hundred Years of Huckleberry Finn: The Boy, His Book & American Culture. Centennial Essays. Ed. by Robert Sattelmeyer & Joseph Donald Crowley. LC 84-19574. 448p. 1985. text 35.00 (*0-8262-0457-0*) U of Mo Pr.

100 Years of Hunting: The Ultimate Tribute to Our Hunting Heritage. Voyageur Press Editors. LC 99-22665. (Illus.). 224p. 1999. 39.95 (*0-89658-414-3*) Voyageur Pr.

100 Years of Illinois State Redbird Basketball. Bryan Bloodworth & Roger Cushman. Ed. by Kenny Mossman & Tom Lamonica. LC 98-38461. (Illus.). 160p. 1998. 29.99 (*1-56478-158-5*) Dalkey Arch.

One Hundred Years of Jazz & Blues. 84p. 1992. write for info. (*0-9632712-0-2*) Six Fifty-One Kings.

100 Years of Kansas Golf. Mal Elliott. (Illus.). 247p. (Orig.). 1996. pap. 19.95 (*0-9652393-0-6*) Elfco.

***100 Years of Kinesiology: History, Research, & Reflections.** Ed. by John L. Haubenstricker & Deborah L. Feltz. 238p. 1999. pap. 10.00 (*0-9667081-4-8*) MSU Lib Comp & Tech.

One Hundred Years of Land Values in Chicago: The Relationship of the Growth of Chicago to the Rise in Its Land Values, 1830-1933. Homer Hoyt. LC 74-112550. (Rise of Urban America Ser.). 1974. reprint ed. 35.95 (*0-405-02456-8*) Ayer.

One Hundred Years of Lynchings. Ralph Ginzburg. 270p. 1988. reprint ed. pap. 14.95 (*0-933121-18-0*) Black Classic.

One Hundred Years of Magic: The Story of Barberton, 1891-1991. Phyllis Taylor. Ed. by Daniel M. Rice. (Illus.). 221p. 1991. pap. write for info. (*0-9621895-7-X*) Summit Cty Hist Soc.

One Hundred Years of Mathematics. George Temple. 316p. 1984. 86.95 (*0-387-91192-8*) Spr-Verlag.

One Hundred Years of Mortality. Edwin C. Hustead. LC 89-26100. (Illus.). 1989. pap. text 10.00 (*0-938959-12-3*) Soc Actuaries.

One Hundred Years of Music in America. Ed. by Paul H. Lang. LC 84-1798. (Music Reprint Ser.). 322p. 1984. reprint ed. lib. bdg. 39.50 (*0-306-76242-0*) Da Capo.

One Hundred Years of Music Publishing in the U. S. W. Fisher. 1973. 59.95 (*0-8490-0768-2*) Gordon Pr.

One Hundred Years of Navajo Rugs. Marian E. Rodee. LC 94-46682. Orig. Title: Old Navajo Rugs. (Illus.). 187p. 1995. pap. 29.95 (*0-8263-1576-3*) U of NM Pr.

One Hundred Years of Negro Freedom. Arna W. Bontemps. LC 80-10828. 276p. 1980. reprint ed. lib. bdg. 59.50 (*0-313-22218-5*, BOOY, Greenwood Pr) Greenwood.

One Hundred Years of Notre Dame Football. Gene Schoor. 416p. 1988. mass mkt. 4.95 (*0-380-70628-8*, Avon Bks) Morrow Avon.

100 Years of Olympic Music: The Music & Musicians of the Modern Olympic Games, 1896-1996. William K. Guegold. LC 96-94402. (Illus.). xxiii, 100p. (Orig.). 1996. pap. 19.95 (*0-9652371-0-9*) Gldn Clef.

One Hundred Years of Operatic in France (ca. 1830-1930) A Descriptive Catalogue of Staging Manuals. H. Robert Cohen & Marie O. Gigou. LC 86-1449. (Musical Life in 19th-Century France Ser.: Vol. 2).Tr. of Cent ans de Mise en Scene Lyrique en France (env. 1830-1930). (FRE & ENG., Illus.). 334p. (C). 1987. text 55.00 (*0-918728-69-X*) Pendragon NY.

One Hundred Years of Oratorio at Augustana: A History of the Handel Oratorio Society, 1881-1980. Conrad Bergendoff. LC 81-52434. (Augustana Historical Society Publications: No. 29). 54p. 1981. 7.50 (*0-910184-00-3*); pap. 5.00 (*0-910184-29-1*) Augustana.

***100 Years of Oz: A Century of Classic Images from the Wizard of Oz.** Ed. by Willard Carroll & John Fricke. LC 99-30777. (Illus.). 160p. 1999. 29.95 (*1-55670-940-4*) Stewart Tabori & Chang.

One Hundred Years of Philippine Paintings. Emmanuel Torres. (Illus.). 86p. 1984. pap. 20.00 (*1-877921-22-X*) Pacific Asia.

***100 Years of Philosophy.** Brian J. Shanley. LC 00-31418. (Studies in Philosophy & the History of Philosophy). 2001. write for info. (*0-8132-0997-8*) Cath U Pr.

One Hundred Years of Photographic History: Essays in Honor of Beaumont Newhall. Ed. by Van Deren Coke. LC 74-83381. 190p. reprint ed. pap. 58.90 (*0-608-12944-5*, 202467900038) Bks Demand.

***100 Years of Planck's Quantum.** Ian Duckworth & E. C .G. Sudarshan. 550p. 2000. 86.00 (*981-02-4309-X*) World Scientific Pub.

One Hundred Years of Poetry for Children's. Ed. by Michael Harrison & Christopher Stuart-Clark. (Illus.). 192p. (YA). 1999. 25.00 (*0-19-276190-0*) OUP.

100 Years of Political Campaign Collectibles. Mark Warda. LC 96-75315. 138p. 1996. pap. 16.95 (*1-888699-00-0*) Galt Pr.

100 Years of Posters of the Folies Bergere & Music Halls of Paris. Alain Weill. 112p. Date not set. write for info. (*0-9664202-5-X*) Posters Please.

One Hundred Years of Progress. Laura L. Benjamin. Ed. by Walter E. Castro. (Illus.). 165p. (C). 1989. text 25.00 (*0-9624328-0-6*) Clemson Univ.

One Hundred Years of Progress: A Photographic Essay on the Development of the California Transportation System. Raymond Forsyth & Joseph Hagwood. Ed. by Wordwrights International Staff et al. LC 96-83760. (Illus.). xiii, 178p. 1996. 28.95 (*0-9652279-0-1*) CA Trans Fnd.

One Hundred Years of Progress: The History of Veterinary Medicine in Minnesota. John P. Arnold & Howard H. Kernkamp. Ed. by Thomas H. Boyd. (Illus.). 260p. (C). 1994. 45.00 (*0-9641872-0-5*) MN Veterinary.

One Hundred Years of Progress: The Oregon Agricultural Experiment Station (1888 to 1988) Ed. by Carol A. Savonen. LC 89-15994. (Illus.). 154p. 1990. 5.00 (*0-9622925-0-8*) OSU AES.

100 Years of Progress in Glaucoma. E. Michael Van Buskirk & M. Bruce Shields. LC 97-13706. 360p. 1997. text 69.50 (*0-7817-1453-2*) Lppncott W & W.

100 Years of Psychoanalysis: Contributions to the History of Psychoanalysis. Ed. by Andre Haynal & Ernst Falzeder. LC 95-127359. 284p. 1994. pap. text 49.95 (*1-85575-090-2*, Pub. by H Karnac Bks Ltd) Brunner-Mazel.

One Hundred Years of Psychological Research in America: G. Stanley Hall & the Johns Hopkins Tradition. Ed. by Stewart H. Hulse & Bert F. Green, Jr. LC 85-8082. (Illus.). 432p. 1986. reprint ed. pap. 134.00 (*0-608-04030-4*, 206476600011) Bks Demand.

One Hundred Years of Public Health in Sutton. Ed. by Jennifer Bray & Michael J. Wilks. 54p. 1987. pap. 20.00 (*0-907335-06-3*, Pub. by Sutton Libs & Arts) St Mut.

One Hundred Years of Public Works Equipment: An Illustrated History. Ed. by Howard Rosen & Joel Mendes. (Illus.). 96p. 1986. pap. text 10.00 (*1-882102-03-7*) Pub Works Hist Soc.

One Hundred Years of Pyrazolone Drugs. Ed. by Kay Brune. (Agents & Actions Supplements Ser.: Vol. 19). 356p. 1986. 77.00 (*0-8176-1814-7*, Pub. by Birkhauser) Princeton Arch.

One Hundred Years of Revolution. Ed. by George Woodcock. LC 73-21627. (World History Ser.: No. 48). 1974. lib. bdg. 75.00 (*0-8383-1799-5*) M S G Haskell Hse.

One Hundred Years of Roads & Rails Around the Solent. David F. Glenn. (C). 1989. 45.00 (*1-85455-043-8*, Pub. by Ensign Pubns & Print) St Mut.

100 Years of Rodeo Stock Contracting. Victoria C. Weiland. LC 97-75411. (Illus.). 308p. 1997. write for info. (*0-9657636-0-9*) Pro Rodeo Stock.

One Hundred Years of Roofing in America. (Illus.). 258p. 1986. 50.00 (*0-934809-02-X*) Natl Roofing Cont.

100 Years of Russian Art: From Private Collections in the U. S. S. R. Ed. by David Elliott. (Illus.). 176p. (C). 1989. pap. 39.95 (*0-85331-549-3*, Pub. by Lund Humphries) Antique Collect.

An Asterisk (*) at the beginning of an entry indicates that the title is appearing for the first time.

One Hundred Years of Sci-Tech Libraries: A Brief History. Ed. by Ellis Mount. LC 87-34567. (Science & Technology Libraries: Vol. 8, No. 1). (Illus.). 193p. 1988. text 39.95 (*0-86656-745-3*) Haworth Pr.

One Hundred Years of Sea Power: The U. S. Navy, 1890-1990. George W. Baer. LC 94-2595. xii, 553p. 1994. 65.00 (*0-8047-2273-0*) Stanford U Pr.

One Hundred Years of Sea Power: The U. S. Navy, 1890-1990. George W. Baer. 566p. 1996. pap. 24.95 (*0-8047-2794-5*) Stanford U Pr.

One Hundred Years of Socialism: The West European Left in the Twentieth Century. Donald Sassoon. 1997. 39.95 (*1-56584-373-8*, Pub. by New Press NY) Norton.

One Hundred Years of Socialism: The West European Left in the Twentieth Century. Donald Sassoon. 992p. 1998. pap. 22.00 (*1-56584-486-6*, Pub. by New Press NY) Norton.

One Hundred Years of Solitude see Cien Anos de Soledad

One Hundred Years of Solitude. Gabriel Garcia Marquez. LC 92-22859. 1976. 25.95 (*0-8488-1429-0*) Amereon Ltd.

One Hundred Years of Solitude. Gabriel Garcia Marquez. 416p. 1995. 20.00 (*0-679-44465-3*) Everymns Lib.

One Hundred Years of Solitude. Gabriel Garcia Marquez. Tr. by Gregory Rabassa. LC 74-83632. 432p. 1970. 30.00 (*0-06-011418-5*) HarperTrade.

***100 Years of Solitude.** Gabriel Garcia Marquez. LC 98-24308. 464p. 1998. pap. 13.50 (*0-06-092979-0*) HarpC.

***One Hundred Years of Solitude.** Joan Mellen. Ed. by Gale Group Publishing Staff. (Literary Masterpieces Ser.: Vol. 5). (Illus.). 210p. 2000. 49.95 (*0-7876-3971-0*) Gale.

One Hundred Years of Solitude. Gabriel Garcia Marquez. 1990. reprint ed. lib. bdg. 24.95 (*0-89966-703-1*) Buccaneer Bks.

One Hundred Years of Solitude: Modes of Reading. Regina Janes. (Twayne's Masterwork Studies: No. 70). 136p. 1991. 29.00 (*0-8057-7989-2*, Twyne) Mac Lib Ref.

One Hundred Years of Solitude Notes. Carl Senna. (Cliffs Notes Ser.). 72p. (C). 1984. pap., text 4.95 (*0-8220-0964-1*, Cliff) IDG Bks.

100 Years of the Cinema. Bruce Hershenson. (Illus.). 104p. 1995. 50.00 (*1-887893-07-5*); pap. 20.00 (*1-887893-06-7*) B Hershenson.

100 Years of the Decorative Arts: Victoriana, Arts & Crafts, Art Nouveau & Art Deco. 264th ed. Eric Knowles. LC 99-164913. (Miller's Antiques Checklist Ser.). (Illus.). 256p. 1998. 35.00 (*1-84000-052-X*, Pub. by Millers Pubns) Antique Collect.

One Hundred Years of the Forth Bridge. Ed. by Roland Paxton. 166p. 1990. text 29.00 (*0-7277-1600-X*, Pub. by T Telford) RCH.

One Hundred Years of the Fourteenth Amendment: Implications for the Future. Jules B. Gerard. xi, 164p. 1973. lib. bdg. 37.50 (*0-89941-599-7*, 500370) W S Hein.

One Hundred Years of the National Formulary: A Symposium. Ed. by Gregory J. Higby. 112p. (Orig.). 1989. pap. 8.00 (*0-931292-21-2*) Am Inst Hist Pharm.

One Hundred Years of the Negro in Show Business. Tom Fletcher. (Music Reprint Ser.). (Illus.). xxii, 337p. 1984. reprint ed. lib. bdg. 45.00 (*0-306-76219-6*) Da Capo.

One Hundred Years of the Sussex Register & County of Sussex. Ed. by Whitfield Gibbs. (Illus.). 108p. 1992. reprint ed. pap. 18.00 (*1-55613-557-2*) Heritage Bk.

***100 Years of the U. S. Open.** John Delery & Greg Garber. LC 99-85983. (Illus.). 168p. 2000. 14.98 (*1-56799-957-3*, Friedman-Fairfax) M Friedman Pub Grp Inc.

100 Years of the Utah State Amateur Championship. Ed. by Jason Wight. (Illus.). 116p. 1998. text 35.00 (*1-57636-060-1*) SunRise Pbl.

One Hundred Years of the "Waterland" Community: A History of Des Moines, Washington. Ed. by Richard T. Kennedy & Grechen F. Schmidt. LC 89-7168. (Illus.). 316p. (Orig.). 1989. pap. 9.25 (*0-9621748-0-7*) City Des Moines WA.

100 Years of the Wimbledon Tennis Championships. James Medlycott. LC 78-309650. 4-93p. 1977. write for info. (*0-600-38768-2*, Pub. by Hamlyn Publishing Group Ltd) Sterling.

One Hundred Years of Theosophy: A History of the Theosophical Society in America. Joy Mills. 245p. 1987. pap. 9.95 (*0-8356-0235-4*, Quest) Theos Pub Hse.

One Hundred Years of Thomism: Aeterni Patris & Afterwards: A Symposium. Ed. by Victor B. Brezik. LC 80-70377. (Center for Thomistic Studies). 210p. 1981. pap. 9.95 (*0-268-01498-1*) Ctr Thomistic.

One Hundred Years of Valentines. Katherine Kreider. LC 98-88527. (Illus.). 128p. (Orig.). 1999. pap. 24.95 (*0-7643-0707-X*) Schiffer.

100 Years of Vienna Secession. (Illus.). 200p. 1998. 55.00 (*3-7757-0712-3*, 810822, Pub. by Gerd Hatje) Dist Art Pubs.

***100 Years of Vintage Farm Tractors: A Century of Tractor Tales & Heartwarming Family Farm Memories.** Ed. by Michael Dregni. LC 99-42237. (Town Square Bks.). (Illus.). 160p. 2000. 29.95 (*0-89658-462-3*) Voyageur Pr.

One Hundred Years of Violoncello: A History of Technique & Performance Practice, 1740-1840. Valerie Walden. LC 96-47436. (Musical Texts & Monographs). (Illus.). 327p. (C). 1998. text 80.00 (*0-521-55449-7*) Cambridge U Pr.

***100 Years of Virology: The Birth & Growth of a Discipline.** Ed. by C. H. Calisher & M. C. Horzinek. (Archives of Virology Ser.: Suppl. 15). (Illus.). 250p. 1999. 146.00 (*3-211-83384-6*) Spr-Verlag.

***100 Years of Wall Street.** Charles R. Geisst. (Illus.). 256p. 1999. 29.95 (*0-07-135619-3*) McGraw.

One Hundred Years of Western Art from Pittsburgh Collections. Peter H. Hassrick. (Illus.). 32p. 1981. pap. text 7.95 (*0-88039-002-6*) Mus Art Carnegie.

100 Years of Women's Wisdom. Criswell Freeman. 1999. pap. text 6.95 (*1-58334-003-3*) Walnut Gr Pr.

One Hundred Years on the Road: The Traveling Salesman in American Culture. Timothy B. Spears. LC 94-6070. 320p. 1995. 42.50 (*0-300-05908-6*) Yale U Pr.

100 Years on the Road: The Traveling Salesman in American Culture. Timothy B. Spears. (Illus.). 320p. 1997. pap. 18.00 (*0-300-07066-7*) Yale U Pr.

One Hundred Years Progress of the United States. LC 70-38257. (Evolution of Capitalism Ser.). 630p. 1972. reprint ed. 39.95 (*0-405-04130-6*) Ayer.

One Hundred Years Young: A History of the Polish Falcons of America, 1887-1987. Donald E. Pienkos. (East European Monographs: No. 231). 348p. 1987. text 79.50 (*0-88033-128-3*, Pub. by East Eur Monographs) Col U Pr.

One Hundred (100's) A Ranking of the Most Influential Persons in History. Michael H. Hart. 572p. 1996. pap. 18.95 (*0-614-21166-2*, 922); pap. 18.95 (*0-614-21714-8*, 922) Kazi Pubns.

One Hundredth Anniversary of Hysteria: Catalog of 1978 International Surrealist Exhibition. Franklin Rosemont. (Illus.). 24p. 1978. pap. 8.00 (*0-941194-11-6*) Black Swan Pr.

One Hundredth Anniversary of Liquid Crystal Research: A Special Issue of the Journal Molecular Crystals & Liquid Crystals. Ed. by S. Kobayashi. vi, 582p. 1988. pap. text 41.00 (*2-88124-325-8*) Gordon & Breach.

One Hundredth Anniversary 1-23 Presentation Box: The World of Beatrix Potter, 23 bks., Set. Beatrix Potter. (Illus.). (J). 1993. text 160.00 (*0-7232-4112-0*, F Warne) Peng Put Young Read.

100th Day of School. Angela S. Medearis. LC 95-13214. (Hello Reader! Ser.: Level 2). (Illus.). 30p. (J). (gr. k-2). 1996. pap. 2.95 (*0-590-25944-X*, Cartwheel) Scholastic Inc.

100th Day of School. Angela Shelf Medearis. (J). 1996. 8.70 (*0-606-08467-3*, Pub. by Turtleback) Demco.

100th Day of School. Teacher Created Materials Staff. 16p. 1997. pap. 2.95 (*1-57690-199-8*) Tchr Create Mat.

***100th Day Worries.** Margery Cuyler. LC 98-562887. (Illus.). 32p. (J). (gr. k-2). 2000. per. 16.00 (*0-689-82979-5*) S&S Trade.

One Hundredth Kill. Charles W. Sasser. Ed. by Paul McCarthy. 288p. (Orig.). 1991. per. 6.50 (*0-671-72713-3*) PB.

One Hundredth Thing about Caroline. Lois Lowry. 160p. (J). (gr. k-6). 1985. pap. 4.50 (*0-440-46625-3*, YB BDD) BDD Bks Young Read.

One Hundredth Thing about Caroline, 001. Lois Lowry. 160p. (J). (gr. 3-6). 1983. 16.00 (*0-395-34829-3*) HM.

One Hundredth Thing about Caroline. Lois Lowry. 1985. 9.09 (*0-606-00972-8*, Pub. by Turtleback) Demco.

One Hundredth Town: Glimpses of Life in Westborough, MA. Harriette M. Forbes. 209p. 1993. reprint ed. lib. bdg. 27.50 (*0-8328-3184-0*) Higginson Bk Co.

100th Boyfriend. Bridget Daly & Janet Skeels. LC 87-4714. (Illus.). 96p. (Orig.). 1987. pap. 5.95 (*0-941104-05-2*) Real Comet.

One Hungry Cat. Joanne Rocklin. LC 96-23043. (Hello Math Reader Ser.). (Illus.). (J). 1997. pap. 3.99 (*0-590-93972-6*) Scholastic Inc.

One Hungry Cat. Joanne Rocklin. (Hello Math Reader Ser.). 1997. 9.19 (*0-606-11708-3*, Pub. by Turtleback) Demco.

***One Hungry Monster.** Holden. 416p. (J). 2001. bds. 5.95 (*0-316-64185-5*, Pub. by Little) Time Warner.

One Hungry Monster: A Counting Book in Rhyme. Susan H. O'Keefe. (Illus.). 32p. (J). (ps-3). 1989. 12.95 (*0-316-63385-2*, Joy St Bks) Little.

One Hungry Monster: A Counting Book in Rhyme. Susan H. O'Keefe. (Illus.). 32p. (J). (gr. k-3). 1992. pap. 5.95 (*0-316-63388-7*, Joy St Bks) Little.

One Hungry Monster: A Counting Book in Rhyme. Susan H. O'Keefe. (J). 1989. 11.15 (*0-606-01417-9*, Pub. by Turtleback) Demco.

1 Hunter. Pat Hutchins. LC 81-6352. (Illus.). 24p. (J). (ps-k). 1982. 17.00 (*0-688-00614-0*, Grenwillow Bks) HarpC Child Bks.

1 Hunter. Pat Hutchins. LC 81-6352. (Illus.). 24p. (J). (ps up). 1986. reprint ed. mass mkt. 4.95 (*0-688-06522-8*, Wm Morrow) Morrow Avon.

***One Husband Needed.** Jeanne Allan. 2000. per. 3.50 (*0-373-15838-6*) Harlequin Bks.

***One Husband Needed.** Jeanne Allan. (Romance Ser.). 2000. mass mkt. 3.50 (*0-373-03592-6*) Harlequin Bks.

***One Husband Required! Wanted: One Wedding Dress.** Sharon Kendrick. 1999. per. 3.75 (*0-373-12023-0*, 1-12023-7, Harlequin) Harlequin Bks.

***One Husband Required! Wanted: One Wedding Dress.** large type ed. Sharon Kendrick. 1999. 21.95 (*0-263-16207-9*, Pub. by Mills & Boon) Ulverscroft.

One Husband Too Many. Jacqueline Diamond. (American Romance Ser.). 1996. per. 3.75 (*0-373-16642-7*, 1-16642-0) Harlequin Bks.

One I Knew the Best of All. Frances Hodgson Burnett. LC 79-8779. (Signal Lives Ser.). 1980. reprint ed. lib. bdg. 39.95 (*0-405-12828-2*) Ayer.

One I Love with Study Guide. Joy Jacobs & Ruth Dourte. (Illus.). 195p. 1993. pap. 12.99 (*0-87509-529-1*) Chr Pubns.

One Impulsive Black Rose. Kathleen F. O'Sullivan. Ed. by Richard S. Danbury, III. LC 94-66579. 160p. (Orig.). 1994. pap. 8.95 (*0-89754-089-1*) Dan River Pr.

One in a Billion. Michael McGoffee & Diane Gard. (Illus.). 29p. (J). (gr. 3-5). 1996. 14.95 (*1-887578-04-8*) SpanPr.

***One in a Hundred.** John W. Leeger. LC 99-91435. 1999. 25.00 (*0-7388-0772-9*); pap. 18.00 (*0-7388-0773-7*) Xlibris Corp.

One in a Million. Harry A. Cole. 352p. 1993. mass mkt. 4.50 (*1-55817-708-6*, Pinncle Kensgtn) Kensgtn Pub Corp.

One in a Million. Ruth J. Dale & Kimberly Raye. (Duets Ser.: No. 4). 1999. per. 5.99 (*0-373-44070-7*, 1-44070-0, Harlequin) Harlequin Bks.

One in a Million. Nicholas Read. (Illus.). 144p. (Orig.). (J). (gr. 3-6). 1996. pap. write for info. (*1-896095-22-4*) Polstar Bk.

***"One in a Million" A Book for Future Jayhawks.** Mark Mallouk. LC 98-75251. (Illus.). (J). (gr. 1-3). 1998. pap. 9.95 (*1-890622-52-4*) Leathers Pub.

One in a Million: Message from the Historic Million Man March. Roberto E. Gibral-Tarik. Tr. by Emmanuel Vedrine. (Mucho Somas Ser.: Vol. 24). (Illus.). 84p. (Orig.). (C). 1997. pap. text 12.95 (*0-914370-74-X*) Mothers Hen.

One in a Minyan & Other Studies. Max J. Routtenberg. 1979. pap. 6.95 (*0-87068-342-X*) Ktav.

***One in Christ: Unity & Diversity in the Church Today.** Basil Hume. (Common Ground Lecture Ser.: Vol. 1). 28p. 1999. pap. 2.50 (*1-881307-22-0*, CGL1) Natl Pastoral LC.

One in Christ Jesus: A Pastoral Response to the Concerns of Women for Church & Society. 1993. 2.95 (*1-55586-359-0*) US Catholic.

One in Eleven: Educational Needs of Catholic Schools in Victoria. Ed. by Ken Dovey & Joe Graffam. 186p. 1995. pap. 40.00 (*0-909184-22-4*, Pub. by Deakin Univ) St Mut.

One in Every Family. Mary L. Friesz. (Illus.). 60p. (Orig.). 1996. per. 9.95 (*0-9650788-6-8*) Mustard Seed CA.

One in Forty - The UFO Epidemic: True Accounts of Close Encounters with UFO's. Preston Dennett. LC 95-46546. 227p. 1996. 25.00 (*1-56072-270-3*, Nova Kroshka Bks) Nova Sci Pubs.

One in Four: America's Youngest Poor. unabridged ed. Jiali Li & Neil Bennett. LC 96-38526. (Illus.). 88p. 1996. pap. 16.95 (*0-926582-20-8*) NCCP.

One in Spirit. Ed. by University of Chicago Archives Staff. (Centennial Publication Ser.). 200p. 1991. pap. 12.95 (*0-226-77720-0*) U Ch Pr.

One in the Faith. Harry N. Huxhold. (Orig.). 1988. pap. 5.95 (*1-55673-060-8*, 8857) CSS OH.

One in the Many: Christian Identity in a Multicultural World. Ed. by Thomas R. Thompson. LC 98-9626. (Calvin Center Ser.). 128p. (C). 1998. 44.00 (*0-7618-1068-4*); pap. 16.00 (*0-7618-1069-2*) U Pr of Amer.

***One in the Middle Is the Green Kangaroo.** 2000. 9.95 (*1-56137-415-6*) Novel Units.

***One in the Middle Is the Green Kangaroo.** (J). 2000. 16.00 (*0-689-84290-2*) Atheneum Yung Read.

One in the Middle Is the Green Kangaroo. Judy Blume. (Illus.). 48p. (J). (gr. k-2). 1982. pap. 3.99 (*0-440-46731-4*, YB BDD) BDD Bks Young Read.

One in the Middle Is the Green Kangaroo. Judy Blume. (Illus.). 32p. (J). (ps-3). 1992. pap. 5.99 (*0-440-40668-4*, YB BDD) BDD Bks Young Read.

One in the Middle Is the Green Kangaroo. Judy Blume. 39p. (J). (gr. k-3). pap. 3.99 (*0-8072-1337-3*) Listening Lib.

One in the Middle is the Green Kangaroo. Judy Blume. 1991. 11.19 (*0-606-00918-3*, Pub. by Turtleback) Demco.

One in the Middle Is the Green Kangaroo. 2nd ed. Judy Blume. LC 80-29664. (Illus.). 32p. (J). (gr. k-2). 1991. reprint ed. text 16.00 (*0-02-711055-9*, Bradbury S&S) S&S Childrens.

One in the Middle Is the Green Kangaroo: A Study Guide. Laurie Diamond. Ed. by Joyce Friedland & Rikki Kessler. (Novel-Ties Ser.). 16p. (J). (gr. 1-3). 1990. pap. text 15.95 (*0-88122-408-1*) Lrn Links.

One in the Spirit. rev. ed. pap. 8.95 (*0-340-71392-5*, Pub. by Hodder & Stought Ltd) Trafalgar.

One in 2000? Towards Catholic-Orthodox Unity. Paul McPartlan. 192p. 1996. pap. 39.95 (*0-85439-439-7*, Pub. by St Paul Pubns) St Mut.

One-Inch Boy. large type ed. Tr. by Donna Tamaki.Tr. of Issun-Boshi. (ENG & JPN., Illus.). 12p. (J). (ps-3). 1996. 35.00 (*1-893533-06-9*, 7) Kamish for Kids.

One Inch from the Fence. Wes Seeliger. LC 72-97821. (Illus.). 160p. 1986. reprint ed. pap. 8.95 (*0-915321-01-7*) Pioneer Vent.

One Indian & Two Chiefs: Short Fiction. Ralph J. Salisbury. 173p. 1994. pap. 14.95 (*0-912586-73-7*) Dine College Pr.

One Indian Summer. Wayne Curtis. 200p. 1994. pap. 12.95 (*0-86492-151-9*, Pub. by Goose Ln Edits) Genl Dist Srvs.

One Industry, Two Chinas. Lynda S. Bell. LC 99-10135. (Illus.). 348p. 1999. 49.50 (*0-8047-2998-0*) Stanford U Pr.

One Interior Life: A Study of the Nature of Wordsworth's Poetic Experience. M. R. Tewari. 188p. 1986. 25.00 (*0-7855-1197-0*) St Mut.

***One Intimate Night.** Penny Jordan. (Presents Ser.). 2000. mass mkt. 3.99 (*0-373-12146-6*, 1121466) Harlequin Bks.

***One Intimate Night.** large type ed. Penny Jordan. (Thorndike Harlequin Romance (Large Print) Ser.). 2000. 22.95 (*0-263-16444-6*) Mac Lib Ref.

***One Is Canada.** Maxine Trottier. LC 99-189175. 24p. (J). 2000. 17.95 (*0-00-224556-6*) HarpC Child Bks.

***One Is Canada.** Maxine Trottier. (Illus.). 32p. 2000. pap. 6.75 (*0-00-638663-6*) HarpCollins.

One Is Enough. Flora Nwapa. 157p. 1992. 24.95 (*0-86543-322-4*); pap. 9.95 (*0-86543-323-2*) Africa World.

1 Is for One. Nadia Wheatley. LC 95-33231. (Illus.). 24p. (J). (ps-2). 1996. pap. 6.95 (*1-57255-133-X*) Mondo Pubng.

One Is Not a Woman, One Becomes: The African Woman in a Transitional Society. Ed. by Daphne W. Ntiri. (Illus.). 143p. (Orig.). 1988. reprint ed. pap. text 15.00 (*0-911557-02-4*) Bedford Publishers.

One Is One. Tasha Tudor. 48p. (J). (ps). 1993. pap. 4.95 (*0-689-71743-1*) Atheneum Yung Read.

***1 Is One.** Tasha Tudor. LC 99-31290. (Illus.). 48p. (J). (ps-3). 2000. per. 16.00 (*0-689-82843-8*) S&S Childrens.

***One Is the Loneliest Number.** Tom Clancy & Steve Pieczenik. (Tom Clancy's Net Force Ser.). (Orig.). (YA). 1999. mass mkt. 4.99 (*0-425-16417-9*, JAM) Berkley Pub.

***One Is the Other.** 247p. (C). 1999. pap. 19.95 (*0-9672316-0-4*) Arch Publishing.

One Is the Sun. 2nd ed. Patricia N. Warren. LC 98-60330. (Illus.). 544p. 2000. reprint ed. pap. 16.95 (*1-889135-02-X*) Wildcat Pr.

1 Is Wonderful. Dayle M. Timmons. (Illus.). 384p. (J). (ps-1). 23.99 (*0-86653-925-5*, FE0925) Fearon Teacher Aids.

One Is Your Master. Tallach. 1994. pap. 1.99 (*1-871676-13-4*, Pub. by Christian Focus) Spring Arbor Dist.

***One Island Many Faiths: The Experience of Religion in Britain.** Rachel Morton. LC 99-66193. (Illus.). 160p. 2000. 27.50 (*0-500-01987-8*, Pub. by Thames Hudson) Norton.

One Jerusalem Is Not Enough. Noble J. Nassar. LC 83-61430. (New American Plays Ser.). (Illus.). 46p. 1983. 18.00 (*0-918266-18-1*) Smyrna.

One Jesuit's Spiritual Journey: Autobiographical Conversations with Jean-Claude Dietsch, S. J. Pedro Arrupe. Tr. by Ruth Bradley. LC 84-81990. Orig. Title: Itineraire d'un Jesuite. Entretiens avec Jean-Claude Dietsch, S. J.. xiv, 160p. 1986. 10.00 (*0-912422-69-6*); 8.00 (*0-912422-68-8*) Inst Jesuit.

One Jesus, Many Christs. Gregory J. Riley. LC 97-3294. 1997. pap. 12.00 (*0-06-066798-2*) HarpC.

One Jesus, Many Christs: The Truth about Christian Origins. Gregory J. Riley. LC 97-3294. 240p. 1997. 23.00 (*0-06-066799-0*, Pub. by Harper SF) HarpC.

***One Jesus, Many Churches: How Jesus Inspired Not One True Christianity, but Many.** Gregory J. Riley. 240p. 2001. pap. 16.00 (*0-8006-3242-7*) Augsburg Fortress.

One Jew's Power, One Jew's Glory. Yechiel Granatstein. 1991. 15.95 (*0-87306-559-X*) Feldheim.

***1 John: Loving Each Other.** Bill Hybels. 96p. 1999. pap. 6.99 (*0-310-22768-2*) Zondervan.

One Jump Ahead. J. Schaeffer. 1997. pap. 39.95 (*0-614-28527-5*) Spr-Verlag.

One Jump Ahead: The Story of Chinook, the World Champion Checkers Computer Program. J. Schaeffer. LC 96-39873. (Copernicus Ser.). (Illus.). 512p. 1997. 34.95 (*0-387-94930-5*) Spr-Verlag.

One Kettle Cookbook with Make It Tasty Spice Blends. Center for Self-Sufficiency, Research Division Sta. 55p. 1985. ring bd. 21.95 (*0-910811-06-7*) Ctr Self Suff.

One Kid at a Time: Mentoring As a Model for Youth Ministry. Miles McPherson & Wayne Rice. Ed. by Randy Southern. (YA). (gr. 6-12). 1997. pap., teacher ed. 8.99 (*0-7814-5205-8*, 29728) Cook.

***One Kind of Freedom: The Economic Consequences of Emancipation.** Roger L. Ransom & Richard Sutch. (Illus.). 450p. 2000. write for info. (*0-521-79169-3*); pap. write for info. (*0-521-79550-8*) Cambridge U Pr.

One King, One Faith: The Parlement of Paris & the Religious Reformations of the Sixteenth Century. Nancy L. Roelker. LC 94-40396. (Centennial Bk.). 532p. (C). 1996. text 68.00 (*0-520-08626-0*, Pub. by U CA Pr) Cal Prin Full Svc.

1 Kings: The Everlasting Covenant: Studies in Hebrew Narrative & Poetry. Jerome T. Walsh. (Berit Olam Ser.). 416p. 1996. 39.95 (*0-8146-5044-9*, M Glazier) Liturgical Pr.

One King's Way. Harry Harrison. 400p. 1996. pap. write for info. (*0-614-05536-9*); mass mkt. 6.99 (*0-8125-3645-2*, Pub. by Tor Bks) St Martin.

One Knee Equals Two Feet (And Everything Else You Need to Know about Football) John Madden & Dave Anderson. 1987. mass mkt. 5.99 (*0-515-09193-6*, Jove) Berkley Pub.

One Known As Seven (Zion) Avi Brenholz. Date not set. pap. 26.00 (*1-889958-02-6*) A Ben Aur.

One Korea? Challenges & Prospects for Reunification. Ed. by Thomas H. Henriksen & Kyongsoo Lho. LC 94-21480. (Publication Ser.: No. 421). 128p. (C). 1994. pap. 18.95 (*0-8179-9292-8*) Hoover Inst Pr.

One Korea via Permanent Neutrality: Peaceful Management of Korean Unification. In K. Hwang. 200p. (Orig.). (C). 1986. text 18.95 (*0-87047-016-7*); pap. text 13.95 (*0-87047-017-5*) Schenkman Bks Inc.

One L: The Turbulent True Story of a First Year at Harvard Law School. Scott Turow. LC KF373.T88A33. 288p. 1997. mass mkt. 12.99 (*0-446-67378-1*, Pub. by Warner Bks) Little.

One L: The Turbulent True Story of a First Year at Harvard Law School. Scott Turow. LC 88-19845. 319p. 1988. reprint ed. 23.00 (*0-374-22647-4*) FS&G.

One Lady at a Time. John Benton. 126p. 1993. pap. text 3.50 (*0-9635411-0-2*) J Benton Bks.

One Land - One Nation. Mabel Johnson. (Illus.). 64p. (J). (gr. 7 up). 1987. pap. 3.95 (*0-9600838-6-3*) M Johnson.

One Land, One Nation. Frank Brennan. 1995. pap. 18.95 (*0-7022-2729-3*, Pub. by Univ Queensland Pr) Intl Spec Bk.

One Land, Three Peoples: A Geography of Robeson County, North Carolina. Thomas E. Ross. LC 94-76044. (Illus.). 130p. (Orig.). 1994. pap. 16.95 (*0-9641628-0-6*) Karo Hollow.

***1 Land 2 Peoples.** 3rd ed. Gerner. 2000. 21.00 (*0-8133-6789-1*, Pub. by Westview) HarpC.

O

One Land, Two Peoples: The Conflict Over Palestine. 2nd ed. Deborah J. Gerner. LC 94-16016. (Dilemmas in World Politics Ser.). (C). 1994. pap. 21.00 (*0-8133-2180-8*, Pub. by Westview) HarpC.

One Language for the World & How to Achieve It. Mario A. Pei. LC 68-56449. 1958. pap. 22.00 (*0-8196-0218-3*) Biblo.

One Language, Two Scripts: The Hindi Movement in Nineteenth Century North India. Christopher King. (Illus.). 244p. 1995. text 26.00 (*0-19-563565-5*) OUP.

One Large Order of Faith to Go. David Willingham. LC 91-38004. (Devotions for Today's Family Ser.). (Illus.). 99p. (Orig.). (J). (gr. 6-8). 1991. pap. text 5.00 (*1-56212-012-3*, 1701-0480) CRC Pubns.

One Last Call; Guide for the Achievement for Lasting Peace, 1. Donnell L Harris. LC 98-66876. 1998. pap. text 12.99 (*0-933451-39-3*) Prescott Pr.

One Last Chance: America Heroes. Justine Davis. (Intimate Moments Ser.). 1993. mass mkt. 3.50 (*0-373-07517-0*, 5-07517-1) Silhouette.

***One Last Dance.** Eileen Goudge. 448p. 2000. mass mkt. 7.50 (*0-451-19948-0*, Sig) NAL.

One Last Dance. Eileen Goudge. LC 98-54891. 384p. 1999. 24.95 (*0-670-88575-4*) Viking Penguin.

One Last Dance. Andrew M. Kelly. LC 98-85022. i, 60p. 1998. pap. 15.00 (*0-9665091-0-2*) Ceres Pubg Inc.

***One Last Dance, Vol. 1.** large type ed. Eileen Goudge. LC 99-27893. 1999. 29.95 (*0-7862-2005-8*) Macmillan Gen Ref.

One Last Dance with Lawrence Welk & Other Stories. Peter Damian Bellis. LC 96-70860. 144p. 1996. pap. 9.00 (*0-9654756-0-3*) River Boat Bks.

One Last Fling! Elizabeth August. 1994. per. 3.50 (*0-373-09871-5*, 5-09871-0) Silhouette.

***One Last Hug Before I Go: The Mystery & Meaning of Deathbed Visions.** Carla Wills-Brandon. 250p. 2000. pap. 11.95 (*1-55874-779-6*) Health Comm.

One Last Kiss. Judith Kelman. 416p. 1994. mass mkt. 5.99 (*0-553-56272-X*) Bantam.

One Last Kiss. Created by Francine Pascal. (Sweet Valley University Ser.: No. 29). 240p. (YA). (gr. 7 up). 1997. mass mkt. 3.99 (*0-553-57053-6*, Sweet Valley) BDD Bks Young Read.

One Last Look: A Sentimental Journey to the Eighth Air Force Heavy Bomber Bases of World War II in England. Philip Kaplan & Rex A. Smith. LC 83-8777. (Illus.). 216p. 1983. 29.98 (*0-89660-012-2*, Artabras) Abbeville Pr.

One Last Shot. Marcia A. Zegar. 1994. 13.95 (*0-9667898-0-6*) KC&S Pubg.

One Last Souvenir. Naomi Church. 80p. (Orig.). pap. text 9.95 (*1-881579-05-0*) Theophilus Pr.

One Last Time. William J. Buchanan. 128p. (Orig.). (YA). 1992. pap. 2.99 (*0-380-76152-1*, Avon Bks) Morrow Avon.

One Last Time: A Psychic Medium Speaks to Those We Have Loved & Lost. John J. Edward. LC 98-29707. 272p. 1998. 21.95 (*0-425-16908-1*) Berkley Pub.

***One Last Time: A Psychic Medium Speaks to Those We Have Loved & Lost.** John J. Edward. 231p. 1999. pap. 12.95 (*0-425-16692-9*) Berkley Pub.

One Last Town. Matt Braun. 1997. mass mkt. 5.99 (*0-312-96236-3*) St Martin.

One Last Waltz. Ethan Mordden. (Stonewall Inn Editions Ser.). 1988. pap. 7.95 (*0-312-01801-0*) St Martin.

One Last Wish: Omnibus, 3 vols. in 1. Lurlene McDaniel. 448p. (YA). 1998. mass mkt. 6.99 (*0-553-57142-7*) BDD Bks Young Read.

One Last Wish: Time to Die, No. 1. Lurlene McDaniel. 192p. (YA). 1992. mass mkt. 4.50 (*0-553-29809-7*) Bantam.

One Leaf Fell. Toby Speed. (Illus.). 32p. (J). (ps up). 1993. 7.50 (*1-55670-271-X*) Stewart Tabori & Chang.

One Leap Forward. Donna J. Napoli. LC 99-23980. (Aladdin Angelwings Ser.: No. 4). (Illus.). 96p. (J). (gr. 2-5). 1999. pap. 3.99 (*0-689-82986-8*) Aladdin.

***One Leap Forward.** Donna Jo Napoli. (Illus.). (J). 1999. 9.34 (*0-606-17907-0*) Turtleback.

***One Leg at a Time: A Short Story about Human Similarities.** Joy Berry. (Superstar Kids' Club Short Stories Ser.: Vol. 1). (Illus.). 48p. (J). (gr. 2-6). 1999. pap. 3.95 (*1-58634-252-5*) Goldstar.

***One-Legged, Bow-Legged Cricket: A Story in a Story.** Joseph R. Pfeiffer & Robert J. Pfeiffer. LC 99-94630. (Illus.). 32p. (J). (gr. k-4). 1999. 14.95 (*0-9659772-3-4*) Chessmore Pub.

One-Legged on Ice. Dannie Abse. LC 82-20055. (Contemporary Poetry Ser.). 64p. (C). 1983. reprint ed. pap. 14.95 (*0-8203-0653-3*) U of Ga Pr.

One Less Fish. Allan Sheather. LC 97-23615. (Illus.). 32p. (J). 1998. pap. 6.95 (*0-88106-323-1*) Charlesbridge Pub.

One Less Fish. Allan Sheather. LC 97-23615. (Illus.). 32p. (J). (ps-3). 1998. 15.95 (*0-88106-322-3*) Charlesbridge Pub.

One Less Fish. Kim Michelle Toft & Alan Sheather. LC 98-217487. (Illus.). 32p. (J). 1997. pap. 14.95 (*0-7022-2947-4*, Pub. by Univ Queensland Pr) Intl Spec Bk.

One Life: An Autobiography of an African American Actress. Ellen Holly. 288p. 1998. pap. 12.00 (*1-56836-197-1*) Kodansha.

One Life: The Autobiography of An African American Actress. Ellen Holly. (Illus.). 320p. 1996. 23.00 (*1-56836-158-0*) Kodansha.

One Life: The Autobiography of Florence Lamborn, Vols. 1 & 2. Florence L. Johnson. (Illus.). 464p. 1997. 27.00 (*0-8059-4048-0*) Dorrance.

One Life: The Free Academic. Max Kaplan. LC 97-26170. 1998. write for info. (*0-8386-3737-X*) Fairleigh Dickinson.

One Life at a Time: Children's Home Society of Minnesota, 1889-1989. Kenneth L. Green. (Illus.). 64p. 1989. 10.00 (*0-685-24268-4*) CHS MN.

One Life at a Time, Please. Edward Abbey. LC 87-8812. 240p. 1995. pap. 9.95 (*0-8050-0603-6*, Owl) H Holt & Co.

***One Life Is Not Enough.** Nellie O. Jackson. LC 99-91626. 2000. 25.00 (*0-7388-1142-4*); pap. 18.00 (*0-7388-1143-2*) Xlibris Corp.

***One Life Moving Toward the Light.** Margaret L. Pegoles. Ed. by Voices of Truths Staff. 96p. 1999. pap. 10.95 (*0-9666777-2-2*) Voice of Truths.

One Life Through Many Facets. Barbara E. Alferieff. (ENG & RUS.). 182p. 1991. pap. write for info. (*0-9660603-0-X*) RE Pub.

One Life to Live: Thirty Years of Memories. Gary Warner. LC 97-32728. (Illus.). 304p. (J). 1998. 29.45 (*0-7868-6367-6*, Pub. by Hyperion) Time Warner.

One Life's Pilgrimage. Gayatri Devi. 1977. pap. 7.95 (*0-911564-27-6*) Vedanta Ctr.

One Lifetime Is Not Enough. large type ed. Zsa Zsa Gabor. (Illus.). 320p. 1993. 27.99 (*0-7089-8694-3*, Charnwood) Ulverscroft.

One Light, One Love. limited ed. Sharon Warren. (Illus.). 136p. 1993. 70.00 (*0-9636074-0-5*) Imagic Unltd.

One Light, One Sun. Illus. by Eugenie Fernandes. LC 87-22256. (Raffi Songs to Read Ser.). 32p. (J). (ps-2). 1990. pap. 5.99 (*0-517-57644-9*, Pub. by Crown Bks Yng Read) Random.

One Lighthouse, One Moon. Anita Lobel. LC 98-50790. (Illus.). 40p. (J). (ps-3). 2000. 15.95 (*0-688-15539-1*, Grenwillow Bks); lib. bdg. 15.89 (*0-688-15540-5*, Grenwillow Bks) HarpC Child Bks.

One Like Jesus: Conversations on the Single Life. Debra K. Farrington. LC 98-36978. 224p. 1999. pap. 12.95 (*0-8294-1267-0*) Loyola Pr.

One-Line Diagrams. (Principles of Steam Generation Ser.: Module 16). (Illus.). 55p. 1982. spiral bd. 20.00 (*0-87683-266-4*) GP Courseware.

One Liners. Alma Heaton. pap. 10.95 (*1-55517-353-5*) CFI Dist.

One-Liners for Business Speeches. Mitch Murray. 1998. 29.95 (*0-572-02268-9*, Pub. by W Foulsham) Trans-Atl Phila.

One-Liners for Speeches on Special Occasions. Mitch Murray. 1998. 14.95 (*0-572-02388-X*, Pub. by W Foulsham) Trans-Atl Phila.

***One-Liners from God: Biblical Affirmations to Lift up the Heart.** Mary C. Macaluso. LC 99-90612. xi, 170p. 1999. pap. 9.95 (*0-9663462-1-1*) Fun Nun.

1 Linux Way to Do DOS, & Windows: Building Microsoft Gates' Business @ the Speed of Thought "Digital Nervous System" Using Oracle 8, NDS, JAVA, & WINE: Get an up to Date 2 CD-ROM Red Hat 5.2 Based Linux O/S with Netscape, DB's & Apps, Real Audio Player, & 2.2 Kernel; Which Runs MS Windows Apps & Has Extra Windofiles & Flaw Proofs. Reginald Burgess. 249p. 1999. mass mkt. 37.95 incl. cd-rom (*1-891950-10-X*) Amer Group Pub.

1 Linux Way to Do DOS, & Windows: Building Microsoft Gates' Business @ the Speed of Thought "Digital Nervous System" Using the Value of Sybase as a Clone to SQL Server: Get an up to Date 2 CD-ROM Red Hat 5.2 Based Linux O/S with Netscape, DB's & Apps, Real Audio Player, & 2.2 Kernel; Which Runs MS Windows Apps & Has Extra Windows Files & Flaw Proofs. Reginald Burgess. 249p. 1999. mass mkt. 37.95 incl. cd-rom (*1-891950-12-6*) Amer Group Pub.

1 Linux Way to Do DOS, & Windows: BuildingMicrosoft Gates' Business @ the Speed of Thought "Digital Nervous System" Using Open Source Postgres SQL, NDS, JAVA & WINE: Get an up to Date 2 CD-ROM Red Hat 5.2 Based Linux O/S with Netscape, SQL DB's & Apps, Real Audio Player, & 2.2 Kernel; Which Runs MS Windows Apps & Has Extra Windows Files & Flaw Proofs. Reginald Burgess. 249p. 1999. mass mkt. 37.95 incl. cd-rom (*1-891950-11-8*) Amer Group Pub.

***One Little Bench, No. 2402.** School Zone Staff. (Lift-Off Ser.). (Illus.). 32p. (J). (ps-3). 1999. pap., wbk. ed. 3.79 (*0-88743-802-4*) Sch Zone Pub Co.

***One Little Butterfly.** Wendy Cheyette Lewison. (Illus.). 14p. (J). (ps-k). 2000. bds. 5.99 (*0-448-42160-7*, G & D) Peng Put Young Read.

One Little Candle. 4th ed. Ruth Adams. xii, 194p. 1994. 10.00 (*0-88053-314-5*, S-251) Macoy Pub.

***One Little Dragonfly.** Wendy Cheyette Lewison. (Finger Puppet Collection Ser.). (Illus.). 14p. (J). (ps-k). 2000. bds. 5.99 (*0-448-42159-3*, G & D) Peng Put Young Read.

One Little Drop of Sunshine. Kathy Poelker. Ed. by Matt Judge. (Rhythms to Reading Ser.). (Illus.). 8p. (Orig.). (J). (ps-3). 1988. pap. text 15.00 (*0-929842-01-4*) Hawthorne Pubs.

One Little Elephant. Colin West. LC 93-36273. (Illus.). 32p. (J). (ps up). 1994. pap. 3.99 (*1-56402-375-3*) Candlewick Pr.

One Little Goat: Had Gadya. Betsy P. Teutsch. LC 89-18298. (Illus.). 32p. (J). 1990. 25.00 (*0-87668-824-5*) Aronson.

One Little Puppy Dog. Janet Morgan Stoeke. LC 98-235164. (J). (ps-1). 1998. pap. 5.99 (*0-525-45740-2*) NAL.

One Little Room. large type ed. Jan Webster. 352p. 1988. 27.99 (*0-7089-1809-3*) Ulverscroft.

One Little Room an Everywhere: The Novels of Barbara Pym. Lotus Snow. Ed. by Constance Hunting. 150p. (Orig.). 1987. pap. text 12.95 (*0-913006-37-8*) Puckerbrush.

One Little Spoonful. Susan Aliki. 14p. pap. 5.95 (*0-694-01502-4*) HarpC.

One Little Voice. Diane Stelling. LC 97-74836. (Illus.). 160p. (J). (ps-6). 1997. pap. 9.95 (*0-9655758-9-6*) Hereami Pub.

One Loaf, One Cup: Ecumenical Studies of 1 Cor 11 & Other Eucharistic Texts. Ben F. Meyer. (New Gospel Studies: No. 6). 180p. 1992. 25.00 (*0-86554-398-4*, MUP/H324) Mercer Univ Pr.

One Lonely Knight: Mickey Spillane's Mike Hammer. Max Allan Collins & James L. Traylor. LC 84-71256. 186p. 1984. 20.95 (*0-87972-301-7*); pap. 11.95 (*0-87972-302-5*) Bowling Green Univ Popular Press.

One Lonely Lion. Rebecca Elgar. (Illus.). (J). (ps-k). bds. 7.99 (*0-590-24918-5*) Scholastic Inc.

One Lonely Lion. Rebecca Elgar. (Lift-the-Flaps Bks.). (Illus.). 10p. (J). 1998. bds. 4.95 (*1-899607-31-5*) Sterling.

One Lonely Night. large type ed. Mickey Spillane, pseud. LC 95-49124. 1996. 21.95 (*0-7838-1229-9*, G K Hall Lrg Type) Mac Lib Ref.

***One Lonely Seahorse.** Saxton Freymann & Joost Elffers. LC 99-33396. (Illus.). 32p. (J). 2000. 15.99 (*0-439-11014-9*, A A Levine) Scholastic Inc.

One Long Argument: Charles Darwin & the Genesis of Modern Evolutionary Thought. Ernst W. Mayr. (Illus.). 192p. (C). 1991. text 19.95 (*0-674-63905-7*) HUP.

One Long Argument: Charles Darwin & the Genesis of Modern Evolutionary Thought. Ernst W. Mayr. (Questions of Science Ser.). (Illus.). 224p. (C). 1993. pap. text 14.95 (*0-674-63906-5*) HUP.

One Long Experiment: Scale & Process in Earth History. Ronald Martin. LC 97-27821. (Perspectives in Paleobiology & Earth History Ser.). (Illus.). 272p. 1998. 85.00 (*0-231-10904-0*) Col U Pr.

One Long Experiment: Scale & Process in Earth History. Ronald Martin. LC 97-27821. (Perspectives in Paleobiology & Earth History Ser.). (Illus.). 272p. 1998. pap. 35.00 (*0-231-10905-9*) Col U Pr.

One Long Poem. fac. ed. William Harmon. LC 82-7213. 64p. 1982. reprint ed. pap. 30.00 (*0-7837-7737-X*, 204749300007) Bks Demand.

One Long Safari. limited ed. Peter W. Hay. LC 97-61794. (Illus.). 350p. 1998. 100.00 (*1-882458-18-4*) Trophy Rm Bks.

One Long War. Netanel Lorch. 1976. 8.00 (*0-685-82597-3*) Herzl Pr.

One Lord, One Church, One Hope, & One God: Mennonite Confessions of Faith. Ed. by Howard J. Loewen. (Text-Reader Ser.: No. 2). 369p. 1985. pap. text 12.00 (*0-936273-08-9*) Inst Mennonite.

One Lord, One Faith. Rex A. Koivisto. LC 92-42715. 408p. (gr. 12). 1993. 19.99 (*0-8010-2126-X*, Bridgept Bks) Baker Bks.

One Lord, One Faith: Writings of the Early Christian Fathers As Evidences of the Restoration. Michael T. Griffith. 248p. (Orig.). 1996. pap. 17.98 (*0-88290-575-9*) Horizon Utah.

One Lord, One Faith, One Church: New Perspectives in Ecumenism. Rene Girault. 160p. (C). 1996. pap. 39.95 (*0-85439-425-7*, Pub. by St Paul Pubns) St Mut.

One Lord One Spirit One Body. Peter Hocken. (Illus.). 140p. (Orig.). 1987. pap. 5.00 (*0-932085-04-0*) Word Among Us.

***One Love.** Earle Davies. 1998. text 35.00 (*0-233-99443-2*, Pub. by Andre Deutsch) Trafalgar.

***One Love.** Earle Davies. 1999. pap. 15.95 (*0-233-99450-5*, Pub. by Andre Deutsch) Trafalgar.

One Love. Lynn Emery. 320p. 1999. mass mkt. 4.99 (*1-58314-046-8*) BET Bks.

One Love: An Unbelievable Journey. Janine Johnson. 150p. 1998. pap. 9.95 (*1-892745-11-9*) Petals of Life.

One Love Forever. large type ed. Meredith B. Brucker. (Linford Romance Library). 368p. 1993. pap. 16.99 (*0-7089-7399-X*, Linford) Ulverscroft.

***One Lucky Fish.** Fran Hurcomb. (Illus.). 32p. (J). (gr. k-5). 1999. pap. 7.95 (*1-894303-15-6*) RRP.

***One Lucky Girl.** George Lyon. LC 98-41149. (Illus.). 32p. (J). (gr. k-3). 2000. 15.95 (*0-7894-2613-7*, D K Ink) DK Pub Inc.

***One Lucky Lord.** Kim D. Bennet. (Wink & a Kiss Ser.). 368p. 2000. mass mkt. 5.50 (*0-505-52363-9*, Love Spell) Dorchester Pub Co.

One Lump or Two. All Childrens Hospital Foundation Staff. LC 88-24638. (Illus.). 1994. spiral bd. 19.95 (*0-87197-243-3*) Favorite Recipes.

One Magic Christmas: A Musical. Bob Fitzsimmons. 31p. (Orig.). (J). (gr. 2-9). 1993. pap. 3.50 (*1-57514-227-9*, 0083) Encore Perform Pub.

***One Magical Kiss.** large type ed. Helen Shelton. 288p. 1999. 25.99 (*0-263-15896-9*, Pub. by Mills & Boon) Ulverscroft.

One Magnificent Cookbook. Junior League of Chicago Staff. 1988. 19.95 (*0-9611622-2-8*) JLC Inc.

One Magnificent Moment. Tryon Lindabury. 140p. (Orig.). 1991. pap. 6.95 (*1-879366-09-6*) Hearthstone OK.

***One Man.** Kerry Johnson. Ed. by Beverly Coney Heirich. (Illus.). 388p. 1999. pap. 13.95 (*0-9669286-0-1*) Harpazo.

One Man - Unconquered. Farris Anderson. (Illus.). 175p. 1998. pap. 19.95 (*0-9663207-1-9*) F Anderson.

One Man Alone: Hemingway & "To Have & Have Not" Toni Knott et al. 224p. 1999. 74.95 (*1-57309-401-3*) Intl Scholars.

***One Man Alone: Hemingway & 'To Have & to Have Not'** Toni D. Knott. LC 99-36277. 272p. 1999. 56.00 (*0-7618-1475-2*); pap. 35.50 (*0-7618-1476-0*) U Pr of Amer.

One Man by Himself: Portraits of Jon Serl. Sam Messer & Red Lips. LC 95-34715. (Profile Ser.: No. 1). 48p. 1995. 39.95 (*0-9638433-6-2*) Hard Pr MA.

One Man Caravan. 2nd ed. Robert E. Fulton, Jr. LC 97-204419. (Incredible Journeys Ser.). (Illus.). 352p. 1996. reprint ed. pap. 24.95 (*1-884313-05-1*, FULT) Whitehorse NH.

One-Man-Collaboration. Mark Sonnenfeld. 28p. 1996. pap. 3.00 (*1-887379-08-8*) M Sonnenfeld.

One Man in His Time. Ellen Glasgow. 386p. Date not set. 27.95 (*0-8488-2623-X*) Amereon Ltd.

One Man in His Time. Serge Obolensky. (Illus.). 1958. 20.00 (*0-8392-1080-9*) Astor-Honor.

One Man in His Time. Ellen Glasgow. (Collected Works of Ellen Glasgow). 379p. 1998. reprint ed. lib. bdg. 98.00 (*1-58201-638-0*) Classic Bks.

One Man in His Time: The Biography of the Laird of Torosay Castle: Traveller, Wartime Escaper & Distinguished Politician. John Robson. 240p. 1997. 100.00 (*1-86227-036-8*, Pub. by Spellmnt Pubs) St Mut.

***One Man One Cross: A Spiritual Journey.** Billy V. Turner. LC 00-103108. 248p. 2000. 22.95 (*0-9663078-7-9*, Pub. by Graystone Pub Co) IPG Chicago.

***One Man, One Rifle, One Land.** J. Y. Jones. (Illus.). 450p. 2000. 59.95 (*1-57157-169-8*) Safari Pr.

One Man, One Vote: America's Most Powerful Black Man - for a Week! Larry Strauss. 224p. 1998. pap. text 12.95 (*0-87067-889-2*) Holloway.

One Man Said No: Fighting Judicial Corruption in New Jersey. Thomas P. Coffey. 144p. 1998. pap. 9.95 (*0-87193-317-9*) Dimension Bks.

One Man Show. Frank Asch. LC 97-7626. (Meet the Author Ser.). (Illus.). 32p. (J). (gr. 2-5). 1997. 14.95 (*1-57274-095-7*, 717) R Owen Pubs.

One Man Tango. Anthony Quinn & Daniel Paisner. 1996. mass mkt. write for info. (*0-614-18003-1*, Harp PBks) HarpC.

One Man to the Altar. Jeanne Allan. (Romance Ser.: Bk. 3584). 187p. 2000. per. 3.50 (*0-373-03584-5*, 1-03584-9) Harlequin Bks.

One Man Who Was Content. Mariana Van Rensselaer. LC 77-94746. (Short Story Index Reprint Ser.). 1977. 16.95 (*0-8369-3126-2*) Ayer.

One-Man Woman. Carole Mortimer. 1997. per. 3.50 (*0-373-11863-5*, 1-11863-7) Harlequin Bks.

One-Man Woman. large type ed. Carole Mortimer. (Harlequin Romance Ser.). 1997. 20.95 (*0-263-14971-4*) Mac Lib Ref.

One Man's America: A Journalist's Search for the Heart of His Country. Henry Grunwald. LC 96-19629. (Illus.). 672p. 1996. 30.00 (*0-385-41408-0*) Doubleday.

One Man's America: A Journalist's Search for the Heart of His Country. Henry Grunwald. (Illus.). 672p. 1998. pap. 14.95 (*0-385-49357-6*) Doubleday.

One Man's Art. Nora Roberts. (NR Flowers Ser.: No. 17). 1992. mass mkt. 3.59 (*0-373-51017-9*, 5-51017-7) Harlequin Bks.

One Man's Blues: The Life & Music of Mose Allison. Patti Jones. (Illus.). 368p. 1998. 25.00 (*0-7043-7086-7*, Pub. by Quartet) Interlink Pub.

One Man's Century: From the Deep South to the Top of the Big Apple. George P. Oslin. LC 98-43917. 144p. 1999. 20.00 (*0-86554-647-9*) Mercer Univ Pr.

One Man's Chorus: The Uncollected Writings. Anthony Burgess. Ed. & Intro. by Benjamin Forkner. 400p. 1998. 25.00 (*0-7867-0568-X*) Carroll & Graf.

One Man's Chorus: The Uncollected Writings. Anthony Burgess. 400p. 2000. pap. text 14.95 (*0-7867-0699-6*) Carroll & Graf.

One Man's Compassion. Fulton Buntain & Hal Donaldson. 256p. 1989. mass mkt. 5.99 (*0-88368-214-1*) Whitaker Hse.

One Man's Destiny. Thomas C. Wilcox. LC 92-80451. (Illus.). 224p. (Orig.). 1992. pap. 9.95 (*1-878893-17-3*) Telcraft Bks.

***One Man's Eye: Photographs from the Alan Siegel Collection.** Intro. by Robert A. Sobieszek. (Illus.). 168p. 2000. 49.50 (*0-8109-6719-7*, Pub. by Abrams) Time Warner.

One Man's Family Album. Carlton E. Morse. (Illus.). 160p. (Orig.). 1988. pap. 8.95 (*0-940249-05-7*) Seven Stones Pr.

One Man's Garden. Henry Mitchell. 1999. pap. 14.00 (*0-395-95769-9*) HM.

One Man's Gold: The Letters & Journals of a Forty-Niner. Enos Christman. (American Biography Ser.). 278p. 1991. reprint ed. lib. bdg. 69.00 (*0-7812-8068-0*) Rprt Serv.

One Man's Gold Rush: A Klondike Album. rev. ed. Murray Morgan. LC 67-13109. (Illus.). 224p. (C). 1995. reprint ed. pap. 24.95 (*0-295-95187-7*) U of Wash Pr.

One Man's Gripes about Golf & Some Player's Attitudes. Hal Foster. LC 95-90161. 130p. 1995. pap. write for info. (*0-9646932-0-8*) New Venture TX.

One Man's Henry Moore. David Finn. (Illus.). 110p. 1993. pap. 19.95 (*0-9876543-2-2*) Yale Ctr Brit Art.

One Man's Initiation 1917: A Novel. John Dos Passos. 146p. (C). 1986. reprint ed. pap. text 17.50 (*0-8191-5360-5*) U Pr of Amer.

One Man's Journey. Kazuo Miyamoto. LC 81-21572. 120p. (Orig.). 1981. pap. 8.95 (*0-938474-01-4*) Buddhist Study.

One Man's Judgment. Lord Wheatley. 240p. 1987. boxed set 50.00 (*0-406-10019-5*, U.K., MICHIE) LEXIS Pub.

One Man's Junk. O. Victor Miller. Ed. by Roberta George & Nancy Phillips. 159p. (Orig.). 1995. pap. 10.00 (*0-9638364-1-2*) Snake Nation.

***One Man's Justice.** Yoshimura. 2001. write for info. (*0-15-100639-3*) Harcourt.

One Man's Law. John Clarkson. 368p. (Orig.). 1994. mass mkt. 5.99 (*0-425-14249-3*) Berkley Pub.

One Man's Life. Don Hummel & Eugenia Hummel. Ed. by Ron Arnold. LC 88-6093. (Americana Bks.). 512p. 1988. 14.95 (*0-939571-03-X*) Free Enter Pr.

O

An Asterisk (*) at the beginning of an entry indicates that the title is appearing for the first time.

One Man's Lincoln: Billy Herndon (Honestly) Represents Abe. Wade Hall. (Illus.). 84p. 1998. pap. 5.00 (*0-9662947-0-X*) KY Humanities.

One Man's Meat. E. B. White. 360p. Date not set. 25.95 (*0-8488-2412-1*) Amereon Ltd.

One Man's Meat. large type ed. E. B. White. LC 97-37435. (Perennial Ser.). 501 p. 1997. lib. bdg. 24.95 (*0-7838-8321-8*, G K Hall Lrg Type) Mac Lib Ref.

One Man's Meat. 13th rev. ed. E. B. White. LC 97-21257. 296p. 1997. pap. 14.95 (*0-88448-192-1*) Tilbury Hse.

One Man's Mission: Twenty Thousand Ships. Contrib. by Kummerman Foundation Staff. 1989. 75.00 (*1-85044-242-8*) LLP.

One Man's Montana: Bob Gilluly's Best Newspaper Yarns. Bob Gilluly. 250p. 1999. pap. 15.00 (*0-915945-03-7*) Heartland Journals.

One Man's Moon: Fifty Haiku by Basho, Buson, Issa, Hakuin, Shiki, Santoka. Matsu Basho et al. Tr. by Cid Corman from JPN. LC 84-80472. 72p. (Orig.). 1984. pap. 10.00 (*0-917788-26-5*) Gnomon Pr.

One Man's Mountains. Tom Patey. LC 97-223983. (Illus.). 294p. 1998. pap. 15.95 (*0-89886-542-5*) Mountaineers.

One Man's Nagasaki: A Personal Sea Odyssey. Kurt Von S. Kynell. LC 98-94248. (Illus.). 464p. 1999. pap. 19.95 (*0-7392-0069-0*, PO2912) Morris Pubng.

One Man's Odyssey. Pearce. 187p. 1986. pap. 13.95 (*0-85207-179-5*, Pub. by C W Daniel) Natl Bk Netwk.

One Man's Odyssey. Ian Pierce. 296p. (Orig.). pap. 20.95 (*0-8464-4263-9*) Beekman Pubs.

One Man's Opinion. C. C. Jobe. Ed. by Susan Coman. 491p. (Orig.). 1993. pap. 12.95 (*0-9625495-3-3*) Magen-J Enterprises.

One Man's Opinion Fix America. Hamner C. Williams. iii, 340p. 1998. 31.60 (*0-9664147-0-5*) Gibraltar Inc.

One Man's Opinion on a Cure for Chronic Back Pain. William C. Gagnon. Ed. by Norman Christenson. (Illus.). 62p. 1998. 19.95 (*0-9663568-0-2*) Our Earths.

One Man's Owl. rev. ed. Bernd Heinrich. LC 93-7167. (Illus.). 264p. 1993. pap. text 14.95 (*0-691-00065-4*, Pub. by Princeton U Pr) Cal Prin Full Svc.

One Man's Poison. John R. Riggs. LC 90-35745. (Garth Ryland Mystery Ser.). 1991. 17.95 (*0-942637-31-3*, Dembner NY) Barricade Bks.

One Man's Poison. large type ed. John R. Riggs. LC 92-11659. 315p. 1992. reprint ed. 16.95 (*1-56054-424-4*) Thorndike Pr.

One Man's Promise. Diana Whitney. (Romance Ser.). 1998. per. 3.50 (*0-373-19307-6*, 1-19307-7) Silhouette.

One Man's San Francisco. Herb Caen. LC 75-14808. 1978. reprint ed. pap. 3.95 (*0-89174-031-7*) Comstock Edns.

One Man's Scrapbook. rev. ed. Compiled by Eddy Joseph. LC 94-42541. 125p. 1995. pap. 19.95 (*0-7734-2738-4*, Mellen Poetry Pr) E Mellen.

One Man's Search: Addresses. Obert C. Tanner. LC 88-28045. 343p. 1989. reprint ed. pap. 106.40 (*0-7837-8570-4*, 204938500011) Bks Demand.

One Man's Secret. large type ed. Miriam Sharman. 400p. 1988. 27.99 (*0-7089-1856-5*) Ulverscroft.

One Man's Story. Charles H. Goyette. (Illus.). 122p. 1996. 19.95 (*0-9654497-5-0*) Transit Pub.

One Man's Trash Is Another Man's Treasure: The Metamorphosis of the European Utensil in the New World. Alexandra Van Dongen et al. (Illus.). 234p. 1996. pap. 45.00 (*90-6918-152-5*, Pub. by Boymans Mus) Dist Art Pubs.

One Man's Universe: The Continuing Chronicles of Arthur Morton McAndrews. Charles Sheffield. 320p. (Orig.). 1993. pap. 9.99 (*0-8125-2399-7*) Tor Bks.

One Man's Vision: The Life of Automotive Pioneer Ralph R. Teetor. Marjorie Meyer. LC 95-77508. (Illus.). 225p. 1995. pap. 16.95 (*1-878208-67-5*) Guild Pr IN.

One Man's Vow. Diana Whitney. (Romance Ser.). 1993. per. 2.75 (*0-373-08940-6*, 5-08940-4) Silhouette.

One Man's Walk with God: A Lifetime of Christian Witness. Herbert R. Cook. LC 94-44920. (Illus.). 304p. (Orig.). 1994. pap. 18.00 (*0-88196-006-3*) Oak Woods Media.

One Man's War. Lindsay McKenna. (Special Edition Ser.: No. 727). 1992. mass mkt. 3.39 (*0-373-09727-1*, 5-09727-4) Harlequin Bks.

One Man's War: A Memoir of World War II. Harold J. Gordon, Jr. Ed. by Nancy M. Gordon. LC 99-17671. (Illus.). 128p. 1999. pap. 11.95 (*0-945257-99-6*) Apex Pr.

One Man's War: Diving As a Guest of the Emperor, 1942. Robert C. Sheats. LC 97-73114. (Illus.). 190p. 1998. pap. 14.95 (*0-941332-60-8*, D936) Best Pub Co.

One Man's War: The Story of the Lafayette Escadrille. Bert Hall & John J. Niles. Ed. by James B. Gilbert. LC 79-7266. (Flight: Its First Seventy-Five Years Ser.). (Illus.). 1980. reprint ed. lib. bdg. 37.95 (*0-405-12176-8*) Ayer.

One Man's West. David Lavender. LC 76-45450. (Illus.). iv, 316p. 1977. pap. 12.50 (*0-8032-5855-0*, Bison Books) U of Nebr Pr.

***One Man's Wilderness: An Alaskan Odyssey.** 26th ed. Richard Proenneke & Sam Keith. LC 98-27704. 223p. 1999. pap. 14.95 (*0-88240-513-6*, Alaska NW Bks) Gr Arts Ctr Pub.

One Man's World. Karan Singh. Ed. by Kishore Gandhi. 1986. 27.50 (*81-7023-090-X*, Pub. by Allied Pubs) S Asia.

One Market, One Money: An Evaluation of the Potential Benefits & Costs of Forming an Economic & Monetary Union. Michael Emerson. (Illus.). 354p. 1992. pap. text 32.00 (*0-19-877324-2*) OUP.

***One Market Under God: Extreme Capitalism, Market Populism & the End of the Economic Democracy.** Thomas Frank. 2000. 26.00 (*0-385-49503-X*) Doubleday.

One Maxi-Martian: GJB-2. Garland R. Girken. 40p. (Orig.). 1997. pap. 6.95 (*0-533-12279-1*) Vantage.

One Meal at a Time: The Only Low-Fat Diet You Need to Lose Weight & Lower Your Cholesterol. Martin Katahn. 544p. 1993. mass mkt. 6.50 (*0-446-36294-8*, Pub. by Warner Bks) Little.

One Meal Cookbook: Cooking for Families with One or More Vegetarians. Debra Diender. LC 98-53839. (Illus.). 240p. 1999. 18.95 (*1-55972-495-1*, Birch Ln Pr) Carol Pub Group.

One Medicine: A Tribute to Kurt Benirschke. Ed. by O. A. Ryder & M. L. Byrd. (Illus.). xiv, 373p. 1984. 86.95 (*0-387-13275-9*) Spr-Verlag.

***One Memory at a Time: Inspiration & Advice for Writing Your Family Story.** D. G. Fulford. LC 00-30320. 224p. 2000. 17.95 (*0-385-49870-5*) Doubleday.

One Mexican Sunday. Mike Oehler. LC 80-82949. (Illus.). 112p. 1981. 8.50 (*0-9604464-1-9*) Mole Pub Co.

One Mezuzah: A Jewish Counting Book. Carol Kitman & Ann Hurwitz. (J). (gr. k). pap. 6.95 (*0-317-70144-4*) Behrman.

One Mezuzah: A Jewish Counting Book. Carol Kitman & Carol Hurwitz. (Illus.). 48p. (J). (ps). 1984. pap. 6.95 (*0-940646-54-4*) Rossel Bks.

1 Microsoft Way . . . A Cookbook to Breaking Bill Gates Windows Monopoly Without Breaking Windows: Available CD-ROM with Linux Files to Build a 95-NT Clone with Mandrake Red Hat 5.3.2 Linux O/S & Wine Included. Reginald P. Burgess. 208p. 1998. pap. 17.95 (*1-891950-08-8*) Amer Group Pub.

One Mighty Torrent: The Drama of Biography. Edgar Johnson. LC CT0034.G7J6. 591p. reprint ed. pap. 183.30 (*0-608-13756-1*, 205167900001) Bks Demand.

One Million Banknote & Other New Stories. Mark Twain, pseud. (Works of Samuel Clemens). 1989. reprint ed. lib. bdg. 79.00 (*0-685-28384-4*) Rprt Serv.

***One Million Children: Success for All.** Robert E. Slavin et al. LC 00-8785. 2000. write for info. (*0-8039-6803-5*) Corwin Pr.

One Million Dollar Desktop Publishing Idea Book. Richard Nodine. 208p. 1994. pap. 29.95 (*0-9641100-0-8*) Pacific Lrning.

$1,000,000 Guide to Wealth & Happiness. 157p. (Orig.). 1997. pap. 26.95 (*0-9657683-0-9*) J M Parker.

One Million Men: The Civil War Draft in the North. Eugene C. Murdock. LC 80-14431. (Illus.). 366p. 1980. reprint ed. lib. bdg. 55.00 (*0-313-22502-8*, MUOM, Greenwood Pr) Greenwood.

One Million One Things That Make You Crabby: The Official Checklist for Complainers, Rant 'n Ravers & Bellyachers & Everybody Else. Natalie Windsor. LC 91-71052. (Illus.). 176p. (Orig.). 1992. pap. 6.95 (*0-944042-06-6*) CorkScrew Pr.

1,000,000 Pound Bank-Note & Other New Stories. Mark Twain, pseud. (Oxford Mark Twain Stories Ser.). (Illus.). 352p. 1996. 22.00 (*0-19-510144-8*) OUP.

One Million Pound Bank-Note & Other New Stories. Mark Twain, pseud. LC 76-121529. (Short Story Index Reprint Ser.). 260p. 1977. 18.95 (*0-8369-3485-7*) Ayer.

One Million Strong: A Photographic Tribute to the Million Man March & Affirmations for the African-American Male. Illus. by Cliff Giles. LC 96-85705. 96p. 1996. 19.95 (*1-878647-29-6*) APU Pub Grp.

One Million Words of Book Notes, 1958-1993. Richard Kostelanetz. LC 93-61167. x, 668p. 1996. 90.00 (*0-87875-451-2*) Whitston Pub.

One Min. Sales Perso M. Spencer Johnson & Larry Wilson. 111p. 1986. mass mkt. 6.50 (*0-380-70151-0*, Avon Bks) Morrow Avon.

One Min. Sales Perso T. Spencer Johnson. 120p. 1991. pap. 9.00 (*0-380-71603-8*, Avon Bks) Morrow Avon.

***One-Minute Academic Functional Assessment & Interventions: "Can't" Do It... Or "Won't" Do It?** Joe Witt & Ray Beck. 212p. 1999. pap. 19.50 (*1-57035-205-4*) Sopris.

One Minute after You Die: A Preview of Your Final Destination. Erwin W. Lutzer. LC 97-147274. 144p. 1997. pap. 8.99 (*0-8024-6322-3*, 237); pap. 11.99 (*0-8024-6323-1*, 238) Moody.

One Minute Answers to Anti-Mormon Questions. Stephen W. Gibson. 208p. 1995. 15.98 (*0-88290-570-8*, 1060) Horizon Utah.

One Minute Asthma: What You Need to Know. 4th ed. Thomas F. Plaut. Ed. by Teresa B. Jones. LC 98-25976. (Illus.). 56p. 1998. 5.00 (*0-914625-20-9*) Pedipress.

One Minute Bible see Biblia al Minuto

One Minute Bible: Men of Character. Lawrence Kimbrough. LC 98-5931. 1998. 19.99 (*0-8054-9267-4*) Broadman.

One Minute Bible: Women of Character. Lawrence Kimbrough. LC 98-5930. 1998. 19.99 (*0-8054-9277-1*) Broadman.

One Minute Bible: 90 Days in the Word for Business Professionals. Lawrence Kimbrough. LC 99-15735. (One Minute Bible Ser.). 1999. 14.99 (*0-8054-9363-8*) Broadman.

One Minute Bible Curriculum. Doug Fields. 1998. pap. 39.00 (*0-310-67948-6*) HarpC.

One Minute Bible Devotions for Kids. Steve Bjorkman. (J). 1998. 16.99 (*0-8054-9297-6*) Broadman.

One-Minute Bible Devotions for Students. John R. Kohlenberger. 1998. pap. 12.99 (*0-8054-9348-4*) Broadman.

***One Minute Bible for Starters: A 90 Days Journey for New Christians, Vol. 1.** Broadman & Holman. LC 99-15734. (One Minute Bible Ser.). 1999. pap. 1.99 (*0-8054-9386-7*, DoorWay TN) Broadman.

One-Minute Bible 4 Students. John R. Kohlenberger, III. (Illus.). 395p. (Orig.). 1993. pap. text 12.99 (*1-881830-14-4*) Garborgs.

One-Minute Bible World. John H. Sailhamer. LC 97-45993. 96p. 1998. pap. 6.99 (*0-310-20393-7*) Zondervan.

One-Minute Biographies & Art Activities: Grades 2-6. Troll Books Staff. 96p. (J). (gr. 2-6). 1999. pap. text 12.95 (*0-8167-3275-2*) Troll Communs.

One-Minute Business Letter. Charles Bury. LC 84-61830. 103p. (Orig.). 1984. pap. 14.95 (*0-9613854-0-5*) Modern Comm Assocs.

One-Minute Christian Theology. John H. Sailhamer. LC 97-45990. 96p. 1998. pap. 6.99 (*0-310-50041-9*) Zondervan.

One-Minute Church History. John H. Sailhamer. LC 97-45992. 96p. 1998. pap. 6.99 (*0-310-20395-3*) Zondervan.

One-Minute Coin Expert. 3rd ed. Scott A. Travers. 304p. 1998. pap. 6.99 (*0-676-60148-0*) Hse Collectbls.

One-Minute Commentary. John H. Sailhamer. LC 97-39133. 96p. 1998. pap. 6.99 (*0-310-50031-1*) Zondervan.

One Minute Communicator: Tips, Techniques & Observations for Better Business Communication. Howard Baker, Jr. LC 91-71063. (Illus.). 75p. (Orig.). (C). 1991. pap. 5.95 (*0-9623660-1-3*) Forum Pr Intl.

One Minute Father: A Father's True Story about the Quickest Way to Teach Your Children How to Like Themselves & Behave Themselves. Spencer Johnson. LC 83-62159. 1983. 15.00 (*0-688-02251-0*, Wm Morrow) Morrow Avon.

One Minute Father: Improve Every Moment You Spend with Your Child. Spencer Johnson. 1995. pap. 7.95 (*0-688-14405-5*, Wm Morrow) Morrow Avon.

One Minute for Yourself. Spencer Johnson. LC 98-35603. 112p. 1998. reprint ed. pap. 9.95 (*0-688-16356-4*, Wm Morrow) Morrow Avon.

One-Minute Game Guide. Seymour Metzner. LC 67-29157. (J). (gr. 1-6). 1968. pap. 6.99 (*0-8224-5070-4*) Fearon Teacher Aids.

One Minute Golfer: Enjoying the Great Game More. Kenneth Blanchard. LC 99-17416. (One Minute Manager Library). 192p. 1999. pap. 9.95 (*0-688-16849-3*, Quil) HarperTrade.

One Minute Guide to Rules of the Road. Charlie Wing. LC 98-17629. (Boating Magazine Book Ser.). (Illus.). 96p. 1998. pap. 14.95 (*0-07-071094-5*) Intl Marine.

One-Minute Healing Experience. Ellen M. Laura. LC 97-14227. 120p. (Orig.). 1997. pap. 11.00 (*1-57733-012-9*) B Dolphin Pub.

One Minute Investor. Robert Clayton. 1998. pap. 5.95 (*1-892937-01-8*) Spec Pubns.

One-Minute Life of Christ. John H. Sailhamer. LC 97-46008. 96p. 1998. pap. 6.99 (*0-310-20392-9*) Zondervan.

One Minute Listener. Howard Baker, Jr. 125p. 1991. pap. write for info. (*0-318-68594-9*) Forum Pr Intl.

One Minute Manager. Kenneth Blanchard & Spencer Johnson. LC 82-8106. 112p. 1982. 20.00 (*0-688-01429-1*, Wm Morrow) Morrow Avon.

One-Minute Manager. 10th ed. Kenneth Blanchard & Spencer Johnson. 112p. 1993. pap. 12.95 (*0-425-09847-8*) Berkley Pub.

One Minute Manager: Putting the One Minute Manager to Work, 2 vols. Kenneth Blanchard. 1993. pap. text, boxed set 21.90 (*0-425-14074-1*) Berkley Pub.

One Minute Manager Balances Work & Life. Kenneth Blanchard. 128p. 1999. pap. 9.95 (*0-688-16850-7*, Quil) HarperTrade.

One Minute Manager Builds High-Performing Teams. Kenneth Blanchard et al. LC 91-18718. (Illus.). 128p. 1991. 18.50 (*0-688-10972-1*, Wm Morrow) Morrow Avon.

One Minute Manager Builds High Performing Teams (revised Edition) rev. abr. ed. Kenneth Blanchard. 128p. 2000. 20.00 (*0-688-17215-6*, Wm Morrow) Morrow Avon.

One Minute Manager Meets the Monkey. Kenneth Blanchard. 1991. pap. 10.00 (*0-688-10380-4*, Quil) HarperTrade.

One-Minute Manager Meets the Monkey. Kenneth Blanchard et al. 1988. 17.00 incl. audio (*0-671-66077-2*) S&S Audio.

One Minute Manager Meets The Monkey. Kenneth Blanchard et al. 137p. 1989. 16.95 (*0-688-06767-0*, Quil) HarperTrade.

One Minute Meditations for Busy People. John Hampsch. 150p. 1996. pap. 9.99 (*0-89283-957-0*) Servant.

One Minute Meeting. Howard Baker, Jr. 135p. 1991. pap. write for info. (*0-318-68593-0*) Forum Pr Intl.

One Minute Methodology. Ken Orr. LC 84-61222. 66p. 1990. pap. 12.95 (*0-932633-17-X*) Dorset Hse Pub Co.

One Minute Mother. Spencer Johnson. LC 83-62158. 1983. 15.00 (*0-688-02250-2*, Wm Morrow) Morrow Avon.

One Minute Mother: Improves Every Moment You Spend with Your Child. Spencer Johnson. LC 95-222410. 112p. 1995. pap. 9.95 (*0-688-14404-7*, Wm Morrow) Morrow Avon.

One Minute Motivators. David M. Blunt. 64p. 1998. 1.00 (*1-893716-01-5*) Church Rk.

One Minute Motivators: Calculator Activities. Ed. by Instructional Fair Staff. 1998. pap. 12.95 (*1-56822-232-7*) Instruct Fair.

One Minute Motivators: Math Motivators. Instructional Fair Staff. (Illus.). 160p. 1998. pap. text 12.95 (*1-56822-277-7*) Instruct Fair.

One Minute Motivators: Primary Math Motivators. Ed. by Instructional Fair Staff. 1998. pap. 12.95 (*1-56822-276-9*) Instruct Fair.

One-Minute Motivators: Rebus Puzzle Activities. Ed. by Instructional Fair Staff. 1998. pap. 12.95 (*1-56822-233-5*); pap. 12.95 (*1-56822-278-5*) Instruct Fair.

One Minute Movies. Summer Brenner. 76p. (Orig.). 1996. pap. 9.95 (*0-614-13245-2*) Bay Area Ctr Art & Tech.

One Minute Nonsense. Anthony De Mello. LC 92-31735. 180p. (C). 1993. pap. 10.95 (*0-8294-0742-1*) Loyola Pr.

One Minute of Your Time: Right from My Heart. Bryant Wright. LC 97-75425. (Illus.). 112p. 1997. pap. 8.95 (*0-9660935-0-X*) Rght From the Hrt.

One-Minute (Or So) Healer: More Wisdom from the Sages, the Rosemarys, & the Times. Dana Ullman. LC 99-88407. 128p. 2000. pap. 9.95 (*1-56170-656-6*, 5003) Hay House.

One Minute Organizing Secret: Finding Electronic Files, Papers, Books & Almost Everything Fast! Girish Parikh. LC 85-62926. 64p. (Orig.). 1985. pap. 11.00 (*0-932888-37-2*, POT) Shetal Ent.

One Minute Parenting: Two Books in One - "The One Minute Mother," "The One Minute Father" Spencer Johnson. LC 92-38932. 1993. 9.99 (*0-517-09282-4*) Random Hse Value.

One-Minute Prophecy. John H. Sailhamer. LC 97-45991. 96p. 1998. pap. 6.99 (*0-310-50051-6*) Zondervan.

One Minute Readings Issues in Science, Technology, & Society. Richard F. Brinkerhoff. 1993. pap. 12.50 (*0-201-23157-3*) Addison-Wesley.

One Minute Reference: Word for Windows, New Edition. Liz Keaffaber. 1993. 7.95 (*1-56761-351-9*, Alpha Ref) Macmillan Gen Ref.

One Minute Sculptures: Cataogue Raisonne 1988-1998. Erwin Wurm. 1999. pap. text 49.95 (*3-89322-977-9*) Dr Cantz sche Druckerei GmbH.

One-Minute Skill Builder: Improving Student Social Skills. Susan Fister & Karen A. Kemp. (Social Skill Builders Ser.). (Illus.). 12p. 1995. pap. text, teacher ed. 45.00 incl. VHS (*1-57035-043-4*, 69VIDEO) Sopris.

One Minute Stewardship Sermons. Charles Cloughen. LC 97-27224. 144p. 1997. pap. 12.95 (*0-8192-1720-4*) Morehouse Pub.

***One Minute Stories.** Istvan Orkeny. 128p. 1999. pap. 21.00 (*963-13-4783-4*, Pub. by Corvina Bks) St Mut.

***1 Minute Stress Stoppers.** Richard Starr. (Illus.). 138p. 2000. pap. 24.95 (*1-888221-32-1*) Results Now.

One Minute Teacher. 2nd ed. Constance Johnson & Spencer Johnson. LC 88-11727. 112p. 1988. reprint ed. pap. 9.95 (*0-688-08249-1*, Quil) HarperTrade.

One-Minute Therapist: Collected Columns. Hugh R. Leavell. 110p. 1999. pap. 12.95 (*0-9668000-0-1*) H R Leavell.

One Minute Thoughts That Bring Wisdom, Harmony & Fulfillment. Richard S. Budzik & Janet K. Budzik. 1990. mass mkt. 4.95 (*0-446-36019-8*) Warner Bks.

One Minute Wisdom. Anthony De Mello. LC 85-29003. 224p. 1988. pap. 11.95 (*0-385-24290-5*, Image Bks) Doubleday.

***One Model's Life (It's Not Easy Being Thin) Send-Up of the Super Model World.** Illus. by Amy Inouye. 128p. 2000. pap. 15.95 (*0-9659754-4-4*, Pub. by Girl Pr) LPC Group.

One Moldavian Summer. Ionel Teodoreanu. Tr. by Eugenia Farca from RUM. 200p. 1993. text 31.00 (*0-88033-238-7*, 341, Pub. by East Eur Monographs) Col U Pr.

One Mom Too Many. Vicki L. Thompson. (Matchmaking Mothers Ser.). 1997. per. 3.50 (*0-373-44017-0*, 1-44017-1) Harlequin Bks.

One Moment in Time: More Inspiring Hits. 48p. (Orig.). (YA). 1988. pap. 7.95 (*0-7692-1061-9*, VF1503) Wrner Bros.

O

One Moment in Time: The Rose & Other Hits. 72p. (Orig.). (YA). 1988. pap. 9.95 (*0-7692-1062-7*, VF1508) Wrner Bros.

One Moment Past Midnight: Men in Blue. Emilie Richards. (Intimate Moments Ser.: No. 949). 1999. mass mkt. 4.25 (*0-373-07949-4*, 1-07949-0) Silhouette.

One Money for Europe. Ed. by Michele U. Fratianni & Theo Peeters. LC 78-67228. (Praeger Special Studies). 238p. 1979. 62.95 (*0-275-90354-0*, C0354, Praeger Pubs) Greenwood.

One Money for Europe? The Economics & Politics of EMU. 2nd ed. Malcolm Crawford. LC 96-2809. 380p. 1996. text 45.00 (*0-312-16115-8*) St Martin.

One Money or Many: Analyzing the Prospects for Monetary Unification in Various Parts of the World. Barry J. Eichengreen & Tamim Bayoumi. LC 94-22966. (Princeton Studies in International Finance: Vol. 76). 44p. 1994. pap. 13.50 (*0-88165-248-2*) Princeton U Int Finan Econ.

One Monkey Don't Stop No Show. Don Evans. 1982. pap. 5.25 (*0-8222-0853-9*) Dramatists Play.

One Monkey Too Many. Jackie F. Koller. LC 96-50350. (Illus.). 32p. (J). 1999. 16.00 (*0-15-200006-2*) Harcourt.

One Monster after Another. Mercer Mayer. (Illus.). 48p. (J). (ps-3). 1993. pap. 5.95 (*1-879920-05-0*) Rain Bird Prods.

One-Month Scriptural Rosary. John A. Hammes. LC 98-67818. 189p. 1999. pap. 6.95 (*0-87973-575-9*) Our Sunday Visitor.

One Moonlit Night. Tr. by Gillian Clark. 107p. (J). (gr. 4). 1991. 38.95 (*0-8464-4831-9*) Beekman Pubs.

One Moonlit Night. Samantha James. 384p. 1998. mass mkt. 5.99 (*0-380-78609-5*, Avon Bks) Morrow Avon.

One Moonlit Night. T. Llew Jones. Tr. by Gillian Clarke. 108p. (J). 1991. 70.00 (*0-86383-627-5*, Pub. by Gomer Pr) St Mut.

One Moonlit Night. Caradog Prichard. LC 96-139705. xv, 76 p. 1995. write for info. (*0-86241-530-6*) Canongate Books.

One Moonlit Night. Caradog Prichard. Tr. by Philip Mitchell from WEL. LC 96-51842. (New Directions Classic). 304p. 1997. pap. 12.95 (*0-8112-1342-0*, NDP835, Pub. by New Directions) Norton.

***One Moose, Twenty Mice.** Claire Beaton. (Illus.). 32p. (J). (ps-k). 2000. pap. 6.99 (*1-84148-129-7*) Barefoot Bks NY.

One Moose, Twenty Mice. Illus. by Clare Beaton. 32p. (J). (ps-k). 1999. 14.95 (*1-902283-37-6*) Barefoot Bks NY.

*One Moose, Twenty Mice. Clare Beaton. (Illus.). 32p. (J). (ps). 2000. reprint ed. bds. 6.99 (*1-84148-285-4*) Barefoot Bks NY.

One More & We're Outnumbered! Baby Blues Scrapbook, Vol. 8. Rick Kirkman & Jerry Scott. LC 96-86650. (Illus.). 128p. (Orig.). 1997. pap. 9.95 (*0-8362-2692-5*) Andrews & McMeel.

One More Border: The True Story of One Family's Wartime Escape from War-Torn Europe. William Kaplan & Shelley Tanaka. LC 99-161924. (Illus.). 64p. (J). (gr. 4-7). 1998. 19.95 (*0-88899-332-3*, Pub. by Gro1undwood-Douglas) Publishers Group.

One More Bridge to Cross: Lowering the Cost of War. John J. Poole. (Illus.). 123p. 1999. pap. 9.40 (*0-9638695-3-1*) Posterity Pr.

*One More Bunny: Adding from One to Ten. Rick Walton. LC 99-27642. (Illus.). 24p. (J). (ps-3). 2000. 15.95 (*0-688-16847-7*) Morrow Avon.

*One More Bunny: Adding from One to Ten. Rick Walton. LC 99-27642. (Illus.). 24p. (YA). (ps-3). 2000. 15.89 (*0-688-16848-5*) Morrow Avon.

One More Chance. Kimberly Comeaux. 1987. mass mkt. 1.99 (*1-57748-427-4*) Barbour Pub.

One More Chance: An Experiment with Human Salvage. Lewis MacBrayne & James P. Ramsey. LC 73-156023. reprint ed. 47.50 (*0-404-09124-5*) AMS Pr.

One More Day: Daily Meditations for the Chronically Ill. large type ed. Sefra K. Pitzele. (Large Print Inspirational Ser.). (Orig.). 1989. pap. 12.95 (*0-8027-2638-0*) Walker & Co.

1 More Elephant. Richard Sobol. 320p. 1999. pap. 4.99 (*0-14-037931-2*) Viking Penguin.

One More for the Road. Tana Reiff. LC 94-79118. (That's Life Ser.: Bk. 2). 96p. (YA). (gr. 6-12). 1994. pap. 4.95 (*0-7854-1087-2*, 40702); audio 10.95 (*0-7854-1096-1*, 40712) Am Guidance.

One More Gift: Total Consecration to the Immaculata According to the Spirituality of Saint Maximilian Kolbe. 2nd ed. Luigi Faccenda. LC 90-81421. (Illus.). 128p. (Orig.). 1994. pap. text 6.95 (*0-9625953-0-6*) Immaculata Pr.

One More Knight. Kathleen Creighton. (Intimate Moments Ser.: No. 890). 1998. per. 4.25 (*0-373-07890-0*, 0-07890-7) Silhouette.

One More Life, Vol. I: 1913-1929. P. N. Haksar. (Illus.). 144p. 1990. 15.95 (*0-19-562574-9*) OUP.

One More Moon. Isabel Hoch. 147p. 1997. pap. 16.95 (*1-875998-32-2*, Pub. by Central Queensland) Accents Pubns.

One More Night. large type ed. Lindsay Armstrong. 1990. reprint ed. lib. bdg. 18.95 (*0-263-12259-X*) Mac Lib Ref.

One More Night with the Frogs. Jesse Duplantis. (Mini-Bks.). 16p. 1993. pap. 1.00 (*0-89274-649-1*, HH-649) Harrison Hse.

*One More Rhyme Before Bedtime. Julia Jamison. (Illus.). 24p. (J). 2000. pap. 7.00 (*0-8059-4734-5*) Dorrance.

One More River. Lynne Reid Banks. 256p. (YA). (gr. 5 up). 1993. mass mkt. 4.99 (*0-380-71563-5*, Avon Bks) Morrow Avon.

One More River. Lynne Reid Banks. 256p. (YA). (gr. 7 up). 1996. mass mkt. 4.50 (*0-380-72755-2*, Avon Bks) Morrow Avon.

One More River. Lynne Reid Banks. 1992. 9.09 (*0-606-05525-8*, Pub. by Turtleback) Demco.

One More River. Karen Blumen. LC 95-21209. (Illus.). (J). (ps). 1995. pap. 6.99 (*0-8066-2759-X*, 9-2759) Augsburg Fortress.

One More River. Fran Striker. 360p. 50.00 (*1-884556-00-0*); pap. 16.00 (*1-884556-01-9*) Quest Wood.

One More River. rev. ed. Lynne Reid Banks. 256p. (YA). (gr. 5 up). 1992. 14.00 (*0-688-10893-8*, Wm Morrow) Morrow Avon.

One More River, No. 25. Suzanne Ellison. (Serenade Serenata Ser.). 1985. pap. 2.50 (*0-310-47022-6*, 15556P) Zondervan.

One More River to Cross. Will Henry, pseud. 256p. 1998. mass mkt. 4.50 (*0-8439-4450-1*, Leisure Bks) Dorchester Pub Co.

*One More River to Cross. Margaret Blair Young & Darius Gray. LC 00-39280. (Standing on the Promises Ser.). 2000. 19.95 (*1-57345-629-2*) Deseret Bk.

One More River to Cross. large type ed. Essie Summers. (Romance Ser.). 336p. 1992. 27.99 (*0-7089-2686-X*) Ulverscroft.

One More River to Cross: An African American Photograph Album. Walter Dean Myers. LC 95-3839. (Illus.). 192p. 1995. 40.00 (*0-15-200089-5*) Harcourt.

One More River to Cross: An African American Photograph Album. Walter Dean Meyers et al. LC 95-3839. (Illus.). 176p. (J). (gr. 4-7). 1999. reprint ed. pap. 18.00 (*0-15-202021-7*, Harcourt Child Bks) Harcourt.

One More River to Cross: Black & Gay in America. Keith Boykin. 288p. 1997. pap. 14.00 (*0-385-47983-2*, Anchor NY) Doubleday.

One More River to Cross: The Stories of Twelve Black Americans. James Haskins. (Scholastic Biography Ser.). 1992. 9.60 (*0-606-05964-4*, Pub. by Turtleback) Demco.

One More River to Cross: The Story of Twelve Black Americans. Jim Haskins. 224p. (J). (gr. 3-7). 1992. 13.95 (*0-590-42896-9*, Scholastic Hardcover) Scholastic Inc.

One More River to Cross: The Story of Twelve Black Americans. Jim Haskins. 224p. (J). (gr. 3-7). 1994. pap. 4.50 (*0-590-42897-7*) Scholastic Inc.

One More Secret. large type ed. Katherine Arthur. 277p. 1993. 27.99 (*0-7505-0573-7*, Pub. by Mgna Lrg Print) Ulverscroft.

One More Spring: A Story of Hope & Friendship. Peter M. Kalellis. LC 95-34098. 216p. 1995. 18.95 (*0-8245-1524-2*) Crossroad NY.

One More Step. Ed. by Wilfred W. Su. (Curriculum Ser.). 110p. 1997. pap. 5.95 (*1-885216-15-7*) Evan Formosan.

One More Story: Contemporary Seneca Tales of the Supernatural. Duwayne Leslie Bowman. 1989. pap. 9.95 (*0-912678-78-X*) Greenfld Rev Lit.

*One More, This Time... Myungkark Park. (Illus.). 100p. 1999. pap. write for info. (*1-877974-37-4*) Prompter Pubns.

One More Time. Carol Burnett. 352p. 1987. mass mkt. 4.95 (*0-380-70449-8*, Avon Bks) Morrow Avon.

One More Time. Edward Orszula. Ed. by Chris Mystery Publishing Staff. 240p. 1999. pap. 12.95 (*0-7392-0298-7*, PO3418) Morris Pubng.

One More Time. Mike Royko. LC 98-46699. (Illus.). 295p. 1999. 22.00 (*0-226-73071-9*) U Ch Pr.

*One More Time: (Just for the Fun of It) Effie Leland Wilder. LC 99-46811. (Illus.). 192p. 1999. 14.95 (*1-56145-213-0*) Peachtree Pubs.

*One More Time: Just for the Fun of It! Notes from Fairacres. large type ed. Effie Leland Wilder. LC 99-462092. (Paperback Ser.). 160p. 2000. pap. 23.95 (*0-7838-8960-7*, G K Hall Lrg Type) Mac Lib Ref.

*One More Time: The Best of Mike Royko. Mike Royko. LC 98-46699. (Illus.). 304p. 1999. pap. 12.00 (*0-226-73072-7*) U Ch Pr.

*One More Time, Mama. Sue Alexander. LC 98-47937. (Illus.). 32p. (J). (ps-k). 1999. 15.95 (*0-7614-5051-3*, Cav Child Bks) Marshall Cavendish.

One More Try, a Story of Entrepreneurial Passion. Thomas A. Ryan. 288p. (Orig.). 1993. pap. write for info. (*0-9638573-3-9*) T A Ryan.

One More Valentine. Anne Stuart. (American Romance Ser.). 1993. per. 3.39 (*0-373-16473-4*, 1-16473-0) Harlequin Bks.

One More Yesterday. J. D. Richards. 230p. 1999. pap. 15.95 (*0-7414-0057-X*) Buy Books.

One Morning. Canna Funakoshi. LC 86-91538. (Illus.). 34p. (J). (ps-3). 1991. pap. 11.95 (*0-88708-033-2*, Picture Book Studio) S&S Childrens.

One Morning in Joseph's Garden: An Easter Story. Barbara Younger & Lisa Flinn. (Illus.). 24p. (J). (ps-3). 1998. 4.95 (*0-687-09550-6*) Abingdon.

One Morning in Maine. Robert McCloskey. (Illus.). (J). (gr. k-3). 1952. 17.99 (*0-670-52627-4*, Viking Child) Peng Put Young Read.

One Morning in Maine. Robert McCloskey. LC no-na6604. (Picture Puffin Ser.). (J). (ps-3). 1976. pap. 5.99 (*0-14-050174-6*, PuffinBks) Peng Put Young Read.

One Morning in Maine. Robert McCloskey. (Picture Puffin Ser.). (Illus.). (J). 1976. 10.19 (*0-606-04247-4*, Pub. by Turtleback) Demco.

*One Mother Wanted: Hope Valley Brides. Jeanne Allan. (Romance Ser.: No. 3576). 1999. per. 3.50 (*0-373-03576-4*, 1-03576-5) Harlequin Bks.

*One Mother Wanted: Hope Valley Brides. large type ed. Jeanne Allan. (Larger Print Ser.: No. 422). 1999. per. 3.50 (*0-373-15822-X*, 1-15822-9) Harlequin Bks.

One Must Wait. Penny Mickelbury. LC 97-29871. 256p. 1998. 21.50 (*0-684-83741-2*) S&S Trade.

One Must Wait. Penny Mickelbury. 304p. 1999. pap. 6.50 (*0-312-97186-9*, St Martins Paperbacks) St Martin.

*One Mykonos: Being Ancients, Being Islands, Being Giants, Being Gay. James Davidson. LC 00-29458. 160p. 2000. text 19.95 (*0-312-26214-0*) St Martin.

One Name but Several Faces: Variety in Popular Christian Denominations in Southeren History. Samuel S. Hill. LC 95-20994. 1996. 20.00 (*0-8203-1792-6*) U of Ga Pr.

One Nation. Capstoen Press Geography Department. 1999. 152.00 (*1-56065-813-4*) Capstone Pr.

One Nation. Capstone Press Geograhy Staff. 1999. 152.00 (*1-56065-658-1*) Capstone Pr.

One Nation. Capstone Press Geography Department Staff. 1999. 152.00 (*0-7368-0122-7*); 114.00 (*0-7368-0150-2*, Cpstone High Low) Capstone Pr.

One Nation?, 6 Vols. Capstone Press Geography Departure Staff. 1999. 114.00 (*1-56065-656-5*) Capstone Pr.

One Nation. Capstone Press Geography Staff. 1999. 152.00 (*1-56065-657-3*) Capstone Pr.

One Nation: An American Government Text with Readings. Capstone Press Geograhpy Department. 1999. 152.00 (*1-56065-812-6*) Capstone Pr.

*One Nation: Patriots & Pirates Portrayed by N. C. Wyeth & Jamie Wyeth. Illus. by N. C. Wyeth & James Wyeth. 128p. 2000. 40.00 (*0-8212-2700-9*) Bulfinch Pr.

*One Nation: Patriots & Pirates Portrayes by N. C. Wyeth & Jamie Wyeth. Jamie Wyeth. 2000. 29.95 (*0-8212-2707-6*, Pub. by Bulfinch Pr) Little.

One Nation, After All: What Middle-Class Americans Really Think about God, Country, Family, Racism, Welfare, Immigration, Homosexuality, Work, the Right, the Left & Each Other. Alan Wolfe. LC 97-36925. 358p. 1999. pap. 13.95 (*0-14-027572-X*) Penguin Putnam.

One Nation, After All: What Middle-Class Americans Really Think about God, Country, Family, Racism, Welfare, Immigration, Homosexuality, Work, the Right, the Left & Each Other. Alan Wolfe. LC 97-36925. 384p. 1998. 24.95 (*0-670-87677-1*) Viking Penguin.

One Nation Again: A Sourcebook on the Civil War. LC 92-16661. (Illus.). 96p. (J). (gr. 5-8). 1995. pap. 8.95 (*1-56294-883-0*) Millbrook Pr.

One Nation Again: A Sourcebook on the Civil War. C. Carter Smith. (American Albums from the Collections of the Library of Congress). 1993. 14.15 (*0-606-07974-2*) Turtleback.

One Nation Again: A Sourcebook on the Civil War. Ed. by Carter Smith. LC 92-16661. (American Albums from the Collections of the Library of Congress). (Illus.). 96p. (J). (gr. 5-8). 1993. lib. bdg. 25.90 (*1-56294-266-2*) Millbrook Pr.

One Nation Becomes Many: The ACCESS Guide to the Former Soviet Union. Ed. by Stephen W. Young et al. (Illus.). 126p. (Orig.). (C). 1992. pap. 17.95 (*1-878597-07-8*) Access Sec Info Serv.

One Nation Divisible: Class, Race & Ethnicity in the United States since 1938. Richard Polenberg. 1993. 25.25 (*0-8446-6676-9*) Peter Smith.

*One Nation Divisible? Ethnic Groups & American National Interests. Tony Smith. LC 00-27288. (Illus.). 224p. 2000. 35.00 (*0-674-00294-6*) HUP.

One Nation, Fifty States: Fifty Interdisciplinary Units Including Content-Based Lessons, Enrichment Projects, & Evaluation Activities. Imogene Forte. Ed. by Jan Keeling. (Illus.). 240p. (Orig.). (J). (gr. 4-7). 1993. pap. text 16.95 (*0-86530-242-1*, 242-1) Incentive Pubns.

*One Nation Indivisible. Sara S. Chapman & Ursula S. Colby. (C). 2001. pap. text. write for info. (*0-7914-4838-X*) State U NY Pr.

*One Nation Indivisible. Sara S. Chapman & Ursula S. Colby. (C). 2001. text. write for info. (*0-7914-4837-1*) State U NY Pr.

One Nation Indivisible: How Ethnic Separatism Threatens America. J. Harvie Wilkinson III. LC 96-39225. 304p. 1997. 24.00 (*0-201-18072-3*) Addison-Wesley.

One Nation, Indivisible: The Civil Rights Challenge for the 1990s. Ed. by Reginald C. Govan & William L. Taylor. LC 89-61199. 500p. (Orig.). (C). 1989. pap. 15.00 (*0-9622865-0-8*) CCCR.

One Nation Indivisible: The Union in American Thought, 1776 to 1861. Paul C. Nagel. LC 80-36682. 328p. 1980. reprint ed. lib. bdg. 35.00 (*0-313-22656-3*, NAON, Greenwood Pr) Greenwood.

One Nation, Many Peoples: Immigration in the United States. Julia Pferdehirt & Dave Schreiner. Ed. by Liza Diprima. (Illus.). 160p. 1997. teacher ed. 79.95 (*1-55933-200-X*, 4026GD) Know Unltd.

One Nation, Many Tribes. Kathleen Krull. (Illus.). 48p. 1999. pap. 5.99 (*0-14-036522-2*) Viking Penguin.

One Nation Series, 30 bks. Incl. Alabama. Capstone Press, Geography Department Staff. LC 97-7068. (Illus.). 48p. (J). (gr. 3-7). 1998. lib. bdg. 19.00 (*1-56065-499-6*, Cpstone High Low); Arizona. Capstone Press Staff. LC 96-23436. (Illus.). 48p. (J). (gr. 3-7). 1996. lib. bdg. 19.00 (*1-56065-440-6*, Cpstone High Low); California. Capstone Press Geography Department Staff. LC 95-45127. (Illus.). 48p. (J). (gr. 3-7). 1996. lib. bdg. 19.00 (*1-56065-354-X*, Cpstone High Low); Colorado. rev. ed. Capstone Press Geography Department Staff. LC 95-49351. (Illus.). 48p. (J). (gr. 3-7). 1996. lib. bdg. 19.00 (*1-56065-356-6*, Cpstone High Low); Connecticut. Ed. by Capstone Press Geography Department Staff. LC 96-46855. (Illus.). 48p. (J). (gr. 3-7). 1997. lib. bdg. 19.00 (*1-56065-472-4*, Cpstone High Low); Florida. rev. ed. Capstone Press Geography Department Staff. LC 95-46663. (Illus.). 48p. (J). (gr. 3-7). 1996. lib. bdg. 19.00 (*1-56065-357-4*, Cpstone High Low); Georgia. Capstone Press Staff. LC 96-35116. (Illus.). 48p. (J). (gr. 3-7). 1997. lib. bdg. 19.00 (*1-56065-473-2*, Cpstone High Low); Hawaii. Patricia K. Kummer. LC 97-7070. (Illus.). 48p. (J). (gr. 3-7). 1998. lib. bdg. 19.00 (*1-56065-525-9*, Cpstone High Low); Illinois. Capstone Press Geography Department Staff. LC 95-49307. (Illus.). 48p. (J). (gr. 3-7). 1996. lib. bdg. 19.00 (*1-56065-353-1*, Cpstone High Low); Indiana. Capstone Press Geography Department Staff. LC 96-46854. (Illus.). 48p. (J). (gr. 3-7). 1997. lib. bdg. 19.00 (*1-56065-474-0*, Cpstone High Low); Louisiana. Capstone Press Geography Department Staff. LC 96-23441. (Illus.). 48p. (J). (gr. 3-7). 1996. lib. bdg. 19.00 (*1-56065-442-2*, Cpstone High Low); Maine. Patricia K. Kummer. LC 97-6328. (Illus.). 48p. (J). (gr. 3-7). 1998. lib. bdg. 19.00 (*1-56065-526-7*, Cpstone High Low); Massachusetts. Capstone Press Geography Department Staff. LC 96-25567. (Illus.). 48p. (J). (gr. 3-7). 1996. lib. bdg. 19.00 (*1-56065-437-6*, Cpstone High Low); Michigan. Capstone Press Geography Department Staff. LC 96-23439. (Illus.). 48p. (J). (gr. 3-7). 1996. lib. bdg. 19.00 (*1-56065-436-8*, Cpstone High Low); Minnesota. Capstone Press Geography Department Staff. LC 96-46870. (Illus.). 48p. (J). (gr. 3-7). 1997. lib. bdg. 19.00 (*1-56065-500-3*, Cpstone High Low); Missouri. Patricia K. Kummer & Capstone Press Staff. LC 97-9497. (Illus.). 48p. (J). (gr. 3-7). 1998. lib. bdg. 19.00 (*1-56065-527-5*, Cpstone High Low); Montana. Patricia K. Kummer & Capstone Press Staff. LC 97-9496. (Illus.). 48p. (J). (gr. 3-7). 1998. lib. bdg. 19.00 (*1-56065-528-3*, Cpstone High Low); Nebraska. Capstone Press Geography Department Staff. LC 96-23440. (Illus.). 48p. (J). (gr. 3-7). 1996. lib. bdg. 19.00 (*1-56065-443-0*, Cpstone High Low); New Jersey. Patricia K. Kummer & Capstone Press Staff. LC 97-6330. (Illus.). 48p. (J). (gr. 3-7). 1998. lib. bdg. 19.00 (*1-56065-529-1*, Cpstone High Low); New Mexico. Patricia K. Kummer & Capstone Press Staff. LC 97-9056. (Illus.). 48p. (J). (gr. 3-7). 1998. lib. bdg. 19.00 (*1-56065-580-1*, Cpstone High Low); New York. Capstone Press Geography Department Staff. LC 95-49400. (Illus.). 48p. (J). (gr. 3-7). 1996. lib. bdg. 19.00 (*1-56065-352-3*, Cpstone High Low); North Carolina. Patricia K. Kummer & Capstone Press Staff. LC 97-7069. (Illus.). 48p. (J). (gr. 3-7). 1998. lib. bdg. 19.00 (*1-56065-530-5*, Cpstone High Low); Ohio. Capstone Press Geography Department Staff. LC 96-23437. (Illus.). 48p. (J). (gr. 3-7). 1996. lib. bdg. 19.00 (*1-56065-439-2*, Cpstone High Low); Oregon. Capstone Press Staff. LC 96-35115. (Illus.). 48p. (J). (gr. 3-7). 1997. lib. bdg. 19.00 (*1-56065-501-1*, Cpstone High Low); Pennsylvania. Capstone Press Geography Department Staff. LC 96-23442. (Illus.). 48p. (J). (gr. 3-7). 1996. lib. bdg. 19.00 (*1-56065-438-4*, Cpstone High Low); South Carolina. Capstone Press Staff. LC 96-35114. (Illus.). 48p. (J). (gr. 3-7). 1997. lib. bdg. 19.00 (*1-56065-502-X*, Cpstone High Low); Texas. rev. ed. Capstone Press Geography Department Staff. LC 95-49345. (Illus.). 48p. (J). (gr. 3-7). 1996. lib. bdg. 19.00 (*1-56065-355-8*, Cpstone High Low); Virginia. Capstone Press Staff. LC 96-35113. (Illus.). 48p. (J). (gr. 3-7). 1997. lib. bdg. 19.00 (*1-56065-503-8*, Cpstone High Low); Washington. Capstone Press Geography Department Staff. LC 96-23438. (Illus.). 48p. (J). (gr. 3-7). 1996. lib. bdg. 19.00 (*1-56065-441-4*, Cpstone High Low); Wisconsin. Capstone Press Geography Department Staff. LC 96-46846. (Illus.). 48p. (J). (gr. 3-7). 1997. lib. bdg. 19.00 (*1-56065-504-6*, Cpstone High Low); (J). 570.00 (*1-56065-655-7*, Cpstone High Low) Capstone Pr.

One Nation, Two Cultures. Gertrude Himmelfarb. LC 99-18922. 192p. 1999. 23.00 (*0-375-40455-4*) Knopf.

*One Nation, Two Cultures. Gertrude Himmelfarb. 2000. pap. write for info. (*0-375-70410-8*) Vin Bks.

One Nation under a Groove: History of Rap. James Haskins. LC 99-39765. 2000. lib. bdg. 16.49 (*0-7868-2414-X*, Pub. by Hyprn Child) Little.

One Nation under a Groove: Motown & American Culture. Gerald Early. 144p. 1995. 17.00 (*0-88001-379-6*) HarpC.

One Nation under a Groove: Motown & American Culture. Gerald Early. 144p. 1996. reprint ed. pap. 12.00 (*0-88001-472-5*) HarpC.

One Nation under God. Kenneth Copeland. 1996. 17.95 incl. VHS (*1-57562-128-2*) K Copeland Pubns.

One Nation under God? Bible Prophecy - When the American Experiment Fails. Clifford Goldstein. LC 95-26114. 1996. pap. 10.99 (*0-8163-1308-3*) Pacific Pr Pub Assn.

One Nation under God? Religion & American Culture. Marjorie B. Garber. LC 98-50482. (Culture Work Ser.). 1999. 75.00 (*0-415-92223-2*); pap. 19.99 (*0-415-92224-0*) Routledge.

One Nation under God: The Rise or Fall of a Nation. Bob Yandian. 126p. 1995. mass mkt. 5.99 (*0-88368-359-8*) Whitaker Hse.

One Nation under God: The Triumph of the Native American Church. Huston Smith & Reuben Snake. LC 95-33980. (Illus.). 176p. 1995. 24.95 (*0-940666-71-5*) Clear Light.

One Nation under God: The Triumph of the Native American Church. Huston Smith & Reuben Snake. LC 95-33980. (Illus.). 176p. 1997. pap. 14.95 (*1-57416-006-0*) Clear Light.

*One Nation under God Facilitator's Guide: Toward Race Reconciliation. Donna Saunders & Jean Leak. 59p. 1999. pap. 12.00 (*1-58119-033-6*) T P Min.

*One Nation under God Group Member's Guide: Toward Race Reconciliation. Donna Saunders & Jean Leak. 53p. 1999. pap. 10.00 (*1-58119-034-4*) T P Min.

One New Man. Reuven Doron. 193p. (Orig.). 1993. pap. 10.00 (*0-9629049-9-6*, RD1-103) Arrow Publications.

One New Man. Witness Lee. 77p. 1986. per. 5.00 (*0-87083-266-2*, 08-014-001) Living Stream Ministry.

One New People: Models for Developing a Multi-Ethnic Church. Manuel Ortiz. LC 96-18504. 150p. (Orig.). 1996. pap. 12.99 (*0-8308-1882-0*, 1882) InterVarsity.

One Night. Debbie Macomber. 336p. 1994. mass mkt. 6.50 (*0-06-108185-X*) HarpC.

*One Night. large type ed. Debbie Macomber. (G. K. Hall Romance Ser.). 2000. 28.95 (*0-7838-8972-0*, G K Hall Lrg Type) Mac Lib Ref.

One Night: A Story from the Desert. Cristina Kessler. (J). 1998. 11.19 (*0-606-13007-1*, Pub. by Turtleback) Demco.

One Night at a Time. Christa Conan. (Intimate Moments Ser.: No. 839). 1998. per. 4.25 (*0-373-07839-0*, 1-07839-3) Silhouette.

One Night Before Christmas. Catherine Leigh. (Romance Ser.: No. 3533). 1998. per. 3.50 (*0-373-03533-0*, 1-03533-6) Harlequin Bks.

One Night Before Christmas. large type ed. Catherine Leigh. (Larger Print Ser.: No. 379). 1998. per. 3.50 (*0-373-15779-7*, 1-15779-1) Harlequin Bks.

*One Night Enjoyed. Beth Andrews. 200p. 2000. 19.95 (*1-929085-32-X*); 17.95 (*1-929085-33-8*); mass mkt. 4.95 (*1-929085-31-1*) Rgncy Pr.

*One Night Enjoyed. large type ed. Beth Andrews. 336p. 2000. 23.95 (*1-929085-34-6*); pap. 19.95 (*1-929085-35-4*) Rgncy Pr.

One Night for Love. Mary Balogh. 384p. 1999. mass mkt. 6.50 (*0-440-22600-7*) Dell.

*One Night for Love. large type ed. Mary Balogh. LC 99-48206. 1999. 22.95 (*1-56895-795-5*, Wheeler) Wheeler Pub.

*One Night in Brazil. Isaac Bashevis Singer. 1999. lib. bdg. 24.95 (*1-56723-163-2*) Yestermorrow.

One Night in His Arms see Noche en Sus Brazos

One Night in His Arms. Penny Jordan. 1998. per. 3.75 (*0-373-12002-8*, 1-12002-1, Mira Bks) Harlequin Bks.

One Night in His Arms. large type ed. 1999. 21.95 (*0-263-15932-9*) Chivers N Amer.

One Night in Payne House. R. L. Stine, pseud. (Give Yourself Goosebumps Special Edition Ser.: No. 4). (J). (gr. 3-7). 1998. pap. 3.99 (*0-590-43378-4*, Pub. by Scholastic Inc) Penguin Putnam.

One Night of Love. Sally Wentworth. 1996. per. 3.50 (*0-373-11810-4*, 1-11810-8) Harlequin Bks.

One Night of Love. large type ed. Sally Wentworth & Patricia Wentworth. 288p. 1995. 23.99 (*0-263-14216-7*, Pub. by Mills & Boon) Ulverscroft.

One Night, One Hanukkah Night. Aidel Backman. (Illus.). 32p. (J). (ps-2). 1990. 9.95 (*0-8276-0368-1*) JPS Phila.

One Night Out Stealing. Alan Duff. LC 95-13244. (Talanoa Ser.). 192p. (Orig.). 1995. pap. 12.95 (*0-8248-1684-6*) UH Pr.

One-Night Stand. Sandra Field. (Presents Ser.). 1993. per. 2.99 (*0-373-11598-9*, 1-11598-9) Harlequin Bks.
One-Night Stand. large type ed. Sandra Field. (Harlequin Ser.). 1993. lib. bdg. 19.95 (*0-263-13352-4*, G K Hall Lrg Type) Mac Lib Ref.
One-Night Stand. large type ed. Sandra Field. 1994. 19.95 (*0-263-13904-2*) Thorndike Pr.
One Night Stand & Other Poems. Jack Spicer. Ed. by Donald Allen. LC 79-28053. 136p. 1980. pap. 4.95 (*0-912516-46-1*) Grey Fox.
One Night Stand Series, 1-1001, Vol. 44. Compiled by Harry Mackenzie & Lothar Polomski. LC 91-7317. (Discographies Ser.: No. 44). 448p. 1991. lib. bdg. 75.00 (*0-313-27729-X*, MKZ, Greenwood Pr) Greenwood.
One Night Stands. Rosa Liksom. (Masks Ser.). 128p. 1994. pap. 11.99 (*1-85242-292-0*) Serpents Tail.
One Night Stands: A Critic's View of British Theatre from 1971-1991. Michael Billington. 382p. 1994. pap. 15.95 (*0-435-08644-8*, 08644) Heinemann.
One Night Stands His. Richard Shenkman & Kurt E. Reiger. LC 79-21771. (Illus.). 1982. pap. 11.00 (*0-688-01399-6*, Quil) HarperTrade.
One Night Stood. Richard Kostelanetz. LC 77-81597. 1977. 10.00 (*0-918406-13-7*); pap. 2.50 (*0-918406-04-8*) Future Pr.
One Night Stood. deluxe ed. Richard Kostelanetz. LC 77-81597. 1977. 50.00 (*0-918406-14-5*) Future Pr.
One Night Stood: Newsprint Edition. Richard Kostelanetz. LC 77-87142. 1977. pap. 1.00 (*0-918406-03-X*) Future Pr.
One Night Stood: Newsprint Edition. deluxe ed. Richard Kostelanetz. LC 77-87142. 1977. 25.00 (*0-918406-06-4*) Future Pr.
One Night Wife. Day Leclaire. 1995. per. 2.99 (*0-373-03376-1*) Harlequin Bks.
One Night with His Wife. Lynne Graham. (Presents Ser.: Bk. 2073). 187p. 2000. per. 3.75 (*0-373-12073-7*, 1-12073-2) Harlequin Bks.
One Nil. Tony Bradman. 80p. (YA). (gr. 6-9). 1984. pap. 7.95 (*0-14-031983-2*, Pub. by Pnguin Bks Ltd) Trafalgar.
1-900 Psychic Speaks. Donna Kenworthy. LC 98-71596. 112p. 1998. pap. 11.95 (*1-57174-113-5*) Hampton Roads Pub Co.
1-900-Sorcery. Mark Hitchcock. 30p. (Orig.). 1993. pap. 2.95 (*1-879366-34-7*) Hearthstone OK.
One Norse Town: The Case of the Suspicious Scrolls. Justin Warner. LC 97-209965. (Kinetic City Super Crew Ser.: No. 3). (Illus.). 192p. (J). (gr. 3-5). 1998. pap. 4.25 (*0-07-006387-7*, Lrning Triangle) McGraw.
One Nurse's Notes: A Personal Journal. Ed. by Creative Nursing Management Staff. 78p. (Orig.). 1988. pap. 5.00 (*0-9621520-6-4*) Creative Nursing.
101 Grouchland Surprises. Shana Corey. 1999. 5.99 (*0-375-80137-5*, Pub. by Random Bks Yng Read) Random.
One Oar in the Brazos. John Young. 215p. Date not set. 12.95 (*0-9649847-0-9*); pap. 8.95 (*0-9649847-1-7*) Waco Tribune-Herald.
One October Night. Pam Jarrell. (HRL Little Bks.). 8p. (J). (ps-k). 1995. pap. text 10.95 (*1-57332-015-3*) HighReach Lrning.
One October Night. Pam Jarrell. (HRL Big Bks.). (Illus.). 8p. (J). (ps-k). 1995. pap. text 10.95 (*1-57332-016-1*) HighReach Lrning.
One Odd Old Owl. Paul Adshead. 28p. (J). (ps-11). 1995. 13.99 (*0-85953-407-3*); pap. 7.99 (*0-85953-408-1*) Childs Play.
One Odd Old Owl. Paul Adshead. (J). 1996. lib. bdg. 16.95 (*0-85953-886-9*) Childs Play.
One of a Kind. Bette Ford. 1998. mass mkt. 4.99 (*0-7860-0619-6*, Pinncle Kensgtn) Kensgtn Pub Corp.
One of a Kind. 7th ed. 436p. 1997. reprint ed. spiral bd. 14.95 (*0-9603054-2-4*) Mobile Jr League Pubns.
One of a Kind: Making the Most of Your Child's Uniqueness. rev. ed. LaVonne Neff. Ed. by Liz Heaney. LC 93-40255. 147p. (Orig.). 1995. pap. 14.00 (*0-935652-20-5*) Ctr Applications Psych.
One of a Kind: Sticker Studies. Paula Rinehart. (Sticker Studies: No. 2). (Illus.). 64p. (Orig.). (J). (gr. 3-7). 1996. pap. 4.99 (*1-57673-007-7*, Gold n Honey) Zondervan.
One-of-a-Kind Mallie. Kim Brubaker Bradley. LC 98-51131. 160p. (J). (gr. 2-7). 1999. 15.95 (*0-385-32694-7*) BDD Bks Young Read.
***One-of-a-Kind Mallie.** Felice Holman. (J). 2000. pap. 4.50 (*0-440-41623-X*, YB BDD) BDD Bks Young Read.
One-of-a-Kind Research Aircraft: A History of In-Flight Simulators, Testbeds & Prototypes. LC 95-67628. (Illus.). 176p. 1995. 45.00 (*0-88740-797-8*) Schiffer.
One of a Kind (the Many Faces & Voices of America) Harry Barba. LC 75-41743. 1976. pap. 9.95 (*0-911906-11-8*) Harian Creative Bks.
One-of-a-Kind Yanky: And Other Stories. Pia Wolcowitz. Ed. by D. L. Rosenfeld. LC 97-74051. (Fun to Read Bks.). (Illus.). 112p. (J). (gr. 2-5). 1997. pap. 6.95 (*0-922613-85-0*) Hachai Pubng.
One of Cleopatra's Nights. Lafcadio Hearn. (Notable American Authors Ser.). 1992. reprint ed. lib. bdg. 75.00 (*0-7812-3067-5*) Rprt Serv.
***One of Custer's Wolverines: The Civil War Letters of Brevet Brigadier General James H. Kidd, 6th Michigan Cavalry.** James Harvey Kidd & Eric J. Wittenberg. LC 00-35635. (Illus.). 2000. write for info. (*0-87338-670-1*) Kent St U Pr.
One of Each. Mary A. Hoberman. LC 96-34831. (Illus.). 32p. (J). (gr. k-3). 1997. 15.95 (*0-316-36731-1*) Little.
***One of Each.** Mary Ann Hoberman. (Illus.). 32p. (J). (ps-3). 2000. pap. 5.95 (*0-316-36644-7*) Little.
One of Fannin's Men. Isabel R. Marvin. LC 97-11719. (Illus.). 104p. (YA). (gr. 4 up). 1997. 15.95 (*1-885777-06-X*); pap. 8.95 (*1-885777-19-1*) Hendrick-Long.
One of God's Children: In the Toe River Valley. Robert B. Phillips. LC 83-70886. (Illus.). 176p. (YA). (gr. 9-12). 1983. 7.00 (*0-9620577-0-3*) R B Phillips Pub.
One of Jackson's Foot Cavalry. John H. Worsham. Ed. by Bell I. Wiley. (Illus.). 215p. 1991. reprint ed. 30.00 (*0-916107-96-5*) Broadfoot.
One of Lee's Best Men: The Civil War Letters of General William Dorsey Pender. Ed. by William W. Hassler. LC 99-12073. (Illus.). 304p. 1999. pap. 16.95 (*0-8078-4823-9*) U of NC Pr.
***One of Many.** Brenda Hodge. 80p. 2000. pap. 16.95 (*1-86368-287-2*, Pub. by Fremantle Arts) Intl Spec Bk.
One of My Totem Poles Is Missing! George E. Weldon. (Illus.). 92p. (Orig.). 1989. pap. 9.95 (*0-943487-20-X*) Sevgo Pr.
One of Our Bombers Is Missing. large type ed. Dan Brennan. (Magna Large Print Ser.). 336p. 1998. 29.99 (*0-7505-1217-2*, Pub. by Mgna Lrg Print) Ulverscroft.
One of Our Conquerors see Works of George Meredith
***One of Our Own.** Diane Salvatore. LC 98-48244. 256p. 1999. pap. 11.95 (*1-56280-243-7*) Naiad Pr.
One of Our Own: (That Special Woman!) Cheryl Reavis. (Special Edition Ser.). 1994. per. 3.50 (*0-373-09901-0*, 1-09901-9) Harlequin Bks.
One of Our Submarines. Darryl Young. (Wordsworth Collection). 352p. 1998. pap. 11.95 (*1-85326-681-7*, Pub. by Wrdsworth Edits) Combined Pub.
One of Ours. Willa Cather. LC 91-50236. (Vintage Classics Ser.). 391p. 1991. pap. 13.00 (*0-679-73744-8*) Vin Bks.
One of Ours. Willa Cather. (Collected Works of Willa Cather). 459p. 1998. reprint ed. lib. bdg. 108.00 (*1-58201-573-2*) Classic Bks.
One of Ours: Timothy McVeigh & the Oklahoma City Bombing. Richard A. Serrano. LC 98-9479. (Illus.). 288p. 1998. 26.95 (*0-393-02743-0*) Norton.
One of the Ancients: The Life & Struggles of a Russian Man of Prayer: Elder Gabriel of Pskov & Kazan. Simeon Kholmogorov. Ed. & Tr. by St. Herman of Alaska Brotherhood Staff from RUS. LC 88-61677. (Acquisition of the Holy Spirit in Russia Ser.). (Illus.). 192p. (Orig.). 1988. pap. 10.00 (*0-938635-27-1*) St Herman Pr.
One of the Boys. Janet Dailey. (Janet Dailey Americana Ser.: No. 880). 1992. per. 3.59 (*0-373-89880-0*, 1-89880-8) Harlequin Bks.
***One of the Boys.** Janet Dailey. LC 00-33500. 2001. write for info. (*0-7838-9119-9*, G K Hall & Co) Mac Lib Ref.
***One of the Boys: Masculinity, Homophobia & Modern Manhood.** David Plummer. LC 99-34431. 364p. (C). 1999. 49.95 (*1-56023-973-5*, Harrington Park); pap. text 24.95 (*1-56023-974-3*, Harrington Park) Haworth Pr.
One of the Children: Gay Black Men in Harlem. William G. Hawkeswood. Ed. by Alex W. Costley. (Men & Masculinity Ser.: Vol. 2). 240p. 1995. 45.00 (*0-520-08112-9*, Pub. by U CA Pr); pap. 16.95 (*0-520-20212-0*, Pub. by U CA Pr) Cal Prin Full Svc.
One of the D-Day Dodgers. Hamilton Tyler. 102p. (C). 1988. pap. 35.00 (*0-7212-0722-7*, Pub. by Regency Pr GBR) St Mut.
***One of the Family.** Susan Floyd. (Superromance Ser.: No. 890). 2000. per. 4.50 (*0-373-70890-4*, 1-70890-8, Harlequin) Harlequin Bks.
***One of the Family.** large type ed. Meredith Webber. 288p. 1999. 25.99 (*0-263-16148-X*, Pub. by Mills & Boon) Ulverscroft.
One of the Family: Telling the Story of a Violent Childhood & the Healing Beyond Pearlie McNeill. LC 90-139767. xii, 268 p. 1990. pap. write for info. (*0-7022-2301-8*, Pub. by Univ Queensland Pr) Intl Spec Bk.
One of the Few: Toward Christian Womanhood. Donna R. Fisher. (Illus.). 77p. (YA). (gr. 9-12). 1995. pap. 6.95 (*0-913717-74-6*, 2167) Hewitt Res Fnd.
***One of the Forgotten Things: Getulio Vargas & Brazilian Social Control, 1930-1954.** R. S. Rose. LC 99-88457. (Contributions in Latin American Studies: Vol. 15). 272p. 2000. 59.95 (*0-313-31358-X*, GM1358, Greenwood Pr) Greenwood.
One of the Gang see Gran Luchadora
One of the Gang. Created by Francine Pascal. (Sweet Valley Twins Ser.: No. 10). 112p. (J). (gr. 3-7). 1987. pap. 3.50 (*0-553-15677-2*) Bantam.
One of the Gang. Jamie Suzanne. (Sweet Valley Twins Ser.: No. 10). (J). (gr. 3-7). 1987. 8.60 (*0-606-03167-7*, Pub. by Turtleback) Demco.
***One of the Good Guys.** Carla Cassidy. 2000. mass mkt. 4.50 (*0-373-82223-5*, 1-82223-8) Harlequin Bks.
One of the Good Guys. Carla Cassidy. (Intimate Moments Ser.). 1993. per. 3.50 (*0-373-07531-6*, 5-07531-2) Silhouette.
One of the Guise. Michael Ramel. 1998. pap. write for info. (*1-57553-781-8*) Watermrk Pr.
One Of The Guys: A Novel. Robert Young. 288p. 2000. pap. 13.00 (*0-06-093189-2*) HarpC.
One of the Guys: A Novel. Robert Clark Young. LC 98-52923. 320p. 1999. 24.00 (*0-06-019365-4*) HarpC.
One of the Many Roses. Gary E. McCormick. 80p. (Orig.). 1991. pap. 9.50 (*0-9630037-0-4*) GEM MI.
One of the Most Beautiful Chapels in the Land. Luc Noppen. (Illus.). 52p. 1988. pap. 16.95 (*0-88884-576-6*, Pub. by Natl Gallery) U Ch Pr.
One of the Most Daring of Men: The Life of Confederate General William T. Wofford. Gerald Smith. (Journal of Confederate History Book Ser.: Vol. 16). (Illus.). 250p. (Orig.). 1997. pap. 16.95 (*1-889332-06-2*) So Herit Pr.
One of the Most Daring of Men: The Life of Confederate General William T. Wofford. Gerald J. Smith. 1997. pap. 16.95 (*1-889332-03-8*) Stackpole.
One of the Presidents' Men: Twenty Years with Eisenhower & Nixon. Maurice H. Stans. 312p. 1995. 25.95 (*1-57488-032-2*) Brasseys.
***One of the Problems of Everett Anderson.** Clifton. 2001. text 15.95 (*0-8050-5201-1*) St Martin.
One of the Third Grade Thinkers. Phyllis Reynolds Naylor. LC 88-3130. (Illus.). 144p. (J). (gr. 3-7). 1988. 15.00 (*0-689-31424-8*) Atheneum Yung Read.
One of the Third Grade Thinkers. Phyllis Reynolds Naylor. LC 88-3130. 144p. (J). (gr. 4-7). 1991. pap. 4.50 (*0-440-40407-X*) Dell.
One of the Third Grade Thinkers. Phyllis Reynolds Naylor. (J). 1988. 8.60 (*0-606-04763-8*, Pub. by Turtleback) Demco.
One of Them. Norene Pavlik. LC 88-61212. (Illus.). 263p. 1988. pap. 8.95 (*0-87973-420-5*, 420) Our Sunday Visitor.
One of These Days, We'll Have to Get Organized: If I Should Die Before I Wake. Donald Upp. LC 92-90627. 64p. 1994. pap. 19.95 (*0-9643499-0-6*) Jadlu Pr.
***One of These Mornings.** Betty Bernard. 224p. 1999. pap. 13.95 (*0-88739-275-X*) Creat Arts Bk.
One of Those Coincidences, & Ten Other Stories. Julian Hawthorne et al. LC 71-116953. (Short Story Index Reprint Ser.). 1977. 24.95 (*0-8369-3456-3*) Ayer.
One of Those Days. Pat Thomson. (J). (gr. k-6). 1987. pap. 2.50 (*0-440-46646-6*, YB BDD) BDD Bks Young Read.
One of Those Who Said "Yes" The Story of a Call. Mariarosa Guerrini. (Illus.). 128p. (C). 1996. pap. 39.95 (*0-85439-257-2*, Pub. by St Paul Pubns) St Mut.
One of Three. Angela Johnson. LC 90-29316. (Illus.). 32p. (J). (ps-1). 1991. 15.95 (*0-531-05955-3*) Orchard Bks Watts.
One of Three. Angela Johnson. LC 90-29316. (Illus.). 32p. (J). (ps-1). 1995. pap. text 5.95 (*0-531-07061-1*) Orchard Bks Watts.
One of Three. Angela Johnson. LC 90-29316. (J). 1995. 11.15 (*0-606-09716-3*, Pub. by Turtleback) Demco.
One of Two see Una de Dos
One of Uncle Billy's Boys: The Civil War Diaries of Cephas B. Hunt. Cephas B. Hunt. LC 93-77126. 192p. 1993. 18.95 (*1-882959-56-6*); per. 12.95 (*1-882959-52-3*) Foxglove TN.
One of Us. Gabrielle Charbonnet. LC 97-80295. (Disney Girls Ser.). 96p. (J). (gr. 2-5). 1998. pap. 3.95 (*0-7868-4156-7*, Pub. by Disney Pr) Time Warner.
One of Us. David Freeman. LC 97-17246. 224p. 1997. 23.00 (*0-7867-0490-X*) Carroll & Graf.
One of Us. David Freeman. LC 98-30513. 288p. 1998. pap. 11.95 (*0-7867-0591-4*) Carroll & Graf.
One of Us, 1. Michael Smith. 368p. 1999. mass mkt. 6.50 (*0-553-58069-8*) Bantam.
One of Us: The Mastery of Joseph Conrad. Geoffrey G. Harpham. LC 96-24571. 192p. 1996. pap. text 14.95 (*0-226-31696-3*) U Ch Pr.
One of Us: The Mastery of Joseph Conrad. Geoffrey G. Harpham. LC 96-24571. 192p. 1999. lib. bdg. 35.00 (*0-226-31695-5*) U Ch Pr.
One of Us Is Lying. Pat Wendorf. 384p. 1997. mass mkt. 10.95 (*0-340-67172-6*, Pub. by Hodder & Stought Ltd) Trafalgar.
101 Divine Healing Facts. T. L. Osborn. 32p. 1983. pap. 1.00 (*0-89274-299-2*, HH-299) Harrison Hse.
One on a Web: Counting Animals at Home. Ginger Wadsworth. LC 96-35946. (Illus.). 32p. (J). (ps-3). 1997. 15.95 (*0-88106-971-X*); pap. 6.95 (*0-88106-973-6*) Charlesbridge Pub.
One on a Web: Counting Animals at Home. Ginger Wadsworth. 1997. 12.15 (*0-606-13681-9*, Pub. by Turtleback) Demco.
One on One. Hank Herman. (Super Hoops Ser.: No. 5). (Illus.). 96p. (J). (gr. 4-6). 1996. pap. 3.50 (*0-553-48277-7*, Skylark BDD) BDD Bks Young Read.
One on One. Hank Herman. (Super Hoops Ser.: No. 5). (J). (gr. 4-6). 1996. 8.60 (*0-606-09916-6*, Pub. by Turtleback) Demco.
One-on-One. Terry Page. (Illus.). 24p. (J). (gr. 2-6). 1996. pap. text 4.00 (*1-887864-56-3*); lib. bdg. 7.00 (*1-887864-12-1*) Boo Bks.
***One on One: A Guide for Establishing Mentor Programs.** Frwd. by Lauro Cavazos. (Illus.). 56p. (C). 2000. reprint ed. pap. text 20.00 (*0-7881-8211-0*) DIANE Pub.
One on One: Conversations with the Shapers of Family Therapy. Richard Simon. LC 91-43238. 192p. 1992. pap. text 16.95 (*0-89862-269-7*) Guilford Pubns.
One on One: Making the Most of Your Mentoring Relationship. Steve Ropp. Ed. by Susan E. Janzen. LC 93-71182. 90p. (Orig.). 1993. pap., spiral bd. 15.95 (*0-87303-206-3*) Faith & Life.
One on One: Poems. Jack Myers. LC 98-74999. v, 90p. 1999. pap. 14.95 (*0-9669419-0-X*) Autumn Hse Pr.
One on One: The Best Men's Monologues for the Nineties. Ed. by Jack Temchin. LC 93-6789. (Acting Ser.). 1992. pap. 7.95 (*1-55783-151-3*) Applause Theatre Bk Pubs.
One on One: The Best Women's Monologues for the Nineties. Ed. by Jack Temchin. LC 93-6790. (Acting Ser.). 1992. pap. 7.95 (*1-55783-152-1*) Applause Theatre Bk Pubs.
One on One: The Imprint Interviews. Ed. by Leanna Crouch. (Illus.). 219p. 1998. pap. text 13.00 (*0-7881-5937-2*) DIANE Pub.
One on One: The Imprint Interviews. Leanna Crouch. (Illus.). 224p. (Orig.). pap. 19.95 (*1-895897-19-X*) Somerville Hse.
One on One: The Secrets of Professional Sales Closing. Ian Seymour. LC 94-8520. (Illus.). 272p. 1996. text 18.95 (*1-56554-213-4*) Pelican.
One-on-One: Where the Real Work in Teamwork Gets Done. Dartnell Editors. (High Performance Teams Ser.). 171p. 1995. pap. 14.95 (*0-85013-235-5*) Dartnell Corp.
One-on-One - Step-by-Step: A Supervisor's Guide to Training in the Workplace. John J. Connor. LC 89-110011. 128p. (Orig.). 1988. pap. 19.95 (*0-945820-03-8*) Harris & Connor.
One-on-One Coloring Book. Terry Page. (Illus.). 32p. (J). (ps-5). 1996. pap. 3.00 (*1-887864-13-X*) Boo Bks.
One-on-One Control: Safe Street Tactics for Law Enforcement. Steven Jimerfield & Timothy Schoenberg. Ed. by Raymond L. Powis. (Illus.). 112p. 1998. pap. text 27.00 (*1-888647-04-3*) Ray & Roo Enter.
***One-on-One Training: How to Effectively Train One Person at a Time.** Dave Arch et al. LC 99-6639. 141p. 2000. 24.95 (*0-7879-5143-9*, Pfiffr & Co) Jossey-Bass.
***One on One with God.** Zondervan Bible Publishers Staff. 28p. (C). 1999. 39.95 (*0-9674725-0-4*) Ortriz.
One One Coco: 509 Jamaican Sayings. (Illus.). 64p. (Orig.). 1996. mass mkt. 6.99 (*1-885778-24-4*, OOC) Seaburn.
1, 1, 1-Trichloroethane. (Environmental Health Criteria Ser.: No. 136). (ENG, FRE & SPA.). 117p. 1992. pap. text 28.00 (*92-4-157136-5*, 1160136) World Health.
One or Two for Christmas see Traditional Christmas Carols: For Piano Solo or Duet
One or Two Love Poems from the White World. Stephen Rodefer. 1976. pap. 2.50 (*0-685-79190-4*) Duende.
***One or Two Things I Remember about Her.** Bernard M. Paeen. 89p. 1999. pap. 10.95 (*0-7414-0007-3*) Buy Books.
One Orleans. Jesse Freeman. 40p. 1999. pap. 8.00 (*1-886094-99-3*) Chicago Spectrum.
One Out of Six: New York Region's New Immigrants. Nancy Foner. (C). (gr. 13). 1999. 55.00 (*0-415-91169-9*) Routledge.
One Out of Ten. Ciwa Griffiths. 270p. 1993. lib. bdg. 12.95 (*0-9630709-5-9*) Wide Range.
One Out of Three: Children Without Health Insurance, 1995-1996. Cynthia Costello & Cheryl Fish-Parcham. (Illus.). 41p. 1998. pap. text 20.00 (*0-7881-7057-0*) DIANE Pub.
One Paddle, Two Paddle: Hawaiian Teen Age Mystery & Suspense Stories. Miriam E. Rappolt. Ed. by Jane W. Pultz. LC 82-24048. (Illus.). 190p. (YA). (gr. 7-12). 1993. pap. 10.95 (*0-916630-69-2*) Pr Pacifica.
One Page Business Plan: Start with a Vision, Build a Company! James T. Horan, Jr. Ed. by Rebecca S. Shaw. LC 97-92653. (Illus.). 98p. 1998. pap. 19.95 (*1-891315-07-2*) One Page Business.
***One Page Financial Statement.** Business Resources, Inc. Staff. 180p. 1999. pap. 15.95 (*1-880394-94-4*) Thomson Learn.
One Page Management. rev. ed. Riaz Khadem & Robert Lorber. LC 97-36685. (Illus.). 160p. 1998. pap. 9.95 (*0-688-15786-6*, Wm Morrow) Morrow Avon.
***1 Page Proposal.** Patrick Riley. 2000. 14.95 (*0-06-039375-0*); pap. 12.00 (*0-06-098860-6*) HarpC.
One Page Strategy Sheet. Curtis E. Sahakian. 12p. 1997. pap. text 39.95 (*1-891765-04-3*) Corp Prtnrg Inst.
One Pair of Boots: A Journey from Georgia to Maine on the Appalachian Trail. Hunter Irvine. 434p. 1999. pap. 17.50 (*1-928590-02-0*) Golden Stone CO.
One Pair of Hands. Monica Dickens. 310p. Date not set. 24.95 (*0-8488-2667-1*) Amereon Ltd.
One Pair of Hands. large type ed. Monica Dickens. LC 94-21544. 361p. 1994. lib. bdg. 17.95 (*0-7862-0249-1*) Thorndike Pr.
One Pair of Hands. Monica Dickens. 220p. 1998. reprint ed. pap. 14.00 (*0-89733-304-7*) Academy Chi Pubs.
One Pale, Fawn Glove. Linda Shaw. 1994. per. 3.59 (*0-373-45167-9*) Silhouette.
***One Palestine Complete.** Tom Segev. 2000. pap. text. write for info. (*0-8050-6587-3*) St Martin.
One Palestine, Complete: Jews & Arabs under the British Mandate. Tom Segev. (Illus.). 592p. 2000. 35.00 (*0-8050-4848-0*, Metropol Bks) H Holt & Co.
One Pan Gourmet. rev. ed. Robert Irwin. 176p. 1991. pap. 12.95 (*0-07-032304-6*) McGraw.
One-Pan Gourmet: Fresh Food on the Trail. Don Jacobson. 176p. 1993. pap. 12.95 (*0-07-032123-X*) McGraw.
One Pan Gourmet: Fresh Food on the Trail. Don Jacobson. LC 93-20071. (Illus.). 192p. 1993. pap. 12.95 (*0-87742-396-2*, Ragged Mntain) McGraw-Hill Prof.
One Pan Gourmet Cooks Lite: A Low-Fat Guide to Outdoor Cooking. Don Jacobson & Don Mauer. 144p. 1996. pap. 11.95 (*1-57034-033-1*) Globe Pequot.
1 Pap Short Hist WW. James L. Stokesbury. LC 80-22207. (Illus.). 352p. 1981. pap. 14.00 (*0-688-00129-7*, Quil) HarperTrade.
One-Parameter Semigroups for Linear Evolution Equations. K. J. Engel & R. Nagel. LC 99-15366. (Graduate Texts in Mathematics Ser.: Vol. 194). 500p. 1999. 49.95 (*0-387-98463-1*) Spr-Verlag.
One Parameter Semigroups of Positive Operators. Ed. by R. Nagel. (Lecture Notes in Mathematics Ser.: Vol. 1184). x, 460p. 1986. 57.30 (*0-387-16454-5*) Spr-Verlag.
One Parent - One Language: An Interactional Approach. Susanne Dopke. (Studies in Bilingualism: No. 3). xviii, 213p. 1992. 59.00 (*1-55619-346-7*) J Benjamins Pubng Co.
One Parent - One Language: An Interactional Approach. Susanne Dopke. LC 92-26142. (Studies in Bilingualism: No. 3). xviii, 213p. 1992. pap. 24.95 (*1-55619-535-4*) J Benjamins Pubng Co.
One-Parent Children: The Growing Minority a Research Guide. Mary N. Gouke & Arline M. Rollins. LC 84-48876. (Reference Books on Family Issues: Vol. 14). 506p. 1990. text 65.00 (*0-8240-8576-0*, SS344) Garland.
One-Parent Families: Healing the Hurts. Howard I. Smith. 104p. 1985. pap. 6.99 (*0-8341-0724-4*) Beacon Hill.
One-Parent Family in the 1980s: Perspectives & Annotated Bibliography. 5th ed. Benjamin Schlesinger. 284p. 1985. pap. 20.95 (*0-8020-6565-1*) U of Toronto Pr.
***One Parent Plus Kids: Children's Curriculum.** Theresa McKenna. 144p. 1999. pap. 14.95 (*1-57921-241-7*) WinePress Pub.

***One Parent Plus Kids: Leadership Manual.** Diana McKenna. 128p. 1999. pap. 15.95 (*1-57921-240-9*) WinePress Pub.

***One Parent Plus Kids: Parent's Workbook.** Theresa McKenna. Ed. by Lucy Nylander. 80p. 1999. pap., wbk. ed. 11.95 (*1-57921-242-5*) WinePress Pub.

One Particular Harbor. Janet L. James. LC 93-33479. 288p. (Orig.). 1994. pap. 13.95 (*1-879360-30-6*) Noble Pr.

One Patch. Karen C. Soltys. LC 95-18466. (Classic American Quilt Collection). (Illus.). 128p. 1995. text 19.95 (*0-87596-684-5*) Rodale Pr Inc.

One Patch & Beyond: A Study in Quilt Making - Shapes, How-To, Lots of Samples. Betty Boyink. (Illus.). 72p. 1997. pap. 14.95 (*0-925623-07-5*) B Boyink.

One Patriot's Saga. James A. Mehring. LC 95-69830. (Illus.). 177p. 1997. 24.95 (*1-57197-039-8*) Pentland Pr.

One Peace. Illus. by Ronda Johnson-Freeman. 49p. Date not set. write for info. (*0-9651384-0-2*) Piper Rain.

***One People.** Guy Kennaway. 2000. pap. 12.95 (*0-86241-829-1*, Pub. by Canongate Books) Interlink Pub.

One People: A Study in Comparative Judaism. Abraham Segal. Ed. by Bernard M. Zlotowitz. 160p. (Orig.). (J). (gr. 7-9). 1983. pap. text 8.95 (*0-8074-0169-2*, 140025) UAHC.

One People: The Ancient Glory of the Black Race. T. Greer. 50p. 1991. pap. 9.95 (*0-9630951-1-0*) Karnak Co.

One People? Tradition, Modernity, & Jewish Unity. Jonathan Sacks. LC 92-38145. (Littman Library of Jewish Civilization). 272p. 1993. 45.00 (*1-874774-00-5*) Intl Spec Bk.

One People? Tradition, Modernity, & Jewish Unity. Jonathan Sacks. LC 92-38145. (Littman Library of Jewish Civilization). 272p. 1993. pap. 19.95 (*1-874774-01-3*) Intl Spec Bk.

One People, One Destiny: The Caribbean & Central America Today. Ed. by Don Rojas. LC 88-62937. 115p. (Orig.). 1988. pap. 11.95 (*0-87348-535-1*); lib. bdg. 35.00 (*0-87348-536-X*) Pathfinder NY.

One People, One Planet: Adventures of a World Citizen. Andre Brugiroux. 288p. (Orig.). 1994. pap. 13.95 (*1-85168-029-2*, Pub. by Onewrld Pubns) Penguin Putnam.

One Percent. Photos by Michael H. Upright. (Optic Nerve Ser.). (Illus.). 88p. 1999. 29.95 (*1-888045-09-4*) Action Publng.

1, Connecting the Community. unabridged ed. Jack Francis & Jacques Bouvier. Ed. by Jerry Cain. LC 98-90957. (Illus.). 64p. 1998. pap. 6.95 (*0-9668900-0-0*) Seat Pants Vis.

One Percent Inspiration, 99 Desperation. Mark Patinkin. 192p. 1996. 19.95 (*0-924771-63-1*, Covered Brdge Pr) Douglas Charles Ltd.

One Patch, Two Patch, Three Patch, Four: A Guide to Making Professional-looking Patchwork Quilts. Carma Beus. LC 83-81177. 52p. 1983. pap. 9.98 (*0-88290-224-5*) Horizon Utah.

One Percent Solution: How to Save Money Without Really Trying. Richard J. Curtis. LC 88-11845. (Illus.). 53p. (Orig.). 1988. pap. 8.95 (*0-945298-04-8*) Curtis Pubns.

One Percent Solution: Leadership Through Action. Bijan Afkami. 1998. pap. 13.95 (*0-9664425-0-4*) SynEM Pr.

One Perfect Knight. Judith Obrien. 380p. 1998. per. 6.50 (*0-671-00040-3*) S&S Trade.

One Perfect Rose. Mary Jo Putney. LC 98-96114. 421p. 1998. mass mkt. 5.99 (*0-449-00018-4*, Crest) Fawcett.

One Perfect Rose. Emilie Richards. (Special Edition Ser.: No. 750). 1992. per. 3.39 (*0-373-09750-6*, 5-09750-6) Harlequin Bks.

One Perfect Rose. large type ed. Mary Jo Putney. LC 97-29620. (Large Print Book Ser.). 1997. 24.95 (*1-56895-476-X*) Wheeler Pub.

One Person & Another. Richard Stern. LC 93-70997. 425p. 1993. 24.00 (*1-880909-06-5*) Baskerville.

One Person Can Make a Difference! Choosing Success. John Haase & H. C. Wolford. (Illus.). 256p. 1998. pap. 19.95 (*0-9654563-3-1*, Haase Hse) Easy Money Pr.

One-Person Development Office. Anita Stangl. LC 90-163685. vii, 43p. 1990. 8.00 (*1-55833-046-1*) Natl Cath Educ.

One-Person Puppet Plays. Denise A. Wright. (Illus.). xiii, 236p. 1990. pap. text 21.50 (*0-87287-742-6*) Teacher Ideas Pr.

One-Person Puppets: A Guide to Writing, Producing & Surviving the One-Person Puppet-Play. Lucy M. Lazenby. 65p. (Orig.). 1996. pap. 12.00 (*0-9648744-0-7*) Southshore Pr.

One Person Shows: Twenty Monologues by Bible Characters. pap. 8.99 (*0-8341-9787-1*) Nazarene.

One Pet Too Many. Gabrielle Charbonnet. LC 98-84793. (Disney Girls Ser.). (J). (gr. 2-5). 1998. pap. 3.95 (*0-7868-4166-4*, Pub. by Disney Pr) Time Warner.

***1 Peter: Standing Strong.** Bill Hybels. 96p. 1999. pap. 6.99 (*0-310-22773-9*) Zondervan.

One-Piece Flow: Cell Design for Transforming the Production Process. Kenichi Sekine. Tr. by Bruce Talbot from JPN. (Illus.). 308p. 1992. 75.00 (*0-915299-33-X*) Productivity Inc.

One Pilot's Log: The Career of E. L. "Slonnie" Sloniger. Jerrold Sloniger. (Illus.). 176p. 1997. 34.95 (*1-57427-048-6*) Howell Pr VA.

One Pink Rose. Julie Garwood. (The Clayborne Brides Ser.). 1997. per. 2.99 (*0-671-01008-5*, Pocket Books) PB.

One Pink Rose. Julie Garwood. 1997. per. 2.66 (*0-671-02019-6*) PB.

1 Pitch Away. Mike Sowell. 1996. 12.95 (*0-02-860846-1*) Macmillan.

One Place. Graham P. Thomas. 38p. 1983. pap. 8.95 (*0-907476-19-8*) Dufour.

One Plus One. David P. Seemuth. 144p. 1995. pap. 6.50 (*1-56476-415-X*, 6-3415, Victor Bks) Chariot Victor.

One Plus One: An Integrated Approach to Communication. 5th ed. James Fullen & John C. Tabor. 288p. 1993. per. 31.95 (*0-8403-8472-6*) Kendall-Hunt.

One Plus One Equals Three - Pairing Man/Woman Strengths: Role Models of Teamwork. Emerson Klees. LC 98-92966. (Role Models of Human Values Ser.: Vol. 1). (Illus.). 232p. 1998. pap. 16.95 (*1-891046-00-4*) Frnds Finger Lks.

One Plus One Makes Marriage Bk. 75: Like Mother, Like Daughter. Marie Ferrarella. (Silhouette Romance Ser.: No. 1328). 1998. per. 3.50 (*0-373-19328-9*, 1-19328-3) Harlequin Bks.

One Point Four Law. K. Abbott. 288p. (C). 1987. 50.00 (*1-870941-06-3*) St Mut.

***One-Point Lessons: Rapid Transfer of Best Practices to the Shopfloor.** Productivity Development Team (Productivity Press) Staff. LC 00-32336. 2000. write for info. (*1-56327-224-5*) Productivity Inc.

1.3 Million Women Marched: Get a Glimpse of the Feeling of the Day. G. D. Dare. LC 99-94396. (Illus.). 54p. 1998. pap. text 16.95 (*0-9672481-0-8*) Buttrfly Press.

One Police Officer's Experiences: Deputy Sheriff to Chief of Police. Harold A. Bastrup. (Illus.). 415p. 1998. reprint ed. pap. 13.95 (*0-9649226-0-6*) Depol Pubn.

One Poor Scruple: A Seven Week's Story. Wilfred Ward. LC 79-8213. reprint ed. 44.50 (*0-404-62159-7*) AMS Pr.

One Possible Basis for a Demonstration of the Existence of God see Einzig Mogliche Beweisgrund

One Possible Basis for a Demonstration of the Existence of God. Immanuel Kant. Tr. & Intro. by Gordon Treash. LC 93-41125.Tr. of Der Einzig Mogliche Beweisgrund. 247p. 1994. reprint ed. pap. 12.95 (*0-8032-7777-6*, Bison Books) U of Nebr Pr.

One Post Farther North. R. J. Hodson. Ed. by Wanda Zimmerman. 57p. 1994. pap. 9.95 (*0-940055-73-2*) Vanessapress.

One-Pot Cakes: 60 Recipes for Cakes from Scratch Using a Pot, a Spoon, & a Pan. Andrew Schloss & Ken Bookman. LC 94-42177. 144p. 1995. 18.95 (*0-688-14138-2*, Wm Morrow) Morrow Avon.

One Pot Chicken Dinners. Peggy Fallon. 1996. 17.50 (*0-614-19376-1*) HarpC.

One-Pot Cookies: 50 Recipes for Making Cookies from Scratch, Using a Pot, a Spoon & a Pan. Andrew Schloss. LC 97-31346. (Illus.). 96p. 1998. 12.95 (*0-7679-0122-3*) Broadway BDD.

One Pot Dishes. 1975. 4.50 (*0-686-23315-8*) Rochester Folk Art.

One-Pot Meals. Time-Life Staff. LC 95-35152. (Great Taste - Low Fat Ser.). (Illus.). 160p. (J). (gr. 7). 1999. spiral bd. 14.95 (*0-7835-4552-5*) Time-Life.

One-Pot Vegetarian Dishes. Amy Cotler. 1996. write for info. (*0-614-96292-7*) HarpC.

One Potato. Diana Pomeroy. 28p. (J). 2000. pap. 6.00 (*0-15-202330-5*) Harcourt.

One Potato: A Counting Book of Potato Prints. Diana Pomeroy. LC 95-10986. (Illus.). 32p. (J). (ps-3). 1996. 16.00 (*0-15-200300-2*) Harcourt.

One Potato, Tu. Gayle Pearson. 112p. (J). (gr. 4-6). 1994. pap. 2.95 (*0-590-47100-7*) Scholastic Inc.

***One Potato, Two Potato.** Jessica Souhami. (Silly Rhymes Ser.). (Illus.). (J). 1999. 7.99 (*0-7112-1244-9*) F Lincoln.

One Potato, Two Potato: A Cookbook & More! Janet Reeves. 256p. 1994. pap. 13.95 (*0-920304-70-2*, Pub. by Gynergy-Ragweed) U of Toronto Pr.

One Potato, Two Potato: The Folklore of American Children. Mary Knapp & Herbert Knapp. (Illus.). (C). 1978. reprint ed. pap. text 12.50 (*0-393-09039-6*) Norton.

One Potato Two Potato Etc. Anita Virgil. LC 90-92149. 133p. (Orig.). 1991. pap. text 12.95 (*0-9628567-0-3*) Peaks Pr.

One Potato, Two Potato, Three Potato, Four! 165 Chants for Children. Mary L. Colgin. Orig. Title: Chants for Children. 77p. 1988. reprint ed. pap. 9.95 (*0-87659-116-0*) Gryphon Hse.

One Potatoe. Sue Porter. 32p. 1989. 12.95 (*0-385-25214-5*) Doubleday.

One-Pound Gospel. Rumiko Takahashi. (Illus.). 240p. 1996. pap. text 16.95 (*1-56931-131-5*) Viz Commns Inc.

One Pound Gospel: Knuckle Sandwich. Rumiko Takahashi. (Illus.). 208p. 1998. pap. text 15.95 (*1-56931-260-5*, Viz Comics) Viz Commns Inc.

One Powerful Mind: The Complete Approach to Emotional Management at Home & at Work. Paul Witz. 288p. 1999. boxed set 29.95 (*0-13-929325-6*) P-H.

One Prayer at a Time: A Day-to-Day Path to Spiritual Growth. Lynne Bundesen. LC 95-37511. 240p. 1995. 19.50 (*0-684-81114-6*) S&S Trade.

One Prayer at a Time: A Day-to-Day Path to Spiritual Growth. Lynne Bundesen. 240p. 1998. pap. 10.00 (*0-684-82546-5*) S&S Trade.

One Prayer at a Time: A Day-to-Day Path to Spiritual Growth. large type ed. Lynne Bundesen. 223p. 1996. 20.95 (*0-7838-1704-5*, G K Hall Lrg Type) Mac Lib Ref.

***One Precious Soul.** Linda Barnhill. 1999. write for info. (*1-58235-451-0*) Watermrk Pr.

One Present from Flekman's. Alan Arkin. LC 98-20346. (Illus.). 32p. (J). (gr. k-3). 1999. 15.95 (*0-06-024530-1*); lib. bdg. 14.89 (*0-06-024531-X*) HarpC Child Bks.

1-Propanol. (Environmental Health Criteria Ser.: No. 102). 98p. 1990. pap. text 23.00 (*92-4-157102-0*, 1160102) World Health.

One Proud Summer. Marsha Hewitt & Claire MacKay. 150p. (YA). reprint ed. pap. 7.95 (*0-88961-048-7*, Pub. by Womens Pr) LPC InBook.

One Purpose of God: An Answer to the Doctrine of Eternal Punishment. Jan Bonda. LC 97-33626. 288p. (Orig.). 1997. pap. 25.00 (*0-8028-4186-4*) Eerdmans.

One Quarter of Humanity: Malthusian Mythology & Chinese Realities, 1700-2000. James Z. Lee. LC 99-11863. 288p. 1999. 47.50 (*0-674-63908-1*) HUP.

One Quest, Hold the Dragons No. 2: Cups & Sorcery. Greg Costikyan. (Cups & Sorcery Ser.: No. 2). 384p. (Orig.). 1995. mass mkt. 4.99 (*0-8125-2269-9*) Tor Bks.

One Quiet Moment. 9p. 1994. pap. 1.30 (*0-8341-9100-8*, AN-3913) Lillenas.

***One Quiet Moment: Prayers & Promises for Each New Day.** Lloyd J. Ogilvie. 365p. 2000. 10.99 (*0-7369-0132-9*) Harvest Hse.

One Quiet Voice. Arthur Geis. (Illus.). 20p. (Orig.). (YA). (gr. 12). 1988. pap. 4.95 (*0-317-93130-X*) Artisan IL.

One Race Many Country Vol. 2: Evolucion De America. Fred J. Jackson, Sr. 24p. 1998. 13.95 (*1-891934-03-1*) Black Rose CA.

1 Ragged Ridge Road. Leonard Foglia. 1998. per. 6.50 (*0-671-00355-0*, Pocket Books) PB.

1 Ragged Ridge Road. Leonard Foglia & David Richards. LC 96-46779. 352p. 1997. 22.00 (*0-671-00354-2*) PB.

One Rainy Night. Doris Gove. LC 93-13900. (Illus.). 32p. (J). (gr. 2-5). 1994. 14.95 (*0-689-31800-6*) Atheneum Yung Read.

***One Rainy Night.** Richard Laymon. 416p. 2000. mass mkt. 5.99 (*0-8439-4690-3*, Leisure Bks) Dorchester Pub Co.

One Real Thing. Laura Peyton Roberts. (Clearwater Crossing Ser.). (YA). (gr. 5-8). 1999. mass mkt. 3.99 (*0-553-49257-8*) BDD Bks Young Read.

One Reckless Night. Sara Craven. (Presents Ser.). 1998. per. 3.75 (*0-373-11944-5*, 1-11944-5) Harlequin Bks.

One Red Rose. Julie Garwood. 1997. mass mkt. 2.99 (*0-614-27767-1*); per. 2.99 (*0-671-01010-7*) PB.

One Red Rose. Julie Garwood. 1997. per. 2.66 (*0-671-02024-2*) PB.

One Red Rose. Leia Stinnett. (Little Angel Bks.). 64p. 1996. pap. text 6.95 (*0-929385-83-7*) Light Tech Pubng.

One Red Rose. Leia A. Stinnett. (Little Angel Bks.). (Illus.). (J). (gr. k-12). 1992. pap. text 6.95 (*1-880737-07-8*) Crystal Jrns.

One Red Sun: A Counting Book. Ezra Jack Keats. (Illus.). 14p. (ps). 1999. pap. 5.99 (*0-670-88478-2*, Viking) Viking Penguin.

One Remains: The White Light Classes, Vol. I. Oreana Asterion. 1992. pap. 14.95 (*0-9631502-1-9*) Gray Wolf Pub.

***One Remarkable Woman.** Robert E. Whelan. vi, 218p. 2000. 21.95 (*0-9678803-0-0*) Intelepub of NV.

One Renegade Cell: How Cancer Begins. Robert A. Weinberg. LC 98-41277. (Illus.). 170p. 1998. 12.00 (*0-465-07275-5*, Pub. by Basic) HarpC.

One Renegade Cell: How Cancer Begins. Robert A. Weinberg. 176p. 1999. pap. 13.00 (*0-465-07276-3*, Pub. by Basic) HarpC.

One Republican's First Campaign for the Legislature: A First-Time Republican Candidate's Step-by-Step Account of How He Organized a Winning Campaign. LC 97-72028. (Illus.). 224p. 1997. pap. 19.95 (*0-9656243-0-7*) Iowa Acad.

One Returned. Robert R. Twitchell. (Illus.). 258p. 1986. 15.95 (*0-9616798-0-8*); pap. 9.95 (*0-318-20167-4*) B Twitchell.

One Revolution: Managing the Academic Medical Practice in an Era of Rapid Change. Ed. by David J. Bachrach & William R. Nicholas. 360p. 1997. pap. 75.00 (*1-56829-083-7*) Med Group Mgmt.

***One Riddle, One Answer.** Illus. by Lauren Thompson & Linda S. Wingerter. LC 99-89308. (J). 2001. pap. write for info. (*0-590-31337-1*) Scholastic Inc.

One Ride Too Many & Twelve Other Action Stories of the Wild West. Frank Bonham. Ed. by Martin H. Greenberg & Bill Pronzini. LC 94-46919. 270p. 1995. pap. 12.00 (*1-56980-034-0*) Barricade Bks.

One Right Reading: A Guide to Irenaeus. Mary A. Donovan. LC 97-37792. 208p. (Orig.). 1997. pap. 18.95 (*0-8146-5875-X*) Liturgical Pr.

One Right Touch. 2nd ed. Katharine Coles. Ed. by Dale K. Boyer. LC 92-81877. (Ahsahta Press Modern & Contemporary Poets of the West Ser.). 60p. (Orig.). 1992. pap. 6.95 (*0-916272-54-0*) Ahsahta Pr.

One River: Explorations & Discoveries in the Amazon Rain Forest. Wade Davis. 544p. 1997. per. 16.00 (*0-684-83496-0*) S&S Trade Pap.

One River: Explorations & Discoveries in the Amazon Rain Forest. Wade Davis. (Illus.). 537p. 1996. 27.00 (*0-684-80886-2*) Simon & Schuster.

One River, Many Currents: A Handbook of Inquiry in the Arts Therapies. Ed. by Helen Payne. 250p. 1993. pap. 29.95 (*1-85302-153-9*) Taylor & Francis.

***One River, Many Wells.** Matthew Fox. 304p. 2000. 24.95 (*1-58542-047-6*, Tarcher Putnam) Putnam Pub Group.

One River More. W. D. Wetherall. LC 98-9180. (Illus.). 240p. 1998. 25.00 (*1-55821-698-7*) Lyons Pr.

One Road. Angus Peter Cambell. LC 98-189657. 1994. write for info. (*0-9520010-1-2*) Fountain Publ.

One Road down from the Wilderness. Julia Bates. LC 89-32035. (Illus.). 80p. (Orig.). 1989. pap. 7.50 (*0-931832-30-6*) Fithian Pr.

One-Room & Consolidated Schools of Connecticut: A Comparative Study of Teachers, Costs & Holding Power. Emil L. Larson. LC 78-176976. (Columbia University. Teachers College. Contributions to Education Ser.: No. 182). reprint ed. 37.50 (*0-404-55182-3*) AMS Pr.

One-Room Country School: South Dakota Stories. Ed. by Norma C. Wilson & Charles L. Woodard. (Illus.). 1999. pap. 9.95 (*0-9632157-5-2*) SD Human Fnd.

One-Room Country Schools: History & Recollections from Wisconsin. Jerry Apps. LC 96-7046. (Illus.). 240p. 1996. pap. 18.95 (*0-942495-53-5*) Palmer Pubns Inc.

One Room in a Castle: Letters from Spain, France & Greece. Karen Connelly. LC 96-112670. 432p. 1995. 24.95 (*0-88801-194-6*, Pub. by Turnstone Pr) Genl Dist Srvs.

One Room School see Historic Communities Series

***One-Room School.** Raymond Bial. LC 98-43241. (Illus.). 48p. (J). (gr. 3-7). 1999. 15.00 (*0-395-90514-1*) HM.

One Room School. Laurence Pringle. LC 96-84154. (Illus.). 32p. (J). (gr. 1-5). 1998. 15.95 (*1-56397-583-1*) Boyds Mills Pr.

One-Room School: Teaching in Nineteen Thirties Western Oklahoma. Donna M. Stephens. LC 90-50240. (Western Frontier Library: Vol. 57). (Illus.). 176p. 1990. 23.95 (*0-8061-2313-3*) U of Okla Pr.

One Room School of Life. Karla B. Whitsitt. LC 97-94894. (Lilac Rose Ser.: Vol. 1). 256p. 15.00 (*1-891452-02-9*) Heart Arbor.

One Room School of Life. Karla B. Whitsitt. LC 97-94894. (Lilac Ser.: Vol. 1). 256p. 2000. pap. 12.00 (*1-891452-03-7*) Heart Arbor.

One Room Schoolhouse: Stories about the Boys. Jim Heynen. 240p. 1994. pap. 12.00 (*0-679-74769-9*) Vin Bks.

One Room Schoolhouses of Arkansas As Seen Through a Pinhole. Photos & Text by Thomas Harding. LC 92-30060. (Illus.). 120p. 1993. 40.00 (*1-55728-271-4*) U of Ark Pr.

One Room Schoolhouses of Florida. 2nd ed. Sandra Dunnavant et al. (Series of Lesson Plans: Ser. 2, No. 20). (Illus.). 16p. (J). (gr. k-12). 1997. write for info. (*1-889030-10-4*) FL Div Hist Res.

One-Room Schools of the Middle West: An Illustrated History. Wayne E. Fuller. LC 94-15799. (Illus.). 176p. 1994. 35.00 (*0-7006-0637-8*) U Pr of KS.

One Round Moon & a Star for Me. Ingrid Mennen. LC 93-9628. (Illus.). 32p. (J). (ps-2). 1994. 15.95 (*0-531-06804-8*); lib. bdg. 16.99 (*0-531-08654-2*) Orchard Bks Watts.

One Round River: The Curse of Gold & the Fight for the Big Blackfoot. Richard Manning. LC 97-27537. 222p. 1998. 25.00 (*0-8050-4792-1*) H Holt & Co.

One-Round War: USMC Scout-Snipers in Vietnam. Peter R. Senich. (Illus.). 384p. 1996. 59.95 (*0-87364-867-6*) Paladin Pr.

One Rubber Duckie. Sesame Street Staff. LC 81-86375. (Board Bks.). (Illus.). (J). (ps). 1982. 4.99 (*0-394-85309-1*, Pub. by Random Bks Yng Read) Random.

One Rule Plan for Family Happiness. Gary Hutchison. 150p. 1994. pap. 20.00 (*1-885631-03-0*) G F Hutchison.

One Sad Day. Bernice Kohn. LC 78-169153. (Illus.). 48p. (J). 1972. 11.95 (*0-89388-026-4*) Okpaku Communications.

***One Sad Ungathered Rose: Schizophrenia - A Mother's Story.** Susan Poole. LC 99-222079. (Illus.). 182p. 2000. pap. 15.95 (*1-898256-62-4*, Pub. by Collins Press) Irish Bks Media.

One Safe Place. Ramsey Campbell. 384p. 1996. 23.95 (*0-312-86035-8*) Forge NYC.

One Safe Place. Ramsey Campbell. 1997. mass mkt. 6.99 (*0-8125-4555-9*, Pub. by Tor Bks) St Martin.

One Samuel: A Literary Reading. Peter D. Miscall. LC 85-42948. (Indiana Studies in Biblical Literature). 224p. (C). 1986. 19.95 (*0-253-34247-3*); pap. 10.95 (*0-253-20365-1*, MB-365) Ind U Pr.

One Saturday Afternoon. Barbara Baker. LC 98-41605. (gr. 1-4). 1999. 13.99 (*0-525-45882-4*) NAL.

One Saturday Afternoon. Barbara Baker. 1999. pap. 3.50 (*0-14-038756-0*) Viking Penguin.

One Saturday Morning. Barbara Baker. (Puffin Easy-To-Read. Level 2 Ser.). (J). 1997. 8.70 (*0-606-11709-1*, Pub. by Turtleback) Demco.

One Saturday Morning. Barbara Baker. (Illus.). (J). (gr. k-3). 1997. pap. 3.50 (*0-14-038605-X*) Viking Penguin.

One Saturday Morning. Tk. (Brainiacs Ser.: No. 4). 112p. (J). (gr. 2-5). 1999. 3.99 (*0-7868-4364-0*, Pub. by Disney Pr) Little.

One School Now: Real Life at Lynn English High. Peter S. Temes. LC 97-11730. (Counterpoints: Vol. 52). 164p. (C). 1998. pap. text 176.00 (*0-8204-3746-8*) P Lang Pubng.

One Score & Two Years of Uncommon Fanfare: Anthology of Award-Winning Poems from the Annual Poetry Contests Sponsored by the North American Mentor Magazine, 1964-1985. Mentor Circle of Poets Staff. LC 85-52334. (Illus.). xii, 244p. 1986. pap. 10.00 (*0-87423-040-3*) Westburg.

One Sea, One Law? Malcolm E. Weiss. LC 81-47535. (Illus.). 120p. (J). (gr. 5 up). 1982. 10.95 (*0-15-258690-3*, Harcourt Child Bks) Harcourt.

One Seal. John Stadler. LC 99-11664. (Illus.). 32p. (J). (ps-2). 1999. 15.95 (*0-531-30195-8*); lib. bdg. 16.99 (*0-531-33195-4*) Orchard Bks Watts.

One Season Here: Poems, 1943-1946. Francis C. Rosenberger. LC 76-150451. 87p. reprint ed. pap. 30.00 (*0-7837-4345-9*, 204405500012) Bks Demand.

One Second in the Arab World. Ronald Codrai. (Illus.). 96p. 75.00 (*1-873544-80-4*, Pub. by Motivate Pubg Ltd) Intl Bk Ctr.

One Seed Makes the Whole Earth Green. Osho. Ed. by Anand Robin. LC 97-221790. (Zen Ser.). 192p. 1992. 14.95 (*3-89338-077-9*, Pub. by Rebel Hse) Oshos.

One Semester Economics: An Introduction for Business & Management Students. Rebecca Harding. LC 97-14137. 250p. (C). 1998. pap. text 29.95 (*0-631-20025-8*) Blackwell Pubs.

One Sensitive Soul to Another. Dale W. Emme. (Illus.). 155p. (Orig.). 1998. pap. 9.95 (*1-889529-13-3*) Two Feathers.

O

An Asterisk (*) at the beginning of an entry indicates that the title is appearing for the first time.

175 Science Experiments to Amuse & Amaze Your Friends: Experiments, Tricks, Things to Make. Brenda Walpole. (J). 1988. 19.09 (0-606-03703-9, Pub. by Turtleback) Demco.

One Sexy Daddy. Vivian Leiber. (American Romance Ser.). 1999. per. 3.99 (0-373-16792-X, 1-16792-3) Harlequin Bks.

One Shahaptan Gathering Fuel. L. Pearne Robbins. (Illus.). 118p. (Orig.). 1994. pap. 8.00 (1-883501-01-6) R Lodges Pub.

One Shahapton Stirring Ashes. rev. ed. L. Pearne Robbins. (Illus.). 135p. 1993. pap. 8.00 (1-883501-00-8) R Lodges Pub.

One Shall Chase a Thousand. Mabel Francis. LC 93-70740. (Jaffray Collection of Missionary Portraits: Bk. 9). (Illus.). 160p. 1993. pap. 9.99 (0-87509-513-5) Chr Pubns.

One Shall Chase a Thousand. Barbara Hibschman. (Junior Jaffray Collection: Bk. 9). 30p. (J). (gr. k-3). 1993. pap. 3.99 (0-87509-516-X) Chr Pubns.

One-Share, One-Vote Controversy. Joel Seligman. 30p. 1986. pap. 10.00 (0-931035-64-3) IRRC Inc DC.

One Sharp & Two Flats. Jane Archer. LC 90-53338. (Orig.). 1990. pap. 5.00 (0-88734-319-8) Players Pr.

One Shenandoah Winter: A Novel. T. Davis Bunn. LC 98-19987. 128p. 1998. 12.99 (0-7852-7217-8) Nelson.

One Shining Moment: Glen Tucket Story. Stephanni Hicken. 5.95 (1-55517-121-4) CFI Dist.

One Shining Season: The Amazing Story of Michigan State University's 1998-99 Men's Basketball Team. Lansing State Journal Staff. (Illus.). 92p. 1999. pap. 12.95 (1-58261-131-9) Sprts Pubng.

One Shining Summer. Quinn Wilder. 1994. per. 2.99 (0-373-03314-1) Harlequin Bks.

One Short Sleep Past. Donald Hoffman. Date not set. write for info. (0-9659632-7-6) Verda Publ.

One Shot-One Kill. Charles W. Sasser & Craig Roberts. 288p. 1990. per. 6.99 (0-671-68219-9) PB.

***One Shots: Five Stand-Alone Scenarios.** John Tynes et al. (Unknown Armies Ser.). (Illus.). 80p. 1999. pap. 14.95 (1-887801-73-1) Trident MN.

***One Show Interactive 2.** Rotovision Staff. 272p. 1999. 45.00 (2-88046-474-9, Rotovision) Watsn-Guptill.

One Show Interactive 1. Rotovision Staff. 192p. 1999. 45.00 (2-88046-430-7, Rotovision) Watsn-Guptill.

***One Show 21.** Rotovision Staff. 409p. 1999. 79.95 (2-88046-475-7, Rotovision) Watsn-Guptill.

One Show 20. Rotovision Staff. 500p. 1999. 79.00 (2-88046-400-5, Rotovision) Watsn-Guptill.

One-Sided Arguments: A Dialectical Analysis of Bias. Douglas Walton. LC 99-15100. (SUNY Series in Logic & Language). 320p. (C). 1999. text 62.50 (0-7914-4267-5, Suny Pr); pap. text 20.95 (0-7914-4268-3, Suny Pr) State U NY Pr.

One-Sided Love Affair. Ethel Porter. 66p. 1999. pap. 6.00 (0-8059-4505-9) Dorrance.

One Silent Night: Men in Blue. Debra Cowan. (Intimate Moments Ser.: No. 899). 1998. per. 4.25 (0-373-07899-4, 1-07899-7) Silhouette.

***One Silent Night: Stories of Christmas Through Women's Eyes.** Janice Chaffee. 160p. 2000. pap. 9.99 (0-7369-0496-4) Harvest Hse.

One Singular Sensation: The Michael Bennett Story. Kevin Kelly. 480p. 1991. mass mkt. 4.95 (0-8217-3310-9, Zebra Kensgtn) Kensgtn Pub Corp.

One Sip at a Time: Making the Best of Swallowing Problems. Ed. by Anna Hollingsworth. (Illus.). 30p. (Orig.). 1995. pap. text 5.25 (0-939838-39-7) Pritchett & Hull.

One Sister Too Many. C. S. Adler. LC 91-15530. 176p. (J). (gr. 3-7). 1991. reprint ed. pap. 3.95 (0-689-71521-8) Aladdin.

168 Seasonal & Holiday Open-Ended Artic Worksheets. M. Thomas Webber, Jr. & Sharon G. Webber. (Illus.). 180p. (J). (ps-3). 1993. spiral bd., wbk. ed. 26.95 (1-58650-030-9, BK-221) Super Duper.

One Size Does Not Fit All. Beverly Naidus. LC 93-30780. 1993. reprint ed. 35.00 (1-883930-01-4); reprint ed. pap. 15.00 (1-883930-00-6) AIGIS Pubns.

One Size Doesn't Fit All. John Madden & Dave Anderson. 256p. 1989. pap. 5.50 (0-515-10146-X, Jove) Berkley Pub.

One Size Doesn't Fit All: Bringing Out the Best in Any Size Church. Gary L. McIntosh. LC 99-18717. (Illus.). 174p. (C). (gr. 13). 1999. pap. 11.99 (0-8007-5699-1) Revell.

One Size Fits All & Other Fables. Liz C. Higgs. LC 93-20672. 1993. 12.99 (0-8407-6333-6) Nelson.

One Size Fits All & Other Holiday Myths. Sam Venable. pap. text 10.75 (0-9615656-9-1) Knoxville News-Sentinel.

One Size Fits Few: The Folly of Educational Standards. Susan Ohanian. LC 98-54482. 154p. 1999. pap. text 16.00 (0-325-00158-8, E00158) Heinemann.

One Size Fits One: Building Commitment One Employee & One Customer at a Time. Gary M. Heil et al. LC 97-112696. (Industrial Engineering Ser.). (Illus.). 250p. 1997. text 25.95 (0-442-02063-5, VNR) Wiley.

One Size Fits One: Building Relationships One Customer & One Employee at a Time. Gary Heil et al. 304p. 1996. 29.95 (0-471-28706-7, VNR) Wiley.

One Size Fits One: Building Relationships One Customer & One Employee at a Time. 2nd ed. Gary Heil et al. LC 98-55216. 321p. 1999. 29.95 (0-471-33167-8) Wiley.

One Slimy Summer. J. R. Black. (Shadow Zone Ser.). 132p. (Orig.). (J). (gr. 3-7). 1994. pap. 3.50 (0-685-71035-1) Random Bks Yng Read.

One Small Blue Bead. 2nd ed. Byrd Baylor. LC 90-28160. (Illus.). 32p. (J). (gr. 2-5). 1992. 16.00 (0-684-19334-5) Scribner.

One Small Dog. Johanna Hurwitz. LC 99-87073. (gr. 2 up). pap. 4.95 (0-380-73293-9) Morrow Avon.

***One Small Dog.** Johanna Hurwitz. LC 99-87073. 128p. (J). (gr. 2 up). 2000. 15.89 (0-06-029220-2); 15.95 (0-688-17382-9, Wm Morrow) Morrow Avon.

One Small Favor. Jerry Parkhurst. 256p. 1997. 22.00 (0-915214-36-9) Prof Pr NC.

One Small Gift. Beverley E. Labrum. (Illus.). 47p. 1997. pap. 6.95 (0-9659639-0-X) B E Labrum.

One Small Girl. Jennifer L. Chan. LC 92-35423. (Illus.). 32p. (J). (gr. k-2). 1993. 12.95 (1-879965-05-4) Polychrome Pub.

One Small Lost Sheep. Claudia Mills. LC 96-18609. (Illus.). 32p. (J). (ps-3). 1997. 16.00 (0-374-35649-1) FS&G.

One Small Miracle. Lance Wubbels. LC 95-480. 8p. 1995. text 11.99 (1-55661-668-6) Bethany Hse.

One Small Place: Tree House. Barbara Brenner. 1924. write for info. (0-688-17180-X, Wm Morrow) Morrow Avon.

One Small Plot of Heaven: Reflections on Family Life by a Quaker Sociologist. Elise Boulding. LC 89-16082. 231p. 1993. pap. 13.00 (0-87574-912-7, 1063) Pendle Hill.

One Small Saga. Bobbie L. Hawkins. LC 84-15612. 112p. (Orig.). 1984. pap. 8.95 (0-918273-05-6) Coffee Hse.

One Small Secret. Meagan McKinney. (Desire Ser.: No. 1222). 1999. per. 3.75 (0-373-76222-4, 1-76222-8) Silhouette.

***One Small Sparrow: The Remarkable True-Life Drama of One Community's Compassionate Response to Save a Little Boy's Life.** Jeff Leeland. (Illus.). 250p. 2000. pap. 9.99 (1-57673-693-8, Pub. by Multnomah Pubs) GL Services.

***One Small Step: A 30th Anniversary Celebration of Project Apollo & the Space Age.** Eugene Fowler. LC 98-68329. (Illus.). 64p. 1999. 14.98 (0-7651-1666-9) Smithmark.

One Small Step: An Education Outreach Guide. 75p. 1993. 19.95 (1-56347-169-8, WS932) AIAA.

One Small Step: Moving Beyond Trauma & Therapy to a Life of Joy. Yvonne Dolan. LC 97-35072. 232p. (Orig.). 1998. pap. 11.95 (1-57601-055-4) Dolan.

***One Smiling Sister.** Lucy Coats. (Toddlers Storybook Ser.). (Illus.). 24p. (ps-k). 2000. pap. 5.95 (0-7894-5622-2) DK Pub Inc.

***One Snowbound Weekend...** Christy Lockhart. (Desire Ser.). 2000. mass mkt. 3.99 (0-373-76314-X, 1-76314-3) Silhouette.

One Snowy Day. Jeffrey Scherer. (Hello, Reader! Ser.). (J). 1997. 8.70 (0-606-12787-9, Pub. by Turtleback) Demco.

One Snowy Eve. deluxe ed. Bruce Talkington. LC 97-81053. (Poky & Friends Ser.). 14p. (J). (ps-1). 1998. 6.99 (0-307-33300-0, Goldn Books) Gldn Bks Pub Co.

***One So Precious among Us.** Dave Landrey & Martha Landrey. Ed. by Cynthia Decker. 96p. 1998. pap. text 6.95 (1-57636-070-9) SunRise Pbl.

One Society Four Systems. Fred Harrison. 100p. 1997. 11.95 (1-901647-04-8, Pub. by Othila Pr) Intl Spec Bk.

One Soldier's Legacy: The National Homestead at Gettysburg. Mary R. Collins & Cindy Stouffer. (Illus.). 128p. (C). 1993. pap. 6.95 (0-939631-67-9) Thomas Publications.

***One Soldier's Memories: World War II.** Steven E. Danish. (Illus.). 202p. 1999. pap. 20.00 (0-913337-35-8) Southfarm Pr.

One Song Hero: The Inward Journey of an Urban Shaman. Marcus S. Robinson. (Illus.). (Orig.). 1994. pap. 38.95 incl. cd-rom (0-9639703-6-4, Wetware New Media) Wetware.

One Song Hero: The Inward Journey of an Urban Shaman. 2nd ed. Marcus S. Robinson. Ed. by Charles Lyons et al. (Illus.). (Orig.). Date not set. pap. 12.95 (0-9639703-5-6, Wetware New Media) Wetware.

One Song, Many Voices. Mark Williams. 25.00 (0-06-662004-X) HarpC.

One Soul, One Struggle. Anton Lucas. (Illus.). 224p. 1991. pap. text 24.95 (0-04-442249-0, Pub. by Allen & Unwin Pty) Paul & Co Pubs.

One Soul's Journey. Linda B. Dallum. (Illus.). (Orig.). 1986. pap. 6.95 (0-9616937-0-3) L B Dallum.

One Source Sacred Journeys: Celebration of Spirit & Art. Ramon Kubicek et al. LC 96-79541. (Illus.). 104p. (Orig.). 1997. 24.95 (0-9655890-1-3) Markowitz Pub.

One South: An Ethnic Approach to Regional Culture. John S. Reed. LC 81-19387. xxii, 218p. (C). 1982. pap. text 17.95 (0-8071-1038-8) La State U Pr.

One South or Many? Plantation Belt & Upcountry in Civil War-Era Tennessee. Robert T. McKenzie. (Illus.). 225p. (C). 1994. text 49.95 (0-521-46270-3) Cambridge U Pr.

One Space Living. Cynthia Inions. (Illus.). 144p. 1999. 24.95 (0-8230-3320-1) Watsn-Guptill.

One Special Child. M. J. Carr. (Cabbage Patch Kids Ser.). (Illus.). 32p. (J). (ps-3). 1992. pap. 2.50 (0-590-45460-9) Scholastic Inc.

One Special Christmas. Irene Hannon. 1999. per. 4.50 (0-373-87077-9, Steeple Hill) Harlequin Bks.

One Special Moment. Brenda Jackson. 256p. 1998. pap. 4.99 (0-7860-0546-7) Kensgtn Pub Corp.

***One Speck of Humanity.** large type ed. Syd Metcalfe. 376p. 2000. 31.99 (0-7089-9130-0) Ulverscroft.

***One Spinning Spider.** Sally Crabtree. (Illus.). (J). 2000. 10.95 (1-86233-167-7) Levinson Bks.

One Spirit, Many Peoples: A Manifesto for Earth Spirituality. Stephen H. Buhner. 288p. 1997. 24.95 (1-57098-120-5) Roberts Rinehart.

One Spirit with the Lord. Merle E. Koepke. 124p. 1995. reprint ed. 24.00 (1-891125-01-X) Hands Jesus.

One Spirit Wrapped in Flesh: A Personal Transformation. Noreen P. Cullen. Ed. by Elizabeth B. La Fond. (Illus.). 146p. (Orig.). 1996. pap. 8.95 (0-9654368-0-2) N Cullen.

One Spiritual Journey. Betty G. Fielder. LC 97-90268. 177p. 1997. pap. 9.95 (0-934426-77-5) NAPSAC Reprods.

One Split Second. Suzan B. Hoppe. (Illus.). 370p. (Orig.). 1993. pap. 15.00 (0-9630608-3-X) R Dean Pr.

One Spring at St. Margaret's. large type ed. Louie Williams. (Linford Romance Library). 304p. 1997. pap. 16.99 (0-7089-5183-X) Ulverscroft.

One Square Mile. Frank O. Braynard. (Illus.). 144p. 1986. 14.00 (0-317-39401-0) F O Braynard.

One Square Mile: An Artist's Journal of America's Heartland. Cathy Johnson. (Illus.). 210p. 1993. 17.95 (0-8027-7393-1) Walker & Co.

***One Square Mile: An Artist's Journal of America's Heartland.** Cathy Johnson. 210p. 1999. reprint ed. pap. text 18.00 (0-7881-6831-2) DIANE Pub.

One Square Mile on the Atlantic Coast: An Artist's Journal of the New Jersey Shore. John R. Quinn. LC 92-38190. (America in Microcosm Ser.). (Illus.). 224p. 1993. pap. 17.95 (0-8027-7395-8) Walker & Co.

One-Stage Prothrombin Time (PT) Test & Activated Partial Thromboplastin Time (APTT) Test: Approved Guideline (1996) 1996. 75.00 (1-56238-301-9, H47-A) NCCLS.

One Star in Sight. Aleister Crowley. 1973. lib. bdg. 250.00 (0-87968-506-9) Krishna Pr.

***One Starry Day in Heaven.** Bill Bell. LC 98-46437. (Illus.). 48p. (J). (ps-3). 1999. 12.98 (0-7651-1056-3) Smithmark.

One Step - Two Step: A Civil War Sequel. Waldron M. McLellon. LC 98-93140. 334p. 1998. pap. 14.95 (1-884489-02-8) Butternut.

One Step Ahead: Early-Intervention Strategies for Adolescent Drug Problems. Joseph A. Muldoon & James F. Crowley. LC 85-73646. (Illus.). 180p. (Orig.). 1986. pap. 14.95 (0-9613416-1-0) Comm Intervention.

One Step Ahead: The Unused Keys to Success. Roger Fritz. LC 98-84654. 168p. 1998. pap. 11.95 (1-890394-19-X, Sage Creek) Rhodes & Easton.

One Step Ahead in China: Guangdong under Reform. Ezra F. Vogel. LC 89-31695. (Interpretations of Asia Ser.). (Illus.). 544p. 1989. 49.95 (0-674-63910-3) HUP.

One Step Ahead in China: Guangdong under Reform. Ezra F. Vogel. (Interpretations of Asia Ser.). (Illus.). 520p. 1990. pap. 19.50 (0-674-63911-1) HUP.

One Step at a Time. Marie Joseph. 1993. 39.95 (0-7066-1005-9, Pub. by Remploy Pr) St Mut.

One Step at a Time. Brian Todd. LC 86-17428. 1988. pap. 13.95 (0-87949-254-6) Ashley Bks.

One Step at a Time: A Definitive Study of Alzheimer's Disease & a Practical Guide for Caregivers. Lorena S. Eaker. LC 96-69044. v, 207p. (Orig.). 1996. pap., per. 15.00 (0-9653000-0-5) S C K Pubns.

***One Step at a Time: An Appalachian Trail Adventure.** Patrick J. Pifher. LC 00-190428. 2000. 25.00 (0-7388-1693-0); pap. 18.00 (0-7388-1694-9) Xlibris Corp.

One Step at a Time: Building a Better Marriage, Family, & You. Joe J. Christensen. LC 96-16342. viii, 152p. 1996. 13.95 (1-57345-188-6) Deseret Bk.

One Step at a Time: Intermediate 1, Bk. 1. Judith D. Garcia. LC 95-46028. (College ESL Ser.). 200p. (J). 1996. pap. 27.95 (0-8384-5030-X) Heinle & Heinle.

One Step at a Time: Intermediate 3, Bk. 2. Judith D. Garcia. LC 95-46059. (College ESL Ser.). 200p. (J). 1996. pap. 27.95 (0-8384-5031-8) Heinle & Heinle.

One Step at a Time: My Walk Across America. Elena J. Hanuse. 232p. 1988. pap. 3.95 (0-380-70623-7, Avon Bks) Morrow Avon.

One Step at a Time: The Remarkable True Story of Bob Wieland. Bob Wieland. 192p. 1989. 12.99 (0-310-51640-4) Zondervan.

One Step Away. Sherryl Woods. (Special Edition Ser.). 1994. per. 3.50 (0-373-09927-4, 1-09927-4) Silhouette.

One Step Away. large type ed. Sherryl Woods. 1996. 19.95 (0-373-59675-8) Thorndike Pr.

One Step Back, Two Steps Forward: On the Language Policy of the Communist Party of the Soviet Union in the National Republics. Michael Bruchis. (East European Monographs: No. 109). 371p. 1982. text 64.50 (0-88033-002-3, Pub. by East Eur Monographs) Col U Pr.

One Step Backwards, Two Steps Forward: Soviet Society & Politics in the New Economic Policy. Roger Pethybridge. (Illus.). 466p. 1990. text 125.00 (0-19-821927-X) OUP.

***One Step Behind Mandela.** Rory Steyn & Debora Patta. (Illus.). 240p. 2000. pap. 19.95 (1-86872-269-4, Pub. by New Holland) BHB Intl.

One Step Between Death & Me. Victor Houston. (Illus.). 68p. (Orig.). 1986. pap. 9.95 (1-55630-019-0) Brentwood Comm.

One Step Beyond. Photos by Alice Wheeler. (Illus.). 216p. 1998. mass mkt. 14.95 (0-9638594-2-0) Zero Hour.

One Step Closer: A Guided Tour of the Spiritual Life. David Edwards. LC 98-20678. 128p. (YA). 1999. pap. 9.99 (1-58229-002-4) Howard Pub LA.

One Step Closer: New Poetry by Women of the West Coast. Ed. by Frances McConnel. 1976. pap. 3.95 (0-915242-09-5) Pygmalion Pr.

One Step Forward? South & West Wales Towards the Year 2000. Ed. by Richard Jenkins & Arwel Edwards. 164p. (C). 1990. pap. 30.00 (0-86383-677-1, Pub. by Gomer Pr) St Mut.

One Step Forward, One Step Back, Human Rights in the People's Republic of China in 1987-88, No. 3. John F. Cooper & Ta-ling Lee. 140p. 1989. 6.00 (0-925153-02-8, 92) Occasional Papers.

One Step from the White House: The Rise & Fall of Senator William F. Knowland. Gayle B. Montgomery et al. LC 97-50545. 400p. 1998. 29.95 (0-520-21194-4, Pub. by U CA Pr) Cal Prin Full Svc.

One Step More: The Life & Work of Father Joseph C. Martin. Jane Maher. (Illus.). 272p. 1998. 35.00 (0-9661760-0-6); pap. 20.00 (0-9661760-1-4) Ashley Press.

***One Step, No Prep, Vol. 3352.** Jo Fitzpatrick. Ed. by Joel Kupperstein. (Illus.). 64p. 1999. pap. text 8.98 (1-57471-411-2, 3352) Creat Teach Pr.

One Step Out of Black Bottom. Walter Wadley. 1988. pap. 4.50 (0-8187-0106-4) Harlo Press.

One-Step Problem Patterns & Their Relation to Problem Solving in Arithmetic. Mary E. Sutherland. LC 76-177734. (Columbia University. Teachers College. Contributions to Education Ser.: No. 925). reprint ed. 37.50 (0-404-55925-5) AMS Pr.

One Step to Spanish, Vol. 1. (SPA., Illus.). 104p. Date not set. pap. write for info. (1-893746-05-4) Visual Teaching.

One Step to Spanish, Vol. 2. (SPA., Illus.). 115p. Date not set. pap. write for info. (1-893746-06-2) Visual Teaching.

One Step to Spanish, Vol. 3. (SPA., Illus.). 107p. Date not set. pap. write for info. (1-893746-07-0) Visual Teaching.

One Step to Spanish, Vol. 4. (SPA., Illus.). 111p. Date not set. pap. write for info. (1-893746-08-9) Visual Teaching.

One Step to Spanish, Vol. 5. (SPA., Illus.). 92p. Date not set. pap. write for info. (1-893746-09-7) Visual Teaching.

***One Step, Two.** Charlotte Zolotow. 2001. text 15.95 (0-8050-6307-2) H Holt & Co.

***One Stick Song.** Sherman Alexie. LC 99-58811. 2000. 25.00 (1-882413-77-6); pap. 15.00 (1-882413-76-8, Pub. by Hanging Loose) SPD-Small Pr Dist.

One-Stop CompuServe for Windows. Michael Banks. 89p. 1995. pap. 34.95 incl. cd-rom (1-55828-463-X, MIS Pr) IDG Bks.

One Stop-Guide to Workshops. Helen L. Rietz & Marilyn Manning. LC 93-13299. 324p. 1993. 40.00 (1-55623-938-6, Irwn Prfssnl) McGraw-Hill Prof.

One Stop Hallelujah Coffee Shop. Jennifer Blood. Ed. by Richard Holst. (Illus.). 150p. (Orig.). 1997. pap., per. write for info. (0-9643280-3-8) Cape Elizabeth.

One-Stop Marketing Book: What Every Small Business Owner Needs to Know. Jonathan Trivers. LC 95-52903. 256p. 1996. 39.95 (0-471-13331-0); pap. 17.95 (0-471-13332-9) Wiley.

One Stop Property Selling: A Guide to the Legal Aspects. Frances Silverman. 220p. 1992. 75.00 (1-85190-162-0, Pub. by Tolley Pubng) St Mut.

***One Stop Shopping Literature & Music for Preschool to K.** Elissa Bludau Engelhardt. (Illus.). 64p. 1999. pap. text, teacher ed. 35.00 (0-9677746-0-8) E B Engelhardt.

One Stormy Day see **Sugar Creek Gang Series**

One-Story Home Plans. Sunset Books Staff. (Best Home Plans Ser.). (Illus.). 224p. 1997. pap. 6.95 (0-376-01193-9) Sunset Books.

One Story Homes: 450 Exceptional Plans from 800 to 4,900 Square Feet. Illus. by Home Planners Staff. LC 98-73697. 384p. 1998. pap. 9.95 (1-881955-53-2) Home Planners.

One-Strike Stopping Power. Frank Albert. (Illus.). 176p. 1993. pap. 15.00 (0-87364-714-9) Paladin Pr.

One-Stroke Design. Dale Swant. 52p. 1993. reprint ed. pap. 5.00 (0-916809-68-4) Scott Pubns MI.

***One Stroke Painting Course.** Plaid. (Illus.). 2000. pap. 14.95 (0-8069-1975-2) Sterling.

One Stubborn Cowboy. Barbara McMahon. (Desire Ser.). 1995. per. 3.25 (0-373-05915-9, 1-05915-3) Silhouette.

One Summer. Albert Drake. LC 79-63672. 1979. pap. 5.00 (0-917976-06-1, White Ewe Pr) Thunder Baas Pr.

One Summer. Fernando Galan. (Literacy Volunteers of America Readers Ser.). 32p. (Orig.). 1988. pap. text 3.00 (0-8428-9605-8) Cambridge Bk.

One Summer. Karen Robards. 400p. 1993. mass mkt. 6.99 (0-440-20829-7) Dell.

One Summer. Nora Roberts. (Language of Love Ser.: No. 31). 1993. per. 3.59 (0-373-51031-4, 1-51031-8) Silhouette.

One Summer Day. Kim Lewis. LC 95-20580. (Illus.). 32p. (J). (ps up). 1996. 15.99 (1-56402-883-6) Candlewick Pr.

One Summer Day. Kim Lewis. LC 95-20580. (Illus.). 32p. (J). (ps). 1998. pap. 5.99 (0-7636-0508-5) Candlewick Pr.

***One Summer Evening.** Mary L. Baxter. 384p. 1999. per. 5.99 (1-55166-523-9, Mira Bks) Harlequin Bks.

One Summer in Lebanon. Lisa Saleh. (Illus.). 90p. (Orig.). 1997. pap. 8.95 (0-9658973-0-3) Saleh Found.

One Summer in Quebec: A. Y. Jackson in 1925. Naomi J. Groves. (Illus.). 144p. 1988. 14.95 (0-921254-02-4, Pub. by Penumbra Pr) U of Toronto Pr.

***One Summer Night.** Gerri Hill. 220p. 2000. pap. 12.00 (1-883061-31-8) Rising AZ.

One Summer's Knight: The Sisters Waskowitz. Kathleen Creighton. (Intimate Moments Ser.: No. 944). 1999. per. 4.25 (0-373-07944-3, 1-07944-1) Silhouette.

***One Summer's Night.** Mary Alice Kruesi. 384p. 2000. mass mkt. 5.99 (0-380-81433-1, Avon Bks) Morrow Avon.

One Sunday Morning. Yumi Heo. LC 98-41161. (Illus.). 32p. (J). (ps-1). 1999. 15.95 (0-531-30156-7); lib. bdg. 16.99 (0-531-33156-3) Orchard Bks Watts.

One Sunny Day: A Child's Memories of Hiroshima. Hideko T. Snider. (Illus.). 214p. 1996. pap. 17.95 (0-8126-9327-2) Open Court.

***1 Sure Way to Relax: Mike Cohen's Journey to Tranquility.** Michael Cohen. 16p. 1999. pap. 16.98 incl. cd-rom (0-9675050-0-3) Audio Educ.

One Surface Learning. Ron Burns & Joey Farris. 76p. (Orig.). 1995. pap. text 21.95 (0-89724-820-1, EL9590CD) Wrner Bros.

An Asterisk (*) at the beginning of an entry indicates that the title is appearing for the first time.

One Surgeon's Private War: Doctor William W. Potter of the 57th New York. Ed. by John M. Priest. LC 96-19886. (Illus.). 158p. 1996. 19.95 (*1-57249-021-7*) White Mane Pub.

One T. Rex over Easy. Bonnie Bader. (Carmen Sandiego Mystery Ser.). (J). (gr. 4-6). 1997. 9.60 (*0-606-11190-5*, Pub. by Turtleback) Demco.

***One Tank Trips Road Food: Finding Great Food on the Road.** Neil Zurcher. (Illus.). 208p. 1999. pap. 13.95 (*1-886228-30-2*) Gray & Co Pubs.

One Taste: The Journals of Ken Wilber. Ken Wilber. LC 98-22970. 396p. 1999. 25.00 (*1-57062-387-2*, Pub. by Shambhala Pubns) Random.

***One Taste: The Journals of Ken Wilber.** Ken Wilber. LC 00-21871. 400p. 2000. pap. 16.95 (*1-57062-547-6*, Pub. by Shambhala Pubns) Random.

One Tattered Angel: A Touching True Story of the Power of Love. Blaine M. Yorgason. LC 98-8352. 1998. 14.95 (*1-57345-392-7*, Shadow Mount) Deseret Bk.

One Teacher in Ten: Gay & Lesbian Educators Tell Their Stories. Ed. by Kevin Jennings. LC 94-13204. 260p. 1994. pap. 11.95 (*1-55583-263-6*) Alyson Pubns.

One Teacher's Classroom: Strategies for Successful Teaching & Learning. Dale Gordon. 140p. (C). (gr. k). 1992. pap. text 18.50 (*0-435-08807-6*, 08807) Heinemann.

One Tear Per Page: Poetry for Lovers & Living. 87p. (Orig.). 1997. pap. 10.00 (*0-9656680-0-2*) Ed Marshall.

One-Ten Pop-Up Surprise! Chuck Murphy. LC 95-159624. (Illus.). 10p. (J). (ps-2). 1995. 13.95 (*0-671-89908-2*) Litle Simon.

One-Term Solution: Ending the Evils of Reelection & Politics As a Career. Kent B. Welton. 233p. (Orig.). (C). 1989. pap. text 9.95 (*0-944361-25-0*) Pandit Pr.

One Terrific Year: Supporting Your Kids Through the Ups & Downs of Their Year. Carole Calladine. (Winston Family Handbooks Ser.). 220p. (Orig.). 1985. 12.10 (*0-86683-862-7*) Harper SF.

One Texas Night. Sylvie Kurtz. 168p. 1999. per. 3.99 (*0-373-22527-X*, 1-22527-5) Harlequin Bks.

One That Got Away. Dan Bolin. LC 99-190194. 1998. pap. 10.00 (*1-57683-074-8*) NavPress.

One That Got Away. Percival Everett. (J). (ps-3). 1992. 14.95 (*0-395-56427-1*, Clarion Bks) HM.

One That Got Away. Percival Everett. (Illus.). 32p. (J). (gr. 1-4). 1992. 14.95 (*0-395-56427-9*, Clarion Bks); lib. bdg. 14.95 (*0-685-52550-3*, Clarion Bks) HM.

***One that Got Away.** Created by Francine Pascal. (Sweet Valley High Senior Year Ser.: No. 9). 192p. (YA). (gr. 7 up). 1999. mass mkt. 4.50 (*0-553-49281-0*) Bantam.

One That Got Away: My SAS Mission Behind Iraqi Lines. Chris Ryan. LC 97-40358. (Illus.). 252p. 1998. reprint ed. pap. 17.95 (*1-57488-156-6*) Brasseys.

One, The Only, The Original Jigsaw Puzzle Book. Francene Sabin & Louis Sabin. LC 76-55658. 110 p. 1977. write for info. (*0-8092-7889-8*) NTC Contemp Pub Co.

One, the Three, & the Many: God, Creation, & the Culture of Modernity. Colin E. Gunton. LC 92-34659. 262p. (C). 1993. pap. text 22.95 (*0-521-42184-5*) Cambridge U Pr.

One They Called "Quiet" L. J. Bolar. LC 94-90383. 269p. 1998. 16.95 (*0-533-11208-7*) Vantage.

***One Thing God Can Never Do.** John Samuel. LC 99-91914. 224p. 2000. pap. 14.95 (*1-56167-595-4*, Five Star Spec Ed) Am Literary Pr.

One Thing I Ask. Hillel Fendel. 1998. 13.95 (*0-87306-881-5*) Feldheim.

One Thing I'm Good At. Karen Lynn Williams. pap. 4.95 (*0-380-73276-9*) Morrow Avon.

***One Thing I'm Good At.** Karen Lynn Williams. LC 99-12855. 144p. (J). (gr. 3-7). 1999. 14.95 (*0-688-16846-9*) Morrow Avon.

One Thing Led to the Next: The Real History of TTYs. Bill Graham. Tr. by Valerie Nelson-Metlay. (Illus.). 64p. (Orig.). 1988. pap. 10.00 (*0-9621715-3-0*) Mosquito Pub.

One Thing Money Can't Buy - The One Thing You Can't Afford to Be Without! Character. Jeff Owens. Date not set. write for info. (*0-9649393-0-4*) Owens Pubns.

One Thing More. Christopher Fry. 1987. pap. 5.25 (*0-8222-0854-7*) Dramatists Play.

One Thing Necessary. Charles Dickinson. (C). 1989. 29.00 (*0-7223-2274-7*, Pub. by A H S Ltd) St Mut.

One Thing Needful. Andrei of Novo-Diveyevo. (Illus.). 160p. 1992. 15.00 (*0-912927-29-1*, X029) St John Kronstadt.

One Thing Needful: A Book of Meditations for the Busy Orthodox Woman. Colette D. Jonopulos. LC 96-77485. 164p. (Orig.). 1996. pap. 14.95 (*1-880971-23-2*) Light&Life Pub Co MN.

One Thing Never Changes. Shawn Strannigan. (I Can Understand Ser.). (Illus.). 24p. (J). (ps-2). 1995. pap. 2.99 (*0-7847-0291-8*, 03458) Standard Pub.

One Thing That Can Save Us. Barry Silesky. LC 93-23691. (Coffee to Go: Short Short Stories Ser.). 128p. (Orig.). 1994. pap. 10.95 (*1-56689-020-9*) Coffee Hse.

One Thing That's True. Cheryl Foggo. 128p. (J). 1997. pap. 16.95 (*1-55074-377-5*) Kids Can Pr.

One Thing That's True. unabridged ed. Cheryl Foggo. 128p. (J). (gr. 6-10). 1998. 16.95 (*1-55074-411-9*, Pub. by Kids Can Pr) Genl Dist Srvs.

One Thing Worse Than Being Alone - Wishing You Were! Craving Solitude & Getting It. Alyce P. Cornyn-Selby. 78p. (Orig.). 1989. pap. 8.95 (*0-941383-07-5*) Beynch Pr.

One Thing Worth Having. Lona B. Kennedy & Allen Bennington. LC 81-83207. 236p. 1982. 12.50 (*0-937884-02-2*, Bennington Bks); pap. 8.50 (*0-937884-03-0*, Bennington Bks) Hystry Mystry.

One Third of a Nation. Lorenzo Morris. 1997. pap. text 54.00 (*0-88258-170-8*) Howard U Pr.

One-Third of a Nation: A New Look at Housing Affordability in America. Michael E. Stone. LC 90-82884. (Illus.). 66p. (Orig.). 1990. pap. 12.00 (*0-944826-31-8*) Economic Policy Inst.

One-Third of a Nation: African American Perspectives. Ed. by Lorenzo Morris & Ura J. Bailey. LC 99-34930. (Illus.). 504p. (C). 1999. pap. text 29.95 (*0-88258-167-8*, MOOT1P) Howard U Pr.

One-Third of a Nation: African American Perspectives, Vol. II. Lorenzo Morris & Ura J. Bailey. (Illus.). 504p. (C). 1997. pap. text 29.95 (*0-88258-168-6*, MOOT2P) Howard U Pr.

One Third of a Nation: Lorena Hickok Reports on the Great Depression. Lorena Hickok. Ed. by Richard Lowitt & Maurine H. Beasley. LC 80-25905. (Illus.). 440p. 1981. reprint ed. 21.95 (*0-252-01096-5*) U of Ill Pr.

One-Third of What Is Known about Natural Philosophy. Paul B. Randolph. 103p. (C). 1989. pap. text 4.50 (*0-317-93248-9*) Randolph Dallas.

One Third Off. Irvin S. Cobb. (Collected Works of Irvin S. Cobb). 148p. 1998. reprint ed. lib. bdg. 88.00 (*1-58201-604-6*) Classic Bks.

134 Sound-Loaded Scenes for Articulation. Illus. by Patti Rishforth. 135p. (J). (gr. k-5). 1997. spiral bd., wbk. ed. 25.95 (*1-58650-054-6*, BK-251) Super Duper.

137 Traditional Crown Moldings: Collection A10. Mike Tecton. (Illus.). 1994. pap. 28.00 (*0-922070-15-6*, COLLECTION A10) M Tecton Pub.

***One Thomas Too Many.** Fay Harbison & Ellen M. Surber. Ed. by Ralph Baber. 208p. 2000. pap. 10.95 (*0-9634733-4-4*) Ogden Pr TX.

One Thought, Eternal Life: The Church in the Hearts of Men. James' Foodland, Inc. Staff & Mitchell E. James, Sr. 317p. (C). 1996. pap. 45.00 (*1-888758-01-5*) Uno Little Pr.

1,911 Best Things Anybody Ever Said. Robert Byrne. (Illus.). 352p. 1988. pap. 12.00 (*0-449-90285-4*) Fawcett.

1000, Vol. 2. rev. ed. Salem Kirban. (Six Six Six/One Thousand Ser.). (Illus.). 1984. pap. 7.99 (*0-89957-901-9*) AMG Pubs.

1000 Airlines in Color. Gerry Manning. LC 98-25176. (Illus.). 144p. 1998. pap. 22.95 (*0-89658-410-0*) Voyageur Pr.

One Thousand American Fungi. Charles McIlvaine & Robert K. MacAdam. LC 72-91857. (Illus.). 1973. reprint ed. pap. 15.00 (*0-87110-094-0*) Ultramarine Pub.

One Thousand & One Affixes & Their Meanings: A Dictionary of Prefixes, Suffixes & Inflections. rev. ed. Raymond E. Laurita. 154p. (YA). (gr. 9-12). 1995. pap. 14.95 (*0-914051-36-9*) Leonardo Pr.

1001 African Names: First & Last Names from the African Continent. Julia Stewart. LC 95-49286. 172p. 1996. pap. 10.95 (*0-8065-1737-9*, Citadel Pr) Carol Pub Group.

***One Thousand & One Arabian Nights.** Geraldine McCaughrean. (Oxford Story Collections). (Illus.). 288p. (YA). 2000. pap. 12.95 (*0-19-275013-5*) OUP.

1001 Baseball Questions. Dom Forker. LC 97-156059. 1997. mass mkt. 5.99 (*0-451-19132-3*, Sig) NAL.

One Thousand & One Broadways: Hometown Talent on Stage. Lorelei F. Eckey et al. LC 82-14806. (Illus.). 173p. 1982. reprint ed. pap. 53.70 (*0-608-00041-8*, 206080700006) Bks Demand.

One Thousand & One Business Leads: The Ultimate Guide to Cutting Through Red Tape & Making. Gale Research Staff. LC 94-229203. 1994. pap. 12.95 (*0-8065-1511-2*, Citadel Pr) Carol Pub Group.

One Thousand & One Business Profit Making Ideas. Allan H. Smith. LC 86-62768. 50p. (Orig.). 1986. pap. 6.00 (*0-931113-06-7*) Success Publ.

One Thousand & One Country Hints. Booksales Staff. 1994. 4.98 (*0-7858-0110-3*) Bk Sales Inc.

One Thousand & One Delights. rev. ed. Nahda Salah. 396p. 1992. 15.95 (*1-887584-03-X*) Intl Prom Art.

1,001 Facts Somebody Screwed Up. Deane Jordan. LC 92-84014. (Illus.). 132p. 1993. pap. 6.95 (*1-56352-064-8*) Longstreet.

One Thousand & One Floral Motifs & Ornaments for Artists & Craftspeople. Ed. by Carol B. Grafton. (Pictorial Archive Ser.). 121p. (Orig.). 1987. pap. 8.95 (*0-486-25352-X*) Dover.

One Thousand & One Great Jokes. Jeff Rovin. 1989. mass mkt. 5.99 (*0-451-15979-9*, Sig) NAL.

One Thousand One High Performance Tech Tips: Engines, Drivetrain, Chassis, Suspension, Power Tuning, Body, Interior, Workshop. Wayne Scraba. LC 94-24716. (Illus.). 169p. (Orig.). 1995. pap. 17.95 (*1-55788-199-5*, HP Books) Berkley Pub.

One Thousand & One Homonyms & Their Meanings: A Dictionary of Homonyms with Defining Sentences. Raymond E. Laurita. 160p. (Orig.). (YA). (gr. 9-12). 1992. pap. 14.95 (*0-914051-29-6*) Leonardo Pr.

One Thousand & One Ideas for English Papers. 2nd ed. Walter J. Miller. 288p. 1994. 10.00 (*0-671-88766-1*) Prntice Hall Bks.

One Thousand & One Ideas for Science Projects. 2nd ed. Marion A. Brisk. 272p. 1994. 12.95 (*0-671-89029-8*) Prntice Hall Bks.

1,001 Lewdest Limericks: An Erotic Collection. Ronald Stanza. 256p. 1996. pap. 9.95 (*0-8065-1774-3*, Citadel Pr) Carol Pub Group.

One Thousand & One Manipulatives for Math. Alison Abrohms. 1993. pap. 16.95 (*0-590-49238-1*) Scholastic Inc.

One Thousand & One Most Asked Questions about the American West. Harry E. Chrisman. LC 82-6337. (Illus.). xiv, 349p. 1982. pap. 19.95 (*0-8040-0383-1*) Swallow.

***1001 Most Useful English Words for Spanish-Speaking People.** Seymour Resnick. 2000. pap. 1.50 (*0-486-41128-1*) Dover.

One Thousand & One Nights. 1970. pap. 37.50 (*0-7100-0206-8*, Routledge Thoemms) Routledge.

1001 Programming Resources. Edward J. Renehan, Jr. LC 97-171645. 528p. 1996. pap. 49.95 incl. cd-rom (*1-884133-50-9*, Jamsa Press) Gulf Pub.

One Thousand & One Questions & Answers about Wine. Henry Walker. 224p. 1976. 7.95 (*0-8184-0214-8*) Carol Pub Group.

One Thousand & One Questions Answered about Birds. Allan D. Cruickshank & Helen Cruickshank. LC 75-41881. (One Thousand & One Questions Ser.). (Illus.). 320p. 1976. reprint ed. pap. 7.95 (*0-486-23315-4*) Dover.

One Thousand & One Questions Answered about Earthquakes, Avalanches, Floods & Other Natural Disasters. Barbara Tufty. (One Thousand & One Questions Ser.). (Illus.). 350p. 1978. reprint ed. pap. 7.95 (*0-486-23646-3*) Dover.

One Thousand & One Questions Answered about the Seashore. N. J. Berrill & Jacquelyn Berrill. LC 76-12889. (One Thousand & One Questions Ser.). (Illus.). 305p. 1976. reprint ed. pap. 8.95 (*0-486-23366-9*) Dover.

One Thousand & One Scrolls, Ornaments & Borders: Ready-to-Use Illustrations for Decoupage & Other Crafts. Ed. by Eleanor H. Rawlings. (Illus.). 128p. 1979. pap. 8.95 (*0-486-23795-8*) Dover.

One Thousand & One-Second Stories. Inagaki Taruho. Tr. by Tricia Vita from JPN. (Sun & Moon Classics Ser.: Vol. 139). 150p. 1997. pap. 12.95 (*1-55713-361-1*) Sun & Moon CA.

One Thousand & One Texas Place Names. Fred Tarpley. LC 80-16828. (Illus.). 256p. 1980. pap. 10.95 (*0-292-76016-7*) U of Tex Pr.

One Thousand & One Things to Do When There's Nothing to Do. Louise Colligan. 128p. (J). (gr. 4-7). 1994. pap. 2.50 (*0-590-46359-4*) Scholastic Inc.

One Thousand & One Ways to Cut Your Expenses. Jonathan D. Pond. 304p. 1992. pap. 10.95 (*0-440-50495-3*) Dell.

One Thousand & One Ways You Can Win at Greyhound Racing. John Braswell. (Illus.). 163p. (Orig.). 1993. pap. 35.00 (*1-883106-00-1*) Key System.

One Thousand Bible Drill Questions. W. Burgess McCreary. 1980. pap. 3.95 (*0-87162-263-7*, WP#D5899) Warner Pr.

1000 Bible Study Outlines. F. E. Marsh. LC 75-125115. 496p. 1970. pap. 17.99 (*0-8254-3247-2*) Kregel.

One Thousand California Place Names: Their Origin & Meaning. 3rd rev. ed. Erwin G. Gudde. LC 68-11311. 1969. pap. 10.95 (*0-520-01432-4*) U CA Pr.

1000 Chairs. Charlotte Fiell. (Klotz Ser.). 1998. pap. 29.99 (*3-8228-7965-7*) Taschen Amer.

One Thousand Chestnut Trees: A Novel of Korea. Mira Stout. LC 97-37521. 336p. 1998. 23.95 (*1-57322-073-6*, Riverhead Books) Putnam Pub Group.

***One Thousand Chestnut Trees: A Novel of Korea.** Mira Stout. 1999. reprint ed. pap. 14.00 (*1-57322-738-2*, Riverhd Trade) Berkley Pub.

One Thousand Chinese Characters with Literary Glosses. Hugh M. Stimson. 1968. 6.95 (*0-88710-054-6*) Yale Far Eastern Pubns.

1,000 Classic Recipes. Lorenz. (Illus.). 19.98 (*0-7548-0255-8*, Pub. by Anness Pub) Random.

One Thousand Cornish Place Names Explained. Julyan Holmes. (C). 1989. 35.00 (*0-907566-76-6*, Pub. by Dyllansow Truran) St Mut.

1,000 Crazy Jokes for Kids. Michael Johnstone. (J). 1987. 10.09 (*0-606-03658-X*, Pub. by Turtleback) Demco.

One Thousand Crazy Jokes for Kids. Michael Johnstone. 192p. 1988. reprint ed. mass mkt. 4.99 (*0-345-34694-7*) Ballantine Pub Grp.

One Thousand Days in Siberia: The Odyssey of a Japanese-American POW. Iwao P. Sano. LC 96-54629. (Illus.). xxii, 216p. 1997. text 30.00 (*0-8032-4262-X*) U of Nebr Pr.

One Thousand Days in Siberia: The Odyssey of a Japanese-American POW. Iwao P. Sano. LC 96-54629. (Illus.). 216p. 1999. pap. 12.00 (*0-8032-9260-0*, Bison Books) U of Nebr Pr.

1000 Design & Ideas. D. M. Campana. 1200p. 1998. 17.00 (*0-939608-39-1*) Campana Art.

1000 Dessous: A History of Lingerie. Gilles Neret. 1998. pap. 29.99 (*3-8228-7629-1*) Taschen Amer.

One Thousand Dollars down Can Make You Rich: Tactics for Real Estate Investors. Jack Cummings. 320p. 1985. 24.95 (*0-317-18450-4*) P-H.

1,000 Dutch Proverbs. Ed. by Gerd De Ley. LC 98-12002. 131p. 1998. pap. 11.95 (*0-7818-0616-X*) Hippocrene Bks.

1,818 Ways to Write Better & Get Published. Scott Edelstein. LC 96-50383. Orig. Title: The Writer's Book of Checklists. 224p. 1997. pap. 14.99 (*0-89879-778-0*, Wrtrs Digest Bks) F & W Pubns Inc.

1836 Facts about the Alamo: And the Texas War for Independence. Mary Deborah Petite. ("Facts About" History Ser.: Vol. 2). (Illus.). 170p. 1999. pap. 11.95 (*1-882810-35-X*) Savas Pub.

1008 Secrets of a Happy Marriage, Wedding Gift Version. Andy Zubko & Andrew William. (Radiant Life Ser.). 205p. (Orig.). 1997. pap. 5.95 (*1-889606-03-0*) Radiant Summit.

1008 Secrets of a Happy Marriage: Best Wishes to the Newlyweds. Andy Zubko & Andrew William. (Radiant Life Ser.). 205p. (Orig.). 1997. pap. 5.95 (*1-889606-05-7*) Radiant Summit.

1080 Degree Snowboarding: Prima's Unauthorized Game Secrets. Tim Bogenn. LC 98-65659. 80p. 1998. per. 12.99 (*0-7615-1592-5*) Prima Pub.

***1000 Families.** Uwe Ommer. 2000. 39.99 (*3-8228-6213-4*) Taschen Amer.

One Thousand Fiddle Tunes: Authentic Country Fiddle Playing--The Fiddler's Bible. Cole, M. M. Publishing Company Editorial Staff. 128p. 1992. spiral bd. 30.00 (*0-8471-0450-8*) M M Cole.

1005 Salt & Pepper Shakers. Larry Carey & Sylvia Tompkins. LC 99-61080. (Illus.). 160p. 1999. pap. 29.95 (*0-7643-0880-7*) Schiffer.

1,500 Ceist Agam Ort t. Cathal Poirteir. (IRI & GAE.). 144p. 1997. pap. 9.95 (*1-85635-142-4*, Pub. by Mercier Pr) Irish Amer Bk.

***1,500 Illustrations for Biblical Preaching.** Ed. by Michael P. Green. LC 99-58160. 450p. (gr. 13 up). 2000. pap. 19.99 (*0-8010-6330-2*) Baker Bks.

1500+ Keywords for $100,000+ Jobs: Tools to Build Winning Resumes. Wendy S. Enelow. LC 97-51728. 1998. pap. text 14.95 (*1-57023-089-7*) Impact VA.

1529 Holy Week & Easter Sermons of Dr. Martin Luther. Martin Luther & Irving L. Sandberg. LC 98-43556. 1999. 20.00 (*0-570-04281-X*) Concordia.

***1000 For 2000: Predictions for the New Millennium.** John Hogue. LC BF1809.H63 1999. 304p. 1999. pap. 8.95 (*0-06-251806-2*) HarpC.

One Thousand Four Hundred & One Things That P*Ss Me Off. I.M. Peeved. 1991. pap. 5.95 (*0-399-51670-0*, Perigee Bks) Berkley Pub.

1475 Conclusions of a Healing Codependent. Dee Frances. 105p. (Orig.). 1994. pap. 9.95 (*0-9635341-8-1*) DDDD Pubns.

1004 Salt & Pepper Shakers. Larry Carey & Sylvia Tompkins. LC 97-81443. 160p. 1998. pap. 29.95 (*0-7643-0553-0*) Schiffer.

1,000 French Words. Berlitz Kids Editors. LC 98-196846. (ENG & FRE., Illus.). 64p. 1998. pap. 12.95 (*2-8315-6549-9*, Berlitz Kids) Berlitz.

One Thousand Fruit Jars Priced. 5th ed. Bill Schroeder. 1996. pap. 5.95 (*0-89145-347-4*, 1782) Collector Bks.

1,000 German Words. Berlitz Kids Editors. LC 98-196843. (ENG & GER., Illus.). 64p. 1998. pap. 12.95 (*2-8315-6550-2*, Berlitz Kids) Berlitz.

1000 Great Guitarists. Hugh Gregory. 164p. 1997. pap. 24.95 incl. audio compact disk (*0-87930-416-2*) Miller Freeman.

***1000 Great Rail-Trails.** Rails-to-Trails Conservancy Staff. LC 99-45628. (Illus.). 256p. 1999. pap. text 14.95 (*0-7627-0598-1*) Globe Pequot.

One Thousand Hour War: Communication in the Gulf, 148. Ed. by Thomas A. McCain & Leonard Shyles. LC 93-12979. (Contributions in Military Studies Ser.: No. 148). 232p. 1993. 57.95 (*0-313-28747-3*, GM8747, Greenwood Pr) Greenwood.

One Thousand Howlers for Kids. Joel Rothman. 224p. 1990. mass mkt. 4.99 (*0-345-36155-5*) Ballantine Pub Grp.

1000 Howlers for Kids. Joel Rothman. (J). 1990. 10.09 (*0-606-01288-5*, Pub. by Turtleback) Demco.

One Thousand Illustrations for Preaching & Teaching. G. Curtis Jones. 400p. 1986. pap. 19.99 (*0-8054-2249-8*, 4222-49) Broadman.

1,000 Indian Recipes. 608p. 2000. 35.00 (*0-02-862588-9*, Pub. by Macmillan) S&S Trade.

1000 Instant Words. Edward Fry. 1996. pap. 8.33 (*0-8092-0880-6*) NTC Contemp Pub Co.

One Thousand Instant Words: The Most Common Words for Teaching Reading, Writing, & Spelling. Edward Fry. 64p. 1994. 6.95 (*0-87673-025-X*) Tchr Create Mat.

One Thousand Islands. John DeVisser & Patsy Fleming. (Illus.). 120p. 1990. 29.95 (*1-55046-044-7*, Pub. by Boston Mills) Genl Dist Srvs.

1,000 Italian Words. Berlitz Kids Editors. (ENG & ITA., Illus.). 64p. 1998. pap. 12.95 (*2-8315-6551-0*, Berlitz Kids) Berlitz.

1,000 Jewish Recipes. Faye Levy. LC 99-55743. 640p. 2000. 32.50 (*0-02-862337-1*) Macmillan.

One Thousand Jokes for Kids of All Ages. Michael Kilgarriff. 240p. (J). (gr. k up). 1986. mass mkt. 4.99 (*0-345-33480-9*) Ballantine Pub Grp.

1,000 Jokes for Kids of All Ages. Michael Kilgarriff. (J). 1974. 10.09 (*0-606-04143-5*, Pub. by Turtleback) Demco.

1000 Keyboard Ideas. Ronald Herder. 244p. 1994. pap. 24.95 (*0-943748-48-8*, PF0724) Ekay Music.

One Thousand Keys to the Truth: Spiritual Guidelines for Latter Days & Second Coming. Mark-Age Staff. LC 75-40976. 156p. 1976. pap. 7.00 (*0-912322-51-9*) Mark-Age.

1,000 Knock Knock Jokes for Kids. Michael Kilgarriff. (J). 1986. 10.09 (*0-606-01287-7*, Pub. by Turtleback) Demco.

One Thousand Knock Knock Jokes for Kids. Ward Lock, Ltd. Staff. 240p. (J). (gr. 4-7). 1986. mass mkt. 4.99 (*0-345-33481-7*) Ballantine Pub Grp.

One Thousand Largest U. S. Banks, 1989. 850p. 1989. 295.00 (*0-317-93791-X*) Sheshunoff.

1000 Makers of the Millennium. DK Publishing Staff. LC 99-14757. 224p. (YA). (gr. 3 up). 1999. 19.95 (*0-7894-4709-6*) DK Pub Inc.

1000 MCQs for Davidson's Principles & Practice of Medicine. Michael J. Ford & A. T. Elder. LC 96-26058. 1997. write for info. (*0-443-05556-4*) Church.

1000 MCQs for Davidson's Principles & Practice of Medicine. 3rd ed. Michael J. Ford & A. T. Elder. LC 96-26058. 1997. pap. text 29.95 (*0-443-05462-2*) Church.

***1000 MCQs for Davidson's Principles & Practice of Medicine.** 4th ed. Ford. 1999. text 29.00 (*0-443-06399-0*) Harcrt Hlth Sci Grp.

***1000 Mexican Recipes.** 640p. 1999. 35.00 (*0-02-863722-4*) S&S Trade.

1,000 Monster Jokes for Kids. Frank N. Stein. (J). 1989. 10.09 (*0-606-01286-9*, Pub. by Turtleback) Demco.

O

One Thousand More Jokes for Kids. Michael Kilgarriff. 224p. (J). (gr. k up). 1987. mass mkt. 4.99 (*0-345-34034-5*) Ballantine Pub Grp.

1,000 More Jokes for Kids. Michael Kilgarriff. (J). 1982. 10.09 (*0-606-04144-3*, Pub. by Turtleback) Demco.

One Thousand Most Important Words. Norman W. Schur. 256p. 1982. mass mkt. 4.99 (*0-345-29863-2*) Ballantine Pub Grp.

1,000 Most Practical Words. Norman W. Schur. 1984. 18.95 (*0-87196-868-1*) Facts on File.

1,999 Facts about Blacks. 2nd rev. ed. Raymond M. Corbin. 228p. 1996. pap. 16.95 (*1-56833-081-2*) Madison Bks UPA.

1938 Geschichte im Gedicht. Mimi Grossberg. (Studies in Austrian Literature, Culture, & Thought). (GER.). 100p. 1994. pap. 9.00 (*0-929497-85-6*) Ariadne CA.

***1912 Facts about Titanic.** Lee W. Merideth. (Illus.). iv, 224p. 1999. pap. 12.95 (*0-9626237-4-1*) Hist Indexes.

1912 Facts about Titanic. Lee W. Merideth. ("Facts About" History Ser.: Vol. 1). (Illus.). 224p. 1999. pap. 11.95 (*1-882810-33-3*) Savas Pub.

1000 Nudes. Uwe Scheid. 756p. 1995. pap. 29.99 (*3-8228-8935-0*) Taschen Amer.

***1000 Objects.** Oliviero Toscani. (Illus.). 2000. pap. 29.99 (*3-8228-5820-X*) Taschen Amer.

1000 on 42nd Street. Tibor Kalman. LC 99-12306. (Illus.). 300p. 1999. pap. 35.00 (*1-57687-045-6*, pwerHse Bks) pwerHse Cultrl.

***1001: A Video Odyssey; Movies to Watch for Your Every Mood.** Steve Tatham. (Illus.). 2000. pap. 15.95 (*1-58065-023-6*) Lone Eagle Pub.

1001 Activities for Children. Rogovin. LC 97-50527. 208p. 1999. 6.99 (*0-517-20283-2*) Random Hse Value.

One Thousand One Advertising Cuts from the Twenties & Thirties. Ed. by Leslie E. Cabarga et al. (Pictorial Archive Ser.). (Illus.). 112p. (Orig.). 1987. pap. 8.95 (*0-486-25490-9*) Dover.

1001 Advertising Tips. Luc Dupont. (Illus.). 290p. 1996. pap. 19.95 (*0-9699834-0-9*) White Rock Pubng.

1001 African Names. Julia Stewart. 224p. 1995. pap. 10.95 (*0-8065-1739-5*, Citadel Pr) Carol Pub Group.

1,001 Afternoons in Chicago. Paul Peditto. 94p. 1998. pap. 5.60 (*0-87129-836-8*, 060) Dramatic Pub.

***1001 All-Time Best-Selling Home Plans.** Home Planners Editors. 704p. 2000. pap. 12.95 (*1-881955-67-2*) Home Planners.

One-Thousand-One Alternatives to Corporal Punishment, Vol. 1. Adah Maurer. (Illus.). 58p. 1984. 5.95 (*0-932141-03-X*) End Violence.

One Thousand One Annees de la Nostalgie. Rachid Boudjedra. (FRE.). 435p. 1988. pap. 16.95 (*0-7859-2104-4*, 2070380874) Fr & Eur.

1,001 Anos de la Lengua Espanola (1,001 Years of the Spanish Language) Antonio Alatorre. (SPA.). 343p. 1989. pap. 16.99 (*968-16-3116-1*, Pub. by Fondo) Continental Bk.

1001 Basketball Trivia Questions. Dale Ratermann & Brian Brosi. 184p. 1999. pap. 12.95 (*1-58382-006-X*) Sports Masters.

1001 Beauty Solutions: The Ultimate One-Step Adviser for Your Everyday Beauty Questions. Beth Barrick-Hickey. LC 95-24937. (Illus.). 160p. 1995. pap. 12.95 (*1-57071-049-X*) Sourcebks.

1001 Best Pick-Up Lines. Don Diebel. 96p. 1999. pap. 14.95 (*0-937164-05-4*) Gemini Pub Co.

1001 Bible Questions Answered. William L. Pettingill. 496p. 1997. 9.99 (*0-88486-165-1*, Bristol Park Bks) Arrowood Pr.

One Thousand One Brilliant Ways to Checkmate. Fred Reinfeld. (Illus.). 1969. reprint ed. pap. 10.00 (*0-87980-110-7*) Wilshire.

1001 Cartoon-Style Illustrations. J. I. Biegeleisen & Dave Ubinas. LC 95-39683. (Pictorial Archive Ser.). (Illus.). 144p. 1996. pap. 8.95 (*0-486-29047-6*) Dover.

***1,001 Chemicals in Everyday Products.** 2nd ed. Grace R. Lewis. LC 98-6419. 400p. 1998. pap. 43.95 (*0-471-29212-5*, Wiley-Interscience) Wiley.

1,001 Chemicals in Everyday Products. Grace Ross Lewis. (Illus.). 344p. 1993. pap. text 26.95 (*0-442-01458-9*, VNR) Wiley.

1001 Chocolate Treats. Gregg R. Gillespie. (Illus.). 440p. 1996. 19.98 (*1-884822-86-X*) Blck Dog & Leventhal.

One Thousand One Christmas Facts & Fancies. Alfred C. Hottes. LC 89-63110. (Illus.). 308p. 1990. reprint ed. lib. bdg. 44.00 (*1-55888-858-6*) Omnigraphics Inc.

One Thousand One Civil War Trivia. rev. ed. Charles B. O'Brien. (Illus.). 156p. (Orig.). 1994. pap. text 8.95 (*0-9637602-0-3*) Neirbo Bks.

One Thousand One Colorado Place Names. Maxine Benson. LC 94-13556. (Illus.). 230p. 1994. 25.00 (*0-7006-0632-7*); pap. 11.95 (*0-7006-0633-5*) U Pr of KS.

1001 Commonly Misspelled Words: What Your Spell Checker Won't Tell You. Robert Magnan & Mary Lou Santovec. 272p. 2000. pap. 12.95 (*0-07-135736-X*) McGraw.

1001 Cosas Que Buscar en la Granja. Usborne Books Staff. (1001 Things to Spot Ser.). 1999. 14.95 (*1-58086-212-8*) EDC.

***1001 Cosas Que Buscar en el Pasado.** Usborne Books Staff. (SPA., Illus.). 32p. (ps up). 2000. 14.95 (*1-58086-286-1*, Usborne) EDC.

***1001 Cosas que Buscar en la Granja (1001 Things to Spot on the Farm)** Gillian Doherty. (One Thousand One Things to Spot Ser.). (SPA., Illus.). 32p. (J). (ps up). 1999. pap. 6.95 (*0-7460-3652-3*, Usborne) EDC.

1001 Craft Verses. Cheryl Phillips. (Illus.). 96p. 1996. write for info. (*0-614-13950-3*) Landmark Pubs Inc.

***1001 Curious Things: Ye Olde Curiosity Shop & Native American Art.** Kate C. Duncan. (Illus.). 248p. 2001. 35.00 (*0-295-98010-9*) U of Wash Pr.

One Thousand One Designs for Whittling & Woodcarving. unabridged ed. Elmer J. Tangerman. (Illus.). 192p. 1995. pap. text 13.95 (*0-486-28362-3*) Dover.

1001 Do-It-Yourself Hints & Tips: Tricks, Shortcuts, How-Tos & Other Nifty Ideas for Inside, Outside & All Around the House. LC 97-22347. 1998. 29.95 (*0-7621-0049-4*, Pub. by RD Assn) Penguin Putnam.

1001 Do-It-Yourself Tips: Hints, Tricks, & Shortcuts for Your Home. Better Homes & Gardens. (Better Homes & Gardens Ser.). (Illus.). 192p. 1995. pap. 19.95 (*0-696-20478-9*) Meredith Bks.

1,001 Easy Tips for Garden & Landscape Design. 352p. 1998. 19.95 (*0-02-862871-3*, Pub. by Macmillan) S&S Trade.

One Thousand One Fascinating Baseball Facts. (Illus.). 384p. 1993. 19.98 (*1-56173-998-7*, 3512600) Pubns Intl Ltd.

One Thousand One Flying Facts & Firsts. Joe Christy. (Illus.). 224p. 1989. 24.95 (*0-8306-9228-2*, 2428); pap. 15.95 (*0-8306-9428-5*, 2428P) McGraw-Hill Prof.

1001 Free Recipes: Directory of Free & Low Cost Recipe Sources. Ed. by Lynn Kerrigan. LC 95-70740. (Illus.). 42p. (Orig.). 1995. pap. text 4.95 (*0-9644757-0-7*) Page One Assocs.

***1001 Funk & Blues Guitar Licks.** Austin Sicard. 216p. 1998. 22.95 (*0-7866-3482-0*, 95378BCD) Mel Bay.

1001 Great Gift Ideas. Jane A. Brody et al. 168p. 1999. 12.99 (*1-57866-064-5*) Galahad Bks.

1001 Great Jokes. Jeff Rovin. 1987. mass mkt. 5.99 (*0-451-16829-1*) NAL.

1001 Great Stories & Quotes. Kent R. Hughes. LC 97-34836. 1998. 14.99 (*0-8423-0409-6*) Tyndale Hse.

1,001 Great Things about Growing Old. 112p. pap. 6.95 (*0-8216-1000-7*) Carol Pub Group.

1,001 Health-Care Questions Women Ask. 3rd ed. Joe S. McIlhaney, Jr. & Susan Nethery. LC 98-3257. (Illus.). 576p. (C). (gr. 13). 1998. pap. 19.99 (*0-8010-5810-4*) Baker Bks.

1001 Hints & Tips for Your Garden. Reader's Digest Editors. LC 96-179. (Illus.). 416p. 1996. 30.00 (*0-89577-860-2*, Pub. by RD Assn) Penguin Putnam.

1001 Humorous Illustrations for Public Speaking: Fresh, Timely & Compelling Illustrations for Preachers, Teachers, & Public Speakers. Michael Hodgin. LC 94-32880. (Illus.). 288p. 1994. pap. 12.99 (*0-310-47391-8*) Zondervan.

1144 Paths to Happiness: The Emerging Science. Francis S. Onderdonk. LC 95-61410. 1997. 24.95 (*0-533-11622-8*) Vantage.

One Thousand One Hundred One Businesses You Can Start from Home. Daryl A. Hall. (Small Business Editions Ser.). 352p. 1994. pap. 19.95 (*0-471-10241-5*) Wiley.

One Thousand One Hundred One Businesses You Can Start from Home. 2nd ed. Daryl A. Hall. (Small Business Editions Ser.). 352p. 1994. 65.00 (*0-471-10237-7*) Wiley.

1101 Ways to Get Published: The Inside Track to Writing & Selling Magazine Articles. (Illus.). 154p. (Orig.). 1996. pap. 16.95 (*0-9653511-0-6*) Stingray Pr.

1,112 Down to Earth Garden Secrets. Reiman Publications Staff. LC 98-65083. 180p. 1998. 16.95 (*0-89821-233-2*) Reiman Pubns.

1100 Words You Need to Know. 3rd ed. Murray Bromberg & Melvin Gordon. LC 93-1014. 280p. 1993. pap. 10.95 (*0-8120-1620-3*) Barron.

***1100 Words You Need to Know.** 4th ed. Murray Bromberg & Melvin Gordon. 280p. 2000. pap. 11.95 (*0-7641-1365-8*) Barron.

1001 Ideas for Science Projects on the Environment. Marion A. Brisk. (Illus.). 256p. 1997. pap. 12.95 (*0-02-861707-X*, Arc) IDG Bks.

1001 Ideas for Science Projects. 3rd ed. Marion Brisk. LC 97-81089. (Illus.). 256p. 1998. 12.95 (*0-02-862513-7*, Arc) IDG Bks.

One Thousand One Ideas for Science Projects. Marion A. Brisk. (Illus.). 224p. 1991. pap. 12.00 (*0-13-633769-4*, Arco) Macmillan Gen Ref.

One Thousand One Ideas to Create Retail Excitement. Edgar A. Falk. LC 94-1050. 320p. (C). 1994. pap. text 19.95 (*0-13-292393-9*) P-H.

One Thousand One Illuminated Initial Letters: Twenty-Seven Full-Color Plates. Owen Jones. (Pictorial Archive Ser.). (Illus.). 32p. 1988. reprint ed. pap. 7.95 (*0-486-25607-3*) Dover.

1001 Incredible Tennis Games, Drills & Tips: A Super Abundance of Information for Every Teaching Professional & Tennis Enthusiast. Tina Hoskins. LC 97-93243. (Illus.). 203p. 1997. pap. 29.95 (*0-9658814-0-7*) Hoskins & Grant.

1001 Ingenious Gardening Ideas: New, Fun & Fabulous That Will Change the Way You Garden - Forever. Ed. by Deborah L. Martin. LC 99-6038. 345p. 1999. text 27.95 (*0-87596-809-0*) Rodale Pr Inc.

1001 Internet Tips. Bill Malone et al. (Illus.). 750p. 2000. pap. 54.95 incl. cd-rom (*1-884133-67-3*, Jamsa Press) Gulf Pub.

1001 Java Programmer's Tips. Steven Griffith et al. LC 97-157844. 624p. 1996. pap. 49.95 incl. cd-rom (*1-884133-32-0*, Jamsa Press) Gulf Pub.

One Thousand One Kansas Place Names. Sondra Van Meter McCoy & Jan E. Hults. LC 89-8885. (Illus.). xvi, 224p. 1989. 25.00 (*0-7006-0392-1*); pap. 9.95 (*0-7006-0393-X*) U Pr of KS.

1,001 Komputer Answers from Kim Komando. Kim Komando. 800p. 1995. pap. 29.99 (*1-56884-460-3*) IDG Bks.

***1001 Linux Tips.** Armand Danesh. (Illus.). 700p. 2000. pap. 54.95 incl. audio compact disk (*1-884133-78-9*, Jamsa Press) Gulf Pub.

1001 Low-Fat Desserts: Delicious, Easy-to-Make Treats for Everyone. Sue Spitler & Linda Yoakam. LC 98-53328. 756p. 1999. pap. 19.95 (*1-57284-028-5*) Surrey Bks.

***1,001 Low-Fat Soups & Stews.** Ed. by Sue Spitler. 850p. 2000. pap. 19.95 (*1-57284-034-X*) Surrey Bks.

***1,001 Low-Fat Vegetarian Recipes.** 2nd ed. Sue Spitler & Linda R. Yoakam. LC 00-26333. (Illus.). 800p. 2000. pap. 19.95 (*1-57284-032-3*) Surrey Bks.

1001 Lowfat Recipes: Quick, Easy, Great Tasting Recipes for the Whole Family. 2nd ed. Ed. by Sue Spitler. 710p. 1998. pap. 19.95 (*1-57284-019-6*) Surrey Bks.

1001 Math Problems. Learning Express Staff. LC 98-49074. 1999. pap. 14.95 (*1-57685-200-8*) LrningExprss.

1001 MCSE Tips. Shane Stigler. 928p. 1998. pap. 54.95 (*1-884133-62-2*, Jamsa Press) Gulf Pub.

One Thousand One Monday Nights: Stories by Twelve Washington Writers. Intro. by Richard Peabody. LC 89-52128. 206p. (Orig.). 1990. pap. 10.00 (*0-9609062-1-5*) WA Expatriates Pr.

1,001 More Facts Somebody Screwed Up. Deane Jordan. LC 96-79794. (Illus.). 144p. (Orig.). 1997. pap. 7.95 (*1-56352-369-8*) Longstreet.

1001 More Humorous Illustrations for Public Speaking: Fresh, Timely, & Compelling Illustrations for Preacher, Teachers, & Speakers. Michael Hodgin. LC 97-17503. (Illus.). 400p. 1998. pap. 15.99 (*0-310-21713-X*) Zondervan.

***1001 More Low-Fat Recipes: Delicious Meals the Whole Family Will Enjoy.** Ed. by Sue Spitler. LC 99-41142. 752p. 2000. pap. 19.95 (*1-57284-031-5*) Surrey Bks.

***1,001 More Secret Codes (1996) for the Hottest Video Games.** Ed. by H. Leigh Davis. (Illus.). 80p. 2000. reprint ed. pap. text 12.00 (*0-7881-9197-7*) DIANE Pub.

***1001 More Things to Do with Your Kids.** Caryl W. Krueger. (Illus.). 2000. pap. 7.99 (*1-57866-081-5*) Galahad Bks.

1001 Most-Asked Texas Gardening Questions. Neil Sperry. LC 96-51263. (Illus.). 282p. 1997. 19.95 (*1-56530-229-X*, Pub. by Summit TX) BookWorld.

1001 Most Useful Spanish Words. Seymour Resnick. (ENG & SPA.). 64p. (Orig.). 1996. pap. text 1.50 (*0-486-29113-8*) Dover.

1001 Muffins, Biscuits, Donuts, Pancakes, Waffles, Popovers, Fritters, Scones, & Other Quick Breads. Gregg R. Gillespie. LC 98-23243. (Illus.). 496p. 1998. 19.98 (*1-57912-042-3*) Blck Dog & Leventhal.

1001 Multiple Choice Questions & Answers in Surgery. 3rd ed. Ed. by H. Rains. (Illus.). 200p. (Orig.). (C). (gr. 13). 1991. pap. text 27.00 (*0-412-40010-3*, Chap & Hall NY) Chapman & Hall.

1001 Multiple Choice Questions & Answers in Surgery: A Companion to Surgical Study Based on "Bailey & Love's Short Practice of Surgery" 4th ed. A. J. Rains. 240p. 1996. pap. 17.99 (*0-412-55560-3*, Pub. by E A) OUP.

1001 Nights Exotica: Erotic Stories & Artwork. Cris Newport. (Illus.). 200p. 1999. pap. 11.00 (*1-886383-82-0*) Pride & Imprints.

***1001 Nights of Drummer Donald McLeod.** Harry Hopkins. 2000. pap. 16.00 (*0-86241-890-9*, Pub. by Canongate Books) Interlink Pub.

1001 Nursing Tips & Timesavers. 3rd ed. Springhouse Publishing Company Staff. Ed. by June Norris. LC 96-69628. (Illus.). 256p. (Orig.). 1996. pap. 18.95 (*0-87434-850-1*) Springhouse Corp.

1001 Office 2000 Tips. Jamsa Press Staff. (Illus.). 750p. 1999. pap. write for info. (*1-884133-71-1*, Jamsa Press) Gulf Pub.

***1001 Pelargoniums.** Hazel Key. (Illus.). 192p. 1999. 24.95 (*0-7134-8268-0*, Pub. by B T B) Branford.

1001 People & Things You Should Know: One Thousand One of the Most Memorable Artists, Entertainers, Inventors & Leaders in Modern History with at Least One Birthday Every Day of the Year. Glenn Thomas. (Illus.). 200p. (YA). 1998. pap. 11.95 (*0-9623944-6-7*) Art & Entertainment.

1001 Perfectly Legal Ways to Get Exactly What You Want, When You Want It, Every Time. FC&A Staff. 560p. 1999. 27.96 (*0-915099-53-5*) FC&A Pub.

1001 Persian-English Proverbs. 2nd ed. Simin K. Habibian. LC 99-10949. (Illus.). 256p. 1999. pap. 16.00 (*0-936347-92-9*) IBEX.

1001 Persian Nights: A Reader's Theater of the Book of Esther. Edward Vander Berg & Robert A. Meyering. (Prime-Time Bible Studies). 84p. 1996. pap., teacher ed. 8.95 (*1-56212-153-7*, 1210-3071) CRC Pubns.

1001 Pitfalls in English Grammar. 3rd ed. Vincent F. Hopper & R. P. Craig. 352p. 1986. pap. 10.95 (*0-8120-3719-7*) Barron.

1001 Pitfalls in French. 3rd ed. James H. Grew. LC 96-86393. (FRE.). 1997. pap. text 10.95 (*0-8120-9651-7*) Barron.

1001 Pitfalls in Spanish. 3rd ed. Marion P. Holt. LC 96-85088. (SPA.). 1997. pap. text 10.95 (*0-8120-9650-9*) Barron.

1001 Plant & Floral Illustrations: From Early Herbals. Richard G. Hatton. (Pictorial Archive Ser.). (Illus.). 256p. 1996. pap. 14.95 (*0-486-29074-3*) Dover.

***1,001 Proverbs for Every Occasion: Wise Thoughts & Insightful Advice from Around the World.** Norma Gleason. LC 99-16392. 1999. 12.95 (*0-8065-2117-1*) Carol Pub Group.

1,001 Proverbs from Tunisia. Isaac Yetiv. (ARA & ENG.). 150p. (Orig.). 1987. 10.00 (*0-89410-615-5*, Three Contnts) L Rienner.

1,001 Questions about Money--Answered. (C). 1998. 19.95 (*0-13-906272-6*, Macmillan Coll) P-H.

1001 Questions & Answers on Pesach. Jeffrey M. Cohen. LC 95-22903. 384p. 1996. 50.00 (*1-56821-523-1*) Aronson.

1,001 Questions & Answers on Rosh Hashanah & Yom Kippur. Jeffrey M. Cohen. LC 97-13022. 1997. 50.00 (*0-7657-9973-1*) Aronson.

1001 Questions Answered About the Mineral Kingdom. unabridged ed. Richard M. Pearl. LC 95-6204. (Illus.). 352p. 1995. reprint ed. pap. text 8.95 (*0-486-28711-4*) Dover.

1001 Questions Answered about Flowers. unabridged ed. Norman Taylor. LC 95-44998. (Illus.). 352p. 1996. reprint ed. pap. text 8.95 (*0-486-29099-9*) Dover.

One Thousand One Questions Answered about Hurricanes, Tornadoes & Other Natural Air Disasters. Barbara Tufty. (Illus.). 416p. 1987. reprint ed. pap. 8.95 (*0-486-25455-0*) Dover.

One Thousand One Questions Answered about Insects. Alexander B. Klots & Elsie B. Klots. (One Thousand & One Questions Ser.). (Illus.). 260p. 1977. reprint ed. pap. 7.95 (*0-486-23470-3*) Dover.

One Thousand One Questions Answered about the Weather. Frank H. Forrester. (Illus.). 448p. 1981. reprint ed. pap. 8.95 (*0-486-24218-8*) Dover.

One Thousand-One Questions Answered about Trees. Rutherford Platt. (Illus.). 352p. 1992. reprint ed. pap. 8.95 (*0-486-27038-6*) Dover.

1001 Questions de Jeu de Sati. rev. ed. Helene Lavoie-Sati. (FRE.). 1994. 19.95 (*2-920083-78-3*) Edns Roseau.

1001 Really Cool Web Sites. Edward J. Renehan, Jr. LC 96-142662. 548p. 1995. pap. 39.95 incl. cd-rom (*1-884133-22-3*, Jamsa Press) Gulf Pub.

1001 Reasons to Think Positive. Ella Patterson. LC 96-29540. 1997. pap. 10.00 (*0-684-83020-5*, Fireside) S&S Trade Pap.

One Thousand One Rhymes & Fingerplays. Totline Staff. LC 93-60788. (Illus.). 312p. (J). (ps). 1994. pap. text, teacher ed. 23.95 (*0-911019-65-0*, WPH 1503) Totline Pubns.

1001 Secret Codes for the Hottest Video Games. BradyGAMES Staff. 96p. 1996. 9.99 (*1-56686-571-9*) Brady Pub.

***1,001 Secret Money Saving Formulas.** Myles Bader. LC 00-27510. 2000. write for info. (*1-58663-000-8*, Friedman-Fairfax) M Friedman Pub Grp Inc.

1001 Secrets for Windows NT Registry. Tim Daniels. LC 97-33918. 500p. (Orig.). 1997. pap. 49.95 incl. cd-rom (*1-882419-68-5*) News Four-Hund.

1001 Sex Secret Every Ma. Chris Allen. LC 94-23333. 352p. 1995. pap. 8.00 (*0-380-72483-9*, Avon Bks) Morrow Avon.

1001 Sex Secret Every Wo. Chris Allen. LC 94-32316. 352p. 1995. pap. 8.00 (*0-380-72484-7*, Avon Bks) Morrow Avon.

One Thousand One Sex Secrets Every Man Should Know. Chris Allen. 340p. (Orig.). 1993. pap. 14.95 (*0-9636454-0-4*) Creat Fire.

One Thousand One Sex Secrets Every Woman Should Know. Chris Allen. 340p. (Orig.). 1993. pap. 14.95 (*0-9636454-1-2*) Creat Fire.

One Thousand One Sex Secrets Set: 1001 Sex Secrets Every Man Should Know; 1001 Sex Secrets Every Woman Should Know, 2 vols., Set. Chris Allen. 680p. 1993. pap. 24.95 (*0-9636454-2-0*) Creat Fire.

1001 Web Site Construction Tips. Kris A. Jamsa & Lars Klander. (Illus.). 700p. (Orig.). 2000. pap. 49.95 incl. cd-rom (*1-884133-19-3*, Jamsa Press) Gulf Pub.

O

***1,001 Skyscrapers.** Eric Howeler & Jeannie Meejin Yoon. LC 99-53587. (Illus.). 64p. 2000. spiral bd. 14.95 (*1-56898-229-1*) Princeton Arch.

1001 Snacks: For Instant Gratification. Gregg R. Gillespie. LC 97-24312. (Illus.). 448p. 1997. 19.98 (*1-884822-97-5*) Blck Dog & Leventhal.

1001 Solved Engineering Fundamentals Problems. 2nd ed. Michael R. Lindeburg. LC 96-51622. 760p. 1997. pap. 35.95 (*1-888577-09-6*, EFPRB2) Prof Pubns CA.

One Thousand One Spot Illustrations of the Lively Twenties. Carol B. Grafton. (Illus.). 123p. (Orig.). 1986. pap. 8.95 (*0-486-25021-0*) Dover.

1,001 Street Fighting Secrets. Sammy Franco. LC 97-170346. (Illus.). 224p. 1997. pap. 39.00 (*0-87364-887-0*) Paladin Pr.

One Thousand One Teaching Props: Simple Props to Make for Working with Young Children. Ed. by Gayle Bittinger & Kathleen Cubley. LC 91-65931. (1001 Ser.). (Illus.). 248p. (Orig.). (J). (ps). 1992. pap. text 19.95 (*0-911019-46-4*, WPH 1501) Totline Pubns.

1001 Teaching Tips: Helpful Hints for Working with Young Children. Totline Staff. Ed. by Kathleen Cubley. LC 93-60118. (1001 Ser.). (Illus.). 208p. (J). (ps). 1993. teacher ed. 17.95 (*0-911019-64-2*, WPH 1502) Totline Pubns.

1,001 Things Every Man Know. Sandler. 1999. pap. text 16.00 (*0-7352-0114-5*) PH Pr.

1001 Things Every Self-Publisher Should Know. Gwendolyn L. Evans. Ed. by Imani Kenyatta. LC 98-66319. (See You at the Top Ser.). 272p. 1998. 15.95 (*1-886580-24-3*) Pinnacle-Syatt.

1,001 Things Everyone Should Know. John A. Garraty. 1996. mass mkt. 15.00 (*0-385-42723-9*) Doubleday.

1001 Things Everyone Should Know about the Universe. William A. Gutsch. (Illus.). 368p. 1999. pap. 15.95 (*0-385-48386-4*) Doubleday.

1001 Things Everyone Should Know about Women's History. Constance Jones. LC 97-44958. (Illus.). 304p. 1998. 24.95 (*0-385-47673-6*) Doubleday.

1001 Things Everyone Should Know about Women's History. Constance Jones. LC 99-56835. 304p. 2000. pap. 15.95 (*0-385-48387-2*, Main St Bks) Doubleday.

***1001 Things Everyone Should Know About Irish-American History.** Ed O'Donnell. 2000. 25.95 (*0-7679-0686-1*) Broadway BDD.

1001 Things Everyone Should Know About the South. John S. Reed. 272p. 1997. pap. 15.95 (*0-385-47442-3*) Doubleday.

An Asterisk (*) at the beginning of an entry indicates that the title is appearing for the first time.

1001 Things Everyone Should Know. Constance Schrader. LC 98-6179. 288p. 1999. pap. 14.95 (0-385-48224-8) Doubleday.

1001 Things Everyone Should Know about African American History. Jeffrey C. Stewart. (Illus.). 416p. 1997. pap. 15.95 (0-385-48576-X, Main St Bks) Doubleday.

***1001 Things Everyone Should Know about the Civil War.** Frank Vandiver. LC 00-26238. 400p. 2000. pap. 15.95 (0-7679-0543-1) Broadway BDD.

1001 Things Everyone Should Know about the Civil War. Frank E. Vandiver. LC 98-22084. 288p. 1999. 24.95 (0-385-47385-0) Doubleday.

One Thousand One Things Everyone Should Know about American History. John A. Garraty. 224p. 1992. pap. 15.95 (0-385-42577-5) Doubleday.

***1,001 Things For Kids on the Internet.** Kurt Nichols. (YA). (gr. k-12). 1999. pap. 9.95 (0-9670123-0-9) Just Child.

One Thousand One Things to Do with Apple II. Mark R. Sawusch. 1991. 24.95 (0-8306-6232-4) McGraw-Hill Prof.

1001 Things to Do with Your Kids. Caryl W. Krueger. LC 87-30794. 320p. (YA). (gr. 9-12). 1988. pap. 4.49 (0-687-29192-5) Abingdon.

1001 Things to Do with Your Kids. Caryl Waller Krueger. 1999. 7.99 (1-57866-044-0) Galahad Bks.

One Thousand One Things to Do with Your Amiga. Dave Prochnow & Knott. 1991. 24.95 (0-8306-6427-0) McGraw-Hill Prof.

One Thousand One Things to Do with Your Apple. Mark R. Sawusch & Tan A. Summers. (Illus.). 256p. (Orig.). 1984. 15.95 (0-8306-0816-8, 1816) McGraw-Hill Prof.

One Thousand One Things to Do with Your Commodore. Mark R. Sawusch. 1991. 24.95 (0-8306-6418-1) McGraw-Hill Prof.

One Thousand One Things to Do with Your IBM. Mark R. Sawusch. 1991. 24.95 (0-8306-6614-1) McGraw-Hill Prof.

One Thousand One Things to Do with Your IBM PC. Mark R. Sawusch & Tan A. Summers. (Illus.). 256p. (Orig.). 1984. pap. 13.95 (0-8306-1826-0) McGraw-Hill Prof.

One Thousand One Things to Do with Your IBM PS-2. Dave Prochnow & Mark R. Sawusch. 1991. 24.95 (0-8306-8686-X) McGraw-Hill Prof.

One Thousand One Things to Do with Your Macintosh. Mark R. Sawusch. (Orig.). 1991. 19.95 (0-8306-6234-0) McGraw-Hill Prof.

1001 Things to Spot Long Ago. Gillian Doherty. (1001 Things to Spot Ser.). 1999. 14.95 (1-58086-194-6) EDC.

1001 Things to Spot Long Ago. Gillian Doherty et al. (One Thousand One Things to Spot Ser.). (Illus.). 32p. (J). (ps-3). 1999. pap. text 6.95 (0-7460-3318-4, Usborne) EDC.

1001 Things to Spot on the Farm. Ed. by Gillian Doherty. (1001 Things to Spot Ser.). (Illus.). 32p. (J). (ps-3). 1999. pap. text 6.95 (0-7460-2955-1, Usborne); lib. bdg. 14.95 (1-58086-152-0, Usborne) EDC.

***1001 Things You Always Wanted to Know about Visual FoxPro.** Marcia Akins et al. Ed. by John Hosier. 588p. 2000. pap. 49.95 (0-9655093-3-8) Hentzenwerke.

1,001 Things You Always Wanted to Know about the Bible but Never Thought to Ask. J. Stephen Lang. LC 98-44531. 504p. 1999. pap. 9.99 (0-7852-7346-8) Nelson.

1,001 Things You Always Wanted to Know about the Holy Spirit. J. Stephen Lang. LC 99-15323. 516p. 1999. pap. 12.99 (0-7852-7046-9) Nelson.

***1,001 Things You Always Wanted to Know about Angels, Demons & the Afterlife.** J. Stephen Lang. 516p. 2000. pap. 12.99 (0-7852-6861-8) Nelson.

1001 Tips & Hints on Ceramics. Dale Swant. 32p. 1995. reprint ed. pap. text 3.95 (0-916809-81-1) Scott Pubns MI.

***1,001 Tips for Better Mail Management.** Allen Curtiss, Jr. Ed. by Timothy J. Riggiero. 300p. 2000. pap. 59.00i (0-615-11384-2) Excelsior Bks PA.

1001 Tips for Garden & Landscape Design. 352p. 1998. 35.00 (0-02-861593-X) Macmillan.

One Thousand One Tips to Increase Your Effectiveness. Bob Miller. Ed. by Jane Morgan. 184p. (Orig.). 1987. pap. 20.00 (0-942227-00-X) Universal Lrn Ctr.

One Thousand One Tips to Increased Effectiveness: PracticalTips Techniques & Ideas to Save You Time & Get More Done in Your Busy Day. Bob Miller. Ed. by Jane Morgan. 192p. (Orig.). 1987. pap. 20.00 (0-318-22828-9) Universal Lrn Ctr.

One Thousand One Toughest TV Trivia Questions of All Time. Vincent Terrace. LC 93-43797. 1994. pap. 9.95 (0-8065-1499-X, Citadel Pr) Carol Pub Group.

1001 Visual Basic Programmer's Tips. Lars Klander & Kris Jamsa. LC 98-112184. 656p. (Orig.). 1997. pap. 54.95 incl. cd-rom (1-884133-56-8, Jamsa Press) Gulf Pub.

1001 Visual Basic Secrets: Shortcuts & Tricks Every Visual Basic Programmer Should Know. David J. Cracas. LC 95-61395. 280p. (Orig.). 2000. pap. 24.95 (0-9640945-9-2) Pierpoint-Martin.

***1001 Vocabulary & Spelling Questions: Fast, Focused Practice to Help You Improve Your Vocabulary.** Learning Express Staff. LC 99-38375. 192p. 1999. pap. 14.95 (1-57685-264-4, Pub. by LrningExprss) Random.

1001 Ways Employees Can Take Initiative. Bob Nelson. LC 99-21940. 304p. 1999. pap. 10.95 (0-7611-1405-X) Workman Pub.

1001 Ways to a Man's Heart. Lori Wilk. 272p. 1995. pap. text 13.95 (0-9649076-0-7) L Wilk.

1001 Ways to Be Romantic. rev. annot. ed. Gregory Godek. LC 99-36946. 368p. 1999. pap. 14.95 (1-57071-481-9) Sourcebks.

***1,001 Ways to Connect with Your Kids.** J. R. Lucas. LC 99-55351. 2000. pap. 10.99 (0-8423-3154-9) Tyndale Hse.

One Thousand One Ways to Energize Employees. Bob Nelson. 1997. pap. 87.60 (0-7611-0861-0) Workman Pub.

One Thousand One Ways to Energize Employees. Bob Nelson. LC 97-10766. (Illus.). 224p. 1997. pap. 10.95 (0-7611-0160-8, 10160) Workman Pub.

1001 Ways to Get Promoted. David E. Rye. LC 99-30192. 288p. 1999. pap. 15.99 (1-56414-430-5) Career Pr Inc.

***1,001 Ways to Have a Dazzling Second Wedding.** Sharon Naylor. 288p. 2001. pap. 13.99 (1-56414-520-4, New Page Bks) Career Pr Inc.

1001 Ways to Improve Your Child's Schoolwork: An A to Z Guide to Common Problems & Practical Solutions'. Lawrence J. Greene. (Illus.). 345p. 1998. pap. text 12.00 (0-7881-5370-6) DIANE Pub.

1001 Ways to Inspire Your Organization, Your Team & Yourself. David E. Rye. LC 97-46188. 272p. 1998. pap. 15.99 (1-56414-348-1) Career Pr Inc.

1,001 Ways to Keep Customers Coming Back: Wow Ideas That Make Customers Happy & Will Increase Your Bottom Line. Donna Greiner & Theodore B. Kinni. LC 99-16904. 272p. 2000. pap. 16.00 (0-7615-2029-5) Prima Pub.

1001 Simple Ways to Lose Weight. Gary L. Rempe. LC 96-47054. 336p. 1997. pap. 14.95 (0-8092-3080-1, 308010, Contemporary Bks) NTC Contemp Pub Co.

1001 Ways to Market Your Books: For Authors & Publishers. 5th rev. ed. John Kremer. (Illus.). 704p. 1998. pap. 27.95 (0-912411-48-1) Open Horizons.

1001 Ways to Market Your Services. Rick Crandall. LC 97-41744. 384p. 1997. pap. 16.95 (0-8092-3158-1, 315810, Contemporary Bks) NTC Contemp Pub Co.

1,001 Ways to Market Yourself & Your Small Business. Lisa Shaw. LC 96-46295. (Peregrine Bk.). 256p. 1997. pap. 12.95 (0-399-52314-6, Perigee Bks) Berkley Pub.

1,001 Ways to Motivate Yourself & Others. Sang H. Kim. 174p. (Orig.). 1995. pap. 9.95 (1-880336-07-3) Turtle CT.

1001 Ways to Pass Organic Chemistry. 2nd ed. S. Banks & J. Bank. (One Thousand One Ways to Pass Ser.). 312p. (C). 1997. pap. text, suppl. ed. 9.50 (0-03-020692-8) SCP.

1001 Ways to Procrastinate. Anthony Rubino. Ed. by Cliff Carle. 1994. pap. 4.99 (0-918259-58-4) CCC Pubns.

One Thousand One Ways to Reward Employees. Bob Nelson. LC 93-14449. (Illus.). 302p. (Orig.). 1994. pap. 9.95 (1-56305-339-X, 3339) Workman Pub.

***1,001 Ways to Save, Grow & Invest Your Money.** David E. Rye. LC 98-55719. 288p. 1999. pap. 15.99 (1-56414-404-6) Career Pr Inc.

One Thousand One Ways to Save Money...& Still Have a Dazzling Wedding. Sharon Naylor. (Illus.). 320p. 1994. pap. 12.95 (0-8092-3657-5, 365750, Contemporary Bks) NTC Contemp Pub Co.

1001 Windows 98 Tips. Kris A. Jamsa. 704p. 1997. pap. text 44.95 (1-884133-61-4, Jamsa Press) Gulf Pub.

1001 Windows 95 Tips. Greg M. Perry. LC 96-142663. 544p. 1996. pap. 39.95 (1-884133-15-0, Jamsa Press) Gulf Pub.

1001 Windows NT Tips. Kris Jamsa. 928p. 1998. pap. 54.95 (1-884133-63-0, Jamsa Press) Gulf Pub.

One Thousand One Winning Chess Sacrifices & Combinations. Fred Reinfeld. 1969. reprint ed. pap. 10.00 (0-87980-111-5) Wilshire.

1001 Wonderful Wonders: Activities for All Children. Anne Rogovin. 208p. (Orig.). 1992. pap. 12.95 (0-687-29193-3) Abingdon.

1001 Word 2000 Tips. Allen L. Wyatt. (Illus.). 720p. 1999. pap. write for info. (1-884133-73-8, Jamsa Press) Gulf Pub.

***1000 Ornamental Designs for Artists & Craftspeople.** Claude Humbert. LC 99-88750. (Pictorial Archive Ser.). (ENG & GER., Illus.). 2000. pap. 16.95 (0-486-40945-7) Dover.

1,000 Palabras en Ingles. Berlitz Editors. (ENG & SPA., Illus.). 64p. 1998. pap. 12.95 (2-8315-6553-7) Berlitz.

***One Thousand Paper Cranes.** Takayuki Ishii. (YA). 2001. mass mkt. 4.99 (0-440-22843-3) BDD Bks Young Read.

***1000 Photos of Aquarium Fish.** Photos by Marie Paule & Christian Piednoir. (One Thousand Photos Ser.). (Illus.). 128p. 2000. 24.95 (0-7641-5217-3) Barron.

***1000 Photos of Minerals & Fossils.** Alain Eid. (One Thousand Photos Ser.). (Illus.). 128p. (J). 2000. 24.95 (0-7641-5218-1) Barron.

1000 Pictures for Teachers to Copy. Andrew Wright. 128p. 1985. spiral bd. 26.09 (0-201-09132-1) Addison-Wesley.

1001 Pitfalls in German. 3rd ed. Henry Strutz. LC 96-86509. 1997. pap. text 10.95 (0-8120-9652-5) Barron.

One Thousand Plus: The Amateur Astronomer's Field Guide to Deep Sky Observing. Tom Lorenzin & Tim Sechler. (Illus.). 168p. 1987. write for info. (0-912081-06-6) Delmar Co.

1,000+ (African) Orisa - Yoruba Names. Fama A. Adewale. LC 98-91283. (ENG & YOR.). 200p. 1998. pap. 16.95 (0-9644247-5-4) ILE Orunmila.

One Thousand Plus Picture Dictionary: One Hundred One Activities. Art Freifeld. (Illus.). 90p. (Orig.). (YA). (gr. 5 up). 1988. teacher ed. 1.95 (0-916177-24-6); pap. text 8.95 (0-916177-06-8) Am Eng Pubns.

1000 Plus Stationery Designs: Dynamic Matching Business Cards, Letterheads & Envelopes. Val Cooper. (Illus.). 200p. (Orig.). 1995. pap. 19.95 (0-9646108-3-3) Point Pac Pr.

1,000 Points of Light: The Public Remains in the Dark. large type rev. ed. Bruce Campbell Adamson. Ed. by Steve Perez et al. (Oswald's Closest Friend Ser.: Vol. 1). (Illus.). 168p. 1996. 18.00 (1-892501-04-X) B C Adamson.

***One Thousand Practical Ideas for Decorating the Home.** Francisco Asensio Cerver. 2000. pap. 29.95 (84-8185-243-0) Watsn-Guptill.

1000 Questions about Home Repair & Maintenance. Al Carrell. LC 97-21210. 504p. 1997. pap. write for info. (1-56530-267-2) Summit TX.

1000 Questions about Women's Health. Jane Chihal & Nancy Brinker. 504p. 1997. pap. 16.99 (1-56530-264-8) Summit TX.

1000 Questions about Your Pregnancy. Jeffrey Thurston. LC 97-33880. (Illus.). 504p. (Orig.). 1997. pap. 16.99 (1-56530-265-6, Pub. by Summit TX) BookWorld.

1000 Questions about Your Wedding. Jaclyn Barrett-Hirschhaut. LC 97-33878. 470p. 1997. pap. 16.99 (1-56530-266-4, Pub. by Summit TX) BookWorld.

One Thousand Questions & Answers about UNIX Systems. Amir H. Majidimehr. 2001. pap. text 30.00 (0-13-119884-X) P-H.

1000 Quotable Poems: An Anthology of Modern Verse. Esther A. Gillespie. 1986. 10.99 (0-517-48121-9) Random Hse Value.

One Thousand Quotable Poems: An Anthology of Modern Verse, 2 Vols. Ed. by Esther A. Gillespie. LC 72-11995. (Granger Index Reprint Ser.). 1980. reprint ed. 24.95 (0-8369-6400-4) Ayer.

One Thousand Reasons to Think: Special Insights to Achieve a Better Life. Ella M. Patterson. LC 94-75365. (Illus.). 200p. (J). (ps-12). 1993. 10.00 (1-884331-00-9) Knowledge Concepts.

1000 Reasons You Might Think She Is My Lover. Angela Costa. (Illus.). 180p. 1997. pap. 10.95 (1-886383-21-9) Pride & Imprints.

1000 Recipe Low-Fat Cookbook. Terry B. Golson. LC 97-28738. 608p. 1997. 29.95 (0-02-860354-0, Pub. by Macmillan) S&S Trade.

1000 Recipe Vegetarian Cookbook. Carol Gelles. LC 96-13606. 640p. 1996. per. 29.95 (0-02-542965-5) Macmillan.

1000 Record Covers. Michael Ochs. (Klotz Ser.). 1996. pap. 29.99 (3-8228-8595-9) Taschen Amer.

***One Thousand Roads to Mecca: Ten Centuries of Travelers Writing about the Muslim Pilgrimage.** Ed. by Michael Wolfe. 656p. 1999. reprint ed. pap. text 17.50 (0-8021-3599-4, Grove) Grove-Atltic.

One Thousand Roads to Mecca: Ten Centuries of Writing about the Pilgrimage to Mecca. Ed. by Michael Wolfe. LC 97-1329. 656p. 1997. 32.50 (0-8021-1611-6, Grove) Grove-Atltic.

1007 Anonymous & Papal Sovereignty: Jewish Perceptions of the Papacy & Papal Policy in the High Middle Ages. Kenneth R. Stow. LC 84-25293. (Hebrew Union College Annual Supplements Ser.: Vol. 4). 99p. 1984. reprint ed. pap. 30.70 (0-608-02084-2, 206273700004) Bks Demand.

One Thousand Silly Sandwiches. Alan Benjamin. (Illus.). 18p. (J). (ps up). 1995. 8.95 (0-671-89830-2) Litle Simon.

***1688: A World History.** John E. Wills, Jr. (Illus.). 352p. 2000. 27.95 (0-393-04744-X) Norton.

***1600 Killers: A Wake-Up Call for Congress.** Andy Jacobs. Ed. by Roger Cook. (Illus.). 240p. 1999. 25.00 (1-889388-04-1) Alistair Pr IN.

1,628 Country Shortcuts...from 1,628 Country People. Ed. by Roy Reiman. LC 95-68774. 196p. 1995. 16.95 (0-89821-148-4, 20102) Reiman Pubns.

***One Thousand Six Salt & Pepper Shakers: Advertising.** Larry Carey & Sylvia Tompkins. (Illus.). 176p. 2000. pap. 29.95 (0-7643-1185-9) Schiffer.

1066 & All That. Yeatman Sellar. pap. 11.95 (0-7493-0964-4, Pub. by Random) Trafalgar.

One Thousand Souls. Aleksei F. Pisemskii. Tr. by Ivy Litvinov. 1970. reprint ed. lib. bdg. 75.00 (0-8371-2239-2, PIOS, Greenwood Pr) Greenwood.

One Thousand Space Monsters Have Landed. Alan Benjamin. (J). 1980. pap. 4.95 (0-590-07667-1) Scholastic Inc.

1000 Spanish Idioms. 2nd ed. J. Dale Miller. LC 71-180253. xii, 173p. (C). 1971. pap. text 8.95 (0-8425-1513-5, Friends of the Library) Brigham.

1,000 Spanish Words. Berlitz Kids Editors. LC 98-18960. (SPA & ENG., Illus.). 64p. 1998. pap. 12.95 (2-8315-6552-9, Berlitz Kids) Berlitz.

One Thousand Strikes of Government Employees. David Ziskind. LC 70-156443. (American Labor Ser., No. 2). 1977. reprint ed. 23.95 (0-405-02951-9) Ayer.

One Thousand Suns: Krishnamurti at Eighty-Five, & the Last Walk. Asit Chandmal. (Illus.). 128p. 1995. 60.00 (0-89381-631-0) Aperture.

1000 Tattoos. Hank Schiffmacher. (Klotz Ser.). 1996. pap. 29.99 (3-8228-8592-4) Taschen Amer.

One Thousand Things You Can Get Free. 1991. lib. bdg. 79.95 (0-8490-4111-2) Gordon Pr.

1000 Thoughts for Funeral Occasions. Intro. by Russell H. Conwell. LC 99-28070. 1999. 48.00 (0-7808-0303-5) Omnigraphics Inc.

***1,003 Great Things about Teachers.** Lisa Birnbach et al. 2000. pap. 8.95 (0-7407-0989-5) Andrews & McMeel.

1,003 Great Things about Kids. Lisa Birnbach. 320p. 1999. 6.98 (1-56731-357-4, MJF Bks) Fine Comms.

1,003 Great Things about Kids. Lisa Birnbach et al. LC 98-7624. (Illus.). 320p. 1998. pap. 8.95 (0-8362-6964-0) Andrews & McMeel.

***1,003 Great Things about Friends.** Hodgman Birnbach. 416p. 2000. 7.98 (1-56731-394-9, MJF Bks) Fine Comms.

***1,003 Great Things about Friends,** Patricia Marx et al. LC 99-21530. 1999. pap. 8.95 (0-7407-0021-9) Andrews & McMeel.

1,003 Great Things about Getting Older. Lisa Birnbach et al. LC 97-3825. 315p. (Orig.). 1997. pap. 8.95 (0-8362-2699-2) Andrews & McMeel.

1,003 Great Things about Getting Older. Hodgman & Lisa Birnbach. 320p. 1999. 7.98 (1-56731-358-2, MJF Bks) Fine Comms.

1,350 Toughest Trivia Questions of All Time. 3rd rev. ed. Vincent Terrace. 416p. 1999. pap. 14.95 (0-8065-2081-7, Citadel Pr) Carol Pub Group.

1,301 Questions & Answers about Judaism. David C. Gross. 448p. 1998. pap. 17.95 (0-7818-0578-3) Hippocrene Bks.

One Thousand Three Hundred Thirty-Seven Spot Illustrations of the Twenties & Thirties. Ed. by Leslie E. Cabarga & Marcie Cabarga. LC 92-9524. (Illus.). 96p. 1992. 8.95 (0-486-27232-X) Dover.

1003 Salt & Pepper Shakers. Larry Carey & Sylvia Tompkins. LC 96-29169. 176p. (gr. 10). 1997. pap. 29.95 (0-7643-0112-8) Schiffer.

1201 Toughest TV Trivia Questions of All Time. Vincent Terrace. 312p. 1995. pap. 9.95 (0-8065-1730-1, Citadel Pr) Carol Pub Group.

1,200 Paint Effects for the Home Decorator. Ray Bradshaw. (Illus.). 192p. 1997. 29.99 (0-89134-816-6, North Lght Bks) F & W Pubns Inc.

***1,200 Paint Effects for the Home Decorator.** Ray Bradshaw. (Illus.). 192p. 2000. pap. 24.99 (1-58180-057-6, North Lght Bks) F & W Pubns Inc.

1002 Salt & Pepper Shakers: Nodders, Fitz & Floyd, Parkcraft with Prices. abr. ed. Larry Carey & Sylvia Tompkins. LC 95-6996. (Illus.). 112p. (Orig.). 1995. pap. 19.95 (0-88740-789-7) Schiffer.

One Thousand Two the Complete Children's Song Book: The Complete Children's Song Book. (Children's Songs Ser.). (J). 1990. 39.95 incl. audio (0-685-32067-7, Z019) Hansen Ed Mus.

1002 Ways to Waste Your Working Time. Diagram Group Staff. (Illus.). 256p. 1996. pap. 9.95 (0-312-14534-9) St Martin.

1000 U. S. Corporate Executives Interested in Russia. 2nd ed. Russian Information & Business Center, Inc. Staff. (Russian Business Library). 400p. 1997. pap. 99.00 (1-57751-327-4) Intl Business Pubns.

One Thousand What's What Jokes for Kids. Michael Johnstone. 240p. (J). (gr. k up). 1987. mass mkt. 4.99 (0-345-34654-8) Ballantine Pub Grp.

1,000 What's What Jokes for Kids. Michael Johnstone. (J). 1986. 10.09 (0-606-04145-1, Pub. by Turtleback) Demco.

One Thousand White Women: The Journals of May Dodd. 3rd ed. Jim Fergus. LC 99-11497. 320p. 1999. pap. 13.95 (0-312-19943-0) St Martin.

One Thousand Windows: A Speaker's Sourcebook of Illustrations. Robert C. Shannon. Ed. by Henrietta Gambill. LC 96-52320. 288p. 1997. pap. 15.99 (0-7847-0621-2, 40001) Standard Pub.

***1,000 Words Is Worth a Picture.** Bruce Bothwell. iii, 147p. 1999. pap. 10.00 (1-929764-03-0) Bothwell Bks.

One Thousand Years: Stories from the History of Christianity in the U. S. S. R., 988-1988. J. Martin Bailey. 1987. pap. 4.95 (0-377-00167-8) Friendship Pr.

1000 Years Ago on Planet Earth. Sneed B. Collard, III. LC 98-43243. (Illus.). 32p. 1999. 15.00 (0-395-90866-3) HM.

One Thousand Years of Bohemian Coinage. Viktor Katz. (Illus.). 1980. reprint ed. pap. 8.00 (0-685-04429-7) S J Durst.

One Thousand Years of Hubbard History, 866 to 1895. E. W. Day. (Illus.). 512p. reprint ed. pap. 76.50 (0-8328-0688-9); reprint ed. lib. bdg. 84.50 (0-8328-0687-0) Higginson Bk Co.

1,000 Years of Irish Poetry. Ed. by Kathleen Hoagland. 800p. 1999. reprint ed. 14.95 (1-56852-235-5, Konecky & Konecky) W S Konecky Assocs.

1000 Years of Irish Poetry: The Celtic & Anglo-Irish Poets from Pagan Times to the Present. Kathleen Hoagland. 830p. 1999. pap. 20.00 (1-56649-010-3) Welcome Rain.

One Thousand Years of Irish Poetry: The Gaelic & Anglo-Irish Poets from Pagan Times to the Present. 9th rev. ed. Ed. by Kathleen Hoagland. 884p. 1999. 18.95 (0-8159-6404-8) Devin.

***One Thousand Years of Philosophy.** Rom Harre. 2000. 59.95 (0-631-21900-5); pap. 24.95 (0-631-21901-3) Blackwell Pubs.

One Thousand Years of Russian Church Music, 988-1988. Ed. by Vladimir Morosan. LC 89-63652. (Monuments of Russian Sacred Music Ser.). (ENG & RUS., Illus.). xlviii, 774p. 1991. lib. bdg. 129.00 (0-9629460-0-1) Musica Russica.

One Thousand Years on Mound Key. rev. ed. Rolfe F. Schell. LC 68-24198. (Illus.). 125p. 1997. 12.95 (0-87208-000-5) Shoeless Pub.

1,000 Years, 1,000 People: Ranking the Men & Women Who Shaped the Millennium. Barbara Bowers et al. LC 98-40381. 331p. 1998. pap. 17.00 (1-56836-253-6) Kodansha.

1000 Years, 1000 People: The Men & Women Who Charted the Course of History for the Last Millennium. Barbara Bowers. 1998. 25.00 (1-56836-273-0) Kodansha.

1, 3-Dichloropropene, 1, 2-Dichloropropane & Mixtures. (Environmental Health Criteria Ser.: No. 146). (ENG, FRE & SPA.). 261p. 1993. pap. text 50.00 (92-4-157146-2, 1160146) World Health.

One, Three-Dipolar Cycloaddition Chemistry, 2 vols., Vol. 2. Albert Padwa. (General Heterocyclic Chemistry Ser.: No. 1-128). 1521p. 1984. 899.00 (0-471-08364-X) Wiley.

One Ticket to New York. Raisa Silver. Ed. by Nataliya Malisova. (RUS., Illus.). 224p. 1997. write for info. (0-9658114-2-5) Mir Collection.

One Ticket to Texas. Jan Hudson. 1997. per. 3.50 (0-373-76071-X, 1-76071-9) Silhouette.

O

An Asterisk (*) at the beginning of an entry indicates that the title is appearing for the first time.

One Tiger Growls: A Counting Book of Animal Sounds. Ginger Wadsworth & James Needham. LC 97-37050. (Illus.). 32p. (J). (ps-3). 1999. 15.95 (*0-88106-273-1*); pap. 6.95 (*0-88106-274-X*) Charlesbridge Pub.

One Time: The Story of a South Central Los Angeles Police Officer. Brian S. Bentley. 235p. (Orig.). 1997. pap. 14.95 (*1-890632-00-7*) Cool Jack Pub.

One Time Around: A Solo World Bicycle Journey. Alan Thompson. Ed. by Ruth Thompson & Janet Rogolsky. LC 91-93068. 263p. 1991. 16.95 (*0-9630747-0-9*) APT Pub.

One Time Around & Beyond. Alfred C. Miller. 591p. 1990. 46.50 (*0-9624215-0-2*) A C Miller.

One Time, I Saw Morning Come Home. Clair Huffaker. 1995. reprint ed. lib. bdg. 28.95 (*1-56849-674-5*) Buccaneer Bks.

One Time, One Place: Mississippi in the Depression: A Snapshot Album. anniversary ed. Photos by Eudora Welty. LC 95-46057. (Illus.). 124p. (C). 1996. reprint ed. 27.50 (*0-87805-866-4*) U Pr of Miss.

One Time, One Place: Mississippi in the Depression: A Snapshot Album. limited ed. Photos by Eudora Welty. LC 95-46057. (Illus.). 124p. (C). 1996. reprint ed. 125.00 (*0-87805-900-8*) U Pr of Miss.

One-Time Warrior. Wolverton. 1999. text. write for info. (*0-312-85657-1*) St Martin.

One Timeless Spring. Ray Bradbury. 24.95 (*0-89190-345-3*) Amereon Ltd.

***One Tiny Hope.** Kari Gilliam Palmer. 240p. 1999. write for info. (*0-9674656-5-6*) Wheeler Holland.

One Tiny Spark. Eva Vogiel. 176p. (YA). (gr. 8-12). 1989. 15.95 (*0-935063-83-8*); pap. 12.95 (*0-935063-84-6*) CIS Comm.

***One to a 100: Manuscript Printing & Bookbinding Design.** John O. Morton. 45p. 2000. 5.95 (*0-9700881-1-6*) ST John.

One to Count Cadence. James Crumley. LC 86-40468. (Vintage Contemporaries Ser.). 352p. 1987. pap. 13.00 (*0-394-73559-5*) Vin Bks.

One to Grow On. Brian Kral. (J). 1993. pap. 6.00 (*0-87602-320-0*) Anchorage.

One to One. G. Manza & F. Newman. pap. 18.95 (*0-87477-948-0*, Tarcher Putnam) Putnam Pub Group.

One to One. 5th ed. Charles W. Dawe & Edward A. Dornan. LC 96-2758. 460p. (C). 1997. pap. text 48.00 (*0-673-98066-5*) Addson-Wesley Educ.

One to One, Bk. 35. Marisa Carroll. (Born in the U. S. A. Ser.). 1997. mass mkt. 4.50 (*0-373-47185-8*, 1-47185-3) Harlequin Bks.

One to One: A Practical Guide to Friendship Evangelism. Terry H. Wardle. 204p. (Orig.). (C). 1989. pap. 7.99 (*0-87509-423-6*) Chr Pubns.

One to One: How to Share Your Faith with a Friend. Michael Green. 128p. 1995. 9.99 (*0-345-40089-5*, Moorings) Ballantine Pub Grp.

One to One: Self-Understanding Through Journal Writing. Christina Baldwin. LC 91-4142. 180p. 1991. pap. 9.95 (*0-87131-652-8*) M Evans.

One to One: The Story of the Big Brothers-Big Sisters Movement in America. George L. Beiswinger. LC 84-20399. (Illus.). 290p. 1985. 15.95 (*0-9613820-0-7*) Big Brothers-Big Sisters.

One to One: Understanding Personal Relationships. Theodore I. Rubin. LC 99-21604. 1999. pap. 11.95 (*0-312-87184-8*, Pub. by Forge NYC) St Martin.

One to One April-May-June, 1997. 82p. (YA). (gr. 8-10). 1997. 20.00 (*0-913585-25-4*) Scripture U Pub.

One to One April-May-June, 1996, Vol. 8. 82p. (YA). (gr. 8-10). 1996. 20.00 (*0-913585-06-8*) Scripture U Pub.

One to One April-May-June, 1998, Vol. 10. 82p. (YA). (gr. 8-10). 1998. 20.00 (*0-913585-42-4*) Scripture U Pub.

***One to One B2B.** Don Peppers. 2001. 22.95 (*0-385-49409-2*) Doubleday.

One to One Fieldbook: The Complete Toolkit for Implementing a Tool Marketing Program. Don Peppers et al. LC 98-38165. 432p. 1999. pap. 19.95 (*0-385-49369-X*) Doubleday.

One to One Future: Building Relationships One Customer at a Time. Don Peppers & Martha Rogers. 464p. 1996. pap. 17.95 (*0-385-48566-2*) Doubleday.

One to One January-February-March, 1998. 82p. (YA). (gr. 8-10). 1997. 20.00 (*0-913585-39-4*) Scripture U Pub.

One to One January-February-March, 1996, Vol. 8. 82p. (YA). (gr. 8-10). 1995. 20.00 (*0-913585-01-7*) Scripture U Pub.

One to One January-February-March, 1997, Vol. 9. 82p. (YA). (gr. 8-10). 1996. 20.00 (*0-913585-21-1*) Scripture U Pub.

One to One July-August-September, 1996, Vol. 8. 82p. (YA). (gr. 8-10). 1996. 20.00 (*0-913585-10-6*) Scripture U Pub.

One to One July-August-September, 1997, Vol. 9. 82p. (YA). (gr. 8-10). 1997. 20.00 (*0-913585-28-9*) Scripture U Pub.

One to One Manager: A Management Guide to Implementing a 1-to-1 Customer Relationship. Don Peppers & Martha Rogers. LC 99-26835. 288p. 1999. 21.95 (*0-385-49408-4*) Doubleday.

One to One October-November-December, 1997. 82p. (YA). (gr. 8-10). 1997. 20.00 (*0-913585-35-1*) Scripture U Pub.

One to One October-November-December, 1996, Vol. 8. 82p. (YA). (gr. 8-10). 1996. 20.00 (*0-913585-15-7*) Scripture U Pub.

One to One Training & Coaching Skills. 2nd ed. Roger Buckley & Jim Caple. 144p. 1997. pap. 25.00 (*0-7494-2065-0*, Kogan Pg Educ) Stylus Pub VA.

One to Ten see Del Uno al Diez

One to Ten. Alan Benjamin & Ellen Appleby. 1991. pap. 9.95 (*0-671-74136-5*) S&S Trade.

One to Ten. Ronne P. Randall. (Happytime Ser.). (Illus.). 24p. (J). (ps). 1987. pap. 1.25 (*0-7214-9554-0*, S871-10, Ladybrd) Penguin Putnam.

One to Ten. Illus. by Fiona Redmond. (Board Counting Bks.). 20p. (J). (ps). 1996. bds. 5.98 (*1-85854-203-0*, 1 85854 203 0) Brimax Bks.

One to Ten - Count Again. Lorna Read. (My Big Little Fat Bks.). (Illus.). 20p. (J). (ps). 1996. bds. 3.49 (*1-85854-174-3*) Brimax Bks.

One to Ten & Back Again. (Rhyme Time Story Time Ser.: No. 9302). (Illus.). 20p. (J). (ps). 1999. bds. write for info. (*1-85854-665-6*) Brimax Bks.

***1 to 10 & Back Again: A Getty Museum Counting Book.** J. Paul Getty Museum Staff. LC 98-9930. 56p. (J). 1998. 16.95 (*0-89236-525-0*, Pub. by J P Getty Trust) OUP.

One to Ten Count Again. James Woodard & Linda Purdy. (Illus.). (J). (ps-k). 1972. lib. bdg. 11.86 (*0-914844-07-5*) J Alden.

One to Ten We Are Counting Again in Iowa. Linda Crockem. (Illus.). 12p. (J). (ps-k). 1997. 14.99 (*0-614-29772-9*) First Bk Prodns.

One to the Many. Anne Hazlewood-Brady. Ed. by Constance Hunting. 1979. pap. text 3.50 (*0-913006-15-7*) Puckerbrush.

***One to Three.** Nancy Griffith. (Illus.). 16p. (J). 2000. pap. 5.95 (*1-891846-15-9*) Busn Word.

1-3 John. Stephen S. Smalley. (Biblical Commentary Ser.: Vol. 51). 29.99 (*0-8499-0250-9*) Word Pub.

One Too Many Candles of Repentance: Poetry & Prose by Linda Mae. Linda Mae. (Illus.). 48p. (Orig.). 1994. pap. 4.95 (*0-9642130-0-1*) Fountain Pen.

One Too Many Marilyns. Ventura. 1950. text 22.50 (*0-8050-3739-X*) St Martin.

***One Touch, Vol. 41.** Vivian Leiber. (Zebra Bouquet Ser.). 2000. mass mkt. 3.99 (*0-8217-6577-9*, Zebra Kensgtn) Kensgtn Pub Corp.

One Touch Guide. William W. Donnelly. 64p. (Orig.). 1997. pap. 19.95 (*0-9658924-9-2*) OTG.

One Touch Healing: Premium Edition. 64p. (C). 1998. pap. 5.95 (*0-13-974197-6*) P-H.

One Touch of Shakespeare: Letters of Joseph Crosby to Joseph Parker Norris, 1875-1878. Ed. by John W. Velz & Frances N. Teague. LC 83-49506. (Illus.). 360p. 1986. 65.00 (*0-918016-74-6*) Folger Bks.

1 Touchdown, Level 1. J. Harmer et al. (Illus.). (YA). 1993. pap. text, teacher ed. 18.50 (*0-582-04058-2*, 79799) Longman.

One Tough Circuit: Midget Racing in America's Heartland. Bill Hill. (Illus.). xxv, 326p. 1998. 49.95 (*0-9662642-0-7*) B Hill Prodns.

***One Tough Cookie.** Vinnie Hansen. LC 00-190417. 196p. 2000. 25.00 (*0-7388-1671-X*); pap. 18.00 (*0-7388-1672-8*) Xlibris Corp.

One Tough Cookie. large type ed. Carole Dean. (Black Satin Romance Ser.). 312p. 1997. 27.99 (*1-86110-038-8*) Ulverscroft.

One Tough Cop: The Bo Dietl Story. Bo Dietl & Ken Cross. 278p. 1998. mass mkt. 6.99 (*0-671-02841-3*) PB.

One Tough Hombre. Joan Hohl. (Mira Bks.). 251p. 1995. per. 4.99 (*1-55166-045-8*, 1-66045-5, Mira Bks) Harlequin Bks.

One Tough Marine. Donald N. Hamblen. 1994. mass mkt. 5.99 (*0-8041-1031-X*) Ivy Books.

One Tough Texan. M. J. Rogers. (Intrigue Ser.: No. 423). 1997. per. 3.75 (*0-373-22423-0*, 1-22423-7) Harlequin Bks.

One Track. Beatrice O'Brien. 1999. pap. text 14.95 (*1-890838-09-8*) Indus Pub.

One Track. Ed. by Tom Taylor & Carol Reilly. 244p. (Orig.). (YA). 1995. pap. 10.00 (*0-9648262-0-8*) Mozart Pk Pr.

***One Track Mind: Photographic Essays on Western Railroading.** Ted Benson. (Illus.). 176p. 2000. 45.00 (*1-55046-273-3*) Boston Mills.

One Train: Poems. Kenneth Koch. LC 94-12088. (Borzoi Reader Ser.). 80p. 1994. 20.00 (*0-679-43417-8*) Knopf.

One Train: Poems. Kenneth Koch. 1996. pap. 13.00 (*0-679-76583-2*) Knopf.

One Trak Mutual Fund Basics & Beyond. 2nd ed. LC 96-13977. 1996. pap. 32.95 (*0-7931-2292-9*, 3924-0102) Dearborn.

One Tree. Stephen R. Donaldson. (Second Chronicles of Thomas Covenant Ser.: Bk. 2). 496p. 1987. mass mkt. 6.99 (*0-345-34869-9*, Del Rey) Ballantine Pub Grp.

One Tree. Stephen R. Donaldson. 1997. pap. 12.00 (*0-345-41847-6*, Del Rey) Ballantine Pub Grp.

One Tree Island. Ed Machado. LC 94-67585. 264p. (J). (gr. 5-10). 1994. pap. 5.99 (*0-9642652-0-6*) Reef Pubng.

One-Trick Rip-Off. Paul Pope. 120p. 1997. 12.95 (*1-56971-244-1*) Dark Horse Comics.

One Trick Short. P. S. Sharma. 1995. pap. 13.95 (*0-533-10844-6*) Vantage.

One Tricky Monkey on Top. 1993. write for info. (*1-56189-376-5*, Am Editions) Amer Educ Pub.

One Tricky Monkey up on Top. Jane Belk Moncure. LC 87-11612. (Magic Castle Readers Ser.). (Illus.). 32p. (J). (ps-2). 1988. lib. bdg. 21.36 (*0-89565-365-6*) Childs World.

One True Doctrine. James Babeckis & Benita Chapman. 148p. 1994. pap. 9.95 (*1-57353-104-9*, Eschaton Bks) Eschaton Prods.

One True Love. Barbara Freethy. 384p. 1998. mass mkt. 5.99 (*0-380-79480-2*, Avon Bks) Morrow Avon.

***One True Thing.** 1999. 9.98 (*0-671-77616-9*) S&S Trade.

One True Thing. Anna Quindlen. 400p. 1995. mass mkt. 6.99 (*0-440-22103-X*) Dell.

One True Thing. Anna Quindlen. 304p. 1997. pap. 11.95 (*0-385-31920-7*) Doubleday.

One True Thing. abr. ed. Anna Quindlen. 1998. 25.00 incl. audio (*0-671-04333-1*, Audioworks) S&S Trade.

One True Thing. large type ed. Anna Quindlen. LC 94-24046. (Large Print Bks.). 1995. 25.95 (*1-56895-168-X*) Wheeler Pub.

One True Thing. Greg Matthews. 320p. 1992. reprint ed. mass mkt. 4.99 (*0-8217-3994-8*, Zebra Kensgtn) Kensgtn Pub Corp.

One TV Blasting & a Pig Outdoors. Deborah Abbott & Henry Kisor. Ed. by Kathy Tucker. LC 94-6649. (Illus.). 40p. (J). (gr. 2-6). 1994. lib. bdg. 14.95 (*0-8075-6075-8*) A Whitman.

***121 North: A Collection of Short Stories by North Texas Professional Writers Association.** Elaine Moore et al. Ed. by C. Kaye Hushour. 199p. 2000. pap. 14.95 (*1-928704-76-X*, Fusion Pr) Authorlink.

***One Twin Too Many.** Megan Stine. (Two of a Kind Ser.: No. 4). (Illus.). 112p. (J). (gr. 3-7). 1999. mass mkt. 3.99 (*0-06-106574-9*) HarpC.

One, Two - Cycloaddition Reactions: The Formation of Three- & Four-Membered Heterocycles. Linda L. Muller & Jan Hamer. LC 67-20265. 372p. reprint ed. pap. 115.40 (*0-7837-3459-X*, 205778500008) Bks Demand.

1, 2 - Dibromoethane. (Environmental Health Criteria Ser.: No. 177). 148p. (C). 1996. pap. text 27.00 (*92-4-157177-2*, 1160177) World Health.

One, Two, & Three: What Does Each One See? Addie Lacoe. (Illus.). 32p. (J). (gr. k-3). 1995. lib. bdg. 21.40 (*1-56294-523-8*) Millbrook Pr.

1, 2 & 3 Color Graphics: Further Imaginative Use of Limited Color in Graphic Design, No. 2. P. I. E. Books Editorial Staff. (Illus.). 224p. 1996. 55.00 (*4-938586-93-2*, Pub. by PIE Bks) Bks Nippan.

1, 2 & 3-Section Sewings Vol. 2: Non-Adhesive Binding, Vol. II. Keith A. Smith. LC 95-92079. (Illus.). 320p. (C). 1995. pap. text 30.00 (*0-9637682-2-0*) K A Smith Bks.

***One, Two, Buckle My Shoe.** (Illus.). 12p. (J). 2001. bds. 2.99 (*0-307-30155-9*, 30155, Goldn Books) Gldn Bks Pub Co.

One, Two, Buckle My Shoe. Agatha Christie. Ed. by Roger Cooper. 240p. 1987. pap. text 5.50 (*0-425-10570-9*) Berkley Pub.

One, Two, Buckle My Shoe. Agatha Christie. (Agatha Christie Collection). 1998. mass mkt. 3.99 (*0-425-16925-1*) Berkley Pub.

One, Two, Buckle My Shoe. Agatha Christie. 1984. 11.09 (*0-606-00968-X*, Pub. by Turtleback) Demco.

One Two Buckle My Shoe. Jessie Hunter. LC 96-51011. 304p. 1997. 22.50 (*0-684-83170-8*) S&S Trade.

One, Two, Buckle My Shoe. Illus. by Liz Loveless. LC 92-40947. 32p. (J). (ps). 1993. 13.95 (*1-56282-477-5*, Pub. by Hyprn Child) Little.

1, 2 Buckle My Shoe. Sherry Neidigh. LC 98-100416. (Illus.). 1997. write for info. (*0-7853-2364-3*) Pubns Intl Ltd.

One, Two, Buckle My Shoe. unabridged ed. Heather Collins. (Illus.). 12p. (J). 1997. bds. 4.95 (*1-55074-410-0*, Pub. by Kids Can Pr) Genl Dist Srvs.

One, Two, Buckle My Shoe: Math Activities for Young Children. Sam E. Brown. (Illus.). 112p. (Orig.). (J). (ps). 1982. pap. 8.95 (*0-87659-103-9*) Gryphon Hse.

One, Two, Buckle My Shoe: Mother Goose. Illus. by Carl Morton. (J). (gr. k-1). 1992. 10.00 (*1-57842-098-9*) Delmas Creat.

One, Two, Buckle My Shoe: Songs & Games for Children. Friedman-Fairfax & Sony Music Staff. (CD Ser.). 1995. pap. 16.98 incl. audio compact disk (*1-56799-126-2*, Friedman-Fairfax) M Friedman Pub Grp Inc.

1,2 Dichloroethane. (Environmental Health Criteria Ser.: Vol. 176). 148p. (C). 1995. pap. 30.00 (*92-4-157176-4*, 1160176) World Health.

One, Two Flea: Level 4, Green. Allan Ahlberg. LC 98-88077. (Reading Together Ser.). (Illus.). 32p. (J). 1999. pap. write for info. (*0-7636-0859-9*) Candlewick Pr.

1, 2, 4, 5-Tetrathiane-I, Synthesen & Reaktionen, Vol. 10. W. Franek. (Sulfur Reports). 85p. 1991. text 240.00 (*3-7186-5131-9*, Harwood Acad Pubs) Gordon & Breach.

One, Two, Four-Trichlorobenzene. Ed. by GDCh-Advisory Committee on Existing Chemicals of E. Tr. by P. Karbe from GER. LC 93-2640. (BUA Report Ser.).Tr. of One, Two, Four-Trichlorobenzol. (ENG & GER.). 1993. 48.00 (*3-527-28557-1*, Wiley-VCH) Wiley.

One, Two, Four-Trichlorobenzol see One, Two, Four-Trichlorobenzene

One 2 Many. Created by Francine Pascal. (Sweet Valley Junior High Ser.: No. 2). 144p. (J). (gr. 3-7). 1999. pap. 4.50 (*0-553-48604-7*) BDD Bks Young Read.

One, Two, One Pair! Bruce McMillan. 32p. (J). (ps-3). 1996. pap. text 4.99 (*0-590-46082-X*) Scholastic Inc.

One Two One Pair. Bruce McMillan. (J). 1991. 10.15 (*0-606-09717-1*, Pub. by Turtleback) Demco.

1-2 Peek-a-Boo! Illus. by Sonja Lamut. LC 96-78085. (Lift & Look Board Bks.). 12p. (J). (ps). 1997. bds. 4.95 (*0-448-41610-7*, G & D) Peng Put Young Read.

***One, Two, Red & Blue.** rev. ed. David La Jars. (Talk Together Ser.). (Illus.). (J). 2000. 9.95 (*1-58728-015-9*); pap. 4.95 (*1-58728-019-1*) Two Can Pub.

One, Two, Skip a Few! First Number Rhymes. Illus. by Roberta Arenson. 32p. (J). (ps-2). 1998. 15.95 (*1-901223-99-X*) Barefoot Bks NY.

***One, Two, Skip a Few! First Number Rhymes.** Roberta Arenson. (Illus.). 32p. (J). (ps-2). 2000. pap. 6.99 (*1-84148-130-0*) Barefoot Bks NY.

One Two Three. LC 94-237082. (Snapshot Concept Board Bks.). (Illus.). 24p. (J). (ps). 1994. bds. 2.95 (*1-56458-534-4*) DK Pub Inc.

1 2 3. (C). 1989. text. write for info. (*0-201-51091-X*) Addison-Wesley.

***123.** Amanda Barlow. (Baby Board Bks.). (Illus.). 12p. (J). (ps up). 2000. bds. 4.95 (*0-7460-4099-7*, Usborne) EDC.

One, Two, Three! Sandra Boynton. LC 93-11288. (Illus.). 24p. (J). 1993. bds. 6.95 (*1-56305-444-2*, 3444) Workman Pub.

***1, 2, 3.** DK Publishing Staff. (Touch & Feel Ser.). 12p. (J). 2000. 6.95 (*0-7894-5220-0*, D K Ink) DK Pub Inc.

1-2-3. Banks Helfrich. (Illus.). 32p. (Orig.). (J). (gr. k-2). 1995. pap. 5.00 (*0-9640647-5-8*) Tossed Salad.

1, 2, 3. Tana Hoban. LC 84-10306. (Illus.). 12p. (J). (ps). 1985. mass mkt. 4.95 (*0-688-02579-X*, Grenwillow Bks) HarpC Child Bks.

One, Two, Three. Lynn Kightley et al. (Little, Brown Primers Ser.). (Illus.). 32p. (J). (ps-1). 1986. mass mkt. 6.95 (*0-316-54004-8*) Little.

1, 2, 3. Tessa Krailing. (Little Bitty Ser.). (Illus.). 20p. (J). (ps). 1991. 3.50 (*0-8120-6264-7*) Barron.

1,2,3. Ladybird Books Staff. (First Steps Ser.). 32p. (J). 1998. 2.50 (*0-7214-1875-9*, Ladybrd) Penguin Putnam.

***1 2 3.** Matt Mitter. (Talking Pages Deluxe Ser.). (Illus.). 14p. (J). 2000. 12.95 (*1-58224-134-1*) Futech Interactive.

1 2 3. Clotilde Olyff. LC 94-1238. (Illus.). 22p. (J). (ps-3). 1994. 13.95 (*0-395-70736-6*, Pub. by Ticknor & Fields) HM.

One Two Three. Jan Pienkowski. (Nursery Board Bks.). (Illus.). 14p. (J). (ps). 1989. 2.95 (*0-671-68136-2*) S&S Trade.

***123.** Quadrillion Media Staff. (J). 1999. pap. 1.99 (*1-84100-284-4*) Quadrillion Media.

***123.** Quadrillion Media Staff. 1999. pap. 3.99 (*1-84100-297-6*) Quadrillion Media.

1 2 3. Illus. by Fiona Redmond. (Brimax Interactive Ser.). 12p. (J). (ps-k). 1996. bds. 6.98 (*1-85854-372-X*) Brimax Bks.

One, Two, Three. Yoshi & Ruth Wells. LC 90-23918. (Illus.). 28p. (J). (ps up). 1991. 15.95 (*0-88708-159-2*, Picture Book Studio) S&S Childrens.

1, 2, 3. large type ed. William Wegman. LC 94-69097. (Illus.). 16p. (J). 1995. 6.70 (*0-7868-0103-4*, Pub. by Hyprn Child) Time Warner.

123, Vol. 1. Sonja Lamut. (Made by Me Ser.). (Illus.). 26p. (ps-k). 1999. pap. 9.99 (*0-8431-7453-6*, Price Stern) Peng Put Young Read.

One, Two, Three: A Through the Window Book of Counting. Janie L. Hunt. LC 96-39408. (Through the Window Ser.). (Illus.). 24p. (J). (ps-k). 1998. 9.95 (*0-7613-0282-4*) Millbrook Pr.

***1, 2, 3: Fun to Learn.** (Illus.). 32p. (J). (ps-3). 1999. pap. 1.99 (*1-58279-008-6*) Trident Pr Intl.

1-2-3: Learn about Counting with Noah & Other Friends. V. Gilbert Beers. (J). 1995. VHS 9.99 (*89-00-88056-X*, Victor Bks) Chariot Victor.

***One, Two, Three! My First Counting Book.** Photos by Chris Shorten. (Illus.). 16p. (J). 1999. reprint ed. 5.95 (*1-892374-19-6*) Weldon Owen.

First Steps Activity 2: 1, 2, 3. Ladybird Staff. (First Steps Ser.). 24p. (J). 1998. pap. 1.99 (*0-7214-2607-7*, Ladybrd) Penguin Putnam.

One Two Three . . . Infinity: Facts & Speculations of Science. George Gamow. (Illus.). 352p. 1988. reprint ed. pap. 8.95 (*0-486-25664-2*) Dover.

One, Two, Three . . . the Toddler Years: A Practical Guide for Parents & Caregivers. 2nd ed. Santa Cruz Toddler Care Center Staff & Irene Van der Zande. (Illus.). 206p. 1995. pap. 11.95 (*0-940953-23-4*) Toddler Ctr Pr.

1-2-3 Art: Open-Ended Art Activities for Young Children. Jean Warren. LC 85-50434. (Totline 1-2-3 Ser.). (Illus.). 160p. (Orig.). (J). (ps-1). 1985. pap. 14.95 (*0-911019-06-5*, 0401) Totline Pubns.

***1-2-3 Be a Phone Sex Operator: A Step-by-Step Guide to the Adult Audiotext Industry for Men.** Ana Loria. 120p. 2000. pap. 21.95 (*0-9651190-3-3*) InfoNet Pubns.

***1-2-3 Be a Porn Star! A Step-by-Step Guide to the Adult Sex Industry for Men & Women.** Ana Loria. 168p. 2000. pap. 24.95 (*0-9651190-2-5*) InfoNet Pubns.

1-2-3 Blocks. Evelyn Petersen. Ed. by Gayle Bittinger. LC 97-62222. (One-Two-Three Ser.). (Illus.). 80p. (J). (ps). 1998. pap. 8.95 (*1-57029-185-3*, 0412) Totline Pubns.

1-2-3 Board Book. Pienkowski. (Illus.). 16p. (J). 1998. 4.99 (*0-689-82096-8*) S&S Childrens.

1 2 3 Boo! Stephanie Peterson. LC 97-204212. (Illus.). (J). 1997. write for info. (*0-7853-2355-4*) Pubns Intl Ltd.

***123 Book.** rev. ed. Cheryl Willis Hudson. (Afro-Bets Ser.). 2000. pap. text 3.95 (*0-940975-98-X*) Just Us Bks.

One-Two-Three Careers for Me: A Career Awareness Program for Preschool-1. Judith A. Sahlin. LC 93-79224. 24p. 1993. 5.95 (*1-884063-02-0*) Mar Co Prods.

1-2-3 Caterpillar. Calino. (Fun-da-mentals Ser.). (Illus.). 30p. (J). 1997. boxed set 6.95 (*0-7892-0304-9*, Abbeville Kids) Abbeville Pr.

1-2-3 Church. Gail Ramshaw. LC 96-35443. (Illus.). 36p. 1996. 15.99 (*0-8066-2335-7*, 10-23357, Augsburg) Augsburg Fortress.

***1, 2, 3, Colores.** Two Can Publishing Ltd. Staff. 2000. mass mkt. 4.95 (*1-58728-952-0*) Two Can Pub.

1-2-3 Colors: Activities for Introducing Color to Young Children. Ed. by Elizabeth S. McKinnon. LC 87-51241. (Totline 1-2-3 Ser.). (Illus.). 160p. (Orig.). (J). (ps-1). 1988. pap. 14.95 (*0-911019-17-0*, 0403) Totline Pubns.

1,2,3 Count Beanies with Me. Dawna Foucht. LC 98-43394. (J). 1998. write for info. (*1-885628-15-3*) Buckaroo Bks.

***1-2-3 Count with Me.** Susan Hood. (Fisher Price Spin & Learn Bks.). (Illus.). 12p. (J). (gr. k-3). 1999. bds. 6.99 (*1-57584-325-0*, Pub. by Rdrs Digest) Random.

1 2 3 Count with Me. Sian Tucker. (J). 12.95 (*0-614-19249-8*) Litle Simon.

1 2 3 Count with Me. Sian Tucker. (Illus.). 24p. (J). (ps-k). 1996. 12.95 (*0-689-80828-3*) S&S Childrens.

One-Two-Three Counting Locally. Wren & Maile. (Keiki's First Bks.). (ENG & HAW., Illus.). 10p. (J). (ps). 1992. bds. 4.95 (*1-880188-01-5*) Bess Pr.

O

An Asterisk (*) at the beginning of an entry indicates that the title is appearing for the first time.

One, Two, Three Echo Me! Ready to Use Songs, Games & Activities to Help Children Sing in Tune. Loretta Mitchell. LC 90-751610. 216p. (C). 1990. pap. text 26.95 (*0-13-636127-7*) P-H.

1-2-3 for DOS: Beginning. 1992. 29.95 (*1-56877-017-0*) Catapult WA.

1-2-3 for DOS: Beginning. 1992. teacher ed. 49.95 (*1-56877-005-7*) Catapult WA.

1-2-3 for Kids, Set. M-USA Video Staff. (LogicNotes Ser.). (Illus.). (Orig.). 1990. pap. text 24.95 (*0-929978-53-6*) M-USA Busn Systs.

One-Two-Three for Rose Lyre. Arnold Logan. pap. 20.00 (*1-889511-04-8*, 1918, WindRose Pub) Rose Harmony.

1-2-3 for Windows: The Visual Learning Guide. David C. Gardner & Grace J. Beatty. 272p. 1994. pap. 19.95 (*1-55958-406-8*) Prima Pub.

1-2-3 for Windows Answers: Certified Technical Support. Kay Y. Nelson. (Certified Tech Support Ser.). 352p. 1994. pap. text 16.95 (*0-07-882068-5*) Osborne-McGraw.

***1-2-3 for Windows Release 5 Smartstart.** Que Education & Training. LC 94-68907. 275p. 1999. pap. text 21.33 (*0-7897-0009-3*) Que.

1-2-3 for Windows 5 for Dummies. 2nd ed. John Walkenbach. LC 94-77752. (For Dummies Ser.). 384p. 1994. pap. 16.95 (*1-56884-216-3*) IDG Bks.

1-2-3 for Windows 95. Que Editors. (Essentials Ser.). 1995. pap. 39.99 (*0-7897-0119-7*) Que.

1-2-3 for Windows Release 5 Essentials. Que Editors. LC 94-69257. (Essentials Ser.). 195p. 1995. 22.99 (*0-7897-0105-7*) Que.

1-2-3 for Windows 95 Essentials. Sue Plumley. Date not set. pap. text 22.99 (*1-57576-004-5*) Que Educ & Trng.

1 2 3 4 5. limited ed. Rona Ponduck. (Illus.). 44p. 1998. pap. 25.00 (*1-892367-00-9*) H Yezerski.

One, Two, Three, Four, Five & Other Favorite Nursery Rhymes. Illus. by Kay Widdowson. (Nursery Rhyme Fun Ser.). 12p. (J). 1995. boxed set 6.95 (*1-884628-24-9*, Flyng Frog) Allied Pub MD.

***1, 2, 3, 4, 5 Once I Caught a Fish Alive!** Alison Boyle. (Illus.). 16p. (J). (ps-k). 2000. 10.95 (*1-86233-116-2*) Levinson Bks.

One, Two, Three, Four, Five, Six, Seven! The Story of Elisha & Naaman. Patricia L. Nederveld. LC 97-32472. (God Loves Me Ser.). (Illus.). 24p. (J). (ps). 1998. pap. 2.45 (*1-56212-290-8*, 1105-0121) CRC Pubns.

1-2-3-4 for the Show: A Guide to Small-Cast One-Act Plays. Lewis W. Heniford. LC 94-42180. 290p. 1995. 41.50 (*0-8108-2985-1*) Scarecrow.

1, 2, 3, 4 Padres! Guia para el Lider: Techicas Efectivas para los Padres de Ninos de la 4 Anos Deedad. Michael H. Popkin et al. (SPA., Illus.). 107p. 1998. 24.95 (*1-880283-21-2*) Active Parenting.

1, 2, 3, 4 Parents! Leader's Guide: Parenting Children Ages 1-to-4 Leader's Guide. Michael H. Popkin et al. (Illus.). 112p. 1996. 24.95 (*1-880283-16-6*) Active Parenting.

One-Two-Three Games: No-Lose Group Games for Young Children. Jean Warren. Ed. by Elizabeth McKinnon. LC 85-50435. (Totline 1-2-3 Ser.). (Illus.). 80p. (Orig.). 1986. pap. 8.95 (*0-911019-09-X*, 0402) Totline Pubns.

***One, Two, Three, Go.** Huyvoun Lee. LC 99-48326. (Illus.). 32p. (ps-4). 2000. pap. text 15.95 (*0-8050-6205-X*) St Martin.

1 2 3 in the Sea: Including Abacus. Marilyn LaPenta. (Illus.). 12p. (J). (ps-1). 1999. boxed set 9.95 (*0-7641-7256-5*) Barron.

***123 Instructions 4 Microsoft PowerPoint 2000.** Alan Roberts & Dylan Fareed. (One Two Three Instructions 4 Learning Guides Ser.). (Illus.). 212p. 2000. pap. 19.95 (*0-9678053-1-7*) OneTwoThr Inst.

***123 Instructions 4 Microsoft Word 2000.** Alan Roberts & Guido Grimaldi. (One Two Three Instructions 4 Learning Guides Ser.). (Illus.). 178p. 2000. pap. 19.95 (*0-9678053-0-9*) OneTwoThr Inst.

***123 Instructions 4 Microsoft Windows 98.** Alan Roberts & Guido Grimaldi. (One Two Three Instructions 4 Learning Guides Ser.). 160p. 2000. pap. 19.95 (*0-9678053-2-5*) OneTwoThr Inst.

***123 Instructions 4 the Internet & Microsoft Outlook 2000.** Alan Roberts & Guido Grimaldi. (One Two Three Instructions 4 Learning Guides Ser.). 172p. 2000. pap. 19.95 (*0-9678053-3-3*) OneTwoThr Inst.

***1, 2, 3 John, Chapters 1-3.** Tyndale House Publishers Staff. (Life Application Bible Studies). 75p. 1999. pap. 5.99 (*0-8423-3412-2*) Tyndale Hse.

***1 2 3 John & Jude.** Jim Starr. (Illus.). 83p. 1999. pap. 1.29 (*1-930264-01-1*) True Jesus.

One, Two, Three, Jump! Penelope Lively. LC 99-76297. (Illus.). 32p. (J). (ps-1). 1999. per. 16.00 (*0-689-82201-4*) S&S Childrens.

One-Two-Three Look at Me. Lisa Meltzer. (Baby Shaped Board Bks.). (Illus.). 28p. (J). (ps). 1990. 2.95 (*0-02-689486-6*) Checkerboard.

123 Louisiana & Me. Linda Crockem. 12p. (J). (ps). 1989. 14.99 (*1-887637-01-X*, TX378468) First Bk Prodns.

1-2-3 Magia: Disciplina Efectiva para Ninos de 2 a 12. Thomas W. Phelan. Tr. by Lois Seijo.Tr. of One-Two-Three Magic: Effective Discipline for Children 2-12. (ENG & SPA., Illus.). 104p. (Orig.). 1996. pap. 9.95 (*1-889140-02-3*) Child Mgmt.

1-2-3 Magic: Effective Discipline for Children 2-12. 2nd rev. ed. Thomas W. Phelan. (Illus.). 180p. 1996. pap. 12.95 (*0-9633861-9-0*) Child Mgmt.

One-Two-Three Magic: Training Your Children to Do What You Want! rev. ed. Thomas W. Phelan. (Illus.). 180p. 1994. pap. 12.95 (*0-9633861-2-3*) Child Mgmt.

One-Two-Three Magic: Effective Discipline for Children 2-12 see 1-2-3 Magia: Disciplina Efectiva para Ninos de 2 a 12.

One-Two-Three Math: Pre-Math Activities for Working with Young Children. Jean Warren. LC 92-80528. (Totline 1-2-3 Ser.). (Illus.). 160p. (Orig.). (J). (ps-1). 1992. 14.95 (*0-911019-52-9*, 0409) Totline Pubns.

1-2-3 Millennium Edition for Dummies. John Walkenbach. LC HF5548.4.L67W3497. (For Dummies Ser.). 408p. 1998. pap. 19.99 (*0-7645-0314-6*) IDG Bks.

1, 2, 3 Monsters on Parade! Marc Tolon Brown. (Arthur Ser.). 24p. (J). (ps-3). 1998. pap. 3.99 (*0-679-89283-4*, Pub. by Random Bks Yng Read) Random.

1, 2, 3 Moose: A Pacific Northwest Counting Book. Photos by Art Wolfe. LC 96-14751. (Illus.). 32p. (J). (ps-3). 1996. 15.95 (*1-57061-078-9*) Sasquatch Bks.

1, 2, 3, Music! Sylvie Auzary-Luton. LC 99-10200. (Illus.). 40p. (J). (ps-2). 1999. 15.95 (*0-531-30188-5*) Orchard Bks Watts.

1 2 3 North Carolina & Me! Linda Crockem. 12p. (J). (ps). 1997. 14.99 (*1-887637-04-4*) First Bk Prodns.

One, Two, Three, Oops! Michael Coleman. LC 98-6476. (Illus.). 32p. (J). (gr. k-2). 1999. 14.95 (*1-888444-45-2*) Little Tiger.

One, Two, Three, Picnic. (Fisher-Price Hideaway Hollow Padded Board Bks.). (Illus.). 16p. (J). (gr. 1). 1998. bds. write for info. (*0-7666-0120-X*, Honey Bear Bks) Modern Pub NYC.

***123 Pop.** Rachel Isadora. LC 99-56686. (Illus.). 32p. (J). (ps-1). 2000. 15.99 (*0-670-88859-1*, Viking Child) Peng Put Young Read.

1-2-3 Puppets: Simple Puppets to Make for Working with Young Children. Jean Warren. Ed. by Gayle Bittinger. LC 89-50122. (Totline 1-2-3 Ser.). (Illus.). 80p. (Orig.). (J). (ps-k). 1989. pap. 8.95 (*0-911019-21-9*, 0404) Totline Pubns.

One, Two, Three, Read! Judith Dettre. LC 79-52661. 1980. pap. 9.99 (*0-8224-5788-1*) Fearon Teacher Aids.

1-2-3 Reading & Writing: Pre-Reading & Pre-Writing Opportunities for Young Children. Jean Warren. Ed. by Gayle Bittinger. LC 91-65932. (Illus.). 160p. (Orig.). (J). (ps). 1992. 14.95 (*0-911019-47-2*, 0407) Totline Pubns.

1-2-3 Release 3.4 QuickStart. Rick Winter. (QuickStart Ser.). 1992. 21.95 (*1-56529-007-0*) Que.

1-2-3 Release 4 for Windows QuickStart. Joyce Nielson. (QuickStart Ser.). 544p. (Orig.). 1993. pap. 9.95 (*0-685-70408-4*) Que.

1-2-3 Revealed. Dan Shaffer. pap. 16.95 (*0-317-06055-4*) P-H.

One-Two-Three Rhymes, Stories, & Songs: Open-Ended Language. Jean Warren. Ed. by Kathleen Cubley. LC 91-67075. (1-2-3 Ser.). (Illus.). 80p. (Orig.). (J). (ps-k). 1992. pap. 8.95 (*0-911019-50-2*, WPH0408) Totline Pubns.

1-2-3 Science: Pre-Science Activities for Young Children. Gayle Bittinger. LC 93-60024. (Totline 1-2-3 Ser.). (Illus.). 160p. (Orig.). (J). (ps-k). 1993. pap. 14.95 (*0-911019-62-6*, 0410) Totline Pubns.

1-2-3 Shapes: Beginning Shape Activities for Young Children. Gayle Bittinger. Ed. by Kathleen Cubley. LC 94-60690. (1-2-3 Ser.). (Illus.). 160p. (J). (ps). 1995. 14.95 (*1-57029-006-7*, WPH 0411) Totline Pubns.

One Two Three Sign with Me. (Illus.). 24p. (J). 1987. pap. 3.95 (*0-939849-01-1*, 104P) Sugar Sign Pr.

***1-2-3 Slide.** Susan Van Metre. (Illus.). 12p. (J). (ps-k). 1999. bds. 12.99 (*0-525-46254-6*, Dutton Child) Peng Put Young Read.

1-2-3 Smoothies: 123 Quick Frosty Drinks - Delicious & Nutritious. Rita Bingham. (Illus.). 200p. 1998. pap. 14.95 (*1-882314-14-X*) Nat Meals Pub.

1, 2, 3 Thanksgiving! W. Nikola-Lisa. Ed. by Abby Levine. LC 90-28638. (Illus.). 32p. (J). (ps-3). 1991. lib. bdg. 14.95 (*0-8075-6109-6*) A Whitman.

1, 2, 3 Thanksgiving! W. Nikola-Lisa. LC 90-28638. 1991. 11.15 (*0-606-10117-9*, Pub. by Turtleback) Demco.

1, 2, 3 Thanksgiving! W. Nikola-Lisa. LC 90-28638. (Illus.). 32p. (J). (ps-1). 1996. reprint ed. pap. 6.95 (*0-8075-6110-X*) A Whitman.

1, 2, 3... The Toddler Years: A Practical Guide for Parents & Caregivers. 3rd rev. ed. Irene Van der Zande & Santa Cruz Toddler Center Staff. Ed. by Sandy Davie. (Illus.). 218p. 1999. pap. 14.50 (*0-940953-22-6*) Toddler Ctr Pr.

One, Two, Three to the Zoo. Eric Carle. LC 81-8609. (Illus.). 32p. (J). (ps-1). 1982. 15.95 (*0-399-61172-X*, Philomel) Peng Put Young Read.

One, Two, Three to the Zoo. Eric Carle. (Illus.). 34p. (J). (ps-2). 1990. pap. 7.95 (*0-399-21970-6*, Sandcastle Bks) Putnam Pub Group.

1, 2, 3 to the Zoo: A Counting Book. Eric Carle. (J). 1968. 13.15 (*0-606-04498-1*, Pub. by Turtleback) Demco.

1, 2, 3, under the Sea: A Little Mermaid Pop-Up Counting Book. Illus. by Vaccaro Associates Staff. LC 94-71789. 20p. (J). (ps-k). 1995. 12.95 (*0-7868-3035-2*, Pub. by Disney Pr) Time Warner.

1 2 3 What Do You See? Big Book. Sherry B. Garr. 24p. (J). (ps-1). 1997. pap. text 17.95 (*1-890566-12-8*) ABCs Unltd.

1 2 3 What Do You See? Trace, Color, Write. Sherry B. Garr. 20p. (J). (ps-1). 1997. pap. text 3.25 (*1-890566-13-6*) ABCs Unltd.

***1-2-3 You Can't Scare Me.** School Zone Publishing Staff. (Illus.). (J). 2000. mass mkt. 4.99 (*0-88743-604-8*) Sch Zone Pub Co.

One, Two, Three, You're Hired. C. James O'Donnell. 160p. 1992. pap. 9.95 (*0-912495-14-6*) San Diego Pub Co.

One-Two-Three Zoo Mystery. Susan Pearson. (J). 1991. pap. 11.95 (*0-671-74052-0*) S&S Trade.

123s. Photos by Sia Aryai. (Baby Bright Board Bks.). (Illus.). 10p. (J). (ps). bds. 5.95 (*1-56565-824-8*, 08248W, Pub. by Lowell Hse Juvenile) NTC Contemp Pub Co.

One Two Threes. Gabriele. (J). 1985. pap. 1.95 (*0-911211-66-7*) Penny Lane Pubns.

One, Two What Did Daddy. Susan R. Cooper. 1996. mass mkt. 5.50 (*0-380-78417-3*, Avon Bks) Morrow Avon.

One-Two-What Will I Do? Claire Jones & Bob Varga. 20p. (J). (gr. k-5). 1995. mass mkt. 4.00 (*1-58193-169-7*) Brown Bag Prods.

One, Two... Where's the Shoe? Victor Ambrus. 1998. 14.95 (*0-86315-261-9*, Pub. by Floris Bks) Anthroposophic.

One Unbelievable Man. Pat Montana. (Romance Ser.). 1994. per. 2.75 (*0-373-08993-7*, 5-08993-3) Silhouette.

One Union in Wood. Jerry Lembcke & William Tattam. LC 84-15808. 210p. 1984. pap. 7.95 (*0-7178-0619-7*) Intl Pubs Co.

One United People: The Federalist & the National Idea. Edward Millican. LC 89-48254. 280p. 1990. text 34.95 (*0-8131-1678-3*) U Pr of Ky.

***One Universe: At Home in the Cosmos.** Neil De Grasse Tyson et al. LC 99-53981. (Illus.). 218 p. 2000. 40.00 (*0-309-06488-0*, Joseph Henry Pr) Natl Acad Pr.

***One up on Wall Street: How to Use What You Already Know to Make Money in the Market.** Peter Lynch & John Rothchild. 304p. 2000. pap. 14.00 (*0-7432-0040-3*, Fireside) S&S Trade Pap.

One up on Wall Street: How to Use What You Already Know to Make Money in the Market. Peter Lynch & John Rothchild. 320p. 1990. pap. 13.95 (*0-14-012792-5*, Penguin Bks) Viking Penguin.

One up, One Down see Uno Arribo, Uno Abajo

One up, One down. Carol Snyder. LC 93-36282. (Illus.). 32p. (J). (ps-3). 1995. 15.00 (*0-689-31828-6*) Atheneum Yung Read.

One-Upmanship. Stephen Potter. LC 96-28937. (Illus.). 177p. 1997. pap. 9.95 (*1-55921-190-3*) Moyer Bell.

One-Upmanship: Being Some Account of the Activities & Teaching of the Lifemanship Correspondence College of One-Upness & Gameslifemastery Stephen Potter. LC 79-304663. 151p. 1977. write for info. (*0-14-001827-1*) Pnguin Bks Ltd.

One upon a Horse: A History of Horses--& How They Shaped Our History. Suzanne Jurmain. LC 88-17522. (Illus.). 176p. (J). (gr. 4 up). 1989. 15.95 (*0-688-05550-8*) Lothrop.

One Vast Page: Essays on the Beat Writers, Their Books, & My Life, 1950-1980. Jeffrey Bartlett. 165p. 1991. pap. 8.95 (*1-889883-00-X*) Provine Pr.

One Very Best Valentine's Day. Joan W. Blos. (Illus.). 32p. (J). (ps-2). 1992. pap. 2.50 (*0-671-75297-9*) Litle Simon.

One Very Best Valentine's Day. Joan W. Blos. 32p. (J). (ps-2). 1998. per. 4.99 (*0-689-81944-7*) S&S Childrens.

One Very Best Valentine's Day. Joan W. Blos. (J). 1998. 10.19 (*0-606-13008-X*, Pub. by Turtleback) Demco.

One Violent Crime: A Testimony. Bruce Shapiro. 256p. 24.00 (*0-465-05249-5*) Basic.

***One Virgin Too Many.** Lindsey Davis. 304p. 2000. 23.95 (*0-89296-716-1*) Mysterious Pr.

One Vision, Many Voices: Lectures Delivered at the Mother Caroline Centenary Celebrations, 1992. Ed. by Virginia Geiger & Patricia McLaughlin. 136p. (Orig.). (C). 1993. pap. text 17.00 (*0-8191-8997-9*); lib. bdg. 43.00 (*0-8191-8996-0*) U Pr of Amer.

One Voice: Music & Stories in the Classroom. Barbara M. Britsch & Amy Dennison-Tansey. LC 95-11838. (Illus.). xxiv, 175p. 1995. pap. text 18.50 (*1-56308-049-4*) Teacher Ideas Pr.

One Voice: Rabbi Jacob M. Rothschild & the Troubled South. Janice R. Blumberg. LC 84-22723. (Illus.). xi, 240p. 1985. 19.95 (*0-86554-150-7*, MUP H141) Mercer Univ Pr.

One Volume Bible Commentary. J. Dummelow. 1993. 39.95 (*0-933062-28-1*) R H Sommer.

One Volume Edition, Regular with Study Guide. Hans C. Ohanian. pap. 62.00 (*0-393-96037-4*) Norton.

One Volume English-Persian Dictionary. Soleyman Haim. 1100p. 1984. lib. bdg. 35.00 (*0-939214-48-2*) Mazda Pubs.

One Volume Persian-English Dictionary. Soleyman Haim. 1039p. 1984. lib. bdg. 35.00 (*0-939214-47-4*) Mazda Pubs.

One Wagon West. Brad E. Hainsworth. 212p. 1995. pap. 11.98 (*1-55517-167-2*) CFI Dist.

One Walked Out of Two & Forgot It. Toby MacLennan. LC 75-189887. 1972. 15.00 (*0-87110-083-5*) Ultramarine Pub.

One War at a Time: The International Dimensions of the American Civil War. Dean B. Mahin. LC 99-29912. 1999. write for info. (*1-57488-209-0*) Brasseys.

***One War at a Time: The International Dimensions of the American Civil War.** Dean B. Mahin. 2000. reprint ed. pap. 21.95 (*1-57488-301-1*) Brasseys.

One Was Johnny see Nutshell Library

One Was Johnny: A Counting Book. Maurice Sendak. (Illus.). 48p. (J). (ps-3). 1962. lib. bdg. 14.89 (*0-06-025540-4*) HarpC Child Bks.

One Was Johnny: A Counting Book. Maurice Sendak. LC 62-13315. (Trophy Picture Bk.). (Illus.). 48p. (J). (ps-3). 1991. pap. 4.95 (*0-06-443251-3*, HarpTrophy) HarpC Child Bks.

One Was Johnny: A Counting Book. Maurice Sendak. (J). 1991. 10.15 (*0-606-04764-6*, Pub. by Turtleback) Demco.

***One Was Not Enough.** Lori Menning. (Illus.). 20p. (J). 2000. pap. 5.95 (*1-891848-81-3*) Busn Word.

One Watermelon Seed. Celia Barker Lottridge. (J). 1986. 13.15 (*0-606-04765-4*, Pub. by Turtleback) Demco.

One Watermelon Seed. Celia Barker Lottridge. (Illus.). 24p. (J). (ps up). 1990. reprint ed. pap. 8.95 (*0-19-540735-0*) OUP.

One Wave Standing. William L. Fox. 80p. 1998. pap. 12.00 (*1-888809-06-X*) La Alameda Pr.

One Way. Marilyn R. Rosenberg. 4p. 1977. pap. 8.00 (*0-317-14975-X*) Marilyn R Rosenberg.

One Way: Bernard Dadie Observes America. Bernard B. Dadie. Tr. by Jo Patterson from FRE. LC 93-27875. 184p. 1994. pap. text 14.95 (*0-252-06408-9*) U of Ill Pr.

One Way: Bernard Dadie Observes America. Bernard B. Dadie. Tr. by Jo Patterson from FRE. LC 93-27875. 184p. 1994. text 29.95 (*0-252-02039-1*) U of Ill Pr.

***One Way Vol. I & II: The Quest for the Truth - Basics & Beyond Recovery, 8 vols.** large type ed. Zoltan Csomoss. 60p. 1998. pap. 10.00 (*0-9702409-1-0*) Zoltan.

One Way & Other Korean Short Stories. Sonu Hwi & Choe In-hun. Ed. by Korean National Commission for UNESCO Staff et al. Tr. by Kim Chong-un et al from KOR. (Modern Korean Short Stories Ser.: No. 5). viii, 204p. 1983. 20.00 (*0-89209-206-8*) Pace Grp Intl.

One Way Free Flow. D. R. Mankekar. 171p. 1978. 11.95 (*0-318-37286-X*) Asia Bk Corp.

1 Way Microsoft Marches Strong... A Case Study of Law, Judicial Power & Constitutional Corruption in America: Includes Coupon for up to Date CD-ROM with Linux Red Hat 5.2 Based O/S with the 2.2 Kernel That Runs MS-Windows Apps. Dylan G. Penal. 268p. 1999. mass mkt. 27.95 (*1-891950-13-4*) Amer Group Pub.

One Way Out. John Clarkson. 400p. (Orig.). 1996. mass mkt. 5.99 (*0-515-11802-8*, Jove) Berkley Pub.

One Way Pockets: The Book of Books on Wall Street Speculation. Don Guyon. LC 65-18336. 1965. reprint ed. pap. 10.00 (*0-87034-013-1*) Fraser Pub Co.

One-Way Relationships Workbook: The 12-Week, Step-by-Step Interactive for Recovery from Codependent Relationships. Alfred H. Ells. 256p. (Orig.). 1992. pap., wbk. ed. 14.99 (*0-8407-3412-3*) Nelson.

One-Way Romance. Patricia Sierra. LC 85-91538. 128p. (J). (gr. 6-10). 1986. pap. 2.50 (*0-380-75107-0*, Avon Bks) Morrow Avon.

One Way Street's Human-Arm Shirt Pattern. (Illus.). 20p. 1989. pap. 6.00 (*1-58302-055-1*, PAT-05) One Way St.

One Way Street's People Puppet Pattern. rev. ed. (Illus.). 16p. 1982. ring bd. 9.00 (*1-58302-056-X*, PAT-01) One Way St.

One-Way Ticket. Ed. by Tricia Hedge. (Illus.). 48p. 1991. pap. text 5.95 (*0-19-422678-6*) OUP.

One-Way Ticket. Zinovy Zinik. LC 96-9568. 192p. 1996. 19.95 (*0-8112-1341-2*, Pub. by New Directions) Norton.

One-Way Ticket. large type ed. James Pattinson. (Ulverscroft Large Print Ser.). 288p. 1998. 29.99 (*0-7089-3918-X*) Ulverscroft.

One Way Ticket: The True Story of Herta Taussig Freitag. Mary A. Johnson. (Illus.). 150p. (Orig.). (J). (gr. 5 up). 1988. pap. 15.95 (*0-9621465-0-1*) Mary Ann Johnson.

One-Way Ticket to Hollywood: Film Artists of Austrian & German Origin in Los Angeles. Doris Angst-Nowik & Jane Sloan. (Illus.). 107p. (Orig.). 1986. pap. 10.00 (*0-318-22296-5*) USC Lib Gifts.

One Way to Die. large type ed. J. B. Dancer. 1990. pap. 16.99 (*0-7089-6854-6*, Linford) Ulverscroft.

One Way to Live . . . for a Month, Vol. 1. Tracy Voigt. 1988. ring bd. write for info. (*0-318-63905-X*) T Voigt.

One Way to Reconstruct the Scene. William V. Davis. LC 79-22810. (Younger Poets Ser.: No. 75). 1980. 18.00 (*0-300-02481-9*); pap. 11.00 (*0-300-02503-3*) Yale U Pr.

One-Way Trail. Max Brand. 240p. 1998. reprint ed. mass mkt. 4.50 (*0-8439-4379-3*, Leisure Bks) Dorchester Pub Co.

One-Way Trail: A Max Brand Western Trio. large type ed. Max Brand. (Sagebrush Large Print Westerns Ser.). 256p. 1996. lib. bdg. 18.95 (*1-57490-014-5*) T T Beeler.

One Way 2 Play. Dal Shealy & Pat Springle. LC 95-8014. 192p. 1995. pap. 9.99 (*0-7852-7676-9*) Nelson.

One Way up Wall Street: The Fred Alger Story. Dilip Mirchandani. LC 99-490605. (Illus.). 496p. 1999. 29.95 (*0-9670128-0-5*) J Charlton.

One Way Weekend. Edith B. Wile. LC 80-22892. 1989. pap. 13.95 (*0-87949-196-5*) Ashley Bks.

1-Ways, Vol. 19. 1996. 310.00 (*0-614-09361-9*) Trans Data Rep.

***One Wedding Required ! (Wanted: One Wedding Dress)** large type ed. Sharon Kendrick. 1999. 21.95 (*0-263-16138-2*) P-H.

One Wedding Required! (Wanted: One Wedding Dress) Sharon Kendrick. (Presents Ser.: No. 2017). 1999. per. 3.75 (*0-373-12017-6*, 1-12017-9) Harlequin Bks.

One-Week Baby. Hayley Gardner. (Yours Truly Ser.). 1997. per. 3.50 (*0-373-52047-6*, 1-52047-7) Silhouette.

One Week in Budapest. P. Buza. (Illus.). 146p. (C). 1990. 55.00 (*0-7855-5220-0*, Pub. by Collets) St Mut.

One Week in Budapest. Peter Buza. 144p. 1989. 30.00 (*963-13-3587-9*, Pub. by Corvina Bks) St Mut.

One-Week Marriage. Renee Roszel. (Romance Ser.: Bk. 3559). 1999. per. 3.50 (*0-373-03559-4*, 1-03559-1) Harlequin Bks.

One-Week Marriage. large type ed. Renee Roszel. (Larger Print Ser.: Bk. 405). 1999. per. 3.50 (*0-373-15805-X*, 1-15805-4) Harlequin Bks.

One-Week Wife. Hayley Gardner. (Yours Truly Ser.). 1997. per. 3.50 (*0-373-52045-X*, 1-52045-1) Silhouette.

One Went to Denver & the Other Went Wrong. Stephen A. Bly. LC 94-38680. (Code of the West Ser.: Bk. 2). 192p. (gr. 8 up). 1995. pap. 9.99 (*0-89107-834-7*) Crossway Bks.

One White Crow. George McMullen. 168p. 1995. pap. 8.95 (*1-57174-007-4*) Hampton Roads Pub Co.

One White Rose. Julie Garwood. (Clayborne Brides Ser.). 1997. per. 2.99 (*0-671-01009-3*) PB.

One White Rose. Julie Garwood. 1997. per. 2.66 (*0-671-02020-X*) PB.

One White Sail. Garne. (J). 1998. 4.95 (*0-87628-978-2*) Ctr Appl Res.

One White Sail. S. T. Garne. (Illus.). 20p. (J). (ps up). 1993. 4.95 (*0-671-87894-8*) Litle Simon.

One White Sail: A Caribbean Counting Book. S. T. Garne. LC 91-24662. (Illus.). 32p. (J). 1992. 14.00 (*0-671-75579-X*, Green Tiger S&S) S&S Childrens.

An Asterisk (*) at the beginning of an entry indicates that the title is appearing for the first time.

One Who Almost Got Away. Alicia Scott. (Intimate Moments Ser.: No. 723). 244p. 1996. per. 3.99 (*0-373-07723-8*, 1-07723-9) Silhouette.

One Who Came Back. Joann Mazzio. 208p. (J). (gr. 5-9). 1992. 16.00 (*0-395-59506-1*) HM.

One Who Did Not Ask. Altaf Fatima. (Asian Writers Ser.). 335p. 1994. pap. 10.95 (*0-435-95084-3*, 95084) Heinemann.

One Who Goes Everywhere: The Ubiquarian's Dictionary. Susanna Cuyler. (Illus.). 160p. (Orig.). 1988. pap. 10.00 (*0-9612018-4-3*) B RUGGED.

One Who Helped see Que Ayuda

One Who Is Legion. Natalie C. Barney. 192p. 1987. reprint ed. 28.00 (*0-915032-83-X*); reprint ed. pap. 14.95 (*0-943373-47-6*) Natl Poet Foun.

One Who Is Standing Apart from Me. Maurice Blanchot. 96p. 1997. pap. text 12.95 (*1-886449-42-2*) Barrytown Ltd.

One Who Knows God. Clement of Alexandria. Tr. by William Wilson from GRE. 160p. (Orig.). 1990. pap. 7.95 (*0-924722-02-9*) Scroll Pub.

One Who Remembers. large type ed. Theresa Charles. 352p. 1988. 27.99 (*0-7089-1862-X*) Ulverscroft.

One Who Walked Alone: Robert E. Howard - The Final Years. Novalyne P. Ellis. 1986. 30.00 (*0-937986-78-X*) D M Grant.

One Who Was Standing Apart from Me. Maurice Blanchot. Ed. by George Quasha. Tr. by Lydia Davis from FRE. Orig. Title: Celui Qui Ne M'Accompagnait Pas. 96p. (C). 1989. 25.00 (*0-88268-053-6*); pap. write for info. (*0-88268-140-0*) Station Hill Pr.

One Whose Eyes Open When You Close Your Eyes. Franz Wright. 54p. 1982. 12.50 (*0-913219-34-7*); pap. 6.50 (*0-913219-35-5*); 17.50 (*0-913219-36-3*) Pym-Rand Pr.

***One Wicked Night.** Shelley Bradley. (Splendor Historical Romances Ser.). 320p. 2000. mass mkt. 4.99 (*0-8217-6467-5*, Zebra Kensgtn) Kensgtn Pub Corp.

One Wicked Night. Jo Leigh. (Temptation Ser.). 1998. per. 3.75 (*0-373-25774-0*, 1-25774-0) Harlequin Bks.

One Wide Sky: Poems by Rhonda Williford. Rhonda Williford. Ed. by R. D. Baker. (Poetry Chapbook Ser.). (Illus.). 28p. (Orig.). 1997. pap. 4.00 (*1-887641-15-7*) Argonne Hotel Pr.

One Wild & Precious Life: Ministering to Adolescents. Fred Herron. LC 96-22716. 112p. 1996. pap. text 16.50 (*0-7618-0417-X*) U Pr of Amer.

One Wild Weekend: Bachelor Auction. Rita C. Estrada. (Temptation Ser.: No. 733). 1999. per. 3.75 (*0-373-25833-X*, 1-25833-4, Harlequin) Harlequin Bks.

One Will - One Purpose - One Economy. Bill Freeman. 25p. (Orig.). 1992. pap. 1.00 (*0-914271-21-0*) Mnstry Pubns.

One Windy Day. Jane Caraway. (Ready-Set-Read Ser.). (Illus.). 32p. (J). (ps-3). 1990. lib. bdg. 21.40 (*0-8172-3579-5*) Raintree Steck-V.

One Windy Day. Jane Caraway. 28p. (J). (ps-3). 1995. pap. text 4.95 (*0-8114-6744-9*) Raintree Steck-V.

One Windy Wednesday. Phyllis Root. LC 96-4237. (Illus.). 24p. (J). (ps-k). 1996. 9.99 (*0-7636-0054-7*) Candlewick Pr.

One Windy Wednesday. Phyllis Root. LC 96-4237. (Giggle Club Ser.). (Illus.). 24p. (J). (ps-1). 1997. reprint ed. pap. 3.29 (*0-7636-0278-7*) Candlewick Pr.

One Winter in the Wilderness. P. Cary Peek. LC 97-26236. (Illus.). 224p. 1998. 24.95 (*0-89301-210-6*) U of Idaho Pr.

One Winter Night: A Hanukkah Story. Eric A. Kimmel. LC 98-46269. (J). 2001. 15.95 (*0-385-32652-1*) Doubleday.

One Winter's Day. Jeffrey Scherer. LC 95-30066. (Hello Reader! Ser.: Level 1). (Illus.). (J). (gr. 1). 1996. write for info. (*0-590-74240-X*) Scholastic Inc.

One Wintry Night. Ruth Bell Graham. LC 91-48107. (Illus.). 72p. (YA). (gr. 11 up). 1995. 16.97 (*0-8010-3848-0*) Baker Bks.

One Wish. C. J. Card. (Magical Love Ser.: Vol. 4). 308p. 1998. mass mkt. 5.99 (*0-515-12354-4*, Jove) Berkley Pub.

***One Wish.** Linda Lael Miller. 368p. 2000. per. 6.99 (*0-671-53786-5*, Pocket Star Bks) PB.

***One Wish.** large type ed. Linda Lael Miller. LC 00-39917. 2000. write for info. (*1-56895-878-1*) Wheeler Pub.

One with Christ. Hudson Taylor. 96p. 1997. mass mkt. 5.99 (*0-88368-061-0*) Whitaker Hse.

One Wobbly Wheelbarrow. (Language of Mathematics Ser.). 1989. 35.92 (*0-8123-6408-2*); pap. 5.36 (*0-8123-6409-0*); audio 7.92 (*0-8123-6411-2*) McDougal-Littell.

One Woman. Susan Fridkin. Date not set. pap. 5.00 (*0-9661402-0-6*) S Fridkin.

One-Woman Crusade. Emma Darcy. (Presents Ser.: No. 1351). 1991. per. 2.75 (*0-373-11351-X*) Harlequin Bks.

One Woman, Five Lives, Five Countries. Eugenia Dallas. Ed. by Paula Silici. LC 98-67925. (Illus.). 257p. 1998. pap. 20.00 (*0-88100-107-4*) Natl Writ Pr.

One-Woman Man. M. L. Gamble. (Intrigue Ser.: Vol. 480). 1998. per. 3.99 (*0-373-22480-X*, 1-22480-7) Harlequin Bks.

One Woman, One Ranch, One Summer. Lucile Bogue. LC 97-18921. (Illus.). 128p. (Orig.). 1997. pap. 10.95 (*0-89407-121-1*, 1211) Strawberry Hill.

One Woman, One Vote: Rediscovering the Woman Suffrage Movement. Ed. by Marjorie S. Wheeler. LC 95-34128. (Illus.). 388p. 1995. 18.95 (*0-939165-26-0*) NewSage Press.

***One Woman Short: A Novel.** George Nelson. LC 00-20400. 256p. 2000. pap. 12.00 (*0-684-86461-4*, Fireside) S&S Trade Pap.

One Woman Show. Cornelia Otis Skinner. 1974. 9.95 (*0-87129-464-8*, O15) Dramatic Pub.

One Woman's Army: A Black Officer Remembers the WAC. Charity A. Earley. LC 88-20181. (Military History Ser.: Vol. 12). (Illus.). 232p. (C). 1996. pap. 15.95 (*0-89096-694-X*) Tex A&M Univ Pr.

One Woman's Charlottetown: Diaries of Margaret Gray Lord, 1863, 1876, 1890. Ed. by Evelyn J. MacLeod. (Mercury Ser.: History No. 42). (Illus.). 212p. 1988. pap. 19.95 (*0-660-10780-5*, Pub. by CN Mus Civilization) U of Wash Pr.

One Woman's Experience: A Collection of Poems. Leigh A. Lombardo. LC 96-24859. 118p. 1997. pap. 19.95 (*0-7734-2702-3*, Mellen Poetry Pr) E Mellen.

One Woman's Feelings: A Poetry Book. Bibliotheca Press Staff. 1981. pap. text 8.95 (*0-939476-13-4*) Prosperity & Profits.

One Woman's Fight. 4th ed. Vashti C. McCollum. (Illus.). 240p. 1993. reprint ed. pap. 15.00 (*1-877733-08-3*) Freedom Rel Found.

One Woman's Gold Rush: Snapshots from Mollie Brackett's Lost Photo Album 1898-1899. Cynthia B. Driscoll. Ed. by David H. Curl. LC 96-12942. (Illus.). 128p. (Orig.). 1996. pap. 12.00 (*0-88196-007-1*) Oak Woods Media.

***One Woman's Jihad: Nana Asma'u, Scholar & Scribe.** Beverly B. Mack & Jean Boyd. LC 99-53817. (Illus.). 192p. 2000. pap. 13.95 (*0-253-21398-3*); lib. bdg. 35.00 (*0-253-33707-0*) Ind U Pr.

One Woman's Liberation: The Story of Fanny Burney. Louis Baldwin & Virginia Baldwin. LC 90-5988. 1991. 29.95 (*0-89341-600-2*, Longwood Academic); pap. 14.95 (*0-89341-601-0*, Longwood Academic) Hollowbrook.

One Woman's Life see Collected Works of Robert Herrick

One Woman's Life. Robert Herrick. (Collected Works of Robert Herrick). 1988. reprint ed. lib. bdg. 59.00 (*0-7812-1274-X*) Rprt Serv.

One Woman's Life in Search of Love & Happiness. Karen L. Walton. (Illus.). 400p. (Orig.). 1997. pap. write for info. (*0-9649785-1-2*) Walton Co.

One Woman's Life, the Steppings of Faith: Edna Gray's Story. Edna Gray. (American Biography Ser.). 352p. 1991. reprint ed. lib. bdg. 79.00 (*0-7812-8153-9*) Rprt Serv.

One Woman's Passion for Peace & Freedom: The Life of Mildred Scott Olmsted. Margaret H. Bacon. LC 92-13755. (Syracuse Studies on Peace & Conflict Resolution). (Illus.). 413p. 1993. reprint ed. pap. 128.10 (*0-608-07590-6*, 205990500010) Bks Demand.

***One Woman's Reflections.** Esther Lester. 80p. 1999. pap. 7.95 (*1-56167-547-4*) Am Literary Pr.

***One Woman's Thoughts: She is You & Me.** Lee Atkinson. 240p. 2000. pap. 14.95 (*0-88347-454-9*, Pub. by T More) BookWorld.

One Woman's War: A Canadian Reporter With the Free French. Gladys Arnold. (Illus.). 222p. 1988. mass mkt. 4.95 (*0-88780-154-4*, Pub. by Formac Publ Co) Formac Dist Ltd.

One Woman's War: Letters Home from the Women's Army Corp, 1944-1946. Anne B. Green. LC 89-13000. (Illus.). xxiv, 308p. 1989. 22.50 (*0-87351-246-4*) Minn Hist.

One Woman's War - Letters Home: From the Women's Army Corps, 1944-1946. Anne B. Green. (Illus.). xxiv, 308p. 1993. pap. 14.95 (*0-87351-286-3*) Minn Hist.

One Woman's West: Recollections of the Oregon Trail & Settling the Northwest Country. 2nd expanded ed. Martha G. Masterson. Ed. by Lois Barton. LC 86-15570. (Illus.). 222p. (Orig.). 1986. pap. 9.95 (*0-9609420-2-5*) S Butte Pr.

One Woman's World War II. Violet A. Kochendoerfer. LC 93-38919. 232p. 1994. 25.00 (*0-8131-1866-2*) U Pr of Ky.

One Wonderful Day at a Time. Irwin Siegel. (Illus.). 32p. (Orig.). (J). (gr. k-4). 1996. pap. 5.95 (*1-886094-43-8*) Chicago Spectrum.

One Wonderful You. Francie Portnoy. LC 97-202671. (Illus.). 48p. (J). (ps-5). 1997. pap. 9.95 (*0-9643051-1-9*) Chldrns Home Soc.

One Woolly Wombat. Kerry Argent & Rod Trinca. (Illus.). 32p. (J). (ps-1). 1987. reprint ed. pap. 6.95 (*0-916291-10-3*) Kane-Miller Bk.

One Word. Marc J. Straus. 80p. 1994. 29.95 (*0-8101-5010-7*, TriQuart); pap. 11.95 (*0-8101-5035-2*, TriQuart) Northwestern U Pr.

One Word at a Time. Trude S. Norman. 256p. 1998. pap. 16.95 (*1-889734-01-2*) Cock-a-Hoop.

One Word at a Time: The Use of Single Word Utterances Before Syntax. Lois Bloom. LC 72-94445. (Janua Linguarum, Ser. Minor: No. 154). 262p. 1973. pap. text 27.70 (*90-279-3375-8*) Mouton.

One Word Deep: Lectures & Readings. Rebecca McClanahan. (Writers-in-Residence Ser.). 112p. 1993. pap. 7.00 (*0-912592-34-6*) Ashland Poetry.

***One Word From God Can Change Your Destiny.** Kenneth Copeland. (One Word From God Ser.). 1999. pap. 6.99 (*1-57794-147-0*) Harrison Hse.

***One Word From God Can Change Your Family.** Kenneth Copeland. (One Word From God Ser.). 1999. pap. 6.99 (*1-57794-148-9*) Harrison Hse.

***One Word From God Can Change Your Finances.** Kenneth Copeland. (One Word From God Ser.). 1999. pap. 6.99 (*1-57794-146-2*) Harrison Hse.

***One Word from God Can Change Your Formula for Success.** Kenneth Copeland. 144p. 1999. pap. text 6.99 (*1-57794-197-7*) Harrison Hse.

***One Word From God Can Change Your Health.** Kenneth Copeland. (One Word From God Ser.). 1999. pap. 6.99 (*1-57794-145-4*) Harrison Hse.

***One Word from God Will Change Your Nation.** Kenneth Copeland. 144p. 1999. pap. text 6.99 (*1-57794-200-0*) Harrison Hse.

***One Word from God Will Change Your Prayer Life.** Kenneth Copeland. 144p. 1999. pap. text 6.99 (*1-57794-198-5*) Harrison Hse.

***One Word from God Will Change Your Relationships.** Kenneth Copeland. 144p. 1999. pap. text 6.99 (*1-57794-199-3*) Harrison Hse.

One Word to the Other. Octavio Paz. (Illus.). 48p. 1991. pap. 10.00 (*0-941179-15-X*) Latitudes Pr.

One Word, Two Words, Hyphenated? 2nd ed. Mary L. Gilman. LC 97-39429. 84p. (Orig.). 1998. pap. 7.95 (*1-881859-01-0*) Natl Ct Report.

One Wore Blue. Heather Graham. 448p. 1991. mass mkt. 6.99 (*0-440-20963-3*) Dell.

One World. enl. rev. ed. John Kiang. Tr. by Michael Zhang & K. Y. Jiang. (CHI.). 870p. 1996. 29.95 (*0-916301-07-9*) One World Pub.

One World, Bk. 3. Tim Priesack & Terry Tomscha. LC 91-45157. (Cassell Secondary English Course Ser.). 1993. wbk. ed. 11.90 (*0-13-635608-7*) P-H.

One World, Coursebook 4. Tim Priesack & Terry Tomscha. LC 94-26090. (English Language Teaching Ser.). 1994. 10.50 (*0-13-635616-8*) P-H.

One World, Level 1. Tim Priesack. 1994. pap. text, teacher ed. 26.80 (*0-13-157140-0*) P-H.

One World, Level 1. Tim Priesack & Terry Tomscha. LC 94-16067. 128p. 1995. pap. text, student ed. 21.20 (*0-13-157132-X*) Prentice ESL.

One World, Level 2. Tim Priesack & Terry Tomscha. 1994. pap. text, teacher ed. 26.80 (*0-13-186008-9*) P-H.

One World, Level 3. Tim Priesack. 1995. pap. text, wbk. ed. 11.00 (*0-13-188145-0*) P-H.

One World, Level 3. Tim Priesack. 1995. pap. text, teacher ed. 26.80 (*0-13-188137-X*) P-H.

One World, Level 4. Tim Priesack & Terry Tomscha. 1995. pap. text, wbk. ed. 11.00 (*0-13-188921-4*) P-H.

***One World: A Beginner's Guide.** Eric Fisher. 752p. 2000. pap. text. write for info. (*0-07-212313-3*) Osborne-McGraw.

One World: American English Student Book+, Level 3. Tim Priesack & Terry Tomscha. 160p. 1995. pap. text, student ed. 21.20 (*0-13-188129-9*) P-H.

One World: American English Student Book, Level 4. Tim Priesack & Terry Tomscha. 160p. 1995. pap. text, student ed. 21.20 (*0-13-188160-4*) P-H.

One World: Multicultural Projects & Activities. (J). (gr. k-6). 1998. teacher ed. 12.95 (*0-8167-2598-5*) Troll Communs.

One World: The Health & Survival of the Human Species in the 21st Century. Ed. by Robert Lanza. 334p. 1996. 25.00 (*0-929173-16-3*) Health Press.

One World: The Interaction of Science & Theology. John Polkinghorne. 128p. 1987. pap. text 13.95 (*0-691-02407-3*, Pub. by Princeton U Pr) Cal Prin Full Svc.

One World Level 2: American English Student Book. Tim Priesack & Terry Tomscha. (Illus.). 128p. 1994. pap. text 21.20 (*0-13-185992-7*) P-H.

One World Level 4, Level 4. Tim Priescha & Terry Tomscha. 1995. pap. text, teacher ed. 26.80 (*0-13-188236-8*) P-H.

One World - Two Views. Richard D. Dobbins. 17p. (Orig.). 1990. pap. 1.00 (*1-890329-13-4*) Totally Alive.

One World & Our Knowledge of It: The Problematic of Realism in Post-Kantian Perspective. Ray F. Rosenberg. (Philosophical Studies: No. 23). 225p. 1980. text 106.00 (*90-277-1136-4*, D Reidel) Kluwer Academic.

One World at a Time. Ted Kooser. LC 84-19636. (Poetry Ser.). 72p. 1985. pap. 10.95 (*0-8229-5366-8*); text 19.95 (*0-8229-3504-X*) U of Pittsburgh Pr.

One World Divisible: A Global History Since 1945. David Reynolds. LC 99-33903. 860p. 2000. text 35.00 (*0-393-04821-7*) Norton.

***One World Divisible: A Global History Since 1945.** David Reynolds. (Illus.). 920p. 2000. pap. 18.95 (*0-393-32108-8*) Norton.

***One World Emerging? Convergence & Divergence in Industrial Societies.** Alex Inkeles. 448p. 1999. pap. 28.00 (*0-8133-6803-0*) Westview.

One World Government a Struggle Between Surrogate Elitism & Popular Will: Uncle Sam or Aunt Geneva? Jule N. Dews. LC 96-67795. (Illus.). 57p. (Orig.). 1996. pap. 16.00 (*0-937300-04-7*) Stoneridge Inst.

One World, Many Cultures. 3rd ed. Stuart Hirschberg & Terry Hirschberg. LC 97-21967. 667p. 1997. pap. text 37.00 (*0-205-26777-7*) P-H.

***One World Many Cultures.** 4th ed. 2000. teacher ed. write for info. (*0-205-32645-5*) Allyn.

***One World, Many Cultures.** 4th ed. Stuart Hirschberg & Terry Hirschberg. LC 99-45189. (Illus.). 624p. 2000. pap. 36.00 (*0-205-31841-X*) Allyn.

One World, Many Cultures: Examination Copy. 3rd rev. ed. Stuart Hirschberg & Terry Hirschberg. 688p. (C). 1997. pap. text. write for info. (*0-205-27664-4*, T7664-0) Allyn.

One World, Many Families. Ed. by Karen Altergott. 81p. (Orig.). (C). 1993. pap. 21.95 (*0-916174-38-7*) Natl Coun Family.

One World Many Issues: Pupils' Book. Ed. by Bernard Williams. (Illus.). 143p. (Orig.). 1997. pap. 22.50 (*0-7487-2981-X*, Pub. by S Thornes Pubs) Trans-Atl Phila.

One World Many Issues: Teacher's Resource Guide. Graham Langtree et al. 96p. (Orig.). 1997. pap., teacher ed. 26.50 (*0-7487-3010-9*, Pub. by S Thornes Pubs) Trans-Atl Phila.

One World, Many Religions. Mary Pope Osborne. LC 96-836. 1996. 25.00 (*0-679-83930-5*) Random.

One World, Many Religions. Mary Pope Osborne. LC 96-836. (Illus.). 1996. lib. bdg. 26.99 (*0-679-93930-X*) Random.

One World, Many Religions: The Ways We Worship. Mary Pope Osborne. (J). (gr. 4-9). 1996. 25.00 (*0-614-19326-5*) Knopf.

One World, Many Worlds: Struggles for a Just World Peace. R. B. Walker. LC 87-30414. 180p. (C). 1988. pap. text 16.95 (*1-55587-109-7*) L Rienner.

One World of Literature. Shirley Lim & Norman K. Spencer. (C). 1992. pap. text 37.56 (*0-395-58880-4*) HM.

***One World of Peace Through Music.** Prod. by Kurt Wahlner. 216p. 2000. write for info. (*0-9700123-0-6*, 12306) Ocean Love.

One World, One Earth: Educating Children for Social Responsibility. Merryl Hammond & Rob Collins. (Illus.). 160p. (Orig.). 1992. pap. 14.95 (*0-86571-247-6*) New Soc Pubs.

One World One Future: New International Strategies for Development. Ed. by Ashok Bapna. 364p. 1985. 65.00 (*0-275-90056-8*, C0056, Praeger Pubs) Greenwood.

One World, One Language: Paving the Way to Better Perspectives for Mental Health. World Congress of Psychiatry Staff. Ed. by Juan J. Lopez-Ibor et al. LC 99-17543. (Illus.). 272p. 1999. pap. 39.00 (*0-88937-214-4*) Hogrefe & Huber Pubs.

One World, One Way. John Benton. 1992. pap. 4.99 (*0-85234-294-2*, Pub. by Evangelical Pr) P & R Pubng.

One World or None. Ed. by Dexter Masters & Katherine Way. LC 71-37858. (Essay Index Reprint Ser.). 1977. reprint ed. 25.95 (*0-8369-2610-2*) Ayer.

One World or None: Prescription for Survival. Errol E. Harris. LC 92-33138. 176p. (Orig.). (C). 1993. pap. 15.00 (*0-391-03801-X*); text 39.95 (*0-391-03812-5*) Humanities.

One World Order: Socialist Dictatorship. John Coleman. LC 98-43399. ii, 229p. 1998. 16.95 (*0-9640104-9-6*) Bridger Hse.

One World Order Is Coming: Who Will Rule? Cathy Burns. LC 98-126763. 116p. (Orig.). 1997. pap. 5.95 (*1-891117-00-9*) Sharing.

***One World, Ready or Not: The Manic Logic of Global Capitalism.** William Greider. 1999. pap. 12.98 (*0-671-04428-1*) PB.

One World, Ready or Not: The Manic Logic of Global Capitalism. William Greider. LC 96-33202. 528p. 1997. 27.00 (*0-684-81141-3*) S&S Trade.

One World, Ready or Not: The Manic Logic of Global Capitalism. William Greider. 528p. 1998. per. 15.00 (*0-684-83554-1*) S&S Trade.

One World: The Approach to Permanent Peace on Earth & General Happiness of Mankind: A Popular Manifesto with Scholarly Annotations. John Kiang. LC 83-63090. (Illus.). 650p. (C). 1984. 24.95 (*0-916301-00-1*) One World Pub.

One World: The Approach to Permanent Peace on Earth & General Happiness of Mankind: A Popular Manifesto with Scholarly Annotations. enl. rev. ed. John Kiang. LC 92-60675. (Illus.). 680p. 1993. 29.95 (*0-916301-04-4*) One World Pub.

One Worm. Jim Kalin. LC 97-66722. 254p. 1997. 19.99 (*0-9653524-5-5*) Russn Hill Pr.

One Worth Waiting For. Alicia Scott. (Intimate Moments Ser.). 1996. per. 3.99 (*0-373-07713-0*, 1-07713-0) Silhouette.

One Writer's Beginnings. Eudora Welty. 17.95 (*0-8488-0659-X*) Amereon Ltd.

One Writer's Beginnings. Eudora Welty. LC 83-18638. (William E. Massey Sr. Lectures in the History of American Civilization). (Illus.). 128p. 1984. text 18.00 (*0-674-63925-1*) HUP.

One Writer's Beginnings. Eudora Welty. (William E. Massey Sr. Lectures in the History of American Civilization). (Illus.). 128p. (C). 1995. pap. 10.95 (*0-674-63927-8*) HUP.

One Writer's Beginnings. Eudora Welty. 1991. mass mkt. 7.99 (*0-446-39328-2*, Pub. by Warner Bks) Little.

One Writer's Reality. Monroe K. Spears. LC 95-43008. 144p. (C). 1995. 29.95 (*0-8262-1049-X*) U of Mo Pr.

One Year after Cairo: Assessing National Action to Implement the International Conference on Population & Development - 65 Country-By-Country Progress Reports. Ed. by Jacqueline Hamilton. (Earth Summit Watch Ser.). 176p. (Orig.). 1996. pap. 8.00 (*0-9644661-1-2*) Earth Summit Watch.

One Year at Yuma. large type ed. Amy Sadler. (Dales Large Print Ser.). 211p. 1996. pap. 18.99 (*1-85389-620-9*, Dales) Ulverscroft.

One Year Bible - Women's Edition see Biblia en un Ano: Mujeres

One Year Bible Companion. LC 92-28480. 400p. 1992. pap. 9.99 (*0-8423-4616-3*) Tyndale Hse.

One Year Bible Devotional. Larry Stockstill. LC 98-12219. 372p. 1998. pap. 9.99 (*0-8307-2195-9*, Regal Bks) Gospel Lght.

One Year Bible Story Book. Virginia J. Muir. (Illus.). 384p. (YA). (gr. 5 up). 1988. 14.99 (*0-8423-2631-6*) Tyndale Hse.

***One Year Book of Bible Prayers.** Compiled by Livingstone Corporation Staff. 2000. 14.99 (*0-8423-3646-X*) Tyndale Hse.

***One Year Book of Bible Promises.** Compiled by Livingstone Corporation Staff. 2000. 14.99 (*0-8423-3553-6*) Tyndale Hse.

One Year Book of Bible Readings. Tyndale House Publishers Staff. LC 99-23019. (One Year Bks.). 1999. 14.99 (*0-8423-3496-3*) Tyndale Hse.

***One Year Book of Devotions for Boys.** Tyndale House Publishers Staff. LC 00-28667. (YA). 2000. write for info. (*0-8423-3620-6*) Tyndale Hse.

***One Year Book of Devotions for Girls.** Tyndale House Publishers Staff. LC 00-29915. 2000. pap. write for info. (*0-8423-3619-2*) Tyndale Hse.

O

An Asterisk (*) at the beginning of an entry indicates that the title is appearing for the first time.

One Year Book of Devotions for Kids. Tyndale House Publishers Staff. 400p. (J). (gr. 4-7). 1993. pap. 10.99 (*0-8423-5087-X*) Tyndale Hse.
One Year Book of Devotions for Kids, Vol. 2. LC 96-114031. 414p. (J). 1995. pap. 10.99 (*0-8423-4592-2*) Tyndale Hse.
One Year Book of Devotions for Kids, Vol. 3. Jill Briscoe. (J). 1997. pap. 10.99 (*0-8423-4662-7*) Tyndale Hse.
One Year Book of Family Devotions, Vol. I. 384p. 1988. pap. 10.99 (*0-8423-2541-7*) Tyndale Hse.
One Year Book of Family Devotions, Vol. 2. 384p. 1989. pap. 10.99 (*0-8423-2510-7*) Tyndale Hse.
One Year Book of Family Devotions, Vol. 3. 384p. 1990. pap. 10.99 (*0-8423-2617-0*) Tyndale Hse.
***One Year Book of Fun & Active Devotions for Kids.** Betsy Rossen Elliot. LC 00-28677. (Illus.). (J). 2000. write for info. (*0-8423-1976-X*) Tyndale Hse.
One Year Book of Hymns. Ed. by Robert K. Brown & Mark R. Norton. LC 94-43726. 1502p. 1995. pap. 19.99 (*0-8423-5095-0*) Tyndale Hse.
One Year Book of Hymns. William J. Petersen & Randy Petersen. Ed. by Robert K. Brown & Mark R. Norton. LC 94-43726. 1995. pap. 14.99 (*0-8423-5072-1*) Tyndale Hse.
One Year Book of Personal Prayer. Corrie Ten Boom. 1998. 12.99 (*0-8423-1557-8*) Tyndale Hse.
One Year Book of Poetry. Phil Comfort. LC 99-38774. 1999. 19.99 (*0-8423-3712-1*) Tyndale Hse.
***One Year Book of Poetry.** Phil Comfort. LC 99-38774. 700p. 1999. pap. text 14.99 (*0-8423-3711-3*) Tyndale Hse.
One Year Book of Psalms. William J. Petersen. LC 99-38571. 1999. pap. text 14.99 (*0-8423-4372-5*) Tyndale Hse.
***One Year Book of Psalms.** William J. Petersen. LC 99-38571. 700p. 1999. 19.99 (*0-8423-4373-3*) Tyndale Hse.
One Year Book of Saints. Clifford Stevens. LC 89-60528. 384p. 1989. pap. 16.95 (*0-87973-417-5*, 417) Our Sunday Visitor.
***One Year Chronological Bible.** One Year Chronological Staff. 2000. 24.99 (*0-8423-3530-7*); pap. 19.99 (*0-8423-3531-5*) Tyndale Hse.
One Year Guide to the Catechism of the Catholic Church. Gerry Rauch. LC 98-48280. 266 p. 1999. pap. 11.99 (*1-56955-026-3*) Servant.
One Year Later: The Homeless Poor in New York City. Kim Hopper et al. LC 82-200214. 92p. (Orig.). 1982. pap. 7.50 (*0-88156-000-6*) Comm Serv Soc NY.
One Year Manual: Twelve Steps to Spiritual Enlightenment. rev. ed. Israel Regardie. LC 92-35344. 96p. 1981. reprint ed. pap. 9.95 (*0-87728-489-X*) Weiser.
One Year of Healthy Hearty & Quick One Dish Meals: 365 Low-Fat Delicious & Time Saving Recipes. Pam Spaude. 400p. 1996. pap. 14.95 (*0-471-34691-8*) Wiley.
One Year of Healthy, Hearty & Simple One-Dish Meals: 365 Low-Fat, Delicious, & Time-Saving Recipes. 2nd rev. ed. Pam Spaude & Jan Owan-McMenainin. 400p. (Orig.). 1996. pap. 14.95 (*1-56561-102-0*) Wiley.
***One Year Off: Leaving It All Behind for a Round-the-World Journey with Our Children.** David E. Cohen. LC 99-21760. (Illus.). 320p. 1999. 24.00 (*0-684-83601-7*) Simon & Schuster.
1 Year Site Licensing - Online Accounting Foundations: A Complete Course on the Web. Klooster. (Accounting - First Year Ser.). 2000. pap. text 141.95 (*0-538-68944-7*) S-W Pub.
One Year to a College Degree. Lynette Long & Eileen Hershberger. LC 91-72905. 208p. (Orig.). 1992. pap. 10.99 (*1-56384-001-4*) Huntington Hse.
One Year with Jesus: New Living Translation James C. Galvin et al. LC 99-26276. 2000. 12.99 (*0-8423-3461-0*) Tyndale Hse.
One Yellow Daffodil: A Hanukkah Story. David A. Adler. LC 94-31374. (Illus.). 32p. (J). (gr. 1-5). 1999. pap. 6.00 (*0-15-202094-2*, Voyager Bks) Harcourt.
One Yellow Lion: Fold-Out Fun with Numbers, Colors, Animals. Matthew Van Fleet. LC 91-11972. (Illus.). 24p. (J). (ps up). 1992. 9.99 (*0-8037-1099-2*, Dial Yng Read) Peng Put Young Read.
One You Love Is Dying: 12 Ideas to Guide You on the Journey. James E. Miller. LC 97-60134. (Illus.). 64p. (Orig.). 1997. pap. text 6.95 (*1-885933-23-1*) Willowgreen Pubng.
One Zillion Valentines. Frank Modell. LC 81-2215. 40p. (J). (ps-3). 1987. reprint ed. mass mkt. 4.95 (*0-688-07329-8*, Wm Morrow) Morrow Avon.
***One Zumwalt Family: Many Descendants of the Eleven Children of Andrew Zumwalt & His Two Wives.** Compiled by Helynn M. Carrier. LC 00-190740. 514p. 2000. pap. text 40.00 (*0-9607550-4-7*) Carriers Bees.
O'Neal & Hazen on Corporations. Thomas L. Hazen & F. Hodge O'Neal. 1989. write for info. (*0-318-63271-3*, Aspen Law & Bus) Aspen Pub.
O'Neal Close Corporations: Law & Practice, 2 vols., No. 12. F. Hodge O'Neal & Robert B. Thompson. 1990. 200.00 (*0-685-33314-0*); write for info. (*0-318-66850-5*); write for info. (*0-318-66851-3*) West Group.
O'Neal's Oppression of Minority Shareholders, 2 vols. 3rd ed. F. Hodge O'Neal & Robert B. Thompson. LC 85-7867. 1990. 230.00 (*0-318-42412-6*); write for info. (*0-318-65004-5*) West Group.
***1CD-9-CM 2000 Codes on Disk.** Ed. by Kathryn Swanson. (Illus.). 1800p. 1999. pap. 149.95 (*1-57066-149-9*, 20028) Practice Mgmt Info.
***Oneida.** L. Gordon McLester. (Indian Nations Ser.). (Illus.). 2000. 25.69 (*0-8172-5457-9*) Raintree Steck-V.
Oneida: Utopian Community to Modern Corporation. Maren L. Carden. LC 98-6533. 1998. pap. text 17.95 (*0-8156-0523-4*) Syracuse U Pr.
Oneida Community. A. Eastlake. 1972. 69.95 (*0-8490-0769-0*) Gordon Pr.
Oneida Community: A Record of an Attempt to Carry Out the Principles of Christian Unselfishnes & Scientific Race-Improvement. Allan Estlake. LC 72-4179. reprint ed. 29.50 (*0-404-10758-3*) AMS Pr.
Oneida County New York 1800 Federal Population Census Schedule Transcript & Index. Ed. by Ralph V. Wood, Jr. iv, 103p. 1962. pap. 4.75 (*0-915184-00-1*) R V Wood.
***Oneida Creation Story.** Harvey Antone & Demus Elm. Ed. by Floyd G. Lounsbury. Tr. by Bryan Gick. LC 00-24446. 178p. 2000. pap. 12.00 (*0-8032-6742-8*) U of Nebr Pr.
Oneida Indian Experience. Ed. by Jack Campisi & Laurence M. Hauptman. 244p. 1988. pap. 18.95 (*0-8156-2453-0*) Syracuse U Pr.
Oneida Indian Experience: Two Perspectives. Ed. by Jack Campisi & Laurence M. Hauptman. LC 88-20110. (Iroquois Book Ser.). (Illus.). 224p. 1988. reprint ed. pap. 69.50 (*0-608-06970-1*, 206717800009) Bks Demand.
Oneida Indian Journey: From New York to Wisconsin, 1784-1860. Laurence M. Hauptman. LC 98-47296. 1999. pap. text 16.95 (*0-299-16144-7*) U of Wis Pr.
Oneida Indian Journey: From New York to Wisconsin, 1784-1860. Gordon L. McLester. 1999. write for info. (*0-299-16140-4*) U of Wis Pr.
Oneida Land Claims: A Legal History. George C. Shattuck. (Iroquois & Their Neighbors Ser.). 288p. 1991. pap. text 19.95 (*0-8156-2525-1*) Syracuse U Pr.
Oneida Verb Morphology. Floyd G. Lounsbury. LC 76-49736. (Yale University Publications in Anthropology Reprints Ser.: No. 48). 111p. 1976. pap. 20.00 (*0-87536-528-0*) HRAFP.
O'Neil Ford, Architect. Mary C. George. LC 91-21193. (Sara & John Lindsey Series in the Arts & Humanities: No. 1). (Illus.). 288p. 1992. 60.00 (*0-89096-433-5*) Tex A&M Univ Pr.
O'Neill. Thomas Kilroy. LC 96-101856. 74p. 1995. pap. 12.95 (*1-85235-163-2*) Dufour.
***O'Neill: Life with Monte Cristo, Vol. 1.** Arthur Gelb & Barbara Gelb. (Illus.). 758p. 2000. 40.00 (*0-399-14609-1*, Pub. by Applause Bks) Putnam Pub Group.
O'Neill: Son & Playwright. Louis Sheaffer. LC 88-47781. 1988. reprint ed. 75.00 (*0-404-20321-3*) AMS Pr.
O'Neill: 3 Plays. Eugene O'Neill. 320p. 1998. mass mkt. 4.95 (*0-451-52667-8*, Penguin Classics) Viking Penguin.
O'Neill on Film. John Orlandello. LC 80-70627. 192p. 1982. 32.50 (*0-8386-2291-7*) Fairleigh Dickinson.
O'Neill, Son & Artist. Louis Sheaffer. LC 88-47779. 1988. reprint ed. 75.00 (*0-404-20322-1*) AMS Pr.
O'Neill Years: Unionist Politics, 1963-1969 David Gordon. LC 89-217921. (Northern Ireland, Contemporary Politics & History Ser.). 168 p. 1989. write for info. (*0-85034-039-X*) Athol Bks.
O'Neill's California Confessions Law: A Comprehensive Outline, Including Detailed Summaries of All Relevant State & Federal Decisions & Statutes. Vincent J. O'Neill, Jr. 1993. ring bd. 124.95 (*1-883952-09-3*) Hse of Steno.
O'Neill's Irish Music: Arranged for Piano or Violin. Francis O'Neill. 192p. 1987. pap. 21.00 (*0-85342-800-X*) Dufour.
O'Neill's Music of Ireland. Miles Krassen. (Illus.). 256p. 1976. pap. 21.95 (*0-8256-0173-8*, OK63206, Oak) Music Sales.
O'Neill's Music of Ireland: Intermediate Level. Ed. by Francis O'Neill. 368p. 1996. spiral bd. 29.95 (*0-7866-2498-1*, 96322) Mel Bay.
***O'Neills of County Cork: The O'Neills in County Cork & Their Descendants from 1666 to 1998.** Germaine C. Grady. LC 99-73644. (Illus.). 346p. 1999. pap. 19.95 (*0-9674771-0-7*) G Grady.
O'Neill's One Thousand One Collection. J. O'Neill. 1986. pap. 20.95 (*0-7866-1603-2*, 95188WW) Mel Bay.
O'Neill's Plays Notes. Peter Clark. (Cliffs Notes Ser.). 112p. (Orig.). 1966. pap. 4.50 (*0-8220-0910-2*, Cliff) IDG Bks.
O'Neill's Shakespeare. Normand Berlin. (Theater: Theory - Text - Performance Ser.). 280p. (C). 1993. text 47.50 (*0-472-10469-1*, 10469) U of Mich Pr.
O'Neill's The Iceman Cometh: Reconstructing the Premiere. Gary Vena. 251p. 1988. pap. 69.95 (*0-7734-1990-X*) E Mellen.
Oneiric Threshold: An Installation by Alastair Noble. Gian F. Mantegna & Steven High. 1993. 5.00 (*0-935519-16-5*) Anderson Gal.
Oneirocritica: The Interpretation of Dreams by Artemidorus. Artemidorus. Tr. by Robert J. White from GRE. 270p. 1990. reprint ed. pap. 36.50 (*0-944558-03-8*) Original Bks.
Oneirocriticon of Achmet: A Medieval Greek & Arabic Treatise on the Interpretation of Dreams. Ed. by Steve M. Oberhelman. 320p. 1991. 39.00 (*0-89672-262-7*) Tex Tech Univ Pr.
Oneirophrenia: The Confusional State. Ladislas J. Meduna. LC 50-6278. (Illus.). 112p. reprint ed. pap. 34.80 (*0-608-30242-2*, 201502300096) Bks Demand.
Oneism. Bonnie Seefeldt. 55p. 1988. pap. 6.00 (*1-884112-01-3*) See More Bks.
Oneity, Equality, Reaching, Glory: Tribute to the 1996 Atlanta Olympics. abr. ed. Eric Fortmeyer. 38p. 1996. pap. 20.00 (*1-928620-03-5*, EFX-699110U0397, Tribute Poet) AGI Prods.
Oneness, Vol. I. Sri Patricia & Gopi Gyan. (Orig.). 1979. pap. 3.95 (*0-935146-11-3*) Morningland.
Oneness, Vol. II. Patricia & Gopi Gyan. (Orig.). 1980. spiral bd. 7.95 (*0-935146-24-5*) Morningland.
Oneness, Vol. III. Sri Donato & Gopi G. Donato. Ed. by Morningland Publications, Inc. Staff. 167p. 1981. pap., spiral bd. 7.95 (*0-935146-58-X*) Morningland.
Oneness: Great Principles Shared by All Religions. Jeffrey Moses. 128p. 1992. pap. 9.00 (*0-449-90760-0*, Columbine) Fawcett.
Oneness: Our Heritage, Our Path, Our Destiny. Bill Bauman. LC 92-85431. 192p. (Orig.). (C). 1992. pap. text 13.00 (*0-9631696-0-2*) Wrld Peace Inst.
***Oneness: Synthesis of Souls.** P. F. Ceaton. LC 99-65229. 125p. 2000. pap. 14.95 (*1-58501-056-1*, Pub. by CeShore Pubg) Natl Bk Netwk.
Oneness & Separateness. Kaplan. 288p. 1998. per. 12.00 (*0-684-85406-6*) S&S Trade.
Oneness & Separateness: From Infant to Individual. Louise J. Kaplan. (Orig.). 1980. pap. 12.00 (*0-671-24061-7*) S&S Trade.
Oneness & The One Accord According to The Lord's Aspiration & The Body Life & Service According to His Pleasure. Witness Lee. 53p. 1990. pap. 3.75 (*0-87083-511-4*, 08-029-001) Living Stream Ministry.
Oneness & Trinity. Samih A. El-Zein. 224p. 1996. 76.50 (*0-7103-0561-3*, Pub. by Kegan Paul Intl) Col U Pr.
Oneness & Trinity, A. D. 100-300: The Doctrine of God in Ancient Christian Writings. David K. Bernard. LC 90-29268. 200p. (Orig.). 1991. pap. 7.99 (*0-932581-81-1*) Word Aflame.
Oneness of All Life. 2nd ed. Marjorie H. Russell. LC 84-50765. (Illus.). 203p. 1984. 3.48 (*0-87159-123-5*) Arcadia Ministry Pubns.
Oneness of God see Unidad de Dios
Oneness of God. David K. Bernard. LC 86-19051. 326p. (Orig.). 1983. pap. 9.99 (*0-912315-12-1*) Word Aflame.
Oneness of God & a Study Guide for the Oneness of God. David Bernard. 504p. 1998. 19.99 (*1-56722-220-X*) Word Aflame.
Oneness of Politics & Religion. Nicholas C. Eliopoulos. 126p. 1970. pap. 9.00 (*0-9605396-1-1*) Eliopoulos.
Oneness of Politics & Religion: Interplay of Matriarchy & Patriarchy in the Growth of Man's Institutions. rev. ed. Nicholas C. Elipoulos. 169p. 1979. text 17.00 (*0-9605396-3-8*) Eliopoulos.
"Oneness Pentecostal" Movement - An Evaluation. Mark A. McNeil. 1993. pap. 3.00 (*1-56186-520-6*) Pilgrim Pubns.
Oneness Pentecostals & the Trinity. Gregory A. Boyd. LC 91-48111. (Christian Research Institute Ser.). 240p. 1992. pap. 16.99 (*0-8010-1019-5*) Baker Bks.
Oneness Remembered - Ultraconsciousness: From: Sananda. Jean Peterson. Ed. by Marilyn J. Wilkinson. (Illus.). (Orig.). 1989. pap. 12.00 (*0-685-29784-5*) Meridian Light.
Oneness, the Trinity & Logic. Robert A. Herrmann. 112p. 1984. pap. 5.95 (*0-912315-80-6*) Word Aflame.
Oneness View of Jesus Christ. David K. Bernard. LC 94-4416. 176p. (Orig.). 1994. pap. 7.99 (*1-56722-020-7*) Word Aflame.
Oneness with God: Where Do I Fit? Bobby Self et al. 23p. (Orig.). 1990. pap. 3.95 (*0-936715-37-5*) Diversity Okla.
***Oneness/Otherness Mystery: Synthesis of Science & Mysticism.** Sutapas Bhattacharya. LC 99-932608. 1999. 44.00 (*81-208-1654-4*, Pub. by Motilal Bnarsidass) S Asia.
Oneonta: The Development of a Railroad Town. 2nd rev. ed. Eugene D. Milener. (Illus.). 600p. 1997. 62.95 (*0-9662095-0-8*) Hartwick Coll.
Oneonta Dine-a-Mate Book. 144p. 1996. pap. text 25.00 (*1-57393-025-3*) Dine-A-Mate.
Oneonta Roundhouse. Jim Loudon. 100p. 1993. pap. 17.95 (*0-9641119-0-X*) LRHS.
Oneota Archaeology: Past, Present, & Future. Ed. & Intro. by William Green. LC 95-25940. (Report Ser.). (Illus.). 200p. (Orig.). 1995. pap. 15.00 (*0-87414-102-8*) U IA Pubns Dept.
Oneota Sites on the Upper Iowa River. Mildred M. Wedel. Ed. by Carl H. Chapman. (Missouri Archaeologist Ser.: Vol. 21, No. 2-4). (Illus.). 181p. (Orig.). 1959. pap. 3.00 (*0-943414-38-5*) MO Arch Soc.
***Oneprince.** Bill Hand. LC 99-90690. (Redaemian Chronicles Ser.: Bks. 1 & 2). 640p. 1999. 25.00 (*0-7388-0478-9*); pap. 18.00 (*0-7388-0479-7*) Xlibris Corp.
Ones & Zeros: Understanding Boolean Algebra, Digital Circuits & the Logic of Sets. John Gregg. LC 97-34932. 296p. 1998. 34.95 (*0-7803-3426-4*, PP5388) Inst Electrical.
Ones That Got Away: A Choctaw Trail of Trials. Mary L. Stahl. LC 96-83954. (Illus.). 176p. (Orig.). 1996. pap. 19.95 (*1-880319-18-7*) Biotech.
Ones We Love. unabridged ed. Viola Erickson. 513p. 1998. pap. 29.95 (*1-892896-76-1*) Buy Books.
Ones Who Got Away. Ralf Mastin. 121p. 1998. pap. write for info. (*0-7541-0028-6*, Pub. by Minerva Pr) Unity Dist.
Ones Who Got Away: Women Who Left Abusive Partners. Ginny NiCarthy. LC 87-20470. (New Leaf Ser.). 329p. (Orig.). 1987. pap. 12.95 (*0-931188-49-0*) Seal Pr WA.
Ones Who Walk Away from Omelas see Creative Short Stories
Ones You Do. Daniel Woodrell. 224p. 1998. pap. 14.00 (*0-671-00135-3*, PB Trade Paper) PB.
Oneself As Another. Paul Ricoeur. Tr. by Kathleen Blamey. LC 92-107. 374p. (C). 1999. 32.95 (*0-226-71328-8*) U Ch Pr.
Oneself as Another. Paul Ricoeur. Tr. by Kathleen Blarney. 374p. 1994. pap. 17.00 (*0-226-71329-6*) U Ch Pr.
Onesicritus: A Study In Hellenistic Historiography. T. S. Brown. 196p. 1981. pap. 20.00 (*0-89005-384-7*) Ares.
O*net Dictionary of Occupational Titles. 39.95 (*0-8239-3031-9*); 49.95 (*0-8239-3032-7*) Rosen Group.
OneTrak: Compliance Answers for Bankers. Dearborn Financial Publishing Staff. LC 94-49129. 189p. 1996. pap. 30.00 (*0-7931-1055-6*, 3925-0101) Dearborn.
Onetti & Others: Comparative Essays on a Major Figure in Latin American Literature. Ed. by Gustavo San Roman. LC 98-42362. (SUNY Series in Latin American & Iberian Thought & Culture). 191p. (C). 1999. pap. text 16.95 (*0-7914-4236-5*) State U NY Pr.
Onetti & Others: Comparative Essays on a Major Figure in Latin American Literature. Ed. by Gustavo San Roman. LC 98-42362. (SUNY Series in Latin American & Iberian Thought & Culture). 224p. (C). 1999. text 49.50 (*0-7914-4235-7*) State U NY Pr.
Onetti y la Fidelidad a las Reglas del Juego. Clark R. Mendez. (SPA.). 188p. (Orig.). (C). 1992. text 46.00 (*0-8191-8889-1*); pap. text 26.50 (*0-8191-8890-5*) U Pr of Amer.
1,25-Dihydroxyvitamin D3 & Its Analogues As Immunomodulators in Autoimmune Type 1 Diabetes: Mechanisms of Action & Preclinical Applications. Kristina Casteels. (Acta Biomedica Lovaniensia Ser.). (Illus.). 160p. 1998. pap. 39.50 (*90-6186-876-9*, Pub. by Leuven Univ) Coronet Bks.
123. Snapshot Staff. LC 97-143372. (Padded Ser.). (Illus.). 10p. (J). 1997. 4.95 (*0-7894-1547-X*) DK Pub Inc.
123-ABC Schoolhouse Fun Phonics Workbook. Lois Torregano. (Illus.). 25p. (J). (ps-1). 1997. lib. bdg., wbk. ed. 10.00 (*0-9660718-0-8*) OneTwoThree-ABC.
1/2/3/4 for the Show Vol. 2: A Guide to Small-Cast One-Act Plays. Lewis W. Heniford. LC 94-42180. (Illus.). 480p. 1999. text 62.00 (*0-8108-3600-9*) Scarecrow.
Oneworld Book of Prayer: A Treasury of Prayers from Around the World. Compiled by Juliet Mabey. 160p. 1999. text 12.95 (*1-85168-203-1*, Pub. by Element MA) Penguin Putnam.
1.2: New Perspectives on Central Appalachian Low-Sulfur Coal Supplies. Jeffrey Price et al. (Illus.). 265p. (Orig.). (C). 1992. pap. 55.00 (*1-878907-63-8*) TechBooks.
Onfim Nos...Finally Us... Escritoras Negras Brasileiras Contemporaneas - Contemporary Black Brazilian Women Writers. Miriam Alves. Tr. by Carolyn R. Durham. (Illus.). 260p. 1995. 35.00 (*0-89410-789-5*, Three Contnts); pap. 16.00 (*0-89410-790-9*, Three Contnts) L Rienner.
Onge. Badal K. Basu. (C). 1990. text 10.00 (*81-7046-074-3*, Pub. by Seagull Bks) S Asia.
Ongoing Crisis in the Great Lakes: Joint Hearing Before the Subcommittee on International Operations & Human Rights & the Subcommittee on Africa of the Committee on International Relations, House of Representatives, 105th Congress, 2nd Session, March 5, 1998. USGPO Staff. LC 98-211364. v, 112p. 1998. pap. write for info. (*0-16-056597-9*) USGPO.
Ongoing Dissertations on Film Series, 8 vols. 1974. write for info. (*0-405-07530-8*) Ayer.
Ongoing Feast: Table Fellowship & Eschatology at Emmaus. Arthur A. Just. 325p. (Orig.). 1994. pap. 21.95 (*0-8146-6013-4*, Pueblo Bks) Liturgical Pr.
***Ongoing Feedback: How to Get It, How to Use It.** Karen Kirkland & Sam Manoogian. (Ideas into Action Guidebook Ser.). 21p. 1998. pap. text 6.95 (*1-882197-36-4*) Ctr Creat Leader.
Ongoing Incarnation: Johann Adam Mohler & the Beginnings of Modern Ecclesiology. Michael J. Himes. LC 96-51963. 384p. (Orig.). 1997. pap. 39.95 (*0-8245-1663-X*, Herdr & Herdr) Crossroad NY.
Ongoing Journey: Awakening Spiritual Life in At Risk Youth. Robert Coles et al. 225p. 1994. pap. 14.95 (*0-938510-48-7*, 32-001) Boys Town Pr.
Ongoing Life: Poems. Myrtle Stedman. LC 92-39429. 128p. (Orig.). 1993. pap. 8.95 (*0-86534-192-3*) Sunstone Pr.
Ongoing Portraits. Walter Pavlich. 52p. (Orig.). 1985. pap. 5.95 (*0-935306-33-1*) Barnwood Pr.
Ongoing Record Review: A Guide to JCAHO Compliance & Best Practice. Jean Clark. (Illus.). 120p. 1998. pap. text 87.00 (*1-57839-038-9*) Opus Communs.
Ongoing State University. James L. Morrill. LC 60-9636. 153p. reprint ed. pap. 47.50 (*0-608-14127-5*, 205589200039) Bks Demand.
***ONI Official Strategies & Secrets.** Bart Farkas. (Illus.). 272p. 2000. pap. 19.99 (*0-7821-2688-X*) Sybex.
ONI-222: Combatants. rev. ed. U. S. Navy Staff. LC 89-80588. (Illus.). (C). 1989. reprint ed. pap. 19.95 (*0-944055-02-8*) Floating Drydock.
Onin War: History of Its Origins & Background with a Selective Translation of the Chronicle of Onin. H. Paul Varley. LC 66-14595. (Studies in Oriental Culture: No. 1). (Illus.). 1966. text 57.50 (*0-231-02943-8*) Col U Pr.
Onion. Kate Braestrup. 1999. pap. write for info. (*0-14-012335-0*, Viking) Viking Penguin.
Onion. Paul Pines. LC 72-83855. (Illus.). 72p. 1972. pap. 3.00 (*0-913142-00-X*) Mulch Pr.
Onion Avenue. Nora S. McNab. 208p. 1991. pap. 11.95 (*0-942323-14-9*) N Amer Heritage Pr.
Onion Book: A Bounty of Culture, Cultivation, & Cuisine. Carolyn Dille & Susan Belsinger. (Illus.). 96p. 1996. pap. 9.95 (*1-883010-10-1*) Interweave.
Onion Chronicles, Pt. 1. James Boyd. 1988. pap. 10.00 (*0-938645-10-2*) In His Steps.
Onion Field. Joseph Wambaugh. 448p. 1987. mass mkt. 7.50 (*0-440-17350-7*) Dell.
Onion Harvest Cookbook. Barbara Ciletti. (Illus.). 176p. 1998. pap. 19.95 (*1-56158-245-X*, 070370) Taunton.
Onion in an Orchid Patch. Algerrie Jones. 90p. 1999. pap. 10.95 (*0-9669179-0-1*) Fifth Wrld.
Onion John. Joseph Krumgold. LC 59-11395. (Trophy Bk.). (Illus.). 248p. (J). (gr. 5 up). 1984. pap. 5.95 (*0-06-440144-8*, HarpTrophy) HarpC Child Bks.
Onion John. Joseph Krumgold. LC 59-11395. (Illus.). 248p. (J). (gr. 4-7). 1987. lib. bdg. 15.89 (*0-690-04698-7*) HarpC Child Bks.

An Asterisk (*) at the beginning of an entry indicates that the title is appearing for the first time.

Onion John. Joseph Krumgold. (Apollo Editions Ser.). (J). 1970. 10.05 (0-606-04251-2, Pub. by Turtleback) Demco.

Onion Juice. Frane Helner. 24p. pap. text 6.00 (1-878173-11-1) Birnham Wood.

Onion Presents: Our Dumb Century. 1999. pap. 11.99 (0-8362-2586-4) Andrews & McMeel.

Onion Ring Theology. Charles E. Taylor, Jr. 172p. (YA). (gr. 10 up). 1993. pap. 9.95 (1-880849-04-6) Chapel Hill NC.

Onion River, Six Vermont Poets. Ed. by Daniel Lusk. LC 97-66698. 99p. (Orig.). 1997. pap. 11.95 (0-9657144-0-3) Onion River Pr.

Onion Storage in the Tropics: A Practical Guide to the Methods of Storage & Their Selection. J. Brice et al. 120p. 1997. pap. 90.00 (0-85954-487-7, Pub. by Nat Res Inst) St Mut.

Onion Sundaes: A Houdini Club Magic Mystery. David A. Adler. (Houdini Club Magic Mystery Ser.). 1994. 9.19 (0-606-07063-X, Pub. by Turtleback) Demco.

Onion Tears. Diana Kidd. LC 92-46601. (Illus.). 62p. (YA). (gr. 5-9). 1993. mass mkt. 3.95 (0-688-11862-3, Wm Morrow) Morrow Avon.

Onion Tears. Diana Kidd. LC 90-43011. (Illus.). 62p. (J). (gr. 2-5). 1991. 15.95 (0-531-05870-0); lib. bdg. 16.99 (0-531-08470-1) Orchard Bks Watts.

Onion Tears. Diana Kidd. (Illus.). (J). 1993. 9.15 (0-606-05965-2, Pub. by Turtleback) Demco.

Onions see NGA Garden Library

Onions. (Magnet Gourmet Ser.). 1997. 5.95 (0-614-27957-7) Sterling.

Onions. Ed. by Smallwood & Stewart Staff. LC 96-86645. (Little Books for Cooks). 80p. 1997. 4.95 (0-8362-2780-8) Andrews & McMeel.

Onions: A Celebration of the Onion Through Recipes, Lore, & History. Mara R. Rogers. 1995. 16.00 (0-201-62680-2) Addison-Wesley.

Onions: A Celebration of the Onion Through Recipes, Lore, & History. Mara R. Rogers. (Illus.). 193p. 1998. text 16.00 (0-7881-5621-7) DIANE Pub.

Onions: Condiment, Nutrient, Medicine. Clarence Meyer. Ed. by David C. Meyer. (Illus.). 115p. (Orig.). 1993. pap. 8.95 (0-916638-16-2) Meyerbooks.

Onions & Allied Crops, 3 vols., Vol. I. Ed. by Haim D. Rabinowitch & James L. Brewster. 288p. 1989. boxed set 240.95 (0-8493-6300-4, SB341) CRC Pr.

Onions & Allied Crops, 3 vols., Vol. II. Ed. by Haim D. Rabinowitch & James L. Brewster. 320p. 1989. lib. bdg. 229.00 (0-8493-6301-2, SB341) CRC Pr.

Onions & Allied Crops, 3 vols., Vol. III. Ed. by Haim D. Rabinowitch & James L. Brewster. 272p. 1989. lib. bdg. 229.00 (0-8493-6302-0, SB341) CRC Pr.

Onions & Cucumbers & Plums: Forty-Six Yiddish Poems. Sarah Betsky-Zweig. LC 80-20914. (ENG & YID.). 285p. reprint ed. pap. 88.40 (0-608-06270-7, 206659900008) Bks Demand.

Onions & Cucumbers & Plums: 46 Yiddish Poems in English. Sarah Bertsky-Zweig. 259p. 1977. 18.95 (0-8369-6002-5) Ayer.

Onions & Garlic: An Old Tale. Eric A. Kimmel. LC 95-32707. (Illus.). 32p. (J). (gr. k-3). 1996. 15.95 (0-8234-1222-9) Holiday.

Onions & Other Vegetable Alliums. James L. Brewster. (Illus.). 256p. 1994. pap. text 45.00 (0-85198-753-2) OUP.

Onions Are My Husband: Survival & Accumulation by West African Market Women. Gracia Clark. LC 94-1907. 488p. 1994. pap. text 22.95 (0-226-10780-9); lib. bdg. 59.95 (0-226-10779-5) U Ch Pr.

***Onion's Finest News Reporting, Vol. 1.** Ed. by Scott Dikkers & Robert A. Siegel. LC 00-28650. 176p. 2000. pap. 16.00 (0-609-80463-4, HUM006000, Three Riv Pr) Crown Pub Group.

Onions in the Stew. Betty MacDonald. Ed. by William Dalzell. 1984. pap. 5.50 (0-87129-383-8, O16) Dramatic Pub.

***Onions in the Stew.** Betty Bard Macdonald. LC 00-31965. (Illus.). 2000. write for info. (0-7838-9107-5, G K Hall & Co) Mac Lib Ref.

Onions in Tropical Regions. L. Currah & F. J. Proctor. 1990. pap. 75.00 (0-85954-283-1, Pub. by Nat Res Inst) St Mut.

Onions, Leeks & Garlic: A Handbook for Gardeners. Marian Coonse. LC 95-16659. (W. L. Moody, Jr. Natural History Ser.: No. 19). (Illus.). 156p. (C). 1995. 29.95 (0-89096-675-3); pap. 16.95 (0-89096-676-1) Tex A&M Univ Pr.

***Onions, Leeks & Garlic: A Handbook for Gardeners.** Marian Coonse. (Illus.). 136p. 2000. reprint ed. text 20.00 (0-7881-6963-7) DIANE Pub.

Onions Love Herbs. Ruth Bass. LC 96-14311. (Illus.). 64p. 1996. 9.95 (0-88266-934-6, Storey Pub) Storey Bks.

Onions, Onions, Onions: Delicious Recipes for the World's Favorite Secret Ingredient. Linda Griffith & Fred Griffith. LC 94-25793. (Illus.). 384p. 1994. pap. 14.95 (1-881527-54-9, Chapters Bks) HM.

***Onions, Onions, Onions: Globe, Spanish, Vidalia, Walla Walla, Shallot & More - In a Wave of Flavor & Aroma.** Rosemary Moon. LC 99-931650. (Illus.). 144p. 2000. pap. 19.95 (1-55209-364-6) Firefly Bks Ltd.

Onipa'a: Five Days in the History of the Hawaiian Nation. Contrib. by Office of Hawaiian Affairs. (Illus.). 208p. 1994. 36.00 (1-56647-051-X) Mutual Pub HI.

Onitsha. J. M. Le Clezio. (Folio Ser.: No. 2472). (FRE.). 1991. pap. 29.95 (2-07-038726-7) Schoenhof.

Onitsha. J. M. Le Clezio. Tr. by Alison Anderson. LC 96-32612. (Illus.). vii, 206p. 1997. pap. 15.00 (0-8032-7966-3); text 40.00 (0-8032-2915-1) U of Nebr Pr.

Onitsha Market Literature. E. N. Obiechina. LC 72-76469. 200p. (C). 1972. 17.50 (0-8419-0122-8, Africana) Holmes & Meier.

Onium Ions. George A. Olah et al. LC 97-43337. 528p. 1998. 110.00 (0-471-14877-6, Wiley-Interscience) Wiley.

Onkwehonwe-Neha. Freire & Lee Maracle. (Illus.). 24p. 1994. per. write for info. (0-920813-93-3) Sister Vis Pr.

Onlie Begetter. Ulric Nisbet. LC 70-121234. (Studies in Shakespeare: No. 24). 1970. reprint ed. lib. bdg. 75.00 (0-8383-1095-8) M S G Haskell Hse.

Onliest One Alive: Surviving Jonestown, Guyana. Catherine H. Thrash. LC 95-90366. (Illus.). 156p. (Orig.). 1998. reprint ed. pap. 10.00 (0-9642666-1-X) M K Towne.

***Onliest Tigger.** Leslie Goldman. (Illus.). 64p. (J). (gr. 2-5). 2000. pap. 4.99 (0-7868-4416-7, Pub. by Disney Pr) Time Warner.

***Online!** 3rd ed. Harnack. 2000. pap. text 15.95 (0-312-24357-X) St Martin.

Online Algorithms: The State of the Art, Vol. 144. Amos Fiat & Gerhard J. Woeginger. LC 98-30694. (Lecture Notes in Computer Science Ser.: Vol. 1442). xviii, 436p. 1998. pap. 59.00 (3-540-64917-4) Spr-Verlag.

***Online Auction Power Selling! I Didn't Know You Could Do That...** Eric Slone. 224p. 2000. pap. 19.99 (0-7821-2708-8) Sybex.

***Online Auctions.** Commerce Net Staff. LC 99-20605. 192p. 1999. pap. 14.95 (0-07-134249-4) McGraw.

***Online Auctions: The Internet Guide for Bargain Hunters & Collectors.** Luanne O'Loughlin et al. 291p. 2000. pap. 14.95 (0-07-135303-8) McGraw.

Online Auctions at E-bay: Bid with Confidence, Sell with Success. Dennis L. Prince. LC 99-70113. (Illus.). 16p. 1999. pap. 19.99 (0-7615-2070-8) Prima Pub.

***Online Auctions at Ebay: Bid with Confidence, Sell with Success.** 2nd ed. Dennis L. Prince. LC 99-65391. 495p. 1999. pap. 19.99 (0-7615-2414-2) Prima Pub.

***Online Broadcasting Solutions: From Stations to Shows.** Ben Sawyer & Dave Greely. 320p. 2000. pap. 29.95 (0-9662889-8-X) Muska Lipman.

Online Business Atlas: The Best Online Sites, Resources & Services in: Management,... Douglas E. Goldstein. 304p. 1996. text 24.95 (0-7863-0888-5, Irwn Prfssnl) McGraw-Hill Prof.

Online Business Guide to Financial Services: The Best Online Sites, Resources & Services in... Douglas E. Goldstein. 304p. 1996. text 24.95 (0-7863-0887-7, Irwn Prfssnl) McGraw-Hill Prof.

Online Business Planning: How to Create a Better Business Plan Using the Internet, Including a Complete Up-to-Date Resource Guide. Robert T. Gorman. LC 98-30984. 224p. 1999. pap. 17.99 (1-56414-369-4) Career Pr Inc.

***Online Business-to-Business Segments & Case Studies.** unabridged ed. Peet Rapp. Ed. by Margaret Gurney. (Illus.). 90p. 1999. 395.00 (1-58637-016-2) ActivMedia.

Online Catalog. COINT Reports Staff. (COINT Reports: Vol. 6, No. 4). 28p. (Orig.). 1986. pap. 3.50 (0-939670-11-9) Info Digest.

Online Catalog: Improving Public Access to Library Materials. Emily G. Fayen. LC 83-12009. (Professional Librarian Ser.). 148p. 1983. 35.00 (0-86729-053-6) Macmillan.

Online Catalog: The Inside Story; Planning & Implementation Guide. 158p. 1983. pap. 14.95 (0-942158-02-4) Ryan Research.

Online Catalog Book: Essays & Examples. Walt Crawford. LC 92-13843. (Professional Librarian Ser.). 230p. 1992. 60.00 (0-8161-1996-1, Hall Reference); 35.00 (0-8161-1995-3, Hall Reference) Macmillan.

Online Catalogue: Developments & Directions. Ed. by Charles R. Hildreth. LC 91-108823. 222p. 1989. reprint ed. pap. 68.90 (0-7837-9272-7, 206001000004) Bks Demand.

Online Christian. Mike Wendland. Ed. by Mike Niederquell. (Illus.). 150p. Date not set. pap. 18.95 (1-889966-01-0) Cyberspacebks.

Online Classroom: Teaching with the Internet. 4th ed. Eileen G. Cotton. Ed. by Christopher Essex. LC 97-33875. (Illus.). 253p. (J). (gr. 1-12). 2000. pap. 29.95 (1-883790-29-8, EDINFO Pr) Grayson Bernard Pubs.

Online College Handbook. 4th ed. Roberts. 1993. text 21.00 incl. 5.25 hd (0-07-832291-X) McGraw.

Online College Handbook: MAC. 4th ed. Roberts. 1992. 21.25 (0-07-832292-8) McGraw.

Online Competitive Intelligence: Move Your Business to the Top Using Cyber-Intelligence. Helen P. Burwell. Ed. by Michael Sankey & Carl R. Ernst. 396p. 1999. pap. 25.95 (1-889150-08-8, Pub. by Facts on Demand) Natl Bk Netwk.

Online Computation & Competitive Analysis. Allan Borodin & Ran El-Yaniv. LC 97-38652. (Illus.). 448p. (C). 1998. text 54.95 (0-521-56392-5) Cambridge U Pr.

***Online Consumer: Profiles & Emerging Markets.** unabridged ed. Julie Shayler & Harry Wolhandler. Ed. by Margaret Gurney. (Illus.). 75p. 2000. ring bd. 495.00 (1-58637-044-8) ActivMedia.

Online Consumer Guide to Healthcare & Wellness: The Best Online Sites, Resources & Services In: Health & Fitness, Diet & Weight Loss, Alternative Medicine, Family Health, Stress Management, Disease & Medical Conditions, Emergency Care & First Aid. Douglas E. Goldstein & Joyce Flory. LC 96-3034. (Best of the Net Ser.). 304p. 1996. text 24.95 (0-7863-0886-9, Irwn Prfssnl) McGraw-Hill Prof.

Online Couch: Psychotherapy & Computer-Mediated Interventions. Jeri Fink. LC 98-6846. 1998. pap. 40.00 (0-7657-0173-1) Aronson.

Online Customer Care: Applying Today's Technology to Achieve World-Class Customer Interaction. Michael Cusack. LC 97-46441. (Illus.). 265p. 1998. 39.50 (0-87389-383-2, H0972) ASQ Qual Pr.

Online Deskbook: Online Magazine's Essential Desk Reference for Online & Internet Searchers. Mary E. Bates. (Illus.). 450p. (Orig.). 1995. pap. 29.95 (0-910965-19-6) Info Today Inc.

Online Diaries: The Lollapalooza '95 Tour Journals. Beck et al. 128p. 1996. 6.00 (1-887128-20-4) Soft Skull Pr.

Online Drug Information Thesaurus. 2nd ed. Martindale. 1990. 110.00 (0-85369-229-7, Pub. by Pharmaceutical Pr) Rittenhouse.

Online Education: Perspectives on a New Environment. Ed. by Linda M. Harasim. LC 89-38987. 302p. 1990. 45.00 (0-275-93448-9, C3448, Greenwood Pr) Greenwood.

Online Epicure: Finding Out Everything You Want to Know about Good Cooking & Eating on the Internet. Neil J. Salkind. LC 96-37792. 230p. 1997. pap. 24.95 (0-471-18019-X) Wiley.

Online Family. Mike Wendland. Ed. by Mike Niederquell. (Illus.). 120p. 1996. pap. 18.95 (1-889966-00-2) Cyberspacebks.

***Online Family: Your Guide to Fun & Discovery in Cyberspace.** Preston Gralla. LC 97-45028. 368p. 1998. pap. 16.95 (0-471-19573-1) Wiley.

Online Family: Your Guide to Fun & Discovery in Cyberspace. Preston Gralla. LC 97-45028. 354p. 1998. 29.95 (0-471-29807-7) Wiley.

Online Games Guide. Joe G. Bell. LC 96-72645. 384p. 1997. per. 19.99 (0-7615-1065-6) Prima Pub.

Online Games Kit. Bradygames Staff. 1995. pap. 59.99 (1-56686-505-0) Brady Pub.

***Online Genealogy Resource Kit.** Sybex, Inc. Staff. (Illus.). 2000. pap. 19.99 (0-7821-2742-8) Sybex.

Online Guide to Healthcare Management & Medicine: The Best Online Sites, Resources & Services in Healthcare Management, Pharmaceuticals, Family Medicine, Patient Education, Emerging Healthcare Trends, Diagnostic Testing, Home Health Care, Financial Management & Telemedicine. Douglas E. Goldstein & Joyce Flory. LC 96-3033. (Best of the Net Ser.). 304p. 1996. pap. 24.95 (0-7863-0885-0, Irwn Prfssnl) McGraw-Hill Prof.

Online Guide to Personal Finance & Investing: The Best Online Sites, Resources & Services in: Investments, Credit Cards, Home Financing & Real Estate, Banking Services, Financial Planning, Taxes. Douglas E. Goldstein & Joyce Flory. LC 96-20395. (Best of the Net Ser.). 304p. 1996. text 24.95 (0-7863-0889-3, Irwn Prfssnl) McGraw-Hill Prof.

***Online Illustrated Abarth Buyer's Guide.** Peter Vack. (Online Buyer's Guides Ser.). (Illus.). 128p. 2000. pap. 34.95 (1-58850-000-4, VelocePress) TheValueGuide.

Online Info Retrieval Systems & Services. Bellardo. 256p. 1997. write for info. (0-12-084795-7) Acad Pr.

Online Information on Hispanics & Other Ethnic Groups. Roberta Medford & Eudora Loh. 324p. 1988. pap. 29.95 (0-915745-07-0) Floricanto Pr.

Online Information Retrieval: An Introductory Manual to Principles & Practice. 4th ed. John Convey. LC 93-150072. (Illus.). 318p. 1992. reprint ed. pap. 98.60 (0-608-07773-9, 206786100010) Bks Demand.

Online Information Retrieval: Concepts, Principles, & Techniques. Stephen P. Harter. (Library & Information Science Ser.). 1986. pap. text 45.00 (0-12-328456-2) Acad Pr.

Online Information Services for Secondary School Students. 2nd ed. Elizabeth S. Aversa et al. 1989. 10.00 (0-8389-0524-2) ALA.

Online Information Sources for Business & Current Affairs: An Evaluation. D. Nicholas & G. Erbach. 320p. 1989. text 130.00 (0-7201-1878-6) Continuum.

Online Investing. Alpha Books Staff. (Teach Yourself in 1 Day). 468p. 1999. pap. 18.95 (0-02-863618-X) Macmillan.

***Online Investing.** Jon D. Markman. LC 99-37221. 352p. 1999. pap. text 24.99 (0-7356-0650-1) Microsoft.

***Online Investing.** 2nd ed. Jon D. Markman. 336p. 2001. 24.99 (0-7356-1123-8) Microsoft.

***Online Investing: The Wall Street Journal Interactive Edition's Complete Guide to Becoming a Successful Internet Investor.** Rich Jaroslovsky & Dave Pettit. LC 99-53668. 320p. 2000. 25.00 (0-8129-3250-1, Times Bks) Crown Pub Group.

***Online Investing the Smart Way.** Stephen Littauer. LC 99-29569. 1999. pap. 19.95 (0-7931-3424-2) Dearborn.

***Online Investing with Quicken 2000.** Susan Price. (Official Guides Ser.). 448p. 2000. pap. 24.99 (0-07-212392-3) McGraw.

Online Investor. Ted Allrich. LC 96-43900. 272p. 1996. pap. 15.95 (0-312-15183-7) St Martin.

***Online Investor.** Provost. 2000. 29.95 (0-07-135884-6) McGraw.

***Online Job Hunting.** Herman Holtz. 304p. 2001. pap. 19.99 (0-7356-1186-6) Microsoft.

***Online Journalism.** Craig. 2002. pap. 35.00 (0-534-53146-6) Thomson Learn.

***Online Journalism.** Mike Ward & Andy Dickinson. 224p. 2000. pap. 39.95 (0-240-51610-9, Focal) Buttrwrth-Heinemann.

***Online Journalism: A Critical Primer.** Jim Hall. 192p. 2000. 59.95 (0-7453-1193-8, Pub. by Pluto GBR); pap. 19.95 (0-7453-1192-X, Pub. by Pluto GBR) Stylus Pub VA.

Online Journalist. 3rd ed. Reddick. (C). 1999. pap. text 37.50 (0-15-506752-4, Pub. by Harcourt Coll Pubs) Harcourt.

Online Journalist: Using the Internet & Other Electronic Resources. Randy Reddick & Elliot King. (Illus.). 240p. (C). 1994. pap. text 27.00 (0-15-502018-8, Pub. by Harcourt Coll Pubs) Harcourt.

***Online Journey Through Astronomy.** Guidry et al. (Astronomy Ser.). 2000. write for info. (0-534-37869-2) Brooks-Cole.

***Online Journey Through Astronomy.** Lee. (Astronomy). 2000. pap. 64.95 (0-534-37410-7) Brooks-Cole.

***Online Journey Through Astronomy: Brief Version.** Guidry et al. (Astronomy Ser.). 2000. write for info. (0-534-37870-6) Brooks-Cole.

***Online Journey Through Astronomy, Solar System.** Guidry et al. (Astronomy Ser.). 2000. write for info. (0-534-37872-2) Brooks-Cole.

***Online Journey Through Astronomy, Stars & Galaxies.** Guidry et al. (Astronomy Ser.). 2000. write for info. (0-534-37871-4) Brooks-Cole.

***Online Kids: A Young Surfer's Guide to Cyberspace.** rev. ed. Gralla. 288p. (C). 1999. 29.95 (0-471-33329-8) Wiley.

***Online Kids: A Young Surfer's Guide to Cyberspace.** rev. ed. Preston Gralla. LC 98-25181. (Illus.). 288p. (J). (gr. 3-9). 1999. pap. text 14.95 (0-471-25312-X) Wiley.

Online Kids: A Young Surfer's Guide to Cyberspace, with Activities. Preston Gralla. LC 96-4667. 288p. (J). 1996. pap. 14.95 (0-471-13545-3) Wiley.

Online Law: The Software Publishers Guide to Electronic Commerce. Thomas Smedinghoff. 576p. (C). 1996. pap. text 39.95 (0-201-48980-5) Addison-Wesley.

***Online Learning Strategies: Association Models for Success.** Don Dea et al. LC 99-32095. (Illus.). 89p. 1999. pap. 28.00 (0-88034-160-2) Am Soc Assn Execs.

Online Manual: A Practical Guide to Business Databases. 2nd ed. Jill Cousins & Lesley Robinson. 837p. 1993. 238.95 (0-631-18931-9) Blackwell Pubs.

Online Market Research: Cost-Effective Searching of the Internet & Online Databases. John F. Lescher. LC 95-4739. 288p. (C). 1995. pap. text 19.95 (0-201-48929-5) Addison-Wesley.

***Online Marketing.** Alexander Hiam. (Getting Started In Ser.). 288p. 2000. pap. 18.95 (0-471-38480-1) Wiley.

Online Marketing Handbook. Daniel S. Janal. (Business Technology Ser.). 1999. pap. text 29.95 (0-442-02703-6, VNR) Wiley.

***Online Markets for Writers: How to Make Money by Selling Your Writing on the Internet.** Anthony Tedesco & Paul Tedesco. LC 99-54938. (Illus.). 192p. 2000. pap. 15.00 (0-8050-6226-2, Owl) H Holt & Co.

***Online Money Management.** Karin Price Mueller. 336p. 2001. pap. 19.99 (0-7356-1111-4) Microsoft.

***Online Newsgathering.** Rawlinson. 256p. 2000. 42.95 (0-240-51608-7, Focal) Buttrwrth-Heinemann.

Online Office: Get Wired with Microsoft. Paul Lavin. (Illus.). 208p. 2001. pap., mass mkt. 34.95 incl. cd-rom (1-85032-269-4) ITCP.

Online Office: Getting Wired with IBM. Paul Lavin. (Illus.). 208p. 2001. pap. 34.99 (1-85032-292-9) ITCP.

Online Office to Get Wired with Oracle. Paul Lavin. (ITCP-UK Computer Science Ser.). (Illus.). 208p. 2001. pap. 34.95 (1-85032-291-0) ITCP.

Online 100: Online Magazine's Field Guide to the 100 Most Important Online Databases. Mick O'Leary. LC 95-189019. 233p. (Orig.). 1995. pap. 22.95 (0-910965-14-5) Info Today Inc.

***Online Pharmacy Rush: Gold Mine or Fool's Gold?** Carl Mercurio & Efrem Sigel. 135p. 1999. pap. 11.95 (0-9662321-3-5) Corp Res Grp.

Online Public Access Catalogs: The User Interface. Charles Hildreth. LC 82-8224. (Library, Information, & Computer Science Ser.: No. 1). (Illus.). 280p. (Orig.). 1982. pap. 18.00 (0-933418-34-5) OCLC Online Comp.

***Online Recruiting: How to Use the Internet to Find Your Best Hires, 1vol.** Donna Graham. LC 99-89260. (Illus.). 216p. 2000. pap. text 22.95 (0-89106-142-8, Davies-Black Pub) Consulting Psychol.

Online Resources for Business (1995) Alfred Glossbrenner & John Rosenberg. 349p. 1999. reprint ed. pap. text 15.00 (0-7881-6503-8) DIANE Pub.

Online Resources for Planners. Sanjay Jeer. LC 98-160083. (Report / American Planning Association, Planning Advisory Service.). 126 p. 1997. 34.00 (1-884829-16-3) Am Plan Assn.

Online Retrieval: A Dialogue of Theory & Practice. Geraldene Walker & Joseph Janes. (Database Searching Ser.). (Illus.). xi, 221p. 1993. pap. text 35.00 (1-56308-157-1) Libs Unl.

Online Retrieval: A Dialogue of Theory & Practice. 2nd ed. Geraldene Walker & Joseph Janes. LC 99-10206. (Database Searching Ser.). 370p. 1999. pap. 55.00 (1-56308-657-3) Libs Unl.

***Online Searcher's Companion.** 152p. 1999. 45.00 (1-85604-293-6, LAP2936, Pub. by Library Association) Bernan Associates.

Online Searching in Public Libraries: A Comparative Study of Performance. Janice H. McCue. LC 88-18482. 288p. 1988. 29.00 (0-8108-2171-0) Scarecrow.

Online Searching in Science & Technology: An Introductory Guide to Equipment, Databases & Search Techniques. 3rd ed. Ed. by David Orton. (Information in Focus Ser.). 128p. 1995. pap. 49.95 (0-7123-0802-4, Pub. by SRIS) L Erlbaum Assocs.

Online Searching on STN. L. Toler. (Illus.). 90p. 1989. 33.95 (0-387-96916-0) Spr-Verlag.

Online Seductions: Falling in Love with Strangers on the Internet. Esther Gwinnell. LC 97-50068. 256p. 1998. 23.00 (1-56836-214-5) Kodansha.

Online Seductions: Falling in Love with Strangers on the Internet. Esther Gwinnell. 1999. pap. 14.00 (1-56836-275-7) Kodansha.

Online Services for Law Enforcement. Timothy Dees. vii, 243p. 1996. 19.95 (1-889373-00-1) Prof Trning.

Online Style Guide: Terms, Usage, & Tips. Karen Pavlicin & Christy Lyon. LC 98-96126. ix, 214p. 1998. spiral bd. 19.95 (0-9657483-3-2) Elva Resa Pub.

Online Superpak: How to Use the Internet; How to Use America Online; Net.Talk. 2nd ed. Ziff Davis Staff. 1995. pap. 37.95 (1-56276-365-2, Ziff-Davis Pr) Que.

O

Online System Migration Guide. Agnew Lambert & Grace Lambert. (LITA Monographs: No. 7). 47p. 1996. pap. 15.00 (0-8389-7832-0) ALA.

Online Systems for Medical Professionals: How to Use & Access Computer Data Base. Harley Bjelland. Ed. by Jill Brittenham. 200p. 1992. 39.95 (1-878487-44-2, ME045) Practice Mgmt Info.

Online Teaching Guide. White & Weight. LC 99-34779. 192p. 1999. pap. text 29.95 (0-205-29531-2) Allyn.

***Online Trading & Brokerage Directory.** Larry Chambers. LC 99-37786. 250p. 1999. pap. 19.95 (0-07-135425-5) McGraw.

***Online Trading for Beginners: Secrets You Need to Know.** P. Robert Butkins. (Illus.). 64p. 1999. pap. 19.95 (0-9678230-0-5) InkManager.

***Online Trading Survival Guide: An Indispensible Handbook for Today's Wired Investor.** 2000. pap. 18.95 (0-7931-3962-7) Dearborn.

***Online Travel.** Ed Perkins. 300p. 2000. pap. 19.99 (0-7356-1110-6) Microsoft.

Online User's Encyclopedia: Bulletin Boards & Beyond. Bernard Aboba. LC 93-13304. 832p. (C). 1993. pap. text 34.95 (0-201-62214-9) Addison-Wesley.

***Online Visit to Africa.** Erin M. Hovanec. LC 00-21996. (Internet Field Trips Ser.). (Illus.). (J). 2000. write for info. (0-8239-5651-2, PowerKids) Rosen Group.

***Online Visit to Antarctica.** Erin M. Hovanec. LC 00-39161. (Internet Field Trips Ser.). (Illus.). (J). 2000. write for info. (0-8239-5656-3, PowerKids) Rosen Group.

***Online Visit to Asia.** Erin M. Hovanec. LC 00-35250. (Internet Field Trips Ser.). (Illus.). (J). 2000. write for info. (0-8239-5652-0, PowerKids) Rosen Group.

***Online Visit to Australia.** Erin M. Hovanec. LC 00-23745. (Internet Field Trips Ser.). (YA). 2000. write for info. (0-8239-5653-9, PowerKids) Rosen Group.

***Online Visit To Europe.** Erin M. Hovanec. LC 00-39169. (Internet Field Trips Ser.). (Illus.). (J). 2000. write for info. (0-8239-5657-1, PowerKids) Rosen Group.

***Online Visit to North America.** Erin M. Hovanec. LC 00-39176. (Illus.). (J). 2000. write for info. (0-8239-5654-7, PowerKids) Rosen Group.

***Online Visit to South America.** Erin M. Hovanec. LC 00-28590. (Illus.). 2001. write for info. (0-8239-5655-5, PowerKids) Rosen Group.

Online vs. Manual Searching in Sci-Tech Libraries. Ed. by Ellis Mount. (Science & Technology Libraries: Vol. 3, No. 1). 83p. 1982. pap. text 29.95 (0-86656-203-6) Haworth Pr.

***Online with the Holy Spirit.** Debbie Eisenbise. (Fast Lane Bible Studies). 49p. (YA). (gr. 7-9). 1999. pap. 9.95 (0-87303-338-8) Faith & Life.

Online-Woerterbuch Englisch-Deutsch 5-1/2 Disks. Heinz-Dieter Wegener. (ENG & GER.). 290p. 1990. 250.00 incl. disk (0-7859-8482-8, 3802304136) Fr & Eur.

Online Writing Classroom. Ed. by Susanmarie Harrington et al. (Written Language Ser.). 416p. 1999. text 79.95 (1-57273-271-7) Hampton Pr NJ.

Online Writing Classroom. Ed. by Susanmarie Harrington et al. (Written Language Ser.). 416p. 2000. pap. text 29.50 (1-57273-272-5) Hampton Pr NJ.

***Online!/A Pocket Style Manual: A Reference Guide to Using Internet Sources.** Andrew Harnack. 1999. pap. 24.95 (0-312-19706-3) St Martin.

Onliness: Novel. Dave Smith. LC 81-255. viii, 248p. 1981. 18.95 (0-8071-0871-5) La State U Pr.

Only. Groom. 1998. per. 6.50 (0-671-52267-1, Pocket Books) PB.

Only. large type ed. Winston Groom. 170p. 1995. lib. bdg. 21.95 (1-57490-027-7, Beeler LP Bks) T T Beeler.

Only a Beginning: The Passionists in China, 1921-31. Caspar Caulfield. LC 90-61190. (Illus.). xvi, 296p. (Orig.). (C). 1990. pap. 14.95 (0-9626119-0-5) Passionist Pr.

Only a Cat. Jutta Ash. (Illus.). 32p. (J). (ps-1). 1998. 17.95 (0-86264-738-X, Pub. by Andersen Pr) Trafalgar.

Only a Clay Vessel. Irene B. Brand. (Illus.). 120p. (Orig.). 1985. pap. 5.00 (0-9615285-0-8) Brand.

Only a Dream Away. Doreen Roberts. (Intimate Moments Ser.). 1993. per. 3.50 (0-373-07513-8, 5-07513-0) Silhouette.

Only a Game: The Diary of a Professional Footballer. Eamon Dunphy. 224p. pap. 13.95 (0-14-010290-6, Pub. by Pnguin Bks Ltd) Trafalgar.

Only a Game? Sport in the Modern World. Tony Mason. (Modern World Issues Ser.). (Illus.). 80p. (C). 1993. pap. text 15.95 (0-521-39992-0) Cambridge U Pr.

Only a Great Rain: A Guide to Chinese Buddhist Meditation. Hsing Yon. Tr. by Tom Graham from CHI. LC 99-19502. 160p. 1999. pap. 14.95 (0-86171-148-3) Wisdom MA.

Only a Little Planet. John Campos. LC 84-90335. (Poems & Drawings of John Campos Ser.). (Illus.). 78p. (Orig.). 1984. pap. 4.95 (0-917021-00-2) Lighthouse Pr.

Only a Memory Away. Madeline St. Claire. (Intrigue Ser.: Vol. 484). 1998. per. 3.99 (0-373-22484-2, 1-22484-9) Harlequin Bks.

Only a Miner: Studies in Recorded Coal-Mining Songs. Archie Green. LC 78-155499. (Music in American Life Ser.). (Illus.). 518p. 1972. text 34.95 (0-252-00181-8) U of Ill Pr.

Only a Mother - Bara en Mor. Ivar Lo-Johansson. Tr. & Afterword by Robert E. Bjork. LC 90-13059. (Modern Scandinavian Literature in Translation Ser.). 513p. 1991. reprint ed. pap. 159.10 (0-608-01838-4, 206248700003) Bks Demand.

Only a Nickel. Michael Walker, Jr. (Amazing English Ser.: Little Bks., Level B). (J). 1995. pap. text 17.64 (0-201-85364-7) Addison-Wesley.

Only a Nickel Big Bks. Pals. 1995. pap. 23.30 (0-201-85350-7) S&S Trade.

Only a Nickel Little Book Level B. Pals. (J). 1995. ring bd. 4.78 (0-201-85358-2) Addison-Wesley.

Only a Paper Moon: The Theatre of Billy Rose. Stephen Nelson. Ed. by Oscar G. Brockett. LC 87-5001. (Theater & Dramatic Studies: No. 42). 183p. reprint ed. 56.80 (0-8357-1796-8, 207074600004) Bks Demand.

Only a Pigeon. Jane Kurtz & Christopher Kurtz. LC 95-44056. (Illus.). 40p. (J). (ps-3). 1997. per. 16.00 (0-689-80077-0) S&S Childrens.

Only a Servant. Kristina Roy. 129p. 1991. pap. 4.50 (0-7399-0143-5, 2331) Rod & Staff.

Only a Sister: Could Be Such a Good Friend. Millie Mackiney. Ed. by Patrick Caton. LC 97-77654. (Illus.). 168p. 1998. pap. 5.95 (1-56245-338-6) Great Quotations.

Only a Star. Margery Facklam. LC 96-1420. (Illus.). 32p. (J). (ps-1). 1996. 15.00 (0-8028-5122-3, Eerdmans Bks) Eerdmans.

Only a Star. Margery Facklam. (Illus.). 32p. (J). (ps-3). 1999. pap. 7.50 (0-8028-5174-6, Eerdmans Bks) Eerdmans.

Only a Toad: A Bilingual Hmong Folktale. Brian Marchant & Heather Marchant. (Illus.). 30p. (Orig.). (J). (ps-7). 1993. pap. 10.50 (1-885298-02-1) Project Chong.

Only a Whisper. Gayle Wilson. (Intrigue Ser.). 1996. per. 3.75 (0-373-22376-5, 1-22376-7) Harlequin Bks.

Only Alien on the Planet. Kristen D. Randle. LC 93-34594. 228p. (J). (gr. 8 up). 1996. pap. 4.99 (0-590-46310-1) Scholastic Inc.

Only Alien on the Planet. Kristen D. Randle. LC 93-34594. (J). 1995. 10.09 (0-606-11710-5, Pub. by Turtleback) Demco.

***Only Alone.** Ynay. LC 99-80023. 119p. 2000. pap. 5.00 (0-9677878-0-7) Rumpl & Mingor.

Only an Excuse? The Scripts. Philip Differ. 192p. 1996. pap. 17.95 (1-85158-699-7, Pub. by Mainstream Pubng) Trafalgar.

Only an Irish Boy. Horatio Alger, Jr. (Works of Horatio Alger Jr.). 1989. reprint ed. lib. bdg. 79.00 (0-685-27578-7) Rprt Serv.

Only an Orphan Girl. Henning Nelms. 1944. pap. 5.25 (0-8222-0855-5) Dramatists Play.

Only Angels Can Wing It: The Rest of Us Have to Practice. Liz C. Higgs. LC 94-43284. 228p. 1995. pap. 10.99 (0-7852-8247-5) Nelson.

Only Angels Have Wings. Arlie J. Blood. LC 98-116756. 234 p. 1997. write for info. (0-9658016-0-8) A Blood.

Only Approved Indians: Stories. Jack D. Forbes. LC 94-24338. (American Indian Literature & Critical Studies: Vol. 12). 188p. 1995. 22.95 (0-8061-2699-X) U of Okla Pr.

Only As Far As Brooklyn. Maurice Kenney. 1977. pap. 4.00 (0-915480-13-1) Good Gay.

Only As One: The Words & Wisdom of Rex Dockery. Wallene T. Dockery. Ed. by Bob Phillips. LC 85-63031. (Motivational Sports Bks.). (Illus.). 112p. 1985. reprint ed. pap. 9.95 (0-936169-00-1) Dockery Enter.

Only Astrology Book You'll Ever Need. Joanna M. Woolfolk. LC 80-5403. 441p. 1990. pap. 14.95 (0-8128-8506-6, Scrbrough Hse) Madison Bks UPA.

Only at the Children's Table. Daria Baron-Hall. (J). (gr. 1-6). 1995. lib. bdg. 22.83 incl. audio (0-8172-2753-9) Raintree Steck-V.

Only Baby: Poems & Notes on Psychiatric Theory. Sheldon Cholst. 72p. (Orig.). 1978. reprint ed. pap. 9.95 (0-931174-01-5) Beau Rivage.

Only Baby Name Book You'll Ever Need. Heidi Overhill. (Illus.). 232p. 1996. pap. 14.95 (1-55013-754-9) Firefly Bks Ltd.

Only Baby-Sitting Book You'll Ever Need: A Guide for Parents. Kimberly Colen. Ed. by Judy Mitchell. (Illus.). 112p. 1997. pap. 10.95 (1-57310-104-4) Teachng & Lrning Co.

Only Bachelors Need Apply. Charlotte Maclay. 1997. per. 3.25 (0-373-19249-5, 1-19249-1) Silhouette.

Only Begotten. unabridged ed. Michael Malone. 455p. 1999. pap. 39.95 (1-885692-06-4) Cath Treas.

Only Begotten Daughter. James Morrow. 312p. 1996. pap. 12.00 (0-15-600243-4, Harvest Bks) Harcourt.

***Only Being There Experience Guide Students Ever Need: Connect Learning, Trips, Kids & School.** Kari Simmons Kling. 32p. 1999. pap. text 9.95 (1-878631-42-X, Pub. by S Kovalik) Bks Educators.

Only Believe: A Spy Story, a Love Story, & a Story of God's Great Miracles in Atheistic Russia. Hannu Haukka. 264p. (Orig.). 1996. pap. 15.00 (1-883893-41-0) WinePress Pub.

Only Believe: Eye Witness Account of the Great Healing Revivals. Don Stewart. 1999. pap. 12.99 (1-56043-340-X, Treasure Hse) Destiny Image.

Only Believe: Russian Language Edition. Smith Wigglesworth. Ed. by Wayne Warner. Tr. by Life Publishers Staff. (RUS.). 1999. pap. write for info. (0-7361-0099-7) Life Pubs Intl.

Only Believe: Ukrainian Language Edition. Smith Wigglesworth. Ed. by Wayne Warner. Tr. by Life Publishers Staff. (UKR.). 1999. pap. write for info. (0-7361-0098-9) Life Pubs Intl.

Only Believe! 180 Daily Devotions by Steve Wigglesworth. Ed. & Compiled by Wayne Warner. LC 96-8674. 200p. (Orig.). 1996. pap. 10.99 (0-89283-949-X, Vine Bks) Servant.

Only Big Show Coming Volume I: 1853-1878. Orin Copple King. LC 00-190844. 25.00 (0-7388-2016-4); pap. 18.00 (0-7388-2017-2) Xlibris Corp.

Only Boobs in the House Are Men. Maxine Berman. LC 94-21814. 140p. (Orig.). 1994. pap. 9.95 (1-879094-34-7) Momentum Bks.

Only Book: A Compendium of One-of-a-Kind Facts. Gerard Del Re & Patricia Del Re. 256p. (Orig.). 1994. pap. 9.00 (0-449-90908-5, Columbine) Fawcett.

***Only Bread, Only Light: Poems.** Stephen Kuusisto. 104p. 2000. pap. 15.00 (1-55659-150-0) Copper Canyon.

Only by Chance. Betty A. Neels. 1998. per. 3.50 (0-373-03537-3, 1-03537-7, Mira Bks) Harlequin Bks.

Only by Chance. large type ed. Betty A. Neels. (Larger Print Ser.). 1999. per. 3.50 (0-373-15783-5, 1-15783-3) Harlequin Bks.

Only by Chance. large type ed. Betty A. Neels. Vol. 431. 251p. 1999. per. 3.50 (0-373-15831-9, 1-15831-0) Harlequin Bks.

Only by Chance. large type ed. Betty A. Neels. (Harlequin Ser.). 1996. 19.95 (0-263-14751-7) Thorndike Pr.

Only by Mistake. P. J. Kavanagh. LC 86-4864. 160p. 1988. pap. 9.95 (0-7145-4085-4) Riverrun NY.

Only by Your Touch. Stella Cameron. 384p. (Orig.). 1992. mass mkt. 4.50 (0-380-76606-X, Avon Bks) Morrow Avon.

Only Chaos & Other Essays. Stanley L. Jaki. 288p. (C). 1990. lib. bdg. 46.50 (0-8191-7895-0) U Pr of Amer.

Only Child. Ricardo Bloch. (Artists' Books Ser.). (Illus.). 48p. (Orig.). 1995. pap. 15.00 (0-89822-112-9) Visual Studies.

Only Child. Carolyn McSparren. 1997. per. 3.99 (0-373-70725-8, 1-70725-6) Silhouette.

Only Child. Frank O'Connor. (Irish Studies). 290p. 1997. pap. 17.95 (0-8156-0450-5) Syracuse U Pr.

Only Child. Jesse Osburn. 256p. (Orig.). (YA). 1996. mass mkt. 3.99 (0-380-78043-7, Avon Bks) Morrow Avon.

Only Child: Being One, Loving One, Understanding One, Raising One. 60th ed. Darrell Sifford. LC 89-45717. 224p. 1990. pap. 13.00 (0-06-097288-2, Perennial) HarperTrade.

Only Children. Alison Lurie. 272p. 1990. pap. 7.95 (0-380-70875-2, Avon Bks) Morrow Avon.

Only Children. A. Rayment. Date not set. 4.99 (1-871676-29-0, Pub. by Christian Focus) Spring Arbor Dist.

***Only Closers Make Big Money.** David E. Plummer & Nancy Crumpton. 160p. 1999. pap. 14.95 (1-881825-24-8) Hist Pubns TX.

Only Companion: Japanese Poems of Love & Longing. expanded ed. Tr. by Sam Hamill from INC. LC 96-24158. (Centaur Editions Ser.). (Illus.). 128p. 1997. pap. 10.00 (1-57062-300-7, Pub. by Shambhala Pubns) Random.

***Only Connect A Cultural History of American Broadcasting.** Michele Hilmes. (Radio/TV/Film Ser.). 2001. 35.00 (0-534-55135-1) Wadsworth Pub.

Only Connect: Art & the Spectator in the Italian Renaissance. John Shearman. 308p. 1992. pap. text 24.95 (0-691-01917-7, Pub. by Princeton U Pr) Cal Prin Full Svc.

Only Connect . . . Art & the Spectator in the Italian Renaissance. John Shearman. (Bollingen Ser.: No. XXXV: 37). (Illus.). 304p. 1992. text 69.50 (0-691-09972-3, Pub. by Princeton U Pr) Cal Prin Full Svc.

Only Connect: Readings on Children's Literature. 3rd ed. Ed. by Sheila Egoff et al. (Illus.). 428p. (C). 1996. pap. text 23.95 (0-19-541024-6) OUP.

***Only Connect: Shaping Networks & Knowledge for the New Millennium** Trevor Haywood. LC 99-36328. 1999. write for info. (1-85739-216-7) Bowker-Saur.

Only Connect: Three Studies in Greek Tragedy. David H. Porter. LC 86-28918. 128p. (Orig.). 1987. pap. text 16.00 (0-8191-5951-4); lib. bdg. 39.00 (0-8191-5950-6) U Pr of Amer.

***Only Connect - Soil, Soul, & Society: The Best of Resurgence Magazine.** John Lane. 320p. 2000. pap. 16.95 (1-870098-90-0) Chelsea Green Pub.

Only Couples Need Apply. Doris M. Disney. 224p. 1988. mass mkt. 2.95 (0-8217-2438-X, Zebra Kensgtn) Kensgtn Pub Corp.

Only Couples Need Apply. Connie Flynn. 1997. per. 3.50 (0-373-52044-1, 1-52044-4) Silhouette.

Only Couples Need Apply. Doris M. Disney. reprint ed. lib. bdg. 18.95 (0-88411-841-X) Amereon Ltd.

Only Cowboy for Caitlin: Family Arch. Lois F. Dyer. (Special Edition Ser.: No. 1253). 1999. per. 4.25 (0-373-24253-0, 1-24253-6) Silhouette.

Only Cure I Know. Charles Atkinson. Ed. by Kathleen Iddings. LC 91-90048. (American Bk.). 71p. 1991. pap. text, per. 10.00 (0-931289-06-8) San Diego Poet Pr.

Only Dance There Is. Ram Dass. LC 73-14054. 192p. 1974. pap. 11.95 (0-385-08413-7, Anchor NY) Doubleday.

Only Diet There Is. Sondra Ray. LC 80-70795. 156p. 1995. pap. 8.95 (0-89087-321-6) Celestial Arts.

Only Don't Know: Selected Teaching Letters of Zen Master Seung Sahn. Seung Sahn. LC 98-39926. 256p. 1999. pap. 14.95 (1-57062-432-1, Pub. by Shambhala Pubns) Random.

Only Don't Know: The Teaching Letters of Zen Master Seung Sahn. 2nd ed. Seung Sahn. 193p. (Orig.). reprint ed. pap. 2.00 (0-942795-03-2) Primary Point Pr.

Only DOS Book You'll Ever Need 6.0. 2nd ed. Doug Lowe. LC 93-859. (Illus.). 610p. 1993. pap. 27.50 (0-911625-71-2) M Murach & Assoc.

Only Drunks & Children Tell the Truth. Drew H. Taylor. 140p. 1998. pap. text 11.95 (0-88922-384-X, Pub. by Talonbks) Genl Dist Srvs.

Only Earth & Sky Last Forever. Nathaniel Benchley. LC 72-82891. (Trophy Bk.). 204p. (YA). (gr. 7 up). 1974. pap. 4.95 (0-06-440049-2, HarpTrophy) HarpC Child Bks.

Only Earth & Sky Last Forever. Nathaniel Benchley. (J). 1972. 10.05 (0-606-02346-1, Pub. by Turtleback) Demco.

Only Earth We Know: Hymn Texts by Fred Kaan. Fred Kaan. LC 99-71815. 144p. 1999. pap. 16.95 (0-916642-66-6, 8064) Hope Pub.

Only EKG Book You'll Ever Need. 3rd ed. Ed. by Lippincott-Raven Staff. 1999. 29.95 (0-7817-1667-5) Lppncott W & W.

Only English? Law & Language Policy in The United States. Billy Platt. LC 89-24968. 199p. 1993. reprint ed. pap. 8.95 (0-8263-1373-6) U of NM Pr.

Only Entertainment. Richard Dyer. (Illus.). 176p. (C). (gr. 13). 1992. pap. 19.99 (0-415-05717-5, A9586) Routledge.

Only Fatherland: Communists, Quit India & the Soviet Union. Arun Shourie. (C). 1991. 17.50 (81-85304-35-1, Pub. by Manohar) S Asia.

Only Fear Dies: A Book of Liberation. 2nd rev. ed. Barry Long. Ed. by Clive Tempest. LC 96-96013. Orig. Title: Ridding Yourself of Unhappiness. 160p. 1994. pap. 12.95 (0-9508050-7-6) B Long Bks.

Only Fiona. Beverly Keller. LC 86-45786. 160p. (J). (gr. 3-7). 1988. 11.95 (0-06-023269-2) HarpC Child Bks.

Only Flesh & Bones. Sarah Andrews. LC 98-14171. 336p. 1998. text 23.95 (0-312-18642-8) St Martin.

Only Flesh & Bones, Vol. 1. Sarah Andrews. 1999. mass mkt. 5.99 (0-312-96702-0, Pub. by Tor Bks) St Martin.

Only Foolproof Way to Stop Smoking: Stop Smoking. Mary Lee. 75p. 1996. pap. 14.95 (1-881242-01-3) Pyramid Educ Inc.

Only for a Day. Barbara J. Crane. (Crane Reading System-English Ser.). (Illus.). (gr. k-2). 1977. pap. text 5.15 (0-89075-101-3) Bilingual Ed Serv.

***Only for a Year.** Ludima Gus Burton. LC 00-190018. 192p. 2000. 18.95 (0-8034-9415-7, Avalon Bks) Bouregy.

Only for Love. Patricia Pellicone. 384p. 1998. pap. 4.99 (0-8217-5927-2) Kensgtn Pub Corp.

Only for the Eye of a Friend: The Poetry of Annis Boudinot Stockton. Annis B. Stockton. Ed. by Carla Mulford. LC 95-7636. 416p. (C). 1995. text 35.00 (0-8139-1613-5) U Pr of Va.

Only for You. Hannah Howell. 380p. 1998. pap. 5.99 (0-8217-5943-4, Zebra Kensgtn) Kensgtn Pub Corp.

Only for You. Hannah Howell. 1995. pap. 4.99 (0-8217-4993-5) NAL.

Only Forever. Kimberly Cates. 1992. mass mkt. 5.99 (0-671-74083-0) PB.

Only Forever. Linda Lael Miller. LC 96-2314. 248p. 1995. per. 4.99 (1-55166-073-3, 1-66073-7, Mira Bks) Harlequin Bks.

***Only Forward.** Michael M. Smith. 352p. 2000. mass mkt. 6.50 (0-553-57970-3) Bantam.

Only Friends see Solo Amigos

Only Friends. Betsy Harris. LC 89-20371. (Hampstead High Ser.). 128p. (J). (gr. 5-9). 1990. pap. text 2.95 (0-8167-1912-8) Troll Communs.

Only Friendship see Solo Amistad

Only Game. large type ed. Patrick Ruell. 467p. 1993. 27.99 (0-7505-0451-X, Pub. by Mgna Lrg Print) Ulverscroft.

Only Game in Town. John Bibee. LC 88-9369. (Spirit Flyer Ser.: Vol. 3). (Illus.). 209p. (Orig.). (J). (gr. 5-8). 1988. pap. 6.99 (0-8308-1202-4, 1202) InterVarsity.

Only Golf Lesson You'll Ever Need: Easy Solutions to Problem Golf Swings. Hank Haney & John Huggan. LC 98-52416. (Illus.). 240p. 1999. 25.00 (0-06-270237-8) HarpC.

Only Good Bear Is a Dead Bear. 2nd ed. Jeanette Prodgers. 224p. 1997. pap. text 9.95 (1-56044-552-1) Falcon Pub Inc.

Only Good Lawyer. Jeremiah Healy. LC 97-52792. 352p. 1998. 23.00 (0-671-00953-2, PB Hardcover) PB.

Only Good Lawyer. Jeremiah Healy. 1999. reprint ed. per. 6.99 (0-671-00954-0, Pocket Books) PB.

Only Good One Is a Dead One. Michael Howard. Ed. by Rozella Heyns. (Illus.). 88p. (Orig.). 1996. pap. 6.00 (1-888529-01-6) Out of Africa Pub.

Only Good Priest. Mark R. Zubro. (Stonewall Inn Mysteries Ser.). 192p. 1992. pap. 8.95 (0-312-07054-3) St Martin.

Only Good Secretary. Jean Potts. 190p. 1998. 19.50 (0-7540-8523-6, Black Dagger) Chivers N Amer.

Only Grace Is Loving God. Lee Lozowick. LC 82-81992. 106p. 1982. pap. 5.95 (0-934252-07-6, Pub. by Hohm Pr) SCB Distributors.

Only Great Changes. Meredith S. Willis. LC 94-14170. 320p. 1997. reprint ed. pap. 10.00 (0-9654043-1-5, 500-1000) Hamilton Stone.

Only Guide to a Winning Investment Strategy You'll Ever Need: Beyond Index Mutual Funds - The Way Smart Money Invests Today. Larry E. Swedroe. LC 97-38908. 304p. 1998. 24.95 (0-525-94435-4, Truman Talley) St Martin.

Only Heaven. R. Gordon & Hu. 88p. 1997. pap. 12.95 (0-7935-8518-X) H Leonard.

Only Heaven Knows. rev. ed. Alex Harding. 1997. reprint ed. pap. 16.95 (0-86819-453-0, Pub. by Currency Pr) Accents Pubns.

Only Henniker on Earth: History of Henniker, NH. Henniker History Committee. LC 79-28597. (Illus.). 376p. 1980. 18.50 (0-914016-67-9) Phoenix Pub.

Only Here: Poems. Joe Salerno. LC 98-71250. (Illus.). 96p. (J). 1998. pap. 7.00 (1-886841-07-1, Ars Poetica) Skylnds Writ & Artists.

Only Hers. Francis Ray. 1996. pap. 4.99 (0-7860-0255-7, Pinncle Kensgtn) Kensgtn Pub Corp.

Only His. Elizabeth Lowell. 400p. (Orig.). 1991. mass mkt. 6.99 (0-380-76338-9, Avon Bks) Morrow Avon.

Only His. large type ed. Elizabeth Lowell. LC 95-49498. (Large Print Bks.). (Orig.). 1996. pap. 22.95 (1-56895-292-9) Wheeler Pub.

Only His Kiss. Sherrie Lord. LC 99-18696. 360p. 1999. pap. 10.99 (1-56476-707-8, Victor Bks) Chariot Victor.

Only Home They Ever Knew: Summit County & the Children's Home. Marilyn W. Merryweather. (Illus.). 112p. 1991. text. write for info. (0-9621895-5-3) Summit Cty Hist Soc.

An Asterisk (*) at the beginning of an entry indicates that the title is appearing for the first time.

Only Hope for America: The Transforming Power of the Gospel of Jesus Christ. Luis Palau & Mike Umlandt. LC 95-44520. 192p. 1996. pap. 10.99 (*0-89107-882-7*) Crossway Bks.

*__Only Human: Martian Independence.__ Neil L. Thompsett. 1999. pap. 12.95 (*1-892412-88-8*) Noggin.

Only Human & Other Stories. Jude Collins. 144p. 1998. pap. 14.95 (*0-85640-622-8*, Pub. by Blackstaff Pr) Dufour.

Only Human Short Stories. Winchinchala. Date not set. pap. write for info. (*1-889768-28-6*) People with Wings.

Only If You Like Cats. Clara Fentress. (Illus.). 60p. 1991. write for info. (*0-9660824-1-9*) C L Fentress.

*__Only in Alaska.__ David R. Stovner. iv, 182p. 1999. pap. 15.00 (*0-9679736-1-9*, 02) Musk Ox.

Only in America. Harry Golden. 25.95 (*0-8488-0080-X*) Amereon Ltd.

Only in America. Harry Golden. LC 72-9917. 317p. 1973. reprint ed. lib. bdg. 69.50 (*0-8371-6607-1*, GOOA, Greenwood Pr) Greenwood.

Only in America: Essays from Public Radio & the New York Times. David Bouchier. 321p. (Orig.). 1999. pap. 14.95 (*0-9652475-1-1*, Pub. by Mid Atlntic) LPC InBook.

Only in America? The Politics of the United States in Comparative Perspective. Graham K. Wilson. LC 98-8861. (Illus.). 176p. (C). 1998. pap. 21.95 (*1-56643-058-5*, Chatham House Pub) Seven Bridges.

Only in America - Opportunity Still Knocks - 1990. Horatio Alger Association of Distinguished America. Ed. by Melissa Herman. (Illus.). 140p. 1990. write for info. (*0-912081-09-0*) Delmar Co.

Only in America Activity Book. Peter Viney & Karen Viney. 1995. pap. text 8.95 (*0-19-458850-5*) OUP.

Only in Arkansas: A Study of the Endemic Plants & Animals of the State. Henry W. Robison & Robert T. Allen. (Illus.). 184p. 1995. text 42.00 (*1-55728-326-5*) U of Ark Pr.

Only in Books: Writers, Readers, & Bibliophiles on Their Passion. J. Kevin Graffagnino. 192p. 1996. 16.95 (*0-945612-49-4*) Madison Hse.

Only in Bridgeport: An Illustrated History of the Park City. 2nd ed. Lennie Grimaldi. 275p. 1993. reprint ed. 24.95 (*0-9632522-1-6*) Harbor Communs.

*__Only in Bridgeport: An Illustrated History of the Park City.__ 3rd ed. Lennie Grimaldi. (Illus.). 275p. 1999. 24.95 (*0-9632522-2-4*, Pub. by Harbor Communs) Bookazine Co Inc.

Only in California. 1989. 17.95 (*0-9622898-0-9*) CHSC.

Only in California: Recipes Which Capture the Spirit & Lifestyles Which Make California Unique. Ed. by Sue Bubnack & Joyce L. Hyde. (Illus.). 272p. 1989. 17.95 (*0-317-93905-X*) CHSC.

Only in Hawaii. Ann Kondo Corum. (Illus.). 106p. 1989. pap. 7.95 (*0-935848-76-2*) Bess Pr.

Only in Heaven: The Life & Campaigns of Sir Arthur Hesilrige, 1601-1661. Barry Denton. (Illus.). 248p. 1997. 27.00 (*1-85075-645-7*, Pub. by Sheffield Acad) CUP Services.

Only in Jerome. Vicky Hunt. LC 94-96163. (Illus.). 128p. (Orig.). 1994. pap. 9.95 (*0-9641785-0-8*) Hub Pubns.

Only in Louisiana: A Guide for the Adventurous Traveler. Keith Odom. 128p. (Orig.). 1994. pap. 6.95 (*0-937552-56-9*) Quail Ridge.

Only in Maine. Vance Bessey. Ed. by Jason B. Raschack. (Illus.). 80p. (Orig.). 1993. pap. 9.95 (*1-885724-00-4*, 01) Edutainment Media.

*__Only in Memory: Crupperneck, West Virginia - Recollections of Rural America.__ Erma Stults. LC 98-61346. 115p. 1998. pap. 11.95 (*1-889332-25-9*) So Herit Pr.

Only in Milford Vol. I: An Illustrated History. DeForest W. Smith. (Illus.). 192p. 1989. 29.95 (*0-9622888-0-2*) G J Smith & Son.

Only in Mississippi: A Guide for the Adventurous Traveler. rev. ed. Lorraine Redd & Jack Davis. LC 93-32607. (Illus.). 112p. 1997. pap. 7.95 (*0-937552-54-2*) Quail Ridge.

Only in My Arms. Jo Goodman. 448p. 1997. mass mkt. 5.50 (*0-8217-5346-0*, Zebra Kensgtn) Kensgtn Pub Corp.

Only in My Dreams. Eve Byron. 384p. 1998. mass mkt. 5.99 (*0-380-79311-3*, Avon Bks) Morrow Avon.

*__Only in New Mexico: An Architectural History of the University of New Mexico: The First Century, 1889-1989.__ Van Dorn Hooker et al. LC 99-6976. 2000. 24.95 (*0-8263-2135-6*) U of NM Pr.

Only in Pittsburgh. S. Trevor Hadley. (Illus.). 264p. 1994. pap. 14.95 (*0-9642251-0-7*) Educ Publng.

Only in Savannah: Stories & Insights on Georgia's Mother City. Thomas F. Coffey, Jr. LC 93-37722. 1993. 22.00 (*0-913720-84-4*) Beil.

Only in Sunshine. Ann Gabhart. (YA). (gr. 7 up). 1988. pap. 2.95 (*0-380-75395-2*, Avon Bks) Morrow Avon.

Only in the Ashes. Maxine O'Callaghan. 320p. 1997. mass mkt. 5.99 (*0-515-12077-4*, Jove) Berkley Pub.

Only in the Moonlight. Vicki L. Thompson. (Men at Work Ser.: Vol. 42). 1998. mass mkt. 4.50 (*0-373-81054-7*, 1-81054-8) Harlequin Bks.

*__Only in Your Arms.__ Tracy Cozzens. 2000. mass mkt. 4.99 (*0-8217-6530-2*, Zebra Kensgtn) Kensgtn Pub Corp.

Only in Your Arms. Lisa Kleypas. 432p. (Orig.). 1992. mass mkt. 5.99 (*0-380-76150-5*, Avon Bks) Morrow Avon.

Only Investment Guide You'll Ever Need. expanded rev. ed. Andrew Tobias. (SPA.). 288p. 1999. pap. 14.00 (*0-15-600599-9*, Harvest Bks) Harcourt.

Only Investment Guide You'll Ever Need. 2nd expanded rev. ed. Andrew Tobias. LC 98-38215. 239p. 1999. pap. 13.00 (*0-15-600560-3*, Harvest Bks) Harcourt.

Only Jealousy of Emer see Eleven Plays of William Butler Yeats

Only Job Hunting Guide You'll Ever Need: The Most Comprehensive Guide for Job Hunters & Career Switchers. rev. ed. Kathryn Petras & Ross Petras. LC 94-47511. 400p. 1995. per. 15.00 (*0-684-80236-8*) S&S Trade.

Only Joking! Laughed the Lobster. Colin West. LC 95-68493. (Illus.). 24p. (J). (ps-2). 1995. 9.95 (*1-56402-647-7*) Candlewick Pr.

"Only Joking!" Laughed the Lobster. Colin West. LC 95-68493. (Giggle Club Ser.). (Illus.). 24p. (J). (ps-1). 1997. reprint ed. pap. 3.29 (*0-7636-0279-5*) Candlewick Pr.

Only Kangaroo among the Beauty: Emily Dickinson & America. Karl Keller. LC 79-10462. 353p. reprint ed. pap. 109.50 (*0-608-06406-8*, 206662000008) Bks Demand.

Only Kid's Party Book You'll Ever Need: Hundreds of Great Ideas Plus a Unique Mix-&-Match Plan. Ed. by Reader's Digest Editors. 1998. 24.95 (*0-7621-0090-7*, Pub. by RD Assn) Penguin Putnam.

Only Land I Know: A History of the Lumbee Indians. Adolph L. Dial & David K. Eliades. (Illus.). 188p. (Orig.). 1995. pap. 17.95 (*0-8156-0360-6*) Syracuse U Pr.

Only Land They Knew: American Indians in the Old South. J. Leitch Wright, Jr. LC 98-51368. (Illus.). 416p. 1999. pap. 19.95 (*0-8032-9805-6*, Bison Books) U of Nebr Pr.

Only Life Gives Life: Revelation, Theology & Christian Living According to Cardinal Newman. Thomas Norris. 256p. 1996. 74.95 (*1-85607-220-7*, Pub. by Columba Press); pap. 54.95 (*1-85607-141-3*, Pub. by Columba Press) Intl Scholars.

Only Light We Read By. Margaret Aho. 36p. 1997. pap. 15.00 (*0-931659-37-X*) Limberlost Pr.

Only Light We Read By. limited ed. Margaret Aho. 36p. 1997. 45.00 (*0-931659-38-8*) Limberlost Pr.

*__Only Living Trust Book You'll Ever Need.__ Bove & Rhodes Staff. 1999. text 24.95 (*0-8050-3931-7*) St Martin.

Only Living Trust Book You'll Ever Need. D. Bovet. 1996. pap. 12.95 (*0-8050-3932-5*) St Martin.

Only Living Witness. Malcolm Forsythe. 224p. 26.00 (*0-7278-5520-4*) Severn Hse.

Only Love. Elizabeth Lowell. 416p. (Orig.). 1995. mass mkt. 6.99 (*0-380-77256-6*, Avon Bks) Morrow Avon.

Only Love. Erich Segal. 1998. mass mkt. 7.50 (*0-425-16440-3*) Berkley Pub.

Only Love. large type ed. Elizabeth Lowell. (Large Print Bks.). (Orig.). 1995. pap. 22.95 (*1-56895-260-0*, Compass) Wheeler Pub.

Only Love. large type ed. Erich Segal. LC 97-43875. (Compass Press Large Print Book Ser.). 1998. 26.95 (*1-56895-520-0*) Wheeler Pub.

Only Love: Living the Spiritual Life in a Changing World. Daya Mata. LC 75-44633. (Illus.). 295p. 1976. 14.00 (*0-87612-215-2*) Self Realization.

Only Love: Living the Spiritual Life in a Changing World. Daya Mata. LC 75-44633. (Illus.). 295p. 1995. pap. 10.50 (*0-87612-216-0*) Self Realization.

Only Love Can Break a Heart, but a Shoe Sale Can Come Close: A Cathy Collection. Cathy Guisewite. (Illus.). 128p. (Orig.). 1992. pap. 9.95 (*0-8362-1893-0*) Andrews & McMeel.

Only Love Can Gain Souls: Personal Evangelism & Nurturalization Handbook. Luke Huang. 200p. 1993. pap. 13.95 (*0-9631789-3-8*) Evan Formosan.

Only Love Can Make It Easy, 2 vols. rev. ed. Bill Coleman & Patty Coleman. LC 80-53335. 160p. 1997. pap., teacher ed. 9.95 (*0-89622-132-6*); pap., student ed. 4.95 (*0-89622-131-8*) Twenty-Third.

Only Love Can Make It Easy: Episcopal Edition. Bill Coleman & Patty Coleman. LC 88-50890. 80p. 1997. pap. 4.95 (*0-89622-383-3*); pap., teacher ed. 9.95 (*0-89622-382-5*) Twenty-Third.

Only Love Is Real: A Story of Soulmates Reunited. Brian L. Weiss. 82p. 1996. 19.95 (*0-446-51945-6*) Warner Bks.

Only Love Is Real: A Story of Soulmates Reunited. Brian Weiss. 192p. 1997. reprint ed. mass mkt. 12.95 (*0-446-67265-3*, Pub. by Warner Bks) Little.

*__Only Love Will Last.__ gif. ed. D. Morgan. 48p. 2000. 14.99 (*0-7369-0338-0*) Harvest Hse.

Only Magic: A Novel. Robert K. Swisher. LC 93-15744. 96p. (Orig.). 1993. pap. 8.95 (*0-86534-198-2*) Sunstone Pr.

Only Man. large type ed. Rosemary Hammond. (Magna Large Print Ser.). 269p. 1997. 27.99 (*0-7505-1129-X*) Ulverscroft.

Only Man for Maggie: Holding Out for a Hero. Leigh Michaels. LC 96-718. (Romance Ser.). 186p. 1996. per. 3.25 (*0-373-03401-6*, 1-03401-6) Harlequin Bks.

Only Man in Wyoming. Kristine Rolofson. (Temptation Ser.). 1997. per. 3.50 (*0-373-25721-X*, 1-25721-1) Harlequin Bks.

Only Man to Trust: Her Protector. Grace Green. (Intrigue Ser.: Vol. 476). 1998. per. 3.99 (*0-373-22476-1*, 1-22476-5) Harlequin Bks.

Only Math Book You'll Ever Need: Practical, Step-by-Step Solutions to Everyday Math Problems. rev. ed. Stanley Kogelman & Barbara R. Heller. LC 93-10539. (Illus.). 290p. 1993. 22.95 (*0-8160-2767-6*) Facts on File.

Only Math Book You'll Ever Need, Revised Edition: Hundreds of Easy Solutions & Shortcuts for Mastering Everyday Numbers. rev. ed. Stanley Kogelman & Barbara R. Heller. 288p. 1995. pap. 15.00 (*0-06-272507-6*, Harper Ref) HarpC.

*__Only Menopause Guide You'll Need.__ Michele Moore. LC 99-54553. (Illus.). 157p. 2000. 42.50 (*0-8018-6407-0*); pap. 13.95 (*0-8018-6408-9*) Johns Hopkins.

Only Mine. Elizabeth Lowell. 400p. 1992. mass mkt. 6.99 (*0-380-76339-7*, Avon Bks) Morrow Avon.

Only Mine. large type ed. Elizabeth Lowell. LC 96-11049. (Large Print Bks.). 1996. pap. 22.95 (*1-56895-322-4*) Wheeler Pub.

Only Moments. Peter Eliason. 287p. (Orig.). 1984. pap. 6.95 (*0-916777-41-3*) W P Allen.

Only Money Guide You'll Ever Need. Petras. 1995. 14.95 (*0-671-75888-8*) S&S Trade.

Only More So: The History of East Hartford, 1783-1976. Lee A. Paquette. LC 92-61362. 372p. 1992. reprint ed. 30.00 (*0-89725-076-1*, 1410) Picton Pr.

Only Morning in Her Shoes: Poems about Old Women. Ed. by Leatrice Lifschitz. 176p. (Orig.). 1990. pap. 4.00 (*0-87421-145-X*) Utah St U Pr.

Only Mothers Know: Patterns of Infant Feeding in Traditional Cultures, 54. Dana Raphael & Flora Davis. LC 84-15742. (Contributions in Women's Studies: No. 54). (Illus.). 159p. 1985. 49.95 (*0-313-24541-X*, RBR/, Greenwood Pr) Greenwood.

Only My Children & Me. Gwendolyn L. Baines. (Illus.). 32p. (Orig.). (YA). 1994. pap. 4.50 (*0-9614505-4-1*) Nevada Pub.

Only My Dreams. large type ed. Rowan Edwards. (Linford Romance Large Print Ser.). 352p. 1998. pap. 17.99 (*0-7089-5258-5*) Ulverscroft.

Only My Dreams. large type ed. Denise Robins. (Dales Large Print Ser.). 435p. 1997. pap. 18.99 (*1-85389-701-9*) Ulverscroft.

Only My Dreams: An English Girlhood. Hilda A. Salusbury. (Illus.). 272p. 1990. 20.00 (*0-89733-276-8*) Academy Chi Pubs.

Only My Life. Louis De Wijze. LC 96-9443. 224p. 1996. 21.95 (*0-312-14697-3*) St Martin.

Only Mystery: Federico Garcia Lorca's Poetry in Word & Image. Sandra Forman et al. (Illus.). 144p. 1992. 34.95 (*0-8130-1133-7*) U Press Fla.

Only Nails Remain. Christopher Merrill. 1995. 20.00 (*0-8050-3049-2*) H Holt & Co.

Only Nature Cures. Benedict Lust. 1983. pap. 5.95 (*0-87904-014-9*) Lust.

Only Necessary Thing: Living a Prayerful Life. Henri J. M. Nouwen. Ed. & Compiled by Wendy Greer. LC 99-43205. 160p. 1999. 18.95 (*0-8245-1833-0*) Crossroad NY.

Only Nine Chairs-A Tall Tale for Passover. Deborah U. Miller. LC 82-80035. (Illus.). 40p. (J). (ps-4). 1982. pap. 5.95 (*0-930494-13-X*) Kar-Ben.

Only Now Are We Aware: Poems. Lloyd Hamlin. LC 91-48461. (Illus.). 64p. (Orig.). 1992. pap. 7.50 (*1-56474-017-X*) Fithian Pr.

Only One. Marc Harshman. LC 92-11349. (Illus.). 32p. (J). (ps-3). 1993. 15.99 (*0-525-65116-0*, Dutton Child) Peng Put Young Read.

Only One: Becoming a Giant Panda. Julia F. Spencer. (Illus.). (J). (ps-5). 1997. 12.95 (*0-614-28718-9*, Dove Audio) NewStar Media.

Only One Author. Albert Krassner. 77p. (Orig.). 1988. pap. 4.95 (*0-912061-16-2*) Veridon Edns.

*__Only One Cowry.__ LC 99-56552. (Illus.). 32p. (J). (gr. k-2). 2000. lib. bdg. 17.99 (*0-531-33288-8*) Orchard Bks Watts.

*__Only One Cowry: A Dahomean Tale.__ Phillis Gershator. LC 99-56552. (Illus.). 32p. (J). (gr. k-2). 2000. 16.95 (*0-531-30288-1*) Orchard Bks Watts.

Only One Cure. large type ed. Grace Read. (Dales Large Print Ser.). 244p. 1997. pap. 18.99 (*1-85389-730-2*) Ulverscroft.

Only One Groom Allowed. Laurie Paige. (Yours Truly Ser.). 1997. per. 3.50 (*0-373-52046-8*, 1-52046-9) Silhouette.

*__Only One Life.__ Jean Vandevenne. 128p. 2000. mass mkt. 5.99 (*0-87508-667-5*, 667) Chr Lit.

Only One Life: A Story of Missionary Resilience. Vera Kuschnir. 378p. (Orig.). 1996. pap. 9.95 (*1-885024-04-5*) Slavic Christian.

Only One Life: My Autobiography. H. Harold Hartzler. 164p. 1992. 9.95 (*1-883294-07-X*) Masthof Pr.

Only One Life: Story of Missionary Resilience. Vera Kushnir. (RUS.). 350p. (Orig.). Date not set. pap. 9.95 (*1-885024-05-3*) Slavic Christian.

Only One Life: The Biography of Stephen F. Olford. John Phillips. LC 94-43087. 352p. 1995. 22.99 (*0-87213-676-0*) Loizeaux.

Only One Ocean. Craig Strang. Date not set. pap. 16.00 (*0-924886-22-6*) Lawrence Science.

Only One Ollie. Denis Roche. LC 96-2851. (Illus.). 14p. (J). 1997. 4.95 (*0-395-81123-6*) HM.

Only One Sky see Tantra: The Supreme Understanding: Discourses on the Tantric Way of Tilopa's Song of Mahamudra

Only One Way Out. Ruth R. Moen. (Kathleen O'Shaughnessy Ser.). (Orig.). (C). 1995. pap. 7.95 (*0-9635653-2-X*) Flying Swan.

Only One Woof. James Herriot. LC 93-21740. (Illus.). 32p. (J). (gr. 1-8). 1993. pap. 6.95 (*0-312-09129-X*) St Martin.

Only One Woof. James Herriot. 1993. 12.15 (*0-606-12462-4*, Pub. by Turtleback) Demco.

Only One Word. James McKeever. 20p. (C). 1979. pap. text 2.99 (*0-86694-001-4*) Omega Pubns OR.

Only One World. 3rd ed. Gerard Piel. (C). 1992. 8.00 (*0-7167-2323-9*) W H Freeman.

Only One World: Our Own to Make & to Keep. 367p. 21.95 (*92-1-100528-0*) UN.

Only Opal. Opal Whiteley & Jane Boulton. LC 91-38581. (Illus.). 32p. (J). (ps up). 1997. pap. 5.99 (*0-698-11564-3*, PapStar) Peng Put Young Read.

Only Opal: The Diary of a Young Girl. Opal Whiteley & Jane Boulton. LC 91-38581. (Illus.). 32p. (J). (ps-3). 1994. 15.95 (*0-399-21990-0*, Philomel) Peng Put Young Read.

Only Opal, the Diary of a Young Girl. Opal Whiteley. (J). 1997. 11.15 (*0-606-11711-3*, Pub. by Turtleback) Demco.

Only Other Crazy Car Book. Sloan Walker & Andrew Vasey. LC 83-6546. (Illus.). 48p. (J). (gr. 4 up). 1984. 10.95 (*0-8027-6504-1*); lib. bdg. 11.85 (*0-8027-6517-3*) Walker & Co.

Only Our Tears: A Book of Poetry. 136p. 1999. pap. write for info. (*0-9663618-1-4*) J Schmidt.

Only Outcast. Julie Johnston. LC 98-60523. 232p. (YA). (gr. 7 up). 1998. 14.95 (*0-88776-441-X*) Tundra Bks.

*__Only Outcast.__ Julie Johnston. 232p. (YA). (gr. 7-12). 1999. reprint ed. pap. 6.95 (*0-88776-488-6*) Tundra Bks.

Only Paradise. large type ed. Marjorie Warby. 480p. 1988. 27.99 (*0-7089-1779-8*) Ulverscroft.

Only Paradoxes to Offer: French Feminists & the Rights of Man. Joan W. Scott. LC 95-31953. 256p. 1996. 27.95 (*0-674-63930-8*) HUP.

Only Paradoxes to Offer: French Feminists & the Rights of Man. Joan W. Scott. 256p. 1997. reprint ed. pap. 17.00 (*0-674-63931-6*) HUP.

Only Paralyzed from the Neck Down: The Life & Ministry of Tom Brewster. Dan Brewster. LC 98-132230. 324p. 1997. pap. 15.95 (*0-87808-275-1*, WCL275-1) William Carey Lib.

Only Personal Letter Book You'll Ever Need. Judi Barton & Nate Rosenblatt. 1994. pap. 19.95 (*0-929543-43-2*) Round Lake Pub.

*__Only Petition at U. S. Tax Court.__ Mariette Do-Nguyen. (Revelations Ser.). (YA). 1999. 35.00 (*0-9652169-3-4*) Rebuild My Church.

Only Piece of Furniture in the House. Diane H. Glancy. LC 96-8425. 124p. 1996. 18.95 (*1-55921-183-0*) Moyer Bell.

Only Problems, Not Solutions! Florentin Smarandache. Ed. by Xiquan Publishing House Staff. (Illus.). 57p. (Orig.). (C). 1991. pap. 5.99 (*1-879585-00-6*) Erhus Univ Pr.

Only Problems, Not Solutions. 4th ed. Florentin Smarandache. LC 92-108051. 113p. reprint ed. pap. 35.10 (*0-608-10476-0*, 207109400008) Bks Demand.

Only Prostitutes Marry in May. Dacia Maraini. 378p. 1994. pap. 18.00 (*0-920717-81-0*) Guernica Editions.

Only Reasons I Mention This: The Best of Daddy Bob. Daddy Bob. Ed. by Bob Fifield. 120p. (Orig.). 1996. pap. 12.95 (*0-9652638-1-9*) Leather Jrnl.

Only Right Solution to Control Sex Offenders & Drug Addicts. Gypsy A. Coolidge. 1990. write for info. (*0-318-66956-0*) Celestial Gems.

Only Rock. Roberta Gould. 1985p. 1985. pap. 7.95 (*0-913152-14-5*) Folder Edns.

Only Rose. unabridged ed. Sarah Orne Jewett. 1994. lib. bdg. 18.95 incl. audio (*1-883049-49-0*) Sound Room.

Only Rose, Set. unabridged ed. Sarah Orne Jewett. (Jewett Ser.). 1994. 16.95 incl. audio (*1-883049-43-1*, 391319, Pub. by Sound Room) Lndmrk Audiobks.

Only Sales Promotion Techniques You'll Ever Need. Ed. by Tamara S. Block. (Illus.). 267p. 1996. 39.95 (*0-85013-255-X*) Dartnell Corp.

Only Servants. Clifford Pond. 1991. pap. 8.99 (*0-946462-24-0*, Pub. by Evangelical Pr) P & R Pubng.

Only Shadows. Lavina M. Hartshoon. 1997. pap. write for info. (*0-7880-0900-1*) CSS OH.

Only Silence Is Shame. John R. Wilder. (Contemporary Poets Ser.: No. 1). (Orig.). 1986. pap. 5.95 (*0-916843-03-3*, 102) Order of Legion.

Only Sin. Julie Ellis. 1994. per. 4.50 (*0-373-83289-3*, 1-83289-8) Harlequin Bks.

Only Soldiers Go to War. Lucinda H. Kennaley. LC 91-65288. (Illus.). 42p. (J). (ps-4). 1991. 14.95 (*0-9628067-1-4*) Thoth MO.

Only Some Big Cats Can Roar: And Other Amazing Facts about Wild Cats. Claire Llewellyn. LC 98-28524. (I Didn't Know That... Ser.). (Illus.). 32p. (J). 1999. 8.95 (*0-7613-0787-7*, Copper Beech Bks); lib. bdg. 21.90 (*0-7613-0900-4*, Copper Beech Bks) Millbrook Pr.

Only Son. Kevin O'Brien. LC 96-77156. 304p. 1997. 21.95 (*1-57566-091-1*, Knsington) Kensgtn Pub Corp.

Only Son. Kevin O'Brien. 352p. 1998. pap. 5.99 (*1-57566-211-6*, Knsington) Kensgtn Pub Corp.

Only Sons. Genaro Gonzalez. LC 91-4679. 126p. (Orig.). 1991. pap. 9.50 (*1-55885-031-7*) Arte Publico.

Only Spring: On Mourning the Death of My Son. Gordon Livingston. LC 99-30985. 256p. 1999. pap. 12.95 (*1-56924-659-9*) Marlowe & Co.

Only St. Nick Knew. Nikki Benjamin. (Special Edition Ser.). 1994. per. 3.50 (*0-373-09928-2*, 1-09928-2) Silhouette.

Only Strangers Travel. Sharon Hawkinson. 1984. 6.95 (*0-88494-533-2*) Bookcraft Inc.

Only Texas Cookbook. Linda W. Eckhardt. LC 99-22657. 284p. 1981. pap. 12.95 (*0-87719-123-9*, 9123) Gulf Pub.

Only the Ashes. Kage. Tr. by Steve Sanfield from JPN. (Illus.). 36p. 1981. pap. 25.00 (*0-940510-02-2*) Tooth of Time.

Only the Ball Was White. Robert Peterson. (Illus.). 416p. 1992. pap. 15.95 (*0-19-507637-0*) OUP.

Only the Ball Was White. Robert Peterson. LC 98-36777. (Illus.). 416p. 1999. 8.99 (*0-517-20501-7*) Random Hse Value.

Only the Ball was White. Robert Peterson. 25.95 (*0-8488-1124-0*) Amereon Ltd.

Only the Best. Beverly Lewis. LC 98-220293. 128p. 1998. pap. 5.99 (*0-7642-2059-4*) Bethany Hse.

Only the Best: Annual Guide to Highest-Rated Education Software-Multimedia for Preschool-Grade 12. Shirley B. Neill & George W. Neill. 144p. 1991. 27.95 (*0-936423-04-8*) Ed News Serv.

*__Only the Best: Masterpieces of the Calouste Gulbenkian Museum, Lisbon.__ Katharine Baetjer et al. LC 99-44794. (Illus.). 176p. 1999. pap. 45.00 (*0-8109-6546-1*, Pub. by Abrams) Time Warner.

O

An Asterisk (*) at the beginning of an entry indicates that the title is appearing for the first time.

***Only the Best Greece.** Ed. by Alexander Kyrtsis. (Illus.). 527p. 1999. pap. 29.95 (*960-377-009-4*, Pub. by Axon Pubns) Pathway Bk Serv.

Only the Best Will Do: The Eddie Stobart Story. Noel Davidson. 1999. pap. text 9.99 (*1-84030-043-4*) Ambassador Prodns Ltd.

Only the Birds Protest: Poems from the Maltese of Mario Azzopardi. Tr. by Grazio Falzon. (Poetry Chapbook Ser.). 1979. 3.00 (*0-932191-02-9*) Mr Cogito Pr.

Only the Cat Saw. Ashley Wolff. LC 96-19046. (Illus.). 32p. (J). (gr. k-3). 1996. pap. 5.95 (*0-8027-7488-1*) Walker & Co.

Only the Dog Knows for Sure: The Best of Thuh Bull. Thuh Bull. LC 96-79803. (Illus.). 128p. (Orig.). 1997. pap. 9.95 (*1-56352-391-4*) Longstreet.

Only the Echoes: The Life of Howard Bass Cushing. Kenneth A. Randall. LC 95-61957. (Illus.). 120p. 1995. 25.00 (*1-881325-17-2*); pap. text 12.95 (*1-881325-19-9*) Yucca Tree Pr.

***Only the End of the World Again.** Neil Gaiman. Ed. by Jamie S. Rich. (Illus.). 48p. 2000. pap. 6.95 (*1-929998-09-0*) Oni Pr Inc.

Only the Enemy in Front: The Recce Corps at War, 1940-1946. Richard Doherty. 288p. 1997. (*1-871085-18-7*) Donovan Pub.

Only the Eyes Say Yes: A Love Story. Philippe Vigand & Stephane Vigand. LC 99-47439. 224p. 2000. 23.95 (*1-55970-508-6*, Pub. by Arcade Pub Inc) Time Warner.

Only the Father Knows: An American Crisis. Robert M. Beaudry. LC 94-77363. 232p. (Orig.). 1995. pap. 12.95 (*0-9642058-0-7*) InChem Pubng.

Only the Good News: On the Law of the Press in India. Rajeev Dhavan. 514p. (C). 1987. 47.50 (*81-85054-38-X*, Pub. by Manohar) S Asia.

Only the Good Parts: A Novel. Daniel Curzon. LC 98-85381. 325p. 1998. 25.00 (*0-9663501-1-1*); pap. 15.00 (*0-7388-0020-1*) Xlibris Corp.

Only the Good Times. Juan Bruce-Novoa. LC 95-9770. 286p. 1995. pap. 9.95 (*1-55885-078-3*) Arte Publico.

Only the Heart. Brian Caswell & David P. Chiem. LC 98-210377. 198p. (YA). 1997. pap. 12.95 (*0-7022-2927-X*, Pub. by Univ Queensland Pr) Intl Spec Bk.

Only, the Last Dinosaur. Jim Dunlap. LC 94-39155. (Illus.). 152p. 1994. pap. 8.95 (*1-55622-382-X*, Rep of TX Pr) Wordware Pub.

Only the Little Bone. David Huddle. LC 85-45962. 256p. 1986. 15.95 (*0-87923-624-8*) Godine.

Only the Lonely: The Roy Orbison Story. 10th ed. Alan Clayson. Date not set. pap. 19.95 (*1-86074-241-6*, SGo0664) Music Sales.

Only the Lover Sings: Art & Contemplation. Josef Pieper. Tr. by Lothar Krauth from GER. LC 90-81771. 76p. (Orig.). 1990. pap. 6.95 (*0-89870-302-6*) Ignatius Pr.

Only the Nails Remain: Scenes from the Balkan Wars. Christopher Merrill. LC 99-16783. 416p. 1999. 27.95 (*0-8476-9820-3*, Pub. by Rowman) Natl Bk Netwk.

Only the Names Remain: The Cherokees & the Trail of Tears. Alex W. Bealer. (Illus.). 80p. (J). (gr. 4-6). 1996. pap. 4.95 (*0-316-08519-7*) Little.

Only the Names Remain: The Cherokees & the Trail of Tears. Alex W. Bealer. 1996. 10.05 (*0-606-08839-3*, Pub. by Turtleback) Demco.

***Only the Names Remain Vol. 6: Tahlequah & Skin Bayou District, Indian Territory, Oklahoma.** Sandi Garrett. 2000. pap. 21.50 (*0-7884-1406-2*, G067) Heritage Bk.

Only the Nude Can Redeem the Landscape. Christy S. Sanford. 75p. (Orig.). 1989. pap. 7.95 (*0-940821-01-X*) Apalachee Pr.

Only the Other Day: A Volume of Essays. Edward V. Lucas. LC 67-28756. (Essay Index Reprint Ser.). 1977. 19.95 (*0-8369-0630-6*) Ayer.

Only the Paranoid Survive: How to Achieve a Success That's Just a Disaster Away. Andrew S. Grove. LC 96-13509. 224p. 1996. 27.50 (*0-385-48258-2*) Doubleday.

Only the Paranoid Survive: How to Achieve a Success That's Just a Disaster Away. Andrew S. Grove. 224p. 1998. mass mkt. 7.99 (*0-385-49327-4*) Doubleday.

Only the Paranoid Survive: How to Achieve a Success That's Just a Disaster Away. Andrew S. Grove. LC 96-13509. (Illus.). 240p. 1999. pap. 15.95 (*0-385-48382-1*) Doubleday.

***Only the Psychics Will Survive: How to Awaken Your Survival Instincts for the New Millennium.** Mahlon Gillis. 144p. 2000. pap. 14.95 (*1-893075-08-7*, Pub. by Spirit Pr OR) ACCESS Pubs Network.

Only the Raw Hands Are Heaven. Naomi Thiers. LC 92-156. 72p. (Orig.). 1992. pap. 10.00 (*0-931846-41-2*) Wash Writers Pub.

***Only the Righteous: Righteous, Righteously, Righteousness, Righteousnesses, 4 vols.** William D. Wade. (Illus.). 356p. 1999. 83.95 (*0-9673679-0-5*) Omega Min.

Only the Ring Was Square. Teddy Brenner & Barney Nagler. LC 81-5940. 164p. 1981. 10.95 (*0-685-03883-1*) P-H.

***Only the River Runs Free.** Bodie Thoene. 1998. pap. 12.99 (*0-7852-7016-7*) Nelson.

Only the River Runs Free. Bodie Thoene. (Galway Chronicles Ser.). 1999. pap. 9.97 (*0-7852-6925-8*) Nelson.

Only the Rivers Run Free, Northern Ireland: The Women's War. Eileen Fairweather et al. (C). pap. 22.00 (*0-86104-668-4*, Pub. by Pluto GBR) Stylus Pub VA.

Only the Salt. Doug Underhill. LC 98-138918. 86p. 1997. pap. 10.50 (*0-921411-35-9*) Genl Dist Srvs.

Only the Strong Survive. James H. Watkins, Sr. LC 94-68972. 129p. (Orig.). 1997. pap. 12.95 (*1-887798-01-3*) WriteMore Pubns.

Only the Strong Survive: Memoirs of a Soul Survivor. Jerry Butler & Earl Smith. xviii, 380p. 1999. 19.95 (*1-893731-00-6*) Mandolin Hse.

***Only the Strong Survive: Memoirs of a Soul Survivor/Jerry Butler, with Earl Smith.** Jerry Butler & Earl Smith. LC 00-32002. 2000. 24.95 (*0-253-33796-8*) Ind U Pr.

Only the Sword of the Spirit. Jacob A. Loewen & Wesley J. Prieb. (Perspectives on Mennonite Life & Thought Ser.: No. 11). 390p. (Orig.). 1997. pap. 15.95 (*0-921788-44-4*) Kindred Prods.

Only the Voice. Hugo Lindo. Tr. by Elizabeth G. Miller. Orig. Title: Solo La Voz. 110p. (Orig.). 1984. pap. 8.00 (*0-939378-04-3*) Mundus Artium.

***Only the Wicked.** Gary Phillips. 352p. 2000. 24.95 (*1-885173-64-4*, Pub. by Write Way) Midpt Trade.

Only the Wind. Enrique C. Menendez. Ed. by Jose Armas. Tr. by Frances Hernandez from SPA. (Illus.). 182p. 1980. 9.00 (*0-918358-05-1*); pap. 7.00 (*0-686-64685-1*) Pajarito Pubns.

Only the Wind & the Sea Were My Friends. Dell O'Neill. 160p. (C). 1989. text 65.00 (*1-872795-99-4*, Pub. by Pentland Pr) St Mut.

Only the Words. Faye George. 20p. 1995. pap. 5.00 (*1-885141-06-8*) Harlequin Ink.

Only the World. Constance Urdang. LC 82-20062. (Poetry Ser.). 60p. 1983. pap. 10.95 (*0-8229-5349-8*) U of Pittsburgh Pr.

Only Thing. Craig Alpaugh. 81p. 1996. pap. 5.50 (*0-87129-661-6*, O57) Dramatic Pub.

Only Thing Holding Me Back Is My Cat: How to Separate Yourself from Your Fears. Turn Obstacles into Opportunities. 2nd ed. Mary R. Franklin. 144p. 1999. pap. 12.95 (*1-893075-09-5*, Pub. by Spirit Pr OR) ACCESS Pubs Network.

Only Thing Holding Me Back Is My Cat: How to Separate Yourself from Your Fears. Turning Obstacles into Opportunities. Mary R. Franklin. (Illus.). 128p. 1997. pap. 14.95 (*0-9662114-0-5*) Organdy Pr.

Only Thing I Fear Is a Cow & a Drunken Man. Mary N. Kratt. (Illus.). 77p. (Orig.). 1991. pap. 10.00 (*0-932112-29-3*) Carolina Wren.

Only Thing That Counts: The Ernest Hemingway - Maxwell Perkins Correspondence. Ernest Hemingway. Ed. by Matthew J. Bruccoli. (Illus.). 365p. 1998. reprint ed. pap. 21.95 (*1-57003-285-8*) U of SC Pr.

Only Thing That Matters: Bringing the Power of the Customer into the Center of Your Business. Karl Albrecht. LC 17-171. 256p. 1992. 23.00 (*0-88730-541-5*, HarpBusn) HarpInfo.

Only Thing That Matters: Bringing the Power of the Customer into the Center of Your Business. Karl Albrecht. LC 92-54853. (Illus.). 256p. 1993. pap. 13.50 (*0-88730-639-X*, HarpBusn) HarpInfo.

Only Thing That Really Matters. Wade Byrd. (Illus.). 180p. (Orig.). 1996. pap. 5.95 (*0-9654192-0-7*) New Day Co.

Only Thing to Fear. Robert Morgan. 256p. 1994. mass mkt. 4.99 (*0-425-14468-2*, Prime Crime) Berkley Pub.

Only Thing to Fear. David Poyer. 480p. 1996. mass mkt. write for info. (*0-614-05527-X*); mass mkt. 6.99 (*0-8125-4815-9*, Pub. by Forge NYC) St Martin.

Only Thing Worse You Could Have Told Me . . . Dan Butler. 1997. pap. 5.25 (*0-8222-1613-2*) Dramatists Play.

***Only This & Nothing More.** 366p. (C). 2000. 40.00 (*0-536-60278-6*) Pearson Custom.

Only 3 Ways to Book Your Show: How to Get Paid Jobs As a Magician, Clown or Other Variety Arts Entertainer. David Ginn. (Illus.). 144p. (Orig.). 1996. pap. 15.00 (*0-9649318-0-X*) Scarlett Green.

Only Time There Is. Jeff Worley. LC 94-45204. (First Poetry Ser.). 80p. (Orig.). 1995. pap. 9.95 (*0-922811-22-9*) Mid-List.

Only Tradition. William W. Quinn, Jr. LC 96-42957. (SUNY Series in Western Esoteric Traditions). 384p. (C). 1997. text 74.50 (*0-7914-3213-0*); pap. text 24.95 (*0-7914-3214-9*) State U NY Pr.

Only True & Incredible Me. Mark Bestmann. LC 98-225933. 24p. (J). 1998. 12.99 (*0-89900-819-4*) College Pr Pub.

Only True People see Colorado Plateau: The Land & the Indians

Only True Power Is in Connection. Andrea K. Willison. 160p. 1998. pap. 9.95 (*0-9664706-0-5*) White Wing Pr.

Only Twice I've Wished for Heaven. Dawn T. Trice. 1997. 23.00 (*0-614-19891-7*) Crown Pub Group.

Only Twice I've Wished for Heaven. large type ed. Dawn T. Trice. LC 97-23291. (Wheeler Large Print Book Ser.). 1997. 23.95 (*1-56895-468-9*) Wheeler Pub.

Only Twice I've Wished for Heaven: A Novel. Dawn T. Trice. LC 97-39733. 320p. 1998. pap. 12.00 (*0-385-49123-9*) Doubleday.

Only Two Hundred Fifty Letters & Memos Managers Will Ever Need. Ronald Tepper. 288p. 1993. pap. 49.95 incl. disk (*0-471-00963-6*) Wiley.

Only Two (Seems Like More) Susan Sturgill. (Illus.). 1990. 18.00 (*0-9626108-4-4*) Laughing Acad Pr.

Only Two Strangers see Solo Dos Extranos: (Only Two Strangers)

Only Victims: A Study of Show Business Blacklisting. Robert Vaughn. 360p. 1996. reprint ed. pap. 17.95 (*0-87910-081-8*) Limelight Edns.

***Only Victor.** Alexander Kent. LC 99-89386. (Richard Bolitho Novels Ser.: No. 18). 384p. 2000. reprint ed. pap. 15.95 (*0-935526-74-9*) McBooks Pr.

Only Virgins Need Apply. Chester Beavon. 1990. 16.95 (*0-9617572-2-1*) Times Journal Pub.

Only Way Home. Robert H. Murray. (Illus.). 159p. 1987. 24.00 (*0-9617970-0-2*) Robert H Murray.

Only Way I Know. Cal Ripken, Jr. & Mike Bryan. 320p. 1998. pap. 12.95 (*0-14-026626-7*) Viking Penguin.

Only Way Out. Deborah Kent. (J). 1997. pap. text 3.99 (*0-590-54081-5*, Apple Paperbacks) Scholastic Inc.

Only Way Out. Deborah Kent. 1997. 9.09 (*0-606-11712-1*, Pub. by Turtleback) Demco.

Only Way Out. Susan Mallery. (Intimate Moments Ser.). 1995. per. 3.75 (*0-373-07646-0*, 1-07646-2) Silhouette.

Only Way Out. large type ed. Susan Mallery. (Silhouette Romance Ser.). 1997. 20.95 (*0-373-59813-0*) Mac Lib Ref.

***Only Way Out Is Through.** Marte Tilton. 2000. pap. 12.99 (*0-88419-727-1*) Creation House.

***Only Way Through It.** Samantha Sayers. LC 00-190642. Orig. Title: Anyone's Path. 112p. 2000. 25.00 (*0-7388-1888-7*); pap. 18.00 (*0-7388-1889-5*) Xlibris Corp.

Only Way to Buy a Car. David J. Hanley. LC 94-69594. 104p. (Orig.). 1994. pap. 8.95 (*0-9644155-0-X*) Roundhse Bks.

Only Way to Fly: The Story of Western Airlines, America's Senior Air Carrier. Robert J. Serling. (Airlines History Project Ser.). (Illus.). reprint ed. 49.50 (*0-404-19334-X*) AMS Pr.

Only Way to Happiness. John MacArthur, Jr. LC 98-209031. (Foundations of the Faith: The Beatitudes Ser.). 1998. pap. 8.99 (*0-8024-3054-6*) Moody.

Only Way to Learn about Horary & Electrical Astrology. Marion D. March & Joan McEvers. (Only Way Ser.: Vol. VI). 256p. (Orig.). 1995. pap. 14.95 (*0-935127-29-1*) ACS Pubns.

Only Way to Learn about Relationships: Synastry Techniques. Marion D. March & Joan McEvers. (Only Way Ser.: Vol. V). 256p. (Orig.). 1994. pap. 14.95 (*0-935127-21-6*) ACS Pubns.

Only Way to Learn about Tomorrow: Current Patterns, Progressions, Directions, Solar & Lunar Returns, Transits. Marion D. March & Joan McEvers. (Only Way Ser.: Vol. IV). 240p. (Orig.). 1992. pap. 14.95 (*0-917086-65-1*) ACS Pubns.

Only Way to Learn Astrology: Basic Principles. Marion D. March & Joan McEvers. (Only Way Ser.: Vol. I). (Illus.). 320p. 1996. pap. 14.95 (*0-917086-00-7*) ACS Pubns.

Only Way to Learn Astrology: Basic Principles. 2nd ed. Marion D. March. (Only Way Ser.: Vol. 1). 320p. 1997. pap. 14.95 (*0-935127-61-5*) ACS Pubns.

Only Way to Learn Astrology: Horoscope Analysis. Marion D. March & Joan McEvers. (Only Way Ser.: Vol. 3). 272p. 1980. pap. 14.95 (*0-917086-43-0*) ACS Pubns.

Only Way to Learn Astrology: Math & Interpretation Techniques. 2nd ed. Marion D. March. (Only Way Ser.: Vol. 2). 288p. 1999. pap. 14.95 (*0-935127-68-2*) ACS Pubns.

Only Way to Learn Astrology: Math & Interpretation Techniques. 2nd rev. ed. Marion D. March & Joan McEvers. (Only Way Ser.: Vol. 2). (Illus.). 264p. 1982. reprint ed. pap. 14.95 (*0-917086-26-0*) ACS Pubns.

Only Way to Walk. S. Brown. Date not set. pap. 6.99 (*1-871676-43-6*, Pub. by Christian Focus) Spring Arbor Dist.

***Only What We Could Carry: The Japanese American Internment Experience.** Ed. by Lawson Inada. (Illus.). 448p. 2000. pap. 18.95 (*1-890771-30-9*) Heyday Bks.

***Only What's Imagined: Poems by Geof Hewitt--Introduction by Hayden Carruth.** Geof Hewitt. 74p. 2000. pap. 12.95 (*0-9676787-0-6*) Kumquat Pr VT.

Only When I Laugh. Elouise Bell. LC 90-48786. 136p. (Orig.). 1990. pap. 9.95 (*1-56085-013-2*) Signature Bks.

Only When I Laugh. Len Deighton. 256p. 1987. 16.45 (*0-89296-175-9*, Pub. by Mysterious Pr) Little.

***Only When I Sleep: My Family's Journey Through Cancer.** Lisa Shaw-Brawley. LC 00-21152. 232p. 2000. pap. 10.95 (*1-55874-774-5*) Health Comm.

Only When The Messengers Come: Poems in Dual Text German/English Language. Olly Komenda-Soentgerath. Tr. by Tom Beck from GER. LC 95-60234. 144p. 1996. pap. 19.95 (*1-85610-040-5*, Pub. by Forest Bks) Dufour.

Only When They're Little: The Story of an Appalachian Family. Kate P. Day. LC 85-3893. 1985. 11.95 (*0-913239-25-9*) Appalach Consortium.

Only Winning Counts: A Practical Guide to Winning Elections in Your Community. Nova Tevis. Ed. by Charlotte Orange. LC 87-63525. 71p. (C). 1988. pap. 6.95 (*0-936026-21-9*) R&M Pub Co.

***Only Wise God: The Compatibility of Divine Foreknowledge & Human Freedom.** William Lane Craig. 157p. 2000. pap. 17.00 (*1-57910-316-2*) Wipf & Stock.

Only with Marx & Jesus. Thomas M. Mongar. LC 97-8605. 1997. write for info. (*0-7618-0775-6*) U Pr of Amer.

***Only with the Heart.** Sherri Szeman. 2000. 24.95 (*1-55970-538-8*, Pub. by Arcade Pub Inc) Time Warner.

ONLY with YOUR. Lisa Kleypas. 416p. 1992. mass mkt. 6.50 (*0-380-76151-3*, Avon Bks) Morrow Avon.

Only Woman in the Room: A Memoir. Beate S. Gordon. 1998. 22.00 (*4-7700-2145-3*, Pub. by Kodansha Intl) Kodansha.

Only Word There Is. Josephine Bridges. 72p. 1999. pap. 12.00 (*0-9670716-0-7*) Mall Street.

Only Words. Catharine A. MacKinnon. LC 93-13600. 112p. 1993. text 14.95 (*0-674-63933-2*) HUP.

Only Words. Catharine A. MacKinnon. 160p. 1996. pap. 10.00 (*0-674-63934-0*) HUP.

***Only Yesterday.** Shmuel Yoseph Agnon. Tr. by Barbara Harshav. 652p. 2000. 35.00 (*0-691-00972-4*, Pub. by Princeton U Pr) Cal Prin Full Svc.

Only Yesterday. Frederick L. Allen. LC 56-13462. 320p. 1942. pap. 8.00 (*0-06-080004-6*, P4, Perennial) HarperTrade.

Only Yesterday. Ed. by Sacks. (C). 1942. pap. text 12.33 (*0-673-97651-3*) Addson-Wesley Educ.

Only Yesterday. large type ed. Syrell R. Leahy. 1991. 27.99 (*0-7089-2448-4*) Ulverscroft.

Only Yesterday: A Quiz on the Sixties. Paul Cowan. 160p. (Orig.). 1990. mass mkt. 7.95 (*0-446-39036-4*, Pub. by Warner Bks) Little.

Only Yesterday: An Informal History of the 1920s. Frederick L. Allen. LC 97-19930. (Investment Classics Ser.). 285p. 1997. 21.95 (*0-471-18952-9*) Wiley.

***Only Yesterday: An Informal History of the 1920s.** Frederick Lewis Allen. LC 00-28345. 352p. 2000. pap. 13.00 (*0-06-095665-8*, Perennial) HarperTrade.

Only Yesterday We Drained the Cup of Sorrow: American Jewish Cemeteries & History. Roberta Halporn. (Illus.). 65p. 2000. pap. 9.95 (*0-930194-22-5*) Ctr Thanatology.

***Only You.** Joye Ames. LC 99-90715. 192p. 1999. 18.95 (*0-8034-9372-X*, Avalon Bks) Bouregy.

Only You. Leigh Greenwood & Peg Sutherland. 1997. per. 3.99 (*0-373-70754-1*, 1-70754-6) Harlequin Bks.

***Only You.** Peggy Lacerra. 2001. 23.00 (*0-609-60558-5*) Harmony Bks.

Only You. Elizabeth Lowell. 384p. 1992. mass mkt. 6.99 (*0-380-76340-0*, Avon Bks) Morrow Avon.

Only You. Angela Winters. 256p. 1997. mass mkt. 4.99 (*0-7860-0352-9*, Pinncle Kensgtn) Kensgtn Pub Corp.

Only You. large type ed. Elizabeth Lowell. LC 96-31679. 1996. pap. 22.95 (*1-56895-363-1*, Compass) Wheeler Pub.

Only You. rev. ed. Timothy Mason. LC 97-208540. 1995. pap. 5.25 (*0-8222-1488-1*) Dramatists Play.

Only You: A Romantic Collection of Inspirational Novellas. Kathleen Yapp et al. 352p. 1998. pap. 4.97 (*1-57748-174-7*) Barbour Pub.

Only You - Sierra. Robin J. Gunn. LC 95-5722. (Sierra Jensen Ser.: Bk. 1). 176p. (YA). (gr. 7-11). 1998. pap. 5.99 (*1-56179-370-1*) Focus Family.

Only You Can Do It: A Personal Guide for Career Planning & Job Searching. rev. ed. Claire Musickant. (Illus.). 1993. pap. text 19.95 (*0-9639752-0-X*) CEM Pubng.

Only You Can Save Mankind. Terry Pratchett. 176p. 1994. mass mkt. 5.99 (*0-552-13926-2*) Bantam.

Only You Can Save Mankind. large type ed. Terry Pratchett. (J). 1996. 16.95 (*0-7451-4957-X*, Galaxy Child Lrg Print) Chivers N Amer.

Only Yours! Susanna My Rose. Robert G. English. 1997. pap. write for info. (*1-57553-601-3*) Watermrk Pr.

***Onlyhouse.** Teresa Toten. (Northern Lights Young Novels Ser.). 112p. (J). (gr. 5-8). 1998. pap. 7.95 (*0-88995-137-3*, Pub. by Red Deer) Genl Dist Srvs.

Onna Rashiku (Like a Woman) The Diary of a Language Learner in Japan. Karen Ogulnick. LC 97-45140. 128p. (C). 1998. text 39.50 (*0-7914-3893-7*); pap. text 12.95 (*0-7914-3894-5*) State U NY Pr.

Ono Ono Girl's Hula. Carolyn Lei-Lanilau. LC 97-7216. 196p. 1997. 34.95 (*0-299-15630-3*); pap. 17.95 (*0-299-15634-6*) U of Wis Pr.

Onomasiological Theory of English Word-Formation. Pavol Stekauer. LC 98-44713. (Studies in Functional & Structural Linguistics: Vol. 46). x, 192p. 1998. 55.00 (*1-55619-897-3*) J Benjamins Pubng Co.

Onomastica Sacra. Paul De Lagarde. x, 368p. 1966. reprint ed. write for info. (*0-318-70777-2*) G Olms Pubs.

Onomasticon Anglo-Saxonicum: A List of Anglo-Saxon Proper Names from the Time of Beda to That of King John. William G. Searle. lvii, 601p. 1969. reprint ed. 109.20 (*0-685-66512-7*, 05102259) G Olms Pubs.

Onomasticon Aristophaneum Sive Index Nominum Quae Apud Aristophanem Ieguntur. Hubert A. Holden. 172p. 1970. reprint ed. write for info. (*0-318-70942-2*) G Olms Pubs.

Onomasticon Aristophaneum Sive Index Nominum Quae Apud Aristophanem Leguntur. Hubert A. Holden. 172p. 1970. reprint ed. write for info. (*0-318-72032-9*) G Olms Pubs.

Onomasticon Goedelicum: An Index, with Identifications, to the Gaelic Names of Places & the Tribes. 2nd ed. Edmund Hogan. 712p. 2000. reprint ed. text 85.00 (*1-85182-126-0*, Pub. by Four Cts Pr) Intl Spec Bk.

Onomasticon Latinogermanicum. T. Golius. (Documenta Linguistica, Reihe II Ser.). xx, 21p. 1972. reprint ed. write for info. (*3-487-04416-1*) G Olms Pubs.

Onomasticon of the Hittite Pantheon, 2 vols. Ben H. Van Gessel. LC 97-32465. 1100p. 1997. 271.75 (*90-04-10809-2*) Brill Academic Pubs.

Onomasticon Taciteum. Philippus Fabia. (GER.). 772p. 1964. reprint ed. write for info. (*0-318-70600-8*) G Olms Pubs.

Onomasticon Tullianum, 3 vols. J. C. Orelli & J. G. Baiter. 1965. reprint ed. write for info. (*0-318-72062-0*) G Olms Pubs.

Onomasticon Tullianum, 3 vols. Johann C. Von Orelli & Johann G. Baiter. cclxii, 1598p. 1965. reprint ed. write for info. (*0-318-71189-3*) G Olms Pubs.

Onomastikon der Biblischen Ortsnamen. Eusebius Caesariensis. (GER.). xxxvi, 207p. 1986. reprint ed. 65.00 (*3-487-01172-7*) G Olms Pubs.

Onomatisches Worterbuch. Joseph Kehrein. vi, 1244p. 1974. reprint ed. write for info. (*3-487-05091-9*) G Olms Pubs.

Onomatopoetics: Theory of Language & Literature. Joseph F. Graham. (Literature, Culture, Theory Ser.: No. 4). 329p. (C). 1992. text 59.95 (*0-521-40078-3*) Cambridge U Pr.

Onondaga: Portrait of a Native People. Ed. by Dennis Connors. LC 85-27686. (Iroquois Bks.). (Illus.). 120p. (Orig.). 1986. pap. 19.95 (*0-8156-0198-0*) Syracuse U Pr.

Onondaga Iroquois Prehistory: A Study in Settlement Archaeology. James Tuck. LC 90-33089. (Iroquois & Their Neighbors Ser.). (Illus.). 256p. (C). 1990. pap. text 16.95 (*0-8156-2511-1*) Syracuse U Pr.

An Asterisk (*) at the beginning of an entry indicates that the title is appearing for the first time.

Onondaga Lake: Limnology & Environmental Management of a Polluted Urban Lake. Ed. by Steven W. Effler & R. S. DeSanto. LC 95-5933. (Springer Series on Environmental Management). (Illus.). 850p. 1996. 109.00 (0-387-94383-8) Spr-Verlag.

Onondaga, or Reminiscences of Earlier & Later Times, Being a Series of Historical Sketches Relative to Onondaga; with Notes on the Several Towns in the County, & Oswego, 2 vols. Joshua V. Clark. (Illus.). 1800p. 1997. reprint ed. lib. bdg. 82.00 (0-8328-6189-8) Higginson Bk Co.

Onondaga's Centennial: Gleanings of a Century. Dwight H. Bruce. (Illus.). 1657p. 1997. reprint ed. lib. bdg. 164.00 (0-8328-6191-X) Higginson Bk Co.

OnRamp: The Traveler's Radio & Entertainment Guide. Manufacturers Group Staff. (Western Edition Ser.). 169p. (Orig.). 1991. pap. 4.95 (1-880126-00-1); pap. 4.95 (1-880126-02-8); pap. 4.95 (1-880126-01-X) Pacif Pr.

Onregmatige Mededinging. H. J. Van Heerden & J. Neethling. (AFR.). 222p. 1983. pap. write for info. (0-409-06021-6, MICHIE) LEXIS Pub.

Onset of Industrialisation. Martin Palmer. (C). 1976. text 45.00 (0-7855-3204-8, Pub. by Univ Nottingham) St Mut.

Onset of Literacy: Cognitive Processes in Reading Acquisition. Ed. by Paul Bertelson. (Cognitive Special Issues Ser.). 192p. (Orig.). 1987. pap. text 15.00 (0-262-52125-3, Bradford Bks) MIT Pr.

Onset Review, Vol. 3, No. 1. Ed. by Susan Pizzolato & Scott Withiam. 72p. 1998. pap. 10.00 (0-9654360-1-2) Word Studio.

Onsets. Mark Dunster. 17p. (Orig.). (YA). (gr. 9-12). 1996. pap. 5.00 (0-89642-333-6) Linden Pubs.

Onshore Pooling & Unitization, Bk. 1. (Mineral Law Ser.). 800p. 1997. ring bd. 82.50 (0-929047-65-6) Rocky Mtn Mineral Law Found.

Onshore Pooling & Unitization, Bk. 2. (Mineral Law Ser.). 450p. 1997. ring bd. 82.50 (0-929047-66-4) Rocky Mtn Mineral Law Found.

Onsite Domestic Sewage Disposal Handbook. Midwest Plan Service Engineers Staff. LC 81-18994. (Illus.). 40p. (Orig.). (C). 1982. pap. 6.00 (0-89373-053-X, MWPS-24) MidWest Plan Serv.

***Onsite Drug Testing.** Ed. by Amanda J. Jenkins & Bruce A. Goldberger. 325p. 2000. 79.50 (0-89603-870-X) Humana.

Onsite Solvent Recovery. Arun R. Gavaskar et al. (Illus.). 84p. (C). 1998. reprint ed. pap. text 30.00 (0-7881-4302-6) DIANE Pub.

Onsite Wastewater Disposal. Richard J. Perkins. (Illus.). 272p. 1989. lib. bdg. 99.95 (0-87371-211-0, L211) Lewis Pubs.

Onsite Wastewater Treatment Systems. Bennette D. Burks & Mary M. Minnis. LC 94-76249. 320p. (C). 1994. pap. text 49.95 (0-9641049-0-3) Hogarth Hse.

Onslaught: Comrades in Arms, Vol. 3. Tom Defalco. (Illus.). 96p. 1997. pap. text 9.95 (0-7851-0282-5) Marvel Entrprs.

Onslaught: Eye of the Storm, Vol. 4. Peter David. (Illus.). 96p. 1997. pap. text 9.95 (0-7851-0283-3) Marvel Entrprs.

Onslaught: Pyarmic Victory, Vol. 6. Scott Lobdell. (Illus.). 144p. 1997. pap. text 12.95 (0-7851-0285-X) Marvel Entrprs.

Onslaught: The Awakening, Vol. 1. Scott Lobdell. (Illus.). 144p. 1997. pap. text 12.95 (0-7851-0280-9) Marvel Entrprs.

Onslaught: The Front Line, Vol. 5. John Ostrander. (Illus.). 112p. 1997. pap. text 9.95 (0-7851-0284-1) Marvel Entrprs.

Onslaught: To the Victor..., Vol. 2. Terry Kavanagh. (Illus.). 96p. 1997. pap. text 9.95 (0-7851-0281-7) Marvel Entrprs.

***Onslaughts: Poems from Hollywood.** Mark Dunster. 11p. 1999. pap. 5.00 (0-89642-963-6) Linden Pubs.

Onslow County: A Brief History. Alan D. Watson. (Illus.). 184p. (Orig.). 1995. pap. 10.00 (0-86526-263-2) NC Archives.

Onstage! Nancy Zelenak & C. Michael Perry. 67p. (Orig.). (YA). (gr. 7-12). 1993. pap. 5.00 (1-57514-118-3, 0062) Encore Perform Pub.

Onstage & Backstage: At the Night Owl Theater. Ann Hayes. LC 96-19934. (Illus.). 32p. (J). (ps-3). 1997. 15.00 (0-15-200782-2) Harcourt.

Onstage & Offstage. Jean G. Edades. (Illus.). 1983. pap. 12.50 (971-10-0051-2, Pub. by New Day Pub) Cellar.

Onstage & Offstage Worlds in Shakespeare's Plays. Anthony Brennan. 352p. 1989. 32.50 (0-685-26089-5, A3529) Routledge.

Onstage Christ: Studies in the Persistence of a Theme. John Ditsky. (Critical Studies). 188p. 1980. 44.00 (0-389-20059-X, N6829) B&N Imports.

Onstage with Grieg: Interpreting His Piano Music. Einar Steen-Nkleberg. LC 96-34512. 448p. 1997. 49.95 (0-253-33248-6) Ind U Pr.

***Ontario.** (Canada in the Twenty First Century Ser.). (Illus.). (J). 2000. 18.95 (0-7910-6068-3) Chelsea Hse.

***Ontario.** Michael Barnes. (Hello Canada Ser.). 1999. pap. 7.95 (1-55041-270-1) Fitzhenry & W Ltd.

Ontario. Michael Barnes. LC 94-20253. (Hello Canada Ser.). (Illus.). 76p. (J). (gr. 4-7). 1995, lib. bdg. 19.95 (0-8225-2754-5, Lerner Publctns) Lerner Pub.

Ontario. Michael Barnes. (Hello Canada Ser.). (Illus.). (J). (gr. 3-6). 1997. pap. 6.95 (0-8225-9801-9) Lerner Pub.

Ontario. Harry Beckett. LC 97-2214. (Journey Across Canada Ser.). 24p. (J). (gr. 3-5). 1997. lib. bdg. 18.60 (1-55916-198-1) Rourke Bk Co.

Ontario. Tanya Lloyd. LC 96-910740. (Illus.). 96p. 17.95 (1-55110-523-3) Whitecap Bks.

Ontario: An Illustrated History. Michael Rounds. LC 97-78256. (Illus.). 1999. 39.95 (1-886483-16-7) Heritge Media.

Ontario: Ulysses Travel Guide. Pascale Couture. Ed. by Ulysses Travel Guide Staff. (Ulysses Travel Guide Ser.). (Illus.). 1999. 19.95 (2-89464-171-2) Ulysses Travel.

Ontario & Quebec with Via Rail. Ed. by Ulysses Travel Guide Staff. (Travel Guides Ser.). (Illus.). 128p. 1998. pap. 7.95 (2-89464-158-3) Ulysses Travel.

Ontario Birds. Chris Fisher & G. Ross. LC 96-205350. (Illus.). 164p. 1996. pap. 14.95 (1-55105-069-2) Lone Pine.

***Ontario Birds.** James Kavanagh. (Pocket Naturalist Ser.). (Illus.). 1999. 5.95 (1-58355-027-5, Pub. by Waterford WA) Falcon Pub Inc.

Ontario Blue-Ribbon Fly Fishing Guide. Scott E. Smith. (Illus.). 94p. 1999. pap. 24.95 (1-57188-162-X) F Amato Pubns.

Ontario Business Corporations Act. annot. ed. Janet Ames & Margot Lettner. 328p. 1990. text 67.00 (0-409-80911-X, MICHIE) LEXIS Pub.

Ontario Business Directory, 1999. American Business Directories Staff. 3856p. 1999. boxed set 595.00 incl. cd-rom (0-7687-0182-1, 1203-5246) Am Busn Direct.

***Ontario Business Directory (2000)** American Business Directories Staff et al. 3,856p. 2000. boxed set 595.00 incl. cd-rom (0-7687-0269-0) Am Busn Direct.

Ontario County: Golden Era of Railroad. Timothy David Munn. (Images of America Ser.). (Illus.). 128p. 1998. pap. 18.99 (0-7524-1222-1) Arcadia Publng.

Ontario County: Pictorial Reflections in the Finger Lakes Region, Vol. 1. Valerie Knoblauch. LC 89-60487. 270p. 1989. 35.00 (0-9622037-0-X) OCFSDC.

Ontario County New York State, 1800 Federal Population Census Schedule, Transcript & Index. Ed. by Ralph V. Wood, Jr. LC 63-52558. (Illus.). vi, 59p. 1963. pap. 3.25 (0-915184-01-X) R V Wood.

Ontario County, New York State, 1810: Federal Population Census Schedule, Transcript & Index. Ed. by Ralph V. Wood, Jr. LC 65-4110. (Illus.). vi, 162p. 1964. pap. 7.25 (0-915184-03-6) R V Wood.

Ontario Estate Administration: A Guide for Legal Secretaries & Law Clerks. 2nd ed. Rintoul. 184p. 1991. spiral bd. 44.00 (0-409-90377-9, MICHIE) LEXIS Pub.

***Ontario Fact Book: Everything You Ever Wanted to Know about Ontario.** Mark Kearney & Randy Ray. (Illus.). 272p. 2000. pap. text 14.95 (1-55285-020-X) Carlton Bks Ltd.

Ontario Family Law Act & Related Statutes: 1994 Consolidation. Butterworth Staff. 858p. 1994. pap. 65.00 (0-433-39137-5, CN, MICHIE) LEXIS Pub.

Ontario for Theatre Lovers: A Theatre - Dining - Lodging Guide to Toronto, Niagara-on-the-Lake, & Stratford. Sharon Watson. LC 94-70729. (Illus.). 320p. (Orig.). 1994. pap. 14.95 (1-882310-01-2) Britain Bks.

Ontario Francais du Sud-Quest: Temoignages Oraux. Andre Lapierre. LC 82-226547. (Cahiers du Centre de Recherche en Civilisation Canadienne-Francaise: Vol. 20). (FRE.). 659p. 1982. reprint ed. pap. 200.00 (0-608-01987-9, 206264300003) Bks Demand.

***Ontario Ghost Stories.** Barbara Smith. (Illus.). 240p. 1998. pap. 11.95 (1-55105-203-2) Lone Pine.

Ontario Hydro at the Millennium: Has Monopoly's Moment Passed? Ed. by Ronald J. Daniels. 409p. 1996. 22.95 (0-7735-1430-9, HD9685, Pub. by McG-Queens Univ Pr); 65.00 (0-7735-1426-0, Pub. by McG-Queens Univ Pr) CUP Services.

Ontario Insurance Act & Regulations. 432p. 1990. pap. 25.00 (0-409-89815-5, MICHIE) LEXIS Pub.

Ontario Lawyers Weekly Bound, Vol. 3. 1984. 98.00 (0-409-80959-4, MICHIE) LEXIS Pub.

Ontario Lawyers Weekly Bound, Vol. 4. 1985. 98.00 (0-409-80960-8, MICHIE) LEXIS Pub.

Ontario Legal Directory, 1999. annuals Ed. by Barry Meikle. (Toronto Legal Directory Ser.). 1000p. 1999. 48.00 (0-8020-4929-X); write for info. (0-8020-4930-3) U of Toronto Pr.

Ontario Legal Directory 1998. Elizabeth Lumley. 950p. 1998. pap. text 48.00 (0-8020-4911-7) U of Toronto Pr.

Ontario Legislature: A Political Analysis. Graham White. 316p. 1989. pap. 20.95 (0-8020-6730-1); text 42.50 (0-8020-5817-5) U of Toronto Pr.

Ontario Loyalist Ancestors. Lindsay S. Reeks. LC 92-73836. (Illus.). 235p. 1992. 30.00 (0-9616950-2-1) L S Reeks.

Ontario Marriage Notices (1830-1856) Thomas B. Wilson. 435p. 1997. reprint ed. pap. 36.50 (0-8063-4683-3) Clearfield Co.

Ontario People, 1796-1803. E. Keith Fitzgerald. (Illus.). 261p. 1998. 25.00 (0-8063-1366-8, 1855) Genealog Pub.

Ontario Place Names. 2nd ed. Ed. by David E. Scott. (Illus.). 256p. 1997. pap. 11.95 (1-55105-087-0) Lone Pine.

Ontario Prehistory: An Eleven-Thousand-Year Archaeological Outline. J. V. Wright. (Canadian Prehistory Ser.). (Illus.). 132p. 1972. pap. 16.95 (0-660-00065-2, Pub. by CN Mus Civilization) U of Wash Pr.

Ontario Retirement Handbook: A Comprehensive Guide to Services & Programs for Retirees. Andrew Dagys. 208p. 1996. pap. 15.00 (1-55022-289-9, Pub. by ECW) Genl Dist Srvs.

Ontario, Uxbridge, Life & Times of Joseph Gould: Reminiscences of Sixty Years of Active Political & Municipal Life. W. H. Higgins. (Illus.). 304p. 1995. reprint ed. pap. 27.50 (0-8328-4608-2); reprint ed. lib. bdg. 37.50 (0-8328-4607-4) Higginson Bk Co.

***Ontario Wildlife.** James Kavanagh. (Pocket Naturalist Ser.). (Illus.). 1999. 5.95 (1-58355-028-3, Pub. by Waterford WA) Falcon Pub Inc.

Ontario's Amazing Museums. Julia Pine. (Illus.). 290p. 1994. pap. 14.95 (1-55022-208-2, Pub. by ECW) Genl Dist Srvs.

***Ontario's Best Hotels & Restaurants.** Pascale Couture. 2000. pap. 12.95 (2-89464-303-9, Pub. by Ulysses Travel) Globe Pequot.

***Ontario's Bike Paths & Railtrails.** John Lynes. 2000. pap. 14.95 (2-89464-263-6, Pub. by Ulysses Travel) Globe Pequot.

Ontario's Educative Society, 6 vols., Vol. 1. W. G. Fleming. LC 77-166928. 396p. reprint ed. pap. 122.80 (0-8357-3968-6, 203575400001) Bks Demand.

Ontario's Educative Society, 6 vols., Vol. 2. W. G. Fleming. LC 77-166928. 579p. reprint ed. pap. 179.50 (0-8357-3969-4, 203575400002) Bks Demand.

Ontario's Educative Society, 6 vols., Vol. 3. W. G. Fleming. LC 77-166928. 636p. reprint ed. pap. 197.20 (0-8357-3970-8, 203575400003) Bks Demand.

Ontario's Educative Society, 6 vols., Vol. 4. W. G. Fleming. LC 77-166928. 785p. reprint ed. pap. 200.00 (0-8357-3971-6, 203575400004) Bks Demand.

Ontario's Educative Society, 6 vols., Vol. 5. W. G. Fleming. LC 77-166928. 320p. reprint ed. pap. 99.20 (0-8357-3972-4, 203575400005) Bks Demand.

Ontario's Educative Society, 6 vols., Vol. 6. W. G. Fleming. LC 77-166928. 559p. reprint ed. pap. 173.30 (0-8357-3973-2, 203575400006) Bks Demand.

Ontario's Heritage Quilts. Marilyn Walker. Ed. by Noel Hudson. (Illus.). 155p. 1992. 50.00 (1-55046-066-8, Pub. by Boston Mills) Genl Dist Srvs.

Ontario's Secret Landscape. Ron Brown. (Illus.). 168p. 1999. pap. 13.95 (1-55046-298-9, Pub. by Boston Mills) Genl Dist Srvs.

***Ontario's Wildlife.** J. David Taylor. Ed. by Noel Hudson. (Illus.). 96p. (Orig.). 1998. pap. 15.00 (0-919783-85-6, Pub. by Boston Mills) Genl Dist Srvs.

Onthebus Issue No. 15/16: A Literary Anthology Double. Ed. by Jack Grapes. pap. 15.00 (0-941017-11-7) Bombshelter Pr.

Ontic: A Knowledge Representation System for Mathematics. David F. McAllister. (Artificial Intelligence Ser.). 174p. 1989. 27.50 (0-262-13235-4) MIT Pr.

Onto the Future. Marsha Daly. pap. 2.95 (0-317-39728-1) St Martin.

Onto the Yellow School Bus & Through the Gates of Hell. Mary Hood. 202p. (Orig.). 1995. pap. 10.95 (0-9639740-3-3) Ambleside Educ.

Ontogenesis of Perception. Ed. by William Epstein. (Special Issue, Journal of Experimental Psychology: Human Perception & Performance Ser.: Vol. 13, No. 4). 107p. 1987. pap. 16.00 (1-55798-008-X) Am Psychol.

Ontogeny & Phylogeny. Stephen Jay Gould. 640p. 1985. pap. text 18.95 (0-674-63941-3) Belknap Pr.

Ontogeny & Phylogeny of Hormone Receptors. G. Csaba. (Monographs in Developmental Biology: Vol. 15). (Illus.). xii, 172p. 1981. 125.25 (3-8055-2174-X) S Karger.

Ontogeny & Sexual Dimorphism of Lower Paleozoic Trilobita see Palaeontographica Americana: Vol. 7

Ontogeny & Systematics. Ed. by Christopher J. Humphries. (Illus.). 288p. 1988. text 68.00 (0-231-06370-9) Col U Pr.

Ontogeny, Cell Differentiation & Structure of Vascular Plants. R. Buvat. (Illus.). 600p. 1989. 281.95 (0-387-19213-1) Spr-Verlag.

***Ontogeny, Functional Ecology & Evolution of Bats.** Rick A. Adams & Scott C. Pedersen. LC 99-57156. 2000. write for info. (0-521-62632-3) Cambridge U Pr.

Ontogeny of Acquired Immunity. CIBA Foundation Staff. LC 72-81001. (CIBA Foundation Symposium: New Ser.: No. 5). 293p. reprint ed. pap. 90.90 (0-608-13513-5, 202213700024) Bks Demand.

Ontogeny of Bonding Attachment. Ed. by P. O. Hubinont. (Progress in Reproductive Biology & Medicine Ser.: Vol. 11). (Illus.). vi, 178p. 1984. 126.25 (3-8055-3862-6) S Karger.

Ontogeny of Communication in the Stumptail Macaque. Suzanne Chevalier-Skolinikoff. (Contributions to Primatology Ser.: Vol. 2). (Illus.). 174p. 1974. 64.50 (3-8055-1647-9) S Karger.

Ontogeny of Creativity. Stanley A. Kuczaj, II & Virginia Kirkpatrick. 224p. 1996. pap. text. write for info. (0-697-15174-3) Brown & Benchmark.

Ontogeny of Immunity. Developmental Immunology Workshop Staff. Ed. by Richard R. Smith et al. LC 66-29457. (Illus.). 222p. reprint ed. pap. 68.90 (0-7837-5003-X, 204467000004) Bks Demand.

***Ontogeny of Information: Developmental Systems & Evolution.** 2nd rev. enl. ed. Susan Oyama. LC 99-34735. (Science & Cultural Theory Ser.). 280p. 2000. pap. text 19.95 (0-8223-2466-0) Duke.

Ontogeny of Receptors & Reproductive Hormone Action. fac. ed. Ed. by Terrell H. Hamilton et al. LC 77-92523. (Illus.). 471p. pap. 146.10 (0-7837-7549-0, 204715800005) Bks Demand.

Ontogeny of the Immune System of the Gut. Thomas T. MacDonald. 128p. 1990. lib. bdg. 142.00 (0-8493-6084-6, QR185) CRC Pr.

Ontogeny of Transmitters & Peptides in the CNS. Anders T. Bjorklund et al. (Handbook of Chemical Neuroanatomy Ser.: Vol. 10). xxii,664p. 1992. 346.00 (0-444-89283-4) Elsevier.

Ontogeny, Phyogeny, & Historical Development. Ed. by Sidney Strauss. LC 87-11481. (Human Development Ser.: Vol. 2). 184p. (C). 1988. text 73.25 (0-89391-384-7) Ablx Pub.

Ontologia de Unamuno. Esteban Tollinchi. LC 77-2955. (Coleccion Mente y Palabra). (SPA.). 239p. 1978. 5.00 (0-8477-0548-X); pap. 4.00 (0-8477-0549-8) U of PR Pr.

Ontological Analysis: The Classical Model. A. Zvie Bar-on. 244p. (C). Date not set. lib. bdg. 42.50 (0-7618-0029-8) U Pr of Amer.

Ontological Argument of Charles Hartshorne. George L. Goodwin. LC 78-2821. (American Academy of Religion. Dissertation Ser.: No. 20). 153p. reprint ed. pap. 47.50 (0-7837-5472-8, 204523700005) Bks Demand.

Ontological Arguments & Belief in God. Graham Oppy. LC 95-6458. 396p. (C). 1996. text 74.95 (0-521-48120-1) Cambridge U Pr.

Ontological Economy: Substitutional Quantification & Mathematics. Dale Gottlieb. (Clarendon Library of Logic & Philosophy). (Illus.). 174p. 1980. 42.00 (0-19-824420-7) OUP.

Ontological Engineering: Papers from the 1997 Symposium. Ed. by Adam Farquhar & Michael Gruninger. (AAAI Technical Reports). (Illus.). 196p. 1997. spiral bd. 25.00 (1-57735-042-1) AAAI Pr.

Ontological Investigations: An Enquiry into the Categories of Nature, Man, & Society. Ingvar Johannson. 368p. 1989. 57.50 (0-415-02588-5) Routledge.

Ontological Relativity & Other Essays. Willard V. Quine. LC 72-91121. (John Dewey Lectures: No. 1). 1977. pap. text 19.50 (0-231-08357-2) Col U Pr.

Ontological Turn: Studies in the Philosophy of Gustav Bergmann. Moltke S. Gram & E. D. Klemke. LC 73-78442. 324p. reprint ed. pap. 100.50 (0-608-15053-3, 202594000047) Bks Demand.

Ontologically Controlled Autonomous Systems: Principles, Operations, & Architecture. George A. Fodor. LC 97-37935. 245p. 1997. text 155.00 (0-7923-8035-5) Kluwer Academic.

Ontologies & Databases. Athman Bouguettaya. LC 98-49398. 1999. write for info. (0-7923-8412-1) Kluwer Academic.

Ontologischen Grundlagen der Freiheitstheorie von Leibniz. Christos Axelos. LC 72-81544. 385p. (C). 1973. 76.15 (3-11-002221-4) De Gruyter.

Ontology. Peter Coffey. 1990. 16.50 (0-8446-1119-0) Peter Smith.

Ontology: The Hermeneutics of Facticity. Martin Heidegger. Tr. by John Van Buren from GER. LC 98-54763. (Studies in Continental Thought). 112p. 1999. text 24.95 (0-253-33507-8) Ind U Pr.

Ontology & Alterity in Merleau-Ponty. Ed. by Galen A. Johnson & Michael B. Smith. (Studies in Phenomenology & Existential Philosophy). 206p. (Orig.). 1990. 49.95 (0-8101-0872-0); pap. 19.95 (0-8101-0873-9) Northwestern U Pr.

Ontology & the Logistic Analysis of Language: An Inquiry into the Contemporary Views on Universals. rev. ed. Guido Kung. Tr. by E. C. Mays from GER. (Synthese Library: No. 13). 221p. 1974. text 96.00 (90-277-0028-1, D Reidel) Kluwer Academic.

Ontology & the Practical Arena. Douglas Browning. LC 89-8369. 180p. 1990. lib. bdg. 35.00 (0-271-00677-3) Pa St U Pr.

Ontology, Causality, & Mind: Essays in Honor of D.M. Armstrong. Ed. by John Bacon et al. LC 92-469. (Illus.). 313p. (C). 1993. text 80.00 (0-521-41562-4) Cambridge U Pr.

***Ontology Management: Papers from the AAAI Workshop.** Ed. by Adam Farquhar & Kilian Stoffel. (Technical Reports: Vol. WS-99-13). (Illus.). 86p. 1999. spiral bd. 25.00 (1-57735-097-9) AAAI Pr.

Ontology of Consciousness. R. Ellis. 214p. (C). 1986. text 111.00 (90-247-3349-9) Kluwer Academic.

Ontology of Construction: On Nihilism of Technology & Theories of Modern Architecture. Gevork Hartoonian & Kenneth Frampton. (Illus.). 192p. 1997. pap. text 18.95 (0-521-58645-3) Cambridge U Pr.

***Ontology of Cyberspace: Law, Philosophy & the Future of Intellectual Property.** David R. Koepsell. 2000. 26.95 (0-8126-9423-6) Open Court.

Ontology of Georg Lukacs: Studies in Materalist Dialectics. Fariborz Shafai. (Avebury Series in Philosophy). 208p. 1996. text 62.95 (1-85972-422-1, Pub. by Avebry) Ashgate Pub Co.

***Ontology of Language: Properties, Individuals & Discourse.** rev. ed. Chris Fox. (Lecture Notes Ser.: No. 105). 192p. (C). 2000. pap. text 22.95 (1-57586-234-4, Pub. by CSLI) Cambridge U Pr.

Ontology of Mind: Events, Processes, & States. Helen Steward. LC 96-52313. (Oxford Philosophical Monographs). 284p. 1997. text 68.00 (0-19-824098-8) OUP.

***Ontology of Mind: Events, Processes, & States.** Helen Steward. LC 96-52313. (Philosophical Monographs). 288p. 2000. pap. 19.95 (0-19-825064-9) OUP.

Ontology of Physical Objects: Four Dimensional Hunks of Matter. Mark Heller. (Studies in Philosophy). 176p. (C). 1990. text 64.95 (0-521-38544-X) Cambridge U Pr.

Ontology of Science. Ed. by John Worrall. (International Research Library of Philosophy). 516p. 1994. 179.95 (1-85521-494-6) Ashgate Pub Co.

Ontology of Social Being Vol. 1: Hegel. Georg Lukacs. (C). 1982. pap. write for info. (0-85036-226-1, Pub. by MRLN) Paul & Co Pubs.

Ontology of Social Being Vol. 2: Marx, Vol. 2. Georg Lukacs. (C). 1982. pap. write for info. (0-85036-227-X, Pub. by MRLN) Paul & Co Pubs.

Ontology of Social Being Vol. 3: Labour, Vol. 3. Georg Lukacs. (C). 1980. pap. write for info. (0-85036-255-5, Pub. by MRLN) Paul & Co Pubs.

Ontology of Socialism. Jadwiga Staniszkis. Tr. by Peggy Watson. (Illus.). 368p. 1992. text 75.00 (0-19-827598-6) OUP.

Ontology of the Analytic Tradition & Its Origins: Realism, Possibility, & Identity in Frege, Russell, Wittgenstein, & Quine. Jan Dejnozka. LC 95-39426. 1996. pap. text 26.95 (0-8226-3053-2) Littlefield.

O

An Asterisk (*) at the beginning of an entry indicates that the title is appearing for the first time.

Ontology of the Anayltic Tradition & Its Origins: Realism, Possibility, & Identity in Frege, Russell, Wittgenstein, & Quine. Jan Dejnozka. LC 95-39426. 1996. lib. bdg. 69.50 (*0-8226-3052-4*) Littlefield.

Ontology of the Middle Way. Peter Fenner. 352p. (C). 1990. lib. bdg. 236.50 (*0-7923-0667-8*, Pub. by Kluwer Academic) Kluwer Academic.

Ontology of the Narrative. Robert Champigny. (De Proprietatibus Litterarum, Ser. Minor: No. 12). 1972. pap. text 22.35 (*90-279-2366-3*) Mouton.

Ontology of the Work of Art: The Musical Work-The Picture-Architect. Roman Ingarden. Tr. by Raymond Meyer. LC 88-22434. (Series in Continental Thought : Vol. 12). 358p. 1989. text 55.00 (*0-8214-0555-1*) Ohio U Pr.

Ontotherapy Handbook: A Philosophical Approach to Mental Health & Self-Improvement. Marvin C. Sterling. Orig. Title: How to Overcome Fear. iv, 195p. 1996. 18.95 (*0-9658614-1-4*, Cope Pub); pap. 13.95 (*0-9658614-0-6*, Cope Pub) COPE.

OnTrak for Sales Assistants. LC 92-36821. 612p. 1994. pap. 49.00 (*0-7931-0596-X*, 3921-0102) Dearborn.

Onward: Contemporary Poetry & Poetics. Ed. by Peter Baker. X, 439p. (C). 1996. pap. text 29.95 (*0-8204-3032-3*) P Lang Pubng.

*__Onward! 25 Years of Advice, Exhortation & Inspiration from America's Best Commencement Speeches.__ Peter J. Smith. 304p. 2000. 25.50 (*0-684-86452-5*) Scribner.

Onward & Upward: Extracts from the Magazine of the Onward & Upward Association Founded by Lady Aberdeen for the Material, Mental & Moral Elevation of Women. Ed. by J. Drummond. 1983. pap. text 3.80 (*0-08-030354-4*, Pergamon Pr) Elsevier.

Onward & Upward in the Garden. Katharine S. White. Ed. & Intro. by E. B. White. LC 96-46922. 6939p. 1997. pap. 13.00 (*0-86547-505-9*) N Point Pr.

Onward & Upward in the Garden. Katharine S. White. 1979. 24.50 (*0-8446-6924-5*) Peter Smith.

Onward & Upward Ourselves. L. D. Beckwith. 181p. 1986. 12.95 (*0-317-68201-6*) L D Beckwith.

Onward Boy Soldiers: The Battle for Milne Bay, 1942. James Henderson. pap. 9.95 (*1-875560-15-7*, Pub. by Univ of West Aust Pr) Intl Spec Bk.

*__Onward Christian Soldiers.__ 2nd ed. Clyde Wilcox. (Dilemmas in American Politics Ser.). 212p. 2000. pap. 19.00 (*0-8133-9759-6*) Westview.

Onward Christian Soldiers: Protestants Affirm the Church. John MacArthur et al. 309p. 1999. pap. 16.95 (*1-57358-102-X*) Soli Deo Gloria.

Onward Christian Soldiers? The Religious Right in American Politics. Clyde Wilcox. LC 96-22561. (Dilemmas in American Politics Ser.). 192p. (C). 1996. pap. text 19.00 (*0-8133-2697-4*, Pub. by Westview) HarpC.

Onward, Christians! Protestants in the Philippine Revolution. Richard L. Schwenk. (Illus.). xiii, 102p. (Orig.). 1986. pap. 8.75 (*971-10-0305-8*, Pub. by New Day Pub) Cellar.

Onward Peregrinos. Myrna Ericksen. LC 97-91068. (Illus.). x, 313p. 1998. pap. 12.95 (*0-9660720-0-6*) Showcase Pubs.

Onward! Through the Fog! Six Dialogues Following the Example of Christ Through Lent. Elizabeth Morris-Pierce. LC 98-44906. 88p. 1999. pap. 8.50 (*0-7880-1310-6*) CSS OH.

Onward to Victory: The Creation of Modern College Sports. Murray Sperber. LC 98-17436. (Illus.). 608p. 1998. text 32.50 (*0-8050-3865-5*) St Martin.

Onward Two Thousand & Beyond: Concepts for Changes. Horace G. Dickerson. (Energy, Transportation, Environment Ser.). 168p. 1991. 27.95 (*0-9631966-1-8*); pap. 22.95 (*0-9631966-4-2*); text 25.95 (*0-9631966-3-4*); pap. text 17.95 (*0-9631966-5-0*); lib. bdg. 37.95 (*0-9631966-2-6*) Univ Pr.

Onychomycoses. Ed. by S. Nolting & H. C. Korting. (Illus.). x, 126p. 1990. 29.95 (*0-387-52132-1*) Spr-Verlag.

*__Onychomycosis: The Current Approach to Diagnosis & Therapy.__ Robert Baran. 74p. 1999. 49.95 (*1-85317-767-9*, Pub. by Martin Dunitz) Blackwell Sci.

Onyourown.Com: E-mail Messages to My Daughter. Bruce Bickel & Stan Jantz. LC 99-211207. 254p. 1999. 12.99 (*1-57748-488-6*) Barbour Pub.

Onyx. large type ed. Jacqueline Briskin. LC 94-31285. 739p. 1995. 24.95 (*0-7838-1133-0*, G K Hall Lrg Type) Mac Lib Ref.

Onza! The Hunt for a Legendary Cat. Neil B. Carmony. LC 95-75822. (Illus.). 208p. 1995. 20.00 (*0-944383-29-7*); pap. 12.95 (*0-944383-28-9*) High-Lonesome.

Onze Etudes sur la Poesie Moderne. J. P. Richard. (FRE.). 1981. pap. 18.95 (*0-7859-2686-0*) Fr & Eur.

Onze Mille Verges: The Amorous Adventures of Prince Mony Vibescu. Guillaume Apollinaire. Tr. by Nina Rootes. 127p. 1992. pap. 17.95 (*0-7206-0735-3*, Pub. by P Owen Ltd) Dufour.

Onzieme Reunion du Sous-Comite Ouest & Centre Africain de Correlation des Sols pour la Mise en Valeur des Terres, Segou, Mali, 1993. (FRE.). 243p. 1994. 30.00 (*92-5-203583-4*, Pub. by FAO) Bernan Associates.

*__Oo.__ Mary Elizabeth Salzmann. LC 00-33206. (Long Vowels Ser.). (Illus.). (J). 2000. write for info. (*1-57765-416-1*) ABDO Pub Co.

Oo-Mah-Ha Ta-Wa-Tha: Omaha City. Fannie R. Giffen. (Modern Reprint Ser.). (Illus.). 94p. 1998. reprint ed. pap. 11.95 (*0-9649315-0-8*) River Junction.

Oobleck: What Do Scientists Do? rev. ed. Cary Sneider. Ed. by Lincoln Bergman & Kay Fairwell. (Great Explorations in Math & Science (GEMS) Ser.). (Illus.). 40p. (J). (gr. 4-8). 1998. pap. 10.50 (*0-924886-09-9*, GEMS) Lawrence Science.

Oocyte Growth & Maturation. T. A. Dettlaff & S. G. Vassetzky. LC 88-3966. (Illus.). 464p. (C). 1988. text 135.00 (*0-306-11013-X*, Kluwer Plenum) Kluwer Academic.

Oodgeroo. Kathie Cochrane. LC 94-233470. 1994. pap. 16.95 (*0-7022-2621-1*, Pub. by Univ Queensland Pr) Intl Spec Bk.

Oodgeroo: A Tribute. Adam Shoemaker. (Australian Literary Studies: Vol. 16, No. 4). 1994. pap. 14.95 (*0-7022-2800-1*, Pub. by Univ Queensland Pr) Intl Spec Bk.

O'odham, Indians of the Sonoran Desert. Ed. by Susan L. Shaffer. (Native Peoples of the Southwest Ser.: Level 5). (Illus.). 1987. student ed. 4.95 (*0-934351-30-9*); teacher ed., ring bd. 197.95 (*0-934351-25-2*) Heard Mus.

O'odham, Indians of the Sonoran Desert, Set. Ed. by Susan L. Shaffer. (Native Peoples of the Southwest Ser.: Level 5). (Illus.). 1987. teacher ed., student ed. 294.43 incl. sl. (*0-934351-14-7*) Heard Mus.

Oodles of Doodles for Hanukkah: A Color, Activity, Sticker Book. Reudor. (Illus.). 35p. (Orig.). (J). (ps up). 1996. pap. 4.95 (*1-886611-08-4*) Atara Publ.

Oodles of Doodles for Passover: A Color, Activity, Sticker Book. Reudor. (Reudor's the Doodle Family Ser.). (Illus.). 34p. (J). (ps-6). 1997. pap. 4.95 (*1-886611-06-8*) Atara Publ.

Oodles of Fun While You Wait. Ed. by Pamela A. Klawitter. LC 95-76635. (Illus.). 128p. (J). (gr. k-6). 1995. pap. 8.95 (*0-88160-232-9*, LW327) Learning Wks.

Oodles of Noodles. Home Library Editors. (Cole's Home Library Cookbooks). (Illus.). 118p. 1999. pap. 11.95 (*1-56426-151-4*, Pub. by Cole Group) ACCESS Pubs Network.

Oodles of Writing Activities. Linda Milliken. 72p. 1992. pap. 7.95 (*1-56472-002-0*) Edupress Inc.

OOER '95: Object-Oriented & Entity-Relationship Modelling: Proceedings, 14th International Conference, Gold Coast, Australia, December 13-15, 1995. Ed. by Michael P. Papazoglou. LC 95-49513. (Lecture Notes in Computer Science Ser.: No. 1021). 451p. 1995. pap. 75.00 (*3-540-60672-6*) Spr-Verlag.

Ooey. E. Farber & J. Sansevere. LC 97-40962. (ps-4). 1998. pap. 3.99 (*0-679-88991-4*, Pub. by Random Bks Yng Read) Random.

*__Ooey Gooey.__ Erica Farber. (Step into Reading Ser.: A Step 1 Book). (J). (ps-1). 1998. 9.19 (*0-606-13966-4*, Pub. by Turtleback) Demco.

Oogenesis, Spermatogenesis & Reproduction. Ed. by R. K. Kinne. (Comparative Physiology Ser.: Vol. 10). (Illus.). x, 222p. 1991. 195.75 (*3-8055-5281-5*) S Karger.

Ooh Aah Paul McGrath: The Black Pearl of Inchicore. Paul McGrath & Cathal Dervan. (Illus.). 237p. 1995. 29.95 (*1-85158-647-4*, Pub. by Mainstream Pubng) Trafalgar.

OOH Activities Teacher's Guide. (OOH Activities Ser.). 24p. 1996. pap. 18.95 (*1-878172-69-7*, 397OOHTG, Wintergreen-Orchard) Riverside Pub Co.

Ooh Ahh Paul McGrath: The Black Pearl of Inchicore. Paul McGrath. (Illus.). 208p. 1994. pap. write for info. (*1-85158-648-2*) Trafalgar.

Ooh Baby Baby. Roberta Batista. 301p. 2000. pap. write for info. (*1-888097-02-7*) Wrd Is Bond.

Ooh Baby, Baby. Diana Whitney. Vol. 3. 1997. per. 4.50 (*0-373-65008-6*, 1-65008-4) Harlequin Bks.

Ooh la la (Max in Love) Maira Kalman. LC 91-50209. (Illus.). (J). (gr. 2 up). 1991. 16.99 (*0-670-84163-3*, Viking Child) Peng Put Young Read.

OOIS '98: 1998 International Conference on Object Oriented Information Systems, 9-11 September 1998, Paris: Proceedings. International Conference on Object Oriented Information Systems Staff et al. LC 98-219182. 496 p. 1998. 99.00 (*1-85233-046-5*) Spr-Verlag.

OOIS '95: 1995 International Conference on Object Oriented Information Systems, 18-20 December 1995, Dublin: Proceedings. Ed. by John Murphy & Brian Stone. 366p. 1995. pap. 75.00 (*3-540-76010-5*) Spr-Verlag.

OOIS '96 Vol. XVII: 1996 International Conference on Object Oriented Information Systems, 16-18 December 1996. Ed. by D. Patel et al. LC 96-37812. (Illus.). 515p. 1997. pap. 79.95 (*3-540-76132-2*) Spr-Verlag.

OOIS'97: 1997 International Conference on Object Oriented Information Systems, Brisbane, 10-12 November 1997. Ed. by M. E. Orlowska & Roberto Zicari. LC 97-35571. xxiv, 520p. 1997. pap. 89.95 (*3-540-76170-5*) Spr-Verlag.

*__Ook the Book.__ Lissa Rovetch & Shannon McNeill. LC 00-8942. 2001. pap. write for info. (*0-8118-2660-0*) Chronicle Bks.

Ooka the Wise: Tales of Old Japan. I. G. Edmonds. LC 93-33410. (Illus.). 96p. (J). (gr. 3 up). 1994. reprint ed. lib. bdg. 16.00 (*0-208-02379-8*, Linnet Bks) Shoe String.

*__Oolesterol.__ A. Geisser-Roever. 1999. pap. text 6.95 (*84-270-2317-0*) Planeta.

Oona: Living in the Shadows: A Biography of Oona O'Neil Chaplin. Jane Scovell. (Illus.). 368p. 1999. mass mkt. 14.99 (*0-446-67541-5*, Pub. by Warner Bks) Little.

Oona: Living in the Shadows: A Biography of Oona O'Neill Chaplin. Jane Scovell. LC 98-21592. (Illus.). 357p. 1998. 25.00 (*0-446-51730-5*, Pub. by Warner Bks) Little.

*__Oonawassee Summer: Something is Lurking Beneath the Surface...__ Melissa Forney. (Illus.). 126p. (J). (gr. 4-8). 2000. pap. 14.95 (*1-928961-04-5*) Barker Creek.

Oonga Boonga. Frieda Wishinsky. LC 98-27477. (Illus.). 32p. (J). (ps-1). 1999. 15.99 (*0-525-46095-0*, Dutton Child) Peng Put Young Read.

Oonts & Others. Julia Older. 72p. 1982. 17.50 (*0-87775-150-1*); pap. 9.95 (*0-87775-151-X*) Unicorn Pr.

Ooo-Cha! Colleen Sydor. (Illus.). 32p. (J). (gr. k-3). 1999. pap. 6.95 (*1-55037-604-7*, Pub. by Annick Pr); lib. bdg. 17.95 (*1-55037-605-5*, Pub. by Annick Pr) Firefly Bks Ltd.

Oooh, You New York Girls! The Urban Pastorale in Ballads & Songs about Sailors Ashore in the Big City. Stuart M. Frank. (Kendall Whaling Museum Monograph: No. 9). (Illus.). 24p. 1996. pap. 8.50 (*0-937854-34-4*) Kendall Whaling.

Ooooh . . . Bit Your Tongue? Gabe Martin. LC 96-84084. (Borderline Cartoons Ser.: Vol. 1). (Illus.). 144p. (Orig.). 1996. pap. 6.95 (*0-9651930-0-4*) Borderline Pub.

Ooops! Suzy Kline. Ed. by Ann Fay. LC 87-25429. (Illus.). 32p. (J). (ps-2). 1988. lib. bdg. 14.95 (*0-8075-6122-3*) A Whitman.

Ooopsy the Clown's Coloring & Activity Book. Amy Tinoco. (ENG & SPA., Illus.). 24p. (J). (ps-3). 1995. pap. 3.99 (*0-9647218-0-5*) Ooopsy the Clown.

OOP in Common Lisp. (C). 1995. pap. text. write for info. (*0-201-41718-9*) Addison-Wesley.

OOP Mit Turbo Pascal. (C). 1990. text. write for info. (*0-201-52268-3*) Addison-Wesley.

Oopletrump's Odyssey, Bk. 4. Alta M. Rymer. LC 85-61861. (Tales of Planet Artembo Ser.). (Illus.). 48p. (Orig.). (J). (gr. 5-7). pap. text 20.00 (*0-9600792-5-4*) Rymer Bks.

Oopra's Gone. David P. Wakeen. (Illus.). 128p. (Orig.). (C). 1993. pap. 9.95 (*0-9634911-9-9*) Waveman Pubs.

Oops! Colin McNaughton. LC 96-44229. (Illus.). 32p. (J). (ps-3). 1997. 14.00 (*0-15-201588-4*, Harcourt Child Bks) Harcourt.

*__Oops!__ Colin McNaughton. (Illus.). (J). (ps-3). 2000. pap. 6.00 (*0-15-202458-1*, Harcourt Child Bks) Harcourt.

Oops. Chris Stroffolino. 64p. 1994. pap. 7.95 (*1-886350-76-0*) Pavement Saw.

Oops. Chris Stroffolino. 64p. 1994. 75.00 (*1-886350-75-2*) Pavement Saw.

Oops! large type ed. John Lutz. LC 98-29242. (Large Print Book Ser.). 1998. 22.95 (*1-56895-653-3*) Wheeler Pub.

Oops! A Nudger Mystery. John Lutz. LC 97-36529. 304p. 1997. text 22.95 (*0-312-18152-3*) St Martin.

Oops! The Manners Guide for Girls. Nancy Holyoke. LC 97-14704. (American Girl Library Ser.). (Illus.). 116p. (Orig.). (J). (gr. 3-7). 1997. pap. text 7.95 (*1-56247-530-4*, Amer Girl Library) Pleasant Co.

Oops: What We Learn When Our Teaching Fails. Ed. by Brenda M. Power & Ruth S. Hubbard. LC 95-46907. (Illus.). 200p. (C). 1996. pap. text 17.00 (*1-57110-027-X*) Stenhse Pubs.

Oops? Common Ceramic Mistakes. Dale Swant. 24p. (Orig.). 1997. pap. 3.95 (*0-916809-79-X*) Scott Pubns MI.

Oops-a-Daisy! And Other Talks for Toddlers. Joyce Dunbar. LC 94-74045. (Illus.). 32p. (J). (ps). 1997. reprint ed. pap. 4.99 (*0-7636-0143-8*) Candlewick Pr.

*__Oops, Clifford!__ Norman Bridwell. LC 98-42693. (Clifford, the Big Red Dog Ser.). (Illus.). 32p. (J). (ps-3). 1999. pap. 15.95 (*0-590-63117-9*, Cartwheel) Scholastic Inc.

Oops! Excuse Me, Please: And Other Mannerly Tales. Bob McGrath. LC 97-4505. (Barron's Educational Ser.). (Illus.). 32p. (J). (ps-2). 1998. 5.95 (*0-7641-5083-9*) Barron.

Oops! I Forgot to Add the Fat to My Recipes! A Guide to Low & No Fat Cooking. Carolyn Fetters. (Illus.). vi, 47p. (Orig.). 1993. pap. 9.95 (*0-9639512-0-3*) C Fetters.

Oops! I Made a Mistake, Level 1. Susan Hood. LC 98-49566. (Fisher-Price All-Star Readers Ser.). (Illus.). 32p. (J). (gr. k-3). 1999. mass mkt. 3.99 (*1-57584-295-5*) Rdrs Digest.

Oops! I Thought This Room Was Vacant. Alden K. Williams. (Illus.). 146p. 1997. 16.95 (*0-9661295-0-4*) Hospitality Mktg.

Oops!!! I'm a Parent. No One Told Me it Would be Hard Work: Learn Effective Parenting. Linda D. Wright-Lee. Ed. by David J. Lee. pap. 23.95 (*0-9673754-6-0*) Wright On Time.

Oops the Join. Fiona Templeton. 110p. 1997. pap. 18.00 (*1-901361-04-7*, Pub. by Rem Pr) SPD-Small Pr Dist.

Oops, Your Manners Are Showing: A Study Course for Ages 8 & Up. 2nd rev. ed. Peggy Norwood & Jan Stabler. (Illus.). 132p. (J). (gr. 2-9). 1997. pap. text, teacher ed. 14.95 (*0-9660287-1-6*); pap. text, wbk. ed. 11.95 (*0-9660287-0-8*) Oops Grp.

Oops, Your Manners Are Showing: Lessons for Ages 4 to 7. Peggy Norwood & Jan Stabler. LC 98-148278. (Illus.). 88p. (J). (ps-2). 1998. pap. text 9.95 (*0-9660287-2-4*) Oops Grp.

Oopsie Otter: A Tale of Playful Otters. Suzanne Tate. LC 96-92952. (Suzanne Tate's Nature Ser.: No. 19). (Illus.). 28p. (J). (gr. k-4). 1997. pap. 4.95 (*1-878405-16-0*) Nags Head Art.

OOPSLA 98: OOPSLA: Conference on Object Oriented Programming Systems Languages & Applications. 1998. 34.00 (*1-58113-005-8*, 548981) Assn Compu Machinery.

OOPSLA 95: Conference on Object-Oriented Programming Systems, Languages & Applications. 483p. 1996. pap. text 31.00 (*0-89791-721-9*, 0) Assn Compu Machinery.

OOPSLA 95: Objected-Oriented Programming Systems Languages & Applications. 496p. 1995. pap. text 39.75 (*0-89791-703-0*, 548951) Assn Compu Machinery.

OOPSLA 94: ACM Conference on Object-Oriented Programming Systems, Languages & Applications. 496p. 1994. pap. text 39.75 (*0-89791-688-3*, 548942) Assn Compu Machinery.

OOPSLA 94 Addendum: ACM Conference on Object-Oriented Programming Systems, Languages & Applications. 148p. 1994. pap. text 20.00 (*0-89791-749-9*, 548943) Assn Compu Machinery.

OOPSLA 97: ACM Conference on Object-Oriented Systemss, Languages & Applications. 1997. pap. 50.00 (*0-89791-908-4*, 548971) Assn Compu Machinery.

OOPSLA 96: ACM Conference on Object-Oriented Programming Systems, Languages & Applications. 470p. 1996. pap. text 34.00 (*0-89791-788-X*, 548961) Assn Compu Machinery.

OOPSLA 93: AMC Conference on Object-Oriented Programming Systems, Languages & Applications. 468p. 1993. pap. text 39.75 (*0-89791-587-9*, 548930) Assn Compu Machinery.

OOPSLA 93 Addendum: ACM Conference on Object-Oriented Programming Systems, Languages & Applications. 144p. 1993. pap. text 19.00 (*0-89791-661-1*, 548941) Assn Compu Machinery.

Oort & the Universe. Ed. by Hugo Van Woerden et al. 210p. 1980. pap. text 58.00 (*90-277-1209-3*); lib. bdg. 82.00 (*90-277-1180-1*) Kluwer Academic.

Oort's Cloud. John Wilkinson. 200p. 2000. pap. 15.00 (*0-9666303-3-5*, Pub. by A A Arts) SPD-Small Pr Dist.

Oosa/Object Life Cycles Combined. Shlaer. 1999. pap. text 42.09 (*0-13-241589-5*) P-H.

Oost-indische Spiegel see Mirror of the Indies: A History of Dutch Colonial Literature

Oostamera. Martin Emanuel. 1991. 18.00 (*0-932526-34-9*) Nexus Pr.

Oosterschelde Estuary: A Case Study of a Changing Ecosystem. Ed. by P. H. Nienhuis & A. C. Smaal. LC 94-14882. (Developments in Hydrobiology Ser.: Vol. 97). 624p. (C). 1994. text 403.50 (*0-7923-2817-5*) Kluwer Academic.

OOTI, a Child of the Nisenan. Terri Ball. Ed. by Jo Smith & ARNHA Publication Committee. (Illus.). 32p. (J). (gr. 3-4). 1996. pap. 4.95 (*1-887815-02-3*) Amer River Nat Hist.

Ooze see Vomito Cosmico

Ooze. R. L. Stine, pseud. (Ghosts of Fear Street Ser.: No. 8). (J). (gr. 4-7). 1996. pap. 3.99 (*0-671-52948-X*, PB Trade Paper) PB.

Ooze. R. L. Stine, pseud. (Ghosts of Fear Street Ser.: No. 8). (J). (gr. 4-9). 1996. 9.09 (*0-606-09321-4*, Pub. by Turtleback) Demco.

*__Oozey Octopus: A Tale of a Clever Critter.__ Suzanne Tate. LC 99-96240. (Suzanne Tate's Nature Ser.: Vol. 22). (Illus.). 28p. (J). (ps-4). 2000. pap. 4.95 (*1-878405-26-8*) Nags Head Art.

OP: Surgery. 3rd ed. D. Das. (C). 1989. 105.00 (*0-7855-6115-3*, Pub. by Current Dist) St Mut.

Op-Amp Circuits Manual. R. M. Marston. 1989. lab manual ed. 32.00 (*0-434-91207-7*) CRC Pr.

OP AMP Workbench. Jerald G. Graeme. 1999. 59.00 (*0-07-134642-2*) Gregg-McGraw.

Op Amps: Design, Application & Troubleshooting. 2nd ed. David L. Terrell. LC 95-26097. (Illus.). 512p. 1996. pap. text 54.95 (*0-7506-9702-4*) Buttrwrth-Heinemann.

Op Amps & Lic for Technology. 2nd ed. Frank R. Dungan. 1992. mass mkt. 56.25 (*0-8273-5086-4*) Delmar.

*__OP, Amps & Linear Integrated Circuits.__ Fiore. (Student Material TV Ser.). (C). 2000. pap. 52.50 (*0-7668-1793-8*); pap., lab manual ed. 22.50 (*0-7668-1794-6*) Delmar.

*__Op Amps & Linear Integrated Circuits.__ 4th ed. 2000. write for info. (*0-13-022811-7*) P-H.

*__Op-Amps & Linear Integrated Circuits.__ 4th ed. Ramakant A. Gayakwad. LC 99-24236. 543p. 1999. 92.00 (*0-13-280868-4*) P-H.

OP Amps & Linear Integrated Circuits for Technicians. 2nd ed. Frank R. Dungan. 1992. teacher ed. 16.00 (*0-8273-5087-2*) Delmar.

Op-Art Quilt Illusions: Fast, Fun & Fabulous 3-D Illusions. Marilyn Doheny. 80p. 1996. reprint ed. pap. 22.95 (*0-945169-18-3*) Doheny Pubns.

Op-Center. Tom Clancy. 1997. pap. 11.95 (*84-08-02019-6*) Planeta.

*__Op-Center: El Silencio del Kremlin.__ Tom Clancy. 1998. pap. 9.95 (*84-08-02117-6*) Planeta.

Op-Center: Juegos del Estado. Tom Clancy. 1998. pap. 9.95 (*84-08-02368-3*) Planeta.

*__Op Center: State of Siege.__ large type ed. Tom Clancy. LC 99-55761. (Basic Ser.). 1999. 29.95 (*0-7862-2318-9*) Thorndike Pr.

Op-Center: Actos de Guerra. Tom Clancy. 1999. 29.95 (*84-08-02717-4*) Planeta.

Op Den Graeff - Updegrove: Indexes & Pedigrees of Known Descendants of Herman Op Den Graeff. Cathy Berger. Ed. by Iris C. Jones. 87p. (Orig.). 1991. pap. text 12.00 (*0-9620067-2-6*) Links Geneal Pubns.

Op-Olympic Peninsula. Seabury Blair, Jr. Ed. by J. Bruce Baumann. (Illus.). 112p. 1994. 19.95 (*1-884850-03-0*) Scripps Howard.

Op To Pop: Furniture of The 1960s. Cara Greenberg. LC 98-46005. 176p. 1999. 40.00 (*0-8212-2516-2*) Little.

Opa-Locka, Baghdad of the South. Carol-Ann Rudy. Ed. by Paul S. George. LC 96-93118. (Hometown Heritage Ser.: Vol. 2). (Illus.). 32p. (Orig.). (J). (gr. 2-4). 1996. pap. 3.50 (*1-889300-01-2*) Dormouse Prods.

Opaa! Greek Cooking Chicago Style. George J. Gekas. 171p. (Orig.). 1991. pap. 15.95 (*0-929387-31-7*) Bonus Books.

Opaa! Greek Cooking Detroit Style. George J. Gekas. 173p. 1993. pap. 14.95 (*0-929387-93-7*) Bonus Books.

Opaa! Greek Cooking New York Style. George J. Gekas. LC 96-37410. 184p. (Orig.). 1997. pap. 12.95 (*1-56625-078-1*) Bonus Books.

OPAC Directory: An Annual Guide to Internet-Accessible Online Public Access Catalogs. rev. ed. Ed. by Bonnie R. Nelson. 500p. 1997. pap. 70.00 (*1-57387-031-5*) Info Today Inc.

An Asterisk (*) at the beginning of an entry indicates that the title is appearing for the first time.

Opacite Referentielle et Quantification: Une Introduction a la Semantique Intensionnelle. Marc M. Matsumakia. (Publications Universitaires Europeennes, Serie 28: Vol. 517). (FRE.). 272p. 1997. 40.95 (*3-906754-74-X*, Pub. by P Lang) P Lang Pubng.

Opacity in the Writings of Robbe-Grillet, Pinter, & Zach: A Study in the Poetics of Absurd Literature. Yoseph Milman. LC 91-43258. (Studies in Comparative Literature: Vol. 18). 148p. 1992. lib. bdg. 69.95 (*0-7734-9701-3*) E Mellen.

Opacity of Spiral Disks: Proceedings of NATO Advanced Research Workshop on the Opacity of Spiral Disks Held 1994, Cardiff, Wales. Ed. by Jonathan I. Davies & David Burstein. LC 95-33174. (NATO ASI Ser.: Ser. C). 379p. (C). 1995. text 191.50 (*0-7923-3638-0*) Kluwer Academic.

Opacity Project, 2 vols. Incl. Vol. 2. Opacity Project (Including the Iron Project) Opacity Project Team Staff. 300p. 1996. 180.00 (*0-7503-0174-0*); Vol. 1. Ed. by Opacity Project Team Staff. (Illus.). 834p. 1995. 206.00 (*0-7503-0288-7*); 360.00 (*0-7503-0175-9*) IOP Pub.

Opacity Project (Including the Iron Project) see Opacity Project

OPACs & Beyond: Proceedings of a Joint Meeting of the British Library, DBMIST, & OCLC. Pref. by Martin Dillon. (Library, Information, & Computer Science Ser.). 100p. (Orig.). 1989. pap. 12.50 (*1-55653-070-6*) OCLC Online Comp.

***Opal.** Elvi Rhodes. 2000. pap. 8.95 (*0-552-12367-6*, Pub. by Transworld Publishers Ltd) Trafalgar.

***Opal Advanced Cutting & Setting.** Paul B. Downing. (Illus.). 144p. 2000. pap. 15.95 (*0-9625311-5-4*) Majestic Pr.

Opal Adventures. 2nd ed. Paul B. Downing. (Illus.). 240p. 1993. 19.95 (*0-9625311-3-8*) Majestic Pr.

Opal & Other Stories. Gustav Meyrink. Tr. by Michael Mitchell. (Studies in Austrian Literature, Culture, & Thought. Translation Ser.). 222p. 1994. pap. 14.95 (*0-929497-89-9*) Ariadne CA.

Opal Cutting Made Easy. 2nd ed. Paul B. Downing. (Illus.). 100p. (Orig.). 1993. pap. 8.95 (*0-9625311-4-6*) Majestic Pr.

Opal Darkness. Cleo Cordell. (Black Lace Ser.). 1995. mass mkt. 5.95 (*0-352-33033-3*, Pub. by Virgin Bks) London Brdge.

Opal Desert: Explorations of Fantasy & Reality in the American Southwest. Peter Wild. LC 99-6113. 231p. 1999. pap. 18.95 (*0-292-79129-1*) U of Tex Pr.

***Opal Desert: Explorations of Fantasy & Reality in the American Southwest.** Peter Wild. LC 99-6113. 231p. 1999. 37.50 (*0-292-79128-3*) U of Tex Pr.

Opal Fire. Sandy Dengler. (Serenade Saga Ser.: No. 27). 1986. pap. 1.49 (*0-310-47412-4*, 15587P) Zondervan.

Opal Fires. Lynda Trent. 320p. 1993. reprint ed. pap. text, mass mkt. 4.50 (*0-8439-3482-4*) Dorchester Pub Co.

Opal Identification & Value. Paul B. Downing. (Illus.). 214p. 1992. 38.95 (*0-9625311-2-X*) Majestic Pr.

Opal in the Closet. Joan Knight. LC 91-659. (Illus.). 28p. (J). (gr. k up). 1992. pap. 14.95 (*0-88708-174-6*, Picture Book Studio) S&S Childrens.

Opal Is a Diamond. John Patrick. 1992. pap. 5.25 (*0-8222-0857-1*) Dramatists Play.

Opal Mystery. Stella Fabian. LC 90-83465. (Boomer Ser.). (Illus.). 192p. (Orig.). (J). (gr. 3-7). 1991. pap. 3.25 (*0-922434-39-5*) Brighton & Lloyd.

Opal Phytoliths in Southeast Asian Flora. Lisa Kealhofer & Dolores R. Piperno. LC 98-38793. (Smithsonian Contributions to Botany Ser.: No. 88). (Illus.). 43p. reprint ed. pap. 30.00 (*0-608-20168-5*, 207143200011) Bks Demand.

Opal Phytoliths of New Zealand. R. Kondo et al. 1994. 40.00 (*0-478-04522-0*, Pub. by Manaaki Whenua) Balogh.

Opal, the Journey of an Understanding Heart. Opal Whitely. LC 95-30753. 1995. pap. 11.00 (*0-517-88516-6*) Crown Pub Group.

Opal Whiteley: The Unsolved Mystery: Together with Opal Whiteley's Diary, The Journal of An Understanding Heart. Opal S. Whiteley. (American Biography Ser.). 294p. 1991. reprint ed. lib. bdg. 69.00 (*0-7812-8413-9*) Rprt Serv.

Opalescent Parrot: Essays. Alfred Noyes. (Essay Index Reprint Ser.). 1977. 20.95 (*0-8369-0748-5*) Ayer.

Opalite Moon. Denise Vitola. 304p. 1997. mass mkt. 5.99 (*0-441-00465-2*) Ace Bks.

Opalka. Text by Bernard Noel et al. LC 97-138747. (Illus.). 128p. 1996. pap. 23.50 (*2-906571-57-1*, 620803, Pub. by Editions Dis Voir) Dist Art Pubs.

Opals. Allan W. Eckert. LC 97-1825. 448p. 1997. 85.00 (*0-471-13397-3*) Wiley.

Opals. Fred Ward. Ed. by Charlotte Ward. LC 97-117456. (Fred Ward Gem Book Ser.). (Illus.). 64p. (Orig.). 1996. pap. 14.95 (*0-9633723-8-6*) Gem Bk Pubs.

Opals. deluxe ed. Rebecca Bingham. (Illus.). 48p. 1982. lthr. 30.00 (*0-88014-042-9*) Mosaic Pr OH.

Opals: With, Rainbows. Olive Custance. (Decadents, Symbolists, Anti-Decadents Ser.). 1996. 49.50 (*1-85477-137-X*) Continuum.

Opal's Baby. John Patrick. 1974. pap. 5.25 (*0-8222-0858-X*) Dramatists Play.

Opal's Husband. John Patrick. 1975. pap. 5.25 (*0-8222-0859-8*) Dramatists Play.

Opal's Million Dollar Duck. John Patrick. 1980. pap. 5.25 (*0-8222-0860-1*) Dramatists Play.

Opals of the Never Never. Robert G. Haill. (Illus.). 160p. 1995. pap. 16.95 (*0-86417-686-4*, Pub. by Kangaroo Pr) Seven Hills Bk.

Opaque Glass. Barbara Roux & Coco Gordon. 30p. (Orig.). 1985. 50.00 (*0-931956-25-0*) Water Mark.

Opaque Nuclear Proliferation: Methodological & Policy Implications. Ed. by Benjamin Frankel. (Journal of Strategic Studies: Vol. 13, No. 3). 216p. 1991. 37.50 (*0-7146-3418-2*, Pub. by F Cass Pubs) Intl Spec Bk.

Opa's Stories. Mary D. Wade. (Illus.). 20p. (J). (gr. 1-3). 1996. pap. 6.95 (*1-882539-20-6*) Colophon Hse.

Opatoula. Mary A. Hood. Ed. by Ellen G. Peppler. 98p. (Orig.). 1993. pap. 7.95 (*0-944206-03-4*) W FL Lit Fed.

OPC: The Miracle Antioxidant. Chris Kilham. LC 98-231775. (Good Health Guides Ser.). pap. 3.95 (*0-87983-862-6*, 38426K, Keats Publng) NTC Contemp Pub Co.

Opcas Pelos Pobres see Bible, the Church, & the Poor

Opcion Mas Segura: Cuaderno de Apuntes. Santiago G. Egana. (SPA., Illus.). 136p. (Orig.). 1988. pap. write for info. (*0-9620622-0-0*) S G Egana.

Opciones para un Parto Suave. Barbara Harper.Tr. of Gentle Birth Choices. (ENG & SPA., Illus.). 298p. 1995. pap. 16.95 (*0-89281-471-3*) Inner Tradit.

***OPCW: The Legal Texts.** Ed. by Lisa Woollomes Tabassi. 604p. 1999. 195.00 (*90-6704-112-2*, Pub. by TMC Asser Pr) Kluwer Law Intl.

OPD Chemical Buyers Directory, 1992. 856p. 1991. pap. 95.00 (*1-878800-00-0*) Schnell Pub.

OPD Chemical Buyers Directory, 1986. 73rd ed. 804p. 1985. pap. 65.00 (*0-9606454-6-6*) Schnell Pub.

OPD Chemical Buyers Directory, 1987. 74th ed. 816p. 1986. pap. 65.00 (*0-9606454-5-4*) Schnell Pub.

Opdyke: Genealogy, Containing the Opdyck-Opdycke-Updike American Descendants of the Wesel & Holland Families. C. W. Opdyke. 499p. 1991. reprint ed. pap. 77.50 (*0-8328-1825-9*); reprint ed. lib. bdg. 87.50 (*0-8328-1824-0*) Higginson Bk Co.

OPEC: The Failing Giant. Mohammed E. Ahrari. LC 85-15040. 272p. 1986. 32.00 (*0-8131-1552-3*) U Pr of Ky.

OPEC: The Rise & Fall of an Exclusive Club. Shukri M. Ghanem. 280p. 1987. 65.00 (*0-7103-0175-8*, 01758) Routledge.

OPEC Aid & the Challenge of Development. Ed. by Abdelkader Benamara & Sam Ifeagwu. 160p. 1987. lib. bdg. 55.00 (*0-7099-1969-7*, Pub. by C Helm) Routldge.

OPEC & Non-OPEC Relations. John Roberts. 20p. 1989. pap. 10.00 (*0-918714-18-6*) Intl Res Ctr Energy.

OPEC & the Market: A Study of Oil Price Rigidity, Determination, & Differentials. Abdul-Razak F. Al-Faris. LC 93-81258. (Illus.). 156p. 1994. 26.00 (*0-918714-41-9*) Intl Res Ctr Energy.

OPEC & the Third World: The Politics of Aid. Shireen T. Hunter. LC 84-47812. (Illus.). 336p. 1984. 31.95 (*0-253-34249-X*) Ind U Pr.

OPEC & the World Oil Market: The Genesis of the 1986 Price Crisis. Ed. by Robert Mabro. (Institute for Energy Studies). (Illus.). 282p. 1987. text 55.00 (*0-19-730003-0*) OUP.

OPEC & the World Oil Market: The March 1983 London Agreement. Wilfred L. Kohl & Carol W. Rendall. (Pew Case Studies in International Affairs). 50p. (C). 1991. pap. text 3.50 (*1-56927-123-2*) Geo U Inst Dplmcy.

OPEC Ascendant? Another Case of Crying Wolf. Eliyahu Kanovsky. LC 90-39561. (Policy Papers: No. 20). 62p. 1990. pap. 8.00 (*0-944029-05-1*) Wash Inst NEP.

OPEC at the Crossroads. Fadhil J. Al-Chalabi. (Illus.). 252p. 1989. 92.00 (*0-08-037526-X*, Pergamon Pr) Elsevier.

OPEC in a Changing World Economy. Abbas Alnasrawi. LC 84-7196. 202p. 1985. reprint ed. pap. 62.70 (*0-608-04074-6*, 206480600011) Bks Demand.

OPEC, the Petroleum Industry, & United States Energy Policy. Arabinda Ghosh. LC 82-13245. (Illus.). 206p. 1983. 55.00 (*0-89930-010-3*, GOU/, Quorum Bks) Greenwood.

OPEC's Investments & the International Financial System. Richard P. Mattione. LC 84-23242. 201p. 1985. 34.95 (*0-8157-5510-4*); pap. 14.95 (*0-8157-5509-0*) Brookings.

Opel Military Vehicles, 1906-1956. Eckhart Bartels. Tr. by Edward Force from GER. LC 97-65444. 176p. 1997. 29.95 (*0-7643-0267-1*) Schiffer.

Opelousas Country: History of Evangeline Prish. Robert Gahn. 1973. 20.00 (*0-87511-053-3*) Claitors.

Open: The British Open Golf Championship since the War Peter Alliss & Michael Hobbs. LC 84-136343. 256p. 1984. write for info. (*0-00-217175-9*) Collins SF.

***Open a Can of Worms.** Debbie Caffrey. 76p. 2000. pap. 23.95 (*0-9645777-4-7*) Debbies Creat.

Open a Door. Susan M. Soong. LC 95-71794. (Illus.). 20p. (Orig.). 1996. pap. 19.95 (*1-888254-00-9*) Contemp Museum.

Open a New Door. Conrad George. (Illus.). 1979. pap. 3.50 (*0-87516-374-2*) DeVorss.

Open Adoption: Research, Theory & Practice. Murray Ryburn. 240p. 1994. 66.95 (*1-85628-692-4*, Pub. by Avebry) Ashgate Pub Co.

Open Adoption Book: A Guide to Making Adoption Work for You. Bruce M. Rappaport. 208p. 1997. 13.95 (*0-02-862170-0*) Macmillan.

Open Adoption Experience: Complete Guide for Adoptive & Birth Families - From Making the Decision Throug. Lois R. Melina & Sharon K. Roszia. LC 92-56254. 416p. 1993. pap. 15.00 (*0-06-096957-1*, Perennial) HarperTrade.

Open-Air Churches of Sixteenth-Century Mexico: Atrios, Posas, Open Chapels, & Other Studies. LC 63-17205. 789p. reprint ed. pap. 200.00 (*0-608-18571-X*, 200300100017) Bks Demand.

Open Airways: An Asthma Self-Management Program. 1991. lib. bdg. 74.95 (*0-8490-4339-5*) Gordon Pr.

Open Alias. Wayne Johnson. Ed. by Edward Mycue. (Took Modern Stories in English Ser.: No. 6). (Illus.). 60p. (Orig.). 1993. pap. 5.00 (*1-879457-08-3*) Norton Coker Pr.

***Open All Night: New Poems.** Charles Bukowski. 375p. 2000. 30.00 (*1-57423-136-7*) Black Sparrow.

***Open All Night: New Poems.** deluxe ed. Charles Bukowski. 375p. 2000. 50.00 (*1-57423-137-5*) Black Sparrow.

Open All Night Ken Miller. Ken Miller. (Illus.). 118p. 1995. 40.00 (*0-87951-571-6*, Pub. by Overlook Pr) Penguin Putnam.

Open All Night Ken Miller. William T. Vollmann & Ken Miller. (Illus.). 118p. 1996. pap. 25.00 (*0-87951-648-8*, Pub. by Overlook Pr) Penguin Putnam.

Open & Clothed: For the Passionate Clothes Lover. unabridged ed. Andrea Lynn Siegel. LC 99-95229. (Illus.). xv, 350p. 1999. pap. 24.00 (*0-9672750-0-8*) Agapanthus Bks.

***Open & Distance Learning in Developing Countries.** H. D. Perraton. LC 99-16902. (Studies in Distance Education). 224p. 2000. pap. write for info. (*0-415-19419-9*) Routledge.

Open & Distance Learning Today. Ed. by Fred Lockwood. LC 95-8130. (Studies in Distance Education). 228p. (C). 1995. pap. 25.99 (*0-415-12759-9*) Routledge.

Open & Flexible Learning in Vocational Education & Training. Judith Calder & Ann McCollum. 192p. 1998. pap. 29.95 (*0-7494-2172-X*, Kogan Pg Educ) Stylus Pub VA.

***Open & Free: Dean Bennett of Chester.** Alex Bruce. (Liverpool Historical Studies: No. 17). 240p. 1999. pap. 19.95 (*0-85323-924-X*, Pub. by Liverpool Univ Pr) Intl Spec Bk.

Open & Industrialised Building. Asko Sarja & International Council for Building Research & Docu. LC 98-220309. (CIB Publication Ser.). 1998. write for info. (*0-419-23840-9*) Routledge.

Open & Innocent: The Gentle, Passionate Art of Not-Knowing. 3rd rev. ed. Scott Morrison. 108p. 1998. pap. 9.00 (*1-882496-11-6*, 003) Twnty Frst Cntry Ren.

Open & Loving Heart: Gentle Words of Self-Endearment. Suzanne Hirabayashi. LC 97-67053. (Illus.). 51p. (YA). 1997. 11.95 (*0-87516-701-2*) DeVorss.

Open & Utility Training: The Motivational Method. Jack Volhard & Wendy Volhard. (Illus.). 240p. 1992. 24.95 (*0-87605-755-5*) Howell Bks.

Open Approach the Information Policymaking: A Case Study of the Moore Universal Telephone Service Act. Robert Jacobson. Ed. by Brenda Dervin. LC 88-24129. (Communication & Information Science Ser.). 192p. 1989. text 73.25 (*0-89391-267-0*) Ablx Pub.

Open Architecture Control Systems & Standards, Vol. 2912. Ed. by Frederick M. Proctor. LC 96-69764. 232p. 1997. 56.00 (*0-8194-2314-9*) SPIE.

***Open Boat.** Stephen Crane. (Short Stories Ser.). 22p. 2000. pap. 3.95 (*1-86092-025-X*, Pub. by Travelman Pub) IPG Chicago.

Open Boat. Stephen Crane. 1999. pap. write for info. (*0-451-52646-5*, Sig Classics) NAL.

Open Boat. Tom Clapp. LC 96-22481. 55p. (Orig.). 1996. reprint ed. pap. 6.00 (*0-88734-200-0*) Players Pr.

Open Boat & Other Stories. Stephen Crane. LC 93-12734. (Thrift Editions Ser.). 112p. 1993. reprint ed. pap. 1.50 (*0-486-27547-7*) Dover.

Open Boat & Other Tales of Adventure. Stephen Crane. LC 06-30865. 65.00 (*0-403-00012-2*) Scholarly.

Open Boat & Other Tales of Adventure. Stephen Crane. (Works of Stephen Crane). 1990. reprint ed. lib. bdg. 79.00 (*0-685-44794-4*) Rprt Serv.

Open Boat Canoeing. Bob Wirth. LC 84-14907. (Illus.). 1985. 18.95 (*0-13-637596-0*); pap. 9.95 (*0-13-637547-2*) P-H.

Open Body: Creating Your Own Yoga. Todd Walton. LC 98-92426. 112p. 1998. pap. 12.00 (*0-380-79535-3*, Avon Bks) Morrow Avon.

***Open Book.** 233p. 2000. pap. 17.00 (*0-9636906-2-0*) Ishnuvu Pub.

Open Book. Monica Dickens. LC 79-313102. xi, 210 p. 1978. write for info. (*0-434-19225-2*) Buttrwrth-Heinemann.

Open Book. John Huston. LC 93-48043. (Illus.). 443p. 1994. reprint ed. pap. 16.50 (*0-306-80573-1*) Da Capo.

Open Book. Jack L. Saunders. 250p. 1998. reprint ed. pap. 10.00 (*1-892590-30-1*) Out Your Bk.

Open Book: Little Thoughts from a Big Head. Mike Bullard. 231p. 1999. text 29.95 (*0-385-25886-0*) Doubleday.

***Open Book: One Publisher's War.** Steve MacDonogh. (Illus.). 288p. 1999. pap. 18.95 (*0-86322-263-3*, Pub. by Brandon Bk Pubs) Irish Bks Media.

***Open Book: The Life & Times of James Barton Preston.** James Barton Preston. LC 00-40016. (YA). 2000. write for info. (*0-87562-113-9*) Spec Child.

Open-Book Experience: Lessons from Over 100 Companies Who Successfully Transformed Themselves. John Case. 256p. 1998. pap. text 14.00 (*0-7382-0040-9*) Perseus Pubng.

Open-Book Management: Creating an Ownership Culture. Thomas L. Barton et al. LC 97-77705. (Illus.). 246p. 1998. pap. 38.50 (*1-885065-12-4*, 098-02) Finan Exec.

Open-Book Management: Getting Started. Catherine Ivancic & Jim Bado. Ed. by Kay Keppler. LC 97-65268. (Fifty-Minute Ser.). 120p. (Orig.). 1997. pap. 10.95 (*1-56052-447-2*) Crisp Pubns.

Open-Book Management: The Coming Business Revolution. John Case. 224p. 1996. pap. 15.00 (*0-88730-802-3*) HarpC.

Open Book Management: You EZ Intro to OBM. 2nd ed. Donald F. Barkman. (Illus.). 52p. 1999. pap. 9.95 (*1-883655-05-6*) Busn Ctr.

Open-Book Management Fieldbook. John P. Schuster et al. LC 97-23164. (Illus.). 256p. 1997. pap. 35.00 (*0-471-18036-X*) Wiley.

***Open Books: Literature in the Curriculum, Kindergarten Through Grade 2.** Carol Otis Hurst. LC 99-39454. 266p. (J). (gr. 2). 1999. 36.95 (*0-938865-77-3*) Linworth Pub.

***Open Borders: The Case Against Immigration Controls.** Teresa Hayter. LC 00-9580. 2001. pap. write for info. (*0-7453-1542-9*, Pub. by Pluto GBR) Stylus Pub VA.

Open Borders? Closed Societies? The Ethical & Political Issues, 226. Ed. by Mark Gibney. LC 88-15484. (Contributions in Political Science Ser.: No. 226). 211p. 1988. 55.00 (*0-313-25578-4*, GWU/, Greenwood Pr) Greenwood.

Open Borders Behind Closed Doors: The European Union & the South. Peter Pennartz. (Illus.). 80p. (Orig.). 1997. pap. 12.95 (*90-5727-005-6*, Pub. by Uitgeverij Arkel) LPC InBook.

Open Borders, Nonalignment & the Political Evolution of Yugoslavia. William Zimmerman. 168p. 1987. text 27.50 (*0-691-07730-4*, Pub. by Princeton U Pr) Cal Prin Full Svc.

Open Boundaries. Ron Schultz. 1998. write for info. (*0-201-32803-8*) Addison-Wesley.

***Open Boundaries: Creating Business Innovation Through Complexity.** Howard Sherman & Ron Schultz. 256p. 1999. pap. text 15.00 (*0-7382-0155-3*, Pub. by Perseus Pubng) HarpC.

Open Boundaries: Creating Business Innovations Through Complexity. Howard J. Sherman & Ron Schultz. LC 98-86418. 256p. 1998. text 26.00 (*0-7382-0005-0*) Perseus Pubng.

Open Boundaries: Jain Communities & Cultures in Indian History. Ed. by John E. Cort. LC 97-46027. (SUNY Series, Hindu Studies). (Illus.). 278p. (C). 1998. text 73.50 (*0-7914-3785-X*); pap. text 24.95 (*0-7914-3786-8*) State U NY Pr.

Open Cage: An Anzia Yezierska Collection. Anzia Yezierska. 280p. 1993. pap. 9.95 (*0-89255-036-8*) Persea Bks.

Open Canoe. Bill Riviere. (Illus.). 288p. 1985. pap. 12.95 (*0-316-74768-8*) Little.

***Open Canoe Technique: A Complete Guide to Paddling the Open Canoe.** Foster. (Illus.). 95p. 2000. pap. 16.95 (*1-898660-26-3*, Pub. by Fernhurst Bks) Motorbooks Intl.

Open Catholicism - The Tradition at Its Best: Essays in Honor of Gerard S. Sloyan. Ed. by Daniel P. Efroymson & John Raines. LC 97-6710. 232p. 1997. pap. 19.95 (*0-8146-5879-2*, M Glazier) Liturgical Pr.

Open-Chain Nitrogen Compounds: Chemistry of Non-Cyclic Nitrogen-Containing Organic Functional Groups. 2nd ed. P. A. Smith. 1982. text. write for info. (*0-318-56716-4*) Addison-Wesley.

Open Championship Golf Courses of Britain. Keith Mackie. (Illus.). 192p. 1997. pap. 49.95 (*1-56554-296-7*) Pelican.

Open Channel Flow. Francis M. Henderson. 544p. (C). 1966. text 75.00 (*0-02-353510-5*, Macmillan Coll) P-H.

***Open Channel Flow.** C. Subhash Jain. LC 99-89638. 350p. 2000. 79.95 (*0-471-35641-7*) Wiley.

Open-Channel Hydraulics. Chow Ven-Te. (Civil Engineering Ser.). 680p. (C). 1959. 113.44 (*0-07-010776-9*) McGraw.

Open-Channel Hydraulics. R. H. French. 1992. 22.50 (*0-07-022144-8*) McGraw.

Open Channel to Babylon. Rex O. Gregory. Ed. by Gwen Costa. LC 91-36326. xx, 360p. 1992. pap. 13.95 (*0-87949-363-1*) Ashley Bks.

***Open Chord Advantage: Play Open String Chords in Any Key Without Returning or Using a Capriccio.** John Bunge. (Illus.). 80p. 1999. pap. 14.95 (*1-56922-197-9*) Creat Cncpts.

Open Chord Cookbook. Date not set. pap. write for info. (*0-7390-0798-X*, 19367); pap. write for info. incl. audio compact disk (*0-7390-0799-8*, 19368) Alfred Pub.

***Open Christianity: Home by Another Road.** Jim Burklo. 2000. pap. write for info. (*0-933670-05-2*) Rising Star.

Open Church. James H. Rutz. LC 92-81563. 182p. (C). pap. text 8.95 (*0-940232-50-2*) Seedsowers.

Open City, Vol. 1. Mary Gaitskill et al. Ed. by Thomas Beller & Daniel Pinchdeck. (Illus.). 75p. (Orig.). 1992. pap. 200.00 (*1-890447-12-9*) Open City Bks.

Open City, Vol. 9. Goeff Dyer et al. 1999. pap. text 8.00 (*1-890447-20-X*) Open City Bks.

Open City: Alphabet City 6. Ed. by John Knechtel. (Illus.). 320p. 1998. pap. 24.95 (*0-88784-621-1*, Pub. by Hse of Anansi Pr) Genl Dist Srvs.

Open City: Seven Writers in Postwar. Ignazio Silone et al. Ed. by William Weaver. LC 99-15666. (Steerforth Italia Ser.). 450p. 1999. pap. 19.00 (*1-883642-82-5*) Steerforth Pr.

Open City No. 10: The Editors' Issue. Thomas Beller et al. 280p. 1999. pap. 8.00 (*1-890447-21-8*, Pub. by Open City Bks) SPD-Small Pr Dist.

Open City Vol. 5: Change or Die. David Foster Wallace et al. Ed. by Thomas Beller & Daniel Pinchdeck. 1997. pap. 15.00 (*1-890447-16-1*) Open City Bks.

Open City Vol. 6: The Only Woman He's Ever Left. Monica S. Lewinsky et al. Ed. by Thomas Beller & Daniel Pinchdeck. 220p. 1998. pap. 8.00 (*1-890447-17-X*, 700002) Open City Bks.

Open City Vol. 7: The Rubbed Away Girl. David Berman et al. Ed. by Thomas Beller & Daniel Pinchdeck. 1999. pap. text 8.00 (*1-890447-18-8*) Open City Bks.

Open City Vol. 8: Beautiful to Strangers. Harvey Shapiro et al. Ed. by Thomas Beller & Daniel Pinchdeck. (Illus.). 200p. 1999. pap. 8.00 (*1-890447-19-6*) Open City Bks.

***Open Closed Open: Poems.** Yehuda Amichai. Tr. by Chana Bloch & Chana Kronfeld from HEB. 2000. 24.00 (*0-15-100378-5*) Harcourt.

Open-Cockpit Kayaks. Bob Beazley. (Nuts-N-Bolt Guides Ser.). (Illus.). 32p. (Orig.). 1996. pap. 4.95 (*0-89732-215-0*) Menasha Ridge.

O

An Asterisk (*) at the beginning of an entry indicates that the title is appearing for the first time.

Open Commonwealth. M. Margaret Ball. LC 78-171937. 300p. reprint ed. 93.00 (*0-8357-9113-0*, 201788200010) Bks Demand.

Open Confession to a Man from a Woman. Marie Corelli. 190p. 1971. reprint ed. spiral bd. 14.00 (*0-7873-0202-3*) Hlth Research.

Open Confession to a Man from a Woman. Marie Corelli. 190p. 1996. reprint ed. pap. 12.95 (*1-56459-737-7*) Kessinger Pub.

Open Connections: The Other Basics. Susan D. Shilcock & Peter A. Bergson. LC 81-116987. 1980. 12.50 (*0-9606434-0-0*) Open Connections.

Open Conspiracy. H. G. Wells. 1979. lib. bdg. 250.00 (*0-8490-2979-1*) Gordon Pr.

Open Conversations: Strategies for Professional Development in Museums. Carolyn P. Blackmon et al. (Illus.). 125p. (Orig.). 1988. pap. 6.00 (*0-914868-10-1*) Field Mus.

Open Corridor Program: Handbook for Parents. (Illus.). 12p. 1971. 0.50 (*0-918374-11-1*) City Coll Wk.

Open Country, Iowa: Rural Women, Tradition, & Change. Deborah Fink. LC 86-967. (SUNY Series in the Anthropology of Work). 275p. (C). 1986. pap. text 21.95 (*0-88706-318-7*) State U NY Pr.

Open Court. Thomas Kinsella. 18p. 1991. pap. 11.95 (*1-873790-13-9*) Dufour.

Open Courtroom: Cameras in New York Courts. New York State Committee to Review Audio-Visual Co. LC 97-16512. xxi, 243p. 1997. 40.00 (*0-8232-1809-0*); pap. 20.00 (*0-8232-1810-4*) Fordham.

Open Covenant: Social Change in Contemporary Society. Christopher B. Doob. LC 87-19882. 128p. 1987. 49.95 (*0-275-92550-1*, C2550, Praeger Pubs); pap. 10.95 (*0-275-92661-3*, B2661, Praeger Pubs) Greenwood.

Open CPI-C Specification: Version 2. 2nd ed. Prentice-Hall Staff. LC 97-162361. 564p. (C). 1996. pap. 59.00 (*0-13-496407-1*) P-H.

Open Cupboard. Barbara Johnston. Ed. by Philip McPeck. Tr. by Vassily Selishchev. LC 99-159984. (Illus.). viii, 72p. 1997. 9.95 (*0-9661106-0-9*) Obagon Pub.

Open Cycle MHD Power Generation: Results Research British MHD Collaborative Committee. J. Heywood & G. Womack. LC 73-79462. 1969. 357.00 (*0-08-006335-7*, Pub. by Pergamon Repr) Franklin.

***Open Day Hearing: Hearing Before the Committee on Rules, House of Representatives, 105th Congress, 2nd on Open Day Hearing for Members to Testify on Proposals To Amend the Rules of the House of Representatives, September 17, 1998.** USGPO Staff. LC 99-170815. iii, 75 p. 1998. pap. write for info. (*0-16-057668-7*) USGPO.

Open Desktop Survival Guide. Stross. (C). 1994. pap. text. write for info. (*0-201-59391-2*) Addison-Wesley.

Open Distributed Processing & Distributed Platforms. Chapman & Hall Staff. text 124.00 (*0-412-81230-4*) Chapman & Hall.

Open Distributed Processing & Multimedia. Gorden Blair. LC 97-17905. 480p. (C). 1998. 44.95 (*0-201-17794-3*) Addison-Wesley.

Open Distributed Systems. Jon Crowcroft. LC 95-48909. 386p. 1996. 60.00 (*0-89006-839-9*) Artech Hse.

O

Open Door. Marcia J. Marlow. 1998. pap. write for info. (*1-58235-016-7*) Watermrk Pr.

Open Door. Floyd Skloot. LC 97-25392. 230p. 1997. pap. text 14.95 (*1-885266-48-0*) Story Line.

Open Door, Bk. 2. Xnadu. LC 78-56655. (Illus.). 57p. (Orig.). 1982. pap. 11.95 (*0-911335-02-1*) Open Door Foun.

Open Door: A Poet Lore Anthology, 1980-1996. Ed. by Philip K. Jason et al. LC 96-61222. 200p. (Orig.). 1997. pap. 16.00 (*0-9654010-0-6*, Writers Ctr Edits) Writers Ctr.

Open Door: The Bradford Bilingual Project. Finbarre Fitzpatrick. 1987. 49.00 (*0-905028-61-9*); 18.00 (*0-905028-60-0*) Taylor & Francis.

Open Door: Thoughts on Acting & Theatre. Peter Brook. 160p. (Orig.). 1995. pap. 10.95 (*1-55936-102-6*) Theatre Comm.

Open Door: When Writers First Learned to Read. Steven Gilbar. 136p. 1989. pap. 10.95 (*0-87923-921-2*) Godine.

Open Door, Book One: Art & Poetry. Xnadu. LC 78-56655. (Illus.). 32p. 1979. 15.95 (*0-911335-01-3*); pap. 8.95 (*0-911335-03-X*) Open Door Foun.

Open Door Diplomat: The Life of W. W. Rockhill, Vol. 33, No., 4--4. Paul A. Varg. LC 74-20342. (Illinois Studies in the Social Sciences: Vol. 33, Pt. 4). (Illus.). 141p. 1975. reprint ed. lib. bdg. 59.50 (*0-8371-7858-4*, VAOD, Greenwood Pr) Greenwood.

Open Door on John. Philip McFadyen. LC 99-210355. 144p. 1998. pap. text 11.95 (*0-281-05147-X*) Abingdon.

Open-Door Policy & the Territorial Integrity of China. Shutaro Tomimas. LC 75-32329. (Studies in Chinese History & Civilization). 149p. 1976. lib. bdg. 59.95 (*0-313-26954-8*, U6954, Greenwood Pr) Greenwood.

Open Door to Poetry. Anne Stokes. LC 73-140118. (Granger Index Reprint Ser.). 1977. 23.95 (*0-8369-6243-5*) Ayer.

Open Door to Reading. W. Murray. (Key Words Readers Ser.: C Series, No. 641-12c). (Illus.). (J). (ps-5). pap. 3.50 (*0-7214-0036-1*, Ladybrd) Penguin Putnam.

Open Door to Spanish, Bk. 1. Margarita Madrigal. (Illus.). 223p. (C). (gr. 7-12). 1980. audio 45.00 (*0-686-77563-5*, 58471) Prentice ESL.

Open Door to Spanish, Bk. 1. Margarita Madrigal. (Illus.). 223p. (YA). (gr. 7-12). 1980. pap. text 5.25 (*0-88345-420-3*, 18469) Prentice ESL.

Open Door to Spanish, Bk. 2. Margarita Madrigal. (Open Door to Spanish Ser.). 222p. (J). (gr. 7-12). 1981. teacher ed. 1.50 (*0-88345-487-4*, 18474); pap. text 5.25 (*0-88345-427-0*, 18470); audio 45.00 (*0-686-77684-4*, 58472) Prentice ESL.

Open Door to Spanish: A Conversation Course for Beginners, Level 1, Bk. 1. 2nd ed. Margarita Madrigal. LC 94-22581. 256p. 1994. pap. 37.60 (*0-13-181520-2*) P-H.

Open Door to Spanish: A Conversation Course for Beginners, Level 2, Vol. 2. 2nd ed. Margarita Madrigal. (Illus.). 272p. (C). 1994. pap. text 39.60 (*0-13-181538-5*) P-H.

***Open Door to the Universe: A Life's Journey.** Maria L. Martinez. 1998. 13.50 (*0-926524-53-4*) Granite WI.

Open Door to the Universe: Finding the Joy of Spirituality along Life's Path. Maria Lupita Martinez. (Illus.). 172p. 1999. pap. 13.50 (*1-893183-00-9*, 505) Granite Pub.

Open Doors. Tr. by Carlos Reyes from SPA. LC 98-54781.Tr. of Puertas Abiertas. 32p. 1999. pap. 7.00 (*0-932264-25-5*) Trask Hse Bks.

Open Doors, 1996-97: Report on International Educational Exchange. annuals Ed. by Todd M. Davis. 224p. 1997. pap. 42.95 (*0-87206-243-0*) Inst Intl Educ.

Open Drawer: More Poems. Rufus Goodwin. 109p. (Orig.). 1992. pap. write for info. (*0-9628429-1-5*) Urban Pr.

Open Ears. Steve Morse. LC 97-185850. (Illus.). 125p. (YA). pap. 14.95 (*0-89524-884-0*, 02503101) Cherry Lane.

Open Ears: Musical Adventures for a New Generation. Sara Debeer. 141p. (J). 1995. pap. text 18.95 (*1-55961-288-6*) Relaxtn Co.

Open Economies: Structural Adjustment & Agriculture. Ed. by Ian Goldin & L. Alan Winters. (Illus.). 342p. (C). 1992. text 69.95 (*0-521-42056-3*) Cambridge U Pr.

Open Economy: Tools for Policymakers in Developing Countries. Ed. by Rudiger Dorbusch & F. Leslie Helmers. (EDI Series in Economic Development). (Illus.). 424p. 1988. pap. text 19.95 (*0-19-520709-2*) OUP.

Open Economy Dynamics. M. Carlberg. (Contributions to Economics Ser.). (Illus.). x, 203p. 1993. 61.95 (*0-387-91456-0*) Spr-Verlag.

***Open Economy Macroeconomics.** Asbjorn Rodseth. (Illus.). 432p. 2000. write for info. (*0-521-78304-6*); pap. write for info. (*0-521-78874-9*) Cambridge U Pr.

Open-Economy Macroeconomics: Proceedings of a Conference Held in Vienna by the International Economic Association. Ed. by Helmut Frisch & Andreas Worgotter. LC 92-26619. (IEA Conference Ser.: No. 105). 350p. 1993. text 55.00 (*0-312-09015-3*) St Martin.

***Open-Economy Macroeconomics for Developing Countries.** Akhtar Hossain & Anis Chowdhury. LC 97-50580. 264p. 1998. 90.00 (*1-85898-227-8*) E Elgar.

***Open-Economy Macroeconomics for Developing Countries.** Akhtar Hossain & Anis Chowdhury. LC 97-50580. 264p. 2000. pap. 30.00 (*1-84064-453-2*) E Elgar.

Open Economy Politics: The Political Economy of the World Coffee Trade. Robert H. Bates. LC 96-20694. 240p. 1997. text 35.00 (*0-691-02655-6*, Pub. by Princeton U Pr) Cal Prin Full Svc.

Open Economy Politics: The Political Economy of the World Coffee Trade. Robert H. Bates. 1999. pap. text 17.95 (*0-691-00519-2*, Pub. by Princeton U Pr) Cal Prin Full Svc.

Open EDI & Law in Europe: A Regulatory Framework. Andreas Mitrakas. LC 97-36841. (Law & Electronic Commerce Ser.: No. 3). 364p. 1997. 115.00 (*90-411-0489-5*) Kluwer Academic.

Open Education Advisor: Training, Role & Function of Advisors to the Open Corridor Program. Descriptions of Specific Help to Teachers. Ed. by Beth Alberty & Ruth Dropkin. 92p. 1975. pap. 3.50 (*0-918374-10-3*) City Coll Wk.

Open Electromagnetic Waveguides. T. Rozzi & M. Mongiardo. (IEE Electromagnetic Waves Ser.: No. 43). 387p. 1997. 95.00 (*0-85296-896-5*) INSPEC Inc.

Open Elite? England 1540-1880. Lawrence Stone. (Illus.). 340p. 1984. pap. text 29.00 (*0-19-820607-0*) OUP.

Open-End Credit see Installment Credit Series

Open-Ended Approach: A New Proposal for Teaching Mathematics. Ed. by Jerry P. Becker & Shigeru Shimada. LC 97-12708. (Illus.). 175p. 1997. pap. 23.95 (*0-87353-430-1*) NCTM.

Open-Ended Art: First Explorations. Kathy Faggella. Ed. by Nina Fondiller. (Illus.). 96p. 1991. pap. 9.95 (*1-878727-06-0*) First Teacher.

Open-Ended Questioning: A Handbook for Educators. Robin L. Freedman. 1993. pap. 16.20 (*0-201-81958-9*) Addison-Wesley.

Open Entrance to the Closed Palace of the King. Eirenaeus Philalethes. 1985. reprint ed. pap. 7.95 (*0-916411-21-4*) Holmes Pub.

Open Eye, Open Heart. Lawrence Ferlinghetti. LC 73-78784. (New Directions Book Ser.). 160p. 1973. reprint ed. pap. 49.60 (*0-608-05909-9*, 206624400008) Bks Demand.

Open Field. John Brodie & James D. Houston. (San Francisco Ser.). 1974. 7.95 (*0-395-19882-8*) HM.

***Open Field Magnetic Resonance Imaging.** Dietrich H. Groenemeyer & Robert B. Lufkin. LC 99-25519. 500p. 1999. 175.00 (*3-540-63781-8*) Spr-Verlag.

Open Field, Understory: New & Selected Poems. James Seay. LC 96-36281. (Southern Messenger Poets Ser.). 160p. 1997. pap. 15.95 (*0-8071-2130-4*); text 22.95 (*0-8071-2129-0*) La State U Pr.

Open Fields: Science in Cultural Encounter. Gillian Beer. (Illus.). 350p. (C). 1996. text 45.00 (*0-19-818369-0*) OUP.

Open Fields: Science in Cultural Encounter. Gillian Beer. (Illus.). 350p. 1999. pap. text 27.50 (*0-19-818635-5*) OUP.

Open Fire: The Open Magazine Pamphlet Series Anthology, Vol. 1. Ed. by Greg Ruggiero & Stuart Sahulka. LC 92-50758. 320p. 1993. pap. 12.95 (*1-56584-056-9*, Pub. by New Press NY) Norton.

Open Fist: An Anthology of Young Illinois Poets. Intro. by Anne Schultz. LC 93-60983. 120p. 1993. pap. 10.95 (*1-882688-01-5*) Tia Chucha Pr.

***Open for Business.** 275p. 2000. 29.99 (*0-7897-2377-8*) Que.

***Open for Business: A Disaster Planning Toolkit for the Small Business Owner.** Institute for Business & Home Safety Staff. (Illus.). 35p. 1999. 10.00 (*1-885312-21-0*) Inst for Busn.

Open for Business: Creating a Transatlantic Marketplace. Ed. by Bruce Stokes. LC 96-3212. 124p. (Orig.). 1996. pap. 16.95 (*0-87609-187-7*) Coun Foreign.

Open for Business: Melbourne's Living Retail History. Ian Krenins. (Illus.). 105p. 1998. pap. 19.95 (*0-86840-433-0*, Pub. by New South Wales Univ Pr) Intl Spec Bk.

Open for Business: Russia's Return to the Global Economy. Ed A. Hewett. 164p. 1992. 32.95 (*0-8157-3620-7*); pap. 12.95 (*0-8157-3619-3*) Brookings.

Open for Business: The Roots of Foreign Ownership in Canada. Gordon Laxer. (Illus.). 256p. 1989. pap. text 17.95 (*0-19-540734-2*) OUP.

Open for Children: For Those Interested in Early Childhood Education. Judith Danoff et al. (Illus.). 225p. (C). 1991. pap. text 21.95 (*0-87411-482-9*) Copley Pub.

Open for Joy. Marcia Hootman. LC 98-27823. 1998. write for info. (*0-943172-98-5*) New Wave Pubns.

Open Form & the Feminine Imagination: The Politics of Reading in Twentieth-Century Innovative Writing. Stephen-Paul Martin. LC PS228.P6M37. (Post Modern Positions Ser.: Vol. 2). 225p. (Orig.). 1988. lib. bdg. 22.95 (*0-944624-02-2*) Maisonneuve Pr.

Open Form & the Shape of Ideas: Literary Structures As Representations of Philosophical Concepts in the 17th & 18th Centuries. Oscar Kenshur. LC 84-45458. 144p. 1986. 30.00 (*0-8387-5081-8*) Bucknell U Pr.

Open Forum: Your Gateway to Open & Distance Learning. Edward M. O'Ferrall. (Illus.). 352p. 1997. pap. 19.95 (*1-86149-014-3*, Pub. by Edition XII) Baker & Taylor.

***Open Forum on Children & Youth Services (1993) Redefining the Federal Role for Libraries.** Intro. by J. Michael Farrell. 218p. (C). 2000. reprint ed. pap. text 35.00 (*0-7881-8951-4*) DIANE Pub.

Open Game in Action. Anatoly Karpov. 1989. pap. 15.95 (*0-02-021811-7*) Macmillan.

Open Games see Comprehensive Chess Openings

Open Gate: Meditations from the High County. Don I. Smith. LC 94-77057. 128p. 1994. reprint ed. pap. 8.99 (*0-932773-05-2*) High Country Bks.

Open Gate: Prayers in the Celtic Tradition. David Adam. LC 94-44757. (Illus.). 128p. 1995. pap. 9.95 (*0-8192-1640-2*) Morehouse Pub.

Open Gate: Teaching in a Foreign Country--a Personal Account. Chris Roerden. LC 90-82649. (Illus.). 288p. (Orig.). (C). 1990. pap. 14.50 (*0-9626859-3-3*) Edit It Pubns.

Open Gates. Susan T. Spaulding & Francis T. Spaulding. LC 78-128158. (Granger Index Reprint Ser.). 1977. 21.95 (*0-8369-6187-0*) Ayer.

Open Gates: The Protest Against the Movement to Restrict European Immigration, 1896-1924. Henry B. Leonard. Ed. by Francesco Cordasco. LC 80-875. (American Ethnic Groups Ser.). 1981. lib. bdg. 35.95 (*0-405-13437-1*) Ayer.

Open Geometry: Open GL & Advanced Geometry. Georg Glaeser & Hellmuth Stachel. LC 98-34428. (Illus.). 360p. 1998. pap. 39.95 incl. cd-rom (*0-387-98599-9*) Spr-Verlag.

Open GL Programming for the X-Window System. Mark J. Kilgard. 576p. (C). 1996. pap. text 44.95 (*0-201-48359-9*) Addison-Wesley.

Open GL Programming for the X Window System. Mark J. Kilgard. 1996. 39.76 (*0-614-20265-5*) Addison-Wesley.

Open GL Programming for Windows 95. Ron Fosner. LC 96-20193. 288p. (C). 1996. pap. text 42.95 incl. cd-rom (*0-201-40709-4*) Addison-Wesley.

Open GL Reference Manual. 2nd ed. Frank Van Gilluwe. LC 96-33409. 1136p. (C). 1996. pap. text 49.95 (*0-201-47950-8*) Addison-Wesley.

Open Government: A Review of the Federal Freedom of Information Act 1982. Australian Law Reform Commission & Australian Administrative Review Council Staff. LC 98-114580. (Parliamentary Paper/Parliament of the Commonwealth of Australia Ser.). 270p. 1995. write for info. (*0-642-24477-4*) Aust Inst Criminology.

Open Government: A Study of the Prospects of Open Government Within the Limitations of the British Political System. Richard A. Chapman & Michael Hunt. LC 87-9176. 194 p. 1987. write for info. (*0-7099-3484-X*) C Helm.

Open Government: The British Interpretation. Ronald Wraith. 74p. (C). 1977. 45.00 (*0-900628-15-4*) St Mut.

Open Guitar Tunings: A Guide to over 75 Tunings, Vol. 1. Ron Middlebrook. (Illus.). 8p. 1991. pap. 4.95 (*0-931759-47-1*) Centerstream Pub.

Open Hands, Open Heart: The Story of Biddy Mason. Deidre Robinson. (Illus.). 48p. (YA). (gr. 4 up). 1997. 15.95 (*0-9660618-0-2*) Sly Fox Pub.

Open Heart. Judith Sornberger. 128p. 1993. 19.95 (*0-934971-32-3*); pap. 9.95 (*0-934971-31-5*) Calyx Bks.

Open Heart. Abraham B. Yehoshua. Tr. by Dalya Bilu. LC 97-2507. 512p. 1997. pap. 14.00 (*0-15-600484-4*) Harcourt.

***Open Heart: A Brief Collection of Wrods, Written from Inside One Man's Heart.** Rob Burger. 48p. 1999. pap. 7.95 (*0-9675717-0-7*) Open Heart IA.

Open Heart: Secret to Happiness. rev. ed. Lester R. Sauvage. 264p. 1998. pap. 12.95 (*0-9663788-0-6*) Better Life Pr.

Open Heart: The Mystic Path of Loving People. Yitzhak Buxbaum. (Jewish Spirit Booklet Ser.: Vol. 2). 96p. (Orig.). 1997. pap. 9.95 (*0-9657112-2-6*) Jewish Spirit.

Open Heart, Clear Mind. Thubten Chodron. LC 90-41454. 224p. 1990. pap. 12.95 (*0-937938-87-4*) Snow Lion Pubns.

Open Heart, Open Home. 1999. 9.99 (*1-55513-374-6*, Victor Bks) Chariot Victor.

Open Heart, Open Home. rev. ed. Karen Mains. Ed. by Laurie Mains. LC 98-100598. 208p. 1997. reprint ed. wbk. ed. 11.00 (*1-57849-036-7*) Mainstay Church.

Open Heart, Open Mind: Practical Lessons in Loving Your Life. 2nd ed. Swami Chetanananda. LC 97-35518. xiv, 208p. 1998. pap. 14.95 (*0-915801-80-9*) Rudra Pr.

Open Heart Surgery: A Second Chance. Nyles V. Reinfeld. 192p. 1983. 22.00 (*0-13-637520-0*); pap. 14.95 (*0-13-637512-X*) P-H.

Open Heart Surgery: Theory & Practice, 7. Ed. by John C. Callaghan & Joseph Wartak. LC 86-5005. (Surgical Science Ser.: Vol. 7). (Illus.). 190p. 1986. 57.95 (*0-275-92088-7*, C2088, Praeger Pubs) Greenwood.

Open Heart Therapy. Bob Mandel. LC 84-45360. 160p. (Orig.). 1995. pap. 8.95 (*0-89087-408-5*) Celestial Arts.

Open Heart/NYILT SZIV. Edith B. Molnar. (ENG & HUN., Illus.). 55p. 1997. pap. 12.95 (*0-9644836-3-7*) Galvart Pub.

Open Hearts: Renewing Relationships with Recovery, Romance & Reality. Patrick Carnes et al. 236p. pap. 19.95 (*1-929866-00-3*, Pub. by Gentle Path Pr) Hazelden.

Open Heavens: Meditations for Advent & Christmas. Eugen Drewermann. Ed. by Joan M. Laflamme & Bernd Marz. Tr. by David J. Krieger. LC 91-28323. 232p. (Orig.). reprint ed. pap. 72.00 (*0-608-20252-5*, 207151100012) Bks Demand.

***Open Here: The Art of Instructional Design.** Paul Mijksenaar & Piet Westendorp. (Illus.). 144p. 1999. pap. 29.95 (*1-55670-962-5*) Stewart Tabori & Chang.

Open Here! The Art of Instructional Design. Paul Mijksenaar & Piet Westendorp. LC 97-33247. 1998. write for info. (*1-55670-617-0*) Stewart Tabori & Chang.

Open-Hole Fishing. 3rd rev. ed. Ed. by Jean T. Pietrobono. (Rotary Drilling Ser.: Unit III, Lesson 2). (Illus.). 56p. 1988. pap. text 16.00 (*0-88698-126-3*, 2.30230) PETEX.

Open-Hole Logging. Ed. by Jeanette Reynolds & Annes McCann. (Oil & Gas Production Ser.). (Illus.). 87p. (Orig.), (C). 1981. pap. text 15.00 (*0-88698-108-5*, 3.30410) PETEX.

Open Holy Bible: The Old & New Testament, a New Translation from the Oldest Known Aramaic Manuscripts into the English Language. Mar M. Yaqira. LC 98-93750. (Illus.). 320p. Date not set. pap. 16.00 (*0-9667572-0-3*) A One Christ Evangel.

Open Horizons. Sigurd F. Olson. LC 98-21095. (Fesler-Lampert Minnesota Heritage Book Ser.). 256p. 1998. pap. 14.95 (*0-8166-3037-2*) U of Minn Pr.

Open House. 1988. mass mkt. 3.95 (*0-446-73682-1*, Pub. by Warner Bks) Little.

Open House. Katey Lehman & Ross Lehman. (Illus.). 1989. 19.50 (*0-685-29451-X*) Bingham Bks.

Open House. Pat Welch. 224p. 1995. pap. 10.95 (*1-56280-102-3*) Naiad Pr.

Open House: A Guided Tour of the American Home, 1637-Present. Merritt Ierley. LC 97-47082. (Illus.). 336p. 1999. 30.00 (*0-8050-4837-5*) H Holt & Co.

***Open House: A Novel.** Elizabeth Berg. LC 99-54258. 256p. 2000. 23.95 (*0-375-50100-2*) Random.

***Open House: Student Book.** Norman Whitney & David McKeegan. LC 97-32714. 1999. 9.95 (*0-19-435842-9*); 9.95 (*0-19-435854-2*) OUP.

***Open House: Student Book.** Norman Whitney & David McKeegan. LC 97-32714. (J). 1999. 9.95 (*0-19-435846-1*); 9.95 (*0-19-435850-X*) OUP.

Open House Butterflies. Ruth Krauss. LC 60-5782. (Illus.). 48p. (J). (ps-3). 1990. 11.00 (*0-06-023445-8*); lib. bdg. 11.89 (*0-06-023446-6*) HarpC Child Bks.

Open House for Butterflies. Ruth Krauss. LC 60-5782. (Carrot Seed Classic Ser.). (Illus.). 48p. (J). (ps-3). 1982. 3.70 (*0-06-029802-2*) HarpC Child Bks.

Open House for Butterflies. Ruth Krauss & Maurice Sendak. LC 60-5782. (Illus.). 48p. (J). 1999. 12.95 (*0-06-028636-9*, Pub. by Harper SF) HarpC.

Open House for Butterflies. Ruth Krauss & Maurice Sendak. LC 60-5782. (Illus.). 48p. (J). 1999. lib. bdg. 12.89 (*0-06-028637-7*, Pub. by Harper SF) HarpC.

Open Implementations & Metaobject Protocols. Gregor Kiczales & Andreas Paepke. 375p. 1994. 45.00 (*0-262-11192-6*) MIT Pr.

***Open in Nine Months.** Leanna Wilson. (American Romance Ser.: Bk. 847). 2000. mass mkt. 4.25 (*0-373-16847-0*, 1-16847-5) Harlequin Bks.

Open Information Interchange Study on Image-Graphics Standards. 94p. (Orig.). (C). 1994. pap. text 50.00 (*0-7881-0724-0*) DIANE Pub.

Open Institutions: The Hope for Democracy. Ed. by John W. Murphy & Dennis L. Peck. LC 92-20048. 224p. 1992. 57.95 (*0-275-94028-4*, C4028, Praeger Pubs) Greenwood.

Open Inventor C++ Reference Manual: The Official Reference Document for Open Inventor, Release 2. OpenInventor Architecture Group Staff. LC 94-8378. 336p. (C). 1994. pap. 33.95 (*0-201-62493-1*) Addison-Wesley.

***Open Issues in European Central Banking** Lorenzo Bini-Smaghi & Daniel Gros. LC 99-40985. 1999. text 69.95 (*0-312-22845-7*) St Martin.

An Asterisk (*) at the beginning of an entry indicates that the title is appearing for the first time.

Open Kitchen: A Chef's Day at the Inn at Bay Fortune. Michael Smith. (Illus.). 168p. 1998. pap. 19.95 (*1-896511-10-4*, Pub. by Callawind) Firefly Bks Ltd.

*Open Land. large type ed. B. M. Bower. LC 00-40275. 2000. write for info. (*1-57490-288-1*, Sagebrush LP West) T T Beeler.

Open Land in Urban Illinois: Roles of the Citizen Advocate. Rutherford H. Platt. LC 78-146641. 132p. 1971. pap. 15.00 (*0-87580-506-X*) N Ill U Pr.

Open Lands: Travels Through Russia's Once Forbidden Places. Mark Taplin. LC 97-26738. (Illus.). 356p. 1997. 29.50 (*1-883642-01-9*) Steerforth Pr.

Open Lands: Travels Through Russia's Once Forbidden Places. Mark Taplin. LC 97-26738. (Illus.). 376p. 1998. reprint ed. pap. 18.00 (*1-883642-87-6*) Steerforth Pr.

Open Learning. David Bosworth. Ed. by Philip Hills. (Issues in Education Ser.). 140p. 1991. text 90.00 (*0-304-32389-6*); pap. text 31.95 (*0-304-32388-8*) Continuum.

Open Learning: Improving Team Performances. Learning Business Staff. 1997. 29.95 (*0-7506-3146-5*) Buttrwrth-Heinemann.

Open Learning Courses for Adults: A Model of Student Progress. David Kember. LC 94-21399. 1995. 39.95 (*0-87778-280-6*) Educ Tech Pubns.

Open Learning Directory, 1993. Employment Department Staff. (Open Learning Directory). 1993. pap. 58.00 (*0-08-041811-2*, Pergamon Pr) Elsevier.

Open Learning for Nurses. Robinson. 1989. pap. text. write for info. (*0-582-04616-5*, Pub. by Addison-Wesley) Longman.

Open Learning in Nursing, Health & Welfare Education. Kate Robinson & Pam Shakespeare. LC 94-43323. 160p. 1995. 114.95 (*0-335-19075-8*); pap. 36.95 (*0-335-19074-X*) OpUniv Pr.

Open Learning in the Mainstream. Ed. by Grugeon Thopre. 1995. pap. write for info. (*0-582-23897-8*) Longman.

Open Lesson to a Bishop. Michael Davies. 1980. pap. 2.00 (*0-89555-142-X*) TAN Bks Pubs.

*Open Letter to a Jehovah's Witness. Roy Zuck. 2000. pap. 15.00 (*0-8024-6438-6*) Moody.

Open Letter to a Southern White Minister on Prejudice: The Eating Cancer of the Soul. R. C. Lawson. 24p. 1995. pap. 3.50 (*1-887939-01-6*, Ohio Minist) VisionQuest Media.

Open Letter to Confused Catholics. 3rd ed. Marcel Lefebvre. Tr. by Society of St. Pius X Staff from FRE. LC 99-19535. 163p. 1992. reprint ed. pap. 8.95 (*0-935952-13-6*) Angelus Pr.

Open Letter to Jesus Christ. D. M. Bennett. LC 90-40422. 23p. 1990. reprint ed. pap. 4.00 (*0-911826-44-0*, 5024) Am Atheist.

Open Letter to Judge Reginald Stanton Vol. 5: The Champion of Legal Lunacy. Thomas P. Coffay. 1998. pap. 4.95 (*0-87193-293-8*) Dimension Bks.

*Open Letter to Pinochet - Miss Kitty: And Other Words from Chile. Charles Phillip Thomas. LC 00-190153. 281p. 2000. 25.00 (*0-7388-1528-4*); pap. 18.00 (*0-7388-1529-2*) Xlibris Corp.

Open Letter to Pope Leo the XIII. Henry George. (Notable American Authors Ser.). 1992. reprint ed. lib. bdg. 75.00 (*0-7812-2918-9*) Rprt Serv.

Open Letters: Selected Writings, 1965-1990. Vaclav Havel. Tr. by Paul Wilson. 1992. pap. 15.00 (*0-679-73811-8*) Vin Bks.

Open Life: Joseph Campbell in Conversation with Michael Toms. Ed. by John Maher & Dennie Briggs. LC 88-51185. (Illus.). 144p. (Orig.). 1988. pap. 9.95 (*0-943914-47-7*) Larson Pubns.

Open Life: Joseph Campbell in conversation with Michael Toms. Michael Toms & Joseph Campbell. LC 89-46078. (Illus.). 144p. 1990. reprint ed. pap. 12.50 (*0-06-097295-5*, Perennial) HarperTrade.

Open Linux Desktop 2.4: US Version. boxed set 39.95 (*1-930651-02-3*) Caldera Systs.

Open Linux Installation & Configuration Handbook. Gary Wilson. 800p. 1999. pap. text 39.99 (*0-7897-2105-8*) Que.

Open Lives, Safe Schools. Ed. by Donovan R. Walling. LC 95-71812. 300p. 1996. pap. 30.00 (*0-87367-485-5*) Phi Delta Kappa.

Open Look Graphical User Interface Application Style Guide. Sun Microsystems, Inc. Staff. 416p. (C). 1990. pap. text 26.95 (*0-201-52364-7*) Addison-Wesley.

Open Look Graphical User Interface Applications Style Guidelines. Sun Microsystems Inc. Staff. (JPN.). (C). 1992. pap. text. write for info. (*0-201-50976-8*) Addison-Wesley.

Open Look Graphical User Interface Functional Specification. Sun Microsystems Inc. Staff. (JPN.). (C). 1992. pap. text. write for info. (*0-201-50977-6*) Addison-Wesley.

Open Mappings on Locally Compact Spaces. G. T. Whyburn. LC 52-42839. (Memoirs of the American Mathematical Society Ser.: No. 1). 26p. 1969. reprint ed. pap. 16.00 (*0-8218-1201-7*, MEMO/1/1) Am Math.

Open Markets Matter. OECD Staff. 176p. 1998. pap. 20.00 (*92-64-16100-7*, 22 98 01 1 P, Pub. by Org for Econ) OECD.

Open Marxism, Vol. 1. Bonefeld. (C). 54.95 (*0-7453-0424-9*, Pub. by Pluto GBR) Stylus Pub VA.

Open Marxism, Vol. 2. Bonefeld. (C). 54.95 (*0-7453-0425-7*, Pub. by Pluto GBR) Stylus Pub VA.

Open Marxism: Theory & Practice, 2. Werner Bonefeld. 1993. pap. 16.95 (*0-7453-0690-X*) LPC InBook.

Open Marxism Vol. 1: Dialectics & History, Vol. 1. Bonefeld. LC 91-8323. 179p. (C). pap. 20.95 (*0-7453-0590-3*, Pub. by Pluto GBR) Stylus Pub VA.

Open Marxism Vol. 2: Theory & Practice, Vol. 2. Bonefeld. LC 91-8323. 172p. (C). pap. 20.95 (*0-7453-0591-1*, Pub. by Pluto GBR) Stylus Pub VA.

Open Me Carefully: Emily Dickinson's Intimate Letters to Susan Huntington Dickinson. Emily Dickinson. Ed. by Ellen L. Hart & Martha N. Smith. LC 98-31033. 352p. 1998. pap. 19.95 (*0-9638183-6-8*, Pub. by Paris Pr MA) Consort Bk Sales.

Open Me Carefully: Emily Dickinson's Intimate Letters to Susan Huntington Dickinson. Emily Dickinson. Ed. by Ellen L. Hart & Martha N. Smith. LC 98-31033. 352p. 1998. 39.95 (*0-9638183-7-6*, Pub. by Paris Pr MA) Consort Bk Sales.

Open Me Now! Herschell Gordon Lewis. (Illus.). 136p. 1995. 40.00 (*1-56625-036-6*) Bonus Books.

Open Meeting Laws. Ann T. Schwing. LC 94-70164. 688p. (Orig.). 1994. pap. text 85.00 (*0-9607358-8-7*) Fathom Pub.

Open Meetings & Local Governments in North Carolina: Some Questions & Answers. 5th ed. David M. Lawrence. LC 98-203566. vii, 61p. (C). 1998. pap. text 13.00 (*1-56011-326-X*) Institute Government.

Open Me...I'm a Dog! Art Spiegelman. LC 98-104768. (Joanna Cotler Bks.). (Illus.). 32p. (J). (ps-3). 1997. 14.95 (*0-06-027320-8*) HarpC Child Bks.

*Open Mike: Handbook for Creation & Operation of a Poetry Reading. Louis Cuneo. 56p. 2000. pap. 9.95 (*0-9647373-1-0*) Marimbo Commun.

Open Mike Night at the Cabaret Voltaire. David Starkey. Ed. by Ruth M. Kempher. (Illus.). 58p. (Orig.). 1996. pap. 13.00 (*1-888832-01-0*) Kings Estate.

Open Mind: Exploring the 6 Patterns of Natural Intelligence. rev. ed. Dawna Markova. (Illus.). 250p. 1996. pap. 14.95 (*1-57324-064-8*) Conari Press.

Open Mind: Women's Daily Inspirations for Becoming Mindful. Diane Mariechild. LC 94-26377. 400p. 1995. pap. 14.00 (*0-06-251093-2*, Pub. by Harper SF) HarpC.

Open Mind & Sociology. Janet Winn. (American University Studies: Philosophy: Ser. V, Vol. 59). VII, 197p. (C). 1988. text 34.50 (*0-8204-0745-3*) P Lang Pubng.

Open Mind-Critical Mind Problem Solving Guide. (Illus.). 31p. (Orig.). 1990. pap. 7.95 (*0-9628230-1-5*) J L Evers Assocs.

Open Mind, Open Heart: The Contemplative Dimension of the Gospel. Thomas Keating. LC 54-11490. 148p. 1994. reprint ed. pap. 12.95 (*0-8264-0696-3*) Continuum.

Open Minded: Working Out the Logic of the Soul. Jonathan Lear. LC 97-41055. 368p. 1999. text 35.00 (*0-674-45533-9*) HUP.

Open Minded: Working Out the Logic of the Soul. Jonathan Lear. 345p. 1999. pap. 15.95 (*0-674-45534-7*) HUP.

Open Minded Heart: Pathway to an Open Hearted Mind. Jacqueline A. Rogers. 100p. (Orig.). 1995. pap. 9.00 (*0-9633540-5-1*) ARC Pub.

Open Minded Kids!, Vol. 22, Bk. 5. Judy Mohr-Stephens. Ed. by Evelyn Riegert. (Please Understand Us Ser.). (Illus.). 1990. write for info. (*0-935323-22-8*) Barrington Hse.

Open Minded Kids!, Vol. 23, Bk. 5. Judy Mohr-Stephens. Ed. by Evelyn Riegert. (Please Understand Us Ser.). (Illus.). 1990. write for info. (*0-935323-23-6*) Barrington Hse.

Open Minded Kids!, Vol. 24, Bk. 5. Judy Mohr-Stephens. Ed. by Evelyn Riegert. (Please Understand Us Ser.). (Illus.). 1990. write for info. (*0-935323-24-4*) Barrington Hse.

Open Minded Kids!, Vol. 25, Bk. 6. Judy Mohr-Stephens. Ed. by Evelyn Riegert. (Please Understand Us Ser.). (Illus.). 1990. write for info. (*0-935323-25-2*) Barrington Hse.

Open Minded Kids!, Vol. 26, Bk. 6. Judy Mohr-Stephens. Ed. by Evelyn Riegert. (Please Understand Us Ser.). (Illus.). 1990. write for info. (*0-935323-26-0*) Barrington Hse.

Open Minded Kids!, Vol. 27, Bk. 6. Judy Mohr-Stephens. Ed. by Evelyn Riegert. (Please Understand Us Ser.). (Illus.). 1990. write for info. (*0-935323-27-9*) Barrington Hse.

Open-Mindedness & Education. William Hare. 178p. 1993. pap. 22.95 (*0-7735-0411-7*, Pub. by McG-Queens Univ Pr) CUP Services.

Open Minds: Exploring Global Issues Through Reading & Discussion. Steven Widdows & Peter Voller. LC 90-60542. 208p. (Orig.). 1996. pap. text 17.95 (*0-472-08358-9*, 08358) U of Mich Pr.

Open Minds & Everyday Reasoning. 2nd ed. Zachary Seech. 288p. (C). 1992. mass mkt. 29.95 (*0-534-17880-4*) Wadsworth Pub.

Open Minds & Everyday Reasoning. 2nd ed. Zachary Seech. (Philosophy Ser.). 1992. 33.25 (*0-534-17882-0*) Wadsworth Pub.

Open Minds to Equality: A Sourcebook of Learning Activities to Affirm Diversity. 2nd ed. Nancy Schniedwind & Ellen Davidson. LC 97-26994. 387p. (C). 1997. pap. text 42.00 (*0-205-16109-X*) Allyn.

*Open Minds Yearbook of Managed Behavioral Health Marketshare in the United States, 1999-2000. 6th rev. ed. Aleta Fox & Keith Garris. Ed. by Monica E. Oss. (Managed Behavioral Health Marketshare in the United States Ser.). (Illus.). 82p. 1999. spiral bd. 195.00 (*1-878586-16-5*, DR-1) Open Minds PA.

Open Minora II & Doubtful Works. Bernard Mandeville. (GER.). 271p. 1999. reprint ed. write for info. (*3-487-10525-X*) G Olms Pubs.

OPEN Modeling Language (OML) Reference Manual. Donald Firesmith et al. LC 97-31448. (SIGS Reference Library: No. 9). 288p. 1998. pap. text 39.95 (*0-521-64823-8*) Cambridge U Pr.

*Open Modeling with UML. Brian Henderson-Sellers. 304p. 2000. pap. 39.95 (*0-201-67512-9*) Addison-Wesley.

Open Moment. Barbara Stone. 400p. (Orig.). 1985. pap. 11.95 (*0-87418-021-X*, 158) Coleman Pub.

Open Moment: Reflections on the Spiritual Life. Swami Chetanananda. LC 95-19822. xi, 90p. 1995. 16.00 (*0-915801-52-3*) Rudra Pr.

*Open Moral Communities. Seymour J. Mandelbaum. LC 99-43445. 415p. 2000. 35.00 (*0-262-13365-2*) MIT Pr.

Open Mouth - Already a Mistake: Talks by Zen Master Wu Kwang. Wu Kwang. 330p. 1997. pap. 18.95 (*0-942795-08-3*) Primary Point Pr.

*Open MRI. Peter Rothschild & Debra Reinking Rothschild. LC 99-42876. 383p. 1999. write for info. (*0-7817-2173-3*, Lippncott) Lppncott W & W.

Open My Eyes: More Children's Object Lessons by Kenneth Mortonson. Kenneth A. Mortonson. LC 95-41492. 124p. 1996. pap. 11.50 (*0-7880-0566-9*, Fairway Pr) CSS OH.

Open Net: A Professional Amateur in the World of Big-Time Hockey. George Plimpton. 288p. 1993. pap. 12.95 (*1-55821-242-6*) Lyons Pr.

Open Night. John Lehmann. LC 72-142654. (Essay Index Reprint Ser.). 1977. reprint ed. 18.95 (*0-8369-2407-X*) Ayer.

Open Organization: The Impact of Secrecy & Disclosure on People & Organizations. Fritz Steele. LC 74-12805. (Illus.). 216p. reprint ed. pap. 67.00 (*0-608-18458-6*, 205632100058) Bks Demand.

Open Organizations: A Model for Effectiveness, Renewal, & Intelligent Change. Oscar G. Mink et al. LC 94-22696. (Management Ser.). 240p. 1994. text. write for info. (*0-7879-0028-1*) Jossey-Bass.

Open Our Eyes: Poetic Meditations, Inspirations & Affirmations. Nanci C. Thomas. LC 99-231073. (Illus.). 64p. 1999. pap. 14.95 (*0-9669663-0-9*) NuB DuB.

Open Papers. Odysseus Elytis. Tr. by Olga Broumas & T. Begley. LC 94-31307. 200p. 1995. pap. 12.00 (*1-55659-070-9*) Copper Canyon.

Open PGP, Specification & Sample Code. 153p. 1999. spiral bd. write for info. (*1-58368-014-4*) Network Assocs.

Open Pit Mine Design Models. 90.00 (*0-87849-083-3*, Pub. by Trans T Pub) Enfield Pubs NH.

Open Pit Mine Planning & Design. Ed. by John T. Crawford, III & William A. Hustrulid. LC 79-52269. (Illus.). 373p. reprint ed. pap. 115.70 (*0-8357-6644-6*, 203531100094) Bks Demand.

*Open-Pit Mining Equipment in Canada: A Strategic Entry Report, 1998. Compiled by Icon Group International Staff. (Illus.). 139p. 1999. ring bd. 1390.00 incl. audio compact disk (*0-7418-1533-8*) Icon Grp.

*Open-pit Mining Equipment in Colombia: A Strategic Entry Report, 1998. Compiled by Icon Group International Staff. (Country Industry Report). (Illus.). 198p. 1999. ring bd. 1980.00 incl. audio compact disk (*0-7418-0514-6*) Icon Grp.

*Open Pit Mining Machinery in Argentina: A Strategic Entry Report, 1996. Compiled by Icon Group International Staff. (Illus.). 134p. 1999. ring bd. 1340.00 incl. audio compact disk (*0-7418-1329-7*) Icon Grp.

Open Plan Office Acoustical Privacy. J. March et al. (Illus.). 1984. pap. text 39.95 (*0-931673-00-3*) J March Pub Grp.

Open Politics. Ed. by Shadow Congress of America Staff. 1986. pap. 5.95 (*0-913290-65-3*) Camaro Pub.

Open Problems in Communication & Computation. Ed. by T. M. Cover & B. Gopinath. (Illus.). 230p. 1987. 58.95 (*0-387-96621-8*) Spr-Verlag.

*Open Problems in Mathematical Systems & Control Theory. Vincent Blondel. LC 98-38067. (Communications & Control Engineering Ser.). 1999. 99.00 (*1-85233-044-9*) Spr-Verlag.

Open Problems in Topology. Ed. by Jan Van Mill & G. M. Reed. 692p. 1990. 140.00 (*0-444-88768-7*, North Holland) Elsevier.

Open Process Specification. Brian Henderson-Sellers. LC 97-26271. 336p. (C). 1997. 42.19 (*0-201-33133-0*) Addison-Wesley.

Open Protocols: Communications Standard for Building Automation Systems. Anna F. Williams & John A. Bernaden. LC 89-1232. 160p. 1989. text 67.00 (*0-88173-084-X*) Fairmont Pr.

Open Public Library: Cleff & Guttman. Beatrice Von Bismarck. Ed. by Achim Konneke & Michael Lingner. 96p. 1995. pap. 22.50 (*3-89322-684-2*) Dist Art Pubs.

Open Quantum Systems & Feynman Integrals. Pavel Charles. 376p. 1984. text 206.50 (*90-277-1678-1*) Kluwer Academic.

Open Query File Magic: A Complete Guide to Maximizing the Power of OPNQRYF. 2nd ed. Ted Holt. (Illus.). 287p. 1998. pap. 69.00 (*1-883884-57-8*) Midrange Comput.

Open Questions: An Introduction to Philosophy. Emmett Barcalow. 476p. (C). 1991. mass mkt. 27.75 (*0-534-16512-5*) Wadsworth Pub.

Open Questions: An Introduction to Philosophy. Emmett Barcalow. 296p. (C). 1992. 23.50 (*0-534-16514-1*) Wadsworth Pub.

Open Questions: An Introduction to Philosophy. 2nd ed. Emmett Barcalow. LC 95-48129. (Philosophy Ser.). (C). 1996. 52.95 (*0-534-50473-6*) Wadsworth Pub.

Open Questions: An Introduction to Philosophy. 3rd ed. Barcalow. (Philosophy Ser.). 2000. pap. text 36.00 (*0-534-51907-5*) Thomson Learn.

Open Questions in Quantum Physics. Gino Tarozzi & Alan VanDerMerwe. 1984. text 206.50 (*90-277-1853-9*) Kluwer Academic.

Open Questions in Relativistic Physics: Proceedings of an International Conference on Special Relativity & Some of Its Applications, June 25-28, 1997. Franco Selleri. LC 98-900498. 375p. 1998. pap. (*0-9683689-1-3*) C Roy Keys.

Open Range & Parking Lots: Southwest Photographs. Gregory McNamee. LC 99-6452. (Illus.). 104p. 1999. pap. 19.95 (*0-8263-2100-3*) U of NM Pr.

Open Range Men. Lauran Paine. 206p. 1990. 19.95 (*0-8027-4105-3*) Walker & Co.

Open Range Men. large type ed. Lauran Paine. LC 90-40665. 304p. 1990. reprint ed. lib. bdg. 16.95 (*1-56054-041-9*) Thorndike Pr.

Open Regionalism in Latin America & the Caribbean. (Libros de la CEPAL: No. 39). 110p. pap. 17.50 (*92-1-121191-3*, E.94.II.G.3) UN.

Open Registry Shipping, Vol. 12. S. R. Tolofari. xii, 382p. 1989. text 237.00 (*2-88124-724-5*) Gordon & Breach.

Open Research Problems in the Life Sciences under Tropical Conditions. Ed. by D. O. Hall et al. 208p. 1987. text 149.00 (*90-6191-683-6*, Pub. by A A Balkema) Ashgate Pub Co.

Open Rhinoplasty. Joseph Leach & Lanny Close. LC 96-14951. (Self-Instructional Package Ser.). 1996. pap. text 25.00 (*1-56772-021-8*) AAO-HNS.

Open Road. (Hot Wheels Coloring Sticker Storybooks Ser.). (Illus.). 24p. (J). (ps-2). 1998. pap. write for info. (*0-7666-0105-6*, Honey Bear Bks) Modern Pub NYC.

Open Road. Douglas McKinley. LC 95-60356. 320p. 1995. 22.00 (*0-9619380-1-3*) Balboa Bks.

Open Road. 7th ed. Compiled by Edward V. Lucas. LC 75-121928. (Granger Index Reprint Ser.). 1977. 19.95 (*0-8369-6169-2*) Ayer.

*Open Road: Poems on Travel. 2000. pap. 3.95 (*0-460-88214-7*, Everyman's Classic Lib) Tuttle Pubng.

Open Road: Walt Whitman on Death & Dying. Walt Whitman. Ed. by Joe Vest. (Illus.). 128p. 1996. 24.95 (*0-9636501-4-9*) Four Crners.

Open Road Trip. Donald Kummings. (Illus.). (Orig.). 1989. 10.50 (*0-9622192-1-5*); pap. 6.00 (*0-9622192-0-7*) Birch Bark WI.

*Open Road West. Joe Blades. 2000. pap. 10.50 (*1-896647-30-8*) Genl Dist Srvs.

Open Roads - Empty Nests. Louise O. Neaderland. (Illus.). 16p. 1988. 5.00 (*0-942561-12-0*) Bone Hollow.

*Open Ruy Lopez. Glenn Flear. 2000. pap. text 19.95 (*1-85744-261-X*) Cadgn Bks.

Open Says-a-Me. Philip E. Caloia. LC 94-92059. (Illus.). 1024p. 1994. pap. 55.00 (*0-9640814-0-7*) Philications.

Open Science: Distance Teaching & Open Learning of Science Subjects. Shelagh Ross & Eileen Scanlon. 288p. 1995. pap. 29.95 (*1-85396-172-8*, Pub. by P Chapman) Taylor & Francis.

Open Sea. Edgar Lee Masters. (Collected Works of Edgar Lee Masters). 302p. 1999. reprint ed. lib. bdg. 88.00 (*1-58201-773-5*, c0773) Classic Bks.

Open Season. Archer Mayor. 320p. 1989. pap. 3.95 (*0-380-70756-X*, Avon Bks) Morrow Avon.

Open Season. Archer Mayor. 320p. 1994. mass mkt. 6.99 (*0-446-40414-4*, Pub. by Warner Bks) Little.

Open Season. David Wolf. 1999. 9.95 (*0-9659748-3-9*) Center Pr Bks.

Open Season: A Survival Guide for Natural Childbirth in the 1990s. Nancy W. Cohen. LC 91-10569. 464p. 1991. pap. 16.95 (*0-89789-272-0*, G272, Bergin & Garvey) Greenwood.

Open Season: A Survival Guide for Natural Childbirth in the 1990s. Nancy W. Cohen. LC 91-10569. 464p. 1991. 29.95 (*0-89789-252-6*, H252, Bergin & Garvey) Greenwood.

Open Season: Selected Poems. Norman Moser. (New 80's Bk.). (Illus.). 60p. (Orig.). 1980. 3.00 (*0-686-29369-X*) Illuminations Pr.

Open Season Guide: Federal Health Benefits & Premiums, 1993. National Association of Retired Federal Employees. Ed. by Gordon F. Brown. 152p. (Orig.). 1992. pap. 9.95 (*0-9631168-2-7*) Natl Ret Fed Emps.

*Open Secret. Photos by Sandi Fellman. (Illus.). 112p. 1999. 70.00 (*3-908163-01-3*) Abbeville Pr.

Open Secret. Tr. by John Moyne & Coleman Books. 96p. 1996. pap. 9.00 (*0-614-21325-8*, 924) Kazi Pubns.

Open Secret. Colin W. Reid. LC 86-63639. (Illus.). 92p. 1987. pap. 12.95 (*0-86140-240-5*, Pub. by Smyth) Dufour.

Open Secret. Jalal Al-Din Rumi. Tr. by John Moyne & Coleman Barks from ENG. LC 99-31399. 1999. pap. 10.95 (*1-57062-529-8*, Pub. by Shambhala Pubns) Random.

Open Secret. Wei Wu-wei. 1982p. (C). 1982. pap. text 22.50 (*962-209-030-3*, Pub. by HK Univ Pr) Coronet Bks.

Open Secret. large type ed. James Leasor. 480p. 1983. 27.99 (*0-7089-8141-0*, Charnwood) Ulverscroft.

Open Secret. rev. ed. Lesslie Newbigin. 192p. 1995. pap. 15.00 (*0-8028-0829-8*) Eerdmans.

Open Secret: Gay Hollywood, 1928-1998. David Ehrenstein. 416p. 1998. 25.00 (*0-688-14992-8*, Wm Morrow) Morrow Avon.

*Open Secret: Gay Hollywood, 1928-1998. David Ehrenstein. LC 98-35526. (Illus.). 400p. 1998. 25.00 (*0-688-15317-8*, Wm Morrow) Morrow Avon.

*Open Secret: Gay Hollywood, 1928-2000. David Ehrenstein. 400p. 2000. pap. 15.00 (*0-688-17585-6*) Morrow Avon.

Open Secret: Versions of Rumi. Melvana Rumi. Tr. by Coleman Barks. LC 83-50052. 96p. 1984. reprint ed. pap. 11.00 (*0-939660-06-7*) Threshold CA.

Open Secret of Strength. Reuben R. Welch. 144p. 1988. pap. 5.95 (*0-310-75281-7*, 17047P) Zondervan.

Open Secrets. Piet Brinton & Roger Worsley. 96p. (C). 1987. text 49.00 (*0-86383-195-8*, Pub. by Gomer Pr) St Mut.

Open Secrets. Carlton Stowers. 1995. mass mkt. 6.50 (*0-671-70997-6*) PB.

Open Secrets: Congressional Money & Politics. 2nd ed. Larry Makinson. LC 92-5802. 1400p. 1992. 169.95 (*0-87187-689-2*) Congr Quarterly.

***Open Secrets: Drawings & Etchings by Paula Rego.** Memory Holloway & Ruth Rosengarten. (Illus.). 72p. 1999. pap. 12.00 (*0-9666437-2-0*) U of MA Art Gallery.

Open Secrets: Israeli Foreign & Nuclear Policies. Shahak. LC 96-34397. 1997. 49.95 (*0-7453-1152-0*); pap. 18.95 (*0-7453-1151-2*, Pub. by Pluto GBR) Stylus Pub VA.

Open Secrets: Seventy Pictures on Paper 1815 to the Present. Ed. by Jeffrey Fraenkel & Matthew Marks. (Illus.). 145p. Date not set. pap. 40.00 (*1-881337-03-0*) Fraenkel Gal.

Open Secrets: Stories. Alice Munro. 1995. pap. 13.00 (*0-679-75562-4*) Vin Bks.

Open Secrets: The Encyclopedia of Congressional Money & Politics. 3rd ed. Larry Makinson & Joshua F. Goldstein. 1362p. 1994. 179.95 (*1-56802-026-0*) Congr Quarterly.

Open Secrets: The Encyclopedia of Congressional Money & Politics. 4th ed. Larry Mackinson & Joshua F. Goldstein. 1348p. 1996. text 120.00 (*1-56802-229-8*) Congr Quarterly.

Open Security Technology & Electronic Data Interchange. Schindler. 1993. 69.00 (*0-387-53478-4*) Spr-Verlag.

Open Sesame. Jean G. Near. LC 82-91113. (Illus.). 78p. 1983. pap. 4.95 (*0-9609166-1-X*) J Near.

Open Sesame. Anna Ross. LC 91-67671. (Lift-&-Peek-A-Board Bks.). (Illus.). 14p. (J). (ps). 1992. 4.99 (*0-679-83063-4*, Pub. by Random Bks Yng Read) Random.

Open Sesame! Poetry & Prose for School-Days, 3 Vols. enl. rev. ed. Blanche W. Bellamy & Maud W. Goodwin. LC 72-451. (Granger Index Reprint Ser.). text 69.95 (*0-8369-9360-8*); 23.95 (*0-8369-6355-5*) Ayer.

Open Sesame: Stage E: Open Sesame Multilevel Book Duplicating Masters. Carol Cellman. (Illus.). 64p. 1989. pap. text 23.95 (*0-19-434264-6*) OUP.

Open Sesame: Understanding American English & Culture Through Folktales & Stories. Planaria J. Price. LC 90-60157. 248p. 1997. pap. text 16.95 (*0-472-08388-0*, 08388) U of Mich Pr.

***Open Sesame: Understanding American English & Culture Through Folktales & Stories.** Planaria J. Price. LC 96-60157. (Illus.). 248p. (C). 1998. pap. text 42.50 incl. audio (*0-472-08506-9*, 08506) U of Mich Pr.

Open Sesame Stage C: Cookie Monster's Blue Book Duplicating Masters. Jane Z. Brauer. 1985. pap. text, teacher ed. 23.95 (*0-19-434193-3*) OUP.

Open Sesame Stage B: Oscar's Bridge to Reading Book Duplicating Masters. Katrin Tiitsman. 1985. pap. text, teacher ed. 28.95 (*0-19-434190-9*) OUP.

Open Sesame Stage F: Ernie & Bert's Red Book Duplicate Masters. Maureen Harris. (Illus.). 64p. 1987. pap. text 23.95 (*0-19-434195-X*) OUP.

Open Sesame Grover. (Illus.). 64p. 1990. pap. text, student ed. 8.50 (*0-19-434415-0*) OUP.

Open Sesame Grover. (Illus.). 84p. 1991. teacher ed. 15.95 (*0-19-434416-9*) OUP.

***Open Sesame Guide to Exploring the Web.** Schane Santore. (C). 1999. pap. 5.00 (*0-8384-1131-2*) Heinle & Heinle.

Open Sesame Multi-Level Book: Activity Book. 1989. pap. text 5.75 (*0-19-434263-8*) OUP.

Open Sesame Multi-Level Book: Teacher's Book. (Illus.). 228p. 1989. pap. text, teacher ed. 15.95 (*0-19-434262-X*) OUP.

Open Sesame Multilevel Book. Illus. by Tom Brannon et al. (Open Sesame Ser.). 96p. (J). 1988. pap. text, student ed. 8.50 (*0-19-434261-1*) OUP.

Open Sesame Octet. T. Brooks. 1995. pap. text 23.00 (*0-7935-4828-4*, 00000678) H Leonard.

Open Sesame Picture Dictionary. Illus. by Tom Cooke. (Open Sesame Ser.). (ENG & JPN.). (J). 1987. pap. text 8.50 (*0-19-434170-4*) OUP.

Open Sesame Picture Dictionary: English/Spanish Version. Jill W. Schimpff. (Illus.). 96p. 1991. pap. text 8.50 (*0-19-434445-2*) OUP.

Open Sesame Picture Dictionary: Featuring Jim Henson's Sesame Street Muppets, Children's Television Workshop. Jill W. Schimpff. (Illus.). 96p. (J). (gr. k-6). 1982. pap. text 8.50 (*0-19-503035-4*) OUP.

Open Sesame Picture Dictionary: Featuring Jim Henson's Sesame Street Muppets, Children's Television Workshop. Jill W. Schimpff. (Illus.). (J). (gr. k-6). 1983. 12.95 (*0-19-503201-2*) OUP.

Open Sesame Picture Dictionary: Featuring Jim Henson's Sesame Street Muppets, Children's Television Workshop. Jill W. Schimpff. (ENG & CHI., Illus.). (J). (gr. k-6). 1988. pap. text 8.50 (*0-19-583744-4*) OUP.

Open Sesame Picture Dictionary: Open Sesame Picture Cards. Jill W. Schimpff. 1984. 49.95 (*0-19-434176-3*) OUP.

Open Sesame Picture Dictionary: Open Sesame Wall Charts. Jill W. Schimpff. (Illus.). 1987. pap. text 45.95 (*0-19-434257-3*) OUP.

Open Sesame Picture Dictionary Activity Book: Featuring Jim Henson's Sesame Street Muppets, Children's Television Workshop. Jill W. Schimpff. (Illus.). 64p. (J). (gr. k-6). 1988. pap. text, student ed. 5.50 (*0-19-434253-0*) OUP.

***Open Session on the Western Hemisphere Today: A Roundtable Discussion: Congressional Hearings.** Ed. by Elton Gallegly. 92p. (C). 1999. pap. text 25.00 (*0-7881-8291-9*) DIANE Pub.

***Open Shop Building Construction Cost Data 2000.** 16th ed. R. S. Means Company Staff. 2000. pap. 89.95 (*0-87629-549-9*) R S Means.

Open Shop Construction Revisited. Herbert R. Northrup. LC 84-48502. (Major Industrial Research Unit Studies: No. 62). 674p. 1984. 38.00 (*0-89546-047-5*) U PA Ctr Hum Res.

Open Shutters: Photographic Impressions by African-Americans in Hampton Roads. Tommy L. Bogger & William B. Wiggins. Ed. by Donna Reiss. (Illus.). 72p. 1995. pap. 15.00 (*1-885163-02-9*) Virginia Beach Ctr.

Open Signs: Language & Society on the U. S. - Mexico Border. Ed. by Harry Polkinhorn et al. (Binational Press Ser.: No. 4). (ENG & SPA.). 310p. 1993. pap. 17.50 (*1-879691-20-5*) SDSU Press.

Open Skies, Arms Control, & Cooperative Security. Ed. by Michael Krepon & Amy E. Smithson. (Henry L. Stimson Center Bk.). (Illus.). 288p. 1992. text 45.00 (*0-312-06603-1*) St Martin.

Open Skies, Closed Minds. Nick Pope. LC 98-48795. (Illus.). 270p. 1999. text 23.95 (*0-87951-916-9*, Pub. by Overlook Pr) Penguin Putnam.

***Open Sky.** Eric Nisenson. 2000. mass mkt. 14.00 (*0-306-80988-5*, Pub. by Da Capo) HarpC.

Open Sky. Paul Virilio. Tr. by Julie Rose. LC 97-11931. 1997. pap. 18.00 (*1-85984-181-3*, Pub. by Verso) Norton.

***Open Sky: Sonny Rollins & His World of Improvisation.** Eric Nisenson. LC 99-55285. 256p. 2000. text 24.95 (*0-312-25330-3*) St Martin.

***Open Society: The Crisis of Global Capitalism Reconsidered.** George Soros. 2000. pap. 26.00 (*1-58648-019-7*) PublicAffairs NY.

Open Society & Its Enemies, 2 vols. 5th rev. ed. Karl R. Popper. Incl. Vol. 1. Spell of Plato. 368p. 1966. pap. text 19.95 (*0-691-01968-1*, Pub. by Princeton U Pr); 1966. write for info. (*0-318-55362-7*) Princeton U Pr.

Open Society & Its Enemies: The High Tide of Prophecy, Vol. II. Karl R. Popper. 432p. 1966. pap. text 19.95 (*0-691-01972-X*, Pub. by Princeton U Pr) Cal Prin Full Svc.

Open Sore of a Continent: A Personal Narrative of the Nigerian Crisis. Wole Soyinka. (C). 1996. 24.00 (*0-614-95756-7*) OUP.

Open Sore of a Continent: A Personal Narrative of the Nigerian Crisis. Wole Soyinka. (The W. E. B. Dubois Institute Ser.). 176p. 1997. pap. 12.95 (*0-19-511921-5*) OUP.

***Open Source: The Unauthorized White Papers.** Donald K. Rosenberg. 250p. 2000. pap. text 19.99 (*0-7645-4660-0*) IDG Bks.

***Open Source Development with CVS.** Karl Franz Fogel. LC 99-48722. 1999. pap. 39.99 (*1-57610-490-7*) Coriolis Grp.

Open Source Intelligence: Selected Reading: Proceedings, Vol. I, 4th international Symposium on [0013]Global Security & Global Competitiveness: Open Source Solutions[0014] 500p. pap. text. write for info. (*0-7881-8980-8*) DIANE Pub.

Open Source Licensing: Building Business & Cooperation with Open Source Intellectual Property. Stig Hackvan. Ed. by Mark Stone. 180p. 2000. pap. 19.95 (*1-56592-560-2*) OReilly & Assocs.

***Open Source Software Development: Adding Clarity to Chaos.** 300p. 2000. 29.99 (*0-672-31989-6*) Sams.

***Open Sources: Voices from the Open Source Revolution.** Chris DiBona & Sam Ockman. Ed. by Mark Stone. (Illus.). 250p. 1999. pap. 27.95 (*1-56592-582-3*) OReilly & Assocs.

Open Space Conservation: Investing in Your Community's Economic Health. John Tibbetts. (Illus.). 36p. 1998. pap. 14.00 (*1-55844-131-X*) Lincoln Inst Land.

Open Space Decision Process: Spatial Allocation of Costs & Benefits. Rutherford H. Platt. LC 72-85930. (University of Chicago, Department of Geography, Research Paper Ser.: No. 142). 204p. 1972. reprint ed. pap. 63.30 (*0-608-02270-5*, 206291100004) Bks Demand.

Open Space Imperative I: Greenspaces & Greenways. Regional Plan Association Staff. (Illus.). 1987. pap. 5.00 (*0-938085-00-X*) Regional Plan Assn.

Open Space Imperative II: II: Where the Pavement Ends. Regional Plan Association Staff. 1987. 5.00 (*0-938085-03-4*) Regional Plan Assn.

Open Space Planning in India. Werner Y. Wolff. Ed. by Schweiz. (Swiss Asian Studies. Research Studies: Vol. 11). (Illus.). VI, 692p. 1991. 76.00 (*3-261-04229-X*) P Lang Pubng.

Open Space, Preservation & Acquisition: Building Sustainable Communities, an Environmental Guide for Local Government. Center for the Study of Law & Politics Staff. 162p. 1991. 40.00 (*1-880386-05-4*) Ctr Study Law.

Open Space Technology: A User's Guide. 2nd rev. ed. Harrison Owen. LC 97-17807. 200p. 1997. pap. 24.95 (*1-57675-024-8*) Berrett-Koehler.

Open Space Values: A Household Survey of Two Philadelphia Parks. David Berry. (Discussion Papers: No. 76). 1974. pap. 10.00 (*1-55869-087-5*) Regional Sci Res Inst.

Open Spaces: Country Poems. David Molitor. (Illus.). 80p. (Orig.). 1996. pap. 10.95 (*0-918292-19-0*) Griggs Print.

***Open Spaces: Lands of the Marin County Open Space District.** Barry Spitz. (Illus.). 272p. 1999. pap. 17.95 (*0-9620715-6-0*) Potrero Meadow Pub.

Open Spaces -Strategien im Offentlichen Raum / Strategies in Public Space. Ed. by Jochem Schneider & Christine Baumgartner. (GER & ENG., Illus.). 240p. 79.00 (*3-930698-99-4*) Edition A Menges.

Open Spaces, City Places: Contemporary Writers on the Changing Southwest. Ed. by Judy N. Temple. LC 93-35926. 144p. (Orig.). 1994. pap. 16.95 (*0-8165-1440-2*) U of Ariz Pr.

Open Spaces in Vienna: A Guide to Contemporary Landscaping. George Lammel. 1998. write for info. (*3-211-83178-9*) Spr-Verlag.

Open Spain - Espana Abierta: Contemporary Documentary Photography in Spain. Ed. by Terry A. Neff. Tr. by Lee Fontanella. (ENG & SPA., Illus.). 264p. 1992. write for info. (*0-932026-27-3*) Columbia College Chi.

***Open Spanish.** Glenn Flear. (Chess Bks.). 1999. pap. text 15.95 (*0-7134-8519-1*) B T B.

Open Spiral of Life: A Book of Poetry. Holly L. Huyck. LC 97-95112. (Illus.). 104p. 1997. pap. 14.95 (*0-9662308-1-7*) Rio Gato Prodns.

***Open States in the Global Economy: The Political Economy of Small-State Macroeconomic Management.** Jonathon W. Moses. LC 99-53014. 2000. text 69.95 (*0-312-23106-7*) St Martin.

Open Stock. Ed. by Henry Kranz. 1980. 3.00 (*0-942582-02-0*) Erie St Pr.

***Open-string Guitar Chords: An Encyclopedia of Over 4,000 Unique & Practical Voicings for All Styles & Levels.** Tom Principato. 104p. 1999. otabind 9.95 (*0-634-00478-6*) H Leonard.

***Open Studio.** Deryck Healey. (Illus.). 115p. 1999. 50.00 (*0-944092-83-7*) Twin Palms Pub.

Open Summer. Jennifer Martin. (Chapbook Series II: No. 4). 24p. 1980. pap. 2.50 (*1-880649-10-1*) Writ Ctr Pr.

Open Superbible. 2nd ed. 700p. 1920. 49.99 (*0-672-31830-X*) Macmillan.

***Open Superbible.** 2nd ed. 700p. 1999. 49.99 (*1-57169-164-2*, Waite Grp Pr) Sams.

Open System: Cooperative Computing in the 1990's. David King. (C). 1996. text. write for info. (*0-201-54835-6*) Addison-Wesley.

Open System Architecture for CIM. Ed. by ESPRIT Consortium AMICE Staff. (Research Reports ESPRIT, Project 688, AMICE: Vol. 1). ix, 212p. 1990. pap. 24.00 (*0-387-52058-9*) Spr-Verlag.

Open System Architecture for CIM. 2nd enl. rev. ed. Ed. by ESPRIT Consortium AMICE Staff. LC 93-1199. (Research Reports ESPRIT, Project 688, AMICE: Vol. 1). xi, 234p. 1993. 42.95 (*0-387-56256-7*) Spr-Verlag.

Open System Environment: Architectural Framework for Information Infrastructure. 1997. lib. bdg. 250.95 (*0-8490-7689-7*) Gordon Pr.

Open System Networking. (C). 1996. write for info. (*0-201-42033-3*) Addison-Wesley.

Open Systems: Setting Sail. Simon Holloway. LC 94-12442. 212p. 1994. 91.95 (*0-291-39810-3*) Ashgate Pub Co.

***Open Systems & Measurement in Relativistic Quantum Theory: Proceedings of the Workshop Held at the Istituto Italiano Per Gli Studi Filosofici, Napoli, April 3-4, 1998.** Ed. by H. P. Breuer et al. (Lecture Notes in Physics Ser.: Vol. 526). viii, 240p. 1999. 68.00 (*3-540-65978-1*) Spr-Verlag.

Open Systems Approach to Quantum Optics: Lectures Presented at the Universite Libre de Bruxelles, October 28 to November 4, 1991. Howard Carmichael. LC 93-19394. (Lecture Notes in Physics, New Series, Monographs: Vol. M18). x, 179p. 1993. 51.95 (*0-387-56634-1*) Spr-Verlag.

Open Systems Engineering: How to Plan & Develop Client-Server Systems. Wendy Rauch. LC 95-50773. 400p. 1996. pap. 54.99 incl. cd-rom (*0-471-13038-9*) Wiley.

Open Systems for Europe. Ed. by A. D. Elliman & C. Sanger. (UNICOM Applied Information Technology Ser.: No. 7). (Illus.). 186p. 1991. mass mkt. 115.50 (*0-412-37850-7*) Chapman & Hall.

Open Systems for Europe. Ed. by T. Elliman & C. Sanger. (UNICOM Applied Information Technology Ser.: No. 6). 176p. 1991. 99.95 (*0-442-30833-7*) Chapman & Hall.

Open Systems Handbook: A Guide to Building Open Systems. James Isaak et al. LC 94-31846. 1994. 69.00 (*1-55937-435-7*) IEEE Standards.

Open Systems in Medicine: The Berlin Approach to Medical Information Processing. Ed. by Eckart Fleck. LC 92-51050. (Studies in Health Technology & Informatics: Vol. 8). 350p. (gr. 12). 1995. 117.00 (*90-5199-123-1*, Pub. by IOS Pr) IOS Press.

Open Systems Interconnection. Intro. by M. R. Tolhurst. (Computer Science Ser.). (Illus.). 237p. (C). 1988. pap. text 35.00 (*0-333-46803-1*) Scholium Intl.

Open Systems Interconnection: Upper Layer Standards & Practices. Baha Hebrawi. 1993. 49.00 (*0-07-033754-3*) McGraw.

Open Systems Networking, TCP - IP & OSI. David M. Piscitello & A. Lyman Chapin. 624p. 1993. 59.95 (*0-201-56334-7*) Addison-Wesley.

Open Systems '93 - Internal Conference on Open Plasma Confinement Systems for Fusion. A. N. Shrinsky. 640p. 1994. text 178.00 (*981-02-1523-1*) World Scientific Pub.

Open Systems Products Directory, 1995. rev. ed. Ed. by UniForum Staff. 1600p. (C). 1995. pap. text 125.00 (*0-936593-30-X*) UniForum.

Open Systems Products Directory, 1996. rev. ed. Ed. by Uniforum Staff. 1600p. (C). 1996. pap. 125.00 (*0-614-10802-0*) UniForum.

Open Systems Standards. Shane McCarron. Ed. by UniForum Staff. (Illus.). 32p. (C). 1995. pap. text. write for info. (*0-936593-31-8*) UniForum.

Open Texts, Partial Maps: A Literary Theory Handbook. Ian Saunders. pap. 13.00 (*0-86422-238-6*, Pub. by Univ of West Aust Pr) Intl Spec Bk.

Open the Barn Door, Find a Cow. Illus. by Christopher Santoro. LC 91-62579. (Chunky Flap Bks. Ser.). 22p. (J). (ps). 1993. 3.99 (*0-679-80901-5*, Pub. by Random Bks Yng Read) Random.

Open the Box: About Television. Janet Root. (Comedia Bks.). 128p. (C). 1988. pap. text 16.99 (*0-906890-78-0*, Pub. by Comedia) Routldge.

Open the Deck. Tanis Knight & Larry Lewin. (Writing Program Ser.). (J). (gr. 6-9). 1982. pap. 11.95 (*0-933282-07-9*); text 15.95 (*0-933282-09-5*) Stack the Deck.

Open the Door! Catherine Carswell. 415p. 1997. pap. 12.95 (*0-86241-644-2*, Pub. by Canongate Books) Interlink Pub.

Open the Door. Osbert Sitwell. LC 75-142277. (Short Story Index Reprint Ser.). 1977. 20.95 (*0-8369-3761-9*) Ayer.

***Open the Door: A Gathering of Poems & Prose Pieces.** Elizabeth Yates. LC 99-22382. (Illus.). 64p. 1999. pap. 11.95 (*1-893894-00-2*) N H Soc.

Open the Door Let's Explore More! Field Trips of Discovery for Young Children. Rhoda Redleaf. LC 96-14294. (Illus.). 368p. (Orig.). 1996. pap. 21.95 (*1-884834-13-2*, 4020) Redleaf Pr.

Open the Door, Little Dinosaur. Katharine Ross. LC 92-80950. (Lift-&-Peek-A-Board Bks.). (Illus.). 14p. (J). (ps). 1993. 3.99 (*0-679-83689-6*, Pub. by Random Bks Yng Read) Random.

Open the Door to Another Language-Spanish see Abra la Puerta a Otro Idioma-Ingles

Open the Door to French. Margarita Madrigal & Dulac. (C). 1987. pap. text 19.20 (*0-13-637232-5*) P-H.

Open the Door to Global Communication. Lee K. Curtis. (Illus.). 32p. (Orig.). 1996. pap. 3.50 (*0-9646390-0-9*) Wind Word Pr.

Open the Frontiers. Leon-Joseph Suenens. 1984. 8.95 (*0-8164-0489-5*) Harper SF.

Open the Lights. Corine Carruthers. 1981. spiral bd. 40.13 (*0-201-10201-3*) Addison-Wesley.

Open the Social Sciences: Report of the Gulbenkian Commission on the Restructuring of the Social Sciences. LC 95-45759. xviii, 105p. 1996. 37.50 (*0-8047-2726-0*) Stanford U Pr.

Open the Social Sciences: Report of the Gulbenkian Commission on the Restructuring of the Social Sciences. Immanuel Wallerstein. LC 95-45759. xviii, 105p. 1996. pap. 10.95 (*0-8047-2727-9*) Stanford U Pr.

Open the Windows: The Popes & Charismatic Renewal. Ed. by Kilian McDonnell. LC 88-83044. xxvii, 67p. (Orig.). 1989. pap. 5.95 (*0-937779-06-7*) Greenlawn Pr.

Open to Closeness. John M. Dettoni. (Groupbuilders Series for Adults). 144p. 1991. pap. 6.50 (*0-89693-881-6*, 6-1881, Victor Bks) Chariot Victor.

Open to Glory. Carol Doran & Thomas H. Troeger. LC 82-18753. 160p. 1993. pap. 14.00 (*0-8170-0981-7*) Judson.

Open to Question: The Art of Teaching & Learning by Inquiry. Walter L. Bateman. LC 90-53089. (Higher Education Ser.). 245p. 1990. 32.95 (*1-55542-268-3*) Jossey-Bass.

Open to the Public: A Guide to the Museums of Northern California. Charlene Akers. (Illus.). 352p. (Orig.). 1994. pap. 14.95 (*0-930588-72-X*) Heyday Bks.

Open to the Public: New & Collected Stories. Muriel Spark. LC 97-20607. 376p. 1997. reprint ed. 24.95 (*0-8112-1367-6*, Pub. by New Directions) Norton.

Open to the Unknown: Dialogues in Delphi. Jean Klein. Ed. by Emma Edwards. LC 92-64317. 130p. (Orig.). 1992. 12.95 (*1-877769-18-5*) Third Millennium.

Open Tomb: A New Approach, Mark's Passover Haggadah (Plus - 72CE) Karel Hanhart. 848p. (Orig.). 1993. 59.95 (*0-8146-5010-4*, M Glazier) Liturgical Pr.

Open Toolbox of Techniques. Brian Henderson-Sellers. LC 98-34616. 448p. (C). 1998. pap. text 49.95 (*0-201-33134-9*) Addison-Wesley.

Open Tubular Column Gas Chromatography in Environmental Sciences. Francis I. Onuska & Francis W. Karasek. LC 84-4806. 294p. 1984. 79.50 (*0-306-41589-5*, Plenum Trade) Perseus Pubng.

Open Tubular Columns in Gas Chromatography. Leslie S. Ettre. LC 65-13583. (Illus.). 184p. 1965. reprint ed. pap. 57.10 (*0-608-05414-3*, 206588300006) Bks Demand.

***Open Tuning Chord Book.** Felix Schell. 48p. 1999. 8.95 (*0-7866-4692-6*, 98286) Mel Bay.

Open Tuning for Solo Guitar: 14 Songs, 9 Tuning. Dorian Michael. (Illus.). 80p. 1997. pap. 19.95 incl. cd-rom (*1-57424-050-1*) Centerstream Pub.

Open Twenty-Four Hours: A Case Study. Mary E. Heim. (Occasional Papers: No. 187). 1990. pap. 2.50 (*0-685-34550-5*) U of Ill Grad Sch.

Open 24 Hours: Featuring 5 Canadian Poets. Anne Burke et al. LC 98-111657. 108p. 1997. pap. text 10.50 (*0-921411-64-2*) Genl Dist Srvs.

Open Universe: An Argument for Indeterminism. Karl R. Popper. 208p. (C). 1992. pap. 27.99 (*0-415-07865-2*) Routledge.

Open Universities: A British Tradition? Robert Bell & Malcolm Tight. LC 92-36208. 1993. 123.00 (*0-335-19126-6*) OpUniv Pr.

Open University. Walter Perry. 320p. 1988. pap. 19.99 (*0-335-15828-5*) OpUniv Pr.

Open University. Walter Perry. LC 76-55917. (Illus.). 316p. reprint ed. pap. 98.00 (*0-8357-4693-3*, 205234800008) Bks Demand.

Open University of America Founder, Mary Columbro Rodgers: Short Bio-Bibliography for Researchers. Mary C. Rodgers. 220p. 1999. pap. 30.00 (*0-89848-381-6*) Open Univ Am.

Open University of America the First Thirty-Five Years, 1965-2000: Memoir of the Founder. Mary C. Rodgers. (Illus.). 350p. 2000. 35.00 (*0-89848-385-9*); pap. 29.00 (*0-89848-386-7*) Open Univ Am.

Open University Opens. Ed. by Jeremy Tunstall. LC 74-78983. 192p. 1974. reprint ed. 27.50 (*0-87023-167-7*); reprint ed. pap. 14.95 (*0-87023-168-5*) U of Mass Pr.

Open Up. Illus. by Bob Ostrom. LC 98-224670. 1998. 4.99 (*0-679-89244-3*, Pub. by Random Bks Yng Read) Random.

An Asterisk (*) at the beginning of an entry indicates that the title is appearing for the first time.

***Open up Words & Understand the World (Decouvrons les Mots et Nous Comprendrons le Monde)** Colette Buvat. LC 99-54. 134p. 1999. spiral bd. 12.96 (*1-55212-303-0*) Trafford Pub.

Open up Your Life: A Woman's Workshop on Christian Hospitality. Latayne C. Scott. 144p. 1984. pap. 5.99 (*0-310-38901-1*, 10451P) Zondervan.

Open Veins of Latin America: Five Centuries of the Pillage of a Continent. Eduardo Galeano. Tr. by Cedric Belfrage from SPA. LC 72-92036. (Illus.). 320p. 1973. pap. 15.00 (*0-85345-308-X*, Pub. by Monthly Rev) NYU Pr.

Open Veins of Latin America: Five Centuries of the Pillage of a Continent, 25th Anniversary Edition. 25th ed. Eduardo Galeano. Tr. by Cedric Belfrage from SPA. LC 97-44750. 360p. 1997. pap. 18.00 (*0-85345-991-6*, Pub. by Monthly Rev) NYU Pr.

Open Veins of Latin America: Five Centuries of the Pillage of a Continent, 25th Anniversary Edition. 25th anniversary ed. Eduardo Galeano. Tr. by Cedric Belfrage from SPA. LC 97-44750. 360p. 1997. 27.00 (*0-85345-990-8*, Pub. by Monthly Rev) NYU Pr.

Open Vistas. Henry Margenau. LC 83-60547. x, 256p. 1983. reprint ed. 26.00 (*0-918024-27-7*); reprint ed. pap. 14.00 (*0-918024-28-5*) Ox Bow.

Open VMS: Architecture, Use, & Migration. Raj Bhargava. 1995. 50.00 (*0-07-005157-7*) McGraw.

Open VMS Alpha Internals & Data Structures: Scheduling & Process Control. Ruth E. Goldenberg et al. LC 97-128795. 580p. 1996. pap. text 64.95 (*1-55558-156-0*, Digital DEC) Buttrwrth-Heinemann.

Open VMS AXP Internals & Data Structures: Version 1.5. Ruth E. Goldenberg & Saro Saravanan. LC 94-11874. 1672p. 1994. text 90.00 (*1-55558-120-X*, Digital DEC) Buttrwrth-Heinemann.

Open VMS Operating System Concepts. 2nd ed. David D. Miller. LC 97-7963. 541p. 1997. pap. text 49.95 (*1-55558-157-9*, Digital DEC) Buttrwrth-Heinemann.

Open VMS Performance Management. Joginder Sethi. (Illus.). 300p. 1995. pap. 47.95 (*1-55558-126-9*, Digital DEC) Buttrwrth-Heinemann.

Open VMS Performance Management. 2nd ed. Joginder Sethi. 1998. pap. 44.95 (*1-55558-206-0*) DEC.

Open VMS System Management Guide. Lawrence Baldwin. LC 95-14965. (Illus.). 416p. 1995. pap. 59.95 (*1-55558-143-9*, Digital DEC) Buttrwrth-Heinemann.

Open Water. Frank Stewart. 64p. 1982. pap. 6.00 (*0-912449-06-3*) Floating Island.

Open Water Cladocera of Ohio. B. Diana Zimmerman & Jerry H. Hubschman. LC 88-60897. (Bulletin New Ser.: Vol. 8, No. 3). (Illus.). 70p. 1990. pap. text 7.00 (*0-86727-106-X*) Ohio Bio Survey.

Open Water Diver: Manual para el Instructor de Buceo en Aguas Abiertas. Robert A. Clark. (SPA.). 140p. 1991. pap. 110.00 (*0-943717-71-X*) Concept Sys.

Open Water Diver Log Book. Jeppesen. 48p. (gr. 13). 1984. spiral bd. 8.95 (*0-8016-9006-4*, 21000) Mosby Inc.

***Open Water Diver Manual.** (DUT., Illus.). 232p. 1998. pap. text 22.95 (*1-880229-47-1*, 2201-D) Concept Sys.

Open Water Diver Manual. Don Freeman. 212p. 1990. pap. text 15.95 (*0-943717-74-4*) Concept Sys.

Open Water Diver Manual. Don Freeman. Tr. by Linda Ferwerda. (DUT.). 212p. 1994. pap. text 21.95 (*1-880229-21-8*) Concept Sys.

Open Water Diver Manual. rev. ed. Karl Shreeves et al. Ed. by Drew Richardson et al. (Illus.). 272p. 1990. pap. text 18.95 (*1-878663-16-X*) PADI.

Open Water Diver Manual. 2nd ed. Don Freeman. 212p. 1992. pap. text 15.95 (*1-880229-08-0*) Concept Sys.

Open Water Diver Manual. 3rd ed. Don Freeman. 218p. 1995. pap. text 12.95 (*1-880229-29-3*) Concept Sys.

Open Water Diver Manual - Metric. rev. ed. Karl Shreeves et al. Ed. by Tonya Talley & Beth Kneeland. (Illus.). 270p. (C). 1990. reprint ed. pap. text 24.95 (*1-878663-17-8*) PADI.

Open Water Diver Manual de Buceo en Aguas Abiertas. Don Freeman. Tr. by Carol A. Stymans & Carlos Duran. (SPA.). 212p. 1991. pap. text 17.25 (*0-943717-79-5*) Concept Sys.

Open Water Diver Manual de Trabajos de Buceo en Aguas Abiertas. Don Freeman. Tr. by Carol A. Stymans & Carlos Duran. 22p. 1991. student ed. 4.50 (*0-943717-80-9*) Concept Sys.

Open Water Diver Study Guide. 3rd ed. Dennis Pulley. 24p. 1995. pap. text 12.95 (*1-880229-30-7*) Concept Sys.

Open Water Diver Workbook. Don Freeman. 22p. 1990. 4.95 (*0-943717-75-2*) Concept Sys.

Open Water Diver Workbook. Don Freeman. Tr. by Linda Ferwerda. (DUT.). 22p. 1994. pap. text 4.95 (*1-880229-22-6*) Concept Sys.

Open Water I Instructor Guide. Dennis Graver. 284p. 1987. ring bd. 69.59 (*0-916974-33-2*, 11006) NAUI.

Open Water Sport Diver, Instructor's Guide. 5th ed. Clinchy. 48p. 1992. teacher ed., spiral bd. 7.95 (*0-8016-9036-6*) Mosby Inc.

Open Water Sport Diver, Workbook. 5th ed. Clinchy. 51p. 1991. pap. text, wbk. ed. 7.95 (*0-8016-9037-4*) Mosby Inc.

Open Water Swimming. Penny Lee Dean. LC 97-38472. (Illus.). 232p. 1998. pap. 18.95 (*0-88011-704-4*, PDEA0704) Human Kinetics.

Open Weave. Devorah Major. LC 95-14834. 176p. (Orig.). 1995. pap. 20.95 (*1-878067-66-4*) Seal Pr WA.

Open Weave. Devorah Major. 256p. (Orig.). 1997. reprint ed. mass mkt. 6.99 (*0-425-15665-6*) Berkley Pub.

Open Wide: Tooth School Inside. Laurie Keller. LC 99-27965. (Illus.). 40p. (J). (gr. k-5). 2000. 16.95 (*0-8050-6192-4*) H Holt & Co.

Open Wide . . . This Won't Hurt a Bit! A Dentist's Guide to Self-Discovery & Self-Management. Doug Siebert. (Illus.). 226p. 1991. 39.95 (*0-9631005-0-5*) D Siebert Co.

***Open Wide : A Visit to the Dentist.** Cecile Schoberle. (Rugrats Ser.: Vol. 14). (Illus.). 24p. (J). (ps-2). 2000. 3.50 (*0-689-82570-6*) S&S Childrens.

***Open Wide : A Visit to the Dentist.** Cecile Schoberle. (Rugrats Ser.). (J). (ps-3). 2000. per. write for info. (*0-671-77361-5*) S&S Childrens.

Open Wide the Doors to Christ: A Framework for Action to Implement "Tertio Millennio Adveniente" 48p. 1997. pap. 4.95 (*1-57455-213-9*) US Catholic.

Open Window. Saki, pseud. 1964. pap. 3.50 (*0-87129-288-2*, O17) Dramatic Pub.

***Open Window: The Cinema of Victor Erice.** Ed. by Linda C. Ehrlich. LC 99-58344. (Filmmakers Ser.). 336p. 2000. 55.00 (*0-8108-3766-8*) Scarecrow.

Open Window - Open Door. Richard Stoker. 192p. 1985. 39.00 (*0-7212-0699-9*, Pub. by Regency Pr GBR) St Mut.

Open Windows: Canadian Short Short Stories. Ed. by Kent Thompson. 112p. 1988. pap. 12.95 (*0-919627-58-7*, Pub. by Quarry Pr) LPC InBook.

Open Windows NT: The Road to DCE Client/Server Systems. Ira Hertzoff. (Illus.). 416p. 1997. text 55.00 (*0-07-028464-4*) McGraw.

Open Work. Umberto Eco. Tr. by Anna Cancogni from ITA. LC 88-21399. 320p. 1989. 42.50 (*0-674-63975-8*); pap. 19.95 (*0-674-63976-6*) HUP.

Open Workings. Iain Bamforth. LC 97-131675. 96p. 1997. pap. 14.95 (*1-85754-257-6*, Pub. by Carcanet Pr) Paul & Co Pubs.

Open World. Hermann Weyl. LC 89-3049. viii, 84p. 1989. reprint ed. 30.00 (*0-918024-71-4*); reprint ed. pap. 14.00 (*0-918024-70-6*) Ox Bow.

Open World: Essays on Leslie Norris. Ed. by Eugene England & Peter Makuck. (ENGL Ser.). xviii, 208p. 1994. 50.00 (*1-879751-82-8*) Camden Hse.

***Open Wound: The Genocide of German Ethnic Minorities in Russia & the Soviet Union, 1915-1949 - And Beyond.** Samuel Sinner.Tr. of Genocid An Russianddeutschen. (ENG & GER.). 375p. 2000. pap. write for info. (*1-891193-08-2*) ND State Univ.

Open Your California Business in 24 Hours: The Complete Start-Up Kit. Peri H. Pakroo. LC 97-37388. (Illus.). 250p. 1998. pap. 24.95 incl. cd-rom (*0-87337-410-X*) Nolo com.

***Open Your California Business in 24 Hours: The Complete Start-Up Kit.** 2nd ed. Peri Pakroo. LC 00-40210. 2000. write for info. (*0-87337-603-X*) Nolo com.

Open Your Ears to Love. Bettine Clemen. 1999. pap. 14.95 (*0-9666770-1-3*) Hovenden Pr.

***Open Your Eyes: 1,000 Simple Ways to Bring Beauty into Your Home & Life Each Day.** Alexandra Stoddard. 336p. 2000. pap. 15.00 (*0-380-73144-4*, HarpRes) HarpInfo.

***Open Your Eyes: 1,000 Simple Ways to Bring Beauty into Your Home & Life Each Day.** Alexandra Stoddard. LC 98-26953. (Illus.). 256p. 1998. 28.00 (*0-688-15904-4*, Wm Morrow) Morrow Avon.

***Open Your Eyes, Sidney Miffet!** Marcie Aboff. (Illus.). 12p. (J). (gr. k-2). 1999. pap. 3.75 (*1-880612-92-5*) Seedling Pubns.

Open Your Eyes, Take a Look at the World. Heng Sure et al. (Illus.). 323p. (Orig.). 1979. pap. 9.00 (*0-917512-32-4*) Buddhist Text.

Open Your Heart. Robin J. Gunn. LC 97-24444. (Sierra Jensen Ser.: Bk. 7). 16p. (J). (gr. 7-9). 1998. pap. 5.99 (*1-56179-562-3*) Focus Family.

Open Your Heart for Love & Your Mind to Harmony. Date not set. pap. write for info. (*1-893637-29-8*) Hlth & Hap.

Open Your Hearts. Michael McColgan. LC 95-72818. 126p. (Orig.). 1996. pap. text 5.95 (*1-882972-62-7*, 3479) Queenship Pub.

Open Your Mind & Be Healed. Johnnie Colemon. LC 97-67757. 96p. 1997. 12.95 (*0-87516-709-8*) DeVorss.

Open Your Mind to Prosperity. rev. ed. Catherine Ponder. LC 70-155720. 184p. 1984. reprint ed. pap. 10.95 (*0-87516-531-1*) DeVorss.

Open Your Mind to Receive. Catherine Ponder. LC 82-74283. 128p. 1983. pap. 10.95 (*0-87516-507-9*) DeVorss.

Open Your Mouth But Don't Say "Ah" Philip Thorek. LC 93-37682. (Illus.). 88p. 1994. pap. 14.95 (*0-89640-252-5*) Igaku-Shoin.

Open Your Mouth for the Dumb. P. Barnes. 1984. pap. 1.45 (*0-85151-390-5*) Banner of Truth.

Open Your Own Bed & Breakfast. 3rd rev. enl. ed. Barbara Notarius & Gail S. Brewer. LC 95-23952. 336p. 1996. pap. 17.95 (*0-471-13044-3*) Wiley.

Openbook Management & Corporate Performance. Jill Maxwell et al. 100p. Date not set. pap. text. write for info. (*0-926902-39-3*) NCEO.

***Opencable Architecture.** Michael Adams. 400p. 1999. 50.00 (*1-57870-135-X*) Cisco Press.

Opencast Mining Technology & Integrated Mechanisation. V. Rzhevsky. 495p. (C). 1987. 110.00 (*0-685-46641-8*, Pub. by Collets) St Mut.

OpenDoc Cookbook. Apple Computer, Inc. Staff. 208p. (C). 1996. pap. text 24.95 (*0-201-47956-7*) Addison-Wesley.

OpenDoc Developers Guide Macintosh Components. Stephen Humphrey. 1996. pap. text 45.00 incl. cd-rom (*1-56830-270-3*) Hayden.

OpenDoc Programming for the Mac. Doug Houseman. 352p. 1995. pap. 39.95 incl. cd-rom (*1-55851-433-3*, M&T Bks) IDG Bks.

***Opened Ground: Selected Poems, 1966-1996.** Seamus Heaney. 464p. 1998. pap. 15.00 (*0-374-52678-8*) FS&G.

***Opened Ground: Selected Poems, 1966-1996.** Seamus Heaney. LC 98-4331. 512p. 1998. 25.00 (*0-374-23517-1*) FS&G.

Opened Mail. Jules Tasca. 74p. 1996. pap. 5.60 (*0-87129-644-6*, O56) Dramatic Pub.

Opened Treasures: A Daily Devotional Reader. Frances R. Havergal. (Orig.). 1991. reprint ed. pap. 8.95 (*1-882701-14-3*) Uplook Min.

Opened Windows. James A. Stewart. 1958. pap. 8.99 (*1-56632-059-3*) Revival Lit.

Opener of the Way. Robert Bloch. 1993. reprint ed. lib. bdg. 18.95 (*0-89968-421-1*, Lghtyr Pr) Buccaneer Bks.

Openers & Temper. Nina Nyhart & Margo Lockwood. LC 78-74232. 88p. 1979. pap. 3.95 (*0-914086-26-X*) Alice James Bks.

Openers of the Gate. L. Adams Beck. 368p. 1986. reprint ed. pap. 11.95 (*0-87516-561-3*) DeVorss.

OpenGL Programming Guide: The Official Guide to Learning OpenGL, Release 1. OpenGL Architecture Review Staff et al. LC 93-3162. 560p. (C). 1993. pap. text 34.95 (*0-201-63274-8*) Addison-Wesley.

***Opengl Programming Guide: The Official Guide to Learning Opengl, Version 1.2.** 3rd ed. Architecture Review Board Opengl Architecture Review Board. LC 99-31356. 784p. 1999. pap. text 49.95 (*0-201-60458-2*) Addison-Wesley.

***OpenGL Reference Manual.** 3rd ed. Robert Ekelund. LC 99-56697. 432p. (C). 1999. pap. text 49.95 (*0-201-65765-1*) Addison-Wesley.

OpenGL Reference Manual: The Official Reference Document for OpenGL, Release 1. OpenGL Architecture Review Staff. 400p. (C). 1992. pap. text 34.95 (*0-201-63276-4*) Addison-Wesley.

OpenGL SuperBible: The Complete Guide to OpenGL Programming for Windows NT & Windows 95. Richard S. Wright, Jr. 768p. 1996. pap. 65.00 incl. cd-rom (*1-57169-073-5*) Sams.

Openhole Well Logging. (SPE Reprint Ser.). 478p. 1987. reprint ed. pap. 20.00 (*1-55563-007-3*, FERPT021) Soc Petrol Engineers.

Opening: Selected Writings of William Segal, 1985-1997. Ed. by Jan Pepper. LC 80-5337. 172p. (C). 1998. 25.00 (*0-8264-1103-7*) Continuum.

Opening a Bank Account. Stuart B. Schwartz. (Life Skills Ser.). (J). 1998. 19.00 (*0-516-21463-2*) Childrens.

Opening a Bank Account. Stuart Schwartz & Craig Conley. LC 98-35115. (Life Skills Ser.). (YA). 1998. 19.00 (*0-7368-0047-6*, Cpstone High Low) Capstone Pr.

Opening a Business, 2 vols. 2nd ed. Kathryn W. Hegar. (C). 1987. pap. text 15.16 (*0-395-45294-5*) HM.

Opening a Can of Words. Scott Simons & Evelyn Simons. (Orig.). (YA). 1994. pap. 3.50 (*0-8125-2948-0*) Tor Bks.

Opening a Can of Worms: Essays on Controversial Issues. Maralene Wesner & Miles Wesner. 131p. (Orig.). 1989. pap. 8.95 (*0-936715-32-4*) Diversity Okla.

Opening a Chestnut Burr. Edward P. Roe. (Notable American Authors Ser.). 1999. reprint ed. lib. bdg. 125.00 (*0-7812-8811-8*) Rprt Serv.

Opening a Dental Practice. R. H. Schaper. 1996. 29.95 (*0-87814-590-7*) PennWell Bks.

Opening a Highway to the Pacific, 1838-1846. James C. Bell, Jr. LC 68-56648. (Columbia University. Studies in the Social Sciences: No. 217). reprint ed. 24.50 (*0-404-51217-8*) AMS Pr.

Opening a New Catholic School: A Series of Case Studies. Timothy J. McNiff et al. Ed. by Robert J. Kealey. LC 97-216084. 69p. 1997. pap. 10.00 (*1-55833-189-1*) Natl Cath Educ.

Opening a Salon. Thomas Kilpatrick. (Illus.). 90p. (C). 1985. reprint ed. pap. text 15.95 (*0-9623429-8-X*) Digits Intl.

Opening Addresses of the American Stage (with William Carey) Laurence Hutton. (Notable American Authors Ser.). 1992. reprint ed. lib. bdg. 75.00 (*0-7812-3308-9*) Rprt Serv.

Opening America's Market: U. S. Foreign Trade Policy since 1776. Alfred E. Eckes. LC 95-2791. (Illus.). 402p. 1995. 39.95 (*0-8078-2213-2*) U of NC Pr.

Opening America's Market: U.S. Foreign Trade Policy Since 1776. Alfred E. Eckes, Jr. LC 95-2791. (Luther Hartwell Hodges Series on Business, Society & the State). (Illus.). 424p. 1999. pap. 19.95 (*0-8078-4811-5*) U of NC Pr.

Opening & Blending of Textile Fibres: Assessment of Some Modern Machinery. Ed. by Wira Staff. 1986. 40.00 (*0-7855-1021-4*) St Mut.

Opening & Closing: Closures. Lois Ericson. Ed. by Lennart Ericson. LC 96-211174. (Illus.). 200p. 1996. pap. 28.00 (*0-911985-09-3*) Erics Pr.

Opening & Closing Bk. 2: How to Present a Case. Roger S. Haydock & John O. Sonsteng. 1994. 12.50 (*0-314-04380-2*) West Pub.

Opening & Operating Offices in Central & Eastern Europe. 1997. 825.00 (*0-614-25462-0*, P814) Econ Intel.

Opening & Operating Offices in Eastern Europe & the CIS. (Research Reports: No. P815). 1997. 625.00 (*0-85058-938-X*, P815) Economist Intell.

Opening & Penetration of Foreign Influence in Samoa to 1880. Joseph W. Ellison. LC 38-28592. (Oregon State Monographs, Studies in History: Vol. 1). 108p. reprint ed. pap. 33.50 (*0-608-17844-6*, 203260600080) Bks Demand.

Opening Arguments: Brief Rhetoric. Carroll. (C). 1993. pap. text, teacher ed. 3.75 (*0-15-501510-9*) Harcourt Coll Pubs.

***Opening Book: Poems.** Patrick Gillespie. LC 99-39132. 1999. pap. 12.50 (*0-87233-125-3*) Bauhan.

***Opening Communications with God Source: Accessing Your Akashic Records.** Arthur H. Martin. Orig. Title: Accessing Your Akashic Record. (Illus.). 220p. 2000. pap. 14.95 (*1-891962-09-4*) Personal Trans.

Opening Day. Dan Bertalan. LC 94-70352. 256p. 1994. pap. 11.95 (*0-9623955-2-8*) Envisage Unlimited.

Opening Day. Colleen Mullins. 1998. 25.00 (*1-893125-04-1*) Womens Studio Wrkshop.

Opening Day. George Stanley. 1993. pap. text 8.95 (*0-88982-050-3*, Pub. by Oolichan Bks) Genl Dist Srvs.

***Opening Day: All Major League Baseball Season Opening Games, by Team, 1876-1998.** Don Kerr. LC 99-18629. 199p. 1999. lib. bdg. 27.50 (*0-7864-0680-1*) McFarland & Co.

Opening Days: Sports Poems. Illus. by Scott Medlock. LC 94-43364. 48p. (J). (gr. 3-7). 1996. 16.00 (*0-15-200270-7*) Harcourt.

Opening Dialogue: Understanding the Dynamics of Language & Learning in the English Classroom. Ed. by Martin Nysrtand et al. LC 96-32840. (Language & Literacy Ser.: Vol. 29). 160p. (C). 1996. text 44.00 (*0-8077-3574-4*); pap. text 19.95 (*0-8077-3573-6*) Tchrs Coll.

Opening Digital Markets: Battle Plans & Business Strategies for Internet Commerce. 2nd ed. Walid Mougayar. LC 97-41318. (Illus.). 336p. 1997. 24.95 (*0-07-043542-1*) McGraw.

Opening Doors. 63p. 1986. write for info. (*0-318-61757-9*); write for info. (*0-318-61758-7*) New Ways Work.

Opening Doors. 3rd ed. Cortina. 2000. 26.25 (*0-07-231496-6*) McGraw.

Opening Doors, Set. 63p. 1986. 23.00 (*0-940173-23-9*) New Ways Work.

Opening Doors: A Facilitator's Handbook. Theodore L. Kowalski. LC 98-48612. 364p. 1998. 57.00 (*0-7618-1299-7*); pap. 37.50 (*0-7618-1300-4*) U Pr of Amer.

Opening Doors: A Job Search Guide for Graduates. Janet G. Revelt. 1996. pap. 27.50 (*0-938609-04-1*) Graduate Group.

***Opening Doors: Connecting Students to Curriculum, Classmates & Learning.** 2nd ed. Ed. by Barbara E. Buswell et al. (Connecting Students Ser.). Orig. Title: Opening Doors: Strategies for Including All Student in Regular Education. 52p. 1999. pap. 13.00 (*1-884720-12-9*) PEAK Parent.

Opening Doors: Idioms in English. Michael Zucaro. 272p. (C). 1992. pap. text 25.00 (*0-13-638669-5*) P-H.

Opening Doors: Learning Support in Higher Education. Ed. by Sheila Wolfendale & Jenny Corbett. (Special Needs in Ordinary Schools Ser.). 144p. 1996. pap. 29.95 (*0-304-33509-6*); text 90.00 (*0-304-33508-8*) Continuum.

Opening Doors: Perspectives on Race Relations in Contemporary America. Ed. by Harry J. Knopke et al. LC 90-36167. 256p. 1991. text 29.95 (*0-8173-0497-5*) U of Ala Pr.

Opening Doors: Perspectives on Race Relations in Contemporary America. Ed. by Harry J. Knopke et al. LC 90-36167. 256p. 1994. pap. text 24.95 (*0-8173-0762-1*) U of Ala Pr.

***Opening Doors: Selling Homes to Multicultural Clients: The Real Estate Agents Guide to Understanding Culturally Diverse Home Buyers & Sellers.** Michael D. Lee. LC 99-50372. (Illus.). 288p. 1999. 34.95 (*1-886939-32-2*, Pub. by OakHill Pr VA) ACCESS Pubs Network.

O

Opening Doors: Strategies for Including All Students in Regular Education. 4th ed. C. Beth Schaffner & Barbara E. Buswell. (Illus.). 55p. 1991. reprint ed. pap. 10.00 (*1-884720-00-5*) PEAK Parent.

Opening Doors: The Life & Work of Joseph Schumpeter, 2 vols., Set. Robert L. Allen. (C). 1990. pap. 44.95 (*1-56000-720-6*) Transaction Pubs.

Opening Doors: The Life & Work of Joseph Schumpeter, 2 vols., Vol. 1: Europe. Robert L. Allen. 335p. (C). 1993. pap. 24.95 (*1-56000-716-8*) Transaction Pubs.

Opening Doors: The Life & Work of Joseph Schumpeter, 2 vols., Vol. 2: America. Robert L. Allen. 340p. (C). 1990. pap. 24.95 (*1-56000-717-6*) Transaction Pubs.

Opening Doors: Understanding College Reading. Joe Cortina & Janet Elder. LC 94-37873. 1995. pap. text 26.25 (*0-07-024004-3*) McGraw.

Opening Doors: Understanding College Reading. 2nd ed. Joe Cortina & Janet Elder. LC 97-16752. 24p. 1997. pap. 34.00 (*0-07-024470-7*) McGraw.

Opening Doors: What Happens in Gestalt Therapy. Daniel Rosenblatt. Date not set. pap. 20.00 (*0-939266-33-4*) Gestalt Journal.

Opening Doors: Your Guide for Accommodating Persons with Disabilities, 10 bks., Set. Building Owners & Managers Association Internation. 15p. (Orig.). 1991. pap. 50.00 (*0-943130-02-6*) Build Own & Man.

Opening Doors: Strategies for Including All Student in Regular Education see Opening Doors: Connecting Students to Curriculum, Classmates & Learning

Opening Doors to College Success. Karen Bergher. 288p. (C). 1992. pap. text 29.95 (*0-8403-8122-0*) Kendall-Hunt.

Opening Doors to Public Health Nursing: A Guidebook. Joyce Zerwekh. (Illus.). 71p. 1998. pap. text 20.00 (*0-9662376-1-7*) WA Public Health.

***Opening Doors to Quaker Religious Education.** Mary Snyder. LC 98-83123. 128p. 1999. 14.95 (*1-888305-09-6*) Friends Genl Conf.

***Opening Doors to Reading: Building School-to-Work Skills.** Dee L. Fabry. 230p. 2000. 32.00 (*1-56308-775-8*, TIP) Libs Unl.

***Opening Doors to the Future: A 12-Session Suport Group for Middle & High School Students Who Are at Risk.** Anna Jean Gaissert. (Illus.). 40p. (YA). (gr. 6-12). 1999. pap. text 8.95 (*1-57543-072-X*) Mar Co Prods.

Opening Doors to Worship. Sally Farneth. (Illus.). 160p. (Orig.). 1993. pap. text 10.00 (*0-9620912-6-X*) Friends Genl Conf.

An Asterisk (*) at the beginning of an entry indicates that the title is appearing for the first time.

Opening Doors Within: 365 Daily Meditations. Eileen Caddy. Ed. by David E. Platts. (Illus.). 204p. 1987. reprint ed. 17.95 (*0-905249-66-6*, Pub. by Findhorn Pr); reprint ed. pap. 12.95 (*0-905249-68-2*, Pub. by Findhorn Pr) Words Distrib.

Opening Education: Policies & Practices from Open & Distance Learning. Ed. by Terry Evans & Daryl Nation. 224p. (C). 1996. 80.00 (*0-415-14182-6*); pap. 24.99 (*0-415-14183-4*) Routledge.

Opening Eye. Frank McGillion. 1991. pap. 10.95 (*0-904575-03-9*) Sigo Pr.

Opening Eyes to Mathematics: Contact & Insight Lessons, 2 vols., Set. Debby Head et al. LC 91-62683. (Illus.). 406p. (C). 1991. teacher ed., spiral bd. 35.00 (*1-886131-38-4*, OEL) Math Lrning.

Opening Eyes to Mathematics: Lessons, Vol. 3. Debby Head et al. (Illus.). 281p. (C). 1995. teacher ed., spiral bd. 25.00 (*1-886131-40-6*, OEL3) Math Lrning.

Opening Eyes to Mathematics: Lessons, Vol. 3, blackline masters. Debby Head et al. (Illus.). 128p. 1995. ring bd. 15.00 (*1-886131-44-9*, OEL3-B) Math Lrning.

Opening Eyes to Mathematics: Lessons & Blackline Masters, 4 vols., Set. Debby Head et al. LC 91-62683. (Illus.). (C). 1995. teacher ed., spiral bd. 95.00 (*1-886131-31-7*, OE) Math Lrning.

Opening Eyes to Mathematics: Sketching Solutions to Algebraic Equations. unabridged ed. Eugene Maier. (Illus.). 57p. 1997. ring bd. 20.00 incl. VHS (*1-886131-43-0*, ME13) Math Lrning.

Opening Eyes to Mathematics: Teaching Reference Manual. Debby Head et al. LC 91-62683. (Illus.). 148p. (C). 1991. spiral bd. 15.00 (*1-886131-30-9*, OEG) Math Lrning.

Opening Eyes to Mathematics Through Musical Array-ngements. Debby Head et al. (Opening Eyes to Mathematics Ser.). (Illus.). 64p. (C). 1991. teacher ed., spiral bd. 10.00 (*1-886131-32-5*, OEMA) Math Lrning.

Opening Financial Markets: Banking Politics on the Pacific Rim. Louis W. Pauly. LC 88-47740. (Cornell Studies in Political Economy). 280p. 1988. 42.50 (*0-8014-2080-6*) Cornell U Pr.

Opening Financial Markets: Banking Politics on the Pacific Rim. Louis W. Pauly. LC 88-47740. (Cornell Studies in Political Economy). (Illus.). 280p. 1990. reprint ed. pap. text 17.95 (*0-8014-9928-3*) Cornell U Pr.

Opening Forbidden Lakes: Fishing Colorado's Watersheds - Without Getting Arrested. Zoltan Malocsay. (Illus.). 144p. 1992. pap. write for info. (*0-9629250-1-2*) Squeezy Pr.

Opening Frontiers in Solar Research: Proceedings of the Topical Meeting of the COSPAR Interdisciplinary Scientific Commission E (Meetings E6 & E9) of the COSPAR 28th Plenary Meeting Held in The Hague, The Netherlands, 25 June-6 July, 1990. Ed. by R. Falciani et al. (Advances in Space Research Ser.: Vol. 11, No. 5). (Illus.). 306p. 1991. pap. 156.50 (*0-08-041159-2*, Pergamon Pr) Elsevier.

***Opening Gambits: The First Session of Psychotherapy.** Peter S. Armstrong. LC 99-41431. 1999. 40.00 (*0-7657-0241-X*) Aronson.

Opening Guns: Fort Sumter to Fredericksburg. Ed. by Albert A. Nofi. (Eyewitness History of the Civil War Ser.). 439p. 1994. pap. 16.95 (*0-938289-41-1*, 289411) Combined Pub.

Opening Guns of World War III: Washington's Assault on Iraq. Jack Barnes & Mary-Alice Waters. (Illus.). 333p. (Orig.). (C). 1991. pap. 12.00 (*0-87348-642-0*) Pathfinder NY.

Opening Guns of World War III. Jack Barnes. (FAR.). 221p. pap. 16.95 (*0-87348-797-4*) Pathfinder NY.

Opening Hearts & Minds: The Joy of Teaching. David E. Moe. (Illus.). (Orig.). 1985. pap. 6.95 (*0-9615797-0-6*) Moe-Tavation.

***Opening Hearts, Minds & Doors: Embodying the Inclusive & Vulnerable Love of God.** Robert Barron & Donald Senior. Ed. by Bernard F. Stratman. 37p. 1999. pap. text 3.00 (*1-893060-02-0*) NFPC.

Opening Heaven's Doors: A Scriptural Guide to Carrying Out God's Plan of Salvation. Paul L. Engstrom. 224p. 1997. 12.95 (*1-884367-02-X*) Winning St Paul.

Opening Hidden Frontiers: The Dragons of Time. J. R. Challacombe. LC 94-68854. Orig. Title: Everyman His Own Frontier. 204p. 1994. pap. 17.95 (*1-886287-03-1*) Clair Studies.

Opening Leads Flipper. Ron Klinger & Mike Lawrence. 30p. 1998. pap. 7.95 (*0-575-06631-8*, Pub. by V Gollancz) Trafalgar.

Opening Leads for ACOL Players. Mike Lawrence & Ron Klinger. 1998. pap. 19.95 (*0-575-06502-8*, Pub. by V Gollancz) Trafalgar.

Opening Leads in Bridge. Tony Sowter. 1998. pap. text 17.95 (*0-7134-7946-9*, Pub. by B T B) Branford.

***Opening Line: The Creative Writer.** Ebele Oseye & Ellease Southerland. 39p. (YA). 2000. pap. text 10.00 (*1-929454-01-5*, 917 863-6528) Eneke.

Opening Mind: A Philosophical Study of Humanistic Concepts. Morris Weitz. LC 77-7387. 292p. 1996. 30.00 (*0-226-89240-9*) U Ch Pr.

Opening Minds: Essays on Fantastic Literature. Brian M. Stableford. LC 95-5020. (I. O. Evans Studies in the Philosophy & Criticism of Literature: No. 14). 144p. 1995. pap. 19.00 (*0-89370-403-2*) Millefleurs.

Opening Moves: Marines Gear up for War. Henry I. Shaw, Jr. (Illus.). 25p. 1996. reprint ed. pap. text 20.00 (*0-7881-3527-9*) DIANE Pub.

Opening Moves: The Making of a Young Chess Champion. Fred Thayer. LC 99-20803. (Illus.). 48p. (J). 2000. 15.95 (*0-316-91339-1*) Little.

Opening Moves: Work in Progress in the Study of Children's Language Development. Ed. by Margaret Meek. 84p. (Orig.). (C). 1985. pap. text 15.00 (*0-435-08250-7*, 08250) Heinemann.

Opening Networks to Competition: The Regulation & Pricing of Access. David Gabel & David F. Weiman. LC 97-35912. (Topics in Regulatory Economics & Policy Ser.). 256p. 1997. lib. bdg. 110.00 (*0-7923-8019-3*) Kluwer Academic.

Opening New Doors: Alternative Careers for Librarians. Ed. by Ellis Mount. LC 92-38494. 1992. 39.00 (*0-87111-408-9*) SLA.

Opening New Doors: Finding Families for Older & Handicapped Children. K. Donley. (C). 1989. 55.00 (*0-903534-33-9*, Pub. by Brit Ag for Adopt & Fost) St Mut.

Opening Night. Thomas Brush. 104p. 1981. pap. 12.00 (*0-937669-05-9*) Owl Creek Pr.

Opening Night. Norm Foster. LC 92-213641. 116p. 1997. pap. text 10.95 (*0-88754-461-4*) Theatre Comm.

Opening Night. Joe Mcdonagh. LC 98-54259. 1999. pap. 5.00 (*0-88734-820-3*) Players Pr.

Opening Night. Cornelia Otis Skinner. 1952. 3.50 (*0-87129-579-2*, O18) Dramatic Pub.

Opening Night Entertaining, 2 vols., Set, Vols. 1-2. Repertory Theatre of St. Louis, Backers Volunteer. (Illus.). (Orig.). 1993. pap. 16.95 (*0-9605504-1-0*) Repertory Theatre SL.

Opening Night Entertaining, 2 vols., Vols. 1-2. Repertory Theatre of St. Louis, Backers Volunteer. (Illus.). 72p. (Orig.). 1993. write for info. (*0-318-72146-5*); write for info. (*0-318-72147-3*) Repertory Theatre SL.

Opening Night on Broadway: A Critical Quotebook of the Golden Era of the Musical Theatre, "Oklahoma!" (1943) to "Fiddler on the Roof" (1964) Steven Suskin. 810p. 1993. pap. 18.00 (*0-02-872628-6*, Schirmer Books) Mac Lib Ref.

Opening Nights: 25 Years of the Manhattan Theatre Club, Vol. 17. John W. Pereira. LC 93-9525. (American University Studies: Series 26, Vol. 17). (Illus.). X, 520p. (C). 1996. 29.95 (*0-8204-2027-1*) P Lang Pubng.

Opening Nights: 25 Years of the Manhattan Theatre Club, Vol. 17. 2nd ed. John W. Pereira. LC 93-9525. (American University Studies: Series 26, Vol. 17). (Illus.). X, 520p. (C). 1996. 18.95 (*0-8204-3381-0*) P Lang Pubng.

Opening of a Rosebud: A Collection of Faith Promoting Stories. Garth T. Harrison. (Let Me Tell You a Story Ser.). vi, 220p. (Orig.). 1996. pap. 12.00 (*0-9653160-0-9*) Bagley Fmly.

Opening of American Society. Robert H. Wiebe. 1985. pap. 12.95 (*0-394-72965-X*, Pub. by Knopf) Random House.

Opening of Japan: A Diary of Discovery in the Far East, 1853-1856. George H. Preble. Ed. by Boleslaw Szczesniak. LC 62-16484. (Illus.). 492p. reprint ed. 152.60 (*0-8357-9737-6*, 201099800073) Bks Demand.

Opening of Korea: A Study of Chinese Diplomacy, 1876-1885. Frederick F. Chien. LC 67-30793. 381p. reprint ed. pap. 118.20 (*0-608-30666-5*, 201021000068) Bks Demand.

Opening of South Lebanon, 1788-1840: A Study of the Impact of the West on the Middle East. William R. Polk. LC 63-13815. (Harvard Middle Eastern Studies: No. 8). 319p. reprint ed. pap. 98.90 (*0-608-30368-2*, 200601900054) Bks Demand.

Opening of Texas to Foreign Settlement, 1801-1821. Mattie A. Hatcher. 1993. reprint ed. lib. bdg. 75.00 (*0-7812-5934-7*) Rprt Serv.

Opening of the American Mind. C. Antonio Provost. LC 89-64102. 1990. 15.95 (*0-87212-246-8*); pap. 9.95 (*0-87212-235-2*) Libra.

Opening of the American Mind: Canons, Culture, & History. Lawrence W. Levine. LC 96-33866. 240p. 1997. pap. 14.00 (*0-8070-3119-4*) Beacon Pr.

Opening of the American West: In Early Photographs & Prints. Ed. by Bill Yenne. (Illus.). 192p. 1993. 19.98 (*1-55521-870-9*) Bk Sales Inc.

Opening of the Apartheid Mind: Options for the New South Africa. Heribert Adam & Kogila A. Moodley. LC 92-36443. (Perspectives on Southern Africa Ser.: No. 50). (C). 1993. 35.00 (*0-520-08199-4*, Pub. by U CA Pr) Cal Prin Full Svc.

Opening of the Chinese Mind: Democratic Changes in China since 1978. Jing Lin. LC 93-50073. 208p. 1994. 49.95 (*0-275-94594-4*, Praeger Pubs) Greenwood.

***Opening of the Civil War.** Eugene M. Wait. LC 99-50324. 379p. 1999. 34.00 (*1-56072-740-3*) Nova Sci Pubs.

Opening of the Cube. James R. Willems. 1975. pap. 7.50 (*0-686-17260-4*) Tree Bks.

Opening of the Field. rev. ed. Robert Duncan. LC 72-93976. 96p. 1973. pap. 6.95 (*0-8112-0480-4*, NDP356, Pub. by New Directions) Norton.

Opening of the Mississippi: A Struggle for Supremacy in the American Interior. Frederic A. Ogg. LC 68-24990. (American History & Americana Ser.: No. 47). (Illus.). 1969. reprint ed. lib. bdg. 75.00 (*0-8383-0223-8*) M S G Haskell Hse.

Opening of the Mississippi: A Struggle for Supremacy in the American Interior. Frederic A. Ogg. (BCL1 - United States Local History Ser.). 670p. 1991. reprint ed. text 109.00 (*0-7812-6304-2*) Rprt Serv.

Opening of the Second World War. David W. Pike. LC 90-15503. (American University Studies: History: Ser. IX, Vol. 105). (Illus.). XL, 387p. (C). 1991. text 62.95 (*0-8204-1524-3*) P Lang Pubng.

Opening of the Third Eye. Douglas M. Baker. 1977. pap. 12.00 (*0-906006-85-6*, Pub. by Baker Pubns) New Leaf Dist.

Opening of the Way: A Practical Guide to the Mystical Teachings of Ancient Egypt. Isha S. De Lubicz. 214p. 1995. pap. 14.95 (*0-89281-572-8*) Inner Tradit.

Opening of the Wisdom Eye. Dalai Lama XIV. LC 70-152732. (Illus.). 178p. 1991. reprint ed. pap. 12.95 (*0-8356-0549-3*, Quest) Theos Pub Hse.

Opening of Tibet: An Account of Lhasa & the Country & People of Central Tibet & of the Mission Sent There by the English Government in the 1903-1904. Perceval Landon. 1990. reprint ed. 68.50 (*81-85326-26-6*, Pub. by Vintage) S Asia.

Opening of Vision: Nihilism & the Postmodern Situation. David M. Levin. 480p. 1988. text 59.95 (*0-415-00412-8*) Routledge.

Opening of Vision: Nihilism & the Postmodern Situation. David M. Levin. 480p. (C). 1988. pap. 25.99 (*0-415-00173-0*) Routledge.

Opening Opportunities for Disadvantaged Learners. Work Conference on Urban Education Staff. Ed. by Harry A. Passow. LC 72-178197. 378p. reprint ed. pap. 117.20 (*0-608-14852-0*, 202605200048) Bks Demand.

Opening Our Doors & Removing the Barriers: Accommodations for Persons with Disabilities. Government Printing Office Staff. 23p. 1996. pap. 2.00 (*0-16-048695-5*) USGPO.

Opening Our Hearts & Homes Group Study Guide. Karen Mains & Adele Calhoun. Ed. by Laurie Mains. (Illus.). 96p. 1998. pap. 7.99 (*1-57849-100-2*) Mainstay Church.

Opening Our Hearts to Men. Susan Jeffers. 240p. 1990. pap. 12.00 (*0-449-90513-6*, Columbine) Fawcett.

Opening Our Moral Eye: Essays, Talks & Poems Embracing Creativity & Community. Mary Caroline Richards. LC 96-41084. (Illus.). 206p. 1996. pap. 19.95 (*0-940262-78-9*, Lindisfarne) Anthroposophic.

***Opening Our Wild Hearts to the Healing Herbs.** Gail Edwards. (Illus.). 296p. 1999. pap. 12.95 (*1-888123-01-X*) Ash Tree.

Opening Play. Chris Ward. 88p. 1995. pap. 11.95 (*0-8050-3579-6*, Pub. by Batsford Chess) H Holt & Co.

Opening Preparation. Assiac. 161p. 1982. 19.95 (*0-08-024095-X*, Pergamon Pr); pap. 11.95 (*0-08-024096-8*, Pergamon Pr) Elsevier.

Opening Preparation. Mark Dvortesky. 1995. pap. 23.95 (*0-8050-3290-8*, Pub. by Batsford Chess) H Holt & Co.

Opening Price Statistical Data on the Futures Markets. R. Earl Hadady. (Illus.). 165p. 1988. 87.50 (*0-9611390-1-3*) Key Bks Pr.

Opening Repertoire for the Attacking Player. Eduard Gufeld. 128p. 1996. text 17.95 (*1-85744-196-6*, Pub. by Cadgn Bks) Macmillan.

Opening Repertoire for the Attacking Player. Raymond Keene. LC 94-76060. 88p. 1995. pap. 14.95 (*0-8050-3582-6*, Pub. by Batsford Chess) H Holt & Co.

Opening Repertoire for the Positional Player. Eduard Gufeld. 128p. 1996. pap. text 19.95 (*1-85744-152-4*, Pub. by Cadgn Bks) Macmillan.

Opening Repertoire for White. Raymond Keene. 1995. pap. 17.00 (*0-8050-4229-6*) H Holt & Co.

Opening Shots: The Unusual, Unexpected, Potentially Career-Threatening First Roles That Launched the Careers of 70 Hollywood Stars. Damien Bona. LC 93-21493. (Illus.). 288p. (Orig.). 1994. pap. 11.95 (*1-56305-279-2*, 3279) Workman Pub.

***Opening Solomon's Gates: Astonishing Archaelogical Discoveries Reveal the History Behind the Bible.** Israel Finkelstein & Neil Asher Silberman. 2001. 26.00 (*0-684-86912-8*) Free Pr.

***Opening Spaces: An Anthology of Contemporary African Women's Writings.** Ed. by Yvonne Vera. LC 99-31512. (African Writers Ser.). 186p. 1999. text 13.95 (*0-435-91010-8*) Heinemann.

***Opening Spaces: Critical Pedagogy & Resistance Theory in Composition.** Joe Marshall Hardin. (C). 2001. pap. text. write for info. (*0-7914-4904-1*) State U NY Pr.

***Opening Spaces: Critical Pedagogy & Resistance Theory in Composition.** Joe Marshall Hardin. (C). 2001. text. write for info. (*0-7914-4903-3*) State U NY Pr.

Opening Spaces: Writing Technologies & Critical Research Practices. Ed. by James Porter & Patricia Sullivan. LC 97-22413. 1997. pap. 24.95 (*1-56750-308-X*) Ablx Pub.

Opening Spaces: Writing Technologies & Critical Research Practices. Ed. by Patricia Sullivan & James Porter. LC 97-22413. 1997. text 73.25 (*1-56750-307-1*) Ablx Pub.

Opening Statement, Closing Argument, & Persuasion in Trial Advocacy. Ed. by Robert M. Krivoshey. LC 93-31985. (Readings in Trial Advocacy & the Social Sciences Ser.: Vol. 2). 320p. 1993. text 20.00 (*0-8153-1420-5*) Garland.

Opening Statements & Closing Arguments. Ronald J. Matlon. LC 92-34211. (Trial Consultant Handbook Ser.: Vol. 1). 1992. 25.00 (*0-9624181-2-9*) Stuart Allen.

Opening Statements, 1980-1990, 1 vol. Alfred Julien. LC 80-15904. 130.00 (*0-685-42756-0*) West Group.

Opening Switches. A. Guenther et al. LC 87-16611. (Advances in Pulsed Power Technology Ser.: Vol. 1). (Illus.). 328p. (C). 1987. 85.00 (*0-306-42664-1*, Plenum Trade) Perseus Pubng.

Opening Texts: Psychoanalysis & the Culture of the Child. Ed. by Joseph H. Smith & William Kerrigan. LC 84-43078. (Psychiatry & the Humanities Ser.: Vol. 8). 166p. 1985. reprint ed. pap. 51.50 (*0-608-07322-9*, 206755000009) Bks Demand.

Opening Texts: Using Writing to Teach Literature. Kathleen D. Andrasick. LC 90-30045. 208p. (Orig.). (C). (gr. 9). 1990. pap. text 21.50 (*0-435-08522-0*, 08522) Heinemann.

Opening the American Mind: Race, Ethnicity, & Gender in Higher Education. Geoffrey M. Sill. LC 92-50856. 1993. 38.50 (*0-87413-473-0*) U Delaware Pr.

Opening the Bible. Roger Ferlo. LC 97-21735. (New Church's Teaching Ser.: Vol. 2). 135p. 1997. pap. 11.95 (*1-56101-144-4*) Cowley Pubns.

Opening the Bible. Thomas Merton. 96p. 1970. pap. 6.95 (*0-8146-0408-0*) Liturgical Pr.

***Opening the Bible: What It Is, Where It Came from, What It Means for You.** Robert Kysar. LC 99-29449. 144p. 1999. pap. 10.99 (*0-8066-3594-0*, Augsburg) Augsburg Fortress.

Opening the Book: New Essays on New Zealand Writing. Ed. by Mark Williams & Michele Leggott. 336p. 1995. pap. 39.95 (*1-86940-115-8*, Pub. by Auckland Univ) Paul & Co Pubs.

Opening the Books: Essays on the Social & Cultural History of British Communism. Andrews. LC 94-42972. pap. 22.95 (*0-7453-0872-4*, Pub. by Pluto GBR) Stylus Pub VA.

Opening the Books: Essays on the Social & Cultural History of British Communism. Andrews. LC 94-42972. (C). 54.95 (*0-7453-0871-6*, Pub. by Pluto GBR) Stylus Pub VA.

Opening the Borders: Inclusivity in Early Modern Studies: Essays in Honor of James V. Mirollo. James V. Mirollo & Peter C. Herman. LC 98-56055. (Illus.). 360p. 1999. 52.50 (*0-87413-675-X*) U Delaware Pr.

Opening the Classroom Door: Teacher, Researcher, Learner. J. John Loughran & Jeffrey Northfield. 192p. 1996. pap. 27.95 (*0-7507-0591-4*, Falmer Pr) Taylor & Francis.

Opening the Clergy Parachute: Soft Landings for Church Leaders Who Are Seeking Change. Christopher C. Moore. 160p. (Orig.). 1995. pap. 14.95 (*0-687-08659-0*) Abingdon.

Opening the Door. Denise Clayton Bryant. 1997. 12.95 (*1-55630-877-9*) Brentwood Comm.

Opening the Door. Peggy R. Neiss. (Illus.). 128p. (Orig.). 1997. pap. 15.95 (*0-9657305-0-6*) P R Neiss.

Opening the Door, Vol. 2. Ed Okonowicz. (Spirits Between the Bays Ser.). (Illus.). 96p. (Orig.). 1995. pap. 8.95 (*0-9643244-3-1*) Myst & Lace.

Opening the Door: A Treatment Model for Therapy with Male Survivors of Sexual Abuse. Adrienne Crowder. LC 94-43270. 224p. 1995. pap. text 22.95 (*0-87630-754-3*) Brunner-Mazel.

***Opening the Door: Improving the Healthy Families/Medi-Cal Application Process - Executive Summary.** (Illus.). 48p. 1998. spiral bd. write for info. (*1-929008-22-8*) CA HlthCare Fnd.

***Opening the Door: Improving the Healthy Families/Medi-Cal Application Process - Full Report.** (Illus.). 98p. 1998. spiral bd. write for info. (*1-929008-23-6*) CA HlthCare Fnd.

Opening the Door to Certainty. Bokar Rinpoche. Tr. by Christiane Buchet from FRE. LC 96-96789. 64p. 1996. pap. 9.95 (*0-9630371-7-X*) ClearPoint.

Opening the Door to Classroom Research. Ed. by Mary W. Olson. LC 89-28255. 166p. 1990. reprint ed. pap. 51.50 (*0-608-00503-7*, 206132300008) Bks Demand.

Opening the Door to the Brain: Granular Cell Neuron Masses. Hyman Olken. (Illus.). 30p. (Orig.). pap. 12.00 (*0-934818-05-3*) Olken Pubns.

Opening the Door to Your Inner Self: My Lessons. Geraldine M. Bennett. LC 91-67122. (Illus.). 122p. (Orig.). (J). (gr. 2 up). 1993. pap. 12.98 (*0-9630718-5-8*, 1-87122) New Dawn NY.

Opening the Doors to Canadian Medical Schools. Rod Elford. (Life Line Ser.). 112p. (Orig.). 1994. pap. 14.95 (*1-55059-084-7*) Temeron Bks.

Opening the Doors to Hollywood: How to Sell Your Idea, Story Book, Screenplay. Carlos De Abreu & Howard J. Smith. LC 94-68044. 416p. 1995. 21.95 (*1-884025-04-8*) Custos Morum.

Opening the Doors to Hollywood: How to Sell Your Idea, Story, Screenplay, Manuscript. Carlos De Abreu. LC 97-14390. 1997. pap. 15.00 (*0-609-80110-4*) Random Hse Value.

Opening the Dragon Gate: The Making of a Modern Taoist Wizard. Chen Kaiguo & Zheng Shunchao. Tr. by Thomas Cleary from CHI. 288p. 1998. pap. 18.95 (*0-8048-3185-8*) Tuttle Pubng.

Opening the Dream Door: Using Your Dreams for Spiritual & Psychic Development. Janice Winsor. 128p. 1998. pap. 14.95 (*1-886708-04-5*) Merrill-West Pub.

Opening the Energy Gates of Your Body: Gain Lifelong Vitality. Bruce K. Frantzis. LC 93-1940. (Illus.). 178p. (Orig.). 1993. pap. 16.95 (*1-55643-164-3*) North Atlantic.

***Opening the Eye of New Awareness.** 2nd rev. ed. Dalai Lama XIV & Donald S. Lopez, Jr. LC 99-28438. 160p. 1999. pap. 14.95 (*0-86171-155-6*) Wisdom MA.

Opening the Eyelid. deluxe ed. David Rattray. LC 90-84027. 96p. (Orig.). 1991. pap. 9.95 (*0-9627430-1-1*); pap. 500.00 (*0-9627430-2-X*) diwan.

Opening the Eyelid. limited ed. David Rattray. LC 90-84027. 96p. (Orig.). 1991. 35.00 (*0-9627430-0-3*) diwan.

Opening the Gates: A Century of Arab Feminist Writing. Ed. by Margot Badran & Miriam Cooke. LC 89-46345. 448p. 1990. 41.95 (*0-253-31121-7*); pap. 19.95 (*0-253-20577-8*, MB 577) Ind U Pr.

Opening the Gates: How Proactive Conversion Can Revitalize the Jewish Community. Gary Tobin & Katherine Simon. LC 98-51233. 240p. 1999. 25.00 (*0-7879-0881-9*) Jossey-Bass.

Opening the Gates of Eighteenth-Century Montreal. Ed. by Phyllis Lambert & Alan Stewart. (Centre Canadien d'Architecture Ser.). (Illus.). 96p. (Orig.). 1992. pap. text 15.95 (*0-262-62086-3*) MIT Pr.

Opening the Gift: Rediscover the Joy of Being Catholic. Ed Eschweiler. 128p. (Orig.). 1993. pap. 8.95 (*0-937997-26-9*) Hi-Time Pflaum.

An Asterisk (*) at the beginning of an entry indicates that the title is appearing for the first time.

Opening the Hand of Thought: Approach to Zen. Kosho Uchiyama. Ed. by Jisho Warner. Tr. by Shohaku Okumura & Tom Wright from JPN. LC 93-10993.Tr. of Seimei no Jitsubutsu, Zen no Jissai, Gendai Bunmei, Zazen, Gudo. 176p. 1993. pap. 13.95 (*0-14-019459-2*, Arkana) Viking Penguin.

Opening the Heart of Compassion: Transform Suffering Through Buddhist Psychology & Practice. Martin Lowenthal & Lar Short. (Illus.). 192p. 1993. pap. 12.95 (*0-8048-1985-8*) Tuttle Pubng.

Opening the Hebrew Scriptures. David E. Johnson. 152p. 1990. pap. 4.95 (*0-88028-102-2*, 1059) Forward Movement.

Opening the Lotus: A Woman's Guide to Buddhism. Sandy Boucher. 208p. 1998. pap. 12.00 (*0-8070-7309-1*) Beacon Pr.

Opening the Lotus: Developing Clarity & Kindness. Sherab G. Amipa. (Basic Book - Orange Ser.). (Illus.). 176p. (Orig.). 1987. pap. 12.95 (*0-86171-049-5*) Wisdom MA.

Opening the Marketplace to Small Enterprise: Where Magic Ends & Development Begins. Ton D. Wilde et al. LC 91-9632. (Kumarian Press Library of Management for Development Ser.). (Illus.). 167p. Date not set. reprint ed. pap. 51.80 (*0-608-20741-1*, 205450000003) Bks Demand.

Opening the Million Dollar Doors of Show Business. large type ed. Mrs. Alistair MacLean, pseud & Sitare Ltd. Staff. (Illus.). 100p. 1999. 10.00 (*0-940178-64-8*) Sitare.

***Opening the Musical Box: A Genesis Chronicle.** Alan Hewitt. 2000. pap. 18.95 (*0-946719-30-6*) Interlink Pub.

Opening the New Testament: A Way to Read the Bible in a Logical & Historical Order; Towards the Recovery of Biblical Literacy. David E. Johnson. 64p. (Orig.). 1989. pap. 2.95 (*0-88028-096-4*, 989) Forward Movement.

Opening the Nursery Door: Reading, Writing & Childhood, 1600-1900. Mary Hilton et al. LC 96-27224. 256p. (C). 1997. 70.00 (*0-415-14898-7*); pap. 22.99 (*0-415-14899-5*) Routledge.

***Opening the Prayer Book.** Jeffrey D. Lee. LC 99-34805. (New Church's Teaching Ser.: Vol. 7). xv, 195p. 1999. pap. 11.95 (*1-56101-166-5*) Cowley Pubns.

Opening the Rainbow Eye, Set. Oscar Ichazo. 162p. 1974. teacher ed., ring bd. 260.00 (*0-916554-22-8*) Arica Inst Pr.

Opening the Seven Seals: The Visions of John the Revelator. Richard D. Draper. LC 91-26254. xii, 308p. 1991. 17.95 (*0-87579-547-1*) Deseret Bk.

Opening the Soviet System. George Soros. 1996. text 19.95 (*0-8133-1205-1*) Westview.

Opening the Space Frontier. Diane K. Moser & Ray Spangenberg. (Space Exploration Ser.). (Illus.). 136p. (YA). 1989. 22.95 (*0-8160-1848-0*) Facts on File.

Opening the Treasures: A Book of Daily Homily Meditations. Charles E. Miller. LC 81-19095. (Illus.). 557p. 1982. pap. 19.95 (*0-8189-0424-0*) Alba.

Opening the West: Federal Internal Improvements Before 1860, 196. Laurence J. Malone. LC 97-43932. (Contributions in Economics & Economic History Ser.: Vol. 196). 176p. 1998. 59.95 (*0-313-30671-0*, Greenwood Pr) Greenwood.

Opening Theory Made Easy: Twenty Strategic Principles to Improve Your Opening Game. Otake Hideo. (Illus.). 170p. 1992. pap. 13.95 (*4-87187-036-7*, G36) Ishi Pr Intl.

Opening to Channel: How to Connect with Your Guide. Sanaya Roman & Duane Packer. Ed. by Gregory Armstrong. (Birth into Light Ser.). 252p. (Orig.). 1987. pap. 12.95 (*0-915811-05-7*) H J Kramer Inc.

Opening to God: A Guide to Prayer. Thomas Green. LC 77-83197. 112p. 1977. pap. 7.95 (*0-87793-136-4*) Ave Maria.

Opening to God: A Guide to Prayer. large type ed. Thomas Hill Green. (Large Print Inspirational Ser.). 176p. 1986. pap. 9.95 (*0-8027-2529-5*) Walker & Co.

Opening to God: Guided Imagery Meditation on Scripture. Carolyn S. Bohler. LC 95-62356. 192p. 1996. pap. 13.00 (*0-8358-0768-1*) Upper Room Bks.

Opening to Grace: Transcending Our Spiritual Malaise. James Leonard Park. LC BT761.2.P37. 64p. 1999. pap. 9.00 (*0-89231-921-6*) Existential Bks.

Opening to Healing Energy. Shepherd Hoodwin. (Summerjoy Michael Book Ser.). 160p. 2000. pap. 13.95 (*1-885469-04-7*) Summerjoy.

***Opening to Love 365 Days a Year.** Judith Sherven & James Sniechowski. LC 99-48223. 425p. 2000. pap. 12.95 (*1-55874-745-1*) Health Comm.

Opening to Reform? An Analysis of China's Revised Criminal Procedure Law. Jonathan Hecht. Ed. by George Black. 87p. (Orig.). 1996. pap. 12.00 (*0-934143-84-6*) Lawyers Comm Human.

Opening to Spirit: Contacting the Healing Power of the Chakras & Honouring African Spirituality. Caroline Shola Arewa. 288p. 1998. pap. 19.95 (*0-7225-3726-3*) Thorsons PA.

Opening to the Infinite: Human Multidimensional Potential. Alice Bryant & Linda Seebach. Ed. by Amy O. Demmon. LC 97-27079. 276p. 1997. per. 15.00 (*0-926524-43-7*) Granite Pub.

Opening to the Quran: Commentary & Vocabulary Reference of Al-Fatiha. Ahmad Z. Hammad. (Quran Ser.: Vol. 1). xx, 120p. 1996. write for info. (*0-9650746-0-9*) QLI.

Opening to Your Higher Self: Manifestations of the Third Kind. Todd Varnum & Fred Fengler. 227p. (Orig.). 1996. pap. 14.95 (*0-9641305-1-3*) Heart Light.

Opening Up: The Healing Power of Confiding in Others. James W. Pennebaker. 240p. 1991. pap. 8.95 (*0-380-70849-3*, Avon Bks) Morrow Avon.

Opening Up: The Healing Power of Expressing Emotions. James W. Pennebaker. LC 97-20544. 249p. 1997. pap. text 15.95 (*1-57230-238-0*, 0238) Guilford Pubns.

Opening up of American Education: A Sampler. Rushkin Teeter. LC 83-3647. 160p. (Orig.). (C). 1983. pap. text 19.00 (*0-8191-3137-7*) U Pr of Amer.

Opening up the Soviet Economy. Jerry F. Hough. LC 87-36835. 100p. 1988. pap. 9.95 (*0-8157-3747-5*) Brookings.

Opening up the Statistical Toolbox: A Practical Guide to Statistical Quality Improvement. Michael Beauregard et al. (Illus.). 400p. 1991. text 64.95 (*0-442-23439-2*) Chapman & Hall.

Opening Way. Dan Wilson. LC 61-11637. (Orig.). 1961. pap. 4.00 (*0-87574-113-4*) Pendle Hill.

Opening Way: Kurozumi Munetada, Founder of Kurozumikyo. Kurozumi Tadaaki. Ed. by Willis Stoesz. Tr. by Julie Iezzi & Harold Wright from JPN. LC 94-16763. (Illus.). 172p. (Orig.). (C). 1994. pap. text 21.50 (*0-8191-9575-8*); lib. bdg. 44.50 (*0-8191-9574-X*) U Pr of Amer.

Opening Windows: Promoting a Fourth Wave of Democracy. Catharin E. Dalpino. 100p. 1998. pap. 14.95 (*0-8157-1701-6*) Brookings.

Opening Windows: Research on Teachers, Students & Schools. Ed. by Kenneth Tobin et al. 225p. 1990. pap. 29.00 (*1-85000-543-5*, Falmer Pr) Taylor & Francis.

***Opening Windows: Spiritual Refreshment for Your Walk with Christ.** Max Lucado et al. LC 99-16440. (Illus.). 269p. 1999. 15.99 (*1-58229-072-5*) Howard Pub LA.

Opening Your Door to Children: How to Start a Family Day Care Program. Kathy Modigliani et al. LC 87-60747. 69p. 1987. pap. 3.50 (*0-935989-06-4*, NAEYC #203) Natl Assn Child Ed.

Openings. Ross Tharaud. 63p. 1976. 3.50 (*0-87886-076-2*, Greenfld Rev Pr) Greenfld Rev Lit.

Openings: A Guide to Psychic Living in the Real World. Joan Pancoe. LC 95-3846. 352p. (Orig.). 1995. pap. 18.95 (*0-9644936-0-8*) Modern Myst.

Openings: A Meditation on History, Method & Sumas Lake. Laura Cameron. (Illus.). 160p. 1997. text 34.95 (*0-7735-1666-2*, Pub. by McG-Queens Univ Pr) CUP Services.

Openings: A Zen Joke Guide for Serious Problem Solving. George A. Katchmer, Jr. Ed. by Mary Holden. LC 96-60386. 192p. (Orig.). 1996. pap. 15.95 (*1-886969-45-0*, B026/450) YMAA Pubn.

Openings: Narrative Beginnings from the Epic to the Novel. A. D. Nuttall. 266p. 1992. text 65.00 (*0-19-811741-8*) OUP.

Openings: Quotations on Spirituality in Everyday Life. Shelley Tucker. LC 97-60002. 95p. (Orig.). 1997. pap. 14.95 (*0-9653800-1-7*) Whiteaker Pr.

Openings & Closings. deluxe ed. Richard Kostelanetz. 1978. reprint ed. pap. 50.00 (*0-932360-75-0*) Archae Edns.

Openings & Closings. Richard Kostelanetz. 1978. reprint ed. pap. 6.00 (*0-932360-18-1*) Archae Edns.

Openings in the Old Trail. Bret Harte. LC 78-113672. (Short Story Index Reprint Ser.). 1977. 21.95 (*0-8369-3401-6*) Ayer.

***Openings in the Old Trail.** Bret Harte. (Works of Bret Harte: Vol. 9). 362p. 1999. reprint ed. lib. bdg. 90.00 (*0-7812-7841-4*) Rprt Serv.

Openings into Ministry. Ed. by Ross Snyder. LC 77-92707. (Studies in Ministry & Parish Life). 1977. 16.95 (*0-913552-10-3*); pap. 9.95 (*0-913552-11-9*) Exploration Pr.

***Openlinux 2.2: Putting Linux to Work for You.** 3rd ed. Caldera Incorporated Staff et al. 1999. pap. text 59.99 (*0-13-015824-0*) P-H.

OpenLinux Web Publishing ToolKit. Caldera Press Staff. 1997. pap. text 69.95 (*0-13-913088-8*) P-H.

Openly Bob. Bob Smith. 272p. 1999. pap. 12.50 (*0-380-73200-9*, Avon Bks) Morrow Avon.

Openly Bob. Bob Smith. LC 97-31007. 1999. 23.00 (*0-688-15120-5*, Wm Morrow) Morrow Avon.

Openly Gay Openly Christian: How the Bible Really is Gay Friendly. Samuel Kader. LC 99-12808. 160p. 1999. pap. 15.95 (*0-943595-78-9*) Leyland Pubns.

***Openmind Wholemind: Parenting & Teaching Tomorrow's Children Today.** Jalmar Press Staff. 1999. pap. 29.95 (*1-880396-64-5*) Jalmar Pr.

Openness & Development: Yearbook of Economic & Social Relations 1996. Ed. by F. P. Lang & R. Ohr. (Studies in Contemporary Economics). (Illus.). 242p. 1996. pap. 71.00 (*3-7908-0958-6*) Spr-Verlag.

Openness for Prosperity: Essays in World Economics. Herbert Giersch. (Illus.). 385p. (C). 1993. 45.00 (*0-262-07148-7*) MIT Pr.

Openness in Adoption: Exploring Family Connections. Harold D. Grotevant & Ruth G. McRoy. LC 98-19745. 229p. 1998. 63.50 (*0-8039-5778-5*); pap. write for info. (*0-8039-5779-3*) Sage.

Openness in Adoption: New Practices, New Issues. Ruth G. McRoy et al. LC 88-2471. 171p. 1988. 55.00 (*0-275-92933-7*, C2933, Praeger Pubs) Greenwood.

Openness Mind. Tarthang Tulku. LC 78-13659. (Nyingma Psychology Ser.). 1978. 30.00 (*0-913546-55-0*); pap. 14.95 (*0-913546-56-9*) Dharma Pub.

Openness of God: A Biblical Challenge to the Traditional Understanding of God. Clark Pinnock et al. LC 94-3575. 192p. (Orig.). 1994. pap. 12.99 (*0-8308-1852-9*, 1852) InterVarsity.

Openpit Mining. Amory B. Lovins. (Earth Island Ser.). 1973. pap. 1.75 (*0-85644-020-5*) Friends of Earth.

***Opens Skies, Closed Minds: For the First Time a Goverment UFO Expert Speaks Out.** Nick Pope. 320p. 2000. mass mkt. 5.99 (*0-440-23489-1*) Dell.

***Opensource Linux Web Programming.** Christopher A. Jones. LC 99-37699. 504p. 1999. pap. 39.99 (*0-7645-4619-8*) IDG Bks.

OpenStep for Enterprises. Nancy L. Craighill. LC 96-1798. 245p. 1996. pap. text 34.95 incl. cd-rom, disk (*0-471-30859-5*) Wiley.

OpenStep Programming. William Ballew & Denise Eatherly. 1997. 49.95 incl. disk (*0-614-20325-2*) Spr-Verlag.

Openstep Programming: Step Two - A New Foundation. William Ballew. 400p. 1997. 44.95 (*0-387-94144-4*) Spr-Verlag.

***Openview Network Node Manager.** John Blommers. 2000. pap. 49.00 (*0-13-019849-8*) P-H.

***OpenVMS System Management Guide.** 2nd ed. Lawrence Baldwin & Steve Hoffman. 480p. 2001. pap. 49.95 (*1-55558-243-5*, Digital DEC) Buttrwrth-Heinemann.

OpenVMS User's Guide. 2nd ed. Patrick Holmay. LC 98-3746. 299p. 1998. pap. text 42.95 (*1-55558-203-6*, Digital DEC) Buttrwrth-Heinemann.

Opera, 5 vols. Ed. by T. W. Allen. Incl. Vol. 1. Iliad, I-XII. 3rd ed. D. B. Monroe. 298p. 1920. text 23.00 (*0-19-814528-4*); Vol. 2. Iliad, XIII-XXIV. 3rd ed. Ed. by D. B. Monroe. 314p. 1920. text 24.95 (*0-19-814529-2*); Vol. 3. Odyssey, I-XII. 2nd ed. Ed. by D. B. Monroe. 242p. 1922. text 22.00 (*0-19-814531-4*); Vol. 4. Odyssey, XIII-XXIV. 2nd ed. Ed. by D. B. Monroe. 228p. 1922. text 22.00 (*0-19-814532-2*); Vol. 5. Hymns, Etc. Ed. by D. B. Monroe. 294p. 1922. text 27.00 (*0-19-814534-9*); (Oxford Classical Texts Ser.). (C). write for info. (*0-318-54864-X*) OUP.

Opera. Ausonius. Ed. by Roger P. H. Green. LC 98-33801. (Oxford Classical Texts Ser.). 354p. 1999. text 55.00 (*0-19-815039-3*) OUP.

Opera. Roy Bennett. (Illus.). 48p. (C). 1996. pap. 10.95 (*0-521-56935-4*) Cambridge U Pr.

Opera, 5 vols. Ed. by John Burnet. Incl. Vol. 2. Parmenides, Philebus, Symposium, Phaedrus, Alcibiades 1 & 2, Hipparchus, Amatores. 2nd ed. 410p. 1922. text 35.00 (*0-19-814541-1*); Vol. 3. Theages, Charmides, Laches, Lysis, Euthydemus, Protagoras, Gorgias, Meno, Hippias Maior, Hippas Minor, Io, Menexenus. Plato. 524p. 1922. text 35.00 (*0-19-814542-X*); Vol. 4. Clitopho, Respublica, Timaeus, Critias. Plato. 554p. 1922. text 35.00 (*0-19-814544-6*); Vol. 5. Minos, Leges, Epinomis, Epistulae, Definitiones. Plato. 610p. 1922. text 55.00 (*0-19-814546-2*); write for info. (*0-318-54865-8*) OUP.

Opera. Robert Donington. (Harbrace History of Musical Forms Ser.). (Illus.). 238p. (C). 1978. pap. text 17.50 (*0-15-567536-2*, Pub. by Harcourt Coll Pubs) Harcourt.

Opera. Robert Donington. LC 77-93589. 1978. pap. text 23.00 (*0-15-504407-9*, Pub. by Harcourt Coll Pubs) Harcourt.

***Opera.** D. L. Gish. LC 99-10872. (World of Music Ser.). (Illus.). 32p. (J). (gr. 2-7). 2001. lib. bdg. 22.60 (*1-58340-045-1*) Smart Apple.

Opera. Johannes Janssen. LC 98-70746. (Crash Course Ser.). (Illus.). 192p. 1998. pap. 13.95 (*0-7641-0438-1*) Barron.

***Opera, 1.** Konemann Inc. Staff. (Illus.). 928p. 2000. 39.95 (*3-8290-3571-3*) Konemann.

Opera. MQ Publications Staff. (Infatuations Ser.). 1998. 12.95 (*1-897954-64-6*, Pub. by Mus Quilts Pub) Sterling.

Opera. Roger A. Mynors. (Oxford Classical Texts Ser.). 468p. 1969. text 21.00 (*0-19-814653-1*) OUP.

Opera. Susan Sutherland. LC 96-72382. (Illus.). 224p. 1998. pap. 10.95 (*0-8442-0026-3*, 00263, Teach Yrslf) NTC Contemp Pub Co.

Opera. Alessandra Taverna. 64p. 1999. 14.95 (*0-7641-5134-7*) Barron.

Opera. Charles Hamm. LC 79-28362. (Music Reprint Ser.). (Illus.). 1980. reprint ed. lib. bdg. 32.50 (*0-306-76013-4*) Da Capo.

Opera, 12 vols. in 13. Libanius. cxi, 6513p. 1985. reprint ed. write for info. (*0-318-70965-1*) G Olms Pubs.

Opera, 2 vols. in 1. Flavius Philostratus. Ed. by C. L. Kayser. lxxxviii, 964p. 1985. reprint ed. write for info. (*3-487-00626-X*) G Olms Pubs.

Opera, 4 vols. in 1. Virgil. Ed. by Otto Ribbeck. viii, 941p. 1966. reprint ed. write for info. (*0-318-71241-5*) G Olms Pubs.

Opera, 4 vols. Virgil. (GER.). viii, 3568p. 1968. reprint ed. write for info. (*0-318-70509-5*); reprint ed. write for info. (*0-318-70510-9*); reprint ed. write for info. (*0-318-70511-7*); reprint ed. write for info. (*0-318-70508-7*) G Olms Pubs.

Opera, 4 vols. Virgil. Ed. by G. P. Wagner. (Illus.). cviii, 3568p. 1968. reprint ed. write for info. (*0-318-71237-7*); reprint ed. write for info. (*0-318-71238-5*); reprint ed. write for info. (*0-318-71239-3*); reprint ed. write for info. (*0-318-71240-7*) G Olms Pubs.

Opera. 2nd ed. H. W. Garrod. (Oxford Classical Texts Ser.). 268p. 1922. text 22.00 (*0-19-814618-3*) OUP.

Opera, 2 vols., Set. Petrus Abaelardus. vi, 1563p. 1970. reprint ed. 385.00 (*0-318-71447-7*) G Olms Pubs.

Opera, 5 vols., Set. Ed. by Harold D. Rosenthal. (Music Reprint Ser.). (Illus.). 1980. reprint ed. lib. bdg. 350.00 (*0-306-79583-3*) Da Capo.

Opera, 4 vols., Set. Virgil. (GER.). viii, 3568p. 1968. reprint ed. write for info. (*0-318-70507-9*) G Olms Pubs.

Opera, 4 vols., Set. Virgil. Ed. by G. P. Wagner. (Illus.). cviii, 3568p. 1968. reprint ed. write for info. (*0-318-71236-9*) G Olms Pubs.

***Opera: A Complete Guide to the Operas, Composers, Artists & Recordings.** 2nd ed. Rough Guides Staff. (Music Reference Ser.). (Illus.). 704p. 1999. pap. 24.95 (*1-85828-456-2*, Pub. by Rough Guides) Penguin Putnam.

Opera: A Concise History. Leslie Orrey. LC 86-51512. (World of Art Ser.). (Illus.). 252p. 1987. pap. 14.95 (*0-500-20217-6*, Pub. by Thames Hudson) Norton.

Opera: A Crash Course. Stephen Pettitt. 144p. 1998. 14.95 (*0-8230-0975-0*) Watsn-Guptill.

Opera: A Pictorial Guide. Quaintance Eaton. 1980. lib. bdg. 45.00 (*0-913870-71-4*) Abaris Bks.

***Opera: A Research & Information Guide.** 2nd ed. Guy A. Marco. (Music Research & Information Guides Ser.). (Illus.). 2000. 95.00 (*0-8153-3516-4*) Garland.

***Opera: An Accident Waiting to Happen (40 Years of Musical Mishaps)** Andrew Foldi. (Illus.). ii, 113p. 1999. pap. 15.00 (*1-878617-28-1*) Leyerle Pubns.

Opera: Dead or Alive; Production, Performance, & Enjoyment of Musical Theatre. Ronald E. Mitchell. LC 73-121772. (Illus.). 350p. 1970. reprint ed. pap. 108.50 (*0-608-07006-8*, 206721400009) Bks Demand.

Opera: Desire, Disease, Death. Linda Hutcheon & Michael Hutcheon. LC 95-18825. (Texts & Contexts Ser.). (Illus.). 296p. 1999. pap. 15.00 (*0-8032-7318-5*, Bison Books) U of Nebr Pr.

Opera: The Extravagant Art. Herbert Lindenberger. LC 84-7092. 298p. 1984. 39.95 (*0-8014-1698-1*); pap. text 17.95 (*0-8014-9425-7*) Cornell U Pr.

Opera: The Undoing of Women. Catherine Clement. Tr. by Betsy Wing.Tr. of L'Opera, ou la Defaite des Femmes. 224p. 1999. pap. 17.95 (*0-8166-3526-9*, Pub. by U of Minn Pr) Chicago Distribution Ctr.

Opera: Tomus IV: Libelli 69-86. Lucian. Ed. by M. D. MacLeod. (Oxford Classical Texts Ser.). 538p. 1987. text 60.00 (*0-19-814596-9*) OUP.

Opera: Tomus One, Libelli 1-25. Ed. by M. D. MacLeod. (Oxford Classical Texts Ser.). 358p. (C). 1972. text 39.95 (*0-19-814656-6*) OUP.

Opera: Tomus Two, Libelli 26-43. Ed. by M. D. MacLeod. (Oxford Classical Texts Ser.). 384p. (C). 1975. text 49.95 (*0-19-814580-2*) OUP.

Opera! What's All the Screaming About? Roger Englander. LC 82-23742. (Illus.). 192p. (J). (gr. 6 up). 1983. 12.95 (*0-8027-6491-6*) Walker & Co.

Opera! What's All the Screaming About? Roger Englander. (Illus.). 192p. 1994. pap. 9.95 (*0-8027-7416-4*) Walker & Co.

Opera! What's All the Screaming About? Roger Englander. (Illus.). 192p. 1994. pap. 19.95 incl. cd-rom (*0-8027-7443-1*) Walker & Co.

***Opera: 100 Essential CDs.** Rough Guides Staff. (Music Reference Ser.). 1999. pap. text 8.95 (*1-85828-451-1*, Pub. by Rough Guides) Penguin Putnam.

Opera Vol. I: Antiquitatum Iudaicarum Libri I-V. Josephus Flavius. lxxxiv, 362p. 1955. write for info. (*3-296-12701-1*) G Olms Pubs.

Opera Vol. I: Enneades I-III cum Vita Porphyrii. Plotinus. Ed. by Paul Henry & H. R. Schwyzer. (Oxford Classical Texts Ser.). 410p. 1964. text 49.95 (*0-19-814561-6*) OUP.

Opera Vol. II: Antiquitatum Ludaicarum Libri VI-X. Josephus Flavius. viii, 392p. 1955. write for info. (*3-296-12702-X*) G Olms Pubs.

Opera Vol. II: Enneades IV-V. Plotinus. Ed. by H. R. Schwyzer & Paul Henry. (Oxford Classical Texts Ser.). 338p. 1977. text 49.95 (*0-19-814582-9*) OUP.

Opera Vol. III: Antiquitatum Ludaicarum Libri XI-XV. Josephus Flavius. lxvii, 410p. 1955. write for info. (*3-296-12703-8*) G Olms Pubs.

Opera Vol. III: Ennead VI. Plotinus. Ed. by H. R. Schwyzer & Paul Henry. 402p. (C). 1983. text 55.00 (*0-19-814591-8*) OUP.

Opera Vol. IV: Antiquitatum Ludaicarum Libri XVI-XX et Vita. Josephus Flavius. x, 390p. 1955. write for info. (*3-296-12704-6*) G Olms Pubs.

Opera Vol. V: De Ludaeorum Vetustate Sive Contra Apionem Libri II. Josephus Flavius. xxviii, 100p. 1955. write for info. (*3-296-12705-4*) G Olms Pubs.

Opera Vol. VI: De Bello Ludaico Libros VII Ediderunt Lustus A. Josephus Flavius. lxxvi, 628p. 1955. write for info. (*3-296-12706-2*) G Olms Pubs.

Opera Vol. VII: Index. Josephus Flavius. viii, 88p. 1955. write for info. (*3-296-12707-0*) G Olms Pubs.

Opera According to Bartalini: A Book of Doggerel Libretti & Comical Illustrati. Gualtiero Bartalini. LC 94-12809. (Illus.). 128p. 1994. pap. 24.00 (*1-56640-994-2*) Pomegranate Calif.

Opera American Style - Arias for Soprano. 80p. 1990. pap. 9.95 (*0-7935-0361-2*, 00660180) H Leonard.

Opera & Concert Singers: An Annotated International Bibliography of Books & Pamphlets. Andrew Farkas. LC 83-49310. 388p. 1984. text 20.00 (*0-8240-9001-2*) Garland.

Opera & Drama. Richard Wagner. Tr. by William Ashton Ellis. LC 95-5263. xx, 416p. 1995. pap. 15.00 (*0-8032-9765-3*, Bison Books) U of Nebr Pr.

Opera & Drama in Russia As Preached & Practiced in the 1860s. Richard F. Taruskin. LC 81-14780. (Russian Music Studies: No. 2). (Illus.). 578p. reprint ed. pap. 179.20 (*0-8357-1245-1*, 207034100085) Bks Demand.

Opera & Drama in Russia as Preached & Practiced in the 1860s. Richard F. Taruskin. LC 93-27441. (Illus.). 582p. (C). 1994. reprint ed. 75.00 (*1-878822-32-2*) Univ Rochester Pr.

Opera & Its Symbols: The Unity of Words, Music, & Staging. Robert Donington. 256p. (C). 1991. 40.00 (*0-300-04713-4*) Yale U Pr.

Opera & Its Symbols: The Unity of Words, Music, & Staging. Robert Donington. (Illus.). 256p. (C). 1992. reprint ed. pap. 16.00 (*0-300-05661-3*) Yale U Pr.

Opera & Shakespeare. Ed. by Holger Klein & Christopher Smith. LC 94-24734. 1994. write for info. (*0-7734-9016-7*) E Mellen.

Opera & Song Books Published in England, 1703-1726: A Descriptive Bibliography. David Hunter. LC 98-234626. (Illus.). 576p. 1999. text 125.00 (*0-948170-10-7*) OUP.

Opera & the Culture of Fascism. Jeremy Tambling. LC 96-13317. 284p. 1996. text 55.00 (*0-19-816566-8*, Clarendon Pr) OUP.

Opera & the Enlightenment. Ed. by Thomas Bauman & Marita P. McClymonds. LC 94-11009. (Illus.). 331p. (C). 1995. text 64.95 (*0-521-46172-3*) Cambridge U Pr.

O

Opera & the Golden West: The Present, Past, & Future of Opera in the U. S. A. Ed. by John L. DiGaetani & Josef P. Sirefman. LC 92-55065. 1994. 45.00 (*0-8386-3519-9*) Fairleigh Dickinson.

Opera & the Librarian, Vol. 25. Compiled by Charles H. Parsons. 1987. write for info. (*0-88946-422-7*) E Mellen.

Opera & the Uses of Language: Mozart, Verdi, & Britten. Sandra Corse. LC 86-45865. (Illus.). 168p. 1987. 32.50 (*0-8386-3300-5*) Fairleigh Dickinson.

Opera & Vocal Masterpieces. 96p. (Orig.). 1993. pap. 10.95 (*0-7692-1144-5*, PF0858) Wrner Bros.

Opera & Vocal Music see Music on Record: A Critical Guide

Opera Anecdotes. Ethan Mordden. 288p. 1988. pap. 12.95 (*0-19-505661-2*) OUP.

Opera Antics & Anecdotes. Stephen B. Tanner. (Illus.). 208p. 1999. pap. 17.95 (*0-920151-32-9*, Pub. by Sound & Vis) Firefly Bks Ltd.

Opera As Drama. rev. ed. Joseph Kerman. 240p. 1988. pap. 15.95 (*0-520-06274-4*, Pub. by U CA Pr) Cal Prin Full Svc.

Opera at the Movies. 80p. 1993. pap. 8.95 (*0-7935-2246-3*, 00292028) H Leonard.

Opera at the Movies, No. 85. 72p. 1994. pap. 7.95 (*0-7935-3176-4*, 00102315) H Leonard.

Opera at the Piano. (World's Great Classical Music Ser.). (Illus.). 240p. 1998. per. 14.95 (*0-7935-8248-2*, HL00310297) H Leonard.

Opera Bibliography, Vol. 17. Compiled by Charles H. Parsons. LC 95-1400. (Mellen Opera Reference Index Ser.). 1987. write for info. (*0-88946-416-2*) E Mellen.

Opera Bibliography, Vol. 18. Compiled by Charles H. Parsons. LC 95-1400. (Mellen Opera Reference Index Ser.). 400p. 1996. text 149.95 (*0-88946-417-0*) E Mellen.

Opera Biographies, 42 vols. Ed. by Andrew Farkas. (Opera Biographies Ser.). 1977. reprint ed. lib. bdg. 1154.00 (*0-405-09666-6*) Ayer.

Opera Brevis. John Wellman. (Illus.). 1977. boxed set 75.00 (*0-685-51278-9*) Heron Pr.

Opera Buffa in Mozart's Vienna. Ed. by Mary Hunter & James Webster. LC 96-50282. (Studies in Opera). (Illus.). 472p. (C). 1997. text 69.95 (*0-521-57239-8*) Cambridge U Pr.

Opera Caravan. Quaintance Eaton. LC 78-9128. (Music Reprint Ser.: 1978). (Illus.). 1978. reprint ed. pap. 6.95 (*0-306-80089-6*); reprint ed. lib. bdg. 42.50 (*0-306-77596-4*) Da Capo.

Opera Choruses for Male Voices. Ed. by John Rutter & Clifford Bartlett. (Oxford Choral Classics Ser.). 72p. 1996. text 7.95 (*0-19-343701-5*) OUP.

Opera Comica Italiana nel Settecento, Studi ed Appunti, 2 vols., Set. Andrea Della Corte. LC 80-2269. reprint ed. 62.50 (*0-404-18830-3*) AMS Pr.

Opera Comique. Nagle Jackson. 1990. pap. 5.25 (*0-8222-0861-X*) Dramatists Play.

Opera Comique. Martin Cooper. 1988. reprint ed. lib. bdg. 75.00 (*0-7812-0105-5*) Rprt Serv.

Opera Comique. Martin Cooper. LC 70-181128. 1949. reprint ed. 45.00 (*0-403-01527-8*) Scholarly.

Opera Comique und ihr Einfluss auf das Europaische Musik-Theater im 19. Jahrhundert. Ed. by Herbert Schneider. (Musikwissenschaftliche Publikationen: Bd. 3). (Illus.). 490p. 1997. 70.00 (*3-487-10250-1*) G Olms Pubs.

Opera Companies & Houses of the United States: A Comprehensive Illustrated Reference. Karyl L. Zietz. LC 94-943. (Illus.). 351p. 1994. lib. bdg. 55.00 (*0-89950-955-X*) McFarland & Co.

Opera Companies & Houses of Western Europe, Canada, Australia & New Zealand: A Comprehensive, Illustrated Reference. Karyl L. Zietz. LC 98-45854. (Illus.). 500p. 1999. lib. bdg. 95.00 (*0-7864-0611-9*) McFarland & Co.

Opera Companies of the World: Selected Profiles. Robert H. Cowden. LC 91-24186. 368p. 1992. lib. bdg. 85.00 (*0-313-26220-9*, CPC, Greenwood Pr) Greenwood.

Opera Composers & Their Works A-D, 22 vols. Compiled by Charles H. Parsons. LC 86-7252. (Mellen Opera Reference Index Ser.: Vol. 1). 534p. 1986. lib. bdg. 149.95 (*0-88946-401-4*) E Mellen.

Opera Composers & Their Works E-K, Vol. 1. Compiled by Charles H. Parsons. LC 86-7252. (Mellen Opera Reference Index Ser.: Vol. 2). 496p. 1986. lib. bdg. 149.95 (*0-88946-402-2*) E Mellen.

Opera Composers & Their Works L-Q. Compiled by Charles H. Parsons. LC 86-7252. (Mellen Opera Reference Index Ser.: Vol. 3). 480p. 1986. lib. bdg. 149.95 (*0-88946-403-0*) E Mellen.

Opera Composers & Their Works R-Z. Compiled by Charles H. Parsons. LC 86-7252. (Mellen Opera Reference Index Ser.: Vol. 4). 512p. 1986. lib. bdg. 149.95 (*0-88946-404-9*) E Mellen.

Opera de la Lune. Jacques Prevert. (FRE., Illus.). 48p. 1986. pap. 10.95 (*0-7859-1381-5*, 2070391418) Fr & Eur.

Opera de Rameau. Paul M. Masson. LC 70-168675. (Music Ser.). (Illus.). 596p. 1972. reprint ed. lib. bdg. 75.00 (*0-306-70262-2*) Da Capo.

Opera, Dictionnaire Chronologique de 1597 a Nos Jours. Livre De Poche Staff. (FRE.). 1986. pap. 16.95 (*0-7859-7852-6*, 2253038687) Fr & Eur.

Opera Discography - Composers A-O, Vol. 10. Compiled by Charles H. Parsons. LC 89-13814. 360p. 1989. lib. bdg. 149.95 (*0-88946-410-3*) E Mellen.

Opera Discography - Composers P-Z, Vol. 11. Compiled by Charles H. Parsons. LC 89-13814. 376p. 1989. lib. bdg. 149.95 (*0-88946-411-1*) E Mellen.

Opera Discography - Performers, Vol. 12. Compiled by Charles H. Parsons. LC 89-13814. 568p. 1989. lib. bdg. 149.95 (*0-88946-497-9*) E Mellen.

Opera et Cetera. LC 96-60342. 96p. (Orig.). 1996. 15.95 (*0-916390-76-4*); pap. 9.95 (*0-916390-75-6*) Wake Forest.

Opera for Beginners. W. Terrence Gordon. (Illus.). 176p. 1996. 11.00 (*0-86316-086-7*) Writers & Readers.

Opera for Dummies. David Pogue & Scott Speck. LC 97-80116. (For Dummies Ser.). (Illus.). 384p. 1997. pap. 24.99 incl. audio compact disk, 3.5 hd (*0-7645-5010-1*) IDG Bks.

Opera for Dummies: Pouge,&David, Set. abr. ed. David Pogue. 1997. audio 18.00 (*0-694-51909-X*, CPN2727) HarperAudio.

Opera for Lovers. Kiti T. Kanawa. 1997. 34.95 (*981-00-7833-1*, Pub. by Merehurst Ltd) Tuttle Pubng.

Opera for the People. Herbert Graf. LC 68-23811. (Music Reprint Ser.). 1973. reprint ed. lib. bdg. 39.50 (*0-306-70984-8*) Da Capo.

Opera Gala: Choruses from Italian Grand Opera. Pref. by Stanley D. Harris. 208p. 1994. 26.25 (*0-9638465-0-7*); pap. 20.00 (*0-9638465-1-5*); spiral bd. 89.00 (*0-9638465-2-3*) Grand Staff.

Opera Gala: Choruses from Italian Grand Opera. Pref. by Stanley D. Harris. 208p. 1994. spiral bd. 444.50 (*0-9638465-3-1*) Grand Staff.

Opera Goers' Complete Guide. Leo L. Melitz. Tr. by Richard Salinger. LC 80-2293. reprint ed. 54.50 (*0-404-18859-1*) AMS Pr.

Opera Guide. abr. ed. Amanda Holden. 1999. pap. 24.95 (*0-14-024138-8*) Viking Penguin.

Opera Handbook. Lazarus. 1987. text. write for info. (*0-582-00107-2*, Pub. by Addison-Wesley) Longman.

Opera Handbook. Ed. by John Lazurus. (Monograph Ser.). 242p. 1990. 30.00 (*0-8161-9094-1*, Hall Reference); 18.95 (*0-8161-1827-2*, Hall Reference) Macmillan.

Opera House Lottery: Zaha Hadid & the Cardiff Bay Project. Nicholas Crickhowell. LC 98-109784. (Illus.). xi, 175p. 1997. 34.50 (*0-7083-1442-2*, Pub. by Univ Wales Pr) Paul & Co Pubs.

Opera Houses of Europe. Andras Kaldor. LC 97-145950. (Illus.). 160p. 1996. 39.50 (*1-85149-248-8*) Antique Collect.

Opera Houses of Iowa. George D. Glenn & Richard L. Poole. LC 93-22793. (Illus.). 204p. 1993. reprint ed. pap. 63.30 (*0-608-06882-9*, 206709000009) Bks Demand.

Opera Houses of the World. Thierry Beauvert. (Illus.). 210p. 1996. text 65.00 (*0-86565-977-X*) Vendome.

Opera in America: A Cultural History. John Dizikes. 1995. pap. 19.00 (*0-300-06101-3*) Yale U Pr.

Opera in Central City. Allen Young. (Illus.). 116p. (Orig.). 1993. pap. 16.95 (*0-9637541-0-6*) Allen Young.

Opera in Context: Essays on Historical Staging from the Late Renaissance to the Time of Puccini. Ed. by Mark A. Radice. LC 97-2712. (Illus.). 450p. 1998. 44.95 (*1-57467-032-8*, Amadeus Pr) Timber.

Opera in Dublin, 1798-1820: Frederick Jones & the Crow Street Theatre. T. J. Walsh. (Illus.). 316p. 1993. 49.95 (*0-19-816397-5*) OUP.

Opera in History: From Monteverdi to Cage. Herbert S. Lindenberger. LC 97-16405. 359p. 1998. 49.50 (*0-8047-3104-7*); pap. write for info. (*0-8047-3105-5*) Stanford U Pr.

Opera in Italy. Naomi Jacob & James C. Robertson. LC 74-140359. (Select Bibliographies Reprint Ser.). 1977. reprint ed. 23.95 (*0-8369-5602-8*) Ayer.

Opera in London: Views of the Press, 1785-1830. Theodore Fenner. LC 93-16279. (Illus.). 784p. (C). 1994. 82.00 (*0-8093-1912-8*) S Ill U Pr.

Opera in Seventeenth-Century Venice: The Creation of a Genre. Ellen Rosand. (Illus.). 710p. 1990. 150.00 (*0-520-06808-4*, Pub. by U CA Pr) Cal Prin Full Svc.

Opera Lexicon: Opern-Lexikon. rev. ed. Horts Seeger. (GER.). 600p. 1986. 110.00 (*0-8288-2178-X*, M6445) Fr & Eur.

Opera Librettists & Their Works A-L, Vol. 5. Compiled by Charles H. Parsons. (Opera Reference Index Ser.). 1987. write for info. (*0-88946-405-7*) E Mellen.

Opera Librettists & Their Works M-Z, Vol. 6. Compiled by Charles H. Parsons. (Opera Reference Index Ser.). 1987. 149.95 (*0-88946-406-5*) E Mellen.

Opera Lover's Guide to Europe. Carol Plantamura. (Illus.). 352p. 1996. pap. text 21.95 (*0-8065-1842-1*, Citadel Pr) Carol Pub Group.

Opera Lovers' Quotations. Helen Exley. 1998. 9.00 (*1-86187-034-5*) Exley Giftbooks.

Opera Mathematica, 3 vols., Set. John Wallis. (GER & LAT., Illus.). 3096p. 1972. reprint ed. lib. bdg. 880.00 (*3-487-04175-8*) G Olms Pubs.

Opera Mediagraphy: Video Recordings & Motion Pictures, 40. Ed. by Sharon G. Almquist. LC 93-28491. (Music Reference Collection: No. 40). 288p. 1993. lib. bdg. 65.00 (*0-313-28490-3*, Greenwood Pr) Greenwood.

Opera Minora. Tacitus. Ed. by Michael Winterbottom & R. M. Ogilive. (Oxford Classical Texts Ser.). 124p. (C). 1975. text 17.95 (*0-19-814658-2*) OUP.

Opera Minora. Francis Hutcheson. Ed. by Bernhard Fabian. (Collected Works: Vol. VII). 1990. reprint ed. 63.70 (*3-487-04040-9*) G Olms Pubs.

Opera Muet. Sylvie Germain. (FRE.). 149p. 1991. pap. 10.95 (*0-7859-2611-9*, 2070383628) Fr & Eur.

Opera Muliebria: Women & Work in Medieval Europe. David Herlihy. (New Perspectives on European History Ser.). 288p. (C). 1989. pap. 20.63 (*0-07-557744-5*) McGraw.

Opera Muliebria: Women & Work in Medieval Europe. David Herlihy. (Illus.). 159p. 1990. 29.95 (*0-87722-714-4*) Temple U Pr.

Opera Observed: Views of a Florentine Impresario in the Early Eighteenth Century. William C. Holmes. LC 93-712. (Illus.). 266p. 1993. pap. text 21.95 (*0-226-34971-3*) U Ch Pr.

Opera Observed: Views of a Florentine Impresario in the Early Eighteenth Century. William C. Holmes. LC 93-712. (Illus.). 266p. 1993. lib. bdg. 62.50 (*0-226-34970-5*) U Ch Pr.

Opera Odyssey: Toward History of Opera in Nineteenth Century America, 32. June C. Ottenberg. LC 93-35861. (Contributions to the Study of Music & Dance Ser.: No. 32). 224p. 1994. 57.95 (*0-313-27841-5*, Greenwood Pr) Greenwood.

Opera of Virus. John Knoll. (Illus.). 58p. 1994. pap. 6.00 (*0-9623013-1-0*) Long Road Pr.

Opera Offstage: Passion & Politics Behind the Great Operas. Milton Brener. LC 96-52636. (Illus.). 256p. 1997. pap. 15.95 (*0-8065-1866-9*, Citadel Pr) Carol Pub Group.

Opera Offstage: Passion & Politics Behind the Great Operas. Milton Brener. (Illus.). 256p. 1996. 24.95 (*0-8027-1313-0*) Walker & Co.

Opera Omnia. Leonhard Euler. Ed. by Swiss Society of Natural Sciences, Euler Committee. (Secundia Ser.: Vol. 17). 312p. (C). 1983. text 85.00 (*3-7643-1447-8*) Birkhauser.

Opera Omnia. Hrotsvitha. Ed. by Walter Berschin. (Illus.). (C). text 69.50 (*3-519-01912-4*) B G Teubner.

Opera Omnia, 4 vols. Ed. by E. C. Marchant. Incl. Vol. 1, Bks. 1-7. Historia Graeca. 2nd ed. 294p. 1922. text 29.95 (*0-19-814552-7*); Vol. 2. Commentarii, Oeconomicus, Convivium, Apologia Socratis. 2nd ed. 292p. 1922. text 29.95 (*0-19-814553-5*); Vol. III. Opera Omnia: Expeditio Cyri. Xenophon. 266p. 1922. text 35.00 (*0-19-814554-3*); Vol. 5. Opuscula. 250p. 1985. text 29.95 (*0-19-814556-X*); (Oxford Classical Texts Ser.). write for info. (*0-318-54866-6*) OUP.

Opera Omnia, 5 vols. Aristotle. Tr. by F. Dubnerum from LAT. (GER.). lvii, 3590p. 1973. reprint ed. 1185.00 (*3-487-05019-6*) G Olms Pubs.

Opera Omnia. Guillaume De Saint-Amour. (GER.). iv, 506p. 1998. reprint ed. write for info. (*3-487-10562-4*) G Olms Pubs.

Opera Omnia, 10 vols. in 11. Desiderius Erasmus. (GER.). 6354p. 1961. reprint ed. write for info. (*0-318-70501-X*) G Olms Pubs.

Opera Omnia, 10 vols. in 11. Desiderius Erasmus. 6354p. 1962. reprint ed. write for info. (*0-318-71258-X*) G Olms Pubs.

Opera Omnia. Guillaume de Saint-Amour. (Illus.). iv, 506p. reprint ed. write for info. (*0-318-71460-4*) G Olms Pubs.

Opera Omnia. Antoni Van Leeuwenhoek. (GER.). 1997. reprint ed. 698.00 (*3-487-04183-9*) G Olms Pubs.

Opera Omnia. Gottfried Wilhelm Leibniz. (GER.). 1990. reprint ed. write for info. (*3-487-09233-6*) G Olms Pubs.

Opera Omnia. Martinus. Ed. by Claude W. Barlow. LC 50-10338. (American Academy in Rome. Papers & Monographs: Vol. 12). 340p. reprint ed. pap. 105.40 (*0-608-16474-7*, 202672800051) Bks Demand.

Opera Omnia, Bd. 5. Johannes Gerson. (GER.). ccii, 3218p. 1987. reprint ed. write for info. (*3-487-07770-1*) G Olms Pubs.

Opera Omnia, 2 vols., Set. Lucius Apuleius. xc, 1820p. 1968. reprint ed. 498.00 (*0-318-71066-8*) G Olms Pubs.

Opera Omnia, 4 vols., Set. Justus Lipsius. (GER.). xii, 5010p. reprint ed. write for info. (*0-318-70500-1*) G Olms Pubs.

Opera Omnia, 2 vols., Set. Giovanni Pico Della Mirandola & Gian F. Pico. xxvi, 2301p. 1969. reprint ed. write for info. (*0-318-71271-7*); reprint ed. write for info. (*0-318-71605-4*) G Olms Pubs.

Opera Omnia, 4 vols. in 2, Set. Francisco Sanchez. viii, 2095p. 1985. reprint ed. write for info. (*3-487-07670-5*) G Olms Pubs.

Opera Omnia: Expeditio Cyri see Opera Omnia

Opera Omnia: Griechisch u. in Lateinischer Uebersetzung, Bd. xx. 2nd ed. Claudis Galenus. Ed. by C. G. Kuehn. (GER.). 1998. reprint ed. write for info. (*3-487-00792-4*) G Olms Pubs.

Opera Omnia Faugues. Ed. by George Schuetze. (Veroffentlichungen Mittelalterlicher Musikhandschriften - Publications of Mediaeval Musical Manuscripts Ser.: Vol. 7). (ENG & GER.). 1963. pap. 40.00 (*0-912024-07-0*) Inst Mediaeval Mus.

Opera Omnia, Figuris Elegantissimis in Aesincisis Illustrata. Marcello Malpighi. (GER.). 1997. reprint ed. 298.00 (*3-487-05639-9*) G Olms Pubs.

Opera Omnia (Griechisch u. in Lateinischer Uebersetzung), 20 vols. in 22. Claudius Galenus. 1986. write for info. (*0-318-70921-X*) G Olms Pubs.

Opera Omnia Philosophica, 2 vols. Franciscus Toletus. 1079p. 1985. reprint ed. write for info. (*0-318-71281-4*); reprint ed. write for info. (*0-318-71282-2*); reprint ed. write for info. (*0-318-71283-0*); reprint ed. write for info. (*0-318-71284-9*) G Olms Pubs.

Opera Omnia Philosophica, 2 vols., Set. Franciscus Toletus. 1079p. 1985. reprint ed. write for info. (*3-487-07493-1*) G Olms Pubs.

Opera on CD: The Essential Guide to the Best Recordings of 100 Operas. 3rd ed. Alan Blyth. 192p. 1995. pap. 19.95 (*1-85626-139-5*, Pub. by Cathie Kyle) Trafalgar.

***Opera on Screen.** Marcia J. Citron. LC 99-48686. 336p. 2000. 35.00 (*0-300-08158-8*) Yale U Pr.

Opera on Screen. Ken Wlaschin. 632p. 1997. lib. bdg. 75.00 (*1-888327-00-6*) Beachwood Pr.

Opera on the Road: Traveling Opera Troupes in the United States, 1825-60. Katherine K. Preston. LC 92-20644. (Music in American Life Ser.). (Illus.). 496p. (C). 1993. text 39.95 (*0-252-01974-1*) U of Ill Pr.

Opera on Video: The Essential Guide. Alan Blyth. 246p. 1996. pap. 19.95 (*1-85626-175-1*, Pub. by Cathie Kyle) Trafalgar.

Opera 101: A Complete Guide to Learning & Loving Opera. Fred Plotkin. LC 94-9477. 512p. (J). 1994. pap. 14.45 (*0-7868-8025-2*, Pub. by Hyperion) Time Warner.

Opera, Past & Present. William F. Apthorp. LC 72-4148. (Select Bibliographies Reprint Ser.). 1977. reprint ed. 21.95 (*0-8369-6870-0*) Ayer.

Opera Performances in Video Format: A Checklist of Commercially Released Recordings. Charles R. Croissant. (Music Library Association Index & Bibliography Ser.: No. 26). 144p. 1991. pap. 15.00 (*0-914954-43-1*) Scarecrow.

Opera Philosophica Quae Latine Scripsit Omnia, 5 Vols. Thomas Hobbes. Ed. by W. Molesworth. 475.00 (*3-511-02230-4*) Adlers Foreign Bks.

Opera Plot Index. David Hamilton & William E. Studwell. LC 89-37920. 480p. 1990. text 20.00 (*0-8240-4621-8*, H1099) Garland.

Opera Plots Made Easy. Robert Deaver. 70p. (Orig.). 1985. pap. 7.95 (*0-932665-00-4*) Deaver Intl.

Opera Politica IV. William Ockham. Ed. by H. S. Offler. (Auctores Britannici Medii Aevi XIV British Academy). 504p. 1997. text 150.00 (*0-19-726127-2*) OUP.

Opera Politica, Historica, Philologica et Epistolica. Willibald Pirckheimer. Ed. by Melchior Goldast. (GER.). 406p. 1969. reprint ed. write for info. (*0-318-70502-8*); reprint ed. write for info. (*0-318-71272-5*) G Olms Pubs.

Opera Premiere Reviews & Re-Assessments: A Listing. Charles H. Parsons. LC 97-29099. (Mellen Opera Reference Index Ser.: Vol. 19). 139p. 1997. 149.95 (*0-88946-172-4*) E Mellen.

Opera Premieres: Reviews, 22 vols., Vols. 15. Compiled by Charles H. Parsons. LC 87-24680. 1987. write for info. (*0-88946-400-6*) E Mellen.

Opera Premieres - Geographical Index A-H. Compiled by Charles H. Parsons. LC 88-12902. (Opera Reference Index Ser.: Vol. 7). 460p. (C). 1988. lib. bdg. 149.95 (*0-88946-407-3*) E Mellen.

Opera Premieres - Geographical Index I-Z. Compiled by Charles H. Parsons. LC 88-12902. (Opera Reference Index Ser.: Vol. 8). 450p. (C). 1988. lib. bdg. 149.95 (*0-88946-408-1*) E Mellen.

Opera Premieres - Performers A-J. Ed. by Charles H. Parsons. LC 93-4741. (Mellen Opera Reference Index Ser.: Vol. 15). 1993. write for info. (*0-88946-414-6*) E Mellen.

Opera Premieres - Performers K-Z, Vol. 15. Ed. by Charles H. Parsons. LC 93-4741. (Mellen Opera Reference Index Ser.: Vol. 16). 1993. write for info. (*0-88946-415-4*) E Mellen.

Opera Premieres/Cast Index A-L. Compiled by Charles H. Parsons. LC 92-9245. (Mellen Opera Reference Index Ser.: Vol. 13). 690p. 1992. lib. bdg. 149.95 (*0-88946-412-X*) E Mellen.

Opera Premieres/Cast Index M-Z. Compiled by Charles H. Parsons. (Mellen Opera Reference Index Ser.: Vol. 14). 686p. 1992. lib. bdg. 149.95 (*0-88946-413-8*) E Mellen.

Opera Production I: A Handbook, Vol. 1. Quaintance Eaton. LC 73-20232. (Music Ser.). 266p. 1974. reprint ed. lib. bdg. 45.00 (*0-306-70635-0*) Da Capo.

Opera Quae Exstant Omnia Poetica, Vols. 1 & 2. Ed. by Ionnes Bocatius & Csonka. (FRE.). 1990. pap. 445.00 (*963-05-5376-7*, Pub. by Akade Kiado) St Mut.

Opera Quae Supersunt, 3 vols. in 2, Set. Marcellinus Ammianus. cxxxiv, 1634p. 1975. reprint ed. 360.00 (*3-487-05654-2*) G Olms Pubs.

Opera Quae Supersunt Omnia. G. Purkircher. (FRE.). 1989. pap. 120.00 (*963-05-4790-2*, Pub. by Akade Kiado) St Mut.

Opera Quiz Book: Everything You Always Wanted to Know about the Greatest Art form Ever Invented. Henry Grossman & Michael Walsh. 200p. 2001. pap. 14.95 (*0-8038-9395-7*, Pub. by Hastings) Midpt Trade.

Opera Scenes for Class & Stage. Mary E. Wallace & Robert Wallace. LC 78-11095. 314p. 1979. 31.95 (*0-8093-0903-3*) S Ill U Pr.

Opera Selecta. Erik Wistrand. (Acta Instituti Romani Regni Sueciae Ser.). (ENG & GER., Illus.). 481p. 1998. pap. 44.50 (*91-7042-006-8*, Pub. by Almqvist Wiksell) Coronet Bks.

Opera Selecta: From Tyre to Tartessos. William Culican. (Studies in Mediterranean Archaeology & Literature: No. 40). (Illus.). 685p. (Orig.). 1986. pap. 97.50 (*91-86098-41-1*, Pub. by P Astroms) Coronet Bks.

Opera since 1800: Opera Listing, 4 Vols., Set, Vols. I-IV. deluxe ed. Dan Woodward. (Opera Since 1800 Ser.). (Illus.). 1998. 200.00 (*1-882935-51-9*) Westphalia.

Opera since 1800 Vol. I: Opera Listing. deluxe ed. Dan Woodward. (Opera Since 1800 Ser.). (Illus.). 1998. 39.95 (*1-882935-03-9*) Westphalia.

Opera since 1800 Vol. II: Composer Listing. deluxe ed. Dan Woodward. (Illus.). 1999. 49.95 (*1-882935-17-9*) Westphalia.

Opera Singers Mediagraphy: Concerts, Recitals & Feature Films, 73. Compiled by Sharon G. Almquist. LC 98-41642. (Music Reference Collection: Vol. 73). 392p. 1999. lib. bdg. 79.50 (*0-313-29592-1*, Greenwood Pr) Greenwood.

Opera Small Talk: Pocket Plots, Crucial Characters, & Amusing Asides. Robert Levine & Elizabeth Lutyens. LC 93-80148. (Illus.). 100p. 1993. pap. 9.95 (*0-9638743-0-6*) Cherubino Pr.

Opera Stars, 1970s-1990s: 200 Photographs by Winnie Klotz. Ed. by James Camner & Carl R. Edwards. LC 98-52669. (Illus.). 128p. 1998. pap. 12.95 (*0-486-40153-7*) Dover.

Opera, State & Society in the Third Republic, 1875-1914. Andre Spies. LC 96-35897. (Studies in Modern European History: Vol. 23). X, 264p. (C). 1998. text 50.95 (*0-8204-3696-8*) P Lang Pubng.

Opera Stories: Random House Books. Adele Geras. LC 97-51795. (J). (gr. 3-7). 1998. lib. bdg. 31.99 (*0-679-99315-0*, Pub. by Random Bks Yng Read) Random.

An Asterisk (*) at the beginning of an entry indicates that the title is appearing for the first time.

Opera Stories: Random House Books. Adele Geras. LC 97-51795. 136p. (YA). (gr. 3-7). 1998. 29.99 (*0-679-89315-6*, Pub. by Random Bks Yng Read) Random.

Opera Stories of To-Day & Yesterday. Edmondstoune Duncan. 227p. 1991. reprint ed. lib. bdg. 79.00 (*0-7812-9334-0*) Rprt Serv.

Opera Subjects, 22 vols., Vol. 9. Compiled by Charles H. Parsons. 1989. 149.95 (*0-88946-409-X*) E Mellen.

Opera That Is Not Opera, 22 vols., Vol. 23. Compiled by Charles H. Parsons. 1987. write for info. (*0-88946-420-0*) E Mellen.

Opera Theater of Count Franz Anton Von Sporck in Prague. Daniel Freeman. LC 91-17971. (Studies in Czech Music: No. 2). 400p. 1993. lib. bdg. 54.00 (*0-945193-17-3*) Pendragon NY.

Opera Through Other Eyes. David J. Levin. (Illus.). 288p. (C). 1994. 39.50 (*0-8047-2239-0*); pap. 15.95 (*0-8047-2240-4*) Stanford U Pr.

Opera Tomus III: Libelli 44-68. Lucian. Ed. by M. D. Macleod. (Oxford Classical Texts Ser.). 406p. (C). 1980. text 55.00 (*0-19-814592-6*) OUP.

Opera Unveiled. Desiree Mayes. LC 99-19508. 1999. pap. 12.00 (*0-942668-53-7*) Katydid Bks.

***Opera Unveiled - 2000: The 2000 Santa Fe Opera Season.** Desiree' Mays. Ed. by Thomas Fitzsimmons. LC 99-53616. (Illus.). 80p. 2000. pap. 12.95 (*0-942668-54-5*) Katydid Bks.

Opera Videography. Compiled by Charles H. Parsons. LC 97-51913. (Mellen Opera Reference Index Ser.: Vol. 20). 368p. 1997. text 199.95 (*0-88946-641-6*) E Mellen.

Opera Without Drama: Currents of Change in Italian Opera, 1675-1725. Robert Freeman. LC 80-29133. (Studies in Musicology: No. 35). 360p. reprint ed. pap. 111.60 (*0-8357-1513-2*, 207028700065) Bks Demand.

Opera Workshop. Raymond Warren. 289p. 1995. 74.95 (*0-85967-970-5*, Pub. by Scolar Pr) Ashgate Pub Co.

***Opera X for Dummies.** Brian Underdahl. (For Dummies Ser.). (Illus.). 360p. 2000. pap. text 24.99 incl. cd-rom (*0-7645-0683-8*) IDG Bks.

Operability of Nuclear Power Systems in Normal & Adverse Environments Topical Meeting: Proceedings American Nuclear Society, Albuquerque, NM September 29 to October 3, 1986. 827p. 95.00 (*0-89448-137-1*, #700130) Am Nuclear Soc.

Operacion Con el Dr. Bip - A Hospital Trip with Dr. Bip. 2nd rev. ed. Christopher F. Tirotta & Conni S. Tirotta. (SPA., Illus.). iii, 29p. (J). (ps-6). 1995. pap. text 1.50 (*1-891359-04-5*) KiDz-Med.

Operacion Estrella: Con Caamano, la Resistencia y la Inteligencia Cubana. Melvin Manon & Jose I. H. (SPA., Illus.). iii, 178p. (Orig.). 1989. pap. 15.00 (*0-89729-524-2*) Ediciones.

***Operacion Exodo: La Profecia Se Cumple, 1vol.** Gustav Scheller. 1999. pap. text 8.99 (*0-88113-556-9*) Caribe Betania.

Operacion Jesucristo y Al Tercer Dia. Mandino Og. (SPA.). 1997. pap. text 23.98 (*968-13-0612-0*) Edit Diana.

Operacion Judas. Carlos J. Bringuier. LC 93-72086. (Coleccion Caniqui). (SPA.). 185p. (Orig.). 1993. pap. 19.00 (*0-89729-694-X*) Ediciones.

***Operacion Multiplicacion: Lider.** Billie Hanks.Tr. of Operation Multiplication. (SPA.). 24p. (YA). 1999. pap. 1.25 (*0-311-13669-9*, Edit Mundo) Casa Bautista.

Operacion Mundo: Guia Diaria de Oracion. P. Johnstone.Tr. of Operation World. (SPA.). 729p. 1994. pap. 15.99 (*958-9149-52-9*, 498493) Editorial Unilit.

Operacion Pedro Pan: El Exodo de los Ninos Cubanos. Josefina Leyva. (SPA.). 305p. 1993. pap. 19.95 (*1-882721-01-2*) Edit Ponce de Leon.

Operacion Raton (Emergency Mouse) Bernard Stone. Tr. by Catalina Dominguez. (SPA., Illus.). 28p. (J). (gr. 1-3). 1993. 12.99 (*968-16-4033-0*, Pub. by Fondo) Continental Bk.

***Operacion y Mantenimiento de Sistemas de Recoleccion de Aguas Residuales.** Kenneth D. Kerri. Tr. by Ruben Robles. (SPA., Illus.). 350p. (C). 1999. pap. text 33.00 (*1-884701-36-1*) CA St U Ofc Water.

Operacion y Seguridad en Buques Tanqueros (Tanker Safety Manual) OCS Marine Staff. (SPA.). (C). 1989. text 395.00 (*0-906314-04-6*, Pub. by Lorne & MacLean Marine) St Mut.

Operacion y Seguridad en Burques Tanqueros: Tanker Safety Manual. (SPA.). (C). 1989. 390.00 (*0-89771-706-6*, Pub. by Lorne & MacLean Marine) St Mut.

Operacion y Seguridad en Burques Tanqueros: Tanker Safety Manual. Lorne & MacLean Marine & Offshore Publications Sta. (SPA.). (C). 1987. 395.00 (*0-7855-4382-1*, Pub. by Lorne & MacLean Marine) St Mut.

***Operaciones de Companias de Seguro de Vida y Salud.** Kenneth Huggins & Robert D. Land. Ed. by Ines Vallenilla. Tr. by Traductoras Asociadas Traductoras from ENG. (PFSL Insurance Education Program Ser.: Vol. 2). (SPA.). 503p. (C). 1998. pap. text. write for info. (*1-57974-057-X*, Pub. by Life Office) PBD Inc.

Operads: Proceedings of Renaissance Conferences, Vol. 202. Jean-Louis Loday et al. LC 96-37049. (Contemporary Mathematics Ser.). 443p. 1996. pap. 85.00 (*0-8218-0513-4*, CONM/202) Am Math.

OperAntics: Fun & Games for the Opera Buff. William J. Brooke. (Illus.). 96p. (Orig.). 1986. pap. 7.95 (*0-930753-02-X*) Spect Ln Pr.

Operantics with Wolfgang Amadeus Mozart: A Workbook. Mary Neidorf. LC 86-14435. 32p. (Orig.). (J). (gr. 3-6). 1987. pap. 4.95 (*0-86534-092-7*) Sunstone Pr.

Operaomnia. 1986. 173.50 (*0-8176-1184-3*) Birkhauser.

Operas, Tome 1, Cadmus et Hermione see Oeuvres Completes de Jean-Baptiste Lully

Operas & Ideas: From Mozart to Strauss. Paul Robinson. LC 86-47637. 288p. 1986. pap. text 15.95 (*0-8014-9428-1*) Cornell U Pr.

Operas & Operatic Style of John Frederick Lampe. Dennis Martin. LC 85-14496. (Detroit Monographs in Musicology: No. 8). xx, 190p. 1985. 40.00 (*0-89990-024-0*) Harmonie Park Pr.

Operas & Plays. Gertrude Stein. LC 98-10554. 400p. 1996. pap. 19.95 (*1-886449-16-3*, P9163) Barrytown Ltd.

Operas II, Tome 2, Alceste see Oeuvres Completes de Jean-Baptiste Lully

Operas Every Child Should Know. Dolores Bacon. 29.95 (*0-8488-0909-2*) Amereon Ltd.

Opera's Great Voices. Nina Beckwith. LC 97-14048. (Life, Times, & Music Ser.). 1997. pap. write for info. (*1-56799-502-0*, Friedman-Fairfax) M Friedman Pub Grp Inc.

Opera's Greatest Melodies. Leonard Hall. 232p. 2000. per. 14.95 (*0-634-00554-5*) H Leonard.

Operas in English: A Dictionary. Margaret R. Griffel. LC 97-11063. 1016p. 1999. lib. bdg. 125.00 (*0-313-25310-2*, Greenwood Pr) Greenwood.

Operas in German: A Dictionary. Margaret R. Griffel. LC 89-17025. 768p. 1990. lib. bdg. 105.00 (*0-313-25244-0*, GGE/, Greenwood Pr) Greenwood.

Operas in One Act: A Production Guide. W. Franklin Summers. LC 96-27775. 400p. 1996. 48.50 (*0-8108-3222-4*) Scarecrow.

Operas, Mysteries of the Great . . . 6th ed. Max Heindel. Ed. by Rosicrucian Fellowship Staff. 176p. 1987. reprint ed. pap. text 12.50 (*0-911274-88-X*) Rosicrucian.

Operas of Alban Berg Vol. II: Lulu. George Perle. LC 76-52033. (Illus.). 352p. 1984. pap. 21.95 (*0-520-06616-2*, Pub. by U CA Pr) Cal Prin Full Svc.

Operas of Alessandro Scarlatti, 1. Alessandro Scarlatti. LC 70-188973. (Harvard Publications in Music: No. 6 & 7). 222p. 1974. reprint ed. pap. 68.90 (*0-7837-3067-5*, 205746000001) Bks Demand.

Operas of Alessandro Scarlatti, Vol. 2. Alessandro Scarlatti. LC 75-765153. (Harvard Publications in Music: No. 6 & 7). 273p. reprint ed. pap. 84.70 (*0-7837-3068-3*, 205746000002) Bks Demand.

Operas of Alessandro Scarlatti, Vol. 4. Alessandro Scarlatti. LC 75-765153. (Harvard Publications in Music: No. 6 & 7). 220p. reprint ed. pap. 68.20 (*0-7837-3078-0*, 205746000006) Bks Demand.

Operas of Alessandro Scarlatti: La Caduta de Decemviri, Vol. 5. Alessandro Scarlatti. Ed. by Hermine W. Williams & Donald J. Grout. (Publications in Music: No. 11). 163p. 1979. pap. 30.00 (*0-674-64031-4*) HUP.

Operas of Alessandro Scarlatti: La Caduta de Decemviri, Vol. 6. Alessandro Scarlatti. Ed. by Hermine W. Williams & Donald J. Grout. (Publications in Music: No. 11). 224p. 1990. pap. 35.00 (*0-674-64032-2*) HUP.

Operas of Alessandro Scarlatti: La Caduta de Decemviri, Vol. 7. Alessandro Scarlatti. Ed. by Hermine W. Williams & Donald J. Grout. (Publications in Music: No. 11). 224p. 1990. 35.00 (*0-674-64033-0*) HUP.

Operas of Alessandro Scarlatti Vol. V: Massimo Puppieno. Alessandro Scarlatti. Ed. by H. Colin Slim. LC 78-11993. (Publications in Music). 1979. pap. text 30.00 (*0-685-02134-3*) HUP.

Operas of Alessandro Scarlatti Vol. VII: Gli Eqivoci nel Sembiante. Alessandro Scarlatti. Ed. by Frank D. Accone. LC 81-7171. (Publications in Music: No. 12). 224p. 1982. pap. text 30.00 (*0-685-05516-7*) HUP.

Operas of Alessandro Scarlatti Vol. VIII: Tigrane. Alessandro Scarlatti. Ed. by Michael Collins. (Publications in Music: No. 13). (Illus.). 288p. 1983. pap. text 40.00 (*0-674-64034-9*) HUP.

Operas of Alessandro Scarlatti Vol. IX: La Statira, Vol. 9. Alessandro Scarlatti. Ed. by Donald J. Grout & William C. Holmes. (Publications in Music: No. 14). 224p. 1985. pap. text 40.00 (*0-674-64035-7*) HUP.

Operas of Benjamin Britten. David Herbert. (Illus.). 384p. (C). 1989. 55.00 (*0-941533-71-9*, NAB) I R Dee.

Operas of Charles Gounod. Steven Hubner. (Illus.). 336p. 1992. reprint ed. pap. text 29.95 (*0-19-816348-7*) OUP.

Operas of Johann Adolf Hasse. Fredrick L. Millner. Ed. by George Buelow. LC 79-11832. (Studies in Musicology: No. 2). (Illus.). 428p. 1979. reprint ed. pap. 132.70 (*0-8357-1006-8*, 207019100064) Bks Demand.

Operas of Michael Tippett: Midsummer Marriage; King Priam; Knot Garden; Ice Break. Michael Tippett. Ed. by Nicholas John. LC 84-1827. (English National Opera Guide Series: Bilingual Libretto, Articles: No. 29). (Illus.). 144p. (Orig.). 1985. pap. 9.95 (*0-7145-4061-7*) Riverrun NY.

Operas of Monteverdi: Includes Orfeo, Return of Ulysses, Coronation of Poppea. Ed. by Nicholas John. (English National Opera Guide Series: Bilingual Libretto, Articles: No. 45). (Illus.). 208p. (Orig.). 1992. pap. 13.95 (*0-7145-4207-5*) Riverrun NY.

Operas of Puccini. William Ashbrook. LC 84-72674. 288p. (Orig.). 1985. reprint ed. pap. text 17.95 (*0-8014-9309-9*) Cornell U Pr.

Operas of Verdi: From Oberto to Rigoletto, Vol. 1. 2nd rev. ed. Julian Budden. (Illus.). 538p. 1992. pap. 22.50 (*0-19-816261-8*) OUP.

Operas of Verdi Vol. 2: From Il Trovatore to La Forza del Destino, Vol. 2. 2nd rev. ed. Julian Budden. (Illus.). 542p. 1992. pap. 22.50 (*0-19-816262-6*) OUP.

Operas, 1684, Tome 3, Amadis see Oeuvres Completes de Jean-Baptiste Lully

Operas That Every Child Should Know. Dolores Bacon. 1911. pap. 25.00 (*0-8196-1385-1*) Biblo.

Operatic Anthology Vol. 1: Soprano Celebrated Arias. 336p. 1986. pap. 19.95 (*0-7935-2582-9*, 50325830) H Leonard.

Operatic Anthology Vol. 2: Piano Celebrated Arias. 288p. 1986. per. 21.95 (*0-7935-2587-X*, 50325840) H Leonard.

Operatic Anthology Vol. 3: Tenor Voice Piano Celebrated Arias. 252p. 1986. per. 18.95 (*0-7935-2612-4*, 50325850) H Leonard.

Operatic Anthology Vol. 4: Baritone Celebrated Arias. 284p. 1986. pap. 18.95 (*0-7935-0504-6*, 50325860) H Leonard.

Operatic Anthology Vol. 5: Bass Voice Piano. 268p. 1986. per. 19.95 (*0-7935-4707-5*, 50325870) H Leonard.

Operatic Lives. Alberto Savinio. Tr. by John Shepley from ITA. LC 88-60730.Tr. of Narrate, uomini, la vostra storia. 311p. (Orig.). 1988. 29.95 (*0-910395-42-X*); pap. 13.95 (*0-910395-43-8*) Marlboro Pr.

Operatics. Michel Leiris. Tr. by Guy Bennett from FRE. (Green Integer Bks.: No. 15). 100p. pap. 9.95 (*1-892295-03-2*, Pub. by Green Integer) Consort Bk Sales.

Operating a Bookstore: Practical Details for Improving Profit. Eliot Leonard. 120p. (Orig.). 1992. pap. 12.95 (*1-879923-04-1*) Booksellers Pub.

Operating a Home Improvement Program: A Complete Overview of the Skills & Finances Need to Run a Successful Program see Program Operations Series

Operating a Really Small Business: An Owner's Guide. Betty Bivins. Ed. by Beverly Manber. LC 92-54350. (Small Business & Entrepreneurship Ser.). 150p. (Orig.). 1993. pap. 15.95 (*1-56052-169-4*) Crisp Pubns.

Operating a Successful Accounting Practice: A Collection of Material from the Journal of Accountancy Practitioners Forum. American Institute of Certified Public Accountants. Ed. by Richard C. Rea. LC 79-117870. 336p. reprint ed. pap. 104.20 (*0-608-15097-5*, 202577300046) Bks Demand.

Operating & Evaluating School Library Media Programs: A Handbook for Administrators & Librarians. Bernice L. Yesner & Hilda L. Jay. LC 98-11469. 424p. 1998. pap. 49.95 (*1-55570-250-3*) Neal-Schuman.

Operating & Financial Performance Profiles of 18-Hole Golf Facilities in the U. S. Daily Fee Facilities. (Illus.). 138p. 1999. pap. 150.00 (*1-57701-150-3*, 99GC057) Natl Golf.

Operating & Financial Performance Profiles of 18-Hole Golf Facilities in the U. S. Municipal Facilities. (Illus.). 138p. 1999. pap. 150.00 (*1-57701-152-X*, 99GC058) Natl Golf.

Operating & Financial Performance Profiles of 18-Hole Golf Facilities in the U. S. Private Facilities. (Illus.). 135p. 1999. pap. 150.00 (*1-57701-151-1*, 99GC059) Natl Golf.

Operating & Financial Performance Profiles of 9-Hole Golf Facilities in the U. S. Combination Package of Public & Private Golf Facilities, 2 vols. 88p. 1995. pap. 150.00 (*1-57701-123-6*, 99GC074) Natl Golf.

Operating & Maintenance Audits. R. Nanayakkara & M. H. Smith. 67p. 1997. pap. 80.00 (*0-86022-477-5*, Pub. by Build Servs Info Assn) St Mut.

Operating & Maintenance Manuals for Building Services Installations. J. H. Armstrong. (C). 1990. pap. 100.00 (*0-86022-179-2*, Pub. by Build Servs Info Assn) St Mut.

Operating at Peak Efficiency: A Technician's Guide to Servicing HVAC-R Equipment. Billy C. Langley. LC 95-15991. 1995. pap. 24.95 (*1-885863-07-1*) Busn News.

Operating Bail - Decision-Making under the Bail Etc. (Scotland) Act 1980. Fiona Peterson & Claire Whittaker. 184p. 1994. pap. 35.00 (*0-11-495173-X*, HM5173X, Pub. by Statnry Office) Bernan Associates.

Operating Budget Handbook for Small Cities & Other Governmental Units. LC 78-71727. (Illus.). 148p. 1978. 15.00 (*0-686-84276-6*) Municipal.

Operating Budget Manual. Lennox L. Moak & Kathryn W. Killian. LC 64-12365. (Illus.). 347p. 1963. 12.00 (*0-686-84284-7*) Municipal.

Operating Cinematography for Film & Video: A Professional & Practical Guide. William E. Hines. LC 97-90057. (Illus.). xvi, 256p. (Orig.). (YA). (gr. 9-12). 1997. pap. 24.95 (*0-935873-01-5*) Ed Venture CA.

Operating Conditions & Hydraulics of Horizontal Settling Tanks. K. V. Gnedin. (Russian Translation Ser.: No. 53). 244p. 1987. 110.00 (*90-6191-489-2*, Pub. by A A Balkema) Ashgate Pub Co.

Operating Controls - Student's Manual: The Molding Process, Module One, Lesson 5. (Illus.). 1997. pap., student ed. write for info. (*1-58677-011-X*) Polymer Train.

Operating Cost Study, 1987. 112p. 1988. pap. text 45.00 (*0-685-34786-9*) Horticult Research.

Operating Costs & Energy Management in Buildings. Moss. LC 97-65933. (Illus.). 200p. (C). 1997. pap. 45.00 (*0-419-21770-3*, E & FN Spon) Routledge.

Operating Criteria for Credit Departments. Credit Research Foundation Staff. 52p. 1989. 40.00 (*0-939050-57-X*) Credit Res NYS.

Operating Data Base for Gas Distribution & Transmission Purposes. 57p. 1974. 2.00 (*0-318-12664-8*, XN0174) Am Gas Assn.

Operating Difficulties on Fine, Kraft & Specialty Paper Machines. 109p. 1991. pap. 18.36 (*1-895288-17-7*) Pulp & Paper.

Operating Difficulties on Newsprint Machines. 69p. 1981. pap. 13.60 (*1-895288-40-1*) Pulp & Paper.

Operating During Strikes: Company Experience, NLRB Policies & Governmental Regulations. Charles R. Perry et al. LC 82-80521. (Labor Relations & Public Policy Ser.: No. 23). 163p. 1982. pap. 20.00 (*0-89546-036-X*) U PA Ctr Hum Res.

Operating Engineer (Stationary) Jack Rudman. (Career Examination Ser.: C-555). 1994. pap. 29.95 (*0-8373-0555-1*) Nat Learn.

Operating Engineers: The Economic History of a Trade Union. Garth L. Mangum. LC 63-19144. (Publications in Industrial Relations). 366p. reprint ed. pap. 113.50 (*0-608-15242-0*, 202917100059) Bks Demand.

***Operating Environment.** Peter Campkin et al. 256p. (Orig.). 1999. pap. 37.50 (*0-273-62876-3*, Pub. by F T P-H) Trans-Atl Phila.

Operating Experience Feedback Report: Assessment of Spent Fuel Cooling. J. G. Ibarra. 48p. 1997. pap. 5.00 (*0-16-062689-7*) USGPO.

Operating Experience with Nuclear Power Stations in Member States in 1994. International Atomic Energy Agency Staff. 854p. 1996. pap. 275.00 (*92-0-104795-9*, STI/PUB/999, Pub. by IAEA) Bernan Associates.

Operating Experiences with Commercial Ground-Source Heat Pump Systems. D. Kane et al. Ed. by Mildred Geshwiler. (Illus.). 124p. 1998. pap. 24.00 (*1-883413-61-3*, 90391) Am Heat Ref & Air Eng.

Operating Factors for Installed HID Luminaires: LM-61-96. (Lighting Measurements Ser.). (Illus.). 8p. 1996. pap. 14.00 (*0-87995-124-9*, LM-61-96) Illum Eng.

***Operating Grants for Nonprofit Organizations.** Oryx Press Staff. 296p. 2000. pap. 29.95 (*1-57356-396-X*) Oryx Pr.

Operating in a Regulated Environment. 2nd ed. Mark Largan. 400p. 1999. pap. 120.00 (*0-85297-508-2*, Pub. by Chartered Bank) St Mut.

Operating in the Dark. Lisa Priest. 2000. pap. write for info. (*0-385-25722-8*) Bantam.

***Operating in the Dark.** Lisa Priest. 336p. 2000. pap. 13.95 (*0-385-25898-4*) Doubleday.

Operating in the Dark: The Accountability Crisis in Canada's Health Care System. Rick Mercer. 336p. 1998. 24.95 (*0-385-25719-8*) Doubleday.

Operating in the Power of the Spirit. Larry Keefauver. LC 97-38120. 64p. 1997. pap., student ed. 6.99 (*0-88419-494-9*) Creation House.

Operating Instructions: A Journal of My Son's First Year. Anne Lamott. 251p. 1994. reprint ed. pap. 9.50 (*0-449-90928-X*, Columbine) Fawcett.

Operating Manual: Qualification Standards for General Schedule Positions. Government Printing Office Staff. 1990. ring bd. 93.00 (*0-16-016692-6*) USGPO.

Operating Manual: The Guide to Personnel Recordkeeping. ring bd. 93.00 (*0-16-016629-2*) USGPO.

Operating Manual: The Guide to Processing Personnel Actions. Government Printing Office Staff. 1987. ring bd. 165.00 (*0-16-016634-9*) USGPO.

Operating Manual - The SF-113 Summary Data Reporting System. Government Printing Office Staff. 1983. ring bd. 60.00 (*0-16-016648-9*) USGPO.

Operating Manual & Workbook to Accompany QuickQuantPlus, Version 4.1 for MacIntosh. 1993. text. write for info. (*0-318-72845-1*) Alamo Pub.

Operating Manual for Spaceship Earth. R. Buckminster Fuller. 18.95 (*0-89190-235-X*) Amereon Ltd.

***Operating Manual for Spaceship Earth.** R. Buckminster Fuller. 128p. 2000. pap. 25.00 (*3-907078-23-3*, Pub. by Lars Muller) Princeton Arch.

Operating Policies & Procedures Manual for Medical Practices. Bette A. Warn & Elizabeth W. Woodcock. 376p. 1999. pap. 125.00 (*1-56829-092-6*) Med Group Mgmt.

Operating Procedures Guidebook: LP-Gas Transportation & Delivery, Vol. 2. 2nd ed. Ed. by John B. Fox. (Illus.). 119p. 1986. reprint ed. pap. 20.00 (*0-88466-006-0*) NPGA.

Operating Results of Independent Supermarkets. 60p. 75.00 (*0-318-14131-0*, P40); 30.00 (*0-318-14132-9*) Food Marketing.

Operating Room Administration Manual: Checklists, Guidelines & Forms. Howard S. Rowland. 650p. 1991. 152.00 (*0-8342-0174-7*, S31) Aspen Pub.

Operating Room Aide. Mary Virgilio. Ed. by Kay Cox. LC 97-67079. (Clinical Allied Healthcare Ser.). (Illus.). 256p. (C). 1997. pap. text 29.95 (*0-89262-433-7*) Career Pub.

Operating Room Aide: Instructor's Guide. Mary Virgilio. Ed. by Kay Cox. (Clinical Allied Healthcare Ser.). (Illus.). 283p. (C). 1997. teacher ed., ring bd. 79.95 (*0-89262-441-8*) Career Pub.

Operating Room & Intensive Care Alarms: Information Transfer. Ed. by John Whyte-Hedley. LC 92-7225. (Special Technical Publication Ser.: No. 1152). (Illus.). 45p. 1992. text 19.00 (*0-8031-1449-4*, STP1152) ASTM.

***Operating Room Management.** Ronald A. Gabel. LC 99-20092. 248p. 1999. text 65.00 (*0-7506-9911-6*) Buttrwrth-Heinemann.

Operating Room Management. Andrew P. Harris & William G. Zitzmann. LC 97-34545. (Illus.). 312p. (C). (gr. 13). 1997. pap. text 44.95 (*0-8151-4178-5*, 26867) Mosby Inc.

Operating Room Policy & Procedures. Nancy Meier. 1993. 145.00 (*1-879575-35-3*) Acad Med Sys.

Operating Room Risk Management, 1996, 3 vols., Set. Ed. by Ronni P. Solomon & Sharon Bayless. 1100p. 1993. 395.00 (*0-941417-05-0*) ECRI.

Operating Section Proceedings: Index: 1950-1969. American Gas Association Operating Section Compres. 90p. 1970. pap. 3.00 (*0-318-12640-0*, X50070) Am Gas Assn.

Operating Section Proceedings, 1979. 1000p. 1979. 20.00 (*0-318-12665-6*, X50379) Am Gas Assn.

Operating Small Shopping Centers. Alan A. Alexander & Richard F. Muhlebach. LC 97-127182. 1997. write for info. (*0-927547-71-6*) Intl Coun Shop.

Operating Styles & Creative Leadership. John G. Young. 77p. (Orig.). 1987. pap. 14.95 (*0-943456-18-5*) Bearly Ltd.

Operating System: PC-DOS see Essential Guide to the Library IBM PC

Operating System Concepts. James L. Peterson & Abraham Silberschatz. LC 82-22766. (Computer Science Ser.). (Illus.). 576p. 1983. write for info. (*0-201-06097-3*) Addison-Wesley.

O

An Asterisk (*) at the beginning of an entry indicates that the title is appearing for the first time.

Operating System Concepts. Abraham Silberschatz & James L. Peterson. (Computer Science Ser.). (Illus.). 640p. (C). 1988. text 34.36 (*0-201-18760-4*) Addison-Wesley.
Operating System Concepts. 2nd ed. James L. Peterson. (C). 1991. pap. text. write for info. (*0-201-50967-9*) Addison-Wesley.
Operating System Concepts. 2nd ed. James L. Peterson & Abraham Silberschatz. (Computer Science Ser.). (C). 1985. teacher ed. write for info. (*0-201-06090-6*); text 34.36 (*0-201-06198-8*) Addison-Wesley.
Operating System Concepts. 3rd ed. Abraham Silverschatz et al. (Illus.). 656p. (C). 1991. text 56.95 (*0-201-51379-X*) Addison-Wesley.
***Operating System Concepts.** 5th ed. Abraham Silberschatz. 912p. 1998. text 80.95 (*0-471-36414-2*) Wiley.
Operating System Concepts (50480) & Unix for the Hyper Impatient. Abraham Silerschatz. (C). 1997. write for info. (*0-201-34041-0*) Addison-Wesley.
Operating System Design: The Xinu Approach. Douglas E. Comer. (Software Ser.). (Illus.). 496p. (C). 1983. 61.00 (*0-13-637539-1*) P-H.
Operating System Design: The Xinu Design, Vol. 1. Douglas E. Comer. LC 88-2543. 528p. 1988. 55.60 (*0-13-638180-4*) P-H.
Operating System Design-Internetworking with XINU, Vol. II. Douglas E. Comer. (Illus.). 640p. 1987. 57.00 (*0-13-637414-X*) P-H.
Operating System Principles. Per B. Hansen. (Illus.). 496p. 1973. text 56.20 (*0-13-637843-9*) P-H.
Operating System Principles: With Multiprocessors & Object Oriented Design. Campbell. 448p. (C). 2002. write for info. (*0-02-318585-6*, Macmillan Coll) P-H.
Operating System Projects for Windows NT. Gary Nutt. LC 98-46037. 256p. (C). 1998. pap. text 38.00 (*0-201-47708-4*) Addison-Wesley.
Operating System Projects for Windows NT. Gary Nutt. 250p. (C). 1999. pap. text. write for info. incl. cd-rom (*0-201-47707-6*) Addison-Wesley.
Operating Systems. Katzan. 1988. 32.95 (*0-07-158725-X*) McGraw.
Operating Systems. Harold Lorin & Harvey M. Deitel. LC 80-10625. (Computer Science: Systems Programming (IBM) Ser.). (Illus.). 480p. (C). 1981. text 41.95 (*0-201-14464-6*) Addison-Wesley.
Operating Systems. C. Ritchie. 226p. 1995. pap. 59.95 (*1-85805-131-2*, Pub. by DP Publns) St Mut.
***Operating Systems.** Simon & Schuster Staff. (C). 1999. 28.00 (*0-13-013159-8*) S&S Trade.
Operating Systems. Taipei Publications Staff. (C). 1992. pap. text. write for info. (*0-201-55654-5*) Addison-Wesley.
Operating Systems. 2nd ed. Milenkovic. 1992. student ed. 27.50 (*0-07-041923-X*) McGraw.
Operating Systems: A Design-Oriented Approach. Charles Crowley. 768p. (C). 1996. text 54.95 (*0-256-15151-2*, Irwn McGrw-H) McGrw-H Hghr Educ.
***Operating Systems: A Modern Perspective.** 2nd ed. Gary Nutt. 611p. (C). 1999. 69.00 (*0-201-61251-8*) Addison-Wesley.
Operating Systems: A Practical Approach. 1992. pap. text 59.00 (*0-13-640152-X*) P-H.
Operating Systems: A Systematic View. 2nd ed. William S. Davis. (Illus.). 448p. 1983. text. write for info. (*0-201-11116-0*) Addison-Wesley.
Operating Systems: A Systematic View. 3rd ed. William S. Davis. LC 86-10898. 539p. (C). 1987. text 47.50 (*0-201-11185-3*) Addison-Wesley.
Operating Systems: A Systematic View. 4th ed. William S. Davis. (Illus.). 672p. (C). 1991. 77.00 (*0-201-56701-6*) Addison-Wesley.
Operating Systems: Communicating with & Controlling the Computer. Laurie S. Keller. 384p. 1988. text, boxed set 44.20 (*0-13-638040-9*) P-H.
***Operating Systems: Design & Implementation.** 2nd ed. Ed. by S & S Trade Staff. (C). 1999. write for info. (*0-13-013747-2*) S&S Trade.
Operating Systems: Design & Implementation. 2nd ed. Andrew S. Tanenbaum & Albert S. Woodhull. LC 96-37153. 940p. 1996. 74.00 (*0-13-638677-6*) P-H.
Operating Systems: Internals & Design Principles. 3rd ed. William Stallings. LC 97-46926. 781p. (C). 1997. 74.00 (*0-13-887407-7*) P-H.
***Operating Systems: Systematic Approach.** (C). 2000. text. write for info. (*0-201-61257-7*) Addison-Wesley.
***Operating Systems & Services** Ragunathan Rajkumar. LC 99-28475. 1999. write for info. (*0-7923-8548-9*, Kluwer Plenum) Kluwer Academic.
Operating Systems API Reference. UNIX System Laboratories Staff. 1088p. 1993. pap. text 39.00 (*0-13-177130-2*, Pub. by P-H) S&S Trade.
Operating Systems Concepts. 5th ed. Abraham Silberschatz. LC 97-28556. (C). 1998. text 64.95 (*0-201-59113-8*) Addison-Wesley.
Operating Systems Engineering, Amagi, Japan 1980: Proceedings. Ed. by M. Maekawa & L. A. Belady. (Lecture Notes in Computer Science Ser.: Vol. 143). 465p. 1982. 40.00 (*0-387-11604-4*) Spr-Verlag.
***Operating Systems for Teams.** McCarthy. (C). 1999. pap. text. write for info. (*0-201-60456-6*) Addison-Wesley.
Operating Systems Handbook: UNIX, Open VMS, OS-400, VM & MVS. Bob DuCharme. 1994. 49.50 (*0-07-017891-7*) McGraw.
Operating Systems of the Nineties & Beyond: International Workshop Dagstuhl Castle, Germany, July 8-12, 1991 Proceedings. Ed. by A. Karshmer et al. (Lecture Notes in Computer Science Ser.: Vol. 563). x, 285p. 1991. 43.00 (*0-387-54987-0*) Spr-Verlag.
Operating Systems Programming: The SR Programming Language. Stephen J. Hartley. (Illus.). 256p. (C). 1995. pap. text 36.95 (*0-19-509579-0*) OUP.
Operating Systems Programming: The SR Programming Language. Stephen J. Hartley. 88p. (C). 1995. text, teacher ed. 40.00 (*0-19-509578-2*) OUP.
Operating Systems Project: An Environment for Operating Systems Projects. Michael Kifer & Scott A. Smolka. (Illus.). 86p. (C). 1991. pap. text 14.67 (*0-201-54887-9*) Addison-Wesley.
Operating Systems Source Code Secrets: Networking Protocol. Lynne G. Jolitz & William F. Jolitz. (Operating System Source Code Secrets Ser.: Vol. 4). 525p. Date not set. 44.95 (*1-57398-007-2*) Annabooks.
Operating Systems Source Code Secrets: Sockets. Lynne G. Jolitz & William F. Jolitz. (Operating System Source Code Secrets Ser.: Vol. 3). 450p. Date not set. 44.95 (*1-57398-003-X*) Annabooks.
Operating Systems Source Code Secrets Vol. 1: The Basic Kernel, Vol. 1. William F. Jolitz & Lynne G. Jolitz. 530p. 1996. 49.95 (*1-57398-026-9*) Annabooks.
Operating Systems Source Code Secrets Vol. 2: The Virtual Memory System, 2. William F. Jolitz & Lynne G. Jolitz. (Operating System Source Code Secrets Ser.). 200p. Date not set. 44.95 (*1-57398-027-7*) Annabooks.
Operating Systems Survey. 2nd ed. Brown. 400p. (C). 1998. pap. text 38.00 (*0-536-01203-2*) S&S Trade.
Operating Systems Vade Mecum. Raphael A. Finkel. 320p. (C). 1986. text 42.00 (*0-13-637455-7*) P-H.
Operating Systems Vade MECUM. 2nd ed. Raphael A. Finkel. (Illus.). 272p. 1988. text 49.00 (*0-13-637950-8*) P-H.
Operating Techniques for the Tractor-Loader-Backhoe. Gary J. Ober. (Illus.). 175p. 1983. pap. 24.95 (*0-911785-00-0*) Equip Trning Res.
Operating Test for Evaluation of the Surface Durability of Gears. T. H. Wickende & G. R. Brophy. (Technical Papers: Vol. P219.01). (Illus.). 24p. 1946. pap. text 30.00 (*1-55589-246-9*) AGMA.
Operating the Dampening System, Instructor Guide. Robert J. Schneider, Jr. 1990. pap. text, teacher ed. 8.00 (*0-88362-141-X*, 0661) GATFPress.
Operating the Inking System . . . Instructor's Guide. Robert J. Schneider, Jr. 1990. pap. text 8.00 (*0-88362-139-8*, 0650) GATFPress.
Operating the Inking System on the Sheetfed Offset Press. Robert J. Schneider, Jr. 1990. pap. text 20.00 (*0-88362-124-X*, 0651) GATFPress.
***Operating Your Own Pet Sitting Business Kit: Lessons Learned from Successful Pet Sitters... What Works & Why!** Vicky Whelan. 20p. 1999. pap. 39.00 (*0-9675533-0-X*) Pet Sitting.
Operation: Baby. Barbara Bretton. 1997. per. 3.75 (*0-373-16689-3*, 1-16689-1) Harlequin Bks.
Operation: Dump the Chump. Barbara Park. 112p. (J). (gr. 3-7). 1983. pap. 2.75 (*0-380-63974-2*, Avon Bks) Morrow Avon.
Operation: Dump the Chump. Barbara Park. (J). 1995. 9.60 (*0-606-08583-1*, Pub. by Turtleback) Demco.
Operation: Dump the Chump. Barbara Park. LC 81-8147. 128p. (J). (gr. 3-9). 1989. reprint ed. pap. 4.99 (*0-394-82592-6*, Pub. by Knopf Bks Yng Read) Random.
Operation: Fast Pass. Phil Taterczynski. 1983. 5.50 (*0-394-53155-8*) Random.
Operation: Hard Sell. (Torg Ser.). 12.00 (*0-87431-321-X*, 20561) West End Games.
Operation: Husband. Barbara Bretton. LC 95-8350. (American Romance Ser.). 250p. 1995. per. 3.50 (*0-373-16581-1*, 1-16581-0) Harlequin Bks.
***Operation: Independence.** Dorothy I. Ansell & Mark J. Kroner. (Illus.). 55p. 1998. spiral bd. 25.00 (*1-878848-52-6*, 240) Natl Res Ctr.
Operation: Rimfire. Michael MacDonald et al. (Mekton Ser.). (Illus.). 104p. (Orig.). 1993. pap. 14.00 (*0-937279-37-4*, MK1501) Talsorian.
Operation: Save the Teacher. Meg Wolitzer. (Wednesday Night Match Ser.). 128p. (Orig.). (J). (gr. 4-8). 1993. pap. 3.50 (*0-380-76461-X*, Avon Bks) Morrow Avon.
Operation: Save the Teacher: Saturday Night Toast. Meg Wolitzer. 128p. (Orig.). (J). 1993. pap. 3.50 (*0-380-76462-8*, Avon Bks) Morrow Avon.
Operation: Save the Teacher: Tuesday Night Pie. Meg Wolitzer. 128p. (Orig.). (J). 1993. pap. 3.50 (*0-380-76460-1*, Avon Bks) Morrow Avon.
Operation: Shoot & Scoot. James Watson, Jr. & Mark Roberts. (Seals - Top Secret Ser.: No. 2). 336p. 1998. mass mkt. 5.99 (*0-380-78713-X*, Avon Bks) Morrow Avon.
Operation - Homefront. Caroline B. Cooney. 1996. 9.09 (*0-606-00717-2*, Pub. by Turtleback) Demco.
***Operation - Rescue in the Redwoods: Readalong - Singalong Pack.** unabridged ed. Sandy Ribar. (Kids on Assignment - The Adventures of Rex & Ruby Ser.: Vol. 1). (J). (ps-5). 1999. pap. 11.49 incl. audio (*1-893401-08-1*, KOA000RR) Pure & Simple.
Operation A. I. M. Greg Cox. (Iron Man Ser.: No. 2). (J). 1996. mass mkt. 5.99 (*1-57297-195-9*) Blvd Books.
Operation Air Traffic Controller: Secrets of Air Traffic Controller Exam. Scott R. O'Hara. 290p. (Orig.). 1991. pap. 14.95 (*0-9629713-0-8*) Intercntl News.
Operation ANADYR: U. S. & Soviet Generals Recount the Cuban Missile Crisis. Anatoli I. Gribkov & William Y. Smith. LC 93-35789. (Illus.). 252p. 1994. 24.95 (*0-86715-266-4*) Edition Q.
Operation & Application of Electrostatic Accelerators: Proceedings of the 31st Symposium of No. F. Dworschak. 350p. 1999. 78.00 (*981-02-3852-5*) World Scientific Pub.
Operation & Care of Residential Hydronic Heating Systems. Hydronics Institute Staff. (Illus.). 8p. (C). 1975. reprint ed. pap. 3.00 (*0-942711-09-2*) Hydronics Inst.
Operation & Control of Water Treatment Processes. C. R. Cox. (Monographs: No. 49). (ENG, FRE, RUS & SPA., Illus.). 390p. 1964. pap. text 52.00 (*92-4-140049-8*, 1140049) World Health.
Operation & Effects of the Generalized System of Preferences: Ninth & Tenth Reviews. 88p. 35.00 (*92-1-112226-0*, E.87.II.D.1) UN.
Operation & Effects of the North American Free Trade Agreement, July 1997. 154p. 1997. per. 15.00 (*0-16-061890-8*) USGPO.
Operation & Efficiency see Modern Power Station Practice
Operation & Maintenance Financial Management Practices: Hearing Before the Military Readiness Subcommittee of the Committee on National Security, House of Representatives, One Hundred Fifth Congress, First Session, Hearing Held July 22, 1997. United States Government. LC 98-142485. iii, 100 p. 1998. write for info. (*0-16-056150-7*) USGPO.
Operation & Maintenance Funding: Trends in Army & Air Force Use of Funds for Combat Forces & Infrastructure. (Illus.). 49p. (Orig.). (C). 1996. pap. text 25.00 (*0-7881-3475-2*) DIANE Pub.
Operation & Maintenance Manual for Commercial & Industrial Steel Boilers. Hydronics Institute Staff. (Illus.). 12p. (C). 1964. reprint ed. pap. 3.50 (*0-942711-08-4*) Hydronics Inst.
Operation & Maintenance of Ground Water Facilities. Com.on Ground Water of Irrigation & Drainage Div. Ed. by Lloyd C. Fowler. (ASCE Manual of Professional Practice Ser.: Vol. 86). 192p. 1996. 48.00 (*0-7844-0139-X*) Am Soc Civil Eng.
Operation & Maintenance of Large Infrastructure Projects: Proceedings of the International Symposium, Copenhagen, Denmark, 10-13 May 1998. Ed. by L. J. Vincentzen & J. S. Jensen. (Illus.). 224p. (C). 1998. text 74.00 (*90-5410-963-7*, Pub. by A A Balkema) Ashgate Pub Co.
Operation & Maintenance of Sludge Dewatering Systems. LC 87-50922. (Manual of Practice, Operations & Maintenance Ser.: No. 8). 235p. 1987. pap. 45.00 (*0-943244-53-6*, MOM8PA) Water Environ.
Operation & Maintenance of Surface Finishing Wastewater Treatment Systems. Clarence H. Roy. 199p. 1988. 60.00 (*0-936569-04-2*); pap. 40.00 (*0-318-35444-6*) Am Electro Surface.
Operation & Maintenance of Urban Water Supply & Sanitation Systems: A Guide for Managers. LC 95-187662. (CHI, ENG & FRE.). ix, 102p. 1994. pap. text 23.00 (*92-4-154471-6*, 1150416) World Health.
Operation & Maintenance of Wastewater Collection Systems, 2 vols., Set. 5th rev. ed. Kenneth D. Kerri. (Illus.). 1226p. (Orig.). (C). 1996. pap. text 44.00 (*1-884701-20-5*) CA St U Ofc Water.
Operation & Maintenance of Wastewater Collection Systems, Vol. 1. 5th rev. ed. Kenneth D. Kerri. (Illus.). 592p. (Orig.). (C). 1996. pap. text 22.00 (*1-884701-19-1*) CA St U Ofc Water.
Operation & Maintenance of Wastewater Collection Systems, Vol. 2. 5th rev. ed. Kenneth D. Kerri. (Illus.). 634p. (Orig.). (C). 1995. pap. text 22.00 (*1-884701-18-3*) CA St U Ofc Water.
Operation & Modeling of the MOS Transistor. Yannis Tsividis. (Electrical Engineering Ser.). 608p. (C). 1987. text 81.00 (*0-07-065381-X*) McGraw.
***Operation & Quality Management.** (C). 2000. text 42.00 (*0-536-60714-1*) Pearson Custom.
***Operation & Quality Management F99 Jit.** (C). 1999. write for info. (*0-536-60210-7*) Pearson Custom.
Operation Artemis. Douglas Scott. LC 79-2077. 1979. 10.95 (*0-672-52610-7*, Bobbs) Macmillan.
Operation Artful Dodger. James Watson, Jr. & Mark Roberts. (Seals - Top Secret Ser.: No. 1). 320p. 1998. mass mkt. 5.99 (*0-380-78712-1*, Avon Bks) Morrow Avon.
Operation Baby-Sitter. Matt Christopher. LC PZ7.C458Op 1999. (Soccer' Cats Ser.: Vol. 2). (Illus.). 64p. (J). (gr. 2-4). 1999. 13.95 (*0-316-13723-5*) Little.
Operation Bad Apple. G. F. Newman. (Royal Court Writers Ser.). 43p. (C). 1988. pap. 6.95 (*0-413-50270-8*, A0198) Heinemann.
Operation Bagration, 1944. Steven J. Zaloga. (Campaign Ser.). (Illus.). 96p. 1995. pap. 14.95 (*1-85532-478-4*, Pub. by Ospry) Stackpole.
Operation Barbarossa: The German Attack on the Soviet Union, June 22, 1941. Ed. by Joseph L. Wieczynski. xvi, 339p. 1993. 60.00 (*1-884445-01-2*) C Schlacks Pub.
Operation Barbarossa in Photographs: The War in Russia As Photographed by the Soldiers, with a New Preface by the Author. Paul Carell. LC 90-62986. (Illus.). 460p. 1991. 49.95 (*0-88740-280-1*) Schiffer.
***Operation Barbarossa, 1941.** Christer Bergstrom & Andrey Mikhailov. (Black Cross/Red Star Ser.: Vol. I). (Illus.). 3340p. 2000. 39.95 (*0-935553-48-7*, Pub. by Pacifica Military) Motorbooks Intl.
Operation Barbary Coast. D. A. Hodgman. (Code Zero Ser.). 1992. per. 3.50 (*0-373-63406-4*, 1-63406-2) Harlequin Bks.
Operation Blockade: A City Divided. Jonathan Fried. Ed. by Melissa K. Elliott. 85p. (Orig.). 1994. pap. 5.00 (*0-910082-26-X*) Am Fr Serv Comm.
Operation Blue Star: The True Story. K. S. Barr. (C). 1993. 16.50 (*81-85944-29-6*, Pub. by UBS Pubs Dist) S Asia.
***Operation Blue Star: The True Story.** K. S. Brar. 1998. reprint ed. pap. 11.50 (*81-7476-068-7*, Pub. by UBS Pubs) S Asia.
Operation Bograt: Fighter Pilot from France to Burma (WW2) Spellmount Ltd. Publishers Staff. (C). 1986. 90.00 (*0-7855-6767-4*, Pub. by Spellmnt Pubs) St Mut.
Operation Bograt: From France to Burma. Ed. by Donald Stones. 192p. (C). 1991. 110.00 (*0-946771-29-4*, Pub. by Spellmnt Pubs) St Mut.
Operation Bookworm: Reading Activities Your Child Will Love. Eileen Zweig & Ellen Gordon. (Illus.). 128p. 1998. pap. 16.00 (*0-9666032-0-6*) Oper Bookworm.
***Operation Bookworm: Let's Read Together: A Parent's Guide to Beginning Reading.** rev. ed. Ellen Gordon & Eileen Zweig. Orig. Title: Operation Bookworm: Reading Activities Your Child Will Love. (Illus.). 128p. 2000. pap. 16.00 (*0-9666032-1-4*) Oper Bookworm.
Operation Bookworm: Reading Activities Your Child Will Love see Operation Bookworm: Let's Read Together: A Parent's Guide to Beginning Reading
Operation Bootstrap: Helping Very Low-Income Households Become Self-Sufficient, 3 vols. (Illus.). 450p. 1996. reprint ed. pap. text 65.00 (*0-7881-3349-7*) DIANE Pub.
Operation C. H. E. S. E. D. & Other Stories. Chayele Kohaine. (Illus.). 139p. (J). (gr. 2-5). 1989. 13.95 (*0-935063-81-1*); pap. text 10.95 (*0-935063-82-X*) CIS Comm.
***Operation, Care & Repair of Farm Machinery: Practical Hints for Handy Men.** John Deere & Company Publishing Staff. 2000. pap. 12.95 (*1-58574-157-4*) Lyon Press.
***Operation Chaos.** Anderson. 1999. mass mkt. 5.99 (*0-8125-7927-5*) Tor Bks.
***Operation Chaos.** Poul Anderson. 256p. 1999. pap. 12.95 (*0-312-87242-9*, Pub. by Tor Bks) St Martin.
Operation Chaos. Poul Anderson. 288p. 1995. reprint ed. 20.00 (*0-7278-4763-5*) Severn Hse.
Operation Charisma: How to Get Charisma & Wind up at the Top. John M. Curtis. 250p. 1999. pap. 14.95 (*0-9670327-0-9*, 0071) Discobolos Pr.
***Operation Cooperation: Discourses on Joint Ventures & Development.** Maximilian Martin. 240p. 1998. pap. text 24.95 (*3-8258-3239-2*, Pub. by CE24) Transaction Pubs.
Operation Crescent Moon: Underground Christians Reaching Muslims in the Land of Mohammed. George John. LC 94-2150. 1994. 5.00 (*0-88264-307-X*) Living Sacrifice Bks.
Operation Crossroads: The Atomic Tests at Bikini Atoll. Jonathan M. Weisgall. LC 93-42134. (Illus.). 446p. 1994. 33.95 (*1-55750-919-0*) Naval Inst Pr.
Operation Damocles. Oscar L. Fellows. 1998. mass mkt. 5.99 (*0-671-57771-9*) Baen Bks.
Operation Desert Shield. Paul J. Deegan. LC 91-730. (J). (gr. 4 up). 1991. lib. bdg. 13.99 (*1-56239-022-8*) ABDO Pub Co.
Operation Desert Shield - Desert Storm: Chronology & Fact Book. Kevin D. Hutchison. LC 95-21530. 320p. 1995. lib. bdg. 69.50 (*0-313-29606-5*, Greenwood Pr) Greenwood.
Operation Desert Shield - Storm: Through the Eyes of a Black Lieutenant. William J. Simmons, Sr. 57p. 1995. pap. 9.00 (*0-9656133-0-5*) Simmons Ent & Servs.
Operation Desert Storm. Paul J. Deegan. LC 91-73078. (War in the Gulf Ser.). (J). (gr. 4 up). 1991. lib. bdg. 13.99 (*1-56239-023-6*) ABDO Pub Co.
Operation Desert Storm: An Assessment of Aerial Refueling Operational Efficiency. 18p. pap. text 30.00 (*0-7881-4128-7*) DIANE Pub.
Operation Desert Storm: Apache Helicopter Fratricide Incident. Ed. by Barbara J. Cart et al. (Illus.). 100p. 1997. reprint ed. pap. text 40.00 (*0-7881-4115-5*) DIANE Pub.
Operation Desert Storm: Evaluation of the Air Campaign. Kwai-Cheung Chan. (Illus.). 235p. (C). 1998. pap. text 40.00 (*0-7881-4769-2*) DIANE Pub.
Operation Desert Storm: Evaluation of the Air War. 26p. (Orig.). (C). 1996. pap. text 15.00 (*0-7881-3555-4*) DIANE Pub.
Operation Desert Storm: Health Concerns of Selected Indiana Persian Gulf War Veterans. 43p. (Orig.). (C). 1995. pap. text 15.00 (*0-7881-2079-4*) DIANE Pub.
Operation Desert Storm: Investigation of a U. S. Army Fratricide Incident. (Illus.). 110p. (Orig.). 1995. pap. text 40.00 (*1-57979-099-2*) DIANE Pub.
Operation Desert Storm: Investigation of a U. S. Army Fratricide Incident. (Illus.). 109p. (Orig.). (C). 1995. pap. text 30.00 (*0-7881-1802-1*) DIANE Pub.
Operation Desert Storm: Problems With Air Force (AF) Medical Readiness. 23p. pap. text 30.00 (*0-7881-4129-5*) DIANE Pub.
Operation Desert Storm: Army Not Adequately Prepared to Deal with Depleted Uranium (DU) Contamination. 42p. pap. text 30.00 (*0-7881-4127-9*) DIANE Pub.
Operation Desert Storm Testimony Report: Investigation of a U. S. Army Fratricide Incident. 6p. 1995. pap. text 10.00 (*1-57979-100-X*) DIANE Pub.
Operation Drumbeat: The Dramatic True Story of Germany's First U-Boat Attacks Along the American Coast in World War II. Michael Gannon. LC 89-46090. (Illus.). 528p. 1991. pap. 16.00 (*0-06-092088-2*, Perennial) HarperTrade.
Operation Dry Dock: Silent Death Annex Book. C. Marek et al. (Silent Death - The Next Millennium Ser.). (Illus.). 92p. 1997. pap. 14.00 (*1-55806-292-0*, 7215) Iron Crown Ent Inc.
***Operation Earth Light: A Glimpse into the World of the Ascended Masters.** Brian C. Keneipp. (Illus.). 156p. 2000. pap. 12.95 (*0-937249-17-3*) Aetherius Soc.
***Operation Eichmann: Pursuit & Capture.** Zvi Aharoni. (Military Classics). 2000. pap. 9.95 (*0-304-35201-2*) Continuum.
Operation Eichmann: The Truth Behind the Pursuit, Capture & Trial of Adolf Eichmann. Zvi Aharoni. Tr. by Helmut Bogler. LC 97-21379. (Illus.). 192p. 1997. 22.95 (*0-471-19377-1*) Wiley.
Operation Elbow Room. Joseph Phillips. 240p. (Orig.). 1995. pap. 11.95 (*1-56474-138-9*) Fithian Pr.

O

An Asterisk (*) at the beginning of an entry indicates that the title is appearing for the first time.

Operation Elrood. (Star Wars Ser.). 15.00 (*0-87431-291-4*, 40132) West End Games.

Operation End Sweep: A History of Minesweeping Operations in North Vietnam. 1994. lib. bdg. 250.00 (*0-8490-8540-3*) Gordon Pr.

Operation End Sweep: A History of Minesweeping Operations in North Vietnam. Ed. by Edward J. Marolda. (Illus.). 129p. (C). 1998. pap. text 30.00 (*0-7881-4802-8*) DIANE Pub.

Operation End Sweep: A History of Minesweeping Operations in North Vietnam. Tensor Industries, Inc. Staff. Ed. by Edward J. Marolda. LC 92-36206. (Illus.). 143p. 1993. 7.50 (*0-945274-14-9*) Naval Hist Ctr.

Operation Epsilon: The Farm Hall Transcripts. Intro. by Charles Frank. 272p. 1993. 35.00 (*0-520-08499-3*, Pub. by U CA Pr) Cal Prin Full Svc.

Operation Esther: Opening the Door for the Last Jews of Yemen. Hayim Tawil et al. LC 98-88644. 340p. 1998. 25.00 (*0-9667575-0-5*) Belkis.

Operation Excalibur. William H. Keith. (Battletech Ser.). 288p. 1996. mass mkt. 5.99 (*0-451-45526-6*, ROC) NAL.

Operation Exodus. 1998. pap. 12.99 (*1-85240-226-1*) SOV5.

*__Operation Exodus II: Answers You Need to Know about Explosive Future Events.__ Steve Lightle. 272p. 1999. pap. 12.99 (*1-890900-05-2*) Insight Intl.

Operation Fantasy Plan. Peter Gilboy. LC 96-29623. 304p. 1998. mass mkt. 5.99 (*0-380-72982-2*, Avon Bks) Morrow Avon.

Operation Fire-Operation Tan. Selwyn Jones et al. 1980. 20.00 (*0-7855-1461-9*, Pub. by NCCL) St Mut.

Operation Fire-Operation Tan. Selwyn Penny & Philip Jones. (C). 1988. 21.00 (*0-7855-6070-X*, Pub. by NCCL) St Mut.

Operation Flood: An Appraisal of Current Indian Dairy Policy. Shanti George. 230p. 1986. 29.95 (*0-19-561679-0*) OUP.

*__Operation Foxley: The British Plan to Kill Hitler.__ Intro. by Mark Seaman. (Illus.). 166p. 1999. pap. text 30.00 (*0-7881-8124-6*) DIANE Pub.

*__Operation Foxley: The British Plan to Kill Hitler.__ Mark Seamen & Ian Kershaw. LC 99-237490. (Illus.). 166p. 1999. pap. 15.95 (*1-873162-72-3*, Pub. by PRO Pubns) Midpt Trade.

Operation Fury. Leo Kessler. 22.00 (*0-7278-4958-1*) Severn Hse.

*__Operation Gadgetman.__ Blackman. (J). 2000. pap. 5.95 (*0-440-86307-4*, Pub. by Transworld Publishers Ltd) Trafalgar.

Operation Getafix. Rene de Goscinny & A. Uderzo. 1992. 24.95 (*0-7859-1051-4*, 0-340-529458) Fr & Eur.

Operation Ghost. Jacques Duquennoy. LC 98-43351. 48p. (J). 1999. 13.00 (*0-15-202182-5*, Harcourt Child Bks); pap. 6.00 (*0-15-202203-1*, Harcourt Child Bks) Harcourt.

Operation Gigolo. Vicki L. Thompson. (Love & Laughter Ser.: Vol. 47). 1998. per. 3.50 (*0-373-44047-2*, 1-44047-8) Harlequin Bks.

Operation Greylord: The Brocton Lockwood Story. Brocton Lockwood & Harlan H. Mendenhall. LC 89-6022. (Illus.). 224p. (C). 1989. 21.95 (*0-8093-1545-9*) S Ill U Pr.

Operation Grizzly Bear. Marian Calabro. LC 88-37497. (Illus.). 112p. (J). (gr. 5 up). 1989. text 13.95 (*0-02-716241-9*, Four Winds Pr) S&S Childrens.

Operation Handbook for Model Railroads. Paul Mallery. (Illus.). 200p. 1991. pap. 12.95 (*0-911868-74-7*, C74) Carstens Pubns.

*__Operation Hangman.__ Mike Martell. (SEALs Strategic Warfare Ser.). 384p. 2000. mass mkt. 6.99 (*0-380-80827-7*) Morrow Avon.

*__Operation Hebron: A Spy Novel.__ Erica Jordan. 2000. 26.95 (*0-88962-777-0*) Mosaic.

Operation Homefront. Marilyn Pappano. (Intimate Moments Ser.: No. 424). 1992. per. 3.39 (*0-373-07424-7*, 5-07424-0) Harlequin Bks.

Operation Iceberg. Gerald Astor. 576p. 1996. mass mkt. 6.50 (*0-440-22178-1*) Dell.

Operation Intercept. Lawrence A. Gooberman. 1975. 103.00 (*0-08-017837-5*, Pub. by Pergamon Repr) Franklin.

Operation Jessica. Herman Weiss. 352p. (Orig.). 1992. mass mkt. 4.99 (*0-446-36288-3*, Pub. by Warner Bks) Little.

Operation Junction City. Lawrence J. Hickey. 65p. 1993. reprint ed. pap. 9.50 (*0-923135-63-4*) Dalley Bk Service.

Operation Just Cause: Lessons for Operations Other Than War. Jennifer M. Taw. LC 96-23125. 55p. 1996. pap. text 13.00 (*0-8330-2405-1*, MR-569-A) Rand Corp.

Operation "Just Cause" The Human Cost of Military Action in Panama. Jane Schaller et al. 45p. 1991. pap. text 6.00 (*1-879707-01-2*) Phy Human Rights.

Operation Just Cause: The Planning & Execution of Joint Operations in Panama, February 1988-January 1990. Ronald H. Cole. 88p. (C). 1996. reprint ed. pap. text 25.00 (*0-7881-3557-0*) DIANE Pub.

Operation Love Match. Kate William. (Sweet Valley High Ser.: No. 103). (YA). (gr. 7 up). 1994. 9.09 (*0-606-06026-X*, Pub. by Turtleback) Demco.

Operation Luna. Poul Anderson. LC 99-24483. 320p. 1999. 22.95 (*0-312-86706-9*, Pub. by Tor Bks) St Martin.

*__Operation Luna.__ Poul Anderson. 416p. 2000. mass mkt. 6.99 (*0-8125-8027-3*) Tor Bks.

Operation Magic Tricks. Ronald Edwards. 108p. (J). (gr. 1-7). 1995. pap. 11.95 (*0-89455-632-0*) Crit Think Bks.

Operation Management. 6th ed. Schonberger. 1996. pap., student ed. 28.75 (*0-256-21534-0*) McGraw.

Operation Manhunt Made Easy. C. S. Lovett. 1961. pap. 4.95 (*0-938148-17-6*) Prsnl Christianity.

Operation Market Garden Orientation. James F. Gabelmann. (Illus.). 76p. (C). 1998. pap. text 15.00 (*1-884680-06-2*) Gabelmann Pr.

Operation Matador: Britain's War Plans Against the Japanese 1918-1941. Ong C. Chung. LC 97-945721. 328p. 1997. 25.00 (*981-210-095-4*, Pub. by Times Academic) Intl Spec Bk.

Operation Melody. Denise O. Pomeraning. LC 94-72210. (Illus.). 64p. (J). (gr. 4-7). 1994. pap. 4.99 (*0-8066-2718-2*, 9-2718, Augsburg) Augsburg Fortress.

Operation Memories: Incredible Stories of World War II Veterans. Evelyn I. Gregory. LC 95-185303. 339p. (C). 1995. text. write for info. (*0-9644435-0-3*) Senior Dist.

Operation Midas. large type ed. Alfred Draper. (Magna Large Print Ser.). 470p. 1996. 27.99 (*0-7505-0954-6*, Pub. by Mgna Lrg Print) Ulverscroft.

Operation Midnight Climax. Neal Bell. 1982. pap. 5.25 (*0-8222-0862-8*) Dramatists Play.

Operation Mindcrime: Selections from Queensryche with Notes & Tablature. 32p. 1994. otabind 19.95 (*0-7935-3776-2*, 00694969) H Leonard.

Operation Mommy. Caroline Cross. (Desire Ser.). 1995. per. 3.25 (*0-373-05939-6*, 1-05939-3) Silhouette.

Operation Moonlight Sonata: The German Raid on Coventry. Allan W. Kurki. LC 94-41798. 200p. 1995. 52.95 (*0-275-95104-9*, Praeger Pubs) Greenwood.

Operation Morningstar. Dorothy L. Harrison. LC 96-48199. (Chronicles of Courage Ser.). 128p. (J). 1997. pap. 4.99 (*0-7814-0242-5*, Chariot Bks) Chariot Victor.

Operation Multiplication see Operacion Multiplicacion: Lider

Operation 'Nestegg: The Liberation of Jersey, 1945. Compiled by Richard Mayne. (Illus.). 80p. (C). 1987. pap. 21.00 (*0-7855-2165-8*, Pub. by Picton) St Mut.

Operation Nestegg: The Liberation of Jersey, 1945. Picton Publishing (Chippenham) Ltd. Staff. (C). 1987. 20.00 (*0-948251-26-3*, Pub. by Picton) St Mut.

Operation New Life: The Untold Story. Richard Mackie. (Illus.). 86p. (Orig.). 1997. pap. 14.95 (*1-885372-09-4*) Solution CA.

Operation Nightfall. John Miles & Tom Morris. LC 74-17665. 224p. 1975. 6.95 (*0-672-52085-0*, Bobbs) Macmillan.

Operation Nighthawk. J. A. Price. 1985. pap. 3.50 (*0-8217-1696-4*) NAL.

*__Operation No Man's Land.__ Mike Martell. (SEALs Strategic Warfare Ser.). 400p. 2000. mass mkt. 6.99 (*0-380-80828-5*) Morrow Avon.

Operation of Broad-Beam Sources. Harold R. Kaufman & Raymond S. Robinson. (Illus.). 201p. (Orig.). 1987. pap. 35.00 (*0-930787-02-1*) Cmnwlth Sci.

Operation of Counterflow Regenerators. Gordan D. Dragutinovic & Branislav S. Baclic. LC 97-81220. (Developments in Heat Transfer Ser.: Vol. 4). 208p. 1998. 95.00 (*1-85312-548-2*, 5482, Pub. by WIT Pr) Computational Mech MA.

Operation of Electrified & Automatic Leases. 2nd ed. Nancy Grona & Mary L. Skinner. Ed. by Mildred Gerding. (Illus.). 114p. (C). 1978. pap. text 15.00 (*0-88698-113-1*, 3.20020) PETEX.

Operation of Extended Aeration Package Plants. Water Pollution Control Federation Staff. LC 85-51395. (Manual of Practice, Operations & Maintenance Ser.: No. 7). 98p. (Orig.). 1985. pap. 32.00 (*0-943244-60-9*, MOPOM7) Water Environ.

*__Operation of Hedge Funds & Their Role in the Financial System: Congressional Hearing.__ Ed. by Richard H. Baker. 141p. (C). 2000. pap. text 35.00 (*0-7567-0036-1*) DIANE Pub.

Operation of Internal Labor Markets: Staffing Practices & Vacancy Chains. Lawrence T. Pinfield. LC 96-34163. (Plenum Studies in Work & Industry). (Illus.). 372p. (C). 1995. 52.50 (*0-306-45046-1*, Kluwer Plenum) Kluwer Academic.

Operation of Municipal Wastewater Treatment Plants. 5th ed. Water Environment Federation Staff. LC 96-41387. (Manual of Practice Ser.). 1996. 138.00 (*1-57278-040-1*) Water Environ.

Operation of Nuclear Power Stations, 1995. EC Staff. 136p. 1996. pap. 17.00 (*92-827-8919-5*, CA99-96-633-3AC, Pub. by Comm Europ Commun) Bernan Associates.

Operation of Rights in the Custodian/Dependent Relationship. Anthony C. Ibbott. 29p. 1992. pap. 1.00 (*0-9625291-3-3*) A C Ibbott Fndtn.

Operation of Small Wastewater Systems, 2 vols., Set. Kenneth D. Kerri. (Illus.). 1020p. (C). 1997. pap. text. write for info. (*1-884701-23-X*) CA St U Ofc Water.

Operation of Small Wastewater Systems, Vol. I. Kenneth D. Kerri. (Illus.). 520p. (C). 1997. pap. text 33.00 (*1-884701-21-3*) CA St U Ofc Water.

Operation of Small Wastewater Systems, Vol. II. Kenneth D. Kerri. (Illus.). 500p. (C). 2000. pap. text. write for info. (*1-884701-22-1*) CA St U Ofc Water.

Operation of Soil-Working Implements in Hilly Regions. Ed. by K. A. Khachatryan. Tr. by K. S. Dhillon from RUS. 239p. (C). 1985. text 130.00 (*0-317-65454-3*, Pub. by A A Balkema) Ashgate Pub Co.

Operation of State & Regional Indicators in Public Policy & Quality of Life Evaluation. Kenneth Meyer et al. 10.00 (*1-55614-075-4*) U of SD Gov Res Bur.

Operation of the Bad Check Laws of Puerto Rico. Frederick K. Beutel. 158p. 1967. 3.00 (*0-8477-2200-7*) U of PR Pr.

Operation of the Fuel System. Peter Novellino. LC 74-734388. 1974. student ed. 7.00 (*0-8064-0079-X*, 407) Bergwall.

Operation of the Offset Press. Theodore F. Makarius. (Illus.). 327p. (C). 1993. pap. 29.50 (*0-911126-07-4*) Perfect Graphic.

Operation of Wastewater Treatment Plants, Vol. I. 4th ed. Kenneth D. Kerri. (Illus.). 528p. (C). 1992. pap. text 22.00 (*1-884701-00-0*) CA St U Ofc Water.

Operation of Wastewater Treatment Plants, Vol. II. 4th ed. Kenneth D. Kerri. (Illus.). 754p. (C). 1993. pap. text 27.00 (*1-884701-01-9*) CA St U Ofc Water.

Operation of Wastewater Treatment Plants, Vols. I & II. Kenneth D. Kerri. (Illus.). 1282p. 1993. pap. text 49.00 (*1-884701-02-7*) CA St U Ofc Water.

Operation Overlord: Gold & Juno Beaches. Christopher Chant. (Order of Battle Ser.). (Illus.). 32p. 1994. pap. 10.95 (*1-898994-01-3*) Stackpole.

Operation Overlord: Omaha Beach & Pointe du Hoc. James Arnold & Roberta Wiener. (Order of Battle Ser.). (Illus.). 32p. 1994. pap. 10.95 (*1-898994-02-1*) Stackpole.

Operation Overlord: Sword Beach & the British 6th Airborne Division. Christopher Chant. (Order of Battle Ser.). (Illus.). 32p. 1994. pap. 10.95 (*1-898994-00-5*) Stackpole.

Operation Overlord: Utah Beach & the U. S. Airborne Divisions. James Arnold & Roberta Wiener. (Order of Battle Ser.). (Illus.). 32p. 1994. pap. 10.95 (*1-898994-03-X*) Stackpole.

Operation Overlord, Design & Reality: The Allied Invasion of Western Europe. Albert Norman. LC 73-100252. 230p. 1970. reprint ed. lib. bdg. 35.00 (*0-8371-2985-0*, NOOO, Greenwood Pr) Greenwood.

Operation Paraquat: The Battle for South Georgia. Ed. by Roger Perkins. 262p. (C). 1986. 75.00 (*0-948251-13-1*, Pub. by Picton) St Mut.

Operation Parterre. George Blagowidow. 286p. 1982. 10.95 (*0-88254-712-7*) Hippocrene Bks.

Operation Pedro Pan: The Untold Exodus of 14,000 Cuban Children. Yvonne Conde. LC 99-17440. (Illus.). 256p. 1999. 27.50 (*0-415-92149-X*) Routledge.

*__Operation Pedro Pan: The Untold Exodus of 14,000 Cuban Children.__ Yvonne M. Conde. 2000. reprint ed. pap. 16.95 (*0-415-92823-0*) Routledge.

Operation Peeg. Jonathon Gathorne-Hardy. LC 74-8908. (J). (gr. 2-5). 1974. 12.95 (*0-397-31594-5*) HarpC Child Bks.

Operation Pressure Point: The Disruption of Street-Level Drug Trade on New York's Lower East Side. Lynn Zimmer. Ed. by Graham Hughes. (Occasional Papers: Vol. II). 26p. (Orig.). (C). 1987. pap. 5.00 (*1-878429-51-5*) NYU Ctr for Rsch in Crime Justice.

Operation Principles of the High Sliding Gears. R. Priti. (Technical Papers: Vol. P109.33). (Illus.). 7p. 1973. pap. text 30.00 (*1-55589-201-9*) AGMA.

Operation: Prosperity: Fixing America's Economy, a Practical & Ecological Guide for Individuals & Governments. Christopher C. Lai. (Illus.). 336p. 1997. pap. 14.95 (*0-9652728-1-8*) Candor Pr.

Operation Provide Comfort: Review of U. S. Air Force Investigation of Black Hawk Fratricide Incident. Barbara W. Alsip et al. (Illus.). 56p. (C). 1998. pap. text 20.00 (*0-7881-7548-3*) DIANE Pub.

*__Operation Pseudo Miranda: A Veteran of the CIA Drug Wars Tells All.__ Kenneth C. Bucchi. 350p. 2000. 23.95 (*1-883955-17-3*, Pub. by Penmarin Bks) Midpt Trade.

Operation Puma: The Air Battle of the Bay of Pigs. Edward B. Ferrer. (Illus.). 242p. 1982. pap. 11.50 (*0-9609000-0-4*) Intl Av Consult.

Operation Pushpak. S. S. Negi. (C). 1987. 45.00 (*81-7136-008-4*, Pub. by Periodical Expert) St Mut.

Operation Quicksilver. Peter Tooley. 1993. pap. 14.00 (*0-86025-415-1*, Pub. by I Henry Pubns) Empire Pub Srvs.

Operation Redemption: A Vision of Hope in an Age of Turmoil. George Trevelan. 1991. pap. 12.95 (*0-904575-57-8*) Sigo Pr.

Operation Remission. Paul Johnson. 344p. 1994. pap. 12.95 (*0-9637974-3-3*) Nefyn & Shaw.

*__Operation-Rescue in the Redwoods: Mini-Musical Production Guide.__ Sandy Ribar. (Kids on Assignment - The Adventures of Rex & Ruby Ser.: Vol. 1). (Illus.). 40p. (J). (gr. k-5). 1999. pap. 7.95 (*1-893401-00-6*, KOA010) Pure & Simple.

*__Operation-Rescue in the Redwoods: Mini-Musical Production Pack.__ Sandy Ribar. (Kids on Assignment - The Adventures of Rex & Ruby Ser.). (Illus.). 40p. (J). (ps-4). 1999. pap. 98.00 (*1-893401-07-3*, KOA00RR) Pure & Simple.

*__Operation-Rescue in the Redwoods: Storybook.__ Sandy Ribar. (Kids on Assignment - The Adventures of Rex & Ruby Ser.: Vol. 8). (Illus.). 40p. (J). 1999. pap. 3.99 (*1-893401-06-5*, KOA081RR) Pure & Simple.

*__Operation-Rescue in the Redwoods: Teacher's Resources.__ Sandy Ribar. Ed. by Henley B. Johnson. (Kids on Assignment - The Adventures of Rex & Ruby Ser.: Vol. 7). (Illus.). 1999. pap., teacher ed. 7.95 (*1-893401-05-7*, KOA061RR) Pure & Simple.

*__Operation Resistance - 2000: The Terrain, Dynamics & Defenses of Antimicrobial Resistance.__ Ed. by Jerome Schonby. 60p. 1999. pap. 13.95 (*0-9668202-2-3*) S Dawson Pubs.

Operation Restore America. rev. ed. Sara Sheldon. LC 96-69540. 445p. (Orig.). 1998. pap. 14.95 (*0-9665654-0-1*) White Sand Lake.

Operation Restore Hope: The Bush Administration's Decision to Intervene in Somalia. Maryann K. Cusimano. (Pew Case Studies in International Affairs). 50p. (C). 1995. pap. text 3.50 (*1-56927-463-0*, GU Schl Foreign) Geo U Inst Dplmcy.

Operation "Restore Hope" The Political & Military Lessons. Ed. by Bruce W. Watson. 1999. pap. 49.00 (*0-8133-1900-5*) Westview.

Operation Rhinoceros. Lee Wardlaw. LC 92-15933. (Illus.). 120p. (Orig.). (J). (gr. 3-6). 1992. pap. 3.50 (*0-931093-14-7*) Red Hen Pr.

*__Operation Rollback.__ Peter Grose. LC 99-89830. (Illus.). 320p. 2000. 25.00 (*0-395-51606-4*) HM.

Operation Sea Angel: A Case Study. Paul A. McCarthy. LC 93-42926. 1994. pap. 13.00 (*0-8330-1492-7*, MR-374-A) Rand Corp.

Operation Sea Lion: German Plans for the Invasion of England, 1939-1942. Ronald Wheatley. LC 78-16322. 201p. 1978. reprint ed. lib. bdg. 35.00 (*0-313-20605-8*, WHOS, Greenwood Pr) Greenwood.

*__Operation Sea Lion: The German Plan to Invade Britain, 1940.__ Egbert Kieser. (Military Classics). 2000. pap. 9.95 (*0-304-35208-X*) Continuum.

Operation Sea Lion: The Projected Invasion of England in 1940: An Account of the German Preparations & the British Countermeasures. Peter Fleming. LC 76-56777. (Illus.). 323p. 1977. reprint ed. lib. bdg. 38.50 (*0-8371-9429-6*, FLOS) Greenwood.

Operation "Sea Lion" & the Role Planned for the Luftwaffe: Study. Karl Klee. (USAF Historical Studies: No. 157). 378p. 1955. reprint ed. pap. text 38.00 (*0-89126-156-7*); reprint ed. 47.00 (*0-89126-155-9*) MA-AH Pub.

Operation Seal Bay. Pat Molloy. 274p. (C). 1989. text 50.00 (*0-86383-542-2*, Pub. by Gomer Pr) St Mut.

*__Operation: Shell Game, No. 4.__ James Watson, Jr. & Mark Roberts. (Seals - Top Secret Ser.). 312p. 1999. mass mkt. 6.50 (*0-380-80575-8*, Avon Bks) Morrow Avon.

Operation Sherlock. Bruce Coville. Ed. by Pat MacDonald. (A. I. Gang Ser.). 224p. (J). 1995. pap. 3.99 (*0-671-89249-5*, Minstrel Bks) PB.

Operation Sherlock. Bruce Coville. (A.I. Gang Ser.). 1995. 9.09 (*0-606-07169-5*, Pub. by Turtleback) Demco.

Operation Shylock. Philip Roth. 1994. pap. 14.00 (*0-679-75029-0*) Vin Bks.

Operation Siberian Crane: The Story Behind the International Effort to Save an Amazing Bird. Judi Friedman. LC 92-13775. (Illus.). 96p. (J). (gr. 5 up). 1992. lib. bdg. 13.95 (*0-87518-515-0*, Dillon Silver Burdett) Silver Burdett Pr.

Operation Skua. R. T. Partridge. 160p. (C). 1990. pap. 35.00 (*0-902633-86-4*, Pub. by Picton) St Mut.

Operation Skua. Picton Publishing (Chippenham) Ltd. Staff. (FAA Ser.). (C). 1987. 39.00 (*0-7855-5334-7*, Pub. by Picton) St Mut.

Operation Smokescreen. large type ed. Michael Judge. (Linford Mystery Library). 432p. 1995. pap. 16.99 (*0-7089-7714-6*, Linford) Ulverscroft.

Operation Snap-Shot: How to Photograph Your Military Service. Kirby L. Vaughn. (Enlistment Planning Ser.). (Illus.). 175p. (Orig.). 1997. pap. write for info. (*0-9644005-7-X*) Essayons Pub.

*__Operation Snowfall.__ Bruce Reaves. 148p. 1999. pap. 13.95 (*0-7414-0128-2*) Buy Books.

Operation Solo: The FBI's Man in the Kremlin. John Barron. (Illus.). 368p. 1997. pap. 12.95 (*0-89526-429-3*) Regnery Pub.

Operation Space Magic - The Cosmic Connection. George King. LC 86-198682. (Illus.). 93p. 1982. pap. 7.95 (*0-937249-10-6*) Aetherius Soc.

Operation Space Power. George King. LC 87-71807. (Illus.). 80p. 1987. pap. 12.95 (*0-937249-12-2*) Aetherius Soc.

Operation Stagecoach Red. J. T. Fitzgerald. 208p. (Orig.). 1994. pap. text 19.95 (*0-930401-73-5*) Artex Pub.

Operation Stagecoach Red. rev. ed. J. T. Fitzgerald. LC 96-71067. 246p. (Orig.). 1997. pap. 15.95 (*1-57197-052-5*) Pentland Pr.

*__Operation Stormbird: Into the Neutral Zone.__ Pocket Books Staff. (Star Trek: The Next Generation Ser.). 2000. per. 16.00 (*0-671-03502-9*) PB.

Operation Stormwind. Duncan Harding. 224p. 1996. 22.00 (*0-7278-4893-3*) Severn Hse.

Operation Survival: The Story of the Battle to Preserve Scotland's Wildlife. Sally Wilson. (Illus.). 192p. 1997. 45.00 (*1-85158-883-3*, Pub. by Mainstream Pubng) Trafalgar.

Operation Systems: Humans - Intelligence - Machines. Ewald Heer. LC 98-92633. (Illus.). xiii, 286p. 1998. pap. 19.80 (*0-9662916-0-3*) HAI-Pubs.

*__Operation Thunder Child.__ Nike Pope. 320p. 2000. per. 12.00 (*0-684-82442-6*) S&S Trade.

Operation Timber: Pages from the Savimbi Dossier. William Minter. LC 88-71419. 200p. (C). 1988. 19.95 (*0-86543-103-5*); pap. 6.95 (*0-86543-104-3*) Africa World.

Operation Timothy. rev. ed. (Illus.). 1995. teacher ed., wbk. ed. write for info. (*0-945292-06-6*) Christ Busn Mens Committee.

Operation Timothy, Set, Bks. 1-4. rev. ed. CBMC Staff. (Illus.). 1995. wbk. ed. write for info. (*0-945292-07-4*) Christ Busn Mens Committee.

Operation Timothy: Series & Leader's Guide, Set, Bks. 1-4. rev. ed. CBMC Staff. (Illus.). 1995. teacher ed., wbk. ed. write for info. (*0-945292-08-2*) Christ Busn Mens Committee.

Operation Timothy Bk. 1: Finding the Way. CBMC Staff. (Illus.). 1995. wbk. ed. write for info. (*0-945292-01-5*) Christ Busn Mens Committee.

Operation Timothy Bk. 2: Knowing the Truth. CBMC Staff. (Illus.). wbk. ed. write for info. (*0-614-11411-X*) Christ Busn Mens Committee.

Operation Timothy Bk. 3: Living with Power. rev. ed. CBMC Staff. (Illus.). wbk. ed. write for info. (*0-945292-03-1*) Christ Busn Mens Committee.

Operation Timothy Bk. 4: Making a Difference. CBMC Staff. (Illus.). 1995. wbk. ed. write for info. (*0-945292-05-8*) Christ Busn Mens Committee.

Operation Titanic. Carolyn Keene. (Nancy Drew & Hardy Boys Super Mystery Ser.: No. 35). (YA). (gr. 6 up). 1998. pap. 3.99 (*0-671-00737-8*, Archway) PB.

Operation Titanic. Carolyn Keene. (Nancy Drew & Hardy Boys Super Mystery Ser.: No. 35). (YA). (gr. 6 up). 1998. 9.09 (*0-606-13650-9*, Pub. by Turtleback) Demco.

Operation Trojan Horse. John A. Keel. LC 96-14564. 288p. 1996. reprint ed. pap. 16.95 (*0-9626534-6-2*) IllumiNet Pr.

Operation Tuscaloosa: 2nd Battalion, 5th Marines, at An Hoa. John J. Culbertson. (Orig.). 1997. mass mkt. 5.99 (*0-8041-1565-6*) Ivy Books.

Operation Wandering Soul. Richard Powers. LC 93-49506. 352p. 1994. reprint ed. pap. 14.00 (*0-06-097611-X*, Perennial) HarperTrade.

Operation Warhawks: How Young People Become Warriors. Terrence Webster-Doyle. (Education for Peace Ser.). (Illus.). 135p. (J). (gr. 5-12). 1993. pap. 14.95 (*0-942941-30-6*) Atrium Soc Educ.

Operation Werwolf. Leon Smith. (World War II Monograph: Vol. 218). 44p. 1997. 17.95 (*1-57638-057-2*, M218H); pap. 7.95 (*1-57638-056-4*, M218S) Merriam Pr.

Operation Wetback: The Mass Deportation of Mexican Undocumented Workers in 1954, 2. Juan R. Garcia. LC 79-6189. (Contributions in Ethnic Studies: No. 2). (Illus.). 268p. 1980. 59.95 (*0-313-21353-4*, GOW/, Greenwood Pr) Greenwood.

Operation World see Operacion Mundo: Guia Diaria de Oracion

Operation World. Patrick Johnstone. 608p. 1993. pap. 14.99 (*0-310-40031-7*) Zondervan.

Operation World. 5th ed. Pat Johnstone. 1995. pap. 12.99 (*0-310-20404-6*); pap. 15.99 (*1-85078-120-6*) O M Lit.

Operational Amplifier Applications. Buck Engineering Staff. Ed. by Buck Engineering Tech. Writers Staff. (F. A. C. E. T. Ser.: Vol. 13). (Illus.). 60p. 1989. pap. text, teacher ed. 11.00 (*0-86657-033-0*); ring bd. 12.00 (*0-86657-032-2*) Lab-Volt.

Operational Amplifier Characteristics & Applications. 3rd ed. Robert G. Irvine. 592p. 1994. 95.00 (*0-13-606088-9*) P-H.

Operational Amplifier Circuits: Analysis & Design. J. C. Nelson. LC 94-32724. (EDN Ser.). 152p. 1994. pap. text 28.95 (*0-7506-9468-8*) Buttrwrth-Heinemann.

Operational Amplifiers. Honeycutt. (Electronics Technology Ser.). 1988. pap., teacher ed. 14.00 (*0-8273-2696-3*) Delmar.

Operational Amplifiers. Arpad Barne. LC 70-150608. (Illus.). 159p. reprint ed. pap. 49.30 (*0-608-10232-6*, 205552500026) Bks Demand.

Operational Amplifiers. I. E. Shepherd. LC 80-40770. (Illus.). 332p. reprint ed. pap. 103.00 (*0-8357-2989-3*, 203925200011) Bks Demand.

Operational Amplifiers. rev. ed. Heath Company Staff. (Electronics Technology Ser.). (Illus.). 368p. (C). 1979. reprint ed. teacher ed. 9.95 (*0-87119-033-8*); reprint ed. pap. text 18.95 (*0-87119-032-X*); reprint ed. ring bd. 44.95 (*0-87119-034-6*) Heathkit-Zenith Ed.

Operational Amplifiers. 2nd ed. Jiri Dostal. (EDN Ser.). (Illus.). 360p. 1993. text 72.95 (*0-7506-9317-7*) Buttrwrth-Heinemann.

*__Operational Amplifiers.__ 4th ed. G. B. Clayton & Steve Winder. 448p. 2000. pap. 49.95 (*0-7506-4643-8*, Newnes) Buttrwrth-Heinemann.

Operational Amplifiers. 4th ed. Bruce W. Newby & George B. Clayton. (Illus.). 350p. 2000. text 44.95 (*0-7506-0640-1*) Buttrwrth-Heinemann.

Operational Amplifiers: 1987 Sourcebook. Technipubs, Inc. Staff. Ed. by Harry L. Helms. 816p. 1987. 42.95 (*0-13-637877-3*) P-H.

*__Operational Amplifiers & Linear Integrated Circuits.__ 6th ed. Robert F. Coughlin & Frederick F. Driscoll. LC 00-40633. 2001. write for info. (*0-13-014991-8*) P-H.

Operational Amplifiers & Linear Integrated Circuits: Theory & Application. James M. Flore. Ed. by Conty. 615p. (C). 1992. text 77.00 (*0-314-90893-5*) West Pub.

Operational Amplifiers & Linear Integrated Circuits: Theory & Applications. Denton J. Dailey. (C). 1989. text 78.92 (*0-07-039931-X*) McGraw.

Operational Amplifiers & Linear Intergrated Circuits. 5th ed. Robert F. Coughlin & Fred F. Driscoll. LC 97-14621. 515p. (C). 1997. 97.00 (*0-13-206541-X*) P-H.

Operational Amplifiers Fundamentals. Buck Engineering Staff. Ed. by Buck Engineering Tech. Writers Staff. (F. A. C. E. T. Ser.: Vol. 12). (Illus.). 68p. 1988. pap. text, teacher ed. 11.00 (*0-86657-031-4*); ring bd. 13.00 (*0-86657-030-6*) Lab-Volt.

Operational Amplifiers, Integrated & Hybrid Circuits. George B. Rutkowski. LC 92-20592. 357p. 1993. 135.00 (*0-471-57718-9*) Wiley.

Operational Amplifiers with Linear Integrated Circuits. 3rd ed. William D. Stanley. (Illus.). 672p. (C). 1993. 120.00 (*0-02-415556-X*, Macmillan Coll) P-H.

Operational & Theoretical Aspects of Intramural-Recreational Sports. Ed. by Thomas P. Sattler et al. LC 86-184773. (Illus.). 368p. 1978. reprint ed. pap. 114.10 (*0-608-07096-3*, 206732300009) Bks Demand.

Operational Approach to Policy Analysis. LC 97-20116. 1997. lib. bdg. 109.00 (*0-7923-9743-6*) Kluwer Academic.

Operational Art: Developments in the Theories of War. Ed. by B. J. McKercher & Michael A. Hennessy. LC 95-52704. 232p. 1996. 65.00 (*0-275-95305-X*, Praeger Pubs) Greenwood.

*__Operational Aspects of Oil & Gas Well Testing.__ Stuart McAleese. LC 00-22084. (Handbook of Petroleum Exploration & Production Ser.). 2000. write for info. (*0-444-50311-0*) Elsevier.

Operational Auditing Handbook: Auditing Business Processes. Andrew D. Chambers & G. K. Rand. LC 96-41459. 546p. 1997. 149.00 (*0-471-97060-3*) Wiley.

Operational Calculus, Vol. 1. 2nd ed. Jan Mikusinski. (International Series on Pure & Applied Mathematics: Vol. 109). (Illus.). 320p. 1983. 151.00 (*0-08-025071-8*, Pub. by Pergamon Repr) Franklin.

Operational Calculus, Vol. 55. Kosaku Yosida. (Applied Mathematical Sciences Ser.). 175p. 1984. 64.95 (*0-387-96047-3*) Spr-Verlag.

Operational Calculus Based on the Two-Sided Laplace Integral. 3rd ed. Balth Van Der Pol & H. Bremmer. LC 86-71694. xiii, 415p. 1987. text 19.95 (*0-8284-0327-9*, 327) Chelsea Pub.

Operational Calculus in Two Variables & Its Applications. V. Ditkin & A. Prudnikov. LC 62-9177. (International Series of Monographs on Pure & Applied Mathematics: Vol. 241). 1962. 85.00 (*0-08-009629-8*, Pub. by Pergamon Repr) Franklin.

Operational Cash Flow Management & Control. Morris A. Nunes. 256p. 1982. 34.95 (*0-13-637470-0*) P-H.

*__Operational Characteristics & Crystal Growth of Nonlinear Optical Materials.__ Ed. by Ravindra B. Lal & Donald O. Frazier. 246p. 1999. pap. text 72.00 (*0-8194-3279-2*) SPIE.

Operational Cloud Seeding Projects in the Western United States: Proceedings of a Session Sponsored by the Irrigation & Drainage Division. Ed. by Daniel F. Kriege. 58p. 1984. 16.00 (*0-87262-413-7*) Am Soc Civil Eng.

Operational Control of Coagulation & Filtration Processes. (Illus.). 112p. 1992. pap. 45.00 (*0-89867-631-2*, 30037) Am Water Wks Assn.

Operational Costs in Acquisitions. Ed. & Intro. by James R. Coffey. LC 90-49254. (Acquisitions Librarian Ser.: Vol. 4). 117p. 1991. text 39.95 (*1-56024-008-3*) Haworth Pr.

Operational Diagnostic Approaches in Psychosomatic Medicine & Psychotherapy. Ed. by H. J. Freyberger & W. Schneider. (Journal Ser.: Vol. 63, No. 2, 1995). (Illus.). 80p. 1995. pap. 42.75 (*3-8055-6133-4*) S Karger.

Operational Distribution Research. Alan D. Mercer et al. 196p. 1978. pap. 31.00 (*0-85066-168-4*) Taylor & Francis.

Operational Effects of Geometrics & Geometric Design. LC 92-32654. (Transportation Research Record Ser.: No. 1356). 1992. write for info. (*0-309-05220-3*) Transport Res Bd.

Operational Efficiency in Forestry Vol. 1: Analysis. U. Sundberg & C. R. Silversides. (Forestry Sciences Ser.). (C). 1988. lib. bdg. 89.00 (*90-247-3683-8*) Kluwer Academic.

Operational Efficiency in Forestry Vol. 2: Practice. C. R. Silversides & U. Sundberg. (Forestry Sciences Ser.). (C). 1988. lib. bdg. 89.00 (*0-7923-0063-7*) Kluwer Academic.

Operational Expert System Applications in Canada. Ed. by Ching Y. Suen & Rajjan Shinghal. LC 91-11584. (Illus.). 192p. 1991. reprint ed. pap. 59.60 (*0-608-04552-7*, 206529400001) Bks Demand.

Operational Expert System Applications in Mexico. Ed. by Francisco J. Cantu-Ortiz. LC 91-17802. (Illus.). 217p. 1991. reprint ed. pap. 67.30 (*0-608-04554-3*, 206529600001) Bks Demand.

Operational Expert System Applications in the Far East. Ed. by Jae Kyu Lee et al. LC 91-25727. (Illus.). 211p. 1991. reprint ed. pap. 65.50 (*0-608-04551-9*, 206529300001) Bks Demand.

Operational Expert System Applications in the United States. Ed. by Jay Liebowitz. LC 91-2280. (Series in Operational Expert Systems Applications Worldwide). (Illus.). 165p. reprint ed. pap. 51.20 (*0-608-04553-5*, 206529500001) Bks Demand.

*__Operational Field Assessments: An Analysis.__ H. Deshong et al. LC 98-29716. (Illus.). 85p. 1999. pap. text 15.00 (*0-8330-2642-9*, MR-982-JS) Rand Corp.

Operational History of Japanese Naval Communications: December 1941-August 1945. Japanese General Staff & War Ministry Staff. 407p. (Orig.). 1995. pap. 28.80 (*0-89412-069-7*) Aegean Park Pr.

Operational Level Productivity Measurement Analysis & Improvement. Ed. by Marvin E. Mundel. (Illus.). 213p. 1985. pap. text 15.00 (*92-833-2026-3*, 320263) Productivity Inc.

Operational Management. Melnyk. 1996. teacher ed. 49.06 (*0-256-23010-2*) McGraw.

Operational Management. 2nd ed. Mark A. Vonderembse. Date not set. pap. text, teacher ed. write for info. (*0-314-81767-0*) West Pub.

Operational Math for Business. Pierce. (Math). 1981. student ed. 7.50 (*0-534-00962-X*) Brooks-Cole.

Operational Math For Business. Pierce. (Math). 1980. 19.75 (*0-534-00789-9*) Brooks-Cole.

Operational Math for Business. 2nd ed. Pierce. (Mathematics Ser.). 1983. student ed. 8.25 (*0-534-01953-6*) Brooks-Cole.

Operational Mathematics. 3rd ed. Ruel V. Churchill. 484p. (C). 1971. 96.56 (*0-07-010870-6*) McGraw.

Operational Mid-Level Management for Police. 2nd ed. John L. Coleman. LC 94-45755. (Illus.). 410p. (C). 1995. text 90.95 (*0-398-05981-0*); pap. text 55.95 (*0-398-05982-9*) C C Thomas.

*__Operational Necessity.__ Gwyn Griffin. 480p. 1999. pap. 15.00 (*1-86046-596-X*, Pub. by Harvill Press) FS&G.

Operational Oceanography: The Challenge for European Co-Operation: Proceedings of the First International Conference on Eurogoos, 7-11 October, 1996, The Hague, The Netherlands. H. W. Behrens. LC 97-39044. (Oceanography Ser.). 777p. 1997. 231.50 (*0-444-82892-3*) Elsevier.

Operational Organic Chemistry: A Problem-Solving Approach to the Laboratory Course. 3rd ed. John W. Lehman. LC 98-7010. 808p. 1998. 90.00 (*0-13-841917-5*) P-H.

Operational Parameters for Hazardous Waste Combustion Devices. Susan Richmond et al. (Illus.). 83p. (C). 1997. reprint ed. pap. text 30.00 (*0-7881-4158-9*) DIANE Pub.

Operational Phenomena Causing Turbine Steam Path Deterioration. William P. Sanders. (Turbomachinery International Publications Monograph: No. S-4). 1988. 19.95 (*0-937506-20-6*) Turbo Intl Pubn.

Operational Planning & Training. IPM Staff. (Training Design & Management Ser.: No. 2). (C). 1994. pap. 93.00 (*0-08-042165-2*, Pub. by IPM Hse) St Mut.

Operational Planning & Training. ITD Staff. (Trainer Development Programme Management & Design 7 Ser.). 1994. pap. text 38.00 (*0-08-042452-X*, Pergamon Pr) Elsevier.

Operational Policy & Procedure Manual. W. H. Heaton. 2000p. 1991. write for info. (*0-683-14203-8*) Heaton Pubns.

Operational Policy & Procedure Manual: Pharmaceutical Services. W. H. Heaton. 300p. ring bd. 125.00 (*1-881057-17-8*) Heaton Pubns.

*__Operational Procedures/Inspection & Quality Control of Duplicate Microforms of Documents & from COM: ANSI/AIIM MS43-1998.__ Association for Information & Image Management Staff. 72p. 1998. 45.00 (*0-89258-348-7*, MS43) Assn Inform & Image Mgmt.

Operational Profitability: Conducting Management Audits. Robert M. Torok & Patrick J. Cordon. LC 96-34964. 272p. 1997. 115.00 (*0-471-17225-1*) Wiley.

Operational Quantum Physics. Paul Busch et al. Ed. by W. Beigbock et al. (Lecture Notes in Physics Ser.: Vol. M31). 230p. 1997. 49.95 (*3-540-59358-6*) Spr-Verlag.

Operational Radiation Safety Program. LC 79-62918. (Report Ser.: No. 59). 68p. 1978. pap. text 25.00 (*0-913392-43-X*) NCRP Pubns.

Operational Radiation Safety Program: Recommendations of the National Council on Radiation Protection & Measurements. National Council on Radiation Protection & Measure. LC 98-4407. (NCRP Reports: Vol. 127). 1998. pap. 30.00 (*0-929600-59-2*) NCRP Pubns.

Operational Radiation Safety-Training. Intro. by Warren K. Sinclair. LC 82-62031. (Report Ser.: No. 71). 54p. 1983. pap. text 25.00 (*0-913392-60-X*) NCRP Pubns.

Operational Reliability & Reliability Testing. (Illus.). 85p. 1977. pap. text 50.00 (*0-915414-52-X*) IEST.

*__Operational Remote Sensing for Sustainable Development: Proceedings of the 18th EARSeL Symposium, Enschede, Netherlands, 11-14 May 1998.__ Ed. by G. J. Nieuwenhuis et al. (Illus.). 540p. (C). 1999. 115.00 (*90-5809-029-9*, Pub. by A A Balkema) Ashgate Pub Co.

Operational Research. Douglas J. White. LC 85-608. (Illus.). 375p. 1985. reprint ed. pap. 116.30 (*0-608-05272-8*, 206581000001) Bks Demand.

Operational Research & Systems: The Systemic Nature of Operational Research. P. Keys. LC 90-19443. (Contemporary Systems Thinking Ser.). (Illus.). 280p. (C). 1990. 75.00 (*0-306-43642-6*, Plenum Trade) Perseus Pubng.

Operational Research & the Social Sciences. Ed. by Michael C. Jackson et al. (Illus.). 742p. (C). 1989. 162.00 (*0-306-43149-1*, Plenum Trade) Perseus Pubng.

*__Operational Research in Industry.__ Tito A. Ciriani. LC 99-26098. 1999. 62.95 (*1-55753-172-2*, Ichor Busn Bks) Purdue U Pr.

Operational Research '90: Selected Papers from the Twelfth International Conference on Operational Research, June 1990. H. E. Bradley. 848p. 1991. pap. 23.50 (*0-08-040239-9*, Pergamon Pr) Elsevier.

Operational Research '90: Selected Papers from the Twelfth International Conference on Operational Research, June 1990. H. E. Bradley & IFORS - International Fed. Op. Res. Societie Staff. LC 91-8520. 848p. 1991. 366.00 (*0-08-040240-2*, Pub. by Pergamon Repr) Franklin.

Operational Review. Ken Impey & Jeff Powell. 250p. 1993. boxed set 96.00 (*0-406-00898-1*, MICHIE) LEXIS Pub.

*__Operational Review: Maximum Results at Efficient Costs.__ Rob Reider. 78p. 1999. pap. 60.00 (*0-471-36134-8*) Wiley.

*__Operational Review: Maximum Results at Efficient Costs.__ 2nd ed. H. Robert Reider. LC 98-23563. 552p. 1998. 135.00 (*0-471-25204-2*) Wiley.

Operational Review, 1994. 1995. pap. 135.00 (*0-85954-399-4*, Pub. by Nat Res Inst) St Mut.

Operational Risk. Wilson. text. write for info. (*0-471-49176-4*) Wiley.

*__Operational Risk & Resilience.__ Chris Frost. 1998. 120.00 (*0-7506-4395-1*) Buttrwrth-Heinemann.

Operational Risk Management: The Integration of Decision, Communications & Multimedia Technologies. Giampiero E. Beroggi & William A. Wallace. LC 98-23721. 1998. 125.00 (*0-7923-8178-5*) Kluwer Academic.

*__Operational Risk Practice & Applications.__ Lore & Borodovsky. 2001. 74.95 (*0-7506-5021-4*) Buttrwrth-Heinemann.

*__Operational Risks.__ Marshall. 350p. 2000. 89.95 (*0-471-84595-7*) Wiley.

Operational Strategy of the Global Environment Facility. Ed. by Mohamed T. El-Ashry. LC 96-219515. 100p. (Orig.). (C). 1996. pap. 6.95 (*1-884122-15-9*) Global Environ.

Operational Subjectives Statistical Methods. Frank Lad. LC 96-6197. (Series in Probability & Statistics, Applied Probability & Statistics). 484p. 1996. 89.95 (*0-471-14329-4*) Wiley.

Operational Techniques for the Hospitality Industry Level 1: A Resource Based Approach. Nick Johns et al. (Resource Based Series for Hospitality & Tourism). 60p. 1994. pap. 23.95 (*0-304-32925-8*) Continuum.

Operational Test & Evaluation: A Systems Engineering Process. Roger T. Stevens. LC 78-21932. (Illus.). 295p. 1979. reprint ed. pap. 91.50 (*0-7837-3476-X*, 205780800008) Bks Demand.

Operational Thermoluminescence Dosimetry. Claudio Furetta. 1998. 48.00 (*981-02-3468-6*) World Scientific Pub.

Operational Thinking for Survival. Lawrence Dennis. LC 73-85338. 1969. 5.95 (*0-87926-003-3*) R Myles.

Operational Tools in the Management of Financial Risks. Ed. by Constantin Zopounidis. LC 97-35193. 344p. 1998. lib. bdg. 125.00 (*0-7923-8055-X*, D Reidel) Kluwer Academic.

Operational Urban Models. David Foot. (Illus.). 1982. pap. 15.95 (*0-416-73330-1*, NO. 3532) Routledge.

Operational Water Management: Proceedings of the International Conference, Copenhagen, 3-7 September 1997. Ed. by J. C. Refsgaard & E. A. Karalis. (Illus.). 486p. (C). 1997. text 110.00 (*90-5410-897-5*, Pub. by A A Balkema) Ashgate Pub Co.

Operationale Entscheidungshilfen fur die Marketingplanung. Ed. by Guenther Haedrich. (Marketing Management Ser.: No. 3). (C). 1977. 84.60 (*3-11-006882-6*) De Gruyter.

Operationalising Sustainable Development: Economic-Ecological Modelling for Developing Countries. Kanchan R. Chopra & Gopal K. Kadekodi. LC 99-17243. (Indo-Dutch Studies on Development Alternatives). 1999. write for info. (*0-7619-9330-4*) Sage.

Operationalization & Research Strategy. J. De Jong-Gierveld & J. J. Hox. 288p. 1990. 47.75 (*90-265-0982-0*) Swets.

Operationalized Psychodynamic Diagnostics (OPD) OPD Working Group. 250p. 2000. 29.50 (*0-88937-188-1*) Hogrefe & Huber Pubs.

Operationen und Regeln Bei Wittgenstein: Vom Logischen Raum Zum Regelraum. Andrej Ule. (GER.). 193p. 1997. 41.95 (*3-631-31339-X*) P Lang Pubng.

Operations Against Irregular Forces. (Guerilla Warfare Ser.). 1986. lib. bdg. 90.00 (*0-8490-3544-9*) Gordon Pr.

Operations Against Irregular Forces. (Military Science Ser.). 1989. lib. bdg. 79.95 (*0-8490-3974-6*) Gordon Pr.

Operations Analysis in the United States Army Eighth Air Force in World War II. C. McArthur. LC 90-829. (History of Mathematics Ser.: Vol. 4). 349p. 1990. text 36.00 (*0-8218-0158-9*, HMATH/4) Am Math.

Operations Analysis of Engineering Sciences: The Case of Lawrence Livermore National Laboratory. Ronald Cutburth. (Illus.). 300p. 1998. spiral bd. 76.00 (*1-878291-27-0*) Love From Sea.

Operations & Fulfillment Handbook. Don Libey et al. Ed. by Judy Evens. (Illus.). 1996. 79.95 (*0-9652607-0-4*) Target Communicators.

Operations & Maintenance. (Illus.). 173p. 1992. pap. 31.00 (*0-913359-69-6*) APPA VA.

Operations & Maintenance Manual for Energy Management. James E. Piper. LC 98-47335. 368p. (C). 1999. text 73.95 (*0-7656-0050-1*, Sharpe Prof) M E Sharpe.

Operations & Maintenance Services in Thailand: A Strategic Entry Report, 1998. Compiled by Icon Group International Staff. (Country Industry Report). (Illus.). 154p. 1999. ring bd. 1540.00 incl. audio compact disk (*0-7418-0520-0*) Icon Grp.

Operations & Maintenance Trainee. Jack Rudman. (Career Examination Ser.: C-554). 1994. pap. 27.95 (*0-8373-0554-3*) Nat Learn.

Operations & Management of Intelligent Transportation Systems. ITS Council Committee. LC 99-182340. 44p. 1998. pap. text 25.00 (*0-935403-21-3*, RP-030) Inst Trans Eng.

Operations & Quality Management. Ho. (ITBP Textbooks Ser.). 1999. pap. text 19.99 (*1-86152-398-X*) Thomson Learn.

Operations & the Management of Change. Vic Gilgeous. 1997. pap. 67.50 (*0-273-62507-1*, Pub. by Pitman Pub) Trans-Atl Phila.

*__Operations & Training SMARTbook: Guide to Operations & the Battlefield Operating Systems.__ 2nd ed. Norman M. Wade. (Illus.). 298p. 1999. spiral bd. 29.95 (*0-9675748-0-3*) Light.

Operations Carried on at the Pyramids of Gizeh in 1837, Vol. 1. Howard Vyse. 1991. pap. text 25.00 (*0-916157-97-0*) African Islam Miss Pubns.

Operations Carried on at the Pyramids of Gizeh in 1837, Vol. 2. Howard Vyse. 1991. pap. text 25.00 (*0-916157-98-9*) African Islam Miss Pubns.

Operations Carried on at the Pyramids of Gizeh in 1837: With a Voyage Account into Upper Egypt. Howard Vyse. (African Studies). reprint ed. 40.00 (*0-938818-30-9*) ECA Assoc.

*__Operations Committee Report: Training, Responsibilities, Staffing, Safety, Quality Assurance.__ Ed. by Patrick N. Kimbrell. 25p. 2000. pap. text 15.00 (*0-930406-16-8*) Undersea & Hyperbaric.

Operations de Reformulation: Analyse du Processus et des Marques Dans Une Perspective Contrastive Francais - Italien. 2nd ed. Corinne Rossari. (Sciences pour la Communication Ser.: Vol. 40). (FRE.). xii, 220p. 1997. 36.95 (*3-906757-86-2*, Pub. by P Lang) P Lang Pubng.

Operations East Africa. Kurt Dichmann. Ed. by Bill Brown. Bk. I. (Illus.). 96p. (Orig.). (YA). (gr. 9-12). 1989. pap. write for info. (*0-318-65532-2*) Ceise Corp.

Operations Flight Clerk. Jack Rudman. (Career Examination Ser.: C-564). 1994. pap. 23.95 (*0-8373-0564-0*) Nat Learn.

Operations for Head Trauma. Peter Gruen. (Illus.). 400p. 1997. write for info. (*0-683-03782-X*) Lppncott W & W.

Operations Guide - Revised for Small 501-C-3 Organizations: Friends of the San Diego Public Library. 5th rev. ed. Betty G. Sherman. Ed. by Frances L. Pierce. 1999. ring bd. 35.00 (*0-9634530-1-7*) B G Sherman.

Operations Handbook for the Small Academic Library. Ed. by Gerard B. McCabe. LC 88-34811. (Library Management Collection). 360p. 1989. lib. bdg. 65.00 (*0-313-26474-0*, MOB/, Greenwood Pr) Greenwood.

O

An Asterisk (*) at the beginning of an entry indicates that the title is appearing for the first time.

Operations in Connective K-Theory. Richard M. Kane. LC 81-14883. (Memoirs of the American Mathematical Society Ser.: No. 34/254). 106p. 1981. pap. 16.00 (*0-8218-2254-3*, MEMO/34/254) Am Math.

Operations in English: 55 Natural & Logical Sequences for Language Acquisition. Gayle Nelson & Thomas Winter. Ed. by Raymond C. Clark. (Supplementary Materials Handbook Ser.: No. 2). (Illus.). 112p. 1993. pap. text 13.00 (*0-86647-074-3*) Pro Lingua.

Operations in Troubled States: Post-Cold War Operations & Peace Talks. Gavin Bulloch et al. 87p. (C). 1998. reprint ed. pap. text 30.00 (*0-7881-3877-4*) DIANE Pub.

Operations Man-Mean Jeans Manufacturing: Business Communication. 2nd ed. Boyer. (GB - Basic Business Ser.). 1990. mass mkt. 31.95 (*0-538-60284-8*) S-W Pub.

Operations Management. 350p. 1989. text 78.95 (*0-566-09011-2*, Pub. by Gower) Ashgate Pub Co.

***Operations Management.** (C). 2000. text. write for info. (*0-536-60712-5*); text. write for info. (*0-536-60713-3*) Pearson Custom.

***Operations Management.** (C). 2002. pap. text 0.00 (*0-201-61547-9*) HEPC Inc.

Operations Management. Callarman. (C). 1997. pap. text, teacher ed. write for info. (*0-03-029394-4*); pap. text, student ed. write for info. (*0-03-029398-7*) Harcourt Coll Pubs.

Operations Management. Green. 1999. 56.00 (*0-07-431759-8*) McGraw.

Operations Management. Morgan Swink. (C). 1993. student ed. 22.00 (*1-881592-01-4*) Hayden-McNeil.

Operations Management. 2nd ed. James B. Dilworth. LC 95-39692. (C). 1995. text 80.50 (*0-07-017021-5*) McGraw.

Operations Management. 2nd ed. Mark A. Vonderembse. (SWC-Management). 1990. pap. text, student ed. 20.50 (*0-314-81768-9*) West Pub.

***Operations Management.** 2nd ed. C. D. J. Waters. (C). 2000. pap. text. write for info. (*0-201-39849-4*) Addison-Wesley.

Operations Management. 3rd ed. (C). 1999. pap. write for info. (*0-13-016463-1*) P-H.

Operations Management. 3rd ed. (C). 2000. text. write for info. (*0-13-016992-7*) S&S Trade.

Operations Management. 3rd ed. Lee J. Krajewski. (C). 1994. pap. text. write for info. (*0-201-59492-7*) Addison-Wesley.

Operations Management. 3rd ed. Joseph G. Monks. (Management Ser.). 800p. (C). 1987. pap. text 69.25 (*0-07-042727-5*) McGraw.

Operations Management. 3rd ed. Ed. by Prentice-Hall Staff. (C). 1999. text. write for info. (*0-13-013866-5*) P-H.

Operations Management. 3rd ed. Ed. by Prentice-Hall Staff. (C). 1999. text. write for info. (*0-13-013867-3*) P-H.

Operations Management. 3rd ed. Ed. by Prentice-Hall Staff. (C). 2000. text. write for info. (*0-13-013865-7*); text. write for info. (*0-13-013864-9*); text. write for info. (*0-13-013868-1*) P-H.

***Operations Management.** 3rd ed. Roberta S. Russell & Bernard W. Taylor. LC 99-25011. 879p. 1999. text 96.00 incl. audio compact disk (*0-13-013092-3*) P-H.

Operations Management. 3rd ed. Voderembrse. (SWC-Management Ser.). Date not set. student ed. 63.00 (*0-324-08725-X*) Sth-Wstrn College.

Operations Management. 3rd ed. Mark A. Vonderembse. Date not set. pap. text, teacher ed. write for info. (*0-314-06341-2*) West Pub.

Operations Management. 4th ed. Lee J. Krajewski. (C). 1996. text. write for info. (*0-201-88950-1*) Addison-Wesley.

Operations Management. 4th ed. Lee J. Krajewski & Larry P. Ritzman. LC 95-22224. 912p. 1995. 103.00 incl. disk (*0-201-82293-8*) Addison-Wesley.

Operations Management. 5th ed. Heizer. LC 98-20778. 880p. 1998. pap. text 97.33 (*0-13-905068-X*) P-H.

Operations Management. 7th ed. Richard J. Schonberger. 2000. 69.74 (*0-07-232059-1*) McGraw.

***Operations Management: A New Approach.** Brown et al. 352p. 2001. pap. 37.95 (*0-7506-4995-X*) Buttrwrth-Heinemann.

Operations Management: A Process-Based Approach with Spreadsheets. Jack Meredith & Scott Shafer. LC 97-46370. 860p. 1998. text 80.95 (*0-471-16545-X*) Wiley.

Operations Management: A Supply Chain Approach. D. L. Waller. (ITBP Textbooks Ser.). 1999. pap. 26.95 (*1-86152-415-3*, Pub. by ITBP) Thomson Learn.

Operations Management: A Value Driven Approach. Steven A. Melnyk & David Denzler. 962p. (C). 1996. text 73.75 (*0-256-12381-0*, Irwn McGrw-H) McGrw-H Hghr Educ.

Operations Management: Advantage. 3rd ed. Robert Fournier & V. Presno. 336p. 1999. pap. 6.64 (*0-13-013862-2*) P-H.

Operations Management: An Active Learning Approach. John Bicheno & Brian B. Elliott. LC 97-44918. 656p. 1997. pap. 68.95 (*0-631-20180-7*) Blackwell Pubs.

***Operations Management: Companion Website.** 3rd ed. 1999. write for info. (*0-13-013974-2*) P-H.

Operations Management: Competing in a Changing Environment. Byron J. Finch & Richard L. Luebbe. 559p. (C). 1995. mass mkt. 99.95 (*0-534-51012-4*) Wadsworth Pub.

Operations Management: Concepts in Manufacturing & Services. 2nd ed. Robert E. Markland et al. LC 97-19602. (SWC-Management Ser.). 1997. pap. 86.95 (*0-538-87831-2*); pap. 21.75 (*0-538-87834-7*) Thomson Learn.

Operations Management: Concepts, Methods & Strategies. 3rd ed. Mark A. Vonderembse & Gregory P. White. LC 95-31418. 850p. (C). 1995. mass mkt. 94.95 (*0-314-06340-4*) West Pub.

***Operations Management: Contemporary Concepts.** Roger G. Schroeder. LC 99-23773. 2000. write for info. (*0-07-236290-1*) McGrw-H Hghr Educ.

***Operations Management: Contemporary Concepts & Cases.** Roger Schroeder. (C). 1999. 55.94 incl. cd-rom (*0-07-233765-6*) McGrw-H Hghr Educ.

***Operations Management: Contemporary Concepts & Cases.** Roger G. Schroeder. LC 99-11077. (Illus.). 2000. write for info. (*0-07-289882-8*) McGrw-H Hghr Educ.

Operations Management: Customer Focused Principles. 6th ed. Edward M. Knod & Richard J. Schonbergerr. LC 96-21354. 1996. write for info. (*0-256-21533-2*, Irwn McGrw-H) McGrw-H Hghr Educ.

Operations Management: Decision Making in the Operations Function. 4th ed. Roger G. Schroeder. LC 92-27873. (Series in Management). (C). 1992. text 98.50 (*0-07-911437-7*) McGraw.

Operations Management: Decision Making in the Operations Function. 4th ed. Roger G. Schroeder. (Management Ser.). (C). 1993. text 69.25 incl. 3.5 ld (*0-07-911644-2*) McGraw.

Operations Management: Improving Customer Service. 4th ed. Richard J. Schonberger & Edward M. Knod, Jr. (C). 1990. disk 18.50 (*0-685-38300-8*, Irwn McGrw-H) McGrw-H Hghr Educ.

Operations Management: Improving Customer Service. 5th ed. Richard J. Schonberger & Edward M. Knod, Jr. LC 93-10644. 1993. teacher ed. write for info. (*0-256-13780-3*, Irwn McGrw-H) McGrw-H Hghr Educ.

Operations Management: Improving Customer Service. 5th ed. Richard J. Schonberger & Edward M. Knod, Jr. LC 93-10644. 680p. (C). 1993. text 73.75 (*0-256-11218-5*, Irwn McGrw-H) McGrw-H Hghr Educ.

Operations Management: Improving Processes & Winning Customers. Karwan. (SWC-Management Ser.). 2001. pap. 55.00 (*0-538-87919-X*) Thomson Learn.

Operations Management: Producing Goods & Services. 2nd rev. ed. Donald Waters. LC 95-26462. (C). 1996. pap. text. write for info. (*0-201-42789-3*) Addison-Wesley.

Operations Management: Strategy Analysis. 4th ed. (C). 1996. 147.00 (*0-201-43194-7*) Addison-Wesley.

***Operations Management: Strategy Analysis.** 5th ed. 480p. (C). 1998. 132.00 (*0-201-33121-7*) Addison-Wesley.

***Operations Management: Strategy Analysis.** 5th ed. 464p. (C). 1998. 24.00 (*0-201-33119-5*) Addison-Wesley.

***Operations Management: Strategy Analysis.** 5th ed. 432p. (C). 1998. text 24.00 (*0-201-33120-9*) Addison-Wesley.

Operations Management: Strategy Analysis. 5th ed. Lee J. Krajewski & Larry P. Ritzman. (C). 1998. pap. text 97.67 (*0-201-35728-3*) S&S Trade.

***Operations Management: Strategy Analysis.** 6th ed. (C). 2001. pap. text 0.00 (*0-201-61545-2*) HEPC Inc.

Operations Management: Strategy & Analysis. Lee J. Krajewski & Larry P. Ritzman. (C). 1987. text. write for info. (*0-201-13480-2*) Addison-Wesley.

***Operations Management: Strategy & Analysis.** 5th ed. (C). 1999. 67.00 (*0-201-33122-5*); write for info. (*0-201-38515-5*) Addison-Wesley.

***Operations Management: Strategy & Analysis.** 5th ed. (C). 1999. write for info. (*0-201-43394-X*) Addison-Wesley.

***Operations Management: Strategy & Analysis.** 5th ed. Lee J. Krajewski. LC 98-17802. 912p. (C). 1998. 97.33 (*0-201-33118-7*) Addison-Wesley.

Operations Management: Study Guide. Steven Melnyk. 192p. (C). 1996. text 26.25 (*0-256-23009-9*, Irwn McGrw-H) McGrw-H Hghr Educ.

Operations Management: Study Guide Plus Diskette. 3rd ed. Krajewski. (C). 1995. pap. text. write for info. (*0-201-59427-7*) Addison-Wesley.

Operations Management: Systems Approach. Starr. (GC - Principles of Management Ser.). 1996. pap., student ed. 17.00 (*0-87709-472-1*) Course Tech.

Operations Management: Teamwork for Customer Service. 6th ed. Edward M. Knod & Richard J. Schonberger. LC 96-21354. 704p. (C). 1996. text 73.75 (*0-256-19406-8*, Irwn McGrw-H) McGrw-H Hghr Educ.

Operations Management: The Basics. R. L. Galloway. LC 96-38890. (Basics of Business Ser.). 127p. 1996. pap. 14.99 (*0-415-12568-5*) Thomson Learn.

Operations Management: WSS Version. 3rd ed. Lee J. Krajewski. (C). 1993. pap. text. write for info. (*0-201-51719-1*) Addison-Wesley.

Operations Management: WSS Version. 4th ed. Lee J. Krajewski. (C). 1995. pap. text. write for info. (*0-201-40016-2*) Addison-Wesley.

Operations Management (Expert) Noori. 1995. 30.50 (*0-07-832599-4*) McGraw.

***Operations Management for Competitive Advantage.** 9th ed. Richard B. Chase et al. LC 00-38321. 2001. write for info. (*0-07-232315-9*) McGraw.

***Operations Management for MBAs.** Jack R. Meredith. LC 98-40650. (Illus.). 380p. 1998. pap. 46.95 (*0-471-29828-X*) Wiley.

Operations Management for Service Industries: Competing in the Service Era. Glenn A. Bassett. LC 92-19835. 272p. 1992. 57.95 (*0-89930-746-9*, BOB, Quorum Bks) Greenwood.

Operations Management for the Hospitality Industry Level 2: A Resource Based Approach. Nick Johns & John S. Edwards. (Resource Based Series for Hospitality & Tourism). 60p. 1994. pap. 23.95 (*0-304-32922-3*) Continuum.

Operations Management Formula Card. 4th ed. (C). 1996. 0.00 (*0-201-88951-X*) HEPC Inc.

Operations Management in a Global Context. Marc J. Scniederjans. LC 97-46648. (Illus.). 208p. 1998. 59.95 (*1-56720-156-3*, Q156, Quorum Bks) Greenwood.

Operations Management in Advanced Manufacture & Services. Ed. by D. K. MacBeth & G. Southern. 300p. 1989. 118.95 (*0-387-51009-5*) Spr-Verlag.

Operations Management in an Information Age. Barry E. King. 348p. (C). 1997. per. 73.95 (*0-7872-4429-5*) Kendall-Hunt.

Operations Management in Business. Andrew Greasley. (Illus.). 320p. 1999. pap. 49.50 (*0-7487-2084-7*, Pub. by S Thornes Pubs) Trans-Atl Phila.

Operations Management in Canada. Don Waters & Ragu Nayak. 1996. text. write for info. (*0-201-82907-X*) Addison-Wesley.

Operations Management in Context. Galloway Et Al. 128p. pap. text. write for info. (*0-7506-4864-3*) Buttrwrth-Heinemann.

***Operations Management in Context.** Galloway Et Al et al. (Illus.). 440p. 2000. pap. text 32.95 (*0-7506-4280-7*) Buttrwrth-Heinemann.

Operations Management in Service Industries & the Public Sector: Teacher's Manual. Christopher Voss et al. LC 85-9339. (Illus.). 109p. reprint ed. pap. 33.80 (*0-608-20224-X*, 207148300012) Bks Demand.

Operations Management in Service Industries & the Public Sector: Text & Cases. Christopher Voss et al. LC 85-9339. 328p. 1985. pap. 129.95 (*0-471-90801-0*) Wiley.

Operations Management in the Forest Products Industry. Richard F. Baldwin. LC 84-61889. (Illus.). 264p. 1984. pap. 45.00 (*0-87930-160-0*) Miller Freeman.

Operations Management Information Systems. Mohsen Attaran. LC 91-44229. 320p. (C). 1992. pap. 62.95 incl. disk (*0-471-52999-0*) Wiley.

Operations Management Information Systems: Text & Software. Mohsen Attaran. 320p. (C). 1992. pap. 62.95 incl. disk (*0-471-57647-6*) Wiley.

Operations Management of Distributed Service Networks: A Practical Quantitative Approach. N. Ahituv & O. Berman. (Applications of Modern Technology in Business Ser.). (Illus.). 310p. (C). 1988. 89.50 (*0-306-42864-4*, Plenum Trade) Perseus Pubng.

Operations Management I. Jack Rudman. (Regents External Degree (REDP) Ser.: Vol. 13). 43.95 (*0-8373-5663-6*) Nat Learn.

Operations Management I. Jack Rudman. (Regents External Degree Ser.: REDP-13). 1994. pap. 23.95 (*0-8373-5613-X*) Nat Learn.

Operations Management Strategy. Mike Harrison. 256p. (Orig.). 1993. pap. 52.50 (*0-273-60119-9*, Pub. by Pitman Pub) Trans-Atl Phila.

Operations Management III. Jack Rudman. (Regents External Degree (REDP) Ser.: Vol. 15). 43.95 (*0-8373-5665-2*) Nat Learn.

Operations Management III. Jack Rudman. (Regents External Degree Ser.: REDP-15). 1994. pap. 23.95 (*0-8373-5615-6*) Nat Learn.

Operations Management II. Jack Rudman. (Regents External Degree (REDP) Ser.: Vol. 14). 43.95 (*0-8373-5664-4*) Nat Learn.

Operations Management II. Jack Rudman. (Regents External Degree Ser.: REDP-14). 1994. pap. 23.95 (*0-8373-5614-8*) Nat Learn.

Operations Management Using Lotus 1-2-3. John H. Blackstone, Jr. & Peter J. Winter. LC 89-84346. 45p. (Orig.). 1990. 105.00 (*1-55822-020-8*) Am Prod & Inventory.

Operations Management Using Microsoft Excel. Andrew Vazsonyi. (Business Statistics Ser.). 2000. pap. 23.95 (*0-534-51739-0*) Wadsworth Pub.

***Operations Management with Multimedia CD.** 3rd ed. Roberta Russell & Bernard Taylor. 900p. 1999. 97.33 (*0-13-030346-1*, Prentice Hall) P-H.

Operations Managemt: Concepts In Manufacturing & Services. Robert E. Markland et al. LC 94-30524. (SWC-Management). 868p. (C). 1995. pap. 69.75 (*0-314-04398-5*) West Pub.

Operations Manager's Desk Book. Murray J. Shainis. 400p. 1982. 49.95 (*0-13-637686-X*) P-H.

Operations Managment (Just in Time Ser.). (C). 1992. pap. write for info. (*0-205-14079-3*) Allyn.

Operations Managment. Callarman. (C). 1997. pap. text. write for info. (*0-03-029393-6*) Harcourt Coll Pubs.

Operations Manual see Manual de Procedimientos

Operations Manual for Machine Tool Technology. Clifford Oliver. LC 82-13489. 272p. (C). 1982. pap. text 29.95 (*0-471-04744-9*) P-H.

Operations of Increasing Order. J. C. Gowan. 408p. (Orig.). 1980. pap. 5.00 (*0-9606822-4-4*) Gowan.

Operations of Life & Health Insurance Companies see Exploitation des Compagnies d'Assurances de Personnes

Operations of the Department of the Treasury's Financial Crimes Enforcement Network: Hearing Before the Subcommittee on General Oversight & Investigations of the Committee on Banking & Financial Services, U. S. House of Representatives, 105th Congress, Second Session, April 1, 1998. LC 98-209598. iii, 143p. 1998. write for info. (*0-16-057152-9*) USGPO.

Operations of the New Bank Act. Thomas Conway, Jr. & Ernest M. Patterson. Ed. by Stuart Bruchey. LC 80-1141. (Rise of Commercial Banking Ser.). 1981. reprint ed. lib. bdg. 42.95 (*0-405-13643-9*) Ayer.

Operations of the Numbers of Arithmetic. rev. ed. Mervin L. Keedy & Marvin L. Bittinger. (Algebra, a Modern Introduction Ser.). (gr. 7-9). 1981. pap. text. write for info. (*0-201-03979-6*) Addison-Wesley.

Operations of United States Affiliates of Foreign Companies. 1995. lib. bdg. 251.95 (*0-8490-6713-8*) Gordon Pr.

Operations of United States Affiliates of Foreign Countries. 1997. lib. bdg. 251.95 (*0-8490-6099-0*) Gordon Pr.

Operations Officer. Jack Rudman. (Career Examination Ser.: C-3069). 1994. pap. 34.95 (*0-8373-3069-6*) Nat Learn.

Operations on Integers see Key to Algebra Series

Operations on Integers, Bk. 10, Square Roots & Quadratic Equations see Key to Algebra Series

Operations Other Than War: Implications for the U. S. Army. Jennifer M. Taw & John E. Peters. LC 95-33170. 52p. 1995. pap. 7.50 (*0-8330-1660-1*, MR-566-A) Rand Corp.

Operations Planning & Control. Joe H. Mize et al. (Illus.). 1971. 46.00 (*0-13-637892-7*) P-H.

Operations Research. 1991. 31.00 (*0-387-54926-9*) Spr-Verlag.

Operations Research. Grundlagen. 1992. 44.00 (*0-387-55294-4*) Spr-Verlag.

Operations Research. Jensen. text. write for info. (*0-471-38004-0*) Wiley.

Operations Research. Wayne L. Winston. (Business Statistics Ser.). (C). 1987. pap. 47.00 (*0-87150-065-5*, 36G0130) PWS Pubs.

Operations Research. 2nd ed. Frederick S. Hillier & Gerald J. Lieberman. LC 73-94383. 816p. (C). 1974. text 32.95 (*0-8162-3856-1*) Holden-Day.

Operations Research. 3rd ed. Winston. 1994. 39.75 (*0-534-23049-0*) Brooks-Cole.

Operations Research. 3rd ed. Wayne L. Winston. (Business Statistics Ser.). 1994. pap. 92.95 (*0-534-20973-4*) Wadsworth Pub.

Operations Research: A First Course. John S. Croucher. (Illus.). 320p. 1980. pap. text 18.00 (*0-08-024797-0*, Pergamon Pr) Elsevier.

***Operations Research: A Practical Introduction.** Michael W. Carter & Camille C. Price. LC 00-31144. 2000. write for info. (*0-8493-2256-1*) CRC Pr.

Operations Research: A Tool for Library Management. Jenny E. Rowley & Peter J. Rowley. LC 81-12899. (Illus.). 151p. (Orig.). 1981. reprint ed. pap. 46.90 (*0-7837-9687-0*, 206041700005) Bks Demand.

Operations Research: An Introduction. 6th ed. Hamdy A. Taha. 916p. (C). 1996. 97.00 (*0-13-272915-6*) P-H.

Operations Research: Applications in Health Care Planning. Ed. by No K. Kwak et al. (Illus.). 360p. (Orig.). 1984. pap. text 34.00 (*0-8191-4168-2*); lib. bdg. 67.50 (*0-8191-4167-4*) U Pr of Amer.

Operations Research: Deterministic Optimization Models. Katta G. Murty. LC 94-19150. 608p. 1994. 58.60 (*0-13-056517-2*) P-H.

Operations Research: Helping Family Planning Programs Work Better. Ed. by Myrna Seidman & Marjorie Horn. (Progress in Clinical & Biological Research Ser.: No. 1922). 578p. 1991. 285.00 (*0-471-56161-4*, Wiley-Liss) Wiley.

Operations Research: Implications for Libraries: The 35th Annual Conference of the Graduate Library School, August 2-4, 1971. Chicago University, Graduate Library School Staff. Ed. by Don R. Swanson & Abraham Bookstein. LC 73-185760. (University of Chicago Studies in Library Science). 166p. reprint ed. pap. 51.50 (*0-608-16376-7*, 202674700051) Bks Demand.

O

Operations Research: Methods, Models, & Applications, 7. Ed. by Jay E. Aronson & Stanley Zionts. LC 95-42161. (IC2 Management & Management Science Ser.: No. 7). 400p. 1998. 69.50 (*1-56720-027-3*, Quorum Bks) Greenwood.

Operations Research: Proceedings, 1998. Ed. by P. Kall & H. J. Luthi. (Illus.). xii, 584p. 1999. pap. 129.00 (*3-540-65381-3*) Spr-Verlag.

Operations Research: Reflexion. 1994. 119.95 (*0-387-57988-5*) Spr-Verlag.

Operations Research Analysis in Quality Test & Evaluation. Donald L. Giadrosich. LC 94-48188. (Education Ser.). 385p. 1995. text 69.95 (*1-56347-112-4*, 12-4) AIAA.

Operations Research Analyst. Jack Rudman. (Career Examination Ser.: C-556). 1994. pap. 34.95 (*0-8373-0556-X*) Nat Learn.

Operations Research & Artificial Intelligence: The Integration of Problem-Solving Strategies. Ed. by Donald B. Brown & Chelsea White, III. (C). 1990. lib. bdg. 157.00 (*0-7923-9106-3*) Kluwer Academic.

Operations Research & Decision Aid Methodologies in Traffic & Transportation Management: Proceedings of the NATO ASI in Balatonfured, March 10-21, 1997. Ed. by M. Labbe et al. (NATO ASI Ser.: Vol. 166). 400p. 1998. 99.00 (*3-540-64652-3*) Spr-Verlag.

Operations Research & Discrete Analysis. Alekseii D. Korshunov. LC 97-121870. (MAIA Mathematics & Its Applications Ser.). 331p. 1997. text 199.00 (*0-7923-4334-4*) Kluwer Academic.

Operations Research & Environmental Management: The FEEN/KLUWER International Series on Economics, Energy & Environment. Ed. by Carlo Carraro & Alain Haurl. LC 95-40367. (Economics, Energy, & Environment Ser.). 304p. (C). 1996. lib. bdg. 136.00 (*0-7923-3767-0*) Kluwer Academic.

Operations Research & Management in Fishing. Ed. by A. Guimaraes Rodrigues. (NATO Advanced Study Institutes Series E, Applied Sciences). (C). 1990. lib. bdg. 201.00 (*0-7923-1051-9*) Kluwer Academic.

Operations Research & the Public Sector. Ed. by S. M. Pollock et al. LC 94-14930. (Handbooks in Operations Research & Management Science: Vol. 6). 740p. 1994. 165.00 (*0-444-89204-4*, North Holland) Elsevier.

Operations Research-apps & Algorithms. 2nd ed. Wayne L. Winston. (Business Statistics). 1262p. (C). 1990. pap. 62.25 (*0-534-92495-6*) Wadsworth Pub.

Operations Research for Libraries & Information Agencies: Techniques for the Evaluation of Management Decision Alternatives. Donald H. Kraft & Bert R. Boyce. (Library & Information Science Ser.). (Illus.). 193p. 1991. text 69.95 (0-12-424520-X) Acad Pr.

Operations Research in Agriculture. Parkash Mehta. 1986. 32.50 (0-8364-1551-5, Pub. by Ashish Pub Hse) S Asia.

Operations Research In Product. Lynwood A. Johnson & Douglas C. Montgomery. 544p. (C). 1974. text 99.95 (0-471-44618-1) Wiley.

Operations Research in Production Planning & Control: Proceedings of a Joint German - U. S. Conference, Hagen Germany, June 25-26, 1992. Ed. by Gunter U. Fandel et al. LC 93-7285. 1993. 169.00 (0-387-56444-6) Spr-Verlag.

Operations Research in Progress. Gustav Feichtinger & Peter Kall. 1982. lib. bdg. 184.00 (90-277-1464-9) Kluwer Academic.

Operations Research in the Airline Industry. Ed. by Gang Yu. LC 97-35539. (International Series in Operations Research & Management Science). 473p. 1998. lib. bdg. 169.95 (0-7923-8039-8) Kluwer Academic.

Operations Research in Transportation Systems: Ideas & Schemes of Optimization Methods for Strategic Planning & Operations Management. Alexander S. Belenky. LC 98-26529. (Applied Optimization Ser.). 1998. 195.00 (0-7923-5157-6) Kluwer Academic.

Operations Research Mathematics & Models. Ed. by Saul I. Gass. LC 81-10849. (Proceedings of Symposia in Applied Mathematics Ser.: Vol. 25). 198p. 1981. reprint ed. pap. 19.00 (0-8218-0029-9, PSAPM/25) Am Math.

Operations Research Method & Practice. C. K. Mustafi. (C). 1988. pap. 20.00 (81-224-0054-X) S Asia.

Operations Research Methods. Stuart S. Nagel & Marian Neef. LC 76-25693. (Quantitative Applications in the Social Sciences Ser.: Vol. 2). 76p. 1976. pap. 10.95 (0-8039-0651-X) Sage.

Operations Research Models in Flexible Manufacturing Systems. Ed. by F. Archetti et al. (CISM Ser.: Vol. 306). (Illus.). vii, 305p. 1989. 75.95 (0-387-82099-X) Spr-Verlag.

Operations Research Models in Quantitative Finance: Proceedings of 13th Meeting, EURO Working Group for Financial Modeling, University of Cyprus, Nicosia, Cyrus. Ed. by R. L. D'Ecclesia & S. A. Zenios. LC 96-137949. (Contributions to Management Science Ser.). 263p. 1995. 61.00 (3-7908-0803-2) Spr-Verlag.

Operations Research '91: Extended Abstracts of the 16th Symposium on Operations Research Held at the University of Trier on September 9-11, 1991. Ed. by P. Gritzmann et al. (Illus.). xxviii, 636p. 1992. pap. 149.00 (0-387-91431-5) Spr-Verlag.

Operations Research '93. A. Bachem & U. Derigs. 555p. 1996. pap. 159.00 (3-7908-0794-X) Spr-Verlag.

Operations Research '92. Ed. by M. Schader et al. (Illus.). xviii, 581p. 1993. pap. 124.00 (0-387-91445-5) Spr-Verlag.

Operations Research Problem Solver. rev. ed. Research & Education Association Staff. LC 83-62276. (Illus.). 1068p. 1996. pap. text 29.95 (0-87891-548-6) Res & Educ.

Operations Research Proceedings. 1984. 93.95 (0-387-13134-5) Spr-Verlag.

Operations Research Proceedings. 1990. 107.95 (0-387-52489-4) Spr-Verlag.

Operations Research Proceedings. 1993. 142.95 (0-387-56642-2) Spr-Verlag.

Operations Research Proceedings DGOR, 1990: Papers of the 19th Annual Meeting. Ed. by W. K. Buhler et al. (Illus.). xiv, 642p. 1992. 154.00 (0-387-55081-X) Spr-Verlag.

Operations Research Proceedings, 1993. H. Dyckhoff et al. 576p. 1994. 143.95 (0-387-57862-5) Spr-Verlag.

Operations Research Proceedings, 1985. Ed. by L. Streitferdt et al. xiv, 580p. 1986. 94.00 (0-387-16506-1) Spr-Verlag.

Operations Research Proceedings, 1996: Selected Papers of the Symposium on Operationa Research (SOR '96), Braunschweig, September 3-6, 1996. Ed. by U. Zimmermann et al. LC 97-15457. (ENG & GER., Illus.). xiv, 524p. 1997. pap. 129.00 (3-540-62630-1) Spr-Verlag.

Operations Research Proceedings, 1997: Selected Papers of the Symposium on Operations Research (SOR '97), Jena, September 3-5, 1997. Ed. by P. Kischka et al. LC 98-19936. xvi, 597p. 1998. pap. 129.00 (3-540-64240-4) Spr-Verlag.

***Operations Research Proceedings, 1999: Selected Papers of the Symposium on Operations Research (SOR 99), Magdeburg, September 1-3, 1999.** Ed. by K. Inderfurth et al. (Illus.). xix, 577p. 2000. pap. 109.00 (3-540-67094-7) Spr-Verlag.

Operations Research Proceedings, 1994: Selected Papers of the International Conference on Operations Research, Berlin, August 30-September 2, 1994. Ed. by Ulrich Derigs et al. LC 94-47366. 1995. 143.00 (3-540-58793-4) Spr-Verlag.

Operations Research Support Methodology. A. Holzman. (Industrial Engineering Ser.: Vol. 2). (Illus.). 664p. 1979. text 195.00 (0-8247-6771-3) Dekker.

Operations Research Windows Lindo/Lingo. 3rd ed. Wayne L. Winston. (Business Statistics Ser.). 1997. pap. 116.95 (0-534-52020-0) Wadsworth Pub.

Operations Research 2. 2nd ed. A. Ravindran et al. LC 86-5561. 656p. 1987. text 99.95 (0-471-08608-8) Wiley.

Operations Review Specialist. Jack Rudman. (Career Examination Ser.: C-3260). 1994. pap. 34.95 (0-8373-3260-5) Nat Learn.

***Operations Scheduling with Applications in Manufacturing & Services.** Xiuli Chao. 1998. 83.75 (0-07-561963-6) McGraw.

Operations Scheduling with Applications in Manufacturing & Services. Michael Pinedo & Xiuli Chao. LC 98-18851. 1998. 64.50 (0-07-289779-1) McGraw.

Operations Strategy. Roth. 2000. 67.00 (0-07-230906-7) McGraw.

Operations Strategy: Focusing Cometitive Excellence. Peter W. Stonebraker & G. Keong Leong. 544p. (C). 1994. text, teacher ed., boxed set 68.20 (0-205-14253-2, H45230) Allyn.

Operations Strategy: Text & Cases. David A. Garvin. 528p. (C). 1992. text 58.60 (0-13-638917-1, 140802) P-H.

Operations Technology: Systems & Evolution. Robert H. Roy. LC 86-7139. (Illus.). 271p. reprint ed. pap. 84.10 (0-608-06137-9, 206647000008) Bks Demand.

Operations Zapata: The "Ultrasensitive" Report & Testimony of the Board of Inquiry on the Bay of Pigs. Maxwell Taylor et al. LC 81-50470. 367p. 1981. lib. bdg. 65.00 (0-313-27052-X, U7052, Greenwood Pr) Greenwood.

Operative Anatomy. Carol E. Scott-Conner & David L. Dawson. (Illus.). 704p. 1993. text 135.00 (0-397-51007-1, Lippnctt) Lppncott W & W.

Operative Anatomy of Abdomen & Pelvis. Edward A. Edwards et al. LC 74-23199. 440p. reprint ed. pap. 136.40 (0-608-17760-1, 205650800069) Bks Demand.

Operative Anatomy of Thorax. Edward A. Edwards et al. LC 79-175458. 263p. reprint ed. pap. 81.60 (0-608-17759-8, 205650700069) Bks Demand.

Operative Approaches in Orthopedic Surgery & Traumatology. Rudolf Bauer. Tr. by Gerhard S. Sharon from GRE. 334p. 1988. 205.00 (0-86577-265-7) Thieme Med Pubs.

Operative Arthroscopy. 2nd ed. Ed. by John B. McGinty et al. LC 95-15899. (Illus.). 1376p. 1995. text 270.00 (0-7817-0294-1) Lppncott W & W.

Operative Atlas for Meningiomas. Ossama Al-Mefty. LC 97-2086. (Illus.). 660p. 1997. text 195.00 (0-7817-0152-X) Lppncott W & W.

Operative Breast Surgery. Dixon. 1999. text 159.00 (0-443-05066-X, W B Saunders Co) Harcrt Hlth Sci Grp.

Operative Challenges in Head & Neck Surgery. Pillsbury. 1991. write for info. (0-8151-6707-5) Mosby Inc.

Operative Colorectal Surgery. George E. Block & A. R. Moosa. LC 92-48340. (Illus.). 640p. 1994. text 155.00 (0-7216-3366-8, W B Saunders Co) Harcrt Hlth Sci Grp.

Operative Endoscopy of the Digestive Tract. G. Bedogni. (Illus.). 274p. 1984. text 106.00 (88-299-0140-7, Pub. by Piccin Nuova) Gordon & Breach.

Operative Endoscopy of the Digestive Tract. G. Bedogni et al. 274p. 1984. text 96.00 (1-57235-014-8, Pub. by Piccin Nuova) Gordon & Breach.

Operative Foot Surgery. John S. Gould. LC 93-1960. (Illus.). 992p. 1993. text 152.00 (0-7216-3196-7, W B Saunders Co) Harcrt Hlth Sci Grp.

Operative Gynecologic Endoscopy. Ed. by Joseph S. Sanfilippo et al. (Clinical Perspectives in Obstetrics & Gynecology Ser.). (Illus.). 250p. 1993. 79.95 (0-387-96881-4) Spr-Verlag.

Operative Gynecologic Endoscopy. 2nd ed. Ed. by Joseph S. Sanfilippo & Ronald L. Levine. LC 95-25735. (Clinical Perspectives in Obstetrics & Gynecology Ser.). 536p. 1996. 115.00 (0-387-94467-2) Spr-Verlag.

Operative Gynecologic Laparascopy: Principles & Techniques. Camran Nezhat et al. 352p. 1995. text 125.00 (0-07-105422-7) McGraw-Hill HPD.

***Operative Gynecologic Laparoscopy: Principles & Techniques.** 2nd ed. Camran Nezhat. LC 99-88759. (Illus.). 352p. 2000. 125.00 (0-07-105431-6) McGraw-Hill Prof.

Operative Gynecology. David M. Gershenson et al. (Illus.). 672p. 1993. text 115.00 (0-7216-3558-X, W B Saunders Co) Harcrt Hlth Sci Grp.

Operative Gynecology. 2nd ed. David M. Gershenson et al. 1215p. 1999. text. write for info. (0-7216-7987-0, W B Saunders Co) Harcrt Hlth Sci Grp.

Operative Hand Surgery, 2 vols., Set. 3rd ed. David P. Green. (Illus.). 2512p. 1993. text 350.00 (0-443-08803-9) Church.

Operative Hand Surgery, Vol. 1. Ed. by David P. Green. LC 82-4208. (Illus.). 978p. 1982. reprint ed. pap. 200.00 (0-8357-6558-X, 203592800001) Bks Demand.

Operative Hand Surgery, Vol. 1. 2nd ed. Ed. by David P. Green. LC 87-22409. (Illus.). 891p. 1988. reprint ed. pap. 200.00 (0-7837-3050-0, 204283800001) Bks Demand.

Operative Hand Surgery, Vol. 2. Ed. by David P. Green. LC 82-4208. (Illus.). 905p. 1982. reprint ed. pap. 200.00 (0-8357-6559-8, 203592800002) Bks Demand.

Operative Hand Surgery, Vol. 2. 2nd ed. Ed. by David P. Green. LC 87-22409. (Illus.). 921p. 1988. reprint ed. pap. 200.00 (0-7837-3051-9, 204283800002) Bks Demand.

Operative Hand Surgery, Vol. 3. 2nd ed. Ed. by David P. Green. LC 87-22409. (Illus.). 883p. 1988. reprint ed. pap. 200.00 (0-7837-3052-7, 204283800003) Bks Demand.

Operative Hand Surgery, Vols. 1-3. Ed. by David P. Green. (Illus.). reprint ed. write for info. (0-608-16099-7) Bks Demand.

Operative Hip Arthroscopy. Byrd. 179.00 incl. vdisk (0-86577-783-7) Thieme Med Pubs.

Operative Hip Arthroscopy. J. W. Byrd. LC 97-30914. (Illus.). 232p. 1997. 129.00 (0-86577-679-2) Thieme Med Pubs.

Operative Hip Arthroscopy. J. W. Byrd. LC 97-30914. 1997. write for info. (3-13-108621-1) Thieme Med Pubs.

Operative Hysteroscopy: A Practical Guide. Thomas Roemer & Wolfgang Straube. (Illus.). viii, 96p. (C). 1997. pap. text 45.35 (3-11-015667-9) De Gruyter.

Operative Laparoscopy: The Masters' Techniques. 2nd ed. Richard M. Soderstrom. LC 97-14251. 275p. 1997. text 125.00 (0-397-51797-1) Lppncott W & W.

Operative Laparoscopy & Hysteroscopy. Ed. by Stephen M. Cohen. 320p. 1996. text 149.00 (0-443-08950-7) Church.

Operative Laparoscopy & Thoracoscopy. Ed. by Bruce V. MacFadyen, Jr. & Jeffrey L. Ponsky. LC 95-20399. (Illus.). 768p. 1996. text 235.00 (0-7817-0279-8) Lppncott W & W.

Operative Laparoscopy for Gynecologist. David Hoffman et al. LC 95-37144. (Illus.). 199p. 1994. text 19.95 (1-880906-05-8) IDI Pub.

Operative Management of Breast Disease. R. Robinson Baker & John Niederhuber. (Illus.). 147p. 1992. text 179.00 (0-7216-2960-1, W B Saunders Co) Harcrt Hlth Sci Grp.

Operative Management of Lower Extremity Fractures in Children. Ed. by Robert Hensinger. 80p. 1992. pap. 35.00 (0-89203-058-5) Amer Acad Ortho Surg.

Operative Management of Upper Extremity Fractures in Children. Ed. by Kaye E. Wilkins. 112p. 1994. pap. 35.00 (0-89203-085-2) Amer Acad Ortho Surg.

Operative Manual of Endoscopic Surgery. Alfred Cuschieri et al. LC 92-2421. (Illus.). 380p. 1992. 175.00 (0-387-53486-5) Spr-Verlag.

Operative Manual of Endoscopic Surgery, Vol. 2. G. F. Buess & A. Cuschieki. 280p. 1994. 198.00 (0-387-56810-7) Spr-Verlag.

Operative Manual of Endoscopic Surgery, Vol. 2. J. Perissat. Ed. by Alfred Cuschieri & G. F. Buess. LC 92-2421. (Illus.). 265p. 1994. text 175.00 (3-540-56810-7) Spr-Verlag.

Operative Maxillofacial Surgery. Ed. by Patel & Langdon. (Illus.). 536p. 1999. text 225.00 (0-412-56000-3, Pub. by E A) OUP.

Operative Nerve Repair & Reconstruction, 2 vols., Set. Richard H. Gelberman. (Illus.). 1760p. 1991. text 289.00 (0-397-51074-8) Lppncott W & W.

Operative Neurosurgery, 2 vols. Ed. by L. G. Kempe. Incl. Vol. 2. Posterior Fossa, Spinal Cord & Peripheral Nerve Disease. (Illus.). viii, 281p. 1986. 368.00 (0-387-04890-1); write for info. (0-318-55798-3) Spr-Verlag.

Operative Neurosurgical Techniques: Indications, Methods, & Results, 2 vols., Set. 3rd ed. Henry H. Schmidek & William H. Sweet. LC 93-42522. (Illus.). 2112p. 1995. text 415.00 (0-7216-5541-6, W B Saunders Co) Harcrt Hlth Sci Grp.

Operative Note: Collected Editorials. Robert M. Goldwyn. LC 92-458. 1992. 38.00 (0-86577-431-5) Thieme Med Pubs.

Operative Obstetrics. Gary D. Hankins et al. 782p. (C). 1995. text 160.00 (0-8385-7409-2, A7409-4, Apple Lange Med) McGraw.

Operative Obstetrics. Ed. by John P. O'Grady et al. LC 95-8734. (Illus.). 512p. 1995. write for info. (0-683-06633-1) Lppncott W & W.

Operative Obstetrics. 2nd ed. (C). 2001. 150.00 (0-8385-7387-8, Medical Exam) Appleton & Lange.

Operative Obstetrics. 2nd ed. Ed. by Leslie Iffy et al. (Illus.). 750p. 1992. text 79.00 (0-07-105395-6) McGraw-Hill HPD.

Operative Occultism see Spiritual Centers in Man

Operative Orthopaedics. Vincent D. Pellegrini & C. McColister Evarts. (C). 2000. 295.00 (0-8385-7400-9) Appleton & Lange.

Operative Orthopaedics, 4 vols., 1. 2nd ed. Ed. by Michael W. Chapman & Michael Madison. LC 92-49608. 1993. 395.00 (0-397-51304-6) Lppncott W & W.

Operative Orthopaedics, 4 vols., 2. 2nd ed. Ed. by Michael W. Chapman & Michael Madison. LC 92-49608. 1993. write for info. (0-397-51305-4) Lppncott W & W.

Operative Orthopaedics, 4 vols., 3. 2nd ed. Ed. by Michael W. Chapman & Michael Madison. LC 92-49608. 1993. write for info. (0-397-51306-2) Lppncott W & W.

Operative Orthopaedics, 4 vols., 4. 2nd ed. Ed. by Michael W. Chapman & Michael Madison. LC 92-49608. 1993. write for info. (0-397-51307-0) Lppncott W & W.

Operative Orthopaedics, 4 vols., Set. 2nd ed. Ed. by Michael W. Chapman & Michael Madison. LC 92-49608. 3,876p. 1993. text 399.00 (0-397-51075-6) Lppncott W & W.

Operative Orthopaedics Cd-Rom Library Institutional. A. W. Crenshaw. 1996. text 495.95 (0-8151-1901-1) Mosby Inc.

Operative Otolaryngology, 2 vols., Set. Eugene N. Myers. Ed. by Larry McGrew. LC 96-16724. (Illus.). 1408p. 1997. text 365.00 (0-7216-3841-4, W B Saunders Co) Harcrt Hlth Sci Grp.

Operative Otorhinolaryngology. Nigel Bleach et al. LC 95-47084. (Illus.). 512p. 1997. 299.95 (0-632-03747-4) Blackwell Sci.

Operative Paediatric Urology. Ed. by J. David Frank & J. H. Johnston. (Illus.). 256p. 1990. text. write for info. (0-443-03478-8) Church.

Operative Pediatric Orthopaedics, No. 2. S. Terry Canale & James H. Beaty. 1994. write for info. (0-8016-7990-7) Mosby Inc.

Operative Pediatric Surgery. Ziegler. (C). 1999. pap. text 195.00 (0-8385-7405-X) Appleton & Lange.

Operative Pediatric Urology. 2nd ed. Frank. 1999. text 145.00 (0-443-05358-8, W B Saunders Co) Harcrt Hlth Sci Grp.

Operative Plastic & Reconstruction Surgery. Evans & Schusterman. LC 99-32189. (Illus.). 1056p. 2000. 295.00 (0-8385-7676-1, Apple Lange Med) McGraw.

Operative Rights. Beth J. Singer. LC 92-39758. 218p. (C). 1993. text 59.50 (0-7914-1657-7); pap. text 19.95 (0-7914-1658-5) State U NY Pr.

Operative Senologie. 1995. 150.00 (3-540-59018-8) Spr-Verlag.

Operative Shoulder Surgery. Stephen Copeland. (Illus.). 1995. text 150.00 (0-443-04640-9) Church.

Operative Skull Base Surgery. Torrens. 1996. text 157.00 (0-443-05079-1, W B Saunders Co) Harcrt Hlth Sci Grp.

Operative Spinal Surgery. Ed. by Michael J. Torrens & Robert A. Dickson. (Practice of Surgery Ser.). (Illus.). 333p. 1991. text 210.00 (0-443-03922-4) Church.

Operative Spine Surgery. William C. Welch. LC 98-22965. 300p. 1999. 150.00 (0-8385-7393-2, Apple Lange Med) McGraw.

Operative Strategies in Inflammatory Bowel Disease. Ed. by F. Michelassi & J. W. Milsom. LC 97-20702. (Illus.). 568p. 1999. 150.00 (0-387-94966-6) Spr-Verlag.

Operative Strategies in Laparoscopic Surgery. Ed. by Edward H. Phillips & Raul J. Rosenthal. 1995. write for info. (0-387-59214-8) Spr-Verlag.

Operative Strategies in Laparoscopic Surgery. Ed. by Edward H. Phillips & Raul J. Rosenthal. 288p. 1995. 110.00 (3-540-59214-8) Spr-Verlag.

Operative Strategy in General Surgery, Vol. 2. J. L. Chassin. (Illus.). 655p. 1984. 109.00 (0-387-90984-2) Spr-Verlag.

Operative Strategy in General Surgery: An Expositive Atlas. 2nd ed. J. L. Chassin. (Illus.). 1055p. 1997. reprint ed. 170.00 (0-387-97968-9) Spr-Verlag.

Operative Surgery: Alimentary Tract & Abdominal Wall-Part 3: Colon, Rectum & Anus. 4th ed. Ed. by Ian P. Todd & L. P. Fielding. (Health Sciences). (Illus.). 672p. 1993. text 175.00 (0-407-00652-4) Thomson Learn.

Operative Surgery & Management. Keen & Farndon. 1998. pap. text 115.00 (0-7506-4238-6) Buttrwrth-Heinemann.

Operative Surgery & Management. 2nd ed. Keen. 896p. 1987. write for info. (0-7236-0836-9, Pub. by John Wright) Macmillan.

Operative Technique in Neonates & Infants. Ed. by T. A. Angerpointner. (Progress in Pediatric Surgery Ser.: Vol. 25). (Illus.). 150p. 1990. 124.00 (0-387-51057-5) Spr-Verlag.

***Operative Techniques in Pediatric Neurosurgery.** Albright. (Illus.). 352p. 2000. 179.00 (0-86577-846-9) Thieme Med Pubs.

Operative Techniques in Shoulder Surgery. Ed. by Lonnie E. Paulos & James E. Tibone. LC 90-1157. (Illus.). 216p. 1991. reprint ed. pap. 67.00 (0-608-07376-8, 206760300009) Bks Demand.

Operative Topographies, 20. Actar Staff. (Quaderns Ser.). 1999. pap. text 25.00 (84-89698-84-8) Dist Art Pubs.

***Operative Trauma Management.** 2nd ed. Erwin R. Thal & Weigelt. 1999. 195.00 (0-8385-7388-6) McGraw.

Operative Trauma Management Atlas. Ed. by C. J. Carrico. LC 97-20619. (Illus.). 335p. (C). 1998. pap. text 185.00 (0-8385-7401-7, A-7401-1, Apple Lange Med) McGraw.

Operative Treatment of the Foot & Ankle. Armen S. Kelikian. LC 98-22076. 784p. 1999. 195.00 (0-8385-7386-X, Apple Lange Med) McGraw.

Operative Urology. Robert J. Krane et al. LC 99-31081. (Foeign Language Ser.). (Illus.). 415p. 1999. text 149.00 (0-443-05580-7, W B Saunders Co) Harcrt Hlth Sci Grp.

Operative Urology Two see Encyclopedia of Urology

Operative Zugangeswege in der Urologie see Approaches in Urologic Surgery

Operator: David Geffen Builds, Buys & Sells the New Hollywood. Tom King. (Illus.). 688p. 2000. 25.95 (0-679-45754-2) Random.

Operator Algebraic Methods in Quantum Field Theory. Hellmut Baumgartel. LC 95-37753. (Series of Lectures). 228p. 1995. text 52.50 (3-05-501655-6, Pub. by Akademie Verlag) Wiley.

Operator Algebras & Applications. Aristides Katavolos. LC 97-19830. (NATO ASI Series. Series C, Mathematical & Physical Sciences). 1997. text 224.50 (0-7923-4625-4) Kluwer Academic.

Operator Algebras & Applications, 2 pts., Pt. 1. Ed. by Richard V. Kadison. LC 82-11561. (Proceedings of Symposia in Pure Mathematics Ser.: Vol. 38). 632p. 1982. text 67.00 (0-8218-1441-9, PSPUM/38.1) Am Math.

Operator Algebras & Applications, 2 pts., Pt. 2. Ed. by Richard V. Kadison. LC 82-11561. (Proceedings of Symposia in Pure Mathematics Ser.: Vol. 38). 625p. 1982. text 67.00 (0-8218-1444-3, PSPUM/38.2) Am Math.

Operator Algebras & Applications, 2 pts., Set. Ed. by Richard V. Kadison. LC 82-11561. (Proceedings of Symposia in Pure Mathematics Ser.: Vol. 38). 1138p. 1982. text 113.00 (0-8218-1445-1, PSPUM/38) Am Math.

Operator Algebras & K-Theory. Ed. by Ronald G. Douglas & Claude Schochet. LC 82-4094. (Contemporary Mathematics Ser.: Vol. 10). 204p. 1982. reprint ed. pap. 23.00 (0-8218-5011-3, CONM/10) Am Math.

Operator Algebras & Mathematical Physics. Ed. by Palle E. Jorgensen & Paul S. Muhly. LC 86-32070. (Contemporary Mathematics Ser.: Vol. 62). 544p. 1987. pap. 57.00 (0-8218-5066-0, CONM/62C) Am Math.

Operator Algebras & Mathematical Physics: Proceedings of a Summer Conference Held June 17-21, 1985 with Support from the National Science Foundation & the University of Iowa. Ed. by Palle E. Jorgensen & Paul S. Muhly. LC 86-32070. (Contemporary Mathematics Ser.: No. 62). 558p. 1987. reprint ed. pap. 173.00 (0-608-03974-8, 205256600012) Bks Demand.

An Asterisk (*) at the beginning of an entry indicates that the title is appearing for the first time.

Operator Algebras & Operator Theory: International Conference on Operator Algebras & Operator Theory, July 4-9, 1997, Shanghai, China. Ed. by Liming Ge et al. LC 98-41143. (Contemporary Mathematics Ser.: Vol. 228). 389p. 1998. pap. 85.00 (*0-8218-1093-6*) Am Math.

Operator Algebras & Operator Theory: Proceedings of the OATE 2 Conference, Romania, 1989. William Arveson. Ed. by A. S. Mishchenko et al. LC 92-234313. (Pitman Research Notes in Mathematics Ser.: Vol. 271). 228p. reprint ed. pap. 70.70 (*0-608-08053-5*, 206901800002) Bks Demand.

Operator Algebras & Operator Theorys. Arveson. 1992. pap. 47.95 (*0-582-09358-9*, Pub. by Addison-Wesley) Longman.

Operator Algebras & Quantum Field Theory. Ed. by S. Doplicher et al. (Illus.). 688p. 1997. 42.00 (*1-57146-047-0*) Intl Pr Boston.

Operator Algebras & Quantum Statistical Mechanics: Equilibrium States, Models in Quantum Statistical Mechanics. 2nd ed. Ola Bratteli. xiii, 505p. 1997. 89.95 (*3-540-61443-5*) Spr-Verlag.

Operator Algebras & Quantum Statistical Mechanics, I: C & W-Algebras, Symmetry Groups, Decomposition of States. 2nd rev. ed. O. Bratteli & D. W. Robinson. (Texts & Monographs in Physics). 500p. 1987. 106.95 (*0-387-17093-6*) Spr-Verlag.

Operator Algebras & Their Applications. Peter A. Fillmore. 170p. 1998. text 46.00 (*0-8218-0908-3*) Am Math.

Operator Algebras & Their Applications. Peter A. Fillmore & James A. Mingo. LC 96-46681. (Fields Institute Communications Ser.: No. 13). 323p. 1996. text 79.00 (*0-8218-0522-3*, FIC/13) Am Math.

Operator Algebras & Their Connections with Topology & Ergodic Theory. Ed. by H. Araki et al. (Lecture Notes in Mathematics Ser.: Vol. 1132). vi, 594p. 1985. 65.95 (*0-387-15643-7*) Spr-Verlag.

***Operator Algebras Generated by Commuting Projections: A Vector Measure Approach.** Werner Ricker. LC 99-42231. (Lecture Notes in Mathematics Ser.: Vol. 1711). (Illus.). i, 159p. 1999. pap. 37.00 (*3-540-66461-0*) Spr-Verlag.

Operator Algebras in Dynamical Systems: The Theory of Unbounded Derivations in C-Algebras. Shoichiro Sakai. (Encyclopedia of Mathematics & Its Applications Ser.: No. 41). 231p. (C). 1991. text 80.00 (*0-521-40096-1*) Cambridge U Pr.

Operator Algebras, Mathematical Physics, & Low Dimensional Topology. Ed. by Richard Herman & Betul Tanbay. LC 93-32230. (Research Notes in Mathematics Ser.). (Illus.). 336p. 1993. text 65.00 (*1-56881-027-X*) AK Peters.

Operator Algebras, Unitary Representations, Enveloping Algebras & Invariant Theory. Alain Connes et al. 1990. 109.00 (*0-8176-3489-4*) Birkhauser.

Operator Approach to Linear Control Systems. A. Cheremensky & V. Fomin. (Mathematics & Its Applications Ser.: Vol. 345). 416p. (C). 1996. text 217.50 (*0-7923-3765-4*) Kluwer Academic.

***Operator "B"** Edward Lee. 150p. 1999. 30.00 (*1-881475-73-5*) Cemetery Dance.

Operator Calculus & Spectral Theory: Symposium on Operator Calculus & Spectral Theory, Lambrecht, Germany, December, 1991. Ed. by M. Demuth et al. LC 92-27729. (Operator Theory, Advances & Applications Ser.: Vol. 57). xi, 359p. 1992. 122.00 (*0-8176-2792-8*, Pub. by Birkhauser) Princeton Arch.

Operator Certification Study Guide. 4th ed. 128p. 1993. spiral bd. 38.00 (*0-89867-303-8*, 20206) Am Water Wks Assn.

Operator Commutation Relations. Palle E. Jorgensen & Robert T. Moore. 1984. text 232.00 (*90-277-1710-9*) Kluwer Academic.

Operator Extensions, Interpolation of Functions, & Related Topics: Proceedings of the 14th International Conference on Operator Theory, Timisoaria, Romania, June 1-5, 1992. Ed. by A. Gheondea Timotin et al. LC 93-17932. (Operator Theory, Advances & Applications Ser.: Vol. 61). 1993. 86.00 (*0-8176-2902-5*) Birkhauser.

Operator Hilbert Space OH, Complex Interpolation, & Tensor Norms, Vol. 122, No. 585. Gilles Pisier. LC 96-13644. (Memoirs of the American Mathematical Society Ser.). 103p. 1996. pap. 36.00 (*0-8218-0474-X*, MEMO/122/585) Am Math.

Operator Licensing Examination Standards for Power Reactors. 470p. 1997. ring bd. 44.00 (*0-16-062685-4*) USGPO.

Operator Limit Distributions in Probability Theory. Zbigniew J. Jurek & David J. Mason. (Hilbert Space Methods in Reliability & Statistical Inference). 312p. 1993. 159.95 (*0-471-58595-5*) Wiley.

Operator Methods for Optimal Control Problems. Ed. by Sung J. Lee. (Lecture Notes in Pure & Applied Mathematics Ser.: Vol. 108). (Illus.). 344p. 1987. pap. text 155.00 (*0-8247-7811-1*) Dekker.

Operator Methods in Quantum Mechanics. O. L. De Lange & R. E. Raab. (Illus.). 392p. 1992. 95.00 (*0-19-853961-4*) OUP.

Operator of Translation along the Trajectories of Differential Equations. Mark A. Krasnosel'skii. LC 67-22349. (Translations of Mathematical Monographs: Vol. 19). 294p. 1968. text 51.00 (*0-8218-1569-5*, MMONO/19) Am Math.

***Operator Spaces.** Edward G. Effros & Zhong-Jin Ruan. (London Mathematical Society Monographs: Vol. 23). 368p. 2000. text 100.00 (*0-19-853482-5*) OUP.

Operator Techniques in Atomic Spectroscopy. Brian R. Judd. LC 98-9450. 302p. 1998. pap. text 19.95 (*0-691-05901-2*, Pub. by Princeton U Pr) Cal Prin Full Svc.

Operator Theorems with Applications to Distributive Problems & Equilibrium Models. Antonio Villar. Ed. by Martin J. Beckmann & W. Krelle. (Lecture Notes in Economics & Mathematical Systems Ser.: Vol. 377). xvi, 160p. 1992. 43.95 (*0-387-55087-9*) Spr-Verlag.

Operator Theory: Proceedings of the 1988 GPOTS - Wabash Conference. Ed. by John B. Conway & B. B. Morrel. LC 89-38852. (Pitman Research Notes in Mathematics Ser.: Vol. 225). 197p. 1990. reprint ed. pap. 61.10 (*0-608-03602-1*, 206442500009) Bks Demand.

Operator Theory - Operator Algebras & Applications. Ed. by William B. Arveson & R. Douglas. LC 90-33771. (Proceedings of Symposia in Pure Mathematics Ser.: Vol. 51). 1025p. 1990. text 190.00 (*0-8218-1486-9*, PSPUM/51) Am Math.

Operator Theory Advances & Applications: Complete Second Order Linear Differential Equations in Hilbert Spaces Vol. 92. A. Ya. Shklyar. LC 96-52340. 232p. 1997. 99.50 (*3-7643-5377-5*) Spr-Verlag.

Operator Theory, Analytic Functions, Matrices & Electrical Engineering. J. William Helton et al. LC 87-1192. (CBMS Regional Conference Series in Mathematics: No. 68). 134p. 1987. pap. 25.00 (*0-8218-0718-8*, CBMS/68) Am Math.

Operator Theory & Arithmetic in H: Infinity Sign. H. Bercovici. LC 88-10344. (Mathematical Surveys & Monographs: Vol. 26). 275p. 1988. text 82.00 (*0-8218-1528-8*, SURV/26) Am Math.

Operator Theory & Boundary Value Problems: International Workshop in Vienna, July 27-30, 1993. Ed. by I. Gohberg & H. Langer. (Operator Theory, Advances, & Applications Ser.: Vol. 80). 313p. 1995. 123.00 (*3-7643-5275-2*) Birkhauser.

Operator Theory & Boundary Value Problems: International Workshop in Vienna, July 27-30, 1993. Ed. by I. Gohberg & H. Langer. LC 95-20689. (Operator Theory, Advances, & Applications Ser.: Vol. 80). 313p. 1995. 123.00 (*0-8176-5275-2*) Birkhauser.

Operator Theory & Complex Analysis. Ed. by T. Ando & I. Gohberg. LC 92-36581. (Operator Theory, Advances & Applications Ser.: Vol. 59). x, 460p. 1992. 117.50 (*0-8176-2824-X*) Birkhauser.

***Operator Theory & Its Applications.** Ed. by A. G. Ramm et al. (FIC Ser.: Vol. 25). 574p. 2000. 130.00 (*0-8218-1990-9*) Am Math.

Operator Theory & Systems: Workshop Proceedings. Ed. by I. Gohberg et al. (Operator Theory Ser.: Vol. 19). 500p. 1986. 156.00 (*0-8176-1783-3*, Pub. by Birkhauser) Princeton Arch.

Operator Theory for Complex & Hypercomplex Analysis: A Conference on Operator Theory & Complex & Hypercomplex Analysis, December 12-17, 1994, Mexico City, Mexico, Vol. 212. Ed. by Enrique R. De Arellano et al. LC 97-28599. (Contemporary Mathematics Ser.: Vol. SALINAS). 298p. 1997. pap. 65.00 (*0-8218-0677-7*) Am Math.

Operator Theory in Function Spaces. Kehe Zhu. (Pure & Applied Mathematics Ser.: Vol. 139). (Illus.). 280p. 1990. text 185.00 (*0-8247-8411-1*) Dekker.

Operator Theory in Function Spaces & Banach Lattices: Essays Dedicated to A. C. Zaanen on the Occasion of His 80th Birthday. A. C. Zaanen. Ed. by C. B. Huijsmans et al. LC 94-44858. (Operator Theory, Advances & Applications Ser.: Vol. 75). 1995. write for info. (*3-7643-5146-2*) Birkhauser.

Operator Theory in Function Spaces & Banach Lattices: Essays Dedicated to A. C. Zaanen on the Occasion of His 80th Birthday. A. C. Zaanen. Ed. by C. B. Huijsmans et al. LC 94-44858. (Operator Theory, Advances & Applications Ser.: Vol. 75). 320p. 1995. 84.50 (*0-8176-5146-2*) Birkhauser.

Operator Theory with a Random Potential, & Some Questions of Statistical Physics. Ed. by V. N. Popov. LC 91-24484. (Proceedings of the Steklov Institute of Mathematics Ser.: Vol. 184). 259p. 1990. reprint ed. pap. 159.00 (*0-8218-3139-9*, STEKLO/184C) Am Math.

Operator Training for Medical & Other Solid Waste Incinerators. Doucet & Mainka Staff. (Illus.). 408p. (Orig.). 1992. pap. 169.00 (*0-87258-596-4*, 055210) Am Hospital.

Operators: Inside 14 Intelligence Company. James Rennie. (Illus.). 256p. 1996. 35.00 (*0-7126-7730-5*, Pub. by CEN3) Trafalgar.

Operators & Function Theory. Ed. by S. C. Power. 1985. text 176.50 (*90-277-2008-8*) Kluwer Academic.

Operator's Guide to Bacteriological Testing. (Illus.). 132p. 1994. pap. 40.00 (*0-89867-719-X*, 20309) Am Water Wks Assn.

Operator's Guide to Water Fluoridation. Glenn M. Tillman. 112p. 1993. lib. bdg. 45.00 (*0-87371-614-0*, L614) Lewis Pubs.

Operator's Handbook. Tenneco Oil Company Staff. LC 61-13964. (Illus.). 227p. 1961. pap. 70.40 (*0-7837-8350-7*, 204913900010) Bks Demand.

Operators in Indefinite Metric Spaces, Scattering Theory & Other Topics. Grigore Arsene. (Operator Theory Ser.: No. 24). 380p. 1987. 113.50 (*0-8176-1843-0*) Birkhauser.

Operator's Manual for Gas Heating Torch Operation (C4.3-83) 1983. pap. 21.00 (*0-87171-233-4*) Am Welding.

Operator's Manual for Oxyfuel Gas Cutting (C4.2-90) (Illus.). 28p. 1990. pap. 21.00 (*0-87171-316-0*) Am Welding.

Operator's Manual for Planet Earth: An Adventure for the Soul. D. Trinidad Hunt. LC 95-38674. 288p. 1996. 19.45 (*0-7868-6177-0*, Pub. by Hyperion) Time Warner.

Operator's Manual for Planet Earth: An Adventure for the Soul. D. Trinidad Hunt. 288p. 1997. pap. 12.45 (*0-7868-8270-0*, Pub. by Hyperion) Time Warner.

Operator's Manual for Successful Living. Nicholas Martin. LC 88-70784. (Illus.). 160p. (Orig.). 1988. pap. 12.95 (*0-87516-608-3*) DeVorss.

Operators of Class C B0S with Spectra in Multiple Connected Regions. Adele Zucchi. LC 97-3959. (Memoirs of the American Mathematical Society Ser.: Vol. 127/607). 52p. 1997. pap. 33.00 (*0-8218-0626-2*, MEMO/127/607) Am Math.

Operators, Oscillations, Waves. Tr. by M. S. Livsic. LC 72-11580. (Translations of Mathematical Monographs: Vol. 34). 274p. (Orig.). 1973. 66.00 (*0-8218-1584-9*, MMONO/34) Am Math.

Operators, Systems & Linear Algebra: Three Decades of Algebraic Systems Theory. Ed. by Uwe Helmke et al. LC 98-164912. (European Consortium for Mathematics in Industry Ser.). 223 p. 1997. write for info. (*3-519-02608-2*) B G Teubner.

Opere Complete di Roberto Longhi see Three Studies: Masolino & Masaccio, Caravaggio & His Forerunners, Carlo Braccesco

Operette Morali see Moral Essays

Operette Morali: Essays & Dialogues. Giacomo Leopardi. Tr. by Giovanni Del Cecchetti from ITA. LC 82-2627. (Biblioteca Italiana Ser.: No. 3). 672p. 1982. pap. 15.95 (*0-520-04928-4*, Pub. by U CA Pr) Cal Prin Full Svc.

Opern-Handbuch. Hugo Riemann. (GER.). 862p. 1979. reprint ed. write for info. (*3-487-06823-0*) G Olms Pubs.

Opern Von Tommaso Trajetta. Jorg Riedlbauer. (GER., Illus.). x, 586p. 1994. write for info. (*3-487-09798-2*) G Olms Pubs.

Opernball. Josef Haslinger. 1999. 21.95 (*3-596-13591-5*) Fischer Taschen.

Opernball. Roman. Josef Haslinger. (GER.). 480p. 1995. 39.75 (*3-10-030053-X*, Pub. by S Fischer) Intl Bk Import.

Opernmetropole Dresden Von der "Festa Teatrale" Zum Modernen Musikdrama. Winfried Hontsch. (GER., Illus.). 360p. 1996. text 115.00 (*90-5705-003-X*) Gordon & Breach.

Operon. 2nd ed. Ed. by Jeffrey H. Miller & William S. Reznikoff. LC 80-15490. (Cold Spring Harbor Monographs). 479p. 1980. reprint ed. pap. 148.50 (*0-608-01813-9*, 206246200003) Bks Demand.

Opersim: An MUS/JES 2 Operator Simulator. 6th ed. Maryhelen H. Hoffman & Lanny L. Hoffman. 50p. 1996. pap. 25.00 (*1-928592-00-7*) MHP Commns.

Opferbereitschaft Israels: Anthropologische und Theologische Voraussetzungen des Opferkultes. Christiane K. Sabmann. (Europaische Hochschulschriften Ser.: Reihe 23, Bd. 529). (GER.). 280p. 1995. 54.95 (*3-631-48247-7*) P Lang Pubng.

Opferritus und Voropfer der Griechen und Romer. Samson Eitrem. v, 493p. 1977. reprint ed. write for info. (*3-487-06381-6*) G Olms Pubs.

OPFur: The Anthropomorphic Supplement for Thundering Steel. Edwin M. Dyer, III. (Illus.). 36p. (Orig.). (C). 1993. pap. text 7.00 (*0-9631504-2-1*) Minds In One Prods.

***Opgang.** Ed. by Joseph Sherman. (Texts & Translations Ser.: Vol. 7). 255p. 1999. pap. 9.95 (*0-87352-787-9*) Modern Lang.

Ophan Train. Judd Cole. (Cheyenne Ser.: No. 16). 176p. (Orig.). 1996. pap. text, mass mkt. 3.99 (*0-8439-3909-5*) Dorchester Pub Co.

Ophelia & Other Poems. Elizabeth Burns. 1991. 12.00 (*0-7486-6096-8*, Pub. by Polygon) Subterranean Co.

Ophelia O. & the Antenatal Mysteries. Tanya Jones. 416p. 1996. mass mkt. 11.95 (*0-7472-4912-1*, Pub. by Headline Bk Pub) Trafalgar.

Ophelia O. & the Mortgage Bandits. Tanya Jones. 448p. 1996. mass mkt. 11.95 (*0-7472-4867-2*, Pub. by Headline Bk Pub) Trafalgar.

Ophelia Paradox: An Inquiry into the Conduct of Our Lives. Mortimer R. Kadish. LC 93-45848. 243p. (C). 1994. 44.95 (*1-56000-162-3*) Transaction Pubs.

Ophelia Speaks: Adolescent Girls Write about Their Search for Self. Ed. by Sara Shandler. LC 99-13534. 304p. (YA). (gr. 7-12). 1999. pap. 12.95 (*0-06-095297-0*) HarpC.

Ophelia's Bedtime Book. Michele Durks Clise. (Illus.). (J). 1999. pap. write for info. (*0-14-055603-6*) NAL.

Ophelia's Great Idea. Deborah Levy. 1999. pap. 6.95 (*0-14-011786-5*, Viking) Viking Penguin.

Ophelia's Legs & Other Poems. Theresa Gillespie. Ed. by Anne Cheney. (Illus.). 136p. (Orig.). 1996. pap. 9.50 (*0-936015-68-3*) Pocahontas Pr.

Ophelia's Shadow Theater. Michael Ende. (Illus.). 32p. (J). (gr. 1 up). 1989. 14.95 (*0-87951-371-3*, Pub. by Overlook Pr) Penguin Putnam.

Ophiolatreia: An Account of the Rites & Mysteries Connected with the Origin, Rise, & Development of Serpent Worship. Hargrave Jennings. 136p. 1996. reprint ed. pap. 13.95 (*1-56459-944-2*) Kessinger Pub.

Ophiolatreia: An Account of the Rites & Mysteries Connected with the Origin, Rise & Development of Serpent Worship. Hargrave Jennings. 129p. 1996. reprint ed. spiral bd. 15.50 (*0-7873-1258-4*) Hlth Research.

Ophiolites - Genesis & Evolution of Oceanic Lithosphere. Ed. by T. J. Peter et al. (C). 1991. text 50.00 (*0-7923-1176-0*) Kluwer Academic.

***Ophiolites & Oceanic Crust: New Insights from Field Studies & Ocean Drilling Program.** Yildirim Dilek. LC 00-30831. (Special Paper Ser.). 2000. pap. write for info. (*0-8137-2349-3*) Geol Soc.

Ophiolites & Their Modern Oceanic Analogues. Ed. by L. M. Parson et al. (Geological Society Special Publications: No. 60). (Illus.). vi, 330p. (C). 1992. 92.00 (*0-903317-69-9*, 262, Pub. by Geol Soc Pub Hse) AAPG.

Ophir. Smadar Samson. (Illus.). 32p. (J). (gr. k-2). 1993. 16.95 (*0-370-31740-8*, Pub. by Bodley Head) Trafalgar.

Ophir-Imogene Loop & Yankee Boy Basin. Brian J. Benzar & Kitty B. Benzar. (Back Roads of the San Juan Mountains Ser.). (Illus.). 32p. 1995. pap. 4.95 (*1-928759-01-7*) Backcountry CO.

Ophiuchi Hotline. John Varley. 1993. mass mkt. 4.99 (*0-441-63484-2*) Ace Bks.

Ophiuroidea of the Hawaiian Islands. A. H. Clark. (BMB Ser.: No. 195). 1974. reprint ed. 25.00 (*0-527-02303-5*) Periodicals Srv.

Ophtalmologie dans l'Egypte d'apres les Papyrus Litteraires Grecs. Marie-Helene Marganne. (Studies in Ancient Medicine: No. 8). (FRE.). 272p. 1994. 100.00 (*90-04-09907-7*, NLG140) Brill Academic Pubs.

Ophthalmic Aide. Jack Rudman. (Career Examination Ser.: C-563). 1994. pap. 23.95 (*0-8373-0563-2*) Nat Learn.

Ophthalmic Anatomy. Merrill J. Reeh et al. (Illus.). 290p. 1981. 25.00 (*0-317-94082-1*) Am Acad Ophthal.

***Ophthalmic & Facial Plastic Surgery: A Compendium of Reconstructive & Aesthetic Techniques.** Frank A. Lesi et al. 400p. (C). 2000. text 130.00 (*1-55642-451-5*) SLACK Inc.

Ophthalmic Anesthesia. 2nd ed. Caroline A. Carr et al. (Illus.). 288p. 1996. pap. text 65.00 (*0-340-56757-0*, Pub. by E A) OUP.

Ophthalmic Assistant: Fundamentals & Clinical Practices, Principles. 6th ed. Harold A. Stein & Bernard J. Slatt. LC 94-226814. (Illus.). 960p. (C). (gr. 13). 1994. pap. text 63.00 (*0-8151-7560-4*, 24208) Mosby Inc.

Ophthalmic Desk Reference. Ed. by James F. Collins et al. LC 91-14969. (Illus.). 702p. 1991. reprint ed. pap. 200.00 (*0-608-07265-6*, 206749300009) Bks Demand.

Ophthalmic Diagnostic Equipment Markets: Industry Focuses on Automated Equipment & Corneal Topography. Market Intelligence Staff. 343p. 1992. 1695.00 (*1-56753-414-7*) Frost & Sullivan.

Ophthalmic Disorders of Children. Ed. by David W. Kaplan. (Journal: Pediatrician: Vol. 17, No. 3, 1990). (Illus.). 84p. 1990. pap. 48.00 (*3-8055-5209-2*) S Karger.

Ophthalmic Disorders Sourcebook. Allan Cook. LC 96-3345. (Health Reference Ser.: Vol. 17). 1996. lib. bdg. 78.00 (*0-7808-0081-8*) Omnigraphics Inc.

Ophthalmic Dispensing. 3rd ed. Russell L. Stimson. (Illus.). 720p. 1979. 94.95 (*0-398-03823-6*) C C Thomas.

Ophthalmic Dispensing: Present Day Realities. Ralph Drew. (Illus.). 304p. 1990. text 74.95 (*0-409-90225-X*) Buttrwrth-Heinemann.

Ophthalmic Drug Delivery: Biopharmaceutical, Technological & Clinical Aspects. Ed. by M. F. Saettone et al. (FIDIA Research Ser.: Vol. 11). 200p. 1988. 118.00 (*0-387-96599-8*) Spr-Verlag.

Ophthalmic Drug Delivery Systems. Ashim K. Mitra. (Drugs & the Pharmaceutical Sciences Ser.: Vol. 58). (Illus.). 536p. 1993. text 215.00 (*0-8247-8806-0*) Dekker.

***Ophthalmic Drug Facts.** Jimmy D. Bartlett. (Illus.). 1999. pap. 54.95 (*1-57439-060-0*) Facts & Comparisons.

Ophthalmic Echography. Cynthia J. Kendall. LC 87-42952. (Ophthalmic Technical Skills Ser.: Vol. II). (Illus.). 200p. (C). 1990. pap. text 40.00 (*1-55642-027-7*) SLACK Inc.

Ophthalmic Echography. Ed. by K. C. Ossoinig. (Documenta Ophthalmologica Proceedings Ser.). (C). 1987. text 389.50 (*0-89838-873-2*) Kluwer Academic.

Ophthalmic Echography No. 13: Proceedings of the SIDUO Congress, 13th, Vienna, Austria, 1990. Ed. by P. Till. LC 92-19775. (Documenta Ophthalmologica Proceedings Ser.: Vol. 55). 560p. (C). 1993. text 264.50 (*0-7923-1808-0*) Kluwer Academic.

Ophthalmic Essentials. M. P. Vrabec. (Illus.). 464p. 1992. pap. 44.95 (*0-86542-202-8*) Blackwell Sci.

***Ophthalmic Fundamentals: Glaucoma.** Joseph W. Sassani. LC 99-16294. (Illus.). 1999. 90.00 (*1-55642-384-5*) SLACK Inc.

Ophthalmic Histopathology. W. R. Lee. (Illus.). 352p. 1993. 255.00 (*0-387-19686-2*) Spr-Verlag.

Ophthalmic Histopathology. William R. Lee. (Illus.). 352p. 1993. 250.00 (*3-540-19686-2*) Spr-Verlag.

Ophthalmic Laser Therapy. Kimiharu Noyori et al. (Illus.). 289p. 1992. 170.00 (*0-89640-199-5*) Igaku-Shoin.

Ophthalmic Lasers: A Primary Care Approach. Wormington. 1998. 50.00 (*0-7506-9572-2*) Buttrwrth-Heinemann.

Ophthalmic Lenses. H. H. Emsley. (Illus.). 340p. 1984. reprint ed. pap. 25.00 (*0-87556-375-9*) Saifer.

Ophthalmic Lenses & Dispensing. Jalie. LC 99-233330. 224p. 1999. pap. text 95.00 (*0-7506-4158-4*) Buttrwrth-Heinemann.

***Ophthalmic Measurements & Optometry: 12-16 May 1997, Kazmierz Dolny, Poland** Maksymilian Pluta et al. LC 99-192200. (Proceedings Ser.). xvi, 202 p. 1998. write for info. (*0-8194-3046-3*) SPIE.

Ophthalmic Medical Assistant: An Independent Study Course. Paul J. Wasson. LC 99-35332. 1999. 110.00 (*1-56055-171-2*) Am Acad Ophthal.

Ophthalmic Medical Assisting: An Independent Study Course. 2nd ed. Ed. by Robert L. Stamper & Paul J. Wasson. LC 94-33317. 1994. pap. write for info. (*1-56055-025-2*) Am Acad Ophthal.

Ophthalmic Medical Assisting: An Independent Study Course. 3rd ed. Tyree Carr. LC 98-33325. 1999. write for info. (*1-56055-041-4*) Am Acad Ophthal.

Ophthalmic Medications & Pharmacology. Brian Duvall & Robert M. Kershner. LC 97-41938. (Basic Bookshelf for Eyecare Professionals Ser.). (Illus.). 144p. 1997. pap. 26.00 (*1-55642-328-4*, 63284) SLACK Inc.

Ophthalmic Microsurgery. Ed. by J. A. Draeger. (Illus.). xii, 184p. 1986. 149.75 (*3-8055-4028-0*) S Karger.

Ophthalmic Microsurgery: Proceedings of the Workshop on Microsurgery, Singapore, May 1977. S. Shan Ratnam & A. S. Lim. (Advances in Ophthalmology Ser.: Vol. 36). (Illus.). 1978. 102.75 (*3-8055-2782-9*) S Karger.

Ophthalmic Nursing. 2nd ed. Rosalind Stollery. LC 96-28897. 288p. 1996. pap. text 39.95 (*0-632-03996-5*) Blackwell Sci.

Ophthalmic Optics. K. Kashik. (C). 1986. 50.00 (*0-521-00105-6*, Pub. by Current Dist) St Mut.

Ophthalmic Optics. K. Kaushik. (C). 1986. 50.00 (*0-89771-352-4*, Pub. by Current Dist) St Mut.

Ophthalmic Optics & Clinical Refraction. David L. Guyton et al. (Illus.). 169p. 1997. spiral bd. 15.00 (*0-9665068-0-4*) Prism MD.

Ophthalmic Pathology. Praema V. Iyer & Robert Rowland. LC 94-137073. (Illus.). 220p. 1993. reprint ed. pap. 68.20 (*0-7837-9745-1*, 206047300005) Bks Demand.

Ophthalmic Pathology, Sect. Eleven. (Basic & Clinical Science Course (1989-90) Ser.). 270p. (C). 1989. pap. text 45.00 (*0-685-26055-0*) Am Acad Ophthal.

Ophthalmic Pathology: An Atlas & Textbook, 4 vols., Set. 4th ed. Ed. by William H. Spencer. Incl. Vol. Four. Ophthalmic Pathology Vol. 3: An Atlas & Textbooks. 4th ed. LC 94-38768. 1995. (*0-7216-6047-9*, W B Saunders Co); Vol. One. Ophthalmic Pathology Vol. 1: An Atlas & Textbooks. 4th ed. LC 94-38768. 1995. (*0-7216-4909-2*, W B Saunders Co); LC 94-38768. (Illus.). 2208p. 1996. Set text 650.00 (*0-7216-4908-4*, W B Saunders Co) Harcrt Hlth Sci Grp.

Ophthalmic Pathology, Vol. 1, An Atlas & Textbooks see Ophthalmic Pathology: An Atlas & Textbook

Ophthalmic Pathology Vol. 2: An Atlas & Textbooks, Vol. Two. 4th ed. Ed. by William H. Spencer. LC 94-38768. 1995. write for info. (*0-7216-4910-6*, W B Saunders Co) Harcrt Hlth Sci Grp.

Ophthalmic Pathology - CD-ROM Single User Version: An Atlas & Textbook. 4th ed. William H. Spencer. Ed. by Richard Zorab. (Illus.). 1997. text 650.00 incl. cd-rom (*0-7216-8193-X*, W B Saunders Co) Harcrt Hlth Sci Grp.

Ophthalmic Pathology of Animals: An Atlas & Reference Book. L. Z. Saunders & L. F. Rubin. (Illus.). 250p. 1975. 141.75 (*3-8055-1580-4*) S Karger.

Ophthalmic Pathology with Clinical Correlations. Ed. by Joseph W. Sassani. (Illus.). 256p. 1997. text 99.00 (*0-397-51469-7*) Lppncott W & W.

Ophthalmic Pharmaceuticals: Successful Laboratory Results Equal Market Success. Market Intelligence Staff. 180p. (Orig.). 1992. 1895.00 (*1-56753-337-X*) Frost & Sullivan.

Ophthalmic Photography: A Textbook of Retinal Photography, Angiography, & Electronic Imaging. Patrick J. Saine & Marshall E. Tyler. LC 96-25989. (Illus.). 334p. 1996. text 155.00 (*0-7506-9793-8*) Buttrwrth-Heinemann.

Ophthalmic Plastic & Reconstructive Surgery. 2nd ed. Nesi & Byron Smith. LC 97-26132. (Illus.). 1248p. (C). (gr. 13). 1997. text 295.00 (*0-8151-6356-8*, 24723) Mosby Inc.

Ophthalmic Plastic & Reconstructive Surgery. 4th ed. William B. Stewart. 486p. 1984. 37.50 (*0-317-94077-5*) Am Acad Ophthal.

Ophthalmic, Plastic, Reconstructive & Orbital Surgery. Ed. by Charles M. Stephenson. LC 96-50457. (Illus.). 590p. 1997. text 199.95 (*0-7506-9081-X*) Buttrwrth-Heinemann.

O

Ophthalmic Plastic Surgery. Della Rocca & Maher. (C). 1999. text 130.00 (*0-8385-7427-0*) P-H.

Ophthalmic Plastic Surgery: Prevention & Management of Complications. Ed. by Richard K. Dortzbach. LC 92-48529. 448p. 1993. text 204.00 (*0-7817-0029-9*) Lppncott W & W.

Ophthalmic Pocket Companion. 4th ed. Dean Dornic. LC 95-38750. 306p. 1995. pap. text 32.00 (*0-7506-9627-3*) Buttrwrth-Heinemann.

Ophthalmic Pocket Companion. 5th ed. Dean Dornic. 368p. 1998. pap. text 32.50 (*0-7506-7120-3*) Buttrwrth-Heinemann.

Ophthalmic Product Markets: Manufacturers Seek Ways to Penetrate Untapped Markets. Market Intelligence Staff. 400p. 1993. 1995.00 (*1-56753-572-0*) Frost & Sullivan.

Ophthalmic Regulatory Manual. 4th rev. ed. Robert M. Portman et al. Orig. Title: Ophthalmic Reimbursement Manual. (Illus.). 252p. 1987. ring bd. write for info. (*1-929196-00-8*) Am Ophthlmc Admin.

Ophthalmic Reimbursement Manual see Ophthalmic Regulatory Manual

Ophthalmic Research & Epidemiology: Evaluation & Application. Stanley W. Hatch. LC 97-45062. 312p. 1998. pap. text 47.50 (*0-7506-9914-0*) Buttrwrth-Heinemann.

Ophthalmic Surgery: Principles & Practice. 3rd ed. George L. Spaeth. 1999. text. write for info. (*0-7216-6972-7*) Harcourt.

Ophthalmic Surgery: Principles & Techniques. Daniel M. Albert & Frederick S. Brightbill. LC 98-34615. (Illus.). 1998. 399.00 (*0-632-04337-7*) Blackwell Sci.

Ophthalmic Surgery Complications: Prevention & Management. Ed. by Judie F. Charlton & George W. Weinstein. LC 94-26149. (Illus.). 524p. 1995. reprint ed. pap. 162.50 (*0-608-07252-4*, 206747900009) Bks Demand.

Ophthalmic Surgical Anatomy: A Clinical Approach. David R. Jordan & Richard L. Anderson. (Ophthalmology Monographs: Vol. 9). 134p. 1995. 70.00 (*1-56055-029-5*) Am Acad Ophthal.

Ophthalmic Surgical Assistant. Regina Boess-Lott & Sharon Stecik. LC 98-45257. (The Basic Bookshelf for Eyecare Professionals). 144p. 1999. pap. 30.00 (*1-55642-403-5*) SLACK Inc.

Ophthalmic Surgical Device Markets: New IDL Technology Improves Reimbursement Outlook. Market Intelligence Staff. 204p. 1992. 1695.00 (*1-56753-418-X*) Frost & Sullivan.

Ophthalmic Surgical Procedures. Peter Hersh. 280p. 1988. 87.95 (*0-316-35865-7*, Little Brwn Med Div) Lppncott W & W.

*__Ophthalmic Technical Skills Handbook.__ Janice K. Ledford. 200p. (C). 2000. pap. text 33.00 (*1-55642-464-7*) SLACK Inc.

*__Ophthalmic Technologies IX.__ Ed. by Pascal O. Rol et al. 480p. 1999. pap. text 103.00 (*0-8194-3061-7*) SPIE.

Ophthalmic Technologies II. Ed. by J. Parel. 1992. 20.00 (*0-8194-0790-9*, 1644) SPIE.

Ophthalmic Technologies VII, Vol. 2971. Ed. by Pascal O. Rol & Karen M. Joos. 226p. 1997. 80.00 (*0-8194-2382-3*) SPIE.

Ophthalmic Technologies VIII, Vol. 3246. Ed. by Pascal O. Rol et al. 324p. 1998. 89.00 (*0-8194-2685-7*) SPIE.

Ophthalmic Technology: A Guide for the Eye Care Assistant. Ed. by Stephen J. Rhode & Stephen P. Ginsberg. (Illus.). 508p. 1987. pap. text 50.00 (*0-88167-276-9*) Lppncott W & W.

Ophthalmic Terminology: Speller & Vocabulary Builder. 3rd ed. Harold A. Stein et al. (Illus.). 384p. (C). (gr. 13). 1991. pap. text 39.00 (*0-8016-6438-1*, 06438) Mosby Inc.

*__Ophthalmic Toxicology.__ 2nd ed. George C. Chiou. LC 99-31971. 500p. 1999. 135.00 (*1-56032-722-7*) Taylor & Francis.

Ophthalmic Tumours. Ed. by Jendo A. Oosterhuis. (Monographs in Ophthalmology). 1985. text 233.50 (*90-6193-528-8*) Kluwer Academic.

Ophthalmic Ultrasonography. Ed. by Jeffrey S. Hillman & Malcolm M. Le May. (Documenta Ophthalmologica Proceedings Ser.). 1983. text 332.00 (*90-6193-734-5*) Kluwer Academic.

Ophthalmic Ultrasound: A Diagnostic Atlas. Cathy Dibernardo et al. LC 98-14389. 1998. 69.00 (*0-86577-765-9*) Thieme Med Pubs.

Ophthalmodouleia: That Is the Service of the Eyes. George Batisch. Tr. by Donald Blanchard from GER. (Hirschberg History of Ophthalmology Ser.: Vol. III). Orig. Title: Ophthalmodouleia, Das ist Augendienst. (Illus.). 600p. 1996. lthr. write for info. (*0-614-30296-X*) Blanchards Brook.

Ophthalmodouleia, Das ist Augendienst see Ophthalmodouleia: That Is the Service of the Eyes

Ophthalmology. Chawla. 354p. 1999. pap. text 37.50 (*0-7506-3963-6*) Buttrwrth-Heinemann.

Ophthalmology. N. R. Galloway & S. A. Vernon. 150p. 1988. 33.95 (*0-387-19516-5*) Spr-Verlag.

Ophthalmology. Jack J. Kanski. LC 96-39720. (Colour Guide Ser.). 1997. write for info. (*0-443-05804-0*) Harcrt Hlth Sci Grp.

Ophthalmology. Emanuel Rosen & William Rosen. LC 97-157872. (Medico-Legal Practitioner Ser.). 304p. 1997. 80.00 (*1-85941-211-4*, Pub. by Cavendish Pubng) Gaunt.

Ophthalmology. Myron Yanoff. 1998. 265.00 (*0-323-00526-8*) Mosby Inc.

Ophthalmology. 2nd ed. Nicholas M. Evans. (Illus.). 296p. 1995. 98.50 (*0-19-262407-5*) OUP.

Ophthalmology. 2nd ed. Fritz Hollwich. Tr. by Frederick C. Blodi from GER. (Flexibook Ser.). (Illus.). 363p. 1985. pap. text 29.90 (*0-86577-184-7*) Thieme Med Pubs.

Ophthalmology. 2nd ed. Kanski. LC 98-14948. (C). 1997. pap. text 16.95 (*0-443-05879-2*, W B Saunders Co) Harcrt Hlth Sci Grp.

Ophthalmology. 2nd ed. Nicholas M. Evans. (Illus.). 296p. 1996. reprint ed. pap. text 49.95 (*0-19-262406-7*) OUP.

Ophthalmology. 3rd ed. Kenneth Wybar. 1984. pap. text 27.95 (*0-7216-0945-7*) Bailliere Tindall.

Ophthalmology: A Clinical Introduction. John W. Gittinger, Jr. 267p. 1984. 31.95 (*0-316-31470-6*, Little Brwn Med Div) Lppncott W & W.

Ophthalmology: A Diagnostic Text. William H. Coles. (Illus.). 424p. 1989. pap. text 35.00 (*0-683-02056-0*) Lppncott W & W.

*__Ophthalmology: A Short Textbook.__ G. K. Lang. (Illus.). 664p. 2000. pap. 39.00 (*0-86577-935-X*) Thieme Med Pubs.

Ophthalmology: A Symptom-Based Approach. 3rd ed. Hector Bryson Chawla. LC 99-19071. 215p. 1999. pap. text 40.00 (*0-7506-3979-2*) Buttrwrth-Heinemann.

Ophthalmology: An Illustration. Mark Batterbury. LC 99-27851. (Illus.). 1999. text 31.00 (*0-443-05537-8*) Harcourt.

Ophthalmology: Concise Medical Textbook. 3rd ed. K. Wybar & M. Kerr Muir. (Illus.). 375p. 1984. pap. text 27.95 (*0-7020-1005-7*, Pub. by W B Saunders) Saunders.

Ophthalmology: Pretest Self-Assessment & Review. H. Jay Wisnicki. (Pretest Specialty Level Ser.). (Illus.). 304p. 1996. pap. text 47.00 (*0-07-052077-1*) McGraw-Hill HPD.

Ophthalmology: Principles & Concepts. 8th ed. Frank W. Newell. (Illus.). 608p. (C). (gr. 13). 1996. text 75.00 (*0-8151-7093-9*, 27525) Mosby Inc.

Ophthalmology Annual, 1988. Ophthalmology Annual Staff. Ed. by Robert D. Reinecke. LC 85-646190. (Illus.). 256p. 1988. pap. 79.40 (*0-7837-8356-6*, 204914600010) Bks Demand.

Ophthalmology Companion. W. Happe. (Illus.). 304p. 1999. pap. text 39.95 (*0-340-74093-0*, Pub. by E A) OUP.

Ophthalmology for Medical Students & Primary Care Physicians. 6th ed. Ed. by Frank G. Berson. LC 93-21474. 1993. write for info. (*1-56055-074-0*) Am Acad Ophthal.

Ophthalmology for Primary Care. Gloria Wu. Ed. by Richard Lampert. LC 96-49580. (Illus.). 176p. 1997. pap. text 35.00 (*0-7216-5078-3*, W B Saunders Co) Harcrt Hlth Sci Grp.

Ophthalmology for the Pediatric Practitioner. Richard M. Robb. 1981. 31.50 (*0-316-74894-3*, Little Brwn Med Div) Lppncott W & W.

Ophthalmology for the Primary Care Practitioner. Palay. (Illus.). 331p. (C). (gr. 13). 1997. pap. text 59.95 (*0-8151-8898-6*, 30318) Mosby Inc.

Ophthalmology Made Ridiculously Simple. Stephen Goldberg. (Illus.). 84p. 1999. pap. text 13.95 (*0-940780-01-1*) MedMaster.

Ophthalmology Office Manual. Frank J. Weinstock. (Office Manual Ser.). 275p. 1993. 145.00 (*1-890018-02-3*) Anadem Pubng.

Ophthalmology Pearls of Wisdom. Mulrooney et al. (Pearls of Wisdom Ser.). 1999. pap. 88.00 (*1-890369-18-7*) Boston Medical.

Ophthalmology Resident Pocket Survival Guide. Shulpa Desai. 100p. (C). 1999. pap. 9.95 (*1-883205-37-9*) Intl Med Pub.

Ophthalmology Review. Myron Yanoff. (C). 1999. text 34.95 (*0-323-00905-0*) Mosby Inc.

Ophthalmology Review Manual. Chern. 560p. pap. text 69.95 (*0-683-30364-3*) Lppncott W & W.

Ophthalmology Secrets. Ed. by James F. Vander. LC 97-52287. (Secrets Ser.). (Illus.). 350p. (Orig.). 1998. pap. text 38.00 (*1-56053-165-7*) Hanley & Belfus.

Ophthalmology Study Guide for Students & Practitioners of Medicine. 5th ed. Ed. by Frank G. Berson. (Illus.). 166p. 1987. 10.00 (*0-317-94084-8*) Am Acad Ophthal.

Ophthamology. 2nd ed. Van Heuven. (C). 1999. text 79.95 (*1-55664-454-X*) Mosby Inc.

Opia. Alan Moore. 84p. 1986. pap. 15.95 (*0-85646-161-X*, Pub. by Anvil Press) Dufour.

Opial Inequalities with Applications in Differential & Difference Equations. Ravi P. Agarwal & Peter Y. Pang. LC 94-48292. (Mathematics & Its Applications Ser.: Vol. 320). 1995. text 180.50 (*0-7923-3365-9*) Kluwer Academic.

Opiate Addiction. Arthur Light et al. Ed. by Gerald N. Grob. LC 80-1257. (Addiction in America Ser.). 1981. reprint ed. lib. bdg. 15.95 (*0-405-13604-8*) Ayer.

Opiate Addiction: Its Handling & Treatment. Edward H. Williams. LC 75-17250. (Social Problems & Social Policy Ser.). 1976. reprint ed. 19.95 (*0-405-07524-3*) Ayer.

Opiate Receptors. Ed. by Gavril W. Pasternak. LC 87-3095. (Receptors Ser.). (Illus.). 520p. 1988. 125.00 (*0-89603-120-9*) Humana.

Opiate Receptors, Neurotransmitters, & Drug Dependence: Basic Science - Clinical Correlates. Ed. by Barry Stimmel. LC 81-7011. (Advances in Alcohol & Substance Abuse Ser.: Vol. 1, No. 1). 129p. 1981. text 39.95 (*0-86656-103-X*) Haworth Pr.

Opiates & Their Alternates for Pain & Cough Relief: Proceedings of the WHO Scientific Group, Geneva, 1971. WHO Staff. (Technical Reports: No. 495). 1972. pap. text 3.00 (*92-4-120495-8*, 1100495) World Health.

Opicinus de Canistris: Weltbild & Bekenntnisse Eines Avignonesischen Klerikers des 14 Jahrhunderts, 2 vols. Richard Salomon. Incl. Vol. 1A. Textband. 1974. Vol. 1B. Tafelband. 1974. (Warburg Institute Studies: Vol. 1). 1974. reprint ed. 100.00 (*0-8115-1378-5*) Periodicals Srv.

Opie Collection of Children's Literature: A Guide to the Microfiche Collection, Unit 1. Compiled by Iona Opie & Peter Opie. v, 79p. 1992. pap. 20.00 (*0-8357-2151-5*) Univ Microfilms.

Opie Collection of Children's Literature: A Guide to the Microfiche Collection, Unit 2. Compiled by Iona Opie & Peter Opie. v, 65p. 1992. pap. 20.00 (*0-8357-2152-3*) Univ Microfilms.

Opie's Pocket Price Guide to Britains Hollowcast Toy Soldiers. James Opie. 128p. 12.95 (*1-872727-82-4*, Pub. by New Cavendish) Pincushion Pr.

Opinion & Evidence: Disease Management. 200p. pap. text 49.95 (*0-86471-052-6*, Pub. by Adis Intl) Lppncott W & W.

Opinion & Evidence: Drug Safety. I. Ralph Edwards. 168p. pap. text 89.95 (*0-86471-044-5*, Pub. by Adis Intl) Lppncott W & W.

Opinion & Evidence: Drug Safety. 2nd ed. I. Ralph Edwards. pap. text 49.95 (*0-86471-065-8*, Pub. by Adis Intl) Lppncott W & W.

Opinion & Evidence: Drug Treatment. 212p. pap. text 89.95 (*0-86471-051-8*, Pub. by Adis Intl) Lppncott W & W.

Opinion & Evidence: Pharmacoeconomics. 208p. pap. text 89.95 (*0-86471-063-1*, Pub. by Adis Intl) Lppncott W & W.

Opinion & Reform in Hume's Political Philosophy. John B. Stewart. 340p. 1992. text 52.50 (*0-691-08626-5*, Pub. by Princeton U Pr) Cal Prin Full Svc.

Opinion Conflict & School Support. Frederick T. Rope. LC 70-177206. (Columbia University. Teachers College. Contributions to Education Ser.: No. 838). viii, 164 p. 1972. reprint ed. 37.50 (*0-404-55838-0*) AMS Pr.

Opinion Connection: Polling, Politics & the Press. Albert H. Cantril. 285p. 1991. 22.95 (*0-87187-583-7*) Congr Quarterly.

Opinion Letters in Securities Matters: Text-Clauses-Law, 3 vols. Arnold S. Jacobs. LC 79-24005. (Securities Law Ser.). 1980. ring bd. 395.00 (*0-87632-301-8*) West Group.

Opinion Polls. Moon. 1999. pap. 24.95 (*0-7190-4224-0*) St Martin.

Opinion Polls & Volatile Electorates: Problems & Issues in Polling European Societies. Matt Henn. LC 98-3177. 268p. 1998. text 68.95 (*1-84014-416-5*, HM261.H397) Ashgate Pub Co.

Opinion Publica y las Aspiraciones de los Puertorriquenos. Luis N. Falcon. 198p. 1978. 4.00 (*0-8477-2479-4*); pap. 3.00 (*0-8477-2486-7*) U of PR Pr.

Opinion Writing. 1996. 16.95 (*1-85431-570-6*, Pub. by Blackstone Pr) Gaunt.

Opinion Writing. Ruggero J. Aldisert. 338p. 1993. reprint ed. text. write for info. (*0-314-84548-8*) West Pub.

Opinion Writing: Inns of Court School of Law, 1996-97. 193p. 1996. pap. 38.00 (*1-954315-70-8*, Pub. by Blackstone Pr) Gaunt.

Opinion Writing & Drafting, 1993-94. 335p. 1994. pap. 48.00 (*1-85431-274-X*, Pub. by Blackstone Pr) Gaunt.

Opinion Writing & Drafting. (Legal Skills for the 1990s Ser.). 1992. pap. 52.00 (*1-85431-233-2*, Pub. by Blackstone Pr) Gaunt.

Opinion Writing & Drafting: Inns of Court School of Law. 347p. 1995. pap. 44.00 (*1-85431-425-4*, Pub. by Blackstone Pr) Gaunt.

Opinion Writing & Drafting in Contract Law. Carron-Ann Russell. 193p. 1996. pap. 22.00 (*1-85941-030-8*, Pub. by Cavendish Pubng) Gaunt.

Opinion Writing & Drafting in Criminal Law. Robert A. Shuster. 250p. 1996. pap. write for info. (*1-85941-031-6*, Pub. by Cavendish Pubng) Gaunt.

Opinion Writing & Drafting in Equity & Trusts. M. Ramjohn. 250p. 1996. pap. write for info. (*1-85941-033-2*, Pub. by Cavendish Pubng) Gaunt.

Opinion Writing & Drafting in Tort. Valerie Beardsmore & Adele Cox. 347p. 1996. pap. 22.00 (*1-85941-032-4*, Pub. by Cavendish Pubng) Gaunt.

Opinion Writing, 1998-99. 3rd ed. Edward Bailey et al. LC 99-199646. (Inns of Court School of Law Ser.). 203p. 1998. pap. 42.00 (*1-85431-772-5*) Gaunt.

Opinion Writing, 1997-98. 2nd ed. Edward Bailey et al. (Inns of Court School of Law Ser.). 197p. 1997. pap. 40.00 (*1-85431-674-5*, Pub. by Blackstone Pr) Gaunt.

Opiniones del Secretario de Justicia de Leyes de Puerto Rico. Ed. by Butterworth Staff. 1992. 50.00 (*0-88063-522-3*, MICHIE) LEXIS Pub.

Opinioni de' Cantori Antichi, e Moderni, o Osservazioni Sopra il Canto Figurato. fac. ed. Pierfrancesco Tosi. (Monuments of Music & Music Literature in Facsimile, II Ser.: Vol. 133). (Illus.). 1968. lib. bdg. 35.00 (*0-8450-2333-0*) Broude.

Opinionmakers. William L. Rivers. LC 83-18529. 207p. 1983. reprint ed. lib. bdg. 59.50 (*0-313-24251-8*, RIOP, Greenwood Pr) Greenwood.

Opinions. Claude C. Washburn. LC 68-29255. (Essay Index Reprint Ser.). 1977. reprint ed. 18.95 (*0-8369-0977-1*) Ayer.

Opinions Banking Commission, 1989: On Queries Relating to Uniform Customs & Practice for Documentary Credits. International Chamber of Commerce Staff. 77p. (Orig.). 1990. pap. text 34.95 (*92-842-1091-7*, 469, Pub. by ICC Pub SA) ICC Pub.

Opinions de Mr. Jerome Coignard. Anatole France, pseud. pap. 9.95 (*0-685-34119-4*) Fr & Eur.

Opinions et Paradoxes. Denis Diderot. 220p. 1963. 14.95 (*0-686-56019-1*) Fr & Eur.

Opinions IV: Philatelic Expertizing. Elizabeth C. Pope. (Opinions Ser.). (Illus.). 250p. 1987. 21.00 (*0-911989-18-8*) Philatelic Found.

Opinions in SEC Transactions. (Corporate Law & Practice Course Handbook, 1985-86 Ser.). 800p. 1994. pap. 99.00 (*0-614-17185-7*, B4-7099) PLI.

Opinions, Literary & Otherwise. Henry W. Taft. LC 68-8499. (Essay Index Reprint Ser.). 1977. 18.95 (*0-8369-0921-6*) Ayer.

Opinions, 1994: 1994 Supplement. Scott Fitzgibbon. 1994. 75.00 (*0-316-28448-3*, Aspen Law & Bus) Aspen Pub.

Opinions of an American Peasant. Thomas Mariano. Ed. by Carrie C. Allison. (Illus.). 256p. (Orig.). 1989. pap. write for info. (*1-877637-01-7*) Mariano Pub.

Opinions of an Old Contrarian. Guy Friddell. (Illus.). 350p. 1997. 9.95 (*1-57380-055-4*) Falcon Pub Inc.

*__Opinions of Different Authors upon the Punishment of Death, 1 vol.__ 2nd ed. Basil Montagu. viii, 310p. 2000. reprint ed. 96.00 (*1-56169-625-0*) Gaunt.

Opinions of Eminent Lawyers on Various Points of English Jurisprudence. George Chalmers. LC 87-80148. (Historical Writings in Law & Jurisprudence Ser.: No. 13). xxvii, 718p. 1987. reprint ed. lib. bdg. 52.00 (*0-89941-545-8*, 305110) W S Hein.

Opinions of Singers Ancient, & Modern, or Observations on Figured Singing. Tosi & Pierfrancesco. Tr. by Edward V. Foreman from ITA. (Masterworks on Singing Ser.: Vol. VI). 1993. text 32.50 (*1-887117-01-6*) Pro musica pr.

Opinions of the Attorney General of California. text 1890.00 (*0-8205-2220-1*) Bender.

Opinions of the Attorney General of the Virgin Islands, 1965-1991, 9 vols., Set, Vols. 1, 3-10 (1935-1986) Ed. by Butterworth Staff. 2000p. 1965. boxed set 315.00 (*0-88063-540-1*, 48973-10, MICHIE) LEXIS Pub.

*__Opinions of the Attorneys General & Judgments of the Supreme Court & the Court of Claims of the United States Relating to the Controversy over Neutral Rights Between the United States & France, 1797-1800.__ Carnegie Endowment for International Peace Staff. LC 99-48343. 2000. write for info. (*1-57588-597-2*) W S Hein.

*__Opinions of the Attorneys General, Decisions of Federal Courts & Diplomatic Correspondence Respecting the Treaties of 1785, 1799 & 1828 Between the United States & Prussia.__ LC 99-48346. 2000. write for info. (*1-57588-598-0*) W S Hein.

Opinions of the Board of Ethical Review, Vol. VII. (Orig.). 1994. pap. text 20.00 (*0-915409-05-4*) Natl Soc Prof Engrs.

Opinions of the Confederate Attorneys General, 1861-1865. Rembert W. Patrick. xxiv, 608p. 1950. lib. bdg. 55.00 (*0-89941-617-9*, 500470) W S Hein.

Opinions of the Ethics Committee on the Principles of Medical Ethics: With Annotations Especially Applicable to Psychiatry. American Psychiatric Association, Ethics Committee. LC RC0455.2.E8. 58p. 1993. reprint ed. pap. 30.00 (*0-608-02019-2*, 206267500003) Bks Demand.

An Asterisk (*) at the beginning of an entry indicates that the title is appearing for the first time.

Opinions of the Ethics Committee on the Principles of Medical Ethics with Annotations Especially Applicable to Psychiatry. APA Ethics Committee. 56p. 1995. pap. text 3.00 (*0-89042-139-0*, 2139) Am Psychiatric.

Opinions of the ICC Banking Commission, 1995-96. rev. ed. International Chamber of Commerce Staff. Ed. by Gary Collyer. 90p. (C). 1997. pap. 49.95 (*92-842-1220-0*, 565) ICC Pub.

Opinions of the Office of Legal Counsel of the United States Department of Justice, 1977-1987, 11 vols. in 9, Set. Ed. by Leon Ulman. 1990. reprint ed. 665.00 (*1-57588-348-1*, 307000) W S Hein.

Opinions on Church Music: Comments & Reports from Four & a Half Centuries. Ed. by Elwyn A. Wienandt. LC 74-75229. 224p. 1974. pap. 14.00 (*0-918954-12-6*) Baylor Univ Pr.

Opinions on Various Subjects: Dedicated to the Industrious Producers, 3 vols. William Maclure. LC 68-18220. 1971. reprint ed. 150.00 (*0-678-00712-8*) Kelley.

Opinions One-Four: The Complete Abstracts & Index. Kenneth J. Kutz & Austin H. Menaker. (Illus.). 1990. 27.50 (*0-911989-20-X*) Philatelic Found.

Opinions-Philatelic Expertizing: An Inside View. Elizabeth C. Pope et al. LC 83-60036. (Illus.). 141p. 1983. 12.00 (*0-911989-00-5*) Philatelic Found.

Opinions, Sage Advise & Words of Wisdom: From Guy Holloway Raymond "Moe" L. Douglas Raymond. (Illus.). 77p. 1997. pap. 21.95 (*0-9661821-0-3*) L Raymond.

Opinions Six: Philatelic Expertizing - An Inside View. Photos by Carl O. Mamay. (Opinions Ser.). (Illus.). ii, 226p. 1992. text 32.50 (*0-911989-25-0*) Philatelic Found.

Opioid Addiction & Treatment: A 12-Year Follow-up. D. Dwayne Simpson. LC 88-29565. 288p. 1990. 32.50 (*0-89464-309-6*) Krieger.

Opioid Analgesia: Recent Advances in Systemic Administration. Ed. by Costantino Benedetti et al. LC 89-24319. (Advances in Pain Research & Therapy Ser.: Vol. 14). 494p. 1990. reprint ed. pap. 153.20 (*0-608-03386-3*, 206408300008) Bks Demand.

Opioid Analgesics: Chemistry & Receptors. A. F. Casy & R. T. Parfitt. LC 86-1520. (Illus.). 534p. (C). 1986. text 145.00 (*0-306-42130-5*, Kluwer Plenum) Kluwer Academic.

Opioid Modulation of Endocrine Function. Ed. by Giuseppe Delitala et al. LC 83-43121. (Frontiers in Neuroscience Ser.). (Illus.). 296p. 1984. reprint ed. pap. 91.80 (*0-608-00623-8*, 206121000007) Bks Demand.

Opioid Peptides. 1992. lib. bdg. 90.00 (*0-8490-5499-0*) Gordon Pr.

Opioid Peptides: Biochemistry & Applied Physiology, Vol. 4. rev. ed. J. Szekely & K. Ramabadran. LC 82-12860. 384p. 1990. 212.00 (*0-8493-6238-5*, QP352) Franklin.

Opioid Peptides: Pharmacology, Vol. II. Ed. by Jozsef I. Szekeley & Andras Z. Ronai. 256p. 1983. 144.00 (*0-8493-6236-9*, QP552, CRC Reprint) Franklin.

Opioid Peptides: Research Methods, Vol. I. Ed. by Jozsef I. Szekely & Andras Z. Ronai. 128p. 1982. 79.00 (*0-8493-6235-0*, QR552, CRC Reprint) Franklin.

Opioid Peptides in Substance Abuse. Ed. by Jozsef I. Szekely. LC 93-9526. (Physiology of Drug Abuse Ser.). 288p. 1993. boxed set 141.95 (*0-8493-7937-7*, RC564) CRC Pr.

***Opioid Sensitivity of Chronic Noncancer Pain.** Ed. by Eija Kalso et al. LC 99-35762. (Progress in Pain Research & Management Ser.: Vol. 14). (Illus.). 406p. 1999. 68.00 (*0-931092-28-0*) Intl Assn Study Pain.

***Opioids & Opioid Receptors: 2nd U.S.-Tawaiin Neuroscience Symposium, Miami, Fla., October 1999 - Proceedings Satellite Symposium of the 29th Annual Meeting of Neuroscience, Miami, Fla, October 1999.** Ed. by L. F. Tseng et al. (Journal of Biomedical Science Ser.: Vol. 7). iv, 104p. 2000. pap. 34.00 (*3-8055-7095-3*) S Karger.

Opioids, Bulimia, & Alcohol Abuse & Alcoholism. Ed. by L. D. Reid. xi, 393p. 1990. 89.95 (*0-387-97242-0*) Spr-Verlag.

Opioids in Pain Control: Basic & Clinical Aspects. Ed. by Christoph Stein. LC 98-19063. (Illus.). 400p. (C). 1999. text 95.00 (*0-521-62269-7*) Cambridge U Pr.

Opioids Peptides: Opiate Receptors & Their Ligands-Experimental & Clinical Aspects, Vol. III. Ed. by Jozsef I. Szekely. 272p. 1983. 139.95 (*0-8493-6237-7*, QP552) CRC Pr.

Opioids 6. Ed. by Albert Herz et al. LC 92-2325. (Handbook of Experimental Pharmacology Ser.: Vol. 104). 1992. 464.00 (*0-387-55397-5*) Spr-Verlag.

Opioids 2. Ed. by G. V. Born et al. (Handbook of Experimental Pharmacology Ser.: Vol. 104/II). (Illus.). 880p. 1993. 510.00 (*0-387-55517-X*) Spr-Verlag.

Opiologia: or A Treatise Concerning the Nature & Safe Use of Opium. Angelo Sala. LC 77-7431. (English Experience Ser.: No. 892). 1977. reprint ed. lib. bdg. 20.00 (*90-221-0892-9*) Walter J Johnson.

Opium. Jean Cocteau. Tr. by Margaret Crosland. LC 90-80804. 176p. 1996. pap. 19.95 (*0-7206-0800-7*, Pub. by P Owen Ltd) Dufour.

Opium. large type ed. Tony Cohan. 736p. 1986. 27.99 (*0-7089-8363-4*, Charnwood) Ulverscroft.

Opium. John P. Gavit. Ed. by Gerald N. Grob. LC 80-1228. (Addiction in America Ser.). 1981. reprint ed. lib. bdg. 30.95 (*0-405-13586-6*) Ayer.

Opium: A History. Martin Booth. LC 98-14951. 381p. 1998. text 24.95 (*0-312-18643-6*) St Martin.

Opium: A History. Martin Booth. 1999. pap. 14.95 (*0-312-20667-4*, St Martins Paperbacks) St Martin.

***Opium: A Portrait of the Heavenly Demon.** Barbara Hodgson. LC 98-53661. 160p. 1999. 22.95 (*0-8118-2411-X*) Chronicle Bks.

Opium: Its Use, Abuse, & Cure; or, from Bondage to Freedom. Leslie E. Keeley. Ed. by Gerald N. Grob. LC 80-1270. (Addiction in America Ser.). (Illus.). 1981. reprint ed. lib. bdg. 15.95 (*0-405-13597-1*) Ayer.

Opium: Journal D'une Desintoxication. Jean Cocteau. 1930. pap. 15.75 (*0-685-11469-4*) Fr & Eur.

Opium: The Poisoned Poppy. Michael Robson. (Illus.). 85p. 1994. 38.00 (*962-7283-08-8*, Pub. by FormAsia) Weatherhill.

Opium Addiction in Chicago. Bingham Dai. LC 72-124503. (Criminology, Law Enforcement, & Social Problems Ser.: No. 126). 1970. 26.00 (*0-87585-126-6*) Patterson Smith.

Opium Addicts & Addiction. John A. Hawkins. Ed. by Gerald N. Grob. LC 80-1262. (Addiction in America Ser.). 1981. reprint ed. lib. bdg. 18.95 (*0-405-13588-2*) Ayer.

Opium & Empire: Chinese Society in Colonial Singapore, 1800-1910. Carl A. Trocki. LC 90-55123. (Asia East by South Ser.). (Illus.). 304p. 1991. text 45.00 (*0-8014-2390-2*) Cornell U Pr.

Opium & Foreign Policy: The Anglo-American Search for Order in Asia, 1912-1954. William O. Walker, III. LC 90-26026. xviii, 346p. (C). 1991. text 19.95 (*0-8078-1970-0*) U of NC Pr.

Opium & the Opium-Appetite. Alonzo Calkins. Ed. by Gerald N. Grob. LC 80-1215. (Addiction in America Ser.). 1981. reprint ed. lib. bdg. 38.95 (*0-405-13571-8*) Ayer.

Opium & the People: Opiate Use & Policy in 19th- & Early 20th-Century Britain. rev. ed. Virginia Berridge. 370p. 1998. 65.00 (*1-85343-413-2*, Pub. by Free Assoc Bks); pap. 25.00 (*1-85343-414-0*, Pub. by Free Assoc Bks) NYU Pr.

Opium As an International Problem: The Geneva Conferences. Westel W. Willoughby. LC 75-17252. (Social Problems & Social Policy Ser.). 1976. reprint ed. 47.95 (*0-405-07526-X*) Ayer.

Opium Clippers. Basil Lubbock. (C). 1987. 150.00 (*0-85174-241-6*) St Mut.

Opium Eating. Ed. by Gerald N. Grob. LC 80-1241. (Addiction in America Ser.). 1981. reprint ed. lib. bdg. 18.95 (*0-405-13611-0*) Ayer.

Opium Empire: Japanese Imperialism & Drug Trafficking in Asia, 1895-1945. John M. Jennings. LC 96-27454. 176p. 1997. 55.00 (*0-275-95759-4*, Praeger Pubs) Greenwood.

***Opium Empire & the Global Political Economy: Study of Asian Opium Trade.** Carl A. Trocki. (Illus.). 232p. (C). 1999. text 90.00 (*0-415-19918-2*) Routledge.

***Opium, Empire & The Global Political Economy: A Study of The Asian Opium Trade.** Carl A. Trocki. LC 99-22499. 1999. pap. 27.99 (*0-415-21500-5*) Routledge.

Opium for the Masses: A Practical Guide to Growing Poppies & Making Opium. Jim Hogshire. LC 94-76105. (Illus.). 116p. (Orig.). (C). 1994. pap. 14.95 (*1-55950-114-6*, 85186) Loompanics.

Opium Habit & Alcoholism. Fred H. Hubbard. Ed. by Gerald N. Grob. LC 80-1232. (Addiction in America Ser.). 1981. reprint ed. lib. bdg. 27.95 (*0-405-13591-2*) Ayer.

Opium Habit, with Suggestions As to the Remedy. Ed. by Horace Day & Gerald N. Grob. LC 80-1224. (Addiction in America Ser.). 1981. reprint ed. lib. bdg. 31.95 (*0-405-13580-7*) Ayer.

Opium of the Intellectuals. Raymond Aron. Tr. by Terence Kilmartin from FRE. LC 77-7400. 324p. 1977. lib. bdg. 69.50 (*0-8371-9672-8*, AROI, Greenwood Pr) Greenwood.

***Opium of the Intellectuals.** rev. ed. Raymond Aron. 467p. 2000. pap. 39.95 (*0-7658-0700-9*) Transaction Pubs.

Opium Poppy: Botany, Chemistry, & Pharmacology. Ed. by L. D. Kapoor. LC 94-20779. (Illus.). 326p. (C). 1995. 49.95 (*1-56024-923-4*) Haworth Pr.

Opium Poppy: Botany, Chemistry, & Pharmacology. Ed. by L. D. Kapoor. LC 94-20779. 326p. (C). 1997. pap. 19.95 (*0-7890-0202-7*) Haworth Pr.

Opium Poppy Garden: The Way of a Chinese Grower. William Griffith. Ed. by Dan Joy et al. (Illus.). 77p. 1993. pap. 14.95 (*0-914171-67-4*) Ronin Pub.

Opium Problem. Charles E. Terry & Mildred Pellens. LC 76-108232. (Criminology, Law Enforcement, & Social Problems Ser.: No. 115). (Illus.). 1970. reprint ed. 65.00 (*0-87585-115-0*) Patterson Smith.

***Opium Regimes: China, Britain & Japan, 1839-1952.** Timothy Brook & Bob T. Wakabayashi. LC 99-35149. (Illus.). 456p. 2000. pap. 22.95 (*0-520-22236-9*, Pub. by U CA Pr) Cal Prin Full Svc.

***Opium Regimes: China, Britain & Japan, 1839-1952.** Timothy Brook & Bob Tadashi Wakabayashi. LC 99-35149. (Illus.). 456p. 2000. 60.00 (*0-520-22009-9*, Pub. by U CA Pr) Cal Prin Full Svc.

Opium Smoking in America & China: A Study of Its Prevalence, & Effects, Immediate & Remote, on the Individual & the Nation. Harry H. Kane. LC 75-17227. (Social Problems & Social Policy Ser.). 1976. reprint ed. 17.95 (*0-405-07497-2*) Ayer.

***Opium, State & Society: China's Narco-Economy & the Guomindang, 1924-1937.** Edward R. Slack. LC 00-42315. 2001. pap. write for info. (*0-8248-2361-3*) UH Pr.

Opium Tea. Bianca Tam. Ed. by Richard L. Weaver & Ron Baron. (Illus.). 300p. 1990. 17.95 (*0-942139-02-X*) Tale Weaver.

Opium the Demon Flower. Sara Graham-Mulhall. Ed. by Gerald N. Grob. LC 80-1229. (Addiction in America Ser.). 1981. reprint ed. lib. bdg. 30.95 (*0-405-13587-4*) Ayer.

Opium to Java: Revenue Farming & Chinese Enterprise in Colonial Indonesia, 1860-1910. James R. Rush. LC 89-45974. (Asia East by South Ser.). (Illus.). 280p. 1990. text 45.00 (*0-8014-2218-3*) Cornell U Pr.

Opium Trade, 1910-1941, 6 vols, Set. LC 74-19745. 1974. 450.00 (*0-8420-1795-X*) Scholarly Res Inc.

Opium War: Barbarians in the Celestial Empire in the Early Part of the Nineteenth Century & the War by Which They Forced Her Gates Ajar. Peter W. Fay. LC 97-35261. 440p. 1998. pap. 18.95 (*0-8078-4714-3*) U of NC Pr.

Opium War Through Chinese Eyes. Arthur Waley. 256p. 1958. pap. 12.95 (*0-8047-0611-5*) Stanford U Pr.

Opium Wars. Phil Taggart. 40p. (Orig.). 1997. pap. 6.00 (*1-890887-01-3*) Mille Grazie.

OPL Optimization Programming Language. Pascal Van Hentenryck. LC 98-34698. (Illus.). 259p. 1999. pap. 30.00 (*0-262-72030-2*) MIT Pr.

OPLL: Ossification of the Posterior Longitudinal Ligament. K. Yonenobu et al. LC 96-27395. 220p. 1996. 175.00 (*4-431-70189-3*) Spr-Verlag.

OPM Comparable Worth - Pay Equity Study Overstates Women's Progress in Federal Workforce. National Committee on Pay Equity & Institute for Women's Policy Research Staff. 10p. 1987. pap. 5.00 (*0-685-29950-3*) Inst Womens Policy Rsch.

OPM Investigations Program: ESOP Transition : Hearing before the Subcommittee on Civil Service of the Committee on Government Reform & Oversight, House of Representatives, One Hundred Fourth Congress, Second Session, October 17, 1996. LC 98-161373. iii, 94 p. 1998. write for info. (*0-16-056025-X*) USGPO.

Opnieuw: Wie Is Jesus? Balans van 150 Jaar Onderzoek naar Jesus see Jesus Matters: 150 Years of Research

OPNQRYF by Example. Mike Dawson & Mike Manto. LC 99-6049. Orig. Title: Desktop Guide to OPNQRYF. 160p. 1999. pap. 39.95 (*1-58304-039-0*) News Four-Hund.

Opossum & the Great Firemaker: A Mexican Legend. Jan M. Mike. LC 92-36459. (Legends of the World Ser.). (Illus.). 32p. (J). (gr. 2-5). 1993. pap., teacher ed. 1.95 (*0-8167-3056-3*) Troll Communs.

Opossum & the Great Firemaker: A Mexican Legend. Jan M. Mike. LC 92-36459. (Legends of the World Ser.). (Illus.). 32p. (J). (gr. 2-5). 1997. lib. bdg. 18.60 (*0-8167-3055-5*) Troll Communs.

Opossum & the Great Firemaker: A Mexican Legend. Jan M. Mike. (Legends of the World Ser.). (J). 1993. 9.15 (*0-606-05526-6*, Pub. by Turtleback) Demco.

Opossum at Sycamore Road. Sally Walker. LC 97-8675. (Smithsonian's Backyard Ser.). (Illus.). 32p. (J). (ps-2). 1997. 15.95 (*1-56899-482-6*) Soundprints.

Opossum at Sycamore Road, Incl. large toy. Sally Walker. (Smithsonian's Backyard Ser.). (Illus.). 32p. (J). (ps-2). 1997. 32.95 (*1-56899-486-9*); 36.95 incl. audio (*1-56899-488-5*) Soundprints.

Opossum at Sycamore Road, Incl. Sm. & Lg. Plush Toy. Sally M. Walker. LC 97-8675. (Smithsonian Backyard Ser.). (Illus.). 32p. (J). (ps-2). 1997. 43.95 incl. audio (*1-56899-635-7*) Soundprints.

Opossum at Sycamore Road, Large Bk. Sally Walker. (Smithsonian Backyard Ser.). (Illus.). 32p. (J). (ps-2). 1997. 19.95 incl. audio (*1-56899-484-2*, BC5014) Soundprints.

Opossum at Sycamore Road, Micro bk. Sally Walker. LC 97-8675. (Smithsonian's Backyard Ser.). (Illus.). 32p. (J). (ps-2). 1997. 4.95 (*1-56899-483-4*); 9.95 incl. audio (*1-56899-490-7*) Soundprints.

Opossum at Sycamore Road, Micro bk., incl. small toy. Sally Walker. (Smithsonian's Backyard Ser.). (Illus.). 32p. (J). (ps-2). 1997. 12.95 (*1-56899-487-7*); 16.95 incl. audio (*1-56899-489-3*) Soundprints.

Opossums. Sandra Lee. LC 97-35222. (Illus.). 32p. (J). 1998. lib. bdg. 22.79 (*1-56766-480-6*) Childs World.

Opossums. Lynn M. Stone. LC 93-10724. (Nighttime Animals Discovery Library). 24p. (J). (gr. k-4). 1993. lib. bdg. 10.95 (*0-86593-295-6*) Rourke Corp.

Opossums, Shrews, & Moles of British Columbia. David W. Nagorsen. LC 97-124283. (Royal British Columbia Museum Handbook Ser.). (Illus.). 176p. 1996. pap. 24.95 (*0-7748-0563-3*) U of Wash Pr.

***Opothleyaholo & the Loyal Muskogee: Their Flight to Kansas in the Civil War.** Lela J. McBride. LC 99-48305. (Illus.). 256p. 1999. lib. bdg. 39.95 (*0-7864-0638-0*) McFarland & Co.

Opowiesc o Wolynskich Belwederczykach. Jozef Wira. LC 92-97279. (POL., Illus.). 280p. 1992. 22.50 (*0-9618215-1-5*) Belweder Pr.

Oppedisano. Joe Oppedisano. 72p. 1999. pap. 19.95 (*88-8158-211-2*, Pub. by Charta) Dist Art Pubs.

Oppenheim Secret Service Omnibus, 2 vols., Vol. 1. E. Phillips Oppenheim. (Spies & Intrigues Ser.: No. 1). 525p. 1984. pap. 8.95 (*0-918172-13-6*) Leetes Isl.

Oppenheim Secret Service Omnibus, 2 vols., Vol. 2. E. Phillips Oppenheim. (Spies & Intrigues Ser.: No. 1). 440p. 1984. pap. 8.95 (*0-918172-14-4*) Leetes Isl.

Oppenheim Toy Portfolio: Baby & Toddler Play Book. Joanne F. Oppenheim. (Oppenheim Toy Portfolio Ser.). 1999. pap. 5.95 (*0-9664823-3-6*) Oppenheim Toy.

***Oppenheim Toy Portfolio 2001: The Best Toys, Books, Videos, Music & Software for Kids. annuals Joanne Oppenheim et al. 378p. 2000. 12.00 (*0-9664823-6-0*) Oppenheim Toy.**

More than 150,000 sold, this annual book has been featured on Oprah, NBC's Today Show & CNN. The experts from the Oppenheim Toy Portfolio, the nationally recognized consumer organization, help guide parents to find the best designed & most educational toys, books, recordings, videos & software for children from infancy to age ten. With reviews of more than 1,000 expert & kid-tested new & classic products, the book also contains features on products for kids with special needs, multicultural toys, books & videos plus the 2001 Platinum Award Lists. The guide is recommended by Family Circle, USA Today, Baby Talk & Working Mother Magazine. For information contact: Oppenheim Toy Portfolio, Inc., 40 East 9th Street, Suite 14M, New York, NY 10003; Phone: 212-598-0502; Fax: 212-598-9709; website: www.toyportfolio.com; e-mail: stephanie@toyportfolio.com. ***Publisher Paid Annotation.***

Oppenheim Toy Portfolio: 2000 Edition: The Best Toys, Books, Video, Music & Software for Kids. 7th rev. ed. Joanne F. Oppenheim et al. (Oppenheim Toy Portfolio Ser.). (Illus.). 342p. 1999. pap. 12.00 (*0-9664823-2-8*) Oppenheim Toy.

Oppenheimer's Diagnostic Neuropathology: A Practical Manual. 2nd ed. Margaret M. Esiri. (Illus.). 480p. 1996. 295.00 (*0-86542-915-4*) Blackwell Sci.

Oppenheims International law V1, Bks. 1& 2. 9th ed. Ed. by Robert Jennings & Arthur Watts. 1500p. (C). 1997. pap. text 132.50 (*0-582-30245-5*, 15707) Gaunt.

Oppermanns. Lion Feuchtwanger. 546p. 1983. pap. 8.95 (*0-88184-063-7*) Carroll & Graf.

Oppianus: Index in Halieutica Oppiani Cilicis et in Cynegetica Poetae Apameensis. Ed. by A. W. James. 132p. 1970. write for info. (*0-318-71966-5*) G Olms Pubs.

Oppianus - Index in Halieutica Oppiani Cilicis et in Cynegetica Poetae Apameensis. Ed. by A. W. James. 132p. 1970. write for info. (*0-318-70651-2*) G Olms Pubs.

Oppianus - Oppiani Apamensis Cynegeticorum Concordantia. Manolis Papathomopoulos. 471p. 1997. write for info. (*3-487-10224-2*) G Olms Pubs.

Opponents of Paul in Second Corinthians. Dieter Georgi. 464p. 1997. pap. 39.95 (*0-567-08539-2*, Pub. by T & T Clark) Bks Intl VA.

Opponents of Third Isaiah: Reconstructing the Cultic History of the Restoration. Brooks Schramm. (JSOT Supplement Ser.: No. 193). 216p. 1995. 60.00 (*1-85075-538-8*, Pub. by Sheffield Acad) CUP Services.

Opponents of War, 1917-1918. Horace C. Peterson & Gilbert C. Fite. LC 85-30570. 402p. 1986. reprint ed. lib. bdg. 89.50 (*0-313-25132-0*, FPOP, Greenwood Pr) Greenwood.

Opportunistic Infections in Patients with the Acquired Immunodeficiency Syndrome. Leoung & Mills. (Infectious Disease & Therapy Ser.: Vol. 3). (Illus.). 476p. 1989. text 155.00 (*0-8247-8080-9*) Dekker.

Opportunistic Intracellular Bacteria & Immunity. Ed. by L. J. Paradise et al. LC 98-42016. (Infectious Agents & Pathogenesis Ser.). (Illus.). 302p. (C). 1998. text 125.00 (*0-306-45894-2*, Kluwer Plenum) Kluwer Academic.

Opportunistic Mycoses of Man & Other Animals. J. M. Smith. 258p. 1989. text 70.00 (*0-85198-638-2*) OUP.

Opportunistic Mycosis. K. R. Joshi. 1995. pap. 180.00 (*81-7233-109-6*, Pub. by Scientific Pubs) St Mut.

Opportunites in Fitness Careers. Jean Rosenbaum & Mary Prine. (Illus.). 146p. 1988. 13.95 (*0-8442-6151-3*, VGM Career) NTC Contemp Pub Co.

Opportunites in Fitness Careers. Jean Rosenbaum & Mary Prine. (Illus.). 146p. 1991. pap. 10.95 (*0-8442-6152-1*, VGM Career) NTC Contemp Pub Co.

***Opportunites in Performing Arts.** rev. ed. Bonnie Bjorguine Bekken. LC 00-39269. (Opportunities Ser.). (Illus.). 2000. pap. 11.95 (*0-658-00471-9*) NTC Contemp Pub Co.

Opportunities. Edward De Bono. 1990. 25.00 (*0-317-90563-5*) Intl Ctr Creat Think.

Opportunities & Challenges: An Administrator's Guide to the New IDEA. Leigh Manasevit et al. Ed. by Ginger R. O'Neil. LC 97-74687. 205p. 1997. pap. 39.95 (*0-87652-230-4*, 760) Am Assn Sch Admin.

Opportunities & Challenges in an Ageing Society: Proceedings of the Colloquium, Amsterdam, the Netherlands, 26-28 October 1989. Ed. by W. J. Van den Heuvel et al. (Verhandelingen der Koninklijke Nederlandse Akademie van Wetenschappen, Afd. Letterkunde, Nieuwe Reeks Ser.: No. 151). 190p. pap. 50.00 (*0-444-85744-3*) Elsevier.

Opportunities & Constraints of Community Language Teaching. Sjaak Kroon. LC 92-20524. 1992. pap. 29.95 (*1-85359-164-5*, Pub. by Multilingual Matters) Taylor & Francis.

Opportunities & Constraints of Parallel Computing. Ed. by J. L. Sanz. (Illus.). xi, 166p. 1989. 39.00 (*0-387-97117-3*) Spr-Verlag.

Opportunities & Dangers of Soviet-Cuban Expansion: Towards a Pragmatic U. S. Policy. Richard J. Payne. LC 87-26778. 261p. (C). 1988. text 21.50 (*0-88706-796-4*) State U NY Pr.

Opportunities & Directions in Antisense & Other Oligonucleotide-Based Technologies. Market Intelligence Staff. 218p. 1993. 1495.00 (*1-56753-603-4*) Frost & Sullivan.

***Opportunities & Hazards of Agricultural Biotechnology.** Evan Schulz. LC 00-9426. 2000. write for info. (*1-888773-04-9*) Econ Strategy.

Opportunities & Limitations in Religious Broadcasting. Peter Elvy. 176p. (C). 1992. pap. 39.00 (*1-870126-15-7*, Pub. by St Andrew) St Mut.

Opportunities & Priorities in Arctic Geoscience. National Research Council Staff. 80p. 1991. pap. text 19.00 (*0-309-04485-5*) Natl Acad Pr.

Opportunities Denied, Opportunities Diminished: Racial Discrimination in Hiring. Margery A. Turner et al. LC 91-21384. (Reports: No. 91-9). (Illus.). 120p. (C). 1991. pap. text 20.50 (*0-87766-554-0*); lib. bdg. 52.00 (*0-87766-553-2*) Urban Inst.

Opportunities Do Not Knock. large type ed. Tom Magee & Ray Hoy. (Illus.). 300p. Date not set. pap. 24.95 (*1-56559-902-0*) HGI-Over Fifty.

Opportunities for Biological Nitrogen Fixation in Rice & Other Non-Legumes. Ed. by Jagdish K. Ladha et al. (Developments in Plant & Soil Sciences Ser.: No. 75). 232p. 1997. text 167.00 (*0-7923-4514-2*) Kluwer Academic.

Opportunities for Biological Nitrogen Fixation in Rice & Other Non-Legumes: Papers Presented at the Second Working Group Meeting of the Frontier Project on Nitrogen Fixation in Rice Held at the National Institute for Biotechnology & Genetic Engineering (Nibge), Faislabad, Pakistan, 13-15 October 1996. J. K. Ladha et al. LC 97-30255. 1997. text. write for info. (*0-7923-4747-1*) Kluwer Academic.

Opportunities for Daily Choice Making. Linda M. Bambara & Freya Koger. Ed. by Diane M. Browder. LC 96-35425. (Innovations Ser.: Vol. 8). (Illus.). 48p. (Orig.). 1996. pap. 21.95 (*0-940898-44-6*) Am Assn Mental.

Opportunities for Energy Investment in Russia & the Republics in the 1990s. Alfred J. Boulos. 24p. 1992. pap. 10.00 (*0-918714-33-8*) Intl Res Ctr Energy.

Opportunities for Excellence: Supporting the Frontline Workforce (for the Mentally Retarded) Ed. by Tecla Jaskulski & William Ebenstein. 158p. (C). 1997. reprint ed. pap. text 25.00 (*0-7881-4254-2*) DIANE Pub.

Opportunities for Innovation: Advanced Manufacturing Technology. 1995. lib. bdg. 273.99 (*0-8490-8364-8*) Gordon Pr.

Opportunities for Innovation: Biotechnology. 1995. lib. bdg. 275.95 (*0-8490-8366-4*) Gordon Pr.

Opportunities for Innovation: Chemical & Biological Sensors. 1995. lib. bdg. 279.95 (*0-8490-8363-X*) Gordon Pr.

Opportunities for Innovation: Optoelectronics. Ed. by David E. Edgerly. 423p. 1995. pap. 59.95 (*1-56676-367-3*, 763673) Technomic.

Opportunities for Innovation: Polymer Composites. 1995. lib. bdg. 275.99 (*0-8490-8365-6*) Gordon Pr.

Opportunities for Innovation Biotechnology. Ed. by Robert M. Busche. 273p. 1994. pap. 44.95 (*1-56676-253-7*, 762537) Technomic.

Opportunities for License, 1994: Research Development Corporation of Japan (JRDC) (Illus.). 71p. (Orig.). (C). 1996. pap. text 45.00 (*0-7881-2555-9*) DIANE Pub.

Opportunities for Newly Released Offenders. Josh Hoekstra. 1996. 27.50 (*0-938609-05-X*) Graduate Group.

Opportunities for Phytochemistry in Plant Biotechnology. Ed. by E. E. Conn. (Recent Advances in Phytochemistry Ser.: Vol. 22). (Illus.). 190p. 1988. 65.00 (*0-306-42936-5*, Plenum Trade) Perseus Pubng.

Opportunities for Plastics in Electronic Components. LC 98-143082. (Illus.). 163p. 1995. 2650.00 (*1-56965-261-9*, P222) BCC.

Opportunities for Plastics in Household Applications. 1993. 1750.00 (*0-89336-932-2*, P-081B) BCC.

O

Opportunities for Plastics in Toys & Outdoor Playground Equipment. 112p. 1992. 1750.00 (*0-89336-912-8*, P-081A) BCC.

Opportunities for Productivity Improvement: One Day RETEC, Ramada Inn Airport, Milwaukee, Wisconsin, March 26, 1985. Society of Plastics Engineers Staff. LC HD9661.. (Illus.). 78p. reprint ed. pap. 30.00 (*0-608-15140-8*, 202580500046) Bks Demand.

Opportunities for Reference Services: The Bright Side of Reference Services in the 1990's. Ed. by Bill Katz. LC 91-3285. (Reference Librarian Ser.: No. 33). (Illus.). 213p. 1991. lib. bdg. 39.95 (*1-56024-137-3*) Haworth Pr.

Opportunities for Transferring Defence Related Advanced Technologies, No. GB-144. Business Communications Co., Inc. Staff. 280p. 1991. 2950.00 (*0-89336-839-3*) BCC.

Opportunities in Accounting Careers. Arthur Lodge. LC 76-42889. (Illus.). (YA). (gr. 8 up). 1985. 13.95 (*0-8442-6341-9*, VGM Career) NTC Contemp Pub Co.

Opportunities in Accounting Careers. Arthur Lodge. LC 76-42889. (Illus.). (YA). (gr. 8 up). 1988. pap. 10.95 (*0-8442-6342-7*, VGM Career) NTC Contemp Pub Co.

Opportunities in Accounting Careers. Martin Rosenberg. (Opportunities in . . . Ser.). (Illus.). 160p. pap. 11.95 (*0-8442-4636-0*, 46360, Natl Textbk Co) NTC Contemp Pub Co.

Opportunities in Accounting Careers. Martin Rosenberg. (Illus.). 160p. 1993. pap. 10.95 (*0-8442-8578-1*, VGM Career) NTC Contemp Pub Co.

Opportunities in Accounting Careers. Martin Rosenberg. (Illus.). 160p. 1994. 13.95 (*0-8442-8577-3*, VGM Career) NTC Contemp Pub Co.

Opportunities in Accounting Careers. Martin Rosenberg. (Opportunities in...Ser.). 160p. 1996. 14.95 (*0-8442-4635-2*, 46352, Natl Textbk Co) NTC Contemp Pub Co.

Opportunities in Acting Careers. rev. ed. Dick Moore. LC 74-25904. (Illus.). (C). 1989. 13.95 (*0-8442-6229-3*, VGM Career) NTC Contemp Pub Co.

*__Opportunities in Adult Education Careers.__ Blythe Camenson. LC 99-37763. (Opportunities in...Ser.). 160p. 1999. pap. 11.95 (*0-658-00109-4*, 001094) NTC Contemp Pub Co.

Opportunities in Advertising. Harry C. Groome, Jr. (Illus.). 160p. 1995. 13.95 (*0-8442-6271-4*, VGM Career) NTC Contemp Pub Co.

Opportunities in Advertising. S. William Pattis. (Illus.). 160p. 1993. pap. 10.95 (*0-8442-6272-2*, VGM Career) NTC Contemp Pub Co.

Opportunities in Advertising Careers. S. William Pattis. LC 94-49545. (Opportunities In . . . Ser.). (Illus.). 160p. pap. 11.95 (*0-8442-4443-0*, 44430, VGM Career) NTC Contemp Pub Co.

Opportunities in Advertising Careers. S. William Pattis. LC 94-49545. (Illus.). 160p. 1995. 14.95 (*0-8442-4442-2*, 44422, VGM Career) NTC Contemp Pub Co.

Opportunities in Aerospace Careers. Wallace R. Maples. (Illus.). 160p. 1991. 13.95 (*0-8442-8650-8*, VGM Career) NTC Contemp Pub Co.

Opportunities in Aerospace Careers. Wallace R. Maples. (Illus.). 160p. 1993. pap. 10.95 (*0-8442-8651-6*, VGM Career) NTC Contemp Pub Co.

Opportunities in Aerospace Careers. rev. ed. Wallace R. Maples. (Opportunities in... Ser.). (Illus.). 160p. 1995. 14.95 (*0-8442-4577-1*, 45771, Natl Textbk Co); pap. 11.95 (*0-8442-4579-8*, 45798, Natl Textbk Co) NTC Contemp Pub Co.

Opportunities in Agriculture Careers. William C. White & Donald N. Collins. (Illus.). 160p. 1993. pap. 10.95 (*0-8442-6555-1*, VGM Career) NTC Contemp Pub Co.

Opportunities in Agriculture Careers. William C. White & Donald N. Collins. (Illus.). 160p. 1995. 13.95 (*0-8442-6554-3*, VGM Career) NTC Contemp Pub Co.

Opportunities in Aircraft Maintenance Careers. Douglas S. Carmody. (Opportunities in... Ser.). 160p. 1999. pap. 11.95 (*0-8442-3581-4*) NTC Contemp Pub Co.

Opportunities in Airline Careers. Adrian A. Paradis. LC 96-27789. (Opportunities in... Ser.). (Illus.). 160p. pap. 11.95 (*0-8442-4652-2*, 46522, Natl Textbk Co) NTC Contemp Pub Co.

Opportunities in Airline Careers. Adrian A. Paradis. (Illus.). 160p. 1989. 13.95 (*0-8442-6028-2*, VGM Career) NTC Contemp Pub Co.

Opportunities in Airline Careers. Adrian A. Paradis. (Illus.). 160p. 1993. pap. 10.95 (*0-8442-6029-0*, VGM Career) NTC Contemp Pub Co.

Opportunities in Airline Careers. Adrian A. Paradis. LC 96-27789. (Opportunities in... Ser.). (Illus.). 160p. 1996. 14.95 (*0-8442-4651-4*, 46514, Natl Textbk Co) NTC Contemp Pub Co.

Opportunities in Alabama Agriculture. Tito Perdue. 222p. 1994. 18.00 (*1-880909-24-3*) Baskerville.

Opportunities in Animal & Pet Care. Mary P. Lee & Richard S. Lee. (Illus.). 160p. 1991. 13.95 (*0-8442-6244-7*, VGM Career) NTC Contemp Pub Co.

Opportunities in Animal & Pet Care. Mary P. Lee & Richard S. Lee. (Illus.). 160p. 1993. pap. 10.95 (*0-8442-6245-5*, VGM Career) NTC Contemp Pub Co.

Opportunities in Animal & Pet Care Careers. Mary P. Lee & Richard S. Lee. LC 93-17661. (Opportunities In . . . Ser.). (Illus.). 160p. pap. 11.95 (*0-8442-4081-8*, 40818, VGM Career) NTC Contemp Pub Co.

Opportunities in Animal & Pet Care Careers. Mary P. Lee & Richard S. Lee. LC 93-17661. (Illus.). 160p. 1994. 14.95 (*0-8442-4079-6*, 40796, VGM Career) NTC Contemp Pub Co.

*__Opportunities in Animation & Cartooning Careers.__ Terence J. Sacks. LC 99-89626. (Opportunities in... Ser.). 160p. 2000. pap. 11.95 (*0-658-00183-3*, 001833) NTC Contemp Pub Co.

*__Opportunities in Animation & Cartooning Careers.__ J. Sacks Terence. LC 99-89626. (Opportunities in... Ser.). 160p. 2000. 14.95 (*0-658-00182-5*, 001825) NTC Contemp Pub Co.

Opportunities in Appraising-Valuation Sciences. Ed. by Dexter MacBride. (Illus.). 149p. 1993. pap. 10.95 (*0-8442-6660-4*, VGM Career) NTC Contemp Pub Co.

Opportunities in Appraising-Valuation Sciences. Ed. by Dexter MacBride. (Illus.). 149p. 1995. 13.95 (*0-8442-6659-0*, VGM Career) NTC Contemp Pub Co.

Opportunities in Aquaculture. (Report Ser.: No. GA-068R). 117p. 1993. 2450.00 (*0-89336-987-X*) BCC.

Opportunities in Aquatics: A Report of the 1984 National Conference, Fort Worth, TX, November 8-11, 1984. Council for National Cooperation in Aquatics Staff. Ed. by Louise Priest & Ann Crowner. LC GV0770.. (Illus.). 137p. reprint ed. pap. 42.50 (*0-8357-3837-X*, 203656300004) Bks Demand.

*__Opportunities in Architectural Careers.__ rev. ed. Robert J. Piper & Richard D. Rush. LC 00-39270. (VGM Opportunities Ser.). 2000. pap. write for info. (*0-658-00475-1*) NTC Contemp Pub Co.

Opportunities in Architecture Careers. Robert J. Piper & Richard D. Rush. LC 92-20018. (Opportunities In . . . Ser.). 160p. pap. 12.95 (*0-8442-4039-7*, 297OIARC, VGM Career) NTC Contemp Pub Co.

Opportunities in Architecture Careers. Robert J. Piper & Richard D. Rush. LC 92-20018. (Opportunities in...Ser.). 160p. 1994. 14.95 (*0-8442-4038-9*, VGM Career) NTC Contemp Pub Co.

Opportunities in Asia: An Assessment of Construction Trends, Needs & Potential Collaboration. Civil Engineering Research Foundation Staff. LC 97-20863. 276p. 1997. 75.00 (*0-7844-0257-4*) Am Soc Civil Eng.

Opportunities in Automotive Service Careers. Ed. by Robert Weber. (Illus.). 160p. 1995. 13.95 (*0-8442-6502-0*, VGM Career) NTC Contemp Pub Co.

Opportunities in Automotive Services. Phillip Perry & Robert M. Weber. LC 96-27797. (Opportunities in... Ser.). (Illus.). 160p. 1996. 14.95 (*0-8442-4672-7*, 46727, Natl Textbk Co) NTC Contemp Pub Co.

Opportunities in Banking. Adrian A. Paradis. (Illus.). 160p. 1988. 13.95 (*0-8442-6213-7*, VGM Career) NTC Contemp Pub Co.

Opportunities in Banking. Adrian A. Paradis. (Illus.). 160p. 1993. pap. 10.95 (*0-8442-6214-5*, VGM Career) NTC Contemp Pub Co.

Opportunities in Banking Careers. Philip Perry. (Opportunities In . . . Ser.). (Illus.). 160p. pap. 11.95 (*0-8442-4050-8*, 40508, VGM Career) NTC Contemp Pub Co.

Opportunities in Banking Careers. Philip Perry. (Opportunities in...Ser.). (Illus.). 160p. 1994. 14.95 (*0-8442-4049-4*, 40494, VGM Career) NTC Contemp Pub Co.

Opportunities in Basic Soil Science Research. G. Sposito & R. J. Reginato. 109p. 1992. 5.00 (*0-89118-799-5*) Soil Sci Soc Am.

Opportunities in Beauty Culture Careers. Susan W. Gearhart. (Illus.). 160p. 1991. 13.95 (*0-8442-6518-7*, VGM Career) NTC Contemp Pub Co.

Opportunities in Beauty Culture Careers. Susan W. Gearhart. (Illus.). 160p. 1993. pap. 10.95 (*0-8442-6519-5*, VGM Career) NTC Contemp Pub Co.

Opportunities in Beauty Culture Careers. rev. ed. Susan W. Gearhart. (Opportunities in... Ser.). 160p. pap. 11.95 (*0-8442-4611-5*, 46115, Natl Textbk Co) NTC Contemp Pub Co.

Opportunities in Beauty Culture Careers. rev. ed. Susan W. Gearhart. (Opportunities in...Ser.). 160p. 1996. 14.95 (*0-8442-4610-7*, 46107, Natl Textbk Co) NTC Contemp Pub Co.

Opportunities in Biological Science. Charles A. Winter. (Illus.). 160p. 1993. 14.95 (*0-8442-8626-5*, VGM Career) NTC Contemp Pub Co.

Opportunities in Biological Science Careers. Charles A. Winter. LC 97-44573. (Opportunities in...Ser.). (Illus.). 160p. 1998. 14.95 (*0-8442-2300-X*, 2300x, VGM Career); pap. 11.95 (*0-8442-2301-8*, 23018, VGM Career) NTC Contemp Pub Co.

Opportunities in Biology. National Research Council Staff. LC 89-13098. (Illus.). 468p. reprint ed. pap. 145.10 (*0-7837-5356-X*, 204511800005) Bks Demand.

Opportunities in Biotechnology Careers. Sheldon S. Brown. 1993. pap. 10.95 (*0-8442-8647-8*, VGM Career) NTC Contemp Pub Co.

Opportunities in Biotechnology Careers. Sheldon S. Brown. 1993. 13.95 (*0-8442-8645-1*, VGM Career) NTC Contemp Pub Co.

Opportunities in Biotechnology Careers. Sheldon S. Brown. Ed. by Julie Han. LC 93-47487. (Opportunities in...Ser.). (Illus.). 160p. 1995. 14.95 (*0-8442-4125-3*, 41253, VGM Career) NTC Contemp Pub Co.

Opportunities in Biotechnology Careers. 2nd ed. Sheldon S. Brown. Ed. by Julie Han. LC 93-47487. (Opportunities In . . . Ser.). (Illus.). 160p. pap. 11.95 (*0-8442-4126-1*, 41261, VGM Career) NTC Contemp Pub Co.

Opportunities in Book Publishing. Robert A. Carter. (Illus.). 160p. 1989. 13.95 (*0-8442-6139-4*, VGM Career) NTC Contemp Pub Co.

Opportunities in Book Publishing. Robert A. Carter. (Illus.). 160p. 1993. pap. 10.95 (*0-8442-6140-8*, VGM Career) NTC Contemp Pub Co.

Opportunities in Broadcasting. Elmo I. Ellis. (Illus.). 151p. 1990. 13.95 (*0-8442-6149-1*, VGM Career) NTC Contemp Pub Co.

Opportunities in Broadcasting. Elmo I. Ellis. (Illus.). 151p. 1993. pap. 10.95 (*0-8442-6150-5*, VGM Career) NTC Contemp Pub Co.

Opportunities in Building Careers. 2nd ed. Michael Sumichrast. LC 98-36773. (Opportunities in...Ser.). 160p. 1998. 14.95 (*0-8442-1816-2*, 18162, VGM Career) NTC Contemp Pub Co.

Opportunities in Building Construction Trades. 2nd ed. Michael Sumichrast. LC 98-36773. (Opportunities Ser.). 160p. 1998. pap. 11.95 (*0-8442-1818-9*, VGM Career) NTC Contemp Pub Co.

Opportunities in Business Communications. Robert Deen. (Illus.). 160p. 1990. 14.95 (*0-8442-6154-8*, 61548, VGM Career) NTC Contemp Pub Co.

Opportunities in Business Management. Irene M. Place. (Illus.). 150p. 1985. 13.95 (*0-8442-6185-8*, VGM Career) NTC Contemp Pub Co.

Opportunities in Business Management. Irene M. Place. (Illus.). 150p. 1988. pap. 10.95 (*0-8442-6186-6*, VGM Career) NTC Contemp Pub Co.

Opportunities in Business Management Careers. rev. ed. Irene M. Place. LC 90-50738. (Opportunities In . . . Ser.). 160p. (YA). (gr. 7 up). pap. 12.95 (*0-8442-8160-3*, 297OIBUM, VGM Career) NTC Contemp Pub Co.

Opportunities in Business Management Careers. rev. ed. Irene M. Place. LC 90-50738. (Opportunities in...Ser.). 160p. (YA). (gr. 7 up). 1994. 14.95 (*0-8442-8158-1*, VGM Career) NTC Contemp Pub Co.

Opportunities in Business Management Careers. rev. ed. Irene M. Place & Lewis Baratz. LC 97-21307. (Opportunities in...Ser.). 160p. 1997. pap. 11.95 (*0-8442-2326-3*, 23263) NTC Contemp Pub Co.

Opportunities in Business Management Careers. rev. ed. Irene M. Place & Lewis Baratz. LC 97-21307. (Opportunities in...Ser.). (Illus.). 160p. 1997. 14.95 (*0-8442-2325-5*, 23255) NTC Contemp Pub Co.

Opportunities in Cable Television. Jan Bone. (Illus.). 160p. 1986. 13.95 (*0-8442-6258-7*, VGM Career) NTC Contemp Pub Co.

Opportunities in Cable Television. Jan Bone. (Illus.). 160p. 1988. pap. 10.95 (*0-8442-6259-5*, VGM Career) NTC Contemp Pub Co.

Opportunities in Cable Television Careers. Jan Bone. LC 92-18317. (Opportunities in...Ser.). (Illus.). 160p. 1994. 14.95 (*0-8442-4026-5*, VGM Career) NTC Contemp Pub Co.

Opportunities in Carpentry Careers. Roger Sheldon. LC 92-15590. (Opportunities In . . . Ser.). (Illus.). 160p. pap. 12.95 (*0-8442-4030-3*, 297OICARP, VGM Career) NTC Contemp Pub Co.

Opportunities in Carpentry Careers. Roger Sheldon. LC 92-15590. (Opportunities in...Ser.). (Illus.). 160p. 1994. 14.95 (*0-8442-4028-1*, VGM Career) NTC Contemp Pub Co.

Opportunities in Carpentry Careers. Roger Sheldon. LC 99-34063. (Opportunities in... Ser.). 160p. 1999. 14.95 (*0-8442-3408-7*) NTC Contemp Pub Co.

Opportunities in Carpentry Careers. rev. ed. Roger Sheldon. LC 99-34063. (Opportunities in... Ser.). 160p. 1999. pap. 11.95 (*0-8442-3424-9*) NTC Contemp Pub Co.

Opportunities in Chemical Engineering. David L. Olsson et al. (Opportunities In . . . Ser.). (Illus.). 160p. pap. 12.95 (*0-8442-6588-8*, 297ICHEME, VGM Career) NTC Contemp Pub Co.

Opportunities in Chemistry. National Research Council Staff. 334p. (C). 1985. text 34.95 (*0-309-03633-X*) Natl Acad Pr.

Opportunities in Chemistry: Today & Tomorrow. George C. Pimentel & Janice A. Coonrod. Ed. by National Research Council Staff. 256p. (Orig.). (C). 1987. pap. text 10.00 (*0-309-03742-5*) Natl Acad Pr.

Opportunities in Chemistry Careers. John H. Woodburn. LC 96-9350. (Opportunities in... Ser.). (Illus.). 160p. 1996. 14.95 (*0-8442-4653-0*, 46530, Natl Textbk Co) NTC Contemp Pub Co.

Opportunities in Chemistry Careers. Jonn H. Woodburn. LC 96-9350. (Opportunities in... Ser.). (Illus.). 160p. pap. 11.95 (*0-8442-4654-9*, 46549, Natl Textbk Co) NTC Contemp Pub Co.

Opportunities in Child Care. Renee Wittenberg. (Illus.). 160p. 1990. 13.95 (*0-8442-6022-3*, VGM Career) NTC Contemp Pub Co.

Opportunities in Child Care. Renee Wittenberg. (Illus.). 160p. 1993. pap. 10.95 (*0-8442-6023-1*, VGM Career) NTC Contemp Pub Co.

Opportunities in Child Care Careers. Renee Wittenberg. (Opportunities In . . . Ser.). (Illus.). 160p. pap. 11.95 (*0-8442-4401-5*, 44015, VGM Career) NTC Contemp Pub Co.

Opportunities in Child Care Careers. Renee Wittenberg. (Opportunities in...Ser.). (Illus.). 160p. 1994. 14.95 (*0-8442-4400-7*, 44007, VGM Career) NTC Contemp Pub Co.

Opportunities in Chiral Technology: Emphasizing Enabling Products. Philip Rotheim. LC 96-143425. 290p. 1995. 2950.00 (*1-56965-031-4*, C079R) BCC.

Opportunities in Chiropractic Careers. R. C. Schafer. 160p. 1994. pap. 10.95 (*0-8442-4132-6*, VGM Career) NTC Contemp Pub Co.

Opportunities in Chiropractic Health Careers. R. C. Shafer. (Opportunities In . . . Ser.). (Illus.). 160p. pap. 12.95 (*0-8442-6566-7*, 297OICHI, VGM Career) NTC Contemp Pub Co.

Opportunities in Chiropractic Health Careers. R. C. Shafer. (Illus.). 160p. 1992. 14.95 (*0-8442-6565-9*, VGM Career) NTC Contemp Pub Co.

Opportunities in Civil Engineering. D. Joseph Hagerty & John E. Heer, Jr. (Illus.). 160p. 1987. 13.95 (*0-8442-6164-5*, VGM Career) NTC Contemp Pub Co.

Opportunities in Civil Engineering. D. Joseph Hagerty & John E. Heer, Jr. (Illus.). 160p. 1994. pap. 10.95 (*0-8442-6165-3*, VGM Career) NTC Contemp Pub Co.

Opportunities in Civil Engineering Careers. Joseph D. Hagerty et al. LC 96-26672. (Opportunities in... Ser.). (Illus.). 160p. pap. 11.95 (*0-8442-4661-1*, 46611, Natl Textbk Co) NTC Contemp Pub Co.

Opportunities in Civil Engineering Careers. Joseph D. Hagerty et al. LC 96-26672. (Opportunities in... Ser.). (Illus.). 160p. 1996. 14.95 (*0-8442-4660-3*, 46603, Natl Textbk Co) NTC Contemp Pub Co.

Opportunities in Commercial Art & Graphic Design. Barbara Gordon. (Illus.). 160p. 1989. pap. 10.95 (*0-8442-6294-3*, VGM Career) NTC Contemp Pub Co.

Opportunities in Commercial Art & Graphic Design. Barbara Gordon. (Illus.). 160p. 1993. 13.95 (*0-8442-6293-5*, VGM Career) NTC Contemp Pub Co.

Opportunities in Commercial Art & Graphic Design Careers. Barbara Gordon. (Opportunities in...Ser.). (Illus.). 160p. 1997. 14.95 (*0-8442-2321-2*, 23212, VGM Career); pap. 11.95 (*0-8442-2322-0*, 23212, VGM Career) NTC Contemp Pub Co.

Opportunities in Commercial Art & Graphic Design Careers. 2nd ed. Barbara Gordon. (Opportunities in...Ser.). (Illus.). 160p. 1994. 14.95 (*0-8442-4005-2*, VGM Career) NTC Contemp Pub Co.

Opportunities in Commercial Art & Graphic Design Careers. 2nd ed. Barbara Gordon. LC 97-35764. (Opportunities In . . . Ser.). (Illus.). 160p. 1997. pap. 12.95 (*0-8442-4006-0*, 297OCA&GD, VGM Career) NTC Contemp Pub Co.

Opportunities in Computer Aided Design & Computer Aided Manufacturing Careers (CAD-CAM) Jan Bone. LC 93-17885. (Opportunities in...Ser.). (Illus.). 160p. 1994. 14.95 (*0-8442-4084-2*, 40842, VGM Career) NTC Contemp Pub Co.

Opportunities in Computer Maintenance Careers. Elliott S. Kanter. LC 94-49351. (Opportunities In . . . Ser.). (Illus.). 160p. pap. 11.95 (*0-8442-4445-7*, 44457, VGM Career) NTC Contemp Pub Co.

Opportunities in Computer Maintenance Careers. Elliott S. Kanter. LC 94-49351. (Opportunities in...Ser.). (Illus.). 160p. 1995. 14.95 (*0-8442-4444-9*, 44449, VGM Career) NTC Contemp Pub Co.

Opportunities in Computer Science. Julie L. Kling. (Illus.). 144p. 1987. pap. 10.95 (*0-8442-6239-0*, VGM Career) NTC Contemp Pub Co.

Opportunities in Computer Science. Julie L. Kling. (Illus.). 144p. 1995. 13.95 (*0-8442-6238-2*, VGM Career) NTC Contemp Pub Co.

An Asterisk (*) at the beginning of an entry indicates that the title is appearing for the first time.

Opportunities in Computer Science Careers. Julie L. Kling. 160p. 1994. 14.95 (*0-8442-8580-3*, VGM Career) NTC Contemp Pub Co.

Opportunities in Computer Systems Careers. rev. ed. Julie K. Burn. (Opportunities In . . . Ser.). (Illus.). 160p. pap. 11.95 (*0-8442-4599-2*, 45992, Natl Textbk Co) NTC Contemp Pub Co.

Opportunities in Computer Systems Careers. rev. ed. Julie K. Burns. (Opportunities in...Ser.). (Illus.). 160p. 1996. 14.95 (*0-8442-4598-4*, 45984, Natl Textbk Co) NTC Contemp Pub Co.

Opportunities in Counseling & Development. Neale J. Baxter. (Illus.). 146p. 1988. 13.95 (*0-8442-6182-3*, VGM Career); pap. 10.95 (*0-8442-6183-1*, VGM Career) NTC Contemp Pub Co.

Opportunities in Counseling & Development Careers. 1989. 13.95 (*0-8442-8656-7*, VGM Career) NTC Contemp Pub Co.

Opportunities in Counseling & Development Careers. 1993. pap. 10.95 (*0-8442-8657-5*, VGM Career) NTC Contemp Pub Co.

Opportunities in Counseling & Development Careers. Neale J. Baxter & Mark U. Toch. LC 93-46078. 160p. 1994. pap. 11.95 (*0-8442-4098-2*, VGM Career) NTC Contemp Pub Co.

Opportunities in Counseling & Development Careers. Neale J. Baxter et al. LC 96-52397. (Opportunities In . . . Ser.). (Illus.). 160p. pap. 11.95 (*0-8442-4689-1*, 46891, VGM Career) NTC Contemp Pub Co.

Opportunities in Counseling & Development Careers. Mark U. Toch et al. LC 96-52397. (Opportunities in... Ser.). (Illus.). 160p. 1997. 14.95 (*0-8442-4688-3*, 46883, Natl Textbk Co) NTC Contemp Pub Co.

Opportunities in Crafts Careers. Marianne F. Munday. (Illus.). 160p. 1987. 13.95 (*0-8442-6015-0*, VGM Career) NTC Contemp Pub Co.

Opportunities in Crafts Careers. Marianne F. Munday. (Illus.). 160p. 1993. pap. 10.95 (*0-8442-6017-7*, VGM Career) NTC Contemp Pub Co.

Opportunities in Culinary Careers. Mary Donovan. LC 97-18166. (Opportunities in... Ser.). 160p. 1998. 14.95 (*0-8442-2333-6*, 23336) NTC Contemp Pub Co.

Opportunities in Culinary Careers. Mary D. Donovan. LC 97-18166. (Opportunities in...Ser.). (Illus.). 160p. 1997. pap. 11.95 (*0-8442-2334-4*, 23344, VGM Career) NTC Contemp Pub Co.

Opportunities in Dance. Paul Denis. (Opportunities In . . . Ser.). (Illus.). 160p. pap. 12.95 (*0-8442-6658-2*, 297OID, VGM Career) NTC Contemp Pub Co.

Opportunities in Dance. Paul Denis. (Illus.). 160p. 1989. 13.95 (*0-8442-6657-4*, VGM Career) NTC Contemp Pub Co.

Opportunities in Data & Word Processing Careers. rev. ed. Marianne Munday. (Opportunities in... Ser.). (Illus.). 160p. 1996. 14.95 (*0-8442-4612-3*, 46123, Natl Textbk Co) NTC Contemp Pub Co.

Opportunities in Data Processing. Norman N. Noerper. (Illus.). 160p. 1989. 14.95 (*0-8442-8637-0*, VGM Career) NTC Contemp Pub Co.

Opportunities in Data Processing. Norman N. Noerper. (Illus.). 148p. 1995. pap. 10.95 (*0-8442-6226-9*, VGM Career) NTC Contemp Pub Co.

Opportunities in Dental Care. Bonnie Kendall. (Illus.). 160p. 1986. 13.95 (*0-8442-6285-4*, VGM Career); pap. 10.95 (*0-8442-6286-2*, VGM Career) NTC Contemp Pub Co.

Opportunities in Dental Care Careers. Noerper. (Opportunities In . . . Ser.). (Illus.). 160p. pap. 11.95 (*0-8442-8576-5*, 85765, VGM Career) NTC Contemp Pub Co.

Opportunities in Dental Care Careers. Noerper. (Illus.). 160p. 1992. 14.95 (*0-8442-8575-7*, 85757, VGM Career) NTC Contemp Pub Co.

***Opportunities in Dental Care Careers.** rev. ed. Bonnie L. Kendall. LC 00-39273. (Opportunities Ser.). 2000. 11.95 (*0-658-00478-6*, VGM Career) NTC Contemp Pub Co.

Opportunities in Desktop Publishing Careers. Kenny Schiff. LC 92-37882. (Opportunities In . . . Ser.). (Illus.). 160p. pap. 11.95 (*0-8442-4065-6*, 40656, VGM Career) NTC Contemp Pub Co.

Opportunities in Direct Marketing Careers. Anne Basye. LC 92-25827. (Opportunities In . . . Ser.). (Illus.). 160p. pap. 12.95 (*0-8442-4037-0*, 297OIDM, VGM Career) NTC Contemp Pub Co.

Opportunities in Direct Marketing Careers. Anne Basye. LC 92-25827. (Opportunities in...Ser.). (Illus.). 160p. 1994. 14.95 (*0-8442-4036-2*, VGM Career) NTC Contemp Pub Co.

***Opportunities in Direct Marketing Careers.** Anne Basye. LC 99-57941. (Opportunities in... Ser.). 160p. 2000. 14.95 (*0-658-00209-0*, 002090) NTC Contemp Pub Co.

***Opportunities in Direct Marketing Careers.** rev. ed. Anne Basye. LC 99-57941. (Opportunities in... Ser.). 160p. 2000. pap. 11.95 (*0-658-00210-4*, 002104) NTC Contemp Pub Co.

Opportunities in Drafting Careers. Mark Rowh. LC 93-10586. (Opportunities In . . . Ser.). (Illus.). 160p. pap. 12.95 (*0-8442-4083-4*, 297OIDR, VGM Career) NTC Contemp Pub Co.

Opportunities in Drafting Careers. Mark Rowh. LC 93-10586. (Opportunities in...Ser.). (Illus.). 160p. 1994. 14.95 (*0-8442-4082-6*, 40826, VGM Career) NTC Contemp Pub Co.

***Opportunities in Education Careers.** Blythe Camenson. LC 99-37763. (Opportunities in... Ser.). 160p. 2000. 14.95 (*0-658-00108-6*, 001086) NTC Contemp Pub Co.

Opportunities in Electrical & Electronic Engineering. S. Paul Shackleton. LC 76-42888. (Illus.). (YA). (gr. 8 up). 1987. 13.95 (*0-8442-6333-8*, VGM Career) NTC Contemp Pub Co.

Opportunities in Electrical & Electronic Engineering. S. Paul Shackleton. LC 76-42888. (Illus.). (YA). (gr. 8 up). 1993. pap. 10.95 (*0-8442-6334-6*, VGM Career) NTC Contemp Pub Co.

Opportunities in Electrical Trades. Robert B. Wood & Kenneth R. Edwards. LC 96-26665. (Opportunities in... Ser.). (Illus.). 160p. pap. 11.95 (*0-8442-4667-0*, 46670, Natl Textbk Co) NTC Contemp Pub Co.

Opportunities in Electrical Trades. Robert B. Wood & Kenneth R. Edwards. LC 96-26665. (Opportunities in... Ser.). (Illus.). 160p. 1996. 14.95 (*0-8442-4666-2*, 46662, Natl Textbk Co) NTC Contemp Pub Co.

Opportunities in Electronics Careers. Mark Rowh. (Opportunities In . . . Ser.). (Illus.). 160p. pap. 12.95 (*0-8442-8184-0*, 297OIEL, VGM Career) NTC Contemp Pub Co.

Opportunities in Electronics Careers. Mark Rowh. (Opportunities in...Ser.). (Illus.). 160p. 1992. 14.95 (*0-8442-8183-2*, VGM Career) NTC Contemp Pub Co.

Opportunities in Electronics Careers. Mark Rowh. LC 98-42440. (Opportunities in...Ser.). 160p. 1999. 14.95 (*0-8442-1841-3*, 18413, VGM Career) NTC Contemp Pub Co.

Opportunities in Electronics Careers. rev. ed. Mark Rowh. LC 98-42440. (Opportunities in...Ser.). 160p. 1999. pap. 11.95 (*0-8442-1845-6*, 18456, VGM Career) NTC Contemp Pub Co.

Opportunities in Energy Careers. Nicholas Basta. (Illus.). 160p. 1993. pap. 10.95 (*0-8442-8584-6*, VGM Career) NTC Contemp Pub Co.

Opportunities in Energy Careers. Nicholas Basta. (Illus.). 160p. 1995. 13.95 (*0-8442-8583-8*, VGM Career) NTC Contemp Pub Co.

Opportunities in Energy Careers. 2nd ed. John H. Woodburn. (Opportunities in... Ser.). (Illus.). 160p. 1992. 14.95 (*0-8442-4009-5*, VGM Career) NTC Contemp Pub Co.

Opportunities in Engineering Careers. rev. ed. Nicholas Basta. LC 95-31373. (Opportunities in... Ser.). (Illus.). 160p. 1995. 14.95 (*0-8442-4591-7*, Natl Textbk Co) NTC Contemp Pub Co.

Opportunities in Engineering Careers. rev. ed. Nick Basta. LC 95-31373. (Opportunities In . . . Ser.). 160p. pap. 11.95 (*0-8442-4592-5*, 45925, Natl Textbk Co) NTC Contemp Pub Co.

Opportunities in Engineering Technology Careers. D. Joseph Hagerty & John E. Heer, Jr. (Opportunities In . . . Ser.). 160p. pap. 12.95 (*0-8442-6163-7*, 297OIENT, VGM Career) NTC Contemp Pub Co.

Opportunities in Engineering Technology Careers. D. Joseph Hagerty & John E. Heer, Jr. 160p. 1990. text 13.95 (*0-8442-6162-9*, VGM Career) NTC Contemp Pub Co.

Opportunities in Entertainment Careers. Jan Goldberg. LC 98-46030. (Opportunities in...Ser.). 160p. 1999. 14.95 (*0-8442-1819-7*, 18197, VGM Career) NTC Contemp Pub Co.

Opportunities in Environmental Careers. Odom Fanning. LC 74-25902. (Illus.). (C). 1988. 13.95 (*0-8442-6176-9*, VGM Career) NTC Contemp Pub Co.

Opportunities in Environmental Careers. Odom Fanning. LC 74-25902. (Illus.). (C). 1990. pap. 10.95 (*0-8442-6177-7*, VGM Career) NTC Contemp Pub Co.

Opportunities in Environmental Careers. rev. ed. Odom Fanning. LC 90-50734. (Opportunities in...Ser.). 160p. (YA). (gr. 7 up). 1993. pap. 10.95 (*0-8442-8163-8*, VGM Career) NTC Contemp Pub Co.

Opportunities in Environmental Careers. rev. ed. Odom Fanning. LC 90-50734. (Opportunities in...Ser.). 160p. (YA). (gr. 7 up). 1994. 13.95 (*0-8442-8161-1*, VGM Career) NTC Contemp Pub Co.

Opportunities in Environmental Careers. 6th rev. ed. Odom Fanning. LC 95-21865. (Opportunities In . . . Ser.). (Illus.). 160p. pap. 11.95 (*0-8442-4584-4*, 45844, VGM Career) NTC Contemp Pub Co.

Opportunities in Environmental Careers. 6th rev. ed. Odom Fanning. LC 95-21865. (VGM Opportunities Ser.). (Illus.). 160p. 1995. 14.95 (*0-8442-4583-6*, 45836, VGM Career) NTC Contemp Pub Co.

Opportunities in Eye Care Careers. Kathleen M. Ahrens. (Opportunities In . . . Ser.). (Illus.). 160p. pap. 12.95 (*0-8442-8594-3*, 297OIEC, VGM Career) NTC Contemp Pub Co.

Opportunities in Eye Care Careers. Kathleen Belikoff. LC 97-39478. (Opportunities in...Ser.). (Illus.). 160p. 1998. 14.95 (*0-8442-2302-6*, 23026, VGM Career); pap. 11.95 (*0-8442-2303-4*, 23034, VGM Career) NTC Contemp Pub Co.

Opportunities in Farming & Agriculture Careers. rev. ed. William C. White & Donald Collins. LC 95-21860. (VGM Opportunities Ser.). (Illus.). 160p. (J). 1995. 14.95 (*0-8442-4580-1*, 45801, VGM Career) NTC Contemp Pub Co.

Opportunities in Fashion. Roslyn Dobler. (Illus.). 160p. 1990. 13.95 (*0-8442-6156-4*, VGM Career) NTC Contemp Pub Co.

Opportunities in Fashion. Roslyn Dobler. (Illus.). 160p. 1993. pap. 10.95 (*0-8442-6157-2*, VGM Career) NTC Contemp Pub Co.

Opportunities in Fashion Careers. Roslyn Dolber. LC 92-16079. (Opportunities In . . . Ser.). (Illus.). 160p. pap. 11.95 (*0-8442-4023-0*, 40230, VGM Career) NTC Contemp Pub Co.

Opportunities in Fashion Careers. Roslyn Dolber. LC 92-16079. (Opportunities in...Ser.). (Illus.). 160p. 1994. 14.95 (*0-8442-4022-2*, VGM Career) NTC Contemp Pub Co.

Opportunities in Fast Food Careers. Ebert. 1989. 13.95 (*0-8442-8643-5*, VGM Career) NTC Contemp Pub Co.

Opportunities in Fast Food Careers. Eberts. 1993. pap. 10.95 (*0-8442-8644-3*, VGM Career) NTC Contemp Pub Co.

Opportunities in Federal Government Careers. 2nd ed. Neale J. Baxter. (Opportunities in...Ser.). (Illus.). 160p. 1994. 14.95 (*0-8442-4000-1*, VGM Career) NTC Contemp Pub Co.

Opportunities in Film. Jan Bone. (Opportunities In . . . Ser.). (Illus.). 160p. pap. 12.95 (*0-8442-8622-2*, 297OIF, VGM Career) NTC Contemp Pub Co.

Opportunities in Film Careers. Jan Bone. LC 97-32180. (Opportunities in...Ser.). (Illus.). 160p. 1998. 14.95 (*0-8442-2337-9*, 23379, VGM Career); pap. 11.95 (*0-8442-2339-5*, 23395, VGM Career) NTC Contemp Pub Co.

Opportunities in Financial Careers. Michael Sumichrast. LC 97-29042. (Opportunities in . . . Ser.). 160p. 1997. pap. 11.95 (*0-8442-2324-7*, 23247, VGM Career) NTC Contemp Pub Co.

Opportunities in Financial Careers. Michael Sumichrast & Dean Crist. LC 97-29042. (Opportunities in...Ser.). (Illus.). 160p. 1997. 14.95 (*0-8442-2323-9*, 23239, VGM Career) NTC Contemp Pub Co.

Opportunities in Financial Careers. Michael J. Sumichrast & Dean Christ. (Illus.). 146p. 1986. 13.95 (*0-8442-6209-9*, VGM Career); pap. 10.95 (*0-8442-6210-2*, VGM Career) NTC Contemp Pub Co.

Opportunities in Financial Careers. rev. ed. Michael J. Sumichrast & Dean Christ. LC 90-50736. (Opportunities In . . . Ser.). 160p. (YA). (gr. 7 up). pap. 12.95 (*0-8442-8167-0*, 297OIFIN, VGM Career) NTC Contemp Pub Co.

Opportunities in Financial Careers. rev. ed. Michael J. Sumichrast & Dean Christ. LC 90-50736. (Opportunities in...Ser.). 160p. (YA). (gr. 7 up). 1991. 14.95 (*0-8442-8166-2*, VGM Career) NTC Contemp Pub Co.

Opportunities in Fire Protection Services. Ron J. Coleman. (Opportunities In . . . Ser.). (Illus.). 160p. pap. 12.95 (*0-8442-8624-9*, 297OIFPS, VGM Career) NTC Contemp Pub Co.

Opportunities in Fire Protection Services. Ron J. Coleman. (Illus.). 160p. 1992. 14.95 (*0-8442-8623-0*, VGM Career) NTC Contemp Pub Co.

Opportunities in Fire Protection Services. Ronny J. Coleman. LC 96-52404. (Opportunities in... Ser.). (Illus.). 160p. 1997. 14.95 (*0-8442-4680-8*, 46808, Natl Textbk Co); pap. 11.95 (*0-8442-4681-6*, 46816, Natl Textbk Co) NTC Contemp Pub Co.

Opportunities in Fitness Careers. Mary Miller. (Opportunities in... Ser.). 160p. 1998. 14.95 (*0-8442-4686-7*, 46867, Natl Textbk Co) NTC Contemp Pub Co.

Opportunities in Fitness Careers. Jean Rosenbaum & Mary Prine. LC 90-50731. (Opportunities in...Ser.). 160p. (YA). (gr. 7 up). 1992. 14.95 (*0-8442-8185-9*, VGM Career) NTC Contemp Pub Co.

Opportunities in Fitness Careers. Jean Rosenbaum & Mary Prine. LC 90-50731. (Opportunities in...Ser.). 160p. (YA). (gr. 7 up). 1994. pap. 11.95 (*0-8442-8186-7*, VGM Career) NTC Contemp Pub Co.

Opportunities in Fitness Careers. 2nd ed. Mary Miller et al. LC 96-48293. (Opportunities in... Ser.). (Illus.). 160p. pap. 11.95 (*0-8442-4687-5*, 46875, Natl Textbk Co) NTC Contemp Pub Co.

Opportunities in Food Service Careers. Carol Caprioni Chemelynski. LC 99-38250. (Opportunities in... Ser.). 160p. 1999. 14.95 (*0-8442-3330-7*); pap. 11.95 (*0-8442-3407-9*) NTC Contemp Pub Co.

Opportunities in Food Service Careers. 2nd ed. Carol C. Chemelynski. (Opportunities In . . . Ser.). (Illus.). 160p. pap. 12.95 (*0-8442-8175-1*, 297OIFS, VGM Career) NTC Contemp Pub Co.

Opportunities in Food Service Careers. 2nd ed. Carol C. Chemelynski. (Opportunities in...Ser.). (Illus.). 160p. 1992. 14.95 (*0-8442-8174-3*, VGM Career) NTC Contemp Pub Co.

Opportunities in Food Services. Carol Caprione. (Illus.). 160p. 1986. 13.95 (*0-8442-6252-8*, VGM Career) NTC Contemp Pub Co.

Opportunities in Food Services. Carol Caprione. (Illus.). 160p. 1988. pap. 10.95 (*0-8442-6253-6*, VGM Career) NTC Contemp Pub Co.

Opportunities in Foreign Language Careers. Wilga M. Rivers. LC 92-15588. (Opportunities In . . . Ser.). (Illus.). 160p. pap. 12.95 (*0-8442-4043-5*, 297OIFL, VGM Career) NTC Contemp Pub Co.

Opportunities in Foreign Language Careers. Wilga M. Rivers. LC 92-15588. (Illus.). 160p. 1994. 14.95 (*0-8442-4042-7*, VGM Career) NTC Contemp Pub Co.

Opportunities in Forestry Careers. Christopher M. Wille. (Opportunities in...Ser.). (Illus.). 160p. (YA). 1994. 14.95 (*0-8442-8571-4*, VGM Career) NTC Contemp Pub Co.

Opportunities in Forestry Careers. Christopher M. Wille. LC 97-40160. (Opportunities in...Ser.). (Illus.). 160p. 1998. 14.95 (*0-8442-2304-2*, 23042, VGM Career); pap. 11.95 (*0-8442-2305-0*, 23050, VGM Career) NTC Contemp Pub Co.

Opportunities in Forestry Careers. rev. ed. Christopher M. Wille. LC 74-25903. (Illus.). (C). 1989. 13.95 (*0-8442-6321-4*, VGM Career) NTC Contemp Pub Co.

Opportunities in Forestry Careers. rev. ed. Christopher M. Wille. LC 74-25903. (Illus.). (C). 1993. pap. text 10.95 (*0-8442-6322-2*, VGM Career) NTC Contemp Pub Co.

Opportunities in Franchising Careers. rev. ed. Kent B. Banning. LC 95-30141. (VGM Opportunities Ser.). (Illus.). 160p. 1995. 14.95 (*0-8442-4433-3*, 44333, VGM Career) NTC Contemp Pub Co.

Opportunities in Funeral Services Careers. Terence J. Sacks. LC 96-47295. (Illus.). 160p. 1997. 14.95 (*0-8442-4558-5*, 45585); pap. 11.95 (*0-8442-4559-3*, 45593, VGM Career) NTC Contemp Pub Co.

Opportunities in Gerontology. Ellen William. (Illus.). 160p. 1993. pap. 10.95 (*0-8442-6168-8*, VGM Career) NTC Contemp Pub Co.

Opportunities in Gerontology. Ellen Williams. (Illus.). 160p. 1988. 13.95 (*0-8442-6166-1*, VGM Career) NTC Contemp Pub Co.

Opportunities in Gerontology & Aging Services Careers. Ellen Williams. LC 95-3220. (Opportunities In . . . Ser.). (Illus.). 160p. pap. 11.95 (*0-8442-4437-6*, 44376, VGM Career) NTC Contemp Pub Co.

Opportunities in Government Service. Neale J. Baxter. (Illus.). 153p. 1980. pap. 10.95 (*0-8442-6619-1*, VGM Career) NTC Contemp Pub Co.

Opportunities in Government Service. Neale J. Baxter. (Illus.). 160p. 1995. 13.95 (*0-8442-6618-3*, VGM Career) NTC Contemp Pub Co.

Opportunities in Health & Medical Careers. I. Donald Snook & Leo D'Orazio. (Opportunities In . . . Ser.). (Illus.). 160p. pap. 12.95 (*0-8442-8574-9*, 297OIH&M, VGM Career) NTC Contemp Pub Co.

Opportunities in Health & Medical Careers. I. Donald Snook & Leo D'Orazio. LC 97-17638. (Opportunities in...Ser.). (Illus.). 160p. 1997. 14.95 (*0-8442-2317-4*, 23174, VGM Career); pap. 11.95 (*0-8442-2318-2*, 23182, VGM Career) NTC Contemp Pub Co.

Opportunities in Health & Medical Careers. I. Donald Snook, Jr. & Leo D'Orazio. (Illus.). 149p. 1987. pap. 10.95 (*0-8442-6263-3*, VGM Career) NTC Contemp Pub Co.

Opportunities in Health & Medical Careers. I. Donald Snook, Jr. & Leo D'Orazio. (Illus.). 149p. 1987. 13.95 (*0-8442-6262-5*, VGM Career) NTC Contemp Pub Co.

Opportunities in Heating, Ventilation, Air-Conditioning, & Refrigeration Careers. Richard S. Budzik. LC 95-648. (Opportunities In . . . Ser.). (Illus.). 160p. pap. 11.95 (*0-8442-4590-9*, 45909, Natl Textbk Co) NTC Contemp Pub Co.

Opportunities in Heating, Ventilation, Air-Conditioning, & Refrigeration Careers. Richard S. Budzik. LC 95-648. (Opportunities in...Ser.). (Illus.). 160p. 1995. 14.95 (*0-8442-4589-5*, 45895, Natl Textbk Co) NTC Contemp Pub Co.

Opportunities in High Tech Careers. Gary D. Golter & Deborah F. Yanuck. LC 94-47113. (Opportunities In . . . Ser.). (Illus.). 160p. pap. 11.95 (*0-8442-4447-3*, 44473, VGM Career) NTC Contemp Pub Co.

Opportunities in High Tech Careers. Gary D. Golter & Deborah F. Yanuck. 160p. 1987. pap. 10.95 (*0-8442-6040-1*, VGM Career); text 13.95 (*0-8442-6037-1*, VGM Career) NTC Contemp Pub Co.

Opportunities in High Tech Careers. Gary D. Golter & Deborah F. Yanuck. LC 94-47113. (Opportunities in...Ser.). (Illus.). 160p. 1995. 14.95 (*0-8442-4446-5*, 44465, VGM Career) NTC Contemp Pub Co.

Opportunities in Holistic Health Care. Gillian Tierney. LC 98-21760. (Opportunities in...Ser.). 160p. 1999. 14.95 (*0-8442-1846-4*, 18464); pap. 11.95 (*0-8442-1851-0*, 18510) NTC Contemp Pub Co.

***Opportunities in Home Economics Careers.** Rhea Shields. LC TX164.S55 2000. (Opportunities in... Ser.). 160p. 2000. 14.95 (*0-658-00201-5*, 002015) NTC Contemp Pub Co.

Opportunities in Home Economics Careers. Rhea Shields & Anna K. Williams. (Opportunities In . . . Ser.). (Illus.). 160p. pap. 12.95 (*0-8442-6347-8*, 297OIHE, VGM Career) NTC Contemp Pub Co.

Opportunities in Home Economics Careers. Rhea Shields & Anna K. Williams. (Illus.). 160p. 1992. 14.95 (*0-8442-6345-1*, VGM Career) NTC Contemp Pub Co.

***Opportunities in Home Economics Careers.** rev. ed. Rhea Shields. LC TX164.S55 2000. (Opportunities in... Ser.). 160p. 2000. pap. 11.95 (*0-658-00202-3*, 002023) NTC Contemp Pub Co.

Opportunities in Homecare Services Careers. Anne Cardoza. LC 92-37879. (Opportunities In . . . Ser.). (Illus.). 160p. pap. 12.95 (*0-8442-4062-1*, 297OIHS, VGM Career) NTC Contemp Pub Co.

Opportunities in Homecare Services Careers. Anne Cardoza. LC 92-37879. (Opportunities in...Ser.). (Illus.). 160p. 1994. 14.95 (*0-8442-4061-3*, 40613, VGM Career) NTC Contemp Pub Co.

Opportunities in Horticultural Careers. Jan Goldberg. LC 94-17800. (Opportunities In . . . Ser.). (Illus.). 160p. pap. 11.95 (*0-8442-4406-6*, 44066, VGM Career) NTC Contemp Pub Co.

Opportunities in Horticultural Careers. Jan Goldberg. LC 94-17800. (Opportunities in...Ser.). (Illus.). 160p. 1994. 14.95 (*0-8442-4405-8*, 44058, VGM Career) NTC Contemp Pub Co.

Opportunities in Hospital Administration Careers. Donald Snook. (Opportunities In . . . Ser.). (Illus.). 160p. pap. 12.95 (*0-8442-6510-1*, 297OIHA, VGM Career) NTC Contemp Pub Co.

Opportunities in Hospital Administration Careers. Donald Snook. (Illus.). 160p. 1988. 14.95 (*0-8442-6509-8*, VGM Career) NTC Contemp Pub Co.

Opportunities in Hospital Administration Careers. I. Donald Snook. LC 96-40277. (VGM Opportunities Ser.). (Illus.). 160p. 1997. 14.95 (*0-8442-4562-3*, 45623); pap. 11.95 (*0-8442-4563-1*, 45631) NTC Contemp Pub Co.

***Opportunities in Hotel & Motel Careers.** rev. ed. Shepard Henkin. LC 00-39271. (VGM Opportunities Ser.). 2000. pap. 11.95 (*0-658-00469-7*) NTC Contemp Pub Co.

Opportunities in Human Resource Management. 3rd ed. William J. Traynor. (Opportunities in...Ser.). (Illus.). 176p. 1989. 13.95 (*0-8442-8639-7*, P114, VGM Career) NTC Contemp Pub Co.

Opportunities in Human Resource Management. 3rd ed. William J. Traynor. (Opportunities in...Ser.). (Illus.). 176p. 1993. pap. 10.95 (*0-8442-8640-0*, VGM Career) NTC Contemp Pub Co.

O

An Asterisk (*) at the beginning of an entry indicates that the title is appearing for the first time.

Opportunities in Human Resource Management Careers. William J. Traynor & J. Steven McKenzie. LC 93-46084. (Opportunities In . . . Ser.). (Illus.). 160p. pap. 11.95 (*0-8442-4093-1*, 40931, VGM Career) NTC Contemp Pub Co.

Opportunities in Human Resource Management Careers. William J. Traynor & J. Steven McKenzie. LC 93-46084. (Illus.). 160p. 1995. 14.95 (*0-8442-4092-3*, 40923, VGM Career) NTC Contemp Pub Co.

Opportunities in Installation & Repair Careers. Mark Rowh. LC 93-47510. (Opportunities In . . . Ser.). (Illus.). 160p. 1994. pap. 11.95 (*0-8442-4136-9*, 41369, VGM Career) NTC Contemp Pub Co.

Opportunities in Installation & Repair Careers. Mark Rowh. LC 93-47510. (Opportunities in...Ser.). (Illus.). 160p. 1995. 14.95 (*0-8442-4135-0*, 41350, VGM Career) NTC Contemp Pub Co.

Opportunities in Insurance. Robert M. Schrayer. (Opportunities in...Ser.). (Illus.). 160p. 1994. 14.95 (*0-8442-4055-9*, VGM Career) NTC Contemp Pub Co.

Opportunities in Insurance. Robert M. Schrayer et al. (Opportunities In . . . Ser.). (Illus.). 160p. pap. 12.95 (*0-8442-4056-7*, 297OII, VGM Career) NTC Contemp Pub Co.

Opportunities in Insurance Careers. Robert M. Schrayer. 160p. 1987. text 13.95 (*0-8442-6008-8*, VGM Career) NTC Contemp Pub Co.

Opportunities in Insurance Careers. Robert M. Schrayer. 160p. 1993. pap. 10.95 (*0-8442-6009-6*, VGM Career) NTC Contemp Pub Co.

Opportunities in Insurance Careers. rev. ed. Robert M. Schrayer. LC 99-30474. (Opportunities in... Ser.). 160p. 1999. pap. 11.95 (*0-8442-2978-4*) NTC Contemp Pub Co.

***Opportunities in Insurance Careers.** rev. ed. Robert M. Schrayer. LC 99-30474. (Opportunities in... Ser.). 160p. 1999. 14.95 (*0-8442-2977-6*) NTC Contemp Pub Co.

Opportunities in Interior Design Careers. Victoria K. Ball. LC 94-47112. (Opportunities In . . . Ser.). (Illus.). 160p. pap. 11.95 (*0-8442-4441-4*, 44414, VGM Career) NTC Contemp Pub Co.

Opportunities in Interior Design Careers. Victoria K. Ball. (Illus.). 144p. 1990. 13.95 (*0-8442-6481-4*, VGM Career) NTC Contemp Pub Co.

Opportunities in Interior Design Careers. Victoria K. Ball. LC 94-47112. (Illus.). 160p. 1995. 14.95 (*0-8442-4440-6*, 44406, VGM Career) NTC Contemp Pub Co.

Opportunities in Interior Design Careers. 2nd ed. Victoria K. Ball. (Illus.). 144p. 1993. pap. 10.95 (*0-8442-6482-2*, VGM Career) NTC Contemp Pub Co.

Opportunities in International Business Careers. Jeffrey S. Arpan. (Illus.). 160p. 1991. 13.95 (*0-8442-6516-0*, VGM Career) NTC Contemp Pub Co.

Opportunities in International Business Careers. Jeffrey S. Arpan. (Illus.). 160p. 1993. pap. 10.95 (*0-8442-6517-9*, VGM Career) NTC Contemp Pub Co.

Opportunities in Journalism Careers. 1989. 13.95 (*0-8442-8660-5*, VGM Career) NTC Contemp Pub Co.

Opportunities in Journalism Careers. 1993. pap. 10.95 (*0-8442-8661-3*, VGM Career) NTC Contemp Pub Co.

Opportunities in Journalism Careers. Jim Patten & Donald L. Ferguson. (Opportunities In . . . Ser.). (Illus.). 160p. pap. 11.95 (*0-8442-4014-1*, 40141, VGM Career) NTC Contemp Pub Co.

Opportunities in Journalism Careers. Jim Patten & Donald L. Ferguson. (Opportunities in...Ser.). 160p. 1995. 14.95 (*0-8442-4013-3*) NTC Contemp Pub Co.

Opportunities in Laser Technology Careers. Jan Bone. (Opportunities In . . . Ser.). (Illus.). 160p. pap. 12.95 (*0-8442-6515-2*, 297OILT, VGM Career) NTC Contemp Pub Co.

Opportunities in Laser Technology Careers. Jan Bone. (Illus.). 160p. 1991. 14.95 (*0-8442-6514-4*, VGM Career) NTC Contemp Pub Co.

***Opportunities in Laser Technology Careers.** rev. ed. Jan Bone. LC 99-52563. (Opportunities in... Ser.). 160p. 2000. 14.95 (*0-658-00203-1*, 002031); pap. 11.95 (*0-658-00204-X*, 00204X) NTC Contemp Pub Co.

***Opportunities in Latin America for PATA Members.** Menlo Consulting Group, Inc. Staff. (Illus.). 56p. 1999. pap. 500.00 (*1-882866-15-0*) Pac Asia Trvl.

Opportunities in Law Careers. Gary A. Munneke. LC 93-25120. (Opportunities In . . . Ser.). (Illus.). 160p. pap. 11.95 (*0-8442-4087-7*, 40877, VGM Career) NTC Contemp Pub Co.

Opportunities in Law Careers. Gary A. Munneke. (Illus.). 160p. 1989. 13.95 (*0-8442-6174-2*, VGM Career) NTC Contemp Pub Co.

Opportunities in Law Careers. Gary A. Munneke. (Illus.). 160p. 1993. pap. 10.95 (*0-8442-6175-0*, VGM Career) NTC Contemp Pub Co.

Opportunities in Law Careers. Gary A. Munneke. LC 93-25120. (Illus.). 160p. 1994. 14.95 (*0-8442-4086-9*, 40869, VGM Career) NTC Contemp Pub Co.

Opportunities in Law Enforcement & Criminal Justice. James A. Stinchcomb. LC 75-32614. (Illus.). 160p. (YA). (gr. 8 up). 1994. 13.95 (*0-8442-8658-3*, VGM Career) NTC Contemp Pub Co.

Opportunities in Law Enforcement & Criminal Justice. rev. ed. James A. Stinchcomb. LC 75-32614. (Illus.). 160p. (YA). (gr. 8 up). 1994. pap. text 10.95 (*0-8442-8659-1*, VGM Career) NTC Contemp Pub Co.

Opportunities in Law Enforcement & Criminal Justice Careers. rev. ed. James A. Stinchcomb. (Opportunities In . . . Ser.). (Illus.). 160p. pap. 11.95 (*0-8442-4609-3*, 46093, Natl Textbk Co) NTC Contemp Pub Co.

Opportunities in Law Enforcement & Criminal Justice Careers. rev. ed. James A. Stinchcomb. (Opportunities in...Ser.). (Illus.). 160p. 1996. 14.95 (*0-8442-4608-5*, 46085, Natl Textbk Co) NTC Contemp Pub Co.

Opportunities in Library & Information Science. Kathleen De La Pena McCook. (Opportunities in... Ser.). (Illus.). 160p. pap. 11.95 (*0-8442-4671-9*, 46719, Natl Textbk Co) NTC Contemp Pub Co.

Opportunities in Library & Information Science. Kathleen De La Pena McCook. (Opportunities in... Ser.). (Illus.). 160p. 1996. 14.95 (*0-8442-4670-0*, 46700, Natl Textbk Co) NTC Contemp Pub Co.

Opportunities in Library & Information Science. Peggy Sullivan & Kathleen M. Heim. (Illus.). 160p. 1989. 13.95 (*0-8442-6145-9*, VGM Career) NTC Contemp Pub Co.

Opportunities in Library & Information Science. Peggy Sullivan & Kathleen M. Heim. (Illus.). 160p. 1993. pap. 10.95 (*0-8442-6146-7*, VGM Career) NTC Contemp Pub Co.

Opportunities in Library & Information Science Careers. Kathleen M. Heim & Margaret Myers. (Opportunities in...Ser.). (Illus.). 160p. 1992. 13.95 (*0-8442-8150-6*, VGM Career) NTC Contemp Pub Co.

Opportunities in Library & Information Science Careers. Kathleen M. Heim & Margaret Myers. (Opportunities in...Ser.). (Illus.). 160p. 1993. pap. 10.95 (*0-8442-8151-4*, VGM Career) NTC Contemp Pub Co.

Opportunities in Machines Shop Trades. John A. Bell. (YA). (gr. 8 up). 1990. 13.95 (*0-8442-6147-5*, VGM Career) NTC Contemp Pub Co.

Opportunities in Machines Shop Trades. John A. Bell. (YA). (gr. 8 up). 1993. pap. 10.95 (*0-8442-6148-3*, VGM Career) NTC Contemp Pub Co.

Opportunities in Magazine Publishing. S. William Pattis. (Illus.). 160p. 1987. 13.95 (*0-8442-6141-6*, VGM Career) NTC Contemp Pub Co.

Opportunities in Magazine Publishing. S. William Pattis. (Illus.). 160p. 1993. pap. 10.95 (*0-8442-6142-4*, VGM Career) NTC Contemp Pub Co.

Opportunities in Magazine Publishing Careers. S. William Pattis. (Opportunities In . . . Ser.). (Illus.). 160p. pap. 12.95 (*0-8442-8180-8*, 297OIMP, VGM Career) NTC Contemp Pub Co.

Opportunities in Magazine Publishing Careers. S. William Pattis. (Opportunities in...Ser.). (Illus.). 160p. 1994. 13.95 (*0-8442-8179-4*, VGM Career) NTC Contemp Pub Co.

Opportunities in Marine & Maritime Careers. William R. Heitzmann. (Opportunities In . . . Ser.). (Illus.). 160p. pap. 12.95 (*0-8442-6351-6*, 297OIM&M, VGM Career) NTC Contemp Pub Co.

Opportunities in Marine & Maritime Careers. William R. Heitzmann. (Illus.). 160p. 1994. 14.95 (*0-8442-6350-8*, VGM Career) NTC Contemp Pub Co.

Opportunities in Marine & Maritime Careers. Wm. Ray Heitzmann. LC 98-40925. (Opportunities in...Ser.). 160p. 1999. pap. 11.95 (*0-8442-1838-3*, 18383, VGM Career) NTC Contemp Pub Co.

Opportunities in Marketing Careers. Margery Steinberg. LC 93-11258. (Opportunities In . . . Ser.). (Illus.). 160p. pap. 12.95 (*0-8442-4078-8*, 297OIM, VGM Career) NTC Contemp Pub Co.

Opportunities in Marketing Careers. Margery Steinberg. (VGM Career Planner Ser.). (Illus.). 160p. 1990. 13.95 (*0-8442-6195-5*, VGM Career) NTC Contemp Pub Co.

Opportunities in Marketing Careers. Margery Steinberg. (VGM Career Planner Ser.). (Illus.). 160p. 1993. pap. 10.95 (*0-8442-6196-3*, VGM Career) NTC Contemp Pub Co.

Opportunities in Marketing Careers. Margery Steinberg. LC 93-11258. (Opportunities in...Ser.). (Illus.). 160p. 1994. 14.95 (*0-8442-4076-1*, VGM Career) NTC Contemp Pub Co.

Opportunities in Marketing Careers. Margery Steinberg. LC 98-48295. (Opportunities in...Ser.). 160p. 1999. 14.95 (*0-8442-1852-9*, 18529, VGM Career); pap. 11.95 (*0-8442-1853-7*, 18537, VGM Career) NTC Contemp Pub Co.

Opportunities in Masonry Careers. Chris Santilli. LC 92-37382. (Opportunities In . . . Ser.). (Illus.). 160p. pap. 11.95 (*0-8442-4067-2*, 40672, VGM Career) NTC Contemp Pub Co.

Opportunities in Masonry Careers. Chris Santilli. LC 92-37382. (Opportunities in...Ser.). (Illus.). 160p. 1994. 14.95 (*0-8442-4066-4*, 40664, VGM Career) NTC Contemp Pub Co.

Opportunities in Mechanical Engineering. Seichi Konzo & James W. Bayne. (Opportunities In . . . Ser.). (Illus.). 160p. pap. 12.95 (*0-8442-6552-7*, 297OIME, VGM Career) NTC Contemp Pub Co.

Opportunities in Medical Imaging Careers. Clifford J. Sherry. LC 93-19679. (Opportunities In . . . Ser.). 160p. pap. 12.95 (*0-8442-4071-0*, 297OIMI, VGM Career) NTC Contemp Pub Co.

Opportunities in Medical Imaging Careers. Clifford J. Sherry. LC 93-19679. (VGM Opportunities Ser.). 160p. 1993. 14.95 (*0-8442-4070-2*, Wiley-VCH) Wiley.

***Opportunities in Medical Imaging Careers.** rev. ed. Sherry Clifford. (Opportunities in... Ser.). 160p. 2000. 14.95 (*0-658-00196-5*, 001965); pap. 11.95 (*0-658-00197-3*, 001973) NTC Contemp Pub Co.

Opportunities in Medical Sales Careers. Chad Ellis. LC 96-45333. (VGM Opportunities Ser.). (Illus.). 160p. 1997. 14.95 (*0-8442-4560-7*, 45607) NTC Contemp Pub Co.

Opportunities in Medical Technology Careers. Karen R. Kami & Jane S. Oliver. 160p. 1994. 13.95 (*0-8442-8671-0*, VGM Career); pap. 10.95 (*0-8442-8672-9*, VGM Career) NTC Contemp Pub Co.

Opportunities in Medical Technology Careers. rev. ed. Karen Karni. (Opportunities In . . . Ser.). (Illus.). 160p. pap. 11.95 (*0-8442-4638-7*, 46387, Natl Textbk Co) NTC Contemp Pub Co.

Opportunities in Medical Technology Careers. rev. ed. Karen Karni. (Opportunities in...Ser.). (Illus.). 160p. 1996. 14.95 (*0-8442-4637-9*, 46379, Natl Textbk Co) NTC Contemp Pub Co.

Opportunities in Mental Health Careers. Philip A. Perry. (VGM Opportunities Ser.). (Illus.). 160p. 1996. 14.95 (*0-8442-4429-5*, 44295, VGM Career) NTC Contemp Pub Co.

Opportunities in Mental Health Careers. Philip A. Perry & Virginia Simons. (Opportunities In . . . Ser.). (Illus.). 160p. pap. 11.95 (*0-8442-4430-9*, 44309, VGM Career) NTC Contemp Pub Co.

Opportunities in Metal Working Careers. Mark Rowh. LC 90-50730. (Opportunities In . . . Ser.). (Illus.). 160p. (YA). (gr. 7 up). pap. 12.95 (*0-8442-8538-2*, 297OIMW, VGM Career) NTC Contemp Pub Co.

Opportunities in Metal Working Careers. Mark Rowh. LC 90-50730. (Opportunities in...Ser.). (Illus.). 160p. (YA). (gr. 7 up). 1994. 14.95 (*0-8442-8537-4*, VGM Career) NTC Contemp Pub Co.

***Opportunities in Metalworking Careers.** Mark Rowh. LC 99-53372. (Opportunities in... Ser.). 160p. 2000. 14.95 (*0-658-00198-1*, 001981, VGM Career) NTC Contemp Pub Co.

***Opportunities in Metalworking Careers.** rev. ed. Mark Rowh. LC 99-53372. (Opportunities in... Ser.). 160p. 2000. pap. 11.95 (*0-658-00200-7*, 002007) NTC Contemp Pub Co.

Opportunities in Microelectronic Careers. Mark Hornung & Richard D. Moran. (Illus.). 160p. 1993. pap. 10.95 (*0-8442-6199-8*, VGM Career) NTC Contemp Pub Co.

Opportunities in Microelectronic Careers. Mark Hornung & Richard D. Moran. (Illus.). 160p. 1995. 13.95 (*0-8442-6197-1*, VGM Career) NTC Contemp Pub Co.

Opportunities in Military Careers. Adrian A. Paradis. 160p. 14.95 (*0-8442-2235-6*, VGM Career) NTC Contemp Pub Co.

Opportunities in Military Careers. Adrian A. Paradis. (Opportunities In . . . Ser.). (Illus.). 160p. pap. 12.95 (*0-8442-8649-4*, 297OIMIL, VGM Career) NTC Contemp Pub Co.

Opportunities in Military Careers. Adrian A. Paradis. (Illus.). 160p. 1994. 14.95 (*0-8442-8648-6*, VGM Career) NTC Contemp Pub Co.

Opportunities in Military Careers: A Guide to Military Occupations & Selected Military Career Paths. Adrian A. Paradis. LC 98-41498. (Opportunities in...Ser.). 160p. 1999. 14.95 (*0-8442-2236-4*, 22364); pap. 11.95 (*0-8442-2238-0*, 22380, VGM Career) NTC Contemp Pub Co.

Opportunities in Modeling. Susan W. Gearhart. (Illus.). 143p. 1986. 13.95 (*0-8442-6236-6*, VGM Career); pap. 10.95 (*0-8442-6237-4*, VGM Career) NTC Contemp Pub Co.

Opportunities in Modeling Careers. Susan W. Gearhart. LC 90-50733. (Opportunities In . . . Ser.). (Illus.). 160p. (YA). (gr. 7 up). pap. 12.95 (*0-8442-8157-3*, 297OIMOD, VGM Career) NTC Contemp Pub Co.

Opportunities in Modeling Careers. Susan Good-Gearhart. LC 98-46530. (Opportunities in...Ser.). 160p. 1999. 14.95 (*0-8442-1753-0*, 17530, VGM Career); pap. 11.95 (*0-8442-1754-9*, 17549, VGM Career) NTC Contemp Pub Co.

Opportunities in Museums Careers. Blythe Camenson. (Opportunities in...Ser.). (Illus.). 160p. 1996. 14.95 (*0-8442-4593-3*, 45933, Natl Textbk Co) NTC Contemp Pub Co.

Opportunities in Museums Careers. Blythe Camerson. (Opportunities In . . . Ser.). (Illus.). 160p. pap. 11.95 (*0-8442-4594-1*, 45941, Natl Textbk Co) NTC Contemp Pub Co.

Opportunities in Music. (Illus.). 144p. 1986. 13.95 (*0-8442-6233-1*, VGM Career) NTC Contemp Pub Co.

Opportunities in Music. (Illus.). 144p. 1991. pap. 10.95 (*0-8442-6235-8*, VGM Career) NTC Contemp Pub Co.

Opportunities in Music Careers. rev. ed. Robert Gerardi. LC 90-50739. (Opportunities in...Ser.). 160p. (YA). (gr. 7 up). 1991. 14.95 (*0-8442-8154-9*, VGM Career) NTC Contemp Pub Co.

Opportunities in Music Careers. 3rd ed. Robert Gerardi. LC 96-46841. (VGM Opportunities Ser.). 160p. 1997. pap. 11.95 (*0-8442-4572-0*, 45720, VGM Career) NTC Contemp Pub Co.

Opportunities in Music Careers. 3rd ed. Robert Gerardi. LC 96-46841. (VGM Opportunities Ser.). (Illus.). 160p. 1997. 14.95 (*0-8442-4571-2*, 45712) NTC Contemp Pub Co.

Opportunities in Music Careers. 1991st rev. ed. Robert Gerardi. LC 90-50739. (Opportunities In . . . Ser.). 160p. (YA). (gr. 7 up). pap. 12.95 (*0-8442-8155-7*, 297OIMUS, VGM Career) NTC Contemp Pub Co.

Opportunities in Nanostructured Materials. 192p. 1997. 3250.00 (*1-56965-453-0*, GB-201) BCC.

Opportunities in Newspaper Publishing Careers. John Tebbel. (Opportunities In . . . Ser.). (Illus.). 160p. pap. 11.95 (*0-8442-8642-7*, 86427, VGM Career) NTC Contemp Pub Co.

Opportunities in Nonprofit Organization Careers. Adrian A. Paradis. LC 93-4667. (Opportunities in...Ser.). (Illus.). 160p. 1994. 14.95 (*0-8442-4088-5*, 40885, VGM Career) NTC Contemp Pub Co.

Opportunities in Nursing Assistant. Joan Fox-Rose. LC 99-31861. (Opportunities in... Ser.). 160p. 1999. 14.95 (*0-8442-3431-1*); pap. 11.95 (*0-8442-3439-7*) NTC Contemp Pub Co.

Opportunities in Nursing Careers. Keville Frederickson. 1992. 13.95 (*0-8442-8635-4*, VGM Career) NTC Contemp Pub Co.

Opportunities in Nursing Careers. Keville Frederickson. 1993. pap. 10.95 (*0-8442-8636-2*, VGM Career) NTC Contemp Pub Co.

Opportunities in Nursing Careers. rev. ed. Keville Frederickson. LC 95-31374. (Opportunities In . . . Ser.). (Illus.). 160p. 1995. pap. 11.95 (*0-8442-4576-3*, 45763, VGM Career) NTC Contemp Pub Co.

Opportunities in Nursing Careers. rev. ed. Keville Frederickson. LC 95-31374. (VGM Opportunities Ser.). (Illus.). 160p. 1995. 14.95 (*0-8442-4575-5*, 45755, VGM Career) NTC Contemp Pub Co.

Opportunities in Nutrition Careers. Carol Caldwell. (Opportunities In . . . Ser.). (Illus.). 160p. pap. 12.95 (*0-8442-8188-3*, 297OINT, VGM Career) NTC Contemp Pub Co.

Opportunities in Nutrition Careers. Carol C. Caldwell. (Illus.). 160p. 1988. 13.95 (*0-8442-6172-6*, VGM Career) NTC Contemp Pub Co.

Opportunities in Nutrition Careers. Carol C. Caldwell. (Illus.). 160p. 1993. pap. 10.95 (*0-8442-6173-4*, VGM Career) NTC Contemp Pub Co.

Opportunities in Nutrition Careers. Carol Coles Caldwell. (Opportunities in... Ser.). 160p. 1999. 14.95 (*0-8442-3240-8*) NTC Contemp Pub Co.

Opportunities in Nutrition Careers. rev. ed. Carol Coles Caldwell. LC 99-34064. (Opportunities in... Ser.). 160p. 1999. pap. 11.95 (*0-8442-3251-3*, 32513) NTC Contemp Pub Co.

Opportunities in Occupational Therapy Careers. Marie-Louis Franciscus et al. LC 94-19969. (Opportunities In . . . Ser.). (Illus.). 160p. pap. 11.95 (*0-8442-4408-2*, 44082, VGM Career) NTC Contemp Pub Co.

Opportunities in Occupational Therapy Careers. Marie-Louis Franciscus et al. LC 94-19969. (VGM Opportunities Ser.). (Illus.). 160p. 1994. 14.95 (*0-8442-4407-4*, 44074, VGM Career) NTC Contemp Pub Co.

***Opportunities in Occupational Therapy Careers.** rev. ed. Marguerite Abbott et al. LC 00-31995. (Opportunities Ser.). 2000. write for info. (*0-658-00473-5*, VGM Career) NTC Contemp Pub Co.

Opportunities in Office Occupations. Blanche Ettinger. LC 94-12511. (Opportunities In . . . Ser.). (Illus.). 160p. pap. 11.95 (*0-8442-4410-4*, 44104, VGM Career) NTC Contemp Pub Co.

Opportunities in Office Occupations. Blanche Ettinger. LC 94-12511. (VGM Opportunities Ser.). (Illus.). 160p. 1994. 14.95 (*0-8442-4409-0*, 44090, VGM Career) NTC Contemp Pub Co.

Opportunities in Office Occupations. Blanche Ettinger & Estelle L. Popham. LC 88-60908. (Illus.). 160p. 1991. 13.95 (*0-8442-6522-5*, VGM Career) NTC Contemp Pub Co.

Opportunities in Office Occupations. Blanche Ettinger & Estelle L. Popham. (Illus.). 176p. 1993. pap. 10.95 (*0-8442-6523-3*, VGM Career) NTC Contemp Pub Co.

Opportunities in Opticianry Today. Bacotti. LC 75-32613. (Illus.). 1993. pap. text 10.95 (*0-8442-6326-5*, VGM Career) NTC Contemp Pub Co.

Opportunities in Opticianry Today. Bacotti. LC 75-32613. (Illus.). 1995. lib. bdg. 13.95 (*0-8442-6325-7*, VGM Career) NTC Contemp Pub Co.

***Opportunities in Options.** Samuel Malkind. (Illus.). 40p. 2000. 10.00 (*0-8059-4844-9*) Dorrance.

Opportunities in Overseas Careers: Blythe Camenson. Blythe Camenson. LC 97-41354. (Opportunities in...Ser.). (Illus.). 160p. 1998. 14.95 (*0-8442-2342-5*, 23425, VGM Career); pap. 11.95 (*0-8442-2343-3*, 23433, VGM Career) NTC Contemp Pub Co.

Opportunities in Paralegal Careers. Alice Fins. (Opportunities In . . . Ser.). (Illus.). 160p. pap. 12.95 (*0-8442-8590-0*, 297OIP, VGM Career) NTC Contemp Pub Co.

Opportunities in Paralegal Careers. Alice Fins. (Illus.). 160p. 1990. 14.95 (*0-8442-8589-7*, VGM Career) NTC Contemp Pub Co.

Opportunities in Paramedical Careers. Alex Kacen. (Illus.). 160p. 1991. 13.95 (*0-8442-6506-3*, VGM Career) NTC Contemp Pub Co.

Opportunities in Paramedical Careers. Alex Kacen. (Illus.). 160p. 1993. pap. 10.95 (*0-8442-6507-1*, VGM Career) NTC Contemp Pub Co.

Opportunities in Paramedical Careers. rev. ed. Alex Kacen. LC 99-26183. (Opportunities in ... (Cloth) Ser.). 160p. 1999. 14.95 (*0-8442-2906-7*); pap. 11.95 (*0-8442-2907-5*) NTC Contemp Pub Co.

Opportunities in Paramedical Careers. 2nd ed. Alex Kacen. (Opportunities In . . . Ser.). (Illus.). 160p. pap. 12.95 (*0-8442-4096-6*, 297OIPARAM, VGM Career) NTC Contemp Pub Co.

Opportunities in Paramedical Careers. 1994th rev. ed. Alex Kacen. LC 93-45609. (Illus.). 160p. 1995. 14.95 (*0-8442-4095-8*, VGM Career) NTC Contemp Pub Co.

Opportunities in Part-Time & Summer Jobs. Adrian A. Paradis. (Opportunities In . . . Ser.). 160p. pap. 12.95 (*0-8442-6302-8*, 297OIPT&SJ, VGM Career) NTC Contemp Pub Co.

Opportunities in Part-Time & Summer Jobs. Adrian A. Paradis. 160p. 1987. 14.95 (*0-8442-6300-1*, VGM Career) NTC Contemp Pub Co.

Opportunities in Part-Time & Summer Jobs. Adrian A. Paradis. LC 97-14945. (Opportunities in...Ser.). (Illus.). 160p. 1997. 14.95 (*0-8442-2315-8*, 23158, VGM Career); pap. 11.95 (*0-8442-2316-6*, 23166, VGM Career) NTC Contemp Pub Co.

Opportunities in Performing Arts Careers. Bonnie B. Bekken. (Opportunities In . . . Ser.). (Illus.). 160p. pap. 11.95 (*0-8442-8567-6*, 85676, VGM Career) NTC Contemp Pub Co.

Opportunities in Performing Arts Careers. Bonnie B. Bekken. (Illus.). 160p. 1992. 14.95 (*0-8442-8566-8*, VGM Career) NTC Contemp Pub Co.

An Asterisk (*) at the beginning of an entry indicates that the title is appearing for the first time.

Opportunities in Personnel Management. William J. Traynor. (Illus.). 160p. 1985. pap. 10.95 (*0-8442-6270-6*, VGM Career) NTC Contemp Pub Co.

Opportunities in Personnel Management. William J. Traynor. (Illus.). 160p. 1991. 13.95 (*0-8442-6269-2*, VGM Career) NTC Contemp Pub Co.

Opportunities in Petroleum Careers. Gretchen Krueger. (Opportunities In . . . Ser.). (Illus.). 160p. pap. 12.95 (*0-8442-8666-4*, 297OIPET, VGM Career) NTC Contemp Pub Co.

Opportunities in Pharmacy Careers. Fred B. Gable. LC 97-35763. (Opportunities In . . . Ser.). (Illus.). 160p. (YA). (gr. 8-12). pap. 12.95 (*0-8442-8592-7*, 297OIPHA, VGM Career) NTC Contemp Pub Co.

Opportunities in Pharmacy Careers. Fred B. Gable. LC 74-82639. (Illus.). 160p. (YA). (gr. 8-12). 1993. 14.95 (*0-8442-8591-9*, VGM Career) NTC Contemp Pub Co.

Opportunities in Pharmacy Careers. Fred B. Gable. (Opportunities in...Ser.). (Illus.). 160p. 1997. 14.95 (*0-8442-2319-0*, 23190, VGM Career); pap. 11.95 (*0-8442-2320-4*, 23204, VGM Career) NTC Contemp Pub Co.

Opportunities in Physical Therapy Careers. Bernice Krumhansl. LC 92-37295. (Opportunities in...Ser.). (Illus.). 160p. 1994. 14.95 (*0-8442-4053-2*, VGM Career) NTC Contemp Pub Co.

Opportunities in Physical Therapy Careers. rev. ed. Bernice Krumhansl. LC 92-37295. (Opportunities In . . . Ser.). (Illus.). 160p. pap. 12.95 (*0-8442-4054-0*, 297OIPHYT, VGM Career) NTC Contemp Pub Co.

Opportunities in Physical Therapy Careers. rev. ed. Bernice R. Krumhansl. LC 99-34065. (Opportunities in... Ser.). 160p. 1999. 14.95 (*0-8442-1804-9*, 18049); pap. 11.95 (*0-8442-1805-7*, 18057) NTC Contemp Pub Co.

Opportunities in Physician Assistant Careers. Terence J. Sacks. LC 94-17799. (Opportunities In . . . Ser.). (Illus.). 160p. 1994. pap. 11.95 (*0-8442-4412-0*, 44120, VGM Career) NTC Contemp Pub Co.

Opportunities in Physician Assistant Careers. Terence J. Sacks. LC 94-17799. (Opportunities in...Ser.). (Illus.). 160p. 1994. 14.95 (*0-8442-4411-2*, 44112, VGM Career) NTC Contemp Pub Co.

Opportunities in Physician Careers. Jan Sugar-Webb. (Opportunities In . . . Ser.). (Illus.). 160p. pap. 12.95 (*0-8442-8597-8*, 297OIPHY, VGM Career) NTC Contemp Pub Co.

Opportunities in Physician Careers. Jan Sugar-Webb. (Illus.). 160p. 1992. 14.95 (*0-8442-8595-1*, VGM Career) NTC Contemp Pub Co.

Opportunities in Physician Careers. rev. ed. Jan Sugar-Webb. LC 99-33038. (Opportunities in... Ser.). 160p. 1999. 14.95 (*0-8442-2979-2*); pap. 11.95 (*0-8442-2984-9*) NTC Contemp Pub Co.

Opportunities in Plastics Careers. Jan Bone. LC 90-50732. (Opportunities In . . . Ser.). (Illus.). 160p. (YA). (gr. 7-12). pap. 12.95 (*0-8442-8674-5*, 297OIPLA, VGM Career) NTC Contemp Pub Co.

Opportunities in Plastics for the 1990's, No. P-2000. Business Communications Co., Inc. Staff. 250p. 1991. 1950.00 (*0-89336-814-8*) BCC.

Opportunities in Plumbing & Pipefitting Careers. Patrick Galvin. (Illus.). 160p. 1990. 13.95 (*0-8442-6187-4*, VGM Career) NTC Contemp Pub Co.

Opportunities in Plumbing & Pipefitting Careers. Patrick Galvin. (Illus.). 160p. 1993. pap. 10.95 (*0-8442-6188-2*, VGM Career) NTC Contemp Pub Co.

Opportunities in Printing Careers. Irvin Borowsky. LC 97-38631. (Opportunities in...Ser.). (Illus.). 160p. 1998. 14.95 (*0-8442-2306-9*, 23069, VGM Career); pap. 11.95 (*0-8442-2307-7*, 23077, VGM Career) NTC Contemp Pub Co.

Opportunities in Printing Careers. Irvin J. Borowsky. (Opportunities In . . . Ser.). (Illus.). 160p. pap. 12.95 (*0-8442-8178-6*, 297OIPRIN, VGM Career) NTC Contemp Pub Co.

Opportunities in Printing Careers. Irvin J. Borowsky. (Opportunities in...Ser.). (Illus.). 160p. 1994. 14.95 (*0-8442-8177-8*, VGM Career) NTC Contemp Pub Co.

Opportunities in Printing Careers. Irving J. Borowsky. (Illus.). 160p. 1987. 13.95 (*0-8442-6189-0*, VGM Career) NTC Contemp Pub Co.

Opportunities in Printing Careers. Irving J. Borowsky. (Illus.). 160p. 1993. pap. 10.95 (*0-8442-6190-4*, VGM Career) NTC Contemp Pub Co.

Opportunities in Property Management Careers. Mariwyn Evans. (Opportunities In . . . Ser.). 160p. pap. 12.95 (*0-8442-8631-1*, 297OIPSYC, VGM Career) NTC Contemp Pub Co.

Opportunities in Property Management Careers. Mariwyn Evans. (Illus.). 160p. 1989. 13.95 (*0-8442-8630-3*, VGM Career) NTC Contemp Pub Co.

***Opportunities in Property Management Careers.** rev. ed. Mariwyn Evans. (Opportunities in... Ser.). 160p. 2000. 14.95 (*0-658-00205-8*, 002058) NTC Contemp Pub Co.

***Opportunities In Property Management Careers / rev.** ed. Mariwyn Evans. LC 99-53681. (Opportunities in...Ser.). 160p. 2000. pap. 11.95 (*0-658-00206-6*, 002066, VGM Career) NTC Contemp Pub Co.

Opportunities in Psychiatry. Fenton Keyes. LC 76-42885. (Illus.). (YA). (gr. 9 up). 1988. 13.95 (*0-8442-6367-2*, VGM Career) NTC Contemp Pub Co.

Opportunities in Psychiatry. Fenton Keyes. LC 76-42885. (Illus.). 160p. (YA). (gr. 9 up). 1994. pap. 10.95 (*0-8442-6368-0*, VGM Career) NTC Contemp Pub Co.

Opportunities in Psychology Careers. Charles M. Super & Donald E. Super. LC 93-46080. (Opportunities In . . . Ser.). (Illus.). 160p. pap. 11.95 (*0-8442-4073-7*, 40737, VGM Career) NTC Contemp Pub Co.

Opportunities in Psychology Careers. Donald E. Super & Charles M. Super. (Illus.). 160p. 1992. 13.95 (*0-8442-6478-4*, VGM Career) NTC Contemp Pub Co.

Opportunities in Psychology Careers. Donald E. Super & Charles M. Super. (Illus.). 160p. 1995. pap. 10.95 (*0-8442-6480-6*, VGM Career) NTC Contemp Pub Co.

Opportunities in Psychology Careers Today. Donald E. Super & Charles M. Super. LC 75-32616. (Illus.). 1995. 13.95 (*0-8442-6327-3*, VGM Career); pap. 10.95 (*0-8442-6328-1*, VGM Career) NTC Contemp Pub Co.

Opportunities in Public Health Careers. George Pickett & Terry W. Pickett. 160p. 1992. text 13.95 (*0-8442-6011-8*, VGM Career) NTC Contemp Pub Co.

Opportunities in Public Health Careers. George Pickett & Terry W. Pickett. 160p. 1993. pap. 10.95 (*0-8442-6012-6*, VGM Career) NTC Contemp Pub Co.

Opportunities in Public Relations Careers. Morris B. Rotman. 1993. pap. 10.95 (*0-8442-6487-3*, VGM Career) NTC Contemp Pub Co.

Opportunities in Public Relations Careers. Morris B. Rotman. LC 94-49547. (Opportunities In . . . Ser.). (Illus.). 160p. 1995. pap. 11.95 (*0-8442-4419-8*, 44198, VGM Career) NTC Contemp Pub Co.

Opportunities in Public Relations Careers. Morris B. Rotman. LC 94-49547. (VGM Opportunities Ser.). (Illus.). 160p. 1995. 14.95 (*0-8442-4417-1*, 44171, VGM Career) NTC Contemp Pub Co.

Opportunities in Publishing Careers. S. William Pattis & Robert A. Carter. LC 94-49618. (Opportunities In . . . Ser.). (Illus.). 160p. pap. 11.95 (*0-8442-4432-5*, 44325, VGM Career) NTC Contemp Pub Co.

Opportunities in Publishing Careers. S. William Pattis & Robert A. Carter. LC 94-49618. (Illus.). 160p. 1995. 14.95 (*0-8442-4431-7*, 44317, VGM Career) NTC Contemp Pub Co.

***Opportunities in Publishing Careers.** rev. ed. S. William Pattis et al. LC 00-39272. (Opportunities Ser.). 2000. pap. 11.95 (*0-658-00484-0*) NTC Contemp Pub Co.

Opportunities in Purchasing Careers. Kent Banning. 160p. 1989. 14.95 (*0-8442-8669-9*, VGM Career) NTC Contemp Pub Co.

Opportunities in Purchasing Careers. Kent Banning. LC 97-29044. (Opportunities in . . . Ser.). 160p. 1997. 14.95 (*0-8442-2327-1*, VGM Career); pap. 12.95 (*0-8442-8670-2*, 297OIPUR, VGM Career); pap. 11.95 (*0-8442-2329-8*, VGM Career) NTC Contemp Pub Co.

Opportunities in Real Estate Careers. Mariwyn Evans. (Opportunities In . . . Ser.). (Illus.). 160p. pap. 12.95 (*0-8442-6477-6*, 297OIRE, VGM Career) NTC Contemp Pub Co.

Opportunities in Real Estate Careers. Mariwyn Evans. (VGM Career Planner Ser.). (Illus.). 160p. 1988. 14.95 (*0-8442-6476-8*, VGM Career) NTC Contemp Pub Co.

Opportunities in Real Estate Careers. Mariwyn Evans. LC 96-47706. (Opportunities in... Ser.). (Illus.). 160p. 1997. 14.95 (*0-8442-4684-0*, 46840, Natl Textbk Co); pap. 11.95 (*0-8442-4685-9*) NTC Contemp Pub Co.

Opportunities in Recreation & Leisure. Clayne R. Jensen & Jay H. Naylor. (Opportunities In . . . Ser.). (Illus.). 160p. pap. 12.95 (*0-8442-8586-2*, 297OIR&L, VGM Career) NTC Contemp Pub Co.

Opportunities in Recreation & Leisure Careers. Clayne Jensen. LC 99-34152. (Opportunities in... Ser.). 160p. 1999. 14.95 (*0-8442-2985-7*) NTC Contemp Pub Co.

Opportunities in Recreation & Leisure Careers. rev. ed. Clayne Jensen. LC 99-34152. (Opportunities in... Ser.). 160p. 1999. pap. 11.95 (*0-8442-3229-7*) NTC Contemp Pub Co.

Opportunities in Refrigeration & Air Conditioning Careers. Richard S. Budzik. 1994. pap. 10.95 (*0-8442-8653-2*, VGM Career) NTC Contemp Pub Co.

Opportunities in Religious Service Careers. John O. Nelson. LC 97-41453. (Opportunities in...Ser.). (Illus.). 160p. 1998. 14.95 (*0-8442-2340-9*, 23409, VGM Career); pap. 11.95 (*0-8442-2341-7*, 23417, VGM Career) NTC Contemp Pub Co.

Opportunities in Religious Service Careers. John Oliver Nelson. (Opportunities In . . . Ser.). (Illus.). 160p. pap. 12.95 (*0-8442-6485-7*, 297OIRS, VGM Career) NTC Contemp Pub Co.

Opportunities in Religious Service Careers. John Oliver Nelson. (Illus.). 160p. 1992. 14.95 (*0-8442-6484-9*, VGM Career) NTC Contemp Pub Co.

Opportunities in Research & Development. Jan Goldberg. (Opportunities in... Ser.). (Illus.). 160p. pap. 11.95 (*0-8442-4650-6*, 46506, Natl Textbk Co) NTC Contemp Pub Co.

Opportunities in Research & Development. Jan Goldberg. (Opportunities in... Ser.). (Illus.). 160p. 1996. 14.95 (*0-8442-4649-2*, 46492, Natl Textbk Co) NTC Contemp Pub Co.

Opportunities in Restaurant Careers. Carol C. Chmelynski. (Opportunities In . . . Ser.). (Illus.). 160p. pap. 12.95 (*0-8442-8664-8*, 297OIREST, VGM Career) NTC Contemp Pub Co.

Opportunities in Restaurant Careers. Carol C. Chmelynski. LC 98-4607. (Opportunities in...Ser.). (Illus.). 160p. 1998. 14.95 (*0-8442-2335-2*, 23352, VGM Career); pap. 11.95 (*0-8442-2336-0*, 23360, VGM Career) NTC Contemp Pub Co.

Opportunities in Restaurant Careers. Carol C. Chmelynsky. (Illus.). 160p. 1992. 14.95 (*0-8442-8662-1*, VGM Career) NTC Contemp Pub Co.

Opportunities in Retailing Careers. Roslyn Dolber. (Illus.). 160p. 1993. pap. 10.95 (*0-8442-6521-7*, VGM Career) NTC Contemp Pub Co.

Opportunities in Retailing Careers. Roslyn Dolber. (Illus.). 160p. 1994. 13.95 (*0-8442-6520-9*, VGM Career) NTC Contemp Pub Co.

Opportunities in Retailing Careers. rev. ed. Roslyn Dolber. (Opportunities in... Ser.). (Illus.). 160p. pap. 11.95 (*0-8442-4642-5*, 46425, Natl Textbk Co) NTC Contemp Pub Co.

Opportunities in Retailing Careers. rev. ed. Roslyn Dolber. (Opportunities in... Ser.). (Illus.). 160p. 1996. 14.95 (*0-8442-4641-7*, 46417) NTC Contemp Pub Co.

Opportunities in Robotics Careers. Jan Bone. 160p. 1993. pap. 10.95 (*0-8442-6021-5*, VGM Career) NTC Contemp Pub Co.

Opportunities in Robotics Careers. Jan Bone. 160p. 1994. text 13.95 (*0-8442-6020-7*, VGM Career) NTC Contemp Pub Co.

Opportunities in Robotics Careers. Jan Bone. (Opportunities in...Ser.). (Illus.). 160p. 1994. 14.95 (*0-8442-4057-5*, 40575, VGM Career) NTC Contemp Pub Co.

Opportunities in Sales Careers. James Brescoll & Ralph M. Dahm. LC 94-49548. (Opportunities In . . . Ser.). 160p. pap. 11.95 (*0-8442-4439-2*, 44392, VGM Career) NTC Contemp Pub Co.

Opportunities in Sales Careers. James Brescoll & Ralph M. Dahm. LC 94-49548. (Opportunities in...Ser.). 160p. 1995. 14.95 (*0-8442-4438-4*, 44384, VGM Career) NTC Contemp Pub Co.

Opportunities in Sales Careers. Ralph Dahm & James Brescoll. (Illus.). 160p. 1993. 13.95 (*0-8442-6498-9*, VGM Career) NTC Contemp Pub Co.

Opportunities in Sales Careers. Ralph Dahm & James Brescoll. (Illus.). 160p. 1994. pap. 10.95 (*0-8442-6499-7*, VGM Career) NTC Contemp Pub Co.

Opportunities in Science Technician Careers. JoAnn Chirico. (Opportunities In . . . Ser.). (Illus.). 160p. pap. 11.95 (*0-8442-4597-6*, 45976, Natl Textbk Co) NTC Contemp Pub Co.

Opportunities in Science Technician Careers. JoAnn Chirico. (Opportunities in...Ser.). (Illus.). 160p. 1996. 14.95 (*0-8442-4596-8*, 45968, Natl Textbk Co) NTC Contemp Pub Co.

Opportunities in Secretarial Careers. Blanche Ettinger. (Opportunities In . . . Ser.). (Illus.). 160p. pap. 12.95 (*0-8442-8173-5*, 297OISEC, VGM Career) NTC Contemp Pub Co.

Opportunities in Secretarial Careers. Blanche Ettinger. (Opportunities in...Ser.). (Illus.). 160p. 1993. 14.95 (*0-8442-8172-7*, VGM Career) NTC Contemp Pub Co.

Opportunities in Secretarial Careers. Blanche Ettinger. (Opportunities in...Ser.). 160p. 1999. pap. 11.95 (*0-8442-1799-9*, 17999, VGM Career) NTC Contemp Pub Co.

Opportunities in Secretarial Careers. Blanche Ettinger & Estelle L. Popham. (Illus.). 147p. 1986. 13.95 (*0-8442-6260-9*, VGM Career) NTC Contemp Pub Co.

Opportunities in Secretarial Careers. Blanche Ettinger & Estelle L. Popham. (Illus.). 147p. 1993. pap. 10.95 (*0-8442-6261-7*, VGM Career) NTC Contemp Pub Co.

Opportunities in Secretarial Careers. 3rd ed. Blanche Ettinger. LC 99-17418. (Opportunities in...Ser.). 160p. 1999. 14.95 (*0-8442-1777-8*, 17778, VGM Career) NTC Contemp Pub Co.

Opportunities in Securities Industry. Edward O'Toole. (Opportunities In . . . Ser.). (Illus.). 160p. pap. 12.95 (*0-8442-6642-6*, 297OISI, VGM Career) NTC Contemp Pub Co.

Opportunities in Securities Industry. Edward O'Toole. (Illus.). 160p. 1987. 13.95 (*0-8442-6641-8*, VGM Career) NTC Contemp Pub Co.

Opportunities in Single-Tenant Retail Properties: Changing Space & Capital Markets. Maury Seldin & Ron M. Donohue. LC 94-233082. 61p. (Orig.). 1994. pap. 12.50 (*0-939653-02-8*, 38-448-390) Couns Real Estate.

Opportunities in Social Science. Rosanne J. Marek. LC 96-47281. (Illus.). 160p. 1997. 14.95 (*0-8442-4573-9*, 45739) NTC Contemp Pub Co.

Opportunities in Social Science Careers. 160p. 1992. 14.95 (*0-8442-8667-2*, VGM Career) NTC Contemp Pub Co.

Opportunities in Social Science Careers. Roseanne J. Marek. 160p. 1994. pap. 11.95 (*0-8442-8668-0*, VGM Career) NTC Contemp Pub Co.

Opportunities in Social Work Careers. Renee Wittenberg. LC 96-27795. (Opportunities in... Ser.). (Illus.). 160p. pap. 11.95 (*0-8442-4675-1*, 46751, Natl Textbk Co) NTC Contemp Pub Co.

Opportunities in Social Work Careers. Renee Wittenberg. (Opportunities in...Ser.). (Illus.). 160p. 1991. 13.95 (*0-8442-6488-1*, VGM Career) NTC Contemp Pub Co.

Opportunities in Social Work Careers. Renee Wittenberg. (Opportunities in...Ser.). (Illus.). 160p. 1993. pap. 10.95 (*0-8442-6490-3*, VGM Career) NTC Contemp Pub Co.

Opportunities in Social Work Careers. Renee Wittenberg. LC 96-27795. (Opportunities in... Ser.). (Illus.). 160p. 1996. 14.95 (*0-8442-4674-3*, 46743, Natl Textbk Co) NTC Contemp Pub Co.

Opportunities in Special Education Careers. Robert Connelly. LC 94-49079. (Opportunities In . . . Ser.). (Illus.). 160p. pap. 11.95 (*0-8442-4426-0*, 44260, VGM Career) NTC Contemp Pub Co.

Opportunities in Special Education Careers. Robert Connelly. LC 94-49079. (Opportunities in...Ser.). (Illus.). 160p. 1995. 14.95 (*0-8442-4425-2*, 44252, VGM Career) NTC Contemp Pub Co.

Opportunities in Speech & Language Pathology Careers. rev. ed. Patricia L. Hicks. LC 95-30194. (Opportunities In . . . Ser.). (Illus.). 160p. 1995. pap. 11.95 (*0-8442-4586-0*, 45860, VGM Career) NTC Contemp Pub Co.

Opportunities in Speech & Language Pathology Careers. rev. ed. Patricia L. Hicks. LC 95-30194. (Illus.). 160p. 1995. 14.95 (*0-8442-4585-2*, 45852, VGM Career) NTC Contemp Pub Co.

Opportunities in Speech-Language Pathology Careers. Patricia Laricino. (Illus.). 160p. 1987. 13.95 (*0-8442-6013-4*, VGM Career) NTC Contemp Pub Co.

Opportunities in Speech-Language Pathology Careers. Patricia Laricino. (Illus.). 160p. 1993. pap. 10.95 (*0-8442-6014-2*, VGM Career) NTC Contemp Pub Co.

Opportunities in Sports & Athletics. William R. Heitzman. (Illus.). 160p. 1993. pap. 10.95 (*0-8442-6224-2*, VGM Career) NTC Contemp Pub Co.

Opportunities in Sports & Athletics Careers. William R. Heitzmann. LC 92-37844. (Opportunities In . . . Ser.). (Illus.). 160p. pap. 11.95 (*0-8442-4052-4*, 40524, VGM Career) NTC Contemp Pub Co.

Opportunities in Sports & Athletics Careers. William R. Heitzmann. LC 92-37844. (Opportunities in...Ser.). (Illus.). 160p. 1994. 14.95 (*0-8442-4051-6*, 40516, VGM Career) NTC Contemp Pub Co.

Opportunities in Sports Medicine Careers. William R. Heitzmann. (Opportunities In . . . Ser.). (Illus.). 160p. 1991. pap. 11.95 (*0-8442-8169-7*, 81697, VGM Career) NTC Contemp Pub Co.

Opportunities in Sports Medicine Careers. William R. Heitzmann. (Opportunities in...Ser.). (Illus.). 160p. 1995. 14.95 (*0-8442-8168-9*, 81689, VGM Career) NTC Contemp Pub Co.

Opportunities in State & Local Government Careers. Neale J. Baxter. (Illus.). 160p. 1987. 13.95 (*0-8442-6193-9*, VGM Career); pap. 10.95 (*0-8442-6194-7*, VGM Career) NTC Contemp Pub Co.

Opportunities in State & Local Government Careers. Neale J. Baxter. LC 92-14629. (Opportunities in...Ser.). (Illus.). 160p. 1994. 14.95 (*0-8442-4040-0*, VGM Career) NTC Contemp Pub Co.

Opportunities in Summer Camp Careers. Blythe Camenson. LC 97-41353. (Opportunities in...Ser.). (Illus.). 160p. 1998. 14.95 (*0-8442-2344-1*, 23441, VGM Career); pap. 11.95 (*0-8442-2345-X*, 2345X, VGM Career) NTC Contemp Pub Co.

Opportunities in Teaching. Janet Fine. (Illus.). 150p. 1987. pap. 10.95 (*0-8442-6250-1*, VGM Career) NTC Contemp Pub Co.

Opportunities in Teaching. Janet Fine. (Illus.). 160p. 1991. 13.95 (*0-8442-6504-7*, VGM Career) NTC Contemp Pub Co.

Opportunities in Teaching Careers. Janet Fine. 1993. pap. 10.95 (*0-8442-6505-5*, VGM Career) NTC Contemp Pub Co.

***Opportunities in Teaching Careers.** rev. ed. Janet Fine. LC 99-87194. (Opportunities in... Ser.). 160p. 2000. 14.95 (*0-658-00194-9*, 001949); pap. 11.95 (*0-658-00195-7*, 001957) NTC Contemp Pub Co.

Opportunities in Teaching English to Speakers of Other Languages. Blythe Camenson. LC 94-49617. (Opportunities In . . . Ser.). (Illus.). 160p. pap. 11.95 (*0-8442-4428-7*, 44287, VGM Career) NTC Contemp Pub Co.

Opportunities in Technical Communications. Jay Gould & Wayne Losano. (Opportunities In . . . Ser.). (Illus.). 160p. pap. 12.95 (*0-8442-6247-1*, 297OITEC, VGM Career) NTC Contemp Pub Co.

Opportunities in Technical Communications. Jay Gould & Wayne Losano. (Illus.). 160p. 1985. 13.95 (*0-8442-6246-3*, VGM Career) NTC Contemp Pub Co.

Opportunities in Technical Communications. Shonan F. Noronha. LC 93-20679. (Opportunities in...Ser.). 1995. 13.95 (*0-8442-4074-5*, VGM Career); pap. 10.95 (*0-8442-4075-3*, VGM Career) NTC Contemp Pub Co.

Opportunities in Technical Education Careers. Robert Connelly. LC 97-29001. (Opportunities in...Ser.). (Illus.). 160p. 1997. 14.95 (*0-8442-2310-7*, 23107, VGM Career) NTC Contemp Pub Co.

Opportunities in Technical Education Careers. Robert Connelly. LC 97-29001. (Opportunities in... Ser.). 160p. 1998. pap. 11.95 (*0-8442-2311-5*, 23115) NTC Contemp Pub Co.

Opportunities in Technical Writing & Communications Careers. Jay Gould. LC 93-46663. (Opportunities In . . . Ser.). (Illus.). 160p. pap. 12.95 (*0-8442-4129-6*, 297OITW&C, VGM Career) NTC Contemp Pub Co.

Opportunities in Technical Writing & Communications Careers. Jay Gould. LC 93-46663. (Opportunities in...Ser.). (Illus.). 160p. 1994. 14.95 (*0-8442-4128-8*, VGM Career) NTC Contemp Pub Co.

***Opportunities in Technical Writing Careers.** rev. ed. Jay Gould. LC 99-56162. (Opportunities in... Ser.). 160p. 2000. 14.95 (*0-658-00207-4*, 002074); pap. 11.95 (*0-658-00208-2*, 002082, VGM Career) NTC Contemp Pub Co.

Opportunities in Telecommunications. Jan Bone. (Illus.). 160p. 1992. 13.95 (*0-8442-8654-0*, VGM Career) NTC Contemp Pub Co.

Opportunities in Telecommunications. Jan Bone. (Illus.). 160p. 1993. pap. 10.95 (*0-8442-8655-9*, VGM Career) NTC Contemp Pub Co.

Opportunities in Telecommunications Careers. rev. ed. Jan Bone. LC 95-24092. (Opportunities In . . . Ser.). 160p. pap. 12.95 (*0-8442-4588-7*, 297OITEL, VGM Career) NTC Contemp Pub Co.

Opportunities in Telecommunications Careers. rev. ed. Jan Bone. LC 95-24092. (VGM Opportunities Ser.). 160p. 1995. 14.95 (*0-8442-4587-9*, VGM Career) NTC Contemp Pub Co.

Opportunities in Telemarketing Careers. Anne Basye. LC 93-48712. (Opportunities In . . . Ser.). (Illus.). 160p. 1994. pap. 11.95 (*0-8442-4134-2*, 41342, VGM Career) NTC Contemp Pub Co.

Opportunities in Telemarketing Careers. Anne Basye. LC 93-48712. (Illus.). 160p. 1995. 14.95 (*0-8442-4133-4*, 41334, VGM Career) NTC Contemp Pub Co.

Opportunities in Television & Video Careers. Shonan Noronha. LC 97-48584. (Opportunities in... Ser.). (Illus.). 160p. 1998. 14.95 (*0-8442-2308-5*, 23085, VGM Career); pap. 11.95 (*0-8442-2309-3*, 23093, VGM Career) NTC Contemp Pub Co.

O

Opportunities in Television & Video Careers. Shonan F. Noronha. (VGM Career Planner Ser.). (Illus.). 160p. 1992. 13.95 (*0-8442-6491-1*, VGM Career) NTC Contemp Pub Co.

Opportunities in Television & Video Careers. Shonan F. Noronha. (VGM Career Planner Ser.). (Illus.). 160p. 1993. pap. 10.95 (*0-8442-6493-8*, VGM Career) NTC Contemp Pub Co.

Opportunities in the Contraceptive & Fertility Markets: Demographic Changes Affect Market Dynamics. 248p. 1992. 1895.00 (*1-56753-002-8*) Frost & Sullivan.

Opportunities in the Deregulated Electric Utilities Market for A-E-P & Environmental Consulting Firms. 128p. 1998. pap. text 195.00 (*1-885002-50-5*) Zweig White.

Opportunities in the Hydrologic Sciences. Committee on Opportunities in the Hydrologic Scien. 368p. 1990. text 29.95 (*0-309-04244-5*) Natl Acad Pr.

Opportunities in the Machine Trades. 1994th rev. ed. Lonny D. Garvey. Ed. by Sarah Kennedy. LC 93-47514. (Opportunities in...Ser.). (Illus.). 160p. 1995. 14.95 (*0-8442-4123-7*, 41237, VGM Career) NTC Contemp Pub Co.

Opportunities in the Machine Trades. 1994th rev. ed. Lonny D. Garvey. LC 93-47514. (Opportunities In . . . Ser.). (Illus.). 160p. pap. 11.95 (*0-8442-4124-5*, 41245, VGM Career) NTC Contemp Pub Co.

Opportunities in the Motion Picture Industry & How to Qualify for Positions in Its Many Branches. Photoplay Research Society Staff. LC 73-124033. (Literature of Cinema, Ser. 1). 1970. reprint ed. 12.95 (*0-405-01633-6*) Ayer.

Opportunities in the Nutrition & Food Sciences: Research Challenges & the Next Generation of Investigators. Ed. by Robert O. Earl et al. 328p. (C). 1994. pap. text 36.95 (*0-309-04884-2*) Natl Acad Pr.

Opportunities in Theatrical Design & Production. Ann Folke & Richard Harden. (Illus.). 160p. 1992. 13.95 (*0-8442-6256-0*, VGM Career) NTC Contemp Pub Co.

Opportunities in Theatrical Design & Production. Ann Folke & Richard Harden. (Illus.). 160p. 1993. pap. 10.95 (*0-8442-6257-9*, VGM Career) NTC Contemp Pub Co.

Opportunities in Tool & Die. George Dudzinski. (Opportunities In . . . Ser.). (Illus.). 160p. pap. 11.95 (*0-8442-4048-6*, 40486, VGM Career) NTC Contemp Pub Co.

Opportunities in Training & Development. Edward Gordon et al. (Opportunities in... Ser.). (Illus.). 160p. pap. 11.95 (*0-8442-4644-1*, 46441, Natl Textbk Co) NTC Contemp Pub Co.

Opportunities in Training & Development. Edward Gordon et al. (Opportunities in... Ser.). 160p. 1996. 14.95 (*0-8442-4643-3*, 46433, Natl Textbk Co) NTC Contemp Pub Co.

Opportunities in Transportation Careers. Adrian A. Paradis. LC 96-47280. (Opportunities in... Ser.). (Illus.). 160p. pap. 11.95 (*0-8442-4683-2*, 46832, Natl Textbk Co) NTC Contemp Pub Co.

Opportunities in Transportation Careers. Adrian A. Paradis. (Illus.). 160p. 1991. 14.95 (*0-8442-6567-5*, VGM Career) NTC Contemp Pub Co.

Opportunities in Transportation Careers. Adrian A. Paradis. (Illus.). 160p. 1993. pap. 11.95 (*0-8442-6568-3*, VGM Career) NTC Contemp Pub Co.

Opportunities in Transportation Careers. Adrian A. Paradis. LC 96-47280. (Opportunities in... Ser.). (Illus.). 160p. 1997. 14.95 (*0-8442-4682-4*, 46824, Natl Textbk Co) NTC Contemp Pub Co.

Opportunities in Travel Careers. Robert Milne. (Opportunities in... Ser.). (Illus.). 160p. pap. 11.95 (*0-8442-4640-9*, 46409, Natl Textbk Co) NTC Contemp Pub Co.

Opportunities in Travel Careers. Robert Milne. (Opportunities in... Ser.). (Illus.). 160p. 1996. 14.95 (*0-8442-4639-5*, 46395, Natl Textbk Co) NTC Contemp Pub Co.

Opportunities in Travel Careers. Robert S. Milne. LC 75-32612. (Illus.). (gr. 8 up). 1985. 13.95 (*0-8442-6215-3*, VGM Career) NTC Contemp Pub Co.

Opportunities in Travel Careers. Robert S. Milne. LC 75-32612. (Illus.). (gr. 8 up). 1986. pap. 10.95 (*0-8442-6216-1*, VGM Career) NTC Contemp Pub Co.

Opportunities in Travel Careers. Robert S. Milne. (Illus.). 160p. 1992. 13.95 (*0-8442-8568-4*, VGM Career) NTC Contemp Pub Co.

Opportunities in Travel Careers. Robert S. Milne. (Illus.). 160p. 1993. pap. 10.95 (*0-8442-8569-2*, VGM Career) NTC Contemp Pub Co.

Opportunities in Travel Careers Robert S. Milne. LC 75-32612. (VGM Career Ser.). 158 p. 1976. write for info. (*0-89022-209-6*) Voc Guidance.

Opportunities in Trucking Careers. Ken Scharnberg. (Opportunities In . . . Ser.). (Illus.). 160p. pap. 12.95 (*0-8442-8182-4*, 297OITRUC, VGM Career) NTC Contemp Pub Co.

Opportunities in Trucking Careers. Ken Scharnberg. (Opportunities in...Ser.). (Illus.). 160p. 1993. 14.95 (*0-8442-8181-6*, VGM Career) NTC Contemp Pub Co.

Opportunities in Veterinary Medicine. Sarah Mikesell. LC 92-43493. (Opportunities In . . . Ser.). (Illus.). 160p. 1993. pap. 11.95 (*0-8442-4060-5*, 40605, VGM Career) NTC Contemp Pub Co.

Opportunities in Veterinary Medicine. Sarah Mikesell. LC 92-43493. (Opportunities in...Ser.). (Illus.). 160p. 1994. 14.95 (*0-8442-4059-1*, 40591, VGM Career) NTC Contemp Pub Co.

Opportunities in Veterinary Medicine Careers. Robert E. Swope. 160p. 1993. pap. 10.95 (*0-8442-6344-3*, VGM Career) NTC Contemp Pub Co.

Opportunities in Veterinary Medicine Careers. Robert E. Swope. 160p. 1993. text 13.95 (*0-8442-6343-5*, VGM Career) NTC Contemp Pub Co.

Opportunities in Visual Arts Careers. Mark Salmon. LC 92-18525. (Opportunities In . . . Ser.). 160p. pap. 11.95 (*0-8442-4033-8*, 297OIVA, VGM Career) NTC Contemp Pub Co.

Opportunities in Visual Arts Careers. Mark Salmon. LC 92-18525. (Opportunities in...Ser.). (Illus.). 160p. 1994. 14.95 (*0-8442-4031-1*, VGM Career) NTC Contemp Pub Co.

Opportunities in Vocational & Technical Careers. Adrian A. Paradis. 160p. 1992. text 13.95 (*0-8442-6018-5*, VGM Career) NTC Contemp Pub Co.

Opportunities in Vocational & Technical Careers. Adrian A. Paradis. 160p. 1993. pap. 10.95 (*0-8442-6019-3*, VGM Career) NTC Contemp Pub Co.

Opportunities in Vocational & Technical Careers. 2nd ed. Adrian A. Paradis. (Opportunities in...Ser.). (Illus.). 160p. 1994. 14.95 (*0-8442-4007-9*, VGM Career) NTC Contemp Pub Co.

Opportunities in Warehousing Careers. Mark Rowh. LC 92-16776. (Opportunities in...Ser.). (Illus.). 160p. 1994. 14.95 (*0-8442-4034-6*, VGM Career) NTC Contemp Pub Co.

Opportunities in Waste Management Careers. Mark Rowh. (Opportunities In . . . Ser.). (Illus.). 160p. pap. 11.95 (*0-8442-4019-2*, 40192, VGM Career) NTC Contemp Pub Co.

Opportunities in Welding Careers. Mark Rowh. LC 96-9351. (Opportunities in... Ser.). (Illus.). 160p. pap. 11.95 (*0-8442-4669-7*, 46697, Natl Textbk Co) NTC Contemp Pub Co.

Opportunities in Welding Careers. Mark Rowh. LC 96-9351. (Opportunities in... Ser.). (Illus.). 160p. 1996. 14.95 (*0-8442-4668-9*, 46689, Natl Textbk Co) NTC Contemp Pub Co.

Opportunities in Word Processing. Marianne F. Mundy. (Illus.). 147p. 1985. 13.95 (*0-8442-6200-5*, VGM Career) NTC Contemp Pub Co.

Opportunities in Word Processing. Marianne F. Mundy. (Illus.). 147p. 1988. pap. 10.95 (*0-8442-6201-3*, VGM Career) NTC Contemp Pub Co.

Opportunities in Word Processing Careers. rev. ed. Marianne F. Mundy. LC 90-50735. (Opportunities In . . . Ser.). 160p. (YA). (gr. 7 up). pap. 12.95 (*0-8442-8165-4*, 297OIWP, VGM Career) NTC Contemp Pub Co.

Opportunities in Word Processing Careers. rev. ed. Marianne F. Mundy. (Opportunities in...Ser.). 160p. (YA). (gr. 7 up). 1993. 14.95 (*0-8442-8164-6*, VGM Career) NTC Contemp Pub Co.

Opportunities in Writing Careers. Elizabeth Foote-Smith. (Opportunities In . . . Ser.). (Illus.). 160p. pap. 12.95 (*0-8442-6513-6*, 297OIWRIT, VGM Career) NTC Contemp Pub Co.

Opportunities in Writing Careers. Elizabeth Foote-Smith. (Illus.). 160p. 1992. 14.95 (*0-8442-6512-8*, VGM Career) NTC Contemp Pub Co.

*__Opportunities in Writing Careers.__ Elizabeth Foote-Smith. LC 98-52484. (Opportunities in...Ser.). 160p. 1999. 14.95 (*0-8442-1810-3*, 18103); pap. 11.95 (*0-8442-1815-4*, 18154, VGM Career) NTC Contemp Pub Co.

Opportunities in Your Own Service Business. Robert McKay. (Opportunities In . . . Ser.). (Illus.). 160p. pap. 12.95 (*0-8442-6232-3*, 297OIYOSB, VGM Career) NTC Contemp Pub Co.

Opportunities in Zoo Careers. Blythe Camenson. LC 97-21798. (Opportunities in...Ser.). (Illus.). 160p. 1997. 14.95 (*0-8442-2312-3*, 23123, VGM Career); pap. 11.95 (*0-8442-2313-1*, 23131, VGM Career) NTC Contemp Pub Co.

Opportunities Industrialization Centers: A Decade of Community - Based Manpower Services. Bernard E. Anderson. LC 76-48860. (Manpower & Human Resources Studies: No. 6). 170p. reprint ed. pap. 52.70 (*0-8357-3159-6*, 203942200012) Bks Demand.

Opportunities Missed, Opportunities Seized: Preventive Diplomacy in the Post-Cold War World. Ed. by Bruce W. Jentleson. LC 99-27300. (Carnegie Commission on Preventing Deadly Conflict Ser.). (Illus.). 456p. 1999. pap. 29.95 (*0-8476-8559-4*) Rowman.

Opportunities Missed, Opportunities Seized: Preventive Diplomacy in the Post-Cold War World. Ed. by Bruce W. Jentleson et al. LC 99-27300. (Carnegie Commission on Preventing Deadly Conflict Ser.). (Illus.). 456p. 1999. 75.00 (*0-8476-8558-6*) Rowman.

Opportunities of a Night. M. De Crebillon. Tr. by Eric Sutton. LC 70-174388. 1972. reprint ed. 23.95 (*0-405-08401-3*) Ayer.

Opportunities of ISO 14,000. Richard K. Miller & Christy H. Gunter. (Market Research Survey Ser.: No. 314). 50p. 1996. 200.00 (*1-55865-337-6*) Future Tech Surveys.

Opportunities to Improve Air Quality Through Transportation Pricing Programs. Ed. by Barry Leonard. (Illus.). 130p. (C). 1998. pap. text 25.00 (*0-7881-3943-6*) DIANE Pub.

Opportunities to Improve Marine Forecasting. Ed. by Committee on Opportunities to Improve Marine Obser. 120p. 1989. pap. text 15.00 (*0-309-04090-6*) Natl Acad Pr.

Opportunities with Industrial Enzymes. Ed. by Robert Heinemann & Bernard Wolnak. LC 92-61636. (Illus.). 160p. 1992. 95.00 (*0-9626769-1-8*) B Wolnak & Assocs.

Opportunity. Sri Chinmoy. (Illus.). 50p. 1998. pap., per. 4.95 (*0-9664613-3-9*) Jharna Kala.

Opportunity & Challenge. Frederick F. Chien. Ed. by Daniel A. Mica & J. Terry Emerson. 1995. 29.95 (*0-614-10452-1*) AZ Hist Foun.

Opportunity & Mobility in Urban Housing Markets. P. C. Emmi & L. Magnusson. (Progress in Planning Ser.: Vol. 43). (Illus.). 88p. 1995. pap. 70.00 (*0-08-042545-3*, Pergamon Pr) Elsevier.

Opportunity, & Other Essays & Addresses. John L. Spalding. LC 68-57339. (Essay Index Reprint Ser.). 1977. 19.95 (*0-8369-0894-5*) Ayer.

Opportunity at Work: The New York City Garment Industry. Mark Levitan. 80p. 1998. 12.00 (*0-88156-216-5*) Comm Serv Soc NY.

Opportunity Cost in Finance & Accounting. H. G. Heymann & Robert Bloom. LC 90-36025. 216p. 1990. 65.00 (*0-89930-400-1*, BMK, Quorum Bks) Greenwood.

Opportunity for Profit. David Gross. (Double Diamond Triangle Saga Ser.). 1998. pap. 2.99 (*0-7869-0868-8*, Pub. by TSR Inc) Random.

Opportunity for Skillful Reading. 5th ed. Irwin L. Joffe. 464p. (C). 1987. pap. write for info. (*0-534-08520-2*) Wadsworth Pub.

Opportunity for Skillful Reading. 6th ed. Irwin L. Joffe. 471p. (C). 1991. pap. 26.95 (*0-534-14664-3*) Wadsworth Pub.

Opportunity for Skillful Reading. 7th ed. Irwin L. Joffe. 459p. (C). 1993. mass mkt. 27.25 (*0-534-21396-0*) Wadsworth Pub.

Opportunity for Skillful Reading. 8th ed. Irwin L. Joffe. LC 96-8980. (Developmental Study/Study Skills Ser.). 1996. pap. 31.00 (*0-534-52326-9*) Wadsworth Pub.

*__Opportunity for Skillful Reading.__ 9th ed. Joffe. (Developmental Study/Study Skills Ser.). 2000. pap. 34.75 (*0-534-52844-9*) Wadsworth Pub.

Opportunity for the Year 2000: Creative Affirmative Action Strategies for a Changing Workforce. 1991. lib. bdg. 79.00 (*0-8490-4355-7*) Gordon Pr.

Opportunity Foregone: Education in Brazil. Ed. by Nancy Birdsall & Richard Sabot. LC 96-77344. (Inter-American Development Bank Ser.). 566p. (C). 1996. pap. 14.50 (*1-886938-03-2*) IADB.

Opportunity House: Ethnographic Stories of Mental Retardation. Michael V. Angrosino. LC 97-33813. (Ethnographic Alternatives Ser.: Vol. 2). 288p. 1997. 65.00 (*0-7619-8916-1*); pap. 23.95 (*0-7619-8917-X*) AltaMira Pr.

Opportunity in Adversity: How Colleges Can Succeed in Hard Times. Janice S. Green et al. LC 85-45062. (Jossey-Bass Higher Education Ser.). 341p. reprint ed. pap. 105.80 (*0-7837-2519-1*, 204267800006) Bks Demand.

Opportunity in Mexico: A Small Business Guide. John L. Manzella & Tony Walker. (Illus.). 1992. write for info. (*0-926566-02-4*) Manzella Trade.

Opportunity in the United States: Social & Individual Responsibility. (Domestic Strategy Group Reports). 90p. 1996. pap. 10.00 (*0-89843-194-8*) The Aspen Inst.

Opportunity Is Calling Vol. 1: How to Start Your Own Successful 900 Number. Robert J. Bentz. (Orig.). 1993. pap. 29.95 (*0-9637758-5-5*) ATS Pubng.

Opportunity Knocks: American Economic Policy after Gorbachev. Robert A. Solo. LC 90-46944. 216p. (gr. 13). 1991. text 79.95 (*0-87332-774-8*) M E Sharpe.

Opportunity Management: Strategic Planning for Small Business. Omer Carey & Dean Olson. write for info. (*0-318-58210-4*) P-H.

Opportunity My Ally. Lewis Cameron. (Illus.). 253p. 1965. 7.50 (*0-227-67706-4*) Attic Pr.

Opportunity of Leisure: The History of the York Railway Institute 1889-1989. Hugh Murray. (C). 1999. pap. text 21.00 (*0-9514452-0-0*, Pub. by W Sessions) St Mut.

Opportunity or Privilege: Labor Legislation in America. Charles W. Baird. (Studies in Social Philosophy & Policy: No. 4). 97p. (Orig.). 1984. pap. 14.95 (*0-912051-02-7*) Transaction Pubs.

Opportunity Programs: Opening the Doors to Higher Education: Hearing of the Committee on Labor & Human Resources, United States Senate, One Hundred Fifth Congress, First Session...June 12, 1997. United States Staff. LC 98-106713. (S. Hrg. Ser.). 87 p. 1997. write for info. (*0-16-055450-0*) USGPO.

Opportunity Reader: Stories, Poetry & Essays from Urban League's Opportunity Magazine. Ed. by Sondra Kathryn Wilson. (Modern Library Harlem Renaissance Ser.). 1999. pap. 14.95 (*0-375-75379-6*) Modern Lib NY.

Opportunity Realized: The Greek Catholic Union's First One Hundred Years 1892-1992. LC 94-75757. 292p. 1994. text 28.95 (*0-9641001-0-X*) Greek Catholic.

Opportunity Scotland. Great Britain Staff. LC 98-229470. (CM Ser.). vi, 74 p. 1998. write for info. (*0-10-140482-4*) U Pr of Amer.

*__Opportunity Spotting.__ Nigel MacLennan. LC 97-32767. 160p. 1998. 29.95 (*0-566-08004-4*, Pub. by Gower) Ashgate Pub Co.

Opportunity Spotting: Creativity for Corporate Growth. Nigel MacLennan. (Illus.). 160p. 1994. 83.95 (*0-566-07497-4*, Pub. by Gower) Ashgate Pub Co.

Opportunity to Learn Standards for Art Education. 64p. (Orig.). 1995. pap. text 15.00 (*0-937652-90-3*, 257) Natl Art Ed.

Opportunity-to-Learn Standards for Music Instruction. LC 94-213063. 32p. (J). (gr. k-12). 1994. pap. 12.00 (*1-56545-040-X*, 1619) MENC.

Opportunity Trove: A Treasure Trove. Melvin P. Espy. LC 88-90658. (Illus.). 160p. 1988. student ed. write for info. (*0-929143-00-0*) RE Dev Inc.

Opportunity 2000: Creative Affirmative Action Strategies for a Changing Workforce. 181p. 1993. pap. text 30.00 (*1-56806-171-4*) DIANE Pub.

Opportunity 2000: Creative Affirmative Action Strategies for a Changing Workforce. 1997. lib. bdg. 250.99 (*0-8490-7669-2*) Gordon Pr.

Opportunity 2000: Creative Affirmative Action Strategies for a Changing Workforce. Kevin R. Hopkins et al. 195p. (Orig.). 1988. pap. 5.00 (*0-16-003889-8*, S/N 029-014-002) USGPO.

Opportunties in Health & Medical Careers. I. Donald Snook & Leo D'Orazio. (Illus.). 160p. 1993. 14.95 (*0-8442-8573-0*, VGM Career) NTC Contemp Pub Co.

Opportunties in Informational Systems Careers. Douglas B. Hoyt. (Illus.). 160p. (YA). 1992. 14.95 (*0-8442-8563-3*, 85633, VGM Career) NTC Contemp Pub Co.

Opportuntities in Entertainment. Jan Goldberg. LC 98-46030. (Opportunities In . . . Ser.). 160p. 1999. pap. 11.95 (*0-8442-1829-4*, 18294, VGM Career) NTC Contemp Pub Co.

Opposing Ambitions: Gender & Identity in an Alternative Organization. Sherryl Kleinman. LC 95-35972. 160p. 1996. pap. 10.95 (*0-226-44005-2*); lib. bdg. 35.00 (*0-226-44004-4*) U Ch Pr.

Opposing Fascion: A Book of Improper Poetry. Stephen Van Eck. LC 92-60513. 97p. 1992. pap. 3.00 (*0-9632612-0-7*) Wet Water.

Opposing Fascism: Community, Authority & Resistance in Europe. Ed. by Tim Kirk & Anthony McElligott. LC 99-212761. 256p. (C). 1999. text 59.95 (*0-521-48309-3*) Cambridge U Pr.

Opposing Poetries: Issues & Institutions. Hank Lazer. (Avant-Garde & Modernism Studies: Pt. 1). 296p. 1996. text 69.95 (*0-8101-1264-7*); pap. text 16.95 (*0-8101-1265-5*) Northwestern U Pr.

Opposing Poetries: Readings. Hank Lazer. (Avant-Garde & Modernism Studies: Pt. 2). 296p. 1996. text 69.95 (*0-8101-1413-5*) Northwestern U Pr.

Opposing Poetries Pt. 2: Readings. Hank Lazer. 296p. 1996. pap. text 16.95 (*0-8101-1414-3*) Northwestern U Pr.

*__Opposing Schools.__ Kathryn M. Neckerman. 1998. 21.00 (*0-226-56960-8*) U Ch Pr.

Opposing Self. Lionel Trilling. LC 79-10362. 256p. 1978. 10.95 (*0-15-170068-0*) Harcourt.

Opposing Self. Lionel Trilling. LC 79-10362. 204p. 1979. pap. 3.95 (*0-15-670065-4*, Harvest Bks) Harcourt.

Opposing Shore. Julien Gracq. Tr. by Richard Howard from FRE. (Twentieth-Century Continental Fiction Ser.). 292p. 1987. pap. text 19.00 (*0-231-05789-X*) Col U Pr.

Opposing Viewpoints in American History, Vol. I. Ed. by Bill Dudley. LC 95-33446. (Illus.). 352p. (J). (gr. 5-12). 1996. pap. text 21.20 (*1-56510-347-5*) Greenhaven.

Opposing Viewpoints in American History, Vol. I. Ed. by Bill Dudley. LC 95-33446. (Illus.). 352p. (J). (gr. 5-12). 1996. lib. bdg. 37.44 (*1-56510-348-3*) Greenhaven.

Opposing Viewpoints in American History, Vol. 2. Ed. by William Dudley. LC 95-33446. (Illus.). 352p. (YA). (gr. 5-12). 1996. lib. bdg. 37.44 (*1-56510-350-5*) Greenhaven.

Opposing Viewpoints in American History, Vol. II. Ed. by William Dudley. LC 95-33446. (Illus.). 352p. (J). (gr. 5-12). 1996. pap. text 21.20 (*1-56510-349-1*) Greenhaven.

*__Opposing Viewpoints in Social Issues.__ William Dudley. LC 99-30912. (Opposing Viewpoints Ser.). 192p. (YA). (gr. 9-12). 2000. 21.96 (*0-7377-0123-4*); pap. 13.96 (*0-7377-0122-6*) Greenhaven.

Opposing Virtues. Famhy Farag. 56p. 1978. pap. 15.95 (*0-85105-323-8*, Pub. by Smyth) Dufour.

*__Opposite Land.__ large type ed. R. Scott Heaton. Ed. by Chris Terrence. (Illus.). 20p. (J). (gr. k-3). 2000. pap. 9.95 (*0-9664880-2-4*) Green Mt Pubng.

Opposite Mirrors: An Essay on the Conventionalist Theory of Institutions. Eerik Lagerspetz. LC 94-42237. (Law & Philosophy Library: Vol. 22). 240p. 1995. lib. bdg. 110.50 (*0-7923-3325-X*, Pub. by Kluwer Academic) Kluwer Academic.

Opposite Oceans. G. Murray Thomas. (Illus.). 24p. (Orig.). 1993. reprint ed. pap. 4.00 (*1-885021-02-X*) Orange Ocean.

Opposite of Letting the Mind Wander: Selected Poems & a Few Songs. Keith Waldrop. (Lost Roads Ser.: No. 36). 128p. (Orig.). 1990. pap. 8.95 (*0-918786-41-X*) Lost Roads.

*__Opposite of Stop Is Go.__ Marcia Leonard. LC 99-64436. (Hanna Bks.). 24p. (J). (ps up). 2000. 7.95 (*0-694-01368-4*, HarpFestival) HarpC Child Bks.

Opposite Poles: Immigrants & Ethnics in Polish Chicago, 1976-1990. Mary P. Erdmans. LC 97-17949. 1998. 50.00 (*0-271-01735-X*); pap. 19.95 (*0-271-01736-8*) Pa St U Pr.

Opposite Religions Still? Interpreting Northern Ireland after the Conflict. Brian K. Lambkin. 224p. (C). 1996. 63.95 (*1-85972-163-X*, Pub. by Avebry) Ashgate Pub Co.

Opposite Sex: Gay Men on Lesbians, Lesbians on Gay Men. Sara Miles & Eric E. Rofes. LC 97-33960. 288p. 1998. text 55.00 (*0-8147-7476-8*); pap. text 17.00 (*0-8147-7477-6*) NYU Pr.

Opposite Song Big Book: Black & White Nellie Edge I Can Read & Sing Big Book. Illus. by Barry Nichols. (J). (ps-2). 1988. pap. text 21.00 (*0-922053-06-5*) N Edge Res.

Opposite the Cross Keys. large type ed. Sylvia Haymon. 1993. 39.95 (*0-7066-1015-6*, Pub. by Remploy Pr) St Mut.

Oppositeness Seminar Kit: How Opposite Personalities Interact. rev. ed. William D. Murray & Rosalie R. Murray. 115p. 1995. ring bd. 119.95 (*1-878287-12-5*) Type & Temperament.

Opposites see Little Mouse's Learn-&-Play

Opposites see Opuestos

Opposites. (Chubby Board Bks.). (Illus.). 16p. (J). (ps). 1988. pap. 2.95 (*0-671-64871-3*) Litle Simon.

Opposites. (Active Minds Ser.). (Illus.). 24p. (J). 1993. 4.98 (*1-56173-484-5*) Pubns Intl Ltd.

Opposites. (Fit-A-Shape Ser.). (Illus.). 10p. (J). 1998. bds. 5.95 (*1-56138-708-8*) Running Pr.

An Asterisk (*) at the beginning of an entry indicates that the title is appearing for the first time.

Opposites. Illus. by Tedd Arnold. (Nursery Rhyme Concept Bks.). 16p. (J). (ps). 1992. pap. 3.95 (*0-671-77823-4*) Litle Simon.

Opposites. Rowan Barnes-Murphy. (Blackboard Bks.). (Illus.). 16p. (J). (ps). 1993. bds. 3.95 (*0-8249-8611-3*, Ideals Child) Hambleton-Hill.

***Opposites.** Almuth Bartl. (Eddie's Finger Quiz Bks.). (Illus.). (J). 2000. pap. 4.95 (*0-7641-1603-7*) Barron.

Opposites. Sandra Boynton. Ed. by Kate Klimo. LC 95-151975. (Boynton Board Bks.). (Illus.). 13p. (J). (gr. k-3). 1982. bds. 4.99 (*0-671-44903-6*) Litle Simon.

Opposites. David A. Carter. (Bug Bks.). (Illus.). 14p. (J). (ps up). 1993. pap. 4.95 (*0-671-86877-2*) Litle Simon.

Opposites. Andy Cooke. (Illus.). 16p. (J). 1996. pap. 4.95 (*0-8120-9611-8*) Barron.

Opposites. Monique Felix. (Mouse Bks.). (Illus.). 32p. (J). (gr. k-3). 1993. 10.60 (*1-56846-002-3*, Creat Educ) Creative Co.

Opposites. Honor Head. (Ed Mouse Finds Out about . . . Ser.). (Illus.). 32p. (J). (ps-2). 1998. pap. 5.95 (*0-8172-8102-9*) Raintree Steck-V.

Opposites. Honor Head. LC 97-34655. (Ed Mouse Finds Out about . . . Ser.). (Illus.). 32 p. (J). (ps-1). 1998. 19.98 (*0-8172-5202-9*) Raintree Steck-V.

Opposites. Laura Hunt. LC 99-462489. (Pooh Ser.). (Illus.). (J). 1999. 4.99 (*0-7364-0034-6*, Pub. by Mouse Works) Time Warner.

Opposites. Lynn Kightley et al. (Little, Brown Primers Ser.). (Illus.). 32p. (J). (ps-1). 1986. mass mkt. 6.95 (*0-316-49931-5*) Little.

Opposites. Murphy. (J). 1998. 4.99 (*0-87628-980-4*) Ctr Appl Res.

Opposites. Ant Parker. (Touch & Feel Ser.). (Illus.). 12p. (J). 1999. pap. 4.95 (*0-7373-0294-1*, 02941W, Pub. by Lowell Hse) NTC Contemp Pub Co.

Opposites. Anna Pomaska. (Illus.). 32p. (J). 1998. pap. 1.00 (*0-486-40354-8*) Dover.

Opposites. Ronne P. Randall. (Happytime Ser.). (Illus.). 24p. (J). (ps). 1987. pap. 1.25 (*0-7214-9556-7*, S871, Ladybrd) Penguin Putnam.

Opposites. Pamela J. Schroeder & Jean M. Donisch. LC 96-735. (What's the Big Idea? Ser.). (Illus.). 32p. (J). (gr. k-2). 1996. lib. bdg. 12.95 (*0-86625-579-6*) Rourke Pubns.

Opposites. J. Tyler & G. Round. (First Learning Ser.). (Illus.). 24p. (J). (ps-3). 1987. pap. 3.95 (*0-7460-0219-X*) EDC.

Opposites. Richard Wilbur. Ed. by Diane D'Andrade. LC 90-39844. (Illus.). 39p. (Orig.). (J). (gr. 1-5). 1991. 11.95 (*0-15-258720-9*) Harcourt.

Opposites: A Beginner's Book of Signs. Angela Bednarczyk & Janet Weinstock. LC 96-67576. (Illus.). 16p. (J). (ps). 1997. bds. 4.95 (*1-887734-06-6*) Star Brght Bks.

Opposites: Active Minds. Photos by George Siede & Donna Preis. (Active Minds-English Ser.). (Illus.). 24p. (J). (ps-3). 1992. lib. bdg. 11.95 (*1-56674-004-5*, HTS Bks) Forest Hse.

Opposites: Flip-&-Find. Candlewick Press Staff. LC 98-87862. (Illus.). 24p. (J). (ps-1). 1999. 7.99 (*0-7636-0894-7*) Candlewick Pr.

***Opposites: Foil Fun Board Books.** Salina Yoon. (Foil Fun Board Bks.). (Illus.). (J). 2000. 4.95 (*1-58117-063-7*, Piggy Toes Pr) Intervisual Bks.

Opposites: Lost & Found Board Book. Mack Thomas. (J). 1995. 3.33 (*0-88070-758-5*, Gold n Honey) Zondervan.

Opposites: Poems from Hollywood. Mark Dunster. 11p. 1999. pap. 5.00 (*0-89642-680-7*) Linden Pubs.

Opposites: Pull & Look Sliding Board Book. Melissa Tyrrell. LC 99-162763. (Pull & Look Sliding Board Bks.). 12p. (J). 1998. bds. 4.95 (*1-888443-87-1*, Piggy Toes Pr) Intervisual Bks.

***Opposites: With over 50 Reusable Stickers.** Lorenz Books Staff. (Sticker Fun Book Ser.). (J). 1998. pap. text 4.95 (*1-85967-773-8*, Lorenz Bks) Anness Pub.

Opposites - English-French. Clare Beaton. (Bilingual First Bks.). (FRE & ENG., Illus.). 24p. 1997. pap. text 3.95 (*0-7641-0030-0*) Barron.

Opposites - English-Spanish. Clare Beaton. LC 96-85819. (Bilingual First Bks.). (SPA & ENG., Illus.). 24p. 1997. pap. text 3.95 (*0-7641-0031-9*) Barron.

Opposites at the Zoo. Abbie Dee & Annie Scott. (Emergent Reader Ser.). 12p. (J). (ps-1). 1991. pap. text 4.25 (*1-56843-077-9*) EMG Networks.

Opposites at the Zoo: Big Book. Abbie Dee & Annie Scott. (Emergent Reader Ser.). 12p. (J). (ps-1). 1991. pap. text 21.00 (*1-56843-029-9*) EMG Networks.

Opposites Attract. Shirley Hailstock. 1999. mass mkt. 4.99 (*1-58314-004-2*) Kensgtn Pub Corp.

***Opposites Attract.** Lynn Kurland et al. 2000. mass mkt. 6.99 (*0-515-12865-1*, Jove) Berkley Pub.

Opposites Attract. Tim F. LaHaye. LC 98-5767. 276p. 1998. 10.99 (*1-56507-952-3*) Harvest Hse.

Opposites Attract. Nora Roberts. (NR Flowers Ser.: No. 9). 1992. per. 3.59 (*0-373-51009-8*, 5-51009-4) Harlequin Bks.

Opposites Class: Aesthetic Realism Class on Opposites. Eli Siegel. 26p. 1975. pap. 3.50 (*0-911492-20-8*) Aesthetic Realism.

Opposites (Los Contrarios), Vol. 6. large type ed. Illus. by Clare Beaton. (English-Spanish Bilingual First Bks.). (ENG & SPA.). 24p. (J). (ps up). 1998. lib. bdg. 14.45 (*1-56674-252-8*) Forest Hse.

***Opposites, More Opposites & a Few Differences.** Richard Wilbur. LC 99-29053. (Illus.). 96p. (J). 2000. pap. 8.00 (*0-15-202347-X*, Harcourt Child Bks) Harcourt.

Opposites of Things. Althea. (Dinosaur Ser.). (Illus.). (J). 1982. pap. 2.95 (*0-85122-714-7*) Parkwest Pubns.

Opposites Sticker Activity Book. Dorling Kindersley Staff. (Illus.). (J). (ps-3). 1993. pap. 6.95 (*1-56458-240-X*) DK Pub Inc.

Opposites Test. Andrew T. Wylie. LC 74-177617. (Columbia University. Teachers College. Contributions to Education Ser.: No. 170). reprint ed. 37.50 (*0-404-55170-X*) AMS Pr.

***Opposites with Funny Friends.** Funny Friends, LLC Staff. (Illus.). 18p. 1999. bds. write for info. (*1-929758-01-4*) Funny Friends.

***Opposites with Funny Friends Value Pack: With Plush Toy.** Funny Friends, LLC Staff. (Illus.). 18p. (J). 1999. bds. write for info. (*1-929758-04-9*) Funny Friends.

Opposition Beyond the Water's Edge: Liberal Internationalists, Pacifists & Containment, 1945-1953, 67. E. Timothy Smith. LC 98-47748. (Contributions to the Study of World History Ser.). 200p. 1999. 57.95 (*0-313-30777-6*) Greenwood.

Opposition Critics: The Antisymbolist Reaction in the Modern Period. Daniel O'Connell. LC 73-80108. (De Proprietatibus Litterarum, Ser. Minor: No. 14). 172p. 1974. pap. text 32.35 (*90-279-3422-3*) Mouton.

Opposition Government in Mexico. Ed. by Victoria E. Rodriguez & Peter M. Ward. LC 94-36197. 270p. 1995. pap. 22.50 (*0-8263-1578-X*) U of NM Pr.

Opposition in Eastern Europe. Ed. by Rudolf L. Tokes. LC 78-32062. 330p. reprint ed. pap. 102.30 (*0-608-06159-X*, 206649200008) Bks Demand.

Opposition in India & the Future of Democracy. J. A. Naik. 236p. 1988. 35.00 (*0-7855-1198-9*) St Mut.

Opposition in South Africa: The Leadership of Z. K. Matthews, Nelson Mandela & Stephen Biko. Tim J. Juckes. LC 94-32918. 240p. 1995. 55.00 (*0-275-94811-0*, Praeger Pubs) Greenwood.

Opposition Poetry in Nazi Germany. Charles W. Hoffman. LC 62-64042. (University of California Publications in Social Welfare: Vol. 67). 206p. reprint ed. pap. 63.90 (*0-608-14169-0*, 2021250000021) Bks Demand.

Opposition Politics in Nepal. Lok R. Baral. 1977. 12.00 (*0-8364-0049-6*) S Asia.

Opposition to the Women's Movement in the United States, 1848-1929. Ed. by Angela Howard & Sasha R. Tarrant. LC 97-38207. (Antifeminism in America Ser.: Vol. 1). 400p. 1997. text 83.00 (*0-8153-2713-7*) Garland.

Opposition Years: Winston Churchill & the Conservative Party, 1945- 1951. Frank A. Mayer. LC 91-4348. (American University Studies: History: Ser. IX, Vols. 116). 187p. (C). 1992. text 36.95 (*0-8204-1661-4*) P Lang Pubng.

Oppositional Imagination: Feminism, Critique & Political Theory. Joan E. Cocks. 288p. 1989. 42.50 (*0-415-01512-X*); pap. 13.95 (*0-415-03206-7*) Routledge.

Oppositional Voices: Women As Writers & Translators in the English Renaissance. Tina Krontiris. 192p. (C). 1997. pap. 27.99 (*0-415-16263-7*) Routledge.

Oppositionist for Life: Memoirs of the Chinese Revolutionary Zheng Chaolin. Ed. & Tr. by Gregor Benton from CHI. LC 95-42652. (Historical Memories Ser.). (C). 1997. text 49.95 (*0-391-03966-0*) Humanities.

Oppositionist for Life: Memoirs of the Chinese Revolutionary Zheng Chaolin. Ed. & Tr. by Gregor Benton. LC 95-42652. (Historical Memories Ser.). (Illus.). 344p. (C). 1997. pap. 18.50 (*0-391-03967-9*) Humanities.

Oppositions in Morphology: As Exemplified in the English Tense System. Irina B. Khlebnikova. LC 72-94476. (Janua Linguarum, Ser. Minor: No. 151). 185p. (Orig.). 1973. pap. text 34.65 (*90-279-2368-X*) Mouton.

Oppositions Reader: Selected Essays, 1973-1984. Ed. by K. Michael Hays. LC 98-33810. (Illus.). 704p. 1998. 65.00 (*1-56898-152-X*); pap. 45.00 (*1-56898-153-8*) Princeton Arch.

Oppression. Tadeusz Grygier. LC 73-14194. (International Library of Sociology & Social Reconstruction: A Study in Social & Criminal Psychology). 362p. 1974. reprint ed. lib. bdg. 69.50 (*0-8371-7145-8*, GROP, Greenwood Pr) Greenwood.

Oppression & Liberty. Simone Weil. Tr. by Arthur Wills & John Petrie from FRE. LC 72-92284. 216p. 1978. pap. 16.95 (*0-87023-251-7*) U of Mass Pr.

Oppression & Resistance: The Struggle of Women in Southern Africa, 29. Richard E. Lapchick & Stephanie Urdang. LC 81-4267. (Contributions in Women's Studies: No. 29). (Illus.). 197p. 1982. 52.95 (*0-313-22960-0*, LWA/, Greenwood Pr) Greenwood.

Oppression & Social Justice. 5th ed. Andrzejewski. 400p. (C). 1995. pap. 36.40 (*0-536-59275-6*) Pearson Custom.

Oppression & Social Justice: Critical Frameworks. Julie R Andrzejewski. 410p. (C). 1993. 45.00 (*0-536-58474-5*) Pearson Custom.

Oppression of Youth. Ted Clark. 1990. 12.50 (*0-8446-5169-9*) Peter Smith.

***Oppressionless.** George Bloomer. 94p. 1998. pap. 9.99 (*1-892352-01-X*) Blooming Bks.

Oppressions of the Sixteenth Century in the Islands of Orkney & Zetland: From Original Documents. Ed. by David Balfour. (Maitland Club, Glasgow. Publications: No. 75). reprint ed. 39.50 (*0-404-53114-8*) AMS Pr.

Oppressive Narrowness: A Study of the Female Community in George Eliot's Early Writings. Barbro A. Norbelie. (Studia Anglistica Upsaliensia Ser.: No. 80). 163p. (Orig.). 1992. pap. 45.00 (*91-554-2982-3*) Coronet Bks.

Oppressive Present: Literature & Social Consciousness in Colonial India. Sudhir Chandra. 204p. 1994. reprint ed. pap. 7.95 (*0-19-563503-5*) OUP.

OPQ: Offbeat Adventures with the Alphabet. rev. ed. Greta Rasmussen. LC 81-82798. (Illus.). 64p. (Orig.). (J). (gr. 2-6). 1994. pap. 8.95 (*0-936110-03-1*) Tin Man Pr.

OPQRS, Etc. Madge Miller. (J). (gr. 4 up). 1984. pap. 6.00 (*0-87602-246-8*) Anchorage.

Oprah. Judith Mahoney Pasternak. LC 99-13865. (Illus.). 120p. 1999. 19.98 (*1-56799-749-X*) M Friedman Pub Grp Inc.

Oprah! Robert Waldron. 1987. 9.05 (*0-606-03883-3*, Pub. by Turtleback) Demco.

Oprah. large type ed. Oprah Winfrey. 1997. pap. 22.00 (*0-679-74948-9*) McKay.

Oprah: An Autobiography. Oprah Winfrey. 1993. 24.00 (*0-679-42688-4*) Knopf.

Oprah! Up Close & down Home. Nellie Bly. 400p. 1994. mass mkt. 4.99 (*0-8217-4613-8*, Zebra Kensgtn) Kensgtn Pub Corp.

***Oprah Winfrey.** (Penguin Readers Lv. 2). (C). 2000. 7.00 (*0-582-41982-4*) Pearson Educ.

***Oprah Winfrey.** Belinda Frederich. (Women of Achievement Ser.). 2000. 19.95 (*0-7910-5891-3*) Chelsea Hse.

***Oprah Winfrey.** Belinda Friedrich. LC 00-21511. (Women of Achievement Ser.). (Illus.). 2000. pap. 9.95 (*0-7910-5892-1*) Chelsea Hse.

Oprah Winfrey. Peg Guilfoyle. LC 98-4214. (Ovations Ser.). (Illus.). 32p. (YA). (gr. 4 up). 1999. lib. bdg. 21.30 (*0-88682-941-0*, Creat Educ) Creative Co.

Oprah Winfrey. Judith J. Presnall. LC 98-23237. (People in the News Ser.). (Illus.). 144p. (YA). (gr. 4-12). 1998. lib. bdg. 23.70 (*1-56006-360-2*) Lucent Bks.

Oprah Winfrey. Jill C. Wheeler. LC 98-29313. (Women of the World Ser.). 2000. lib. bdg. 13.95 (*1-57765-319-X*) ABDO Pub Co.

Oprah Winfrey: A Voice for the People. Philip Brooks. LC 98-35382. (Book Report Biography Ser.). 128p. (J). (gr. 6-8). 1999. 22.00 (*0-531-11563-1*) Watts.

***Oprah Winfrey: A Voice for the People.** Philip Brooks. (Illus.). 2000. pap. 6.95 (*0-531-16406-3*) Watts.

Oprah Winfrey: Entertainer. Lois P. Nicholson. Ed. by Nathan I. Huggins. (Black Americans of Achievement Ser.). (Illus.). 124p. (YA). (gr. 5 up). 1994. lib. bdg. 19.95 (*0-7910-1886-5*) Chelsea Hse.

Oprah Winfrey: Entertainer. Lois P. Nicholson. Ed. by Nathan I. Huggins. (Black Americans of Achievement Ser.). 124p. (YA). (gr. 5 up). 1994. pap. 8.95 (*0-7910-1915-2*) Chelsea Hse.

Oprah Winfrey: Entertainer. Lois P. Nicholson. (Junior Black Americans of Achievement Ser.). (Illus.). 76p. (J). (gr. 1-4). 1997. pap. 4.95 (*0-7910-4460-2*) Chelsea Hse.

Oprah Winfrey: Entertainer. Lois P. Nicholson. LC 96-43736. (Junior Black Americans of Achievement Ser.). (Illus.). 76p. (J). (gr. 4-7). 1997. lib. bdg. 15.95 (*0-7910-2390-7*) Chelsea Hse.

Oprah Winfrey: Entertainer. Marianne Ruuth. (Black American Ser.). (Illus.). 208p. (Orig.). (YA). (gr. 6-12). 1996. mass mkt. 4.95 (*0-87067-796-9*, BH-796-9, Melrose Sq) Holloway.

Oprah Winfrey: Queen of Daytime TV. Ann Weil. LC 96-37293. (Business Whizzes Ser.). (J). 1998. 22.00 (*0-382-39503-4*, Crstwood Hse); write for info. (*0-382-39504-2*, Crstwood Hse) Silver Burdett Pr.

Oprah Winfrey: Talk Show Legend. Sara McIntosh-Wooten. LC 98-27770. (African-American Biographies Ser.). 128p. (YA). (gr. 6 up). 1999. lib. bdg. 20.95 (*0-7660-1207-7*) Enslow Pubs.

Oprah Winfrey: Television Star. Steven Otfinoski. LC 93-21540. (Library of Famous Women). (Illus.). 64p. (J). (gr. 4-7). 1993. lib. bdg. 17.95 (*1-56711-015-0*) Blackbirch.

Oprah Winfrey: The Real Story. George Mair. LC 94-18112. (Illus.). 352p. 1994. 21.95 (*1-55972-250-9*, Birch Ln Pr) Carol Pub Group.

Oprah Winfrey: The Real Story. abr. ed. George Mair. 1995. 16.95 incl. audio (*1-882071-56-5*) B&B Audio.

Oprah Winfrey: The Real Story. rev. ed. George Mair. (Citadel Stars Ser.). (Illus.). 404p. 1996. mass mkt. 5.99 (*0-8065-8003-8*, Citadel Pr) Carol Pub Group.

Oprah Winfrey: The Real Story. rev. ed. George Mair. (Illus.). 416p. 1998. mass mkt. 6.99 (*0-8065-8017-8*, Citadel Pr) Carol Pub Group.

Oprah Winfrey Speaks: Insights from the World's Most Influential Voice. Janet C. Lowe & Oprah Winfrey. LC 98-36572. 512p. 1998. 16.95 (*0-471-29864-6*) Wiley.

Oprah Winfrey Story. Geraldine Woods. LC 91-7818. (Taking Part Ser.). (Illus.). 80p. (J). (gr. 3 up). 1991. lib. bdg. 13.95 (*0-87518-463-4*, Dillon Silver Burdett) Silver Burdett Pr.

***Opryland Insider's Guide to Nashville.** Susan Chappell. LC 99-40371. (Illus.). 176p. 2000. pap. 10.00 (*0-345-40883-7*) Ballantine Pub Grp.

Opryland Plantation Recipes & Kountry Kooking. Phila R. Hach. 1983. 10.95 (*0-9606192-2-4*) Hach.

Opso . . . Toward the Marshes. Ruth Specht. 148p. (Orig.). 1987. pap. 7.95 (*0-931889-06-5*) Epistemology Pubs.

Opsomer, Carmelia: Index de la Pharmacopee Latine du Ler Au Xe Siecle, 2 vols., Set. Carmelia Opsomer. (Alpha-Omega, Reihe A Ser.: Bd. CV). (GER.). lxxxviii, 824p. 1989. write for info. (*3-487-09190-9*) G Olms Pubs.

OPSpecs Manual: Operating Specifications for Precision, Accuracy, & Quality Control. expanded ed. James O. Westgard. LC 95-90486. (Illus.). 234p. 1996. spiral bd. 75.00 (*1-886958-03-3*) Westgard Qual.

Opt: An Illusionary Tale. Arline Baum & Joseph Baum. (Illus.). 32p. (J). (ps-3). 1989. pap. 5.99 (*0-14-050573-3*, PuffinBks) Peng Put Young Read.

Optatus: Against the Donatists. Tr. & Intro. by Mark J. Edwards. LC 98-117302. (Translated Texts for Historians Ser.). 304p. (C). 1997. pap. 19.95 (*0-85323-752-2*, Pub. by Liverpool Univ Pr) U of Pa Pr.

Optcheskie Solitony see Optical Solitons

Optic Fiber Communications Link Design. (Fiber Optics User's Manual & Design Ser.: Vol. XVII). 1984. 75.00 (*0-614-18473-8*, 152U17) Info Gatekeepers.

Optic Fundus Signs of Developmental & Neurological Disorders in Children: A Manual for Clinicians. Lois J. Martyn et al. LC 65-80492. (Clinics in Developmental Medicine Ser.: No. 89). (Illus.). 80p. (C). 1991. text 34.95 (*0-521-41209-9*, Pub. by Mc Keith Pr) Cambridge U Pr.

Optic Nerve Disorders. Lanning B. Kline. LC 96-28344. (Ophthalmology Monographs). 1996. write for info. (*1-56055-037-6*) Am Acad Ophthal.

Optic Nerve in Clinical Practice. Andrew S. Gurwood & Bruce G. Muchnick. LC 97-2671. 312p. 1997. text 82.00 (*0-7506-9557-9*) Buttrwrth-Heinemann.

Optic Nerve in Glaucoma. Ed. by S. M. Drance. LC 95-8861. 1995. 91.50 (*90-6299-123-8*) Kugler Pubns.

Optic Nerve in Glaucoma. Rohit Varma & George L. Spaeth. (Illus.). 365p. 1992. text 99.00 (*0-397-51014-4*) Lppncott W & W.

Optic Nerve in Glaucoma. Ed. by Rohit Varma et al. LC 92-10299. (Illus.). 382p. reprint ed. pap. 118.50 (*0-608-09735-7*, 206989800007) Bks Demand.

***Optic of Walter Benjamin: De-, Dis-, Ex-, 3.** Alex Coles. (Illus.). 240p. 1999. pap. 21.95 (*1-901033-41-4*, Pub. by Black Dog Pubg) RAM Publications.

Optic Pathway Gliomas. Ed. by V. M. Riccardi. (Journal: Neurofibromatosis: Vol. 1, No. 4). (Illus.). 60p. 1989. pap. 33.25 (*3-8055-4945-8*) S Karger.

Optica Electromegentica Fundamentos. Jose M. Cabrera. (SPA.). 272p. (C). 1992. pap. text 14.33 (*0-201-60132-X*) Addison-Wesley.

Optica Tradicional y Moderna. Daniel Malcara. (Ciencia para Todos Ser.). (SPA.). pap. 6.99 (*968-16-3240-0*, Pub. by Fondo) Continental Bk.

Optical Access Networks, Nague, the Netherlands. 1997. 125.00 (*0-614-26546-0*, E93OPR) Info Gatekeepers.

Optical Activity & Chiral Discrimination. Ed. by Stephen F. Mason. (NATO Advanced Study Institutes Series C, Mathematical & Physical Sciences: No. 48). 1979. text 135.00 (*90-277-0982-3*) Kluwer Academic.

Optical Allusions. Aperture Staff. 1999. pap. text 18.50 (*0-89381-858-5*) Aperture.

Optical Allusions: An Art Photographer's Poems. unabridged ed. Ivy Bigbee. (Illus.). 119p. 1998. 47.50 (*0-9663161-0-X*) Reddi-Arts.

Optical Amplifiers. (Fiber Optics Reprint Ser.: Vol. 38). 308p. 1996. 75.00 (*0-614-18433-9*) Info Gatekeepers.

Optical Amplifiers & Their Applications. LC 94-65369. (Nineteen Ninety-Four Technical Digest Ser.: Vol. 14). 300p. (Orig.). 1994. pap. 75.00 (*1-55752-356-8*) Optical Soc.

***Optical Amplifiers & Their Applications.** Ed. by Douglas M. Baney et al. LC 98-85587. (Trends in Optics & Photonics Ser.: Vol. 25). (Illus.). 318p. 1998. pap. 55.00 (*1-55752-559-5*) Optical Soc.

Optical Amplifiers & their Applications. Ed. by H. Ishio & S. Shimada. Tr. by F. R. Apps from JPN. 288p. 1994. 235.00 (*0-471-94005-4*) Wiley.

Optical Amplifiers & Their Applications. Ed. by Mikhail N. Zervas et al. LC 97-69105. (Trends in Optics & Photonics Ser.: Vol. 16). (Illus.). 523p. 1997. pap. 55.00 (*1-55752-505-6*) Optical Soc.

Optical Amplifiers & Their Applications, Vol. 15. LC 94-65369. (Nineteen Ninety-Four Technical Digest Ser.: Vol. 14). 300p. (Orig.). 1994. pap. text 48.00 (*1-55752-357-6*) Optical Soc.

Optical Amplifiers & Their Applications: Trends in Optics & Photonics. Ed. by Robert Jopson. LC 95-72774. (TOPS Ser.: Vol. 5). 276p. (Orig.). 1996. pap. 55.00 (*1-55752-453-X*) Optical Soc.

Optical Amplifiers, 1994. 1994. 1995.00 (*0-614-18344-8*, IGIC-70) Info Gatekeepers.

Optical & Acoustic Waves in Solids - Modern Topics: Proceedings of the International School on Condensed Matter Physics, 2nd, Varna, Bulgaria Sept. 23-30, 1982. Ed. by M. Borissov. 490p. 1983. 108.00 (*9971-950-61-8*) World Scientific Pub.

Optical & Electrical Active Polymers Market. 186p. 1991. 2250.00 (*0-89336-866-0*, GB-150) BCC.

Optical & Electrical Properties. Ed. by P. A. Lee. (Physics & Chemistry of Materials with Layered Structures Ser.: No. 4). 1976. text 211.50 (*90-277-0676-X*) Kluwer Academic.

Optical & Electrical Properties of Polymers Vol. 214: Materials Research Society Symposium Proceedings. Ed. by J. A. Emerson & J. M. Torkelson. 197p. 1991. text 30.00 (*1-55899-106-9*) Materials Res.

Optical & Electrical Properties of Semiconductors. Ed. by Yu V. Kopaev. 250p. 1996. pap. 111.00 (*1-898326-37-1*, Pub. by CISP) Balogh.

***Optical & Electronic Properties of Fullerenes & Fullerene-Based Materials.** J. Shinar et al. LC 99-51467. 1999. write for info. (*0-8247-8257-7*) Dekker.

Optical & Fiber Optic Sensor Systems. Ed. by Shangliang Huang et al. LC 98-227290. (Proceedings of SPIE Ser.: Vol. 3555). 506p. 1998. 116.00 (*0-8194-3016-1*) SPIE.

Optical & Geometric Patterns & Designs. Spyros Horemis. (Illus.). 97p. 1970. pap. 8.95 (*0-486-22214-4*) Dover.

Optical & Geometrical Allover Patterns: 70 Original Drawings. Jean Larcher. LC 78-72985. (Pictorial Archive Ser.). (Illus.). 70p. 1979. pap. 7.95 (*0-486-23758-3*) Dover.

Optical & Imaging Techniques for Biomonitoring II. Ed. by Hans-Jochen Foth et al. (Europto Ser.: Vol. 2927). 236p. 1996. 66.00 (*0-8194-2329-7*) SPIE.

Optical & Imaging Techniques for Biomonitoring III. Ed. by Hans-Jochen Foth et al. LC 98-172805. (Europto Ser.: Vol. 3196). 244p. 1998. 69.00 (*0-8194-2628-8*) SPIE.

Optical & Imaging Techniques for Biomonitoring IV. Ed. by Marco D. Fante et al. (Europto Ser.: Vol. 3567). 1998. 80.00 (*0-8194-3029-3*) SPIE.

*__Optical & Infrared Spectroscopy of Circumstellar Matter.__ Ed. by Eike Guenther et al. LC 99-67268. (Conference Series Proceedings: Vol. 188). 365p. 1999. text 52.00 (*1-58381-014-5*) Astron Soc Pacific.

Optical & Spectroscopic Properties of Glass. G. Fuxi. (Illus.). viii, 283p. 1992. 238.95 (*0-387-54071-7*) Spr-Verlag.

Optical Anecdotes, Vol. X40. Ed. by D. J. Lovell. 148p. 1981. 15.00 (*0-89252-353-0*) SPIE.

Optical Art. Illus. by Ruth Heller. (Designs for Coloring Ser.). 64p. (J). 1992. pap. 4.99 (*0-448-03143-4*, G & D) Peng Put Young Read.

Optical Art: Theory & Practice. Rene Parola. LC 95-45369. (Illus.). 144p. 1998. reprint ed. pap. 13.95 (*0-486-29054-9*) Dover.

Optical Astronomical Instrumentation. Ed. by Sandro D'Odorico. LC 98-226769. (Proceedings of SPIE Ser.: Vol. 3355). 1008p. 1998. 149.00 (*0-8194-2802-7*) SPIE.

Optical Astronomical Spectroscopy. C. R. Kitchin. (Illus.). 272p. 1995. 138.00 (*0-7503-0345-X*); pap. 40.00 (*0-7503-0346-8*) IOP Pub.

Optical Astronomy from the Earth & Moon, No. 55. Ed. by Diane M. Pyper & Ronald Angione. 320p. 1994. 34.00 (*0-937707-74-0*) Astron Soc Pacific.

Optical Bi-Stability, Dynamical Nonlinearity & Photonic Logic: Proceedings of a Royal Society Discussion Meeting Held on 21-22, March 1984, Organized by S. D. Smith, A. Miller & B. S. Wherrett. Royal Society of London Staff et al. Ed. by Arthur Miller et al. (Illus.). 261p. 1985. text 86.50 (*0-85403-239-8*) Royal Soc London.

Optical Biopsies & Microscopic Techniques. Ed. by Irving J. Bigio et al. (Europto Ser.: Vol. 2926). 326p. 1996. 85.00 (*0-8194-2328-9*) SPIE.

Optical Biopsies & Microscopic Techniques II. Ed. by Irving J. Bigio et al. (Europto Ser.: Vol. 3197). 324p. 1997. 89.00 (*0-8194-2629-6*) SPIE.

Optical Biopsies & Microscopic Techniques III, Vol. 3568. Ed. by Irving J. Bigio et al. LC 99-226903. (Europto Ser.). 1998. 69.00 (*0-8194-3030-7*) SPIE.

Optical Biopsy II, Vol. 3250. Ed. by Robert R. Alfano. LC 98-227289. 226p. 1998. 69.00 (*0-8194-2689-X*) SPIE.

Optical Bistability, Instability & Optical Computing: Proceedings of the Int'l Topical Meeting on Optical Bistability, Instability & Optical Computing, 1987. Ed. by H-Y Zhang & K-K Lee. 400p. (C). 1988. pap. 45.00 (*9971-5-0578-9*); text 105.00 (*9971-5-0547-9*) World Scientific Pub.

Optical Bistability 3. Ed. by H. M. Gibbs et al. (Proceedings in Physics Ser.: Vol. 8). (Illus.). xiv, 364p. 1986. 62.00 (*0-387-16512-6*) Spr-Verlag.

Optical Channels: Fibers, Clouds, Water, & the Atmosphere. S. Karp et al. (Applications of Communications Theory Ser.). (Illus.). 420p. (C). 1988. 125.00 (*0-306-42654-4*, Plenum Trade) Perseus Pubng.

Optical Chaos. Ed. by F. T. Arecchi & Robert G. Harrison. 736p. 1994. pap. 50.00 (*0-8194-1216-3*) SPIE.

Optical Character Recognition. Shunji Mori. LC 98-23908. (Microwave & Optical Engineering Ser.). 560p. 1999. 125.00 (*0-471-30819-6*, Wiley-Interscience) Wiley.

*__Optical Character Recognition: An Illustrated Guide to the Frontier.__ Steven V. Rice et al. LC 99-20879. (Kluwer International Series in Engineering & Computer Science). 1999. write for info. (*0-7923-8492-X*) Kluwer Academic.

Optical Characterization in Microelectronics Manufacturing. S. Perkowitz et al. (Illus.). 34p. (Orig.). (C). 1994. pap. text 25.00 (*0-7881-1539-1*) DIANE Pub.

Optical Characterization of Epitaxial Semiconductor Layers. Ed. by Gunther Bauer & Wolfgang Richter. LC 95-44724. 436p. 1995. 82.95 (*3-540-59129-X*) Spr-Verlag.

Optical Characterization of Semiconductors. Ed. by D. B. Kushev. 260p. 1992. text 100.00 (*0-87849-632-7*, Pub. by Trans T Pub) Enfield Pubs NH.

Optical Characterization of Semiconductors. S. Perkowitz. (Techniques of Physics Ser.). (Illus.). 220p. 1993. text 81.00 (*0-12-550770-4*) Acad Pr.

Optical Characterization Techniques for High-Performance Microelectronic Device Manufacturing III, Vol. 2877. Ed. by Damon K. DeBusk & Ray T. Chen. 228p. 1996. 56.00 (*0-8194-2275-4*) SPIE.

Optical Coatings: Proceedings of the International Symposium, 23-25 May 1989, Shanghai, China. Ed. by Jinfa Tang & Yixun Yan. (International Academic Publishers Ser.). 347p. 1989. 105.00 (*0-08-037871-4*, Pergamon Pr) Elsevier.

Optical Coherence & Quantum Optics. Leonard Mandel & Emil Wolf. (Illus.). 1192p. (C). 1995. text 54.95 (*0-521-41711-2*) Cambridge U Pr.

Optical Coherence Tomography of Ocular Diseases. Carmen A. Puliafito et al. LC 95-20538. (Illus.). 384p. 1995. 175.00 (*1-55642-295-4*, 62954) SLACK Inc.

Optical Communication Engineering Dictionary in Four Languages: English-German-French-Russian. Jens P. Rehahn. (ENG, FRE, GER & RUS.). 156p. 1992. 49.00 (*0-7859-8912-9*) Fr & Eur.

Optical Communication Networks. Biswanath Mukherjee. LC 97-16145. (Computer Communications Ser.). (Illus.). 576p. 1997. 60.00 (*0-07-044435-8*) McGraw.

Optical Communication Receiver Design. S.B. Alexander. (Telecommunications Ser.: No. 37). 328p. 1997. 48.00 (*0-85296-900-7*, TE037) INSPEC Inc.

Optical Communication Receiver Design. Stephen B. Alexander. LC 95-46526. (Tutorial Texts in Optical Engineering Ser.: Vol. TT22). 1996. pap. 48.00 (*0-8194-2023-9*) SPIE.

Optical Communication Technology: Optische Kommunikationstechnik. Jens P. Rehahn & Natalja Schafer. (ENG, FRE, GER & RUS.). 176p. 1988. 95.00 (*0-8288-0874-0*, F18820) Fr & Eur.

Optical Communications. 2nd ed. Robert M. Gagliardi & Sherman Karp. (Telecommunications & Signal Processing Ser.: 2). 347p. 1995. 89.95 (*0-471-54287-3*) Wiley.

Optical Communications Systems. John Gowar. 1996. 18.95 (*0-614-18452-5*, B25005) Info Gatekeepers.

Optical Components Techniques, & Systems in Engineering. Rajpal S. Sirohi & Mahendra P. Kothiyal. (Optical Engineering Ser.: Vol. 28). (Illus.). 456p. 1990. text 175.00 (*0-8247-8395-6*) Dekker.

Optical Computer Architectures: The Application of Optical Concepts to Next Generation Computers. Alastair D. McAulay. LC 90-42103. 560p. 1991. 135.00 (*0-471-63242-2*) Wiley.

Optical Computers: The Next Frontier in Computing, 2 vols. Richard K. Miller. (Illus.). 276p. 1991. pap. text 285.00 (*0-89671-113-7*) SEAI Tech Pubns.

Optical Computing. LC 92-62843. (Nineteen Ninety-Three Technical Digest Ser.: Vol. 7). 350p. (Orig.). 1993. pap. 75.00 (*1-55752-290-1*); pap. text 48.00 (*1-55752-289-8*) Optical Soc.

Optical Computing. LC 95-67805. (1995 Technical Digest Ser.: Vol. 10). 316p. (Orig.). 1995. pap. 75.00 (*1-55752-390-8*) Optical Soc.

Optical Computing. Richard K. Miller & Terri C. Walker. LC 88-81641. (Survey on Technology & Markets Ser.: No. 50). 50p. 1989. pap. text 200.00 (*1-55865-049-0*) Future Tech Surveys.

Optical Computing. Ed. by F. A. Tooley & Brian S. Werrett. (Scottish Universities Summer School in Physics, a NATO Advanced Study Institute Ser.: No. 34). 400p. 1989. 189.00 (*0-905945-17-4*) IOP Pub.

Optical Computing: A Survey for Computer Scientists. Dror G. Feitelson. (Illus.). 416p. 1992. reprint ed. pap. text 27.50 (*0-262-56062-3*) MIT Pr.

Optical Computing: An Introduction. Mohammad A. Karim & Abdul A. Awwal. LC 91-30533. (Series in Microwave & Optical Engineering). 384p. 1992. 128.00 (*0-471-52886-2*) Wiley.

Optical Computing: Digital & Symbolic. Arrathoon. (Optical Engineering Ser.: Vol. 19). (Illus.). 432p. 1989. text 170.00 (*0-8247-7644-5*) Dekker.

Optical Computing: Proceedings of the International Conference, Heriot-Watt University, Edinburgh, U. K., August 22-25, 1994. Ed. by Brian S. Wherrett & P. Chavel. LC 95-6175. (Institute of Physics Publishing Conference Ser.: No. 139). (Illus.). 660p. 1995. 300.00 (*0-7503-0126-0*) IOP Pub.

Optical Computing in Japan. Ed. by S. Ishihara. (Illus.). 525p. (C). 1990. text 225.00 (*0-941743-85-3*) Nova Sci Pubs.

Optical Constants of Bulk Materials & Films. 2nd ed. L. Ward. LC 94-13114. (Optics & Optoelectronics Ser.). (Illus.). 312p. 1994. 168.00 (*0-7503-0324-7*) IOP Pub.

Optical Constants of Inorganic Glasses. Andrei M. Efimov. LC 94-47106. (Laser & Optical Science & Technology Ser.). 224p. 1995. boxed set 119.95 (*0-8493-3783-6*, 3783) CRC Pr.

Optical Control of Microwave Devices. Rainee N. Simons. LC 89-49101. (Artech House Microwave Library). (Illus.). 254p. 1990. reprint ed. pap. 78.80 (*0-7837-9773-7*, 206050200005) Bks Demand.

*__Optical Control of Molecular Dynamics.__ Stuart A. Rice & Meishan Zhao. LC 99-49631. 420p. 2000. text 89.95 (*0-471-35423-6*, Wiley-Interscience) Wiley.

Optical Corrections in the Sculpture of Donatello. Robert Munman. LC 84-71080. (Transactions Ser.: Vol. 75, Pt. 2). 1985. pap. 18.00 (*0-87169-752-1*, T752-MUR) Am Philos.

*__Optical Crystallography.__ F. Donald Bloss. (Monograph Ser.). (Illus.). 239p. 1999. 32.00 (*0-939950-49-9*) Mineralogical Soc.

Optical Data Display, Processing & Storage: 2nd SPSE Symposium, Advance Printing of Paper Summaries, the Aladdin Hotel, Las Vegas, Nevada, March 15-19, 1981. Society of Photographic Scientists & Engineers Staff. LC TA1630.S6. 133p. reprint ed. pap. 41.30 (*0-608-30573-1*, 201586100007) Bks Demand.

Optical Data Processing: Applications. Ed. by David Casasent. (Topics in Applied Physics Ser.: Vol. 23). (Illus.). 1978. 70.95 (*0-387-08453-3*) Spr-Verlag.

Optical Data Storage. LC 94-65357. (Nineteen Ninety-Four Technical Digest Ser.: Vol. 10). 350p. (Orig.). 1994. pap. 75.00 (*1-55752-345-2*); pap. text 48.00 (*1-55752-344-4*) Optical Soc.

*__Optical Data Storage.__ (Nineteen Ninety-Eight OSA Technical Digest Ser.: Vol. 8). 400p. (Orig.). (C). 1999. pap. 75.00 (*1-55752-544-7*) Optical Soc.

Optical Data Storage 1997 Topical Meeting, Vol. 3109. Ed. by Henryk Birecki & James Z. Kwiecien. LC 98-122078. 262p. 1997. 69.00 (*0-8194-2530-3*) SPIE.

Optical Data Storage '98: 10-13 May, 1998, Aspen, Colorado. Topical Meeting on Optical Data Storage et al. LC 99-169804. (Proceedings / the International Society for Optical Engineering). 292 p. 1998. write for info. (*0-8194-2851-5*) SPIE.

Optical Data Transmission Technology for Space Payloads. (Fiber Optics User's Manual & Design Ser.: Vol. VII). 110p. 1981. 75.00 (*0-614-18463-0*, 152U07) Info Gatekeepers.

*__Optical Design & Analysis Software.__ Ed. by Richard C. Juergens. 1999. pap. text 72.00 (*0-8194-3266-0*) SPIE.

Optical Design Fundamentals for Infrared Systems. Max J. Riedl. LC 95-20201. (Tutorial Texts in Optical Engineering Ser.: Vol. TT 20). 1995. pap. 42.00 (*0-8194-1935-4*) SPIE.

Optical Designs in Motion: With 3 Different Moire Screens. Craig Cassin. LC 96-54604. (Clip-Art Ser.). (Illus.). 1997. pap. 8.95 (*0-486-29571-0*) Dover.

Optical Designs in Motion with Moire Overlays. Carol B. Grafton. (Illus.). 32p. (Orig.). 1976. pap. 8.95 (*0-486-23284-0*) Dover.

Optical Detectors for Astronomy: October 8-10, 1996, Garching, Germany. Ed. by James W. Beletic & Paolo D'Amico. LC 97-49807. (Astrophysics & Space Science Library). 228p. 1998. 72.00 (*0-7923-4925-3*) Kluwer Academic.

*__Optical Devices & Methods for Microwave/Millimeter Wave & Frontier Applications, Vol. 3464.__ Ed. by Mario N. Armenise et al. LC 99-193803. 1998. 80.00 (*0-8194-2919-8*) SPIE.

*__Optical Devices for Fiber Communication.__ Ed. by Michel J. Digonnet. 1999. pap. text 72.00 (*0-8194-3440-X*) SPIE.

Optical Diagnostic Methods for Inorganic Transmissive Materials, Vol. 3425. Ed. by Raju U. Datla. LC 99-170354. 1998. 59.00 (*0-8194-2880-9*) SPIE.

Optical Diagnostics for Flow Processes. L. Lading et al. (Illus.). 406p. (C). 1994. text 132.00 (*0-306-44817-3*, Kluwer Plenum) Kluwer Academic.

*__Optical Diagnostics for Fluids, Heat, Combustion & Photomechanics for Solids.__ Ed. by Soyoung S. Cha et al. 1999. pap. text 103.00 (*0-8194-3269-5*) SPIE.

Optical Diagnostics for Thin Film Processing. Irving Herman. LC 95-16540. (Illus.). 783p. 1995. text 100.00 (*0-12-342070-9*) Acad Pr.

Optical Diagnostics of Biological Fluids & Advanced Techniques in Analytical Cytology, Vol. 2982. Ed. by Alexander V. Priezzhev et al. LC 97-175337. 510p. 1997. 107.00 (*0-8194-2393-9*) SPIE.

Optical Diagnostics of Biological Fluids III. Ed. by Alexander V. Priezzhev et al. LC 98-227283. (Proceedings of SPIE Ser.: Vol. 3252). 204p. 1998. 69.00 (*0-8194-2691-1*) SPIE.

*__Optical Diagnostics of Biological Fluids IV.__ Ed. by Alexander V. Priezzhev et al. 206p. 1999. pap. text 72.00 (*0-8194-3069-2*) SPIE.

*__Optical Diagnostics of Living Cells II.__ Ed. by Daniel L. Farkas et al. 296p. 1999. pap. text 72.00 (*0-8194-3074-9*) SPIE.

Optical Diagnostics of Materials & Devices for Opto-, Micro- & Quantum Electronics, 1997, Vol. 3359. Ed. by Sergei V. Svechnikov & Mikhail Y. Valakh. LC 98-171718. 579p. 1998. 99.00 (*0-8194-2808-6*) SPIE.

Optical Discs in Libraries: Use & Trends. Ching-chih Chen. 240p. 1991. 79.50 (*0-938734-49-0*) Info Today Inc.

Optical Disk Systems for Records Management. 2nd ed. William Saffady. 54p. 1995. 55.00 (*0-933887-54-X*, A4537) ARMA Intl.

Optical Disk Technology: A Source Guide. 1991. lib. bdg. 79.00 (*0-8490-4854-0*) Gordon Pr.

Optical Disks. Jonathan L. Mayo. (Illus.). 208p. 1990. pap. 15.95 (*0-8306-3372-3*, 3372, Windcrest) TAB Bks.

Optical Document Security. Ed. by Rudolf L. Van Renesse. LC 93-6123. 396p. 1994. pap. 122.80 (*0-608-03157-7*, 206361000007) Bks Demand.

Optical Document Security. 2nd ed. Ed. by Rudolf L. Van Renesse. LC 97-48421. 468p. 1997. 109.00 (*0-89006-982-4*) Artech Hse.

Optical Effects Associated with Small Particles. R. K. Chang & P. W. Barber. (Advanced Series in Applied Physics: Vol. 1). 360p. (C). 1988. pap. 51.00 (*9971-5-0462-6*); text 109.00 (*9971-5-0412-X*) World Scientific Pub.

Optical Effects in Amorphous Semiconductors (Snowbird, Utah, 1984) Ed. by P. C. Taylor & S. G. Bishop. LC 84-72419. (AIP Conference Proceedings Ser.: No. 120). 486p. 1984. lib. bdg. 45.50 (*0-88318-319-6*) Am Inst Physics.

Optical Effects in Liquid Crystals. Ed. by I. Janossy. (C). 1991. text 185.50 (*0-7923-1277-5*) Kluwer Academic.

Optical Effects of Ion Implantation. P. D. Townsend et al. (Cambridge Studies in Modern Optics: No. 13). (Illus.). 294p. (C). 1994. text 64.95 (*0-521-39430-9*) Cambridge U Pr.

Optical, Electric, & Magnetic Properties of Molecules: A Review of the Work of A. D. Buckingham. A. D. Buckingham et al. LC 97-10467. (Illus.). 362p. 1997. 201.00 (*0-444-82596-7*) Elsevier.

Optical-Electronic Publishing Directory. Richard A. Bowers. 110p. 1986. pap. 30.00 (*0-937665-00-2*) Info Arts.

Optical Electronics. 4th ed. Ammon Yariv. 736p. 1995. teacher ed. 31.00 (*0-03-053239-6*) OUP.

Optical Electronics in Modern Communications. 5th ed. Amnon Yariv. (Electrical & Computer Engineering Ser.). (Illus.). 768p. 1997. text 87.00 (*0-19-510626-1*) OUP.

*__Optical Emission Lines of the Elements.__ R. Payling & Peter L. Larkins. LC 99-56527. 760p. 2000. 750.00 (*0-471-62378-4*) Wiley.

Optical Encoders & Resolvers. Richard K. Miller & Terri C. Walker. LC 88-84061. (Survey on Technology & Markets Ser.: No. 86). 50p. 1989. pap. text 200.00 (*1-55865-113-6*) Future Tech Surveys.

*__Optical Engineering for Sensing & Nanotechnology (ICOSN '99)__ Ed. by Ichirou Yamaguchi. 684p. 1999. pap. text 120.00 (*0-8194-3214-8*) SPIE.

Optical Engineering Fundamentals. Bruce H. Walker. LC 97-42884. (Tutorial Texts in Optical Engineering). 1998. pap. 48.00 (*0-8194-2764-0*) SPIE.

Optical Fabrication & Testing. LC 92-60858. (Nineteen Ninety-Two Technical Digest Ser.: Vol. 24). 200p. 1992. pap. 66.00 (*1-55752-260-X*) Optical Soc.

Optical Fabrication & Testing. LC 95-72757. (Nineteen Ninety-Six Technical Digest Ser.: No. 7). 196p. 1996. pap. 75.00 (*1-55752-437-8*) Optical Soc.

*__Optical Fabrication & Testing.__ (Nineteen Ninety-Eight OSA Technical Digest Ser.: Vol. 12). 200p. (C). 1998. pap. 75.00 (*1-55752-556-0*) Optical Soc.

*__Optical Fabrication & Testing.__ Ed. by Roland Geyl & Jonathan Maxwell. (Europto Ser.). 568p. 1999. pap. text 120.00 (*0-8194-3213-X*) SPIE.

Optical FDM Network Technologies. Kiyoshi Nosu. LC 97-8687. (Optoelectronics Engineering Ser.). 184p. 1997. 83.00 (*0-89006-769-4*) Artech Hse.

Optical Fiber Amplifiers: Materials, Devices, & Applications. Makoto Shimizu et al. Ed. by Shoichi Sudo & Yasutake Ohishi. LC 97-23661. (Optoelectronics Engineering Ser.). 640p. 1997. 113.00 (*0-89006-809-7*) Artech Hse.

Optical Fiber Cable Raceway, UL 2024. (C). 1995. pap. text 95.00 (*1-55989-951-4*) Underwrtrs Labs.

Optical Fiber Communication. Ed. by Winston I. Way et al. LC 98-226768. (Proceedings of SPIE Ser.: Vol. 3420). 388p. 1998. 89.00 (*0-8194-2874-4*) SPIE.

Optical Fiber Communication. 2nd ed. Keiser. 1991. student ed. 24.06 (*0-07-033618-0*) McGraw.

*__Optical Fiber Communication Conference (OFC) - International Conference on Integrated Optics & Optical Fiber Communication (IOOC)__ (Nineteen Ninety-Nine OSA Technical Digest Ser.). 400p. (C). 1999. pap. 92.00 (*1-55752-582-X*) Optical Soc.

Optical Fiber Communication Conference, 1994. IEEE, Lasers & Electro-Optics Society & Communicat. Ed. by Institute of Electrical & Electronics Engineers, I. LC 93-87348. 336p. 1994. lib. bdg. write for info. (*0-7803-1875-7*, 94CH3422-3) Inst Electrical.

Optical Fiber Communication Conference, 1994. IEEE, Lasers & Electro-Optics Society & Electron D. Ed. by Institute of Electrical & Electronics Engineers, I. LC 93-87348. 336p. 1994. fiche. write for info. (*0-7803-1876-5*) Inst Electrical.

Optical Fiber Communication Systems. Leonid G. Kazovsky et al. LC 96-27860. 690p. 1996. 99.00 (*0-89006-756-2*) Artech Hse.

Optical Fiber Communications. 2nd ed. Gerd E. Keiser. 368p. (C). 1991. 92.50 (*0-07-033617-2*) McGraw.

Optical Fiber Communications. 3rd ed. Keiser. LC 99-37108. 1999. 72.50 (*0-07-232101-6*) McGraw.

Optical Fiber Communications Link Design Performance Standards for Long Haul Telecommunications. (Fiber Optics User's Manual & Design Ser.: Vol. IX). 118p. 1985. 75.00 (*0-614-18465-7*, 152U09) Info Gatekeepers.

Optical Fiber Connectors: An Interlaboratory Comparison of Measurements of Endface Geometry. Timothy J. Drapala. 36p. 1998. pap. 3.00 (*0-16-056684-3*) USGPO.

Optical Fiber Data Transfer System for Helicopters. 135p. 1988. 85.00 (*0-614-18479-7*, 135P45) Info Gatekeepers.

Optical Fiber Interferometer to Study Surface Charges Produced by Triboelectric Forces. 45p. 1986. 65.00 (*0-614-18480-0*, 135P46) Info Gatekeepers.

Optical Fiber Materials & Processing Vol. 172: Materials Research Society Symposium Proceedings. Ed. by S. Takahashi et al. 360p. 1990. text 17.50 (*1-55899-060-7*) Materials Res.

Optical Fiber Materials & Properties: Symposium Held December 3-5, 1986, Boston, Massachusetts, U. S. A. Materials Research Society Staff. Ed. by Suzanne R. Nagel. LC 87-7852. (Materials Research Society Symposia Proceedings Ser.: No. 88). (Illus.). 261p. reprint ed. pap. 81.00 (*0-7837-1929-9*, 204214400001) Bks Demand.

*__Optical Fiber Reliability & Testing.__ Ed. by M. John Matthewson. 1999. pap. text 72.00 (*0-8194-3441-8*) SPIE.

Optical Fiber Rotation Sensing. Ed. by William K. Burns. (Quantum Electronics Ser.). (Illus.). 390p. 1993. text 94.00 (*0-12-146075-4*) Acad Pr.

*__Optical Fiber Sensor Technology: Applications & Systems.__ Ed. by K. T. V. Grattan & B. T. Meggitt. (Optoelectronics, Imaging & Sensing Ser.: Vol. 3). 350p. 1999. write for info. (*0-412-82570-8*) Kluwer Academic.

*__Optical Fiber Sensor Technology: Fundamentals.__ K. T. V. Grattan & B. T. Meggitt. LC 00-42668. 2000. write for info. (*0-7923-7852-0*) Kluwer Academic.

Optical Fiber Sensors. Arthur N. Chester et al. (C). 1987. text 278.50 (*90-247-3518-1*) Kluwer Academic.

Optical Fiber Sensors, Vol. III. Ed. by Brian Culshaw & John Dakin. (Optoelectronics Engineering Ser.). 237p. 1996. 89.00 (*0-89006-932-8*) Artech Hse.

Optical Fiber Sensors Vol. IV: Applications, Analysis, & Future Trends. Ed. by Brian Culshaw & John Dakin. (Optoelectronics Engineering Ser.). 540p. 1997. 109.00 (*0-89006-940-9*) Artech Hse.

Optical Fiber Sensors '90: Sydney, Australia. 1990. 195.00 (*0-614-26523-1*, O90PRC) Info Gatekeepers.

Optical Fiber Sensors '93: Florence, Italy. 1993. 195.00 (*0-614-26549-5*, O93PRC) Info Gatekeepers.

Optical Fiber Splices & Connectors. Calvin M. Miller. 1996. 119.00 (*0-614-18458-4*, B25006) Info Gatekeepers.

Optical Fiber Splices & Connectors: Theory & Methods. Calvin M. Miller et al. LC 86-1439. (Optical Engineering Ser.: No. 10). (Illus.). 440p. reprint ed. pap. 136.40 (*0-7837-4424-2*, 205248400012) Bks Demand.

Optical Fiber Systems: Technology, Design & Applications. C. K. Kao. 1996. 64.95 (*0-614-18454-1*, B08003) Info Gatekeepers.

Optical Fiber Technology. Ed. by D. B. Keck. (Milestone Ser.). 1992. 45.00 (*0-8194-0736-4*, MS38HC); pap. 35.00 (*0-8194-0737-2*) SPIE.

Optical Fiber Telecommunications, 2 vols. Miller. 1998. 229.00 (*0-12-497349-3*) Acad Pr.

Optical Fiber Telecommunications. Miller & Alan G. Chynoweth. 1996. 79.50 (*0-614-18457-6*, B01027) Info Gatekeepers.

Optical Fiber Telecommunications, Vol. II. Ed. by Stewart E. Miller & Ivan P. Kaminow. 768p. 1988. text 114.00 (*0-12-497351-5*) Acad Pr.

O

An Asterisk (*) at the beginning of an entry indicates that the title is appearing for the first time.

Optical Fiber Telecommunications III. Ed. by Ivan P. Kaminow & Thomas L. Koch. Incl. Vol. A. LC 96-43812. (Illus.). 608p. 1997. text 98.00 (*0-12-395170-4*); Vol. B. LC 96-43812. (Illus.). 515p. 1997. text 98.00 (*0-12-395171-2*); 178.00 (*0-12-395169-0*) Acad Pr.

Optical Fiber Theory: A Supplement to Applied Electromagnetics. Pierre-Andre Belanger. 244p. 1993. text 52.00 (*981-02-1491-X*) World Scientific Pub.

Optical Fiber Transmission. E. E. Basch. 1996. 79.95 (*0-614-18453-3*, B11021) Info Gatekeepers.

Optical Fiber Transmission Systems. S. D. Personick. LC 80-20684. (Applications of Communications Theory Ser.). (Illus.). 192p. (C). 1981. text 59.50 (*0-306-40580-6*, Kluwer Plenum) Kluwer Academic.

Optical Fibers: Materials & Fabrication. Tatsuo Izawa & Shoichi Sudo. 1987. text 201.00 (*90-277-2378-8*) Kluwer Academic.

Optical Fibers & Applications. (Fiber Optics Reprint Ser.: Vol. 2, 1990-1994). 318p. 1996. 75.00 (*0-614-18427-4*) Info Gatekeepers.

Optical Fibers & Applications, No. 1, 1985-1989. rev. ed. IGIC, Inc. Staff. (Fiber Optics Reprint Ser.: Vol. 2). (Illus.). 390p. 1994. pap. 75.00 (*1-56851-051-9*) Info Gatekeepers.

***Optical Fibers & Their Applications VI.** Ed. by Jan Dorosz & Ryszard S. Romaniuk. 342p. 1999. pap. text 84.00 (*0-8194-3205-9*) SPIE.

Optical Fibers for Transmission. John E. Midwinter. LC 91-4636. 428p. 1992. reprint ed. 66.50 (*0-89464-595-1*) Krieger.

Optical Fibers in Medicine. Ed. by A. Katzir. 1992. 20.00 (*0-8194-0795-X*, 1649) SPIE.

Optical Fibre. C. K. Kao. (Materials & Devices Ser.: No. 6). 168p. 1988. boxed set 59.00 (*0-86341-125-8*, ED006) INSPEC Inc.

Optical Fibre Communication: 1st, London, September 16-18, 1975. European Conference on Optical Fibre Communication. LC TK5103.59.E9. (Institution of Electrical Engineers Conference Report Ser.: No. 132). 224p. reprint ed. pap. 69.50 (*0-608-11049-3*, 201212700080) Bks Demand.

Optical Fibre Communication Systems. Ed. by C. P. Sandbank. LC 79-40822. (Illus.). 355p. reprint ed. pap. 110.10 (*0-7837-5206-7*, 204493400005) Bks Demand.

Optical Fibre Communications. 2nd ed. John M. Senior. 922p. (C). 1992. pap. text 105.00 (*0-13-635426-2*) P-H.

Optical Fibre Communications: Devices, Circuits, & Systems. M. J. Howes. LC 79-40512. (Wiley Series in Solid State Devices & Circuits). (Illus.). 316p. reprint ed. pap. 98.00 (*0-8357-4553-8*, 203745200008) Bks Demand.

Optical Fibre Lasers & Amplifiers. P. W. France. 1991. 165.00 (*0-8493-7716-1*, TA1677) CRC Pr.

Optical Fibre Sensing & Signal Processing. B. Culshaw. Ed. by J. E. Flood & C. J. Hughes. 256p. 1984. boxed set 99.00 (*0-906048-99-0*, TE904) INSPEC Inc.

***Optical Fibre Sensor Technology** K. T. Grattan & B. T. Meggitt. LC 99-14196. 1999. write for info. (*0-412-84420-6*) Chapman & Hall.

Optical Fibres, Vol. 5. G. L. Beaven et al. (EPO Applied Technology Ser.). (Illus.). 650p. 1986. 280.00 (*0-08-030577-6*, Pub. by Pergamon Repr) Franklin.

Optical Fibres & Sources for Communications. M. J. Adams & I. D. Henning. LC 90-47279. (Updates in Applied Physics & Electrical Technology Ser.). (Illus.). 192p. (C). 1990. text 75.00 (*0-306-43711-2*, Kluwer Plenum) Kluwer Academic.

Optical Filter Design & Analysis: A Signal Processing Approach. C. K. Madsen & J.H. Zhao. LC 98-34993. (Wiley Series in Microwave & Optical Engineering). 432p. 1999. 84.95 (*0-471-18373-3*) Wiley.

Optical Formulas Tutorial. Ellen D. Stoner & Patricia Perkins. LC 97-14338. 232p. 1997. pap. text 32.50 (*0-7506-9913-2*) Buttrwrth-Heinemann.

Optical Glass. T. S. Izumitani. LC 86-22236. (Translation Ser.).Tr. of Kogaku Garasu. (Illus.). 208p. 1986. text 79.95 (*0-88318-506-7*) Spr-Verlag.

Optical Ground Wire - U. S. Markets, Competitors, & Opportunities: 1997-2002 Analysis & Forecasts. Julie Perangelo. 45p. 1998. pap. text 2400.00 (*1-878218-86-7*) World Info Tech.

Optical Guided Waves & Devices. Richard Syms. 500p. 1992. pap. 59.00 (*0-07-707425-4*) McGraw.

Optical Holography: Principles, Techniques & Applications. 2nd ed. P. Hariharan. (Studies in Modern Optics: No. 20). (Illus.). 422p. (C). 1996. text 100.00 (*0-521-43348-7*); pap. text 44.95 (*0-521-43965-5*) Cambridge U Pr.

Optical Illusion Book. Houghton Mifflin Company Staff. (Literature Experience 1993 Ser.). (J). (gr. 8). 1992. pap. 11.04 (*0-395-61857-6*) HM.

Optical Illusion Book. Seymour Simon. LC 83-43222. (Illus.). 80p. (J). (gr. 3-7). 1984. pap. 6.95 (*0-688-03254-0*, Wm Morrow) Morrow Avon.

Optical Illusion Book. Seymour Simon. 1991. 12.15 (*0-606-02505-7*, Pub. by Turtleback) Demco.

***Optical Illusion Magic: Visual Tricks & Amusements** Michael A. DiSpezio. LC 99-21113. 1999. 17.95 (*0-8069-6581-9*) Sterling.

Optical Illusion Puzzles. Tr. by Paul Kuttner. LC 83-18198. (Illus.). 96p. (Orig.). (J). (gr. 7 up). 1984. 12.95 (*0-8069-6868-0*) Sterling.

Optical Illusions. Stan Gibilisco. (Puzzles, Paradoxes & Brain Teasers Ser.: No. 4). (Illus.). 140p. 1990. pap. 8.95 (*0-8306-3464-9*) McGraw-Hill Prof.

Optical Illusions. Barrie Henderson. (J). (gr. 4-7). 1994. 2.95 (*0-590-20836-5*) Scholastic Inc.

Optical Illusions. Smithmark Staff. (CD ROM Factfinders Ser.). (Illus.). 32p. 1997. 4.98 (*0-7651-9316-7*) Smithmark.

***Optical Illusions.** Ed. by Sterling Publishing Staff. (Pocket Puzzlers Ser.). (Illus.). (J). 2000. pap. 2.95 (*0-8069-4993-7*) Sterling.

Optical Illusions Coloring Book. Sato. (Illus.). pap. 2.95 (*0-486-28330-5*) Dover.

Optical Illusions for Quilters. Karen Combs. LC 97-30330. (Illus.). 144p. 1997. pap. 22.95 (*0-89145-892-1*, 4831, Am Quilters Soc) Collector Bks.

Optical Illusions in Art: Or - Discover How Paintings Aren't Always What They Seem to Be. Alexander Sturgis. (Illus.). 32p. (J). (gr. 3 up). 1996. 14.95 (*0-8069-6135-X*) Sterling.

Optical Illusions Lab: The Ultimate Optical Illusions Pack. Ronnie Randall. (Science Lab Ser.). (Illus.). 32p. (J). (gr. 3-7). 1999. 19.95 (*1-57145-383-0*, Silver Dolph) Advantage Pubs.

Optical Illusions Quilt Designs. Sharon C. Odgen. LC 93-32469. (Design Library). 48p. 1994. 4.95 (*0-486-27932-4*) Dover.

Optical Imaging & Propagation with Emphasis on Aberration Theory. Virendra N. Mahajan. LC 97-7721. 469p. 1997. write for info. (*0-8194-2515-X*) SPIE.

Optical Imaging of Brain Function & Metabolism. U. Dirnagl et al. LC 93-24703. (Advances in Experimental Medicine & Biology Ser.: Vol. 333). (Illus.). 308p. (C). 1993. text 95.00 (*0-306-44528-X*, Kluwer Plenum) Kluwer Academic.

Optical Imaging of Brain Function & Metabolism No. 2: Physiological Basis & Comparison to Other Functional Neuroimaging Methods, Vol. 2. Ed. by A. Villringer & Ulrich Dirnagl. LC 97-7513. (Advances in Experimental Medicine & Biology Ser.: Vol. 413). (Illus.). 260p. (C). 1997. text 85.00 (*0-306-45585-4*, Kluwer Plenum) Kluwer Academic.

***Optical Information Processing.** Ed. by Yuri V. Gulyaev. 364p. 1999. pap. text 92.00 (*0-8194-3505-8*) SPIE.

Optical Information Processing. Francis T. Yu. LC 89-39413. 576p. 1990. reprint ed. 63.50 (*0-89464-422-X*) Krieger.

Optical Information Processing & Holography. W. Thomas Cathey. 414p. (C). 1974. text 54.50 (*0-471-14078-3*) Krieger.

Optical Information Science & Technology (OIST97) Vol. 3347: Optical Recording Mechanisms & Media. Ed. by Andrei L. Mikaelian. LC 98-172299. 432p. 1998. 89.00 (*0-8194-2794-2*) SPIE.

Optical Information Science & Technology (OIST97) Vol. 3348: Computer & Holographic Optics & Image Processing. Ed. by Andrei L. Mikaelian. LC 98-172301. 368p. 1998. 80.00 (*0-8194-2795-0*) SPIE.

Optical Information Science & Technology (OIST97) Vol. 3402: Optical Memory & Neural Networks. Ed. by Andrei L. Mikaelian. LC 98-172300. 532p. 1998. 99.00 (*0-8194-2852-3*) SPIE.

Optical Information Technology: Workshop Proceedings. Ed. by S. Desmond Smith & Roderick F. Neale. LC 93-2199. (ESPRIT Basic Research Ser.). 1993. 71.95 (*0-387-56563-9*) Spr-Verlag.

Optical Inorganic Dielectric Materials & Devices, Vol. 2967. Ed. by Andris Krumins et al. LC 96-72056. 292p. 1997. 69.00 (*0-8194-2373-4*) SPIE.

Optical Inspection & Micromeasurements. Ed. by Christophe Gorecki. 82p. 1997. pap. 124.00 (*0-8194-2518-4*) SPIE.

Optical Inspection & Testing: Proceedings of a Conference Held, 17-18 November 1992, Boston, Massachusetts. Ed. by James D. Trolinger. LC 93-18556. (Critical Reviews of Optical Science & Technology Ser.: Vol. CR46). 1993. 30.00 (*0-8194-1040-3*); pap. 30.00 (*0-8194-1039-X*) SPIE.

Optical Instruments for Weather Forecasting, Vol. 2832. Ed. by Gary W. Kamerman. 188p. 1996. 46.00 (*0-8194-2220-7*) SPIE.

Optical Integrated Circuits. Hiroshi Nishihara et al. 454p. 1989. 55.00 (*0-07-046092-2*) McGraw.

Optical Interconnection: Foundations & Applications. Ed. by Christopher Tocci & H. John Caulfield. LC 94-5943. 383p. 1994. 93.00 (*0-89006-632-9*) Artech Hse.

Optical Interconnections & Parallel Processing: Trends at the Interface. Ed. by Pascal Berthome & Afonso Ferreira. LC 97-42015. 410p. 1997. 182.00 (*0-7923-4817-6*) Kluwer Academic.

Optical Interconnects for Computer System Design. Patrick W. Dowd. (C). 2001. 25.33 (*0-13-124637-2*, Macmillan Coll) P-H.

Optical Interference Coatings. LC 95-68681. (1995 Technical Digest Ser.: Vol. 17). 471p. (Orig.). 1995. pap. 75.00 (*1-55752-404-1*) Optical Soc.

***Optical Interference Coatings & Applications.** (Nineteen Ninety-Eight OSA Technical Digest Ser.: Vol. 9). 200p. (C). 1998. pap. 75.00 (*1-55752-550-1*) Optical Soc.

Optical Interferograms - Reduction & Interpretation, Vol. STP 666. 168p. 1979. pap. 22.50 (*0-8031-0709-9*, STP666) ASTM.

Optical Investigations of Cells in Vitro & in Vivo, Vol. 3260. Ed. by Daniel L. Farkas et al. LC 98-227303. 316p. 1998. 80.00 (*0-8194-2699-7*) SPIE.

Optical Isolators, UL 1577. 3rd ed. (C). 1995. pap. text 95.00 (*1-55989-832-1*) Underwrtrs Labs.

Optical Line Systems: Transmission Aspects. D. J. MacLean. LC 95-4908. 642p. 1996. 210.00 (*0-471-95083-1*) Wiley.

***Optical Manufacturing & Testing III.** Ed. by H. Philip Stahl. 1999. pap. text 120.00 (*0-8194-3268-7*) SPIE.

Optical Manufacturing & Testing II. Ed. by H. Philip Stahl. LC 98-122609. 58p. 1997. pap. 99.00 (*0-8194-2556-7*) SPIE.

***Optical Materials.** Simmons. LC 99-65137. 391p. (C). 1999. text 79.95 (*0-12-644140-5*) Acad Pr.

Optical Materials. R. Wood. 160p. 1993. 50.00 (*0-901716-44-8*, Pub. by Inst Materials) Ashgate Pub Co.

Optical Materials: An Introduction to Selection & Application. Solomon Musikant. (Optical Engineering Ser.: Vol. 6). (Illus.). 272p. 1985. text 145.00 (*0-8247-7309-8*) Dekker.

Optical Materials Vol. 1: A Series of Advances. Ed. by Solomon Musikant. (Illus.). 424p. 1990. text 190.00 (*0-8247-8131-7*) Dekker.

Optical Materials - Processing & Science Vol. 152: Materials Research Society Symposium Proceedings. Ed. by D. B. Poker & C. Ortiz. 298p. 1989. text 17.50 (*1-55899-025-9*) Materials Res.

Optical Materials & Engineering Industry Review. 297p. 1997. 1500.00 (*1-56965-427-1*, DOP96) BCC.

Optical Materials, Fabrication, Lasers, Microscopes, & Basic Products - U. S. Markets, Technologies, & Opportunities: 1992-1997 Analysis. Frank Kuzler. (Illus.). 160p. 1992. pap. text 1295.00 (*1-878218-32-8*) World Info Tech.

Optical materials Technology for Energy Efficiency & Solar Energy. Ed. by Carl M. Lampert et al. LC 98-122052. 24p. 1997. pap. 59.00 (*0-8194-2560-5*) SPIE.

***Optical Measurement Systems for Industrial Inspection.** Ed. by Malgorzata Kujawinska & Wolfgang Osten. 404p. 1999. pap. text 103.00 (*0-8194-3310-1*) SPIE.

Optical Measurement Techniques & Applications. Ed. by Pramod K. Rastogi. LC 97-12547. 456p. 1997. 103.00 (*0-89006-516-0*) Artech Hse.

Optical Measurements: Techniques & Applications. Ed. by Franz Mayinger. LC 94-20066. 1994. 131.95 (*0-387-56765-8*) Spr-Verlag.

***Optical Memory & Optical Data Storage, ISOMODS 1999.** Ed. by Shigeo Kubota et al. 418p. 1999. pap. text 84.00 (*0-8194-3458-2*) SPIE.

Optical Methods & Physics of Colloidal Dispersions. Ed. by T. Palberg et al. (Progress in Colloid & Polymer Science Ser.: No. 104). viii, 204p. 1997. text 79.95 (*3-7985-1085-7*) Spr-Verlag.

Optical Methods for Information Technologies. Andrei L. Mikaelian. LC 94-11785. 1994. 125.00 (*0-89864-070-9*) Allerton Pr.

Optical Methods for Time & State-Resolved Chemistry. Ed. by C. Ng. 1992. 20.00 (*0-8194-0784-4*, 1638) SPIE.

***Optical Methods for Tumor Treatment & Detection.** Ed. by Thomas J. Dougherty. 120p. 1999. pap. text 62.00 (*0-8194-3062-5*) SPIE.

Optical Methods for Tumor Treatment & Detection: Mechanisms & Techniques in Photodynamic Therapy. Ed. by T. J. Dougherty. 1992. 20.00 (*0-8194-0791-7*, 1645) SPIE.

Optical Methods for Tumor Treatment & Detection Vol. 2972: Mechanisms & Techniques in Photodynamic Therapy VI. Ed. by Thomas J. Dougherty. 194p. 1997. 69.00 (*0-8194-2383-1*) SPIE.

Optical Methods for Tumor Treatment & Detections Vol. 3247: Mechanisms & Techniques in Photodynamic Therapy VII. Ed. by Thomas J. Dougherty. 162p. 1998. 69.00 (*0-8194-2686-5*) SPIE.

Optical Methods in Biomedical & Environmental Sciences: Selected Contributions to the Third International Conference on Optics within Life Sciences, OWLS III, Tokyo, Japan, 10-14 April 1994. International Conference on Optics within Life Sci. Ed. by Hitoshi Ohzu & Shinichi Komatsu. LC 94-27064. (Series of the International Society on Optics Within Life Sciences: Vol. 3). 388p. 1994. 210.50 (*0-444-81817-0*) Elsevier.

Optical Methods of Engineering Analysis. Gary L. Cloud. (Illus.). 503p. (C). 1998. reprint ed. pap. text 36.95 (*0-521-63642-6*) Cambridge U Pr.

Optical Methods of Measurement R. S. Sirohi & F. S. Chau. LC 99-15000. (Optical Engineering Ser.). (Illus.). 328p. 1999. text 165.00 (*0-8247-6003-4*) Dekker.

Optical Metrology. Kjell J. Gasvik. LC 86-16003. 241p. reprint ed. pap. 74.80 (*0-7837-4514-1*, 204429300001) Bks Demand.

Optical Metrology. 2nd ed. Kjell J. Gasvik. LC 95-4095. 332p. 1996. 220.00 (*0-471-95474-8*) Wiley.

Optical Metrology. 2nd ed. Kjell J. Gasvik. LC 95-4095. 332p. 1999. pap. 89.95 (*0-471-95528-0*) Wiley.

Optical Metrology: Coherent & Incoherent Optics for Metrology, Sensing & Control in Science, Industry & Biomedicine. Ed. by Oliverio D. Soares. (C). 1987. text 389.50 (*90-247-3517-3*) Kluwer Academic.

***Optical Metrology: Proceedings of a Conference, Held July 18-19,1999, Denver, Colorado** Ghanim A. Al-Jumaily & SPIE Staff. LC 99-32250. (Critical Reviews of Optical Science & Technology Ser.). 1999. write for info. (*0-8194-3235-0*) SPIE.

Optical Microlithography XI. Ed. by Luc Van den Hove. LC 98-233147. (Proceedings of SPIE Ser.: Vol. 3334). 1106p. 1998. 158.00 (*0-8194-2779-9*) SPIE.

***Optical Microlithography XII.** Ed. by Luc Van den Hove. 1214p. 1999. pap. text 171.00 (*0-8194-3153-2*) SPIE.

Optical Microlithography X, Vol. 3051. Ed. by Gene E. Fuller. LC 98-122035. 996p. 1997. 132.00 (*0-8194-2465-X*) SPIE.

Optical Microscopy: Emerging Methods & Applications. Ed. by Brian Herman & John J. Lemasters. (Illus.). 441p. 1992. text 84.00 (*0-12-342060-1*) Acad Pr.

Optical Microscopy for Biology. Ed. by Brian Herman & Ken Jacobson. 690p. 1990. 275.00 (*0-471-56762-0*) Wiley.

Optical Microscopy for the Materials Science. James H. Richardson. LC 79-179481. (Monographs & Textbooks in Material Science: Vol. 3). 702p. reprint ed. pap. 200.00 (*0-608-30280-5*, 205501700007) Bks Demand.

Optical Microscopy of Carbon Steels. Leonard E. Samuels. LC 80-16341. (Illus.). 614p. reprint ed. pap. 190.40 (*0-608-16000-8*, 203307300083) Bks Demand.

***Optical Microstructural Characterization of Semiconductors Vol. 588: Materials Research Society Symposium Proceedings.** Ed. by J. Piqueras et al. LC 00-28177. 333p. 2000. text 90.00 (*1-55899-496-3*) Materials Res.

***Optical Microsystems in Silicon Based on a Fabry-Perot Resonance Cavity: Application for Spectral Analysis of Visible Light.** Jose Higino G. Correia. (Illus.). 196p. 1999. pap. 46.50 (*90-407-1870-9*, Pub. by Delft U Pr) Coronet Bks.

Optical Mineralogy. 4th ed. Paul E. Kerr. (Illus.). 492p. (C). 1977. 108.44 (*0-07-034218-0*) McGraw.

Optical Mineralogy: Mineral Descriptions, Vol. 2. Ernest G. Ehlers. (Illus.). 275p. 1988. 75.00 (*0-86542-324-5*) Blackwell Sci.

Optical Minerology. (C). 1980. write for info. (*0-8087-9060-9*) Pearson Custom.

Optical Modeling & Characterization of Hydrogenated Amorphous Silicon Solar Cells. G. Tao. 144p. 1994. pap. 42.50 (*90-407-1063-5*, Pub. by Delft U Pr) Coronet Bks.

***Optical Monitoring of Myenteric Neuronal Activity: A Confocal fluorescent Ca2+-Indicator Study.** Pieter Vanden Berghe. (Acta Biomedica Lovaniensia Ser.: 21). (Illus.). 149p. 2000. pap. 55.00 (*90-5867-023-6*, Pub. by Leuven Univ) Coronet Bks.

Optical Network Design & Modelling, 001. Chapman & Hall Staff. text 124.00 (*0-412-84260-2*) Chapman & Hall.

***Optical Networking.** Alberto Bononi. LC 99-34588. xiv, 402p. 1999. pap. 119.00 (*1-85233-641-2*, Pub. by Spr-Verlag) Spr-Verlag.

***Optical Networking.** Peter Tomsu & Christian Schmutzer. 300p. 2000. pap. 59.99 (*0-13-028226-X*) Pearson Pubns.

Optical Networks. Rajiv Ramaswami & Kumar Sivarajan. LC 97-46057. 600p. 1998. text 72.95 (*1-55860-445-6*) Morgan Kaufmann.

***Optical Networks & Their Applications.** Ed. by Richard A. Barry. LC 98-86314. (Trends in Optics & Photonics Ser.: Vol. 20). (Illus.). 380p. 1998. pap. 55.00 (*1-55752-545-5*) Optical Soc.

Optical Neural Networks. Ed. by Suganda Jutamulia. 710p. 1994. pap. 50.00 (*0-8194-1577-4*) SPIE.

Optical Nonlinearity & Bistability of Semiconductors. Ed. by H. J. Hansch. 583p. 1989. pap. 100.00 (*1-56081-007-6*, Wiley-VCH) Wiley.

***Optical On-Line Industrial Process Monitoring.** Ed. by Robert J. Nordstrom & Wim A. De Groot. 1999. pap. text 50.00 (*0-8194-3452-3*) SPIE.

Optical Organic & Semiconductor Inorganic Materials, Vol. 2968. Ed. by Edgar A. Silinsh et al. LC 97-203563. 334p. 1997. 80.00 (*0-8194-2374-2*) SPIE.

Optical Oscillators with Degenerate Four-Wave Mixing, Dynamic Grating Lasers. S. Odoulov. (Laser Science & Technology Ser.). 152p. 1991. pap. text 123.00 (*3-7186-4972-1*, Harwood Acad Pubs) Gordon & Breach.

Optical Parametric Generation & Amplification. J. Y. Zhang & Jung Y. Huang. (Laser Science & Technology Ser). 56p. 1995. pap. text 53.00 (*3-7186-5743-0*, Harwood Acad Pubs) Gordon & Breach.

Optical Particle Sizing: Theory & Practice. Ed. by G. Gouesbet & G. Grehan. LC 87-29148. (Illus.). 654p. 1988. 155.00 (*0-306-42781-8*, Plenum Trade) Perseus Pubng.

Optical Pattern Recognition. Ed. by J. L. Horner & Bahram Javidi. (Critical Reviews Ser.). 1992. 30.00 (*0-8194-0759-3*, CR40HC); pap. 30.00 (*0-8194-0760-7*) SPIE.

Optical Pattern Recognition. B. Kumar. (C). 2000. 42.01 (*0-13-099912-1*) P-H.

Optical Pattern Recognition. Ed. by Francis T. Yu & Suganda Jutamulia. LC 97-36651. (Illus.). 464p. (C). 1998. 105.00 (*0-521-46517-6*) Cambridge U Pr.

Optical Pattern Recognition, No. 8. Ed. by David P. Casasent & Tien-Hsin Chao. 55p. 1997. pap. 99.00 (*0-8194-2488-9*) SPIE.

Optical Pattern Recognition IX, Vol. 3386. Ed. by David P. Casasent & Tien-Hsin Chao. 410p. 1998. 99.00 (*0-8194-2835-3*) SPIE.

***Optical Pattern Recognition X.** Ed. by David P. Casasent & Tien-Hsin Chao. 424p. 1999. pap. text 92.00 (*0-8194-3189-3*) SPIE.

Optical Performance of the Light Microscope, 14. H. Wolfgang Zieler. LC 72-85238. (Illus.). 1974. 25.00 (*0-904962-02-4*) Microscope Pubns.

Optical Performance of the Light Microscope, 15. H. Wolfgang Zieler. LC 72-85238. (Illus.). 1974. 30.00 (*0-904962-01-6*) Microscope Pubns.

Optical Phase Conjugation. Robert A Fisher. (Quantum Electronics - Principles & Applications Ser.). 612p. 1983. text 99.00 (*0-12-257740-X*) Acad Pr.

Optical Phase Conjugation. M. Gower & D. Proch. LC 93-4996. 1994. 181.95 (*0-387-56703-8*) Spr-Verlag.

Optical Phenomena in Semiconductor Structures of Reduced Dimensions: Proceedings of the NATO Advanced Research Workshop on Frontiers of Optical Phenomena in Semiconductor Structures of Reduced Dimensions, Yountville, California, U. S. A. July 27-31, 1992. Ed. by David J. Lockwood & Aron Pinczuk. LC 93-31755. (NATO Advanced Study Institutes Series E, Applied Sciences: No. 248). 466p. (C). 1993. text 294.00 (*0-7923-2512-5*) Kluwer Academic.

Optical Physics. S. G. Lipson et al. (Illus.). 515p. (C). 1995. pap. text 39.95 (*0-521-43631-1*) Cambridge U Pr.

Optical Physics. 3rd ed. S. G. Lipson et al. (Illus.). 515p. (C). 1995. text 95.00 (*0-521-43047-X*) Cambridge U Pr.

Optical Polarization of Molecules, 4 vols. Marcis Auzinsh & Ruvin Ferber. (Monographs on Atomic, Molecular, & Chemical Physics: No. 4). (Illus.). 322p. (C). 1995. text 90.00 (*0-521-44346-6*) Cambridge U Pr.

O

***Optical Power Limiting.** Ed. by Francois Kajzar. 552p. 1999. pap. text 125.00 (*90-5699-262-7*) Gordon & Breach.

Optical Principles & Technology for Engineers. James E. Stewart. (Mechanical Engineering Series of Reference Books & Textbooks: Vol. 104). (Illus.). 360p. 1996. text 135.00 (*0-8247-9705-1*) Dekker.

Optical Principles of the Diffraction of X-Rays. R. W. James. LC 82-80706. 1982. reprint ed. 85.00 (*0-918024-23-4*) Ox Bow.

Optical Probes of Conjugated Polymers, Vol. 3145. Ed. by Z. Valy Vardeny & Lewis J. Rothberg. LC 98-160776. 558p. 1997. 107.00 (*0-8194-2567-2*) SPIE.

Optical Probes of Organic Thin Films: Photons-In & Photons-Out. Ed. by M. K. Debe. (Progress in Surface Science Ser.: Vol. 24). (Illus.). 285p. 1989. pap. 149.50 (*0-08-036384-9*, Pergamon Pr) Elsevier.

Optical Probing of Single Molecules. Ed. by T. Basche. 250p. 1996. 305.00 (*3-527-29316-7*) Wiley.

Optical Processes & Systems. J. Shamir. LC 99-13754. 450p. 1999. 80.00 (*0-8194-3226-1*) SPIE.

Optical Processes in Liquid Junction Photovoltaics Holger Streckert & Lynda Kennedy. LC 98-88596. 219 p. 1982. write for info. (*0-9668123-2-8*) Mission Pr.

Optical Processes in Microcavities. Ed. by Richard K. Chang & Anthony J. Campillo. LC 95-46571. (Advanced Series in Applied Physics: Vol. 3). 400p. 1996. text 78.00 (*981-02-2344-7*) World Scientific Pub.

Optical Processes in Semiconductors. 2nd ed. Jacques I. Pankove. LC 75-16756. (Illus.). 428p. 1976. reprint ed. pap. text 13.95 (*0-486-60275-3*) Dover.

Optical Properties & Remote Sensing of Inland & Coastal Waters. Robert P. Bukata et al. LC 95-15157. (Illus.). 384p. 1995. boxed set 99.95 (*0-8493-4754-8*, 4754) CRC Pr.

Optical Properties & Structure of Tetrapyrroles: Proceedings of a Symposium, University of Konstanz, West Germany, August 12-17, 1984. Ed. by Gideon Blauer & Horst Sund. (Illus.). xiv, 536p. 1985. 211.55 (*3-11-010054-1*) De Gruyter.

***Optical Properties of Crystaline & Amorphous Semiconductors: Materials & Fundamental Principles** Sadao Adachi. LC 99-23738. 1999. write for info. (*0-7923-8563-2*) Kluwer Academic.

Optical Properties of Excited States in Solids. B. Di Bartolo. LC 92-30374. (NATO ASI Ser.: Vol. 301). (Illus.). 766p. (C). 1993. text 165.00 (*0-306-44316-3*, Kluwer Plenum) Kluwer Academic.

Optical Properties of Glass. Ed. by Norbert J. Kreidl & Donald R. Uhlmann. 266p. 1991. 91.00 (*0-944904-35-1*, G020) Am Ceramic.

Optical Properties of Low-Dimensional Materials. T. Ogawa & Y. Kanemitsu. 400p. 1996. text 99.00 (*981-02-2231-9*) World Scientific Pub.

Optical Properties of Low-Dimensional Materials, 2. 400p. 1997. 60.00 (*981-02-3048-6*) World Scientific Pub.

Optical Properties of Low Dimensional Silicon Structures: Proceedings of the NATO Advanced Research Workshop, Meylan, France, March 1-3, 1993. Ed. by Daniel C. Bensahel. (NATO Advanced Science Institutes Series C: Mathematical & Physical Sciences). 254p. (C). 1993. text 174.50 (*0-7923-2446-3*) Kluwer Academic.

***Optical Properties of Materials Vol. 579: Materials Research Society Symposium Proceedings.** Ed. by J. R. Chelikowsky et al. 2000. text 86.00 (*1-55899-487-4*) Materials Res.

Optical Properties of Metal Clusters. U. Kreibig & M. Vollmer. (Material Science Ser.: Vol. 25). 1994. write for info. (*3-540-57836-6*) Spr-Verlag.

Optical Properties of Metal Clusters. U. Kreibig & M. Vollmer. (Material Science Ser.: Vol. 25). 536p. 1995. 74.95 (*0-387-57836-6*) Spr-Verlag.

Optical Properties of Narrow-Gap Low-Dimensional Structures. Ed. by C. M. Torres et al. (NATO ASI Series B, Physical Sciences: Vol. 152). (Illus.). 354p. 1987. 95.00 (*0-306-42566-1*, Plenum Trade) Perseus Pubng.

Optical Properties of Semiconductor Nanocrystals. S. V. Gaponenko. LC 97-35237. (Studies in Modern Optics: No. 23). (Illus.). 242p. (C). 1998. 59.95 (*0-521-58241-5*) Cambridge U Pr.

***Optical Properties of Semiconductor Nanostructures.** Marcin L. Sadowski et al. LC 00-37546. (NATO Science Ser.). 2000. pap. write for info. (*0-7923-6317-5*, Kluwer Plenum) Kluwer Academic.

Optical Properties of Semiconductor Quantum Dots. Ulrike Woggon. LC 96-44746. (Springer Tracts in Modern Physics Ser.). (Illus.). 260p. 1996. 159.00 (*3-540-60906-7*) Spr-Verlag.

Optical Properties of Semiconductors. Ed. by G. Martinez. 1992. text 208.00 (*0-7923-2058-1*) Kluwer Academic.

Optical Properties of Semiconductors. enl. rev. ed. Ed. by M. Balkanski & T. S. Moss. (Handbook on Semiconductors Ser.: Vol. 2). 874p. 1994. 340.25 (*0-444-89101-3*) Elsevier.

Optical Properties of Semiconductors. Ed. by N. G. Basov. Tr. by Albin Tybulewicz from RUS. LC 75-37609. (Proceedings of the P. N. Lebedev Physics Institute Ser.: No. 75). (Illus.). 189p. 1976. reprint ed. pap. 58.60 (*0-608-05534-4*, 206600200006) Bks Demand.

Optical Properties of Solids. Ed. by K. C. Lee et al. 350p. (C). 1991. text 104.00 (*981-02-0596-1*) World Scientific Pub.

Optical Properties of Thin Solid Films. O. S. Heavens. (Illus.). 288p. 1991. reprint ed. pap. 9.95 (*0-486-66924-6*) Dover.

Optical Properties of III-V Semiconductors: The Influence of Multi-Valley Bandstructures. H. Kalt. Ed. by M. Cardona et al. LC 95-24949. (Series in Solid-State Sciences: Vol. 121). (Illus.). 240p. 1995. 79.95 (*3-540-60229-1*) Spr-Verlag.

Optical Publishing Industry Assessment. 9th ed. Julie B. Schwerin & Ted Pine. 1997. pap. text 1295.00 (*0-9637052-7-X*) InfoTech.

***Optical Pulse & Beam Propagation.** Ed. by Yehuda B. Band. 302p. 1999. pap. text 92.00 (*0-8194-3079-X*) SPIE.

Optical Radiation & Visual Health. M. Waxler & V. Hitchins. LC 86-12933. 232p. 1986. 130.00 (*0-8493-5752-7*, CRC Reprint) Franklin.

Optical Radiation Detectors. E. L. Dereniak & D. G. Crowe. LC 84-7356. (Pure & Applied Optics Ser.: No. 1-349). 320p. 1984. 120.00 (*0-471-89797-3*) Wiley.

Optical Radiation Measurements III, Vol. 2815. Ed. by James M. Palmer. 192p. 1996. 56.00 (*0-8194-2203-7*) SPIE.

Optical Radiations in Medicine. Edwin C. McCullough. (AAPM Reports: No. 3). 28p. (Orig.). 1997. pap. 10.00 (*1-888340-06-1*) AAPM.

Optical Recording, Storage & Retrieval Systems, Vol. 2890. Ed. by Baogen Feng & Yoshito Tsunoda. 162p. 1996. 46.00 (*0-8194-2291-6*) SPIE.

Optical Remote Sensing for Environmental & Process Monitoring, Vol. 2883. Ed. by Robert R. Romano. 721p. 1996. 80.00 (*0-8194-2281-9*) SPIE.

Optical Remote Sensing for Industry & Environmental Monitoring. Ed. by Upendra N. Singh et al. LC 98-227296. (Proceedings of SPIE Ser.: Vol. 3504). 602p. 1998. 141.00 (*0-8194-2963-5*) SPIE.

Optical Remote Sensing of the Atmosphere. LC 95-67219. (1995 Technical Digest Ser.: Vol. 2). 260p. (Orig.). 1995. pap. 92.00 (*1-55752-374-6*) Optical Soc.

Optical Remote Sensing of the Atmosphere. (Nineteen Ninety-Nine OSA Technical Digest Ser.). 200p. (Orig.). (C). 1999. pap. 92.00 (*1-55752-599-4*) Optical Soc.

Optical Remote Sensing of the Atmosphere & Clouds. Ed. by Jinxue Wang et al. LC 99-159847. (Proceedings of SPIE Ser.: Vol. 3501). 626p. 1998. 124.00 (*0-8194-2960-0*) SPIE.

Optical Resolution Procedures for Chemical Compounds: Alcohols, Phenols, Thiols, Aldehydes & Ketones, Vol. 3. Paul Newman. 738p. 1984. lib. bdg. 57.50 (*0-9601918-4-4*) Optical Resolution.

Optical Resolution Procedures for Chemical Compounds Vol. 1: Amines & Related Compounds. Compiled by Paul Newman. 1978. 52.50 (*0-9601918-0-1*) Optical Resolution.

Optical Resolution Procedures for Chemical Compounds Vol. 2: Acids, 2 pts. Paul Newman. LC 78-61452. 1981. write for info. (*0-9601918-1-X*); write for info. (*0-9601918-2-8*) Optical Resolution.

Optical Resolution Procedures for Chemical Compounds Vol. 2: Acids, 2 pts., Set. Paul Newman. LC 78-61452. 1981. 79.00 (*0-9601918-3-6*) Optical Resolution.

Optical Resolution Procedures for Chemical Compounds Vol. 4, Pt. 1: Compounds Containing a Sulfur or Selenium Stereocenter. Paul Newman. 1611p. 1993. write for info. (*0-9601918-5-2*) Optical Resolution.

Optical Resolution Procedures for Chemical Compounds Vol. 4, Pt. 2: Compounds Containing a Sulfur or Selenium Stereocenter. Paul Newman. 1611p. 1993. write for info. (*0-9601918-6-0*) Optical Resolution.

Optical Resonance & Two-Level Atoms. Joseph H. Eberly. (Illus.). 256p. 1987. reprint ed. pap. 8.95 (*0-486-65533-4*) Dover.

Optical Resonators: Fundamentals, Advanced Concepts & Applications. Norman Hodgson & Horst Weber. LC 97-3957. 1997. pap. 139.00 (*3-540-76137-3*) Spr-Verlag.

Optical Resonators: Science & Engineering. Ram Kossowsky et al. LC 97-51920. (NATO ASI Series, Partnership Sub-Series 3, High Technology). 516p. 1998. 239.00 (*0-7923-4962-8*) Kluwer Academic.

Optical Rheometry of Complex Fluids. Gerald G. Fuller. (Topics in Chemical Engineering Ser.). (Illus.). 288p. 1995. text 70.00 (*0-19-509718-1*) OUP.

***Optical Rocks & Crystals.** Martin Schwabacker. Ed. by Cathy Nichols. (Illus.). 16p. (YA). 2000. write for info. (*1-884270-17-4*) Nancy Hall.

***Optical Scanning.** Ed. by Leo Beiser et al. 280p. 1999. pap. text 72.00 (*0-8194-3273-3*) SPIE.

Optical Scanning Systems: Design & Apllications. Ed. by Leo Beiser & Stephen F. Sagan. LC 98-125246. 35p. 1997. pap. 69.00 (*0-8194-2553-2*) SPIE.

Optical Scattering Vol. PM24: Measurement & Analysis. 2nd abr. ed. John C. Stover. LC 95-14620. 321p. 1995. 65.00 (*0-8194-1934-6*) SPIE.

Optical Security & Counterfeit Deterrence Techniques: 1-2 February, 1996, San Jose, California. Rudolf L. Van Renesse et al. LC 95-72254. x, 238 p. 1996. pap. write for info. (*0-8194-2033-6*) SPIE.

Optical Security & Counterfeit Deterrence Techniques II, Vol. 3314. Ed. by Rudolf L. Van Renesse. LC 98-217157. 336p. 1998. 69.00 (*0-8194-2754-3*) SPIE.

Optical Semiconductor Devices. Mitsuo Fukuda. LC 98-16423. (Microwave & Optical Engineering Ser.). 440p. 1998. 105.00 (*0-471-14959-4*) Wiley.

Optical Sensor. David Savage. 130p. 1999. pap. 1995.00 (*0-471-36370-7*) Wiley.

Optical Sensors, Vol. 6. Ed. by R. Dandliker et al. 658p. 1992. lib. bdg. 300.00 (*0-89573-678-0*, Wiley-VCH) Wiley.

***Optical Sensors & Microsystems: New Concepts, Materials, Technologies.** S. Martellucci et al. LC 00-23898. 2000. write for info. (*0-306-46380-6*, Kluwer Plenum) Kluwer Academic.

Optical Shop Testing. 2nd ed. Daniel Malacara. LC 91-16856. (Series In Pure & Applied Optics: No. 1349). 792p. 1992. 150.00 (*0-471-52232-5*) Wiley.

Optical Signal Processing. Ed. by M. A. Fiddy & M. Nieto-Vesperinas. 112p. 1991. text 102.00 (*0-7923-9215-9*) Kluwer Academic.

Optical Signal Processing. Anthony Vanderlugt. LC 91-23378. (Pure & Applied Optics Ser.: No. 1349). 632p. 1992. 175.00 (*0-471-54682-8*) Wiley.

Optical Signal Processing: Fundamentals. P. K. Das. (Illus.). 488p. 1991. 79.95 (*0-387-51476-7*) Spr-Verlag.

Optical Signal Processing, Computing, & Neural Networks. Francis T. Yu & S. Jutamulia. LC 92-6525. (Series in Microwave & Optical Engineering). 432p. 1992. 139.00 (*0-471-53654-7*) Wiley.

***Optical Signal Processing, Computing & Neural Networks.** Francis T. S. Yu & Suganda Jutamulia. LC 00-42027. 2000. reprint ed. pap. write for info. (*1-57524-158-7*) Krieger.

***Optical Signal Processing, Computing & Neural Networks.** Francis T. S. Yu & Suganda Jutamulia. (Illus.). 2000. reprint ed. text. write for info. (*1-57524-157-9*) Krieger.

Optical Signal Processing Model for the Interferometric Fiber Optic Gyro Vol. 1: Deterministic Model. Joseph M. Aein. LC 95-13803. 62p. 1995. pap. text 7.50 (*0-8330-1642-3*, MR-482/1-ARPA) Rand Corp.

Optical Signals: Animal Communication & Light. Jack P. Hailman. LC 76-48501. 381p. reprint ed. pap. 118.20 (*0-7837-3710-6*, 205788800009) Bks Demand.

Optical Solitons. Fatkhulla K. Abdullaev et al. LC 93-13774. (Nonlinear Dynamics Ser.).Tr. of Optcheskie Solitony. 1993. 86.95 (*0-387-51985-8*) Spr-Verlag.

Optical Solitons: Proceedings of the Workshop on Optical Solitons, Chipman-Tashkent, U. S. S. R., May 1989. Ed. by Fatkhulla K. Abdullaev. 216p. (C). 1991. text 101.00 (*981-02-0303-9*) World Scientific Pub.

Optical Solitons: Theory & Experiment. Ed. by J. R. Taylor. (Studies in Modern Optics: No. 13). 472p. (C). 1992. text 109.95 (*0-521-40548-3*) Cambridge U Pr.

***Optical Solitons: Theoretical Challenges & Industrial Perspectives: Les Houches Workshop, September 28-October 2, 1998.** Ed. by V. E. Zakharov & S. Wabnitz. (Les Houches Winter School Ser.: Vol. 12). xvi, 390p. 1999. pap. 76.00 (*3-540-66314-2*) Spr-Verlag.

Optical Sources, Detectors & Systems: Fundamentals & Applications. Robert H. Kingston. LC 95-12389. (Optics & Photonics Ser.). (Illus.). 198p. 1995. text 53.00 (*0-12-408655-1*) Acad Pr.

Optical Spanish Manual. Stanley S. Laburna. LC 96-36007. 176p. 1996. pap. text 16.50 (*0-7506-9674-5*) Buttrwrth-Heinemann.

Optical Spectrometric Measurements of High Temperatures. Optical Spectrometric Measurements of High Tempera. Ed. by Philip J. Dickerman. LC 61-5607. 397p. reprint ed. pap. 123.10 (*0-608-30369-0*, 200513900050) Bks Demand.

***Optical Spectroscopic Techniques & Instrumentation for Atmospheric & Space Research II.** Ed. by Allen M. Larar. 1999. pap. text 111.00 (*0-8194-3242-3*) SPIE.

Optical Spectroscopic Techniques & Instrumentation for Atmospheric & Space Research II, Vol. 2830. Ed. by Paul B. Hays & Jinxue Wang. 382p. 1996. 76.00 (*0-8194-2218-5*) SPIE.

Optical Spectroscopies of Electronic Absorption. J. R. Lalanne. (World Scientific Series in Contemporary Chemical Physics - Vol. 17: Vol. 17). 300p. 1999. 58.00 (*981-02-3861-4*) World Scientific Pub.

Optical Spectroscopy. Paul Bouis. (C). 2001. pap. text 14.95 (*0-13-123225-8*) P-H.

Optical Spectroscopy: Quantitative Methods. Earl L. Wehry. 150p. (C). 2001. pap. 14.95 (*0-13-102658-5*) P-H.

Optical Spectroscopy of Low Dimensional Semiconductors: Proceedings of the NATO Advanced Study Intstitute, Ankara & Antalya, Turkey, 9-20 September 1996. Ed. by Gerhard Abstreiter et al. LC 97-33653. (NATO Advanced Science Institutes Ser.: No. 344). 400p. 1997. text 217.50 (*0-7923-4728-5*) Kluwer Academic.

Optical Storage. Ed. by Glenn T. Sincerbox & James M. Zavislan. 702p. 1992. 65.00 (*0-8194-0890-5*); pap. 50.00 (*0-8194-0891-3*) SPIE.

Optical Storage: An Overview of the Technology & Its Use within the United Nations System. 114p. 25.00 (*92-1-100390-3*) UN.

Optical Storage & Retrieval. Ed. by Francis T. S. Yu & Suganoda Jutamulia. LC 96-18091. (Optical Engineering Ser.: Vol. 54). (Illus.). 344p. 1996. text 150.00 (*0-8247-9707-8*) Dekker.

***Optical Storage Devices & Software in Netherlands: A Strategic Entry Report, 1995.** Compiled by Icon Group International Staff. (Illus.). 126p. 1999. ring bd. 1260.00 incl. audio compact disk (*0-7418-1544-3*) Icon Grp.

Optical Storage for Computers: Technology & Applications. Alan Bradley. 1989. text 49.95 (*0-470-21488-0*) P-H.

Optical Storage Technology. Ed. by Duanyi Xu & Seiva Ogawa. LC 98-227291. (Proceedings of SPIE Ser.: Vol. 3562). 190p. 1998. 69.00 (*0-8194-3023-4*) SPIE.

Optical Studies in Liquids & Solids. Ed. by D. V. Skobel'tsyn. LC 69-12523. (Proceedings of the P. N. Lebedev Physics Institute Ser.: No. 39). (Illus.). 276p. 1969. reprint ed. pap. 85.60 (*0-608-05506-9*, 206597400006) Bks Demand.

Optical Studies of Muscle Cross-Bridges. Ed. by Ronald J. Baskin & Yin Yeh. 256p. 1987. 120.00 (*0-8493-6157-5*, QP321, CRC Reprint) Franklin.

Optical Switching. (Fiber Optics Reprint Ser.: Vol. 40). 197p. 1996. 75.00 (*0-614-18435-5*) Info Gatekeepers.

Optical Switching in Low-Dimensional Systems. Ed. by Hartmut Haug & L. Banyai. (NATO ASI Series B, Physics: Vol. 194). (Illus.). 394p. 1989. 115.00 (*0-306-43155-6*, Plenum Trade) Perseus Pubng.

Optical System Contamination V & Stray Light & System Optimization, Vol. 2864. Ed. by A. Peter Glassford et al. 498p. 1996. 85.00 (*0-8194-2252-5*) SPIE.

Optical System Design. Allen Nussbaum. LC 97-43430. 224p. (C). 1997. 84.00 (*0-13-901042-4*) P-H.

***Optical System Design Primer.** Robert E. Fischer. (Primer Ser.). (Illus.). 800p. 2000. 99.50 (*0-07-134916-2*) McGraw-Hill Prof.

Optical System Layout. Warren J. Smith. LC 97-12535. (Illus.). 224p. 1997. 65.00 (*0-07-059254-3*) McGraw.

Optical Systems Contamination & Degradation, Vol. 3427. Ed. by Philip T. Chen et al. 1998. 89.00 (*0-8194-2882-5*) SPIE.

Optical Systems for Soft X-Rays. A. G. Michette. (Illus.). 344p. (C). 1986. text 110.00 (*0-306-42320-0*, Kluwer Plenum) Kluwer Academic.

Optical Techniques for Industrial Inspection. Ed. by P. Cielo. 606p. 1988. text 138.00 (*0-12-174655-0*) Acad Pr.

Optical Techniques in Fluid, Thermal & Combustion Flow, 10-13 July, 1995, San Diego, California. Soyoung S. Cha et al. LC 95-68561. xi, 590p. 1995. write for info. (*0-8194-1905-2*) SPIE.

Optical Technologies for Aerospace Sensing: Proceedings of a Conference Held 16-17 November 1992, Boston, Massachusetts. Ed. by James E. Pearson. LC 93-18557. (Critical Reviews of Optical Science & Technology Ser.: Vol. CR47). 1993. 30.00 (*0-8194-1042-X*); pap. 30.00 (*0-8194-1041-1*) SPIE.

Optical Technologies in the Humanities: Selected Contributions to the International Conference on New Technologies in the Humanities & Fourth International Conference on Optics Within Life Sciences, Owls IV, Munster, Germany, 9-13 July 1996. Ed. by D. Dirksen & G. Von Bally. LC 97-30664. (Optics Within Life Sciences Ser.: Vol. 4). (Illus.). x, 267p. 1997. 99.95 (*3-540-63280-8*) Spr-Verlag.

Optical Technology for Microwave Applications VII. Ed. by Anastasios P. Goutzoulis. 24p. 1997. pap. 59.00 (*0-8194-2582-6*) SPIE.

Optical Technology in Fluid, Thermal & Combustion Flow III, Vol. 3172. Ed. by Soyoung S. Cha et al. LC 98-122619. 740p. 1997. 124.00 (*0-8194-2594-X*) SPIE.

Optical Telecommunications Network. Capmany. text. write for info. (*0-471-81850-X*) Wiley.

Optical Telescopes of Today & Tomorrow, Vol. 2871. Ed. by Arne L. Ardeberg. LC 97-175314. 1401p. 1997. 195.00 (*0-8194-2268-1*) SPIE.

***Optical Testing.** Daniel Malacara. 568p. 1999. 105.00 (*0-8194-3216-4*) SPIE.

Optical Testing & Metrology. Stahl. 1995. pap. text 45.00 (*0-07-060691-9*) McGraw.

Optical-Thermal Response of Laser-Irradiated Tissue. Ed. by Ashley J. Welch & Martin J. Van Gemert. (Lasers, Photonics, & Electro-Optics Ser.). 952p. (C). 1995. text 159.50 (*0-306-44926-9*, Kluwer Plenum) Kluwer Academic.

Optical Thin Film Deposition. Michael R. Jacobson. 1991. text 48.95 (*0-07-032209-0*) McGraw.

Optical Thin Films: Users Handbook. James D. Rancourt. LC 96-28046. 289p. 1996. 60.00 (*0-8194-2285-1*) SPIE.

Optical Thin Films V: New Developments. Ed. by Randolph L. Hall. LC 98-122099. 39p. 1997. pap. 80.00 (*0-8194-2555-9*) SPIE.

Optical Time-Domain Reflectometry. Duwayne Anderson & Florian Bell. (Illus.). 395p. 1997. 59.95 (*0-927489-01-5*, 001-1134-00) Tektronix.

Optical Tomography & Spectroscopy of Tissue Vol. 2979: Theory, Instrumentation Model, & Human Studies II. Ed. by Britton Chance & Robert R. Alfano. LC 98-122045. 878p. 1997. 149.00 (*0-8194-2390-4*) SPIE.

***Optical Tomography & Spectroscopy of Tissue III.** Ed. by Britton Chance et al. 720p. 1999. pap. text 153.00 (*0-8194-3067-6*) SPIE.

Optical Transfer Function. Williams. LC 88-14904. (Pure & Applied Optics Ser.). 412p. 1989. 135.00 (*0-471-94770-9*) Wiley.

Optical Transfer Function of Imaging Systems. Tom L. Williams. (Optics & Optoelectronics Ser.). 504p. 1999. 145.00 (*0-7503-0599-1*) IOP Pub.

***Optical Trapping & Manipulation of Neutral Particles Using Lasers: A Reprint Volume with Commentaries.** Arthur Ashkin. 800p. 2000. 98.00 (*981-02-4057-0*); pap. 58.00 (*981-02-4058-9*) World Scientific Pub.

Optical Unconscious. Rosalind E. Krauss. (Illus.). 365p. 1994. pap. text 20.00 (*0-262-61105-8*) MIT Pr.

***Optical Vortices.** Ed. by Mikhail Vasnetsov & K. Staliunas. (Horizons in World Physics Ser.: Vol. 228). 218p. 1999. lib. bdg. 89.00 (*1-56072-671-7*) Nova Sci Pubs.

Optical Waveguide Analysis. Masanori Koshiba. 173p. 1992. 59.95 (*0-07-035368-9*) McGraw.

Optical Waveguide Concepts. C. Vassallo. (Optical Wave Sciences & Technology Ser.: Vol. 1). 322p. 1991. 165.50 (*0-444-88684-2*) Elsevier.

Optical Waveguide Materials. Ed. by George H. Sigel et al. (Symposium Proceedings Ser.: Vol. 244). 397p. 1992. text 64.00 (*1-55899-138-7*) Materials Res.

Optical Waveguide Theory by the Finite Element Method. Masanori Koshiba. LC 92-38965. (Advances in Optoelectronics Ser.). 272p. (C). 1993. text 196.50 (*0-7923-2080-8*) Kluwer Academic.

Optical Waves in Crystals: Propagation & Control of Laser Radiation. Amnon Yariv & Pochi Yeh. LC 83-6892. (Pure & Applied Optics Ser.). 608p. 1983. 175.00 (*0-471-09142-1*, 1-349) Wiley.

Optical Waves in Layered Media. Pochi Yeh. LC 88-78. (Pure & Applied Optics Ser.). 416p. 1988. 148.00 (*0-471-82866-1*) Wiley.

***Optical WDM Networks: Principles & Practice.** Krishna M. Sivalingam & Suresh Subramaniam. 368p. 2000. 125.00 (*0-7923-7825-3*) Kluwer Academic.

Optical Wideband Transmission Systems. Ed. by Clemens Baack. 288p. 1986. 128.00 (*0-8493-6152-4*, TK5103, CRC Reprint) Franklin.

An Asterisk (*) at the beginning of an entry indicates that the title is appearing for the first time.

***Optical Wireless Communications, Vol. 353.** Ed. by Eric J. Korevaar. LC 99-227068. 142p. 1999. 48.00 (*0-8194-2993-7*) SPIE.

***Optical Wireless Communications II.** Ed. by Eric J. Korevaar. 1999. pap. text 50.00 (*0-8194-3443-4*) SPIE.

Opticianry: The Practice & the Art, 4 vols., Set. William A. Borover. Incl. Vol. I. Introduction to Dispensing. (Illus.). 259p. 1981. per. 48.00 (*0-9606398-0-2*); Vol. II. Science of Opticianry. (Illus.). 300p. 1982. per. 48.00 (*0-9606398-2-9*); Vol. III. Dynamics of Dispensing. (Illus.). 1983. per. 48.00 (*0-9606398-3-7*); Vol. IV. Business of Opticianry. 1984. per. 48.00 (*0-9606398-4-5*); (Illus.). Set pap. 192.00 (*0-9606398-1-0*) Gracie Ent.

Optick Glasse of Humors. Thomas Walkington. LC 81-16630. 216p. 1982. reprint ed. 50.00 (*0-8201-1371-9*) Schol Facsimiles.

Opticks. Sir Isaac Newton. 532p. 1952. pap. text 12.95 (*0-486-60205-2*) Dover.

Opticrom Four Percent in Clinical Practice. Robert N. Ross. LC 84-72911. (Illus.). 43p. 1984. write for info. (*0-914132-05-9*) Fisons Corp.

Optics. (Lectures on Theoretical Physics Ser.: Vol. 4). 1964. pap. text 52.00 (*0-12-654676-2*) Acad Pr.

Optics. Ludwig Bergmann & Clemens Schaefer. LC 99-22303. 1400p. 1999. 99.95 (*3-11-014318-6*) De Gruyter.

Optics. Robert Gardner. (Yesterday's Science, Today's Technology Ser.). (Illus.). 96p. (J). (gr. 5-8). 1995. lib. bdg. 20.40 (*0-8050-2852-8*) TFC Bks NY.

Optics. Eugene Hecht. 256p. (C). 1974. pap. 14.95 (*0-07-027730-3*) McGraw.

Optics. Eugene Hecht & Alfred Zajac. 1974. 39.95 (*0-201-02835-2*) Addison-Wesley.

Optics, 2 pts. Jean P. Mathieu. Incl. Pt. 1. Electromagnetic Optics. LC 73-10408. 1975. Pt. 2. Quantum Optics. LC 73-10408. 1975. LC 73-10408. 1975. 243.00 (*0-08-017157-5*, Pub. by Pergamon Repr) Franklin.

Optics. Alan Tunnacliffe & Gordon Hirst. (C). 1989. 150.00 (*0-900099-15-1*, Pub. by Assn Brit Dispen Opticians) St Mut.

Optics. 2nd ed. Miles V. Klein & Thomas E. Furtak. LC 85-22598. 672p. 1986. text 106.95 (*0-471-87297-0*) Wiley.

Optics. 2nd ed. F. Graham Smith & J. H. Thomson. (Manchester Physics Ser.). 336p. 1988. pap. 89.95 (*0-471-91535-1*) Wiley.

Optics. 2nd ed. Francis Graham-Smith & J. H. Thomson. LC 87-22174. (The Manchester Physics Ser.). (Illus.). 336p. 1988. reprint ed. pap. 104.20 (*0-608-07296-6*, 206752400009) Bks Demand.

Optics. 3rd ed. Eugene Hecht. Ed. by Karen Guardino. LC 96-3253. 644p. (C). 1997. 100.00 (*0-201-83887-7*) Addison-Wesley.

Optics. 3rd ed. Francis W. Sears. 1949. text 60.00 (*0-201-06915-6*) Addison-Wesley.

Optics. 10th ed. M. H. Freeman. 536p. 1990. text 80.00 (*0-7506-2210-5*) Buttrwrth-Heinemann.

***Optics.** 11th ed. Michael H. Freeman & Christopher Hull. (Illus.). 546p. 2000. 115.00 (*0-7506-4248-3*) Buttrwrth-Heinemann.

Optics see Electron Optics

Optics: An Introduction for Technicians & Technologists. Maher Awad et al. LC 99-17279. (Illus.). 229p. (C). 1999. 87.00 (*0-13-227794-8*) P-H.

Optics: Light for a New Age. Jeff Hecht. LC 87-23398. (Illus.). 44p. (J). (gr. 5-9). 1988. 15.95 (*0-684-18879-1*) Scribner.

Optics: The Science of Vision. Vasco Ronchi. (Illus.). ix, 360p. 1991. reprint ed. pap. 11.95 (*0-486-66846-0*) Dover.

Optics & Focus for Camera Assistants: Art, Science & Zen. Fritz L. Hershey. (Illus.). 312p. 1996. pap. 46.95 (*0-240-80200-4*, Focal) Buttrwrth-Heinemann.

Optics & Information Theory. Francis T. Yu. LC 76-23135. (Illus.). 217p. reprint ed. pap. 67.30 (*0-7837-3485-9*, 205781800008) Bks Demand.

Optics & Lasers. Ed. by G. G. Petrash. (Proceedings of the Lebedev Physics Institute Ser.: Vol. 211). 247p. 1994. lib. bdg. 165.00 (*1-56072-197-9*) Nova Sci Pubs.

Optics & Lasers. 3rd rev. ed. M. Young. (Optical Sciences Ser.: Vol. 5). 300p. 1986. pap. 48.00 (*0-387-16127-9*) Spr-Verlag.

Optics & Lasers: Including Fibers & Optical Waveguides. 4th rev. ed. M. Young. (Illus.). 344p. 1993. 37.95 (*0-387-55010-0*) Spr-Verlag.

***Optics & Lasers: Including Fibers & Optical Waveguides.** 5th rev. enl. ed. Matt Young. (Advanced Texts in Physics Ser.). (Illus.). xx, 500p. 1999. 59.95 (*3-540-65741-X*) Spr-Verlag.

***Optics & Lasers in Biomedicine & Culture: Contributions to the 5th International Conference on Optics Within Life Sciences Owls V, Crete, 13-16 October, 1998.** International Conference on Optics within Life Sci. Ed. by C. Fotakis et al. LC 99-53478. (Optics Within Life Ser.: Vol. 5). (Illus.). xii, 337p. 2000. 119.00 (*3-540-66648-6*) Spr-Verlag.

Optics & Nonlinear Optics of Liquid Crystals. Iam-Choon Khoo & S. T. Wu. (Series in Nonlinear Optics: No. 1). 440p. 1993. text 81.00 (*981-02-0934-7*); pap. text 40.00 (*981-02-0935-5*) World Scientific Pub.

Optics & Optical Instrumentation: Dictionary, Vol. 1: E to G. Ed. by Werner Bindmann. (ENG & GER.). 450p. 1974. 59.50 (*3-7684-6411-3*) Adlers Foreign Bks.

Optics & Optical Instrumentation: Dictionary, Vol. 2: G to E. Ed. by Werner Bindmann. (ENG & GER.). 450p. 1974. 59.50 (*3-7684-6512-8*) Adlers Foreign Bks.

Optics & Optical Instruments. 1996. lib. bdg. 253.95 (*0-8490-8302-8*) Gordon Pr.

Optics & Optical Instruments. 3rd ed. B. K. Johnson. Orig. Title: Practical Optics. 224p. 1960. pap. 7.95 (*0-486-60642-2*) Dover.

***Optics & Optoelectronics '98.** Ed. by Kehar Singh et al. 532p. 1999. pap. text 103.00 (*0-8194-3203-2*) SPIE.

Optics & Spectroscopy Undergraduate Laboratory Resource Book: A Collection of Experiments for Undergraduates Illustrating Some Basic Principles of Physics & Their Technological Applications. Ed. by Kevin M. Jones & Jefferson Strait. 143p. (Orig.). 1993. pap. 29.95 (*1-55752-270-7*) Optical Soc.

Optics & Vision. Frank L. Pedrotti & Leon S. Pedrotti. LC 97-26179. 395p. (C). 1997. 78.00 (*0-13-242223-9*) P-H.

Optics, Astronomy & Logic: Studies in Arabic Science & Philosophy. A. I. Sabra. (Collected Studies: No. CS 444). 335p. 1994. 109.95 (*0-86078-435-5*, Pub. by Variorum) Ashgate Pub Co.

Optics at the Nanometer Scale: Imaging & Storing with Photonic Near Fields. Ed. by M. Nieto-Vesperinas & N. Garcia. (NATO ASI Ser.: Series E, Vol. 319). 1996. text 180.50 (*0-7923-4020-5*) Kluwer Academic.

***Optics Book: Fun Experiments with Light, Vision & Color.** Shar Levine. (J). 1999. pap. text 9.95 (*0-8069-9942-X*) Sterling.

Optics Book: Fun Experiments with Light, Vision & Color. Sharon Levine et al. LC 98-26732. (Illus.). 80p. (J). (gr. 4-7). 1998. 19.95 (*0-8069-9947-0*) Sterling.

Optics Cooke Book. 2nd ed. Ed. by Stephen M. Fantone. 1984. pap. 25.00 (*1-55752-212-X*) Optical Soc.

Optics Eighty-Four, Vol. 32, No. 2. Ed. by S. Bennett. (Journal of Modern Optics Ser.). 1985. 55.00 (*0-85066-956-1*) Taylor & Francis.

Optics for Clinicians. 25th anniversary ed. Melvin L. Rubin. LC 72-97862. (Illus.). 1993. 38.00 (*0-937404-34-9*) Triad Pub FL.

Optics for High-Brightness Synchrotron Radiation Beamlines II, Vol. 2856. Ed. by Lonny E. Berman & John R. Arthur. 368p. 1996. 66.00 (*0-8194-2244-4*) SPIE.

Optics for Ophthalmologists. A. A. Sadun & J. D. Brandt. (Illus.). 115p. 1987. pap. 28.00 (*0-387-96623-4*) Spr-Verlag.

Optics for Protection of Man & Environment Against Natural & Technological Disasters: Proceedings of the Second International Conference on Optics Within Life Sciences, Munster, Germany, 4-9 October 1992. Second International Conference on Optics in Life. Ed. by Gert Von Bally & Hans I. Bjelkhagen. LC 93-20864. 346p. 1993. 238.50 (*0-444-89861-1*) Elsevier.

Optics for Science & New Technology: Proceedings of the 17th Congress of the International Commission for Optics, August 19-23, 1996, Hotal Riviera (Yusong), Taejon, Korea, 2 vols. International Commission for Optics et al. LC 96-69902. xli, 1241 p. 1996. pap. write for info. (*0-8194-2164-2*) SPIE.

Optics for Sportsmen. Al Aiken & Stuart Williams. 1993. 49.50 (*1-879356-26-0*) Wolfe Pub Co.

***Optics for Technology Students.** Robert O. Naess. 2000. teacher ed. write for info. (*0-13-018880-8*) P-H.

***Optics for Technology Students.** Robert O. Naess. LC 99-89482. (Illus.). 384p. 2000. 88.00 (*0-13-011294-1*) P-H.

Optics for the Hunter: An Evaluation of Binoculars, Scopes, Range Finders & Spotting Scopes. John Barsness. (Illus.). 225p. 1999. 24.95 (*1-57157-156-6*, Pub. by Safari Pr) Natl Bk Netwk.

Optics in Agriculture, Forestry & Biological Processing II, Vol. 2907. Ed. by George E. Meyer & James A. DeShazer. 284p. 1996. 66.00 (*0-8194-2309-2*) SPIE.

Optics in Astronomy: The Thirty-Second Herstmonceux Conference Celebrating C. G. Wynne's 80th Birthday. Ed. by J. V. Wall. (Illus.). 300p. (C). 1993. text 69.95 (*0-521-44511-6*) Cambridge U Pr.

Optics in Atmospheric Propagation, Adaptive Systems & Lidat Techniques for Remote Sensing. Ed. by Adam D. Devir et al. (Europto Ser.: Vol. 2956). 262p. 1997. 94.00 (*0-8194-2360-2*) SPIE.

***Optics in Atmospheric Propagation & Adaptive Systems.** Ed. by Anton Kohnle & John D. Gonglewski. 1999. pap. text 72.00 (*0-8194-3461-2*) SPIE.

Optics in Atmospheric Propagation & Adaptive Systems II. Ed. by Anton Kohnle & Adam D. Devir. LC 98-161683. (Europto Ser.: Vol. 3219). 166p. 1998. 69.00 (*0-8194-2651-2*) SPIE.

Optics in Biomedical Sciences: Graz Austria, 1981 Proceedings. G. V. Bally & P. Greguss. (Optical Sciences Ser.: Vol. 31). (Illus.). 274p. 1982. 73.95 (*0-387-11666-4*) Spr-Verlag.

***Optics in Computing.** (Nineteen Ninety-Nine OSA Technical Digest Ser.). 200p. (C). 1999. pap. 75.00 (*1-55752-588-9*) Optical Soc.

Optics in Computing. Compiled by Optical Society of America Staff. LC 97-65498. (Nineteen Ninety-Seven Technical Digest Ser.: Vol. 8). (Illus.). 298p. 1997. pap. 75.00 (*1-55752-491-2*) Optical Soc.

Optics in Computing '98, Vol. 3490. Ed. by Pierre H. Chavel et al. LC 98-234083. 616p. 1998. 107.00 (*0-8194-2949-X*) SPIE.

Optics in Four Dimensions, 1980: ICO Ensenada. Ed. by M. A. Machado & L. M. Narducci. LC 80-70771. (AIP Conference Proceedings Ser.: No. 65). 745p. 1981. lib. bdg. 40.75 (*0-88318-164-9*) Am Inst Physics.

Optics in Medicine, Biology, & Environmental Research: Proceedings of the International Conference on Optics in Life Sciences, Partenkirchen, Germany, 12-16 August 1990. Ed. by Gert Von Bally & Shyam Hkanna. LC 93-24585. 392p. 1993. 238.50 (*0-444-89860-3*) Elsevier.

Optics in Photography. Ed. by R. Kingslake. 1992. 44.00 (*0-8194-0763-1*, PM06) SPIE.

Optics in the Age of Euler: Conceptions of the Nature of Light, 1700-1795. Casper Hakfoort. (Illus.). 253p. (C). 1995. text 69.95 (*0-521-40471-1*) Cambridge U Pr.

Optics in the Health Sciences: Index of New Information for Research & State of Current Progress. Fred O. Crowder. 150p. 1997. 47.50 (*0-7883-1380-0*); pap. 44.50 (*0-7883-1381-9*) ABBE Pubs Assn.

Optics Index, 1990-1993: Journal of the Optical Society of America A: Optics, Image Science & Vision, Journal of the Optical Society of America B: Optical Physics, Journal of Lightwave Technology, Applied Optics, Optics Letters. 592p. 1994. pap. 50.00 (*1-55752-319-3*) Optical Soc.

Optics of Charged Particle Beams. David C. Carey. (Accelerators & Storage Rings Ser.: Vol. 6). xviii, 298p. 1987. text 209.00 (*3-7186-0350-0*) Gordon & Breach.

Optics of Contact Lenses. Ed. by Austin Bennett. (C). 1989. 125.00 (*0-900099-22-4*, Pub. by Assn Brit Dispen Opticians) St Mut.

Optics of Diffractive & Gradient: Index Elements & Systems. G. I. Greisukh et al. LC 96-37422. 391p. 1997. pap. 55.00 (*0-8194-2451-X*) SPIE.

Optics of Excitons in Confined Systems: Proceedings of the International Meeting, Italy, 24-27 September 1991. Ed. by A. D'Andrea et al. (Institute of Physics Conference Ser.: No. 123). (Illus.). 376p. 1992. 170.00 (*0-85498-413-5*) IOP Pub.

Optics of Femtosecond Laser Pulses. Ed. by S. A. Akhmanov et al. 384p. 1992. 75.00 (*0-88318-851-1*) Am Inst Physics.

***Optics of Light Scattering Media: Problems & Solutions.** Alex A. Kokhanovsky. LC 98-53555. (Wiley-Praxis Series in Atmospheric Physics). 228p. 1999. 165.00 (*0-471-97260-6*) Wiley.

***Optics of Liquid Crystal Displays.** Pochi Yeh & Claire Gu. LC TK7872.L56Y44 1999. 438p. 1999. 79.95 (*0-471-18201-X*) Wiley.

Optics of Liquid Crystals: Optics & Interfacial Phenomena in Liquid Crystals & Polymers: Proceedings of the 2nd International Topical Meeting, Italy, October 1988, A Special Issue of the Journal Molecular Crystals & Liquid Crystals. Ed. by G. Barbero et al. xiv, 470p. 1990. pap. text 1382.00 (*2-88124-403-3*) Gordon & Breach.

Optics of Nanostructured Materials. Ed. by Vadim Markel & Thomas George. 576p. 2000. text 145.00 (*0-471-34968-2*) Wiley.

Optics of Semiconductor Nanostructures. Ed. by F. Henneberger et al. 590p. 1993. 183.75 (*3-05-501544-4*) Wiley.

***Optics of the Human Eye.** David Atchinson & G. Smith. (Illus.). 288p. 2000. pap. 60.00 (*0-7506-3775-7*) Buttrwrth-Heinemann.

Optics of Thermotropic Liquid Crystals. Ed. by S. J. Elston & J. R. Sambles. LC 98-130248. 256p. 1997. 145.00 (*0-7484-0629-8*, Pub. by Tay Francis Ltd) Taylor & Francis.

Optics of Thin Films: An Optical Multilayer Theory. Zdenek Knittl. LC 73-20896. (Wiley Series in Pure & Applied Optics). (Illus.). 548p. reprint ed. pap. 169.90 (*0-608-17542-0*, 203052000069) Bks Demand.

Optics, Physiology & Vision. Ed. by Suzanne P. McKee. (Vision Research Ser.: No. VR 263). 400p. 1990. 45.00 (*0-08-040692-0*, Pub. by PPI) Elsevier.

Optics Problem Solver. rev. ed. Research & Education Association Staff. LC 81-50899. 832p. 1994. pap. 29.95 (*0-87891-526-5*) Res & Educ.

Optics, Refraction, & Contact Lenses, Sect. 2. (Basic & Clinical Science Course (1989-90) Ser.). 296p. (C). 1989. pap. text 45.00 (*0-685-26046-1*) Am Acad Ophthal.

***Optics, Retinoscopy & Refractometry.** Al Lens. LC 98-50141. (Basic Bookshelf for Eyecare Professionals Ser.). (Illus.). 144p. 1999. pap. 30.00 (*1-55642-397-7*, 63977) SLACK Inc.

Optics Today. Ed. by John N. Howard. LC 86-71346. (Readings from Physics Today Ser.). (Illus.). 352p. (Orig.). 1987. pap. text 45.00 (*0-88318-499-0*) Am Inst Physics.

Optilex Chinese - English General Dictionary Database. Ceta Group Staff. 1993. cd-rom 425.00 (*1-881265-03-X*) Dunwoody Pr.

Optima & Equilibria: An Introduction to Nonlinear Analysis. Jean P. Aubin. Tr. by Stephen Wilson from FRE. LC 92-45828. (Graduate Texts in Mathematics Ser.: Vol. 130). (Illus.). 417p. 1993. 65.95 (*0-387-52121-6*) Spr-Verlag.

Optima & Equilibria: An Introduction to Nonlinear Analysis. 2nd ed. Jean P. Aubin. LC 98-39225. (Graduate Texts in Mathematics Ser.: Vol. 140). 1998. 69.95 (*3-540-64983-2*) Spr-Verlag.

Optima for Animals. rev. ed. R. McNeil Alexander. LC 96-12454. 1996. pap. 28.95 (*0-691-02798-6*, Pub. by Princeton U Pr) Cal Prin Full Svc.

Optima Suavidad. Sal Salasin. LC 99-71502. 81p. 1999. pap. 9.95 (*1-891408-08-9*, GBP-9) Green Bean.

Optimal Aging: Get over Getting Older. Albert Ellis & Emmett Velten. LC 98-4017. 296p. 1998. pap. 17.95 (*0-8126-9383-3*) Open Court.

Optimal Algorithms. Ed. by H. Djidjev. (Lecture Notes in Computer Science Ser.: Vol. 401). vi, 308p. 1989. 40.00 (*0-387-51859-2*) Spr-Verlag.

Optimal & Adaptive Signal Processing. Peter M. Clarkson. 560p. 1993. boxed set 104.95 (*0-8493-8609-8*, TK) CRC Pr.

Optimal Bundling: Marketing Strategies for Improving Economic Performance. H. Hennig-Schmidt. LC 98-55584. (Illus.). viii, 299p. 1999. 99.00 (*3-540-65247-7*) Spr-Verlag.

Optimal Commodity Investing. Gary Antonacci. 1983. pap. 35.00 (*0-930233-20-4*) Windsor.

Optimal Consumption & Investment with Bankruptcy. Suresh P. Sethi. LC 96-38797. 448p. (C). 1996. lib. bdg. 156.00 (*0-7923-9755-X*) Kluwer Academic.

Optimal Control. J. Stoer. Ed. by R. Bulirsch et al. (Lecture Notes in Control & Information Sciences: Vol. 95). xii, 321p. 1987. 59.95 (*0-387-17900-3*) Spr-Verlag.

***Optimal Control.** Richard Vinter. LC 99-57788. (Systems & Control Ser.). 365p. 1999. 79.95 (*0-8176-4075-4*) Birkhauser.

Optimal Control. V. M. Alekseev et al. Tr. by V. M. Volosov from RUS. LC 87-6935. (Contemporary Soviet Mathematics Ser.). 322p. 1987. reprint ed. pap. 99.90 (*0-608-09370-X*, 205411500002) Bks Demand.

Optimal Control. 2nd ed. Frank L. Lewis & Vassilis L. Syrmos. LC 95-15649. 560p. 1995. 120.00 (*0-471-03378-2*) Wiley.

Optimal Control: An Introduction to the Theory with Application. Leslie M. Hocking. (Oxford Applied Mathematics & Computing Science Ser.). (Illus.). 268p. 1991. pap. text 39.95 (*0-19-859682-0*) OUP.

Optimal Control: Basics & Beyond. Peter Whittle. LC 95-22113. (Wiley-Interscience Series in Systems & Optimization). 474p. 1996. 185.00 (*0-471-95679-1*); pap. text 84.95 (*0-471-96099-3*) Wiley.

Optimal Control: Calculus of Variations, Optimal Control Theory, & Numerical Methods. R. Bulirsch et al. LC 93-1951. (International Series of Numerical Mathematics). 360p. 1993. 110.00 (*0-8176-2887-8*) Birkhauser.

Optimal Control: Theory, Algorithms, & Applications. William W. Hager & Panos M. Pardalos. LC 98-6568. (Applied Optimization Ser.). 1998. 227.00 (*0-7923-5067-7*) Kluwer Academic.

Optimal Control & Differential Games. Ed. by Lev S. Pontryagin. LC 90-42913. (Proceedings of the Steklov Institute of Mathematics Ser.: Vol. 185). 278p. 1990. pap. 138.00 (*0-8218-3134-8*, STEKLO/185) Am Math.

Optimal Control & Estimation. Robert F. Stengel. LC 94-20406. Orig. Title: Stochastic Optimal Control. (Illus.). xv, 639p. 1994. reprint ed. pap. text 16.95 (*0-486-68200-5*) Dover.

Optimal Control & System Theory in Dynamic Economic Analysis. Masahiko Aoki. (Dynamic Economics Ser.: Vol. 1). 402p. 1976. write for info. (*0-7204-8603-3*, North Holland) Elsevier.

Optimal Control & the Calculus of Variations. Enid R. Pinch. (Illus.). 242p. (C). 1995. pap. text 39.95 (*0-19-851489-1*) OUP.

Optimal Control & Viscosity Solutions of Hamilton-Jacobi-Bellman Equations. M. Bardi & I. Dolcetta. Ed. by C. I. Byrnes. LC 97-23275. (Systems & Control). 500p. 1996. 89.50 (*0-8176-3640-4*) Birkhauser.

Optimal Control & Viscosity Solutions of Hamilton-Jacobi-Bellman Equations. M. Bardi & I. C. Dolcetta. LC 97-23275. (Systems & Control). 500p. 1997. write for info. (*3-7643-3640-4*) Birkhauser.

Optimal Control Applications in Electric Power Systems. G. S. Christensen et al. (Mathematical Concepts & Methods in Science & Engineering Ser.: Vol. 35). (Illus.). 208p. (C). 1987. 75.00 (*0-306-42517-3*, Plenum Trade) Perseus Pubng.

Optimal Control, Expectations & Uncertainty. Sean Holly & Andrew H. Hallett. 256p. 1989. text 64.95 (*0-521-26444-8*) Cambridge U Pr.

Optimal Control Methods for Linear Discrete-Time Economic Systems. Yasuo Murata. (Illus.). 175p. 1982. 102.95 (*0-387-90709-2*) Spr-Verlag.

Optimal Control of Differential Equations. Ed. by Nicolae H. Pavel. (Lecture Notes in Pure & Applied Mathematics Ser.: Vol. 160). (Illus.). 352p. 1994. pap. text 145.00 (*0-8247-9234-3*) Dekker.

Optimal Control of Distributed Nuclear Reactors. G. S. Christensen et al. LC 95-25531. (Mathematical Concepts & Methods in Science & Engineering Ser.: Vol. 41). (Illus.). 232p. (C). 1990. text 85.00 (*0-306-43305-2*, Kluwer Plenum) Kluwer Academic.

***Optimal Control of Distributed Systems: Theory & Applications.** A. V. Fursikov. LC 99-48377. (Translations of Mathematical Monographs: Vol. 187). 305p. 1999. 121.00 (*0-8218-1382-X*) Am Math.

Optimal Control of Drug Administration in Cancer Chemotherapy. R. M. Martin & K. L. Teo. 204p. 1993. text 61.00 (*981-02-1428-6*) World Scientific Pub.

Optimal Control of Hydrosystems. Larry W. Mays. LC 96-29981. (Illus.). 384p. 1997. text 160.00 (*0-8247-9830-9*) Dekker.

***Optimal Control of Mechanical Oscillations.** A. S. Kovaleva. Ed. by V. I. Babitsky & J. Wittenburg. Tr. by V. Silberschmidt from RUS. LC 99-17773. (Foundations of Engineering Mechanics Ser.). (Illus.). 265p. 1999. 81.00 (*3-540-65442-9*) Spr-Verlag.

Optimal Control of Nonlinear Parabolic Systems: Theory, Algorithms & Applications. Pekka Neittaanmaki & D. Tiba. LC 93-45312. (Pure & Applied Mathematics Ser.: Vol. 179). (Illus.). 424p. 1994. text 165.00 (*0-8247-9081-2*) Dekker.

Optimal Control of Nonsmooth Distributed Parameter Systems. D. Tiba. (Lecture Notes in Mathematics Ser.: Vol. 1459). vii, 159p. 1991. 36.95 (*0-387-53524-1*) Spr-Verlag.

Optimal Control of Partial Differential Equations. K. H. Hoffmann et al. (International Series of Numerical Mathematics: Vol. 68). (ENG & GER.). 264p. 1984. 49.95 (*3-7643-1598-9*) Birkhauser.

***Optimal Control of Partial Differential Equations: International Conference in Chemnitz, Germany, April 20-25, 1998.** Ed. by K. H. Hoffmann et al. LC 99-37066. (International Series in Numerical Mathematics: Vol. 133). 336p. 1999. 125.00 (*3-7643-6151-4*, Pub. by Birkhauser) Spr-Verlag.

***Optimal Control of Partial Differential Equations: International Conference in Chemnitz, Germany, April 20-25, 1998** K.H. Hoffmann et al. LC 99-37066. (International Series of Numerical Mathematics). 1999. write for info. (*0-8176-6151-4*) Birkhauser.

O

An Asterisk (*) at the beginning of an entry indicates that the title is appearing for the first time.

Optimal Control of Partial Differential Equations: Proceedings of IFIP (W.G. 7.2) International Conference, Irsee, April 9-12, 1990. Ed. by K. H. Hoffmann & W. Krabs. (Lecture Notes in Control & Information Sciences: Vol. 149). (Illus.). vi, 247p. 1991. 65.95 (*0-387-53591-8*) Spr-Verlag.

Optimal Control of Partial Differential Equations II: Theory & Applications. K. H. Hoffman & W. Krabs. (International Series of Numerical Mathematics: Vol. 78). 240p. 1986. 80.50 (*0-8176-1846-5*) Birkhauser.

Optimal Control of Random Sequences in Problems with Constraints. A. B. Piunovskiy. LC 97-16602. 1997. text 197.50 (*0-7923-4571-1*) Kluwer Academic.

Optimal Control of Soil Venting: Mathematical Modeling & Applications. H. H. Gerke et al. LC 99-211193. (International Series in Numerical Mathematics: Vol. 127). 184p. 1999. 79.50 (*3-7643-6041-0*) Birkhauser.

Optimal Control of Systems Governed by Partial Differential Equations. Ed. by A. Bermudez. (Lecture Notes in Control & Information Sciences: Vol. 114). (Illus.). 331p. 1989. 71.95 (*0-387-50495-8*) Spr-Verlag.

Optimal Control of Systems Governed by Partial Differential Equations. J. L. Lions. Tr. by S. K. Mitter. LC 78-113638. (Grundlehren der Mathematischen Wissenschaften Ser.: Vol. 170). (Illus.). 1971. 86.95 (*0-387-05115-5*) Spr-Verlag.

Optimal Control of Viscous Flow. Ed. by S. S. Sritharan. (Miscellaneous Titles in Applied Mathematics Ser.: Vol. 59). (Illus.). xi, 198p. 1998. pap. 55.00 (*0-89871-406-0*, BKOT0059) Soc Indus-Appl Math.

Optimal Control System R & D in the Soviet Union: Moscow Institute of Control Problems & Linear Time-Lag System Research. Rafael Yanushevsky. Ed. by Andreas Tamberg. 155p. (Orig.). 1989. pap. text 75.00 (*1-55831-090-8*) Delphic Associates.

***Optimal Control Theory: Applications to Management Science & Economics.** Suresh P. Sethi & Gerald L. Thompson. LC 00-40540. 2000. write for info. (*0-7923-8608-6*) Kluwer Academic.

Optimal Control Theory & Static Optimization in Economics. Daniel Leonard & Ngo V. Long. (Illus.). 365p. (C). 1992. text 85.00 (*0-521-33158-7*); pap. text 39.95 (*0-521-33746-1*) Cambridge U Pr.

Optimal Control Theory for Infinite Dimensional Systems. Xungjing Li & Jiongmin Yong. LC 94-37168. (Systems & Control Ser.). 1994. 115.00 (*0-8176-3722-2*) Birkhauser.

Optimal Control Theory with Economic Applications. A. Seierstad & K. Sydsaeter. (Advanced Textbooks in Economics Ser.: No. 24). 466p. 1987. 79.50 (*0-444-87923-4*, North Holland) Elsevier.

Optimal Control Via Nonsmooth Analysis. Philip D. Loewen. LC 93-4143. (CRM Proceedings & Lecture Notes Ser.: Vol. 2). 153p. 1993. pap. 45.00 (*0-8218-6996-5*, CRMP/2) Am Math.

Optimal Control with a Worst-Case Performance Criterion & Applications. M. B. Subrahmanyam & M. Thoma. Ed. by A. Wyner. (Lecture Notes in Control & Information Sciences: Vol. 145). (Illus.). 143p. 1990. 31.95 (*0-387-52822-9*) Spr-Verlag.

Optimal Decisions. Oskar Lange. LC 76-143810. 304p. 1972. 139.00 (*0-08-016053-0*, Pub. by Pergamon Repr) Franklin.

Optimal Decisions under Uncertainty. J. K. Sengupta. (Universitext Ser.). x, 286p. 1985. 39.95 (*0-387-15032-3*) Spr-Verlag.

Optimal Decisions under Uncertainty. Jati K. Sengupta. (Lecture Notes in Economics & Mathematical Systems Ser.: Vol. 193). 156p. 1981. 30.00 (*0-387-10869-6*) Spr-Verlag.

Optimal Design. S. D. Silvey. 1980. 22.50 (*0-412-22910-2*, NO. 6396) Chapman & Hall.

***Optimal Design: Theory & Applications to Materials & Structures.** Valery V. Vasiliev & Zafer Ghurdal. LC 98-88627. x, 320p. 1999. 149.95 (*1-56676-686-9*) Technomic.

Optimal Design & Control: Proceedings of the Workshop on Optimal Design & Control, Blacksburg, Virginia, April 8-9, 1994. Workshop on Optimal Design & Control Staff. Ed. by Jeffrey Borggaard et al. LC 95-1023. (Progress in Systems & Control Theory Ser.: Vol. 18). 1995. 71.00 (*0-8176-3808-3*) Birkhauser.

***Optimal Design of Control Systems: Stochastic & Deterministic Problems** G. E. Kolosov. LC 99-30940. (Monographs & Textbooks in Pure & Applied Mathematics). (Illus.). 424p. 1999. text 165.00 (*0-8247-7537-6*) Dekker.

Optimal Design of Experiments. Friedrich Pukelsheim. LC 00-279. (Probability & Mathematical Statistics: Applied Probability & Statistics Section Ser.). 480p. 1993. 109.95 (*0-471-61971-X*) Wiley.

Optimal Design of Flexible Manufacturing Systems. U. Tetzlaff. (Contributions to Management Science Ser.). (Illus.). xii, 190p. 1991. 61.95 (*0-387-91395-5*) Spr-Verlag.

Optimal Design of Flexural Systems. George I. Rozvany. 200p. 1976. 136.00 (*0-08-020517-8*, Pub. by Pergamon Repr) Franklin.

Optimal Design of Thermal Systems & Components. (HTD Ser.: Vol. 279). 136p. 1994. 37.50 (*0-7918-1278-2*, H00910) ASME.

***Optimal Digestion: New Strategies for Achieving Digestive Health.** Trent W. Nichols. LC 99-29600. (Illus.). 624p. 1999. pap. 16.00 (*0-380-80498-0*, Avon Bks) Morrow Avon.

Optimal Dynamic Investment Policies of a Value Maximizing Firm. Peter M. Kort. (Lecture Notes in Economics & Mathematical Systems Ser.: Vol. 330). (Illus.). viii, 185p. 1989. 39.95 (*0-387-51152-0*) Spr-Verlag.

Optimal Edge Detection & Digital Picture Processing. 3rd rev. ed. James A. Green. LC 94-77824. (Engineering Ser.: Vol. 1). (Illus.). 86p. 1997. pap. text 43.20 (*1-890121-50-9*, 03/01/02) Grnwd Resch.

Optimal Edge Detection & Digital Picture Processing. 3rd rev. ed. James A. Green. LC 94-77824. (Engineering Ser.: Vol. 1). (Illus.). 86p. 1999. 50.00 (*1-890121-17-7*, 03-01-02) Grnwd Resch.

Optimal Engineering Design: Principles & Applications. Siddall. (Mechanical Engineering Ser.: Vol. 14). (Illus.). 536p. 1982. text 175.00 (*0-8247-1633-7*) Dekker.

Optimal Estimation with an introduction to Stachastic Control Theory. Frank L. Lewis. LC 85-26554. 400p. 1986. 130.00 (*0-471-83741-5*) Wiley.

Optimal Experience: Psychological Studies of Flow in Consciousness. Ed. by Mihaly Csikszentmihalyi & Isabella S. Csikszentmihalyi. (Illus.). 430p. (C). 1992. pap. text 22.95 (*0-521-43809-8*) Cambridge U Pr.

Optimal Filtering. V. N. Fomin. LC 98-39157. (Mathematics & Its Applications Ser.). 1998. 173.00 (*0-7923-5286-6*); spiral bd. 173.00 (*0-7923-5287-4*) Kluwer Academic.

Optimal Firm Behaviour in the Context of Technological Progress & a Business Cycle. Onno Van Hilten. (Lecture Notes in Economics & Mathematical Systems Ser.: Vol. 352). (Illus.). xii, 229p. 1991. 38.95 (*0-387-53563-2*) Spr-Verlag.

Optimal Flow Control in Manufacturing Systems: Production Planning & Scheduling. Oded Z. Maimon et al. LC 98-21517. (Applied Optimization Ser.). 346p. 1998. write for info. (*0-7923-5106-1*) Kluwer Academic.

Optimal Gear Design for Equal Strength Teeth Using Addendum Modification Coefficients. C. H. Suh. (Nineteen Ninety-Three Fall Technical Meeting Ser.: Vol. 93FTM5). (Illus.). 12p. 1993. pap. text 30.00 (*1-55589-598-0*) AGMA.

Optimal Health: How to Get It - How to Keep It. Randy W. Martin. Ed. by Sara B. Rhodes. LC 98-83056. (Illus.). 200p. 1999. pap. 19.95 (*1-891850-16-4*) Med Bear.

***Optimal Health Guidelines.** 4th rev. ed. John R. Lee. (Illus.). xv, 211p. 1999. pap. 14.00 (*0-9643737-0-X*) BLL Pubng.

***Optimal Hydraulic Control of Groundwater Systems.** David Ahlfeld & Ann Mulligan. 500p. 1999. 54.95 (*0-12-044830-0*) Acad Pr.

Optimal Imperfection? Domestic Uncertainty & Institutions in International Relations. George W. Downs. 215p. 1996. pap. text 17.95 (*0-691-01625-9*, Pub. by Princeton U Pr) Cal Prin Full Svc.

Optimal Imperfection? Domestic Uncertainty & Institutions in International Relations. George W. Downs & David M. Rocke. 159p. 1996. text 45.00 (*0-691-04460-0*, Pub. by Princeton U Pr) Cal Prin Full Svc.

Optimal Implementation of Functional Programming Languages. Andrea Asperti & Stefano Guerrini. (Tracts in Theoretical Computer Science Ser.: Vol. 45). 404p. (C). 1998. text 69.95 (*0-521-62112-7*) Cambridge U Pr.

Optimal Income Tax & Redistribution. Matti Tuomala. (Illus.). 206p. 1990. text 59.00 (*0-19-828605-8*) OUP.

Optimal Interprocedural Program Optimization: A New Framework & Its Application. J. Knoop. (Lecture Notes in Computer Science Ser.: Vol. 1428). xxv, 288p. 1998. pap. 55.00 (*3-540-65123-3*) Spr-Verlag.

Optimal Inventory Modeling of Systems: Multi-Echelon Techniques. Craig C. Sherbrooke. LC 91-43613. (New Dimensions in Engineering Ser.). (Illus.). 304p. 1992. pap. 94.30 (*0-608-05163-2*, AU0048600005) Bks Demand.

Optimal Learning in the Primary Classroom. Trevor Hawes. 1998. pap., teacher ed. write for info. (*1-899836-25-X*, Pub. by Crown Hse) Empowerment Tech.

Optimal Load Balancing in Distributed Computer Systems, Vol. XX. H. Kameda et al. LC 96-37813. (Telecommunication Networks & Computer Systems Ser.). (Illus.). 251p. 1997. pap. 69.95 (*3-540-76130-6*) Spr-Verlag.

Optimal Long-Term Operation of Electric Power Systems. G. S. Christensen & S. A. Soliman. LC 88-15268. (Mathematical Concepts & Methods in Science & Engineering Ser.: Vol. 38). (Illus.). 324p. (C). 1988. text 95.00 (*0-306-42875-X*, Kluwer Plenum) Kluwer Academic.

Optimal Monetary Policy. Richard T. Froyen. 320p. (C). 2000. text 50.00 (*0-8133-1162-4*) Westview.

Optimal Monetary Unit. Wolfram Engels. 136p. 1982. text 18.50 (*3-593-32843-7*) Irvington.

Optimal Muscle Recovery: Your guide to Achieving Peak Physical Perfromance. Edmund R. Burke. 224p. 1999. pap. text 14.95 (*0-89529-884-8*, Avery) Penguin Putnam.

Optimal Performance in Tennis: Mental Skills for Maximum Achievement in Athletics & Life. R. Christopher Barden & Bruce K. Jackson. Ed. by Martin E. Ford. (Illus.). 204p. 1993. 59.95 incl. audio (*0-9640543-0-2*) Optimal Perform.

Optimal Performance of Civil Infrastructure Systems: Proceedings of the International Workshop on Optimal Performance of Civil Infrastructure Systems Held in Conjunction with the ASCE Technical Committee on Optimal Structural Design Meeting at the Structural Congress XV. Ed. by Dan M. Frangopol. LC 97-48535. (Illus.). 222p. 1997. pap. text 35.00 (*0-7844-0315-5*, 40315-5) Am Soc Civil Eng.

Optimal Periodic Control. F. Colonius. (Lecture Notes in Mathematics Ser.: Vol. 1313). vi, 177p. 1988. 35.95 (*0-387-19249-2*) Spr-Verlag.

Optimal Planning for Economic Stabilization. Robert S. Pindyck. (Contributions to Economic Analysis Ser.: Vol. 81). 168p. 1983. 59.00 (*0-7204-3183-2*, North Holland) Elsevier.

Optimal Portfolios - Stochastic Models for Optimal Investment & Risk Management in Continuous Time. R. Korn. LC 97-36352. 300p. 1997. text 48.00 (*981-02-3215-2*) World Scientific Pub.

Optimal, Predictive, & Adaptive Control. Edoardo Mosca. LC 94-6082. 480p. 1994. text 67.00 (*0-13-847609-8*) P-H.

Optimal Pricing, Inflation, & the Cost of Price Adjustment. Ed. by Eytan Sheshinski & Yoram Weiss. LC 92-35198. (Illus.). 534p. 1993. 52.50 (*0-262-19332-9*) MIT Pr.

Optimal Recovery. Ed. by B. Bojanov & H. Wozniakowski. 292p. 1992. 175.00 (*1-56072-016-6*) Nova Sci Pubs.

***Optimal Recovery of Analytic Functions.** K. Yu Osipenko. 220p. 2000. lib. bdg. 89.00 (*1-56072-821-3*) Nova Sci Pubs.

Optimal Regulation: The Economic Theory of Natural Monopoly. Kenneth E. Train. LC 91-4361. 360p. 1991. 52.50 (*0-262-20084-8*) MIT Pr.

Optimal Relay & Saturating Control System Synthesis. E. P. Ryan. (Control Engineering Ser.: No. 14). 352p. 1982. boxed set 145.00 (*0-906048-56-7*, CE014) INSPEC Inc.

***Optimal Reliability Design: Fundamentals & Applications.** Way Kuo et al. (Illus.). 450p. 2000. write for info. (*0-521-78127-2*) Cambridge U Pr.

Optimal Responsiveness: How Therapists Heal Their Patients. Howard Bacal. LC 97-24483. 416p. 1998. 55.00 (*0-7657-0114-6*) Aronson.

Optimal Sampled-Data Control Systems. Tongwen Chen & Bruce A. Francis. LC 95-6882. (Communications & Control Engineering Ser.). (Illus.). 374p. 1996. 89.95 (*3-540-19949-7*) Spr-Verlag.

Optimal Sequentially Planned Decision Procedures. Norbert Schmitz et al. Ed. by J. O. Berger et al. LC 92-29504. (Lecture Notes in Statistics Ser.: Vol. 79). (Illus.). xii, 209p. 1993. 52.95 (*0-387-97908-5*) Spr-Verlag.

Optimal Set Covering for Biological Classification: Theory of Conditional Clustering & Its Use in Biological Classification & Identification. L. P. Lefkovitch. (Illus.). 454p. (Orig.). 1993. pap. 32.50 (*0-660-14821-8*, Pub. by Canadian Govt Pub) Accents Pubns.

Optimal Shape Design for Elliptic Systems. O. Pironneau. (Computational Physics Ser.). (Illus.). 190p. 1983. 75.95 (*0-387-12069-6*) Spr-Verlag.

Optimal Signal Processing. Sophocles J. Orfanidis. 1985. 34.95 (*0-02-949860-0*) Free Pr.

***Optimal Solution of Nonlinear Equations.** Krzysztof A. Sikorski. LC 99-45246. (Illus.). 256p. 2000. text 55.00 (*0-19-510690-3*) OUP.

Optimal Spatial Interaction & the Gravity Model. S. Erlander. (Lecture Notes in Economics & Mathematical Systems Ser.: Vol. 173). (Illus.). 107p. 1980. 28.00 (*0-387-09729-5*) Spr-Verlag.

Optimal Stabilization Policies of Dynamic Economic Systems under Decentralized Information & Control-Regulation Structures. Hajime Myoken. (Collection des Theses de la Faculte des Sciences Economiques et Sociales de l'Universite de Geneve). (Illus.). XIV, 293p. 1990. pap. 55.00 (*3-261-04261-3*) P Lang Pubng.

Optimal Strategy For Pai Gow Poker. 2nd ed. Stanford Wong. (Illus.). 160p. 1992. reprint ed. pap. 14.95 (*0-935926-17-8*) Pi Yee Pr.

Optimal Structural Design under Stability Constraints. Antoni Gajewski & Michal Zyczkowski. (C). 1988. text 266.50 (*90-247-3612-9*) Kluwer Academic.

Optimal Surgical Approach for Elective Reconstruction of the Infra- & Juxta-Renal Abdominal Aorta: A Randomised Prospective Study. Hendrik Lacroix. (Acta Biomedica Lovaniensia Ser.: No. 157). 127p. 1997. pap. 37.50 (*90-6186-841-6*, Pub. by Almqvist Wiksell) Coronet Bks.

Optimal Taxation of Interest Income: A Comparative View of Interest Taxation in Germany, the Netherlands, Switzerland, & the United States. Jacqueline Hess-Ingrassia. (Law Ser.: Vol. 4). 81p. (Orig.). 1995. pap. 36.50 (*90-6186-691-X*, Pub. by Leuven Univ) Coronet Bks.

Optimal Temperature Conditions in the Design of Diesel Engines. M. V. Stradomskii & Ye A. Maksimov. 1995. write for info. (*1-56700-048-7*) Begell Hse.

Optimal Thinking Vol. 1: How to Maximize Your Life with Minimum Effort. Rosalene A. Glickman. LC 96-61206. (Illus.). ix, 256p. (Orig.). 1997. 23.00 (*0-9653823-2-X*) Wrld Acad Prsnl Dev.

Optimal Thinking Vol. 1: How to Maximize Your Life with Minimum Effort. Rosalene A. Glickman. LC 96-61206. (Illus.). ix, 256p. (Orig.). 1998. pap. 17.95 (*0-9653823-3-8*) Wrld Acad Prsnl Dev.

Optimal Unbiased Estimation of Variance Components. James D. Malley. (Lecture Notes in Statistics Ser.: Vol. 39). ix, 146p. 1986. 47.95 (*0-387-96449-5*) Spr-Verlag.

Optimal Use of Sandimmun in Endogenous Uveitis. D. Benezra et al. (Illus.). 30p. 1988. 39.95 (*0-387-18878-9*) Spr-Verlag.

Optimal Use of Sandimmun in Organ Transplantation. Ed. by W. Land. (Illus.). 40p. 1987. 40.95 (*0-387-17865-1*) Spr-Verlag.

Optimal Use of the Clinical Laboratory. Ed. by Oren Zinder. (Illus.). viii, 140p. 1986. 77.50 (*3-8055-4328-X*) S Karger.

Optimal VLSI Architectural Synthesis: Area Performance & Testability. Catherine H. Gebotys & Mohamed I. Elmasry. (C). 1991. text 122.00 (*0-7923-9223-X*) Kluwer Academic.

Optimal Wellness: Where Mainstream & Alternative Medicine Meet. Ralph Golan. 576p. 1995. pap. 20.00 (*0-345-35874-0*, Ballantine Epiphany) Ballantine Pub Grp.

Optimale Kontrolle Okonomischer Prozesse: Anwendungen des Maximumprinzips in Den Wirtschaftswissenschaften. Gustav Feichtinger & Hartl. xvi, 631p. (C). 1986. lib. bdg. 169.25 (*3-11-010432-6*) De Gruyter.

Optimality in Biological & Artificial Networks. Ed. by Daniel S. Levine & Wesley R. Elsberry. (INNS Series of Texts, Monographs, & Proceedings). 400p. (C). 1996. 89.95 (*0-8058-1561-9*) L Erlbaum Assocs.

Optimality in Infinite Horizon Economies, Vol. 269. A. Borglin. 188p. 1986. 25.95 (*0-387-16475-8*) Spr-Verlag.

Optimality Pays: An Introduction to Linear Programming. Jeganathan Sriskandarajh. (Hi Map Ser.: No. 20). (Illus.). 60p. pap. text 11.99 (*0-614-05305-6*, HM 5620) COMAP Inc.

Optimality Theory. Ed. by Diana B. Archangeli & D. Terence Langendoer. LC 97-16853. 250p. (Orig.). (C). 1997. 72.95 (*0-631-20225-0*); pap. 29.95 (*0-631-20226-9*) Blackwell Pubs.

Optimality Theory. Rene Kager. LC 98-39103. (Textbooks in Linguistics). (Illus.). 400p. (C). 1999. 64.95 (*0-521-58019-6*); pap. 24.95 (*0-521-58980-0*) Cambridge U Pr.

Optimality Theory: Phonology, Syntax & Acquisition. Ed. by J. Dekkers et al. 640p. 2000. pap. text 45.00 (*0-19-823844-4*) OUP.

Optima++ Developer's Toolkit. Peter J. Horwood. LC 97-15384. (Client/Server Computing Ser.). (Illus.). 427p. 1997. pap., pap. text 49.95 incl. cd-rom (*0-07-913255-3*) McGraw.

Optimisation. Dorothy M. Greig. LC 79-42892. (Longman Mathematical Texts Ser.). 191p. reprint ed. pap. 59.30 (*0-7837-4033-6*, 204386200011) Bks Demand.

Optimised Radar Processors. Ed. by A. Farina. (Radar, Sonar, Navigation & Avionics Ser.: No. 1). 200p. 1987. 85.00 (*0-86341-118-5*, RA001) INSPEC Inc.

Optimising Pesticide Use. Wilson. text. write for info. (*0-471-49075-X*) Wiley.

Optimism: The Biology of Hope. Lionel Tiger. Ed. by Philip Turner. (Kodansha Globe Trade Paperback Ser.). 336p. 1995. pap. 15.00 (*1-56836-072-X*, Kodansha Globe) Kodansha.

***Optimism & Pessimism: Implications for Theory, Research & Practice.** Edward C. Chang. LC 00-31310. 2000. write for info. (*1-55798-691-6*) Am Philos.

Optimism at Armageddon: Voices of American Participants in World War One. Mark Meigs. 280p. (C). 1997. text 45.00 (*0-8147-5548-8*) NYU Pr.

Optimism Gap: The I'm OK, They're Not Syndrome & the Myth of American Decline. David Whitman. LC 98-15694. 128p. 1998. 22.00 (*0-8027-1334-3*) Walker & Co.

Optimism in the Works of St. Francis De Sales. William C. Marceau. LC 89-29359. (Toronto Studies in Theology: Vol. 41). 336p. 1989. lib. bdg. 99.95 (*0-88946-990-3*) E Mellen.

Optimism of Ralph Waldo Emerson. William F. Dana. 1972. 59.95 (*0-8490-0771-2*) Gordon Pr.

Optimism of Youth. Jack Jackson. 120p. 1991. pap. 12.95 (*1-56097-067-7*) Fantagraph Bks.

Optimist - Pessimist's Guide to the Millenium. Barbara A. Kiefer & Ed Strnad. LC 95-23115. 160p. (Orig.). 1996. pap. 10.00 (*0-399-52191-7*, Perigee Bks) Berkley Pub.

Optimist in Hell. Stephen Spotte. LC 97-65996. 200p. 1998. pap. 13.95 (*0-88739-158-3*) Creat Arts Bk.

Optimist Racing: A Manual for Sailors, Parents & Coaches. Phil Slater. (Illus.). 95p. 1998. pap. 16.95 (*1-898660-12-3*) Motorbooks Intl.

Optimistic Child: A Proven Program to Safeguard Children Against Depression & Build Lifelong Resilience. Martin E. Seligman et al. LC 96-16770. 352p. 1996. pap. 14.00 (*0-06-097709-4*, Perennial) HarperTrade.

Optimistic Classroom: Creative Ways to Give Children Hope. Debbie Hewitt & Sandra Heidemann. LC 98-30927. 1998. 22.95 (*1-884834-60-4*) Redleaf Pr.

Optimistic Life. Orison S. Marden. 316p. 1997. pap. 28.00 (*0-89540-351-X*, SB-351) Sun Pub.

Optimistic Organizations: How to Get, Grow, Keep Positive Power in Your Company. Jean A. Hollands. (Illus.). 152p. (Orig.). 1992. pap. 12.95 (*0-9632556-3-0*) Select Bks CA.

Optimistic Thinking: The Key to Success. Rob McCarter. 96p. 1994. pap. 9.95 (*1-57087-073-X*) Prof Pr NC.

Optimist's Daughter. Eudora Welty. 21.95 (*0-8488-0660-3*) Amereon Ltd.

Optimist's Daughter. Eudora Welty. LC 98-54720. 1999. pap. 20.00 (*0-375-70688-7*) Random Hse Lrg Prnt.

Optimist's Daughter. Eudora Welty. 1978. 16.10 (*0-606-01698-8*, Pub. by Turtleback) Demco.

Optimist's Daughter. Eudora Welty. LC 89-40630. (Vintage International Ser.). 208p. 1990. pap. 11.00 (*0-679-72883-X*) Vin Bks.

***Optimist's Daughter.** large type ed. Eudora Welty. 192p. 2000. pap. 22.00 (*0-06-095587-2*, Ecco Press) HarperTrade.

Optimization. Ed. by M. Dolecki. (Lecture Notes in Mathematics Ser.: Vol. 1405). viii, 220p. 1989. 33.00 (*0-387-51970-X*) Spr-Verlag.

Optimization. David G. Luenberger. 344p. 1997. pap. 80.00 (*0-471-18117-X*) Wiley.

***Optimization.** Spall. 400p. 2000. write for info. (*0-471-33052-3*) Wiley.

Optimization. Spode Group Staff. 1991. pap. 13.95 (*1-871315-26-3*) Ashgate Pub Co.

Optimization: A Simplified Approach. William Conley. (Illus.). 272p. 1981. text 21.95 (*0-89433-121-3*) Petrocelli.

Optimization: A Theory of Necessary Conditions. Lucien W. Neustadt. LC 76-3010. 439p. 1976. reprint ed. pap. 136.10 (*0-7837-9401-0*, 206014600004) Bks Demand.

An Asterisk (*) at the beginning of an entry indicates that the title is appearing for the first time.

***Optimization: Foundations & Applications.** Miller. LC 99-21921. 653p. 1999. pap. 89.95 (0-471-35169-5) Wiley.

Optimization: Foundations & Applications, 1. Miller. LC 99-21921. 570p. 1999. text 150.00 (0-471-32242-3) Wiley.

***Optimization: Proceedings of the 9th Belgian-French-German Conference on Optimization, Namur, September 7-11, 1998.** French-German Conference on Optimization Staff. Ed. by Van Hien Nguyen et al. LC 99-59997. (Lecture Notes in Economics & Mathematical Systems Ser.: 481). x, 498p. 2000. pap. 96.00 (3-540-66905-1) Spr-Verlag.

Optimization: Techniques & Applications (ICOTA '95) 1200p. 1995. 104.00 (981-02-2282-3) World Scientific Pub.

Optimization: Theory & Algorithms. Jean-Baptiste Hiriart-Urruty et al. (Lecture Notes in Pure & Applied Mathematics Ser.: Vol. 86). (Illus.). 272p. 1983. pap. text 135.00 (0-8247-7019-6) Dekker.

Optimization Algorithms for Networks & Graphs. 2nd expanded rev. ed. Edward Minier. Ed. by James R. Evans & Edward Minieka. (Illus.). 488p. 1992. text 69.75 (0-8247-8602-5) Dekker.

Optimization & Artificial Intelligence in Civil & Structural Engineering, 2 vols., 1. Ed. by B. H. V. Topping. LC 92-26741. 1992. lib. bdg. 270.50 (0-7923-1955-9) Kluwer Academic.

Optimization & Artificial Intelligence in Civil & Structural Engineering, 2 vols., 2. Ed. by B. H. V. Topping. LC 92-26741. 1992. lib. bdg. 153.00 (0-7923-1956-7) Kluwer Academic.

Optimization & Artificial Intelligence in Civil & Structural Engineering, 2 vols., Set. Ed. by B. H. V. Topping. LC 92-26741. 1992. text 293.00 (0-7923-1957-5) Kluwer Academic.

***Optimization & Chaos.** Ed. by M. Majumdar et al. (Studies in Economic Theory: Vol. 11). (Illus.). x, 454p. 2000. 79.00 (3-540-67030-0) Spr-Verlag.

Optimization & Computational Logic. Kenneth Mcaloon & Carol Tretkoff. LC 96-23734. (Discrete Mathematics & Optimization Ser.). 560p. 1996. 84.95 (0-471-11533-9, Wiley-Interscience) Wiley.

***Optimization & Control in Civil & Structural Engineering.** Ed. by B. H. V. Topping & B. Kumar. 244p. 1999. pap. 295.00 (0-948749-62-8, Pub. by Civil-Comp) St Mut.

Optimization & Decision-Making in Radiological Protection. ICRP Staff. (International Commission on Radiological Protection Ser.: Vol. 55). 69p. 1989. 41.50 (0-08-037388-7, Pergamon Pr) Elsevier.

Optimization & Decision Support Systems in Civil Engineering. A. B. Templeman. 92p. 1991. text 263.00 (2-88124-823-3) Gordon & Breach.

Optimization & Design of Geodetic Networks. Ed. by E. W. Grafarend & F. Sanso. LC 85-14683. (Illus.). 600p. 1985. 114.95 (0-387-15739-5) Spr-Verlag.

Optimization & Discrete Choice in Urban Systems. Michael Batty et al. Ed. by Peter Nijkamp. (Lecture Notes in Economics & Mathematical Systems Ser.: Vol. 247). vi, 371p. 1985. 47.50 (0-387-15660-7) Spr-Verlag.

Optimization & Dynamical Systems. Uwe Kelmke & John B. Moore. LC 93-38669. (Communications & Control Engineering Ser.). 1994. 99.00 (0-387-19857-1) Spr-Verlag.

Optimization & Economic Evaluation of Granular Activated Carbon for Organic Removal. 610p. 1989. pap. 60.00 (0-89867-469-7, 90550) Am Water Wks Assn.

Optimization & Nonsmooth Analysis. F. H. Clarke. LC 90-35113. (Classics in Applied Mathematics Ser.: No. 5). xii, 308p. 1990. pap. 38.00 (0-89871-256-4) Soc Indus-Appl Math.

Optimization & Nonstandard Analysis. J. E. Rubio. LC 94-21446. (Pure & Applied Mathematics Ser.: Vol. 184). (Illus.). 376p. 1994. text 175.00 (0-8247-9281-5) Dekker.

Optimization & Operations Research: Proceedings of a Workshop Held at the University of Bonn, October 2-8, 1977. Ed. by R. Henn et al. (Lecture Notes in Econometrics & Operations Research Ser.: Vol. 157). 1978. 26.00 (0-387-08842-3) Spr-Verlag.

Optimization & Related Fields. Ed. by R. Conti et al. (Lecture Notes in Mathematics Ser.: Vol. 1190). vii, 419p. 1986. 53.95 (0-387-16476-6) Spr-Verlag.

Optimization-Based Computer-Aided Modelling & Design. Ed. by A. J. Beulens & H. J. Sebastian. (Lecture Notes in Control & Information Sciences: Vol. 174). (Illus.). 268p. 1992. 90.95 (0-387-55135-2) Spr-Verlag.

***Optimization Concepts & Applications in Engineering.** 90p. 2000. teacher ed. write for info. (0-13-018655-4) P-H.

Optimization Concepts & Applications in Engineering. Chandrupatla. LC 98-44441. 432p. 1998. 105.00 (0-13-031279-7) P-H.

***Optimization, Dynamics & Economic Analysis: Essays in Honor of Gustav Feichtinger.** Ed. by Engelbert J. Dockner et al. LC 00-38558. (Illus.). x, 428p. 2000. 94.00 (3-7908-1295-1, Pub. by Physica-Verlag) Spr-Verlag.

Optimization for Profit: A Decision Maker's Guide to Linear Programming. Filmore E. Bender et al. LC 91-6615. (Illus.). 540p. 1992. pap. 17.95 (1-56022-015-5); lib. bdg. 89.95 (1-56022-014-7) Haworth Pr.

***Optimization in Computational Chemistry & Molecular Biology: Local & Global Approaches.** Christodoulos A. Floudas & P. M. Pardalos. LC 99-89296. (Nonconvex Optimization & Its Applications). 2000. write for info. (0-7923-6155-5) Kluwer Academic.

Optimization in Control Theory & Practice. Igor Gumowski & C. Mira. LC 68-12059. 252p. reprint ed. pap. 71.90 (0-608-12507-5, 2024456) Bks Demand.

Optimization in Economic Theory. 2nd ed. Avinash Dixit. (Illus.). 196p. 1990. pap. text 23.00 (0-19-877210-6) OUP.

***Optimization in Elliptic Problems with Applications to Mechanics of Deformable Bodies & Fluid Mechanics.** W. G. Litnivov. (Operator Theory: Vol. 119). 544p. 2000. 145.00 (3-7643-6199-9, Pub. by Birkhauser) Spr-Verlag.

***Optimization in Elliptic Problems with Applications to Mechanics of Deformable Bodies & Fluid Mechanics.** William G. Litvinov. LC 00-30398. 2000. write for info. (0-8176-6199-9) Birkhauser.

Optimization in Industry, 1997: Proceedings. Ed. by Ashok D. Belegundu & Farrokh Mistree. LC 98-760034. 283p. 1998. pap. 90.00 (0-7918-1248-0) ASME Pr.

Optimization in Operations Research. Ronald L. Rardin. LC 97-27030. 919p. (C). 1997. 97.00 (0-02-398415-5) P-H.

Optimization in Planning & Operation of Electric Power Systems. Ed. by K. Frauendorfer et al. 365p. 1993. 87.95 (0-387-91471-4) Spr-Verlag.

Optimization in Quality Control. Khaled S. Al-Sultan & M. A. Rahim. LC 97-150. 1997. lib. bdg. 143.00 (0-7923-9889-0) Kluwer Academic.

Optimization in Solving Elliptic Problems. Eugene G. D'yakonov. Ed. by Steve McCormick. 592p. 1995. lib. bdg. 89.95 (0-8493-2872-1, 2872) CRC Pr.

Optimization in Structural Design: Proceedings of the International Union of Theoretical & Applied Mechanics Symposium, Warsaw, Aug. 21-24, 1973. International Union of Theoretical & Applied Mecha. Ed. by A. Sawczuk & Z. Mroz. (International Union of Theoretical & Applied Mechanics Symposia Ser.). (Illus.). 600p. 1975. 157.95 (0-387-07044-3) Spr-Verlag.

Optimization Issues in the Design & Control of Large Space Structures: Proceedings of a Session Sponsored by the Structural Division. Ed. by Manohar P. Kamat. 62p. 1985. 16.00 (0-87262-452-8) Am Soc Civil Eng.

Optimization Methods. O. V. Vasiliev. LC 95-54153. (Advanced Series in Mathematical Science & Engineering). 1996. write for info. (1-885978-24-3) Wrld Fed Pubs.

Optimization Methods for Engineering Design. Richard L. Fox. LC 78-127891. (Engineering Ser.). (C). 1971. write for info. (0-201-02078-5) Addison-Wesley.

Optimization Methods for Material Design of Cement-Based Composites. A.M. Brandt. 1998. pap. 110.00 (0-419-21790-8) Thomson Learn.

Optimization Methods in Partial Differential Equations: Proceedings from the 1996 Joint Summer Research Conference, June 16-20, 1996, Mt. Holyoke College. Ed. by Steven Cox & Irena Lasiecka. LC 97-22252. (Contemporary Mathematics Ser.: Vol. 209). 349p. 1997. pap. 69.00 (0-8218-0604-1) Am Math.

Optimization Methods in Structure Design. Ed. by H. A. Eschenauer & Neils Olhoff. 460p. (C). 1983. text 24.95 (3-411-01654-X) Birkhauser.

***Optimization Modeling for Supply Chain Management.** Shapiro. 2000. pap. 40.00 (0-534-37363-1) Thomson Learn.

Optimization Modeling with LINDO. 5th ed. Linus E. Schrage. LC 96-49946. 1997. pap. 97.95 (0-534-34857-2) Brooks-Cole.

Optimization Modeling with Lingo. 3rd rev. ed. Lindo Systems, Inc. Staff. (Illus.). 550p. (C). 1998. pap. text 71.95 (1-893355-00-4) Lindo Systs.

Optimization Models & Concepts in Production Management. Ed. by P. Brandimarte. xiv, 339p. 1995. text 88.00 (2-88449-020-5) Gordon & Breach.

Optimization Models Using Fuzzy Sets & Possibility Theory. Ed. by Janusz Kacprzyk & Sergei A. Orlovski. (C). 1987. text 253.00 (90-277-2492-X) Kluwer Academic.

Optimization of Cam Mechanisms. J. Angeles & C. S. Lopez-Cajun. (C). 1991. lib. bdg. 145.00 (0-7923-1355-0) Kluwer Academic.

Optimization of Cancer Radiotherapy: Proceedings of the 2nd International Conference on Dose, Time Fractionation in Radiation Oncology Held at the University of Wisconsin, Madison, Wisconsin, September 12-14, 1984. Ed. by Bhudatt R. Paliwal et al. (American Association of Physicists in Medicine Symposium Ser.: No. 5). 560p. 1985. 45.00 (0-88318-483-4, Pub. by Am Inst Physics) Med Physics Pub.

Optimization of Chemical Processes. T. F. Edgar & David M. Himmelblau. (Chemical Engineering Ser.). 652p. (C). 1987. 99.38 (0-07-018991-9) McGraw.

Optimization of Chemical Processes. 2nd ed. Edgar. 2000. 66.00 (0-07-039359-1) McGraw.

Optimization of Chromatographic Selectivity: A Guide to Method Development. Peter J. Schoenmakers. (Journal of Chromatography Library: No. 35). 346p. 1986. 199.50 (0-444-42681-7) Elsevier.

Optimization of Composite Structures Design. Antonio Miravete. 256p. 1996. 531.00 incl. disk (1-85573-208-4, Pub. by Woodhead Pubng) Am Educ Systs.

Optimization of Discrete Time Systems: The Upper Boundary Approach. Z. Nahorski et al. (Lecture Notes in Control & Information Sciences: Vol. 51). 137p. 1983. 18.95 (0-387-12258-3) Spr-Verlag.

Optimization of Distributed Parameter Structures, Vol. 1. Edward J. Haug & J. Cea. 1981. text 306.00 (90-286-2791-X) Kluwer Academic.

Optimization of Dynamic Systems. Sunil K. Agrawal & Brian C. Fabien. LC 99-21107. (Solid Mechanics & Its Applications Ser.: 221p. 1999. write for info. (0-7923-5681-0) Kluwer Academic.

Optimization of Filtration for Cyst Removal. Nancy L. Patania et al. LC 96-131392. (Illus.). 158p. 1995. pap. 115.00 (0-89867-825-0, 90699) Am Water Wks Assn.

Optimization of Highway Concrete Technology. Mohamad Nagi et al. 275p. (C). 1994. pap. text 15.00 (0-309-05751-5, SHRP-C-373) SHRP.

Optimization of Industrial Unit Processes. 2nd ed. Bela G. Liptak. LC 98-20091. 432p. 1998. boxed set 94.95 (0-8493-9873-8, CH9873) CRC Pr.

Optimization of Irrigation & Drainage Systems: Proceedings. Irrigation & Drainage Specialty Conference Staff. LC 73-158127. 634p. reprint ed. pap. 196.60 (0-608-11468-5, 200490600047) Bks Demand.

Optimization of Large Structural Systems: Proceedings of the NATO - DFG Advanced Study Institute, Berchtesgaden, Germany, 23 September-4 October 1991, 2 vols., Set. Ed. by George I. Rozvany. LC 92-43799. (NATO Advanced Science Institutes Series: Mathematical & Physical Sciences: No. 231). 1244p. (C). 1993. lib. bdg. 481.00 (0-7923-2130-8) Kluwer Academic.

Optimization of Large Structural Systems: Proceedings of the NATO - DFG Advanced Study Institute, Berchtesgaden, Germany, 23 September-4 October 1991, 2 vols., Vol. I. Ed. by George I. Rozvany. LC 92-43799. (NATO Advanced Science Institutes Series: Mathematical & Physical Sciences: No. 231). 1244p. (C). 1993. lib. bdg. 580.50 (0-7923-2128-6) Kluwer Academic.

Optimization of Large Structural Systems: Proceedings of the NATO - DFG Advanced Study Institute, Berchtesgaden, Germany, 23 September-4 October 1991, 2 vols., Vol. II. Ed. by George I. Rozvany. LC 92-43799. (NATO Advanced Science Institutes Series: Mathematical & Physical Sciences: No. 231). 1244p. (C). 1993. lib. bdg. write for info. (0-7923-2129-4) Kluwer Academic.

Optimization of Linear Control Systems: Analytical Methods & Computational Algorithms. 272p. 1998. text 76.00 (90-5699-113-2) Gordon & Breach.

Optimization of Mechanical Properties of Thermoplastics Through Alloying. 246p. 1991. 2450.00 (0-89336-602-1, PO75U) BCC.

Optimization of Methods for Approximate Solution of Operator Equations. Sergei V. Pereverzev. LC 93-25889. (Computational Mathematics & Analysis Ser.). 330p. (C). 1994. lib. bdg. 145.00 (1-56072-140-5) Nova Sci Pubs.

Optimization of Observation & Control Processes. V. V. Malyshev et al. (Educ Ser.). (Illus.). 349p. 1992. 69.95 (1-56347-040-3, 40-3) AIAA.

Optimization of Plant Nutrition: Proceedings of the VIII International Colloquium for the Optimization of Plant Nutrition, Lisbon, Portugal, 1-8 September 1992. Ed. by M. A. Fragoso. (Developments in Plant & Soil Sciences Ser.). 696p. (C). 1993. text 535.50 (0-7923-2519-2) Kluwer Academic.

***Optimization of Powdered Activated Carbon Application for Geosmin & MIB Removal.** Mark Graham & AWWA Research Foundation Staff. LC 99-50343. 1999. write for info. (1-58321-019-9) Am Water Wks Assn.

Optimization of Processing, Properties, & Service Performance Through Microstructural Control - STP 792. Ed. by Halle Abrams et al. LC 82-71748. 341p. 1983. text 37.95 (0-8031-0240-2, STP792) ASTM.

Optimization of Radiotherapy, Particularly in Developing Countries: Report of a WHO Meeting of Investigators. (Technical Report Ser.: No. 644). 89p. 1980. pap. text 6.00 (92-4-120644-6, 1100644) World Health.

Optimization of SQL Queries for Parallel Machines. W. Hasan. LC 96-39704. (Lecture Notes in Computer Science Ser.: Vol. 1182). 133p. 1996. pap. 30.00 (3-540-62065-6) Spr-Verlag.

Optimization of Static Gaskets. Hans J. Tuckmantel. 1993. 75.00 (3-88432-020-3, 9KE1) Gulf Pub.

Optimization of Stochastic Models: The Interface Between Simulation & Optimization. George C. Pflug. LC 96-27381. (Discrete Event Dynamic Systems in Engineering & Computer Science Ser.). 400p. (C). 1996. lib. bdg. 193.50 (0-7923-9780-0) Kluwer Academic.

Optimization of Stochastic Systems: Topics in Discrete-Time Dynamics. 2nd ed. Masanao Aoki. (Economic Theory, Econometrics & Mathematical Economics Ser.). 400p. 1989. text 104.00 (0-12-058851-X) Acad Pr.

Optimization of Structural Systems & Applications: Computer Aided Optimum Design of Structures III. Ed. by Carlos A. Brebbia & S. Hernandez. LC 93-71019. (OPTI Ser.: Vol. 3). 696p. 1993. 299.00 (1-56252-166-7, 2432) Computational Mech MA.

Optimization of Structural Systems & Applications: Computer-Aided Optimum Design of Structures III. Ed. by S. Hernandez & Carlos A. Brebbia. 696p. 280.00 (1-85166-841-1) Elsevier.

Optimization of Structural Systems & Industrial Applications. Ed. by S. Hernandez & Carlos A. Brebbia. LC 91-71738. (OPTI Ser.: Vol. 2). 692p. 1991. 233.00 (1-56252-068-7, 1401) Computational Mech MA.

Optimization of Structural Topology Shape & Material. Martin Philip Bendsoe. LC 95-13005. 1995. write for info. (0-387-59057-9) Spr-Verlag.

Optimization of Structural Topology Shape & Material. Martin Philip Bendsoe. LC 95-13005. 288p. 1995. 107.95 (3-540-59057-9) Spr-Verlag.

Optimization of Transport Networks. Peter A. Steenbrink. LC 73-2793. 341p. reprint ed. pap. 105.80 (0-8357-6243-2, 203423800089) Bks Demand.

Optimization of Unit Operations. Bela G. Liptak. LC 86-47960. 432p. 1987. lib. bdg. 79.95 (0-8019-7706-1) NP-Chilton.

Optimization of Weighted Monte Carlo Methods. G. A. Mikhailov. Ed. by Roland Glowinski et al. Tr. by K. K. Sabelfeld from RUS. (Computational Physics Ser.). 220p. 1992. 103.95 (0-387-53005-3) Spr-Verlag.

Optimization on Low Rank Nonconvex Structures. Hiroshi Konno et al. LC 96-37405. (Nonconvex Optimization & Its Applications Ser.). 1997. lib. bdg. 212.00 (0-7923-4308-5) Kluwer Academic.

Optimization, Optimal Control, & Partial Differential Equations: First Franco-Romanian Conference, Iasi, September 7-11, 1992. Ed. by Viorel Barbu et al. LC 92-25607. (International Series of Numerical Mathematics: Vol. 107). xiii, 347p. 1992. 122.00 (0-8176-2788-X, Pub. by Birkhauser) Princeton Arch.

Optimization over Time: Dynamic Programming & Stochastic Control, Vol. 2. fac. ed. Peter Whittle. LC 81-16401. (Wiley Series in Probability & Mathematical Statistic. Applied Probability & Statistics Staff). 327p. 1983. pap. 101.40 (0-7837-8643-3, 204385300012) Bks Demand.

Optimization over Time Vol. 1: Dynamic Programming & Stochastic Control. Peter Whittle. LC 81-16401. (Wiley Series in Probability & Mathematical Statistics). 342p. 1982. reprint ed. pap. 106.10 (0-7837-4023-9, 204385300011) Bks Demand.

Optimization, Parallel Processing & Applications. Ed. by Alexander B. Kurzhanski et al. (Lecture Notes in Economics & Mathematical Systems Ser.: Vol. 304). vi, 292p. 1988. pap. 44.80 (0-387-19053-8) Spr-Verlag.

Optimization Problems. Lothar Collatz & W. Wetterling. Tr. by P. R. Hadsack from GER. (Applied Mathematical Sciences Ser.: Vol. 17). (Illus.). 370p. (Orig.). 1975. 72.95 (0-387-90143-4) Spr-Verlag.

Optimization Software Guide. Jorge J. More & S. J. Wright. LC 93-33771. (Frontiers in Applied Mathematics Ser.: No. 14). xii, 154p. 1993. pap. 31.00 (0-89871-322-6) Soc Indus-Appl Math.

Optimization Statistics & Designs in Pharmaceutics. N. R. Bohidar. 465p. 1999. 73.95 (0-8493-9421-X) CRC Pr.

***Optimization Techniques.** Ed. by Cornelius T. Leondes. 284p. 1998. text 120.00 (90-5699-644-4, Harwood Acad Pubs) Gordon & Breach.

Optimization Techniques: An Introduction. L. R. Foulds. (Undergraduate Texts in Mathematics Ser.). (Illus.). 502p. 1981. 69.95 (0-387-90586-3) Spr-Verlag.

Optimization Techniques: Modeling & Optimization in the Service of Man, Pt. 1. Ed. by J. Cea. LC 76-9857. (Lecture Notes in Computer Science Ser.: Vol. 40.). 1976. 46.00 (0-387-07622-0) Spr-Verlag.

Optimization Techniques: Proceedings the IFIP Technical Conference, Novosibirsk, 1974. IFIP Technical Conference Staff. Ed. by Gurii I. Marchuk. (Lecture Notes in Computer Science Ser.: Vol. 27). 515p. 1975. 28.95 (0-387-07165-2) Spr-Verlag.

Optimization Techniques & Applications: International Conference, 2 vols., Set. K. H. Phua et al. 1200p. 1992. text 190.00 (981-02-1062-0) World Scientific Pub.

Optimization Techniques in Statistics. Ed. by Jagdish Rustagi. (Statistical Modeling & Decision Science Ser.). (Illus.). 359p. 1994. text 78.00 (0-12-604555-0) Acad Pr.

Optimization Theory & Algorithms, Vol. 124. E. Polak. LC 97-2158. (Applied Mathematical Sciences Ser.). 784p. 1997. 69.95 (0-387-94971-2) Spr-Verlag.

Optimization Theory & Applications: Problems with Ordinary Differential Equations. Lamberto Cesari. (Applications of Mathematics Ser.: Vol. 17). (Illus.). 544p. 1983. 161.95 (0-387-90676-2) Spr-Verlag.

Optimization Theory with Applications. Donald A. Pierre. 640p. 1998. reprint ed. pap. 16.95 (0-486-65205-X) Dover.

Optimization under Constraints: Theory & Applications of Nonlinear Programming. Peter Whittle. LC 75-149574. (Wiley Series in Probability & Mathematical Statistics). 251p. reprint ed. pap. 77.90 (0-608-18642-2, 202428800036) Bks Demand.

Optimization with Disjunctive Constraints. H. D. Sherali & C. M. Shetty. (Lecture Notes in Economics & Mathematical Systems Ser.: Vol. 181). (Illus.). 156p. 1980. 18.00 (0-387-10228-0) Spr-Verlag.

Optimize Barrier Coextrusion: A Regional Technical Conference, September 5 & 6, 1985, Pheasant Run Resort, St. Charles, Illinois-Sponsored by the Chicago Section & the Extrusion Division of SPE. Society of Plastics Engineers Staff. LC TP1175.E9S6. (Coetrusion III Ser.). 209p. pap. 64.80 (0-608-17147-6, 202769000056) Bks Demand.

Optimize the Magic of Your Mind. Sidney J. Parnes et al. LC 98-138866. 196p. 1997. pap. 18.95 (0-943456-41-X) Bearly Ltd.

Optimize Your Cruising Sailboat. Roberts. LC 00-22835. (Illus.). 192p. 2000. 25.95 (0-07-134114-5) McGraw.

***Optimize Your Operation: Stories, Tools & Lessons for Using the Principles of Process Management to Improve Your Quality.** James C. Abbott. LC 99-62121. (Walkabout Ser.). (Illus.). 306p. 2000. 39.95 (1-887355-04-9) R H Smith Pubs.

Optimized LCAO Method & the Electronic Structure of Extended Systems. Helmut Eschrig. (Research Reports in Physics). (Illus.). 225p. 1989. 64.95 (0-387-50740-X) Spr-Verlag.

Optimized-Motion Planning: Theory & Implementation. Cherif Ahrikencheikh & Ali A. Seireg. 366p. 1994. 110.00 incl. disk (0-471-01903-8) Wiley.

Optimized Vibration Testing & Analysis. Edward A. Szymkowiak. LC 62-38584. 107p. 1983. pap. text 60.00 (0-915414-70-8) IEST.

Optimizing & Troubleshooting Retention & Drainage Short Course, 1994: San Francisco Marriott, San Francisco, CA, April 27-29. Technical Association of the Pulp & Paper Industry. LC TS1120.R47. (TAPPI Course Notes Ser.). (Illus.). 134p. 1994. pap. 41.60 (0-608-05375-9, 208242600010) Bks Demand.

O

Optimizing Bandwidth. Michele J. Petrovsky. LC 98-16887. (McGraw Hill Series on Computer Communication). 500p. 1998. pap. 44.95 (*0-07-049889-X*) McGraw.

Optimizing Brown: An Indigenous Examination of Latino Roots, Values, & Rights. Ricardo Duenez. LC 97-106895. (Illus.). 60p. (Orig.). 1996. pap. 4.95 (*0-9655220-0-8*) Tlacatlihua Communs.

Optimizing C++ Steve Heller. LC 98-24381. 464p. 1998. pap. text 44.99 (*0-13-977430-0*) P-H.

Optimizing C with Assembly Code. Peter Gulutzan & Trudy Pelzer. 432p. 1995. pap. 29.95 incl. disk (*0-87930-447-2*) C M P Books.

Optimizing Cash Flow. Institute of Credit Management Staff. LC 99-164571. 126p. 1998. write for info. (*0-87622-759-0*) Aspen Pub.

Optimizing Chloramine Treatment. (Illus.). 358p. 1993. pap. 75.00 (*0-89867-687-8*, 90620) Am Water Wks Assn.

Optimizing Cleaning Techniques for Copper Alloy Condenser Tubing in Seawater Service. LaQue Center for Corrosion Technology, Inc. Staff. 48p. 1984. write for info. (*0-318-60405-1*) Intl Copper.

Optimizing Client/Server Networks. Coletta Witherspoon & Comaq. LC 95-81092. 528p. 1996. pap. 29.99 (*1-56884-593-6*) IDG Bks.

Optimizing Development Profits in Large Scale Real Estate Projects. Michael D. Wilburn & Robert M. Gladstone. LC 72-79135. (Urban Land Institute, Technical Bulletin Ser.: No. 67). (Illus.). 64p. reprint ed. pap. 30.00 (*0-8357-8255-7*, 203395100087) Bks Demand.

Optimizing Early Child Care & Education, Vol. 13. A. S. Honig. (Special Aspects of Education Ser.). vii, 207p. 1990. text 71.00 (*2-88124-769-5*) Gordon & Breach.

***Optimizing Filtration in Biological Filters: Final Report.** Peter M. Huck. LC 00-22037. 2000. write for info. (*1-58321-065-2*) Am Water Wks Assn.

Optimizing Hob Accuracy for Hob Life. W. C. Smith. (Technical Papers: Vol. P129.18). (Illus.). 7p. 1969. pap. text 30.00 (*1-55589-163-2*) AGMA.

Optimizing Housing for the Elderly: Homes Not Houses. Intro. by Leon A. Pastalan. (Journal of Housing for the Elderly). 163p. 1991. text 39.95 (*1-56024-076-8*) Haworth Pr.

***Optimizing Human Development: Existential Meaning Across the Life Span.** Gary T. Reker & Kerry Chamberlain. LC 99-6281. 1999. write for info. (*0-7619-0994-X*) Sage.

Optimizing HVAC Systems. Albert Thumann. LC 87-45326. 250p. 1987. text 59.00 (*0-88173-042-4*) Fairmont Pr.

Optimizing INFORMIX Applications. Robert D. Schneider. LC 95-3656. 352p. (C). 1995. pap. text 67.00 (*0-13-149238-1*) P-H.

Optimizing Jet Transport Efficiency: Performance, Operations, & Economics. Carlos E. Padilla. LC 96-16573. (Illus.). 205p. 1996. pap. 49.95 (*0-07-048208-X*) McGraw.

Optimizing Learning: The Integrative Education Model in the Classroom. Barbara Clark. 256p. (C). 1990. pap. 45.80 (*0-675-20482-8*, Merrill Coll) P-H.

Optimizing Light Microscopy for Biological & Clinical Laboratories. ASCLS Staff. LC 97-207224. 208p. 1997. per. 24.95 (*0-7872-3538-5*) Kendall-Hunt.

Optimizing Liquid Crystal. Mostafa Hedayatnia. LC 92-25872. (Six Sigma Research Institute Ser.). 1993. pap. text 10.95 (*0-201-63417-1*) Addison-Wesley.

Optimizing Microsoft C Library, 5.25. Len Dorfman. 1991. 34.95 (*0-8306-2567-4*) McGraw-Hill Prof.

Optimizing Microsoft C Library, 3.5. Len Dorfman. 1991. 34.95 (*0-8306-2568-2*) McGraw-Hill Prof.

Optimizing Microsoft SQL Server. Robert Schneider. LC 97-104433. 608p. (C). 1996. pap. text 39.95 (*0-13-266222-1*) P-H.

Optimizing Network Traffic: Notes from the Field. Microsoft Corporation Staff. LC 98-52138. 400p. 1999. pap. 39.99 (*0-7356-0648-X*) Microsoft.

Optimizing Networks for the 21st Century. 1998. write for info. (*0-7897-9808-5*) Que.

Optimizing Ocean Current Crossings. Gerald Marcus & Edward Marcus. 16p. 1993. pap. text 15.00 (*1-882502-18-3*) US Sail Assn.

Optimizing OP AMP Performance. Jerald E. Graeme. LC 96-41207. (Illus.). 226p. 1996. 55.00 (*0-07-024522-3*) McGraw.

Optimizing Ozonation for Turbidity & Organics (TOC) Removal by Coagulation & Filtration. William C. Becker & Charles R. O'Melia. (Illus.). 236p. 1996. pap. 195.00 (*0-89867-878-1*, 90703) Am Water Wks Assn.

Optimizing Performance, Motor Selection & Design Concepts. Jerry Irvine. (Advanced Information Reports: No. 6). 16p. 1984. 3.95 (*0-912468-04-1*, AIR-6) CA Rocketry.

Optimizing Performance of Energy Systems. Saul Stricker. LC 84-18470. (Illus.). 153p. (C). 1984. 32.95 (*0-02-948940-7*) Free Pr.

***Optimizing Post-Earthquake Lifeline System Reliability: 5th U. S. Conference on Lifeline Earthquake Engineering.** U. S. Conference on Lifeline Earthquake Engineering Staff et al. LC 99-35328. 1040p. 1999. 110.00 (*0-7844-0449-6*) Am Soc Civil Eng.

Optimizing Programs. C. F. Schofield. 1989. text 49.95 (*0-470-21533-X*) P-H.

Optimizing Quality in Electronics Assembly: A Heretical Approach. Jim Smith. LC 96-29182. (Illus.). 502p. 1996. 54.95 (*0-07-059229-2*) McGraw.

Optimizing Reservoir Resources: A New Model for Reservoir Reliability. Charles ReVelle. LC 98-38927. 200p. 1999. 69.95 (*0-471-18877-8*) Wiley.

Optimizing Resources: A Manager's Guide to Success. AORN Staff. 107p. (Orig.). 1993. pap. text 43.75 (*0-939583-82-8*) Assn Oper Rm Nurses.

Optimizing SQL: Embedded SQL in C. Peter Gulutzan & Trudy Pelzer. (Illus.). 230p. 1997. pap. 34.95 incl. disk (*0-87930-448-0*) C M P Books.

Optimizing Structure in Context: Scrambling & Information Structure. Hye-Won Choi. LC 99-20043. (Dissertations in Linguistics Ser.: No. 16). 256p. (C). 1999. text 59.95 (*1-57586-157-7*); pap. text 22.95 (*1-57586-156-9*) CSLI.

Optimizing Surface Texture of Concrete Pavement. Portland Cement Association Staff. 112p. 1995. 40.00 (*0-89312-134-7*, RD111T) Portland Cement.

Optimizing the Clinical Devlopment of Antipsychotic Drugs. Neal R. Cutler et al. LC 97-3041. 216p. 1998. 79.95 (*0-471-97011-5*) Wiley.

Optimizing the Desktop. (C). 2000. pap. 36.00 (*0-13-977752-0*) P-H.

Optimizing the Machine Controls - Student's Manual: Working with the Machine, Module Three, Lesson 3. (Illus.). 1997. pap., student ed. write for info. (*1-58677-027-6*) Polymer Train.

Optimizing the Organization: How to Link People & Technology. Emily Schultheiss. 224p. 1988. text 29.95 (*0-88730-305-6*, HarpBusn) HarpInfo.

Optimizing the Resources for Water: Proceedings of the 17th Annual Conference. Ed. by Reza M. Khanbilvardi & Thomas C. Gooch. LC 90-451. 839p. 1990. pap. text 81.00 (*0-87262-756-X*) Am Soc Civil Eng.

Optimizing the Shape of Mechanical Elements & Structures. A. A. Seireg & Jorge Rodriguez. LC 96-5420. (Mechanical Engineering Ser.: No. 105). (Illus.). 616p. 1997. text 165.00 (*0-8247-9555-5*) Dekker.

Optimizing the Windows Registry. Kathy Ivens. LC 97-77544. (Infraworld Networking Ser.). 384p. 1998. pap. 39.99 (*0-7645-3159-X*) IDG Bks.

Optimizing Theory & Experiments. Randall R. Robey & Martin C. Schultz. LC 92-25260. (Illus.). 186p. (Orig.). (C). 1993. pap. text 34.95 (*1-56593-078-9*, 0382) Thomson Learn.

Optimizing Unix for Performance. Amir H. Majidimehr. LC 95-40312. 352p. (C). 1995. pap. 47.00 (*0-13-111551-0*) P-H.

***Optimizing Windows for Games, Graphics & Multimedia.** David L. Farquhar. Ed. by Robert Denn. LC 99-88626. (Illus.). 280p. 1999. pap. 24.95 (*1-56592-677-3*) OReilly & Assocs.

Optimizing Windows 95. B. J. Sineath. LC 95-81431. 400p. 1996. pap. 34.99 incl. disk (*1-56884-594-4*) IDG Bks.

Optimizing Windows NT. Sean K. Daily. LC 97-74804. 1032p. 1998. pap. 49.99 (*0-7645-3110-7*) IDG Bks.

Optimizing Windows NT, Vol. 4. Microsoft Corporation Staff. 608p. write for info. incl. disk (*1-55615-655-3*) Microsoft.

Optimizing Wireless /RF Circuits. John D. Lenk. (Electronics Workbench Circuit Solution Ser.). 300p. 1999. 60.00 (*0-07-134376-8*) McGraw-Hill Prof.

Optimizing Work Performance: A Look Beyond the Bottom Line. Martin Morf. LC 85-23232. 205p. 1986. 49.95 (*0-89930-143-6*, MWK/, Quorum Bks) Greenwood.

Optimizing Your Multimedia PC. L. J. Skibbe. LC 95-81105. 384p. 1995. pap. 34.99 (*1-56884-595-2*) IDG Bks.

Optimum Backwash of Dual Media Filters & GAC Filter-Adsorbers with Air Scour. 126p. 1991. pap. 59.00 (*0-89867-576-6*, 90584) Am Water Wks Assn.

Optimum Calcium Intake. 1996. lib. bdg. 251.75 (*0-8490-6016-8*) Gordon Pr.

Optimum Child: Developing Your Child's Fullest Potential Through Astrology. Gloria Star. LC 87-45745. (Modern Astrology Library). 352p. 1987. pap. 9.95 (*0-87542-740-5*) Llewellyn Pubns.

Optimum Cruise Performance of Subsonic Transport Aircraft. E. Torenbeek. (Series 02 - Flight Mechanics: No. 03). (Illus.). 60p. 1998. pap. 18.95 (*90-407-1579-3*, Pub. by Delft U Pr) Coronet Bks.

Optimum Currency Areas: New Analytical & Policy Developments. Mario I. Blejer et al. LC 97-13514. 1997. pap. write for info. (*1-55775-652-X*) Intl Monetary.

Optimum Delegation. Didactic Systems Staff. (Simulation Game Ser.). 1973. pap. 26.25 (*0-89401-019-0*) Didactic Syst.

Optimum Design of High Loaded Case Carburized Large Gears. Manfred Hirt & E. Jahnel. (Technical Papers: Vol. P229.23). (Illus.). 20p. 1982. pap. text 30.00 (*1-55589-290-6*) AGMA.

Optimum Designs for Multi-Factor Models. Rainer Schwabe. LC 96-14776. (Lecture Notes in Statistics Ser.: Vol. 113). 124p. 1996. pap. 32.95 (*0-387-94745-0*) Spr-Verlag.

***Optimum Disposal Methods for Use on the Gulf Intracoastal Waterway.** Ed. by Charles P. Giammona & Roy W. Hann, Jr. (Illus.). 111p. (C). 1999. reprint ed. pap. text 25.00 (*0-7881-8316-8*) DIANE Pub.

Optimum Experimental Designs. A. C. Atkinson & A. N. Donev. LC 92-8342. (Oxford Statistical Science Ser.: Vol. 7). (Illus.). 344p. (C). 1992. text 75.00 (*0-19-852254-1*, Clarendon Pr) OUP.

***Optimum Healing.** Craig Brown. 1998. pap. 19.95 (*0-7126-7107-2*, Pub. by Random) Trafalgar.

Optimum Health: A Cardiologist's Prescription. unabridged ed. Stephen T. Sinatra. LC 95-80607. (Illus.). 368p. 1996. 24.95 (*1-879111-81-0*) Lincoln-Bradley.

Optimum Health: A Natural Lifesaving Prescription for Your Body & Mind. Stephen T. Sinatra. 352p. 1998. reprint ed. pap. 13.95 (*0-553-37922-4*) Bantam.

Optimum Health for the New Millennium. Ernestine Townsend. 250p. 1999. pap. 19.95 (*0-7392-0283-9*, PO3381) Morris Pubng.

Optimum Home Designs: A105. Randy Bynre. Ed. by National Plan Service Staff. (Illus.). 32p. 1992. 4.95 (*0-934039-36-4*) Hme Dsgn Altntves.

Optimum Inductive Methods: A Study in Inductive Probability, Bayesian Statistics, & Verisimilitude. Roberto Festa. LC 93-11840. (Synthese Library: Vol. 232). 208p. (C). 1993. lib. bdg. 112.00 (*0-7923-2460-9*, Pub. by Kluwer Academic) Kluwer Academic.

Optimum Inventory Levels. L. Catalano. 34p. 1990. reprint ed. pap. 28.50 (*0-938648-24-1*) T-C Pr CA.

***Optimum Kayak: How to Choose, Maintain, Repair & Customize the Right Boat for You.** Andy Knapp. LC 99-32854. 144p. 1999. pap. 16.95 (*0-07-038298-0*) McGraw.

***Optimum Lifeskills for Stress Management.** Darrell Franken. 350p. 2000. pap. (*0-934957-28-2*) Wellness Pubns.

Optimum Methods in Statistics. F. Steiner. LC 98-110086. 370p. 1997. 222.00 (*963-05-7439-X*, Pub. by Akade Kiado) St Mut.

Optimum Number of Teeth for Span Measurement. John R. Colbourne. (1985 Fall Technical Meeting Ser.: Vol. 85FTM9). (Illus.). 9p. 1985. pap. text 30.00 (*1-55589-102-0*) AGMA.

***Optimum Nutrition Bible.** Patrick Holford. LC 98-53510. 340p. 1999. pap. 16.95 (*1-58091-015-7*) Crossing Pr.

Optimum Physical Performance Capacity in Adults: Proceedings of the WHO Scientific Group, Geneva, 1968. WHO Staff. (Technical Reports: No. 436). 1969. pap. text 5.00 (*92-4-120436-2*, 1100436) World Health.

Optimum Pipe Size Selection. Claude B. Nolte. (Illus.). 304p. (C). 1978. 60.00 (*0-87849-024-8*, Pub. by Trans T Pub) Enfield Pubs NH.

Optimum Separation Design for Subsea & Floating Production Systems. K. Bassiti. 1989. 150.00 (*90-6314-568-3*, Pub. by Lorne & MacLean Marine) St Mut.

Optimum Shape: Automated Structural Design. Ed. by James A. Bennett & Mark E. Botkin. (General Motors Research Symposia Ser.). 410p. 1986. 95.00 (*0-306-42419-3*, Plenum Trade) Perseus Pubng.

Optimum Sports Nutrition: Your Competitive Edge - A Nutritional Guide for Optimizing Athletic Performance. Michael Colgan. 562p. 1993. pap. 24.95 (*0-9624840-5-9*) Advanced Research Pr.

Optimum Staffing Mix in Australian Nursing Homes: A Review of the Literature (DINROO) Alan Pearson. 92p. 1993. pap. 39.00 (*0-7300-1550-5*, Pub. by Deakin Univ) St Mut.

Optimum Steam Curing Procedure in Precasting Plants. (PCI Journal Reprints Ser.). 25p. 1985. pap. 12.00 (*0-318-19736-7*, JR8) P-PCI.

Optimum Structural Design: Theory & Applications. Ed. by R. H. Gallagher & O. C. Zienkiewicz. LC 72-8600. (Illus.). 372p. reprint ed. pap. 115.40 (*0-8357-4564-3*, 203746600008) Bks Demand.

Optimum Use of Primary Energy Resources. (ECE Energy Ser.: No. 4). 227p. 60.00 (*92-1-100354-7*, GV.90.0.8) UN.

Optimum Use of Space: Time Spent in Alaska. Belinda D. LaFluer. LC 98-65167. 64p. 1998. pap. 9.95 (*1-888125-25-X*) Publ Consult.

Optimus Princeps: Saggio Sulla Storia & Sui Tempi Dell' Imperatore Traiano. Roberto Paribeni. LC 75-7334. (Roman History Ser.). (ITA., Illus.). 1975. reprint ed. 58.95 (*0-405-07051-9*) Ayer.

Optimystic's Handbook. Terry Lynn Taylor. LC 97-6076. pap. 15.00 (*0-06-251464-4*) HarpC.

Optimystic's Handbook: Using Mystical Wisdom to Discover Hope, Happiness, & the Wonder of Spiritual Living. Terry L. Taylor & Mary B. Crain. 192p. 1998. text 22.00 (*0-7881-5823-6*) DIANE Pub.

Optina Hermitage & It's Time see **Optina Pustin' i Jeja Vremja**

Optina Pustin' i Jeja Vremja. I. M. Kontsevich.Tr. of Optina Hermitage & It's Time. (Illus.). 604p. 1970. 25.00 (*0-317-29246-3*); pap. 20.00 (*0-317-29247-1*) Holy Trinity.

Optina Pustyn Monastery in the Russian Literary Imagination: Iconic Vision in Works by Dostoevsky, Gogol, Tolstoy, & Others, Vol. 3. Leonard J. Stanton. (Middlebury Studies in Russian Language & Literature). XVI, 308p. (C). 1995. 54.95 (*0-8204-1697-5*) P Lang Pubng.

Opting for Change: A Handbook for Evaluation & Planning for Theological Education by Extension. Ed. by Ross Kinsler & James H. Emery. LC 91-65731. 112p. (Orig.). (C). 1992. pap. text 7.95 (*0-87808-229-8*, WCL229-8) William Carey Lib.

Opting for Oil: The Political Economy of Technological Change in the West German Chemical Industry, 1945-1961. Raymond G. Stokes. 273p. (C). 1994. text 59.95 (*0-521-45124-8*) Cambridge U Pr.

Opting for the Poor: A Challenge for North Americans. Peter J. Henriot. (Energies for Social Transformation Ser.). 64p. (Orig.). 1990. pap. text 5.95 (*0-934255-09-1*) Center Concern.

Opting Out: Choice & the Future of Schools. Martin Rogers. 200p. (C). 1992. pap. 18.50 (*0-85315-769-3*, Pub. by Lawrence & Wishart) NYU Pr.

Opting Out of Medicare: Private Medical Markets in Ontario. Alan D. Wolfson & Carolyn Tuohy. LC 81-114075. (Ontario Economic Council Research Studies: No. 19). (Illus.). 260p. reprint ed. pap. 80.60 (*0-7837-4279-7*, 204397100012) Bks Demand.

Option: Click. Dave McKean. Ed. by Clare Haythornwaite. (Illus.). 88p. 1998. 40.00 (*0-9642069-1-9*) A Spiegel Fine Arts.

Option Delta. Richard Marcinko & John Weisman. (Rogue Warrior Ser.). 416p. 2000. reprint ed. per. 6.99 (*0-671-00073-X*, Pocket Star Bks) PB.

Option Embedded Bonds: Price Analysis, Credit Risk, & Investment Strategies. Israel Nelken. 312p. 1996. 75.00 (*0-7863-0818-4*, Irwn Prfssnl) McGraw-Hill Prof.

Option Fool: Hundreds & Hundreds of Real World Answers from the Online Option Forum. Hubert Lee. LC 97-9621. 1997. 24.95 (*0-7863-1212-2*, Irwn Prfssnl) McGraw-Hill Prof.

Option for the Poor: A Hundred Years of Vatican Social Teaching. Donal Dorr. LC 92-20785. 300p. (Orig.). (C). 1992. pap. 19.00 (*0-88344-827-0*) Orbis Bks.

Option for the Poor: The Basic Principle of Liberation Theoloy in the Light of the Bible. 2nd ed. Norbert Lohfink. Ed. by Duane L. Christensen. Tr. by Linda M. Maloney. LC 95-25305. (Berkeley Lectures: Vol. 1). 1996. 8.95 (*0-941037-38-X*, BIBAL Press) D & F Scott.

Option Lock. Justin Richards. (Doctor Who Ser.). 1998. pap. 5.95 (*0-563-40583-X*) BBC.

Option Market Making: Trading & Risk Analysis for the Financial & Commodity Option Markets. Allen J. Baird. LC 92-12010. (Wiley Finance Editions Ser.). 224p. 1992. 69.95 (*0-471-57832-0*) Wiley.

Option Nucleaire et les Entreprises Suisses. Claude Meylan. (European University Studies: Economics & Management: Ser. 5, Vol. 446). (FRE.). XIV, 272p. 1983. 35.80 (*3-261-03281-2*) P Lang Pubng.

Option of Prison Privatization: A Guide for Community Deliberations. David N. Ammons et al. LC 92-23148. 60p. 1993. pap. 11.95 (*0-89854-159-X*) U of GA Inst Govt.

Option Players Advanced Guidebook: Turning the Tables on the Options Markets. Kenneth R. Trester. LC 80-83175. (Illus.). 275p. 1980. pap. 35.00 (*0-9604914-1-4*) Inst Options.

***Option Pricing.** Richard Rendleman. 350p. 2000. 74.95 (*0-631-21589-1*); pap. 34.95 (*0-631-21590-5*) Blackwell Pubs.

Option Pricing: Mathematical Models & Computation. rev. ed. Paul Wilmott et al. 457p. 1997. 165.00 (*0-9522082-0-2*, Pub. by Oxford Finan) Am Educ Systs.

Option Pricing: Numerical Methods. Les Clewlow. LC 97-36998. 330p. 1998. 89.95 (*0-471-96651-7*) Wiley.

Option Pricing & Investment Strategies. 3rd ed. Richard M. Bookstaber. 1991. text 45.00 (*1-55738-145-3*, Irwn Prfssnl) McGraw-Hill Prof.

Option Pricing & Strategies in Investing. Richard M. Bookstaber. LC 80-15013. 256p. 1981. text 24.95 (*0-201-00123-3*) Addison-Wesley.

Option Strategies: A Portfolio Approach. Ed. by Michael Himick. 250p. 1998. 65.00 (*0-8144-0438-3*) AMACOM.

Option Strategies: Profit-Making Techniques for Stock Index & Commodity Options. 2nd ed. Courtney D. Smith. LC 96-909. 336p. 1996. 69.95 (*0-471-11555-X*) Wiley.

Option Strategies for Beginners. Samuel Malkind. (Illus.). 32p. 1997. 10.00 (*0-8059-4186-X*) Dorrance.

Option Valuation. John O'Brien & Sanjay Srivastava. LC 94-44758. 1995. write for info. (*0-538-84810-3*) S-W Pub.

Option Valuation & Hedging: A Trader's Perspective. Marti G. Subrahmanyam. 256p. 1996. 65.00 (*0-471-04467-9*) Wiley.

Option Valuation & Implied Volatility in Lotus 123(TM) OVIV. SAH Research, Inc., Staff. (Illus.). 1990. student ed. 695.00 incl. disk (*0-9626417-0-7*) Sah Research.

Option Valuation in the Presence of Market Imperfections, Vol. 1369. Andreas Bell. Vol. 5. write for info. (*0-318-69980-X*) P Lang Pubng.

***Option Valuation under Stochastic Volatility: With Mathematica Code.** Alan L. Lewis. LC 99-91935. (Illus.). 360p. (C). 2000. pap. 97.50 (*0-9676372-0-1*) Finance Pr.

Option Volatility & Pricing: Advanced Trading Strategies & Techniques. rev. ed. Sheldon Natenberg. 350p. 1994. text 50.00 (*1-55738-486-X*, Irwn Prfssnl) McGraw-Hill Prof.

Optional Implant Positioning & Soft Tissue Management for the Branemark System. Patrick Palacci. LC 95-15503. (Illus.). 83p. 1995. text 68.00 (*0-86715-308-3*) Quint Pub Co.

Optional Options: Work Design & Manufacturing Automation. Joe Benders. 272p. 1993. 67.95 (*1-85628-490-5*, Pub. by Avebry) Ashgate Pub Co.

Optionen auf Futures Verstehen (German Making Sense of Futures Options) Robert Sennholz. (GER.). 1997. pap. 3.50 (*0-915513-84-6*) Ctr Futures Ed.

Options. Beene. (C). 1992. pap., wbk. ed. 21.56 (*0-395-59963-6*) HM.

Options. 3rd ed. Robert Kolb. 464p. 1997. 64.95 (*1-57718-081-X*) Blackwell Pubs.

Options. 3rd ed. Michael C. Thomsett. LC 96-49244. (Getting Started Ser.). (Illus.). 241p. 1997. pap. 18.95 (*0-471-17758-X*) Wiley.

Options. 3rd rev. ed. Robert W. Kolb. LC 96-34107. (Illus.). 464p. 1997. text 69.95 (*1-57718-064-X*) Blackwell Pubs.

Options: A Communication Skills Series, 3 bks., Set. Durlynn Aneman & Vickie Sanders. LC 92-84129. 1993. mass mkt. 12.95 (*0-538-62153-2*) S-W Pub.

Options: A Personal Seminar. Scott Fullman. LC 92-19109. 1992. pap. text 26.00 (*0-13-643578-5*) P-H.

Options: An Introduction. 2nd ed. Robert W. Kolb. LC 93-80417. 353p. 1993. pap. 35.00 (*1-878975-36-6*) Blackwell Pubs.

Options: Comprehensive Guide to Options. Martin Torosian. 1986. 44.00 (*0-9603592-1-4*) MTA Financial Servs.

Options: Essential Concepts & Trading Strategies. 2nd ed. Options Institute Staff. 430p. 1994. text 55.00 (*0-7863-0272-0*, Irwn Prfssnl) McGraw-Hill Prof.

***Options: Essential Concepts & Trading Strategies.** 3rd ed. Options Institute Staff. LC 99-18006. (Illus.). 441p. 1999. 55.00 (*0-07-134169-2*) McGraw.

An Asterisk (*) at the beginning of an entry indicates that the title is appearing for the first time.

Options: Expanding Educational Services for Adults. National Center for Research in Vocational Educati. 1987. 174.00 (*0-318-35280-X*, SP 500) Ctr Educ Trng Employ.

Options: Making the Decisions That Touch the Heart, Mind & Soul of a Woman. Karla Gottry. 128p. 1996. pap. 4.95 (*1-886158-11-8*) Macalester.

Options: Perception & Deception: Superior Results Through Position Analysis & Risk Control. Charles M. Cottle. 308p. 1996. text 60.00 (*1-55738-907-1*, Irwn Prfssnl) McGraw-Hill Prof.

Options: The Alternative Cancer Therapy Book. Richard Walters. LC 92-49901. 416p. (Orig.). pap. 13.95 (*0-89529-510-5*, Avery) Penguin Putnam.

Options: The Fundamentals. Glenn Satty & Joe Troccolo. 100p. 1994. pap. 12.99 (*0-9641112-0-9*) Swiss Bank.

Options: The International Guide to Valuation & Trading Strategies. Gordon Gemmill. 288p. 1993. 37.95 (*0-07-707497-1*) McGraw.

Options: Trading Strategies That Work. William F. Eng. (Finance & Taxation Ser.). 1992. 50.00 (*0-7494-0919-3*) Kogan Page Ltd.

Options Vol. II: A Directory of Child & Senior Services (Arizona Edition) Linda F. Radke. 1989. pap. 9.95 (*0-9619853-4-8*) Five Star AZ.

Options - A Directory of Child & Senior Services. Linda F. Radke. 1987. pap. 6.00 (*0-9619853-1-3*) Five Star AZ.

Options - Journal 1. Anema. (EC - HS Communication/ English Ser.). 1993. mass mkt. 2.95 (*0-538-62154-0*) S-W Pub.

Options - Journal 3. Anema. (EC - HS Communication/ English Ser.). 1993. mass mkt. 2.95 (*0-538-62156-7*) S-W Pub.

Options - Journal 2. Anema. (EC - HS Communication/ English Ser.). 1993. mass mkt. 2.95 (*0-538-62155-9*) S-W Pub.

Options - Plain & Simple: Successful Investment Strategies Without the Rocket Science. Lenny Jordon. 288p. 2000. 29.00 (*0-273-63878-5*) F T P H.

Options, a Communication Skills Series, Bk. 1. Anema. LC 92-84129. (EC - HS Communication/English Ser.). 1993. mass mkt. 12.95 (*0-538-62151-6*) S-W Pub.

Options, a Communications Skills Series, Bk. 2. Anema. LC 92-84129. (EC - HS Communication/English Ser.). 1993. mass mkt. 12.95 (*0-538-62152-4*) S-W Pub.

Options Advantage: Gaining a Trading Edge over the Markets. David L. Caplan. 250p. 1991. 40.00 (*1-55738-214-X*, Irwn Prfssnl) McGraw-Hill Prof.

Options & Futures. French. text. write for info. (*0-471-57577-1*) Wiley.

Options & Futures: A Tutorial. Roger G. Clarke. 1992. pap. text 20.00 (*0-943205-16-6*) RFICFA.

Options & Futures in International Portfolio Management. Terry J. Watsham. LC 92-5850. 392p. 1992. mass mkt. 52.95 (*0-412-42690-0*) Chapman & Hall.

Options & Opportunities: Overcoming Barriers to Worklife Education & Training. Ivan Charner & Nancy K. Schlossberg. 33p. 1989. 7.50 (*0-86510-066-7*) Natl Inst Work.

Options & Perspectives: A Sourcebook of Innovative Foreign Language Programs in Action, K-12. William D. Love & Lucille J. Honig. LC 73-78994. 381p. reprint ed. pap. 118.20 (*0-608-16280-9*, 202655300053) Bks Demand.

Options & the Management of Financial Risk. Phelim Boyle. 1992. text 25.00 (*0-938959-26-3*) Soc Actuaries.

Options Are Easy to Understand. Samuel N. Malkind. 1995. 11.95 (*0-533-11500-0*) Vantage.

***Options As a Strategic Investment.** Lawrence G. McMillan. 4p. 2001. 55.00 (*0-7352-0197-8*) PH Pr.

Options As a Strategic Investment. 3rd ed. Lawrence G. McMillan. LC 92-23160. 882p. (C). 1993. text 49.95 (*0-13-636002-5*) P-H.

Options Course: A Winning Program for Investors & Traders. Rudi Binneweis. LC 96-109673. 300p. 1995. 50.00 incl. disk (*1-55738-871-7*, Irwn Prfssnl) McGraw-Hill Prof.

Options Course: High Profit & Low Stress Trading Methods. George A. Fontanills. LC 97-50522. (Wiley Trading Advantage Ser.). 320p. 1998. 49.95 (*0-471-24950-5*) Wiley.

***Options Course Workbook.** George A. Fontanills. 137p. 1998. pap. 34.95 (*0-471-24949-1*) Wiley.

Options Edge: Winning the Volatility Game with Options on Futures. William R. Gallacher. LC 98-11804. 273p. 1998. 34.95 (*0-07-038296-4*) McGraw.

Options, Experience & Trends in Spent Nuclear Fuel Management. I.A.E.A. Staff. LC 96-117310. (Technical Reports: Vol. 378). 72p. 1995. pap. text 35.00 (*92-0-101095-8*, STI/DOC/378, Pub. by IAEA) Bernan Associates.

Options for a New Canada. Ed. by Ronald L. Watts & Douglas M. Brown. 358p. 1991. text 50.00 (*0-8020-5921-X*); pap. text 19.95 (*0-8020-6901-0*) U of Toronto Pr.

Options for Britain. David Halpern et al. 392p. 1996. 79.95 (*1-85521-715-5*, Pub. by Dartmth Pub); pap. 32.95 (*1-85521-831-3*, Pub. by Dartmth Pub) Ashgate Pub Co.

***Options for Closed Water Systems.** Ed. by H. Aalderink et al. (Water Science & Technology Ser.). 272p. 1999. pap. 163.00 (*0-08-043641-2*, Pergamon Pr) Elsevier.

Options for Community Response to the Safe Drinking Water Act, No. 35. David J. Eaton. (Policy Research Project Report). 120p. 1979. pap. 4.95 (*0-89940-635-1*) LBJ Sch Pub Aff.

Options for Conservation: The Different Roles of Nongovernmental Conservation Organizations. Sarah Fitzgerald. LC 90-24078. 166p. 1990. reprint ed. pap. 51.50 (*0-608-04233-1*, 206499000012) Bks Demand.

Options for Electronic Mail. Libby Trudell et al. LC 84-15418. (Professional Librarian Ser.). 172p. 1986. 35.00 (*0-86729-105-2*, Hall Reference) Macmillan.

Options for Expanding Health Insurance Coverage in New York State. United Hospital Fund of New York Staff. LC 98-21242. 1998. 25.00 (*1-881277-41-0*) United Hosp Fund.

***Options for Expanding the Health Families Program: Estimates.** Elias Lopez & Richard A. Figueroa. 12p. 1999. pap. write for info. (*1-58703-101-9*, CRB-99-004) CA St Libry.

Options for Girls: A Door to the Future: An Anthology on Science & Math Education. Ed. by Meg Wilson. LC 91-37557. 1992. pap. 20.00 (*0-89079-543-6*, 9995) PRO-ED.

***Options for Leak & Break Detection & Repair of Drinking Water Systems.** Lawrence A. Smith & K. A. Fields. LC 00-27513. 180p. 2000. 57.50 (*1-57477-091-8*) Battelle.

Options for Reaching Water Quality Goals: Proceedings of a Symposium Held in Washington, D. C. at the Twentieth Annual Conference of the American Water Resources Association - Co-Sponsored by Tennessee Valley Authority. American Water Resources Association Staff. Ed. by Theodore M. Schad. LC 85-71658. (American Water Resources Association Technical Publication Ser.: No. TPS 84-2). (Illus.). 225p. reprint ed. pap. 69.80 (*0-7837-5566-X*, 204534100005) Bks Demand.

***Options for Remote Monitoring & Control of Small Drinking Water Facilities.** Albert J. Pollack. LC 99-14431. 1999. pap. 57.50 (*1-57477-072-1*) Battelle.

Options for Rural Telecommunications Development. Rogati A. Kayani & Andrew Dymond. (World Bank Technical Paper Ser.: No. 359). 144p. 1997. pap. 22.00 (*0-8213-3948-6*, 13948) World Bank.

Options for Social Welfare Policy: The Public's View. John Doble & Keith Melville. 52p. (Orig.). 1986. pap. 6.50 (*1-889483-04-4*) Public Agenda.

Options for Tax Reform. Ed. by Joseph A. Pechman. LC 84-72269. (Dialogues on Public Policy Ser.). 149p. 1984. pap. 11.95 (*0-8157-6995-4*) Brookings.

Options for the Control of Influenza No. III: Proceedings of the 3rd International Conference on Options for the Control of Influenza, Cairns, Australia, 4-9 May, 1996. Lorena Brown et al. LC 96-47465. (International Congress Ser.: 1123). 880p. 1996. 273.00 (*0-444-82461-8*) Elsevier.

Options for the 80s: Proceedings of the Second National Conference of the Association of College & Research Libraries, October 1-4, 1981, Minneapolis, Minnesota, 2 vols. Ed. by Michael D. Kathman & Virgil F. Massman. LC 82-7721. (Foundations in Library & Information Science: Vol. 17). 687p. 1982. 157.00 (*0-89232-276-4*) Jai Pr.

Options for the Management of Tuna Fisheries in the Indian Ocean. 79p. 1991. 9.00 (*92-5-103016-2*, Pub. by FAO) Bernan Associates.

Options for the 90's: Employer Support for Child Care. National Council of Jewish Women Staff. 22p. 1991. 10.00 (*0-685-62939-2*) NCJW.

Options for the Stock Investor: How Any Investor Can Use Options to Enhance & Protect Their Return. James Bittman. LC 95-21707. 225p. 1995. 29.95 incl. disk (*1-55738-872-5*, Irwn Prfssnl) McGraw-Hill Prof.

Options for Tunnelling, 1993. Ed. by H. Robert Burger. LC 93-15219. (Developments in Geotechnical Engineering Ser.: Vol. 74). 936p. 1993. 220.00 (*0-444-89935-9*) Elsevier.

Options for U. S. Energy Policy. Ed. by Henry S. Rowen. 317p. 1977. pap. text 24.95 (*0-917616-20-0*) Transaction Pubs.

Options for U. S. Military Support to the United Nations. fac. ed. Martha Bills et al. LC JX1981.P7O6. (Illus.). 47p. 1992. reprint ed. pap. 30.00 (*0-608-00957-1*, 206180400011) Bks Demand.

Options for Undergraduate Foreign Language Programs: Four-Year & Two-Year Colleges. Renate A. Schulz. LC 78-71999. (Options for Teaching Ser.: No. 3). 125p. 1979. pap. 38.80 (*0-608-05591-3*, 206605100006) Bks Demand.

Options from Within: Learning to Love Yourself & Be Loved. Jacques Weisel. 192p. 1994. pap. text, per. 10.00 (*0-8403-8096-8*) Kendall-Hunt.

Options, Futures & Exotic Derivative Assets. Eric C. Briys & Mondher Bellalah. LC 97-44712. 472p. 1998. pap. 64.95 (*0-471-96908-7*) Wiley.

Options, Futures & Exotic Derivatives Assets. Eric C. Briys. LC 97-44712. (Frontiers in Finance Ser.). 472p. 1998. 89.95 (*0-471-96909-5*) Wiley.

Options, Futures & Other Derivative Securities. 3rd ed. John C. Hull. LC 96-13389. 592p. 1996. text 86.00 (*0-13-186479-3*, Pub. by P-H) S&S Trade.

Options, Futures, & Other Derivatives. 3rd ed. John C. Hull. 1998. 89.75 (*0-13-887498-0*) P-H.

***Options, Futures, & Other Derivatives.** 4th ed. John C. Hull. LC 99-26609. 698p. (C). 1999. 94.00 (*0-13-022444-8*) P-H.

Options in Corporate Finance. 2nd ed. Moore. 1998. 23.00 (*0-07-232707-3*) McGraw.

Options in Roman Catholicism: An Introduction. Ed. by Nathan R. Kollar. LC 82-21823. 224p. (Orig.). 1983. pap. text 22.00 (*0-8191-2959-3*) U Pr of Amer.

Options in Teaching English to Adult Speakers of Other Languages: (A Collection of Essays) Christopher Corbel. 131p. (C). 1989. 80.00 (*0-7300-0697-2*, Pub. by Deakin Univ) St Mut.

Options Laboratory: A Course in Options. 2nd rev. ed. Roger E. Ison. (Illus.). 160p. (Orig.). 1995. 89.95 incl. disk (*0-9650375-0-9*, OL-A17-CP) Mantic Sftwre.

Options Markets. John C. Cox & Mark Rubinstein. (Illus.). 432p. (C). 1985. 66.00 (*0-13-638205-3*, Pub. by P-H) S&S Trade.

Options on Foreign Exchange. David F. DeRosa. (Institutional Investor Publications). 250p. 1992. text 65.00 (*1-55738-249-2*, Irwn Prfssnl) McGraw-Hill Prof.

Options on Foreign Exchange. 2nd rev. ed. David F. DeRosa. LC 99-38491. (Series in Financial Engineering). 240p. 2000. 69.95 (*0-471-31641-5*) Wiley.

Options on Futures: A Hands-On Workbook of Real World Trading Simulations & Money Making Strategies, Revised Edition. Ronald J. Frost. LC 94-171573. 1993. text 50.00 (*1-55738-516-5*, Irwn Prfssnl) McGraw-Hill Prof.

Options Pricing. Ingersoll. 1998. 65.74 (*0-07-231689-6*) McGraw.

Options Primer. Robert W. Kolb. LC 96-39149. (Illus.). 320p. (Orig.). (C). 1997. pap. text 49.95 (*1-57718-071-2*) Blackwell Pubs.

Options Strategies: A Portfolio Approach. Ed. by Michael Himick. 375p. 1999. 65.00 (*1-57958-066-1*) Fitzroy Dearborn.

Options Strategist: High-Profit Techniques for Every Market Condition. Kenneth H. Shaleen. 275p. 1995. 29.95 (*1-55738-890-3*, Irwn Prfssnl) McGraw-Hill Prof.

Options Traders. 3rd ed. 912p. (C). 1998. lib. bdg. 9.85 (*0-13-099661-0*) S&S Trade.

Options Trading & Volatiligy Trading: Options Trading & Volatility Trading. Ed. by Laurence A. Connors. (Best of the Professional Traders Journal Ser.). 64p. 1999. pap. 39.95 (*0-9650461-7-6*) M Gordon Pubng.

Options Trading Strategy of a Lifetime. William Grandmill. 268p. 1995. 60.00 (*0-930233-56-5*) Windsor.

***Options Workbook: Proven Strategies from a Market Wizard.** Anthony J. Saliba. 2001. pap. 40.00 (*0-7931-4097-8*) Dearborn.

***Optionsewertung Und Asicherungsstrategien.** Jurgen Bar. (Illus.). IX, 220p. 1999. 45.95 (*3-631-33546-6*) P Lang Pubng.

Optique de Claude Ptolemee. 2nd ed. Albert Lejeune. LC 89-9858. (Collection de Travaux de l'Academie Internationale d'Histoire des Sciences: Vol. 31). (FRE & LAT.). viii, 414p. 1989. reprint ed. 260.00 (*90-04-09126-2*) Brill Academic Pubs.

Optique et Mathematiques: Recherches Sur l'Historie de la Pensee Scientifique en Arabe. Roshdi Rashed. (Collected Studies: Vol. CS378). 352p. 1992. 124.95 (*0-86078-330-8*, Pub. by Variorum) Ashgate Pub Co.

Optiques: La Vie Quotidienne. (FRE.). (C). pap., teacher ed. 35.95 (*0-8442-1470-1*, VF1470-1) NTC Contemp Pub Co.

Optische Bestimmung der Gesteinsbildenden Minerale Teil 1: Bestimmungstabellen. H. U. Bambauer et al. 188p. 1982. 32.00 (*3-510-65106-5*, Pub. by E Schweizerbartsche) Balogh.

Optizmation: Handbooks in Operations Research & Management Science, Vol. 1. Ed. by George L. Nemhauser et al. 710p. 1989. 165.00 (*0-444-87284-1*, North Holland) Elsevier.

Opto-Contact Vol. 3414: Workshop on Technology Transfers, Start-Up Opportunities & Strategic Alliances. Ed. by Robert J. Corriveau et al. LC 99-170367. 1998. 89.00 (*0-8194-2868-X*) SPIE.

Opto-Mechanical Systems Design. 2nd rev. ed. Paul R. Yoder, Jr. LC 92-26044. (Optical Engineering Ser.: Vol. 35). (Illus.). 686p. 1992. text 159.50 (*0-8247-8754-4*) Dekker.

***Optoelectronic & Electronic Sensors III.** Ed. by Antoni Nowakowski & Bogdan Chachulski. 248p. 1999. pap. text 72.00 (*0-8194-3204-0*) SPIE.

Optoelectronic & Electronic Sensors II. Ed. by Zdzislaw Jankiewicz & Henryk Madura. LC 97-203564. 250p. 1997. pap. 69.00 (*0-8194-2469-2*) SPIE.

***Optoelectronic Devices.** Safa Kasap. 600p. (C). 2000. 87.00 (*0-201-61087-6*) Addison-Wesley.

Optoelectronic Devices. S. Desmond Smith. 416p. 1995. pap. 78.00 (*0-13-143769-0*) P-H.

Optoelectronic Devices & Optical Imaging Techniques. Douglas A. Ross. (Electrical & Electronic Engineering Ser.). (Illus.). 137p. 1979. pap. text 32.00 (*0-333-25335-3*) Scholium Intl.

Optoelectronic Devices & Systems for Processing: 8-9 August 1996, Denver, Colorado. Kristina M. Johnson et al. LC 96-23000. (Critical Reviews of Optical Science & Technology Ser.). 1996. pap. 70.00 (*0-8194-2257-6*, CR65) SPIE.

Optoelectronic Information Processing: 2-5 June 1997, Barcelona, Spain. Bahram Javidi et al. LC 97-32250. 1997. 48.00 (*0-8194-2675-X*) SPIE.

Optoelectronic Integrated Circuits, Vol. 3006. Ed. by Yoon-Soo Park & Ramu V. Ramaswamy. LC 97-200943. 498p. 1997. 89.00 (*0-8194-2417-X*) SPIE.

***Optoelectronic Integrated Circuits & Packaging III.** Ed. by Michael R. Feldman et al. 262p. 1999. pap. text 72.00 (*0-8194-3101-X*) SPIE.

Optoelectronic Integrated Circuits II, Vol. 3290. Ed. by Shih-Yuan Wang & Yoon S. Park. LC 98-160781. 384p. 1997. 80.00 (*0-8194-2729-2*) SPIE.

Optoelectronic Integration: Physics, Technology & Applications. Ed. by Osamu Wada. LC 94-6977. (International Series in Engineering & Computer Science, VLSI, Computer Architecture, & Digital Screen Processing). 472p. (C). 1994. text 183.50 (*0-7923-9453-4*) Kluwer Academic.

Optoelectronic Interconnects & Packaging IV, Vol. 3005. Ed. by Ray T. Chen & Peter S. Guilfoyle. LC 97-175324. 370p. 1997. 89.00 (*0-8194-2416-1*) SPIE.

Optoelectronic Interconnects & Packaging, 1996: Proceedings of a Conference Held 30-31 January 1996, San Jose, California. Ed. by Ray T. Chen & Peter S. Guilfoyle. LC 95-49833. (Critical Reviews of Optical Science & Technology Ser.: Vol. CR62). 1996. pap. 80.00 (*0-8194-2017-4*) SPIE.

***Optoelectronic Interconnects VI.** Ed. by Julian P. Bristow & Suning Tang. 394p. 1999. pap. text 84.00 (*0-8194-3102-8*) SPIE.

Optoelectronic Interconnects III: 8-9 February, 1995, San Jose, California Ray T. Chen et al. LC 94-69345. (Proceedings Ser.). viii, 366p. 1995. pap. write for info. (*0-8194-1747-5*) SPIE.

Optoelectronic Interconnects V, Vol. 3288. Ed. by Ray T. Chen & Julian P. Bristow. 298p. 1998. 69.00 (*0-8194-2727-6*) SPIE.

Optoelectronic Materials - Ordering, Composition Modulation, & Self-Assembled Structures: Materials Research Society Symposium Proceedings, Vol.417. Ed. by E. D. Jones et al. 426p. 1996. 73.00 (*1-55899-320-7*) Materials Res.

Optoelectronic Materials & Device Concepts. Ed. by M. Razeghi. 1991. pap. 20.00 (*0-8194-0533-7*, PM05) SPIE.

Optoelectronic Materials & Devices. Ed. by Marek Osinski & Yan K. Su. (Proceedings of SPIE Ser.: Vol. 3419). 474p. 1998. 107.00 (*0-8194-2873-6*) SPIE.

Optoelectronic Packaging. Ed. by Yung-Cheng Lee et al. LC 96-44716. (Microwave & Optical Engineering Ser.). 261p. 1997. 87.95 (*0-471-11188-0*) Wiley.

Optoelectronic Properties of Inorganic Compounds. D. M. Roundhill & J. P. Fackler. LC 98-7495. (Modern Inorganic Chemistry Ser.). (Illus.). 416p. (C). 1998. text 115.00 (*0-306-45557-9*, Kluwer Plenum) Kluwer Academic.

Optoelectronic Switching Systems in Telecommunications & Computers. Herbert A. Elion & Morozov. (Electro-Optics Ser.: Vol. 4). (Illus.). 272p. 1984. text 135.00 (*0-8247-7163-X*) Dekker.

Optoelectronic Techniques for Microwave & Millimeter-Wave Engineering. William M. Robertson. LC 95-21286. 244p. 1995. 93.00 (*0-89006-711-2*) Artech Hse.

Optoelectronics. Heath Company Staff. (Electronics Technology Ser.). (Illus.). 495p. (C). 1981. teacher ed. 9.95 (*0-87119-073-7*); student ed. 9.95 (*0-87119-072-9*); pap. text 14.95 (*0-87119-071-0*, EB-605); ring bd. 59.95 (*0-87119-070-2*, EE-105) Heathkit-Zenith Ed.

OptoElectronics. Vaughn D. Martin. LC 96-72184. (Illus.). 264p. 1997. pap. 34.95 (*0-7906-1091-4*) Prompt Publns.

***Optoelectronics.** Savage. 120p. 1999. pap. 1995.00 (*0-471-37872-0*) Wiley.

Optoelectronics. Endel Uiga. LC 94-31912. 352p. 1995. 91.00 (*0-02-422170-8*, Macmillan Coll) P-H.

***Optoelectronics: An Introduction.** 3rd ed. John Wilson. 480p. 1998. pap. 86.00 (*0-13-103961-X*) P-H.

Optoelectronics: An Introduction to Materials & Devices. Jasprit Singh. (Illus.). 537p. (C). 1995. 77.19 (*0-07-057650-5*) McGraw.

Optoelectronics: Intermediate Study, Vol. 2. Vaughn D. Martin. (Illus.). 258p. 1997. pap. 34.95 (*0-7906-1110-4*) Prompt Publns.

Optoelectronics: Technologies & Applications. Vijai K. Tripathi & A. Selvarajan. LC 92-41330. 1993. 30.00 (*0-8194-1209-0*, PM11) SPIE.

Optoelectronics Vol. 3: Experimental Study. Vaughn D. Martin. (Illus.). 435p. 1998. pap. 44.95 (*0-7906-1122-8*) Prompt Publns.

Optoelectronics Circuits Manual. R. M. Marston. LC 97-181139. 190p. 1999. pap. text 32.95 (*0-7506-0157-4*, Newnes) Buttrwrth-Heinemann.

Optoelectronics Circuits Manual. Raymond Micheal Marston. 1988. 32.00 (*0-434-91211-5*) CRC Pr.

Optoelectronics Circuits Manual. 2nd ed. R. M. Marston. LC 99-20871. 1999. 29.95 (*0-7506-4166-5*) Buttrwrth-Heinemann.

Optoelectronics, Fiber Optics & Lasers: A Text-Lab Manual. 2nd ed. Morris Tischler. 256p. 1991. lib. bdg. 52.20 (*0-07-064792-5*) McGraw.

Optoelectronics, Fiber Optics & Lasers: A Text-Lab Manual. 2nd ed. Morris Tischler. 256p. 1991. teacher ed. 13.32 (*0-07-064793-3*) McGraw.

Optoelectronics, Fiberoptics, & Laser Cookbook. Thomas Petruzzellis. LC 97-423. (Illus.). 300p. 1997. 39.95 (*0-07-049839-3*) McGraw.

Optoelectronics, Fiberoptics, & Laser Cookbook. Thomas Petruzzellis. LC 97-423. (Illus.). 322p. 1997. pap. 29.95 (*0-07-049840-7*) McGraw.

Optoelectronics for Data Communication. Ed. by Ronald C. Lasky et al. (Illus.). 338p. 1995. text 73.00 (*0-12-437160-4*) Acad Pr.

Optoelectronics for Environmental Science. Ed. by S. Martellucci & Arthur N. Chester. LC 90-22278. (Ettore Majorana International Science Series, Life Sciences: Vol. 54). (Illus.). 302p. (C). 1990. 132.00 (*0-306-43806-2*, Plenum Trade) Perseus Pubng.

Optoelectronics in Japan & the United States. unabridged ed. Stephen R. Forrest. (JTEC Panel Report Ser.). (Illus.). 359p. (Orig.). 1996. pap. write for info. (*1-883712-39-4*) Intl Tech Res.

***Optogalvanic Effect in Ionized Gas.** N. G. Preobrazhensky et al. 216p. 1999. text 95.00 (*90-6994-001-9*, Lebedev Physical) Gordon & Breach.

Optogalvanic Spectroscopy, 1990. Ed. by R. S. Stewart & J. E. Lawler. (Institute of Physics Conference Ser.: Vol. 113). (Illus.). 352p. 1991. 158.00 (*0-85498-047-4*) IOP Pub.

Optokinetics: A Treatise on the Motions of Lights. Harry H. Mark. LC 81-71626. (Illus.). 150p. 1982. 9.95 (*0-9608152-0-1*) H Mark-Corbett.

Optomechanical Design: Proceedings of a Conference Held 22-23 July 1992, San Diego, California. Ed. by Paul R. Yoder, Jr. LC 92-16833. (Critical Reviews of Optical Science & Technology Ser.: Vol. CR43). 1992. 85.00 (*0-8194-0952-9*); pap. 70.00 (*0-8194-0953-7*) SPIE.

Optomechanical Design & Precision Instruments. Ed. by Alson E. Hatheway. LC 98-122611. 21p. 1997. pap. 59.00 (*0-8194-2554-0*) SPIE.

Optomechanical Engineer Handbook. Ahmad. 416p. 1998. 129.00 incl. cd-rom (*0-8493-9753-7*) CRC Pr.

*__Optomechanical Engineering & Vibration Control.__ Ed. by Eddy A. Derby et al. 1999. pap. text 111.00 (*0-8194-3272-5*) SPIE.

Optometric Case Analysis. rev. ed. Leonard C. Emery. Ed. by Sally M. Corngold. (Introduction to Behavioral Optometry Ser.). 117p. (C). 1993. lib. bdg. 18.00 (*0-943599-66-0*) OEPF.

Optometric Guide to Surgical Co-Management. Debra Bezan et al. LC 92-23818. (Illus.). 118p. 1992. spiral bd. 37.50 (*0-7506-9329-0*) Buttrwrth-Heinemann.

Optometric Management of Learning Related Vision D. Mitchell M. Scheiman & Michael Rouse. (Illus.). 606p. (C). (gr. 13). 1994. text 71.95 (*0-8016-6385-7*, 06385) Mosby Inc.

Optometric Management of Learning Related Vision Problems. Mitchell M. Scheiman & Michael W. Rouse. LC 94-3010. 1994. write for info. (*0-08-151638-X*) Mosby Inc.

Optometric Management of Nearpoint Vision Disorders. Martin H. Birnbaum. 416p. 1992. text 92.50 (*0-7506-9193-X*) Buttrwrth-Heinemann.

Optometric Management of Reading Disfunction. Ed. by John R. Griffin et al. LC 96-43032. 254p. 1996. pap. text 45.00 (*0-7506-9516-1*) Buttrwrth-Heinemann.

*__Optometric Products in Singapore: A Strategic Entry Report, 1995.__ Compiled by Icon Group International Staff. (Illus.). 115p. 1999. ring bd. 1150.00 incl. audio compact disk (*0-7418-1614-8*) Icon Grp.

Optometric Vision Therapy. rev. ed. J. Baxter Swartwout. Ed. by Sally M. Corngold. (Introduction to Behavioral Optometry Ser.). (Illus.). 172p. 1988. reprint ed. pap. text 18.00 (*0-943599-03-2*) OEPF.

Optometric Vision Therapy Manual: Procedures & Forms. J. Baxter Swartwout. Ed. by Conkey et al. (Illus.). 419p. (C). 1991. spiral bd. 55.00 (*0-943599-20-2*) OEPF.

Optometrist. Jack Rudman. (Career Examination Ser.: C-557). 1994. pap. 29.95 (*0-8373-0557-8*) Nat Learn.

Optometrist's & Ophthalmologist's Guide to Pilot's Vision. Warren V. DeHaan. LC 81-69431. 200p. 1982. 33.00 (*0-941388-00-X*) Am Trend Pub.

Optometry. Frank M. Kitchell. (Opportunities In . . . Ser.). (Illus.). 160p. pap. 12.95 (*0-8442-6497-0*, 297OIO, VGM Career) NTC Contemp Pub Co.

Optometry. Frank M. Kitchell. (Opportunities in...Ser.). (Illus.). 160p. 1988. 13.95 (*0-8442-6496-2*, VGM Career) NTC Contemp Pub Co.

Optometry Admission Test. Jack Rudman. (Admission Test Ser.: ATS-27). 1997. reprint ed. pap. 23.95 (*0-8373-5027-1*) Nat Learn.

Optometry Admission Test (OAT) Jack Rudman. (Admission Test Ser.: Vol. 27). 43.95 (*0-8373-5127-8*) Nat Learn.

Optometry Admission Test Student Guide. David M. Tarlow. (Illus.). 1993. pap. 16.95 (*0-931572-04-5*) Datar Pub.

Optometry Admissions Test: Core Content. David M. Tarlow. (Medical Examinations Ser.). 592p. (Orig.). (C). 1996. pap. 49.95 (*1-57774-002-5*) Educ Tsting Cnslts.

Optometry & Health Sciences: Index of New Information with Authors & Subjects. Marshal D. Shantzman. 161p. 1997. 47.50 (*0-7883-1632-X*); pap. 44.50 (*0-7883-1633-8*) ABBE Pubs Assn.

Optometry & the Health Sciences: Index of New Information for Research & Clinical Practice. Fred O. Crowder. 150p. 1997. 47.50 (*0-7883-1378-9*); pap. 44.50 (*0-7883-1379-7*) ABBE Pubs Assn.

Optometry Clinics. John G. Classe. (C). 1991. 65.00 (*0-8385-7407-6*) Appleton & Lange.

Optometry Examination Review (MEPC) 4th ed. Linda Casser. (Illus.). 416p. (C). 1999. pap. text 36.95 (*0-8385-7449-1*, A7449-0, Apple Lange Med) McGraw.

Optometry in America: A History of the Illinois College of Optometry (1872-1997) Anistatia R. Miller & Jared M. Brown. LC 96-77258. (Illus.). 160p. 1996. 45.00 (*0-9652759-1-4*) IL Coll Optometry.

OptoSource '94. Market Intelligence Staff. 396p. 1994. 595.00 (*1-56753-959-9*) Frost & Sullivan.

Optronic Techniques in Diagnostic & Therapeutic Medicine. Ed. by R. Pratesi. (Illus.). 328p. (C). 1991. text 114.00 (*0-306-43938-7*, Kluwer Plenum) Kluwer Academic.

Optyical Toys. Basil Harley. 1989. pap. 30.00 (*0-85263-923-6*, Pub. by Shire Pubns) St Mut.

Opuestos. large type ed. Brian Wildsmith. Tr. by Maria Fiol. LC 96-72564.Tr. of Opposites. (SPA., Illus.). 16p. (J). (ps). 1998. bds. 4.95 (*1-887734-18-X*) Star Brght Bks.

Opulent Interiors of the Gilded Age: All 203 Photographs from Artistic Houses, with New Text. Arnold Lewis et al. (Illus.). 192p. 1987. pap. 15.95 (*0-486-25250-7*) Dover.

Opus. Barry Windsor-Smith. (Illus.). 1999. 39.95 (*1-56097-367-6*) Fantagraph Bks.

*__Opus.__ Barry Windsor-Smith. (Opus Ser.: Vol. 2). 2000. 49.95 (*1-56097-393-5*, Pub. by Fantagraph Bks) Seven Hills Bk.

*__Opus: Poems from Hollywood.__ Mark Dunster. 11p. 1999. pap. 5.00 (*0-89642-821-4*) Linden Pubs.

Opus: The Making of Musical Instruments in Canada. Carmelle Begin & Constance Nebel. (Illus.). 148p. 1992. 29.95 (*0-660-14006-3*, Pub. by CN Mus Civilization) U of Wash Pr.

Opus Americanus. Gloria Chavez-Vasquez. (ENG & SPA., Illus.). 192p. 1993. pap. 12.95 (*0-9650774-0-3*) White Owl Edits.

Opus Astronomicum, 3 vols. in 1. Mohammed I. Battani. cxvii, 162p. 1977. reprint ed. 400.00 (*3-487-06262-3*) G Olms Pubs.

Opus Dei: Leadership & Vision in Today's Catholic Church. Vittorio Messori. Tr. by Gerald Malsbary from ITA. LC 97-28110. 186p. 1997. 27.50 (*0-89526-450-1*) Regnery Pub.

Opus Dei: Who? How? Why? Giuseppe Romano. Tr. by Edmund C. Lane from ITA. LC 95-23355. 214p. (Orig.). 1995. pap. 9.95 (*0-8189-0739-8*) Alba.

Opus Dei in the Church. Fernando Ocariz. (SPA.). 253p. 1994. pap. 19.95 (*0-933932-79-0*) Scepter Pubs.

Opus Deorum: Photography by Jim French. Jim French. (Illus.). 100p. 1993. 45.00 (*1-880777-05-3*, AMN4) State Man.

Opus Epistolarum Des. Erasmi Roterodami: Complete letters of Erasmus, 12 vols., Set. Desiderius Erasmus. Ed. by P. S. Allen et al. (Illus.). 6684p. 1992. 1100.00 (*0-19-820353-5*) OUP.

Opus Epistolarum Des. Erasmi Roterodami Vol. XII: Indices. Desiderius Erasmus. Ed. by Barbara Flower & Elisabeth Rosenbaum. 200p. 1992. 59.00 (*0-19-818305-4*) OUP.

Opus Epistolarum Des. Erasmi Roterodami, 1484-1514, Vol. I. Desiderius Erasmus. Ed. by P. S. Allen. (Illus.). 654p. 1992. 120.00 (*0-19-820341-1*) OUP.

Opus Epistolarum Des. Erasmi Roterodami, 1514-1517, Vol. II. Desiderius Erasmus. Ed. by P. S. Allen. (Illus.). 636p. 1992. 120.00 (*0-19-820342-X*) OUP.

Opus Epistolarum Des. Erasmi Roterodami, 1517-1519, Vol. III. Desiderius Erasmus. Ed. by P. S. Allen. (Illus.). 688p. 1992. 120.00 (*0-19-820343-8*) OUP.

Opus Epistolarum Des. Erasmi Roterodami, 1519-1521, Vol. IV. Desiderius Erasmus. Ed. by P. S. Allen. (Illus.). 680p. 1992. 120.00 (*0-19-820344-6*) OUP.

Opus Epistolarum Des. Erasmi Roterodami, 1522-1524, Vol. V. Desiderius Erasmus. Ed. by P. S. Allen & H. M. Allen. (Illus.). 664p. 1992. 120.00 (*0-19-820345-4*) OUP.

Opus Epistolarum Des. Erasmi Roterodami, 1525-1527, Vol. V. Desiderius Erasmus. Ed. by P. S. Allen & H. M. Allen. (Illus.). 552p. 1992. 110.00 (*0-19-820346-2*) OUP.

Opus Epistolarum Des. Erasmi Roterodami, 1527-1528, Vol. VII. Desiderius Erasmus. Ed. by P. S. Allen & H. M. Allen. (Illus.). 590p. 1992. 110.00 (*0-19-820347-0*) OUP.

Opus Epistolarum Des. Erasmi Roterodami, 1529-1530, Vol. VIII. Desiderius Erasmus. Ed. by P. S. Allen & H. M. Allen. (Illus.). 584p. 1992. 110.00 (*0-19-820348-9*) OUP.

Opus Epistolarum Des. Erasmi Roterodami, 1530-1532, Vol. IX. Desiderius Erasmus. Ed. by P. S. Allen et al. (Illus.). 528p. 1992. 110.00 (*0-19-820349-7*) OUP.

Opus Epistolarum Des. Erasmi Roterodami, 1532-1534, Vol. X. Desiderius Erasmus. Ed. by P. S. Allen et al. (Illus.). 468p. 1992. 89.00 (*0-19-820350-0*) OUP.

Opus Epistolarum Des. Erasmi Roterodami, 1534-1536, Vol. XI. Desiderius Erasmus. Ed. by P. S. Allen et al. (Illus.). 400p. 1992. 89.00 (*0-19-820351-9*) OUP.

OPUS Fifty. Nelson White & Anne White. LC 85-51521. 70p. (Orig.). 1985. pap. 30.00 (*0-939856-52-2*) Tech Group.

Opus Historicum: Praefatio see Hilary of Poitier's Preface to His Opus Historicum: Translation & Commentary

*__Opus Majus of Roger Bacon, 2 vols.__ Tr. by Robert B. Burke. (Medieval & Renaissance Philosophy Ser.). 854p. 2000. 280.00 (*1-85506-856-7*) Thoemmes Pr.

Opus Majus of Roger Bacon. Robert B. Burke. (Illus.). 876p. 1998. reprint ed. pap. 75.00 (*0-7661-0421-4*) Kessinger Pub.

Opus Maledictorum: Insults, Curses, Slurs, & Other Bad Words from Around the World. Ed. by Reinhold Aman. 350p. (Orig.). 1996. pap. 14.95 (*1-56924-836-2*) Marlowe & Co.

Opus Mixtum: Essays in Ancient Art & Society. Ed. by Tullia Linders et al. (Acta Instituti Romani Regni Sueciae, Series in 4 Degrees). (Illus.). 176p. 1994. pap. 49.50 (*91-7042-150-1*, Pub. by P Astroms) Coronet Bks.

Opus No. 1 No. 1: A Chapbook. M. B. Weltz. LC 98-173122. 22p. 1997. pap. 8.95 (*0-533-12421-2*) Vantage.

Opus O. Theodore Enslin. 68p. (Orig.). 1981. pap. 5.00 (*0-87924-039-3*) Membrane Pr.

Opus One Piano Tutor. Nina Dalby. 84p. Date not set. 9.95 (*0-946005-11-7*, OS 10125, Pub. by Ossian) Music Sales.

Opus Pistorum see Under the Roofs of Paris

Opus Posthumous. Wallace Stevens. 1990. pap. 17.00 (*0-679-72534-2*) Vin Bks.

Opuscula, 5 vols. Johann U. Von Cramer. (GER.). 4084p. 1996. write for info. (*3-487-10145-9*) G Olms Pubs.

Opuscula. Gian V. Gravina. 205p. reprint ed. write for info. (*0-318-71598-8*) G Olms Pubs.

Opuscula, 3 vols., Set. Moritz Haupt. Ed. by Ulrich Von Wilamowitz-Moellendorff. 1601p. 1967. reprint ed. write for info. (*0-318-70757-8*) G Olms Pubs.

Opuscula, 8 vols., Set. J. Gottfried Hermann. lvi, 3318p. 1970. reprint ed. write for info. (*0-318-70934-1*) G Olms Pubs.

Opuscula see Opera Omnia

Opuscula: A Supplement to the Opera Omnia. Desiderius Erasmus. Ed. by Wallace K. Ferguson. xiii, 373p. 1978. reprint ed. 76.70 (*3-487-06576-2*) G Olms Pubs.

Opuscula Academica. Johan N. Madvig. xi, 779p. 1977. reprint ed. write for info. (*3-487-06456-1*) G Olms Pubs.

Opuscula Academica, 2 vols., Set. Johannes Vahlen. xv, 1157p. 1967. reprint ed. write for info. (*0-318-70839-6*) G Olms Pubs.

Opuscula Acadmica Collecta et Animadversionibus Locupletata, 6 vols. Christian G. Heyne. (GER.). xcvi, 2841p. 1997. reprint ed. 1195.00 (*3-487-10421-0*) G Olms Pubs.

Opuscula Altaica: Essays Presented in Honor of Henry Schwarz. Ed. by Edward H. Kaplan & Donald W. Whisenhunt. (Studies on East Asia). (Illus.). 700p. (C). 1994. 85.00 (*0-914584-19-7*) WWUCEAS.

Opuscula Atheniensia XVIII. Ed. by Tullia Linders. (Acta Instituti Atheniensis Regni Sueciae Ser.: Series 4, XXXIX). (Illus.). 249p. (Orig.). 1990. pap. 97.50 (*91-7916-020-4*, Pub. by P Astroms) Coronet Bks.

Opuscula Atheniensia XI. Ed. by Par G. Gierow et al. (Acta Instituti Atheniensis Regni Sueciae Ser.: Vol. XXII). (Illus.). 201p. 1975. pap. 69.50 (*91-85086-09-6*, Pub. by P Astroms) Coronet Bks.

Opuscula Atheniensia XV. Lennart Palmqvist. (Acta Instituti Atheniensis Regni Sueciae Ser.: Vol. XXXI). (Illus.). 200p. 1984. pap. 87.50 (*91-85086-59-2*, Pub. by P Astroms) Coronet Bks.

Opuscula Atheniensia XIV. Ed. by Berit Wells. (Acta Instituti Atheniensis Regni Sueciae Ser.: Vol. XXIX). (Illus.). 132p. 1982. pap. 79.50 (*91-85086-44-4*, Pub. by P Astroms) Coronet Bks.

Opuscula Atheniensia XIX. Ed. by Paul Astrom. (Acta Instituti Atheniensis Regni Sueciae Ser.: Series 4, XLI). (Illus.). 203p. (Orig.). 1992. pap. 78.00 (*91-7916-023-9*, Pub. by P Astroms) Coronet Bks.

Opuscula Atheniensia XVII. Brita Alroth. (Acta Instituti Atheniensis Regni Sueciae Ser.: Vol. XXXVII). (Illus.). 238p. 1988. pap. 97.50 (*91-7916-000-X*, Pub. by P Astroms) Coronet Bks.

Opuscula Atheniensia XVI. Ed. by Brita Alroth & Acta Instituti Atheniensis Staff. (Acta Instituti Atheniensis Regni Sueciae Ser.: Vol. XXXIV). (Illus.). 130p. (Orig.). 1986. pap. 57.50 (*91-85086-80-0*, Pub. by P Astroms) Coronet Bks.

Opuscula Atheniensia X. Ed. by Sture Brunnsaker. (Acta Instituti Atheniensis Regni Sueciae Ser.: Vol. XVIII). (Illus.). 90p. 1971. pap. 33.50 (*91-85086-01-0*, Pub. by P Astroms) Coronet Bks.

Opuscula Atheniensia XIII. Berit Wells. (Acta Instituti Atheniensis Regni Sueciae Ser.: Vol. XXVII). (Illus.). 259p. 1980. pap. 85.00 (*91-85086-25-8*, Pub. by P Astroms) Coronet Bks.

Opuscula Atheniensia XII. Ed. by Robin Hagg & Berit Wells. (Acta Instituti Atheniensis Regni Sueciae Ser.: Vol. XXV). (Illus.). 147p. 1978. pap. 55.00 (*91-85086-12-6*, Pub. by P Astroms) Coronet Bks.

Opuscula Atheniensia XX. Ed. by Paul Astrom. (Acta Instituti Atheniensis Regni Sueciae Series in 4: Vol. XLIII). (Illus.). 295p. (Orig.). 1994. pap. 97.50 (*91-7916-030-1*, Pub. by P Astroms) Coronet Bks.

Opuscula Omnia. Thomas De Vio Cajetanus. (GER.). 307p. 1995. reprint ed. 210.00 (*3-487-10034-7*) G Olms Pubs.

Opuscula Philologica, 5 vols., Set. Friedrich Ritschl. lxxxiv, 4122p. 1978. reprint ed. write for info. (*3-487-06642-4*) G Olms Pubs.

Opuscula Rhetorica. Theodorus II Ducas. Ed. by L. Tartaglia. (Illus.). 320p. (C). text 100.00 (*3-519-01863-2*) B G Teubner.

Opuscula Romana, Vol. VIII. Ed. by Institutum Romanum Regni Sueciae Staff. (Acta Instituti Romani Regni Sueciae, Series in 4 Degrees: Vol. XXXI). (Illus.). 115p. 1974. pap. 35.00 (*91-7042-003-3*, Pub. by P Astroms) Coronet Bks.

Opuscula Romana, Vol. IX. Ed. by Per G. Gierow. (Acta Instituti Romani Regni Sueciae, Series in 4 Degrees: Vol. XXXIII). (Illus.). 224p. 1973. pap. 49.50 (*91-7042-013-0*, Pub. by P Astroms) Coronet Bks.

Opuscula Romana XVIII. Ed. by Tullia Linders et al. (Acta Instituti Romani Regni Sueciae Ser.: Series 4, XLVII). (Illus.). 239p. (Orig.). 1990. pap. 97.50 (*91-7042-136-6*, Pub. by P Astroms) Coronet Bks.

Opuscula Romana XI. Ed. by Robin Hagg & Berit Wells. (Acta Instituti Romani Regni Sueciae, Series in 4 Degrees: Vol. XXXV). (Illus.). 140p. 1976. pap. 62.50 (*91-7042-051-3*, Pub. by P Astroms) Coronet Bks.

Opuscula Romana XV. Ed. by Brita Alroth. (Acta Instituti Romani Regni Sueciae, Series in 4 Degrees: Vol. XLII). (Illus.). 120p. 1985. pap. 87.50 (*91-7042-099-8*, Pub. by P Astroms) Coronet Bks.

Opuscula Romana XIV. Ed. by Lennart Palmqvist. (Acta Instituti Romani Regni Sueciae, Series in 4 Degrees: Vol. XXXIX). (Illus.). 102p. 1983. pap. 67.50 (*91-7042-085-8*, Pub. by P Astroms) Coronet Bks.

Opuscula Romana XIX. Ed. by Tullia Linders et al. (Acta Instituti Romani Regni Sueciae Ser.: Series 4, LI). (Illus.). 119p. (Orig.). 1993. pap. 57.50 (*91-7042-146-3*, Pub. by P Astroms) Coronet Bks.

Opuscula Romana XVII. Ed. by Brita Alroth. (Acta Instituti Romani Regni Sueciae, Series in 4 Degrees: Vol. XLVI). (Illus.). 247p. 1989. pap. 97.50 (*91-7042-135-8*, Pub. by P Astroms) Coronet Bks.

Opuscula Romana XVI. Ed. by Brita Alroth. (Acta Instituti Romani Regni Sueciae, Series in 4 Degrees: Vol. XLIV). (Illus.). 166p. 1987. pap. 92.50 (*91-7042-120-X*, Pub. by P Astroms) Coronet Bks.

Opuscula Romana XIII. Ed. by Berit Wells. (Acta Instituti Romani Regni Sueciae, Series in 4 Degrees: Vol. XXXVII). (Illus.). 104p. 1981. pap. 67.50 (*91-7042-070-X*, Pub. by P Astroms) Coronet Bks.

Opuscula Romana XII. Ed. by Paul Astrom. (Acta Instituti Romani Regni Sueciae Ser.: Series 4, XXXVI). (Illus.). 65p. (Orig.). 1978. pap. 22.50 (*91-7042-064-5*, Pub. by P Astroms) Coronet Bks.

Opuscula Romana XX. Ed. by Robin Hagg et al. (Acta Instituti Romani Regni Sueciae Ser.: Series 4, LII). (Illus.). 290p. (Orig.). 1996. pap. 87.00 (*91-7042-152-8*, Pub. by P Astroms) Coronet Bks.

Opuscula Selecta. Porphyrius. xxiii, 320p. 1977. reprint ed. write for info. (*3-487-00421-6*) G Olms Pubs.

Opuscules et Fragments Inedits. Gottfried Wilhelm Leibniz. xiv, 682p. 1988. reprint ed. write for info. (*3-487-01197-2*); reprint ed. pap. write for info. (*3-487-00099-7*) G Olms Pubs.

Opuscules Spirituels. Jeanne M. Guion, pseud. 560p. 1978. reprint ed. write for info. (*3-487-06537-1*) G Olms Pubs.

Opusculum de Musica Ex Traditione Iohannis Hollandrini. Ed. by Alexander Rausch. (Theorists in Translation Ser.: Vol. 15). (ENG, GER & LAT.). 182p. 1997. 48.00 (*1-896926-00-2*) Inst Mediaeval Mus.

*__Opusculum Fabularum: Die Fabelsammlung Der Berliner Handschrift Theol. Lat. Fol. 142.__ Christina Meckelnborg & Bernd Schneider. 208p. 1999. 68.00 (*90-04-11333-9*) Brill Academic Pubs.

Oqua. Thomas Blair. LC 79-15861. 1990. pap. 13.95 (*0-87949-163-9*) Ashley Bks.

Oquirrh Fault Zone, Tooele County, Utah: Surficial Geology & Paleoseismicity. B. J. Solomon et al. Ed. by William R. Lund. (Special Study of the Utah Geological Survey Ser.: Vol. 88, Pt. 6). (Illus.). 64p. (Orig.). 1996. pap. 14.50 (*1-55791-370-6*, SS-88) Utah Geological Survey.

Or. Blaise Cendrars. (FRE.). 1973. pap. 10.95 (*0-7859-1733-0*, 2070363317) Fr & Eur.

*__Or.__ Madison Morrison. 100p. 1999. pap. 9.00 (*81-86847-02-2*) Tiger Moon Pubns.

*__Or.__ Arthur Schechter. 2000. pap. 8.95 (*0-7407-1022-2*) Andrews & McMeel.

Or & Argent. Bruno B. Heim. LC 95-135838. (Illus.). 133p. 1994. 70.00 (*0-905715-24-1*, Pub. by Smyth) Dufour.

OR at Work: Case Studies on the Application of OR in Industry, Service, Agriculture & Healthcare. Ed. by Leonard Fortuin et al. LC 96-209122. 374p. 1996. 79.95 (*0-7484-0455-4*, Pub. by Tay Francis Ltd); pap. 39.95 (*0-7484-0456-2*, Pub. by Tay Francis Ltd) Taylor & Francis.

Or dans la Nuit: Chroniques et Prefaces Litteraires, 1910-1943. Jean Giraudoux. 11.50 (*0-685-33922-X*) Fr & Eur.

Or de la Republique. Jean Duvignaud. (FRE.). 1984. pap. 17.95 (*0-7859-1995-3*, 2070375641) Fr & Eur.

"Or Does It Explode?" Black Harlem in the Great Depression. Cheryl Greenberg. LC 96-51559. (Illus.). 336p. 1997. reprint ed. pap. 19.95 (*0-19-511584-8*) OUP.

Or Else, the Lightning God & Other Stories. Catherine Lim. (Writing in Asia Ser.). 194p. (Orig.). (C). 1980. pap. 5.00 (*0-435-00251-1*, 00251) Heinemann.

*__OR Evidence Code Handbook, 99 Edition.__ Laird Kirkpatrick. 271p. 1999. pap. 56.50 (*0-327-10131-8*, 8227613) LEXIS Pub.

Or Go down in Flame: A Navigator's Death over Schweinfurt. W. Raymond Wood. (Illus.). 248p. 1993. 24.95 (*0-9627613-9-7*) Sarpedon.

Or Hadash: Let a New Light Shine. Betsy Doglin Katz. LC 96-141768. 1987. pap. 18.00 (*0-8074-0560-4*, 571204) UAHC.

Or Hatorah: Vayikro, Vol. 3. Menachem M. Schneerson. (HEB.). 328p. 1993. 30.00 (*0-8266-5373-1*) Kehot Pubn Soc.

Or Hatorah Bamidbar Volz, Vol. 2. Menachem M. Tzedek. Ed. by Aaron Chitrick & Gavriel Shapiro.Tr. of Light of the Torah. (HEB.). 712p. 1997. 30.00 (*0-8266-5375-8*) Kehot Pubn Soc.

Or Hatoran Megilas Esther (The Light of Torah on Megilas Esther) Menachem M. Schneersohn. (HEB.). 348p. 1990. 15.00 (*0-8266-5370-7*) Kehot Pubn Soc.

Or Learn to Walk on Water: Poems by Daisy Aldan. Daisy Aldan. (Illus.). 1971. 4.50 (*0-913152-15-3*) Folder Edns.

Or Nerev: Hebrew Text. Moses Cordavero. 100p. 1980. 10.00 (*0-943688-17-5*) Res Ctr Kabbalah.

. . . Or Not to Be: A Collection of Suicide Notes. Marc Etkind. LC 96-28863. 112p. 1997. pap. 10.00 (*1-57322-580-0*, Riverhd Trade) Berkley Pub.

OR on the Micro. David L. Whitaker. LC 82-17463. (Illus.). 205p. reprint ed. pap. 63.60 (*0-608-16014-8*, 203309200083) Bks Demand.

Ora Con los Ojos Abiertos. Richard L. Pratt, Jr. (SPA.). 200p. pap. 10.95 (*1-55883-111-8*, 6784-1602) Libros Desafio.

Ora Maritima. 2nd ed. Lucius F. Avienus. Ed. by Murphy & Miller. (Ancient Greek & Roman Writers Ser.). xii, 180p. 1977. pap. 15.00 (*0-89005-175-5*) Ares.

Oracao see Prayer - Bringing Heaven to Earth

Oracle 8 Certified Professional DBA Certification Exam Guide. Jason S. Couchman. (Illus.). 1187p. 1999. 99.99 incl. cd-rom (*0-07-212087-8*) Osborne-McGraw.

Oracion. John Bunyan. (SPA.). 148p. 1990. pap. 4.99 (*0-85151-408-1*) Banner of Truth.

Oracion: Su Fundamento Para el Exito. Kenneth Copeland. Ed. by Copeland, Kenneth, Publications Staff. (SPA.). 106p. (Orig.). 1984. pap. 5.95 (*0-88114-311-1*) K Copeland Pubns.

Oracion - Clave del Avivamiento. Paul Y. Cho & R. Whitney Manzano. Tr. by Juan S. Araujo from ENG.Tr. of Prayer - Key to Revival. (SPA.). 128p. 1987. pap. 8.99 (*0-88113-241-1*) Caribe Betania.

Oracion Acerca de la Dignidad del Hombre. Giovanni Pico Dela Mirandola. 33p. 1992. pap. 1.50 (*0-8477-0712-1*) U of PR Pr.

Oracion Acerca de la Dignidad del Hombre. Giovanni Pico Della Mirandola. (SPA.). 38p. 1986. pap. 1.50 (*0-8477-0730-X*) U of PR Pr.

Oracion Cristiana - Privilegio y Responsabilidad: The Christian Prayer - Privilege & Responsibility. James D. Crane. (SPA.). 96p. (Orig.). 1991. pap. 7.50 (*0-311-40048-5*) Casa Bautista.

*__Oracion de los Fieles, 2000: Para los Domingos, Solemnidades, Fiestas y Otros Eventos.__ Ed. by James Wilde. 112p. 1999. pap. 5.95 (*1-57992-073-X*) OR Catholic.

Oracion de Poder. Lowell Lundstrom.Tr. of How You Can Pray with Power. (SPA.). 160p. 1983. pap. 5.99 (*0-8297-1361-1*) Vida Pubs.

Oracion de Una Oracion. Clemente Bobonis. (SPA.). 97p. 1996. pap. write for info. (*0-929441-01-X*) Pubns Puertorriquenas.

Oracion Intercesora. Donald Sheets.Tr. of Intercessory Prayer. 10.99 (*0-7899-0395-4*, 496624) Editorial Unilit.

Oracion Intercesora, Set. Kenneth Copeland. Tr. by Kenneth Copeland Publications Staff from ENG. (SPA.). 1984. pap., student ed. 20.00 incl. audio (*0-88114-318-9*) K Copeland Pubns.

Oracion Invade lo Imposible. Jack W. Hayford. Ed. by Angel Carrodeguas. Tr. by Eliezer Oyola. Orig. Title: Prayer Is Invading the Impossible. (SPA.). 160p. 1985. pap. 4.99 (*0-8297-1457-X*) Vida Pubs.

Oracion la una Perspectiva Biblica: La una Perspectiva Biblica. Charles R. Swindoll. (Serie Realidades - Realities Ser.).Tr. of Prayer: A Biblical Perspective. (SPA.). 32p. 1990. pap. 1.79 (*1-56063-029-9*, 498113) Editorial Unilit.

Oracion Poderosa Que Prevalece. Wesley L. Duewel.Tr. of Mighty Prevailing Prayer. (SPA.). 400p. 1995. 10.99 (*1-56063-635-1*, 497729) Editorial Unilit.

Oracion Que da Resultados. Victor Ricardo. (Serie Realidades - Realities Ser.).Tr. of Prayer That Produces Results. (SPA.). 36p. 1989. pap. 1.99 (*0-945792-67-0*, 498105) Editorial Unilit.

Oracion Que Prevalece. Kenneth E. Hagin.Tr. of Prevailing Prayer to Peace. (SPA.). 1986. pap. 5.95 (*0-89276-186-5*) Faith Lib Pubns.

Oracion y los Cultos de Oracion. 2nd ed. Carlos H. Mackintosh. Ed. by Roger P. Daniel. Tr. by Sara Bautista from ENG. (Serie Diamante).Tr. of Prayer & the Prayer Meeting. (SPA., Illus.). 40p. 1982. pap. 0.85 (*0-942504-08-9*) Overcomer Pr.

Oracional Bilingue: A Prayer Book for Spanish-English Communities. Ed. by Jorge Perales. (ENG & SPA.). 96p. 1994. pap. 7.95 (*0-8146-2094-9*) Liturgical Pr.

Oracional Bilingue Para Ninos: A Children's Prayerbook in Spanish-English. Jorge Peralas. (ENG & SPA.). 1998. pap. text 4.95 (*0-8146-2459-6*) Liturgical Pr.

Oraciones - Prayers. 2nd ed. Ed. by James Socias. (ENG & SPA.). 64p. Date not set. pap. 2.95 (*1-890177-00-8*) Midwest Theol.

Oraciones a la Hora de Dormir. E. Reeves.Tr. of Prayer at Bedtime. (SPA.). (J). 1.89 (*0-7899-0478-0*, 498665) Editorial Unilit.

Oraciones con Poder. World Ministries Staff.Tr. of Prayers That Avail Much. (SPA.). 128p. 1997. pap. 7.99 (*0-89274-480-4*, HH-480) Harrison Hse.

***Oraciones con Poder, Vol. 1.** G. A. Copeland.Tr. of Prayers That Avail Much. (SPA.). 2000. 8.99 (*0-7899-0539-6*, 550104) Editorial Unilit.

***Oraciones Con Ponder.** Germaine Copeland. Vol. 2. (SPA.). 2000. pap. 8.99 (*0-7899-0691-0*) Spanish Hse Distributors.

Oraciones de la Biblia. Joseph Frank. (SPA.). 1997. pap. text 7.98 (*968-403-918-2*) Selector.

Oraciones de los Fieles, 1999: Para los Domingos, Solemnidades, Fiestas y Otros Eventos de la Parroquia. Ed. by James E. Wilde. (Illus.). 112p. 1995. pap. 5.95 (*1-57992-021-7*) OR Catholic.

Oraciones de los Fieles, 1997: Para los Domingos, Solemnidades, Fiestas y Otros Eventos de la Parroquia. rev. ed. 111p. 1996. pap. 5.95 (*0-915531-52-6*) OR Catholic.

Oraciones de los Fieles, 1998: Para los Domingos, Solemnidades, Fiestas y Otros Eventos de la Parroquia. rev. ed. (Illus.). 111p. 1997. pap. 5.95 (*0-915531-93-3*) OR Catholic.

Oraciones del Corazon (Prayers of the Heart) M.A.C.C. Team Staff. (SPA.). 34p. 1992. write for info. (*0-614-04892-3*) Mex Am Cult.

Oraciones para Corazoncitos. E. Kucharik.Tr. of Prayers for Little Hearts. (SPA.). (J). 6.99 (*0-7899-0437-3*, 497769) Editorial Unilit.

***Oraciones Para los Pequenitos with Other.** MacLean Staff. (SPA.). (J). (ps-k). 2000. 10.99 (*0-7899-0744-5*) Spanish Hse Distributors.

Oraciones Para Sanar. Intro. by John Columbus Taylor.Tr. of Moments of Silence. (SPA., Illus.). 207p. (Orig.). 1997. pap. text 10.98 (*968-403-764-3*) Selector.

Oraciones para Todas las Ocasiones. Francis Evans. (SPA.). 1993. pap. 7.50 (*0-89942-916-5*, 916/S) Catholic Bk Pub.

Oraciones Pora Ti (Prayers for You) Elpa Soler. Ed. by Palma Real. (SPA., Illus.). 95p. 1998. pap. 6.50 (*0-9664941-0-5*) Edic Palma Real.

***Oraciones Que las Mujeres Oran.** Quin Sherrer & Ruthanne Garlock. (SPA.). 1999. pap. 7.99 (*0-7899-0603-1*) Spanish Hse Distributors.

Oracle. (C). 1989. text. write for info. (*0-201-51097-9*) Addison-Wesley.

Oracle. (C). 1990. text. write for info. (*0-201-52297-7*) Addison-Wesley.

Oracle. Altenhofen. (C). 1990. text. write for info. (*0-201-52276-4*) Addison-Wesley.

***Oracle.** Katherine Greyle. 400p. 1998. mass mkt. 6.99 (*1-57343-022-6*) LionHearted.

Oracle. Mike Resnick. 256p. (Orig.). 1992. mass mkt. 4.99 (*0-441-58694-5*) Ace Bks.

Oracle. Watson. 1998. pap. text 11.95 (*0-575-60226-0*) Gollehon Pr.

Oracle. Ian Watson. 256p. 1998. 27.00 (*0-575-06487-0*, Pub. by V Gollancz) Trafalgar.

Oracle. Wojkowski. (C). 1994. text. write for info. (*0-318-70367-X*) S-W Pub.

Oracle: A Beginner's Guide. Michael Abbey & Michael J. Corey. (Oracle Press Ser.). 522p. 1995. pap. 29.95 (*0-07-882122-3*) McGraw.

***Oracle: A Beginner's Guide.** Michael Abbey et al. 765p. 1999. pap. 44.99 (*0-07-212204-8*) Osborne Bks.

Oracle: A Database Developer's Guide. 2nd ed. Ulka Rodgers. 400p. (C). 1998. pap. text 49.99 (*0-13-841420-3*) P-H.

Oracle: A Text for African American Youth Ministry. Oralisa Martin. 268p. (Orig.). 1994. pap. text 39.95 (*0-9642067-0-6*) Maranatha Pr.

Oracle: Building High Performance Online Systems. William H. Inmon. 272p. 1993. 64.99 (*0-471-56740-X*) Wiley.

***Oracle: DBA.** Frank Lynch. (Oracle Manuals Ser.). 180p. 1999. 150.00 (*1-930245-09-2*) Pinnacle Soft Solut.

***Oracle: Discoverer - 2000.** rev. ed. Pinnacle Software Solutions, Inc. Staff. (Oracle Manuals Ser.). 180p. 1999. 100.00 (*1-930245-08-4*) Pinnacle Soft Solut.

Oracle: Forms Developer's Companion. Steve Muench et al. 596p. (Orig.). (C). 1994. pap. text 44.50 (*0-9637526-5-0*) Maverick CA.

***Oracle: Forms 4.5.** rev. ed. Pinnacle Software Solutions, Inc. Staff. (Oracle Manuals Ser.). 320p. 1998. 100.00 (*1-930245-04-1*) Pinnacle Soft Solut.

***Oracle: Forms 5.0.** rev. ed. Pinnacle Software Solutions, Inc. Staff. (Oracle Manuals Ser.). 320p. 1999. 100.00 (*1-930245-05-X*) Pinnacle Soft Solut.

***Oracle: PL/SQL.** rev. ed. Pinnacle Software Solutions, Inc. Staff. (Oracle Manuals Ser.). 180p. 1998. 100.00 (*1-930245-03-3*) Pinnacle Soft Solut.

***Oracle: Reports 2.5.** rev. ed. Pinnacle Software Solutions, Inc. Staff. (Oracle Manuals Ser.). 180p. 1998. 100.00 (*1-930245-06-8*) Pinnacle Soft Solut.

***Oracle: Reports 3.0.** rev. ed. Pinnacle Software Solutions, Inc. Staff. (Oracle Manuals Ser.). 180p. 1999. 100.00 (*1-930245-07-6*) Pinnacle Soft Solut.

***Oracle: Reports 6.0.** Pinnacle Software Solutions Staff. (Oracle Manuals Ser.). (Illus.). 450p. 2000. 100.00 (*1-930245-16-5*) Pinnacle Soft Solut.

Oracle: Special Edition. 2nd ed. (C). 1989. text. write for info. (*0-201-56204-9*) Addison-Wesley.

***Oracle: SQL.** Pinnacle Software Solutions, Inc. Staff. (Oracle Manuals Ser.). 280p. 1998. 100.00 (*1-930245-02-5*) Pinnacle Soft Solut.

Oracle: The Complete Reference Electronic Edition. George B. Koch & Kevin Loney. LC 97-131303. 1150p. 1996. pap., pap. text 54.99 incl. cd-rom (*0-07-882285-8*) Osborne-McGraw.

***Oracle Advanced PL/SQL Programming.** Scott Urman. 812p. 2000. pap. 49.99 incl. cd-rom (*0-07-212146-7*) Osborne-McGraw.

Oracle & Networking. Hugo Toledo, Jr. (Oracle Press Ser.). 560p. 1999. pap. 44.99 (*0-07-882408-7*, Oracle Press) Osborne-McGraw.

***Oracle & SQL Server Integration.** Stephen Chelack. (Illus.). 400p. 2001. pap. text 39.99 (*0-7645-4699-6*) IDG Bks.

Oracle & Unix Performance Tuning. Ahmed Alomari. LC 97-13114. 288p. (C). 1997. pap. text 44.95 (*0-13-849167-4*) P-H.

Oracle & Unix Performance Tuning. 2nd ed. Ahmed Alomari. LC 98-22873. 352p. 1998. pap. text 39.99 (*0-13-907676-X*) P-H.

***Oracle & Visual Basic Developer's Handbook.** 4th ed. mark Tomlinson et al. (Developer's Handbks.). (Illus.). 800p. 2000. 49.99 (*0-7821-2476-3*) Sybex.

Oracle Application Server Web Toolkit Reference. Richard J. Niemiec et al. 924p. 1998. pap. text 44.99 (*0-07-882433-8*) Osborne-McGraw.

***Oracle Applications Performance Tuning Handbook.** Andy Tremayne. 2000. pap. 59.99 (*0-07-212549-7*) Osborne-McGraw.

Oracle at the Supermarket: The American Preoccupation with Self-Help. Steven Starker. 224p. 1988. 34.95 (*0-88738-233-9*) Transaction Pubs.

Oracle Backup & Recovery Handbook. Rama Velpuri. (Oracle Press Ser.). 300p. 1995. pap. text 29.95 (*0-07-882106-1*) McGraw.

Oracle Backup & Recovery Handbook: 7.3 Edition. Rama Velpuri. LC 97-139616. 1997. pap. 34.99 (*0-07-882323-4*) Osborne-McGraw.

Oracle Bone Collections in the United States. Hung-hsiang Chou. LC 74-34551. (University of California Publications, Occasional Papers: No. 10). (Illus.). 188p. reprint ed. pap. 58.30 (*0-8357-6864-3*, 203556200095) Bks Demand.

Oracle Bone Diviners of the Vin Dynasty, 1. Tsung-I Jao. LC DS0744.. (CHI.). 704p. reprint ed. pap. 200.00 (*0-8357-6662-4*, 203533100001) Bks Demand.

Oracle Bone Diviners of the Vin Dynasty, 2. Tsung-I Jao. LC DS0744.. (CHI.). 710p. reprint ed. pap. 200.00 (*0-8357-6663-2*, 203533100002) Bks Demand.

Oracle Bones. Houghton Mifflin Company Staff. (Literature Experience 1991 Ser.). (J). (gr. 7). 1990. pap. 11.04 (*0-395-55180-3*) HM.

Oracle Bones from the White & Other Collections. Hsu Chin-Hsiung. (Illus.). 280p. 37.14 (*0-88854-231-3*) Brill Academic Pubs.

Oracle Built-In Packages. Steve Feuerstein. 956p. 1998. pap. 46.95 (*1-56592-375-8*) OReilly & Assocs.

Oracle Case: Method Function & Process Modelling. Richard Barker. 400p. (C). 1992. 64.95 (*0-201-56525-0*) Addison-Wesley.

***Oracle Certified DBA Test Prep Guide.** Sima Yazdani. LC 99-46829. 400p. 2000. pap. 29.99 (*0-13-014271-9*) P-H.

Oracle Certified Professional Application Developer Exam Guide. Jason S. Couchman et al. (Illus.). 1351p. 1999. pap. 99.99 incl. cd-rom (*0-07-211975-6*) McGraw.

Oracle Certified Professional DBA Certification Exam Guide. Jason S. Couchman. 1257p. 1998. pap. 99.99 (*0-07-882549-0*) Osborne-McGraw.

***Oracle Certified Professional DBO Certification Exam Guide.** Jason S. Couchman. 543p. 2000. 59.99 (*0-07-212361-3*) McGraw.

Oracle Corporation: The WetFeet.com Insider Guide. 5th ed. WetFeet.com Staff. (Insider Guides Ser.). 36p. 1998. spiral bd. 25.00 (*1-58207-043-1*) WetFeet.

Oracle Data Warehousing: The Practical Guide to Building a Data Warehouse. Michael J. Corey & Michael Abbey. LC 97-107179. 560p. 1996. pap. text 34.95 (*0-07-882242-4*) Osborne-McGraw.

Oracle Database Administration. Synec Technology Staff. 350p. 1998. 29.99 (*0-07-134431-4*) McGraw.

***Oracle Database Administration: The Essential Reference.** David C. Kreines & Brian Laskey. Ed. by Deborah Russell. (Illus.). 560p. 1999. pap. 34.95 (*1-56592-516-5*) OReilly & Assocs.

Oracle Database Administration on UNIX Systems. Lymnwood Brown. LC 97-183203. 224p. (C). 1997. pap. text 39.95 incl. cd-rom (*0-13-244666-9*) P-H.

Oracle Database Construction Kit. John A. Palinski. LC 97-68697. 1997. 49.99 incl. cd-rom (*0-7897-1419-1*) Que.

Oracle Databases on the Web. 10th ed. Donald K. Burleson. LC 97-154645. 592p. (C). 1997. mass mkt. 39.99 (*1-57610-099-5*) Coriolis Grp.

Oracle Databases on Windows NT. Lillian Hobbs. LC 97-46516. 367p. 1998. pap. text 39.95 (*1-55558-190-0*, Digital DEC) Buttrwrth-Heinemann.

Oracle DBA: Proven Techniques to Pass the Oracle Certified Professional Exam. Michael R. Ault. LC 98-16072. (Exam Cram Ser.). 1998. pap. text 29.99 (*1-57610-262-9*) Coriolis Grp.

Oracle DBA: Tips & Techniques. Rich Niemiec. 1999. pap. 39.99 (*0-07-882432-X*) Osborne-McGraw.

Oracle DBA Exam Cram: Test 3 & Test 4. Michael R. Ault. LC 98-29351. (Exam Cram Ser.). xxiii, 385 p. 1999. pap. 29.99 (*1-57610-331-5*) Coriolis Grp.

Oracle DBA Handbook. Kevin Loney. (Oracle Press Ser.). 608p. 1994. pap. text 34.95 (*0-07-881182-1*) McGraw.

Oracle DBA Handbook: 7.3 Edition. 2nd ed. Kevin Loney. LC 97-132496. 1996. pap. text 39.99 (*0-07-882289-0*) Osborne-McGraw.

Oracle Dba Interactive Workbook. (C). 1999. write for info. (*0-13-016125-X*) P-H.

Oracle DBA Reference Library. Ahmed Alomari. (C). 1997. pap. text 119.95 incl. cd-rom (*0-13-894742-2*) P-H.

***Oracle DBA 7.3 to 8 Upgrade Exam Cram.** Robert Freeman. LC 99-54512. (Exam Cram Ser.). 2000. pap. 29.99 (*1-57610-543-1*) Coriolis Grp.

Oracle Design. Ian Stevenson & Dave Ensor. LC 97-146805. 546p. 1997. pap. write for info. (*1-56592-268-9*) Thomson Learn.

***Oracle Designer: A Template for Developing an Enterprise Standards Document.** Mark A. Kramm & Kent Graziano. LC 99-40531. (PTR Oracle Ser.). (Illus.). 300p. 1999. pap. text 44.99 (*0-13-015343-5*) P-H.

Oracle Designer - 200 Handbook. Carrie Anderson & David Wendelken. 624p. (C). 1996. pap. 41.95 (*0-201-63445-7*) Addison-Wesley.

Oracle Designer - 2000. Albert Lulushi. LC 97-44451. 992p. (C). 1997. pap. text 49.95 (*0-13-849753-2*, Pub. by P-H) S&S Trade.

Oracle Designer - 2000 Handbook: Master Oracle's Powerful CASE Tools. Paul Dorsey & Peter Koletzke. LC 97-138981. 512p. 1996. pap. text 34.95 (*0-07-882229-7*) Osborne-McGraw.

Oracle Designer Generation. Kenneth R. Atkins et al. (Illus.). 1154p. 2000. pap. 64.99 incl. cd-rom (*0-07-882475-3*) Osborne-McGraw.

Oracle Designer Handbook - 2nd Edition. 2nd ed. Paul Dorsey & Peter Koletzke. LC 99-174707. (Illus.), 1075p. 1998. pap. 44.99 (*0-07-882417-6*, Oracle Press) Osborne-McGraw.

***Oracle Desk Reference: The Professional's Companion.** Guy Harrison. LC 99-38904. 400p. 1999. pap. text 34.99 (*0-13-013294-2*) P-H.

***Oracle Developer: Advanced Forms & Reports.** Paul Dorsey & Peter Koletzke. 835p. 2000. pap. text 59.99 (*0-07-212048-7*) Osborne-McGraw.

Oracle Developer - 2000 Handbook. Robert J. Muller. LC 96-133415. (Oracle Press Ser.). (Illus.). 504p. 1996. pap. text 39.95 (*0-07-882180-0*) McGraw.

Oracle Developer - 2000. Michael W. Stowe. LC 95-36300. 304p. 1995. pap. 48.00 (*0-13-227968-1*) P-H.

***Oracle Developer Advanced Form Builder Vol. 1: Instructor Guide.** (Illus.). 2000. pap., teacher ed. write for info. (*0-7423-0456-6*, ODAFRM50IGV1) ComputerPREP.

***Oracle Developer Advanced Form Builder Vol. 1: Learning Guide.** (Illus.). (YA). 2000. pap. write for info. (*0-7423-0454-X*, ODAFRM50LGV1) ComputerPREP.

***Oracle Developer Advanced Form Builder Vol. 2: Instructor Guide.** (Illus.). 2000. pap., teacher ed. write for info. (*0-7423-0457-4*, ODAFRM50IGV2) ComputerPREP.

***Oracle Developer Advanced Form Builder Vol. 2: Learning Guide.** (Illus.). (YA). 2000. pap. write for info. (*0-7423-0455-8*, ODAFRM50LGV2) ComputerPREP.

***Oracle Developer Advanced Form Builder Set: Instructor Guide, 2 vols., Set.** Orig. Title: tp. (Illus.). 2000. pap., teacher ed. write for info. (*0-7423-0465-5*, ODAFRM50IGSET) ComputerPREP.

***Oracle Developer Advanced Form Builder Set: Learning Guide, 2 vols., Set.** (Illus.). (YA). 2000. pap. write for info. (*0-7423-0464-7*, ODAFRM50LGSET) ComputerPREP.

***Oracle Developer Form Builder Vol. 1: Instructor Guide.** (Illus.). 2000. pap., teacher ed. write for info. (*0-7423-0452-3*, ODFRM50IGV1) ComputerPREP.

***Oracle Developer Form Builder Vol. 1: Learning Guide.** (Illus.). (YA). 2000. pap. write for info. (*0-7423-0450-7*, ODFRM50LGV1) ComputerPREP.

***Oracle Developer Form Builder Vol. 2: Instructor Guide.** (Illus.). 2000. pap., teacher ed. write for info. (*0-7423-0453-1*, ODFRM50IGV2) ComputerPREP.

***Oracle Developer Form Builder Vol. 2: Learning Guide.** (Illus.). (YA). 2000. pap. write for info. (*0-7423-0451-5*, ODFRM50LGV2) ComputerPREP.

***Oracle Developer Form Builder Vol. 3: Instructor Guide.** (Illus.). 2000. pap., teacher ed. write for info. (*0-7423-0478-7*, ODFRM50IGV3) ComputerPREP.

***Oracle Developer Form Builder Vol. 3: Student Guide.** (Illus.). (YA). 2000. pap., student ed. write for info. (*0-7423-0477-9*) ComputerPREP.

***Oracle Developer Form Builder Set: Instructor Guide, 2 vols., Set.** (Illus.). 2000. pap., teacher ed. write for info. (*0-7423-0463-9*, ODFRM50IGSET) ComputerPREP.

***Oracle Developer Form Builder Set: Learning Guide, 2 vols., Set.** (Illus.). (YA). 2000. pap. write for info. (*0-7423-0462-0*, ODFRM50LGSET) ComputerPREP.

***Oracle Developer Forms Techniques.** Bulusu Lakshman. LC 99-68916. 248p. 2000. 34.99 (*0-672-31846-6*) Sams.

***Oracle Developer Report Builder Vol. 1: Instructor Guide.** (Illus.). 2000. pap., teacher ed. write for info. (*0-7423-0460-4*, ODRPT30IGV1) ComputerPREP.

***Oracle Developer Report Builder Vol. 1: Learning Guide.** (Illus.). (YA). 2000. pap. write for info. (*0-7423-0458-2*, ODRPT30LGV1) ComputerPREP.

***Oracle Developer Report Builder Vol. 2: Instructor Guide.** (Illus.). 2000. pap., teacher ed. write for info. (*0-7423-0461-2*, ODRPT30IGV2) ComputerPREP.

***Oracle Developer Report Builder Vol. 2: Learning Guide.** (Illus.). (YA). 2000. pap. write for info. (*0-7423-0459-0*, ODRPT30LGV2) ComputerPREP.

***Oracle Developer Report Builder Set: Instructor Guide, 2 vols., Set** (Illus.). 2000. pap., teacher ed. write for info. (*0-7423-0467-1*, ODRPT30IGSET) ComputerPREP.

***Oracle Developer Report Builder Set: Learning Guide, 2 vols., Set.** (Illus.). (YA). 2000. pap. write for info. (*0-7423-0466-3*, ODRPT30LGSET) ComputerPREP.

Oracle Developer Starter Kit. Robert J. Muller. 792p. 1999. pap. text 49.99 incl. cd-rom (*0-07-212047-9*) McGraw.

Oracle Developer/2000 Forms. Albert Lulushi. LC 98-30448. 1000p. 1998. pap. text 49.99 (*0-13-949033-7*) P-H.

Oracle Developer/2000 Handbook. 2nd ed. Robert J. Muller. LC 97-209033. 728p. 2000. pap. 44.99 (*0-07-882326-9*) Osborne-McGraw.

***Oracle Developer/2000 Handbook.** 2nd ed. Michael W. Stowe. LC 98-34644. 304p. 1998. pap. text 44.99 (*0-13-918111-3*) P-H.

Oracle Developers Research Library. Lulushi & Harriet Beecher Stowe. 1998. boxed set 119.99 (*0-13-010620-8*) P-H.

***Oracle Discoverer Handbook.** Michael Armstrong-Smith. (Illus.). 2000. pap. 44.99 (*0-07-212635-3*) Osborne-McGraw.

Oracle Distributed System, 3.5. Lafreniere Webb. 1991. 24.95 (*0-8306-1652-7*) McGraw-Hill Prof.

Oracle Distributed System, 5.25. Lafreniere Webb. 1991. 24.95 (*0-8306-1647-0*) McGraw-Hill Prof.

***Oracle Distributed Systems.** Charles Dye. Ed. by Deborah Russell. (Illus.). 548p. 1999. pap. 39.95 incl. disk (*1-56592-432-0*) OReilly & Assocs.

***Oracle Ed1 Internal Services: For Waits, Latches, Locks & Memory.** Steve Adams. Ed. by Deborah Russell. (Illus.), 150p. 1999. pap. 19.95 (*1-56592-598-X*) OReilly & Assocs.

Oracle Edge. Stuart Read. LC 99-35387. 256p. 1999. 19.95 (*1-58062-165-1*) Adams Media.

***Oracle 8 DBA; Database Administration Exam Cram.** Paul Collins. LC 00-22938. (Oracle Certified Professional Ser.). (Illus.). 404p. 2000. pap. text 29.99 (*1-57610-603-9*) Coriolis Grp.

***Oracle 8.** ENI Publishing Ltd. Staff. (Keeping Ahead Ser.). 1999. pap. 24.95 (*2-7460-0560-3*) ENI Publng.

Oracle 8: A Beginner's Guide. Michael Abbey & Michael J. Corey. (Illus.). 767p. 1997. pap. text 39.99 (*0-07-882393-5*, Oracle Press) Osborne-McGraw.

Oracle 8: The Complete Reference. George K. Koch & Kevin Loney. LC 97-207566. (Illus.). 1300p. 1997. 59.99 incl. cd-rom (*0-07-882396-X*, Oracle Press) Osborne-McGraw.

***Oracle 8 Advanced PL/SQL.** (Illus.). 220p. (C). 1999. pap. write for info. (*0-7423-0351-9*) ComputerPREP.

Oracle 8 Architecture. Steven M. Bobrowski. LC 97-220323. 356p. 1997. pap. text 34.99 (*0-07-882274-2*) Osborne-McGraw.

Oracle8 Backup & Recovery Handbook. Rama Velpuri & Anand Adkoli. LC 98-130867. (Illus.). 628p. (Orig.). 1998. pap. text 44.99 (*0-07-882389-7*, Oracle Press) Osborne-McGraw.

Oracle 8 Bible. Carol McCullough. LC 98-70265. 1176p. 1998. pap. 49.99 (*0-7645-3198-0*) IDG Bks.

***Oracle 8 Database Administration.** (Illus.). (YA). 1999. pap. write for info. (*0-7423-0411-6*, ODBA85D00TL) ComputerPREP.

Oracle 8 Database Administration on Windows NT. Lynnwood Brown. LC 98-11705. 400p. 1998. pap. text 39.99 (*0-13-927443-X*) P-H.

Oracle 8 DBA Handbook. Kevin Loney. (Illus.). 822p. (Orig.). 1997. pap. text 44.99 (*0-07-882406-0*, Oracle Press) Osborne-McGraw.

Oracle 8 How-To: Intermediate - Advanced. Paul Dalberth et al. LC 97-40533. 720p. 1998. pap. 39.99 (*1-57169-123-5*) Sams.

***Oracle 8i DBA's Bible.** Jonathan Gennick. (Illus.). 1152p. 2000. pap. text 49.99 (*0-7645-4623-6*) IDG Bks.

***Oracle 8i for Dummies.** rev. ed. Carol McCullough. (For Dummies (Computers) Ser.). (Illus.). 400p. 1999. pap. 24.99 incl. cd-rom (*0-7645-0570-X*) IDG Bks.

O

Oracle 8 PL-BQL Programming. 2nd ed. Scott Urman. LC 97-228979. (Illus.). 848p. (Orig.). 1997. pap. text 44.99 (*0-07-882305-6*, Oracle Press) Osborne-McGraw.

Oracle 8 Tuning. Michael J. Corey et al. LC 98-113989. (Illus.). 293p. (Orig.). 1997. pap. text 44.99 (*0-07-882390-0*, Oracle Press) Osborne-McGraw.

***Oracle 8/8i DBA Certification.** Paul Lane. (Oracle Bks.). (Illus.). 1400p. 2000. pap. 99.99 (*0-672-31785-0*) Sams.

***Oracle 8i & UNIX Performance Tuning.** Ahmed Alomari. (PTR Oracle Ser.). (Illus.). 450p. 2000. pap. 49.99 (*0-13-018706-2*) P-H.

***Oracle 8I Data Migration Handbook.** Paul Dorsey. 576p. 2000. pap. text. write for info. (*0-07-212391-5*, Oracle Press) Osborne-McGraw.

***Oracle 80 From Scratch.** Dan Hotka. (Illus.). 400p. 2000. pap. 39.99 (*0-7897-2369-7*) Que.

***Oracle 8I: Complete Reference.** Koch Loney. (Illus.). 1392p. 2000. pap. text 69.99 (*0-07-212364-8*, Oracle Press) Osborne-McGraw.

Oracle Electronic Resource Kit. Publishing Sams. 1997. pap. text, boxed set 99.99 incl. cd-rom (*0-672-31097-X*) Sams.

***Oracle Essentials: Oracle 8 & Oracle 8i.** Rick Greenwald et al. Ed. by Deborah Russell. (Illus.). 300p. 1999. pap. 29.95 (*1-56592-708-7*) OReilly & Assocs.

Oracle Financials Handbook. David James et al. LC 99-218917. (Illus.). 723p. (Orig.). 1999. pap. 49.99 (*0-07-882375-7*, Oracle Press) Osborne-McGraw.

Oracle for Delfi. Jerome Rothenberg. LC 95-206573. 1995. pap. 8.00 (*0-87924-065-2*) Membrane Pr.

Oracle for Visual Basic Developers. Nick Snowdown. LC 98-86743. 752p. 1998. pap. 39.99 (*0-7821-2322-8*) Sybex.

***Oracle Forms: Interactive Workbook.** Baman Motivala. 467p. 2000. pap., wbk. ed. 39.99 (*0-13-015808-9*) P-H.

***Oracle Forms & Reports.** Andy Yao. 200p. (C). 1999. 30.00 (*1-930360-01-0*) Unitd Tech.

Oracle Forms Interactive Workbook. (C). 2000. pap. write for info. (*0-13-086329-7*) P-H.

Oracle Glass. Judith M. Riley. 528p. 1995. pap. 12.50 (*0-449-91006-7*) Fawcett.

Oracle in der Anwendung. (C). 1990. text. write for info. (*0-201-52298-5*) Addison-Wesley.

Oracle J Developer 2. Cary Jensen. 1999. pap. 49.99 (*0-07-212098-3*) Osborne-McGraw.

***Oracle Java Developer 2.** Jensen. 1999. write for info. (*0-07-212100-9*) McGraw.

Oracle JDeveloper. Cary Jensen et al. LC 98-208681. 688p. 2000. pap. 44.99 (*0-07-211863-6*) Osborne-McGraw.

Oracle Lips: A Collection. aut. limited num. ed. Storm Constantine. 398p. 1999. 45.00 (*0-9667848-0-4*, Pub. by Stark Hse Pr) Firebird Dist.

Oracle Mystery of Life & Destiny (1931) L. W. De Laurence. 194p. 1999. reprint ed. pap. 17.95 (*0-7661-0736-1*) Kessinger Pub.

Oracle Networking. Hugo Toledo, Jr. LC 97-138545. (Oracle Press Ser.). 512p. (Orig.). 1996. pap. text 34.95 (*0-07-882165-7*) Osborne-McGraw.

Oracle NT Handbook. Rama Velpuri & Anand Adkoli. LC 99-162558. 500p. 1998. 44.99 (*0-07-211917-9*, Oracle Press) Osborne-McGraw.

Oracle of Clarion: Unveiling the Goddess - A Story to Awaken the Heart of Humanity. unabridged ed. Paula Peterson. 205p. 1996. pap. 12.95 (*0-9653235-0-1*) Rainbow Pyramid.

Oracle of Geomancy: Techniques of Earth Divination. Stephen Skinner. 400p. 1987. pap. write for info. (*0-907061-82-6*, Pub. by Prism Pr) Assoc Pubs Grp.

Oracle of Geomancy: The Divinatory Arts of Raml, Geomantia, Sikidy, & the I Ching. Nigel Pennick. 1995. pap. 19.95 (*1-898307-16-4*) Holmes Pub.

***Oracle of Kabbalah: Mystical Teachings of the Hebrew Letters.** Richard Seidman. LC 00-40231. 192p. 2000. 29.95 (*0-312-24173-9*, Thomas Dunne) St Martin.

Oracle of Leadership, 2 Bk. Kit. William J. Cox. 128p. (Orig.). 1995. pap. 12.95 (*0-963847I-4-7*) WJC Pr.

Oracle of Love. Jim Mele. 24p. 1976. pap. 1.00 (*0-916696-01-4*) Cross Country.

Oracle of Rama: An Adaptation of Rama Ajna Prashna of Goswami Tulsidas. David Frawley. (Illus.). 208p. 1997. pap., per. 12.95 (*1-878423-19-3*) Morson Pub.

***Oracle of Rama: An Adaptation of Rama Ajna Prashna of Goswami Tulsidas.** Comment by David Frawley. 194p. 1999. 100.00 (*81-208-1558-0*, Pub. by Motilal Bnarsidass) St Mut.

***Oracle of Rama: An Adaptation of Rama Ajna Prashna of Goswami Tulsidas with Commentary.** David Frawley. 194p. 1999. pap. 45.00 (*81-208-1559-9*, Pub. by Motilal Bnarsidass) St Mut.

Oracle of the Coffee House: John Dunton's Athenian Mercury. Gilbert D. McEwen. LC 78-171109. (Huntington Library Publications). 265p. 1972. reprint ed. pap. 82.20 (*0-608-03171-2*, 206362400007) Bks Demand.

Oracle of the Dreamtime: Aboriginal Dreamings Offer Guidance for Today. Donni Hakanson. (Illus.). 168p. 1998. pap. 24.95 (*1-885203-65-9*) Jrny Editions.

Oracle of the Goddess. Monte Farber & Amy Zerner. 80p. 1998. 27.95 (*0-312-19179-0*, Thomas Dunne) St Martin.

Oracle of the Heart: Selected Poems. Muriel T. Stackley. (Illus.). 68p. 1998. pap. 9.95 (*0-945530-19-6*) Wordsworth KS.

Oracle of Tyre: The Septuagint of Isaiah XXIII As Version & Vision. Arie Van Der Kooij. LC 98-16843. (Vetus Testamentum Ser.). 224p. 1998. 76.50 (*90-04-11152-2*) Brill Academic Pubs.

Oracle Performance Tuning. 2nd ed. Mark Gurry & Peter Corrigan. LC 97-159805. (Illus.). 964p. 1996. pap. 47.95 (*1-56592-237-9*) Thomson Learn.

Oracle Performance Tuning: Tips & Techniques. Richard J. Niemiec et al. (Illus.). 894p. 1999. pap. 49.99 (*0-07-882434-6*) Osborne-McGraw.

Oracle Performance Tuning & Optimization. Ed Whalen. LC 95-72345. 720p. 1996. 49.99 incl. cd-rom (*0-672-30886-X*) Sams.

Oracle Pl Sql Interactive Workbook. (C). 1999. write for info. (*0-13-016126-8*) P-H.

***Oracle Pl Sql Interactive Workbook.** Douglas Scherer et al. 472p. 2000. pap. text 39.99 (*0-13-015743-0*) P-H.

Oracle PL/SQL. Scott Urman & Tim Smith. 1999. text. write for info. (*0-07-212144-0*) McGraw.

Oracle PL/SQL: Tips & Techniques. Richard J. Niemiec et al. 942p. 1999. pap. 49.99 (*0-07-882438-9*) McGraw.

Oracle PL/SQL Built-Ins Pocket Reference. Steven Feuerstein et al. Ed. by Debby Russell & Gigi Estabrook. (Illus.). 76p. 1998. reprint ed. pap. 8.95 (*1-56592-456-8*) OReilly & Assocs.

***Oracle PL/SQL CD Bookshelf.** O'Reilly & Associates, Inc. Staff. Ed. by Linda Walsh. (Illus.). 272p. 2000. pap. 89.95 incl. cd-rom (*1-56592-849-0*) OReilly & Assocs.

Oracle PL/SQL Language Pocket Reference. Stephen Feuerstein et al. Ed. by Gigi Estabrook. 110p. 1999. reprint ed. pap. 8.95 (*1-56592-457-6*) OReilly & Assocs.

Oracle PL/SQL Programming. Steven Feuerstein. Ed. by Deborah Russell. LC 96-140775. (Illus.). (Orig.). 1995. pap. 44.95 (*1-56592-142-9*) Thomson Learn.

Oracle PL/SQL Programming. Scott Urman. LC 96-168887. (Oracle Press Ser.). 564p. 1996. pap. 34.95 (*0-07-882176-2*) McGraw.

Oracle PL/SQL Programming. 2nd ed. Steven Feuerstein. Ed. by Debby Russell. 1028p. (Orig.). 1997. pap. 46.95 (*1-56592-335-9*) OReilly & Assocs.

***Oracle PL/SQL Programming: A Developer's Workbook.** Steven Feuerstein. Ed. by Deborah Russell. (Illus.). 500p. 2000. pap. 36.95 (*1-56592-674-9*) OReilly & Assocs.

Oracle Power Objects Handbook. Bruce Kolste. (Oracle Press Ser.). 512p. 1995. pap. text 32.95 (*0-07-882089-8*) Osborne-McGraw.

***Oracle Programming.** 2nd ed. Andy Yao. 150p. (C). 2000. 25.00 (*1-930360-02-9*) Unitd Tech.

Oracle Programming: A Primer. 2nd ed. Rajshekhar Sunderraman. LC 99-47984. 334p. (C). 1999. pap. 30.80 (*0-201-61258-5*) Addison-Wesley.

***Oracle Quickstart Guide.** (C). 1999. write for info. incl. cd-rom (*0-201-61214-3*) Addison-Wesley.

Oracle Reporting: Queries with SQL Objects. Gary M. Lewis. LC 95-94198. (Illus.). (Orig.). 1995. pap. 36.00 (*0-9644912-3-0*) Komenda Pub.

Oracle Resource Guide, 1994-1995. David Pepin & Susan Pepin. 1168p. 1994. pap. 30.00 (*0-9643092-3-8*) Visionary Sftware.

Oracle SAP Administration. Donald K. Burleson. Ed. by Virginia Estabrook & Deborah Russell. (Illus.). 352p. 1999. pap. 32.95 (*1-56592-696-X*) OReilly & Assocs.

Oracle Scripts. Brian Lomasky & David Kreines. (Illus.). 208p. 1998. pap. 29.95 incl. cd-rom (*1-56592-438-X*) OReilly & Assocs.

Oracle Security. Marlene Theriault & William Heney. Ed. by Debby Russell. (Illus.). 446p. 1998. pap. 34.95 (*1-56592-450-9*) OReilly & Assocs.

Oracle Server Programming. Froese. (C). 1997. pap. text. write for info. (*0-201-87750-3*) Addison-Wesley.

Oracle 7: A User's & Developer's Guide, Including Version 7.1. Gunter Sturner & George Staw. LC 94-31174. 425p. 1994. pap. 36.95 (*0-442-01962-9*, VNR) Wiley.

***Oracle 7 Administration in a Box.** Brown. (C). 1998. pap. text 145.00 (*0-13-011932-6*) P-H.

***Oracle Seven Administration in a Box: Professor Sample Pk.** 1999. write for info. (*0-13-017558-7*) P-H.

Oracle SQL: High-Performance Tuning. Guy Harrison. LC 97-1168. 512p. (C). 1997. pap. text 49.95 incl. cd-rom (*0-13-614231-1*) P-H.

Oracle SQL: Learning the Craft. (Illus.). Date not set. pap. write for info. (*0-9644912-5-7*) Komenda Pub.

Oracle SQL: 101 Frequently Asked Questions. Gary M. Lewis & Alex Sirota. LC 96-94143. (Illus.). (Orig.). 1997. pap. 30.00 (*0-9644912-7-3*) Komenda Pub.

Oracle SQL & PL/SQL Annotated Archives. Kevin Loney & Rachel Carmichael. LC 99-158016. 585p. 1998. pap. text 49.95 (*0-07-882536-9*) Osborne-McGraw.

Oracle SQL Applikationen. (SPA.). (C). 1990. pap. text. write for info. (*0-201-52284-5*) Addison-Wesley.

Oracle SQL Developer's Guide. Carolyn J. Hursch & Jack L. Hursch. 1991. 32.95 (*0-07-158197-9*) McGraw.

Oracle SQL Developer's Guide. Carolyn J. Hursch & Jack L. Hursch. 240p. 1991. 32.95 (*0-8306-2566-6*, 1560, Windcrest) TAB Bks.

***Oracle SQL Interactive Workbook.** Alexandrea Morrison. (Interactive Workbook Ser.). 544p. 2000. pap. text, wbk. ed. 39.99 (*0-13-015745-7*) P-H.

***Oracle SQL* Plus Pocket Reference.** Jonathan Gennick. (Illus.). 96p. 2000. pap. 8.95 (*1-56592-941-1*) OReilly & Assocs.

***Oracle SQL*Plus: The Definitive Guide.** Jonathan Gennick. Ed. by Deborah Russell. (Illus.). 350p. 1999. pap. 34.95 (*1-56592-578-5*) OReilly & Assocs.

Oracle Troubleshooting. Rama Velpuri & Anand Adkoli. (Illus.). 464p. (Orig.). 1997. pap. text 44.99 (*0-07-882388-9*, Oracle Press) Osborne-McGraw.

Oracle Unleashed. Advanced Information Systems, Inc. Staff et al. LC 95-72326. (Illus.). 1404p. 1996. 59.99 incl. cd-rom (*0-672-30872-X*) Sams.

Oracle Unleashed. 2nd ed. Advanced Information Systems, Inc. Staff et al. LC 97-67500. 1500p. 1997. 59.99 (*0-672-31148-8*) Mac USA.

Oracle Unleashed. 3rd ed. Comment by Advanced Informations Staff. 1999. pap. text 49.99 (*0-672-31575-0*) Sams.

Oracle User's Handbook. Larry E. Towner. 350p. 1991. 39.95 (*0-8493-7408-1*, CRC Reprint) Franklin.

Oracle Web Application Server Handbook: The Complete Guide to Using Oracle's Powerful Web Solutions. abr. ed. Barry Johnson. LC 98-126689. 684p. 1998. pap. 39.99 (*0-07-882215-7*) McGraw.

Oracle Web Applications: PL/SQL Developer's Introduction. Andrew Odewahn. Ed. by Deborah Russell. (Illus.). 275p. 1999. pap. 29.95 (*1-56592-687-0*) OReilly & Assocs.

Oracle Web Server Handbook. Steve Johnson. 1997. pap. 39.99 (*0-614-28516-X*, Oracle Press) Osborne-McGraw.

***Oracle WebDB Bible.** Rick Greenwald. LC 99-35434. (Bible Ser.). 800p. 1999. pap. 49.99 (*0-7645-3326-6*) IDG Bks.

Oracle Websystem 2.0 Unleashed. Matthew Bennett. 600p. Date not set. pap. text 49.99 incl. cd-rom (*1-57521-179-3*) Sams.

Oracle Within. Dick Sutphen. Ed. by Claire Zion. 288p. (Orig.). 1991. pap. 10.00 (*0-671-72360-X*) PB.

***Oracle XML Handbook.** Ben Chang. 2000. pap. 59.99 (*0-07-212489-X*) Osborne-McGraw.

Oracle 24x7 Tips & Techniques. Venkat S. Devraj & Ravi Balwada. 1008p. 2000. pap. text 49.99 (*0-07-211999-3*) Osborne-McGraw.

Oracle 8 Administration & Management. Michael Ault. LC 97-36223. 880p. 1997. pap., pap. text 54.99 incl. cd-rom (*0-471-19234-1*) Wiley.

Oracle 8 Black Book. Michael R. Ault. LC 97-37926. (C). 1998. mass mkt. 49.99 (*1-57610-187-8*) Coriolis Grp.

***Oracle 8 DBA: Backup & Recovery Exam Cram.** Debbie Wong. (Oracle Certified Professional Ser.). 2000. pap. text. write for info. (*1-57610-623-3*) Coriolis Grp.

Oracle 8 Design Using UML Object Modeling. Paul Dorsey & Joseph R. Hudicka. LC 99-185351. 496p. 1998. pap. 49.99 (*0-07-882474-5*) Intl Marine.

***Oracle 8i DBA Handbook.** Kevin Loney & Marlene Theriault. 979p. 1999. pap. text 49.99 incl. cd-rom (*0-07-212188-2*, Oracle Press) Osborne-McGraw.

Oracle8 Data Warehousing. 5th ed. Gary Dodge & Tim Gorman. LC 97-42035. 672p. 1998. pap. 44.99 (*0-471-19952-4*) Wiley.

***Oracle8 DBA Tips & Techniques.** Sumit Sarin. (Tips & Techniques Ser.). 608p. 2000. pap. 49.99 (*0-07-212245-5*) Osborne-McGraw.

***Oracle8 DBA: Network Administration Exam Cram.** Barbara A. Pascavage. LC 99-52992. (Exam Cram Ser.). (Illus.). 2000. pap. 29.99 (*1-57610-578-4*) Coriolis Grp.

***Oracle8 DBA: Performance Tuning Exam Cram.** Josef Brinson. (Exam Cram Ser.). (Illus.). 2000. pap. 29.99 (*1-57610-602-0*) Coriolis Grp.

***Oracle8 DBA: SQL & PL/SQL Exam Cram.** Michael R. Ault. (Exam Cram Ser.). 2000. pap. 29.99 (*1-57610-577-6*) Coriolis Grp.

Oracle8 Design Tips. Dave Ensor & Ian Stevenson. (Illus.). 130p. 1997. pap. 14.95 (*1-56592-361-8*) OReilly & Assocs.

Oracle8 Developer's Guide. Jim Hobuss & Carol McCullough Dieter. LC QA76.9.D3M39428 1999. (Developer's Guide Ser.). (Illus.). 624p. 1999. pap. 49.99 incl. cd-rom (*0-7645-3197-2*) IDG Bks.

Oracle8 Troubleshooting. Rama Velpuri & Anand Adkoli. 656p. 1999. pap. 49.99 (*0-07-882580-6*) Osborne-McGraw.

***Oracle8i Administration & Management.** Michael R. Ault. LC 99-53657. 1024p. 1999. pap. 59.99 incl. cd-rom (*0-471-35453-8*) Wiley.

***Oracle8i Data Warehousing.** Susan Hillson. 381p. 1999. pap. 44.95 (*1-55558-205-2*, Digital DEC) Buttrwrth-Heinemann.

***Oracle8i for Linus.** Robert Farrington. 400p. 2000. pap. 34.95 (*1-55558-247-8*, Digital DEC) Buttrwrth-Heinemann.

***Oracle8i for Linux Starter Kit.** Steve M. Bobrowski. 528p. 2000. 49.99 (*0-07-212442-3*, Oracle Press) Osborne-McGraw.

Oracle8i PL/SQL Programming: A Guide to New Features. Steven Feuerstein. Ed. by Debby Russell. (Illus.). 250p. 1999. pap. 29.95 (*1-56592-675-7*) OReilly & Assocs.

***Oracle8i Tips & Techniques.** Douglas Scherer et al. 545p. 2000. pap. 49.99 (*0-07-212103-3*) Osborne-McGraw.

***Oracle81 for Windows NT Starter Kit.** Steve M. Bobrowski. 481p. 2000. pap. 49.99 incl. cd-rom (*0-07-212248-X*) McGraw.

Oracles Against Babylon in Jeremiah 50-51: A Horror among the Nations. David J. Reimer. LC 92-29514. 340p. 1992. text 99.95 (*0-7734-9821-4*) E Mellen.

Oracles & Demons of Tibet. Rene De Nebesky-Wojkowitz. 1974. 300.00 (*0-87968-463-1*) Gordon Pr.

Oracles & Demons of Tibet. Rene De Nebesky-Wojkowitz. (Illus.). 666p. 1990. reprint ed. pap. 45.00 (*957-9482-19-5*) Oriental Bk Store.

Oracles & Demons of Tibet: The Cult & Iconography of the Tibetan Protective Deities. Rene De Nebesky-Wojkowitz. (C). 1993. 68.00 (*0-8364-2866-8*, Pub. by Book Faith) S Asia.

Oracles & Hierophants: Constructions of Romantic Authority. David G. Riede. LC 91-55074. 288p. 1991. text 42.50 (*0-8014-2626-X*) Cornell U Pr.

Oracles & Mysteries. Tr. by Thomas Taylor. (Thomas Taylor Ser.: Vol. 7). 1995. 32.00 (*1-898910-06-5*, Pub. by Prometheus) Minerva CA.

Oracles & Sibyls: Telling the Future in the Past. Robert Wilhelm. (Ancient Greek & Roman Resource Ser.). (Illus.). 100p. 24.95 (*1-56696-132-7*) Jackdaw.

Oracles, Bones, Stars & the Wheelbarrows: Ancient Chinese Science & Technology. Frank Ross, Jr. 192p. (YA). (gr. 7-12). 1989. pap. 6.95 (*0-395-54967-1*) HM.

Oracle's Cooperative Development Environment: A Reference User's Guide. Kevin E. Kline. LC 94-48197. (Datamation Ser.: Vol. 1). 366p. 1995. pap. 44.95 (*0-7506-9500-5*, Digital DEC) Buttrwrth-Heinemann.

***Oracles 8i Database Administration.** Noel Yuhanna. LC 99-27790. 450p. 1999. pap. 42.95 (*1-884777-78-3*) Manning Pubns.

Oracles for Dummies. Carol McCullough. LC 97-80356. 384p. 1997. pap. 29.99 incl. cd-rom (*0-7645-0239-5*) IDG Bks.

Oracles of Empire: Poetry, Politics, & Commerce in British America, 1690-1750. David S. Shields. LC 90-10836. 310p. 1990. 35.95 (*0-226-75298-4*) U Ch Pr.

***Oracles of God: The Old Testament Canon.** Andrew Steinmann. LC 99-30819. 240p. 1999. pap. 19.95 (*0-570-04282-8*) Concordia.

***Oracles of God: The Roman Catholic Church & Irish Politics, 1922-37.** Patrick Murray. 2000. 69.95 (*1-900621-27-4*, Pub. by Univ Coll Dublin Pr); pap. 32.95 (*1-900621-28-2*, Pub. by Univ Coll Dublin Pr) Dufour.

Oracles of Light. Virginia Pagliore. LC 84-61992. 96p. 1986. pap. 8.00 (*0-918618-26-6*) Pella Pub.

Oracles of Nostradamus. Charles Ward. xxix, 375 p. 1974. 250.00 (*0-87968-232-9*) Gordon Pr.

Oracles of Nostradamus. Charles A. Ward. 400p. 1981. pap. 28.00 (*0-89540-084-7*, SB-084) Sun Pub.

Oracles of Nostradamus. Charles A. Ward. 375p. 1996. reprint ed. spiral bd. 18.50 (*0-7873-0933-8*) Hlth Research.

Oracles of the Law. John P. Dawson. 520p. 1968. pap. 40.00 (*0-685-39008-X*, 73-008) U MI Law CLE.

Oracles of the Law. John P. Dawson. LC 78-7. 520p. 1978. reprint ed. lib. bdg. 85.00 (*0-313-20260-5*, DAOL, Greenwood Pr) Greenwood.

Oracles of the Law. John P. Dawson. (Michigan Legal Publications). xix, 520p. 1986. reprint ed. lib. bdg. 55.00 (*0-89941-541-5*, 304700) W S Hein.

Oracles on Man & Government. John M. Morley. LC 68-22933. (Essay Index Reprint Ser.). 1977. reprint ed. 19.95 (*0-8369-0720-5*) Ayer.

Oracle's Screen. William Spencer-Hale & Dave Newton. (Illus.). (Orig.). 1995. pap. 10.00 (*0-9648726-1-7*) Quintessential Mercy.

Oracle8 Advanced Tuning & Administration. Kevin Loney et al. 660p. 1998. pap. text 49.99 (*0-07-882534-2*) Osborne-McGraw.

***Oracle8 Certified Professional Financial Applications Consultant Exam Guide.** Christopher Allen. 1072p. 2000. 99.99 (*0-07-212358-3*) McGraw.

Oracle8 Data Warehousing. Michael Corey et al. LC 98-161689. 686p. 1998. pap. text 44.99 (*0-07-882511-3*) Osborne-McGraw.

Oracle8 JSQL Programming. Scott Urman. 608p. 1998. pap. text 49.99 (*0-07-882498-2*) Osborne-McGraw.

Oracle8i SQLJ Programming. Nirva Morisseau-Leroy et al. 557p. 1999. 49.99 (*0-07-212160-2*) McGraw.

ORACLS: A Design System for Linear Multivariable Control. Ernest S. Armstrong. (Control & Systems Theory Ser.: Vol. 10). (Illus.). 256p. 1980. text 135.00 (*0-8247-1239-0*) Dekker.

Oracula Sibyllina. John Geffcken. Ed. by W. R. Connor. LC 78-18576. (Greek Texts & Commentaries Ser.). (Illus.). 1979. reprint ed. lib. bdg. 25.95 (*0-405-11419-2*) Ayer.

Oraculo del Dilogun. Dimas P. Meret. (SPA.). 881p. 1997. 175.00 (*0-9661781-1-4*) Edit Osha.

Oracy Matters. Margaret MacLure et al. 224p. 1988. pap. 34.95 (*0-335-15855-2*) OpUniv Pr.

Oradour: Massacre & Aftermath. large type ed. Robin Mackness. (Illus.). 1991. 11.50 (*0-7089-2503-0*) Ulverscroft.

Orage Immobile. Francoise Sagan. (FRE.). 1992. pap. 10.95 (*0-7859-3238-0*, 2266043056) Fr & Eur.

Orage with Gurdjieff in America. Louise Welch. 200p. (Orig.). pap. 12.95 (*0-7100-9016-1*, Routledge Thoemms) Routledge.

Orages: Poemes. Francois Mauriac. 9.50 (*0-685-34298-0*) Fr & Eur.

Orages au Paradis. Pamela Burford. (Rouge Passion Ser.: No. 485). (FRE.). 1998. mass mkt. 3.50 (*0-373-37485-2*, 1-37485-9) Harlequin Bks.

Orages D'Acier. Ernst Junger. (FRE.). 448p. 1974. pap. 10.95 (*0-7859-2334-9*, 2070365395) Fr & Eur.

Oraibi Marau Ceremony: The Stanley McCormick Hopi Expedition. Henry R. Voth. LC E 0099.H7.V6. (Field Museum of Natural History Anthropological Ser.: Vol. 11, No. 1). (Illus.). 220p. 1912. reprint ed. pap. 68.20 (*0-608-02721-9*, 206338600004) Bks Demand.

Oraibi Oaqol Ceremony: The Stanley McCormick Hopi Expedition. Henry R. Voth. LC 04-12952. (Field Columbian Museum Anthropological Ser.: Vol. 6, No. 1). (Illus.). 165p. 1903. reprint ed. pap. 51.20 (*0-608-02695-6*, 206334800004) Bks Demand.

Oraibi Soyal Ceremony, & Oraibi Powamu Ceremony, & Mishongnovi Ceremonies of the Snake & Antelope Fraternities, & Oraibi Summer Snake Ceremony, 4 wks. in 1 vol. 1901-03. G. A. Dorsey & H. R. Voth. (Chicago Field Museum of Natural History Fieldiana Anthropology Ser.: Vol. 3). 1974. 80.00 (*0-527-01863-5*) Periodicals Srv.

Oraibi Summer Snake Ceremony: The Stanley McCormick Hopi Expedition. Henry R. Voth. LC 04-12951. (Field Columbian Museum, Publication 83, Anthropological Ser.: Vol. 3, No. 4). 378p. 1903. reprint ed. pap. 117.20 (*0-608-02111-3*, 206276000004) Bks Demand.

Oraibu Marau Ceremony - Brief Miscellaneous Hopi Papers. H. R. Voth. (Chicago Field Museum of Natural History Fieldiana Anthropology Ser.: Vol. 11). 1912. 55.00 (*0-527-01871-6*) Periodicals Srv.

Oraison Funebres. Jacques-Benigne Bossuet. (Class. Hatier Ser.). pap. 6.95 (*0-685-34206-9*, F35542) Fr & Eur.

Oraison Funebre de Gorgias. Carl W. Vollgraff. Ed. by Gregory Vlastos. LC 78-14601. (Morals & Law in Ancient Greece Ser.). 1979. reprint ed. lib. bdg. 17.95 (*0-405-11580-6*) Ayer.

O

An Asterisk (*) at the beginning of an entry indicates that the title is appearing for the first time.

Oraisons Funebres. Jacques-Benigne Bossuet. 461p. 1961. 19.95 (*0-8288-7470-0*) Fr & Eur.

Oraisons Funebres: Discours Prononces par l'Auteur, 1958-1965. Andre Malraux. (Coll. Soleil). 13.50 (*0-685-34270-0*) Fr & Eur.

Oral AIDS: Manifestations, Safety Measures & Questions of Transmissibility. Ed. by D. Ajdukovic. 256p. 1990. 95.00 (*0-444-01576-0*) P-H.

Oral Anatomy, Embryology & Histology. B. K. Berkovitz & B. J. Moxham. LC 94-46127. (Self-Assessment Picture Tests in Dentistry Ser.). 144p. (C). (gr. 13). 1994. text 25.50 (*0-7234-2007-6*) Mosby Inc.

Oral Anatomy 3. 3rd ed. B. K. Berkovitz. 2001. text 79.95 (*0-323-00873-9*) Mosby Inc.

Oral & Dental Trauma in Children & Adolescents. Graham Roberts & Peter Longhurst. (Illus.). 112p. (C). 1996. text 115.00 (*0-19-262055-X*); pap. text 59.95 (*0-19-262049-5*) OUP.

***Oral & Literate Culture in England, 1500-1700.** Adam Fox. (Oxford Studies in Social History). (Illus.). 350p. 2000. text 74.00 (*0-19-820512-0*) OUP.

Oral & Maxillofacial Infections. 3rd ed. Ed. by Richard G. Topazian & Morton H. Goldberg. LC 92-48356. (Illus.). 672p. 1993. text 142.00 (*0-7216-4845-2*, W B Saunders Co) Harcrt Hlth Sci Grp.

Oral & Maxillofacial Pathology. Brad W. Neville et al. LC 94-20442. (Illus.). 688p. 1995. text 62.95 (*0-7216-6695-7*, W B Saunders Co) Harcrt Hlth Sci Grp.

Oral & Maxillofacial Radiology: Radiologic - Pathologic Correlations. Dale A. Miles et al. (Illus.). 352p. 1991. text 65.00 (*0-7216-3070-7*, W B Saunders Co) Harcrt Hlth Sci Grp.

***Oral & Maxillofacial Radiology Today: Proceedings of the 12th International Congress of Dentomaxillofacial Radiology, Osaka, Japan, June 26-July 1, 1999.** International Congress of Dento-Maxillo-Facial Radiology Staff et al. LC 00-28786. 2000. write for info. (*0-444-50405-2*) Elsevier.

Oral & Maxillofacial Surgery. Ed. by E. Hjorting-Hansen. (Illus.). 584p. 1985. text 138.00 (*0-86715-154-4*) Quint Pub Co.

Oral & Maxillofacial Surgery. 7th ed. Raymond J. Fonseca. LC 99-11886. 2000. text. write for info. (*0-7216-9631-7*, W B Saunders Co) Harcrt Hlth Sci Grp.

Oral & Maxillofacial Trauma. 2nd ed. Raymond J. Fonseca & Robert V. Walker. Ed. by Larry McGrew. LC 96-42342. (Illus.). 1376p. 1997. text 335.00 (*0-7216-6213-7*, W B Saunders Co) Harcrt Hlth Sci Grp.

Oral & Maxillofacial Traumatology, Vol. I. Eberhard Kruger & Wilfried Schilli. (Illus.). 402p. 1982. text 174.00 (*0-931386-68-3*) Quint Pub Co.

Oral & Maxillofacial Traumatology, Vol. 2. Wilfried Schilli. Ed. by Eberhard Kruger. (Illus.). 605p. 1986. text 194.00 (*0-931386-69-1*) Quint Pub Co.

Oral & Nonverbal Expression. Ivan Muse. (School Leadership Library). (Illus.). 160p. 1996. 29.95 (*1-883001-27-7*) Eye On Educ.

Oral & the Written Gospel: The Hermeneutics of Speaking & Writing in the Synoptic Tradition, Mark, Paul, & Q. Werner H. Kelber. LC 96-43119. (Voices in Performance & Text Ser.). 1997. 35.00 (*0-253-33230-3*); pap. 17.95 (*0-253-21097-6*) Ind U Pr.

Oral & the Written Gospel: The Hermeneutics of Speaking & Writing in the Synoptic Tradition, Mark, Paul, & Q. Werner H. Kelber. LC 82-7450. 272p. reprint ed. pap. 84.40 (*0-608-18359-8*, 203304200083) Bks Demand.

Oral & Written Communication: Historical Approaches. Ed. by Richard L. Enos. LC 86-655578. (Written Communication Annual Ser.: Vol. 4). 264p. 1990. reprint ed. pap. 81.90 (*0-608-03006-6*, 206345600006) Bks Demand.

Oral & Written Composition: Historical Approaches. Richard L. Enos. (Written Communication Annual Ser.: Vol. 4). (Illus.). 272p. (C). 1990. 62.00 (*0-8039-3107-7*) Sage.

Oral & Written Poetry in African Literature Today. Ed. by Eldred D. Jones et al. LC 88-83635. (African Literature Today Ser.). 170p. (C). 1989. 29.95 (*0-86543-125-6*); pap. 9.95 (*0-86543-126-4*) Africa World.

Oral Antecedents of Greek Librarianship. H. Curtis Wright. LC 77-73645. xxvi, 237p. 1978. 19.95 (*0-8425-0623-3*, Friends of the Library) Brigham.

Oral Antibiotics Education Course. Competence Assurance Systems Staff. (Illus.). 1984. pap. text 60.00 (*0-89147-061-1*) CAS.

Oral Anticoagulants: Chemical & Biological Properties & Clinical Applications. Ed. by Leon Poller & Jack Hirsch. (Arnold Publication). 356p. (C). 1996. text 125.00 (*0-340-55266-2*) OUP.

Oral Antidiabetics. Ed. by Jochen Kuhlman & W. Puls. (Handbook of Experimental Pharmacology Ser.: Vol. 119). (Illus.). 712p. 1995. 514.95 (*3-540-58990-2*) Spr-Verlag.

Oral Art & Literature of Kazakhs of Russian Central Asia. Thomas G. Winner. Ed. by Richard M. Dorson. LC 80-799. (Folklore of the World Ser.). 1981. reprint ed. lib. bdg. 31.95 (*0-405-13339-1*) Ayer.

***Oral Bacterial Ecology: The Molecular Basis.** Howard K. Kuramitsu & Richard P. Ellen. 314p. 2000. 149.99 (*1-898486-22-0*, Pub. by Horizon Sci) Intl Spec Bk.

Oral Biblical Criticism: The Influence of the Principles of Orality on the Literary Structure of Paul's Epistle to the Philippians. Casey W. Davis. LC 99-179315. (JSNTS Ser.: Vol. 172). 196p. 1999. 57.50 (*1-85075-972-3*, Pub. by Sheffield Acad) CUP Services.

***Oral Biofilms & Plaque Control.** Ed. by H. J. Busscher & L. V. Evans. (Illus.). 480p. 1999. text 125.00 (*90-5702-391-1*, Harwood Acad Pubs) Gordon & Breach.

Oral Biology. B. G. Van Rensburg. (Illus.). 524p. 1995. pap. text 78.00 (*0-86715-271-0*) Quint Pub Co.

Oral Biology at the Turn of the Century: Misconceptions, Truths, Challenges & Prospects, Congress, Interlaken, August 1998 (30th Anniversary of the European Research Group for Oral Biology, ERGOB) Ed. by B. Guggenheim & S. Shapiro. (Illus.). 262p. 1999. pap. 121.75 (*3-8055-6795-2*) S Karger.

Oral Biology for Dental Hygienist. Mary Bath-Balogh. 1997. pap. text, wbk. ed. 20.95 (*0-7216-6903-4*, W B Saunders Co) Harcrt Hlth Sci Grp.

Oral Biology for Dental Hygienists. Mary Bath-Balogh & Margaret J. Fehrenbach. Ed. by Selma Kaszczuk. LC 96-16729. (Illus.). 416p. 1996. pap. text 44.00 (*0-7216-6687-6*, W B Saunders Co) Harcrt Hlth Sci Grp.

***Oral Bioscience.** D. B. Ferguson. LC 98-32450. 1999. write for info. (*0-443-05373-1*) Church.

Oral Book Reviewing to Stimulate Reading: A Practical Guide in Technique for Lecture & Broadcast. Evelyn Oppenheimer. LC 80-20006. 168p. 1980. 21.00 (*0-8108-1352-1*) Scarecrow.

***Oral Cancer.** Robert A. Ord & Remy H. Blanchaert. LC 99-40839. 244p. 1999. write for info. (*0-86715-357-1*) Quint Pub Co.

Oral Cancer 3rd ed. Sol Silverman & American Cancer Society Staff. LC 90-199. xi, 148 p. 1990. write for info. (*0-944235-05-0*) Am Cancer NY.

***Oral Cancer.** 4th ed. Sol Silverman, Jr. 174p. 1998. pap. 59.95 incl. cd-rom (*1-55009-050-X*) DEKR.

Oral Cancer: Epidemiology, Etiology & Pathology. Ed. by Colin J. Smith et al. 125p. 1990. 68.95 (*0-89116-541-X*) Hemisp Pub.

Oral Cancer: Synopsis of Pathology & Management. Dimitroulis & Avery. LC 98-4825. 176p. 1998. pap. text 42.50 (*0-7236-1022-3*) Buttrwrth-Heinemann.

Oral Cancer Clinical & Pathological Considerations: Clinical & Pathological Considerations. Ed. by Bruce A. Wright et al. LC 87-23892. 240p. 1988. 115.00 (*0-8493-6774-3*, RC280, CRC Reprint) Franklin.

Oral Care: The Mouth in Terminal & Critical Illness. Ed. by Austin H. Kutscher et al. LC 79-48046. 1980. lib. bdg. 23.95 (*0-405-12642-5*) Ayer.

Oral Caress: The Loving Guide to Exciting a Woman. Robert William Birch. 150p. 1996. 19.95 (*1-57074-307-X*) Greyden Pr.

Oral Cepahlosporins. Ed. by Robert C. Moellering, Jr. (Antibiotics & Chemotherapy Ser.: Vol. 47). (Illus.). x, 190p. 1995. 188.00 (*3-8055-6163-6*) S Karger.

Oral Colon - Specific Drug Delivery. David R. Friend. 288p. 1992. lib. bdg. 189.00 (*0-8493-6688-7*, RM355) CRC Pr.

Oral Communication. 11th ed. Samovar. 2000. 23.00 (*0-07-231565-2*) McGraw.

Oral Communication: Speaking Across Cultures. 9th ed. Larry A. Samovar & Jack Mills. LC 93-73884. 400p. (C). 1994. text. write for info. (*0-697-20158-9*) Brown & Benchmark.

Oral Communication: Speaking Across Cultures. 10th ed. Larry A. Samovar & Jack Mills. LC 96-86800. 448p. (C). 1997. text. write for info. (*0-697-29909-0*, WCB McGr Hill) McGraw-H Hghr Educ.

Oral Communication: Speaking Across Cultures. 10th ed. Larry A. Samovar & Lisa Stefani. 112p. (C). 1997. text, wbk. ed. 13.75 (*0-697-36906-4*, WCB McGr Hill) McGraw-H Hghr Educ.

Oral Communication: Speaking Across Cultures. 11th rev. ed. Larry A. Samovar. LC 99-34763. (Illus.). 434p. (C). 2000. pap. text. write for info. (*1-891487-28-0*) Roxbury Pub Co.

Oral Communication for Business: Charting the Path. Sherry H. Humphrey & Donald E. Nelson. 111p. (C). 1991. pap. text 12.95 (*0-89641-202-4*) American Pr.

Oral Communication Problems in Children & Adolescents. 2nd ed. Ed. by Sol Adler & Deborah A. King. LC 93-10741. 240p. (C). 1993. 54.00 (*0-205-15089-6*) Allyn.

Oral Communication Skills for Vo-Tech Students: A Competency-Based Approach. Cathy S. Mester & R. T. Tauber. (Orig.). 1991. pap. 10.75 (*0-911168-79-6*) Prakken.

Oral Communications. 2nd ed. Hendrix. 1998. 8.25 (*0-07-154178-0*) McGraw.

Oral Complications of Cancer Chemotherapy. Ed. by Douglas E. Peterson. 1983. lib. bdg. 54.50 (*0-89838-563-6*) Kluwer Academic.

Oral Contraceptives: A Guide for Programs & Clinics. 4th ed. Cedric W. Porter, Jr. et al. (ENG, POR & SPA.). 56p. 1982. 3.50 (*0-933853-12-2*) Pathfinder Fund.

Oral Contraceptives: Technical & Safety Aspects. WHO Staff. (WHO Offset Publications: No. 64). 45p. 1982. 4.00 (*92-4-170064-5*) World Health.

Oral Contraceptives & Breast Cancer. Institute of Medicine Staff. 198p. 1991. text 24.95 (*0-309-04493-6*) Natl Acad Pr.

Oral Contraceptives & Breast Cancer: The Implications of the Present Findings for Informed Consent & Informed Choice. Ed. by R. D. Mann. (Illus.). 406p. 1990. 65.00 (*1-85070-282-9*) Prthnon Pub.

Oral Contraceptives & Cardiovascular Disease: An Analysis of the Recent Discussions on the Safety of the Pill. Ed. by Jean Cohen. LC 96-39337. (Illus.). 88p. 1997. text 32.00 (*1-85070-787-1*) Prthnon Pub.

Oral Contraceptives & Neoplasia: Report of a WHO Scientific Group. (Technical Reports: No. 817). (CHI, ENG, FRE & SPA.). vi, 46p. 1992. pap. text 9.00 (*92-4-120817-1*, 1100817) World Health.

Oral Contraceptives Education Course. Competence Assurance Systems Staff. (Illus.). 1985. pap. text 85.00 (*0-89147-109-X*) CAS.

Oral Controlled Release Products. U. Gundert-Remey. 1990. 105.00 (*3-8047-1042-5*) CRC Pr.

Oral Development & Histology. 2nd ed. James K. Avery. LC 94-30332. (Illus.). 416p. 1994. 59.00 (*0-86577-553-2*) Thieme Med Pubs.

***Oral Diagnosis: The Clinician's Guide.** William S. Birnbaum & Stephen M. Dunne. (Illus.). 314p. 2000. pap. 35.00 (*0-7236-1040-1*) Buttrwrth-Heinemann.

Oral Diagnosis, Oral Medicine & Treatment Planning. 2nd ed. Steven L. Bricker et al. (Illus.). 854p. 1994. pap. text 59.95 (*0-8121-1605-4*) Lppncott W & W.

Oral Discourse & Education. Bronwyn Davies & David Corson. LC 97-30202. (Encyclopedia of Language & Education Ser.). 1997. lib. bdg. write for info. (*0-7923-4639-4*) Kluwer Academic.

Oral Disease. 2nd ed. Crispian Scully & R. A. Cawson. LC 99-10154. (Colour Guide Ser.). 1999. write for info. (*0-443-06170-X*) Harcrt Hlth Sci Grp.

Oral Diseases: An Illustrated Guide to Diagnosis & Management. Crispian Scully. (Illus.). 1996. text. write for info. (*1-85317-202-2*, Pub. by Martin Dunitz) Mosby Inc.

Oral Diseases: Textbook & Atlas. Ed. by T. M. Lotti et al. LC 98-26502. (Illus.). 400p. 1998. 219.00 (*3-540-62416-3*) Spr-Verlag.

Oral Diseases in the Tropics. Ed. by S. R. Prabhu et al. (Illus.). 824p. 1992. 175.00 (*0-19-262008-8*) OUP.

***Oral Embryology & Pathohistology.** Hironori Kitamura. 483p. 1998. 125.00 (*4-900978-05-1*) Med Dent Media.

Oral Enteric Bacterial Vaccines: Proceedings of the WHO Scientific Group, Geneva, 1971. WHO Staff. (Technical Reports: No. 500). 1972. pap. text 4.00 (*92-4-120500-8*, 1100500) World Health.

Oral Enteric Vaccines: Report on a WHO Working Group. (Euro Reports & Studies Ser.: No. 63). 42p. 1982. pap. text 4.00 (*92-890-1229-3*) World Health.

Oral Epics from Africa: Vibrant Voices from a Vast Continent. Ed. by John W. Johnson et al. LC 96-47367. (African Epic Ser.). 1997. 35.00 (*0-253-33257-5*); pap. 14.95 (*0-253-21110-7*) Ind U Pr.

Oral Evidence & the Family Historian. (C). 1987. 35.00 (*0-7855-2127-5*, Pub. by Birmingham Midland Soc) St Mut.

Oral Examinations in Medical Specialty Board Certification. 1983. 29.95 (*0-934277-02-8*) Am Bd Med Spec.

Oral-Formulaic Theory: A Folklore Casebook. Ed. by John M. Foley. LC 89-16911. (Folklore Casebks.: Vol. 5). 432p. 1990. text 62.00 (*0-8240-8485-3*, 739) Garland.

Oral Health - Diet & Other Factors: The Report of the British Nutrition Foundation's Task Force. Ursula Arens & British Nutrition Foundation Staff. LC 98-39770. 240p. 1999. 139.50 (*0-444-50025-1*) Elsevier.

Oral Health & Hygiene: Subject Analysis, Reference & Research Guidebook. Martha R. Segal. LC 87-47652. 160p. 1987. 47.50 (*0-88164-604-0*); pap. 44.50 (*0-88164-605-9*) ABBE Pubs Assn.

Oral Health & the Older Adult. Kerschbaum. 1999. pap. text. write for info. (*0-7216-4068-0*, W B Saunders Co) Harcrt Hlth Sci Grp.

Oral Health Care for the Geriatric Patient in a Long Term Care Facility. 11.13 (*0-934510-13-X*, J010) Am Dental.

Oral Health Promotion. Ed. by Lone Schou & Anthony S. Blinkhorn. LC 92-48851. (Illus.). 296p. 1993. text 57.50 (*0-19-262003-7*) OUP.

Oral Health Promotion & Disease Prevention: Disease Prevention. Malvitz. 1996. pap. write for info. (*0-7216-4008-7*, W B Saunders Co) Harcrt Hlth Sci Grp.

Oral Health Services in Europe. J. Kostlan. (WHO Regional Publications, European Ser.). 141p. 1979. 16.00 (*92-9020-105-3*, 1310005) World Health.

Oral Health Sourcebook. Ed. by Allan Cook. LC 97-28301. (Health Reference Ser.: Vol. 30). 1997. lib. bdg. 78.00 (*0-7808-0082-6*) Omnigraphics Inc.

Oral Health Surveys. 4th ed. LC 98-169533. 66p. 1997. pap. 19.00 (*92-4-154493-7*, 1154275) World Health.

Oral Health Surveys: Basic Methods. 51p. 1987. pap. text 12.60 (*92-4-154216-0*, 1150275) World Health.

Oral Histology: Inheritance & Development. 2nd ed. Dominic V. Provenza. LC 84-20140. 497p. reprint ed. pap. 154.10 (*0-7837-2740-2*, 204312000006) Bks Demand.

Oral Histology & Embryology. Leslie P. Gartner. (Illus.). 246p. (C). 1989. pap. text 28.57 (*0-910841-06-3*) Jen Hse Pub Co.

***Oral Histology & Embryology.** 2nd ed. Leslie P. Gartner. LC 99-36859. (Illus.). 227p. (C). 1999. pap. 35.95 (*0-910841-09-8*) Jen Hse Pub Co.

***Oral Histories & Analysis of Nontraditional Women Studies: A Study of Unconventional Strengths.** Catherine Coogan Ward & Karen Westbrooks. LC 00-32454. (Women's Studies: Vol. 26). 252p. 2000. 89.95 (*0-7734-7759-4*) E Mellen.

Oral Histories & the 1960s. 2nd ed. Angie Lewellyn et al. Ed. by Vicki Cole. (Series of Lesson Plans: Ser. 2, No. 23). (Illus.). 16p. (J). (gr. k-12). 1997. write for info. (*1-889030-05-8*) FL Div Hist Res.

Oral Histories of Children Who Survived the Holocaust. Brana Gurewitsch & Center for Holocaust Studies Staff. LC 88-70082. 23p. 1986. write for info. (*0-9609970-4-0*) Mus Jew Heritage.

Oral Histories of Rural Utah: Generations Sanpete, 16 vols., Set. Dixie D. Bond. 230p. (Orig.). 1989. pap. 200.00 (*0-685-28902-8*) Violet Pr UT.

Oral Histories of Three Secondary School Students in Tanzania. Ed. & Tr. by Sara J. Talis. LC 87-5768. (African Studies: Vol. 2). 264p. 1987. lib. bdg. 89.95 (*0-88946-179-1*) E Mellen.

Oral History. Stephen Caunce. LC 93-26417. (Approaches to Local History Ser.). 1994. pap. text. write for info. (*0-582-07295-6*, Pub. by Addison-Wesley) Longman.

Oral History: A Complete Guide to Interviewing & Transcription. Kevin W. Sandifer. Ed. by Rowland P. Gill. 48p. 1985. pap. text 8.95 (*0-910653-30-5*) Archival Servs.

Oral History: A Guide for Teachers (And Others) Thad Sitton et al. LC 83-3483. 175p. reprint ed. pap. 54.30 (*0-608-20114-6*, 207138600011) Bks Demand.

Oral History: A Handbook. Ken Howarth. LC 99-206293. (Illus.). 224p. 1998. 39.95 (*0-7509-1756-3*, Pub. by Sutton Pub Ltd) Intl Pubs Mktg.

Oral History: A Novel. Lee Smith. 1996. pap. 11.00 (*0-345-41028-9*) Ballantine Pub Grp.

Oral History: An Interdisciplinary Anthology. 2nd ed. Ed. by David K. Dunaway & Willa K. Baum. LC 96-25385. (American Association for State & Local History Book Ser.). (Illus.). 432p. 1996. 65.00 (*0-7619-9188-3*); pap. 24.95 (*0-7619-9189-1*) AltaMira Pr.

Oral History: An Introduction for Students. James Hoopes. LC 78-9956. ix, 155p. 1979. pap. 14.95 (*0-8078-1344-3*) U of NC Pr.

Oral History: From Tape to Type. Cullom Davis et al. LC 77-4403. 151p. reprint ed. pap. 46.90 (*0-608-14976-4*, 202569600045) Bks Demand.

Oral History & Delinquency: The Rhetoric of Criminology. James Bennett. LC 81-7514. (C). 1981. 32.00 (*0-226-04245-6*) U Ch Pr.

Oral History & Delinquency: The Rhetoric of Criminology. James Bennett. LC 81-7514. 380p. (C). 1988. pap. text 19.50 (*0-226-04246-4*) U Ch Pr.

Oral History & Literature of the Wolof People of Waalo, Northern Senegal: The Master of the Word (Griot) in the Wolof Tradition. Samba Diop. (African Studies: Vol. 36). 1995. write for info. (*0-7734-9031-0*) E Mellen.

Oral History & the Law. John A. Neuenschwander. LC 85-13686. (Oral History Association Pamphlet Ser.: No. 1). 1993. pap. 8.00 (*0-317-01097-2*) Oral Hist.

Oral History Cataloging Manual. Compiled by Marion Matters. LC 95-8672. 112p. 1995. pap. 25.00 (*0-931828-97-X*) Soc Am Archivists.

Oral History Collection. Ed. by Shirley E. Stephenson. 1985. 12.00 (*0-930046-06-4*) CSUF Oral Hist.

Oral History Collection of Columbia University. 4th ed. Elizabeth B. Mason & Louis M. Starr. LC 79-11527. (Illus.). xxx, 306p. 1979. text 22.50 (*0-9602492-0-6*) Columbia U Oral Hist Res.

Oral History Evaluation Guidelines. Oral History Association Staff. (Pamphlet Ser.: Vol. 3). (Orig.). 1992. pap. text 5.00 (*0-614-32271-5*) Oral Hist.

Oral History for the Local Historical Society. 3rd rev. ed. Willa K. Baum. LC 95-42556. (American Association for State & Local History Book Ser.). 80p. 1987. reprint ed. pap. 13.95 (*0-7619-9133-6*) AltaMira Pr.

***Oral History Health & Welfare** Joanna Bornat. LC 99-20476. 1999. text. write for info. (*0-415-19156-4*) Routledge.

Oral History in Social Work: Research, Assessment & Intervention. Ruth R. Martin. LC 95-17009. (Human Services Guides Ser.: Vol. 69). 144p. 1995. 42.00 (*0-8039-4382-2*); pap. 18.95 (*0-8039-4383-0*) Sage.

Oral History in South Dakota: A Rich Tradition. Julin et al. 1979. 1.00 (*1-55614-076-2*) U of SD Gov Res Bur.

Oral History in the Secondary School Classroom. Barry A. Lanman & George L. Mehaffy. (Oral History Association Pamphlet Ser.: No. 2). 39p. (Orig.). 1988. pap. 8.00 (*0-317-03929-6*) Oral Hist.

***Oral History LA Dodgers.** Steve Delsohn. 2001. write for info. (*0-380-97755-9*) Morrow Avon.

***Oral History of Christianity: Eye Witness Accounts of the Dramatic Turning Points in the Story of the Church.** Robert Backhouse. Ed. by Owen Collins. 474p. 1998. pap. 14.95 (*0-00-628098-6*, Pub. by HarpC) Trafalgar.

Oral History of Contemporary Jewry: An Annotated Catalog. Institute of Contemporary Jewry Staff. LC 90-2859. 272p. 1990. text 10.00 (*0-8240-5683-3*, SS565) Garland.

Oral History of Gestalt Therapy: Interviews with Laura Perls, Isadore From, Erving Polster, Miriam Polster & Elliott Shapiro. 2nd ed. Joe Wysong & Edward Rosenfeld. 96p. 1989. pap. 10.00 (*0-939266-08-3*) Gestalt Journal.

***Oral History of Modern Architecture: Interviews with the Greatest Architects of the Twentieth Century.** John Peter. 320p. 2000. pap. 34.95 (*0-8109-2746-2*, Pub. by Abrams) Time Warner.

Oral History of Saturday Night Live. Tom M. Shales. 2001. Price not set. (*0-316-78146-0*) Little.

Oral History of West Southern Pines, North Carolina. Nancy Mason. 192p. (Orig.). 1987. 23.45 (*0-9617019-0-0*); pap. 14.95 (*0-9617019-1-9*) Southern Pines.

Oral History Reader. Robert Perks & Alistair Thomson. LC 97-12846. 486p. (C). 1998. 90.00 (*0-415-13351-3*); pap. 25.99 (*0-415-13352-1*) Routledge.

Oral Hst & Local Historian. Stephen Caunce. LC 93-26417. (Approaches to Local History Ser.). (C). 1994. text 52.50 (*0-582-07294-8*, Pub. by Addison-Wesley) Longman.

Oral Hygiene: Products & Practice. Olga F. Pader. (Cosmetic Science & Technology Ser.: Vol. 6). (Illus.). 552p. 1987. text 250.00 (*0-8247-7701-8*) Dekker.

Oral Hygiene for the Orthodontic Patient. Siegward D. Heintze et al. LC 98-8476. (Illus.). 170p. 1998. pap. text 58.00 (*0-86715-295-8*) Quint Pub Co.

Oral Implantology. S. Otobe. 1990. text 80.00 (*1-57235-013-X*) Piccin Nuova.

Oral Implantology. S. Otobe. (Illus.). 264p. 1990. text 88.00 (*88-299-0263-2*, Pub. by Piccin Nuova) Gordon & Breach.

O

Oral Implantology. 2nd ed. A. Schroeder. (Illus.). 510p. 1996. pap. text 29.90 (*0-86577-545-1*) Thieme Med Pubs.

Oral Inspection see D.A.E Project: Instructional Materials for Dental Health Professions

Oral Interpretation. (C). 1970. write for info. (*0-8087-5448-3*) Pearson Custom.

Oral Interpretation, 8 vols. 8th ed. Charlotte I. Lee & Timothy Gura. (C). 1991. text 62.76 (*0-395-59329-8*) HM.

Oral Interpretation, 9 vols. 9th ed. Lee. LC 96-76923. (C). 1996. pap. text 36.76 (*0-395-79485-4*) HM.

Oral Interpretation Literature. William Poschman. 200p. (C). 1995. 46.95 (*0-7872-1118-4*) Kendall-Hunt.

Oral Language Across the Curriculum. David Corson. 1988. 54.00 (*0-905028-97-X*, Pub. by Multilingual Matters); pap. 24.95 (*0-905028-96-1*, Pub. by Multilingual Matters) Taylor & Francis.

Oral Language Activities for Special Children. Darlene Mannix. 280p. (C). 1986. pap. text 29.95 (*0-87628-637-6*) P-H.

Oral Language for Today's Classroom. Claire Staab. (Pippin Teacher's Library Ser.). 126p. 1992. pap. text 15.00 (*0-88751-046-9*, 00719) Heinemann.

Oral Law. Schimmel. 18.95 (*0-87306-088-1*) Feldheim.

Oral Leukoplakia. J. Banoczy. 1982. text 137.50 (*90-247-2655-7*) Kluwer Academic.

Oral Life Histories of One-Room Schoolhouse Teachers: Voices from the Recitation Bench. Gretchen A. Duling. LC 97-29258. 316p. 1997. text 99.95 (*0-7734-4250-2*) E Mellen.

***Oral Literature & Performance in Southern Africa.** Duncan Brown. LC 99-16622. 256p. 2000. pap. 22.95 (*0-8214-1309-0*, Ohio U Ctr Intl) Ohio U Pr.

***Oral Literature & Performance in Southern Africa.** Ed. by Duncan Brown. LC 99-16622. 256p. 2000. text 44.95 (*0-8214-1308-2*, Ohio U Ctr Intl) Ohio U Pr.

Oral Literature & the Formula. Ed. by Benjamin A. Stolz & Richard S. Shannon. LC 76-29202. 290p. (Orig.). 1976. pap. 10.00 (*0-89824-426-9*) Trillium Pr.

Oral Literature in Africa. Ruth H. Finnegan. LC 96-109467. (Oxford Library of African Literature Ser.). (Illus.). 570p. 1976. reprint ed. pap. text 35.00 (*0-19-572413-5*) OUP.

Oral Literature in African Libraries: Implications for Ghana. A. Anaba Alemna. 45p. 1993. 6.00 (*0-941934-64-0*) Indiana Africa.

Oral Manifestations of HIV Infection: Proceedings of the 2nd International Workshop on the Oral Manifestations of HIV Infection, January 31-February 3, 1993, San Francisco, California. International Workshop on the Oral Manifestation o. Ed. by John S. Greenspan et al. LC 94-37145. (Illus.). 374p. 1995. pap. text 64.00 (*0-86715-286-9*) Quint Pub Co.

Oral Mechanism Examination for Children & Young Adults: What Comes after "Ahhh" John E. Riski & Mary A. Witzel. 1997. 110.00 incl. VHS (*1-58041-015-4*, 0112088) Am Speech Lang Hearing.

Oral Medicine. David Wray & J. Gibson. LC 97-10853. (Color Guide, Picture Tests Ser.). 1997. pap. text 17.95 (*0-443-05301-4*) Church.

Oral Medicine. 4th ed. William R. Tyldesley & Anne E. Field. (Illus.). 178p. 1995. text 105.00 (*0-19-262626-4*); pap. text 61.50 (*0-19-262625-6*) OUP.

Oral Medicine: A Pocket Guide. Lewis R. Eversole. LC 94-47441. (Illus.). 208p. 1995. pap. text 36.00 (*0-7216-4973-4*, W B Saunders Co) Harcrt Hlth Sci Grp.

Oral Medicine: Diagnosis & Treatment. Drore Eisen & Denis P. Lynch. LC 97-4386. (Illus.). 320p. (C). (gr. 13). 1997. text 79.95 (*0-8151-3105-4*, 29157) Mosby Inc.

Oral Medicine & Hospital Practice. 4th rev. ed. Peter Lockhart. Orig. Title: A Practical Guide to Hospital Dental Practice. (Illus.). 550p. 1997. pap. text 30.00 (*0-9657191-0-3*) FSCOD.

Oral Method of Latin Teaching. H. Loehry. (C). 1982. pap. text 55.00 (*0-900269-10-3*, Pub. by Old Vicarage) St Mut.

Oral Microbiology. 2nd ed. Michael Martin & Philip D. Marsh. LC QR0047.. (Aspects of Microbiology Ser.: No. 1). 128p. reprint ed. pap. 39.70 (*0-7837-4043-3*, 204387300011) Bks Demand.

***Oral Microbiology.** 4th ed. Philip D. Marsh & Michael Martin. LC 99-38298. 192p. 2000. pap. text 50.00 (*0-7236-1051-7*) Buttrwrth-Heinemann.

Oral Microbiology & Immunology. 2nd ed. Ed. by Russell J. Nisengard & Michael G. Newman. (Illus.). 512p. 1993. pap. text 54.50 (*0-7216-6753-8*, W B Saunders Co) Harcrt Hlth Sci Grp.

Oral Morphology of Anuran Larvae: Terminology & General Description. Richard J. Wassersug. (Occasional Papers: No. 48). 23p. 1976. pap. 1.00 (*0-317-04575-X*) U KS Nat Hist Mus.

***Oral-Motor Analysis & Remediation Techniques.** 2nd rev. ed. Char Boshart. (Illus.). 156p. 1998. pap. 37.00 (*0-9666844-4-3*) Speech Dyn Inc.

Oral Motor Assessment & Treatment. (C). 2000. text 44.95 (*0-205-29786-2*, Longwood Div) Allyn.

Oral Motor Assessment & Treatment: Improving Syllable Production. Glyndon D. Riley & Jeanna Riley. 64p. (Orig.). 1985. pap. text 79.00 (*0-685-12077-5*, 2983) PRO-ED.

Oral-Motor Techniques in Articulation Therapy. Pamela Marshalla. Ed. by Char Boshart. (Illus.). 95p. 1992. pap. 39.00 (*0-9666844-3-5*) Speech Dyn Inc.

Oral Mucosal Drug Delivery. Michael J. Rathbone. (Drugs & the Pharmaceutical Sciences Ser.: Vol. 74). (Illus.). 464p. 1996. text 185.00 (*0-8247-9744-2*) Dekker.

Oral Narrative in Afghanistan: The Individual in Tradition. Margaret A. Mills. LC 90-2960. (Folklore & Oral Tradition Ser.). 288p. 1990. text 30.00 (*0-8240-2871-6*) Garland.

Oral Narrative Research with Black Women. Ed. by Kim M. Vaz. LC 97-4842. 272p. 1997. 41.95 (*0-8039-7428-0*); pap. 19.95 (*0-8039-7429-9*) Sage.

Oral Nature of the Homeric Simile. William C. Scott. LC 74-168778. (Mnemosyne, Bibliotheca Classica Batava Ser.). ix, 212p. 1974. write for info. (*90-04-03789-6*) Brill Academic Pubs.

Oral OB GYN Board Exam: How to Prepare for the Exam, How to Take the Exam, How to Pass the Exam. Anita K. Das. LC 98-24808. 1998. 19.95 (*1-56053-303-X*) Hanley & Belfus.

Oral Oncology. Gordon B. Snow & Isaac Van Der Waal. (Developments in Oncology Ser.). 1984. text 161.00 (*0-89838-631-4*) Kluwer Academic.

Oral Pathology. R. A. Cawson & J. W. Odell. (Colour Guide Ser.). (Illus.). 152p. 1993. pap. text 16.95 (*0-443-04800-2*) Harcrt Hlth Sci Grp.

Oral Pathology. Van Der Kwast. (Illus.). 392p. 1988. text 106.00 (*0-86715-197-8*, 1978) Quint Pub Co.

Oral Pathology. 2nd ed. R. A. Cawson & E. W. Odell. LC 99-11698. (Colour Guide Ser.). (Illus.). 1999. write for info. (*0-443-06171-8*, W B Saunders Co) Harcrt Hlth Sci Grp.

Oral Pathology. 2nd ed. J. V. Soames & J. C. Southam. LC 92-16493. (Oxford Medical Publications). (Illus.). 336p. 1993. pap. 30.00 (*0-19-262214-5*) OUP.

Oral Pathology. 2nd ed. J. V. Soames & J. C. Southam. LC 92-16493. (Oxford Medical Publications). (Illus.). 336p. 1993. text 98.00 (*0-19-262215-3*) OUP.

Oral Pathology. 3rd ed. J. V. Soames & J. C. Southam. (Illus.). 352p. 1998. pap. text 62.50 (*0-19-262894-1*) OUP.

***Oral Pathology.** 3rd ed. James V. Soames. (Illus.). 304p. 1998. text 135.00 (*0-19-262895-X*) OUP.

Oral Pathology: Actual Diagnostic & Prognostic Aspects. Gerhard Seifert & Arne Burkhardt. LC 96-18025. (Current Topics in Pathology Ser.). 320p. 1996. 179.50 (*3-540-60987-3*) Spr-Verlag.

Oral Pathology: Clinical Pathology Correlations. 3rd ed. Joseph A. Regezi & James Sciubba. Ed. by Judy Fletcher. LC 97-51667. (Illus.). 688p. (C). 1999. text 63.95 (*0-7216-7731-2*, W B Saunders Co) Harcrt Hlth Sci Grp.

Oral Pathology: Mucous Membrane Lesions. Joseph V. Mauro & Michael R. Meyrowitz. 64p. 1984. 30.00 (*0-318-17795-1*); write for info. (*0-318-17796-X*) Am Dental Hygienists.

Oral Pathology Dental Hygienist. 2nd ed. Ibsen. 1995. 350.00 (*0-7216-6545-4*) Harcourt.

Oral Pathology for the Dental Hygienist. 2nd ed. Olga A. Ibsen & Joan A. Phelan. Ed. by Selma Ozmat. LC 95-30945. (Illus.). 560p. 1996. text 54.00 (*0-7216-6051-7*, W B Saunders Co) Harcrt Hlth Sci Grp.

Oral Pathology for the Dental Hygienist. 3rd ed. Olga A. C. Ibsen. LC 99-35202. (Illus.). 460p. 2000. text. write for info. (*0-7216-8574-9*, W B Saunders Co) Harcrt Hlth Sci Grp.

Oral Pathology, Intestinal Pathology, Hypobaric Pathology: Proceedings of the International Society of Geographical Pathology, 11th Conference, Newcastle-upon-Tyne, August, 1972. International Society of Geographical Pathology St. Ed. by J. R. Ruettner. (Pathologia et Microbiologica Ser.: Vol. 39, No. 3-4). 1973. reprint ed. pap. 47.50 (*3-8055-1370-4*) S Karger.

***Oral Pleasure.** Terry Smith. 160p. 2000. reprint ed. pap. 5.95 (*1-930535-01-5*) Star Dists.

Oral Poetics in Middle English Poetry. Ed. by Mark C. Amodio. LC 94-9803. (Albert Bates Lord Studies in Oral Tradition: Vol. 13). 304p. 1994. text 15.00 (*0-8153-0830-2*, H1595) Garland.

Oral Poetry: An Introduction. Paul Zumthor. Tr. by Kathy Murphy-Judy. (Theory & History of Literature Ser.: Vol. 70). 271p. (C). 1990. pap. 19.95 (*0-8166-1725-2*) U of Minn Pr.

Oral Poetry: Its Nature, Significance & Social Context. Ruth H. Finnegan. LC 91-27008. (Illus.). 324p. 1992. text 36.95 (*0-253-32200-6*); pap. text 15.95 (*0-253-20708-8*, MB-708) Ind U Pr.

***Oral Presentation in Medicine.** A. Fingerhut & F. Lacaine. 100p. 2000. pap. 27.00 (*2-287-59686-0*, Pub. by Spl France Editions) Spr-Verlag.

***Oral Presentations for Technical Communication.** Laura J. Gurak. LC 99-46796. 263p. 1999. pap. text 42.00 (*0-205-29415-4*) Allyn.

Oral Presentations for Technical Communications. (C). 1999. pap. text. write for info. (*0-205-31452-X*) Allyn.

Oral Presentations from Thesis Defenses. 321p. (Orig.). 1995. pap. 40.00 (*1-888947-16-0*) Sudbury Valley.

Oral Proficiency Evaluation Manual. EMC Staff et al. text 19.95 (*0-8219-0940-1*) EMC-Paradigm.

Oral Psychophysiology: Stress, Pain & Behavior in Dental Care. Ilana Eli. 240p. 1992. lib. bdg. 89.95 (*0-8493-0159-9*, RK53) CRC Pr.

Oral Radiology: Principles & Interpretation. 4th ed. Paul W. Goaz & Stuart C. White. LC 98-53444. (Illus.). 752p. 1999. text 67.95 (*0-8151-9491-9*, 30605) Mosby Inc.

Oral Radiology No. 3: Principles & Interpretation. 3rd ed. Paul W. Goaz & Stuart C. White. LC 93-45306. (Illus.). 752p. (C). (gr. 13). 1994. text 74.00 (*0-8016-7295-3*, 07295) Mosby Inc.

Oral Rehabilitation: Clinical Determination of Occlusion. Sumiya Hobo & Hisao Takayama. 168p. 1997. text 55.00 (*4-87417-532-5*) Quint Pub Co.

Oral Rehabilitation with Implant-Supported Prostheses Vicente Jimenez-Lopez. LC 99-10978. 1999. write for info. (*0-86715-358-X*) Quint Pub Co.

Oral Retinoids in Dermatology Workshop Held on the 15th International Congress of Dermatology, Mexico City, October 1977. Ed. by C. E. Orfanos & R. Schuppli. 1978. pap. 22.75 (*3-8055-2950-3*) S Karger.

Oral Road: Phonetics, Phonology, & Practice with the Sounds of Spanish see Camino Oral: Fonetica, Fonologia y Practica de los Sonidos del Espanol

Oral Roberts: An American Life. David E. Harrell, Jr. LC 84-48484. (Illus.). 640p. 1985. 12.95 (*0-253-15844-3*) Ind U Pr.

Oral Sadism & the Vegetarian Personality: Readings from the Journal of Polymorphous Perversity. Glenn C. Ellenbogen. 320p. 1987. mass mkt. 5.99 (*0-345-34700-5*) Ballantine Pub Grp.

Oral Self Care: Strategies for Preventative Dentistry. Philip Weinstein et al. 230p. (C). 1991. pap. text 28.00 (*1-880291-00-2*) Cont Dental Educ.

Oral Sensorimotor Function. Douglas Junge. (Illus.). ix, 182p. 1998. pap. text 30.00 (*1-891949-04-7*, Ishiyaku EuroAmerica) Med Dent Media.

Oral Sensory Mechanisms. Ed. by Yojiro Kawamura. (Frontiers of Oral Physiology Ser.: Vol. 4). (Illus.). x, 130p. 1983. 85.25 (*3-8055-3576-7*) S Karger.

Oral Sex for Dodos. Les Deux. (Illus.). 59p. 1999. pap. 9.95 (*1-892896-40-0*) Buy Books.

Oral Structural Biology. Hubert E. Schroeder. Tr. by Richard Jacobi from GER. (Flexibook Ser.). (Illus.). 424p. (Orig.). 1991. pap. text 29.90 (*0-86577-387-4*) Thieme Med Pubs.

Oral Style: Marcel Jousse. Tr. by Edgard Sienaert & Richard Whitaker. LC 90-3320. (Albert Bates Lord Studies in Oral Tradition: Vol. 6). 294p. 1990. text 10.00 (*0-8240-6892-0*, 1352) Garland.

Oral Surgery for the General Dentist. H. F. Sailer & G. F. Pajarola. LC 98-8414. (Illus.). 372p. 1998. 199.00 (*0-86577-707-1*) Thieme Med Pubs.

Oral Surgery for the General Dentist. Hermann F. Sailer & Gion F. Pajarola. LC 98-8414. (Color Atlas of Dental Medicine Ser.). 1998. 199.00 (*3-13-108241-0*) Thieme Med Pubs.

Oral Surgery in General Dentistry: A Self-Instructional Guide, 9 bks., Set. James R. Hooley & Robert J. Whitacre. 1021p. 1984. pap. 129.50 (*0-89939-001-3*) Stoma Pr.

Oral Tolerance: Mechanisms & Applications. Ed. by Howard L. Weiner & Lloyd F. Mayer. (Annals of the New York Academy of Sciences Ser.: Vol. 778). 453p. 1996. pap. 115.00 (*0-89766-996-7*) NY Acad Sci.

Oral Tradition. Jewelle Gomez. LC 95-31481. 80p. 1995. pap. 9.95 (*1-56341-063-X*); lib. bdg. 20.95 (*1-56341-064-8*) Firebrand Bks.

Oral Tradition & Hispanic Literature: Essays in Honor of Samuel G. Armistead, Vol. 15. Ed. by Mishael M. Caspi. LC 95-7724. (Albert Bates Lord Studies in Oral Tradition: Vols. 15 & 1919). 647p. 1995. text 75.00 (*0-8153-2062-0*, H1919) Garland.

Oral Tradition & the Gospels: The Problem of Mark 4. Barry W. Henaut. (JSNTS Ser.: Vol. 82). 335p. 1993. 85.00 (*1-85075-407-1*, Pub. by Sheffield Acad) CUP Services.

Oral Tradition & Written Record in Classical Athens. Rosalind Thomas. (Cambridge Studies in Oral & Literate Culture: No. 18). 328p. (C). 1989. text 65.00 (*0-521-35025-5*) Cambridge U Pr.

Oral Tradition & Written Record in Classical Athens. Rosalind Thomas. (Cambridge Studies in Oral & Literate Culture: No. 18). 335p. (C). 1992. pap. text 25.95 (*0-521-42518-2*) Cambridge U Pr.

Oral Tradition As History. Jan Vansina. LC 84-40504. (Illus.). 268p. 1985. pap. 17.95 (*0-299-10214-9*) U of Wis Pr.

Oral Tradition from the Indus. rev. ed. John F. McNair & Thomas L. Barlow. Ed. by Richard M. Dorson. LC 77-70609. (International Folklore Ser.). (Illus.). 1977. reprint ed. lib. bdg. 17.95 (*0-405-10108-2*) Ayer.

Oral Tradition in Judaism: The Case of the Mishnah. Jacob Neusner. LC 87-12056. (Albert Bates Lord Studies in Oral Tradition: Vol. 1). 176p. 1987. text 10.00 (*0-8240-7849-7*, H764) Garland.

Oral Tradition in the Middle Ages: Selected Papers from the 1988 CEMERS Conference. Ed. by W. F. Nicolaisen. LC 93-14340. (Medieval & Renaissance Texts & Studies: Vol. 112). (Illus.). 240p. 1995. 24.00 (*0-86698-165-9*, MR112) MRTS.

Oral Tradition in the South. Waldo W. Braden. LC 82-20827. 147p. 1983. reprint ed. pap. 45.60 (*0-608-00863-X*, 2061654000010) Bks Demand.

Oral Tradition of Yangzhou Storytelling. Vibeke Bordahl. (NIAS Monographs in Asian Studies: No. 73). 495p. (C). 1996. text 65.00 (*0-7007-0436-1*, Pub. by Curzon Pr Ltd) UH Pr.

Oral Traditional Literature: A Festschrift for Albert Bates Lord. Ed. by John M. Foley. (Illus.). 461p. 1981. 34.95 (*0-89357-073-7*) Slavica.

Oral Traditions & the Verbal Arts: Guide to Research Methods. Ruth H. Finnegan. (ASA Research Methods Ser.). 240p. (C). 1991. pap. 25.99 (*0-415-04841-9*) Routledge.

Oral Traditions from the Gambia Vol. 1: Mandinka Griots. Donald R. Wright. LC 79-14855. (Papers in International Studies: Africa Ser.: No. 37). 198p. reprint ed. pap. 61.40 (*0-7837-1326-6*, 204147400001) Bks Demand.

Oral Traditions of Anuta: A Polynesian Outlier in the Solomon Islands. Richard Feinberg. LC 97-6246. (Oxford Studies in Anthropological Lingusitics: No. 15). (Illus.). 304p. 1998. text 85.00 (*0-19-510683-0*) OUP.

Oral Tragedy. Dorothy Lusk. 20p. 1988. pap. 4.00 (*0-921331-08-8*) SPD-Small Pr Dist.

***Oral Tumoractivated Chemotherapy: A New Effective & Convenient Treatment in Oncology: Satellite Symposium Held at the 23rd ESMO Congress Athens, Greece, November 6, 1998.** Ed. by Stan Kaye. (Oncology Ser.). iv,32p. 1999. write for info. (*3-8055-6877-0*) S Karger.

Oral Versions of Personal Experience - Three Decades of Narrative Analysis: A Special Issue of the Journal of Narrative & Life History. Ed. by Michael G. Bamberg. 415p. 1997. pap. write for info. (*0-8058-9865-4*) L Erlbaum Assocs.

Oral World & Written Word: Ancient Israelite Literature. Susan Niditch. Ed. by Douglas A. Knight. LC 96-21497. (Library of Ancient Israel). 176p. 1996. 19.00 (*0-664-21946-2*) Westminster John Knox.

Oralite et Litterature-Orality & Literature: Actes du XIe Congres de L'Aaaociation Internationale de Litterature Comparee-Proceedings of the XIth Congress of the International Comparative Association. Ed. by Hans R. Runte & Roseann Runte. 260p. 1991. 39.80 (*0-8204-1372-0*) P Lang Pubng.

Orality & Literacy: The Technologizing of the World. Walter J. Ong. 212p. 1982. pap. 18.99 (*0-415-02796-9*, NO. 6526) Routledge.

Orality & Literacy in Hellenic Greece. Tony M. Lentz. LC 88-14152. 232p. (C). 1989. text 26.95 (*0-8093-1359-6*) S Ill U Pr.

Orality & Performance in Early French Romance. Evelyn Birge Vitz. LC 98-36154. 328p. 1998. 90.00 (*0-85991-538-7*, DS Brewer) Boydell & Brewer.

Orality, Literacy, & Modern Media. Ed. by Dietrich Scheunemann. (GERM Ser.). xiv, 212p. (C). 1996. 55.00 (*1-57113-032-2*) Camden Hse.

Orality, Literacy & the Fictive Imagination: African American & African Diasporan Literatures, Vol. 1. Tom Spencer-Walters. Ed. by Jacquelyn Brice-Finch. 350p. (Orig.). 1998. pap. 30.00 (*0-911557-16-4*) Bedford Publishers.

Oralpathologie I. 1996. 465.00 (*3-540-61036-7*) Spr-Verlag.

Orando con Cristo. Paul Y. Cho.Tr. of Praying with Jesus. (SPA.). 176p. 1990. pap. 6.99 (*0-8297-0389-6*) Vida Pubs.

Orando Con Jesus. David Y. Cho.Tr. of Praying with Jesus. (POR.). 116p. 1991. pap. 5.95 (*0-8297-1662-9*) Vida Pubs.

Orando la Oracion del Senor, el Padre Nuestro. E. Towns.Tr. of Praying the Lord's Prayer. write for info. (*0-7899-0450-0*, 495019) Editorial Unilit.

Orando los Unos por los Otros. W. Robert Bruce. (Serie Discipulo - Discipleship Ser.).Tr. of Praying for One Another. (SPA.). 1.79 (*1-56063-896-6*, 498250) Editorial Unilit.

Orando los Unos por los Otros - Praying for One Another. F. F. Bruce. (Serie Discipulado Ser.). (SPA.). 26p. 1996. write for info. (*0-614-24383-1*) Editorial Unilit.

Orando Para Lograr Resultados. Victor Ricardo. 32p. 1992. pap. 1.15 (*1-885630-20-4*) HLM Producciones.

Orando por las 100 Ciudades de Acceso. P. Wagner.Tr. of Praying Through the 100 Gateway Cities. (SPA.). 148p. 1995. 7.99 (*0-7899-0145-5*, 498627) Editorial Unilit.

Orando por los Hijos de los Misioneros. F. F. Bruce. (Serie Discipulado - Discipleship Ser.).Tr. of Praying for Missionary Kids. (SPA.). 20p. 1996. 1.99 (*1-56063-895-8*, 498249) Editorial Unilit.

***Orando por Usted.** Howard Tryon, Jr. (SPA.). 128p. 1999. pap. 6.99 (*0-8254-1774-0*, Edit Portavoz) Kregel.

***Orando Solos y Juntos.** Arthur R. Baranowski. Tr. by Jerry Frank. (Llamados a ser Iglesia Ser.). 120p. 2000. pap. 6.95 (*0-86716-403-4*) St Anthony Mess Pr.

***Orang Asli Now: The Orang Asli in the Malaysian Political World.** Roy D. Jumper. LC 99-23613. (Illus.). 224p. 1999. 48.00 (*0-7618-1441-8*) U Pr of Amer.

***Orang Utan's Playtime.** Laura Gates Galvin. (Let's Go to the Zoo! Ser.: Vol. 2). (Illus.). 16p. (J). 1999. bds. 5.95 (*1-56899-796-5*) Soundprints.

Orang Utan's Playtime: Including Toy. Laura Gates Galvin. (Let's Go to the Zoo! Ser.: Vol. 2). (Illus.). 16p. (J). 1999. bds. 9.95 (*1-56899-797-3*) Soundprints.

Oranga Wheanau: The Whanau Well-Being Project: The Ora Toa Health Unit & the Whaioranga Trust. LC 97-135889. 24 p. 1994. write for info. (*0-478-04331-7*, Pub. by Manaaki Whenua) Balogh.

Orange see Spectrum of English

Orange. Orange Historical Society Staff. (Images of America Ser.). (Illus.). 128p. 1998. pap. 16.99 (*0-7524-0892-5*) Arcadia Publng.

Orange. Mary E. Salzmann. LC 98-26681. (What Color Is It? Ser.). (Illus.). 24p. (J). 2000. lib. bdg. 18.50 (*1-57765-158-8*, SndCastle) ABDO Pub Co.

Orange: A Manual. Nico Vassilakis. (Illus.). 30p. (Orig.). 1997. pap. 7.00 (*0-945085-11-7*) Sub Rosa.

Orange: The City 'Round the Plaza. Phil Brigandi. Ed. by Lori Parks. LC 97-71127. (Illus.). 200p. 1997. 39.95 (*1-886483-11-6*) Heritge Media.

Orange & Lemons of India & Ceylon Text. E. Boniva. (C). 1988. text 750.00 (*0-89771-561-6*, Pub. by Intl Bk Distr) St Mut.

Orange Balloon. Penny Harter. (Xtras Ser.: No. 8). 36p. (Orig.). 1980. pap. 2.00 (*0-89120-012-6*) From Here.

Orange Blobs, Yellow Fluff & Green Spaghetti. Louise Harris. LC 94-65904. (Illus.). 37p. (Orig.). (J). 1994. pap. 9.95 (*0-9640674-0-4*) New World SC.

Orange Blossom Trails: Walks in the Natural Areas of Florida. Phillip Manning. LC 97-25696. (Afoot in the South Ser.). (Illus.). (Orig.). 1997. pap. 13.95 (*0-89587-201-3*) Blair.

***Orange Blossoms: 50 Years of Growth in Orange County.** Ed. by John Sorenson & Lori Parks. LC 99-76565. (Illus.). 300p. 2000. 49.95 (*1-886483-35-3*) Heritge Media.

Orange Book see Miquon Math Lab Series: Complete Home School

Orange Book. Richard McGuire. LC 94-15031. 1994. 10.19 (*0-606-06640-3*, Pub. by Turtleback) Demco.

An Asterisk (*) at the beginning of an entry indicates that the title is appearing for the first time.

***Orange Book: Learning Language Arts Through Literature.** 2nd ed. Debbie Strayer & Susan S. Simpson. (Learning Language Arts Through Literature Ser.). 244p. (J). (gr. 4). 1998. pap., teacher ed. 25.00 (*1-880892-84-7*) Com Sense FL.

Orange Cat Bistro. Nancy Linde. 192p. 1996. 18.95 (*1-57566-050-4*, Knsington) Kensgtn Pub Corp.

Orange Cat Bistro. Nancy Linde. 1997. pap. 5.50 (*1-57566-132-2*, Knsington); pap. 12.00 (*1-57566-151-9*, Knsington) Kensgtn Pub Corp.

Orange Cheeks. Jay O'Callahan. LC 92-43509. (Illus.). 40p. (J). (ps-3). 1983. 15.95 (*1-56145-073-1*) Peachtree Pubs.

***Orange Cookbook: 200 Citrus Recipes from Around the World.** Frank Thomas & Marlene Leopold. 176p. 2000. pap. 14.95 (*1-57416-056-7*) Clear Light.

Orange County. A. D. Skies. (Business Start-Up Quick Guide). 1997. pap. text 5.95 (*1-890998-05-2*) Mixed Bag.

Orange County: A Centennial Celebration. Doris Walker. 368p. 1989. 25.00 (*1-881547-08-6*) Pioneer Pubns.

Orange County: A Narrative History. Compiled by Almet S. Moffat. 87p. 1997. reprint ed. pap. 16.00 (*0-8328-6193-6*) Higginson Bk Co.

Orange County: A Photographic Collection. MaryAnn Hemphill. Ed. by Jane Freeburg. Tr. by Eliane LeBeck et al. LC 96-69862. (Pictorial Bks.). (ENG, FRE, GER, JPN & SPA., Illus.). 80p. 1996. 19.95 (*0-932653-22-7*) Sunbelt Pubns.

Orange County: Through an Artist's Eye. Ed. & Photos by Steven Simon. (Illus.). 112p. 1997. 34.95 (*0-9652771-1-9*) Simon Fine Art.

Orange County Adventures with Children: A Guide for Parents, Grandparents & Teachers. Doris I. Walker. LC 96-90634. (Illus.). 256p. 1997. pap. 12.95 (*0-9606476-7-8*) To-the-Point.

Orange County Annual Report, 1999. 4th ed. Ed. by Jennifer Knight. 1999. pap. 12.95 (*1-928646-04-2*) BenchMark Pubg OR.

Orange County Beaches. Randy Vogel. (Twelve Short Hikes Ser.). (Illus.). 32p. 1997. pap. 4.95 (*1-57540-102-9*) Falcon Pub Inc.

Orange County Business Directory 1999. 8th ed. 578p. 1999. pap. 75.00 (*1-57541-089-3*) Database Pub Co.

Orange County, California Retirement & Relocation Guide. large type ed. Dorris Walker. (Retirement & Relocation Guides Ser.). (Illus.). 350p. Date not set. pap. 24.95 (*1-56559-117-8*) HGI-Over Fifty.

Orange County Children's Directory. 100p. 1996. write for info. (*0-614-97109-8*) Riviera Pubns.

Orange County Children's Directory. Ed. by Elizabeth A. Nelson. 110p. 1989. pap. 4.95 (*1-877609-00-5*) Riviera Pubns.

Orange County Children's Directory. Riviera Publications Staff. Ed. by Elizabeth A. Nelson. 110p. 1990. pap. 4.95 (*1-877609-01-3*) Riviera Pubns.

Orange County Children's Directory, 1992. Elizabeth A. Nelson. 1991. pap. 4.95 (*1-877609-05-6*) Riviera Pubns.

***Orange County, 1889.** (Illus.). v, 40p. 2000. pap. 14.95 (*1-891030-14-0*) Paragon Agency.

***Orange County Entertainment, 2000.** (Illus.). 822p. 1999. pap. 48.00 (*1-880248-56-5*, 0014) Enter Pubns.

Orange County Experience. 2nd ed. Diane E. Rulien et al. (Orange County Centennial Edition Ser.). (Illus.). 250p. 1989. pap. text 27.95 (*0-932967-13-2*) Pacific Shoreline.

Orange County Experience: A Pictorial History of Orange County California. Diane E. Rulien & Gary Cardinale. (Illus.). 228p. 1987. pap. 23.95 (*0-932967-07-8*) Pacific Shoreline.

Orange County Explore Map AAA. Auto Club, Southern California Editors Staff. (Illus.). 1997. pap. 3.95 (*1-56413-397-4*) Auto Club.

Orange County Genealogical Society Quarterlies with Indices, Set. 1986. pap. text 65.00 (*0-937135-14-3*) Orange County Genealog.

Orange County Genealogical Society Quarterlies with Indices, Set, Vols. 1-10. 1986. pap. text 40.00 (*0-937135-13-5*) Orange County Genealog.

Orange County Genealogical Society Quarterly, Vols. 1-14. 1986. pap. text 1.00 (*0-937135-11-9*) Orange County Genealog.

Orange County Genealogical Society Quarterly Index, Vol. 15. 1986. pap. text 2.00 (*0-937135-10-0*) Orange County Genealog.

Orange County Hills, Vol. 1. Randy Vogel. (Twelve Short Hikes Ser.). (Illus.). 32p. 1997. pap. 4.95 (*1-57540-100-2*) Falcon Pub Inc.

Orange County Hills, Vol. 2. Randy Vogel. (Twelve Short Hikes Ser.). (Illus.). 32p. 1997. pap. 4.95 (*1-57540-101-0*) Falcon Pub Inc.

Orange County Marriages, 1747-1850. 2nd rev. ed. John Vogt & T. William Kethley, Jr. 410p. 1991. pap. 20.00 (*0-935931-61-9*) Iberian Pub.

Orange County New York Atlas. Orange County Genealogical Society Staff et al. 85p. (Orig.). 1984. reprint ed. lib. bdg. 30.00 (*0-9604116-7-4*) Orange County Genealog.

Orange County, North Carolina Taxpayers, 1784-1793. T.L.C. Genealogy Staff. LC 91-65575. 97p. (Orig.). 1991. pap., spiral bd. 12.00 (*1-886633-32-0*) TLC Genealogy.

Orange County Quarterlies with Indices, Set, Vols. 1-12. 1986. pap. text 45.00 (*0-937135-15-1*, 86-39) Orange County Genealog.

Orange County Scene: A Look at Orange County: Colorful Past. Michael C. Kilroy. LC 96-90911. (Illus.). 100p. (Orig.). 1997. pap. 15.95 (*0-9655832-0-1*) MacPherson.

Orange County Sheriff's Office (1845-1995) Turner Publishing Company Staff. LC 94-61702. (Illus.). 144p. 1994. 39.95 (*1-56311-160-8*) Turner Pub KY.

Orange County Street Guide & Directory: 1999 Edition. Thomas Bros. Maps Staff. (Illus.). 144p. 1998. pap. 16.95 (*1-58174-031-X*) Thomas Bros Maps.

***Orange County Street Guide & Directory: 2000 Edition.** (Illus.). 144p. 1999. pap. 16.95 (*1-58174-137-5*) Thomas Bros Maps.

Orange County Street Guide & Directory ZIP Code Edition: 1999 Edition. Thomas Bros. Maps Staff. (Illus.). 146p. 1998. pap. 23.95 (*1-58174-032-8*) Thomas Bros Maps.

***Orange County Street Guide & Directory Zip Code Edition: 2000 Edition.** (Illus.). 144p. 1999. pap. 23.95 (*1-58174-138-3*) Thomas Bros Maps.

***Orange County 2000.** Ed. by Don McCormack. (Illus.). 1999. pap. 13.95 (*1-929365-04-7*, Pub. by McCormacks Guides) Bookpeople.

***Orange County 2000 - The Millennium Book.** unabridged ed. Pat Mott. (Illus.). 256p. 1999. 49.95 (*0-9670270-0-4*, Pub. by Orange Coast Kom) Sunbelt Pubns.

Orange County, Virginia, Court Orders, 1734-1741: An Every-Name Index. T.L.C. Genealogy Staff. 116p. 1994. pap., spiral bd. 20.00 (*1-886633-97-5*) TLC Genealogy.

Orange County, Virginia, Marriages, 1747-1818. Catherine L. Knorr. 132p. 1982. reprint ed. 17.50 (*0-89308-252-X*, VA 15) Southern Hist Pr.

Orange County, Virginia Marriages, 1747-1850. John Vogt & T. William Kethley, Jr. (Illus.). 320 p. 1991. pap. 20.00 (*0-935931-10-4*) Iberian Pub.

Orange County, Virginia, Order Book One 1734-1739, Pt. 1. Barbara V. Little. 114p. (Orig.). 1990. pap. 15.00 (*0-9624041-2-8*) Dominion Market.

Orange County, Virginia, Tithables, 1734-1782. rev. ed. Barbara V. Little. 281p. (Orig.). 1990. pap. text 29.50 (*0-9624041-1-X*) Dominion Market.

Orange Cum, Techno-Stress, American Sex. Jessica Flemming & Bill Tyson. LC 93-85263. (Illus.). 160p. (Orig.). 1993. pap. 12.95 (*1-883445-02-7*) Plain Brown.

Orange Fairy Book. Ed. by Andrew Lang. 26.95 (*0-89190-083-7*) Amereon Ltd.

Orange Fairy Book. Ed. by Andrew Lang. (Illus.). 358p. (J). (gr. 1-6). 1968. pap. 7.95 (*0-486-21909-7*) Dover.

Orange Fairy Book. Ed. by Andrew Lang. (Illus.). (J). (gr. 4-12). 1990. 22.00 (*0-8446-4770-5*) Peter Smith.

Orange Fish. Carol Shields. 208p. 1992. pap. 11.95 (*0-14-015282-2*, Penguin Bks) Viking Penguin.

Orange Fragrantis Encyclopaedia. Scentouri Staff. 1985. ring bd. 27.95 (*0-318-03764-5*) Prosperity & Profits.

Orange Grove & Other Stories: Reading Level 2. 1993. audio 17.95 (*0-88336-561-8*) New Readers.

Orange Grove & Other Stories: Reading Level 2. Rosanne Keller. 1993. 7.95 (*0-88336-558-8*) New Readers.

***Orange Illustrated: And Described.** (Illus.). vii, 75p. 2000. pap. 15.95 (*1-891030-13-2*) Paragon Agency.

***Orange in My World.** Joanne Winne. (Welcome Bks.). (Illus.). (J). 2000. 13.50 (*0-516-23125-1*) Childrens.

***Orange in My World.** Joanne Winne. LC 00-24381. (World of Color Ser.). (Illus.). 24p. (J). (ps-2). 2000. pap. write for info. (*0-516-23050-6*) Childrens.

Orange in the Orange: A Novella & Two Stories. Fielding Dawson. LC 94-45314. 172p. (C). 1994. 25.00 (*0-87685-963-5*); pap. 13.50 (*0-87685-962-7*) Black Sparrow.

Orange Juice. Betsey Chessen & Pamela Chanko. LC 97-34206. (Science Emergent Readers Ser.). (Illus.). (J). (ps-3). 1997. pap. 2.50 (*0-590-14999-7*) Scholastic Inc.

***Orange Laughter.** Leone Ross. 240p. 2000. 23.00 (*0-374-22676-8*) FS&G.

Orange Messiahs. Scott A. Sonders. 168p. 1999. pap. 14.95 (*0-912159-06-5*) Center Pr CA.

Orange Mofit: Journal. Sterling. 1994. 6.95 (*1-897954-11-5*) M Q Pubns.

***Orange Parades: The Politics of Ritual, Tradition & Control.** Dominic Bryan. (Anthropology, Culture & Society Ser.). 2000. pap. 22.50 (*0-7453-1413-9*) Pluto GBR.

***Orange Parades: The Politics of Ritual, Tradition & Control.** Dominic Bryan. LC 00-8816. (Anthropology, Culture & Society Ser.). 2000. write for info. (*0-7453-1418-X*, Pub. by Pluto GBR) Stylus Pub VA.

***Orange Pony.** Wendy Douthwaite. (J). 2000. mass mkt. 4.99 (*0-330-33631-2*) Mcm Child Bks.

***Orange Pulp: Stories of Mayhem, Murder, & Mystery.** Ed. by Maurice J. O'Sullivan & Steve Glassman. 2000. 24.95 (*0-8130-1803-X*) U Press Fla.

Orange Riots: Irish Political Violence in New York City, 1870 & 1871. Michael A. Gordon. LC 93-9847. (Illus.). 280p. (C). 1993. text 39.95 (*0-8014-2754-1*) Cornell U Pr.

***Orange Student Activity Book: Learning Language Arts Through Literature.** 2nd rev. ed. Debbie Strayer & Susan S. Simpson. (Learning Language Arts Through Literature Ser.). 253p. (J). 1998. pap. 20.00 (*1-880892-19-7*) Com Sense FL.

Orange Teasers: A Compilation of Puzzles for Vol Fans. John Stephens. (Illus.). 68p. 1997. pap. 9.95 (*1-882194-30-6*) TN Valley Pub.

Orange Tree. Carlos Fuentes. Tr. by Alfred MacAdam. LC 93-33608. (SPA.). 256p. 1994. 21.00 (*0-374-22683-0*) FS&G.

Orange Uses: Uses for the Orange. rev. ed. Recycling Consortium Staff. 1992. ring bd. 19.95 (*0-317-04796-5*) Prosperity & Profits.

Orange You Glad? Parent. (Captain Kangaroo Ser.). 32p. (J). (gr. k-1). 2000. pap. 3.99 (*0-06-107157-9*, HarpEntertain) Morrow Avon.

Orangeburg Massacre. rev. ed. Jack Bass & Jack Nelson. LC 84-9092. xviii, 248p. 1996. pap. 17.95 (*0-86554-552-9*) Mercer Univ Pr.

Orangeism: The Canadian Phase. Frontenac Library Cataloging Department Staff. Ed. by William King, Jr. 1976. text. write for info. (*0-07-092998-X*) McGraw.

Orange/Los Angeles Counties Street Guide & Directory: 1999 Edition. Thomas Bros. Maps Staff. (Illus.). 480p. 1998. pap. 29.95 (*1-58174-034-4*) Thomas Bros Maps.

***Orange/Los Angeles Counties Street Guide & Directory: 2000 Edition.** (Illus.). 480p. 1999. pap. 29.95 (*1-58174-139-1*) Thomas Bros Maps.

Orangerien in Westfalen. Claudia S. Linten. (Europaische Hochschulschriften Ser.: Reihe 28, Vol. 327). (Illus.). 382p. 1998. pap. 56.95 (*3-631-33087-1*) P Lang Pubng.

Orangeries. Michel Saudan. LC 98-173781. (Evergreens Ser.). 1998. 29.99 (*3-8228-7765-4*) Taschen Amer.

Orangery. Gilbert Sorrentino. (Sun & Moon Classics Ser.: No. 91). 104p. 1995. pap. 10.95 (*1-55713-225-9*) Sun & Moon CA.

Oranges. Jason Cooper. LC 97-13232. (Farm to Market Discovery Library). 24p. (J). (gr. k-4). 1997. lib. bdg. 15.93 (*0-86625-621-0*) Rourke Pubns.

Oranges. Claire Llewellyn. LC 99-28942. (What's for Lunch? Ser.). 32p. (J). (gr. k-2). 1999. 20.50 (*0-516-21548-5*) Childrens.

Oranges. John McPhee. LC 66-20125. 149p. 1967. 20.00 (*0-374-22688-1*) FS&G.

Oranges. John McPhee. LC 66-20125. 152p. 1975. pap. 10.00 (*0-374-51297-3*) FS&G.

Oranges Are Not the Only Fruit. Jeanette Winterson. 192p. 1997. pap. 12.00 (*0-8021-3516-1*, Grove) Grove-Atltic.

Oranges de Sang. John Hawkes. (FRE.). 370p. 1976. pap. 11.95 (*0-7859-2377-2*, 2070368459) Fr & Eur.

Oranges for Health - California for Wealth: The Billion-Dollar Navel & the California Dream. Vincent Moses. (Illus.). vii, 34p. (Orig.). 1992. pap. 6.00 (*0-9603586-1-7*) Chaffey Commun Cult Ctr.

Oranges for Orange Juice, Vol. 3912. Rozanne L. Williams. (Social Studies Learn to Read Ser.). (Illus.). 8p. (J). (ps-2). 1996. pap. 1.75 (*1-57471-131-8*, 3912) Creat Teach Pr.

Oranges for Orange Juice, Vol. 3970. Rozanne L. Williams. (Social Studies Big Bks.). (Illus.). 8p. (J). (ps-2). 1997. pap. 8.98 (*1-57471-177-6*, 3969) Creat Teach Pr.

Oranges for the Son of Alexander Levy. Nella Bielski. 133p. 1981. 11.95 (*0-906495-70-9*) Writers & Readers.

Oranges from Santo Domingo: Selected Poems, 1950-1990. Guy B. Stiles. (Poetry Ser.). 71p. (Orig.). 1991. pap. text 10.00 (*0-916611-04-3*) Antilles Pr.

Oranges in Eastern Mexico: An Economic Analysis of Production & Marketing Channels. Juan P. Mondragon et al. LC 97-43526. (Illus.). 129p. 1998. pap. 30.00 (*0-944961-04-5*) FL Sci Source.

***Oranges on Golden Mountain.** Elizabeth Partridge. LC 99-462287. (Illus.). (J). 2000. write for info. (*0-525-46453-0*, Dutton Child) Peng Put Young Read.

Orangi Pilot Project: Reminiscences & Reflections. Akhtar H. Khan. (Illus.). 198p. 1997. text 24.95 (*0-19-577689-5*) OUP.

Orangutan. Ruth Ashby. (Illus.). 60p. (J). (gr. 4-7). 1996. pap. text 5.95 (*0-382-39484-4*) Silver Burdett Pr.

Orangutan. Ruth Ashby. LC 93-5754. (Remarkable Animals Ser.). (Illus.). 60p. (YA). (gr. 5 up). 1994. lib. bdg. 13.95 (*0-87518-600-9*) Silver Burdett Pr.

***Orangutan.** Stephen Brend. (Natural World Ser.). (Illus.). (J). 2000. 9.95 (*0-7398-3126-7*) Raintree Steck-V.

***Orangutan.** Stuart P. Levine. LC 99-37697. (Overview Ser.). (Illus.). 128p. (YA). (gr. 6-9). 2000. lib. bdg. 23.70 (*1-56006-560-5*) Lucent Bks.

***Orangutan: Habitats, Life Cycles, Food Chains, Threats.** Stephen Brend. LC 00-27459. (Natural World Ser.). (Illus.). (J). 2000. 27.12 (*0-7398-2765-0*) Raintree Steck-V.

Orangutan Biology. Ed. by Jeffrey H. Schwartz. (Illus.). 400p. 1988. text 110.00 (*0-19-504371-5*) OUP.

***Orangutan Odyssey.** Birute M. Galdikas & Nancy E. Briggs. LC 99-25446. (Illus.). 144p. 1999. 39.95 (*0-8109-3694-1*, Pub. by Abrams) Time Warner.

Orangutan 1b4. Bill Wall. 90p. (Orig.). 1989. pap. 6.00 (*0-931462-92-4*) Chess Ent.

Orangutans see Zoobooks

Orangutans. M. C. Helldorfer. LC 98-67961. (Animal Safari Ser.). (Illus.). 10p. (J). (ps-k). 1999. bds. 5.95 (*0-7922-7106-8*, Pub. by Natl Geog) Publishers Group.

***Orangutans.** Gisela Kaplan & Lesley J. Rogers. (Illus.). 192p. 2000. text 23.00 (*0-7382-0290-8*) Perseus Pubng.

Orangutans Patricia A. Martin. LC 99-17065. (Illus.). 48p. (gr. 3-5). 2000. 21.50 (*0-516-21571-X*) Childrens.

***Orangutans.** Patricia A. Fink Martin. (True Bks.). (Illus.). 48p. (J). (gr. 3-5). 2000. pap. 6.95 (*0-516-27020-6*) Childrens.

Orangutans. Lynn M. Stone. (Monkey Discovery Library). (Illus.). 24p. (J). (gr. k-5). 1990. lib. bdg. 10.95 (*0-86593-065-1*); lib. bdg. 8.95 (*0-685-36319-8*) Rourke Corp.

Orangutans. Wildlife Education, Ltd. Staff. (Zoobooks Ser.). (Illus.). 20p. (YA). (gr. 5 up). 1996. pap. 2.75 (*0-937934-02-X*) Wildlife Educ.

Orangutans. Wildlife Education, Ltd. Staff & John B. Wexo. (Zoobooks Ser.). (Illus.). 24p. (J). (gr. 5 up). 1993. 13.95 (*0-937934-83-6*) Wildlife Educ.

Orangutans. Mae Woods. LC 96-313. (J). 1997. lib. bdg. 13.95 (*1-56239-600-5*) ABDO Pub Co.

***Orangutans: Wizards of the Rain Forest.** Anne E. Russon. LC QL737.P96R87 1999. (Illus.). 224p. 2000. 29.95 (*1-55209-453-7*) Firefly Bks Ltd.

Oranizational Behav Lect Guide. Miles. 1998. pap. 12.50 (*0-07-234134-3*) McGraw.

Oranizational Learning Pt. II: Theory Method & Practice. 2nd ed. Argyris Schon. Ed. by Michael Payne. 305p. (C). 1995. pap. text 40.00 (*0-201-62983-6*) Addison-Wesley.

Oran's Dictionary of the Law. 2nd ed. Daniel Oran. 500p. (C). 1991. mass mkt. 24.75 (*0-314-84690-5*) West Pub.

Orar. Mother Teresa of Calcutta. 1999. pap. text 9.95 (*84-08-02841-3*) Planeta.

***Orar.** Juan Pablo, II. 1999. 19.95 (*84-08-02482-5*) Planeta Edit.

Orary Authors. rev. ed. Dear. (Contemporary Authors Revised Ser.: Vol. 49). 1995. 140.00 (*0-8103-9340-9*) Gale.

O'Rathaille. Michael Hartnett. LC 99-181617. 80p. 1997. 24.95 (*1-85235-210-8*, Pub. by Gallery Pr); pap. 14.95 (*1-85235-209-4*, Pub. by Gallery Pr) Dufour.

***Oratio: Mittelalterliche Redekunst in lateinischer Sprache.** Thomas Haye. (Mittellateinische Studien und Texte Ser.: 27). 240p. 1999. text 145.00 (*90-04-11335-5*) Brill Academic Pubs.

Oratio Catechetica: Opera Dogmatica Minora, Pars 4. Gregorius Nyssenus. Ed. by E. Muhlenberg. (Gregorii Nysseni Opera Ser.: Nos. 3 & 4). (GRE.). 216p. 1996. 73.00 (*90-04-10348-1*) Brill Academic Pubs.

***Oratio Obliqua, Oratio Recta: An Essay on Metarepresentation.** Francois Recanati. (Representation & Mind Ser.). (Illus.). 450p. (C). 2000. pap. 24.95 (*0-262-68116-1*, Bradford Bks) MIT Pr.

Oration: All Power Resides in the People. 2nd ed. Hugh B. Grigsby. Ed. by Calvert W. Tazewell. LC 91-76376. (Illus.). 77p. 1992. reprint ed. pap. 9.00 (*1-878515-89-6*) W S Dawson.

Oration on the Dignity of Man. Giovanni Pico Della Mirandola. Tr. by A. Robert Caponigri. 72p. 1996. pap. 8.95 (*0-89526-713-6*, Gateway Editions) Regnery Pub.

Oration upon the Most Recent Death of Christopher Columbus. Robert Viscusi. (VIA Folios Ser.: Vol. 1). 20p. 1993. pap. 4.00 (*1-884419-00-3*) Bordighera.

Orationes, 3 vols. in 4 pts. Incl. Vol. 1. Nos. 1-19. Ed. by S. H. Butcher. 422p. 1922. text 39.95 (*0-19-814518-7*); Vol. 3. Nos. 41-60. Ed. by S. H. Butcher. 541p. 1931. text 35.00 (*0-19-814521-7*); Vol. 2, Pt. 2. Nos. 27-40. Ed. by W. Rennie. 214p. 1988. text 39.95 (*0-19-814520-9*); Vol. 2, Pt. 1. Nos. 20-26. Ed. by S. H. Butcher. 370p. 1985. text 39.95 (*0-19-814519-5*); (Oxford Classical Texts Ser.). write for info. (*0-318-54868-2*) OUP.

Orationes, 6 vols. Incl. Vol. 1. Pro Sex. Roscio, De Imperio, Cn. Pompei, Pro Cluentio, in Catilinam, Pro Murena, Pro Caelio. Ed. by A. C. Clark. 350p. 1922. text 32.00 (*0-19-814605-1*); Vol. 2. Pro Milone, Pro Marcello, Pro Ligario, Pro Rege Deiotaro, Philip Picae, 1-14. 2nd ed. Ed. by A. C. Clark. 356p. 1922. text 35.00 (*0-19-814606-X*); Vol. 3. Divinatio in Q. Caecilium, in C. Verrem. 2nd ed. Ed. by William Peterson. 486p. 1922. text 42.00 (*0-19-814607-8*); Vol. 4. Pro P. Quincto, Pro Q. Roscio Comoedo, Pro A. Caecina, De Lege Agraria Contra Rullum, Pro C. Rabirio Perduellionis Reo, Pro L. Flacco, In L. Pisonem, Pro C. Rabirio Postumo. Ed. by A. C. Clark. 341p. 1922. text 29.95 (*0-19-814608-6*); Vol. 5. Cum Senatui Gratias Egit, Cum Populo Gratias Egit, De Domo Sua, De Haruspicum Responso, Pro Sestio, in Vatinium, De Provinciis Consularibus, Pro Balbo. Ed. by William Peterson. 308p. 1922. text 29.95 (*0-19-814609-4*); Vol. 6. Pro Tullio, Pro Fonteio, Pro Sulla, Pro Archia, Pro Plancio. Pro Scauro. A. C. Clark. 190p. 1922. text 29.95 (*0-19-814610-8*); (Oxford Classical Texts Ser.). write for info. (*0-318-54867-4*) OUP.

Orationes. Lysias. Ed. by Karl Hude. (Oxford Classical Texts Ser.). (GRE.). 290p. 1979. reprint ed. text 29.95 (*0-19-814538-1*) OUP.

Orationes Homeri des Leonardo Bruni Aretino: Kritische Edition der Lateinischen und Kastilianischen Uberstzung Mit Prolegomena und Kommentar. Peter Thiermann. LC 93-27164. (Mnemosyne Ser.: Supplement 126). (GER.). viii, 251p. 1993. 107.00 (*90-04-09719-8*) Brill Academic Pubs.

Orationes (XXXIV) Ex Codice Mediolanensi (Ed. Aug. Maio) Themistius. xvi, 756p. 1974. reprint ed. write for info. (*3-487-05402-7*) G Olms Pubs.

Orations. Isaeus. (Loeb Classical Library: No. 202). 506p. 1927. 19.95 (*0-674-99222-9*) HUP.

Orations. Lysias. (Loeb Classical Library: No. 244). 734p. 1930. 19.95 (*0-674-99269-5*) HUP.

Orations, 3 vols., 1. Tr. by George Norlin. (Loeb Classical Library: No. 209, 229, 373). 466p. 1928. 18.95 (*0-674-99231-8*) HUP.

Orations, 3 vols., 2. Isocrates. (Loeb Classical Library: No. 209, 229, 373). 550p. 1929. 19.95 (*0-674-99252-0*) HUP.

Orations, 3 vols., 3. Tr. by La Rue Van Hook. (Loeb Classical Library: No. 209, 229, 373). 534p. 1945. 18.95 (*0-674-99411-6*) HUP.

Orations & Addresses. Harriot Curtis. (Works of Harriot Curtis). 1990. reprint ed. lib. bdg. 79.00 (*0-685-44764-2*) Rprt Serv.

Orations & Speeches, on Various Occasions. Edward Everett. LC 72-4963. (Romantic Tradition in American Literature Ser.). 642p. 1980. reprint ed. 47.95 (*0-405-04634-0*) Ayer.

Orations of American Orators, 2 vols. rev. ed. Intro. by Julian Hawthorne. 1997. reprint ed. 195.00 (*1-56169-306-5*) Gaunt.

Orations of Arsanes Agaynst Philip: Of the Embassadors of Venice. Arsanes. LC 70-26068. (English Experience Ser.: No. 233). 164p. 1970. reprint ed. 20.00 (*90-221-0233-5*) Walter J Johnson.

Orations of Demosthenes, 2 vols., Set. Demosthenes. Ed. by C. R. Kennedy. 1977. lib. bdg. 250.00 (*0-8490-2378-5*) Gordon Pr.

Orations of Mohammad. Sam L. Pool. 1994. pap. 3.50 (*1-56744-175-0*) Kazi Pubns.

Orations of Muhhamad, the Prophet of Islam. M. M. Akbar. 106p. 1991. 8.50 (*81-7151-047-7*) Asia Bk Corp.

Orations on the Freedom of the Press. Theophilus Fisk. LC 73-125692. (American Journalists Ser.). 1971. reprint ed. 17.95 (*0-405-01669-7*) Ayer.

Orations VIII, XII & XXXVI. Dio Chrysostomus. Ed. by D. A. Russell. (Greek & Latin Classics - Imperial Library). 274p. (C). 1992. text 65.00 (*0-521-37548-7*); pap. text 24.95 (*0-521-37696-3*) Cambridge U Pr.

Orator. Marcus Tullius Cicero. Ed. by Wilhelm Kroll. vii, 228p. 1971. 55.00 (*3-296-11600-1*) G Olms Pubs.

Orator Hunt: Henry Hunt & English Working-Class Radicalism. John Belchem. 320p. 1985. 59.00 (*0-19-822759-0*) OUP.

Oratores Attici. 531p. 1968. reprint ed. 120.00 (*0-318-70991-0*) G Olms Pubs.

Oratorical Culture in Nineteenth-Century America: Transformations in the Theory & Practice of Rhetoric. Ed. by Gregory Clark & S. Michael Halloran. LC 92-42230. (Illus.). 304p. (C). 1993. 36.95 (*0-8093-1739-7*) S Ill U Pr.

Oratorical Encounters: Selected Studies & Sources of Twentieth-Century Political Accusations & Apologies, 9. Ed. by Halford R. Ryan. LC 87-23662. (Contributions to the Study of Mass Media & Communications Ser.: No. 9). 354p. 1988. 69.50 (*0-313-25568-7*, ROR/) Greenwood.

Oratorio ad Graecos & Fragments. Tatian. Ed. & Tr. by Molly Whittaker. (Oxford Early Christian Texts Ser.). 118p. 1982. text 34.50 (*0-19-826809-2*) OUP.

Oratorio Anthology: Alto Mezzo Soprano. 232p. 1994. per. 18.95 (*0-7935-2506-3*, 00747059) H Leonard.

Oratorio Anthology: Baritone Bass. 272p. 1994. per. 18.95 (*0-7935-2508-X*, 00747061) H Leonard.

Oratorio Anthology: Soprano. 224p. 1994. per. 19.95 (*0-7935-2505-5*, 00747058) H Leonard.

Oratorio Anthology: Tenor. 216p. 1994. per. 19.95 (*0-7935-2507-1*, 00747060) H Leonard.

***Oratorio in Bologna 1650-1730.** Victor Crowther. LC 98-33456. (Oxford Monographs on Music). (Illus.). 208p. 2000. text 74.00 (*0-19-816635-4*) OUP.

Oratorio in Venice. Denis Arnold & Elsie Arnold. (Royal Musical Association Monographs: Vol. 2). 118p. 1993. 24.95 (*0-947854-01-0*) U Ch Pr.

Oratorios of Handel: Music Book Index. Percy M. Young. 244p. 1993. reprint ed. lib. bdg. 79.00 (*0-7812-9717-6*) Rprt Serv.

Orators: An English Study. W. H. Auden. reprint ed. lib. bdg. 39.00 (*0-7812-0289-2*) Rprt Serv.

Orators: An English Study. W. H. Auden. LC 77-131613. 116p. 1932. reprint ed. 39.00 (*0-403-00500-0*) Scholarly.

Orators & Philosophers. Bruce A. Kimball. (C). 1995. pap. 14.00 (*0-87447-514-7*) H Holt & Co.

Orator's Manual: A Practical & Philosophical Treatise on Vocal Culture, Emphasis & Gesture. rev. ed. George L. Raymond. LC 72-434. (Granger Index Reprint Ser.). 1977. reprint ed. 23.95 (*0-8369-6368-7*) Ayer.

Orators of the American Revolution. 2nd ed. E. L. Magoon. 456p. 1993. reprint ed. 47.50 (*0-8377-2442-2*, Rothman) W S Hein.

Oratorum et Rhetorum Sententiae, Divisiones, Colores (Scripta Quae Manserunt: L. Annaei Senecae) Lucius Annaeus Seneca. Ed. by H. J. Muller. xliv, 628p. 1990. reprint ed. write for info. (*3-487-09348-0*) G Olms Pubs.

Oratory. Bob Jones, Jr. (Illus.). iv, 70p. (Orig.). (YA). (gr. 7-12). 1992. pap. text 17.00 (*1-889510-16-5*) Chmpionship Debate.

Oratory & Rhetoric in the Nineteenth-Century South: A Rhetoric of Defense. W. Stuart Towns. LC 98-13544. 232p. 1998. 59.95 (*0-275-96223-7*, Praeger Pubs) Greenwood.

***Oratory & Rhetoric in the Nineteenth-Century South: A Rhetoric of Defense.** W. Stuart Towns. LC 98-13544. 232p. 2000. pap. 24.95 (*0-275-96969-X*, Praeger Pubs) Greenwood.

Oratory in the New South. fac. ed. Ed. by Waldo W. Braden. LC 78-25909. 296p. 1979. reprint ed. pap. 91.80 (*0-7837-7937-2*, 204769300008) Bks Demand.

Oratory of Negro Leaders, 1900-1968, 1. Marcus H. Boulware. LC 72-90794. 312p. 1970. 65.00 (*0-8371-1849-2*, BOO&, Greenwood Pr) Greenwood.

Orature in African Literature Today. Ed. by Eldred D. Jones et al. LC 70-2505. (African Literature Today Ser.: Vol. 18). 200p. (C). 1992. 45.00 (*0-86543-350-X*); pap. 14.95 (*0-86543-351-8*) Africa World.

Orayvi Revisited: Social Stratification in an "Egalitarian" Society. Jerrold E. Levy & Barbara Pepper. (Resident Scholar Ser.). (Illus.). 216p. 1992. 35.00 (*0-933452-33-0*) Schol Am Res.

Orazio Gentileschi & the Poetic Tradition in Caravaggesque Painting. R. Ward Bissell. LC 80-11452. (Illus.). 404p. 1982. 75.00 (*0-271-00263-8*) Pa St U Pr.

Orban's Oral Histology & Embryology. 11th ed. Bhaskar. (Illus.). 512p. (C). (gr. 13). 1990. text 61.95 (*0-8016-0239-4*, 00239) Mosby Inc.

ORBE. Jorge L. Morales. (Poetry Ser.). 160p. 1992. 50.00 (*0-317-05418-X*); pap. 40.00 (*0-317-05419-8*) Instit Nacional.

***Orbe Indiano.** David A. Brading. 770p. 1999. 21.99 (*968-16-3657-0*) Fondo CA.

Orbis 100. 100th ed. Ed. by Mike Shields. 1996. pap. 12.95 (*0-9529013-0-7*) Intl Spec Bk.

Orbis Pictus (1887) John A. Comenius. 236p. 1999. reprint ed. pap. 24.95 (*0-7661-0825-2*) Kessinger Pub.

Orbit: NASA Astronauts Photograph the Earth. National Geographic Society Staff. LC 96-24428. 1996. write for info. (*0-7922-3715-3*) Natl Geog.

Orbit: NASA Astronauts Photograph the Earth. National Geographic Society Staff. (Illus.). 224p. 1996. 40.00 (*0-7922-3714-5*) Natl Geog.

Orbit & Sellar Region: Microsurgical Anatomy & Operative Approaches. Albert L. Rhoton, Jr. & Yoshihiro Natori. (Illus.). 380p. 1996. text 189.00 (*0-86577-531-1*) Thieme Med Pubs.

Orbit & the Visual Pathway: Anatomical & Pathological Aspects & Detailed Clinical Accounts. Ed. by Dieter Voth & Paul Glees. ix, 367p. (C). 1994. pap. text 190.80 (*3-11-012803-9*) De Gruyter.

Orbit Correction & Analysis in Circular Accelerators. L. V. Luccio. Ed. by J. A. Niederer et al. (AIP Conference Proceedings Ser.: No. 315). 200p. 1994. text 95.00 (*1-56396-373-6*) Am Inst Physics.

Orbit Determination & Analysis. J. M. Dow. (Advances in Space Research Ser.: Vol. 19). 108.00 (*0-08-043288-3*, Pergamon Pr) Elsevier.

Orbit Determination & Analysis: Proceedings of the PSD Meeting of the COSPAR Technical Panel on Satellite Dynamics Which Was Held During the 30th COSPAR Scientific Assembly, Hamburg, Germany, 11-21 July, 1994. Ed. by J. B. Zielinski. (Advances in Space Research Ser.: Vol. 16). 156p. 1995. pap. 97.75 (*0-08-042637-9*, Pergamon Pr) Elsevier.

Orbit, Eyelids, & Lacrimal System, Sect. 9. (Basic & Clinical Science Course (1989-90) Ser.). 252p. (C). 1989. pap. text 45.00 (*0-685-26053-4*) Am Acad Ophthal.

Orbit Method in Representation Theory. Ed. by M. Duflo et al. (Progress in Mathematics Ser.: No. 82). 225p. 1990. 60.50 (*0-8176-3474-6*) Birkhauser.

Orbit Theory. Applied Mathematics Symposium Staff. Ed. by Garrett D. Birkhoff & R. E. Langer. LC 50-1183. (Proceedings of Symposia in Applied Mathematics Ser.). 195p. 1959. text 35.00 (*0-8218-1309-9*, PSAPM/9) Am Math.

Orbit Wipeout! Tony Abbott. (J). 1995. mass mkt. 4.75 (*0-553-54235-4*) BDD Bks Young Read.

Orbital Debris: A Technical Assessment. National Research Council Staff. 224p. (C). 1995. text 39.95 (*0-309-05125-8*) Natl Acad Pr.

Orbital Debris from Upper-Stage Breakup. Ed. by Joseph P. Loftus, Jr. (PAAS Ser.: Vol. 121). 227p. 1989. 65.95 (*0-930403-58-4*, V-121) AIAA.

Orbital Disease: Imaging & Analysis. Daniel S. Casper et al. LC 92-49784. (Illus.). 1992. 142.00 (*0-86577-430-7*) Thieme Med Pubs.

Orbital Disorders. Ed. by G. M. Bleeker et al. (Illus.). 1978. text 268.50 (*90-6193-570-9*) Kluwer Academic.

Orbital Disorders: Proceedings of the International Symposium, 2nd, Amsterdam, May, 1973. International Symposium on Orbital Disorders Staff. Ed. by G. M. Bleeker et al. (Modern Problems in Ophthalmology Ser.: Vol. 14). 300p. 1975. 213.25 (*3-8055-2051-4*) S Karger.

Orbital Express Project of Bristol Aerospace & Microsat Launch Systems, Inc. Geoffrey V. Hughes. LC 96-52648. 84p. 1997. pap. 30.00 (*1-56347-192-2*) AIAA.

Orbital Forcing Timescales & Cyclostratigraphy. Ed. by M. R. House & A. S. Gale. (Geological Society Special Publication Ser.: No. 85). (Illus.). 204p. 1995. 100.00 (*1-897799-23-3*, 250, Pub. by Geol Soc Pub Hse) AAPG.

Orbital Fractures: Diagnosis, Operative Treatment, Secondary Corrections. B. Hammer. (Illus.). 112p. 1995. text 112.00 (*0-88937-139-3*) Hogrefe & Huber Pubs.

Orbital Hodograph Analysis. Ed. by Samuel P. Altman. (Science & Technology Ser.: Vol. 3). 150p. 1965. 20.00 (*0-87703-031-6*, Am Astronaut Soc) Univelt Inc.

Orbital Interaction Theory of Organic Chemistry. Arvi Rauk. 336p. 1994. 82.50 (*0-471-59389-3*) Wiley.

Orbital Interactions in Chemistry. Thomas A. Albright et al. LC 84-15310. 464p. 1985. 99.95 (*0-471-87393-4*) Wiley.

Orbital International Laboratory, 3rd & 4th IAF/OIL Symposia, Oct. 5-6, 1970, Constance, Germany, Sept. 24-25, 1971, Brussels, Belgium: 3rd & 4th IAF/OIL Symposia, Constance, Germany, Oct. 5-6, 1970, Brussels, Belgium, Sept, 24-25, 1971. Ed. by Ernst A. Steinhoff. (Science & Technology Ser.: Vol. 33). 322p. 1974. 30.00 (*0-87703-068-5*, Am Astronaut Soc) Univelt Inc.

Orbital Management: Beyond the Hierarchy. Jay H. Lehr & Jose E. Rodriguez. LC 87-143. (Illus.). 120p. (Orig.). (C). 1987. pap. 9.95 (*0-8191-6265-5*); lib. bdg. 19.95 (*0-8191-6264-7*) U Pr of Amer.

Orbital Mechanics. Vladimir A. Chobotov. (Educ Ser.). 375p. 1991. 89.95 (*1-56347-007-1*, 07-1) AIAA.

Orbital Mechanics. Richard G. Madonna. LC 88-29051. (Foundation Ser.). 126p. (C). 1997. 52.50 (*0-89464-010-0*) Krieger.

Orbital Mechanics. John E. Prussing & Bruce A. Conway. LC 92-41505. (Illus.). 208p. (C). 1993. text 52.95 (*0-19-507834-9*) OUP.

Orbital Mechanics. 2nd rev. ed. Ed. by Vladimir A. Chobotov. 375p. 1996. 89.95 (*1-56347-179-5*) AIAA.

Orbital Mechanics: Theory & Applications. Tom Logsdon. LC 97-6507. 288p. 1997. 80.00 (*0-471-14636-6*) Wiley.

Orbital Mechanics & Mission Design, Apr. 24-27, 1989, Greenbelt, MD. Ed. by Jerome Teles. LC 57-43769. (Advances in the Astronautical Sciences Ser.: Vol. 69). (Illus.). 862p. 1989. 95.00 (*0-87703-311-0*, Am Astronaut Soc); pap. 80.00 (*0-87703-312-9*, Am Astronaut Soc) Univelt Inc.

Orbital Motion. 3rd rev. ed. A. E. Roy. (Illus.). 548p. 1988. 239.00 (*0-85274-228-2*); pap. 56.00 (*0-85274-229-0*) IOP Pub.

Orbital Resonance. John Barnes. (Illus.). 256p. (YA). (gr. 7 up). pap. 3.99 (*0-8125-1623-0*, Pub. by Tor Bks) St Martin.

Orbital Resonance. John Barnes. 256p. 1992. mass mkt. 4.99 (*0-8125-3238-4*, Pub. by Tor Bks) St Martin.

Orbital Surgery: A Conceptual Approach. Jack Rootman et al. (Illus.). 416p. 1995. text 225.00 (*0-7817-0254-2*) Lppncott W & W.

Orbital Symmetry & Reaction Mechanism: The OCAMS View. E. A. Halevi. (Illus.). 352p. 1992. 54.95 (*0-387-50164-9*) Spr-Verlag.

Orbital Transport - Technical, Meteorological & Chemical Aspects: Third Aerospace Symposium Braunschweig 26-28 August, 1991. Ed. by H. Oertel & H. Korner. (Illus.). 492p. 1993. 191.95 (*0-387-56318-0*) Spr-Verlag.

Orbital Tumors. 3rd ed. John W. Henderson et al. LC 93-11033. 464p. 1993. text 151.00 (*0-7817-0096-5*) Lppncott W & W.

***Orbitals in Chemistry: A Modern Guide for Students.** Victor Gil. (Illus.). 324p. 2000. write for info. (*0-521-66167-6*); pap. write for info. (*0-521-66649-X*) Cambridge U Pr.

Orbitals, Terms & States. Malcolm Gerloch. LC 85-26432. 188p. reprint ed. pap. 58.30 (*0-7837-6730-7*, 204635800011) Bks Demand.

Orbiting the Giant Hairball: A Corporate Fool's Guide to Surviving with Grace. Gordon MacKenzie. LC 96-92018. (Illus.). 224p. 1996. 44.40 (*0-9650249-0-3*) OpusPocus.

Orbiting the Giant Hairball: A Corporate Fool's Guide to Surviving with Grace. Gordon MacKenzie. LC 97-52991. (Illus.). 224p. 1998. 22.00 (*0-670-87983-5*) Viking Penguin.

Orbiting the Sun: Planets & Satellites of the Solar System. Fred L. Whipple. (Books on Astronomy). (Illus.). 344p. 1981. pap. text 11.50 (*0-674-64126-4*) HUP.

Orbiting the Sun: Planets & Satellites of the Solar System. Fred L. Whipple. (Books on Astronomy). (Illus.). 344p. 1981. 42.00 (*0-674-64125-6*) HUP.

Orbitoid Foraminifera of the Genus Orthrophragmina from Georgia & Florida. C. W. Cooke & J. A. Cushman. (USGS Professional Paper Ser.: No. 108G). (Illus.). 1972. reprint ed. spiral bd. 10.00 (*0-934454-02-7*) Lubrecht & Cramer.

Orbitones, Spoonharps & Bellowphones. Bart Hopkin. 1998. pap. 19.95 (*1-55961-481-1*, Ellipsis Arts) Relaxtn Co.

Orbits. Brett Hursey. (Dog River Review Poetry Ser.: Ser. 19). 24p. (Orig.). 1995. pap. 3.00 (*0-916155-32-3*) Trout Creek.

***Orbits: Poems from Hollywood.** Mark Dunster. 11p. 1999. pap. 5.00 (*0-89642-813-3*) Linden Pubs.

Orbits: The Ancient Mediterranean Tradition of Urban Networks. J. Gottman. 7.00 (*0-904920-10-0*) David Brown.

Orbits Voyagers. Ndir. 1989. text 58.36 (*0-395-52131-9*) HM.

***Orborgon Vol. 2: The Last Legacy Tetralogy.** Grace Chetwin. (Illus.). 334p. 1999. pap. 25.00 (*1-930094-03-5*, Rivet Bks) Feral Press.

Orbs of Jade. large type ed. Barbara Masterton. 1991. 27.99 (*0-7089-2372-0*) Ulverscroft.

Orca. BBN Staff. (MS - Middle School Science Ser.). 1998. teacher ed. 70.00 (*0-538-66312-X*) S-W Pub.

Orca. BBN Staff. (MS - Middle School Science Ser.). 1998. pap., student ed. 13.95 (*0-538-66313-8*) S-W Pub.

Orca. Steven Brust. 304p. (Orig.). 1996. mass mkt. 5.99 (*0-441-00196-3*) Ace Bks.

***Orca: Commander of the Sea.** Jbercome Julienne & Renbee Le Bloas. LC 00-38373. (Animal Close-Ups Ser.). (Illus.). 2001. pap. write for info. (*1-57091-427-3*) Charlesbridge Pub.

Orca: The Whale Called Killer. rev. ed. Erich Hoyt. Ed. by Susan Brody et al. (Illus.). 292p. 1984. pap. 12.95 (*0-920656-25-0*, Pub. by Camden Hse) Firefly Bks Ltd.

Orca: Visions of the Killer Whale. Peter Knudtson. LC 96-14387. 128p. 1996. 27.00 (*0-87156-906-X*, Pub. by Sierra) Random.

Orca Pocket Guide. Mary Getten. (Illus.). 32p. (Orig.). 1996. pap. 1.95 (*0-945092-40-7*) EZ Nature.

Orca Project: A Meeting of Nations. Randall L. Eaton. 228p. 1999. pap. 20.00 (*0-9663696-0-2*) Sacred Pr.

Orca Song. Michael C. Armour. LC 94-927. (Smithsonian Oceanic Collection). (Illus.). 32p. (J). (ps-2). 1994. 15.95 (*1-56899-069-3*) Soundprints.

Orca Song. unabridged ed. Michael C. Armour. LC 94-927. (Smithsonian Oceanic Collection). (Illus.). 32p. (J). (ps-2). 1994. 19.95 incl. audio (*1-56899-073-1*) Soundprints.

Orca Song, Incl. large toy. Michael C. Armour. LC 94-927. (Smithsonian Oceanic Collection). (Illus.). 32p. (J). (ps-2). 1994. 29.95 (*1-56899-071-5*) Soundprints.

Orca Song, Micro-Book. Michael C. Armour. LC 94-927. (Smithsonian Oceanic Collection). (Illus.). 32p. (J). (ps-2). 1994. 4.95 (*1-56899-070-7*) Soundprints.

Orca Song, Micro-Book, incl. small toy. Michael C. Armour. LC 94-927. (Smithsonian Oceanic Collection). (Illus.). 32p. (J). (ps-2). 1994. 9.95 (*1-56899-072-3*) Soundprints.

Orca Whale: With Plush Animal. Betsy Girard. (Alphabet Zoop Ser.). 1997. 12.95 (*1-888170-09-3*) Advent Quest.

Orcas Around Me: My Alaskan Summer. Debra Page. LC 95-52647. (Illus.). 40p. (J). (gr. 1-4). 1997. lib. bdg. 15.95 (*0-8075-6137-1*) A Whitman.

Orcas, Eagles & Kings. Steve Yates. (Illus.). 224p. 1993. 29.95 (*1-882175-00-X*) Primavera FL.

Orca's Family: And More Northwest Coast Stories. Robert James Challenger. 48p. 1997. pap. 9.95 (*1-895811-39-2*) Heritage Hse.

***Orcas Island: Mystery.** Jan G. Johnson. 1999. pap. 7.99 (*0-8280-1314-4*) Review & Herald.

Orcas of the Gulf: A Natural History. Gerard Gurmley. (Illus.). 205p. (Orig.). 1997. reprint ed. pap. text 15.00 (*0-7881-5042-1*) DIANE Pub.

Orchard. Harry Mathews. 48p. (Orig.). (C). 1988. pap. 7.00 (*0-917453-18-2*) Bamberger.

Orchard. Drusilla Modjeska. 268p. 1998. pap. 15.95 (*0-7043-4514-5*, Pub. by Womens Press) Trafalgar.

Orchard. Isidro Sanchez & Carme Peris. (Discovering Nature Ser.). (Illus.). 32p. (J). (ps). 1991. pap. 5.95 (*0-8120-4710-9*) Barron.

Orchard: A Memoir. Adele C. Robertson. 256p. 1997. pap. 11.95 (*0-553-37859-7*) Bantam.

Orchard: A Memoir. Adele C. Robertson. LC 95-17187. 234p. 1995. 20.00 (*0-8050-4092-7*) H Holt & Co.

Orchard & a Garden. Dudley Laufman. 1974. pap. 10.00 (*0-87233-026-5*) Bauhan.

Orchard Book of Nursery Rhymes. Illus. by Faith Jaques. LC 89-71002. 96p. (ps-3). 1999. 22.95 (*0-531-05903-0*) Orchard Bks Watts.

Orchard Fire. Shena Mackay. LC 97-18478. 1997. pap. 12.00 (*0-15-600532-8*, Harvest Bks) Harcourt.

Orchard Hill. Elizabeth Seifert. 1973. reprint ed. lib. bdg. 21.95 (*0-88411-013-3*) Amereon Ltd.

Orchard Keeper. Cormac McCarthy. 1994. 24.00 (*0-8446-6751-X*) Peter Smith.

Orchard Keeper. Cormac McCarthy. LC 92-56360. 1993. pap. 12.00 (*0-679-72872-4*) Vin Bks.

Orchard Keeper. Cormac McCarthy. 1997. reprint ed. lib. bdg. 29.95 (*1-56849-686-9*) Buccaneer Bks.

Orchard King. Miriam MacGregor. 1993. per. 2.89 (*0-373-03255-2*, 1-03255-6) Harlequin Bks.

Orchard King. large type ed. Miriam Macgregor. 1993. reprint ed. lib. bdg. 18.95 (*0-263-13182-3*) Mac Lib Ref.

Orchard Lamps. Ivan Drach. Ed. by Stanley Kunitz. LC 77-95136. (Illus.). 79p. 1978. pap. 12.95 (*0-8180-1541-1*, Pub. by Sheep Meadow); text 25.00 (*0-8180-1538-1*, Pub. by Sheep Meadow) U Pr of New Eng.

Orchard Mason Bee: The Life History-Biology-Propagation. Brian L. Griffin.Tr. of Osmia Lignaria Propinqua Cresson. 1993. pap. text 9.95 (*0-9635841-1-1*) Knox Cellars.

***Orchard Mason Bee: The Life History, Biology, Propagation & Use of a North American Native Bee.** 2nd rev. ed. Brian L. Griffin. (Illus.). 144p. 1999. pap. 12.00 (*0-9635841-2-X*) Knox Cellars.

Orchard of Tears. Sax Rohmer, pseud. 1969. 8.50 (*0-685-22716-2*) Bookfinger.

Orchard of the Crescent Moon. Jenny Nimmo. 170p. (J). (gr. 5-9). 1997. pap. 2.95 (*0-8167-2265-X*) Troll Communs.

Orchard on Fire. Shena Mackay. LC 96-8420. 215p. 1996. 19.95 (*1-55921-175-X*) Moyer Bell.

***Orchard Pest Monitoring Guide for Pears: A Resource Book for the Pacific Northwest.** Philip D. VanBuskirk et al. LC 99-35574. 64p. (Orig.). 1999. pap. text 10.00 (*0-9630659-9-8*) Good Fruit Grow.

***Orchard Prairie: The First Hundred Years 1879-1979.** Kathryn Treffrey Highberg. (Illus.). 216p. 1998. pap. 14.95 (*0-87770-679-4*) Ye Galleon.

Orchard Safety: Specialty Safety Training. Richard Bruce. (ENG & SPA.). 1996. 29.95 (*0-913702-60-9*) Thomson Pubns.

Orchard Tractors. Hans Halbestadt. LC 96-18751. (Farm Tractor Color History Ser.). (Illus.). 128p. 1996. pap. 9.98 (*0-7603-0141-7*) MBI Pubg.

***Orchard Valley.** Debbie Macomber. 1999. per. 5.99 (*1-55166-308-2*, 1-66308-7, Mira Bks) Harlequin Bks.

Orchard Valley Trilogy: Nora; Stephanie; Valérie, 3 bks. Debbie Macomber. 1997. mass mkt. write for info. (*0-373-15269-8*, 1-15269-3) Harlequin Bks.

Orchard Valley Weddings. Debbie Macomber. (By Request Ser.). 1997. mass mkt. 5.99 (*2-273-20156-7*, 1-20156-5) Harlequin Bks.

***Orchards.** Adele Richardson. LC 99-23825. (Let's Investigate Ser.). 2001. lib. bdg. write for info. (*1-58341-081-3*) Creative Co.

Orchards: 7 Adaptations of Chekhov. Anton Chekhov. 1987. pap. 6.95 (*0-88145-055-3*) Broadway Play.

Orchards, Berry Patches & Garden Cookbook. B. Carlson. (Illus.). 230p. 1997. spiral bd. 11.95 (*1-57166-082-8*) Hearts N Tummies.

Orchards, Gardens & Pieces of Sky. Helena S. Brand. 60p. (Orig.). 1994. pap. text 10.00 (*0-914435-23-X*) Marylhurst Art.

Orchard's Little Blue Book of Nursery Rhymes. Nila Aye. LC 97-12370. (Illus.). 32p. (J). (ps-1). 1998. 5.95 (*0-531-30063-3*) Orchard Bks Watts.

Orchard's Little Green Book of Nursery Rhymes. Nila Aye. LC 97-12371. (Illus.). 32p. (J). (ps-1). 1998. 5.95 (*0-531-30060-9*) Orchard Bks Watts.

Orchard's Little Red Book of Nursery Rhymes. Nila Aye. LC 97-12372. (Illus.). 32p. (J). (ps-1). 1998. 5.95 (*0-531-30061-7*) Orchard Bks Watts.

Orchard's Little Yellow Book of Nursery Rhymes. Illus. by Nila Aye. LC 97-12369. 32p. (J). (ps-1). 1998. 5.95 (*0-531-30062-5*) Orchard Bks Watts.

***Orchards of Perseverance: Conversations with Trappist Monks about God, Their Lives & the World.** David D. Perata. (Illus.). 224p. 2000. pap. 17.95 (*0-9672135-0-9*) St Thereses Pr.

Orcherd of Syon Vol. I: Text, Vol. I, Text. Ed. by P. Hodgson & G. M. Liegey. (EETS Original Ser.: No. 258). 1966. 50.00 (*0-19-722258-7*, Pub. by EETS) Boydell & Brewer.

Orchesographie. Thoinot Arbeau. 104p. 1989. reprint ed. 80.00 (*3-487-06697-1*) G Olms Pubs.

Orchesography. Thoinot Arbeau. Ed. by Julia Sutton. Tr. by Mary S. Evans. (Illus.). 266p. 1966. pap. 6.00 (*0-486-21745-0*) Dover.

Orchestra. 1994. 43.59 (*1-57251-022-6*) TWI.

Orchestra. Mark Rubin & Alan Daniel. (Illus.). 48p. (J). (gr. 1-3). 1992. pap. 8.95 (*0-920668-99-2*) Firefly Bks Ltd.

Orchestra. Peter Ustinov. (J). (ps up). 19.98 incl. audio MFLP CA.

Orchestra. Ebenezer Prout. 1990. reprint ed. lib. bdg. 140.00 (*0-7812-9151-8*) Rprt Serv.

O

An Asterisk (*) at the beginning of an entry indicates that the title is appearing for the first time.

Orchestra, 2 vols. Ebenezer Prout. (Illus.). 577p. reprint ed. 59.00 (*0-403-00322-9*) Scholarly.

***Orchestra: Origins & Transformations.** Ed. by Joan Peyser. LC 00-23681. 672p. 2000. pap. write for info. (*0-8230-8385-3*, Billboard Bks) Watsn-Guptill.

Orchestra: The Works of Ebenezer Prout, 2 vols. Ebenezer Prout. reprint ed. lib. bdg. 99.00 (*0-7812-0781-9*) Rprt Serv.

Orchestra & Its Instruments. Esther Singleton. 1977. lib. bdg. 69.95 (*0-8490-2379-3*) Gordon Pr.

Orchestra Board-Executive Connection: Selecting, Enabling, & Evaluating the Executive Director. Ellen C. Hirzy. Ed. by Ann Meier. 80p. 1992. pap. 30.00 (*0-614-04619-X*) Am Symphony Orch.

Orchestra Conductor's Secret to Health & Long Life: Conducting & Other Easy Things to Do to Feel Better, Keep Fit, Lose Weight, Increase Energy & Live Longer. Dale L. Anderson. LC 99-160713. 128p. (Orig.). 1997. pap. 11.95 (*1-56561-103-9*) Wiley.

Orchestra Conductor's Secret to Health & Long Life: Conducting & Other Easy Things to Do to Feel Better, Keep Fit, Lose Weight, Increase Energy & Live Longer. Dale L. Anderson. 128p. (Orig.). 1997. pap. 11.95 (*0-471-34693-4*) Wiley.

Orchestra from Beethoven to Berlioz. Adam Carse. 400p. (C). 1996. reprint ed. pap. text 35.00 (*0-87556-832-7*) Saifer.

Orchestra from Beethoven to Berlioz. Adam Von Ahn Carse. 1988. reprint ed. lib. bdg. 79.00 (*0-685-55956-4*) Rprt Serv.

Orchestra from Beethoven to Berlioz. Adam Von Ahn Carse. LC 79-181122. 514p. 1948. reprint ed. 69.00 (*0-403-01521-9*) Scholarly.

Orchestra in England: A Social History. LC 75-181219. 272p. 1956. reprint ed. 29.00 (*0-685-38427-6*) Scholarly.

Orchestra in England: A Social History. Reginald Nettel. 1988. reprint ed. lib. bdg. 49.00 (*0-7812-0774-6*) Rprt Serv.

Orchestra in the XVIIIth Century. Adam Carse. (Illus.). 184p. 1941. lib. bdg. 27.50 (*0-8450-2551-1*) Broude.

Orchestra Musician's Odyssey - a View from the Rear. Milan Yancich. (Illus.). xix, 367p. 1996. 28.00 (*0-9653890-0-6*) Wind Music.

***Orchestra of Voices: Making the Argument for Greater Speech & Press Freedom in the People's Republic of China.** Elizabeth Michel. Ed. by Sun C. Xupei. LC 00-32375. 2000. write for info. (*0-275-96956-8*, Praeger Pubs) Greenwood.

Orchestra on Record, 1896-1926: An Encyclopedia of Orchestral Recordings Made by the Acoustical Process, 73. Claude G. Arnold. LC 97-2740. (Discographies Ser.: Vol. 173). 728p. 1997. lib. bdg. 135.00 (*0-313-30099-2*, Greenwood Pr) Greenwood.

Orchestra: or a Poem of Dancing. John Davies. 1988. reprint ed. lib. bdg. 49.00 (*0-7812-0025-3*) Rprt Serv.

Orchestra: or a Poem of Dancing. John Davies. LC 70-161962. 1947. reprint ed. 45.00 (*0-403-01333-X*) Scholarly.

Orchestra Speaks. Bernard Shore. LC 71-177966. (Essay Index Reprint Ser.). 1977. reprint ed. 20.95 (*0-8369-2570-X*) Ayer.

Orchestral Accents. Richard Korn. LC 79-156673. (Essay Index Reprint Ser.). 1977. reprint ed. 23.95 (*0-8369-2320-0*) Ayer.

Orchestral & Band Instruments. G. F. Broadhead. 1976. lib. bdg. 49.00 (*0-403-03788-3*) Scholarly.

Orchestral & Band Instruments. G. F. Broadhead. 1988. reprint ed. lib. bdg. 49.00 (*0-7812-0256-6*) Rprt Serv.

Orchestral Bowings & Routines. 10th ed. Elizabeth Green. 107p. 1990. 20.60 (*0-89917-606-2*) Am String Tchrs.

Orchestral Clarinet. Kalman Bloch. (Study of Symphonic Repertoire Ser.: Vol. 3). 75p. (Orig.). 1989. pap. text 14.00 (*0-9620014-1-4*) Clarion Music Assn.

Orchestral Clarinet, Vol. I. Kalman Bloch. (Study of Symphonic Repertoire Ser.). 1989. pap. text 17.95 (*0-317-94094-5*) Clarion Music Assn.

Orchestral Clarinet, Vol. II. Kalman Bloch. (Study of Symphonic Repertoire Ser.). 1989. pap. text 12.00 (*0-317-94095-3*) Clarion Music Assn.

Orchestral Conducting: A Textbook for Students & Amateurs. Adam von Ahn Carse. LC 78-109716. (Illus.). 100p. 1971. reprint ed. lib. bdg. 59.50 (*0-8371-4206-7*, CAOC, Greenwood Pr) Greenwood.

Orchestral Conducting: A Textbook for Students & Amateurs. Adam Von Ahn Carse. 100p. 1990. reprint ed. lib. bdg. 59.00 (*0-7812-9153-4*) Rprt Serv.

Orchestral Excerpts: A Comprehensive Index. Carolyn Rabson. LC 92-46475. (Reference Books in Music: No. 25). xi, 221p. 1993. 35.00 (*0-914913-26-3*, Fallen Lef Pr) Scarecrow.

Orchestral Instruments & What They Do: A Primer for Concert-Goers. Daniel G. Mason. 104p. 1990. reprint ed. lib. bdg. 59.00 (*0-7812-9155-0*) Rprt Serv.

Orchestral Library Series, No. 1. Prod. by Zobeida Perez. (Orig.). 1994. pap. 189.00 (*0-89898-773-3*, BMR05111) Wrner Bros.

Orchestral Library Series, No. 2. Zobeida Perez. (Orig.). (YA). 1994. pap. 189.00 (*0-89898-774-1*) Wrner Bros.

Orchestral Music see Music on Record: A Critical Guide

Orchestral Music, Vol. 1. Irving Kolodin. LC 78-95. (Guide to Long-Playing Records Ser.: Vol. 1). 268p. 1978. reprint ed. lib. bdg. 55.00 (*0-313-20297-4*, GULP01, Greenwood Pr) Greenwood.

Orchestral Music: A Handbook. 3rd ed. David Daniels. LC 96-34819. 632p. 1996. 50.00 (*0-8108-3228-3*) Scarecrow.

Orchestral Music Catalog: Scores. Oscar G. Sonneck. LC 69-12692. (Music Reprint Ser.). 1969. reprint ed. lib. bdg. 75.00 (*0-306-71228-8*) Da Capo.

Orchestral Music in Print. Ed. by Margaret K. Farish. LC 79-24450. (Music in Print Ser.: Vol. 5). 1016p. 1979. lib. bdg. 195.00 (*0-88478-010-4*) Musicdata.

***Orchestral Music in Print: Master Index 1999.** (Music in Print Ser.: Vol. 5x). 583p. 2000. lib. bdg. 95.00 (*0-88478-052-X*) Musicdata.

Orchestral Music in Print: 1983 Supplement. Ed. by Margaret K Farish. LC 83-13336. (Music in Print Ser.: Vol. 5S). 237p. 1983. lib. bdg. 95.00 (*0-88478-014-7*) Musicdata.

Orchestral Music in Print: 1994 Supplement. Ed. by Margaret K. Farish. LC 94-16889. (Music-in-Print Ser.: Vol. 5t). 1994. 110.00 (*0-88478-033-3*) Musicdata.

***Orchestral Music in Print: 1999 Supplement.** Ed. by Robert W. Cho et al. (Music in Print Ser.: Vol. 5u). 272p. 2000. lib. bdg. 95.00 (*0-88478-051-1*) Musicdata.

Orchestral Music in Salzburg, 1750-1780. Leopold Mozart et al. Ed. by Cliff Eisen. (Recent Researches in Music of the Classic Era Ser.: Vol. RRC40). xxiii, 118p. 1994. pap. 45.00 (*0-89579-287-7*) A-R Eds.

Orchestral Performance: A Guide for Conductors &Players. Christopher Adey. 450p. 1998. pap. 42.95 (*0-571-17724-7*) Faber & Faber.

Orchestral Repertoire for Bass Drum & Cymbals. Raynor Carroll. 90p. 1997. pap. 14.95 (*0-9650322-5-6*) Batterie Music.

Orchestral Repertoire for the Glockenspiel, Vol. 1. Raynor Carroll. 60p. 1996. pap. 12.95 (*0-9650322-2-1*) Batterie Music.

Orchestral Repertoire for the Glockenspiel, Vol. 2. Raynor Carroll. 60p. 1996. pap. 12.95 (*0-9650322-3-X*) Batterie Music.

Orchestral Repertoire for the Snare Drum. Raynor Carroll. 112p. 1997. pap. 16.95 (*0-9650322-4-8*) Batterie Music.

Orchestral Repertoire for the Tambourine, Triangle & Castanets, Vol. II. Raynor Carroll. 1998. pap. 16.95 (*0-9650322-8-0*) Batterie Music.

Orchestral Repertoire for the Xylophone. Raynor Carroll. 68p. 1998. pap. 16.95 (*0-9650322-6-4*); pap. 16.95 (*0-9650322-7-2*) Batterie Music.

Orchestral Technique: A Manual for Students. 3rd ed. Gordon Jacob. (Illus.). 104p. 1983. text 23.95 (*0-19-318204-1*) OUP.

Orchestral Wind Instruments, Ancient & Modern. Ulric Daubeny. (Select Bibliographies Reprint Ser.). 1977. 18.95 (*0-8369-5597-8*) Ayer.

Orchestral Wind Instruments, Ancient & Modern. Ulric Daubeny. 1977. lib. bdg. 59.95 (*0-8490-2380-7*) Gordon Pr.

Orchestral Wind Instruments, Ancient & Modern. Ulric Daubeny. 147p. 1990. reprint ed. lib. bdg. 59.00 (*0-7812-9113-5*) Rprt Serv.

Orchestral Works of Antonin Dvorak. Otakar Sourek. Tr. by Roberta F. Samsour. LC 77-109851. (Illus.). 351p. 1971. reprint ed. lib. bdg. 35.00 (*0-8371-4342-X*, SOOW, Greenwood Pr) Greenwood.

Orchestranimals. large type ed. Van Lampen. (J). (ps up). 1989. 19.95 (*0-590-73163-7*) Scholastic Inc.

Orchestrated Death. Cynthia Harrod-Eagles. 272p. 1993. mass mkt. 5.50 (*0-380-71967-3*, Avon Bks) Morrow Avon.

Orchestrated Death: A Mystery Introducing Inspector Bill Slider. Cynthia Harrod-Eagles. 256p. 1992. text 19.95 (*0-684-19388-4*, Scribners Ref) Mac Lib Ref.

Orchestrated Death: A Mystery Introducing Inspector Bill Slider. large type ed. Cynthia Harrod-Eagles. LC 92-11071. 459p. 1992. reprint ed. lib. bdg. 17.95 (*1-56054-451-1*) Thorndike Pr.

Orchestrating Learning with Quality. David P. Langford & Barbara A. Cleary. LC 94-45285. 187p. 1995. pap. 24.00 (*0-87389-321-2*, H0867) ASQ Qual Pr.

Orchestrating 1-2-3: Notes for Advanced Users. David C. Rier & Edmund S. Fine. LC 84-20436. 1985. pap. write for info. (*0-201-16901-0*) Addison-Wesley.

Orchestrating Revival: A Story of Missions in Mexico. T. Wynn Drost. LC 96-5118. (Illus.). 132p. (Orig.). 1996. pap. 6.99 (*1-56722-142-4*) Word Aflame.

Orchestrating Sales Success: The Art & Process of Appointment Generation. aut. ed. Charlie Van Hecke. (Illus.). 65p. 1998. pap. 24.95 incl. audio (*0-9670965-0-2*) Sales Support.

Orchestrating Success: Improve Control of the Business with Sales & Operations Planning. Richard C. Ling & Walter E. Goddard. LC 88-50483. 157p. 1988. 116.00 (*0-939246-11-2*) Wiley.

Orchestrating Success: Improve Control of the Business with Sales & Operations Planning. Richard C. Ling & Walter E. Goddard. 176p. 1995. 55.00 (*0-471-13227-6*) Wiley.

Orchestrating Your Career. William E. Perry. 1997. 10.00 (*0-614-29666-8*) Quality Assurance.

***Orchestration** Samuel Adler. (C). 1999. text, wbk. ed. 45.25 (*0-393-98214-9*) Norton.

Orchestration. Walter Piston. (Illus.). (C). 1955. text 43.75 (*0-393-09740-4*) Norton.

Orchestration. Cecil Forsyth. (Music Ser.). (Illus.). 576p. 1982. reprint ed. pap. 13.95 (*0-486-24383-4*) Dover.

Orchestration see Score Reading

Orchestration: Music Book Index. Cecil Forsyth. 530p. 1993. reprint ed. lib. bdg. 99.00 (*0-7812-9667-6*) Rprt Serv.

Orchestration & Orchestral Style of Major Symphonic Works: Analytical Perspectives. Leonard Ott. LC 97-25667. (Studies in the History & Interpretation of Music). 344p. 1997. 99.95 (*0-7734-8601-1*) E Mellen.

***Orchestration of the Arts: A Creative Symbiosis of Existential Powers: The Vibrating Interplay of Sound, Color, Image, Gesture, Movement, Rhythm, Fragrance, Word & Touch.** Marlies Kronegger & American Society for Phenomenology Fine Arts Staff. LC 99-52076. (Analecta Husserliana Ser.). (Illus.). 2000. write for info. (*0-7923-6008-7*) Kluwer Academic.

Orchestration Quick Reference Book for Musicians & Visual Artists, Vol. 1. Illus. by Robert Trondsen. ii, 160p. 1997. pap. 19.95 (*0-9660925-0-3*) All Notes Incl.

Orchestration Theory: A Bibliography, 52. James E. Perone. LC 95-52948. (Music Reference Collection: Vol. 52). 200p. 1996. lib. bdg. 67.95 (*0-313-29596-4*, Greenwood Pr) Greenwood.

Orchestre see Nouvelles Pieces Grincantes

Orchestre Rouge. Gilles Perrault. (FRE.). 573p. 1989. pap. 65.00 (*0-7859-3451-0*, 2213023883) Fr & Eur.

Orchid. Jayne Castle, pseud. 327p. 1998. per. 6.99 (*0-671-56902-3*) PB.

***Orchid.** Jayne Castle, pseud. LC 98-48130. 1999. write for info. (*1-57490-174-5*) T T Beeler.

Orchid. Illus. by Nick Hawken. LC 99-231309. (Magnet Gardener Ser.). 10p. 1998. pap. 4.95 (*0-8069-1871-3*) Sterling.

Orchid. Robert Grant. LC 68-57527. (Muckrakers Ser.). (Illus.). 229p. reprint ed. lib. bdg. 22.50 (*0-8398-0664-7*) Irvington.

Orchid. Robert Grant. (Muckrakers Ser.). (Illus.). 229p. (C). 1986. reprint ed. pap. text 6.95 (*0-8290-2386-0*) Irvington.

Orchid Art & the Orchid Isle. John Thomas & Harvey Hess. Ed. by Jerre E. Tanner. (Illus.). 92p. 1985. reprint ed. 19.95 (*0-931909-02-3*); reprint ed. pap. 12.00 (*0-931909-03-1*); reprint ed. 150.00 (*0-931909-00-7*); reprint ed. 55.00 (*0-931909-01-5*) Malama Arts.

***Orchid Beach.** Stuart Woods. LC 98-23628. 336p. (YA). (gr. 10 up). 1998. 25.00 (*0-06-019181-3*) HarpC.

Orchid Beach. Stuart Woods. 416p. 1999. mass mkt. 7.50 (*0-06-101341-2*) HarpC.

***Orchid Beach.** large type ed. Stuart Woods. LC 99-46169. 1999. 26.95 (*1-56895-774-2*, Wheeler) Wheeler Pub.

***Orchid Beach: Monk,&Debra, Set.** abr. ed. Stuart Woods. 1998. audio 25.00 (*0-694-52058-6*, 694524, Pub. by HarperAudio) Lndmrk Audiobks.

Orchid Biology: Reviews & Perspectives, Vol. III. Ed. by Joseph Arditti. LC 76-25648. (Comstock Bk.). (Illus.). 416p. 1983. text 72.50 (*0-8014-1512-8*) Cornell U Pr.

Orchid Biology: Reviews & Perspectives, Vol. IV. Ed. by Joseph Arditti. LC 76-25648. (Comstock Bk.). (Illus.). 352p. 1987. text 72.50 (*0-8014-1777-5*) Cornell U Pr.

Orchid Biology: Reviews & Perspectives, Vol. V. Ed. by Joseph Arditti. (Illus.). 432p. 1991. 58.00 (*0-88192-170-X*) Timber.

Orchid Biology Vol. 6: Reviews & Perspectives, Vol. 6. Ed. by Joseph Arditti. 610p. 1994. 195.00 (*0-471-54907-X*, Wiley-Liss) Wiley.

Orchid Biology Vol. 7: Reviews & Perspectives, Vol. VII. Ed. by Joseph Arditti & Alec M. Pridgeon. 424p. 1997. text 220.50 (*0-7923-4516-9*) Kluwer Academic.

Orchid Boat see Women Poets of China

Orchid Book: A Guide to the Identification of Cultivated Orchid Species. Ed. by James Cullen. (Illus.). 555p. (C). 1992. text 57.95 (*0-521-41856-9*) Cambridge U Pr.

Orchid Fever: A Horticultural Tale of Love, Lust, & Lunacy. Eric Hansen. LC 99-44582. 288p. 2000. 23.00 (*0-679-45141-2*) Pantheon.

Orchid Flora of Puerto Rico & the Virgin Islands. James D. Ackerman. LC 95-3660. (Memoirs Ser.: Vol. 73). (ENG & SPA.). 1995. 35.00 (*0-89327-394-5*) NY Botanical.

Orchid Genus Book: A Study Guide for the Orchid Family. Patsy Webster. 206p. 1992. pap. 30.00 (*0-9634148-0-1*) Orchid Educ Srvs.

Orchid Growers Manual. 7th ed. B. S. Williams & H. Williams. 1973. reprint ed. 175.00 (*3-7682-0043-4*) Lubrecht & Cramer.

***Orchid Growing.** Peter Black. LC 98-212488. 160p. 1998. pap. 17.95 (*0-7063-7743-5*, Pub. by WrLock) Sterling.

Orchid Growing. Storey Publishing Staff. pap. 17.95 (*0-676-57356-8*) Random.

Orchid Growing Basics. Gustav Schoser. LC 93-24785. (Illus.). 128p. 1993. pap. 12.95 (*0-8069-0362-7*) Sterling.

Orchid Growing Basics. Storey Publishing Staff. 1997. pap. 12.95 (*0-676-57207-3*) Random.

Orchid Growing in the Tropics. Ed. by Orchid Society of South East Asia Staff. (Illus.). 208p. 1994. 32.95 (*981-204-108-7*) Timber.

Orchid Growing Outside in the Kingdom of the Coconut Palm. 16th ed. Richard C. Paul. 24p. 1984. pap. 5.00 (*1-888089-20-2*) Green Nature Bks.

Orchid Herbarium of Oakes Ames Botanical Museum Index. 225p. 1989. write for info. (*0-88736-010-6*) Chadwyck-Healey.

Orchid House. Phyllis S. Allfrey. LC 96-20720. 250p. (C). 1996. pap. 16.95 (*0-8135-2332-X*) Rutgers U Pr.

***Orchid House.** Kathleen Comstock. LC 99-75262. 272p. 2000. pap. 16.95 (*1-57197-201-3*, Pub. by Pentland Pr) Assoc Pubs Grp.

Orchid House. large type ed. Phyllis S. Allfrey. 320p. 1992. 22.95 (*1-85089-599-6*) Transaction Pubs.

***Orchid Hunter.** Jill Marie Landis. 400p. 2000. mass mkt. 6.99 (*0-515-12768-X*, Jove) Berkley Pub.

Orchid Hunting in the Lost World (And Elsewhere in Venezuela) G. C. Dunsterville & E. Dunsterville. (Illus.). 280p. (C). 1988. write for info. (*0-923096-00-0*) Amer Orchid Soc Inc.

***Orchid in Lore & Legend.** Luigi Berliocchi. Ed. by Mark Griffiths. (Illus.). 224p. 2000. 29.95 (*0-88192-491-1*) Timber.

Orchid Island. large type ed. Dorothy E. Miller. 190p. (Orig.). 1999. pap. 8.00 (*0-9638844-4-1*) Miller & Seymour.

***Orchid Isle.** Sally Fairchild. 2000. mass mkt. 5.99 (*1-55166-604-9*, 1-66604-9, Mira Bks) Harlequin Bks.

Orchid Names & Their Meanings. Hubert Mayr. Tr. by M. Schmucker. pap. 50.00 (*3-904144-07-3*) Gantner Verlag.

Orchid Paintings of Franz Bauer. Joyce Stewart & William T. Stearn. (Illus.). 160p. 1993. 39.95 (*0-88192-243-9*) Timber.

***Orchid Pavilion Gathering: Chinese Painting from the University of Michigan Museum of Art, 2 vols.** Marshall P. S. Wu. LC 99-67186. (Illus.). 2000. pap., boxed set. write for info. (*1-930561-00-8*, Pub. by Michigan Mus) U of Wash Pr.

***Orchid Pavilion Gathering: Chinese Painting from the University of Michigan Museum of Art, 2 vols.** Marshall P. S. Wu. LC 99-67186. (Illus.). 400p. 2000. pap. 60.00 (*0-295-97931-3*) U of Wash Pr.

Orchid Species Culture: Dendrobium. Charles Baker & Margaret Baker. 875p. 1996. pap. 59.95 (*0-88192-366-4*) Timber.

Orchid Species Culture: Dendrobium. Charles O. Baker & Margaret L. Baker. LC 96-4992. 875p. 1996. 99.95 (*0-88192-360-5*) Timber.

Orchid Species Culture: Pescatorea to Pleione. Margaret L. Baker & Charles O. Baker. LC 90-22011. 264p. 1991. 32.95 (*0-88192-189-0*); pap. 19.95 (*0-88192-208-0*) Timber.

Orchid Stud Book: Enumeration of Hybrid Orchids of Artificial Origin: With Historical Introduction. R. A. Rolfe & C. C. Hurst. (Illus.). 327p. 1986. reprint ed. text 50.00 (*81-211-0003-8*) Lubrecht & Cramer.

***Orchid Thief.** Susan Orlean. 304p. 2000. pap. 14.00 (*0-449-00371-X*) Ballantine Pub Grp.

Orchid Thief: A True Story of Beauty & Obsession. Susan Orlean. LC 98-16829. 284p. 1998. 25.00 (*0-679-44739-3*) Random.

Orchid Tree. large type ed. Virginia Coffman. 592p. 1987. 27.99 (*0-7089-1638-4*) Ulverscroft.

Orchidaceae: Studies in the Family, Set, Vols. 1-7. Oakes Ames. (Illus.). 1547p. (C). 1988. 500.00 (*0-7855-3294-3*) St Mut.

Orchidaceae: Studies in the Family, Vol. 1. Oakes Ames. (Illus.). 156p. (C). 1988. write for info. (*0-7855-2583-1*, Pub. by Scientific) St Mut.

Orchidaceae: Studies in the Family, Vol. 2. Oakes Ames. (Illus.). 288p. (C). 1988. write for info. (*0-7855-2584-X*, Pub. by Scientific) St Mut.

Orchidaceae: Studies in the Family, Vol. 3. Oakes Ames. (Illus.). 99p. (C). 1988. write for info. (*0-7855-2585-8*, Pub. by Scientific) St Mut.

Orchidaceae: Studies in the Family, Vol. 4. Oakes Ames. (Illus.). 288p. (C). 1988. write for info. (*0-7855-2586-6*, Pub. by Scientific) St Mut.

Orchidaceae: Studies in the Family, Vol. 5. Oakes Ames. (Illus.). 271p. (C). 1988. write for info. (*0-7855-2587-4*, Pub. by Scientific) St Mut.

Orchidaceae: Studies in the Family, Vol. 6. Oakes Ames. (Illus.). 27p. (C). 1988. write for info. (*0-7855-2588-2*, Pub. by Scientific) St Mut.

Orchidaceae: Studies in the Family, Vol. 7. Oakes Ames. (Illus.). 174p. (C). 1988. write for info. (*0-7855-2589-0*, Pub. by Scientific) St Mut.

Orchidaceae Belgicae: Orchids of Belgium, Vols. 1-5. E. Klopfenstein & P. Toussaint. (Illus.). 1987. 250.00 (*1-878762-92-3*) Balogh.

Orchidaceae in Flora of the Presidency of Madras. J. S. Gamble. 208p. (C). 1978. 45.00 (*0-7855-3289-7*, Pub. by Scientific) St Mut.

Orchidaceae in Flora of Tropical Africa. R. A. Rolfe. 595p. (C). 1984. 50.00 (*0-7855-3283-8*, Pub. by Scientific) St Mut.

Orchidaceae of Mexico. Williams. (Illus.). 343p. 1986. text 35.00 (*0-945345-71-2*, Pub. by B Singh) Lubrecht & Cramer.

Orchidaceae Perrierianae: Ein Beitrag Zur Orchideenkunde der Insel Madagascar. Richard R. Schlechter. (Feddes Repertorium Specierum Novarum Regni Vegetabilis Ser.: No. 33). (GER.). 391p. 1981. reprint ed. 107.95 (*3-87429-183-9*, 008675, Pub. by Koeltz Sci Bks) Lubrecht & Cramer.

Orchidacearum Genera et Species. F. W. Kraenzlin. (Plant Monograph: No. 6). (Illus.). 1969. reprint ed. 130.00 (*3-7682-0649-1*) Lubrecht & Cramer.

Orchidaceous Plants. John Lindley. 553p. (C). 1983. 80.00 (*0-7855-3287-0*, Pub. by Scientific) St Mut.

Orchideen Europas (The Orchids of Europe) D. Aichele & A. Schwegler. (Kosmos Naturfuehrer (Nature Guides) Ser.). (GER., Illus.). 192p. 1988. pap. 40.00 (*3-440-05829-8*, Pub. by Franckh-Kosmos) Balogh.

Orchideen Fuer zu Hause. J. Pinske. (GER., Illus.). 127p. 1984. pap. text 15.00 (*3-405-12923-0*) Lubrecht & Cramer.

Orchideen von Java, Vol. 1. J. J. Smith. 672p. (C). 1984. 250.00 (*0-7855-3282-X*, Pub. by Scientific) St Mut.

Orchideenkultur: Botanische Grundlagen Pflanzenbeschreibungen. 2nd ed. Gertrud Fast. (Illus.). 1981. 75.00 (*3-8001-6133-8*, Pub. by Eugen Ulmer) Balogh.

Orchideenkultur (Orchid Culture) Botanische Grundlagen, Kulturverfahren, Pflanzenbeschreibungen (Botanical Basis, Culture, & Descriptions) 3rd ed. Gertrude Fast. (GER., Illus.). 416p. 1995. 112.00 (*3-8001-6451-5*, Pub. by Eugen Ulmer) Balogh.

Orchideentafeln aus Curtis's Botanical Magazine (Orchid Plates from Curtis' Botanical Magazine) S. Sprunger. (GER., Illus.). 525p. 1986. 240.00 (*3-8001-6183-4*) Balogh.

Orchidees Dictionnaire Iconographique, 2 vols. Alfred Cogniaux. (FRE.). 1990. 995.00 (*0-7859-8241-8*, 2908041049) Fr & Eur.

Orchids. Frank Anderson. (Illus.). 1996. pap. 4.95 (*0-89659-122-0*) Abbeville Pr.

Orchids. Ray Bilton & Mike Tibbs. LC 99-170945. (Growing Classic Ser.). (Illus.). 96p. 1998. pap. 12.95 (*0-8069-6285-2*) Sterling.

Orchids. Alex Bristow. (Wisley Handbooks Ser.). (Illus.). 64p. (Orig.). 1989. pap. 5.95 (*0-304-31097-2*, Pub. by Cassell) Sterling.

O

An Asterisk (*) at the beginning of an entry indicates that the title is appearing for the first time.

Orchids. P. Delforge. (Illus.). 480p. 1995. 29.95 (*0-00-220024-4*, Pub. by HarpC) Trafalgar.
Orchids. Derek Fell. LC 99-11607. (Let's Investigate Ser.). (Illus.). 1999. 19.95 (*1-58341-003-1*, Creat Educ) Creative Co.
Orchids. Rick Imes. 80p. 1993. 6.98 (*1-55521-839-3*) Bk Sales Inc.
***Orchids.** Andrew Mikolajski. (New Plant Library). 1999. 11.95 (*0-7548-0125-X*, Lorenz Bks) Anness Pub.
Orchids. S. K. Mukherjee. (C). 1988. 30.00 (*0-7855-3273-0*, Pub. by Scientific) St Mut.
Orchids. Peter Murray. LC 95-906. (Nature Books Ser.). (Illus.). 32p. (J). (gr. 2-6). 1995. lib. bdg. 22.79 (*1-56766-194-7*) Childs World.
***Orchids.** Douglas Nash. (Illus.). 2000. 19.98 (*1-57145-265-6*, Thunder Bay) Advantage Pubs.
Orchids. Michel Paul. 1998. 19.99 (*3-8228-7762-X*) Taschen Amer.
Orchids. John F. Prevost. LC 96-3800. (Illus.). 24p. (J). (ps-4). 1996. lib. bdg. 13.98 (*1-56239-609-9*) ABDO Pub Co.
***Orchids.** 2nd rev. ed. Joyce Stewart. (Illus.). 124p. 2000. 19.95 (*0-88192-481-4*) Timber.
Orchids. 3rd rev. ed. Sunset Books Staff. LC 97-80063. (Illus.). 112p. 1998. pap. 12.95 (*0-376-03556-0*) Sunset Books.
Orchids: A Splendid Obsession. Brian Rittershausen & Wilma Rittershausen. LC 99-35327. (Illus.). 224p. 1999. 50.00 (*1-57959-054-3*, SOMA) BB&T Inc.
Orchids: An Iconography. (Exotic Miniatures Ser.). (Illus.). 88p. 1994. 12.50 (*981-00-3832-1*) Heian Intl.
Orchids: Natural History & Classification. Robert L. Dressler. LC 80-24561. (Illus.). 344p. (C). 1990. 51.95 (*0-674-87525-7*) HUP.
Orchids: Natural History & Classification. Robert L. Dressler. (Illus.). 344p. 1990. pap. text 15.95 (*0-674-87526-5*) HUP.
Orchids: Scientific Studies. Ed. by Carl L. Withner. LC 84-19435. 618p. (C). 1985. reprint ed. lib. bdg. 69.50 (*0-89874-809-7*) Krieger.
Orchids: Scientific Survey. Carl L. Withner. LC 87-27548. (Illus.). 660p. 1990. reprint ed. 72.50 (*0-89464-262-6*) Krieger.
Orchids: Status Survey & Conservation Action Plan. Eric Hagsater et al. LC 97-189392. (ENG & FRE.). 153 p. 1996. write for info. (*2-8317-0325-5*) IUCN.
***Orchids: The Complete Grower's Guide.** Wilma Rittershausen & Brian Rittershausen. (Illus.). 176p. 2000. 49.50 (*1-870673-34-4*, Pub. by Garden Art Pr) Antique Collect.
Orchids: Their Culture & Management. deluxe ed. W. Watson. LC 79-52705. (Illus.). 1979. 39.95 (*0-87850-036-7*) Darwin Pr.
***Orchids, a Care Manual.** Brian Rittershausen & Sara Rittershausen. (Illus.). 2000. 19.95 (*1-57145-676-7*, Laurel Glen Pub) Advantage Pubs.
Orchids & Daffodils: A Lyrical Bouquet. Lincoln B. Young. 287p. 1988. 22.95 (*0-911666-40-0*) Fine Arts Pr.
Orchids As Houseplants. rev. ed. Rebecca T. Northen. (Illus.). 160p. 1976. reprint ed. pap. 4.95 (*0-486-23261-1*) Dover.
Orchids for Love. large type ed. Janet Beaton. (Linford Romance Library). 1991. pap. 16.99 (*0-7089-7110-5*) Ulverscroft.
Orchids for the Collector. Jack Kramer. 1996. 49.50 (*1-870673-18-2*, Pub. by Garden Art Pr) Antique Collect.
Orchids for the Home & Greenhouse. Ed. by Charles M. Fitch. (Plants & Gardens Ser.). (Illus.). 95p. 1990. pap. 7.95 (*0-945352-05-0*) Bklyn Botanic.
Orchids for the South. Jack Kramer. LC 94-4992. 176p. 1994. 28.95 (*0-87833-857-8*) Taylor Pub.
Orchids from Seed. P. A. Thompson. (Illus.). iv, 30p. 1996. pap. 10.00 (*0-947643-96-6*, Pub. by Royal Botnic Grdns) Balogh.
Orchids from the Botanical Register, 1815-1847, 2 vols., Set. Ed. by Samuel Sprunger. (Illus.). 650p. 1991. 398.00 (*0-8176-2479-1*) Birkhauser.
Orchids Growers Manual. B. S. William. (C). 1988. 250.00 (*0-7855-3266-8*, Pub. by Scientific) St Mut.
Orchids in India. J. K. Maheshwari. 1995. pap. 240.00 (*81-7233-330-7*, Pub. by Scientific Pubs) St Mut.
Orchids in Moonlight. large type ed. Patricia Hagan. LC 93-47351. 1994. 22.95 (*1-56895-059-4*) Wheeler Pub.
Orchids in the Mud: Personal Accounts by Veterans of the 132nd Infantry Regiment. Joseph G. Micek. Ed. by Robert C. Muehrcke. (Illus.). 464p. 1985. 22.00 (*0-9615127-0-9*) J G Micek.
Orchids, 1989. Robert Mapplethorpe. 1991. 30.00 (*0-8212-1874-3*, Pub. by Bulfinch Pr) Little.
Orchids, 1995: Official Calendar of the American Orchid Society. Judy White. (Illus.). 24p. 1994. 10.95 (*0-9639596-2-X*) Judd Pubng.
Orchids of Borneo Vol. 1: Introduction & a Selection of Species. C. L. Chan et al. (Illus.). xviii, 322p. 1994. 60.00 (*967-99947-3-2*, Pub. by Royal Botnic Grdns) Balogh.
Orchids of Borneo Vol. 2: Bulbophyllum. J. J. Vermeulen. (Illus.). x, 342p. 1991. 60.00 (*0-9504876-9-4*, Pub. by Royal Botnic Grdns) Balogh.
Orchids of Burma. B. Grant. 432p. (C). 1982. 50.00 (*0-7855-3288-9*, Pub. by Scientific) St Mut.
Orchids of East Africa. Frank Piers. 304p. (C). 1984. 80.00 (*0-7855-3284-6*, Pub. by Scientific) St Mut.
Orchids of East Africa. 2nd rev. ed. Frank Piers. (Illus.). 1984. pap. 50.00 (*3-7682-0569-X*) Lubrecht & Cramer.
Orchids of Greece. J. D. Lepper. 60p. 1982. 35.00 (*0-7223-1450-7*, Pub. by A H S Ltd) St Mut.
Orchids of Guatemala, 2 vols., Set. Oakes Ames. 13793p. (C). 1985. 150.00 (*0-7855-3292-7*, Pub. by Scientific) St Mut.
***Orchids of Guatemala: A Revised Annotated Checklist.** rev. annot. ed. Margaret A. Dix & Michael W. Dix. iii, 62p. 2000. pap. 20.00 (*0-915279-66-5*) Miss Botan.
Orchids of Guatemala & Belize. Oakes Ames & Donovan S. Correl. (Nature Ser.). 800p. 1985. reprint ed. pap. 19.95 (*0-486-24834-8*) Dover.
Orchids of India. T. K. Bose. (C). 1988. 200.00 (*0-7855-3280-3*, Pub. by Scientific) St Mut.
Orchids of Indiana. Michael A. Homoya. LC 92-34139. 308p. 1993. 34.95 (*0-253-32864-0*) Ind U Pr.
Orchids of Java. J. B. Comber. (Illus.). vi, 407p. 1990. 60.00 (*0-947643-21-4*, Pub. by Royal Botnic Grdns) Balogh.
Orchids of Kenya. Joyce Stewart. (Illus.). 191p. 1996. 55.00 (*0-88192-357-5*) Timber.
***Orchids of Madagascar.** David Du Puy et al. (Illus.). 376p. 1999. 98.00 (*1-900347-70-9*, Pub. by Royal Botnic Grdns) Balogh.
Orchids of Maine. Jean W. Cameron. 1976. pap. 8.95 (*0-89101-001-7*) U Maine Pr.
Orchids of Malawi. I. F. La Croix et al. (Illus.). 277p. 1991. 99.00 (*90-6191-808-1*, Pub. by A A Balkema) Ashgate Pub Co.
Orchids of Malaya: Description of More Than 130 Species Including a Comprehensive Botanic Glossary. L. B. Segerback. (Illus.). 190p. (C). 1987. 80.00 (*90-6191-700-X*, Pub. by A A Balkema) Ashgate Pub Co.
Orchids of Mexico, Pt. 1. E. Hagsater. (Icones Orchidacearum Ser.: Fascicle 1). (ENG & SPA., Illus.). 1990. 40.00 (*1-878762-78-8*) Balogh.
Orchids of Minnesota. Welby R. Smith. LC 92-47478. (Illus.). 179p. 1993. 24.95 (*0-8166-2309-0*) U of Minn Pr.
Orchids of Mussorie. M. B. Raizada. (C). 1988. 250.00 (*0-7855-3269-2*, Pub. by Scientific) St Mut.
Orchids of Nepal. M. L. Banerjee. (International Bioscience Ser.: No. 4). 134p. (C). 1978. 24.00 (*0-7855-3291-9*, Pub. by Scientific) St Mut.
Orchids of Nepal. M. L. Banerji. (Illus.). 135p. (Orig.). 1982. text 15.00 (*0-934454-95-7*) Lubrecht & Cramer.
Orchids of Nepal Himalaya. M. L. Banerji & Prabha Pradhan. (Illus.). 640p. 1983. lib. bdg. 385.00 (*3-7682-1366-8*) Lubrecht & Cramer.
Orchids of Nigeria. L. B. Segerback. 130p. (C). 1983. text 91.00 (*90-6191-217-2*, Pub. by A A Balkema) Ashgate Pub Co.
Orchids of North Western Himalaya. Tr. by J. F. Duthie. (C). 1988. 200.00 (*0-7855-3278-1*, Pub. by Scientific) St Mut.
***Orchids of Papua New Guinea.** Andree Millar. LC 99-38929. (Illus.). 128p. 1999. 34.95 (*0-88192-438-5*) Timber.
Orchids of Peru, No. 2. Charles Schweinfurth. LC 58-10546. (Chicago Natural History Museum, Publication 868, Botany Ser.: Vol. 30, No. 2). 279p. 1959. reprint ed. pap. 86.50 (*0-608-03772-9*, 206459500009) Bks Demand.
Orchids of Peru, Vol. N4. Charles Schweinfurth. LC 58-10546. (Chicago Natural History Museum, Publication 814, Fieldiana, Anthropology Ser.: Vol. 30, No. 4). 226p. 1961. reprint ed. pap. 70.10 (*0-608-02118-0*, 206276700004) Bks Demand.
Orchids of Puerto Rico & the Virgin Islands: Orquideas de Puerto Rico y las Islas Virgenes. James D. Ackerman & Maruja Del Castillo De Mayada. (ENG & SPA., Illus.). 168p. 1993. 39.95 (*0-8477-2342-9*) U of PR Pr.
Orchids of Samoa. P. J. Cribb & W. Arthur Whistler. (Illus.). vii, 144p. 1996. pap. 40.00 (*1-900347-01-6*, Pub. by Royal Botnic Grdns) Balogh.
Orchids of Sikkim Himalaya. G. King. (C). 1988. 400.00 (*0-7855-3275-7*, Pub. by Scientific) St Mut.
***Orchids of South Africa.** H. P. Linder & H. Kurzweil. (Illus.). 600p. (C). 1999. 97.50 (*90-5410-445-7*, Pub. by A A Balkema) Ashgate Pub Co.
Orchids of South-West Australia. rev. ed. Noel Hoffman & Andrew Brown. LC 99-221419. (Illus.). 480p. 1998. pap. 59.95 (*1-876268-18-2*, Pub. by Univ of West Aust Pr) Intl Spec Bk.
Orchids of South-West Australia. 2nd ed. Noel Hoffman & Andrew Brown. 1992. 59.95 (*1-875560-13-0*, Pub. by Univ of West Aust Pr) Intl Spec Bk.
Orchids of South-West Australia. 2nd ed. Noel Hoffman & Andrew Brown. LC 96-175808. (Illus.). 432p. 1995. reprint ed. pap. 49.95 (*1-875560-51-3*, Pub. by Univ of West Aust Pr) Intl Spec Bk.
***Orchids of Tasmania.** David Jones et al. 550p. 2000. 79.95 (*0-522-84851-6*, Pub. by Melbourne Univ Pr) Paul & Co Pubs.
Orchids of the Central African Republic: A Provisional Checklist. P. J. Cribb & J. M. Fay. 26p. 1987. reprint ed. 10.00 (*1-878762-56-7*, Pub. by Royal Botnic Grdns) Balogh.
Orchids of the High Mountains of New Guinea. P. Van Royen. (Illus.). 784p. 1980. 130.00 (*3-7682-1261-0*) Lubrecht & Cramer.
Orchids of the Northeast: A Field Guide. William K. Chapman. LC 96-5733. (Illus.). 200p. (C). 1996. pap. 17.95 (*0-8156-0342-8*, CHONP); text 39.95 (*0-8156-2697-5*, CHON) Syracuse U Pr.
Orchids of the Solomon Islands & Bougainville. B. A. Lewis & P. J. Cribb. (Illus.). ix, 335p. 1991. pap. 40.00 (*0-947643-27-3*, Pub. by Royal Botnic Grdns) Balogh.
Orchids of the Western Great Lakes Region. Frederick W. Case, Jr. Ed. by Christine E. Bartz. LC 86-70869. (Bulletin Ser.: No. 48). (Illus.). 252p. 1987. reprint ed. 29.00 (*0-87737-036-2*) Cranbrook.
Orchids of the World. V. Elbert. 1983. pap. text 3.50 (*0-486-24585-3*) Dover.
Orchids of Vanuatu. B. A. Lewis & P. J. Cribb. (Illus.). 171p. 1989. pap. 24.00 (*0-947643-16-8*, Pub. by Royal Botnic Grdns) Balogh.
Orchids of Victoria. Gary Backhouse & Jeffrey Jeans. (Miegunyah Press Ser.: 2:4). (Illus.). 412p. 1995. text 59.95 (*0-522-84393-X*, Pub. by Melbourne Univ Pr) Paul & Co Pubs.
Orchids on Stamps. Peggy Alrich. (Illus.). 88p. 1991. pap. 9.00 (*0-935991-12-3*) Am Topical Assn.
Orchids Organic. 3rd ed. Richard C. Paull. (Illus.). 86p. 1996. pap. 39.95 (*1-888089-15-6*) Green Nature Bks.
Orchids Simplified. Henry Jaworski. (Illus.). 144p. 1997. pap. 21.00 (*0-395-91327-6*) HM.
Orchids Simplified. Storey Publishing Staff. 1997. pap. 21.00 (*0-676-57069-0*) Random.
Orchos Chaim of the Rosh. A. Sternbuch. 1992. 17.99 (*0-89906-548-1*); pap. 14.99 (*0-89906-549-X*) Mesorah Pubns.
Orchot tzadikim see Ways of the Righteous: Orchoth Tzaddikim
Orc's Opal. Piers Anthony & Robert E. Margroff. 1991. mass mkt. 4.99 (*0-8125-1177-8*) Tor Bks.
***Ord & the Shining Star.** Margaret Snyder. (Dragon Tales Ser.). 24p. 2000. pap. 3.25 (*0-375-80546-X*) Random.
***Ord Eats a Pizza.** Irene Trimble. (Step into Reading Ser.). (Illus.). (J). 2000. 11.99 (*0-375-91085-9*) Random Bks Yng Read.
***Ord Eats a Pizza.** Irene Trimble. (Early Step into Reading Ser.). (Illus.). (J). (ps-k). 2000. pap. 3.99 (*0-375-81085-4*) Random Bks Yng Read.
Ordained: An Owen Keane Mystery. Terence Faherty. 1998. per. 4.99 (*0-373-26296-5*, 1-26296-3, Mira Bks) Harlequin Bks.
Ordained: An Owen Keane Mystery. Terence Faherty. LC 97-23062. 240p. 1997. text 21.95 (*0-312-16958-2*) St Martin.
Ordained to Be a Jew: A Catholic Priest's Conversion to Judaism. Scalamonti. LC 92-25994. xi, 180 p. 1992. 25.00 (*0-88125-412-6*) Ktav.
Ordained to Preach: A Theology & Practice of Preaching. Charles E. Miller. LC 92-16295. 236p. (Orig.). 1992. pap. 12.95 (*0-8189-0637-5*) Alba.
Ordained Women in the Church of the Nazarene: The First Generation. Rebecca Laird. 167p. (Orig.). 1993. pap. 10.99 (*0-8341-1452-6*, 85257) Beacon Hill.
Ordaining Women. rev. ed. B. T. Roberts. LC 98-129481. 106p. 1992. reprint ed. pap. 5.95 (*0-89367-176-2*) Light & Life Comm.
Ordaining Women: Culture & Conflict in Religious Organizations. Mark Chaves. LC 97-12518. (Illus.). 240p. 1997. 31.00 (*0-674-64145-0*) HUP.
Ordaining Women: Culture & Conflict in Religious Organizations. Mark Chaves. 249p. 1999. pap. text 16.95 (*0-674-64146-9*) HUP.
Ordalie dans la Grece Primitive. Gustave Glotz. Ed. by Gregory Vlastos. LC 78-19352. (Morals & Law in Ancient Greece Ser.). 1979. reprint ed. lib. bdg. 15.95 (*0-405-11545-8*) Ayer.
Ordance Survey Complete Guide to Battlefields of Britain. D. Smurthwaite. 1988. 19.95 (*0-86350-005-6*) Viking Penguin.
Ordbok for Tekstbehandling: Norwegian Dictionary of Data Processing. Knut Hofstad. (NOR.). 70p. 1992. pap. 65.00 (*0-7859-3666-1*, 8200029719) Fr & Eur.
Orde Wingate & the Historians. Petr Mead. (C). 1989. 50.00 (*0-86303-318-0*, Pub. by Merlin Bks) St Mut.
Ordeal. William W. Johnstone. 320p. 1998. pap. 5.99 (*0-7860-0554-8*, Pinncle Kensgtn) Kensgtn Pub Corp.
Ordeal. Linda Lovelace & Mike McGrady. 1980. 10.00 (*0-8065-0687-3*, Citadel Pr) Carol Pub Group.
Ordeal. Deanie F. Mills. 1997. 22.95 (*0-614-27902-X*) NAL.
***Ordeal.** Deanie F. Mills. 464p. 1998. mass mkt. 6.99 (*0-451-18894-2*, Sig) NAL.
Ordeal. Nevil Shute. lib. bdg. 23.95 (*0-8488-2030-4*) Amereon Ltd.
Ordeal. Mary N. Murfree. (Notable American Authors Ser.). 1999. reprint ed. lib. bdg. 125.00 (*0-7812-4612-1*) Rprt Serv.
Ordeal: My Ten Years in a Malaysian Prison. Beatrice Saubin. Tr. by Barbara Brister from FRE. LC 93-47090. 272p. 1994. 22.45 (*1-55970-230-3*, Pub. by Arcade Pub Inc) Time Warner.
Ordeal by Fire. Incl. Vol. 1. Coming of War. James M. McPherson. 208p. (C). 1985. pap. text 15.82 (*0-07-553947-0*); Vol. 2. Civil War. 389p. (C). 1985. pap. text (*0-07-553949-7*); 1986. pap. text. write for info. (*0-318-59832-9*) McGraw.
Ordeal by Fire. 2nd ed. James M. McPherson. LC 92-23635. 208p. (C). 1993. 38.44 (*0-07-045837-5*) McGraw.
Ordeal by Fire. 3rd ed. James M. McPherson. 2000. 49.00 (*0-07-231736-1*) McGraw.
Ordeal by Fire, Vol. 2. 2nd ed. James M. McPherson. LC 92-23635. (C). 1993. 38.44 (*0-07-045838-3*) McGraw.
Ordeal by Fire: Civil War, Vol. 2. 3rd ed. James M. McPherson. 480p. 2000. pap. 38.44 (*0-07-232065-6*) McGraw.
Ordeal by Fire: Coming of War, Vol. 1. 3rd ed. James M. McPherson. 224p. 2000. pap. 38.44 (*0-07-232064-8*) McGraw.
Ordeal by Fire: The Civil War & Reconstruction. 2nd ed. James M. McPherson. LC 81-11832. 800p. (C). 1991. 62.50 (*0-07-045842-1*) McGraw.
Ordeal by Hunger. George R. Stewart. 24.95 (*0-8488-0636-0*) Amereon Ltd.
Ordeal by Hunger: The Story of the Donner Party. George R. Stewart. 416p. 1992. pap. 13.95 (*0-395-61159-8*) HM.
Ordeal by Hunger: The Story of the Donner Party. George R. Stewart. 1992. reprint ed. lib. bdg. 75.00 (*0-7812-5092-7*) Rprt Serv.
Ordeal by Innocence. Agatha Christie. 272p. 1991. mass mkt. 5.99 (*0-06-100278-X*, Harp PBks) HarpC.
Ordeal by Innocence. Agatha Christie. 1991. 11.09 (*0-606-12463-2*, Pub. by Turtleback) Demco.
Ordeal by Labyrinth: Conservations with Claude-Henri Rocquet. Mircea Eliade. Tr. by Derek Coltman. LC 81-21796. (Illus.). x, 226p. 1984. pap. 8.95 (*0-226-20388-3*) U Ch Pr.
Ordeal by Labyrinth: Conversations with Claude-Henri Rocquet. Mircea Eliade. Tr. by Derek Coltman from FRE. LC 81-21796. (Illus.). 240p. 1982. 17.50 (*0-226-20387-5*) U Ch Pr.
Ordeal in Space. Robert A. Heinlein. 22.95 (*0-89190-848-X*) Amereon Ltd.
Ordeal in Space. Robert A. Heinlein. 1990. reprint ed. lib. bdg. 18.95 (*0-89968-517-X*) Buccaneer Bks.
Ordeal of Andy Dean. large type ed. Douglas Hirt. LC 94-8002. (Western Ser.). 316p. 1994. lib. bdg. 18.95 (*0-7862-0220-3*) Thorndike Pr.
Ordeal of Arms, Air Combat, Europe & the Balkans, WW Two: Foggia, 1944. Merle L. Perkins. LC 93-84457. (Illus.). 180p. (Orig.). 1993. pap. 26.39 (*0-9637220-4-2*); lib. bdg. 38.39 (*0-9637220-3-4*) S H A P E WI.
Ordeal of Change. Eric Hoffer. 124p. 1990. reprint ed. 25.95 (*0-89966-748-1*) Buccaneer Bks.
Ordeal of Coexistence. Willy Brandt. LC 63-15113. 120p. reprint ed. pap. 37.20 (*0-7837-2228-1*, 205731800004) Bks Demand.
Ordeal of Community: Hagiography & Discipline in Merovingian Convents. JoAnn McNamara. Tr. by John Halborg. (Translation Ser.). 103p. 1993. pap. 10.00 (*0-920669-04-2*, Pub. by Peregrina Pubng) Cistercian Pubns.
Ordeal of Convoy NY 119. 2nd ed. Charles D. Gibson. LC 92-70532. (Illus.). 180p. 1992. lib. bdg. 28.00 (*0-9608996-5-0*) Ensign Pr.
Ordeal of Edward Bushell. Godfrey D. Lehman. 276p. (Orig.). 1988. pap. 14.95 (*1-879563-04-5*) Lexicon CA.
Ordeal of Gilbert Pinfold. Evelyn Waugh. 1979. 15.95 (*0-316-92624-8*); pap. 11.95 (*0-316-92622-1*) Little.
Ordeal of Herbert Hoover. Carl N. Degler. (Irvington Reprint Series in American History). (C). 1991. reprint ed. pap. text 1.90 (*0-8290-2606-1*, H-52) Irvington.
Ordeal of Integration: Progress & Resentment in America's "Racial" Crisis, 3 vols., Vol. 1. Orlando Patterson. 248p. 1998. reprint ed. pap. 15.00 (*1-887178-97-X*, Pub. by Counterpt DC) HarpC.
Ordeal of Love: C. F. Andrews & India. Hugh Tinker. (Oxford India Paperbacks Ser.). (Illus.). 356p. 1998. reprint ed. pap. text 17.95 (*0-19-564377-1*) OUP.
Ordeal of Mark Twain. Van Wyck Brooks. LC 75-41039. (BCL Ser. II). reprint ed. 37.50 (*0-404-14512-4*) AMS Pr.
Ordeal of Nationalism in Modern Europe, 1789-1945. Endre B. Gastony. LC 92-1008. 380p. 1992. 99.95 (*0-7734-9478-2*) E Mellen.
Ordeal of Olive Oatman: A True Story of the American West. Margaret Rau. LC 97-28182. (Illus.). 112p. (YA). (gr. 5 up). 1998. lib. bdg. 18.95 (*1-883846-21-8*) M Reynolds.
Ordeal of Richard Feverel: A History of a Father & Son. George Meredith. LC 99-461805. 524p. 1999. pap. 11.95 (*0-14-043483-6*, PuffinBks) Peng Put Young Read.
Ordeal of Richard Feverel: A History of a Father & Son see Works of George Meredith
Ordeal of Robert Frost: The Poet & His Poetics. Mark Richardson. LC 96-51279. 288p. 1997. 24.95 (*0-252-02338-2*) U of Ill Pr.
***Ordeal of Robert Frost: The Poet & His Poetics.** Mark Richardson. 288p. 2000. reprint ed. pap. 16.95 (*0-252-06899-8*) U of Ill Pr.
Ordeal of Running Standing. Thomas Fall. LC 93-13384. 1993. 15.95 (*0-8061-2571-3*) U of Okla Pr.
Ordeal of the Constitution: The Anti-Federalists & the Ratification Struggle of 1787-1788. Robert A. Rutland. LC 83-19295. 342p. 1983. reprint ed. pap. text 17.95 (*0-930350-50-2*) NE U Pr.
Ordeal of the Hermitage: The Siege of Leningrad, 1941-1944. T. Varshavsky & D. Rest. (C). 1990. 300.00 (*0-7855-4487-9*, Pub. by Collets) St Mut.
Ordeal of the Longhouse: The Peoples of the Iroquois League in the Era of European Colonization. Daniel K. Richter. LC 92-53621. (Institute of Early American History & Culture Ser.). (Illus.). xviii, 436p. (C). 1992. 59.95 (*0-8078-2060-1*); pap. 19.95 (*0-8078-4394-6*) U of NC Pr.
Ordeal of the Mountain Man. William W. Johnstone. 288p. 1996. mass mkt. 4.99 (*0-8217-5373-8*, Zebra Kensgtn) Kensgtn Pub Corp.
Ordeal of the Presidency. David C. Coyle. LC 72-10691. (Illus.). 408p. 1973. reprint ed. lib. bdg. 35.00 (*0-8371-6612-8*, COOP, Greenwood Pr) Greenwood.
Ordeal of the Seventh Carrier. Peter Albano. 384p. 1992. mass mkt. 3.99 (*0-8217-3932-8*, Zebra Kensgtn) Kensgtn Pub Corp.
Ordeal of Thomas Hutchinson. Bernard Bailyn. LC 73-76379. 458p. 1976. pap. 17.95 (*0-674-64161-2*) Belknap Pr.
Ordeal of Three Doctors. Elizabeth Seifert. 1974. reprint ed. lib. bdg. 23.95 (*0-88411-053-2*) Amereon Ltd.
Ordeal of Total War, 1939-1945. Gordon Wright. (Illus.). 314p. (C). 1997. reprint ed. pap. text 15.95 (*0-88133-972-5*) Waveland Pr.
Ordeal of Woodrow Wilson. Herbert Hoover. (Woodrow Wilson Center Press Ser.). (Illus.). 350p. 1992. reprint ed. pap. text 12.95 (*0-943875-41-2*) Johns Hopkins.
Ordeal Therapy: Unusual Ways to Change Behavior. Jay Haley. LC 83-49262. (Social & Behavioral Science Ser.). 227p. 1984. 36.95 (*0-87589-595-6*) Jossey-Bass.
Orden de Dios para la Familia. 2nd ed. Larry Christenson & Howard Hendricks. Tr. by Angel Carrodeguas from ENG.Tr. of Families Go Better. (SPA.). 80p. (C). 1989. pap. 6.99 (*0-88113-242-X*) Caribe Betania.
Ordenamiento Juridico del Acuerdo de Cartagena, 3 vols. LC 96-78985. 1996. reprint ed. text 595.00 (*1-57588-197-7*, 310880) W S Hein.

Ordenamjentos Dados a la Villa de Penafiel, 10 de Abril de 1345. Juan Manuel. Tr. & Intro. by Richard P. Kinkade. (Spanish Ser.: No. 112). xii, 143p. 1996. 25.00 (*1-56954-052-7*) Hispanic Seminary.

Ordenanza del Senor Cuauhtemoc: Paleografia Traduccion, & Noticia Introdutoria see Philological & Documentary Studies

Ordenes Ejecutivas I. Tom Clancy. 1998. 34.95 (*84-08-02448-5*) Planeta.

Ordenes Ejecutivas II. Tom Clancy. 1998. 29.95 (*84-08-02449-3*) Planeta.

Order. NADINE SOMERS. 2000. mass mkt. 6.95 (*0-352-33460-6*) London Brdge.

Order - Disorder: Paintings by Natalie Alper, Lydia Dona, Mary Heilmann & Jacqueline Humphries. Barry Schwabsky & Diana L. Johnson. (Illus.). 16p. (Orig.). 1996. pap. 12.00 (*0-933519-34-6*) D W Bell Gallery.

Order - Preserving Maps & Integration Processes. E. J. McShane. (Annals of Mathematics Studies: No. 31). 1974. reprint ed. 25.00 (*0-527-02747-2*) Periodicals Srv.

Order Against Chaos: Business Culture & Labor Ideology in America, 1880-1915, 32. Sarah L. Watts. LC 90-43383. (Contributions in Labor Studies: No. 32). 208p. 1991. 55.00 (*0-313-27588-2*, WOA/, Greenwood Pr) Greenwood.

***Order Against Progress: Goverment, Foreign Investment & Railroads in Brazil, 1854-1913.** William R. Summerhill. 2000. 55.00 (*0-8047-3224-8*) Stanford U Pr.

Order Amid Chaos: Jeremiah As Symbolic Tapestry. Louis Stulman. (Biblical Seminar Ser.: Vol. 57). 204p. 1998. pap. 23.75 (*1-85075-976-6*, Pub. by Sheffield Acad) CUP Services.

Order & Artifice in Hume's Political Philosophy. Frederick G. Whelan. LC 84-42554. 406p. 1985. reprint ed. pap. 125.90 (*0-7837-9479-7*, 206022100004) Bks Demand.

Order & Cause of Salvation & Damnation Chart. John Bunyan. pap. 3.99 (*0-87377-028-5*) GAM Pubns.

Order & Chaos: An International Collection of Literature, Philosophy, & Poetry Specially Selected for Book Discussion Groups by the Great Books Foundation. Ed. & Intro. by Great Bks. Foundation Staff. LC 97-31626. (Fiftieth Anniversary Ser.). 328p. (Orig.). 1997. pap. 14.95 (*1-880323-78-8*) Great Bks Found.

***Order & Chaos: An Introduction to Differential Equations.** Florin Diacu. 2000. pap. text. write for info. (*0-7167-3296-3*) W H Freeman.

Order & Chaos in Nonlinear Physical Systems. S. Lundqvist et al. LC 88-15113. (Physics of Solids & Liquids Ser.). (Illus.). 488p. (C). 1988. text 135.00 (*0-306-42847-4*, Kluwer Plenum) Kluwer Academic.

Order & Conflict in Contemporary Capitalism: Studies in the Political Economy of West European Nations. Ed. by John H. Goldthorpe. 386p. 1985. 65.00 (*0-19-878008-7*) OUP.

Order & Connexion: Studies in Bibliography & Book History - Selected Papers from the Munby Seminar, Cambridge, July, 1994. Ed. by R. C. Alston. LC 96-42403. (Illus.). 224p. 1997. 75.00 (*0-85991-506-9*) Boydell & Brewer.

Order & Design: Henry James' Titled Story Sequences. Richard P. Gage. (American University Studies: American Literature: Ser. XXIV, Vol. 1). 323p. 1988. 42.95 (*0-8204-0687-2*) P Lang Pubng.

Order & Discipline in China: The Shanghai Mixed Court, 1911-1927. Thomas B. Stephens. LC 91-36748. (Asian Law Ser.: No. 9). 168p. 1991. text 40.00 (*0-295-97123-1*) U of Wash Pr.

***Order & Disorder.** Lucy Hutchinson. Ed. by David Norbrook. 2001. 64.95 (*0-631-22060-7*); pap. 29.95 (*0-631-22061-5*) Blackwell Pubs.

***Order & Disorder.** David Z. Rich. 288p. 2001. 64.00 (*0-275-96787-5*, Praeger Pubs) Greenwood.

Order & Disorder after the Cold War. Ed. by Brad Roberts. LC 95-35117. (Washington Quarterly Reader Ser.). 457p. 1995. pap. text 22.00 (*0-262-68088-2*) MIT Pr.

Order & Disorder in Matter. Giorgio Careri. 162p. (C). 1984. write for info. (*0-8053-1700-7*); pap. 25.95 (*0-8053-1725-2*) Addison-Wesley.

Order & Diversity in the Living World: Teaching Taxonomy & Systematics in Schools. Jorge V. Crisci et al. 1993. 3.00 (*0-941212-11-4*) Natl Assn Bio Tchrs.

Order & Freedom: The Conservative Vision of Community. Ed. by George Carey & Bruce Frohnen. LC 98-23398. 216p. (Orig.). 1998. 53.00 (*0-8476-8660-4*); pap. 22.95 (*0-8476-8661-2*) Rowman.

Order & Innovation in the Middle Ages: Essays in Honor of Joseph R. Strayer. Ed. by William C. Jordan et al. LC 75-30196. (Illus.). 594p. reprint ed. pap. 184.20 (*0-7837-0562-X*, 204090600019) Bks Demand.

Order & Integration of Knowledge. William O. Martin. LC 68-54425. (Illus.). 355p. 1969. reprint ed. lib. bdg. 69.50 (*0-8371-0161-1*, MAKN, Greenwood Pr) Greenwood.

Order & Life. Joseph Needham. 1968. pap. text 11.50 (*0-262-64001-5*) MIT Pr.

Order & Might. Nathan Rotenstreich. LC 87-9980. (SUNY Series in Philosophy). 238p. (C). 1988. pap. text 19.95 (*0-88706-630-5*) State U NY Pr.

Order & Ministry. Dorothea Hall & Robert Hannaford. 165p. 1996. pap. 19.95 (*0-85244-279-3*, 955, Pub. by Gra1cewing) Morehouse Pub.

Order & Non-Order: Proceedings of the 19th Nihon University International Symposium Tokyo, Japan 10 - 12 March 1997. Ed. by Y. Ito et al. LC 98-222940. 250p. 1998. 66.00 (*981-02-3397-3*) World Scientific Pub.

Order & Partialities: Theory, Pedagogy & the "Postcolonial" Ed. by Kostas Myrsiades & Jerry McGuire. LC 94-41282. (SUNY Series, Interruptions). 415p. (C). 1995. pap. text 19.95 (*0-7914-2640-8*) State U NY Pr.

Order & Partialities: Theory, Pedagogy & the "Postcolonial" Ed. by Kostas Myrsiades & Jerry McGuire. LC 94-41282. (SUNY Series, Interruptions). 415p. (C). 1995. text 59.50 (*0-7914-2639-4*) State U NY Pr.

Order & Phase Stability in Alloys. Ed. by F. Ducastelle. (Cohesion & Structure Ser.: Vol. 3). xiv, 512p. 1991. 216.50 (*0-444-86973-5*, North Holland) Elsevier.

Order & Progress. Frederic Harrison. Ed. by Martha S. Vogeler. LC 74-497. 395p. 1975. 38.50 (*0-8386-1541-4*) Fairleigh Dickinson.

Order & Progress: Brazil from Monarchy to Republic. Gilberto Freyre. Tr. by Rod W. Horton from POR. LC 80-11440. (Illus.). 422p. 1980. reprint ed. lib. bdg. 75.00 (*0-313-22363-7*, FROP, Greenwood Pr) Greenwood.

Order & Reality: Supplemental Science Experiments & Activities. Renee Citron. (Illus.). 45p. (J). (gr. k-7). 1997. pap. text 5.95 (*1-57896-011-8*, 2409) Hewitt Res Fnd.

Order & Skepticism: Human Geography & the Dialectic of Science. Richard Szymanski & John A. Agnew. Ed. by C. Gregory Knight. LC 81-69238. (Resource Publications in Geography). (Orig.). 1981. pap. 15.00 (*0-89291-160-3*) Assn Am Geographers.

Order & Surprise. Martin Gardner. LC 83-61117. (Illus.). 396p. 1983. 30.95 (*0-87975-219-X*) Prometheus Bks.

Order & Time. Ronald Christensen. (Entropy Minimax Sourcebook Ser.: Vol. 10). (Illus.). x, 134p. (C). 1984. lib. bdg. 19.95 (*0-938876-19-8*) Entropy Ltd.

Order & Violence: Hedley Bull & International Relations. Ed. by J. D. Miller & R. J. Vincent. (Illus.). 228p. 1990. text 59.00 (*0-19-827555-2*) OUP.

Order Book & Related Papers of the Common Hall of the Borough of Norfolk, Virginia, 1736-1798. Ed. by Brent Tarter. LC 78-13714. xvi, 448p. 1979. 19.95 (*0-88490-072-X*) Library of VA.

***Order by Accident.** Miller. 176p. 2000. 60.00 (*0-8133-6794-8*, Pub. by Westview) HarpC.

Order Clerk see Gregg Office Job Training Program, Classroom Installation

Order, Concord & Constituency. Ed. by Gerard Gazdar et al. (Linguistic Models Ser.). xii, 219p. 1983. pap. 50.00 (*90-70176-77-7*) Mouton.

Order, Disorder & Chaos in Quantum Systems. P. Exner & H. Neidhardt. (Operator Theory Ser.: Vol. 46). 360p. 1990. 114.00 (*0-8176-2492-9*) Birkhauser.

Order, Empiricism & Politics: Two Traditions of English Political Thought, 1500-1700. W. H. Greenleaf. LC 80-10499. (University of Hull Publications). 299p. 1980. reprint ed. lib. bdg. 52.50 (*0-313-22324-6*, GROE, Greenwood Pr) Greenwood.

Order, Family, & Community in Buenos Aires, 1810-1860. Mark D. Szuchman. LC 87-34479. (Illus.). 336p. 1988. 47.50 (*0-8047-1461-4*) Stanford U Pr.

***Order for the Oceans at the Turn of the Century.** Davor Vidas & Willy Streng. LC 99-18552. xxxiii, 577 p. 1999. 138.00 (*90-411-1172-7*) Kluwer Law Intl.

Order for the Solemn Exposition of the Holy Eucharist: People's Edition. 144p. 1993. pap. 4.95 (*0-8146-2200-3*) Liturgical Pr.

Order for the Solemn Exposition of the Holy Eucharist: Presider's Edition. 240p. 1993. 34.95 (*0-8146-2039-6*) Liturgical Pr.

Order, Freedom, & the Polity: Critical Essays on the Open Society. Ed. by George W. Carey. 196p. (Orig.). 1986. pap. text 20.00 (*0-8191-5156-4*); lib. bdg. 45.00 (*0-8191-5155-6*) U Pr of Amer.

Order from Confusion Sprung: Studies in Eighteenth-Century Literature from Swift to Cowper. Claude Rawson. LC 92-5336. 448p. (C). 1992. reprint ed. pap. 25.00 (*0-391-03745-5*) Humanities.

Order from Confusion Sprung: Studies in 18th Century Literature from Swift to Cowper. Claude Rawson. 272p. 1985. text 19.95 (*0-04-800019-1*) Routledge.

Order in Chaos: Proceedings of the International Conference, Los Alamos, NM, U. S. A., 24-28 May, 1982. Ed. by David R. Campbell & Harvey Rose. x, 362p. 1983. reprint ed. 111.50 (*0-444-86727-9*, I-299-84, North Holland) Elsevier.

Order in Living Organisms: A Systems Analysis of Evolution. Rupert Riedl. Tr. by R. P. Jefferies. LC 77-28245. (Illus.). 333p. reprint ed. pap. 103.30 (*0-608-17654-0*, 203051300069) Bks Demand.

Order in Multiplicity: Aristotle's Theory of Homonymy. Christopher Shields. LC 98-27571. (Oxford Aristotle Studies Ser.). 304p. 1999. text 72.00 (*0-19-823715-4*) OUP.

Order in Paradox: Myth, Ritual, & Exchange among Nepal's Tamang. David H. Holmberg. LC 88-43238. 288p. 1989. 39.95 (*0-8014-2247-7*) Cornell U Pr.

Order in Paradox: Myth, Ritual, & Exchange among Nepal's Tamang. David H. Holmberg. LC 88-43238. 288p. 1992. pap. text 16.95 (*0-8014-8055-8*) Cornell U Pr.

Order in the Amorphous "State" of Polymers. Ed. by Steven E. Keinath et al. 448p. 1987. 115.00 (*0-306-42548-3*, Plenum Trade) Perseus Pubng.

***Order in the Court: A Writer's Guide to the Legal System.** David Mullally. LC 99-46123. (Behind the Scenes Ser.). (Illus.). 288p. 1999. pap. 17.99 (*0-89879-858-2*, 10601, Wrtrs Digest Bks) F & W Pubns Inc.

Order in the Court: Crafting a More Just World in Lawless Times; Reflections on the Essence of the Law. Benjamin Sells. LC 98-31402. 216p. 1999. 21.95 (*1-86204-443-0*, Pub. by Element MA) Penguin Putnam.

Order in the Court: History & Society in la Princesse de Cleves. Laurence A. Gregorio. (Stanford French & Italian Studies: Vol. 47). 128p. 1987. pap. 56.50 (*0-915838-63-X*) Anma Libri.

Order in the Offices: Essays Defining the Roles of Church Officers. Ed. by Mark R. Brown. LC 93-73703. 312p. 1993. pap. 11.95 (*0-9638961-0-5*) Classic Presby.

Order in the Twilight. Bernhard Waldenfels. Tr. by David J. Parent from GER. LC 96-30875. (Series in Continental Thought : Vol. 24). Orig. Title: Ordnung im Zwielicht. 207p. (C). 1996. text 36.95 (*0-8214-1168-3*) Ohio U Pr.

Order in the Universe: The Films of John Carpenter. Robert C. Cumbow. (Filmmakers Ser.). (Illus.). 251p. 1990. 31.00 (*0-8108-2344-6*) Scarecrow.

***Order in the Universe: The Films of John Carpenter.** 2nd ed. Robert C. Cumbow. (Filmmakers Ser.: No. 70). (Illus.). 295p. 2000. 35.00 (*0-8108-3719-6*) Scarecrow.

Order in Thin Organic Films. R. H. Tredgold. (Illus.). 211p. (C). 1994. text 57.95 (*0-521-39484-8*) Cambridge U Pr.

Order in Variety: Essays & Poems in Honor of Donald E. Stanford. Ed. by R. W. Crump. LC 90-50934. 224p. 1991. 38.50 (*0-87413-420-X*) U Delaware Pr.

Order Is Given. Andrew A. Green. (Illus.). 118p. (Orig.). 1993. pap. 5.95 (*0-9639356-0-7*) A A Green.

Order, Law & Crime. Michalowski. 1985. 14.50 (*0-07-553915-2*) McGraw.

Order, Law & Crime. Raymond J. Michalowski. 512p. (C). 1985. pap. 56.56 (*0-07-554450-4*) McGraw.

***Order, Legitimacy & Wealth in Ancient States.** Janet E. Richards & Mary Van Buren. LC 99-56316. 2000. write for info. (*0-521-77212-5*); write for info. (*0-521-77671-6*) Cambridge U Pr.

Order Microsauria. Robert Carroll & Pamela Gaskill. LC 78-56735. (Memoirs Ser.: Vol. 126). (Illus.). 1978. pap. 20.00 (*0-87169-126-4*, M126-CAR) Am Philos.

Order My Steps in Thy Word: Contentment in Psalm over 600 Scriptures. Christie S. Careathers. LC 95-69872. 80p. 1995. pap. write for info. (*1-57502-022-X*, P00411) Morris Pubng.

Order of Americans of Armorial Ancestry Lineage of Members. Order of Americans of Armorial Ancestry Staff. LC 97-215271. 690 p. 45.00 (*0-8063-4719-8*) Clearfield Co.

Order of Assassins. Marshall G. Hodgson. LC 78-63343. (Crusades & Military Orders Ser.: Second Series). reprint ed. 46.00 (*0-404-17018-8*) AMS Pr.

Order of Battle: Allied Ground Forces of Operation Desert Storm. Thomas D. Dinackus. LC 99-29407. (Illus.). 408p. 2000. pap. 17.95 (*1-55571-493-5*) PSI Resch.

Order of Battle of the United States Land Forces in the World War Vol. 3: Zone of the Interior, 3 bks., Set. LC 87-600306. 1633p. 1996. reprint ed. boxed set 47.00 (*0-16-001968-0*, S/N 008-029-001) USGPO.

Order of Battle of United States Land Forces in the World War Vol. 1: American Expeditionary Forces, General Headquarters, Armies, Army Corps, Services of Supply, Separate Forces. LC 87-600306. (Center for Military History Publication German Report Series, DA Pam: No. 23-1). 426p. (C). 1988. reprint ed. 21.00 (*0-16-001966-4*, 008-029-00164-1) USGPO.

Order of Battle of United States Land Forces in the World War Vol. 2: American Expeditionary Forces, Divisions. (Center for Military History Publication German Report Series, DA Pam: No. 23-2). 457p. 1988. reprint ed. 29.00 (*0-16-001967-2*, S/N 008-029-00165-9) USGPO.

Order of Boatmen. Kenn Sealey. (C). 1990. 50.00 (*1-86305-001-9*, Pub. by Pascoe Pub) St Mut.

Order of Books: Readers, Authors & Libraries in Europe Between the 14th & 18th Centuries. Roger Chartier. LC 93-84986. xii, 126p. 1994. 45.00 (*0-8047-2266-8*) Stanford U Pr.

Order of Books: Readers, Authors & Libraries in Europe Between the 14th & 18th Centuries. Roger Chartier. LC 93-84986. xii, 126p. 1994. pap. 12.95 (*0-8047-2267-6*) Stanford U Pr.

Order of Chivalry. Ramon Lull, pseud. Ed. by F. S. Ellis. Tr. by William Caxton from FRE. LC 79-8368. reprint ed. 45.00 (*0-404-18352-2*) AMS Pr.

Order of Christian Funerals: General Introduction & Pastoral Notes. (Liturgy Documentary Ser.: No. 8). 75p. (Orig.). 1989. pap. 5.95 (*1-55586-990-4*) US Catholic.

Order of Christian Funerals: Minister's Edition. 488p. 1989. 39.95 (*0-8146-1500-7*) Liturgical Pr.

Order of Christian Funerals: Rite of Committal. Vatican Congregation for Divine Worship Staff. Ed. by Bishops' Committee on the Liturgy, National Confer. Tr. by International Committee on English in the Liturgy from LAT. 111p. 1989. 18.00 (*0-929650-13-1*, OCFCOM) Liturgy Tr Pubns.

Order of Christian Funerals: Ritual Edition. Vatican Congregation for Divine Worship Staff. Ed. by Bishops' Committee on the Liturgy, National Confer. Tr. by International Committee on English in the Liturgy. 387p. 1989. 39.00 (*0-929650-12-3*, OCF/RE) Liturgy Tr Pubns.

Order of Christian Funerals: Study Edition. 400p. 1990. pap. 9.95 (*0-8146-1937-1*) Liturgical Pr.

Order of Christian Funerals: Study Edition. Vatican Congregation for Divine Worship Staff. Ed. by Bishops' Committee on the Liturgy, National Confer. Tr. by International Committee on English in the Liturgy. 387p. 1990. pap. 13.00 (*0-930467-68-X*, OCF/SE) Liturgy Tr Pubns.

Order of Christian Funerals: Wake Leader's Edition. Vatican Congregation for Divine Worship Staff. Ed. by Bishops' Committee on the Liturgy, National Confer. Tr. by International Committee on English in the Liturgy from LAT. (Illus.). 256p. 1990. 24.00 (*0-929650-21-2*, WAKLDR) Liturgy Tr Pubns.

Order of Christian Funerals Appendix 2: Cremation. Committee On The Litur Bishops. 16p. 1997. pap. 2.95 (*0-89942-352-3*, 352/04) Catholic Bk Pub.

Order of Christian Funerals Including Appendix 2: Cremation. Orig. Title: Rite of Funerals. 320p. 1989. lthr. 27.95 (*0-89942-351-5*, 350/13) Catholic Bk Pub.

Order of Christian Funerals Including Appendix 2: Cremation. rev. ed. Tr. by International Committee on English in the Liturgy,. 320p. 1998. 21.95 (*0-89942-350-7*, 350/22) Catholic Bk Pub.

Order of Darkness Greene. 2002. write for info. (*0-15-100559-1*) Harcourt.

Order of Deacon: Its Origin & History in the Early Church. unabridged ed. LaRue H. Velott. LC 96-90502. 61p. (Orig.). 1996. pap. text 6.95 (*0-9653373-0-8*) Vellott Assocs.

Order of Deaths Head. Heinz Hohne. 1979. mass mkt. 2.95 (*0-345-28333-3*, Ballantine) Ballantine Pub Grp.

Order of Death's Head. Heinz Hohne. 1977. mass mkt. 2.50 (*0-345-25882-7*) Ballantine Pub Grp.

Order of Death's Head. Heinz Hohne. 1983. mass mkt. 4.95 (*0-345-31024-1*) Ballantine Pub Grp.

Order of Economic Liberalization: Financial Control in the Transition to a Market Economy. 2nd ed. Ronald I. McKinnon. (Johns Hopkins Studies in Development). 224p. (C). 1993. pap. text 16.95 (*0-8018-4743-5*) Johns Hopkins.

Order of Knowledge. Geoffrey Powell. (Avebury Series in Philosophy). 160p. 1993. 72.95 (*1-85628-555-3*, Pub. by Avebury) Ashgate Pub Co.

Order of Learning: Essays on the Contemporary University. Edward Shils. LC 96-47503. 292p. 1997. text 34.95 (*1-56000-298-0*) Transaction Pubs.

Order of Liberalization of the External Sector in Developing Countries. Sebastian Edwards. LC 85-21. (Essays in International Finance Ser.: No. 156). 28p. 1984. pap. 10.00 (*0-88165-088-9*) Princeton U Int Finan Econ.

Order of Minims in Seventeenth-Century France. P. J. Whitmore. (International Archives of the History of Ideas Ser.: No. 20). 376p. 1967. lib. bdg. 106.00 (*90-247-0196-1*, Pub. by M Nijhoff) Kluwer Academic.

Order of Montaigne's Essays: Selected Papers from the Proceedings of the International Montaigne Colloquium Held at UMass-Amherst in Oct. 1988. Pref. by Daniel R. Martin. 247p. 1989. 16.95 (*1-878417-00-2*) Hestia Pr.

Order of My Free Names: The Self-Revelation of the Incarnate Divine Person, Adi Da, & How to Call Him by Name. Adi Da. LC 97-149387. 200p. 1996. pap. text 17.95 (*1-57097-024-6*) Dawn Horse Pr.

Order of Nature. Lawrence J. Henderson. LC 70-150186. (Select Bibliographies Reprint Ser.). 1977. 20.95 (*0-8369-5699-0*) Ayer.

Order of Nature in Aristotle's Physics: Place & the Elements. Helen S. Lang. LC 97-51317. 352p. (C). 1998. 64.95 (*0-521-62453-3*) Cambridge U Pr.

Order of Operations: Following the Order of Operation for Fun & Profit. Abigail Silver. (Textworks Ser.). (Illus.). ix, 106p. (YA). (gr. 6-12). 1995. ring bd. 39.95 (*1-58284-015-6*, Thoughtful Educ) Silver Strong.

Order of Orthodox Divine Services: According to the Slavonic Typicon of the Orthodox Church. Matthew Williams & Peter Fekula. 1997. pap., spiral bd. 30.00 (*0-912927-90-9*, X054) St John Kronstadt.

Order of Presentation in Persuasion. Carl I. Hovland. LC 57-11917. (Yale Studies in Attitude & Communication: Vol. 1). 202p. reprint ed. pap. 62.70 (*0-608-30823-4*, 200616000061) Bks Demand.

***Order of Reason.** Brian Campbell. (Mage Ser.). 2000. pap. 22.00 (*1-56504-469-X*) White Wolf.

Order of Rituals: The Interpretation of Everyday Life. Hans-Georg Soeffner. LC 96-41532. 244p. (C). 1997. text 32.95 (*1-56000-184-4*) Transaction Pubs.

Order of St. George: Bible Memory. Bristol House Staff. 47p. 1992. pap. 29.95 (*0-917851-32-3*) Bristol Hse.

Order of St. John of Jerusalem: Past & Present. Rose G. Kingsley. LC 76-29842. reprint ed. 41.50 (*0-404-15422-0*) AMS Pr.

Order of Terror. Wolfgang Sofsky. 1999. pap. 16.95 (*0-691-00685-7*, Pub. by Princeton U Pr) Cal Prin Full Svc.

Order of Terror: The Concentration Camp. Wolfgang Sofsky. Tr. by William Templer from GER. LC 96-1921. (Illus.). 352p. 1997. 29.95 (*0-691-04354-X*, Pub. by Princeton U Pr) Cal Prin Full Svc.

Order of the Arrow. Michael T. Hinkemeyer. 320p. 1993. mass mkt. 4.99 (*0-8125-0968-4*) Tor Bks.

***Order of the Coif.** Alexander Pulling. LC 99-37829. 2000. 75.00 (*1-58477-025-2*) Lawbk Exchange.

Order of the Coif. Alexander Pulling. Ed. by Roy M. Mersky & J. Myron Jacobstein. LC 75-15318. (Classics in Legal History Reprint Ser.: Vol. 28). 288p. 1975. reprint ed. lib. bdg. 45.00 (*0-89941-027-8*, 301220) W S Hein.

Order of the Cross. John T. Ferrier. (Illus.). 24p. 1988. pap. text 6.00 (*0-900235-61-6*) Order Of The Cross.

Order of the Day. Andrew Greig. LC 90-80807. 64p. 1990. pap. 14.95 (*1-85224-102-0*, Pub. by Bloodaxe Bks) Dufour.

Order of the Day: An Unidentified Flying Opus. Marcio Souza. 240p. 1986. mass mkt. 4.50 (*0-380-89765-2*, Avon Bks) Morrow Avon.

Order of the Day: Political Speeches of Two Decades. Thomas Mann. LC 79-80389. (Essay Index Reprint Ser.). 1977. 31.95 (*0-8369-1060-5*) Ayer.

Order of the Death's Head. Heinz Hohne. 1985. mass mkt. 5.95 (*0-345-32995-3*) Ballantine Pub Grp.

Order of the Divine & Holy Liturgy. Alkiviadis C. Calivas et al. Ed. by Nomikos M. Vaporis. (ENG & GRE., Illus.). 95p. 1987. ring bd. 12.95 (*0-917651-41-3*) Holy Cross Orthodox.

***Order of the Garter, 1348-1461: Chivalry & Politics in Late Medieval England.** Hugh E. L. Collins. LC 99-57223. 336p. 2000. write for info. (*0-19-820817-0*) OUP.

Order of the Star. Evelyn Hart. 320p. 1998. 25.00 (*0-7278-5258-2*) Severn Hse.

Order of the Synoptics: Why Three Synoptic Gospels? Bernard Orchard & Harold Riley. LC 87-5593. 384p. 1987. 38.95 (*0-86554-222-8*, MUP H-199) Mercer Univ Pr.

Order of the Universe: The Spiralic Concept of Man. George Ohsawa. Ed. by Jim Poggi. (Illus.). 103p. 1986. pap. 7.95 (*0-918860-46-6*) G Ohsawa.

Order of the Universe: Who is the Messiah? Asalia Rasheed. 52p. (Orig.). (C). 1991. pap. text 10.00 (*0-317-04219-X*) Darby Pub.

Order of Things. Michel Foucault. 1994. pap. 14.00 (*0-679-75335-4*) Random.

Order of Things. Barbara A. Kipfer. 1998. pap. 16.00 (*0-375-70164-8*) Random Ref & Info.

***Order of Things.** Barbara Ann Kipfer. LC 00-23552. (Illus.). 416p. 2000. 10.99 (*0-517-20868-7*) Random.

Order of Things: A Life of Joseph Furphy. John Barnes. (Illus.). 472p. 1991. 55.00 (*0-19-553187-6*) OUP.

Order of Woodcraft Chivalry, 1916-1949: As a New Age Alternative to the Boy Scouts. Derek Edgell. LC 92-38019. (Illus.). 724p. 1993. text 139.95 (*0-7734-9197-X*) E Mellen.

Order of Words in the Ancient Languages Compared with That of the Modern Languages. Henri Weil. Tr. by Charles W. Super. (Amsterdam Classics in Linguistics Ser.: No. 14). xxxix, 114p. 1978. 43.00 (*90-272-0975-8*) J Benjamins Pubng Co.

Order on the Court: Lon Kruger & the Revitalization of Florida Gator Basketball. Bob McClellan. 176p. 1995. 35.00 (*0-9648680-0-8*) Heritage Spts.

Order, or Disorder. Amy Newman. (CSU Poetry Ser.: Vol. XLVIII). 75p. (Orig.). 1995. 15.00 (*1-880834-18-9*); pap. 10.00 (*1-880834-17-0*) Cleveland St Univ Poetry Ctr.

Order or the Hospital of St. John of Jerusalem. William K. Bedford. LC 76-29831. reprint ed. 44.50 (*0-404-15412-3*) AMS Pr.

Order Out of Chaos. John T. Reeve. 96p. (Orig.). 1996. pap. text 5.95 (*1-57087-205-8*) Prof Pr NC.

Order Out of Chaos: How to Simplify Your Life & Housework. Marilyn E. Cannaday. LC 97-92199. (Illus.). 128p. 1997. pap. 6.95 (*1-890826-02-2*) Rock Creek Pr.

Order Out of Chaos: John Shaw Billings & America's Coming of Age. Carleton B. Chapman. (Illus.). xvl, 420p. 1994. 28.95 (*0-88135-187-3*, Countway Lib Med) Watson Pub Intl.

Order Placement Guide. Lyn M. Sennholz. 28p. 1997. pap. 3.00 (*0-915513-79-X*) Ctr Futures Ed.

***Order Restored: A Biblical Interpretation of Health, Medicine & Healing.** Garth D. Ludwig. LC 99-21264. 272p. 1999. pap. 19.95 (*0-570-04272-0*) Concordia.

Order Statistics. 2nd ed. David. 360p. 1995. pap. text 129.95 (*0-471-13728-6*) Wiley.

Order Statistics. 2nd ed. Ed. by Herbert A. David. LC 80-6928. (Probability & Mathematical Statistics Ser.). 384p. 1981. 198.50 (*0-471-02723-5*) Wiley.

Order Statistics: Applications. N. Balakrishnan & C. R. Rao. LC 98-226116. (Handbook of Statistics Ser.: No. 17). 800p. 1998. write for info. (*0-444-82922-9*) Elsevier.

Order Statistics: Theory & Methods. N. Balakrishnan & C. R. Rao. LC 98-220801. (Handbook of Statistics Ser.: No. 16). 1998. write for info. (*0-444-82091-4*) Elsevier.

Order Statistics & Inference Estimation Methods. N. Balakrishnan. LC 96-2811. (Statistical Modeling & Decision Science Ser.). 377p. 1990. text 116.00 (*0-12-076948-4*) Acad Pr.

Order under Law: Readings in Criminal Justice. 5th rev. ed. Ed. by Robert G. Culbertson & Ralph A. Weisheit. LC 97-204852. (Illus.). 352p. (C). 1996. pap. text 18.95 (*0-88133-926-1*) Waveland Pr.

Order War. L. E. Modesitt, Jr. 480p. 1995. 23.95 (*0-312-85569-9*) Tor Bks.

Order War. L. E. Modesitt, Jr. 480p. 1996. pap., student ed. 4.99 (*0-614-05524-5*); mass mkt. 4.99 (*0-8125-3404-2*, Pub. by Tor Bks) St Martin.

Order Within Chaos: Towards a Deterministic Approach to Turbulence. Pierre Berge et al. LC 86-9097. 380p. 1987. reprint ed. 175.00 (*0-471-84967-7*) Wiley.

Order Without Design: Information Production & Policy Making. Martha S. Feldman. (Illus.). 213p. 1989. 35.00 (*0-8047-1724-9*); pap. 13.95 (*0-8047-1726-5*) Stanford U Pr.

Order without Government: The Society of the Pemon Indians of Venezuela. David J. Thomas. LC 81-1818. (Illinois Studies in Anthropology: No. 13). (Illus.). 280p. 1982. pap. text 17.50 (*0-252-00888-X*) U of Ill Pr.

Order Without Law: How Neighbors Settle Disputes. Robert C. Ellickson. 312p. (C). 1991. 49.95 (*0-674-64168-X*) HUP.

Order Without Law: How Neighbors Settle Disputes. Robert C. Ellickson. 320p. 1994. pap. 22.95 (*0-674-64169-8*) HUP.

Order Without Rules: Critical Theory & the Logic of Conversation. David Bogen. LC 98-7242. (SUNY Series in the Philosophy of the Social Sciences). 192p. (C). 1999. text 59.50 (*0-7914-4055-9*); pap. text 19.95 (*0-7914-4056-7*) State U NY Pr.

Orderable Groups. Roberta Mura & Akbar Rhemtulla. LC 76-56702. (Lecture Notes in Pure & Applied Mathematics Ser.: Vol. 27). 175p. reprint ed. pap. 54.30 (*0-608-08967-2*, 206960200005) Bks Demand.

Ordered Algebraic Structures. LC 96-52348. 1997. text 164.00 (*0-7923-4377-8*) Kluwer Academic.

Ordered Algebraic Structures. Ed. by Jorge Martinez. (C). 1989. text 191.50 (*0-7923-0489-6*) Kluwer Academic.

Ordered Algebraic Structures. Tsinakis. Ed. by Wayne B. Powell. (Lecture Notes in Pure & Applied Mathematics Ser.: Vol. 99). (Illus.). 216p. (C). 1985. pap. text 125.00 (*0-8247-7342-X*) Dekker.

Ordered Algebraic Structures: The 1991 Conrad Conference. Ed. by Jorge Martinez & C. Holland. LC 93-18855. 1993. text 169.50 (*0-7923-2258-4*) Kluwer Academic.

Ordered Alloys. 3rd ed. Bolton Landing Conference Staff et al. 1970. 45.00 (*0-87511-600-0*) Claitors.

Ordered & Turbulent Patterns in Taylor-Couette Flow. C. D. Andereck & F. Hayot. LC 92-18440. (NATO ASI Ser.: Vol. 297). (Illus.). 370p. (C). 1992. text 125.00 (*0-306-44238-8*, Kluwer Plenum) Kluwer Academic.

Ordered by Words: Language & Narration in the Novels of William Faulkner. Judith Lockyer. LC 90-39842. 224p. (C). 1991. 29.95 (*0-8093-1702-8*) S Ill U Pr.

Ordered Chaos: The Interpretation of English Noun-Noun Compounds. Mary E. Ryder. LC 94-9527. 1994. 55.00 (*0-520-09777-7*, Pub. by U CA Pr) Cal Prin Full Svc.

Ordered Cones & Approximation. Klaus Keimel & Walter Roth. Ed. by A. Dold et al. LC 92-12015. (Lecture Notes in Mathematics Ser.: Vol. 1517). vi, 134p. 1992. 30.95 (*0-387-55445-9*) Spr-Verlag.

***Ordered Exponential Fields.** Contrib. by Salma Kuhlmann. LC 99-49502. (FIM Ser.: Vol. 12). 166p. 2000. 50.00 (*0-8218-0943-1*) Am Math.

Ordered Fields & Real Algebraic Geometry. Ed. by D. W. Dubois & T. Recio. LC 82-3951. (Contemporary Mathematics Ser.: Vol. 8). 360p. 1982. pap. 33.00 (*0-8218-5007-5*, CONM/8) Am Math.

Ordered Fields & Real Algebraic Geometry. American Mathematical Society Special Session Staf. Ed. by D. W. Dubois & T. Recio. LC 82-3951. (Contemporary Mathematics Ser.: No. 8). 368p. 1982. reprint ed. pap. 114.10 (*0-608-03973-X*, 205256500012) Bks Demand.

Ordered Fluids & Liquid Crystals: A Symposium Sponsored by the Division of Colloid & Surface Chemistry at the 150th Meeting of the American Chemical Society, Atlantic City, NJ, September 14-15, 1965. American Chemical Society Staff. LC 67-19831. (Advances in Chemistry Ser.: No. 63). (Illus.). 342p. 1967. reprint ed. pap. 106.10 (*0-608-06797-0*, 206699400009) Bks Demand.

Ordered Groups: Proceedings of the Boise State Conference. Conference on Ordered Groups (1978: Boise, ID) Sta. Ed. by Jo E. Smith et al. LC 80-24251. (Lecture Notes in Pure & Applied Mathematics Ser.: No. 62). (Illus.). 192p. 1980. reprint ed. pap. 59.60 (*0-608-05898-X*, 206623300007) Bks Demand.

Ordered Groups & Infinite Permutation Groups. Ed. by W. Charles Holland. LC 95-47424. (Mathematics & Its Applications Ser.: Vol. 354). 256p. (C). 1995. text 136.00 (*0-7923-3853-7*) Kluwer Academic.

Ordered Intermetallics - Physical Metallurgy & Mechanical Behaviour: Proceedings of the NATO Advanced Research Workshop, Irsee, Germany, June 23-28, 1991. Ed. by C. T. Liu et al. LC 92-10360. (NATO Advanced Study Institutes Series E, Applied Sciences: Vol. 213). 712p. (C). 1992. text 332.00 (*0-7923-1726-2*) Kluwer Academic.

Ordered Liberty: A Constitutional History of New York. Peter J. Galie. x, 409p. (C). 1995. pap. 19.00 (*0-8232-1652-7*); text 39.00 (*0-8232-1651-9*) Fordham.

Ordered Liberty & the Constitutional Framework: The Political Thought of Friedrich A. Hayek, 176. Barbara M. Rowland. LC 87-278. (Contributions in Political Science Ser.: No. 176). 156p. 1987. 49.95 (*0-313-25609-8*, RLI/, Greenwood Pr) Greenwood.

Ordered Love: Sex Roles & Sexuality in Victorian Utopias--the Shakers, the Mormons, & the Oneida Community. Louis J. Kern. LC 80-10763. xv, 430p. 1981. pap. 22.50 (*0-8078-4074-2*) U of NC Pr.

Ordered Media in Chemical Separations. Ed. by Willie L. Hinze & Daniel W. Armstrong. LC 87-13563. (Symposium Ser.: No. 342). (Illus.). 312p. 1987. 60.95 (*0-8412-1402-6*) Am Chemical.

Ordered Media in Chemical Separations. Ed. by Willie L. Hinze & Daniel W. Armstrong. LC 87-13563. (ACS Symposium Ser.: Vol. 342). 306p. 1987. reprint ed. pap. 94.90 (*0-608-03535-1*, 206425400008) Bks Demand.

Ordered Phases in Metallic Systems. N. M. Matveeva & E. V. Kozlov. (Illus.). 237p. (C). 1996. lib. bdg. 135.00 (*1-56072-357-2*) Nova Sci Pubs.

Ordered Pluralism: A Philosophical Plan of Action for Teaching. George E. Barton. 2.50 (*0-8156-7022-2*, NES 42) Syracuse U Cont Ed.

Ordered Profusion: Studies in Dictionaries & the English Lexicon. Thomas Finkenstaedt & Dieter Wolff. 166p. 1973. 54.95 (*3-533-02253-6*) Adlers Foreign Bks.

Ordered Sets. Ed. by Ivan Rival. 1982. text 346.50 (*90-277-1396-0*) Kluwer Academic.

Ordered Sets & Lattices. K. Drashkovicheva et al. LC 88-38112. (Translations Ser.: Series 2, Vol. 141). 203p. 1989. 82.00 (*0-8218-3121-6*, TRANS2/141) Am Math.

Ordered Sets & Lattices II. LC 88-38112. (Translations Ser.: Series 2, Vol. 152). 246p. 1992. text 128.00 (*0-8218-7501-9*, TRANS2/152C) Am Math.

Ordered Society: Gender & Class in Early Modern England. Susan D. Amussen. LC 93-38125. 1994. pap. 19.50 (*0-231-09979-7*) Col U Pr.

Ordered Steps. LaJoyce Martin. LC 96-18966. (Path of Promise Ser.). 208p. (Orig.). 1996. pap. 8.99 (*1-56722-190-4*) Word Aflame.

Ordered Structure & Algebra of Computer Languages: Proceedings of the Conference. K. P. Shum. 368p. 1993. text 109.00 (*981-02-1240-2*) World Scientific Pub.

Ordered Structures & Partitions. Richard Stanley. LC 52-42839. (Memoirs Ser.: No. 1/119). 104p. 1972. pap. 16.00 (*0-8218-1819-8*, MEMO/1/119) Am Math.

Ordered to Care: The Dilemma of American Nursing, 1850-1945. Susan M. Reverby. (Cambridge History of Medicine Ser.). (Illus.). 320p. 1987. pap. text 19.95 (*0-521-33565-5*) Cambridge U Pr.

***Ordered to Die: A History of the Ottoman Army in the First World War, 201.** Edward J. Erickson. (Contributions in Military Studies: Vol. 201). 244p. 2000. 62.00 (*0-313-31516-7*, GM1516, Greenwood Pr) Greenwood.

Ordered to Return: My Life after Dying. 2nd ed. George C. Ritchie, Jr. LC 98-70607. 184p. 1998. reprint ed. pap. 12.95 (*1-57174-096-1*) Hampton Roads Pub Co.

Ordered Universes: Approaches to the Anthropology of Religion. Morton Klass. LC 94-41434. 192p. (C). 1995. pap. 24.00 (*0-8133-1214-0*, Pub. by Westview) HarpC.

Ordered Weighted Averaging Operators: Theory & Applications. Ronald R. Yager & Janusz Kacprzyk. LC 97-13170. 1997. text 150.50 (*0-7923-9934-X*) Kluwer Academic.

***Ordering Anarchy: International Law in International Society.** R. A. Mullerson. LC 00-41583. 2000. write for info. (*90-411-1408-4*) Kluwer Law Intl.

***Ordering Anarchy: Leaders & Armies in Tacitus' "Histories"** Rhiannon Ash. LC 99-47172. 246p. 1999. text 49.50 (*0-472-11113-2*, 11113) U of Mich Pr.

Ordering & Organisation in Ionic Solutions: The 19th Yamada Conference (Kyoto, Japan) Ed. by Norio Ise. 704p. (C). 1988. pap. 59.00 (*9971-5-0503-7*); text 138.00 (*9971-5-0502-9*) World Scientific Pub.

Ordering & Phase Transitions in Charged Colloids. Ed. by A. K. Arora et al. LC 95-30600. (Complex Fluids & Fluid Microstructures Ser.). (Illus.). 400p. 1996. 125.00 (*1-56081-917-0*, Wiley-VCH) Wiley.

Ordering & Phase Transitions in Charged Colloids. Ed. by A. K. Arora & B. V. Tata. 361p. 1996. 169.00 (*0-471-18630-9*) Wiley.

Ordering at Surfaces & Interfaces: Proceedings of the 3rd NEC Symposium Hakone, Japan, October 7-11, 1990. Ed. by A. Yoshimori et al. (Materials Science Ser.: Vol. 17). (Illus.). x, 379p. 1992. 75.95 (*0-387-53924-7*) Spr-Verlag.

Ordering Demons. John Wheatcroft. LC 78-75343. 108p. 1981. 9.95 (*0-8453-4720-9*, Cornwall Bks) Assoc Univ Prs.

Ordering Disorder: Prospect & Retrospect in Condensed Matter Physics. Ed. by D. Naugle. (AIP Conference Proceedings Ser.: No. 286). (Illus.). 352p. 1993. text 125.00 (*1-56396-255-1*, AIP Pr) Spr-Verlag.

Ordering from Catalogs & Dining Out. Northwest Regional Educational Laboratory Staff. (Lifeworks Ser.). (Illus.). 1980. text 13.96 (*0-07-047305-6*) McGraw.

Ordering in Macromolecular Systems: Proceedings of the OUMS'93, Toyonaka, Osaka, Japan, 3-6 June 1993. Ed. by A. Teramoto et al. LC 94-8717. 1994. 133.00 (*0-387-57817-X*) Spr-Verlag.

Ordering in Two Dimensions: Proceedings of an International Conference Held at Lake Geneva, Wisconsin, U. S. A., May 28-30. Ed. by Sunil K. Sinha. LC 80-26060. 516p. reprint ed. pap. 160.00 (*0-608-16364-3*, 202627100049) Bks Demand.

***Ordering Medieval Society: Perspectives on Intellectual & Practical Modes of Shaping Social Relations.** Bernhard Jussen. LC 00-39284. (Middle Ages Ser.). 2000. write for info. (*0-8122-3561-4*) U of Pa Pr.

Ordering Mirror: Readers & Contexts. Phillip Lopate. LC 93-2065. (Ben Belitt Lectureships Ser.). xxiii, 304p. 1993. 30.00 (*0-8232-1515-6*) Fordham.

Ordering of Bees. John Levett. LC 70-171773. (English Experience Ser.: No. 398). 96p. 1971. reprint ed. 35.00 (*90-221-0398-6*) Walter J Johnson.

Ordering of Justice: A Study of Accused Persons as Defendants in the Criminal Process. Richard V. Ericson & Patricia M. Baranek. (Canadian Studies in Criminology). 288p. 1982. pap. text 18.95 (*0-8020-6463-9*) U of Toronto Pr.

Ordering of the Arts in Eighteenth-Century England. Lawrence I. Lipking. LC 76-90953. 523p. reprint ed. pap. 162.20 (*0-8357-2780-7*, 203990600014) Bks Demand.

Ordering of Time: From the Ancient Computus to the Modern Computer. Arno Borst. Tr. by Andrew Winnard from GER. LC 93-27993.Tr. of Computus. 178p. 1993. lib. bdg. 39.95 (*0-226-06658-4*) U Ch Pr.

Ordering Phenomena in Condensed Matter Physics: Twenty-Sixth Karpacz. Z. M. Galasiewicz & A. Pekalski. (Winter School of Theorteical Physics Ser.). 496p. 1990. text 130.00 (*981-02-0248-2*) World Scientific Pub.

Ordering Space: Types in Architecture & Design. Karen A. Franck & Lynda H. Scheneekloth. (Architecture Ser.). 383p. 1994. pap. 54.95 (*0-471-28505-6*, VNR) Wiley.

Ordering Space: Types in Architecture & Design. Ed. by Karen A. Franck & Lynda H. Schneekloth. 1994. pap. 47.95 (*0-442-01233-0*, VNR) Wiley.

Ordering Systems: An Introduction to Architectural Design. Edward T. White. (Illus.). 185p. 1972. pap. 12.00 (*1-928643-06-X*) Archit Media.

Ordering the Oceans: The Law of the Sea in Practice. Clyde Sanger. 1987. pap. 18.95 (*0-8020-6635-6*) U of Toronto Pr.

Ordering the Oceans: The Making of the Law of the Sea. Clyde Sanger. LC 87-208478. 237p. reprint ed. pap. 73.50 (*0-7837-1226-X*, 204136200020) Bks Demand.

Ordering the World: Approaches to State & Society in Sung Dynesty China. Ed. by Robert P. Hymes & Conrad Schirokauer. (Studies on China: No. 16). 447p. 1993. 58.00 (*0-520-07691-5*, Pub. by U CA Pr) Cal Prin Full Svc.

Ordering Time: From the Ancient Computus to the Modern Computer. Arno Borst. Tr. by Andrew Winnard. x, 178p. 1993. pap. text 17.95 (*0-226-06659-2*) U Ch Pr.

Ordering Your Private World see Ponga Orden en Su Mundo Interior

Ordering Your Private World. Gordon MacDonald. LC 97-6545. 228p. 1997. pap. 12.99 (*0-7852-7161-9*) Nelson.

Ordering Your Private World. Gordon MacDonald. 1995. pap. 12.95 (*1-880828-94-4*) Touch Pubns.

Ordering Your Steps. Dwayne Stone. LC 97-90737. 71p. 1998. pap. 8.95 (*0-533-12468-9*) Vantage.

Orderings, Valuations & Quadratic Forms. T. Y. Lam. LC 83-11729. (CBMS Regional Conference Series in Mathematics: No. 52). 143p. 1983. pap. 25.00 (*0-8218-0702-1*, CBMS/52) Am Math.

***Orderly & Effective Insolvency Procedures: Key Issues.** International Monetary Fund Staff. LC 99-36851. 1999. write for info. (*1-55775-820-4*) Intl Monetary.

Orderly Book of Captain Benjamin Taliaferro, 2nd Virginia Detachment, Charleston, South Carolina, 1780. Ed. by Lee A. Wallace, Jr. LC 79-24547. ix, 185p. 1980. 15.00 (*0-88490-071-1*) Library of VA.

Orderly Chaos: The Mandala Principle. Chogyam Trungpa. LC 91-52527. (Dharma Ocean Ser.). 128p. (Orig.). 1991. pap. 18.00 (*0-87773-636-7*, Pub. by Shambhala Pubns) Random.

Orderly Cricket. Rae Oetting. LC 68-16395. (Illus.). 32p. (J). (gr. 2-3). 1967. lib. bdg. 9.95 (*0-87783-028-2*) Oddo.

Orders, Algorithms, & Applications: International Workshop ORDAL '94. Ed. by Vincent Bouchitte & Michael Morvan. LC 94-3555. (Lecture Notes in Computer Science Ser.: Vol. 831). 1994. 39.95 (*0-387-58274-6*) Spr-Verlag.

Orders & Badges of the White Armies in the Civil War. limited ed. P. Pashkov. (Illus.). 31p. 1983. pap. 10.00 (*0-317-06616-1*) Quaker.

Orders & Directions for the Better Administration of Justice. LC 72-38176. (English Experience Ser.: No. 451). 1972. reprint ed. 15.00 (*90-221-0451-6*) Walter J Johnson.

Orders & Families of Seed Plants of China. Hsuan Keng et al. 464p. 1993. text 112.00 (*981-02-1481-2*) World Scientific Pub.

Orders & Instructions. (Open Learning for Supervisory Management Ser.). 1986. pap. text 19.50 (*0-08-070079-9*, Pergamon Pr) Elsevier.

Orders & Instructions. Nebsm Staff. (Open Learning for Supervisory Management Ser.). 1986. pap. text 19.50 (*0-08-033964-6*, Pergamon Pr) Elsevier.

Orders & Their Applications. Ed. by Irving Reiner & Klaus W. Roggenkamp. (Lecture Notes in Mathematics Ser.: Vol. 1142). x, 306p. 1985. 46.95 (*0-387-15674-7*) Spr-Verlag.

Orders, Decorations & Badges of the Socialist Republic of Vietnam: And the National Front for the Liberation of South Vietnam - A Photographic Reference. Edward J. Emering. LC 96-70000. (Illus.). 96p. 1997. pap. 24.95 (*0-7643-0143-8*) Schiffer.

Orders, Decorations & Medals of Sir Winston Churchill. Douglas S. Russell. Ed. by Richard M. Langworth. (Educational Ser.: No. 3). (Illus.). 108p. 1990. pap., per. 10.00 (*0-943879-06-X*) Churchill Ctr.

Orders from France: The Americans & the French in a Revolutionary World. Roger G. Kennedy. LC 90-33174. (Illus.). 540p. (C). 1990. reprint ed. pap. 21.95 (*0-8122-1328-9*) U of Pa Pr.

Orders of a Quartic Field, Vol. 122, No. 583. Jin Nakagawa. LC 96-12849. (Memoirs of the American Mathematical Society Ser.). 75p. 1996. pap. 34.00 (*0-8218-0472-3*, MEMO/122/583) Am Math.

Orders of Affection. Arthur Smith. LC 95-67962. (Poetry Ser.). 1996. pap. 11.95 (*0-88748-223-6*) Carnegie-Mellon.

Orders of Affection. Arthur Smith. LC 95-67962. (Poetry Ser.). 72p. (C). 1996. 20.95 (*0-88748-222-8*) Carnegie-Mellon.

Orders of Change: Building Value-Driven Organizations. Rose L. Kennedy. (C). 1995. pap. text 20.50 (*0-07-034081-1*) McGraw.

Orders of Chivalry, Foreign Decorations & Awards to Natal, Cape Colony & Union Defence Forces. Ed. by Roberts Staff. (C). 1989. 90.00 (*1-873058-90-X*, Pub. by Roberts) St Mut.

Orders of Discourse: Philosophy, Social Science, & Politics. John G. Gunnell. LC 98-18013. 270p. 1998. 68.00 (*0-8476-9202-7*); pap. 24.95 (*0-8476-9203-5*) Rowman.

Orders of Knighthood & of Merit: The Pontifical, Religious & Secularised Catholic-Founded Orders & Their Relationship to the Apostolic See. Peter B. Van Duren. (Colin Symthe Publication). (Illus.). 784p. 1996. text 135.00 (*0-86140-371-1*) OUP.

Orders of Light. Martha Lang-Wescott. (Illus.). 320p. (Orig.). 25.00 (*0-9619852-3-2*) Treehouse Mtn.

Orders of Ministry: Reflections on Direct Ordination, 1996. Ed. by Edwin F. Hallenbeck. LC 96-72279. 100p. (Orig.). 1997. pap. text 8.00 (*1-886136-02-5*) N Am Assn Diaconate.

Orders of the Dreamed: George Nelson on Cree & Northern Ojibwa Religion & Myth, 1823. Jennifer S. Brown & Robert Brightman. (Illus.). 226p. 1998. pap. 15.95 (*0-87351-370-3*) Minn Hist.

Orders of the Great Work - Alchemy. Manly P. Hall. (Adepts Ser.). 10.95 (*0-89314-534-3*) Philos Res.

Orders of the Quest - the Holy Grail. Manly P. Hall. (Adepts Ser.). (Illus.). 101p. 1999. 10.95 (*0-89314-533-5*) Philos Res.

Orders of the Retina. Thomas M. Disch. LC 82-4728. 45p. (Orig.). 1982. pap. 30.00 (*0-915124-61-0*) Coffee Hse.

O

An Asterisk (*) at the beginning of an entry indicates that the title is appearing for the first time.

Orders of Universal Reformation - Utopias. Manly P. Hall. (Adepts Ser.). 10.95 (*0-89314-535-1*) Philos Res.

Orders of Universal Reformation - Utopias. Manly P. Hall. (Adepts Ser.). (Illus.). 102p. 1999. pap. 8.50 (*0-89314-380-4*) Philos Res.

Orders, Production & Investment: A Cyclical & Structural Analysis. Victor Zarnowitz. (Business Cycles Ser.: No. 22). 785p. 1973. 160.00 (*0-87014-215-1*) Natl Bur Econ Res.

Orders to Kill: The Truth about the Murder of Martin Luther King. William Pepper. (Illus.). 576p. 1995. 28.00 (*0-7867-0253-2*) Carroll & Graf.

Orders to Kill: The Truth Behind the Murder of Martin Luther King. William F. Pepper. LC 97-26202. 592p. 1998. mass mkt. 16.00 (*0-446-67394-3*, Pub. by Warner Bks) Little.

Ordin on Contesting Confirmation 3rd ed. Sally M. Henry & Robert L. Ordin. LC 98-51351. 1998. ring bd. 183.00 (*1-56706-663-1*) Aspen Law.

Ordinal & Symbolic Data Analysis: Proceedings of the International Conference on Ordinal & Symbolic Data Analysis--Osda '95, Paris, June 20-23, 1995. Ed. by Otto Opitz et al. LC 96-23140. (Studies in Classification, Data Analysis, & Knowledge Organization). 372p. 1996. 99.50 (*3-540-61081-2*) Spr-Verlag.

Ordinal Data Modeling. James H. Albert & Valen E. Johnson. Ed. by S. Fienberg et al. LC 98-51801. 312p. 1999. 65.00 (*0-387-98718-5*) Spr-Verlag.

Ordinal Invariants in Topology. V. Kannan. LC 81-7969. (Memoirs of the American Mathematical Society Ser.: No. 32/245). 164p. 1981. pap. 19.00 (*0-8218-2245-4*, MEMO/32/245) Am Math.

Ordinal Log - Linear Models. Masako Ishii-Kuntz. (Quantitative Applications in the Social Sciences Ser.: Vol. 97). (C). 1994. pap. text 10.95 (*0-8039-4376-8*) Sage.

Ordinal Methods for Behavioral Data Analysis. Norman Cliff. LC 96-22689. 224p. 1996. 45.00 (*0-8058-1333-0*) L Erlbaum Assocs.

*__Ordinal of the Abbey of the Holy Trinity Fecamp: Fecamp, Musee de la Benedictine, MS 186, Pt. 1.__ Ed. by David Chadd. (Henry Bradshaw Society Ser.). 256p. 2000. 60.00 (*1-870252-13-6*, Henry Bradshaw Soc) Boydell & Brewer.

Ordinal Time Series Analysis: Methodology & Applications in Management Strategy & Policy, 1. Timothy Ruefli. LC 90-30011. 280p. 1990. 55.00 (*0-89930-571-7*, Quorum Bks) Greenwood.

Ordinals of Christ from Their Origins to the Twelfth Century. Roger E. Reynolds. (C). 1978. 110.00 (*3-11-007058-8*) De Gruyter.

Ordinance Enforcement Officer. Jack Rudman. (Career Examination Ser.: C-3068). 1994. pap. 29.95 (*0-8373-3068-8*) Nat Learn.

Ordinance Inspector. Jack Rudman. (Career Examination Ser.: C-2852). 1994. pap. 29.95 (*0-8373-2852-7*) Nat Learn.

Ordinance-Making Powers of the President of the United States. James Hart. LC 78-151595. reprint ed. 27.50 (*0-404-03139-0*) AMS Pr.

Ordinance Making Powers of the President of the United States. James Hart. LC 78-87482. (Law, Politics & History Ser.). 1970. reprint ed. lib. bdg. 39.50 (*0-306-71487-6*) Da Capo.

Ordinance of Freedom. Robert V. Van Trees. LC 86-50013. 112p. (Orig.). 1986. pap. 3.95 (*0-9616282-1-9*) R Van Trees.

Ordinance of 1787 - The Nation Begins. William D. Ellis. LC 87-61575. 128p. 1987. pap. 6.95 (*0-913428-64-7*) Landfall Pr.

Ordinance Power of the Japanese Emperor. Tomio Nakano. LC 71-173009. reprint ed. 31.50 (*0-404-04650-9*) AMS Pr.

Ordinances. Naomi Lazard. (Poetry Chapbook Ser.). 58p. (Orig.). 1984. pap. 12.00 (*0-937669-11-3*) Owl Creek Pr.

Ordinances. Naomi Lazard. 60p. (Orig.). 1995. pap. 12.00 (*1-887478-04-3*, WiseAcre) Red Sea NY.

Ordinances: What Are They? David R. Plaster. 1985. pap. 7.99 (*0-88469-164-0*) BMH Bks.

*__Ordinances of Government: Al-Ahkam al-Sultaniyya.__ Al-Ahkam A. Al-Mawardi. Tr. by Wafaa Wahba. (Great Books of Islamic Civilization Ser.). 312p. 2000. pap. 25.00 (*1-85964-140-7*) Garnet Publishing Co.

Ordinances of Heaven: The Quickening. Michael Shimpach. LC 96-68791. (Illus.). 387p. (Orig.). 1996. pap. 17.95 (*1-57502-209-5*, P0848) Morris Pubng.

Ordinances of Manu. Ed. by Edward W. Hopkins. (C). 1995. reprint ed. 22.50 (*81-215-0667-0*, Pub. by M Manoharial) Coronet Bks.

Ordinances of the New Testament. William G. Schell. 67p. pap. 2.00 (*0-686-29158-1*) Faith Pub Hse.

Ordinarily Sacred. Lynda Sexson. LC 92-12892. (Studies in Religion & Culture). 144p. (C). 1992. pap. text 12.50 (*0-8139-1416-7*) U Pr of Va.

Ordinary Albert. Nancy Antle. 1998. 16.00 (*0-207-19047-X*) HarpC.

Ordinary Albert. Nancy Antle. 1998. pap. 6.95 (*0-207-19158-1*) HarpC.

Ordinary Americans. Ed. by Linda R. Monk & Charles Sass. 190p. 1994. teacher ed., ring bd. 14.95 (*0-614-14108-7*) Close Up Fnd.

Ordinary Americans: U. S. History Through the Eyes of Everyday People. Ed. by Linda R. Monk & Charles Sass. LC 93-33401. 296p. 1994. pap. 15.95 (*0-932765-47-5*, 1304-94) Close Up Fnd.

Ordinary & Delay. Wiener. 1992. pap. 51.95 (*0-582-09113-6*, Pub. by Addison-Wesley) Longman.

Ordinary & Differential Equations & Stability Theory: An Introduction. David A. Sanchez. 164p. 1979. pap. text 6.95 (*0-486-63828-6*) Dover.

Ordinary & Extraordinary Fruits & Vegetables. Mary Z. Silverzweig. (Illus.). 130p. (Orig.). 1990. pap. 3.62 (*0-9626779-0-6*) Silverzweig Assocs.

Ordinary & Partial Differential Equations. Ed. by R. J. Jarvis & Brian D. Sleeman. (Lecture Notes in Mathematics Ser.: Vol. 1151). 357p. 1985. pap. 46.20 (*0-387-15694-1*) Spr-Verlag.

Ordinary & Partial Differential Equations, Vol. 3. Ed. by B. D. Sleeman & R. J. Jarvis. LC 91-648883. (Pitman Research Notes in Mathematics Ser.: No. 254). 231p. 1991. pap. 71.70 (*0-608-05228-0*, 206576500003) Bks Demand.

Ordinary & Partial Differential Equations, Vol. 4. B. D. Sleeman. 1993. lib. bdg. 65.95 (*0-582-09137-3*, Pub. by Addison-Wesley) Longman.

Ordinary & Partial Differential Equations, Vol. 5. R. J. Jarvis. (Pitman Research Notes in Mathematics Ser.). 1997. pap. 47.95 (*0-582-30589-6*, Pub. by Addison-Wesley) Longman.

Ordinary & Sacred as Blood: Alabama Women Speak. Ed. by Mary C. Moran. LC 99-63719. xii, 244p. 1999. pap. 11.95 (*0-9672676-0-9*) Rivers Edge Pubg Co.

Ordinary & Stochastic Differential Geometry As a Tool for Mathematical Physics. Yuri Gliklikh. LC 96-28675. (Mathematics & Its Applications Ser.). 208p. (C). 1996. text 121.50 (*0-7923-4154-6*) Kluwer Academic.

Ordinary & the Extraordinary: An Anthropological Study of Chinese Reform & the 1989 People's Movement in. Frank N. Pieke. LC 95-35861. 280p. (C). 1996. 110.00 (*0-7103-0540-0*, Pub. by Kegan Paul Intl) Col U Pr.

Ordinary Angers. Steve DeFrance. 96p. 1993. pap. 12.50 (*0-9624205-4-9*) Inevitable Pr.

Ordinary Baby. Gloria Gaither. 14.99 (*0-310-23086-1*) Zondervan.

*__Ordinary Callling, Extraordinary Challenge: Women & Ministry Rules.__ Norma C. Everist. 176p. 2000. pap. 16.00 (*0-687-08757-0*) Abingdon.

Ordinary Cat. Christine Kettner. LC 90-19441. (Illus.). 32p. (J). (ps-3). 1991. 13.95 (*0-06-023172-6*); lib. bdg. 13.89 (*0-06-023173-4*) HarpC Child Bks.

Ordinary Cause Rules. 2nd rev. ed. William McCulloch et al. 224p. 1998. pap. 53.00 (*1-85811-175-7*, Pub. by CLT Prof) Gaunt.

Ordinary Children, Extraordinary Teachers. Marva Collins. 264p. 1992. pap. 12.95 (*1-878901-41-9*) Hampton Roads Pub Co.

*__Ordinary Courage: The Revolutionary War Adventures of Joseph Plumb Martin.__ 2nd ed. Ed. by James K. Martin. (Illus.). 192p. (C). 1999. pap. text 16.50 (*1-881089-47-9*) Brandywine Press.

Ordinary Courage: The Revolutionary War Adventures of Private Joseph Plumb Martin. Ed. by James K. Martin. (Illus.). 192p. (C). 1993. pap. text 16.50 (*1-881089-12-6*) Brandywine Press.

Ordinary Day. Vivian Leiber. (American Romance Ser.: No. 712). 1998. per. 3.75 (*0-373-16712-1*, 1-16712-1) Harlequin Bks.

Ordinary Days. Orval Lund. 31p. 1996. 3.50 (*0-941127-18-4*) Dacotah Terr Pr.

Ordinary Differential Equations W/apps. Bernard J. Rice & Jerry D. Strange. LC 85-29901. (Math). 325p. (C). 1986. mass mkt. 40.00 (*0-534-06366-7*) Brooks-Cole.

Ordinary Differential Equations W/apps. 2nd ed. Bernard J. Rice & Jerry Strange. LC 88-21725. (Math). (Illus.). 465p. (C). 1988. mass mkt. 58.50 (*0-534-09906-8*) Brooks-Cole.

Ordinary Differential Equa 3rd. 3rd ed. Leighton. (Math). 1970. 13.50 (*0-534-01956-0*) Brooks-Cole.

Ordinary Differential Equat W /mod Apps. Finizio. (Math). 1978. mass mkt. 22.25 (*0-534-00552-7*) Brooks-Cole.

Ordinary Differential Equat W /mod Apps. 2nd ed. Norman Finizio & Gerasimos Ladas. (Math). 432p. (C). 1982. mass mkt. 34.00 (*0-534-00898-4*) PWS Pubs.

Ordinary Differential Equations. 1996. 16.95 (*0-340-63203-8*, Pub. by E A) Routldge.

Ordinary Differential Equations. Dieter Armbruster. (C). 1997. pap. text, lab manual ed. write for info. (*0-201-82476-0*) Addison-Wesley.

Ordinary Differential Equations. V. I. Arnold. (Illus.). 270p. (C). 1978. pap. text 25.00 (*0-262-51018-9*) MIT Pr.

Ordinary Differential Equations. V. I. Arnol'd. Tr. by R. Cooke from RUS. (Universitext Ser.). (Illus.). xiv, 322p. 1997. text 59.95 (*0-387-54813-0*) Spr-Verlag.

Ordinary Differential Equations. William Bolton. 1996. pap. 15.95 (*0-582-23399-2*) Addison-Wesley.

Ordinary Differential Equations. George F. Carrier & Carl E. Pearson. LC 91-2642. (Classics in Applied Mathematics Ser.: No. 6). x, 220p. 1991. pap. 34.50 (*0-89871-265-3*) Soc Indus-Appl Math.

Ordinary Differential Equations. Edward L. Ince. (Illus.). 558p. 1956. pap. text 13.95 (*0-486-60349-0*) Dover.

Ordinary Differential Equations. L. B. Jones. (Mathematical Topics for Engineering & Science Students Ser.). (Illus.). 1976. 22.00 (*0-8464-0689-6*) Beekman Pubs.

Ordinary Differential Equations. Lebovitz. (Mathematics Ser.). 2002. pap. 60.00 (*0-534-36552-3*) Brooks-Cole.

Ordinary Differential Equations. T. Myint-U. 296p. 1977. 45.75 (*0-444-00233-2*) P-H.

Ordinary Differential Equations. Otto Plaat. LC 70-156869. 350p. 1971. 33.95 (*0-8162-6844-4*) Holden-Day.

Ordinary Differential Equations. Lev S. Pontryagin & L. Kacinskas. LC 62-17075. 1962. 142.00 (*0-08-009699-9*, Pub. by Pergamon Repr) Franklin.

Ordinary Differential Equations. W. Walter & R. Thompson. Ed. by S. Axler et al. (Graduate Texts in Mathematics Ser.: Vol. 182). 366p. 1998. 49.95 (*0-387-98459-3*) Spr-Verlag.

Ordinary Differential Equations. Morris Tenenbaum & Harry Pollard. (Illus.). 818p. 1985. reprint ed. pap. 18.95 (*0-486-64940-7*) Dover.

Ordinary Differential Equations. 2nd ed. Jack K. Hale. LC 79-17238. (Pure & Applied Mathematics Ser.: Vol. 21). 380p. 1980. lib. bdg. 47.50 (*0-89874-011-8*) Krieger.

Ordinary Differential Equations. 4th ed. Garrett D. Birkhoff & Gian-Carlo Rota. LC 88-14231. 416p. 1989. text 117.95 (*0-471-86003-4*) Wiley.

Ordinary Differential Equations: An Introduction to Nonlinear Analysis. Herbert Amann. Tr. by Gerhard Metzen. (Studies in Mathematics: Vol. 13). (Illus.). xiii, 458p. (C). 1990. lib. bdg. 84.95 (*3-11-011515-8*) De Gruyter.

Ordinary Differential Equations & Calculus of Variations. M. V. Makarets & Reshetnyak. 384p. 1995. text 86.00 (*981-02-2191-6*) World Scientific Pub.

Ordinary Differential Equations & Operators. Ed. by W. Norrie Everitt & R. T. Lewis. (Lecture Notes in Mathematics Ser.: Vol. 1032). 521p. 1983. 57.95 (*0-387-12702-X*) Spr-Verlag.

Ordinary Differential Equations & Smooth Dynamical Systems. D. V. Anosov. LC 98-175523. 233p. 1997. pap. text 54.50 (*3-540-61220-3*) Spr-Verlag.

Ordinary Differential Equations in R to the Nth Power. Livio C. Piccinini et al. (Applied Mathematical Sciences Ser.: Vol. 39). 386p. 1984. 79.95 (*0-387-90723-8*) Spr-Verlag.

Ordinary Differential Equations in the Complex Domain. unabridged ed. Einar Hille. LC 97-70. (Illus.). 496p. 1997. reprint ed. pap. text 14.95 (*0-486-69620-0*) Dover.

Ordinary Differential Equations Using Matlab. 2nd ed. John C. Polkinghorne & David Arnold. LC 99-462614. (C). 1999. pap. text 15.00 (*0-13-011381-6*) P-H.

Ordinary Differential Equations with Applications. 2nd ed. Rice & Strange. (Mathematics Ser.). 1988. student ed. 20.00 (*0-534-09907-6*) Brooks-Cole.

Ordinary Differential Equations with Constant Coefficient. S. K. Godunov. Tr. by Tamara Rozhkovskaya from RUS. LC 97-20182. (Translations of Mathematical Monographs Ser.: No. 169). 284p. 1997. text 99.00 (*0-8218-0656-4*, MMONO/169) Am Math.

Ordinary Differential Equations with Mathematica: A Media Approach. A. Gray et al. LC 96-54732. (TELOS - the Electronic Library of Science). (Illus.). 920p. 1997. 69.95 incl. cd-rom (*0-387-94481-8*) Spr-Verlag.

Ordinary Differential Equations with Mathematica: A Media Approach. Alfred Gray. (Illus.). 502p. 1995. 49.95 (*0-387-94480-X*) Spr-Verlag.

*__Ordinary Differential Equations with Modern Applications.__ 3rd ed. 444p. (C). 1998. text 42.00 (*0-536-01852-9*) S&S Trade.

Ordinary Differential Equations with Numerical Techniques. John Van Iwaarden. 526p. (C). 1985. student ed. 0.90 (*0-15-567551-6*); disk. write for info. (*0-318-59003-4*) SCP.

*__Ordinary Enlightenment.__ John Robinson. 175p. 2000. pap. 12.95 (*0-87159-261-4*) Unity Bks.

Ordinary Events. Carl Sesto. 32p. 1995. 40.00 (*1-880515-50-4*) Schl Mus Fine.

Ordinary Families, Special Children: A Systems Approach to Childhood Disability. 2nd ed. Milton Seligman & Rosalyn B. Darling. LC 96-38683. 324p. 1997. lib. bdg. 32.00 (*1-57230-155-4*, 0155) Guilford Pubns.

*__Ordinary Families, Special Children: A Systems Approach to Childhood Disability.__ 2nd ed. Milton Seligman & Rosalyn B. Darling. 324p. 1999. pap. text 20.00 (*1-57230-466-9*) Guilford Pubns.

Ordinary Genius: The Story of Albert Einstein. Stehpanie S. McPherson. (Illus.). 96p. (J). 1997. pap. text 6.95 (*1-57505-067-6*, Carolrhoda) Lerner Pub.

Ordinary Genius: The Story of Albert Einstein. Stephanie S. McPherson. LC 93-1408. (Trailblazers Ser.). 96p. (J). (gr. 3-7). 1995. lib. bdg. 22.60 (*0-87614-788-0*, Carolrhoda) Lerner Pub.

*__Ordinary German Lives During the Holocaust.__ Heidi Scriba & Janet Barton Speer. (Illus.). 224p. 2000. pap. 24.00 (*0-913337-38-2*) Southfarm Pr.

Ordinary Grace: An Examination of the Roots of Compassion, Altruism & Empathy, & the Ordinary Individuals Who Help Others in Extraordinary Ways. Kathleen A. Brehony. LC 98-31876. 256p. 1999. 24.95 (*1-57322-108-2*, Riverhead Books) Putnam Pub Group.

*__Ordinary Grace: Lessons from Those Who Help Others in Extraordinary Ways.__ Kathleen A. Brehony. 2000. pap. 12.95 (*1-57322-786-2*, Riverhd Trade) Berkley Pub.

*__Ordinary Graces: Christian Teachings on the Interior Life.__ Ed. by Lorraine Kisly. 256p. 2000. 22.00 (*0-609-60674-3*) Bell T.

Ordinary Heart. unabridged ed. Carol G. Kaplan. 58p. 1997. pap. 12.00 (*1-56439-069-1*) Ridgeway.

Ordinary Hero. Yves Bertrand. LC 98-19392.Tr. of Le Heros Ordinaire. 143p. 1998. pap. text 23.95 (*1-891859-25-0*) Atwood Pub LLC.

Ordinary Heroes: When the Walls of Life Are Crumbling. David R. Walls. LC 90-85033. 192p. 1991. pap. 8.99 (*0-89636-271-X*, LifeJourney) Chariot Victor.

*__Ordinary Horror.__ David Searcy. 2001. 24.95 (*0-670-89476-1*, Viking) Viking Penguin.

Ordinary Justice: A Zoe Kergulin Mystery. Trudy Labovitz. LC 99-19045. 248p. 1999. pap. 12.00 (*1-883523-31-1*, Pub. by Spinsters Ink) SPD-Small Pr Dist.

Ordinary Knowledge: An Introduction to Interpretative Sociology. Michel Maffesoli. Tr. by David Macey. 192p. 1996. 76.95 (*0-7456-1118-4*) Blackwell Pubs.

Ordinary Lessons: Girlhoods of the 1950s. Susan Douglas Franzosa. LC 96-47028. (Counterpoints Ser.: Vol. 43). (Illus.). XIV, 315p. (C). 1999. pap. text 32.95 (*0-8204-3669-0*) P Lang Pubng.

Ordinary Life: A Memoir of Illness. Kathlyn Conway. LC 96-273316. 250p. 1996. pap. text 22.95 (*0-7167-3036-7*) W H Freeman.

Ordinary Life: L3. Jerry Messec. Ed. by Jean A. McConochie. (Regents Readers Ser.). (Illus.). 68p. (gr. 7-12). 1987. pap. text 3.50 (*0-13-639816-2*, 20886) Prentice ESL.

Ordinary Life . . . Touched by an Extraordinary God. Arlene M. Gray. LC 98-115490. (Illus.). 218p. 1997. pap. 8.95 (*1-880726-12-2*) Turnage Pub.

Ordinary Life, Festival Days: Aesthetics in the Midwestern County Fair. Leslie Prosterman. LC 93-49385. (Illus.). 352p. 1994. pap. text 24.95 (*1-56098-408-2*) Smithsonian.

Ordinary Life of Extraordinary People: An Attempt at Literary Anecdotes with Elements of Literary Plagiarism. Vadim Shamarin. (RUS., Illus.). 86p. 1999. pap. write for info. (*0-9670766-0-9*) Russian Radio.

Ordinary Lives: Platoon 1005 & the Vietman War. W. D. Ehrhart. LC 98-39963. (Illus.). 344p. 1999. 29.50 (*1-56639-674-3*) Temple U Pr.

Ordinary Love & Good Will. Jane Smiley. 208p. 1996. pap. 10.00 (*0-449-90794-5*, Columbine) Fawcett.

Ordinary Love & Good Will. Jane Smiley. 224p. 1991. mass mkt. 5.99 (*0-8041-0714-9*) Ivy Books.

Ordinary Magic. Malcolm Bosse. LC 93-7956. Orig. Title: Ganesh. 192p. (J). 1993. pap. 5.95 (*0-374-42517-5*) FS&G.

Ordinary Magic. Malcolm Bosse. Orig. Title: Ganesh. 1994. 17.75 (*0-8446-6774-9*) Peter Smith.

Ordinary Magic. Meeka Walsh. 1997. pap. 7.95 (*0-88801-136-9*, Pub. by Turnstone Pr) Genl Dist Srvs.

Ordinary Magic: And Other Ceremonies. Gwenana. Ed. by Jonnie Taylor-Leidt. LC 87-83379. (Illus.). 111p. (Orig.). 1987. per. 6.95 (*0-931721-06-7*) La Jolla Poets.

Ordinary Magic: Everyday Life As Spiritual Path. Ed. by John Welwood. LC 92-50125. 296p. (Orig.). 1992. pap. 17.00 (*0-87773-597-2*, Pub. by Shambhala Pubns) Random.

Ordinary Man. Mel Arrighi. 1969. pap. 5.25 (*0-8222-0863-6*) Dramatists Play.

Ordinary Men Called by God: A Study of Abraham, Moses & David. James M. Boice. LC 97-47515. 144p. 1998. pap. 9.99 (*0-8254-2075-X*) Kregel.

Ordinary Men RI. Christopher R. Browning. LC 91-50471. (Illus.). 304p. 1998. pap. 14.00 (*0-06-099506-8*, Perennial) HarperTrade.

Ordinary Messengers. Michael Hannon. 96p. 1991. pap. 10.00 (*0-912449-33-0*) Floating Island.

Ordinary Miracles. Stephanie S. Tolan. Date not set. pap. 4.95 (*0-380-73322-6*, Wm Morrow) Morrow Avon.

*__Ordinary Miracles.__ Stephanie S. Tolan. LC 99-13658. 160p. 1999. 16.00 (*0-688-16269-X*, Wm Morrow) Morrow Avon.

Ordinary Miracles: Life in a Small Church. Nick Taylor. LC 92-597. 288p. 1993. 21.00 (*0-671-70944-5*) S&S Trade.

*__Ordinary Miracles: True Stories of an Extraordinary God Who Works in Our Everyday Lives.__ Rebekah Montgomery. 2000. 12.99 (*1-57748-744-3*) Barbour Pub.

Ordinary Objects. Hans Deichmann. Tr. by Peter Constantine & Peter Glassgold. LC 97-32567. 1997. 22.00 (*1-56886-048-X*) Marsilio Pubs.

Ordinary of the Mass in Eight Languages. 48p. (Orig.). 1992. pap. 4.95 (*0-8146-2125-2*, Liturg Pr Bks) Liturgical Pr.

Ordinary Paradise: A Memoir. Laura Furman. LC 98-27467. (Illus.). 160p. 1998. 22.95 (*0-9657468-4-4*) Winedale Pub.

Ordinary Parents, Exceptional Children. Robert A. Naseef. LC 96-49752. 256p. 1997. 21.95 (*1-55972-377-7*, Birch Ln Pr) Carol Pub Group.

Ordinary Partial Differential Equation. Sleeman & Jarvis. 1987. pap. text. write for info. (*0-582-98892-6*, Pub. by Addison-Wesley) Longman.

Ordinary People. Judith Guest. 1983. 5.50 (*0-87129-500-8*, O39) Dramatic Pub.

Ordinary People. Judith Guest. LC 82-9834. 1982. 13.05 (*0-606-10277-9*, Pub. by Turtleback) Demco.

Ordinary People. Judith Guest. 263p. 1982. pap. 8.95 (*0-14-006517-2*, Penguin Bks) Viking Penguin.

Ordinary People: Family Life & Global Values. Michael True. LC 90-22590. 160p. reprint ed. pap. 49.60 (*0-608-20249-5*, 207150800012) Bks Demand.

Ordinary People - Extraordinary Marriages: Reclaiming God's Original Design. Brian Nystrom. Ed. by Debbie Jensen. (Illus.). 200p. 1997. 18.95 (*0-9655512-5-3*) Life Res Am.

Ordinary People - Study Guide. Crystal Norris. Ed. by Joyce Friedland & Rikki Kessler. (Novel-Ties Ser.). (YA). (gr. 9-12). 1993. pap. text 15.95 (*0-88122-122-8*) Lrn Links.

Ordinary People & Extraordinary Evil: A Report on the Beguilings of Evil. Fred Emil Katz. LC 92-15578. 154p. (C). 1993. text 57.50 (*0-7914-1441-8*); pap. text 18.95 (*0-7914-1442-6*) State U NY Pr.

Ordinary People & The tin Can Tree: Curriculum Unit. Center for Learning Network Staff et al. (Novel Ser.). 62p. (YA). (gr. 9-12). 1996. spiral bd. 18.95 (*1-56077-369-3*) Ctr Learning.

Ordinary People As Monks & Mystics: Lifestyles for Self-Discovery. Marsha Sinetar. LC 85-62932. 192p. 1986. pap. 11.95 (*0-8091-2773-3*) Paulist Pr.

Ordinary People Can Do the Extraordinary. Ed. by Bennie E. Goodwin & Colleen Birchett. 64p. (Orig.). 1993. pap., teacher ed. 6.95 (*0-940955-23-7*); pap. text 7.95 (*0-940955-22-9*) Urban Ministries.

Ordinary People Dancing: Essays on Kate O'Brien. Eibhear Walshe. 1993. 45.00 (*0-902561-65-0*) Cork Univ.

O

An Asterisk (*) at the beginning of an entry indicates that the title is appearing for the first time.

Ordinary People Extraordinary Lives: A Book of Possibilities. Rahul Patel. LC 98-100939. (Illus.). 56p. 1997. pap. 14.99 (*0-9661493-0-0*) R Patel.

***Ordinary People, Extraordinary Lives: A Pictorial History of Working People in New York City.** Debra E. Bernhardt & Rachel Bernstein. LC 99-50742. (Illus.). 221p. 2000. 34.95 (*0-8147-9866-7*) NYU Pr.

Ordinary People, Extraordinary Lives: Political & Economic Change in a Tohoku Village. Jackson H. Bailey. LC 91-15781. (Illus.). 272p. 1991. text 35.00 (*0-8248-1299-9*) UH Pr.

***Ordinary People, Extraordinary Money: The 8 Secrets of How 5,000 Ordinary Americans Became Successful Investors--and How You Can Too.** Ric Edelman. LC 99-53998. 336p. 2000. 25.00 (*0-06-270247-5*) HarpC.

Ordinary People, Extraordinary Wealth. Ric Edelman. pap. 14.00 (*0-06-273686-8*) HarpC.

Ordinary People in Public Policy: A Behavioural Analysis. Richard Rose. 208p. (C). 1989. text 45.00 (*0-8039-8135-X*); pap. text 17.95 (*0-8039-8136-8*) Sage.

Ordinary Relationship: American Opposition to Republican Revolution in China. Daniel M. Crane & Thomas A. Breslin. LC 85-26452. 256p. 1986. 32.95 (*0-8130-0800-X*) U Press Fla.

***Ordinary Ressurections: Children in the Years of Hope.** Jonathan Kozol. 2000. pap. 14.00 (*0-06-095645-3*) HarpC.

***Ordinary Resurrections: Children in the Years of Hope.** Jonathan Kozol. Ed. by Doug Pepper. LC 99-59808. 336p. 2000. 25.00 (*0-517-70000-X*) Crown Pub Group.

Ordinary Seaman. Francisco Goldman. 400p. 1998. reprint ed. pap. 12.00 (*0-8021-3548-X*, Grove) Grove-Atltic.

Ordinary Snake Dance. Phoebe MacAdams. 62p. 1994. pap. 10.00 (*0-9649240-3-X*) Cahuenga Pr.

Ordinary Social Occasions Sandcastles & Structural Reproduction: A Sociology of Everybody's Social Life. Howard N. Boughey. LC 95-6676. 200p. (C). 1995. text 39.95 (*0-391-03938-5*) Humanities.

Ordinary Songs. Lisa Steinman. 26p. 1996. 5.00 (*0-614-30123-8*) Skydog OR.

***Ordinary Splendors: Tales of Virtues & Wisdom.** Toni Knapp. (Illus.). 43p. (J). (gr. 5-7). 2000. reprint ed. text 16.00 (*0-7881-6845-2*) DIANE Pub.

Ordinary Story. Ivan A. Goncharov. Tr. by Marjorie L. Hoover from RUS.Tr. of Obyknovennaia Istoriia. 1994. 27.95 (*0-87501-088-1*) Ardis Pubs.

Ordinary Stuff: A Simple Guide for Abundant Living. Joan Betts. LC 97-66588. 112p. 1997. pap. 12.00 (*1-888604-04-2*) SunShine CO.

***Ordinary Suffering of Extraordinary Saints.** Vincent J. O'Malley. LC 99-75034. 272p. 2000. pap. 12.95 (*0-87973-893-6*) Our Sunday Visitor.

Ordinary Things: Poems from a Walk in Early Spring. Ralph Fletcher. LC 96-3393. (Illus.). 48p. (J). (gr. 7 up). 1997. 15.00 (*0-689-81035-0*) Atheneum Yung Read.

Ordinary Time see Daily Homilies

Ordinary Time: Cycles in Marriage, Faith, & Renewal. Nancy Mairs. 256p. 1994. pap. 15.00 (*0-8070-7057-2*) Beacon Pr.

Ordinary Time: For the Three Year Lectionary. Alan Smith. (Psalm Songs Ser.: No. 3). 1998. pap. 17.95 (*0-225-66855-6*) Continuum.

Ordinary Time: Praying with Children & Families. Center for Learning Network Staff. (Religion Ser.). 179p. 1996. spiral bd. 19.95 (*1-56077-458-4*) Ctr Learning.

Ordinary Time - Weeks 18 to 34 see St. Joseph Liturgy of the Hours: Liturgy of the Hours

Ordinary Time - Weeks 1 to 17 see St. Joseph Liturgy of the Hours: Liturgy of the Hours

Ordinary Time Weeks 1-12 see In Conversation with God

Ordinary Time Weeks 12-23 see In Conversation with God

Ordinary Time Weeks 24-34 see In Conversation with God

***Ordinary to Extraordinary: Exploring Visual Design Problems.** Ken Vieth. (Illus.). 148p. 1999. pap. 19.95 (*0-87192-387-4*) Davis Mass.

Ordinary Vices. Judith N. Shklar. LC 84-531. 280p. 1984. 39.00 (*0-674-64175-2*) Belknap Pr.

Ordinary Vices. Judith N. Shklar. 280p. 1995. pap. text 14.95 (*0-674-64176-0*) Belknap Pr.

Ordinary Wisdom. Eloise K. Healy. (Illus.). (Orig.). 1981. 25.00 (*0-940806-01-0*); pap. 10.00 (*0-940806-00-2*) Paradise Press.

Ordinary Wisdom: And Other Pleasures. Gwenana. Ed. by Jonnie Taylor-Leidt. (Illus.). 100p. (Orig.). 1987. per. 6.95 (*0-931721-05-9*) La Jolla Poets.

***Ordinary Wisdom: Biographical Aging & the Journey of Life.** William L. Randall & Gary M. Kenyon. LC 00-22889. 240p. 2000. 59.00 (*0-275-96556-2*, C6556, Praeger Pubs) Greenwood.

***Ordinary Wisdom: Sakya Pandita's Treasury of Good Advice.** Sakya Pandita. Tr. by John T. Davenport. 384p. 2000. pap. 21.95 (*0-86171-161-0*) Wisdom MA.

Ordinary Woman. Miriam E. Giles. 1997. pap. 56.95 (*1-57553-545-9*) Watermrk Pr.

***Ordinary Woman: The Remarkable Story of the First American Woman in California.** Cecelia Holland. LC 98-48929. 1999. 21.95 (*0-312-86528-7*, Pub. by Forge NYC) St Martin.

Ordinary Woman's Extraordinary Faith: The Autobiography of Patricia St. John. Patricia M. St. John. LC 95-44552. 312p. 1996. pap. 11.99 (*0-87788-751-9*, H Shaw Pubs) Waterbrook Pr.

***Ordinary Women.** Susan Sallis. (J). 2000. pap. 10.95 (*0-552-13756-1*, Pub. by Transworld Publishers Ltd) Trafalgar.

Ordinary Women . . . Extraordinary Circumstances. Bonnie Lang et al. 134p. 1995. 10.00 (*1-879908-09-3*) Milton Pub.

***Ordinary Women, Extraordinary Lives: Women in American History.** Ed. by Kriste Lindenmeyer. LC 00-25659. (Human Tradition in America Ser.: No. 6). 320p. 2000. 55.00 (*0-8420-2752-1*); pap. 18.95 (*0-8420-2754-8*, SR Bks) Scholarly Res Inc.

Ordinary Wonders: Living Recovery from Sexual Abuse. Lilian Green. 264p. pap. 13.95 (*0-88961-172-6*, Pub. by Womens Pr) LPC InBook.

Ordinary Words. Ruth Stone. LC 99-29931. 1999. 17.95 (*0-9638183-9-2*, Pub. by Paris Pr MA); pap. 13.95 (*0-9638183-8-4*, Pub. by Paris Pr MA) Consort Bk Sales.

***Ordination.** U. Bernell Baldwin. LC 99-93692. (Illus.). vii, 210p. 1999. pap. 15.00 (*0-9670514-0-1*) U & W Pub.

Ordination: A Biblical-Historical View. Marjorie Warkentin. LC 82-8908. 212p. reprint ed. pap. 65.80 (*0-608-14516-5*, 202534800043) Bks Demand.

Ordination Anointings in the Western Church Before 1000 A. D. Gerald G. Ellard. (Mediaeval Academy of America Publications: Vol. 16). 1932. 30.00 (*0-527-01688-8*) Periodicals Srv.

Ordination for Deacons. J. R. Mosley. 4p. (Orig.). 1997. pap. 4.00 (*0-9627958-3-6*) J R Mosleys Pr.

Ordination in the Study of Morphology, Evolution & Systematics of Insects: Application & Quantitative Genetic Rationals. Ed. by J. T. Sorensen & R. Foottit. LC 92-32305. 418p. 1992. 200.00 (*0-444-89801-8*) Elsevier.

Ordination of Plant Communities. Robert H. Whittaker. 1982. pap. text 97.50 (*90-6193-565-2*) Kluwer Academic.

Ordination of Women: An Essay on the Office of Christian Ministry. Paul K. Jewett. 148p. 1992. reprint ed. pap. 7.95 (*1-881266-07-9*) Fuller Seminary.

Ordination of Women As Rabbis: Studies & Responsa. Ed. by Simon Greenberg. (Moreshet Studies in Jewish History, Literature & Thought: Vol. XIV). 1988. 19.95 (*0-87334-041-8*) Ktav.

Ordination Rites of the Ancient Churches of East & West. Paul F. Bradshaw. 288p. 1992. pap. 19.95 (*0-8146-6000-2*, Pueblo Bks) Liturgical Pr.

Ordinations of U. S. Catholic Bishops, 1790-1989: A Chronological List. Charles Bransom. 288p. 1990. boxed set 59.95 (*1-55586-323-X*) US Catholic.

Ordines Coronationis Franciae: Texts & Ordines for the Coronation of Frankish & French Kings & Queens in the Middle Ages, Vol. I. Ed. by Richard A. Jackson. LC 94-48121. (Middle Ages Ser.). 320p. 1995. text 49.95 (*0-8122-3263-1*) U of Pa Pr.

***Ordiness Coronationis Franciae: Texts & Ordines for the Coronation of Frankish & French King.** Richard A. Jackson. (Middle Ages Ser). 2000. 69.95 (*0-8122-3542-8*) U of Pa Pr.

Ordnance Gazeteer of Scotland: A Graphic & Accurate Description of Every Place in Scotland, 3 vols., Set. Ed. by Francis H. Groome. (Illus.). 1762p. 1995. reprint ed. lib. bdg. 150.00 (*0-8328-4598-1*) Higginson Bk Co.

Ordnance Survey Guide to Historic Houses in Britain. Nathaniel Harris & Paul Pettit. (Ordnance Survey Guides Ser.). (Illus.). 320p. (Orig.). 1987. pap. 14.95 (*0-393-30401-9*) Norton.

Ordnance Survey Leisure Guide: Lake District. Automobile Association Staff. Date not set. pap. text 15.95 (*0-7495-1195-8*, Pub. by Auto Assn Guides) Hunter NJ.

Ordnance Survey Memoirs of Ireland Vol. 1: County Armagh. Ed. by Angelique Day & Patrick McWilliams. LC 91-154915. (Illus.). 150p. 1990. pap. 15.99 (*0-85389-341-1*, Pub. by Inst Irish Studies) Irish Bks Media.

Ordnance Survey Memoirs of Ireland Vol. 2: County Antrim I: Newtownabbey & District. Ed. by Angelique Day & Patrick McWilliams. (Illus.). 150p. 1990. pap. 15.99 (*0-85389-347-0*, Pub. by Inst Irish Studies) Irish Bks Media.

Ordnance Survey Memoirs of Ireland Vol. 3: County Down I: South Down. Ed. by Angelique Day & Patrick McWilliams. (Illus.). 150p. 1990. pap. 15.99 (*0-85389-358-6*, Pub. by Inst Irish Studies) Irish Bks Media.

Ordnance Survey Memoirs of Ireland Vol. 4: Fermanagh I: Enniskillen & Upper Loch Erne. Ed. by Angelique Day & Patrick McWilliams. (Illus.). 150p. 1990. pap. 15.99 (*0-85389-360-8*, Pub. by Inst Irish Studies) Irish Bks Media.

Ordnance Survey Memoirs of Ireland Vol. 5: Tyrone I: South West & South Tyrone (Omagh) Ed. by Angelique Day & Patrick McWilliams. (Illus.). 150p. 1990. pap. 15.99 (*0-85389-362-4*, Pub. by Inst Irish Studies) Irish Bks Media.

Ordnance Survey Memoirs of Ireland Vol. 6: Londonderry 1: Magherafelt & District. Ed. by Angelique Day & Patrick McWilliams. (Illus.). 150p. 1990. pap. 15.99 (*0-85389-364-0*, Pub. by Inst Irish Studies) Irish Bks Media.

Ordnance Survey Memoirs of Ireland Vol. 7: Down II: North Down & the Ards. Ed. by Angelique Day & Patrick McWilliams. (Illus.). 150p. 1991. pap. 15.99 (*0-85389-374-8*, Pub. by Inst Irish Studies) Irish Bks Media.

Ordnance Survey Memoirs of Ireland Vol. 8: Antrim II: Lisburn & South Antrim. Ed. by Angelique Day & Patrick McWilliams. (Illus.). 150p. 1991. pap. 15.99 (*0-85389-376-4*, Pub. by Inst Irish Studies) Irish Bks Media.

Ordnance Survey Memoirs of Ireland Vol. 9: Antrim II: Larne & Island Magee. Ed. by Angelique Day & Patrick McWilliams. (Illus.). 150p. 1991. pap. 15.99 (*0-85389-378-0*, Pub. by Inst Irish Studies) Irish Bks Media.

Ordnance Survey Memoirs of Ireland Vol. 10: Antrim III: Larne & Island Magee. Ed. by Angelique Day & Patrick McWilliams. (Illus.). 150p. 1991. pap. 15.99 (*0-85389-389-6*, Pub. by Inst Irish Studies) Irish Bks Media.

Ordnance Survey Memoirs of Ireland Vol. 11: Londonderry III: Roe Valley Lower (Magilligan) Ed. by Angelique Day & Patrick McWilliams. (Illus.). 150p. 1991. pap. 15.99 (*0-85389-390-X*, Pub. by Inst Irish Studies) Irish Bks Media.

Ordnance Survey Memoirs of Ireland Vol. 12: Down III: Mid-Down. Ed. by Angelique Day & Patrick McWilliams. (Illus.). 150p. 1991. pap. 15.99 (*0-85389-391-8*, Pub. by Inst Irish Studies) Irish Bks Media.

Ordnance Survey Memoirs of Ireland Vol. 13: Antrim IV: The Glens. Angelique Day. Ed. by Patrick McWilliams. (Illus.). 150p. 1991. pap. 15.99 (*0-85389-392-6*, Pub. by Inst Irish Studies) Irish Bks Media.

Ordnance Survey Memoirs of Ireland Vol. 14: Fermanagh II: Lower Lough Erne. Ed. by Angelique Day & Patrick McWilliams. (Illus.). 150p. 1991. pap. 15.99 (*0-85389-393-4*, Pub. by Inst Irish Studies) Irish Bks Media.

Ordnance Survey Memoirs of Ireland Vol. 15: Londonderry IV: Roe Balley Upper (Dungiven) Ed. by Angelique Day & Patrick McWilliams. (Illus.). 150p. 1991. pap. 15.99 (*0-85389-394-2*, Pub. by Inst Irish Studies) Irish Bks Media.

Ordnance Survey Memoirs of Ireland Vol. 16: County Antrim V: Giant's Causeway & Ballymoney. Ed. by Angelique Day & Patrick McWilliams. (Illus.). 125p. 1991. pap. 15.99 (*0-85389-388-8*, Pub. by Inst Irish Studies) Irish Bks Media.

Ordnance Survey Memoirs of Ireland Vol. 17: Down IV: East Down & Lecale. Ed. by Angelique Day & Patrick McWilliams. (Illus.). 150p. 1992. pap. 15.99 (*0-85389-439-6*, Pub. by Inst Irish Studies) Irish Bks Media.

Ordnance Survey Memoirs of Ireland Vol. 18: County Londonderry V: Maghera & Tamlaght O'Crilly. Ed. by Angelique Day & Patrick McWilliams. (Illus.). 144p. 1993. pap. 18.50 (*0-85389-441-8*, Pub. by Inst Irish Studies) Irish Bks Media.

Ordnance Survey Memoirs of Ireland Vol. 19: County Antrim VI: Southwest Antrim. Ed. by Angelique Day & Patrick McWilliams. (Illus.). 138p. 1993. pap. 18.50 (*0-85389-458-2*, Pub. by Inst Irish Studies) Irish Bks Media.

Ordnance Survey Memoirs of Ireland Vol. 20: Tyrone II: Mid & East Tyrone (Cookstown & Dungannon) Ed. by Angelique Day & Patrick McWilliams. (Illus.). 150p. 1993. pap. 18.50 (*0-85389-460-4*, Pub. by Inst Irish Studies) Irish Bks Media.

Ordnance Survey Memoirs of Ireland Vol. 21: County Antrim VII. Ed. by Angelique Day & Patrick McWilliams. (Illus.). 150p. 1990. pap. 15.99 (*0-85389-462-0*, Pub. by Inst Irish Studies) Irish Bks Media.

Ordnance Survey Memoirs of Ireland Vol. 22: County Londonderry VI: Northeast Londonderry. Ed. by Angelique Day & Patrick McWilliams. (Illus.). 122p. 1993. pap. 18.50 (*0-85389-464-7*, Pub. by Inst Irish Studies) Irish Bks Media.

Ordnance Survey Memoirs of Ireland Vol. 24: County Antrim IX: North Antrim Coast & Rathlin. Ed. by Angelique Day & Patrick McWilliams. (Illus.). 134p. 1994. pap. 18.50 (*0-85389-468-X*, Pub. by Inst Irish Studies) Irish Bks Media.

Ordnance Survey Memoirs of Ireland Vol. 25: Londonderry VII: North-West Londonderry. Ed. by Angelique Day & Patrick McWilliams. (Illus.). 125p. 1994. pap. 18.50 (*0-85389-510-4*, Pub. by Inst Irish Studies) Irish Bks Media.

Ordnance Survey Memoirs of Ireland Vol. 26: County Antrim X: East Antrim (Glynn, Inver, Kilroot & Templecorran) Ed. by Angelique Day & Patrick McWilliams. (Illus.). 132p. 1996. pap. 18.50 (*0-85389-512-0*, Pub. by Inst Irish Studies) Irish Bks Media.

Ordnance Survey Memoirs of Ireland Vol. 27: County Londonderry VIII: East Londonderry. Ed. by Angelique Day & Patrick McWilliams. (Illus.). 130p. 1994. pap. 18.50 (*0-85389-514-7*, Pub. by Inst Irish Studies) Irish Bks Media.

Ordnance Survey Memoirs of Ireland Vol. 28: County Londonderry IX: West Londonderry. Ed. by Angelique Day & Patrick McWilliams. (Illus.). 127p. 1995. pap. 18.50 (*0-85389-516-3*, Pub. by Inst Irish Studies) Irish Bks Media.

Ordnance Survey Memoirs of Ireland Vol. 29: County Antrim XI: Antrim Town & Ballyclare. Ed. by Angelique Day & Patrick McWilliams. (Illus.). 157p. 1995. pap. 18.50 (*0-85389-518-X*, Pub. by Inst Irish Studies) Irish Bks Media.

Ordnance Survey Memoirs of Ireland Vol. 30: County Londonderry X: Mid-Londonderry. Ed. by Angelique Day & Patrick McWilliams. (Illus.). 132p. 1995. pap. 18.50 (*0-85389-520-1*, Pub. by Inst Irish Studies) Irish Bks Media.

Ordnance Survey Memoirs of Ireland Vol. 31: County Londonderry XI: South Londonderry. Ed. by Angelique Day & Patrick McWilliams. (Illus.). 144p. 1995. pap. 18.50 (*0-85389-550-3*, Pub. by Inst Irish Studies) Irish Bks Media.

Ordnance Survey Memoirs of Ireland Vol. 32: County County Antrim XII: Ballynure & District. Ed. by Angelique Day & Patrick McWilliams. (Illus.). 141p. 1995. pap. 18.50 (*0-85389-552-X*, Pub. by Inst Irish Studies) Irish Bks Media.

Ordnance Survey Memoirs of Ireland Vol. 33: County Londonderry XII: Coleraine & Mouth of the Bann. Ed. by Angelique Day & Patrick McWilliams. (Illus.). 173p. 1995. pap. 18.50 (*0-85389-554-6*, Pub. by Inst Irish Studies) Irish Bks Media.

Ordnance Survey Memoirs of Ireland Vol. 34: County Londonderry XIII: Clondermot & the Waterside. Ed. by Angelique Day & Patrick McWilliams. (Illus.). 133p. 1996. pap. 18.50 (*0-85389-556-2*, Pub. by Inst Irish Studies) Irish Bks Media.

Ordnance Survey Memoirs of Ireland Vol. 35: County County Antrim XIII: Templepatrick & District. Ed. by Angelique Day & Patrick McWilliams. (Illus.). 160p. 1996. pap. 18.50 (*0-85389-560-0*, Pub. by Inst Irish Studies) Irish Bks Media.

Ordnance Survey Memoirs of Ireland Vol. 36: County Londonderry XIV: Faughanvale. Ed. by Angelique Day & Patrick McWilliams. (Illus.). 120p. 1996. pap. 18.50 (*0-85389-558-9*, Pub. by Inst Irish Studies) Irish Bks Media.

Ordnance Survey Memoirs of Ireland Vol. 37: County Antrim XIV: Carrickfergus. Ed. by Angelique Day & Patrick McWilliams. (Illus.). 195p. 1996. pap. 18.50 (*0-85389-563-5*, Pub. by Inst Irish Studies) Irish Bks Media.

Ordnance Survey Memoirs of Ireland Vol. 38: County Donegal: North-East Donegal. Ed. by Angelique Day & Patrick McWilliams. LC 91-154915. (Illus.). 152p. 1997. pap. 18.50 (*0-85389-564-3*, Pub. by Inst Irish Studies) Irish Bks Media.

Ordnance Survey Memoirs of Ireland Vol. 39: County Donegal II: West & South Donegal. Ed. by Angelique Day & Patrick McWilliams. (Illus.). 199p. 1997. pap. 18.50 (*0-85389-659-3*, Pub. by Inst Irish Studies) Irish Bks Media.

Ordnance Survey Memoirs of Ireland Vol. 40: Counties Cavan, Leitrim, Louth, Mnaghan & Sligo. Ed. by Angelique Day & Patrick McWilliams. (Illus.). 150p. 1998. pap. 18.50 (*0-85389-661-5*, Pub. by Inst Irish Studies) Irish Bks Media.

Ordnance Went up Front. 417p. 1993. 35.00 (*1-884849-09-1*) R&R Bks.

Ordnung Coleoptera (Larven) Bernhard Klausnitzer. (Bestimmungsbucher Zur Bodenfauna Europas, Band 10). 1978. text 234.00 (*90-6193-569-5*) Kluwer Academic.

Ordnung der Woerter: Kognitive und Lexikalische Strukturen. Ed. by Gisela Harris. (Institut fuer Deutsche Sprache - Jahrbuch, 1993 Ser.). (GER.). v, 403p. (C). 1995. lib. bdg. 118.45 (*3-11-014438-7*) De Gruyter.

Ordnung des Terrors: Das Konzentrationslager. Wolfgang Sofsky. (GER.). 390p. 1993. 45.00 (*3-10-072704-5*, Pub. by S Fischer) Intl Bk Import.

Ordnung im Zwielicht see Order in the Twilight

Ordnung und Chaos: Das Englishce Restaurationsdrama, 1660-1685. Elmar Lehmann. (Beihefte zu Poetica Ser.: Vol. 19). (GER.). 194p. 1988. 56.00 (*90-6032-307-6*, Pub. by B R Gruner) Humanities.

***Ordnungsschwund Ordnungswandel: Par Lagerkvist und der deutsche Expressionismus.** Piotr Bukowski. 2000. 37.95 (*3-631-35508-4*) P Lang Pubng.

Ordo ab Chao: The Original & Complete Rituals 4-33 Degree of the First Supreme Council, 33 Degree at Charleston, South Carolina. 426p. 1996. reprint ed. pap. 75.00 (*1-56459-999-X*) Kessinger Pub.

Ordo Initationis Christianae Adulorum see Rite of Christian Initiation of Adults

***Ordo Nobilis.** Michael De Verteuil et al. (Ars Magica Ser.). 224p. 2000. pap. 25.95 (*1-887801-82-0*, Atlas Games) Trident MN.

Ordo Virtutum of Hildegard of Bingen: Critical Studies. Ed. by Audrey E. Davidson. (Early Drama, Art & Music Monograph: No. 18). 1992. pap. 13.00 (*1-879288-18-4*); boxed set 25.00 (*1-879288-17-6*) Medieval Inst.

Ordonnance for the Five Kinds of Columns after the Method of the Ancients. Claude Perrault. Tr. by Indra K. McEwen. LC 92-4649. (Texts & Documents Ser.). (Illus.). 208p. 1993. 34.95 (*0-89236-232-4*, Pub. by J P Getty Trust); pap. 19.95 (*0-89236-233-2*, Pub. by J P Getty Trust) OUP.

***Ordos Plateau of China: An Endangered Environment.** Hong Jiang. LC 99-6751. 210p. 1999. 29.95 (*92-808-1035-9*) UN Univ Pr.

Ordovician & Siluvian Faunas from Arctic Canada, Vol. 1. Curt Teichert. LC 76-21347. (Thule Expedition, 5th, 1921-1924 Ser.: No. 5). (Illus.). reprint ed. 71.50 (*0-404-58305-9*) AMS Pr.

Ordovician Basin in the Puna of NW-Argentina & N-Chile Geodynamic Evolution from Back-Arc to Foreland Basin. Heinrich Bahlburg. (Geotektonische Forschungen Ser.: Vol. 75). (GER.). 107p. 1990. pap. 52.00 (*3-510-50041-5*, Pub. by E Schweizerbartsche) Balogh.

Ordovician (Caradoc) Marginal Basin Volcanism in Snowdonia (North-West Wales) M. F. Howells et al. (British Geological Survey Ser.). (Illus.). 203p. 1991. pap. 80.00 (*0-11-884465-2*, Pub. by Statnry Office) Balogh.

Ordovician Deicke & Millbring K-Bentonite Beds of the Cincinnati Arch & Southern Valley & Ridge Province. James T. Hayes. LC 94-3151. (Special Papers: No. 290). 1994. pap. 24.00 (*0-8137-2290-X*) Geol Soc.

Ordovician K-Bentonites of Eastern North America. Ed. by Dennis R. Kolata et al. LC 96-34502. (Special Papers: No. 313). 1997. pap. 46.00 (*0-8137-2313-2*) Geol Soc.

Ordovician Odyssey: Short Papers for the 7th International Symposium on the Ordovician System, Las Vegas, Nevada. Ed. by J. D. Cooper et al. 498p. 1995. 30.00 (*1-878861-70-0*) Pac Section SEPM.

An Asterisk (*) at the beginning of an entry indicates that the title is appearing for the first time.

Ordovician of the Great Basin: Fieldtrip Guidebook & Volume for the 7th International Symposium on the Ordovician System, Las Vegas, Nevada. Ed. by J. D. Cooper. 151p. 1995. 12.00 (*1-878861-71-9*) Pac Section SEPM.

Ordovician System in Greenland & South Africa: Correlation Charts & Explanatory Notes. Ed. by S. Henry Williams. LC 94-1653. (IUGS Publication Ser.: Vol. 29). 1994. pap. 25.00 (*0-8137-7429-2*) Geol Soc.

Ordovician System of the East European Platform & Tuva-Southeastern Russia: Correlation Charts & Explanatory Notes. Ed. by Barry D. Webby et al. LC 94-10370. (IUGS Publication Ser.: No. 28). 1994. pap. 25.00 (*0-8137-7428-4*) Geol Soc.

Ordre du Discours. Michel Foucault. (Gallimard Ser.). (FRE.). 84p. 1971. pap. 17.95 (*2-07-027774-7*) Schoenhof.

Ord's Bothy Songs & Ballads. Alexander Fenton. 400p. (C). 1996. reprint ed. pap. 36.00 (*0-85976-303-X*, Pub. by J Donald) St Mut.

Ordways. William Humphrey. LC 96-45593. (Voices of the South Ser.). 376p. 1997. pap. 14.95 (*0-8071-2161-4*) La State U Pr.

Ore-Bearing Granite Systems: Petrogenesis & Mineralizing Processes. Ed. by H. J. Stein & J. L. Hannah. (Special Papers: No. 246). (Illus.). 380p. 1990. pap. 30.00 (*0-8137-2246-2*) Geol Soc.

Ore Deposition Associated with Magmas. (Reviews in Economic Geology Ser.: Vol. 4). (Illus.). 250p. (C). 1989. pap. text 25.00 (*0-9613074-3-9*) Soc Econ Geol.

Ore Deposits of the United States, 1933-1967: The Graton-Sales Volume, Vol. 1. Ed. by John D. Ridge. LC 68-24170. (Rocky Mountain Fund Ser.). (Illus.). 1023p. 1970. reprint ed. pap. 200.00 (*0-7837-9171-2*, 204987100001) Bks Demand.

Ore Deposits of the United States, 1933-1967: The Graton-Sales Volume, Vol. 2. Ed. by John D. Ridge. LC 68-24170. (Rocky Mountain Fund Ser.). (Illus.). 895p. 1970. reprint ed. pap. 200.00 (*0-7837-9172-0*, 204987100002) Bks Demand.

Ore Dust in Her Shoes. 2nd ed. Claire W. Schumacher. LC 80-52920. (Illus.). 194p. (Orig.). 1991. 8.00 (*0-917378-05-9*) Zenith City.

Ore Elements in Arc Lavas, No. 29. R. L. Stanton. LC 93-42959. (Oxford Monographs on Geology & Geophysics: No. 24). (Illus.). 404p. 1994. text 145.00 (*0-19-854050-7*, Clarendon Pr) OUP.

Ore Geology & Industrial Minerals. 3rd ed. A. M. Evans. (Geoscience Texts Ser.). (Illus.). 400p. 1992. pap. 54.95 (*0-632-02953-6*) Blackwell Sci.

Ore Microscopy & Ore Petrography. 2nd ed. James R. Craig & David Vaughan. 448p. 1994. 140.00 (*0-471-55175-9*) Wiley.

Ore Minerals & Intergrowth. Paul Ramdohr. 1980. 97.00 (*0-08-011635-3*, Pergamon Pr) Elsevier.

Ore Minerals & Their Inter-Growths Vol. 1: English Translation of 4th Edition, 2 vols., Set. 2nd ed. Paul Ramdohr & D. Ingerson. LC 79-40745. (International Series in Earth Science: Vol. 35). (Illus.). 1269p. 1980. 203.00 (*0-08-023801-7*, Pub. by Pergamon Repr) Franklin.

Ore Mobilization in the Alps & in SE-Europe. Ed. by W. E. Petrascheck. (Schriftenreihe der Erdwissenschaftlichen Kommissionen Ser.: Band 6). (ENG & GER.). 106p. 1983. 36.95 (*0-387-86511-X*) Spr-Verlag.

Ore Processing. S. K. Jain. 530p. (C). 1987. text 142.00 (*90-6191-485-X*, Pub. by A A Balkema) Ashgate Pub Co.

Ore Processing. S. K. Jain. 1987. 47.00 (*81-204-0140-9*, Pub. by Oxford IBH) S Asia.

Oregon see From Sea to Shining Sea

Oregon see Atlas of Historical County Boundaries

Oregon see Celebrate the States - Group 2

Oregon see One Nation Series

***Oregon.** (Switched on Schoolhouse Ser.). (Illus.). (J). 2000. pap. 24.95 (*0-7403-0289-2*) Alpha AZ.

Oregon. Gretchen Bratvold. (Hello U. S. A. Ser.). (Illus.). 72p. (J). (gr. 3-6). 1991. lib. bdg. 19.95 (*0-8225-2704-9*, Lerner Publctns) Lerner Pub.

Oregon. Gretchen Bratvold. (Hello U. S. A. Ser.). (Illus.). 72p. (J). 1997. pap. text 5.95 (*0-8225-9765-9*) Lerner Pub.

Oregon. Dennis B. Fradin. (From Sea to Shining Sea Ser.). (Illus.). 64p. (J). 1995. pap. 7.95 (*0-516-43837-9*) Childrens.

Oregon Scott Ingram. LC 99-20967. (America the Beautiful Ser.). 2000. 32.00 (*0-516-20996-5*) Childrens.

Oregon. Paul Joseph. LC 97-21421. (United States Ser.). (Illus.). 32p. 1998. lib. bdg. 19.93 (*1-56239-878-4*, Checkerboard Library) ABDO Pub Co.

***Oregon.** Rhonda Ostertag. LC 99-29579. (Camping Guides Ser.). 1999. pap. 16.95 (*1-56044-707-9*) Falcon Pub Inc.

Oregon. Rand McNally Staff. 1997. pap. 5.95 (*0-528-96682-0*) Rand McNally.

Oregon. R. Conrad Stein. LC 88-38528. (America the Beautiful Ser.). (Illus.). 144p. (J). (gr. 4 up). 1989. lib. bdg. 28.00 (*0-516-00483-2*) Childrens.

Oregon. Kathleen Thompson. LC 85-9973. (Portrait of America Library). 48p. (J). (gr. 4-8). 1996. pap. 5.95 (*0-8114-7463-1*) Raintree Steck-V.

Oregon. Kathleen Thompson. LC 85-9973. (Portrait of America Library). (Illus.). 48p. (J). (gr. 3-6). 1996. lib. bdg. 22.83 (*0-8114-7382-1*) Raintree Steck-V.

Oregon. WHITECAP BOOKS. 1999. 14.95 (*1-55110-864-X*) Gr Arts Ctr Pub.

Oregon. Charlotte Wilcox. (One Nation Ser.). 1997. 19.00 (*0-516-20531-5*) Childrens.

***Oregon.** 2nd ed. Ed. by Fodors Travel Publications, Inc. Staff. 192p. (Orig.). 2000. pap. 13.50 (*0-679-00403-3*) Fodors Travel.

Oregon. 3rd ed. (Compass American Guides Ser.). 320p. 1998. pap. 19.95 (*0-679-00033-X*, Compass Amrcn) Fodors Travel.

Oregon: A Postcard Book. Larry Geddis. 1994. pap. text 7.95 (*1-56044-278-6*) Falcon Pub Inc.

Oregon: A Short History of a Long Journey. John B. Wyeth. 1974. 19.95 (*0-87770-027-3*) Ye Galleon.

Oregon: A Statistical Overview, 1996. Rebecca L. Reid & William R. Flagg. 140p. 1996. per. 30.00 (*0-9653878-0-1*) Sthrn Oregon Reg.

Oregon: End of the Trail. Federal Writers' Project Staff. (American Guidebook Ser.). 548p. 1941. reprint ed. 79.00 (*0-403-02186-3*) Somerset Pub.

Oregon: End of the Trail. Federal Writers' Project Staff & Writers Program-WPA Staff. (American Guide Ser.). 1989. reprint ed. lib. bdg. 79.00 (*0-7812-1036-4*, 1036) Rprt Serv.

Oregon: Facts & Symbols. Emily McAuliffe. LC 98-41526. 1999. 14.00 (*0-531-11804-5*) Capstone Pr.

Oregon: Facts & Symbols. Emily Mcauliffe. LC 98-41526. (States & Their Symbols Ser.). (J). 1999. write for info. (*0-7368-0216-9*, Hlltop Bks) Capstone Pr.

Oregon: Its History, Condition & Prospects. Gustavus Hines. LC 72-9450. (Far Western Frontier Ser.). (Illus.). 444p. 1973. reprint ed. 29.95 (*0-405-04978-1*) Ayer.

Oregon: Off the Beaten Path: A Guide to Unique Places. 4th ed. Myrna Oakley. LC 99-33142. (Off the Beaten Path Ser.). (Illus.). 224p. 1999. pap. text 12.95 (*0-7627-0405-5*) Globe Pequot.

Oregon: The Struggle for Possession. William Barrows. LC 72-3766. (American Commonwealths Ser.: No. 2). reprint ed. 39.50 (*0-404-57202-2*) AMS Pr.

***Oregon: Then & Now.** Thomas Robinson & John Daniel. (Illus.). 184p. 2000. 60.00 (*1-56579-380-3*) Westcliffe Pubs.

Oregon: There & Back in 1877. Wallis Nash. Ed. by J. Kenneth Munford. LC 76-9770. (Illus.). 348p. 1976. reprint ed. 19.95 (*0-87071-077-X*) Oreg St U Pr.

Oregon - California Trail. Ed. by O. J. Fargo. (Western History Ser.). (Illus.). 55p. (Orig.). (YA). (gr. 5 up). 1990. pap. 1.50 (*0-924702-30-3*) Grn Valley Area.

Oregon - Collected Works of Federal Writers Project. Federal Writers' Project Staff. 1991. reprint ed. lib. bdg. 98.00 (*0-7812-5778-6*) Rprt Serv.

Oregon, a Report. Neil M. Howison. 36p. 1976. reprint ed. pap. 9.95 (*0-87770-053-2*) Ye Galleon.

***Oregon Almanac: Facts about Oregon.** Andrea Jarvela. (Illus.). 2000. pap. 12.95 (*1-55868-472-7*, West Winds Pr) Gr Arts Ctr Pub.

Oregon Alphabet Book. 2nd ed. Susan Torrence & Leslie Polansky. (Illus.). 32p. (J). (ps-6). 1983. 5.95 (*0-914281-00-3*) Torrence Pubns.

Oregon & Applegate Trail Diary of Welborn Beeson in 1853: The Unabridged Diary with Introduction & Contemporary Comments by Bert Webber. exp. rev. ed. Ed. by Bert Webber. LC 87-8170. Orig. Title: Welborn Beeson on the Oregon Trail in 1853. (Illus.). 82p. 1987. pap. 7.50 (*0-936738-21-9*) Webb Research.

Oregon & California in 1848, 2 vols. J. Quinn Thornton. LC 72-9471. (Far Western Frontier Ser.). (Illus.). 802p. 1973. reprint ed. 54.95 (*0-405-04998-6*) Ayer.

Oregon & California Trail Diary of Jane Gould in 1862: The Unabridged Diary with Introduction & Contemporary Comments by Bert Webber. Ed. by Bertram Weber. LC 87-14249. (Illus.). 92p. 1987. pap. 7.50 (*0-936738-22-7*) Webb Research.

Oregon & El Dorado. Thomas Bulfinch. (Works of Thomas Bulfinch). 1989. reprint ed. lib. bdg. 79.00 (*0-7812-2168-4*) Rprt Serv.

Oregon & Other Short Plays. Peter Hedges. 1999. pap. 5.25 (*0-8222-1639-6*) Dramatists Play.

Oregon & Other State Greats (Biographies) Carole Marsh. (Carole Marsh Oregon Bks.). (Illus.). (J). 1994. pap. 19.95 (*0-7933-1914-5*); lib. bdg. 29.95 (*0-7933-1913-7*); disk 29.95 (*0-7933-1915-3*) Gallopade Intl.

Oregon & Overland Trail Diary of Mary Louisa Black in 1865: The Unabridged Diary with Introduction & Contemporary Comments by Bert Webber, Includes Genealogy. Ed. by Marguerite Black. LC 87-8170. (Illus.). 86p. 1989. pap. 7.50 (*0-936738-36-7*) Webb Research.

Oregon & Washington National Forest Campground Directory & Recreation Guide. 2nd rev. ed. Dale Farley. Ed. by Shirley T. Moore. (Illus.). 212p. 1990. pap. text 4.95 (*0-914019-25-2*) NW Interpretive.

Oregon & Washington Parks Guide. Barbara Sinotte & Peggy DeLay. (State & National Parks Ser.). (Illus.). 240p. (Orig.). 1996. pap. 11.95 (*1-55650-736-4*) Hunter NJ.

Oregon Appellate Manual, 1986-1992. George W. Kelly. 280p. 1992. ring bd. 70.00 (*0-409-20129-4*, MICHIE) LEXIS Pub.

Oregon Atlas & Gazetteer. 3rd ed. Delorme Publishing Staff. LC 99-464314. 88p. 1998. pap. 16.95 (*0-89933-258-7*) DeLorme Map.

Oregon Automotive Directory. Ed. by T. L. Spelman. 1985. 24.95 (*1-55527-027-1*) Auto Contact Inc.

Oregon Bach Festival, 1970-1994. Marian C. Donnelly. LC 94-17193. 1994. pap. 10.00 (*0-87114-116-7*) U of Oreg Bks.

Oregon Bandits, Bushwackers, Outlaws, Crooks, Devils, Ghosts, Desperadoes & Other Assorted & Sundry Characters! Carole Marsh. (Carole Marsh Oregon Bks.). (Illus.). (J). 1994. pap. 19.95 (*0-7933-0937-9*); lib. bdg. 29.95 (*0-7933-0938-7*); disk 29.95 (*0-7933-0939-5*) Gallopade Intl.

Oregon Bankruptcy Law. Richard Slottee. 1994. spiral bd. 175.00 (*1-56257-765-4*, 82263-10, MICHIE) LEXIS Pub.

Oregon Biennial, 97. Kathryn Kanjo. (Illus.). 47p. 1997. pap. 15.00 (*1-883124-07-7*) Portland Art Mus.

Oregon Bill: The Collected Yarns of a Northwest Icon. Rod Fielder. (Illus.). 169p. (Orig.). 1996. pap. 12.00 (*1-885266-47-2*) Story Line.

Oregon "BIO" Bingo! 24 Must Know State People for Kids to Learn about While Having Fun! Carole Marsh. (Bingo! Ser.). (Illus.). (J). (gr. 2-8). 1998. pap. 14.95 (*0-7933-8633-0*) Gallopade Intl.

Oregon Birds. James Kavanagh. (Pocket Naturalist Ser.). (Illus.). 1998. 5.95 (*1-889903-70-1*, Pub. by Waterford WA) Falcon Pub Inc.

Oregon Blue Book, 1997-1998. Oregon Secretary of State Staff. (Illus.). 480p. (Orig.). 1997. pap. 14.00 (*0-924540-02-8*) Oregon Secy.

Oregon Blue Book, 91-92. Ed. by Phil Keisling. 1991. pap. 10.00 (*0-924540-11-7*) Oregon Secy.

Oregon Blue-Ribbon Fly Fishing Guide. John Shewey. (Illus.). 94p. 1998. pap. 24.95 (*1-57188-133-6*) F Amato Pubns.

Oregon Book: Information A to Z. Connie H. Battaile. LC 98-90263. xi, 677p. 1998. pap. 24.95 (*0-9657638-2-X*) Saddle Mtn.

Oregon Bookstore Book: A Surprising Guide to Our State's Bookstores & Their Specialties for Students, Teachers, Writers & Publishers. Carole Marsh. (Oregon Bks.). (Illus.). 1994. pap. 19.95 (*0-7933-2967-1*); lib. bdg. 29.95 (*0-7933-2966-3*); disk 29.95 (*0-7933-2968-X*) Gallopade Intl.

Oregon Boy in the Yukon: An Alaska Highway Story. Willis Grafe. LC 91-78007. (Illus.). 163p. (Orig.). 1992. pap. 9.95 (*0-9631813-0-0*) Chesnimnus Pr.

***Oregon Business Directory, 1999-2000.** American Business Directories Staff. 1520p. 1999. boxed set 450.00 incl. cd-rom (*0-7687-0148-1*, 1047-8809) Am Busn Direct.

***Oregon Business Directory (2000-2001)** American Business Directories Staff et al. 1,520p. 2000. boxed set 450.00 incl. cd-rom (*0-7687-0233-X*) Am Busn Direct.

Oregon, California & Mormon Trails by Air: A Pilot's Guide to the Immigrant Trails. William W. White. (Illus.). 208p. 1997. pap. 16.95 (*0-9655085-9-5*) Western Airtrails.

Oregon Campgrounds Hiking Guide. Rhonda Ostertag & George Ostertag. LC 97-24352. 256p. 1997. 14.95 (*0-89886-547-6*) Mountaineers.

Oregon Cattleman, Governor, Congressman: Memoirs & Times of Walter M. Pierce. Walter M. Pierce. Ed. by Arthur H. Bone. LC 80-81718. (Illus.). 528p. 1981. pap. 14.95 (*0-87595-098-1*) Oregon Hist.

Oregon Census Index, 1880: Mortality Schedules. (Illus.). 1981. lib. bdg. 35.00 (*0-89593-462-0*, Accel Indexing) Genealogical Srvcs.

Oregon Census Index, 1850: Mortality Schedules. (Illus.). 1980. lib. bdg. 30.00 (*0-89593-458-2*, Accel Indexing) Genealogical Srvcs.

Oregon Census Index, 1851-1859, Vol. 1. Ronald V. Jackson. (Illus.). lib. bdg. 48.00 (*0-89593-764-6*, Accel Indexing) Genealogical Srvcs.

Oregon Census Index, 1841-1849. Ronald V. Jackson. (Illus.). 1984. lib. bdg. 55.00 (*0-89593-763-8*, Accel Indexing) Genealogical Srvcs.

Oregon Census Index, 1890: Union Veterans. (Illus.). lib. bdg. 50.00 (*0-89593-463-9*, Accel Indexing) Genealogical Srvcs.

Oregon Census Index, 1870: Mortality Schedules. (Illus.). 1981. lib. bdg. 34.00 (*0-89593-460-4*, Accel Indexing) Genealogical Srvcs.

Oregon Census Index, 1860: Mortality Schedules. (Illus.). lib. bdg. 30.00 (*0-89593-459-0*, Accel Indexing) Genealogical Srvcs.

Oregon City, (by Way of the Barlow Road) at the End of the National Historic Oregon Trail. Bert Webber & Margie Webber. LC 92-33561. (Illus.). 120p. 1993. pap. 12.95 (*0-936738-71-5*) Webb Research.

Oregon Classic Christmas Trivia: Stories, Recipes, Activities, Legends, Lore & More! Carole Marsh. (Carole Marsh Oregon Bks.). (Illus.). (J). 1994. pap. 19.95 (*0-7933-0940-9*); lib. bdg. 29.95 (*0-7933-0941-7*); disk 29.95 (*0-7933-0942-5*) Gallopade Intl.

Oregon Coast. Mark Hoy & John Maher. LC 93-27488. (Illus.). 104p. (Orig.). 1994. pap. 9.95 (*1-56037-043-2*) Am Wrld Geog.

Oregon Coast. Photos by Steve Terrill. (Illus.). 64p. 1995. 14.95 (*1-56579-120-7*) Westcliffe Pubs.

Oregon Coast: America's Most Scenic Coastline. (Illus.). 48p. (Orig.). 1996. pap. text 9.95 (*1-884958-24-9*) Am Prods.

Oregon Coast Aquarium Seafood Cookbook. Leslie J. Mansfield. 144p. 1997. pap. 14.95 (*0-89288-262-X*) Maverick.

Oregon Coast Best Places. 2nd ed. Stephanie Irving. (Illus.). 152p. 1999. pap. 11.95 (*1-57061-174-2*) Sasquatch Bks.

Oregon Coast Impressions, Vol. 1. Larry Geddis. (Illus.). 48p. (Orig.). 1997. pap. 11.95 (*0-9655963-0-3*) Arts of Earth.

Oregon Coast Recreational Atlas: A Guide to Natural Resources & Recreational Opportunities. Timothy J. Sullivan. LC 91-72792. (Orig.). 1991. pap. 11.95 (*1-880062-21-6*) E&S Geog & Info Servs.

Oregon Coast Visitors Guide. Pat McNemar. 110p. (Orig.). 1997. pap. 8.95 (*1-57502-478-0*, P01432) Morris Pubng.

Oregon Coastal Salmon Spawning Surveys, 1994-1995. Steven E. Jacobs & Cedric X. Cooney. 214p. 1997. reprint ed. 28.80 (*0-89904-676-2*, Cascade Geog Soc); reprint ed. pap. 22.80 (*0-89904-662-2*, Cascade Geog Soc) Crumb Elbow Pub.

Oregon Coastales. Carole Marsh. (Carole Marsh Oregon Bks.). (Illus.). (J). 1994. lib. bdg. 29.95 (*0-7933-1907-2*) Gallopade Intl.

Oregon Coastales. Carole Marsh. (Carole Marsh Oregon Bks.). (Illus.). (J). 1997. pap. 19.95 (*0-7933-1908-0*) Gallopade Intl.

Oregon Coastales! Carole Marsh. (Oregon Bks.). (J). 1994. lib. bdg. 29.95 (*0-7933-7302-6*) Gallopade Intl.

Oregon Coloring Book. (Illus.). 24p. (Orig.). (J). (gr. k-2). 1995. pap. 2.99 (*1-886462-29-1*) J & H Sales.

Oregon Comprehensive Index, 1994, 2 vols., Set. 1200p. Date not set. 100.50 (*0-614-10382-7*, MICHIE) LEXIS Pub.

Oregon Constitution & Proceedings & Debates of the Constitutional Convention of 1857. Ed. by Charles Henry Carey. 543p. 1926. 14.95 (*0-87595-092-2*) Oregon Hist.

Oregon Consumer Health Care Scorecard Project: Final Report. Pamela Hanes & Merwyn Greenlick. (Illus.). 129p. (Orig.). 1997. pap. text 30.00 (*0-7881-4490-1*) DIANE Pub.

Oregon Cook Book. Janet Walker. (Illus.). 128p. (Orig.). 1995. ring bd. 6.95 (*1-885590-03-2*) Golden West Pub.

Oregon Cooking. B. Carlson. (Illus.). 176p. 1998. spiral bd. 5.95 (*1-57166-112-3*) Hearts N Tummies.

Oregon Corporation Law & Practice. Sandra L. Rich & Roy W. Tucker. LC 91-30641. (National Corporation Law Ser.). 1991. ring bd. 126.00 (*0-13-640129-5*) Aspen Law.

Oregon County Missouri Deed Abstracts, 1845-1868. Nona S. Williams. 326p. (Orig.). 1994. pap. text 27.00 (*1-55613-945-4*) Heritage Bk.

Oregon Covered Bridges: An Oregon Documentary. Bert Webber. LC 90-13064. (Illus.). 162p. 1991. 24.95 (*0-936738-65-0*) Webb Research.

Oregon Covered Bridges: Expanded Edition. expanded ed. Bert Webber & Margie Webber. LC 95-12050. (Illus.). 108p. 1995. pap. 12.95 (*0-936738-86-3*) Webb Research.

***Oregon Crime in Perspective 2000.** Ed. by Kathleen O'Leary Morgan & Scott E. Morgan. 22p. 2000. spiral bd. 19.00 (*0-7401-0336-9*) Morgan Quitno Corp.

Oregon Crime Perspective, 1998. Ed. by Kathleen O'Leary Morgan & Scott E. Morgan. 20p. 1998. pap. 19.00 (*1-56692-936-9*) Morgan Quitno Corp.

Oregon Crime Perspectives, 1999. Kathleen O'Leary Morgan. 22p. 1999. spiral bd. 19.00 (*0-7401-0136-6*) Morgan Quitno Corp.

Oregon Criminal Practice. Wayne T. Westling. LC 96-69191. 900p. 1996. 95.00 (*1-55834-360-1*, 82308-10, MICHIE) LEXIS Pub.

Oregon Criminal Practice, 1998 Supplement. Wayne T. Westling. 151p. 1998. write for info. (*0-327-00862-8*, 8230911) LEXIS Pub.

Oregon "Crinkum-Crankum" A Funny Word Book about Our State. Carole Marsh. (Oregon Bks.). (Illus.). (J). (gr. 3-12). 1994. 29.95 (*0-7933-4919-2*); pap. 19.95 (*0-7933-4920-6*); disk 29.95 (*0-7933-4921-4*) Gallopade Intl.

Oregon Crisis. John M'Duffee. 30p. 1999. reprint ed. pap. 5.95 (*0-87770-063-X*) Ye Galleon.

Oregon Debtor-Creditor Law. 2nd ed. Brian A. Blum. 570p. 1992. ring bd. 95.00 (*0-88063-996-2*, MICHIE) LEXIS Pub.

Oregon Descents: A Backcountry Ski Guide to the Southern Cascades. David Waag. (Illus.). 160p. 1997. pap. 17.95 (*0-9661746-0-7*, Pub. by Free Heel) Alpenbooks.

Oregon Desert. E. R. Jackman & R. A. Long. LC 64-15389. (Illus.). 1964. 19.95 (*0-87004-074-X*) Caxton.

***Oregon Desert Guide: 70 Hikes.** Andy Kerr. LC 99-50933. (Illus.). 272p. 2000. pap. 14.95 (*0-89886-602-2*) Mountaineers.

Oregon Detour. Nard Jones. LC 89-16355. (Northwest Reprints Ser.). 320p. 1990. pap. 13.95 (*0-87071-501-1*); text 24.95 (*0-87071-500-3*) Oreg St U Pr.

Oregon Dingbats! Bk. 1: A Fun Book of Games, Stories, Activities & More about Our State That's All in Code! for You to Decipher. Carole Marsh. (Oregon Bks.). (Illus.). (J). (gr. 3-12). 1994. pap. 19.95 (*0-7933-3885-9*); lib. bdg. 29.95 (*0-7933-3884-0*); disk 29.95 (*0-7933-3886-7*) Gallopade Intl.

Oregon Divided: A Regional Geography. Samuel N. Dicken & Emily F. Dicken. LC 80-84480. (Two Centuries of Oregon Geography Ser.: Vol. 2). (Illus.). 192p. 1982. 17.95 (*0-87595-082-5*); pap. 10.95 (*0-87595-064-7*) Oregon Hist.

Oregon Ducks Football: 100 Years of Glory. Michael C. McCann. LC 95-79214. (Illus.). 160p. 1995. 28.95 (*0-9648244-7-7*) McCann Communs.

Oregon Earthquake Handbook: An Easy-to-Understand Information & Survival Guide. Vern Cope. LC 92-97560. (Illus.). 152p. (Orig.). 1993. pap. text 11.95 (*0-9635564-3-6*) V Cope.

Oregon East, Oregon West: Travels & Memoirs by Theodor Kirchoff, 1863-1872. Ed. by Frederic Trautmann. LC 85-26573. (Illus.). 220p. 1987. 19.95 (*0-87595-174-0*) Oregon Hist.

Oregon Environmental Law Handbook. Preston, Thorgrimson, Shidler, Gates & Ellis Staff. 201p. 1992. pap. text 79.00 (*0-86587-285-6*) Gov Insts.

Oregon Events Guide: 1998-99 Edition. rev. ed. Gail Folgedalen. (Illus.). 130p. 1998. pap. 9.95 (*1-881005-22-4*) Gails Guides.

Oregon Evidence. 3rd ed. Laird C. Kirkpatrick. 980p. 110.00 (*1-55834-366-0*) LEXIS Pub.

Oregon Evidence Code Handbook, 1995. 400p. (Orig.). 1995. 39.50 (*0-614-10379-7*, MICHIE) LEXIS Pub.

Oregon Evidence Code Handbook, 1992. 400p. 1994. pap. 39.50 (*0-409-20125-1*, MICHIE) LEXIS Pub.

Oregon Evidence Code with Objections. Anthony J. Bocchino et al. 231p. 1997. pap. 25.95 (*1-55681-551-4*) Natl Inst Trial Ad.

Oregon Evidence, 1989-1993. 2nd ed. Laird C. Kirkpatrick. 971p. Date not set. text 110.00 (*0-409-20382-3*, 82271-11, MICHIE) LEXIS Pub.

Oregon Evidence, 1989-1993. 2nd ed. Laird C. Kirkpatrick. 980p. 1994. ring bd., suppl. ed. 47.50 (*0-685-74296-2*, MICHIE) LEXIS Pub.

O

An Asterisk (*) at the beginning of an entry indicates that the title is appearing for the first time.

Oregon Evidence, 1990. 2nd ed. Laird Kirkpatrick. 1995. text. write for info. (*0-409-20385-8*, 82271-10, MICHIE) LEXIS Pub.

Oregon Evidence, 1998 Supplement. 3rd ed. Kirkpatrick. 66p. 1998. suppl. ed. 42.50 (*0-327-00357-X*, 8227213) LEXIS Pub.

***Oregon Evidence, 1999 Supplement.** Laird C. Kirkpatrick. 50p. 1999. write for info. (*0-327-01574-8*, 8227214) LEXIS Pub.

Oregon Experience. Bernard Freemesser. Ed. by George Beltran. LC 78-73426. (Illus.). 1979. 19.95 (*0-918966-04-3*) Image West.

Oregon Experiment. Christopher Alexander. (Illus.). 202p. 1975. 39.95 (*0-19-501824-9*) OUP.

Oregon Express Companies. Dale E. Forster. 231p. 1985. 32.50 (*0-9619690-0-8*) D E Forster.

Oregon Facts & Factivities. Carole Marsh. (Carole Marsh State Bks.). (Illus.). (J). (gr. 4-7). 1996. pap., teacher ed. 19.95 (*0-7933-7921-0*, C Marsh) Gallopade Intl.

Oregon Family Adventure Guide: Great Things to See & Do for the Entire Family. Cheryl McLean. LC 95-7741. (Family Adventure Guide Ser.). (Illus.). 176p. (Orig.). 1995. pap. 9.95 (*1-56440-647-4*) Globe Pequot.

Oregon Farmer's Market Cookbook. Kris Wetherbee. (Illus.). 200p. 1998. pap. 14.95 (*0-89288-272-7*) Maverick.

Oregon Federal Census Index, 1880. (Illus.). 1986. lib. bdg. 112.00 (*0-89593-461-2*, Accel Indexing) Genealogical Srvcs.

Oregon Federal Census Index, 1850. Ronald V. Jackson & Gary R. Teeples. LC 77-86104. (Illus.). 1978. lib. bdg. 55.00 (*0-89593-114-1*, Accel Indexing) Genealogical Srvcs.

Oregon Federal Census Index, 1870. Ronald V. Jackson. (Illus.). 1985. lib. bdg. 80.00 (*0-89593-766-2*, Accel Indexing) Genealogical Srvcs.

Oregon Federal Census Index, 1860. Ronald V. Jackson. LC 99-198555. (Illus.). 1985. lib. bdg. 75.00 (*0-89593-765-4*, Accel Indexing) Genealogical Srvcs.

Oregon Festival Fun for Kids! Carole Marsh. (Oregon Bks.). (Illus.). (YA). (gr. 3-12). 1994. pap. 19.95 (*0-7933-4038-1*); lib. bdg. 29.95 (*0-7933-4037-3*); disk 29.95 (*0-7933-4039-X*) Gallopade Intl.

Oregon Firsts: Oregon's Trailblazing Past & Present. James A. Long. (Illus.). 224p. (Orig.). (YA). 1993. pap. 24.95 (*1-882635-00-0*) Pumpkin Ridge.

Oregon for the Curious. Ralph Friedman. LC 75-151057. (Illus.). 1972. pap. 9.95 (*0-87004-222-X*) Caxton.

Oregon Fossils. Orr. 390p. 1998. per. 40.95 (*0-7872-5454-1*) Kendall-Hunt.

Oregon "GEO" Bingo! 38 Must Know State Geography Facts for Kids to Learn While Having Fun! Carole Marsh. (Bingo! Ser.). (Illus.). (J). (gr. 2-8). 1998. pap. 14.95 (*0-7933-8634-9*) Gallopade Intl.

Oregon Geographic Names. 6th ed. Lewis McArthur. 968p. 1992. pap. 19.95 (*0-87595-237-2*) Oregon Hist.

Oregon Geographic Names. 6th ed. Lewis L. McArthur. 920p. 1992. 29.95 (*0-87595-236-4*) Oregon Hist.

Oregon Golf. Paul Linnman. LC 99-25224. 1999. 29.95 (*1-55868-474-3*) Gr Arts Ctr Pub.

Oregon Government! The Cornerstone of Everyday Life in Our State! Carole Marsh. (Carole Marsh Oregon Bks.). (Illus.). (J). (gr. 3-12). 1996. pap. 19.95 (*0-7933-6293-8*); lib. bdg. 29.95 (*0-7933-6292-X*); disk 29.95 (*0-7933-6294-6*) Gallopade Intl.

Oregon Government Law Deskbook. 300p. 1991. ring bd. 65.00 (*0-685-40833-7*, 403-51) Oregon Law Inst.

Oregon Government Law Deskbook. 125p. 1993. ring bd. 35.00 (*0-614-04694-7*) Oregon Law Inst.

Oregon, Greyhound of the Atlantic: A Diver's Scrapbook. Intro. by S. Bielenda. (Illus.). 185p. (Orig.). 1993. pap. 20.00 (*0-9635879-0-0*) H F Kaasmann.

Oregon Gulch Gold Mining Company of Butte County, California, 1852. Ed. by Norman Tanis. (American Classics Facsimile Ser.: Pt. V). 1976. pap. 10.00 (*0-937048-04-6*) Santa Susana.

Oregon Gull Identification Workbook. Kathy Merrifield. 38p. 1991. pap. 9.95 (*0-9630692-0-9*) Selaginella.

***Oregon Health Care in Perspective 2000.** Ed. by Kathleen O'Leary Morgan & Scott E. Morgan. 21p. 2000. spiral bd. 19.00 (*0-7401-0236-2*) Morgan Quitno Corp.

Oregon Health Care Perspective, 1998. Ed. by Kathleen O'Leary Morgan & Scott E. Morgan. 20p. 1998. pap. 19.00 (*1-56692-836-2*) Morgan Quitno Corp.

Oregon Health Care Perspective 1999. Ed. by Kathleen O'Leary Morgan. 21p. 1999. spiral bd. 19.00 (*0-7401-0086-6*) Morgan Quitno Corp.

Oregon High: A Climbing Guide to Nine Cascade Volcanoes. Jeff Thomas. 128p. (Orig.). 1991. pap. 11.95 (*0-9629042-0-1*) Keep Climbing.

Oregon "HISTO" Bingo! 42 Must Know State History Facts for Kids to Learn While Having Fun! Carole Marsh. (Bingo! Ser.). (Illus.). (J). (gr. 2-8). 1998. pap. 14.95 (*0-7933-8635-7*) Gallopade Intl.

Oregon Historical & Biographical Index, Vol. 1. Ronald V. Jackson. LC 78-53713. (Illus.). 1984. lib. bdg. 30.00 (*0-89593-196-6*, Accel Indexing) Genealogical Srvcs.

Oregon Historical Quarterly Index, 1961-1980. Ed. by Rick Harmon. 500p. (Orig.). 1990. pap. text 20.00 (*0-87595-127-9*) Oregon Hist.

Oregon Historical Quarterly Index, 1900-1939, Vol. 1. Ed. by Rick Harmon. 838p. 1990. reprint ed. pap. text 20.00 (*0-87595-221-6*) Oregon Hist.

Oregon Historical Quarterly Index, 1940-1960, Vol. 2. LC 06-13601. 712p. 25.00 (*0-87595-079-5*); pap. 20.00 (*0-87595-078-7*) Oregon Hist.

Oregon Historical Society Microfilm Guide. LC 73-79868. (Research & Bibliography Ser.: No. 4). 162p. pap. 7.50 (*0-87595-041-8*) Oregon Hist.

Oregon Historical Vignettes. Paul Keller & Jack Pement. (Illus.). 104p. 1974. 14.95 (*0-8323-0247-3*) Binford Mort.

Oregon History! Surprising Secrets about Our State's Founding Mothers, Fathers & Kids! Carole Marsh. (Carole Marsh Oregon Bks.). (Illus.). (J). (gr. 3-12). 1996. pap. 19.95 (*0-7933-6140-0*); lib. bdg. 29.95 (*0-7933-6139-7*); disk 29.95 (*0-7933-6141-9*) Gallopade Intl.

Oregon Hot Air Balloon Mystery. Carole Marsh. (Carole Marsh Oregon Bks.). (Illus.). (J). (gr. 2-9). 1994. 29.95 (*0-7933-2651-6*); pap. 19.95 (*0-7933-2652-4*); disk 29.95 (*0-7933-2653-2*) Gallopade Intl.

Oregon Hot Zones! Viruses, Diseases, & Epidemics in Our State's History. Carole Marsh. (Hot Zones! Ser.). (Illus.). (J). (gr. 3-12). 1998. pap. 19.95 (*0-7933-8940-2*); lib. bdg. 29.95 (*0-7933-8939-9*) Gallopade Intl.

Oregon in Perspective, 1998. Ed. by Kathleen O'Leary Morgan & Scott E. Morgan. 24p. 1998. pap. 19.00 (*1-56692-886-9*) Morgan Quitno Corp.

***Oregon in Perspective, 1999.** Kathleen O'Leary Morgan. 26p. 1999. spiral bd. 19.00 (*1-56692-986-5*) Morgan Quitno Corp.

***Oregon in Perspective 2000.** Ed. by Kathleen O'Leary Morgan & Scott E. Morgan. 26p. 2000. spiral bd. 19.00 (*0-7401-0286-9*) Morgan Quitno Corp.

Oregon Indian Dictionary for Kids! Carole Marsh. (Carole Marsh State Bks.). (Illus.). (J). (gr. 2-9). 1996. 29.95 (*0-7933-7755-2*, C Marsh); pap. 19.95 (*0-7933-7756-0*, C Marsh) Gallopade Intl.

Oregon Indians Culture. Jeff Zucker. 1983. pap. text 24.95 (*0-87595-109-0*) Oregon Hist.

***Oregon Insurance Laws.** Oregon. LC 98-66068. 1999. write for info. (*0-89246-496-8*) NILS Pub.

***Oregon Investment & Business Guide: Business, Investment, Export-Import Opportunities, 50, 37.** Global Investment Center, USA Staff. (U. S. Regional Investment & Business Library-99: Vol. 37). (Illus.). 350p. (Orig.). 1999. pap. 59.95 (*0-7397-1136-9*) Intl Business Pubns.

Oregon Jeopardy! Answers & Questions about Our State! Carole Marsh. (Oregon Bks.). (Illus.). (J). (gr. 3-12). 1994. pap. 19.95 (*0-7933-4191-4*); lib. bdg. 29.95 (*0-7933-4190-6*); disk 29.95 (*0-7933-4192-2*) Gallopade Intl.

Oregon "Jography" A Fun Run Thru Our State. Carole Marsh. (Carole Marsh Oregon Bks.). (Illus.). (J). 1994. pap. 19.95 (*0-7933-1891-2*); lib. bdg. 29.95 (*0-7933-1890-4*); disk 29.95 (*0-7933-1892-0*) Gallopade Intl.

Oregon Kid's Cookbook: Recipes, How-to, History, Lore & More! Carole Marsh. (Carole Marsh Oregon Bks.). (Illus.). (J). 1994. pap. 19.95 (*0-7933-0949-2*); lib. bdg. 29.95 (*0-7933-0950-6*); disk 29.95 (*0-7933-0951-4*) Gallopade Intl.

Oregon Land, Rural or Urban? Wayne A. Leeman. LC 96-94975. xiv, 178p. 1997. pap. 12.95 (*0-9654913-2-3*) Millwright Pr.

Oregon Law Review, 1921-1994, 72 vols. 1921. mic. film 3960.00 (*0-318-57453-5*) W S Hein.

Oregon Law Review, 1921-1994, 75 vols., Set. 1995. 3562.50 (*0-8377-9128-6*, Rothman) W S Hein.

Oregon Legacy. large type ed. Dana Fuller Ross. 482p. 1991. lib. bdg. 21.95 (*0-8161-4989-5*, G K Hall Lrg Type) Mac Lib Ref.

Oregon Library Book: A Surprising Guide to the Unusual Special Collections in Libraries Across Our State for Students, Teachers, Writers & Publishers - Includes Reproducible Mailing Labels Plus Activities for Young People! Carole Marsh. (Oregon Bks.). (Illus.). 1994. pap. 19.95 (*0-7933-3117-X*); lib. bdg. 29.95 (*0-7933-3116-1*); disk 29.95 (*0-7933-3118-8*) Gallopade Intl.

Oregon Local Government Law Deskbook. 425p. 1991. ring bd. 75.00 (*0-685-40834-5*, 403-57) Oregon Law Inst.

Oregon Local Government Law Supplement. 160p. 1993. ring bd. 35.00 (*0-614-04695-5*) Oregon Law Inst.

Oregon Logging Pioneer: George Shroyer's Life, Work & Humor. Joyce M. Hall. Ed. by Lee Wood. LC 98-22697. (Illus.). 1998. pap. 24.95 (*1-878815-12-1*) Reflected Images.

Oregon Main Street: A Rephotographic History. James Norton. 100p. 1994. pap. 19.95 (*0-87595-256-9*) Oregon Hist.

Oregon Manufacturers Register 1999. 6th ed. 630p. 1998. pap. 110.00 (*1-57541-080-X*) Database Pub Co.

Oregon Math! How It All Adds up in Our State. Carole Marsh. (Carole Marsh Oregon Bks.). (Illus.). (YA). (gr. 3-12). 1996. pap. 19.95 (*0-7933-6599-6*); lib. bdg. 29.95 (*0-7933-6598-8*) Gallopade Intl.

Oregon Media Book: A Surprising Guide to the Amazing Print, Broadcast & Online Media of Our State for Students, Teachers, Writers & Publishers - Includes Reproducible Mailing Labels Plus Activities for Young People! Carole Marsh. (Oregon Bks.). (Illus.). 1994. pap. 19.95 (*0-7933-3273-7*); lib. bdg. 29.95 (*0-7933-3272-9*); disk 29.95 (*0-7933-3274-5*) Gallopade Intl.

Oregon Meeting: Proceedings of the Annual Meeting of the Division of Eugene, Oregon, August 12-15, 1985. Ed. by R. C. Hwa. 800p. 1986. pap. 63.00 (*9971-5-0046-9*); text 181.00 (*9971-5-0041-8*) World Scientific Pub.

Oregon Mountain Ranges. George Wuerthner. (Oregon Geographic Ser.: No. 1). (Illus.). 104p. (Orig.). 1987. pap. 6.95 (*0-938314-30-0*) Am Wrld Geog.

Oregon My Oregon. Ray Atkeson & Catherine Glass. LC 98-19322. (Illus.). 128p. 1998. 29.50 (*1-55868-321-6*) Gr Arts Ctr Pub.

Oregon Mystery Van Takes Off! Bk. 1: Handicapped Oregon Kids Sneak Off on a Big Adventure. Carole Marsh. (Oregon Bks.). (Illus.). (J). (gr. 3-12). 1994. 29.95 (*0-7933-5072-7*); pap. 19.95 (*0-7933-5073-5*); disk 29.95 (*0-7933-5074-3*) Gallopade Intl.

Oregon Names: How to Say Them & Where Are They Located? Bert Webber. LC 92-33559. (Illus.). 112p. 1995. pap. 9.95 (*0-936738-72-3*) Webb Research.

***Oregon Nature Weekends.** James A. Yuskavitch. LC 00-39385. (Illus.). 2000. pap. write for info. (*1-56044-964-0*) Falcon Pub Inc.

Oregon Nonprofit Corporation Handbook. 2nd rev. ed. Cynthia Cumfer & Kay Sohl. 760p. 1996. pap. 45.00 (*0-9654614-0-8*) Tech Assist.

Oregon Notary Law Primer. 2nd rev. ed. National Notary Association Editors. 124p. 1998. pap. 16.00 (*1-891133-04-7*, 5128) Natl Notary.

Oregon Objections at Trial. Ronald L. Carlson & Myron H. Bright. LC 92-13850. 190p. 1992. pap. 39.50 (*1-56257-163-X*, MICHIE) LEXIS Pub.

Oregon on My Mind. LC 94-71772. (On My Mind Ser.). (Illus.). 120p. 1995. 29.95 (*1-56044-307-3*) Falcon Pub Inc.

Oregon Outlaws. Gary Meier & Gloria Meier. LC 97-165187. (Illus.). 254p. (Orig.). 1996. pap. 17.95 (*1-886609-05-5*) Tamarack Bks.

Oregon Outrider, 206. Jon Sharpe. 176p. 1999. mass mkt. 4.99 (*0-451-19581-7*, Sig) NAL.

Oregon Painters, the First Hundred Years (1859-1959) Index & Biographical Dictionary. Ginny Allen et al. LC 99-23461. 341p. 1999. 40.00 (*0-87595-271-2*) Oregon Hist.

Oregon Parks Guide. Barbara McCaig. Ed. by Chris Boyce. 100p. (Orig.). 1988. pap. text 5.95 (*0-935201-41-6*) Affordable Adven.

Oregon Pioneers. Maria L. Hidden. (Shorey Historical Ser.). 18p. reprint ed. pap. 10.00 (*0-8466-0073-0*, S73) Shoreys Bkstore.

Oregon Question: Essays in Anglo-American Diplomacy & Politics. Frederick Merk. LC 67-14345. 443p. reprint ed. pap. 137.40 (*0-7837-2300-8*, 205738800004) Bks Demand.

Oregon Quiz Bowl Crash Course! Carole Marsh. (Carole Marsh Oregon Bks.). (Illus.). (J). 1994. pap. 19.95 (*0-7933-1905-6*); lib. bdg. 29.95 (*0-7933-1904-8*); disk 29.95 (*0-7933-1906-4*) Gallopade Intl.

Oregon Real Estate Law. 4th ed. David L. Rockwell et al. (Illus.). 245p. (Orig.). 1995. pap. 32.95 (*0-915799-96-0*) Rockwell WA.

Oregon Real Estate Practices. 4th ed. David L. Rockwell et al. (Illus.). 296p. (Orig.). 1995. pap. 32.95 (*0-915799-97-9*) Rockwell WA.

Oregon Real Estate Practices, Finance, Law. Ralph A. Palmer & Gregory J. Frank. 468p. (C). 1996. pap. text 33.60 (*0-13-777681-0*) P-H.

Oregon Rediscovered. Bianco. 1994. 16.95 (*0-9643408-0-1*) Bianco Pub.

Oregon Reflections: Littlebook. Photos by Steve Terrill. (Illus.). 64p. 1996. 14.95 (*1-56579-146-0*) Westcliffe Pubs.

Oregon Regulations: Containing Insurance Division Regulations. Oregon. Insurance Division & National Insurance Law Service. LC 97-67933. (Illus.). 1997. write for info. (*0-89246-475-5*) NILS Pub.

Oregon Related Regulations. NILS Publishing Company. LC 97-69597. (Illus.). 1997. write for info. (*0-89246-483-6*) NILS Pub.

Oregon Retirement & Relocation Guide. large type ed. Phil Dubina & Babara Dubina. LC 97-33597. (Retirement & Relocation Guides Ser.). (Illus.). 350p. (Orig.). 1999. pap. 24.95 (*1-56559-106-2*) HGI-Over Fifty.

Oregon Revised Statutes Annotated: 1998 Supplement, 9 vols. 8906p. 1998. pap. 575.00 (*0-327-05356-9*, 47265-12) LEXIS Pub.

Oregon Revised Statutes Annotated: 1998 Supplement, Pt. 1, Chapters 1-70, ORSA Vols. 1-4. 982p. 1998. pap., suppl. ed. write for info. (*0-327-05357-7*, 84291-12) LEXIS Pub.

Oregon Revised Statutes Annotated: 1998 Supplement, Pt. 2, Vols. 5-10. 1134p. 1998. pap., suppl. ed. write for info. (*0-327-05358-5*, 84292-12) LEXIS Pub.

Oregon Revised Statutes Annotated: 1998 Supplement, Pt. 3, Vols. 11-18. 1155p. 1998. pap., suppl. ed. write for info. (*0-327-05359-3*, 84293-12) LEXIS Pub.

Oregon Revised Statutes Annotated: 1998 Supplement, Pt. 4, Vols. 19-25. 831p. 1998. pap., suppl. ed. write for info. (*0-327-05360-7*, 84294-12) LEXIS Pub.

Oregon Revised Statutes Annotated: 1998 Supplement, Pt. 5, Vols. 26-30. 686p. 1998. pap., suppl. ed. write for info. (*0-327-05361-5*, 84295-12) LEXIS Pub.

Oregon Revised Statutes Annotated: 1998 Supplement, Pt. 6, Vols. 31-35. 943p. 1998. pap., suppl. ed. write for info. (*0-327-05362-3*, 84296-12) LEXIS Pub.

Oregon Revised Statutes Annotated: 1998 Supplement, Pt. 7, Vols. 36-43. 1039p. 1998. pap., suppl. ed. write for info. (*0-327-05363-1*, 84297-12) LEXIS Pub.

Oregon Revised Statutes Annotated: 1998 Supplement, Pt. 8, Vols. 44-48. 950p. 1998. pap., suppl. ed. write for info. (*0-327-05364-X*, 84298-12) LEXIS Pub.

Oregon Revised Statutes Annotated: 1998 Supplement, Pt. 9, Vols. 49-52. 897p. 1998. pap., suppl. ed. write for info. (*0-327-05365-8*, 84299-12) LEXIS Pub.

Oregon Revised Statutes Annotated: 1998 Supplement - Constitution. 289p. 1998. pap., suppl. ed. write for info. (*0-327-05366-6*, 84300-12) LEXIS Pub.

Oregon Revised Statutes Annotated, 1998-1999 Interim Annotation Service. annot. ed. (Oregon Revised Statutes Annotated Ser.: No. 1). 150p. 1998. pap. write for info. (*0-327-06450-1*, 4727113) LEXIS Pub.

Oregon Revised Statutes Annotated 1998-1999 Interim Annotation Service Pamphlet, No. 2. annot. ed. 200p. 1999. pap. write for info. (*0-327-08619-X*, 47272-14) LEXIS Pub.

***Oregon Revised Statutes Annotationed Vol. 3: 1998-1999 Interim Annotation Service.** 400p. 1999. write for info. (*0-327-09900-3*, 4727314) LEXIS Pub.

Oregon River Watch: A Contemporary History of Oregon's Waterways, Vol. 1. Ed. by Michael P. Jones. (Oregon River Watch Ser.). (Illus.). 48p. (Orig.). (J). 1985. text 9.95 (*0-89904-143-4*); pap. text 5.00 (*0-89904-144-2*); 8.00 (*0-89904-145-0*) Crumb Elbow Pub.

Oregon River Watch: A Contemporary History of Oregon's Waterways, Vol. 2. Ed. by Michael P. Jones. (Oregon River Watch Ser.). (Illus.). 50p. (Orig.). (J). 1985. text 9.95 (*0-89904-146-9*); pap. text 5.00 (*0-89904-147-7*); 8.00 (*0-89904-148-5*) Crumb Elbow Pub.

Oregon Rivers. John Daniel. LC 97-8933. (Illus.). 166p. 1997. 45.00 (*1-56579-229-7*) Westcliffe Pubs.

***Oregon Road & Recreation Atlas.** Benchmark Maps Staff. (Illus.). 27p. 1998. pap. 18.95 (*0-929591-50-X*, Benchmark Maps) Map Link.

***Oregon Road Map & Travel Guide.** William L. Sullivan. 1999. pap. text 9.95 (*0-9665345-0-6*) Navillus Pr.

Oregon Rollercoasters! Carole Marsh. (Oregon Bks.). (Illus.). (YA). (gr. 3-12). 1994. pap. 19.95 (*0-7933-5336-X*); lib. bdg. 29.95 (*0-7933-5335-1*); disk 29.95 (*0-7933-5337-8*) Gallopade Intl.

Oregon Rules of Civil Procedure: 1994 Handbook. Lisa Kloppenberg. 600p. 1993. pap. 39.50 (*0-614-05939-9*, MICHIE) LEXIS Pub.

Oregon Rules of Civil Procedure: 1995 Handbook. Lisa A. Kloppenberg. 600p. (Orig.). Date not set. 41.00 (*0-614-10380-0*, MICHIE) LEXIS Pub.

Oregon Rules of Civil Procedure Annotated. Butterworth Staff. 500p. 1994. pap. 68.00 (*0-250-44848-3*, MICHIE) LEXIS Pub.

Oregon Rules of Civil Procedure Annotated (1999) Oregon 1999 Rules of Civil Procedure. 490p. 1998. pap. write for info. (*0-327-06502-8*, 4728014) LEXIS Pub.

Oregon Rules of Civil Procedure Annotated 1999 Supplement: Pocket Part. 40p. 1999. write for info. (*0-327-08644-0*, 47281-13) LEXIS Pub.

***Oregon Rules of Civil Procedure Annotated (2000)** 500p. 1999. pap. 115.00 (*0-327-09899-6*, 4728015) LEXIS Pub.

Oregon Rules of Civil Procedure Handbook: 1997-1998 Edition. Lisa Kloppenberg. Ed. by Frederic Merrill. 620p. (Orig.). 1997. pap. text 45.50 (*0-409-24969-6*, 82281-12, MICHIE) LEXIS Pub.

Oregon Rules of Civil Procedure in the Courts. Fredric R. Merrill. 194p. (Orig.). 1988. pap. text 18.50 (*0-317-92497-4*) Oregon Law Inst.

***Oregon Rules of Civil Procedure, 1999 Edition.** Lisa A. Kloppenberg. 620p. 1999. pap. 52.50 (*0-327-10132-6*, 8228113) LEXIS Pub.

Oregon Rules of Professional Responsibility: Annotated. Peter R. Jarvis et al. 300p. 1994. pap., suppl. ed. 35.00 (*0-685-40835-3*, 426) Oregon Law Inst.

Oregon Saltwater Fishing Guide. 2nd ed. Frank Haw & Raymond M. Buckley. Ed. by Stanton L. Jones. (Illus.). 200p. (C). reprint ed. pap. 8.95 (*0-939936-03-8*) Jones Pub.

Oregon Sampler: Resorts & Recipes: Featuring a Sampling of Recipes from the Resorts & People of Oregon. Assistance League of Corvallis Staff. (Illus.). 318p. 1985. 14.95 (*0-9616597-0-X*) Assistance League of Corvallis.

Oregon School Trivia: An Amazing & Fascinating Look at Our State's Teachers, Schools & Students. Carole Marsh. (Carole Marsh Oregon Bks.). (Illus.). (J). 1994. pap. 19.95 (*0-7933-0946-8*); lib. bdg. 29.95 (*0-7933-0947-6*); disk 29.95 (*0-7933-0948-4*) Gallopade Intl.

Oregon Schoolma'am: From Rimrocks to Tidelands. Grace B. Martin. (Illus.). 144p. 1981. pap. 7.95 (*0-934784-25-6*) Calapooia Pubns.

Oregon Schoolma'am Bk. 2: The Depression Years. Grace B. Martin. (Illus.). 200p. pap. 7.95 (*0-934784-26-4*) Calapooia Pubns.

Oregon Scroll. Rodney Nelson. 1976. pap. 3.00 (*0-914974-11-4*) Holmgangers.

Oregon Shipwrecks. Don B. Marshall. LC 84-71477. (Illus.). 250p. 1984. 24.95 (*0-8323-0430-1*) Binford Mort.

Oregon Silly Basketball Sportsmysteries, Vol. 1. Carole Marsh. (Carole Marsh Oregon Bks.). (Illus.). (J). 1994. pap. 19.95 (*0-7933-0943-3*); lib. bdg. 29.95 (*0-7933-0944-1*); disk 29.95 (*0-7933-0945-X*) Gallopade Intl.

Oregon Silly Basketball Sportsmysteries, Vol. 2. Carole Marsh. (Carole Marsh Oregon Bks.). (Illus.). (J). 1994. pap. 19.95 (*0-7933-1917-X*); lib. bdg. 29.95 (*0-7933-1916-1*); disk 29.95 (*0-7933-1918-8*) Gallopade Intl.

Oregon Silly Football Sportsmysteries, Vol. 1. Carole Marsh. (Carole Marsh Oregon Bks.). (Illus.). (J). 1994. pap. 19.95 (*0-7933-1896-3*); lib. bdg. 29.95 (*0-7933-1895-5*); disk 29.95 (*0-7933-1897-1*) Gallopade Intl.

Oregon Silly Football Sportsmysteries, Vol. 2. Carole Marsh. (Carole Marsh Oregon Bks.). (Illus.). (J). 1994. pap. 19.95 (*0-7933-1899-8*); lib. bdg. 29.95 (*0-7933-1898-X*); disk 29.95 (*0-7933-1900-5*) Gallopade Intl.

Oregon Silly Trivia! Carole Marsh. (Carole Marsh Oregon Bks.). (Illus.). (J). 1994. pap. 19.95 (*0-7933-1888-2*); lib. bdg. 29.95 (*0-7933-1887-4*); disk 29.95 (*0-7933-1889-0*) Gallopade Intl.

O

An Asterisk (*) at the beginning of an entry indicates that the title is appearing for the first time.

Oregon Spelling Bee! Score Big by Correctly Spelling Our State's Unique Names. Carole Marsh. (Carole Marsh Oregon Bks.). (Illus.). (YA). (gr. 3-12). 1996. pap. 19.95 (0-7933-6752-2); lib. bdg. 29.95 (0-7933-6751-4) Gallopade Intl.

***Oregon State Credit Directory, 2000 Edition.** rev. ed. American Business Directories Staff. 368p. 1999. boxed set 145.00 incl. cd-rom (0-7687-0318-2) Am Busn Direct.

Oregon State Parks: A Complete Recreation Guide. Jan Bannon. LC 93-41780. (State Parks Ser.). 250p. 1994. pap. 14.95 (0-89886-380-5) Mountaineers.

***Oregon Story, 1850-2000.** Compiled by Oregonian Staff. 2000. 29.95 (1-55868-543-X) Gr Arts Ctr Pub.

Oregon Studies in Chinese & Russian Culture. Ed. by Albert Leong. LC 90-5520. (American University Studies: Slavic Languages & Literature: Ser. XII, Vol. 13). (Illus.). XVIII, 376p. (C). 1990. text 72.95 (0-8204-1309-7) P Lang Pubng.

Oregon Survival. Betty L. Hall & Colin Dunkeld. 160p. (Orig.). (gr. 10-12). 1979. pap. text 5.84 (0-03-050816-9) Westwood Pr.

Oregon Sweet Oregon. Kathleen Karr. (Petticoat Party Ser.: No. 3). 160p. (YA). (gr. 5 up). 1997. 14.95 (0-06-027233-3); lib. bdg. 14.89 (0-06-027234-1) HarpC Child Bks.

Oregon Sweet Oregon. Kathleen Karr. LC 97-31151. (Petticoat Party Ser.: Vol. 3). 160p. (J). (gr. 5 up). 1998. pap. 4.95 (0-06-440497-8, HarpTrophy) HarpC Child Bks.

Oregon Territory. Aaron V. Brown. 24p. 1968. reprint ed. pap. 4.95 (0-87770-034-6, A825) Ye Galleon.

Oregon Territory: Its History & Discovery. Travers Twiss. 1998. 24.95 (0-87770-670-0); pap. 15.95 (0-87770-671-9) Ye Galleon.

Oregon, the Way It Was. Edwin D. Culp. LC 81-1266. (Illus.). 235p. 1981. pap. 15.95 (0-87004-285-8) Caxton.

Oregon III. Photos by Ray Atkeson. LC 86-83247. (Illus.). 160p. 1987. 39.95 (0-932575-28-5) Gr Arts Ctr Pub.

Oregon Timeline: A Chronology of Oregon History, Mystery, Trivia, Legend, Lore & More. Carole Marsh. (Oregon Bks.). (Illus.). (J). (gr. 3-12). 1994. pap. 19.95 (0-7933-5987-2); lib. bdg. 29.95 (0-7933-5986-4); disk 29.95 (0-7933-5988-0) Gallopade Intl.

Oregon Trade Tokens. James Hemphill. (Illus.). 592p. 1991. 49.95 (0-912317-13-2); pap. 39.95 (0-912317-14-0); lib. bdg. 59.95 (0-912317-18-3) World Exo.

***Oregon Trail.** Jean F. Blashfield. (We the People Ser.). (Illus.). 48p. (J). 2000. write for info. (0-7565-0045-1) Compass Point.

Oregon Trail. Carol Cohen. 39.00 (1-56696-145-9) Jackdaw.

Oregon Trail. Leonard Everett Fisher. LC 90-55103. (Illus.). 64p. (J). (gr. 4-6). 1990. lib. bdg. 18.95 (0-8234-0833-7) Holiday.

Oregon Trail. Lynda Hatch. (Pathways of America Ser.). (Illus.). 96p. (J). (gr. 4-8). 1994. 10.99 (0-86653-798-8, GA1473) Good Apple.

Oregon Trail. Kimmel. 1999. pap. write for info. (0-670-84539-6); pap. 3.99 (0-14-036085-9) Viking Penguin.

***Oregon Trail.** Francis Parkman. Ed. by Bernard Rosenthal. (Oxford World's Classics Ser.). (Illus.). 384p. 2000. pap. 10.95 (0-19-283912-8) OUP.

Oregon Trail. Francis Parkman. Ed. by E. N. Feltskog. LC 94-19303. (Illus.). xviii, 758p. 1994. pap. 25.00 (0-8032-8739-9, Bison Books) U of Nebr Pr.

Oregon Trail. Francis Parkman. Ed. & Intro. by David Levin. (American Library). 500p. 1982. pap. 11.95 (0-14-039042-1, Penguin Classics) Viking Penguin.

Oregon Trail. Rick Steber. (Tales of the Wild West Ser.: Vol. 1). (Illus.). 60p. 1986. pap. 4.95 (0-945134-01-0); lib. bdg. 14.95 (0-945134-79-7) Bonanza Pub.

Oregon Trail. R. Conrad Stein. LC 93-36994. (Cornerstones to Freedom Ser.). (Illus.). 32p. (J). (gr. 3-6). 1994. lib. bdg. 19.50 (0-516-06674-9) Childrens.

Oregon Trail. R. Conrad Stein. (Illus.). 32p. (J). (gr. 3-6). 1994. pap. 5.95 (0-516-46674-7) Childrens.

***Oregon Trail.** large type ed. Ralph Compton. 360p. 2000. 31.99 (0-7089-9135-1) Ulverscroft.

Oregon Trail. Francis Parkman. Ed. by E. N. Feltskog. LC 68-9017. 854p. reprint ed. pap. 200.00 (0-608-15032-0, 202594800047) Bks Demand.

Oregon Trail: Essays on Life & Death, & Survival. Michael P. Jones. (Illus.). 50p. 1988. 11.00 (0-89904-278-3); pap. 8.00 (0-89904-279-1) Crumb Elbow Pub.

Oregon Trail: Last of the Pioneers. Rick Steber. (Heart of the West Ser.). (Illus.). 182p. (Orig.). 1993. 24.95 (0-945134-28-2); pap. 15.95 (0-945134-29-0) Bonanza Pub.

Oregon Trail: Ruts, Rogues & Reminiscences. Ellen Carney. (Illus.). 322p. (Orig.). 1993. pap. 17.50 (0-9636479-0-3) Traildust Pub.

Oregon Trail: Sketches of Prairie & Rocky Mountain Life. Francis Parkman. 1996. reprint ed. lib. bdg. 26.95 (0-8488-1768-0) Amereon Ltd.

Oregon Trail: The Missouri River to the Pacific Ocean. Federal Writers' Project Staff. LC 70-145012. (American Guidebook Ser.). (Illus.). 1971. reprint ed. 59.00 (0-403-01290-2) Somerset Pub.

Oregon Trail: The Missouri River to the Pacific Ocean. Federal Writers' Project Staff & Writers Program-WPA Staff. (American Guide Ser.). 1989. reprint ed. lib. bdg. 59.00 (0-7812-1065-8, 1065) Rprt Serv.

Oregon Trail: The Sketches of Prairie & Rocky - Mountain Life. Francis Parkman. 479p. 1980. reprint ed. 34.95 (0-87928-103-0) Corner Hse.

Oregon Trail: Trail Drive, No. 9. Ralph Compton. 1995. mass mkt. 5.99 (0-312-95547-2) St Martin.

Oregon Trail: Voyage of Discovery. Dan Murphy. LC 92-70247. (Illus.). 64p. (Orig.). 1992. pap. 7.95 (0-88714-064-5) KC Pubns.

Oregon Trail: Voyage of Discovery. Dan Murphy. Tr. by Brigitte Morales. (GER., Illus.). 48p. (Orig.). 1993. pap. 8.95 (0-88714-749-6) KC Pubns.

Oregon Trail & Its Pioneers: Essays, Diary Excerpts & Other Writings. Ed. by Michael P. Jones. (Illus.). 190p. 1990. 19.95 (0-89904-298-8) Crumb Elbow Pub.

Oregon Trail & Its Pioneers: Essays, Diary Excerpts, & Other Writings. Ed. by Michael P. Jones & Robert K. Brown. (Illus.). 298p. 1988. pap. 15.00 (0-89904-299-6) Crumb Elbow Pub.

Oregon Trail & the Conspiracy of Pontiac. Francis Parkman. Ed. by William R. Taylor. 951p. 1991. 35.00 (0-940450-54-2, Pub. by Library of America) Penguin Putnam.

***Oregon Trail & the Days of '49.** Janet Gray. (Historic Cookbooks Ser.: Vol. 2). (Illus.). 128p. 1999. mass mkt. 5.00 (1-885507-13-5) Fundco Printers.

Oregon Trail Center: The Story Behind the Scenery. Joyce B. Hunsaker. LC 95-75096. (Illus.). 48p. (Orig.). 1995. pap. 7.95 (0-88714-089-0) KC Pubns.

Oregon Trail Cookbook. Leslie J. Whipple. 192p. 1992. pap. 14.95 (0-89288-234-4) Maverick.

Oregon Trail Cookbook: A Historical View of Cooking, Traveling & Surviving on the Trail. Scott Morris. LC 93-78500. 200p. 1993. 10.95 (0-9631249-3-5, Cookbks by Morris) Morris Pubng.

Oregon Trail Cooking. Mary Gunderson. LC 99-27054. (Exploring History Through Simple Recipes Ser.). 32p. (J). (gr. 2-7). 2000. lib. bdg. 22.60 (0-7368-0355-6, Blue Earth Bks) Capstone Pr.

***Oregon Trail Cooking.** Mary Gunderson. (Exploring History Through Simple Recipes Ser.). 32p. (gr. 2-7). 1999. 14.60 (0-516-21866-2) Childrens.

Oregon Trail Diaries Gift Set of Six Diaries with Separate Index & Fold-Out Color Map. Ed. by Bert Webber. (Illus.). 604p. (Orig.). 1992. pap. 48.95 (0-936738-59-6) Webb Research.

Oregon Trail Diary of James Akin, Jr. in 1852: The Unabridged Diary with Introduction & Contemporary Comments by Bert Webber, Includes Genealogies of Akin, Booth, Ingram & Richey Families. Ed. by Bert Webber. LC 89-5327. (Illus.). 102p. 1989. pap. 7.50 (0-936738-35-9) Webb Research.

Oregon Trail Diary of Rev. Edward Evans Parrish in 1844: The Unabridged Diary with Introduction & Contemporary Comments by Bert Webber, Includes Genealogy. LC 88-20489. (Illus.). 96p. 1988. pap. 7.50 (0-936738-28-6) Webb Research.

Oregon Trail Diary of Twin Sisters Cecilia Adams & Parthenia Blank in 1852: The Unabridged Diary with Introduction & Contemporary Comments by Bert Webber. Cecilia Adams & Parthenia Blank. LC 90-12057. (Illus.). 86p. 1990. pap. 7.50 (0-936738-48-0) Webb Research.

Oregon Trail Emigrant Massacre, 1862 & Port-Neuf Muzzle Loaders Rendezvous, Massacre Rocks, Idaho. Bert Webber. LC 87-14731. (Illus.). 70p. 1987. pap. 6.95 (0-936738-23-5) Webb Research.

Oregon Trail in American History. Rebecca Stefoff. LC 97-7271. (In American History Ser.). (Illus.). 112p. (YA). (gr. 5 up). 1997. lib. bdg. 20.95 (0-89490-771-9) Enslow Pubs.

Oregon Trail Is Still Alive. Kenneth H. Jones & Laura B. Jones. LC 97-20934. (Illus.). 202p. 1997. 48.00 (1-56216-037-0); pap. 23.00 (1-56216-038-9) Systems Co.

Oregon Trail Is Still Alive: A Photographic Retracement of the Oregon Trail. Ken Jones & Laura Jones. LC TXU 673 921. (Illus.). xii, 198p. 1997. pap. 19.95 (0-9656614-0-7) K & L Jones.

Oregon Trail Memorial Half-Dollar, 1926-1939. Bert Webber. LC 85-27917. (Illus.). 54p. 1986. pap. 4.95 (0-936738-16-2) Webb Research.

Oregon Trail Revisited. 5th ed. Gregory M. Franzwa. (Illus.). 1997. pap. 19.95 (1-880397-23-4) Patrice Pr.

Oregon Trail Souvenir Book. Rick Steber. (Illus.). 32p. (Orig.). 1992. pap. 2.50 (0-945134-97-5) Bonanza Pub.

Oregon Trail II: Official Strategy Guide. Prima Publication Staff. 1995. pap. text 19.95 (0-7615-0376-5) Prima Pub.

Oregon Trail, Yesterday & Today. William Hill. LC 86-6134. (Illus.). (Orig.). 1987. pap. 11.95 (0-87004-319-6) Caxton.

Oregon Trail, Yesterday & Today: A Curriculum Guide for K-12. Eleanor J. Hall. (Illus.). 205p. 1992. 29.95 (0-931056-10-1) Jefferson Natl.

Oregon Travail, 1, 7. Doug Hawkins. (Kit Carson Ser.). 176p. 1999. mass mkt. 3.99 (0-8439-4548-6) Dorchester Pub Co.

Oregon Trivia. Ted Magnuson. LC 98-15449. 192p. 1998. pap. 6.95 (1-55853-601-9) Rutledge Hill Pr.

Oregon Trunk. large type ed. Wayne D. Overholser. LC 98-15050. (Sagebrush Large Print Westerns Ser.). 1998. 18.95 (1-57490-127-3) T T Beeler.

Oregon 2000! Coming Soon to a Calendar Near You - The 21st Century! - Complete Set of AL 2000 Items. Carole Marsh. (Two Thousand! Ser.). (Illus.). (J). (gr. 3-12). 1998. pap. 75.00 (0-7933-9383-3); lib. bdg. 85.00 (0-7933-9384-1) Gallopade Intl.

Oregon 2000! Coming Soon to a Calendar near You-The 21st Century! Carole Marsh. (Two Thousand! Ser.). (Illus.). (J). (gr. 3-12). 1998. pap. 19.95 (0-7933-8787-6); lib. bdg. 29.95 (0-7933-8786-8) Gallopade Intl.

Oregon UFO's & Extraterrestrials! A Look at the Sightings & Science in Our State. Carole Marsh. (Carole Marsh Oregon Bks.). (Illus.). (J). (gr. 3-12). 1997. pap. 19.95 (0-7933-6446-9); lib. bdg. 29.95 (0-7933-6445-0) Gallopade Intl.

Oregon Uniform Commercial Code, 3 vols. Henry J. Bailey, III. 1680p. 1990. boxed set 225.00 (0-409-24954-8, MICHIE) LEXIS Pub.

Oregon Uniform Commercial Code, 3 vols. Henry J. Bailey, III. 1680p. 1993. suppl. ed. 55.00 (0-685-74297-0, MICHIE) LEXIS Pub.

Oregon Uniform Commercial Code, 3 vols. 2nd ed. Henry Bailey. 1990. text 235.00 (0-327-01042-8, 82286, MICHIE) LEXIS Pub.

Oregon Uniform Commercial Code, 3 vols., Set. Henry J. Bailey, III. 1993. boxed set 225.00 (0-614-05940-2, MICHIE) LEXIS Pub.

Oregon Uniform Commercial Code, 3 vols., Set. Henry J. Bailey. 1680p. 1995. 225.00 (0-614-10381-9, MICHIE) LEXIS Pub.

Oregon Uniform Commercial Code, 1998 Cumulative Supplement. Bailey. 320p. 1998. pap., suppl. ed. write for info. (0-327-00398-7, 8229012) LEXIS Pub.

Oregon Uniform Trial Court Rules. LLP Staff. 431p. 1998. ring bd. write for info. (0-327-00584-X, 8229821) LEXIS Pub.

***Oregon Uniform Trial Court Rules, Issue 33.** Ed. by LLP Staff. 600p. 1999. ring bd. write for info. (0-327-01283-8, 8229822) LEXIS Pub.

Oregon Uniform Trial Court Rules & Supplementary Local Rules, 1985-1993. Ed. by Butterworth Staff. 460p. 1995. ring bd. 80.00 (0-409-24951-3, 82297-10, MICHIE) LEXIS Pub.

Oregon Uniform Trial Court Rules & Supplementary Local Rules, 1985-1993. Butterworths Staff. 460p. 1993. suppl. ed. 32.50 (1-56257-283-0, MICHIE) LEXIS Pub.

Oregon Votes, 1858-1972. Burton W. Onstine. LC 73-88980. 395p. 1973. pap. 9.95 (0-87595-043-4) Oregon Hist.

***Oregon Watersheds: Many Activities Contribute to Increased Turbidity During Large Storms.** Ed. by Barry T. Hill. (Illus.). 69p. 1999. pap. text 20.00 (0-7881-8077-0) DIANE Pub.

Oregon Weather Book: A State of Extremes. George H. Taylor & Raymond R. Hatton. LC 99-35418. (Illus.). 256p. 1999. pap. 19.95 (0-87071-467-8) Oreg St U Pr.

***Oregon Wild & Beautiful: Coast.** Photos by Fred Pflughoft. (Illus.). 120p. 2000. 29.95 (1-56037-152-8) Am Wrld Geog.

***Oregon Wild & Beautiful: Mountains.** Photos by Fred Pflughoft. (Illus.). 120p. 2000. 29.95 (1-56037-154-4) Am Wrld Geog.

Oregon Wildflowers. Photos by Steve Terrill. (Illus.). 64p. 1995. 14.95 (1-56579-121-5) Westcliffe Pubs.

Oregon Wildflowers: Beginner's Field Guide. Beverly Magley. LC 91-77419. (Interpreting the Great Outdoors Ser.). (Illus.). 32p. 1992. pap. 6.95 (1-56044-035-X) Falcon Pub Inc.

Oregon Wildlife Viewing Guide. rev. ed. James A. Yuskavitch. LC 93-46140. (Watchable Wildlife Ser.). (Illus.). 96p. 1994. reprint ed. pap. 8.95 (1-56044-271-9) Falcon Pub Inc.

Oregon Wine Country. Judy Peterson-Nedry. LC 97-80275. 1998. pap. text 23.95 (1-55868-318-6) Gr Arts Ctr Pub.

Oregon Winegrape Grower's Guide. 4th ed. (Illus.). 256p. 1992. write for info. (0-942367-08-1) Oreg Winegrowers Assn.

Oregon Women: A Bio-Bibliography. Compiled by Evelyn Leasher. (Bibliographic Ser.: No. 18). 64p. 1981. pap. 9.95 (0-87071-138-5) Oreg St U Pr.

Oregon's Best Jokes. Elliot Maxx. (Illus.). 96p. (Orig.). 1995. pap. 7.95 (0-935735-03-8) Fiasco Productions.

Oregon's Changing Coastal Fishing Communities. Ed. by Jennifer Gilden. 73p. 1999. pap. 5.00 (1-881826-17-1) OR Sea Grant.

Oregon's Coast - Best Family Attractions: From Brookings to Astoria. David Gabbe & Carolyn Gabbe. 224p. 1992. pap. 11.95 (1-881409-00-7) Jhnstn Assocs.

Oregon's Experience with Minimum Wage Legislation. Victor P. Morris. LC 68-58609. (Columbia University. Studies in the Social Sciences: No. 320). reprint ed. 27.50 (0-404-51320-4) AMS Pr.

Oregon's Fading Past. Lawrence E. Nielsen & Donald S. Galbreath. 200p. 1993. pap. 19.95 (0-89288-240-9) Maverick.

Oregon's Ghosts & Monsters. Mike Helm. LC 81-51427. (Oregon Country Library: Vol. 5). (Illus.). 176p. 1983. pap. 9.95 (0-931742-03-X) Rainy Day Oreg.

Oregon's Golden Years. Miles F. Potter. LC 75-12292. 185p. 1976. pap. 14.95 (0-87004-254-8) Caxton.

Oregon's Golden Years: Bonanza of the West. Miles F. Potter. LC 75-12292. 194p. 1976. reprint ed. pap. 60.20 (0-608-00727-7, 206150200009) Bks Demand.

Oregon's Great Train Holdup. Bert Webber. (Illus.). 32p. 1974. pap. 4.95 (0-87770-124-5) Ye Galleon.

Oregon's Great Train Holdup Bandits Murder 4 - Didn't Get a Dime! The Last Great Train Holdup in the West, Documentary. Bert Webber & Margie Webber. LC 87-27285. (Illus.). 86p. 1988. pap. 8.95 (0-936738-31-6) Webb Research.

Oregon's Historic Portland: A Brief Glimpse from Early Beginnings to Early 1950's. Works Progress Administration Staff & Michael P. Jones. (Illus.). 50p. 1995. 11.00 (0-89904-331-3, Silhouette Imprints); pap. 8.00 (0-89904-332-1, Silhouette Imprints) Crumb Elbow Pub.

Oregon's History: A Brief Glimpse Backwards. Michael P. Jones. (Illus.). 50p. 1995. 11.00 (0-89904-337-2, Silhouette Imprints) Crumb Elbow Pub.

Oregon's Journey. Illus. by Louis Joos. LC 93-11796. 40p. (J). (gr. k-4). 1995. pap. 4.95 (0-8167-3306-6, Troll Medallion) Troll Communs.

Oregon's Journey. Illus. by Rascal Louis Joos. LC 93-11796. 40p. (J). (gr. k-4). 1997. 15.95 (0-8167-3305-8) BrdgeWater.

Oregon's Journey. Louis Joos Rascal. (J). 1993. 10.15 (0-606-07976-9) Turtleback.

Oregon's Living Landscape: Strategies & Opportunities to Conserve Biodiversity. Oregon Biodiversity Project Staff. LC 98-15394. (Illus.). 220p. 1998. pap. 29.95 (0-926549-01-4) Defend Wildlife.

Oregon's (Most Devastating!) Disasters & (Most Calamitous!) Catastrophies! Carole Marsh. (Carole Marsh Oregon Bks.). (Illus.). (J). 1994. pap. 19.95 (0-7933-0934-4); lib. bdg. 29.95 (0-7933-0935-2); disk 29.95 (0-7933-0936-0) Gallopade Intl.

Oregon's National Forests. Photos by Robert W. Reynolds. LC 89-81617. (Illus.). 84p. 1990. 26.50 (1-55868-016-0) Gr Arts Ctr Pub.

Oregon's Natural Setting: From Early History to Early 1950's. Michael P. Jones. (Illus.). 50p. 1995. 12.00 (0-89904-428-X, Silhouette Imprints); pap. 9.00 (0-89904-429-8, Silhouette Imprints) Crumb Elbow Pub.

Oregon's Outback. Russell Baehr. Ed. by Verne Reaves. (Illus.), 250p. (Orig.). 1985. pap. 15.95 (0-89288-108-9) Maverick.

Oregon's Outback. Donna Ikenberry. LC 96-196246. (Illus.). 87p. 1995. pap. 14.95 (1-57188-043-7) F Amato Pubns.

Oregon's Quiet Waters: A Guide to Lakes for Canoeists & Other Paddlers. 2nd ed. Cheryl McLean & Clint Brown. (Illus.). 176p. (Orig.). 1996. pap. 14.95 (0-943097-03-7) Jackson Creek Pr.

Oregon's Salty Coast. James A. Gibbs & Bert Webber. LC 94-9939. (Illus.). 176p. 1994. pap. 12.95 (0-936738-82-0) Webb Research.

Oregon's Seacoast Lighthouses: An Oregon Documentary. James A. Gibbs & Bert Webber. LC 92-3682. (Illus.). 268p. 1992. pap. 14.95 (0-936738-57-X) Webb Research.

Oregon's South Coast in a Nutshell. Leslie D. Cole. (In a Nutshell Ser.). (Illus.). 1994. pap. 5.95 (1-884497-02-0) Nutshell TourMaps.

Oregon's Swimming Holes. Relan Colley. LC 94-28360. 320p. (Orig.). 1994. pap. 14.95 (0-89997-169-5) Wilderness Pr.

Oregon's Unsolved Mysteries (And Their "Solutions") Includes Scientific Information & Other Activities for Students. Carole Marsh. (Oregon Bks.). (Illus.). (J). (gr. 3-12). 1994. pap. 19.95 (0-7933-5834-5); lib. bdg. 29.95 (0-7933-5833-7); disk 29.95 (0-7933-5835-3) Gallopade Intl.

Oregon's Wallowa Valley. (Illus.). 36p. (Orig.). 1997. pap. 9.95 (0-9656831-0-9) Wallowa Vly Photo.

Oreille Cassee see Broken Ear

Oreille Cassee. Herge.Tr. of Broken Ear. (FRE., Illus.). 62p. (J). 19.95 (0-8288-5054-2) Fr & Eur.

***Oreille Cassee.** Herge.Tr. of Broken Ear. (FRE.). (gr. 4-7). 1999. 19.95 (2-203-00105-4) Midwest European Pubns.

Oreilles de Jungle. Pierre Boulle. (FRE.). 240p. 1972. 24.95 (0-7859-1163-4, 2080605739) Fr & Eur.

O'Reilly Book. Michael C. O'Laughlin. (Irish Family Histories Ser.). (Illus.). 50p. 1981. 15.00 (0-940134-21-7) Irish Genealog.

***O'Reilly Factor: The Good, the Bad, & the Completely Ridiculous in American Life.** Bill O'Reilly. 224p. 2000. 23.00 (0-7679-0528-8) Broadway BDD.

O'Reilly Java Toolkit. Shawn P. Wallace. 200p. 1999. pap. 79.95 (1-56592-603-X) OReilly & Assocs.

O'Reilly Nutshell Assortment. RSI Promotion Staff. 1997. pap. 19.95 (1-56592-374-X) OReilly & Assocs.

O'Reilly Utilities - Quick Solutions for Windows 98 Annoyances. Mark Bracewell & David Karp. Ed. by Gina Blaber. 1998. pap. 39.95 (1-56592-549-1) OReilly & Assocs.

Oreja Rota. Herge. (SPA., Illus.). 62p. (J). 19.95 (0-8288-5055-0) Fr & Eur.

Orejana Bull: For Cowboys Only. 7th ed. Gail I. Gardner. 48p. 1987. pap. 8.95 (0-927579-14-6) Sharlot Hall Mus Pr.

Orel Hershiser. Carl R. Green. LC 93-28044. (Sports Headliners Ser.). (J). (gr. 5 up). 1994. text 13.95 (0-89686-836-2) Macmillan.

Orem Postal People. Clyde E. Weeks, Jr. (Illus.). 96p. 1988. 24.95 (0-9643423-3-2) Magnif Mormon.

Oremos. T. S. Nee.Tr. of Let Us Pray. (SPA.). 120p. 1980. pap. 4.99 (0-8297-1046-9) Vida Pubs.

***Oremos Con Poder.** C. Peter Wagner. 1998. pap. text 8.99 (0-88113-505-4) Caribe Betania.

Oremos, Oremos: New Mexican Midwinter Masquerades. Peggy V. Beck. (Illus.). (Orig.). 1987. pap. text 5.95 (0-9609818-2-9) M Rogers Mus.

Oremus: Speaking with God in the Words of the Roman Rite. Tr. by Martin D. O'Keefe. LC 93-61062. (Series V: No. 2). (LAT.). viii, 390p. 1993. pap. 32.95 (1-880810-28-X) Inst Jesuit.

Oren Con el Corazon. Slavko Barbaric.Tr. of Pray with the Heart. 55p. 1988. pap. 4.50 (0-940535-15-7, UP113) Franciscan U Pr.

Orenburg Oblast: Economy, Industry, Government, Business. 2nd rev. ed. Russian Information & Business Center, Inc. Staff. (Russian Regional Business Directories Ser.). (Illus.). 200p. 1997. pap. 99.00 (1-57751-404-1) Intl Business Pubns.

***Orenburg Oblast Regional Investment & Business Guide.** Global Investment & Business Center, Inc. Staff. (Russian Regional Investment & Business Guides Ser.: Vol. 56). (Illus.). 350p. 1999. pap. 99.00 (0-7397-0855-4) Intl Business Pubns.

***Orenburg Oblast Regional Investment & Business Guide.** Contrib. by Global Investment & Business Center, Inc. Staff. (Russian Regional Investment & Business Guides Ser.: Vol. 14). (Illus.). 350p. 2000. pap. 99.95 (0-7397-3004-5) Intl Business Pubns.

Orendel: Ein Deutsches Spielmannsgedicht. Ed. by Arnold E. Berger. (GER.). cxxxiv, 191p. (C). 1974. reprint ed. text 84.60 (3-11-003399-2) De Gruyter.

***Oren's World.** Mark A. Lindsley. 296p. 1999. pap. 16.95 (0-7414-0184-3) Buy Books.

O

*Oreo. Fran Ross. (Northeastern Library of Black Literature). 224p. 2000. pap. 15.95 (1-55553-464-3) NE U Pr.
Oreo with a Twist. LC 98-68025. (Illus.). 96p. 1999. text 12.95 (0-696-20956-X) Meredith Bks.
Ores & Industry in South America. Foster H. Bain & Thomas T. Read. Ed. by Stuart Bruchey & Eleanor Bruchey. LC 76-4767. (American Business Abroad Ser.). (Illus.). 1976. reprint ed. 35.95 (0-405-09265-2) Ayer.
Ores & Minerals: Introducing Economic Geology. J. W. Barnes. 192p. 1991. pap. 80.00 (0-471-93203-5) Wiley.
Ores to Metals: The Rocky Mountain Smelting Industry. James E. Fell. LC 79-9093. (Illus.). 357p. reprint ed. pap. 110.70 (0-7837-0991-9, 204129700020) Bks Demand.
Oresme's Livre de Politiques & the France of Charles V. Susan Babbitt. LC 84-71076. (Transactions Ser.: Vol. 75, Pt. 1). 156p. 1985. pap. 15.00 (0-87169-751-3, T751-BAS) Am Philos.
Orest Adamovich Kiprenskii, 1782-1980. D. V. Sarab'ianov. 208p. 1982. 130.00 (0-7855-1643-3) St Mut.
Oresteia. Aeschylus. Tr. by Hugh Lloyd-Jones. LC 93-15929. 1994. 15.95 (0-520-08328-8, Pub. by U CA Pr) Cal Prin Full Svc.
Oresteia. Aeschylus. Tr. & Notes by Peter Meineck. LC 98-37825. (HPC Classics Ser.). 288p. (C). 1998. pap. 8.95 (0-87220-390-5); lib. bdg. 32.95 (0-87220-391-3) Hackett Pub.
Oresteia. Ed. by Michael Ewans. LC 74-489. 256p. (Orig.). 1995. pap. 7.50 (0-460-87548-5, Everyman's Classic Lib) Tuttle Pubng.
Oresteia. Tr. by Wendy D. O'Flaherty. LC 88-20492. 262p. 1989. pap. 12.95 (0-226-00772-3) U Ch Pr.
Oresteia. Illus. by Wendy D. O'Flaherty & David Grene. LC 88-20492. 262p. 1997. lib. bdg. 39.00 (0-226-00771-5) U Ch Pr.
Oresteia, 2 vols., Set. 2nd ed. Aeschylus. Ed. by G. Thomson. LC 74-489. 277p. 1966. lib. bdg. 98.50 (0-317-54488-8, Pub. by AM Hakkert) Coronet Bks.
Oresteia: Agamemnon, the Libation Bearers, the Eumenides. Aeschylus. Tr. by Robert Fagles. (Classics Ser.). 352p. 1984. pap. 9.95 (0-14-044333-9, Penguin Classics) Viking Penguin.
Oresteia of Aeschylus. Ted Hughes. 256p. 1999. text 25.00 (0-374-22721-7) FS&G.
*Oresteia of Aeschylus: A New Translation. Ted Hughes. 208p. 2000. pap. 11.00 (0-374-52705-9) FS&G.
Oresteia of Aeschylus: Agamemnon, the Libation Bearers, the Eumenides, Fragments. Tr. by Edward W. Haile from GRE. 182p. (Orig.). (C). 1994. pap. text 27.50 (0-8191-9320-8) U Pr of Amer.
Oresteia Trilogy: Agamemnon, the Libation - Bearers & the Furies. unabridged ed. Aeschylus. Tr. by E. D. Morshead. LC 96-13715. (Thrift Editions Ser.). 160p. 1996. reprint ed. pap. text 1.50 (0-486-29242-8) Dover.
Oresteia/Apollo & Bacchus. Aeschylus et al. Tr. & Illus. by William Whallon. LC 96-44037. (Oleander Language & Literature Ser.: Vol. 18). vi, 115p. 1997. 22.50 (0-906672-58-9); pap. 14.95 (0-906672-59-7) Oleander Pr.
Oresteian Trilogy. Aeschylus. Tr. by Philip Vellacott. Incl. Agamemnon. 1956. pap. Choephori. 1956. pap. Eumenides. (YA). (gr. 9 up). 1956. pap. (Classics Ser.). 208p. (Orig.). (YA). (gr. 9 up). 1956. Set pap. 9.95 (0-14-044067-4, Penguin Classics) Viking Penguin.
Orestes. Tr. by William Arrowsmith. LC 55-5787. 1968. write for info. U Ch Pr.
Orestes. Euripides. 442p. 1989. pap. text 28.00 (0-19-814396-6) OUP.
Orestes. Frank J. Nisetich & Euripides. Tr. by John Peck. (Greek Tragedy in New Translations Ser.). 128p. 1995. pap. text 7.95 (0-19-509659-2) OUP.
Orestes: Plays of Aeschylus. Tr. by Paul Roche. 1996. pap. 10.95 (0-452-01166-3, Plume) Dutton Plume.
Orestes A. Brownson: A Bibliography, 1826-1876. annot. ed. Anno. & Compiled by Patrick W. Carey. LC 96-45810. (Orestes A. Brownson's Collected Works: No. 10). 212p. (Orig.). 1996. pap. 25.00 (0-87462-634-X) Marquette.
Orestes A. Brownson: Selected Writings. Ed. by Patrick Carey. (Sources of American Spirituality Ser.). 1991. 24.95 (0-8091-0433-4) Paulist Pr.
Orestes A. Brownson: The Pope's Champion in America. Thomas R. Ryan. 1984. 49.50 (0-8290-0333-9); pap. 10.95 (0-8290-1608-2) Irvington.
Orestes Brownson: Selected Political Essays. Intro. by Russell Kirk. 230p. (C). 1990. pap. 21.95 (0-88738-825-6) Transaction Pubs.
Orestes Brownson: Sign of Contradiction. R. A. Herrera. LC 99-71453. 1999. 24.95 (1-882926-33-1) ISI Books.
Orestes Brownson & the American Republic: An Historical Perpective. Hugh Marshall. LC 74-142187. 316p. reprint ed. pap. 98.00 (0-608-15255-2, 202949300061) Bks Demand.
Orestes in Progress. Roberta Kalechofsky. LC 76-12977. 233p. 1976. pap. 10.00 (0-916288-02-1) Micah Pubns.
Orestie. Paul Claudel. (FRE.). 256p. 1961. 8.95 (0-7859-1132-4, 2070215393) Fr & Eur.
Orestie Aischylos. Ulrich Von Wilamowitz-Moellendorff. (GER.). vi, 268p. 1969. write for info. (3-296-16040-X, Pub. by Weidmann) Lubrecht & Cramer.
Orexis. Kenneth Irby. 32p. 1981. pap. write for info. (0-930794-17-6) Station Hill Pr.
Orf. David Meltzer. 1993. reprint ed. mass mkt. 6.95 (1-56333-110-1) Masquerade.
Orfe. Cynthia Voigt. LC 91-46058. 128p. (YA). (gr. 9 up). 1992. 12.95 (0-689-31771-9) Atheneum Yung Read.
Orfe. Cynthia Voigt. 128p. (J). (gr. 7-9). 1994. pap. 3.95 (0-590-47442-1) Scholastic Inc.
Orfe. Cynthia Voigt. (Point Signature Ser.). 1992. 9.05 (0-606-06641-1, Pub. by Turtleback) Demco.
Orfeo Ed Euridice in Full Score. Christoph W. Gluck. 160p. pap. text 10.95 (0-486-27324-5) Dover.
Orfevrerie Francaise. deluxe ed. Veronique Alemany-Dessaint. (FRE.). 216p. 1991. 195.00 (0-8288-7301-1, 2705900357) Fr & Eur.
Orff Re-Echoes Vol. 1: Selections from "The Orff Echo", 1969-1974 & the Supplements. 2nd ed. 164p. 1983. 5.25 (0-614-04178-3) Amer Orff.
Orff-Schulwerk: Applications for the Classroom. Brigitte Warner. 304p. (C). 1990. text 31.60 (0-13-639824-3) P-H.
Orff-Schulwerk: Background & Commentary. Tr. & Compiled by Mary Stringham. 56p. 1976. pap. 1.95 (0-918812-05-4, SE 0062) MMB Music.
Orff, Twenty-Seven Dragons & a Snarkel. Betty Waterton. (Illus.). 32p. (J). (ps-8). 1984. pap. 4.95 (0-920303-03-X, Pub. by Annick) Firefly Bks Ltd.
Orff, Twenty-Seven Dragons & a Snarkel. Kulyn Waterton. (Illus.). 24p. (J). (ps-8). 1984. 12.95 (0-920303-02-1, Pub. by Annick) Firefly Bks Ltd.
Orfield's Criminal Procedure under the Federal Rules, 7 vols., Set. 2nd ed. Mark S. Rhodes. LC 85-50534. 1985. 710.00 (0-685-59839-X) West Group.
Orfordness: Secret Site. Gordon Kinsey. 192p. 1990. 39.00 (0-86138-006-1, Pub. by T Dalton) St Mut.
Org Theory & Design 4e. 4th ed. Richard L. Daft. Ed. by Fenton & Craig. (SWC-Management). 558p. (C). 1991. mass mkt. 62.50 (0-314-93365-4) West Pub.
Org Theory & Design 5e. 5th ed. Richard L. Daft. LC 94-34070. (SWC-Management). 750p. (C). 1994. pap. 65.75 (0-314-04452-3) West Pub.
Organ. rev. ed. Peter Williams. 1997. pap. 16.95 (0-393-30362-4) Norton.
Organ, Vol. 1. Young Gordon. (Preludes For Worship Ser.). 1997. pap. 9.95 (0-634-00340-2) H Leonard.
Organ: A Brief Guide to Its Construction, History, Usage & Music. David Baker. (Illus.). 96p. 1991. pap. 10.50 (0-7478-0131-2, Pub. by Shire Pubns) Parkwest Pubns.
Organ: Its Evolution, Principles of Construction & Use. William L. Sumner. 1988. reprint ed. lib. bdg. 59.00 (0-7812-0572-7) Rprt Serv.
Organ: Its Evolution, Principles of Construction & Use. 3rd ed. William L. Sumner. LC 73-181272. 544p. 1962. reprint ed. 95.00 (0-403-01695-9) Scholarly.
Organ: King of Instruments. Peter Williams et al. (Illus.). 43p. 1995. pap. write for info. (0-9616755-7-8) Westfield Ctr.
Organ Allocation: Organized by Fondation Marcel Merieux & Universite Claude Bernard - Lyon 1 Proceedings of the 30th International Conference on Transplantation & Clinical Immunology, June 2-4, 1998. Ed. by Jean-Louis Touraine et al. (Transplantation & Clinical Immunology Ser.). 309p. 1998. 146.00 (0-7923-5077-4) Kluwer Academic.
Organ & Harpsichord Music by Women Composers: An Annotated Catalog, 30. Compiled by Adel Heinrich. LC 91-3210. (Music Reference Collection: No. 30). 392p. 1991. lib. bdg. 75.00 (0-313-26802-9, HOH, Greenwood Pr) Greenwood.
Organ & Tissue Donation & Transplantation: A Humanities Curriculum for Medical Students. Phillip V. Davis & Bethany J. Speilman. 166p. 1997. ring bd. 25.00 incl. cd-rom (0-931369-32-0) Southern IL Univ Sch.
Organ & Tissue Donation for Transplantation. Ed. by Jeremy R. Chapman et al. LC 97-25104. (An Arnold Publication). (Illus.). 488p. 1997. text 115.00 (0-340-61394-7) OUP.
Organ & Tissue Transplantation: Nursing Care from Procurement Through Rehabilitation. M. K. Norris & Mary A. House. LC 90-14141. 346p. (C). 1991. 39.95 (0-8036-6587-3) Davis Co.
Organ & Tissue Transplantation in the European Union: Management of Difficulties & Health Risks Linked to Donors. Ed. by Yvon Englert. LC 94-30823. 1994. write for info. (0-614-03068-4, Pub. by M Nijhoff) Kluwer Academic.
*Organ Anthology, , Vol. 1. 136p. 1999. 19.95 (1-57992-009-8) OR Catholic.
*Organ Anthology, Vol. 2. 136p. 1999. 19.95 (1-57992-010-1) OR Catholic.
Organ Based Autoimmune Diseases. Ed. by J. M. Cruse & R. E. Lewis. (Concepts in Immunopathology Ser.: Vol. 2). (Illus.). x, 278p. 1985. 129.75 (3-8055-3929-0) S Karger.
Organ Behavior, 5 vols. 5th ed. Moorhead. LC 97-72522. (C). 1997. text 72.76 (0-395-84196-8) HM.
Organ Building for Amateurs. Mark Wicks. (Illus.). 1988. pap. 35.00 (0-913746-01-0) Organ Lit.
Organ Building in New York City, 1700 to 1900. John Ogasapian. LC 78-300889. (Illus.). 1977. pap. text 30.00 (0-913746-10-X) Organ Lit.
Organ-Cases & Organs of the Middle Ages & Renaissance. A. G. Hill. (Illus.). xii, 261p. 1988. reprint ed. pap. 60.00 (0-913746-22-3) Organ Lit.
Organ Chord Dictionary. Morton Manus. (Alfred Handy Guide Ser.). 48p. 1978. 4.95 (0-88284-156-4, 283) Alfred Pub.
Organ Conservation in Curative Cancer Treatment: Indications, Contraindications, Methods. Ed. by J. L. Meyer & J. M. Vaeth. (Frontiers of Radiation Therapy & Oncology Ser.: Vol. 27). (Illus.). xii, 256p. 1993. 216.75 (3-8055-5663-2) S Karger.
Organ Construction. enl. ed. J. W. Hinton. (Illus.). xv, 180p. 1910. pap. 70.00 (0-913746-36-3) Organ Lit.
Organ Construction. 3rd enl. ed. J. W. Hinton. (Illus.). xv, 180p. 1910. 95.00 (0-913746-35-5) Organ Lit.
Organ Directed Toxicities of Anticance Drugs. Ed. by Miles P. Hacker & John Lazo. (Developments in Oncology Ser.). 272p. (C). 1988. text 130.50 (0-89838-356-0) Kluwer Academic.
Organ-Directed Toxicity: Symposium on Chemical Indices & Mechanisms of Organ-Directed Toxicity, Barcelona, Spain, 4-7 March 1981. S. S. Brown & D. S. Davies. (IUPAC Symposium Ser.). (Illus.). 400p. 1981. 160.00 (0-08-026197-3, Pub. by Pergamon Repr) Franklin.
Organ Donation & Transplantation: Psychological & Behavioral Factors. Ed. by James Shanteau & Richard J. Harris. 214p. 1990. 19.95 (1-55798-079-9) Am Psychol.
Organ Donations & Procurements: Index of Authors & Subjects. American Health Research Institute Staff. 180p. 1993. 47.50 (1-55914-936-1); pap. 44.50 (1-55914-937-X) ABBE Pubs Assn.
*Organ Fifty Years Hence. Francis Burgess. 176p. 2000. reprint ed. lib. bdg. 59.00 (0-7812-9314-6) Rprt Serv.
Organ Grinders. Bill Fitzhugh. LC 98-4492. 352p. 1998. 20.00 (0-380-97651-X, Avon Bks) Morrow Avon.
*Organ Grinders. Bill Fitzhugh. 384p. 1999. mass mkt. 6.50 (0-380-79835-2, Avon Bks) Morrow Avon.
Organ Handbook, 1985. Ed. by Alan Laufman. 100p. 1985. 5.00 (0-913499-52-8) Organ Hist Soc.
Organ Handbook, 1984. Ed. by Alan Laufman. 112p. 1984. 5.00 (0-913499-51-X) Organ Hist Soc.
Organ Handbook, 1987. Ed. by Alan Laufman. (Illus.). 100p. (Orig.). 1987. pap. 5.00 (0-913499-54-4) Organ Hist Soc.
Organ Handbook, 1983. Ed. by Alan Laufman. 136p. 1983. 5.00 (0-913499-50-1) Organ Hist Soc.
Organ Histology. LC 97-160089. 235p. 1997. 29.00 (981-02-2612-8); pap. 17.00 (981-02-2613-6) World Scientific Pub.
Organ Hymns for Praise & Worship: Music for Advent & Christmas, 3. John Innes. 1997. pap. 7.95 (0-634-01187-1) H Leonard.
Organ in Western Culture. Peter Williams. LC 92-19196. (Studies in Medieval & Renaissance Music). (Illus.). 415p. (C). 1993. text 89.95 (0-521-41843-7) Cambridge U Pr.
Organ, Its History & Construction: A Comprehensive Treatise on the Structure & Capabilities of the Organ with Specifications & Suggestive Details for Instruments of All Sizes, 3 vols., Set. 3rd ed. Edward J. Hopkins & Edward F. Rimbault. (Illus.). xxxii, 796p. 1988. reprint ed. 195.00 (0-913746-28-2); reprint ed. pap. 150.00 (0-913746-29-0) Organ Lit.
Organ Literature: A Comprehensive Survey, 2 vols. 3rd ed. Corliss R. Arnold. 1995. 110.00 (0-8108-2970-3) Scarecrow.
Organ Literature: A Comprehensive Survey, Vol. 1. 3rd ed. Corliss R. Arnold. 398p. 1995. 55.00 (0-8108-2964-9) Scarecrow.
Organ Literature: A Comprehensive Survey, Vol. 2. 3rd ed. Corliss R. Arnold. 922p. 1995. 85.00 (0-8108-2965-7) Scarecrow.
Organ, May, 1892-April, 1894 Vols. I & II: A Centennial Facsimile Edition with a Biography of Everett E. Truette & a List of Subscribers. Everett E. Truett. 606p. 1995. 59.95 (0-9610092-3-3) Boston Organ Club.
Organ Metabolism & Nutrition: Ideas for Future Critical Care. Ed. by John M. Kinney & Hugh N. Tucker. LC 93-41120. 528p. 1994. text 61.00 (0-7817-0160-0) Lppncott W & W.
Organ Metabolism & Nutrition: Ideas for Future Critical Care. Ed. by John M. Kinney & Hugh N. Tucker. LC 93-41120. 544p. reprint ed. pap. 168.70 (0-608-09734-9, 206989700007) Bks Demand.
Organ Method for Young Beginners. Andrew Scott. (Progressive Ser.: Bk. 1). (Illus.). 1997. pap. text 7.95 incl. cd-rom (0-947183-31-0) Koala Pubns.
Organ Music. Johann Sebastian Bach. 357p. 1970. pap. 13.95 (0-486-22359-0) Dover.
Organ Music for Celebration & Praise. James H. Conely. LC 74-236614. 48p. reprint ed. pap. 30.00 (0-7837-5882-0, 204560200006) Bks Demand.
Organ Music for Lent & Easter. Ed. by Dale Tucker. 48p. (C). 1997. pap. text 8.95 (0-7692-1694-3, EL9755) Wrner Bros.
Organ Music in Print. 2nd ed. Ed. by Walter A. Frankel & Nancy K. Nardone. LC 83-26956. (Music in Print Ser.: Vol. 3). 354p. 1984. lib. bdg. 110.00 (0-88478-015-5) Musicdata.
Organ Music in Print: 1990 Supplement. Ed. by Mark Daugherty. LC 90-6438. (Music in Print Ser.: Vol. 3S). 284p. 1990. lib. bdg. 95.00 (0-88478-026-0) Musicdata.
Organ Music in Print: 1997 Supplement. Ed. by Robert W. Cho et al. LC 83-26956. (Music-in-Print Ser.: Vol. 3t). 228p. 1997. lib. bdg. 95.00 (0-88478-043-0) Musicdata.
Organ Music of Fred Bock, Vol. 1. Fred Bock. 1997. pap. 10.95 (0-634-00357-7) H Leonard.
Organ Music of Fred Bock: Ten Christmas Melodies, 2. 1997. pap. 9.95 (0-634-01196-0) H Leonard.
Organ Part see I'm Getting Frustrated!!!
Organ-Piano Duets Praise & Worship Organ Piano Duets: Arrangements Bock, Bolks, Sanborn, Wyrtzen. 1997. pap. 10.95 (0-634-00365-8) H Leonard.
Organ Pipe Cactus National Monument: Where Edges Meet. Bill Broyles. LC 96-42360. 64p. 1996. pap. 9.95 (1-877856-69-X) SW Pks Mnmts.
Organ Pipe Cactus National Monument, AZ. rev. ed. Ed. by Trails Illustrated Staff. 1996. 8.99 (0-925873-71-3) Trails Illustrated.
Organ Playing: Its Technique & Expression. A. Eaglefield Hull. LC 81-1474. (Music Ser.). (Illus.). viii, 256p. 1981. reprint ed. lib. bdg. 32.50 (0-306-76134-3) Da Capo.
Organ Playing & Design: A Plea for Exuberance. Donald Willing. (Illus.). v, 55p. (Orig.). 1976. pap. 7.50 (0-913746-31-2) Organ Lit.
Organ Playing & Organ Building in France & Germany, 1906. Albert Schweitzer. Tr. by William D. Turner. 35p. 1984. pap. text 7.50 (0-913746-17-7) Organ Lit.
Organ Praise & Worship Organ. Fred Bock. 1997. pap. 10.95 (0-634-00360-7) H Leonard.
Organ Praises. Contrib. by Rick Parks. 52p. 1983. 10.99 (0-8341-9360-4, MB-524) Lillenas.
Organ Preludes of Johann Sebastian Bach. George B. Stauffer. LC 80-15519. (Studies in Musicology: No. 27). 273p. reprint ed. pap. 84.70 (0-8357-1562-0, 207028300065) Bks Demand.
Organ Preservation for Transplantation. 2nd enl. rev. ed. Ed. by Armand M. Karow, Jr. & David E. Pegg. LC 81-5432. (Illus.). 719p. reprint ed. pap. 200.00 (0-7837-3376-3, 204333400008) Bks Demand.
Organ Preservation Surgery for Laryngeal Cancer. Gregory S. Weinstein et al. LC 98-40983. (Illus.). 272p. 1999. pap. 378.95 (1-56593-903-4, 1788) Thomson Learn.
*Organ Preservation Surgery of the Larynx: 1999 Singular Catalog. Weinstein. 1999. write for info. (1-56593-956-5) Thomson Learn.
Organ Procurement & Preservation. Goran B. Klintmalm & Marlon F. Levy. LC 98-55261. (Vademecum Ser.). 250p. 1999. spiral bd. 45.00 (1-57059-498-8) Landes Bioscience.
*Organ Procurement & Transplantation: Assessing Current Policies & the Potential Impact. Institute of Medicine Staff. 254p. 1999. pap. 44.00 (0-309-06578-X) Natl Acad Pr.
Organ Registration: A Comprehensive Treatise on the Distinctive Quality of Tone & Organ. Everett E. Truett. 1988. reprint ed. lib. bdg. 49.00 (0-7812-0797-5) Rprt Serv.
Organ Registration: A Comprehensive Treatise on the Distintive Quality of Tone & Organ Stops. Everett E. Truett. LC 78-181284. 264p. 1919. reprint ed. 29.00 (0-403-01707-6) Scholarly.
Organ Replacement Therapy: Ethics, Justice & Commerce: First Joint Meeting of ESOT & EDTA - ERA Munich, December 1990. Ed. by W. Land & J. B. Dossetor. (Illus.). xxiii, 578p. 1991. 185.00 (0-387-53687-6) Spr-Verlag.
Organ-Selective Actions of Steroid Hormones. Ed. by D. T. Baird et al. LC 95-42665. (Ernst Schering Research Foundation Workshop Ser.: No. 16). 1995. write for info. (0-387-60338-7); 68.95 (3-540-60338-7) Spr-Verlag.
Organ Shortage - The Solutions: Proceedings of the 26th Conference on Transplantation & Clinical Immunology 13-15 June 1994. Ed. by J. L. Touraine et al. LC 94-37471. (Transplantation & Clinical Immunology Ser.: Vol. 26). 360p. (C). 1995. text 166.00 (0-7923-3179-6) Kluwer Academic.
Organ Sonatas. Alexandre Guilmant. 1999. pap. text 13.95 (0-486-40620-2) Dover.
Organ Symphonies No. 01-No. 03. Louis Vierne. 160p. 1996. 10.95 (0-486-29405-6, 278499Q) Dover.
Organ Technique: A Historical Approach. Sandra Soderlund. 200p. (Orig.). (C). 1980. pap. 27.95 (0-937276-00-6, HMO140) Hinshaw Mus.
*Organ Technique: Modern & Early. George H. Ritchie & George B. Stauffer. (Illus.). 384p. 2000. pap. text 35.00 (0-19-513745-0) OUP.
Organ Theory Tension Change. Jaffee. 2000. 32.00 (0-07-234166-1) McGraw.
*Organ Transplant: The Debate over Who, How & Why. Adam Winters. LC 00-21863. (Focus on Science & Society Ser.). 2000. lib. bdg. write for info. (0-8239-3209-5) Rosen Group.
Organ Transplantation. Frank P. Stuart & Michael M. Abecassis. LC 99-57056. (Vademecum Ser.). 592p. 2000. spiral bd. 45.00 (1-57059-529-1) Landes Bioscience.
Organ Transplantation: A Manual for Nurses. Ed. by Barbara Williams et al. 376p. 1991. 49.95 (0-8261-7230-X) Springer Pub.
Organ Transplantation: Long-Term Results. Ed. by Paul & Kim Solez. LC 92-18547. (Illus.). 432p. 1992. text 190.00 (0-8247-8599-1) Dekker.
Organ Transplantation: Meanings & Realities. Ed. by Stuart J. Youngner et al. LC 95-2995. 298p. 1996. pap. 22.95 (0-299-14964-1) U of Wis Pr.
Organ Transplantation & Tissue Grafting. Herve. 289p. 289.00 (0-86196-383-0, Pub. by J Libbey Med) Bks Intl VA.
Organ Transplantation in Rats & Mice: Microsurgical Techniques & Immunological Principles. Ed. by W. Timmermann et al. LC 98-18910. (Illus.). 550p. 1998. 219.00 (3-540-64081-9) Spr-Verlag.
Organ Transplantation in Religious, Ethical & Social Context: No Room for Death. Intro. by William R. DeLong. LC 93-29164. (Journal of Health Care Chaplaincy: Vol. 5, Nos. 1/2). (Illus.). 175p. 1993. lib. bdg. 39.95 (1-56024-470-4) Haworth Pr.
Organ Transplantation, 1990. Ed. by George M. Abouna et al. (Developments in Surgery Ser.). (C). 1991. text 341.00 (0-7923-1191-4) Kluwer Academic.
Organ Transplantation Policy: Issues & Prospects. Ed. by James F. Blumstein & Frank A. Sloan. LC 89-16928. 265p. (C). 1989. text 37.95 (0-8223-0939-4) Duke.
*Organ Transplants. Mary Kittredge. (21st Century Health & Wellness Ser.). (Illus.). 128p. (YA). 1999. 24.95 (0-7910-5522-1) Chelsea Hse.
Organ Transplants: A Patient's Guide. Massachusetts General Hospital Organ Transplant Staff & H. F. Pizer. (Illus.). 256p. (C). 1991. text 24.95 (0-674-64235-X) HUP.
Organ Transplants: How to Boost Supply & Ensure Equitable Distribution. (Illus.). 94p. (Orig.). (C). 1993. pap. text 30.00 (0-7881-0078-5) DIANE Pub.
*Organ Transplants: Making the Most of Your Gift of Life. Robert Finn. Ed. by Linda Lamb. 320p. 2000. pap. 19.95 (1-56592-634-X, Patient-Centered) OReilly & Assocs.

O

An Asterisk (*) at the beginning of an entry indicates that the title is appearing for the first time.

Organ Transplants & Ethics. David Lamb. (Avebury Series in Philosophy). 172p. 1996. text 68.95 (*1-85972-507-4*, Pub. by Avebury) Ashgate Pub Co.

Organ Transplants from Executed Prisoners: An Argument for the Creation of Death Sentence Organ Removal Statutes. Louis J. Palmer, Jr. LC 99-15655. 166p. 1999. lib. bdg. 35.00 (*0-7864-0673-9*) McFarland & Co.

Organ Voicing & Tuning: A Guide to Amateurs. (Illus.). 39p. 1992. reprint ed. pap. 4.95 (*0-913499-11-0*) Organ Hist Soc.

Organ Voluntaries, Vol. 3. Alexander Schreiner. Ed. by Charles R. Cronham & Dale Tucker. 120p. (Orig.). 1985. reprint ed. pap. 14.95 (*0-7692-0336-1*, FE09800) Wrner Bros.

Organ Works. Johannes Brahms et al. 176p. 1991. pap. 11.95 (*0-486-26828-4*) Dover.

Organ Works. Dietrich Buxtehude. 320p. 1988. pap. 14.95 (*0-486-25682-0*) Dover.

Organ Works. Cesar Franck. 208p. 1987. pap. 12.95 (*0-486-25517-4*) Dover.

Organ Works. Johann J. Froberger. 224p. 1994. pap. text 12.95 (*0-486-28093-4*) Dover.

Organ Works. Franz Liszt. 176p. 1996. pap. 13.95 (*0-486-29083-2*) Dover.

Organ Works. Johann Pachelbel. 160p. pap. text 10.95 (*0-486-27858-1*) Dover.

***Organ Works of Marcel Dupre, Vol. 4.** Graham Steed. LC 99-30299. (Complete Organ Ser.). 271p. 1999. 64.00 (*1-57647-007-5*) Pendragon NY.

Organ Works of Russell Schulz-Widmar: From the Organist's Companion. Ed. by Dale Tucker. 68p. (C). 1997. pap. text 9.95 (*0-7692-1586-6*, DM9702) Wrner Bros.

Organa Britannica, Vol. 4. (C). write for info. (*0-8387-5045-1*) Bucknell U Pr.

Organa Britannica: Organs Built in England, 1660-1860, 3 vols., 1. James Boeringer. LC 78-72492. (Illus.). 1200p. 1983. 95.00 (*0-8387-1894-9*) Bucknell U Pr.

Organa Britannica: Organs Built in England, 1660-1860, 3 vols., 2. James Boeringer. LC 78-72492. (Illus.). 1200p. 1987. 95.00 (*0-8387-5043-5*) Bucknell U Pr.

Organa Britannica: Organs Built in England, 1660-1860, 3 vols., 3. James Boeringer. LC 78-72492. (Illus.). 1200p. 1990. 125.00 (*0-8387-5044-3*) Bucknell U Pr.

Organelle Diseases. Applegarth. 688p. 1997. text 150.00 (*0-412-54910-7*, Pub. by E A) OUP.

Organelle Genes & Genomes. Nicholas W. Gillham. LC 93-33374. (Illus.). 440p. (C). 1994. pap. text 51.00 (*0-19-508248-6*) OUP.

Organelle Heredity. fac. ed. Nicholas W. Gillham. LC 75-43195. (Illus.). 618p. pap. 191.60 (*0-7837-7176-2*, 204712300005) Bks Demand.

Organelles. Mark Carroll. LC 88-24625. (Molecular Cell Biology Ser.). 202p. 1989. pap. text 26.95 (*0-89862-526-2*) Guilford Pubns.

Organelles in Eukaryotic Cells: Molecular Structure & Interactions. Ed. by J. M. Tager et al. LC 89-25545. (Illus.). 278p. 1990. 79.50 (*0-306-43388-5*, Plenum Trade) Perseus Pubng.

Organelles in Tumor Diagnosis: An Ultrastructural Atlas. Brian Eyden. LC 96-1857. (Illus.). 192p. 1996. 79.50 (*0-89640-311-4*) Igaku-Shoin.

Organic. 7th ed. T. W. Graham Solomons. 624p. 1999. pap., student ed. 58.95 (*0-471-35196-2*) Wiley.

Organic: Selected Experiments. 3rd ed. Mayo. (C). 1998. pap. text 39.00 (*0-471-32863-4*) Wiley.

Organic - Inorganic Hybrid Materials Vol. 519: Proceedings Materials Research Society Symposium. Ed. by R. M. Laine et al. 415p. 1998. text 81.00 (*1-55899-425-4*) Materials Res.

Organic Acids see Rohstoffe des Pflanzenreichs

Organic Acids in Aquatic Ecosystems. Ed. by E. M. Perdue & E. T. Gjessing. LC 89-29728. 360p. 1990. 335.00 (*0-471-92631-0*) Wiley.

Organic Acids in Geological Processes. Ed. by E. D. Pittman & M. D. Lewan. LC 94-3819. 1994. 111.95 (*0-387-56953-7*) Spr-Verlag.

Organic Acids in Man. R. A. Chalmers & A. M. Lawson. LC 81-11342. 1982. 82.50 (*0-412-14890-0*, NO. 6573) Chapman & Hall.

Organic Acidureas. Ed. by G. M. Addison et al. 1984. text 124.00 (*0-85200-875-9*) Kluwer Academic.

Organic Additives & Ceramic Processing: With Applications in Powder Metallurgy, Ink, & Paint. 2nd ed. Ed. by Daniel J. Shanefield. LC 96-28177. 335p. (C). 1996. text 137.50 (*0-7923-9765-7*) Kluwer Academic.

Organic Additives & Ceramic Processing: With Applications in Powder Metallurgy, Ink, & Print. Daniel J. Shanefield. LC 95-8313. 328p. (C). 1995. text 119.00 (*0-7923-9574-3*) Kluwer Academic.

Organic Alchemy. 2nd ed. R. P. Kaushik. LC 77-94471. (Orig.). 1978. pap. 5.95 (*0-918038-07-3*) Journey Pubns.

Organic Alchemy: The Universal Law of Soul Progression, Lessons 209-15. C. C. Zain. (Brotherhood of Light Home Study Ser.: Course 19). (Illus.). 137p. 1998. pap. 16.95 (*0-87887-353-8*) Church of Light.

Organic Analysis Using Atomic Absorption Spectrometry (AAS) Saad S. Hassan. (Analytical Chemistry Ser.: 1-118). 384p. 1984. text 120.00 (*0-470-27498-0*) P-H.

Organic & Biochemistry. David G. Lygre. (Chemistry Ser.). 1995. pap., lab manual ed. 28.95 (*0-534-34253-1*) Brooks-Cole.

Organic & Biochemistry for Today. 2nd ed. Spencer L. Seager & Michael R. Slabaugh. Ed. by Westby. LC 93-33035. (Chemistry). 475p. (C). 1994. mass mkt. 33.25 (*0-314-02854-4*) West Pub.

Organic & Biochemistry for Today. 3rd ed. Spencer L. Seager & Michael R. Slabaugh. LC 96-43515. 475p. 1997. mass mkt. 33.25 (*0-314-21627-8*) West Pub.

***Organic & Biochemistry for Today.** 4th ed. Slabaugh Seager. LC 99-42016. (Chemistry Ser.). 1999. 47.50 (*0-534-37288-0*) Brooks-Cole.

***Organic & Biochemistry for Today.** 4th ed. Spencer L. Seager & Michael R. Slabaugh. LC 99-42016. (Chemistry Ser.). 444p. 1999. pap. 63.95 (*0-534-37289-9*) Brooks-Cole.

***Organic & Biochemistry in the Lab.** 5th ed. (C). 1998. write for info. (*0-8087-5699-0*) Pearson Custom.

Organic & Biological Chemistry. John R. Holum. LC 95-32942. 528p. 1995. text 81.95 (*0-471-12972-0*) Wiley.

Organic & Biological Chemistry. John R. Holum. 360p. 1996. pap., student ed. 25.95 (*0-471-13756-1*) Wiley.

Organic & Biological Chemistry. Mundy. (C). 1993. text 79.50 (*0-03-029013-9*) Harcourt Coll Pubs.

Organic & Biological Chemistry: Intro. Experiments & Exercises. 2nd ed. Claudia Hein. 184p. (C). 1998. pap. text 30.95 (*0-7872-2534-7*, 41253402) Kendall-Hunt.

Organic & Biological Chemistry: Introductory Experiments & Exercises. 2nd ed. Claudia Hein. 184p. (C). 1996. 22.95 (*0-7872-2363-8*) Kendall-Hunt.

Organic & Compost-Based Growing Media for Tree Seedling Nurseries. Joan H. Miller & Norman Jones. LC 94-23707. (Technical Papers: No. 264). 90p. 1995. pap. 22.00 (*0-8213-3039-X*, 13039) World Bank.

Organic & Inorganic Coatings for Corrosion Prevention - Research & Experiences. Ed. by L. Fedrizzi & P. L. Bonora. (European Federation of Corrosion Publications: No. 20). (Illus.). 368p. 1997. 150.00 (*1-86125-030-4*) Ashgate Pub Co.

Organic & Inorganic Fertilizers. Robert Parnes. 167p. (Orig.). 1996. pap. text 39.95 (*0-9603554-3-X*) Woods End.

Organic & Inorganic Low-Dimensional Crystalline Materials. Ed. by P. Delhaes & M. Drillon. LC 87-28561. (NATO ASI Series B, Physics: Vol. 168). (Illus.). 496p. 1988. 125.00 (*0-306-42783-4*, Plenum Trade) Perseus Pubng.

***Organic & Inorganic Photochemsitry.** Ed. by V. Ramamurthy & Kirk S. Schanze. LC 98-35550. (Molecular & Supramolecular Photochemistry Ser.). (Illus.). 368p. 1998. text 175.00 (*0-8247-0174-7*) Dekker.

Organic & Polymer Materials for Nonlinear Optics. Ed. by S. Kobayashi. v, 176p. 1990. text 757.00 (*2-88124-440-8*) Gordon & Breach.

Organic & Whole Foods. Andre Domine. (Culinaria Ser.). (Illus.). 460p. 1997. 39.95 (*3-89508-472-7*, 520074) Konemann.

Organic Architecture. Sharp. 176p. 1999. text 79.95 (*0-7506-1364-5*) Buttrwrth-Heinemann.

Organic Brain Pathology. Mary L. Marley. 264p. 1989. 86.00 (*0-205-10142-9*) P-H.

Organic Brain Pathology & the Bender-Gestalt Test: A Differential Diagnostic. Mary L. Marley. 264p. 1983. text 38.00 (*0-8089-1425-1*, 792683, Grune & Strat) Harcrt Hlth Sci Grp.

Organic Building Blocks of the Chemical Industry. H. Harry Szmant. (C). 1988. write for info. (*0-318-57087-4*) Macmillan.

Organic Building Blocks of the Chemical Industry. H. Harry Szmant. LC 89-30001. 736p. 1989. 165.00 (*0-471-85545-6*) Wiley.

Organic Building up of the Church As the Body of Christ to Be the Organism of the Processed & Dispensing Triune God. Witness Lee. 82p. 1989. per. 5.25 (*0-87083-497-5*, 08-015-001) Living Stream Ministry.

Organic C-Centered Radicals see Atomic & Molecular Physics: Group II

Organic Chef. Jane Hernan. 256p. 1993. pap. 19.95 (*0-385-25408-3*) Doubleday.

Organic Chem. 3rd ed. Carey. 1996. 89.74 (*0-07-844757-7*) McGraw.

Organic Chem Lab Survival Manual: A Student's Guide to Techniques. 4th ed. James W. Zubrick. LC 96-35813. 400p. (C). (gr. 13). 1997. pap. 39.95 (*0-471-12948-8*) Wiley.

***Organic Chem Lab Survival Manual: A Student's Guide to Techniques.** 5th ed. James W. Zubrick. 320p. (C). 2000. pap. write for info. (*0-471-38732-0*) Wiley.

Organic Chemical. 3rd ed. Vollhardt. 1998. student ed. 105.00 incl. cd-rom (*0-7167-3460-5*); student ed. 95.00 incl. cd-rom (*0-7167-3461-3*) W H Freeman.

Organic Chemical Chemistry. Ed. by J. Garbarczyk & D. W. Jones. (IUCr Crystallographic Symposia Ser.: No. 4). (Illus.). 224p. 1991. 59.00 (*0-19-855383-8*) OUP.

Organic-Chemical Drugs & Their Synonyms: An International Survey, 4 vols., Set. 7th ed. Martin Negwer. LC 94-27326. 3952p. 1994. text 925.00 (*3-527-40040-0*, Pub. by Akademie Verlag) Wiley.

Organic Chemical Nomenclature. Philipp Fresenius. (Organic Chemistry Ser.). 304p. 1989. text 69.95 (*0-470-21098-2*) P-H.

***Organic Chemicals: An Environmental Perspective.** Alasdair H. Neilson. LC 99-52061. 912p. 1999. boxed set 99.95 (*1-56670-376-X*) Lewis Pubs.

Organic Chemicals from Biomass. Irving S. Goldstein. 320p. 1981. 181.00 (*0-8493-5531-1*, TP247, CRC Reprint) Franklin.

Organic Chemicals in Natural Water: Applied Monitoring & Impact Assessment. J. W. Moore & S. Ramamoorthy. (Environmental Management Ser.). (Illus.). 290p. 1984. 117.00 (*0-387-96034-1*) Spr-Verlag.

Organic Chemicals in the Soil Environment, Vol. 1. Ed. by Cleve A. Goring & John W. Hamaker. LC 71-179384. (Books in Soils & the Environment). 456p. reprint ed. pap. 141.40 (*0-8357-6244-0*, 205508400001) Bks Demand.

Organic Chemicals in the Soil Environment, Vol. 2. Ed. by Cleve A. Goring & John W. Hamaker. LC 71-179384. (Books in Soils & the Environment). (Illus.). 543p. reprint ed. pap. 168.40 (*0-8357-6245-9*, 203453500002) Bks Demand.

Organic Chemistry, 9 vols. (C). 1995. pap., teacher ed. 11.96 (*0-395-72403-1*) HM.

Organic Chemistry. (C). 1996. lab manual ed. write for info. (*0-8087-9567-8*) Pearson Custom.

Organic Chemistry. (C). 1996. lab manual ed. write for info. (*0-8087-5684-2*) Pearson Custom.

Organic Chemistry. David Baker & Robert Engel. Ed. by Pullins. (Chemistry). 1200p. (C). 1992. pap. 82.25 (*0-314-93000-0*) West Pub.

Organic Chemistry. Roger D. Barry. LC 74-79834. (Allied Health Ser.). 1975. student ed. 5.10 (*0-672-61379-4*, Bobbs); pap. text 8.35 (*0-672-61378-6*, Bobbs) Macmillan.

Organic Chemistry. Robert J. Boxer. 1997. pap., student ed. 81.56 (*0-07-290404-6*) McGraw.

Organic Chemistry. Cesare. 1999. lab manual ed. 12.49 (*0-07-228897-3*) McGraw.

***Organic Chemistry.** Jonathan Clayden et al. (Illus.). 1568p. (C). 2000. pap. text 49.95 (*0-19-850346-6*) OUP.

***Organic Chemistry.** Jonathan Claydon et al. (Illus.). 1408p. 2000. text 85.00 (*0-19-850347-4*) OUP.

Organic Chemistry. Timothy S. Eckert. 1104p. 1995. text. write for info. (*0-697-16348-2*, WCB McGr Hill) McGrw-H Hghr Educ.

Organic Chemistry. Fessenden. (Chemistry Ser.). 1979. 29.00 (*0-87150-724-2*); student ed. 6.75 (*0-87150-730-7*) PWS Pubs.

Organic Chemistry. Maryanne Fox & James K. Whitesell. (Chemistry Ser.). 896p. 1994. 77.50 (*0-86720-207-6*) Jones & Bartlett.

Organic Chemistry, 8 vols. Hart. (C). Date not set. text, teacher ed., suppl. ed. write for info. (*0-395-57235-5*) HM.

Organic Chemistry. Hornback. 1997. pap. text, student ed. 37.00 (*0-534-35258-8*) Brooks-Cole.

Organic Chemistry. Hornback. LC 97-46609. 1998. pap. 72.75 (*0-534-35254-5*) Brooks-Cole.

Organic Chemistry. Hornback. (Chemistry Ser.). 1998. mass mkt. 70.00 (*0-534-36283-4*) Brooks-Cole.

Organic Chemistry. Hornback. (Chemistry Ser.). 1998. pap., student ed. 37.00 (*0-534-35259-6*) Brooks-Cole.

Organic Chemistry. Maitland Jones. (C). 1997. pap. text, student ed. 54.25 (*0-393-97080-9*) Norton.

Organic Chemistry. Daniel S. Kemp & Frank Vellaccio. 1980. 77.95 (*0-87901-123-8*) Worth.

Organic Chemistry. Daniel S. Kemp & Frank Vellaccio. 1980. pap., teacher ed. 29.95 (*0-87901-124-6*) Worth.

Organic Chemistry. G. Marc Loudon. LC 83-7075. (Chemistry Ser.). 1150p. 1984. text. write for info. (*0-201-14438-7*); student ed. write for info. (*0-201-14436-0*) Addison-Wesley.

Organic Chemistry. John McMurry. LC 83-7744. (Chemistry). 1051p. (C). 1984. mass mkt. 48.50 (*0-534-01204-3*) Brooks-Cole.

Organic Chemistry. Herbert Meislich. 1999. pap. text 8.95 (*0-07-052718-0*) McGraw-Hill Pubng.

Organic Chemistry. Ed. by Merken. (C). 1986. text, teacher ed. write for info. (*0-321-40544-7*) Addson-Wesley Educ.

Organic Chemistry. Donald L. Pavia. (C). 1999. text 47.50 (*0-03-063986-7*) Harcourt Coll Pubs.

Organic Chemistry. Raber. Date not set. pap. text, teacher ed. write for info. (*0-314-35233-3*) West Pub.

Organic Chemistry. Douglas Raber & Nancy Raber. (Chemistry). 1445p. (C). 1988. mass mkt. 69.50 (*0-314-28508-3*) West Pub.

Organic Chemistry. Neil E. Schore. (C). 1994. pap. text, teacher ed. 24.00 (*0-7167-2571-1*) W H Freeman.

Organic Chemistry. Smith. 2001. text. write for info. (*0-13-640251-8*) P-H.

Organic Chemistry. Thomas N. Sorrell. LC 98-47383. (Illus.). 1352p. (C). 1999. text 92.00 (*0-935702-47-4*) Univ Sci Bks.

Organic Chemistry. Svoronos-Sarlo. 1994. 10.00 (*0-697-24698-1*, WCB McGr Hill) McGrw-H Hghr Educ.

Organic Chemistry. K. Peter Vollhardt. (Chemistry Ser.). (Illus.). 1275p. (C). 1987. text 49.60 (*0-7167-1786-7*) W H Freeman.

Organic Chemistry. K. Peter Vollhardt. (Chemistry Ser.). (Illus.). 1275p. (C). 1987. trans. 280.00 (*0-7167-1883-9*) W H Freeman.

Organic Chemistry. K. Peter Vollhardt. LC 93-15648. (C). 1993. text 64.80 (*0-7167-3546-6*) W H Freeman.

Organic Chemistry. K. Peter Vollhardt & Neil E. Schore. LC 93-15648. (C). 1993. pap. text. write for info. (*0-7167-2451-0*) W H Freeman.

Organic Chemistry. 2nd ed. (C). 1991. 19.46 (*0-13-642612-3*, Macmillan Coll) P-H.

Organic Chemistry. 2nd ed. Norman L. Allinger et al. LC 75-18431. 1976. text 77.95 (*0-87901-050-9*) Worth.

Organic Chemistry. 2nd ed. Norman L. Allinger et al. LC 75-18431. 1976. pap. text, student ed. 14.95 (*0-87901-078-9*) Worth.

Organic Chemistry. 2nd ed. Atkins. 1996. 26.88 (*0-07-011339-4*) McGraw.

Organic Chemistry. 2nd ed. Philip S. Bailey, Jr. & Christina A. Bailey. 1997. pap. text, student ed. 37.00 (*0-13-850348-6*) P-H.

Organic Chemistry. 2nd ed. Brown. (C). 1997. pap. 114.00 (*0-03-023137-X*); pap. 114.00 (*0-03-023144-2*) Harcourt.

Organic Chemistry. 2nd ed. Brown. (C). 1997. 118.50 (*0-03-023182-5*) Harcourt.

Organic Chemistry. 2nd ed. Brown. (C). 1997. 441.50 (*0-03-020694-4*) Harcourt.

Organic Chemistry. 2nd ed. Brown. (C). 1997. pap. text 31.00 (*0-03-024301-7*, Pub. by Harcourt Coll Pubs) Harcourt.

Organic Chemistry. 2nd ed. Brown. 848p. (C). 1997. text, student ed. 60.50 (*0-03-020453-4*, Pub. by SCP) Harcourt.

Organic Chemistry. 2nd ed. Brown & Foote. LC 97-65257. (Illus.). 1232p. (C). 1997. text 106.00 (*0-03-020458-5*, Pub. by SCP) Harcourt.

Organic Chemistry. 2nd ed. Bruice. LC 97-29107. 1362p. 1997. 112.00 (*0-13-841925-6*) P-H.

Organic Chemistry. 2nd ed. Francis A. Carey. (C). 1991. text 78.50 (*0-07-009934-0*); pap. text, student ed. 45.00 (*0-07-009935-9*) McGraw.

Organic Chemistry. 2nd ed. Daley. 1998. 14.50 (*0-697-24100-9*) McGraw.

Organic Chemistry. 2nd ed. Daley. 2000. 28.25 (*0-697-24040-1*, WCB McGr Hill) McGrw-H Hghr Educ.

Organic Chemistry. 2nd ed. Durst. 1987. teacher ed. 23.12 (*0-07-018399-6*) McGraw.

Organic Chemistry. 2nd ed. Fessenden. (Chemistry Ser.). Date not set. teacher ed. 1.00 (*0-87150-369-7*) PWS Pubs.

Organic Chemistry. 2nd ed. Fessenden. (Chemistry Ser.). 1982. 41.75 (*0-87150-752-8*); student ed. 12.00 (*0-87150-753-6*) PWS Pubs.

Organic Chemistry. 2nd ed. Maryanne Fox & James K. Whitesell. LC 96-46985. 1248p. 1997. 88.75 (*0-7637-0178-5*) Jones & Bartlett.

Organic Chemistry. 2nd ed. Grahame Jones & Ovaska. pap. text. write for info. (*0-393-97556-8*) Norton.

Organic Chemistry. 2nd ed. Lewis. 2000. 17.74 (*0-697-14370-8*) McGraw.

Organic Chemistry. 2nd ed. Marc Loudon. (Illus.). 1300p. (C). 1988. trans. 100.00 (*0-8053-6645-8*) Benjamin-Cummings.

Organic Chemistry. 2nd ed. John McMurry. LC 87-15835. (Chemistry). 1241p. (C). 1987. mass mkt. 60.75 (*0-534-07968-7*) Brooks-Cole.

Organic Chemistry. 2nd ed. Boris Pavlov & Alexander Terentyev. Tr. by Mir Publishers Staff from RUS. (Illus.). 616p. (C). 1975. 29.95 (*0-8464-0690-X*) Beekman Pubs.

Organic Chemistry. 2nd ed. Neil E. Schore. 1993. student ed. 24.00 (*0-7167-2172-4*) W H Freeman.

Organic Chemistry. 2nd ed. Svoronos. 1996. teacher ed. 14.68 (*0-697-33924-6*) McGraw.

Organic Chemistry. 2nd ed. Paris Svoronos et al. 352p. (C). 1996. text, lab manual ed. write for info. (*0-697-33923-8*, WCB McGr Hill) McGrw-H Hghr Educ.

***Organic Chemistry.** 3rd ed. (C). 2000. write for info. (*0-13-031012-3*) P-H.

***Organic Chemistry.** 3rd ed. (C). 2000. text. write for info. (*0-13-017863-2*) P-H.

***Organic Chemistry.** 3rd ed. (C). 2001. text. write for info. (*0-13-017859-4*); text. write for info. (*0-13-017861-6*); text. write for info. (*0-13-017862-4*); text. write for info. (*0-13-017865-9*); text. write for info. (*0-13-017866-7*); text. write for info. (*0-13-017850-0*) P-H.

Organic Chemistry. 3rd ed. (C). 1995. pap. text 424.66 (*0-8053-6662-8*) Benjamin-Cummings.

Organic Chemistry. 3rd ed. 128p. (C). 1995. pap. text 24.00 (*0-8053-6652-0*) Benjamin-Cummings.

Organic Chemistry. 3rd ed. 112p. (C). 1996. pap. text 24.00 (*0-8053-6663-6*) Benjamin-Cummings.

Organic Chemistry. 3rd ed. Atkins. 2001. student ed. 18.00 (*0-07-231945-3*) McGraw.

Organic Chemistry. 3rd ed. Carey. 1995. pap., student ed. 50.94 (*0-07-011223-1*) McGraw.

Organic Chemistry. 3rd ed. Francis A. Carey. LC 95-25237. 1151p. (C). 1995. 102.81 (*0-07-011212-6*) McGraw.

Organic Chemistry. 3rd ed. Ralph J. Fessenden & Joan S. Fessenden. LC 86-17200. (Chemistry). 1100p. (C). 1986. mass mkt. 52.75 (*0-534-05088-3*) Brooks-Cole.

Organic Chemistry. 3rd ed. G. Marc Loudon. 1994. 94.25 (*0-8053-6550-8*) Benjamin-Cummings.

Organic Chemistry. 3rd ed. Marc Loudon. 1390p. (C). 1994. 115.00 (*0-8053-6650-4*) Benjamin-Cummings.

Organic Chemistry. 3rd ed. Marc Loudon. (C). 1996. text 135.00 (*0-8053-6667-9*) Benjamin-Cummings.

Organic Chemistry. 3rd ed. McMurry. (Chemistry Ser.). 1992. pap., teacher ed. write for info. (*0-534-16223-1*) Brooks-Cole.

Organic Chemistry. 3rd ed. John McMurry. (Chemistry Ser.). 1992. pap., student ed. 37.00 (*0-534-16219-3*) Brooks-Cole.

Organic Chemistry. 3rd ed. Vollardt. 1998. pap. text, student ed. 38.95 (*0-7167-3165-7*) W H Freeman.

Organic Chemistry. 3rd ed. K. Peter Vollhardt. 1998. pap. 24.00 (*0-7167-3163-0*) W H Freeman.

Organic Chemistry. 3rd ed. K. Peter Vollhardt. 1998. teacher ed. 160.00 (*0-7167-3424-9*) W H Freeman.

Organic Chemistry. 3rd ed. Leroy G. Wade, Jr. LC 94-24693. 1300p. 1994. text 105.67 (*0-13-301631-5*) P-H.

Organic Chemistry. 4th ed. (C). 1999. text 16.00 (*0-13-016191-8*) Aspen Law.

***Organic Chemistry.** 4th ed. 112p. (C). 2000. pap. 20.00 (*0-13-030432-8*) P-H.

Organic Chemistry. 4th ed. Carey. LC 99-45791. 2000. 84.00 (*0-07-290501-8*) McGraw.

***Organic Chemistry.** 4th ed. Francis A. Carey. LC 99-45791. 2000. write for info. (*0-07-117499-0*) McGraw.

Organic Chemistry. 4th ed. Seyhan N. Ege. 1998. pap. text, teacher ed. 14.97 (*0-395-92326-3*) HM.

Organic Chemistry. 4th ed. Ralph J. Fessenden. (Chemistry). 1990. student ed. 36.50 (*0-534-12257-4*) Brooks-Cole.

O

Organic Chemistry. 4th ed. Ralph J. Fessenden & Joan S. Fessenden. (Chemistry). 1216p. (C). 1990. mass mkt. 75.50 (*0-534-12252-3*) Brooks-Cole.
Organic Chemistry. 4th ed. Mcmurry. text 88.31 (*0-534-33276-5*); text 81.00 (*0-534-33255-2*) Brooks-Cole.
Organic Chemistry. 4th ed. Robert T. Morrison. 1982. pap. text 30.60 (*0-205-17802-2*) Allyn.
Organic Chemistry. 4th ed. Robert T. Morrison & Robert N. Boyd. 1408p. (C). 1982. text 48.00 (*0-205-05838-8*, EDP 685838) Allyn.
Organic Chemistry. 4th ed. Robert T. Morrison & Robert N. Boyd. (C). 1983. pap. text 11.20 (*0-205-07984-9*) Allyn.
Organic Chemistry. 4th ed. Wade. LC 98-45643. 1256p. 1998. 112.00 (*0-13-922741-5*) P-H.
*__Organic Chemistry.__ 4th ed. Wade. 1999. suppl. ed. write for info. (*0-13-018818-2*) P-H.
Organic Chemistry. 5th ed. (C). 1995. write for info. (*0-8087-9558-9*) Pearson Custom.
Organic Chemistry. 5th ed. Philip S. Bailey, Jr. & Christina A. Bailey. 1995. pap. text, student ed., suppl. ed. 38.00 (*0-13-180324-7*) P-H.
Organic Chemistry. 5th ed. Fessenden. student ed. 106.20 (*0-534-31844-4*) Thomson Learn.
Organic Chemistry. 5th ed. Ralph J. Fessenden & Joan S. Fessenden. LC 93-28377. 1168p. 1993. pap. 77.25 (*0-534-20028-1*) Brooks-Cole.
Organic Chemistry. 5th ed. McMurry. LC 99-16981. (Chemistry). 1999. pap. 70.00 (*0-534-36274-5*); pap. text, student ed. 42.00 (*0-534-37192-2*) Brooks-Cole.
*__Organic Chemistry.__ 5th ed. McMurry. LC 99-16981. 1284p. 1999. pap. 78.00 (*0-534-37366-6*) Thomson Learn.
Organic Chemistry. 5th ed. Robert T. Morrison & A. W. Boyd. 1987. pap., student ed. 35.00 (*0-685-18128-6*, H8454-4); write for info. (*0-318-61878-8*, H0524-2); trans. 70.00 (*0-685-18129-4*, H0525-9) P-H.
Organic Chemistry. 5th ed. Stanley H. Pine. (C). 1987. pap. text, student ed. write for info. (*0-07-050119-X*) McGraw.
*__Organic Chemistry.__ 6th ed. (C). 1999. write for info. (*0-8087-2411-8*) Pearson Custom.
*__Organic Chemistry.__ 6th ed. Philip S. Bailey, Jr. & Christina A. Bailey. LC 99-52987. 570p. 1999. pap. text 69.00 (*0-13-924119-1*) P-H.
Organic Chemistry. 6th ed. Fessenden. (Chemistry Ser.). 1998. pap., student ed. 16.75 (*0-534-35201-4*) Brooks-Cole.
Organic Chemistry. 6th ed. Fessenden. 1998. pap., student ed. 38.00 (*0-534-35200-6*) Brooks-Cole.
Organic Chemistry. 6th ed. Ralph J. Fessenden. LC 97-43828. 1998. mass mkt. 85.50 (*0-534-35199-9*) Brooks-Cole.
Organic Chemistry. 6th ed. Robert T. Morrison & A. W. Boyd. (C). 1992. pap. text, student ed. 52.00 (*0-13-643677-3*) P-H.
Organic Chemistry. 6th ed. Robert T. Morrison & Robert K. Boyd. 1360p. 1992. 114.00 (*0-13-643669-2*) P-H.
Organic Chemistry. 6th ed. Robert T. Morrison & Robert N. Boyd. (C). 1992. 62.00 (*0-205-12042-3*, Macmillan Coll) P-H.
Organic Chemistry. 6th ed. Solomons. 1995. text, student ed. 100.00 (*0-471-13755-3*) Wiley.
Organic Chemistry. 6th ed. T. W. Graham Solomons. LC 95-16672. 1328p. (C). 1995. text 117.95 (*0-471-01342-0*) Wiley.
Organic Chemistry. 6th ed. T. W. Graham Solomons & Darrell Woodman. 1997. cd-rom 84.95 (*0-471-17285-5*) Wiley.
Organic Chemistry. 7th ed. Brown. 1997. text. write for info. (*0-13-578378-X*) Allyn.
Organic Chemistry. 7th ed. Morrison. 2000. pap. text, student ed., suppl. ed. 46.67 (*0-13-800160-X*) P-H.
*__Organic Chemistry.__ 7th ed. Morrison. 2000. pap. text, teacher ed. write for info. (*0-13-800210-X*) P-H.
Organic Chemistry. 7th ed. Robert T. Morrison & Robert N. Boyd. 1998. text 85.33 (*0-13-267816-0*) P-H.
Organic Chemistry. 7th ed. Solomons. text 114.00 (*0-471-37326-5*); text 112.00 (*0-471-37771-6*) Wiley.
Organic Chemistry. 7th ed. T. W. Graham Solomons & Craig B. Fryhle. LC 98-46357. 1344p. 1999. 117.95 incl. cd-rom (*0-471-19095-0*) Wiley.
Organic Chemistry. 7th ed. T. W. Graham Solomons & Craig B. Fryhle. 1999. pap. text 14.95 (*0-471-36322-7*) Wiley.
Organic Chemistry, 8 vols. 8th ed. Hart. (C). 1991. pap. text 73.16 (*0-395-62838-5*) HM.
Organic Chemistry, 9 vols. 9th ed. (C). 1995. pap. text, student ed. 33.16 (*0-395-72402-3*) HM.
Organic Chemistry, 9 vols. 9th ed. Hart. LC 94-76506. (C). 1994. text 74.36 (*0-395-70838-9*) HM.
Organic Chemistry, 9 vols. 9th ed. Hart. (C). 1995. pap. text, lab manual ed. 37.16 (*0-395-72401-5*) HM.
Organic Chemistry. 10th ed. Hart. LC 98-72038. 1998. text 63.87 (*0-395-90225-8*) HM.
Organic Chemistry 10th ed. Hart. 1999. pap., lab manual ed. 8.97 (*0-395-92346-8*) HM.
Organic Chemistry, Chapter 17. 2nd ed. Maryanne Fox & James Whitesell. (Chemistry Ser.). 1997. pap. 6.25 (*0-7637-0389-3*) Jones & Bartlett.
Organic Chemistry, Chapter 18. 2nd ed. Maryanne Fox & James Whitesell. (Chemistry Ser.). 1997. pap. 6.25 (*0-7637-0390-7*) Jones & Bartlett.
Organic Chemistry, Chapter 19. 2nd ed. Maryanne Fox & James Whitesell. (Chemistry Ser.). 1997. pap. 6.25 (*0-7637-0391-5*) Jones & Bartlett.
Organic Chemistry, Chapter 20. 2nd ed. Maryanne Fox & James Whitesell. (Chemistry Ser.). 1997. pap. 6.25 (*0-7637-0392-3*) Jones & Bartlett.
Organic Chemistry, Chapter 21. 2nd ed. Maryanne Fox & James Whitesell. (Chemistry Ser.). 1997. pap. 6.25 (*0-7637-0393-1*) Jones & Bartlett.
Organic Chemistry, Chapter 22. 2nd ed. Maryanne Fox & James Whitesell. (Chemistry Ser.). 1997. pap. 6.25 (*0-7637-0394-X*) Jones & Bartlett.
Organic Chemistry, Chapter 23. 2nd ed. Maryanne Fox & James Whitesell. (Chemistry Ser.). 1997. pap. 6.25 (*0-7637-0395-8*) Jones & Bartlett.
Organic Chemistry, Set. 7th ed. T. W. Graham Solomons. (Study Guide Set). text, student ed. write for info. (*0-471-36369-3*) Wiley.
Organic Chemistry, Vol. I. Roger Macomber. LC 96-60221. (Illus.). 319p. (C). 1996. pap. text 36.50 (*0-935702-90-3*) Univ Sci Bks.
Organic Chemistry, Vol. 1. K. Peter Vollhardt. 2000. student ed. 83.00 (*0-7167-2638-6*) St Martin.
Organic Chemistry, Vol. 2. Roger Macomber. (Illus.). 410p. (C). 1996. pap. text 38.50 (*0-935702-93-8*) Univ Sci Bks.
Organic Chemistry, Vol. 4. 7th ed. Solomons. text 136.00 (*0-471-37887-9*) Wiley.
Organic Chemistry: A Brief Course. Robert C. Atkins & Frank A. Carey. (C). 1989. text, student ed. 23.75 (*0-07-009921-9*) McGraw.
Organic Chemistry: A Brief Course. Robert C. Atkins & Frank A. Carey. (C). 1989. trans. 240.00 (*0-07-074455-6*) McGraw.
Organic Chemistry: A Brief Course. 2nd ed. Robert C. Atkins & Frank A. Carey. LC 96-79060. 524p. (C). 1996. 81.56 (*0-07-011337-8*) McGraw.
Organic Chemistry: A Brief Course. 3rd ed. Robert C. Atkins. 2001. 48.74 (*0-07-231944-5*) McGraw.
Organic Chemistry: A Brief Course. 5th ed. Walter W. Linstromberg & Henry E. Baumgarten. 448p. (C). text 71.96 (*0-669-05525-5*) HM Trade Div.
Organic Chemistry: A Brief Course. 6th ed. Walter W. Linstromberg & Henry E. Baumgarten. LC 86-81385. 517p. (C). 1987. text 71.96 (*0-669-12660-8*); pap. text, student ed. 28.76 (*0-669-12661-6*); 2.66 (*0-669-17411-4*) HM Trade Div.
Organic Chemistry: A Brief Introduction. Robert J. Ouellette. (Illus.). 624p. (C). 1994. write for info. (*0-318-69913-3*) Macmillan.
Organic Chemistry: A Brief Introduction. 2nd ed. Robert J. Ouellette. LC 97-25850. 559p. (C). 1997. pap. text 79.67 (*0-13-841933-7*) P-H.
Organic Chemistry: A Brief Survey of Concepts & Applications. 4th ed. Philip S. Bailey, Jr. & Christina A. Bailey. 1989. student ed. 21.00 (*0-318-40087-1*, H1781-7) P-H.
Organic Chemistry: A Comprehensive Degree Text & Source Book. Hans Beyer & Wolfgang Walter. Ed. & Tr. by Douglas Lloyd. LC 97-178950. 1038p. 1997. pap. 45.00 (*1-898563-37-3*, Pub. by Horwood Pub) Paul & Co Pubs.
Organic Chemistry: A Concise Text for First Year Students. John F. Elsworth. (Illus.). 231p. (C). 1992. pap. text 42.00 (*0-7021-2797-3*, Pub. by Juta & Co) Intl Spec Bk.
Organic Chemistry: A Modern Perspective. David E. Lewis. 1152p. (C). 1996. text. write for info. (*0-697-35091-6*, WCB McGr Hill) McGrw-H Hghr Educ.
Organic Chemistry: An Intermediate Text. Robert V. Hoffman. (Topics in Organic Chemistry Ser.). (Illus.). 336p. (C). 1996. text 57.95 (*0-19-509618-5*) OUP.
*__Organic Chemistry: Brief Survey Concept & Applications.__ 6th ed. 1999. write for info. (*0-13-015480-6*) P-H.
Organic Chemistry: Chemistry 315. 2nd ed. Roth et al. 76p. (C). 1997. spiral bd., lab manual ed. 17.95 (*0-7872-2721-8*, 41272102) Kendall-Hunt.
Organic Chemistry: Preliminary Version. Richard Daley & Sally Daley. 1424p. (C). 1996. text. write for info. (*0-697-35090-8*, WCB McGr Hill) McGrw-H Hghr Educ.
Organic Chemistry: Short. Boxer. 396p. 1997. pap., student ed. 24.69 (*0-697-14062-8*) McGraw.
Organic Chemistry: Solutions Manual. Maryanne Fox & James K. Whitesell. (Chemistry Ser.). 408p. 1994. pap., student ed. 35.00 (*0-86720-879-1*) Jones & Bartlett.
Organic Chemistry: Solutions Manual. 2nd ed. Maryanne Fox & James K. Whitesell. (Chemistry Ser.). 400p. 1997. pap., student ed. 43.75 (*0-7637-0413-X*) Jones & Bartlett.
Organic Chemistry: Solutions Manual. 5th ed. Ralph J. Fessenden. (Chemistry Ser.). 1993. mass mkt., student ed. 45.50 (*0-534-20029-X*) Brooks-Cole.
Organic Chemistry: Structure & Function. 3rd ed. K. P. Vollhardt & Neil E. Schore. LC 97-22455. 1300p. 1998. pap. text 100.95 (*0-7167-2721-8*) W H Freeman.
Organic Chemistry: Structure & Reactivity, 3 Vols. 3rd ed. Seyhan N. Ege. 1355p. (C). 1994. text 92.36 (*0-669-34161-4*) HM Trade Div.
Organic Chemistry: Structure & Reactivity, 3 Vols. 3rd ed. Seyhan N. Ege et al. 1097p. (C). 1994. pap. text, student ed. 49.96 (*0-669-34162-2*) HM Trade Div.
Organic Chemistry: Structure & Reactivity. 4th ed. Seyhan N. Efge. LC 98-72019. xxxii, 1148p. 1999. text 79.17 (*0-395-90223-1*) HM.
Organic Chemistry: Student Manual & Solution Manual. John McMurry. LC 83-7744. (Chemistry). 1051p. (C). 1984. mass mkt., student ed. 23.25 (*0-534-02675-3*) Brooks-Cole.
Organic Chemistry: Study Guide & Solutions Manual. 4th ed. John McMurray. (Chemistry Ser.). 1328p. 1995. student ed. 43.50 (*0-534-23833-5*) Brooks-Cole.
Organic Chemistry: Study Guide with Drill Problems. 5th ed. Ralph J. Fessenden. (Chemistry Ser.). 1994. mass mkt., student ed. 32.75 (*0-534-20030-3*) Brooks-Cole.
Organic Chemistry: Test Bank. Maryanne Fox & James K. Whitesell. (Chemistry Ser.). 115p. 1994. pap., teacher ed. 50.00 (*0-86720-891-0*) Jones & Bartlett.
Organic Chemistry: Test Bank. 2nd ed. Maryanne Fox & James Whitesell. (Chemistry Ser.). Date not set. pap. 10.00 (*0-7637-0492-X*) Jones & Bartlett.
Organic Chemistry: The Basis of Life. B. Miller. 1980. text 28.75 (*0-8053-7071-4*) Addison-Wesley.
Organic Chemistry: The Fundamental Principles, Vol. 1. 6th ed. I. L. Finar. 1986. pap. 38.95 (*0-582-44257-5*, Pub. by Addison-Wesley) Longman.
Organic Chemistry: UCLA Version. 2nd ed. Maryanne Fox & James Whitesell. (Chemistry Ser.). 1997. pap. 6.25 (*0-7637-0476-8*) Jones & Bartlett.
Organic Chemistry Pt. 1. 3rd ed. (C). 1997. lab manual ed. write for info. (*0-8087-9622-4*) Pearson Custom.
Organic Chemistry - An Alphabetical Guide. Bradford P. Mundy & Michael G. Ellerd. 416p. 1996. 44.95 (*0-471-52445-X*) Wiley.
Organic Chemistry & SG Student Manual. 3rd ed. Carey. 1997. 65.50 (*0-07-561227-5*) McGraw.
Organic Chemistry & Study Guide/Solutions Manual. 2nd ed. K. Peter Vollhardt. 2000. student ed. 83.00 (*0-7167-2736-6*) W H Freeman.
Organic Chemistry by Leroy Wade: Solutions Manual & Study Guide. Melvin L. Druelinger & Allen M. Schoffstall. 752p. (C). 1987. pap. text. write for info. (*0-318-62491-5*) P-H.
Organic Chemistry Digest Victoria Ukachukwu. 366p. (C). 1995. text, wbk. ed. 32.00 (*0-536-58854-6*) Pearson Custom.
Organic Chemistry Exam File. Ed. by Robert J. Boxer. (Exam File Ser.). 534p. 1988. pap. 24.50 (*0-910554-66-8*) Engineering.
Organic Chemistry for Health & Life Sciences. 4th ed. Paul W. Groundwater. (C). 1998. pap. text 26.25 (*0-582-29765-6*, Pub. by Addison-Wesley) Longman.
Organic Chemistry for Higher Education. John Brockington & Peter Stamper. LC 81-17118. (Longman Technician Series, Mathematics & Sciences). 349p. reprint ed. pap. 108.20 (*0-8357-2977-X*, 203923900011) Bks Demand.
Organic Chemistry for Students of Biology & Medicine. 3rd ed. G. A. Taylor. 1987. pap. 27.95 (*0-582-44708-9*, Pub. by Addison-Wesley) Longman.
Organic Chemistry Hypercard. Ed. by George H. Schmid. (C). 1996. text 14.95 (*0-8016-7494-8*) Mosby Inc.
*__Organic Chemistry I: Laboratory Manual to Chemistry 233.__ 2nd ed. Dorothy Mazzocchi. 166p. (C). 1999. spiral bd. 16.95 (*0-7872-6374-5*, 41637401) Kendall-Hunt.
Organic Chemistry I & II: Lecture Notes & Workbook. Kurt Donaldson & Jamie Scott. 686p. (C). 1996. pap. text, per. 135.95 (*0-7872-1917-7*, 41191701) Kendall-Hunt.
Organic Chemistry I Quick Review. Frank Pellegrini. (Cliffs Quick Reviews Ser.). (Illus.). 101p. (C). 1997. pap. text 9.95 (*0-8220-5326-8*, Cliff) IDG Bks.
Organic Chemistry in Action: The Design of Organic Synthesis. Felix Serratosa. (Studies in Organic Chemistry: No. 41). 396p. 1990. 224.50 (*0-444-88345-2*) Elsevier.
Organic Chemistry in Action: The Design of Organic Synthesis. 2nd ed. Felix Serratosa & Josep Xicart. LC 96-13632. (Studies in Organic Chemistry: Vol. 51). 566p. 1996. text 284.00 incl. disk (*0-444-81935-5*) Elsevier.
Organic Chemistry in Colour. 1986. 51.95 (*0-387-17260-2*) Spr-Verlag.
Organic Chemistry Lab. John Marx. 80p. (C). 1995. spiral bd. 19.95 (*0-7872-1239-3*, 41123901) Kendall-Hunt.
Organic Chemistry Lab. Oscar R. Rodig. (C). 1990. pap. text, teacher ed. 34.00 (*0-03-012648-7*) Harcourt Coll Pubs.
Organic Chemistry Lab Manual. Ronald L. Halterman & Mark C. Morvant. (C). 1995. pap. 17.06 (*1-56870-180-2*) RonJon Pub.
Organic Chemistry Lab Manual. Albert Sneden. 196p. (C). 1996. pap. text, spiral bd. 23.95 (*0-7872-0403-X*) Kendall-Hunt.
Organic Chemistry Laboratory. 2nd ed. Oscar R. Rodig. LC 96-68142. (C). 1996. pap. text, lab manual ed. 76.50 (*0-03-011648-1*, Pub. by Harcourt Coll Pubs) Harcourt.
*__Organic Chemistry Laboratory: Standard & Microscale Experiments.__ 3rd ed. Charles E. Bell et al. LC 00-30100. (Illus.). 2000. pap. write for info. (*0-03-029272-7*) SCP.
Organic Chemistry Laboratory Manual. Paris Svoronos & Edward Sarlo. 352p. (C). 1993. text. write for info. (*0-697-14799-1*, WCB McGr Hill) McGrw-H Hghr Educ.
Organic Chemistry Laboratory Manual with Waste Management & Molecular Modeling. 2nd ed. Yousry Martin-Sayed. 124p. 1994. spiral bd. 16.95 (*0-8403-8727-X*) Kendall-Hunt.
Organic Chemistry Made Easy. J. Nentwig & M. Kreuder. 576p. 1992. pap. 89.95 (*0-471-18827-1*, Wiley-VCH) Wiley.
Organic Chemistry Made Easy. Joachim Nentwig et al. 558p. (C). 1992. pap. text 59.95 (*1-56081-548-5*, Wiley-VCH) Wiley.
*__Organic Chemistry MCAT Set.__ 7th ed. Solomons. 1999. text 80.00 (*0-471-37062-2*) Wiley.
Organic Chemistry Name Game. A. Nickon. 1987. 55.00 (*0-08-035549-8*, Pergamon Pr) Elsevier.
Organic Chemistry of Aliphatic Nitrogen Compounds. Ben R. Brown. LC 93-31645. (International Series of Monographs on Chemistry: No. 28). (Illus.). 794p. 1994. text 225.00 (*0-19-855753-2*, Clarendon Pr) OUP.
Organic Chemistry of B (Beta)-Lactams. Ed. by Gunda I. Georg. LC 92-34461. 382p. 1993. 115.00 (*1-56081-083-1*, Wiley-VCH) Wiley.
Organic Chemistry of Coal. Ed. by John W. Larsen. LC 78-8114. (ACS Symposium Ser.: Vol. 71). 335p. 1978. reprint ed. pap. 103.90 (*0-608-03930-6*, 206437700009) Bks Demand.
Organic Chemistry of Drug Design & Drug Action. Richard B. Silverman. (Illus.). 422p. 1992. text 65.00 (*0-12-643730-0*) Acad Pr.
*__Organic Chemistry of Drug Synthesis,, 6 Vol.Set.__ Daniel Lednicer & Lester A. Mitscher. 2120p. 1998. 699.00 (*0-471-33370-0*) Wiley.
Organic Chemistry of Drug Synthesis, 4 vols., Set. Daniel Lednicer & Lester A. Mitscher. 1616p. 1990. 349.00 (*0-471-53176-6*) Wiley.
Organic Chemistry of Drug Synthesis, 4 vols., Vol. 1. Daniel Lednicer & Lester A. Mitscher. LC 76-28387. 496p. 1977. 165.00 (*0-471-52141-8*) Wiley.
Organic Chemistry of Drug Synthesis, 4 vols., Vol. 2. Daniel Lednicer & Lester A. Mitscher. LC 76-28387. 544p. 1980. 165.00 (*0-471-04392-3*) Wiley.
Organic Chemistry of Drug Synthesis, 4 vols., Vol. 3. Daniel Lednicer & Lester A. Mitscher. 304p. 1984. 165.00 (*0-471-09250-9*) Wiley.
Organic Chemistry of Drug Synthesis, 4 vols., Vol. 4. Daniel Lednicer & Lester A. Mitscher. 272p. 1990. 165.00 (*0-471-85548-0*) Wiley.
Organic Chemistry of Drug Synthesis, Vol. 5. Daniel Lednicer & Lester A. Mitscher. 240p. 1994. 165.00 (*0-471-58959-4*) Wiley.
Organic Chemistry of Drug Synthesis, 5 vols., Vol. 5. Daniel Lednicer & Lester A. Mitscher. 1856p. 1996. 430.00 (*0-471-16990-0*) Wiley.
*__Organic Chemistry of Drug Synthesis, Vol. 6.__ Daniel Lednicer & Lester A. Mitscher. LC 76-28387. 264p. 1998. 98.95 (*0-471-24510-0*) Wiley.
*__Organic Chemistry of Enzyme Catalyzed Reactions.__ Richard Silverman. LC 99-66034. 717p. 1999. 79.95 (*0-12-643745-9*) Acad Pr.
Organic Chemistry of Lactams. Ed. by Gunda I. George. 381p. 1992. 175.00 (*0-471-18799-2*, Wiley-VCH) Wiley.
Organic Chemistry of Macromolecules: An Introductory Textbook. Abe Ravve. LC 67-17006. (Illus.). 512p. reprint ed. pap. 158.80 (*0-7837-0902-1*, 204120700019) Bks Demand.
Organic Chemistry of Museum Objects. 2nd ed. John S. Mills & Raymond White. LC 93-32082. (Series in Conservation & Museology). 224p. 1994. 74.95 (*0-7506-1693-8*) Buttrwrth-Heinemann.
*__Organic Chemistry of Museum Objects.__ 2nd ed. John S. Mills & Raymond White. LC 93-32082. (Illus.). 206p. 2000. pap. 42.95 (*0-7506-4693-4*) Buttrwrth-Heinemann.
Organic Chemistry of Peptides. Harry D. Law. LC 75-126888. 243p. reprint ed. pap. 75.40 (*0-608-14049-X*, 202401500035) Bks Demand.
Organic Chemistry of Polycoordinated Iodine. A. Varvoglis. LC 92-14164. 414p. 1992. 115.00 (*1-56081-538-8*, Wiley-VCH) Wiley.
Organic Chemistry of Polycoordinated Iodine. A. Varvoglis. 414p. 1992. 185.00 (*0-471-18825-5*, Wiley-VCH) Wiley.
Organic Chemistry of Sulfur: The Tetra Covalent Sulfur Compounds. C. M. Suter. vi, 858p. (C). 1971. text 536.00 (*0-677-65130-9*) Gordon & Breach.
Organic Chemistry of the Atmosphere. Lee D. Hansen. 288p. 1991. lib. bdg. 99.95 (*0-8493-8834-1*, QC879) CRC Pr.
Organic Chemistry of the Earth's Atmosphere. V. A. Isidorov. (Illus.). 228p. 1990. 142.95 (*0-387-51731-6*) Spr-Verlag.
Organic Chemistry (Preview Edition) 2nd ed. Brown & Foote. 320p. 1997. text. write for info. (*0-03-024563-X*) SCP.
Organic Chemistry Problem Solver. rev. ed. Research & Education Association Staff. LC 77-19370. 1408p. 1998. pap. text 29.95 (*0-87891-512-5*) Res & Educ.
Organic Chemistry Rescue Kit. 2nd ed. Kimberly N. Jones. (Illus.). 215p. (C). 1997. pap. text 23.50 (*0-9651162-2-0*) Wysteria Ltd.
Organic Chemistry (Softlock CD not Included) 6th ed. T. W. Graham Solomons. 1998. text 117.95 (*0-471-29026-2*) Wiley.
Organic Chemistry SSG Student Manual. Schmid. 1997. 104.25 (*0-07-561234-8*) McGraw.
Organic Chemistry Study Guide. George H. Schmid. 600p. (C). 1996. text 51.25 (*0-8016-7491-3*) Mosby Inc.
Organic Chemistry Study Guide & Alchemy III Workbook. 2nd ed. K. Peter Vollhardt. 2000. student ed., wbk. ed. 82.00 (*0-7167-2914-8*) W H Freeman.
Organic Chemistry Survival Manual. Suzanne T. Mabrouk. LC 94-47102. 115p. (C). 1996. pap. text 17.96 (*0-395-83869-X*) HM.
*__Organic Chemistry 2425: Take Home Quizzes.__ Ralph Logan. 1999. pap. text 9.28 (*1-56870-351-1*) RonJon Pub.
*__Organic Chemistry 2423: Take Home Quizzes.__ Ralph Logan. 1999. pap. text 9.28 (*1-56870-350-3*) RonJon Pub.
*__Organic Chemistry II.__ Ed. by Cliffs Notes Staff. (Cliffs Quick Reviews Ser.). (Illus.). 240p. 2000. pap. 9.99 (*0-7645-8616-5*) IDG Bks.
Organic Chemistry Using Clays. M. Balogh & Pierre Laszlo. LC 92-38522. (Reactivity & Structure Ser.: Vol. 29). 1993. 151.95 (*0-387-55710-5*) Spr-Verlag.
Organic Chemistry W/infotrac W/online Cd. 4th ed. McMurry. (Chemistry). 1998. pap. 75.25 incl. cd-rom (*0-534-36355-5*) Brooks-Cole.
Organic Chemistry W/infotrac W/online Cd. 6th ed. Fessenden. (Chemistry). 1998. pap. 77.00 incl. cd-rom (*0-534-36340-7*) Brooks-Cole.
Organic Chemistry with InfoTrac. Hornback. 1998. pap. 73.75 (*0-534-36346-6*) Brooks-Cole.
Organic Chemistry/Darling Mode. M. Jones. (C). Date not set. pap. write for info. (*0-393-10210-6*) Norton.

O

An Asterisk (*) at the beginning of an entry indicates that the title is appearing for the first time.

Organic Chemistry/Molecular Models. Volhardt. 2000. 90.00 (*0-7167-2647-5*) W H Freeman.

Organic Chemistry/Molecular Models. K. Peter Vollhardt. 1995. 90.00 (*0-7167-2791-9*) W H Freeman.

Organic Chemistry/Preview, Vol. 1. 3rd ed. K. Peter Vollhardt. 1997. write for info. (*0-7167-3085-5*) St Martin.

Organic Chemists Compounds. 1991. ring bd. write for info. (*0-412-64410-X*) Chapman & Hall.

Organic Chemists Desk Reference. 6th ed. P. H. Rhodes. 174p. (gr. 13). 1995. lib. bdg. 40.00 (*0-412-54100-9*) Chapman & Hall.

Organic Chlorine Solvents: Health Risk to Workers. Royal Society of Chemistry Staff. (Orig.). 1987. 153.00 (*0-85186-078-8*) CRC Pr.

Organic City: Urban Definition & Community Organization, 1880-1920. Patricia M. Melvin. LC 87-13322. 240p. 1987. 29.95 (*0-8131-1585-X*) U Pr of Ky.

Organic Coating: Properties & Evaluation. 2nd ed. F. Konstandt. (C). 2000. write for info. (*0-8206-0356-2*) Chem Pub.

Organic Coating: Science & Technology, 2 vols., Vol. 2. Zeno W. Wicks et al. 784p. 1994. 195.00 (*0-471-30828-5*) Wiley.

Organic Coating Technology, Vol. 1. Henry F. Payne. LC 54-5971. 70.00 (*0-471-67286-6*) Wiley.

Organic Coating Technology, Vol. 2. Henry F. Payne. 72.00 (*0-471-67353-6*) Wiley.

Organic Coating Technology, 2 vols., Vol. 2. Henry F. Payne. Incl. Vol. 1. Oils, Resins, Varnishes & Polymers. LC 54-5971. 674p. 1954. pap. 200.00 Vol. 1. Pigments, & Pigmented Coatings for Architectural & Industrial Applications., **2 vols.** LC 54-5971. 674p. pap. 200.00 (*0-608-16081-4*, 205553600001); LC 54-5971. (Illus.). 725p. reprint ed. Set pap. 200.00 (*0-608-18687-2*, 205553600002) Bks Demand.

Organic Coatings: Proceedings of the International Meeting of Physical Chemistry, Paris, France 1995. Ed. by Pierre-Camille Lacaze. (AIP Conference Proceedings Ser.: No. 354). (Illus.). 560p. 1996. 145.00 (*1-56396-535-6*, AIP Pr) Spr-Verlag.

***Organic Coatings: Science & Technolgy.** 2nd ed. Zeno W. Wicks, Jr. et al. LC 98-25870. 646p. 1999. 125.00 (*0-471-24507-0*) Wiley.

Organic Coatings for Corrosion Control. Ed. by Gordon P. Bierwagen. (ACS Symposium Ser.: No. 689). (Illus.). 468p. 1998. text 145.00 (*0-8412-3549-X*) OUP.

Organic Coatings for Steel Enclosures for Outdoor Use Electrical Equipment, UL 1332. 3rd ed. (C). 1995. pap. text 95.00 (*1-55989-753-8*) Underwrtrs Labs.

Organic Colorants: A Handbook of Data of Selected Dyes for Electro-Optical Applications. M. Okawara et al. (Physical Sciences Data Ser.: No. 35). 504p. 1989. 404.50 (*0-444-98884-X*) Elsevier.

Organic Complexants & Microparticulates in the Facilitated Transport of Radionuclides. A. J. Schilk. 110p. 1996. per. 10.00 (*0-16-062792-3*) USGPO.

Organic Compounds. University of Michigan, Department of Chemistry St. (C). 1993. student ed. 9.00 (*1-881592-15-4*) Hayden-McNeil.

Organic Compounds in Aquatic Environment. Ed. by Samuel D. Faust & Joseph V. Hunter. LC 72-172938. (Illus.). 660p. reprint ed. pap. 200.00 (*0-608-30259-7*, 205501300007) Bks Demand.

Organic Compounds of Sulphur, Selenium & Tellurium, Vol. 6. Royal Society of Chemistry Staff. 1989. 194.00 (*0-85186-299-3*) CRC Pr.

Organic Compounds of Sulphur, Selenium & Tellurium, Vols. 1-5. Ed. by D. R. Hogg. Incl. Vol. 1. 1969-70 Literature. LC 72-78527. 1971. 47.00 (*0-85186-259-4*); 1970-72 Literature. LC 72-78527. 1973. 52.00 (*0-85186-269-1*); 1972-74 Literature. 1975. 63.00 (*0-85186-279-9*); Vol. 4. 1974-76 Literature. LC 72-78527. 1977. 88.00 (*0-85186-289-6*); 1976-78 Literature. LC 72-78527. 1979. 98.00 (*0-85186-620-4*); LC 72-78527. write for info. (*0-318-50476-6*) Am Chemical.

Organic Conductors: Fundamentals & Applications. Ed. by Jean-Pierre Farges. LC 94-16958. (Applied Physics Ser.: Vol. 4). (Illus.). 872p. 1994. text 215.00 (*0-8247-9216-5*) Dekker.

***Organic Conformational Analysis & Stereochemistry Form Circular Dichroism Spectroscopy.** David A Lightner & Jerome E. Gurst. LC 99-38864. 480p. 2000. text 94.95 (*0-471-35405-8*, Wiley-VCH) Wiley.

Organic Constituents of Higher Plants. 6th ed. Trevor Robinson. (Illus.). iv, 346p. 1991. 18.50 (*0-935118-03-9*) Cordus Pr.

Organic Cooking for (Not-So-Organic) Mothers. Marlene A. Bumgarner. LC 80-23089. (Illus.). 160p. 1984. spiral bd. 7.95 (*0-938006-00-2*) Chesbro.

Organic Dairy Farming: Kickapoo Organic Resource Network. Laura Lee Benson & Robert Zirkel. LC 95-67281. (Illus.). 87p. (Orig.). pap. 6.00 (*0-9637982-1-9*) Orang-Utan Pr.

Organic Design in Home Furnishings. Eliot F. Noyes. LC 70-86424. (Museum of Modern Art Publications in Reprint). (Illus.). 1969. reprint ed. 10.95 (*0-405-01540-2*) Ayer.

Organic Disease & Pest Control. (Taylor's Weekend Gardening Guide Ser.). 1997. write for info. (*0-614-27233-5*) HM.

Organic Diseases see Encyclopedia of Urology

Organic Divers. 1994. 21.79 (*1-57251-019-6*) TWI.

Organic Dusts: Exposure, Effects, & Prevention. Ranner Rylander. 320p. 1994. lib. bdg. 99.95 (*0-87371-699-X*, L699) Lewis Pubs.

Organic Electrochemistry: An Introduction & a Guide. 3rd ed. Ed. by Henning Lund & Manuel M. Baizer. (Illus.). 1576p. 1991. text 295.00 (*0-8247-8154-6*) Dekker.

Organic Electroluminescent Materials & Devices. Ed. by Seizo Miyata & Hari S. Nalwa. 496p. 1997. text 117.00 (*2-919875-10-8*) Gordon & Breach.

Organic Electronic Spectral Data. Ed. by John P. Phillips et al. (Organic Electronic Spectral Data Ser.: Vol. 30). 929p. 1994. 275.00 (*0-471-10971-1*) Wiley.

Organic Electronic Spectral Data, Vol. 5: 1960-61. Ed. by John P. Phillips et al. LC 60-16428. 1029p. pap. 200.00 (*0-608-11732-3*, 200636100058) Bks Demand.

Organic Electronic Spectral Data, Vol. 6: 1962-63. Ed. by John P. Phillips et al. LC 60-16428. 1340p. reprint ed. pap. 200.00 (*0-608-11733-1*, 200636100059) Bks Demand.

Organic Electronic Spectral Data, Vol. 9: 1967. Ed. by John P. Phillips et al. LC 60-16428. 976p. reprint ed. pap. 200.00 (*0-608-11734-X*, 200636100060) Bks Demand.

Organic Electronic Spectral Data, Vol. 25. Ed. by John P. Phillips et al. 1020p. 1989. 325.00 (*0-471-51505-1*) Wiley.

Organic Electronic Spectral Data, Vol. 26. Ed. by John P. Phillips et al. 932p. 1990. 385.00 (*0-471-51941-3*) Wiley.

Organic Electronic Spectral Data, Vol. 28, 1986. Henry Feuer et al. Ed. by John P. Phillips et al. LC 60-16428. (Organic Electronic Spectral Data Ser.). 960p. 1992. 385.00 (*0-471-58588-2*) Wiley.

Organic Electronic Spectral Data, Vol. 29. Henry Feuer et al. 936p. 1993. 275.00 (*0-471-31121-9*) Wiley.

Organic Electronic Spectral Data, Vol. 31. Ed. by John P. Phillips et al. LC 60-16428. 887p. 1995. 235.00 (*0-471-14093-7*) Wiley.

Organic Electronic Spectral Data, 1985, Vol. 27. John P. Phillips et al. 944p. 1991. 385.00 (*0-471-55553-3*) Wiley.

Organic Energetic Compounds. Ed. by Paul L. Marinkas. (Illus.). 298p. (C). 1994. lib. bdg. 145.00 (*1-56072-201-0*) Nova Sci Pubs.

Organic Evolution. Diana Lipscomb. 200p. (C). 1994. spiral bd. 26.95 (*0-8403-9478-0*) Kendall-Hunt.

Organic Experiments, 8 vols. Williamson. (C). Date not set. pap. 11.96 (*0-395-86520-4*) HM.

Organic Experiments. 6th ed. Walter W. Linstromberg & Henry E. Baumgarten. 404p. (C). 1987. pap. text 37.96 (*0-669-12662-4*); teacher ed. 2.66 (*0-669-12663-2*) HM Trade Div.

Organic Experiments. 7th ed. Louis E. Fieser & Kenneth L. Williamson. 645p. (C). 1992. text 69.96 (*0-669-24344-2*); teacher ed. 2.66 (*0-669-24345-0*) HM Trade Div.

Organic Experiments, 8 vols. 8th ed. Williamson. LC 97-72467. (C). 1997. text 69.96 (*0-395-86519-0*) HM.

Organic Faith: A Call to Authentic Christianity. Ron Mitchell. LC 97-45634. 175p. 1998. pap. 10.95 (*0-940895-40-4*) Cornerstone IL.

Organic Farming. Nicolas Lampkin. (Illus.). 720p. 1990. 49.95 (*0-85236-191-2*, Pub. by Farming Pr) Diamond Farm Bk.

Organic Farming: Current Technology & Its Role in a Sustainable Agriculture. Ed. by D. F. Bezdicek et al. (ASA Special Publications: No. 46). 192p. 1984. 8.00 (*0-89118-076-1*) Am Soc Agron.

Organic Fertilizer: The Truth & the B. S. Craig C. Dremann. LC 86-30225. 40p. (Orig.). 1987. pap. 6.00 (*0-933421-17-6*) Redwood Seed.

Organic Fluorine Chemistry. Milos Hudlicky. LC 76-131889. (Illus.). 212p. 1971. reprint ed. pap. 65.80 (*0-608-05451-8*, 206592000006) Bks Demand.

Organic Foods for Health. Raymond W. Bernard. 1996. spiral bd. 9.00 (*0-7873-1008-5*) Hlth Research.

Organic Foundations of Animal Behavior. Joseph Altman. LC 65-18350. (Illus.). 1966. text 39.50 (*0-03-052230-7*) Irvington.

Organic Free Radicals. Ed. by William A. Pryor. LC 78-1672. (ACS Symposium Ser.: Vol. 69). 495p. 1978. reprint ed. pap. 153.50 (*0-608-03928-4*, 206437500009) Bks Demand.

Organic Functional Group Analysis. F. Critchfield & R. Belcher. LC 62-22068. (International Series of Monographs on Analytical Chemistry: Vol. 8). 1963. 83.00 (*0-08-013500-5*, Pub. by Pergamon Repr) Franklin.

Organic Functional Group Preparations, 3 vols. 2nd ed. Sandler. 1989. 407.00 (*0-12-618600-6*) Acad Pr.

Organic Functional Group Preparations, Vol. I. 2nd ed. Stanley R. Sandler. (Organic Chemistry Ser.). 1983. text 146.00 (*0-12-618601-4*) Acad Pr.

Organic Functional Group Preparations, Vol. 2. 2nd ed. Ed. by Stanley R. Sandler & Wolf Karo. 576p. 1986. text 146.00 (*0-12-618602-2*) Acad Pr.

Organic Functional Group Preparations, Vol. 3. 2nd ed. Ed. by Stanley R. Sandler & Wolf Karo. (Organic Chemistry Ser.). 552p. 1989. text 146.00 (*0-12-618603-0*) Acad Pr.

Organic Garden Book: The Complete Guide to Growing Flowers, Fruit & Vegetables Naturally. Geoff Hamilton. LC 93-34259. (Illus.). 288p. 1994. reprint ed. pap. 19.95 (*1-56458-528-X*) DK Pub Inc.

Organic Gardener see Building Healthy Gardens: A Safe & Natural Approach

Organic Gardener. Catherine O. Foster. pap. 8.95 (*0-685-04274-X*, V-785) Vin Bks.

Organic Gardener Handbook of Nature. Storey Publishing Staff. 1997. pap. 17.95 (*0-676-57179-4*) Random.

Organic Gardener's Basics. Barbara P. Lawton & George F. Van Patten. Ed. by Stevie O. Daniels. (Organic Gardener's Ser.). (Illus.). 208p. (Orig.). 1993. pap. 12.95 (*1-878823-01-9*) Van Patten Pub.

Organic Gardener's Composting. Steve O. Solomon. Ed. by Stevie O. Daniels. (Organic Gardener's Ser.). (Illus.). 144p. (Orig.). 1993. pap. 9.95 (*1-878823-06-X*) Van Patten Pub.

Organic Gardener's Handbook of Natural Insect & Disease Control: A Complete, Problem-Solving Guide to Keeping Your Garden & Yard Healthy Without Chemicals. rev. ed. Barbara W. Ellis & Fern M. Bradley. (Illus.). 544p. 1996. pap. 17.95 (*0-87596-753-1*) Rodale Pr Inc.

Organic Gardener's Home Reference: A Plant-by-Plant Guide to Growing Fresh, Healthy Food. Tanya Denckla. LC 93-22835. Orig. Title: Gardening at a Glance. (Illus.). 304p. 1994. reprint ed. 29.95 (*0-88266-840-4*, Garden Way Pub); reprint ed. pap. 21.95 (*0-88266-839-0*, Garden Way Pub) Storey Bks.

Organic Gardening. 192p. 2000. pap. text 25.00 (*0-02-862315-0*, Pub. by Macmillan) S&S Trade.

Organic Gardening. 60p. (C). 1996. text, student ed., wbk. ed. 10.60 (*0-536-59935-1*) Pearson Custom.

Organic Gardening: Vegetable Growth in Simple Terms. 130p. (C). 1997. 27.60 (*0-536-00731-4*) Pearson Custom.

***Organic Gardening in Basic Lawns.** Organic Gardening Magazine Staff. LC 99-50442. (Illus.). 112p. 2000. pap. 14.95 (*0-87596-837-6*) Rodale Pr Inc.

Organic Gardening in the American West: A Guide. rev. ed. Robert F. Smith, Jr. LC 98-29430. 96p. 1998. pap. 10.00 (*0-86534-282-2*) Sunstone Pr.

***Organic Gardening with Roses.** Organic Gardening Magazine Staff. LC 99-50445. (Illus.). 112p. 2000. pap. text 14.95 (*0-87596-839-2*) Rodale Pr Inc.

***Organic Gardening with Soil.** Organic Gardening Magazine Staff. LC 99-50443. (Illus.). 2000. pap. 14.95 (*0-87596-838-4*) Rodale Pr Inc.

***Organic Gardening with Vegetables.** Organic Gardening Magazine Staff. LC 99-50444. (Illus.). 112p. 2000. pap. text 14.95 (*0-87596-840-6*) Rodale Pr Inc.

Organic Gardening Workbook 4th ed. 160p. (C). 1999. pap. text, student ed. 20.20 (*0-536-02464-2*) Pearson Custom.

Organic Geochemistry: An Introduction. S. D. Killops. (C). 1993. pap. text 49.69 (*0-582-08040-1*, Pub. by Addison-Wesley) Longman.

Organic Geochemistry: Principles & Applications. M. Engel & S. Macko. LC 93-28298. (Topics in Geobiology Ser.: Vol. 11). (Illus.). 884p. (C). 1993. 89.50 (*0-306-44378-3*, Plenum Trade) Perseus Pubng.

Organic Geochemistry No. 2: A Selection of Papers from the Second Australian Geochemistry Conference, University of Melbourne, 28-29 May 1984. Ed. by E. W. Baker. 98p. 1985. pap. 40.00 (*0-08-032640-4*, Pub. by PPL) Elsevier.

Organic Geochemistry in Petroleum Exploration. Colin Baker. LC TN0870.5.A44. (AAPG Continuing Education Course Note Ser.: Vol. 10). (Illus.). 168p. reprint ed. pap. 52.10 (*0-608-08726-2*, 206936500004) Bks Demand.

Organic Geochemistry of Natural Waters. E. M. Thurman. (Developments in Biogeochemistry Ser.). 1985. text 214.50 (*90-247-3143-7*) Kluwer Academic.

Organic Gourmet: Feast of Fields. Tracy Kett. (Illus.). 192p. 1999. pap. 17.95 (*1-896503-83-7*, Pub. by R Rose Inc) Firefly Bks Ltd.

Organic Gourmet: Recipes & Resources from a Seasonal Kitchen. Barbara Kahn. LC 95-3368. (Illus.). 300p. (Orig.). (C). 1995. pap. 16.95 (*1-883319-32-3*) Frog Ltd CA.

Organic Greenhouse Gardening: Gardening in the 21st Century. Ted M. Taylor. Ed. by Sara Patton. (Illus.). 320p. (Orig.). 1998. pap. 19.95 (*0-614-13806-X*) Green Erth Pub.

***Organic Indoor Air Pollutants: Occurrence, Measurement, Evaluation.** Ed. by Tunga Salthammer. 328p. 1999. 154.95 (*3-527-29622-0*) Wiley.

Organic Industrial Chemicals in Australia: A Strategic Entry Report, 1997. Compiled by Icon Group International Staff. (Country Industry Report). (Illus.). 136p. 1999. ring bd. 1360.00 incl. audio compact disk (*0-7418-0230-9*) Icon Grp.

Organic Inhibitors or Corrosion of Metals. Y. I. Kuznetsov. (Illus.). 300p. (C). 1996. text 114.00 (*0-306-45169-7*, Kluwer Plenum) Kluwer Academic.

Organic-Inorganic Hybrid Materials for Photonics. Ed. by Liliane G. Hubert-Pfalzgraf & S. I. Najafi. LC 98-226771. (Proceedings of SPIE Ser.: Vol. 3469). 212p. 1998. 59.00 (*0-8194-2924-4*) SPIE.

Organic Lab Techniques: Small-Scale Approach. Pavia. LC 97-19525. (Saunders Golden Sunburst Ser.). (Illus.). 976p. (C). 1997. text 84.00 (*0-03-024519-2*, Pub. by SCP) Harcourt.

Organic Laboratory Techniques. Fessenden. (Chemistry Ser.). 1984. 25.50 (*0-87150-703-X*) PWS Pubs.

Organic Laboratory Techniques. 2nd ed. Ralph J. Fessenden & Joan S. Fessenden. LC 92-38632. 254p. 1993. mass mkt. 34.00 (*0-534-20160-1*) Brooks-Cole.

***Organic Laboratory Techniques.** 3rd ed. Ralph J. Fessenden et al. LC 00-33718. (Illus.). 2000. pap. write for info. (*0-534-37981-8*) Brooks-Cole.

Organic Leadership Vol. 1: Browing People & Profits. Charles A. Waters. 170p. 1997. pap. 16.75 (*0-9660987-0-6*) C A Waters.

Organic Light-Emitting Materials & Devices, Vol. 3148. Ed. by Zakya H. Kafafi. LC 98-171719. 424p. 1997. 99.00 (*0-8194-2570-2*) SPIE.

Organic Light-Emitting Materials & Devices II, Vol. 3476. Ed. by Zakya H. Kafafi. LC 99-206515. 1998. 99.00 (*0-8194-2931-7*) SPIE.

Organic Liquids: Structure, Dynamics, & Chemical Properties. Ed. by Amyand D. Buckingham et al. LC 78-8462. 362p. reprint ed. pap. 112.30 (*0-608-15580-2*, 202964200062) Bks Demand.

Organic Living Designs. Ed. by Patricia L. Mackenzie. (Illus.). Date not set. pap. write for info. (*0-9657552-9-0*) P L Mackenzie.

Organic Machine: The Remaking of the Columbia River. Richard White. 144p. 1996. 8.00 (*0-8090-1583-8*) Hill & Wang.

Organic Marine Geochemistry. Ed. by Mary L. Sohn. LC 86-3429. (ACS Symposium Ser.: No. 305). (Illus.). x, 428p. 1986. 82.95 (*0-8412-0965-0*, PA 410) Am Chemical.

Organic Marine Geochemistry. Ed. by Mary L. Sohn. LC 86-3429. (ACS Symposium Ser.: Vol. 305). 440p. 1986. reprint ed. pap. 136.40 (*0-608-03851-2*, 206429800008) Bks Demand.

Organic Materials & Fullerenes: Proceedings of Symposium K on Fullerenes - from New Molecules to New Materials & Symposium M on New Prospects on Electronic Properties of Organic Materials of the 1995 E-MRS Spring Conference, Strasbourg, France, May 22-26, 1995. Ed. by C. Taliani et al. LC 96-229409. (European Materials Research Society Symposia Proceedings Ser.: Vol. 58). 680p. 1996. 296.00 (*0-444-82415-4*, North Holland) Elsevier.

Organic Materials for Electronics: Proceedings of Symposium D of the 1994 E-MRS Spring Conference, Strasbourg, France, 24-27 May 1994. Ed. by J.L. Bredas et al. (European Materials Research Society Symposia Proceedings Ser.: Vol. 49). 340p. 1994. 228.00 (*0-444-82168-6*, North Holland) Elsevier.

Organic Materials for Non-Linear Optics. Ed. by R. A. Hann & D. Bloor. 400p. 1989. 126.00 (*0-85186-806-1*, R6806) CRC Pr.

Organic Materials for Non-Linear Optics II. Ed. by Geoffrey J. Ashwell & David Bloor. 362p. 1993. 142.00 (*0-85186-625-5*, Q) CRC Pr.

Organic Materials for Non-Linear Optics, II, No. 91. Richard Hann & D. Bloor. 1991. 132.00 (*0-85186-397-3*) CRC Pr.

Organic Materials for Photonics: Science & Technology. Ed. by G. Zerbi. LC 93-17753. (European Materials Research Society Monographs: Vol. 6). 430p. 1993. 234.75 (*0-444-89916-2*, North Holland) Elsevier.

Organic Materials in Aquatic Ecosystems. Ed. by H. Seki. 208p. 1982. 123.00 (*0-8493-6446-9*, QH541, CRC Reprint) Franklin.

Organic Mathematics: Proceedings of the Organic Mathematics Workshop, December 12-14, 1995, Simon Fraser University. Jonathan M. Borwein. LC 97-179. (Conference Proceedings, Canadian Mathematical Society Ser.: Vol. 20). 412p. 1997. pap. 79.00 (*0-8218-0668-8*, CMSAMS/20) Am Math.

Organic Matter: Productivity, Accumulation, & Preservation in Recent & Ancient Sediments. Ed. by Jean K. Whelan & John W. Farrington. 550p. 1992. text 97.00 (*0-231-07162-0*) Col U Pr.

Organic Matter Accumulation: The Organic Cyclicities of the Kimmeridge Clay Formation (Yorkshire, GB) & the Recent Maar Sediments (Lac du Bouchet, France) P. Bertrand et al. (Lecture Notes in Earth Sciences Ser.: Vol. 57). (Illus.). 200p. 1995. 85.95 (*3-540-59170-2*) Spr-Verlag.

Organic Matter Accumulation: The Organic Cyclicities of the Kimmeridge Clay Formation (Yorkshire, GB) & the Recent Maar Sediments (Lac du Bouchet, France) Ed. by Elisabeth Lallier-Verges et al. LC 95-12984. (Lecture Notes in Earth Sciences Ser.: Vol. 57). 1995. write for info. (*0-387-59170-2*) Spr-Verlag.

Organic Matter in Natural Waters. Ed. by D. W. Hood. (Occasional Publications: No. 1). 625p. 3.00 (*0-914500-00-7*) U of AK Inst Marine.

***Organic Matters & Mineralisation: Thermal Alteration, Hydrocarbon Generation & Role in Metallogenesis.** Miryam Glirkson & Maria Mastalerz. LC 99-40884. 1999. write for info. (*0-412-73330-7*) Kluwer Academic.

Organic Memory: History & the Body in the Late Nineteenth & Early Twentieth Centuries. Laura Otis. LC 93-47280. (Texts & Contexts Ser.: No. 11). xiii, 300p. 1994. text 50.00 (*0-8032-3561-5*) U of Nebr Pr.

Organic Mental Disease. Frank R. Freemon. LC 79-23180. (Illus.). 248p. 1981. text 37.00 (*0-88331-169-0*) R B Luce.

Organic Metamorphism & Geothermal History. Paul Robert. (C). 1987. pap. text 104.50 (*90-277-2501-2*) Kluwer Academic.

Organic Method Primer Basics: The Basics: Special Edition. Bargyla Rateaver & Gylver Rateaver. (Conservation Gardening & Farming Ser.). (Illus.). 100p. 1994. pap. 25.00 (*0-915966-04-2*) Rateavers.

Organic Method Primer Update: Special Edition. Bargyla Rateaver & Gylver Rateaver. (Conservation Gardening & Farming Ser.). (Illus.). 700p. 1993. 200.00 (*0-915966-01-8*) Rateavers.

Organic Micropollutants in the Aquatic Environment. Ed. by G. Angeletti & Alf Bjorseth. (C). 1988. text 234.00 (*90-277-2738-4*) Kluwer Academic.

Organic Micropollutants in the Aquatic Environment. Ed. by G. Angeletti & Alf Bjorseth. (C). 1991. text 257.50 (*0-7923-1104-3*) Kluwer Academic.

Organic Micropollutants in the Aquatic Environment. Ed. by A. Bjrseth & G. Angeletti. 1986. text 237.50 (*90-277-2242-0*) Kluwer Academic.

***Organic Modeling with Organica.** Bill Fleming. (Conquering 3D Graphics Ser.). 450p. 1999. pap. 49.95 incl. cd-rom (*0-12-260499-7*, Pub. by Morgan Kaufmann) Harcourt.

Organic Molecular Crystals: Interaction, Localization, & Transport Phenomena. Edgar A. Silinsh & Vladislav Capek. LC 94-17192. 1994. 84.95 (*1-56396-069-9*) Spr-Verlag.

Organic Molecular Crystals: Their Electronic States. Edgar A. Silinsh. (Solid-State Sciences Ser.: Vol. 16). (Illus.). 410p. 1980. 78.95 (*0-387-10053-9*) Spr-Verlag.

Organic Molecular Photophysics, Vol. 1. Ed. by John B. Birks. LC 72-8594. 618p. reprint ed. pap. 191.60 (*0-608-09944-9*, 203048100001) Bks Demand.

O

An Asterisk (*) at the beginning of an entry indicates that the title is appearing for the first time.

Organic Molecular Photophysics, Vol. 2. Ed. by John B. Birks. LC 72-8594. (Wiley Monographs in Chemical Physics). 673p. 1975. reprint ed. pap. 200.00 (*0-608-09945-7*, 203048100002) Bks Demand.

Organic Molecular Solids: Properties & Applications. W. Jones. LC 96-35232. 448p. 1997. boxed set 154.95 (*0-8493-9428-7*) CRC Pr.

Organic Molecules. Helms. 1997. 1.50 (*0-7167-9308-3*) W H Freeman.

Organic Molecules for Nonlinear Optics & Photonics. Ed. by J. Messier et al. (C). 1991. text 257.50 (*0-7923-1181-7*) Kluwer Academic.

Organic Nature of the Church. Bill Freeman. 250p. (Orig.). Date not set. pap. 6.00 (*0-914271-63-6*) Mnstry Pubns.

Organic '92: Proceedings of the Organic Farming Symposium. Ed. by Shirley Humphrey. LC 95-62463. viii, 223p. 1996. pap. 15.00 (*1-879906-16-3*, 3356) ANR Pubns CA.

Organic Nitrogen Compounds for Use As Fertilizers. T. P. Murray & R. C. Horn. (Technical Bulletin Ser.: No. T-14). 64p. (Orig.). 1979. pap. 4.00 (*0-88090-013-X*) Intl Fertilizer.

Organic Nomenclature: A Programmed Introduction. 5th ed. James G. Traynham. LC 96-45238. 145p. (C). 1996. pap. text 31.20 (*0-13-270752-7*, Prentice Hall) P-H.

*__Organic Nonlinear Optical Materials.__ Ed. by Manfred Eich & Mark G. Kuzyk. 1999. pap. text 84.00 (*0-8194-3282-2*) SPIE.

Organic Nonlinear Optical Materials. P. Gunter. 256p. 1995. text 99.00 (*2-88124-975-2*); pap. text 42.00 (*2-88449-007-8*) Gordon & Breach.

Organic Nonlinear Optical Materials & Devices Vol. 561: Materials Research Society Symposium Proceedings. Ed. by B. Kippelen et al. LC 99-37090. 224p. 1999. text 72.00 (*1-55899-468-8*) Materials Res.

Organic Pages: Organic Trade Association's 1998 North American Resource Directory. Compiled by Organic Trade Association Staff. 270p. 1998. spiral bd. 44.95 (*1-881427-99-4*) OTA Press.

*__Organic Pages: Organic Trade Association's 1999 North American Resource Directory.__ Pratt. 272p. 1999. pap. 34.95 (*1-881427-91-9*, Pub. by OTA Press) Chelsea Green Pub.

*__Organic Pages: Organic Trade Association's 1999 North American Resource Directory.__ Ed. by Dan Pratt. 322p. 1999. spiral bd. (*1-881427-90-0*) OTA Press.

Organic Peroxides, Vol. 1. Ed. by Daniel Swern. LC 72-84965. 654p. reprint ed. pap. 200.00 (*0-608-13328-0*, 205572500033) Bks Demand.

Organic Peroxygen Chemistry. Ed. by W. A. Hermann. (Topics in Current Chemistry Ser.: Vol. 164). (Illus.). xi, 130p. 1993. 107.95 (*0-387-56252-4*) Spr-Verlag.

Organic Pest Control Handbook. rev. ed. Pest Publications Staff. LC 97-48311. (Illus.). 96p. 1998. pap. 10.95 (*1-57067-052-8*) Book Pub Co.

Organic Pesticides in the Environment: A Symposium Co-Sponsored by the Division of Water, Air, & Waste Chemistry & the Pesticide Subdivision of the Division of Agricultural & Food Chemistry at the 150th Meeting of the American Chemical Society, Atlantic City, NJ, Sept. 13-15, 1965. American Chemical Society Staff. LC 66-30613. (Advances in Chemistry Ser.: No. 60). (Illus.). 319p. 1966. reprint ed. pap. 98.90 (*0-608-06799-7*, 206699600009) Bks Demand.

Organic Petrography & Organic Geochemistry of Texas Tertiary Coals in Relation to Depositional Environment & Hydrocarbon Generation. P. K. Mukhopadhyay. (Reports of Investigations: RI 188). (Illus.). 118p. 1989. pap. 9.00 (*0-317-03121-X*) Bur Econ Geology.

Organic Petrology: A New Handbook Incorporating Some Revised Parts of Stach's Textbook of Coal Petrology. G. H. Taylor et al. LC 98-205664. (Illus.). xvi, 704p. 1998. 116.00 (*3-443-01036-9*, Pub. by Gebruder Borntraeger) Balogh.

Organic Philosophy of Education. Frank C. Wegener. LC 73-9213. 472p. 1974. reprint ed. lib. bdg. 75.00 (*0-8371-6979-8*, WEOP, Greenwood Pr) Greenwood.

Organic Photochemistry, Vol. 2. Ed. by Orville L. Chapman. LC 66-11283. 244p. reprint ed. pap. 75.70 (*0-608-09947-3*, 202782500002) Bks Demand.

Organic Photochemistry, Vol. 11. Ed. by Albert Padwa. (Illus.). 456p. 1991. text 225.00 (*0-8247-8561-4*) Dekker.

Organic Photochemistry: A Visual Approach. Jan Kopecky. 285p. 1991. 110.00 (*0-471-18717-8*, Wiley-VCH) Wiley.

Organic Photochemistry: A Visual Approach. Jan Kopecky. 285p. 1992. text 65.00 (*0-89573-296-3*, Wiley-VCH) Wiley.

Organic Photochemistry: Principles & Applications. Jacques Kagan. (Illus.). 234p. 1993. text 76.00 (*0-12-394320-5*) Acad Pr.

Organic Photochemistry Vol. 1: Molecular & Supramolecular Photochemistry. Ed. by V. Ramaurthy & Kirk S. Schanze. LC 97-186938. 608p. 1997. text 195.00 (*0-8247-0012-0*) Dekker.

Organic Photochemistry of Benezene-1. D. Bryce-Smith & A. Gilbert. 18p. 1976. pap. 15.50 (*0-08-020464-3*, Pergamon Pr) Elsevier.

Organic Photochromes. A. V. El'tsov. (Illus.). 280p. (C). 1990. text 110.00 (*0-306-11012-1*, Kluwer Plenum) Kluwer Academic.

Organic Photochromic & Thermochromic Compounds, Vol. 2. Ed. by J. C. Crano & R. Guglielmetti. LC 98-31170. (Topics in Applied Chemistry Ser.). (Illus.). 450p. (C). 1998. text. write for info. (*0-306-45883-7*, Kluwer Plenum) Kluwer Academic.

Organic Photochromic & Thermochromic Compounds Vol. 1: Photochromic Families. Ed. by John C. Crano & Robert Guglielmetti. (Topics in Applied Chemistry Ser.). (Illus.). 400p. (C). 1998. text 125.00 (*0-306-45882-9*, Kluwer Plenum) Kluwer Academic.

*__Organic Photonic Materials & Devices.__ Ed. by Bernard Kippelen. 292p. 1999. pap. text 92.00 (*0-8194-3093-5*) SPIE.

Organic Photoreceptors for Imaging Systems. Ed. by Borsenberger & David S. Weiss. (Optical Engineering Ser.: Vol. 39). (Illus.). 472p. 1993. text 185.00 (*0-8247-8926-1*) Dekker.

Organic Photoreceptors for Xerography. Paul M. Borsenberger & David S. Weiss. LC 98-2799. (Optical Engineering Ser.). (Illus.). 792p. 1998. text 195.00 (*0-8247-0173-9*) Dekker.

Organic Photorefractive Materials & Xerographic Photoreceptors, Vol. 2850. Ed. by Stephen Ducharme & James W. Stasiak. 218p. 1996. 56.00 (*0-8194-2238-X*) SPIE.

Organic Phototransformations in Nonhomogeneous Media. Ed. by Marye A. Fox. LC 85-7471. (ACS Symposium Ser.: Vol. 278). 320p. 1985. reprint ed. pap. 99.20 (*0-608-03909-8*, 206435600009) Bks Demand.

*__Organic, Physical & Materials Photochemistry.__ V. Ramamurthy & Kirk S. Schanze. LC 00-40476. (Molecular & Supramolecular Photochemistry Ser.). 2000. write for info. (*0-8247-0404-5*) Dekker.

Organic Pigments. 2nd ed. Peter A. Lewis. (Illus.). 43p. 1995. pap. 30.00 (*0-934010-34-X*) Fed Soc Coat Tech.

Organic Pigments. 3rd ed. (Illus.). Date not set. pap. 30.00 (*0-934010-35-8*) Fed Soc Coat Tech.

Organic Pollutants in the Environment. (CMS Workshop Lectures: Vol. 8). (Illus.). 200p. (C). 1996. pap. text 20.00 (*1-881208-10-9*) Clay Minerals.

Organic Pollutants in Water. Ed. by M. Malaiyandi & Irwin H. Suffet. LC 86-22218. (Advances in Chemistry Ser.: No. 214). (Illus.). xv, 797p. 1986. 99.95 (*0-8412-0951-0*, Pub. by Am Chemical) OUP.

Organic Pollutants in Water: Sampling, Analysis, & Toxicity Testing. Ed. by Murugan Malaiyandi & Irwin H. Suffet. LC 86-22218. (Advances in Chemistry Ser.: Vol. 214). 816p. 1987. reprint ed. pap. 200.00 (*0-608-03893-8*, 206434000008) Bks Demand.

Organic Polymer Chemistry. K. J. Saunders. (Illus.). 500p. (C). 1988. text 47.50 (*0-412-27570-8*) Chapman & Hall.

Organic Polymer Chemistry: A Primer : Supplement to Organic Chemistry. Boone. (C). 1994. pap. text, suppl. ed. 12.50 (*0-03-010633-8*) Harcourt Coll Pubs.

Organic Power. Barry Oshry. LC 80-4780. (Notes on Power Ser.). (Orig.). 1976. pap. text 7.50 (*0-910411-03-4*) Power & Sys.

Organic Practice of the New Way. Witness Lee. 80p. 1989. per. 4.25 (*0-87083-477-0*, 12-015-001) Living Stream Ministry.

Organic Prayer: Cultivating Your Relationship with God. Nancy Roth. LC 93-12653. (Illus.). 167p. 1993. pap. 12.95 (*1-56101-077-4*) Cowley Pubns.

Organic Psychiatry: The Psychological Consequences of Cerebral Disorder. 3rd ed. William A. Lishman. LC 97-7107. 1997. pap. 99.95 (*0-86542-820-4*) Blackwell Sci.

Organic Psychiatry: The Psychological Consequences of Cerebral Disorder. 3rd ed. William A. Lishman. LC 97-7107. (Illus.). 1998. 99.95 (*0-86542-842-5*) Blackwell Sci.

Organic Psychoses: A Guide to Diagnosis. John G. Dewan & William B. Spaulding. LC RC0528.O7D49. (Illus.). 184p. reprint ed. pap. 57.10 (*0-608-30249-X*, 201418600096) Bks Demand.

Organic Puppet Theatre: Children's Activities in Health Awareness. Terry L. Schultz & Linda M. Sorenson. (Illus.). 92p. (Orig.). 1984. pap. text 15.95 (*0-9612902-0-X*) Night Owl Pr.

Organic Radiation Chemistry. Ed. by V. K. Milinchuk & V. I. Tupikov. 1989. text 185.00 (*0-470-21452-X*) P-H.

Organic Reaction Mechanisms. Knipe. text. write for info. (*0-471-49017-2*) Wiley.

*__Organic Reaction Mechanisms__ 19th ed. Knipe. 578p. 1999. 475.00 (*0-471-97364-5*) Wiley.

Organic Reaction Mechanisms: An Annual Survey of Literature, 1995, Vol. 95. Ed. by A. C. Knipe & W. E. Watts. 622p. 1997. 600.00 (*0-471-97106-5*) Wiley.

Organic Reaction Mechanisms: An Introduction. 2nd ed. Ronald Breslow. LC 73-80663. (Organic Chemistry Monograph Ser.). xv, 272 p. 1969. write for info. (*0-8053-1252-8*) Benjamin-Cummings.

*__Organic Reaction Mechanisms: Selected Problems & Solutions.__ William C. Groutas. 279p. 1999. pap. 29.95 (*0-471-28251-0*) Wiley.

Organic Reaction Mechanisms, 1987: An Annual Survey Covering the Literature Dated December, 1986 to November 1987. Organic Reaction Mechanisms Staff. Ed. by A. C. Knipe & W. E. Watts. LC 66-23143. 666p. reprint ed. pap. 200.00 (*0-608-20227-4*, 207148600012) Bks Demand.

Organic Reaction Mechanisms, 1988: An Annual Survey Covering the Literature Dated December, 1987 to November 1988. Organic Reaction Mechanisms Staff. Ed. by A. C. Knipe & W. E. Watts. LC 66-23143. (Illus.). 754p. reprint ed. pap. 200.00 (*0-608-20226-6*, 207148500012) Bks Demand.

Organic Reaction Mechanisms, 1989: An Annual Survey Covering the Literature Dated December, 1988 to November 1989. Organic Reaction Mechanisms Staff. Ed. by A. C. Knipe & W. E. Watts. LC 66-23143. (Illus.). 721p. reprint ed. pap. 200.00 (*0-608-20225-8*, 207148400012) Bks Demand.

Organic Reaction Mechanisms, 1990: An Annual Survey Covering the Literature Dated December, 1989 to November 1990. Organic Reaction Mechanisms Staff. Ed. by A. C. Knipe & W. E. Watts. LC 66-23143. (Illus.). 664p. reprint ed. pap. 200.00 (*0-608-20229-0*, 207148800012) Bks Demand.

Organic Reaction Mechanisms, 1991: An Annual Survey Covering the Literature Dated December, 1990 & November 1991. Organic Reaction Mechanisms Staff. Ed. by A. C. Knipe & W. E. Watts. LC 66-23143. (Illus.). 626p. reprint ed. pap. 194.10 (*0-608-20228-2*, 207148700012) Bks Demand.

Organic Reaction Mechanisms, 1974: An Annual Survey Covering the Literature Dated December 2973 Through November 1974. Ed. by A. R. Butler & M. John Perkins. LC 66-23143. 668p. reprint ed. pap. 200.00 (*0-608-14051-1*, 202401700035) Bks Demand.

Organic Reaction Mechanisms, 1969: An Annual Survey Covering the Literature Dated December 1968 Through November 1969. Ed. by B. Capon & C. W. Rees. LC 66-23143. 720p. reprint ed. pap. 200.00 (*0-608-13714-6*, 205161800069) Bks Demand.

Organic Reaction Mechanisms, 1973: An Annual Survey Covering the Literature Dated December 1972 Through November 1973. Ed. by A. R. Butler & M. John Perkins. LC 66-23143. 587p. reprint ed. pap. 182.00 (*0-608-14050-3*, 202401600035) Bks Demand.

Organic Reaction Mechanisms, 1975: An Annual Survey Covering the Literature Dated December 1974 Through November 1975. Ed. by A. R. Butler & M. John Perkins. LC 66-23143. 630p. reprint ed. pap. 195.30 (*0-608-14052-X*, 202401800035) Bks Demand.

Organic Reaction Mechanisms, 1976: An Annual Survey Covering the Literature Dated December 1975 Through November 1976. Ed. by A. R. Butler & M. John Perkins. LC 66-23143. 695p. reprint ed. pap. 200.00 (*0-608-14053-8*, 202401900035) Bks Demand.

Organic Reaction Mechanisms, 1977: An Annual Survey Covering the Literature Dated December, 1976 Through November, 1977. Ed. by A. C. Knipe & W. E. Watts. LC 66-23143. (Illus.). 749p. reprint ed. pap. 200.00 (*0-608-17561-7*, 203054300069) Bks Demand.

Organic Reaction Mechanisms, 1978: An Annual Survey Covering the Literature Dated December, 1977 Through November, 1978. Ed. by A. C. Knipe & W. E. Watts. LC 66-23143. (Illus.). 730p. reprint ed. pap. 200.00 (*0-608-17562-5*, 203054400069) Bks Demand.

Organic Reaction Mechanisms, 1979: An Annual Survey Covering the Literature Dated December, 1978 Through November, 1979. Ed. by A. C. Knipe & W. E. Watts. LC 66-23143. (Illus.). 769p. reprint ed. pap. 200.00 (*0-608-17563-3*, 203054500069) Bks Demand.

Organic Reaction Mechanisms, 1980: An Annual Survey Covering the Literature Dated December, 1979 Through November, 1980. A. C. Knipe & W. E. Watts. LC 66-23143. (Illus.). 728p. 1981. reprint ed. pap. 200.00 (*0-608-18405-5*, 203054600069) Bks Demand.

Organic Reactions, Vol. 1. R. J. Adams. (Organic Reactions Ser.). 402p. 1942. 99.95 (*0-471-00462-6*) Wiley.

Organic Reactions, Vol. 2. R. J. Adams. (Organic Reactions Ser.). 460p. 1944. 99.95 (*0-471-00495-2*) Wiley.

Organic Reactions, Vol. 3. R. J. Adams. (Organic Reactions Ser.). 461p. 1946. 99.95 (*0-471-00528-2*) Wiley.

Organic Reactions, Vol. 4. R. J. Adams. (Organic Reactions Ser.). 428p. 1948. 99.95 (*0-471-00561-4*) Wiley.

Organic Reactions, Vol. 5. R. J. Adams. (Organic Reactions Ser.). 446p. 1949. 99.95 (*0-471-00594-0*) Wiley.

Organic Reactions, Vol. 6. R. J. Adams. (Organic Reactions Ser.). 528p. 1951. 99.95 (*0-471-00627-0*) Wiley.

Organic Reactions, Vol. 7. (Organic Reactions Ser.). 440p. 1953. 99.95 (*0-471-00660-2*) Wiley.

Organic Reactions, Vol. 8. R. J. Adams. (Organic Reactions Ser.). 437p. 1954. 99.95 (*0-471-00693-9*) Wiley.

Organic Reactions, Vol. 9. R. J. Adams. (Organic Reactions Ser.). 476p. 1957. 99.95 (*0-471-00726-9*) Wiley.

Organic Reactions, Vol. 10. R. J. Adams. (Organic Reactions Ser.). 563p. 1959. 99.95 (*0-471-00759-5*) Wiley.

Organic Reactions, Vol. 11. A. C. Cope. (Organic Reactions Ser.). 501p. 1960. 99.95 (*0-471-17127-1*) Wiley.

Organic Reactions, Vol. 12. A. C. Cope. (Organic Reactions Ser.). 538p. 1962. 99.95 (*0-471-17160-3*) Wiley.

Organic Reactions, Vol. 13. A. C. Cope. (Organic Reactions Ser.). 382p. 1963. 99.95 (*0-471-17163-8*) Wiley.

Organic Reactions, Vol. 14. A. C. Cope. (Organic Reactions Ser.). 512p. 1965. 99.95 (*0-471-17166-2*) Wiley.

Organic Reactions, Vol. 15. A. C. Cope. (Organic Reactions Ser.). 592p. 1967. 99.95 (*0-471-17168-9*) Wiley.

Organic Reactions, Vol. 16. A. C. Cope. (Organic Reactions Ser.). 444p. 1968. 99.95 (*0-471-17169-7*) Wiley.

Organic Reactions, Vol. 17. Ed. by William G. Dauben. (Organic Reactions Ser.). 352p. 1969. 98.95 (*0-471-19615-0*) Wiley.

Organic Reactions, Vol. 18. Ed. by William G. Dauben. (Organic Reactions Ser.). 475p. 1970. 98.95 (*0-471-19618-5*) Wiley.

Organic Reactions, Vol. 19. Ed. by William G. Dauben. (Organic Reactions Ser.). 434p. 1972. 98.95 (*0-471-19619-3*) Wiley.

Organic Reactions, Vol. 20. Ed. by William G. Dauben. (Organic Reactions Ser.). 494p. 1973. 98.95 (*0-471-19621-5*) Wiley.

Organic Reactions, Vol. 24. Ed. by William G. Dauben. 431p. 1976. 98.95 (*0-471-19625-8*) Wiley.

Organic Reactions, Vol. 27. (Organic Reactions Ser.). 405p. 1982. 98.95 (*0-471-09657-1*) Wiley.

Organic Reactions, Vol. 28. Ed. by William G. Dauben. (Organic Reactions Ser.). 347p. 1982. 99.95 (*0-471-86141-3*) Wiley.

Organic Reactions, Vol. 29. William G. Dauben. LC 79-642486. 480p. (C). 1983. reprint ed. 99.95 (*0-471-87490-6*) Wiley.

Organic Reactions, Vol. 30. Ed. by William G. Dauben. (Organic Reactions Ser.). 592p. 1984. 99.95 (*0-471-89013-8*) Wiley.

Organic Reactions, Vol. 31. Ed. by William G. Dauben. LC 42-20265. (Organic Reaction Mechanisms Ser.: No. 2-201). 416p. 1984. 99.95 (*0-471-88671-8*) Wiley.

Organic Reactions, Vol. 32. Ed. by William G. Dauben. (Organic Reactions Ser.). 544p. 1984. 99.95 (*0-471-88101-5*) Wiley.

Organic Reactions, Vol. 35. Ed. by Andrew S. Kende. 672p. 1988. 99.95 (*0-471-83253-7*) Wiley.

Organic Reactions, Vol. 36. Ed. by Andrew S. Kende. 602p. 1988. 99.95 (*0-471-85748-3*) Wiley.

Organic Reactions, Vol. 37. Andrew S. Kende. 588p. 1989. 99.95 (*0-471-50169-7*) Wiley.

Organic Reactions, Vol. 38. Ed. by Leo A. Paquette. 832p. 1990. 125.00 (*0-471-51594-9*) Wiley.

Organic Reactions, Vol. 39. Leo A. Paquette. 608p. 1990. 120.00 (*0-471-52632-0*) Wiley.

Organic Reactions, Vol. 40. Ed. by Leo A. Paquette. 528p. 1991. 110.00 (*0-471-53841-8*) Wiley.

Organic Reactions, Vol. 41. Leo A. Paquette. 672p. 1992. 99.95 (*0-471-54409-4*) Wiley.

Organic Reactions, Vol. 42. Leo A. Paquette. 696p. 1992. 99.95 (*0-471-54410-8*) Wiley.

Organic Reactions, Vol. 43. Leo A. Paquette. 832p. 1993. 105.00 (*0-471-58479-7*) Wiley.

Organic Reactions, Vol. 44. Ed. by Leo A. Paquette. 624p. 1993. 105.00 (*0-471-30302-X*) Wiley.

Organic Reactions, Vol. 45. Leo A. Paquette. 688p. 1994. 105.00 (*0-471-03161-5*) Wiley.

Organic Reactions, Vol. 46. Ed. by Leo A. Paquette et al. 416p. 1994. 105.00 (*0-471-08619-3*) Wiley.

Organic Reactions, Vol. 47. Ed. by Leo A. Paquette et al. LC 42-20265. 592p. 1995. 99.95 (*0-471-11737-4*) Wiley.

Organic Reactions, Vol. 48. Ed. by Leo A. Paquette et al. LC 42-20265. 880p. 1996. 105.00 (*0-471-14699-4*) Wiley.

Organic Reactions, Vol. 49. Leo A. Paquette. LC 42-20265. (Organic Reactions Ser.). 700p. 1996. 98.95 (*0-471-15655-8*) Wiley.

Organic Reactions, Vol. 50. Ed. by Leo A. Paquette. LC 42-20265. (Organic Reactions Ser.). 704p. 1997. 105.00 (*0-471-15657-4*) Wiley.

Organic Reactions, Vol. 51. Leo A. Paquette. LC 42-20265. (Organic Reactions Ser.). 502p. 1997. 98.95 (*0-471-18394-6*) Wiley.

Organic Reactions, Vol. 52. Ed. by Leo A. Paquette. 600p. 1998. 95.00 (*0-471-18395-4*) Wiley.

Organic Reactions, Vol. 54. Leo Paquette & Robert Bittman. 442p. 1999. 89.95 (*0-471-34888-0*) Wiley.

*__Organic Reactions, Vol. 55.__ Leo Paquette. 654p. 1999. 95.00 (*0-471-37614-0*) Wiley.

Organic Reactions: Equilibria, Kinetics, & Mechanism. Ferenc Ruff & I. G. Csizmadia. LC 94-6367. (Studies in Organic Chemistry: Vol. 50). 482p. 1994. 249.00 (*0-444-88174-3*) Elsevier.

Organic Reactions: Simplicity & Logic. Pierre Laszlo. 716p. 1996. pap. 74.95 (*0-471-95278-8*) Wiley.

Organic Reactions in Aqueous Media. Chao-Jun Li & Tak-Hang Chan. LC 96-29886. 216p. 1997. 64.95 (*0-471-16395-3*) Wiley.

Organic Reactions, Vol. 33, Vol. 33. Ed. by Andrew S. Kende. (Organic Reactions Ser.). 368p. 1985. 99.95 (*0-471-80229-8*) Wiley.

Organic Reactions, Vol. 34, Vol. 34. Ed. by Andrew S. Kende. LC 42-20265. 412p. 1985. 99.95 (*0-471-80673-0*) Wiley.

Organic Reactivity: Physical & Biological Aspects. Ed. by Bernard T. Golding et al. 470p. 1995. 139.95 (*0-85404-710-7*, R4710) CRC Pr.

Organic Remains of a Former World, 3 vols. James Parkinson. Ed. by Claude C. Albritton, Jr. LC 77-6534. (History of Geology Ser.). (Illus.). 1978. lib. bdg. 108.95 (*0-405-10454-5*) Ayer.

Organic Revolution in Nutrition: The Future of Vitamins, Natural Versus Synthetic. Raymond W. Bernard. 20p. 1996. reprint ed. spiral bd. 9.00 (*0-7873-1213-4*) Hlth Research.

Organic Rose Garden. Liz Druitt. LC 95-51682. 176p. 1996. 19.95 (*0-87833-906-X*) Taylor Pub.

Organic Semiconducting Polymers. Ed. by J. E. Katon. LC 68-54854. (Monographs in Macromolecular Chemistry: Vol. 1). 325p. reprint ed. 100.80 (*0-8357-9089-4*, 205504400008) Bks Demand.

Organic Semiconductors, 2 vols., Pt. B. Felix Gutmann & Lawrence Lyons. LC 78-25782. 742p. (C). 1983. reprint ed. 80.00 (*0-89874-316-8*) Krieger.

Organic Small Farming. Hugh Corley. Ed. by Bargyla & Gylver Rateaver. LC 74-33122. (Conservation Gardening & Farming Ser.: Ser. C). (C). 1975. reprint ed. pap. 35.00 (*0-9600698-4-4*) Rateavers.

Organic Spectroscopy. fac. ed. David W. Brown et al. LC 87-36005. (Illus.). 258p. 1988. reprint ed. pap. 80.00 (*0-608-00984-9*, 206184000012) Bks Demand.

Organic Spectroscopy: An Introduction. 2nd ed. Stanley F. Dyke. LC 78-40163. (Illus.). 290p. reprint ed. pap. 89.90 (*0-8357-6585-7*, 203598000097) Bks Demand.

*__Organic Spirituality: A Sixfold Path for Contemplative Living.__ Nicki Verploegen Vandergrift. 120p. 2000. pap. 13.00 (*1-57075-326-1*) Orbis Bks.

Organic Stereochemistry. Shelia Buxton. (C). 1996. pap. text 32.81 (*0-582-23932-X*, Pub. by Addison-Wesley) Longman.

Organic Structural Spectroscopy. Joseph B. Lambert et al. LC 97-40522. 568p. (C). 1997. 94.67 (*0-13-258690-8*) P-H.

Organic Structure Analysis. Phillip Crews et al. LC 97-31686. (Topics in Organic Chemistry). (Illus.). 576p. (C). 1998. text 89.00 (*0-19-510102-2*) OUP.

Organic Structure Determination. Daniel G. Pasto & Carl R. Johnson. (C). 1969. text 55.00 (*0-13-640854-0*) P-H.

Organic Structures from Spectra. 2nd rev. ed. L. D. Field et al. 220p. 1995. pap. 49.95 (*0-471-95631-7*) Wiley.

An Asterisk (*) at the beginning of an entry indicates that the title is appearing for the first time.

Organic Substances & Sediments in Water Vol. 1: Huumics/Soils. Robert A. Baker. 408p. 1991. lib. bdg. 110.00 (*0-87371-342-7*) CRC Pr.

Organic Substances in Soil & Water: Natural Constituents & Their Influences on Contaminant Behaviour. Ed. by A. J. Beck et al. 200p. 1993. 126.00 (*0-85186-635-2*) CRC Pr.

Organic Substances/Sediments in Water Vol. 2: Processes/Analysis. Ed. by Robert A. Baker. 560p. 1991. lib. bdg. 110.00 (*0-87371-528-4*) CRC Pr.

Organic Substances/Sediments in Water Vol. 3: Biological. Robert A. Baker. 344p. 1991. lib. bdg. 110.00 (*0-87371-529-2*) CRC Pr.

Organic Sulfur Chemistry: Structure & Mechanism. Shigeru Oae & Joyce T. Doi. (Illus.). 288p. 1991. lib. bdg. 225.00 (*0-8493-4739-4*, QD412) CRC Pr.

Organic Sulfur Compounds from Marine Organisms, Vol. 4. C. Christophersen & U. Anthoni. Ed. by Alexander Senning. (Sulfer Reports: Vol. 4, No. 9). 91p. 1986. pap. text 98.00 (*3-7186-0337-3*) Gordon & Breach.

Organic Sulfur Compounds of Petroleum, Vol. 5. Bolshakov. 290p. 1986. text 277.00 (*3-7186-0355-1*) Gordon & Breach.

Organic Sulphur Chemistry: Biochemical Aspects. Shigeru Oae. 288p. 1992. lib. bdg. 199.00 (*0-8493-4740-8*, QP535) CRC Pr.

Organic Superconductivity. Ed. by Vladimir Z. Kresin & W. A. Little. LC 90-22264. (Illus.). 398p. (C). 1990. text 150.00 (*0-306-43730-9*, Kluwer Plenum) Kluwer Academic.

Organic Superconductors. T. Ishiguro & K. Yamaji. (Solid-State Sciences Ser.: Vol. 88). (Illus.). 312p. 1990. 64.00 (*0-387-51321-3*) Spr-Verlag.

Organic Superconductors. 2nd ed. T. Ishiguro et al. LC 98-8807. (Springer Series in Solid-State Sciences: Vol. 88). xii, 288p. 1998. pap. 54.95 (*3-540-63025-2*) Spr-Verlag.

Organic Syntheses, Vol. 68. Ed. by James D. White. 318p. 1990. 84.95 (*0-471-53789-6*) Wiley.

Organic Syntheses, Vol. 69. Leo A. Paquette. 328p. 1991. 78.95 (*0-471-54560-0*) Wiley.

Organic Syntheses, Vol. 71. Larry Overman. 320p. 1993. 69.95 (*0-471-30531-6*) Wiley.

Organic Syntheses, Vol. 74. Ed. by Ichiro Shinkai. (Organic Synthesis Ser.). 341p. 1997. 54.95 (*0-471-15656-6*) Wiley.

Organic Syntheses: An Annual Publication of Satisfactory Methods for the Preparation of Organic Chemicals, 75. Amos B. Smith. 296p. 1998. 44.95 (*0-471-18372-5*) Wiley.

Organic Syntheses: An Annual Publication of Satisfactory Methods for the Preparation of Organic Chemicals, Vol. 53. Ed. by Arnold Brossi & Richard E. Benson. LC 21-17747. 207p. reprint ed. pap. 64.20 (*0-608-13716-2*, 205528300013) Bks Demand.

Organic Syntheses: An Annual Publication of Satisfactory Methods for the Preparation of Organic Chemicals, Vol. 67. Ed. by Bruce E. Smart. 289p. 1989. 74.95 (*0-471-51379-2*) Wiley.

Organic Syntheses: An Annual Publication of Satisfactory Methods for the Preparation of Organic Chemicals, Vol. 72. David L. Coffen. 333p. 1994. 68.50 (*0-471-30727-0*) Wiley.

Organic Syntheses: Collective Volumes. H. Gilman. Ed. by Wayland E. Noland. (Organic Syntheses Collective Volumes Ser.: Vols. 1-9). 592p. 1941. 99.95 (*0-471-30030-6*) Wiley.

Organic Syntheses: Collective Volumes, Vol. 2. Ed. by A. H. Blatt. 644p. 1943. 135.00 (*0-471-07986-3*) Wiley.

Organic Syntheses: Collective Volumes, Vol. 3, Vols. 20-29. Ed. by E. C. Horning & Wayland E. Noland. (Organic Syntheses Collective Volumes Ser.). 902p. 1955. 120.00 (*0-471-40953-7*) Wiley.

Organic Syntheses: Collective Volumes, Vol. 6, Vols. 50-59. Ed. by Wayland E. Noland. (Organic Synthesis Ser.). 1232p. 1988. 135.00 (*0-471-85243-0*) Wiley.

Organic Syntheses: Reaction Guide. Dennis C. Liotta & Mark Volmer. (Organic Syntheses Collective Volumes Ser.). 872p. 1991. 98.95 (*0-471-54261-X*) Wiley.

Organic Syntheses Based on Name Reactions & Unnamed Reactions. Alfred Hassner & C. Stumer. LC 93-21414. (Teubner in Computer Science Ser.: No. 11). 462p. 1994. pap. 50.00 (*0-08-040279-8*, Pergamon Pr) Elsevier.

Organic Syntheses by Oxidation with Metal Compounds. Ed. by W. J. Mijs & C. R. H. De Jonge. (Illus.). 936p. (C). 1986. text 222.00 (*0-306-41999-8*, Kluwer Plenum) Kluwer Academic.

***Organic Syntheses Collective Volumes, Vol. 9.** Freeman. 840p. 1998. 98.95 (*0-471-24248-9*) Wiley.

Organic Syntheses Collective Volumes: Organic Syntheses New Indices, Reaction Guide, 1-69 vols. , Vol. 1. Ed. by Freeman. 8540p. 1994. text 925.00 (*0-471-12429-X*) Wiley.

Organic Syntheses Collective Volumes Vol. 1: Organic Syntheses Cumulative Indices for Collective Volumes 1-8. Ed. by Jeremiah P. Freeman. 648p. 1995. 94.95 (*0-471-31192-8*) Wiley.

Organic Syntheses Collective Volumes, Vol. 4, Vols. 30-39, Vol. 4, Vols. 30-39. N. Rabjohn. Ed. by Wayland E. Noland. 1056p. 1963. 145.00 (*0-471-70470-9*, 2-203) Wiley.

Organic Syntheses Collective Volumes, Vol. 5, Vols. 40-49, Vol. 5, Vols. 40-49. Henry E. Baumgarten. 1248p. 1973. 149.00 (*0-471-05707-X*) Wiley.

Organic Syntheses, Vol. 65, Vol. 65. Ed. by Edwin Vedejs. 278p. 1987. 78.95 (*0-471-63637-1*) Wiley.

Organic Synthesis. (Topics in Current Chemistry Ser.: Vol. 59). (Illus.). 160p. 1976. 43.00 (*0-387-07440-6*) Spr-Verlag.

Organic Synthesis. Smith. 1994. student ed. 28.13 (*0-07-059234-9*) McGraw.

Organic Synthesis. Michael B. Smith. 1250p. (C). 1994. 101.56 (*0-07-048716-2*) McGraw.

Organic Synthesis. Christine L. Willis & Martin Wills. (Oxford Chemistry Primers Ser.: Vol. 31). (Illus.). 96p. (C). 1996. pap. text 12.95 (*0-19-855791-4*) OUP.

***Organic Synthesis.** 2nd ed. M. B. Smith. 2001. 9.50 (*0-07-048242-X*) McGraw.

Organic Synthesis, Vol. 70. Ed. by Albert Meyers. 336p. 1992. 74.95 (*0-471-57743-X*) Wiley.

Organic Synthesis, Vol. 73. Ed. by Robert K. Boeckman. LC 21-17747. (Organic Synthesis Ser.). 353p. 1996. 44.95 (*0-471-14701-X*) Wiley.

Organic Synthesis, Vol. 76. Stephen F. Martin. 340p. 1999. 49.95 (*0-471-34886-4*) Wiley.

Organic Synthesis: Concepts, Methods, Starting Materials. 2nd ed. Jurgen-Hinrich Fuhrhop & Gustav Penzlin. 432p. 1993. pap. 69.95 (*3-527-29074-5*, Wiley-VCH) Wiley.

Organic Synthesis: Modern Trends. Ed. by Oleg Chizhov. 1991. 66.00 (*0-632-02014-8*) CRC Pr.

Organic Synthesis: The Disconnection Approach. Stuart Warren. 550p. 1983. pap., student ed. 59.95 (*0-471-90082-6*) Wiley.

Organic Synthesis: The Disconnection Approach. Stuart Warren. LC 81-19694. 404p. 1984. pap., student ed. 69.95 (*0-471-10161-3*) Wiley.

Organic Synthesis: The Role of Boron & Silicon. Susan E. Thomas. (Oxford Chemistry Primers Ser.: No. 1). (Illus.). 96p. (C). 1992. pap. text 12.95 (*0-19-855662-4*) OUP.

Organic Synthesis: The Science Behind the Art. W. A. Smit et al. 486p. 1998. pap. 52.95 (*0-85404-544-9*) Spr-Verlag.

Organic Synthesis: Theory & Applications, Vol. 1. Ed. by Tomas Hudlicky. 242p. 1989. 109.50 (*0-89232-865-7*) Jai Pr.

Organic Synthesis: Theory & Applications, Vol. 2. Ed. by Tomas Hudlicky. 188p. 1993. 109.50 (*1-55938-185-X*) Jai Pr.

Organic Synthesis: Theory & Applications, Vol. 3. Ed. by Tomas Hudlicky. 1996. 109.50 (*1-55938-834-X*) Jai Pr.

Organic Synthesis: Theory & Applications, Vol. 4. Ed. by Tomas Hudlicky. 1999. 109.50 (*0-7623-0444-8*) Jai Pr.

Organic Synthesis Vols. 60-64: Collective Volumes, Vol. 7. Ed. by Jeremiah P. Freeman. LC 21-17747. 624p. 1990. 99.95 (*0-471-51559-0*) Wiley.

Organic Synthesis Vols. 65-69: Collective Volumes, Vol. 8, Vols. 65-69. Ed. by Jeremiah P. Freeman. 720p. 1993. 99.95 (*0-471-58565-3*) Wiley.

Organic Synthesis at High Pressures. Kiyoshi Matsumoto & Roy M. Acheson. LC 90-31171. 456p. 1991. 175.00 (*0-471-62761-5*) Wiley.

***Organic Synthesis Engineering.** L. K. Doraiswamy. (Topics in Chemical Engineering Ser.). (Illus.). 720p. 2000. text 125.00 (*0-19-509689-4*) OUP.

Organic Synthesis Highlights II. Ed. by H. Waldmann. 424p. 1997. pap. 95.00 (*3-527-29378-7*) Wiley.

Organic Synthesis Highlights III. Johann Mulzer. 460p. 1998. pap. 105.00 (*3-527-29500-3*, Wiley-VCH) Wiley.

***Organic Synthesis in Water.** Ed. by Paul A. Greico. LC 97-74074. 328p. 1998. write for info. (*0-7514-0410-1*) Kluwer Academic.

Organic Synthesis, Reactions & Mechanisms. (Topics in Current Chemistry Ser.: Vol. 137). (Illus.). 250p. 1987. 95.00 (*0-387-16904-0*) Spr-Verlag.

Organic Synthesis under Extreme Conditions. Tse-Lok Ho. LC 98-8006. 386p. 1998. 48.00 (*981-02-3252-7*) World Scientific Pub.

Organic Synthesis Via Metal Carbonyls, Vol. 1. Ed. by Irving Wender & Piero Pino. LC 67-13965. 531p. reprint ed. pap. 164.70 (*0-608-10891-X*, 200631400058) Bks Demand.

Organic Synthesis with Oxidative Enzymes. H. L. Holland. 463p. 1991. 170.00 (*0-471-18762-3*) Wiley.

Organic Synthesis with Oxidative Enzymes. Herbert L. Holland. 463p. 1992. text 95.00 (*0-89573-779-5*, Wiley-VCH) Wiley.

Organic Sythesis: An Interdisciplinary Challenge. Streith & Prinzba. 1991. 61.00 (*0-632-01441-5*) CRC Pr.

Organic Thin Films: Structure & Applications. Curtis W. Frank. LC 98-6368. (Illus.). 416p. 1998. text 135.00 (*0-8412-3564-3*, Pub. by Am Chemical) OUP.

Organic Thin Films for Photonic Applications. LC 92-62927. (Nineteen Ninety-Three Technical Digest Ser.: Vol. 17). 200p. (Orig.). 1993. pap. 75.00 (*1-55752-316-9*) Optical Soc.

Organic Thin Films for Photonic Applications. LC 92-62927. (Technical Digest Ser.: Vol. 17, 1993). 200p. (Orig.). 1993. pap. text 48.00 (*1-55752-315-0*) Optical Soc.

Organic Thin Films for Photonic Applications, Vol. 2. LC 95-68689. (Nineteen Ninety-Four Technical Digest Ser.: Vol. 21). 536p. (Orig.). 1995. pap. 75.00 (*1-55752-412-2*) Optical Soc.

Organic Thin Films for Photonics Applications. Compiled by Optical Society of America Staff. LC 97-68770. (Nineteen Ninety-Seven Technical Digest Ser.: Vol. 14). (Illus.). 269p. 1997. pap. 74.00 (*1-55752-511-0*) Optical Soc.

Organic Thin Films for Waveguiding Nonlinear Optics. F. Kajzar & J. D. Swalen. (Advances in Nonlinear Optics Ser). 817p. 1996. text 165.00 (*2-88449-070-1*) Gordon & Breach.

Organic Thinking: A Study in Rabbinic Thought. Max Kadushin. 1976. pap. 16.95 (*0-8197-0018-5*) Bloch.

***Organic Traveler's Guide: Exploring Organics in Northern California's Sonoma, Napa &...** Patricia Dines. (Illus.). 2000. pap. 9.95 (*0-9700941-0-8*) Comnity Actn.

Organic Union in God's Relationship with Man. Witness Lee. 94p. 1993. pap. 4.50 (*0-87083-736-2*, 04-022-001) Living Stream Ministry.

Organic Unity in Coleridge. Gordon McKenzie. LC 75-30008. reprint ed. 27.50 (*0-404-14014-9*) AMS Pr.

Organic Vegetable Gardening. Time-Life Books Editors. Ed. by Janet Cave. LC 95-48919. (Complete Gardener Ser.). (Illus.). 160p. (gr. 11). 1999. pap. 16.95 (*0-7835-4108-2*) Time-Life.

Organic Voice Disorders: Assessment & Treatment. Ed. by William S. Brown et al. LC 96-23807. (Illus.). 398p. (C). 1996. 55.00 (*1-56593-268-4*, 0590) Thomson Learn.

Organic Waste Recycling. Chongrak Polprasert. LC 88-20722. (Illus.). 371p. 1989. reprint ed. pap. 115.10 (*0-608-04000-2*, 206473700011) Bks Demand.

Organic Waste Recycling: Technology & Management. 2nd ed. Chongrak Polprasert. 426p. 1996. pap. 75.00 (*0-471-96482-4*) Wiley.

Organic Way to Health, Pt. III. Raymond W. Bernard. (Science of Organic Dietetics Ser.). 1996. spiral bd. 9.00 (*0-7873-0995-8*) Hlth Research.

Organic Way to Health Pt. 1: Nutritional Value of Organic Foods & Sea Vegetation. Raymond W. Bernard. (Science of Organic Dietetics Ser.). 1996. spiral bd. 9.00 (*0-7873-0997-4*) Hlth Research.

Organic Way to Health Pt. 2: Seed Protein vs. Animal Proteins. Raymond W. Bernard. (Science of Organic Dietetics Ser.). 1996. spiral bd. 9.00 (*0-7873-0996-6*) Hlth Research.

Organic Way to Health Pt. 4: Latest Advances in Nutrition from the New Organic Viewpoint. Raymond W. Bernard. (Science of Organic Dietetics Ser.). 1996. spiral bd. 11.00 (*0-7873-0994-X*) Hlth Research.

***Organic Wine Guide.** Monty Waldin. 2000. pap. 12.95 (*0-7225-3833-2*) Thorsons PA.

***Organic 7e Chemistry Lab 4e Se.** 7th ed. T. W. Graham Solomons. (Chemistry Lab: 4). 1999. text 96.00 (*0-471-36368-5*) Wiley.

Organichem Model Set (FC No. 207), Set. 1989. 11.25 (*0-86720-140-1*) Jones & Bartlett.

***Organic/Inorganic Hybrid Materials -- 2000: Materials Research Society Symposium Proceedings, Vol. 628.** Ed. by R. M. Laine et al. 2000. text 82.00 (*1-55899-536-6*) Materials Res.

Organic/Inorganic Hybrid Materials II Vol. 576: Materials Research Society Symposium Proceedings. Ed. by L. C. Klein et al. LC 99-46950. 465p. 1999. text 74.00 (*1-55899-483-1*) Materials Res.

Organicism: Origin & Development, Life & Publications of the Author. Archie J. Bahm. LC 96-90092. 569p. 1996. pap. 25.00 (*0-911714-23-5*) World Bks.

Organicism As Reenchantment: Whitehead, Prigogine, & Barth. James Kirk. LC 92-40986. (American University Studies: Philosophy: Ser. V, Vol. 167). XIII, 138p. 1994. 35.95 (*0-8204-2110-3*) P Lang Pubng.

Organics & the Rockies - Field Guide. Ed. by Romeo M. Flores et al. (Public Information Circular Ser.: No. 33). 184p. (Orig.). (C). 1994. pap. 15.00 (*1-884589-06-5*) Wyoming St Geol.

Organics Removal by Granular Activated Carbon. 286p. 1989. pap. 51.00 (*0-89867-475-1*, 20033) Am Water Wks Assn.

Organics Syntheses, Vol. 64. Ed. by Andrew S. Kende. 308p. 1986. 89.95 (*0-471-84742-9*) Wiley.

Organicum: A Practical Handbook of Organic Chemistry. B. J. Hazzard et al. 1973. 340.00 (*0-08-012789-4*, Pub. by Pergamon Repr) Franklin.

Organisation. 3rd ed. Alfred Kieser & Herbert Kubicek. (GER.). 545p. 1992. 44.65 (*3-11-013499-3*) De Gruyter.

Organisation & Bureaucracy: An Analysis of Modern Theories. Nicos P. Mouzelis. LC 68-11361. 239p. 1967. pap. text 25.95 (*0-202-30078-1*) Aldine de Gruyter.

Organisation & Economic Change. Ed. by Alan Mabin. 220p. (Orig.). 1989. pap. text 17.95 (*0-86975-382-7*, Pub. by Ravan Pr) Ohio U Pr.

Organisation & Management of Intensive Care: A Prospective Study in 12 European Countries. D. Reis Miranda. Ed. by J. L. Vincent et al. LC 97-13204. (Update in Intensive Care & Emergency Medicine Ser.: Vol. 29). (Illus.). 220p. 1998. 105.00 (*3-540-62581-X*) Spr-Verlag.

Organisation & Scientific Discovery. John Hurley. LC 96-25877. 186p. 1997. 85.00 (*0-471-96963-X*) Wiley.

Organisation Corporative de la France d'Ancien Regime. Felix Oliver-Martin. xiii, 565p. reprint ed. write for info. (*0-318-71385-3*) G Olms Pubs.

Organisation for Japanese Technology: The Japanese Style of Management in the New Generation. Koji Okubayashi et al. (Series on Technology Management). 230p. 1999. 38.00 (*1-86094-142-7*, Pub. by Imperial College) World Scientific Pub.

Organisation in Plants. 3rd ed. W. M. Baron. (Illus.). 272p. 1992. pap. text 35.95 (*0-521-42751-7*) Cambridge U Pr.

Organisation Militaire de l'Egypt Byzantine. Jean Maspero. (Bibliotheque Des Hautes Etudes Ser.: No. 201). 157p. 1974. reprint ed. write for info. (*3-487-05282-2*) G Olms Pubs.

Organisation of Integrated Product Development. Victor Paashuis. Ed. by D. T. Pham. LC 97-44699. (Advanced Manufacturing Ser.). (Illus.). xi, 266p. 1997. 84.95 (*3-540-76225-6*) Spr-Verlag.

Organisation of Maternity Care: A Guide to Evaluation. Campbell & Garcia. 160p. 1997. pap. text 30.00 (*1-898507-37-6*) Buttrwrth-Heinemann.

Organisation of Mountain Search & Rescue Operations. Anthony S. G. Jones. 76p. 1988. pap. 7.50 (*0-913724-34-3*) Emerg Response Inst.

Organisation of Political Parties. 2nd ed. Central Office of Info. LC 95-140361. (Aspects of Britain Ser.). (Illus.). 66p. 1997. pap. 11.95 (*0-11-701838-4*, HM18384, Pub. by Statnry Office) Bernan Associates.

Organisation of the Firm: International Business Perspectives. Ram Mudambi & Martin J. Ricketts. LC 97-8357. (Illus.). 232p. (C). 1997. 85.00 (*0-415-14298-9*) Routledge.

Organisation of Thought, Educational & Scientific. Alfred North Whitehead. LC 76-106727. 228p. 1974. reprint ed. lib. bdg. 69.50 (*0-8371-3448-X*, WHOT, Greenwood Pr) Greenwood.

Organisation System. (Open Learning for Supervisory Management Ser.). 1986. pap. text 19.50 (*0-08-070016-0*, Pergamon Pr) Elsevier.

Organisation von Vertraulichkeit: Eine Empirische Analyse der Compliance-Systeme Deutscher Universalbanken. Hans P. Pirner. (GER., Illus.). 252p. 1996. 44.95 (*3-631-30771-3*) P Lang Pubng.

Organisational & Financial Management of Religious Institutions. V. K. Rao. (C). 1992. 34.00 (*0-8364-2807-2*, Pub. by Deep & Deep Pubns) S Asia.

Organisational Behavior: An Australian Perspective. (C). 1991. pap. text. write for info. (*0-201-50041-8*) Addison-Wesley.

Organisational Behaviour. G. A. Cole. 300p. 1995. pap. 59.95 (*1-85805-135-5*, Pub. by DP Publns) St Mut.

Organisational Behaviour. Wood. 864p. write for info. (*0-471-33769-2*) Wiley.

Organisational Behaviour. 3rd ed. Roger Bennett. 310p. 1994. pap. 44.50 (*0-273-63424-0*, Pub. by Pitman Pub) St Mut.

Organisational Behaviour: An Introductory Text. 2nd ed. David A. Buchanan & Andrzej A. Hucyznski. 637p. (C). 1991. pap. 120.00 (*0-13-639899-5*, Pub. by IPM Hse) St Mut.

***Organisational Behaviour: Individual, Group & Organisation.** Ian Brooks. 320p. 1999. pap. 38.50 (*0-273-63286-8*, Pub. by F T P-H) Trans-Atl Phila.

Organisational Behaviour & Gender. Fiona Wilson. LC 94-29854. 1995. write for info. (*0-07-707615-X*) McGraw.

Organisational Capability & Competitive Advantage. Ed. by Charles Harvey & Geoffrey Jones. 204p. 1992. text 42.50 (*0-7146-3457-3*, Pub. by F Cass Pubs) Intl Spec Bk.

Organisational Change: Sociological Perspectives. David Collins. LC 97-42959. 256p. (C). 1998. pap. 25.99 (*0-415-17156-3*) Routledge.

Organisational Change: Sociological Perspectives. David Collins. LC 97-42959. 232p. (C). 1998. 85.00 (*0-415-17155-5*) Routledge.

***Organisational Change & Retail Finance.** Richard Harper et al. LC 99-37474. 232p. 1999. 90.00 (*0-415-20264-7*) Routledge.

Organisational Culture. 2nd ed. Andrew Brown. 320p. 1998. pap. 54.50 (*0-273-63147-0*, Pub. by Pitman Pub) Trans-Atl Phila.

***Organisational Culture & the Psychological Contract.** 56p. 2000. pap. 35.95 (*0-8464-5180-8*) Beekman Pubs.

Organisational Decision Making: Student Book. Clifford. 1992. pap. text, student ed. write for info. (*0-582-08118-1*, Pub. by Addison-Wesley) Longman.

Organisational Design: The Work Levels Approach. Ralph Rowbottom & David Billis. 1987. text 78.95 (*0-566-05408-6*, Pub. by Avebry) Ashgate Pub Co.

Organisational Effectiveness in a Multinational Bureaucracy. Hans J. Michelmann. LC 78-60532. 271p. 1979. 55.00 (*0-275-90394-X*, C0394, Praeger Pubs) Greenwood.

***Organisational Health: Diagnosis & Treatment.** Perrin & T. Webber. (Financial Times Management Briefings Ser.). 1998. pap. 94.50 (*0-273-63396-1*, Pub. by F T P-H) Trans-Atl Phila.

Organisational Learning & Effectiveness. John Denton. (Illus.). 224p. (C). (gr. 13). 1998. 85.00 (*0-415-19214-5*, D6249); pap. 27.99 (*0-415-19215-3*, D6253) Routledge.

***Organisational Learning & Management Accounting Systems: A Study of Local Government.** Louise Kloot et al. 64p. 1999. pap. 19.95 (*0-86840-713-5*, Pub. by New South Wales Univ Pr) Intl Spec Bk.

***Organisational Learning in the Automotive Sector.** Penny West. LC 00-22535. (Advances in Management & Business Studies). 2000. write for info. (*0-415-21986-8*) Routledge.

Organisational Structure & the Care of the Mentally Retarded. Norma V. Raynes et al. LC 79-83740. (Praeger Special Studies). 240p. 1979. 62.95 (*0-275-90411-3*, C0411, Praeger Pubs) Greenwood.

***Organisations: A Strategic Perspective.** Paul R. Ferguson & Glenys J. Ferguson. LC 99-59237. 2000. write for info. (*0-312-23282-9*) St Martin.

***Organisations & Development: Strategies, Structures & Processes.** Dale Reidar. LC 00-33278. 2000. pap. write for info. (*0-7619-9430-0*) Sage.

***Organisations in Action: Competition Between Contexts** Peter A. Clark. LC 99-17479. 1999. pap. write for info. (*0-415-18231-X*) Routledge.

***Organisations in Action: Competition Between Contexts.** Peter A. Clark. LC 99-17479. 256p. (C). 1999. text. write for info. (*0-415-18230-1*) Routledge.

Organisations Internationales, le Regionalisme International, le Regionalisme International Africain: Presentation Generale, Evolution et Perspectives d'Avenir. Innocent Semuhire. (Publications Universitaires Europeennes: Series 2: Vol. 2070). (FRE.). 430p. 1996. pap. 60.95 (*3-906754-87-1*) P Lang Pubng.

***Organisationslernen Durch Wissensmanagement.** Projektgruppe Wissenschaftliche Beratung. (Illus.). 184p. 1999. 34.00 (*3-631-35029-5*) P Lang Pubng.

Organisationstheoretische & Okonomische Grundlagen der Kommunalen Verwaltungsreform in Nordrhein-Westfalens Grobstadten. Friedhelm Knorr. (GER., Illus.). 272p. 1996. 54.95 (*3-631-30989-9*) P Lang Pubng.

O

An Asterisk (*) at the beginning of an entry indicates that the title is appearing for the first time.

Organisationstheorien Von Weber Bis Weick. Emil Walter-Busch. (Wirtschaftswissenschaftliche Studienbuch Ser.). (GER.). 368p. 1996. text 43.00 (90-5708-019-2); pap. text 22.00 (90-5708-020-6) Gordon & Breach.

Organisationstransformation und Transformationsmanagement. Miriam Luckhardt. (Wirtschaftspsychologie Ser.: Bd. 4). (GER., Illus.). 180p. 1996. pap. 42.95 (3-631-30787-X) P Lang Pubng.

Organisch-Chemische Nomenklatur. Hans Reimlinger. (GER.). 620p. (C). 1997. lib. bdg. 87.40 (3-11-014863-3) De Gruyter.

Organise Your Mind. Ronald Dingwall. 72p. (C). 1986. 50.00 (0-86236-001-3, Pub. by Granary) St Mut.

Organised Abuse. Ed. by Peter Bibby. LC 96-83248. 304p. 1996. 64.95 (1-85742-284-8, Pub. by Arena) Ashgate Pub Co.

Organised Capital: Employers' Associations & Industrial Relations in Northern England. Arthur McIvor. (Illus.). 323p. (C). 1996. text 64.95 (0-521-55094-7) Cambridge U Pr.

***Organised Crime in Antiquity.** Ed. by Keith Hopwood. 278p. 1999. 49.50 (0-7156-2905-0, Pub. by Classical Pr) David Brown.

Organised Molecular Assemblies in the Solid State. Whitesell. 268p. 1999. 199.00 (0-471-95232-X) Wiley.

Organised Monolayers. Kuhn. text. write for info. (0-471-49018-0); pap. text. write for info. (0-471-49019-9) Wiley.

Organised "Plastic" Counterfeiting. Newton John. LC 96-217963. 196p. 1995. pap. 75.00 (0-11-341128-6, HM11286, Pub. by Statnry Office) Bernan Associates.

Organising a Plain-Language Project. Mark Duckworth & Gordon Mills. 67p. 1996. pap. 29.00 (1-86287-243-0, Pub. by Federation Pr) Gaunt.

Organising Development Through Participation Co-Operative Organisation & Services for Land Settlement. Liam E. Pickett. 176p. 1988. lib. bdg. 57.50 (0-7099-5607-X, Pub. by C Helm) Routldge.

Organising Effective Training: How to Plan & Run Successful Courses & Seminars. James Chalmers. (Business Basics Ser.). 127p. 1996. pap. 19.95 (1-85703-329-9, Pub. by How To Bks) Trans-Atl Phila.

Organising Feminisms. Morley. LC 98-20861. 1999. pap. 21.95 (0-312-21678-5) St Martin.

***Organising Feminisms.** Morley. LC 98-20861. 1999. text 65.00 (0-312-21676-9) St Martin.

Organising for Improved Sales Effectiveness. David Senton & Peter Kirby. 138p. 1983. text 53.95 (0-566-02379-2) Ashgate Pub Co.

Organising for Learning: Staff Development Strategies for Residential & Day Services Work: A Theoretical & Practical Guide. Robin Douglas & Chris Payne. (C). 1988. 50.00 (0-7855-3733-3, Pub. by Natl Inst Soc Work) St Mut.

Organising for Learning: Staff Development Strategies for Residential & Day Services Work. A Theoretical & Practical Guide. Robin Douglas & Chris Payne. (C). 1988. 95.00 (0-7855-0077-4, Pub. by Natl Inst Soc Work) St Mut.

Organising for Learning: Staff Development Strategies for Residential & Day Services Work. A Theoretical & Practical Guide. Ed. by Robin Douglas & Chris Payne. (C). 1988. 50.00 (0-7855-5883-7, Pub. by Natl Inst Soc Work) St Mut.

Organising Innovation Research: The Inner Life of University. Li Bennich-Bjorkman. LC 97-27903. (Issues in Higher Education Ser.). 250p. 1997. 85.00 (0-08-043072-4, Pergamon Pr) Elsevier.

Organising Innovative Manufacturing Systems. Harry Boer. (Business School Library). 284p. 1991. text 82.95 (1-85628-273-2, Pub. by Avebry) Ashgate Pub Co.

Organising Public Social Services. Challis. 1990. pap. 34.95 (0-582-06302-7) Ashgate Pub Co.

Organising Strategy: Sun Tzu Business Warcraft. Peter H. Grinyer. 579p. 2000. text 46.95 (0-409-99683-1) Buttrwrth-Heinemann.

Organising the Farmers: Cocoa Politics & National Development in Ghana. Bjorn Beckman. 299p. 1976. write for info. (91-7106-101-0, Pub. by Nordic Africa) Transaction Pubs.

Organising the Unorganised Workers. Ed. by Ruddar Datt. LC 98-906101. (C). 1997. 39.00 (81-259-0342-9, Pub. by Vikas) S Asia.

Organising Unorganised Labour: A Study of NLI Rural Camps. Ed. by Vidhut Joshi. (C). 1990. 12.50 (81-204-0539-0, Pub. by Oxford IBH) S Asia.

Organising Women's Protest: A Study of Political Styles in Two South Indian Activist Groups. Eldrid Mageli. LC 96-229335. (NIAS Monographs in Asian Studies: No. 72). 288p. (C). 1996. text 48.00 (0-7007-0431-0, Pub. by Curzon Pr Ltd); pap. text 24.95 (0-7007-0440-X, Pub. by Curzon Pr Ltd) UH Pr.

Organising Your Second Marriage. Carole Chapman. 160p. (Orig.). 1994. pap. 11.95 (0-572-01987-4, Pub. by W Foulsham) Trans-Atl Phila.

***Organism.** Kurt Goldstein. 424p. 2000. pap. text 20.00 (0-942299-97-3) Zone Bks.

Organism: A Holistic Approach to Biology. Kurt Goldstein. LC 94-40858. 422p. (C). 1995. reprint ed. 28.00 (0-942299-96-5) Zone Bks.

Organism & the Origins of Self. Ed. by Alfred I. Tauber. 400p. (C). 1991. lib. bdg. 194.00 (0-7923-1185-X, Pub. by Kluwer Academic) Kluwer Academic.

Organism, Medicine, & Metaphysics. Ed. by Stuart F. Spicker. (Philosophy & Medicine Ser.: No. 7). 357p. 1978. text 98.50 (90-277-0823-1, D Reidel) Kluwer Academic.

Organism of the triune God in the Organic Union of His Divine Trinity see Organismo del Dios Triuno en la Union Organica de Su Trinidad Divina

Organism of the Triune God in the Organic Union of the Divine Trinity. Witness Lee. 64p. 1988. pap. 4.00 (0-87083-399-5, 08-016-001) Living Stream Ministry.

***Organism Structure & Function.** 3rd ed. (C). 1998. 16.00 (0-8087-9852-9) Pearson Custom.

Organismal Biology. James Riopel. 222p. (C). 1998. spiral bd. 28.95 (0-7872-5663-3, 41566304) Kendall-Hunt.

Organismal Biology Laboratory Exercises. Joan Bray et al. 132p. (C). 1997. pap. text, per. 33.95 (0-7872-3312-9, 41331201) Kendall-Hunt.

Organismo del Dios Triuno en la Union Organica de Su Trinidad Divina. Witness Lee.Tr. of Organism of the triune God in the Organic Union of His Divine Trinity. (SPA.). 65p. 1989. pap. 4.00 (0-87083-432-0, 08-016-002) Living Stream Ministry.

***Organisms: Hands on Elementary School Science.** 2nd ed. (Illus.). 44p. 2000. teacher ed. 35.00 (1-883410-34-7) L Poore.

Organisms & Populations. Alexandra Dickerman. 1998. text 5.25 (0-07-229413-2) McGraw.

Organisms Student Notebook. National Science Resources Center Staff. (Science & Technology for Children Ser.). (Illus.). 18p. (J). (gr. 1). 1996. pap. text, student ed., wbk. ed. write for info. (0-89278-736-8, 97-1103) Carolina Biological.

Organisms Teacher's Guide. National Science Resources Center Staff. (Science & Technology for Children Ser.). (Illus.). 243p. 1996. pap. text. write for info. (0-89278-735-X, 97-1102) Carolina Biological.

Organismus und Umwelt. Rudolf Langthaler. (Studien und Materialien Zur Geschichte der Philosophie Ser.: Bd. 34). (GER.). 270p. 1992. write for info. (3-487-09638-2) G Olms Pubs.

Organismuskonzept und Sprachgeschichtsschreibung: Die "Geschichte der Deutschen Sprache" Von Jacob Grimm. Maria Herrlich. (GER.). 222p. 1998. write for info. (3-487-10648-5) G Olms Pubs.

Organist As Scholar: Essays in Honor of Russell Saunders. Russell Saunders. Ed. by Kerala J. Snyder. LC 94-12811. (Festschrift Ser.: No. 12). 1994. 54.00 (0-945193-44-0) Pendragon NY.

Organists & Organ Playing in Nineteenth-Century France & Belgium. Orpha C. Ochse. LC 94-2589. 512p. 1994. 39.95 (0-253-34161-2) Ind U Pr.

Organist's Guide to Resources for the Hymnal, 1982, Vol. I. Ed. by Dennis Schmidt. (Hymnal Studies: No. 7). 181p. 1987. pap. 17.95 (0-89869-151-6) Church Pub Inc.

Organist's Guide to Resources for the Hymnal, 1982, Vol. 2. Ed. by Dennis Schmidt. (Hymnal Studies: No. 7). 259p. 1991. pap. 21.95 (0-89869-192-3) Church Pub Inc.

Organists' Manual: Technical Studies & Selected Compositions for the Organ. Roger E. Davis. (C). 1985. 53.50 (0-393-95461-7) Norton.

Organist's Picture Chords. Howard Brown. (Illus.). 32p. 1977. pap. 8.95 (0-86001-500-9, AM20843) Music Sales.

***Organist's Reader: Essays.** Robert Noehren. LC 99-13271. 1999. write for info. (0-89990-086-0) Harmonie.

Organist's Treasury, Bk. 2. (Kevin Mayhew Ser.). 200p. 1996. 34.95 (0-7866-2287-3, MB96156) Mel Bay.

Organizacion & Liderazgo. Lee G. Bolman. (SPA.). 512p. (C). 1995. pap. text 13.33 (0-201-60106-0) Addison-Wesley.

Organizacion Marca una Diferencia: Educacion y Salud en America Latina. Ed. by William Savedoff. (SPA.). 322p. 1998. pap. text 21.50 (1-886938-31-8) IADB.

Organizaciones, Comportamiento, Estructura & Processes. James L. Gibson. (SPA.). (C). 1994. pap. text. write for info. (0-201-60109-5) Addison-Wesley.

Organizar para Evangelizar - Manual para el Crecimiento de la Iglesia (Organize to Evangelize - A Manual for Church Growth) Larry L. Lewis. Tr. by Josie H. Smith from ENG. (SPA.). 112p. (Orig.). 1992. pap. 6.50 (0-311-13857-8) Casa Bautista.

Organizatal Behavr CANDA. 4th ed. Usher. 352p. (C). 1996. pap. text 23.44 (0-673-98145-2) Addson-Wesley Educ.

Organization. 3rd ed. Bobko. 1995. 25.94 (0-07-042788-7) McGraw.

Organization: A Guide to Problems & Practice. John Child. 316p. (C). 1984. pap. 70.00 (0-06-318275-0, Pub. by P Chapman) St Mut.

Organization: Text, Cases & Readings in the Management of Organizational Design & Change. 3rd ed. Leonard A. Schlesinger et al. 640p. (C). 1991. text 71.35 (0-256-09184-6, Irwn McGrw-H) McGrw-H Hghr Educ.

Organization - Communication: Emerging Perspectives. Contrib. by Randall K. Stutman et al. (Communication & Information Science Ser.: Vol. 3). (Illus.). 256p. (C). 1996. text 73.25 (0-89391-621-8) Ablx Pub.

Organization - Communication: Emerging Perspectives. Lee Thayer. LC 85-6159. (People, Communication, Organization Ser.: Vol. 1). 296p. 1986. text 78.50 (0-89391-274-3) Ablx Pub.

Organization - Communication: Emerging Perspectives. Ed. by Lee Thayer. LC 85-6159. (People, Communication, Organization Ser.: Vol. 2). 256p. 1988. text 73.25 (0-89391-425-8) Ablx Pub.

Organization - Communication: Emerging Perspectives. Lee Thayer & George Barnett. (Emerging Perspectives: Vol. 5). 291p. 1997. pap. 39.50 (1-56750-275-X) Ablx Pub.

Organization - Communication: Emerging Perspectives, Vol. 4. John F. Stone. Ed. by Lee Thayer & George A. Barnett. (Illus.). 256p. 1994. text 73.25 (0-89391-995-0) Ablx Pub.

Organization - Communication: Emerging Perspectives, Vol. 5. Ed. by George Barnett & Lee Thayer. (Illus.). 291p. 1997. text 78.50 (1-56750-195-8) Ablx Pub.

Organization - Communication: Emerging Perspectives, Vol. 6. Ed. by George A. Barnett. 300p. 1998. pap. 39.50 (1-56750-315-2); text 73.25 (1-56750-314-4) Ablx Pub.

Organization - The Extracellular Matrix: A Polarz Microsc. Appr. Lazslo Modis. 296p. 1990. lib. bdg. 239.00 (0-8493-5786-1, QM563) CRC Pr.

Organization Analysis & Development: A Social Construction of Organizational Behaviour. Ed. by Iain L. Mangham. LC 86-26713. (Industrial Psychology & Organization Behaviour Ser.). 283p. reprint ed. pap. 87.80 (0-7837-6162-7, 204588400009) Bks Demand.

Organization & Administration of Maternal & Child Health Services: Proceedings of the WHO Expert Committee on Maternal & Child Health, Geneva, 1968. WHO Staff. (Technical Reports: No. 428). 1969. pap. text 5.00 (92-4-120428-1, 1100428) World Health.

Organization & Administration of Practice-Teaching in Privately Endowed Colleges of Liberal Arts. Jacob I. Baugher. LC 72-176543. (Columbia University. Teachers College. Contributions to Education Ser.: No. 487). reprint ed. 37.50 (0-404-55487-3) AMS Pr.

Organization & Administration of Smaller College Athletics: A Handbook for Athletic Directors & Administrators. Richard C. Cosby. LC 89-82049. 1990. pap. 14.95 (0-938991-50-7) Colonial Pr AL.

Organization & Administration of Substitute-Teaching Service in City-School Systems. Clare C. Baldwin. LC 75-176533. (Columbia University. Teachers College. Contributions to Education Ser.: No. 615). reprint ed. 37.50 (0-404-55615-9) AMS Pr.

Organization & Administration of the Union Army, 1861-1865, 2 vols., Set. Fred A. Shannon. (History - United States Ser.). 1992. reprint ed. lib. bdg. 150.00 (0-7812-6186-4) Rprt Serv.

***Organization & Aesthetics.** Antonio Strati. LC 98-75046. 216p. 1999. write for info. (0-7619-5238-1) Sage.

Organization & Change in Complex Systems. Ed. by Marcelo Alonso. 278p. 1989. 34.95 (0-89226-059-9) Paragon Hse.

Organization & Chaos: Defining the Methods of Nonlinear Management. H. Richard Priesmeyer. LC 92-7486. 272p. 1992. 59.95 (0-89930-630-6, PMM, Quorum Bks) Greenwood.

Organization & Control of American Schools. 6th ed. Ronald Campbell et al. 512p. (C). 1990. 125.00 (0-675-21126-3, Merrill Coll) P-H.

Organization & Decision Theory. Ira Horowitz. (C). 1989. lib. bdg. 113.50 (0-7923-9050-4) Kluwer Academic.

***Organization & Economic Behaviour.** Anna Grandori. LC 00-38261. 2000. pap. write for info. (0-415-16408-7) Routledge.

Organization & Environment. Lawrence. 296p. 1986. pap. 14.36 (0-07-103246-0) McGraw.

Organization & Governance in Higher Education. 4th ed. Ed. by Marvin W. Peterson et al. (ASHE Reader Ser.). 476p. (C). 1991. pap. text 48.00 (0-536-57981-4) Pearson Custom.

***Organization & Governance in Higher Education.** 5th ed. 624p. (C). 2000. 48.00 (0-536-60749-4) Pearson Custom.

Organization & History of the Chicago, Milwaukee & St. Paul Railway Company. John W. Cary. Ed. by Stuart Bruchey. LC 80-1296. (Railroads Ser.). 1981. reprint ed. lib. bdg. 38.95 (0-405-13766-4) Ayer.

Organization & Identities. Clark et al. 1994. pap. write for info. (1-86152-529-X) Thomson Learn.

Organization & Identities: Text & Readings in Organizational Behavior. Ed. by Heather Clark et al. LC 94-70255. 456p. 1994. mass mkt. 34.95 (0-412-56410-6) Chapman & Hall.

Organization & Information Systems. Ed. by Zdravko Kaltnekar & Tone Ljubic. (Production Economics & Logistics Forum Ser.: Vols. 1-2). (Illus.). 500p. 1996. text 158.00 (3-908450-15-2, Pub. by Trans T Pub) Enfield Pubs NH.

Organization & Its Ecosystem Vol. 2: A Theory of Structuring in Organizations. Charles E. Bidwell & John D. Kasarda. LC 85-7992. (Monographs in Organizational Behavior & Industrial Relations: Vol. 2). 364p. 1985. 78.50 (0-89232-500-3) Jai Pr.

Organization & Leadership: A Parish Assessment & Formation Workbook. Maureen Gallagher. (Follow Me! Ser.). 1998. pap. 9.95 (1-881307-16-6, B7166) Natl Pastoral LC.

Organization & Leadership in the Local Church. Kenneth Kilinski & Jerry Wolfert. 1973. 17.95 (0-310-26810-9, 18132) Zondervan.

Organization & Management. Ullrich. Date not set. pap. 58.00 (0-324-00607-1) Sth-Wstrn College.

Organization & Management. Patrick Williams & Bonnie Best. (C). 1993. pap. text 21.50 (0-07-070417-1) McGraw.

Organization & Management: A Contingency Approach. Gary Dessler. (Illus.). 1976. 22.95 (0-685-03884-X) P-H.

Organization & Management: A Systems & Contingency Approach. 4th ed. Fremont Kast & James Rosenzweig. (Management Ser.). 720p. (C). 1985. text 40.00 (0-07-033443-9) McGraw.

Organization & Management: Theory & Practice. Catheryn Seckler-Hudson. LC 55-11617. 324p. 1955. 22.00 (0-686-58000-1); fiche 9.00 (0-685-03092-X) Lomond.

Organization & Management in China, 1979-1990. Ed. by Oded Shenkar. LC 91-6387. 188p. (C). (gr. 13). 1991. text 66.95 (0-87332-818-3) M E Sharpe.

Organization & Management of Advanced Manufacturing. Ed. by Gavriel Salvendy & Waldemar Karwowski. LC 92-36731. 426p. 1994. 130.00 (0-471-55508-8) Wiley.

Organization & Management of Construction. Ed. by D. A. Langford. (Illus.). 1768p. (C). 1996. 375.00 (0-419-21030-X, E & FN Spon) Routledge.

Organization & Management of Construction: Managing Construction Information. Ed. by David Langford. 358p. (C). (gr. 13). 1997. 160.00 (0-419-22250-2) Routledge.

Organization & Management of Construction: Managing the Construction Enterprise. Ed. by David Langford. 430p. (C). (gr. 13). 1996. 160.00 (0-419-22230-8) Routledge.

Organization & Management of Construction: Shaping Theory & Practice. Ed. by David Langford. 908p. (C). (gr. 13). 1996. 160.00 (0-419-22240-5) Routledge.

Organization & Management of Public Transport Projects: Proceedings of a Conference Sponsored by the Public Transport Committee of the Urban Transportation Division. Ed. by George V. Marks & Bhagirath Lall. 32p. 1985. 34.00 (0-87262-458-7) Am Soc Civil Eng.

Organization & Management of the Truck Dealership. F. R. Gaylord. 1979. 15.50 (0-685-07173-1) Northwood Univ.

Organization & Management Structure of American Furniture Companies. Christopher Tonelli. LC 98-24196. (Illus.). 57p. 1998. spiral bd. 450.00 (0-921577-81-8) AKTRIN.

Organization & Management Theory & Practice. Gathorne V. Butler. 464p. (C). 1986. 90.00 (0-13-641754-X, Pub. by IPM Hse) St Mut.

Organization & Methods for Endocrinology Laboratory Services: Report on a Working Group. (Euro Reports & Studies Ser.: No. 51). 18p. 1981. pap. text 4.00 (92-890-1217-X) World Health.

Organization & Objectives of State Teachers' Associations. John E. Granrud. LC 70-176817. (Columbia University. Teachers College. Contributions to Education Ser.: No. 234). reprint ed. 37.50 (0-404-55234-X) AMS Pr.

Organization & Operation of the Small Business Administration. U. S. House of Representatives Select Committee on. Ed. by Stuart Bruchey & Vincent P. Carosso. LC 78-19005. (Small Business Enterprise in America Ser.). (Illus.). 1979. reprint ed. lib. bdg. 31.95 (0-405-11501-6) Ayer.

Organization & Planning of Adult Education. Theodore J. Kowalski. LC 87-34014. 218p. (C). 1988. pap. text 21.95 (0-88706-799-9) State U NY Pr.

Organization & Procedures of the Federal Regulatory Commissions & Agencies & Their Effect on Small Business, 2 vols. U. S. House of Representatives Select Committee on. Ed. by Stuart Bruchey & Vincent P. Carosso. LC 78-19001. (Small Business Enterprise in America Ser.). (Illus.). 1979. reprint ed. lib. bdg. 78.95 (0-405-11497-4) Ayer.

Organization & Promotion of World Peace: A Study of Universal-Regional Relationships. R. A. Akindale. LC 74-79987. 223p. reprint ed. pap. 69.20 (0-608-09958-9, 202642000049) Bks Demand.

Organization & Replication of Viral DNA. Albert S. Kaplan. 208p. 1982. 124.95 (0-8493-6405-1, QR394) CRC Pr.

Organization & Staffing of Corporate Public Affairs. Seymour Lusterman. (Report: No. 894). (Illus.). v, 31p. (Orig.). 1987. pap. text 60.00 (0-8237-0336-3) Conference Bd.

Organization & Structure of FAO Including Titles of Staff. Incl. No. 15. 88p. 1974. pap. 7.50 (Terminology Bulletins Ser.). write for info. (0-318-62068-5) Bernan Associates.

Organization & Structure of FAO Including Titles of Staff. (Terminology Bulletins: No. 15, Rev. 3). 100p. 1978. pap. 7.50 (0-686-72312-0, F2055) Bernan Associates.

Organization & Structure of FAO Including Titles of Staff. 6th rev. ed. (Terminology Bulletins Ser.: No. 15). 205p. 1992. pap. 25.00 (92-5-003170-X, F170X) Bernan Associates.

Organization & Technology in Capitalist Development. William Lazonick. LC 92-2430. (Economists of the Twentieth Century Ser.). 320p. 1992. 110.00 (1-85278-742-2) E Elgar.

Organization & Time Management. rev. ed. Herman Ohme. Ed. by Jean Ohme. (Illus.). 48p. 1989. pap. 5.00 (0-936047-03-8) CA Educ Plan.

Organization, Authority & Programs of State Fish & Wildlife Agencies. 40p. 1987. 10.00 (0-318-23695-8) Wildlife Mgmt.

***Organization Behavior: Lecture Guide.** Kreitner. 1999. 12.50 (0-07-238602-9) McGraw.

***Organization Behavior & Change: Managing Human Resources for Organizational Effectiveness.** 11th ed. Ed. by Thomas C. Head. 653p. 1998. pap. text 26.90 (0-87563-827-9) Stipes.

***Organization Behavior 2000-2001.** Fred H. Maidment. (Annual Editions Ser.). 240p. (C). 1999. pap. 16.56 (0-07-233376-6) McGrw-H Hghr Educ.

***Organization Charts.** 3rd ed. Gale Group Staff. 260p. 1999. 155.00 (0-7876-2452-7) Gale.

Organization, Class & Control. Stewart Clegg & David Dunkerley. 1980. pap. 20.00 (0-7100-0435-4, Routledge Thoemms) Routledge.

Organization Communication. Andrews. (C). 1996. text, suppl. ed. 49.16 (0-395-78242-2) HM.

Organization Communication Profile. John Eric Adair. (C). 1985. pap. 75.00 (0-85171-083-2, Pub. by IPM Hse) St Mut.

Organization Design. Jay R. Galbraith. LC 76-10421. (Illus.). (C). 1977. text 68.00 (0-201-02558-2) Addison-Wesley.

An Asterisk (*) at the beginning of an entry indicates that the title is appearing for the first time.

Organization Design: A Practical Guide. Margaret R. Davis & David A. Weckler. Ed. by Janis Paris. LC 95-83228. 151p. (Orig.). 1996. pap. 12.95 (*1-56052-388-3*) Crisp Pubns.

Organization Development: A Practitioner's Tool Kit. Lenny Ralphs. LC 97-83114. (Fifty-Minute Ser.). 114p. (Orig.). 1996. pap. 10.95 (*1-56052-359-X*) Crisp Pubns.

Organization Development: Behavior Science Interventions for Organization Improvement. 6th ed. French & Bell. 343p. 1998. pap. 48.00 (*0-13-242231-X*) P-H.

Organization Development: Ideas & Issues. Robert T. Golembiewski. 250p. 1989. 34.95 (*0-88738-245-2*) Transaction Pubs.

Organization Development: Interventions & Strategies. S. Ramnarayan et al. LC 97-41760. 1998. write for info. (*0-7619-9223-5*); pap. write for info. (*0-7619-9224-3*) Sage.

Organization Development: Principles & Practices. fac. ed. Wyatt W. Burke. LC 81-83134. (Illus.). 416p. 1982. reprint ed. pap. 129.00 (*0-7837-8214-4*, 204791400008) Bks Demand.

Organization Development: Strategies for Changing Environments. Robert D. Smither et al. LC 95-21446. 656p. (C). 1997. 92.00 (*0-673-99418-X*) Addson-Wesley Educ.

Organization Development & Change. 6th ed. Thomas G. Cummings & Christopher G. Worley. LC 96-50329. 725p. 1997. mass mkt. 87.95 (*0-314-20149-1*) S-W Pub.

***Organization Development & Change.** 7th ed. Thomas G. Cummings & Christopher G. Worley. LC 00-41276. 2001. write for info. (*0-324-01987-4*) Sth-Wstrn College.

Organization Development & Change. 5th ed. Thomas Cummings & Christopher G. Worley. Ed. by Fenton. LC 92-41858. (SWC-Management). 600p. (C). 1993. mass mkt. 64.25 (*0-314-01253-2*) West Pub.

Organization Development & Transformation: Managing Effective Change. 4th ed. Ed. by Wendell L. French et al. LC 93-38865. 624p. (C). 1994. text 48.50 (*0-256-10339-9*, Irwn McGrw-H) McGrw-H Hghr Educ.

Organization, Development & Transformation: Managing Effective Change. 4th ed. Robert A. Zawacki et al. 560p. 1994. pap. write for info. (*0-256-10449-2*, Irwn McGrw-H) McGrw-H Hghr Educ.

***Organization Development & Transformation: Managing Effective Change.** 5th ed. Wendell L. French. LC 99-27906. 1999. pap. text 49.00 (*0-256-24116-3*, Irwn McGrw-H) McGrw-H Hghr Educ.

Organization Development Annual Vol. II: Contracting for Organization Development Consultation. Ed. & Intro. by Conrad N. Jackson. LC 94-78641. 107p. 1994. reprint ed. pap. 20.00 (*1-56286-011-9*) Am Soc Train & Devel.

Organization Development Annual Vol. III: Diagnosing Client Organizations. Ed. by Conrad N. Jackson & Michael R. Manning. LC 94-78642. 133p. 1994. reprint ed. pap. 20.00 (*1-56286-012-7*) Am Soc Train & Devel.

Organization Development Classics: A History of the Future of Change. Donald F. Van Eynde. LC 97-25665. 1997. 34.95 (*0-7879-0866-5*) Jossey-Bass.

Organization Development for Academic Libraries: An Evaluation of the Management Review & Analysis Program, 28. Edward R. Johnson & Stuart H. Mann. LC 79-8289. (Contributions in Librarianship & Information Science Ser.: No. 28). (Illus.). 199p. 1980. 49.95 (*0-313-21373-9*, JMA/) Greenwood.

Organization Development for Operating Managers. Michael E. McGill. LC 76-50051. 189p. reprint ed. pap. 58.60 (*0-608-12404-4*, 205213900040) Bks Demand.

Organization Development in Health Care Settings: A Special Issue of Consultation: An International Journal. Ed. by R. Wayne Boss. 76p. 1988. pap. 12.95 (*0-89885-425-3*, Kluwer Acad Hman Sci) Kluwer Academic.

Organization Development in Public Administration, Vol. 5. Ed. by William B. Eddy & Robert Golembieski. (Public Administration & Public Policy: A Comprehensive Publication Program Ser.). (Illus.). 280p. 1978. text 125.00 (*0-8247-6667-9*) Dekker.

Organization Development in Public Administration: Public Sector Applications of Organization Development Technology, Pt. 2. Ed. by Robert T. Golembiewski & William B. Eddy. LC 77-27574. (Public Administration & Public Policy Ser.: Vol. 5). 336p. reprint ed. pap. 104.20 (*0-608-14175-5*, 202150700022) Bks Demand.

Organization Development in the Mining Industry: Theory & Practice. James Gavin. LC 85-24400. 210p. 1986. 55.00 (*0-275-92061-5*, C2061, Praeger Pubs) Greenwood.

Organization Dissonance & Change. Jan Koolhaas. LC 81-16368. (Illus.). 226p. reprint ed. pap. 70.10 (*0-8357-4561-9*, 203746300008) Bks Demand.

***Organization Ethics in Health Care.** Ed. by Edward M. Spencer et al. LC 99-31080. (Illus.). 256p. 2000. text 39.95 (*0-19-512980-6*) OUP.

Organization Executive Course, 9 vols. Incl. Vol. 0. Basic Staff. 1991. 175.00 (*0-88404-591-9*); Vol. 1. Hubbard Communications Office Division One of the Organization Executive Course. 1991. 175.00 (*0-88404-592-7*); Vol. 2. Dissemination Division Two of the Organization Executive Course. 1991. 175.00 (*0-88404-593-5*); Vol. 3. Treasury Division Three of the Organization Executive Course. 1991. 175.00 (*0-88404-594-3*); Vol. 4. Technical Division Four of the Organization Executive Course. 1991. 175.00 (*0-88404-595-1*); Vol. 5. Qualifications Division Five of the Organization Executive Course. 1991. 175.00 (*0-88404-596-X*); Vol. 6. Distribution Division Six of the Organization Executive Course. 1991. 175.00 (*0-88404-597-8*); Vol. 7. Executive Division Seven: The Executive's Handbook of the Organization Executive Course. 1991. 175.00 (*0-88404-598-6*); 1991. write for info. (*0-318-55378-3*) Bridge Pubns Inc.

Organization Executive Course. L. Ron Hubbard. 840.00 (*0-686-30798-4*) Church Scient NY.

Organization Family: Work & Family Linkages in the U. S. Military. Ed. by Gary L. Bowen & Dennis K. Orthner. LC 88-32440. 218p. 1989. 55.00 (*0-275-92813-6*, C2813, Praeger Pubs) Greenwood.

Organization for Change: A Systems Analysis of Family Planning in Rural India. B. D. Misra et al. (Michigan Papers on South & Southeast Asia: No. 21). xxiv, 444p. (C). 1982. 5.00 (*0-89148-019-6*) Ctr S&SE Asian.

Organization for Manufacturing. Donald L. Bowman. Ed. by Ivan R. Vernon. LC 79-110568. (Manufacturing Management Ser.: No. 2). (Illus.). 262p. reprint ed. pap. 81.30 (*0-8357-6482-6*, 203585300097) Bks Demand.

Organization for National Security. Victor H. Krulak. (Illus.). 141p. 1983. pap. 8.00 (*0-913187-00-3*) U S Strat Inst.

Organization for Program Management. Cyril Davies et al. LC 78-27660. 252p. reprint ed. pap. 78.20 (*0-608-17664-8*, 203037800069) Bks Demand.

Organization for Radiation Protection: The Operations of the ICRP & NCRP, 1928. DOE Technical Information Center Staff & Lauriston S. Taylor. LC 79-607999. 2062p. 1979. lib. bdg. 59.75 (*0-87079-116-8*, DOE/TIC-10124) DOE.

Organization for the Care of Handicapped Children, National, State, Local. White House Conference on Child Health & Protectio. LC 74-1715. (Children & Youth Ser.: Vol. 14). 390p. 1974. reprint ed. 34.95 (*0-405-05990-6*) Ayer.

Organization Game. 2nd ed. Robert H. Miles & W. Alan Randolph. (C). 1985. text 25.00 (*0-673-16654-6*) Addson-Wesley Educ.

Organization Game: A Simulation Participant's Manual. 3rd ed. W. Alan Randolph et al. 120p. (C). 1997. pap. text 42.00 (*0-673-46861-5*) Addson-Wesley Educ.

Organization Game: An Interactive Buisness Game Where You Make or Break the Company. Craig R. Hickman. 372p. (C). 1995. pap. text 12.95 (*0-13-231812-1*) P-H.

Organization in a Changing Environment: Unionization of Welfare Employees. Russell K. Schutt. LC 84-26787. (SUNY Series in the Sociology of Work). 243p. (C). 1985. text 64.50 (*0-88706-044-7*); pap. text 21.95 (*0-88706-045-5*) State U NY Pr.

Organization in the Spinal Cord. A. G. Brown. (Illus.). 260p. 1983. 157.00 (*0-387-10549-2*) Spr-Verlag.

Organization in Vision. G. Kanizsa. LC 79-11851. 267p. 1979. 38.50 (*0-275-90373-7*, C0373, Praeger Pubs) Greenwood.

Organization in Vision: Essays on Gestalt Perception. Gaetano Kanizsa. 1979. 38.95 (*0-03-049071-5*) Holt R&W.

Organization Learning & Knowledge Technologies in a Dynamic Environment. W. R. Baets. LC 98-21025. xiv, 275 p. 1998. 89.95 (*0-7923-8170-X*) Kluwer Academic.

Organization Man, Organization Woman: Calling, Leadership, & Culture. Shirley J. Roels et al. Ed. by Rex Matthews. LC 97-19990. (Studies in Christian Ethics & Economic Life: No. 4). 176p. 1997. pap. 17.95 (*0-687-00964-2*) Abingdon.

Organization Management. 4th ed. Kast. 1985. teacher ed. 37.50 (*0-07-033444-7*) McGraw.

Organization, Management, & Expert Systems: Models of Automated Reasoning. Ed. by Michael Masuch. (Studies in Organization: No. 23). x, 249p. (C). 1990. lib. bdg. 54.95 (*3-11-011942-0*) De Gruyter.

Organization, Management, & Tactics of Social Research. Ed. by Richard O'Toole. LC 71-138996. 330p. 1971. reprint ed. pap. 102.30 (*0-608-05345-7*, 206505000012) Bks Demand.

Organization Matters: Agency Problems in Health & Education in Latin America. Ed. by William D. Savedoff. (Inter-American Development Bank Ser.). 300p. 1998. pap. 21.50 (*1-886938-19-9*) IADB.

Organization Modeling: Innovative Architectures of the 21st Century. Joseph Morabito et al. 300p. (C). 1999. 48.00 (*0-13-257552-3*) P-H.

Organization of a Bank: Study of the Nature of Organization & the Fusion Process. Chris Argyris. Ed. by Leon Stein. LC 77-70479. 1977. reprint ed. lib. bdg. 29.95 (*0-405-10153-8*) Ayer.

Organization of a Seasonal Range of Knitted Fabrics. R. W. Herbert. 1979. 85.00 (*0-7855-7210-4*) St Mut.

Organization of Academic Work. 2nd ed. Peter Blau. LC 94-7215. 312p. (C). 1994. pap. 24.95 (*1-56000-756-7*) Transaction Pubs.

Organization of Action: A New Synthesis. Charles R. Gallistel. 432p. 1980. 49.95 (*0-89859-009-4*) L Erlbaum Assocs.

Organization of Afferents from the Brain Stem Nuclei to the Cerebellar Cortex in the Cat. B. Brown Gold. (Advances in Anatomy, Embryology & Cell Biology Ser.: Vol. 62). (Illus.). 100p. 1980. 37.00 (*0-387-09960-3*) Spr-Verlag.

Organization of African Unity: An Analysis of Its Role. Gino J. Naldi. 328p. 1989. text 130.00 (*0-7201-2006-3*) Continuum.

Organization of African Unity: An Analysis of Its Role 2nd ed. Gino J. Naldi. LC 99-15336. 2000. 99.95 (*0-7201-2243-0*) Mansell Pub.

Organization of African Unity: An Annotated Bibliography. Compiled by Gordon Harris. LC 93-42579. (International Organizations Ser.: Vol. 7). 135p. (C). 1994. text 59.95 (*1-56000-153-4*) Transaction Pubs.

Organization of African Unity after Thirty Years. Ed. by Yassin El-Ayouty. LC 93-24830. 232p. 1993. 55.00 (*0-275-94439-5*, C4439, Praeger Pubs) Greenwood.

Organization of American Culture, 1700-1900: Private Institutions, Elites, & the Origins of American Nationality. Peter Hall. (Education & Socialization in American History Ser.). 304p. (C). 1984. pap. text 20.00 (*0-8147-3425-1*) NYU Pr.

Organization of American States. Ann V. Thomas & A. J. Thomas. LC 63-9754. 542p. reprint ed. pap. 168.10 (*0-8357-8978-0*, 203343000086) Bks Demand.

Organization of American States. 2nd ed. O. Carlos Stoetzer. LC 92-1752. 464p. 1993. 69.50 (*0-275-93633-3*, C3633, Praeger Pubs) Greenwood.

Organization of American States, Vol. 11. David Sheinin. (International Organizations Ser.). 240p. (C). 1995. text 69.95 (*1-56000-243-3*) Transaction Pubs.

Organization of American States & Human Rights, 1960-1967. Inter-American Commission on Human Rights. (ENG & SPA.). 1972. 15.00 (*0-8270-2520-3*) OAS.

Organization of American States Directory & Chiefs of State & Cabinet Minister of the American Republics. 157p. 1974. ring bd. 10.00 (*0-8270-1763-4*) OAS.

***Organization of American States in its 50th Year Overview of a Regional Commitment.** Christopher R. Thomas. LC 98-46229. 1998. write for info. (*0-8270-3876-3*) OAS.

Organization of an Alaskan Expedition. Boyd N. Everett, Jr. LC 84-80852. 112p. (Orig.). 1984. pap. 9.95 (*0-918803-00-4*) Gorak Bks.

Organization of Arab Petroleum Exporting Countries: History, Policies & Prospects, 40. Mary A. Tetreault. LC 80-24722. (Contributions in Economics & Economic History Ser.: No. 40). 215p. 1981. 62.95 (*0-313-22558-3*, TAP/, Greenwood Pr) Greenwood.

***Organization of Attachment Relationships: Maturation, Culture & Context.** Ed. by Patricia McKinsey Crittenden & Angelika Hartl Claussen. (Illus.). 432p. (C). 2000. 69.95 (*0-521-58002-1*) Cambridge U Pr.

Organization of Behavior in Face-to-Face Interaction. Ed. by Adam Kendon et al. (World Anthropology Ser.). xiv, 510p. 1975. 51.55 (*90-279-7569-8*) Mouton.

Organization of Biochemical Systems: Structural & Regulatory Aspects. Ed. by Boris I. Kurganov & A. E. Lyubarev. 245p. (C). 1994. lib. bdg. 105.00 (*1-56072-092-1*) Nova Sci Pubs.

Organization of Cell Metabolism. Ed. by G. Rickey Welch & James S. Clegg. LC 87-2468. (NATO ASI Series A, Life Sciences: Vol. 127). 380p. 1987. 105.00 (*0-306-42554-8*, Plenum Trade) Perseus Pubng.

Organization of Communities. J. Gee & Paul S. Giller. 1987. pap. 59.95 (*0-632-02143-8*) Blackwell Sci.

Organization of Competitive Wholesale Power Markets & Spot Price Pools. Ed. by Dianna Gordon. LC 97-168770. (Restructure? What Then? Ser.). 52p. 1996. 15.00 (*1-55516-812-4*, 4121) Natl Conf State Legis.

Organization of Corporate Crime: An Inquiry into the Dynamics of Antitrust Violation. Katherine M. Jamieson. LC 93-48821. (Studies in Crime, Law, & Justice: Vol. 11). 114p. (C). 1994. text 52.00 (*0-8039-5199-X*); pap. text 21.95 (*0-8039-5200-7*) Sage.

Organization of Courts. Roscoe Pound. LC 79-12700. (Judicial Administration Ser.). 322p. 1980. reprint ed. lib. bdg. 35.00 (*0-313-21998-2*, POOC, Greenwood Pr) Greenwood.

Organization of Debt into Currency: And Other Papers. Charles H. Carroll. Ed. by Edward C. Simmons. LC 70-172207. (Right Wing Individualist Tradition in America Ser.). 1972. reprint ed. 33.95 (*0-405-00418-4*) Ayer.

Organization of Economic Innovation in Europe. Ed. by Alfonso Gambardella & Franco Malerba. LC 98-39111. (Illus.). 416p. (C). 1999. 74.95 (*0-521-64303-1*) Cambridge U Pr.

Organization of Emergency Medical Care. Ed. by Leonid B. Shapiro & I. A. Ostrovskii. LC 75-24873. 175p. reprint ed. pap. 54.30 (*0-608-30506-5*, 202075400018) Bks Demand.

Organization of Europe. David M. Harrison. LC 94-28757. 224p. (C). 1995. pap. 17.99 (*0-415-11071-8*, C0044) Thomson Learn.

Organization of Health Workers & Labor Conflict. Ed. by Samuel Wolfe. LC 77-94410. (Policy, Politics, Health & Medicine Ser.: Vol. 2). 161p. 1978. pap. 22.00 (*0-89503-009-8*) Baywood Pub.

Organization of Hope. Howell S. Baum. LC 96-5109. (SUNY Series in Urban Public Policy). 336p. (C). 1997. text 75.50 (*0-7914-3193-2*); pap. text 25.95 (*0-7914-3194-0*) State U NY Pr.

Organization of Hypocrisy: Talk, Decisions & Actions in Organizations. Nils Brunsson. Tr. by Nancy Adler. LC 89-14785. 250p. 1989. reprint ed. pap. 77.50 (*0-608-03997-7*, 206473400011) Bks Demand.

Organization of Illegal Markets: An Economic Analysis. 43p. (C). 1993. pap. text 20.00 (*1-56806-883-2*) DIANE Pub.

Organization of Illegal Markets: An Economic Analysis. 1991. lib. bdg. 65.95 (*0-8490-4800-1*) Gordon Pr.

Organization of Industry. George J. Stigler. LC 82-20013. viii, 336p. 1983. pap. text 14.95 (*0-226-77432-5*) U Ch Pr.

Organization of Industry. 2nd ed. Shughart. LC \\. 1997. 77.95 (*0-87393-414-8*) Dame Pubns.

Organization of Industry. 2nd ed. Thomas C. Banfield. LC 68-55469. (Reprints of Economic Classics Ser.). 1973. reprint ed. 35.00 (*0-678-00964-3*) Kelley.

Organization of Information. Arlene G. Taylor. LC 98-53625. (Library & Information Science Text Ser.). 275p. 1999. 50.00 (*1-56308-493-7*); pap. 40.00 (*1-56308-498-8*) Libs Unl.

Organization of Innovation: East-West Perspectives. Ed. by John Child & Paul Bate. (Studies in Organization: No. 11). 238p. (C). 1987. lib. bdg. 84.65 (*3-11-010700-7*) De Gruyter.

Organization of Inquiry. Gordon Tullock. LC 66-26026. 242p. reprint ed. pap. 75.10 (*0-608-12824-4*, 202346100033) Bks Demand.

Organization of Inquiry. Gordon Tullock. 242p. (C). 1987. reprint ed. pap. text 23.00 (*0-8191-5775-9*) Univ Pub Assocs.

Organization of Interest: A Thesis Presented to Department of Philosophy, Harvard University, for the Degree Doctor of Philosophy, 1917. Henry N. Wieman & Cedric L. Hepler. LC 84-22202. (Monograph Series of the Foundation for Philosophy of Creativity). 196p. (Orig.). 1985. lib. bdg. 49.50 (*0-8191-4378-2*) U Pr of Amer.

Organization of Interests: Incentives & the Internal Dynamics of Political Interests Groups. Terry M. Moe. LC 79-13238. 1980. lib. bdg. 14.95 (*0-226-53351-4*) U Ch Pr.

Organization of Interests: Incentives & the Internal Dynamics of Political Interests Groups. Terry M. Moe. 292p. 1988. pap. text 19.95 (*0-226-53353-0*, Midway Reprint) U Ch Pr.

Organization of International Business: Studies in the Economics of Trust, Vol. 2. Mark Casson. LC 94-48432. (Illus.). 224p. 1995. 85.00 (*1-85898-230-8*) E Elgar.

Organization of Interoceanic Trade in European Expansion, 1450-1800. Ed. by Pieter Emmer & Femme Gaastra. LC 96-3759. (Expanding World Ser.: Vol. 13). 456p. 1996. text 147.95 (*0-86078-505-X*, Pub. by Variorum) Ashgate Pub Co.

Organization of Islamic Conference: Theory & Practice of Pan-Islamic Cooperation. Noor A. Baba. (C). 1995. write for info. (*81-207-1617-5*) Sterling Pubs.

Organization of Knowledge in Modern America, 1860-1920. Ed. by Alexandra Oleson & John Voss. LC 78-20521. 503p. reprint ed. pap. 156.00 (*0-608-15187-4*, 202737500055) Bks Demand.

Organization of Language. Janice Moulton & George M. Robinson. LC 80-19052. 400p. 1981. pap. text 29.95 (*0-521-29851-2*) Cambridge U Pr.

Organization of Local & Intermediate Health Administrations: Proceedings of the WHO Expert Committee, Geneva, 1971. WHO Staff. (Technical Reports: No. 499). 1972. pap. text 3.00 (*92-4-120499-0*, 1100499) World Health.

Organization of Manpower Training in International Package Deals: Temporary Organizations for Transfer of Technology. A. Hadjikhani. 230p. (Orig.). 1985. pap. text 36.00 (*91-554-1752-3*) Coronet Bks.

Organization of Mental Health Services: Societal & Community Systems. Ed. by W. Richard Scott & Bruce L. Black. LC 85-19582. (Sage Focus Editions Ser.: No. 78). 311p. 1986. reprint ed. pap. 96.50 (*0-608-01498-2*, 205954200001) Bks Demand.

Organization of Mental Health Services in Developing Countries: Proceedings of the WHO Expert Committee on Mental Health, 16th, Geneva, 1974. WHO Staff. (Technical Reports: No. 564). 1975. pap. text 6.00 (*92-4-120564-4*, 1100564) World Health.

Organization of North American Prehistoric Chipped Stone Tool Technologies. Ed. by Philip J. Carr. LC 94-1508. (Archaeological Ser.: No. 7). (Illus.). vi, 136p. 1994. pap. 18.50 (*1-879621-14-2*); lib. bdg. 30.00 (*1-879621-15-0*) Intl Mono Prehstry.

Organization of Perception & Action. D. G. Mackay. (Cognitive Science Ser.). (Illus.). xxii, 233p. 1987. 60.95 (*0-387-96509-2*) Spr-Verlag.

Organization of Political Parties in Southern Europe. Ed. by Piero Ignazi & Colette Ysmal. LC 97-40888. 328p. 1998. 69.50 (*0-275-95612-1*, Praeger Pubs) Greenwood.

Organization of Power: Aspects of Bureaucracy in the Ancient Near East. 2nd rev. ed. Ed. by Mcguire Gibson & R. D. Biggs. LC 91-60541. (Studies in Ancient Oriental Civilization: No. 46). (Illus.). xii, 168p. 1991. pap. text 25.00 (*0-918986-72-9*) Orient Inst.

Organization of Programming Languages. B. Teufel. (Illus.). xi, 208p. 1991. 44.85 (*0-387-82315-8*) Spr-Verlag.

Organization of Prokaryotic Cell Membrane, Vol. I. Ed. by Bijan K. Ghosh. 272p. 1981. 119.00 (*0-8493-5653-9*, QR77, CRC Reprint) Franklin.

Organization of Prokaryotic Cell Membrane, Vol. II. Ed. by Bijan K. Ghosh. 224p. 1981. 127.00 (*0-8493-5654-7*, CRC Reprint) Franklin.

Organization of Prokaryotic Cell Membranes, Vol. III. Ed. by Bijan K. Ghosh. 280p. 1985. 159.00 (*0-8493-5659-8*, QR77, CRC Reprint) Franklin.

Organization of Public Education in South Carolina. MIchael Richardson. 408p. 1992. pap., per. 35.95 (*0-8403-8190-5*) Kendall-Hunt.

Organization of Public Health Care: An Economic Analysis of the Swedish Health Care System. Clas Rehnberg. (Linkoping Studies in Arts & Sciences: No. 58). 172p. (Orig.). 1991. pap. 55.00 (*91-7870-728-5*) Coronet Bks.

Organization of Reduction Data Flow & Control Flow Systems. Werner Kluge. LC 92-3192. (Computer Systems Ser.). (Illus.). 512p. 1992. pap. text 55.00 (*0-262-61081-7*) MIT Pr.

Organization of School Health Programs. 2nd ed. Kerry J. Redican et al. 496p. (C). 1992. text. write for info. (*0-697-13129-7*) Brown & Benchmark.

Organization of Science & Technology at the Watershed: The Academic & Industrial Perspective. Ed. by G. Reger & U. Schmoch. LC 96-185352. (Technology, Innovation, & Policy Ser.: Vol. 3). (Illus.). xii, 426p. 1996. pap. 95.00 (*3-7908-0910-1*) Spr-Verlag.

O

An Asterisk (*) at the beginning of an entry indicates that the title is appearing for the first time.

Organization of Space in Developing Countries. Edgar A. Johnson. LC 74-122216. 470p. 1970. reprint ed. pap. 145.70 (*0-7837-2280-X*, 205736800004) Bks Demand.

Organization of the Bacterial Genome. Ed. by Robert L. Charlebois. LC 99-32407. (Illus.). 378p. 1999. 79.95 (*1-55581-151-5*) ASM Pr.

Organization of the Boot & Shoe Industry in Massachusetts Before 1875. Blanche E. Hazard. LC 67-29512. (Library of Early American Business & Industry: No. 18). (Illus.). x, 293p. 1969. reprint ed. 45.00 (*0-678-00457-9*) Kelley.

Organization of the British Army in the American Revolution. Edward E. Curtis. (BCL1 - U. S. History Ser.). 223p. 1991. reprint ed. lib. bdg. 79.00 (*0-7812-6118-X*) Rprt Serv.

Organization of the British Army in the American Revolution. Edward E. Curtis. LC 72-131679. 223p. 1972. reprint ed. 39.00 (*0-403-00566-3*) Scholarly.

Organization of the Cerebral Cortex. Ed. by Francis O. Schmitt et al. (Illus.). 614p. 1981. 80.00 (*0-262-19189-X*) MIT Pr.

Organization of the Cytoplasm, Pt. 1. Cold Spring Harbor Symposia on Quantitative Biolog. LC 34-8174. (Cold Spring Harbor Symposia on Quantitative Biology Ser.: Vol. 46). (Illus.). 513p. 1982. pap. 159.10 (*0-7837-8984-X*, 204976400001) Bks Demand.

Organization of the Cytoplasm, Pt. 2. Cold Spring Harbor Symposia on Quantitative Biolog. LC 34-8174. (Cold Spring Harbor Symposia on Quantitative Biology Ser.: Vol. 46). (Illus.). 566p. 1982. pap. 175.50 (*0-7837-8985-8*, 204976400002) Bks Demand.

Organization of the Cytoplasm, Vol. 1. Ed. by Stephen Rothman & E. Edward Bittar. Date not set. 128.50 (*0-7623-0395-6*) Jai Pr.

***Organization of the Early Christian Churches: Eight Lectures Delivered before the University of Oxford, in the Year 1880.** Edwin M. A. Hatch. 246p. 1999. pap. 20.00 (*1-57910-245-X*) Wipf & Stock.

Organization of the Early Vertebrate Embryo: Proceedings of a NATO ASI Held in Spetsai, Greece, September 16-26, 1994. Ed. by Nikolas Zagris et al. (NATO ASI Ser.: Vol. A279). (Illus.). 344p. (C). 1995. text 110.00 (*0-306-45132-8*) Plenum.

Organization of the English Customs System, 1696-1786. Elizabeth E. Hoon. LC 68-17686. (Reprints of Economic Classics Ser.). xxxii, 322p. 1968. reprint ed. 39.50 (*0-678-05604-8*) Kelley.

***Organization of the Future.** Frances Hesselbein. 288p. 2000. pap. 18.00 (*0-7879-5203-6*) Jossey-Bass.

Organization of the Future: New Visions, Strategies & Practices for the Next Era. Frances Hesselbein. LC 96-45826. (Drucker Foundation Future Ser.: Vol. 2). 1997. mass mkt. 25.00 (*0-7879-0303-5*) Jossey-Bass.

Organization of the German Air Force High Command & Higher Echelon Headquarters within the German Air Force. Bruno Maass. (USAF Historical Studies: No. 190). 247p. 1955. reprint ed. pap. text 38.95 (*0-89126-151-6*) MA-AH Pub.

Organization of the Government under the Constitution. David M. Matteson. LC 72-118201. (American Constitutional & Legal History Ser). 1970. reprint ed. lib. bdg. 47.50 (*0-306-71935-5*) Da Capo.

Organization of the Required Physical Education for Women in State Universities. Georgia B. Johnson. LC 73-176913. (Columbia University. Teachers College. Contributions to Education Ser.: No. 253). reprint ed. 37.50 (*0-404-55253-6*) AMS Pr.

Organization of the School Year: A Comparative Study. UNESCO Staff. (Education Studies & Documents: No. 43). 1974. reprint ed. pap. 25.00 (*0-8115-1367-X*) Periodicals Srv.

Organization of the United Methodist Church: Revised 1997-2000 Edition. rev. ed. Jack M. Tuell. LC 98-115235. 160p. 1997. pap. 9.95 (*0-687-05665-9*) Abingdon.

Organization of the United Methodist Church: 1993 Edition. rev. ed. Jack M. Tuell. LC 92-37620. 176p. 1993. pap. 8.95 (*0-687-29448-7*) Abingdon.

Organization of Trade in Food Products: Three Early Food & Agriculture Organizations Proposals. United Nations Food & Agriculture Organization Staff. (World Food Supply Ser.). 1976. 19.95 (*0-405-07799-8*, 19106) Ayer.

Organization of Transnational Corporations. Ed. by Gunnar Hedlund. (Readings in Transnational Corporations Ser.). 396p. 1996. pap. 29.95 (*0-415-14108-7*) Routledge.

Organization of Work: A Comparative Analysis of Production Among Nonindustrial Peoples. Stanley H. Udy, Jr. LC 59-9547. (Comparative Studies). 198p. 1967. pap. 10.00 (*0-87536-314-8*) HRAFP.

Organization, Performance & Equity: Perspectives on the Japanese Economy. Ed. by Ryuzo Sato. LC 96-32770. (Current Issues Series in Japan-U. S. Business & Economics). 464p. (C). 1996. lib. bdg. 157.50 (*0-7923-9772-X*) Kluwer Academic.

Organization, Policy & Practice in the Human Services. Bernard Neugeboren. 319p. 1991. pap. 19.95 (*1-56024-159-4*) Haworth Pr.

***Organization, Power & Change.** Finn Borum. LC 95-211656. 1999. 29.00 (*87-16-13248-3*) Mksgaard.

Organization Research on Health Institutions. Ed. by Basil S. Georgopoulos. LC 72-619554. 432p. reprint ed. pap. 134.00 (*0-7837-5248-2*, 204498400005) Bks Demand.

Organization Skills see Career Skills Library

Organization-Society Nexus: A Critical Review of Models & Metaphors, 67. Ronald G. Corwin. LC 87-7552. (Contributions in Sociology Ser.: No. 67). 358p. 1987. 55.00 (*0-313-25582-2*, CLU/, Greenwood Pr) Greenwood.

Organization Space: Landscapes, Houses & Highways in America. Keller Easterling. LC 99-40790. (Illus.). 224p. 1999. 35.00 (*0-262-05061-7*) MIT Pr.

Organization Staffing & Work Adjustment. Aharon Tziner. LC 90-32404. 224p. 1990. 55.00 (*0-275-93499-3*, C3499, Praeger Pubs) Greenwood.

Organization Strategy: A Marketing Approach. E. Raymond Corey & Steven H. Star. LC 79-132151. (Illus.). 447p. reprint ed. pap. 138.60 (*0-8357-6307-2*, 203558000096) Bks Demand.

Organization Systems. GMBATU Staff. (Open Learning for Supervisory Management Ser.). 1986. pap. text 19.50 (*0-08-034052-0*, Pergamon Pr) Elsevier.

Organization Teams: Building Continuous Quality Improvement Facilitator's Guide. Peter Mears. (Illus.). 120p. 1994. teacher ed., per. 57.95 (*1-884015-44-1*) St Lucie Pr.

Organization, the Effect on Large Corporations. Barry C. Harris. LC 83-3589. (Research in Business Economics & Public Policy Ser.: No. 2). 137p. reprint ed. pap. 42.50 (*0-8357-1435-7*, 207038700088) Bks Demand.

Organization Theories & Public Administration. Charles R. Davis. LC 95-53000. 160p. 1996. 52.95 (*0-275-95576-1*, Praeger Pubs) Greenwood.

Organization Theory. 2nd ed. Gortner. (Public Administration Ser.). 1997. text 41.95 (*0-534-26610-X*) Wadsworth Pub.

Organization Theory: A Public Perspective. 2nd ed. Harold F. Gortner et al. LC 96-76555. 448p. (C). 1996. pap. text 66.50 (*0-03-019387-7*, Pub. by Harcourt Coll Pubs) Harcourt.

Organization Theory: A Strategic Approach. V. K. Narayanan & Raghu Nath. LC 92-31180. 608p. (C). 1993. text 71.35 (*0-256-08778-4*, Irwn McGrw-H) McGrw-H Hghr Educ.

Organization Theory: Cases & Applications. 3rd ed. Richard L. Daft & Mark P. Sharfman. Ed. by Fenton. 379p. (C). 1990. pap. text 35.50 (*0-314-66769-5*) West Pub.

Organization Theory: From Chester Barnard to the Present & Beyond. Ed. by Oliver E. Williamson. (Illus.). 288p. 1995. pap. text 19.95 (*0-19-509830-7*) OUP.

Organization Theory: Modern, Symbolic, & Postmodern Perspective. Mary J. Hatch. LC 97-170130. (Illus.). 416p. (C). 1997. pap. text 42.95 (*0-19-877490-7*) OUP.

Organization Theory: Readings & Cases. Penny L. Wright & Stephen P. Robbins. (Illus.). 320p. (C). 1987. pap. text 15.00 (*0-13-641119-3*) P-H.

Organization Theory: Selected Readings. 4th ed. Ed. by D. S. Pugh. 608p. 1997. reprint ed. pap. 24.95 (*0-14-025024-7*, Pub. by Pnguin Bks Ltd) Trafalgar.

Organization Theory: Structures, Designs, & Applications. 3rd ed. Stephens P. Robbins. 560p. 1990. 84.00 (*0-13-642471-6*) P-H.

Organization Theory & Class Analysis: New Approaches & New Issues. Ed. by Stewart R. Clegg. (Studies in Organization: No. 17). xiv, 529p. (C). 1990. lib. bdg. 74.95 (*3-11-012003-8*) De Gruyter.

Organization Theory & Design. 7th ed. Daft. (SWC-General Business). 2000. pap. text 85.95 (*0-324-02100-3*) Thomson Learn.

Organization Theory & Management. Lynch. (Public Administration & Public Policy Ser.: Vol. 20). (Illus.). 280p. 1983. text 75.00 (*0-8247-7021-8*) Dekker.

Organization Theory & Public Organizations. Florence Heffron. 384p. (C). 1988. 50.00 (*0-13-642208-X*) P-H.

Organization Theory & Technocratic Consciousness: Rationality, Ideology, & Quality of Work. Mats Alvesson. (Studies in Organization: No. 8). x, 286p. 1987. lib. bdg. 74.95 (*3-11-010574-8*) De Gruyter.

Organization Theory for Long-Range Planning. Eric Rhenman. LC 72-5724. 222p. reprint ed. pap. 68.90 (*0-8357-6246-7*, 203423600089) Bks Demand.

Organization Theory for Public Administration. Michael M. Harmon & Richard T. Mayer. LC 94-74920. (Illus.). 436p. (C). text 39.95 (*0-9639874-0-2*) Chatelaine.

Organization Theory for Public Administration. 2nd rev. ed. Michael M. Harmon & Richard T. Mayer. LC 94-74920. (Illus.). 436p. (C). 1996. pap. text 25.95 (*0-9639874-9-6*) Chatelaine.

Organization, Training, Search & Recovery Procedures for the Underwater Unit. 2nd ed. Thomas R. Lewis. LC 79-83668. (Illus.). 54p. 1979. 6.95 (*0-918616-04-2*) Northern Mich.

Organization Transformation Theorists & Practitioners: Profiles & Themes. Beverly R. Fletcher. LC 90-34367. 184p. 1990. 59.95 (*0-275-93584-1*, C3584, Praeger Pubs) Greenwood.

Organization Transitions & Innovation Design. Peter Clark & Ken Starkey. 252p. 1993. 49.95 (*0-86187-646-6*, Pub. by P P Pubs) Cassell & Continuum.

***Organization 2005: Four Steps Companies Must Take to be Successful in Dynamic Times.** Leslie Bendaly. Ed. by Lori Cates. LC 99-39270. (Illus.). 192p. 1999. pap. 14.95 (*1-57112-102-1*, P1021) Park Ave.

Organization Without Authority: Dilemmas of Social Control in Free Schools. Ann Swidler. LC 79-16575. 213p. reprint ed. pap. 66.10 (*0-7837-2339-3*, 205742700004) Bks Demand.

Organization Woman: Building a Career - An Inside Report Surveys by Arthur Highman. Edith L. Highman. 204p. 1985. 20.95 (*0-89885-237-4*, Kluwer Acad Hman Sci) Kluwer Academic.

Organizational Acceptance of Human Resource Management Innovcation: Strategic Lessons for HRM. Ellen E. Kossek. LC 88-32143. 175p. 1989. 52.95 (*0-89930-374-9*, KOZ, Quorum Bks) Greenwood.

***Organizational Achievement & Failure in Information Technology Management.** Ed. by Mehdi Khosrowpour. LC 99-57182. (Illus.). 2650p. (C). 2000. pap. 165.00 (*1-878289-83-7*) Idea Group Pub.

Organizational Adaptation by Public Libraries, 47. Snunith Shoham. LC 83-22738. (Contributions in Librarianship & Information Science Ser.: No. 47). (Illus.). 163p. 1984. 49.95 (*0-313-24406-5*, SOA/, Greenwood Pr) Greenwood.

Organizational Alternatives in Soviet-Type Economics. Nicolas Spulber. LC 78-68378. 300p. reprint ed. pap. 85.50 (*0-608-17529-3*, 2030622) Bks Demand.

Organizational Analysis As Deconstructive Practice. Robert K. Chia. LC 96-18620. (Studies in Organization: Vol. 77). xiv, 245p. (C). 1996. text 59.95 (*3-11-014559-6*) De Gruyter.

Organizational & Budgetary Slack. Ahmed Riahi-Blekaoui. LC 93-30990. 144p. 1994. 55.00 (*0-89930-884-8*, Quorum Bks) Greenwood.

***Organizational & Communicational 1997.** Ed. by White & Chapman Staff. 1999. pap. text 24.15 (*0-536-00203-7*) P-H.

Organizational & Community Response to Domestic Abuse & Homelessness. Marjorie Bard. LC 93-47244. (Children of Poverty Ser.). 192p. 1994. text 20.00 (*0-8153-1597-X*) Garland.

Organizational & Human Resources Sourcebook. 2nd ed. Douglas B. Gutknecht & Janet R. Miller. LC 89-20352. (Illus.). 426p. (Orig.). (C). 1990. pap. text 46.00 (*0-8191-7623-0*); lib. bdg. 74.00 (*0-8191-7622-2*) U Pr of Amer.

Organizational & Interorganizational Dynamics: An Annotated Bibliography. Jacob Peters & Doreen L. Smith. LC 92-10773. (Library of Sociology: Vol. 25). 288p. 1992. text 20.00 (*0-8240-5304-4*, SS641) Garland.

***Organizational & Social Perspectives on Information Technology: IFIP TC8 WG8.2 International Working Conference on the Social & Organizational Perspective on Research & Practice in Information Technology, June 9-11, 2000, Aalborg, Denmark.** IFIP TC8 WG8.2 International Working Conference on New Information Technologies in Organizational Processes: Field Studies & Theoretical Reflections on the Future of Work Staff et al. LC 00-35236. 2000. write for info. (*0-7923-7836-9*) Kluwer Academic.

Organizational Approach to Environmental Control. Sherry Sabbarwal. 1990. 24.00 (*81-7024-316-5*, Pub. by Ashish Pub Hse) S Asia.

Organizational Approaches to Strategy. Ed. by Glenn R. Carroll & David Vogel. 224p. 1988. text 26.95 (*0-88730-267-X*, HarpBusn) HarpInfo.

Organizational Architecture: A Managerial Economics Approach. James Brickley et al. 448p. (C). 1995. text 21.95 (*0-256-20224-9*, Irwn McGrw-H) McGrw-H Hghr Educ.

Organizational Architecture: Designs for Changing Organizations. David A. Nadler et al. LC 92-4071. (Management Ser.). 304p. 1992. text 34.95 (*1-55542-443-0*) Jossey-Bass.

Organizational Arrangements to Facilitate Global Management of Fisheries. Edward L. Miles. LC 73-20844. (Resources for the Future, Program of International Studies of Fishery Arrangements, Paper: No. 4). 35p. reprint ed. pap. 30.00 (*0-608-12542-3*, 202380800034) Bks Demand.

Organizational Aspects of Health Communication Campaigns. Ed. by Thomas E. Backer & Everett M. Rogers. (Illus.). 280p. (C). 1993. text 49.95 (*0-8039-4997-9*); pap. text 24.00 (*0-8039-4998-7*) Sage.

Organizational Aspects of Health Informatics: Managing Technological Change. Nancy M. Lorenzi & Robert T. Riley. LC 94-19977. (Computers in Health Care Ser.). (Illus.). 312p. 1994. 54.00 (*0-387-94226-2*) Spr-Verlag.

***Organizational Behavior.** (Person Oriented Fit Ser.). 1998. write for info. (*0-13-011011-6*) P-H.

Organizational Behavior. Baack. LC 97-67106. 1998. 78.95 (*0-87393-636-1*) Dame Pubns.

Organizational Behavior. David J. Cherrington. 650p. 1989. teacher ed. write for info. (*0-318-63902-5*, H1960-7); write for info. (*0-318-63903-3*, H1961-5) P-H.

Organizational Behavior. Kemery. 602p. (C). 1998. pap. text 44.00 (*0-536-01204-0*) S&S Trade.

Organizational Behavior. John Martin. 768p. 1998. pap. 24.95 (*1-86152-180-4*) Thomson Learn.

***Organizational Behavior** Steven Lattimore McShane & Mary A. Young Von Glinow. LC 99-37328. 2000. write for info. (*0-256-22896-5*, Irwn McGrw-H) McGrw-H Hghr Educ.

Organizational Behavior. Dennis R. Middlemist. Date not set. pap. text, student ed. 20.00 (*0-314-79361-5*) West Pub.

Organizational Behavior. Peck. 588p. (C). 1998. pap. text 59.75 (*0-536-01490-6*) Pearson Custom.

Organizational Behavior. Jack Rudman. (ACT Proficiency Examination Program (PEP) Ser.: Vol. 19). 43.95 (*0-8373-5569-9*) Nat Learn.

Organizational Behavior. Jack Rudman. (Dantes Subject Standardized Tests (DANTES) Ser.: Vol. 49). 43.95 (*0-8373-6549-X*) Nat Learn.

Organizational Behavior. Jack Rudman. (ACT Proficiency Examination Program Ser.: PEP-19). 1994. pap. 23.95 (*0-8373-5519-2*) Nat Learn.

Organizational Behavior. Jack Rudman. (Dantes Subject Standardized Tests (DANTES) Ser.: Vol. DANTES-49). 1994. pap. 23.95 (*0-8373-6649-6*) Nat Learn.

Organizational Behavior. Verser. (C). 1999. text 65.00 (*0-03-098286-3*, Pub. by Harcourt Coll Pubs) Harcourt.

Organizational Behavior. 2nd ed. Champoux. Date not set. pap. 58.00 (*0-324-00605-5*) Sth-Wstrn College.

Organizational Behavior. 2nd ed. Gary Johns. (C). 1988. text 57.00 (*0-673-18418-8*) Addson-Wesley Educ.

Organizational Behavior. 2nd ed. Kemery. 575p. (C). 1998. pap. text 44.00 (*0-536-01248-2*) Pearson Custom.

***Organizational Behavior.** 2nd ed. John Martin. 2000. pap. write for info. (*1-86152-583-4*) Thomson Learn.

Organizational Behavior. 2nd ed. Gregory Moorhead & Ricky W. Griffin. LC 88-81348. 1989. teacher ed. 3.16 (*0-318-36899-4*); student ed. write for info. (*0-318-63322-1*); trans. write for info. (*0-318-63323-X*) HM.

Organizational Behavior. 2nd ed. Denis D. Umstot. Date not set. pap. text, teacher ed. write for info. (*0-314-79015-2*) West Pub.

***Organizational Behavior.** 3rd ed. Nelson & Quick. 2000. pap., student ed. 13.00 (*0-324-07176-0*) Sth-Wstrn College.

Organizational Behavior. 3rd ed. Robert P. Vecchio. 752p. (C). 1994. text 92.00 (*0-03-098917-5*) Dryden Pr.

Organizational Behavior. 3rd ed. Robert P. Vecchio et al. 480p. (C). 1994. pap. text, teacher ed. 49.75 incl. trans. (*0-03-098918-3*) Dryden Pr.

Organizational Behavior. 4th ed. Gary Johns. LC 95-5562. (Illus.). 631p. (C). 1997. 98.00 (*0-673-99562-3*) Addson-Wesley Educ.

Organizational Behavior. 4th ed. Kreitner. 1997. pap., student ed. 84.06 (*0-07-561638-6*) McGraw.

Organizational Behavior. 4th ed. Kreitner. 1999. write for info. (*0-07-236833-0*) McGraw.

Organizational Behavior. 4th ed. Robert Kreitner & Angelo Kinicki. LC 97-5076. 672p. (C). 1997. text 67.95 (*0-256-22512-5*, Irwn McGrw-H) McGrw-H Hghr Educ.

Organizational Behavior. 5th ed. (C). 1997. text 11.00 (*0-673-55597-6*, GoodYrBooks) Addson-Wesley Educ.

Organizational Behavior. 5th ed. (C). 1997. text 11.00 (*0-673-55208-X*) S&S Trade.

***Organizational Behavior.** 5th ed. (C). 2000. text 0.00 (*0-321-02109-6*) HEPC Inc.

Organizational Behavior. 6th ed. J. Stewart Black. Ed. by Richard M. Steers. (C). 1998. text. write for info. (*0-321-01404-9*) Addson-Wesley Educ.

Organizational Behavior. 6th ed. Don Hellriegel et al. Ed. by Fenton & Craig. 779p. (C). 1991. text 64.75 (*0-314-92684-4*) West Pub.

Organizational Behavior. 6th ed. David A. Kolb & Joyce S. Osland. LC 94-42475. 672p. 1994. pap. 66.00 (*0-13-151010-X*) P-H.

***Organizational Behavior.** 6th ed. Dorothy Marcic. (SWC-General Business Ser.). 2000. pap. 34.00 (*0-324-04850-5*) Thomson Learn.

Organizational Behavior. 7th ed. Hellriegel & Slocum. (GI - Organizational Behavior Ser.). (C). 1994. mass mkt., student ed. 20.95 (*0-314-05870-2*) S-W Pub.

Organizational Behavior. 7th ed. Fred Luthans. 1995. write for info. incl. VHS (*0-07-911790-2*) McGraw.

***Organizational Behavior.** 7th ed. John R. Schermerhorn et al. LC 99-41455. (Series in Management). 585p. (C). 1999. text 98.95 (*0-471-33287-9*) Wiley.

Organizational Behavior. 8th ed. Hellriegel. (GI - Organizational Behavior Ser.). (C). 1997. pap., student ed. 18.95 (*0-538-88027-9*) S-W Pub.

Organizational Behavior. 8th ed. Hellriegel et al. LC 97-13217. (GI - Organizational Behavior Ser.). (C). 1997. text 79.95 (*0-538-88024-4*) S-W Pub.

Organizational Behavior. 8th ed. Fred Luthans. LC 97-15805. 704p. 1997. 84.06 (*0-07-039184-X*) McGraw.

Organizational Behavior. 9th ed. Hellriegel. (Management Ser.). 2000. pap. write for info. (*0-324-00977-1*) Sth-Wstrn College.

Organizational Behavior. 9th ed. Hellriegel & Slocum. (SWC-Management Ser.). 2000. pap., student ed. 15.50 (*0-324-00980-1*) Thomson Learn.

Organizational Behavior. 9th ed. Luthans. 2001. 65.74 (*0-07-231288-2*) McGraw.

Organizational Behavior. 12th ed. Thompson. 2000. 65.74 (*0-07-231499-0*) McGraw.

Organizational Behavior, Test bank. 3rd ed. Robert P. Vecchio & William Bommer. 488p. (C). 1994. pap. text 40.00 (*0-03-010739-3*) Dryden Pr.

***Organizational Behavior: A Critical Text.** Knights & Wilmott. 2001. pap. 19.99 (*1-86152-359-9*) Thomson Learn.

Organizational Behavior: A Diagnostic Approach. 6th ed. Judith R. Gordon. LC 98-10500. 640p. 1998. 87.00 (*0-13-922824-1*) P-H.

Organizational Behavior: A Management Challenge. 2nd ed. Gregory B. Northcraft & Margaret A. Neale. LC 97-72827. 726p. (C). 1994. text 68.00 (*0-03-074611-6*) Dryden Pr.

Organizational Behavior: A Manager's View. R. Bruce McAfee & Paul J. Champagne. LC 86-24745. (Illus.). 489p. (C). 1987. pap. text, teacher ed. write for info. (*0-314-35226-0*) West Pub.

Organizational Behavior: An Applied Perspective. Andrew J. Durbin. LC 96-42472. (GI - Organizational Behavior Ser.). 1996. pap. 49.95 (*0-538-85776-5*) S-W Pub.

***Organizational Behavior: An Experiential Approach.** 7th ed. Joyce S. Osland et al. LC 00-27648. 592p. 2000. pap. 61.33 (*0-13-017610-9*) P-H.

***Organizational Behavior: Concepts Controversial & Application.** 9th ed. (C). 2000. write for info. (*0-13-018042-4*) P-H.

***Organizational Behavior: Concepts, Controversies, Applications.** 9th ed. Stephen P. Robbins. LC 99-49448. 750p. 2000. 96.00 (*0-13-016680-4*) P-H.

Organizational Behavior: Concepts, Controversies, Applications, Vol. 2. 8th ed. Stephens P. Robbins. LC 97-5407. 675p. 1997. 90.67 (*0-13-857459-6*, Pub. by P-H) S&S Trade.

Organizational Behavior: Concepts, Controversies, Applications D-Cart. 8th ed. Robbins. 1998. 77.00 (*0-13-011088-4*) P-H.

***Organizational Behavior: Core Concepts.** 4th ed. Robert P. Vecchio. LC 99-63504. (Illus.). 2000. write for info. (*0-03-025856-1*) Holt R&W.

Organizational Behavior: Course Study Guide. R. Currier. 208p. 1994. spiral bd. Price not set. (*0-933195-08-7*) CA College Health Sci.

An Asterisk (*) at the beginning of an entry indicates that the title is appearing for the first time.

Organizational Behavior: Exams, 4 vols. Gregory Moorhead. (C). Date not set. text. write for info. (*0-395-71681-0*) HM.

Organizational Behavior: Experiential Approach 126p. (C). 1996. text 21.40 (*0-536-59491-0*) Pearson Custom.

***Organizational Behavior: Foundations, Realitie & Challenges.** 3rd ed. Debra L. Nelson & James C. Quick. LC 99-23693. 641p. 1999. pap. 86.95 (*0-324-00637-3*) Thomson Learn.

Organizational Behavior: Foundations, Realities & Challenges. Debra L. Nelson & James C. Quick. Ed. by Leyh. LC 93-27987. 650p. (C). 1993. pap. 68.50 (*0-314-02640-1*) West Pub.

Organizational Behavior: Foundations, Realities & Challenges. 2nd ed. Debra L. Nelson & James C. Quick. 1997. teacher ed. write for info. (*0-314-20558-6*) West Pub.

Organizational Behavior: Foundations, Realities & Challenges. 2nd ed. Debra L. Nelson & James C. Quick. LC 96-35205. 1997. mass mkt. 61.25 (*0-314-20567-5*) West Pub.

Organizational Behavior: Foundations, Realities & Challenges. 2nd ed. Debra L. Nelson & James C. Quick. LC 96-35205. 650p. 1997. mass mkt. 70.25 (*0-314-09626-4*) West Pub.

Organizational Behavior: Human Behavior at Work. 9th ed. John W. Newstrom & Keith Davis. LC 92-22097. (Series in Management). (C). 1993. text 78.25 (*0-07-015603-4*) McGraw.

Organizational Behavior: Human Behavior at Work. 10th ed. John W. Newstrom & Keith Kavis. LC 96-25597. 624p. (C). 1996. 84.38 (*0-07-046504-5*) McGraw.

Organizational Behavior: Individuals, Groups, & Processes. Joseph E. Champoux. Ed. by Horan. LC 95-16979. 668p. (C). 1996. mass mkt. 95.95 (*0-314-06242-4*) West Pub.

Organizational Behavior: Lecturers Resource Manual. John Martin. (ITBP Textbooks Ser.). 768p. 1998. pap., teacher ed. 19.99 (*1-86152-163-4*) Thomson Learn.

Organizational Behavior: Managing People & Organizations, 4 vols. 4th ed. Gregory Moorhead & Ricky W. Griffin. 736p. (C). 1994. text 72.76 (*0-395-70898-2*) HM.

Organizational Behavior: Managing People & Organizations, 4 vols. 4th ed. Gregory Moorhead & Ricky W. Griffin. (C). 1995. text, teacher ed. 11.96 (*0-395-71233-5*) HM.

Organizational Behavior: MGMT 237. Kathryn Hegar. (C). 1994. pap. text 26.41 (*1-56870-106-3*) RonJon Pub.

Organizational Behavior: Securing Competitive Advantage. 3rd ed. John A. Wagner. LC 97-14578. 444p. 1997. 74.00 (*0-13-859810-X*) P-H.

Organizational Behavior: Study Guide. Baack. LC \\. 1998. student ed. 24.95 (*0-87393-664-7*) Dame Pubns.

Organizational Behavior: The Essentials. Debra L. Nelson & James C. Quick. LC 95-23788. 375p. (C). 1995. mass mkt. 46.95 (*0-314-06436-2*) West Pub.

Organizational Behavior: The Management of Individual & Organizational Performance. 2nd ed. David J. Cherrington. LC 93-33568. 784p. (C). 1993. text 50.00 (*0-205-15550-2*) Allyn.

Organizational Behavior: The Person-Organization Fit. Afsaneh Nahavandi & Ali R. Malekzadeh. LC 98-21488. 609p. 1998. 96.00 (*0-13-285982-3*) P-H.

Organizational Behavior: The State of the Science. Ed. by Jerald Greenberg. (Applied Psychology Ser.). 312p. 1994. pap. 29.95 (*0-8058-1215-6*); text 69.95 (*0-8058-1214-8*) L Erlbaum Assocs.

Organizational Behavior: Update Edition. 6th ed. John R. Schermerhorn et al. 656p. 1997. text 97.95 (*0-471-24651-4*) Wiley.

Organizational Behavior & Change: Managing Diversity, Cross-Cultural Dynamics & Ethics. Joseph W. Weiss. 375p. (C). 1995. mass mkt. 68.95 (*0-314-06929-1*) West Pub.

***Organizational Behavior & Change: Managing Diversity, Cross-cultural Dynamics & Ethics.** 2nd ed. Joseph W. Weiss. LC 00-38800. 2000. 66.95 (*0-324-02709-5*) Sth-Wstrn College.

Organizational Behavior & Management. 3rd ed. John M. Invancevich & Michael T. Matteson. LC 92-17938. 816p. (C). 1992. teacher ed. write for info. (*0-256-11032-8*, Irwn McGrw-H) McGrw-H Hghr Educ.

Organizational Behavior & Management. 4th ed. John M. Ivancevich & Michael T. Matteson. LC 95-12638. 672p. (C). 1995. text 67.95 (*0-256-16209-3*, Irwn McGrw-H) McGrw-H Hghr Educ.

Organizational Behavior & Management. 5th ed. John M. Ivancevich & Michael T. Matteson. LC 98-23635. 704p. 1998. 84.06 (*0-256-26906-8*) McGraw.

Organizational Behavior & Management. 5th ed. Kreitner. LC 99-86384. 2000. 65.74 (*0-07-231500-8*) McGraw.

Organizational Behavior & Performance. Ed. by Szilagyi. (C). 1995. text. write for info. (*0-321-01402-2*) Addson-Wesley Educ.

Organizational Behavior & Public Management. 3rd ed. Michael L. Vasu et al. LC 97-52353. (Public Administration & Public Policy Ser.). (Illus.). 424p. 1998. text 150.00 (*0-8247-0135-6*) Dekker.

Organizational Behavior & the Psychology of Unions. Julian Barling et al. (Industrial-Organizational Psychology Ser.). (Illus.). 264p. 1992. text 70.00 (*0-19-507336-3*) OUP.

Organizational Behavior Casebook: Cases & Concepts in Organizational Behavior. Alan Thomas. 256p. 1996. pap. 20.99 (*0-415-11851-4*) Thomson Learn.

Organizational Behavior Casebook: Cases & Concepts in Organizational Behavior. Alan Thomas. 256p. 1997. pap., teacher ed. 61.95 (*1-86152-013-1*) Thomson Learn.

Organizational Behavior: Experiences & Cases. 4/e. 4th ed. Dorothy Marcic. LC 95-140273. (SWC-Management). 459p. (C). 1995. pap. 34.25 (*0-314-04596-1*) West Pub.

Organizational Behavior in Chinese Society. Ed. by Sidney L. Greenblatt et al. LC 80-26728. 274p. 1981. 69.50 (*0-275-90638-8*, C0638, Praeger Pubs) Greenwood.

Organizational Behavior in Education. 6th ed. Robert G. Owens. LC 97-23120. 368p. 1997. 71.33 (*0-205-26909-5*) P-H.

***Organizational Behavior in Education: Instructional Leadership & School Reform.** 7th ed. Robert G. Owens. 368p. 2000. 71.33 (*0-205-32198-4*) Allyn.

Organizational Behavior in Insurance, 2 vols. George A. White et al. LC 92-71749. (C). 1992. pap. 41.00 (*0-89462-068-1*, 4502/4503) IIA.

Organizational Behavior in Schools & School Districts. Samuel B. Bacharach. LC 81-5138. 532p. 1981. 45.50 (*0-275-90579-9*, C0579, Praeger Pubs) Greenwood.

Organizational Behavior in the Marine Corps: Three Interpretations. Frank Marutollo. LC 89-70913. 232p. 1990. 59.95 (*0-275-93493-4*, C3493, Greenwood Pr) Greenwood.

Organizational Behavior, International. 2nd ed. Robert Kreitner & Angelo Kinicki. (C). 1991. text, student ed. 32.50 (*0-256-11394-7*, Irwn McGrw-H) McGrw-H Hghr Educ.

Organizational Behavior Lecture Notes. Rowland Baughman. 64p. (C). 1993. student ed. 15.63 (*1-56870-059-8*) RonJon Pub.

Organizational Behavior Management & Developmental Disabilities Services: Accomplishments & Future Directions. Ed. by Dennis H. Reid. LC 98-39134. 258p. 1998. 49.95 (*0-7890-0662-6*) Haworth Pr.

Organizational Behavior Management & Statistical Process Control: Theory, Technology & Research. Ed. by Thomas C. Mawhinney. LC 87-32520. (Journal of Organizational Behavior Management: Vol. 9, No. 1). (Illus.). 159p. 1988. text 49.95 (*0-86656-751-8*) Haworth Pr.

***Organizational Behavior 1.** 2nd ed. Ed. by Kemery. 536p. 1999. pap. text 47.00 (*0-536-02695-5*) P-H.

Organizational Behavior Reader. 6th ed. Ed. by David A. Kolb et al. LC 94-47064. 560p. (C). 1995. pap. 60.00 (*0-13-186487-4*) P-H.

***Organizational Behavior 2.** 2nd ed. Ed. by Kemery. 558p. 1999. pap. text 48.00 (*0-536-02696-3*) S&S Trade.

Organizational Behavior, 6E. 6th ed. John R. Schermerhorn et al. LC 96-35434. (Wiley Series in Management). 624p. 1996. text 97.95 (*0-471-15416-4*) Wiley.

Organizational Behavior 7e. Don Hellriegel et al. LC 94-32601. (SWC-Management). 848p. (C). 1995. pap. 68.50 (*0-314-04472-8*) West Pub.

***Organizational Behaviour.** Martin. (Illus.). 608p. 1999. mass mkt. 32.95 (*0-412-60960-6*, Chap & Hall NY) Chapman & Hall.

Organizational Behaviour. Nelson. 1994. pap., teacher ed. write for info. (*0-314-03553-2*); text. write for info. (*0-314-03498-6*) West Pub.

Organizational Behaviour. 3rd ed. Robert Kreithner & Angelo Kinicki. LC 94-19883. 605p. (C). 1994. text 67.95 (*0-256-14056-1*, Irwn McGrw-H) McGrw-H Hghr Educ.

Organizational Behaviour. 3rd annot. ed. Robert Kreithner & Angelo Kinicki. LC 94-19883. 1994. teacher ed. write for info. (*0-256-17505-5*, Irwn McGrw-H) McGrw-H Hghr Educ.

***Organizational Behaviour.** 5th ed. 2000. teacher ed. write for info. (*0-201-64383-9*) Addison-Wesley.

Organizational Behaviour. 5th ed. Jhons Saks. 640p. (C). 2000. 84.95 (*0-201-64381-2*) Addison-Wesley.

Organizational Behaviour: A Critical Introduction. Fiona Wilson. LC 99-24521. (Illus.). 288p. 2000. text 80.00 (*0-19-878256-X*) OUP.

***Organizational Behaviour: A Critical Introduction.** Fiona M. Wilson. LC 99-24521. 1999. write for info. (*0-19-878257-8*) OUP.

Organizational Behaviour: A Psychological Approach to Behaviour in the Workplace. Ita O'Donovan. (Contemporary Psychology Ser.). 192p. 1996. 75.00 (*0-7484-0358-2*); pap. 24.95 (*0-7484-0359-0*) Taylor & Francis.

Organizational Behaviour: An Introductory Text. B. Buchanan et al. 488p. (C). 1989. 220.00 (*0-7855-4621-9*, Pub. by Inst Pur & Supply) St Mut.

Organizational Behaviour: An Introductory Text. 3rd ed. Huczynski. 617p. 1997. pap. 65.00 (*0-13-207259-9*) P-H.

***Organizational Behaviour: Cbc Video Lib.** 5th ed. 2000. VHS. write for info. (*0-201-70935-X*) S&S Trade.

***Organizational Behaviour: Concepts,controversies, Applications Cdn: Cbc Phc Vid Lib Phc.** 2nd ed. 2000. text. write for info. (*0-13-014470-3*) P-H.

***Organizational Behaviour: Experimental Approach.** 7th ed. 2000. teacher ed. write for info. (*0-13-030880-3*) P-H.

Organizational Behaviour: Foundation, Realities & Challenges. 2nd ed. Nelson & Quick. 1997. 26.50 (*0-314-20566-7*) West Pub.

Organizational Behaviour: Integrated Readings. David Buchanan. 1997. pap. 28.00 (*0-13-234345-2*) P-H.

Organizational Behaviour: Text & Cases. M. Gangadhar Rao et al. 584p. 1990. text 40.00 (*81-220-0040-1*, Pub. by Konark Pubs Pvt Ltd) Advent Bks Div.

Organizational Behaviour & Change in Europe: Case Studies. Ed. by Francoise Chevalier & Michael Segalla. LC 96-190442. (Contemporary European Management Ser.: Vol. 2). 320p. 1996. 85.00 (*0-8039-7909-6*); pap. 29.95 (*0-8039-7910-X*) Sage.

Organizational Behaviour & Introductory Text. A. Buchanan et al. 488p. (C). 1985. 170.00 (*0-7855-5690-7*, Pub. by Inst Pur & Supply) St Mut.

Organizational Behaviour Casebook: Cases & Concepts in Organizational Behaviour. Ed. by Alan Thomas. 256p. 1996. pap. 69.95 (*0-415-11850-6*) Thomson Learn.

Organizational Behaviour for Hospitality Management. Roy Wood. 264p. 1993. pap. 32.95 (*0-7506-1830-2*) Buttrwrth-Heinemann.

***Organizational Behaviour in Hotels & Restaurants: An International Perspective.** Yvonne Guerrier. LC 99-13331. 256p. 1999. pap. 39.95 (*0-471-98650-X*) Wiley.

Organizational Behaviour in International Management. Terence Jackson. LC 93-242222. (BH Contemporary Business Ser.). (Illus.). 373p. 1993. reprint ed. pap. 115.70 (*0-608-07930-8*, 206790400012) Bks Demand.

Organizational Capability: Competing from the Inside Out. Dave Ulrich & Dale Lake. LC 90-31355. 352p. 1990. 39.95 (*0-471-61807-1*) Wiley.

Organizational Capability & Competitive Advantage. Ed. by William Lazonick & William Mass. LC 94-44343. (International Library of Critical Writings in Economics: Vol. 11). 672p. 1995. 265.00 (*1-85278-776-7*) E Elgar.

Organizational Capital: The Path to Higher Productivity & Well-Being. John F. Tomer. LC 87-16828. 205p. 1987. 55.00 (*0-275-92582-X*, C2582, Praeger Pubs) Greenwood.

Organizational Career Development: Benchmarks for Building a World-Class Workforce. Thomas G. Gutteridge et al. LC 93-29. (Management Ser.). 300p. 1993. text 38.95 (*1-55542-526-7*) Jossey-Bass.

Organizational Careers: Some New Perspectives. Ed. by John Van Maanen. LC 76-13537. (Wiley Series on Individuals, Groups & Organizations). 210p. reprint ed. pap. 65.10 (*0-608-30191-4*, 201489900094) Bks Demand.

Organizational Change: Sourcebook I: Cases in Organizational Development. Ed. by Bernard Lubin et al. 1979. pap. text 19.95 (*0-88390-150-1*) L Erlbaum Assocs.

Organizational Change: Sourcebook II: Cases in Conflict Management. Ed. by Leonard D. Goodstein et al. 1979. pap. text 19.95 (*0-88390-151-X*) L Erlbaum Assocs.

Organizational Change: The Political Economy of the YMCA. Mayer N. Zald. Ed. by David P. Street. LC 77-101494. (Studies of Urban Society). 1970. lib. bdg. 22.00 (*0-226-97850-8*) U Ch Pr.

Organizational Change & Development in Human Service Organizations: Administration in Social Work, Vol. 16, Nos. 3/4. Ed. by David Bergal & Hillel Schmid. LC 92-41586. (Illus.). 223p. 1993. lib. bdg. 49.95 (*1-56024-373-2*) Haworth Pr.

Organizational Change & Drug-Free Workplaces: Templates for Success. Thomas E. Backer & Kirk B. O'Hara. LC 90-23117. 208p. 1991. 59.95 (*0-89930-434-6*, BDU, Quorum Bks) Greenwood.

Organizational Change & Redesign: Ideas & Insights for Improving Performance. Ed. by George P. Huber & William H. Glick. LC 92-27456. (Illus.). 464p. 1993. text 70.00 (*0-19-507285-5*) OUP.

Organizational Change & Redesign: Ideas & Insights for Improving Performance. Ed. by George P. Huber & William H. Glick. (Illus.). 464p. 1995. pap. text 24.95 (*0-19-510115-4*) OUP.

Organizational Change & the Management of Expertise. Janette Webb & David Cleary. LC 95-131541. 208p. (C). 1993. pap. 72.95 (*0-415-09189-6*) Thomson Learn.

Organizational Change & the Third World: Designs for the Twenty-First Century. Allen Jedlicka. LC 87-13252. 150p. 1987. 55.00 (*0-275-92317-7*, C2317, Praeger Pubs) Greenwood.

Organizational Change, Evolution, Structuring & Awareness: Organizational Computing Systems. Ed. by N. Guimaraes & European Commission. LC 98-4657. (Research Reports Esprit: No. 1). 150p. 1998. pap. 24.00 (*3-540-62863-0*) Spr-Verlag.

Organizational Change in Japanese Factories. Robert M. Marsh & Hiroshi Manari. LC 88-19810. (Monographs in Organizational Behavior & Industrial Relations: Vol. 9). 313p. 1989. 78.50 (*0-89232-777-4*) Jai Pr.

Organizational Change in Post-Communist Europe: Management & Transformation in the Czech Republic. Ed Clark & Anna Soulsby. LC 98-35445. (Studies of Societies in Transition). 1998. write for info. (*0-415-20333-3*) Routledge.

***Organizational Change Processes: Theory & Methods for Research.** Marshal Scott Poole et al. (Illus.). 768p. 2001. text 45.00 (*0-19-513500-8*) OUP.

***Organizational Change Processes: Theory & Methods for Research.** Marshall Scott Poole et al. (Illus.). 400p. 2000. text 45.00 (*0-19-513198-3*) OUP.

Organizational Change Through Effective Leadership. 2nd ed. Robert H. Guest et al. 240p. (C). 1986. pap. text 49.00 (*0-13-641390-0*) P-H.

Organizational Charts & Job Descriptions for the Advancement Office. Judith Phair & Roland King. Ed. by Cathryn Dorsey. LC 99-183050. 191p. 1998. pap. 42.00 (*0-89964-330-2*, 28119) Coun Adv & Supp Ed.

Organizational Citizenship Behavior & Contextual Performance: A Special Issue of "Human Performance" Ed. by Walter C. Borman & Stephan J. Motowidlo. 120p. 1997. pap. 20.00 (*0-8058-9875-1*) L Erlbaum Assocs.

***Organizational Commitment & Conflict: Studies in Healthy Organizational Processes.** Omer Bin Sayeed. LC 99-89252. 2000. pap. write for info. (*81-7036-866-9*) Sage.

Organizational Communication. (C). 2000. text 38.67 (*0-205-29578-9*, Longwood Div) Allyn.

Organizational Communication. Peggy Yunas Byers. LC 96-24912. 382p. 1996. pap. text 50.00 (*0-205-17443-4*) Allyn.

Organizational Communication. Timothy Downs. (C). 2001. 40.00 (*0-205-26523-5*, Macmillan Coll) P-H.

Organizational Communication. Eisenberg. 1993. pap. text, teacher ed. 0.81 (*0-312-06848-4*) St Martin.

Organizational Communication. Eisenberg. 1996. pap. 51.95 (*0-312-13692-7*) St Martin.

Organizational Communication. Peter K. Manning. (Communication & Social Order Ser.). 260p. 1992. pap. text 25.95 (*0-202-30402-7*); lib. bdg. 49.95 (*0-202-30401-9*) Aldine de Gruyter.

Organizational Communication. 2nd ed. Ed. by Sherry D. Ferguson & Stewart Ferguson. 544p. 1987. 49.95 (*0-88738-164-2*); pap. 29.95 (*0-88738-699-7*) Transaction Pubs.

Organizational Communication. 3rd ed. Eisenberg. 1999. pap. text 51.95 (*0-312-20175-3*) St Martin.

Organizational Communication. 3rd ed. Gary L. Kreps. (C). 1998. text 50.25 (*0-8013-1187-X*) Longman.

***Organizational Communication.** 3rd ed. Miller. 2001. text 39.25 (*0-534-56144-6*) Thomson Learn.

Organizational Communication. 3rd ed. R. Wayne Pace & Don F. Faules. LC 93-31436. 386p. 1993. 63.00 (*0-13-643800-8*) P-H.

Organizational Communication. 6th ed. Gerald M. Goldhaber. 480p. (C). 1993. text. write for info. (*0-697-12921-7*) Brown & Benchmark.

Organizational Communication. 6th ed. Gerald M. Goldhaber. 480p. (C). 1996. per. write for info. (*0-697-37866-7*) Brown & Benchmark.

Organizational Communication: A Bibliography. Henry Voos. LC 67-63681. 259p. reprint ed. pap. 80.30 (*0-608-11139-2*, 205068400089) Bks Demand.

Organizational Communication: A Strategic Approach. 5th ed. Wells & Spinks. LC 97-67093. 1997. 65.95 (*0-87393-717-1*) Dame Pubns.

Organizational Communication: A Strategic Approach (Study Guide) 5th ed. Wells & Spinks. 1997. student ed. 24.95 (*0-87393-718-X*) Dame Pubns.

Organizational Communication: Abstracts, Analysis & Overview, 4 vols., 7. Howard H. Greenbaum et al. LC HF5718.G744. 400p. pap. 124.00 (*0-8357-8421-5*, 203468500007) Bks Demand.

Organizational Communication: Abstracts, Analysis & Overview, 4 vols., 8. Howard H. Greenbaum et al. LC HF5718.G744. 384p. pap. 119.10 (*0-8357-8422-3*, 203468500008) Bks Demand.

Organizational Communication: Abstracts, Analysis & Overview, 4 vols., 9. Howard H. Greenbaum et al. LC HF5718.G744. 383p. pap. 118.80 (*0-8357-8423-1*, 203468500009) Bks Demand.

Organizational Communication: Abstracts, Analysis & Overview, Vol. 5. Howard H. Greenbaum et al. LC HF5718.G744. 288p. reprint ed. pap. 89.30 (*0-8357-4717-4*, 203468500005) Bks Demand.

Organizational Communication: Abstracts, Analysis & Overview, 4 vols., Vol. 6. Howard H. Greenbaum et al. LC HF5718.G744. 357p. pap. 110.70 (*0-8357-8420-7*, 203468500006) Bks Demand.

Organizational Communication: Approaches & Processes. Katherine Miller. LC 94-28667. 353p. 1994. pap. 36.25 (*0-534-20790-1*) Wadsworth Pub.

Organizational Communication: Approaches & Processes. 2nd ed. Katherine Miller. LC 98-16390. 1998. pap. 56.95 (*0-534-52227-0*) Wadsworth Pub.

Organizational Communication: Challenges of Change, Diversity, & Continuity. William W. Neher. 382p. 1996. 59.00 (*0-205-15006-3*) Allyn.

Organizational Communication: Connectedness in Action. Cynthia Stohl. LC 95-2521. (Interpersonal CommTexts Ser.: Vol. 5). 176p. 1995. text 44.00 (*0-8039-3424-6*) Sage.

Organizational Communication: Connectedness in Action. Cynthia Stohl. LC 95-2521. (Interpersonal CommTexts Ser.: No. 5). 203p. 1995. pap. 21.00 (*0-8039-3425-4*) Sage.

Organizational Communication: Empowerment in a Technological Society. Patricia H. Andrews & Richard T. Herschel. 416p. (C). 1995. text 49.16 (*0-395-72800-2*); text, teacher ed. 11.96 (*0-395-72801-0*) HM.

Organizational Communication: The Essence of Effective Management. 3rd ed. Phillip V. Lewis. LC 86-5571. 345p. 1987. text 38.95 (*0-471-84131-5*) P-H.

Organizational Communication: The Process. Lea Hall. 230p. (Orig.). (C). 1991. pap. text 21.95 (*0-89641-218-0*) American Pr.

Organizational Communication: Theory & Behavior: Instructor's Manual & Test Bank. Peggy Y. Byers. (C). 1996. pap. text, teacher ed. write for info. (*0-205-26466-2*, T6466-1) Allyn.

Organizational Communication: Theory & Practice. 2nd ed. Gary L. Kreps. 331p. (C). 1990. 76.00 (*0-8013-0155-6*, 75817) Longman.

Organizational Communication: Traditional Themes & New Directions. Ed. by Robert D. McPhee & Phillip K. Tompkins. LC 85-14488. (Sage Annual Reviews of Communications Research Ser.: No. 13). 296p. 1985. reprint ed. pap. 91.80 (*0-608-01189-4*, 205948700001) Bks Demand.

Organizational Communication Abstracts '75. Raymond L. Falcione & Howard H. Greenbaum. 1976. pap. 4.90 (*0-931874-02-5*) Assn Busn Comm.

Organizational Communication Abstracts, 1974. Howard H. Greenbaum & Raymond L. Falcione. 1975. pap. 3.90 (*0-931874-01-7*) Assn Busn Comm.

Organizational Communication & Change. Ed. by Philip Salem. LC 99-36048. (Hampton Press Communication Ser.). 400p. (C). 1998. text 75.00 (*1-57273-116-8*); pap. text 28.50 (*1-57273-117-6*) Hampton Pr NJ.

Organizational Communication & Cultural Vision: Approaches for Analysis. Mary L. Mohan. LC 92-30247. (SUNY Series, Human Communication Processes). 202p. (C). 1993. text 64.50 (*0-7914-1537-6*); pap. text 21.95 (*0-7914-1538-4*) State U NY Pr.

O

Organizational Communication & Management: A Global Perspective. Ed. by Andrzej K. Kozminski & Donald P. Cushman. LC 91-47620. (SUNY Series, Human Communication Processes). 234p. (C). 1993. text 64.50 (*0-7914-1305-5*); pap. text 21.95 (*0-7914-1306-3*) State U NY Pr.

Organizational Communication Consulting: An Introductory Workbook. Bonnie Kay. 156p. 1992. pap., wbk. ed. 18.95 (*0-7872-8066-6*) Kendall-Hunt.

*__Organizational Communication for Survival.__ 224p. (C). 2000. pap. 37.00 (*0-205-31693-X*) Allyn.

Organizational Communication for Survival: Making Work, Work. Virginia P. Richmond & James C. McCroskey. 168p. (C). 1991. pap. text 38.00 (*0-13-640079-5*) P-H.

Organizational Communication Imperatives: Lessons of the Space Program. Phillip K. Tompkins. LC 92-12079. (Illus.). 248p. (C). 1993. pap. text. write for info. (*0-935732-40-3*) Roxbury Pub Co.

Organizational Communication in the Personal Context: From Interview to Retirement. Hickson. LC 97-44740. 307p. (C). 1998. 55.00 (*0-205-19775-2*) Allyn.

Organizational Communication Simulation. Van Grace. 180p. (Orig.). (C). 1994. pap. text 25.00 (*0-9643249-6-2*) Bliss-Veinotte.

Organizational Communication Simulation. 2nd ed. (C). 1996. pap. text 27.50 (*0-9643249-7-0*) Bliss-Veinotte.

Organizational Communication Structure. J. David Johnson. Ed. by Brenda Dervin. (Communication & Information Science Ser.). 240p. (C). 1993. pap. 39.50 (*1-56750-069-2*); text 73.25 (*0-89391-721-4*) Ablx Pub.

*__Organizational Communication Textlink.__ 1p. (C). 1999. pap. 17.00 (*0-536-02241-0*) Pearson Custom.

Organizational Communication 91. 2nd ed. James W. Gibson. 494p. (C). 1997. pap. 90.00 (*0-06-042315-3*) Addson-Wesley Educ.

*__Organizational Communications: Introduction to Communication & Human Relations.__ 216p. (C). 1999. 21.00 (*0-536-60256-5*) Pearson Custom.

Organizational Communiction. Eisenberg. 464p. 1996. pap. text 5.00 (*0-312-15017-2*) St Martin.

Organizational Conflict. V. Venkaiah. (C). 1991. 25.50 (*81-7141-142-8*) S Asia.

Organizational Conflict & Cooperation: A Theoretical Approach Illustrated by a Case Study from the Hungarian Construction Industry. L. Hethy. (Illus.). 218p. (C). 1988. 60.00 (*963-05-4700-7*, Pub. by Akade Kiado) St Mut.

Organizational Conflicts of Interest in Government Contracting. 174p. 1991. pap. 12.50 (*0-89707-726-1*, 539-0106, ABA Pub Contract) Amer Bar Assn.

Organizational Consultation: A Casebook. Ed. by Robert K. Conyne & James M. O'Neil. LC 92-20917. (Counseling Psychologist Casebook Ser.: Vol. 1). (Illus.). 232p. (C). 1992. 42.00 (*0-8039-4201-X*) Sage.

Organizational Consultation: A Casebook. Ed. by Robert K. Conyne & James M. O'Neil. LC 92-20917. (Counseling Psychologist Casebook Ser.: Vol. 1). 220p. 1992. reprint ed. pap. 68.20 (*0-608-07684-8*, 206777400010) Bks Demand.

Organizational Consultation: A Casebook, No. 1. Ed. by Robert K. Conyne & James M. O'Neil. LC 92-20917. (Counseling Psychologist Casebook Ser.: Vol. 1). (Illus.). 232p. (C). 1992. pap. 19.95 (*0-8039-4202-8*) Sage.

Organizational Consulting: A Gestalt Approach. Edwin C. Nevis. (Gestalt Institute of Cleveland Press Book Ser.). 225p. 1987. pap. 22.50 (*0-88163-249-X*) Analytic Pr.

*__Organizational Culture.__ Karel De Witte. 112p. 2000. pap. 39.95 (*0-86377-997-2*) Psychol Pr.

Organizational Culture. fac. ed. Ed. by Peter J. Frost et al. LC 85-2172. (Illus.). 419p. 1985. reprint ed. pap. 129.90 (*0-608-01002-2*, 206186000012) Bks Demand.

Organizational Culture & Leadership. Edgar H. Schein. LC 84-43034. (Joint Publication in the Jossey-Bass Management Series & the Jossey-Bass Social & Behavioral Science Ser.). 380p. 1985. reprint ed. pap. 117.80 (*0-7837-6505-3*, 204561700007) Bks Demand.

Organizational Culture & Leadership. 2nd ed. Edgar H. Schein. LC 92-23849. (Management-Social & Behavioral Science Ser.). 440p. 1992. text 34.45 (*1-55542-487-2*) Jossey-Bass.

Organizational Culture & Leadership. 2nd ed. Edgar H. Schein. 1996. pap. text 26.95 (*0-7879-0362-0*) Jossey-Bass.

Organizational Culture & Performance. R. K. Divedi. 330p. 1995. pap. 225.00 (*81-85880-59-X*, Pub. by Print Hse) St Mut.

Organizational Culture in the Management of Mergers. Afsaneh Nahavandi & Ali R. Malekzadeh. LC 92-44685. 200p. 1993. 55.00 (*0-89930-669-1*, NAU, Quorum Bks) Greenwood.

Organizational Culture, Rule-Governed Behavior & Organizational Behavior Management: Theoretical Foundations & Implications for Research & Practice. Ed. by Thomas C. Mawhinney. LC 92-30026. (Journal of Organizational Behavior Management: Vol. 12, No. 2). (Illus.). 137p. 1993. 39.95 (*1-56024-359-7*) Haworth Pr.

Organizational Culture, Rule-Governed Behavior & Organizational Behavior Management: Theoretical Foundations & Implications for Research & Practice. Ed. by Thomas C. Mawhinney. LC 92-30026. (Journal of Organizational Behavior Management: Vol. 12, No. 2). 137p. 1996. pap. 17.95 (*0-7890-0068-7*) Haworth Pr.

Organizational Cultures: Types & Transformations. Diana C. Pheysey. LC 92-30809. 328p. (C). 1996. pap. 25.99 (*0-415-08292-7*, A9685) Thomson Learn.

Organizational Cultures: Types & Transformations. Diana C. Pheysey. LC 92-30809. 328p. (C). (gr. 13). 1996. pap. 70.00 (*0-415-08291-9*, A9681) Thomson Learn.

Organizational Cultures in Theory & Practice. Ed. by Jesper S. Pedersen & Jesper S. Sorensen. (Illus.). 135p. 1989. text 72.95 (*0-566-07090-1*, Pub. by Avebry) Ashgate Pub Co.

Organizational Decision Making. Ed. by Zur B. Shapira. (Series on Judgment & Decision Making). (Illus.). 407p. (C). 1996. text 59.95 (*0-521-48107-4*) Cambridge U Pr.

Organizational Decision Making & Information. Mairead Browne. LC 92-42684. 272p. 1993. pap. 39.50 (*1-56750-017-X*); text 73.25 (*0-89391-870-9*) Ablx Pub.

Organizational Decision-Making under Different Economic & Political Conditions. Ed. by P. J. Drenth et al. LC 97-104977. 248p. pap. 47.00 (*0-444-85810-5*) Elsevier.

Organizational Democracy & Political Processes. Ed. by Colin Crouch & Frank A. Heller. LC 83-209112. (International Yearbook of Organizational Democracy Ser.: No. 1). (Illus.). 736p. reprint ed. pap. 200.00 (*0-608-18144-7*, 203283100081) Bks Demand.

Organizational Design. Jeffrey Pfeffer. Ed. by Kenneth D. Mackenzie. LC 77-86024. (Organizational Behavior Ser.). (Illus.). (C). 1978. pap. text 15.95 (*0-88295-453-9*) Harlan Davidson.

Organizational Design: The Organizational Audit & Analysis Technology. Kenneth D. Mackenzie. Ed. by Melvin J. Voigt. LC 85-13454. (Communication & Information Science Ser.). 304p. 1986. text 73.25 (*0-89391-348-0*) Ablx Pub.

Organizational Design: The Organizational Audit & Analysis Technology. Kenneth D. Mackenzie. 304p. 1993. pap. 39.50 (*1-56750-072-2*) Ablx Pub.

Organizational Design & Research: Approaches to Organizational Design & Methods of Organizational Research. Ed. by James D. Thompson & Victor H. Vroom. LC 70-137859. 463p. (C). reprint ed. 143.60 (*0-8357-9759-7*, 201915100010) Bks Demand.

*__Organizational Determinants of Budgetary Influence & Involvement__ Noah P. Barsky. LC 99-36250. 1999. write for info. (*0-8153-3550-4*) Garland.

Organizational Development. W. Warner Burke. (C). 1998. text 44.00 (*0-673-39018-7*) Addison-Wesley Educ.

Organizational Development. 5th ed. Cummings. Date not set. pap. text, teacher ed. write for info. (*0-314-01983-9*) West Pub.

Organizational Development: A Normative View. W. Warner Burke. LC 86-26474. 189p. (C). 1987. pap. text 26.95 (*0-201-10697-3*) Addison-Wesley.

Organizational Development: A Normative View. 2nd ed. W. Warner Burke. LC 93-14813. 240p. (C). 1993. pap. text 37.00 (*0-201-50835-4*) Addison-Wesley.

Organizational Development: Case Studies in the Printing Industry. Philip J. Sadler & Bernard Barry. LC 73-850844. 248p. reprint ed. pap. 76.90 (*0-608-11220-8*, 200455500043) Bks Demand.

Organizational Development in Health Care. R. Wayne Boss. (Organization Development Ser.). (Illus.). 150p. (C). 1989. pap. text 26.95 (*0-201-18364-1*) Addison-Wesley.

Organizational Development in the U. K., U. S. A. A Joint Evaluation. Ed. by Cary L. Cooper. LC 77-15084. 1978. text 12.00 (*0-89433-069-1*) Petrocelli.

Organizational Development Tools. Mary E. Paul. 84p. 1993. student ed. 25.00 (*1-883542-01-4*) ResourceWomen.

Organizational Diagnosis. Harry Levinson et al. LC 71-168429. (Illus.). 575p. 1976. pap. 21.00 (*0-674-64346-1*) HUP.

Organizational Diagnosis: A Workbook of Theory & Practice. Marvin R. Weisbord. LC 77-93328. (Illus.). 180p. 1978. pap. 28.00 (*0-201-08357-4*) Addison-Wesley.

Organizational Diagnosis & Assessment: Models for Bridging Theory & Practice. Michael I. Harrison & Arie Shirom. LC 98-9070. 486p. 1998. 65.00 (*0-8039-5510-3*); pap. write for info. (*0-8039-5511-1*) Sage.

Organizational Dilemmas. Robert I. McLaren. LC 81-19745. (Illus.). 140p. reprint ed. pap. 43.40 (*0-8357-4601-1*, 203753400008) Bks Demand.

Organizational Dimensions of Global Change: No Limits to Cooperation. David L. Cooperrider & Jane E. Dutton. LC 98-40069. (Human Dimensions of Global Change Ser.). 432p. 1999. 65.00 (*0-7619-1528-1*); pap. 34.95 (*0-7619-1529-X*) Sage.

Organizational Downsizing, Discrimination & Corporate Social Responsibility. Zeinab A. Karake-Shalhoub. LC 98-51668. 176p. 1999. 55.00 (*1-56720-251-9*, Quorum Bks) Greenwood.

Organizational Dynamics: Diagnosis & Intervention. John P. Kotter. 99p. (C). 1978. pap. text 37.00 (*0-201-03890-0*) Addison-Wesley.

Organizational Ecology. Michael T. Hannan & John Freeman. 384p. Date not set. pap. 21.50 (*0-674-64349-6*) HUP.

Organizational Ecology. Michael T. Hannan & John Freeman. LC 88-15470. (Illus.). 384p. 1989. 47.95 (*0-674-64348-8*) HUP.

Organizational Effectiveness. Harris et al. LC 96-42219. (Leadership & Management in Education Ser.). 1997. 103.95 (*0-335-19844-9*) OpUniv Pr.

Organizational Effectiveness. Harris et al. LC 96-42219. (Leadership & Management in Education Ser.). 1997. pap. 32.95 (*0-335-19843-0*) Taylor & Francis.

Organizational Effectiveness: Theory Research Utilization. Ed. by S. Lee Spray. LC 75-36534. 195p. reprint ed. pap. 60.50 (*0-608-13547-X*, 202545100044) Bks Demand.

Organizational Elan. Louis C. Schroeter. LC 75-113191. 192p. reprint ed. pap. 59.60 (*0-608-11088-4*, 205169700002) Bks Demand.

Organizational Engineering: A New Method of Creating High Peformance Human Structures. Gary J. Salton. (Illus.). 277p. (C). 1996. 34.95 (*0-9649369-3-3*) Prfssnl Comns.

Organizational Engineering Approach to Team Building. Gary J. Salton. 1997. spiral bd. 350.00 (*0-9649369-4-1*) Prfssnl Comns.

Organizational Entry. Ed. by Gerald R. Ferris & Kendrith M. Rowland. LC 90-4582. (Research in Personnel & Human Resources Management Ser.). 320p. 1990. pap. 25.75 (*1-55938-228-7*) Jai Pr.

Organizational Entry. 3rd ed. (C). 2001. pap. text. write for info. (*0-201-35722-4*) S&S Trade.

Organizational Environments: Ritual & Rationality. John W. Meyer & W. Richard Scott. LC 91-18467. 308p. 1992. pap. 95.50 (*0-608-07788-7*, 205266300010) Bks Demand.

Organizational Environments: Ritual & Rationality. John W. Meyer & W. Richard Scott. (Illus.). 312p. (C). 1992. 48.00 (*0-8039-4468-3*); pap. 23.50 (*0-8039-4469-1*) Sage.

Organizational Ethics & the Good Life. Edwin M. Hartman. (Ruffin Series in Business Ethics). 232p. 1996. 55.00 (*0-19-509678-9*); pap. 24.95 (*0-19-510077-8*) OUP.

*__Organizational Ethics in the Compliance Context.__ John Abbott Worthley. LC 99-28710. 370p. 1999. pap. 48.00 (*1-56793-110-3*) Health Admin Pr.

Organizational Ethnography: An Illustrative Application in the Study of Indian R & D Settings. V. Suchitra Mouly & Jayaram K. Sankaran. LC 94-33425. 180p. 1995. text 22.95 (*0-8039-9211-4*) Sage.

Organizational Evolution: New Directions. Ed. by Jitendra V. Singh. (Illus.). 360p. (C). 1990. 48.00 (*0-8039-3658-3*); pap. 23.50 (*0-8039-3659-1*) Sage.

Organizational Evolution: New Directions. Ed. by Jitendra V. Singh. LC 90-33468. (Illus.). 336p. 1990. reprint ed. pap. 104.20 (*0-608-07683-X*, 206777300010) Bks Demand.

Organizational Excellence: Achieving Excellence by Building Leaders & Improving Processes. Samuel E. Dotson & James A. Griffin. (Illus.). 370p. 1997. ring bd. 275.00 (*0-9662588-3-5*) DaySpring Lrdrship.

Organizational Form & Business Strategy in the U. S. Petroleum Industry. Michael Ollinger. LC 92-41876. 166p. (C). 1993. lib. bdg. 39.50 (*0-8191-8990-1*) U Pr of Amer.

Organizational Forms for the Closely Held Corporation. Harry J. Haynsworth, IV. 502p. 1989. ring bd. 37.25 (*0-8318-0560-9*, B560); ring bd. 57.75 incl. disk (*0-8318-0642-7*, B560/B642) Am Law Inst.

Organizational Gameboard: Winning the Game at Work in Changing Times. Barbara E. Kovach. LC 88-31070. (Illus.). 226p. 1989. pap. 27.95 (*0-87778-215-6*) Educ Tech Pubns.

Organizational Goals & Environment: Goal Setting As an Interactive Process. James D. Tompson & William J. McEwen. (Reprint Series in Social Sciences). (C). 1993. reprint ed. pap. text 5.00 (*0-8290-3038-7*, S-291) Irvington.

Organizational Guide to Telecommuting: Setting up & Running a Successful Telecommuter Program George M. Piskurich. LC 98-70650. 175 p. 1998. write for info. (*1-56286-086-0*) Am Soc Train & Devel.

Organizational Hologram: The Effective Management of Organizational Change. Kenneth D. MacKenzie. 528p. 1990. lib. bdg. 186.00 (*0-7923-9082-2*) Kluwer Academic.

Organizational Illusions. A. W. McEachern. LC 84-51382. (Illus.). 200p. 1984. 25.00 (*0-930237-00-5*); pap. 12.50 (*0-930237-01-3*) Shale Bks.

Organizational Innovation. Ed. by Jerald Hage. LC 97-45886. (History of Management Thought Ser.). 409p. 1998. text 144.95 (*1-85521-972-7*, Pub. by Ashgate Pub) Ashgate Pub Co.

Organizational Issues in High Technology Management. Ed. by Luis R. Gomez-Mejia et al. LC 90-38799. (Monographs in Organizational Behavior & Industrial Relations: Vol. 11). 303p. 1990. 78.50 (*1-55938-104-3*) Jai Pr.

Organizational Issues in Indian Agriculture. K. N. Raj. 236p. 1990. 28.00 (*0-19-562520-X*) OUP.

Organizational Justice & Human Resource Management. Robert Folger & Russell Cropanzano. LC 98-8895. (Foundations for Organizational Science Ser.). 304p. 1998. 34.00 (*0-8039-5686-X*) Sage.

Organizational Leadership. 222p. (C). 1997. 23.60 (*0-536-59783-9*) Pearson Custom.

Organizational Leadership of Human Resources: The Knowledge & the Skills, 3 pts. John M. Brion. LC 88-35766. 1989. 225.00 (*0-89232-778-2*) Jai Pr.

Organizational Leadership of Human Resources Pt. I: The Individual. John M. Brion. LC 88-35766. 415p. 1989. 86.25 (*0-89232-779-0*) Jai Pr.

Organizational Leadership of Human Resources Pt. II: The Organization. John M. Brion. LC 88-35766. 398p. 1989. 86.25 (*0-89232-780-4*) Jai Pr.

Organizational Leadership of Human Resources Pt. III: Integration. John M. Brion. LC 88-35766. 231p. 1989. 86.25 (*0-89232-781-2*) Jai Pr.

Organizational Learning. Ed. by Michael D. Cohen & Lee S. Sproull. LC 95-35478. (Organizational Science Ser.: Vol. 2). (Illus.). 432p. 1995. 69.95 (*0-8039-7088-9*); pap. 32.95 (*0-8039-7089-7*) Sage.

*__Organizational Learning: Creating, Retaining & Transferring Knowledge.__ Linda Argote. LC 98-51375. 1999. write for info. (*0-7923-8420-2*) Kluwer Academic.

*__Organizational Learning: From World Class Theories to Global Best Practices.__ David R. Schwandt & Michael J. Marquardt. LC 99-28722. 280p. 1999. boxed set 34.95 (*1-57444-259-7*) St Lucie Pr.

Organizational Learning & Competitive Advantage. Ed. by Bertrand Moingeon & Amy Edmondson. 224p. 1996. 75.00 (*0-7619-5166-0*); pap. 26.95 (*0-7619-5167-9*) Sage.

Organizational Learning & Technological Change. Ed. by C. Zucchermaglio et al. (NATO ASI F Computer & Systems Sciences Ser.: Vol. 141). 408p. 1995. 107.00 (*3-540-58917-1*) Spr-Verlag.

*__Organizational Learning & the Learning Organization.__ Ed. by Mark Easterby-Smith et al. 256p. 1998. 78.00 (*0-7619-5915-7*); pap. 27.95 (*0-7619-5916-5*) Sage.

Organizational Learning at Work: Embracing the Challenges of the New Workplace. Ed. by Editors of The Systems Thinker Newsletter. LC 98-8601. (Illus.). 142p. 1998. pap. 24.95 (*1-883823-26-9*) Pegasus Comm.

Organizational Learning Capability: Generating & Generalizing Ideas with Impact. Arthur K. Yeung et al. LC 98-3797. (Illus.). 232p. 1999. 29.95 (*0-19-510204-5*) OUP.

Organizational Learning Cycle: How We Can Learn Collectively. Nancy M. Dixon. LC 94-17076. 176p. 1994. pap. 24.95 (*0-07-707937-X*) McGraw.

Organizational Learning Cycle: How We Can Learn Collectively. 2nd ed. Nancy M. Dixon. LC 98-30675. xxiv, 240 p. 1999. 74.95 (*0-566-08058-3*) Ashgate Pub Co.

Organizational Learning in Schools. Kenneth Leithwood & Karen S. Louis. LC 98-52440. 394p. 1999. 83.00 (*90-265-1539-1*); pap. 29.00 (*90-265-1540-5*) Swets.

*__Organizational Learning, Performance & Change: An Introduction to Strategic Human Resource Development.__ Jerry W. Gilley & Ann Maycunich. 408p. 2000. text 45.00 (*0-7382-0248-7*, Pub. by Perseus Pubng) HarpC.

Organizational Learning Process: A Systems Dynamics Approach. Jac Vennix. LC 96-11166. 312p. 1996. 70.00 (*0-471-95355-5*) Wiley.

Organizational Life: Learning to Be Self-Directed. Edward Cell. LC 98-16033. 352p. (C). 1998. 62.00 (*0-7618-1112-5*); pap. 34.50 (*0-7618-1113-3*) U Pr of Amer.

Organizational Life Cycle: Issues in the Creation, Transformation, & Decline of Organizations. Ed. by John R. Kimberly et al. LC 79-92466. (Jossey-Bass Social & Behavioral Science Ser.). 516p. reprint ed. pap. 160.00 (*0-7837-0177-2*, 204047400017) Bks Demand.

Organizational Life on Television. Leah R. Vande Berg & Nick Trujillo. Ed. by Lee Thayer. LC 88-7558. (People, Communication, Organization Ser.). 320p. (C). 1989. pap. 39.50 (*0-89391-567-X*); text 78.50 (*0-89391-489-4*) Ablx Pub.

Organizational Linkages: Understanding the Productivity Paradox. National Research Council, Panel on Organizational. Ed. by Douglas H. Harris. 320p. (Orig.). 1994. text 44.95 (*0-309-04934-2*) Natl Acad Pr.

*__Organizational Literacy for Educators.__ Jason Earle & Sharon D. Kruse. LC 98-29684. (Topics in Educational Leadership Ser.). 272p. 1999. pap. 24.95 (*0-8058-2639-4*) L Erlbaum Assocs.

Organizational Maintenance Military Petroleum Pipelines, Tanks, & Related Equipment. 1991. lib. bdg. 79.95 (*0-8490-4204-6*) Gordon Pr.

*__Organizational Management Administration for Athletic Programs.__ 4th ed. Thomas Kinder. 350p. 1998. pap. 32.95 (*0-945483-80-5*) E Bowers Pub.

Organizational Marketing. Wilson. (ITBP Textbooks Ser.). 468p. 1999. pap. 19.99 (*1-86152-480-3*) Thomson Learn.

*__Organizational Mastery with Integrated Management Systems: Controlling the Dragon.__ Michael T. Noble. 500p. 2000. 79.95 (*0-471-38928-5*) Wiley.

*__Organizational Measurement Manual.__ David Wealleans. 208p. 2000. 84.95 (*0-566-08349-3*, Pub. by Ashgate Pub) Ashgate Pub Co.

Organizational Membership: Personal Development in the Workplace. Howell S. Baum. LC 89-29799. (SUNY Series in the Sociology of Work). 290p. 1990. text 29.50 (*0-7914-0385-8*) State U NY Pr.

Organizational Memory Systems: A Special Double Issue of the Journal of Organizational Computing & Electronic Commerce. Ed. by Lorne Olfman. 136p. 1999. pap. 34.50 (*0-8058-9796-8*) L Erlbaum Assocs.

Organizational Morale. Robert Hershey. LC 84-82616. 89p. (Orig.). 1985. pap. text 12.95 (*0-318-22787-8*) Kings Point Pr.

Organizational Needs Assessment: Design, Facilitation & Analysis. Samuel B. McClelland. LC 95-14606. 336p. 1995. 69.50 (*0-89930-950-X*, Quorum Bks) Greenwood.

Organizational Oversight: Planning & Scheduling for Effectiveness. David A. Erlandson et al. LC 96-15147. (School Leadership Library). (Illus.). 160p. 1996. 29.95 (*1-883001-26-9*) Eye On Educ.

Organizational Paradigm Shifts. LC 95-54020. 1996. 60.00 (*1-56972-001-0*) NACUBO.

Organizational Paradoxes: Clinical Approaches to Management. 2nd ed. Manfred F. De Vries. LC 94-15858. (Illus.). 240p. (C). (gr. 13). 1994. pap. 16.99 (*0-415-11073-4*, B4781) Thomson Learn.

Organizational Participation: Myth & Reality. Frank Heller et al. LC 98-2531. 304p. 1998. text 85.00 (*0-19-828851-4*) OUP.

*__Organizational Participation: Myth & Reality.__ Frank Heller et al. 304p. 1998. pap. text 24.95 (*0-19-829378-X*) OUP.

Organizational Pattern & the Penal Code of the Qumran Sect: A Comparison with Guilds & Religious Associations of the Hellenistic-Roman Period. Moshe Weinfeld. (Novum Testamentum et Orbis Antiquus Ser.: Vol. 2). 104p. 1986. text 20.50 (*3-7278-0363-0*, Pub. by Presses Univ Fribourg) Eisenbrauns.

An Asterisk (*) at the beginning of an entry indicates that the title is appearing for the first time.

Organizational Performance & Measurement in the Public Sector: Toward Service, Effort & Accomplishment Reporting. Arie Halachmi & Geert Bouckaert. LC 95-19466. 368p. 1996. 79.50 (*0-89930-958-5*, Quorum Bks) Greenwood.

Organizational Performance & Rewards: 663 Experiences in Making the Link. Jerry L. McAdams & Elizabeth J. Hawk. (Illus.). 1994. 150.00 (*1-57963-073-1*) Am Compensation.

Organizational Performance & Rewards: 663 Experiences in Making the Link (Executive Summary) Jerry L. McAdams & Elizabeth J. Hawk. (Illus.). 1994. 25.00 (*1-57963-074-X*) Am Compensation.

Organizational Phase of Project Open Book: A Report to the Commission on Preservation & Access. Shari Weaver & Donald Waters. 11p. 1992. pap. 5.00 (*1-887334-18-1*) Coun Lib & Info.

Organizational Politica. Charles Cachenmeyer. (Analysis Ser.). 74p. (Orig.). 1979. pap. text 18.00 (*0-938526-00-6*) Inst Analysis.

Organizational Politics, Justice & Support: Managing the Social Climate of the Workplace. Ed. by Russell S. Cropanzano & K. Michele Kacmar. LC 95-7700. 256p. 1995. 65.00 (*0-89930-906-2*, Quorum Bks) Greenwood.

Organizational Portfolio: A Theory of Performance-Driven Organizational Change. Lex Donaldson. LC 98-25383. 320p. 1998. 32.00 (*0-7619-0354-2*) Sage.

Organizational Power Politics: Tactics in Organizational Leadership. Gilbert W. Fairholm. LC 92-20066. 256p. 1993. 59.95 (*0-275-94420-4*, C4420, Praeger Pubs) Greenwood.

Organizational Practice of Democracy. Ed. by Robert N. Stern & Sharon McCarthy. LC 85-14719. (International Yearbook of Organizational Democracy Ser.: No. 3). (Illus.). 523p. reprint ed. pap. 162.20 (*0-7837-6397-2*, 204611000010) Bks Demand.

Organizational Processes. Francis D. Tuggle. Ed. by Kenneth D. Mackenzie. LC 77-86001. (Organizational Behavior Ser.). (Illus.). (C). 1978. pap. text 15.95 (*0-88295-455-5*) Harlan Davidson.

Organizational Productivity & Performance Quality: What to Do for Continuing Improvement. Herbert Heaton. LC 98-111655. 65p. 1998. pap. 19.95 (*0-9661640-1-6*) Lorenzo Imprints.

Organizational Project & Diagnosis, Module 2. Deborah Ancona et al. (GI - Organizational Behavior Ser.). 1995. mass mkt. 7.95 (*0-538-85878-8*) S-W Pub.

***Organizational Psychology.** Cary L. Cooper. (Manchester Business & Management Series). 432p. 2000. pap. 54.95 (*0-631-20992-1*) Blackwell Pubs.

***Organizational Psychology.** Ed. by Cary L. Cooper & Ronald J. Burke. (Manchester Business & Management Series). 432p. 2000. 74.95 (*0-631-20991-3*) Blackwell Pubs.

Organizational Psychology. Jex. text 55.00 (*0-471-37420-2*) Wiley.

Organizational Psychology. Ed. by Lynn R. Offermann & Marilyn K. Gowing. (Special Issue American Psychologist Ser.: Vol. 45, No. 2). 224p. 1990. pap. 16.00 (*1-55798-092-6*) Am Psychol.

Organizational Psychology. 2nd ed. P. J. D. Drenth. LC 98-186244. (Work & Organizational Psychology Handbks.). 1998. 79.95 (*0-86377-526-8*, Pub. by Psychol Pr) Taylor & Francis.

Organizational Psychology. 3rd ed. Edgar G. Schein. (Foundations of Modern Psychology Ser.). (Illus.). 272p. 1979. pap. text 46.00 (*0-13-641332-3*) P-H.

Organizational Psychology, Vols. I, II & III. Philip Stone & Mark Cannon. (International Library of Management). 1900p. 1998. text 599.95 (*1-85521-351-6*, Pub. by Ashgate Pub) Ashgate Pub Co.

Organizational Psychology: A Book of Readings. David A. Kolb et al. (Behavior Sciences in Business Ser.). 1979. text 16.95 (*0-685-03886-6*) P-H.

Organizational Psychology: An Experimental Approach. 3rd ed. David A. Kolb et al. 1979. pap. 19.95 (*0-685-03887-4*) P-H.

Organizational Psychology: Foundations & Applications. Robert Lawson & Zheng Shen. LC 96-29599. (Illus.). 288p. (C). 1997. text 57.95 (*0-19-511069-2*) OUP.

Organizational Psychology: Its Origins, Assumptions, & Implications for Educational Administration. Adrian Carr. 80p. (C). 1995. pap. 50.00 (*0-7300-0682-4*, Pub. by Deakin Univ) St Mut.

Organizational Public Relations: A Political Perspective. Christopher Spicer. LC 96-23822. (Communication Ser.). 372p. (C). 1996. pap. text 36.00 (*0-8058-1838-3*) L Erlbaum Assocs.

Organizational Report Cards. William T. Gormley & David L. Weimer. LC 98-39374. 1999. 39.95 (*0-674-64350-X*) HUP.

Organizational Response to Changing Community Systems. David F. Gillespie et al. LC 76-25890. 83p. reprint ed. pap. 30.00 (*0-608-17129-8*, 202730300055) Bks Demand.

Organizational Restructuring in the Emergency Department. Nancy S. Donatelli et al. Ed. by Linda Greenberg. 102p. 1995. pap. text 35.00 (*0-935890-53-X*) Emerg Nurses IL.

Organizational Revolution: Presbyterians & American Denominationalism. Ed. by John M. Mulder et al. (Presbyterian Presence Ser.). 300p. (Orig.). 1991. pap. 24.95 (*0-664-25197-8*) Westminster John Knox.

Organizational Risk Factors for Job Stress. Ed. by Steven L. Sauter & Lawrence R. Murphy. LC 95-31599. 400p. 1995. pap. 19.95 (*1-55798-297-X*) Am Psychol.

Organizational Role of Management Accountants. Patrick J. Keating & Shahid Ansari. 1997. pap. 7.50 (*0-256-26395-7*, Irwn Prfssnl) McGraw-Hill Prof.

Organizational Role of Supervisors. Jack Asgar. 94p. 1989. write for info. (*0-9622797-0-6*) Practical Mgmt.

Organizational Rules: A Framework for Understanding Organizational Action. Albert J. Mills & Stephen J. Murgatroyd. 240p. 1990. 118.00 (*0-335-09908-4*); pap. 34.95 (*0-335-09907-6*) OpUniv Pr.

Organizational Science Abroad: Constraints & Perspectives. C. A. Osigweh. LC 88-28572. (Illus.). 364p. (C). 1989. 75.00 (*0-306-42969-1*, Plenum Trade) Perseus Pubng.

Organizational Scientists: Their Professional Careers. Barney G. Glaser. LC 68-25515. 1964. 32.50 (*0-672-51186-X*) Irvington.

Organizational Scientists: Their Professional Careers. Barney G. Glaser. LC 63-12180. 1964. pap. 2.50 (*0-672-60835-9*, Bobbs) Macmillan.

Organizational Scientists: Their Professional Careers. Barney G. Glaser. 140p. 1964. pap. 22.00 (*1-884156-05-3*) Sociology Pr.

Organizational Sentencing Guidelines. 115.00 (*0-929576-94-2*, No.117) Busn Laws Inc.

Organizational Sentencing Guidelines: Compliance & Mitigation. Ed. by Jed S. Rakoff et al. 1993. ring bd. 85.00 (*0-317-05401-5*, 00619) NY Law Pub.

Organizational Sociology. Ed. by W. Richard Scott. (International Library of Management). 692p. 1994. 249.95 (*1-85521-406-7*, Pub. by Dartmth Pub) Ashgate Pub Co.

Organizational State: Social Change in National Policy Domains. Edward O. Laumann & David Knoke. LC 87-40142. (Illus.). 592p. 1987. pap. text 21.95 (*0-299-11194-6*) U of Wis Pr.

Organizational Strategies for Older Workers. P. K. Robinson. (Work in America Institute Studies in Productivity: No. 31). (Illus.). 36p. pap. 39.00 (*0-317-66850-1*, Pergamon Pr) Elsevier.

Organizational Strategies for Older Workers. Pauline K. Robinson. (Studies in Productivity: Vol. 31). 88p. 1983. pap. 55.00 (*0-08-030954-2*) Work in Amer.

Organizational Strategies for Small-Farm Agriculture in Jamaica. Ed. by Harvey Blustain & Elsie LeFranc. 217p. (Orig.). (C). 1981. pap. text 8.00 (*0-86731-013-8*) Cornell CIS RDC.

Organizational Strategies for Small Farm Development in Jamaica. Ed. by Harvey Blustain & Elsie LaFranc. (RDC Bks.). 200p. 1982. 8.00 (*0-86731-119-3*) Cornell CIS RDC.

Organizational Strategy: Structure & Process. Raymond E. Miles & Charles C. Snow. (Management Ser.). (Illus.). (C). 1978. text 66.00 (*0-07-041932-9*) McGraw.

Organizational Strategy & Change. Johannes M. Pennings et al. LC 84-47994. (Jossey-Bass Social & Behavioral Science Ser.). 597p. reprint ed. pap. 185.10 (*0-7837-0186-1*, 204048200017) Bks Demand.

Organizational Structure of Calvin's Theology. Ed. by Richard C. Gamble. LC 92-28975. (Articles on Calvin & Calvinism Ser.: Vol. 7). 400p. 1992. text 72.00 (*0-8153-1048-X*) Garland.

Organizational Structure of Libraries. Lowell A. Martin. (Library Administration: No. 12). 1996. 39.50 (*0-8108-3123-6*) Scarecrow.

Organizational Structure of the Kibbutz. Amitai Etzioni. Ed. by Harriet Zuckerman & Robert K. Merton. LC 79-8996. (Dissertations on Sociology Ser.). 1980. lib. bdg. 28.95 (*0-405-12967-X*) Ayer.

Organizational Structure, Problem Solving, & Effectiveness: A Comparative Study of Hospital Emergency Services. Basil S. Georgopoulos. LC 86-81398. (Joint Publication in the Jossey-Bass Health Series & the Jossey-Bass Management Ser.). 417p. reprint ed. pap. 129.30 (*0-7837-2552-3*, 204271100006) Bks Demand.

***Organizational Studies: Critical Perspectives on Business & Management.** Warwick Organizational Behaviour Staff. LC 00-38260. 2000. pap. write for info. (*0-415-21553-6*) Routledge.

Organizational Studies in Higher Education see Contemporary Higher Education: Issues for the Twenty-First Century

Organizational Surveys: Tools for Assessment & Change. Ed. by Allen J. Kraut. (Business & Management Ser.). 417p. 1996. 41.95 (*0-7879-0234-9*) Jossey-Bass.

Organizational Symbolism. Ed. by Louis R. Pondy et al. LC 83-13542. (Monographs in Organizational Behavior & Industrial Relations: Vol. 1). 307p. 1983. 78.50 (*0-89232-366-3*) Jai Pr.

Organizational Symbolism. Ed. by Barry A. Turner. (Studies in Organization: No. 19). xii, 315p. (C). 1990. lib. bdg. 54.95 (*3-11-011051-2*) De Gruyter.

Organizational Systematic Study of State Regulation. Leigh B. Boske. (Working Paper Ser.: No. 57). 25p. 1990. pap. 5.50 (*0-89940-538-X*) LBJ Sch Pub Aff.

Organizational Systems & Engineering Groups: A Comparative Study of Two Technical Groups in Industry. Louis B. Barnes. LC 60-13102. 210p. reprint ed. pap. 65.10 (*0-608-11548-7*, 200220800019) Bks Demand.

Organizational Team Building. Earl J. Ends & Curtis W. Page. (Illus.). 218p. 1984. reprint ed. pap. text 21.50 (*0-8191-3754-5*) U Pr of Amer.

Organizational Teamwork in High-Speed Management. Yanan Ju & Donald P. Cushman. LC 94-814. (SUNY Series, Human Communication Processes). 150p. (C). 1994. text 44.50 (*0-7914-2237-2*); pap. text 14.95 (*0-7914-2238-0*) State U NY Pr.

Organizational Theory. Gareth R. Jones. (C). 1995. pap. text. write for info. (*0-201-84554-7*) Addison-Wesley.

Organizational Theory: A Strategic Approach. 5th ed. B. J. Hodge et al. 704p. (C). 1996. 87.00 (*0-205-15274-0*) Allyn.

Organizational Theory: Cases & Applications. 4th ed. Richard L. Daft & Mark P. Sharfman. LC 95-112704. 516p. (C). 1994. mass mkt. 50.95 (*0-314-04453-1*) West Pub.

Organizational Theory: Research & Design. William M. Evan. (Illus.). 496p. (C). 1993. reprint ed. teacher ed. write for info. (*0-318-69796-3*) Macmillan.

Organizational Theory: Text & Cases. 2nd ed. 512p. (C). 1997. text 24.00 (*0-201-84876-7*) Addison-Wesley.

Organizational Theory: Text & Cases. 2nd ed. Gareth Jones. LC 97-19744. 734p. (C). 1997. 91.00 (*0-201-84875-9*, Prentice Hall) P-H.

Organizational Theory & Design. 6th ed. Richard L. Daft. LC 97-20922. (Miscellaneous/Catalogs Ser.). (C). 1997. mass mkt. 85.95 (*0-538-87902-5*) S-W Pub.

Organizational Theory & Inquiry. Yvonna S. Lincoln. (Focus Editions Ser.: Vol. 75). 320p. 1985. 59.95 (*0-8039-2494-1*); pap. 26.00 (*0-8039-2495-X*) Sage.

Organizational Theory & Public Policy. Ed. by Richard H. Hall & Robert E. Quinn. LC 83-9704. (Sage Focus Editions Ser.: No. 63). 304p. 1983. reprint ed. pap. 94.30 (*0-608-01188-6*, 205948600001) Bks Demand.

Organizational Theory of Education. Clark. 2000. 55.00 (*0-07-011161-8*) McGraw.

Organizational Theory of Education. Clark. 2001. 55.00 (*0-07-011162-6*) McGraw.

Organizational Training & Development. ITD Staff. (Trainer Development Programme Management & Design 7 Ser.). 1994. pap. text 38.00 (*0-08-042450-3*, Pergamon Pr) Elsevier.

Organizational Training & Development Needs. IPM Staff. (C). 1994. pap. 100.00 (*0-08-042164-4*, Pub. by IPM Hse) St Mut.

Organizational Transformation: Approaches, Strategies, & Theories. Amir Levy & Uri Merry. LC 86-9389. 347p. 1986. 65.00 (*0-275-92147-6*, C2147, Praeger Pubs) Greenwood.

Organizational Transformation & Learning: A Cybernetic Approach to Management. Raul Espejo et al. LC 95-43598. 364p. 1996. 79.95 (*0-471-96182-5*) Wiley.

Organizational Transformation & Process Reengineering. Johnson A. Edosomwan. 224p. 1995. lib. bdg. 49.95 (*1-884015-56-5*) St Lucie Pr.

Organizational Transformation Through Business Process Reengineering. Ed. by William King & Vikram Sethi. LC 97-32092. 575p. (C). 1997. 73.00 (*0-13-897877-8*) P-H.

Organizational Transitions: Managing Complex Change. 2nd ed. Richard Beckhand & Reubin T. Harris. (Organization Development Ser.). (Illus.). 117p. (C). 1987. pap. text 40.00 (*0-201-10887-9*) Addison-Wesley.

Organizational Troubleshooting: Asking the Right Questions, Finding the Right Answers. Reed E. Nelson. LC 95-51414. 184p. 1997. 55.00 (*1-56720-046-X*, Quorum Bks) Greenwood.

Organizational Unconscious: How to Create the Corporate Culture You Want & Need. 2nd ed. Robert F. Allen et al. 229p. 1987. reprint ed. pap. 8.95 (*0-941703-00-2*) Healthyculture.

Organizational Values in America. William G. Scott & David K. Hart. 282p. 1989. 34.95 (*0-88738-279-7*) Transaction Pubs.

Organizational Violence: Creating a Prescription for Change. Lloyd C. Williams. LC 93-27711. 208p. 1994. 57.95 (*0-89930-808-2*, Quorum Bks) Greenwood.

Organizational Vision, Values & Mission. Dennis T. Jaffe et al. Ed. by Philip Gerould. LC 92-70921. (Fifty-Minute Ser.). 100p. 1993. pap. 10.95 (*1-56052-210-0*) Crisp Pubns.

Organizational Weapon: A Study of Bolshevik Strategy & Tactics. Philip Selznick. Ed. by Lewis A. Coser & Walter W. Powell. LC 79-7020. (Perennial Works in Sociology). 1980. reprint ed. lib. bdg. 31.95 (*0-405-12119-9*) Ayer.

Organizational Woman: Power & Paradox. Beth Haslett et al. Ed. by Brenda Dervin. (Communication & Information Science Ser.). 272p. (C). 1992. pap. 39.50 (*0-89391-845-8*); text 73.25 (*0-89391-837-7*) Ablx Pub.

Organizationl Behavior. 4th ed. Dunham. (C). 1997. pap. text, teacher ed., suppl. ed. 22.50 (*0-673-55994-7*) Addson-Wesley Educ.

Organization/Representation: Work & Organizations in Popular Culture. Ed. by John Hassard & Ruth Holliday. LC 97-69195. 288p. 1997. 45.00 (*0-7619-5391-4*); pap. 15.99 (*0-7619-5392-2*) Sage.

Organizations. Hage. (C). 1997. text 52.00 (*0-15-500126-4*) Harcourt Coll Pubs.

Organizations. 7th ed. James L. Gibson et al. (C). 1990. text 60.95 (*0-256-08046-1*, Irwn McGrw-H) McGrw-H Hghr Educ.

Organizations. 10th ed. Gibson. LC 99-24416. 544p. 1999. 84.06 (*0-07-229587-2*) McGraw.

Organizations: Behavior, Structure, Processes. 7th ed. James L. Gibson et al. (C). 1991. text 44.95 (*0-685-38296-6*, Irwn McGrw-H) McGrw-H Hghr Educ.

Organizations: Behavior, Structure, Processes. 9th ed. James L. Gibson et al. 736p. (C). 1996. text 67.95 (*0-256-19268-5*, Irwn McGrw-H) McGrw-H Hghr Educ.

Organizations: Multiple Agents with Multiple Criteria, Newark, 1980. Proceedings. Ed. by J. N. Morse. (Lecture Notes in Economics & Mathematical Systems Ser.: Vol. 190). (Illus.). 509p. 1981. 55.50 (*0-387-10821-1*) Spr-Verlag.

Organizations: Rational, Natural, & Open Systems. 4th ed. W. Richard Scott. LC 97-9352. 416p. 1997. pap. text 51.00 (*0-13-266354-6*) P-H.

Organizations: Structure & Behavior. 3rd ed. Joseph A. Litterer. LC 80-15645. (Series in Management). 638p. 1980. pap. text 37.50 (*0-471-07786-0*) Krieger.

Organizations: Structure & Behavior, Vol. 1. 2nd ed. Joseph A. Litterer. LC 77-88314. 510p. 1969. reprint ed. pap. 158.10 (*0-608-13611-5*, 205516000001) Bks Demand.

Organizations: Structure & Behavior, Vol. 2. 2nd ed. Joseph A. Litterer. LC 77-88314. (Wiley Series in Management & Administration). (Illus.). 431p. 1969. reprint ed. pap. 133.70 (*0-7837-3421-2*, 205516000002) Bks Demand.

Organizations: Structures, Processes, & Outcomes. 7th ed. Richard H. Hall. LC 98-16393. 340p. (C). 1998. pap. text 47.00 (*0-13-903394-7*) P-H.

Organizations: Theory & Design. Arthur G. Bedeian & Raymond F. Zammuto. (Illus.). 624p. (C). 1991. text 56.00 (*0-03-012583-9*) Dryden Pr.

***Organizations, Agencies & Institutions.** 11th ed. Gale Group Staff. (Medical & Health Information Directory Ser.). 4200p. 1999. 255.00 (*0-7876-3480-8*) Gale.

Organizations & Associations: Resource Directory for Local Elected Officials. 31p. 1994. 10.00 (*1-886152-03-9*, No. 2007) Natl League Cities.

Organizations & Communication Technology. Ed. by Janet Fulk & Charles W. Steinfeld. (Illus.). 320p. (C). 1990. 49.95 (*0-8039-3530-7*); pap. 23.95 (*0-8039-3531-5*) Sage.

Organizations & Ethical Individualism. Ed. by Konstantin Kolenda. LC 87-32673. 193p. 1988. 49.95 (*0-275-92760-1*, C2760, Praeger Pubs) Greenwood.

Organizations & Management: Toward the Future. Arye Globerson & Edgar Krau. 208p. 1993. 72.95 (*1-85628-530-8*, Pub. by Avebry) Ashgate Pub Co.

Organizations & National Culture: A Comparative Analysis. Monir H. Tayeb. 192p. (C). 1988. text 35.00 (*0-8039-8166-X*) Sage.

Organizations & Nutritional Methods of Life Forms see Biology of Nutrition

Organizations & Organization Theory. Jeffrey Pfeffer. LC 82-10154. 400p. 1986. text 24.95 (*0-88730-201-7*, HarpBusn) HarpInfo.

***Organizations & People.** Amed. 1999. pap. 113.95 (*0-566-08188-1*) Ashgate Pub Co.

Organizations & Practitioners of Natural Hygiene & a Brief History of Natural Hygiene. Arthur M. Baker. 24p. (Orig.). 1994. pap. 5.95 (*1-883989-03-5*) Self Hlth Care.

Organizations & Technical Change: Strategy, Objectives, & Involvement. rev. ed. David A. Preece. LC 94-34917. (The Routledge Series in the Management of Technology). 272p. (C). 1995. pap. 80.95 (*0-415-12514-6*, B4890); pap. 18.99 (*0-415-10186-7*, C0296) Thomson Learn.

Organizations & the Psychological Contract: Managing People at Work. Peter J. Makin et al. LC 96-7011. 416p. 1996. pap. 32.95 (*0-275-95685-7*, Praeger Pubs) Greenwood.

Organizations & the Psychological Contract: Managing People at Work. Peter Makin et al. LC 96-7011. 416p. 1996. 75.00 (*1-56720-091-5*, Quorum Bks) Greenwood.

Organizations & Their Environments Vol. 3: Essays in the Sociology of Organizations. Charles K. Warriner. LC 83-48086. (Contemporary Studies in Sociology: Vol. 3). 207p. 1984. 78.50 (*0-89232-382-5*) Jai Pr.

Organizations As Bargaining & Influence Systems. Peter Abell. LC 74-15208. (Illus.). 189p. 1975. write for info. (*0-470-00160-7*) Halsted Pr.

Organizations As Systems. Ed. by Martin Lockett & Roger Spear. 244p. 1980. pap. 38.00 (*0-335-00263-3*) OpUniv Pr.

Organizations As Theatre: A Social Psychology of Dramatic Appearances. Iain L. Mangham & Michael A. Overington. LC 86-19199. 224p. reprint ed. pap. 69.50 (*0-7837-6163-5*, 204588500009) Bks Demand.

***Organizations, Competition, & the Business Environment.** 2000. teacher ed. write for info. (*0-201-64857-1*) P-H.

Organizations for Policy Analysis: Helping Government Think. Ed. by Carol H. Weiss. LC 91-12233. 305p. 1992. reprint ed. pap. 94.60 (*0-608-04325-7*, 206510500012) Bks Demand.

Organizations in a World Economy. Walter W. Powell. 128p. Date not set. pap. 18.95 (*0-8039-9020-0*) Pine Forge.

Organizations in America: A Portrait of Their Structures & Human Resource Practices. Arne L. Kalleberg et al. 480p. (C). 1996. 58.00 (*0-8039-5815-3*); pap. 27.95 (*0-8039-5816-1*) Sage.

Organizations in Industry: Strategy, Structure & Selection. Ed. by Glenn R. Carroll & Michael T. Hannan. LC 94-9011. (Illus.). 400p. (C). 1995. text 59.95 (*0-19-508309-1*); pap. text 39.95 (*0-19-508310-5*) OUP.

Organizations in Modern Life: Cities & Other Large Networks. Herman Turk. LC 76-50710. (Jossey-Bass Behavioral Science Ser.). 296p. reprint ed. pap. 91.80 (*0-608-16899-8*, 202777100056) Bks Demand.

Organizations in Society. Morgan. 1997. pap. 24.95 (*0-333-43855-8*) St Martin.

Organizations in the Body. Benjamin M. Freeman. (Illus.). (Orig.). 1996. pap. 20.00 (*0-9654275-1-X*) Lively Bks.

Organizations in the Network Age. Nicky Gunson & David Boddy. LC 95-14281. 304p. (C). 1995. pap. 18.99 (*0-415-13223-1*) Thomson Learn.

Organizations in the Network Age. Nicky Gunson & David Boddy. LC 95-14281. 288p. (C). (gr. 13). 1995. pap. 78.95 (*0-415-05325-0*) Thomson Learn.

Organizations in Transition: Opportunities & Challenges for Evaluation. Ed. by Colleen L. Larson & Hallie Preskill. LC 85-644749. (New Directions for Evaluation Ser.: No. PE 49). 1991. pap. 22.00 (*1-55542-795-2*) Jossey-Bass.

Organizations Management & Control: An Annotated Bibliography. Russell Stout, Jr. & Richard A. Steele. LC 79-3639. 208p. 1980. 21.95 (*0-253-14448-5*) Ind U Pr.

O

Organizations of State Government Officials Directory, 1992. 60p. 1993. pap. 25.00 (*0-87292-976-0*, D-021-92) Coun State Govts.

Organizations, Programs, & Activities of the Geologic Division, U. S. Geological Survey. Robert E. Davis. (Illus.). 40p. 1998. reprint ed. pap. 5.00 (*0-89904-902-8*, Ecosytems Resrch) Crumb Elbow Pub.

Organizations with Incomplete Information: Essays in Economic Analysis Tribute to Roy Radner. Ed. by Mukul Majumdar. LC 98-226794. (Illus.). 356p. (C). 1998. text 64.95 (*0-521-55300-8*) Cambridge U Pr.

Organizations Working Together: Coordination in Interorganizational Networks. Catherine Alter & Jerald Hage. (Library of Social Research: Vol. 191). (Illus.). 240p. (C). 1992. 59.95 (*0-8039-4826-3*); pap. 26.00 (*0-8039-4827-1*) Sage.

***Organizatn Devlopmt: Strats Chang Env 2 Edt.** 2nd ed. (C). 2001. pap. text 0.00 (*0-321-02837-6*) HEPC Inc.

Organizatonal Communication. 6th ed. Goldhaber. 1992. 13.75 (*0-697-12922-5*, WCB McGr Hill) McGrw-H Hghr Educ.

***Organize & De-Stress the Christmas Season: Put the "Merry" Back in Your Christmas!** Helen D. Volk. 33p. 1999. pap. 8.50 (*1-930155-00-X*) Beyond Clutr.

Organize Guidance Program Development Team Module, Competency-Based Career Guidance (CBCG) - Category A: Guidance Program Planning. National Center for Research in Vocational Educati. 1985. 7.95 (*0-317-04753-1*, CG100A02) Ctr Educ Trng Employ.

Organize or Perish: America's Independent Progressives, 1913-1933, 114. Eugene M. Tobin. LC 85-11452. (Contributions in American History Ser.: No. 114). 293p. 1986. 55.00 (*0-313-25013-8*, TOR/, Greenwood Pr) Greenwood.

Organize the Chaos! The Achiever Ethic. J. R. Challacombe. LC 95-92531. 173p. (Orig.). (C). 1995. pap. 17.95 (*1-886287-33-3*) Clair Studies.

Organize the Disorganized: Tips & Techniques to Reduce Stress. Linda Herr. 111p. (Orig.). 1994. pap. 10.95 (*0-9645348-0-0*) L M Herr.

Organize Your Books in 6 Easy Steps: A Workbook for the Sole Proprietor Service-Oriented Business. Donna M. Murphy. Ed. by Sue Maksen. (Illus.). 152p. 1998. pap. 16.95 (*0-9664848-0-0*) IRIE Pubng.

***Organize Your Business Finances with QuickBooks 99 in a Weekend.** Prima Pub Staff. LC 98-68643. (In a Weekend Ser.). (Illus.). 342p. 1999. pap. 19.99 (*0-7615-2031-7*) Prima Pub.

Organize Your Closet: And Other Storage Ideas. (Illus.). 64p. 1993. spiral bd. 5.98 (*1-56173-740-2*, 3615300) Pubns Intl Ltd.

Organize Your Family! Simple Routines for You & Your Kids. Ronnie Eisenberg & Kate Kelly. 144p. 1993. pap. 7.70 (*1-56282-871-1*, Pub. by Hyperion) Time Warner.

Organize Your Finances: Deluxe 98 in a Weekend. Diane Tinney. LC 97-67393. 416p. 1998. per. 19.99 (*0-7615-1186-5*) Prima Pub.

***Organize Your Finances in a Weekend with Quicken Deluxe 2000.** Diane Tinney. 1999. pap. 19.99 (*0-7615-2324-3*) Prima Pub.

Organize Your Finances in a Weekend with Quicken Deluxe 99. rev. ed. Diane Tinney. LC 98-67610. (In a Weekend Ser.). 396p. 1998. per. 19.99 (*0-7615-1786-3*) Prima Pub.

Organize Your Home! Simple Routines for Managing Your Household. Ronnie Eisenberg & Kate Kelly. LC 93-26498. 144p. (Orig.). (J). 1994. pap. 7.70 (*0-7868-8006-6*, Pub. by Hyperion) Time Warner.

***Organize Your Home! Simple Routines for Managing Your Household.** rev. ed. Ronni Eisenberg & Kate Kelly. LC 98-41636. 160p. (J). 1999. pap. 9.70 (*0-7868-8382-0*, Pub. by Hyperion) Time Warner.

Organize Your Home Office! Simple Routines for Setting up an Office at Home. Ronnie Eisenberg & Kate Kelley. LC 99-34677. 224p. 2000. pap. 10.95 (*0-7868-8465-7*, Pub. by Hyperion) Time Warner.

Organize Your Job Search: Simple Solutions for Finding the Job You Want. Ronnie Eisenberg & Kate Kelley. LC 99-17003. 176p. 2000. pap. 10.95 (*0-7868-8467-3*, Pub. by Hyperion) Time Warner.

Organize Your Office! Simple Routines for Managing Your Workspace. Ronnie Eisenberg & Kate Kelly. LC 93-49528. 160p. (J). 1995. pap. 8.70 (*0-7868-8037-6*, Pub. by Hyperion) Time Warner.

***Organize Your Office! Simple Routines for Managing Your Workspace.** rev. ed. Ronni Eisenberg & Kate Kelly. LC 98-41318. 176p. (J). 1999. pap. 9.70 (*0-7868-8381-2*, Pub. by Hyperion) Time Warner.

***Organize Your Personal Finances: Know What You've Got.** J. B. Hudson. 176p. 1998. pap. 24.95 (*0-9666460-0-2*, 630) South Lakes Pub.

Organize Your Space! 1995. pap. 149.00 incl. audio, VHS (*1-56052-340-9*); pap. 24.95 incl. audio (*1-56052-345-X*) Crisp Pubns.

Organize Yourself! Ronnie Eisenberg & Kate Kelly. 224p. 1986. pap. 8.95 (*0-02-028420-9*) Macmillan.

Organize Yourself! rev. ed. Ronni Eisenberg & Kate Kelly. LC 96-44615. 320p. 1997. 9.95 (*0-02-861507-7*) Macmillan.

Organized Activity & Its Support by Computer. Anatol W. Holt. LC 97-26714. 1997. text 97.50 (*0-7923-4708-0*) Kluwer Academic.

Organized Actor: A Ready-to-Use Workbook for the Serious Actor. 3rd ed. Leslie Becker. 100p. 1994. spiral bd., wbk. ed. 16.95 (*0-9667365-0-8*) Pizazz Prods.

Organized Actor: The Workbook & Planner for the Serious Actor. 3rd ed. Leslie Becker. 139p. 1998. pap. text, wbk. ed. 17.95 (*0-9667365-1-6*) Pizazz Prods.

Organized Anarchy in Europe: The Role of States & Intergovernmental Organizations. Jaap De Wilde & Hakan Wiberg. LC 95-62311. 350p. 1996. text 65.00 (*1-86064-062-1*) St Martin.

Organized & Corporate Crime in Europe: Offers That Can't be Refused. Vincenzo Ruggiero. (Socio-Legal Studies). (Illus.). 208p. 1996. 83.95 (*1-85521-522-5*, Pub. by Dartmth Pub) Ashgate Pub Co.

Organized Anti-Semitism in America: The Rise of Group Prejudice During the Decade 1930-1940. Donald S. Strong. LC 78-26198. 191p. 1979. reprint ed. lib. bdg. 55.00 (*0-313-20883-2*, STOA, Greenwood Pr) Greenwood.

Organized Assemblies in Chemical Analysis, Vol. 2. Ed. by Willie L. Hinze. Date not set. 109.50 (*0-7623-0059-0*) Jai Pr.

Organized Assemblies in Chemical Analysis Vol. 1: Reversed Micelles. Ed. by Willie L. Hinze. 186p. 1994. 109.50 (*1-55938-336-4*) Jai Pr.

Organized at Last Vol. I: Step by Step. 2nd rev. ed. Char Miller & Stephanie Grantham. 118p. 1996. pap. text 7.95 (*0-9636982-0-6*, 9270) G & R Pub.

***Organized Business & the New Global Order: Edited by Justin Greenwood & Henry Jacek; Foreword by Philippe C. Schmitter.** Justin Greenwood & Henry J. Jacek. LC 99-36940. (Advances in Political Science Ser.). 2000. text 75.00 (*0-312-22796-5*) St Martin.

Organized Business, Economic Change & Democracy in Latin America. Ed. by Francisco Durand & Eduardo Silva. ii, 297p. 1998. pap. 24.95 (*1-57454-048-3*) U Miami N-S Ctr.

Organized Business in France. Henry W. Ehrmann. LC 81-4161. (Illus.). 514p. 1981. reprint ed. lib. bdg. 79.50 (*0-313-23035-8*, EHOB, Greenwood Pr) Greenwood.

Organized Chaos: The Key to Decluttering, Organizing & Simplifying Your Life. Sylvia Jessy. Ed. by Teri Flatley. (Illus.). 140p. 1998. pap. 13.95 (*0-9664199-0-1*) Organized Chaos.

Organized Crime. Ronald G. Iacovetta. 1998. write for info. (*0-89089-796-4*) Carolina Acad Pr.

Organized Crime. Ed. by Nikos Passas. (International Library of Criminology & Criminal Justice). 612p. 1995. 199.95 (*1-85521-437-7*, Pub. by Dartmth Pub) Ashgate Pub Co.

Organized Crime. Patric J. Ryan. LC 95-12100. (Contemporary World Issues Ser.). 297p. (YA). (gr. 10 up). 1995. lib. bdg. 39.50 (*0-87436-746-8*) ABC-CLIO.

***Organized Crime.** Ed. by James Torr. LC 98-24228. (Contemporary Issues Ser.). 192p. (YA). (gr. 9-12). 1998. pap. 17.45 (*1-56510-890-6*); lib. bdg. 27.45 (*1-56510-891-4*) Greenhaven.

Organized Crime. Josh Wilker. LC 98-47954. (Crime, Justice, & Punishment Ser.). (Illus.). (YA). (gr. 7 up). 1999. lib. bdg. 19.95 (*0-7910-4271-5*) Chelsea Hse.

***Organized Crime.** 2nd ed. Lyman & Potter. LC 99-13095. (Illus.). 536p. 1999. 71.00 (*0-13-010020-X*) P-H.

Organized Crime. 6th ed. Abadinsky. LC 99-42094. (Criminal Justice Ser.). 1999. pap. text 60.95 (*0-534-54380-4*) Thomson Learn.

Organized Crime: A Compilation of U. N. Documents, 1975-1998. Ed. by M. Cherif Bassiouni & Eduardo Vetere. LC 98-39562. 664p. 1998. lib. bdg. 125.00 (*1-57105-084-1*) Transnatl Pubs.

Organized Crime: A Global Perspective. Ed. by Robert J. Kelly. LC 82-71041. 312p. (C). 1986. pap. 24.95 (*0-8476-7559-9*) Rowman.

Organized Crime: Uncertainties & Dilemmas. Ed. by Stanley Einstein & Menachem Amir. (Illus.). 1999. write for info. (*0-942511-90-5*); pap. write for info. (*0-942511-89-1*) OICJ.

Organized Crime & Cocaine Trafficking. 1997. lib. bdg. 600.95 (*0-8490-7602-1*) Gordon Pr.

Organized Crime & Heroin Trafficking, 2 vols. 1997. lib. bdg. 605.95 (*0-8490-7605-6*) Gordon Pr.

Organized Crime & Money Laundering. 1997. lib. bdg. 250.99 (*0-8490-7601-3*) Gordon Pr.

Organized Crime Around the World. Sabrina Adamoli et al. 177p. 1998. pap. 30.00 (*951-53-1746-0*) Willow Tree NY.

Organized Crime in America. Dennis J. Kenney & James O. Finckenauer. LC 94-18081. 398p. 1994. 50.95 (*0-534-24702-4*) Wadsworth Pub.

Organized Crime in America. 3rd ed. Jay S. Albanese. LC 95-76762. (Illus.). 265p. (C). 1995. pap. 31.95 (*0-87084-028-2*) Anderson Pub Co.

Organized Crime in Chicago see Illinois Crime Survey

Organized Crime in Chicago (Unexpurgated) John Landesco. 1968. reprint ed. write for info. (*0-318-62185-1*) Patterson Smith.

Organized Crime in Europe. Petrus C. Van Duyne. 247p. (C). 1995. lib. bdg. 125.00 (*1-56072-244-4*) Nova Sci Pubs.

Organized Crime in Pennsylvania. (Illus.). 364p. (Orig.). (C). 1993. pap. text 45.00 (*1-56806-884-0*) DIANE Pub.

Organized Crime in the Americas: Beyond the Mafia. Sue Mahan & Katherine O'Neil. LC 98-19692. 257p. 1998. write for info. (*0-7619-1358-0*); pap. write for info. (*0-7619-1359-9*) Sage.

Organized Crime in the Netherlands. Cyrille Fijnaut. LC 98-27179. 1998. pap. 41.00 (*90-411-1027-5*) Kluwer Law Intl.

Organized Democracy: Political Institutions in a Welfare State - The Case of Norway. Johan P. Olsen. 246p. 1985. pap. 32.00 (*82-00-06442-5*) Scandnvan Univ Pr.

Organized Executive. abr. ed. Stephanie Winston. 1986. 11.00 incl. audio (*0-671-62568-3*, Sound Ideas) S&S Audio.

Organized Executive: A Program for Productivity - New Ways to Manage Time, Paper, People, & the Electronic Office. rev. ed. Stephanie Winston. LC 94-15676. 352p. 1994. mass mkt. 14.99 (*0-446-39528-5*, Pub. by Warner Bks) Little.

Organized Executive: New Ways to Manage Time, Paper, & People. Stephanie Winston. 1985. mass mkt. 9.99 (*0-446-38384-8*, Pub. by Warner Bks) Little.

Organized for Action: Commitment in Voluntary Associations. David Knoke & James R. Wood. LC 80-26927. 281p. reprint ed. pap. 87.20 (*0-7837-5674-7*, 205910100005) Bks Demand.

Organized for Success! 95 Tips for Taking Control of Your Time, Your Space, & Your Life. Nanci McGraw. Ed. by Kelly Scanlon. LC 95-74769. (Self-Study Sourcebook Ser.). (Illus.). 188p. 1996. pap. 15.95 (*1-878542-79-6*, 13-0012) SkillPath Pubns.

***Organized Garage Sale: The Step-by-Step Guidebook for a Stress-less Garage Sale.** Helen D. Volk. 21p. 1999. pap. 6.50 (*1-930155-01-8*) Beyond Clutr.

Organized German Settlement & Its Effects on the Frontier of South-Central Texas. Hubert G. Wilhelm. Ed. by Francesco Cordasco. LC 80-905. (American Ethnic Groups Ser.). (Illus.). 1981. lib. bdg. 30.95 (*0-405-13464-9*) Ayer.

Organized Industrial Relations in Europe: What Future? Colin Crouch & Franz Traxler. LC 94-74469. x, 331 p. 1995. 87.95 (*1-85972-061-7*, Pub. by Avebry) Ashgate Pub Co.

Organized Interests & Self-Regulation: An Economic Approach. Ed. by Bernardo Bortolotti & Gianluca Fiorentini. 288p. 2000. text 68.00 (*0-19-829652-5*) OUP.

Organized Interests & the European Community. Justin Greenwood et al. (Studies in Neo-Corporatism). (Illus.). 256p. (C). 1992. text 69.00 (*0-8039-8701-3*) Sage.

Organized Interests & the State: Studies in Neo-Corporatism. Ed. by Alan Cawson. 192p. (Orig.). (C). 1985. pap. text 20.95 (*0-8039-9719-1*) Sage.

Organized Labor. Harry A. Millis. LC 74-22752. (Labor Movement in Fiction & Non-Fiction Ser.). reprint ed. 57.50 (*0-404-58504-3*) AMS Pr.

Organized Labor: Its Problems, Purposes & Ideals & the Present & Future of American Wage Earners. John Mitchell. LC 68-56263. (Library of American Labor History). (Illus.). xii, 436p. 1973. reprint ed. 49.50 (*0-678-00733-0*) Kelley.

Organized Labor & American Politics, 1894-1994: The Labor-Liberal Alliance. Ed. by Kevin Boyle. LC 97-47472. (Series in American Labor History). 320p. (C). 1998. pap. text 23.95 (*0-7914-3952-6*) State U NY Pr.

Organized Labor & American Politics, 1894-1994: The Labor-Liberal Alliance. Ed. by Kevin Boyle. LC 97-47472. (Series in American Labor History). 320p. (C). 1998. text 71.50 (*0-7914-3951-8*) State U NY Pr.

Organized Labor & Production: Next Steps in Industrial Democracy. Morris L. Cooke & Philip Murray. LC 73-156409. (American Labor Ser., No. 2). 1971. reprint ed. 23.95 (*0-405-02918-7*) Ayer.

Organized Labor & the Church: Reflections of a "Labor" Priest. George G. Higgins & William Bole. LC 92-36139. 256p. 1993. pap. 12.95 (*0-8091-3374-1*) Paulist Pr.

Organized Labor & the Law. Alpheus T. Mason. LC 73-89755. (American Labor, from Conspiracy to Collective Bargaining Ser., No. 1). 265p. 1972. reprint ed. 18.95 (*0-405-02142-9*) Ayer.

Organized Labor at the Crossroads. Ed. by Wei-Chiao Huang. LC 89-9113. 162p. 1989. text 20.00 (*0-88099-076-7*); pap. text 10.00 (*0-88099-075-9*) W E Upjohn.

Organized Labor Education & Training Programs. John R. MacKenzie. 45p. 1984. 5.50 (*0-318-22163-2*, IN286) Ctr Educ Trng Employ.

Organized Labor in the Asia-Pacific Region: A Comparative Study of Trade Unionism in Nine Countries. Ed. by Stephen Frenkel. LC 92-42494. (Cornell International Industrial & Labor Relations Reports: No. 24). 432p. (Orig.). 1993. pap. text 29.95 (*0-87546-198-0*, ILR Press) Cornell U Pr.

Organized Labor in the Twentieth-Century South. Ed. by Robert H. Zieger. LC 90-22448. 296p. (C). 1991. text 32.00 (*0-87049-697-2*) U of Tenn Pr.

Organized Labor in Venezuela, 1958-1991: Behavior & Concerns in a Democratic Setting. Steve Ellner. LC 92-44554. (Latin American Silhouettes Ser.). 312p. 1993. 50.00 (*0-8420-2443-3*) Scholarly Res Inc.

Organized Labor Movement in Puerto Rico. Miles Galvin. LC 77-74389. 248p. 1979. 34.50 (*0-8386-2009-4*) Fairleigh Dickinson.

Organized Labor's Linkage with Vocational Education. Dorothy Shields. 20p. 1986. 3.00 (*0-318-22164-0*, OC 110); VHS 125.00 (*0-317-01418-8*, VS105VHS, VS105UM) Ctr Educ Trng Employ.

Organized Labour & Pressure Politics: The Canadian Labour Congress, 1956-1968. David Kwavnick. 256p. 1972. 24.95 (*0-7735-0089-8*, Pub. by McG-Queens Univ Pr) CUP Services.

Organized Labour & Pressure Politics: The Canadian Labour Congress, 1956-1968. David Kwavnick. LC 72-82247. 295p. reprint ed. pap. 91.50 (*0-7837-6923-7*, 204675200003) Bks Demand.

Organized Living. Dawn Walters & Helen Chislett. (Illus.). 165p. 30.00 (*1-85029-894-7*, Pub. by Conran Octopus) Antique Collect.

Organized Medicine in the Progressive Era: The Move Towards Monopoly. James G. Burrow. LC 77-894. 232p. reprint ed. pap. 72.00 (*0-608-14681-1*, 202584000046) Bks Demand.

Organized Method of String Playing: Double Bass Exercises for the Left Hand. Ed. by Murray Grodner. 1965. pap. 6.00 (*0-318-19431-7*, 60870-906) Peermusic Classical.

Organized Miracles: A Study of a Contemporary, Youth, Communal, Fundamentalist Organization. James T. Richardson et al. LC 78-55937. 368p. 1979. 34.95 (*0-87855-284-7*) Transaction Pubs.

Organized Obsessions: 1,001 Offbeat Associations, Fan Clubs, & Micro-Societies You Can Join. 250p. 1992. pap. 9.95 (*0-8103-9415-4*) Visible Ink Pr.

Organized Religion & Seniors' Mental Health. Anthony J. Blasi. LC 99-11322. 128p. 1999. 37.00 (*0-7618-1347-0*); pap. 22.50 (*0-7618-1348-9*) U Pr of Amer.

Organized Religion in the Political Transformation of Latin America. Ed. by Satya R. Pattnayak. LC 95-3402. 252p. (Orig.). (C). 1995. pap. text 29.50 (*0-7618-0040-9*); lib. bdg. 54.00 (*0-7618-0039-5*) U Pr of Amer.

Organized Social Complexity: Challenge to Politics & Policy. Ed. by Todd R. La Porte. LC 74-25606. 388p. 1975. reprint ed. pap. 120.30 (*0-7837-9366-9*, 206010900004) Bks Demand.

Organized Solutions: Surfactants in Science & Technology. Ed. by Stig E. Friberg & Bjorn Lindman. (Surfactant Science Ser.: Vol. 44). (Illus.). 410p. 1992. text 199.00 (*0-8247-8698-X*) Dekker.

***Organized Sports Betting: How to Even the Score with Your Bookmaker.** Jerry Bleiman. 60p. 2000. pap. write for info. (*0-9701535-0-3*) J & J Pubng.

Organized Technology: Networks & Innovation in Technical Systems. Wesley Shrum. LC 85-3553. (Science & Society: Series in Science, Technology, & Human Values: Vol. 6). (Illus.). 292p. 1985. pap. 19.95 (*0-911198-74-1*) Purdue U Pr.

Organized to Be the Best! New Timesaving Ways to Simplify & Improve How You Work. 3rd ed. Susan Silver. LC 95-22391. (Illus.). 384p. 1995. 24.95 (*0-944708-46-3*) Adams Hall.

***Organized to Be Your Best! Simplify & Improve How You Work.** 4th ed. Susan Silver. 288p. 2000. 27.95 (*0-944708-61-7*); pap. 17.95 (*0-944708-60-9*) Adams Hall.

Organized Womanhood: Cultural Politics in the Pacific Northwest, 1840-1920. Sandra L. Haarsager. LC 97-12710. 442p. 1997. 39.95 (*0-8061-2974-3*); pap. 19.95 (*0-8061-3001-6*) U of Okla Pr.

Organized Writer: A Brief Rhetoric. Edward Proffitt. LC 91-36782. 191p. (C). 1992. pap. text 28.95 (*1-55934-118-1*, 1118) Mayfield Pub.

Organized Writer: Instructor's Manual. Edward Proffitt. (C). 1992. pap. text, teacher ed. write for info. (*1-55934-129-7*, 1129) Mayfield Pub.

Organizer: Kent Rowley: A Canadian Union Life. Rick Salutin. 163p. 1980. 24.95 (*0-88862-242-2*, Pub. by J Lorimer); pap. 14.95 (*0-88862-241-4*, Pub. by J Lorimer) Formac Dist Ltd.

Organizer: Secrets & Systems from the World's Top Executive Assistants. Anna-Carin Jean. LC 98-43020. (Illus.). 160p. 1999. 12.00 (*0-06-039229-0*) HarpC.

***Organizer for Readers: So Many Books So Little Time.** Dolores Judd. 73p. 1998. spiral bd. 9.95 (*0-9673399-0-1*) D Judd.

Organizer Principles of Economics. Gordon Staff. (C). 2000. pap. text 129.00 (*0-03-002452-8*) Harcourt Coll Pubs.

Organizer Principles of Macroeconomics. Gordon Staff. (C). 2000. pap. text 129.00 (*0-03-002587-7*) Harcourt Coll Pubs.

Organizer Principles of Microeconomics. Gordon Staff. (C). 2000. pap. text 129.00 (*0-03-002442-0*) Harcourt Coll Pubs.

Organizer's Manual. Ed. by Ed Hedemann. (Illus.). 220p. 1981. 10.00 (*0-940862-00-X*) War Res League.

Organizing: A Guide for Grassroots Leaders. rev. ed. Si Kahn. LC 91-24243. 345p. 1991. 32.95 (*0-87101-197-2*) Natl Assn Soc Wkrs.

***Organizing a Conference: How to Plan & Run an Outstanding & Effective Event.** Pauline Appleby. (Illus.). 144p. (Orig.). 1999. pap. 19.95 (*1-85703-382-5*, Pub. by How To Bks) Trans-Atl Phila.

Organizing a Conference on National Security. Betsy Reid et al. 1986. spiral bd. 7.50 (*0-937115-00-2*) Comm Natl Security.

Organizing a Healthcare Financial Services Division. Russell A. Caruana. 225p. 1989. 50.00 (*0-930228-36-7*, Irwn Prfssnl) McGraw-Hill Prof.

Organizing a Healthcare Financial Services Division. 3rd ed. Russell A. Caruana. 170p. 1989. 50.00 (*0-930228-69-3*) Hlthcare Fin Mgmt.

Organizing A Home Filing System. Pam L. Opperman & Connie S. Wedge. (Illus.). 28p. 1998. pap. 9.95 (*0-9669466-3-4*) Hope River.

Organizing a School Projectionist Club. Philip Mannino. pap. 0.75 (*0-685-48118-2*) Sch Proj Club.

Organizing a Small Business Entity. Harry J. Haynesworth & Banking & Business Law American Bar Association Staff. LC 85-73716. (Small Business Ser.). 498p. 1988. suppl. ed. 21.50 (*0-8318-0518-8*, B518/B578) Am Law Inst.

Organizing a Small Business Entity: 1988 Supplement. Harry J. Haynsworth. 101p. (Orig.). 1988. pap. text 7.76 (*0-8318-0578-1*, B578) Am Law Inst.

Organizing a Support Group. 1992. write for info. (*0-944093-19-1*) Am Brain Tumor.

Organizing a Wisconsin Business Corporation: Articles, Bylaws, & Other Forms. 2nd ed. Joseph W. Boucher et al. LC 98-15027. 1998. ring bd. 165.00 incl. disk (*1-57862-011-2*) State Bar WI.

Organizing African Unity. Jon Woronoff. LC 72-16716. 703p. 1979. lib. bdg. 52.00 (*0-8108-0321-6*) Scarecrow.

Organizing Against Crime: Redeveloping the Neighborhood. Anthony Sorrentino. LC 76-21840. 272p. 1977. 42.95 (*0-87705-301-4*, Kluwer Acad Hman Sci) Kluwer Academic.

Organizing AIDS: Workplace & Organizational Responses to the HIV - AIDS Epidemic. David Goss & Derek Adam-Smith. LC 95-12253. (Social Aspects of AIDS Ser.). 168p. 1995. 85.00 (*0-7484-0258-6*); pap. 29.95 (*0-7484-0259-4*) Taylor & Francis.

An Asterisk (*) at the beginning of an entry indicates that the title is appearing for the first time.

Organizing an Anarchy: Belief, Bureaucracy, & Politics in the National Institute of Education. Lee S. Sproull et al. LC 77-15411. (Illus.). 1995. 27.95 (*0-226-76992-5*) U Ch Pr.

Organizing & Maintaining a Successful A. D. D. Support Group: A Practical Guide. William J. Hayes. 48p. 1994. pap. 8.00 (*1-885988-01-X*) Add Resources.

Organizing & Managing an Installment Loan Department see Installment Credit Series

Organizing & Managing Digital Product Companies. Barua Anitash. (C). 2000. text. write for info. (*0-201-32792-9*) Addison-Wesley.

Organizing & Managing Resources. Learning Business Staff. 1997. 32.95 (*0-7506-3156-2*) Buttrwrth-Heinemann.

Organizing & Managing Special Education Programs in Regular Class Settings: A Guide for Special Educators. Ada L. Vallecorsa & Laurie U. Debettencourt. LC 98-33186. (Illus.). 290p. (C). 1999. pap. text 39.00 (*0-02-422371-9*, Macmillan Coll) P-H.

Organizing & Managing the Classroom Enviroment. Wocholz. 626p. 1998. pap. text 63.50 (*0-536-01329-2*) Pearson Custom.

Organizing & Organizations: An Introduction. David Sims et al. (Illus.). 336p. (C). 1993. text 55.00 (*0-8039-8702-1*); pap. text 19.95 (*0-8039-8703-X*) Sage.

Organizing & Staffing Loan Review. John A. Davis, Jr. Ed. by Joan H. Behr. LC 88-33045. (Illus.). 68p. 1989. pap. text 48.00 (*0-936742-63-1*) Robt Morris Assocs.

Organizing & Staffing the Presidency, Vol. III. Bradley D. Nash et al. (Proceedings Ser.). (Orig.). 1980. 11.00 (*0-938204-01-7*) Ctr Study Presidency.

Organizing & the Law. 4th ed. Stephen I. Schlossberg & Judith A. Scott. LC 91-3252. 487p. 1991. trans. 45.00 (*0-87179-672-4*, 0672) BNA Books.

Organizing Artists: A Document & Directory of the National Association of Artists' Organizations, 1998. Ed. by Roberto Bedoya. LC 98-66539. (Illus.). 163p. 1998. pap. 25.00 (*0-927851-05-9*) NAAO.

Organizing Asian American Labor: The Pacific Coast Canned-Salmon Industry, 1870-1942. Chris Friday. LC 93-29471. (Asian American History & Culture Ser.). 368p. (C). 1994. text 44.95 (*1-56639-139-3*) Temple U Pr.

Organizing Asian American Labor: The Pacific Coast Canned-Salmon Industry, 1870-1942. Chris Friday. LC 93-29471. (Asian American History & Culture Ser.). 368p. (C). 1995. pap. text 22.95 (*1-56639-398-1*) Temple U Pr.

Organizing Asian Pacific Workers in Southern California. Ed. by June McMahon. (Current Issues Ser.: No. 9). 42p. 1993. reprint ed. pap. 7.00 (*0-89215-149-8*) U Cal LA Indus Rel.

*__Organizing Bodies: Policy, Institutions & Work.__ Linda McKiernan-Allen & Nick Watson. LC 00-26979. 2000. write for info. (*0-312-23476-7*) St Martin.

Organizing Business: Trade Associations in America & Japan. Leonard H. Lynn & Timothy J. McKeown. LC 87-17468. (AEI Studies: No. 459). 214p. (Orig.). (C). 1988. lib. bdg. 21.75 (*0-8447-3629-5*) U Pr of Amer.

Organizing Business for War: Corporatist Economic Organization During the Second World War. Ed. by Wyn Grant et al. 320p. 1991. 19.50 (*0-85496-655-2*) Berg Pubs.

Organizing China: The Problem of Bureaucracy, 1949-1976. Harry Harding. LC 79-67772. 432p. 1981. 52.50 (*0-8047-1080-5*) Stanford U Pr.

Organizing Civil Society: The Popular Sectors & the Struggle for Democracy. Philip Oxhorn. LC 94-34682. 448p. 1995. 60.00 (*0-271-01435-0*); pap. 19.95 (*0-271-01436-9*) Pa St U Pr.

Organizing Community Resources in Sexuality Counseling & Family Planning for the Retarded: A Community Workers' Manual. Karin Rolett. 1976. pap. 3.00 (*0-89055-118-9*) Carolina Pop Ctr.

Organizing Corporate & Other Business Enterprises. 5th ed. Chester Rohrlich & Bender's Editors. 1975. ring bd. 240.00 (*0-8205-1595-7*) Bender.

Organizing Corporations in California. 2nd ed. Keith R. McBride. Ed. by Donald R. Briggs. LC 82-74145. 260p. 1996. ring bd. 76.00 (*0-88124-989-0*, BU-37761) Cont Ed Bar-CA.

Organizing Corporations in California. 2nd ed. Keith W. McBride. Ed. by Donald R. Briggs. LC 82-74145. 370p. 1997. ring bd. 65.00 (*0-7626-0102-7*, BU-37763) Cont Ed Bar-CA.

Organizing Corporations in California: May, 1992 Update. 2nd ed. Hilary H. Cohen & Doug Gummerman. Ed. by Edward D. Giacomini et al. LC 82-74145. 615p. 1992. ring bd. 60.00 (*0-88124-502-X*, BU-37767) Cont Ed Bar-CA.

Organizing Corporations in California: May, 1994 Update. 2nd ed. Hilary H. Cohen & Doug Gummerman. Ed. by Donald R. Briggs. LC 82-74145. 184p. 1994. 49.00 (*0-88124-759-6*, BU-37768) Cont Ed Bar-CA.

*__Organizing Corporations in California - 5-99 Update.__ 2nd ed. Keith W. McBride. Ed. by David Peyerwold. LC 82-74145. 440p. 1999. ring bd. 77.00 (*0-7626-0319-4*, BU-37765) Cont Ed Bar-CA.

*__Organizing Corporations in California - 5/98 Update.__ 2nd ed. Keith W. McBride. Ed. by Donald R. Briggs. LC 82-74145. 290p. 1998. ring bd. 67.00 (*0-7626-0229-5*, BU-37764) Cont Ed Bar-CA.

Organizing Crime: Essays in Opposition. Alan A. Block. 254p. 1991. lib. bdg. 98.50 (*0-7923-1033-0*) Kluwer Academic.

Organizing Data for CIM Applications. Charles S. Knox. LC 87-15740. (Mechanical Engineering Ser.: Vol. 60). (Illus.). 373p. reprint ed. pap. 115.70 (*0-608-08948-6*, 206958300005) Bks Demand.

Organizing Democracy in Eastern Germany: Interest Groups in Post-Communist Society. Stephen Padgett. LC 99-12130. (Illus.). 216p. (C). 2000. 57.95 (*0-521-65170-0*); pap. 21.95 (*0-521-65703-2*) Cambridge U Pr.

Organizing Deviance. 2nd ed. Joel Best & David F. Luckenbill. LC 93-19690. 292p. (C). 1993. pap. text 25.20 (*0-13-336355-4*) P-H.

Organizing Dissent: Dissenting Social Movements in Theory & Practice. 2nd ed. Ed. by William K. Carroll. LC 97-190921. 350p. 1997. pap. 24.95 (*1-55193-002-1*) Garamond Pr.

Organizing Dissent: The Politics of Protest in the Mexican Teachers' Union. Maria L. Cook. LC 95-26109. 1996. 60.00 (*0-271-01560-8*); pap. 19.95 (*0-271-01561-6*) Pa St U Pr.

Organizing Dixie: Organizing Alabama Workers in the Industrial Era, 9. Philip Taft. LC 80-546. (Contributions in Labor History Ser.: No. 9). (Illus.). 228p. 1981. 59.95 (*0-313-21447-6*, TAL/, Greenwood Pr) Greenwood.

Organizing Early Experience: Imagination & Cognition in Childhood. Ed. by D. C. Morrison. 247p. 1988. pap. 31.95 (*0-89503-051-9*) Baywood Pub.

Organizing Effective Institutional Research Offices. Ed. by Jennifer B. Presley. LC 85-645339. (New Directions for Institutional Research Ser.: No. IR 66). 1990. pap. 22.00 (*1-55542-829-0*) Jossey-Bass.

*__Organizing Electronic Materials for Access: A Cataloging & Management Guide.__ Ingrid Hsieh-Yee. LC 99-52467. 255p. 2000. 40.00 (*1-56308-629-8*) Libs Unl.

Organizing Europe: The Institutions of Integration. 2nd ed. Clive Archer. LC 93-23351. (An Arnold Publication). (Illus.). 320p. 1998. pap. text 22.00 (*0-340-59039-4*, Pub. by E A) OUP.

Organizing Families & Reunions. Randall K. Mehew. (Personal Enrichment Ser.). 125p. (Orig.). 1991. pap. write for info. (*0-929985-76-1*) Jackman Pubng.

Organizing for Agricultural Development: Human Aspects in the Utilization of Science & Technology. William F. Whyte. LC 75-16479. 72p. (Orig.). 1975. pap. text 14.95 (*0-87855-598-6*) Transaction Pubs.

Organizing for Better Meetings: Classic Handbook for Meeting Planners. Homer B. Smith. (Illus.). 105p. 1976. spiral bd. 9.95 (*0-9621285-2-X*) Mktg Educ Assocs.

Organizing for Collective Action: The Political Economies of Associations. David Knoke. (Social Institutions & Social Change Ser.). 272p. 1990. lib. bdg. 49.95 (*0-202-30412-4*) Aldine de Gruyter.

Organizing for Community Action. Stephen Burghardt. LC 82-6034. (Sage Human Services Guides Ser.: No. 27). 120p. 1982. reprint ed. pap. 37.20 (*0-608-01190-8*, 205948800001) Bks Demand.

Organizing for Defense: The American Military Establishment in the Twentieth Century. Paul Y. Hammond. LC 76-51422. 403p. 1977. reprint ed. lib. bdg. 38.50 (*0-8371-9442-3*, HAOD, Greenwood Pr) Greenwood.

Organizing for Democracy: NGOs, Civil Society, & the Philippine State. Ed. by G. Sidney Silliman & Lela G. Noble. LC 97-38490. 360p. 1998. text 55.00 (*0-8248-1947-0*); pap. text 34.95 (*0-8248-2043-6*) UH Pr.

*__Organizing for Dummies.__ Eileen Roth. 384p. 2000. pap. 19.99 (*0-7645-5300-3*) IDG Bks.

Organizing for Empire: Edwardian Ladies & Imperial Power. Julia Bush. LC 99-12380. (Women, Power & Politics Ser.). 242p. 1999. 75.00 (*0-7185-0061-X*) Bks Intl VA.

Organizing for Equality: The Evolution of Women's & Racial-Ethnic Organizations in America, 1955-1985. Debra C. Minkoff. LC 94-46688. (Arnold & Caroline Rose Book Series of the American Sociological Association). 150p. (C). 1995. text 48.00 (*0-8135-2208-0*) Rutgers U Pr.

Organizing for Foreign Policy Crises: Presidents, Advisers, & the Management of Decision-Making. Patrick J. Haney. LC 97-4582. 200p. (C). 1997. text 42.50 (*0-472-10704-6*, 10704) U of Mich Pr.

Organizing for Global Competitiveness: The Asia-Pacific Regional Design. Robert J. Kramer. (Report: No. 1133-95-RR). (Illus.). 58p. (Orig.). 1995. pap. 100.00 (*0-8237-0581-1*) Conference Bd.

Organizing for Global Competitiveness: The Business Unit Design. Robert J. Kramer. (Report: No. 1110-95-RR). (Illus.). 55p. (Orig.). 1995. pap. text 100.00 (*0-8237-0557-9*) Conference Bd.

Organizing for Global Competitiveness: The European Regional Design. Robert J. Kramer. (Report Ser.: No. 1151-96-RR). (Illus.). 50p. (Orig.). 1996. pap. text 100.00 (*0-614-19413-X*) Conference Bd.

Organizing for Growth. Robert D. Noble. 51p. 1987. 10.00 (*0-944687-10-5*) Gather Family Inst.

Organizing for Higher Productivity: An Analysis of Japanese Systems & Practices. 2nd ed. Koji Matsumoto. (Illus.). 75p. 1986. reprint ed. text 18.00 (*92-833-1065-9*, 310659); reprint ed. pap. text 13.75 (*92-833-1066-7*, 310667) Productivity Inc.

Organizing for Instruction. Ted Kowalski. (C). 1994. pap. text. write for info. (*0-8013-1360-0*) Longman.

Organizing for Interdependence: The Role of Government. Adam Yarmolinsky. 20p. (Orig.). 1976. pap. text 12.00 (*0-8191-5858-5*) U Pr of Amer.

*__Organizing for Justice: Central Labor Councils & the Revival of American Unionism.__ Ed. by Immanuel Ness & Stuart Eimer. (Illus.). 256p. 2000. 64.95 (*0-7656-0599-6*) M E Sharpe.

Organizing for Learning: Staff Development Strategies for Residential & Day Services Work: a Theoretical & Practical Guide. Robin Douglas & Chris Payne. (C). 1988. 70.00 (*0-902789-53-8*, Pub. by Natl Inst Soc Work) St Mut.

Organizing for Learning: Toward the 21st Century. Ed. by Herbert J. Walberg & John J. Lane. 112p. (Orig.). 1989. pap. 12.00 (*0-88210-223-0*) Natl Assn Principals.

Organizing for Learning in the Primary Classroom: A Balanced Approach to Classroom Management. Janet R. Moyles. LC 92-5706. 208p. 1993. 103.95 (*0-335-15660-6*); pap. 28.95 (*0-335-15659-2*) Taylor & Francis.

Organizing for Local Governmental Planning in North Carolina. 2nd rev. ed. Philip P. Green, Jr. 168p. (C). 1989. pap. text 14.00 (*1-56011-123-2*) Institute Government.

Organizing for National Security, 3 vols., Set. U. S. Congress, Senate Committee on Government Ope. LC 78-22404. (American Military Experience Ser.). (Illus.). 1980. reprint ed. lib. bdg. 139.95 (*0-405-11879-1*) Ayer.

Organizing for Neighbourhood Development: A Comparative Study of Community Based Development. 2nd ed. Alan Twelvetrees. 179p. 1996. text 74.95 (*1-85972-283-0*, Pub. by Avebry) Ashgate Pub Co.

Organizing for Our Lives: New Voices from Rural Communities. Richard S. Street & Samuel Orozco. (Illus.). 120p. 1993. pap. 24.95 (*0-939165-18-X*) NewSage Press.

Organizing for Political Victory. Loren B. Belker. LC 82-7855. 208p. (C). 1982. text 30.95 (*0-88229-727-9*) Burnham Inc.

Organizing for Power & Empowerment. Jacqueline B. Mondros & Scott M. Wilson. LC 93-31676. (Empowering the Powerless Ser.). 279p. 1994. 61.50 (*0-231-06718-6*); pap. 26.50 (*0-231-06719-4*) Col U Pr.

Organizing for Science: The Making of an Industrial Research Laboratory. Shiv Visvanathan. 1985. 24.00 (*0-19-561715-0*) OUP.

Organizing for Small Business Crime Prevention. Ed. by Jean O'Neil. 12p. 1988. pap. 5.95 (*0-934513-43-0*, M13B) Natl Crime DC.

Organizing for Social Change: A Manual for Activists in the 1990s. Kimberly A. Bobo et al. LC 90-4767. 271p. 1991. pap. 19.95 (*0-932020-93-3*) Seven Locks Pr.

Organizing for Social Change: A Manual for Activists in the 1990s. 2nd ed. Kim Bobo et al. LC 90-47467. 1996. pap. text 19.95 (*0-929765-41-9*) Seven Locks Pr.

Organizing for Social Research. Ed. by Burkart Holzner et al. 386p. 1982. pap. text 11.95 (*0-87073-835-6*) Schenkman Bks Inc.

Organizing for Successful School-Based Management. Priscilla Wohlstetter. LC 97-21199. 1997. pap. 13.95 (*0-87120-289-1*) ASCD.

Organizing for the Creative Person: How to Find the Organizing Style That Works for You. Dorothy Lehmkuhl. 1993. pap. 14.00 (*0-517-88164-0*, Crown) Crown Pub Group.

Organizing for the Future: The New Logic for Managing Complex Organizations. Jay Galbraith & Edward E. Lawler. LC 92-39634. (The Management Ser.). 336p. (C). 1993. text 32.95 (*1-55542-528-3*) Jossey-Bass.

Organizing for the Use of Space: Historical Perspectives on a Persistent Issue. Ed. by Roger D. Launius. LC 96-103619. (AAS History Ser.: Vol. 18). (Illus.). 234p. 1995. 60.00 (*0-87703-403-6*, Am Astronaut Soc); pap. 40.00 (*0-87703-404-4*, Am Astronaut Soc) Univelt Inc.

Organizing for Whole Language. Ed. by Yetta M. Goodman et al. LC 90-21918. 389p. (C). 1991. pap. text 25.00 (*0-435-08541-7*, 08541) Heinemann.

Organizing Friends Groups: A How-to-Do-It Manual for Librarians. Mark Y. Herring. (How-to-Do-It Ser.). 150p. 1992. pap. text 45.00 (*1-55570-062-4*) Neal-Schuman.

Organizing from the Inside Out: The Foolproof System for Organizing Your Home, Your Office & Your Life. Julie Morgenstern. LC 98-16292. (Illus.). 256p. 1998. pap. 15.00 (*0-8050-5649-1*, Owl) H Holt & Co.

*__Organizing from the Inside Out for the New World of Work.__ Julie Morgenstern. 2001. pap. 14.00 (*0-8050-6470-2*) H Holt & Co.

Organizing Genius. Warren Bennis & Patricia W. Biederman. 256p. 1998. pap. 13.00 (*0-201-33989-7*) Addison-Wesley.

Organizing God's Work. Harris. LC 98-13513. 1998. text 59.95 (*0-312-21501-0*) St Martin.

Organizing Hints & Tips. Deni Bown. LC 97-14618. 144p. 1997. 19.95 (*0-7894-1998-X*) DK Pub Inc.

*__Organizing Immigrants: The Challenge for Unions in Contemporary California.__ Ed. by Ruth Milkman. LC HD6490.O72U657 2000. 2000. pap. 18.95 (*0-8014-8617-3*) Cornell U Pr.

Organizing in Hard Times: Labor & Neighborhoods in Hartford. Louise B. Simmons. LC 93-33184. (Labor & Social Change Ser.). 208p. (C). 1994. pap. 22.95 (*1-56639-156-3*); text 69.95 (*1-56639-155-5*) Temple U Pr.

Organizing Independence: The Artists' Federation of the Paris Commune & Its Legacy, 1871-1889. Gonzalo J. Sanchez, Jr. LC 96-18582. (Illus.). xii, 245p. 1997. text 55.00 (*0-8032-4255-7*) U of Nebr Pr.

Organizing Industrial Activities Across Firm Boundaries. Anna Dubois. LC 97-21645. 176p. (C). 1998. 75.00 (*0-415-14707-7*) Routledge.

Organizing Industrial Development. Ed. by Rolf Wolff. (Studies in Organization: No. 7). xii, 391p. 1986. lib. bdg. 84.95 (*3-11-010669-8*) De Gruyter.

Organizing Information see Skillbooster Series

Organizing Information: Principles & Practice. Christopher Turner. LC Z 0693.T86. (Illus.). 164p. 1987. reprint ed. pap. 50.90 (*0-608-08870-6*, 206950900004) Bks Demand.

Organizing Information: Principles of Data Base & Retrieval Systems. Dagobert Soergel. LC 83-15741. (Library & Information Science Ser.). (C). 1985. pap. text 54.00 (*0-12-654261-9*) Acad Pr.

Organizing Jainism in India & England. Marcus Banks. (Oxford Studies in Social & Cultural Anthropology). (Illus.). 282p. 1992. text 75.00 (*0-19-827388-6*) OUP.

Organizing Knowledge. Needham. (C). 1977. text 23.00 (*0-233-95836-3*) Westview.

Organizing Knowledge. 2nd ed. Jennifer Rowley. 450p. 1992. pap. 34.95 (*1-85742-005-5*, Pub. by Gower) Ashgate Pub Co.

*__Organizing Knowledge: An Introduction to Managing Access to Information.__ 3rd ed. Jennifer Rowley & John Farrow. LC 99-45648. 416p. 2000. pap. 39.95 (*0-566-08047-8*, Pub. by Gower) Ashgate Pub Co.

Organizing Knowledge for Environmentally & Socially Sustainable Development. Ed. by Ismail Serageldin et al. (ESD Studies & Monographs). 100p. 1998. pap. 22.00 (*0-8213-4250-9*, 14250) World Bank.

Organizing Lake Users: A Practical Guide. 84p. 1991. pap. 12.95 (*1-880686-15-5*, H2) Terrene Inst.

Organizing Manual. Donna L. Ciangio & Karen S. Smith. (Follow Me! Ser.). 32p. 1997. pap. 15.95 (*1-881307-03-4*, B7034) Natl Pastoral LC.

Organizing Mexican Undocumented Farm Workers on Both Sides of the Border. Guadalupe L. Sanchez & Jesus Romo. (Research Reports: No. 27). 12p. (Orig.). (C). 1981. pap. 5.00 (*0-935391-26-6*, RR-27) UCSD Ctr US-Mex.

Organizing Modernity: New Weberian Perspectives on Work, Organizations, & Society. Larry Ray & Michael Reed. LC 94-7259. 320p. (C). 1994. pap. 24.99 (*0-415-08917-4*, B4466) Routledge.

Organizing Multimedia Information: Principles & Practice of Information Retrieval. Mary A. Burke. LC 98-36866. 250p. 1999. 78.95 (*0-566-08171-7*) Ashgate Pub Co.

*__Organizing My Learning: Daily Student Planner Teacher's Manual.__ 12p. (Orig.). 1999. pap. text, teacher ed. 2.95 (*0-89455-680-0*) Crit Think Bks.

Organizing My Learning: Daily Student Planner Using Graphic Organizers. Sandra Parks & Howard Black. 108p. (J). (gr. 5-9). 1999. pap. 12.95 (*0-89455-678-9*, MP6501) Crit Think Bks.

Organizing Nonprint Materials. 2nd ed. Jay E. Daily. (Books in Library & Information Science: Vol. 48). (Illus.). 320p. 1986. text 115.00 (*0-8247-7504-X*) Dekker.

*__Organizing Organizations.__ Nils Brunsson. 1999. 42.00 (*87-16-13427-3*) Mksgaard.

Organizing Outdoor Volunteers: A Step-by-Step Program for Grassroots Environmental Action Groups. 2nd ed. Roger L. Moore et al. LC 92-22621. (Illus.). 128p. 1992. pap. 4.95 (*1-878239-16-3*) AMC Books.

*__Organizing Political Institutions: Essays for Johan P. Olsen.__ Ed. by Morten Egeberg & Per Laegreid. 388p. (C). 1999. 37.00 (*82-00-12960-8*, Pub. by Scand Univ Pr) IBD Ltd.

Organizing Projects for Success. Vijay K. Verma. (Human Aspects of Project Management Ser.: Vol. 1). 201p. 1995. pap. 32.95 (*1-880410-40-0*) Proj Mgmt Inst.

*__Organizing Property of Communication.__ Francois Cooren. LC 99-52671. (Pragmatic & Beyond New Ser.: Vol. 65). xvi, 255p. 2000. 50.00 (*1-55619-943-0*) J Benjamins Pubng Co.

Organizing Puerto Rican Migrant Farmworkers: The Experience of Puerto Ricans in New Jersey. Gloria B. Santiago. Ser. XI, Vol. 15. X, 260p. (C). 1988. text 42.50 (*0-8204-0582-5*) P Lang Pubng.

Organizing Rescue: Jewish National Solidarity in the Modern Period. Ed. by Selwyn I. Troen & Benjamin Pinkus. 1992. text 57.50 (*0-7146-3413-1*, Pub. by F Cass Pubs) Intl Spec Bk.

Organizing, Role Enactment, & Disaster: A Structural Theory. Gary A. Kreps et al. LC 92-56767. 1994. 38.50 (*0-87413-468-4*) U Delaware Pr.

Organizing Rural Business: Policy, Planning & Management. Rajagopal et al. LC 94-32848. 180p. (C). 1995. 22.95 (*0-8039-9200-9*) Sage.

Organizing Rural Workers: The Gujarat Government Experience. Indira Hirway & Joseph Abraham. 1990. 17.50 (*81-204-0476-9*, Pub. by Oxford IBH) S Asia.

Organizing Schools. William J. Bailey. LC 96-61758. (Educational Leadership for the 21st Century Ser.: Vol. 4). 243p. 1996. text 44.95 (*1-56676-486-6*) Scarecrow.

Organizing Scientific Meetings. August Epple. LC 96-37969. (Illus.). 198p. (C). 1997. pap. 17.95 (*0-521-58919-3*); text 54.95 (*0-521-56351-8*) Cambridge U Pr.

Organizing Scientific Research for War: The Administrative History of the Office of Scientific Research & Development. Irvin Stewart. Ed. by I. Bernard Cohen. LC 79-7999. (Three Centuries of Science in America Ser.). 1980. reprint ed. lib. bdg. 33.95 (*0-405-12587-9*) Ayer.

Organizing Silence: A World of Possibilities. Robin P. Clair. LC 97-47048. (Series in Speech Communication). 288p. (C). 1998. text 59.50 (*0-7914-3941-0*); pap. text 19.95 (*0-7914-3942-9*) State U NY Pr.

Organizing So All Children Can Learn: Applying the Principles of Learning. 1995. 8.00 (*1-889630-50-0*) Natl Ctr & Econ.

Organizing Societies for War: The Process & Consequences of Societal Militarization. Patrick M. Regan. LC 93-8621. 208p. 1994. 55.00 (*0-275-94670-3*, C4670, Praeger Pubs) Greenwood.

An Asterisk (*) at the beginning of an entry indicates that the title is appearing for the first time.

Organizing Special Events & Conferences: A Practical Guide for Busy Volunteers & Staff. Darcy C. Devney. LC 89-30179. 130p. 1990. pap. 18.95 (*0-910923-63-9*) Pineapple Pr.

Organizing Strangers: Poor Families in Guatemala City. Bryan R. Roberts. LC 72-3513. (Texas Pan-American Ser.). 378p. reprint ed. pap. 117.20 (*0-8357-7759-6*, 203611700002) Bks Demand.

Organizing Successful Tournaments. 2nd ed. John Byl. LC 98-11714. (Illus.). 184p. 1998. pap. 19.95 (*0-88011-955-1*, PBYL0955) Human Kinetics.

Organizing TAPP: Useful Forms for Teen Parenting Programs. Jeanne Lindsay. (YA). 1997. pap. 4.95 (*1-885356-23-4*) Morning Glory.

Organizing the Breathless: Cotton Dust, Southern Politics, & the Brown Lung Association. Robert E. Botsch. (Illus.). 240p. 1993. text 32.50 (*0-8131-1818-2*) U Pr of Ky.

Organizing the Ethnic Community: An Account of the Origin, History, & Development of the Joint Civic Committee of Italian Americans (1952-1995) Anthony Sorrentino. LC 95-31271. (Illus.). 184p. 1995. pap. 14.95 (*0-934733-89-9*) CMS.

Organizing the Executive Branch: The Johnson Presidency. Emmette S. Redford & Marlan Blissett. LC 81-1142. (Administrative History of the Johnson Presidency Ser.). (C). 1995. 30.00 (*0-226-70675-3*) U Ch Pr.

Organizing the Executive Branch: The Johnson Presidency. Emmette S. Redford & Marlan Blissett. LC 81-1142. (Administrative History of the Johnson Presidency Ser.). 287p. reprint ed. pap. 89.00 (*0-608-09510-9*, 205431100005) Bks Demand.

Organizing the Finance Function. T. Sheridan. (Financial Times Management Briefings Ser.). 1997. pap. 152.50 (*0-273-63240-X*, Pub. by F T P-H) Trans-Atl Phila.

Organizing the Future: Matrix Models for the Postindustrial Polity. Walter F. Baber. LC 82-7009. 146p. 1983. pap. 45.30 (*0-608-05181-0*, 206568900006) Bks Demand.

Organizing the Lakota: The Political Economy of the New Deal on the Pine Ridge & Rosebud Reservations. Biolsi. LC 92-182. 280p. 1998. pap. 17.95 (*0-8165-1885-8*) U of Ariz Pr.

Organizing the Lakota: The Political Economy of the New Deal on the Pine Ridge & Rosebud Reservations. Thomas Biolsi. LC 92-182. (Illus.). 240p. 1992. 38.50 (*0-8165-1127-6*) U of Ariz Pr.

Organizing the Landscape: Geographical Perspectives on Labor Unionism. Andrew Herod. LC 98-10856. 1998. 62.95 (*0-8166-2970-6*); pap. 24.95 (*0-8166-2971-4*) U of Minn Pr.

Organizing the Library's Support: Donors, Volunteers, Friends. Allerton Park Institute Staff. Ed. by Donald W. Krummel. LC 80-14772. 125p. reprint ed. pap. 38.80 (*0-7837-1234-0*, 204137100020) Bks Demand.

Organizing the Multinational Enterprise: An Information Processing Perspective. William G. Egelhoff. 320p. 1988. text 34.95 (*0-88730-170-3*, HarpBusn) HarpInfo.

Organizing the Nonprofit Sector: A Replication Guide or Crafting a State Nonprofit Policy Agenda. Carol E. Wayman. Ed. by Deborah S. Koch. (Orig.). 1996. pap. 15.00 (*1-886949-05-0*) Union Inst.

Organizing the Presidency. rev. ed. Stephen Hess. 273p. 1988. 36.95 (*0-8157-3626-6*); pap. 16.95 (*0-8157-3625-8*) Brookings.

Organizing the Shipyards: Union Strategy in Three Northeast Ports, 1933-1945. David Palmer. LC 98-26635. (Illus.). 272p. 1998. 39.95 (*0-8014-2734-7*, ILR Press) Cornell U Pr.

Organizing the South Bronx. Jim Rooney. LC 93-49671. (SUNY Series, the New Inequalities). 283p. (C). 1994. text 57.50 (*0-7914-2209-7*); pap. text 23.95 (*0-7914-2210-0*) State U NY Pr.

Organizing the Unemployed: Community & Union Activists in the Industrial Heartland. James J. Lorence. LC 95-33412. (SUNY Series in American Labor History). 407p. (C). 1996. text 68.50 (*0-7914-2987-3*); pap. text 22.95 (*0-7914-2988-1*) State U NY Pr.

Organizing Thinking Book 1: Graphic Organizers. Sandra Parks & Howard Black. 307p. (Orig.). (J). (gr. 2-5). 1992. pap. 34.95 (*0-89455-354-2*) Crit Think Bks.

Organizing Thinking Book 2: Graphic Organizers. Sandra Parks & Howard Black. 342p. (Orig.). (J). (gr. 4-8). 1990. pap. 34.95 (*0-89455-355-0*) Crit Think Bks.

Organizing Time: Understanding Rhythm - A Method For... William C. Cutter. Ed. by Scott Foss. 47p. (C). 1999. pap. text 6.00 (*0-89328-152-2*, 30/1373R) Lorenz Corp.

Organizing to Count: Change in the Federal Statistical System. Janet L. Norwood. 150p. (C). 1995. pap. text 25.50 (*0-87766-635-0*); lib. bdg. 48.50 (*0-87766-634-2*) Urban Inst.

Organizing to Win: New Research on Union Strategies. Ed. by Kate Bronfenbrenner et al. LC 97-28827. 368p. 1998. pap. 19.95 (*0-8014-8446-4*) Cornell U Pr.

Organizing, Training, & Equipping the Air Force for Crises & Lesser Conflicts. Carl H. Builder & Theodore W. Karasik. 115p. 1995. pap. text 15.00 (*0-8330-2320-9*, MR-626-AF) Rand Corp.

Organizing Travel, Accommodation & Meetings. Learning Business Staff. 1997. 32.95 (*0-7506-3157-0*) Buttrwrth-Heinemann.

Organizing Unions. Mary Cornish & Lynn Spink. (Illus.). 350p. 1994. pap. 19.95 (*0-929005-55-4*, Pub. by Sec Story Pr) LPC InBook.

Organizing Women: Formal & Informal Women's Groups in the Middle East. Ed. by Dawn Chatty. LC 97-204030. 1997. 55.00 (*1-85973-910-5*, Pub. by Berg Pubs); pap. 19.50 (*1-85973-915-6*, Pub. by Berg Pubs) NYU Pr.

Organizing Women in Contemporary Russia: Engendering Transition. Valerie Sperling. LC 98-43642. (Illus.). 304p. (C). 1999. 59.95 (*0-521-66017-3*); pap. 22.95 (*0-521-66963-4*) Cambridge U Pr.

Organizing Women Office Workers: Dissatisfaction, Consciousness & Action. Roberta Goldberg. LC 82-18907. 152p. 1983. 49.95 (*0-275-90990-5*, C0990, Praeger Pubs) Greenwood.

Organizing Wonder: Making Inquiry Science Work in the Elementary School. Heinemann Staff. LC 98-10306. 1998. pap. text 17.00 (*0-325-00045-X*) Heinemann.

Organizing Your Family History Search: Efficient & Effective Ways to Gather & Protect Your Genealogical Research. Sharon DeBartolo Carmack. LC 99-21643. (Illus.). 176p. 1999. pap. 16.99 (*1-55870-511-2*, 70425, Betrwy Bks) F & W Pubns Inc.

Organizing Your Future: A Guide to Decisionmaking in Your Later Years. Legal Counsel for the Elderly Staff. 102p. 1993. pap. 50.00 (*0-933945-04-3*) Legal Coun Elderly.

Organizing Your Home Office for Success. 2nd rev. ed. Lisa Kanarek. LC 98-93232. (Illus.). 240p. 1998. pap. 14.95 (*0-9643470-1-6*) Blakely Press.

Organizing Your Office & Staff for Your Fund-Raising Efforts: Creating Materials to Streamline the Fund-Raising Process see Fund Raising Series

Organizing Your Practice Through Automation: Managing Information & Data. American Psychological Association Practice Direct. (APA Practitioner's Toolbox Ser.). 72p. 1996. pap. 29.95 (*1-55798-359-3*) Am Psychol.

Organizing Your Practices: A New Swimming Manual. 3rd rev. ed. Charles E. Bird. (Illus.). 416p. (C). 1988. pap. 19.95 (*0-317-93356-6*) Bird Pub Co.

Organizing Your Workspace: A Guide to Personal Productivity. Odette Pollar. Ed. by Michael G. Crisp. LC 91-76238. (Fifty-Minute Ser.). 92p. 1992. pap. 10.95 (*1-56052-125-2*) Crisp Pubns.

Organizing Your Workspace: A Guide to Personal Productivity. Odette Pollar. Ed. by Debbie Woodbury. LC 98-74378. (Crisp 50-Minute Bks.). 120p. 1998. pap. 10.95 (*1-56052-522-3*) Crisp Pubns.

Organizing Your Youth Soccer Team: Swedish Soccer Federation. 2nd ed. Lars-Ake Backstrom et al. LC 87-22535. (Illus.). 216p. reprint ed. pap. 67.00 (*0-608-20836-1*, 207193500003) Bks Demand.

*__Organobismuth Chemistry.__ Hitomi Suzuki. LC 99-46573. 1999. write for info. (*0-444-20528-4*) Elsevier.

Organoboranes in Organic Synthesis. Gordon M. Cragg. LC 72-90962. (Studies in Organic Chemistry: No. 1). (Illus.). 438p. reprint ed. pap. 135.80 (*0-7837-0726-6*, 204105000019) Bks Demand.

Organoboron Compounds in Organic Synthesis. B. M. Mikhailov & Yu N. Bubnov. xxxiv, 781p. 1984. text 634.00 (*3-7186-0113-3*) Gordon & Breach.

Organocopper Reagents: A Practical Approach. Ed. by R. J. Taylor. (Practical Approach Series in Chemistry: No. 1). (Illus.). 376p. 1995. spiral bd. 45.00 (*0-19-855758-2*) OUP.

Organoderivatives of Rare Earth Elements. M. N. Bochkarev et al. LC 94-31169. (Topics in F-Element Chemistry Ser.: Vol. 3). 556p. (C). 1995. text 254.00 (*0-7923-3153-2*) Kluwer Academic.

Organoflourine Chemistry: Structure, Reactivity & Synthesis. W. R. Dolbier & B. Smart. Date not set. write for info. (*0-8247-9539-3*) Dekker.

Organofluorine Chemistry: Fluorinated Alkenes & Reactive Intermediates. Ed. by R. D. Chambers. (Topics in Current Chemistry Ser.: Vol. 192). (Illus.). 260p. 1997. 139.00 (*3-540-63171-2*) Spr-Verlag.

Organofluorine Chemistry: Principles & Commercial Applications. R. E. Banks et al. (Topics in Applied Chemistry Ser.). (Illus.). 670p. (C). 1994. text 135.00 (*0-306-44610-3*, Kluwer Plenum) Kluwer Academic.

Organofluorine Chemistry: Techniques & Synthons. Ed. by R. D. Chambers. (Topics in Current Chemistry Ser.: Vol. 193). (Illus.). 265p. 1997. 139.00 (*3-540-63170-4*) Spr-Verlag.

*__Organofluorine Compounds: Chemistry & Applications.__ Tamejiro Hiyama et al. Ed. by H. Yamamoto. LC 99-87168. (Illus.). xii, 272p. 2000. 109.00 (*3-540-66689-3*) Spr-Verlag.

Organofluorine Compounds in Medicinal Chemistry & Biomedical Applications. Ed. by Robert Filler et al. LC 93-26998. (Studies in Organic Chemistry: Vol. 48). 394p. 1993. 268.00 (*0-444-89768-2*) Elsevier.

Organogenesis see Illustrated Human Embryology

Organogenesis of the Kidney. Lauri Saxen. (Developmental & Cell Biology Monographs: No. 19). (Illus.). 184p. 1987. text 80.00 (*0-521-30152-1*) Cambridge U Pr.

Organogermanium Compounds, Pt. 4. John Drake. (Gmelin Handbook of Inorganic & Organometallic Chemistry Ser.: Vol. 4). 364p. 1994. 1600.00 (*0-387-93696-3*) Spr-Verlag.

*__Organolithium Chemistry: A Synthetic Perspective.__ Clayden. (Tetrahedron Organic Chemistry Ser.). 2000. 114.50 (*0-08-043262-X*, Pergamon Pr); pap. 49.50 (*0-08-043261-1*, Pergamon Pr) Elsevier.

Organomagnesium Methods in Organic Chemistry. Ed. by B. D. Wakefield. (Best Synthetic Methods Ser.). (Illus.). 249p. 1995. text 79.00 (*0-12-730945-4*) Acad Pr.

Organomercury Compounds in Organic Synthesis. R. C. Larock. (Reactivity & Structure Ser.: Vol. 22). 420p. 1985. 299.95 (*0-387-13749-1*) Spr-Verlag.

*__Organometallic Bonding & Reactivity: Fundamental Studies.__ Ed. by John M. Brown & P. Hofmann. LC 99-33293. (Topics in Organometallic Chemistry Ser.: Vol. 4). (Illus.). 220p. 1999. 125.00 (*3-540-64253-6*) Spr-Verlag.

Organometallic Chemistry. Gary O. Spessard. 561p. 1996. 90.00 (*0-13-640178-3*) P-H.

Organometallic Chemistry, Vol. 8. Edward W. Abel & Stone. 1991. 164.00 (*0-85186-690-5*) CRC Pr.

Organometallic Chemistry, Vol. 9. Abel & Stone. 1991. 274.00 (*0-85186-571-2*) CRC Pr.

Organometallic Chemistry, Vol. 10. Abel & Stone. 1989. 274.00 (*0-85186-581-X*) CRC Pr.

Organometallic Chemistry, Vol. 11. Abel & Stone. 1989. 274.00 (*0-85186-591-7*) CRC Pr.

Organometallic Chemistry, Vol. 12. Abel & Stone. 1989. 263.00 (*0-85186-601-8*) CRC Pr.

Organometallic Chemistry, Vol. 13. Abel & Stone. 1988. 263.00 (*0-85186-611-5*) CRC Pr.

Organometallic Chemistry, Vol. 15. Abel. 1988. 296.00 (*0-85186-631-X*) CRC Pr.

Organometallic Chemistry, Vol. 17. E. W. Abel & F. G. Stone. 502p. 1989. 330.00 (*0-85186-651-4*) CRC Pr.

Organometallic Chemistry, Vol. 18. Royal Society of Chemistry Staff. 1989. 362.00 (*0-85186-661-1*) CRC Pr.

Organometallic Chemistry, Vol. 19. Abel & Stone. 1990. 362.00 (*0-85186-671-9*) CRC Pr.

Organometallic Chemistry, Vol. 20. Stone & Able. 1991. 330.00 (*0-85186-681-6*) CRC Pr.

Organometallic Chemistry, Vol. 22. E. W. Abel. 506p. 1993. 341.00 (*0-85186-701-4*, R6701) CRC Pr.

Organometallic Chemistry, Vol. 23. Edward W. Abel. 456p. 1994. 341.00 (*0-85186-711-1*, R6711) CRC Pr.

Organometallic Chemistry: A Unified Approach. Ram C. Mehrotra & Anirudh Singh. LC 87-29632. 634p. 1991. text 105.00 (*0-470-21019-2*) Halsted Pr.

Organometallic Chemistry: An Overview. John S. Thayer. 170p. 1988. 69.95 (*0-471-18652-X*) Wiley.

Organometallic Chemistry: An Overview. John S. Thayer. LC 87-21654. (Illus.). xii, 170p. 1988. 45.00 (*0-89573-121-5*, Wiley-VCH) Wiley.

Organometallic Chemistry of the Transition Elements. F. P. Pruchnik. (Modern Inorganic Chemistry Ser.). (Illus.). 774p. (C). 1990. text 165.00 (*0-306-43192-0*, Kluwer Plenum) Kluwer Academic.

Organometallic Chemistry of the Transition Metals. 2nd ed. Robert H. Crabtree. LC 93-9498. 512p. 1994. 74.95 (*0-471-59240-4*) Wiley.

*__Organometallic Chemistry of the Transition Metals.__ 3rd ed. Robert Crabtree. 500p. 2001. 69.95 (*0-471-18423-3*) Wiley.

Organometallic Compounds, Vol. 1, Pt. 1, Groups I-III. 4th ed. G. E. Coates & K. Wade. 1985. text 75.00 (*0-412-23120-4*, NO. 6530) Chapman & Hall.

Organometallic Compounds in the Environment: Principles & Reactions. Ed. by P. J. Craig. 368p. 1986. 265.00 (*0-471-84727-5*) Wiley.

Organometallic Compounds of Germanium, Tin, & Lead. P. G. Harrison. (Chemistry Sourcebook Ser.). 192p. 1985. lib. bdg. 35.00 (*0-412-26810-8*, 9542) Chapman & Hall.

Organometallic Compounds of Iron. G. R. Knox. (Chemistry Sourcebook Ser.). 488p. 1985. lib. bdg. 49.95 (*0-412-26820-5*, 9547) Chapman & Hall.

Organometallic Compounds of Silicon. D. R. Walton. (Chemistry Sourcebook Ser.). 330p. 40.00 (*0-412-26860-4*, 9543) Chapman & Hall.

Organometallic Compounds of the Group Four Elements, Vol. 1 Part 2: The Bond to Carbon. Ed. by Alan G. MacDiarmid. LC 68-11573. 275p. 1968. reprint ed. pap. 85.30 (*0-608-08448-4*, 202783100054) Bks Demand.

Organometallic Compounds of the Group Four Elements, Vol. 2, Pt. 2: The Bond of Halogens & Halogenoids. Ed. by Alan G. MacDiarmid. LC 68-11573. 248p. 1972. reprint ed. pap. 76.90 (*0-608-08449-2*, 202707600054) Bks Demand.

Organometallic Compounds of the Group Four Elements Vol. 1, Pt. 1: The Bond to Carbon. Ed. by Alan G. MacDiarmid. LC 68-11573. (Illus.). 619p. reprint ed. pap. 191.90 (*0-608-18013-0*, 202900200001) Bks Demand.

Organometallic Compounds of Zinc, Cadmium & Mercury. J. L. Wardell. (Chemistry Sourcebook Ser.). 220p. 35.00 (*0-412-26870-1*, 9546) Chapman & Hall.

Organometallic Ion Chemistry. Ed. by Ben S. Freiser. LC 95-12379. (Understanding Chemmical Reactivity Ser.: Vol. 15). 352p. (C). 1996. text 213.50 (*0-7923-3478-7*) Kluwer Academic.

Organometallic Reagents in Organic Synthesis. Ed. by John E. Bateson & M. B. Mitchell. (Smith Kline Beecham Symposium Ser.). (Illus.). 304p. 1994. text 83.00 (*0-12-499150-5*) Acad Pr.

Organometallic Reagents in Synthesis. Paul R. Jenkins. (Oxford Chemistry Primers Ser.: No. 3). (Illus.). 96p. (C). 1992. pap. text 12.95 (*0-19-855666-7*) OUP.

Organometallic Vapor-Phase Epitaxy: Theory & Practice. Ed. by Gerald B. Stringfellow. 398p. 1989. text 100.00 (*0-12-673840-8*) Acad Pr.

Organometallic Vapor-Phase Epitaxy: Theory & Practice. 2nd ed. G. B. Stringfell. LC 98-27187. 634p. 1999. 120.00 (*0-12-673842-4*) Acad Pr.

Organometallics: A Concise Introduction. 2nd ed. Ed. by Christoph Elschenbroich & Albrecht Salzer. 495p. (C). 1992. pap. 39.50 (*3-527-28164-9*, Wiley-VCH) Wiley.

Organometallics in Cancer Chemotherapy, Vol. 1. Ionel Haiduc & Cristian Silvestru. 264p. 1989. boxed set 171.00 (*0-8493-5867-1*, RC271) CRC Pr.

Organometallics in Cancer Chemotherapy, Vol. 2. Ionel Haiduc. 384p. 1990. boxed set 230.00 (*0-8493-5868-X*, RC271) CRC Pr.

Organometallics in Organic Synthesis. Ed. by Armin De Meijere & H. Tom Dieck. (Illus.). 355p. 1988. 103.95 (*0-387-18592-5*) Spr-Verlag.

Organometallics in Organic Synthesis 2. Ed. by H. W. Werner & G. Erker. (Illus.). 320p. 1989. 82.95 (*0-387-50531-8*) Spr-Verlag.

Organometallics in Synthesis: A Manual. Schlosser. text 189.00 (*0-471-98416-7*) Wiley.

Organometallics in Synthesis: A Manual. Ed. by Manfred Schlosser. 614p. 1996. pap. 79.95 (*0-471-96961-3*) Wiley.

Organometallics in Synthesis: A Manual. Ed. by Manfred Schlosser. LC 93-2193. 613p. 1994. reprint ed. pap. 190.10 (*0-608-04599-3*, 206536900003) Bks Demand.

Organometallics of the F-Elements. Ed. by Tobin J. Marks & Dieter Fischer. (NATO Advanced Study Institutes Ser.: C-44). 1979. lib. bdg. 146.00 (*90-277-0990-4*) Kluwer Academic.

Organometallics 1: Complexes with Transition Metal-Carbons-Bonds. Manfred Bochmann. (Oxford Chemistry Primers Ser.: Vol. 12). (Illus.). 96p. (C). 1994. pap. text 12.95 (*0-19-855750-7*, 7848) OUP.

Organometallics 2: Complexes with Transition Metal-Carbon p-Bonds. Manfred Bochmann. (Oxford Chemistry Primers Ser.: No. 13). (Illus.). 96p. (C). 1994. text 29.95 (*0-19-855814-7*); pap. text 12.95 (*0-19-855813-9*) OUP.

Organometals & Organometalloids: Occurrence & Fate in the Environment. Ed. by F. E. Brinckman & J. Michael Bellama. LC 78-24316. (ACS Symposium Ser.: No. 82). 1978. 49.95 (*0-8412-0461-6*) Am Chemical.

Organometals & Organometalloids: Occurrence & Fate in the Environment. Ed. by F. E. Brinckman & J. Michael Bellama. LC 78-24316. (ACS Symposium Ser.: Vol. 82). 463p. 1978. reprint ed. pap. 143.60 (*0-608-03944-6*, 206439100009) Bks Demand.

Organomolybdenum Compounds Pt. 12: Mo Molybdenum. 333p. 1994. 1505.00 (*0-387-93692-0*) Spr-Verlag.

Organon of Medicine. Samuel Hahnemann. Tr. by Naude Kunzli & Pendleton. (Illus.). 1980. 16.95 (*0-87477-223-0*) Formur Intl.

Organon of Medicine. Samuel Hahnemann. Tr. by Alain Naude et al. LC 82-3244. pap. 7.95 (*0-685-43165-7*) St Martin.

Organon of Medicine. 6th ed. Samuel Hahnemann. Tr. by Jost Kunzli et al from GER. 270p. 1993. reprint ed. pap. 16.95 (*0-9636312-0-9*) Cooper Pub.

Organon of the Medical Art. unabridged ed. Samuel Hahnemann. Ed. by Wenda Brewster O'Reilly. Tr. by Steven Decker. 430p. 1996. 55.00 (*1-889613-01-0*); pap. 29.95 (*1-889613-00-2*) Birdcage Bks.

Organonickel Compounds. Planck, Max, Society for the Advancement of Scienc. (Gmelin Handbuch der Anorganischen Chemie Ser.: Vol. 16, Pt. 1). (Illus.). 419p. 1975. 630.00 (*0-387-93294-1*) Spr-Verlag.

Organonitrogen Chemistry. Patrick D. Bailey. (Oxford Chemistry Primers Ser.: Vol. 38). (Illus.). 94p. (C). 1996. pap. text 12.95 (*0-19-855775-2*) OUP.

Organonitrogen Stereodynamics, 2 vols., Set, Pts. I & II. Ed. by Joseph B. Lambert & Yoshito Takeuchi. (Methods in Stereochemical Analysis Ser.). 692p. 1992. text 195.00 (*1-56081-556-6*, Wiley-VCH) Wiley.

Organopgraphy of Plants, Especially of the Archegoniatae & Spermatophyta, 2 vols. K. Goebel. Tr. by Issac B. Balfour from GER. (Illus.). 977p. 1969. reprint ed. lib. bdg. 75.00 (*0-02-845320-4*) Lubrecht & Cramer.

Organophosphates: Chemistry, Fate, & Effects. Ed. by Janice E. Chambers & Patricia E. Levi. (Illus.). 443p. 1992. text 94.00 (*0-12-167345-6*) Acad Pr.

Organophosphorous Chemistry, Vol. 25. D. W. Allen & B. J. Walker. (Specialist Periodical Reports). 350p. 1994. 310.00 (*0-85186-390-6*, R6390) CRC Pr.

Organophosphorous Stereochemistry, 2 pts. Ed. by W. E. McEwen & K. Darrell Berlin. Incl. Pt. 1. Origins of (P3&4) Compounds. 387p. 1975. 77.00 (*0-12-787031-8*); Pt. 2. P(5) Compounds. 1975. 70.00 (*0-12-787032-6*); (Benchmark Papers in Organic Chemistry: Vols. 3 & 4). 1975. write for info. (*0-318-50321-2*) Acad Pr.

Organophosphorus Chemistry, Vol. 11. Walker. 1988. 219.00 (*0-85186-980-7*) CRC Pr.

Organophosphorus Chemistry, Vol. 12. Walker. 1988. 219.00 (*0-85186-106-7*) CRC Pr.

Organophosphorus Chemistry, Vol. 14. Walker. 1988. 208.00 (*0-85186-126-1*) CRC Pr.

Organophosphorus Chemistry, Vol. 15. Walker. 1988. 274.00 (*0-85186-136-9*) CRC Pr.

Organophosphorus Chemistry, Vol. 16. Walker. 1988. 219.00 (*0-85186-146-6*) CRC Pr.

Organophosphorus Chemistry, Vol. 17. Walker. 1988. 241.00 (*0-85186-156-3*) CRC Pr.

Organophosphorus Chemistry, Vol. 19. Walker. 1989. 296.00 (*0-85186-176-8*) CRC Pr.

Organophosphorus Chemistry, Vol. 20. B. J. Walker. 1989. 296.00 (*0-85186-186-5*) CRC Pr.

Organophosphorus Chemistry, Vol. 21. Walker. Ed. by J. B. Hobbs. 1990. 296.00 (*0-85186-196-2*) CRC Pr.

Organophosphorus Chemistry, Vol. 22. Walker & Allen. 1991. 303.00 (*0-85186-206-3*) CRC Pr.

Organophosphorus Chemistry, Vol. 24. D. W. Allen & B. J. Walker. 432p. 1993. 310.00 (*0-85186-320-5*, R6320) CRC Pr.

Organophosphorus Chemistry, Vols. 1-10. Incl. 1969-70 Literature. LC 73-268317. 1971. 38.00 (*0-85186-016-8*); 1971-72 Literature. LC 73-268317. 1973. 38.00 (*0-85186-036-2*); 1972-73 Literature. LC 73-268317. 1974. 41.00 (*0-85186-046-X*); 1973-74 Literature. LC 73-268317. 1975. 41.00 (*0-85186-056-7*); 1974-75 Literature. LC 73-268317. 1976. 50.00 (*0-85186-066-4*); 1975-76 Literature. LC 73-268317. 1977. 56.00 (*0-85186-076-1*); 1977-78 Literature. Ed. by S. Trippett. LC 73-268317. 1979. 72.00 (*0-85186-096-6*); 1968-69 Literature. LC 73-268317. 1970. 34.00 (*0-85186-006-0*); 1970-71 Literature. LC 73-268317. 1972. 38.00 (*0-85186-026-5*); 1976-77 Literature. LC 73-268317. 1978. 61.00 (*0-85186-086-9*); LC 73-268317. write for info. (*0-318-50478-2*) Am Chemical.

Organophosphorus Insecticides. A. W. Hayes. 76p. 1990. text 82.00 (*2-88124-474-2*) Gordon & Breach.

An Asterisk (*) at the beginning of an entry indicates that the title is appearing for the first time.

Organophosphorus Insecticides: A General Introduction. (Environmental Health Criteria Ser.: No. 63). 181p. 1986. pap. text 26.00 (*92-4-154263-2*, 1160063) World Health.

Organophosphorus Pesticides Criteria (Dose-Effect Relationships) for Organophosphorus Compounds. Commission of the European Communities. Ed. by R. Derache. 1977. pap. 95.00 (*0-08-021993-4*, Pub. by Pergamon Repr) Franklin.

Organoselenium Chemistry. Dennis C. Liotta. LC 86-5582. 422p. 1987. 215.00 (*0-471-88867-2*) Wiley.

Organoselenium Chemistry: A Practical Approach. Ed. by Thomas G. Back. LC 99-28970. (The Practical Approach in Chemistry Ser.). (Illus.). 310p. 1999. text 140.00 (*0-19-850141-2*) OUP.

*__Organoselenium Chemistry: Modern Developments in Organic Synthesis.__ Ed. by T. Wirthlin. (Topics in Current Chemistry Ser.). 260p. 2000. 178.00 (*3-540-66516-1*) Spr-Verlag.

Organosilicon & Bioorganosilicon Chemistry: Structure, Bonding, Reactivity & Synthetic Application. Ed. by Hideki Sakurai. LC 85-926. 298p. 1985. text 62.95 (*0-470-20188-6*) P-H.

Organosilicon & Organogermanium Derivatives of Furan, Vol. 12. E. Lukevics & L. M. Ignatovich. (Chemistry Reviews Ser.: SSR Sec. B, Vol. 12, Pt. 3). 106p. 1988. pap. text 87.00 (*3-7186-4854-7*) Gordon & Breach.

Organosilicon Chemistry. Stephan Pawlenko. (Illus.). xii, 186p. 1986. 153.85 (*3-11-010329-X*) De Gruyter.

*__Organosilicon Chemistry Four: From Molecules to Materials.__ 4th ed. Ed. by Morbert Auner & Johann Weis. 852p. 2000. 155.00 (*3-527-29854-1*) Wiley.

Organosilicon Chemistry III: From Molecules to Materials. Ed. by Norbert Auner & Johann Weis. 742p. 1998. 195.00 (*3-527-29450-3*, Wiley-VCH) Wiley.

Organosilicon Heteropolymers & Hetercompounds. Sergei N. Borisov et al. Tr. by Nigel Turton & Tatiani I. Turton from RUS. LC 68-13393. (Monographs in Inorganic Chemistry). 655p. 1970. reprint ed. pap. 200.00 (*0-608-05410-0*, 206587900006) Bks Demand.

Organosulfur Antioxidants in Hydrocarbon Oils, Vol. 4. D. N. Harpp & J. Robertson. 35p. 1985. pap. text 41.00 (*3-7186-0296-2*) Gordon & Breach.

Organosulfur Chemistry. Gordon H. Whitham. (Oxford Chemistry Primers Ser.: No. 33). (Illus.). 96p. (C). 1995. pap. text 12.95 (*0-19-855899-6*) OUP.

Organosulfur Chemistry Vol. 2: Synthetic & Stereochemical Aspects. Ed. by Philip Page. (Organosulfur Chemistry Ser.: Vol. 2). (Illus.). 328p. 1997. text 135.00 (*0-12-543562-2*) Morgan Kaufmann.

*__Organosulfur Chemistry I.__ Ed. by P. C. B. Page et al. (Topics in Current Chemistry Ser.: Vol. 204). (Illus.). 210p. 1999. 135.00 (*3-540-65787-8*) Spr-Verlag.

*__Organosulfur Chemistry II.__ Ed. by P. C. B. Page et al. (Topics in Current Chemistry Ser.: Vol. 205). (Illus.). 200p. 1999. 149.00 (*3-540-65729-0*) Spr-Verlag.

Organosulphur Chemistry: Synthetic Aspects. Ed. by P. Page. (Illus.). 277p. 1995. text 87.00 (*0-12-543560-6*) Acad Pr.

Organotin Chemistry. A. G. Davies. LC 97-194256. 340p. 1997. 270.00 (*3-527-29049-4*, Wiley-VCH) Wiley.

Organotin Compounds. 8th ed. Planck, Max, Society for the Advancement of Scienc. (Gmelin Handbuch der Anorganischen Chemie Ser.: Vol. 26, Pt. 1). 182p. 1975. 290.00 (*0-387-93291-7*) Spr-Verlag.

Organotin Compounds, Vol. 2. Ed. by Albert K. Sawyer. LC 71-142895. 388p. 1971. reprint ed. pap. 120.30 (*0-608-08451-4*, 202710000002) Bks Demand.

Organotin Compounds, Vol. 3. Ed. by Albert K. Sawyer. LC 71-142895. 470p. 1972. reprint ed. pap. 145.70 (*0-608-08452-2*, 202901300003) Bks Demand.

Organotin Compounds: New Chemistry & Applications; A Symposium Sponsored by the Division of Inorganic Chemistry, at the 171st Meeting of the American Chemical Society, New York, N. Y., April 6-7, 1976. Ed. by Jerold J. Zuckerman. LC 76-54338. (Advances in Chemistry Ser.: No. 157). 309p. 1976. reprint ed. pap. 95.80 (*0-608-08450-6*, 202423800035) Bks Demand.

Organotin Compounds, 1971, Vol. 1. Ed. by Albert K. Sawyer. LC 71-142895. (Illus.). 270p. 1971. reprint ed. pap. 83.70 (*0-7837-0956-0*, 204126100001) Bks Demand.

Organotitanium Compounds, Pt. 1. 1977. 415.00 (*0-387-93334-4*) Spr-Verlag.

Organotitanium Reagents in Organic Synthesis. M. T. Reetz. (Reactivity & Structure Ser.: Vol. 24). (Illus.). 240p. 1986. 149.95 (*0-387-15784-0*) Spr-Verlag.

Organotransition Metal Chemistry: Applications to Organic Synthesis. Ed. by S. G. Davies. (Organic Chemistry Ser.: Vol. 2). (Illus.). 428p. 1983. text 190.00 (*0-08-026202-3*, CRC Reprint); pap. text 48.00 (*0-08-030714-0*, CRC Reprint) Franklin.

Organotransition Metal Chemistry: Fundamental Concepts & Applications. Akio Yamamoto. 480p. 1986. 135.00 (*0-471-89171-1*) Wiley.

Organozinc Reagents: A Practical Approach. Ed. by Paul Knochel & Philip Jones. LC 98-34161. (Practical Approach Series in Chemistry). (Illus.). 370p. 1999. text 135.00 (*0-19-850121-8*) OUP.

Organozinc Reagents in Organic Systhesis. Ender Erdik. LC 95-49095. (New Directions in Organic & Biological Chemistry Ser.). 432p. 1996. boxed set 124.95 (*0-8493-9151-2*) CRC Pr.

Organs I Have Met. Edwin H. Lemare. (Illus.). 137p. 1992. 25.00 (*0-913746-32-0*) Organ Lit.

Organs of Equilibrium & Orientation As a Control System. Ed. by M. Valentinuzzi. (Biomedical Engineering & Computation Ser.: Vol. 2). xiv, 194p. 1980. text 322.00 (*3-7186-0014-5*) Gordon & Breach.

Organs of Mexico City Cathedral. Dirk A. Flentrop. Tr. by John Fesperman. LC 85-600240. (Smithsonian Studies in History & Technology: No. 47). 59p. reprint ed. pap. 30.00 (*0-608-15435-0*, 202936200060) Bks Demand.

Organs of Our Time II. Ed. by Homer D. Blanchard. LC 81-185580. (Illus.). 176p. (Orig.). 1981. pap. 20.00 (*0-930112-05-9*) Organ Lit.

Organum Deitatis: Die Christologie des Thomas de Vio Cajetan. Marcel Nieden. (Studies in Medieval & Reformation Thought: Vol. 62). (GER.). 288p. 1997. text 99.50 (*90-04-10801-7*) Brill Academic Pubs.

Organum, Hoc est Libri Omnes Ad Logicam Pertinentes, Graece et Latine. Aristotle. (GER.). 895p. 1967. reprint ed. write for info. (*0-318-70450-1*) G Olms Pubs.

Organum, Hoc Est, Libri Omnes Ad Logicam Pertinentes, Graece et Latine. Aristotle. 895p. 1967. reprint ed. write for info. (*0-318-70862-0*) G Olms Pubs.

Organversagen in der Intensivmedizin. Ed. by W. Behrendt et al. (Beitraege zur Intensiv und Notfallmedizin Ser.: Vol. 1). (Illus.). xii, 182p. 1983. pap. 55.00 (*3-8055-3794-8*) S Karger.

OrganWise Guys Vol. 2: Basic Training for Better Health, 2 vols. Michelle Lombardo. (Illus.). 35p. (J). (gr. 2-5). 1998. write for info. (*0-9648438-3-8*) Wellness GA.

Organran Extending the Frontiers of Venous Thrombosis Prophylaxis. Ed. by J. Hirsh. (Journal: Haemostasis: Vol. 22, No. 2, 1992). (Illus.). 60p. 1992. pap. 47.00 (*3-8055-5626-8*) S Karger.

Orgasm Is a Vacuum, Tension-in-Repose, the Fountain of Youth Foundation: Unifying the Body in the Universal Field of Unification Through Tension-in-Repose. Millicent Linden. (Illus.). 1985. 8.00 (*0-912628-11-1*) M Linden NY.

Orgasmo Adulto Escapes from the Zoo. 1985. pap. 6.95 (*0-88145-028-6*) Broadway Play.

Orgasms: Homosexual Encounters from First Hand, Vol. 2. Ed. by Winston Leyland. (Illus.). 192p. (Orig.). 1985. pap. 10.95 (*0-917342-12-7*) Leyland Pubns.

*__Orgasms of History: 3000 Years of Spontaneous Insurrection.__ AK Press Staff. 2000. pap. 16.00 (*1-902593-34-0*) AK Pr.

Orgelwerke Johann Sebastian Bachs: Die Vorworte Zu Den "Samtlichen Orgelwerken" Albert Schweitzler. (GER.). 270p. 1995. write for info. (*3-487-09710-9*) G Olms Pubs.

Orgia Perpetua (The Perpetual Orgy) Mario Vargas Llosa. (SPA.). 260p. 1995. pap. 23.99 (*84-375-0412-0*, Pub. by Fondo) Continental Bk.

Orgies Unlimited. E. Adam. 6.95 (*0-7472-4528-2*, Pub. by Headline Bk Pub) Trafalgar.

Orgies Unlimited. John Marbeck. 44.95 (*1-893263-06-1*) Ipso Facto.

Orgins of Terrorism: Psychologies, Ideologies, Theologies, States of Mind. Walter Reich. LC 98-24652. 302p. 1998. pap. text 18.95 (*0-943875-89-7*) W Wilson Ctr Pr.

Orgone Accumulator Handbook: Construction Plans, Experimental Use & Protection Against Toxic Energy. James DeMeo. 155p. 1989. pap. 12.95 (*0-9621855-0-7*) Natural Energy.

Orgotek T-Shirt (XL-Only) 17.95 (*1-56504-594-7*) White Wolf.

Orgy. rev. ed. Muriel Rukeyser. LC 97-23632. 216p. 1997. reprint ed. pap. 14.95 (*0-9638183-2-5*) Paris Pr MA.

Orgy Bound. Daniel Clowes. 80p. 1996. pap. 14.95 (*1-56097-302-1*) Fantagraph Bks.

Orgy Room: And Other Stories. Mon Roes. 118p. (C). 1988. pap. 1.95 (*0-9618960-2-7*) M M Fain.

Ori Tahiti, Vol. II, Bk. 17. Vicki Corona. (Celebrate the Cultures Ser.). (Illus.). 32p. 1989. pap. 14.95 (*1-58513-007-9*) Dance Fantasy.

Oria & Valesio: Dutch Archaeological Investigations in the Brindisi Region of Southern Italy. J. S. Boersma. (Mededelingen der Koninklijke Nederlandse Akademie van Wetenschappen, Afd. Letterkunde Ser.: No. 53(3)). 56p. 1990. pap. text 22.50 (*0-444-85717-6*) Elsevier.

Oriana Don't You Cry Vol. XXI: Complete Plays 21; The Infant; Agatha; Elijah; F. A. T. H. E. R. S. Manual Pererias Garcia. 90p. 1998. pap. 4.95 (*1-885901-71-2*) Presbyters Peartree.

Oriana Fallaci: The Rhetoric of Freedom. John Gatt-Rutter. (New Directions in European Writing Ser.). 212p. 1996. 49.50 (*1-85973-069-8*) Berg Pubs.

Oriana Fallaci: The Rhetoric of Freedom. John Gatt-Rutter. Ed. by John E. Flowers. (New Directions in European Writing Ser.). 224p. 1996. pap. 19.50 (*1-85973-074-4*) Berg Pubs.

Oriana Fallaci: The Woman & the Myth. Santo L. Arico. LC 97-14420. 320p. 1998. 29.95 (*0-8093-2153-X*) S Ill U Pr.

Oribatid Mites: A Catalogue of Australian Genera & Species. M. J. Colloff & B. Halliday. (Monographs on Invertebrate Taxonomy: Vol. 6). 224p. 120.00 (*0-643-06371-4*, Pub. by CSIRO) Accents Pubns.

Oriens. Ed. by R. Sellheim. Vol. 34. (GER., Illus.). Vi, 574p. 1994. pap. text (*90-04-10160-8*) Brill Academic Pubs.

Oriens. Ed. by Rudolf Sellheim & Gerhard Endreb. (Milletlerarasi Sark Tetkikleri Cemiyeti Mecmuasi - Journal of the International Society for Oriental Research Ser.: Vol. 35). 296p. 1996. pap. 93.75 (*90-04-10634-0*, NLG135) Brill Academic Pubs.

Oriens-Occidens, Band 1. Willy Hartner. (GER.). xx, 537p. 1968. write for info. (*0-318-70479-X*) G Olms Pubs.

Oriens-Occidens Vol. 1: 2 Aufl. Hildesheim. Willy Hartner. (Collectanea Ser.: Vol. III, 1 & 2). (GER.). xx, 537p. 1980. write for info. (*3-487-01912-4*) G Olms Verlag.

Oriens-Occidens Vol. 2: Schriften zur Wissenschafts und Kulturgeschichte, 2 vols., Set. Willy Hartner. Ed. by Y. Maeyama. Vol. III, 1-2. (GER.). 450p. write for info. (*3-487-07356-0*) G Olms Pubs.

Oriens-Occidens Vol. 2: Schriften zur Wissenschafts-und Kulturgeschichte, 1983. Willy Hartner. Ed. by Y. Maeyama. (GER.). 450p. write for info. (*0-318-70481-1*) G Olms Pubs.

Oriens-Occidens, 1968 Vol. 1. Willy Hartner. Ed. by Y. Maeyama. (GER.). xx, 537p. write for info. (*0-318-70480-3*) G Olms Pubs.

Orient. Judith Samson & Denis Maryk. (Family Library of World Travel). (Illus.). 64p. 1985. pap. 4.95 (*0-933521-18-9*) AGT Pub.

Orient, 12 vols., Set. (GER.). 9231p. 1992. write for info. incl. fiche (*0-318-70565-6*) G Olms Pubs.

Orient: Hero Guide Dog of the Appalachian Trail. Tom McMahon. (Illus.). 32p. (J). (ps-3). 1995. 14.95 (*1-56796-006-5*) WRS Group.

Orient Gateway. Vittorio Giardino. Tr. by Jeff Lisle from ITA. LC 98-178850. (Illus.). 64p. 1997. pap. 13.95 (*1-56163-184-1*, Comics Lit) NBM.

Orient of Style: Modernist Allegories of Conversion. Beryl Schlossman. LC 90-38620. (Illus.). 312p. (C). 1990. text 54.95 (*0-8223-1076-7*); pap. text 21.95 (*0-8223-1094-5*) Duke.

Orient of the Boulevards: Exoticism, Empire, & Nineteenth-Century French Theater. Angela C. Pao. LC 97-29126. (New Cultural Studies). (Illus.). 256p. (C). 1997. 39.95 (*0-8122-3425-1*) U of Pa Pr.

Orient Out the Window: Places & Things Asian. Eugene N. Laughridge. 149p. (Orig.). 1993. pap. 7.95 (*0-9639455-0-5*) MLH Bks.

*__Orient Strikes Back: A Global View of Cultural Display.__ Joy Hendry. (Materializing Culture Ser.). (Illus.). 256p. 2000. 65.00 (*1-85973-328-X*, Pub. by Berg Pubs); pap. 19.50 (*1-85973-333-6*, Pub. by Berg Pubs) NYU Pr.

Orient Sunbeams: From the Porte to the Pyramids, by Way of Palestine. Samuel S. Cox. Ed. by Moshe Davis. LC 77-70665. (America & the Holy Land Ser.). (Illus.). 1977. reprint ed. lib. bdg. 36.95 (*0-405-10238-0*) Ayer.

Orient und Okzident Nach den Hauptwerken des Jakob von Vitry. Ilse Schondorfer. (Europaische Hochschulschriften Ser.: Reihe 3, Bd. 743). (GER.). 256p. 1997. 51.95 (*3-631-31662-3*) P Lang Pubng.

Orient under the Caliphs: With 4 Additional Chapters. Alfred Kremer. LC 77-25110. (Studies in Islamic History: No. 9). xii, 554p. 1978. reprint ed. lib. bdg. 57.50 (*0-87991-458-0*) Porcupine Pr.

Orientacion en Instituciones Educativas. Ana C. Caceres. LC 76-10359. 226p. (Orig.). 1976. pap. 3.50 (*0-8477-2737-8*) U of PR Pr.

Oriental Acquaintance see Collected Works of John W. De Forest

Oriental Acquaintance. John W. De Forest. (Collected Works of John W. De Forest). 1988. reprint ed. lib. bdg. 59.00 (*0-7812-1154-9*) Rprt Serv.

Oriental & Biblical Studies: Collected Writings of E. A. Speiser. Ephraim A. Speiser. Ed. by Moshe Greenberg & Jacob J. Finkelstein. LC 65-21779. 616p. reprint ed. pap. 191.00 (*0-608-30320-8*, 200380200034) Bks Demand.

Oriental & Islamic Art in the Isabella Stewart Gardner Museum. Walter B. Denny et al. LC 75-22427. (Illus.). 136p. (Orig.). 1975. pap. 5.00 (*0-914660-01-2*) I S Gardner Mus.

Oriental & Linguistic Studies, Vol. I. William D. Whitney. 417p. 1981. 25.00 (*0-8290-0529-3*) Irvington.

Oriental & Linguistic Studies, Vol. 1. William D. Whitney. LC 72-8581. (Essay Index Reprint Ser.). 1977. reprint ed. 25.95 (*0-8369-7342-9*) Ayer.

Oriental & Linguistic Studies, Vol. II. William D. Whitney. LC 72-8581. 418p. 1981. 22.00 (*0-8290-0825-X*) Irvington.

Oriental & Western Siberia: A Narrative of Seven Years' Explorations & Adventures in Siberia, Mongolia, the Kirghissteppes, Chinese Tartary & Part of Central Asia. Thomas W. Atkinson. LC 75-115504. (Russia Observed Ser., No. 1). 1978. reprint ed. 33.95 (*0-405-03002-9*) Ayer.

Oriental Annual Containing a Series of Tales, Legends, & Historical Romances. Meadows Taylor & Thomas Bacon. (C). 1995. reprint ed. 34.00 (*81-206-1118-7*, Pub. by Asian Educ Servs) S Asia.

Oriental Antiques & Art: An Identification & Value Guide. Sandra Andacht. LC 87-50296. (Illus.). 428p. (Orig.). 1987. pap. 21.95 (*0-87069-485-5*, Wllce-Homestd) Krause Pubns.

Oriental Architecture I: India, Indonesia, Indochina. Mario Bussagli. LC 88-43458. (History of World Architecture Ser.). (Illus.). 224p. 1989. reprint ed. pap. 29.95 (*0-8478-1056-9*, Pub. by Rizzoli Intl) St Martin.

Oriental Architecture II: China, Korea, Japan. Mario Bussagli. LC 88-43458. (History of World Architecture Ser.). (Illus.). 224p. 1989. reprint ed. pap. 29.95 (*0-8478-1055-0*, Pub. by Rizzoli Intl) St Martin.

Oriental Art: A Quarterly Journal Devoted to All Forms of Oriental Art. Incl. Vols. 1-17, London, 1955-1971. 1986. 1284.00 Vols. 1-3, London, 1948-49-1950-51. 1986. 177.00 Vols. 1-3, London, 1948-49-1950-51. 1986. pap. text 168.00 1986. write for info. (*0-318-60648-8*) Periodicals Srv.

Oriental Art & Culture: A Study of Indian Chinese & Japanese Art, 2 vols., Set. Ed. by A. Waley. (C). 1988. 395.00 (*0-7855-0059-6*, Pub. by Print Hse) St Mut.

Oriental Birth Dreams. Fred J. Seligson. LC 89-83651. (Illus.). 237p. (Orig.). 1989. pap. 22.95 (*0-930878-67-1*) Hollym Intl.

Oriental Caravan. S. I. Shah. 322p. 1984. 150.00 (*1-85077-015-8*, Pub. by Darf Pubs Ltd) St Mut.

Oriental Carpet & Textile Studies, Vol. 6. Ed. by Walter B. Denny et al. 1986. 49.95 (*1-889666-04-1*, 04) Phila Eighth ICOC.

Oriental Carpet Design. P. R. Ford. LC 91-67305. (Illus.). 352p. 1992. reprint ed. pap. 34.95 (*0-500-27664-1*, Pub. by Thames Hudson) Norton.

Oriental Carpet Designs in Full Color. Friedrich Sarre & Trenkwald Sarre. (Illus.). 48p. 1980. pap. 8.95 (*0-486-23835-0*) Dover.

Oriental Carpets. Volkmar Gantzhorn Taschen. (J). 1998. 29.99 (*3-8228-0545-9*, Pub. by Benedikt Taschen) Bks Nippan.

Oriental Carpets. Taschen Staff. 1996. pap. text 29.95 (*3-8228-9631-4*) Taschen Amer.

Oriental Carpets: A Buyer's Guide. Essie Sakhai. (Illus.). 144p. 1995. pap. 16.95 (*1-55921-146-6*) Moyer Bell.

Oriental Carpets: A Complete Guide, Vol. 1. Murray L. Eiland. LC 98-66218. (Illus.). 352p. (gr. 8). 1998. 75.00 (*0-8212-2548-0*) Little.

Oriental Carpets in Miniature: Charted Designs for Needlepoint, Cross-Stitch, or What You Will. Frank M. Cooper. Ed. by Linda C. Ligon. (Illus.). 120p. 1994. pap. 16.95 (*0-934026-98-X*) Interweave.

Oriental Carpets in the Philadelphia Museum of Art. Charles G. Ellis. LC 87-32713. (Illus.). 304p. (Orig.). 1988. pap. 32.00 (*0-87633-070-7*) Phila Mus Art.

Oriental Children in American Homes: How Do They Adjust? Frances M. Koh. LC 81-66194. 132p. 1984. reprint ed. pap. 14.95 (*0-9606090-0-8*) EastWest Pr.

*__Oriental Coins & Their Values Vol. I: The World of Islam.__ M. Mitchener. (Illus.). 510p. 1998. lib. bdg. 265.00 (*0-904173-15-1*) S J Durst.

Oriental Collection: 20 Original Needlepoint Designs. Shelley F. Lazar. 1992. 24.95 (*0-316-88902-4*) Little.

*__Oriental Commerce Vol. 1: Containing a Geographical Description of the Principal Places in the East Indies, China & Japan.__ 2nd ed. William Milburn. (Illus.). 1150p. 1999. reprint ed. 137.50 (*81-215-0895-9*, Pub. by M Manoharial) S Asia.

*__Oriental Commerce Vol. 2: Containing a Geographical Description of the Principal Places in the East Indies, China & Japan.__ 2nd ed. William Milburn. 1999. reprint ed. 99.50 (*81-215-0896-7*, Pub. by M Manoharial) S Asia.

Oriental, Continental & British Porcelain. Robert L. Hobson. LC 76-40888. (Illus.). 1979. 29.95 (*0-89344-023-X*) Ars Ceramica.

Oriental Cooking Class Cookbook. (Illus.). 192p. 1993. 19.98 (*1-56173-024-6*, 2006300) Pubns Intl Ltd.

Oriental Cooking in the Adirondacks. Sudjai N. Bentley. LC 92-90200. 1992. pap. 10.00 (*0-9600902-1-5*) R P Bentley.

Oriental Cross Stitch: 25 Exquisite Designs Inspired by the Far East. Debbie Minton. (Illus.). 128p. 1999. 24.95 (*1-85585-675-1*, Pub. by Collins & Br) Sterling.

Oriental Design Stained Glass Pattern Book. Richard Ott. 64p. 1986. pap. 4.95 (*0-486-25229-9*) Dover.

*__Oriental Designs.__ (Electronic Clip Art Ser.). (Illus.). 64p. 1999. 9.95 incl. cd-rom (*0-486-99964-5*) Dover.

Oriental Despotism: A Comparative Study of Total Power. Karl A. Wittfogel. LC 56-10873. 576p. reprint ed. pap. 178.60 (*0-8357-8256-5*, 203392500087) Bks Demand.

Oriental Dragon, No. 1. G. John Juray. Ed. by Charlotte Taylor. LC 92-90169. 256p. 1992. pap. 12.95 (*0-9632497-0-3*) Juray-Hse Gd Bks.

Oriental Enlightenment: The Encounter Between Asian & Western Thought. LC 96-41067. 272p. (C). 1997. 80.00 (*0-415-13375-0*) Routledge.

Oriental Enlightenment: The Encounter Between Asian & Western Thought. J. J. Clarke. LC 96-41067. 272p. (C). 1997. pap. 22.99 (*0-415-13376-9*) Routledge.

Oriental Essays. Arthur J. Arberry. LC 95-163904. 220p. (C). 1996. 65.00 (*0-7007-0289-X*, Pub. by Curzon Pr Ltd) Paul & Co Pubs.

Oriental Explorations & Studies, 6 vols. , Set. American Geographical Society of New York Staff. reprint ed. 438.00 (*0-404-60230-4*) AMS Pr.

Oriental Floral Designs & Motifs for Artists, Needleworkers & Craftspeople. Ming-Ju Sun. (Illus.). 96p. (Orig.). 1985. pap. 7.95 (*0-486-24903-4*) Dover.

Oriental Flower Arrangements. I. Kong. 1996. 26.95 (*4-07-972714-3*) Shufu No.

Oriental Fortune Telling. Jimmei Shimano. LC 65-18960. (Illus.). 170p. (YA). (gr. 9 up). 1965. pap. 9.95 (*0-8048-0448-6*) Tuttle Pubng.

Oriental Gardening. Maureen Sanchez & Kate Jerome. (American Garden Guides Ser.). 224p. 1996. pap. 25.00 (*0-679-75861-5*) Pantheon.

Oriental Geography of Ibn Hawqal, an Arabian Traveller of the Tenth Century. Ibn Hawqal. Tr. by William G. Ouseley. (ARA.). xxxvi, 327p. reprint ed. lib. bdg. 75.00 (*0-89241-182-1*) Caratzas.

Oriental Girls Desire Romance. Catherine Liu. LC 94-74872. 280p. 1997. pap. 13.95 (*1-885030-24-X*) Kaya Prod.

Oriental Herbal Cookbook for Good Health, Vol. 1. Ed. & Tr. by Pailly W. L. Su from CHI. Tr. by Eileen Wang et al from CHI.Tr. of Han Zang Shi Yang Shen Wang Mu. (Illus.). 155p. 1993. 45.95 (*0-9675483-0-6*) C H Image.

Oriental Images. Intro. by Columbus Museum of Art Staff & Budd H. Bishop. (Illus.). 20p. (Orig.). 1985. pap. 3.50 (*0-918881-13-7*) Columbus Mus Art.

Oriental Insects: Annual Periodical, 1983-1998, Vols. 17-32. 1996. 55.00 (*1-877711-21-7*) Assoc Pubs FL.

Oriental Insects: Quarterly Journal, 1967-82, Vols. 1-16. 1982. pap. 55.00 (*1-877711-20-9*) Assoc Pubs FL.

*__Oriental Insects Vol. 33: An International Journal of Insect Taxonomy of Old World Tropics.__ Ed. by V. K. Gupta. (Illus.). 434p. (C). 1999. text 60.00 (*1-877711-23-3*) Assoc Pubs FL.

Oriental Institute Excavations at Selenkahiye, Syria: Terra-Cotta Figurines & Model Vehicles. Harold Liebowitz. Ed. by Maurits Nanning Van Loon. LC 81-71738. (Bibliotheca Mesopotamica Ser.: Vol. 22). (Illus.). xiv, 60p. 1988. 23.00 (*0-89003-105-3*); pap. 16.00 (*0-89003-104-5*) Undena Pubns.

O

Oriental Institute Hawana Papyri: Demotic & Greek Texts from an Egyptian Family Archive in the Fayum (Fourth to Third Century B. C.) R. Jasnow & G. R. Hughes. LC 96-67506. (Publications: Vol. 113). (Illus.). xxvii, 101p. 1997. text 45.00 (*1-885923-02-3*) Orient Inst.

Oriental Institute Museum Teacher's Kit: Advanced Level. J. D. Barghusen. (Museum Publications). 195p. 1991. 12.00 (*0-918986-81-8*) Orient Inst.

Oriental Institute Museum Teacher's Kit: Elementary Level. J. D. Barghusen. (Museum Publications). 166p. 1991. 12.00 (*0-918986-80-X*) Orient Inst.

Oriental Lacquer. Oliver R. Impey & Mary Tregear. (Illus.). 32p. 1995. pap. 7.25 (*0-900090-88-X*, 088-XX, Pub. by Ashmolean Mus) A Schwartz & Co.

Oriental Learning & Western Knowledge: The Encounter of Educational Traditions in Bengal 1781-1835. Arabella W. Nylund. (Uppsala Studies in Education: No. 38). 186p. (Orig.). 1991. pap. 39.00 (*91-554-2778-2*) Coronet Bks.

Oriental Literature. fac. ed. Incl. Literature of Arabia. Ed. by Epiphanius Wilson. 1977. 13.95 (*0-8369-8229-0*); Literature of China. Ed. by Epiphanius Wilson. 1971. 20.95 (*0-8369-8228-2*); Literature of India. Ed. by Epiphanius Wilson. 1977. 27.95 (*0-8369-8226-6*); Literature of Japan. Ed. by Epiphanius Wilson. 1977. 18.95 (*0-8369-8227-4*); Literature of Persia. Intro. by Richard J. Gottheil. 1977. 28.95 (*0-8369-8225-8*); (Play Anthology Reprint Ser.). 1900. write for info. (*0-318-50865-6*) Ayer.

Oriental Magic. 2nd ed. Idries Shah. (Illus.). 206p. 1992. 48.00 (*0-86304-017-9*, Pub. by Octagon Pr) ISHK.

Oriental Magic: Described & Explained. Harry Kellar et al. (Illus.). 44p. 1992. pap. 9.50 (*0-916638-49-9*) Meyerbooks.

Oriental Materia Medica. Hong-yen Hsu et al. 932p. 1986. 59.95 (*0-941942-22-8*) Orient Heal Arts.

Oriental Mealybug Parasitoids of the Anagyrini. John S. Noyes & M. Hayat. (Illus.). 560p. 1994. text 150.00 (*0-85198-895-4*) OUP.

Oriental Medicine: A Modern Interpretation. Tr. by Kihyon Kim from KOR. (Illus.). xii, 318p. (Orig.). 1996. pap. 29.95 (*0-915649-00-4*) Yuin Univ Pr.

Oriental Medicine: An Illustrated Guide to the Asian Arts of Healing. J. Van Alphen & A. Aris. 1997. pap. 39.95 (*1-57062-317-1*, Pub. by Shambhala Pubns) Random.

Oriental Medicine & Cancer. Myung C. Kim. LC 96-92634. (Illus.). 350p. (Orig.). 1997. pap. 19.95 (*1-890016-00-4*, 96-1001) Seven Galaxy.

Oriental, Medieval, & Renaissance Music see Historical Anthology of Music

Oriental Memoirs: Selected from a Series of Familiar Letters Written During Seventeen Years Residence in India, 4 vols., Set. James Forbes. 1988. reprint ed. 575.00 (*81-212-0111-X*, Pub. by Gian Publng Hse) S Asia.

Oriental Modern: Lin Yutang Translating China & America. Quian Suoqiao. 200p. 1999. 50.00 (*0-8153-3283-1*) Garland.

Oriental Mysticism: A Treatise on Sufistic & Unitarian Theosophy of the Persians. E. H. Palmer. (PER.). 84p. 1974. 18.00 (*0-900860-34-0*, Pub. by Octagon Pr) ISHK.

Oriental Mysticism: A Treatise on Sufistic & Unitarian Theosophy of the Persians. Ed. by Edward H. Palmer. 84p. 1969. reprint ed. 30.00 (*0-7146-2576-0*, Pub. by F Cass Pubs) Intl Spec Bk.

Oriental Orthodox Churches in the United States. Ed. by Robert F. Taft. 32p. 1986. pap. 2.95 (*1-55586-987-4*) US Catholic.

Oriental Orthodox-Roman Catholic Interchurch Marriages & Other Pastoral Relationships. Aelred Cody et al. 164p. (Orig.). 1995. pap. text 17.95 (*1-55586-097-4*) US Catholic.

Oriental Painting Course: A Structured, Practical Guide to Painting Skills & Techniques of... Wang Jainan. LC 96-29557. (Illus.). 224p. 1996. 32.50 (*0-8230-3389-9*) Watsn-Guptill.

Oriental Party Food. Paul Bloomfield. 160p. 1995. 8.95 (*0-316-09923-6*) Little.

Oriental Philosophy: A Westerner's Guide to Eastern Thought. Stuart C. Hackett. LC 78-65010. 251p. reprint ed. pap. 77.90 (*0-8357-4748-4*, 203767000009) Bks Demand.

Oriental Pleasure Troves. 7th ed. Martin Ancel. LC 85-61264. (Illus.). 246p. 1985. pap. 19.95 (*0-685-04064-X*); per. 29.95 (*0-685-57741-4*) Pleasure Trove.

Oriental Policy of the United States. Henry Chung. LC 70-111737. (American Imperialism: Viewpoints of United States Foreign Policy, 1898-1941 Ser.). 1977. reprint ed. 23.95 (*0-405-02008-2*) Ayer.

Oriental Porcelain Painting: A Tour of the Birthplace of Porcelain. Pauline A. Salyer. LC 83-50654. (Illus.). 175p. 1983. lib. bdg. 29.95 (*0-911298-02-9*) Salyer.

Oriental Religions & Their Relation to Universal Religion, 3 vols. Samuel Johnson. (Notable American Authors Ser.). 1992. reprint ed. lib. bdg. 225.00 (*0-7812-3498-0*) Rprt Serv.

Oriental Religions in Roman Paganism, 1911. Franz Cumont. 325p. 1996. reprint ed. pap. 24.95 (*1-56459-537-4*) Kessinger Pub.

Oriental Responses to the West: Comparative Essays in Select Writers from the Muslim World. Nasrin Rahimieh. x, 124p. 1990. pap. 49.50 (*90-04-09177-7*) Brill Academic Pubs.

Oriental Rug Collection of Jerome & Mary Jane Straka. Jerome A. Straka & Louise W. Mackie. LC 78-57955. (Illus.). 136p. 1978. pap. 16.50 (*0-87405-010-3*) Textile Mus.

Oriental Rug Lexicon. Peter F. Stone. LC 96-19139. (Illus.). 288p. 1997. pap. 29.95 (*0-295-97574-1*); text 50.00 (*0-295-97573-3*) U of Wash Pr.

***Oriental Rug Repair.** 2nd rev. ed. Peter F. Stone. (Illus.). 184p. 2000. pap. 39.50 (*0-940582-03-1*) Greenleaf Co.

Oriental Rug Symbols: The Figure in the Carpet. John Train. (Illus.). 128p. 1996. 40.00 (*0-85667-464-8*, Pub. by P Wilson) Scala Books.

Oriental Rugs: A Bibliography. George W. O'Bannon. LC 94-11116. 757p. 1994. 83.50 (*0-8108-2899-5*) Scarecrow.

Oriental Rugs: A Complete Guide. Charles W. Jacobsen. LC 62-14117. (Illus.). 279p. 1962. 49.95 (*0-8048-0451-6*) Tuttle Pubng.

Oriental Rugs: A Practical Guide. Lee Allane. LC 88-50227. (Illus.). 146p. 1988. pap. 14.95 (*0-500-27517-3*, Pub. by Thames Hudson) Norton.

***Oriental Rugs: An Introduction.** Gordon Redford Walker. (Illus.). 256p. 2000. 24.95 (*1-85375-316-5*, Pub. by Prion) Trafalgar.

Oriental Rugs: Care & Repair. Majid Amini. 1995. pap. write for info. (*0-316-03785-0*, Pub. by Little Brown) Trafalgar.

Oriental Rugs Vol. 1: Caucasian. Ian Bennett. (Illus.). 376p. 1981. 89.50 (*0-902028-58-8*) Antique Collect.

Oriental Rugs Vol. 2: Persian. Erich Aschenbrenner. (Illus.). 268p. 1981. 69.50 (*0-907462-12-X*) Antique Collect.

Oriental Rugs Vol. 4: Turkish. C. Fritzche & K. Zipper. (Illus.). 260p. 1990. 69.50 (*1-85149-091-4*) Antique Collect.

Oriental Rugs Vol. 5: Turkoman. Uwe Jourdan. (Illus.). 320p. 1994. 69.50 (*1-85149-136-8*) Antique Collect.

Oriental Rugs, Antique & Modern. Walter A. Hawley. (Illus.). 320p. 1970. reprint ed. pap. 12.95 (*0-486-22366-3*) Dover.

Oriental Rugs from Atlantic Collections. Ed. by Dennis R. Dodds & Murray L. Eiland, III. (Illus.). 304p. 1996. 95.00 (*1-889666-02-5*, 02) Phila Eighth ICOC.

***Oriental Rugs of the Silk Route: Cultural, Process & Selections.** John Gregorian. (Illus.). 176p. 2000. text 50.00 (*0-8478-2221-4*) Rizzoli Intl.

Oriental Rugs Today: A Guide to the Best in New Carpets from the East. Emmett Eiland. LC 99-39180. (Illus.). 208p. 1999. pap. 34.95 (*1-893163-03-2*) Berkeley Hills.

Oriental Scenes. Prod. by Zobeida Perez. 16p. (Orig.). 1994. pap. 17.00 (*0-89898-785-7*) Wrner Bros.

Oriental Secrets to Weight Loss. Yutopian Enterprises Staff. LC 99-177071. 1997. pap. text 14.95 (*1-889554-29-4*) Yutopian Ent.

Oriental 7-Day, Quick Weight-Off Diet, Revised & Expanded. 2nd rev. ed. John Heinerman. 204p. (C). 1996. text 24.95 (*0-13-254905-0*) P-H.

Oriental Shorthair Cats. Stuart A. Kallen. LC 95-48188. (Cats Ser.: Set 2). (J). 1998. lib. bdg. 13.98 (*1-56239-582-3*) ABDO Pub Co.

Oriental Silverwork: Malay & Chinese. H. Ling Roth. (Oxford in Asia Hardback Reprints Ser.). (Illus.). 336p. 1994. 95.00 (*0-19-588605-4*) OUP.

Oriental Tales. Marguerite Yourcenar. Tr. by Alberto Manguel from FRE. 147p. 1986. pap. 11.00 (*0-374-51997-8*) FS&G.

Oriental Tales. large type ed. Marguerite Yourcenar. (Illus.). 200p. 1991. 22.95 (*1-85290-018-0*, Pub. by ISIS Lrg Prnt) Transaction Pubs.

Oriental, the Ancient & the Primitive. Jack Goody. (Studies in Literacy, Family, Culture & the State). (Illus.). 562p. (C). 1990. pap. text 22.95 (*0-521-36761-1*) Cambridge U Pr.

Oriental Theories of Human Development: Scriptural & Popular Beliefs from Hinduism, Buddhism, Confucianism, Shinto, & Islam. R. Murray Thomas. (American University Studies Anthropology & Sociology: Ser. XI, Vol. 19). XX, 345p. 1988. text 45.95 (*0-8204-0681-3*) P Lang Pubng.

Oriental Thought: An Introduction to the Philosophical & Religious Thought of Asia. Yong C. Kim. (Quality Paperback Ser.: No. 365). 144p. 1981. reprint ed. pap. 14.25 (*0-8226-0365-9*) Littlefield.

Oriental Trade Ceramics in South-East Asia: Ninth to Sixteenth Centuries. with a Catalogue of Chinese, Vietnamese & Thai Wares in Australia. Ed. by John S. Guy. (Oxford in Asia Studies in Ceramics). (Illus.). 180p. 1990. pap. text 65.00 (*0-19-588963-0*) OUP.

Oriental U. K. Restaurants, 1997. Egon Ronay Staff. (Travel Guides 1997 Ser.). (Illus.). 360p. (Orig.). 1997. pap. 14.95 (*1-898718-64-4*, Pub. by Ringpr Bks) Seven Hills Bk.

Oriental Vegetables: The Complete Guide for the Gardening Cook. Joy Larkcom. (Illus.). 240p. 1994. pap. 17.00 (*1-56836-017-7*) Kodansha.

Oriental Vegetarian Cooking. Gail Duff. (Illus.). 160p. (Orig.). 1989. pap. 12.95 (*0-89281-344-X*) Inner Tradit.

***Oriental Watercolor Techniques: For Contemporary Painting.** Frederick Wong. (Illus.). 2000. pap. 14.95 (*0-486-40949-X*) Dover.

Orientales: Les Feuilles d'Automne. Victor Hugo. (FRE.). 1981. pap. 19.95 (*0-7859-2783-2*) Fr & Eur.

Orientales: Les Feuilles d'Automne. Victor Hugo. (Poesie Ser.). (FRE.). 384p. 1981. pap. 15.95 (*2-07-032206-8*) Schoenhof.

Orientalia Journal Annual of Articles, Vol. 1. Sandra Andacht. (Illus.). 144p. (Orig.). 1981. pap. 9.95 (*0-9607616-0-8*) S Andacht.

Orientalische Kultur und Europaisches Mittelalter. Ed. by I. Craemer-Ruegenberg & Albert Zimmermann. (Miscellanea Mediaevalia Ser.: Band 17). ix, 440p. 1985. 203.85 (*3-11-010531-4*) De Gruyter.

Orientalische Pferd und das Privatgestute Seiner Majestat Des Konigs (Wilhelm II) von Wurttemberg. August Jager. (Documenta Hippologica Ser.). (Illus.). 216p. 1983. reprint ed. write for info. (*3-487-08056-7*) G Olms Pubs.

Orientalische Skizzen. Theodor Noldeke. (GER.). ix, 304p. 1974. reprint ed. 65.00 (*3-487-05207-5*) G Olms Pubs.

Orientalische und Griechische Bronzereliefs aus Olympia. Brigitte Borell & Dessa Rittig. 368p. 1998. text 200.00 (*3-11-015091-3*) De Gruyter.

Orientalischen Handschriften der Herzoglichen Bibliothek Zu Gotha, 5 vols. Wilhelm Pertsch. xlviii, 2601p. reprint ed. write for info. (*0-318-71551-1*) G Olms Pubs.

Orientalism. Edward W. Said. 180p. 1996. pap. 10.50 (*0-614-21630-3*, 927) Kazi Pubns.

Orientalism. Edward W. Said. LC 79-10497. 1979. pap. 15.00 (*0-394-74067-X*) Vin Bks.

Orientalism Ziauddin Sardar. LC 99-21097. (Concepts in the Social Sciences Ser.). 1999. 19.95 (*0-335-20206-3*) OpUniv Pr.

Orientalism & Modernism: The Legacy of China in Pound & Williams, 1913-1923. Zhaoming Qian. LC 95-6130. (Illus.). 216p. 1995. text 49.95 (*0-8223-1657-9*); pap. text 16.95 (*0-8223-1669-2*) Duke.

Orientalism & Religion: Post-Colonial Theory, India & 'the Mystic East' Richard King. LC 98-46343. 1999. pap. 24.99 (*0-415-20258-2*) Routledge.

***Orientalism & Religion Post-Colonial Theory, India & the Mystic East.** Richard King. LC 98-46343. 1999. write for info. (*0-415-20257-4*) Routledge.

Orientalism & the Postcolonial Predicament: Perspectives on South Asia. Peter Van Der Veer. Ed. by Carol A. Breckenridge. LC 93-18290. (New Cultural Studies). 300p. (Orig.). (C). 1993. text 45.00 (*0-8122-3168-6*); pap. text 20.95 (*0-8122-1436-6*) U of Pa Pr.

Orientalism, Evangelicalism, & the Military Cantonment in Early Nineteenth Century India. Ed. by Nancy G. Cassels. LC 91-34611. 164p. 1991. lib. bdg. 79.95 (*0-7734-9686-6*) E Mellen.

Orientalism in Art. Christine Peltre. LC 98-28579. (Illus.). 295p. 1998. 95.00 (*0-7892-0459-2*) Abbeville Pr.

Orientalism in Lord Byron's "Turkish Tales" "The Giaour (1813), "The Bride of Abydos" (1813), "The Cosair" (1814) & "The Siege of Corinth" (1816) Abdur R. Kidwai. LC 94-37608. 324p. 1995. text 99.95 (*0-7734-8988-6*) E Mellen.

Orientalism, Islam & Islamists. Ed. by Asaf Hussain et al. LC 84-72244. 300p. (Orig.). 1985. 17.50 (*0-915597-15-2*) Amana Bks.

Orientalism, Modernism, & the American Poem. Robert W. Kern. (Studies in American Literature & Culture: No. 97). 329p. (C). 1996. text 59.95 (*0-521-49613-6*) Cambridge U Pr.

Orientalism, Poetry & Millenium. Rosane Rocher. 1983. 44.00 (*0-8364-0870-5*) S Asia.

Orientalism, Postmodernism, & Globalism. Bryan S. Turner. LC 94-4968. 240p. (C). 1994. pap. 24.99 (*0-415-10862-4*, B4648) Routledge.

Orientalism Transposed: The Impact of the Colonies on British Culture. Ed. by Julie F. Codell & Dianne Sachko Macleod. LC 98-70163. (Illus.). 250p. 1998. text 86.95 (*1-85928-454-X*, Pub. by Ashgate Pub) Ashgate Pub Co.

Orientalisms of the Bible, Vol. 2. K. C. Pillai. 1974. 4.95 (*0-912178-04-3*) Mor-Mac.

Orientalizing Revolution: Near Eastern Influence on Greek Culture in the Early Archaic Age. Walter Burkert. (Revealing Antiquity Ser.: No. 5). (Illus.). 256p. 1992. 35.00 (*0-674-64363-1*) HUP.

Orientalizing Revolution: Near Eastern Influence on Greek Culture in the Early Archaic Age. Walter Burkert. Tr. by Margaret E. Pinder. (Revealing Antiquity Ser.: No. 5). (Illus.). 240p. (C). 1995. pap. text 16.50 (*0-674-64364-X*) HUP.

Orientals: Asian Americans in Popular Culture. Robert G. Lee. LC 98-25853. (Asian American History & Culture Ser.). (Illus.). 288p. 2000. text 59.50 (*1-56639-658-1*) Temple U Pr.

***Orientals: Asian Americans in Popular Culture.** Robert G. Lee. (Asian American History & Culture Ser.). (Illus.). 288p. 2000. pap. 19.95 (*1-56639-753-7*) Temple U Pr.

Orientatcion Basica Para Recien Convertidos. Wilfredo Calderon. (SPA.). 116p. 1986. pap. 2.50 (*0-938127-00-4*) Publ Senda de Vida.

Orientation & Communication in Arthropods. M. Lehrer. LC 98-118531. (Experientia Supplementum Ser.: Vol. 84). (Illus.). 350p. 1997. text 160.00 (*3-7643-5693-6*) Birkhauser.

Orientation & Development: Supervisors. Ad Wittemann. 33p. 1974. pap. 25.00 (*0-938481-14-2*) Camelot Consult.

Orientation & Mobility Primer for Families & Young Children. Bonnie Dobson-Burk & Everett W. Hill. LC 89-14878. 48p. 1989. pap. 14.95 (*0-89128-157-6*) Am Foun Blind.

Orientation & Mobility Teaching Manual. 2nd ed. William Allen et al. 120p. (C). 1997. pap. text 24.00 (*1-890786-04-7*) Visions-Srvs.

Orientation & Mobility Techniques: A Guide for the Practitioner. Everett W. Hill & Purvis Ponder. LC 76-15678. 119p. 1976. pap. 22.95 (*0-89128-001-4*) Am Foun Blind.

Orientation & Study Skills. 2nd ed. Williams. 1997. text 19.25 (*0-07-007020-2*) McGraw.

Orientation & Study Skills. 2nd ed. Williams. 1998. 24.00 (*0-07-230126-0*) McGraw.

Orientation & the Leray-Schauder Theory for Fully Nonlinear Elliptic Boundary Value Problems. Patrick Fitzpatrick & Jacobo Pejsachowicz. LC 92-33383. (Memoirs Ser.: No. 483). 131p. 1993. pap. 27.00 (*0-8218-2544-5*, MEMO/101/483) Am Math.

Orientation by Disorientation: Studies on Literary Criticism & Biblical Literary Criticism Presented in Honor of William A. Beardslee. Ed. by Richard A. Spencer. (Pittsburgh Theological Monographs: No. 35). 1980. pap. text 15.00 (*0-915138-44-1*) Pickwick.

Orientation Effects in the Mechanical Behavior of Anisotropic Structural Materials. American Society for Testing & Materials Staff. LC 66-29104. (American Society for Testing & Materials Special Technical Publication Ser.: Special Technical Publication, No. 405). 97p. reprint ed. pap. 30.10 (*0-608-11589-4*, 200070300039) Bks Demand.

Orientation for Offshore Crane Operations. 2nd ed. Ed. by Kathryn Roberts. LC 97-18616. (Rotary Drilling Ser.: Unit V, Lesson 8). (Illus.). 80p. 1997. pap. text 16.00 (*0-88698-179-4*, 2.50820) PETEX.

Orientation in Birds. Ed. by P. Berthold. (Experientia Supplementa Ser.: No. 60). 344p. 1991. 174.50 (*0-8176-2618-2*) Birkhauser.

Orientation Manual for Long-Term Care Facilities: A Program for Developing & Retaining Vital Employees. 2nd ed. Joan M. Iannone & Margaret G. Bye. LC 93-25297. 216p. 1993. 33.95 (*0-8261-8280-1*) Springer Pub.

Orientation of Single Crystals by Back Reflection Laue Pattern Simulation. C. Martin & E. Dieguez. LC 98-54444. 164p. 1998. lib. bdg. 27.00 (*981-02-2871-6*) World Scientific Pub.

Orientation on Quantitative IR-Thermografy in Wall-Shear Stress Measurements. R. Mayer. (Series 01 - Aerodynamics: No. 09). (Illus.). 102p. 1998. pap. 22.50 (*90-407-1572-6*, Pub. by Delft U Pr) Coronet Bks.

Orientation Relating to Exploration & Exploration Drilling for Petroleum Deposits on Svalbard. Norwegian Petroleum Directorate Staff. 1998. pap. text 60.00 (*82-7257-376-8*, Pub. by Oljedirektoratet) St Mut.

Orientation Tips for Returning Students. Margie Sherman. (Illus.). 8p. 1994. pap. 2.50 (*1-884241-22-0*, PO314) Energeia Pub.

Orientation to Cinema - The Complete Guide to Career Planning: A Survey of the Industry for Beginning TV & Film Students, Vols. 1 & 2. 2nd ed. W. Milton Timmons. LC 88-71932. (Illus.). 419p. (C). 1988. pap. text 46.00 (*0-918260-02-7*) Acad Assoc.

Orientation to College: A Reader on Becoming an Educated Person. Jane Shipton & Sharon Villines. Ed. by Elizabeth Steltenpohl. LC 95-30478. 225p. (C). 1995. pap. 36.95 (*0-534-26484-0*) Wadsworth Pub.

Orientation to College Learning. Dianna L. Van Blerkom. LC 94-9682. 298p. 1994. 22.25 (*0-534-24528-5*) Wadsworth Pub.

Orientation to College Learning. Vanblerkom. (Freshman Orientation Ser.). 1994. suppl. ed. 11.25 (*0-534-24531-5*) Wadsworth Pub.

Orientation to College Learning. 2nd ed. Vanblerkom. LC 98-50283. (Freshman Orientation/College Success Ser.). 1999. 34.95 (*0-534-52389-7*) Wadsworth Pub.

Orientation to Counseling. 4th ed. Peterson & Nisenholz. LC 98-12731. 448p. 1998. 71.00 (*0-205-27539-7*) P-H.

Orientation to Deafness. Nanci A. Scheetz. LC 92-11985. 336p. 1992. 76.00 (*0-205-13438-6*, H34382) Allyn.

Orientation to Health Services. Ruth M. Lee. LC 77-15094. 1978. teacher ed. write for info. (*0-672-61435-9*); pap. write for info. (*0-672-61434-0*) Macmillan.

Orientation to Higher Education in California. Susan Moore et al. 176p. (C). 1994. pap. text, per. 11.95 (*0-8403-9689-9*) Kendall-Hunt.

Orientation to Home Care Nursing. Carolyn J. Humphrey & Paula Milone-Nuzzo. LC 95-21181. 326p. 1995. 37.00 (*0-8342-0706-0*, 20706) Aspen Pub.

Orientation to Inquiry in a Reflective Professional Psychology. Lisa L. Hoshmand. LC 93-39602. (SUNY Series, Alternatives in Psychology). 307p. (C). 1994. pap. text 19.95 (*0-7914-2116-3*) State U NY Pr.

Orientation to Inquiry in a Reflective Professional Psychology. Lisa L. Hoshmand. LC 93-39602. (SUNY Series, Alternatives in Psychology). 307p. (C). 1994. text 59.50 (*0-7914-2115-5*) State U NY Pr.

Orientation to Language & Learning Disorders in Children. Mitchell R. Burkowsky. LC 75-176182. 304p. 1973. 16.50 (*0-87527-098-0*) Green.

***Orientation to Nursing in the Rural Community.** Angeline Bushy. LC 00-8364. 2000. pap. write for info. (*0-7619-1157-X*) Sage.

Orientation to Options: Expanding Educational Services for Adults. National Center for Research in Vocational Educati. 1987. 25.00 (*0-317-03905-9*, SP500BVHS) Ctr Educ Trng Employ.

Orientation to the Community College. Linda Aguilar et al. 356p. (C). 1996. pap. text, per. 37.95 (*0-7872-2475-8*) Kendall-Hunt.

Orientation to the Theater. 5th ed. Theodore W. Hatlen. 416p. (C). 1991. pap. text 68.00 (*0-13-638883-3*) P-H.

Orientation to the Trance Experience. Ronald A. Havens & Catherine R. Walters. 1989. 11.95 incl. audio (*0-87630-571-0*) Brunner-Mazel.

Orientation to the World of Work Module, Connections: School & Work Transitions - Work Skills. National Center for Research in Vocational Educati. 1987. write for info. (*0-318-67179-4*, SP100CB01) Ctr Educ Trng Employ.

Orientation to Total Fitness. 5th ed. Vincent J. Melograno & James E. Klinzing. 240p. 1993. per. 19.95 (*0-8403-6745-7*) Kendall-Hunt.

Orientational Optical Nonlinearity of Liquid Crystals: A Special Issue of the Journal Molecular Crystals & Liquid Crystals. N. V. Tabiryan et al. (Molecular Crystals & Liquid Crystals Ser.). iv, 140p. 1986. pap. text 142.00 (*2-88124-147-6*) Gordon & Breach.

Orientational Phenomena in Polymers. Ed. by L. Myasnikova & V. A. Marikhin. (Progress in Colloid & Polymer Science Ser.). 142p. 1994. 83.95 (*0-387-91453-6*) Spr-Verlag.

Orientations. Pierre Boulez. Ed. by Jean-Jacques Nattiez. Tr. by Martin Cooper. 544p. 1986. 39.95 (*0-674-64375-5*) HUP.

Orientations: Collected Writings. Pierre Boulez. Ed. by Jean-Jacques Nattiez. Tr. by Martin Cooper. 544p. 1990. pap. 20.50 (*0-674-64376-3*) HUP.

O

An Asterisk (*) at the beginning of an entry indicates that the title is appearing for the first time.

Orientations in Special Education. Ed. by K. Wedell. LC 74-6660. 220p. reprint ed. pap. 68.20 (*0-8357-3093-X*, 203935000012) Bks Demand.

Oriented Crystallization on Amorphous Substrates. E. I. Givargizov. LC 90-45319. (Microdevices: Physics & Fabrication Technologies Ser.). (Illus.). 382p. (C). 1990. 115.00 (*0-306-43122-X*, Plenum Trade) Perseus Pubng.

Oriented Leadership: Why All Christians Need It. Benjamin D. Williams & Michael T. McKibben. LC 94-4422. 1994. pap. 12.95 (*0-86642-052-5*) Ortho Church Am.

***Oriented Matroids.** Anders Bjorner et al. (Encyclopedia of Mathematics & Its Applications Ser.: No. 46). (Illus.). 550p. (C). 2000. pap. 49.95 (*0-521-77750-X*) Cambridge U Pr.

Oriented Matroids. Bernd Sturmfels et al. (Encyclopedia of Mathematics & Its Applications Ser.: No. 46). (Illus.). 528p. (C). 1993. text 110.00 (*0-521-41836-4*) Cambridge U Pr.

Oriented Polymer Materials. Ed. by Stoyko Fakirov. 1998. 140.00 (*3-527-29693-X*) Wiley.

Orienteering. Boy Scouts of America. (Illus.). 40p. (YA). (gr. 6-12). 1992. pap. 2.90 (*0-8395-3385-3*, 33385) BSA.

Orienteering. Carol McNeill. (Skills of the Game Ser.). (Illus.). 128p. 1996. pap. 19.95 (*1-85223-990-5*, Pub. by Crolwood) Trafalgar.

Orienteering. Tom Renfrew. LC 96-10885. (Outdoor Pursuits Ser.). (Illus.). 136p. (Orig.). 1996. pap. 14.95 (*0-87322-885-5*, PREN0885) Human Kinetics.

Orienteering: The Sport of Navigating with Map & Compass. Steven Boga. LC 96-24380. (Illus.). 208p. 1997. pap. 17.95 (*0-8117-2870-6*) Stackpole.

Orienteering Book. Steve Andreson. LC 77-73875. (Illus.). 100p. 1977. reprint ed. pap. 3.95 (*0-89037-118-0*) Anderson World.

Orienteering Handbook. Anne Anthony. (Illus.). 48p. 1981. pap. 5.95 (*0-88839-047-5*) Hancock House.

Orientierungsversuche: Evangelische Christenheit in Politik, Gesellschaft und Staat. Martin Honecker. 384p. 1998. 124.00 (*3-11-015635-0*) De Gruyter.

Orienting & Habituation: Perspectives in Human Research. Ed. by David Siddle. LC 83-6455. 538p. reprint ed. pap. 166.80 (*0-608-15632-9*, 203176200076) Bks Demand.

Orienting Masculinity, Orienting Nation: Somerset Maugham's Exotic Fiction, 68. Philip Holden. LC 95-46130. (Contributions to the Study of World Literature Ser.: Vol. 68). 176p. 1996. 55.00 (*0-313-29812-2*, Praeger Pubs) Greenwood.

Orienting Polymers: Proceedings of a Workshop Held at the IMA, University of Minnesota, Minneapolis, March 21-26, 1983. Ed. by J. L. Erickson. (Lecture Notes in Mathematics Ser.: Vol. 1063). vii, 166p. 1984. 34.95 (*0-387-13340-2*) Spr-Verlag.

Orienting the Student in College, with Special Reference to Freshman Week. Jay C. Knode. LC 77-176949. (Columbia University. Teachers College. Contributions to Education Ser.: No. 415). reprint ed. 37.50 (*0-404-55415-6*) AMS Pr.

***Orientis Graeci Inscriptiones Selectae, 2 vols.; set.** Ed. by Wilhelm Dittenberger. 1408p. 2000. reprint ed. 150.00 (*0-89005-587-4*) Ares.

Orientis Graeci Inscriptiones Selectae, 2 vols., Set. Wilhelm Dittenberger. (GER.). x, 1408p. 1986. reprint ed. write for info. (*3-487-00030-X*) G Olms Pubs.

Orientreise Vom Jahre 1881. Rudolf Von Habsburg-Lothringen, pseud. (Illus.). 364p. reprint ed. write for info. (*0-318-71514-7*) G Olms Pubs.

Orifice Metering of Natural Gas. (Gas Measurement Committee Reports: No. 3). 85p. 1978. pap. 4.00 (*0-318-12666-4*, XQ0178) Am Gas Assn.

Orifice Metering of Natural Gas. 2nd ed. (Manual of Petroleum Measurement Standards Ser.: Chap. 14.3, Pt. 1). 126p. 1985. 50.00 (*0-317-33090-X*, 852-30350) Am Petroleum.

Oriflamb. Isabel Zuber. (Poetry Chapbook Ser.). 36p. (Orig.). 1987. pap. write for info. (*0-9624274-1-1*) NC Writers Network.

Origami. Paul Jackson. 1999. 9.95 (*1-85967-988-9*, Lorenz Bks) Anness Pub.

Origami. Paula Mulathino. 80p. 1995. 10.98 (*0-7858-0262-2*) Bk Sales Inc.

Origami. Eileen O'Brien & Kate Needham. Ed. by Fiona Watt. (How to Make Ser.). (Illus.). 32p. (Orig.). (J). (gr. 3-7). 1997. pap. 6.95 (*0-7460-2719-2*, Usborne); lib. bdg. 14.95 (*0-88110-938-X*, Usborne) EDC.

Origami. Hidaki Sakata. (Illus.). 66p. (Orig.). 1984. pap. 11.00 (*0-87040-580-2*) Japan Pubns USA.

***Origami.** Jill Smolinski. LC 99-76525. (First-Timers Guides Ser.). (Illus.). 80p. (J). (gr. 1-4). 2000. pap. 8.95 (*0-7373-0370-0*, 03700W, Pub. by Lowell Hse Juvenile) NTC Contemp Pub Co.

Origami: Balloon, Airplane, No. 2. Atsuko Nakata. (Illus.). 16p. 1986. pap. 4.95 (*0-89346-273-X*) Heian Intl.

Origami: Coaster, Birdmobile, No. 7. Atsuko Nakata. (Illus.). 16p. 1986. pap. 4.95 (*0-89346-278-0*) Heian Intl.

Origami: Crab, Dinosaur, No. 10. (Illus.). 16p. 1988. pap. 4.95 (*0-89346-308-6*) Heian Intl.

Origami: Creative Ideas for Paperfolding. Gay M. Gross. LC 95-209803. 72p. 1994. pap. 8.95 (*1-56799-068-1*, Friedman-Fairfax) M Friedman Pub Grp Inc.

Origami: Elephant, Shrimp, No. 11. (Illus.). 16p. 1988. pap. 4.95 (*0-89346-309-4*) Heian Intl.

Origami: Flower, Rocket, No. 3. Atsuko Nakata. (Illus.). 16p. 1986. pap. 4.95 (*0-89346-274-8*) Heian Intl.

Origami: Fox, Ladybug, Crown, No. 6. Atsuko Nakata. (Illus.). 16p. 1986. pap. 4.95 (*0-89346-277-2*) Heian Intl.

Origami: Giraffe, Owl, Tree, No. 9. (Illus.). 16p. 1988. pap. 4.95 (*0-89346-307-8*) Heian Intl.

Origami: Goldfish, Butterfly, No. 15. (Illus.). 16p. (J). (gr. 1-9). 1992. pap. 4.95 (*0-89346-381-7*) Heian Intl.

Origami: House, Hat, Organ, No. 1. Atsuko Nakata. (Illus.). 16p. 1986. pap. 4.95 (*0-89346-272-1*) Heian Intl.

Origami: Inspired by Japanese Prints. Steve Biddle. 48p. 1998. 22.00 (*0-670-88206-2*) Viking Penguin.

Origami: Japanese Paper Folding, Florence Sakade. LC 57-10685. (Illus.). 32p. (Orig.). (J). (gr. 2 up). 1957. pap. 6.95 (*0-8048-0456-7*) Tuttle Pubng.

Origami: Japanese Paper Folding, 3 vols., Vol. 2. Florence Sakade. LC 57-10685. (Illus.). 32p. (Orig.). (J). (gr. 2 up). 1957. pap. 6.95 (*0-8048-0455-9*) Tuttle Pubng.

Origami: Japanese Paper Folding, 3 vols., Vol.1. Florence Sakade. LC 57-10685. (Illus.). 32p. (Orig.). (J). (gr. 2 up). 1957. pap. 6.95 (*0-8048-0454-0*) Tuttle Pubng.

Origami: Mushroom, Gondola, No. 5. (Illus.). 16p. 1986. pap. 4.95 (*0-89346-276-4*) Heian Intl.

Origami: Penguin, Peacock, No. 13. (Illus.). 16p. (J). (gr. 1-9). 1992. pap. 4.95 (*0-89346-379-5*) Heian Intl.

Origami: Purse, Tulip, Umbrella, No. 8. Atsuko Nakata. (Illus.). 16p. 1986. pap. 4.95 (*0-89346-279-9*) Heian Intl.

Origami: Rabbit, Dog, Whale, No. 4. Atsuko Nakata. (Illus.). 16p. 1986. pap. 4.95 (*0-89346-275-6*) Heian Intl.

Origami: Rokoan Style. Masako Sakai & Michie Sahara. (Illus.). 32p. 1998. 22.50 (*0-89346-875-4*) Heian Intl.

Origami: Sailboat, Ice Cream, No. 16. (Illus.). 16p. (J). (gr. 1-9). 1992. pap. 4.95 (*0-89346-382-5*) Heian Intl.

Origami: Sombero, Snail, No. 12. (Illus.). 16p. 1988. pap. 4.95 (*0-89346-310-8*) Heian Intl.

Origami: Sun UFO, Fish, No. 14. (Illus.). 16p. (J). (gr. 1-9). 1992. pap. 4.95 (*0-89346-380-9*) Heian Intl.

Origami ABC's. Hideaki Sakata. (Illus.). 48p. 1997. pap. text 9.95 (*0-87040-999-9*) Japan Pubns USA.

Origami American Style. John Montroll. (Illus.). 32p. (J). (gr. 2 up). 1990. pap. 6.00 (*0-9627254-0-4*) Zenagraf.

Origami & Papercraft. Paul Jackson & Vivian Frank. (Illus.). 128p. 1996. write for info. (*1-57215-146-3*) World Pubns.

Origami Animals. Keiji Kitamura. (Illus.). 80p. 1994. 18.00 (*0-87040-941-7*) Japan Pubns USA.

Origami Animals. Hector Rojas. LC 91-18266. (Illus.). 160p. (YA). (gr. 7 up). 1993. pap. 14.95 (*0-8069-8649-2*) Sterling.

Origami Boxes. Tomoko Fuse. (Illus.). 64p. (Orig.). 1989. pap. 15.00 (*0-87040-821-6*) Japan Pubns USA.

Origami Boxes: For Gifts, Treasures & Trifles. Alexandra Dirk. LC 96-46685. (Illus.). 64p. 1997. pap. 10.95 (*0-8069-9495-9*) Sterling.

Origami Classroom, Vol. I. Dokuotei Nakano. (Illus.). 24p. 1993. pap. 12.95 (*0-87040-912-3*) Japan Pubns USA.

Origami Classroom, Vol. 2. Dokuotei Nakano. (Illus.). 24p. 1994. boxed set 12.95 (*0-87040-938-7*) Japan Pubns USA.

Origami Dinosaurs. Yoshihide Momotani. Ed. by Chikako Noma & Barbara Einzig. (Illus.). 68p. 1993. pap. 12.00 (*1-56836-008-8*) Kodansha.

***Origami-Do: The Art of Paper Folding,** Michael LaFosse. 2000. 35.00 (*1-56496-639-9*) Rockport Pubs.

***Origami Extravaganza: Folding Paper, a Book & a Box.** Tuttle Publishing Firm Staff. LC 00-28709. (Illus.). 2000. 22.95 (*0-8048-3242-0*) Tuttle Pubng.

Origami Flowers. James M. Sakoda. LC 98-27754. (Illus.). 80p. 1999. pap. 6.95 (*0-486-40285-1*) Dover.

Origami for Beginners. Vicente Palacios. LC 98-42549. (Illus.). 96p. 1999. pap. 4.95 (*0-486-40284-3*) Dover.

Origami for Beginners: The Creative World of Paperfolding. Florence Temko. (Illus.). 48p. 1991. pap. 8.95 (*0-8048-1688-3*) Tuttle Pubng.

Origami for Christmas. Chiyo Araki. LC 82-80736. (Illus.). 140p. 1987. pap. 19.00 (*0-87011-807-2*) Kodansha.

Origami for Displays: Ornaments. Toshie Takahama. (Illus.). 32p. (Orig.). pap. 5.95 (*4-07-975428-0*, Pub. by Shufunomoto Co Ltd) Tuttle Pubng.

Origami for Fun: Thirty-One Basic Models. Toshie Takahama. (Illus.). 32p. (Orig.). 1980. reprint ed. pap. 6.95 (*4-07-975339-X*, Pub. by Shufunomoto Co Ltd) Tuttle Pubng.

Origami for the Connoisseur. Kunihiko Kasahara & Toshie Takahama. (Illus.). 1998. pap. 19.00 (*4-8170-9002-2*, Pub. by Japan Pubn Trad) Bks Nippan.

Origami for the Enthusiast: Step-by-Step Instructions in over 700 Diagrams. Montroll. (Illus.). 80p. pap. 7.95 (*0-486-23799-0*) Dover.

Origami from Angelfish to Zen. Peter Engel. LC 93-46659. 1994. 12.95 (*0-486-28138-8*) Dover.

Origami Greeting Cards: A Guide to Making Unique, Attractive Cards for Any Occasion. Isamu Asahi. Tr. by Yuko S. Tomita. (Illus.). 32p. (Orig.). 1990. pap. 7.95 (*0-8048-1587-9*) Tuttle Pubng.

Origami Hearts. Francis M. Ow. (Illus.). 112p. (Orig.). 1996. pap. 15.00 (*0-87040-957-3*) Japan Pubns USA.

Origami in King Arthurs Court: An Adventure in Folding. Lew Rozelle. LC 97-5636. 1997. pap. 15.95 (*0-312-15619-7*, St Martin Griffin) St Martin.

Origami in the Classroom, Bk. 1. Chiyo Araki. LC 65-13412. (Illus.). 40p. (J). (gr. 1 up). 1968. bds. 14.95 (*0-8048-0452-4*) Tuttle Pubng.

Origami in the Classroom, Bk. 2. Chiyo Araki. LC 65-13412. (Illus.). 40p. (J). (gr. 1 up). 1968. bds. 14.95 (*0-8048-0453-2*) Tuttle Pubng.

Origami Insects & Their Kin: Step-by-Step Instructions in over 1500 Diagrams. Robert J. Lang. LC 95-50. (Illus.). 160p. 1995. pap. 9.95 (*0-486-28602-9*) Dover.

Origami Inside-Out. John Montroll. LC 95-90214. (Illus.). 120p. (YA). 1993. pap. 9.95 (*1-877656-08-9*) Antroll Pub.

Origami Inside-Out. John Montroll. LC 93-4147. 1993. reprint ed. pap. 9.95 (*0-486-27674-0*) Dover.

Origami Made Easy. Kunihiko Kasahara. LC 73-83956. (Illus.). 128p. 1973. pap. 9.00 (*0-87040-253-6*) Japan Pubns USA.

Origami Magic. Florence Temko. 72p. (J). (gr. 4-7). 1993. pap. 7.95 (*0-590-47124-4*) Scholastic Inc.

Origami Monsters. Isamu Asahi. (Illus.). 32p. 1992. pap. 8.95 (*0-8048-1867-3*) Tuttle Pubng.

Origami Omnibus: Paper-Folding for Everybody. Kunihiko Kasahara. (Illus.). 384p. 1998. pap. 22.00 (*4-8170-9001-4*, Pub. by Japan Pubn Trad) Bks Nippan.

***Origami Ornaments.** Lew Rozelle. (Illus.). 160p. 2000. pap. 17.95 (*0-312-26369-4*) St Martin.

Origami, Plain & Simple. Robert Neale & Thomas Hull. LC 93-44067. (Illus.). 112p. (Orig.). 1994. pap. 10.95 (*0-312-10516-9*) St Martin.

Origami Playtime Bk. 1: Animals. Nobuyoshi Enomoto. (Illus.). 32p. (Orig.). (J). (gr. 2-8). 1992. pap. 6.95 (*0-8048-1726-X*) Tuttle Pubng.

Origami Playtime Bk. 2: Toys & Knick-Knacks. N. Enomoto. (Illus.). 32p. (Orig.). (J). (gr. 2-8). 1992. pap. 4.95 (*0-8048-1727-8*) Tuttle Pubng.

Origami Rockets: Spinners, Zoomers, Floaters & More. Lew Rozelle. LC 98-31678. 192p. 1999. pap. 17.95 (*0-312-19944-9*) St Martin.

Origami Safari. Steve Biddle & Megumi Biddle. (Illus.). 80p. (YA). (gr. 4 up). 1994. pap. 8.95 (*0-688-13570-6*, Wm Morrow) Morrow Avon.

Origami Sculptures. 2nd ed. John Montroll. Ed. by Andrew Montroll. LC 89-81888. (Illus.). 120p. (Orig.). (YA). 1990. pap. text 9.95 (*1-877656-02-X*) Antroll Pub.

Origami Sculptures. 2nd ed. John Montroll. 144p. (Orig.). 1990. pap. 9.95 (*0-486-26587-0*) Dover.

Origami Sea Life. John Montroll. 256p. 1991. pap. 10.95 (*0-486-26765-2*) Dover.

Origami Sea Life. 2nd ed. John Montroll & Robert Lang. Ed. by Andrew Montroll. LC 90-80778. (Illus.). 192p. 1991. pap. text 10.95 (*1-877656-05-4*) Antroll Pub.

Origami Step by Step. Robert Harbin. (Illus.). 64p. 1998. pap. 3.95 (*0-486-40136-7*) Dover.

***Origami to Astonish & Amuse.** JEREMY SHAFER. (Illus.). 208p. 2000. pap. 19.95 (*0-312-25404-0*) St Martin.

Origami Toys: Fifteen Simple Models. Toshie Takahama. (Illus.). 32p. (Orig.). 1973. pap. 6.95 (*4-07-975210-5*, Pub. by Shufunomoto Co Ltd) Tuttle Pubng.

Origami Treasure Chest. Keiji Kitamura. (Illus.). 80p. (Orig.). (J). 1991. pap. 18.00 (*0-87040-868-2*) Japan Pubns USA.

Origami Workshop. Gay M. Gross & Nancy Palubniak. LC 94-26921. (Illus.). 120p. 1995. pap. text 11.95 (*1-56799-148-3*, Friedman-Fairfax) M Friedman Pub Grp Inc.

***Origami Wreaths & Rings.** David Petty. LC 98-61606. (Illus.). 123p. 1998. pap. 19.95 (*0-9627254-1-2*) Zenagraf.

Origami Zoo. Robert J. Lang. 1990. pap. 15.95 (*0-312-04015-6*) St Martin.

Origamic Architecture: Tour of Nara, Ancient Capital of Japan. Masahiro Chatani. 82p. 1993. pap. 39.95 (*4-395-27043-3*, Pub. by Shokokusha) Bks Nippan.

Origamic Architecture Around the World. 2nd ed. Ed. by Masahiro Chatani. (Illus.). 66p. 1989. pap. 29.95 (*4-395-27017-4*, Pub. by Shokokusha) Bks Nippan.

Origamic Architecture Goes Modern: Building Masterpieces. Masahiro Chatani. (Illus.). 96p. 1991. pap. 39.95 (*4-395-27040-9*, Pub. by Shokokusha) Bks Nippan.

Origanum (Labiate) rev. ed. J. H. Ietswaart. (Leiden Botanical Ser.: No. 4). (Illus.). 153p. 1980. pap. 31.00 (*90-6021-463-3*, Pub. by Rijksherbarium) Balogh.

Origen. Henri Crouzel. 1996. 49.95 (*0-567-09500-2*) Bks Intl VA.

Origen. Henri Crouzel. Tr. by A. S. Worrall. 296p. pap. 29.95 (*0-567-08639-9*) T&T Clark Pubs.

Origen. Joseph W. Trigg. LC 97-23338. (Early Church Fathers Ser.). 264p. (C). 1998. 75.00 (*0-415-11835-2*, D4878); pap. 24.99 (*0-415-11836-0*, D4882) Routledge.

Origen. Jean Danielou. Tr. by Walter Mitchell. LC 82-48698. (Orthodoxies & Heresies in the Early Church Ser.). reprint ed. 36.00 (*0-404-62381-6*) AMS Pr.

Origen: Selected Writings. Ed. by Rowan A. Greer. LC 79-84886. (Classics of Western Spirituality Ser.). 334p. 1979. pap. 23.95 (*0-8091-2198-0*) Paulist Pr.

Origen: Treatise on the Passover & Dialogue with Heraclides. Ed. & Tr. by Robert J. Daly. (Ancient Christian Writers Ser.: No. 54). 1992. 16.95 (*0-8091-0452-0*) Paulist Pr.

Origen & the Life of the Stars: A History of an Idea. Alan B. Scott. (Oxford Early Christian Studies). 206p. 1994. reprint ed. pap. text 26.00 (*0-19-826361-9*) OUP.

Origen de la Leyenda. S. R. Curtis. (Zorro Ser.). (SPA.). 1998. pap. text 9.95 (*1-58105-166-2*) Santillana.

Origen de las Especies. Charles Darwin. Ed. by Jaume Jose. Tr. by Antonio De Zulueta. (Nueva Austral Ser.: Vol. 16). (SPA.). 1991. pap. text 34.95 (*84-239-1816-5*) Elliots Bks.

Origen, Prayer, Exhortation to Martyrdom. Ed. by Walter J. Burghardt et al. LC 78-62467. (Ancient Christian Writers Ser.: No. 19). 261p. 1954. 29.95 (*0-8091-0256-0*) Paulist Pr.

Origen, Spirit & Fire: A Thematic Anthology of His Writings. Ed. by Hans U. Von Balthasar. Tr. by Robert J. Daly. LC 83-14368. 434p. 1984. reprint ed. pap. 134.60 (*0-7837-9110-0*, 204991200004) Bks Demand.

Origen, the Song of Songs: Commentary & Homilies. Ed. by Walter J. Burghardt et al. LC 57-11826. (Ancient Christian Writers Ser.: No. 26). 491p. 1957. 24.95 (*0-8091-0261-7*) Paulist Pr.

Origen y Formacion del Estado en Mesoamerica. Ed. by Andres Medina et al. 198p. 1986. pap. 9.14 (*968-837-959-X*, UN029) UPLAAP.

Origenes de la Burguesia en la Espana Medieval. Luis Garcia de Valdeavellano. Ed. by Jose M. Perez-Prendes. (Nueva Austral Ser.: Vol. 231). (SPA.). 1991. pap. text 24.95 (*84-239-7231-3*) Elliots Bks.

Origenes de la Ciencia Moderna. Elias Trabulse. (Breviarios Ser.). (SPA.). pap. 11.99 (*968-16-4378-X*, Pub. by Fondo) Continental Bk.

Origenes de la Civilizacion. V. Childe. (Breviarios Ser.). (SPA.). pap. 8.99 (*968-16-0178-5*, Pub. by Fondo) Continental Bk.

Origenes de la Civilizacion Maya. Richard Adams. (SPA.). 19.99 (*968-16-3254-0*, Pub. by Fondo) Continental Bk.

Origenes de la Guerra Con Mexico (Origins of the War with Mexico) Glenn W. Price. (SPA.). 290p. 1974. pap. 8.99 (*968-16-2417-3*, Pub. by Fondo) Continental Bk.

Origenes de la Nacionalidad Mexicana (Origins of the Mexican Nationality) Peggy K. Liss. (SPA.). 273p. 1986. pap. 13.99 (*968-16-1937-4*, Pub. by Fondo) Continental Bk.

Origenes de un Barrio Chicano (Origin of a Chicano Barrio) Bruce Johansen & Roberto Maestas. (SPA.). 184p. 1989. pap. 9.99 (*968-16-2867-5*, Pub. by Fondo) Continental Bk.

Origenes del Correo Terrestre en Guatemala. Walter B. Bose. (Guatemala Postal History Pamphlet Ser.: No. 1). 1984. reprint ed. pap. 4.25 (*0-913129-03-8*) La Tienda.

Origenes del Costumbrismo Etico-Social, Addison y Steele: Antecedentes del Articulo Costumbrista Espanol y Argentino. Gioconda Marun. LC 83-80966. (SPA.). 167p. (Orig.). 1983. pap. 19.95 (*0-89729-278-2*) Ediciones.

Origenes y Desarrollo de la Aficion Teatral en Puerto Rico. Emilio J. Pasarell. Incl. Bk. 2. Siglo XX. pap. 3.50 (*0-8477-3144-8*); (Illus.). (C). Set pap. 6.00 (*0-8477-3142-1*) U of PR Pr.

Origenes y Desarrollo del Espanol en Puerto Rico: Siglos XVI y XVII. Manuel A. Nazario. LC 80-21477. 470p. 1982. 15.00 (*0-8477-3197-9*); pap. 12.00 (*0-8477-3198-7*) U of PR Pr.

Origeniana Quinta, No. Betl 105. E. Peters. 1998. 84.95 (*90-6831-423-8*, Pub. by Peeters Pub) Bks Intl VA.

Origeniana Sexta, No. Betl 118. E. Peters. LC 96-204051. 1998. 122.00 (*90-6831-725-3*, Pub. by Peeters Pub) Bks Intl VA.

Origenist Controversy: The Cultural Construction of an Early Christian Debate. Elizabeth Ann Clark. 352p. 1992. text 52.50 (*0-691-03173-8*, Pub. by Princeton U Pr) Cal Prin Full Svc.

Origen's Hexapla & Fragments: Papers Presented at the Rich Seminar on the Hexapla, Oxford Centre for Hebrew & Jewish Studies, 25th-3rd August 1994. Ed. by Alison Salvesen. (Texte und Studien Zum Antiken Judentum Ser.: No. 58). (Illus.). 516p. 1998. 157.50 (*3-16-146575-X*, Pub. by JCB Mohr) Coronet Bks.

Origin & Antiquity of Freemasonry. Albert Churchward. 75p. (Orig.). 1992. reprint ed. pap. 12.95 (*1-56459-107-7*) Kessinger Pub.

Origin & Authority in Seventeenth-Century England: Bacon, Milton, Butler. Alvin Snider. 288p. 1994. text 55.00 (*0-8020-2865-9*) U of Toronto Pr.

Origin & Cause: A Crime Novel. Shelly Reuben. 352p. 1994. 20.00 (*0-684-19702-2*, Scribners Ref) Mac Lib Ref.

Origin & Conclusion of the Paris Pact. Denys P. Myers. LC 75-147608. (Library of War & Peace; Kellogg Pact & the Outlawry of War). 1975. lib. bdg. 46.00 (*0-8240-0368-3*) Garland.

Origin & Destination. Alighiero E. Boetti. 1998. pap. text 35.00 (*2-930246-00-6*, Pub. by Soc Exposit) Dist Art Pubs.

Origin & Destiny of Humanity. William E. Key-Nee. LC 89-51874. 160p. (C). 1990. pap. 9.95 (*0-924608-00-5*, Whitford) Schiffer.

Origin & Development of a Philosophy of Long-Range Planning in American Business. David I. Cleland. LC 75-41751. (Companies & Men: Business Enterprises in America Ser.). (Illus.). 1976. 35.95 (*0-405-08068-9*) Ayer.

Origin & Development of Dhrupad & Its Bearing on Instrumental Music. E. S. Perera. LC 94-902446. (C). 1995. 28.50 (*81-7074-111-4*, Pub. by KP Bagchi) S Asia.

Origin & Development of Dramatic Criticism in the New York Times, 1851-1880. John Rothman. LC 78-126346. 1971. 12.95 (*0-405-02560-2*) Ayer.

Origin & Development of Islam. Asghar Ali Engineer. 248p. 1980. 19.95 (*0-940500-33-7*) Asia Bk Corp.

Origin & Development of Jazz. 3rd ed. Otto Werner. 256p. (C). 1994. per. 29.95 (*0-8403-9567-1*) Kendall-Hunt.

Origin & Development of Language. Roy Wilkinson. (Learning Resources Ser.). 64p. (Orig.). 1992. pap. 12.95 (*1-869890-35-3*, Pub. by Hawthorn Press) Anthroposophic.

Origin & Development of Light Opera. Sterling Mackinlay. 1972. 59.95 (*0-8490-0772-0*) Gordon Pr.

Origin & Development of One Henry Sixth in Relation to Shakespeare, Marlowe, Peele & Greene. Allison Gaw. LC 75-144614. vi, 180 p. 1971. reprint ed. 20.00 (*0-404-02689-3*) AMS Pr.

Origin & Development of Psychoanalysis. Sigmund Freud. 108p. 1960. pap. 8.95 (*0-89526-919-8*) Regnery Pub.

Origin & Development of the Army Security Agency, 1917-1947. U. S. Army Security Agency Staff. 51p. 1994. pap. 12.80 (*0-89412-025-5*) Aegean Park Pr.

Origin & Development of the Bengali Language. Suniti K. Chatterji. 1993. reprint ed. 29.00 (*81-7167-117-9*, Pub. by Rupa) S Asia.

Origin & Development of the Christian Church in Gaul During the First Six Centuries of the Christian Era. T. Scott Holmes. 1977. lib. bdg. 59.95 (*0-8490-2382-3*) Gordon Pr.

Origin & Development of the Law of the Sea. R. P. Anand. 1982. lib. bdg. 114.00 (*90-247-2617-4*) Kluwer Academic.

Origin & Development of the Moral Ideas, 2 vols., Set. Edward A. Westermarck. LC 78-22241. (Gay Experience Ser.). reprint ed. 64.50 (*0-404-61532-5*) AMS Pr.

O

Origin & Development of the Moral Ideas, 2 Vols., Set. Edward A. Westermarck. LC 74-37359. (Select Bibliographies Reprint Ser.). 1977. reprint ed. 89.95 (*0-8369-6706-2*) Ayer.

Origin & Development of the National Security Agency. George A. Brownell. 98p. 1981. pap. 20.80 (*0-89412-054-9*) Aegean Park Pr.

Origin & Development of the Playa Basins, Sources of Recharge to the Ogallala Aquifer, Southern High Plains, Texas & New Mexico. T. C. Gustavson et al. (Reports of Investigations: No. 229). (Illus.). 44p. 1995. pap. 6.00 (*0-614-11623-6*) Bur Econ Geology.

Origin & Development of the Pueblo Katsina Cult. E. Charles Adams. LC 90-48047. 235p. 1993. reprint ed. pap. 17.95 (*0-8165-1358-9*) U of Ariz Pr.

Origin & Development of the Story of Troilus & Criseyde. K. Young. 1972. 250.00 (*0-8490-0773-9*) Gordon Pr.

Origin & Development of the Study of Language in the West. Vivien Law. (C). 1997. text 90.00 (*0-485-11498-4*) Humanities.

Origin & Development of Troilus & Criseyde. Karl O. Young. LC 68-8342. 200p. (C). 1968. reprint ed. 50.00 (*0-87752-125-5*) Gordian.

Origin & Development of Vaisnaivism. Suvira Jaiswal. 1981. 23.50 (*0-8364-2611-8*, Pub. by M Manoharial) S Asia.

Origin & Development of Western Cuisine. Emma Grandy. (Illus.). 630p. (Orig.). 1994. 24.95 (*0-9644078-0-9*) Emma Grandy.

Origin & Diagenesis of Cap Rock, Gyp Hill & Oakwood Salt Domes, Texas. C. W. Kreitler & S. P. Dutton. (Reports of Investigations: RI 131). (Illus.). 58p. 1983. pap. 3.50 (*0-318-03284-8*) Bur Econ Geology.

Origin & Distribution of Tell el Yahudiyeh Ware. Maureen F. Kaplan. (Studies in Mediterranean Archaeology: Vol. LXII). (Illus.). 476p. (Orig.). 1980. pap. 97.50 (*91-85058-49-1*, Pub. by P Astroms) Coronet Bks.

Origin & Distribution of the Elements: Proceedings of the Symposium (New Orleans) G. J. Mathews. 780p. (C). 1988. text 138.00 (*9971-5-0455-3*) World Scientific Pub.

Origin & Diversification of Language. Ed. by Nina G. Jablonski & Leslie C. Aiello. LC 98-71454. (Memoirs of the California Academy of Sciences Ser.: No. 24). (Illus.). 204p. 1998. 19.95 (*0-940228-44-0*, Pub. by Calif Acad Sci); pap. 19.95 (*0-940228-46-7*, Pub. by Calif Acad Sci) U CA Pr.

Origin & Doctrines of Early Indian Buddhist Schools. Vasu-Mitra. Tr. by Jiryo Masuda. LC 78-70133. reprint ed. 32.50 (*0-404-17403-5*) AMS Pr.

Origin & Early Development of the Chinese Writing System. William G. Boltz. (American Oriental Ser.: Vol. 78). ix, 205p. 1994. 47.50 (*0-940490-78-1*) Am Orient Soc.

Origin & Early Diversification of Land Plants: A Cladistic Study. Paul Kenrick & Peter R. Crane. LC 97-24710. (Series in Comparative Evolutionary Biology). (Illus.). 592p. 1997. text 55.00 (*1-56098-730-8*); pap. text 27.50 (*1-56098-729-4*) Smithsonian.

Origin & Early Evolution of Angiosperms. Charles B. Beck. 1976. text 97.00 (*0-231-03857-7*) Col U Pr.

Origin & Early Evolution of Animals. Earl D. Hanson. LC 76-41480. (Illus.). 680p. 1977. reprint ed. pap. 200.00 (*0-8357-6247-5*, 205682100090) Bks Demand.

Origin & Early Evolution of the Metazoa. J. H. Lipps & P. W. Signor. (Topics in Geobiology Ser.: Vol. 10). (Illus.). 578p. (C). 1992. text 120.00 (*0-306-44067-9*, Kluwer Plenum) Kluwer Academic.

Origin & Early History of Christianity in Britain: From Its Dawn to the Death of Augustine. Andrew Gray. LC 90-86205. 144p. (Orig.). 1991. reprint ed. pap. 7.00 (*0-934666-43-1*) Artisan Pubs.

Origin & Early History of Engraving in France. Andre Blum. LC 77-73881. (Illus.). 1978. reprint ed. lib. bdg. 60.00 (*0-87817-216-5*) Hacker.

Origin & Early History of the Office of Notary. James C. Brown. 1976. lib. bdg. 59.95 (*0-8490-2383-1*) Gordon Pr.

Origin & Education of a Doctor. Brooks Ranney. LC 90-92020. (Illus.). 396p. 1990. pap. 12.00 (*0-9618939-2-3*) B Ranney.

Origin & Evaluation of Formation Pressures. Bhagwan Sahay & Walter H. Fertl. (C). 1989. text 207.50 (*0-7923-0126-9*) Kluwer Academic.

Origin & Evolution of Biological Energy Conversion. Ed. by H. Baltscheffsky. 328p. 1997. 135.00 (*0-471-18581-7*) Wiley.

Origin & Evolution of Biological Energy Conversion. Ed. by Herrick Baltscheffsky. (Illus.). 350p. 1996. 125.00 (*1-56081-614-7*, Wiley-VCH) Wiley.

Origin & Evolution of Birds. 2nd ed. Alan Feduccia. LC 95-46758. (Illus.). 534p. (C). 1996. 55.00 (*0-300-06460-8*) Yale U Pr.

Origin & Evolution of Birds. 2nd ed. Alan Feduccia. LC 98-43737. (Illus.). 480p. 1999. pap. text 29.95 (*0-300-07861-7*) Yale U Pr.

Origin & Evolution of Deserts. Ed. by Stephen G. Wells & Donald R. Haragan. LC 83-1340. (Contributions of the Committee on Desert & Arid Zones Research of the Southwestern & Rocky Mountain Division of the American Association for the Advancement of Science Ser.). 240p. reprint ed. pap. 74.40 (*0-608-15403-2*, 202931600060) Bks Demand.

Origin & Evolution of Earth. Kent Condie & Robert Sloan. LC 97-43759. 498p. 1998. 80.00 (*0-13-491820-7*) P-H.

Origin & Evolution of Freemasonry Connected with the Origin & Evolution of the Human Race. Albert Churchward. Ed. by Al I. Obaba. (Illus.). 250p. 1990. pap. text 25.00 (*0-916157-48-2*) African Islam Miss Pubns.

Origin & Evolution of Freemasonry Connected with the Origin & Evolution of the Human Race. Albert Churchward. (African Heritage Classical Research Studies). pap. 25.00 (*0-938818-59-7*) ECA Assoc.

Origin & Evolution of Freemasonry Connected with the Origin & Evolution of the Human Race. Albert Churchward. 239p. 1996. reprint ed. spiral bd. 38.00 (*0-7873-0172-8*) Hlth Research.

Origin & Evolution of Freemasonry Connected with the Origin & Evolution of the Human Race. Albert Churchward. 239p. 1992. reprint ed. pap. 19.95 (*1-56459-104-2*) Kessinger Pub.

Origin & Evolution of Galaxies. B. J. Jones & J. E. Jones. 1982. pap. text 88.00 (*90-277-1517-3*); lib. bdg. 146.00 (*90-277-1507-6*) Kluwer Academic.

Origin & Evolution of Galaxies: Proceedings of the Course of the International School of Cosmology & Gravitation, 7th, Erice, Trapani, Scicily, May 11-23, 1981. Ed. by Venzo De Sabbata. 222p. 1982. 70.00 (*9971-950-05-7*) World Scientific Pub.

Origin & Evolution of Gymnosperms. Ed. by Charles B. Beck. (Illus.). 552p. 1988. text 91.00 (*0-231-06358-X*) Col U Pr.

Origin & Evolution of Humans & Humanness. Ed. by D. Tab Rasmussen & Schopf. LC 93-6741. 160p. 1993. pap. text 37.50 (*0-86720-857-0*) Jones & Bartlett.

Origin & Evolution of Intelligence. J. William Schopf & Arnold B. Scheibel. LC 96-49305. (Life Science Ser.). 296p. 1997. 38.75 (*0-7637-0365-6*) Jones & Bartlett.

Origin & Evolution of Interplanetary Dust. Ed. by A. C. Levasseur-Regourd & H. Hasegawa. 450p. (C). 1992. text 226.50 (*0-7923-1365-8*) Kluwer Academic.

Origin & Evolution of Larval Forms. Brian K. Hall. LC 98-86239. 1998. 79.95 (*0-12-730935-7*) Acad Pr.

Origin & Evolution of Life: On the Theory of Action, Reaction & Interaction of Energy. Henry F. Osborn. Ed. by Stephen Jay Gould. LC 79-8340. (History of Paleontology Ser.). (Illus.). 1980. reprint ed. lib. bdg. 36.95 (*0-405-12728-6*) Ayer.

Origin & Evolution of Life on Earth. David W. Hollar. (Magill Bibliographies Ser.). 235p. 1992. 42.00 (*0-8108-2797-2*) Scarecrow.

Origin & Evolution of Man. Cold Spring Harbor Symposia on Quantitative Biolog. LC 34-8174. (Cold Spring Harbor Symposia on Quantitative Biology Ser.: Vol. 15). (Illus.). 439p. 1951. pap. 136.10 (*0-7837-8973-4*, 204975400003) Bks Demand.

Origin & Evolution of Neutron Stars. Ed. by D. J. Helfand & J. H. Huang. (C). 1987. lib. bdg. 197.00 (*90-277-2537-3*) Kluwer Academic.

Origin & Evolution of Neutron Stars. Ed. by D. J. Helfand & J. H. Huang. xx, 572p. (C). 1987. pap. text 83.00 (*90-277-2538-1*) Kluwer Academic.

Origin & Evolution of Pacific Island Biotas, New Guinea to Eastern Polynesia: Patterns & Processes. Ed. by Allen Keast & Scott E. Miller. (Illus.). 531p. 1996. 230.00 (*90-5103-136-X*, Pub. by SPB Acad Pub) Balogh.

Origin & Evolution of Planetary & Satellite Atmospheres. Ed. by S. K. Atreya et al. LC 89-4651. (Space Science Ser.). 881p. 1989. 67.50 (*0-8165-1105-5*) U of Ariz Pr.

Origin & Evolution of Planetary Atmospheres. fac. ed. A. Henderson-Sellers. LC 83-124743. (Monographs on Astronomical Subjects: No. 9). (Illus.). 256p. 1983. reprint ed. pap. 79.40 (*0-7837-8003-6*, 204775900008) Bks Demand.

Origin & Evolution of Planetary Nebulae. Sun Kwok. LC 99-21392. (Cambridge Astrophysics Ser.: No. 33). (Illus.). 320p. (C). 2000. 69.95 (*0-521-62313-8*) Cambridge U Pr.

Origin & Evolution of Primitive Man (1912) Albert Churchward. 136p. 1999. reprint ed. pap. 24.95 (*0-7661-0831-7*) Kessinger Pub.

Origin & Evolution of Prokaryotic & Eukaryotic Cells. Koichiro Matsuno & H. Hartman. 442p. 1993. text 106.00 (*981-02-1262-3*) World Scientific Pub.

Origin & Evolution of Religion. Albert Churchward. 421p. 1996. reprint ed. spiral bd. 62.00 (*0-7873-0174-4*) Hlth Research.

Origin & Evolution of Religion. Albert Churchward. 422p. 1992. reprint ed. pap. 37.00 (*1-56459-203-0*) Kessinger Pub.

Origin & Evolution of Religion, Vol. 1. Albert Churchward. Ed. by Al I. Obaba. (Illus.). 172p. 1924. pap. text 22.00 (*0-916157-27-X*) African Islam Miss Pubns.

Origin & Evolution of Religion, Vol. 2. Albert Churchward. Ed. by Al I. Obaba. (Illus.). 114p. 1924. pap. text 12.00 (*0-916157-28-8*) African Islam Miss Pubns.

Origin & Evolution of Religion, Vol. 3. Albert Churchward. Ed. by Al I. Obaba. 250p. 1924. pap. text 30.00 (*0-685-38272-9*) African Islam Miss Pubns.

Origin & Evolution of Sedimentary Basins & Their Energy & Mineral Resources, IUGG 3. Ed. by R. W. Hutchinson & Roger W. Macqueen. (Geophysical Monograph Ser.: Vol. 48). 202p. 1989. 30.00 (*0-87590-452-1*) Am Geophysical.

Origin & Evolution of the Calls & Facial Expressions of the Primates see Evolution of Facial Expression: Two Accounts

Origin & Evolution of the Elements. S. Kubono & T. Kajino. 300p. 1993. text 95.00 (*981-02-1394-8*) World Scientific Pub.

Origin & Evolution of the Gastropod Family Pomatiopsidae, with Emphasis on the Mekong River Triculinae. George M. Davis. (Monograph: No. 20). (Illus.). 120p. 1979. pap. 5.00 (*0-910006-28-8*) Acad Nat Sci Phila.

Origin & Evolution of the Human Race. Albert Churchward. (Illus.). 600p. 1994. reprint ed. pap. 39.95 (*1-56459-427-0*) Kessinger Pub.

Origin & Evolution of the Human Race, Vol. I. Albert Churchward. Ed. by Al I. Obaba. (Illus.). 146p. 1990. pap. text 22.00 (*0-916157-39-3*) African Islam Miss Pubns.

Origin & Evolution of the Human Race, Vol. II. Albert Churchward. Ed. by Al I. Obaba. (Illus.). 144p. 1990. pap. text 22.00 (*0-916157-40-7*) African Islam Miss Pubns.

Origin & Evolution of the Human Race, Vol. III. Albert Churchward. Ed. by Al I. Obaba. (Illus.). 142p. 1990. pap. text 22.00 (*0-916157-41-5*) African Islam Miss Pubns.

Origin & Evolution of the Human Race, Vol. IV. Albert Churchward. Ed. by Al I. Obaba. (Illus.). 224p. 1990. pap. text 22.00 (*0-916157-42-3*) African Islam Miss Pubns.

Origin & Evolution of the Human Race, Vol. V. Albert Churchward. Ed. by Al I. Obaba. (Illus.). 116p. 1990. pap. text 22.00 (*0-916157-43-1*) African Islam Miss Pubns.

Origin & Evolution of the Universe. Ed. by Ben Zuckerman & Matthew A. Malkan. LC 96-4260. 152p. 1996. pap. 36.25 (*0-7637-0030-4*) Jones & Bartlett.

Origin & Evolution of the Universe: Evidence for Design? Ed. by John Robson. 318p. 1987. 65.00 (*0-7735-0617-9*, Pub. by McG-Queens Univ Pr); pap. 22.95 (*0-7735-0618-7*, Pub. by McG-Queens Univ Pr) CUP Services.

***Origin & Evolution of the Vertebrate Immune System.** Ed. by L. Du Pasquier & G. W. Litman. (Current Topics in Microbiology & Immunology Ser.: Vol. 248). (Illus.). 340p. 2000. 199.00 (*3-540-66414-9*) Spr-Verlag.

***Origin & Evolution of Tropical Rain Forests.** Robert J. Morley. LC 99-29654. 272p. 2000. 140.00 (*0-471-98326-8*) Wiley.

Origin & Evolution of Viruses. Esteban Domingo. 496p. 1999. 120.00 (*0-12-220360-7*) Acad Pr.

Origin & Evolutionary Radiation of the Mollusca. Ed. by John D. Taylor. (Illus.). 406p. (C). 1996. text 135.00 (*0-19-854980-6*) OUP.

Origin & Function of Human Feelings. Victor S. Johnston. 1998. write for info. (*0-201-36084-5*) Addison-Wesley.

Origin & Goal of History. Karl Jaspers. Tr. by Michael Bullock from GER. LC 76-21246. 294p. 1977. reprint ed. lib. bdg. 41.50 (*0-8371-8983-7*, JAOG, Greenwood Pr) Greenwood.

Origin & Growth of Caste in India. N. K. Dutt. 340p. 1986. reprint ed. 18.00 (*0-8364-1677-5*) S Asia.

Origin & Growth of Christianity in Tripura. Sukhendu Debbarma. (C). 1996. 18.00 (*81-7387-038-1*, Pub. by Indus Pub) S Asia.

Origin & Growth of Plato's Logic: With an Account of Plato's Style & of the Chronology of His Writings. Wincenty Lutoslawski. xviii, 547p. 1983. reprint ed. 89.70 (*3-487-07336-6*) G Olms Pubs.

Origin & Growth of Plato's Logic: With an Account of Plato's Style & the Chronology of His Writings. Wincenty Lutoslawski. (Classical Studies). reprint ed. lib. bdg. 62.00 (*0-697-00041-9*) Irvington.

Origin & Growth of the American Constitution: An Historical Treatise in Which the Documentary Evidence As to the Making of the Entirely New Plan of Federal Government Embodied in the Existing Constitution of the United States Is, for the First Time, Set Forth As a Complete & Consistent Whole. Hannis Taylor. LC 98-24693. xliv, 676p. 1998. reprint ed. 75.00 (*0-8377-2677-8*, Rothman) W S Hein.

Origin & Growth of the English Constitution, an Historical Treatise, 2 vols. Hannis Taylor. 1992. write for info. (*0-318-68966-9*); write for info. (*0-318-68967-7*) W S Hein.

Origin & Growth of the English Constitution, an Historical Treatise, 2 vols., Set. Hannis Taylor. 1992. reprint ed. lib. bdg. 150.00 (*0-8377-2636-0*, Rothman) W S Hein.

Origin & Growth of the Moral Instinct, 2 vols. Alexander Sutherland. LC 73-14182. (Perspectives in Social Inquiry Ser.). 822p. 1974. reprint ed. 51.95 (*0-405-05525-0*) Ayer.

Origin & Growth of Village Communities in India. Baden H. Baden-Powell. 155p. 1985. reprint ed. 125.00 (*81-85046-14-X*, Pub. by Scientific) St Mut.

Origin & History of Contract in Roman Law down to the End of the Republican Period: Being the York Prize Essay for the Year 1893. W. W. Buckler. xi, 228p. 1983. reprint ed. 35.00 (*0-8377-0341-7*, Rothman) W S Hein.

Origin & History of Irish Names of Places. Patrick W. Joyce. 611p. 1998. reprint ed. pap. 41.00 (*0-7884-0972-7*, J591) Heritage Bk.

Origin & History of Marginal & Inland Seas: Proceedings of the 27th International Geological Congress, Vol. 23. International Geological Congress Staff. 230p. 1984. lib. bdg. 84.00 (*90-6764-032-8*, Pub. by VSP) Coronet Bks.

Origin & History of the Earth see Proceedings of the 30th International Geological Congress

Origin & History of the English Language. G. P. Marsh. 1972. 59.95 (*0-8490-0774-7*) Gordon Pr.

Origin & History of the Name of Bennett. Crescent Family. (Illus.). 112p. 1988. reprint ed. pap. 20.00 (*0-8328-0239-5*); reprint ed. lib. bdg. 28.00 (*0-8328-0238-7*) Higginson Bk Co.

Origin & History of the New York Employing Printers' Association. Charlotte E. Morgan. LC 68-58608. (Columbia University. Studies in the Social Sciences: No. 319). reprint ed. 27.50 (*0-404-51319-0*) AMS Pr.

Origin & Ideals of the Modern School. Francisco Ferrer Y Guardia. Tr. by Joseph McCabe. LC 73-161328. (Atheist Viewpoint Ser.). 126p. 1979. reprint ed. 16.95 (*0-405-03809-7*) Ayer.

Origin & Influence of the Thoroughbred Horse. William Ridgeway. LC 73-174446. (Illus.). 1972. reprint ed. 30.95 (*0-405-08890-6*, Pub. by Blom Pubns) Ayer.

Origin & Meaning of Hasidism. Martin Buber. LC 87-26192. 264p. (C). 1988. reprint ed. pap. 19.95 (*0-391-03549-5*) Humanities.

Origin & Mineralogy of Clays: Clays & the Environment. Ed. by Bruce Velde. (Illus.). x, 360p. 1995. 108.95 (*0-387-58012-3*) Spr-Verlag.

Origin & Mineralogy of Clays Vol. 1: Clay & the Environment. Ed. by Bruce Velde. LC 95-24195. 1995. write for info. (*3-540-58012-3*) Spr-Verlag.

Origin & Nature of Our Institutional Models. rev. ed. Wolf Wolfensberger. (Illus.). 1975. 8.50 (*0-937540-03-X*, HPP-4) Human Policy Pr.

Origin & Originality in Renaissance Literature: Versions of the Source. David Quint. LC 82-24789. 275p. reprint ed. pap. 85.30 (*0-7837-4528-1*, 208019100003) Bks Demand.

***Origin & Originality in Rushdie's Fiction.** Dutheil De la Rochere & Martine Hennard. LC 99-35311. xxxvi, 232p. (C). 1999. pap. text 41.95 (*0-8204-4241-0*) P Lang Pubng.

***Origin & Originality in Rushdie's Fiction.** Martine Hennard Dutheil de la Rochere. xxxvi, 232p. 1999. pap. 41.95 (*3-906762-63-7*, Pub. by P Lang) P Lang Pubng.

Origin & Past of Homo Sapiens. S. Brenner & K. Hanihara. (Human Biology Ser.). 316p. 1995. text 61.00 (*981-02-1912-1*) World Scientific Pub.

Origin & Prevention of Major Wars. Ed. by Robert I. Rotberg & Theodore K. Rabb. (Studies in Interdisciplinary History). 360p. (C). 1989. pap. text 21.95 (*0-521-37955-5*) Cambridge U Pr.

Origin & Principles of the American Revolution, Compared with the Origin & Principles of the French Revolution. Friedrich Von Gentz. Ed. by Richard Loss. LC 77-16175. 96p. 1977. reprint ed. lib. bdg. 50.00 (*0-8201-1302-6*) Schol Facsimiles.

Origin & Progress of the American Party in Politics: Embracing a Complete History of the Philadelphia Riots in May & July of 1844. John H. Lee. LC 79-117881. (Select Bibliographies Reprint Ser.). 1977. reprint ed. 26.95 (*0-8369-5334-7*) Ayer.

Origin & Progress of Writing. 2nd ed. Thomas Astle. LC 76-161701. reprint ed. lib. bdg. 84.50 (*0-404-00413-X*) AMS Pr.

Origin & Refining of Petroleum. Ed. by H. G. McGrath & M. E. Charles. LC 73-164409. (Advances in Chemistry Ser.: No. 103). 1971. 24.95 (*0-8412-0120-X*) Am Chemical.

Origin & Refining of Petroleum. American Chemical Society, Division of Petroleum Chemistry Staff. LC 73-164409. (Advances in Chemistry Ser.: No. 103). (Illus.). 240p. 1971. reprint ed. pap. 74.40 (*0-608-03276-X*, 206379400007) Bks Demand.

Origin & Resolution of an Urban Crisis: Baltimore, 1890. Alan D. Anderson. LC 77-4553. (Johns Hopkins Studies in Urban Affairs). 155p. reprint ed. pap. 48.10 (*0-608-14630-7*, 202582300046) Bks Demand.

Origin & Role of the European Bank for Reconstruction & Development. Paul A. Menkveld. 192p. (C). 1991. lib. bdg. 100.50 (*1-85333-626-2*, Pub. by Graham & Trotman) Kluwer Academic.

Origin & Signification of Scottish Surnames. Clifford S. Sims. 122p. 2000. reprint ed. 17.50 (*0-8063-0314-X*, 5400) Genealog Pub.

Origin & Spread of Oriental Words in European Languages. Arnaldo Steiger. 1963. 15.95 (*0-913298-32-8*) S F Vanni.

Origin & Treatment of Schizophrenic Disorders. Theodore Lidz. 158p. 1990. reprint ed. pap. 26.95 (*0-8236-8206-4*, BN 23895) Intl Univs Pr.

Origin & Use of the Word Africa. Manu Ampim. (Illus.). 1995. pap. write for info. (*0-9636447-5-0*) Advan The Res.

Origin by Design. Harold G. Coffen. LC 82-21445. (Illus.). 494p. 1983. pap. 16.99 (*0-8280-0131-6*) Review & Herald.

Origin, Derivation & Diminutive Forms of Jewish Personal Names. Shmuel Gorr. Ed. by Chaim Freedman. LC 92-24934. 128p. 1992. reprint ed. 15.00 (*0-9626373-2-7*) Avotaynu.

Origin, Diagenesis, & Petrophysics of Clay Minerals in Sandstone. Ed. by David W. Houseknecht & Edward H. Pittman. (Special Publications Ser.: No. 47). (Illus.). 1992. 92.00 (*0-918985-95-1*) SEPM.

Origin, Evolution & Modern Aspects of Biomineralization in Plants & Animals. Ed. by R. E. Crick. (Illus.). 548p. (C). 1990. text 180.00 (*0-306-43498-9*, Kluwer Plenum) Kluwer Academic.

***Origin, Expansion & Demise of Plant Species.** Donald A. Levin. LC 99-34861. (Oxford Series in Ecology & Evolution). (Illus.). 240p. 2000. text 70.00 (*0-19-512728-5*); pap. text 35.00 (*0-19-512729-3*) OUP.

Origin Legend of the Navaho Enemy Way. Berard Haile. LC 76-43725. (Yale Univ. Publications in Anthropology: No. 17). 328p. 1983. reprint ed. 37.50 (*0-404-15781-5*) AMS Pr.

Origin Legend of the Navajo Flintway. Berard Haile. LC 74-7972. reprint ed. 49.50 (*0-404-11859-3*) AMS Pr.

Origin Like Water: Collected Poems, 1967-1987. Eavan Boland. 206p. 1997. pap. 12.00 (*0-393-31601-7*) Norton.

Origin Myth of Acoma & Other Records. Matthew W. Stirling. (Bureau of American Ethnology Bulletins Ser.). 123p. 1995. lib. bdg. 79.00 (*0-7812-4135-9*) Rprt Serv.

Origin, Occurrence & Behaviour of Sediments in Sewer Systems. M. A. Verbanck. (Water Science & Technology Ser.: Vol. 25). 234p. 1992. 105.75 (*0-08-042185-7*, Pergamon Pr) Elsevier.

Origin of Adaptations. Verne Grant. LC 63-11695. (Illus.). 606p. 1963. text 111.50 (*0-231-02529-7*) Col U Pr.

An Asterisk (*) at the beginning of an entry indicates that the title is appearing for the first time.

Origin of Adaptations. Verne Grant. LC 63-11695. (Illus.). 606p. 1971. pap. text 34.50 (*0-231-08648-2*) Col U Pr.

Origin of American Black English: Be-Forms in Hoodoo Texts. Traute Ewers. (Topics in English Linguistics Ser.: No. 15). xi, 327p. (C). 1995. lib. bdg. 121.55 (*3-11-014586-3*) Mouton.

Origin of Animal Body Plans: A Study in Evolutionary Developmental Biology. Wallace Arthur. (Illus.). 352p. (C). 1997. text 74.95 (*0-521-55014-9*) Cambridge U Pr.

Origin of Animal Body Plans: A Study in Evolutionary Developmental Biology. Wallace Arthur. (Illus.). 352p. (C). 2000. pap. write for info. (*0-521-77928-6*) Cambridge U Pr.

Origin of Arithmetic Skills: A Phenomenographic Approach. Dagmar Neuman. (Goteborg Studies in Educational Sciences: No. 62). 352p. 1987. pap. 59.50 (*91-7346-194-6*, Pub. by Acta U Gothenburg) Coronet Bks.

Origin of Attic Comedy. Francis M. Cornford. LC 92-38813. (Ann Arbor Paperbacks Ser.). 344p. 1993. pap. text 16.95 (*0-472-08195-0*, 08195) U of Mich Pr.

Origin of Biblical Traditions. Albert T. Clay. LC 78-63556. (Yale Oriental Series: Researches: No. 12). reprint ed. 37.50 (*0-404-60282-7*) AMS Pr.

Origin of Birds & the Evolution of Flight. Ed. by Kevin Padian. (Memoirs of the California Academy of Sciences Ser.: No. 8). 98p. 1986. pap. text 13.00 (*0-940228-14-9*) Calif Acad Sci.

Origin of Bombay. J. Gerson Da Cunha. (C). 1993. reprint ed. text 48.00 (*81-206-0815-1*, Pub. by Asian Educ Servs) S Asia.

Origin of British Field Systems: An Interpretation. Robert A. Dodgshon. LC 80-49987. 1980. text 111.00 (*0-12-219260-5*) Acad Pr.

***Origin of Capitalism.** Ellen M. Wood. 132p. 1999. 30.00 (*1-58367-007-6*, Pub. by Monthly Rev) NYU Pr.

Origin of Capitalism. Ellen Meiksins Wood. LC 98-48940. 2p. 1999. pap. text 13.00 (*1-58367-000-9*, Pub. by Monthly Rev) NYU Pr.

Origin of Cells: Causes & Cures of Cancer: Bone, Face, Lungs, Prostate. Betty Zorotovich. (Illus.). 254p. (Orig.). 1980. pap. 19.95 (*0-9605084-0-6*) McCall-Faure.

Origin of Certain Place Names in the United States. Henry Gannett. 280p. 1996. pap. 22.00 (*0-7884-0579-9*, 6055) Heritage Bk.

Origin of Certain Place Names in the United States. Henry Gannett. 280p. 1978. reprint ed. 24.95 (*0-87928-097-2*) Corner Hse.

Origin of Certain Place Names in the United States. 2nd ed. Henry Gannett. 334p. 1996. pap. 31.50 (*0-8063-0544-4*, 2135) Genealog Pub.

Origin of Chinese Culture. Hong Jia. (CHI.). 158p. (Orig.). 1996. pap. 4.95 (*0-9644818-3-9*) Waymont Intl.

Origin of Chinese Deities. Cheng Manchao. 240p. 1995. 9.95 (*7-119-00030-6*, Pub. by Foreign Lang) China Bks.

Origin of Chinese Festivals. Ed. by Goh P. Ki. Tr. by Koh K. Kiang. (Illus.). 228p. 1997. pap. 14.95 (*981-3068-61-2*) China Bks.

Origin of Civilisation & the Primitive Condition of Man. John L. Avebury. LC 72-1280. (Select Bibliographies Reprint Ser.). 1977. reprint ed. 31.95 (*0-8369-6819-0*) Ayer.

Origin of Civilization & Language. Premsukh Poonai. LC 94-65864. (Illus.). 247p. (C). 1994. 29.00 (*1-883122-03-1*) Pearce Pub.

Origin of Competitive Strength: Fifty Years of the Auto Industry in Japan & the U. S. A. Kawahara. (Illus.). xxxiv, 278p. 1998. 59.95 (*4-431-70223-7*) Spr-Verlag.

Origin of Consciousness: An Attempt to Conceive the Mind As a Product of Evolution. Charles A. Strong. LC 75-3402. reprint ed. 46.50 (*0-404-59398-4*) AMS Pr.

Origin of Consciousness in the Breakdown of the Bicameral Mind. Jolian Jaynes. 1978. pap. 18.95 (*0-8020-6511-2*) U of Toronto Pr.

Origin of Consciousness in the Breakdown of the Bicameral Mind. Julian Jaynes. 480p. 1990. pap. 18.00 (*0-395-56352-6*) HM.

***Origin of Consciousness in the Breakdown of the Bicameral Mind.** Julian Jaynes. (Illus.). 512p. 2000. pap. 17.95 (*0-618-05707-2*) HM.

Origin of Continents & Oceans. A. Wegener. 1977. pap. 69.95 (*0-8490-2384-X*) Gordon Pr.

Origin of Continents & Oceans. Alfred Wegener. Tr. by John Biram. (Illus.). 246p. 1999. pap. 8.95 (*0-486-61708-4*) Dover.

Origin of Cosmic Rays. Ed. by J. L. Osborne & Arnold W. Wolfendale. LC 75-2436. (NATO Advanced Study Institutes Ser.: No. C14). x, 466p. 1975. lib. bdg. 146.00 (*90-277-0585-2*) Kluwer Academic.

Origin of Cosmic Rays. Ed. by Giancarlo Setti et al. 1981. pap. text 73.00 (*90-277-1272-7*) Kluwer Academic.

Origin of Death: Studies in African Mythology. Hans Abrahamsson. Ed. by Robert J. Kastenbaum. LC 76-19555. (Death & Dying Ser.). 1979. reprint ed. lib. bdg. 25.95 (*0-405-09551-1*) Ayer.

Origin of Egyptian Symbolism. Iamblichus. Tr. by Alexander Wilder from GRE. 1991. reprint ed. pap. 3.95 (*1-55818-141-5*, Sure Fire) Holmes Pub.

Origin of English Surnames. P. H. Reaney. 1980. pap. 12.95 (*0-7100-0353-6*, Routledge Thoemms) Routledge.

Origin of Ethnography in Japan: Yanagita Kunio & His Times. Minoru Kawada. (Japanese Studies). 220p. 1993. 89.95 (*0-7103-0450-1*, A9888) Routledge.

Origin of Everyday Moods: Managing Energy, Tension & Stress. Robert E. Thayer. 1996. 19.95 (*0-614-97010-5*) OUP.

Origin of Everyday Moods: Managing Energy, Tension & Stress. Robert E. Thayer. (Illus.). 288p. 1996. 35.00 (*0-19-508791-7*) OUP.

Origin of Everyday Moods: Managing Energy, Tension & Stress. Robert E. Thayer. (Illus.). 288p. 1997. reprint ed. pap. 14.95 (*0-19-511805-7*) OUP.

Origin of Everything: The Cosmos, the Earth & You. Carl Carrozza. (Textworks Ser.). (Illus.). ix, 91p. (YA). (gr. 6-12). 1995. ring bd. 39.95 (*1-58284-014-8*, Thoughtful Educ) Silver Strong.

Origin of Evil. John Fiske. (Notable American Authors Ser.). 1992. reprint ed. lib. bdg. 75.00 (*0-7812-2857-3*) Rprt Serv.

Origin of Finger-Printing. William J. Herschel. LC 78-156019. (Criminal Justice Ser.). (Illus.). 178p. 1974. reprint ed. 36.50 (*0-404-09119-9*) AMS Pr.

Origin of Formalism in Social Science. Jeffrey T. Bergner. LC 80-17484. 160p. 1981. 19.50 (*0-226-04362-2*) U Ch Pr.

Origin of Formalism in Social Science. Jeffrey T. Bergner. LC 80-17484. 174p. reprint ed. pap. 54.00 (*0-608-09386-6*, 205413100004); reprint ed. pap. 53.70 (*0-608-21010-2*, 2054538) Bks Demand.

Origin of Freemasonry & Knight Templar (1907) John R. Bennett. 215p. 1996. reprint ed. pap. 17.95 (*1-56459-557-9*) Kessinger Pub.

Origin of German Tragic Drama. Walter Benjamin. 256p. 1998. 22.00 (*1-85984-899-0*, Pub. by Verso) Norton.

Origin of Human Characteristics & Behavior. Charles W. Stiehl. (Enlightenment of Man Ser.). 128p. pap. text 29.95 (*0-9701997-0-8*, I) Scholars Libr.

Origin of Humankind. Richard Leakey. LC 94-3617. (Science Masters Ser.). (Illus.). 171p. 1994. 20.00 (*0-465-03135-8*, Pub. by Basic) HarpC.

Origin of Humankind. Richard Leakey. 192p. 1996. pap. 12.00 (*0-465-05313-0*) HarpC.

Origin of Intelligence in the Child see Jean Piaget

Origin of Jagannath Deity. Jitamitra P. Singh Deo. (C). 1991. 22.00 (*81-212-0352-X*, Pub. by Gian Publng Hse) S Asia.

Origin of Land Plants. Linda E. Graham. 304p. 1993. 140.00 (*0-471-61527-7*) Wiley.

Origin of Language. Ed. by Roy Harris & Andrew Pyle. (Key Issues Ser.). 300p. 1996. 72.00 (*1-85506-438-3*) Bks Intl VA.

Origin of Language. Ed. by Roy Harris & Andrew Pyle. (Key Issues Ser.: Vol. 7). 300p. 1996. pap. 24.00 (*1-85506-437-5*) Bks Intl VA.

Origin of Language: Tracing the Evolution of the Mother Tongue. Merrit Ruhlen. 239p. 1994. 27.95 (*0-471-58426-6*) Wiley.

Origin of Language: Tracing the Evolution of the Mother Tongue. Merritt Ruhlen. LC 93-39009. (Illus.). 256p. 1996. pap. 17.95 (*0-471-15963-8*) Wiley.

Origin of Laws, Arts, & Sciences & Their Progress among the Most Ancient Nations, 3 vols. Antoine Y. Goguet & A. C. Fugere. LC 72-1630. (Illus.). reprint ed. 210.00 (*0-404-08230-0*) AMS Pr.

Origin of Life. Wolman. 1981. lib. bdg. 171.00 (*90-277-1229-8*) Kluwer Academic.

Origin of Life: A Panoramic History of the Known & the Unknown. Edmond B. Szekely. (Illus.). 80p. 1988. 7.50 (*0-89564-079-1*) IBS Intl.

Origin of Life & Death: African Creation Myths. Ulli Beier. (African Writers Ser.). 65p. (C). 1966. pap. 7.95 (*0-435-90023-4*, 90023) Heinemann.

Origin of Life on Earth: An African Creation Myth. David A. Anderson-Sankofa. (Illus.). 32p. (YA). 1991. lib. bdg. 18.95 (*0-9629978-5-4*) Sights Prods.

Origin of Life on Earth: An African Creation Myth. David A. Anderson-Sankofa. (Illus.). 32p. (YA). 1996. pap. 9.95 (*1-886366-09-8*) Sights Prods.

Origin of Marine Ooids & Grapestones. Frank H. Fabricius. (Contributions to Sedimentology Ser.: No. 7). (Illus.). iv, 112p. 1977. pap. 37.00 (*3-510-57007-3*, Pub. by E Schweizerbartsche) Balogh.

Origin of Matter & Evolution of Galaxies. 450p. 1997. 68.00 (*981-02-3012-5*) World Scientific Pub.

Origin of Matter & Evolution of Galaxies, 97: Atami, Japan 5-7 November 1997. Ed. by S. Kubono et al. 450p. 1999. 88.00 (*981-02-3677-8*) World Scientific Pub.

Origin of Mattole: Through the Eyes of a Salmon. George B. Miner. (Illus.). 192p. (Orig.). 1996. pap. 10.00 (*0-9653673-0-4*, M-0001) G B Miner.

Origin of Medieval Scientific: 300 A. D. Through 1300 A. D. Tacham. 1994. 24.95 (*0-8057-9515-4*, Twyne) Mac Lib Ref.

Origin of Modern Calculating Machines. J. A. Turck. LC 72-5081. (Technology & Society Ser.). (Illus.). 200p. 1977. reprint ed. 19.95 (*0-405-04730-4*) Ayer.

Origin of Modern Humans. Roger Lewin. 1998. pap. 19.95 (*0-7167-6023-1*) W H Freeman.

Origin of Modern Humans & the Impact of Chronometric Dating. Ed. by M. J. Aitken et al. (Illus.). 288p. 1993. text 49.50 (*0-691-03242-4*, Pub. by Princeton U Pr) Cal Prin Full Svc.

Origin of Perspective. Hubert Damisch. Tr. by John Goodman. LC 93-21895. 504p. 1994. 55.00 (*0-262-04139-1*) MIT Pr.

Origin of Perspective. Hubert Damisch. Tr. by John Goodman. (Illus.). 504p. 1995. pap. text 26.50 (*0-262-54077-0*) MIT Pr.

***Origin of Philosophy.** Jose Ortega y Gasset. LC 99-56002. 2000. pap. 10.00 (*0-252-06896-3*) U of Ill Pr.

Origin of Phyla. James Valentine. 1997. pap. text 29.95 (*0-226-84549-4*); lib. bdg. 65.00 (*0-226-84548-6*) U Ch Pr.

Origin of Prejudice in Children. Mario A. Benitez. 36p. (Orig.). 1996. pap. 5.95 (*0-9654217-0-8*) Fndtn of Educ Soc.

Origin of Races & Color: With an Archeological Compendium of Ethiopian & Egyptian Civilization. Martin R. Delany. LC 90-82685. 100p. 1991. reprint ed. 19.95 (*0-933121-51-2*); reprint ed. pap. 8.95 (*0-933121-50-4*) Black Classic.

Origin of Radar. Robert M. Page. LC 78-25844. (Illus.). 196p. 1979. reprint ed. lib. bdg. 38.50 (*0-313-20781-X*, PAOR, Greenwood Pr) Greenwood.

Origin of Raga. Sekhar Bandyopadhyaya. (C). 1995. 12.50 (*81-215-0261-6*, Pub. by M Manoharial) Coronet Bks.

Origin of Russia, Vol. I. Omeljan Pritsak. (Series in Ukrainian). 850p. (C). 1982. 50.00 (*0-674-64465-4*) HUP.

Origin of Russian Communism. Nicolas Berdyaev. 192p. 1960. pap. text 16.95 (*0-472-06034-1*, 06034, Ann Arbor Bks) U of Mich Pr.

Origin of Saivism & Its Development in the Tamil Land. K. R. Subramaniam. 88p. 1986. reprint ed. 15.00 (*0-8364-1715-1*, Pub. by Usha) S Asia.

Origin of Satan. Frederick K. Price. 32p. 1988. pap. 1.00 (*0-89274-544-4*, HH-544) Harrison Hse.

Origin of Satan: The New Testament Origins of Christianity's Demonization of Jews, Pagans & Heretics. Elaine H. Pagels. Date not set. 23.00 (*0-614-32354-1*) Random.

Origin of Satan: The New Testament Origins of Christianity's Demonization of Jews, Pagans & Heretics. Elaine H. Pagels. 1996. pap. 12.00 (*0-679-73118-0*) Random.

Origin of Species. Charles Darwin. 1976. 31.95 (*0-8488-0975-0*) Amereon Ltd.

Origin of Species. Charles Darwin. 432p. 1999. mass mkt. 5.95 (*0-553-21463-2*) Bantam.

Origin of Species. Charles Darwin. 1986. mass mkt. 6.99 (*0-451-62776-8*) NAL.

Origin of Species. Charles Darwin. Ed. by Appleman. (Illus.). 0.00 (*0-393-05549-3*) Norton.

Origin of Species. Charles Darwin. Ed. & Intro. by Gillian Beer. (Oxford World's Classics Ser.). (Illus.). 472p. 1998. pap. 8.95 (*0-19-283438-X*) OUP.

Origin of Species. Charles Darwin. LC 90-63888. (Great Minds Ser.). 444p. (C). 1991. pap. 10.95 (*0-87975-675-6*) Prometheus Bks.

Origin of Species. Charles Darwin. Ed. by J. W. Burrow. (Classics Ser.). 480p. 1982. pap. 10.95 (*0-14-043205-1*, Penguin Classics) Viking Penguin.

Origin of Species. Charles Darwin. (Classics of World Literature Ser.). 480p. 1998. pap. 5.95 (*1-85326-780-5*, 7805WW, Pub. by Wrdsworth Edits) NTC Contemp Pub Co.

Origin of Species. abr. ed. Charles Darwin. (C). 1975. pap. text 11.25 (*0-393-09219-4*) Norton.

Origin of Species: Complete & Fully Illustrated. Charles Darwin. (Illus.). 544p. 1995. 9.99 (*0-517-12320-7*) Random Hse Value.

***Origin of Species: Darwin's Theory of Evolution.** Don Nardo. LC 00-9681. (Words That Changed History Ser.). 2001. lib. bdg. write for info. (*1-56006-801-9*) Lucent Bks.

Origin of Species by Means of Natural Selection. Charles Darwin. LC 93-3598. 714p. 1993. 20.00 (*0-679-60070-1*) Modern Lib NY.

Origin of Species by Means of Natural Selection. Charles Darwin. LC 98-21225. 1998. pap. 8.95 (*0-375-75146-7*) Modern Lib NY.

Origin of Speech. Eugen Rosenstock-Huessy. LC 81-20527. 1981. pap. 15.00 (*0-912148-13-6*) Argo Bks.

***Origin of Stars & Planetary Systems.** Charles J. Lada & N. Kylafis. LC 99-40948. (NATO Science Ser.). (Illus.). 1999. write for info. (*0-7923-5908-9*) Kluwer Academic.

Origin of Structure in the Universe: Proceedings of the NATO Advanced Research Workshop, Chateau du Pont d'Oye, Belgium, April 27-May 2, 1992. Ed. by E. Gunzig. (NATO Advanced Science Institutes Series C: Mathematical & Physical Sciences). 288p. (C). 1993. text 188.00 (*0-7923-2234-7*) Kluwer Academic.

Origin of Subjectivity: An Essays on Descartes. Hiram Caton. LC 72-91291. 264p. reprint ed. pap. 81.90 (*0-608-10173-7*, 201055700069) Bks Demand.

Origin of Symmetries. C. D. Froggatt et al. 500p. (C). 1991. text 90.00 (*9971-966-30-1*); pap. text 48.00 (*9971-966-31-X*) World Scientific Pub.

Origin of Table Manners Vol. 3: Mythologiques. Claude Levi-Strauss. Tr. by John Weightman & Doreen Weightman. (Illus.). 552p. 1990. pap. text 23.95 (*0-226-47493-3*) U Ch Pr.

Origin of Tarzan: The Mystery of the Creation of Tarzan Solved. Sarkis Atamian. LC 97-65127. 128p. (Orig.). 1997. pap. 14.95 (*1-888125-12-8*) Publ Consult.

Origin of Terror, Vol. 1. R. Mathews-Danzer. Ed. by Rinaldo Mathews. (Wizard, Ghost & Heroes Ser.). (Illus.). 170p. 2000. pap. 18.00 (*1-888417-02-1*) Dimefast.

***Origin of the American Indigenes.** Charles Hallock. (LC History-America-E). 18p. 1999. reprint ed. lib. bdg. 69.00 (*0-7812-4328-9*) Rprt Serv.

Origin of the Arab-Israeli Arms Race: Arms, Embargo, Military Power & Decision in the 1948 Palestine War. Amitzur Ilan. LC 95-2923. 288p. (C). 1996. text 45.00 (*0-8147-3758-7*) NYU Pr.

Origin of the Aryans. Isaac Taylor. 1972. 250.00 (*0-8490-0776-3*) Gordon Pr.

Origin of the Bible. Phil Comfort. 320p. 1992. 15.99 (*0-8423-4735-6*) Tyndale Hse.

***Origin of the Bible.** Philip Wesley Comfort. LC 99-51648. (Quiknotes Ser.). 2000. pap. 6.99 (*0-8423-3555-2*) Tyndale Hse.

Origin of the Book of Sindbad. B. E. Perry. (C). 1960. 35.00 (*3-11-000538-7*) De Gruyter.

***Origin of the Brunists.** Robert Coover. 2000. pap. 12.00 (*0-8021-3743-1*, Grove) Grove-Atltic.

Origin of the Chemical Elements. Roger J. Tayler & A. S. Everest. (Wykeham Science Ser.: No. 23). 176p. (C). 1975. reprint ed. 18.00 (*0-8448-1150-5*, Crane Russak) Taylor & Francis.

Origin of the Communist Autocracy: Political Opposition in the Soviet State, First Phase, 1917-1922. 2nd ed. Leonard B. Schapiro. LC 55-8644. 421p. reprint ed. pap. 130.60 (*0-608-17495-5*, 202999500067) Bks Demand.

Origin of the Concept of Nuclear Forces. Laurie M. Brown & Helmut Rechenberg. LC 96-31758. (Illus.). 384p. 1996. 87.00 (*0-7503-0373-5*) IOP Pub.

Origin of the Cross. George Hammond. LC 87-80586. (Illus.). 80p. (Orig.). 1987. pap. write for info. (*0-940915-02-2*) Hammond Psych Pubns.

***Origin of the Cult of Aphrodite.** J. Rendel Harris. (Illus.). 1999. pap. 9.95 (*1-55818-464-3*) Holmes Pub.

Origin of the Distinction of Ranks: 1806 Edition. John Millar. 450p. 1996. reprint ed. 75.00 (*1-85506-080-9*) Bks Intl VA.

Origin of the Earth. Ed. by Horton E. Newsom & John H. Jones. (Illus.). 384p. (C). 1990. text 65.00 (*0-19-506619-7*) OUP.

***Origin of the Earth & Moon.** Robin M. Canup. (Space Science Ser.). 2000. 50.00 (*0-8165-2073-9*) U of Ariz Pr.

Origin of the Earth & Moon. A. E. Ringwood. (Illus.). 1979. 73.00 (*0-387-90369-0*) Spr-Verlag.

Origin of the Egyptians. Augustus Le Plongeon. 1985. 18.50 (*0-89314-418-5*) Philos Res.

Origin of the English Constitution. George B. Adams. xii, 378p. 1986. reprint ed. 42.50 (*0-8377-1901-1*, Rothman) W S Hein.

Origin of the English Nation. H. Munro Chadwick. 232p. (C). 1983. reprint ed. pap. 18.00 (*0-941694-09-7*) Cliveden Pr.

Origin of the Family, Private Property, & the State. Friedrich Engels. LC 72-85711. 259p. 1972. pap. 17.95 (*0-87348-261-1*) Pathfinder NY.

Origin of the Family, Private Property, & the State. 2nd ed. Friedrich Engels. Ed. by Eleanor B. Leacock. LC 79-184309. 274p. (C). 1972. pap. 7.95 (*0-7178-0359-7*) Intl Pubs Co.

Origin of the Fittest: Essays on Evolution & the Primary Factors of Organic Evolution, 2 vols. Edward D. Cope. LC 73-17813. (Natural Sciences in America Ser.). 1066p. 1974. reprint ed. 76.95 (*0-405-05729-6*) Ayer.

Origin of the Gods: A Psychoanalytic Study of Greek Theogonic Myth. Richard S. Caldwell. (Illus.). 224p. (C). 1993. reprint ed. pap. text 19.95 (*0-19-507266-9*) OUP.

***Origin of the Guyanian Indians Ascertained: or The Aborigines of America, (Especially of the Guyanas,) & the East Indian Coolie Immigrants Compared: Being Articles Published in "The Colonist" Newspaper, with an Additional Section on the Hindu Coolies.** H. Bronkhurst. (LC History-America-E). 67p. 1999. reprint ed. lib. bdg. 69.00 (*0-7812-4313-0*) Rprt Serv.

Origin of the Icelanders. Barthi Guthmundsson. Tr. by Lee M. Hollander. LC 66-19265. 183p. 1967. reprint ed. pap. 56.80 (*0-608-03369-3*, 200198300011) Bks Demand.

Origin of the Idea of Crusade. Carl Erdmann. Tr. by Marshall W. Baldwin & Walter A. Goffart from GER. LC 77-71980. 483p. reprint ed. pap. 149.80 (*0-8357-2781-5*, 203990700014) Bks Demand.

Origin of the Illinois Juvenile Court Law: Juvenile Courts & What They Have Accomplished. 3rd ed. Compiled by Timothy D. Hurley. LC 74-2681. reprint ed. 37.50 (*0-404-09159-8*) AMS Pr.

Origin of the Indian Civilizations in South America. Erland Nordenskiold. LC 75-46063. (Comparative Ethnographical Studies: Vol. 9). reprint ed. 55.00 (*0-404-15149-3*) AMS Pr.

Origin of the Inequality of the Social Classes. Gunnar Landtman. LC 75-100511. reprint ed. 37.50 (*0-404-00623-X*) AMS Pr.

Origin of the Inequality of the Social Classes. Gunnar Landtman. LC 68-56332. (Illus.). 444p. 1969. reprint ed. lib. bdg. 79.50 (*0-8371-0522-6*, LASC, Greenwood Pr) Greenwood.

Origin of the Jesuits. James Broderick. LC 96-31317. 274p. (C). 1997. reprint ed. pap. 13.95 (*0-8294-0930-0*, Jesuit Way) Loyola Pr.

Origin of the Jesuits. James Brodrick. LC 83-45590. reprint ed. 33.50 (*0-404-19883-X*) AMS Pr.

Origin of the Jesuits. James Brodrick. LC 70-138604. 274p. 1971. reprint ed. lib. bdg. 65.00 (*0-8371-5523-1*, BROJ, Greenwood Pr) Greenwood.

Origin of the Modern Jewish Woman Writer: Romance & Reform in Victorian England. Michael Galchinsky. (Illus.). 276p. 1996. 39.95 (*0-8143-2612-9*); pap. 18.95 (*0-8143-2613-7*) Wayne St U Pr.

Origin of the Moving School in Massachusetts. Harlan Updegraff. LC 78-177685. (Columbia University. Teachers College. Contributions to Education Ser.: No. 17). reprint ed. 37.50 (*0-404-55017-7*) AMS Pr.

Origin of the Moving School in Massachusetts. Harlan Updegraff. LC 70-89249. (American Education: Its Men, Institutions & Ideas, Ser. 1). 1970. reprint ed. 11.95 (*0-405-01487-2*) Ayer.

Origin of the National Banking System. A. M. Davis. Ed. by Stuart Bruchey. LC 80-1142. (Rise of Commercial Banking Ser.). 1981. reprint ed. lib. bdg. 26.95 (*0-405-13644-7*) Ayer.

Origin of the Royal Arch: English Royal Arch Degree (1867) George Oliver. 242p. 1999. reprint ed. pap. 17.95 (*0-7661-0814-7*) Kessinger Pub.

Origin of the Second Amendment: A Documentary History of the Bill of Rights in Commentaries on Liberty, Free Government & an Armed Populace 1787-1792. 2nd ed. Ed. & Intro. by David E. Young. LC 94-73724. liii, 838p. (C). 1995. pap. 29.95 (*0-9623664-3-9*) Gold Oak Bks.

O

Origin of the Serif: Brush Writings & Roman Letters. Edward M. Catich. Ed. by Mary W. Gilroy. (Illus.). 311p. 1991. write for info. (*0-9629740-0-5*); pap. write for info. (*0-9629740-1-3*) St Ambrose U.

Origin of the Solar System. NATO Advanced Study Institute on the Origin of the. Ed. by S. F. Dermott. LC 77-7547. (Illus.). 686p. reprint ed. pap. 200.00 (*0-608-17678-8*, 203039500069) Bks Demand.

Origin of the Solar System: Soviet Research, 1925-1991. Stephen G. Brush & A. E. Levin. (Illus.). 400p. 1994. text 69.95 (*1-56396-281-0*, AIP Pr) Spr-Verlag.

Origin of the Solar System: The Capture Theory. John R. Dormand & Michael M. Woolfson. 1989. text 49.95 (*0-470-21466-X*) P-H.

Origin of the Soul in St. Augustine's Later Works. Robert J. O'Connell. LC 86-82222. xiii, 363p. (C). 1987. 40.00 (*0-8232-1172-X*) Fordham.

Origin of the Species. Barbara Barg. 1994. pap. 7.00 (*1-57027-007-4*) Autonomedia.

Origin of the Species: Playscript. Curtis Zahn. LC 90-53082. (Orig.). 1990. pap. 5.00 (*0-88734-314-7*) Players Pr.

Origin of the Strategic Cruise Missile. Ronald Huisken. LC 81-4921. 202p. 1981. 55.00 (*0-275-90650-7*, C0650, Praeger Pubs) Greenwood.

Origin of the Theater: An Essay. Benjamin Hunninghers. LC 77-20684. 114p. 1978. reprint ed. lib. bdg. 52.50 (*0-313-20007-6*, HUOT, Greenwood Pr) Greenwood.

Origin of the Third Family. C. S. Wu et al. LC 97-20205. (World Scientific Series in the 20th Century Physics). 1997. write for info. (*981-02-3163-6*) World Scientific Pub.

Origin of the Universe. Andres L. Ruiz. Tr. by Natalia Tizon. LC 96-37980. (Sequences of Earth & Space Ser.). (Illus.). 32p. (J). 1997. 12.95 (*0-8069-9744-3*) Sterling.

Origin of the Upper Jurassic Limestones of the Swabian Alb (Southwest Germany) Manfred P. Gwinner. (Contributions to Sedimentology Ser.: No. 5). (Illus.). iv, 75p. 1976. pap. 31.00 (*3-510-57005-7*, Pub. by E Schweizerbartsche) Balogh.

Origin of the Vampire: How It All Started. John Walker. 16p. (YA). (gr. 6-12). 1998. pap. 6.00 (*0-8059-4262-9*) Dorrance.

Origin of the Vineyard Black Dog. Edwin B. Athearn. (Illus.). 1993. pap. 3.50 (*1-883154-00-6*) E B Athearn.

Origin of the Young God Kalidasa's "Kumarasambhava" Tr. by Hank Heifetz. 192p. 1985. pap. 14.95 (*0-520-07126-3*, Pub. by U CA Pr) Cal Prin Full Svc.

Origin of Tragedy. William Ridgeway. LC 65-19621. (Illus.). 238p. 1972. 23.95 (*0-405-08891-4*, Pub. by Blom Pubns) Ayer.

Origin of Values. Ed. by Michael Hechter et al. LC 92-27888. (Sociology & Economics Ser.). 352p. 1993. pap. text 29.95 (*0-202-30447-7*); lib. bdg. 57.95 (*0-202-30446-9*) Aldine de Gruyter.

***Origin of Values: Essays in the Sociology & Philosophy of Beliefs.** Raymond Boudon. 248p. 2000. 39.95 (*0-7658-0043-8*) Transaction Pubs.

Origin of Variation of Races of Mankind & the Cause of Evolution. Betty J. Y. Ho. LC 68-57933. (System of Government in the Living Body Ser.). (Illus.). 169p. 1969. pap. 15.00 (*0-9600148-1-0*) Juvenescent.

Origin of Weight. J. R. McClean. (Illus.). 1979. pap. 5.00 (*0-916710-46-7*) Obol Intl.

***Origin of Western Mysticism: Selected Writings of Plotinus.** S. Abhayananda. LC 99-38569. (Classics of Mystical Literature). 198p. 2000. pap. 19.95 (*0-914557-13-0*, Pub. by Atma Bks) ACCESS Pubs Network.

***Origin of Western Mysticism: Selected Writings of Plotinus.** Plotinus & Abhayananda. LC 99-38569. 2000. write for info. (*0-914557-12-2*) Atma Bks.

Origin of Williamstown, MA. 2nd ed. Arthur L. Perry. (Illus.). 650p. reprint ed. lib. bdg. 65.00 (*0-8328-2554-9*) Higginson Bk Co.

Origin, Persecutions, & Doctrines of the Waldenses from Documents: Many Now for the First Time Collected & Edited. Pius Melia. LC 77-84716. reprint ed. 37.50 (*0-404-16122-7*) AMS Pr.

Origin, Progress & Prospects of the Catholic Mission to the Rocky Mountains. Pierre-Jean De Smet. 1971. reprint ed. pap. 1.00 (*0-87770-044-3*) Ye Galleon.

Origin, Progress & Vicissitudes of the Mohawk & Hudson Railroad. Joel Munsell. 20p. 1993. reprint ed. lib. bdg. 69.00 (*0-7812-5218-0*) Rprt Serv.

Origin Russian Civil War. Geoffrey Swain. LC 95-13287. (Origins of Modern Wars Ser.). 336p. (C). 1995. text 57.75 (*0-582-05967-4*, Pub. by Addison-Wesley); pap. text 22.25 (*0-582-05968-2*, Pub. by Addison-Wesley) Longman.

Origin, Structure & Evolution of Galaxies: Proceedings of the Yellow Mountain Summer School of Astrophysics. Ed. by Fang Lizhi. 344p. (Orig.). (C). 1988. pap. 47.00 (*9971-5-0522-3*); text 108.00 (*9971-5-0521-5*) World Scientific Pub.

Origin Tradition of Ancient Israel: The Literary Formation of Genesis & Exodus 1-23. Thomas L. Thompson. (Journal for the Study of the Old Testament Supplement Ser.: Vol. 55). 221p. 1987. 50.00 (*1-85075-084-X*, Pub. by Sheffield Acad); pap. 19.95 (*1-85075-083-1*, Pub. by Sheffield Acad) CUP Services.

Origin, Variation, Immunity & Breeding of Cultivated Plants: Phytogeographic Basis of Plant Breeding. N. I. Vavilov. Tr. by K. Starr Chester. 60p. 1987. reprint ed. pap. 11.75 (*0-933421-18-4*) Redwood Seed.

Original - How to Beat a Parking Ticket - NYC Edition. Joel Peskoff. Ed. by Judy Ornstein. 40p. (Orig.). 1991. pap. write for info. (*0-931579-16-3*) J F Caroll Pub.

Original AC, Ace & Cobra: The Restorers Guide to AC, Bristol, & Ford Engined Cars. Rinsey Mills. (Full Color Restoration Guides Ser.). (Illus.). 96p. 1990. text 34.95 (*1-870979-14-1*, Bay View Bks) MBI Pubg.

Original Accounts of the Lone Women of San Nicholas Island. Contrib. by Andrea Liss. (Illus.). 16p. 1998. pap. 9.95 (*0-9666963-2-8*) Side Street Pr.

***Original Acta of St. Peter's Abbey, Gloucester C. 1122 to 1263.** Ed. by Robert B. Patterson. LC 98-227796. (Illus.). 1998. write for info. (*0-900197-47-1*) Bristol Gloucestershire Archaeological Soc.

Original Adventure Story. Lester Schulman. (Small Soldiers Ser.). 128p. (J). (gr. 2-6). 1998. mass mkt. 3.99 (*0-448-41882-7*, G & D) Peng Put Young Read.

***Original Adventures of Hank the Cowdog.** John R. Erickson. (Hank the Cowdog Ser.: No. 1). (Illus.). (J). (gr. 2-5). 1999. pap. 12.25 (*0-8335-6815-9*) Econo-Clad Bks.

Original Adventures of Hank the Cowdog. John R. Erickson. (Hank the Cowdog Ser.: No. 1). (Illus.). 105p. (J). (gr. 2-5). 1983. pap. 6.95 (*0-9608612-2-X*) Maverick Bks.

Original Adventures of Hank the Cowdog. John R. Erickson. LC 98-41813. (Hank the Cowdog Ser.: No. 1). (Illus.). 144p. (J). (gr. 2-5). 1998. pap. 4.99 (*0-14-130377-8*, PuffinBks) Peng Put Young Read.

Original Adventures of Hank the Cowdog. John R. Erickson. (Hank the Cowdog Ser.: No. 1). (Illus.). (J). (gr. 2-5). 1988. 12.05 (*0-606-01391-1*, Pub. by Turtleback) Demco.

Original Adventures of Hank the Cowdog. John R. Erickson. (Hank the Cowdog Ser.: No. 1). (Illus.). 144p. (J). (gr. 3-7). 1998. 13.99 (*0-670-88408-1*) Viking Penguin.

Original Adventures of Hank the Cowdog. unabridged ed. John R. Erickson. (Hank the Cowdog Audio Ser.: No. 1). (Illus.). 105p. (J). (gr. 2-5). 1983. 13.95 incl. audio (*0-916941-01-9*) Maverick Bks.

***Original Adventures of Hank the Cowdog: Deluxe Edition.** John R. Erickson. (Hank the Cowdog Ser.: No. 1). (Illus.). (J). (gr. 2-5). 1998. 12.99 (*0-670-88439-1*) Viking Penguin.

***Original Allis-Chalmers, 1933-1957.** Guy Fay & Andy Kraushaar. (Original Ser.). (Illus.). 128p. 2000. 29.95 (*0-7603-0439-4*, 130127AP, Pub. by MBI Pubg) Motorbooks Intl.

Original Ambivalence: Autobiography & Violence in Thomas De Quincey, Vol. 11. Matthew T. Schneider. LC 94-30419. (Age of Revolution & Romanticism Ser.). X, 197p. (C). 1995. text 48.95 (*0-8204-2632-6*) P Lang Pubng.

Original American Wheat Dolly. Mary Lomen. (Illus.). 224p. (Orig.). 1992. pap. 19.95 (*0-942323-15-7*) N Amer Heritage Pr.

Original Analects: Sayings of Confucius & His Successors. Tr. by E. Bruce Brooks & A. Taeko Brooks. LC 97-25748. 368p. 1997. 29.50 (*0-231-10430-8*) Col U Pr.

Original & Authentic Journal of Occurrences During the Late American War. Roger Lamb. LC 67-29033. (Eyewitness Accounts of the American Revolution Ser.). 1968. reprint ed. 19.95 (*0-405-01118-0*) Ayer.

Original & Spryrnge of All Sectes & Orders by Whome, Wha or Where (Sic) They Beganne. Tr. by M. Coverdale from DUT. LC 79-84127. (English Experience Ser.: No. 946). 140p. 1979. reprint ed. lib. bdg. 20.00 (*90-221-0946-1*) Walter J Johnson.

Original & the Pretenders. Saul S. Solowey. 293p. write for info. (*0-9618098-0-9*) Land Pub FL.

Original Anecdotes of Peter the Great, Collected from the Conversation of Several Persons of Distinction at Petersburg & Moscow. Jakob Von Storcksburg Staehlin. LC 74-115587. (Russia Observed, Series I). 1970. reprint ed. 23.95 (*0-405-03064-9*) Ayer.

Original Angus Young. Arti Funaro. (Illus.). 80p. 1985. pap. 14.95 (*0-8256-2344-8*, AM38555) Music Sales.

Original Anthology: Eyewitness to Early American Telegraphy. Alfred Vail. LC 74-4698. (Telecommunications Ser.). (Illus.). 268p. 1974. 34.84 (*0-405-06043-2*) Ayer.

Original Arizona Cookin' Wes Medley. Ed. by Tim Mohanna. (Illus.). 1992. pap. write for info. (*0-9633651-1-8*) Orig Western.

Original Arno Press Anthology for Saint Paul's Magazine. Anthony Trollope. LC 80-1908. (Selected Works of Anthony Trollope). 1981. lib. bdg. 38.95 (*0-405-14116-5*) Ayer.

Original Arno Press Anthology Miscellaneous Essays & Reviews. Anthony Trollope. LC 80-1907. (Selected Works of Anthony Trollope). 1981. lib. bdg. 66.95 (*0-405-14115-7*) Ayer.

Original Art Deco Allover Patterns. William Rowe. (Illus.). 48p. 1989. pap. 5.95 (*0-486-26139-5*) Dover.

Original Art Deco Designs. William Rowe. (Pictorial Archive Ser.). (Illus.). (Orig.). 1973. pap. 7.95 (*0-486-22567-4*) Dover.

Original Art of Music. Dorothy Ling. LC 88-19117. 190p. 1990. 38.50 (*0-8191-7117-4*); pap. 20.00 (*0-8191-7118-2*) U Pr of Amer.

Original Audition Scenes for Actors: A Collection of Professional-Level Short Scenes. Garry M. Kluger. Ed. by Arthur L. Zapel. LC 87-61894. 128p. (Orig.). (YA). (gr. 9 up). 1987. pap. 12.95 (*0-916260-45-3*, B129) Meriwether Pub.

Original Azusa Street Devotional. Larry Keefauver. LC 97-22328. (Chrisma Classics Devotional Ser.). 180p. 1997. mass mkt. 6.99 (*0-88419-481-7*) Creation House.

Original B. B. King. Jesse Gress. (Illus.). 80p. 1989. pap. 14.95 (*0-8256-2540-8*, AM63504) Music Sales.

Original Backyard Scientist. Jane Hoffman. (Illus.). 58p. (Orig.). (J). (gr. k-6). 1987. per. 8.50 (*0-9618663-1-4*) Backyard Scientist.

Original Bad Boy: Meet Dennis Rodman's Father. Philander Rodman, Jr. & Tom Storm. (Illus.). 64p. 1997. pap. 11.95 (*1-880047-57-8*) Creative Des.

Original Baltimore Neighborhood Cookbook. Ann Hazan & Irina Smith. LC 91-8913. (Illus.). 256p. 1991. pap. 14.95 (*0-940159-13-9*) Camino Bks.

Original Banjo Case Chord Book. Larry Sandberg. 48p. pap. 5.95 (*0-8256-2377-4*, AM34885) Music Sales.

Original Basement Waterproofing Handbook. Jack Masters. (Illus.). 120p. 1996. pap. 31.95 (*0-9664036-0-6*) Mstr Jack Pubs.

Original Bassini Operation for Inguinal Hernia. A. Chinaglia. (Illus.). 116p. 1988. text 44.00 (*88-299-0229-2*, Pub. by Piccin Nuova) Gordon & Breach.

Original Bassini Operation for Inguinal Hernia: Centenary Edition. A. Chinaglia. 116p. 1988. text 40.00 (*1-57235-038-5*) Piccin Nuova.

Original Behavior. Nelson. Date not set. pap. text, teacher ed. write for info. (*0-314-03367-X*) West Pub.

Original Belle. Edward P. Roe. (Notable American Authors Ser.). 1999. reprint ed. lib. bdg. 125.00 (*0-7812-8820-7*) Rprt Serv.

Original Bible Restored. 2nd ed. Ernest L. Martin. (Illus.). 336p. (YA). (gr. 10). 1991. pap. text 14.95 (*0-945657-89-7*) Acad Scriptural Knowledge.

Original Biography of Abbie Burgess, Lighthouse Heroine. 6th ed. Ruth Sargent & Dorothy Jones. 190p. 1998. reprint ed. pap. 10.95 (*0-9629882-5-1*) Adfax Pubns.

Original Black Sabbath. Steve Tarshis. (Illus.). 48p. 1985. pap. 14.95 (*0-8256-2416-9*, AM39009) Music Sales.

***Original Blessing.** Matthew Fox. 368p. 2000. pap. 15.95 (*1-58542-067-0*, Tarcher Putnam) Putnam Pub Group.

***Original Bliss: A Novel.** A. L. Kennedy. LC 98-15887. 224p. 1999. 21.00 (*0-375-40272-1*) Knopf.

Original Bliss: A Novel. A. L. Kennedy. 224p. 1999. 12.00 (*0-375-70278-4*, Vin) Random.

***Original Bluegrass Spectacular: Mandolin Edition.** Tr. by Richard Kriehn. 80p. 1998. pap. 15.00 (*0-7866-1671-7*, 97018) Mel Bay.

***Original Bluegrass Spectacular - Mandolin Edition.** CMH Records Staff. 80p. 1998. pap. 29.95 incl. audio compact disk (*0-7866-4073-1*, 97018CDP) Mel Bay.

***Original Bluegrass Spectacular/Guitar Edition.** CMH Records Staff. 108p. 1998. spiral bd. 32.95 incl. audio compact disk (*0-7866-4071-5*, 96665CDP) Mel Bay.

***Original Bluegrass Spectacular/Guitar Edition.** Tr. by Tommy Flint. 108p. 1998. pap. 17.95 (*0-7866-0568-5*, 96665) Mel Bay.

Original Book of Ecclesiastes. Ed. & Intro. by Charles Siegel. 64p. (Orig.). 1996. pap. 6.95 (*0-9648397-5-X*) Northbrae Bks.

Original Book of Horse Treats: Cookbook of Recipes for Horse Treats. Ed. by June V. Evers. LC 94-96042. (Illus.). 1994. 19.95 (*0-9638814-1-8*) Horse Hollow.

Original Boston Cooking School Cookbook, 1896. 100th anniversary ed. Fanny M. Farmer. 580p. 1996. pap. 18.96 (*0-88363-196-2*) S&S Trade.

Original Buckwheat. Reg E. Gaines. 128p. 1998. pap. 10.00 (*0-9654738-1-3*) Lng Shot Prods.

Original Bulletin Boards on Jewish Themes. Nachama S. Moskowitz. xii, 477 p. 1986. pap. 13.50 (*0-86705-019-5*) A R E Pub.

Original Calculus, Vol. 1. Stewart. (Adaptable Courseware Ser.). 1996. 33.25 (*0-534-49738-1*) Brooks-Cole.

Original Cameron Aurameter Book: Dowsing Auras, Invisible Energies & Thoughtforms. 2nd abr. rev. ed. Verne L. Cameron et al. Ed. by Bill Cox & Davina Cox. Orig. Title: The Cameron Aurameter. (Illus.). 68p. 1997. pap. 17.50 (*0-88234-014-X*) Life Understanding.

***Original Carter Family.** 44p. 1999. pap. 9.95 (*0-634-00381-X*) H Leonard.

Original Casting of Moliere's Plays. Roger W. Herzel. Ed. by Bernard Beckerman. LC 81-7538. (Theater & Dramatic Studies: No. 1). 121p. 1981. reprint ed. pap. 37.60 (*0-8357-1209-5*, 207007400063) Bks Demand.

Original Chicago Trivia Book. Joseph A. DeBartolo. (Illus.). 250p. 1985. pap. 8.95 (*0-930281-03-9*) Sarsaparilla.

Original Code in the Bible: Using Science & Mathematics to Reveal God's Fingerprints. Del Washburn. LC 98-24243. 200p. 1998. 19.95 (*1-56833-115-0*) Madison Bks UPA.

Original Collector's Price Guide to PEZ. 10th ed. Michael E. Edelman & John J. LaSpina. 59p. 1999. pap. 10.00 (*0-9670243-0-7*) Toys in Attic.

Original College Adventure Aide see College Survival Instruction Book

Original Color: A Novel. Chun Zhang. (CHI.). 396p. (Orig.). 1996. pap. 9.95 (*0-9644818-8-X*) Waymont Intl.

Original Comic Art: Identification & Price Guide. Jerry Weist. (Confident Collector Ser.). (Illus.). 520p. (Orig.). 1992. pap. 15.00 (*0-380-76965-4*, Avon Bks) Morrow Avon.

Original Coming Out Stories. 2nd enl. rev. ed. Ed. by Julia Penelope & Susan J. Wolfe. (Illus.). 312p. 1989. pap. 14.95 (*0-89594-339-5*) Crossing Pr.

Original Compositions Vol. 1: 2 Pianos 4 Hands. F. Schubert. 112p. 1986. per. 14.00 (*0-7935-5199-4*, 50261660) H Leonard.

Original Computer Idiot PC User's Guide. Martin J. Duran. (Idiot Ser.). (Illus.). 192p. (Orig.). pap. 15.95 (*1-879986-40-X*) SoftMark CA.

Original Computer Idiot PC User's Guide: For IBM PC's & Compatibles. Martin J. Duran. (Idiot Ser.). (Illus.). 192p. (Orig.). 1992. pap. 15.95 (*1-879986-00-0*) SoftMark CA.

Original Confederate Colt. rev. ed. William S. Albaugh, III & Richard D. Steuart. (William Albaugh Collection). (Illus.), 62p. 1993. reprint ed. 25.00 (*1-56837-262-0*) Broadfoot.

Original Confession of Nat Turner: The Complete Text of the Confessions of the Leader of the Most Successful Slave Revolt in United States History. H. Khalif Khalifah. 32p. (Orig.). 1992. pap. 3.95 (*1-56411-059-1*) Untd Bros & Sis.

Original Corvette, 1953-62: The Restorers Guide. Tom Falconer. (Illus.). 96p. 1997. 35.95 (*1-870979-90-7*, Bay View Bks) MBI Pubg.

***Original Corvette Sting Ray 1963, 67.** 112p. 2000. 34.95 (*1-901432-14-9*, Pub. by MBI Pubg) Motorbooks Intl.

Original Cowboy Cookbook. Wes Medley. (Illus.). 106p. pap. text 12.95 (*0-9633651-0-X*) Orig Western.

Original Critoen DS: The Restorer's Guide to All DS & ID Models 1955-75. John Reynolds & Jan DeLange. (Illus.). 144p. 1996. 36.95 (*1-870979-71-0*, Bay View Bks) MBI Pubg.

Original Curious George: Collector's Edition. H. A. Rey & Margret Rey. LC 98-71472. (Curious George Ser.). (Illus.). 64p. (J). (ps-2). 1998. 25.00 (*0-395-92272-0*) HM.

Original Dances, Waltzes & Hornpipes for the Violin, Composed by M. Higgins. M. Higgins. 16p. 1991. pap. 8.00 (*0-9637812-0-0*) MO St Old Time.

Original Dating Questionnaire for Teens: A Great Way to Get to Know Each Other. Lorilyn Bailey. (Illus.). 128p. (Orig.). (YA). (gr. 7-12). pap. write for info. (*0-9641239-7-5*) Lormax Commun.

***Original Designs for Silk Ribbon Embroidery.** Jenny Bradford. (Illus.). 2000. pap. 12.95 (*1-86351-237-3*) Sally Milner.

Original Dictionary of Modern Hairstyling for Beauty Salons. Eileen M. Murphy. (Illus.). 67p. 1981. spiral bd. 12.95 (*0-9609792-0-4*) Eileens Beautique.

Original "Do-It-Yourself" Guide to Wardrobe Planning. Barbara J. Kenzik. LC 98-93441. (Illus.). v, 80p. 1998. pap. 14.95 (*0-9667355-0-1*) Bookworm Pr.

***Original Documents Controversy: From Glencoe to the ICC Decision.** James E. Byrne. viii, 160p. 1999. pap. 49.95 (*1-888870-21-4*) Inst Intl Bnking.

Original Dr. Shade (& Other Stories) Kim Newman. 1998. mass mkt. 48.93 (*0-671-71562-3*) S&S Trade.

Original Dwelling Place: Zen Buddhist Essays. Robert Aitken. 256p. 1997. pap. text 13.50 (*1-887178-41-4*, Pub. by Counterpt DC) HarpC.

Original 1896 Boston Cooking-School Cookbook. Fannie M. Farmer. LC 97-15. (Illus.). 618p. 1997. reprint ed. pap. text 12.95 (*0-486-29697-0*) Dover.

Original Enlightenment & the Transformation of Medieval Japanese Buddhism. Jacqueline I. Stone. LC 98-54333. (Studies in East Asian Buddhism: 12). (Illus.). 600p. 1999. 55.00 (*0-8248-2026-6*) UH Pr.

Original Feminist Attack on the Bible. Elizabeth C. Stanton. LC 74-9343. 258p. 1974. 6.95 (*0-405-05997-3*) Ayer.

Original Ferrari V8: Restoration Guide for All Models 1974-1994, Vol. 8. Keith Bluemel. (Original Ser.). (Illus.). 128p. 1996. 35.95 (*1-870979-78-8*, Bay View Bks) MBI Pubg.

Original Ferrari V12, 1965-73: The Restorers Guide to Front Engined Road Cars. Keith Blueme. LC 99-56957. (Illus.). 128p. 1999. text 35.95 (*1-901432-22-X*, 128276AE) Motorbooks Intl.

Original Freddie Ackerman. Hadley Irwin. (Illus.). 192p. (YA). (gr. 7 up). 1996. per. 3.99 (*0-689-80389-3*) Aladdin.

Original Freddie Ackerman. Hadley Irwin. LC 91-43145. (Illus.). 192p. (YA). (gr. 5 up). 1992. 15.00 (*0-689-50562-0*) McElderry Bks.

Original Freddie Ackerman. Hadley Irwin. LC 91-43145. (J). 1996. 9.09 (*0-606-09718-X*, Pub. by Turtleback) Demco.

Original Fun-Way Bandsman: C Flute. 1990. 4.95 (*0-685-32115-0*, N057) Hansen Ed Mus.

Original Goodness: Eknath Easwaran on the Beatitudes. 2nd ed. Eknath Easwaran. LC 89-15931. (Classics of Christian Inspiration Ser.). 288p. 1996. 22.00 (*0-915132-92-3*); pap. 12.95 (*0-915132-91-5*) Nilgiri Pr.

Original Guitar Case Chord Book. Peter Pickow. 48p. pap. 5.95 (*0-8256-2367-7*, AM35841) Music Sales.

Original Guitar Case Scale Book. Peter Pickow. (Illus.). 48p. 1996. pap. 4.95 (*0-8256-2588-2*, AM 76217) Music Sales.

Original Handbook for the Recently Deceased. Claude Needham. (Illus.). 144p. 1992. 100.00 (*0-89556-093-3*) Gateways Bks & Tapes.

Original Handbook for the Recently Deceased. Claude Needham. (Illus.). 144p. 1993. pap. 12.50 (*0-89556-068-2*) Gateways Bks & Tapes.

Original Historical Mystery Anthology. Miriam G. Morfreds & Sharon Newman. 1997. mass mkt. write for info. (*0-614-18901-2*, Prime Crime) Berkley Pub.

***Original Homeowner's Remodeling Price Guide.** Mark B. Constantian & Richard Hammersley. 43p. 1998. pap. 15.00 (*0-9676899-0-2*) Beacon Data Serv.

***Original Honda CB750.** Wyatt. 128p. 2000. 35.95 (*1-901432-13-0*, Pub. by MBI Pubg) Motorbooks Intl.

Original Ideas of Jesus That Are Changing the World. George Drew. 45p. (Orig.). 1980. pap. 7.95 (*0-940754-05-3*) Ed Ministries.

Original Illustrated Arthur Conan Doyle. Arthur Conan Doyle. 1992. 7.98 (*0-89009-391-1*) Bk Sales Inc.

Original Illustrated Sherlock Holmes. Arthur Conan Doyle. 636p. 1985. 7.98 (*0-89009-057-2*) Bk Sales Inc.

Original Illustrated Sherlock Holmes. Arthur Conan Doyle. (Illus.). 656p. 1996. pap. 12.95 (*1-879582-25-2*) Platinum Pr.

***Original Illustrated 'Strand' Sherlock Holmes: The Complete Facsimile Edition.** Arthur Conan Doyle. (Illus.). 1126p. 2000. reprint ed. pap. text 25.00 (*0-7881-9173-X*) DIANE Pub.

Original Instrumental Music. David Winters. 100p. (Orig.). 1996. pap. 15.00 (*0-9616283-5-9*) D Winters.

An Asterisk (*) at the beginning of an entry indicates that the title is appearing for the first time.

Original Intent: Chief Justice Rehnquist & the Course of American Church-State Relations. Derek Davis. LC 90-27447. 222p. 1991. 32.95 (*0-87975-649-7*) Prometheus Bks.

Original Intent: The Courts, the Constitution & Religion. 2nd large type ed. David Barton. 550p. (Orig.). 1997. pap. 12.95 (*0-925279-57-9*) Wallbuilders.

Original Intent & the Constitution: A Philosophical Study. Gregory Bassham. LC 91-44467. 256p. (C). 1992. text 55.00 (*0-8476-7737-0*) Rowman.

Original Intent & the Framer's Constitution. Leonard W. Levy. 288p. 1988. text 19.95 (*0-02-918791-5*) Free Pr.

***Original Intent & the Framers' Constitution.** Leonard W. Levy. 544p. 2000. reprint ed. pap. 19.95 (*1-56663-312-5*, Pub. by I R Dee) Natl Bk Netwk.

Original Intent & the Framer's of the Constitution: A Disputed Question. Harry Jaffa. LC 93-5881. 432p. 1993. 24.00 (*0-89526-496-X*) Regnery Pub.

Original Intent of the First Amendment - According to the Founding Fathers: The Profane Wresting of United States Federal Law. 2nd ed. Michael E. Citriniti & Michael D. Juzwick. (Illus.). 128p. 1997. pap. 13.25 (*1-887412-00-X*) Light Eternal Pubns.

Original Internet Address Book. Mesa Group Staff. LC 96-32050. 160p. (C). 1996. pap. text 5.95 (*0-13-260431-0*) P-H.

Original Jaguar E Type. Philip Porter. (Original Jaguar Ser.). (Illus.). 9128p. 1990. text 34.95 (*1-870979-12-5*, Bay View Bks) MBI Pubg.

Original Jaguar MK1-MK2. Nigel Thorley. (Original Jaguar Ser.). (Illus.). 128p. 1990. text 34.95 (*1-870979-15-X*, Bay View Bks) MBI Pubg.

***Original Jaguar XJ.** 128p. 2000. 35.95 (*1-901432-11-4*, Pub. by MBI Pubg) Motorbooks Intl.

Original Jaguar XK: The Restorers Guide to XK120, XK140 & XK150 Roadster, Drophead Coupe & Fixed-Head Coupe. Philip Porter. (Illus.). 144p. 1998. 36.95 (*1-901432-02-5*, Bay View Bks) MBI Pubg.

Original Jazz Classics Buyers Guide. (Illus.). (Orig.). 1995. pap. 12.95 (*0-9637421-3-2*) Fantasy CA.

Original Jeff Beck. Mark Michaels. (Illus.). 80p. 1985. pap. 14.95 (*0-8256-2340-5*, AM38357) Music Sales.

Original Jerry Donahue: Guitar Styles of Jerry Donahue. Doc Rossi. (Illus.). 80p. 1993. pap. 15.95 (*0-7119-2948-3*, AM88360) Music Sales.

Original Jesus: Life & Vision. Wright. 160p. 1997. pap. 15.00 (*0-8028-4283-6*) Eerdmans.

Original Jesus: The Buddhist Sources of Christianity. Elmar R. Gruber. 288p. 1996. pap. 14.95 (*1-85230-835-4*, Pub. by Element MA) Penguin Putnam.

Original Jesus: The Buddhist Sources of Christianity. Holger Kersten & Elmar R. Gruber. 1995. text 29.95 (*1-85230-628-9*, Pub. by Element MA) Penguin Putnam.

Original Jewish Cookbook. Mildred G. Bellin. 470p. 1984. reprint ed. 17.95 (*0-8197-0058-4*) Bloch.

Original John G. Lake Devotional. Larry Keefauver. LC 97-23310. (Charisma Classic Ser.). 180p. 1997. mass mkt. 6.99 (*0-88419-479-5*) Creation House.

Original Journals of the Lewis & Clark Expedition, 8 vols., Set. Ed. by Reuben G. Thwaites. LC 72-88223. reprint ed. 224.00 (*0-405-00030-8*) Ayer.

Original Joy Journal. 2nd rev. ed. Valla D. Fotiades. Ed. by John M. Fotiades & Christina Bergenholtz. (Illus.). 128p. 1999. pap. write for info. (*0-926565-04-4*) Edgeworth & North.

Original Kawasaki Z1, Z900 & K2900. David Marsden. 128p. 1999. 35.95 (*0-7603-0775-X*, Pub. by MBI Pubg) Motorbooks Intl.

Original Land Entries in Montgomery County. Harris B. Dickey. (Illus.). 45p. 1997. reprint ed. pap. 9.00 (*0-8328-6853-1*) Higginson Bk Co.

Original Land Rover Series 1: The Restorer's Guide to Civil & Military Models 1948-58. James Taylor. (Illus.). 128p. 1996. 24.98 (*1-870979-72-9*, Bay View Bks) MBI Pubg.

***Original Lebonese & Middle East Cookbook: Lebanese Middle East Cookbook.** rev. large type ed. Agnes Johns. Ed. by Joseph Johns et al. Tr. by Kimberly Johns et al from ARA. LC 83-90402. (Illus.). 130p. 2000. pap. 24.95 (*0-9612148-1-3*) A N Johns.

Original Letters. John Colville. Ed. by David Laing. LC 72-976. (Bannatyne Club, Edinburgh. Publications: No. 104). reprint ed. 62.50 (*0-404-52859-7*) AMS Pr.

Original Letters Illustrative of English History, 11 vols. Ed. by Henry Ellis. reprint ed. 566.50 (*0-404-02310-X*) AMS Pr.

Original Letters of Alexander Botts. William H. Upson. 127p. Date not set. 17.95 (*0-8488-2501-2*) Amereon Ltd.

Original Letters of Eminent Literary Men of the 16th, 17th & 18th Centuries. Ed. by Henry Ellis. LC 71-166022. (Camden Society, London. Publications, First Ser.: No. 23). reprint ed. 95.00 (*0-404-50123-0*) AMS Pr.

Original Letters Relating to the Ecclesiastical Affairs of Scotland, 2 vols. Ed. by David Laing. LC 73-171637. (Bannatyne Club, Edinburgh. Publications: No. 92). reprint ed. 95.00 (*0-404-52833-3*) AMS Pr.

Original Love. Molly Peacock. 96p. 1996. pap. 10.00 (*0-393-31466-9*, Norton Paperbks) Norton.

Original Lovers' Questionnaire Book. Lorilyn Bailey. 128p. 1994. pap. 9.95 (*0-9641239-9-1*) Lormax Commun.

Original Malt Whisky Almanac: A Taster's Guide. Wallace Milroy. 1998. pap. 15.00 (*1-897784-68-6*, Pub. by N Wilson Pubng) Interlink Pub.

Original Man. Osho. LC 97-208943. (Zen Ser.). xii, 231p. 1997. 12.95 (*3-89338-056-6*, Pub. by Rebel Hse) Oshos.

Original Man: The Life & Times of Elijah Muhammad. Claude Andrew Clegg, III. (Illus.). 400p. 1998. pap. 14.95 (*0-312-18153-1*) St Martin.

***Original Maple Kids.** large type ed. Derrick M. Dandridge. (Maple Kids Ser.). (Illus.). 28p. (ps-2). 1999. pap. 5.00 (*1-928694-00-4*, Pub. by Modern Star Bks) Allnce Hse.

Original Maria Woodworth-Etter Devotional. Larry Keefauver. LC 97-23287. (Charisma Classic Ser.). 180p. 1997. mass mkt. 6.99 (*0-88419-480-9*) Creation House.

Original Martial Arts Encyclopedia: Tradition - History - Pioneers. rev. ed. John Corcoran & Emil Farkas. Ed. by Stuart Sobel. LC 92-81677. (Illus.). 450p. 1993. reprint ed. 29.95 (*0-9615126-3-6*) Pro Action Pub.

Original Marxism. Richard Mongar. (C). 1996. pap. text 21.50 (*0-7453-0592-X*) Westview.

Original Marxism. Thomas Mongar. (C). 1996. text 57.95 (*0-7453-0426-5*) Westview.

Original McGuffey's Eclectic Series, 8 vols., William H. McGuffey. 1982. reprint ed. teacher ed., boxed set 109.99 (*0-88062-029-3*) Mott Media.

Original McGuffey's Eclectic Series, 7 Vols. William H. McGuffey. (J). (gr. k-12). 1982. reprint ed. 99.99 (*0-88062-014-5*) Mott Media.

***Original Meanings: Politics & Ideas in the Making of the Constitution.** Jack N. Rakove. 439p. 2000. pap. text 17.00 (*0-7881-9199-3*) DIANE Pub.

Original Meanings: Politics & Ideas in the Making of the Constitution. Jack N. Rakove. 448p. 1996. 35.00 (*0-394-57858-9*) Knopf.

Original Meanings: Politics & Ideas in the Making of the Constitution. Jack N. Rakove. 1997. pap. 17.00 (*0-679-78121-8*) Vin Bks.

Original Members & Other Officers Eligible to the Society of the Cincinnati 1783-1938. Bryce Metcalf. Ed. by Robert R. Davenport. 390p. 1994. text 45.00 (*1-885943-03-2*) Historic Trust.

Original MGA: Restorer's Guide to 1500, 1600, MKII, Twin Cam & Roadsters & Coups. A. D. Clausager. (Bayview Ser.). (Illus.). 120p. 1993. 34.95 (*1-870979-31-1*) MBI Pubg.

Original MGT Series: Restorer's Guide to MG, TA, TB, TC, TD & TF. Anders D. Clausager. (Illus.). 96p. 1989. text 34.95 (*1-870979-06-0*, Bay View Bks) MBI Pubg.

***Original Michael Frayn: Comic Essays about Modern Life.** Michael Frayn. 226p. 2000. pap. 12.95 (*0-413-63970-3*) Methn.

Original Mind: The Practice of Zen in the West. Richard Bakerroshi. 256p. 1999. 23.95 (*1-57322-110-4*, Riverhead Books) Putnam Pub Group.

Original Mini Coop: The Restorer's Guide to 997 & 998 Cooper & 970, 1071 & 1275 Cooper S. John Parnell. (Bayview Ser.). (Illus.). 120p. 1993. 34.95 (*1-870979-32-X*) MBI Pubg.

Original Misunderstanding: The English, the Americans, & the Dialectic of Federalist Jurisprudence. Stephen B. Presser. LC 90-85344. 284p. 1991. lib. bdg. 34.95 (*0-89089-425-6*) Carolina Acad Pr.

Original Monologues for Men. Robes Kossez. 42p. (Orig.). 1987. pap. 5.95 (*0-939641-01-1*) Special Bks.

Original Monologues for Women. Robes Kossez. 47p. (Orig.). 1986. pap. 5.95 (*0-939641-00-3*) Special Bks.

Original Monster Truck: Bigfoot see Cruisin'

Original Monster Truck: Bigfoot. Scott Johnston. (Cruisin' Ser.). (Illus.). 48p. (J). (gr. 3-6). 1994. 19.00 (*0-516-35200-8*) Childrens.

Original Morgan, 1936-1991: The Restorers Guide to 4/4, Plus 4 & Plus 8. John Worrall & Liz Turner. (Illus.). 128p. 1992. text 35.95 (*1-870979-29-X*, Bay View Bks) MBI Pubg.

Original Morris Minor: Restorers Guide to All Saloon Tourer/Convertible, Traveller & Light Commercial Models. Ray Newell. (Illus.). 126p. 1993. text 35.95 (*1-870979-43-5*, Bay View Bks) MBI Pubg.

Original Mother Goose. deluxe ed. Ed. by Running Press Staff. LC 91-50157. (Illus.). 136p. (J). (ps-3). 1992. 15.95 (*1-56138-113-6*) Running Pr.

Original Mountain Bike Book. Rob Van der Plas. LC 97-46364. (Bicycle Bks.). (Illus.). 192p. 1998. pap. 19.95 (*0-933201-86-9*, Bicycle Bks) MBI Pubg.

Original Mr. Jacobs: Startling Expose. Telemachus T. Timayenis. Ed. by Gerald Grob. LC 76-46107. (Anti-Movements in America Ser.). 1977. reprint ed. lib. bdg. 26.95 (*0-405-09978-9*) Ayer.

Original Music for Men's Voices: A Selected Bibliography. 2nd ed. William Tortolano. LC 80-25917. 206p. 1981. 30.00 (*0-8108-1386-6*) Scarecrow.

Original Native New Mexico Cooking: Recipes. Yolanda Ortiz y Pino. LC 93-29047. 32p. (Orig.). 1993. pap. 5.95 (*0-86534-210-5*) Sunstone Pr.

Original Naturalism: An Introduction to the Philosophy of Justus Buchler. Beth J. Singer. 360p. 1983. 40.00 (*0-8387-5038-9*) Bucknell U Pr.

Original New Testament: The First Definitive Translation of the New Testament in 2000 Years. Hugh Schonfield. LC 97-33524. 1998. pap. 29.95 (*1-86204-252-7*, Pub. by Element MA) Penguin Putnam.

Original Nexus, No. 2. Mike Baron & Steve Rude. Ed. by Richard Bruning. (Illus.). 106p. 1986. 29.95 (*0-936211-00-8*); pap. 6.95 (*0-915419-03-3*) Graphitti Designs.

Original 1973-1977 Corvette Fact Manual. 2nd ed. Peter J. Licastro. (Illus.). 148p. 1994. pap. 35.95 (*0-9630555-7-7*) Just The Facts.

Original NO-NO-NO Cookbook: No Sugar, No Salt, No Fats. rev. ed. Jeri Kallison & Penny Stoliar. spiral bd. 6.50 (*0-9615954-0-X*) D&S Publishing.

Original Olympics. Stewart Ross. (Ancient Greece Ser.). 48p. (J). 1999. 18.95 (*0-87226-596-X*, 6596XB, P Bedrick Books) NTC Contemp Pub Co.

Original One & Two Minute Monologues for Auditions. Robes Kossez. 29p. (Orig.). 1993. pap. 6.95 (*0-939641-06-2*) Special Bks.

Original Order of Shakespeare's Sonnets. William Shakespeare. Ed. by Denys Bray. LC 76-30699. (Studies in Shakespeare: No. 24). 1977. lib. bdg. 75.00 (*0-8383-2140-2*) M S G Haskell Hse.

Original Papal Documents in England & Wales from the Accession of Pope Innocent III to the Death of Pope Benedict XI (1198-1304) Ed. by Jane E. Sayers. LC BX1210.O75 1999. 798p. 1999. text 210.00 (*0-19-820204-0*) OUP.

Original Papers Illustrative of the Life & Writings of John Milton. Ed. by William D. Hamilton. (Camden Society, London. Publications, First Ser.: No. 75). reprint ed. 34.00 (*0-404-50175-3*) AMS Pr.

Original Papers of the Wisconsin History Commission, 8 vols. Wisconsin History Commission. LC 74-19613. reprint ed. write for info. (*0-404-12404-6*) AMS Pr.

Original Papers Regarding Trade in England & Abroad. John Keymer. Ed. by M. F. Lloyd-Prichard. LC 67-29746. 64p. 1967. 25.00 (*0-678-00342-4*) Kelley.

Original Patentees of Land at Washington Prior to 1700. Bessie W. Gahn. LC 77-79982. 85p. 1998. reprint ed. pap. 10.95 (*0-8063-0155-4*) Clearfield Co.

Original Peace: Restoring God's Creation. David Burrell & Elena Malits. LC 97-17543. 128p. (Orig.). 1997. pap. 8.95 (*0-8091-3733-X*, 3733-X) Paulist Pr.

Original People. unabridged ed. T. B. Foley. 64p. (Orig.). (J). 1997. pap. 12.00 (*1-887159-10-X*) Preston-Speed.

Original People, 5 bks., Set I, Reading Level 5. Robyn Holder et al. (Illus.). 288p. (J). (gr. 4-8). 1987. 62.50 (*0-685-58808-4*) Rourke Corp.

Original People, 5 bks., Set I, Reading Level 5. Robyn Holder et al. (Illus.). 288p. (J). (gr. 4-8). 1987. lib. bdg. 83.35 (*0-86625-256-8*) Rourke Pubns.

Original People, 4 bks., Set II, Reading Level 5. Muhammad Alotaibi et al. (Illus.). 288p. (J). (gr. 4-8). 1989. 50.00 (*0-685-58809-2*) Rourke Corp.

Original People, 4 bks., Set II, Reading Level 5. Muhammad Alotaibi et al. (Illus.). 288p. (J). (gr. 4-8). 1989. lib. bdg. 66.68 (*0-86625-269-X*) Rourke Pubns.

Original People: Native Americans in the Champlain Valley. Ray Gonyea. 32p. 1988. pap. 7.95 (*1-890402-13-3*) Clinton Cnty Hist.

Original Peter Rabbit Books: 13-23 Presentation Box. Beatrix Potter. (J). 1990. text 65.00 (*0-7232-5178-9*, F Warne) Peng Put Young Read.

Original Peter Rabbit Miniature Collection, No. I. Beatrix Potter. (Picture Bks.: Vol. I). (Illus.). (J). (ps-3). 1991. pap. 5.95 (*0-7232-3982-7*, F Warne) Peng Put Young Read.

Original Peter Rabbit Miniature Collection, No. III. Beatrix Potter. (Illus.). (J). (ps-3). 1989. pap. 5.95 (*0-7232-3984-3*, F Warne) Peng Put Young Read.

Original Peter Rabbit Miniature Collection, Vol. II. Beatrix Potter. Vol. II. (J). (ps-3). 1988. pap. 5.95 (*0-7232-3983-5*, F Warne) Peng Put Young Read.

***Original Peter Rabbit Storybook Playset.** Beatrix Potter. (J). 1999. pap. 18.99 (*0-7232-4557-6*) Peng Put Young Read.

Original Philadelphia Neighborhood Cookbook. Ann Hazan & Irina Smith. LC 87-16656. (Illus.). 300p. (Orig.). 1988. pap. 14.95 (*0-940159-02-3*) Camino Bks.

Original Photoplay Movie Reviews of Famous Silent Films (1914-1928) Reproductions, Including Photos & Advertisements, from Microfilm. Intro. by David A. Weiss. (Illus.). (Orig.). 1997. pap. 17.50 (*0-9634299-4-9*) Cumberland Ent.

Original Piano Chord Finder. Leo Alfassy. (Illus.). 40p. 1979. pap. 5.95 (*0-8256-2389-8*, AM24860) Music Sales.

Original Piano Scale Finder. Darryl Winston. (Illus.). 48p. 1993. pap. 5.95 (*0-8256-1360-4*, AM91300) Music Sales.

Original Plane Watcher's Mini Field Guide. 2nd rev. ed. Sean F. Broderick & James F. Switzer. 2p. 1997. pap. 4.95 (*0-9649462-1-1*) FishBelly White.

Original Plane Watchers Mini-Field Guide: D. C./Baltimore Edition. Sean F. Broderick & James F. Switzer. 1995. 3.95 (*0-9649462-0-3*) FishBelly White.

Original Poems. Verda M. Heimann. 1997. pap. 56.95 (*1-57553-659-5*) Watermrk Pr.

Original Pooh Treasury, Vol. 1, Set. unabridged ed. A. A. Milne, pseud. (J). 1996. 17.00 incl. audio (*1-57375-456-0*, 71294) Audioscope.

Original Pooh Treasury: Eeyore Has a Birthday, Kanga & Baby Roo Come to the Forest, Christopher Robin Gives a Pooh Party, Vol. 2. A. A. Milne, pseud. (Illus.). (J). 1996. 20.00 incl. digital audio (*1-57375-458-7*) Audioscope.

Original Porsche 911: The Guide to All Production Models 1963-98. Peter Morgan. (Illus.). 144p. 1998. 36.95 (*1-901432-16-5*, Bay View Bks) MBI Pubg.

Original Porsche 924/944/968: The Guide to All Models 1975-95 Including Turbos & Limited Edition. Peter Morgan. (Illus.). 128p. 1998. 35.95 (*1-901432-05-X*, Bay View Bks) MBI Pubg.

Original Porsche 356: The Restoration Guide to All Coupe, Cabriolet, Roadster & Speedster Models 1950-65. Laurence Meredith. (Illus.). 112p. 1995. pap. 34.95 (*1-870979-58-3*, Bay View Bks) MBI Pubg.

Original Prints: New Writing from Scottish Women, Vol. II. Ed. by Kasia Boddy & Jane Sillars. LC 87-63209. 156p. (Orig.). 1988. pap. 9.95 (*0-948275-30-8*) Dufour.

Original Prints 4: New Writing from Scottish Women. Ed. by Elizabeth Burns et al. 1992. pap. 10.95 (*0-7486-6129-8*, Pub. by Edinburgh U Pr) Col U Pr.

Original Programme of the Theosophical Society. Helena P. Blavatsky. 1931. 3.00 (*0-8356-7150-X*, Quest) Theos Pub Hse.

***Original Pronouncements.** 1500p. 1999. pap. 51.95 (*0-471-35522-4*) Wiley.

Original Pronouncements, Vol. 1. 7th ed. Gerhard Mueller et al. (C). 1997. 56.50 (*0-256-18105-5*, Irwn McGrw-H) McGrw-H Hghr Educ.

Original Pronouncements, Vol. 2. 7th ed. Ron Guerrette. (C). 1999. 57.90 (*0-256-17752-X*, Irwn McGrw-H) McGrw-H Hghr Educ.

Original Pronouncements: Accounting Standards As of June 1, 1993, Vol. 1. Financial Accounting Standards Board Staff. LC HF5616.U5.F5. 1581p. 1993. pap. 200.00 (*0-7837-8482-1*, 204928600001) Bks Demand.

Original Pronouncements: Accounting Standards As of June 1, 1993, Vol. 2. Financial Accounting Standards Board Staff. LC HF5616.U5.F5. 1746p. 1993. pap. 200.00 (*0-7837-8483-X*, 204928600002) Bks Demand.

Original Pronouncements Through June, 1973 see Accounting Standards: Original Pronouncements, July 1973-June 1986

Original publisher: The Yonan Codex Foundation see Enlightenment from the Aramaic: Words & Phrases in Estrangel Script

Original Randy Rhoads. Wolf Marshall. (Illus.). 48p. 1986. pap. 14.95 (*0-8256-1065-6*, AM63850) Music Sales.

***Original Range Rover 1970-1986.** James Taylor. (Illus.). 128p. 1999. 35.95 (*0-7603-0777-6*, 128943AP, Pub. by MBI Pubg) Motorbooks Intl.

Original Recitations with Lesson-Talks. enl. ed. Ed. by Emma D. Banks. LC 79-51959. (Granger Poetry Library). 1980. reprint ed. 20.00 (*0-89609-176-7*) Roth Pub Inc.

Original Records of Entry: Criminal Justice Information Policy. 69p. (Orig.). (C). 1994. pap. text 25.00 (*0-7881-0387-3*) DIANE Pub.

Original Recyclers. Don A. Franco. Ed. by Winfield Swanson. 252p. 1996. 25.00 (*0-9654660-0-0*) Natl Renderers.

***Original Reiki-Handbook of Dr. Mikao Usui.** Mikao Usui & Frank Arjava Petter. (Illus.). 2000. pap. 14.95 (*0-914955-57-8*) Lotus Pr.

Original Retreater's Bibliography. Don Stephens & Barbie Stephens. 1967. 10.00 (*0-686-21856-6*) Stephens Pr.

***Original Revolution: Essays on Christian Pacifism.** John Howard Yoder. 190p. 1998. pap. 18.00 (*1-57910-137-2*) Wipf & Stock.

Original Roadkill Cookbook. B. R. Peterson. 53p. (Orig.). 1987. pap. 4.95 (*0-89815-200-3*) Ten Speed Pr.

***Original Rolls-Royce & Bentley 1946-65.** James Taylor. LC 99-40956. 160p. 1999. 36.95 (*1-901432-18-1*) Motorbooks Intl.

Original Rules of Golf. 4p. 1998. 19.95 (*0-9631709-4-5*) W Busn Forum.

Original San Francisco Giants: The Giants of '58. Steve Bitker. LC 98-84764. (Illus.). 295p. 1998. 29.95 (*1-57167-182-X*) Sports Pub.

Original Sceptics: A Controversy. Ed. by Myles F. Burnyeat & Michael Frede. LC 95-514551. 192p. (Orig.). (C). 1997. pap. text 14.95 (*0-87220-347-6*); lib. bdg. 34.95 (*0-87220-348-4*) Hackett Pub.

Original Scots Colonists of Early America: Supplement, 1607-1707. David Dobson. LC 97-77224. 211p. 1997. suppl. ed. 22.50 (*0-8063-1442-7*) Genealog Pub.

***Original Scots Colonists of Early America, Caribbean Supplement.** David Dobson. 147p. 1999. 20.00 (*0-8063-1612-8*) Genealog Pub.

Original Scots Colonists of Early America, 1612-1783. David Dobson. 370p. 1999. 28.50 (*0-8063-1239-4*) Genealog Pub.

Original Scroll Saw Shelf Patterns. Patricia Spielman & Loren Raty. LC 92-39062. (Illus.). 128p. 1993. pap. 14.95 (*0-8069-8714-6*) Sterling.

***Original Self: Living with Paradox & Originality.** Thomas Moore. LC 99-45049. (Illus.). 160p. 2000. 22.00 (*0-06-019542-8*) HarpC.

Original Shaker Music, Vol. II. 1992. reprint ed. 12.95 (*0-915836-24-6*) United Soc Shakers.

Original Shirley Temple Dolls in Full Color. 81st ed. Children's Museum Staff. (Illus.). 32p. (J). (gr. 2 up). 1988. pap. 4.95 (*0-486-25461-5*) Dover.

Original Signs: Gesture, Sign & the Sources of Language. David F. Armstrong. LC 98-49671. (Illus.). 181p. 1999. text 39.95 (*1-56368-075-0*) Gallaudet Univ Pr.

Original Sin, 1 vol. Nina Bangs. (Love Spell Ser.). 400p. 1999. mass mkt. 5.99 (*0-505-52324-8*) Dorchester Pub Co.

***Original Sin.** Michael Daley. 36p. 2000. pap. 8.00 (*0-9651413-6-5*) Pleasure Boat.

Original Sin. Jonathan Edwards. Ed. by Clyde A. Holbrook. (Works of Jonathan Edwards: Vol. 3). 448p. 1970. 80.00 (*0-300-01198-9*) Yale U Pr.

Original Sin. Marius Gabriel. 704p. 1993. mass mkt. 6.50 (*0-553-29649-3*) Bantam.

Original Sin. P. D. James. 560p. 1996. mass mkt. 7.99 (*0-446-60234-5*, Pub. by Warner Bks) Little.

Original Sin. large type ed. Rosalie Ash. (Harlequin Ser.). 1994. lib. bdg. 19.95 (*0-263-13774-0*) Thorndike Pr.

Original Sin: Illuminating the Riddle. Henri Blocher. LC 98-53406. (New Studies in Biblical Theology). 158p. 1999. pap. 18.00 (*0-8028-4411-1*) Eerdmans.

Original Sin: (Secrets . . .) Rosalie Ash. (Presents Ser.). 1995. per. 3.25 (*0-373-11723-X*, 1-11723-3) Harlequin Bks.

Original Sin: The Visionary Art of Joe Coleman. Joe Coleman et al. LC 96-77596. (Illus.). 144p. 1997. 45.00 (*0-9638129-9-8*); pap. 29.95 (*0-9638129-6-3*, 620231) Heck Editions.

Original Sin? Today: We Will Call It Genetic Engineering. Arlen Edward Ingram. pap. write for info. (*0-9667499-1-X*) Angel Pure.

Original Sin in the Light of Modern Science. Patrick O'Connell. 128p. 1973. pap. 3.00 (*0-912414-15-4*) Lumen Christi.

O

Original Sins: And Other Poems from Afterlife. Stephanie S. Anderson. (Orig.). (C). 1995. pap. 6.00 (0-9645709-0-4) Selene River Pr.

Original Sins: Reflections on the History of Zionism & Israel. Benjamin Beit-Hallahmi. LC 93-13551. 240p. 1993. 29.95 (1-56656-130-2, Olive Branch Pr); pap. 14.95 (1-56656-131-0, Olive Branch Pr) Interlink Pub.

Original Six: Old-Time Hockey Trivia. Don Weekes. LC 95-225863. (Illus.). 128p. (YA). 1995. pap. 9.95 (1-55054-453-5, Pub. by DGL) Sterling.

Original Six: True Stories from Hockey's Classic Era. Ed. by Paul Quarrington. LC 98-108671. (Illus.). 160p. 21.99 (0-433-39752-7) Buttrwrth-Heinemann.

Original Smith Wigglesworth Devotional. Larry Keefauver. LC 97-23286. (Charisma Classic Ser.). 180p. 1997. pap. 6.99 (0-88419-482-5) Creation House.

Original Snow Village Collector's Album: 1990 Edition. Department 56, Inc., Staff. 116p. 1990. 24.95 (0-9622603-3-9) Dept Fifty Six.

Original Social Stories. 2nd rev. ed. Carol Gray. Ed. by Sue Jonker. 425p. 1993. pap. 39.95 (1-885477-19-8) Fut Horizons.

Original Staging Manuals for Ten Parisian Operatic Premieres. H. Robert Cohen. (Musical Life in Nineteenth Century France Ser.: No. 6). 1998. 55.00 (0-945193-61-0) Pendragon NY.

Original Standards. Mike Garson. Ed. by Andrew D. Gordon. 68p. 1998. spiral bd. 19.95 incl. cd-rom (1-882146-65-4) A D G Prods.

Original Star Wars & the Age of Ice. Dennis G. Lindsay. (Creation Science Ser.: Vol. 6). 1992. per. 8.95 (0-89985-284-X) Christ for the Nations.

Original Steam-Boat Supported: or Reply to Mr. James Rumsey's Pamphlet. John A. Fitch. LC 73-165631. (Select Bibliographies Reprint Ser.). 1977. reprint ed. 18.95 (0-8369-5938-8) Ayer.

Original Steelmakers. John R. Stubbles. LC HD9510.5.S78. (Illus.). 52p. 1984. reprint ed. pap. 30.00 (0-608-05893-9, 206622800007) Bks Demand.

Original Stories. Mary Wollstonecraft Shelley. 1972. 59.95 (0-8490-0779-8) Gordon Pr.

***Original Story By: A Memoir of Broadway & Hollywood.** Arthur Laurents. LC 99-40733. (Illus.). 400p. 2000. 30.00 (0-375-40055-9) Knopf.

Original Story of Santa Claus. Robert T. Stout. (Illus.). 56p. (J). (ps-8). 1981. 6.95 (0-911049-00-2) Yuletide Intl.

Original Study Smart Audio & Workbook Set. Henry E. Florey, Jr. Ed. by John W. Ross. (Illus.). 50p. (gr. 8-12). 1985. write for info. (0-9624330-0-4) Learning Skills.

Original Sunday Dinner: Meals from Family Kitchens. Lora L. Parrott. 304p. 1979. kivar 18.99 (0-8341-0594-2) Beacon Hill.

Original Survey & Land Subdivision. Norman J. Thrower. LC 66-13454. (Monographs: No. 4). 1966. 15.00 (0-89291-083-6) Assn Am Geographers.

***Original Tao: Inward Training (Nei-Yeh) & the Foundations of Taoist Mysticism.** Harold D. Roth. LC 99-20737. (Translations from the Asian Classics). 272p. 1999. 29.50 (0-231-11564-4) Col U Pr.

Original Tarot & You. Richard Roberts. 210p. (Orig.). 1987. pap. 8.95 (0-942380-06-1) Vernal Equinox.

Original Tavern Theatre. John Thomas & Robert W. Service. Ed. by Donna Duffy. (Illus.). 76p. (Orig.). (C). 1988. pap. 5.00 (0-9620982-0-5) J T Thomas.

***Original Text Solar Pons Omnibus.** Derleth. (August Derleth Library). 2000. 60.00 (1-55246-077-0) Battered Silicon.

Original Three Little Pigs Re-Told. Marilyn J. Shearer. LC 90-60398. (Illus.). 16p. (J). (ps-6). 1990. pap. 10.95 (1-878389-03-3) L Ashley & Joshua.

Original Torah: The Political Intent of the Bible's Writers. S. David Sperling. (Reappraisals in Jewish Social & Intellectual History Ser.). 208p. 1998. text 42.50 (0-8147-8094-6) NYU Pr.

***Original Triumph Bonneville.** Gerard T. Kane & David Marsden. LC 99-51836. (Illus.). 128p. 1999. pap. 35.95 (0-7603-0776-8, 128942AP, Pub. by MBI Pubg) Motorbooks Intl.

***Original Triumph Stag: The Restorers Guide.** James Taylor. LC 99-52112. (Illus.). 96p. 1999. 34.95 (1-901432-24-6, 128278AE) Motorbooks Intl.

***Original Triumph TR4/4A/5/6.** Piggott. 128p. 2000. 35.95 (1-901432-04-1, Pub. by MBI Pubg) Motorbooks Intl.

***Original Triumph TR7 & TR8.** Bill Piggott. (Illus.). 96p. 2000. 35.95 (0-7603-0972-8, 130765AP, Pub. by MBI Pubg) Motorbooks Intl.

Original Triumph TR2/3/3A: The Restorers Guide to All Sidescreen Models Including the Francorchamps, Italia & TR3B Versions. Bill Pigott. (Illus.). 128p. 1998. 35.95 (1-901432-03-3, Bay View Bks) MBI Pubg.

Original Trivia Treasury: One Thousand & One Questions for Competitive Play. R. Wayne Schmittberger. LC 90-42285. 208p. 1990. pap. 15.95 (0-471-52759-9) Wiley.

Original Vegetarian Food Combining Cookbook: Recipes for Health & Healing. Dana Britton. Orig. Title: Hidden Treasures Cookbook. (Illus.). 55p. (Orig.). 1997. pap., spiral bd. 6.00 (0-944478-14-X) Dock Pub Co.

Original Vermonters: Native Inhabitants, Past & Present. expanded rev. ed. William A. Haviland & Marjory W. Power. LC 93-35978. (Illus.). 362p. 1994. pap. 22.95 (0-87451-667-6) U Pr of New Eng.

Original Version of Office Copier Humor. L. Edwin Rauch. (Illus.). 98p. 1996. spiral bd. 9.95 (0-9668402-0-8) Spittin Image.

Original Victory Garden Book. E. G. Kains. LC 77-21121. 1978. pap. 3.95 (0-8128-2428-8, Scrbrough Hse) Madison Bks UPA.

Original Vincent Motorcycle. Jacqueline Bickerstaff. (Original Ser.). (Illus.). 128p. 1997. 35.95 (1-870979-83-4, Bay View Bks) MBI Pubg.

Original Vision: A Study of the Religious Experience of Childhood. Edward Robinson. 192p. (Orig.). 1984. 7.95 (0-8164-2439-X) Harper SF.

Original Visions: Shifting the Paradigm, Women's Art, 1970-1996. Alston Conley & Katherine Nahum. (Illus.). 72p. (Orig.). (C). 1997. pap. text 12.95 (0-9640153-6-6) McMullen Mus Art.

Original Visions: The Religions of Oral Peoples. Denise L. Carmody & John T. Carmody. (Illus.). 176p. (Orig.). (C). 1992. pap. text 19.40 (0-02-319395-6, Macmillan Coll) P-H.

Original VW Beetle, Updated ed. The Guide to European Models 1945-1978. rev. ed. Laurence Meredith. LC 99-40953. (Illus.). 144p. 1999. 36.95 (1-901432-27-0) MBI Pubg.

Original VW Bus: The Restorers Guide to All Bus, Panel Van & Pick up Models 1950-79. Laurence Meredith. (Original Ser.). (Illus.). 128p. 1997. 35.95 (1-870979-84-2, Bay View Bks) MBI Pubg.

Original Walker's Diary: Your Personal Walking Record. Jerry W. Stanley. 130p. 1988. spiral bd. 7.95 (0-685-21916-X) Sports Diary Pub.

Original Warm Fuzzy Tale. Claude Steiner. LC 77-77981. (Illus.). 48p. (J). (gr. k up). 1977. pap. 9.95 (0-915190-08-7, JP9008-7) Jalmar Pr.

Original White House Cookbook. Hugo Ziemann & F. L. Gillette. 626p. 1983. 24.95 (0-8159-6413-7) Devin.

Original Word Teaching Series Vol. I: Introduction to New Testament Greek. Charles D. Goodwin & William D. McBrayer. LC 89-92390. 192p. 1989. pap., student ed. 24.95 (0-9626544-0-X) Original Word.

Original Word Teaching Series Vol. II: New Testament Greek for Bible Study, 3 videos 1 audio. Charles D. Goodwin & W. David McBrayer. (GRE.). 133p. 1997. pap. 149.00 incl. audio, vdisk (0-614-30448-2); pap. 24.95 (0-9626544-6-9) Original Word.

Original Writings of Edward Bach. Judy Howard & John Ramsell. 109p. 1991. pap. 13.95 (0-85207-230-9, Pub. by C W Daniel) Natl Bk Netwk.

Original Writings of Edward Bach. Nora Weeks & Victor Bullen. (Illus.). 216p. (Orig.). pap. 20.95 (0-8464-4264-7) Beekman Pubs.

***Original Yoga: As Expounded in Sivasamhita, Gherandasamhita & Patanjala Yogasutra.** 2nd rev. ed. Shyam Ghosh. LC 99-935070. 1999. 29.50 (81-215-0891-6, Pub. by M Manoharial) Coronet Bks.

Originale Fensterentwurfe Des Jugendstils: Art Nouveau Stained-Glass Window Designs. Erhard Remmert. Tr. by Lynn Hattery-Beyer. (ENG & GER., Illus.). 272p. (C). 1991. 228.00 (3-8170-2020-1, Pub. by Knstvrlag Weingrtn) Intl Bk Import.

Originality & Imagination. Thomas McFarland. LC 84-47949. 247p. reprint ed. pap. 76.60 (0-608-07397-0, 206762400009) Bks Demand.

Originality, & Other Essays. William H. McMasters. LC 67-28759. (Essay Index Reprint Ser.). 1977. 16.95 (0-8369-0656-X) Ayer.

Originality As Vengeance in Philippine Literature. Lucilla Hosillos. 171p. (Orig.). (C). 1984. pap. 15.00 (971-10-0131-4, Pub. by New Day Pub) Cellar.

Originality in Byzantine Literature, Art & Music. Ed. by A. R. Littlewood. (Oxbow Monographs in Archaeology: No. 50). (Illus.). 240p. 1995. 45.00 (0-946897-87-5, Pub. by Oxbow Bks) David Brown.

Originality of Japanese Civilization. Arthur Waley. 1980. lib. bdg. 60.00 (0-8490-3199-0) Gordon Pr.

Originality of the Avant-Garde & Other Modernist Myths. Rosalind E. Krauss. (Illus.). 319p. 1986. pap. text 19.50 (0-262-61046-9) MIT Pr.

Originality of Thomas Jones. Lawrence Gowing. LC 85-50606. (Walter Neurath Memorial Lectures). (Illus.). 1986. 12.95 (0-500-55017-4, Pub. by Thames Hudson) Norton.

Originally Published as Part of Vol. 2 of the Civil War, a Narrative see Beleaguered City: The Vicksburg Campaign, Dec. 1862-July 1863

Originalmusik und Musikbearbeitung. Hermann Riedel. 259p. 1971. 24.00 (3-8059-0813-X) Theodore Front.

Originals. Jane Yolen. LC 96-6220. (Illus.). 32p. (J). (ps-3). 1998. 15.95 (0-399-23007-6, Philomel) Peng Put Young Read.

Originals. 2nd rev. ed. Ed. by Bonnie G. McLennaghan. (Illus.). 266p. 1997. reprint ed. pap. 24.95 (0-9625396-3-5) Lindal Cedar.

***Originals: American Women Artists.** Eleanor Munro. (Illus.). 608p. 2000. pap. text 22.50 (0-306-80955-9, Pub. by Da Capo) HarpC.

Originals: American Women Artists. Eleanor Munro. 1982. pap. 19.00 (0-671-42812-8, Touchstone) S&S Trade Pap.

Originals: One Thousand One Proverbs for Today. Raymond P. Brunk. LC 92-73780. 128p. (Orig.). 1992. pap. 4.25 (0-9634038-2-6) Anthony Pubs.

***Originals: The New York Celtics Invent Modern Basketball.** Murry Nelson. LC 99-22733. 225p. 1999. 51.95 (0-87972-793-4); pap. 25.95 (0-87972-794-2) Bowling Green Univ Popular Press.

Originals: Who's Really Who in Fiction. William E. Amos. 1986. 19.95 (0-316-03741-9) Little.

Originals for Quilts: New Expressive Quilting Designs Presents. Ruth Fuleki & Barbra Brausch. (Illus.). 55p. 1997. pap. 16.95 (0-9660729-0-1) Central Pr.

Originary Thinking: Elements of Generative Anthropology. Eric Gans. LC 92-34035. 240p. (C). 1993. 35.00 (0-8047-2114-9) Stanford U Pr.

***Origination of Something Glorious: A Study of Luke 1:1-6:49.** Charles R. Swindoll. 1998. pap., student ed. 5.95 (1-57972-193-1) Insight Living.

Originations of Life from Volcanoes & Petroleum: A Scientific Theory Opposed to Evolution. Donald E. Tyler. 130p. 1983. pap. 10.95 (1-884981-01-7) Discov Bks.

Origine des Instruments de Musique: Introduction Ethnologique a l'Histoire de la Musique Instrumentale. 2nd ed. Andre Schaeffner. (Reeditions Ser.: No. 3). (Illus.). 1980. 41.55 (90-279-6085-2); pap. 40.00 (0-686-21788-8) Mouton.

Origine et l'Evolution du Concept Crec de Phusis. Gerard Naddaf. LC 92-43280. (FRE.). 616p. 1993. text 129.95 (0-7734-9937-7) E Mellen.

Origines & Retraites dans La Nouvelle Heloise. Laurence Mall. LC 96-22117. (Eighteenth-Century French Intellectual History Ser.: No. 5). (FRE.). 211p. (C). 1997. text 45.95 (0-8204-3349-7) P Lang Pubng.

Origines Celticae: And Other Contributions to the History of Britain, 2 vols., 1. Edwin Guest. LC 70-118474. 1979. reprint ed. lib. bdg. 62.00 (0-8290-1858-1) Irvington.

Origines Celticae: And Other Contributions to the History of Britain, 2 vols., 2. Edwin Guest. LC 70-118474. 1979. reprint ed. lib. bdg. 62.00 (0-8290-1859-X) Irvington.

Origines Celticae: And Other Contributions to the History of Britain, 2 vols., Set. Edwin Guest. LC 70-118474. 1979. reprint ed. lib. bdg. 127.00 (0-8046-1223-4) Irvington.

Origines de Chant Liturgique de l'Eglise Latin. Francois A. Gevaert. 93p. 1971. reprint ed. write for info. (0-318-71129-X) G Olms Pubs.

Origines de la Civilisation Technique see Histoire Generale des Techniques

Origines de la Legende Troyenne de Rome (281-31) Jacques Perret. xxxii, 678p. reprint ed. write for info. (0-318-71387-X) G Olms Pubs.

Origines de la Monnaie a Athenes. Ernest Babelon. (FRE., Illus.). 92p. 1979. reprint ed. 20.00 (0-916710-59-9) Obol Intl.

Origines de la Reforme des Carmes en France au XVIlieme Siecle. P. W. Janssen. (International Archives of the History of Ideas Ser.: No. 4). 298p. 1964. lib. bdg. 73.50 (90-247-0180-5, Pub. by M Nijhoff) Kluwer Academic.

Origines de l'Ancienne France, 4 vols. Jacques Flach. xix, 2294p. reprint ed. write for info. (0-318-71339-X) G Olms Pubs.

Origines de l'Empire Ottoman. Mehmet F. Koprulu. LC 78-2453. (Studies in Islamic History: No. 8). 146p. 1978. reprint ed. lib. bdg. 29.50 (0-87991-457-2) Porcupine Pr.

Origines de l'Opera Francais. C. Nuitter & E. Thoinan. LC 77-4106. (Music Reprint Ser.). 1977. reprint ed. lib. bdg. 42.50 (0-306-70895-7) Da Capo.

Origines du Chant Romain: L'Antiphonaire Gregorien. Amedee Gastoue. (FRE.). reprint ed. 55.00 (0-404-56609-X) AMS Pr.

Origines du Culte des Martyrs. 2nd rev. ed. Hippolyte Delehaye. LC 78-63459. (Crusades & Military Orders Ser.: Second Series). reprint ed. 52.50 (0-404-16518-4) AMS Pr.

Origines du Theatre Lyrique Moderne. Romain Rolland. 332p. 1971. 85.00 (0-7859-5566-6) Fr & Eur.

Origines et les Caracteres de la Premier Croisade. Paul Rousset. LC 76-29837. reprint ed. 37.50 (0-404-15428-X) AMS Pr.

Origines Parochiales Scotiae, 2 vols. in 3. Ed. by Cosmo N. Innes et al. LC 76-170804. (Bannatyne Club, Edinburgh. Publications: No. 97). reprint ed. 210.00 (0-404-52850-3) AMS Pr.

Origini del Melodramma, 3 vols. Angelo Solerti. iv, 262p. 1969. reprint ed. write for info. (0-318-71589-9) G Olms Pubs.

Origini e Dottrina del Fascismo. Niccolo D. Evola. LC 79-180385. (Studies in Fascism). reprint ed. 39.50 (0-404-56121-7) AMS Pr.

Originial Alice. Sally Browning. (Illus.). 64p. 1997. pap. text 9.95 (0-7123-4533-7) U of Toronto Pr.

Origins. Ed. by Andrew C. Fabian. (Darwin College Lectures). (Illus.). 184p. (C). 1989. text 36.95 (0-521-35189-8) Cambridge U Pr.

Origins. Morton Marcus. (Illus.). (Orig.). 1973. pap. 10.00 (0-87711-045-X) Story Line.

Origins. Robert Winner. (Slow Loris Poetry Ser.). 24p. 1982. pap. 4.95 (0-918366-24-0) Slow Loris.

Origins. Ed. by Charles E. Woodward et al. LC 98-72564. (Conference Series Proceedings: Vol. 148). 482p. 1998. 52.00 (1-886733-68-6) Astron Soc Pacific.

Origins. 4th ed. Morton Marcus. (Illus.). 80p. (Orig.). (C). 1988. reprint ed. pap. 6.95 (0-9621321-2-8) Brown Bear.

Origins: A Guide to the Place Names of Grand Teton National Park & Surrounding Area. Elizabeth W. Hayden & Cynthia Nielsen. Ed. by GTNP Staff. (Illus.). 44p. 1988. pap. 1.95 (0-931895-11-1) Grand Teton NHA.

Origins: Brain & Self Organization. Ed. by Karl H. Pribram. (INNS Ser.). 728p. 1994. text 135.00 (0-8058-1786-7) L Erlbaum Assocs.

Origins: Contemporary Vedic Library Series Based on the Teachings of A. C. Bhaktivedanta Swami Prabhupada. Richard L. Thompson. (Illus.). 64p. 1984. pap. 2.95 (0-89213-137-3, 0) Bhaktivedanta.

Origins: Cosmos, Earth & Mankind. Hubert Reeves et al. LC 97-27830.Tr. of Plus Belle Histoire du Monde. 192p. 1998. 22.45 (1-55970-408-X, Pub. by Arcade Pub Inc) Time Warner.

Origins: Cosmos, Earth, & Mankind. Hubert Reeves et al. 1999. pap. 12.95 (1-55970-458-6, Pub. by Arcade Pub Inc) Time Warner.

Origins: Creation or Evolution. Richard B. Bliss. LC 92-190747. (Illus.). 80p. (YA). (gr. 6 up). 1988. pap. 9.95 (0-89051-132-2) Master Bks.

Origins: Creation Texts from the Ancient Mediterranean. Harris Lenowitz. Ed. by Charles Doria. LC 74-18844. 1976. lib. bdg. 32.50 (0-404-14849-2) AMS Pr.

Origins: Linking Science & Scripture. Ariel Roth. LC 98-226799. (Illus.). 320p. 1998. 29.99 (0-8280-1328-4) Review & Herald.

Origins: Our Place in Hubble's Universe. John R. Gribbin & Simon Goodwin. LC 97-21833. (Illus.). 160p. 1998. 29.95 (0-87951-813-8, Pub. by Overlook Pr) Penguin Putnam.

Origins: The Ancient Near Eastern Background of Some Modern Western Institutions. William W. Hallo. (Studies in the History & Culture of the Ancient Near East: Vol. 6). xviii, 362p. 1996. 68.50 (90-04-10328-7) Brill Academic Pubs.

Origins: The Lives & Worlds of Modern Cosmologists. Alan P. Lightman & Roberta Brawer. (Illus.). 576p. 1990. text 42.00 (0-674-64470-0) HUP.

Origins: The Lives & Worlds of Modern Cosmologists. Alan P. Lightman & Roberta Brawer. (Illus.). 576p. 1992. pap. text 16.95 (0-674-64471-9) HUP.

Origins: What Is at Stake? Wilbert H. Rusch, Sr. (Creation Research Society Monographs: No. 5). (Illus.). 73p. (Orig.). 1991. pap. text 8.00 (0-940384-10-8) Creation Research.

Origins - Today's Science, Tomorrow's Myth. 2nd rev. ed. James E. Strickling. LC 96-92210. (Illus.). xvii, 265p. 1996. pap. 19.95 (0-9651717-0-1) Peripheral Vsn Ent.

Origins & Adaptations: A Philosophy of Practice. Estelle B. Breines. 281p. 1986. text 32.95 (0-941930-03-3) Geri-Rehab.

Origins & Ancient History of Wine. Ed. by Patrick McGovern et al. (Food & Nutrition in History & Anthropology Ser.: Vol. II). 409p. 1996. pap. text 45.00 (90-5699-552-9, ECU38) Gordon & Breach.

Origins & Ancient History of Wine, Vol. 11. Ed. by Patrick McGovern. (Food & Nutrition in History & Anthropology Ser.). 409p. 1996. text 55.00 (2-88124-577-3) Gordon & Breach.

Origins & Aspects of Olympism. John T. Powell. 239p. (Orig.). (C). 1994. pap. text 17.20 (0-87563-502-4) Stipes.

Origins & Career Consequences of Sex Differences in High School Mathematics Achievement. Lauress L. Wise et al. 128p. 1979. pap. 13.00 (0-89785-656-2) Am Inst Res.

Origins & Causes of the Savings & Loan Debacle: A Blueprint for Reform. 1996. lib. bdg. 250.95 (0-8490-6040-0) Gordon Pr.

Origins & Characteristics of Anabaptism. M. Lienhard. (International Archives of the History of Ideas Ser.: No. 87). 1977. lib. bdg. 191.50 (90-247-1896-1) Kluwer Academic.

Origins & Components of Behaviorology. Stephen F. Ledoux. LC 96-84449. 368p. 1997. 50.00 (1-882508-07-6) ABCs.

Origins & Consequences of Obesity: Symposium No. 201. CIBA Foundation Staff. LC 96-24161. (CIBA Foundation Symposium Ser.). 288p. 1996. 128.00 (0-471-96506-5) Wiley.

Origins & Demise of South African Apartheid: A Public Choice Analysis. Anton D. Lowenberg & William H. Kaempfer. (Illus.). 296p. (C). 1998. text 54.50 (0-472-10905-7, 10905) U of Mich Pr.

Origins & Destinations: 41 Essays on Chinese America. Ed. by Munson Kwok et al. LC 94-67955. ix, 507p. (Orig.). 1994. pap. 20.00 (0-930377-03-6) Chinese Hist CA.

Origins & Destinies: Immigration, Race & Ethnicity in America. Silvia Pedraza & Ruben Rumbaut. 575p. (C). 1995. 48.95 (0-534-21444-4) Wadsworth Pub.

***Origins & Development of African Theology.** Gwinyai H. Muzorewa. 160p. (Orig.). 2000. pap. 18.00 (1-57910-339-1) Wipf & Stock.

Origins & Development of African Theology. Gwinyai H. Muzorewa. LC 84-14769. 160p. (Orig.). reprint ed. pap. 49.60 (0-8357-4068-4, 203675800005) Bks Demand.

Origins & Development of Agriculture in East Africa: The Ethnosystems Approach to the Study of Early Food Production in Kenya. Ed. by Richard E. Leakey & Leendert J. Slikkerveer. (Studies in Technology & Social Change: No. 19). (Illus.). 302p. (Orig.). (C). 1991. pap. 20.00 (0-945271-28-X) ISU-CIKARD.

Origins & Development of Agriculture in the Lowland Neotropics of Latin America. Dolores R. Piperno & Deborah M. Pearsall. LC 98-84003. (Illus.). 400p. 1998. boxed set 99.00 (0-12-557180-1) Morgan Kaufmann.

Origins & Development of Ancient Greek Democracy. James L. O'Neil. (Greek Studies: Interdisciplinary Approaches). 195p. 1995. pap. 23.95 (0-8476-7957-8); lib. bdg. 60.50 (0-8476-7956-X) Rowman.

Origins & Development of Applied Chemistry. James R. Partington. LC 74-26284. (History, Philosophy & Sociology of Science Ser.). 1975. reprint ed. 50.95 (0-405-06611-2) Ayer.

Origins & Development of Classical Hinduism. A. L. Basham. Ed. by Kenneth G. Zysk. (Illus.). 208p. 1991. pap. text 13.95 (0-19-507349-5) OUP.

Origins & Development of European Integration: A Reader & Companion. Peter Stirk & David Weigall. LC 98-20773. 6p. 1998. 89.50 (1-85567-516-1, Pub. by P P Pubs); pap. 29.95 (1-85567-517-X, Pub. by P P Pubs) Cassell & Continuum.

Origins & Development of Federal Crime Control Policy: Herbert Hoover's Initiatives. James D. Calder. LC 93-20298. 328p. 1993. 65.00 (0-275-94284-8, C4284, Praeger Pubs) Greenwood.

Origins & Development of Food Policies in Europe. Ed. by John Burnett & Derek J. Oddy. LC 93-5647. 1994. 64.00 (0-7185-1474-2) St Martin.

Origins & Development of Food Policies in Europe. Dereka J. Oddy. Ed. by John Burnett. 256p. 1994. pap. 25.00 (0-7185-1694-X) St Martin.

O

An Asterisk (*) at the beginning of an entry indicates that the title is appearing for the first time.

Origins & Development of High Ability: Symposium No. 178. Ed. by Gregory R. Bock & Kate Ackrill. LC 93-29488. (CIBA Foundation Symposium Ser.: Vol. 178). 266p. 1993. 134.95 (*0-471-93945-5*) Wiley.

Origins & Development of Labor Economics. Paul J. McNulty. 1984. reprint ed. pap. text 12.95 (*0-262-63097-4*) MIT Pr.

Origins & Development of Medical Imaging. T. Doby & G. Alker. LC 96-8134. (Medical Humanities Ser.). (Illus.). 176p. (C). 1996. 29.95 (*0-8093-2010-X*) S Ill U Pr.

Origins & Development of Professional Football, 1890-1920. rev. ed. Marc S. Maltby. LC 97-10251. (Studies in American Popular History & Culture). 256p. 1997. text 54.00 (*0-8153-2797-8*) Garland.

***Origins & Development of Pure Land Buddhism: A Study & Translation of Gyonen's Jodo Homon Genrusho.** Mark Laurence Blum. LC 99-49558. (Illus.). 336p. 2000. text 45.00 (*0-19-512524-X*) OUP.

Origins & Development of Schizophrenia: Advances in Experimental Psychopathology. Ed. by Mark F. Lenzenweger & Robert H. Dworkin. LC 97-52362. 557p. 1998. 49.95 (*1-55798-497-2*, 431-8730) Am Psychol.

Origins & Development of the Arab-Israeli Conflict. Ann M. Lesch & Dan Tschirgi. LC 97-49481. 240p. 1998. 39.95 (*0-313-29970-6*) Greenwood.

Origins & Development of the English Language. 3rd ed. Thomas Pyles & John Algeo. 383p. (C). 1982. teacher ed. write for info. (*0-318-52971-8*) Harcourt Coll Pubs.

Origins & Development of the English Language. 4th ed. Thomas Pyles & John Algeo. (Illus.). 425p. (C). 1992. text. write for info. (*0-318-68953-7*) Harcourt Coll Pubs.

Origins & Development of the English Language. 4th ed. Thomas Pyles & John Algeo. 416p. (C). 1993. text 59.00 (*0-15-500168-X*, Pub. by Harcourt Coll Pubs) Harcourt.

Origins & Development of the European Community: A Student Reader & Companion. Ed. by David Weigall & Peter M. Stirk. 256p. (C). 1992. pap. text 19.50 (*0-7185-1461-0*, Pub. by Leicester U Pr) Cassell & Continuum.

Origins & Development of the European Community: A Student Reader & Companion. Ed. by David Weigall & Peter M. Stirk. 256p. (C). 1992. text 59.00 (*0-7185-1428-9*) St Martin.

Origins & Development of the European Union. Martin J. Dedman. 160p. (C). 1996. pap. 17.99 (*0-415-11161-7*) Routledge.

Origins & Development of the Second Amendment. David T. Hardy. 96p. 1986. 14.95 (*0-941540-13-8*, 3300) Blacksmith Corp.

Origins & Development of the Turkish Novel. Ahmet O. Evin. (Studies in Middle Eastern Literatures: No. 11). 1983. pap. 16.00 (*0-88297-040-2*) Bibliotheca.

Origins & Development of West German Military Thought, 1949-1966, Vol. 1. Julian Lider. 1986. text 133.95 (*0-566-00946-3*, Pub. by Dartmth Pub) Ashgate Pub Co.

Origins & Development of West German Military Thought, 1966-1985, Vol. 2. Julian Lider. 500p. 1988. text 133.95 (*0-566-05236-9*, Pub. by Dartmth Pub) Ashgate Pub Co.

Origins & Diversity of Axial Age Civilizations. Ed. by Samuel N. Eisenstadt. LC 86-14515. (SUNY Series in Near Eastern Studies). 600p. (C). 1986. text 24.50 (*0-88706-094-3*) State U NY Pr.

Origins & Early Development of the Antichrist Myth. Gregory C. Jenks. (Beiheft zur Zeitschrift fuer die Neuetestamentliche Wissenschaft Ser.: Vol. 59). xxviii, 416p. (C). 1990. lib. bdg. 121.55 (*3-11-012405-X*) De Gruyter.

Origins & Early Development of Witham, Essex. Warwick Rodwell. (Illus.). 128p. 1993. pap. 48.00 (*0-946897-50-6*, Pub. by Oxbow Bks) David Brown.

Origins & Early History, 1675-1835 see Greenwich Observatory

***Origins & Economic Impact of the First Bank of the United States, 1791-1797.** David Jack Cowen. LC 00-39315. (Financial Sector of the American Economy Ser.). (Illus.). 2000. write for info. (*0-8153-3837-6*) Garland.

Origins & English Predecessors of the New England Primer. Gillian Avery. (Illus.). 28p. 1999. pap. write for info. (*0-944026-95-8*) Am Antiquarian.

Origins & Evolution of Behavior Disorders: From Infancy to Adult Life. Stella Chess & Alexander Thomas. LC 87-7582. 344p. 1987. pap. 19.50 (*0-674-64477-8*) HUP.

Origins & Evolution of New Businesses. Amar Bhide. LC 99-38239. (Illus.). 432p. 2000. 35.00 (*0-19-513144-4*) OUP.

Origins & Evolution of Religion. Albert Churchward. (African Heritage Classical Research Studies). 422p. reprint ed. 60.00 (*0-938818-61-9*) ECA Assoc.

Origins & Evolution of the Arab-Zionist Conflict. Michael J. Cohen. 1987. pap. 13.95 (*0-520-06598-0*, Pub. by U CA Pr) Cal Prin Full Svc.

Origins & Evolution of the Field of Industrial Relations in the United States. Bruce E. Kaufman. LC 92-19055. (Cornell Studies in Industrial & Labor Relations: No. 25). 304p. (Orig.). (C). 1993. pap. text 19.95 (*0-87546-192-1*, ILR Press) Cornell U Pr.

***Origins & Evolution of the Single Market in Europe.** Bill Lucarelli. LC 99-72654. 206p. 1999. text 65.95 (*0-7546-1108-6*, Pub. by Ashgate Pub) Ashgate Pub Co.

Origins & Extinctions. Donald E. Osterbrock & Peter H. Raven. LC 88-1396. (C). 1988. 25.00 (*0-300-04260-4*) Yale U Pr.

Origins & Growth of Communication. Ed. by Lynne Feagans et al. LC 83-10041. 356p. 1984. text 73.25 (*0-89391-164-X*) Ablx Pub.

Origins & Growth of Criminology: Essays on Intellectual History, 1760-1945. Ed. by Piers Beirne. (International Library of Criminology & Criminal Justice). 416p. 1994. 159.95 (*1-85521-418-0*, Pub. by Dartmth Pub) Ashgate Pub Co.

Origins & History of Consciousness. Erich Neumann & R. F. C. Hull. (Works by Erich Neumann: Vol. 42). (Illus.). 520p. 1954. pap. 17.95 (*0-691-01761-1*, Pub. by Princeton U Pr) Cal Prin Full Svc.

Origins & Implications of Kant's Critical Philosophy: NC-PK. Mark Glouberman. LC 90-24214. (Studies in the History of Philosophy: Vol. 19). 312p. 1991. lib. bdg. 99.95 (*0-88946-732-3*) E Mellen.

Origins & Method - Towards a New Understanding of Judaism & Christianity: Essays in Honour of John C. Hurd. Ed. by Bradley H. McLean. (JSNT Supplement Ser.: Vol. 86). 409p. 1993. 85.00 (*1-85075-441-1*, Pub. by Sheffield Acad) CUP Services.

Origins & Nature of Language. Giorgio Fano. Tr. by Susan Petrilli. LC 90-23963. (Advances in Semiotics Ser.). (Illus.). 372p. 1992. 15.00 (*0-253-32121-2*) Ind U Pr.

Origins & Past of Modern Humans: Towards Reconciliation. Ed. by Philip V. Tobias & Keiichi Omoto. LC 98-210063. 300p. 1997. text 76.00 (*981-02-3203-9*) World Scientific Pub.

Origins & Psychodynamics of Creativity: A Psychoanalytic Perspective. Jerome D. Oremland. LC 96-43194. 224p. 1997. 32.50 (*0-8236-3905-3*, 03905) Intl Univs Pr.

Origins & Relationships of Lower Invertebrates. Ed. by S. Conway Morris et al. (Illus.). 1985. 125.00 (*0-19-857181-X*) OUP.

Origins & Rise of Associate Degree Nursing Education. Patricia T. Haase. LC 89-13405. 210p. (Orig.). (C). 1990. text 49.95 (*0-8223-0978-5*); pap. text 16.95 (*0-8223-0991-2*) Duke.

Origins & Rise of Ethology. W. H. Thorpe. 186p. 1979. 49.95 (*0-275-90431-8*, C0431, Praeger Pubs) Greenwood.

Origins & Rise of the British Distillery. William T. Harper. LC 99-14292. (Studies in British History: Vol. 53). 320p. 1999. text 99.95 (*0-7734-8007-2*) E Mellen.

Origins & Scope of Roe vs. Wade: Hearing Before the Committee on the Judiciary, U. S. House of Representatives. Composed by Diane Publishing Staff. 125p. (C). 1998. pap. text 35.00 (*0-7881-4919-9*) DIANE Pub.

Origins & Spread of Agriculture & Pastoralism in Eurasia. Ed. by David R. Harris. (Illus.). 594p. 1996. text 55.00 (*1-56098-676-X*); pap. text 26.95 (*1-56098-675-1*) Smithsonian.

Origins & Teachings of Freemasonry. Robert A. Morey. 144p. (Orig.). 1990. pap. write for info. (*0-925703-28-1*) Crown MA.

Origins, Content, & Future of AACRTwo. rev. ed. Ed. by Richard P. Smiraglia & Edward Swanson. LC 91-39734. (ALCTS Papers on Library Technical Services & Collections). 139p. (C). 1992. pap. text 25.00 (*0-8389-3405-6*) ALA.

Origins Controversy: Creation or Chance. Dennis G. Lindsay. (Creation Science Ser.: Vol. 3). 1991. 6.95 (*0-89985-280-7*) Christ for the Nations.

Origins Crimean War. David M. Goldfrank. LC 93-14826. (Origins of Modern Wars Ser.). 320p. (C). 1994. pap. text 30.00 (*0-582-49055-3*, Pub. by Addison-Wesley) Longman.

***Origins Diet: How Eating in Tune with Your Evolutionary Roots Can Prevent Disease, Boost Vitality & Help You Stay Lean & Fit.** Elizabeth Somer. (Illus.). 288p. 2001. text 23.00 (*0-8050-6335-8*) H Holt & Co.

Origins Early Development of Shi'a Islam. S. H. Jafri. 332p. 1979. 45.00 (*0-86685-595-5*, LDL5955, Pub. by Librairie du Liban) Intl Bk Ctr.

Origins, Evolution, & Destinies of Binary Stars in Clusters. Ed. by E. F. Milone & J. C. Mermilliod. (ASP Conference Series Proceedings: Vol. 90). 508p. 1996. 34.00 (*1-886733-11-2*) Astron Soc Pacific.

Origins, Evolution & Nature of the Cold War: An Annotated Bibliography. Norman Hillmer et al. LC 85-15032. (War-Peace Bibliography Ser.: No. 19). 174p. 1985. lib. bdg. 49.00 (*0-87436-391-8*) ABC-CLIO.

Origins for World War I, 1871-1914. 2nd ed. Joachim Remak. LC 94-77240. (Illus.). 170p. (C). 1994. pap. text 29.50 (*0-15-501438-2*, Pub. by Harcourt Coll Pubs) Harcourt.

Origins Greek Civil War. David H. Close. LC 94-39794. (Origins of Modern Wars Ser.). 248p. (C). 1995. pap. 72.00 (*0-582-06472-4*) Longman.

Origins Greek Civil War. David H. Close. LC 94-39794. (Origins of Modern Wars Ser.). 256p. (C). 1995. pap. text 33.53 (*0-582-06471-6*) Longman.

Origins, Icons & Illusions. Harold R. Booher. LC 98-159250. 17p. 1997. pap. 29.95 (*0-87527-515-X*) Green.

Origins in Acoustics: The Science of Sound from Antiquity to the Age of Newton. Frederick V. Hunt. LC 78-5032. (Illus.). 224p. 1992. 20.00 (*0-300-02220-4*) Acoustical Soc Am.

Origins in Acoustics: The Science of Sound from Antiquity to the Age of Newton. Frederick V. Hunt. LC 78-5032. 218p. reprint ed. pap. 67.60 (*0-7837-3301-1*, 205770300006) Bks Demand.

Origins in Williamstown, Massachusetts, 2 vols. Arthur L. Perry. (Illus.). viii, 631p. 1993. reprint ed. pap. text 36.50 (*1-55613-766-4*) Heritage Bk.

Origins, Initiations. Kirk Robertson. (Illus.). 1980. 100.00 (*0-918824-19-2*) Turkey Pr.

Origins Modern Economics: Paradigmatic Approach. Ley Robert & Lowell E. Johnson. 218p. (C). 1990. text 49.00 (*0-536-57844-3*) Pearson Custom.

Origins of a Catastrophe: Yugoslavia & it's Destroyers. Warren Zimmermann. 320p. 1999. pap. 14.00 (*0-8129-3303-6*, Times Bks) Crown Pub Group.

Origins of Action: Interdisciplinary & International Perspectives. Ed. by L. Oppenheimer & Jaan Valsiner. (Illus.). xv, 265p. 1991. 79.95 (*0-387-97510-1*) Spr-Verlag.

Origins of African Plant Domestication. Ed. by Jack R. Harlan et al. (World Anthropology Ser.). (Illus.). xiv, 498p. 1976. 69.25 (*90-279-7819-0*) Mouton.

Origins of Afro-American Fiction. Maryemma Graham. 12p. 1990. pap. 2.50 (*0-944026-27-3*) Am Antiquarian.

Origins of Aggression. Willard W. Hartup & Jan De Wit. (Psychological Studies: No. 10). 1978. 60.00 (*90-279-7673-2*) Mouton.

Origins of Agnosticism: Victorian Unbelief & the Limits of Knowledge. Bernard V. Lightman. LC 87-2690. 264p. 1987. reprint ed. pap. 81.90 (*0-608-03722-2*, 206454700009) Bks Demand.

Origins of Agriculture. Ed. by Charles A. Reed. (World Anthropology Ser.). (Illus.). xvi, 1014p. 1977. 113.85 (*90-279-7919-7*) Mouton.

Origins of Agriculture. Harold J. Peake. LC 76-44776. reprint ed. 27.50 (*0-404-15960-5*) AMS Pr.

Origins of Agriculture: An International Perspective. Ed. by C. Wesley Cowan & Patty J. Watson. LC 91-32767. (Series in Archaeological Inquiry). (Illus.). 250p. (C). 1992. pap. text 21.95 (*0-87474-991-3*) Smithsonian.

Origins of Agriculture & Settled Life. Richard S. MacNeish. LC 91-50304. (Illus.). 448p. 1992. text 75.00 (*0-8061-2364-8*) U of Okla Pr.

Origins of Agriculture in Europe. I. J. Thorpe. (Illus.). 240p. (C). 1996. 85.00 (*0-415-08009-6*) Routledge.

Origins of Algae & Their Plastids. Ed. by D. Bhattacharya. (Illus.). 320p. 1998. 179.00 (*3-211-83036-7*) Spr-Verlag.

Origins of Algae & Their Plastids. Debashish Bhattacharya. LC 97-48872. (Plant Systematics & Evolution Ser.). 1997. write for info. (*3-211-83035-9*) Spr-Verlag.

Origins of Alliances. Stephen M. Walt. LC 87-47606. (Cornell Studies in Security Affairs). 336p. (C). 1987. text 45.00 (*0-8014-2054-7*) Cornell U Pr.

Origins of Alliances. Stephan M. Walt. LC 87-47606. (Cornell Studies in Security Affairs). 336p. 1990. reprint ed. pap. text 16.95 (*0-8014-9418-4*) Cornell U Pr.

Origins of American Academic Librarianship. Orvin L. Shiflett. LC 81-14969. (Libraries & Information Science). 308p. (C). 1981. text 73.25 (*0-89391-082-1*) Ablx Pub.

Origins of American Banking, 7 vols., Set. Ed. by John F. Chown. 1800p. (C). 1997. 745.00 (*0-415-14450-7*) Routledge.

Origins of American Capitalism: Collected Essays. James A. Henretta. 224p. 1991. text 47.50 (*1-55553-109-1*) NE U Pr.

Origins of American Constitutionalism. Donald S. Lutz. LC 88-6415. 178p. 1988. pap. text 14.95 (*0-8071-1506-1*) La State U Pr.

Origins of American Critical Thought, 1810-1835. William Charvat. (BCL1-PS American Literature Ser.). 218p. 1993. reprint ed. lib. bdg. 79.00 (*0-7812-6564-9*) Rprt Serv.

Origins of American Film Criticisms, 1909-1939. Myron O. Lounsbury. LC 72-556. (Dissertations on Film Ser.). 560p. 1974. reprint ed. 36.95 (*0-405-04099-7*) Ayer.

Origins of American Government & Citizenship: Political Parties & Elections see American Government

Origins of American Linguistics, 1643-1914, 13 vols. Intro. by Ray Harris. 5590p. (C). 1997. text, boxed set 1565.00 (*0-415-14955-X*) Routledge.

Origins of American National Security Policy: Sea Power, Air Power & Foreign Policy, 1900-1941. Lester H. Brune. 348p. 1981. pap. text 36.95 (*0-89126-075-7*) MA-AH Pub.

Origins of American Political Parties, 1789-1803. John F. Hoadley. LC 85-15787. 269p. 1986. reprint ed. pap. 83.40 (*0-608-02126-1*, 206277500004) Bks Demand.

Origins of American Politics. Bernard Bailyn. LC 68-12665. 1970. pap. 5.56 (*0-394-70865-2*, V604) Vin Bks.

Origins of American Public Finance: Debates over Money, Debt & Taxes in the Constitutional Era, 1776-1836, 198. Donald R. Stabile. LC 98-11163. (Contributions in Economics & Economic History Ser.: Vol. 198). 224p. 1998. 59.95 (*0-313-30754-7*, Greenwood Pr) Greenwood.

Origins of American Slavery: Freedom & Bondage in the English Colonies. Betty Wood. LC 96-36025. 1997. 18.00 (*0-8090-7456-7*) Hill & Wang.

Origins of American Social Science. Dorothy Ross. (Ideas in Context Ser.: No. 19). 532p. (C). 1990. text 54.95 (*0-521-35092-1*) Cambridge U Pr.

Origins of American Social Science. Dorothy Ross. (Ideas in Context Ser.: No. 19). 533p. (C). 1992. pap. text 20.95 (*0-521-42836-X*) Cambridge U Pr.

Origins of American Trancendalism. Nathaniel Kaplan & Thomas Katsaros. 1975. pap. 17.95 (*0-8084-0415-6*) NCUP.

Origins of America's Civil War. Bruce Collins. LC 81-81340. 165p. (C). 1981. 29.50 (*0-8419-0714-5*) Holmes & Meier.

Origins of an Heroic Image: Sun Yat-sen in London, 1896-1897. John Y. Wong. (East Asian Historical Monographs). (Illus.). 320p. (C). 1986. 34.50 (*0-19-584080-1*) OUP.

Origins of Analytical Philosophy. Michael Dummett. LC 93-3772. 208p. 1994. 40.50 (*0-674-64472-7*) HUP.

Origins of Analytical Philosophy. Michael Dummett. 208p. 1996. pap. 17.95 (*0-674-64473-5*) HUP.

Origins of Anatomically Modern Humans. M. H. Nitecki & D. V. Nitecki. (Interdisciplinary Contributions to Archaeology Ser.). (Illus.). 356p. (C). 1994. 52.50 (*0-306-44675-8*, Plenum Trade) Perseus Pubng.

Origins of Ancrene Wisse. E. J. Dobson. (Illus.). 450p. (C). 1976. text 49.00 (*0-19-811864-3*) OUP.

Origins of Angling: And a New Printing of "The Treatise of Fishing with an Angle" 3rd ed. John McDonald et al. LC 97-4452. (Illus.). 288p. 1997. reprint ed. 40.00 (*1-55821-587-5*) Lyons Pr.

Origins of Anglo-American Radicalism. Ed. by Margaret C. Jacob & James Jacob. 368p. (C). 1983. text 44.95 (*0-04-909015-1*) Routledge.

Origins of Anglo-American Radicalism. 2nd ed. Ed. by Margaret C. Jacob & James R. Jacob. LC 90-23163. 352p. (C). 1991. pap. 18.50 (*0-391-03703-X*) Humanities.

Origins of Anglo Saxon Kingdoms. Steven Bassett. 300p. 1989. text 59.00 (*0-7185-1317-7*, Pub. by Leicester U Pr) Cassell & Continuum.

Origins of Anglo-Saxon Kingdoms. Ed. by Steven Bassett & Nicholas Brooks. (Studies in the Early History of Britain). (Illus.). 312p. 1994. pap. text 25.00 (*0-7185-1367-3*) St Martin.

Origins of Anti-Semitism: Attitudes Towards Judaism in Pagan & Christian Antiquity. John G. Gager. 312p. 1985. pap. text 19.95 (*0-19-503607-7*) OUP.

***Origins of Apocalypticism in Judaism & Christianity.** Ed. by John J. Collins. (Encyclopedia of Apocalypticism Ser. : Vol. 1). 520p. 2000. pap. text 39.95 (*0-8264-1253-X*) Continuum.

Origins of Arab Nationalism. Ed. by L. Anderson et al. 1991. text 57.50 (*0-231-07434-4*) Col U Pr.

Origins of Arab Nationalism. Ed. by Rashid Khalidi et al. 312p. 1993. pap. 20.00 (*0-231-07435-2*) Col U Pr.

Origins of Arab Nationalism. Ed. by Rashid Khalidi et al. 325p. (C). 1998. text 30.00 (*0-7881-5504-0*) DIANE Pub.

Origins of Architectural Pleasure. Grant Hildebrand. LC 98-8213. 185p. 1999. 35.00 (*0-520-21505-2*, Pub. by U CA Pr) Cal Prin Full Svc.

Origins of Art: A Psychological & Sociological Inquiry. Yrjo Hirn. LC 78-17311. 340p. 1979. reprint ed. 26.95 (*0-405-08623-7*, Pub. by Blom Pubns) Ayer.

Origins of Australia's Capital Cities. Ed. by Pamela Statham. (Studies in Australian History). (Illus.). 384p. (C). 1991. pap. text 27.95 (*0-521-40832-6*) Cambridge U Pr.

Origins of Backwardness in Eastern Europe: Economics & Politics from the Middle Ages until the Early Twentieth Century. Ed. by Daniel Chirot. 269p. 1991. reprint ed. pap. 17.95 (*0-520-07640-0*, Pub. by U CA Pr) Cal Prin Full Svc.

Origins of Beowulf: And Their Pre-Viking Kingdom of East Anglia. Sam Newton. (Illus.). 192p. 1999. pap. 24.95 (*0-85991-472-0*) Boydell & Brewer.

Origins of Beowulf & the Pre-Viking Kingdom of East Anglia. Sam Newton. (Illus.). 192p. (C). 1994. 75.00 (*0-85991-361-9*) Boydell & Brewer.

Origins of Biblical Law: The Decalogues & the Book of the Covenant. Calum M. Carmichael. LC 92-6908. 272p. 1992. text 37.50 (*0-8014-2712-6*) Cornell U Pr.

***Origins of Biblical Monotheism: Israel's Polytheistic Background & the Ugaritic Texts.** Mark S. Smith. LC 99-58180. 384p. 2000. text 60.00 (*0-19-513480-X*) OUP.

Origins of Central Banking in the United States. Richard H. Timberlake, Jr. LC 78-4622. (Illus.). 284p. 1978. 27.50 (*0-674-64480-8*) HUP.

Origins of Certainty: Means & Meanings in Pascal's "Pensees" Hugh M. Davidson. LC 78-12768. 1993. 16.00 (*0-226-13716-3*) U Ch Pr.

Origins of Certainty: Means & Meanings in Pascal's Pensees. Hugh M. Davidson. LC 78-12768. 170p. reprint ed. pap. 52.70 (*0-608-09443-9*, 205424300005) Bks Demand.

Origins of Chemistry. Robert P. Multhauf. (Classics in the History & Philosophy of Science Ser.: Vol. 3). 424p. 1993. pap. text 64.00 (*2-88124-594-3*) Gordon & Breach.

Origins of Cheshire. N. J. Higham. (Origins of the Shire Ser.). 1944. write for info. (*0-7910-3159-4*, Pub. by Manchester Univ Pr) St Martin.

Origins of Cheshire. N. J. Higham. (Origins of the Shire Ser.). 200p. 1994. pap. 32.00 (*0-7190-3160-5*) St Martin.

Origins of Chinese Bolshevism: An Ideology in the Making, 1921-1928. Michael Y. Luk. (South-East Asian Historical Monographs). (Illus.). 376p. (C). 1990. text 35.00 (*0-19-584209-X*) OUP.

Origins of Chinese Communism. Arif Dirlik. (Illus.). 315p. (C). 1989. pap. text 23.95 (*0-19-505454-7*) OUP.

Origins of Chinese Law: Penal & Administrative Law in Its Early Development. Yongping Liu. 374p. 1999. text 45.00 (*0-19-590344-7*) OUP.

Origins of Christian Faith. Terrance Callan. LC 93-23465. 160p. (Orig.). 1994. pap. 9.95 (*0-8091-3459-4*) Paulist Pr.

Origins of Christian Morality. Wayne A. Meeks. 1995. pap. 14.00 (*0-300-06513-2*) Yale U Pr.

Origins of Christianity: A Critical Introduction. Ed. by R. Joseph Hoffmann. LC 85-62744. 326p. (Orig.). 1985. pap. 23.95 (*0-87975-308-0*) Prometheus Bks.

Origins of Christianity: A Historical Introduction to the New Testament. 2nd rev. ed. Schuyler Brown. (Oxford Bible Ser.). 190p. (Orig.). (C). 1993. pap. text 16.95 (*0-19-826207-8*) OUP.

Origins of Christianity: An Exploration. Etienne Nodet & Justin Taylor. LC 98-5539. 1998. pap. 39.95 (*0-8146-5862-8*) Liturgical Pr.

Origins of Christianity in Bohemia. Marvin Kantor. (Illus.). 299p. 1990. 35.95 (*0-8101-0874-7*) Northwestern U Pr.

Origins of Cities in Dry-Farming Syria & Mesopotamia in the Third Millennium B. C. Ed. by Harvey Weiss. LC 86-2087. 167p. 1986. text 27.50 (*0-931500-08-7*) Eisenbrauns.

O

An Asterisk (*) at the beginning of an entry indicates that the title is appearing for the first time.

Origins of Citizenship in Ancient Athens. Philip Brook Manville. 279p. 1990. pap. text 17.95 (*0-691-01593-7*, Pub. by Princeton U Pr) Cal Prin Full Svc.

Origins of Civic Universities: Manchester, Leeds & Liverpool. David R. Jones. LC 88-5102. 239p. reprint ed. pap. 74.10 (*0-608-20353-X*, 207160600001) Bks Demand.

Origins of Class Struggle in Louisiana: A Social History of White Farmers & Laborers During Slavery & After, 1840-1875. Roger W. Shugg. LC 74-1055. 388p. reprint ed. pap. 120.30 (*0-608-13748-0*, 205166600004) Bks Demand.

Origins of Cognitive Skills: The 18th Annual Carnegie Mellon Symposium on Cognition. Ed. by Catherine Sophian. (Carnegie Mellon Symposia on Cognition Ser.). 442p. (C). 1984. text 89.95 (*0-89859-390-5*) L Erlbaum Assocs.

Origins of Complex Language: An Inquiry into the Evolutionary Beginnings of Sentences, Syllables & Truth. Andrew Carstairs-McCarthy. (Illus.). 272p. 1999. text 80.00 (*0-19-823822-3*); pap. text 19.95 (*0-19-823821-5*) OUP.

Origins of Complex Societies in Late Prehistoric Iberia. Ed. by Katina T. Lillios. LC 95-1561. (Archaeological Ser.: Vol. 8). (Illus.). vii, 183p. 1995. pap. text 25.00 (*1-879621-18-5*) Intl Mono Prehstry.

Origins of Complex Societies in Late Prehistoric Iberia. Ed. by Katina T. Lillios. LC 95-1561. (Archaeological Ser.: No. 8). (Illus.). vii, 183p. 1995. lib. bdg. 39.50 (*1-879621-19-3*) Intl Mono Prehstry.

Origins of Composition Studies in the American College, 1875-1925: A Documentary History. John C. Brereton. (Series in Composition, Literacy, & Culture). 584p. (C). 1996. pap. 24.95 (*0-8229-5535-0*); text 59.95 (*0-8229-3783-2*) U of Pittsburgh Pr.

Origins of Conflict: The United States in Central America, Selected Essays. Thomas B. Adams. Ed. by Melden E. Smith. 68p. (Orig.). 1989. pap. text 3.00 (*0-685-27234-6*) N Shore Cmnty Coll Pr.

Origins of Containment: A Psychological Explanation. Deborah W. Larson. LC 85-42691. 420p. 1985. pap. text 20.95 (*0-691-02303-4*, Pub. by Princeton U Pr) Cal Prin Full Svc.

Origins of Contemporary France. Hippolyte A. Taine. Ed. by Edward T. Gargan. LC 73-87311. (Classic European Historians Ser.). xlvi, 446p. 1974. lib. bdg. 25.00 (*0-226-78934-9*) U Ch Pr.

Origins of Contemporary France. Hippolyte A. Taine. Ed. by Edward T. Gargan. LC 73-87311. (Classic European Historians Ser.). 1994. pap. text 12.00 (*0-226-78935-7*) U Ch Pr.

Origins of Controversy. 2nd ed. Dennis Lindsay. (RUS., Illus.). (Orig.). 1997. mass mkt. write for info. (*1-890863-02-5*) Wrld Wide Print.

Origins of Crime: A New Evaluation of the Cambridge-Sommerville Youth Study. William J. McCord & Joan McCord. LC 69-14939. (Criminology, Law Enforcement, & Social Problems Ser.: No. 49). (C). 1969. reprint ed. 30.00 (*0-87585-049-9*); reprint ed. pap. 12.00 (*0-87585-908-9*) Patterson Smith.

Origins of Cultural Differences & Their Impact on Management. Jack Scarborough. LC 97-13404. 288p. 1998. 59.95 (*1-56720-123-7*, Quorum Bks) Greenwood.

Origins of Culture & Anarchy: Matthew Arnold & Popular Education in England. Fred G. Walcott. LC 76-485471. 185p. reprint ed. pap. 57.40 (*0-608-30534-0*, 201918500011) Bks Demand.

***Origins of Democratic Culture: Printing, Petitions & the Public Sphere in Early-Modern England** David Zaret. LC 99-25810. (Studies in Cultural Sociology). 2000. 45.00 (*0-691-00694-6*, Pub. by Princeton U Pr) Cal Prin Full Svc.

Origins of Democratization in Poland: Workers, Intellectuals, & Oppositional Politics, 1976-1980. Michael H. Bernhard. 400p. (C). 1993. pap. 21.00 (*0-231-08093-X*) Col U Pr.

Origins of Desire: Modern Spanish Short Stories. Juan A. Masoliver. (Modern European Short Stories Ser.). 208p. 1994. pap. 13.99 (*1-85242-187-8*) Serpents Tail.

Origins of Digital Computers. 3rd ed. Ed. by Brian Randell. (Texts & Monographs in Computer Science). (Illus.). 598p. 1982. 87.00 (*0-387-11319-3*) Spr-Verlag.

Origins of Dispensationalism: The Darby Factor. Larry Crutchfield. 254p. (Orig.). (C). 1991. lib. bdg. 52.50 (*0-8191-8467-5*) U Pr of Amer.

Origins of Dispensationalism: The Darby Factor. Larry Crutchfield. 254p. (Orig.). (C). 1992. pap. text 28.50 (*0-8191-8468-3*) U Pr of Amer.

Origins of Dracula: The Background to Bram Stoker's Gothic Masterpiece. Clive Leatherdale. LC 95-220634. 239p. 1995. 29.95 (*1-874287-07-4*, Pub. by Desert Island Bks) Firebird Dist.

Origins of Drama in Scandanavia. Terry Gunnell. (Illus.). 440p. (C). 1995. text 125.00 (*0-85991-458-5*, DS Brewer) Boydell & Brewer.

Origins of Early Semitic Ritual. Samuel H. Hooke. (British Academy, London, Schweich Lectures on Biblical Archaeology Series, 1930). 1974. reprint ed. pap. 25.00 (*0-8115-1277-0*) Periodicals Srv.

Origins of Economic Growth: The Fundamental Interaction Between Material & Nonmaterial Values. Arvid Aulin. LC 97-1231. 1997. write for info. (*3-540-62517-8*) Spr-Verlag.

Origins of Economic Inequality Between Nations: Critique of Western Theories & Underdevelopement. C. Ramirez-Faria. 334p. (C). 1990. pap. text 22.50 (*0-04-445843-6*) Routledge.

Origins of Economic Thought & Justice. Joseph J. Spengler. LC 79-27026. (Political & Social Economy Ser.). 192p. 1980. 21.95 (*0-8093-0947-5*) S Ill U Pr.

***Origins of English Nonsense.** Noel Malcolm. 1998. pap. 13.95 (*0-00-638844-2*, Pub. by HarpC) Trafalgar.

Origins of English Words: A Discursive Dictionary of Indo-European Roots. Joseph T. Shipley. LC 83-8415. 671p. 1984. reprint ed. pap. 200.00 (*0-608-00813-3*, 206160100010) Bks Demand.

Origins of Entrepreneurship in Meiji Japan. Johannes Hirschmeier. LC 64-20973. (Harvard East Asian Ser.: No. 17). 368p. reprint ed. pap. 114.10 (*0-7837-2274-5*, 205736200004) Bks Demand.

Origins of Epistemology in Early Greek Thought: A Study of Psyche & Logos in Heraclitus. Joel Wilcox. LC 93-49635. (Studies in the History of Philosophy: Vol. 34). 192p. 1994. 79.95 (*0-7734-9122-8*) E Mellen.

Origins of Europe: Four New Studies in Archaeology & History. Desmond Collins. LC 75-313261. 347p. 1975. 6.95 (*0-04-940045-2*) Allen & Unwn AT.

Origins of European Dissent. R. I. Moore. (MART Thirty Medieval Academy Reprints for Teaching Ser.: No. 30). 322p. 1994. reprint ed. pap. text 17.95 (*0-8020-7566-5*) U of Toronto Pr.

Origins of European Individualism. Aaron Gurevich. Tr. by Katherine Judelson. (Making of Europe Ser.). 320p. (C). 1995. 31.95 (*0-631-17963-1*) Blackwell Pubs.

Origins of European Thought About the Body, the Mind, the Soul, the World, Time, & Fate. Richard B. Onians. LC 72-9298. (Philosophy of Plato & Aristotle Ser.). 1980. reprint ed. 43.95 (*0-405-04853-X*) Ayer.

Origins of European Thought about the Body, the Mind, the Soul, the World, Time, & Fate: New Interpretations of Greek, Roman, & Kindred Evidence, Also of Some Basic Jewish & Christian Beliefs. 2nd ed. Richard B. Onians. (Illus.). 608p. 1988. pap. text 32.95 (*0-521-34794-7*) Cambridge U Pr.

Origins of Evening. Gibb. LC 97-39454. 108p. 1999. pap. 11.00 (*0-393-31964-4*) Norton.

Origins of Evening: Poems. Robert Gibb. LC 97-39454. 96p. 1998. 21.00 (*0-393-04644-3*) Norton.

Origins of Everyday Things. Ed. by Reader's Digest Editors & Ruth Binney. LC 98-55992. 320p. 1999. 29.95 (*0-276-42320-8*); 29.95 (*0-7621-0141-5*, Pub. by RD Assn) Penguin Putnam.

Origins of Evil in Hindu Mythology. Wendy D. O'Flaherty. (Hermeneutics: Studies in the History of Religions: No. 6). 1977. pap. 18.95 (*0-520-04098-8*, Pub. by U CA Pr) Cal Prin Full Svc.

Origins of Faith & Life: Genesis A. (New Horizons Bible Study Ser.). 1981. pap., student ed. 1.50 (*0-89367-053-7*) Light & Life Comm.

Origins of Fear. Ed. by Michael Lewis & Leonard A. Rosenblum. LC 74-9565. (Origins of Behavior Ser.: Vol. 2). 298p. reprint ed. pap. 92.40 (*0-608-30793-9*, 201262100082) Bks Demand.

Origins of Federal Support for Higher Education: George W. Atherton & the Land-Grant College Movement. Roger L. Williams. (Illus.). 256p. 1991. 40.00 (*0-271-00730-3*) Pa St U Pr.

Origins of Form. rev. ed. Christopher Williams. (Illus.). 144p. (Orig.). 1995. pap. 18.95 (*0-942655-10-9*) Archit CT.

Origins of Free Verse. H. T. Kirby-Smith. 320p. 1998. pap. text 17.95 (*0-472-08565-4*, 08565) U of Mich Pr.

Origins of Freemasonry: Scotland's Century, 1590-1710. David Stevenson. (Illus.). 263p. (C). 1990. pap. text 19.95 (*0-521-39654-9*) Cambridge U Pr.

Origins of French Art Criticism: From the Ancient Regime to the Restoration. Richard Wrigley. (Illus.). 440p. 1995. pap. text 35.00 (*0-19-817409-8*) OUP.

Origins of French-Canadian Families: Extracted from the French Civil Statistics, First Series. Archange Godbout. LC 98-161944. 1997. write for info. (*0-88545-060-4*) Elysee Edns.

Origins of Futuristic Fiction. Paul K. Alkon. LC 86-25026. (Illus.). 354p. 1987. 35.00 (*0-8203-0932-X*) U of Ga Pr.

Origins of Genius: Darwinian Perspectives on Creativity. Dean K. Simonton. LC 98-45044. (Illus.). 320p. 1999. 27.50 (*0-19-512879-6*) OUP.

Origins of Geometry. Serres Staff. (Illus.). (C). text. write for info. (*0-472-10697-X*) U of Mich Pr.

Origins of Grammar: Evidence from Early Language Comprehension. Kathy Hirsh-Pasek & Roberta M. Golinkoff. (Language, Speech & Communication Ser.). (Illus.). 240p. 1996. 33.00 (*0-262-08242-X*, Bradford Bks) MIT Pr.

Origins of Grammar: Evidence from Early Language Comprehension. Kathy Hirsh-Pasek & Roberta Michnick Golinkoff. (Language, Speech & Communication Ser.). (Illus.). 230p. 1999. reprint ed. pap. 17.50 (*0-262-58180-9*, Bradford Bks) MIT Pr.

Origins of Graphic Design in America, 1870-1920. Burton Raffel. LC 96-52342. 1997. 27.50 (*0-300-06835-2*) Yale U Pr.

Origins of Greek Civilization (NCHS) (J). 13.50 (*0-382-40948-5*); 18.00 (*0-382-40949-3*) Cobblestone Pub Co.

Origins of Greek Civilization, 100-650 B.C. Chester G. Starr, Jr. 1991. pap. 15.95 (*0-393-30779-4*) Norton.

Origins of Greek Religion. B. C. Dietrich. 314p. (C). 1973. 165.40 (*3-11-003982-6*) De Gruyter.

Origins of Greek Thought. Jean-Pierre Vernant. LC 81-15247. 144p. 1982. reprint ed. pap. text 9.95 (*0-8014-9293-9*) Cornell U Pr.

Origins of Group Psychoanalysis. Ed. by Harold I. Kaplan & Benjamin J. Sadock. 160p. 1986. 30.00 (*0-87668-077-5*) Aronson.

Origins of Hamilton's Fiscal Policies. Donald F. Swanson. LC 63-63264. (University of Florida Monographs: Social Sciences: No. 17). 95p. reprint ed. pap. 30.00 (*0-7837-4996-1*, 204466300004) Bks Demand.

Origins of Health & Disease, Vol. 1. Peter W. Nathanielsz. Date not set. pap. text. write for info. (*0-7167-2999-7*); pap. text. write for info. (*0-7167-3024-3*) W H Freeman.

Origins of Hertfordshire. Tom Williamson. text. write for info. (*0-7190-4491-X*, Pub. by Manchester Univ Pr) St Martin.

Origins of Human Aggression: Dynamics & Etiology. Gerard G. Neuman. LC 86-15370. 200p. 1987. 35.95 (*0-89885-324-9*, Kluwer Acad Hman Sci) Kluwer Academic.

Origins of Human Cancer: A Comprehensive Review. fac. ed. Ed. by Joan Brugge et al. LC 91-13383. (Illus.). 922p. 1991. reprint ed. pap. 200.00 (*0-7837-8112-1*, 204791900008) Bks Demand.

Origins of Human Diet & Medicine: Chemical Ecology. Timothy Johns. LC 96-20505. (Arizona Studies in Human Ecology). 356p. 1996. pap. 19.95 (*0-8165-1687-1*) U of Ariz Pr.

Origins of Human Potential: Evolution, Development, & Psychology. Ken Richardson. LC 97-14925. 240p. (C). 1998. write for info. (*0-415-17369-8*); pap. 24.99 (*0-415-17370-1*) Routledge.

Origins of Human Society. Peter Bogtucki. LC 98-56285. (History of the World Ser.). (Illus.). 352p. 1999. text 62.95 (*1-55786-349-0*) Blackwell Pubs.

***Origins of Human Society.** Peter Bogucki. (History of the World Ser.). (Illus.). 352p. 1999. pap. 29.95 (*1-57718-112-3*) Blackwell Pubs.

Origins of Hydraulic Mining in California. limited ed. Philip R. May. (Illus.). 88p. 1970. 6.95 (*0-910740-17-8*) Holmes.

Origins of Ice Dance Music. Muriel Kay. 44p. 1992. pap. text 12.00 (*0-9631758-6-6*) Platoro Pr.

Origins of Igneous Rocks. Paul C. Hess. LC 88-28389. (Illus.). 384p. 1989. 88.00 (*0-674-64481-6*) HUP.

Origins of Indian Psychology. N. Ross Reat. LC 90-48484. 400p. (C). 1990. pap. 25.00 (*0-89581-924-4*); text 30.00 (*0-89581-923-6*) Asian Humanities.

Origins of Industrial Capitalism in India: Business Strategies & the Working Classes in Bombay, 1900-1940. Rajnarayan Chandavarkar. (Cambridge South Asian Studies: No. 51). (Illus.). 489p. (C). 1994. text 74.95 (*0-521-41496-2*) Cambridge U Pr.

Origins of Industrial Engineering: The Early Years of a Profession. Howard Emerson & Douglas Naehring. 121p. 1988. 19.95 (*0-89806-097-4*, ORGINE) Eng Mgmt Pr.

Origins of Instability in Early Republican Mexico. Donald F. Stevens. LC 90-25357. 199p. 1991. text 37.95 (*0-8223-1136-4*) Duke.

Origins of Intelligence: Infancy & Early Childhood. Ed. by Michael Lewis. LC 75-31530. 423p. reprint ed. pap. 131.20 (*0-608-14054-6*, 202402000035) Bks Demand.

Origins of Intelligence: Infancy & Early Childhood. 2nd ed. Ed. by Michael Lewis. 552p. 1983. 47.50 (*0-306-41225-X*, Plenum Trade) Perseus Pubng.

Origins of Intelligence: The Evolution of Cognitive Development in Monkeys, Apes & Humans. Sue T. Parker & Michael L. McKinney. LC 98-37428. (Illus.). 404p. 1999. 55.00 (*0-8018-6012-1*) Johns Hopkins.

Origins of Intelligence in Children. Jean Piaget. 418p. (Orig.). 1974. pap. 27.95 (*0-8236-8207-2*, 23900) Intl Univs Pr.

Origins of Intelligence Services: The Ancient Near East Persia, Greece, Rome, Byzantium, the Arab Muslim Empires, the Mongol Empire, China, Muscovy. Francis Dvornik. LC 73-17098. (Illus.). 350p. reprint ed. pap. 108.50 (*0-608-30766-1*, 205051200084) Bks Demand.

Origins of International Economic Disorder: A Study of United States International Monetary Policy from World War Two to the Present. Fred L. Block. LC 75-7190. 1977. pap. 16.95 (*0-520-03729-4*, Pub. by U CA Pr) Cal Prin Full Svc.

Origins of International Rivalry in Samoa, 1845-1884. Sylvia Masterman. LC 75-35205. reprint ed. 32.50 (*0-404-14228-1*) AMS Pr.

Origins of Invention: A Study of Industry among Primitive Peoples. Otis T. Mason. LC 77-38362. (Select Bibliographies Reprint Ser.). 1977. reprint ed. 29.95 (*0-8369-6779-8*) Ayer.

***Origins of Irish Convict Transportation to Australia.** Bob Reece. LC 00-27250. 308p. 2000. text 69.95 (*0-312-23211-X*) St Martin.

Origins of Islamic Jurisprudence. M. Y. Guraya. 1992. 18.00 (*1-56744-176-9*) Kazi Pubns.

Origins of Isma'ilism: A Study of the Historical Background of the Fatimid Caliphate. Bernard Lewis. LC 74-180357. reprint ed. 29.50 (*0-404-56289-2*) AMS Pr.

Origins of Japanese Industrial Power: Strategies, Institutions & the Development of Organizational Capability. Ed. by E. Abe & R. Fitzgerald. 186p. 1995. pap. 19.50 (*0-7146-4157-X*, Pub. by F Cass Pubs) Intl Spec Bk.

Origins of Japanese Industrial Power: Strategies, Institutions & the Development of Organizational Capability. Ed. by Etsuo Abe & Robert Fitzgerald. LC 94-38512. 140p. 1995. 42.50 (*0-7146-4623-7*, Pub. by F Cass Pubs) Intl Spec Bk.

Origins of Japanese Trade Supremacy: Development & Technology in Asia from 1540 to the Pacific War. Christopher Howe. LC 95-3400. 500p. 1996. 49.95 (*0-226-35485-7*) U Ch Pr.

***Origins of Japan's Democratic Constitution.** Theodore McNelly. LC 99-87956. 240p. 2000. 52.00 (*0-7618-1636-4*); pap. 29.50 (*0-7618-1637-2*) U Pr of Amer.

Origins of Japan's Medieval World: Courtiers, Clerics, Warriors, & Peasants in the Fourteenth Century. Jeffrey P. Mass. LC 97-2475. 544p. 1997. 65.00 (*0-8047-2894-1*) Stanford U Pr.

***Origins of Japanese Trade Supremacy: Development & Technology in Asia from 1540 to the Pacific.** Christopher Howe. 1999. pap. text 25.00 (*0-226-35486-5*) U Ch Pr.

Origins of Judaism: Religion, History, & Literature in Late Antiquity, 13 vols., Set. Intro. by Jacob Neusner. 1992. 1425.00 (*0-8240-7499-8*) Garland.

Origins of Knowledge & Imagination. Jacob Bronowski. LC 77-13209. (Silliman Lectures: Vol. 44). 1979. pap. 12.00 (*0-300-02409-6*) Yale U Pr.

Origins of Kuwait. B. J. Slot. (Illus.). 127p. 1991. 60.50 (*90-04-09409-1*) Brill Academic Pubs.

Origins of Language. Charles Li. 224p. 2001. 23.00 (*0-06-039196-0*, ReganBks) HarperTrade.

***Origins of Language: What Nonhuman Primates Can Tell Us.** Ed. by Barbara J. King. LC 99-28268. (Advanced Seminar Ser.). 450p. 1999. 60.00 (*0-933452-59-4*); pap. 24.95 (*0-933452-60-8*) Schol Am Res.

Origins of Language Disorders: A Special Issue of Developmental Neuropsychology. Ed. by Donna J. Thal & Judith S. Reilly. 248p. 1997. pap. 20.00 (*0-8058-9853-0*) L Erlbaum Assocs.

Origins of Latin Love-Elegy. Archibald A. Day. 148p. 1983. reprint ed. lib. bdg. 36.50 (*3-487-04307-6*) G Olms Pubs.

Origins of Law & Economics: The Economists' New Science of Law, 1830-1930. Heath Pearson. (Historical Perspectives on Modern Economics Ser.). 210p. (C). 1997. text 64.95 (*0-521-58143-5*) Cambridge U Pr.

***Origins of Left-Libertarianism: Anthology of Historical Writings.** Peter Vallentyne & Hillel Steiner. LC 00-41516. 2000. write for info. (*0-312-23591-7*) St Martin.

Origins of Legislative Sovereignty & the Legislative State: Modern Origins, Developments & Perspectives Against the Background of 'machiavellism': Modern Major 'isms' (19th-20th Centuries), 5. A. London Fell. 520p. 1999. 79.50 (*0-275-96753-0*, Praeger Pubs) Greenwood.

Origins of Legislative Sovereignty & the Legislative State Vol. 5: Modern Origins, Developments & Perspectives Against the Background of 'Machiavellism' Book II: Modern Major 'Isms' (17th-18th Centuries) A. London Fell. 488p. 1996. 79.50 (*0-275-95689-X*, Praeger Pubs) Greenwood.

Origins of Liberal Dictatorship in Central America: Guatemala, 1865-1873. Wayne M. Clegern. 192p. (C). 1994. text 34.95 (*0-87081-317-X*) Univ Pr Colo.

***Origins of Liberal Dominance: State, Church & Party in Nineteenth-Century Europe.** Andre Gould. LC 99-33446. 176p. (C). 1999. text 39.50 (*0-472-11015-2*, 11015) U of Mich Pr.

Origins of Liberty: Political & Economic Liberalization in the Modern World. Paul W. Drake & Mathew D. McCubbins. LC 97-37205. 208p. 1998. text 55.00 (*0-691-05753-2*, Pub. by Princeton U Pr); pap. text 17.95 (*0-691-05755-9*, Pub. by Princeton U Pr) Cal Prin Full Svc.

Origins of Life. David W. Deamer & Gail R. Fleischaker. 448p. (C). 1994. pap. 42.50 (*0-86720-181-9*) Jones & Bartlett.

***Origins of Life.** Roy A. Gallant. LC 99-86435. (Story of Science Ser.). (Illus.). 2000. 28.50 (*0-7614-1151-8*) Marshall Cavendish.

***Origins of Life.** John Maynard Smith & Eors Szathmary. (Illus.). 192p. 2000. pap. 13.95 (*0-19-286209-X*) OUP.

***Origins of Life.** Anna-Teresa Tymieniecka. LC 00-28393. 2000. write for info. (*0-7923-6246-2*) Kluwer Academic.

Origins of Life. Christopher Wills. 1999. write for info. (*0-201-38627-5*) Addison-Wesley.

Origins of Life. 2nd ed. Freeman Dyson. LC 99-21079. (Illus.). 125p. 1999. pap. 12.95 (*0-521-62668-4*) Cambridge U Pr.

Origins of Life: From the Birth of Life to the Origin of Language. John Maynard Smith & Eors Szathmary. (Illus.). 190p. 1999. 25.00 (*0-19-850493-4*) OUP.

Origins of Life: Proceedings of the Seventh International Conference, Mainz, July 10-15, 1983 (A Special Issue of a Journal) Ed. by Klaus Dose et al. 1984. text 364.50 (*90-277-1694-3*) Kluwer Academic.

Origins of Life on the Earth & in the Cosmos. Geoffrey L. Zubay. LC 95-76545. 448p. (C). 1995. text 42.50 (*0-697-22117-2*, WCB McGr Hill) McGrw-H Hghr Educ.

Origins of Lincoln's Inn. Ronald F. Roxburgh. LC 85-81798. (Cambridge Studies in English Legal History). 102p. 1986. reprint ed. 35.00 (*0-912004-52-5*) Gaunt.

Origins of Literary Studies in America: A Documentary Anthology. Ed. by Gerald Graff & Michael Warner. 292p. 1988. 45.00 (*0-415-90024-7*) Routledge.

Origins of Literary Studies in America: A Documentary Anthology. Ed. by Gerald Graff & Michael Warner. 292p. (C). 1988. pap. 19.99 (*0-415-90025-5*) Routledge.

Origins of Logical Empiricism. Ed. by Ronald N. Giere & Alan W. Richardson. LC 96-19926. (Minnesota Studies in the Philosophy of Science: Vol. 16). 384p. 1996. 49.95 (*0-8166-2834-3*) U of Minn Pr.

Origins of Lonergan's Notion of the Dialectic of History: A Study of Lonergan's Early Writings on History. Michael Shute. 232p. (C). 1992. lib. bdg. 48.50 (*0-8191-8838-7*) U Pr of Amer.

***Origins of Major War: Hegemonic Rivalry & the Fear of Decline.** Dale C. Copeland. LC 00-24040. (Studies in Security Affairs). 2000. write for info. (*0-8014-3750-4*) Cornell U Pr.

Origins of Malay Nationalism. William R. Roff. (Illus.). 352p. 1995. pap. 29.95 (*967-65-3059-X*) OUP.

Origins of Man: Physical Anthropology. John Buettner-Janusch. LC 66-14128. 701p. reprint ed. pap. 200.00 (*0-608-13614-X*, 205513800008) Bks Demand.

An Asterisk (*) at the beginning of an entry indicates that the title is appearing for the first time.

Origins of Man & the Universe: The Myth That Came to Life. 2nd rev. ed. Barry Long. Ed. by Clive Tempest & Jade Bell. LC 97-93601. (Illus.). 381p. 1998. pap. 19.95 (*1-899324-12-7*) B Long Bks.

***Origins of Mark: The Markan Community in Current Debate.** Dwight N. Peterson. 224p. 2000. text 85.00 (*90-04-11755-5*) Brill Academic Pubs.

Origins of Marvel Comics. Stan Lee. (Illus.). 240p. 1997. pap. text 24.95 (*0-7851-0551-4*) Marvel Entrprs.

Origins of Marvel Comics. Stan Lee. LC 74-11141. 254p. 1974. write for info. (*0-671-21864-6*) S&S Trade.

***Origins of Mass Communications During the American Cold War: Educational Effects & Contemporary Implications.** Timothy Glander. LC 99-38568. (Volume in Sociocultural, Political, Historical Studies in Education Ser.). 237p. 1999. write for info. (*0-8058-2734-X*); pap. write for info. (*0-8058-2735-8*) L Erlbaum Assocs.

Origins of Materialism: The Evolution of a Scientific View of the World. rev. ed. George Novack. LC 76-160511. 300p. 1965. reprint ed. pap. 19.95 (*0-87348-022-8*) Pathfinder NY.

***Origins Of Mathematics.** V. Lakshmikantham & S. Leela. 104p. 2000. 44.00 (*0-7618-1736-0*); pap. 24.50 (*0-7618-1737-9*) U Pr of Amer.

Origins of Maya Art: Monumental Stone Sculpture of Kaminaljuyu, Guatemala, & the Southern Pacific Coast. Lee A. Parsons. LC 85-31148. (Studies in Pre-Columbian Art & Archaeology: No. 28). (Illus.). 224p. (Orig.). 1986. pap. text 30.00 (*0-88402-148-3*, PAORP) Dumbarton Oaks.

Origins of Meaning. Donn Welton. 348p. 1983. lib. bdg. 184.00 (*90-247-2618-2*, Pub. by M Nijhoff) Kluwer Academic.

Origins of Medical Attitudes Toward Drug Addiction in America: Eight Studies, 1791 to 1858, an Original Anthology. Ed. by Gerald N. Grob. LC 80-1203. (Addiction in America Ser.). 1981. lib. bdg. 35.95 (*0-405-13563-7*) Ayer.

Origins of Medieval Jurisprudence: Pavia & Bologna, 850-1150. Charles M. Radding. LC 87-14237. 272p. reprint ed. pap. 84.40 (*0-7837-4539-7*, 208028600004) Bks Demand.

Origins of Mendelism. Robert C. Olby. LC 84-2491. (Illus.). xviii, 328p. 1996. pap. text 18.00 (*0-226-62592-3*) U Ch Pr.

Origins of Mental Illness: Temperament, Deviance & Disorder. 2nd ed. Gordon Claridge. 293p. 1995. pap. 15.00 (*1-883536-01-4*, Malor Bks) ISHK.

Origins of Metrology. Daniel M. McDonald. (Illus.). 143p. 1992. 27.00 (*0-9519420-0-X*) David Brown.

Origins of Metropolitan Manila: A Political & Social Analysis. Manuel A. Caoili. (Illus.). 299p. (Orig.). (C). 1989. pap. 18.75 (*971-10-0385-6*, Pub. by New Day Pub) Cellar.

Origins of Mexican National Politics, 1808-1847. Ed. by Jaime E. Rodriguez O. LC 97-17583. (Latin American Silhouettes Ser.). 144p. 1997. pap. 16.95 (*0-8420-2723-8*, SR Bks) Scholarly Res Inc.

Origins of Middle-Class Culture: Halifax, Yorkshire, 1660-1780. John Smail. (Illus.). 264p. 1994. text 42.50 (*0-8014-2990-0*) Cornell U Pr.

Origins of Military Thought: From the Enlightenment to Clausewitz. Azar Gat. (Oxford Historical Monographs). (Illus.). 296p. 1991. reprint ed. pap. 24.95 (*0-19-820257-1*, 8946) OUP.

Origins of Mod Sculpture. Albert E. Elsen. pap. 18.95 (*0-8076-1470-X*, Pub. by Braziller) Norton.

Origins of Modern Arab Political Thought. Khaldun S. Al-Husry. LC 80-11794. 184p. 1980. reprint ed. 25.00 (*0-88206-037-6*) Caravan Bks.

Origins of Modern Arabic Fiction. 2nd rev. ed. Matti Moosa. LC 97-21883. 458p. 1997. 59.95 (*0-89410-683-X*, Three Contnts) L Rienner.

Origins of Modern Architecture. Ed. by Eric Uhlfelder. LC 98-38522. 299p. 1998. pap. 16.95 (*0-486-40145-6*) Dover.

Origins of Modern Consciousness: Essays by John Higham (And Others) Intro. by John Weiss. LC 65-10145. (Wayne Bks.: No. 18). (Illus.). 206p. reprint ed. pap. 63.90 (*0-7837-3639-8*, 204350600009) Bks Demand.

Origins of Modern English Society. Harold Perkin. (Studies in Social History). 480p. (C). 1985. pap. 24.99 (*0-415-05922-4*) Routledge.

Origins of Modern English Society, 1780-1880. Harold J. Perkin. 480p. pap. 13.95 (*0-7448-0026-9*) Routledge.

Origins of Modern English Society, 1780-1880. Harold J. Perkin. LC 76-384509. (Canadian University Paperbooks Ser.: No. 115). 479p. reprint ed. pap. 148.50 (*0-8357-4165-6*, 203693900007) Bks Demand.

Origins of Modern Europe: The Medieval Heritage of Western Civilization. R. Allen Brown. LC 96-212595. 264p. 1996. pap. 24.95 (*0-85115-665-7*, Boydell Pr) Boydell & Brewer.

Origins of Modern Freedom in the West. Ed. by R. W. Davis. LC 94-20717. (Making of Modern Freedom Ser.). xvi, 384p. 1995. 49.50 (*0-8047-2474-1*) Stanford U Pr.

Origins of Modern German Colonialism, 1871-1885. Mary E. Townsend. LC 74-2493. (Columbia University Studies in History, Economics & Public Law). 205p. 1975. reprint ed. 35.00 (*0-86527-144-5*) Fertig.

Origins of Modern Germany. Geoffrey Barraclough. 504p. 1984. reprint ed. pap. 15.95 (*0-393-30153-2*) Norton.

Origins of Modern Irish Socialism, 1881-1896. Fintan Lane. 172p. 1997. 64.95 (*1-85918-151-1*, Pub. by Cork Univ); pap. 24.95 (*1-85918-152-X*, Pub. by Cork Univ) Intl Spec Bk.

Origins of Modern Japanese Literature. Kojin Karatani. Tr. by Brett De Bary. LC 92-33670. (Post-Contemporary Interventions Ser.). 240p. 1993. pap. text 17.95 (*0-8223-1323-5*) Duke.

Origins of Modern Literary Yiddish. Dov-Ber Kerler. LC 94-45337. (Oxford Modern Languages & Literature Monographs). (ENG & YID., Illus.). 347p. 1999. 120.00 (*0-19-815166-7*, Clarendon Pr) OUP.

Origins of Modern Musical Criticism: French & Italian Music, 1600-1750. Georgia Cowart. LC 81-641. (Studies in Musicology: No. 38). 228p. reprint ed. pap. 70.70 (*0-8357-1166-8*, 207026500065) Bks Demand.

Origins of Modern Philosophy of Science, 1830-1914, 12 vols., Set. Ed. by Andrew Pyle. 2715p. (C). 1996. 1485.00 (*0-415-13267-3*) Routledge.

Origins of Modern Psychiatry. Ed. by C. Thompson. LC 87-8163. (Wiley Medical Publication Ser.). (Illus.). 289p. 1987. reprint ed. pap. 89.60 (*0-608-02607-7*, 206326500004) Bks Demand.

Origins of Modern Russia. Jan Kucharzewski. 503p. 1943. 8.00 (*0-940962-19-5*) Polish Inst Art & Sci.

Origins of Modern Russian Education: An Intellectual Biography of Count Sergei Uvarov, 1786-1855. Cynthia H. Whittaker. LC 84-7471. 348p. 1984. 35.00 (*0-87580-100-5*) N Ill U Pr.

Origins of Modern Science. Herbert Butterfield. 1997. 16.95 (*0-684-83637-8*) Free Pr.

Origins of Modern Science. rev. ed. Herbert Butterfield. 1965. pap. 16.95 (*0-02-905070-7*) Free Pr.

Origins of Modern Treatment & the Education of Physically Handicapped Children: An Original Anthology. Ed. by William R. Phillips & Janet Rosenberg. LC 79-6010. (Physically Handicapped in Society Ser.). 1980. lib. bdg. 44.95 (*0-405-13102-X*) Ayer.

***Origins of Modern Witchcraft: The Evolution of a World Religion.** Ann Moura. 2000. pap. 14.95 (*1-56718-648-3*) Llewellyn Pubns.

Origins of Modernism in Russian Architecture. William C. Brumfield. LC 90-34093. (Illus.). 400p. 1991. 95.00 (*0-520-06929-3*, Pub. by U CA Pr) Cal Prin Full Svc.

Origins of Moral Theology in the United States: Three Different Approaches. Charles E. Curran. Ed. by James F. Keenan. LC 96-46601. (Moral Traditions & Moral Agruments Ser.). 224p. 1997. 55.00 (*0-87840-634-4*); pap. 24.95 (*0-87840-635-2*) Georgetown U Pr.

Origins of Music. Nils L. Wallin et al. LC 98-54088. (Illus.). 585p. 1999. 65.00 (*0-262-23206-5*) MIT Pr.

Origins of Mycenaean Civilisation. O. T. Dickinson. (Studies in Mediterranean Archaeology: Vol. XLIX). (Illus.). 127p. 1977. pap. 49.50 (*91-85058-74-2*, Pub. by P Astroms) Coronet Bks.

Origins of Narcotic Control in the U. S. 1991. lib. bdg. 79.95 (*0-8490-4633-5*) Gordon Pr.

Origins of Narrative: The Romantic Appropriation of the Bible. Stephen Prickett. (Illus.). 304p. (C). 1996. text 64.95 (*0-521-44543-4*) Cambridge U Pr.

Origins of National Interests. Ed. by Glenn Chafetz et al. LC 99-38155. (Series on Security Studies). 400p. 1999. 57.50 (*0-7146-4985-6*, Pub. by F Cass Pubs); pap. 19.50 (*0-7146-8048-6*, Pub. by F Cass Pubs) Intl Spec Bk.

Origins of Nationality in South Asia: Patriotism & Ethical Government in the Making of Modern India. A. C. Bayly. LC 99-932096. 350p. 1999. text 35.00 (*0-19-564457-3*) OUP.

Origins of Native Americans: Evidence from Anthropological Genetics. Michael H. Crawford. LC 97-7474. (Illus.). 326p. (C). 1998. text 64.95 (*0-521-59280-1*) Cambridge U Pr.

Origins of Nativism in the United States, 1800-1844. Ray A. Billington. LC 73-19129. (Politics & People Ser.). (Illus.). 716p. 1979. reprint ed. 57.95 (*0-405-05854-3*) Ayer.

Origins of NATO. Ed. by Joseph Smith. (Exeter Studies in History: No. 28). 189p. 1990. pap. text 19.95 (*0-85989-352-9*, Pub. by Univ Exeter Pr) Northwestern U Pr.

Origins of Natural Science. Rudolf Steiner.Tr. of Der Entstehungsoment der Naturwissenschaft in der Weltgeschichte und ihre seitherige Entwickelung. 159p. 1985. 20.00 (*0-8001-0140-5*) Anthroposophic.

Origins of Natural Science. Rudolf Steiner.Tr. of Der Entstehungsoment der Naturwissenschaft in der Weltgeschichte und ihre seitherige Entwickelung. 159p. 1985. pap. 10.95 (*0-88010-140-7*) Anthroposophic.

***Origins of Nature's Beauty.** Alexander F. Skutch. (Illus.). 292p. 1999. reprint ed. text 30.00 (*0-7881-6797-9*) DIANE Pub.

Origins of Nature's Beauty: Essays by Alexander F. Skutch. Alexander F. Skutch. LC 91-884. (Corrie Herring Hooks Ser.). (Illus.). 318p. 1992. 29.95 (*0-292-76037-X*) U of Tex Pr.

Origins of Nazi Genocide: From Euthanasia to the Final Solution. Henry Friedlander. LC 94-40941. (Illus.). 448p. 1995. 45.00 (*0-8078-2208-6*) U of NC Pr.

Origins of Nazi Genocide: From Euthanasia to the Final Solution. Henry Friedlander. (Illus.). 448p. 1997. pap. 18.95 (*0-8078-4675-9*) U of NC Pr.

Origins of Neuroscience: A History of Explorations into Brain Function. Stanley Finger. LC 92-48265. (Illus.). 480p. (C). 1994. text 90.00 (*0-19-506503-4*) OUP.

Origins of New Mexico Families: A Genealogy of the Spanish Colonial Period. Fray A. Chavez. 442p. 1992. pap. 45.00 (*0-89013-239-9*) Museum NM Pr.

Origins of Nonviolence: Tolstoy & Gandhi in Their Historical Setting. Martin Green. LC 85-12138. 264p. 1986. text 27.50 (*0-271-00414-2*) Pa St U Pr.

Origins of Nurturance: Developmental, Biological & Cultural Perspectives on Caregiving. Ed. by Alan Fogel & Gail F. Melson. 304p. (C). 1986. text 69.95 (*0-89859-643-2*) L Erlbaum Assocs.

Origins of Old Germanic Studies in the Low Countries. Cornelis Dekker. LC 98-41715. (Studies in Intellectual History). xii, 484p. 1998. 141.50 (*90-04-11031-3*) Brill Academic Pubs.

Origins of Open Field Agriculture. Ed. by Trevor Rowley. (Illus.). 258p. 1981. 44.00 (*0-389-20102-2*, OROPEC) B&N Imports.

Origins of Order: Self-Organization & Selection in Evolution. Stuart A. Kauffman. (Illus.). 734p. 1993. pap. text 39.95 (*0-19-507951-5*) OUP.

Origins of Organic Chemistry, 1800-1900. Russell. 1992. 18.00 (*0-85186-440-6*) CRC Pr.

Origins of Pacific War & the Importance of Magic. Komatsu. LC 98-4390. 360p. 1999. text 65.00 (*0-312-17385-7*) St Martin.

Origins of Palestinian Nationalism. Muhammad Y. Muslih. (Institute for Palestine Studies). 288p. 1989. pap. text 20.00 (*0-231-06509-4*) Col U Pr.

Origins of Philosophy. D. Hyland. LC 89-15450. 383p. (C). 1973. reprint ed. pap. 18.50 (*0-391-03217-8*) Humanities.

Origins of Philosophy: Its Rise in Myth & the Pre-socratics : a Collection of Early Writings. Drew A. Hyland. LC 98-54408. 1998. 16.95 (*1-57392-350-8*, Humanity Bks) Prometheus Bks.

Origins of Photography. 3rd rev. ed. Helmut Gernsheim. LC 82-80979. (Illus.). 1983. 50.00 (*0-500-54080-2*, Pub. by Thames Hudson) Norton.

Origins of Photojournalism in America. Michael L. Carlebach. LC 91-40145. (Illus.). 208p. (Orig.). 1992. pap. 29.95 (*1-56098-159-8*) Smithsonian.

Origins of Piaget's Concept of Decentration: Developmental Theory in Piaget & Habermas. Barbara S. Peterman. LC 96-72015. 104p. (Orig.). (C). 1997. pap. text 12.95 (*1-889767-00-X*) Custos Pr.

Origins of Planets & Life. Ed. by H. J. Melosh. LC 98-110021. 354p. 1997. pap. 15.00 (*0-8243-2098-0*) Annual Reviews.

Origins of Poe's Critical Theory. Margaret Alterton. (BCL1-PS American Literature Ser.). 191p. 1992. reprint ed. lib. bdg. 69.00 (*0-7812-6833-8*) Rprt Serv.

Origins of Popular Style: Antecedents of Twentieth-Century Popular Music. Peter Van der Merwe. (Illus.). 366p. 1992. pap. text 21.00 (*0-19-816305-3*) OUP.

***Origins of Popular Superstitions.** T. Sharper Knowlson. 242p. 2000. reprint ed. pap. text 17.00 (*0-7881-6876-2*) DIANE Pub.

Origins of Postmodern Youth: Informal Youth Movements in a Comparative Perspective. Reuven Kahane. LC 97-13319. 266p. 1997. text 49.95 (*3-11-015432-3*) De Gruyter.

Origins of Postmodernity. Perry Anderson. LC 99-237049. 160p. 1998. 65.00 (*1-85984-864-8*, Pub. by Verso); pap. 18.00 (*1-85984-222-4*, Pub. by Verso) Norton.

Origins of Pre-Columbian Art. Terence Grieder. LC 81-12966. (Texas Pan American Ser.). (Illus.). 251p. reprint ed. pap. 77.90 (*0-8357-4279-2*, 203707800007) Bks Demand.

Origins of Programming. A. P. Ershov. (Illus.). 324p. 1990. 131.95 (*0-387-97061-4*) Spr-Verlag.

Origins of Protective Labor Legislation for Women, 1905-1925. Susan Lehrer. LC 87-6485. (SUNY Series on Women & Work). 318p. (C). 1987. text 64.50 (*0-88706-506-6*); pap. text 21.95 (*0-88706-505-8*) State U NY Pr.

Origins of Prussia. Francis L. Carsten. LC 81-17868. 309p. 1982. reprint ed. lib. bdg. 35.00 (*0-313-23220-2*, CAOP, Greenwood Pr) Greenwood.

Origins of Psychopathology: Problems in Research & Public Policy. Ed. by David F. Ricks & Barbara S. Dohrenwend. LC 82-14638. 295p. reprint ed. pap. 84.10 (*0-608-15605-1*, 2031717) Bks Demand.

Origins of (P3&4) Compounds see Organophosphorous Stereochemistry

Origins of Ptolemy's Astronomical Parameters. Robert R. Newton. (Technical Publications of the Center for Archaeoastronomy: No. 4). (Illus.). 228p. (Orig.). 1982. pap. 12.00 (*0-912025-02-6*) JHU Applied Physics.

Origins of Ptolemy's Astronomical Tables. Robert R. Newton. (Technical Publications of the Center for Archaeoastronomy: No. 5). (Illus.). 264p. (Orig.). 1985. pap. 12.00 (*0-912025-03-4*) JHU Applied Physics.

Origins of Public Health in America: Selected Essays, 1820-1855. 1977. 19.95 (*0-405-03963-8*, 15715) Ayer.

Origins of Public High Schools: A Reexamination of the Beverly High School Controversy. Maris A. Vinovskis. LC 85-40380. 208p. 1986. text 29.95 (*0-299-10400-1*) U of Wis Pr.

Origins of Renaissance Art: The Baptistery Doors, Florence. Antonio Paolucci. Tr. by Francoise Pouncey Chiarini. LC 96-28403. (Illus.). 176p. 1996. 60.00 (*0-8076-1413-0*) Braziller.

Origins of Rhetoric in Ancient Greece. Thomas Cole. LC 90-36983. (Ancient Society & History Ser.). 208p. 1995. pap. text 16.95 (*0-8018-5118-1*) Johns Hopkins.

Origins of Satan. Elaine H. Pagels. 1996. pap. 12.00 (*0-614-97751-7*) Vin Bks.

Origins of Science: An Inquiry into the Foundations of Western Thought. Ernest H. Hutten. LC 77-13633. 241p. 1978. reprint ed. lib. bdg. 62.50 (*0-313-20003-3*, HUOR, Greenwood Pr) Greenwood.

Origins of Scientific Economics. William Letwin. LC 75-8721. 316p. 1975. reprint ed. lib. bdg. 65.00 (*0-8371-8038-4*, LEOS, Greenwood Pr) Greenwood.

***Origins of Scottish Nationhood.** Neil Davidson. LC 99-89799. 2000. write for info. (*0-7453-1609-3*, Pub. by Pluto GBR) Stylus Pub VA.

Origins of Sea Terms. John G. Rogers. (American Maritime Library: Vol. 11). xv, 220p. 1984. 20.00 (*0-913372-31-5*) Mystic Seaport.

***Origins of Second World War Reconsidered: A. J. P. Taylor & Historians.** 2nd ed. Gordon Martel. LC 99-18880. 1999. pap. 25.99 (*0-415-16325-0*) Routledge.

***Origins of Second World War Reconsidered: A. J. P. Taylor & Historians.** 2nd ed. Ed. by Gordon Martel. LC 99-18880. 304p. (C). 1999. text. write for info. (*0-415-16324-2*) Routledge.

Origins of Self & Identity: Living & Dying in Freud's Psychoanalysis. John A. Friedman. LC 97-44520. 240p. 1998. 40.00 (*0-7657-0154-5*) Aronson.

Origins of Semiosis: Sign Evolution in Nature & Culture. Ed. by Winfried Noth. LC 94-21517. (Approaches to Semiotics Ser.: Vol. 116). x, 480p. 1994. 198.50 (*3-11-014196-5*) Mouton.

Origins of Sex: Three Billion Years of Genetic Recombination. Lynn Margulis & Dorion Sagan. 259p. (Orig.). (C). 1990. pap. 20.00 (*0-300-04619-7*) Yale U Pr.

Origins of Sexuality & Homosexuality. Michael G. Shively. Ed. by John P. De Cecco. LC 84-22563. (Journal of Homosexuality Ser.: Vol. 9, Nos. 2 & 3). 174p. 1994. reprint ed. pap. text 19.95 (*0-918393-00-0*, Harrington Park) Haworth Pr.

Origins of Southern Radicalism: The South Carolina Upcountry, 1800-1860. Lacy K. Ford, Jr. (Illus.). 432p. 1991. reprint ed. pap. text 19.95 (*0-19-506961-7*) OUP.

Origins of Southern Sharecropping. Edward Royce. LC 93-18076. (Labor & Social Change Ser.). 288p. 1993. 69.95 (*1-56639-069-9*) Temple U Pr.

Origins of Southwestern Agriculture. R. G. Matson. LC 91-14054. (Illus.). 356p. 1991. 66.00 (*0-8165-1196-9*) U of Ariz Pr.

Origins of Spanish Romanticism: A Selective Annotated Bibliography. Margaret D. Jacobson. LC 83-51784. 96p. 1985. pap. 25.00 (*0-89295-033-1*) Society Sp & Sp-Am.

Origins of Specialization in American Medicine: An Anthology of Sources. Ed. by Charles E. Rosenberg. (Medical Care in the United States Ser.: Vol. 13). 200p. 1989. reprint ed. lib. bdg. 15.00 (*0-8240-8342-3*) Garland.

***Origins of Species.** Margulus. 2000. 28.00 (*0-465-04391-7*, Pub. by Basic); pap. 15.00 (*0-465-04392-5*, Pub. by Basic) HarpC.

Origins of Spontaneous Revolution: East Germany, 1989. Peter Voss et al. LC 95-8860. (Economics, Cognition, & Society Ser.). 296p. (C). 1995. text 57.50 (*0-472-10575-2*, 10575) U of Mich Pr.

Origins of Stalinsim: From Leninist Revolution to Stalinist Society. Pavel Campeanu. LC 84-18410. 200p. (gr. 13). 1986. text 70.95 (*0-87332-363-7*) M E Sharpe.

Origins of Statecraft in China: The Western Chou Empire, Vol. 1. Herrlee G. Creel. LC 73-110072. (Illus.). xiv, 560p. 1995. pap. text 14.50 (*0-226-12044-9*) U Ch Pr.

Origins of Statics: The Sources of Physical Theory. Pierre M. Duhem. Tr. by Grant F. Leneaux et al. (Boston Studies in the Philosophy of Science). 632p. 1991. lib. bdg. 287.50 (*0-7923-0898-0*, Pub. by Kluwer Academic) Kluwer Academic.

***Origins of Story.** Ed. by Barbara Harrison & Gregory Maguire. LC 98-45300. (Illus.). 224p. (J). 1999. per. 18.00 (*0-689-82604-4*) McElderry Bks.

Origins of Suffolk. Peter Warner. LC 95-33402. (Origins of the Shires). (Illus.). 200p. (C). 1996. text 29.95 (*0-7190-3817-0*, Pub. by Manchester Univ Pr) St Martin.

Origins of Teacher Education at Calvin College, 1900-1930: And Gladly Teach. Peter P. DeBoer. LC 91-27032. (Mellen Studies in Education: Vol. 18). 120p. 1991. lib. bdg. 59.95 (*0-7734-9670-X*) E Mellen.

Origins of Teapot Dome: Progressive Parties & Petroleum. James L. Bates. LC 78-5265. (Illus.). 278p. 1978. reprint ed. lib. bdg. 65.00 (*0-313-20383-0*, BAOT, Greenwood Pr) Greenwood.

Origins of Terrorism: Psychologies, Ideologies, Theologies, States of Mind. Ed. by Walter Reich. (Woodrow Wilson Center Ser.). 300p. (C). 1990. pap. text 21.95 (*0-521-38589-X*) Cambridge U Pr.

Origins of the Ainu Language: The Ainu Indo-European Controversy. Ed. by Kirsten Refsing. (Ainu Library Collection: Vol. 2). 1998. lib. bdg. 695.00 (*0-7007-1034-5*, Pub. by Curzon Pr Ltd) UH Pr.

Origins of the American Business Corporation. Oscar Handlin & Mary Handlin. (Irvington Reprint Series in American History). (C). 1991. reprint ed. pap. text 1.90 (*0-8290-2607-X*, H-95) Irvington.

Origins of the American Business Corporation, 1784-1855: Broadening the Concept of Public Service During Industrialization, 19. Ronald E. Seavoy. LC 81-1017. (Contributions in Legal Studies: No. 19). (Illus.). 314p. 1982. 65.00 (*0-313-22885-X*, SBC/) Greenwood.

Origins of the American Civil War. Brian H. Reid. (Origins of Modern Wars Ser.). 416p. (C). 1996. pap. 34.60 (*0-582-49178-9*) Longman.

Origins of the American Civil War. Brian H. Reid. (Origins of Modern Wars Ser.). 416p. (C). 1996. 83.00 (*0-582-49177-0*) Longman.

Origins of the American Constitution: A Documentary History. Ed. by Michael G. Kammen. 400p. 1986. pap. 14.95 (*0-14-008744-3*, Penguin Bks) Viking Penguin.

Origins of the American Film. Ed. by Gordon Hendricks. LC 74-169345. (Arno Press Cinema Program Ser.). (Illus.). 600p. 1978. reprint ed. 38.95 (*0-405-03919-0*) Ayer.

Origins of the American High School. William J. Reese. LC 94-24975. 352p. 1995. 35.00 (*0-300-06384-9*) Yale U Pr.

***Origins of the American High School.** William J. Reese. (Illus.). 352p. 1999. 18.00 (*0-300-07943-5*) Yale U Pr.

Origins of the American Revolution: With a New Introduction & Bibliography. 2nd ed. John C. Miller. (Illus.). xxii, 530p. 1959. 67.50 (*0-8047-0593-3*); pap. 18.95 (*0-8047-0594-1*) Stanford U Pr.

O

Origins of the Anastasian Currency Reform. D. M. Metcalf. (Illus.). vii, 105p. 1969. text 36.50 (*0-317-54491-8*, Pub. by AM Hakkert) Coronet Bks.

Origins of the Ancient Israelite States. Volkmar Fritz & Philip R. Davies. LC 96-219580. (JSOTS Ser.: No. 228). 219p. 1996. pap. 23.75 (*1-85075-798-4*, Pub. by Sheffield Acad) CUP Services.

Origins of the Ancient Israelite States. Ed. by Volkmar Fritz & Philip R. Davies. LC 96-219580. (JSOTS Ser.: No. 228). 219p. 1996. 65.00 (*1-85075-629-5*, Pub. by Sheffield Acad) CUP Services.

Origins of the Anglo-American Missionary Enterprise in China, 1807. Murray A. Rubinstein. Ed. by Kenneth E. Rowe. (ATLA Monographs: No. 33). 400p. 1996. 59.50 (*0-8108-2770-0*) Scarecrow.

Origins of the Arab Israeli Wars. 3rd ed. Ritchie Ovendale. LC 99-12400. (Origins of Modern Wars Ser.). 360p. 1999. pap. 30.73 (*0-582-36895-2*) Longman.

Origins of the Arab-Israeli Wars: Origins of Modern Wars. 2nd ed. Ritchie Ovendale. (Origins of Modern Wars Ser.). (Illus.). 264p. (C). 1992. pap. text 33.25 (*0-582-06369-8*) Longman.

Origins of the Ashkenazic Jews. 1996. lib. bdg. 253.75 (*0-8490-5937-2*) Gordon Pr.

Origins of the Authoritarian Welfare State in Prussia: Conservatives, Bureaucracy & the Social Question, 1815-70. Hermann Beck. (Social History, Popular Culture, & Politics in Germany Ser.). 320p. 1995. text 54.50 (*0-472-10546-9*, 10546) U of Mich Pr.

Origins of the Authoritarian Welfare State in Prussia: Conservatives, Bureaucracy & the Social Question, 1815-70. Hermann Beck. 320p. (C). 1997. reprint ed. pap. text 24.95 (*0-472-08428-3*, 08428) U of Mich Pr.

Origins of the Baha'i Community of Canada, 1898-1948. Will C. Van den Hoonaard. LC 96-229355. (Illus.). 368p. 1996. 39.95 (*0-88920-272-9*) W Laurier U Pr.

Origins of the Bible: Rethinking Canon History. John W. Miller. LC 94-33902. (Theological Inquiries Ser.). 272p. 1995. pap. 18.95 (*0-8091-3522-1*) Paulist Pr.

Origins of the Bill of Rights. Leonard W. Levy. LC 98-44965. (Contemporary Law Ser.). (Illus.). 304p. 1999. 30.00 (*0-300-07802-1*) Yale U Pr.

Origins of the Bolero School. Ed. by Javier Suarez-Pajares et al. Tr. by Lynn Garafola et al from SPA. (Studies in Dance History). (Illus.). 139p. 1993. pap. 21.95 (*0-9653519-5-5*, Wesleyan Univ Pr) U Pr of New Eng.

Origins of the Boxer Uprising. Joseph W. Esherick. 410p. 1987. pap. 18.95 (*0-520-06459-3*, Pub. by U CA Pr) Cal Prin Full Svc.

Origins of the British Israelites: The Lost Tribes. O. Michael Friedman. LC 92-42338. 184p. 1993. text 79.95 (*0-7734-2306-0*) E Mellen.

Origins of the British Labour Party. J. H. Reid. LC 55-11709. 272p. reprint ed. pap. 84.40 (*0-608-14618-8*, 205589900039) Bks Demand.

Origins of the Bronze Age Oasis Civilization in Central Asia. Fredrik T. Hiebert. LC 94-66685. (American School of Prehistoric Research Bulletins Ser.: Vol. 42). (Illus.). 240p. 1994. pap. 40.00 (*0-87365-545-1*) Peabody Harvard.

Origins of the Center for Hellenic Studies. Eric N. Lindquist. (Illus.). 96p. 1991. text 16.95 (*0-691-03174-6*, Pub. by Princeton U Pr) Cal Prin Full Svc.

Origins of the Chancellorship: The Buried Report of 1948. Eugene C. Lee. LC 94-24409. (Chapters in the History of the University of California Ser.). 77p. (Orig.). 1995. pap. 10.00 (*0-87772-360-5*) UCB IGS.

Origins of the Changs. Dumitru Martinas. LC 99-195242. 200p. 1998. 42.00 (*973-98391-4-2*, Pub. by Ctr Romanian Studies) Intl Spec Bk.

Origins of the Chavin Culture. Chiaki Kano. LC 79-89241. (Studies in Pre-Columbian Art & Archaeology: No. 22). (Illus.). 87p. 1979. pap. 10.00 (*0-88402-092-4*) Dumbarton Oaks.

Origins of the Children's Song Cycle As a Musical Genre with Four Case Studies & an Original Cycle. Gloria Shafer. LC 89-9427. (Studies in the History & Interpretation of Music: Vol. 14). 150p. 1989. lib. bdg. 69.95 (*0-88946-439-1*) E Mellen.

Origins of the Chinese Revolution, 1915-1949. Lucien Bianco. Tr. by Muriel Bell from FRE. LC 75-150321. xvii, 220p. 1971. reprint ed. pap. 12.95 (*0-8047-0827-4*) Stanford U Pr.

*__Origins of the Chosfon Dynasty.__ John B. Duncan. LC 00-29876. (Korean Studies of the Henry M. Jackson School of International Studies). (Illus.). 400p. 2000. 60.00 (*0-295-97985-2*) U of Wash Pr.

Origins of the Christian Doctrine of Sacrifice. Robert J. Daly. LC 77-78628. 160p. (Orig.). reprint ed. pap. 49.60 (*0-608-16321-X*, 202687500053) Bks Demand.

Origins of the Christian Mystical Tradition: From Plato to Denys. Andrew Louth. 232p. (C). 1983. pap. text 22.00 (*0-19-826668-5*) OUP.

Origins of the Civil Rights Movement: Black Communities Organizing for Change. Aldon D. Morris. 1986. pap. 16.95 (*0-02-922130-7*) Free Pr.

Origins of the Cold War. Arthur Meier Schlesinger, Jr. (Irvington Reprint Series in American History). (C). 1991. reprint ed. pap. text 2.60 (*0-8290-2614-2*, H-464) Irvington.

Origins of the Cold War. 2nd ed. Thomas G. Paterson. (Problems in European Civilization Ser.). (C). 1990. pap. text 18.36 (*0-669-91447-9*) HM Trade Div.

Origins of the Cold War. 3rd ed. Ed. by Thomas G. Paterson & Robert J. McMahon. LC 90-82002. (Problems in American Civilization Ser.). 367p. (C). 1991. pap. text 18.36 (*0-669-24445-7*) HM Trade Div.

Origins of the Cold War. 4th ed. McMahon. LC 98-72061. 1998. pap. text 14.07 (*0-395-90430-7*) HM.

Origins of the Cold War: An International History. Ed. by Melvyn P. Leffler & David S. Painter. LC 93-23298. (Illus.). 336p. (C). 1994. pap. 24.99 (*0-415-09694-4*) Routledge.

Origins of the Cold War: The Novikov, Kennan, & Roberts "Long Telegrams" of 1946. rev. ed. Ed. by Kenneth M. Jensen. LC 93-43921. (Orig.). 1991. reprint ed. pap. text 10.95 (*1-878379-27-5*) US Inst Peace.

Origins of the Cold War in Europe: International Perspectives. Ed. by David Reynolds. LC 93-61583. 352p. 1994. 35.00 (*0-300-05892-6*) Yale U Pr.

Origins of the Cold War in the Near East: Great Power Conflict & Diplomacy in Iran, Turkey, & Greece. Bruce R. Kuniholm. LC 79-83999. 533p. reprint ed. pap. 165.30 (*0-608-06332-0*, 206669300008) Bks Demand.

Origins of the Cold War, 1941-1948. 2nd ed. Martin McCauley. LC 95-9846. (Seminar Studies in History). 168p. (C). 1995. pap. 15.93 (*0-582-27659-4*) Longman.

Origins of the Common Law. Arthur R. Hogue. LC 85-15949. 287p. (C). 1986. reprint ed. 10.00 (*0-86597-053-X*); reprint ed. pap. 5.00 (*0-86597-054-8*) Liberty Fund.

Origins of the Crimean Alliance. Ann P. Saab. LC 76-30526. 235p. reprint ed. pap. 72.90 (*0-8357-3138-3*, 203940100012) Bks Demand.

Origins of the Crisis in the U. S. S. R. Essays on the Political Economy of a Disintegrating System. Hillel Ticktin. LC 91-4282. 204p. (C). (gr. 13). 1992. pap. text 42.95 (*0-87332-888-4*) M E Sharpe.

Origins of the Crisis in the USSR: Essays on the Political Economy of a Disintegrating System. Hillel Ticktin. LC 91-4282. 204p. (C). (gr. 13). 1992. text 69.95 (*0-87332-861-2*) M E Sharpe.

Origins of the Cultural Revolution Vol. 1: Contradictions Among the People, 1956-1957. Roderick MacFarquhar. LC 73-15793. (Studies of the East Asian Institute). (Illus.). 470p. 1987. pap. text 25.50 (*0-231-08385-8*, King's Crown Paperbacks) Col U Pr.

Origins of the Cultural Revolution Vol. 2: The Great Leap Forward, 1958-1960. Roderick MacFarquhar. (Studies of the East Asian Institute). (Illus.). 439p. 1987. pap. text 29.00 (*0-231-05717-2*) Col U Pr.

Origins of the Cultural Revolution Vol. III: The Coming of the Cataclysm, Vol. 3. Roderick MacFarquhar. 480p. 1997. 50.00 (*0-231-11082-0*) Col U Pr.

Origins of the Cultural Revolution Vol. III: The Coming of the Cataclysm, 1961-1966. Roderick MacFarquhar. 1999. pap. 18.50 (*0-231-11083-9*) Col U Pr.

Origins of the Czech National Renascence. Hugh L. Agnew. LC 92-36909. (Russian & East European Studies). 338p. (C). 1994. text 49.95 (*0-8229-3742-5*) U of Pittsburgh Pr.

Origins of the Druze People & Religion, with Extracts from Their Sacred Writings. Philip K. Hitti. LC 30-27674. (Columbia University. Oriental Studies: No. 28). reprint ed. 27.50 (*0-404-50518-X*) AMS Pr.

*__Origins of the Eisenhower Doctrine: The U. S., Britain & Nasser's Egypt, 1953-57.__ Ray Takeyh. LC 99-51696. 2000. text 65.00 (*0-312-23085-0*) St Martin.

Origins of the English Civil War: Conspiracy, Crusade, or Class Conflict? Ed. by Philip A. Taylor. (Problems in European Civilization Ser.). 107p. (C). 1960. pap. text 16.36 (*0-669-24174-1*) HM Trade Div.

Origins of the English Language: A Social & Linguistic History. Joseph M. Williams. LC 74-12596. (Illus.). 440p. 1986. pap. 18.95 (*0-02-934470-0*) Free Pr.

Origins of the English Library. Raymond Irwin. LC 81-7105. 255p. 1981. reprint ed. lib. bdg. 65.00 (*0-313-23149-4*, IROE, Greenwood Pr) Greenwood.

Origins of the English Novel, 1600-1740. Michael McKeon. LC 86-18495. 544p. 1988. reprint ed. pap. text 21.95 (*0-8018-3746-4*) Johns Hopkins.

Origins of the Equal Rights Amendment: American Feminism Between the Wars, 23. Susan D. Becker. LC 80-23633. (Contributions in Women's Studies: No. 23). 300p. 1981. 55.00 (*0-313-22818-3*, BOE/, Greenwood Pr) Greenwood.

Origins of the Eucharistic Prayer. Enrico Mazza. 376p. (Orig.). 1995. pap. text 34.95 (*0-8146-6119-X*, Pueblo Bks) Liturgical Pr.

Origins of the European Legal Order. Maurizio Lupoi. LC 98-8258. 656p. (C). 2000. text 125.00 (*0-521-62107-0*) Cambridge U Pr.

Origins of the Europeans: Classical Observations in Culture & Personality. William S. Shelley. LC 97-35167. 324p. 1998. 74.95 (*1-57309-221-5*); pap. 54.95 (*1-57309-220-7*) Intl Scholars.

Origins of the Federal Judiciary: Essays on the Judiciary Act of 1789. Ed. by Maeva Marcus. (Illus.). 320p. 1992. text 60.00 (*0-19-506721-5*, 1528) OUP.

Origins of the Federal Reserve System: Money, Class & Corporate Capitalism, 1890-1913. pap. text. write for info. (*0-7881-9191-8*) DIANE Pub.

Origins of the Federal Reserve System: Money, Class, & Corporate Capitalism, 1890-1913. James Livingston. LC 85-48199. 272p. 1986. pap. text 16.95 (*0-8014-9681-0*) Cornell U Pr.

Origins of the Federal Theology in Sixteenth-Century Reformation Thought. D. A. Weir. (Illus.). 264p. 1990. 59.00 (*0-19-826690-1*) OUP.

Origins of the Fifth Amendment: The Right Against Self-Incrimination. Leonard W. Levy. LC 99-34149. 561p. 1999. pap. 18.95 (*1-56663-270-6*, Pub. by I R Dee) Natl Bk Netwk.

Origins of the Fifth Amendment: The Right Against Self-Incrimination. Leonard W. Levy. 576p. 1986. reprint ed. pap. 14.95 (*0-02-919580-2*); reprint ed. text 23.99 (*0-02-919570-5*) Free Pr.

Origins of the First & Second World Wars. Frank McDonough. (Perspectives in History Ser.). 128p. (C). 1998. pap. 13.95 (*0-521-56861-7*) Cambridge U Pr.

Origins of the First United Front in China: The Role of Sneevliet (Alias Maring), 2 pts., Set. Tony Saich. LC 90-2583. (Illus.). xxvii, 941p. 1991. 223.00 (*90-04-09173-4*) Brill Academic Pubs.

Origins of the 1st World War. (C). 1987. pap. text 12.50 (*0-582-22382-2*, 70931) Longman.

Origins of the First World War. Ruth B. Henig. 80p. 1989. pap. 7.95 (*0-415-01513-8*, A3724) Routledge.

Origins of The First World War. James Joll. (Origins of Modern Wars Ser.). (Illus.). 228p. (C). 1989. pap. text 19.00 (*0-582-49016-2*, 73443) Longman.

Origins of the First World War. L. C. Turner. (Foundations of Modern History Ser.). (Illus.). 120p. (C). 1970. pap. text 10.50 (*0-393-09947-4*) Norton.

*__Origins of the First World War.__ 2nd ed. James Joll. 1999. pap. 32.00 (*0-582-41866-6*) Longman.

Origins of the First World War. 2nd ed. Gordon Martel. LC 95-4505. (Seminar Studies in History). 152p. (C). 1996. pap. text 14.06 (*0-582-28697-2*, Pub. by Addison-Wesley) Longman.

Origins of the First World War. 2nd rev. ed. Ruth B. Henig. LC 93-3376. (Lancaster Pamphlets Ser.). 80p. (C). 1993. pap. 11.99 (*0-415-10233-2*, B2467) Routledge.

Origins of the First World War: Profiles in Power Series. 2nd ed. James Joll. (Origins of Modern Wars Ser.). 264p. (C). 1995. pap. 33.93 (*0-582-08920-4*, 79200) Longman.

*__Origins of the Fourth World War.__ Jeff Nyquist. 280p. 1999. pap. 14.99 (*1-58275-010-6*, Pub. by Black Forest Pr) Epic Bk Promo.

*__Origins of the Fourth World War.__ Jeffrey R. Nyquist. 254p. 1998. pap. 15.00 (*1-58538-004-0*) Prophecy Club.

Origins of the Fourth World War: And the Coming Wars of Mass Destruction. unabridged ed. Jeffrey R. Nyquist. vi, 254p. 1998. pap. 20.00 (*0-9666877-0-1*) J Nyquist.

Origins of the Franciscan Order. Cajétan Esser. 289p. (Orig.). 1970. 12.50 (*0-8199-0408-2*, Frncscn Herld) Franciscan Pr.

Origins of the French Revolution. 2nd ed. William Doyle. 256p. (C). 1988. pap. text 21.00 (*0-19-822284-X*) OUP.

Origins of the French Revolution. 3rd ed. William Doyle. LC 98-39031. 248p. 1999. text 65.00 (*0-19-873175-2*); pap. text 19.95 (*0-19-873174-4*) OUP.

Origins of the French Revolution: Popular Misery, Social Ambitions, or Philosophical Ideas? 3rd ed. Ed. by Brian Tierney et al. (Historical Pamphlets Ser.). (C). 1977. pap. text 9.50 (*0-07-553614-5*) McGraw.

Origins of the French Revolutionary Wars: Origins of Modern Wars. Timothy C. W. Blanning. (Origins of Modern Wars Ser.). (Illus.). 226p. (C). 1986. pap. text 26.50 (*0-582-49051-0*, 73460) Longman.

Origins of the Gandharan Style: A Study of Contributory Influences. Lolita Nehru. (Illus.). 252p. 1990. 55.00 (*0-19-562472-6*) OUP.

Origins of the Gods. James S. Hans. LC 90-40941. (SUNY Series, The Margins of Literature). 227p. (C). 1991. pap. text 21.95 (*0-7914-0661-X*) State U NY Pr.

Origins of the Gods see Florentine Codex, A General History of the Things of New Spain

Origins of the Gospel Traditions. Birger Gerhardsson. LC 78-19634. 95p. reprint ed. pap. 30.00 (*0-608-15329-X*, 202961500061) Bks Demand.

Origins of the GULAG: The Soviet Prison-Camp System, 1917-1934. Michael Jakobson. LC 92-10711. (Illus.). 192p. (C). 1992. text 29.95 (*0-8131-1796-8*) U Pr of Ky.

Origins of the Higher Groups of Tetrapods: Controversy & Consensus. Ed. by Hans-Peter Schultze & Linda Trueb. LC 90-55752. (Illus.). 576p. 1991. text 99.95 (*0-8014-2497-6*) Cornell U Pr.

Origins of the Holocaust see Nazi Holocaust

Origins of the Holocaust: Christian Anti-Semitism. Ed. by Randolph L. Braham. 85p. 1986. text 40.00 (*0-88033-953-5*, 204, Pub. by East Eur Monographs) Col U Pr.

Origins of the Human Brain. Ed. by Jean-Pierre Changeux & Jean Chavaillon. (Fyssen Foundation Symposium Ser.). (Illus.). 334p. 1996. reprint ed. pap. text 40.00 (*0-19-852390-4*) OUP.

Origins of the Hundred Years War: The Angevin Legacy, 1250-1340. Malcolm Vale. (Illus.). 342p. 1996. pap. text 32.00 (*0-19-820620-8*) OUP.

Origins of the Indian Planetary Deities. Stephen Markel. LC 93-41911. (Studies in Asian Thought & Religion: Vol. 16). (Illus.). 284p. 1994. text 89.95 (*0-7734-9401-4*) E Mellen.

Origins of the Indo-European Races & Peoples, 2 vols. V. C. Pillai. 1990. reprint ed. 110.00 (*81-85326-25-8*, Pub. by Vintage) S Asia.

Origins of the Infinitesimal Calculus. M. Grace Baron. LC 68-21382. 1969. 141.00 (*0-08-012513-1*, Pub. by Pergamon Repr) Franklin.

Origins of the Infinitesimal Calculus. Margaret E. Baron. viii, 304p. 1987. reprint ed. pap. 9.95 (*0-486-65371-4*) Dover.

*__Origins of the Inquisition in Fifteenth Century Spain.__ B. Netanyahu. 2000. pap. 29.95 (*0-940322-39-0*) NY Rev Bks.

Origins of the International Competitiveness of Firms: The Impact of Location & Ownership in the Professional Service Industries. Lilach Nachum. LC 98-42883. (New Horizons in International Business Ser.). 256p. 1999. 85.00 (*1-84064-012-X*) E Elgar.

Origins of the Iranian-American Alliance, 1941-1953. Mark H. Lytle. 254p. 1987. 49.50 (*0-8419-1060-X*) Holmes & Meier.

Origins of the Islamic State, 2 vols. Incl. Vol. 1. Tr. by Philip K. Hitti. LC 76-82247. reprint ed. (*0-404-51694-7*); Vol. 2. Tr. by Francis C. Murgotten. LC 76-82247. reprint ed. (*0-404-51695-5*); LC 76-82247. (Columbia University. Studies in the Social Sciences: No. 163 & No. 163a). 82.50 (*0-404-51163-5*) AMS Pr.

Origins of the Israeli Polity: Palestine under the Mandate. Dan Horowitz & Moshe Lissak. Tr. by Charles Hoffman. LC 78-3175. (Illus.). 320p. 1994. lib. bdg. 24.00 (*0-226-35366-4*) U Ch Pr.

Origins of the Israeli Polity: Palestine under the Mandate. Dan Horowitz & Moshe Lissak. Tr. by Charles Hoffman from HEB. LC 78-3175. 304p. reprint ed. pap. 94.30 (*0-608-09404-8*, 205420500004) Bks Demand.

Origins of the Italian Veduta. Brown University, Department of Art Staff. LC 78-52897. (Illus.). 105p. (Orig.). 1978. pap. text 20.00 (*0-933519-07-9*) D W Bell Gallery.

Origins of the Jump Shot: Eight Men Who Shook the World of Basketball. John Christgau. LC 98-37508. (Illus.). xii, 220p. 1999. pap. 15.00 (*0-8032-6394-5*) U of Nebr Pr.

Origins of the Kabbalah. Gershom Scholem. Ed. by R. J. Wernblowsky. Tr. by Allan Arkush from GER. 503p. (C). 1987. text 75.00 (*0-691-07314-7*, Pub. by Princeton U Pr) Cal Prin Full Svc.

Origins of the Kabbalah. Gershom Scholem. Ed. by R. J. Werblowsky. Tr. by Allan Arkush from GER. 503p. (C). 1987. pap. text 19.95 (*0-691-02047-7*, Pub. by Princeton U Pr) Cal Prin Full Svc.

Origins of the Koran: Classic Essays on Islam's Holy Book. Ibn Warraq. LC 98-6075. 420p. 1998. 32.95 (*1-57392-198-X*) Prometheus Bks.

Origins of the Korean War Vol. 2: The Roaring of the Cataract, 1947-1950. Bruce Cumings. LC 80-8543. (Studies of the East Asian Institute, Columbia University: No. 1). (Illus.). 986p. reprint ed. pap. 200.00 (*0-608-09569-9*, 2054371) Bks Demand.

Origins of the Liberal Party & Liberal Imperialism: The Career of Charles Buller, 1806-1848. David A. Haury. Ed. by Peter Stansky. (Modern European History Ser.). 392p. 1987. text 15.00 (*0-8240-7814-4*) Garland.

Origins of the Liturgical Year. 2nd ed. Thomas J. Talley. 255p. 1992. pap. 19.95 (*0-8146-6075-4*, Pueblo Bks) Liturgical Pr.

Origins of the Maritime Strategy: American Naval Strategy in the First Postwar Decade. Michael A. Palmer. (Contributions to Naval History Ser.: No. 1). (Illus.). 129p. (C). 1988. pap. 7.50 (*0-945274-01-7*) Naval Hist Ctr.

Origins of the Maritime Strategy: The Development of American Naval Strategy, 1945-1955. Michael A. Palmer. LC 90-30117. (Illus.). 192p. 1990. 24.95 (*0-87021-667-8*) Naval Inst Pr.

Origins of the Marshall Plan. John Gimbel. LC 75-39334. xiv, 344p. 1976. 45.00 (*0-8047-0903-3*) Stanford U Pr.

Origins of the Marshall Plan. fac. ed. John Gimbel. LC 75-39334. 358p. pap. 30.00 (*0-7837-7264-5*, 204704100005) Bks Demand.

Origins of the Medieval World. William C. Bark. xiv, 162p. 1958. pap. 12.95 (*0-8047-0514-3*) Stanford U Pr.

Origins of the Mithraic Mysteries: Cosmology & Salvation in the Ancient World. David Ulansey. (Illus.). 168p. 1991. reprint ed. pap. 12.95 (*0-19-506788-6*) OUP.

Origins of the Modern Chinese Movement in Indonesia. Tek H. Kwee. Ed. by Lea E. Williams. LC 70-16525. (Cornell University, Southeast Asia Program, Data Paper Ser.). 74p. reprint ed. pap. 30.00 (*0-7837-1666-4*, 204196500024) Bks Demand.

Origins of the Modern European State System, 1494-1618. Matthew S. Anderson. LC 97-31324. (C). 1998. text 68.44 (*0-582-22945-6*, Pub. by Addison-Wesley) Longman.

Origins of the Modern Jew: Jewish Identity & European Culture in Germany, 1749-1824. Michael A. Meyer. LC 67-12384. (Waynebooks Ser.: No. 32). 250p. (C). 1972. reprint ed. pap. 16.95 (*0-8143-1470-8*) Wayne St U Pr.

Origins of the Modern Mind: Three Stages in the Evolution of Culture & Cognition. Merlin Donald. (Illus.). 448p. (C). 1991. text 38.50 (*0-674-64483-2*) HUP.

Origins of the Modern Mind: Three Stages in the Evolution of Culture & Cognition. Merlin Donald. (Illus.). 424p. (C). 1993. pap. text 16.95 (*0-674-64484-0*) HUP.

Origins of the Modern West: Essays & Sources in Early Modern European History to Accompany a Series of Fims Entitled Renaissance. Theodore K. Rabb. Ed. by Sherrin D. Marshall. LC 92-43374. 320p. (C). 1993. pap. 36.25 (*0-07-041231-6*) McGraw.

Origins of the Modern West: Essays & Sources in Early Modern European History to Accompany a Series of Fims Entitled Renaissance. Theodore K. Rabb. Ed. by Sherrin D. Marshall. LC 92-43374. (C). 1994. pap., student ed. 10.31 (*0-07-041232-4*) McGraw.

Origins of the Muslim Consciousness in India: A World-System Perspective, 29. Syed N. Ahmad. LC 91-2529. (Contributions to the Study of World History Ser.: No. 29). 328p. 1991. 65.00 (*0-313-27331-6*, ASH, Greenwood Pr) Greenwood.

Origins of the National Forests: A Centennial Symposium. Ed. by Harold K. Steen. LC 92-1236. 334p. (C). 1992. 31.95 (*0-8223-1252-2*); pap. 16.95 (*0-8223-1272-7*) Forest Hist Soc.

Origins of the National Recovery Administration: Business, Government & the Trade Association Issue, 1921-1933. 2nd rev. ed. Robert F. Himmelberg. LC 93-23761. xx, 232p. 1993. 30.00 (*0-8232-1540-7*); pap. 20.00 (*0-8232-1541-5*) Fordham.

*__Origins of the Navy Judge Advocate General's Corps 1775-1967: A History of Legal Administration in the United States Navy.__ Jay M. Siegel. LC 97-73190. 912p. 1998. boxed set 51.00 (*0-16-049135-5*) USGPO.

An Asterisk (*) at the beginning of an entry indicates that the title is appearing for the first time.

Origins of the New Churches' Movement in Southern Ethiopia, 1927-1944. Brian L. Fargher. LC 96-24803. (Studies of Religion in Africa). xvi, 329p. 1996. 123.00 (*90-04-10661-8*) Brill Academic Pubs.

Origins of the New South, 1877-1913. rev. ed. C. Vann Woodward. LC 77-14582. (History of the South Ser.: Vol. 9). xiv, 656p. 1951. text 60.00 (*0-8071-0009-9*) La State U Pr.

Origins of the New South, 1877-1913. rev. ed. C. Vann Woodward. LC 77-14582. (History of the South Ser.: Vol. 9). xiv, 656p. 1981. pap. text 24.95 (*0-8071-0019-6*) La State U Pr.

Origins of the Number Concept. Charles J. Brainerd. LC 78-21223. 227p. 1979. 65.00 (*0-275-90334-6*, C0334, Praeger Pubs) Greenwood.

Origins of the Old Rus' Weights & Monetary Systems: Two Studies in Western Eurasian Metrology & Numismatics in the Seventh to Eleventh Centuries. Omeljan Pritsak. LC 92-54345. (Harvard Series in Ukrainian Studies). (Illus.). 160p. (C). 1998. text 29.00 (*0-916458-48-2*) Harvard Ukrainian.

Origins of the Ottoman Empire. M. Fuad Koprulu. Ed. & Tr. by Gary Leiser from TUR. LC 90-22723. (SUNY Series in the Social & Economic History of the Middle East). 155p. (C). 1991. pap. text 21.95 (*0-7914-0820-5*) State U NY Pr.

Origins of the Ottoman Empire. M. Fuad Koprulu. Ed. & Tr. by Gary Leiser from TUR. LC 90-22723. (SUNY Series in the Social & Economic History of the Middle East). 155p. (C). 1992. text 64.50 (*0-7914-0819-1*) State U NY Pr.

Origins of the Pacific War. Akira Iriye. LC 98-87529. 1999. pap. text 11.95 (*0-312-14788-0*) St Martin.

Origins of the Pacific War & the Importance of "Magic" Keiichiro Komatsu. 360p. 1998. text 55.00 (*1-873410-66-2*, Pub. by Curzon Pr Ltd) UH Pr.

Origins of the Pact of Steel. Mario Toscano. LC 67-24276. 431p. reprint ed. pap. 133.70 (*0-608-10772-7*, 202074500018) Bks Demand.

Origins of the Partition of India, 1936-1947. Anita I. Singh. (Oxford University South Asian Studies Ser.). 286p. 1990. reprint ed. pap. text 6.95 (*0-19-562541-2*) OUP.

Origins of the Philippine Republic: Extracts from the Diaries & Records of Francis Burton Harrison. Francis B. Harrison. LC 74-186457. (Cornell University, Southeast Asia Program, Data Paper Ser.: No. 95). 268p. reprint ed. pap. 83.10 (*0-608-14379-0*, 202184500023) Bks Demand.

Origins of the Platonic Academy of Florence. Arthur Field. LC 88-9952. 318p. reprint ed. pap. 98.60 (*0-608-06317-7*, 206667900008) Bks Demand.

***Origins of the Professional Roman Soldier.** M. C. J. Miller. (Illus.). 250p. 2000. write for info. (*0-89005-584-X*) Ares.

Origins of the Republican Party, 1852-1856. William E. Gienapp. 582p. 1988. pap. text 29.95 (*0-19-505501-2*) OUP.

Origins of the Restoration Movement. Richard Tristano. LC 88-83888. 1988. 11.95 (*0-914422-17-0*) Glenmary Res Ctr.

Origins of the Romanesque: Near Eastern Influences on European Art Fourth to Twelfth Centuries. V. I. Atroshenko & Judith Collins. LC 85-21635. (Illus.). 176p. 1986. 60.00 (*0-87951-247-4*, Pub. by Overlook Pr) Penguin Putnam.

Origins of the Russian Intelligensia: The Eighteenth-Century Nobility. Marc Raeff. LC 66-19152. 256p. (Orig.). (C). 1966. pap. 8.95 (*0-15-670150-2*, Harvest Bks) Harcourt.

Origins of the Russian Revolution. 2nd rev. ed. Alan Wood. LC 93-13451. (Lancaster Pamphlets Ser.). 50p. (C). 1993. pap. 11.99 (*0-415-10232-4*, B2470) Routledge.

Origins of the Salvation Army. Norman H. Murdoch. LC 94-9334. (Illus.). 256p. (C). 1996. pap. text 16.00 (*0-87049-955-6*) U of Tenn Pr.

Origins of the Science of Crystals. John G. Burke. LC 66-13584. 208p. reprint ed. pap. 64.50 (*0-608-15837-2*, 203142700074) Bks Demand.

Origins of the Second Arab-Israel War: Egypt, Israel & the Great Powers, 1952-56. Michael B. Oren. 199p. 1993. 49.50 (*0-7146-3430-1*, Pub. by F Cass Pubs) Intl Spec Bk.

Origins of the Second World War. Maurice Baumont. Tr. by Simone D. Ferguson. LC 77-16652. 327p. 1978. 45.00 (*0-300-02215-8*) Yale U Pr.

Origins of the Second World War. Patrick Finney. LC 97-3795. (Arnold Readers in History Ser.). 480p. 1997. pap. text 19.95 (*0-340-67640-X*) OUP.

Origins of the Second World War. Ed. by Patrick Finney. LC 97-3795. (Arnold Readers in History Ser.). 480p. 1997. text 65.00 (*0-340-67641-8*) OUP.

Origins of the Second World War. A. J. P. Taylor. 320p. 1996. per. 14.00 (*0-684-82947-9*) S&S Trade Pap.

Origins of the Second World War. 2nd ed. R. J. Overy. LC 97-38405. (Seminar Studies in History). (C). 1998. pap. text 13.13 (*0-582-29085-6*, Drumbeat) Longman.

Origins of the Second World War: American Foreign Policy & World Politics, 1917-1941. Arnold A. Offner. LC 85-23928. 288p. (C). 1986. reprint ed. pap. 19.50 (*0-89464-320-7*); reprint ed. text 23.50 (*0-89874-924-7*) Krieger.

Origins of the Second World War in Asia & the Pacific. Akira Iriye. (Origins of the Modern Wars Ser.). 216p. (Orig.). (C). 1989. pap. 35.66 (*0-582-49349-8*, 73585) Longman.

Origins of the Second World War in Europe. 2nd ed. P. M. Bell. LC 96-52074. (Origins of Modern Wars Ser.). 1p. (C). 1997. pap. text 22.50 (*0-582-30470-9*) Longman.

Origins of the Second World War Reconsidered: The A. J. P. Taylor Debate after Twenty-Five Years. Ed. by Gordon Martel. 292p. 1986. text 75.00 (*0-04-940084-3*); pap. text 19.95 (*0-04-940085-1*) Routledge.

Origins of the Second World War Reconsidered: The A. J. P. Taylor Debate after Twenty-Five Years. Ed. by Gordon Martel. LC 85-20097. (Illus.). 288p. (C). 1986. pap. 24.99 (*0-415-08420-2*) Routledge.

Origins of the Second World War, 1933-1939. Ruth Henig. (Lancaster Pamphlets Ser.). 50p. (C). 1985. pap. 11.99 (*0-415-06590-9*) Routledge.

Origins of the Shakers: From the Old World to the New World. Clarke Garrett. LC 97-39244. 304p. 1998. reprint ed. pap. text 16.95 (*0-8018-5923-9*) Johns Hopkins.

Origins of the South African War, 1899-1902. Iain R. Smith. Ed. by Harry Hearder. (Origins of Modern Wars Ser.). 480p. (C). 1995. pap. 36.93 (*0-582-49520-2*) Addison-Wesley.

Origins of the State in Italy, 1300-1600. Ed. by Julius Kirshner. (Studies in European History from the Journal of Modern History). 216p. 1996. pap. text 15.95 (*0-226-43770-1*); lib. bdg. 27.95 (*0-226-43769-8*) U Ch Pr.

Origins of the State Mental Hospital in America: Six Documentary Studies, 1837-1856. LC 73-2409. (Mental Illness & Social Policy; the American Experience Ser.). 1979. 29.95 (*0-405-05219-7*) Ayer.

Origins of the Synagogue & the Church. Kaufmann Kohler. Ed. by H. G. Enelow. LC 73-2213. (Jewish People; History, Religion, Literature Ser.). 1979. reprint ed. 26.95 (*0-405-05277-4*) Ayer.

Origins of the Tainan Culture, West Indies. Sven Loven. LC 76-44753. (Taino Indians of Hispaniola & Eastern Cuba Ser.). (Illus.). reprint ed. 95.00 (*0-404-15948-6*) AMS Pr.

Origins of the Tiandihui: The Chinese Triads in Legend & History. Dian H. Murray & Qin Baoqi. xiv, 350p. Date not set. 42.50 (*0-8047-2125-4*) Stanford U Pr.

Origins of the Tiandihui: The Chinese Triads in Legend & History. Diane H. Murray & Qin Baoqi. LC 93-24514. xiv, 350p. 1994. 49.50 (*0-8047-2324-9*) Stanford U Pr.

Origins of the Turbojet Revolution. fac. ed. Edward W. Constant. LC 80-11802. (Johns Hopkins Studies in the History of Technology; New Ser.: No. 5). (Illus.). 327p. 1980. pap. 101.40 (*0-7837-7636-5*, 204738900007) Bks Demand.

Origins of the TVA: The Muscle Shoals Controversy, 1920-1932. Preston J. Hubbard. (C). 1968. reprint ed. pap. 3.50 (*0-393-00467-8*) Norton.

Origins of the Twelfth Amendment: The Electoral College in the Early Republic, 1787-1804, 344. Tadahisa Kuroda. LC 93-44508. (Contributions in Political Science Ser.: No. 344). 256p. 1994. 65.00 (*0-313-29151-9*, Greenwood Pr) Greenwood.

Origins of the University: The Schools of Paris & Their Critics, 1100-1215. Stephen C. Ferruolo. LC 84-40445. 392p. 1985. 49.50 (*0-8047-1266-2*) Stanford U Pr.

Origins of the Urban Crisis: Race & Inequality in Postwar Detroit. Thomas J. Sugrue. LC 96-13694. (Princeton Studies in American Politics). 408p. 1997. text 49.50 (*0-691-01101-X*, Pub. by Princeton U Pr); pap. text 16.95 (*0-691-05888-1*, Pub. by Princeton U Pr) Cal Prin Full Svc.

Origins of the Urban School: Public Education in Massachusetts, 1870-1915. Marvin Lazerson. LC 77-168433. (Joint Center for Urban Studies Publications). 302p. reprint ed. pap. 93.70 (*0-608-16109-8*, 201768600007) Bks Demand.

Origins of the Vigilant State: The London Metropolitan Police Special Branch Before the First World War. Bernard Porter. 272p. 1991. reprint ed. 60.00 (*0-85115-283-X*) Boydell & Brewer.

Origins of the Volga Bulghars. I. Zimonyi. (Studia Uralo-altaica Ser.). 211p. 1990. pap. 76.00 (*0-685-53308-5*) J Benjamins Pubng Co.

Origins of the Western Legal Tradition: From Thales to the Tudors. Ellen Goodman. LC 96-123041. 400p. 1995. pap. 45.00 (*1-86287-181-7*, Pub. by Federation Pr) Gaunt.

Origins of the Whig Party: A Dissertation. Malcolm E. Carroll. LC 72-112705. (Law, Politics & History Ser.). 1970. reprint ed. lib. bdg. 37.50 (*0-306-71917-7*) Da Capo.

Origins of the Yiddish Language. Katz. 1987. 26.25 (*0-08-034765-7*, Pergamon Pr) Elsevier.

Origins of the Yiddish Language: Papers from the First Annual Oxford Winter Symposium in Yiddish Language & Literature, Oxford, 16-17 December 1985. Ed. by David Katz. LC 87-8891. 146p. 1987. 66.25 (*0-08-034156-X*, Pergamon Pr) Elsevier.

Origins of Theoretical Population Genetics. William B. Provine. LC 73-153711. (Chicago History of Science & Medicine Ser.). xii, 214p. 1999. pap. text 19.00 (*0-226-68466-0*) U Ch Pr.

Origins of Thoracic Anaesthesia. William W. Mushin & Leslie Rendell-Baker. Orig. Title: Principles of Thoracic Anaesthesia. (Illus.). xx, 172p. 1991. reprint ed. write for info. (*0-9614932-2-4*) Wood Lib-Mus.

Origins of Totalitarianism. Hannah Arendt. LC 68-3757. 574p. 1973. pap. 17.00 (*0-15-670153-7*, HB244, Harvest Bks) Harcourt.

Origins of Totalitarianism Pt. 2 see Imperialism

Origins of Totalitarianism Pt. 3 see Totalitarianism

Origins of Trade Union Power. Henry Phelps-Brown. LC 83-1920. 336p. 1983. 39.95 (*0-19-877115-0*) OUP.

Origins of Trade Union Power. Henry Phelps-Brown. LC 83-1920. 336p. 1986. pap. 16.95 (*0-19-285156-X*) OUP.

Origins of Ulster Unionism: The Formation of Popular Protestant Politics & Ideology in Nineteenth-century Ireland. Peter Gibbon. LC 76-360466. viii, 163p. 1975. write for info. (*0-7190-0613-9*) Manchester Univ Pr.

Origins of Vicente Huidobro's Creacionismo (1911-1916) & Its Evolution (1917-1947) Luisa M. Perdigo. LC 93-39318. 360p. 1993. text 99.95 (*0-7734-2299-4*) E Mellen.

Origins of Violence: Approaches to the Study of Conflict. rev. ed. Anatol Rapoport. LC 94-12483. 589p. (C). 1994. pap. 29.95 (*1-56000-783-4*) Transaction Pubs.

Origins of Violence in Mexican Society. Christina J. Johns. LC 94-32917. 240p. 1995. 59.95 (*0-275-94838-2*, Praeger Pubs) Greenwood.

Origins of Virasaiva Sects: A Typological Analysis of Ritual & Associational Patterns in the Sunyasampadane. R. Blake Michael. (C). 1992. 25.00 (*81-208-0776-6*, Pub. by Motilal Bnarsidass) S Asia.

Origins of Virtue: Human Instincts & the Evolution of Cooperation. Matt Ridley. (Illus.). 295p. 1997. text 24.95 (*0-670-86357-2*) Viking Penguin.

Origins of Virtue: Human Instincts & the Evolution of Cooperation. Matt Ridley. LC 96-44907. 295p. 1998. pap. 13.95 (*0-14-026445-0*) Viking Penguin.

Origins of Walter Rauschenbusch's Social Ethics. Donovan E. Smucker. 184p. 1994. 60.00 (*0-7735-1163-6*, Pub. by McG-Queens Univ Pr) CUP Services.

Origins of War: From the Stone Age to Alexander the Great. rev. ed. Arther Ferrill. LC 97-1420. (History & Warfare Ser.). 240p. (C). 1997. pap. text 25.00 (*0-8133-3302-4*, Pub. by Westview) HarpC.

***Origins of War in South Asia: Indo-Pakistani Conflicts since 1947.** Sumit Ganguly. 1999. pap. 18.00 (*81-7094-333-7*, Pub. by Vision) S Asia.

Origins of War Prevention: The British Peace Movement & International Relations, 1730-1854. Martin Caedel. 598p. 1996. text 110.00 (*0-19-822674-8*) OUP.

Origins of Waves. Austin Clarke. LC 96-932212. 1997. pap. 19.99 (*0-7710-2127-5*) McCland & Stewart.

***Origins of Welfare State in Britain, 8 vols., set.** Ed. & Intro. by Nicholas Deakin. (Illus.). 2600p. (C). 2000. text 980.00 (*0-415-21222-7*) Routledge.

Origins of Western Warfare: Militarism & Morality in the Ancient World. Doyne Dawson. (History & Warfare Ser.). 216p. (C). 1997. pap. 24.00 (*0-8133-3392-X*, Pub. by Westview) HarpC.

Origins of World War II. 2nd ed. Keith Eubank. (European History Ser.). 200p. 1990. pap. text 11.95 (*0-88295-871-2*) Harlan Davidson.

Origins of Writing. Ed. by Wayne M. Senner. LC 89-30400. (Illus.). viii, 247p. 1989. reprint ed. pap. text 22.00 (*0-8032-9167-1*, Bison Books) U of Nebr Pr.

Origins of Zionism. David Vital. (Illus.). 412p. 1980. pap. text 31.00 (*0-19-827439-4*) OUP.

Origin's Official Guide to Wing Commander III. Frase et al. (Illus.). 256p. (Orig.). 1995. pap. 24.95 (*0-929373-44-8*) Origin Syst.

Origins Official Guide to Wing Commander IV. Origin Systems Inc. Staff. 1996. pap. text 19.95 (*0-929373-37-5*) Elect Arts.

Origins Reconsidered: In Search of What Makes Us Human. Richard Leakey & Roger Lewin. 400p. 1993. pap. 16.95 (*0-385-46792-3*, Anchor NY) Doubleday.

Origins Russo Japan War. Ian H. Nish. (Origins of Modern Wars Ser.). 274p. (C). 1989. pap. 39.06 (*0-582-49114-2*, 73483) Longman.

Origins Second World War. 129p. (C). 1989. pap. text 19.00 (*0-582-35378-5*, 72209) Longman.

Origins Solution: An Answer in the Creation-Evolution Debate. Dick Fischer. 1996. pap. 14.95 (*1-55673-188-4*, Fairway Pr) CSS OH.

Origins, Transformations, Limitations: Scientific Culture in the Natural & Social Sciences. William M. Wentworth. (Illus.). 52p. (Orig.). (C). 1997. pap. text 19.95 (*1-890230-00-6*, 001-01) Counseling Arts Pr.

Origins Wars German Unification. William Carr. (Origins of Modern Wars Ser.). (Illus.). 256p. (C). 1995. pap. 39.06 (*0-582-49148-7*, 78818) Longman.

***Origmai & Papercraft: 60 Beautiful Paper Creations.** Paul Jackson. (Illus.). 2000. 14.95 (*0-7548-0117-9*, Lorenz Bks) Anness Pub.

Origo Gentis Romanae: De Viris Illustribus, Concordantiae et Indices. Luca Cardinali. (Alpha-Omega, Reihe A Ser.: Bd. CLXXXVI). (GER.). 549p. 1997. write for info. (*3-487-10494-6*) G Olms Pubs.

Oriki of a Grasshopper, & Other Plays. Femi Osofisan. LC 95-6636. 195p. 1995. pap. 19.95 (*0-88258-181-3*) Howard U Pr.

Orilla Inminenre. Saul Sosnowski. (SPA.). 171p. 1987. pap. 14.00 (*950-600-092-1*) Ediciones Norte.

Orilla Oscura (The Dark Edge of the Water) Jose M. Merino. 352p. 1995. pap. 16.95 (*0-679-76348-1*) Vin Bks.

Orillas del rio Piedra me sente y llore. Paulo Coelho. LC 96-34273. (SPA.). 224p. 1996. pap. 11.00 (*0-06-251462-8*, Pub. by Harper SF) HarpC.

Orillas del Rio Plum (On the Banks of Plum Creek) Laura Ingalls Wilder. 1996. pap. text 7.95 (*84-279-3208-1*) Lectorum Pubns.

Orimili: One Man's Struggle for Power in Pre-Colonial Nigeria. Amechi Akwanga. (African Writers Ser.). 186p. (C). 1991. pap. 8.95 (*0-435-90670-4*, 90670) Heinemann.

Orin Orisa: Songs for Selected Heads. 2nd rev. ed. John Mason. LC 97-61174. (Illus.). 496p. (Orig.). 1997. pap. text 25.00 (*1-881244-06-7*) Yoruba Theol Arch.

***Orinoco-Parima: Indian Societies in Venezuela.** Luiz Boglar. (Cisneros Collections). (Illus.). 2000. 55.00 (*3-7757-0873-1*) Gerd Hatje.

Orinoco River. Carol Rawlins. LC 99-10816. (Watts Library). 1999. 24.00 (*0-531-11740-5*) Watts.

***Orinoco River.** Carol B. Rawlins. (Watts Library). (Illus.). (J). 2000. pap. 8.95 (*0-531-16429-2*) Watts.

Orinoco, Rosa de Dos Aromas y Otras Piezas Dramaticas (Orinoco, Rose of Two Fragrances & Other Dramatic Pieces) Emilio Carballido. (SPA.). 270p. 1994. pap. 8.99 (*968-16-4161-2*, Pub. by Fondo) Continental Bk.

***Orioles.** Matt Silverman. 96p. 2000. mass mkt. 2.50 (*1-892129-51-5*) Total Sprts.

Orioles. L. M. Stone. LC 98-2726. (Backyard Birds Ser.). (J). 1998. (*0-86593-474-6*) Rourke Corp.

Orioles, Blackbirds, & Their Kin: A Natural History. Alexander F. Skutch. (Illus.). 291p. 1996. pap. text 22.95 (*0-8165-1601-4*) U of Ariz Pr.

Orioles, Blackbirds, & Their Kin: Natural History of the New World's Most Diverse Avian Family. Alexander F. Skutch. LC 95-4431. (Illus.). 291p. 1996. 52.00 (*0-8165-1584-0*) U of Ariz Pr.

Orioles Memories. Rex Barney. 1994. 19.95 (*0-9625427-0-9*) Goodwood Pr.

Orioles Yearbook, 1993: An All Star Season. 96p. (Orig.). 1993. pap. 10.00 (*0-87295-000-X*) French-Bray.

Oriomo Papuans: Ecology of Sago-Eaters in Lowland Papua. Ryutaro Ohtsuka. (Illus.). 197p. 1983. 30.00 (*0-86008-327-6*, Pub. by U of Tokyo) Col U Pr.

Orion. Jerald Bullis. LC 76-40995. (Orig.). 1976. pap. 5.00 (*0-917492-03-X*) Jackpine Pr.

Orion. Dyson. 1999. write for info. (*0-8050-5985-7*) H Holt & Co.

Orion. W. D. Everman. LC 75-322771. (Ithaca House Fiction Ser.). 94p. 1975. 4.50 (*0-87886-055-X*, Greenfld Rev Pr) Greenfld Rev Lit.

Orion. Donal Heffernam. (Illus.). 1993. pap. 10.00 (*1-883477-02-6*) Lone Oak MN.

Orion. deluxe limited num. ed. Jerald Bullis. LC 76-40995. (Orig.). 1976. 10.00 (*0-917492-02-1*) Jackpine Pr.

Orion. Ben Bova. 432p. 1992. reprint ed. mass mkt. 4.99 (*0-8125-3247-3*, Pub. by Tor Bks) St Martin.

Orion. 2nd ed. Masamune Shirow. (Illus.). 272p. 1994. pap. 17.95 (*1-56971-148-8*) Dark Horse Comics.

Orion: The Gold Beater. George L. Aiken. (Works of George Aiken (1830-1876)). 1989. reprint ed. lib. bdg. 90.00 (*0-7812-1589-7*) Rprt Serv.

Orion: The Story of a Rape. Ralph Graves. LC 92-35527. 1993. 21.95 (*0-942637-81-X*) Barricade Bks.

Orion among the Stars. Ben Bova. 320p. 1995. 22.95 (*0-312-85637-7*) Tor Bks.

Orion among the Stars. Ben Bova. 1996. mass mkt. 5.99 (*0-8125-3511-1*, Pub. by Tor Bks) St Martin.

Orion & the Conqueror. Ben Bova. 352p. 1995. 5.99 (*0-8125-2376-8*, Pub. by Tor Bks) St Martin.

Orion Arm Bk. 2: The Rampart Worlds. Julian May. 2000. mass mkt. 6.99 (*0-345-39519-0*, Del Rey) Ballantine Pub Grp.

Orion Blinded: Essays on Claude Simon. Ed. by Randi Birn & Karen Gould. LC 79-17687. 320p. 1981. 38.50 (*0-8387-2420-5*) Bucknell U Pr.

Orion Complex. C. Goudis. 1982. text 199.50 (*90-277-1298-0*) Kluwer Academic.

Orion Computer Blue Book Consumer Edition, 1992. 1992. 200.00 (*0-932089-84-4*) Orion Res.

***Orion Conspiracy.** Ron Edwards. LC 00-190166. 2000. 25.00 (*0-7388-1599-3*); pap. 18.00 (*0-7388-1600-0*) Xlibris Corp.

Orion Conspiracy: A Story of the End. Kenneth R. Wade. LC 93-41100. 1994. pap. 10.99 (*0-8163-1195-1*) Pacific Pr Pub Assn.

Orion in the Dying Time. Ben Bova. 1991. mass mkt. 4.99 (*0-8125-1429-7*, Pub. by Tor Bks) St Martin.

Orion Mystery. Gilbert Bauval. 352p. 1994. mass mkt. 29.95 (*0-385-25483-0*) Doubleday.

Orion Mystery. Robert Bauval & Adrian Gilbert. (Illus.). 336p. 1996. pap. write for info. (*0-385-25542-X*) Doubleday.

Orion Mystery: Unlocking the Secrets of the Pyramids. Adrian Gilbert & Robert Bauval. 1995. pap. 14.00 (*0-517-88454-2*) Random Hse Value.

Orion Piano & Organ Blue Book, 1992. 1992. 200.00 (*0-932089-80-1*) Orion Res.

Orion Property. Kate Saundby. LC 98-89500. 375p. 1998. text 25.00 (*0-7388-0199-2*); pap. text 15.00 (*0-7388-0200-X*) Xlibris Corp.

Orion Rising: An Owen Keane Mystery. Terence Faherty. LC 99-22068. (Owen Keane Mysteries Ser.). 256p. 1999. text 22.95 (*0-312-20351-9*) St Martin.

Orion Shall Rise. Poul Anderson. 1991. reprint ed. per. 4.99 (*0-671-72090-2*) Baen Bks.

Orion, the Hunter. Necia H. Apfel. LC 94-44268. (Illus.). 48p. (J). (gr. 4-7). 1995. 16.95 (*0-395-68962-7*, Clarion Bks) HM.

Orion Thebanus: Etymologicon. Orion Thebanus. viii, 255p. 1973. reprint ed. write for info. (*3-487-04539-7*) G Olms Pubs.

Orione, Ossia Diana Vendicata & Zanaida. Ed. by Ernest Warburton. (Johann Christian Bach Ser.). 1989. text 165.00 (*0-8240-6053-9*) Garland.

Orion's Belt. Denby Montana. Ed. by Owen Mould. 85p. (Orig.). 1994. pap. 8.00 (*0-9644856-9-9*, Celtic Butterfly) Spellman-Tris.

Orion's Belt. large type ed. Jon Michelet. 528p. 1987. 27.99 (*0-7089-1689-9*) Ulverscroft.

Orion's Belt & Other Writings. Gemino H. Abad. LC 96-946490. 168p. 1997. pap. text 18.00 (*971-542-109-1*, Pub. by U of Philippines Pr) UH Pr.

***Orion's Gold.** Franklin C. Fetter, Jr. LC 99-95378. (Illus.). 171p. 1999. pap. 10.00 (*0-9673219-0-5*) Bl Goose Exped.

***Orion's Legacy: A Cultural History of Man As Hunter.** Charles Bergman. 359p. 2000. reprint ed. pap. text 14.00 (*0-7881-6951-3*) DIANE Pub.

Oris. Mark Dunster. 13p. (Orig.). 1991. pap. 4.00 (*0-89642-199-6*) Linden Pubs.

O

An Asterisk (*) at the beginning of an entry indicates that the title is appearing for the first time.

Orishatukeh Faduma: Liberal Theology & Evangelical Pan-Africanism, 1857-1946. Moses Moore. LC 95-39630. (ATLA Monographs: No. 40). 320p. 1996. 49.50 (*0-8108-3091-4*) Scarecrow.

Orissa: Its Golden Epoch. K. P. Padhy. (C). 1994. 50.00 (*81-85151-85-7*) S Asia.

Orissa & Her Remains Ancient & Medieval. Mano M. Ganguly. (Illus.). 540p. 1986. 225.00 (*0-318-36257-0*) Asia Bk Corp.

***Orissan History, Culture & Archaeology: Reconstructing Indian History & Culture.** S. A. Pradhan. LC 98-909202. xix, 477 p. 1998. write for info. (*81-246-0117-8*, Pub. by D K Printwrld) S Asia.

Orissers. Leopold H. Myers. 1971. reprint ed. 59.00 (*0-403-01125-6*) Scholarly.

Oritumbre. Arthur De Lima. 194p. 1987. 35.00 (*0-7223-1539-2*, Pub. by A H S Ltd) St Mut.

Orixas: Os Deuses Vivos da Africa. Abdias D. Nascimento. 170p. 1997. 79.95 (*85-85853-01-8*) Temple U Pr.

Oriya Nationalism: Quest for a United Orissa. Nivedita Mohanty. 1983. 21.00 (*0-8364-0954-X*, Pub. by Manohar) S Asia.

Orkney. RIAS Staff. 104p. (C). 1991. pap. 75.00 (*1-873190-02-6*, Pub. by Royal Inc Architects) St Mut.

Orkney - A Historical Guide. Caroline Wickam-Jones. (Illus.). 156p. 1998. pap. 15.95 (*1-874744-71-8*, Pub. by Birlinn Ltd) Dufour.

Orkney All the Way Through. George Garson. 128p. (C). 1996. pap. 40.00 (*0-85976-362-5*, Pub. by J Donald) St Mut.

Orkney & Shetland Records, 3 vols., Set. Ed. by Alfred W. Johnston & Amy Johnston. (Viking Society for Northern Research: Old Lore Ser.). reprint ed. 82.50 (*0-404-60221-5*) AMS Pr.

***Orkney Days.** deluxe ed. Lucy Dougall. Tr. by Dixie Peaslee. LC 00-610. (Illus.). 45p. 2000. pap. 12.95 (*0-9660092-8-2*) Puget Sound.

Orkney Eighty Years Ago: With Special Attention to Evie. James Omond. LC 77-87683. reprint ed. 27.50 (*0-404-16479-X*) AMS Pr.

Orkney from Old Photographs. Gordon Wright. 144p. (C). 1989. 60.00 (*0-903065-36-3*, Pub. by G Wright Pub) St Mut.

Orkney Norn. Hugh Marwick. LC 78-72635. (Celtic Language & Literature Ser.: Goidelic & Brythonic). reprint ed. 27.50 (*0-404-17568-6*) AMS Pr.

Orkneyinga Saga. Joseph Anderson. 368p. (C). 1989. 44.00 (*0-901824-25-9*, Pub. by Mercat Pr Bks) St Mut.

Orkneyinga Saga: The History of the Earls of Orkney. Hermann Palsson. (Classics Ser.). 250p. 1981. pap. 13.95 (*0-14-044383-5*, Penguin Classics) Viking Penguin.

Orkneyinga Saga & Magnus Saga see Icelandic Sagas, & Other Historical Documents on the British Isles

Orkneyingers' Saga (Translation) see Icelandic Sagas, & Other Historical Documents on the British Isles

***Orkneymen in Canada.** John Murray Gibbon. 13p. 2000. pap. 4.00 (*1-886560-80-3*) Quintin Pub RI.

Orla. Bridget Brian. 112p. 1984. 40.00 (*0-7212-0641-7*, Pub. by Regency Pr GBR) St Mut.

***Orlan: Millennial Female.** Kate Ince. (Dress, Body, Culture Ser.). (Illus.). 256p. 2000. 65.00 (*1-85973-334-4*, Pub. by Berg Pubs); pap. 19.50 (*1-85973-339-5*, Pub. by Berg Pubs) NYU Pr.

Orlan: This Is My Body . . . This Is My Software . . . Orlan. (ENG & FRE., Illus.). 80p. 1996. pap. 39.95 incl. cd-rom (*0-9521773-6-6*, Pub. by Art Bks Intl) Partners Pubs Grp.

Orlanda. Jacqueline Harpman. Tr. by Ross Schwartz from FRE. LC 99-41328. 224p. 1999. text 24.95 (*1-58322-011-9*, Pub. by Seven Stories) Publishers Group.

Orlande de Lassus: Chansons 107-145. Ed. by Jane A. Bernstein. LC 87-750544. (Sixteenth-Century Chanson Ser.: Vol. 14). 202p. 1988. text 30.00 (*0-8240-3113-X*) Garland.

Orlande de Lassus: Chansons 34-71. Ed. by Jane A. Bernstein. LC 87-750544. (Sixteenth-Century Chanson Ser.: Vol. 11). 208p. 1987. text 30.00 (*0-8240-3110-5*) Garland.

Orlande de Lassus: Chansons 34-71. Ed. by Jane A. Bernstein. LC 87-750544. (Sixteenth-Century Chanson Ser.: Vol. 12). 208p. 1988. text 30.00 (*0-8240-3111-3*) Garland.

Orlando see Winter Simulation Conference Proceedings

Orlando. Roger St. Pierre. LC 94-74969. (Illustrated Travel Guides from Thomas Cook Ser.). (Illus.). 192p. 1995. pap. text 12.95 (*0-8442-9094-7*, Passprt Bks) NTC Contemp Pub Co.

Orlando. Tripbuilder, Inc. Staff. 1998. pap. text 5.95 (*1-56621-525-0*) TripBuilder.

Orlando. Virginia Woolf. 284p. 1995. 24.95 (*1-85695-317-3*, Pub. by ISIS Lrg Prnt) Transaction Pubs.

Orlando. Virginia Woolf. Ed. by Rachel Bowlby. (World's Classics Ser.). (Illus.). 400p. 1992. pap. write for info. (*0-19-281825-2*) OUP.

Orlando. Virginia Woolf. LC 73-5729. (Illus.). 336p. 1973. reprint ed. pap. 12.00 (*0-15-670160-X*, Harvest Bks) Harcourt.

Orlando. 2nd ed. (Passport's Illustrated Travel Guides Ser.). (Illus.). 192p. 1998. pap. 14.95 (*0-8442-4822-3*, 48223, Passprt Bks) NTC Contemp Pub Co.

***Orlando: A Trip Abroad.** Kathleen Hale. 32p. (YA). (gr. k up). 1999. text (*0-7232-4456-1*) F Warne Pubs.

Orlando: The City Beautiful. Glenda E. Hood & Donna Jones. LC 97-35678. (Urban Tapestry Ser.). (Illus.). 368p. 1997. 44.95 (*1-881096-46-7*) Towery Pub.

Orlando & Central Florida. (Landmark Visitors Guide Ser.). (Illus.). 256p. (Orig.). 1999. pap. 15.95 (*1-901522-22-9*) Hunter NJ.

Orlando & Central Florida. 5th ed. Access Press Staff. (Access Guides Ser.). 224p. 1999. pap. 19.00 (*0-06-277282-1*, HarpRes) HarpInfo.

Orlando & Central Florida: Including Disney World, the Space Coast, Tampa & Daytona. Jim Tunstall. (Adventure Guide). 296p. 1998. pap. text 15.95 (*1-55650-825-5*) Hunter NJ.

Orlando & Central Florida Street Guide. Kelly King. 230p. (Orig.). 1988. pap. 14.95 (*0-943983-02-9*) Natl Direct.

Orlando & Disney World. NTC Publishing Group Staff. (Passport Essential Guide Ser.). 128p. 1998. pap. 8.95 (*0-8442-0135-9*, 01359, Passprt Bks) NTC Contemp Pub Co.

***Orlando & Southern Florida.** 208p. 2000. spiral bd. 16.95 (*1-56251-331-1*, Pub. by AAA) S&S Trade.

Orlando Area Street Atlas: Covering Alta Monte Springs, Kissimmee, St. Cloud & Walt Disney World. (Illus.). 130p. 1996. pap. 29.95 (*1-877651-73-7*) Trakker Maps.

Orlando Cepeda: The Baby Bull. Rich Keller. Ed. by Laura Thorpe. 28p. (Orig.). 1987. pap. write for info. (*0-942627-03-2*) Woodford Pubng.

Orlando Chefs Book. William Struns. Ed. by R. McMinn. 120p. (Orig.). 1989. pap. text 6.95 (*0-935201-92-0*) Affordable Adven.

Orlando De Lassus, 72-106, Vol. 13. Jane A. Berstein. LC 87-750544. (Sixteenth-Century Chanson Ser.). 210p. 1988. text 30.00 (*0-8240-3112-1*) Garland.

Orlando Di Lasso: Complete Motets 17: Motets from Printed Anthologies & Manuscripts, 1555-69. (Recent Researches in the Music of the Renaissance Ser.: Vol. RRR115). (Illus.). xxxii, 183p. 1999. pap. 75.00 (*0-89579-416-0*) A-R Eds.

Orlando Di Lasso: Seven Penitential Psalms with Two Laudate Psalms; An Edition of Munich, Bayerische Staatsbibliothek. Ed. by Charlotte Smith. LC 82-49091. 296p. 1983. 45.00 (*0-87413-238-X*) U Delaware Pr.

Orlando Di Lasso: The Complete Motets I: Il Primo Libro de Mottetti a Cinque et a Sei Voici (Antwerp, 1556) Orlando Di Lasso. Ed. by James Erb. (Recent Researches in Music of the Renaissance Ser.: No. RRR114). (Illus.). xxxv, 116p. 1998. pap. 55.00 (*0-89579-415-2*) A-R Eds.

Orlando di Lasso: The Complete Motets 10: The Four-Language Print for Four & Eight Voices (Munich, 1573) Orlando Di Lasso. Ed. by Peter Bergquist et al. (Recent Researches in Music of the Renaissance Ser.: Vol. RRR102). (Illus.). xxiv, 125p. 1995. pap. 50.00 (*0-89579-323-7*) A-R Eds.

Orlando Di Lasso: The Complete Motets 14. Orlando Di Lasso. Ed. by David Crook & Peter Bergquist. (Recent Researches in Music of the Renaissance Ser.: Vol. RRR111). (Illus.). xxiii, 120p. 1997. pap. 50.00 (*0-89579-392-X*) A-R Eds.

Orlando di Lasso: The Complete Motets 7. Orlando Di Lasso. Ed. by Peter Bergquist. (Recent Researches in Music of the Renaissance Ser.: Vol. RRR112). (Illus.). xxxii, 219p. 1998. pap. 85.00 (*0-89579-410-1*) A-R Eds.

***Orlando di Lasso: The Complete Motets 9, Patrocinium Musices Prima Parts (Munich 1573)** Orlando Di Lasso. Ed. by Peter Bergquist. (Recent Researches in the Music of the Renaissance Ser.: Vol. R120). (Illus.). xxviii, 189p. 2000. pap. 55.00 (*0-89579-455-1*) A-R Eds.

Orlando Di Lasso: The Seven Penitential Psalms & Laudate Dominum de Caelis. Orlando Di Lasso. Ed. by Peter Bergquist. (Recent Researches in Music of the Renaissance Ser.: Vols. RRR86-87). (Illus.). xxviii, 200p. 1990. pap. 70.00 (*0-89579-247-8*) A-R Eds.

Orlando Di Lasso: Two Motet Cycles for Matins for the Dead. Orlando Di Lasso. Ed. by Peter Bergquist. (Recent Researches in Music of the Renaissance Ser.: No. RRR55). (Illus.). 110, xxip. 1983. pap. 45.00 (*0-89579-164-1*) A-R Eds.

***Orlando di Lasso - The Complete Motets 8: Moduli Quinis Vocibus Nunquam Hactenus Editi (Paris, 1571)** Orlando Di Lasso. Ed. by Peter Bergquist. (Recent Researches in Music of the Renaissance Ser.: Vol. RRR118). (Illus.). xxiv, 140p. 1999. pap. 55.00 (*0-89579-442-X*) A-R Eds.

***Orlando di Lasso - The Complete Motets 15: Cantica Sacra Sex et Octo Vocibus (Munich, 1585)** Orlando Di Lasso. Ed. by David Crook. (Recent Researches in the Music of the Renaissance Ser.: Vol. RRR117). (Illus.). xxii, 138p. 1999. pap. 55.00 (*0-89579-440-3*) A-R Eds.

Orlando di Lasso - The Complete Motets 11: Liber Motte Tarum Trium Vocum (Munich, 1575); Novae Aliquot, Ad Duas Voces Cantiones (Munich, 1577) Orlando Di Lasso. Ed. by Peter Bergquist et al. (Recent Reserches in Music of the Renaissance Ser.: Vol. RRR103). (Illus.). xx, 119p. 1995. pap. 50.00 (*0-89579-327-X*) A-R Eds.

Orlando di Lasso - The Complete Motets 5: Motets for Quinque et Sex Vocibus Peronatae Sacrae Cantiones (Venice, 1565); Motets for Five to Eight Voices from Sacrae Cantiones, Liber Secundus, Tertius, Quartus (Venice, 1566) Orlando Di Lasso. Ed. by Peter Bergquist et al. (Recent Researches in Music of the Renaissance Ser.: Vol. RRR109). (Illus.). xxix, 306p. 1997. pap. 105.00 (*0-89579-385-7*) A-R Eds.

Orlando di Lasso - The Complete Motets 6: Motets for Four to Eight Voices from Selectissimae Cantiones (Nuremberg, 1568) Orlando Di Lasso. Ed. by Peter Bergquist et al. (Recent Researches in Music of the Renaissance Ser.: Vol. RRR110). (Illus.). xxxvii, 206p. 1997. pap. 80.00 (*0-89579-389-X*) A-R Eds.

Orlando di Lasso & Others: Canzoni Villanesche & Villanelle. Orlando Di Lasso et al. Ed. by Donna C. Jackson. (Recent Researches in Music of the Renaissance Ser.: Vol. RRR82-83). (Illus.). lviii, 149p. 1991. pap. 65.00 (*0-89579-245-1*, RRR82-83) A-R Eds.

Orlando di Lasso Studies. Ed. by Peter Bergquist. LC 98-11734. (Genres in American Cinema Ser.). (Illus.). 275p. (C). 1999. text 64.95 (*0-521-59387-5*) Cambridge U Pr.

Orlando di Lasso: The Complete Motets 4: Motets for Six Voices from Primus Liber Concentuum Sacrorum (Paris, 1564); Motets for Four to Ten Voices from Modulorum Secundum Volumen (Paris, 1565) Orlando Di Lasso. Ed. by Peter Bergquist et al. (Recent Researches in Music of the Renaissance Ser.: Vol. RRR105). (Illus.). xxiv, 224p. 1996. pap. 75.00 (*0-89579-335-0*) A-R Eds.

Orlando di Lasso's Imitation Magnificats for Counter-Reformation Munich. David Crook. LC 93-33537. 312p. 1994. text 57.50 (*0-691-03614-4*, Pub. by Princeton U Pr) Cal Prin Full Svc.

***Orlando Entertainment, 2000.** (Illus.). 630p. 1999. pap. 35.00 (*1-58553-047-6*, 00P7) Enter Pubns.

***Orlando, Florida.** Rand McNally Staff. 1999. pap. text 19.95 (*0-528-97875-6*) Rand McNally.

Orlando, Florida: A Pictorial Guide to Florida's Magical City. (Illus.). 32p. Date not set. pap. text. write for info. (*1-56944-147-2*) Terrell Missouri.

***Orlando for Less Compact Guide.** (For Less Compact Guides Ser.). (Illus.). 72p. 1999. pap. 9.95 (*1-901811-46-8*, Pub. by Metropolis International) IPG Chicago.

Orlando Furioso. Ludovico Ariosto. Tr. & Intro. by Guido Waldman. (Oxford World's Classics Ser.). 656p. 1999. pap. 16.95 (*0-19-283677-3*) OUP.

Orlando Furioso: A Stoic Comedy. Clare Carroll. LC 97-11628. (Medieval & Renaissance Texts & Studies: Vo. 174). 256p. 1997. 26.00 (*0-86698-215-9*, MR174) MRTS.

Orlando Furioso: An English Translation with Introductions, Notes & Index by Allan Gilbert, 2 vols. Ludovico Ariosto. (C). 1954. 45.00 (*0-913298-31-X*) S F Vanni.

Orlando Furioso: The Frenzy of Orlando: A Romantic Epic, Vol. 1. Ludovico Ariosto. Tr. & Intro. by Barbara Reynolds. (Classics Ser.). 832p. 1975. pap. 16.95 (*0-14-044311-8*, Penguin Classics) Viking Penguin.

Orlando Furioso in English Heroical Verse. Ludovico Ariosto. Tr. by John Harrington. LC 77-25638. (English Experience Ser.: No. 259). (Illus.). 424p. 1970. reprint ed. 75.00 (*90-221-0259-9*) Walter J Johnson.

Orlando Gibbons see Tudor Church Music

***Orlando Gibbons & the Gibbons Family of Musicians.** John Harley. LC 99-31935. (Illus.). 340p. 1999. text 78.95 (*1-84014-209-X*, Pub. by Ashgate Pub) Ashgate Pub Co.

***Orlando Group & Friends: A Collection of Writings & Art.** Ed. by Christine Blackwell et al. (Illus.). 2000. write for info. (*0-9621385-2-5*) Arbiter Pr.

Orlando Innamorato. Matteo M. Boiardo. Tr. & Intro. by Charles S. Ross. (World's Classics Ser.). (Illus.). 454p. 1995. pap. 13.95 (*0-19-282438-4*) OUP.

Orlando Legend in Nineteenth Century French Literature. Dana A. Kress. (Age of Revolution & Romanticism Ser.: Vol. 10). XI, 173p. (C). 1996. text 43.95 (*0-8204-2617-2*) P Lang Pubng.

Orlando Like a Pro. 3rd ed. Ed. by Robert Fisher. 1999. 12.00 (*0-679-00450-5*) Fodors Travel.

Orlando Magic see Pro Basketball Today

Orlando Magic. Paul Joseph. LC 97-19598. (Inside the NBA Ser.). (Illus.). 32p. (J). (gr. 3-8). 1997. lib. bdg. 16.95 (*1-56239-768-0*) ABDO Pub Co.

***Orlando Metro Business Directory, 1999-2000.** rev. ed. American Business Directories Staff. 3328p. 1999. boxed set 495.00 incl. cd-rom (*0-7687-0197-X*) Am Busn Direct.

Orlando's Littlewhile Friends. Audrey Wood. LC 90-45723. (Illus.). 32p. (J). (ps-2). 1989. 13.99 (*0-85953-111-2*); pap. 6.99 (*0-85953-106-6*) Childs Play.

Orlando's Littlewhile Friends. Audrey Wood. (J). 1996. lib. bdg. 15.95 (*0-85953-847-8*) Childs Play.

Orlando's Other Theme Parks: What to Do When You've Done Disney. 2nd rev. ed. Kelly Monaghan. LC 98-72666. (Illus.). 480p. 1998. pap. 16.95 (*1-887140-09-3*, Pub. by Intrepid Trvlr) Natl Bk Netwk.

Orlando's Sleep: An Autobiography of Gender. Jennifer Spry. LC 96-45119. (Illus.). 200p. (Orig.). 1997. pap. 12.95 (*0-934678-80-4*) New Victoria Pubs.

Orleanais ont la Parole. P. Biggs & C. Dalwood. (Illus.). 1977. teacher ed. 7.95 (*0-582-33122-6*); pap. text 8.95 (*0-582-33121-8*); audio 14.00 (*0-582-37885-0*) Longman.

Orleans City Plan. (Grafocarte Maps Ser.). 1995. 8.95 (*2-7416-0031-7*, 80031) Michelin.

Orleans Digest of Laws (with Moreau Lislet Notes) Vergne De Le. 1971. 45.00 (*0-87511-022-3*) Claitors.

Orleans Gallery: The Founders. Historic New Orleans Collection Staff. (Illus.). 48p. (Orig.). 1982. pap. 10.00 (*0-917860-10-1*) Historic New Orleans.

Orley Farm. Anthony Trollope. Ed. by David Skilton. (World's Classics Ser.). 860p. 1985. pap. 9.95 (*0-19-281713-2*) OUP.

Orley Farm. Anthony Trollope. 450p. 2000. pap. 10.95 (*0-19-283856-3*) OUP.

Orley Farm. Anthony Trollope. (Illus.). 736p. 1981. reprint ed. pap. 11.95 (*0-486-24181-5*) Dover.

Orley Farm: (trollope 1993) Skilton. 1993. 48.00 (*1-870587-27-8*) Ashgate Pub Co.

Orlicky's Material Requirements Planning. 2nd ed. George W. Plossl. LC 93-41951. 311p. 1993. 49.00 (*0-07-050459-8*) McGraw.

Orlicz Spaces & Modular Spaces. J. Musielak. (Lecture Notes in Mathematics Ser.: Vol. 1034). 222p. 1983. 35.95 (*0-387-12706-2*) Spr-Verlag.

Orlif, the Friendly Giant. Ethel Kanganas & Margaret Sauer. (Illus.). 40p. (J). 1997. 19.95 (*1-875560-79-3*, Pub. by Univ of West Aust Pr) Intl Spec Bk.

***Orlo & Leini.** Rafael Alvarez. LC 99-87708. (Illus.). 176p. 2000. pap. 14.95 (*1-891521-07-1*) Woodholme Hse.

Orloff & His Wife: Tales of the Barefoot Brigade. 15th ed. Maxim Gorky. Tr. by Isabel F. Hapgood from RUS. LC 72-11934. (Short Story Index Reprint Ser.). 1977. reprint ed. 31.95 (*0-8369-4232-9*) Ayer.

Orloff (Chana) Catalogue Raisonne of the Sculptures. Felix Marcilhac. (FRE., Illus.). 256p. 1991. 150.00 (*1-55660-191-3*) A Wofsy Fine Arts.

Orlov Legacy. Robert Marcum. LC 96-873. 386p. (Orig.). 1996. pap. 13.95 (*1-57345-146-0*) Deseret Bk.

Orm. John Dashney. (J). 1998. 12.95 (*0-9641357-8-7*) Storm Peak.

Ormanville: Life on the Iowa Frontier, 1850-1900. Silvano A. Wueschner. (Illus.). 204p. (Orig.). 1993. 22.95 (*0-9636151-1-4*); pap. 12.95 (*0-9636151-0-6*) St Andrews IA.

Orme Alternatives Vol. I: The Archaeological Resources of Roosevelt Lake & Horseshoe Reservoir. Steven L. Fuller. (Archaeological Ser.: No. 98). (Illus.). 305p. 1976. pap. 9.95 (*1-889747-03-3*) Ariz St Mus.

Orme du Mail. Anatole France, pseud. (FRE.). 192p. 1965. pap. 10.95 (*0-7859-0055-1*, M11055) Fr & Eur.

Orme du Mail. Anatole France, pseud. 188p. 1986. pap. 11.95 (*0-7859-5629-8*, 2266017888) Fr & Eur.

Orme du Mail see Romans et Contes

Orme du Mail: Avec: Le Mannequin d'Osier. Anatole France, pseud. 360p. 1966. 9.95 (*0-686-55871-5*) Fr & Eur.

Ormee of Bordeaux: A Revolution During the Fronde. Sal A. Westrich. LC 79-166485. (Johns Hopkins University Studies in Historical & Political Science: Ser. 89, No. 2). 172p. reprint ed. pap. 53.40 (*0-608-14697-8*, 202584900046) Bks Demand.

Ormond. Charles Brockden Brown. Ed. by Mary Chapman. (Literary Texts Ser.). 400p. 1999. pap. 12.95 (*1-55111-091-1*) Broadview Pr.

***Ormond Beach.** Ormond Beach Historical Trust Staff. (Images of America Ser.). (Illus.). 128p. 2000. pap. 18.99 (*0-7385-0257-X*) Arcadia Publng.

***Ormond Beach: A Historic Tour in Picture Postcards.** Donald D. Spencer. LC 00-21199. 2000. write for info. (*0-89218-325-X*) Camelot Pub.

Ormond: or The Secret Witness. Charles Brockden Brown. (Works of Charles Brockden Brown). 1989. reprint ed. lib. bdg. 79.00 (*0-7812-2067-X*) Rprt Serv.

Ormond: or The Secret Witness: Bicentennial Edition. Charles Brockden Brown. LC 82-14904. (Novels & Related Works of Charles Brockden Brown Ser.: Vol. 2). 492p. 1982. reprint ed. pap. 152.60 (*0-608-07346-6*, 206757400009) Bks Demand.

Ormsbee Odyssey. Nora Coppage. 350p. 1990. 38.00 (*0-317-02848-0*); 32.50 (*0-317-02849-9*) A M Coppage.

Ormulum, with the Notes & Glossary of Dr. Robert Meadows White, 2 vols. Ormulum. Ed. by Robert Holt. LC 72-178548. reprint ed. 85.00 (*0-404-56654-5*) AMS Pr.

Orn. Piers Anthony. 1978. pap. 3.95 (*0-380-00266-3*, Avon Bks) Morrow Avon.

Ornament see Geometric Design & Ornament

Ornament: A Social History since 1450. Michael Snodin & Maurice Howard. LC 95-39597. 232p. 1996. 50.00 (*0-300-06455-1*) Yale U Pr.

Ornament - Eight Thousand Years: An Illustrated Handbook of Motifs. Eva Wilson. LC 93-48252. (Illus.). 320p. 1994. 39.95 (*0-8109-3260-1*, Pub. by Abrams) Time Warner.

Ornament & Amulet: Rings of the Islamic Lands. Marian Wenzel. (Nassar D. Khalili Collection of Islamic Art: Vol. XVI). (Illus.). 304p. 1993. text 260.00 (*0-19-727614-8*) OUP.

Ornament & Architecture: Renaissance Drawings, Prints, & Books. Brown University, Department of Art Staff. (Illus.). 175p. (Orig.). 1980. pap. 20.00 (*0-933519-05-2*) D W Bell Gallery.

Ornament & Crime: Selected Essays. Adolf Loos. Tr. by Michael Mitchell. (Studies in Austrian Literature, Culture, & Thought). 204p. 1998. pap. 19.95 (*1-57241-046-9*) Ariadne CA.

Ornament & Object: Canadian Jewellery & Metal Art, 1946-1996. Anne Barros. LC 98-118747. 176p. 1997. 28.00 (*1-55046-218-0*, Pub. by Boston Mills) Genl Dist Srvs.

Ornament & Silence: Essays on Women's Lives. Kennedy Fraser. 272p. 1998. pap. 13.00 (*0-375-70112-5*) Vin Bks.

Ornament, Fantasy, & Desire in Nineteenth-Century French Literature. Rae B. Gordon. (Illus.). 288p. 1992. text 45.00 (*0-691-06927-1*, Pub. by Princeton U Pr) Cal Prin Full Svc.

Ornament in European Folk Art. R. Peesch. (Illus.). 210p. (C). 1982. text 303.00 (*0-7855-5872-1*, Pub. by Collets) St Mut.

Ornament in European Folk Art. R. Peesch. (Illus.). 210p. (C). 1988. 300.00 (*0-569-19823-2*, Pub. by Collets) St Mut.

Ornament in Indian Architecture. Margaret P. Allen. LC 89-40766. (Illus.). 504p. 1992. 65.00 (*0-87413-399-8*) U Delaware Pr.

Ornament to His Profession. Ed. by Priscilla Olson. (NESFA's Choice Ser.). 537p. 1998. 25.00 (*1-886778-09-4*) New Eng SF Assoc.

Ornament to the City: Historic Architecture in Downtown Fairmont. Debra B. McMillan. LC 96-78848. (Illus.). 304p. 1996. 34.90 (*0-929915-18-6*) Headline Bks.

Ornament Tree. Jean Thesman. LC 95-17102. 240p. (J). (gr. 5-9). 1996. 16.00 (*0-395-74278-1*) HM.

Ornament Tree. Jean Thesman. LC 95-17102. 176p. (YA). (gr. 7-12). 1998. mass mkt. 4.50 (*0-380-72912-1*, Avon Bks) Morrow Avon.

Ornament Tree. Jean Thesman. 1998. 9.60 (*0-606-13682-7*, Pub. by Turtleback) Demco.

An Asterisk (*) at the beginning of an entry indicates that the title is appearing for the first time.

***Ornamental.** (Ironworking Lev 3 Ser.). 2000. teacher ed., ring bd. 12.00 (*0-13-031252-5*) P-H.

Ornamental Bedding Plants. Allan M. Armitage. (CAB International Publication Ser.: 4). 186p. 1994. pap. text 40.00 (*0-85198-901-2*) OUP.

Ornamental Borders, Scrolls & Cartouches for Artists & Craftspeople. Syracuse Ornamental Company Staff. (Pictorial Archive Ser.). (Illus.). 128p. 1987. reprint ed. pap. 8.95 (*0-486-25489-5*) Dover.

Ornamental Branches: Needlework Arts from Lititz Moravian Girls' School Between 1800 & 1965. Patricia T. Herr. 1996. pap. 20.00 (*0-89865-968-X*) Donning Co.

Ornamental Bulbs, Corms & Tubers. A. R. Rees. (Crop Production Science in Horticulture Ser.: No. 1). (Illus.). 220p. 1992. pap. text 40.00 (*0-85198-656-0*) OUP.

Ornamental Calligraphy. George J. Becker. LC 93-2454. (Illus.). 64p. 1993. reprint ed. pap. text 5.95 (*0-486-27678-3*) Dover.

Ornamental Carpentry of Nineteenth-Century American Houses: One Hundred Sixty-Five Photographs. rev. ed. Ben Karp. Orig. Title: Wood Motifs in American Domestic Architecture. (Illus.). 144p. 1981. reprint ed. pap. 9.95 (*0-486-24144-0*) Dover.

Ornamental Cartouches. Johann U. Krauss. (Design Library). (Illus.). 48p. (Orig.). 1988. pap. 4.95 (*0-486-25665-0*) Dover.

Ornamental Coffers: Eight Centuries of European Craftsmanship. Ewald Berger. 1999. 110.00 (*3-925369-83-X*) Arnoldsche Art Pubs.

Ornamental Conifers for Australian Gardens. Raymond J. Rowell. (Illus.). 320p. 1996. 44.95 (*0-86840-239-7*, Pub. by New South Wales Univ Pr) Intl Spec Bk.

Ornamental Designs. Jacob Broschart. (Illus.). 96p. 1992. pap. 9.95 (*0-486-27039-4*) Dover.

Ornamental Designs & Illustrations. 4th ed. John M. Bergling. LC 63-22578. 1992. 24.95 (*0-910222-05-3*) Gem City Coll.

***Ornamental Designs & Illustrations: 100th Anniversary Collector's Edition.** 5th deluxe ed. J. M. Bergling & C. M. Bergling. LC 99-76682. (Encyclopedias of Technical Art Bks.: Vol. III). (Illus.). 110p. 2000. text 64.95 (*0-9677808-3-7*) Bergling Prodns.

Ornamental Flower Stained Glass Pattern Book: 83 Designs for Workable Projects. Ed Sibbett, Jr. (Illus.). 64p. 1984. pap. 6.95 (*0-486-24738-4*) Dover.

Ornamental Flowering Shrubs in Australia. Raymond J. Rowell. (Illus.). 334p. 1991. 37.95 (*0-86840-084-X*, Pub. by New South Wales Univ Pr) Intl Spec Bk.

Ornamental Flowering Trees in Australia. Raymond J. Rowell. (Illus.). 321p. 1991. 37.95 (*0-86840-124-2*, Pub. by New South Wales Univ Pr) Intl Spec Bk.

Ornamental French Hardware Designs. Selected by Carol B. Grafton. LC 95-40826. (Pictorial Archive Ser.). 128p. 1995. pap. 8.95 (*0-486-28851-X*) Dover.

Ornamental Gardener: Creative Ideas for Every Gardener. Miranda Innes. (Illus.). 160p. 1992. 35.00 (*0-88045-123-8*) Stemmer Hse.

Ornamental Grass Gardening see Ornamental Grasses: Design Ideas, Uses, & Varieties

Ornamental Grasses. (Taylor's Weekend Gardening Guide Ser.). 1997. pap. 19.95 (*0-614-27238-6*) HM.

Ornamental Grasses. Rick Drake. 72p. 1996. pap. text 12.95 (*1-56799-323-0*, Friedman-Fairfax) M Friedman Pub Grp Inc.

Ornamental Grasses, No. 117. Ed. by Peter H. Loewer. (Plants & Gardens Ser.). (Illus.). 104p. 1989. pap. 7.95 (*0-945352-48-4*) Bklyn Botanic.

Ornamental Grasses: Design Ideas, Uses, & Varieties. Thomas A. Reinhardt et al. LC 95-13522. Orig. Title: Ornamental Grass Gardening. (Illus.). 128p. 1995. pap. 14.95 (*1-56799-219-6*, Friedman-Fairfax) M Friedman Pub Grp Inc.

Ornamental Grasses: The Amber Wave. 2nd ed. Carole Ottesen. 288p. 1995. pap. 24.95 (*0-07-048021-4*) McGraw.

Ornamental Grasses & Design Ideas. Storey Publishing Staff. 1997. pap. 14.95 (*0-676-57048-8*) Random.

Ornamental Grasses & Grasslike Plants. A. J. Oakes. LC 92-42440. 624p. (C). 1993. reprint ed. lib. bdg. 79.50 (*0-89464-826-8*) Krieger.

Ornamental Horticulture. Jack Rudman. (Occupational Competency Examination (OCE) Ser.: Vol. 28). 47.95 (*0-8373-5778-0*) Nat Learn.

Ornamental Horticulture. Jack Rudman. (Occupational Competency Examination Ser.: OCE-28). 1994. pap. 27.95 (*0-8373-5728-4*) Nat Learn.

Ornamental Horticulture. 3rd ed. Ingels. 2000. pap. 49.50 (*0-7668-1417-3*) Delmar.

Ornamental Horticulture: Principles & Practices. Jack E. Ingels. LC 84-26010. 550p. (C). 1985. text 44.50 (*0-8273-1943-6*) Delmar.

Ornamental Horticulture: Principles & Practices. Jack E. Ingels. LC 84-26010. 550p. (C). 1985. teacher ed. 12.00 (*0-8273-1944-4*) Delmar.

Ornamental Horticulture: Science, Operations & Management. 2nd ed. Jack E. Ingels. LC 93-28344. (C). 1994. pap. 49.00 (*0-8273-6364-8*) Delmar.

Ornamental Horticulture: Science, Operations & Management. 2nd ed. Jack E. Ingels. 29p. 1994. teacher ed. 12.75 (*0-8273-6365-6*) Delmar.

Ornamental Horticulture As a Vocation. 2nd ed. Stanley B. Moore. (Illus.). (J). 1988. text 11.95 (*0-912178-01-9*) Mor-Mac.

Ornamental Horticulture in India. G. S. Randhawa. (Illus.). 144p. 1973. 8.00 (*1-55528-089-7*, Pub. by Today Tomorrow) Scholarly Pubns.

Ornamental Horticulture Review CTB. Hobar Staff. (Agriculture Ser.). 1993. 59.95 (*1-55797-548-5*, VNR) Wiley.

Ornamental Ironwork. A. Durenne. LC 98-167579. (Illus.). 128p. 1998. pap. 10.95 (*0-486-29811-6*) Dover.

Ornamental Ironwork. Susan Southwork. 224p. 1992. pap. 39.95 (*0-07-059804-5*) McGraw.

Ornamental Ironwork: Two Centuries of Craftsmanship in Albany & Troy, New York. Diana S. Waite. LC 90-60011. (Illus.). 140p. (Orig.). 1990. pap. 24.95 (*0-9625368-0-6*) Mount Ida Pr.

Ornamental Kitchen Garden. Geoff Hamilton. (Illus.). 254p. 1996. pap. 21.95 (*0-563-36763-6*, BBC-Parkwest) Parkwest Pubns.

Ornamental Kitchen Garden. George Hamilton. (Illus.). 1996. 28.95 (*0-563-36017-8*, BBC-Parkwest) Parkwest Pubns.

Ornamental Landscape Grasses. Steven M. Still. Ed. by Muriel N. King. (Ornamental Landscape Grasses - Slide Ser.). (Illus.). 92p. 1994. pap. text 17.95 (*1-56502-005-7*, 2129N) Ohio Agri Educ.

Ornamental Metal Casting. 1996. lib. bdg. 250.75 (*0-8490-8349-4*) Gordon Pr.

Ornamental Metal Casting. R. E. Whitmoyer. 1986. pap. 9.95 (*0-917914-43-0*) Lindsay Pubns.

***Ornamental Palm Horticulture.** Timothy K. Broschat & Alan W. Meerow. LC 00-36403. 2000. write for info. (*0-8130-1804-8*) U Press Fla.

Ornamental Pen Designs & Flourishes. Carol Grafton. LC 96-25993. (Dover Pictorial Archives Ser.). 48p. 1996. pap. 5.95 (*0-486-29388-2*) Dover.

Ornamental Penmanship. William Milns & William Tomkins. (Illus.). 75p. 1983. pap. 7.95 (*0-486-24449-0*) Dover.

Ornamental Plants for Subtropical Regions: A Handbook for Reference. Roland S. Hoyt. (Illus.). 485p. 1999. text. write for info. (*0-9601746-1-3*) Livngston Pr.

Ornamental Plants in Australia. 4th ed. Raymond J. Rowell. (Illus.). 244p. 1992. 37.95 (*0-86840-372-5*, Pub. by New South Wales Univ Pr) Intl Spec Bk.

Ornamental Shrubs, Climbers & Bamboos. Graham S. Thomas. 544p. 1992. 49.95 (*0-88192-250-1*) Timber.

Ornamental Turning. T. D. Walshaw. (Illus.). 208p. 1990. pap. 26.50 (*1-85486-108-5*, Pub. by Nexus Special Interests) Trans-Atl Phila.

Ornamental Turning. John H. Evans. (Illus.). 344p. 1993. reprint ed. pap. 22.50 (*1-879335-35-2*) Astragal Pr.

Ornamental Vegetable Garden. Diana Anthony. (Illus.). 120p. 1999. pap. 19.95 (*1-894020-55-3*) Warwick Publ.

Ornamental Water Gardening: How & What to Grow. John Mirgon et al. Ed. by Gayle Weinstein. (Illus.). 33p. (Orig.). 1991. pap. 7.95 (*0-9629743-0-7*) Shereth Grp.

Ornamental Waterfowl. H. Kolbe. 262p. 1980. 45.00 (*0-905418-49-2*, Pub. by Gresham Bks) St Mut.

Ornamental Woodcarving in the Norwegian Tradition. Johan Amrud. 105p. (C). 1995. 35.00 (*82-00-41978-9*, Pub. by Scand Univ Pr) IBD Ltd.

Ornamentation: A Question & Answer Manual. Lloyd-Watts Valery et al. LC 94-76938. 64p. (C). 1995. pap. text 8.95 (*0-88284-549-7*, 6000) Alfred Pub.

Ornamentation & Illustrations from the Kelmscott Chaucer. William Morris. 128p. 1973. pap. 8.95 (*0-486-22970-X*) Dover.

Ornamentation & Improvisation in Mozart. Frederick Neumann. LC 90-31538. 316p. 1986. reprint ed. pap. 98.00 (*0-608-07638-4*, 205995400010) Bks Demand.

Ornamentation in Baroque & Post-Baroque Music. Frederick Neumann. LC 77-72130. (Illus.). 630p. 1978. pap. text 45.00 (*0-691-02707-2*, Pub. by Princeton U Pr) Cal Prin Full Svc.

Ornamented Bags for Tallit & Tefillin of the Judah L - Magnes Museum: Catalog of the Collection. Ruth Eis. Ed. by Nelda Cassuto. LC 83-83059. (Magnes Museum Collection Ser.). 99p. (Orig.). 1984. pap. text 22.50 (*0-943376-20-3*) Magnes Mus.

Ornamented Jewish Oil-Lamps from the Destruction of the 2nd Temple Through Bar-Kakhba. Sussman. 1983. pap. 60.00 (*0-85668-164-4*, Pub. by Aris & Phillips) David Brown.

***Ornaments: Creating Handmade Tree Decorations.** Carol Endler Sterbenz. LC 00-38959. 2000. 19.95 (*0-7407-1023-0*) Andrews & McMeel.

Ornaments: Lace, Fans, Gloves, Walking-Sticks, Parasols, Jewelry, & Trinkets. Modes & Manners Supplement. Max Von Boehn. LC 70-148467. (Illus.). 293p. 1972. reprint ed. 30.95 (*0-405-08286-X*, Pub. by Blom Pubns) Ayer.

Ornaments: Twelve Tales of Christmas. Karen Engelmann. LC 98-19564. (Illus.). 72p. 1998. 12.98 (*0-7651-0869-0*) Smithmark.

Ornaments & Evergreens, Vol. 1, No. 2. unabridged ed. Ed. by Lard M. Wegeng & Jenn Wilson. 65p. 1997. pap. 9.95 (*0-9659454-3-X*) Columbia Pubns.

Ornaments for the Daughters of Zion. Cotton Mather. LC 78-8588. 128p. 1978. 50.00 (*0-8201-1311-5*) Schol Facsimiles.

Ornaments in Classical & Modern Music. Clarence G. Hamilton. reprint ed. 27.50 (*0-404-12947-1*) AMS Pr.

Ornaments in Jade. Arthur Machen. 54p. 1997. 29.95 (*1-872621-24-4*, Pub. by Tartarus Pr) Firebird Dist.

Ornaments of Christmas. Ed. by Bill Thompson. LC 89-64421. 60p. 1990. pap. text 9.95 (*0-916809-43-9*) Scott Pubns MI.

Ornaments of Fire: The World's Best 101 Short Poems & Fragments. Ed. by Edd Wheeler. LC 93-26419. (Illus.). 136p. (Orig.). 1994. pap. 9.95 (*1-56474-071-4*) Fithian Pr.

Ornaments of Orissa. Ramesh Prasad Mohapatra. Ed. by Thomas Donaldson. LC 98-908308. 1998. 148.00 (*81-7646-031-1*, Pub. by BR Pub) S Asia.

Ornamentum. Veronica Biermann & Leon Battista Alberti. (Studien Zur Kunstgeschichte Ser.: Band 111). (GER.). 232p. 1997. 60.00 (*3-487-10260-9*) G Olms Pubs.

Ornate Pictorial Calligraphy: Instructions & over 150 Examples. E. A. Lupfer. (Lettering, Calligraphy, Typography Ser.). (Illus.). 80p. 1982. pap. 4.95 (*0-486-21957-7*) Dover.

Ornate with Smoke. Sterling Plumpp. LC 97-22954. 1997. write for info. (*0-88378-193-X*); pap. 12.95 (*0-88378-198-0*) Third World.

Ornery Bunch: Tales & Anecdotes Collected by the WPA Montana Writers Project. Writers Program of the Work Project Staff. LC 99-26427. 1999. pap. 14.95 (*1-56044-842-3*, Two Dot) Falcon Pub Inc.

Ornette Coleman: His Life & Music. Peter N. Wilson. Tr. by Robert Dobbin from GER. LC 99-21581.Tr. of Ornette Coleman: Sein Leben, Seine Musik, Seine Schallplatten. (Illus.). 216p. 1999. pap. 15.95 (*1-893163-04-0*) Berkeley Hills.

Ornette Coleman: Sein Leben, Seine Musik, Seine Schallplatten see Ornette Coleman: His Life & Music

Orniflle Ou le Courant d'Air see Pieces Grincantes

Orniflle Ou le Courant d'Air. Jean Anouilh. (FRE.). 224p. 1974. pap. 10.95 (*0-7859-2206-7*, M2959) Fr & Eur.

Orniflle Ou le Courant d'Air. Jean Anouilh. (Folio Ser.: No. 545). (FRE.). 1974. pap. 8.95 (*2-07-036545-X*) Schoenhof.

Ornithischia. R. Steel. (Encyclopedia of Paleoherpetology Ser.: Pt. 15). (Illus.). 84p. 1969. pap. text 52.50 (*3-437-30028-8*) Lubrecht & Cramer.

Ornitholestes: A Dinosaur from the Jurassic Period see New Dinosaur Collection

Ornithological Bibliography. Compiled by Elliot Coues. 859p. 1995. reprint ed. 95.00 (*1-57898-023-2*) Martino Pubng.

Ornithological Books in the Yale University Library. S. Dillon Ripley & Lynette Scribner. (Illus.). 338p. 1993. reprint ed. 85.00 (*1-888262-61-3*) Martino Pubng.

Ornithological Gazetteer of Argentina. 2nd ed. Raymond A. Paynter, Jr. (Illus.). 1045p. 1995. pap. 68.00 (*0-910999-31-7*) Mus Comp Zoo.

Ornithological Gazetteer of Bolivia. 2nd ed. Raymond A. Paynter, Jr. (Illus.). vi, 187p. 1992. pap. 14.00 (*0-910999-28-7*) Mus Comp Zoo.

Ornithological Gazetteer of Brazil. Raymond A. Paynter, Jr. & Melvin A. Traylor, Jr. (Ornithological Gazetteers of the Neotropics Ser.). (Illus.). xiii, 789p. (Orig.). 1991. pap. 53.00 (*0-910999-27-9*) Mus Comp Zoo.

Ornithological Gazetteer of Chile. Raymond A. Paynter, Jr. (Illus.). v, 331p. 1988. pap. 22.00 (*0-910999-25-2*) Mus Comp Zoo.

Ornithological Gazetteer of Colombia. 2nd rev. ed. Raymond A. Paynter, Jr. (Ornithological Gazetteers of the Neotropics Ser.). (Illus.). 537p. 1997. pap. text 40.00 (*0-910999-32-5*) Mus Comp Zoo.

Ornithological Gazetteer of Ecuador. 2nd ed. Raymond A. Paynter, Jr. (Illus.). xi, 249p. 1993. pap. 20.00 (*0-910999-29-5*) Mus Comp Zoo.

Ornithological Gazetteer of Paraguay. 2nd ed. Raymond A. Paynter, Jr. (Illus.). iv, 61p. 1989. pap. 8.00 (*0-910999-26-0*) Mus Comp Zoo.

Ornithological Gazetteer of Peru. Lorain Stephens & Melvin A. Traylor, Jr. (Illus.). vi, 273p. 1983. pap. 20.00 (*0-910999-22-8*) Mus Comp Zoo.

Ornithological Gazetteer of the Guianas. Lorain Stephens & Melvin A. Traylor, Jr. v, 123p. 1985. pap. 12.00 (*0-910999-24-4*) Mus Comp Zoo.

Ornithological Gazetteer of Uruguay. 2nd ed. Raymond A. Paynter, Jr. (Illus.). vi, 113p. 1994. pap. 14.00 (*0-910999-30-9*) Mus Comp Zoo.

Ornithological Gazetteer of Venezuela. Raymond A. Paynter, Jr. (Illus.). iii, 245p. 1982. pap. 18.00 (*0-910999-21-X*) Mus Comp Zoo.

Ornithologists of the United States Army Medical Corps: Thirty-Six Biographies. Edgar E. Hume. Ed. by Keir B. Sterling. LC 77-81131. (Biologists & Their World Ser.). (Illus.). 1978. reprint ed. lib. bdg. 54.95 (*0-405-10729-3*) Ayer.

Ornithology. F. Brooks et al. (Science & Nature Ser.). (Illus.). 48p. (J). (gr. 5-11). 1993. pap. 7.95 (*0-7460-0685-3*, Usborne); lib. bdg. 15.95 (*0-88110-514-7*, Usborne) EDC.

Ornithology. Ellen Doris. LC 93-61888. (Real Kids - Real Science Ser.). (Illus.). 63p. (J). 1994. 16.95 (*0-500-19008-9*, Pub. by Thames Hudson) Norton.

Ornithology. Frank B. Gill. 512p. (C). 1989. text 43.20 (*0-7167-2065-5*) W H Freeman.

Ornithology. Peter Rabbit. (Illus.). 57p. (Orig.). 1983. pap. 12.00 (*0-9615914-0-4*) Minor Heron.

Ornithology: Land Birds. James G. Copper. Ed. by Spencer F. Baird & J. D. Whitney. LC 73-17812. (Natural Sciencs in America Ser.). (Illus.). 608p. 1974. reprint ed. 51.95 (*0-405-05728-8*) Ayer.

Ornithology: United States Geological Exploration of the Fortieth Parallel. Robert Ridgway. LC 73-17839. (Natural Sciences in America Ser.: Pt. 3). (Illus.). 370p. 1974. reprint ed. 28.95 (*0-405-05761-X*) Ayer.

Ornithology at the University of Michigan Biological Station & the Birds of the Region. Olin S. Pettingill, Jr. (Illus.). viii, 118p. 1974. pap. text 5.00 (*0-939294-00-1*, QL-684-M5-P4) Beech Leaf.

Ornithology for Africa. Gordon L. Maclean. 310p. 1991. 45.00 (*0-86980-737-4*, Pub. by Univ Natal Pr); pap. 35.00 (*0-86980-771-4*, Pub. by Univ Natal Pr) Intl Spec Bk.

Ornithology in Laboratory & Field. 5th ed. Olin S. Pettingill, Jr. 1985. text 45.00 (*0-12-552455-2*) Acad Pr.

Ornithology of the Indian Subcontinent, 1872-1992: An Annotated Bibliography. Charles G. Burg et al. 330p. (C). 1994. pap. 20.00 (*0-9644592-0-5*) Natl Mus Nat Hist.

Ornithomimids, the Fastest Dinosaur. Don Lessem. LC 93-10264. (Special Dinosaurs Ser.). (Illus.). (J). (gr. 2-5). 1993. lib. bdg. 19.95 (*0-87614-813-5*, Carolrhoda) Lerner Pub.

Ornitomimo (Ornithomimus) Laura Alden. (Libros Sobre Dinosaurios! Ser.). (SPA., Illus.). 32p. (J). (gr. k-4). 1994. lib. bdg. 21.36 (*1-56766-145-9*) Childs World.

Oro Blanco Nugget. Richard S. Wheeler. 352p. 1996. mass mkt. 4.99 (*0-8125-5021-8*, Pub. by Forge NYC) St Martin.

Oro de los Suenos, Level 4. Adapted by Jose Maria Merino. (Leer en Espanol Ser.). (SPA.). (C). 1998. pap. 6.95 (*84-294-3489-5*) Santillana.

Oro Plata. Daniele Carbonel. Date not set. 100.00 (*2-908228-14-9*, Pub. by Assouline) Rizzoli Intl.

Oro Plata: Embroidered Costumes of the Bullfight. Daniele C. Pedro. LC 98-116084. (Illus.). 162p. 1997. 75.00 (*2-84323-035-7*, Pub. by Assouline) Rizzoli Intl.

Oro Puro. Crystal Lewis.Tr. of Gold. 1998. pap. text 6.99 (*0-88113-521-6*) Caribe Betania.

Oro Solar y Otras Fuentes de Energia. Juan Tonda. (Ciencia para Todos Ser.). (SPA.). pap. 6.99 (*968-16-4286-4*, Pub. by Fondo) Continental Bk.

Oro Vos Faciatis . . . an Election Unit. Lorraine A. Strasheim. 7p. (YA). (gr. 9-12). 1991. spiral bd. 1.95 (*0-939507-32-3*, B11) Amer Classical.

Oro y el Futuro Del Pueblo. Ed. by Rose De Tevis et al. (Illus.). 155p. 1979. pap. 5.00 (*0-918358-11-6*) Pajarito Pubns.

Orobanche. C. A. Kreutz. 160p. 1995. 99.00 (*90-74508-05-7*, Pub. by A A Balkema) Ashgate Pub Co.

Orofacial Growth & Development. Ed. by Albert A. Dahlberg & Thomas M. Graber. (World Anthropology Ser.). (Illus.). xiv, 354p. 1977. 52.35 (*90-279-7889-1*) Mouton.

Orofacial Myology: Beyond Tongue Thrust. Robert M. Mason et al. 63p. 1994. pap. text 40.00 (*0-910329-81-8*, 0111904) Am Speech Lang Hearing.

Orofacial Pain: Guidelines for Assessment, Classification, & Management. American Academy of Orofacial Pain Staff. Ed. by Jeffrey P. Okeson. LC 96-4651. (Illus.). 300p. 1996. pap. text 28.00 (*0-86715-312-1*) Quint Pub Co.

Orofacial Pain: Understanding Temporomandibular (TMJ) Disorders. Joseph Gibilisco et al. (Illus.). 60p. (Orig.). 1994. pap. 28.00 (*0-86715-211-7*) Quint Pub Co.

Orofacial Pain & Temporomandibular Disorders. Ed. by James R. Fricton & Ronald B. Dubner. (Advances in Pain Research & Therapy Ser.: Vol. 21). (Illus.). 556p. 1994. text 125.00 (*0-7817-0237-2*) Lppncott W & W.

Orogenic Belts & Geological Mapping see Proceedings of the 30th International Geological Congress

Orogeny Through Time. Ed. by J. P. Burg & M. Ford. (Geological Society Special Publication Ser.: No. 121). vi, 272p. 1997. 99.00 (*1-897799-75-6*, 362, Pub. by Geol Soc Pub Hse) AAPG.

Orokaiva Society. Francis E. Williams. LC 82-25129. (Illus.). 355p. 1983. reprint ed. lib. bdg. 85.00 (*0-313-23846-4*, WIOR, Greenwood Pr) Greenwood.

***Oromia: An Introduction to the History of the Oromo People.** rev. ed. Gadaa Melbaa. LC 99-33590. 150p. 1999. pap. 12.00 (*1-886513-18-X*) Kirk Hse Pubs.

Oromia & Ethiopia: State Formation & Ethnonational Conflict, 1868-1992. Asafa Jalata. LC 93-32. 221p. 1993. lib. bdg. 48.00 (*1-55587-425-8*) L Rienner.

Oromo Nationalism & the Ethiopian Discourse: The Search for Freedom & Democracy. Ed. by Asafa Jalata. LC 97-46970. 430p. 1997. 79.95 (*1-56902-065-5*); pap. 21.95 (*1-56902-066-3*) Red Sea Pr.

Oromo Newspaper Reader. Yigazu Tucho & R. David Zorc. LC 95-83384. 1996. 54.00 (*1-881265-32-3*) Dunwoody Pr.

Oromo of Ethiopia: A History, 1570-1860. Mohammed Hassen. LC 93-44124. 272p. 1994. reprint ed. 49.95 (*0-932415-94-6*); reprint ed. pap. 16.95 (*0-932415-95-4*) Red Sea Pr.

Oron No. 4: The Valley of Ogrum. David C. Smith. (Orig.). 1982. mass mkt. 2.75 (*0-685-05673-2*, Zebra Kensgtn) Kensgtn Pub Corp.

Oron No. 5: The Ghost Army. David C. Smith. mass mkt. 2.75 (*0-685-08780-8*, Zebra Kensgtn) Kensgtn Pub Corp.

Orondo los Unos por los Otros. Bruce. (Serie Discipulado - Discipleship Ser.).Tr. of Praying for One Another. (SPA.). 26p. 1996. write for info. (*0-614-27089-8*) Editorial Unilit.

Oroonako & Other Stories. Behn Aphra. (Cloth Bound Pocket Ser.). 320p. 1999. 7.95 (*3-8290-0902-X*, 520665) Konemann.

***Oroonoko.** Aphra Behn. 368p. 1999. text 39.95 (*0-312-21065-5*) St Martin.

Oroonoko. fac. ed. Thomas Southerne. Ed. by Maximillian E. Novak & David S. Rodes. LC 75-38054. (Regents Restoration Drama Ser.). 185p. 1976. reprint ed. pap. 57.40 (*0-7837-8309-4*, 204909500010) Bks Demand.

Oroonoko: A Tragedy. Thomas Southern. LC 75-93420. (Black Heritage Library Collection). 1977. 14.95 (*0-8369-8659-8*) Ayer.

Oroonoko & Other Prose Narratives. Aphra Behn. LC 67-25151. 1993. 14.95 (*0-88143-154-0*) Ayer.

Oroonoko & Other Prose Narratives. Aphra Behn. LC 67-25151. 1972. 40.95 (*0-405-08252-5*, Pub. by Blom Pubns) Ayer.

Oroonoko, & Other Writings. Aphra Behn. Ed. & Intro. by Paul Salzman. LC 99-186652. (Oxford World's Classics Ser.). 320p. 1998. pap. 8.95 (*0-19-283460-6*) OUP.

Oroonoko: or The Royal Slave. Aphra Behn. 96p. 1997. pap. 8.95 (*0-393-31205-4*) Norton.

Oroonoko or, The Royal Slave. Ed. by Joanna Lipking. LC 96-47186. (Norton Critical Editions Ser.). (C). 1997. pap. text 9.25 (*0-393-97014-0*) Norton.

Oroonoko, the Rover & Other Works. Aphra Behn. Ed. & Intro. by Janet Todd. 384p. 1999. pap. text 6.00 (*0-14-043338-4*) Addson-Wesley Educ.

Orot. Abraham I. Kook. Tr. & Intro. by Bezalel Naor. LC 92-43822. 312p. 1993. pap. 30.00 (*1-56821-017-5*) Aronson.

O

Orot: A Multidisciplinary Journal of Judaism. Ed. by Bezalel Naor. v, 119p. 1991. 17.95 (*0-9674512-0-5*) Orot Inc.

Orotic Acid. Ed. by Werner Reutter. 1981. text 84.00 (*0-85200-294-7*) Kluwer Academic.

O'Rourke Corrugation. X-Canada Staff. 1995. write for info. (*0-394-25976-9*) Random Ref & Info.

***O'Rourkes: An Toiseach (The Beginning)** Bob Shea. LC 99-91128. 1999. 25.00 (*0-7388-0642-0*); pap. 18.00 (*0-7388-0643-9*) Xlibris Corp.

Oroz Codex: or Relation of the Description of the Holy Gospel Province in New Spain, & the Lives of the Founders & Other Note-Worthy Men of Said Province Composed by Fray Pedro Oroz, 1584-1586. Ed. by Angelico Chavez. (Documentary Ser.). 1972. 35.00 (*0-88382-011-0*) AAFH.

Orozco: A Small Tribute. Text by Hayden Herrera. (Illus.). 24p. 1996. pap. 15.00 (*1-930191-02-2*) M Martin Fine Art.

***Orozco in Gringoland: The Years in New York.** Alejandro Anreus. LC 00-9645. (Illus.). 2001. pap. write for info. (*0-8263-2068-6*) U of NM Pr.

Orp. Suzy Kline. 96p. (J). (gr. 3-7). 1989. 13.95 (*0-399-21639-1*, G P Putnam) Peng Put Young Read.

Orp. Suzy Kline. 96p. (J). 1990. reprint ed. pap. 3.50 (*0-380-71038-2*, Avon Bks) Morrow Avon.

Orp & the Chop Suey Burgers. Suzy Kline. 96p. (J). (gr. 4). 1992. pap. 3.50 (*0-380-71359-4*, Avon Bks) Morrow Avon.

Orp & the Chop Suey Burgers. Suzy Kline. (Illus.). 112p. (J). (gr. 4-8). 1990. 14.95 (*0-399-22185-9*, G P Putnam) Peng Put Young Read.

***Orp & the Chop Suey Burgers.** Suzy Kline. LC 99-36115. (J). 2000. 4.99 (*0-698-11781-6*, PuffinBks) Peng Put Young Read.

Orp & the FBI. Suzy Kline. LC 94-24552. 100p. (J). 1995. 14.95 (*0-399-22664-8*, G P Putnam) Peng Put Young Read.

***Orp Goes to the Hoop.** Suzy Kline. LC 99-36114. 112p. (J). 2000. pap. 4.99 (*0-698-11803-0*) Putnam Pub Group.

Orp Goes to the Hoop. Suzy Kline. 96p. (J). (gr. 4). 1993. reprint ed. pap. 3.50 (*0-380-71829-4*, Avon Bks) Morrow Avon.

Orphan. Chet Hosac. LC 98-75296. (Illus.). 192p. 1999. pap. 17.95 (*1-887747-23-0*) Legendary Pub.

Orphan. Faith McNulty. 40p. (J). 1992. 11.95 (*0-590-43838-7*, Scholastic Hardcover) Scholastic Inc.

Orphan. Shashi Warrier. LC 98-905860. 340p. 1998. 16.00 (*0-14-027118-X*, PuffinBks) Peng Put Young Read.

Orphan. Era Zistel. (Illus.). 64p. (Orig.). (J). (gr. 4 up). 1990. pap. 11.95 (*0-9617426-5-8*) J N Townsend.

Orphan. Clarence Mulford. 308p. 1974. reprint ed. lib. bdg. 27.95 (*0-88411-225-X*) Amereon Ltd.

Orphan. Thomas Otway. Ed. by Aline M. Taylor. LC 75-13067. (Regents Restoration Drama Ser.). 148p. 1976. reprint ed. pap. 45.90 (*0-7837-8910-6*, 204962100002) Bks Demand.

***Orphan: A True Story of Abandonment, Abuse & Redemption.** Roger Dean Kiser, Sr. 256p. 2000. pap. 10.95 (*1-58062-448-0*) Adams Media.

Orphan Reissue Edition. Suzy Kline. 96p. (J). (gr. 3-7). 1999. pap. 4.99 (*0-698-11780-8*, PuffinBks) Peng Put Young Read.

Orphan & the Doll. Tracy Friedman. (J). 1988. pap. text 2.50 (*0-590-41218-3*) Scholastic Inc.

Orphan Boy. Tololwa M. Mollel. (Illus.). (J). 1991. 14.95 (*0-685-53587-8*, Clarion Bks) HM.

Orphan Boy. Tololwa M. Mollel. (Illus.). 32p. (J). (gr. k-3). 1991. 16.00 (*0-89919-985-2*) HM.

Orphan Boy. Tololwa M. Mollel. LC 90-2358. (J). (ps-3). 1995. pap. 5.95 (*0-395-72079-6*, Clarion Bks) HM.

Orphan Boy: A Maasai Story. Tololwa M. Mollel. (J). 1990. 11.40 (*0-606-07977-7*) Turtleback.

Orphan Brigade: The Kentucky Confederates Who Couldn't Go Home. William C. Davis. LC 82-18700. (Illus.). xvi, 318p. 1983. pap. 17.95 (*0-8071-1077-9*) La State U Pr.

Orphan Brigade: The Kentucky Confederates Who Couldn't Go Home. 2nd ed. William C. Davis. LC 93-16359. (Illus.). 352p. 1993. reprint ed. 19.95 (*0-8117-1182-X*) Stackpole.

Orphan Child. Mariagorretti Okoro. (Orig.). (J). (gr. 2-6). 1997. pap. 6.95 (*0-533-12111-6*) Vantage.

Orphan Conducts the Dovehouse Orchestra. Deborah Woodard. (Illus.). 41p. 1999. pap. 7.00 (*0-9657177-2-0*) Bear Star.

Orphan Country: Children of Scotland's Broken Homes, 1845 to the Present. Lynn Abrams. 250p. 1998. pap. 60.00 (*0-85976-497-4*, Pub. by J Donald) St Mut.

Orphan Factory: Essays & Memoirs. Charles Simic. LC 97-23678. 128p. (C). 1997. pap. 13.95 (*0-472-06663-3*, 06663) U of Mich Pr.

Orphan Factory: Essays & Memoirs. Charles Simic. LC 97-23678. 128p. (C). 1997. text 39.50 (*0-472-09663-X*, 09663) U of Mich Pr.

Orphan for Nebraska. Charlene J. Talbot. LC 78-12179. (Illus.). 216p. (J). (gr. 4-6). 1979. 14.95 (*0-689-30698-9*) Atheneum Yung Read.

***Orphan Game.** large type ed. Ann Darby. LC 99-39089. 521p. 1999. 27.95 (*0-7838-8749-3*, G K Hall Lrg Type) Mac Lib Ref.

***Orphan Game: A Novel.** Ann Darby. 336p. 2000. pap. 13.00 (*0-688-17782-4*, Quil) HarperTrade.

Orphan Game: A Novel. Ann Darby. LC 98-43778. 336p. 1999. 24.00 (*0-688-16778-0*, Wm Morrow) Morrow Avon.

Orphan Girl: The Memoir of a Chicago Bag Lady. Jane Hertenstein. LC 97-45653. 208p. 1998. pap. text 12.95 (*0-940895-39-0*) Cornerstone IL.

Orphan Girl & Other Stories: West African Folk Tales. Compiled & Retold by Buchi Offodile. (Illus.). Date not set. pap. 15.00 (*1-56656-375-5*) Interlink Pub.

Orphan Gospel. Dean W. Chapman. (Biblical Seminar Ser.: No. 16). 235p. (C). 1993. pap. 28.50 (*1-85075-346-6*, Pub. by Sheffield Acad) CUP Services.

Orphan Has Many Parents. Friedland Kraft. 1998. 29.50 (*0-88125-650-1*) Ktav.

***Orphan in New York City: Life with a Thousand Brothers & Sisters.** Seymour Siegel & Laura Edwards. LC 00-190073. 2000. 25.00 (*0-7388-1474-1*); pap. 18.00 (*0-7388-1475-X*) Xlibris Corp.

Orphan in the Attic: Photographs by James Baker Hall. Roger Rawlings. (Illus.). 28p. (C). 1995. pap. 12.00 (*0-614-13241-X*) Univ KY Art Mus.

Orphan in the Movie House. Carole Stone. 1997. pap. 5.00 (*0-916897-26-5*) Andrew Mtn Pr.

Orphan in the Sands. Virginia Haroutunian. Ed. by Eric Ninneman. (Illus.). 178p. (YA). 1995. reprint ed. pap. 19.00 (*0-9664381-0-8*) V Haroutunian.

Orphan Island. Rose Macaulay. 1971. reprint ed. 39.00 (*0-403-01081-0*) Scholarly.

***Orphan Journey Home.** Liza Ketchum. 2001. pap. write for info. (*0-380-80988-5*) Morrow Avon.

***Orphan Journey Home.** Liza Ketchum & C. B. Mordan. LC 99-42649. (Illus.). 176p. (J). (gr. 3-7). 2000. 15.00 (*0-380-97811-3*, Avon Bks) Morrow Avon.

Orphan Lamb. Ann Purser. 320p. 1997. pap. 8.95 (*0-7528-0245-3*, Pub. by Orion Pubng Grp) Trafalgar.

Orphan Lamb. large type ed. Ann Purser. LC 96-9843. 1996. pap. 20.95 (*0-7862-0802-3*) Thorndike Pr.

Orphan Objects: Facets of the Textiles Collection of the Joods Historisch Museum, Amsterdam. Daniel M. Swetschinski et al. LC 97-217740. (Illus.). 248p. 1999. 75.00 (*90-400-9953-7*, Pub. by Waandrs) Consort Bk Sales.

Orphan of Ellis Island: A Time Travel Adventure. Elvira Woodruff. LC 95-45613. 160p. (J). (gr. 4-7). 1997. 14.95 (*0-590-48245-9*) Scholastic Inc.

Orphan of Gold City. Frederick V. Fisher. Ed. by Emma M. Weston. (Illus.). 133p. 1998. pap. 4.95 (*1-883179-11-4*) Weston Bible.

Orphan Road: The Railroad Comes to Seattle, 1853-1911. Kurt Armbruster. LC 99-37058. (Illus.). 280p. 1999. 39.95 (*0-87422-185-4*) Wash St U Pr.

Orphan Road: The Railroad Comes to Seattle, 1853-1911. Kurt Armbruster. LC 99-37058. (Illus.). 280p. 1999. pap. 29.95 (*0-87422-186-2*) Wash St U Pr.

Orphan Runaways. Kristiana Gregory. LC 97-4345. 144p. (J). (gr. 3-7). 1998. 15.95 (*0-590-60366-3*) Scholastic Inc.

***Orphan Seal: A True Story.** Fran Hadgkins. (Illus.). 32p. (J). (gr. 1-5). 2000. pap. 9.95 (*0-89272-471-4*) Down East.

Orphan Stone: The Minnesinger Dream of Reich, 15. Richard J. Berleth. LC 89-17238. 288p. 1990. 62.95 (*0-313-26856-8*, BOA/, Greenwood Pr) Greenwood.

Orphan Swaggy: Australian Lifestyle in the 1930's. James Maizey & Claire Williams. LC 97-106290. (Illus.). 179p. 1996. pap. 16.95 (*1-875998-12-8*, Pub. by Central Queensland) Accents Pubns.

Orphan Train. Aurand Harris. 1998. pap. 6.50 (*0-87602-360-X*) Anchorage.

***Orphan Train Adventures, 6 bks.** large type ed. Joan Lowery Nixon. Incl. Caught in the Act. large type ed. LC 99-89431. (J). (gr. 4 up). 1999. lib. bdg. 21.27 (*0-8368-2639-6*); Dangerous Promise. large type ed. LC 99-55938. (J). (gr. 4). 1999. lib. bdg. 21.27 (*0-8368-2642-6*); Family Apart. large type ed. LC 99-55932. (J). (gr. 4 up). 1999. lib. bdg. 21.27 (*0-8368-2638-8*); In the Face of Danger. large type ed. LC 99-55933. (J). 1999. lib. bdg. 21.27 (*0-8368-2640-X*); Keeping Secrets. large type ed. LC 99-55931. (J). 1999. lib. bdg. 21.27 (*0-8368-2643-4*); Place to Belong. large type ed. LC 99-55934. (J). 1999. lib. bdg. 21.27 (*0-8368-2641-8*); (J). (gr. 4 up). 1999. Set lib. bdg. 127.62 (*0-8368-2637-X*) Gareth Stevens Inc.

Orphan Train Rider: One Boy's True Story. Andrea Warren. LC 94-43688. (Illus.). 80p. (J). (gr. 3-5). 1996. 16.00 (*0-395-69822-7*) HM.

Orphan Train Rider: One Boy's True Story. Andrea Warren. 80p. (J). (gr. 3-5). 1998. pap. 7.95 (*0-395-91362-4*) HM.

Orphan Train West Pack, 4. Jane Peart. (Orphan Train West Ser.). (gr. 13 up). pap. 29.95 (*0-8007-6403-X*) Revell.

***Orphan Train West Series for Young Readers 4 vols.** Jane Peart. (Illus.). (J). 2000. pap. 19.96 (*0-8007-6442-0*) Chosen Bks.

Orphan Trains. Annette R. Fry. LC 93-29723. (American Events Ser.). (Illus.). 96p. (YA). (gr. 6 up). 1994. lib. bdg. 14.95 (*0-02-735721-X*, New Dscvry Bks) Silver Burdett Pr.

Orphan Trains: Leaving the Cities Behind see Perspectives on History Series

Orphan Trains: Placing Out in America. Marilyn I. Holt. LC 91-29155. (Illus.). ix, 264p. 1992. text 45.00 (*0-8032-2360-9*) U of Nebr Pr.

Orphan Trains: Placing Out in America. Marilyn I. Holt. LC 91-29155. (Illus.). ix, 264p. 1992. pap. 12.00 (*0-8032-7265-0*, Bison Books) U of Nebr Pr.

***Orphan Trains: The Story of Charles Loring Brace & the Children He Saved & Failed, 1853-1929.** Stephen O'Connor. (Illus.). 320p. 2001. 26.00 (*0-395-84173-9*) HM.

Orphan Trains to Missouri. Michael D. Patrick & Evelyn G. Trickel. LC 97-12244. (Illus.). 144p. (J). 1997. pap. 9.95 (*0-8262-1121-6*) U of Mo Pr.

Orphan Trees. George Peffer & Terry Murcko. LC 79-91911. (Midwest Writer Ser.). 80p. 1980. pap. 4.95 (*0-917530-08-X*) Pig Iron Pr.

Orphanage. Hubert Fichte. Tr. by Martin Chalmers from GER. 176p. (Orig.). 1991. pap. 10.95 (*1-85242-161-4*) Serpents Tail.

Orphanage Miss. large type ed. Clare Rossiter. (Nightingale Ser.). 1996. pap. 17.95 (*0-7838-1623-5*, G K Hall Lrg Type) Mac Lib Ref.

Orphanages: Index of New Information. Benny B. Augustine. 150p. 1998. 47.50 (*0-7883-2026-2*); pap. 44.50 (*0-7883-2027-0*) ABBE Pubs Assn.

Orphanages Reconsidered: Child Care Institutions in Progressive Era Baltimore. Nurith Zmora. LC 93-14640. 352p. 1993. 64.95 (*1-56639-071-0*) Temple U Pr.

Orphanages Reconsidered: Child Care Institutions in Progressive Era Baltimore. Nurith Zmora. (Illus.). 352p. 1996. pap. 19.95 (*1-56639-465-1*) Temple U Pr.

Orphaned Adult: Confronting the Death of a Parent. Marc Angel. LC 86-20161. 162p. 1987. 26.95 (*0-89885-334-6*, Kluwer Acad Hman Sci) Kluwer Academic.

***Orphaned Adult: Understanding & Coping with Grief & Change After the Death of Our Parents.** Alexander Levy. 208p. 2000. reprint ed. pap. text 14.00 (*0-7382-0361-0*, Pub. by Perseus Pubng) HarpC.

Orphaned Capital: Adopting the Right Revenues for the District of Columbia. Carol O'Cleireacain. LC 97-4634. 214p. (Orig.). 1997. pap. 16.95 (*0-8157-6425-1*) Brookings.

Orphaned Imagination: Melancholy & Commodity Culture in English Romanticism. Guinn Batten. LC 97-49691. 1998. 59.95 (*0-8223-2205-6*); pap. 19.95 (*0-8223-2221-8*) Duke.

***Orphans.** Peter Mullany. 1999. pap. 12.95 (*1-901680-30-4*) Screen Test Pub.

Orphans. Gerald Pearce. 192p. 1990. 18.95 (*0-8027-5764-2*) Walker & Co.

Orphans. Leslie Russell. LC 96-90982. 222p. 1998. 17.95 (*0-533-12526-X*) Vantage.

Orphans. Jean Simon. 320p. 1992. mass mkt. 4.50 (*0-8217-3929-8*, Zebra Kensgtn) Kensgtn Pub Corp.

***Orphans.** V. C. Andrews. 672p. 2000. reprint ed. mass mkt. 7.99 (*0-7434-0361-4*, Pocket Books) PB.

Orphans: A Play in Two Acts. James Prideaux. 1980. pap. 5.25 (*0-8222-0864-4*) Dramatists Play.

***Orphans: The Journey of the Six Reuter Children.** Ollie Kirby. LC 99-91666. 2000. 25.00 (*0-7388-1178-5*); pap. 18.00 (*0-7388-1179-3*) Xlibris Corp.

Orphans & Incentives: Developing Technology to Address Emerging Infections. Ed. by Polly F. Harrison & Joshua Lederberg. LC 98-101323. 112p. (C). 1997. text 22.00 (*0-309-05941-0*) Natl Acad Pr.

Orphans in Babylon: Abortion in America. Where Are We Now? How Did We Get Here? Where Should We Be? How Can We Get There? Roger Domingo. LC 98-94109. 312p. 1998. pap. 29.95 (*0-9668541-0-1*) Turnstyle.

Orphans in Gethsemane: A Novel of the Past in the Present. Vardis Fisher. (Testament of Man Ser.). 987p. 1960. 80.00 (*0-614-22020-3*, Idaho Center for the Bk) Heming W Studies.

Orphans of Petrarch: Poetry & Theory in the Spanish Renaissance. Ignacio Navarrete. LC 93-4559. (Publications of the Center for Medieval & Renaissance Studies: Vol. 25). 1994. 48.00 (*0-520-08373-3*, Pub. by U CA Pr) Cal Prin Full Svc.

Orphans of the Cold War: America & the Tibetan Struggle for Survival. John Kenneth Knaus. LC 99-11836. 416p. 1999. 27.50 (*1-891620-18-5*, Pub. by PublicAffairs NY) HarpC.

***Orphans of the Cold War: America & the Tibetan Struggle for Survival.** John Kenneth Knaus. 416p. 2000. pap. 16.00 (*1-891620-85-1*, Pub. by PublicAffairs NY) HarpC.

Orphans of the Empire: The Shocking Story of Child Migration to Australia. Alan P. Gill. LC 98-156008. xv, 701 p. 1997. write for info. (*1-86429-062-5*) Millennium Bks.

Orphans of the Living. Jennifer Toth. LC 96-40316. 1997. 22.50 (*0-684-80097-7*) S&S Trade.

Orphans of the Living. Jennifer Toth. 320p. 1998. pap. 13.00 (*0-684-84480-X*, Touchstone) S&S Trade Pap.

Orphans of the Night. Ed. by Josepha Sherman. 160p. (J). (gr. 6-10). 1995. 16.95 (*0-8027-8368-6*) Walker & Co.

Orphans of the Storm. large type ed. Alan Evans. 1991. 27.99 (*0-7089-2515-4*) Ulverscroft.

Orphans of the Storm: Stories on the Partition of India. Ed. by Saros Cowasjee & K. S. Duggal. LC 94-906939. (C). 1995. text 28.00 (*81-7476-017-2*, Pub. by UBS Pubs Dist); pap. text 12.00 (*81-85944-92-X*, Pub. by UBS Pubs Dist) S Asia.

Orphans of the Wild. Vivian Wilson. (Illus.). 320p. 1988. 22.50 (*0-935632-65-4*) Wolfe Pub Co.

Orphans of Versailles: The German Minority in Western Poland, 1918-1939. Richard Blanke. LC 92-19216. 328p. (C). 1993. 39.95 (*0-8131-1803-4*) U Pr of Ky.

Orphans on the River: Little Red, White & Mississippi Rivers Were Their Home. Norman R. Martin. Ed. by Judy C. Mullins. (Illus.). 113p. (YA). 1998. pap. 10.00 (*0-9646489-7-0*) Martain Pub.

Orphan's Preferred. large type ed. James V. Miller. (Linford Western Library). 304p. 1988. pap. 16.99 (*0-7089-6493-1*, Linford) Ulverscroft.

Orphan's Survival Guide. Wolf White Wolf Publishing Staff. (Mage Ser.). (Illus.). 1998. pap. 16.00 (*1-56504-436-3*, 4252) White Wolf.

Orphan's Tent. Tom DeHaven. (Illus.). (YA). (gr. 7 up). 1996. pap. 18.00 (*0-318-40133-9*) S&S Childrens.

Orphant Annie Story Book. 3rd ed. Johnny Gruelle. LC 89-80852. 100p. (J). (gr. k-5). 1989. reprint ed. 22.95 (*0-9617367-9-8*) Guild Pr IN.

Orpharion; Greens Groatsworth of Wit; The Repentance of Robert Greene; Greenes Vision, 1592-1599 see Life & Complete Works in Prose & Verse of Robert Greene

Orphean Passages: The Drama of Faith. Walter Wangerin, Jr. 320p. 1996. pap. 12.99 (*0-310-20568-9*) Zondervan.

Orphee. Jean Cocteau. (FRE.). 116p. 1961. 8.95 (*0-8288-9130-3*, M3314) Fr & Eur.

Orphee Data-Base of Guitar Records. Jacques Chaine. Ed. by Matanya Ophee. LC 89-80418. 1990. 25.00 (*0-936186-30-5*, RTFT-6); pap. 15.00 (*0-936186-35-6*, RTFT-6A) Edit Orphee.

Orphee Data-Base of Guitar Records: 1991 Supplement. Jacques Chaine. Ed. by Matanya Ophee. LC 89-80418. 128p. (Orig.). 1991. pap. 8.00 (*0-936186-58-5*, RTFT-6-91) Edit Orphee.

***Orphee de Ballanche Vol. 4: Genese et Signification.** Alan J. L. Busst. (Le Romantisme et Apres en France Ser.). 343p. 1999. 52.95 (*3-906763-81-1*, Pub. by P Lang) P Lang Pubng.

Orphee et l'Orphisme dans l'Antiquite Greco-Romaine. Luc Brisson. (Collected Studies: Vol. CS476). 320p. 1995. 109.95 (*0-86078-453-3*, Pub. by Variorum) Ashgate Pub Co.

Orphei Hymni - Orphei Hymnorum Concordantia. Ed. by Albertus Bernabe. (Alpha-Omega, Reihe A Ser.: Bd. LXXXIV). (GER.). 184p. 1988. 55.00 (*3-487-07872-4*) G Olms Pubs.

Orphelin de Mer, Ou, Les Memoires de Monsieur Non. Eric Ollivier. (FRE.). 1984. pap. 10.95 (*0-7859-4200-9*) Fr & Eur.

Orpheus. Aleister Crowley. 1973. lib. bdg. 250.00 (*0-87968-176-4*) Krishna Pr.

Orpheus. Hutton. (J). 1996. 16.00 (*0-689-80148-3*) McElderry Bks.

Orpheus. Kenneth McLeish. 80p. 1998. pap. 12.95 (*1-84002-016-4*) Theatre Comm.

Orpheus. abr. ed. Charles Mikolaycak. LC 91-27440. (Illus.). 32p. (YA). (gr. 7 up). 1992. 19.95 (*0-15-258804-3*, Harcourt Child Bks) Harcourt.

Orpheus. G. R. Mead. 208p. 1996. reprint ed. pap. 19.95 (*1-56459-611-7*) Kessinger Pub.

Orpheus: A History of Religions. Salomon Reinach. Tr. by Florence Simmonds. 497p. 1996. reprint ed. pap. 39.00 (*1-56459-568-4*) Kessinger Pub.

Orpheus: A Masque. Annie Fields. (Notable American Authors Ser.). 1992. reprint ed. lib. bdg. 75.00 (*0-7812-2822-0*) Rprt Serv.

Orpheus: A Poetic Drama. Owen Barfield. LC 82-83247. 160p. (Orig.). 1983. pap. 6.95 (*0-940262-01-0*, Lindisfarne) Anthroposophic.

Orpheus: Myths of the World. Padraic Colum. 1996. pap. text 21.95 (*0-86315-519-7*, Pub. by Floris Bks) Anthroposophic.

Orpheus: The Metamorphoses of a Myth. Ed. by John Warden. LC 82-189058. 254p. reprint ed. pap. 78.80 (*0-608-16797-5*, 202640400049) Bks Demand.

Orpheus: The Metamorphosis of a Myth: Studies in the Orpheus Myth from Antiquity to the Renaissance. Ed. by John Warden. 251p. 1985. pap. 16.95 (*0-8020-6593-7*) U of Toronto Pr.

Orpheus: The Myth of the Poet. Charles Segal. (Softshell Bks.). 250p. (C). 1993. pap. text 16.95 (*0-8018-4720-6*) Johns Hopkins.

Orpheus: The Myth of the Poet. Charles Segal. LC 88-45411. 253p. reprint ed. pap. 78.50 (*0-7837-2200-1*, 204253800004) Bks Demand.

Orpheus - Das Alter der Kitharoden. Robert Bohme. 140p. write for info. (*3-296-10900-5*) G Olms Pubs.

Orpheus - The Fisher: Comparative Studies in Orphic & Early Christian Cult Symbolism. Robert Eisler. 315p. 1992. reprint ed. pap. 22.95 (*1-56459-029-1*) Kessinger Pub.

Orpheus & Company: Contemporary Poems on Greek Mythology. Ed. by Deborah DeNicola. LC 98-49534. 354p. 1999. pap. 19.95 (*0-87451-918-7*); text 50.00 (*0-87451-917-9*) U Pr of New Eng.

Orpheus & Euridice: Vocal Score. C. Gluck. (ENG & FRE.). 1986. pap. 24.95 (*0-7935-1243-3*, 50338110) H Leonard.

Orpheus & Eurydice see Greek Mythology

***Orpheus & Eurydice: A Lyric Sequence.** Gregory Orr. 80p. 2001. pap. 12.00 (*1-55659-151-9*) Copper Canyon.

Orpheus & Greek Religion: A Study of the Orphic. W. K. Guthrie. (Princeton - Bollingen Series in World Mythology). 308p. 1993. pap. text 17.95 (*0-691-02499-5*, Pub. by Princeton U Pr) Cal Prin Full Svc.

Orpheus & Power: The Movimento Negro of Rio de Janeiro & Sao Paulo, Brazil, 1945-1988. Michael G. Hachard. LC 93-38137. 216p. 1994. text 39.50 (*0-691-03292-0*, Pub. by Princeton U Pr) Cal Prin Full Svc.

Orpheus & Power: The Movimento Negro of Rio de Janeiro & Sao Paulo, Brazil, 1945-1988. Michael George Hanchard. 203p. 1998. pap. 15.95 (*0-691-00270-3*, Pub. by Princeton U Pr) Cal Prin Full Svc.

Orpheus at Eighty. Vincent Sheean. LC 75-8175. 372p. 1975. reprint ed. lib. bdg. 69.50 (*0-8371-8129-1*, SHOE, Greenwood Pr) Greenwood.

Orpheus Britannicus. fac. ed. Henry Purcell. (Monuments of Music & Music Literature in Facsimile, I Ser.: Vol. 1). (Illus.). 1965. lib. bdg. 75.00 (*0-8450-2001-3*) Broude.

Orpheus C. Kerr Papers, 3 vols. Robert H. Newell. LC 78-169922. reprint ed. 115.00 (*0-404-03670-8*) AMS Pr.

Orpheus C. Kerr Papers. Robert H. Newell. (BCL1-PS American Literature Ser.). 1992. reprint ed. lib. bdg. 79.00 (*0-7812-6805-2*) Rprt Serv.

O

Orpheus C. Kerr Papers. Robery H. Newell. (Notable American Authors Ser.). 1999. reprint ed. lib. bdg. 125.00 (*0-7812-4629-6*) Rprt Serv.

Orpheus Caledonius, Vol. 1. Ed. by Peter Holman. 1991. pap. 65.00 (*0-946868-09-3*, Pub. by Hardie Pr) St Mut.

Orpheus Caledonius, Vol. 11. Ed. by Peter Holman. 1991. pap. 70.00 (*0-946868-10-7*, Pub. by Hardie Pr) St Mut.

Orpheus Descending see Best American Plays: Fifth Series, 1958-1963

Orpheus Descending see Four Plays

Orpheus Descending. Tennessee Williams. 1958. pap. 5.25 (*0-8222-0865-2*) Dramatists Play.

Orpheus Dis(re)membered: Milton & the Myth of the Poet-Hero. Rachel Falconer. (SAP Publications). 300p. 1996. 55.00 (*1-85075-609-0*, Pub. by Sheffield Acad) CUP Services.

Orpheus. Eurydice. Hermes: Notations on a Landscape. deluxe limited ed. Rainer Maria Rilke. Tr. by Stephen Mitchell. (ENG & GER., Illus.). 35p. 1996. 500.00 (*0-89304-057-6*) Cross-Cultrl NY.

Orpheus, Eurydice, Hermes: Notations on a Landscape. limited ed. Rainer Maria Rilke. Tr. by Stephen Mitchell. (ENG & GER., Illus.). 35p. 1996. 150.00 (*0-89304-058-4*) Cross-Cultrl NY.

Orpheus in Brooklyn: Orphism, Rimbaud, & Henry Miller Bertrand Mathieu. LC 77-366292. xii, 230p. 1976. write for info. (*90-279-3036-8*) Mouton.

Orpheus in Nineteenth-Century Symbolism. Dorothy M. Kosinski. Ed. by Stephen Foster. LC 89-4732. (Studies in the Fine Arts: The Avant-Garde: No. 61). 448p. reprint ed. 138.90 (*0-8357-1868-9*, 207072800004) Bks Demand.

***Orpheus in the Middle Ages.** rev. ed. John Block Friedman. LC 99-53213. (Illus.). 265p. 2000. pap. 29.95 (*0-8156-2825-0*) Syracuse U Pr.

Orpheus in Winter: Morley Callaghan's The Loved & the Lost. John Orange. (Canadian Fiction Studies: No. 22). 120p. (C). 1993. pap. text 14.95 (*1-55022-123-X*, Pub. by ECW) Genl Dist Srvs.

Orpheus Programme. Roger Cottrell. 515p. (Orig.). (YA). (gr. 10). 1995. pap. 21.00 (*1-85863-203-X*) AK Pr Dist.

Orpheus with His Lute: Poetry & the Renewal of Life. Elizabeth Henry. 288p. (C). 1992. 31.95 (*0-8093-1769-9*) S Ill U Pr.

Orphic Fragments. S. Ronan. 150p. (C). 1988. text 95.00 (*0-948366-22-2*, Pub. by Chthonios Bks) St Mut.

Orphic Moment: Shaman to Poet-Thinker in Plato, Nietzsche, & Mallarme. Robert McGahey. LC 93-46495. (SUNY Series, The Margins of Literature). 209p. (C). 1994. text 59.50 (*0-7914-1941-X*); pap. text 19.95 (*0-7914-1942-8*) State U NY Pr.

Orphic Mysteries in Syria & Early Christianity. Vacher Burch. 1990. pap. 4.95 (*1-55818-125-3*) Holmes Pub.

Orphic Pantheon. G. R. Mead. 1984. pap. 8.95 (*0-916411-18-4*) Holmes Pub.

Orphic Poems. M. L. West. (Illus.). 1984. 75.00 (*0-19-814854-2*) OUP.

Orphic Songs. Dino Campana. Tr. by I. L. Salomon from ITA. LC 98-9893. (Pocket Poets Ser.: Vol. 54).Tr. of Canti Orfici. 176p. 1998. pap. 12.95 (*0-87286-340-9*) City Lights.

Orphic Songs. Dino Campana. Tr. by Charles Wright from ITA. LC 83-63448. (Field Translation Ser.).Tr. of Canti Orfici. 130p. 1984. 11.50 (*0-932440-16-9*); pap. 6.50 (*0-932440-17-7*) Oberlin Coll Pr.

Orphica. lxiv, 952p. 1971. reprint ed. 200.00 (*3-487-04024-7*) G Olms Pubs.

Orphicorum Fragmenta. Ed. by Otto Kern. x, 408p. 1972. write for info. (*3-296-13900-1*) G Olms Pubs.

Orphische Weltanschauung der Antike und Ihr Erbe Bei Den Dichtern Nietzsche, Holderlin, Novalis und Rilke, Vol. 10. Johanna J. Aulich. . (Illus.). 204p. 1997. 37.95 (*3-631-32568-1*) P Lang Pubng.

Orphydice. Janet Rodney. 56p. (Orig.). 1986. 17.50 (*0-938535-76-5*); pap. 7.00 (*0-938535-75-7*) Salt-Works Pr.

ORPLID: Analyse und Diskussion des Literarischen Kommunikationsraumes der "Katholischen" Zeitschrift ORPLID. Evelyn Viehoff-Kamper. Ed. by Helmut Kreuzer & Karl Riha. (Forschungen Zur Literatur- und Kulturgeschichte Ser.: Bd. 36). 242p. 1993. 40.80 (*3-631-45749-9*) P Lang Pubng.

***Orquideas a la Luz de la Luna.** Michel Paul. 1998. 25.99 (*3-8228-8036-1*) Benedikt Taschen.

Orquideas a la Luz de la Luna. 3rd ed. Carlos Fuentes. 116p. 1988. pap. 14.95 (*0-7859-5179-2*) Fr & Eur.

Orr White Hitchcock, 1796-1863. Ed. by Christina M. Cohen. (Illus.). 16p. 1992. pap. 8.00 (*0-9632800-0-7*) Deerfield Acad.

Orra Phelps, M. D. Adirondack Naturalist & Mountaineer. Mary Arakelian. (Illus.). 2000. 30.00 (*0-925168-66-1*) North Country.

***Orrefors: A Century of Swedish Glassmaking.** Kerstin Wickman. (Illus.). 256p. 1999. 75.00 (*91-7988-152-1*, Pub. by Byggforlaget) U of Wash Pr.

Orrefors Glass. Alastair Duncan. LC 96-145363. (Illus.). 320p. 1996. 89.50 (*1-85149-224-0*) Antique Collect.

***Orrery: Computer Models of Astronomical Systems.** Caxton C. Foster. LC 99-54574. 1999. write for info. (*0-943396-65-4*) Willmann-Bell.

Orrible Synne. E. J. Burford. LC 74-172023. (Illus.). 220p. 1979. pap. 7.95 (*0-7145-1126-9*) M Boyars Pubs.

Orrin Porter Rockwell: Man of God, Son of Thunder. 2nd ed. Harold Schindler. LC 82-23747. (Publications in the American West: Vol. 15). (Illus.). 440p. (C). 1993. reprint ed. pap. 19.95 (*0-87480-440-X*) U of Utah Pr.

***Orrington, Penobscot County, Maine Vol. 7: Wiswell Journals & Account Books, 1787-1866.** David Livingstone Swett. 579p. 1999. 99.00 (*0-89725-369-8*) Picton Pr.

Orrorsh Sourcebook: Torg. (Torg Ser.). 18.00 (*0-87431-319-8*, 20510) West End Games.

ORSANCO Story: Water Quality Management in the Ohio Valley under an Interstate Compact. Edward J. Cleary. LC 67-16036. 351p. reprint ed. pap. 108.90 (*0-7837-3140-X*, 202308700032) Bks Demand.

Orsini Inventories. Gisela Rubsamen. LC 80-83121. 224p. 1980. pap. 46.00 (*0-89236-010-0*, Pub. by J P Getty Trust) OUP.

Orsinian Tales. Ursula K. Le Guin. 6.99 (*0-06-105606-5*) HarpC.

Orsinian Tales. Ursula K. Le Guin. 224p. 1991. mass mkt. 4.50 (*0-06-100182-1*, Harp PBks) HarpC.

***Orson Hyde: The Olive Branch of Israel.** Myrtle Stevens Hyde. LC 99-67645. 500p. 2000. 29.95 (*1-888106-71-9*) Agreka Bks.

***Orson Scott Card: A Reader's Checklist & Reference Guide.** CheckerBee Publishing Staff. 1999. pap. text 4.95 (*1-58598-009-9*) CheckerBee.

Orson Welles. write for info. (*0-8386-3119-3*) Fairleigh Dickinson.

***Orson Welles.** Paul Duncan. 2000. pap. 5.95 (*1-903047-04-8*, Pub. by Pocket Essentials) Trafalgar.

Orson Welles. John Russell Taylor. (Legends Ser.). (Illus.). 156p. 2000. pap. 9.95 (*1-55783-349-4*) Applause Theatre Bk Pubs.

Orson Welles. 2nd expanded rev. ed. Joseph McBride. (Illus.). 320p. 1996. pap. 14.95 (*0-306-80674-6*) Da Capo.

Orson Welles: A Bio-Bibliography, 8. Bret Wood. LC 89-25625. (Bio-Bibliographies in the Performing Arts Ser.: No. 8). 377p. 1990. lib. bdg. 49.95 (*0-313-26538-0*, WOR/, Greenwood Pr) Greenwood.

Orson Welles: A Biography. Barbara Leaming. (Illus.). 592p. 1995. reprint ed. pap. 20.00 (*0-87910-199-7*) Limelight Edns.

Orson Welles: A Critical View. Andre Bazin. Tr. by Jonathan Rosenbaum. (Illus.). 138p. 1991. reprint ed. pap. 13.95 (*0-918226-28-7*) Acrobat.

Orson Welles: The Road to Xanadu. Simon Callow. (Illus.). 680p. 1997. pap. 14.95 (*0-14-025456-0*) Viking Penguin.

Orson Welles on Shakespeare: The W. P. A. & Mercury Theatre Playscripts, 30. Orson Welles. Ed. & Intro. by Richard France. LC 90-32464. (Contributions in Drama & Theatre Studies: No. 30). 312p. 1990. 59.95 (*0-313-27334-0*, FOW, Greenwood Pr) Greenwood.

***Orson Welles, Shakespeare, & Popular Culture.** Michael Anderegg. LC 98-24770. (Film & Culture Ser.). (Illus.). 216p. 1998. lib. bdg. 42.50 (*0-231-11228-9*) Col U Pr.

***Orson Welles, Shakespeare, & Popular Culture.** Michael Anderegg. LC 98-24770. (Film & Culture Ser.). (Illus.). xiv, 213 p. 1999. pap. 16.50 (*0-231-11229-7*) Col U Pr.

Ort Bran. Daniel Ort. LC 90-34158. 128p. (Orig.). 1990. pap. 14.95 (*0-914061-15-1*); boxed set 20.00 (*0-914061-18-6*) Orchises Pr.

ORT Cooks Around the World. Members of Women's American ORT Staff. (Illus.). 229p. (Orig.). 1994. pap. 12.95 (*0-9652450-0-4*) Wom Am ORT.

Ortega y Gasset: Un Humanista Para Nuestro Tiempo. Ed. by Ciriaco M. Arroyo. (Monografias De ALDEEU Ser.). (SPA.). 176p. (C). 1992. pap. 22.00 (*0-9626630-2-6*) Spanish Profs Amer.

Ortega y Gasset & the Question of Modernity. Intro. by Patrick H. Dust. (Hispanic Issues Ser.: No. 5). 387p. (Orig.). 1989. pap. 12.95 (*0-910235-34-1*) Prisma Bks.

Ortega y Gasset en la Cultura Hispanoamerican (Ortega y Gasset in Hispanomarican Culture) Tzvi Medin. (SPA.). 318p. 1994. pap. 14.99 (*968-16-4251-1*, Pub. by Fondo) Continental Bk.

Ortho Asia. 3rd ed. Larry D. Iversen. 1986. 10.95 (*0-316-43434-5*, Little Brwn Med Div) Lppncott W & W.

Ortho-Bionomy: A Practical Manual. Kathy Kain. LC 97-19837. (Illus.). 194p. (Orig.). 1997. pap. 19.95 (*1-55643-250-X*) North Atlantic.

Ortho Book of Gardening Basics. Susan Lang. Ed. by Norman Rae. LC 90-86169. (Illus.). 504p. 1991. 24.95 (*0-89721-233-9*, Ortho Bks) Meredith Bks.

Ortho Dump Bin. Date not set. write for info. (*0-676-52107-X*, Ortho Bks) Meredith Bks.

Ortho Garden Planner 95-MID-NE. Ortho Books Staff. 1995. pap. 10.95 (*0-89721-262-2*, Ortho Bks) Meredith Bks.

Ortho Garden Planner 96-SE. Ortho Books Staff. 1995. pap. 10.95 (*0-89721-278-9*, Ortho Bks) Meredith Bks.

Ortho Garden Planner 96-West. Ortho Books Staff. 1995. pap. 10.95 (*0-89721-277-0*, Ortho Bks) Meredith Bks.

Ortho Home Gardener's Problem Solver. Rick Bond et al. Ed. by Cheryl Smith. (Illus.). 400p. 1996. 39.95 (*0-89721-358-0*, Ortho Bks) Meredith Bks.

Ortho Home Gardener's Problem Solver. L. Patricia Kite. Ed. by Cheryl Smith. LC 92-61734. (Illus.). 400p. (Orig.). 1993. pap. 24.95 (*0-89721-255-X*, 06030, Ortho Bks) Meredith Bks.

***Ortho Problem Solver.** (Illus.). 1140p. 1999. 150.00 (*0-89721-453-6*, Ortho Bks) Meredith Bks.

Ortho Problem Solver. 3rd ed. Michael Smith & Ortho Books-Reference Staff. LC 88-63838. 1993. pap. 180.00 (*0-89721-199-5*, Ortho Bks) Meredith Bks.

Ortho Problem Solver. 4th rev. ed. Ortho Books-Reference Staff. Ed. by Michael D. Smith. LC 94-65696. (Illus.). 960p. 1994. 225.00 (*0-89721-268-1*, UPC 06021, Ortho Bks) Meredith Bks.

***Ortho Side of PCBS.** L. G. Hansen. LC 99-27960. 269p. 1999. write for info. (*0-7923-8541-1*) Kluwer Academic.

Ortho Wood Podium. Date not set. write for info. (*0-676-52108-8*, Ortho Bks) Meredith Bks.

Orthobionomics: Hygienic System. 2nd ed. Herbert M. Shelton. 352p. 1996. reprint ed. spiral bd. 21.00 (*0-7873-1303-3*) Hlth Research.

Orthodontic Cephalometry. Athanasiou. 1995. 143.00 (*0-7234-2045-9*) Mosby Inc.

Orthodontic Diagnosis. Thomas Rakosi & Irmtrud Jonas. LC 92-49147. (Color Atlas of Dental Medicine Ser.). 1993. 179.00 (*0-86577-450-1*) Thieme Med Pubs.

***Orthodontic Materials: Scientific & Clinical Aspects.** William A. Brantley & Theodore Eliades. (Illus.). 256p. 2000. 79.00 (*0-86577-929-5*) Thieme Med Pubs.

Orthodontic Treatment: Management of Unfavorable Sequelae. Ed. by J. A. McNamara, Jr. & Carroll-Ann Trotman. (Craniofacial Growth Ser.: Vol. 31). (Illus.). 437p. 1996. 69.00 (*0-929921-27-5*) UM CHGD.

Orthodontic Treatment: Outcome & Effectiveness. Ed. by Carroll-Ann Trotman & James A. McNamara. (Craniofacial Growth Ser.: Vol. 30). (Illus.). 387p. 1995. 59.00 (*0-929921-26-7*) UM CHGD.

Orthodontic Treatment Mechanics & the Pre-Adjusted Appliance. John C. Bennett. (Illus.). 265p. (C). (gr. 13). 1993. text 142.00 (*0-8151-0673-4*, 23026) Mosby Inc.

Orthodontics. 2nd ed. Spiro J. Chaconas. (Illus.). 356p. 1989. boxed set. write for info. (*0-8151-1612-8*) Mosby Inc.

Orthodontics: Current Principles & Techniques. 3rd ed. (Illus.). 976p. 1999. text 169.00 (*0-8151-9363-7*, 31746) Mosby Inc.

***Orthodontics: Pciture Test Atlas.** Claire Nightingale & Jonothan Sandy. (Illus.). 192p. 2000. pap. text 32.50 (*0-7236-1072-X*, Pub. by John Wright) Buttrwrth-Heinemann.

Orthodontics No. 2: Current Principles & Techniques. 2nd ed. Thomas M. Graber et al. (Illus.). 976p. (C). (gr. 13). 1994. text 180.00 (*0-8016-6590-6*, 06590) Mosby Inc.

***Orthodontics & Paediatric Dentistry.** Declan T. Millett & Richard Welbury. LC 99-53892. (Colour Guide Ser.). (Illus.). 1999. write for info. (*0-443-06287-0*) Church.

Orthodontics in an Aging Society. W. Andrew Achenbaum et al. Ed. by David S. Carlson. LC 88-71195. (Craniofacial Growth Ser.: Vol. 22). (Illus.). 199p. 1989. 49.00 (*0-929921-18-6*) UM CHGD.

Orthodontics with Fixed Appliances. Frans P. Van Der Linden. Tr. by John F. Jefferys. LC 97-3037. (Van der Linden Orthodontic Ser.). (Illus.). 567p. 1997. pap. text 120.00 (*1-85097-044-0*) Quint Pub Co.

Orthodox, 7. Thomas E. Fitzgerald. LC 94-21685. (Denominations in America Ser.: Vol. 7). 184p. 1995. lib. bdg. 75.00 (*0-313-26281-0*, Greenwood Pr) Greenwood.

Orthodox Alaska: A Theology of Mission. Michael J. Oleksa. LC 92-37026. 1993. pap. 11.95 (*0-88141-092-6*) St Vladimirs.

Orthodox & Catholic Sister Churches: East Is West & West Is East, Vol. 27. Michael A. Fahey. LC 96-4522. (Pere Marquette Lectures: No. 1996). (Illus.). 1996. 15.00 (*0-87462-576-9*) Marquette.

***Orthodox & Complementary Medicine: An Alliance for a Changing World.** W. H. Kirkaldy-Willis & A. A. Swartz. 200p. (C). 2000. pap. 18.95 (*1-55643-355-7*) North Atlantic.

Orthodox Apologetic Theology. I. M. Andreyev. LC 94-67834. (Illus.). 216p. 1995. pap. 10.00 (*0-938635-48-4*) St Herman Pr.

Orthodox Approach to Philosophy. Apostolos Makrakis. Ed. by Orthodox Christian Educational Society Staff. Tr. by Denver Cummings. (Logos & Holy Spirit in the Unity of Christian Thought Ser.: Vol. 1). 82p. 1977. reprint ed. pap. 5.00 (*0-938366-06-8*) Orthodox Chr.

Orthodox Christian Alphabet Coloring Book. Moses Armstrong. 35p. (J). (gr. k-3). Date not set. pap. 5.00 (*1-879038-45-5*, 9013) Synaxis Pr.

Orthodox-Christian Apologetics see Pravoslavno-Khristijanskaja Apologetika

Orthodox Christian Meditations: Spiritual Discourses for the Orthodox Christians. Apostolos Makrakis. Ed. by Orthodox Christian Educational Society Staff. Tr. by Denver Cummings. 143p. (Orig.). 1965. pap. 3.95 (*0-938366-22-X*) Orthodox Chr.

Orthodox-Christian Moral Theology see Pravoslavno-Khristijanskoe Nravstvennoje Bogoslovije

Orthodox Christian Terminology: A Discussion of the Subject of Developing a Satisfactory, Acceptable, Standardised English Language Terminology in Eastern Orthodox Theology, Hagiology, Church Services, & the Sacred Arts, Together with Greek-English & English Greek Glossaries. Constantine Cavarnos. LC 97-77265. 80p. 1997. pap. 5.95 (*0-914744-98-4*) Inst Byzantine.

Orthodox Christian Theological Language & World Religions. Anastasios Zavales. (Illus.). 127p. (Orig.). (C). 1995. pap. text 49.95 (*1-884090-03-6*) Ecumenics Intl.

Orthodox Christians & Moslems. Ed. by Nomikos M. Vaporis. 203p. 1986. pap. 6.95 (*0-917651-34-0*, Pub. by Holy Cross Orthodox) BookWorld.

***Orthodox Christians in America.** John A. Erickson. LC 99-19901. (Religion in American Life Ser.). (Illus.). 144p. (YA). (gr. 7 up). 1999. lib. bdg. 22.00 (*0-19-510852-3*) OUP.

Orthodox Christians in North America, 1794-1994. Mark Stokoe & Leonid Kishkovsky. LC 95-32128. 1995. pap. 12.95 (*0-86642-053-3*) Ortho Church Am.

Orthodox Church. Thomas E. FitzGerald. LC 94-21685. 184p. 1998. pap., student ed. 18.95 (*0-275-96438-8*, Praeger Pubs) Greenwood.

Orthodox Church. rev. ed. Sergius Bulgakov. Tr. by Lydia W. Kesich from RUS. LC 88-1851.Tr. of Pravoslavie. 200p. (Orig.). 1988. pap. 11.95 (*0-88141-051-9*) St Vladimirs.

Orthodox Church: Four Hundred & Fifty-Five Questions & Answers. Stanley S. Harakas. 1988. pap. 16.95 (*0-937032-56-5*) Light&Life Pub Co MN.

Orthodox Church: Its Past & Its Role in the World Today. 3rd ed. John Meyendorff. LC 81-4978. 196p. 1996. reprint ed. pap. 11.95 (*0-913836-81-8*) St Vladimirs.

Orthodox Church: New Edition. Timothy Ware. (Illus.). 368p. (Orig.). 1993. pap. 14.95 (*0-14-014656-3*, Penguin Bks) Viking Penguin.

Orthodox Church - A Well-Kept Secret: A Journey Through Church History. George Nicozisin. 192p. (Orig.). 1997. pap. 11.95 (*1-880971-33-X*) Light&Life Pub Co MN.

Orthodox Church & the Ecumenical Movement During the Period 1920-1969. George P. Macris. (Illus.). 196p. (Orig.). 1986. pap. 12.50 (*0-913026-74-3*) St Nectarios.

Orthodox Church in the Byzantine Empire. Joan M. Hussey. (Oxford History of the Christian Church Ser.). (Illus.). 440p. 1990. reprint ed. pap. text 39.95 (*0-19-826456-9*) OUP.

Orthodox Church in the History of Russia. Dimitry Pospielovsky. LC 98-26971. 1998. 19.95 (*0-88141-179-5*) St Vladimirs.

Orthodox Church of India: History. David Daniel. 1986. 14.95 (*0-318-36664-9*) Asia Bk Corp.

Orthodox Church of the East in the Eighteenth Century. Tr. by George Williams. LC 73-131028. reprint ed. 45.00 (*0-404-06977-0*) AMS Pr.

Orthodox Church's Vision of Unity. Jane M. De Vyver. (Illus.). 36p. 1995. pap. 3.50 (*1-881211-24-X*) Firebird Videos.

Orthodox Clip Art. John Matusiak. (Illus.). 87p. 1987. pap. 17.95 (*1-880971-55-0*) Light&Life Pub Co MN.

Orthodox Conference Proceedings, 1990. limited ed. Ed. by St. Nectarios Press Staff. 80p. (Orig.). 1990. pap. 6.00 (*0-913026-26-3*) St Nectarios.

Orthodox Corruption of Scripture: The Effect of Early Christological Controversies on the Text of the New Testament. Brad D. Ehrman. 328p. 1996. pap. text 19.95 (*0-19-510279-7*) OUP.

Orthodox Daily Prayers. Ed. by St. Tikhon's Seminary Press Staff. 169p. (Orig.). 1982. 10.95 (*1-878997-26-2*); pap. 8.95 (*1-878997-25-4*) St Tikhons Pr.

Orthodox Definition of Political Science see Political Philosophy of the Orthodox Church

Orthodox Definition of Political Science. Apostolos Makrakis. Ed. by Orthodox Christian Educational Society Staff. Tr. by Denver Cummings. 163p. 1968. reprint ed. pap. 4.95 (*0-938366-31-9*) Orthodox Chr.

Orthodox Doctrine of the Apostolic Eastern Church. Platon. 1973. 5.00 (*0-89981-066-7*) Eastern Orthodox.

Orthodox Doctrine of the Apostolic Eastern Church: A Compendium of Christian Theology. Platon. LC 70-81772. reprint ed. 42.50 (*0-404-05058-1*) AMS Pr.

Orthodox Dogmatic Theology: A Concise Exposition. 2nd ed. Michael Pomazansky. Tr. by Hieromonk S. Rose from RUS. LC 84-51294. (Orthodox Theological Texts Ser.). 426p. (Orig.). (C). 1997. reprint ed. pap. 19.95 (*0-938635-69-7*) St Herman Pr.

Orthodox Eastern Church. 3rd ed. Adrian Fortescue. LC 70-179520. (Select Bibliographies Reprint Ser.). 1977. reprint ed. 29.95 (*0-8369-6649-X*) Ayer.

Orthodox Evangelist see Library of American Puritan Writings: The Seventeenth Century

Orthodox Faith & Life in Christ: Translation, Preface, & Introduction by Asterios Gerostergios, et Al. Justin Popovich et al. LC 94-79270. (Illus.). 248p. 1994. pap. 17.50 (*1-884729-02-9*) Inst Byzantine.

Orthodox Fathers, Orthodox Faith. Touma Al-Khouri. LC 96-135457. (Trilogy for Christ Ser.: Pt. 1). 392p. 1994. per. 10.95 (*1-879038-20-X*) Oakwood Pubns.

***Orthodox Feasts of Jesus Christ & the Virgin Mary.** Hugh Wybrew. LC 00-38720. 2000. pap. write for info. (*0-88141-203-1*) St Vladimirs.

Orthodox Fundamentalists: A Critical View. John W. Morris. LC 98-67944. 103p. 1998. pap. 10.95 (*1-880971-40-2*) Light&Life Pub Co MN.

Orthodox House of Worship: Informative & Interpretative Homilies on Liturgical Themes. Augoustinos N. Kantiotes & Asterios Gerostergios. LC 94-77475. (Illus.). 232p. 1994. 17.50 (*1-884729-01-0*) Inst Byzantine.

Orthodox Iconography: Four Essays Dealing with the History of Orthodox Iconography, the Iconographic Decoration of Churches, the Functions of Icons, & the Theology & Aesthetics of Byzantine Iconography, in Addition Three Appendices Containing Early Christian Texts on Icons, Etc. 3rd ed. Constantine Cavarnos. LC 77-74606. (Illus.). 100p. 1992. pap. 5.95 (*0-914744-37-2*) Inst Byzantine.

Orthodox Jewish Brit Chadasha. Tr. by Phillip E. Goble from GRE. LC 97-72602. 723p. (Orig.). 1997. pap. 29.95 (*0-939341-03-4*) AFI Intl Pubs.

Orthodox Judaism in America. Moshe D. Sherman. LC 95-20932. (Jewish Denominations in America Ser.). 304p. 1996. lib. bdg. 85.00 (*0-313-24316-6*, Greenwood Pr) Greenwood.

Orthodox Lent, Holy Week, & Easter: Liturgical Texts with Commentary. Hugh Wybrew. LC 97-5317. 1997. 9.95 (*0-88141-162-0*) St Vladimirs.

Orthodox Liturgical Dress. Chrysostomos. 73p. 1998. reprint ed. pap. 8.95 (*1-886412-22-7*) Preserv Press.

Orthodox Liturgy. 1984. 21.95 (*0-685-08597-X*) OUP.

Orthodox Liturgy: The Development of the Eucharistic Liturgy in the Byzantine Rite. Hugh Wybrew. LC 90-37967. (Illus.). (Orig.). 1990. pap. 11.95 (*0-88141-100-0*) St Vladimirs.

Orthodox Missionary Society of Russia: An Historical Account of Its Foundation. C. R. Hales. 1994. pap. 1.50 (*0-89981-146-9*) Eastern Orthodox.

***Orthodox New Testament No. 1: The Holy Gospels: Evangelistarion.** Holy Apostles Convent Staff. Ed. & Illus. by Dormition Skete. LC 99-73026.Tr. of Evangelistarion. 640p. 1999. 36.50 (*0-944359-13-2*) Holy Apostles Convent.

O

***Orthodox New Testament No. 2: Acts, Epistles, & Revelation: Praxapostolos.** Holy Apostles Convent Staff. Ed. & Illus. by Dormition Skete. LC 99-73025.Tr. of Praxapostolos. 672p. 1999. 36.50 (*0-944359-14-0*) Holy Apostles Convent.

Orthodox Perspectives on Baptism, Eucharist & Ministry. Ed. by Gennadios Limouris & Nomikos M. Vaporis. LC 85-27298. Vol. 128. xii, 168p. (Orig.). 1985. pap. 6.95 (*0-917651-22-7*, Pub. by Holy Cross Orthodox) BookWorld.

Orthodox Perspectives on Pastoral Praxis: Papers of the Intra-Orthodox Conference on Pastoral Praxis (24-25 September, 1986) Celebrating the 50th Anniversary of Holy Cross Greek Orthodox School of Theology (1937-1987) Ed. by Theodore G. Stylianopoulos. 202p. (Orig.). (C). 1988. pap. 6.95 (*0-917651-19-7*, Pub. by Holy Cross Orthodox) BookWorld.

Orthodox Pomjanyk of the Seventeenth-Eighteenth Centuries. Ihor Sevcenko et al. LC 89-84703. (Harvard Series in Ukrainian Studies). xii, 292p. (C). 1989. text 19.95 (*0-916458-32-6*) Harvard Ukrainian.

***Orthodox Prayer Book.** Ephrem Lash. 118p. 1999. pap. 12.00 (*0-19-122447-2*) OUP.

Orthodox Prayer Book. Russian Day Committee Staff. (ENG & SLA.). 606p. 1991. 14.95 (*1-878997-16-5*); 14.95 (*1-878997-29-7*) St Tikhons Pr.

***Orthodox Prophecy on the Pontificate of John Paul II & the Oracle of Kremna: The WWIII.** Helen Tzima Otto. Ed. by Gordon H. Otto. LC 98-90545. (Orthodox Prophecy on the End Times: Vol. 1). (Illus.). 216p. 2000. pap. 12.00 (*1-891663-00-3*) Verenikia Pr.

Orthodox-Protestant Debate. Apostolos Makrakis. Tr. by Denver Cummings. 101p. 1949. reprint ed. pap. 5.95 (*0-938366-37-8*) Orthodox Chr.

Orthodox Saints, Vol. 1. George Poulos. 1992. pap. 13.95 (*0-917651-64-2*, Pub. by Holy Cross Orthodox) BookWorld.

Orthodox Saints, Vol. 2. George Poulos. 1992. pap. 13.95 (*0-917651-65-0*, Pub. by Holy Cross Orthodox) BookWorld.

Orthodox Saints, Vol. 3. George Poulos. 1992. pap. 13.95 (*0-917651-66-9*, Pub. by Holy Cross Orthodox) BookWorld.

Orthodox Saints, Vol. 4. George Poulos. 1992. pap. 13.95 (*0-917651-67-7*, Pub. by Holy Cross Orthodox) BookWorld.

***Orthodox Social Ethics, Vol. 3.** Stanley S. Harakas. LC 98-56047. (Wholeness of Faith & Life Ser.). 140p. 1999. pap. 12.95 (*1-885652-30-5*, Pub. by Holy Cross Orthodox) BookWorld.

Orthodox Spiritual Life. Giorgios I. Mantzarides. LC 94-13034. 1994. pap. text 12.95 (*0-916586-69-3*, Pub. by Holy Cross Orthodox) BookWorld.

***Orthodox Spiritual Life According to Saint Silouan of Mount Athos.** Harry M. Boosalis. LC 00-22089. 2000. pap. write for info. (*1-878997-60-2*) St Tikhons Pr.

Orthodox Spirituality. 1987. pap. 0.50 (*0-89981-067-5*) Eastern Orthodox.

Orthodox Spirituality: An Outline of the Orthodox Ascetical & Mystical Tradition. Monk of the Eastern Church Staff. LC 96-26144. 111p. 1978. pap. 8.95 (*0-913836-51-6*) St Vladimirs.

Orthodox Synthesis: The Unity of Theological Thought. Ed. by Joseph J. Allen. LC 81-5674. 231p. (Orig.). 1981. pap. 10.95 (*0-913836-84-2*) St Vladimirs.

Orthodox Theology: An Introduction. Vladimir Lossky. LC 78-1853. 137p. 1978. pap. 9.95 (*0-913836-43-5*) St Vladimirs.

Orthodox Theology & Diakonia: Trends & Prospects. Intro. by Demetrios J. Constantelos. 398p. (C). 1981. 17.95 (*0-916586-79-0*, Pub. by Hellenic Coll Pr) BookWorld.

Orthodox Union Story: A Centenary Portrayal. Saul Bernstein. 400p. 1997. pap. 40.00 (*0-7657-9953-7*) Aronson.

Orthodox Veneration of Mary the Birthgiver of God: Orthodox Theological Texts. 4th rev. ed. John Maximovitch. Ed. by St. Herman of Alaska Brotherhood Staff. Tr. & Intro. by Seraphim Rose. LC 94-66189. (Illus.). 88p. 1994. pap. 7.00 (*0-938635-68-9*) St Herman Pr.

Orthodox View on Abortion. John Kowalczyk. 1979. pap. 4.95 (*0-686-27070-3*) Light&Life Pub Co MN.

Orthodox Way. Kallistos T. Ware. 196p. 1979. pap. 9.95 (*0-913836-58-3*) St Vladimirs.

Orthodox Worship: A Living Continuity with the Synagogue, the Temple & the Early Church. H. Anstall & B. Williams. 1990. pap. 12.95 (*0-937032-72-7*) Light&Life Pub Co MN.

Orthodoxies in Massachusetts: Rereading America Puritanism. Janice Knight. LC 93-6398. 312p. 1994. 51.95 (*0-674-64487-5*) HUP.

Orthodoxies in Massachusetts: Rereading American Puritanism. Janice Knight. 330p. 1997. reprint ed. pap. 19.50 (*0-674-64488-3*) HUP.

Orthodoxy. G. K. Chesterton. 160p. Date not set. 160.00 (*0-8488-2648-5*) Amereon Ltd.

Orthodoxy. G. K. Chesterton. 160p. 1991. pap. 9.95 (*0-385-01536-4*, Image Bks) Doubleday.

Orthodoxy. G. K. Chesterton. LC 95-75659. 168p. 1995. pap. 10.95 (*0-89870-552-5*) Ignatius Pr.

Orthodoxy. G. K. Chesterton. LC 94-18847. (Wheaton Literary Ser.). 188p. 1994. 14.99 (*0-87788-630-X*, H Shaw Pubs) Waterbrook Pr.

Orthodoxy: A Creed for Today: Talks on the Nicene Creed. Anthony M. Coniaris. 1972. pap. 11.95 (*0-937032-19-0*) Light&Life Pub Co MN.

Orthodoxy & Heresy in Earliest Christianity. Walter Bauer. LC 71-141252. 352p. reprint ed. pap. 109.20 (*0-608-17174-3*, 202787600056) Bks Demand.

Orthodoxy & Heresy in Earliest Christianity. Walter Bauer. Ed. by Robert Kraft & Gerhard A. Krodel. Tr. by Philadelphia Seminar on Christian Origins Staff from GEH. 352p. 1996. reprint ed. pap. 24.00 (*0-9623642-7-4*) Sigler Pr.

Orthodoxy & Heresy in Religious Movements: Discipline & Dissent. Ed. by Malcolm R. Greenshields & Thomas A. Robinson. LC 92-35171. 196p. 1992. text 79.95 (*0-7734-9183-X*) E Mellen.

Orthodoxy & Modern Society. Sergius Bulgakov. Ed. & Tr. by Robert Bird. (Readings in Russian Philosophy Ser.: Vol. 4). 62p. 1995. pap. 3.50 (*1-929829-03-5*) Variable Pr.

Orthodoxy & Nationality: Andreiu Saguna & the Rumanians of Transylvania, 1846-1873. Keith Hitchins. (Historical Studies: No. 94). 336p. 1977. 25.00 (*0-674-64491-3*) HUP.

***Orthodoxy & Reform: The Clergy in Seventeenth Century Rostock.** Jonathan Strom. (Beitraege Zur Historischen Theologie Ser.: Vol. 111). 300p. 1999. 225.00 (*3-16-147191-1*, Pub. by JCB Mohr) Coronet Bks.

Orthodoxy & the Religion of the Future. Seraphim Rose. 272p. 1996. pap. 10.00 (*1-887904-00-X*) St Herman Pr.

Orthodoxy Confronts Modernity. Ed. by Jonathan Sacks. 19.95 (*0-88125-363-4*) Ktav.

***Orthodoxy, Difference & Scales: Essayson the Plitical Geography of Russian Orthodox Church(es) in the 20th Century.** Dmitri Sidorov. (Princeton Theological Monograph Ser.: 46). 2000. pap. write for info. (*1-55635-038-4*) Pickwick.

Orthodoxy, Heresy, & Schism in Early Christianity. Ed. by Everett Ferguson. LC 92-41867. (Studies in Early Christianity: Vol. 4). 376p. 1993. text 77.00 (*0-8153-1064-1*) Garland.

Orthodoxy, Heterodoxy & Dissent in India. Ed. by Samuel N. Eisenstadt et al. LC 83-26910. (Religion & Society Ser.: No. 23). viii, 179p. 1984. 67.70 (*3-11-009659-5*) Mouton.

Orthodoxy in Australia. H. Simmons. 1986. pap. 4.95 (*0-917653-20-3*, Pub. by Hellenic Coll Pr) BookWorld.

Orthodoxy of the Church. Watchman Nee. 102p. 1973. per. 7.25 (*0-87083-007-4*, 08-017-001) Living Stream Ministry.

Orthodoxy, Roman-Catholicism, Protestatism & Sectarianism see Pravoslavije, Rimo-Katolichestvo, Protenstatizm i Sektantstvo

Orthoepic Dictionary of the Russian Language. 4th ed. S. N. Borunova et al. Ed. by R. I. Avanesova. (RUS.). 704p. 1988. reprint ed. 21.95 (*0-8285-5375-0*) Firebird NY.

Orthogeriatrics: Comprehensive Orthopedic Care for the Elderly Patient. Raymond J. Newman. (Illus.). 224p. 1992. text 150.00 (*0-7506-1371-8*) Buttrwrth-Heinemann.

Orthognathic Surgery: A Synopsis of Basis Principles & Surgical Techniques. George Dimitroulis et al. (Illus.). 198p. 1994. pap. text 52.50 (*0-7236-1017-7*) Buttrwrth-Heinemann.

Orthogonal & Symplectic Clifford Algebras: Spinor Structures. Albert Crumeyrolle. (C). 1990. text 248.50 (*0-7923-0541-8*) Kluwer Academic.

Orthogonal Arrays. A. S. Hedayat et al. Ed. by P. Bickel et al. LC 99-30377. 440p. 1999. 64.95 (*0-387-98766-5*) Spr-Verlag.

Orthogonal Decompositions & Functional Limit Theorems for Random Graph Statistics. Svante Janson. LC 94-17088. (Memoirs Ser.: No. 534). 78p. 1994. pap. 31.00 (*0-8218-2595-X*, MEMO/111/534) Am Math.

Orthogonal Decompositions & Integral Lattices. A. A. Kostrikin & P. H. Tiep. (De Gruyter Expositions in Mathematics Ser.: 15). 534p. (C). 1994. lib. bdg. 109.95 (*3-11-013783-6*) De Gruyter.

Orthogonal Frequency Division Multiplexing for Wireless Communications. (C). 1999. text 70.00 (*0-13-010640-2*) P-H.

Orthogonal Functions. G. Sansone. 411p. 1991. pap. 9.95 (*0-486-66730-8*) Dover.

Orthogonal Functions, Moment Theory & Continued Fractions: Theory & Applications. Ed. by William B. Jones & A. Sri Ranga. LC 98-24470. (Lecture Notes in Pure & Applied Mathematics Ser.). (Illus.). 440p. 1998. pap. text 165.00 (*0-8247-0207-7*) Dekker.

Orthogonal Matrix-Valued Polynomials & Applications. Ed. by I. Gohberg. (Operator Theory Ser.: Vol. 34). 232p. 1988. 114.00 (*0-8176-2242-X*) Birkhauser.

***Orthogonal Polarization Spectral Imaging (OPS Imaging) - a New Tool for the Observation & Measurement of the Human Microcirculation: 16th Bodensee Symposium on Microcirculation, Lindau, September 1999.** Ed. by K. Messmer. (Progress in Applied Microcirculation Ser.: Vol. 24). (Illus.). 118p. 2000. 111.50 (*3-8055-7065-1*) S Karger.

Orthogonal Polynomials. Geza Freud. LC 76-134028. 1971. text 140.00 (*0-08-016047-6*, Pub. by Pergamon Repr) Franklin.

Orthogonal Polynomials. Paul G. Nevai. LC 78-32112. (Memoirs of the American Mathematical Society Ser.: No. 213). 185p. 1991. reprint ed. pap. 18.00 (*0-8218-2213-6*, MEMO/18/213) Am Math.

Orthogonal Polynomials. Gabor Szego. LC 39-33497. (Colloquium Publications: Vol. 23). 432p. 1975. reprint ed. pap. 34.00 (*0-8218-1023-5*, COLL/23) Am Math.

Orthogonal Polynomials: Estimates, Asymptotic Formulas, & Series of Polynomials Orthogonal on the Unit Circle & on an Interval. L. Ya Geronimus. LC 60-53450. 248p. reprint ed. pap. 76.90 (*0-608-13318-3*, 205580100038) Bks Demand.

Orthogonal Polynomials - Theory & Practice: Proceedings of the NATO Advanced Study Institute on "Orthogonal Polynomials & Their Applications" Held in Columbus, Ohio, U. S. A. May 22 - June 3, 1989. Paul G. Nevai. (C). 1989. text 255.50 (*0-7923-0569-8*) Kluwer Academic.

***Orthogonal Polynomials & Random Matrices: A Riemann-Hilbert Approach.** P. A. Deift. LC 98-74666. (Lecture Notes in Mathematics Ser.). 273p. 1999. write for info. (*0-9658703-2-4*) NYU Courant.

Orthogonal Polynomials & Special Functions. Richard Askey. (CBMS-NSF Regional Conference Series in Applied Mathematics: No. 21). vii, 110p. 1975. pap. text 29.50 (*0-89871-018-9*) Soc Indus-Appl Math.

Orthogonal Polynomials & Their Applications: Proceedings of the International Congress. Ed. by Jaime Vinuesa. (Lecture Notes in Pure & Applied Mathematics Ser.: Vol. 117). (Illus.). 240p. 1989. pap. text 165.00 (*0-8247-8161-9*) Dekker.

Orthogonal Polynomials for Engineers & Physicists. Petr Beckmann. LC 72-87318. 1973. 35.00 (*0-911762-14-0*) Golem.

***Orthogonal Polynomials in Two Variables.** P. K. Suetin. (Analytical Methods & Special Functions Ser.). 368p. 1999. 130.00 (*90-5699-167-1*) Gordon & Breach.

Orthogonal Rational Functions. Adhemar Bultheel et al. LC 98-11646. (Monographs on Applied & Computational Mathematics: No. 5). (Illus.). 384p. (C). 1999. text 59.95 (*0-521-65006-2*) Cambridge U Pr.

Orthogonal Series. B. Kashin & A. Saakyan. LC 89-333. (Translations of Mathematical Monographs: Vol. 75). 451p. 1989. text 170.00 (*0-8218-4527-6*, MMONO/75) Am Math.

Orthogonal Series & Approximation of Functions. LC 85-20001. (Steklov Institute of Mathematics Ser.: Vol. 164). 273p. 1985. pap. 121.00 (*0-8218-3091-0*, STEKLO/164) Am Math.

***Orthogonal Sets & Polar Methods in Linear Algebra: Applications to Matrix Calculations, Systems of Equations, Inequalities, & Linear Programming.** Enrique Castillo et al. LC 98-38391. (Pure & Applied Mathematics: A Wiley-Interscience Series of Texts, Monographs & Tracts). 422p. 1999. 99.95 (*0-471-32889-8*) Wiley.

Orthogonale Polynome. Geza Freud. (Mathematische Reihe Ser.: No. 33). (GER., Illus.). 294p. 1980. 76.00 (*0-8176-0127-9*) Birkhauser.

Orthogonality & Spacetime Geometry. Robert Goldblatt. (Universitext Ser.). (Illus.). 210p. 1987. 63.95 (*0-387-96519-X*) Spr-Verlag.

Orthograhic Dictionary of the Russian Language. 25th ed. Ed. by S. G. Barkhudarova et al. (RUS.). 400p. 1987. reprint ed. 12.95 (*0-8285-5444-7*) Firebird NY.

Orthograhie Als Sprachkultur. Horst H. Munske. VIII, 336p. 1997. 44.95 (*3-631-31142-7*) P Lang Pubng.

Orthographe Francaise a l'Epoque de la Renaissance. Catach. (Publ. Romanes et Franc.). 87.40 (*0-685-36649-9*, F134160) Fr & Eur.

Orthographe Francaise a l'Epoque de la Renaissance. Catach. (FRE.). 498p. 1968. pap. 150.00 (*0-7859-5219-5*) Fr & Eur.

Orthographe pour Tous. Bescherelle. (FRE.). 256p. 1990. 22.95 (*0-7859-9237-5*) Fr & Eur.

Orthographe Sans Peine: Orthography for French Speakers. Assimil Staff. (FRE.). 28.95 (*0-8288-4396-1*, M10747) Fr & Eur.

Orthographic Codes & Code-Switching: A Study in 16th Century Swedish Orthography. Alexander Zheltukhin. LC 96-225833. (Stockholm Studies in Scandinavian Philology: No. 21). 298p. 1996. pap. 54.50 (*91-22-01738-0*) Coronet Bks.

Orthographic Dictionary of the Lettish (Latvian) Language. L. Ceplitis. (LAV.). 358p. 1981. 14.95 (*0-8288-1624-7*, F58240) Fr & Eur.

Orthographic Projection Simplified. 4th ed. Charles Quinlan. 128p. 1986. text 11.59 (*0-02-668490-X*) Glencoe.

Orthographic Projection Simplified. 5th ed. Charles Quinlan. (Illus.). 128p. (YA). (gr. 6-12). 1999. pap., student ed. 11.48 (*0-02-677320-1*) Glencoe.

Orthographic Way of Writing English Prosody. 1976. reprint ed. pap. 1.95 (*0-934982-10-4*) Primary Pr.

Orthographical Dictionary of the Russian Language. S. Barkhudarov. (RUS.). 480p. (C). 1980. 90.00 (*0-7855-5048-8*, Pub. by Collets) St Mut.

Orthographie. Pierre Burney. 128p. 1967. 9.95 (*0-8288-7462-X*) Fr & Eur.

***Orthographieerwerb: Qualitative Fehleranalysen Zum Aufbau der Orthographischen Kompetenz.** Gunther Thome. (Illus.). 338p. 1998. 51.95 (*3-631-34221-7*) P Lang Pubng.

Orthographies & Reading: Perspectives from Cognitive Psychology, Neuropsychology, & Linguistics. Ed. by Leslie Henderson. 144p. 1984. text 29.95 (*0-86377-009-6*) L Erlbaum Assocs.

Orthography & Phonology. Ed. by Phillip A. Luelsdorff. LC 87-9361. xi, 238p. (C). 1987. 74.00 (*90-272-2039-5*) J Benjamins Pubng Co.

Orthography, Phonology, Morphology, & Meaning. Ed. by Ram Frost & Leonard Katz. LC 92-29646. (Advances in Psychology Ser.: Vol. 94). viii,436p. 1992. 166.50 (*0-444-89140-4*, North Holland) Elsevier.

***Orthokeratology: A Practical Approach.** David Ruston et al. (Illus.). 224p. 2000. pap. 52.50 (*0-7506-4007-3*) Buttrwrth-Heinemann.

Orthokeratology Handbook. Todd D. Winkler & Rodger T. Kame. LC 94-33552. (Illus.). 112p. 1994. spiral bd. 40.00 (*0-7506-9595-1*) Buttrwrth-Heinemann.

Orthomodular Lattices. Ladislav Beran. 1985. text 220.00 (*90-277-1715-X*) Kluwer Academic.

Orthomodular Lattices. G. Kalmbach. (London Mathematical Society Monographs: No. 18). 1983. text 173.00 (*0-12-394580-1*) Acad Pr.

Orthomodular Structures As Quantum Logics: Intrinsic Properties, State Space & Probabilistic Topics. Pavel Ptak & Sylvia Pulmannova. (C). 1991. text 166.50 (*0-7923-1207-4*) Kluwer Academic.

Orthomolecular Treatment for Schizophrenia. Abram Hoffer. (Good Health Guides Ser.). 48p. 1999. pap. 3.95 (*0-87983-910-4*, 39104K, Keats Publng) NTC Contemp Pub Co.

Orthomorphism Graphs of Groups. Anthony B. Evans. LC 92-41123. (Lecture Notes in Mathematics Ser.: Vol. 1535). 1993. 30.95 (*0-387-56351-2*) Spr-Verlag.

Orthongonal Functions in Systems & Control. K. B. Datta & B. M. Mohan. 288p. 1995. text 68.00 (*981-02-1889-3*) World Scientific Pub.

Orthonormal Systems & Banach Space Geometry. Albrecht Pietsch & Jorg Wenzel. LC 98-227912. (Encyclopedia of Mathematics & Its Applications Ser.: No. 70). (Illus.). 554p. (C). 1998. text 80.00 (*0-521-62462-2*) Cambridge U Pr.

Orthopaed Physiother. Tidswell. 1998. 29.95 (*0-7234-2592-2*) Mosby Inc.

Orthopaedic. Brotzma. 1996. text 130.00 (*0-8151-1011-1*, 29167) Mosby Inc.

Orthopaedic Allograft Surgery. Andrei A. Czitrom & Heinz Winkler. LC 96-15022. (Illus.). 300p. 1996. 215.00 (*3-211-82647-5*) Spr-Verlag.

Orthopaedic Anaesthesia. 2nd ed. A. Loach. 192p. 1994. text 75.00 (*0-340-56438-5*, Pub. by E A) OUP.

Orthopaedic & Sports Physical Therapy. James A. Gould, III. (Mosby-Year Book Publication Ser.). (Illus.). 718p. 1990. 61.95 (*0-685-48371-1*, M2908, CRC Reprint) Franklin.

Orthopaedic Anesthesia. Ed. by Denise J. Wedel. (Illus.). 441p. 1992. text 114.00 (*0-443-08873-X*) Church.

Orthopaedic Assessment & Treatment of the Geriatric Patient. Carole B. Lewis & Karen A. Knortz. (Illus.). 424p. (C). (gr. 13). 1993. text 69.00 (*0-8016-6512-4*, 06512) Mosby Inc.

Orthopaedic Basic Science. Sheldon R. Simon. 704p. 1994. 150.00 (*0-89203-079-8*) Amer Acad Ortho Surg.

Orthopaedic Basic Science. Ed. by Sheldon R. Simon. 704p. 1994. pap. 120.00 (*0-89203-059-3*) Amer Acad Ortho Surg.

Orthopaedic Biomechanics: The Application of Engineering to the Musculoskeletal System. Victor H. Frankel & Albert H. Burstein. LC 77-78537. 196p. reprint ed. pap. 60.80 (*0-608-14437-1*, 205185200010) Bks Demand.

Orthopaedic Board Review. Ed. by Timothy S. Loth. LC 92-22708. (Illus.). 648p. (C). (gr. 13). 1992. pap. text 62.00 (*0-8016-2740-0*, 02740) Mosby Inc.

Orthopaedic Case Studies. Nancy Gann. LC 97-43309. 176p. 1998. 35.00 (*0-8342-1077-0*) Aspen Pub.

Orthopaedic Decision Making. 2nd ed. Robert W. Bucholz. (Illus.). 480p. (C). (gr. 13). 1996. text 92.95 (*0-8016-7356-9*, 07356) Mosby Inc.

Orthopaedic Diagnosis: Clinical, Radiological & Pathological Coordinates. H. A. Sissons et al. (Illus.). 420p. 1984. 79.95 (*0-387-12795-X*) Spr-Verlag.

Orthopaedic Diagnosis & Management: A Guide to the Care of Orthopaedic Patients. B. S. Goldie & D. C. Dunn. (Illus.). 272p. 1991. pap. 44.95 (*0-632-03043-7*) Blackwell Sci.

Orthopaedic Dictionary. Stanley Hoppenfeld. 456p. 1993. spiral bd. 89.00 (*0-397-51311-9*) Lppncott W & W.

Orthopaedic Infection: Diagnosis & Treatment. Ramon B. Gustilo. 1989. text 142.00 (*0-7216-2341-7*, W B Saunders Co) Harcrt Hlth Sci Grp.

Orthopaedic Injuries of the Civil War: An Atlas of Orthopaedic Injuries & Treatments During the Civil War. Julian E. Kuz & Bradley P. Bengston. LC 96-75433. (Illus.). 76p. (Orig.). 1996. 9.95 (*0-9635861-7-3*) North South Trader.

***Orthopaedic Knowledge Update.** Elizabeth A. Arendt et al. LC 99-26597. 1999. write for info. (*0-89203-205-7*) Amer Acad Ortho Surg.

Orthopaedic Knowledge Update. 2nd ed. Mark S. Mizel & American Orthopaedic Foot & Ankle Society Staff. LC 98-38633. 1998. write for info. (*0-89203-178-6*) American Academic Assn for Peace in the Middle East.

Orthopaedic Knowledge Update, No. 5. Ed. by James R. Kasser. (Illus.). 720p. 1996. pap. 165.00 (*0-89203-114-X*) Amer Acad Ortho Surg.

Orthopaedic Knowledge Update: Foot & Ankle. Glenn B. Pfeffer & Mark S. Mizel. LC 94-77974. (Illus.). 324p. 1994. pap. 115.00 (*0-89203-112-3*) Amer Acad Ortho Surg.

Orthopaedic Knowledge Update: Hip & Knee Reconstruction. Ed. by John J. Callaghan. LC 95-39517. 334p. 1995. pap. 115.00 (*0-89203-117-4*) Amer Acad Ortho Surg.

Orthopaedic Knowledge Update: Pediatrics. Ed. by B. Stephens Richards. 352p. 1996. pap. 115.00 (*0-89203-159-X*) Amer Acad Ortho Surg.

Orthopaedic Knowledge Update: Shoulder & Elbow. American Academy of Orthopaedic Surgeons Staff. Ed. by Tom R. Norris. LC 97-43921. (OKU Specialty Ser.). (Illus.). 424p. 1997. pap. 115.00 (*0-89203-170-0*) Amer Acad Ortho Surg.

Orthopaedic Knowledge Update: Trauma. Alan M. Levine. 350p. 1996. pap. 115.00 (*0-89203-126-3*) Amer Acad Ortho Surg.

Orthopaedic Management in Childhood. 2nd ed. Ed. by P. F. Williams & W. G. Cole. LC 91-33901. 377p. 1991. 119.95 (*0-442-31496-5*) Chapman & Hall.

Orthopaedic Management of Spina Bifida Cystica. 2nd ed. Malcolm B. Menelaus. LC 79-40044. (Current Problems in Orthopaedics Ser.). 227p. reprint ed. pap. 70.40 (*0-8357-3375-0*, 203962100013) Bks Demand.

Orthopaedic Medicine: A Practical Approach. Monica Kesson & Elaine Atkins. LC 97-26142. 480p. 1998. pap. text 57.50 (*0-7506-2543-0*) Buttrwrth-Heinemann.

O

An Asterisk (*) at the beginning of an entry indicates that the title is appearing for the first time.

Orthopaedic MRI: A Teaching File. Stephen J. Pomeranz. (Illus.). 416p. 1991. text 106.00 (*0-397-51105-1*) Lppncott W & W.

Orthopaedic Neurology: A Diagnostic Guide to Neurologic Levels. Stanley Hoppenfeld. LC 65-2199. (Illus.). 131p. 1977. text 51.00 (*0-397-50368-7*, Lippnctt) Lppncott W & W.

Orthopaedic Nursing. Leona A. Mourad. LC 94-16955. (Plans of Care for Specialty Practice Ser.). 360p. (C). 1994. pap. 32.75 (*0-8273-5944-6*) Delmar.

Orthopaedic Nursing. 2nd ed. Ann B. Maher et al. LC 97-37502. (Illus.). 944p. 1998. text 99.00 (*0-7216-6952-2*, W B Saunders Co) Harcrt Hlth Sci Grp.

Orthopaedic Nursing. 6th ed. Edward C. Pinney. (Illus.). 368p. 1983. text 22.00 (*0-7216-0933-3*, W B Saunders Co) Harcrt Hlth Sci Grp.

Orthopaedic Nursing & Rehabilitation. 9th ed. Mary Powell. (Illus.). 640p. 1986. 53.00 (*0-443-03238-6*) Church.

***Orthopaedic Nursing Care Competencies: Adult Acute Care.** Gail A. Bryant et al. Ed. by Susan Smith. 102p. 1999. pap. 45.00 (*1-892665-04-2*) Natl Assn Ortho Nurse.

Orthopaedic Nursing in Developing Countries. M. Powell. (WHO Regional Publications, South-East Asia Ser.: No. 3). 147p. 1977. pap. text 16.00 (*92-9022-103-8*) World Health.

Orthopaedic Patient Education Resource Manual. Sandra J. Painter. LC 94-1342. ring bd. 189.00 (*0-8342-0545-9*, S126) Aspen Pub.

Orthopaedic Physical Examination. Bruce Reider. Ed. by Richard Lampert. LC 98-38025. (Illus.). 525p. 1999. text. write for info. (*0-7216-7437-2*, W B Saunders Co) Harcrt Hlth Sci Grp.

Orthopaedic Physical Therapy. Ed. by Robert Donatelli & Michael J. Wooden. LC 88-25675. (Illus.). 613p. reprint ed. pap. 190.10 (*0-7837-6259-3*, 204597100010) Bks Demand.

Orthopaedic Physical Therapy. 2nd ed. Ed. by Robert A. Donatelli & Michael J. Wooden. (Illus.). 864p. 1993. text 95.00 (*0-443-08835-7*) Church.

Orthopaedic Physical Therapy. 3rd ed. Robert Donatelli. (C). 1999. text. write for info. (*0-443-07993-5*) Church.

Orthopaedic Physician's Assistant Techniques. Charles E. Lambert & Donald Stone. LC 74-77819. (Allied Health Ser.). 1975. pap. 7.05 (*0-672-61388-3*, Bobbs) Macmillan.

Orthopaedic Radiography. Bruce W. Long & John A. Rafert. LC 94-14941. (Illus.). 560p. 1994. text 75.00 (*0-7216-6649-3*, W B Saunders Co) Harcrt Hlth Sci Grp.

Orthopaedic Rehabilitation. 2nd ed. Ed. by Vernon L. Nickel & Michael J. Botte. (Illus.). 939p. 1992. text 155.00 (*0-443-08726-1*) Church.

Orthopaedic Sports Medicine, 2 vols., Set. Ed. by Jesse C. DeLee, Jr. & David Drez. (Illus.). 1888p. 1993. text 280.00 (*0-7216-2836-2*, W B Saunders Co) Harcrt Hlth Sci Grp.

Orthopaedic Surgery. Edward L. Compere. LC 73-93801. (Handbook of Operative Surgery Ser.). 323p. reprint ed. pap. 100.20 (*0-608-15498-9*, 202973500064) Bks Demand.

Orthopaedic Surgery: Basic Science & Clinical Science. Juan J. Rodrigo. 770p. 1985. 80.00 (*0-316-75369-6*, Little Brwn Med Div) Lppncott W & W.

Orthopaedic Surgical Pathology. Forest. (C). 1998. text 295.00 (*0-443-05540-8*) Church.

Orthopaedic Testing: A Rational Approach to Diagnosis. Steven L. Kleinfield & Hanet A. Gerard. (Illus.). 688p. 1993. text 152.00 (*0-443-08876-4*) Church.

Orthopaedic Trauma Protocols. Ed. by Sigvard T. Hansen, Jr. & Marc F. Swiontkowski. LC 92-48788. 416p. 1993. text 165.00 (*0-88167-994-1*) Lppncott W & W.

***Orthopaedics.** 2nd ed. Frank V. Aluisio et al. LC 97-41655. (House Officer Ser.). (Illus.). 300p. 1998. write for info. (*0-683-18213-7*) Lppncott W & W.

Orthopaedics. 2nd ed. Hooper. (Orig.). (C). 1998. pap. text 16.95 (*0-443-05888-1*, W B Saunders Co) Harcrt Hlth Sci Grp.

Orthopaedics: A Problem Solving Approach for Physiotherapists. K. Percival et al. (Illus.). 288p. (C). 1998. pap. write for info. (*0-443-05074-0*) Church.

Orthopaedics: A Review Book. Edward V. Craig. Date not set. write for info. (*0-683-30243-4*) Lppncott W & W.

Orthopaedics: A Study Guide. Ed. by Jeffrey M. Spivak & Joseph D. Zuckerman. (Illus.). 936p. 1999. pap. text, student ed. 75.00 (*0-07-060355-3*) McGraw-Hill HPD.

Orthopaedics: Essentials of Diagnosis & Treatment. Ed. by Charles R. Clark & Michael Bonfiglio. (Illus.). 1994. text 74.00 (*0-443-08807-1*) Church.

Orthopaedics: PreTest Self-Assessment & Review. Ed. by Frank C. Wilson & Patrick P. Lin. LC 95-21405. (Pretest Specialty Level Ser.). (Illus.). 320p. 1996. pap. text 48.00 (*0-07-052076-3*) McGraw-Hill HPD.

Orthopaedics: Problems in Primary Care. Randall E. Marcus. Ed. by Melanie C. Karaffa. (Illus.). 400p. (C). 1991. text 49.95 (*1-878487-33-7*, 5907M) Practice Mgmt Info.

Orthopaedics & Trauma. Ronald L. Huckstep & Eugene Sherry. LC 94-5218. (Color Guide Ser.). 158p. 1994. pap. text 18.95 (*0-443-04980-7*) Church.

Orthopaedics & Trauma: An Illustrated Colour Text. Ronald K. McRae & A. W. Kinninmonth. LC 96-39211. (Illus.). 152p. 1997. pap. text 34.95 (*0-443-05135-6*) Church.

Orthopaedics for the House Officer. William J. Mallon et al. (Illus.). 200p. 1990. 21.95 (*0-683-05420-1*) Lppncott W & W.

Orthopaedics in General Practice. Andrew Carr & Anthony Harnden. LC 96-37668. (Illus.). 240p. 1997. pap. text 52.50 (*0-7506-2219-9*) Buttrwrth-Heinemann.

Orthopaedics in Primary Care. 3rd ed. Gerald G. Steinberg et al. LC 98-41147. (Illus.). 450p. 1998. write for info. (*0-683-30258-2*) Lppncott W & W.

Orthopaedics Principles of Basic & Clinical Science. Felix Bronner & Richard V. Worrell. LC 99-20513. 312p. 1999. boxed set 79.95 (*0-8493-9237-3*) CRC Pr.

Orthopaedics Two Thousand & One. Clement Sledge. 2001. 83.00 (*0-8151-1465-6*, 31715) Mosby Inc.

Orthopaedics Two Thousand & Two. Sledge Clement. 2002. 83.00 (*0-8151-1555-5*, 31716) Mosby Inc.

***Orthopathic Medicine: The Unification of Orthopedics with Osteopathy Through the Fascial Distortion Model.** 3rd rev. ed. Stephen Typaldos. (Illus.). 250p. 1999. text 120.00 (*0-9659641-2-4*) Ortho Global.

Orthopathy, Teaching New Science of Health & Natural Healing. Shelton & Clements. 200p. 1996. reprint ed. spiral bd. 31.50 (*0-7873-0777-7*) Hlth Research.

Orthopedia: Spine, Back, & Neck. (Illus.). 928p. 1991. lib. bdg. 149.00 (*1-879952-01-7*) Inst Spine.

***Orthopedic - Neurology Words & Phrases.** 2nd ed. Health Professions Institute Staff. 700p. 1999. pap. write for info. (*0-934385-03-3*) Hlth Prof Inst.

Orthopedic - Neurology Words & Phrases, 1994: A Quick Reference Guide. LC 94-176954. 630p. 1994. pap. 40.00 (*0-934385-55-6*) Hlth Prof Inst.

Orthopedic & Sports Physical Therapy. 3rd ed. Malone. Ed. by Thomas G. Mcpoil. (Illus.). 656p. (C). (gr. 13). 1996. text 64.00 (*0-8151-5886-6*, 24514) Mosby Inc.

Orthopedic Boards Review No. II: A Case Study Approach. Ed. by Timothy S. Loth. (Illus.). 480p. (C). (gr. 13). 1995. pap. text 80.00 (*0-8151-5322-8*, 24693) Mosby Inc.

Orthopedic Dictionary. R. I. Avaanesov. (RUS.). 704p. 1983. 35.00 (*0-8288-2002-3*, M15155) Fr & Eur.

***Orthopedic Diseases of the Joints of the Dog.** Robert L. Leighton. 230p. 2000. write for info. (*1-58692-029-4*) Copyright Mgmt.

Orthopedic Flash. Carole Lewis et al. 725p. 1997. text 249.00 (*0-9643582-4-7*) Learn Pubns.

Orthopedic Imaging: Techniques & Applications. Ed. by A. M. Davies et al. LC 97-49118. (Medical Radiology Ser.). (Illus.). 350p. 1998. 189.00 (*3-540-63187-9*) Spr-Verlag.

Orthopedic Infection. Ed. by David L. Schlossberg. (Clinical Topics in Infectious Disease Ser.). (Illus.). 295p. 1988. 115.00 (*0-387-96719-2*) Spr-Verlag.

Orthopedic Joint Implants Markets: Update 621. (Market Research Reports: No. 326). 125p. 1996. 795.00 (*0-317-05481-3*) Theta Corp.

Orthopedic Management of Cerebral Palsy. 2nd ed. Eugene E. Bleck. LC 65-80559. (Clinics in Developmental Medicine Ser.: No. 99-100). (Illus.). 497p. (C). 1991. text 85.00 (*0-521-41218-8*) Mc Keith Pr.

Orthopedic, Neurological & Chiropractic Physical Examinations. Barry Creighton. (Illus.). 80p. 1986. pap. 39.50 (*0-911110-57-7*, MICHIE) LEXIS Pub.

Orthopedic Nurse. Jack Rudman. (Certified Nurse Examination (CN) Ser.: Vol. 27). 43.95 (*0-8373-6177-X*) Nat Learn.

Orthopedic Nurse. Jack Rudman. (Certified Nurse Examination Ser.: Vol. CN-27). 1997. pap. 23.95 (*0-8373-6127-3*) Nat Learn.

Orthopedic Pathology. Michael J. Klein. Ed. by Debra S. Heller. (Blackwell Pathology CD-ROM Ser.: Vol. II). 1995. 299.95 (*0-86542-473-X*) Blackwell Sci.

Orthopedic Pathology. Schiller. 1997. text. write for info. (*0-7216-4355-8*, W B Saunders Co) Harcrt Hlth Sci Grp.

Orthopedic Pathophysiology in Diagnosis & Treatment. Jonathan Cohen et al. (Illus.). 526p. 1989. text 140.00 (*0-443-08070-4*) Church.

Orthopedic Pathophysiology in Diagnosis & Treatment. Jonathan Cohen & Michael Bonfiglio. LC 89-22215. (Illus.). 538p. reprint ed. pap. 166.80 (*0-7837-8849-5*, 204949400012) Bks Demand.

Orthopedic Pearls. Leon Benson & Jeffrey Visotsky. LC 99-14699. (Illus.). 402p. (C). 1999. pap. text 21.95 (*0-8036-0185-9*) Davis Co.

Orthopedic Physical Assessment. 3rd ed. David J. Magee. LC 96-41121. (Illus.). 815p. 1997. text 51.95 (*0-7216-6290-0*, W B Saunders Co) Harcrt Hlth Sci Grp.

Orthopedic Prosthesis-Appliances. (Market Research Reports: No. 911). (Illus.). 164p. 1990. 295.00 (*0-317-05016-8*) Theta Corp.

Orthopedic Radiology. Adam Greenspan. LC 65-40140. (Illus.). 448p. 1988. text 210.00 (*0-397-44660-8*, Lippnctt) Lppncott W & W.

Orthopedic Radiology. 2nd ed. Barbara Weissman. 1999. text. write for info. (*0-7216-3791-4*, W B Saunders Co) Harcrt Hlth Sci Grp.

Orthopedic Radiology: A Practical Approach. 2nd ed. Adam Greenspan. 728p. 1995. 236.50 (*0-563-75023-5*) Lppncott W & W.

Orthopedic Radiology: A Practical Approach. 3rd ed. Adam Greenspan. LC 99-10897. 954p. 1999. write for info. (*0-7817-1589-X*) Lppncott W & W.

Orthopedic Radiology: A Practical Approach, Set. 2nd ed. Adam Greenspan. 1993. sl. 1890.00 (*1-56375-167-4*) Lppncott W & W.

Orthopedic Rehabilitation Review. Loth & Wadsworth. (Illus.). 440p. (C). (gr. 13). 1997. pap. text 46.95 (*0-8151-2526-7*, 31050) Mosby Inc.

***Orthopedic Rehabilitation Science: Principles for Clinical M.** Katie Lundon. LC 99-39419. (Illus.). 224p. 1999. pap. text 52.50 (*0-7506-7155-6*) Buttrwrth-Heinemann.

Orthopedic Research Procedures & Techniques Pt. 2: A Special Issue of the Journal Automedica. Ed. by M. H. Krag & M. H. Pope. 12p. 1989. text 306.00 (*0-677-25800-3*) Gordon & Breach.

Orthopedic Secrets. 2nd rev. ed. David E. Brown & Randall D. Neumann. LC 99-11421. (Secrets Ser.). (Illus.). 400p. 1999. pap. text 39.00 (*1-56053-302-1*) Hanley & Belfus.

Orthopedic Secrets: Questions You Will Be Asked on Rounds, in the Clinic, on Oral Exams. Ed. by David E. Brown & Randall D. Neumann. (Secrets Ser.). (Illus.). 400p. (Orig.). 1994. pap. text 39.00 (*1-56053-106-1*) Hanley & Belfus.

Orthopedic Sports Medicine, 3 Vols. Delee. 1993. text 320.00 (*0-7216-5602-1*) Harcourt.

Orthopedic Sports Medicine, 3 Vols. Delee. 1993. text 350.00 (*0-7216-4194-6*, W B Saunders Co) Harcrt Hlth Sci Grp.

Orthopedic Surgery: Elastic Compression. 2nd rev. ed. H. F. Boggiano. (Illus.). 650p. 1996. 85.00 (*0-9654469-0-5*) H F Boggiano.

Orthopedic Surgery: The Essentials. Mark E. Baratz. LC 98-45052. 1999. 125.00 (*3-13-116291-0*) Thieme Med Pubs.

Orthopedic Surgery: The Essentials. Mark E. Baratz et al. LC 98-45052. (Illus.). 992p. 1999. 99.00 (*0-86577-779-9*) Thieme Med Pubs.

Orthopedic Surgery Manual. Association of Surgical Technologists Staff. (Allied Health Ser.). 2000. pap. 40.00 (*0-7668-1128-X*) Delmar.

Orthopedic Therapy of the Shoulder. Ed. by Martin J. Kelley & William A. Clark. LC 94-28214. (Illus.). 480p. 1994. text 49.95 (*0-397-54830-3*) Lppncott W & W.

Orthopedic Transfusion Therapy. Ed. by Mark E. Brecher & Leigh C. Jefferies. LC 95-44616. (Illus.). 107p. (C). 1995. 40.00 (*1-56395-046-4*) Am Assn Blood.

Orthopedics. (Medical Ser.). (Illus.). 138p. 1983. pap. text 12.95 (*0-935920-06-4*, Ntl Pubs Blck) P-H.

Orthopedics. 2nd ed. Geoffrey Hooper. LC 96-29577. (Colour Guide Ser.). 1997. write for info. (*0-443-05806-7*) Harcrt Hlth Sci Grp.

Orthopedics. 3rd ed. P. H. Regents. 130p. 1993. pap. 20.17 (*0-13-156845-0*) P-H.

Orthopedics: A History & Iconography. Leonard F. Peltier. (Illus.). 305p. 1993. 225.00 (*0-930405-47-1*) Norman SF.

Orthopedics & Medicine: Research & Subject Analysis with Reference Bibliography. Gloria L. Zander. LC 85-48107. 150p. 1987. 47.50 (*0-88164-486-2*); pap. 44.50 (*0-88164-487-0*) ABBE Pubs Assn.

Orthopedics in Infancy & Childhood. 2nd ed. G. C. Lloyd-Roberts & John A. Fixsen. 226p. 1990. pap. text 180.00 (*0-7506-1030-1*) Buttrwrth-Heinemann.

Orthopedist. Lee Jacobs. LC 98-3901. (Doctors in Action Ser.). (Illus.). 24p. (J). (gr. 3-5). 1998. lib. bdg. 15.95 (*1-56711-236-6*) Blackbirch.

Orthopedist's Guide to Plain Film Imaging. Helene Pavlov. (Illus.). 336p. 1998. 65.00 (*0-86577-717-9*) Thieme Med Pubs.

Orthopsychiatry: Index of Modern Information. Peter J. Kasnevitch. LC 88-47972. 150p. 1990. 47.50 (*1-55914-028-3*); pap. 44.50 (*1-55914-029-1*) ABBE Pubs Assn.

Orthoptera - Acriidae. W. F. Kirby. (Fauna of British India Ser.). x, 278p. 1973. reprint ed. 20.00 (*0-88065-147-4*) Scholarly Pubns.

Orthoptera Species File No. 1: Crickets (Grylloidea) Daniel Otte. 120p. (Orig.). 1994. pap. 55.00 (*0-9640101-2-7*) Orthopterists.

Orthoptera Species File No. 2: Grasshoppers (Acridomorpha) A. Daniel Otte. 162p. (Orig.). 1994. pap. 35.00 (*0-9640101-3-5*) Orthopterists.

Orthoptera Species File No. 3: Grasshoppers (Acridomorpha) B. Daniel Otte. 241p. (Orig.). 1994. pap. 45.00 (*0-9640101-4-3*) Orthopterists.

Orthoptera Species File No. 4: Grasshoppers (Acridomorpha) C. Daniel Otte. 518p. (Orig.). 1995. pap. 65.00 (*0-9640101-5-1*) Orthopterists.

Orthoptera Species File No. 5: Grasshoppers (Acridomorpha) D. Daniel Otte. 630p. (Orig.). 1995. pap. 65.00 (*0-9640101-6-X*) Orthopterists.

Orthoptera Species File No. 6: Tetrigoidea & Tridactyloidea: (Orthoptera: Caelifera) & Addenda to OSF Vols. 1-5. Daniel Otte. 261p. 1997. pap. 25.00 (*0-9640101-7-8*) Orthopterists.

Orthoptera Species File No. 7: Tettigonioidea. Daniel Otte. 373p. 1997. pap. 50.00 (*0-9640101-8-6*) Orthopterists.

Orthoptera Species File Series, Set, Nos. 1-5. Daniel Otte. (Illus.). (Orig.). 1995. pap. text 265.00 (*0-9640101-1-9*) Orthopterists.

Orthopters of Europe, Vol. 3. H. Harz & A. Kaltenbach. (Entomalogica Ser.: Vol. 12). 1976. text 255.50 (*90-6193-122-3*) Kluwer Academic.

Orthoptic Assessment & Management. David Stidwell. LC 97-51262. (Modern Optometry Ser.). 1998. pap. 75.00 (*0-632-05012-8*) Blackwell Sci.

Orthoptics: A Syllabus of Ocular Motility. Ed. by Paula M. Edelman. (Illus.). 104p. 1987. 25.00 (*0-317-94089-9*) Am Acad Ophthal.

Orthoptics: A Syllabus of Ocular Motility. 2nd ed. Ed. by Paula M. Edelman. LC 92-17635. (Illus.). 1992. write for info. (*1-56055-023-6*) Am Acad Ophthal.

Ortho's All about Bathroom Remodeling. Larry Hodgson & Linda M. Hunter. LC 97-76219. (Illus.). 96p. 1998. pap. 11.95 (*0-89721-414-5*, Ortho Bks) Meredith Bks.

Ortho's All about Home Offices. Jeff Beneke & Douglas Ross. LC 97-76214. (Illus.). 96p. 1998. pap. 11.95 (*0-89721-416-1*, Ortho Bks) Meredith Bks.

Ortho's All about Houseplants. Kate Jerome. LC 98-66919. (Ortho's All about Ser.). (Illus.). 96p. 1998. pap. 11.95 (*0-89721-427-7*, Ortho Bks) Meredith Bks.

Ortho's All about Kitchen Remodeling. Larry Hodgson & John Riha. LC 97-76213. (Illus.). 96p. 1998. pap. 11.95 (*0-89721-415-3*, Ortho Bks) Meredith Bks.

Ortho's All about Sprinklers & Drip Systems. Ortho Staff. LC 97-75856. (Illus.). 96p. 1998. pap. 11.95 (*0-89721-413-7*, Ortho Bks) Meredith Bks.

Ortho's All about Storage Solutions. Dave Toht & Jim Sanders. LC 97-76218. (Illus.). 96p. 1998. pap. 11.95 (*0-89721-418-8*, Ortho Bks) Meredith Bks.

Ortho's Complete Guide to Successful Houseplants. rev. ed. Larry Hodgson et al. Ed. by Marianne Lipanovich. LC 92-70582. (Illus.). 320p. 1992. 24.95 (*0-89721-249-5*, UPC 05610A, Ortho Bks) Meredith Bks.

Ortho's Complete Guide to Vegetables. Pamela J. Manley. Ed. by Ben Allen. LC 96-67631. (Illus.). 320p. 1997. 29.95 (*0-89721-317-3*, Ortho Bks) Meredith Bks.

Ortho's Complete Guide to Vegetables. Pamela J. Manley. LC 96-67631. (Illus.). 320p. 1993. pap. 24.95 (*0-89721-314-9*) Meredith Bks.

Ortho's Deck Plans. Ortho Staff. LC 97-75854. (Illus.). 96p. 1996. pap. 11.95 (*0-89721-411-0*, Ortho Bks) Meredith Bks.

Ortho's 50 Quick Home Improvements. Sharon Ross & Dave Toht. LC 97-76217. (Illus.). 96p. 1998. pap. 11.95 (*0-89721-417-X*, Ortho Bks) Meredith Bks.

Ortho's Guide to Creative Home Landscaping. rev. ed. Ortho Books Staff. 336p. 1991. pap. 24.95 (*0-89721-279-7*) Meredith Bks.

Ortho's Guide to Decks & Patios. LC 96-67630. (Illus.). 304p. 1992. pap. 24.95 (*0-89721-312-2*) Meredith Bks.

Ortho's Guide to Decks & Patios. LC 96-67630. (Illus.). 304p. 1996. 29.95 (*0-89721-315-7*) Meredith Bks.

Ortho's Guide to Enjoying Birds. Ortho Books Staff. (Illus.). 352p. 1991. pap. 24.95 (*0-89721-280-0*) Meredith Bks.

Ortho's Guide to Enjoying Roses. Ann Reilly. LC 92-70585. (Illus.). 352p. 1996. 29.95 (*0-89721-293-2*, Ortho Bks) Meredith Bks.

Ortho's Guide to Herbs. Monica Brandies. LC 96-67629. (Illus.). 304p. 1992. 29.95 (*0-89721-316-5*); pap. 24.95 (*0-89721-313-0*) Meredith Bks.

Ortho's Guide to Successful Flower Gardening. LC 94-67706. (Illus.). 352p. 1995. pap. 24.95 (*0-89721-272-X*, UPC05608) Meredith Bks.

Ortho's Guide to Successful Flower Gardening. Rick Bond. Ed. by Barbara F. Stremple. LC 90-80072. (Illus.). 352p. 1996. 29.95 (*0-89721-291-6*, Ortho Bks) Meredith Bks.

Ortho's Guide to Successful Houseplants. rev. ed. Larry Hodges & Charles C. Powell. Ed. by Marianne Lipanovich. LC 94-66707. (Illus.). 320p. 1995. pap. 24.95 (*0-89721-273-8*, UPC05609) Meredith Bks.

Ortho's Guide to the Birds Around Us. Alice E. Mace. Ed. by Suzanne Sherman. LC 95-68607. (Illus.). 352p. 1996. 29.95 (*0-89721-290-8*, Ortho Bks) Meredith Bks.

Ortho's Home Improvement Encyclopedia. Robert J. Beckstrom. Ed. by Karin Shakery. LC 85-70877. (Illus.). 512p. 1985. 24.95 (*0-89721-066-2*, Ortho Bks) Meredith Bks.

Ortho's Home Improvement Encyclopedia. rev. ed. Robert J. Beckstrom & Ortho Books-How to Staff. Ed. by Alan Ahlstrand. LC 94-65698. (Illus.). 512p. 1994. 29.95 (*0-89721-270-3*, UPC 05620A) Meredith Bks.

Ortho's Home Repair Problem Solver. LC 94-69604. (Illus.). 320p. (Orig.). 1995. pap. 24.95 (*0-89721-260-6*, 06035) Meredith Bks.

Ortho's Patio Plans. Sharon Ross & Barbara Sabella. LC 97-75855. (Illus.). 96p. 1998. pap. 11.95 (*0-89721-412-9*, Ortho Bks) Meredith Bks.

Ortho's Shrubs & Hedges. Penelope O'Sullivan. LC 98-66912. (Ortho's All about Ser.). (Illus.). 96p. 1998. pap. 11.95 (*0-89721-432-3*, Ortho Bks) Meredith Bks.

Ortho's Vegetable Gardening. Ortho Books Staff. Date not set. write for info. (*0-89721-324-6*, Ortho Bks) Meredith Bks.

Orthosilicates. Ed. by W. A. Deer et al. (Rock-Forming Minerals Ser.: No. 1A). (Illus.). 932p. 1997. 125.00 (*1-897799-88-8*, Pub. by Geol Soc Pub Hse) AAPG.

Orthostatic Disorders of the Circulation: Mechanisms, Manifestations & Treatment. D. H. Streeten. LC 86-18748. (Illus.). 286p. (C). 1986. text 89.50 (*0-306-42322-7*, Kluwer Plenum) Kluwer Academic.

***Orthotics: A Comprehensive Clinical Approach.** Joan E. Edelstein & Jan Bruckner. 300p. (C). 2000. text 39.00 (*1-55642-416-7*) SLACK Inc.

Orthotics: Clinical Practice & Rehabilitation Technology. Ed. by John B. Redford et al. LC 95-35492. 337p. 1995. pap. text 48.00 (*0-443-08992-2*) Church.

Orthotics & Prosthetics in Rehabilitation. Michelle M. Lusardi & Caroline Nielsen. 600p. 2000. 99.00 (*0-7506-9807-1*) Buttrwrth-Heinemann.

Orthotics in Functional Rehabilitation of the Lower Limb. Deborah A. Nawoczenski & Marcia E. Epler. LC 96-25618. (Illus.). 315p. 1997. text 47.00 (*0-7216-6134-3*, W B Saunders Co) Harcrt Hlth Sci Grp.

Orthotics in Neurologic Rehabilitation. Ed. by Mindy L. Aisen. 160p. 1992. pap. 34.95 (*0-939957-47-7*) Demos Medical.

Orthotics in Rehabilitation: Splinting the Hand & Body. Pat McKee. LC 97-48427. 340p. 1998. pap. text 32.95 (*0-8036-0351-7*) Davis Co.

Orthotics, Prosthetics & Mobility Aids. 1994. lib. bdg. 250.00 (*0-8490-8406-7*) Gordon Pr.

Orthpaedic Knowledge Update: Sports Medicine. Ed. by Letha Y. Griffin. LC 94-77973. (Illus.). 400p. 1994. 115.00 (*0-89203-113-1*) Amer Acad Ortho Surg.

Ortlich Betaubt see Local Anaesthetic

***Ortner & Ortner: Primer of Architecture.** Laurids Ortner & Ortner & Ortner Hrsg. Staff. (Illus.). 240p. 2000. 79.95 (*3-7643-6068-2*) Birkhauser.

***Ortner & Ortner: 3 Buildings for European Culture.** Laurids Ortner. 1999. 45.00 (*3-88375-349-1*) Walther Konig.

Ortnit & Wolfdietrich: Two Medieval Romances. J. W. Thomas. LC 85-72929. (GERM Ser.: Vol. 23). (Illus.). 98p. (C). 1986. 29.95 (*0-938100-40-8*) Camden Hse.

O

Ortnit und die Wolfdietriche. Arthur Amelung & Oskar Janicke. (Deutsches Heldenbuch Ser.: Band 1). (GER.). lxxii, 302p. 1968. write for info. (*3-296-17103-7*, Pub. by Weidmann) Lubrecht & Cramer.

Ortnit und die Wolfdietriche. Arthur Amelung & Oskar Janicke. (Deutsches Heldenbuch Ser.: Band 2). (GER.). l, 352p. 1968. write for info. (*3-296-17104-5*, Pub. by Weidmann) Lubrecht & Cramer.

Ortografia Acitib: Letros. Fernandez. (SPA.). (C). 1997. text 10.00 (*0-673-19234-2*) Addison-Wesley.

Ortografia Practica. rev. unabridged ed. Jose Escarpanter. (SPA., Illus.). 144p. 1992. pap. 5.95 (*0-9648426-2-9*) Brickell Commun.

Ortografia Practica. 5th ed. Suazo Pascual. (SPA.). 195p. 1996. pap. 14.00 (*84-7640-553-7*, Pub. by Edaf Edit) IBD Ltd.

Ortography Rules for the Spanish Language: For Students of Spanish As a Second Language & Spanish G.E.D. Students. Hector G. Sorzano. 1991. pap. text 5.00 (*0-9631066-0-0*) H G Sorzano.

Orton Diaries. John Lahr. Date not set. pap. 11.99 (*0-7493-2183-0*) Heinemann.

Orton Diaries: Including the Correspondence of Edna Welthorpe & Others. Ed. by Joe Orton & John Lahr. LC 96-18361. (Illus.). 332p. 1996. pap. 14.95 (*0-306-80733-5*) Da Capo.

***Ortona: Canada's Epic World War Two Battle.** Mark Zuehlke. (Illus.). 320p. 1999. text 32.95 (*0-7737-3198-9*, Pub. by Stoddart Publ) Genl Dist Srvs.

Ortswuestungen des Havellandes: Historisch-Archaeologische Beitraege Zur Wuestungkunde der Mark Brandenburg. Guenter Mangelsdorf. Bd. 86. (GER.). 338p. (C). 1994. lib. bdg. 110.80 (*3-11-014086-1*) De Gruyter.

O'Ruddy. Stephen Crane. (Works of Stephen Crane). 1990. reprint ed. lib. bdg. 79.00 (*0-685-44788-X*) Rprt Serv.

Oruga Muy Hambrienta (The Very Hungry Caterpillar) Eric Carle. LC 79-13202. (SPA., Illus.). 32p. (J). (ps-2). 1994. 18.95 (*0-399-22780-6*, Philomel) Peng Put Young Read.

Oruga, Oruga Vol. 3: Pasitos Spanish Language Development Books. Darlyne F. Schott. (Pasitos Hacia la Lectura Ser.). 15p. (J). (gr. k-1). 1990. pap. text 11.50 (*1-56537-052-X*) D F Schott Educ.

Orvie: The Dictator of Dearborn. David L. Good. LC 89-30495. (Great Lakes Bks.). (Illus.). 450p. (C). 1989. 39.95 (*0-8143-2289-1*) Wayne St U Pr.

***Orvis Cookbook: Fifty Complete Menus for Fish & Game.** Romi Perkins. (Illus.). 1999. pap. 29.95 (*1-55821-954-4*) Lyons Pr.

Orvis Fly-Fishing Guide. Tom Rosenbauer. (Illus.). 272p. 1988. 32.95 (*0-941130-91-6*); pap. 17.95 (*0-941130-92-4*) Lyons Pr.

Orvis Fly Pattern. John Harder. 1990. pap. 29.95 (*0-452-26743-9*, Plume) Dutton Plume.

***Orvis Guide to Beginning Fly Tying.** Eric Leiser. (Illus.). 2000. pap. 14.95 (*1-58574-096-9*) Lyons Pr.

***Orvis Guide to Prospecting for Trout.** Tom Rosenbauer. (Illus.). 2000. pap. 19.95 (*1-58574-090-X*) Lyons Pr.

***Orvis Guide to Reading Trout Streams.** Tom Rosenbauer. LC 99-29589. 1999. 17.95 (*1-55821-933-1*) Lyons Pr.

Orvis Guide to Saltwater Fly Fishing. Nick Curcione. LC 93-44243. (Illus.). 256p. 1993. 24.95 (*1-55821-252-3*) Lyons Pr.

Orvis Guide to Saltwater Fly Fishing. Nick Curcione. 1996. pap. text 18.95 (*1-55821-491-7*) Lyons Pr.

***Orvis Pocket Guide to Dry-Fly Fishing.** Tom Rosenbauer. (Illus.). 2001. 16.95 (*1-58574-158-2*) Lyons Pr.

***Orvis Pocket Guide to Fly Fishing for Bonefish & Permit.** Jack Samson. (Illus.). 2000. 16.95 (*1-58574-075-6*) Lyons Pr.

***Orvis Pocket Guide to Fly Fishing for Striped Bass & Bluefish.** Lou Tabory. (Illus.). 2000. 16.95 (*1-58574-076-4*) Lyons Pr.

***Orvis Pocket Guide to Nymphing Techniques.** Tom Rosenbauer. (Illus.). 2000. 16.95 (*1-58574-077-2*) Lyons Pr.

***Orvis Pocket Guide to Stillwater Fly-Fishing Techniques.** Tom Rosenbauer. (Illus.). 2000. 16.95 (*1-58574-078-0*) Lyons Pr.

***Orvis Shooting School Method of Wingshooting: An Orvis Guide.** Orvis Shooting School Staff. (Orvis Guides Ser.). (Illus.). 128p. 2000. 16.95 (*1-57223-314-1*) Willow Creek Pr.

***Orvis Streamside Guide to Approach & Presentation.** Tom Rosenbauer. (Orvis Streamside Guides Ser.). (Illus.). 2000. 16.95 (*1-55821-985-4*) Lyons Pr.

***Orvis Streamside Guide to Fly Casting.** Tom Deck. LC 99-47874. 2000. 16.95 (*1-55821-987-0*) Lyons Pr.

***Orvis Streamside Guide to Leaders, Lines & Tippets.** Tom Rosenbauer. LC 99-45681. (Orvis Streamside Guides Ser.). 2000. 16.95 (*1-55821-984-6*) Lyons Pr.

***Orvis Streamside Guide to Trout Foods & Their Imitations.** Tom Rosenbauer. (Orvis Streamside Guides Ser.). (Illus.). 2000. 16.95 (*1-55821-986-2*) Lyons Pr.

Orvis Wing-Shooting Handbook: Proven Techniques for Better Shotgunning. Bruce Bowlen. LC 85-17084. (Illus.). 96p. (Orig.). 1985. pap. 10.95 (*0-941130-05-3*) Lyons Pr.

***Orvol Oblast Regional Investment & Business Guide.** Global Investment & Business Center, Inc. Staff. (Russian Regional Investment & Business Guides Ser.: Vol. 57). (Illus.). 350p. 1999. pap. 99.00 (*0-7397-0856-2*) Intl Business Pubns.

Orwell: The Lost Writings. George Orwell. Ed. by W. J. West. 352p. 1988. mass mkt. 5.95 (*0-380-70118-9*, Avon Bks) Morrow Avon.

***Orwell: Wintry Conscience of a Generation.** Jeffrey Meyers. (Illus.). 320p. 2000. 27.95 (*0-393-04792-X*) Norton.

Orwell & Gissing. Mark Connelly. LC 97-8499. (American University Studies: Vol. 185, No. IV). 126p. (C). 1997. text 30.95 (*0-8204-3330-6*) P Lang Pubng.

Orwell for Beginners. David Smith. (Illus.). 192p. 1999. pap. 11.95 (*0-86316-292-4*) Writers & Readers.

Orwell in Athens. Van De Donk. LC 95-75769. 1995. 82.00 (*90-5199-219-X*) IOS Press.

Orwell Mystique: A Study in Male Ideology. Daphne Patai. LC 84-8488. 344p. 1984. pap. 19.95 (*0-87023-447-1*); lib. bdg. 40.00 (*0-87023-446-3*) U of Mass Pr.

Orwell Reader: Fiction, Essays, & Reportage. George Orwell. LC 61-1439. 480p. 1961. pap. 15.00 (*0-15-670176-6*, Harvest Bks) Harcourt.

Orwell Remembered Vol. II: The Town of Orwell & America's Wars. Betty D. Martin. 230p. 1993. pap. 12.50 (*1-886303-01-0*) Write to Print.

Orwellian World of Jehovah's Witnesses. Heather Botting & Gary Botting. (Illus.). 224p. 1984. pap. 16.95 (*0-8020-6545-7*) U of Toronto Pr.

Orwellian World of Jehovah's Witnesses. Heather D. Botting. LC 84-196541. (Illus.). 247p. reprint ed. pap. 76.60 (*0-8357-8257-3*, 203397600088) Bks Demand.

Orwell's 1984: Text, Sources, Criticism. 2nd ed. George Orwell. Ed. by Irving Howe & David Levin. (Harbrace Sourcebooks Ser.). 450p. (C). 1982. pap. text 32.50 (*0-15-565811-5*, Pub. by Harcourt Coll Pubs) Harcourt.

Oryol Oblast: Economy, Industry, Government, Business. 2nd rev. ed. Russian Information & Business Center, Inc. Staff. (Russian Regional Business Directories Ser.). (Illus.). 200p. 1997. pap. 99.00 (*1-57751-405-X*) Intl Business Pubns.

***Oryol Oblast Regional Investment & Business Guide.** Contrib. by Global Investment & Business Center, Inc. Staff. (Russian Regional Investment & Business Guides Ser.: Vol. 57). (Illus.). 350p. 2000. pap. 99.95 (*0-7397-3005-3*) Intl Business Pubns.

Oryx American Family Tree, 12 vols. Incl. Student's Guide to African American Genealogy. Anne E. Johnson & Adam M. Cooper. Ed. by Roger Rosen. LC 95-41357. (Illus.). 176p. (YA). (gr. 6-12). 1995. 24.95 (*0-89774-972-3*); Student's Guide to British American Genealogy. Anne E. Johnson. LC 95-38165. (Illus.). 176p. (YA). (gr. 6-12). 1995. 24.95 (*0-89774-982-0*); Student's Guide to Chinese American Genealogy. Colleen She. LC 96-17158. (Illus.). 168p. (YA). (gr. 6-12). 1996. 24.95 (*0-89774-980-4*, ACE-Oryx); Student's Guide to German American Genealogy. Gregory Robl. LC 95-45217. (Illus.). 176p. (YA). (gr. 6-12). 1996. 24.95 (*0-89774-983-9*); Student's Guide to Irish American Genealogy. Erin McKenna. LC 96-26070. (Illus.). 176p. (YA). (gr. 6-12). 1996. 24.95 (*0-89774-976-6*); Student's Guide to Italian American Genealogy. Terry C. Brockman. LC 95-47314. (Illus.). 176p. (YA). (gr. 6-12). 1996. 24.95 (*0-89774-973-1*); Student's Guide to Japanese American Genealogy. Yoji Yamaguchi. LC 95-36130. (Illus.). 176p. (YA). (gr. 6-12). 1996. 24.95 (*0-89774-979-0*); Student's Guide to Jewish American Genealogy. Jay Schleifer. LC 96-937. (Illus.). 176p. (YA). (gr. 6-12). 1996. 24.95 (*0-89774-977-4*); Student's Guide to Mexican American Genealogy. George Ryskamp & Peggy Ryskamp. LC 96-19127. (Illus.). 176p. (YA). (gr. 6-12). 1996. 24.95 (*0-89774-981-2*); Student's Guide to Native American Genealogy. E. Barrie Kavasch. LC 96-10196. (Illus.). 176p. (YA). (gr. 6-12). 1996. 24.95 (*0-89774-975-8*); Student's Guide to Polish American Genealogy. Carl S. Rollyson & Lisa O. Paddock. Ed. by Roger Rosen. LC 95-41416. (Illus.). 176p. (YA). (gr. 6-12). 1996. 24.95 (*0-89774-974-X*); Student's Guide to Scandinavian American Genealogy. Lisa O. Paddock & Carl S. Rollyson. LC 95-43086. (Illus.). 176p. (YA). (gr. 6-12). 1996. 24.95 (*0-89774-978-2*); 1996. 299.40 (*1-57356-071-5*) Oryx Pr.

Oryx Guide to Natural History: The Earth & All Its Inhabitants. Patricia L. Barnes-Svarney & Thomas E. Svarney. LC 99-41783. (Illus.). 252p. 1999. 69.95 (*1-57356-159-2*) Oryx Pr.

***Oryx Higher Education Service Learning Source Book.** Robin J. Crews. (Illus.). 240p. 2001. boxed set 64.50 (*1-57356-253-X*) Oryx Pr.

***Oryx Holocaust Sourcebook.** William R. Fernekes. 416p. 2001. text 55.00 (*1-57356-295-5*) Oryx Pr.

***Oryx Nanotechnology Directory & Sourcebook.** David E. Newton. (Illus.). 352p. 2001. text 125.00 (*1-57356-307-2*) Oryx Pr.

Oryza: From Molecule to Plant. Ed. by Takuji Sasaki & Graham Moore. LC 97-18394. 240p. 1997. text 167.00 (*0-7923-4455-3*) Kluwer Academic.

OS JCL & Utilities: A Comprehensive Treatment. Michael Trombetta & Sue C. Finkelstein. LC 83-6333. (Illus.). 1984. 33.50 (*0-201-07970-4*) Addison-Wesley.

Os Judeus, Vossa Majestade! 2nd rev. ed. Goran Larsson. Tr. by Paulo R. Pereira & Maria D. Barros.Tr. of Jews! Your Majesty. (POR., Illus.). 40p. 1997. pap. 3.00 (*1-888235-23-3*) AMI-Jerusalem.

Os Lusiadas. Tommaso Campanella. (POR.). 378p. 1985. reprint ed. lib. bdg. 97.50 (*3-487-07486-9*) G Olms Pubs.

Os Meus Amores: Poemas. unabridged ed. Emilia Lopes. (Poetry/ Poesia Ser.: No. 6). (POR & ENG.). 96p. 1996. boxed set 12.95 (*1-889358-02-9*, 18) Peregrinacao.

OS-9 Insights: An Advanced Programmers Guide to OS-9. Peter C. Dibble. Ed. by Eileen Beck et al. 645p. (C). 1994. write for info. (*0-918035-05-8*, INS68TE68MO) Microware Systs.

OS-9 Insights: An Advanced Programmers Guide to OS-9. 2nd ed. Peter C. Dibble. Ed. by David F. Davis. 542p. (C). 1992. write for info. (*0-918035-03-1*, INS68SE68MO) Microware Systs.

OS-9 Primer. Mark A. Heilpern. 645p. (C). 1995. write for info. (*0-918035-04-X*, PRI68RA68MO) Microware Systs.

QS 9000: Quality Systems Handbook. David Hoyle. 554p. 1996. 49.00 (*1-56091-925-6*, R-195) Soc Auto Engineers.

Os Organoosmium Compounds. M. Keber-Ludwig et al. (Gmelin Handbook of Inorganic & Organometallic Chemistry Ser.: Supp. Vol. B9). 379p. 1995. 1529.00 (*3-540-93715-3*) Spr-Verlag.

Os Organoosmium Compounds. 8th ed. Gmelin Institute for Inorganic Chemistry of the Ma. (Gmelin Handbook of Inorganic & Organometallic Chemistry Ser.: Pt. B 6). (Illus.). xi, 248p. 1993. 1080.00 (*0-387-93671-8*) Spr-Verlag.

Os Organoosmium Compounds see Gmelin: Handbook of Inorganic & Organometallic Chemistry

Os Organoosmium Compounds: Mononuclear Compounds. 8th ed. Gmelin Institute for Inorganic Chemistry of the Ma. (Gmelin Handbook of Inorganic & Organometallic Chemistry Ser.,: Pt. 2). (Illus.). xi, 410p. 1993. 1665.00 (*0-387-93679-3*) Spr-Verlag.

Os Organoosmium Compounds, Pt. B, Tetranuclear Compounds see Gmelin: Handbook of Inorganic & Organometallic Chemistry

Os-Osmium. 1980. 700.00 (*0-387-93420-0*) Spr-Verlag.

Os Osmium, Pt. A/1. (Gmelin Handbook of Inorganic & Organometallic Chemistry Ser.). (Illus.). xi, 283p. 1992. 1165.00 (*0-387-93647-5*) Spr-Verlag.

OS Utilities. Doug Lowe. LC 80-84103. (Illus.). 185p. 1981. pap. 22.50 (*0-911625-11-9*) M Murach & Assoc.

Osa Menor: Una Historia del Ferrocarril Subterraneo. F. N. Monjo. Tr. by Teresa Mlawer. LC 95-26309. (Ya Se Leer Ser.).Tr. of Drinking Gourd. (SPA., Illus.). 64p. (J). (gr. k-3). 1997. pap. 4.95 (*0-06-444217-9*, HpArco Iris) HarpC Child Bks.

Osa Menor: Una Historia del Ferrocarril Subterraneo. F. N. Monjo.Tr. of Drinking Gourd. 1997. 10.15 (*0-606-10860-2*, Pub. by Turtleback) Demco.

Osage: An Ethnohistorical Study of Hegemony on the Prairie-Plains. Willard H. Rollings. (Illus.). 336p. 1995. pap. 17.95 (*0-8262-1006-6*) U of Mo Pr.

Osage & the Invisible World: From the Works of Francis La Flesche. Francis La Flesche. Ed. & Intro. by Garrick A. Bailey. LC 95-17999. (Civilization of the American Indian Ser.: Vol. 217). (Illus.). 344p. 1995. 29.95 (*0-8061-2743-0*) U of Okla Pr.

***Osage & the Invisible World: From the Works of Francis La Flesche, Vol. 217.** Garrick Bailey. 1999. pap. text 16.95 (*0-8061-3132-2*) U of Okla Pr.

Osage Ceremonial Dance I'n-Lon-Schka. Alice A. Callahan. LC 90-50230. (C). 1993. pap. 11.95 (*0-8061-2486-5*) U of Okla Pr.

Osage County Kansas Cemeteries & Old Soldiers & Obituaries. Compiled by Arleen Bayless & Jill Herzog. LC 96-105263. 669p. (Orig.). 1996. 76.00 (*0-943259-15-0*) Topeka Geneal Soc.

Osage County Kids: A True Story. Lou Dean. 160p. 1999. pap. 11.95 (*0-9671208-2-9*) Clinescot Pubg.

***Osage Destiny.** Florence B. Smith. 273p. 1999. pap. 7.00 (*1-893463-26-5*) F B Smith.

Osage in Missouri. Kristie C. Wolferman. LC 97-10975. (Missouri Heritage Readers Ser.). (Illus.). 144p. 1997. pap. 9.95 (*0-8262-1122-4*) U of Mo Pr.

Osage Indian Murders: A True Crime Story. Lawrence J. Hogan. LC 97-95334. (Illus.). 296p. 1998. pap. 16.95 (*0-9659174-1-X*) Amlex.

Osage Life & Legends: Earth People - Sky People. Robert M. Liebert. LC 89-3359. (Illus.). 144p. 1987. pap. 8.95 (*0-87961-169-3*) Naturegraph.

***Osage Society & Culture: The First 125 Years of Post European Contact, 1700-1825.** Michael Tatham. 23p. 1999. pap. text 7.95 (*0-9647895-8-2*) FLPB Pr.

Osages: Children of the Middle Waters. John J. Mathews. LC 61-9006. (Civilization of the American Indian Ser.: No. 60). (Illus.). 848p. 1981. reprint ed. pap. 27.95 (*0-8061-1770-2*) U of Okla Pr.

***Osaka Municipal Projects in Japan: A Strategic Entry Report, 1999.** Compiled by Icon Group International. (Illus.). 170p. 1999. ring bd. 1700.00 incl. audio compact disk (*0-7418-1777-2*) Icon Grp.

Osaka Prefectural Government Construction Projects in Japan: A Strategic Entry Report, 1996. Compiled by Icon Group International Staff. (Country Industry Report). (Illus.). 166p. 1999. ring bd. 1660.00 incl. audio compact disk (*0-7418-0591-X*) Icon Grp.

***Osaka, the Merchant's Capital of Early Modern Japan.** Ed. & Pref. by James L. McClain. LC 98-45675. (Illus.). 295p. 1999. 49.95 (*0-8014-3630-3*) Cornell U Pr.

***OSBA Desk Manual.** Denny L. Ramey et al. LC 99-64023. 329p. 1999. ring bd. 49.95 (*0-9664544-2-1*) OSBACLE Institute.

Osbert & Lucy. Ronald Ferns. LC 88-21359. (Illus.). 32p. (J). (gr. k-3). 1989. 13.95 (*0-06-021835-5*) HarpC Child Bks.

Osbert Sitwell. Philip Ziegler. LC 99-47108. (Illus.). 464p. 1999. 30.00 (*0-679-44650-8*) Knopf.

Osborn Festival of Phobias. Robert Osborn. LC 78-162432. (Illus.). 1971. pap. 2.95 (*0-87140-250-5*, Pub. by Liveright) Norton.

Osborn Festival of Phobias. Eve Wengler. (Illus.). 1971. pap. text 2.95 (*0-87140-056-1*) Liveright.

***Osborne: Four Plays.** John Osborne. (Oberon Bks.). 240p. 2000. pap. 20.95 (*1-84002-074-1*) Theatre Comm.

***Osborne: Plays One.** John Osborne. 240p. 1998. pap. 18.95 (*1-84002-037-7*, Pub. by Oberon Bks Ltd) Consort Bk Sales.

Osborne: Thomas Osborne of Ashford, Kent, England & Some of His American Descendants. Daniel J. Weeks. 32p. 1994. reprint ed. pap. 7.00 (*0-8328-4072-6*) Higginson Bk Co.

Osborne & Little: The Decorated Room. Lorraine Johnson & Gabrielle Townsend. 176p. 1988. 35.00 (*0-87951-304-7*, Pub. by Overlook Pr) Penguin Putnam.

Osborne & Little Style: Decorating Themes & Combinations. Jackie Cole. LC 97-72787. (Illus.). 176p. 1997. 40.00 (*0-8212-2385-2*, Pub. by Bulfinch Pr) Little.

Osborne County Hall of Fame. Von Rothenberger. LC 98-71236. xv, 221p. 1998. per. 29.95 (*1-55856-273-7*, 257) Closson Pr.

Osborne County, Kansas. Von Rothenberger. (Images of America Ser.). (Illus.). 128p. 1999. pap. 18.99 (*0-7385-0164-6*) Arcadia Publng.

Osborne-McGraw-Hill 16-Bit CP-M User's Guide. F. Dolinar & S. Schmitt. (Osborne Books). 500p. 1984. pap. 18.95 (*0-88134-130-4*) McGraw.

***Osborne's NetWare 5 Administration Answers! Tech Support.** Billie Pierce et al. (Answers! Ser.). (Illus.). 490p. 1998. pap. 29.99 (*0-07-211885-7*) Osborne-McGraw.

***Oscar.** Laura Joy Lustig. (Illus.). 24p. 2000. pap. 3.95 (*0-9676660-3-1*, Pick Pocket Pr) Phony Lid Pubns.

Oscar: An Inquiry into the Nature of Sanity? P. Wilson. (Illus.). 142p. (C). 1992. reprint ed. pap. text 10.95 (*0-88133-669-6*) Waveland Pr.

Oscar! Furry Faces. Carol Nicklaus. (Illus.). 5p. (J). 1999. 7.99 (*0-679-89489-6*) Random.

***Oscar: His Story.** Oscar Hoffman Coen & Mildred Coen Robeck. (Illus.). 152p. 1999. pap. 16.00 (*0-8059-4710-8*) Dorrance.

Oscar & Lucinda. Laura Jones. 1998. pap. 13.95 (*0-571-19470-2*) Faber & Faber.

Oscar & Lucinda. large type ed. Peter Carey. 818p. 1989. reprint ed. 20.95 (*1-85089-318-7*, Pub. by ISIS Lrg Prnt) Transaction Pubs.

Oscar & Lucinda: Movie Tie-in. Peter Carey. LC 97-6669. 1997. pap. 13.00 (*0-679-77750-4*) Vin Bks.

Oscar Caliber Gun. Henry Baum. 189p. 1997. pap. 9.95 (*1-887128-21-2*) Soft Skull Pr.

Oscar, Cat-about-Town. James Herriot. LC 93-21746. (Illus.). 32p. (J). (gr. 1-3). 1993. pap. 7.95 (*0-312-09130-3*) St Martin.

Oscar, Cat-about-Town. James Herriot. (J). (gr. 1-3). 1993. 12.15 (*0-606-12466-7*, Pub. by Turtleback) Demco.

***Oscar de La Hoya.** Robert J. Quinn. (Latinos in the Limelight Ser.). (Illus.). 2000. 17.95 (*0-7910-6098-5*) Chelsea Hse.

Oscar de la Hoya. Bob Taylor. LC 93-7813. (Winning Spirit Ser.). 48p. (J). (gr 4-8). 1993. lib. bdg. 21.27 (*0-86592-175-X*) Rourke Enter.

Oscar de la Hoya: Champion Boxer. Valene Menard. LC 97-43509. (Real-Life Reader Biographies Ser.). (Illus.). 32p. (J). (gr. 3-8). 1998. lib. bdg. 15.95 (*1-883845-58-0*) M Lane Pubs.

Oscar de la Hoya: Gold-Medal Boxer see Reading Power Set 2: Hot Shots

Oscar de la Renta. Louis Carrillo. LC 95-19537. 48p. (J). (gr. 5-7). 1994. pap. 5.95 (*0-8114-9787-9*) Raintree Steck-V.

Oscar de la Renta. Louis Carrillo. (Contemporary Hispanic Americans Ser.). (Illus.). 48p. (J). (gr. 4-8). 1995. lib. bdg. 24.26 (*0-8172-3980-4*) Raintree Steck-V.

Oscar de la Renta. large type ed. Louis Carrillo. 54p. (J). (gr. 4-8). pap. 13.50 (*0-614-20573-5*, L-86297-00 APHB) Am Printing Hse.

Oscar de Mejo: The Naive Surrealist. Oscar De Mejo. (Illus.). 143p. 1992. 49.50 (*0-8109-3209-1*, Pub. by Abrams) Time Warner.

Oscar de Mejo's ABC. Oscar De Mejo. LC 91-28768. (Laura Geringer Bks.). (Illus.). 32p. (J). (ps up). 1992. 17.00 (*0-06-020516-4*); pap. 16.89 (*0-06-020517-2*) HarpC Child Bks.

Oscar Encyclopedia. Charles Matthews. LC 94-47288. 1280p. 1995. pap. 24.95 (*0-385-47364-8*, Main St Bks) Doubleday.

***Oscar Fever: The History & Politics of the Academy Awards.** Emanuel Levy. 384p. 2000. 19.95 (*0-8264-1284-X*) Continuum.

Oscar from Africa: The Biography of O. F. Watkins. Elizabeth Watkins. 1995. text 45.00 (*1-85043-948-6*, Pub. by I B T) St Martin.

Oscar Got the Blame. Tony Ross. (J). Date not set. pap. text. write for info. (*0-05-004405-2*) Addison-Wesley.

Oscar Hammerstein II: The Collection. 19.95 (*0-7935-5066-1*, 00313026) H Leonard.

Oscar, King of the Harbor. Marilynn Heddell. (ENG.). 12p. (J). 1994. pap. text 5.00 (*1-57833-032-7*) Todd Commns.

Oscar Montelius 150 Years: Proceedings of a Colloquium Held in the Royal Academy Letters, History & Antiquities, Stockholm, 13 May 1993. Ed. by Paul Astrom. (Konferenser: No. 32). (Illus.). 112p. (Orig.). 1995. pap. 32.50 (*91-7402-244-X*) Coronet Bks.

Oscar Needs a Friend. Joan Stimson. (Illus.). 32p. (J). (ps-1). 1998. pap. 5.95 (*0-7641-0746-1*) Barron.

Oscar Niemeyer. Joseph M. Botey. (Illus.). 240p. 1996. pap. text 19.95 (*84-252-1576-5*) Watsn-Guptill.

Oscar Niemeyer & Brazilian Free-Form Modernism. David Underwood. LC 93-39301. (Illus.). 128p. 1994. pap. 14.95 (*0-8076-1336-3*, Pub. by Braziller) Norton.

Oscar Niemeyer & Brazilian Free-Form Modernism. David K. Underwood. LC 93-39301. (Illus.). 128p. 1994. 22.50 (*0-8076-1335-5*) Braziller.

Oscar Niemeyer & the Architecture of Brazil. David Underwood. LC 94-11866. 208p. 1994. 60.00 (*0-8478-1686-9*, Pub. by Rizzoli Intl); pap. 40.00 (*0-8478-1687-7*, Pub. by Rizzoli Intl) St Martin.

Oscar Otter. Nathaniel Benchley. LC 66-11499. (I Can Read Bks.). (Illus.). 64p. (J). (ps-3). 1966. lib. bdg. 15.89 (*0-06-020472-9*) HarpC Child Bks.

Oscar Otter. Nathaniel Benchley. LC 66-11499. (I Can Read Bks.). (Illus.). 64p. (J). (ps-3). 1980. pap. 3.95 (*0-06-444025-7*, HarpTrophy) HarpC Child Bks.

Oscar Otter. Nathaniel Benchley. (I Can Read Bks.). (J). (ps-1). 1980. 8.95 (*0-606-12467-5*, Pub. by Turtleback) Demco.

An Asterisk (*) at the beginning of an entry indicates that the title is appearing for the first time.

Oscar Otter. Nathaniel Benchley & Arnold Lobel. (I Can Read Bks.). (Illus.). (J). (ps-1). 1966. 14.89 (*0-06-020471-0*, 108548) HarpC Child Bks.

Oscar Otters Sticker Stories. Maurice Pledger. (Illus.). 96p. (J). (ps). 1999. pap. 10.95 (*1-57145-385-7*, Silver Dolph) Advantage Pubs.

***Oscar Peterson: Note for Note Transcriptions of Classic Recordings.** 1999. 39.95 incl. cd-rom H Leonard.

Oscar Peterson: The Will to Swing. Gene Lees. (Illus.). 304p. 1991. pap. 14.95 (*1-55958-111-5*) Prima Pub.

***Oscar Peterson: The Will to Swing.** rev. ed. Gene Lees. (Illus.). 2000. pap. 18.95 (*0-8154-1021-2*) Cooper Sq.

Oscar Plays Out in the Rain see Qetun'am Ellallugmi Aquilla

Oscar Romero: Martyr for the Poor. Ann Daly. 1989. pap. 22.00 (*1-85390-093-1*, Pub. by Veritas Pubns) St Mut.

***Oscar Romero: Memories in Mosaic.** Maria Lopez Vigil. LC 99-462256. (Illus.). 2000. write for info. (*0-918346-24-X*) EPICA.

***Oscar Romero: Reflections on His Life & Writings.** Marie Dennis et al. LC 99-52262. (Modern Spiritual Masters Ser.). 144p. 2000. pap. 13.00 (*1-57075-309-1*) Orbis Bks.

Oscar Satellite Revue. Dave Ingram. (Illus.). 43p. 1988. pap. 7.95 (*1-891237-16-0*, MFJ-31) MFJ Ent.

Oscar Sonneck & American Music. Ed. by William Lichtenwanger. LC 82-13670. (Music in American Life Ser.). 304p. 1983. text 29.95 (*0-252-01021-3*) U of Ill Pr.

Oscar Stars from A to Z. Roy Pickard. (Illus.). 448p. 1998. pap. 19.95 (*0-7472-7690-0*, Pub. by Headline Bk Pub) Trafalgar.

Oscar the Fancy Rat, Tessa Krailing. LC 98-31032. (Petsitters Club Ser.: No. 7). (Illus.). 96p. (J). (gr. 1-4). 1999. pap. 3.95 (*0-7641-0692-9*) Barron.

Oscar Wilde see Notable Biographies

Oscar Wilde. (Little Brown Notebooks). 1998. 9.99 (*1-897954-79-4*, Pub. by Mus Quilts Pub) Sterling.

Oscar Wilde. Ed. by Karl Beckson. (Critical Heritage Ser.). 448p. (C). 1997. 140.00 (*0-415-15952-0*) Routledge.

Oscar Wilde. Richard Ellmann. 1988. pap. 18.95 (*0-394-75984-2*) Vin Bks.

Oscar Wilde. Donald H. Ericksen. (English Authors Ser.: No. 211). 176p. 1977. 28.95 (*0-8057-6680-4*, Twyne) Mac Lib Ref.

Oscar Wilde. Andre Gide. pap. 8.95 (*0-685-34152-6*) Fr & Eur.

Oscar Wilde. Frank Harris. 368p. 1992. pap. 10.95 (*0-88184-759-3*) Carroll & Graf.

Oscar Wilde. Frank Harris. LC 97-17482. 368p. 1997. pap. 12.95 (*0-7867-0479-9*) Carroll & Graf.

Oscar Wilde. Ed. by Robert Mighall. (Everyman's Poetry Ser.). 116p. 1997. pap. 1.95 (*0-460-87803-4*, Everyman's Classic Lib) Tuttle Pubng.

Oscar Wilde. Sheridan Morley. (Illus.). 160p. 1998. pap. 18.95 (*1-55783-330-3*) Applause Theatre Bk Pubs.

Oscar Wilde. Oscar Wilde. Ed. by Isobel M. Murray. (Oxford Authors Ser.). 660p. 1989. pap. text 21.00 (*0-19-281978-X*) OUP.

Oscar Wilde. Katharine Worth. Ed. by Bruce King & Adele King. (Modern Dramatists Ser.). 207p. 1992. pap. 11.95 (*0-333-30423-3*) St Martin.

Oscar Wilde. enl. rev. ed. Edouard Roditi. LC 86-8578. 224p. 1986. pap. 10.95 (*0-8112-0995-4*, NDP633, Pub. by New Directions) Norton.

Oscar Wilde. Vyvyan Holland. LC 87-51291. (Literary Lives Ser.). (Illus.). 144p. 1998. reprint ed. pap. 12.95 (*0-500-26031-1*, Pub. by Thames Hudson) Norton.

Oscar Wilde. Robert Merle. LC 79-8071. (FRE.). reprint ed. 43.50 (*0-404-18381-6*) AMS Pr.

Oscar Wilde. Robert H. Sherard. LC 73-133282. (English Biography Ser.: No. 31). 1970. reprint ed. lib. bdg. 75.00 (*0-8383-1181-4*) M S G Haskell Hse.

Oscar Wilde. 2nd ed. Richard Pine. (Gill's Irish Lives Ser.). (Illus.). 151p. 1998. reprint ed. pap. 13.95 (*0-7171-2690-0*, Pub. by Gill & MacMill) Irish Bks Media.

***Oscar Wilde: A Certain Genius.** Barbara Belford. (Illus.). 416p. 2000. 29.95 (*0-679-45734-8*) Random.

Oscar Wilde: A Collection of Critical Essays. Ed. by Jonathan Freedman. LC 95-12411. (New Century Views Ser.). 257p. (C). 1995. pap. text 12.95 (*0-13-146044-7*) P-H.

Oscar Wilde: A Critical Study. Arthur Ransom. LC 79-151283. (English Literature Ser.: No. 33). 1971. reprint ed. lib. bdg. 75.00 (*0-8383-1230-6*) M S G Haskell Hse.

Oscar Wilde: A Life in Letters, Writings & Wit. Ed. by Juliet Gardiner. (Illustrated Letters Ser.). (Illus.). 160p. 1998. pap. 17.95 (*1-85585-242-X*, Pub. by Collins & Br) Trafalgar.

Oscar Wilde: A Long & Lovely Suicide. Melissa Knox. LC 94-276. (Illus.). 240p. 1994. 35.00 (*0-300-05905-1*) Yale U Pr.

Oscar Wilde: A Long & Lovely Suicide. Melissa Knox. (Illus.). 240p. 1996. pap. 16.00 (*0-300-06873-5*) Yale U Pr.

Oscar Wilde: A Study. Andre Gide. Tr. by L. Gordon. 1975. 250.00 (*0-87968-229-9*) Gordon Pr.

Oscar Wilde: A Writer for the Nineties. Michael Cadden & Mary A. Jensen. (Illus.). 76p. 1995. pap. 10.00 (*0-87811-039-9*) Princeton Lib.

Oscar Wilde: An Annotated Bibliography, 38. Compiled by Thomas A. Mikolyzk. LC 93-14052. (Bibliographies & Indexes in World Literature Ser.: No. 38). 512p. 1993. lib. bdg. 85.00 (*0-313-27597-1*, MOT/, Greenwood Pr) Greenwood.

***Oscar Wilde: An Exquisite Life.** Stephen Calloway & David Colvin. (Illus.). 112p. 1999. pap. 19.95 (*1-56649-074-X*) Welcome Rain.

Oscar Wilde: An Idler's Impression. Edgar E. Saltus. LC 68-54293. reprint ed. 37.50 (*0-404-05542-7*) AMS Pr.

Oscar Wilde: Art & Morality. Stuart Mason. LC 79-174694. (English Literature Ser.: No. 33). 1971. reprint ed. lib. bdg. 75.00 (*0-8383-1334-5*) M S G Haskell Hse.

Oscar Wilde: Myths, Miracles & Imitations. John Stokes. (Illus.). 230p. (C). 1996. text 59.95 (*0-521-47537-6*) Cambridge U Pr.

Oscar Wilde: The Complete Works. Oscar Wilde. LC 95-111358. (Collins Classics Ser.). 1344p. 1998. pap. 17.95 (*0-00-470473-8*) Collins SF.

***Oscar Wilde: The Critic As Humanist.** Bruce Bashford. LC 98-54801. 200p. 1999. 36.00 (*0-8386-3769-8*) Fairleigh Dickinson.

Oscar Wilde: The Double Image. George Woodcock. 308p. 1989. 48.99 (*0-921689-43-8*, Pub. by Black Rose); pap. 19.99 (*0-921689-42-X*, Pub. by Black Rose) Consort Bk Sales.

Oscar Wilde: The Fisherman & His Soul & Other Fairy Tales. Oscar Wilde. (Bloomsbury Poetry Classics Ser.). 1998. text 9.95 (*0-312-19086-7*) St Martin.

Oscar Wilde: The Importance of Being Irish. Davis Coakley. (Illus.). 256p. 1996. pap. 13.95 (*1-57098-083-7*) Roberts Rinehart.

***Oscar Wilde: The Major Works.** Oscar Wilde. Ed. by Isobel Murray. (Oxford World's Classics Ser.). 636p. 2000. pap. 15.95 (*0-19-284054-1*) OUP.

***Oscar Wilde: Trial & Punishment, 1895-1897.** Ed. by Barry Leonard. (Illus.). 52p. 1999. pap. text 25.00 (*0-7881-8126-2*) DIANE Pub.

***Oscar Wilde: Trial & Punishment 1895-1897.** Michael Taylor. 1999. 19.95 (*1-873162-50-2*) PRO Pubns.

Oscar Wilde & His Literary Circle. Compiled by John C. Finzi. LC 79-8059. reprint ed. 28.50 (*0-404-18370-0*) AMS Pr.

Oscar Wilde & His Mother. Contesse De Bremont Anna. LC 72-2155. (English Biography Ser.: No. 31). 1972. reprint ed. lib. bdg. 75.00 (*0-8383-1457-0*) M S G Haskell Hse.

Oscar Wilde & the Aesthetic Movement. Stuart Mason. LC 75-119081. (English Literature Ser.: No. 33). 1970. reprint ed. lib. bdg. 75.00 (*0-8383-1077-X*) M S G Haskell Hse.

Oscar Wilde & the Poetics of Ambiguity. Michael P. Gillespie. LC 96-14579. 208p. (C). 1996. 49.95 (*0-8130-1453-0*) U Press Fla.

Oscar Wilde & the Yellow '90s. Frances Grebanier. LC 79-8062. reprint ed. 37.00 (*0-404-18373-5*) AMS Pr.

Oscar Wilde Chronology. Norman Page. (Author Chronologies Ser.). 128p. 1991. 40.00 (*0-8161-7298-6*, Hall Reference) Macmillan.

Oscar Wilde Discovers America, 1882. Lloyd Lewis & Henry J. Smith. LC 67-12459. (Illus.). 1972. reprint ed. 24.95 (*0-405-08746-2*) Ayer.

Oscar Wilde (1854-1900) Selected Poems. Ed. by Malcolm Hicks. pap. write for info. (*0-85635-984-X*, Pub. by Carcanet Pr) Paul & Co Pubs.

Oscar Wilde Encyclopedia. Karl E. Beckson. LC 97-36303. (Studies in the Nineteenth Century). 456p. 1998. 125.00 (*0-404-61498-1*) AMS Pr.

Oscar Wilde File. Jonathan Goodman. 160p. 1995. pap. 14.95 (*0-7490-0217-4*) Allison & Busby.

Oscar Wilde in the 1990's: Critic As Creator. Melissa Knox. LC 98-37818. 2001. 60.00 (*1-57113-042-X*) Camden Hse.

Oscar Wilde Quotations. Oscar Wilde. 1999. 7.00 (*0-7117-1045-7*) Seven Hills Bk.

Oscar Wilde Revalued: An Essay on New Materials & Methods of Research. Ian Small. LC 90-96297. (British Authors, 1880-1920 Ser.: No. 8). 320p. 1993. lib. bdg. 30.00 (*0-944318-07-X*) ELT Pr.

Oscar Wilde's America: Counterculture in the Gilded Age. Mary W. Blanchard. LC 97-39628. (Illus.). 320p. 1998. 45.00 (*0-300-07460-3*) Yale U Pr.

***Oscar Wilde's Decorated Books.** Nicholas Frankel. LC 99-59553. 240p. (C). 1999. text 47.50 (*0-472-11069-1*, 11069) U of Mich Pr.

Oscar Wilde's Last Stand: Decadence, Conspiracy, & the Most Outrageous Trial of the Century. Philip Hoare. LC 97-52311. (Illus.). 256p. 1998. 25.95 (*1-55970-423-3*, Pub. by Arcade Pub Inc) Time Warner.

Oscar Wilde's Last Stand: Decadence, Conspiracy, & the Most Outrageous Trial of the Century. Philip Hoare. 256p. 1999. 14.95 (*1-55970-472-1*, Pub. by Arcade Pub Inc) Time Warner.

Oscar Wilde's the Importance of Being Earnest. rev. ed. Graham Handley. (Brodie's Notes Ser.). 51p. 1994. pap. 5.95 (*0-333-58219-5*, Pub. by Macmillan) Trans-Atl Phila.

Oscar Wilde's The Importance of Being Earnest: A Reconstructive Critical Edition of the Text of the First Production, St. James Theatre, London, 1895. Oscar Wilde. Ed. by Joseph Donohue & Ruth Berggren. (Illus.). 384p. 1996. text 70.00 (*0-86140-378-9*) OUP.

***Oscar Wilde's the Selfish Giant.** Oscar Wilde. LC 99-32495. (Illus.). 32p. (J). 2000. 16.95 (*0-375-80319-X*, Pub. by Knopf Bks Yng Read) Random.

***Oscar Wilde's the Selfish Giant.** Oscar Wilde. LC 99-32495. 32p. 2000. lib. bdg. 18.99 (*0-375-90319-4*, Pub. by Knopf Bks Yng Read) Random.

Oscar Wilde's Wit & Wisdom: A Book of Quotations. Oscar Wilde. LC 98-13741. 60p. 1998. pap. 1.00 (*0-486-40146-4*) Dover.

Oscar Williams: Selected Poems. Oscar Williams. 1964. pap. 3.95 (*0-8079-0136-9*) October.

Oscar Zariski - Collected Papers Vol. 1: Foundations of Algebric Geometry & Resolution of Singularities. Ed. by H. Hironaka & D. Mumford. (Mathematicians of Our Time Ser.). 1972. 60.00 (*0-262-08049-4*) MIT Pr.

Oscar Zariski - Collected Papers Vol. 2: Holomorphic Functions & Linear Systems. Ed. by M. Artin & D. Mumford. (Mathematicians of Our Time Ser.). 1973. 60.00 (*0-262-01038-0*) MIT Pr.

Oscar Zariski - Collected Papers Vol. 4: Equisingularity on Algebraic Varieties. Ed. by J. Lipman & B. Teissier. (Mathematicians of Our Time Ser.). 1979. 85.00 (*0-262-24022-X*) MIT Pr.

Oscar "Zeta" Acosta: The Uncollected Works. Ed. by Ilan Stavans. LC 95-33398. 368p. (Orig.). 1996. pap. 14.95 (*1-55885-099-6*) Arte Publico.

Oscars. Neal Pronek. 96p. 1972. 11.95 (*0-86622-212-X*, PS-687) TFH Pubns.

Oscars: An Unauthorized History of Hollywood's Academy Awards. Anthony Holden. (Illus.). 400p. 1993. 25.00 (*0-671-70129-0*) S&S Trade.

Oscars: Keeping & Breeding Them in Captivity. Richard F. Stratton. (Illus.). 64p. 1997. pap. 6.95 (*0-7938-0370-5*, RE-620) TFH Pubns.

Oscar's Bridge to Reading Book: Activity Book. 1985. pap. text 5.75 (*0-19-434189-5*) OUP.

Oscar's Bridge to Reading Book: Student Book. 1985. pap. text, student ed. 7.95 (*0-19-434171-2*) OUP.

Oscar's Bridge to Reading Book: Teacher's Book. 1985. pap. text, teacher ed. 15.95 (*0-19-434177-1*) OUP.

Oscar's Dreamland Yesteryear Museum: The Story of Oscar O. Cooke & His Collection. Marcie A. Limpp. (Illus.). 144p. (Orig.). 1997. pap. 17.95 (*0-9656378-0-8*) Hayseed Pub.

Oscar's Grouch Jamboree. write for info. (*0-307-47721-5*) Gldn Bks Pub Co.

Oscar's Spots. Janet Robertson. LC 93-22199. (Illus.). 32p. (J). (ps-2). 1996. pap. 3.95 (*0-8167-3134-9*, Troll Medallion) Troll Communs.

***Oscar's Starry Night.** Joan Stimson. (Illus.). 32p. (J). (ps-1). 1999. 12.95 (*0-7641-5207-6*) Barron.

OSCE in the Maintenance of Peace & Security: Conflict Prevention, Crisis Management & Peaceful Settlement of Disputes. Ed. by Michael Bothe et al. LC 97-44704. 580p. 1997. 182.00 (*90-411-0446-1*) Kluwer Academic.

OSCE Meeting on Human Dimension Issues (1997) Ed. by Michael R. Hathaway. 67p. (C). 1999. text 20.00 (*0-7881-7933-0*) DIANE Pub.

Osceola. R. P. Johnson. LC 72-91158. (Story of an American Indian Ser.). 90 p. 1973. write for info. (*0-87518-055-8*, Dillon Silver Burdett) Silver Burdett Pr.

Osceola. Herman J. Viola. 1996. 10.15 (*0-606-12468-3*, Pub. by Turtleback) Demco.

Osceola: Jewel of Tug Hill, 1844-1984. Lola Moore & Elizabeth Quinn. (Illus.). 400p. 1985. pap. 14.95 (*0-685-43033-2*) Moore & Quinn.

Osceola: Memories of a Sharecropper's Daughter. Osceola Mays & Alan Govenar. LC 98-40411. (Illus.). 64p. (J). (gr. 3-7). 2000. 15.99 (*0-7868-0407-6*, Pub. by Disney Pr) Time Warner.

Osceola: Memories of a Sharecropper's Daughter. Osceola Mays et al. Ed. by Alan Govenar. LC 98-40411. 64p. (J). (gr. 3-7). 2000. lib. bdg. 16.00 (*0-7868-2357-7*, Pub. by Disney Pr) Time Warner.

Osceola: Seminole Rebel see North American Indians of Achievement

Osceola, Patriot & Warrior. Moses Jumper & Ben Sonder. Ed. by Alex Haley. LC 92-25209. (Stories of America Ser.). (Illus.). 76p. (J). (gr. 2-5). 1992. lib. bdg. 24.26 (*0-8114-7225-6*) Raintree Steck-V.

Osceola, Patriot & Warrior. Moses Jumper & Ben Sonder. Ed. by Alex Haley. LC 92-25209. (Stories of America Ser.). (Illus.). 76p. (J). (gr. 4-7). 1992. pap. 4.95 (*0-8114-8065-8*) Raintree Steck-V.

Osceola, Seminole Warrior. Joanne Oppenheim. (J). 1979. 8.70 (*0-606-01695-3*, Pub. by Turtleback) Demco.

Osceola, Seminole Warrior. Joanne F. Oppenheim. LC 78-60116. (Illus.). 48p. (J). (gr. 4-6). 1979. pap. 3.50 (*0-89375-148-0*) Troll Communs.

Osceola's Legacy. Patricia R. Wickman. LC 89-20551. 288p. 1991. pap. 22.95 (*0-8173-0483-5*) U of Ala Pr.

***OSCE's in Paediatrics.** A. Khan & H. Pandya. (Illus.). 192p. 1998. pap. write for info. (*0-443-05728-1*) Church.

Oscillate Wildly: Space, Body, & Spirit of Millennial Materialism. Peter Hitchcock. LC 98-36588. 232p. 1998. 49.95 (*0-8166-3149-2*); pap. 19.95 (*0-8166-3150-6*) U of Minn Pr.

Oscillating Heterogeneous Catalytic Systems. Marina M. Slin'ko & Nils I. Jaeger. LC 94-27696. 408p. 1994. 291.50 (*0-444-88891-8*) Elsevier.

Oscillating Pressure Fields on a Free Surface. T. Francis Ogilvie. LC VM0363.O344. (University of Michigan, Dept. of Naval Architecture & Marine Engineering, Report Ser.: No. 30). 64p. reprint ed. pap. 30.00 (*0-608-12982-8*, 202386800034) Bks Demand.

Oscillation & Dynamics in Delay Equations: (Proceedings of the Special Session Held at the 97th Annual Meeting of the American Mathematical Society on January 16-19, 1991 in San Francisco, California) Ed. by John R. Graef & Jack K. Hale. LC 92-12229. (Contemporary Mathematics Ser.: Vol. 129). 263p. 1992. pap. 36.00 (*0-8218-5140-3*, CONM/129) Am Math.

Oscillation, Bifurcation & Chaos: Proceedings of the Canadian Mathematical Society Annual Seminar, 1986. Ed. by W. F. Langford et al. LC 87-11402. (Conference Proceedings of the Canadian Mathematical Society Ser.: Vol. 8). 711p. 1988. reprint ed. pap. 93.00 (*0-8218-6013-5*, CMSAMS/8) Am Math.

Oscillation Theory, Computation, & Methods of Compensated Compactness. Ed. by C. M. Dafermos et al. (IMA Volumes in Mathematics & Its Applications Ser.: Vol. 2). (Illus.). 415p. 1986. 65.95 (*0-387-96401-0*) Spr-Verlag.

***Oscillation Theory for Difference & Functional Differential.** Ravi P. Agarwal et al. 352p. 2000. 152.00 (*0-7923-6289-6*, Kluwer Plenum) Kluwer Academic.

Oscillation Theory for Functional Differential Equations. L. H. Erbe et al. LC 94-38757. (Pure & Applied Mathematics Ser.: Vol. 190). (Illus.). 504p. 1994. text 195.00 (*0-8247-9598-9*) Dekker.

Oscillation Theory for Neutral Differential Equations with Delay. D. D. Bainov & D. P. Mishev. (Illus.). 288p. 1991. 149.00 (*0-7503-0142-2*) IOP Pub.

Oscillation Theory of Delay Differential Equations: With Applications. I. Gyori. Ed. by G. Ladas. (Oxford Mathematical Monographs). 384p. 1992. 95.00 (*0-19-853582-1*) OUP.

Oscillation Theory of Operator - Differential Equations. Drumi D. Bainov. (Soviet & East European Mathematics Ser.). 280p. 1995. text 61.00 (*981-02-1100-7*) World Scientific Pub.

Oscillation Theory of Two-Term Differential Equations. Uri Elias. LC 97-3731. 1997. text 124.00 (*0-7923-4447-2*) Kluwer Academic.

Oscillations & Traveling Waves in Chemical Systems. Ed. by Richard J. Field & Maria Burger. LC 84-15382. 681p. 1985. 359.00 (*0-471-89384-6*) Wiley.

Oscillations & Waves. R. Buckley. (Student Monographs in Physics). (Illus.). 64p. 1985. pap. 15.00 (*0-85274-793-4*) IOP Pub.

Oscillations & Waves. F. K. Kneubyhl. LC 97-30399. (Illus.). 400p. 1997. 69.00 (*3-540-62001-X*) Spr-Verlag.

Oscillations & Waves. M. I. Rabinovich & D. I. Trubetskov. (C). 1989. text 382.50 (*0-7923-0445-4*) Kluwer Academic.

Oscillations & Waves: In Strong Gravitational & Electromagnetic Fields. N. R. Sibgatullin. Ed. by W. Beiglbock et al. Tr. by N. M. Queen from RUS. (Texts & Monographs in Physics). (Illus.). 384p. 1991. 108.95 (*0-387-19461-4*) Spr-Verlag.

Oscillations & Waves: Versatility of Maxwell Equations. V. I. Zubov. (Series on Optimization). 600p. 1998. text 109.00 (*981-02-0977-0*) World Scientific Pub.

Oscillations in Chemical Reactions. Okan Gurel. (Topics in Current Chemistry Ser.: Vol. 118). (Illus.). 130p. 1983. 53.95 (*0-387-12575-2*) Spr-Verlag.

Oscillations in Finite Quantum Systems. George F. Bertsch & Ricardo A. Brogila. LC 92-40596. (Cambridge Monographs on Mathematical Physics). (Illus.). 224p. (C). 1994. text 54.95 (*0-521-41148-3*) Cambridge U Pr.

Oscillations in Nonlinear Systems. rev. unabridged ed. Jack K. Hale. LC 92-24840. ix, 180p. 1993. pap. text 7.95 (*0-486-67362-6*) Dover.

Oscillations in Planar Phase-Space Dynamic Systems. Ronald E. Mickens. LC 95-44982. (Series on Advances in Mathematics for Applied Sciences). 250p. 1996. text 48.00 (*981-02-2292-0*) World Scientific Pub.

Oscillations in Rail Vehicle Traction Drives: Analysis of Electromechanics. M. W. Winterling. (Illus.). 210p. 1997. pap. 57.50 (*90-407-1514-9*, Pub. by Delft U Pr) Coronet Bks.

Oscillations, Waves, & Chaos in Chemical Kinetics. Stephen K. Scott. (Illus.). 96p. (C). 1994. text 31.95 (*0-19-855832-5*); pap. text 12.95 (*0-19-855844-9*) OUP.

Oscillator Circuit & Projects. Stephen Kamichik. LC 97-65789. (Illus.). 249p. 1997. pap. 24.95 (*0-7906-1111-2*) Prompt Publns.

Oscillator Circuits. Rudolf F. Graf. LC 96-43977. 192p. 1996. pap. text 24.95 (*0-7506-9883-7*) Buttrwrth-Heinemann.

Oscillator Design & Computer Simulation. 2nd ed. Randall W. Rhea. (Illus.). 320p. 1996. 65.00 (*0-07-052415-7*) McGraw.

Oscillator Design & Computer Simulation. 2nd ed. Randall W. Rhea. (Illus.). 320p. 1995. 64.00 (*1-884932-30-4*) Noble Pubng.

Oscillator Duality Correspondence for the Pair 0(2,2), SP(2,R) T. Przebinda. LC 89-6540. (Memoirs Ser.: No. 79/403). 105p. 1989. pap. 20.00 (*0-8218-2464-3*, MEMO/79/403) Am Math.

Oscillator Representation in Quantum Physics. M. Dineykhan et al. Ed. by J. Ehlers et al. LC 95-7855. (Lecture Notes in Physics - Monographs: Vol. m26). ix, 279p. 1995. 57.95 (*3-540-59085-4*) Spr-Verlag.

Oscillators, North American Markets, Applications & Competitors: 1992-1996 Analysis. Tim Archdeacon. 250p. 1900.00 (*1-883742-02-1*) Allied Busn.

Oscillators Simplified, with 61 Projects. Delton T. Horn. LC 87-13882. (Illus.). 238p. 1987. 17.95 (*0-8306-0375-1*, 2875); pap. 11.95 (*0-8306-2875-4*) McGraw-Hill Prof.

Oscillatory Event-Related Brain Dynamics. C. Pantev et al. LC 94-48769. (NATO ASI Ser.: Vol. 271). (Illus.). 478p. (C). 1995. text 130.00 (*0-306-44894-7*, Kluwer Plenum) Kluwer Academic.

Oscillatory Evolution Processes: Quantitative Analyses Arising from Applied Science. Igor Gumowski. (Nonlinear Science: Theory & Applications Ser.). 272p. 1989. text 95.00 (*0-7190-2212-6*, Pub. by Manchester Univ Pr) St Martin.

Oscillatory Evolution Processes: Quantitative Analyses Arising from Applied Science. Igor Gumowski. (Nonlinear Science: Theory & Applications Ser.). 336p. 1992. 579.50 (*0-471-93516-6*) Wiley.

Oscilloscope Guide. Arnold J. Banks. (Illus.). 336p. 1997. pap. 29.95 (*0-7906-1124-4*) Prompt Publns.

Oscilloscopes. Ian Hickman. 1988. 22.00 (*0-434-90738-3*) CRC Pr.

Oscilloscopes: Selecting & Restoring a Classic. Stan Griffiths. 372p. 1992. 19.95 (*0-9633071-5-0*) S A Griffiths.

Oscura Noticia - Hombre y Dios. Damaso Alonso. Ed. by Antonio Chicharro Chamorro. (Nueva Austral Ser.: No. 247). (SPA.). 1991. pap. text 24.95 (*84-239-7247-X*) Elliots Bks.

O

An Asterisk (*) at the beginning of an entry indicates that the title is appearing for the first time.

Oseas & Amos. G Cohen. (SPA.). 208p. 1997. pap. 7.99 (0-8254-1128-9) Kregel.

Oseberg Skiff. Rebecca Newth. (Illus.). 64p. (Orig.). 1991. pap. 6.95 (0-9630310-0-7) Will Hall.

Oseh Shalom. Lori Sagarin & James J. Sagarin. (Illus.). (J). (gr. 4-6). 1990. pap., student ed. 6.00 (0-8074-0351-2, 123703) UAHC.

Osei Bonsu: Warrior King of Asante. Kwami Segbawu. LC 79-300764. (Makers of African History Ser.). (Illus.). 63p. 1977. pap. 30.00 (0-608-05247-7, 206578400001) Bks Demand.

***Osem Storoci Slovenskej Heraldiky (Eight Centuries of the Slovak Heraldry)** Ladislav Vrtel. (SLO & ENG., Illus.). 296p. 1999. 34.95 (0-86516-458-4) Bolchazy-Carducci.

Osen' Na Vindzorskoi Doroge: Zapiski Massazhista. Grigorii Ryskin. LC 86-9773. (RUS.). 164p. 1986. pap. 8.50 (0-938920-71-5) Hermitage Pubs.

Osen' V Amerike. Bakhyt Kenzheev. LC 88-24305. (Russian Ser.). 128p. (Orig.). 1988. pap. 8.00 (1-55779-006-X) Hermitage Pubs.

Osen' Veka. Valery Petrochenkov. LC 82-84747. (RUS., Illus.). 152p. (Orig.). 1983. 8.00 (0-911971-00-9) Effect Pub.

Osennie Prikoly: Almanakh. Tr. of Nearing of Fall. 180p. 1998. pap. text 26.00 (0-914265-59-8) New Eng Pub MA.

Osenniye List'ya: Autumn Leaves. N. Perelman. (RUS.). 64p. (Orig.). 1994. pap. 10.00 (0-929647-05-X) H A Frager & Co.

Oseola McCarty's Simple Wisdom for Rich Living. Oseola McCarty. LC 96-76509. 112p. 1996. 9.95 (1-56352-341-8) Longstreet.

Oser Inventer l'Avenir (Daring to Invent the Future) La Parole de Sankara (Sankara Speaks) Thomas Sankara. LC 88-61827. (FRE., Illus.). 290p. (Orig.). (C). 1991. pap. 35.95 (2-7384-0761-7) Pathfinder NY.

OSF - Motif Programmer's Guide Release 1.2. Open Software Foundation Staff. 650p. 1992. pap. 65.00 (0-13-643107-0) P-H.

OSF - Motif Programmer's Reference Release 1.2. Open Software Foundation Staff. 1260p. 1992. pap. 86.00 (0-13-643115-1) P-H.

OSF - Motif Style Guide Release 1.2. Open Software Foundation Staff. 400p. 1992. pap. 46.00 (0-13-643123-2) P-H.

OSF - Motif User's Guide Release 1.2. Open Software Foundation Staff. 176p. 1992. pap. 31.60 (0-13-643131-3) P-H.

Osf Dce: Guide to Developing Distributed Applications. Harold Lockhart. 1994. pap. 59.95 (0-07-911481-4) McGraw.

Osf Dce Administration Guide Core Components. Open Software Foundation Staff. 800p. 1995. pap. 60.00 (0-13-185844-0, Prentice Hall) P-H.

OSF DCE Application Development Guide, Vol. 2. Open Software Foundation Staff. 912p. 1995. pap. 65.00 (0-13-185885-8) P-H.

OSF DCE Application Development Guide, Vol. 3. Open Software Foundation Staff. 640p. 1995. pap. 64.00 (0-13-185893-9) P-H.

OSF DCE Application Development Guide 1.1, Vol. 1. Open Software Foundation Staff. 416p. 1995. pap. 57.00 (0-13-185877-7) P-H.

OSF DCE Application Development Reference. Open Software Foundation Staff. 880p. 1995. pap. 65.00 (0-13-185869-6) P-H.

OSF DCE Command Reference. Open Software Foundation Staff. 740p. 1996. pap. 62.00 (0-13-185851-3) P-H.

OSF DCE DFS Adm. Guide & Reference 1.1. Open Software Foundation Staff. 1056p. 1996. pap. 72.00 (0-13-185828-9) P-H.

OSF Dce. Gds. Admin. Guide & Reference. Open Software Foundation Staff. 704p. 1995. pap. 46.60 (0-13-185901-3) P-H.

OSF DCE User's Guide & Reference. Open Software Foundation Staff. 208p. 1998. pap. 28.60 (0-13-643842-3) P-H.

OSF Motif. Berlage. (C). 1990. text. write for info. (0-201-55906-4) Addison-Wesley.

OSF/Motif Version 1.1 Einfuhrung in Server und Clients. Klaus Eickemeyer. (GER.). (C). 1992. text. write for info. (0-201-57859-X) Addison-Wesley.

OSF/Motif Version 1.1 Server und Clients Zum Nachschlagen. Klaus Eickemeyer. (GER.). (C). 1992. text. write for info. (0-201-57860-3) Addison-Wesley.

Osgodby School, 1863-1923. Alan Wilkinson & Rosemary West. 1985. 30.00 (0-946270-14-7, Pub. by Pentland Pr) St Mut.

Osgood & Anthony Perkins: A Comprehensive History of Their Work in Theatre, Film & Other Media, with Credits & an Annotated Bibliography. Laura K. Palmer. LC 90-53518. (Illus.). 423p. 1991. lib. bdg. 49.95 (0-89950-577-5) McFarland & Co.

Osh Riot: A First-Hand Account. Karl A. Krippes. 55p. (Orig.). 1996. pap. 7.50 (0-9651505-1-8) Hierogly Pr.

OSHA: History, Law & Policy. Benjamin W. Mintz. LC 84-11333. 800p. reprint ed. pap. 200.00 (0-7837-4593-1, 204431200002) Bks Demand.

***OSHA: Secrets of the Yoruba Lucumi Santeria Religion in the United States & the Americas.** Julio Garcia Cortez. Ed. by Roger Francis. LC 00-132518. (Illus.). 473p. (C). 2000. pap. 34.95 (1-890157-22-8) Athelia-Henrietta.

OSHA & EPA Process Safety Management Requirements: A Practical Guide for Compliance. Mark S. Dennison. (Industrial Health & Safety Ser.). 416p. 1994. 98.95 (0-471-28641-9, VNR) Wiley.

OSHA & EPA Process Safety Management Requirements: A Practical Guide to Compliance. Mark S. Dennison. LC 94-12507. 416p. 1994. text 76.95 (0-442-01876-2, VNR) Wiley.

OSHA & State Employee Hazard Communications Program. rev. ed. Hobart G. Miller et al. 325p. 1988. teacher ed. 295.00 (0-940394-29-4) Labelmaster.

OSHA & State Employee Hazard Communications Program, 2 vols., Vols. 1-2. H. G. Miller et al. Ed. by Knowles-McFarland. 622p. 1985. 395.00 (0-940394-16-2) Labelmaster.

OSHA & the Politics of Health Regulation: Organizational & Political Changes in a Regulatory Agency. Ed. by David P. McCaffrey. LC 82-11201. 210p. 1982. 42.50 (0-306-41050-8, Plenum Trade) Perseus Pubng.

OSHA Answer Book: The Employers Manual That Answers Every OSHA Question. 4th rev. ed. Mark M. Moran. 316p. 1999. pap. 59.95 (0-9632296-7-2) Moran Assocs.

OSHA Answer Book: The Employers Manual That Answers Every Osha Question. 4th rev. large type ed. Mark Moran. 320p. 1993. pap. 59.95 (1-890966-52-5) Moran Assocs.

OSHA Bloodborne Pathogens Exposure Control Plan. Neal Langerman. 382p. 1992. lib. bdg. 120.00 (0-87371-802-X, L802) Lewis Pubs.

OSHA Compendium for Health Care Professional. Neilsen. LC 99-11382. (Allied Health Ser.). (C). 1999. pap. 40.95 (0-7668-0478-X) Delmar.

OSHA Compliance & Management Handbook. Charleston C. Wang. LC 93-26691. (Illus.). 456p. 1993. 109.00 (0-8155-1334-8) Noyes.

OSHA Compliance Encyclopedia. 1995. 495.00 incl. cd-rom (0-614-08797-X, 154001) Busn Legal Reports.

OSHA Compliance Encyclopedia, 3 vols., Set. rev. ed. 1993. ring bd. 459.95 (1-55645-594-1, OCB) Busn Legal Reports.

OSHA Compliance Encyclopedia: Construction Edition, 2 vols., Set. rev. ed. 1989. ring bd. 325.00 (1-55645-592-5, 110008) Busn Legal Reports.

***OSHA Compliance Guide: Regulations - Sample Plans - Forms.** 9th ed. H. Ray Kirk. Ed. by Summers Press Staff. 508p. 2000. ring bd. 92.50 (1-56759-060-8) Summers Pr.

OSHA Compliance Handbook. Reed, Smith, Shaw & McClay Staff. 364p. 1992. pap. text 89.00 (0-86587-290-2) Gov Insts.

OSHA Construction Manual. Merritt Company Staff. 1995. ring bd. 397.00 (1-56343-069-X) Silver Lake.

OSHA Crane Safety Handbook. J. J. Keller & Assoc., Inc. Staff. 38p. 1995. per. 1.90 (1-877798-35-5, 179-H) J J Keller.

OSHA Electrical Regulations Simplified. James G. Stallcup. LC 94-183718. (Illus.). 352p. (Orig.). (C). 1994. pap., student ed. 40.75 (1-885341-00-8) Thomson Learn.

OSHA Electrical Regulations Simplified, 1996 Edition. rev. ed. James G. Stallcup. Ed. by James W. Stallcup. LC 96-75164. (Illus.). 400p. (C). 1996. pap., wbk. ed. 39.95 (1-885341-09-1) Grayboy Pubng.

OSHA Environmental Compliance Handbook, 1997. Anthony J. Thompson. (Clark Boardman Callaghan Environmental Law Ser.). 378p. 1997. pap. 125.00 (0-8366-1128-4) West Group.

OSHA Excavation Standard Handbook. 22p. 1997. per. 1.99 (1-877798-91-6, 100-H) J J Keller.

OSHA Facilities Marking Manual. Keller, J. J., & Associates, Inc. Staff. LC 90-64429. 383p. 2000. ring bd. 125.00 (0-934674-89-2, 42-M) J J Keller.

OSHA Field Inspection Reference Manual. Occupational Safety & Health Administration Staff. 144p. 1995. pap. text 69.00 (0-86587-426-3) Gov Insts.

OSHA Field Operations Manual. 6th ed. U. S. Department of Labor, Occupational Safety & Health Staff. 456p. 1994. pap. text 89.00 (0-86587-380-1) Gov Insts.

OSHA 500. 2nd rev. ed. Mark M. Moran & Robert D. Moran. (Illus.). 313p. 1995. ring bd. 99.95 (0-9632296-6-4) Moran Assocs.

OSHA for Transportation: Key Compliance Topics. Keller, J. J., & Associates, Inc. Staff. LC 92-73678. 780p. 2000. ring bd. 125.00 (1-877798-19-3, 58-M) J J Keller.

Osha Handbook. R. Barth. (C). 1995. pap. text 29.50 (0-07-005374-X) McGraw.

OSHA Handbook for Small Businesses. x, 64p. 1996. pap. 30.00 (0-9656560-8-X) DIANE Pub.

OSHA Handbook for Small Businesses. (Illus.). 65p. 1997. pap. text 20.00 (0-7881-4200-3) DIANE Pub.

OSHA Handbook for Small Businesses. Government Printing Office Staff. 74p. 1996. pap. 7.00 (0-16-048832-X) USGPO.

OSHA Handbook for Small Businesses. rev. ed. 57p. 1993. pap. text 25.00 (1-56806-392-X) DIANE Pub.

OSHA High Voltage Electrical Systems Simplified. James G. Stallcup. Ed. by James W. Stallcup. LC 94-78613. (Illus.). 392p. (Orig.). (C). 1995. pap., student ed. 38.95 (1-885341-03-2) Thomson Learn.

OSHA in the Real World: How to Maintain Workplace Safety While Keeping Your Competitive Edge. John Hartnett. LC 95-79499. (Taking Control Ser.). 391p. (Orig.). 1995. 29.95 incl. disk (1-56343-113-0) Silver Lake.

OSHA Index Compliance & Safety Regulations & Job Classifications. Jacob D. Paz et al. 1999. 49.95 (1-56670-285-2, L1285) Lewis Pubs.

***OSHA Inspection Book: What Every Employer Needs to Know about OSHA Inspections.** Robert D. Moran. 250p. 1999. pap. 59.95 (1-890966-54-1) Moran Assocs.

OSHA Inspections: Preparation & Response: Updated for 2000. rev. ed. Rick Kaletsky. (Illus.). 438p. 1996. 64.95 (0-07-033160-X) McGraw.

OSHA Laboratory Standard Implementation Guide. Leo C. Hearn, Jr. et al. 152p. 1991. lib. bdg. 115.00 (0-87371-532-2, L532) Lewis Pubs.

OSHA Made Easy: A Guide to Recordkeeping, Reporting, & Compliance. Robert D. Moran & Mark M. Moran. LC 94-12508. 471p. 1994. text 120.95 (0-442-01908-4, VNR) Wiley.

OSHA Made Easy: A Guide to Recordkeeping, Reporting, & Compliance. Robert D. Moran & Mark M. Moran. (Industrial Health & Safety Ser.). 471p. 1994. 149.00 (0-471-28653-2, VNR) Wiley.

OSHA-NFPA Standards see NFPA Guide to OSHA Fire Protection Regulations

OSHA, 1988. 333p. 1988. 17.50 (0-685-69469-0) PLI.

***OSHA 1910 Compliance Manual for General Industry, 3 vols., Set.** Ed. by Amy Gordon. 1800p. 1999. 397.00 (0-940394-81-2) Labelmaster.

***OSHA 1926 Compliance Manual for the Construction Industry, 3 Vols., Set.** Ed. by Amy Gordon. 1800p. 1999. 397.00 (0-940394-82-0) Labelmaster.

OSHA Problem-Solver. LC 96-164806. 1995. ring bd. 149.95 (1-55645-031-1, 100001) Busn Legal Reports.

OSHA PSM Compliance Without Going Bankrupt: The Zero-Base Strategy That Works & Saves Money. Max Ansari. LC 97-60911. (Illus.). 274p. 1997. 50.00 (0-9656888-1-X) WA Indust Mgmt.

OSHA Publication 8-1.7 Guidelines for Laser Safety, No. 118. 120p. 1991. pap. text 55.00 (0-685-57322-2) Laser Inst.

OSHA Quick Guide for Residential Builders & Contractors. Jonathan F. Hutchings. 400p. 1998. 54.95 (0-07-913763-6) McGraw.

***OSHA Quick Guide for Residential Builders & Contractors.** Jonathan F. Hutchings. 400p. 1998. pap. 39.95 (0-07-913764-4) McGraw.

OSHA Quick Guide for Residential Builders & Contractors. Jonathan F. Hutchings. LC 98-9801. (Illus.). 450p. 1998. 54.95 (0-07-031836-0); pap. 39.95 (0-07-031837-9) McGraw.

OSHA Recordkeeping Software. rev. ed. Jordan Suhrstedt. (Illus.). 110p. 1999. per. 119.50 incl. disk (1-56759-032-2) Summers Pr.

***OSHA Recordkeeping Software.** rev. ed. Jordan Suhrstedt. (Illus.). 110p. 2000. pap. 119.50 (1-56759-064-0) Summers Pr.

OSHA Reference Manual. Merritt Company Staff. 1995. ring bd. 397.00 (0-930868-03-X) Silver Lake.

OSHA Regulated Hazardous Substances: Health, Toxicity, Economic & Technological Data, 2 vols., Set. Occupational Safety & Health Administration Staff. LC 90-6751. (Illus.). 2294p. 1990. 195.00 (0-8155-1240-6) Noyes.

OSHA Standards Digest. Ed. & Pref. by C. Ray Asfahl. 162p. 1985. pap. 49.95 (0-945709-04-8) New Cent Media.

OSHA Standards for the construction Industry. Ed. by CCH Editorial Staff Publication. (Safety Professional Series). 700p. pap. text 37.50 (0-8080-0474-3) CCH INC.

***OSHA Standards for the General Industry.** Ed. by CCH Editorial Staff Publication. (Safety Professional Series). 1100p. 2000. pap. 45.95 (0-8080-0473-5) CCH INC.

***OSHA Technical Manual.** 5th ed. OSHA Staff. 474p. 1999. pap. 89.00 (0-86587-674-6) Gov Insts.

***OSHA Training Guide: Repros, Programs, Tests.** H. Ray Kirk. Ed. by Charles B. Lewis. LC 99-45503. (Illus.). 414p. 1999. ring bd. 119.50 (1-56759-037-3) Summers Pr.

***Oshanet: Installation Guide.** Media Magic Staff. 1999. pap. write for info. (0-7668-2012-2) Delmar.

OSHA's Bloodborne Pathogen Procedures Made Cost Effective: FED-OSHA Mandated Exposure Control for Occupational Exposure Control to Bloodborne Pathogens. rev. ed. Med-Facts, Inc. Staff. 118p. 1993. student ed. 495.00 (1-884006-25-6) Med-Facts.

OSHA's Bloodborne Pathogens Standard: Compliance in Clinical Laboratory. Peggy P. Luebbert. 1992. 50.00 incl. VHS (0-89189-349-0) Am Soc Clinical.

OSHA's Electrical Safety & Lockout/Tagout Standards: Proven Written Programs for Compliance. Mark M. Moran. LC 96-193899. 182p. 1996. pap. text 69.00 incl. disk (0-86587-502-2) Gov Insts.

OSHA's Final Bloodborne Pathogens Standard: Implications for Health Care Environmental Services. Pamela L. Blyth. 96p. (Orig.). 1993. pap. 40.00 (0-87258-632-4, 057014) Am Hospital.

OSHA's Hazard Communication Standard: A Proven Written Program for Compliance. Mark M. Moran. LC 96-189435. 161p. (Orig.). 1996. pap. 69.00 incl. disk (0-86587-499-9) Gov Insts.

OSHA's Process Safety Management Standard: A Proven Written Program for Compliance. Mark M. Moran. LC 96-182419. 235p. 1996. pap. text 69.00 incl. disk (0-86587-500-6) Gov Insts.

OSHA's Right to Know Hazardous Chemicals: A Consolidated List. 2nd ed. Inter-Face Associates Staff. LC 86-20836. 250p. 1986. ring bd. 70.00 (0-938135-06-6) Interface Assocs.

Oshkosh & Winnebago County: Land Rich Enough: An Illustrated History. Michael Goc. 128p. (YA). (gr. 7 up). 1988. 27.95 (0-89781-253-0) Am Historical Pr.

Oshkosh Woodworkers' Strike of 1898: A Wisconsin Community in Crisis. Virginia Glenn Crane. (Illus.). xi, 569p. 1998. pap. 15.00 (0-9669195-0-5) Virginia Crane.

Osho Neo Tarot. Osho. (Illus.). 85p. 1986. pap. 19.95 (3-89338-129-5, Pub. by Rebel Hse) Oshos.

OSHO No Book. Osho. 150p. 1989. 12.95 (3-89338-047-7, Pub. by Rebel Hse) Oshos.

Osho Rajaneesh & His Disciples: Some Western Perceptions. Harry Aveling. LC 99-931099. xl, 441 p. 1999. pap. 160.00 (81-208-1599-8, Pub. by Motilal Bnarsidass) St Mut.

***Osho Rajneesh & His Disciples: Some Western Perceptions.** Harry Aveling. LC 99-931099. 442p. 1999. 265.00 (81-208-1598-X, Pub. by Motilal Bnarsidass) St Mut.

Osho Transformation Tarot: Insights & Parables for Renewal in Everyday Life. Osho. LC 99-38828. 180p. 1999. text 24.95 (0-312-24530-0) St Martin.

Oshodi Sentence Completion Index (OSCI) John E. Oshodi. 23p. (C). 1996. reprint ed. pap. text. write for info. (0-9644455-1-4) Oshodi Fnd.

Oshun: Ifa & the Spirit of the River. Fa'lokum Fatunmbi. 30p. 1993. pap. 4.95 (0-942272-32-3) Original Pubns.

OSI: A Model for Computer Communications Standards. Ulysses D. Black. 336p. (C). 1990. text 54.75 (0-13-637133-7) P-H.

OSI Conformance Testing Methodology & TTCN. Bernd Baumgarten & Alfred Giessler. LC 94-36819. 340p. 1994. 194.50 (0-444-89712-7) Elsevier.

OSI-Conformant Networks. Eduard A. Yakubaitis. Tr. by Martin Morell from RUS. (Illus.). x, 246p. 1992. 75.00 (0-89864-055-5) Allerton Pr.

OSI Explained: End to End Computer Communication Standards. John Henshall. 260p. (C). 1990. pap. text 83.00 (0-13-639451-5) P-H.

OSI Explained: End-to-End Computer Communications Standards. John Henshall & Sandy Shaw. 224p. 1988. text 36.95 (0-470-21100-8) P-H.

OSI95 Transport Service with Multimedia Support. Ed. by A. Danthine. (Research Reports ESPRIT: Vol. 1). 1994. 75.95 (0-387-58316-5) Spr-Verlag.

Osiander in Preussen (1549-1552) Martin Stupperich. (Arbeiten zur Kirchengeschichte Ser.: Vol. 44). 402p. (C). 1973. 95.40 (3-11-004221-5) De Gruyter.

Osillations in Neural Systems. Ed. by Daniel S. Levine et al. LC 99-39666. 448p. 1999. 99.95 (0-8058-2066-3) L Erlbaum Assocs.

Osios Machkimos: Beginner's Guide to Hebrew Script. 1992. pap. 6.95 (0-87306-960-9) Feldheim.

Osip Mandel'shtam Vols. 1 & 2: Istoriia i Poetika. Dimitrii Segal. (Slavica Hierosolymitana Ser.: Vols. 8 & 9). (RUS.). 818p. 1998. pap. 80.00 (1-57201-050-9) Berkeley Slavic.

Osip Mandelstam. Jane G. Harris. (World Authors Ser.: No. 799). 184p. 1988. 32.00 (0-8057-8230-3, Twyne) Mac Lib Ref.

Osip Mandelstam & His Age. Steven Broyde. LC 74-16801. (Slavic Monographs: No. 1). 264p. 1975. 34.95 (0-674-64492-1) HUP.

Osip Mandelstam & the Modernist Creation of Tradition. Clare Cavanagh. LC 94-11248. 376p. 1995. text 49.50 (0-691-03682-9, Pub. by Princeton U Pr) Cal Prin Full Svc.

Osip Mandelstam's Stone. Osip Mandelshtam. LC 80-7545. (Lockert Library of Poetry in Translation). 268p. reprint ed. pap. 83.10 (0-8357-6930-5, 203798900009) Bks Demand.

Osip Senkovsky's the Fantastic Journey of Baron Brambeus. Osip I. Senkovskii. Tr. by Louis Pedrotti from RUS. LC 93-9985. (Middlebury Studies in Russian Language & Literature: Vol. 5).Tr. of Fantasticheskie Puteshestviia Barona Brambeusa. XVII, 232p. (C). 1994. text 32.95 (0-8204-2203-7) P Lang Pubng.

Osiris. Ed. by Arnold W. Thackray. (Second Ser.: 6). 368p. 1990. 39.00 (0-685-34250-6); 29.00 (0-685-45294-8) Hist Sci Soc.

Osiris. Ed. by Arnold W. Thackray. (Second Ser.: Vol. 6). 368p. 1990. pap. 20.00 (0-685-45295-6) Hist Sci Soc.

Osiris. Ed. by Arnold W. Thackray. (Second Series: 2). 368p. 1991. lib. bdg. 39.00 (0-934235-04-X) Hist Sci Soc.

Osiris. H. P. Cooke. 180p. 1979. reprint ed. pap. 15.00 (0-89005-287-5) Ares.

***Osiris, Vol. 1.** Sally Kohlstedt. 2000. pap. text 25.00 (0-934235-03-1) U Ch Pr.

Osiris, Vol. 1. Sally G. Kohlstedt. 1991. lib. bdg. 39.00 (0-934235-02-3) U Ch Pr.

Osiris, Vol. 3. Arnold W. Thackray. 1991. pap. text 25.00 (0-934235-09-0); lib. bdg. 39.00 (0-934235-08-2) U Ch Pr.

***Osiris, Vol. 4.** Arthur Donovan. 2000. lib. bdg. 39.00 (0-934235-10-4) U Ch Pr.

Osiris, Vol. 5. Olesko. 1991. lib. bdg. 39.00 (0-934235-12-0) U Ch Pr.

Osiris, Vol. 5. Olesko. 1993. pap. text 25.00 (0-934235-13-9) U Ch Pr.

Osiris: God of Stone. Gozo Yoshimasu. LC 88-61337. 69p. 1989. 20.00 (0-932662-75-7) St Andrews NC.

Osiris Vol. 8: Research Schools: Historical Reappraisals. Ed. by Gerald L. Geison & Frederic L. Holmes. (Osiris Ser.). 256p. 1993. pap. text 25.00 (0-226-28546-4) U Ch Pr.

Osiris Vol. 8: Research Schools: Historical Reappraisals. Ed. by Gerald L. Geison & Frederic L. Holmes. (Osiris Ser.). 256p. 1993. lib. bdg. 39.00 (0-226-28545-6) U Ch Pr.

Osiris & Appolo: Encounters Between Ancient Egypt & Greece. Anthony Preus. 1998. pap. 17.00 (1-883058-44-9, Intl Medieval) Global Pubns.

Osiris & Isis. Patricia. (Illus.). 267p. (Orig.). 1980. pap. 7.95 (0-935146-19-9) Morningland.

Osiris & the Egyptian Resurrection, 2 vols., Vol. 1. E. A. Wallis Budge. LC 72-81534. (Illus.). 906p. 1973. reprint ed. pap. 10.95 (0-486-22780-4) Dover.

Osiris & the Egyptian Resurrection, 2 vols., Vol. 2. 2nd ed. E. A. Wallis Budge. LC 72-81534. (Illus.). 906p. 1973. reprint ed. pap. 9.95 (0-486-22781-2) Dover.

Osiris Chip. Thomas M. Kane. (Cyberpunk Ser.). 32p. 1992. pap. 8.00 (1-887801-35-9, Atlas Games) Trident MN.

Osiris Complex: Case Studies in Multiple Personality Disorder. Colin A. Ross. LC 93-95100. 296p. (C). 1994. pap. 17.95 (0-8020-7358-1); text 50.00 (0-8020-2858-6) U of Toronto Pr.

O

An Asterisk (*) at the beginning of an entry indicates that the title is appearing for the first time.

Osiris N: The Victim & the American Novel. Biyot K. Tripathy. xii, 282p. (Orig.). 1985. pap. write for info. (*90-6032-264-9*) B R Gruner.

Osiris, the God of Stone. Gozo Yoshimasu. 68p. Date not set. 14.00 (*0-932662-70-6*) St Andrews NC.

Osito. Else H. Minarik. LC 69-14452. (Spanish I Can Read Bk.).Tr. of Little Bear. (SPA., Illus.). 64p. (J). (ps-3). 1969. lib. bdg. 10.89 (*0-06-024244-2*) HarpC Child Bks.

Osito. Else H. Minarik.Tr. of Little Bear. (J). 1980. 15.15 (*0-606-10488-7*, Pub. by Turtleback) Demco.

***Osito de Peluche y Otros Animales.** Michael Ende. (SPA., Illus.). 2000. 12.95 (*84-241-3350-1*) Everest SP.

Osito! Donde Estas? (Teddy! Where Are You?) Ralph Steadman. Tr. by Catalina Dominguez. (SPA., Illus.). 32p. (J). (gr. 1-3). 1994. 12.99 (*968-16-4556-1*, Pub. by Fondo) Continental Bk.

Osito Encantador - Bear Magic. Chris Cahill. LC 90-62628. (Finger Magic Bk.). (Illus.). 12p. (J). 1991. bds. 5.95 (*1-877779-19-9*) Schneider Educational.

Osito, Osito: Black & White Nellie Edge I Can Read & Sing Big Book. Tr. by Marissa Zamora-Pearson from ENG. (SPA., Illus.). (J). (ps-2). 1993. pap. text 21.00 (*0-922053-26-X*) N Edge Res.

Osito Polar. Hans De Beer. LC 94-40894.Tr. of Polar Bear. (SPA., Illus.). 26p. (J). (gr. k-3). 1995. pap. 6.95 (*1-55858-390-4*, Pub. by North-South Bks NYC) Chronicle Bks.

Osito Polar. Hans De Beer. Tr. by Agustin Antreasyan.Tr. of Polar Bear. (SPA., Illus.). 14p. (J). (ps). 1998. bds. 6.95 (*0-7358-1092-3*, Pub. by North-South Bks NYC) Chronicle Bks.

Osito Polar. Hans De Beer.Tr. of Polar Bear. (J). 1995. 12.40 (*0-606-08736-2*) Turtleback.

***Osito Polar Libro Grande.** Hans De Beer.Tr. of Little Polar Bear Big Bear. (SPA., Illus.). 32p. (J). (gr. k-3). 1999. pap. 19.95 (*0-7358-1217-9*, Pub. by North-South Bks NYC) Chronicle Bks.

***Osito Polar y el Conejito Valiente.** Hans De Beer. Tr. by Agustin Antreasyan. (SPA., Illus.). 32p. (gr. k-3). 2000. 15.95 (*0-7358-1004-4*); pap. 6.95 (*0-7358-1005-2*) North-South Bks NYC.

Osito Polar y Su Nueva Amiga. Hans De Beer. LC 94-40894.Tr. of Polar Bear & His New Friend. (SPA., Illus.). 32p. (J). (gr. k-3). 1996. pap. 6.95 (*1-55858-639-3*, Pub. by North-South Bks NYC) Chronicle Bks.

***Osito Usado.** Clay Carmichael. Tr. by Elena Moro.Tr. of Used-Up Bear. (SPA., Illus.). 48p. (J). (gr. 1-3). 2000. pap. 5.95 (*0-7358-1306-X*, Pub. by North-South Bks NYC) Chronicle Bks.

***Osito Usado.** Clay Carmichael.Tr. of Used-Up Bear. (SPA., Illus.). (J). 2000. 11.40 (*0-606-18319-1*) Turtleback.

***Ositolandia - Teddyland.** Phil Roxbee Cox. (Illus.). 32p. (YA). (ps up). 2000. pap. 6.95 (*0-7460-3892-5*, Usborne) EDC.

Ositos Nada Mas - Primarily Bears. A. Berdugo et al. (ENG & SPA.). 159p. (J). (gr. k-6). 1992. 16.95 (*1-881431-30-4*, 1432) AIMS Educ Fnd.

Oskar Klein Memorial Lectures Volume Vol. 1: Lectures by C. N. Yang & S. Weinberg. Ed. by Gosta Ekspong. 140p. (C). 1991. text 40.00 (*981-02-0352-7*); pap. text 21.00 (*981-02-0353-5*) World Scientific Pub.

Oskar Klein Memorial Lecutres. Gosta Ekspong. 164p. 1994. text 43.00 (*981-02-1450-2*) World Scientific Pub.

Oskar Kokoschka. (Illus.). 1958. pap. 5.00 (*0-910810-09-5*) Johannes.

Oskar Kokoschka. Ed. by Klaus Albrecht et al. (Illus.). 230p. 1991. 65.00 (*3-7913-1132-8*, Pub. by Prestel) te Neues.

Oskar Kokoschka. Richard Calvocoressi. (Illus.). 1986. 38.00 (*0-89207-060-9*); pap. 26.00 (*0-89207-059-5*) S R Guggenheim.

Oskar Kokoschka: Drawings & Watercolors, 1906-1926. (Illus.). 140p. 1983. 50.00 (*3-921561-32-9*, Pub. by Edition Cantz) Dist Art Pubs.

Oskar Kokoschka: Drawings, 1906-1965. Ernest G. Rathenau. 1993. pap. 22.95 (*0-87024-333-0*) U of Miami Pr.

Oskar Kokoschka: Literary Graphic Works, 1906-1923. expanded rev. ed. Richard S. Field. (Illus.). 86p. 1977. 3.50 (*0-918386-20-9*) W Benton Mus.

Oskar Kokoschka: Postcard Book. Prestel Staff. 1997. 8.95 (*3-7913-1768-7*, Pub. by Prestel) te Neues.

Oskar Kokoschka: The Painter As Playwright. Henry I. Schvey. LC 82-2871. (Illus.). 165p. reprint ed. pap. 51.20 (*0-608-16055-5*, 203318500084) Bks Demand.

Oskar Panizza: His Life & Works. Peter D. Brown. LC 83-48749. (American University Studies: Germanic Languages & Literature: Ser. I, Vol. 27). 232p. (C). 1983. pap. text 24.65 (*0-8204-0038-6*) P Lang Pubng.

Oskar Pfisters Analytische Seelsorge: Theorie & Praxis des Ersten Pastoralpsychologen, Dargestellt an Zwei Fallstudien. Eckart Nase. (Arbeiten zur Praktischen Theologie Ser.: Bd. 3). (GER., Illus.). xviii, 622p. (C). 1993. lib. bdg. 167.70 (*3-11-013235-4*) De Gruyter.

Oskar Schindler. Jack L. Roberts. LC 95-11712. (Importance of Ser.). (Illus.). 112p. (YA). (gr. 7 up). 1996. lib. bdg. 22.45 (*1-56006-079-4*) Lucent Bks.

***Oskar Schindler.** Jeremy Roberts. LC 00-27846. (Holocaust Biographies Ser.). 2000. write for info. (*0-8239-3310-5*) Rosen Group.

Oskar Schindler & His List: The Man, the Book, the Film, the Holocaust & Its Survivors. Ed. & Pref. by Thomas Fensch. LC 95-13696. (Illus.). 288p. 1995. 24.95 (*0-8397-6472-3*) Eriksson.

Oskar Schlemmer, Tanz Theatre Buhne. Oskar Schlemmer. 1995. 65.00 (*3-7757-0521-X*, Pub. by Gerd Hatje) Dist Art Pubs.

Oskar Waelterlin: Ein Profil. M. P. Loeffler. (GER.). 256p. 1979. 16.95 (*0-8176-1133-9*) Birkhauser.

Oskforder Yiddish: A Yearbook of Yiddish Studies I. David Katz. 401p. 1990. text 107.00 (*3-7186-4979-9*, Harwood Acad Pubs) Gordon & Breach.

Oski's Pediatrics: Principles & Practice. 3rd ed. Julia A. McMillan & Frank A. Oski. LC 98-50639. 2446p. 1999. 150.00 (*0-7817-1618-7*) Lppncott W & W.

Oski's Pediatrics: Principles & Practice. 3rd ed. Julia A. McMillan et al. 2848p. 150.00 (*0-7817-2012-5*) Lppncott W & W.

OSL Handbook. Hung & Rom. (QM - Quantitative Methods Ser.). (C). 1994. pap. 53.95 (*0-87709-757-7*) Course Tech.

Osler: Inspirations from a Great Physician. Charles S. Bryan. LC 96-30172. (Illus.). 280p. (C). 1997. 39.95 (*0-19-511251-2*) OUP.

Osler, & Other Papers. William S. Thayer. LC 78-84342. (Essay Index Reprint Ser.). 1977. 23.95 (*0-8369-1111-3*) Ayer.

Oslerian Pathology: An Assessment & Annotated Atlas of Museum Specimens. Intro. by Alvin E. Rodin. (Illus.). 250p. (C). 1981. 25.00 (*0-87291-144-6*) Coronado Pr.

***Osler's Web: Inside the Labyrinth of the Chronic Fatigue Syndrome Epidemic.** Hillary Johnson. 720p. 2000. reprint ed. text 30.00 (*0-7881-6980-7*) DIANE Pub.

***Oslo Accords: International Law & the Israeli-Palestinian Peace Agreements.** Geoffrey R. Watson. 320p. 2000. text 72.00 (*0-19-829891-9*) OUP.

Oslo & Bergen. Insight Guides Staff. (Insight Guides). 1998. pap. text 12.95 (*0-88729-334-4*) Langenscheidt.

Osm Dni see Eight Days: An Elegy for Thomas Garrigue Masaryk

Osma a Skupina Vytvarnych Umelcu, 1907-1917, Cesky Kubismus. Miroslav Lamac. (CZE., Illus.). 544p. 1988. 70.00 (*0-317-03838-9*) Szwede Slavic.

Osmanisch-Tuerkische Im Seventeen, Jahrhundert: Untersuchungen an Den Transkriptionstexten Von Jakab Nagy De Harsany. G. Hazai. (Near & Middle East Monographs: No. 15, Pt. 1). 1973. 152.30 (*90-279-2415-5*) Mouton.

Osmanischen Reiches Staatsverfassung und Staatsverwaltung. Joseph F. Von Hammer-Purgstall. (GER.). xlii, 1031p. 1974. reprint ed. write for info. (*3-487-00460-7*) G Olms Pubs.

Osmia Lignaria Propinqua Cresson see Orchard Mason Bee: The Life History-Biology-Propagation

Osmin's Rage: Philosophical Reflections on Opera, Drama & Text, with a New Final Chapter Peter Kivy. LC 98-54953. 1999. 17.95 (*0-8014-8589-4*) Cornell U Pr.

Osmium. 1976. 145.00 (*0-387-93150-3*) Spr-Verlag.

Osmond Family Trivia Book: Celebrating 40 Years in Entertainment. Ed. by Cathy Kinsella & Olive Osmond. LC 99-180389. (Illus.). 257p. 1998. pap. 19.95 (*1-888106-72-7*) Agreka Bks.

Osmo's Autobearography. Joseph Albert. (Who's There Bears? Ser.: Vol. 1). (Illus.). 24p. (J). (ps-2). 1997. write for info. (*1-891376-00-4*) Fluffyville USA.

Osmo's Who's Playing Where? Joseph Albert. (Who's There Bears? Ser.: Vol. 2). (Illus.). 24p. (J). (ps-2). 1997. write for info. (*1-891376-01-2*) Fluffyville USA.

Osmosis: Ettore Spalletti & Haim Steinbach. Ettore Spalletti. 1993. 34.95 (*0-89207-105-2*) S R Guggenheim.

Osmosis & Dialysis. Gayle N. Sauer & Conrad L. Stanitski. (Modular Laboratory Program in Chemistry Ser.). 12p. (C). 1995. pap. text 1.50 (*0-87540-454-5*, PROP 454-5) Chem Educ Res.

Osmosis & Diffusion. Helms. 1997. 1.50 (*0-7167-9311-3*) W H Freeman.

Osmosis & Glassfibre Yacht Construction. 2nd ed. Tony Staton-Bevan. 1996. pap. text 19.95 (*0-07-061033-9*) McGraw.

Osmosis & Glassfibre Yacht Construction. 2nd ed. Tony Staton-Bevan. (Illus.). 150p. 1995. pap. 19.95 (*0-924486-83-X*) Sheridan.

Osmosis, Care & Repair of the Glassfibre Yacht. Staton-Bevan. (Illus.). 1991. pap. write for info. (*0-7136-3513-4*) Adlard Coles.

Osnovy Teorii Igr see Foundations of Game Theory: Noncooperative Games

Oso - Chirinchinchina: Spanish Take-Home Parent Pack, Set. (Take-Home Parent Packs Ser.). (SPA., Illus.). (Orig.). 1993. pap. 16.95 (*1-56334-383-5*) Hampton-Brown.

Oso Llamado Paddington (A Bear Called Paddington) Michael Bond. (SPA.). (J). 1996. pap. text 7.50 (*84-279-3701-6*) Lectorum Pubns.

Oso Mas Elegante (Big Book) Alma F. Ada. (Cuento Mas Ser.). (SPA., Illus.). 24p. (Orig.). (J). (gr. k-3). 1989. pap. text 29.95 (*0-917837-10-X*) Hampton-Brown.

***Oso Polar, Oso Polar, Que Es Ese Ruido?** Bill Martin, Jr. LC 99-40728. (SPA., Illus.). 32p. (ps-k). 2000. text 15.95 (*0-8050-6427-3*) H Holt & Co.

Oso Que No Lo Era (The Bear That Wasn't) Else H. Minarik & Frank Tashlin. (SPA., Illus.). (J). (gr. 2-4). 1995. pap. 10.95 (*958-24-0002-1*, Pub. by Santillana) T R Bks.

Osoriinae (Insecta: Coleoptera: Staphylinidae) see Fauna of New Zealand Series

Osos. Lynn M. Stone. (Depredadores Ser.).Tr. of Bears. (SPA.). 24p. (J). (gr. k-4). 1994. lib. bdg. 10.95 (*0-86593-315-4*) Rourke Corp.

Osos. Lynn M. Stone. (Animales Norteamericanos Ser.).Tr. of Bears. (SPA.). 24p. (J). (gr. k-4). 1991. lib. bdg. 14.60 (*0-86592-833-9*) Rourke Enter.

Osos Berenstain & el Cuarto Desordenado. Stan Berenstain & Jan Berenstain. Tr. by Rita Guibert from ENG. LC 91-50191. (Berenstain Bears First Time Bks.).Tr. of Berenstain Bears & the Messy Room. (SPA., Illus.). 32p. (J). (ps-3). 1992. pap. 3.25 (*0-679-83470-2*, Pub. by Random Bks Yng Read) Random.

Osos Berenstain & la Ninera. Stan Berenstain & Jan Berenstain. Tr. by Rita Guibert from ENG. LC 92-46719. (Berenstain Bears First Time Bks.).Tr. of Berenstain Bears & the Sitter. (SPA., Illus.). 32p. (J). (ps-3). 1993. pap. 3.25 (*0-679-84746-4*, Pub. by Random Bks Yng Read) Random.

Osos Berenstain & las Paleas Entre Amigos. Stan Berenstain & Jan Berenstain. Tr. by Rita Guibert from ENG. LC 92-14807. (Berenstain Bears First Time Bks.).Tr. of Berenstain Bears & the Trouble with Friends. (SPA., Illus.). 32p. (J). (gr. k-2). 1993. pap. 3.25 (*0-679-84006-0*, Pub. by Random Bks Yng Read) Random.

Osos Berenstain Dia de Mudanza. Stan Berenstain & Jan Berenstain. Tr. by Rita Guibert from ENG. LC 93-37312. (Berenstain Bears First Time Bks.). Orig. Title: Berenstain Bears' Moving Day. (SPA., Illus.). 32p. (J). (gr. k-2). 1994. pap. 3.25 (*0-679-85430-4*, Pub. by Random Bks Yng Read) Random.

Osos Berenstain en la Oscuridad. Stan Berenstain & Jan Berenstain. Tr. by Rita Guibert from ENG. LC 91-51092. (Berenstain Bears First Time Bks.).Tr. of Berenstain Bears In The Dark. (SPA., Illus.). 32p. (J). (ps-3). 1992. pap. 3.25 (*0-679-83471-0*, Pub. by Random Bks Yng Read) Random.

Osos Berenstain, No Se Permiten Ninas. Stan Berenstain & Jan Berenstain. LC 93-29904. (Berenstain Bears First Time Bks.).Tr. of Berenstain Bears, No Girls Allowed. (SPA.). 32p. (J). (gr. k-2). 1994. pap. 3.25 (*0-679-85431-2*, Pub. by Random Bks Yng Read) Random.

Osos Berenstain y Demasiada Fiesta. Stan Berenstain & Jan Berenstain. Tr. by Rita Guibert from ENG. LC 92-45874. (Berenstain Bears First Time Bks.).Tr. of Berenstain Bears & Too Much Birthday. (SPA., Illus.). 32p. (J). (ps-3). 1993. pap. 3.25 (*0-679-84745-6*, Pub. by Random Bks Yng Read) Random.

Osos Polares. Sarah Palmer. (Mamifero Marino Ser.).Tr. of Polar Bears. 24p. (J). (gr. k-4). 1991. lib. bdg. 14.60 (*0-86592-673-5*) Rourke Enter.

Osos Por Aji. Joanne Ryder. Tr. by Sandra M. Dorros.Tr. of Bears Out There. (SPA., Illus.). 32p. (J). (ps-3). 1995. 15.00 (*0-689-31982-7*) Atheneum Yung Read.

Osos Salvajes y Mansos. Arthur Morton. Tr. by Angelita L. Aguilar. (SPA.). (J). (gr. k-3). 1994. 12.50 (*1-57842-020-2*) Delmas Creat.

Osos Scouts Berenstain & el Complot de la Gran Calabaza. Stan Berenstain & Jan Berenstain. (Berenstain Bear Scouts Ser.).Tr. of Berenstain Bear Scouts & the Humongous Pumpkin. (SPA.). 64p. (J). (gr. 3-6). 1995. pap. 2.99 (*0-590-59750-7*) Scholastic Inc.

Osos Scouts Berenstain enla Cueva del Murcielago Gigante. Jan Berenstain & Stan Berenstain. (Berenstain Bear Scouts Ser.).Tr. of Berenstain Bear Scouts & the Giant Bat Cave. (SPA.). 64p. (J). (gr. 3-6). 1995. pap. 2.99 (*0-590-59749-3*) Scholastic Inc.

***Osos Scouts Berenstain Gritan de Terror.** Stan Berenstain & Jan Berenstain. (Berenstain Bear Scouts Ser.).Tr. of Berenstain Bear Scouts Scream Their Heads Off. (SPA.). (J). (gr. 3-6). 1998. 8.60 (*0-606-13580-4*, Pub. by Turtleback) Demco.

Osos Scouts Berenstain Salvan a Rascaespaldas. Stan Berenstain & Jan Berenstain. (Berenstain Bear Scouts Ser.).Tr. of Berenstain Bear Scouts Save that Backscratcher. (SPA., Illus.). (J). (gr. 4-7). 1996. mass mkt. 2.99 (*0-590-69766-8*) Scholastic Inc.

Osos Scouts Berenstain Salvan a Rascaespaldas. Stan Berenstain & Jan Berenstain. (Berenstain Bear Scouts Ser.).Tr. of Berenstain Bear Scouts Save that Backscratcher. (SPA.). (J). (gr. 3-6). 1996. 8.19 (*0-606-09575-6*, Pub. by Turtleback) Demco.

Osos Scouts Berenstain Se Encuentran Con Patagrande. Stan Berenstain & Jan Berenstain. (Berenstain Bear Scouts Ser.).Tr. of Berenstain Bear Scouts Meet BigPaw. (SPA.). (J). (gr. 3-6). 1996. pap. 2.99 (*0-590-67664-4*) Scholastic Inc.

Osos Scouts Berenstain Se Encuentran Con Patagrande. Stan Berenstain & Jan Berenstain. (Berenstain Bear Scouts Ser.).Tr. of Berenstain Bear Scouts Meet BigPaw. (SPA.). (J). (gr. 3-6). 1995. 8.09 (*0-606-08563-7*, Pub. by Turtleback) Demco.

Osos Scouts Berenstain y el Bagre Que Tose. Stan Berenstain & Jan Berenstain. (Berenstain Bear Scouts Ser.).Tr. of Berenstain Bear Scouts & the Coughing Catfish. (SPA.). (J). (gr. 3-6). 1996. pap. text 2.99 (*0-590-87729-1*) Scholastic Inc.

Osos Scouts Berenstain y el Bagre Que Tose. Stan Berenstain & Jan Berenstain. (Berenstain Bear Scouts Ser.).Tr. of Berenstain Bear Scouts & the Coughing Catfish. (SPA.). (J). (gr. 3-6). 1996. 8.09 (*0-606-09719-8*, Pub. by Turtleback) Demco.

Osos Scouts Berenstain y El Complot de La Gran Calabaza. Stan Berenstain & Jan Berenstain. (Berenstain Bear Scouts Ser.).Tr. of Berenstain Bear Scouts & the Humongous Pumpkin. (SPA.). (J). (gr. 3-6). 1995. 8.09 (*0-606-07805-3*, Pub. by Turtleback) Demco.

Osos Scouts Berenstain y el Desastre Colosal. Stan Berenstain & Jan Berenstain. (Berenstain Bear Scouts Ser.).Tr. of Berenstain Bear Scouts & the Really Big Disaster. (SPA.). (J). (gr. 3-6). 1998. pap. text 3.50 (*0-590-94482-7*, Little Apple) Scholastic Inc.

***Osos Scouts Berenstain y el Desastre Colosal, 1.** Stan Berenstain & Jan Berenstain. (Berenstain Bear Scouts Ser.).Tr. of Berenstain Bear Scouts & the Really Big Disaster. (SPA.). (J). (gr. 3-6). 1998. 8.60 (*0-606-13581-2*, Pub. by Turtleback) Demco.

Osos Scouts Berenstain y el Monstruo De Hielo. Stan Berenstain & Jan Berenstain. (Berenstain Bear Scouts Ser.).Tr. of Berenstain Bear Scouts & the Ice Monster. (SPA.). (J). (gr. 3-6). 1997. pap. text 3.50 (*0-590-94480-0*) Scholastic Inc.

Osos Scouts Berenstain y el Monstruo De Hielo. Stan Berenstain & Jan Berenstain. (Berenstain Bear Scouts Ser.).Tr. of Berenstain Bear Scouts & the Ice Monster. (SPA.). (J). (gr. 3-6). 1997. 8.60 (*0-606-12760-7*, Pub. by Turtleback) Demco.

Osos Scouts Berenstain y la Bola de Cristal Magica. Stan Berenstain & Jan Berenstain. (Berenstain Bear Scouts Ser.).Tr. of Berenstain Bear Scouts & the Magic Crystal Ball. (SPA.). (J). (gr. 3-6). 1997. pap. text 3.50 (*0-590-94476-2*) Scholastic Inc.

Osos Scouts Berenstain y la Bola de Cristal Magica. Stan Berenstain & Jan Berenstain. (Berenstain Bear Scouts Ser.).Tr. of Berenstain Bear Scouts & the Magic Crystal Ball. (SPA.). (J). (gr. 3-6). 1997. 8.60 (*0-606-11577-3*, Pub. by Turtleback) Demco.

Osos Scouts Berenstain y la Guerra de los Fantasmas. Stan Berenstain & Jan Berenstain. (Berenstain Bear Scouts Ser.).Tr. of Berenstain Bear Scouts & the War of the Ghosts. (SPA.). (J). (gr. 3-6). 1996. pap. text 2.99 (*0-590-93381-7*) Scholastic Inc.

Osos Scouts Berenstain y la Guerra de los Fantasmas. Stan Berenstain & Jan Berenstain. (Berenstain Bear Scouts Ser.).Tr. of Berenstain Bear Scouts & the War of the Ghosts. (SPA.). (J). (gr. 3-6). 1996. 8.09 (*0-606-10480-1*, Pub. by Turtleback) Demco.

Osos Scouts Berenstain y la Pizza Voladora. Stan Berenstain & Jan Berenstain. (Berenstain Bear Scouts Ser.).Tr. of Berenstain Bear Scouts & the Sci-Fi Pizza. (SPA.). (J). (gr. 3-6). 1996. 8.09 (*0-606-10481-X*, Pub. by Turtleback) Demco.

Osos Scouts Berenstain y la Terrible Termita Habladora. Stan Berenstain & Jan Berenstain. (Berenstain Bear Scouts Ser.).Tr. of Berenstain Bear Scouts & the Terrible Talking Termite. (SPA.). (J). (gr. 3-6). 1996. mass mkt. 2.99 (*0-590-73850-X*) Scholastic Inc.

Osos Scouts Berenstain y la Terrible Termita Habladora. Stan Berenstain & Jan Berenstain. (Berenstain Bear Scouts Ser.).Tr. of Berenstain Bear Scouts & the Terrible Talking Termite. (SPA.). (J). (gr. 3-6). 1996. 8.09 (*0-606-09576-4*, Pub. by Turtleback) Demco.

Osos Scouts Berenstain y los Siniestros Anillos de Humo. Stan Berenstain & Jan Berenstain. (Berenstain Bear Scouts Ser.).Tr. of Berenstain Bear Scouts & the Sinister Smoke Rings. (SPA.). (J). (gr. 3-6). 1997. pap. 3.50 (*0-590-94474-6*) Scholastic Inc.

Osos Scouts Berenstain y los Siniestros Anillos de Humo. Stan Berenstain & Jan Berenstain. (Berenstain Bear Scouts Ser.).Tr. of Berenstain Bear Scouts & the Sinister Smoke Rings. (SPA., Illus.). (J). (gr. 3-6). 1997. pap. 3.50 (*0-614-29041-4*) Scholastic Inc.

Osos Scouts Berenstain y los Siniestros Anillos de Humo. Stan Berenstain & Jan Berenstain. (Berenstain Bear Scouts Ser.).Tr. of Berenstain Bear Scouts & the Sinister Smoke Rings. (J). (gr. 3-6). 1997. 8.70 (*0-606-11578-1*, Pub. by Turtleback) Demco.

OSPF: Anatomy of an Internet Routing Protocol. John T. Moy. LC 97-39463. 368p. (C). 1998. 47.95 (*0-201-63472-4*) Addison-Wesley.

OSPF Complete Implementation. John T. Moy. (C). 2000. 44.95 incl. cd-rom (*0-201-30966-1*) Addison-Wesley.

Osprey. Dorothy H. Patent. LC 92-30103. (Illus.). 64p. (J). (gr. 4-9). 1993. 14.95 (*0-395-63391-5*, Clarion Bks) HM.

Osprey: The Fish Hawk. Stephen D. Carpenteri. LC 96-46821. (Wildlife Ser.). 144p. 1997. pap. 14.95 (*1-55971-590-1*, NorthWord Pr) Creat Pub Intl.

Osprey Illustrated Military Diary, 1999. (Illus.). 72p. 1999. 18.95 (*1-85532-816-X*, Pub. by Ospry) Stackpole.

Osprey Illustrated Military Diary, 2000. Osprey Staff. (Illus.). 72p. 1999. 18.95 (*1-85532-869-0*, Pub. by Ospry) Stackpole.

Ospreys. Roy Dennis. (Illus.). 48p. 1994. pap. 11.95 (*0-948661-19-4*, Pub. by Colin Baxter Ltd) Voyageur Pr.

***Ospreys.** Doug Wechsler. LC 99-59410. (Really Wild Life of Birds of Prey Ser.). (Illus.). (J). 2000. lib. bdg. write for info. (*0-8239-5597-4*) Rosen Group.

***Osru: A Tale of Many Incarnations.** Justin Sterns. LC 99-76091. 208p. 1999. write for info. (*1-893766-08-X*) Aeon Pub Co.

OSS Against the Reich: The World War II Diaries of Colonel David K. E. Bruce. Ed. by Nelson D. Lankford. LC 90-47719. (Illus.). 256p. 1991. 28.50 (*0-87338-427-X*) Kent St U Pr.

OSS Agents in Hitler's Heartland: Destination Innsbruck. Gerald Schwab. LC 95-42505. 208p. 1996. 57.95 (*0-275-95470-6*, Praeger Pubs) Greenwood.

OSS Crossbows. John W. Brunner. (Illus.). 162p. 1991. 14.95 (*0-932572-15-4*) Phillips Pubns.

OSS in China: Prelude to Cold War. Maochun Yu. LC 96-22593. 368p. 1997. 40.00 (*0-300-06698-8*) Yale U Pr.

***Ossawattomie Brown: or The Insurrection at Harper's Ferry.** J. C. Swayze. (Americana Series). 35p. 2000. reprint ed. pap. 3.95 (*0-937657-54-9*) Feedbk Theabks & Prospero.

Osseo-Integrated Implants Vol. I: Basics, Materials, & Joint Replacements. Ed. by Gunther Heimke. 374p. 1990. lib. bdg. 210.00 (*0-8493-5958-9*, RD132) CRC Pr.

Osseo-Integrated Implants Vol. II: Implants in Oral & Ent Surgery. Ed. by Gunther Heimke. 380p. 1990. lib. bdg. 239.00 (*0-8493-5959-7*, RD132) CRC Pr.

Osseointegrated Dental Technology. Graham E. White. (Illus.). 233p. 1993. text 100.00 (*1-85097-031-9*, B8809) Quint Pub Co.

Osseointegrated Implant Manual. Nippon Dental University Staff. (Illus.). 159p. 1994. pap. 150.00 (*1-56386-014-7*, Ishiyaku EuroAmerica) Med Dent Media.

Osseointegration & Occlusal Rehabilitation. Sumiya Hobo et al. (Illus.). 478p. 1989. text 158.00 (*4-87417-274-1*) Quint Pub Co.

O

An Asterisk (*) at the beginning of an entry indicates that the title is appearing for the first time.

Osseointegration in Craniofacial Reconstruction. B. R. Anemark. Ed. by Per-Ingvar Branemark & Dan E. Tolman. LC 98-21397. (Illus.). 337p. 1998. text 156.00 (*0-86715-337-7*) Quint Pub Co.

Osseointegration in Dentistry: An Introduction. Ed. by Philip Worthington et al. LC 94-5464. (Illus.). 120p. 1994. pap. text 28.00 (*0-86715-281-8*) Quint Pub Co.

Osseointegration in Oral Rehabilitation: An Introductory Textbook. Ed. by Ignace Naert et al. (Illus.). 211p. (Orig.). 1993. pap. text 45.00 (*1-85097-030-0*, B8807) Quint Pub Co.

Osseointegration in Skeletal Reconstruction & Joint Replacement: 2nd International Workshop on Osseointegration in Skeletal Reconstruction & Joint Replacement, Rancho Santa Fe, California, October 27-29, 1994. Ingvar Branemark et al. LC 96-51486. 232p. 1997. pap. text 98.00 (*0-86715-325-3*) Quint Pub Co.

Osseous Development in the Hand As an Index of Skeletal Development. Charles D. Flory. (Society for Research in Child Development Monographs: Vol. 1, No. 3). 1936. 25.00 (*0-527-01488-5*) Periodicals Srv.

Osseous Reconstruction of the Maxilla & the Mandible: Surgical Techniques Using Titanium Mesh & Bone Mineral. Philip J. Boyne & Michael Peetz. LC 96-26147. (Illus.). 116p. 1996. text 68.00 (*0-86715-319-9*) Quint Pub Co.

Ossi di Seppia see Bones of Cuttlefish

Ossian & Ossianic Literature. Alfred T. Nutt. LC 70-139166. (Popular Studies in Mythology, Romance & Folklore: No. 3). reprint ed. 27.50 (*0-404-53503-8*) AMS Pr.

Ossian Bingley Hart, Florida's Loyalist Reconstruction Governor. Canter Brown, Jr. LC 97-16763. (Southern Biography Ser.). (Illus.). 336p. 1997. text 40.00 (*0-8071-2137-1*) La State U Pr.

Ossian House. A. C. Stewart. LC 76-9645. (J). (gr. 6 up). 1976. lib. bdg. 26.95 (*0-87599-219-6*) S G Phillips.

Ossian, Ou les Bardes see Chefs-d'Oeuvre Classiques de l'Opera Francais

Ossian Revisited. Ed. by Howard Gaskill. 1991. text 68.00 (*0-7486-0247-X*, Pub. by Edinburgh U Pr) Col U Pr.

Ossian's Fingal, 1792. James Macpherson & Ossian. LC 96-2989. (Revolution & Romanticism, 1789-1834 Ser.). 224p. 1996. 75.00 (*1-85477-208-2*) Continuum.

***Ossining.** Carl Oechsner. (Images of America Ser.). 128p. 1998. pap. 18.99 (*0-7524-0983-2*) Arcadia Publng.

Ossining, NY, 1950's. Historical Briefs, Inc. Staff. Ed. by Thomas Antonucci & Michael Antonucci. 200p. 1994. pap. 19.95 (*0-89677-056-7*) Hist Briefs.

Ossining, NY, 1940's. Historical Briefs, Inc. Staff. Ed. by Thomas Antonucci & Michael Antonucci. 176p. 1994. pap. 19.95 (*0-614-03689-5*) Hist Briefs.

Ossoul Faghr va Tassavof: Principles of Faghr & Sufism. Shah Maghsoud Sadegh Angha. LC 87-60094. (PER.). 173p. 1987. 110.00 (*0-910735-10-7*) MTO Printing & Pubn Ctr.

Ost - West. Christian Boltanski. LC 98-180816. (Illus.). 64p. 1998. pap. 19.95 (*3-929078-33-3*, Kehayoff) te Neues.

Ostade (Adriaen Van) Catalogue Raisonne of the Engraved Work. rev. ed. Louis Godefroy. (ENG & FRE., Illus.). 1989. 150.00 (*1-55660-040-2*) A Wofsy Fine Arts.

Ostafrika-Bibliographie: Kenya-Tanzania-Uganda, 1945-1993. (Bibliographienzur Regionalen Geographie und Landeskunde Ser.). 300p. 1995. 125.00 (*3-598-21140-6*) K G Saur Verlag.

Ostalpen-Tektonik I. Alexander Tollmann. (Geotektonische Forschungen Ser.: Vol. 24). (GER.). ii, 90p. 1970. pap. 23.00 (*3-510-50925-0*, Pub. by E Schweizerbartsche) Balogh.

Ostalpen-Tektonik III. Andreas Thurner. (Geotektonische Forschungen Ser.: Vol. 39). (GER.). ii, 124p. 1971. 27.00 (*3-510-50005-9*, Pub. by E Schweizerbartsche) Balogh.

Ostalpen-Tektonik II. Reinhard Schoenenberg. (Geotektonische Forschungen Ser.: Vol. 35). (GER.). ii, 93p. 1970. 30.00 (*3-510-50001-6*, Pub. by E Schweizerbartsche) Balogh.

Ostankino Palace Museum: A Guide. A. Chervyakov. (Illus.). 144p. (C). 1985. 40.00 (*0-7855-5191-3*, Pub. by Collets) St Mut.

Ostdeutschen Kietze. Herbert Ludat. (GER.). viii, 220p. 1984. reprint ed. write for info. (*3-487-07573-3*) G Olms Pubs.

Ostend. Francois Gravel. Tr. by Sheila Fischman. LC 97-142896. 306p. 1996. pap. text 18.95 (*0-920953-93-X*) Stoddart Publ.

Osten's Bay. Zenobia N. Vole. 208p. 1988. pap. 8.95 (*0-941483-15-0*) Naiad Pr.

Osteoarthritic Disorders: Workshop, Monterey, California, April 1994. Ed. by Klaus E. Kuettner & Victor M. Goldberg. LC 95-7068. 507p. 1995. 105.00 (*0-89203-129-8*) Amer Acad Ortho Surg.

Osteoarthritis. Ed. by Kenneth D. Brandt et al. LC 97-11747. (Illus.). 612p. (C). 1998. text 129.50 (*0-19-262735-X*) OUP.

Osteoarthritis. 2nd ed. Moskowitz. 1992. text 170.00 (*0-7216-6581-0*, W B Saunders Co) Harcrt Hlth Sci Grp.

Osteoarthritis: A Step-by-Step Sucess Story to Show Others They Can Help Themselves. Fred L. Savage. 96p. 1989. pap. 11.95 (*0-88268-086-2*) Station Hill Pr.

Osteoarthritis: Clinical & Experimental Aspects. Ed. by J. P. Pelletier et al. LC 98-33430. (Illus.). 480p. 1999. pap. 99.00 (*3-540-65127-6*) Spr-Verlag.

Osteoarthritis: Current Research & Prospects for Pharmacological Intervention. R. G. Russell & P. A. Dieppe. 232p. (C). 1991. 300.00 (*1-85271-093-4*, Pub. by IBC Tech Srvs) St Mut.

***Osteoarthritis: Fundamentals & Strategies for Joint-Preserving Treatment.** Ed. by J. Grifka & J. D. Ogilvie-Harris. (Illus.). 240p. 2000. 89.00 (*3-540-66309-6*) Spr-Verlag.

***Osteoarthritis: Nature's Cure.** Karolyn A. Gazella. 32p. 1998. pap. 3.95 (*1-890694-09-6*) IMPAKT Communs.

Osteoarthritis: Public Health Implications for an Aging Population. Ed. by David Hamerman. LC 96-45259. 272p. 1997. text 45.00 (*0-8018-5561-6*) Johns Hopkins.

Osteoarthritis in Rhesus Monkeys & Gibbons: A Locomotor Model of Joint Degeneration. C. J. DeRousseau. (Contributions to Primatology Ser.: Vol. 25). (Illus.). xiv, 146p. 1988. 83.50 (*3-8055-4700-5*) S Karger.

Osteochondral Allografts. Gary E. Friedlander et al. 403p. 1983. 120.00 (*0-316-29346-6*, Little Brwn Med Div) Lppncott W & W.

Osteoclast - Osteoblast, Vol. 1. Ed. by Mone Zaidi. Date not set. 128.50 (*0-7623-0396-4*) Jai Pr.

Osteolathyrismus: Quantitativ-Morphologische Untersuchungen der Experimentellen Skeletterkrankungen bei der Ratte. H. Plenk. Ed. by G. Wolf-Heidegger. (Bibliotheca Anatomica Ser.: No. 14). (Illus.). 104p. 1976. 41.75 (*3-8055-2306-8*) S Karger.

Osteology for Radiographers. Shillingford. (Illus.). 144p. 1985. pap. 29.95 (*0-632-01349-4*) Blackwell Sci.

Osteology for the Archaeologist: The American Mastodon & the Woolly Mammoth; North American Birds: Skulls & Mandibles & Postcranial Skeletons. rev. ed. Stanley J. Olsen. LC 79-65654. (Peabody Museum Papers: Vol. 56, Nos. 3, 4, & 5). (Illus.). 196p. 1979. pap. 35.00 (*0-87365-197-9*) Peabody Harvard.

Osteology of Pteranodon. George F. Eaton. (Connecticut Academy of Arts & Sciences Ser., Trans.: Vol. 2). 1910. pap. 300.00 (*0-685-22871-1*) Elliots Bks.

Osteology of Some Maya Mammals. Stanley J. Olsen. LC 81-85463. (Peabody Museum Papers: No. 73). (Illus.). 92p. 1982. pap. 18.00 (*0-87365-199-5*) Peabody Harvard.

Osteology of the Reptiles. Alfred S. Romer. LC 97-5401. (Illus.). 800p. Date not set. reprint ed. 96.50 (*0-89464-985-X*) Krieger.

Osteonecrosis: Etiology, Diagnosis, & Treatment. American Orthopaedic Association Staff. Ed. by James R. Urbaniak & John P. Jones, Jr. LC 97-41931. (Illus.). 453p. 1997. 120.00 (*0-89203-174-3*) Amer Acad Ortho Surg.

Osteopathic Approach to Diagnosis & Treatment. 2nd ed. Eileen Digiovanna. LC 96-41775. 500p. 1996. text 75.00 (*0-397-51581-2*, Lppncttl) Lppncott W & W.

Osteopathic Considerations in Systemic Disease. William Kuchera & Michael Kuchera. 294p. (C). 1994. pap. text 34.75 (*1-57074-154-9*) Greyden Pr.

Osteopathic Considerations in Systemic Dysfunction. Michael Kuchera & William Kuchera. (C). 1996. write for info. (*1-57074-348-7*) Greyden Pr.

Osteopathic Diagnosis. Emanuel Sammut & Patrick Searle-Barnes. (Illus.). 272p. 1998. pap. 72.50 (*0-7487-3296-9*, Pub. by S Thornes Pubs) Trans-Atl Phila.

Osteopathic Mechanics. Edythe F. Ashmore. 237p. 1996. reprint ed. pap. 22.00 (*0-7873-0043-8*) Hlth Research.

Osteopathic Mechanics: A Textbook. E. F. Ashmore. 1991. lib. bdg. 79.95 (*0-8490-4104-X*) Gordon Pr.

***Osteopathic Medicine Careers.** Terence J. Sacks. (Opportunities in . . . Ser.). 2000. 14.95 (*0-658-00184-1*, VGM Career); pap. 11.95 (*0-658-00186-8*, VGM Career) NTC Contemp Pub Co.

Osteopathic Principles in Practice. Michael Kuchera & William Kuchera. (C). 1996. write for info. (*1-57074-347-9*) Greyden Pr.

Osteopathic Principles in Practice. William Kuchera & Michael Kuchera. 763p. (C). 1994. pap. text 42.50 (*1-57074-151-4*) Greyden Pr.

Osteopathy: Index of New Developments & Modern Research. Stanley X. Garrett. 200p. 1993. 47.50 (*1-55914-514-5*); pap. 44.50 (*1-55914-515-3*) ABBE Pubs Assn.

Osteopathy: Is It for You? Chris Belshaw. (Illus.). 128p. 1993. pap. 11.95 (*0-906540-95-X*, Pub. by Element MA) Penguin Putnam.

Osteopathy (Original Osteopathic Moves As Taught by Still) 9th ed. Frederick W. Collins. 11p. 1997. reprint ed. spiral bd. 8.00 (*0-7873-0191-4*) Hlth Research.

Osteopathy Research & Practice. A. T. Still. LC 92-70915. 293p. (C). 1992. reprint ed. text 34.95 (*0-939616-14-9*) Eastland.

Osteopontin: Role in Cell Signalling & Adhesion. Ed. by David T. Denhardt et al. LC 95-11516. (Annals Ser.: Vol. 760). 1995. pap. 110.00 (*0-89766-940-1*) NY Acad Sci.

Osteoporose: Grundlagen, Diagnostik und Therapiekonzepte. Ed. by H. Broell & M. A. Dambacher. (Illus.). viii, 314p. 1995. 259.25 (*3-8055-6192-X*) S Karger.

Osteoporosis see Atlas of Clinical Endocrinology

Osteoporosis. Annemarie Colbin. 256p. 1999. pap. 23.95 (*0-525-94286-6*) NAL.

Osteoporosis. Ed. by Robert Marcus et al. (Illus.). 1373p. 1996. text 149.95 (*0-12-470860-9*) Acad Pr.

Osteoporosis. Ed. by Robert Marcus. (Illus.). 352p. 1994. 99.95 (*0-86542-266-4*) Blackwell Sci.

Osteoporosis. Ed. by David J. Sartoris. (Illus.). 432p. 1996. text 165.00 (*0-8247-9507-5*) Dekker.

Osteoporosis. Tony Smith. (ACP Home Medical Guides). 96p. 2000. pap. 6.95 (*0-7894-4172-1*, D K Ink) DK Pub Inc.

Osteoporosis. Ed. by John C. Stevenson & Robert Lindsay. (Illus.). 402p. 1999. text 98.50 (*0-412-48870-1*, Pub. by E A) OUP.

Osteoporosis. Woodland Publishing Staff. (Woodland Health Ser.). 1997. pap. text 3.95 (*1-58054-006-6*) Woodland UT.

Osteoporosis: A Clinical Guide. Anthony D. Woolf et al. 1995. pap. 9.95 (*0-614-06227-6*); pap. 9.95 (*0-614-07395-2*, M Dunitz) Scovill Paterson.

Osteoporosis: A Guide to Diagnostic & Treatment. Ed. by H. Broell & M. Dambacher. (Rheumatology Ser.: Vol. 18). (Illus.). viii, 292p. 1996. 259.25 (*3-8055-5624-1*) S Karger.

Osteoporosis: A Guide to Prevention & Treatment. John F. Aloia. LC 88-13819. (Illus.). 248p. (Orig.). 1989. reprint ed. pap. 76.90 (*0-608-06461-0*, 206729900009) Bks Demand.

Osteoporosis: A Natural Approach to Prevention. Westeron Stephens, III. 57p. 1995. 12.95 (*0-9644215-1-8*) W Stephens.

Osteoporosis: A Source Guide. 1991. lib. bdg. 69.95 (*0-8490-4903-2*) Gordon Pr.

Osteoporosis: An Exercise Guide. Margie Bissinger. (Illus.). 27p. 1998. pap., wbk. ed. 9.95 (*0-9668792-0-1*) Workfit Consult.

***Osteoporosis: Ancient Truths, Natural Remedies & the Latest Findings for Your Health Today.** Don Colbert. (Bible Cure Ser.). 2000. pap. 5.99 (*0-88419-681-X*) Creation House.

Osteoporosis: Diagnostic & Therapeutic Principles. Ed. by Clifford J. Rosen. (Current Clinical Practice Ser.). 312p. 1996. 99.50 (*0-89603-374-0*) Humana.

Osteoporosis: Etiology, Diagnosis & Management. 2nd ed. Ed. by B. Lawrence Riggs & L. Joseph Melton, III. LC 95-7020. 560p. 1995. text 134.00 (*0-7817-0275-5*) Lppncott W & W.

Osteoporosis: Fundamentals of Clinical Practice. Murray J. Favus et al. LC 97-30731. 1996. pap. text. write for info. (*0-397-51823-4*) Lppncott W & W.

Osteoporosis: Genetics, Prevention & Treatment. John S. Adams & Barbara P. Lukert. LC 98-46837. (Endocrine Update Ser.). 308p. 1999. write for info. (*0-7923-8366-4*) Kluwer Academic.

Osteoporosis: How to Make Your Bones Last a Lifetime. Wanda S. Lyon & Cynthia E. Sutton. 240p. 1993. pap. 10.99 (*1-56943-005-5*) NTC Contemp Pub Co.

Osteoporosis: Medical Blunders & Treatment Strategies. William N. Taylor. LC 96-21046. 117p. 1996. pap. 25.00 (*0-7864-0229-6*) McFarland & Co.

Osteoporosis: Medical Subject Index of Progress with Reference Bibliography. Jennifer H. Houston. LC 88-47597. 150p. 1987. 47.50 (*0-88164-750-0*); pap. 44.50 (*0-88164-751-9*) ABBE Pubs Assn.

Osteoporosis: Nutritional Aspects. Ed. by A. P. Simopoulos & C. Galli. (World Review of Nutrition & Dietetics Ser.: Vol. 73). (Illus.). xii, 108p. 1993. 139.25 (*3-8055-5751-5*) S Karger.

Osteoporosis: Pathogenesis & Management. R. M. Francis. (C). 1990. text 89.50 (*0-7923-8933-6*) Kluwer Academic.

***Osteoporosis: Pocketbook Edition.** 2nd ed. Woolf. 2000. 14.95 (*1-85317-678-8*, Pub. by Martin Dunitz) Blackwell Sci.

Osteoporosis: Prevention & Treatment. Felix Kolb et al. Ed. by Nancy Wiltsek. (Illus.). 1986. pap. 2.50 (*0-933161-07-7*) Better H Prog.

***Osteoporosis: Prevention, Diagnosis & Management.** 3rd rev. ed. Morris Notelovitz. 244p. 1999. pap. text 19.95 (*1-884735-50-9*) Prof Comms.

Osteoporosis: Proceedings of an International Symposium Held at the Jerusalem Osteoporosis Center in June, 1981. Ed. by J. Menczel et al. LC 81-19822. (Illus.). 452p. reprint ed. pap. 140.20 (*0-608-15575-6*, 202963700062) Bks Demand.

***Osteoporosis: The Alternatives.** Evan L. Snead. LC 99-47037. 456p. 1999. pap. 19.95 (*1-893157-00-8*) Bridger Hse.

***Osteoporosis: Unmask a Silent Thief.** Raymond E. Cole. Ed. by Donna Kehoe. (Illus.). 240p. 2000. 19.95 (*0-917073-03-7*) Wellpower.

Osteoporosis - Phases, Conditions & Therapy: Index of New Information with Authors, Subjects & References. Florence M. Connors. 150p. 1994. 47.50 (*1-55914-724-5*); pap. 44.50 (*1-55914-725-3*) ABBE Pubs Assn.

Osteoporosis - Questions & Answers. John Stevenson & Michael C. Ellerington. (Questions & Answers Ser.). (Illus.). 968p. 1993. 12.95 (*1-873413-50-5*); pap. 10.95 (*1-873413-55-6*) Merit Pub Intl.

Osteoporosis & You. Elizabeth K. White et al. (Illus.). 40p. 1994. pap. 3.60 (*0-317-59867-8*) Budlong.

Osteoporosis Book. Ed. by Nancy E. Lane. LC 98-19650. (Illus.). 224p. 1999. 27.50 (*0-19-511602-X*) OUP.

Osteoporosis, Critique & Practicum. Richard D. Wasnich et al. (Illus.). 225p. (Orig.). 1989. pap. text 36.95 (*0-9623265-1-8*) Banyan Pr HI.

Osteoporosis Cure: Reverse the Crippling Effects with New Treatments. Harris McIlwain. LC 97-94411. 208p. 1998. mass mkt. 5.99 (*0-380-79336-9*, Avon Bks) Morrow Avon.

Osteoporosis Handbook. 2nd ed. Sydney L. Bonnick. LC 97-204669. (Illus.). 216p. (Orig.). 1997. pap. 14.95 (*0-87833-978-7*) Taylor Pub.

Osteoporosis in Asia: Crossing the Frontiers. LC 98-162311. 200p. 1997. lib. bdg. 34.00 (*981-02-2730-2*) World Scientific Pub.

Osteoporosis in Clinical Practice: A Practical Guide for Diagnosis & Treatment. Ed. by Piet Geusens. LC 97-41383. xvii, 188p. 1997. pap. 39.00 (*3-540-76223-X*) Spr-Verlag.

***Osteoporosis in Men.** J. M. Kaufman. 2001. write for info. (*1-84214-033-7*) Prthnon Pub.

Osteoporosis in Men: The Effects of Gender on Skeletal Health. Bruce Orwoll & Eric S. Orwoll. LC 98-83125. (Illus.). 582p. 1999. 99.95 (*0-12-528640-6*) Acad Pr.

Osteoporosis, 1996: Proceedings of the 1996 World Congress on Osteoporosis, Amsterdam, the Netherlands, 18-23 May 1996. World Congress on Osteoporosis Staff & S. Papapoulos. LC 96-38652. (International Congress Ser.). 422p. 1996. 206.25 (*0-444-82276-3*) Elsevier.

***Osteoporosis Primer.** Ed. by Janet E. Henderson & David Goltzman. (Illus.). 388p. 2000. pap. write for info. (*0-521-64446-1*) Cambridge U Pr.

Osteoporosis Research, Education & Health Promotion. 68p. (Orig.). (C). 1993. pap. text 30.00 (*0-7881-0063-7*) DIANE Pub.

Osteoporosis Solution. Carl Germano. LC 98-66722. 1999. text 22.00 (*1-57566-391-0*) Kensgtn Pub Corp.

***Osteoporosis Solution.** Carl Germano. 2000. pap. 14.00 (*1-57566-496-8*) Kensgtn Pub Corp.

***Osteoporosis Sourcebook.** Ed. by Allan R. Cook. (Health Reference Ser.). (Illus.). 600p. 2000. lib. bdg. 78.00 (*0-7808-0239-X*) Omnigraphics Inc.

Osteoporosis, the Silent Stalker: A Woman's Illustrated Guide to the Prevention & Treatment of Osteoporosis. Timothy J. Gray. LC 94-70320. (Illus.). 188p. (Orig.). 1994. pap. 15.95 (*0-9622269-8-X*) BookPartners.

***Osteoporotic Syndrome: Detection, Prevention & Treatment.** Louis V. Avioli. 2000. pap. text 59.95 (*0-12-068705-4*) Acad Pr.

Osteosarcoma in Adolescents & Young Adults: New Developments & Controversies. Ed. by G. Bennett Humphrey et al. LC 92-49668. (Cancer Treatment & Research Ser.: Vol. 62). (C). 1993. text 307.00 (*0-7923-1905-2*) Kluwer Academic.

Osteosynthesis in Spinal Surgery. Ed. by E. Ascani et al. (Progress in Spinal Pathology Ser.: Vol. 4). (Illus.). 185p. 1990. 62.95 (*0-387-82150-3*) Spr-Verlag.

Osterman Weekend. Robert Ludlum. 336p. 1984. mass mkt. 7.99 (*0-553-26430-3*) Bantam.

***Osterreich Und der Tourismus Von Opatija (Abbazia) Vor Dem Ersten Weltkrieg Und Zur Mitte der 1990ER Jahre.** Peter Jordan & Milena Persic. (Illus.). XII, 397p. 1998. 67.95 (*3-631-30449-8*) P Lang Pubng.

Osterreichische Galerie Belvedere, Vienna. (Museum Guides Ser.). (Illus.). 192p. (Orig.). 1996. pap. 14.95 (*3-7913-1622-2*, Pub. by Prestel) te Neues.

Osterreichische Munzpragungen, 1519-1938, 2 vols. V. Miller Zu Aichholz et al. (GER., Illus.). 1981. 195.00 (*0-86723-000-2*) Obol Intl.

Osterreichische Pferdeankaufmission Unter Dem K. K. Obersten Ritter v. Brudermann in Syrien, Palastina und der Wuste In Den Jahren 1856 und 1857. Eduard Loffler. (Documenta Hippologica Ser.). xv, 240p. 1978. reprint ed. write for info. (*3-487-08174-1*) G Olms Pubs.

Osterreichische Regierung Und Verwaltung Im Weltkriege. Joseph Redlich. (Wirtschafts-Und Sozialgeschichte des Weltkrieges (Osterreichische Und Ungarische Serie)). (GER.). 1925. 100.00 (*0-317-27532-1*) Elliots Bks.

***Osterreichischer Hno-Kongress, 1999.** 84p. 1999. 34.00 (*3-8055-6954-8*) S Karger.

Osterreichs erstes Reformationsjubilaum: Jakob Glatz und die Gemeinden Augsburgischer Konfession 1817/1818 - Ein Modell des Verhaltnisses von Kirchenleitung und Verkundigung. Wichmann Von Meding. (Kontexte Ser.: Band 23). (GER., Illus.). 215p. 1998. 37.95 (*3-631-33250-5*) P Lang Pubng.

Osteuropa: Reformen & Wandel. 2nd ed. Christoph Royen. (GER.). 168p. 1990. pap. 23.00 (*3-7890-1948-8*, Pub. by Nomos Verlags) Intl Bk Import.

Ostfriesische Kuestengebiet: Nordsee, Inseln, Watten und Marschen. Hansjorg Streif. (Sammlung Geologischer Fuehrer Ser.: Band 57). (GER., Illus.). vii, 376p. 1990. spiral bd. 29.00 (*3-443-15051-9*, Pub. by Gebruder Borntraeger) Balogh.

***Ostfront: Hitler's War on Russia, 1941-1945.** Charles Winchester. (Illus.). 180p. 2000. pap. 22.95 (*1-84176-066-8*) Ospry.

Ostfront: The Russian Front, 1941-45. LC 90-62982. (Illus.). 256p. 1991. 29.95 (*0-88740-282-8*) Schiffer.

Ostfront: The Russian Front, 1941-45. Charles Winchester. 1998. 39.95 (*1-85532-711-2*) Osprey.

Osthandel & Ostpolitik: German Foreign Trade Policies in Eastern Europe from Bismarck to Adenauer. Robert M. Spaulding. LC 96-20811. (Monographs in German History). (Illus.). 552p. (C). 1997. 89.00 (*1-57181-039-0*) Berghahn Bks.

Ostheimer's Manual of Obstetric Anesthesia. 3rd ed. David J. Birnbach. LC 99-35204. (Illus.). 315p. 2000. pap. text. write for info. (*0-443-06554-3*, W B Saunders Co) Harcrt Hlth Sci Grp.

Ostjakologische Arbeiten, Band 2. Wolfgang Steinitz. 1977. 150.00 (*90-279-3314-6*) Mouton.

Ostlere & Bryce-Smith's Anaesthetics for Medical Students. 10th ed. Thomas B. Boulton & Colin E. Blogg. (Illus.). 276p. 1989. pap. text. write for info. (*0-443-02821-4*) Church.

Ostomies & Continent Diversions: Nursing Management. Beverly G. Hampton. (Illus.). 400p. (C). (gr. 13). 1992. text 45.00 (*0-8016-2041-4*, 02041) Mosby Inc.

Ostomy & Incontinence Products. (Market Research Reports: No. 270). (Illus.). 133p. 1992. 295.00 (*0-317-05017-6*) Theta Corp.

Ostomy Book: Living Comfortably with Colostomies, Ileostomies & Urostomies. 2nd rev. ed. Barbara D. Mullen & Kerry A. McGinn. 252p. 1991. pap. 16.95 (*0-923521-12-7*) Bull Pub.

***Ostraca.** Gabriel Levin. 70p. 2000. pap. 18.95 (*0-85646-317-5*, Pub. by Anvil Press) Dufour.

Ostracism: A Social & Biological Phenomenon. Ed. by Margaret Gruter & Roger D. Masters. 247p. (Orig.). (C). 1986. pap. 20.00 (*0-317-55376-3*) Gruter Inst.

An Asterisk (*) at the beginning of an entry indicates that the title is appearing for the first time.

Ostracod Family Entocytheridae. Dabney G. Hart & C. W. Hart, Jr. (Monograph: No. 18). (Illus.). 239p. 1974. pap. 15.00 (*0-910006-26-1*) Acad Nat Sci Phila.

Ostracoda: The Henry V. Howe Memorial Volume. Ed. by W. A. Van den Bold. LC 78-621997. (Geoscience & Man Ser.: Vol. 6). (Illus.). 190p. 1974. pap. 15.00 (*0-938909-05-3*) Geosci Pubns LSU.

Ostracoda & Biostratigraphy: Proceedings of the 12th International Symposium, Prague, 26-30 July 1994. Ed. by Riha Jaroslav. (Illus.). 464p. (C). 1995. text 110.00 (*90-5410-540-2*, Pub. by A A Balkema) Ashgate Pub Co.

Ostracoda from the Late Permian of Greece (Thaumatocyprididae & Polycopidae) Israel G. Sohn & Louis S. Kornicker. LC 98-6127. (Smithsonian Contributions to Paleobiology Ser.: Vol. 87). (Illus.). 38p. reprint ed. pap. 30.00 (*0-608-10498-1*, 207114000009) Bks Demand.

Ostracoda (Halocypridina, Cladocopina) from an Anchialine Lava Tube in Lanzarote, Canary Islands. Louis S. Kornicker & Thomas M. Iliffe. LC 94-44428. (Smithsonian Contributions to Zoology Ser.: Vol. 568). 36p. 1995. reprint ed. pap. 30.00 (*0-608-00505-3*, 206132500008) Bks Demand.

Ostracoda in the Earth & Life Sciences: Proceedings of the 11th International Symposium, Warrnambool, July 1991. K. G. McKenzie & P. J. Jones. (Illus.). 740p. (C). 1994. 168.00 (*90-5410-306-X*, Pub. by A A Balkema) Ashgate Pub Co.

Ostracoda (Myodocopina) from Shallow Waters of the Northern Territory & Queensland, Australia. Louis S. Kornicker. LC 95-35606. (Smithsonian Contributions to Zoology Ser.: Vol. 578). (Illus.). 101p. 1995. reprint ed. pap. 31.40 (*0-608-01768-X*, 206242600003) Bks Demand.

Ostracoda (Myodocopina) of the Southeast Australian Continental Slope, Pt. 1. fac. ed. Louis S. Kornicker. LC 93-38048. (Smithsonian Contributions to Zoology Ser.: No. 553). 204p. 1994. reprint ed. pap. 63.30 (*0-7837-8263-2*, 204904400001) Bks Demand.

Ostracoda (Myodocopina) of the Southeast Australian Continental Slope, Pt. 2. Louis S. Kornicker. LC 93-38048. (Smithsonian Contributions to Zoology Ser.: Vol. 562). 101p. 1995. reprint ed. pap. 31.40 (*0-608-00278-X*, 204904400002) Bks Demand.

Ostracoda (Myodocopina) of the Southeast Australian Continental Slope, Pt. 3. Louis S. Kornicker. LC 93-38048. (Smithsonian Contributions to Zoology Ser.: No. 573). (Illus.). 190p. 1996. reprint ed. pap. 58.90 (*0-608-02959-9*, 206342400003) Bks Demand.

Ostracoda of Ohio. Norma C. Furtos. (Bulletin Ser.: No. 29). 1933. pap. text 2.00 (*0-86727-028-4*) Ohio Bio Survey.

Ostracodes from the Late Neogene of Cuba see Bulletins of American Paleontology: Vol. 68

Ostraka. Mabel L. Lang. LC 90-46998. (Athenian Agora Ser.: Vol. 25). (Illus.). xvi, 188p. 1990. 55.00 (*0-87661-225-7*) Am Sch Athens.

Ostraka & Name Stones from the Tomb of Sen-Mut (No. 71) at Thebes: Metropolitan Museum of Art Publications in Reprint. William C. Hayes. LC 76-168406. (Illus.). 136p. 1973. reprint ed. 24.95 (*0-405-02239-5*) Ayer.

Ostraka Varia (O. Varia 1-60) Tax Receipts & Legal Documents on Demotic, Greek, & Greek-Demotic Ostraka, Chiefly of the Early Ptolemaic Period, from Various Collections. S. P. Vleeming. LC 94-26020. 294p. 1994. 132.00 (*90-04-10132-2*) Brill Academic Pubs.

Ostrava-Pillage see Grande Encyclopedie

***Ostrich.** Michael A. Thomas. LC 00-8599. (Western Literature Ser.). 288p. 2000. pap. 17.00 (*0-87417-351-5*) U of Nev Pr.

Ostrich: Biology, Production & Health. Ed. by Denis C. Deeming. LC 99-17680. (CABI Publishing Ser.). 368p. 1999. 100.00 (*0-85199-350-8*) OUP.

Ostrich & the EMU: Policy Choices Facing the UK. Contrib. by Rupert Pennant-Rea. 112p. 1997. pap. 12.00 (*1-898128-31-6*, Pub. by Ctr Econ Policy Res) Brookings.

Ostrich Christianity: Self-Deception in Popular Christianity. Van B. Weigel. LC 85-17981. 254p. (Orig.). (C). 1986. lib. bdg. 49.00 (*0-8191-4974-8*) U Pr of Amer.

Ostrich Communal Nesting. Brian C. Bertram. (Monographs in Behavior & Ecology). (Illus.). 208p. 1992. text 42.50 (*0-691-08785-7*, Pub. by Princeton U Pr) Cal Prin Full Svc.

Ostrich Cookbook. Ginger Kight et al. (Illus.). 128p. 2000. pap. 9.95 (*1-58063-060-X*) Renaissance.

Ostrich Factor: Our Population Myopia. Garrett Hardin. LC 97-39272. (Illus.). 176p. 1999. 22.00 (*0-19-512274-7*) OUP.

Ostrich Farms. Lynn M. Stone. LC 99-25302. (Funky Farms Ser.). 24p. 1999. lib. bdg. write for info. (*0-86593-539-4*) Rourke Corp.

Ostrich Position. Carol Lee. pap. 5.95 (*0-86316-057-3*) Writers & Readers.

Ostriches see Avestruces

***Ostriches.** Caroline Arnold. LC 99-45703. (Early Bird Nature Ser.). (Illus.). 32p. (J). (ps-3). 2000. 22.60 (*0-8225-3044-9*, Lerner Publctns) Lerner Pub.

Ostriches. Emilie U. Lepthien. LC 93-3407. (New True Books Ser.). (Illus.). 48p. (J). (gr. k-4). 1993. pap. 5.50 (*0-516-41193-4*) Childrens.

Ostriches. Thane Maynard. (Nature Books Ser.). (Illus.). 32p. (J). (gr. 2-6). 1996. lib. bdg. 22.79 (*1-56766-274-9*) Childs World.

Ostriches. Lynn M. Stone. (Illus.). 24p. (J). (gr. k-4). 1989. lib. bdg. 10.95 (*0-86592-323-X*) Rourke Enter.

Ostriches & Other Flightless Birds. Caroline Arnold. (Nature Watch Bks.). (Illus.). 48p. (J). (gr. 2-5). 1990. lib. bdg. 19.95 (*0-87614-377-X*, Carolrhoda) Lerner Pub.

Ostriches & other Ratites. Wildlife Education, Ltd. Staff. (Zoobooks Ser.). (Illus.). (J). 1994. pap. 2.75 (*0-937934-60-7*) Wildlife Educ.

Ostriches, Emus, Rheas, Kiwis & Cassowaries see Zoobooks

Ostroemische Plastik der Theodosianischen Zeit. Johannes Kollwitz. (Studien zur Spaetantiken Kunstgeschichte: Vol. 12). (Illus.). vi, 208p. (C). 1978. reprint ed. 292.35 (*3-11-004998-8*) De Gruyter.

Ostroporose: Moderne Diagnostik - Therapeutische Konsequenzen Fuer Klinik und Praxis. Ed. by M. J. Seibel & M. E. Kraenzlin. (Illus.). viii, 128p. 1995. pap. 35.00 (*3-8055-6248-9*) S Karger.

Ostrovsky: The Storm. Ed. by A. V. Knowles. (Bristol Russian Texts Ser.). (RUS.). 142p. 1988. pap. 16.95 (*0-631-15452-3*) Blackwell Pubs.

Ostrovsky: Four Plays. Alexander Ostrovsky. Tr. by Stephen Mulrine. (Absolute Classics Ser.). 128p. 1997. pap. 16.95 (*1-899791-05-1*) Theatre Comm.

Ostwald Ripening. S. Marsh. 1999. write for info. (*0-08-042141-5*, Pergamon Pr) Elsevier.

OS/2 Warp Presentation Manager API. Joel L. Barnum. LC 95-1222. 475p. 1995. pap. 29.95 (*0-471-03873-3*) Wiley.

OS/2 at Work. Edelhart. 1990. pap. 24.95 (*0-13-642620-4*) P-H.

OS/2 Data Processing with Review of OS-VS. Harry Carroll. LC 74-2047. 298p. reprint ed. pap. 92.40 (*0-608-10300-4*, 201388100087) Bks Demand.

OS/2 Environment, Changes & Enhancements to the SAS System, Release 6.11. 64p. (C). 1995. pap. 12.00 (*1-55544-270-6*, BR55267) SAS Publ.

OS/2 Environment, Changes & Enhancements to the SAS System, Version 6.10. 80p. (C). 1994. pap. 7.00 (*1-55544-633-7*, BR55137) SAS Publ.

OS/2 Environment: Changes & Enhancements to the SAS System, Release 6.10. SAS Institute, Inc. Staff. 80p. 1994. pap. 19.95 (*1-58025-426-8*, BR56629) SAS Publ.

OS/2 for Dummies. Andy Rathbone. 375p. 1993. pap. 19.95 (*1-878058-76-2*) IDG Bks.

OS/2 for the Impatient. Paul W. Abrahams. (C). 1997. pap. text. write for info. (*0-201-59146-4*) Addison-Wesley.

OS/2 1.3 Fundamental: End User. 1993. 29.95 (*1-56877-051-0*); teacher ed. 49.95 (*1-56877-052-9*) Catapult WA.

OS/2 Power Tools. David Moskowitz & Kathy Ivens. 400p. 1989. pap. 44.95 incl. disk (*0-13-643065-1*) P-H.

OS/2 Presentation Manager User's Guide. Bud Aaron. (Illus.). 380p. 1989. 28.95 (*0-8306-0736-6*, 3036); pap. 19.95 (*0-8306-9336-X*, 3036P) McGraw-Hill Prof.

OS/2 Programmer's Guide, Vol. 1. 2nd ed. Ed Lacobucci. 1990. pap. text 29.95 (*0-07-881533-9*) McGraw.

OS/2, the Workplace Shell: A User's Guide & Tutorial for Release 2.0. Maria E. Tyne. 361p. (Orig.). 1992. reprint ed. pap. 24.95 (*0-89435-442-6*) Wiley.

OS/2 2.1: IBM PC Quick Reference Guide. George Lynch. 1993. pap. 12.00 (*1-56243-119-6*, Y-18) DDC Pub.

OS/2 2.1 Presentation Manager GPI. 2nd ed. Graham C. Winn. (Computer Science Ser.). 1994. pap. 39.95 (*0-442-01891-6*, VNR) Wiley.

OS/2 2.1 "Red Book" for Developers. IBM Staff. (Illus.). 800p. (Orig.). 1994. 34.99 (*1-56529-287-1*) Que.

OS/2 2.3 Presentation Manager Programming for COBOL Programmers. rev. ed. Robert B. Chapman. LC 96-134078. 504p. 1993. pap. 39.95 incl. disk (*0-471-56140-1*) Wiley.

OS/2 2 Quick Reference Guide. George Lynch. 1993. pap. 12.00 (*1-56243-091-2*, OS-17) DDC Pub.

OS/2 Warp: Easy Installation Guide. Jonathan Kamin. LC 95-68179. 1995. pap. text 12.95 (*0-7615-0099-5*) Prima Pub.

OS/2 Warp for Dummies. 2nd ed. Andy Rathbone. 384p. 1995. pap. 19.99 (*1-56884-205-8*) IDG Bks.

OS/2 Warp for the SoHo Environment: Making the Most of the Small Office Home Office PC. Michael Price. LC 95-41544. 1995. write for info. (*0-07-709200-7*) McGraw.

Os/2 Warp Internet Express. Deborah Morrison. 256p. 1995. pap. 24.99 (*1-56884-465-4*) IDG Bks.

OS/2 Warp Presentation Manager Mentor: Foundations of PM Programming. Michael Drapkin. LC 95-35268. 368p. 1995. pap. text 39.95 incl. disk (*0-471-13167-9*) Wiley.

OS/2 Warp Professional Reference. John W. Little et al. LC 95-34180. (Professional Ser.). 900p. 1995. pap. 55.00 (*1-56205-502-X*) New Riders Pub.

OS/2 Warp Programmer's Sidekick: Functions & Structures: A Quick-Reference to OS/2 Functions, Macros & Structures. Glade Diviney & Keith Murray. 592p. (Orig.). 1995. pap. 39.95 (*0-9647472-8-6*) Quarter Horse.

OS/2 Warp Programming for Dummies. Blake Watson. 480p. 1995. pap. 19.99 (*1-56884-337-2*) IDG Bks.

OS/2 Warp Toolkit for System Developers. Maurice Viscuso. 1996. 29.95 (*0-614-14492-2*) P-H.

OS/2 Warp Uncensored. Peter G. Magid. 848p. 1995. pap. 39.99 (*1-56884-474-3*) IDG Bks.

Osugi Sakae, Anarchist in Taisho Japan: The Creativity of the Ego. Thomas A. Stanley. (East Asian Monographs: No. 102). 300p. 1982. 30.00 (*0-674-64493-X*) HUP.

O'Sullivan Book. Michael C. O'Laughlin. (Irish Family Histories Ser.). (Illus.). 50p. 1981. 15.00 (*0-940134-18-7*) Irish Genealog.

O'Sullivan Stew. Hudson Talbott. LC 98-5721. (Illus.). 48p. (YA). (gr. k up). 1999. 15.99 (*0-399-23162-5*, G P Putnam) Peng Put Young Read.

Osun Seegesi: The Elegant Deity of Wealth, Power, & Femininity. Diedre Badejo. LC 95-51678. 248p. 1996. text 59.95 (*0-86543-354-2*) Africa World.

Osun Seegesi: The Elegant Deity of Wealth, Power & Femininity. Diedre Badejo. LC 95-51678. 248p. 1996. pap. 18.95 (*0-86543-355-0*) Africa World.

Oswald & the CIA. John Newman. 608p. 1995. 28.00 (*0-7867-0131-5*) Carroll & Graf.

Oswald & the CIA. John Newman. (Illus.). 627p. 1998. text 28.00 (*0-7881-5487-7*) DIANE Pub.

Oswald Chambers. David W. Lambert. LC 97-4646. (Men of Faith Ser.). 128p. 1997. mass mkt. 4.99 (*1-55661-942-1*) Bethany Hse.

Oswald Chambers: Abandoned to God: The Life Story of the Author of My Upmost for His Highest. David McCasland. LC 98-43187. (Illus.). 336p. 1998. pap. 14.99 (*1-57293-050-0*) Discovery Hse Pubs.

Oswald Hoot: The Owl Who Was Scared of the Dark. Elizabeth Gullander. (Illus.). 64p. (J). (ps-6). 1982. pap. 4.95 (*0-940828-05-7*); lib. bdg. 7.95 (*0-940828-06-5*) D Youra Studios.

Oswald in New Orleans: Case for Conspiracy with the CIA. Harold Weisberg. 1967. 25.00 (*0-911606-04-1*) Weisberg.

Oswald Mathias Ungers. Martin Kieren. (Studio Paperback Ser.). 1997. pap. 29.95 (*3-7643-5585-9*, Pub. by Birkhauser) Princeton Arch.

Oswald Mosley & British Fascism. James Drennan. 1976. lib. bdg. 69.95 (*0-8490-2388-2*) Gordon Pr.

***Oswald Oberhuber: Written Pictures, up Until Now.** Ed. by P. Noever. (Illus.). 157p. 1999. pap. 36.00 (*3-211-83352-8*) Spr-Verlag.

Oswald Spengler. H. Stuart Hughes. 196p. (C). 1991. pap. text 21.95 (*1-56000-576-9*) Transaction Pubs.

Oswald Talked: The New Evidence in the JFK Assassination. Ray LaFontaine & Mary LaFontaine. LC 94-45945. (Illus.). 456p. 1996. reprint ed. 25.00 (*1-56554-029-8*) Pelican.

Oswald the Monkey. Egon Mathiesen. (Illus.). (J). (gr. k-3). 1959. 9.95 (*0-8392-3025-7*) Astor-Honor.

Oswald Von Wolkenstein - Handschrift A. fac. ed. Comment by F. Delbono. (Codices Selecti B Ser.: Vol. LIX). (GER., Illus.). 122p. 1977. 254.00 (*3-201-00995-4*, Pub. by Akademische Druck-und) Balogh.

Oswald's Closest Friend: The George de Mohrenschildt Story, 9 vols., Set. 2nd rev. ed. Bruce C. Adamson. Ed. by Dennis McDonough et al. (Illus.). 1202p. 1996. 196.00 (*1-892501-03-1*) B C Adamson.

Oswego Movement in American Education. Ned H. Dearborn. LC 74-89171. (American Education: Its Men, Institutions, & Ideas. Series 1: Its Men, Institutions & Ideas, Ser. 1). 1974. reprint ed. 18.95 (*0-405-01409-0*) Ayer.

***Oswego Speedway: The First Fifty Years.** George Caruso, Jr. (Illus.). 542p. 2000. 49.95 (*0-9677438-1-8*) Speedway.

Osynliga Barnet see Tales from Moominvalley

OS/2. (C). 1990. text. write for info. (*0-201-52300-0*) Addison-Wesley.

OS/2 Presentation Manager Developer's Guide. Bud Aaron. (Illus.). 480p. 1989. 34.95 (*0-8306-0346-8*, 3046); pap. 24.95 (*0-8306-9346-7*, 3046P) McGraw-Hill Prof.

Os/2 Warp PowerPc: New Frontie. Ken W. Christopher & Mary P. Wright. 476p. 1995. pap. 29.99 (*1-56884-458-1*) IDG Bks.

OS/2 Warp Survival Kit Pk, Set. Brian Proffit. 144p. 1995. 19.95 incl. disk (*0-201-40915-1*) Addison-Wesley.

OT Goals: Occupational Therapy Goals & Objectives Associated with Learning. Michelle Tobias et al. 185p. 1991. pap. text 52.50 (*0-7616-4244-7*) Commun Skill.

Ot Khodasevicha do Nabokova. Inna Broude. LC 90-49449. (RUS.). 180p. (Orig.). 1990. pap. 10.00 (*1-55779-024-8*) Hermitage Pubs.

Ot La-Ba'ot, 5 bks., Set. Yosi Gordon. (Illus.). 120p. (J). (gr. 3-4). 1991. student ed. 7.50 (*0-933873-54-9*) Torah Aura.

OT Survey Study Guide. B. Poinsett. 1994. pap., student ed. 12.99 (*0-8054-1086-4*, 4210-86) Broadman.

OTA Children's Coloring Book. Teresa Rosen. (Illus.). 24p. (J). (ps-8). 1989. pap. 3.95 (*0-944227-04-X*) Prac Psych Pr.

Otage: Le Pain Dur - Le Pere Humilie. Paul Claudel. (FRE.). pap. 13.95 (*0-8288-3630-2*, F94322) Fr & Eur.

Otage: Le Pain Dur - Le Pere Humilie. Paul Claudel. (Folio Ser.: No. 170). (FRE.). pap. 10.95 (*2-07-036170-5*) Schoenhof.

Otages du Desir. Elizabeth Power. 1998. mass mkt. 3.50 (*0-373-34718-9*, 1-34718-6) Harlequin Bks.

Otago: The University. Roger Hall. 1994. 24.95 (*0-908569-85-8*, Pub. by Univ Otago Pr) Intl Spec Bk.

Otahki, Trail of Tears Princess. A. Lorberg. 1967. pap. 1.00 (*0-911208-13-5*) Ramfre.

Otan Iyebiye: Las Piedras Preciosas. Lydia Cabrera. (Coleccion del Chicherekú). (SPA.). 113p. 1986. pap. 6.95 (*0-89729-397-5*) Ediciones.

Otarie, Espiegle Sirene see Sea Lion

Otayahuk Ungazimi (Otayahuk in Siberia) J. Otayahuk & V. Kaneshiro. (ESK.). 17p. 1973. pap. 2.00 (*0-933769-72-5*) Alaska Native.

OTC Derivatives: Additional Oversight Could Reduce Costly Sales Practice Disputes. Cecile O. Trop. Ed. by Thomas J. McCool. (Illus.). 230p. (C). 1998. pap. text 40.00 (*0-7881-7329-4*) DIANE Pub.

OTC Diagnostics Markets. (Market Research Reports: No. 244). 103p. 1992. 795.00 (*0-317-05466-X*) Theta Corp.

OTC Medications: Symptoms & Treatment of Common Illnesses. A. Li Wan Po & G. Li Wan Po. (Illus.). 256p. 1991. pap. 31.95 (*0-632-02954-4*) Blackwell Sci.

OTC Medications: Symptoms & Treatments of Common Illnesses. 2nd ed. Alain Wan Po Li & G. Wan Po Li. LC 97-11878. 1997. pap. 34.95 (*0-632-04046-7*) Blackwell Sci.

Otce Nas. 2nd ed. Vladimir Uhri. (SLO.). 60p. 1996. pap. 3.00 (*1-56983-015-0*) New Creat WI.

***Otchum: A Companion in a World of Ice.** Konemann Inc. Staff. (Illus.). 176p. 2000. pap. 20.00 (*3-8290-4104-7*) Konemann.

Otello. Giuseppe Verdi. Ed. & Tr. by Nicholas John from ITA. Tr. by Andrew Porter from ITA. (English National Opera Guide Series: Bilingual Libretto, Articles: No. 7). (Illus.). (Orig.). 1981. pap. 9.95 (*0-7145-3850-7*) Riverrun NY.

Otello in Full Score. Giuseppe Verdi. 576p. 1986. 22.95 (*0-486-25040-7*) Dover.

Otello, Ossia il Moro di Venezia: Dramma per Musica in Three Acts by Francesco Berio de Salsa, 3 vols. Gioachino Rossini. Ed. by Michael Collins. (Critical Edition of the Worlds of Gioachino Rossini, Section 1: Operas: Vol. 19). 1130p. 1995. lib. bdg. 195.00 (*0-226-72850-1*) U Ch Pr.

Otero, 3 vols. Miguel A. Otero. LC 73-14420. (Mexican American Ser.). 1036p. 1977. reprint ed. 75.95 (*0-405-05685-0*) Ayer.

Otey, Ringgold & Davidson Virginia Artillery. Michael A. Cavanaugh. (Virginia Regimental Histories Ser.). (Illus.). 118p. 1993. 19.95 (*1-56190-045-1*) H E Howard.

Otfrid Von Weissenburg: Narrator or Commentator. Donald A. Mackenzie. (Stanford University. Stanford Studies in Language & Literature: Vol. 6, Pt. 3). reprint ed. 27.50 (*0-404-51812-5*) AMS Pr.

Otglagol"nye Sushchestvitel"nye s Suffiksom -k(a) v Russkom Iazyke XI-XVII Vekov. Valentina Pichugina. LC 95-35739. (RUS.). 174p. (Orig.). 1995. pap. 17.50 (*1-55779-085-X*) Hermitage Pubs.

***Othello.** (Globe Adapted Classics Ser.). 1999. write for info. (*0-8359-5555-9*); teacher ed. write for info. (*0-8359-4999-0*) Globe Fearon.

***Othello.** Ed. by Cliffs Notes Staff. (Cliffs Complete Ser.). 240p. 2000. pap. 9.99 (*0-7645-8573-8*) IDG Bks.

***Othello.** Ed. by Cliffs Notes Staff. (Cliffs Notes Ser.). 128p. 2000. pap. 4.99 (*0-7645-8587-8*) IDG Bks.

Othello. Mark Dunster. 24p. (Orig.). 1995. pap. 5.00 (*0-89642-261-5*) Linden Pubs.

***Othello.** Gloria Levine. 32p. 1999. 9.95 (*1-56137-520-9*) Novel Units.

***Othello.** Gloria Levine. 40p. (YA). 1999. wbk. ed. 11.95 (*1-56137-521-7*) Novel Units.

***Othello.** Barbara A. Mowat & Paul Werstine. 1999. per. 9.95 (*0-671-04289-0*) S&S Trade.

Othello. Pechter. 1998. 29.00 (*0-8057-7849-7*) Mac Lib Ref.

Othello. Contrib. by Garmini Salgado & Fenella Salgado. (Penguin Critical Studies). 96p. 2000. pap. 9.95 (*0-14-077194-8*, Pub. by Pnguin Bks Ltd) Trafalgar.

Othello. William Shakespeare. Ed. by Alvin B. Kernan. 288p. 1999. pap. text 2.67 (*0-451-52132-3*) Addson-Wesley Educ.

Othello. William Shakespeare. (Illustrated Classics Shakespeare Collection). 64p. 1994. pap. 4.95 (*0-7854-0810-X*, 40612) Am Guidance.

Othello. William Shakespeare. 1987. 40.00 (*0-8453-4521-4*) Assoc Univ Prs.

Othello. William Shakespeare. Ed. by David Bevington et al. (Classics Ser.). 208p. 1988. mass mkt. 3.95 (*0-553-21302-4*, Bantam Classics) Bantam.

Othello. William Shakespeare. Ed. by Norman Sanders. (New Cambridge Shakespeare Ser.). (Illus.). 223p. 1984. text 44.95 (*0-521-22339-3*); pap. text 11.95 (*0-521-29454-1*) Cambridge U Pr.

Othello. William Shakespeare. Ed. by Jane Coles. (Cambridge School Shakespeare Ser.). (Illus.). 240p. (C). 1992. pap. 11.95 (*0-521-39576-3*) Cambridge U Pr.

Othello. William Shakespeare. 1989. lib. bdg. 27.95 (*0-7910-0926-2*) Chelsea Hse.

Othello. William Shakespeare. Ed. by Harold Bloom. (Bloom's Notes Ser.). 1998. pap. 4.95 (*0-7910-4145-X*) Chelsea Hse.

Othello. William Shakespeare. Ed. & Tr. by Angel-Luis Pujante. (Nueva Austral Ser.: Vol. 185). (SPA.). 1991. pap. text 24.95 (*84-239-1985-4*) Elliots Bks.

Othello. William Shakespeare. Ed. by Roma Gill. (Oxford School Shakespeare Ser.). (C). 1994. text 10.72 (*0-669-40353-9*) HM Trade Div.

Othello. William Shakespeare. LC 96-17306. (Shorter Shakespeare Ser.). 1996. 9.95 (*0-02-861231-0*) Macmillan.

***Othello.** William Shakespeare. (Big Works Collection). (Illus.). 1p. 1999. 29.95 (*1-929142-13-7*) One Page Bk.

Othello. William Shakespeare. Ed. by Paul Werstine & Barbara Mowat. (New Folger Library Ser.). (Illus.). 368p. 1993. per. 3.99 (*0-671-72281-6*, Folger Shake Ser) PB.

Othello. William Shakespeare. 1996. 18.00 incl. audio (*0-679-44927-2*) Random Hse Value.

Othello. William Shakespeare. Ed. by John Andrews. 256p. 1997. 3.95 (*0-460-87517-5*, Everyman's Classic Lib) Tuttle Pubng.

Othello. William Shakespeare. Ed. by Smith. (Exeter French Texts Ser.: Vol. 80). (FRE.). 116p. Date not set. pap. text 19.95 (*0-85989-362-6*, Pub. by Univ Exeter Pr) Northwestern U Pr.

Othello. William Shakespeare. Ed. by Gerald E. Bentley, Jr. (Pelican Shakespeare Ser.). 160p. 1958. pap. 3.95 (*0-14-071410-3*, Pelican Bks) Viking Penguin.

Othello. William Shakespeare. Ed. by Kenneth Muir. (New Penguin Shakespeare Ser.). 240p. 1981. pap. 5.95 (*0-14-070707-7*, Penguin Classics) Viking Penguin.

Othello. William Shakespeare. LC 83-12538. (Illus.). 130p. (YA). (gr. 7 up). 1999. pap. 7.95 (*0-89480-611-4*, 611) Workman Pub.

Othello. William Shakespeare. (Classics Library). 160p. 1997. pap. 3.95 (*1-85326-018-5*, 0185WW, Pub. by Wrdsworth Edits) NTC Contemp Pub Co.

O

Othello. William Shakespeare. Ed. by John R. Brown. (Shakespeare Library). 192p. 2000. pap. 7.95 (*1-55783-386-9*) Applause Theatre Bk Pubs.

Othello. deluxe limited ed. William Shakespeare. (Illus.). 128p. 1973. boxed set 1650.00 (*1-55660-239-1*) A Wofsy Fine Arts.

Othello. large type ed. William Shakespeare. 1991. pap. 24.95 (*0-7089-4504-X*, Charnwood) Ulverscroft.

Othello see New Variorum Edition of Shakespeare

Othello. unabridged ed. William Shakespeare. (Dover Thrift Editions Ser.). 112p. 1996. reprint ed. pap. 1.00 (*0-486-29097-2*) Dover.

Othello. rev. ed. William Shakespeare. Ed. by Alvin Kernan. (Signet Classics Ser.). 246p. 1998. mass mkt. 3.95 (*0-451-52685-6*, Sig Classics) NAL.

Othello. 2nd rev. ed. William Shakespeare. Ed. by Roma Gill. (Oxford School Shakespeare Ser.). (Illus.). 162p. (YA). (gr. 6 up). 1994. pap. text 7.95 (*0-19-831978-9*) OUP.

Othello. 3rd ed. William Shakespeare. Ed. by E. A. J. Honigmann. LC 95-42926. (English). 300p. 1996. pap. 9.95 (*0-415-01515-4*) Thomson Learn.

Othello. 3rd ed. William Shakespeare. Ed. by E. A. Honigmann. (Arden Shakespeare Ser.). 1996. 9.95 (*0-17-443464-2*) Thomson Learn.

Othello. 3rd ed. William Shakespeare. (English). (C). 1997. lib. bdg. 45.00 (*0-17-443465-0*) Wadsworth Pub.

Othello. 7th ed. William Shakespeare. 1958. pap. 9.95 (*0-415-02701-2*); pap. 45.00 (*0-416-47440-3*) Thomson Learn.

Othello. 7th rev. ed. William Shakespeare. Ed. by Maurice R. Ridley & E. A. J. Honigmann. LC 95-42926. (English). 1996. pap. 45.00 (*0-415-01514-6*, NO. 2484) Thomson Learn.

Othello, Set. abr. ed. William Shakespeare. 1995. audio 18.00 (*1-55994-730-6*, CPN 225) HarperAudio.

Othello: A Contextual History. Virginia M. Vaughan. 257p. 1997. pap. text 19.95 (*0-521-58708-5*) Cambridge U Pr.

Othello: A Guide to the Play. Ed. by Joan Lord Hall. LC 98-46817. (Guides to Shakespeare Ser.). 240p. 1999. lib. bdg. 49.95 (*0-313-30263-4*) Greenwood.

Othello: A Novel. William Shakespeare. 176p. (YA). (gr. 7-12). 1998. mass mkt. 3.99 (*0-590-41966-8*) Scholastic Inc.

Othello: A Novel. William Shakespeare. 1998. 9.09 (*0-606-13009-8*, Pub. by Turtleback) Demco.

Othello: A Unit Plan. Mary B. Collins. 170p. 1994. teacher ed., ring bd. 26.95 (*1-58337-111-7*) Teachers Pet Pubns.

Othello: An Historical & Comparative Study. Elmer E. Stoll. LC 67-21714. 70p. 1967. reprint ed. 30.00 (*0-87752-108-5*) Gordian.

Othello: An Historical & Comparative Study. Elmer E. Stoll. LC 65-15888. (Studies in Shakespeare: No. 24). (C). 1969. reprint ed. lib. bdg. 75.00 (*0-8383-0630-6*) M S G Haskell Hse.

Othello: An Historical & Comparative Study. Elmer E. Stoll. (BCL1-PR English Literature Ser.). 70p. 1992. reprint ed. lib. bdg. 59.00 (*0-7812-7273-4*) Rprt Serv.

Othello: Curriculum Unit. Center for Learning Network Staff & William Shakespeare. (Shakespeare Ser.). 83p. (YA). (gr. 9-12). 1992. reprint ed. spiral bd. 18.95 (*1-56077-254-9*) Ctr Learning.

O

Othello: Dual Edition. James Scott. 112p. 1998. wbk. ed. 6.75 (*1-58049-503-6*, SBS15) Prestwick Hse.

Othello: Granville Barkers Preface to Shakespeare. William Shakespeare. Ed. by Granville Barker. 224p. 1995. pap. 6.95 (*0-435-08655-3*, 08655) Heinemann.

Othello: Modern Text with Introduction. William Shakespeare. Ed. & Intro. by A. L. Rowse. (Contemporary Shakespeare Ser.: Vol. IV). 154p. (Orig.). (C). 1986. pap. text 3.45 (*0-8191-3925-4*) U Pr of Amer.

Othello: Nabil Kanso Paintings. limited ed. Nabil Kanso. LC 96-67929. (Illus.). 92p. 1996. 55.00 (*1-888536-19-5*) Nev Editions.

Othello: New Essays by Black Writers. Ed. by Mythili Kaul. LC 96-47192. 232p. (Orig.). (C). 1997. pap. text 19.95 (*0-88258-191-0*, KAONP) Howard U Pr.

Othello: New Perspectives. Ed. by Virginia M. Vaughan & Kent Cartwright. LC 89-46413. 280p. 1996. pap. 18.95 (*0-8386-3708-6*) Fairleigh Dickinson.

Othello: New Swan Shakespeare Advanced Series. William Shakespeare. Ed. by Gamini Salgado. (New Swan Shakespeare Ser.). 1990. pap. 9.95 (*0-582-52748-1*, Drumbeat) Longman.

Othello: Reproducible Teaching Unit. rev. ed. James Scott. 43p. (YA). (gr. 7-12). 1995. teacher ed., ring bd. 29.50 (*1-58049-074-3*, TU35/U) Prestwick Hse.

Othello: The Moor of Venice. William Shakespeare. LC 73-14771. (Shakespeare Ser.). 1974. pap. 7.50 (*0-672-61106-6*, Bobbs) Macmillan.

***Othello: The New Variorum Edition.** William Shakespeare. Ed. by Horace Howard Furness. LC 00-29515. 2000. pap. 14.95 (*0-486-41467-1*) Dover.

Othello: The World's Great Drama: Drama Centered Language Arts Activities. abr. ed. James Scott. 56p. (YA). (gr. 7-12). 1999. wbk. ed. 3.50 (*1-58049-373-4*, GD04A) Prestwick Hse.

Othello, a Critical Study. William R. Turnbull. LC 73-177578. xii, 392p. reprint ed. 52.50 (*0-404-06529-5*) AMS Pr.

"Othello" & Interpretive Traditions. Edward Pechter. LC 99-20943. (Studies in Theatre History & Culture). (Illus.). 272p. 1999. text 32.95 (*0-87745-685-2*) U of Iowa Pr.

Othello & Other Stories from Shakespeare's Plays. William Shakespeare. Ed. by D. H. Howe. (Illus.). 110p. 1993. pap. text 5.95 (*0-19-585465-9*) OUP.

Othello Complete Study Edition. Ed. by Sidney Lamb. (Cliffs Notes Ser.). 101p. 1966. pap. 6.95 (*0-8220-1434-3*, Cliff) IDG Bks.

Othello in Wonderland & Mirror-Polishing Storytellers. Gholamboseyn Sa'edi. Ed. by Mohammad R. Ghanoonparvar. Tr. by Michael Phillips from PER. LC 96-44025. (Bibliotheca Iranica Ser.: No. 2). 160p. (Orig.). 1996. pap. 13.95 (*1-56859-046-6*) Mazda Pubs.

Othello Notes. Gary Carey & Paul A. Jorgenson. (Cliffs Notes Ser.). 88p. 1959. pap. 4.95 (*0-8220-0063-6*, Cliff) IDG Bks.

Othello or Tracking the Green-Eyed Monster. Nancy Linehan Charles. 48p. Date not set. pap. 5.60 (*1-58342-027-4*, O63) Dramatic Pub.

Othello Readalong. William Shakespeare. (Illustrated Classics Shakespeare Collection). 64p. 1994. pap. 14.95 incl. audio (*0-7854-0826-6*, 40614) Am Guidance.

Othello, the Moor of Venice. William Shakespeare. Ed. & Illus. by Diane Davidson. LC 83-60730. (Shakespeare on Stage Ser.: Vol. 8). 142p. (YA). (gr. 8-12). 1985. pap. 6.95 (*0-934048-16-9*) Lrn Links.

Othello, the Moor of Venice. William Shakespeare. (C). 3.95 (*0-671-00640-1*, Arco) Macmillan Gen Ref.

Othello, the Moor of Venice & Taming of the Shrew see Shakespeare Yesterday - Today, 1989-1998

Othello's Sacrifice: Essays on Shakespeare & Romantic Tradition. John O'Meara. LC 95-81892. 128p. Date not set. pap. 10.00 (*1-55071-040-0*) Guernica Editions.

Other see Otra: Marriage Meltdown

Other see Otro

***Other.** K. A. Applegate. (Animorphs Ser.: Vol. 40). (Illus.). (J). 2000. 10.34 (*0-606-18511-9*) Turtleback.

Other. Gordon Rupert Dickson. 576p. 1995. mass mkt. 6.99 (*0-8125-1599-4*, Pub. by Tor Bks) St Martin.

Other. Thomas Tryon. 1993. reprint ed. lib. bdg. 27.95 (*0-89968-443-2*, Lghtyr Pr) Buccaneer Bks.

Other: British & Irish Poetry since 1970. Ed. by Richard Caddel & Peter Quartermain. LC 98-39557. (Wesleyan Poetry Ser.). 312p. 1999. pap. 19.95 (*0-8195-2258-9*, Wesleyan Univ Pr) U Pr of New Eng.

Other Alice: The Story of Alice Liddell & Alice in Wonderland. Christina Bjork. Tr. by Joan Sandlin from SWE. LC 93-662. (Illus.). 100p. (J). 1993. 18.00 (*91-29-62242-5*, Pub. by R & S Bks) FS&G.

***Other Alice: The Story of Alice Liddell & Alice in Wonderland.** Christina Bjork & Inga-Karin Erikkson. (Illus.). 93p. 1999. reprint ed. text 18.00 (*0-7881-6848-7*) DIANE Pub.

Other Amanda. Lynn Leslie. (Loving Dangerously Ser.). 1997. per. 3.99 (*0-373-70735-5*, 1-70735-5) Harlequin Bks.

Other America. Harrington. 1997. per. 10.00 (*0-684-82678-X*) S&S Trade.

Other America. Carl Stegmann. Tr. by Maria St. Goar from GER.Tr. of Das Andere Amerika. xvi, 280p. 1997. pap. 21.95 (*0-945803-28-1*, 00129) R Steiner Col.

Other America: Art & the Labour Movement in the United States. Ed. by Philip S. Foner & Reinhard Schultz. 176p. (Orig.). 1990. pap. text 14.95 (*0-685-31952-0*) Routledge.

Other America: Caribbean Literature in a New World Context. J. Michael Dash. LC 97-38884. (New World Studies Ser.). 224p. 1998. text 42.50 (*0-8139-1763-8*); pap. text 18.50 (*0-8139-1764-6*) U Pr of Va.

Other America: Poverty in the United States. Michael Harrington. LC 93-10798. 231p. 1994. pap. 9.00 (*0-02-020763-8*) Macmillan.

***Other American: The Life of Michael Harrington.** Maurice Isserman. LC 99-56654. (Illus.). 464p. 2000. 27.50 (*1-891620-30-4*, Pub. by PublicAffairs NY) HarpC.

Other American Drama. Marc Robinson. LC 96-53224. 216p. 1997. pap. 14.95 (*0-8018-5630-2*) Johns Hopkins.

Other American Traditions: Nineteenth-Century Women Writers. Ed. by Joyce W. Warren. LC 92-10879. 380p. (C). 1993. 45.00 (*0-8135-1910-1*); pap. 16.95 (*0-8135-1911-X*) Rutgers U Pr.

Other Americans: How Immigrants Renew Our Country, Our Economy, & Our Values. Joel Millman. LC 96-49265. 369p. 1998. pap. 13.95 (*0-14-024217-1*) Viking Penguin.

Other Americans: Sexual Variance in the National Past. Charles O. Jackson. LC 95-52995. 280p. 1996. 65.00 (*0-275-95550-8*, Praeger Pubs); pap. 27.95 (*0-275-95551-6*, Praeger Pubs) Greenwood.

Other Americans, Other Americas: The Politics & Poetics of Multiculturalism. Ed. by Magdalena J. Zaborowska. LC 99-163793. (Dolphin Ser.: Vol. 28). (Illus.). 215p. 1998. pap. 19.95 (*87-7288-379-0*, Pub. by Aarhus Univ Pr) David Brown.

Other Anna. Barbara Esstman. LC 92-33107. 1993. 22.95 (*0-15-170410-4*) Harcourt.

Other Anna: A Novel. Barbara Esstman. LC 98-50457. 384p. 1999. pap. 13.00 (*0-06-097767-1*) HarpC.

Other Annapolis. Philip L. Brown. (Illus.). 148p. 1994. 27.50 (*1-884878-00-8*) Annapol Pubng.

Other Apostolates Today: Selected Letters & Addresses - III. Pedro Arrupe. Ed. by Jerome Aixala. LC 81-80741. xvi, 365p. 1981. 4.50 (*0-912422-81-5*); pap. 4.00 (*0-912422-80-7*) Inst Jesuit.

Other Approaches to Civil-Military Integration: The Chinese & Japanese Arms Industries. (Illus.). 141p. (Orig.). (C). 1995. pap. text 30.00 (*0-7881-2492-7*) DIANE Pub.

Other Approaches to Civil-Military Integration: The Chinese & Japanese Arms Industries. (Orig.). 1996. lib. bdg. 251.95 (*0-8490-5988-7*) Gordon Pr.

Other Arab-Israeli Conflict: Making America's Middle East Policy, from Truman to Reagan. Steven L. Spiegel. LC 84-16253. xvi, 538p. 1986. pap. text 39.00 (*0-226-76962-3*) U Ch Pr.

Other Arab-Israeli Conflict: Making America's Middle East Policy, from Truman to Reagan. Steven L. Spiegel. LC 84-16253. xvi, 522p. 1993. 24.95 (*0-226-76961-5*) U Ch Pr.

Other Argentina: The Interior & National Development. Larry Sawers. LC 95-45573. (C). 1996. pap. 79.00 (*0-8133-2750-4*, Pub. by Westview) HarpC.

Other Argentina: The Interior & National Development. Larry Sawers. 336p. 1996. pap. 28.00 (*0-8133-3548-5*, Pub. by Westview) HarpC.

Other Art. John Harris. LC 98-140379. 240p. 1997. pap. 12.00 (*0-921586-58-2*, Pub. by New Star Bks) Genl Dist Srvs.

Other Atlantis. Robert J. Scrutton. reprint ed. write for info. (*0-85978-021-X*, Pub. by C W Daniel) Natl Bk Netwk.

Other Australia: Experiences of Migration. Brian Murphy. LC 92-42536. (Illus.). 284p. (C). 1993. text 64.95 (*0-521-44194-3*) Cambridge U Pr.

Other Austrians: Post-1945 Austrian Women's Writing: Proceedings of the Conference Held at Nottingham from 18-20 April, 1996. Ed. by Allyson Fiddler. LC 98-24078. 247p. (C). 1998. pap. text 52.95 (*0-8204-3446-9*) P Lang Pubng.

"Other" Austrians: Post-1945 Austrian Women's Writing: Proceedings of the Conference Held at Nottingham from 18-20 April, 1996. Ed. by Allyson Fiddler. 247p. 1998. pap. 52.95 (*3-906756-40-8*) P Lang Pubng.

Other Battle: Luftwaffe Night Aces vs. Bomber Command. Peter Hinchliffe. LC 97-100843. (Illus.). 352p. 1996. 29.95 (*0-7603-0265-0*) MBI Pubg.

Other Battle of the Bulge. Charles Whiting. LC 90-42276. (Illus.). 200p. 1990. 19.95 (*0-8128-4004-6*, Scrbrough Hse) Madison Bks UPA.

Other Battle of the Bulge: Operation Northwind. Charles Whiting. 240p. 1992. mass mkt. 4.99 (*0-380-71628-3*, Avon Bks) Morrow Avon.

***Other Bells for Us to Ring.** Robert Cormier. 2000. mass mkt. 4.99 (*0-440-22862-X*, LE) Dell.

Other Bells for Us to Ring. Robert Cormier. 1990. 9.09 (*0-606-02821-8*, Pub. by Turtleback) Demco.

Other Bible. Ed. by Willis Barnstone. LC 83-48416. 768p. 1984. pap. 28.00 (*0-06-250030-9*, CN 4087, Pub. by Harper SF) HarpC.

Other Boston: A Vision for the Future. Ed. by Yohel Camayd-Freixas et al. LC 88-51167. 180p. (Orig.). 1988. pap. 25.00 (*0-923206-01-9*) Boston UR & DG.

Other Bostonians: Poverty & Progress in the American Metropolis, 1880-1970. Stephan A. Thernstrom. LC 73-77469. (Studies in Urban History). 360p. (C). 1973. pap. 15.95 (*0-674-64496-4*) HUP.

Other Brahmins: Boston's Black Upper Class, 1750-1950. Adelaide M. Cromwell. LC 93-41949. 216p. 1994. text 32.00 (*1-55728-301-X*) U of Ark Pr.

Other Britain, Other British: Essays in Contemporary Multicultural Fiction. Lee. 1996. pap. 18.95 (*0-7453-0646-2*, Pub. by Pluto GBR) Stylus Pub VA.

Other Brother. Melody Carlson. LC 99-16674. (Illus.). 40p. (J). (gr. 3-6). 1999. 9.99 (*1-58134-122-9*) Crossway Bks.

Other Brother. large type ed. Sherry Lynn Ferguson. (Dales Large Print Ser.). 209p. 1997. pap. 18.99 (*1-85389-684-5*) Ulverscroft.

Other California: The Great Central Valley in Life & Literature. rev. ed. Gerald W. Haslam. LC 93-30734. (Western Literature Ser.). 208p. 1993. pap. 13.95 (*0-87417-225-X*) U of Nev Pr.

Other Californians: Prejudice & Discrimination under Spain, Mexico, & the United States to 1920. Robert F. Heizer & Alan J. Almquist. LC 76-121186. 1971. pap. 14.95 (*0-520-03415-5*, Pub. by U CA Pr) Cal Prin Full Svc.

Other Canadas: An Anthology of Science Fiction & Fantasy. John Robert Colombo. LC 80-487461. 360 p. 1979. write for info. (*0-07-082952-7*) McGraw.

Other Candidates: Third Parties in Presidential Elections. Frank Smallwood. LC 82-40478. 333p. reprint ed. pap. 103.30 (*0-7837-6206-2*, 204592700009) Bks Demand.

Other Capri. Kelly F. Cook & Dwain L. Kitchel. (Illus.). 201p. (Orig.). 1992. pap. 10.00 (*1-882194-00-4*) TN Valley Pub.

Other Carl Sandburg. Philip R. Yannella. LC 96-17019. 264p. 1996. 27.00 (*0-87805-941-5*) U Pr of Miss.

Other Casanova: A Contribution to 18th-Century Music & Manners. Paul Nettl. LC 73-107872. (Music Ser.). (Illus.). 1970. reprint ed. lib. bdg. 39.50 (*0-306-71896-0*) Da Capo.

Other Catholics. Keith P. Dyrud et al. 1978. 36.95 (*0-405-10820-6*) Ayer.

Other Cats: Six Handmade Books of Poems about Cats. Ed. by Malachi McCormick. (Illus.). 120p. 1983. pap., boxed set 24.00 (*0-943984-06-8*) Stone St Pr.

Other Cheek. large type ed. Genevieve Lyons. LC 98-41738. 411p. 1998. pap. write for info. (*0-7540-2163-7*, G K Hall Lrg Type) Mac Lib Ref.

Other Cheek. large type ed. Genevieve Lyons. LC 98-41738. 1998. 25.95 (*0-7838-0389-3*, G K Hall Lrg Type) Mac Lib Ref.

Other Children. Lawrence Raab. LC 86-70208. (Poetry Ser.). 80p. (C). 1987. 20.95 (*0-88748-028-4*); pap. 11.95 (*0-88748-029-2*) Carnegie-Mellon.

Other Children, Other Languages: Issues in the Theory of Language Acquisition. Ed. by Yonata Levy. 424p. 1994. text 79.95 (*0-8058-1330-6*) L Erlbaum Assocs.

Other China: Journeys Around Taiwan. Douglas Fetherling. LC 96-138616. 128p. 1996. pap. 12.95 (*1-55152-025-7*, Pub. by Arsenal Pulp) LPC InBook.

***Other Chinas: The Yao & the Politics of National Belonging.** Ralph A. Litzinger. LC 99-87369. (Illus.). 344p. 2000. pap. 21.95 (*0-8223-2549-7*) Duke.

***Other Chinas: The Yao & the Politics of National Belonging.** Ralph A. Litzinger. LC 99-87369. (Illus.). 344p. 2000. lib. bdg. 64.95 (*0-8223-2525-X*) Duke.

Other Choices for Becoming a Woman. Joyce Mitchell. (YA). (gr. 7 up). 1975. pap. 6.00 (*0-912786-34-5*) Know Inc.

Other City: People & Politics in New York & London. Ed. by Susanne MacGregor & Arthur Lipow. LC 94-24212. 256p. (C). 1995. pap. 18.50 (*0-391-03885-0*) Humanities.

Other City: People & Politics in New York & London. Ed. by Susanne MacGregor & Arthur Lipow. LC 94-24212. 256p. (C). 1995. text 49.95 (*0-391-03852-4*) Humanities.

***Other Civil War: American Women in the Nineteenth Century.** rev. ed. Catherine Clinton. LC 98-52075. 12p. 1999. pap. 13.00 (*0-8090-1622-2*) Hill & Wang.

***Other Colombia: Conversations with Rebels, Warlords & Doves.** Ann Carrigan. (Open Media Pamphlet Ser.: Vol. 19). 80p. 2000. pap. 6.95 (*1-58322-043-7*, Pub. by Seven Stories) Publishers Group.

Other Concerns & Brother Clark. Hollis S. Summers. LC 88-19655. 77p. 1988. 17.95 (*0-8214-0910-7*); pap. 8.95 (*0-8214-0911-5*) Ohio U Pr.

Other Correspondence of Lavrou & Varic (Russian Text) see Lavrou-Years of Emigration: Letters & Documents

Other Council Fires Were Here Before Ours: A Classic Native American Creation Story As Retold by a Seneca Elder & Her Granddaughter. Twylah H. Nitsch & Jamie Sams. LC 90-55307. (Illus.). 160p. (Orig.). 1991. pap. 17.00 (*0-06-250763-X*, Pub. by Harper SF) HarpC.

Other Country. Carol A. Duffy. 56p. 1993. pap. 14.95 (*0-85646-226-8*, Pub. by Anvil Press) Dufour.

Other Country: Patterns in the Writings of Alice Munro. James Carslallen. 560p. (C). 1993. pap. text 40.00 (*1-55022-163-9*, Pub. by ECW) Genl Dist Srvs.

Other Creations. Christopher Manes. 1910. mass mkt. 14.95 (*0-385-48368-6*) Doubleday.

Other Criteria: Confrontations with Twentieth-Century Art. Leo Steinberg. LC 72-77502. (Illus.). 436p. 1975. pap. 32.50 (*0-19-501846-X*) OUP.

Other Cultures, Elder Years: An Introduction to Cultural Gerontology. 2nd ed. Ellen R. Holmes & Lowell D. Holmes. LC 95-3737. (Illus.). 324p. 1995. 52.00 (*0-8039-5133-7*) Sage.

Other Cultures, Elder Years: An Introduction to Cultural Gerontology. 2nd ed. Ellen R. Holmes & Lowell D. Holmes. LC 95-3737. (Illus.). 288p. 1995. pap. 24.00 (*0-8039-5134-5*) Sage.

Other Dancers. Justin Spring. Ed. by Robert Bixby. 24p. (Orig.). 1991. pap. 6.00 (*0-9624453-5-5*) March Street Pr.

Other Darker Ned. large type ed. Anne Fine. (J). 1997. 16.95 (*0-7451-5494-8*, Galaxy Child Lrg Print) Chivers N Amer.

Other Daughter. Lisa Gardner. 404p. 1999. mass mkt. 6.50 (*0-553-57679-8*) Bantam.

***Other Daughter, Lp.** 2000. 30.00 (*0-7862-2290-5*) Mac Lib Ref.

Other Days. William Winter. LC 77-121513. (Essay Index Reprint Ser.). 1977. 26.95 (*0-8369-1816-9*) Ayer.

Other Days: Being Chronicles & Memories of the Stage. William Winter. (Notable American Authors Ser.). 1999. reprint ed. lib. bdg. 125.00 (*0-7812-7777-9*) Rprt Serv.

Other Days: Selected Poems. rev. ed. Donald E. Sharp. (Illus.). 132p. 1988. pap. 5.95 (*0-9620273-0-8*) Donano Pr.

Other Days Around Me: A Memoir. Richard Hough. (Illus.). 288p. 1992. 45.00 (*0-340-55221-2*, Pub. by Hodder & Stought Ltd) Trafalgar.

Other Days in Greenwich [CT]. Frederick A. Hubbard. (Illus.). xviii, 346p. 1997. reprint ed. pap. 23.50 (*0-7884-0637-X*, H801) Heritage Bk.

Other Days in Greenwich or Tales & Reminiscences of an Old New England Town. F. A. Hubbard. (Illus.). 363p. 1989. reprint ed. lib. bdg. 37.50 (*0-8328-0558-0*) Higginson Bk Co.

Other Desert War: British Special Forces in North Africa, 1940-1943, 56. John W. Gordon. LC 86-9969. (Contributions in Military Studies Ser.: No. 56). (Illus.). 264p. 1987. 65.00 (*0-313-25240-8*, GSP/, Greenwood Pr) Greenwood.

Other Destinies: Understanding the American Indian Novel. Louis Owens. LC 92-3507. (American Indian Literature & Critical Studies: Vol. 3). 302p. (Orig.). 1994. pap. 13.95 (*0-8061-2673-6*) U of Okla Pr.

Other Devil's Name. large type ed. E. X. Ferrars. 320p. 1988. 5.99 (*0-7089-1833-6*) Ulverscroft.

Other Diabetes: Living & Eating Well with Type 2 Diabetes. Elizabeth Hiser. LC 98-47490. 256p. 1999. 23.00 (*0-688-15329-1*, Wm Morrow) Morrow Avon.

***Other Dickens: Pickwick to Chuzzlewit.** John Bowen. LC 99-16104. 240p. 2000. text 70.00 (*0-19-818506-5*) OUP.

Other Door: Stories. Karen Heuler. 168p. (C). 1995. pap. 17.95 (*0-8262-1041-4*) U of Mo Pr.

Other Dreams. 2nd rev. ed. Nicholas Ifkovits. LC 98-93360. 227p. 1999. pap. 11.95 (*0-9651700-3-9*) Counter-Force Pr.

Other Economy: Pastoral Husbandry on a Medieval Estate. Kathleen Biddick. 274p. (C). 1989. 50.00 (*0-520-06388-0*, Pub. by U CA Pr) Cal Prin Full Svc.

Other Edens. Christopher Evans & Robert Holdstock. LC 88-108796. ix, 237p. 1987. pap. write for info. (*0-04-823378-1*, Pub. by Allen & Unwin Pty) Paul & Co Pubs.

Other Edens. Nick Waplington. (Illus.). 88p. 1994. 60.00 (*0-89381-587-X*) Aperture.

Other Edens: The Sketchbook of an Artist Naturalist. John H. Dick. LC 79-67270. (Illus.). 1979. 19.95 (*0-8159-6412-9*) Devin.

Other 18th Century: English Women of Letters, 1660-1800. Ed. by Robert W. Uphaus & Gretchen M. Foster. 475p. 1991. 29.95 (*0-937191-39-6*) Mich St U Pr.

Other 18th Century: English Women of Letters, 1660-1800. Ed. by Robert W. Uphaus & Gretchen M. Foster. 475p. 1994. pap. text 19.95 (*0-937191-40-X*) Mich St U Pr.

***"Other" Eighteenth Century: English Women of Letters, 1660-1800.** Robert W. Uphaus & Gretchen M. Foster. LC 99-88851. 2000. write for info. (*0-87013-438-8*) Mich St U Pr.

Other Elites: Women, Politics, & Power in the Executive Branch. Maryanne Borrelli & Janet M. Martin. LC 96-43234. 1997. 55.00 (*1-55587-658-7*) L Rienner.

Other Emily. Gibbs Davis. (Illus.). 32p. (J). (gr. k-3). 1990. pap. 4.95 (*0-395-54947-7*) HM.

"Other Eminent Men of Wilford Woodruff" Vicki J. Anderson. 413p. 1994. 17.95 (*0-9642524-0-6*) Zichron Histrcl.

Other End of Time. Frederik Pohl. 1997. mass mkt. 6.99 (*0-614-27805-8*); mass mkt. 6.99 (*0-8125-3519-7*, Pub. by Tor Bks) St Martin.

***Other Enemy? Australian Soldiers & the Military Police.** Glen Wahlert. (Australian Army History Ser.). 256p. 2000. 39.95 (*0-19-551189-1*) OUP.

Other Energy Crisis: Firewood. Erik P. Eckholm. (Worldwatch Papers). 1975. pap. 5.00 (*0-916468-00-3*) Worldwatch Inst.

***Other Esteem: Meaningful Life in a Multicultural Society.** Philip O. Hwang. LC 00-25013. (Illus.). 192p. 2000. pap. 19.95 (*1-56032-876-2*) Taylor & Francis.

Other Europe: Eastern Europe to 1945. E. Garrison Walters. (Illus.). 512p. (C). 1988. pap. 18.50 (*0-8156-2440-9*) Syracuse U Pr.

Other Europe: Eastern Europe to 1945. E. Garrison Walters. LC 87-28560. 448p. reprint ed. pap. 138.90 (*0-608-06971-X*, 206717900009) Bks Demand.

***Other Eye.** Jerry Kennealy. 2000. mass mkt. 6.99 (*0-451-40926-4*, Onyx) NAL.

***Other Eye of Isiris.** R. Austin Freeman. (R. Austin Freeman Omnibus Edition Ser.: Vol. 12). 254p. 1999. 28.00 (*1-55246-184-X*) Battered Silicon.

***Other Eye, Other Ear: An Epic Prose Poem.** Will Inman. Ed. by Eleanor Watson-Gove. 2000. 6.00 (*1-879457-86-5*) Norton Coker Pr.

***Other 'F' Word.** Barry Seltzer & Erwin Seltzer. 108p. 1998. pap. write for info. (*0-9664313-0-8*) Prism Pubng.

Other Face of India. M. V. Kamath. 150p. 1988. text 18.95 (*81-220-0088-6*, Pub. by Konark Pubs Pvt Ltd) Advent Bks Div.

Other Face of Love: Dialogues with the Prison Experience of Albert Speer. Miriam Pollard. 180p. 1996. 17.95 (*0-8245-1562-5*) Crossroad NY.

Other Fellow. Francis H. Smith. LC 77-98595. (Short Story Index Reprint Ser.). 1977. 20.95 (*0-8369-3170-X*) Ayer.

Other Feminists: Activists in the Liberal Establishment. Susan M. Hartmann. LC 98-15218. (Illus.). 224p. 1998. 30.00 (*0-300-07464-6*) Yale U Pr.

Other 50's: Interrogating Midcentury American Icons. Ed. by Joel Foreman. 336p. 1996. 17.95 (*0-252-06574-3*) U of Ill Pr.

Other 50 Percent: Multicultural Perspectives on Gender Relations. Ed. by Mari Womack & Judith Marti. (Illus.). 381p. (C). 1993. pap. text 17.95 (*0-88133-722-6*) Waveland Pr.

Other Floors, Other Voices: A Textography of a Small University Building. John M. Swales. LC 98-12631. (Rhetoric, Knowledge, & Society Ser.). 225p. 1998. write for info. (*0-8058-2087-6*); pap. write for info. (*0-8058-2088-4*) L Erlbaum Assocs.

Other Florida. 2nd rev. ed. Gloria Jahoda. LC 67-21339. (Florida Classics Ser.). (Illus.). 348p. 1984. reprint ed. pap. 12.95 (*0-912451-04-1*) Florida Classics.

Other Flute: A Performance Manual of Contemporary Techniques with 33.3 RPM Mono Record. 2nd ed. Robert Dick. LC 88-92275. 144p. 1989. spiral bd. 39.95 (*0-939407-02-7*) Multiple Breath Music.

Other Followers of Jesus: Minor Characters as Major Figures in Mark's Gospel. Joel F. Williams. LC 94-212063. (JSNTS Ser.: Vol. 102). 231p. 1994. 70.00 (*1-85075-489-6*, Pub. by Sheffield Acad) CUP Services.

Other Fools & Their Doings. H. N. Goff. LC 70-38651. (Black Heritage Library Collection). 1977. reprint ed. 21.95 (*0-8369-9009-9*) Ayer.

Other Foot see Creative Short Stories

Other Forty Niners: A Topical History of Sanpete Country, Utah 1849-1983. Sanpete County Commission. Ed. by Albert C. Antrei et al. (Illus.). 500p. 1982. 17.50 (*0-914740-26-1*) Western Epics.

Other Founders: Anti-Federalism & the Dissenting Tradition in America, 1788-1828. Saul Cornell. LC 99-13685. 352p. 1999. 55.00 (*0-8078-2503-4*); pap. 19.95 (*0-8078-4786-0*) U of NC Pr.

Other 1492: Jewish Settlement in the New World. Norman H. Finkelstein. LC 89-6253. (Illus.). 96p. (J). (gr. 5-9). 1989. lib. bdg. 13.95 (*0-684-18913-5*) Scribner.

Other Freud: Religion, Culture & Psychoanalysis. James DiCenso. LC 98-23772. 192p. (C). 1999. pap. 24.99 (*0-415-19659-0*, D6256) Routledge.

Other Freud: Religion, Culture & Psychoanalysis. James DiCenso. LC 98-23772. 192p. (C). (gr. 13). 1999. 75.00 (*0-415-19658-2*, D6252) Routledge.

Other Fronts. (World War One Ser.). Date not set. pap. text. write for info. (*0-582-22094-7*, Pub. by Addison-Wesley) Longman.

Other Gate, & Other Stories. Vere Hutchinson. LC 78-160935. (Short Story Index Reprint Ser.). 1977. reprint ed. 20.95 (*0-8369-3914-X*) Ayer.

Other Germanies: Questioning Identity in Women's Literature & Art. Ed. by Karen Jankowsky & Carla Love. LC 97-9844. (SUNY Series in Postmodern Culture). 318p. (C). 1997. text 59.50 (*0-7914-3449-4*); pap. text 19.95 (*0-7914-3450-8*) State U NY Pr.

***Other Gettysberg.** Creighton. 2000. 27.50 (*0-465-01456-9*, Pub. by Basic) HarpC.

***Other Gettysburg.** Creighton. 2000. pap. 16.00 (*0-465-01457-7*, Pub. by Basic) HarpC.

Other Gettysburg Addresses. Christina Glatfelter et al. (Illus.). 80p. (Orig.). 1988. pap. 6.50 (*0-9620686-0-8*) Off The Track Pr.

Other Girls. Ayres. 1999. pap. 16.95 (*0-9666750-3-7*, Pub. by Nocturnum Pr) Consort Bk Sales.

***Other God: Dualist Religions from Antiquity to the Cathar Heresy.** Yuri Stoyanov. 352p. 2000. pap. 14.95 (*0-300-08253-3*) Yale U Pr.

Other God that Failed: Hans Freyer & the Deradicalization of German Conservatism. Jerry Z. Muller. LC 87-18781. 465p. 1987. reprint ed. pap. 144.20 (*0-608-02577-1*, 206322300004) Bks Demand.

Other Gospels see Otros Evangelios

Other Gospels: Non-Canonical Gospel Texts. Ed. by Ron Cameron. LC 82-8662. 192p. 1982. pap. 19.95 (*0-664-24428-9*) Westminster John Knox.

Other Gospels: Non-Canonical Gospel Texts. Paul B. Smith. LC 76-867848. 160 p. 1970. write for info. (*0-551-05256-2*) M Pickering.

Other Government. Mark Green. 318p. 1975. 12.50 (*0-686-36548-8*) Ctr Responsive Law.

Other Government: Power & the Washington Media. William L. Rivers. LC 81-40694. 210p. 1982. text 15.00 (*0-87663-365-3*, Pub. by Universe) St Martin.

***Other Great Depression: How I'm Overcoming, on a Daily Basis, at Least a Million Addictions & Dysfunctions & Finding a Spiritual (Sometimes) Life.** Richard Lewis. 2001. 23.00 (*1-891620-93-2*) PublicAffairs NY.

Other Greeks: The Family Farm & the Agrarian Roots of Western Civilization. Victor D. Hanson. 350p. 1995. 28.00 (*0-02-913751-9*) Free Pr.

Other Greeks: The Family Farm & the Agrarian Roots of Western Civilization. Victor D. Hanson. LC 99-18181. 580p. 1999. pap. 18.95 (*0-520-20935-4*, Pub. by U CA Pr) Cal Prin Full Svc.

Other Guest. Sue Welford. LC 94-79398. (Ten-Minute Mysteries Ser.). 32p. (YA). (gr. 6-12). 1994. pap. 2.95 (*0-7854-0846-0*, 40769) Am Guidance.

Other Guest Readalong. Sue Welford. LC 94-79398. (Ten-Minute Mysteries Ser.). 32p. (YA). (gr. 6-12). 1994. pap. 12.95 incl. audio (*0-7854-1055-4*, 40771) Am Guidance.

Other Guy's Sperm: The Cause of Cancers & Other Diseases. Donald E. Tyler. LC 94-94234. 131p. 1994. pap. 14.95 (*1-884981-05-4*) Discov Bks.

Other Half: Glimpses of Grassroots Asia. Peter C. Stuart. LC 89-83723. 141p. (Orig.). 1989. pap. 9.95 (*0-9622350-4-0*) Far Horizon.

Other Half: Wives of Alcoholics. Jacqueline P. Wiseman. (Communication & Social Order Ser.). 310p. 1991. pap. text 25.95 (*0-202-30383-7*); lib. bdg. 47.95 (*0-202-30382-9*) Aldine de Gruyter.

Other Half of My Soul: Bede Griffiths & the Hindu-Christian Dialogue. Beatrice Bruteau. (Illus.). 300p. 1996. pap. 16.00 (*0-8356-0717-8*, Quest) Theos Pub Hse.

Other Half of the Truth about the Holocaust & Other Things. John Mertens. LC 99-164312. iv, 29p. 1997. pap. 12.00 (*1-891211-02-1*) Gazelle Books.

Other Half West Civilizat, Vol. 1. Hunter. 67.50 (*0-07-031375-X*) McGraw.

Other Half West Civilizat, Vol. 2. Hunter. 67.50 (*0-07-031376-8*) McGraw.

Other Hand Clapping. Marco Vassi. LC 86-62448. 160p. 1987. 22.00 (*0-932966-78-0*) Permanent Pr.

Other Heart. Jeff Worley. 36p. 1991. pap. 5.00 (*1-889806-03-X*) Devils Millhopper.

Other Heidegger. Fred Dallmayr. (Contestations Ser.). 248p. 1995. pap. text 15.95 (*0-8014-8140-6*) Cornell U Pr.

Other Hemisphere: Selected Poems. Jan Kemp. (Orig.). (YA). (gr. 10 up). 1991. pap. 10.00 (*1-57889-032-2*) Passeggiata.

Other Henry James. John C. Rowe. LC 98-18977. (New Americanists Ser.). 1998. 49.95 (*0-8223-2128-9*); pap. 17.95 (*0-8223-2147-5*) Duke.

Other High Crimes. David A. Gordon. 1994. 23.00 (*1-885823-00-2*) Macaulay & Wittenstein.

Other Histories. Ed. by Kirsten Hastrup. LC 92-984. (European Association of Social Anthropologists Ser.). 144p. (C). (gr. 13). 1992. 85.00 (*0-415-06122-9*, A5985) Routledge.

Other Hong Kong Report, 1995. Ed. by Stephen Y. Cheung & Stephen M. Sze. (Hong Kong Ser.). 486p. (C). 1997. pap. text 34.50 (*962-201-681-2*, Pub. by Chinese Univ) U of Mich Pr.

Other Hong Kong Report, 1998. Ed. by Yiu-Kwan Fan & Larry C. Chow. 450p. 1998. pap. 34.50 (*962-201-829-7*, Pub. by Chinese Univ) U of Mich Pr.

Other Hong Kong Report, 1994. Ed. by Donald H. McMillen & Man Si-Wai. (Hong Kong Ser.). 502p. 1994. pap. 49.50 (*962-201-633-2*, Pub. by Chinese Univ) Coronet Bks.

Other Hong Kong Report, 1996. Ed. by Nyaw Mee-kau & Li Si-ming. (Illus.). 537p. (Orig.). 1997. pap. text 34.50 (*962-201-715-0*, Pub. by Chinese Univ) U of Mich Pr.

Other Hong Kong Report 1997. Ed. by Joseph Y. Cheng. 1997. pap. 32.50 (*962-201-778-9*, Pub. by Chinese Univ) U of Mich Pr.

Other House. Henry James. LC 77-17499. (J). 1978. write for info. (*0-89244-083-X*) Queens Hse-Focus Serv.

Other House. Henry James. Ed. by Tony Tanner. 224p. 1996. 4.95 (*0-460-87806-9*, Everyman's Classic Lib) Tuttle Pubng.

Other House. Henry James. 228p. 1976. reprint ed. lib. bdg. 27.95 (*0-89190-317-8*, Queens House) Amereon Ltd.

Other House. Henry James. LC 75-32756. (Literature of Mystery & Detection Ser.). 1976. reprint ed. 33.95 (*0-405-07880-3*) Ayer.

Other House. Henry James. LC 99-15893. 220p. 1999. reprint ed. pap. 12.95 (*0-940322-32-3*, Pub. by NY Rev Bks) Midpt Trade.

Other Housing Crisis: Sheltering the Poor in Rural America. Housing Assistance Council & Center on Budget & Policy Priorities Staff. 69p. 1989. 8.00 (*1-58064-078-8*) Housing Assist.

***Other Husserl: The Horizons of Transcendental Phenomenology.** Donn Welton. LC 00-38906. (ENG.). 2000. write for info. (*0-253-33795-X*) Ind U Pr.

Other I: The Fictions of Clark Blaise. Robert Lecker. 246p. (C). 1988. text 28.00 (*1-55022-083-7*, Pub. by ECW); pap. text 16.00 (*1-55022-082-9*, Pub. by ECW) Genl Dist Srvs.

Other Image: A Collection of New Translations & Articles about Translation. Ed. by Rich Ives. 87p. (Orig.). 1984. pap. 7.00 (*0-937669-14-8*) Owl Creek Pr.

Other in Jewish Thought & History: Constructions of Jewish Culture & Identity. Ed. by Laurence J. Silberstein & Robert L. Cohn. LC 94-10880. (New Perspectives on Jewish Studies). 520p. (C). 1994. text 55.00 (*0-8147-7989-1*); pap. text 20.00 (*0-8147-7990-5*) NYU Pr.

Other India. Bahadur I. Singh. 263p. 1979. 14.95 (*0-318-36943-5*) Asia Bk Corp.

Other India: Seven Contemporary Indian Photographers. Intro. by David Elliott. 1982. pap. 20.00 (*0-905836-31-6*, Pub. by Museum Modern Art) St Mut.

Other Inquisitions, 1937-1952. Jorge Luis Borges. Tr. by Ruth L. Simms from SPA. (Texas Pan American Ser.). 223p. 1964. pap. 14.95 (*0-292-76002-7*) U of Tex Pr.

Other Instrument. Guy De Furia. (Interpersonal Trust Surveys Ser.). 1997. pap. 3.95 (*0-7879-0898-3*) Jossey-Bass.

Other Intentions: Cultural Contexts & the Attribution of Inner States. Ed. by Lawrence Rosen. LC 94-27115. (Advanced Seminar Ser.). 264p. 1995. pap. 24.95 (*0-933452-89-6*) Schol Am Res.

Other Intentions: Cultural Contexts & the Attribution of Inner States. Lawrence Rosen & Jennifer Harris. Ed. by Richard Ziegfeld. LC 94-27115. (Advanced Seminar Ser.). 264p. 1995. text 55.00 (*0-933452-88-8*) Schol Am Res.

Other Islands of New York City: A Historical Companion. Sharon Seitz & Stuart Miller. LC 96-11597. 280p. 1996. pap. 17.00 (*0-88150-336-3*, Pub. by Countryman) Norton.

Other Japan: Conflict, Compromise, & Resistance since 1945. rev. ed. Ed. & Intro. by Joe Moore. LC 96-35872. (Japan in the Modern World Ser.). 422p. (C). (gr. 13). 1996. text 85.95 (*1-56324-867-0*, East Gate Bk) M E Sharpe.

Other Japan: Conflict, Compromise, & Resistance since 1945. rev. ed. Ed. & Intro. by Joe Moore. LC 96-35872. (Japan in the Modern World Ser.). (Illus.). 424p. (gr. 13). 1996. pap. text 24.95 (*1-56324-868-9*, East Gate Bk) M E Sharpe.

Other Japan: Postwar Realities. Ed. by Patricia E. Tsurumi. LC 87-23365. 176p. (C). (gr. 13). 1988. pap. text 30.95 (*0-87332-451-X*, East Gate Bk) M E Sharpe.

Other Japan: Voices Beyond the Mainstream. David T. Suzuki & Keibo Oiwa. LC 98-47560. (Illus.). 336p. 1999. pap. 18.95 (*1-55591-417-9*) Fulcrum Pub.

Other Jews: Portraits in Poverty. Dorothy Rabinowitz. LC 77-183251. (Institute of Human Relations Press Paperback Ser.). 64p. (Orig.). 1972. 1.25 (*0-87495-015-5*) Am Jewish Comm.

Other John Logan: Colonel John Logan & the 32nd Illinois. Tom Emery. LC 99-165685. 12p. 1998. pap. 3.99 (*0-9661637-1-0*) Hist In Print.

Other Kind: A Cultural Connection. Eleni Paidoussi. 200p. 1995. pap. 12.95 (*1-885778-03-1*) Seaburn.

Other Kinds of Dreams: Black Women's Organizations & the Politics of Transformation. Julia Sudbury. (Gender, Racism, Ethnicity Ser.). 304p. (C). 1998. 85.00 (*0-415-16731-0*); pap. 25.99 (*0-415-16732-9*) Routledge.

Other Kinds of Treason. large type ed. Ted Allbeury. (Adventure Suspense Ser.). 336p. 1992. 27.99 (*0-7089-8649-8*, Charnwood) Ulverscroft.

Other Kingdom. Victor Price. LC 97-141035. 240p. 1996. pap. text 14.95 (*1-55821-451-8*, 14518, Pub. by Breakaway Bks) Consort Bk Sales.

Other Kingdom. Hubert Van Zeller. LC 68-55377. 123p. 1969. pap. 4.95 (*0-87243-032-4*) Templegate.

Other Kitten. Patricia M. St. John. 8p. (J). (gr. 2-4). 1990. reprint ed. pap. 3.99 (*1-55661-152-8*) Bethany Hse.

Other Kuwait: An American Father & Daughter's Personal Impressions. Lee R. Lambert & Erin Lambert. Ed. by Connie Berry & Nan Wampler. (Illus.). 250p. (Orig.). (C). 1992. pap. text 16.95 (*0-9626397-1-0*) L R Lambert & Assocs.

Other Land of Beautiful Things. Abbabus Acturi. (Illus.). 250p. (Orig.). 1992. pap. 12.95 (*1-880601-39-7*) Danon Pub.

Other Landscape. Neil M. Gunn. 318p. 1990. 19.95 (*0-8027-1108-1*) Walker & Co.

Other Laura. Sheryl Lynn Postman. (Intrigue Ser.). 1996. per. 3.75 (*0-373-22367-6*, 1-22367-6) Harlequin Bks.

Other Leaders, Other Heroes: West Point's Legacy to America Beyond the Field of Battle. James R. Endler. LC 98-24033. 264p. 1998. 35.00 (*0-275-96369-1*, Praeger Pubs) Greenwood.

***Other Life.** Andrea Hollander Budy. 64p. 2001. pap. 12.95 (*1-885266-98-7*, Pub. by Story Line) Consort Bk Sales.

Other Lives. Laurie Blauner. (Poetry Chapbook Ser.). 64p. 1984. pap. 12.00 (*0-937669-13-X*) Owl Creek Pr.

Other Lives. Christopher Buckley. LC 85-5545. 75p. (Orig.). 1985. pap. 6.00 (*0-87886-125-4*, Greenfld Rev Pr) Greenfld Rev Lit.

Other Lives. Patricia Hooper. Ed. by Jack Galef. LC 84-71700. (Contemporary Writers Ser.). 72p. (Orig.). 1984. pap. 10.00 (*0-910323-01-1*) Elizabeth St Pr.

Other Lives. Sarah Woodhouse. LC 96-31789. 1996. 21.95 (*0-312-15185-3*) St Martin.

Other Lives. large type ed. Sarah Woodhouse. (Charnwood Large Print Ser.). 336p. 1997. 27.99 (*0-7089-8972-1*) Ulverscroft.

Other Lives, Other Selves: A Jungian Psychotherapist Discovers Past Lives. Roger J. Woolger. LC 88-47683. 408p. 1988. pap. 14.95 (*0-553-34595-8*) Bantam.

Other Log of Phileas Fogg. Philip Jose Farmer. 304p. 1993. mass mkt. 4.99 (*0-8125-2468-3*, Pub. by Tor Bks) St Martin.

***Other Love.** large type ed. Denise Robins. 352p. 1999. pap. 20.99 (*1-85389-957-7*, Dales) Ulverscroft.

***Other Lover.** Bruce Smith. LC 99-22588. 96p. 2000. pap. 13.00 (*0-226-76408-7*) U Ch Pr.

Other Lovers. Jackie Kay. 62p. 1994. pap. 12.95 (*1-85224-253-1*, Pub. by Bloodaxe Bks) Dufour.

Other Machiavelli: Republican Writings by the Author of "The Prince" Niccolo Machiavelli. Ed. by Quentin P. Taylor. LC 97-43868. 136p. (C). 1998. text 46.00 (*0-7618-1014-5*); pap. text 24.50 (*0-7618-1015-3*) U Pr of Amer.

Other Machine. Dion Farquhar. 256p. (C). 1996. pap. 18.99 (*0-415-91279-2*) Routledge.

Other Machine. Dion Farquhar. 256p. (C). 1996. 65.00 (*0-415-91278-4*) Routledge.

Other Main Traveled Roads see Collected Works of Hamlin Garland

Other Main Traveled Roads. Hamlin Garland. (Collected Works of Hamlin Garland). 1988. reprint ed. lib. bdg. 59.00 (*0-7812-1241-3*) Rprt Serv.

Other Man. Francis Durbridge. 21.95 (*0-7540-8542-2*, Black Dagger) Chivers N Amer.

Other Man. large type ed. Francis Durbridge. 1977. 12.00 (*0-85456-547-7*) Ulverscroft.

Other Man Was Me: A Voyage to the New World. Rafael Campo. LC 94-8659. 90p. 1994. pap. 8.00 (*1-55885-111-9*) Arte Publico.

Other Man's Guide to (And from) Infidelity. Elissa Gough. 120p. 1998. pap. 19.95 (*1-891863-04-5*) Face Reality.

Other Man's Wife see Esposa de Otro Hombre: A Married Woman?

Other Margaret. large type ed. Jill Murray. 1990. 27.99 (*0-7089-2255-4*) Ulverscroft.

Other Mary Shelley: Beyond Frankenstein. Audrey A. Fisch et al. LC 92-14568. (Illus.). 312p. 1993. text 70.00 (*0-19-507740-7*) OUP.

Other Me. Leia Stinnett. (Little Angel Bks.). (Illus.). (J). (gr. k-8). Date not set. pap. text. write for info. (*1-880737-18-3*) Crystal Jrns.

Other Me: Poetic Thoughts on ADD for Adults, Kids, & Parents. Wilma R. Fellman. LC 97-7215. (Illus.). 136p. (Orig.). 1997. pap. 16.00 (*1-886941-16-5*, 0924) Spec Pr FL.

Other Men's Minds. Jay Lewis. LC 70-134108. (Essay Index Reprint Ser.). 1977. 19.95 (*0-8369-1974-2*) Ayer.

Other Mexico: The North American Triangle Completed. John Warnock. (Illus.). 321p. 1995. 52.99 (*1-55164-029-5*, Pub. by Black Rose); pap. 23.99 (*1-55164-028-7*, Pub. by Black Rose) Consort Bk Sales.

Other Mid-Life Crisis: Everything You Need to Know about Wills, Hospitals, Life-&-Death Decisions, & Final Matters (but Were Never Taught) Adeline Rosemire. LC 94-22698. 98p. (Orig.). 1994. pap. 14.95 (*0-9640044-0-2*) Meridian Calif.

Other Middle Ages: Witnesses at the Margins of Medieval Society. Dyan Elliott. LC 98-13308. (Middle Ages Ser.). 304p. 1998. 39.95 (*0-8122-3448-0*) U of Pa Pr.

Other Middle Ages: Witnesses at the Margins of Medieval Society. Dyan Elliott. LC 98-13308. (Middle Ages Ser.). 288p. 1998. pap. 18.50 (*0-8122-1654-7*) U of Pa Pr.

Other Mind: A Study of Dance in South India. Beryl De Zoete. 1988. reprint ed. lib. bdg. 49.00 (*0-7812-0216-7*) Rprt Serv.

Other Mind, a Study of Dance in South India. Beryl De Zoete. reprint ed. 69.00 (*0-403-08185-8*) Scholarly.

Other Minds. Alec Hyslop. LC 94-41364. (Synthese Library SYLI: Vol. 246). 168p. (C). 1995. lib. bdg. 92.50 (*0-7923-3245-8*, Pub. by Kluwer Academic) Kluwer Academic.

Other Minds: Critical Essays, 1969-1994. Thomas Nagel. 240p. 1995. text 35.00 (*0-19-509008-X*) OUP.

Other Minds: Critical Essays 1969-1994. Thomas Nagel. 229p. 1999. pap. 17.95 (*0-19-513246-7*) OUP.

***Other Mind's Eye: The Gateway to the Hidden Treasures of Your Mind.** Allen Sargent. (Illus.). 221p. 1999. pap. 14.95 (*0-9674831-0-7*) Success Desgn.

Other Minneapolis. David L. Rosheim. (Illus.). (Orig.). pap. 6.50 (*0-9602996-0-2*) Andromeda.

***Other Mirror: Grand Theory Through the Lens of Latin America.** Miguel Angel Centeno. (Illus.). 360p. 2001. 59.50 (*0-691-05016-3*) Princeton U Pr.

***Other Mirror: Grand Theory Through the Lens of Latin America.** Miguel Angel Centeno & Fernando Lopez-Alves. LC 00-32625. 360p. 2000. 15.95 (*0-691-05017-1*) Princeton U Pr.

Other Mirror: Women's Narrative in Mexico, 1980-1995, 80. Kristine Ibsen. LC 96-30580. (Contributions to the Study of World Literature Ser.). 216p. 1997. 59.95 (*0-313-30180-8*, Greenwood Pr) Greenwood.

Other Miss Derwent. large type ed. Patricia M. Ashley. (Dales Romance Ser.). 286p. 1993. pap. 18.99 (*1-85389-397-8*, Dales) Ulverscroft.

Other Missiles of October: Eisenhower, Kennedy & the Jupiters, 1957-1963. Philip Nash. LC 96-43691. 232p. (gr. 13). 1997. pap. 19.95 (*0-8078-4647-3*); lib. bdg. 49.95 (*0-8078-2339-2*) U of NC Pr.

Other Mississippi. Carney. 1994. pap. 14.95 (*0-938252-01-1*) Coffeetable.

O

Other Modernism: F. T. Marinetti's Futurist Fiction of Power. Cinzia S. Blum. LC 96-3604. (Illus.). 250p. (C). 1996. 50.00 (0-520-20048-9, Pub. by U CA Pr); pap. 17.95 (0-520-20049-7, Pub. by U CA Pr) Cal Prin Full Svc.

Other Modernities: Gendered Yearnings in China After Socialism. Lisa Rofel. LC 98-38034. 321p. 1998. 40.00 (0-520-21078-6, Pub. by U CA Pr); pap. 16.95 (0-520-21079-4, Pub. by U CA Pr) Cal Prin Full Svc.

***Other Mother: A Lesbian's Fight for Her Daughter.** Nancy Abrams. LC 99-13125. (Living Out Ser.). 282p. 1999. text 50.00 (0-299-16490-X) U of Wis Pr.

Other Mother: A Lesbian's Fight for Her Daughter. Nancy Abrams. LC 99-13125. (Living Out Ser.). 269p. 1999. pap. 19.95 (0-299-16494-2) U of Wis Pr.

Other Mother: A Woman's Love for the Child She Gave up for Adoption. Carol Schaefer. LC 90-39201. 296p. 1992. pap. 12.95 (0-939149-75-3) Soho Press.

Other Mothers Have Problems Too, Pt. 1. Anand Shah. (Illus.). 48p. (Orig.). 1988. pap. 4.95 (0-929417-00-3) Analisa Enterprises.

Other Mountains to Climb. Ruth Strang. 64p. (Orig.). 1987. pap. text 1.95 (0-937580-95-3) Sumrall Pubng.

Other Mrs. Kennedy. 4th ed. Jerry Oppenheimer. 752+16p. 1995. mass mkt. 7.99 (0-312-95600-2) St Martin.

Other Nation: The Poor in English Novels of the 1840s & 1850s. Sheila M. Smith. (Illus.). 1980. 55.00 (0-19-812642-5) OUP.

Other Nations, 1. Chaosium, Inc. Staff. 1998. pap. text 12.95 (1-56882-128-X) Chaosium.

Other Nature. Stephanie A. Smith. 256p. 1997. pap. 13.95 (0-312-86352-7) St Martin.

Other Nevada, As Painted by Fred Boyce: Nevada Paintings. Fred J. Boyce. (Illus.). 97p. Date not set. write for info. (0-9630399-0-3) Boyce Art.

Other New York Jewish Intellectuals. Ed. by Carole S. Kessner. LC 94-17491. (Reappraisals in Jewish Social & Intellectual History Ser.). (C). 1994. text 55.00 (0-8147-4659-4); pap. text 20.00 (0-8147-4660-8) NYU Pr.

Other Nietzsche. Joan Stambaugh. LC 93-18455. (SUNY Series in Philosophy). 160p. (C). 1994. pap. text 18.95 (0-7914-1700-X) State U NY Pr.

***Other 99The Conservation & Biodiversity of Invertabrates.** Ed. by Surrey Beatty Staff. 462p. 1999. pap. 360.00 (0-9586085-1-2, Pub. by Surrey Beatty & Sons) St Mut.

Other One. Sidonie-Gabrielle Colette. Tr. by Elizabeth Tait & Roger Senhouse. LC 70-178783. 160p. 1972. reprint ed. lib. bdg. 55.00 (0-8371-6295-5, COTO, Greenwood Pr) Greenwood.

***Other Ones.** Jean Thesman. LC 98-45711. 208p. (YA). (gr. 5-9). 1999. 15.99 (0-670-88594-0, Viking) Viking Penguin.

Other Paris: Stories. Mavis Gallant. LC 74-116951. (Short Story Index Reprint Ser.). 1977. 20.95 (0-8369-3454-7) Ayer.

***Other Pasts: Women, Gender & History in Early Modern Southeast Asia.** Ed. by Barbara Watson Andaya. (Southeast Asia Papers). 384p. 2000. pap. text 30.00 (1-930734-00-X) Ctr for SE.

Other Paths. Price. 1999. mass mkt. 3.95 (0-445-40276-8, Pub. by Warner Bks) Little.

Other People: A Mystery Story. Martin Amis. LC 93-42062. 1994. pap. 13.00 (0-679-73589-5) Vin Bks.

Other People, Other Lands. Elayne Clift. 72p. 1999. pap. 6.95 (0-9634827-5-0) OGN Pubns.

Other People, Other Places. (Illus.). 96p. 1991. 19.95 (0-9666723-0-5) Eldredge Pr.

Other People, Other Places. Marzieh Gail. 288p. 1982. 18.50 (0-85398-122-1); pap. 10.50 (0-85398-123-X) G Ronald Pub.

Other People, Other Places, Vol. 2. (Illus.). 96p. 1998. 19.95 (0-9666723-1-3) Eldredge Pr.

Other People's Business: A Guidebook to Ohio Company & Industrial Tours. Jane Ware. LC 93-84273. 192p. 1993. pap. 12.95 (1-882203-01-1) Orange Frazer.

***Other People's Children.** Joanna Trollope. 352p. 2000. pap. 13.95 (0-425-17437-9) Berkley Pub.

Other People's Children. Joanna Trollope. LC 98-40004. 304p. 1999. 23.95 (0-670-88513-4, Viking) Viking Penguin.

***Other People's Children.** Joanna Trollope. LC 99-31998. 1999. write for info. (1-56895-753-X, Compass) Wheeler Pub.

Other People's Children: Cultural Conflict in the Classroom. Lisa Delpit. 224p. 1995. 21.00 (1-56584-179-4, Pub. by New Press NY) Norton.

Other People's Children: Cultural Conflict in the Classroom. Lisa Delpit. 224p. 1996. pap. 14.95 (1-56584-180-8, Pub. by New Press NY) Norton.

Other People's Dirt: A Housecleaner's Curious Adventures. Louise Rafkin. LC 97-43673. 210p. 1998. 17.95 (1-56512-162-7, 72162) Algonquin Bks.

***Other People's Dirt: A Housecleaner's Curious Adventures.** Louise Rafkin. 208p. 1999. pap. 11.95 (0-452-28081-8, Plume) Dutton Plume.

Other Peoples' Gardens. Christopher Lloyd. 224p. 1997. pap. 22.95 (0-14-023860-3, Pub. by Pnguin Bks Ltd) Trafalgar.

***Other People's Habits.** R. Anthony Daniele. 224p. 2000. pap. 21.95 (0-07-135915-X) McGraw.

Other People's Houses. Susan R. Cooper. 1993. per. 3.99 (0-373-26112-8, 1-26112-2) Harlequin Bks.

Other People's Houses. Susan R. Cooper. pap. 3.99 (0-373-05139-5) St Martin.

***Other People's Houses.** Vona Groarke. LC 99-198445. 58p. 2000. 24.95 (1-85235-241-8, Pub. by Gallery Pr); pap. 13.95 (1-85235-240-X, Pub. by Gallery Pr) Dufour.

Other People's Houses. Lore Segal. 320p. 1994. pap. 11.95 (1-56584-143-3, Pub. by New Press NY) Norton.

Other People's Lives. Catherine N. Parke. LC 93-48034. 64p. (Orig.). 1994. pap. 9.00 (0-933532-97-0) BkMk.

Other People's Mail: An Anthology of Letter Stories. Ed. & Intro. by Gail Pool. LC 99-49609. 286p. 2000. pap. 16.95 (0-8262-1246-8) U of Mo Pr.

Other People's Marriages. large type ed. Rosie Thomas. LC 94-22930. 654p. 1994. lib. bdg. 24.95 (0-7862-0327-7) Thorndike Pr.

Other People's Marriages. Rosie Thomas. 416p. 1995. reprint ed. mass mkt. 5.99 (0-380-72238-0, Avon Bks) Morrow Avon.

Other People's Money. Arthur Lyons. 1989. 17.45 (0-89296-218-6, Pub. by Mysterious Pr) Little.

Other People's Money: A Study in the Social Psychology of Embezzlement (With New Intro. by Author Added) Donald R. Cressey. LC 73-7907. (Criminology, Law Enforcement, & Social Problems Ser.: No. 202). 204p. 1973. reprint ed. lib. bdg. 26.50 (0-87585-202-5) Patterson Smith.

***Other People's Money: The Basics of Asset Misappropriation.** Association of Certified Fraud Examiners Staff. 300p. 1999. 169.00 (1-889277-18-5) Assn Certified Fraud.

Other People's Money: The Ultimate Seduction. Jerry Sterner. (Illus.). 96p. 1990. 14.95 (1-55783-062-2); pap. 7.95 (1-55783-061-4) Applause Theatre Bk Pubs.

Other People's Money & How the Bankers Use It. Ed. by Louis D. Brandeis & Melvyn I. Urofsky. 192p. 1995. pap. text 15.95 (0-312-10314-X) St Martin.

Other People's Money & How the Bankers Use It. 2nd ed. Louis D. Brandeis. LC 86-7463. (Reprints of Economic Classics Ser.). lxii, 223p. 1986. reprint ed. lib. bdg. 35.00 (0-678-00856-6) Kelley.

Other People's Myths: The Cave of Echoes. Wendy D. O'Flaherty. xiv, 226p. 1995. pap. 15.00 (0-226-61857-9) U Ch Pr.

Other People's Pets. Tana Reiff. LC 94-76143. (Working for Myself Ser.). 80p. 1994. pap. 4.95 (0-7854-1113-5, 40833) Am Guidance.

***Other People's Rules.** Julia Hamilton. 2000. 24.95 (0-312-26627-8) St Martin.

Other People's Secrets: A Techno-Expose' on the Legal Invasion of Privacy by Computers. 2nd ed. Todd A. McNutt. 60p. (YA). (gr. 11 up). 1999. pap. 9.95 (1-885037-06-6) SEEBIC Pubng.

Other People's Skeletons. Julie Smith. (Northern California Mysteries Ser.). 1993. mass mkt. 5.99 (0-8041-1086-7) Ivy Books.

***Other People's Skeletons.** Julie Smith. LC 99-25261. 1999. 19.95 (0-7862-1953-X) Mac Lib Ref.

Other People's Troubles. Jason Sommer. LC 96-48627. (Phoenix Poets Ser.). 80p. 1997. pap. 12.95 (0-226-76816-3); lib. bdg. 26.00 (0-226-76815-5) U Ch Pr.

Other People's Words: The Cycle of Low Literacy. Victoria Purcell-Gates. LC 94-31073. (Illus.). 256p. 1995. text 31.00 (0-674-64497-2, PUROTH) HUP.

Other People's Words: The Cycle of Low Literacy. Victoria Purcell-Gates. (Illus.). 256p. 1997. pap. text 18.00 (0-674-64511-1) HUP.

Other People's Worlds. William Trevor. LC 80-501879. 242p. 1980. write for info. (0-370-30312-1) Bodley Head.

Other People's Worlds. William Trevor. 240p. 1991. pap. 10.95 (0-14-010669-3, Penguin Bks) Viking Penguin.

***Other People's Worlds: An Introduction to Cultural & Social Anthropology.** Joy Hendry. LC 98-53610. 249p. 1999. pap. text 17.50 (0-8147-3602-5) NYU Pr.

***Other People's Worlds: An Introduction to Social Anthropology.** Joy Hendry. LC 98-53610. 1999. text 55.00 (0-8147-3601-7) NYU Pr.

Other Person's Shoes: One Act Musical. Hank Beebe. (Illus.). 20p. (YA). (gr. 6-12). 1992. pap. 3.25 (0-88680-366-7) I E Clark.

Other Perspective in Gender & Culture: Rewriting Woman & the Symbolic. Juliet F. MacCannell. 1990. text 46.00 (0-231-07256-2) Col U Pr.

***Other Pictures: Amateur Photographs from the Collection of Thomas Walther.** (Illus.). 178p. (C). 1999. 50.00 (0-944092-82-9) Twin Palms Pub.

***Other Place.** Monica Hughes. 2000. pap. 14.95 (0-00-648176-0) HarpC.

***Other Place.** Ibrahim Abedel Meguid. 316p. 1999. 29.50 (977-424-456-7, Pub. by Am Univ Cairo Pr) Col U Pr.

Other Place: And Other Stories of the Same Sort. J. B. Priestley. LC 72-167467. (Short Story Index Reprint Ser.). 1977. reprint ed. 20.95 (0-8369-3993-X) Ayer.

Other Places. Judy Schrafft. LC 98-67434. (Illus.). 144p. 1999. pap. 19.95 (1-57197-141-6) Pentland Pr.

Other Places: Three Plays; A Kind of Alaska; Victoria Station; Family Voices. Harold Pinter. LC 82-24185. 96p. 1983. pap. 6.95 (0-8021-5189-2, Grove) Grove-Atltic.

Other Places: Three Short Plays. Harold Pinter. 1984. pap. 5.25 (0-8222-0866-0) Dramatists Play.

Other Places in the Turnings of a Mind: Poetry Collection. Leialoha A. Perkins. 48p. 1987. pap. write for info. (1-892174-04-9) Kamalu uluolele.

Other Planet. Ascher-Straus. LC 88-4991. 256p. 1988. 15.95 (0-914232-93-2) McPherson & Co.

Other Planets Other Men: Gay Short Stories. Ed. by John Savage. LC 82-1621. 1991. text 22.95 (0-87949-185-X) Ashley Bks.

Other Poetry of Keats. Gerald B. Kauvar. LC 69-18836. 238p. 1975. 34.50 (0-8386-7434-8) Fairleigh Dickinson.

Other Policy: The Influence of Policies on Technology Choice & Small Enterprise Development. Ed. by Ton De Wilde et al. 512p. (Orig.). 1990. 47.50 (1-85339-063-1, Pub. by Intermed Tech) Stylus Pub VA.

Other Powers: The Age of Suffrage, Spiritualism, & the Scandalous Victoria Woodhull. Barbara Goldsmith. LC 98-33315. (Illus.). 560p. 1999. pap. 16.00 (0-06-095332-2) HarpC.

Other Powers: The Age of Suffrage, Spiritualism, & the Scandalous Victoria Woodhull. Barbara Goldsmith. LC 97-49464. 512p. 1998. 30.00 (0-394-55536-8) Knopf.

Other Price of Hitler's War: German Military & Civilian Losses Resulting from World War II, 55. Martin K. Sorge. LC 86-409. (Contributions in Military Studies Ser.: No. 55). 195p. 1986. 52.95 (0-313-25293-9, SGO/, Greenwood Pr) Greenwood.

Other Print Tradition: Essays on Chapbooks, Broadsides, & Related Ephemera. Ed. by Cathy L. Preston & Michael J. Preston. LC 95-23141. (New Perspectives in Folklore Ser.: Vol. 3). (Illus.). 312p. 1995. text 25.00 (0-8153-0376-9, H1470) Garland.

Other Prussia: Royal Prussia, Poland & Liberty, 1569-1772. Karin Friedrich. LC 99-21652. (Cambridge Studies in Early Modern History). (Illus.). 306p. (C). 2000. 64.95 (0-521-58335-7) Cambridge U Pr.

Other Puerto Rico. Kathryn Robinson. (Illus.). 164p. (Orig.). 1984. pap. 11.95 (0-915393-19-0) Perm Pr.

Other Pushkin: A Study of Alexander Pushkin's Prose Fiction. Paul Debreczeny. LC 81-85449. xiv, 386p. 1983. 47.50 (0-8047-1143-7) Stanford U Pr.

***Other Race Desire.** Jane Gaines. 1999. pap. text 18.00 (0-226-27875-1); lib. bdg. 47.00 (0-226-27874-3) U Ch Pr.

***Other Rebecca.** Maureen Freeley. LC 99-51852. 304p. 2000. 23.00 (0-89733-477-9) Academy Chi Pubs.

Other Reconstruction: Where Violence & Womanhood Meet in the Writings of Ida B. Wells-Barnett, Angelina Weld Grimke, & Nella Larsen. rev. ed. Ericka M. Miller. LC 99-29874. (Studies in African American History & Culture). 176p. 1999. 48.00 (0-8153-3495-8) Garland.

***Other Revolution: NGO & Feminist Perspectives from South Asia** Renuka M. Sharma & Purusottama Bilimoria. LC 99-933676. (Naari Series on Women Studies). xv, 364p. 1999. write for info. (81-7030-629-9, Pub. by Sri Satguru Pubns) S Asia.

Other Revolution: Russian Evangelical Awakenings. Geoffrey Ellis & Wesley Jones. LC 96-85782. 230p. (Orig.). 1996. pap. 16.95 (0-89112-022-X) Abilene Christ U.

Other Road. Jack D. Kendall. LC 97-199153. 240p. (Orig.). 1996. pap. 9.95 (0-9650361-0-3) Beacon of Truth.

Other Rooms. Shirley Powell. 112p. 1997. pap. 19.95 (0-922558-02-7) Poets Pr.

***Other Rooms, Other Houses: A Memoir of Facts & Dreams.** Virginia O. Earle. LC 98-43042. (Illus.). 126p. 1999. 20.00 (0-87233-122-9) Bauhan.

Other Rope Book. Monika Dalkin & Mignonne Hollis. 30p. (J). (gr. 2-6). 10.95 (0-9644524-0-5) Jolly Geranium.

Other Routes: Part-Time Higher Education Policy. David M. Smith & Michael R. Saunders. (Cutting Edge Ser.). 160p. 1991. 113.00 (0-335-15199-X); pap. 41.95 (0-335-15198-1) OpUniv Pr.

Other Rules: Never Wear Panties on a First Date & Other Tips. Ann Blakeley & Julia Moore. 1998. mass mkt. 6.95 (1-56333-658-8) Masquerade.

Other Samuel Johnson: A Psychohistory of Early New England. Peter N. Carroll. LC 77-74413. 247p. 1979. 34.50 (0-8386-2059-0) Fairleigh Dickinson.

Other Sappho. Ellen Frye. LC 89-23607. 218p. (Orig.). 1989. pap. 8.95 (0-932379-68-0); lib. bdg. 18.95 (0-932379-69-9) Firebrand Bks.

Other Scene: Psychoanalytic Readings in Modern Spanish & Latin-American Literature. Stephen M. Hart. LC 91-62080. (ENG & SPA.). 164p. 1992. pap. 40.00 (0-89295-065-X) Society Sp & Sp-Am.

Other Schools of Thought: Three Dramatic Pieces. Morris Panych. LC 94-234169. (Illus.). 140p. 1994. pap. 12.95 (0-88922-346-7, Pub. by Talonbks) Genl Dist Srvs.

Other Selves. Dino Minni. 98p. pap. 8.00 (0-919349-54-4) Guernica Editions.

Other Selves. Rosanne Wasserman. LC 98-50719. 120p. 1999. pap. 12.00 (1-891305-04-2) Painted Leaf.

Other Selves: Aristotle on Personal & Political Friendship. Paul C. Schollmeier. LC 93-18102. (SUNY Series in Ethical Theory). 222p. (C). 1994. text 57.50 (0-7914-1683-6); pap. text 20.95 (0-7914-1684-4) State U NY Pr.

Other Selves: Autobiography & Biography in Cross-Cultural Perspective. Ed. by Phyllis Granoff & Koichi Shinohara. 250p. 1996. text 21.95 (0-88962-581-6) Mosaic.

Other Selves: Philosophers on Friendship. Ed. by Michael Pakaluk. 288p. (C). 1991. pap. text 12.95 (0-87220-113-9); lib. bdg. 32.95 (0-87220-114-7) Hackett Pub.

Other Sexes: Rewriting Difference from Woolf to Winterson. Andrea L. Harris. LC 99-23584. (C). 1999. text 47.50 (0-7914-4455-4); pap. text 15.95 (0-7914-4456-2) State U NY Pr.

Other Shakespeare. Laura A. Shamas. 74p. 1981. pap. 5.50 (0-87129-762-0, O34) Dramatic Pub.

Other Shakespeare: Romeo & Juliet. William Shakespeare. Ed. by William T. Betken. 531p. 1984. 29.95 (0-941672-04-2); pap. 12.95 (0-941672-05-0) Valentine Pub.

Other Shakespeare: The Two Gentlemen of Verona. unexpurgated ed. William Shakespeare. Ed. by William T. Betken. LC 81-52512. 284p. (C). 1982. 13.95 (0-941672-00-X); pap. 7.95 (0-941672-01-8) Valentine Pub.

Other Sheep I Have: The Autobiography of Father Paul M. Washington. Paul M. Washington & David M. Gracie. LC 93-34730. (Illus.). 240p. (C). 1994. pap. 19.95 (1-56639-178-4); text 69.95 (1-56639-177-6) Temple U Pr.

Other Shepards. Adele Griffin. LC 98-12609. 218p. (J). 1998. lib. bdg. 15.49 (0-7868-2370-4, Pub. by Disney Pr) Little.

***Other Shepards.** Adele Griffin. LC 98-12609. 224p. (J). (gr. 5-8). 1998. 14.95 (0-7868-0423-8, Pub. by Disney Pr) Time Warner.

Other Shepards. Adele Griffin. LC 98-12609. 224p. (J). (gr. 5-9). 1999. pap. 5.99 (0-7868-1333-4, Pub. by Hyprn Child) Time Warner.

Other Shepherd. William S. Deal. 1982. pap. 1.95 (0-686-38053-3) Crusade Pubs.

Other Shore. Antonio D'Alfonso. 164p. 1989. pap. 8.00 (0-920717-32-2) Guernica Editions.

Other Shore. unabridged ed. Larry Reiner. LC 97-50517. 288p. 1998. lib. bdg. 24.75 (0-9626148-4-X) Integra Pr.

Other Shore: Plays by Gao Xingjian. Gao Xingjian. (Illus.). 350p. (C). pap. text 24.50 (962-201-862-9, Pub. by Chinese Univ) U of Mich Pr.

Other Shore: 100 Poems by Rafael Alberti. Rafael Alberti. Ed. by Kosrof Chantikian. Tr. by Jose A. Elgorriaga & Martin Paul from SPA. LC 80-84602. (Modern Poets in Translation Ser.: Vol. I). xiii, 234p. (C). 1981. 25.95 (0-916426-05-X); pap. 15.95 (0-916426-06-8) KOSMOS.

Other Side. Julia Alvarez. Orig. Title: El Otro Lado. 176p. 1996. pap. 10.95 (0-452-27341-2, Plume) Dutton Plume.

Other Side. Alejandro Aura. (Illus.). 32p. (YA). (gr. k up). 1995. lib. bdg. 16.95 (1-55037-405-2, Pub. by Annick) Firefly Bks Ltd.

Other Side. Larry Burchall. 120p. 1991. per. write for info. (0-8187-0149-8) Harlo Press.

Other Side. Mary Gordon. 400p. 1990. pap. 13.95 (0-14-014408-0, Penguin Bks) Viking Penguin.

Other Side. Cynthia Holz. LC 98-111669. 238p. 1998. pap. 12.95 (1-896764-01-0, Pub. by Sec Story Pr) LPC InBook.

***Other Side.** Alfred Kubin. Tr. by Mike Mitchell from GER. (Dedalus European Classics Ser.). (Illus.). 288p. 2000. pap. 15.99 (1-873982-69-0, Pub. by Dedalus) Subterranean Co.

***Other Side.** Kevin McColley. LC 00-29161. 384p. 2000. 24.00 (0-684-85762-6) S&S Trade.

Other Side. Marga Minco et al. Tr. by Ruth Levitt et al from DUT. 118p. 1994. 30.00 (0-7206-0908-9, Pub. by P Owen Ltd) Dufour.

Other Side. large type ed. Mary Gordon. LC 94-8053. 1994. 23.95 (1-56895-072-1) Wheeler Pub.

Other Side. Maxwell S. Burt. LC 70-134064. (Essay Index Reprint Ser.). 1977. reprint ed. 23.95 (0-8369-2218-2) Ayer.

Other Side: How Soviets & Americans Perceive Each Other. Ed. by Jonathan J. Halperin. (Illus.). (Orig.). 1987. pap. text 14.95 (0-317-59572-5) Comm Natl Security.

Other Side: How Soviets & Americans Perceive Each Other. Ed. by Jonathan J. Halperin & Robert D. English. (Beyond the Kremlin Ser.). 160p. (Orig.). (C). 1987. pap. 24.95 (0-88738-687-3) Transaction Pubs.

Other Side: Journeys in Baja, California. Judy G. Botello. LC 98-22892. (Illus.). 178p. 1997. pap. 12.95 (0-932653-25-1) Sunbelt Pubns.

Other Side: Shorter Poems. Angela Johnson. LC 98-13736. 64p. (YA). (gr. 5-7). 1998. 16.99 (0-531-33114-8) Orchard Bks Watts.

Other Side: Shorter Poems. Angela Johnson. LC 98-13736. 64p. (YA). (gr. 5-7). 1998. 15.95 (0-531-30114-1) Orchard Bks Watts.

***Other Side: Shorter Poems.** Angela Johnson. LC 98-13736. (Illus.). 64p. (YA). (gr. 5-9). 2000. pap. 6.95 (0-531-07167-7) Orchard Bks Watts.

Other Side: The Fault Lines, Guerrilla Saints & True Heart of Rock 'n' Roll. Ruben Martinez. 192p. 1993. pap. 11.00 (0-679-74591-2) Vin Bks.

***Other Side: The True Story of the Boy Who Sees Ghosts.** Denice Jones. LC 00-132569. 320p. 2000. 25.95 (0-88282-198-9, Pub. by New Horizon NJ) Natl Bk Netwk.

***Other Side & Back: A Psychic's Guide to Our World & Beyond.** Sylvia Browne. 2000. mass mkt. 7.50 (0-451-19863-8, Sig) NAL.

Other Side & Back: A Psychic's Guide to Our World & Beyond. Sylvia Browne & Lindsay Harrison. LC 99-18283. 304p. 1999. 23.95 (0-525-94504-0) NAL.

***Other Side & Back: A Psychic's Guide to Our World & Beyond.** large type ed. Sylvia Browne. (Core Ser.). 343p. 2000. 29.95 (0-7838-9018-4, G K Hall Lrg Type) Mac Lib Ref.

Other Side Makes Chocolate. Joan M. McCartney. (Illus.). 88p. (Orig.). 1981. pap. 2.95 (0-9609788-0-1) J M McCartney.

Other Side of a Memory. Dean Bathelter. (Illus.). viii, 228p. 1996. write for info. (0-9654636-0-5) Kenlex Pub.

Other Side of Arms Control: Soviet Objectives in the Gorbachev Era. Alan B. Sherr. 384p. 1988. 49.95 (0-04-445061-3) Routledge.

Other Side of Caesar's Coin: Selected Papers. Robert V. Vaughn. LC Z695.9.V34 1995. 149p. 1995. pap. 15.00 (0-9627257-0-6) Aye-Aye Arts.

Other Side of Calvinism. Laurence M. Vance. LC 91-90818. 475p. (Orig.). 1991. pap. 16.95 (0-9628898-0-6) Vance FL.

Other Side of Calvinism. rev. ed. Laurence M. Vance. LC 99-71074. 800p. (Orig.). 1999. pap. 27.95 (0-9628898-7-3) Vance FL.

Other Side of Charleston: Archaeological Survey of the Saks Fifth Avenue Location, Charleston, South Carolina. Michael Trinkley et al. LC 93-37292. (Research Ser.: No. 45). (Illus.). xiii, 181p. 1996. pap. 45.00 (1-58317-039-1) Chicora Found.

Other Side of Dailiness. Lorraine M. York. 176p. (C). 1988. pap. text 15.00 (1-55022-002-0, Pub. by ECW) Genl Dist Srvs.

An Asterisk (*) at the beginning of an entry indicates that the title is appearing for the first time.

Other Side of Dailiness. Lorraine M. York. (Illus.). 176p. (C). 1988. text 25.00 (*1-55022-003-9*, Pub. by ECW) Genl Dist Srvs.

Other Side of Dark. Joan Lowery Nixon. (Laurel-Leaf Suspense Ser.). 192p. (YA). (gr. 7-12). 1987. mass mkt. 4.50 (*0-440-96638-8*, LLL BDD) BDD Bks Young Read.

Other Side of Dark. Joan Lowery Nixon. (YA). 1992. 8.84 (*0-606-03631-8*, Pub. by Turtleback) Demco.

Other Side of Death. Jan Price. 192p. 1996. pap. 10.00 (*0-449-90992-1*) Fawcett.

Other Side of Death. Judith Van Gieson. LC 90-55575. 224p. 1991. 18.95 (*0-06-016581-2*) HarperTrade.

Other Side of Death: Scientifically Examined & Carefully Described. C. W. Leadbeater. 864p. 1996. reprint ed. pap. 45.00 (*1-56459-624-9*) Kessinger Pub.

Other Side of Death: What the Bible Teaches about Heaven & Hell. J. Sidlow Baxter. LC 96-46396. 256p. 1997. pap. 12.99 (*0-8254-2158-6*) Kregel.

Other Side of Delinquency. Waln K. Brown. LC 82-23162. (Crime, Law, & Deviance Ser.). 204p. 1983. reprint ed. pap. 63.30 (*0-7837-5658-5*, 205908400005) Bks Demand.

Other Side of Desire: Lacan's Theory of the Registers. Tamise Van Pelt. LC 99-43545. (C). 2000. text 57.50 (*0-7914-4475-9*); pap. text 18.95 (*0-7914-4476-7*) State U NY Pr.

***Other Side of Eden: Life with John Steinbeck.** John Steinbeck, IV & Nancy Steinbeck. 350p. 2001. 27.00 (*1-57392-858-5*) Prometheus Bks.

***Other Side of Ethel Mertz.** Frank Castelluccio. 2000. mass mkt. 6.99 (*0-425-17609-6*) Blvd Books.

Other Side of Ethel Mertz: The Life Story of Vivian Vance. Frank Castelluccio & Alvin Walker. (Illus.). 300p. 1998. 24.95 (*1-879198-26-6*) Knwldg Ideas & Trnds.

***Other Side of Everest.** Matt Dickinson. (Illus.). 272p. 2000. pap. 13.00 (*0-8129-3340-0*, Times Bks) Crown Pub Group.

***Other Side of Everest: Climbing the North Face Through the Killer Storm.** Pref. by Matt Dickinson. LC 98-48850. (Illus.). 240p. 1999. 23.00 (*0-8129-3159-9*, Times Bks) Crown Pub Group.

Other Side of Everest: Climbing the North Face Through the Killer Storm. large type ed. Matt Dickinson. LC 99-22830. (Basic Ser.). 1999. pap. 25.95 (*0-7862-1965-3*) Mac Lib Ref.

Other Side of Evolution Its Effect & Fallacy (1903) Alexander Patterson. 178p. 1998. reprint ed. pap. 17.95 (*0-7661-0569-5*) Kessinger Pub.

Other Side of Green. Peter A. Gagliano. LC 97-15556. 224p. 1997. 17.95 (*0-944957-72-2*) Rivercross Pub.

Other Side of Grief. George E. Vandeman. (Outreach Ser.). 48p. 1986. pap. 1.49 (*0-8163-0660-5*) Pacific Pr Pub Assn.

***Other Side of Haight.** James Fadiman. 320p. 2001. 25.95 (*0-89087-984-2*) Celestial Arts.

Other Side of Heaven: Postwar Fiction by Vietnamese & American Writers. Ed. by Wayne Karlin et al. 412p. 1995. pap. 17.95 (*1-880684-31-4*) Curbstone.

Other Side of Heroism: The U. S. Military & Humanitarian Operations. Joyce Starr. 320p. Date not set. 24.00 (*0-02-881100-3*) Brasseys.

Other Side of History see Takeover: How Euroman Changed the World

Other Side of Hope. William H. Bruce. 245p. (Orig.). 1995. per. 14.95 (*0-9644967-2-0*) Bruce Intl.

Other Side of International Development Policy: Non-Aid Economic Relations with Developing Countries in Canada, Denmark, The Netherlands, Norway, & Sweden. G. K. Helleiner. 240p. 1990. text 45.00 (*0-8020-2646-X*) U of Toronto Pr.

Other Side of Jordan. LaJoyce Martin. LC 92-14091. 246p. (Orig.). 1992. pap. 8.99 (*0-932581-98-6*) Word Aflame.

Other Side of Joy: Religious Melancholy among the Bruderhof. Julius H. Rubin. LC 97-24740. 288p. 2000. text 45.00 (*0-19-511943-6*) OUP.

Other Side of Justice: A Novel. Hal B. Coleman. LC 92-32567. 288p. (Orig.). 1993. pap. 14.95 (*0-86534-183-4*) Sunstone Pr.

Other Side of Language: A Philosophy of Listening. Gemma C. Fiumara. LC 95-21338. 256p. (C). 1995. pap. 22.99 (*0-415-04927-X*) Routledge.

Other Side of Love. large type ed. Denise Robins. 432p. 1995. 27.99 (*0-7089-3437-4*) Ulverscroft.

Other Side of Love: Handling Anger in a Godly Way. Gary Chapman. 183p. 1999. pap. 11.99 (*0-8024-6777-6*) Moody.

***Other Side of Love: Handling Anger in a Godly Way.** Ed. by Jim Vincent. 1999. audio 14.99 (*0-8024-6778-4*) Moody.

Other Side of Midnight. Sidney Sheldon. 1991. 5.99 (*0-446-77478-2*) Warner Bks.

Other Side of Midnight. Sidney Sheldon. LC 98-19558. 432p. 1998. mass mkt. 12.00 (*0-446-67468-0*, Pub. by Warner Bks) Little.

Other Side of Midnight. Ed. by Cynthia Stevens. 1997. 69.95 (*1-57553-408-8*) Watermrk Pr.

Other Side of Midnight. Sidney Sheldon. 288p. 1988. reprint ed. mass mkt. 7.50 (*0-446-35740-5*, Pub. by Warner Bks) Little.

Other Side of Midnight, 2000: An Executive Guide to the Year 2000 Problems. Barbara J. Taylor & Martha V. Daniel. LC 98-227061. 192p. 1998. lib. bdg. 29.95 (*0-9643853-9-2*) Stargazer.

***Other Side of Nothingness: Toward a Theology of Radical Openness.** Beverly J. Lanzetta. (C). 2001. pap. text. write for info. (*0-7914-4950-5*) State U NY Pr.

***Other Side of Nothingness: Toward a Theology of Radical Openness.** Beverly J. Lanzetta. (C). 2001. text. write for info. (*0-7914-4949-1*) State U NY Pr.

Other Side of Now. Sharon Negri. LC 88-26870. 72p. (Orig.). 1989. pap. 7.00 (*0-931846-35-8*) Wash Writers Pub.

Other Side of Oasis. (Piano-Vocal-Guitar Ser.). Date not set. pap. 14.95 (*0-7935-8568-6*) H Leonard.

Other Side of Oasis. 144p. 1997. otabind 19.95 (*0-7935-8570-8*) H Leonard.

Other Side of Oregon. Ralph Friedman. LC 92-19731. (Orig.). 1993. pap. 12.95 (*0-87004-352-8*) Caxton.

Other Side of Organizing: Personal Dilemmas & Political Demands. Steve Burghardt. 248p. 1982. 22.95 (*0-87073-630-2*); pap. 15.95 (*0-87073-631-0*) Schenkman Bks Inc.

Other Side of Oz. Buddy Ebsen. Ed. by Steven Cox. LC 93-73697. (Illus.). 1994. 24.95 (*1-880538-08-3*) Donovan Pub.

Other Side of Paradise see Otra Cara del Paraiso: Verdad/Sectas

Other Side of Paradise. large type ed. Maynah Lewis. 288p. 1985. 27.99 (*0-7089-1379-2*) Ulverscroft.

Other Side of Pastoral Ministry: Using Process Leadership to Transform Your Church. Daniel A. Brown. LC 96-22620. 160p. 1996. pap. 9.99 (*0-310-20602-2*) Zondervan.

***Other Side of Psychology: How Experimental Psychologists Find Out about the Way We Think & Act.** Denise D. Cummins. 240p. 2000. reprint ed. text 23.00 (*0-7881-6968-8*) DIANE Pub.

Other Side of Raymond Chandler. Raymond Chandler. 23.95 (*0-88411-421-X*) Amereon Ltd.

Other Side of Reading. Joe Wayman. 144p. (J). (gr. k-8). 1980. 13.99 (*0-916456-64-1*, GA 183) Good Apple.

Other Side of River. Charles Wright. 1984. mass mkt. 6.95 (*0-394-72367-8*) Random.

Other Side of Sex: An Open Letter to My Grandchildren. Dean Guest. 50p. (Orig.). (J). (gr. 5-10). 1991. pap. 2.50 (*1-879667-00-2*) Dove Pr TX.

Other Side of Silence. Joan M. Drury. LC 93-26211. 256p. (Orig.). 1993. pap. 9.95 (*0-933216-92-0*) Spinsters Ink.

Other Side of Silence. Margaret Mahy. 1997. 10.09 (*0-606-13010-1*, Pub. by Turtleback) Demco.

Other Side of Silence. Margaret Mahy. LC 95-8615. 192p. (J). 1995. 14.99 (*0-670-86455-2*, Viking) Viking Penguin.

Other Side of Silence. Arden Neisser. LC 89-71507. 316p. 1990. pap. 15.95 (*0-930323-64-5*) Gallaudet Univ Pr.

Other Side of Silence: Meditation for the Twenty-First Century. 2nd rev. ed. Morton T. Kelsey. LC 97-2256. 384p. 1997. pap. 22.95 (*0-8091-3700-3*) Paulist Pr.

Other Side of Silence: Men's Lives & Gay Identities - A Twentieth-Century History. John Loughery. (Illus.). 544p. 1999. pap. 16.95 (*0-8050-6124-X*, Pub. by H Holt & Co) VHPS.

Other Side of Silence: Men's Lives & Gay Identities - A Twentieth-Century History. John Loughery. LC 97-42575. 507p. 1998. text 35.00 (*0-8050-3896-5*) St Martin.

***Other Side of Silence: Voices from the Partition of India.** Urvashi Butalia. LC 99-50297. (Illus.). 278p. 2000. pap. 17.95 (*0-8223-2494-6*) Duke.

***Other Side of Silence: Voices from the Partition of India.** Urvashi Butalia. LC 99-921581. 1999. write for info. (*0-19-579054-5*) OUP.

***Other Side of Silence: Voices from the Partition of India.** Urvashi Butalia. LC 98-905436. xi, 278 p. 1998. 24.00 (*0-670-87892-8*) Viking Penguin.

Other Side of Silence: Women Tell about Their Experiences with Date Rape. Ed. by Christine Carter. 257p. 1995. 19.95 (*0-9627671-9-0*) Avocus Pub.

Other Side of Sleep: Selected Poems of Maxine Cassin. 2nd ed. Maxine Cassin. LC 95-71175. (Illus.). 144p. 1995. pap. 11.00 (*0-916620-50-6*) Portals Pr.

Other Side of the Asian American Success Story. Wendy Walker-Moffat. (Education Ser.). 231p. 1995. text 29.95 (*0-7879-0122-9*) Jossey-Bass.

Other Side of the Bridge. Wolfram Hanel. LC 96-21748. (Illus.). 48p. (J). (gr. 2-4). 1996. 13.95 (*1-55858-626-1*, Pub. by North-South Bks NYC); lib. bdg. 13.88 (*1-55858-627-X*, Pub. by North-South Bks NYC) Chronicle Bks.

***Other Side of the Bridge.** Wolfram Hanel. LC 96-21748. (Illus.). 48p. (J). (gr. 2-4). 1999. pap. 5.95 (*0-7358-1203-9*, Pub. by North-South Bks NYC) Chronicle Bks.

Other Side of the Bridge. Ted Levering. LC 91-91144. (Illus.). 400p. (Orig.). 1990. pap. 14.95 (*0-9640957-7-7*) Willowmead.

Other Side of the Canyon. Romer Zane Grey. (Zane Grey's Laramie Nelson Ser.). 224p. 1989. reprint ed. pap. text, mass mkt. 2.95 (*0-8439-2886-7*) Dorchester Pub Co.

Other Side of the Closet: The Coming-Out Crisis for Straight Spouses & Families. expanded rev. ed. Amity P. Buxton. 352p. 1994. pap. 17.95 (*0-471-02152-0*) Wiley.

Other Side of the Coin. Ruth K. Hall. 98p. (Orig.). 1996. pap. 5.95 (*1-57502-280-X*, PO980) Morris Pubng.

Other Side of the Coin. Edward C. Rochette. LC 85-24442. (Illus.). 200p. (Orig.). 1986. pap. 10.00 (*0-939650-24-X*) S J Durst.

Other Side of the Coin: Causes & Consequences of Men's Oppression. Roy U. Schenk. LC 82-209050. 256p. 1982. pap. 10.00 (*0-9613177-0-1*) MPC Pr.

Other Side of the Coin: The Nonmonetary Characteristics of Jobs. Lauri Perman. LC 90-29089. (Harvard Studies in Sociology: Outstanding Dissertations & Monographs Twenty-Two Distinguished Works from the Past Fifty Years). 392p. 1991. text 30.00 (*0-8240-9265-1*) Garland.

***Other Side of the Dale.** large type unabridged ed. Gervase Phinn. 310p. 2000. pap. 19.95 (*0-7531-5079-4*, 150794, Pub. by ISIS Lrg Prnt) ISIS Pub.

Other Side of the Dark: I Am Yours, the Crackerwalker, Pink. Judith Thompson. 1997. text 19.95 (*0-88754-537-8*) Theatre Comm.

Other Side of the Desk. Sandra K. Bunt. LC 90-71374. (Illus.). 135p. (Orig.). (J). (gr. 3-6). 1992. pap. 7.95 (*0-932433-80-4*) Windswept Hse.

Other Side of the Door. Joy N. Hulme. LC 90-41020. 168p. (J). (gr. 3-6). 1990. pap. 4.95 (*0-87579-412-2*) Deseret Bk.

Other Side of the Error Term: Aging & Development As Model Systems in Cognitive Neuroscience, Vol. 125. Naftali Raz. LC 98-3180. (Advances in Psychology Ser.). 458p. 1998. 135.00 (*0-444-82522-3*) Elsevier.

Other Side of the Frontier: Economic Explorations into Native American History. Ed. by Linda Barrington. LC 98-27900. (American & European Economic History Ser.). 320p. (C). 1998. pap. 28.00 (*0-8133-3396-2*, Pub. by Westview) HarpC.

***Other Side of the Frontier: Economic Explorations into Native American History.** Ed. by Linda Barrington. LC 98-27900. (American & European Economic History Ser.). 320p. (C). 1998. 75.00 (*0-8133-3395-4*, Pub. by Westview) HarpC.

***Other Side of the Gray: A Poet's Journey.** T. Stanley Lannon. 20p. 1999. pap. 3.00 (*0-9673765-0-5*, 001) Lemming Line.

Other Side of the Hill: Poems by the Capitol Hill Poetry Group. Jean Nordhaus et al. Ed. by Cindy Comitz. 100p. (Orig.). 1996. pap. 10.00 (*0-938572-18-0*) Bunny Crocodile.

Other Side of the Hudson: A Jewish Immigrant Adventure. Kenneth D. Roseman. (Do-It-Yourself Jewish Adventure Ser.). (J). (gr. 4-6). 1993. pap. 7.95 (*0-8074-0506-X*, 140061) UAHC.

Other Side of the Invisible Fence. Trevor Romain. Ed. by Benne Willerman. LC 94-72241. 96p. (J). (gr. 3-11). 1994. pap. 7.95 (*1-880092-17-4*) Bright Bks TX.

Other Side of the Island: Stories. Yvonne N. Perry. LC 93-45278. (Illus.). 112p. (Orig.). 1994. pap. 10.00 (*1-880284-06-5*) J Daniel.

Other Side of the Jordan. 2nd ed. Nelson Glueck. xxii, 260p. 1970. 20.00 (*0-685-65118-5*) Am Sch Orient Res.

Other Side of the Medal. Edward J. Thompson. LC 78-144848. 142p. 1974. reprint ed. lib. bdg. 49.75 (*0-8371-5979-2*, THOS, Greenwood Pr) Greenwood.

Other Side of the Medal: A Paleobiologist Reflects on the Art & Serendipity of Science. Everett C. Olson. LC 90-5612. (Illus.). xiv, 182p. 1990. 19.95 (*0-939923-13-0*) M & W Pub Co.

Other Side of the Mirror. Marion Zimmer Bradley. (Darkover Ser.). 304p. 1987. pap. 4.50 (*0-88677-185-4*, Pub. by DAW Bks) Penguin Putnam.

Other Side of the Mirror. Maggi Charles. 1993. mass mkt. 3.39 (*0-373-09795-6*, 5-09795-1) Silhouette.

Other Side of the Mountain. Michel Bernanos. Tr. by Elaine P. Halperin from FRE. LC 90-46018. 107p. 1990. reprint ed. 18.95 (*0-87797-180-3*) Cherokee.

Other Side of the Mountain: The End of the Journey: 1967-1968. Thomas Merton. Ed. by Patrick Hart. LC 98-12655. (Journals of Thomas Merton: Vol. 7). 368p. 1998. 30.00 (*0-06-065486-4*, Pub. by Harper SF) HarpC.

Other Side of the Mountain: The End of the Journey, 1967-1968, Vol. 7, 1967-1968. Thomas Merton. Ed. by Patrick Hart. LC 98-12655. (Journals of Thomas Merton: Vol. 7). (Illus.). 368p. 1999. pap. 15.00 (*0-06-065487-2*, Pub. by Harper SF) HarpC.

Other Side of the Picture. Eva Szabo. LC 96-227350. (Illus.). iv, 248p. (Orig.). 1996. pap. 12.50 (*0-9653972-0-3*) Medallion WI.

***Other Side of the Rainbow.** J. Palmer Barney. 1999. pap. 12.95 (*1-929985-01-0*) Angel Hrt Pub.

Other Side of the River. large type ed. Jessica Blair. (Magna Large Print Ser.). 496p. 1998. 29.99 (*0-7505-1181-8*, Pub. by Mgna Lrg Print) Ulverscroft.

Other Side of the River: A Novel of the American Civil War. Robert D. Halpert. 254p. 1996. pap. 12.95 (*0-9661018-3-9*) Breacon Pub.

Other Side of the River: A Story of Two Towns, a Death, & America's Dilemma. Alex Kotlowitz. 336p. 1999. pap. 14.95 (*0-385-47721-X*, Anchor NY) Doubleday.

Other Side of the '60s: Young Americans for Freedom & the Rise of Conservative Politics. John Andrew. LC 96-48088. (Perspectives on the Sixties Ser.). 280p. (C). 1997. text 50.00 (*0-8135-2400-8*); pap. text 19.95 (*0-8135-2401-6*) Rutgers U Pr.

Other Side of the Stone: Releasing Resurrectional Power in Your Life. John H. Hampsch. 16p. 1997. pap. 1.25 (*1-57918-027-2*, 7155) Queenship Pub.

Other Side of the Story. 18.99 (*0-89906-519-8*, OTHH); pap. 15.99 (*0-89906-520-1*, OTHP) Mesorah Pubns.

Other Side of the Story. Barbara Greenwood & Pat Hancock. (J). 1993. mass mkt. 7.95 (*0-590-73643-4*) Scholastic Inc.

Other Side of the Story. Richard Shelton. LC 87-70926. (Confluence Press Short Fiction Ser.). 96p. (Orig.). 1987. 15.00 (*0-917652-61-4*); pap. 8.00 (*0-917652-62-2*) Confluence Pr.

Other Side of the Story: Structures & Strategies of Contemporary Feminist Narratives. Molly Hite. LC 89-776. 184p. 1992. pap. text 14.95 (*0-8014-8017-5*) Cornell U Pr.

Other Side of the Sun. large type ed. Madeleine L'Engle. LC 93-35731. 1993. lib. bdg. 20.95 (*0-7862-0089-8*) Thorndike Pr.

Other Side of the Sun: A Novel. Madeleine L'Engle. (Wheaton Literary Ser.). 384p. 1996. 19.99 (*0-87788-615-6*, H Shaw Pubs) Waterbrook Pr.

Other Side of the Table. Robby Cohn. Ed. by Debrah L. Kearns. 144p. 1996. 13.95 (*1-877804-12-6*) Chandler White.

Other Side of the Table: The Soviet Approach to Arms Control. Ed. by Michael Mandelbaum. LC 89-22239. 215p. 1990. reprint ed. pap. 66.70 (*0-608-02004-4*, 206266000003) Bks Demand.

Other Side of the Wall. Stanley Ellin. 1976. 20.95 (*0-89190-499-9*) Amereon Ltd.

Other Side of the Wall. Madeena B. Nolan. 1973. 3.50 (*0-87129-397-8*, O21) Dramatic Pub.

***Other Side of Twilight: A Story of Intrigue & Betrayal.** Geoffrey Parrish. LC 99-91800. 2000. 25.00 (*0-7388-1278-1*); pap. 18.00 (*0-7388-1279-X*) Xlibris Corp.

Other Side of War. Eugene Fazekas. LC 97-91004. (Illus.). iv, 148p. 1997. pap. 21.95 (*0-9660085-0-2*) Fazekas Pub.

***Other Side of War.** Herbert Youngdahl. 90p. 2000. pap. 9.95 (*1-885003-57-9*, Pub. by R D Reed Pubs) Midpt Trade.

Other Side of War: On the Hospital Transports with the Army of the Potomac. 2nd unabridged ed. Katharine P. Wormeley. Ed. by Christine T. Heidorf. 244p. 1998. reprint ed. pap. 16.95 (*0-87928-118-9*) Corner Hse.

Other Side of Welcome. Sue E. Johnson. LC 97-76423. 80p. 1998. pap. 10.00 (*1-880222-30-2*) Red Apple Pub.

***Other Side of Western Civilization.** 5th ed. Stearns. LC 99-60750. (C). 1999. text 34.00 (*0-15-507850-X*) Harcourt Coll Pubs.

Other Side of Western Civilization Vols. I & II: Readings in Everyday Life, Vol. I: Ancient World-Reformation. 4th ed. Marci Sortor & Peter N. Stearns. 416p. (C). 1992. pap. text 29.50 (*0-15-567653-9*, Pub. by Harcourt Coll Pubs) Harcourt.

Other Side of Western Civilization Vols. I & II: Readings in Everyday Life, Vol. II: 16th Century-Present. 4th ed. Marci Sortor & Peter N. Stearns. 415p. (C). 1991. pap. text 29.50 (*0-15-567654-7*, Pub. by Harcourt Coll Pubs) Harcourt.

***Other Side of Yellow.** 3rd ed. Jessie Redding Hull. (Illus.). 64p. 1999. reprint ed. pap. 5.95 (*1-893916-12-X*) Project Pr.

***Other Side of Yesterday: The China Maya Connection.** Carol Miller. LC 00-190632. 116p. 2000. 25.00 (*0-7388-1870-4*); pap. 18.00 (*0-7388-1871-2*) Xlibris Corp.

Other Side River: Free Verse. Ed. by Leza Lowitz & Miyuki Aoyama. LC 95-14440. (Rock Spring Collection of Japanese Literature). (Illus.). 256p. (Orig.). 1995. pap. 14.00 (*1-880656-16-7*) Stone Bridge Pr.

Other Side Speaks: Survival Manual for Mankind. Jerry Dennon. 86p. (Orig.). 1992. pap. 10.00 (*0-9633049-0-9*) Burdette Bks.

***Other Simon: An Eye Witness Account by the Man Who Carried the Cross.** Danford L. Crane. 192p. 1998. pap. 9.95 (*1-57636-062-8*) SunRise Pbl.

Other Sisterhoods: Literary Theory & U. S. Women of Color. Sandra K. Stanley. LC 97-4689. 360p. 1998. 49.95 incl. audio (*0-252-02361-7*) U of Ill Pr.

Other Sisterhoods: Literary Theory & U. S. Women of Color. Sandra K. Stanley. LC 97-4689. 360p. 1998. text 19.95 (*0-252-06666-9*) U of Ill Pr.

***Other Six Days: Vocation, Work & Ministry in Biblical Perspective.** Paul Stevens. 298p. 2000. pap. 24.00 (*0-8028-4800-1*) Eerdmans.

Other Sky & the House in November. Keith Laumer. 256p. 1985. pap. 2.95 (*0-8125-4377-7*, Pub. by Tor Bks) St Martin.

Other Sleep. Julian Green. Tr. by Evan W. Cameron from FRE. 160p. (Orig.). 1999. pap. 12.95 (*1-885586-08-6*, Pub. by Turtle Point Pr) Dist Art Pubs.

Other Solitudes: Multicultural Fiction & Interviews. Ed. by Linda Hutcheon & Marion Richardson. 352p. 1990. pap. text 14.95 (*0-19-540756-3*) OUP.

Other Song Book. Dave Anderson. 264p. 1991. reprint ed. spiral bd. 12.95 (*0-9628303-2-1*); reprint ed. per. 10.95 (*0-9628303-3-X*) Fellow Minist.

Other Songbook - Words Only. large type ed. Dave Anderson. 264p. 1992. pap. 15.00 (*0-9628303-4-8*) Fellow Minist.

***Other South: Southern Dissenters in the Nineteenth Century.** Carl N. Degler. 2000. reprint ed. pap. 19.95 (*0-8130-1830-7*) U Press Fla.

Other Species: Observations by Women on the Study of Men. Marlene Rimler. Ed. by Patrick Caton. LC 96-78977. 168p. 1997. pap. 5.95 (*1-56245-281-9*) Great Quotations.

***Other States' Incentives to Attract or Encourage Aerospace Manufacturing.** Rosa Maria Moller. 47p. 1999. pap. write for info. (*1-58703-109-4*, CRB-99-010) CA St Libry.

Other Story of Lutherans at Worship: Reclaiming Our Heritage of Diversity. David S. Luecke. 126p. (Orig.). 1995. pap. 7.00 (*0-9628303-7-2*) Fellow Minist.

Other Struggle for Equal Schools: Mexican-Americans During the Civil Rights. Ruben Donato. LC 97-13021. (SUNY Series, the Social Context of Education). 210p. (C). 1997. text 59.50 (*0-7914-3519-9*); pap. text 19.95 (*0-7914-3520-2*) State U NY Pr.

Other Taiwan, 1945 to the Present. Ed. by Murray A. Rubinstein. LC 94-16058. 496p. (C). (gr. 13). 1994. text 88.95 (*1-56324-192-7*, East Gate Bk); pap. text 34.95 (*1-56324-193-5*, East Gate Bk) M E Sharpe.

Other Tan Identity. Steyn. LC 96-17958. 288p. 1997. pap. 29.95 (*0-7190-4463-4*, Pub. by Manchester Univ Pr) St Martin.

Other Texas Frontier. Harry H. Ransom. Ed. by Hazel H. Ransom. (Illus.). 75p. 1984. 19.95 (*0-292-71101-8*) U of Tex Pr.

Other Theatres: A History of Experimental Theatre in Britain. Andrew Davis. 272p. 1987. 53.00 (*0-389-20706-3*, N8264); pap. 16.00 (*0-389-20707-1*, N8265) B&N Imports.

O

Other Theory of Nuclear Structure. James Carter. LC 93-73894. (Illus.). 96p. (Orig.). (C). 1993. pap. 32.00 (*0-9636592-0-0*) Absolute Motion.

Other Theory of Physics: A Unified Non-Field Theory of Mass, Space, Time & Gravity. James Carter. (Illus.). 208p. (Orig.). (C). 1994. pap. text 22.00 (*0-9636592-1-9*) Absolute Motion.

Other Times: Philosophical Perspectives on Past, Present & Future. David Cockburn. LC 96-50077. (Studies in Philosophy). 370p. (C). 1997. text 59.95 (*0-521-59214-3*) Cambridge U Pr.

Other Times & Other Places. Rudy Pinola. 116p. 1999. pap. 8.75 (*1-883428-03-3*) Econ Res Srv.

Other Times & Other Seasons. Laurence Hutton. (Notable American Authors Ser.). 1992. reprint ed. lib. bdg. 75.00 (*0-7812-3314-3*) Rprt Serv.

Other Times Fading Faces. unabridged ed. Edward E. MacDonald. 1996. mass mkt. 9.95 (*1-891371-01-0*) Angel Ministries.

Other Times, Other Places: Macroeconomic Lessons from U. S. & European History. Charles L. Schultze. LC 86-14759. 88p. 1986. 28.95 (*0-8157-7766-3*); pap. 10.95 (*0-8157-7765-5*) Brookings.

Other Times, Other Realities: Toward A Theory of Psychoanalytic Treatment. Arnold H. Modell. 192p. 1996. pap. text 17.95 (*0-674-64499-9*) HUP.

Other Times, Other Realities: Toward a Theory of Psychoanalytic Treatment. Arnold H. Modell. 208p. 1990. text 27.50 (*0-685-32245-9*) HUP.

Other Times, Other Realities: Toward a Theory of Psychoanalytic Treatment. Arnold H. Modell. 208p. (C). 1990. 40.50 (*0-674-64498-0*) HUP.

***Other Times, Other Women.** Dorothy Dilts Swartz. LC 99-97514. 2000. pap. 7.95 (*0-533-13423-4*) Vantage.

Other Tongue: English Across Cultures. 2nd ed. Ed. by Braj B. Kachru. (English in the Global Context Ser.). 416p. 1992. text 44.95 (*0-252-01869-9*); pap. text 21.95 (*0-252-06200-0*) U of Ill Pr.

Other Tongue: Nation & Ethnicity in the Linguistic Borderlands. Ed. by Alfred Arteaga. LC 93-45755. 336p. 1994. text 54.95 (*0-8223-1458-4*); pap. text 18.95 (*0-8223-1462-2*) Duke.

***Other Topics in Women's Health.** (Ultrasound & Women's Health Ser.: Vol. 4). 1998. write for info. (*1-930047-53-3*, 98IV-P); pap. write for info. (*1-930047-49-5*, 98IV) Am Inst Ultrasound.

Other Tradition of Modern Architecture: The Uncompleted Project. Colin St. John Wilson. (Illus.). 128p. (Orig.). 1995. 38.00 (*1-85490-412-4*) Academy Ed UK.

***Other Traditions.** John Ashbery. LC 00-39648. (Charles Eliot Norton Lectures). 192p. 2000. 22.95 (*0-674-00315-2*) HUP.

Other Tribological Problems see Eurotrib, '81: Proceedings of the Third International Tribology Congress, Warsaw

"Other Tuscany" Essays in the History of Lucca, Pisa, & Siena During the Thirteenth, Fourteenth & Fifteenth Centuries. Ed. by Thomas W. Blomquist & Maureen F. Mazzaoui. LC 94-4664. (Studies in Medieval Culture: Vol. 34). 1994. pap. 15.00 (*1-879288-42-7*); boxed set 35.00 (*1-879288-41-9*) Medieval Inst.

Other Twenty-Three Hours: Child-Care Work with Emotionally Disturbed Children in a Therapeutic Milieu. Albert E. Trieschman et al. LC 70-75052. (Modern Applications of Social Work Ser.). 256p. (C). 1969. pap. text 27.95 (*0-202-26086-0*) Aldine de Gruyter.

Other Two. unabridged ed. Edith Wharton. (Edith Wharton Ser.). 1994. 16.95 incl. audio (*1-883049-12-1*) Sound Room.

Other Two: Library Edition. unabridged ed. Edith Wharton. 1994. lib. bdg. 18.95 incl. audio (*1-883049-35-0*) Sound Room.

Other Victim. D. Kessler. mass mkt. 13.95 (*0-340-68901-3*, Pub. by Hodder & Stought Ltd) Trafalgar.

Other Victim: How Caregivers Survive a Loved One's Chronic Illness. Alan Drattell. LC 96-7742. 116p. 1996. pap. 17.95 (*0-929765-43-5*) Seven Locks Pr.

Other Victims: First-Person Stories of Non-Jews Persecuted by the Nazis. Ina R. Friedman. 214p. (YA). (gr. 7 up). 1995. pap. 6.95 (*0-395-74515-2*, Sandpiper) HM.

Other Victims: First-Person Stories of Non-Jews Persecuted by the Nazis. Ina R. Friedman. 1990. 12.30 (*0-606-07978-5*) Turtleback.

Other Victims of Suicide. Sharon Craft. 115p. (Orig.). 1998. pap. 9.50 (*1-879366-18-5*) Hearthstone OK.

Other Visions, Other Voices: Women Political Artists in Greater Los Angeles. Paul Von Blum. LC 94-5197. (Illus.). 200p. (Orig.). 1994. pap. 34.50 (*0-8191-9475-1*); lib. bdg. 66.00 (*0-8191-9492-1*) U Pr of Amer.

Other Visualized: Depictions of the Mongoloid Peoples. Ed. by Takeru Akazawa et al. (Illus.). 274p. 1993. pap. 33.50 (*0-86008-509-0*, Pub. by U of Tokyo) Col U Pr.

Other Voice. Ed. by Moira Burgess. LC 87-63413. 1988. 27.50 (*0-948275-39-1*); pap. 12.95 (*0-948275-31-6*) Dufour.

Other Voice: A Companion to the Text of the Course, Chapter 1-15. Brent Haskell. LC 97-77527. 416p. 1998. pap. 21.95 (*0-87516-715-2*) DeVorss.

***Other Voice: A Portrait of Hilda of Whitby in Words & Music.** Gail Godwin & Robert Starer. 84p. 1999. pap. 12.00 (*0-9622553-7-8*, 650-001) Selah Pub Co.

Other Voice: Essays on Modern Poetry. Octavio Paz. Tr. by Helen Lane. 1991. 16.95 (*0-15-170449-X*) Harcourt.

Other Voice: Essays on Modern Poetry. Octavio Paz. Tr. by Helen Lane. 176p. 1992. pap. 9.95 (*0-15-670455-2*, Harvest Bks) Harcourt.

Other Voice: Scottish Women's Writing since 1808. Ed. by Moira Burgess. LC 87-63413. 290p. 1988. 27.50 (*0-318-39994-6*) Dufour.

Other Voice: Scottish Women's Writing since 1808. Moira Burgess. LC 87-63143. 290p. 1988. 27.50 (*0-685-31955-5*); pap. 12.95 (*0-685-31956-3*) Dufour.

Other Voices: A History of Homosexuality & Popular Music. Richard Smith. (Lesbian & Gay Studies Ser.). 224p. 1997. 69.95 (*0-304-32860-X*, Pub. by Cassell) LPC InBook.

Other Voices: Essays on Italian Regional Culture & Language. Ed. by John Staulo. 1990. 35.50 (*0-916379-73-6*) Scripta.

Other Voices from Pakistan: Collection of Essays, News Reports, & Literary Writing. Compiled by Pakistan - Indian People's Forum for Peace & Democ. (C). 1995. pap. 14.00 (*81-224-0735-8*) S Asia.

Other Voices, Other Rooms. Truman Capote. 1994. lib. bdg. 24.95 (*1-56849-388-6*) Buccaneer Bks.

Other Voices, Other Rooms. Truman Capote. LC 98-48265. 245 p. 1999. write for info. (*0-7540-3681-2*) Chivers N Amer.

***Other Voices, Other Rooms.** Truman Capote. LC 98-48265. 1999. 25.95 (*0-7838-8491-5*) Macmillan Gen Ref.

Other Voices, Other Rooms. Truman Capote. 1994. pap. 12.00 (*0-679-74564-5*) Vin Bks.

Other Voices, Other Views: An International Collection of Essays from the Bicentennial, 34. Ed. by Robin W. Winks. LC 77-84751. (Contributions in American Studies: No. 34). 428p. 1978. 69.50 (*0-8371-9844-5*, WAO/, Greenwood Pr) Greenwood.

***Other Voices, Other Views: Expanding the Canon in English Renaissance Studies.** Ed. by Helen Ostovich et al. LC 99-18368. (Illus.). 328p. 1999. 47.50 (*0-87413-680-6*) U Delaware Pr.

Other Voices, Other Vistas: Short Stories from Africa, China, India, Japan, & Latin America. Barbara H. Solomon. 1992. 13.09 (*0-606-01492-6*, Pub. by Turtleback) Demco.

Other Voices, Other Vistas: Stories from Africa, China, India, Japan, & Latin America. Ed. by Barbara H. Solomon. 424p. (Orig.). 1992. mass mkt. 7.99 (*0-451-62845-4*, Ment) NAL.

Other Walker: A Book of Poems. Kenneth Fields. 1971. 3.95 (*0-934614-00-8*) Talisman Research.

Other Walls: The Arab-Israeli Peace Process in a Global Perspective. rev. ed. Harold H. Saunders. (Illus.). 288p. 1991. pap. text 16.95 (*0-691-02337-9*, Pub. by Princeton U Pr) Cal Prin Full Svc.

Other Walls: The Politics of the Arab-Israeli Peace. Harold H. Saunders. LC 85-20095. (AEI Studies: No. 432). (Illus.). 200p. reprint ed. pap. 62.00 (*0-8357-4519-8*, 203737800008) Bks Demand.

Other War. Geoffrey Vitale. LC 97-151280. 220p. 1996. pap. text 16.95 (*0-920953-98-0*) Stoddart Publ.

Other Way: An Alternative Approach to Acting & Directing. Charles Marowitz. LC 97-23967. (Illus.). 241p. 1999. 24.95 (*1-55783-303-6*) Applause Theatre Bk Pubs.

Other Way: Meditation Experiences Based on the I Ching. Carol K. Anthony. 288p. (Orig.). 1990. pap. 12.95 (*0-9603832-5-5*) Anthony Pub Co.

Other Way Around. Frank P. Verdon. 256p. 1996. text 45.00 (*1-86064-030-3*) St Martin.

Other Way to Listen. Byrd Baylor. 32p. 1997. per. 5.99 (*0-689-81053-9*) S&S Childrens.

Other Way to Listen. Byrd Baylor. LC 78-23430. (Illus.). 32p. (J). (ps-3). 1978. 15.00 (*0-684-16017-X*) Scribner.

Other Way to Listen. Byrd Baylor. 1997. 11.19 (*0-606-13683-5*, Pub. by Turtleback) Demco.

Other Ways & Other Flesh. Edith L. O'Shaughnessy. LC 70-150482. (Short Story Index Reprint Ser.). 1977. reprint ed. 18.95 (*0-8369-3823-2*) Ayer.

Other Ways of Growing Old: Anthropological Perspectives. Ed. by Pamela T. Amoss & Stevan Harrell. LC 79-66056. xxiv, 270p. 1981. 42.50 (*0-8047-1072-4*); pap. 15.95 (*0-8047-1153-4*) Stanford U Pr.

Other Ways of Knowing: Recharting Our Future with Ageless Wisdom. John Broomfield. LC 97-7876. 224p. 1997. pap. 14.95 (*0-89281-614-7*) Inner Tradit.

Other Ways to Win: Creating Alternatives for High School Graduates. Kenneth C. Gray & Edwin L. Herr. LC 95-18302. 208p. 1995. pap. 24.95 (*0-8039-6246-0*) Corwin Pr.

Other Ways to Win: Creating Alternatives for High School Graduates. Kenneth C. Gray & Edwin L. Herr. LC 95-18302. 208p. 1995. text 55.95 (*0-8039-6245-2*) Cofwin Pr.

Other Weapons. Luisa Valenzuela. Tr. by Deborah Bonner from SPA. 135p. 1985. pap. 10.00 (*0-910061-22-X*, 1204) Ediciones Norte.

Other Wife: A Novel. Emery Barrus. LC 91-10871. 288p. 1991. text 22.95 (*0-931832-87-X*) Fithian Pr.

Other-Wise: Alterity, Materiality & Meditation. Per Otnes. 202p. (C). 1997. text 33.00 (*82-00-22558-5*) Scandnvan Univ Pr.

Other Wise Man. Henry Van Dyck. 64p. 1995. pap. 10.95 (*1-869890-66-3*, Pub. by Hawthorn Press) Anthroposophic.

Other Wise Man. Henry Van Dyke. LC 89-7590. (Illus.). 32p. (J). (ps-3). 1992. pap., per. 6.95 (*0-8249-8564-8*, Ideals Child) Hambleton-Hill.

Other Within Us: Feminist Perspectives on Women & Aging. Ed. by Marilyn Pearsall. 1997. 59.00 (*0-614-27690-X*); pap. 18.00 (*0-614-27689-6*) Westview.

Other Woman. Sidonie-Gabrielle Colette. LC 79-173201. Orig. Title: Mon Ami Valentine. 1972. write for info. (*0-672-51651-9*) Macmillan.

***Other Woman.** Joy Fielding. LC 99-50155. 1999. 25.95 (*1-57490-242-3*, Beeler LP Bks) T T Beeler.

Other Woman. Laurie John. (Sweet Valley University Ser.: No. 16). (YA). (gr. 7 up). 1995. 9.09 (*0-606-08636-6*, Pub. by Turtleback) Demco.

Other Woman. Ann O'Leary. LC 98-31633. 208p. 1999. pap. 11.95 (*1-56280-234-8*) Naiad Pr.

Other Woman. Created by Francine Pascal. (Sweet Valley University Ser.: No. 16). 240p. (YA). (gr. 7 up). 1995. mass mkt. 3.99 (*0-553-56696-2*, Sweet Valley) BDD Bks Young Read.

***Other Woman.** Pashonia S. Robinson. (Illus.). 152p. 1999. pap. 11.95 (*0-9666100-2-4*) Black Ink.

Other Woman. large type ed. Jill McGown. 477p. write for info. (*0-7505-1065-X*, Pub. by Mgna Lrg Print) Ulverscroft.

Other Woman: A Life of Violet Trefusis, Including Previously Unpublished Correspondence with Vita Sackville-West. Philippe Jullian et al. LC 76-25141. xii, 256p. 1976. write for info. (*0-395-20539-5*) HM.

Other Woman: Feminism & Femininity in the Work of Marguerite Duras. Trista Selous. (C). 1988. 42.50 (*0-300-04287-6*) Yale U Pr.

Other Woman: My Years with O. J. Simpson: Story of Love, Trust & Betrayal. Paula Barbieri. LC 97-73861. (Illus.). 304p. 1997. 23.45 (*0-316-65113-3*) Little.

Other Woman: Stories of Two Women & a Man. Ed. & Intro. by Susan Koppelman. LC 84-10099. 384p. 1984. pap. 12.95 (*0-935312-25-0*) Feminist Pr.

Other Woman: The Real Truth about Women & Their Secret Relationships. Rosie Milligan. 216p. (Orig.). 1997. pap. 14.95 (*1-881524-07-8*) Milligan Bks.

Other Woman: True Stories of Love, Betrayal, & the Men Women Have Shared as Husbands & Lovers. Leigh Cato. 240p. 1996. pap. 12.95 (*1-56352-336-1*) Longstreet.

Other Woman: Women of Colour in Contemporary Canadian Literature. Ed. by Makeda Silvera. LC 95-230419. (Illus.). 472p. 1994. pap. 19.95 (*0-920813-47-X*) Sister Vis Pr.

Other Woman & Other Stories. Dina Mehta. 121p. 1981. 16.95 (*0-685-21572-5*) Asia Bk Corp.

Other Woman's Guide to (And from) Infidelity. Elissa Gough. 110p. 1998. pap. 19.95 (*1-891863-03-7*) Face Reality.

Other Women. Lisa Alther. 1996. pap. 13.95 (*0-452-27678-0*, Plume) Dutton Plume.

Other Women. Margaret Bacon. 320p. 1994. mass mkt. 11.95 (*0-7472-4532-0*, Pub. by Headline Bk Pub) Trafalgar.

Other Women: A Workbook for Women Who Work with Women. Carolyn S. Duff et al. (Illus.). (Orig.). 1989. pap. write for info. (*0-318-65968-9*) WomenWorks.

Other Women: Challenge in the Workplace. Carolyn S. Duff. (Illus.). (Orig.). 1990. pap. write for info. (*0-9624823-0-7*) WomenWorks.

Other Women: Lesbian Experience & Psychoanalytic Theory of Women. Beverly Burch. LC 96-41400. 190p. 1997. 41.50 (*0-231-10602-5*); pap. 16.50 (*0-231-10603-3*) Col U Pr.

Other Women: The Writing of Class, Race & Gender, 1832-1898. Anita Levy. (Illus.). 250p. 1991. pap. text 11.95 (*0-691-01493-0*, Pub. by Princeton U Pr) Cal Prin Full Svc.

Other Women: The Writing of Class, Race, & Gender, 1832-1898. Anita Levy. LC 90-42210. 184p. 1991. reprint ed. pap. 57.10 (*0-608-04593-4*, 206536300003) Bks Demand.

Other Women, Other Men. Willard Manus. 1988. pap. 9.95 (*0-915572-38-9*) Panjandrum.

Other Women's Children. Perri Klass. 320p. 1992. mass mkt. 5.99 (*0-8041-0857-9*) Ivy Books.

Other Women's Children. large type ed. Perri Klass. 1991. 27.99 (*0-7089-8614-5*, Charnwood) Ulverscroft.

***Other Words: Essays on Poetry & Translation.** Joseph P. Clancy. 146p. 2000. 39.95 (*0-7083-1558-5*, Pub. by U Wales Pr) Paul & Co Pubs.

Other Words, Other Worlds: Language in Culture. Ed. by James W. Dodge. 1972. pap. 10.95 (*0-915432-72-2*) NE Conf Teach Foreign.

Other World. John Wynne. 180p. (Orig.). 1994. pap. 9.95 (*0-87286-290-9*) City Lights.

***Other World.** 4th ed. Joseph Weatherby, Jr. LC 99-29897. 343p. (C). 1999. pap. 41.40 (*0-8013-3266-4*) Longman.

***Other World: Issues & Politcs of Developing World.** 4th ed. (C). 2000. text. write for info. (*0-321-06982-X*); text. write for info. (*0-321-06984-6*) Addson-Wesley Educ.

Other World: Issues & Politics in the Developing World. 2nd ed. Joseph Weatherby, Jr. et al. LC 93-12745. 256p. (C). 1994. pap. text 34.75 (*0-8013-0702-3*, 78730) Longman.

Other World: Issues & Politics of the Developing World. 3rd ed. Joseph N. Weatherby et al. LC 96-10554. 303p. (C). 1996. pap. text 47.00 (*0-8013-1670-7*) Longman.

Other World: Spiritualism & Psychical Research in England, 1850-1914. Janet Oppenheim. (Illus.). 504p. 1985. text 80.00 (*0-521-26505-3*) Cambridge U Pr.

Other World: Spiritualism & Psychical Research in England, 1850-1914. Janet Oppenheim. (Illus.). 518p. 1988. pap. text 21.95 (*0-521-34767-X*) Cambridge U Pr.

Other Worlds. Paul Davies. LC 97-209250. 208p. 1997. pap. 12.95 (*0-14-013877-3*) Viking Penguin.

Other Worlds. Robert Holman. (Methuen New Theatrescripts Ser.). 181p. (C). 1990. pap. 12.95 (*0-413-62190-1*) Heinemann.

Other Worlds. Robert Holman. (Royal Court Writers Ser.). 56p. (C). 1988. pap. write for info. (*0-413-52260-1*, A0199, Methuen Drama) Methn.

Other Worlds. Torkom Saraydarian. LC 89-51506. (Illus.). 648p. (Orig.). 1990. pap. 27.00 (*0-929874-05-6*) TSG Pub Found.

Other Worlds. James S. Trefil. LC 99-14601. 1999. write for info. (*0-7922-7490-3*) Natl Geog.

Other Worlds. limited ed. Torkom Saraydarian. LC 89-51506. (Illus.). 648p. (Orig.). 1990. 38.00 (*0-929874-04-8*) TSG Pub Found.

Other Worlds: A Beginner's Guide to Planets & Moons. Terence Dickinson. (Illus.). 64p. (J). (gr. 5-9). 1995. pap. 9.95 (*1-895565-70-7*); lib. bdg. 19.95 (*1-895565-71-5*) Firefly Bks Ltd.

Other Worlds: Arishima Takeo & the Bounds of Modern Japanese Fiction. Paul Anderer. LC 84-12171. 224p. 1984. text 46.00 (*0-231-05884-5*) Col U Pr.

Other Worlds: Images of the Cosmos from Earth & Space. James Trefil. LC 99-14601. (Illus.). 240p. 1999. per. 34.50 (*0-7922-7491-1*, Pub. by Natl Geog) S&S Trade.

Other Worlds: Notions of Self & Emotion among the Lohorung Rai. Charlotte Hardman. Ed. by John Gledhill et al. (Explorations in Anthropology Ser.). 320p. 1996. 55.00 (*1-85973-150-3*); pap. 19.50 (*1-85973-155-4*) Berg Pubs.

***Other Worlds: Rosenblat,&Barbara.** abr. ed. Barbara Michaels, pseud. 1999. audio 18.00 (*0-694-52082-9*, 396222, Pub. by HarperAudio) Lndmrk Audiobks.

Other Worlds: Society Seen Through Soap Opera. Dorothy Anger. LC 99-209467. 216p. 1999. pap. 16.95 (*1-55111-103-9*) Broadview Pr.

Other Worlds: The Bell Witch & the Stratford Haunting. Barbara Michaels, pseud. LC 98-39204. 224p. 1999. 23.00 (*0-06-019235-6*) HarpC.

***Other Worlds: The Bell Witch & the Stratford Haunting.** Barbara Michaels, pseud. 304p. 2000. mass mkt. 6.99 (*0-06-109749-7*) HarpC.

Other Worlds: The Bell Witch & the Stratford Haunting. large type ed. Barbara Michaels, pseud. LC 98-53490. (Paperback Bestsellers Ser.). 280p. 1950. pap. 27.95 (*0-7838-8557-1*, G K Hall Lrg Type) Mac Lib Ref.

Other Worlds: The Bell Witch & the Stratford Haunting. large type ed. Barbara Michaels, pseud. LC 98-53490. 1999. 29.95 (*0-7838-8556-3*, G K Hall Lrg Type) Mac Lib Ref.

Other Worlds: The Bell Witch & the Stratford Haunting. large type ed. Barbara Michaels, pseud. LC 98-53490. 1999. write for info. (*0-7862-1770-7*) Thorndike Pr.

Other Worlds: The Endless Possibilities of Literature. Trevor H. Cairney. LC 90-30709. (Illus.). 152p. (Orig.). (C). 1990. pap. 15.00 (*0-435-08531-X*, 08531) Heinemann.

Other Worlds: The Fantasy Genre. John H. Timmerman. LC 83-72015. 1983. 17.95 (*0-87972-241-X*) Bowling Green Univ Popular Press.

Other Worlds: The Search for Life in the Universe. Michael Lemonick. (Illus.). 272p. 1999. pap. 14.00 (*0-684-85313-2*, Touchstone) S&S Trade Pap.

Other Worlds: The Search for Life in the Universe. Michael D. Lemonick. LC 97-49006. 272p. 1998. 24.50 (*0-684-83294-1*) S&S Trade.

Other Worlds Vol. 1: Called. Lauren Zimmerman. 1998. pap. 14.95 (*0-9666593-0-9*) Aquarian Concpts.

Other Worlds & Other Seas: Art & Vision in Saint-Amant's Nature Poetry. Robert T. Corum, Jr. LC 78-73094. (French Forum Monographs: No. 13). (Illus.). 174p. (Orig.). 1979. pap. 10.95 (*0-917058-12-7*) French Forum.

Other Worlds, Other Beings. Lathel F. Duffield & Camilla L. Duffield. LC 97-90860. 1998. pap. 10.95 (*0-533-12496-4*) Vantage.

Other Worlds, Other Lives - Discover Your True Cosmic Origins. Brad Steiger. 160p. 1995. pap. 14.95 (*0-938294-51-2*) Inner Light.

Other Worlds, Other Universes. Ed. by Brad Steiger & John White. 242p. 1986. reprint ed. spiral bd. 17.50 (*0-7873-1291-6*) Hlth Research.

Other Worlds Than This. Tr. by Rachel Hadas. LC 93-33530. (Illus.). 152p. (C). 1994. pap. 12.95 (*0-8135-2068-1*); text 32.00 (*0-8135-2067-3*) Rutgers U Pr.

Other Writing: Postcolonial Essays in Latin America's Writing Culture. Djelal Kadir. LC 92-27622. 240p. 1993. 37.95 (*1-55753-031-9*); pap. 19.95 (*1-55753-032-7*) Purdue U Pr.

Other You. Vernon Johnson. pap. 7.25 (*0-931841-10-0*) Satchells Pub.

***Othermindedness: The Emergence of Network Culture.** Michael Joyce. LC 99-6770. (Studies in Literature & Science). 264p. 2000. text 34.50 (*0-472-11082-9*, 11082) U of Mich Pr.

Otherness: Collected Stories by a Modern Master of Science Fiction. David Brin. 368p. 1994. mass mkt. 6.99 (*0-553-29528-4*) Bantam.

Otherness & the Media: The Ethnography of the Imagined & the Imaged, Vol. 3. Ed. by Hamid Naficy & Teshome Gabriel. 256p. 1993. pap. text 12.00 (*3-7186-0569-4*) Gordon & Breach.

Otherness of God. Ed. by Orrin F. Summerell. LC 97-44953. (Studies in Religion & Culture). 304p. 1998. pap. 37.50 (*0-8139-1771-9*) U Pr of Va.

Others see Drugie: Anthology of Modern Poetry

***Others.** James Herbert. LC 99-33576. 504p. 1999. 25.95 (*0-312-87293-3*, Pub. by Forge NYC) St Martin.

***Others.** James Herbert. 2000. mass mkt. 6.99 (*0-8125-7904-6*) Tor Bks.

Others. D. M. Wind. 368p. (Orig.). 1993. pap. text, mass mkt. 4.50 (*0-8439-3530-8*) Dorchester Pub Co.

Others: How Animals Made Us Human. Paul Shepard. LC 95-32313. (Illus.). 390p. 1995. text 27.50 (*1-55963-433-2*) Island Pr.

Others: How Animals Made Us Human. Paul Shepard. (Illus.). 374p. 1997. pap. 17.95 (*1-55963-434-0*, Shearwater Bks) Island Pr.

Others Before You . . . The History of Wisconsin Dells. Ed. by Michael J. Goc. LC 95-39319. 324p. (Orig.). 1995. pap. 40.00 (*0-938627-30-9*) New Past Pr.

Others, Including Morstive Sternbump: A Novel. Marvin Cohen. LC 76-11615. 247p. 1976. 15.00 (*0-672-52145-8*) Ultramarine Pub.

O

An Asterisk (*) at the beginning of an entry indicates that the title is appearing for the first time.

Others Knowing Others: Perspectives on Ethnographic Careers. Ed. by Don D. Fowler & Donald L. Hardesty. LC 93-29354. (Series in Ethnographic Inquiry). 256p. (Orig.). (C). 1994. pap. text 16.95 (*1-56098-336-1*) Smithsonian.

Others' Lines. David Giannini. (Spike Ser.: No. 10). (Illus.). 1997. pap. 6.00 (*1-885089-07-4*) Cityful Pr.

Others Must Dance for the Lord Dionysus Now: A Poetic Memoir. Kostas Myrsiades. LC 93-85993. (Illus.). 72p. (Orig.). 1993. pap. text 10.00 (*0-918618-55-X*) Pella Pub.

Others of Light: Awakening of Life Essence & Planetary Renewal. Norma Hobaugh. 121p. 1992. pap. 8.50 (*0-9635135-0-8*) N Hobaugh.

Others See Us. William Sleator. 163p. (YA). (gr. 7 up). 1995. pap. 4.99 (*0-14-037514-7*, PuffinBks) Peng Put Young Read.

Others See Us. William Sleator. LC 93-18940. 1995. 9.09 (*0-606-09721-X*, Pub. by Turtleback) Demco.

Others Unknown: The Oklahoma City Bombing & Conspiracy. Stephen Jones & Peter Israel. 352p. 1998. text 25.00 (*1-891620-07-X*, Pub. by PublicAffairs NY) HarpC.

Otherside of Paradise: Tourism, Conservation & Development in the Bay Islands. Susan C. Stonich. LC 99-54930. (Illus.). 225p. 2000. pap. text 30.00 (*1-882345-31-2*) Cognizant Comm.

***Otherside of Paradise: Tourism, Conservation & Development in the Bay Islands.** Susan C. Stonich. LC 99-54930. (Illus.). 225p. 2000. text 38.00 (*1-882345-30-4*) Cognizant Comm.

Otherspace. (Star Wars Ser.). 10.00 (*0-87431-128-4*, 40028) West End Games.

Otherspace: Martian Typography. Johanna Drucker & Brad Freeman. 1992. 35.00 (*0-932526-41-1*) Nexus Pr.

Otherspace II. (Star Wars Ser.). 10.00 (*0-87431-106-3*, 40028) West End Games.

Otherwere: Stories of Transformation. Laura A. Gilman. Ed. by Keith R. DeCandido. 272p. 1996. mass mkt. 5.99 (*0-441-00363-X*) Ace Bks.

Otherwhere . . . One Step Beyond: Anthology. large type ed. Ed. by Marilyn R. Riddle. (Illus.). 48p. (Orig.). 1988. pap. 10.00 (*0-9603748-5-X*) Sandpiper OR.

Otherwise. Eleanor Wilner. LC 93-18038. (Phoenix Poets Ser.). 144p. 1993. pap. 11.95 (*0-226-90030-4*); lib. bdg. 30.50 (*0-226-90029-0*) U Ch Pr.

Otherwise: New & Selected Poems. Jane Kenyon. LC 95-80894. 228p. 1996. 23.95 (*1-55597-240-3*) Graywolf.

Otherwise: New & Selected Poems. Jane Kenyon. 230p. 1997. pap. 16.00 (*1-55597-266-7*) Graywolf.

Otherwise Engaged. Suzanne Finnamore. LC 98-49998. 209p. 1999. 22.00 (*0-375-40652-2*) Knopf.

***Otherwise Engaged.** Suzanne Finnamore. LC 98-49998. (Contemporaries Ser.). 224p. 2000. pap. 12.00 (*0-375-70642-9*) Vin Bks.

Otherwise Engaged. Carolyn Keene. (Nancy Drew on Campus Ser.: No. 23). (YA). (gr. 8 up). 1997. per. 3.99 (*0-671-00215-5*) PB.

Otherwise Engaged: The Private Lives of Successful Career Women. Srully Blotnick. LC 84-28708. 310p. reprint ed. pap. 96.10 (*0-608-16043-1*, 203317000084) Bks Demand.

Otherwise Known As Murder. Neil McGaughey. LC 94-1527. 224p. 1994. text 20.00 (*0-684-19674-3*, Scribners Ref) Mac Lib Ref.

Otherwise Known As Sheila the Great see Judy Blume

Otherwise Known As Sheila the Great see Judy Blume Collection

Otherwise Known As Sheila the Great. Judy Blume. 128p. (J). (gr. 4-7). 1976. pap. 4.99 (*0-440-46701-2*, YB BDD) BDD Bks Young Read.

Otherwise Known As Sheila the Great. Judy Blume. 166p. pap. 4.99 (*0-8072-1497-3*) Listening Lib.

Otherwise Known As Sheila the Great. Judy Blume. (J). (gr. 3-6). 1972. 15.99 (*0-525-36455-2*, Dutton Child) Peng Put Young Read.

Otherwise Known As Sheila the Great. Judy Blume. (J). 1972. 9.60 (*0-606-00739-3*, Pub. by Turtleback) Demco.

***Otherwise Known as Sheila the Great.** Judy Blume. (Illus.). (J). (gr. 4-7). 2000. mass mkt. 2.99 (*0-375-80679-2*, Pub. by Random Bks Yng Read) Random.

Otherwise Perfect History. Julia Wendell. LC 87-81731. (Ithaca House Ser.). 84p. 1988. pap. 7.95 (*0-87886-127-0*, Greenfld Rev Pr) Greenfld Rev Lit.

Otherwise Than Being or Beyond Essence. Emmanuel Levinas. Tr. by Alphonso Lingis from FRE. LC 98-19597. 205p. 1998. pap. text 22.50 (*0-8207-0299-4*) Duquesne.

Otherwise Than Being or Beyond Essence. Emmanuel Levinas. Tr. by Alphonso Lingis. (Martinus Nijhoff Phaenomenologica Ser.: No. 3). 273p. 1981. lib. bdg. 85.50 (*90-247-2374-4*, Pub. by M Nijhoff) Kluwer Academic.

Otherworld. Sarah Dreher. LC 93-6977. (Stoner McTavish Mystery Ser.). 256p. (Orig.). 1993. pap. 10.95 (*0-934678-44-8*) New Victoria Pubs.

***Otherworld.** Mercedes Lackey et al. 640p. 2000. per. 6.99 (*0-671-57852-9*) Baen Bks.

Otherworld. F. S. Flint. LC 78-64028. (Des Imagistes: Literature of the Imagist Movement Ser.). reprint ed. 30.00 (*0-404-17107-9*) AMS Pr.

Otherworld in Irish Literature & History. Ed. by Jonathan Wooding. 256p. 1999. 50.00 (*1-85182-246-1*, Pub. by Four Cts Pr) Intl Spec Bk.

Otherworld Journeys: Accounts of Near-Death Experience in Medieval & Modern Times. Carol G. Zaleski. 288p. 1987. reprint ed. text 30.00 (*0-19-503915-7*) OUP.

Otherworld Journeys: Accounts of Near-Death Experience in Medieval & Modern Times. Carol G. Zaleski. 288p. 1988. reprint ed. pap. 11.95 (*0-19-505665-5*) OUP.

Otherworldly Hamlet: Four Essays. John O'Meara. 112p. 1991. pap. 10.00 (*0-920717-50-0*) SPD-Small Pr Dist.

Othman, the Third Caliph of Islam. Fazl Ahmad. (Heroes of Islam Ser.: Bk. 4). 95p. (Orig.). (YA). (gr. 7-12). 1984. pap. 3.50 (*1-56744-242-0*) Kazi Pubns.

Othmar H. Ammann: Sein Beitrag zur Entwicklung des Bruckenbaus. Fritz Stuessi. (Geschichte und Theorie der Architektur Ser.: No. 7). (GER., Illus.). 150p. 1980. 36.00 (*0-8176-0692-0*) Birkhauser.

Othniel see People of the Promise Series

Otho Stubbs, a Lasting Legacy: Western & Indian Art. Dora B. Stubbs. (Illus.). vi, 84p. 1992. pap. 44.95 (*0-9702163-1-9*) Stubbs.

Otho Stubbs, a Lasting Legacy: Western & Indian Art. deluxe ed. Dora B. Stubbs. (Illus.). vii, 84p. 1992. 54.95 (*0-9702163-0-0*) Stubbs.

Otia Sacra. Mildmay F. Westmorland. LC 75-31684. 200p. 1975. reprint ed. lib. bdg. 50.00 (*0-8201-1162-7*) Schol Facsimiles.

Otilia's Body. Sergio Galindo. Tr. by Carolyn Brushwood & John S. Brushwood. LC 93-44121. (Texas Pan American Ser.). (Illus.). 240p. (Orig.). 1994. pap. 15.95 (*0-292-72770-4*); text 37.50 (*0-292-72769-0*) U of Tex Pr.

Otimum & Equilibrium for Regional Economics: Collected Papers of Noboru Sakashita. Ed. by Komei Sasaki. LC 96-10508. 210p. 1996. 98.50 (*3-540-60884-2*) Spr-Verlag.

***Otis.** Janie Bynum. LC 99-6087. 36p. (J). (ps-2). 2000. 14.00 (*0-15-202153-1*, Harcourt Child Bks) Harcourt.

Otis Dunn-Manhunter. Nat Richards. Ed. by Billie Young. LC 73-83919. 150p. 1974. 21.95 (*0-87949-018-7*) Ashley Bks.

Otis Ferguson Reader. Otis Ferguson. Ed. by Dorothy Chamberlain & Robert Wilson. LC 82-71391. 327p. 1982. pap. 20.00 (*0-913204-14-5*) December Pr.

Otis Guernsey - Burns Mantle Theater Yearbook: The Best Plays of 1997-1998. Ed. by Otis L. Guernsey, Jr. (Illus.). 496p. 1998. 47.50 (*0-87910-271-3*) Limelight Edns.

Otis Guernsey-Burns Mantle Theater Yearbook: The Best Plays of 1993-1994. Ed. by Otis L. Guernsey, Jr. & Jeffrey Sweet. (Illus.). 648p. 1994. 45.00 (*0-87910-183-0*) Limelight Edns.

Otis Guernsey-Burns Mantle Theater Yearbook: The Best Plays of 1994-1995. Ed. by Otis L. Guernsey, Jr. & Jeffrey Sweet. (Illus.). 608p. 1995. 45.00 (*0-87910-196-2*) Limelight Edns.

Otis Guernsey-Burns Mantle Theater Yearbook: The Best Plays of 1995-1996. Ed. by Otis L. Guernsey & Jeffrey Sweet. (Illus.). 587p. 1996. 47.50 (*0-87910-089-3*) Limelight Edns.

Otis Guernsey-Burns Mantle Theater Yearbook: The Best Plays of 1996-1997. Ed. by Otis Guernsey, Jr. (Theater Yearbook: No. 78). (Illus.). 496p. 1997. 47.50 (*0-87910-097-4*) Limelight Edns.

***Otis Orchards the First Fifty Years.** Mary Hanley Berglund. 266p. 1998. reprint ed. pap. 15.95 (*0-87770-683-2*) Ye Galleon.

Otis Redding, Vol. 8. CPP Belwin Staff. (Legendary Performer Ser.). 1989. pap. 14.95 (*0-89898-617-6*, TPF0149) Wrner Bros.

Otis Rush Collection. 128p. 1997. otabind 19.95 (*0-7935-6569-3*) H Leonard.

Otis Spofford. Beverly Cleary. LC 53-6660. (Illus.). 192p. (J). (gr. 4-7). 1953. 16.00 (*0-688-21720-6*, Wm Morrow) Morrow Avon.

Otis Spofford. Beverly Cleary. (J). 1953. 9.60 (*0-606-04766-2*, Pub. by Turtleback) Demco.

Otis Spofford (repackage) Beverly Cleary. (Illus.). 192p. (J). (gr. 3-7). 1990. reprint ed. mass mkt. 4.99 (*0-380-70919-8*, Avon Bks) Morrow Avon.

Otisco Lake Community. Roger Trendowski. (Images of America Ser.). (Illus.). 128p. 1998. pap. 16.99 (*0-7524-1269-8*) Arcadia Publng.

Otisfield, Harrison, Naples & Sebago Town Register, 1906 (Town Histories & Directories) Compiled by Mitchell & Davis. 169p. 1997. reprint ed. pap. 24.00 (*0-8328-5885-4*) Higginson Bk Co.

Otitis Media: Coping with the Effects in the Classroom. Dorinne S. Davis. 138p. (C). 1989. 26.20 (*0-9622326-0-2*) The Davis Ctr.

Otitis Media & Child Development. Ed. by James F. Kavanagh. LC 86-50578. 232p. 1986. text 28.50 (*0-912752-12-2*) York Pr.

Otitis Media in Children: A Controversial Issue. Ed. by Jean-Philippe Guyot. (Oto-Rhino-Laryngologia Nova Ser.: Vol. 8, No. 3, Pt. 121-122, 1998). (Illus.). 48p. 1999. pap. 25.25 (*3-8055-6835-5*) S Karger.

Otitis Media in Infants & Children. 2nd ed. Charles D. Bluestone & Jerome O. Klein. LC 93-40646. (Illus.). 310p. 1994. text 69.00 (*0-7216-4818-5*, W B Saunders Co) Harcrt Hlth Sci Grp.

Otitis Media in Young Children: Medical, Developmental & Educational Considerations. Joanne E. Roberts et al. LC 96-42315. 1997. 48.95 (*1-55766-278-9*) P H Brookes.

Otitis Media Toad. M. Tos et al. (Illus.). xvi, 728p. 1999. 255.00 (*90-6299-165-3*) Kugler Pubns.

Otitis Media with Effusion in Young Children. 1995. lib. bdg. 251.95 (*0-8490-6779-0*) Gordon Pr.

Otitis Media with Effusion in Young Children: Clinical Practice Guideline. 1997. lib. bdg. 250.95 (*0-8490-8141-6*) Gordon Pr.

Otitis Media with Effusion in Young Children: Clinical Practice Guideline. Sylvan E. Stool & Alfred O. Berg. (Illus.). 108p. (C). 1998. pap. text 30.00 (*0-7881-4822-2*) DIANE Pub.

Otitis Media with Effusion in Young Children 12: Clinical Practice Guideline. Sylvan E. Stool. 124p. 1994. per. 5.00 (*0-16-061524-0*) USGPO.

Otitus Media with Effusion in Children. David Chalmers et al. (Clinics in Developmental Medicine Ser.: No. 108). (Illus.). 167p. (C). 1991. text 49.95 (*0-521-41224-2*, Pub. by Mc Keith Pr) Cambridge U Pr.

Otloh Von St. Emmeram Liber de Temptatione Cuiusdam Monachi: Untersuchung, Kritische Edition und Ubersetzung. Sabine Gabe. (Lateinische Sprache und Literatur des Mittelalters: Bd. 29). 384p. 1999. 55.95 (*3-906759-45-8*, Pub. by P Lang) P Lang Pubng.

Oto. William Whitman. LC 78-82348. (Columbia Univ. Contributions to Anthropology Ser.: Vol. 28). reprint ed. 31.50 (*0-404-50578-3*) AMS Pr.

Otoacoustic Emissions. Jan Maurer et al. LC 96-50973. (Self-Instructional Ser.). (Illus.). 60p. (Orig.). 1997. pap. text 25.00 (*1-56772-055-2*, 5506305) AAO-HNS.

Otoacoustic Emissions: A Manual for Clinical Applications. Brenda L. Lonsbury-Martin. 100p. 2000. pap. 49.95 (*1-56593-952-2*, 1882) Thomson Learn.

Otoacoustic Emissions: Basic Science & Clinical Applications. Charles I. Berlin. LC 97-50307. (Illus.). 124p. 1998. pap. 55.00 (*1-56593-975-1*, 1930) Thomson Learn.

Otoacoustic Emissions: Clinical Applications. Martin S. Robinette & Theodore J. Glattke. (Illus.). 368p. 1997. 49.00 (*0-86577-579-6*) Thieme Med Pubs.

Otoacoustic Emissions: From Research to Practice. Beth Priever & Martin Robinette. (Illus.). 75p. 1997. pap. 45.00 incl. audio (*0-910329-92-3*, 0112021) Am Speech Lang Hearing.

Otoacoustic Emissions: Theory Application & Techniques. Susan J. Norton & David T. Kemp. 300p. 1998. 34.95 (*1-56593-270-6*, 0592) Singular Publishing.

Otoendoscopically Guided Surgery. J. M. Thomassin. (Illus.). xvi, 87p. 1995. 104.00 (*3-540-59626-7*) Spr-Verlag.

Otogeny of the Immune System. Ed. by B. H. Waksman. (Progress in Allergy Ser.: Vol. 29). (Illus.). xii, 268p. 1981. 126.25 (*3-8055-2434-X*) S Karger.

Otoimmunology. Ed. by Jan E. Veldman & Brian F. McCabe. LC 87-17148. (Illus.). 196p. 1987. lib. bdg. 86.00 (*90-6299-033-9*, Pub. by Kugler) Kugler Pubns.

Otokahekagapi (First Beginnings) Sioux Creation Story. Thomas E. Simms. (Illus.). 36p. (Orig.). (J). 1987. pap. 4.50 (*1-877976-06-7*, 406-0005) Tipi Pr.
The first in a series of Lakota legends, is written & illustrated to foster greater respect for a proud people's tradition. This account in English & Lakota presents the profundity of the creation mystery. The pictures are Indian pictures, because this is the beginning of the Sioux Creation account. But it is for all children everywhere, because everyone asks about how things got started & how the World began. "So this picture book is like a little ball game. We shall learn that the book is a ball. Wakantanka will throw this ball to us, which is this book, & we shall catch it. Then we shall understand it. And we shall enjoy ourselves. Bring the ball -- this book -- to the Center, which is your Heart, then you will receive a present. The present is invisible, like a little secret. Good. That's all. Now I shall throw the ball to you. Catch it!" ***Publisher Paid Annotation.***

Otolaryngologist's Guide to Allergy. Hueston C. King. (Illus.). 312p. 1990. text 59.00 (*0-86577-338-6*) Thieme Med Pubs.

Otolaryngology, 5 vols. English. (C). 1993. ring bd. 585.00 (*0-397-57244-1*) Lppncott W & W.

Otolaryngology, 5 vols. Loose Leaf Reference Services Staff. Ed. by Gerald M. English. ring bd. 525.00 (*0-06-148010-X*) Lppncott W & W.

Otolaryngology, 5 vols. rev. ed. Loose Leaf Reference Services Staff. Ed. by Gerald M. English. 85.00 (*0-686-86019-5*) Lppncott W & W.

Otolaryngology, 4 vols., 1. 3rd ed. Michael M. Paparella & Donald A. Shumrick. Ed. by William L. Meyerhoff. LC 77-25566. (Illus.). 3536p. 1990. text 195.00 (*0-7216-1505-8*, W B Saunders Co) Harcrt Hlth Sci Grp.

Otolaryngology, 4 vols., 2. 3rd ed. Michael M. Paparella & Donald A. Shumrick. Ed. by William L. Meyerhoff. LC 77-25566. (Illus.). 3536p. 1990. text 195.00 (*0-7216-1506-6*, W B Saunders Co) Harcrt Hlth Sci Grp.

Otolaryngology, 4 vols., 3. 3rd ed. Michael M. Paparella & Donald A. Shumrick. Ed. by William L. Meyerhoff. LC 77-25566. (Illus.). 3536p. 1990. text 195.00 (*0-7216-1507-4*, W B Saunders Co) Harcrt Hlth Sci Grp.

Otolaryngology, 4 vols., 4. 3rd ed. Michael M. Paparella & Donald A. Shumrick. Ed. by William L. Meyerhoff. LC 77-25566. (Illus.). 3536p. 1990. text 195.00 (*0-7216-3446-X*, W B Saunders Co) Harcrt Hlth Sci Grp.

Otolaryngology, 4 vols., Set. 3rd ed. Michael M. Paparella & Donald A. Shumrick. Ed. by William L. Meyerhoff. LC 77-25566. (Illus.). 3536p. 1990. text 625.00 (*0-7216-1504-X*, W B Saunders Co) Harcrt Hlth Sci Grp.

Otolaryngology: A Case Study Approach. Thomas A. Tami. LC 97-51988. 1998. pap. 69.00 (*0-86577-773-X*); pap. 69.00 (*3-13-111541-6*) Thieme Med Pubs.

Otolaryngology: Head & Neck Surgery. Charles W. Cummings. 1996. text 495.00 incl. cd-rom (*0-8151-2071-0*); text 895.00 incl. cd-rom (*0-8151-2076-1*) Mosby Inc.

Otolaryngology: Head & Neck Surgery. Keatjin Lee. 951p. (C). 1992. pap. text 155.00 (*0-8385-9067-5*, A9067-8, Apple Lange Med) McGraw.

***Otolaryngology: Head & Neck Surgery.** Pasha. 2000. pap. 59.95 (*0-7693-0053-7*) Singular Publishing.

Otolaryngology: Head & Neck Surgery. 3rd ed. Charles W. Cummings et al. (Illus.). 3000p. (C). (gr. 13). 1998. text 495.00 (*0-8151-2067-2*, 29857) Mosby Inc.

***Otolaryngology: Head & Neck Surgery Review.** Charles W. Cummings, Jr. et al. 320p. (C). 1998. text. write for info. (*0-323-00688-4*) Mosby Inc.

Otolaryngology: Head/Neck Surgery. William L. Meyerhoff. (C). 1992. text 215.00 (*0-7216-3623-3*) Harcourt.

Otolaryngology: Pediatric Head & Neck Surgery, Vol. 3. Mark Richardson. (Illus.). 608p. (C). (gr. 13). 1998. text 150.00 (*0-8151-2135-0*, 29855) Mosby Inc.

***Otolaryngology: Self-Assessment & Board Review.** Charles A. Syms et al. (Illus.). 352p. 2001. pap. 49.00 (*0-86577-917-1*) Thieme Med Pubs.

***Otolaryngology: The Essentials.** Ed. by Allen M. Seiden et al. (Illus.). 1216p. 2000. pap. 69.00 (*0-86577-854-X*) Thieme Med Pubs.

***Otolaryngology Head & Neck Surgery.** 16th ed. John Jacob Ballenger. 2002. pap. 236.00 (*0-7693-0172-X*, Pub. by Singular Publishing) Thomson Learn.

***Otolaryngology Head & Neck Surgery Pocket Manual.** 16th ed. John Jacob Ballenger. 2002. pap. 64.00 (*0-7693-0173-8*, Pub. by Singular Publishing) Thomson Learn.

Otolaryngology in ASEAN Countries: 6th ASEAN Congress, Chiang, Rai, Thailand, November 1994. Ed. by Sujitra Prasansuk et al. LC 96-44296. (Advances in OtoRhinoLaryngology Ser.: Vol. 51, 1996). (Illus.). viii, 128p. 1996. 85.25 (*3-8055-6336-1*) S Karger.

Otolith Function in Spatial Orientation & Movement. Bernard Cohen & Bernhard J. M. Hess. LC 99-24766. (Annals of the New York Academy of Science Ser.). 1999. write for info. (*1-57331-218-5*) NY Acad Sci.

Otolith Microstructure Examination & Analysis. Ed. by David K. Stevenson. 126p. (Orig.). 1992. pap. 37.95 (*0-660-14747-5*, Pub. by Canadian Govt Pub) Accents Pubns.

Otolithi Piscium. D. Nolf. (Handbook of Paleoichthyology: Vol. 10). (Illus.). 145p. 1985. pap. text 128.70 (*3-437-30399-6*) Lubrecht & Cramer.

Otologic Medicine & Surgery, Vol. 1. Ed. by Peter W. Alberti & Robert J. Ruben. LC 88-1022. (Illus.). 1037p. reprint ed. pap. 200.00 (*0-7837-6824-9*, 204665600001) Bks Demand.

Otologic Medicine & Surgery, Vol. 2. Ed. by Peter W. Alberti & Robert J. Ruben. LC 88-1022. (Illus.). 949p. reprint ed. pap. 200.00 (*0-7837-6825-7*, 204665600002) Bks Demand.

Otologic Surgery. Ed. by Derald E. Brackmann et al. LC 93-40738. (Illus.). 1994. text 173.00 (*0-7216-6639-6*, W B Saunders Co) Harcrt Hlth Sci Grp.

Otologic Surgery: Core Workbook & Update Service. Goin. 1991. write for info. (*0-8151-3707-9*) Mosby Inc.

Otologic Surgery: Manual of Oto-Surgical Techniques. Michel Portmann & Didier Portmann. LC 97-45064. (Illus.). 298p. 1998. pap. 185.95 (*1-56593-939-5*, 1860) Thomson Learn.

Otological Significance of the Round Window. Y. Nomura. (Advances in OtoRhinoLaryngology Ser.: Vol. 33). (Illus.). x, 162p. 1984. 100.00 (*3-8055-3806-5*) S Karger.

Otology Today. Ed. by G. Babighian. (Advances in OtoRhinoLaryngology Ser.: Vol. 37). (Illus.). viii, 200p. 1987. 152.25 (*3-8055-4498-7*) S Karger.

Otomi de Ixtenxo. Yolanda Lastra. (SPA.). 453p. 1997. pap. 37.00 (*968-36-6000-2*, UN048, Pub. by Instit de Invest) UPLAAP.

Otoneurology. Ed. by Wilhelmus J. Oosterveld. LC 84-3717. (Wiley-Medical Publication). (Illus.). 284p. reprint ed. pap. 88.10 (*0-8357-7929-7*, 205232900002) Bks Demand.

Otoneurosurgery. W. Pellett et al. (Illus.). 256p. 1990. 238.00 (*0-387-50979-8*) Spr-Verlag.

Otoneurosurgery-Latral Skull Base. Salvinelli. 1996. text 93.00 (*0-7216-7051-2*, W B Saunders Co) Harcrt Hlth Sci Grp.

***Otono.** Karen Bryant-Mole. (Picture This! Ser.).Tr. of Fall. (SPA., Illus.). 24p. (J). (gr. k-2). 1999. lib. bdg. 12.95 (*1-57572-909-1*) Heinemann Lib.

Otono. Judy Nayer. Ed. by Don Curry. Tr. by Leyla Torres from ENG. (Spanish Discovery Links Ser.). (SPA.). 8p. (J). (gr. k). 1997. pap. text 2.75 (*1-56784-964-4*) Newbridge Educ.

Otono. J. M. Parramon et al. (Four Seasons Ser.). (SPA., Illus.). 32p. 1985. pap. 6.95 (*0-8120-3646-8*) Barron.

Otono. Lynn M. Stone. (Mientras la Tierra Gira Ser.).Tr. of Fall. 24p. (J). (gr. k-4). 1994. lib. bdg. 17.27 (*1-55916-061-6*) Rourke Bk Co.

Otono del Patriarca. Gabriel Garcia Marquez. (SPA.). 301p. 1980. 10.00 (*0-8288-8588-5*) Fr & Eur.

Otono del Patriarca. Gabriel Garcia Marquez. (SPA.). 263p. 1987. pap. 24.95 (*0-7859-4984-4*) Fr & Eur.

Otono del Patriarca. Gabriel Garcia Marquez. (SPA.). 297p. 1997. pap. text 24.98 (*968-13-1707-6*) Edit Diana.

Otophysiology: Proceedings of the International Symposium, Ann Arbor, 1971. International Symposium on Otophysiology Staff. Ed. by J. E. Hawkins et al. (Advances in OtoRhinoLaryngology Ser.: Vol. 20). 1973. 182.75 (*3-8055-1338-0*) S Karger.

Otoplasty: Aesthetic & Reconstructive Techniques. 2nd ed. Jack Davis. LC 96-35161. (Illus.). 1525p. 1997. 165.00 (*0-387-94878-3*) Spr-Verlag.

Otorhinolaryngology: Head & Neck Surgery. 15th rev. ed. Ed. by John J. Ballenger & James B. Snow. LC 95-7241. (Illus.). 1296p. 1996. 179.00 (*0-683-00315-1*) Lppncott W & W.

Otorhinolaryngology, Head & Neck Surgery: Proceedings of the XIV World Congress, Madrid, Spain, Sept. 10-15, 1989, Vols. 1 & 2. Ed. by T. Sacristan et al. LC 91-6998. (Illus.). 1991. lib. bdg. 514.50 (*90-6299-071-1*, Pub. by Kugler) Kugler Pubns.

Otosclerosis. Ed. by R. Filipo. LC 90-5230. (Illus.). 178p. 1990. lib. bdg. 51.50 (*90-6299-061-4*, Pub. by Kugler) Kugler Pubns.

Otosclerosis: Diagnosis & Treatment. 2nd ed. Anthony F. Jahn & David M. Vernick. (Self-Instructional Package Ser.). (Illus.). 79p. 1993. pap. text 25.00 (*1-56772-007-2*) AAO-HNS.

Otoscopy. Browning. write for info. (*0-340-61376-9*, Pub. by E A) Routldge.

Otoscopy: A Structured Approach. P. J. Wormald & G. G. Browning. (Illus.). 104p. (Orig.). (C). 1996. pap. text 70.00 (*1-56593-706-6*, 1390) Singular Publishing.

Otot Ha-Shamayim: Samuel Ibn Tibbon's Hebrew Version of Aristotle's Meteorology: A Critical Edition. Aristotle. Tr. & Intro. by Resianne Fontaine. LC 94-48198. (Aristoteles Semitico-Latinus Ser.: Vol. 8). 1995. 114.50 (*90-04-10258-2*) Brill Academic Pubs.

Ototoxicity: Basic Science & Clinical Applications. Ed. by Donald Henderson et al. 410p. 1999. lib. bdg. 120.00 (*1-57331-204-5*) NY Acad Sci.

Otra: Marriage Meltdown. Emma Darcy. (Bianca Ser.: Vol. 455).Tr. of Other. (SPA.). 1998. per. 3.50 (*0-373-33455-9*, 1-33455-6) Harlequin Bks.

Otra Broma de Elmer. David McKee.Tr. of Elmer Again. (SPA.). 28p. (J). (gr. 1-3). 1994. 12.99 (*968-16-4560-X*, Pub. by Fondo) Continental Bk.

Otra Cara: La Vida de un Maya. 3rd ed. Gaspar P. Gonzalez. (SPA.). 256p. 1998. pap. 12.95 (*1-886502-21-8*) Yax Te Found.

Otra Cara de la Moneda. Beltran De Quiros. LC 83-82388. (Coleccion Caniqui). (SPA.). 62p. (Orig.). 1984. pap. 5.95 (*0-89729-342-8*) Ediciones.

Otra Cara del Paraiso: Verdad/Sectas. C. Mazanares.Tr. of Other Side of Paradise. (SPA.). 272p. 1995. 7.99 (*1-56063-462-6*, 498442) Editorial Unilit.

***Otra Historia de los Estados Unidos.** Howard Zinn. Orig. Title: A People's History of the United States. (SPA.). 520p. 2000. pap. 19.95 (*1-58322-054-2*, Pub. by Seven Stories) Publishers Group.

Otra Mujer en Su Matrimonio. Penny Vincenzi. 1999. pap. text 13.95 (*84-08-02252-0*) Planeta.

Otra Mujer en Su Matrimonio. Norman Wright. (SPA.). 224p. 1996. pap. 8.99 (*0-8254-1889-5*, Edit Portavoz) Kregel.

Otra Oportunidad. Laurie John. Tr. by Maruja Del Pozo. (Sweet Valley University Ser.: No. 6).Tr. of The Love of Her Life. (YA). (gr. 7 up). 1995. 15.60 (*0-606-10534-4*, Pub. by Turtleback) Demco.

Otra Oportunidad de Amar, Vol. 162. Cindy Gerard. (Silhouette Deseo Ser.). 1999. per. 3.50 (*0-373-35292-1*) Harlequin Bks.

Otra Orilla: Comedia en Tres Actos. Jose Lopez-Rubio. Ed. by Anthony M. Pasquariello & John V. Falconieri. LC 58-12829. (SPA.). 1977. reprint ed. pap. text 7.95 (*0-89197-324-9*) Irvington.

Otra Sintaxis. Armando Zarate & Hugo Bastos. (Illus.). 28p. (Orig.). 1981. pap. 4.00 (*0-935350-06-3*) Luna Bisonte.

Otra Vez . . . - Prohibido . . . - Arboles . . . Alejandro Casona. (SPA.). 172p. 1985. 7.95 (*0-8288-7030-6*, S30189) Fr & Eur.

Otra Vez el Diablo Nuestra Natacha: Arboles Mueren de Pie. Alejandro Casona. (SPA.). pap. 8.95 (*968-432-252-6*, Pub. by Porrua) Continental Bk.

Otranto. Maria Corti. Tr. by Jessie Bright from ITA. LC 93-32681. 288p. (Orig.). 1993. pap. 12.50 (*0-934977-29-1*) Italica Pr.

Otras Inquisiciones. Jorge Luis Borges. (SPA.). pap. 13.95 (*84-206-1604-4*, Pub. by Alianza Editorial) Continental Bk.

Otritsanije Vmesto Utverzhdenije. George Grabbe.Tr. of Denial Instead of Affirmation. 48p. 1971. pap. 2.00 (*0-317-30377-5*) Holy Trinity.

***Otro.** Miranda Lee.Tr. of Other. (ENG & SPA.). 2000. per. 3.50 (*0-373-33540-7*) Harlequin Bks.

Otro Amor, Otra Cluded. Barbara Taylor Bradford. 1999. pap. text 9.95 (*84-08-02522-8*) Planeta.

Otro Borges, el Primer Borges (The Other Borges, the First Borges) Rafael O. Franco. (SPA.). 300p. 1995. reprint ed. pap. 10.99 (*950-557-187-9*, Pub. by Fondo) Continental Bk.

Otro en Tu Corazon. Emma Darcy. (Bianca Ser.: No. 171). (SPA.). 1999. per. 3.50 (*0-373-33521-0*) Harlequin Bks.

Otro Hombre (The Other Man) Karen Van der Zee. (SPA.). 1997. per. 3.50 (*0-373-33411-7*, 1-33411-9) Harlequin Bks.

Otro Lado. Alejandro Aura. (Illus.). 44p. 1995. 12.99 (*968-16-3672-4*) Fondo.

***Otro Lado.** Luis De la Paz. LC 99-67260. (Coleccion Caniqui). (SPA.). 133p. 1999. pap. 13.00 (*0-89729-914-0*) Ediciones.

Otro Lado de la Biblia (The Other Side of the Bible) Lo Que la Teologia No Ha Revelado - What Theology Has Not Revealed - un Amanecev a la Realidad - a Dawn to Reality. Jacob Principe. (SPA.). 250p. (Orig.). pap. write for info. (*0-9641776-0-9*) El Otro Lado.

Otro Lado (The Other Side) The True Story of Marcus Hooks--Smuggler. Jack Malmin. LC 90-70919. (Illus.). 1991. 19.95 (*0-9627198-0-3*) Trailblazer Pub.

Otro Lope de Vega, No. 114. Sainz De Robles & Federico Carlos Corriente Cordoba. (SPA.). 150p. 1973. write for info. (*0-8288-8577-X*) Fr & Eur.

***Otro Problema!** Susan F. Tierno. Tr. by Ana M. Alvarado. (Think-Kids Book Collection).Tr. of It Was Just Another Problem. (SPA., Illus.). 16p. (J). 2000. pap. 2.95 (*1-58237-044-3*) Creat Think.

Otros - Columbus & the Three Who Made His Enterprise of the Indies Succeed. John Frye. LC 92-32974. (Illus.). 128p. 1992. text 59.95 (*0-7734-9196-1*) E Mellen.

Otros Diaz: Memories of "Other Days"...from Mexico in Revolution to a Life of Medicine in Texas. Octavio Garcia. Ed. by Virginia Kimball. LC 84-82265. (Illus.). 400p. 1985. 15.95 (*0-9614037-0-5*) Grey Home Pr.

Otros Evangelios. P. Hoff.Tr. of Other Gospels. (SPA.). 192p. 1993. pap. 9.99 (*0-8297-1904-0*) Vida Pubs.

Otros Extranjeros En la Revolucion Norteamericana. Herminio Portell-Vila. LC 77-88537. (Coleccion de Estudios Hispanicos - Hispanic Studies Collection). 1978. pap. 8.00 (*0-89729-173-5*) Ediciones.

Otsego County New York State, 1800: Federal Population Census Schedule, Transcript & Index. Ed. by Ralph V. Wood, Jr. LC 65-4697. vii, 68p. 1965. pap. 4.50 (*0-915184-04-4*) R V Wood.

Otsego County Reminiscences: Personal & Other Incidents; Early Settlement of Otsego County Etc. Levi Beardsley. (Illus.). 575p. 1997. reprint ed. lib. bdg. 59.50 (*0-8328-6197-9*) Higginson Bk Co.

Otsu-e: Japanese Folk Paintings: From the Harriet & Edison Spencer Collection. Matthew Welch. (Illus.). 80p. 1997. pap. 25.00 (*0-912964-55-3*) Minneapolis Inst Arts.

Otsutstvie. Derieva Regina. LC 92-46143. (RUS.). 122p. (Orig.). 1993. pap. 8.00 (*1-55779-053-1*) Hermitage Pubs.

Ottaviani Intervention: Short Critical Study of the New Order of Mass. Alfredo C. Ottaviani & Antonio C. Bacci. Tr. by Anthony Cekada. LC 92-60956. 63p. (Orig.). 1992. pap. 7.00 (*0-89555-470-4*) TAN Bks Pubs.

Ottavio Bariolla: Caprici, Overo Canzoni a Quattro...Libro Terzo (Milan, 1594) Ed. by James Ladewig. LC 94-47251. (Italian Instrumental Music of the Sixteenth & Seventeenth Centuries Ser.: Vol. 12). 216p. 1995. text 94.00 (*0-8240-4511-4*) Garland.

Ottavo Libro de Madrigali a Cinque Voci (1598) Luca Marenzio. (Secular Works: Vol. 15). (Illus.). 1986. pap. 50.00 (*0-8450-7115-7*) Broude.

Ottawa. Kathi Howes. (Native American People Ser.: Set III). 32p. (J). (gr. 4-8). 1992. lib. bdg. 21.27 (*0-86625-394-7*) Rourke Pubns.

Ottawa. Elaine Landau. (First Bks.). (Illus.). 64p. (J). (gr. 5-8). 1996. lib. bdg. 22.00 (*0-531-20226-7*) Watts.

Ottawa. Elaine Landau. (First Bks.). (Illus.). 64p. (J). (gr. 5-8). 1996. pap. 6.95 (*0-531-15783-0*) Watts.

Ottawa. Tanya Lloyd. LC 96-910736. (Illus.). 96p. 17.95 (*1-55110-527-6*) Whitecap Bks.

Ottawa. Ed. by Carol Martin. LC 97-950011. (Colour Guides Ser.). (Illus.). 200p. 1997. pap. 16.95 (*0-88780-396-2*, Pub. by Formac Publ Co) Seven Hills Bk.

***Ottawa.** 2nd ed. Pascale Couture. (Travel Guide Ser.). (Illus.). 2001. pap. 12.95 (*2-89464-331-4*) Ulysses Travel.

Ottawa: A Contemporary Portrait. Sue Baker et al. LC 97-36178. 224p. 1997. 39.00 (*1-885352-74-3*) Community Comm.

Ottawa: A Kid's Eye View. Laurel Aziz & Frank B. Edwards. (Illus.). 72p. (YA). (gr. 5 up). 1993. pap. 9.95 (*0-921285-26-4*, Pub. by Bungalo Books) Firefly Bks Ltd.

Ottawa: An Illustrated History. John H. Talor. 232p. pap. 19.95 (*0-88862-980-X*, Pub. by J Lorimer) Formac Dist Ltd.

Ottawa: An Illustrated History. John H. Talor. (Illus.). 232p. 34.95 (*0-88862-981-8*, Pub. by J Lorimer) Formac Dist Ltd.

Ottawa: Ulysses Travel Guide. Pascale Couture. Ed. by Ulysses Travel Guide Staff. (Ulysses Travel Guide Ser.). (Illus.). 192p. pap. 12.95 (*2-89464-170-2*, 862588Q) Ulysses Travel.

Ottawa: Where Rivers Meet - An Illustrated History. Courtney C. Bond. LC 84-19571. 192p. 1984. 24.95 (*0-89781-111-9*) Am Historical Pr.

Ottawa & Chippewa Indians of Michigan, 1870-1909. Raymond C. Lantz. 296p. 1991. pap. 21.00 (*1-55613-531-9*) Heritage Bk.

Ottawa & the Outer Provinces: The Challenge of Regional Integration in Canada. Stephen Tomblin. LC 96-112525. 214p. 29.95 (*1-55028-477-0*, Pub. by J Lorimer); pap. 19.95 (*1-55028-476-2*, Pub. by J Lorimer) Formac Dist Ltd.

***Ottawa County Historical Atlas & Gazetteer.** Ed. by Kit Lane. 1999. pap. 9.50 (*1-877703-46-X*) Pavilion Pr.

Ottawa County, OK, News-Papers: 1895-1922 Vital Statistics Index. Ed. by Hildred Hughes Ables & Audrey Topliff. 429p. 1980. 35.00 (*1-892744-07-4*, A-107) Maloy.

***Ottawa Entertainment, 2000.** (Illus.). 550p. 1999. pap. 30.00 (*1-58553-048-4*, 0067) Enter Pubns.

Ottawa Indian Cemetery, 1870-1995. Compiled by Gerald L. Housman. 112p. write for info. (*0-9640706-7-7*) Cock-a-Hoop.

Ottawa Men: The Civil Service Mandarins, 1935-1957. 2nd ed. Jack L. Granatstein. LC 98-141306. (Illus.). 368p. 1998. reprint ed. pap. 24.95 (*0-8020-8181-9*) U of Toronto Pr.

Ottawa, 1974 see Chemistry of Natural Products: Proceedings

Ottawa River Canals & the Defence of British North America. Robert F. Legget. (Illus.). 308p. 1988. text 35.00 (*0-8020-5794-2*) U of Toronto Pr.

***Ottawa River Whitewater: A Paddler's Guide to the Middle & Main Channels.** Jim Hargreaves. (Illus.). 168p. 2000. pap. 13.95 (*1-55046-317-9*) Boston Mills.

Ottawa Senators see NHL Today

Ottawa Senators. Morgan Hughes & Paul Joseph. LC 98-13894. (Inside the NHL Ser.). (J). 1998. 16.48 (*1-57765-057-3*) ABDO Pub Co.

Ottawa Valley Portfolio. Pat Keough & Rosemarie Keough. (Illus.). 180p. 1987. 75.00 (*0-9692557-0-5*) Genl Dist Srvs.

Ottawa Waterway: Gateway to a Continent. Robert F. Legget. LC 75-6780. (Illus.). 303p. reprint ed. pap. 94.00 (*0-8357-8258-1*, 203405000088) Bks Demand.

Ottawa with Kids. James Hale & Joanne Milner. LC 97-160240. (Illus.). 184p. 1996. pap. 16.95 (*0-921912-98-6*) MW&R.

Ottawan. John C. Wright, Jr. (Illus.). 80p. 1984. reprint ed. pap. 7.00 (*0-912382-31-7*) Black Letter.

Ottemiller's Index to Plays in Collections: An Author & Title Index to Plays Appearing in Collections Published Between 1900 & 1985. 7th ed. Billie M. Connor & Helene Machedlover. LC 87-34160. 576p. 1988. 52.00 (*0-8108-2081-1*) Scarecrow.

Otter. Kenneth Meadows. LC 97-42267. (Little Earth Medicine Library). 64p. 1998. 8.95 (*0-7894-2882-2*) DK Pub Inc.

Otter. Sandy Ransford. LC 98-40378. (Animal Lives Ser.). (Illus.). 32p. (gr. k-3). 1999. teacher ed. 9.95 (*0-7534-5176-X*) LKC.

Otter & Twin Otter. Sean Rossiter. 208p. 1999. 34.95 (*1-55054-637-6*, Pub. by DGL) Orca Bk Pubs.

Otter Creek: The Indian Road. James E. Peterson. LC 90-82089. (Illus.). 176p. (Orig.). (YA). (gr. 5 up). 1990. pap. 15.00 (*0-914960-83-0*) Academy Bks.

Otter Hound Champions, 1952-1994. Camino E. E. & Bk. Co. Staff. LC 96-212446. (Illus.). 70p. 1992. pap. 36.95 (*1-55893-020-5*) Camino E E & Bk.

Otter Nonsense. Norman Juster. LC 93-22041. (Illus.). 64p. (J). 1994. 9.95 (*0-688-12282-5*, Wm Morrow) Morrow Avon.

Otter on His Own: The Story of a Sea Otter. Doe Boyle. LC 94-28696. (Smithsonian Oceanic Collection). (Illus.). 32p. (J). (ps-2). 1995. 15.95 (*1-56899-129-0*); 19.95 incl. audio (*1-56899-133-9*, BC4005) Soundprints.

Otter on His Own: The Story of a Sea Otter, Incl. 12" plush toy. Doe Boyle. LC 94-28696. (Smithsonian Oceanic Collection). (Illus.). 32p. (J). (ps-2). 1995. 32.95 (*1-56899-131-2*) Soundprints.

Otter on His Own: The Story of a Sea Otter, Micro bk. Doe Boyle. LC 94-28696. (Smithsonian Oceanic Collection). (Illus.). 32p. (J). (ps-2). 1995. 4.95 (*1-56899-130-4*) Soundprints.

Otter on His Own: The Story of a Sea Otter, Micro bk., incl. 7" plush toy. Doe Boyle. LC 94-28696. (Smithsonian Oceanic Collection). (Illus.). 32p. (J). (ps-2). 1995. 12.95 (*1-56899-132-0*) Soundprints.

Otter Play. Nancy Luenn. LC 96-34026. 32p. (ps-4). 1998. 16.00 (*0-689-81126-8*) S&S Childrens.

***Otter Skins, Boston Ships & China Goods: The Maritime Fur Trade of the Northwest Coast, 1785-** James R. Gibson. (Illus.). 448p. 1999. pap. text 22.50 (*0-295-97900-3*) U of Wash Pr.

Otter Skins, Boston Ships, & China Goods: The Maritime Fur Trade of the Northwest Coast, 1785-1841. James R. Gibson. (Illus.). 448p. 1992. text 60.00 (*0-7735-0829-5*, Pub. by McG-Queens Univ Pr) CUP Services.

***Otter Skins, Boston Ships & China Goods: The Maritime Fur Trade of the Northwest Coast, 1785-1841.** James R. Gibson. 448p. 1999. pap. 27.95 (*0-7735-2028-7*) McG-Queens Univ Pr.

Otter Swims see Sierra Club's Growing up Books

Otterbury Incident. Day C. Lewis. 1961. pap. 12.95 (*0-14-030163-1*, Pub. by Pnguin Bks Ltd) Trafalgar.

Otterhound: AKC Rank #142. Hugh R. Monat. (Rare Breed Ser.). (Illus.). 96p. 1998. 19.95 (*0-7938-0775-1*, RX-125) TFH Pubns.

Otters see Welcome to the World of Animals

Otters. Paul Chanin. (Illus.). 128p. text 19.95 (*0-905483-90-1*, Pub. by Whittet Bks) Diamond Farm Bk.

Otters. Emilie U. Lepthien. LC 93-33515. (New True Books Ser.). (Illus.). 48p. (J). (gr. 2-4). 1994. pap. 5.50 (*0-516-41056-3*) Childrens.

Otters. David Stone. (Illus.). 32p. 1992. pap. 8.00 (*2-8317-0096-5*, Pub. by IUCN) Island Pr.

Otters: An Action Plan for Their Conservation. Sheila Macdonald & Chris Mason. Ed. by Pat Foster-Turley et al. (Illus.). 130p. (Orig.). 1991. pap. 20.00 (*2-8317-0013-2*, Pub. by IUCN) Island Pr.

Otters, Octopuses & Odd Creatures of the Deep: A Tale of History, Science, & Mystery. Randall A. Reinstedt. Ed. by John Bergez. LC 87-82106. (History & Happenings of California Ser.). (Illus.). 64p. (J). (gr. 3-6). 1987. 13.95 (*0-933818-21-1*); pap. 9.95 (*0-933818-76-9*) Ghost Town.

Otters on the Loose: An Otter's Adventure Story. Louis Dorfman. LC 98-60174. 147p. (J). (gr. 2-9). 1998. pap. 8.95 (*1-881636-35-6*) Windsor Hse Pub Grp.

Otters under Water. Jim Arnosky. (Illus.). 32p. (J). (ps-1). 1992. 14.95 (*0-399-22339-8*, G P Putnam) Peng Put Young Read.

***Otters under Water, 1 vol.** Jim Arnosky. 1999. pap. 5.99 (*0-698-11556-2*) Putnam Pub Group.

Ottoman Survey Register of Podolia (ca. 1681) Pt. 1: Defter-i Mufassal-i Eyalet-i-Kamanice. Dariusz Kolodziejczyk. (Ottoman Documents Pertaining to Ukraine & the Black Sea Countries Ser.). (Illus.). 224p. (C). 2000. pap. text 75.00 (*0-916458-78-4*) Harvard Ukrainian.

Ottoman Survey Register of Podolia (ca. 1681) Pt. 2: Defter-i Mufassal-i Eyalet-i-Kamanice. Dariusz Kolodziejczyk. (Ottoman Documents Pertaining to Ukraine & the Black Sea Countries Ser.). (Illus.). 192p. (C). 2000. pap. text 75.00 (*0-916458-79-2*) Harvard Ukrainian.

Ottmar Liebert. Nouveau Flamenco. 1997. pap. text 14.95 (*1-56922-137-5*) Creat Cncpts.

Ottmar Liebert: Borrasca - Tab Guitar. 1998. 14.95 (*1-56922-179-0*, 07-4084) Creat Cncpts.

***Ottmar Mergenthaler: The Man & His Machine: A Biographical Appreciation of the Inventor on His Centennial.** Basil Kahan. LC 99-45557. (Illus.). 264p. 2000. 55.00 (*1-58456-007-X*, 56711) Oak Knoll.

Otto. Charlotte V. Dunn. LC 99-189022. (Illus.). 240p. 1998. pap. 20.00 (*1-57502-867-0*, PO2362, SchlMate) Morris Pubng.

***Otto: Biography of a Teddy Bear.** Tomi Ungerer. LC 99-16773. (Illus.). 32p. (J). (gr. 1-5). 1999. 16.95 (*1-57098-304-6*, Pub. by Roberts Rinehart) Publishers Group.

Otto Cartoons. Jay Piersanti. LC 93-80698. (Illus.). 96p. 1994. pap. 5.95 (*0-87341-296-6*, OS01) Krause Pubns.

Otto Dix: Life & Work. Fritz Loffler. Tr. by R. J. Hollingdale from GER. LC 81-2947. (Illus.). 424p. 1982. 95.00 (*0-8419-0578-9*) Holmes & Meier.

Otto Dix: Watercolors & Gouaches. (GER., Illus.). 296p. 1991. 275.00 (*3-7757-0334-9*, Pub. by Gerd Hatje) Dist Art Pubs.

Otto Dix, 1891-1969. Ed. by Keith Hartley. (Illus.). 232p. 1992. 75.00 (*1-85437-094-4*, Pub. by Tate Gallery) U of Wash Pr.

Otto Ernst Schweizer, 1890-1965: Bauten und Projekte. Immo Boyken. (Illus.). 304p. 1997. 79.00 (*3-930698-01-3*) Edition A Menges.

Otto Furth, das Dramatische Werk der Wiener Jahre und Prosa im Exil, Vol. 10. Ursula Macris. (Austrian Culture Ser.). (GER.). VIII, 182p. (C). 1995. 45.95 (*0-8204-2230-4*) P Lang Pubng.

Otto Gross, Freudian Psychoanalyst, 1877-1920: Literature & Ideas. Martin Green. LC 98-53713. 372p. 1999. text 99.95 (*0-7734-8164-8*) E Mellen.

Otto Haendler - Leben und Werk: Eine Untersuchung der Strukturen Seines Seelsorgeverstandnisses. Kerstin Voigt. (Erfahrung und Theologie Ser.: Bd. 21). (GER.). 354p. 1993. 55.80 (*3-631-45188-1*) P Lang Pubng.

***Otto Hahn: Achievement & Responsibility.** Klaus Hoffmann. LC 00-40045. 2000. pap. write for info. (*0-387-95057-5*) Spr-Verlag.

Otto Hahn & the Rise of Nuclear Physics. Ed. by William R. Shea. (University of Western Ontario Series in Phylosophy of Science: 22). 261p. 1983. lib. bdg. 162.50 (*90-277-1584-X*) Kluwer Academic.

Otto Jespersen: Facets of His Life & Work. Ed. by Arne Juul & Hans F. Nielsen. LC 89-17797. (Studies in the History of the Language Sciences: No. 52). xviii, 154p. 1989. 35.00 (*90-272-4537-1*) J Benjamins Pubng Co.

Otto Klemperer: His Life & Times, 2 vols. Peter Heyworth. LC 97-111686. (C). 1996. text 75.00 (*0-521-56538-3*) Cambridge U Pr.

Otto Klemperer: His Life & Times, Vol. 1: 1885-1933. Peter Heyworth. 512p. 1996. 42.95 (*0-521-49509-1*) Cambridge U Pr.

Otto Klemperer: His Life & Times, Vol. 2: 1933-1973. Peter Heyworth. (Illus.). 500p. (C). 1996. 42.95 (*0-521-24488-9*) Cambridge U Pr.

Otto Kunzli: Oh, Say. Klaus Ottmann. (Illus.). 32p. (C). 1992. 10.00 (*0-929687-10-8*) E & C Zilkha Gal.

Otto Laske: Navigating New Musical Horizons, 53. Ed. by Jerry Tabor. LC 98-42709. (Contributions to the Study of Music & Dance Ser.: 53). 232p. 1999. 59.95 (*0-313-30632-X*) Greenwood.

Otto Learns about His Medicine: A Story about Medication for Children with ADHD. rev. ed. Matthew R. Galvin. LC 95-34553. (Illus.). 32p. (J). (ps-3). 1995. 11.95 (*0-945354-71-1*) Am Psychol.

Otto Ludwig: Das Literarische und Musikalische Werk Mit Einer Vollstandigen Otto-Ludwig-Bibliographie. Claudia Pilling. 567p. 1998. 79.95 (*3-631-33149-5*) P Lang Pubng.

Otto Luening: A Bio-Bibliography, 35. Ralph Hartsock. LC 90-22926. (Bio-Bibliographies in Music Ser.: No. 35). 288p. 1991. lib. bdg. 62.95 (*0-313-24320-4*, HAO, Greenwood Pr) Greenwood.

Otto Neumann: A Rediscovered Artist. Stephen P. Breslow & David M. Sokol. (Illus.). 85p. (Orig.). (C). 1987. pap. 18.00 (*1-878293-01-X*) Tampa Mus Art.

Otto Neurath: Philosophy Between Science & Politics. Nancy Cartwright et al. (Ideas in Context Ser.: No. 38). (Illus.). 304p. (C). 1996. text 59.95 (*0-521-45174-4*) Cambridge U Pr.

Otto of the Silver Hand. Howard Pyle. (Illus.). 173p. (J). (gr. 5-9). 1967. pap. 6.95 (*0-486-21784-1*) Dover.

Otto Perry: Master Railroad Photographer. Charles Albi & William C. Jones. LC 82-4201. (Illus.). 336p. 1982. 30.00 (*0-918654-32-7*) CO RR Mus.

***Otto Piene: Retrospektive 1952, 1996.** Otto Piene. (Illus.). 208p. 2000. 65.00 (*3-87909-468-3*, Pub. by Wienand) Nazraeli Press.

Otto Ping: Photographer of Brown County, Indiana, 1900-1940. W. Douglas Hartley. LC 94-22242. (Illus.). x, 95p. 1994. pap. 10.95 (*0-87195-105-3*) Ind Hist Soc.

Otto Selz: His Contribution to Psychology. Adriaan de Groot. Ed. by Nico H. Frijda. (Illus.). 306p. 1981. 57.70 (*90-279-3438-X*) Mouton.

Otto Skorzeny: My Commando Operations: The Memoirs of Hitler's Most Daring Commando. Otto Skorzeny. Tr. by David Johnston from GER. LC 94-68031. (Illus.). 496p. 1995. 35.00 (*0-88740-718-8*) Schiffer.

Otto Steidle: Structures for Living. Ed. by Florian Kossak. (Illus.). 152p. 1994. pap. 45.00 (*3-7643-5545-X*, Pub. by Birkhauser) Princeton Arch.

Otto the Cat. Gail Herman. (All Aboard Reading Picture Readers Ser.). (Illus.). 32p. (J). (ps-1). 1995. pap. 3.95 (*0-448-40968-2*, G & D) Peng Put Young Read.

Otto Von Bismarck & Imperial Germany. 3rd ed. Theodore S. Hamerow. LC 93-76066. (Problems in European Civilization Ser.). 170p. (C). 1994. pap. text 18.36 (*0-669-29444-6*) HM Trade Div.

O

An Asterisk (*) at the beginning of an entry indicates that the title is appearing for the first time.

Otto Wagner: Reflections on the Raiment of Modernity. Ed. by Harry F. Mallgrave. LC 93-3808. (Issues & Debates Ser.). (Illus.). 436p. 1993. 55.00 (*0-89236-258-8*, Pub. by J P Getty Trust); pap. 29.95 (*0-89236-257-X*, Pub. by J P Getty Trust) OUP.

*__Otto Weininger: Sex, Science & Self in Imperial Vienna.__ Chandak Sengoopta. LC 99-88081. (Series on Sexuality, History & Society). 1999. 29.00 (*0-226-74867-7*) U Ch Pr.

Ottobeuren, Benediktiner-Abtei, Bibliothek und Musik-Archiv MO 1037. Alexander Silbiger. LC 88-752059. (Seventeenth-Century Keyboard Music Ser.: Vol. 23). 184p. 1989. text 25.00 (*0-8240-8022-X*) Garland.

Ottocento: Romanticism & Revolution in 19th-Century Italian Painting. Roberta J. Olson. LC 92-30898. (Illus.). 296p. 1992. 67.95 (*0-917418-94-8*) Am Fed Arts.

Ottocento: Romanticism & Revolution in 19th-Century Italian Painting. Roberta J. Olson. LC 92-30898. (Illus.). 296p. (C). 1993. text 69.95 (*0-8122-3207-0*, Pub. by Centro Di) U of Pa Pr.

Ottoline Morrell: Life on the Grand Scale. Miranda Seymour. LC 92-37079. 451p. 1993. 30.00 (*0-374-22818-3*) FS&G.

Ottoman Almanacs of the Arab Provinces, 1888-1902, 7 vols. Ed. by Selim Deringil. (ENG & TUR.). 1999. reprint ed. lib. bdg. 1495.00 (*1-85207-850-2*, Pub. by Archive Editions) N Ross.

Ottoman & Persian Odysseys, Vol. 1. Johnston. 258p. 1998. text 49.50 (*1-86064-330-2*, Pub. by I B T) St Martin.

Ottoman & Spanish Empires in the 16th & 17th Centuries. Leopold Von Ranke. LC 78-153628. reprint ed. 29.50 (*0-404-09266-7*) AMS Pr.

Ottoman & Turkish Jewry: Community & Leadership. (Turkish Studies). 16.95 (*0-614-04313-1*) IN Univ Turkish.

Ottoman & Turkish Jewry: Community & Leadership. Ed. by Aron Rodrigue. LC 91-77684. (Turkish Studies: Vol. 12). 292p. (C). 1992. pap. 18.95 (*1-878318-03-9*) IN Univ Turkish.

Ottoman Army, 1914-18. David Nicolle. (Men-at-Arms Ser.). (Illus.). 48p. 1994. pap. 11.95 (*1-85532-412-1*, 9240, Pub. by Ospry) Stackpole.

Ottoman Army of Napoleonic War. Nicolle. 1998. 12.95 (*1-85532-697-3*, 847844Q, Pub. by Ospry) Stackpole.

Ottoman Art in the Service of Empire. Zdzislaw Zygulski, Jr. (Hagop Kevorkian Series on Near Eastern Art & Civilization). (Illus.). 192p. (C). 1991. text 55.00 (*0-8147-9671-0*) NYU Pr.

Ottoman Centuries. Lord Kinross. LC 76-28498. (Illus.). 1979. reprint ed. pap. 15.95 (*0-688-08093-6*, Quil) HarperTrade.

Ottoman Century: The District of Jerusalem in the 1600s. Dror Ze'evi. LC 95-30362. (SUNY Series in Medieval Middle East History). 258p. (C). 1996. text 73.50 (*0-7914-2915-6*) State U NY Pr.

Ottoman Century: The District of Jerusalem in the 1600s. Dror Zeevi. LC 95-30362. (SUNY Series in Medieval Middle East History). 258p. (C). 1996. pap. text 24.95 (*0-7914-2916-4*) State U NY Pr.

Ottoman City & Its Parts: Urban Structure & Social Order. Ed. by Irene A. Bierman et al. (Subsidia Balcanica, Islamica et Turcica Ser.: No. 3). (Illus.). x, 256p. 1991. text 60.00 (*0-89241-473-1*) Caratzas.

Ottoman City Between East & West: Aleppo, Izmir & Istanbul. Edhem Eldem et al. LC 98-43855. (Cambridge Studies in Islamic Civilization). (Illus.). 258p. (C). 1999. 59.40 (*0-521-64304-X*) Cambridge U Pr.

Ottoman Civil Officialdom: A Social History. Carter V. Findley. LC 88-17810. (Illus.). 423p. reprint ed. pap. 131.20 (*0-608-06371-1*, 206673200008) Bks Demand.

Ottoman Diplomacy in Hungary: Letter from the Pashas of Buda, 1590-1593. Gustav Bayerle. LC 74-188493. (Uralic & Altaic Ser.: Vol. 101). 196p. (Orig.). 1972. pap. text 16.00 (*0-87750-169-6*) Res Inst Inner Asian Studies.

Ottoman Embroidery. Roderick Taylor. LC 92-46405. (Illus.). 224p. 1993. 59.95 (*1-56656-134-5*) Interlink Pub.

Ottoman Empire. (YA). (gr. 10-12). 1975. 6.00 (*0-317-56397-1*) UM Ctr MENAS.

Ottoman Empire, Vol. 5. Israel Zinberg. 25.00 (*0-87068-241-5*) Ktav.

Ottoman Empire: Its Record & Legacy. Wayne S. Vucinich. LC 78-11514. (Anvil Ser.). 192p. 1979. reprint ed. pap. 11.50 (*0-88275-785-7*) Krieger.

Ottoman Empire: The Classical Age, 1300-1600. 2nd ed. Halil Inalcik. (Late Byzantine & Ottoman Studies: No. 1). (Illus.). xii, 258p. 1989. lib. bdg. 50.00 (*0-89241-388-3*) Caratzas.

Ottoman Empire & Islamic Tradition. Norman Itzkowitz. LC 79-23386. 136p. 1980. reprint ed. pap. text 9.00 (*0-226-38806-9*, P869) U Ch Pr.

Ottoman Empire & the World Economy: The Nineteenth Century. Resat Kasaba. LC 88-3039. (SUNY Series in Middle Eastern Studies). 191p. (C). 1988. text 74.50 (*0-88706-804-9*); pap. text 24.95 (*0-88706-805-7*) State U NY Pr.

Ottoman Empire from 1720 to 1734: As Revealed in Despatches from the Venetian Baili, Vol XXVII, No. 3--3. Mary L. Shay. LC 75-18363. (Illinois Studies in the Social Sciences: Vol. XXVII, No. 3). 165p. 1978. reprint ed. lib. bdg. 38.50 (*0-8371-8319-7*, SHOTE) Greenwood.

Ottoman Empire: German Sphere of Action: the Economic Interests of the German Empire in Turkey 1871-1908) see Aktionsfeld Osmanisches Reich: Die Wirtschaftsinteressen des Deutschen Kaiserreiches in der Turkei 1871-1908 (Unter Besonderer Berucksichtigung Europaischer Literatur)

*__Ottoman Empire, 1700 - 1922.__ Donald Quataert. (New Approaches to European History Ser.: Vol. 17). (Illus.). 232p. 2000. 54.95 (*0-521-63328-1*); pap. 19.95 (*0-521-63360-5*) Cambridge U Pr.

Ottoman Garrisons on the Middle Danube. Ed. by Asparuch Velkov & Evgenity Radushev. LC 97-134688. 548p. 1996. pap. 110.00 (*963-05-7391-1*, Pub. by Akade Kiado) St Mut.

Ottoman Greeks in the Age of Nationalism: Politics, Economy & Society in the Nineteenth Century. Ed. by Dimitri Gondicas & Charles P. Issawi. LC 99-28792. 256p. (C). 1999. text 34.95 (*0-87850-096-0*) Darwin Pr.

Ottoman Gulf: The Creation of Kuwait, Saudi Arabia, & Qatar, 1870-1914. Frederick F. Anscombe. LC 97-12680. 288p. 1997. pap. 18.50 (*0-231-10839-7*); lib. bdg. 50.00 (*0-231-10838-9*) Col U Pr.

Ottoman Lady: A Social History from 1718-1918, 70. Fanny Davis. LC 85-14717. (Contributions in Women's Studies: No. 70). (Illus.). 336p. 1986. 75.00 (*0-313-24811-7*, DOL, Greenwood Pr) Greenwood.

*__Ottoman Law of War & Peace.__ Viorel Panaite. 240p. 2000. text 30.00 (*0-88033-461-4*) Col U Pr.

Ottoman Literature. Elias Gibb. 1972. 59.95 (*0-8490-0781-X*) Gordon Pr.

Ottoman Lyric Poetry: An Anthology. Tr. by Walter G. Andrews et al from TUR. LC 96-24262. (Illus.). 328p. 1997. 40.00 (*0-292-70471-2*); pap. 14.95 (*0-292-70472-0*) U of Tex Pr.

Ottoman Melodies: Hebrew Hymns. Andreas Tietze & Joseph Yahalom. LC 95-168187. (Bibliotheca Orientalis Hungarica Ser.: No. XLIII). 208p. 1995. pap. 110.00 (*963-05-6864-0*, Pub. by Akade Kiado) St Mut.

Ottoman Military Administration in Eighteenth-Century Bosnia. Michael R. Hickok. LC 97-16890. (Ottoman Empire & Its Heritage Ser.: Vol. 13). (Illus.). 160p. 1997. text 61.00 (*90-04-10689-8*) Brill Academic Pubs.

*__Ottoman Past & Today's Turkey.__ Kemal H. Karpat. LC 00-37935. (Social, Economic & Political Studies of the Middle East & Asia). 320p. 2000. 96.00 (*90-04-11562-5*) Brill Academic Pubs.

*__Ottoman Peoples & the End of Empire.__ Justin McCarthy. (Historical Endings). 224p. 2000. pap. 24.95 (*0-340-70657-0*); text 72.00 (*0-340-70656-2*) OUP.

*__Ottoman-Polish Diplomatic Relations (15th-18th Century) An Annotated Edition of Names & other Documents.__ annot. ed. Ko Odziejczyk Dariusz. LC 98-44347. (Ottoman Empire & Its Heritage Ser.). 1999. write for info. (*90-04-11280-4*) Brill Academic Pubs.

Ottoman Population, 1830-1914: Demographic & Social Characteristics. Kemal H. Karpat. LC 83-47762. (Turkish & Ottoman Studies). (Illus.). 259p. 1985. reprint ed. pap. 80.30 (*0-608-07474-8*, 206769600009) Bks Demand.

Ottoman Province of Damascus in the 16th Century. Muhammad A. Bakit. 308p. 1982. 48.00 (*0-86685-322-7*, LDL3227) Intl Bk Ctr.

Ottoman Seapower & Levantine Diplomacy in the Age of Discovery. Palmira Brummett. LC 92-44704. (SUNY Series in the Social & Economic History of the Middle East). 285p. (C). 1993. text 64.50 (*0-7914-1701-8*); pap. text 21.95 (*0-7914-1702-6*) State U NY Pr.

Ottoman Slave Trade & Its Suppression, 1840-1890. Ehud R. Toledano. LC 82-47618. (Princeton Studies on the Near East). 327p. 1982. reprint ed. pap. 101.40 (*0-608-02592-5*, 206324900004) Bks Demand.

Ottoman Statesman in War & Peace: Ahmed Resmi Efendi, 1700-1783. Virginia H. Aksan. xviii, 253p. 1995. 107.00 (*90-04-10116-0*) Brill Academic Pubs.

Ottoman Steam Navy, 1828-1923. Bernd Langensiepen & Ahmet Guleryuz. Tr. by J. Cooper. LC 94-69766. (Illus.). 208p. 1995. 55.00 (*1-55750-659-0*) Naval Inst Pr.

Ottoman Tributes in Hungary According to Sixteenth Century Tapu Registers of Novigrad. Gustav Bayerle. (Near & Middle East Monographs: No. 8). 1973. text 76.95 (*90-279-2437-6*) Mouton.

Ottoman Turkish Writers: A Biographical Dictionary of Significant Ottoman Literature. Louis Mitler. (American University Studies: General Literature: Ser. XIX, Vol. 15). XVI, 203p. (C). 1988. text 31.50 (*0-8204-0633-3*) P Lang Pubng.

Ottoman Turks. Justin McCarthy. LC 96-16824. 1p. (C). 1996. pap. text 24.38 (*0-582-25655-0*, Pub. by Addison-Wesley) Longman.

Ottoman Turks: A History to 1923. Justin McCarthy. LC 96-16824. (C). 1996. text 52.95 (*0-582-25656-9*, Pub. by Addison-Wesley) Longman.

Ottoman Warfare, 1500-1700. Rhoads Murphey. LC 98-45274. 288p. (C). 1999. text 55.00 (*0-8135-2684-1*); pap. text 25.00 (*0-8135-2685-X*) Rutgers U Pr.

Ottomans. Andrew Wheatcroft. 1994. write for info. (*0-201-62715-9*) Addison-Wesley.

Ottomans: Dissolving Images. Andrew Wheatcroft. (Illus.). 368p. 1996. pap. 13.95 (*0-14-016879-6*, Penguin Bks) Viking Penguin.

Ottomans Et la Mort: Permanences Et Mutations. Ed. by Gilles Veinstein. Vol. 9. (FRE., Illus.). lv, 324p. 1996. text (*90-04-10505-0*) Brill Academic Pubs.

*__Ottomans, Hungarians & Habsburgs in Central Europe: The Military Confines in the Era of Ottoman Conquest.__ Pal Fodor & Geza David. LC 00-34284. 2000. write for info. (*90-04-11907-8*) Brill Academic Pubs.

Ottomans in Syria: A History of Justice & Oppression. Douwes. 224p. 1999. text 55.00 (*1-86064-031-1*) St Martin.

Ottomans, Turks & the Jewish Polity: A History of the Jews of Turkey. Walter F. Weiker. 386p. (C). 1992. lib. bdg. 59.00 (*0-8191-8644-9*) U Pr of Amer.

Ottoneum Theater: An English Survivor from Seventeenth-Century Germany. Graham C. Adams. LC 91-57961. (Studies in the Renaissance: No. 32). 1992. 39.50 (*0-404-62332-8*) AMS Pr.

Ottonian Book Illumination: An Historical Study. Henry Mayr-Harting. (Illus.). 500p. 1999. text 75.00 (*1-872501-74-5*) Gordon & Breach.

Ottonian Book Illumination: An Historical Study. Henry Mayr-Harting. (Illus.). 544p. 1999. pap. text 38.00 (*1-872501-79-6*) Gordon & Breach.

Otto's Box of Bad Feelings. James Molnar. (Kid Safe Ser.). (Illus.). (Orig.). (J). (ps-3). 1995. pap. 5.00 (*0-9644142-1-X*) Open Book Pubng.

Otto's Boy. Walter Wager. 1995. mass mkt. 6.99 (*0-8125-4355-6*, Pub. by Forge NYC) St Martin.

Ottos Boy. Walter Wager. 1985. 16.95 (*0-02-622510-7*) Macmillan.

Otto's Rainy Day. Pamela R. Levy. LC 99-19695. (Illus.). (J). 2000. write for info. (*1-57091-400-1*) Charlesbridge Pub.

Ottsovstvo. Epshtein M. Naumovich. LC 92-17804. (RUS.). 160p. (Orig.). 1992. pap. 12.00 (*1-55779-045-0*) Hermitage Pubs.

Otway & Lee: Biography from a Baroque Age. Roswell G. Ham. LC 69-13923. (Illus.). 250p. 1969. reprint ed. lib. bdg. 59.50 (*0-8371-0462-9*, HAOL, Greenwood Pr) Greenwood.

Otzar Hazmiros. 7.50 (*0-87559-089-6*); pap. 5.00 (*0-87559-088-8*) Shalom.

Otzar Pisgame Chabad. Eliyahu Friedman. (HEB.). 472p. 1993. 17.00 (*0-8266-5280-8*) Kehot Pubn Soc.

Ou Comment s'en Debarrasser see Theatre

Ou Es-Tu, Catherine? - Something Good. Robert Munsch. (Droles D'Histories Ser.). (FRE., Illus.). 24p. (J). (ps up). 1991. pap. 6.95 (*2-89021-155-X*, Pub. by La Courte Ech) Firefly Bks Ltd.

Ou Est Ce Poisson? see Ou' Est Ce Poisson?

Ou' Est Ce Poisson? Barbara Brenner et al.Tr. of Ou Est Ce Poisson?. (FRE., Illus.). (J). pap. 6.99 (*0-590-24226-1*) Scholastic Inc.

OU Men: Work Through Learning. Patricia Lunneborg. 140p. 1998. pap. 24.95 (*0-7188-2972-7*, Lutterworth-Parkwest) Parkwest Pubns.

Ou Sont Passes les Dinosaures? Sylvie Desrosiers. (Novels in the Roman Jeunesse Ser.). (FRE.). 96p. (J). (gr. 4-7). 1990. pap. 7.95 (*2-89021-119-3*, Pub. by La Courte Ech) Firefly Bks Ltd.

Ouabache Adventure - Canoeing the Wabash. Allen L. Johnson. LC 91-90625. (Illus.). 200p. 1991. 13.95 (*1-880675-00-5*) Creat Enter.

Ouachita County, Arkansas Census, 1860. annot. ed. Bobbie J. McLane. 130p. (Orig.). 1987. pap. 18.00 (*0-929604-43-1*) Arkansas Ancestors.

Ouachita Mountains: A Guide for Fishermen, Hunters, & Travelers. Milton D. Rafferty. LC 90-50695. 1993. pap. 19.95 (*0-8061-2360-5*) U of Okla Pr.

Ouachita Parish, Louisiana Cemeteries, Vol. 3. Claudie Hodges & Betty B. Hodges. 206p. 1993. pap. 19.00 (*1-57088-060-3*) J&W Ent.

Ouachita Parish, Louisiana Cemeteries, Vol. 5. Claudie Hodges & Betty B. Hodges. 288p. 1993. pap. 22.00 (*1-57088-062-X*) J&W Ent.

Ouachita Parish, Louisiana Cemetery Records, Vol. 1. Claudie Hodges & Betty B. Hodges. 254p. 1993. pap. 20.00 (*1-57088-058-1*) J&W Ent.

Ouachita Parish, Louisiana Cemetery Records, Vol. 2. Claudie Hodges & Betty B. Hodges. 206p. 1993. pap. 19.00 (*1-57088-059-X*) J&W Ent.

Ouachita Parish, Louisiana Cemetery Records, Vol. 4. Claudie Hodges & Betty B. Hodges. 215p. 1993. pap. 19.00 (*1-57088-061-1*) J&W Ent.

Ouachita Parish, Louisiana Cemetery Records, Vol. 6. Claudie Hodges & Betty B. Hodges. 205p. 1993. pap. 25.00 (*1-57088-063-8*) J&W Ent.

Ouachita Parish, Louisiana Marriage Records, 1803-1899. John C. Head. 145p. 1993. pap. text 18.00 (*1-57088-011-5*) J&W Ent.

Ouachita System. Peter T. Flawn et al. (Publication Ser.: PUB 6120). (Illus.). 401p. 1961. reprint ed. pap. 12.00 (*0-318-03315-1*) Bur Econ Geology.

Ouachita Trail Guide. 2nd rev. ed. Tim Ernst. LC 96-60332. (Illus.). 136p. (Orig.). 1996. pap. 16.95 (*1-882906-34-9*) CLOUDLAND.

*__Ouarkxpress 4: An Introduction to Electronic Mechanicals, R.__ Against the Clock, Inc. Staff. 328p. 1999. pap. text 35.00 (*0-13-022656-4*, Prentice Hall) P-H.

Oublie. Elie Wiesel. (FRE.). 1991. pap. 14.95 (*0-7859-2722-0*) Fr & Eur.

*__Ouch!__ Natalie Babbitt. LC 97-78382. (Illus.). 32p. (J). 1998. lib. bdg. 15.89 (*0-06-205067-2*) HarpC Child Bks.

Ouch! Natalie Babbitt et al. LC 97-78382. (Illus.). 32p. (J). 1998. 14.95 (*0-06-205066-4*) HarpC Child Bks.

Ouch! Teacher Created Materials Staff. (Go Bks.). 8p. (J). (gr. k-1). 1997. pap. 2.49 (*1-57690-795-3*) Tchr Create Mat.

*__Ouch! Life Can Hurt, but Healing is Your Choice.__ Susan R. Germanson. 2000. pap. 16.95 (*0-533-13481-1*) Vantage.

Ouderen in Het Jaar 2005 see Elderly in 2005: Health & Care: Updated Scenarios on Health & Aging, 1990-2005

Ought American Slavery to Be Perpetuated. William G. Brownlow & Abram Pryne. LC 79-83959. (Black Heritage Library Collection). 1977. 22.95 (*0-8369-8520-6*) Ayer.

Oui: The Paranoid-Critical Revolution, Writings, 1927-1933. Salvador Dali. Tr. by Yvonne Shafir. 192p. 1998. pap. text 13.95 (*1-878972-22-7*) Exact Change.

Ouija. Stoker Hunt. 176p. 1992. pap. 12.00 (*0-06-092350-4*) HarpC.

Ouija Board: A Doorway to the Occult. Edmond C. Gruss. 208p. (Orig.). 1994. pap. 8.99 (*0-87552-247-5*) P & R Pubng.

Oukele la Tele. Susie Morgenstern. (Folio - Cadet Bleu Ser.: No. 190). (FRE., Illus.). 54p. (J). (gr. 1-5). 1991. pap. 9.95 (*2-07-031190-2*) Schoenhof.

Ould Fields, New Corne: The Personal Memoirs of a Twentieth Century Lawyer. Erwin N. Griswold. LC 91-35927. (Illus.). 444p. (C). 1991. 31.50 (*0-314-92951-7*) West Pub.

Oulipo: A Primer of Potential Literature. Ed. & Tr. by Warren F. Motte, Jr. LC 97-51428. 224p. 1998. pap. 14.95 (*1-56478-187-9*) Dalkey Arch.

Oulipo Compendium. Mathews & Brotchie. 320p. 1998. pap. 19.99 (*0-947757-96-1*, Pub. by Atlas Pr) Serpents Tail.

Ounce of Pollution Prevention: Analysis & Rating of Ten State Pollution Prevention Laws. Bill Ryan & Richard Schrader. 60p. 1990. 15.00 (*0-685-56588-2*) CPA Washington.

Ounce of Preservation: A Guide to the Care of Papers & Photographs. Craig A. Tuttle. LC 94-23044. (Illus.). 112p. (Orig.). 1995. pap. 12.95 (*1-56825-021-5*) Rainbow Books.

Ounce of Prevention: A Parent's Guide to Moral & Spiritual Growth in Children. Bruce S. Narramore. 160p. 1973. pap. 5.95 (*0-310-30301-X*, 11035P) Zondervan.

Ounce of Prevention: How Parents Can Stop Childhood Behavioral & Emotional Problems Before They Start. Lawrence E. Shapiro. LC 00-38324. 256p. 2000. 24.00 (*0-06-019301-8*) HarpC.

Ounce of Prevention: Jobsite Safety & Insurance for Builders & Remodelers. Quenda B. Story. Ed. by Sharon Lamberton. LC 94-44964. (Illus.). 96p. 1995. pap. 7.50 (*0-86718-397-7*) Home Builder.

Ounce of Prevention: Preventing the Homosexual Condition in Today's Youth. Don Schmierer. LC 99-167493. 1998. pap. text 12.99 (*0-8499-3716-7*) Word Pub.

Ounce of Prevention: The Urban Dweller's Guide to Being Safe. John Steel. 97p. 1994. pap., per. 9.95 (*0-9643345-0-X*) Wrath & Ire.

Ounce of Prevention: Waste Reduction Strategies for Health Care Facilities. Glen McRae et al. (Illus.). 222p. (Orig.). 1993. pap. 50.00 (*0-87258-637-5*, 057007) Am Hospital.

Ounce of Prevention, a Pound of Uncertainty: The Cost-Effectiveness of School-Based Drug Prevention Programs. Jonathan Caulkins et al. LC 99-19931. (Illus.). 150p. 1999. pap. 15.00 (*0-8330-2560-0*, MR-923-RWJ, Pub. by Rand Corp) Natl Bk Netwk.

Oundle & the English Public School. Raymond Flower. 1976. 29.95 (*0-905743-56-3*, Pub. by Stacey Intl) Intl Bk Ctr.

Ouo Vaditis. Ed. by John Broadhurst. 160p. 1997. pap. 14.95 (*0-85244-382-X*, 958, Pub. by Gra1cewing) Morehouse Pub.

*__Our Accountability to God.__ Arthur W. Pink. 478p. 1999. pap. 21.99 (*0-8024-6572-2*) Moody.

Our Accustomed Discourse on the Antique: Cesare Gonzaga & Gerolamo Garimberto, Two Renaissance Collectors of Greco-Roman Art. Clifford M. Brown. LC 92-29917. (Reference Library of the Humanities: Vol. 1438). 336p. 1993. text 35.00 (*0-8153-0228-2*) Garland.

Our Actors & Actresses: The Dramatic List. 2nd enl. rev. ed. Ed. by Charles E. Pascoe. LC 70-91911. 1972. 30.95 (*0-405-08838-8*) Ayer.

Our Africa. Edward Knapp. 240p. (Orig.). 1989. pap. 12.00 (*0-9622519-0-9*) Dolphin Pubs.

Our African Connection: What We Brought from Home. Wallace Y. McNair. 250p. (Orig.). (C). 1997. pap. text. write for info. (*0-9627600-5-6*) Wstrn Images.

Our African Journal, 1945-1950. Allen H. Bilderback & Lillian A. Bilderback. 156p. (Orig.). (YA). (gr. 8 up). 1993. pap. text 10.00 (*0-9630710-2-5*) ABCO Pub.

Our Age: The Historic New Era of Christian-Jewish Understanding. Jack Bemporad & Michael Shevack. (Today's Issues Ser.). 96p. (Orig.). 1996. pap. 6.95 (*1-56548-081-3*) New City.

*__Our Aging Brain: Changing & Growing.__ Harold W. Nash. Ed. by Timothy A. Nash. LC 98-92099. (Illus.). 162p. 1999. pap. 15.00 (*0-9666162-0-0*) Ontarolina.

Our Aging Population: The Social Security Crisis. Ed. by Carol C. Collins. LC 83-1413. (Illus.). 224p. reprint ed. pap. 69.50 (*0-8357-4241-5*, 203702900007) Bks Demand.

Our Aging Society. Alan Pifer. 1986. pap. 12.95 (*0-03-930334-9*) H Holt & Co.

Our Aging Society: Paradox & Promise. Ed. by Alan Pifer & Lydia Bronte. 1986. pap. 15.95 (*0-393-30334-9*) Norton.

Our Ailing Health Care System: Health Care Is Bankrupting America & Leaving Us Increasingly Diseased. Arthur M. Baker. LC 93-93556. 50p. (Orig.). 1994. pap. 8.95 (*1-883989-11-6*) Self Hlth Care.

Our Air/Nuestro Aire: Canticle/Cantico. Jorge Guillen. Tr. by Carl W. Cobb from SPA. LC 97-34364. (Hispanic Literature Ser.: Vol. 40). (SPA.). 272p. 1997. text 89.95 (*0-7734-8420-5*) E Mellen.

Our Air/Nuestro Aire: Clamor/Clamor Homage/ Homenaje. Jorge Guillen. Tr. by Carl W. Cobb from SPA. LC 97-34364. (Hispanic Literature Ser.: Vol. 41). (SPA.). 278p. 1997. text 89.95 (*0-7734-8422-1*) E Mellen.

Our Amazing Animal Friends. National Geographic Society Staff. (Kids Want to Know Ser.). (Illus.). 32p. (J). (ps-3). pap. 4.95 (*0-7922-3408-1*, Pub. by Natl Geog) Publishers Group.

O

Our Amazing Bodies: A Supplement to Childcraft - The How & Why Library. World Book Staff. LC 65-25105. (Illus.). 224p. (J). (gr. 1-6). 1995. write for info. (0-7166-0695-X) World Bk.

Our Amazing World. 18.99 (0-89906-313-6, AMAH); pap. 15.99 (0-89906-314-4, AMAP) Mesorah Pubns.

Our America. Marilyn LaPenta. Ed. by Susan Evento. (Macmillan Early Skills Program - Conversion Ser.). 64p. (J). (ps-2). 1995. pap. 9.95 (1-56784-513-4) Newbridge Educ.

Our America. Waldo D. Frank. LC 73-105512. reprint ed. 37.50 (0-404-02547-1) AMS Pr.

Our America. Waldo D. Frank. (BCL1 - U. S. History Ser.). 232p. 1991. reprint ed. lib. bdg. 79.00 (0-7812-6019-1) Rprt Serv.

Our America! Land of the Free. Ed. by Ideals Magazine Staff. (Illus.). 80p. (Orig.). 1991. pap. 7.95 (0-8249-1099-0) Ideals.

Our America: Life & Death on the South Side of Chicago. Lealan Jones et al. 208p. 1998. per. 14.00 (0-671-00464-6) Simon & Schuster.

Our America: Nativism, Modernism, & Pluralism. Walter B. Michaels. LC 95-12117. (Post-Contemporary Interventions Ser.). 208p. 1995. text 29.95 (0-8223-1700-1) Duke.

Our America: Nativism, Modernism, & Pluralism. Walter B. Michaels. LC 95-12117. (Post-Contemporary Interventions Ser.). 200p. 1997. pap. text 12.95 (0-8223-2064-9) Duke.

Our American Artists: With Portraits, Studios & Engravings of Paintings, Repr. of 1879 Ed. S. G. Benjamin. LC 75-28870. (Art Experience in Late 19th Century America Ser.: Vol. 6). (Illus.). 1977. lib. bdg. 70.00 (0-8240-2230-0) Garland.

Our American Brethren: A History of Letters in the British Press During the American Revolution, 1775-1781. Alfred Grant. LC 95-1194. 222p. 1995. lib. bdg. 34.50 (0-7864-0086-2) McFarland & Co.

Our American Cardinals. J. J. Walsh. 1972. 59.95 (0-8490-0782-8) Gordon Pr.

Our American Cardinals. James J. Walsh. LC 68-58815. (Essay Index Reprint Ser.). 1977. 26.95 (0-8369-1072-9) Ayer.

Our American Cousin. Ed. by W. D. Taylor. (Illus.). 108p. 1990. pap. 21.00 (0-933833-20-2) Beacham Pub Corp.

Our American Cousins: Being Personal Impressions of the People & Institutions of the United States, 1883. W. E. Adams. LC 92-12083. 388p. 1992. lib. bdg. 99.95 (0-7734-9521-5) E Mellen.

Our American Economy. Elaine Schwartz. 1990. pap. text 59.96 (0-8013-0129-7, 75793) Longman.

Our American Government. 1997. lib. bdg. 250.95 (0-8490-6186-5) Gordon Pr.

Our American Government: An Introductory Guide for American Citizens. (Illus.). 124p. (Orig.). 1994. pap. text 25.00 (0-7881-0740-2) DIANE Pub.

Our American Government, 1993. 130p. 1993. pap. 7.50 (0-16-063255-2, Congress) USGPO.

Our American Humorists. Thomas L. Masson. LC 67-23245. (Essay Index Reprint Ser.). 1977. 26.95 (0-8369-0692-6) Ayer.

Our American Music. John Howard. 713p. 1993. reprint ed. lib. bdg. 109.00 (0-7812-5274-1) Rprt Serv.

Our American Theatre. Oliver M. Sayler. LC 70-89600. (Illus.). 1972. reprint ed. 30.95 (0-405-08925-2, Pub. by Blom Pubns) Ayer.

Our Amish Neighbors. William I. Schrieber. LC 62-17137. (Illus.). xii, 228p. 1978. pap. 9.95 (0-226-74035-8) U Ch Pr.

Our Ancestors. Ellen Davies-Rogers. 1986. write for info. (0-318-59202-9) Plantation.

Our Ancestors & Us. Myra Bennett. LC 98-72265. 1998. pap. 36.99 (0-9666972-0-0, OAAU-1) Intl Pub & Dist.

Our Ancient Liberties. Leon Whipple. LC 73-175723. (Civil Liberties in American History Ser.). 1972. reprint ed. lib. bdg. 19.50 (0-306-70419-6) Da Capo.

Our Angry Earth. Frederik Pohl & Isaac Asimov. 448p. 1993. mass mkt. 5.99 (0-8125-2096-3, Pub. by Tor Bks) St Martin.

Our Anniversary. Ed. by Helen Exley. (So-Much-More-Than-a-Card Ser.). (Illus.). 28p. 1997. pap. 2.99 (1-85015-844-4) Exley Giftbooks.

Our Apostolic Mandate: Letter to the French Archbishops & Bishops on the "Sillon" Pius, X, pseud. Tr. by Yves Dupont from FRE.Tr. of Notre Charge Apostolique. 58p. 1998. pap. 4.45 (0-935952-49-7) Angelus Pr.

Our Appalachia: An Oral History. Ed. by Laurel Shackelford & Bill Weinberg. LC 76-48625. 408p. 1988. pap. 22.00 (0-8131-0184-0) U Pr of Ky.

Our Appointment with Life: The Buddha's Teaching on Living in the Present. Thich Nhat Hanh. Tr. by Annabel Laity from VIE. 55p. (Orig.). 1990. pap. 6.00 (0-938077-36-8) Parallax Pr.

Our Araby: Palm Springs & the Garden of the Sun. J. Smeaton Chase. LC 87-18318. (Illus.). 86p. 1987. reprint ed. 9.95 (0-9618724-0-3) Palm Springs CA.

*__Our Arcadia.__ Robin Lippincott. 2000. 21.95 (0-670-89273-4) Viking Penguin.

Our Arctic Year. Vivian Staender & Gil Staender. LC 83-8815. (Alaska Geographic Ser.: Vol. 12, No. 4). (Illus.). 150p. 1985. pap. 19.95 (0-88240-176-9) Alaska Geog Soc.

Our Arizona Heritage: Memories of Jessie & Ray Killian, 1896-1989. rev. ed. Ray Killian. 600p. 1992. write for info. (0-9633640-0-6) C M Killian.

Our Army Nurses: Stories from Women in Civil War. Mary G. Holland. LC 97-60189. (Illus.). 320p. 1998. pap. 19.95 (1-889020-04-4) Edinbrugh Pr.

Our Art, Our Voices: Native American Cultural Perspectives. Denni D. Woodward. LC 95-68805. (Illus.). 48p. (Orig.). 1995. pap. text 10.00 (0-937031-05-4) Stanford Art.

Our Asian Journey: A Novel. Dallas Wiebe. 450p. 1998. pap., per. 30.00 (0-9692539-9-0) Cinc Writers Proj.

Our Awesome God. Campbell. 1997. pap. 9.99 (1-85792-318-9, Pub. by Christian Focus) Spring Arbor Dist.

*__Our Awesome God: The God Many Christians Claim to Know Is Not the God of the Bible.__ Reinder Bruinsma. Ed. by B. Russell Holt. LC 99-87385. 159p. 2000. pap. 11.99 (0-8163-1781-X) Pacific Pr Pub Assn.

Our Babies, Ourselves: How Biology & Culture Shape the Way We Parent. Meredith F. Small. (Illus.). 320p. 1999. pap. 14.95 (0-385-48362-7) Doubleday.

Our Baby see Nuestro Bebe

Our Baby. (Illus.). 64p. 23.00 (0-614-01772-6) Gibson.

Our Baby. Nancy C. Akmon. (Illus.). 56p. 1997. 35.00 (1-884807-17-8, EC7) Blushing Rose.

*__Our Baby.__ Four Seasons Staff. 1998. 12.95 (1-85645-102-X) Four Seasons Publishing Ltd.

Our Baby. Lawrence G. Lovasik. (Illus.). 1995. 10.95 (0-89942-266-7, 266/97) Catholic Bk Pub.

Our Baby. Robyn McIlhenny. LC 92-27268. (Voyages Ser.). (Illus.). (J). 1993. 3.75 (0-383-03646-1) SRA McGraw.

Our Baby: A Journal. (Illus.). 96p. 1994. pap. 19.95 (0-00-255447-X) Collins SF.

Our Baby: The First Year. D. Von Cramm et al. LC 97-26565. (Illus.). 288p. 1997. pap. 16.95 (0-8120-9778-5) Barron.

Our Baby Book. C. Mackenzie. 9.99 (1-85792-026-0, Pub. by Christian Focus) Spring Arbor Dist.

*__Our Baby Book.__ Jan Slob. 2000. 19.99 (1-56245-420-X) Great Quotations.

Our Baby Book: Gift see Nuestro Bebe: Regalo

Our Baby from China: An Adoption Story. Nancy D'Antonio. LC 96-32327. 24p. (J). (ps-2). 1997. lib. bdg. 13.95 (0-8075-6162-2) A Whitman.

Our Baby's Being Baptized. Marilyn Perry. (Illus.). 16p. (J). Date not set. pap. 3.95 (0-929032-70-5, Pub. by Wood Lake Bks) Logos Prods.

*__Our Baby's Book.__ Martha Rohrer. (Illus.). 32p. 1999. pap. 5.25 (0-7399-0250-4, 2124) Rod & Staff.

Our Baby's First Seven Years. 1985. 20.00 (0-937970-07-7) Gibson.

Our Baby's First Seven Years. 1989. 32.00 (0-8378-8180-3) Gibson.

*__Our Baby's First Seven Years: A Record Book.__ 7th ed. Mothers' Aid Staff. Ed. by Liza Brown. (Illus.). 76p. 2000. 40.00 (0-9703011-0-3) Mothers Aid.

Our Baby's First Year: A Baby Record Calendar. Meadowbrook Creations Staff. 30p. 1983. pap. 10.00 (0-88166-003-5) Meadowbrook.

Our Baby's Record Book. Ed. by Helen Exley. (Record Bks.). (Illus.). 80p. 1993. 12.00 (1-85015-445-7) Exley Giftbooks.

Our Backyard see Under the Microscope

Our Baldridge Forbears. Chester C. Kennedy. (Illus.). 625p. 1993. 59.95 (1-56869-026-6) Oldbuck Pr.

Our Baptist Tradition. William P. Tuck. LC 93-714. 112p. 1993. pap. 10.00 (1-880837-29-3) Smyth & Helwys.

Our Beautiful America: A Christian-Oriented United States History Text. Juanita C. Houston. Ed. by Carla B. Perez. (Illus.). (J). (gr. 5-8). 1999. pap., wbk. ed. 17.95 (0-88280-138-4); text, student ed. 23.95 (0-88280-136-8); pap. text, teacher ed. 21.95 (0-88280-137-6) ETC Pubns.

Our Beautiful America: A Christian-Oriented United States History Text, Student Test Booklet. Juanita C. Houston. Ed. by Carla B. Perez. (Illus.). (J). (gr. 5-8). 1999. pap. text 19.95 (0-88280-139-2) ETC Pubns.

Our Beautiful Baby: Photo Frame & Memory Album. 30p. 1998. 14.95 (1-888443-78-2, Pop-Up Pr) Intervisual Bks.

*__Our Beautiful, Dry & Distant Texts: Art History as Writing.__ James Elkins. (Illus.). 2000. pap. 22.00 (0-415-92663-7) Routledge.

Our Beautiful Dry & Distant Texts: On the History of Art As Writing. James Elkins. LC 96-22842. 1997. 55.00 (0-271-01630-2) Pa St U Pr.

Our Beginning: Genesis Through the Eyes of a Woman. Kay S. McKean. 152p. 1996. pap. 8.99 (1-57782-001-0) Discipleshp.

Our Beginnings: The History of the Epworth United Methodist Church. Wallace Y. Ponce. (Orig.). 1988. 10.00 (0-9620308-3-X); pap. 10.00 (0-9620308-8-0); text 10.00 (0-9620308-2-1); lib. bdg. 10.00 (0-9620308-9-9) Epworth United Methodist Church.

Our Beloved Jock. James A. Stewart. 1964. pap. 0.99 (1-56632-070-4) Revival Lit.

Our Beloved Sweden: Food, Flowers, Festivals & Faith. Janet L. Martin & Ilene L. Lorenz. 1996. pap. 17.95 (1-886627-02-9, Sentel) Redbird Prods.

Our Best Advice: The Multiage Problem Solving Handbook. Jim Grant et al. Ed. by Aldene Fredenburg. LC 96-83279. 112p. 1996. pap. 12.95 (1-884548-04-0, 4762) Soc Dev Educ.

Our Best Baby Afghans. LC 96-76049. 144p. 1996. pap. text 14.95 (1-57486-042-9) Oxmoor Hse.

Our Best Cookbook 2: A Second Serving. Wisconsin Restaurant Association Education Foundat. LC 95-61352. (Illus.). 144p. (Orig.). 1995. pap. 14.95 (0-942495-47-0) Palmer Pubns Inc.

Our Best Days. Sandy Coleman & Nancy Hull-Mast. LC 90-61371. (Meditation Ser.). 400p. pap. 10.00 (1-56838-114-X, 7813 A) Hazelden.

Our Best Friends. Gyo Fujikawa. (Illus.). 16p. (J). (ps). 1989. reprint ed. bds. 6.95 (1-55987-009-5, Sunny Bks) J B Comns.

Our Best Friends: Wagging Tales to Warm the Heart. Michael Capuzzo & Teresa Banik Capuzzo. 304p. 1999. mass mkt. 6.50 (0-553-58104-X) Bantam.

Our Best Hope: Early Intervention with Prenatally Drug-Exposed Infants & Their Families. Jane Stump. 1992. pap. 9.95 (0-87868-493-X, 4930) Child Welfare.

*__Our Best Seasonal Quilts.__ Marianne Fons & Liz Porter. (Illus.). 144p. 2000. pap. 19.95 (0-8487-2362-7) Leisure AR.

Our Best Thread Crochet. Leisure Arts Staff. LC 96-77624. 128p. 1996. pap. 14.95 (1-57486-055-0, 2889) Leisure AR.

Our Best to You. Ed. by Kathleen Callahan. (Illus.). 268p. (Orig.). 1984. pap. 7.50 (0-9615563-0-7) K J Callahan.

Our Best 200+ Holiday Quickies. Leisure Arts Staff. LC 97-70453. 144p. 1997. pap. 19.95 (1-57486-061-5) Oxmoor Hse.

*__Our Bible & the Ancient Manuscripts: Eyre & Spottiswoode, Longdon, England.__ Frederic G. Kenyon. 1999. pap. 60.00 (1-58329-013-3) Lazarus Minist.

Our Bible Chronology Established, the Sealed Book of Daniel Opened: A Book of Reference for Those Who Wish to Examine the Sure Word of Prophecy. 5th ed. William C. Thurman. 350p. 1996. reprint ed. spiral bd. 30.00 (0-7873-0870-6) Hlth Research.

*__Our Big Home: An Earth Poem.__ Linda Glaser. LC 99-45775. 32p. (J). (gr. k-3). 2000. 21.90 (0-7613-1650-7) Millbrook Pr.

*__Our Big Home: An Earth Poem.__ Linda Glaser. LC 99-45775. 32p. (J). (ps-3). 2000. 14.95 (0-7613-1292-7) Millbrook Pr.

Our Bird Friends & Foes. William A. Dupuy. (Illus.). 1990. 15.00 (0-8446-0601-4) Peter Smith.

Our Black Heritage, 8 vols. (J). (gr. 4-12). 1994. pap. 19.95 (0-7933-6794-8); lib. bdg. 29.95 (0-7933-6793-X); disk 29.95 (0-7933-6795-6) Gallopade Intl.

*__Our Black Seminarians: And Black Clergy Without a Black Theology.__ Intro. by John Henrik Clarke. LC 96-84728. (Illus.). 109p. 1998. reprint ed. pap. 14.95 (0-933121-62-8) Black Classic.

Our Blessed Mother. Therese Johnson Borchard. LC 99-16159. 1999. pap. 9.95 (0-8245-1819-5) Crossroad NY.

Our Blessed Mother. George Brundage. (Illus.). 16p. (J). 1993. bds. 2.75 (0-89942-846-0, 846/22) Catholic Bk Pub.

Our Blessed Mother Leads Her Children Out of Sarajevo. Johannes M. Stromberg. 41p. 1994. pap. 3.95 (1-882972-27-9) Queenship Pub.

Our Blind Children: Growing & Learning with Them. 3rd ed. Berthold Lowenfeld. (Illus.). 260p. 1977. 39.95 (0-398-02200-3); pap. 27.95 (0-398-06249-8) C C Thomas.

Our Blood & His Guts. Eugene W. Luciano. 212p. 1995. 22.00 (1-57087-187-6) Prof Pr NC.

Our Bodies see Child's First Library of Learning

Our Bodies see Under the Microscope

Our Bodies. Gakken Co. Ltd. Editors. Tr. by Time-Life Books Editors. (Child's First Library of Learning). (Illus.). 90p. (J). (gr. k-3). 1991. pap. write for info. (0-8094-9453-1); text. write for info. (0-8094-9452-3); lib. bdg. write for info. (0-8094-9451-5) Time-Life.

Our Bodies: Hands-On Minds-On Science. 1997. pap. 11.95 (1-55734-618-6) Tchr Create Mat.

Our Bodies: Learning to Use Them to Please God. Brena Price. (BMC Teaching Bks.). (Illus.). 20p. (J). (gr. 1-8). 1983. pap. 4.50 (0-86508-157-3) BCM Pubn.

Our Bodies, Our Cells: Children's Activities in Body Systems. Marilyn Cahn. LC 92-15985. (Children's Activity Ser.). (Illus.). 1992. 14.95 (1-56071-087-X) ETR Assocs.

Our Bodies, Ourselves see Nuestros Cuerpos, Nuestras Vidas: Our Bodies, Ourselves

Our Bodies, Ourselves. Boston Women's Health Staff. 1998. 34.00 (0-8446-6981-4) Peter Smith.

Our Bodies, Ourselves for the New Century: A Book for & by Women. rev. ed. Boston Women's Health Book Collective Staff. LC 98-12725. (Illus.). 784p. 1998. per. 24.00 (0-684-84231-9, Touchstone) S&S Trade Pap.

*__Our Bodies Remember: Poems.__ Dana Wildsmith. 60p. 1999. pap. 12.00 (1-885912-21-8) Sows Ear Pr.

Our Body see Human Body

Our Body . . . God's Temple: A Study of Nutrition from a Biblical Perspective. Patrick V. McClure. (Illus.). 224p. (Orig.). 1995. pap. text 12.95 (0-9646792-0-5) P McClure.

Our Bones Are Scattered. Ward. 1999. pap. 16.00 (0-8050-5218-6) St Martin.

Our Bones Are Scattered: The Cawnpore Massacres & the Indian Mutiny of 1857. Andrew Ward. (Illus.). 703p. 1996. 30.00 (0-317-52485-2, J Macrae Bks) H Holt & Co.

*__Our Book of Asia.__ Jamilah Kolocotronis. Ed. by Heidi Liddle & Huseyin Abiva. LC 98-88208. (Muslims Around The World Ser.). (Illus.). (J). (gr. 5-6). 1999. pap. text. write for info. (1-56316-450-7) Iqra Intl Ed Fdtn.

Our Book of Du'a' for Children. Ed. & Tr. by Fadel I. Abdallah from ARA. (Illus.). 25p. (Orig.). (J). (ps-1). 1994. pap. 5.00 (1-56316-317-9) Iqra Intl Ed Fdtn.

*__Our Book 2000.__ Text by William K. Hickey. 135p. 2000. 6.00 (0-615-11667-1) Hickey Ad.

Our Boundless Self: A Call to Awake. John A. Price. 2000. pap. write for info. (1-887884-07-6) Wings of Spirit.

Our Boys Have Won the Cup. David Potter. 184p. 1996. pap. 59.00 (0-85976-454-0, Pub. by J Donald) St Mut.

*__Our Boys Speak: Adolescent Boys Write About Their Inner Lives.__ John Nikkah. LC 00-26415. 192p. 2000. pap. 12.95 (0-312-26280-9) St Martin.

Our Brilliant Heritage. Oswald Chambers. 334p. 1999. pap. 13.95 (0-87508-494-X, 494) Chr Lit.

Our Brilliant Heritage: And, If You Will Be Perfect, with Disciples Indeed. Oswald Chambers. LC 98-26759. 336p. 1998. pap. 14.99 (1-57293-042-X) Discovery Hse Pubs.

Our Brink Heritage, 1998, 2 vols. Wanda L. Gines & Ronald L. Gines. Incl. Vol. I. LC 98-71249. 248p. 1998. pap. Not sold separately (1-57502-784-4, PO2167); Vol. II. LC 98-71249. 304p. 1998. pap. Not sold separately (1-57502-785-2, PO2168); LC 98-71249. x, 484p. 1998. 45.00 (1-57502-786-0) Morris Pubng.

Our Brother Has Down's Syndrome. Shelly Cairo et al. (Illus.). 24p. (J). (ps-3). 1985. pap. 5.95 (0-920303-31-5, Pub. by Annick); lib. bdg. 15.95 (0-920303-30-7, Pub. by Annick) Firefly Bks Ltd.

Our Brother in Black: His Freedom & His Future. Atticus G. Haygood. LC 77-107806. (Select Bibliographies Reprint Ser.). 1977. 18.95 (0-8369-5214-6) Ayer.

Our Brother in Black: His Freedom & His Future. Atticus G. Haygood. LC 72-78994. (Black Heritage Library Collection). 1996. 14.50 (0-8369-8697-0) Ayer.

Our Brothers' War. Ed. by John S. Moremen. 152p. 1993. pap. 14.95 (0-9624086-5-4) Sulgrave Pr.

Our Burden of Shame: Japanese-American Internment see First Books

Our Business Civilization: Some Aspects of Our American Culture. James T. Adams. (BCL1 - U. S. History Ser.). 306p. 1991. lib. bdg. 89.00 (0-7812-6018-3) Rprt Serv.

Our Business Civilization: Some Aspects of Our American Culture. James T. Adams. LC 75-92608. reprint ed. 32.50 (0-404-00288-9) AMS Pr.

*__Our Call to Serve Others: Award-Winning, Student Initiated Service Projects - A Resource for Schools.__ Ed. by Russell P. Boniface. (Illus.). 1999. write for info. (0-88210-333-4) Natl Assn Principals.

Our Cambria. Irina Wilson & Art Wilson. (Illus.). (Orig.). 1985. pap. 6.95 (0-935733-00-0) Dead Reckoning.

*__Our Camelot.__ Jasmu Heen. 1999. pap. 17.00 (1-876341-00-9) Kodansha Intl.

Our Campaigns: Second Regiment Pennsylvania Reserve Volunteers 1861-1864. Ed. by Stanley W. Zamonski. LC 94-41967. (Civil War Classics Ser.). (Illus.). 304p. 1995. pap. 17.99 (0-942597-84-2, Burd St Pr) White Mane Pub.

Our Cancer Year. Harvey Pekar & Joyce Brabner. LC 94-10523. (Illus.). 252p. (Orig.). 1994. pap. 17.95 (1-56858-011-8) FWEW.

Our Captured Moments. Charles J. Palmer & Jacqueline Palmer. LC 96-86077. (Illus.). 250p. 1996. 49.95 (1-881808-29-7) Creat Arts & Sci.

Our Casualty & Other Stories. James O. Hannay. LC 74-122713. (Short Story Index Reprint Ser.). 1977. 19.95 (0-8369-3546-2) Ayer.

Our Catholic Devotions: A Popular Guidebook. Therese J. Borchard. LC 97-43776. 144p. 1998. pap. 9.95 (0-8245-1739-3) Crossroad NY.

Our Catholic Heritage in Texas, 1519-1936, 7 vols., Set. Carlos Castaneda. 1993. reprint ed. lib. bdg. 525.00 (0-7812-5963-0) Rprt Serv.

Our Catholic Heritage in Texas, 1519-1936, 7 vols., Set. Carlos E. Castenada. LC 76-1471. (Chicano Heritage Ser.). (Illus.). 1976. reprint ed. 272.95 (0-405-09488-4) Ayer.

Our Catholic Identity Spanish Grade Two Workbook Grade Two: Catechism Workbook. annot. ed. (SPA., Illus.). (J). (gr. 2). 1998. pap. text, teacher ed., wbk. ed. 2.95 (0-7829-0800-4) Tabor Pub.

Our Catholic Prayer: A Popular Guidebook. Therese J. Borchard. LC 98-46462. 144p. 1999. pap. 9.95 (0-8245-1606-0) Crossroad NY.

Our Catskill Mountains. H. A. Haring. 350p. 1993. reprint ed. lib. bdg. 89.00 (0-7812-5124-9) Rprt Serv.

*__Our Century: The Palm Beach Post.__ (Illus.). 240p. 2000. write for info. (0-9657200-3-9) Mega Bks.

Our Chalet Songbook. 2nd ed. Girl Scouts of the U. S. A., Our Chalet Committee. (FIN, FRE, GER, GRE & ITA.). 94p. 1978. 3.50 (0-88441-364-0, 23-929) Girl Scouts USA.

Our Chancellor: Sketches for a Historical Picture, 2 Vols, Set. Moritz Busch. Tr. by W. Beatty-Kingston. LC 76-109615. (Select Bibliographies Reprint Ser.). 1977. 54.95 (0-8369-5225-1) Ayer.

Our Changing Constitution: How & Why We Have Amended It. Isobel V. Morin. LC 97-26909. (Illus.). 176p. (YA). (gr. 7 up). 1998. lib. bdg. 22.90 (0-7613-0222-0) Millbrook Pr.

Our Changing Geopolitical Premises. Thomas P. Rona. LC 81-16192. 364p. reprint ed. pap. 112.90 (0-608-13016-8, 202415900035) Bks Demand.

Our Changing Land. Thomas-Cochran. (What a Wonderful World Ser.). 1991. pap. text. write for info. (0-582-90956-2, Pub. by Addison-Wesley) Longman.

Our Changing Lives. Kenneth Sollitt. (Ann of the Prairie Ser.: Pt. II). 182p. (J). 1986. reprint ed. pap. 6.95 (0-940652-04-8) Inhtce Pubns.

Our Changing Morality, a Symposium. Ed. by Freda Kirchwey. LC 78-169389. (Family in America Ser.). 254p. 1977. reprint ed. 18.95 (0-405-03866-6) Ayer.

Our Changing Planet. Gallimard Jeunesse. Tr. by Nicole Valaire. LC 95-53839. (Scholastic Voyages of Discovery Ser.: Vol. 17). 48p. (J). 1996. 19.95 (0-590-47651-3, Scholastic Ref) Scholastic Inc.

Our Changing Planet. 2nd ed. Fred T. MacKenzie. LC 97-31347. 486p. 1997. pap. text 46.00 (0-13-271321-7) P-H.

Our Changing Planet: The Fiscal Year 1996 U. S. Global Change Research Program. Robert C. Correll. (Illus.). 152p. (C). 1998. pap. text 35.00 (0-7881-7540-8) DIANE Pub.

Our Changing Planet: The Fiscal Year 1997 U. S. Global Change Research Program. Robert W. Correll & Robert C. Harris. (Illus.). 162p. (C). 1998. pap. text 35.00 (0-7881-7538-6) DIANE Pub.

*__Our Changing Planet: The FY 1995 U. S. Global Change Research Program.__ Ed. by John H. Gibbons. (Illus.). 132p. (C). 2000. reprint ed. pap. text 25.00 (0-7881-8607-8) DIANE Pub.

An Asterisk (*) at the beginning of an entry indicates that the title is appearing for the first time.

Our Changing Planet: The FY 1998 U. S. Global Change Research Program. John H. Gibbons. (Illus.). 118p. 1997. pap. text 35.00 (*0-7881-4688-2*) DIANE Pub.

Our Changing Planet: The FY 1999 U. S. Global Change Research Program. Rick Piltz. (Illus.). 130p. (C). 1999. pap. text 35.00 (*0-7881-7589-0*) DIANE Pub.

***Our Changing Planet: The FY 2000 U. S. Global Change Research Program - Implementation Plan & Budget Overview.** Ed. by Neal Lane. (Illus.). 100p. (C). 1999. pap. text 20.00 (*0-7881-8253-6*) DIANE Pub.

Our Changing Population. Richard Gill et al. 512p. (C). 1991. 52.60 (*0-13-642661-1*) P-H.

Our Changing Population. Glazer. 1992. pap. text, student ed. 22.67 (*0-13-642687-5*) P-H.

Our Changing White House. Ed. by Wendell Garrett. (Illus.). 256p. 1995. text 45.00 (*1-55553-222-5*) NE U Pr.

Our Character, Our Future: Reclaiming America's Moral Destiny. Alan Keyes. 160p. 1996. 9.99 (*0-310-20816-5*) Zondervan.

Our Chemical Culture: Drug Use & Misuse. Marcia Summers et al. LC 81-5271. 120p. (gr. 10-12). 1982. text 18.95 (*0-87073-337-0*); pap. text 12.95 (*0-87073-336-2*) Schenkman Bks Inc.

Our Chiefs & Elders: Words & Photographs of Native Leaders. David Neel. LC 92-24652. (Illus.). 160p. 1992. pap. 25.95 (*0-7748-0502-1*) U of Wash Pr.

Our Chiefs & Elders: Words & Photographs of Native Leaders. David Neel. LC 92-24652. (Illus.). 192p. 1992. 39.95 (*0-295-97217-3*) U of Wash Pr.

Our Child? Sally T. Hayes. 1995. per. 3.75 (*0-373-07671-1*, 1-07671-0) Silhouette.

Our Child: Preparation for Parenting in Adoption - Instructor's Guide. Carol A. Hallenbeck. LC 84-90588. (Illus.). 240p. 1988. teacher ed., per. 24.95 (*0-9611872-0-4*) Our Child Pr.

Our Children see Raising Nuestros Ninos

Our Children: An Ornament of the Life of This World. LC 96-95114. 176p. 1996. pap. 10.00 (*0-9617422-1-6*) A Khalid.

Our Children: Coming to Terms with the Loss of a Child: Parents' Own Stories. Ed. by Ena Mirren & Compassionate Friends Staff. 204p. 1996. pap. 14.95 (*0-340-62863-4*, Pub. by Hodder & Stought Ltd) Trafalgar.

Our Children Are Alcoholics: Coping with Children Who Have Addictions. Sally B. & David B. Ed. by Mary J. Graham. LC 97-70959. xiv, 174p. 1997. per. 14.95 (*1-888461-02-0*) Islewest Pub.

Our Children at Risk. LC 96-117518. (CERI Ser.). 125p. (Orig.). 1995. pap. 34.00 (*92-64-14430-7*, Pub. by Org for Econ) OECD.

Our Children at Risk: The 5 Worst Environmental Threats to Their Health. Lawrie Mott. (Illus.). 124p. 1997. pap. 14.00 (*1-893340-11-2*) Natl Resources Defense Coun.

Our Children Forever. Joel Martin. 400p. 1996. reprint ed. mass mkt. 7.50 (*0-425-15343-6*) Berkley Pub.

Our Children Forever: George Anderson's Message from Children on the Other Side. Joel Martin & Patricia Romanowski. 336p. (Orig.). 1994. pap. 12.00 (*0-425-14138-1*) Berkley Pub.

Our Children Free & Happy: Letters from Black Settlers in Africa in the 1760s. Ed. by Christopher Fyfe. 122p. 1992. 35.00 (*0-7486-0270-4*, Pub. by Edinburgh U Pr) Col U Pr.

Our Children from Latin America: Making Adoption Part of Your Life. Laurel Strassberger. LC 91-67207. (Illus.). 144p. 1992. pap. text 10.95 (*0-913292-24-9*) Tiresias Pr.

Our Children, Our Future. Tim Burns. 15.00 (*0-614-19153-X*) Marco Polo Pubs.

Our Children, Our Future: Defining the Stakes in a Battle We Must Not Lose. E. Timothy Burns. (Illus.). 1991. pap. 14.95 (*1-56374-000-1*) Marco Polo Pubs.

Our Children Today: A Guide to Their Needs from Infancy Through Adolescence. Ed. by Child Study Association of America Staff. LC 72-4512. (Essay Index Reprint Ser.). 1977. reprint ed. 23.95 (*0-8369-2938-1*) Ayer.

Our Children's Heritage: A History of Clarkston-Independence Township. Rosemary Lewis et al. (Illus.). 81p. (J). (gr. 2-4). 1995. 25.00 (*0-9621749-2-0*); text 8.79 (*0-9621749-1-2*) Clarkston CHS.

Our Children's Toxic Legacy: How Science & Law Fail to Protect Us from Pesticides. 2nd ed. John Wargo. (Illus.). 402p. 1998. pap. 18.00 (*0-300-07446-8*) Yale U Pr.

Our Children's Toxic Legacy: How Science & Law Failed to Protect Us from Pesticides. John Wargo. (Illus.). 402p. 1996. 37.00 (*0-300-06686-4*) Yale U Pr.

Our Choice of Gods. Richard Parrish. Ed. by Stewart Richardson. 464p. 1989. 19.95 (*1-55972-002-6*, Birch Ln Pr) Carol Pub Group.

Our Choices: Women's Personal Decisions about Abortion. Sumi Hoshiko. LC 92-19605. 1993. 14.95 (*1-56023-025-8*, Harrington Park); lib. bdg. 39.95 (*1-56024-333-3*) Haworth Pr.

Our Chosen Faith see Fe Que Hemos Escogido: Una Introduccion al Unitario Universalismo

Our Christian Symbols. Friedrich O. Rest. LC 53-9923. (Illus.). 96p. 1954. pap. 5.95 (*0-8298-0099-9*) Pilgrim OH.

Our Christmas. Ed. by Jane Kozlovski & Mark Jacobsen. (Illus.). 8p. 1991. pap. 4.95 (*0-9623800-6-7*) Madison Pk Grtings.

Our Christmas Memories Book. Ed. by Talus Corporation Staff. (Illus.). 1997. 25.99 (*0-927510-98-7*) Terrapin.

Our Christmas Memories Book. Sheryl Whalen. (Illus.). 80p. 1999. 24.95 (*0-9668930-1-8*) Whalen Innov.

Our Christmas Memories Book. Talus Corporation Staff. (Illus.). 23p. 1997. reprint ed. 25.99 (*1-892953-01-3*) Terrapin.

Our Church. R. D. Kernolhan. 112p. (C). 1988. pap. text 45.00 (*0-7152-0587-0*) St Mut.

Our Church: The 100th Anniversary Osman Immanuel Lutheran Church. Centennial Committee Staff. LC 95-60510. (Illus.). 334p. 1995. pap. 17.95 (*1-878044-25-7*, Wld Rose) Mayhaven Pub.

Our Church: There's More to It Than You Think. Gordon G. Johnson. LC 83-82990. (Illus.). 72p. (J). (gr. 5-6). 1993. student ed. 5.99 (*0-935797-33-5*) Harvest IL.

Our Church Music. Richard S. Willis. LC 72-1662. reprint ed. 34.50 (*0-404-08336-6*) AMS Pr.

Our Cities: Their Role in the National Economy. National Resources Committee. LC 73-11923. (Metropolitan America Ser.). (Illus.). 108p. 1974. reprint ed. 18.95 (*0-405-05406-8*) Ayer.

Our Cities Today & Tomorrow: A Survey of Planning & Zoning Progress in the United States. Theodora Hubbard & Henry V. Hubbard. LC 73-11919. (Metropolitan America Ser.). (Illus.). 466p. 1974. reprint ed. 29.95 (*0-405-05396-7*) Ayer.

Our City: The Jews of San Francisco. Irena Narell. 1981. 25.00 (*0-317-61576-9*) Akiba Pr.

Our Class Memory Album. Ed. by Scholastic, Inc. Staff. 1993. pap. 4.95 (*0-590-49416-3*) Scholastic Inc.

Our Classical Judeo Christian & Medieval Heritage. 2nd ed. Turner. (C). 1991. pap. text 20.60 (*0-536-57949-0*) Pearson Custom.

Our Classroom: We Can Learn Together. rev. ed. Chick Moorman & Dee Dishon. (Illus.). 218p. 1986. reprint ed. 19.95 (*0-9616046-1-1*) Prsnl Power Pr.

Our Classroom Is Wild America. Michael J. Cohen. LC 74-76019. (Illus.). 1978. pap. 10.00 (*0-89166-011-9*) Cobblesmith.

***Our Cloth Life.** Christina Wilson. 152p. 1999. pap. 13.00 (*0-8059-4544-X*) Dorrance.

Our Coal & Our Coal-Pits. John R. Leifchild. (Illus.). 243p. 1968. reprint ed. 30.00 (*0-7146-1401-7*, Pub. by F Cass Pubs) Intl Spec Bk.

Our Colonial Period. Bill Yenne. (Making of America Ser.). 1996. pap. text 6.95 (*0-912517-20-4*) Bluewood Bks.

Our Colorado Immortals in Stained Glass. Elaine A. Clearfield. (Illus.). pap. 7.95 (*0-9617471-0-2*) E A Clearfield.

Our Colorful Family Tree. Sherrie A. Styx. (Illus.). 10p. (J). (ps-2). 1989. 3.00 (*1-882121-00-7*) Styx Enter.

Our Common Affairs: Texts from Women in the Old South. Ed. by Joan E. Cashin. LC 95-51431. (Illus.). 352p. (C). 1996. text 39.95 (*0-8018-5306-0*) Johns Hopkins.

Our Common African Genesis: Evidence from Genetics, Linguistics, Archaeology, Genesis, & Pre-Egyptian History & How Christian Mythology Tried to Erase It. Larry West. LC 98-90485. (Illus.). 65p. 2000. pap. 10.95 (*0-533-12815-3*) Vantage.

Our Common Future. Don Hinrichsen. 1986. 10.00 (*1-85383-010-0*, Pub. by Escan Pubns) Island Pr.

Our Common Future. World Commission on Employment & Development Staff. (Illus.). 398p. 1987. pap. text 16.95 (*0-19-282080-X*) OUP.

Our Common Herd. Sue Sanders. Ed. by Annette K. Baxter. LC 79-8811. (Signal Lives Ser.). 1980. reprint ed. lib. bdg. 30.95 (*0-405-12856-8*) Ayer.

Our Common Journey De Jongh. LC 99-20787. 1999. pap. 25.00 (*1-85649-739-9*) St Martin.

Our Common Journey CAPTAIN DE JONGH. LC 99-20787. 1999. text 65.00 (*1-85649-738-0*) St Martin.

***Our Common Journey: A Transition Toward Sustainability.** National Research Council Staff. 360p. 1999. pap. 60.00 (*0-309-06783-9*) Natl Acad Pr.

Our Common Lands: Defending the National Parks. Ed. by David J. Simon. LC 88-16977. 567p. (C). 1988. text 50.00 (*0-933280-58-0*) Island Pr.

Our Common Lands: Defending the National Parks. Ed. by David J. Simon. LC 88-16977. 567p. (Orig.). (C). 1988. pap. text 32.00 (*0-933280-57-2*) Island Pr.

Our Common Life: Reflections on Being a Spouse. Mary Glover & Rob Glover. 119p. 1999. pap. 5.95 (*0-87946-201-9*, 284) ACTA Pubns.

Our Common Oneness. Bill Freeman. LC 94-75759. 284p. 1995. pap. 7.50 (*0-914271-58-X*) Mnstry Pubns.

Our Common Oneness. Bill Freeman. 1998. pap. text 10.95 (*0-914271-98-9*) Mnstry Pubns.

Our Common School System. Mary A. Dodge. (Notable American Authors Ser.). 1992. reprint ed. lib. bdg. 75.00 (*0-7812-2661-9*) Rprt Serv.

Our Common Shores & Our Common Challenge: Environmental Protection of the Pacific. Ed. by D. Shaw. (Illus.). 142p. (Orig.). (C). 1995. pap. text 5.00 (*1-56612-027-6*) AK Sea Grant CP.

Our Communion, Our Peace, Our Promise see Guide for the Assembly

Our Communion, Our Peace, Our Promise see Guia para la Asamblea

Our Community. Kathryn T. Hegeman. (Illus.). (Orig.). (J). (gr. k-3). 1982. pap., teacher ed. 10.00 (*0-89824-034-4*); pap., student ed. 4.99 (*0-89824-035-2*) Trillium Pr.

***Our Companion Animals: Tales of Transformation from Farm Sanctuary.** Ed. by Gene Bauston & Lorri Bauston. 2001. pap. 14.00 (*1-930051-23-9*) Lantern Books.

Our Congress. Michael Weber. (I Know America Ser.). (Illus.). 48p. (J). (gr. 2-4). 1994. pap. 6.95 (*0-7613-0091-0*) Millbrook Pr.

Our Congress. Michael Weber. LC 94-7639. (I Know America Ser.). (Illus.). 48p. (J). (gr. 2-4). 1996. lib. bdg. 20.90 (*1-56294-443-6*) Millbrook Pr.

Our Congress. Michael Weber. LC 94-7639. (I Know America Ser.). (J). 1994. 12.15 (*0-606-09722-8*, Pub. by Turtleback) Demco.

Our Conscious Universe: And the Mysteries Thereof. Raymond A. Decker. LC 98-65015. 165p. 1998. pap. 9.95 (*0-9660847-0-5*) OCU Bks.

Our Constitution. Linda C. Johnson. LC 91-43232. (I Know America Ser.). (Illus.). 48p. (J). (gr. 2-4). 1992. pap. 8.95 (*1-56294-813-X*); lib. bdg. 20.90 (*1-56294-090-2*) Millbrook Pr.

Our Constitution. Linda Carlson Johnson. LC 91-43232. (I Know America Ser.). 1992. 14.15 (*0-606-06642-X*, Pub. by Turtleback) Demco.

Our Constitution: The Myth That Binds Us. Eric Black. 192p. (C). 1988. pap. 25.00 (*0-8133-0695-7*, Pub. by Westview) HarpC.

Our Constitution: The Way It Was. rev. ed. Madalyn M. O'Hair. 70p. 1988. 6.00 (*0-910309-41-8*, 5400) Am Atheist.

Our Constitution, Our Government. Robert Field. 1984. pap. text, student ed., wbk. ed. 10.95 (*0-87594-282-2*) Book-Lab.

Our Constitution, Our Government. 3rd rev. ed. Robert J. Field. (Illus.). 158p. (J). (gr. 4-12). 1998. pap. text, wbk. ed. 10.95 (*0-87594-378-0*) Book-Lab.

Our Constitution, Our Government: Teacher's Guide. 3rd rev. ed. Robert J. Field. 86p. 1997. pap. text, teacher ed. 7.95 (*0-87594-283-0*) Book-Lab.

Our Constitutional Heritage. James J. Carroll. LC 98-179838. 67p. 1991. 15.75 (*1-56256-006-9*) Peoples Pub Grp.

Our Contemporary Composers. John T. Howard, Jr. & Arthur Mendel. (New Reprints in Essay & General Literature Index Ser.). 1977. reprint ed. 34.95 (*0-518-10201-7*, 10201) Ayer.

Our Context: The Cosmos & the Flow of History: Measurement & Uncertainty: Perspectives on the Present. Richard L. Crews. 43p. (C). 1988. pap. text. write for info. (*0-945864-03-5*) Columbia Pacific U Pr.

Our Context: The Cosmos & the Flow of History: Origins: Perspectives on the Past. Richard L. Crews. 70p. (C). 1988. pap. text. write for info. (*0-945864-02-7*) Columbia Pacific U Pr.

Our Context: The Cosmos & the Flow of History: Probabilities & Possibilities: Perspectives on the Future. Richard L. Crews. 62p. (C). 1988. pap. text. write for info. (*0-945864-04-3*) Columbia Pacific U Pr.

Our Continent, Our Future: African Perspectives on Structural Adjustment. Thandika Mkandawire & Charles C. Soludo. LC 98-41439. 224p. 1998. 79.95 (*0-86543-704-1*); pap. 21.95 (*0-86543-705-X*) Africa World.

Our Convicts, 2 vols. in 1. Mary Carpenter. LC 69-16229. (Criminology, Law Enforcement, & Social Problems Ser.: No. 88). 1969. reprint ed. 30.00 (*0-87585-080-4*) Patterson Smith.

Our Cool Field Trip. Pawnee Elementary, Mrs. Salisbury's Third Grade Cl. (WeWrite Kids! Ser.: No. 13). (Illus.). 35p. (J). (ps-3). 1995. pap. 3.95 (*1-884987-43-5*) WeWrite.

Our Cooperative Classroom. David W. Johnson et al. (Illus.). 94p. (Orig.). 1988. pap. text, teacher ed. 10.00 (*0-939603-05-5*) Interaction Bk Co.

Our Cops - Their Stories. Ed. by Iris Gadd & Roger Gadd. 347p. 1987. pap. 5.95 (*0-7736-7135-8*) Genl Dist Srvs.

Our Coral Reefs. S. M. Soule. (ICLARM Education Ser.: No. 15). 27p. 1994. write for info. (*971-8709-40-1*, Pub. by ICLARM) Intl Spec Bk.

Our Core Democratic Values: Civic Virtue in Action. Jean Shafer. (Illus.). 32p. (J). (gr. 3-7). 1999. wbk. ed. 14.95 (*0-938682-54-7*) River Rd Pubns.

Our Corner of the World: Seventeen Illinois Artists. Diane Cox et al. (Illus.). 32p. 1989. 7.00 (*0-945558-05-8*) ISU Univ Galls.

Our Cosmic Ancestors. rev. ed. Maurice Chatelain. Ed. by Marlene Donovan. (Illus.). 226p. 1988. reprint ed. pap. 9.95 (*0-929686-00-4*) Temple Golden Pubns.

***Our Cosmic Connection: What is the True Meaning of Life?** unabridged ed. R. Wayne Stewart. (Illus.). 148p. 2000. pap. text 14.95 (*0-9679818-0-8*) Tri-Tron Global.

***Our Cosmic Future: Humanity's Fate in the Universe.** Nikos Prantzos. Tr. by Stephen Lyle. (Illus.). 320p. 2000. 24.95 (*0-521-77098-X*) Cambridge U Pr.

***Our Cosmic Origins: From the Big Bang to the Emergence of Life & Intelligence.** Armand H. Delsemme. (Illus.). 342p. 2001. pap. 14.95 (*0-521-79480-3*) Cambridge U Pr.

Our Cosmic Origins: From the Big Bang to the Emergence of Life & Intelligence. rev. ed. Armand H. Delsemme. LC 97-33010. (Illus.). 320p. (C). 1998. 24.95 (*0-521-62038-4*) Cambridge U Pr.

Our Cosmic Universe. John Kraus. 281p. 1980. write for info. (*1-882484-01-0*); pap. write for info. (*1-882484-02-9*) CYGNUS-QUASAR Bks.

Our Country: Its Land & People. Laurel R. Singleton & Douglas R. Superka. (Illus.). 192p. 1986. 125.00 (*0-87746-031-0*); teacher ed. 90.00 (*0-87746-032-9*) Graphic Learning.

Our Country: The Shaping of America from Roosevelt to Reagan. Michael Barone. 1992. pap. 19.95 (*0-02-901862-5*) Free Pr.

Our Country Cookin' Ed. by Junior Social Workers Staff. 320p. 1984. 14.95 (*0-9613296-0-2*) Jr Soc Workers.

Our Country, Our Culture: The Politics of Political Correctness. Ed. by Edith Kurzweil & William Phillips. 300p. 1995. pap. 12.50 (*0-9644377-3-2*) Partisan Rev Pr.

Our Countrymen. . . Benson J. Lossing. (Notable American Authors Ser.). 1999. reprint ed. lib. bdg. 125.00 (*0-7812-3859-5*) Rprt Serv.

Our Country's Birds & How-To Know Them. W. J. Gordon. (Illus.). 152p. 1998. pap. 25.00 (*0-87556-849-1*) Saifer.

***Our Country's Founders: Words of Advice from the Founders in Stories, Letters, Poems & Speeches.** William J. Bennett. 1998. 17.00 (*0-8054-1600-5*) Broadman.

Our Country's Good. Timberlake Wertenbaker. (Orig.). 1988. pap. 5.95 (*0-87129-342-0*, O42) Dramatic Pub.

Our Country's Good. Timberlake Wertenbaker. (Methuen Modern Plays Ser.). 91p. (Orig.). (C). 1991. pap. write for info. (*0-413-65900-3*, AO590, Methuen Drama) Methn.

Our County & Its People: A Descriptive & Biographical Record of Madison County. Ed. by John E. Smith. (Illus.). 888p. 1997. reprint ed. lib. bdg. 89.50 (*0-8328-6170-7*) Higginson Bk Co.

Our County & Its People: A Descriptive Work on Jefferson County. Ed. by Edgar C. Emerson. (Illus.). 1254p. 1997. reprint ed. lib. bdg. 130.00 (*0-8328-6157-X*) Higginson Bk Co.

Our County & Its People: A History of the Valley & County of Chemung from the Closing Years of the 18th Century. With Biographies & Personal References. Ausburn Towner. (Illus.). 862p. 1995. reprint ed. lib. bdg. 88.00 (*0-8328-6547-8*) Higginson Bk Co.

Our County & Its People: Historical & Memorial Record of Crawford Co. Samuel P. Bates. (Illus.). 972p. 1997. reprint ed. lib. bdg. 97.50 (*0-8328-6404-8*) Higginson Bk Co.

Our County & Its People Vol. 1: A Descriptive Work on Erie County, N.Y. Truman C. White. (Illus.). 906p. 1992. reprint ed. lib. bdg. 91.00 (*0-8328-2584-0*) Higginson Bk Co.

Our County & Its People Vol. 2: A Descriptive Work on Erie County, New York. Truman C. White. 617p. 1992. reprint ed. lib. bdg. 62.00 (*0-8328-2587-5*) Higginson Bk Co.

Our County, Our Story: Portage County. Malcolm Rosholt. (Illus.). 600p. 1999. reprint ed. lib. bdg. 62.50 (*0-8328-9792-2*) Higginson Bk Co.

Our Court System. Zachary A. Kelly. LC 99-28687. (Law & Order Ser.). 1999. write for info. (*0-86593-575-0*) Rourke Corp.

Our Courts on Trial. V. R. Iyer. 1987. 19.95 (*81-7018-448-7*) Asia Bk Corp.

Our Covenant God: Learning to Trust Him. Kay Arthur. LC 99-11808. 288p. 1999. 19.95 (*1-57856-182-5*); pap. 12.95 (*1-57856-261-9*) Waterbrook Pr.

Our Covenant of Prosperity: Crossing the Threshold to Supernatural Abundance. Markus Bishop. LC 97-213780. 112p. 1997. pap. 6.99 (*0-89274-959-8*) Harrison Hse.

Our Covenant with God. Copelan. 1988. pap. 2.95 (*0-938458-02-7*) K Copeland Pubns.

Our Covenant with God. Kenneth Copeland. 32p. 1976. mass mkt. 2.95 (*0-88114-742-7*) K Copeland Pubns.

***Our Covenant with God.** Kenneth Copeland. 66p. 1999. pap. 4.99 (*1-57562-242-4*) K Copeland Pubns.

Our Covenant with God: What It Provides. Keith Hershey. (Christian Life Ser.). 28p. (Orig.). 1992. pap. 1.95 (*0-940487-04-7*) Jubilee CA.

Our Criminal Courts. Raymond Moley. LC 74-3835. (Criminal Justice in America Ser.). 1974. reprint ed. 25.95 (*0-405-06181-1*) Ayer.

Our Criminal Courts. Raymond Moley. xxiii, 271p. 1997. reprint ed. 88.50 (*1-56169-341-3*) Gaunt.

Our Crowd: The Great Jewish Families of New York. Stephen Birmingham. LC 96-32954. 404p. 1996. reprint ed. pap. 17.95 (*0-8156-0411-4*, BIOCP) Syracuse U Pr.

Our Crowded Planet: Essays on the Pressures of Population. Ed. by Fairfield Osborn. LC 82-21145. 240p. 1983. reprint ed. lib. bdg. 65.00 (*0-313-22639-3*, OSOC, Greenwood Pr) Greenwood.

Our Croze's Nest. John Gould. 192p. (Orig.). 1997. pap. 13.95 (*0-942396-79-0*) Blackberry ME.

Our Cry for Life: Feminist Theology from Latin America - Nuestra Clamor por la Vida. Maria P. Aquino. Tr. by Dinah Livinstone from SPA. LC 93-33087. 200p. 1993. reprint ed. pap. 18.00 (*0-88344-895-5*) Orbis Bks.

Our Cuban Colony: A Study in Sugar. Leland H. Jenks. LC 70-111718. (American Imperialism: Viewpoints of United States Foreign Policy, 1898-1941 Ser.). 1976. reprint ed. 25.95 (*0-405-02028-7*) Ayer.

Our Cuban Colony: A Study in Sugar. Leland H. Jenks. (BCL1 - U. S. History Ser.). 341p. 1991. reprint ed. lib. bdg. 89.00 (*0-7812-6049-3*) Rprt Serv.

Our Cuban Colony: A Study in Sugar. Leland H. Jenks. Ed. by Harry E. Barnes. LC 74-145111. (Illus.). xxi, 341p. 1972. reprint ed. 21.00 (*0-403-01050-0*) Scholarly.

Our Cultural Agony. Vincent Vycinas. 213p. 1973. lib. bdg. 85.50 (*90-247-1355-2*, Pub. by M Nijhoff) Kluwer Academic.

Our Cultural Cancer & Its Cure. Howard A. Slaatte. 224p. (C). 1995. lib. bdg. 39.00 (*0-8191-9787-4*) U Pr of Amer.

Our Culture "Left" or "Right" Litterateurs Confront Nihilism. Paul Eidelberg & Will Morrisey. 232p. 1992. text 89.95 (*0-7734-9171-6*) E Mellen.

Our Currency, Our Country. John Redwood. LC 98-115526. 240p. pap. 15.95 (*0-14-026523-6*, Pub. by Pnguin Bks Ltd) Trafalgar.

Our Czeck-ered Past. Bessie A. Sisson. 196p. Date not set. pap. 14.95 (*1-887150-07-2*) Millennia Bks.

Our Daily Bread. Martin Ralph DeHaan & Henry G. Bosch. LC 88-20791. 384p. 1959. 14.99 (*0-310-23410-7*, 9505) Zondervan.

***Our Daily Bread.** G. J. Zondervan. 208p. 1999. 9.97 (*0-310-97897-1*) Zondervan.

Our Daily Bread: A Selection of Daily Readings from the Popular Devotional. LC 96-40858. 384p. 1997. pap. 17.99 (*1-57293-019-5*) Discovery Hse Pubs.

*__Our Daily Bread: Socialist Distribution & the Art of Survival in Stalin's Russia, 1927-1941.__ Ed. by Elena Osokina et al. LC 99-86153. (The New Russian History Ser.). (Illus.). 288p. 2000. 64.95 (*1-56324-904-9*) M E Sharpe.

Our Daily Bread Favorites. Ed. by Richard W. DeHaan & Henry G. Bosch. 384p. 1971. 14.95 (*0-310-23590-1*, 18042) Zondervan.

Our Daily Fix: Drugs in Australia. V. A. Brown et al. (Illus.). 320p. 1986. pap. text 18.50 (*0-08-033044-4*, Pub. by Aberdeen U Pr) Macmillan.

Our Daily Times with God. Discovery House Staff. 432p. 1988. pap. 12.99 (*0-929239-01-6*) Discovery Hse Pubs.

Our Daily Times with God. large type ed. Discovery House Staff. LC 96-17993. 432p. 1988. pap. 14.99 (*0-929239-03-2*) Discovery Hse Pubs.

Our Daily Walk. F. B. Meyer. 16.99 (*1-85792-048-1*, Pub. by Christian Focus) Spring Arbor Dist.

Our Daily Walk. F. B. Meyer. 1982. pap. 9.95 (*0-310-29141-0*) Zondervan.

Our Daughter Learns to Read & Write: A Case Study from Birth to 3. Marcia Baghban. LC 84-10868. 170p. reprint ed. pap. 52.70 (*0-8357-2637-1*, 204012500014) Bks Demand.

*__Our Daughters' Health: Practical & Invaluable Advice for Raising Confident Girls Ages 6-16.__ Shari Roan. 2001. pap. 14.95 (*0-7868-8500-9*, Pub. by Disney Pr) Time Warner.

Our Dawson Family. Sally M. Patin. 232p. 1981. 20.00 (*0-89308-215-5*) Southern Hist Pr.

Our Day Family, 1597-1990. Doyle Day. ix, 356p. 1990. 40.00 (*0-944619-51-7*) Gregath Pub Co.

Our Day in the Light of Prophecy (1918) W. A. Spicer. 380p. 1998. reprint ed. pap. 27.95 (*0-7661-0627-6*) Kessinger Pub.

Our Day Out. Willey Russell. 56p. (C). 1988. pap. 7.95 (*0-413-54870-8*, A0201) Heinemann.

Our Day Out & Other Plays. Wiley Russell. 160p. 1989. pap. 11.95 (*0-09-172882-7*) Dufour.

Our Dead Behind Us: Poems. Audre Geraldine Lorde. 88p. 1994. pap. 9.00 (*0-393-31238-0*) Norton.

Our Deadly Addiction: Overconsumption. Levi Keidel. LC 98-67424. 79p. 1999. pap. 9.95 (*1-57197-130-0*) Pentland Pr.

Our Dear Mother the Spirit: An Investigation of Count Zinzendorf's Theology & Praxis. Gary S. Kinkel. 258p. (C). 1990. lib. bdg. 46.00 (*0-8191-7743-1*) U Pr of Amer.

Our Debt & Duty to the Farmer. Henry C. Wallace. Ed. by Dan C. McCurry & Richard E. Rubenstein. LC 74-30661. (American Farmers & the Rise of Agribusiness Ser.). 1975. reprint ed. 25.95 (*0-405-06838-7*) Ayer.

Our December Hearts: Meditations for Advent & Christmas. Anne McConney. LC 99-31259. 112p. 1999. pap. 10.95 (*0-8192-1786-7*, 5979) Morehouse Pub.

Our Decentralized Literature: Cultural Mediations in Selected Jewish & Southern Writers. Jules Chametzky. LC 86-1259. 168p. 1986. pap. text 15.95 (*0-87023-540-0*) U of Mass Pr.

Our Declaration of Independence. Jay Schleifer. LC 91-43229. (I Know America Ser.). (Illus.). 48p. (J). (gr. 2-4). 1992. lib. bdg. 20.90 (*1-56294-205-0*) Millbrook Pr.

Our Declaration of Independence. Jay Schleifer. LC 91-43229. (I Know America Ser.). (Illus.). 48p. (J). (gr. 2-4). 1992. pap. 8.95 (*1-56294-814-8*) Millbrook Pr.

Our Demographically Divided World. Lester R. Brown & Jodi L. Jacobson. LC 86-51475. (Worldwatch Papers: No. 74). 64p. (Orig.). (C). 1986. pap. 5.00 (*0-916468-75-5*) Worldwatch Inst.

Our Destiny: A Treasury of Travellers Verse. Compiled by Shamus McPhee. 128p. 1998. pap. 24.00 (*1-898218-82-X*) St Mut.

Our Destiny: Biblical Teaching on the Last Things. Stanley M. Horton. (Logion Press Ser.). 304p. 1996. 19.95 (*0-88243-322-9*, 02-0322) Gospel Pub.

Our Destiny: Biblical Teachings on the Last Things. Stanley M. Horton. (RUS.). 300p. 1998. text. write for info. (*1-890219-93-2*) Life Pubs Intl.

Our Destiny: Biblical Teachings on the Last Things. Stanley M. Horton. (UKR.). 330p. 1998. text. write for info. (*1-890219-94-0*) Life Pubs Intl.

Our Destiny: The Child. Linda M. Mutz. LC 96-84392. (Illus.). 60p. 1996. 14.95 (*1-888024-06-2*) Ahead Desktop.

Our Destiny: The Child. Linda M. Mutz. LC 96-85822. 80p. 1996. pap. 14.95 (*1-888024-10-0*) Ahead Desktop.

Our Destiny We Know: Essays in Honor of Edwin K. Gedney. Ed. by Freeman Barton. 269p. (Orig.). 1996. pap. 9.99 (*1-881909-24-7*) Advent Christ Gen Conf.

Our Dhammapada. Wayne Lord, Sr. 112p. (Orig.). 1993. pap. 8.95 (*0-9636577-0-4*) Trego-Hill.

Our Dinosaurs Are Dying: New American Poems. Kenan Heise. (Illus.). 124p. (Orig.). 1994. pap. 9.95 (*0-924772-26-3*) CH Bookworks.

Our Divided World: Poverty, Hunger, & Overpopulation. Micki McKisson & Linda MacRae-Campbell. (Our Only Earth Ser.). (J). (gr. 4-12). 1990. pap. 25.00 (*0-913705-52-7*) Zephyr Pr AZ.

Our Divine Legacy - Christ & the International Vipers: Helleno-Christianity Versus the Figment of Judeo-Christianity. rev. ed. Nicholas C. Eliopoulos. 444p. 1999. pap. text 37.00 (*1-893760-30-8*) Eliopoulos.

Our Double Time, 1. Michael O'Siadhail. LC 98-189163. 1999. pap. text 17.95 (*1-85224-450-X*) Bloodaxe Bks.

Our "Downriver" River: Nautical History & Tales of the Lower Detroit River. Rockne P. Smith. (Illus.). ix, 132p. 1997. pap. 19.50 (*0-9660349-0-2*) R P Smith.

Our Dramatic Heritage, Vol. 1. Ed. by Philip G. Hill. LC 81-65294. 368p. 1983. 45.00 (*0-8386-3106-1*) Fairleigh Dickinson.

Our Dramatic Heritage: The 18th Century, Vol. 3. Ed. by Philip G. Hill. LC 81-65294. 1987. 45.00 (*0-8386-3108-8*) Fairleigh Dickinson.

Our Dramatic Heritage Vol. 2: The Golden Age. Ed. by Philip G. Hill. LC 81-65294. 624p. 1985. 60.00 (*0-8386-3107-X*) Fairleigh Dickinson.

Our Dramatic Heritage Vol, 3: The 18th Century. Ed. by Philip G. Hill. 308p. 1988. 50.00 (*0-8386-3266-1*) Fairleigh Dickinson.

Our Dramatic Heritage Vol. 4: Romanticism & Realism. Ed. by Philip G. Hill. LC 81-65294. 504p. 1989. 65.00 (*0-8386-3267-X*) Fairleigh Dickinson.

Our Dramatic Heritage Vol. 5: Reactions to Realism. Ed. by Philip G. Hill. LC 81-65294. 384p. 1991. 55.00 (*0-8386-3411-7*) Fairleigh Dickinson.

Our Dramatic Heritage Vol. 6: Expressing the Inexpressible. Ed. by Philip G. Hill. LC 81-65294. 336p. 1992. 55.00 (*0-8386-3421-4*) Fairleigh Dickinson.

*__Our Dream: A World Free of Poverty.__ Sandra Granzow. LC 00-28329. 160p. 2000. 40.00 (*0-8213-4702-0*, 14702) World Bank.

Our Dreaming Mind. Robert L. Van de Castle. LC 95-94192. 576p. 1995. pap. 15.00 (*0-345-39666-9*) Ballantine Pub Grp.

Our Drowning World. Antony Milne. 192p. 1988. write for info. (*1-85327-004-0*, Pub. by Prism Pr) Assoc Pubs Grp.

Our Dudley Heritage. James H. Mason & Mary S. Mason. LC 82-60822. 96p. 1982. 16.50 (*0-9609032-0-8*) J H Mason.

*__Our Dumb Century: The Onion Presents One Hundred Years of Headlines from America's Finest New s Source.__ abr. ed. Scott Dikkers. 1999. audio 12.00 (*0-694-52199-X*) HarperAudio.

Our Dumb Century: The Onion Presents 100 Years of Headlines from America's Finest News Source. Scott Dikkers & Onion Writers Staff. (Illus.). 164p. 1999. pap. 16.00 (*0-609-80461-8*, Three Riv Pr) Crown Pub Group.

Our Earliest Ancestors. Bjorn Kurten. Tr. by Erik J. Friis from SWE. LC 93-6516.Tr. of Vara Aldsta f Orf Ader. 1993. 27.50 (*0-231-08061-1*) Col U Pr.

Our Early Ancestors: An Introductory Study of Mesolithic, Neolithic, & Copper Age Cultures in Europe & Adjacent Regions. Miles C. Burkitt. LC 72-80142. (Illus.). 1972. reprint ed. 18.95 (*0-405-08331-9*, Pub. by Blom Pubns) Ayer.

*__Our Earth.__ Brighter Vision Staff. (Learning Adventures Ser.). (Illus.). (J). (gr. k-1). 1999. pap. text 2.25 (*1-55254-061-8*) Brighter Vision.

Our Earth. Craig Chisholm. (Explainers Ser.). (Illus.). 24p. (J). (gr. 2-4). 1982. pap. 4.95 (*0-86020-582-7*, Usborne) EDC.

Our Earth. Anne Rockwell. 24p. (J). 2000. pap. 6.00 (*0-15-202383-6*, Voyager Bks) Harcourt.

Our Earth. Anne F. Rockwell. LC 97-1247. (Illus.). 24p. (J). (gr. k-1). 1998. 13.00 (*0-15-201679-1*) Harcourt.

Our Earth Vol. 1: The Water Planet: An Introduction. Debra S. Dixon & Susan V. Henry. Ed. by Lundie Spence & Christine San Jose. (Illus.). 45p. (Orig.). (J). (gr. 3-7). 1992. pap. 14.95 (*0-9609506-2-1*) Prescott Durrell & Co.

Our Earth, Our Cure: A Handbook of Natural Medicine for Today. Raymond Dextreit. Ed. & Tr. by Michel Abehsera from FRE. (Illus.). 210p. 1993. reprint ed. pap. 15.95 (*0-8065-1013-7*, Citadel Pr) Carol Pub Group.

Our Ecological Footprint: Reducing Human Impact on the Earth. William Rees & Mathis Wackernagel. (Illus.). 176p. (Orig.). 1995. pap. 14.95 (*0-86571-312-X*) New Soc Pubs.

Our Economic Predicament in Perspective. Fred C. Armstrong. LC 77-91219. 1978. 10.00 (*0-87212-100-3*) Libra.

Our Economy: Why It's Not Working & How to Fix It. 2nd ed. John Field & Ralph Pressel. 562p. (Orig.). (C). 1993. pap. text 39.50 (*0-8191-9227-9*); lib. bdg. 67.50 (*0-8191-9226-0*) U Pr of Amer.

Our Ecosystem. Doris Roettger. 1993. pap. 8.99 (*0-86653-936-0*) Fearon Teacher Aids.

Our Educational Melting Pot: Have We Reached the Boiling Point? Ed. by Carlos A. Bonilla et al. LC 97-71584. (Illus.). 100p. (Orig.). 1997. pap. text 19.95 (*1-879774-07-0*) ICA Pub Co.

Our Eight Nights of Hanukkah. Michael J. Rosen & DyAnne DiSalvo-Ryan. LC 99-11001. 32p. (J). 2000. 16.95 (*0-8234-1476-0*) Holiday.

Our Elders Understand Our Rights: Evolving International Law Regarding Indegenous, 1. Drew Taylor. LC 98-230738. 1999. pap. 18.95 (*0-919441-66-1*) O R C A.

Our Elections. Richard Steins. LC 94-8537. (I Know America Ser.). (Illus.). 48p. (J). (gr. 2-4). 1994. lib. bdg. 20.90 (*1-56294-446-0*) Millbrook Pr.

Our Elections. Richard Steins. (I Know America Ser.). (Illus.). 48p. (J). (gr. 2-4). 1996. pap. 6.95 (*0-7613-0092-9*) Millbrook Pr.

Our Elections. Richard Steins. LC 94-8537. (I Know America Ser.). (J). 1994. 12.15 (*0-606-09723-6*, Pub. by Turtleback) Demco.

Our Elephant & That Child. Judith Kroll. (QRL Poetry Bks.: Vol. XXX). 1991. 20.00 (*0-614-06440-6*) Quarterly Rev.

Our Eleven Chief Justices: A History of the Supreme Court in Terms of Their Personalities. Kenneth B. Umbreit. LC 91-55365. xiv, 539p. 1991. reprint ed. 135.00 (*0-912004-91-6*) Gaunt.

Our Elusive Constitution: Silences, Paradoxes, Priorities. Daniel N. Hoffman. LC 96-48971. (SUNY Series in American Constitutionalism). 297p. (C). 1997. text 59.50 (*0-7914-3501-6*); pap. text 19.95 (*0-7914-3502-4*) State U NY Pr.

Our Emergent Civilization. Ed. by Ruth N. Anshen. LC 70-134048. (Essay Index Reprint Ser.). 1977. 23.95 (*0-8369-2101-1*) Ayer.

*__Our Emily.__ Mary Jane Staples. (J). 2000. pap. 10.95 (*0-552-13444-9*, Pub. by Transworld Publishers Ltd) Trafalgar.

Our Eminent Friend Edmund Burke, Six Essays. Thomas W. Copeland. LC 76-104217. 251p. 1970. reprint ed. lib. bdg. 49.50 (*0-8371-3334-3*, COEB, Greenwood Pr) Greenwood.

Our Endangered Parks. LC 63-62002. 1994. 9.95 (*0-614-10446-7*, L114) Natl Parks & Cons.

Our Endangered Planet: Air. Lisa Yount & Mary M. Rodgers. LC 95-5375. (J). 1995. lib. bdg. 22.60 (*0-8225-2510-0*) Lerner Pub.

Our Endangered Planet: Antarctica. Suzanne Winckler & Mary M. Rodgers. 64p. (J). (gr. 4 up). 1991. lib. bdg. 22.60 (*0-8225-2506-2*, Lerner Publctns) Lerner Pub.

Our Endangered Planet: Groundwater. Mary K. Hoff & Mary M. Rodgers. (Illus.). 64p. (J). (gr. 4 up). 1991. lib. bdg. 22.60 (*0-8225-2500-3*, Lerner Publctns) Lerner Pub.

Our Endangered Planet: Oceans. Mary M. Rodgers & Mary K. Hoff. (Illus.). 72p. (J). (gr. 4 up). 1991. lib. bdg. 22.60 (*0-8225-2505-4*, Lerner Publctns) Lerner Pub.

Our Endangered Planet: Population Growth. Mary K. Hoff & Mary M. Rodgers. (Illus.). 64p. (J). (gr. 4 up). 1991. lib. bdg. 22.60 (*0-8225-2502-X*, Lerner Publctns) Lerner Pub.

Our Endangered Planet: Rivers & Lakes. Mary K. Hoff & Mary M. Rodgers. (Illus.). 64p. (J). (gr. 4 up). 1991. lib. bdg. 22.60 (*0-8225-2501-1*, Lerner Publctns) Lerner Pub.

Our Endangered Planet: Soil. Suzanne Winckler & Mary M. Rodgers. LC 92-39902. (Our Endangered Planet Ser.). (J). 1993. lib. bdg. 22.60 (*0-8225-2508-9*, Lerner Publctns) Lerner Pub.

Our Endangered Planet: Tropical Rain Forests. Cornelia F. Mutel. 64p. (J). (gr. 4 up). 1991. lib. bdg. 22.60 (*0-8225-2503-8*, Lerner Publctns) Lerner Pub.

Our Endangered Planet: Tropical Rain Forests. Cornelia F. Mutel. (J). (gr. 4 up). 1993. pap. 8.95 (*0-8225-9629-6*, Lerner Publctns) Lerner Pub.

*__Our Enduring Values: Librarianship in the 21st Century.__ Michael Gorman. LC 00-27127. 2000. write for info. (*0-8389-0785-7*) ALA.

Our Enemy Destroyed. Donald Duren. LC 90-93244. 196p. 1990. per. write for info. (*0-8187-0124-2*) Harlo Press.

Our Enemy, the Child. Agnes De Lima. LC 78-89172. (American Education: Its Men, Institutions, & Ideas. Series 1). 1975. reprint ed. 23.95 (*0-405-01410-4*) Ayer.

Our Enemy, the State. Albert J. Nock. LC 76-172222. (Right Wing Individualist Tradition in America Ser.). 1979. reprint ed. 23.95 (*0-405-00431-1*) Ayer.

Our Enemy, the State. 9th ed. Albert J. Nock. LC 82-83561. 112p. 1998. pap. 9.95 (*0-87319-023-8*) Hallberg Pub Corp.

Our Enemy, the State: Including "On Doing the Right Thing" Albert J. Nock. xxv, 117p. 1994. 19.95 (*0-930073-11-8*) Fox & Wilkes.

Our English Heritage. Gerald W. Johnson. LC 72-12627. 253p. 1973. reprint ed. lib. bdg. 65.00 (*0-8371-6676-4*, JOEH, Greenwood Pr) Greenwood.

*__Our Environment.__ Time-Life Books Editors. Ed. by Karin Kinney. LC 99-56070. (Student Library: Vol. 9). 128p. (J). 1999. 24.95 (*0-7835-1358-5*) Time-Life.

Our Environment: An Introduction to Physical Geography. 3rd ed. Donald K. Fellows. LC 84-22165. 486p. 1985. pap. 80.95 (*0-471-88193-7*) Wiley.

Our Environment: Book & Poster. Rebecca Stark. Date not set. teacher ed. 12.95 (*0-910857-89-X*, 089-XAPS) Educ Impress.

Our Environment: Thematic Unit. Mary E. Sterling. (Thematic Units Ser.). (Illus.). 80p. (J). (gr. k-3). 1991. student ed. 9.95 (*1-55734-272-5*) Tchr Create Mat.

Our Environment Theme Set, 7 bks. (Beginners Ser.). 1991. pap. 10.52 (*0-8123-6955-6*); pap. 10.52 (*0-8123-6961-0*); pap. 10.52 (*0-8123-6967-X*); pap. 10.52 (*0-8123-6968-8*); pap. 10.52 (*0-8123-6969-6*); pap. 10.52 (*0-8123-6970-X*); pap. 10.52 (*0-8123-6975-0*) McDougal-Littell.

*__Our Evolution.__ Waldo Vieira. 1999. pap. 11.95 (*85-86019-42-9*) Intl Inst Proj.

Our Evolving Curriculum Pt. I: A Special Issue of the Peabody Journal of Education, Vol. 69, No. 3, 1996. Ed. by Allan C. Ornstein & Unda S. Behar. 1996. reprint ed. pap. 20.00 (*0-8058-9897-2*) L Erlbaum Assocs.

Our Evolving Earth: Geology 1103. 322p. (C). 1995. text 42.00 (*0-536-59182-2*) Pearson Custom.

Our Evolving Universe. Malcolm S. Longair. (Illus.). 197p. (C). 1996. text 39.95 (*0-521-55091-2*) Cambridge U Pr.

Our Evolving Universe. Malcolm S. Longair. (Illus.). 224p. 1997. pap. 20.95 (*0-521-62975-6*) Cambridge U Pr.

Our Ewing Heritage, 2 vols., Set. Betty J. Durbin Carson & Doris M. Durbin Wooley. (Illus.). 944p. (Orig.). 1995. pap. text 60.50 (*0-7884-0236-6*) Heritage Bk.

Our Ewing Heritage with Related Families, 2 vols., Set. Betty J. Carson & Doris M. Wooley. LC 96-216331. 1057p. (Orig.). 1996. pap. 72.00 (*0-7884-0475-X*, C068) Heritage Bk.

Our Exciting World. (Barbie Preschool Workbks.: Vol. 3). (Illus.). 72p. (J). 1998. pap. write for info. (*0-7666-0212-5*, Honey Bear Bks) Modern Pub NYC.

Our Existential Predicament: Loneliness, Depression, Anxiety, & Death. rev. ed. James L. Park. LC B819.P37 1995. 308p. (Orig.). 1996. pap. text 50.00 (*0-89231-900-3*) Existential Bks.

*__Our Exium Universe: Theory For the New Millennium.__ Burghard Sonntag. 1999. pap. text 11.95 (*1-889131-32-6*) CasAnanda.

*__Our Expectations for Preservation.__ large type ed. Janet R. Reinhold. (Illus.). 8p. 1999. 5.00 (*1-891406-26-4*) Future Pubg.

Our Exploits at West Poley. Thomas Hardy. 1990. reprint ed. lib. bdg. 25.95 (*0-89966-699-X*) Buccaneer Bks.

Our Eyes Can Be Opened: Preaching the Miracle Stories of the Synoptic Gospels Today. Ronald J. Allen. LC 81-43679. 146p. (C). 1983. pap. text 17.00 (*0-8191-2671-3*) U Pr of Amer.

Our Eyes Reveal a Nation in Crisis . . . And the Way Out! What Every Parent, Counselor & Educator Should Know about the Iris of the Eyes! unabridged ed. William M. Scott. (Illus.). 78p. 1998. pap. 12.95 (*0-9665795-0-X*) Growth Adventures.

Our Fair City. Ed. by Robert S. Allen. LC 73-19124. (Politics & People Ser.). 396p. 1974. reprint ed. 29.95 (*0-405-05851-9*) Ayer.

*__Our Faith: God's Great Gift.__ Sister Mary Eligia et al. (Our Holy Faith Ser.: Vol. VI). (Illus.). 350p. (YA). (gr. 6-7). 1998. text 20.00 (*0-911845-82-8*) Neumann Pr.

Our Faith & Fellowship. G. Carlson. LC 77-75023. (Radiant Life Ser.). 128p. 1977. pap. 4.99 (*0-88243-908-1*, 02-0908) Gospel Pub.

Our Faith & Fellowship. G. Raymond Carlson. LC 77-75023. (Radiant Life Ser.). 128p. 1977. pap., teacher ed. 5.50 (*0-88243-178-1*, 32-0178) Gospel Pub.

Our Faith & Strength. Naftali Hoffner. 1994. 8.95 (*1-58330-106-2*) Feldheim.

Our Faith & Worship, Vol. 1. Abidullah Ghazi & Tasneema K. Ghazi. Ed. by Noura Durkee & Fadel Abdallah. (Illus.). 71p. 1993. pap. text 6.00 (*1-56316-055-2*) Iqra Intl Ed Fdtn.

Our Faith & Worship Vol. 2: Textbook of Islamic 'Aqa'id & Arkan. unabridged ed. Abidullah Ghazi & Tasneema Ghazi. Ed. by Carolyn Baugh & Suhaib Ghazi. LC 94-65696. 58p. (Orig.). (J). (gr. 1-3). 1996. pap. text 6.00 (*1-56316-060-9*) Iqra Intl Ed Fdtn.

Our Faith & Worship Workbook, Vol. 1. Tasneema Ghazi. Ed. by Samina Mustapha. (Illus.). 91p. 1994. student ed. 6.00 (*1-56316-057-9*) Iqra Intl Ed Fdtn.

Our Faithful Friend: Building Intimacy with God. John D. Sloan. (Knowing God Ser.). 64p. 1994. 5.99 (*0-310-48301-8*) Zondervan.

Our Falklands War. Maritime Books Staff. (C). 1986. text 60.00 (*0-907771-08-4*, Pub. by Maritime Bks) St Mut.

Our False Christianity, How It Started. Harold Kaisersatt. 136p. (Orig.). 1988. pap. 8.00 (*0-930401-18-2*) Artex Pub.

Our Familiar Songs & Those Who Made Them. Helen K. Johnson. LC 74-15743. (Popular Culture in America Ser.). 676p. 1975. reprint ed. 50.95 (*0-405-06378-4*) Ayer.

Our Families, Our Values: Snapshots of Queer Kinship. Ed. by Robert E. Goss & Amy A. Strongheart. LC 97-1311. 290p. 1997. pap. 19.95 (*1-56023-910-7*, Harrington Park) Haworth Pr.

Our Families, Our Values: Snapshots of Queer Kinship. Ed. by Robert E. Goss & Amy A. Strongheart. LC 97-1311. 290p. 1997. 49.95 (*0-7890-0234-5*) Haworth Pr.

Our Families/Our Stories: From the African American Community, Riverside, California. Ed. by H. Vincent Moses & Celena Turney. (Illus.). 20p. (Orig.). 1997. mass mkt. 5.00 (*0-935661-25-5*) Riverside Mus Pr.

Our Family. L. V. D'Agostino. (Illus.). 1973. 6.95 (*0-9601076-1-4*) L V D'Agostino.

Our Family: Facts & Fancies: The Crary & Related Families. Regina M. Mandrell. Ed. by William S. Coker et al. (Southern History & Genealogy Ser.). (Illus.). 276p. 1993. pap. text 27.50 (*1-882695-05-4*) Patagonia Pr.

Our Family Album: The Unfinished Story of the Christian Reformed Church. James Schaap. LC 98-36521. 423p. 1998. 24.95 (*1-56212-361-0*, 1700-7200) CRC Pubns.

Our Family & Toys Two One-Act Plays. Mario Fratti. 1986. pap. 4.95 (*0-918680-31-X*) Griffon House.

Our Family Babysitting Guide. Julie Young & Woody Young. Orig. Title: Babysitting Wise. 64p. 1992. reprint ed. spiral bd. 8.95 (*0-939513-32-3*) Joy Pub SJC.

*__Our Family Book of Days: A Record Through the Years.__ Kathleen Finley. 224p. 2000. 24.95 (*0-88489-646-3*) St Marys.

Our Family Can Read, 2 bks. Reginald Oxendine. (Illus.). 76p. (Orig.). (J). (gr. k up). 1992. 29.95 (*0-944049-01-X*); 29.95 (*0-944049-02-8*) Arrow Pub NC.

Our Family Can Read, 2 bks., Set. Reginald Oxendine. (Illus.). 76p. (Orig.). (J). (gr. k up). 1992. pap. text 29.95 incl. audio (*0-944049-00-1*) Arrow Pub NC.

Our Family Diary: A Keepsake Diary for the Entire Family. Russell D. Earnest, Jr. LC TX98-92744. 128p. 1998. pap. 19.95 (*1-879311-13-5*) R D Earnest.

Our Family Foods: A Journal. Lynne O'Dell. (Illus.). 107p. 1996. 19.95 (*0-9651043-0-3*) Kings Mtn.

Our Family Has Cancer, Too! Christine Clifford. LC 97-4771. (Illus.). 64p. (J). (gr. k-6). 1997. pap. 6.95 (*1-57025-144-4*) Pfeifer-Hamilton.

Our Family History. Randall K. Mehew. (Personal Enrichment Ser.). 27p. (Orig.). 1991. write for info. (*0-929985-74-5*) Jackman Pubng.

*__Our Family History.__ Thomas Ray Woodard. (Illus.). xvi, 205p. 2000. 48.95 (*0-9679573-1-1*); pap. 19.95 (*0-9679573-0-3*) T R Woodard.

*__Our Family History.__ deluxe ed. Random House Value Publishing Staff. 160p. 2000. 14.99 (*0-517-43636-1*) Random Hse Value.

Our Family History: Record Book, Photograph Album & Family Tree. Reader's Digest Editors. 1999. 24.95 (*0-7621-0232-2*, Readers Digest) Login Bros.

Our Family History & Album Waterlane Edition, 2 vols. Rutledge Hill Press Staff. 1999. boxed set 19.99 (*1-55853-708-2*) Rutledge Hill Pr.

O

An Asterisk (*) at the beginning of an entry indicates that the title is appearing for the first time.

Our Family History & Records. George L. Allerton. (Illus.). 352p. 1988. pap. 13.95 (*0-945620-00-4*); ring bd. 19.95 (*0-945620-01-2*) Associated Specialties.

Our Family Is Divorcing: A Read-Aloud Book for Families Experiencing Divorce. Patricia P. Johnson & Donna R. Williams. LC 96-26335. (Helping Children Who Hurt Ser.). (Illus.). 80p. (Orig.). (J). 1996. pap. 11.95 (*0-89390-391-4*) Resource Pubns.

***Our Family... Just Recipes & Memories.** Erma Wells Huso. (Illus.). 96p. 2001. pap. write for info. (*1-892668-26-2*) Prospect Pr.

Our Family Memories: Highlights of Our Times Together. Judy M. Lawrence. Ed. by Victor M. Spadaccini & Susan Schreifels. (Illus.). 96p. 1995. 9.95 (*0-911493-14-X*) Blue Sky.

***Our Family Organizer.** Gina Glidewell. 1999. ring bd. 35.00 (*0-9669471-1-8*) Live Oak Pr.

Our Family, Our Friends, Our World: An Annotated Guide to Significant Multicultural Books for Children & Teenagers. Lyn Miller-Lachmann. 710p. 1992. 46.00 (*0-8352-3025-2*) Bowker.

Our Family, Our Strength. Tehilla Abramov & Yirmyohu Abramov. 153p. 1997. 17.95 (*1-56871-126-3*, Pub. by Targum Pr) Feldheim.

Our Family, Our Town: Essays on Family & Local History Sources in the National Archives. Compiled by Timothy Walch. LC 86-600230. (Illus.). 223p. 1987. 5.00 (*0-911333-50-9*, 100012) National Archives & Recs.

***Our Family Saga: The True Story of My Life, 1930-1965.** Martin Lackner. LC 99-91798. 2000. 25.00 (*0-7388-1274-9*); pap. 18.00 (*0-7388-1275-7*) Xlibris Corp.

Our Family Shares Advent: Scripture, Prayer, & Activities for Families. Mary Y. Nilsen. (Illus.). 64p. (Orig.). (J). (gr. 1-8). 1981. 7.95 (*0-86683-637-3*, 8129) Harper SF.

Our Family Songs. Connie Winter-Eulberg & Steven B. Eulberg. (Illus.). 34p. 1995. pap. 5.00 (*0-9639663-5-9*) Owl Mtn Music.

Our Family Story. Grant. 1996. 16.95 (*0-7459-3380-7*, Pub. by Lion Pubng) Trafalgar.

Our Family Tree. Julie Hausner. 144p. 1989. 7.98 (*0-89009-136-6*) Bk Sales Inc.

Our Family Tree. Lisa Peters. 2002. write for info. (*0-15-201772-0*) Harcourt.

***Our Family Tree: Level B.** Steck-Vaughn Company Staff. (Read All about It Ser.). (Illus.). (J). 2000. pap. 4.95 (*0-8114-3803-1*) Raintree Steck-V.

Our Family Tree Record Book. Deni Bown. 64p. 1997. 17.95 (*0-7894-2076-7*) DK Pub Inc.

Our Famous Women: An Authorized Record of the Lives & Deeds of Distinguished American Women of Our Times. Elizabeth S. Phelps et al. LC 73-1192. (Essay Index Reprint Ser.). (Illus.). 1977. reprint ed. 38.95 (*0-518-10060-X*) Ayer.

***Our Farm of Four Acres & the Money We Made by It.** A. Coulton. Ed. by Nathan Griffith. LC 99-80033. (Illus.). 101p. 2000. pap. 10.00 (*0-9665103-2-1*) Cobblemead Publications.

Our Fascinating Past: Charlotte Harbor Early Years. Lindsey Williams. Ed. by U. S. Cleveland. (Illus.). 448p. 1993. write for info. (*0-614-18968-3*) Charlotte Harbor.

Our Fascinating Past: Charlotte Harbor Later Years. Lindsey Williams. Ed. by U. S. Cleveland. (Illus.). 480p. 1996. write for info. (*0-614-18969-1*) Charlotte Harbor.

Our Fate: The Zodiac (1900) Margaret Mayo. 154p. 1998. reprint ed. pap. 11.00 (*0-7661-0638-1*) Kessinger Pub.

Our Fate & the Zodiac. Margaret Mayo. 135p. 1996. reprint ed. spiral bd. 12.00 (*0-7873-0592-8*) Hlth Research.

Our Father see Learning My Prayers

Our Father. (Illus.). 32p. (Orig.). (J). (ps-3). 1990. pap. 0.99 (*0-89942-696-4*, 696/00) Catholic Bk Pub.

Our Father. (Alice in Bibleland Ser.). (Orig.). (J). Date not set. 5.95 (*0-88271-526-7*, 10113) Regina Pr.

Our Father. (Orig.). 1998. 3.95 (*0-88271-628-X*) Regina Pr.

Our Father. Date not set. 0.99 (*0-88271-546-1*, 10341); bds. 3.95 (*0-88271-562-3*, 12012) Regina Pr.

Our Father. Lily Cavell. (Illus.). 24p. 1990. spiral bd. 7.95 (*1-885038-01-1*) Uriel Press.

Our Father. Marilyn French. 448p. 1995. mass mkt. 6.99 (*0-345-38490-3*) Ballantine Pub Grp.

Our Father. Marilyn French. 1996. mass mkt. 6.99 (*0-345-91020-6*) Fawcett.

Our Father. Carolyn J. Griffin. (Lyrics on Matters Relating to Ser.). 10p. 1985. 8.00 (*1-929388-00-4*) Griffin Pubg Co Inc.

Our Father. Bernard Haring. Tr. by Gwen Griffith-Dickson. 104p. 1996. pap. 7.95 (*0-88489-483-5*) St Marys.

Our Father. John Harkes. 176p. 1996. pap. 39.95 (*0-85439-529-6*, Pub. by St Paul Pubns) St Mut.

Our Father. Lawrence G. Lovasik. LC 98-170511. 1993. 7.95 (*0-89942-375-2*, 375/09) Catholic Bk Pub.

Our Father. David Nichols. 1999. write for info. (*0-201-57010-6*) Addison-Wesley.

Our Father. Cliffor Pond. 1997. pap. 7.99 (*0-946462-43-7*, Pub. by Evangelical Pr) P & R Pubng.

Our Father. Lois Veals. 2.99 (*0-906731-41-0*, Pub. by Christian Focus) Spring Arbor Dist.

Our Father . . . Stefan Wyszynski. (C). 1988. 49.00 (*0-85439-216-5*, Pub. by St Paul Pubns) St Mut.

Our Father. Illus. by Helmut Zechner. 1996. pap. 39.95 (*0-85439-432-X*, Pub. by St Paul Pubns) St Mut.

Our Father: A Play. Michael G. Stephens. LC 98-38034. 57p. 1996. pap. 10.00 (*1-881471-15-2*) S Duyvil.

Our Father: A Play. Michael G. Stephens. LC 96-38034. 1997. write for info. (*1-881471-14-4*) S Duyvil.

Our Father: A Tribute to Dermot Morgan Don Morgan. LC 99-158444. 206 p. 1998. 19.95 (*1-874597-96-0*) New Island Books.

***Our Father: Four Commentaries on the Lord's Prayer.** Bill McCarthy. (Illus.). 122p. 1999. pap. 8.95 (*1-891903-15-2*) St Andrew Prodns.

Our Father: Matthew Six. (Illus.). 48p. 1983. 8.20 (*0-86683-745-0*, AY8398) Harper SF.

***Our Father: Reflections on the Lord's Prayer.** Adrian Simonis. (Illus.). 112p. 1999. pap. 14.00 (*0-8028-4675-0*) Eerdmans.

Our Father: Sonnet Symphony. Benito F. Reyes. 28p. (Orig.). 1994. pap. 3.00 (*0-939375-39-7*) World Univ Amer.

***Our Father: The Prayer Jesus Taught.** Mary Joslin. 2000. 15.95 (*0-8294-1504-1*) Loyola Pr.

Our Father Abe: The Story of a Deaf Shoe Repairman. Harvey L. Barash & Eva B. Dicker. (Illus.). 272p. (Orig.). 1991. 12.95 (*0-9629634-1-0*) Abar Pr.

Our Father Abraham: Jewish Roots of the Christian Faith. Marvin R. Wilson. 395p. 1990. pap. 20.00 (*0-8028-0423-3*) Eerdmans.

Our Father & Hail Mary. Lawrence G. Lovasik. (Saint Joseph Picture Bks.). (Illus.). 1987. pap. 1.25 (*0-89942-389-2*, 389-00) Catholic Bk Pub.

Our Father, Friend of Little Children: Children's Object Lessons Based on the Lord's Prayer. 2nd ed. Wesley T. Runk. 24p. (Orig.). 1995. pap. 4.95 (*0-7880-0372-0*) CSS OH.

Our Father in Heaven: Christian Faith & Inclusive Language for God. John W. Cooper. LC 98-40633. 304p. (C). (gr. 13). 1999. pap. 19.99 (*0-8010-2188-X*) Baker Bks.

Our Father, Our King: Drawings by Saul Raskin. Saul Raskin. 96p. 1966. 39.95 (*0-8197-0603-5*) Bloch.

Our Father, Our Mother: Mary & the Faces of God. George T. Montague. 175p. 1990. pap. 3.48 (*0-940535-28-9*, UP128) Franciscan U Pr.

***Our Father Speaks.** C. Alan Ames. 1999. pap. 11.95 (*1-890137-40-5*) One Hund-One Fnd.

Our Father Who Art on Earth. Richard D. Dobbins. 19p. 1990. pap. 1.00 (*1-890329-10-X*) Totally Alive.

Our Father/Hail Mary. Lawrence Lovasik. (St. Joseph Beginner Ser.). (Illus.). 32p. (J). (gr. k-3). 1996. 3.50 (*0-89942-228-4*, 228/22) Catholic Bk Pub.

Our Fathers. Andrew O'Hagan. LC 99-25486. 304p. 1999. 23.00 (*0-15-100494-3*, Harvest Bks) Harcourt.

***Our Fathers.** Andrew O'Hagan. 304p. 2000. pap. 13.00 (*0-15-601202-2*) Harcourt.

Our Fathers: Manners & Customs of the Ancient Victorians. Alan Bott & Irene Clephane. LC 75-160614. (Illus.). 1972. 30.95 (*0-405-08292-4*, Pub. by Blom Pubns) Ayer.

***Our Fathers & Mothers: A Family Story, 1800-2000 A. D.** Jack Meyer. (Illus.). 125p. 2000. pap. 10.00 (*0-9672197-1-X*) CrocusplusDBR.

Our Father's Before Us. Martin Calvin. 305p. (Orig.). 1983. pap. 4.95 (*0-914397-00-1*) Cornell Des.

Our Father's Family. Allen D. Peterson. LC 95-68674. 57p. 1995. pap. 7.50 (*0-9646503-0-4*) A D Peterson.

Our Fathers' Fields: A Southern Story. James E. Kibler. LC 97-50376. (Illus.). 352p. 1998. 29.95 (*1-57003-214-9*) U of SC Pr.

Our Fathers Have Told Us. S. Beck. 224p. 1993. write for info. (*1-883704-01-4*) Cleaveland.

Our Father's Plan. rev. ed. Boyd K. Packer. LC 84-72516. 62p. 1994. 12.95 (*0-87579-820-9*) Deseret Bk.

Our Father's Plan: God's Arrangements & Our Response. William G. Most. 276p. 1993. reprint ed. pap. 7.95 (*0-931888-50-6*) Christendom Pr.

Our Father's Promises . . . to Us! Paul E. Paino. 64p. 1992. pap. 6.95 (*1-882357-00-0*) P E Paino Minist.

***Our Father's World.** Michael J. McHugh & David K. Arwine. 1999. teacher ed. 5.95 (*1-930092-06-7*) Christian Liberty.

***Our Father's World.** Michael J. McHugh & David K. Arwine. (Illus.). 112p. (J). (gr. 1-2). 1999. pap. text 8.95 (*1-930092-05-9*) Christian Liberty.

***Our Father's World: Test Booklet.** Michael J. McHugh & David K. Arwine. 1999. 2.95 (*1-930092-07-5*) Christian Liberty.

Our Faust? Roots & Ramifications of a Modern German Myth. Ed. by Reinhold Grimm & Jost Hermand. LC 86-40452. (Monatshefte Occasional Volumes Ser.: Vol. 5). (Illus.). 199p. reprint ed. pap. 61.70 (*0-608-20433-1*, 207168600002) Bks Demand.

Our Favorite Birds. Lenore H. Hughes. LC 86-91359. (Illus.). 88p. (Orig.). 1986. 8.50 (*0-9604772-3-3*) Hughes Pub.

Our Favorite Folksongs: Five Finger. 24p. 1995. pap. 5.95 (*0-7935-4883-7*, 00310068) H Leonard.

Our Favorite Recipes Vol. 1: Gracious Southern Recipes from the Garden Patch Company. Betty Gray et al. 100p. 1994. pap. 9.95 (*0-9651762-0-7*) Grdn Patch.

***Our Favorite Things to Do.** Lisa Trumbauer & Gail Saunders-Smith. LC 00-36490. (Illus.). (J). 2000. write for info. (*0-7368-0739-X*) Capstone Pr.

Our Favorite Things Way Back Then & Now. Burr E. Fancher & Jacob W. Fancher. Ed. & Illus. by Ada Fancher. 114p. (Orig.). (YA). (gr. 7 up). 1995. pap. 6.00 (*1-887335-01-3*) Fancher & Assocs.

Our Favorites, Vol. 4473. Michelle W. Nechaer. Ed. by Joel Kupperstein. (Learn to Read Math Ser.). (Illus.). 16p. (J). 1998. pap. 2.75 (*1-57471-380-9*, 4473) Creat Teach Pr.

Our Federal & State Constitution see Nuestras Constituciones Federal y Estatal

Our Federal & State Constitutions. Alex J. Schmidt. 65p. (YA). (gr. 7-11). 1997. reprint ed. pap. text 4.25 (*0-931298-00-8*) A J S Pubns.

***Our Federal Constitution, Our Alabama Constitution.** rev. ed. Alex Schmidt & Steve Schmidt. Ed. & Illus. by Dennis Schmidt. 64p. 1999. pap. text 6.00 (*1-892291-08-8*) RJS Pubns.

Our Federal Constitution, Our Florida Constitution. rev. ed. Alex Schmidt & Steve Schmidt. Ed. & Illus. by Dennis Schmidt. 64p. 1974. pap. text 6.00 (*1-892291-07-X*) RJS Pubns.

Our Federal Constitution, Our Michigan Constitution. rev. ed. Alex Schmidt & Steve Schmidt. Ed. & Illus. by Dennis Schmidt. 64p. 1997. pap. text 6.00 (*1-892291-01-0*) RJS Pubns.

***Our Federal Constitution, Our Missouri Constitution.** rev. ed. Alex Schmidt & Steve Schmidt. Ed. & Illus. by Dennis Schmidt. 64p. 1999. pap. text 6.00 (*1-892291-00-2*) RJS Pubns.

Our Federal Constitution, Our New Jersey Constitution. rev. ed. Alex Schmidt & Steve Schmidt. Ed. & Illus. by Dennis Schmidt. 64p. 1997. pap. text 6.00 (*1-892291-02-9*) RJS Pubns.

Our Federal Constitution, Our New York Constitution. rev. ed. Alex Schmidt & Steve Schmidt. Ed. & Illus. by Dennis Schmidt. 64p. 1996. pap. text 6.00 (*1-892291-03-7*) RJS Pubns.

***Our Federal Constitution, Our State Constitution.** rev. ed. Alex Schmidt & Steve Schmidt. Ed. & Illus. by Dennis Schmidt. 64p. 1999. pap. text 6.00 (*1-892291-09-6*) RJS Pubns.

***Our Federal Constitution, Our Texas Constitution.** rev. ed. Alex Schmidt & Steve Schmidt. Ed. & Illus. by Dennis Schmidt. 64p. 1999. pap. text 6.00 (*1-892291-06-1*) RJS Pubns.

***Our Federal Constitution, Our Wisconsin Constitution.** rev. ed. Alex Schmidt & Steve Schmidt. Ed. & Illus. by Dennis Schmidt. 64p. 1999. pap. text 6.00 (*1-892291-04-5*) RJS Pubns.

Our Feet Are the Feet of Dogs. Camilla Beck. 1997. 12.00 (*1-891051-08-3*) Back Cover Pr.

Our Feet Walk the Sky: Women of the South Asian Diaspora. Ed. by Women of South Asian Descent Collective Staff. LC 93-36354. 392p. (Orig.). 1998. pap. 14.95 (*1-879960-32-X*) Aunt Lute Bks.

Our Fiery Trial: Abraham Lincoln, John Brown, & the Civil War Era. Stephen B. Oates. LC 78-16286. 160p. 1983. pap. 15.95 (*0-87023-397-1*) U of Mass Pr.

Our Fifty States. Janet Hale & Richard Rayburn. Ed. by Karen J. Goldfluss. (Illus.). 288p. 1994. student ed. 24.95 (*1-55734-470-1*) Tchr Create Mat.

Our 50 States. Ed. by Instructional Fair Staff. 1998. pap. 10.95 (*0-88012-852-6*) Instruct Fair.

Our Fifty States & Their Flags. Illus. by TNT Stone & Associates Staff & Petertil Design Partners Staff. (Powertools for Kids Ser.: No. 15). 4p. (J). (gr. 2-5). 1998. pap., wbk. ed. 4.95 (*1-58220-014-9*, 32505, PowerTools for Kids) Navigator.

Our Fight: Writings by Veterans of the Abraham Lincoln Brigade, Spain 1936-1939. Ed. by Alvah C. Bessie & Albert Prago. LC 87-5562. 320p. (C). 1987. pap. 12.00 (*0-85345-724-7*, Pub. by Monthly Rev) NYU Pr.

Our Fight for Russia. Paul N. Butkoff. LC 98-26933. 256p. 1998. 45.00 (*1-56072-554-0*) Nova Sci Pubs.

Our Fight with Tammany. Charles H. Parkhurst. 1970. 25.95 (*0-405-02470-3*, 18944) Ayer.

Our Fight with Tammany. Charles H. Parkhurst. LC 70-119941. (Select Bibliographies Reprint Ser.). reprint ed. 16.50 (*0-8369-5384-3*) Ayer.

Our Fighting Men & Women. Harry Knill. (J). (gr. 1-9). 1992. pap. 2.50 (*0-88388-172-1*) Bellerophon Bks.

Our Films, Their Films. Satyajit Ray. 219p. 1983. 19.95 (*0-86125-637-9*) Asia Bk Corp.

Our Films, Their Films. Satyajit Ray. 224p. (J). 1994. 22.45 (*0-7868-6122-3*, Pub. by Hyperion) Time Warner.

Our Finest Hour: Will Clayton, the Marshall Plan, & the Triumph of Democracy. Gregory A. Fossedal. LC 92-33108. (Publication Ser.: No. 412). (Illus.). 350p. (C). 1993. text 34.95 (*0-8179-9201-4*); pap. text 18.95 (*0-8179-9202-2*) Hoover Inst Pr.

Our Firemen: History of the New York Fire Departments. Augustine E. Costello. (Illus.). 1112p. 1997. reprint ed. 24.95 (*1-57715-013-9*) Knckerbocker.

***Our First Hundred Years.** Archibald McKinlay. LC 99-41274. 1999. write for info. (*1-57864-086-5*) Donning Co.

Our First Pony. Marguerite Henry. LC 96-31717. (Illus.). 64p. (J). (gr. 1-4). 1997. mass mkt. 6.99 (*0-689-81026-1*) S&S Trade.

Our First Pony. Marguerite Henry. 1997. 12.19 (*0-606-11713-X*, Pub. by Turtleback) Demco.

Our First Republicans: Social Writings of John Dunmore Lang, Charles Harpur & Daniel Henry Deniehy. Ed. by David Headon & Elizabeth Perkins. 196p. 1998. pap. 34.00 (*1-86287-265-1*, Pub. by Simmonds & Hill Pubng) Gaunt.

Our First Sukkah. Norma Simon. (Festival Series of Picture Storybooks). (Illus.). (J). (ps). 1959. spiral bd. 4.50 (*0-8381-0703-6*) USCJE.

Our First Year: Sticker Calendar. Jane Koziouski & Mark Jacobsen. Ed. by Judi Jacobsen. (Wedding Ser.). (Illus.). 36p. 1990. 9.95 (*0-685-31316-6*) Madison Pk Grtings.

Our Fish Missing, Bk. 1. R. Kingsland. (Illus.). (J). 1995. mass mkt. 6.95 (*0-340-61965-1*, Pub. by Hodder & Stought Ltd) Trafalgar.

***Our Flag.** 52p. 1999. pap. 2.50 (*0-16-063287-0*, Congress) USGPO.

Our Flag. Eleanor Ayer. LC 91-38892. (I Know America Ser.). (Illus.). 48p. (J). (gr. 2-4). 1992. pap. 8.95 (*1-878841-86-6*) Millbrook Pr.

Our Flag. Eleanor H. Ayer. LC 91-38892. (I Know America Ser.). 1992. 14.15 (*0-606-06644-6*, Pub. by Turtleback) Demco.

***Our Flag.** Ed. by John W. Warner. (Illus.). 51p. 2000. reprint ed. pap. text 20.00 (*0-7881-8804-6*) DIANE Pub.

Our Flag: Born Through Valor. Wanda Z. Larson. (Illus.). 75p. (J). (gr. 4-12). 1999. pap. 12.00 (*0-9628584-1-2*) Blue Uncrn.

Our Flag: How to Honor It, How to Display It. 7th ed. 1995. 1.50 (*0-934021-03-1*) Natl Flag Foun.

Our Flag: Its History, Practices & Observances. (Illus.). 52p. (Orig.). 1994. pap. text 20.00 (*0-7881-0219-2*) DIANE Pub.

Our Flag in Verse & Prose: Its History, Origin, & Celebration As Related in Song & Story. Ed. by Robert H. Schauffler. 225p. 2000. reprint ed. lib. bdg. 40.00 (*0-7808-0195-4*) Omnigraphics Inc.

Our Flight. rev. ed. Kathryn C. Moore. Ed. by Ronald Hutson. Orig. Title: My First Flight. (Illus.). (J). (ps-4). 1991. lib. bdg. 3.95 (*0-9633295-0-2*) K Cs Bks N Stuff.

***Our Florida: Heritage of the Sunshine State in Stories & Photos.** Ed. by Michael Dregni. LC 00-44771. (Illus.). 160p. 2000. 29.95 (*0-89658-483-6*) Voyageur Pr.

Our Florida Cranes & Their Neighbors - A Love Story. Katie Roberts & Earle Roberts. (Illus.). 56p. (Orig.). (J). (gr. 4-8). 1995. pap. 8.48 (*0-9647812-0-4*) K & E Roberts.

Our Food see Under the Microscope

Our Food see World Agriculture

Our Food, Our Common Ground. Linda Rocawich. (Southern Exposure Ser.). (Illus.). 112p. (Orig.). 1983. pap. 4.00 (*0-943810-16-7*) Inst Southern Studies.

Our Forefathers. Steinmetz. Ed. by Grunberger. (HEB & YID.). Date not set. text 11.00 (*1-890899-74-7*) Bks Plus NY.

Our Forefathers: The Gothonic Nations: Manual of the Ethnography of the Gothic, German, Dutch, Anglo-Saxon, Frisian & Scandinavian Peoples, 2 vols. G. Schutte. Tr. by J. Young. 1977. lib. bdg. 200.00 (*0-8490-2389-0*) Gordon Pr.

Our Forests, Our Future. World Commission on Forestry & Sustainable Development. (Illus.). 200p. (C). 1999. text 74.95 (*0-521-66021-1*); pap. text 32.95 (*0-521-66956-1*) Cambridge U Pr.

***Our Forgotten Arts & Crafts.** John Seymour. LC 99-86448. (Illus.). (J). 2000. write for info. (*0-7894-5847-0*) DK Pub Inc.

Our Forgotten History: The Early Map Makers. John Booth. (C). 1986. pap. text 60.00 (*0-906853-05-2*, Pub. by Cambdge Hse Bks) St Mut.

Our Four Boys: Foster Parenting Retarded Teenagers. Martha U. Dickerson. LC 78-5642. 246p. reprint ed. pap. 76.30 (*0-8357-3976-7*, 203667400005) Bks Demand.

Our Freedom in Christ: A Lay Bible Study in Romans. Reuben R. Welch. (Lay Bible Study Ser.). 144p. (Orig.). 1988. pap. 5.95 (*0-310-75251-5*, 17045P) Zondervan.

Our French-Canadian Ancestors. Gerard Lebel. Ed. & Tr. by Thomas J. LaForest from FRE. LC 83-81941. (Illus.). 1997. pap. 20.00 (*0-914163-25-6*) L I S I Pr.

***Our French Canadian Ancestors.** Gerard Lebel & Jacques Saintonge. Tr. by Thomas J. LaForest from FRE. LC 83-81941. 1999. pap. 20.00 (*0-914163-28-0*) L I S I Pr.

***Our French-Canadian Ancestors.** Gerard Lebel & Jacques Saintonge. Tr. by Thomas J. LaForest from FRE. LC 83-81941. 1999. pap. 20.00 (*0-914163-29-9*) L I S I Pr.

***Our French-Canadian Ancestors.** Gerard Lebel & Jacques Saintonge. Tr. by Thomas J. LaForest from FRE. LC 83-81941. 2000. pap. 20.00 (*0-914163-30-2*) L I S I Pr.

Our French Canadian Ancestors. R. P. Lebel. LC 83-81941.Tr. of Now Ancetres. (FRE., Illus.). 288p. 1996. pap. write for info. (*0-914163-23-X*) L I S I Pr.

Our French Canadian Ancestors, Vol. I. rev. ed. Gerard Lebel. Ed. & Tr. by Thomas J. Leforest from FRE. LC 83-81941. (Illus.). 300p. 1983. reprint ed. pap. 20.00 (*0-914163-01-9*) L I S I Pr.

Our French Canadian Ancestors, Vol. II. rev. ed. Gerard Lebel. Ed. & Tr. by Thomas J. Laforest. LC 83-81941. (Illus.). 290p. 1984. pap. 20.00 (*0-914163-02-7*) L I S I Pr.

Our French Canadian Ancestors, Vol. III. rev. ed. Gerard Lebel. Ed. & Tr. by Thomas J. Laforest. LC 83-81941. (Illus.). 296p. 1985. pap. 20.00 (*0-914163-03-5*) L I S I Pr.

Our French Canadian Ancestors, Vol. IV. rev. ed. Jacques Saintonge. Ed. & Tr. by Thomas J. Laforest from FRE. LC 83-81941. (Illus.). 296p. 1986. pap. 20.00 (*0-914163-04-3*) L I S I Pr.

Our French Canadian Ancestors, Vol. V. Jacques Saintonge. Ed. & Tr. by Thomas J. Laforest. LC 83-81941. (Illus.). 288p. 1987. pap. 20.00 (*0-914163-05-1*) L I S I Pr.

Our French Canadian Ancestors, Vol. VI. Jacques Saintonge. Ed. & Tr. by Thomas J. Laforest from FRE. LC 83-81941. (Illus.). 312p. 1988. pap. 20.00 (*0-914163-06-X*) L I S I Pr.

Our French Canadian Ancestors, Vol. VII. Jacques Saintonge. Ed. & Tr. by Thomas J. Laforest from FRE. LC 83-81914. (Illus.). 298p. 1988. pap. 15.00 (*0-914163-07-8*) L I S I Pr.

Our French Canadian Ancestors, Vol. VIII. Jacques Saintonge. Ed. & Tr. by Thomas J. Laforest from FRE. LC 83-81914. (Illus.). 284p. 1989. pap. 20.00 (*0-914163-08-6*) L I S I Pr.

Our French Canadian Ancestors, Vol. IX. Gerard Lebel. Ed. & Tr. by Thomas J. Laforest. LC 83-81941. (Illus.). 321p. 1986. pap. 20.00 (*0-914163-09-4*) L I S I Pr.

Our French Canadian Ancestors, Vol. X. rev. ed. Gerard Lebel. Ed. & Tr. by Thomas J. Laforest. LC 83-81941. (Illus.). 312p. 1990. pap. 20.00 (*0-914163-10-8*) L I S I Pr.

Our French Canadian Ancestors, Vol. XI. Gerard Lebel. Ed. & Tr. by Thomas J. Laforest from FRE. LC 83-81941. (Illus.). 310p. 1990. pap. 20.00 (*0-914163-11-6*) L I S I Pr.

Our French Canadian Ancestors, Vol. XII. Gerard Lebel. Ed. & Tr. by Thomas J. Laforest. LC 83-81941. (Illus.). 300p. 1991. pap. 20.00 (*0-914163-12-4*) L I S I Pr.

O

An Asterisk (*) at the beginning of an entry indicates that the title is appearing for the first time.

Our French Canadian Ancestors, Vol. XIII. Jacques Saintonge. Ed. & Tr. by Thomas J. Laforest from FRE. LC 83-81941. (Illus.). 310p. 1991. pap. 20.00 (0-914163-13-2) L I S I Pr.

Our French Canadian Ancestors, Vol. XIV. Gerard Lebel. Ed. & Tr. by Thomas J. Leforest. LC 83-81941. (Illus.). 310p. 1992. pap. 20.00 (0-914163-14-0) L I S I Pr.

Our French Canadian Ancestors, Vol. XV. Gerard Lebel. Ed. & Tr. by Thomas J. Laforest. LC 83-81941. (Illus.). 284p. 1992. pap. 20.00 (0-914163-15-9) L I S I Pr.

Our French Canadian Ancestors, Vol. XVI. Gerard Lebel. Ed. & Tr. by Thomas J. Laforest. LC 83-81941. (Illus.). 280p. 1993. pap. 20.00 (0-914163-16-7) L I S I Pr.

Our French Canadian Ancestors, Vol. XVII. Jacques Saintonge. Ed. & Tr. by Thomas J. Laforest. LC 83-81941. (Illus.). 280p. 1993. pap. 20.00 (0-914163-17-5) L I S I Pr.

Our French Canadian Ancestors, Vol. XVIII. Gerard Lebel. Ed. & Tr. by Thomas J. Laforest. LC 83-81941. (Illus.). 290p. 1994. pap. 20.00 (0-914163-18-3) L I S I Pr.

Our French Canadian Ancestors, Vol. XIX. Gerard Lebel. Ed. & Tr. by Thomas J. Laforest. LC 83-81941. (Illus.). 270p. 1994. pap. text 20.00 (0-914163-19-1) L I S I Pr.

Our French Canadian Ancestors, Vol. XX. Gerard Lebel. Ed. & Tr. by Thomas J. Laforest from FRE. LC 83-81941. (Illus.). 249p. 1995. pap. 20.00 (0-914163-20-5) L I S I Pr.

Our French Canadian Ancestors, Vol. XXI. Gerard Lebel. Ed. & Tr. by Thomas J. Laforest from FRE. LC 83-81941. (Illus.). 285p. 1995. pap. 20.00 (0-914163-21-3) L I S I Pr.

Our French Canadian Ancestors, Vol. XXII. Jacques Saintonge. Ed. & Tr. by T. J. Laforest from FRE. LC 83-81941. (Illus.). 288p. 1996. pap. 20.00 (0-914163-22-1) L I S I Pr.

Our French Canadian Ancestors, Vol. XXIV. R. P. Lebel. Ed. & Tr. by Thomas J. LaForest from FRE. LC 83-81941.Tr. of Now Ancetres. 275p. 1997. pap. 20.00 (0-914163-24-8) L I S I Pr.

***Our French-Canadian Ancestors: Index of Names.** Gerard Lebel & Jacques Saintonge. Tr. by Thomas J. LaForest from FRE. LC 83-81941. 2000. pap. 20.00 (0-914163-31-0) L I S I Pr.

***Our French-Canadian Ancestors: 1 Aug 98.** Gerard Lebel & Jacques Saintonge. Tr. by Thomas J. LaForest from FRE. LC 83-81941. 1998. pap. 20.00 (0-914163-27-2) L I S I Pr.

Our French-Canadian Ancestors: 1 May 98. Gerard Lebel & Jacques Saintonge. Tr. by Thomas J. LaForest from FRE. LC 83-81941. 1998. pap. 20.00 (0-914163-26-4) L I S I Pr.

Our Friend, John Burroughs. Clara Barrus. LC 76-130262. (American Biography Ser.: No. 32). 1970. reprint ed. lib. bdg. 75.00 (0-8383-1169-5) M S G Haskell Hse.

Our Friend Manso. Benito Perez Galdos. Tr. by Robert H. Russell from SPA. LC 86-14758.Tr. of El/Amigo Manso. 224p. 1987. text 41.00 (0-231-06404-7) Col U Pr.

Our Friend the Charlatan see Works of George Gissing

Our Friend the Charlatan. George R. Gissing. LC 78-80631. reprint ed. 52.00 (0-404-02815-2) AMS Pr.

Our Friend, the Earth. JoAnne Nelson. LC 92-37716. (Primarily Health Ser.). (Illus.). (J). (gr. k-2). 1995. pap. 6.00 (0-935529-59-4) Wright Group.

Our Friend the Sun. Janet Palazzo. LC 81-11460. (Now I Know Ser.). (Illus.). 32p. (J). (gr. k-2). 1997. pap. 3.50 (0-89375-651-2) Troll Communs.

Our Friends see Critter Sitters Board Books

Our Friends. (Key Words Readers Ser.: A Series, No. 641-6a). (Illus.). (J). (ps-5). pap. 3.50 (0-7214-0508-8, Ladybrd) Penguin Putnam.

Our Friends. (Key Words Readers Ser.: Series S05, Set 1). (Illus.). (J). (ps-5). 4.75 (0-317-03987-3, Ladybrd) Penguin Putnam.

Our Friends: The Navajos. Ed. by Broderick H. Johnson. LC 76-13397. (Illus.). 151p. 1976. pap. 8.00 (0-912586-22-2) Dine College Pr.

Our Friends the Saints. George Brundage. (Illus.). 16p. (J). (ps-3). 1994. bds. 2.75 (0-89942-844-4, 844/22) Catholic Bk Pub.

Our Friendship Gives Me a Feeling of Belonging. Pauline Smith. (C). 1990. pap. 30.00 (0-908175-70-1, Pub. by Boolarong Pubns) St Mut.

Our Fundamental Rights & How We Can Reclaim Them: A Psychological Approach. Bill Boushka. LC 98-96799. 91p. 1998. pap. 9.95 (0-9656744-2-8) High Productivity.

Our Future Homes - Opportunity, Choice & Responsibility. (Command Papers: Ser. 2901). 60p. 1995. pap. 17.00 (0-10-129012-8, HM90128, Pub. by Statnry Office) Bernan Associates.

Our Future in Light of Twentieth-Century Evil: Hope, History & Human Culture. Robert S. Frey. (Jewish Scholars Press Ser.). 120p. (Orig.). 1996. 69.95 (1-57309-015-8); pap. 39.95 (1-57309-014-X) Intl Scholars.

Our Future in Space. Ed. by Steven Anzovin. (Reference Shelf Ser.: Vol. 63, No. 2). 175p. 1991. pap. 25.00 (0-8242-0812-9) Wilson.

Our Future Selves: Love, Life, Sex, & Aging. Merrily Weisbord. 220p. 1993. pap. 12.95 (1-55643-145-7) North Atlantic.

Our Future Together. Bishops' Committee for Pastoral Research Staff & Practices National Conference of Catholic Bishops. (Marriage Is a Sacrament Ser.). 72p. (C). 1990. pap. 3.95 (1-55586-351-5) US Catholic.

Our Future's Past: Documenting Australia's Federation. Compiled by Raymond Evans et al. LC 97-166070. (Illus.). 295p. 1997. write for info. (0-7329-0891-4, Pub. by Macmill Educ) Paul & Co Pubs.

Our Game. John Le Carre, pseud. 1996. mass mkt. 6.99 (0-345-40000-3) Ballantine Pub Grp.

Our Game. John Le Carre, pseud. 1997. pap. 12.00 (0-345-41831-X) Ballantine Pub Grp.

Our Game: A Novel. John Le Carre, pseud. 1995. 24.00 (0-679-44189-1) Knopf.

Our Game: An American Baseball History. Charles C. Alexander. (Illus.). 448p. 1995. pap. 14.95 (0-8050-2094-2, Owl) H Holt & Co.

Our Game - An American Baseball History. Charles C. Alexander. (Illus.). 392p. 1997. 9.98 (1-56731-130-X, MJF Bks) Fine Comms.

Our Gang: Jewish Crime & the New York Jewish Community, 1900-1940. Jenna W. Joselit. LC 82-49287. (Modern Jewish Experience Ser.). 223p. reprint ed. pap. 69.20 (0-7837-3714-9, 205789200009) Bks Demand.

Our Garage see Set 3

Our Garden: Reflections on Nature. Francis Neilson. 1971. 250.00 (0-87700-015-8) Revisionist Pr.

Our Garden Book: The Garden Planner & Record Keeper. Illus. by Jenny Norton. 142p. 1988. 14.95 (0-948751-01-0) Interlink Pub.

Our Garden Our Friend. Kamil Bednar. Tr. by Ludmila Velinsky-Ondrujova from CZE. (Illus.). 180p. 1994. pap. 9.95 (0-685-71273-7) Kabel Pubs.

Our Garden Our Friend. Kamil Bednar. (Illus.). 182p. 1994. text 29.50 (0-930329-65-1) Kabel Pubs.

Our Gardens, Ourselves: Reflections on an Ancient Art. Jennifer Bennett. (Illus.). 176p. 1994. pap. 14.95 (0-921820-91-7) Firefly Bks Ltd.

Our Generation Against Nuclear War. Ed. by Dimitrios I. Roussopoulos. 476p. 1983. 43.99 (0-920057-15-2, Pub. by Black Rose); pap. 14.99 (0-920057-04-7, Pub. by Black Rose) Consort Bk Sales.

Our Genial Enemy, France. E. D. Schoonmaker. 1972. 69.95 (0-8490-0783-6) Gordon Pr.

Our Geologic Environment. Harvey Blatt. LC 96-30973. 541p. 1997. pap. text 70.67 (0-13-371022-X) P-H.

Our Geologic Environment. Jane Boger & Phillip Boger. 244p. (C). 1996. ring bd. 31.95 (0-7872-2718-8, 41271801) Kendall-Hunt.

Our George. H. A. Rey. (J). 1974. pap. 1.95 (0-590-02043-9) Scholastic Inc.

Our Girls. Conrad Seiler. 1939. pap. 5.25 (0-8222-0868-7) Dramatists Play.

Our Girls. Dio Lewis. LC 74-3958. (Women in America Ser.). 388p. 1974. reprint ed. 34.95 (0-405-06106-4) Ayer.

Our Glass. Louise O. Neaderland. (Illus.). 1984. 25.00 (0-942561-04-X) Bone Hollow.

Our Global Environment: A Health Perspective. 4th rev. ed. Anne Nadakavukaren. (Illus.). 711p. (C). 1995. pap. text 32.95 (0-88133-831-1) Waveland Pr.

***Our Global Environment: A Health Perspective.** 5th ed. Anne Nadakavukaren. (Illus.). 697p. (C). 2000. pap. 34.95 (1-57766-098-6) Waveland Pr.

Our Global Neighborhood: The Report of the Commission on Global Governance. Global Governance Commission Staff. (Illus.). 432p. 1995. pap. 15.95 (0-19-827997-3) OUP.

Our Global Past. Newman. 1998. pap. text, wbk. ed. 6.50 (0-312-17190-0) St Martin.

Our Global Village. 2nd ed. Labarca. LC 98-87493. (C). 1999. pap. text 24.00 (0-03-022256-7, Pub. by Harcourt Coll Pubs) Harcourt.

Our Globe, Our World. Kate Petty. (Around & About Ser.). (Illus.). 32p. (J). (gr. 2-4). 1993. pap. 5.95 (0-8120-1236-4) Barron.

Our Globe under Siege III. Robert Morris. 200p. 1988. pap. 9.95 (0-936676-75-2) Inst Achieve Human Pot.

Our Glorious Century. Reader's Digest Editors. LC 94-14328. (Illus.). 512p. 1994. 40.00 (0-89577-616-2, Pub. by RD Assn) Penguin Putnam.

Our Glorious Future: The Interpretation of "Light on the Path" Mabel Collins. 115p. 1995. reprint ed. pap. 15.95 (1-56459-503-X) Kessinger Pub.

Our Glorious Inheritance: Deliverance from the Occult-Audio. Michael R. Shreve. 1991. 5.95 (0-942507-15-0) Deeper Revelation.

Our Glorious Inheritance: Deliverance from the Occult-Video. Michael R. Shreve. 1991. 19.95 (0-942507-16-9) Deeper Revelation.

Our Glorious Inheritance: Syllabus-Questionnaire, 2 vols. Incl. Vol. 1, Pt. 1. Our Glorious Inheritance: Syllabus-Questionnaire. Mike Shreve. 1993. 10.00 (0-942507-22-3); Vol. 1, Pt. 2. Our Glorious Inheritance: Syllabus-Questionnaire. 1993. 10.00 (0-942507-24-X); 1993. 10.00 (0-942507-23-1) Deeper Revelation.

Our Glorious Inheritance: Syllabus-Questionnaire see Our Glorious Inheritance: Syllabus-Questionnaire

Our Glorious Inheritance: The Revelation of the Titles of the Children of God, Vol. 1. rev. ed. Michael R. Shreve. 1987. pap. text 11.95 (0-942507-00-2) Deeper Revelation.

Our Glorious Inheritance: The Revelation of the Titles of the Children of God, Vol. 2. rev. ed. Michael R. Shreve. 1987. pap. 11.95 (0-942507-01-0) Deeper Revelation.

Our Glorious Inheritance: The Revelation of the Titles of the Children of God, Vol. 3. (Orig.). 1988. pap. 11.95 (0-942507-02-9) Deeper Revelation.

Our Glorious Inheritance: The Revelation of the Titles of the Children of God, Vol. 4. Michael R. Shreve. 1991. pap. text 11.95 (0-942507-03-7) Deeper Revelation.

Our Glorious Inheritance: The Revelation of the Titles of the Children of God, Vol. 5. Michael R. Shreve. 1991. pap. text 11.95 (0-942507-11-8) Deeper Revelation.

Our Glorious Inheritance: The Revelation of the Titles of the Children of God, 8 vols., Vol. 6. Michael R. Shreve. 1991. pap. 11.95 (0-942507-12-6) Deeper Revelation.

Our Glorious Inheritance Study Guide: The Revelation of the Titles of the Children of God, 8 vols., Set. Michael R. Shreve. 1991. pap. 14.95 (0-942507-04-5) Deeper Revelation.

Our Glorious Lord. John Ritchie. 1996. pap. 8.99 (0-946351-08-2, Pub. by John Ritchie) Loizeaux.

Our Glorious Lord. large type ed. F. B. Meyer. 6.99 (1-85792-103-8, Pub. by Christian Focus) Spring Arbor Dist.

Our Glorious Lord: Beholding God's Majesty. Jack Kuhatschek. (Knowing God Ser.). 64p. 1994. 5.99 (0-310-48361-1) Zondervan.

Our Glorious Tomorrow. Burton W. Pierce. 207p. (Orig.). 1991. pap. 9.95 (0-9628973-0-2) Daybreak Pubs.

Our Goal Is Gold: A Pictorial Profile of the 1998 U. S. A. Hockey Team. U. S. A. Hockey Staff & NHL Staff. (Illus.). ix, 160p. 1998. 49.95 (1-891613-01-4) Everett Sports.

Our Goal Is Gold: A Pictorial Profile of the 1998 U. S. A. Hockey Team. U. S. A. Hockey Staff & NHL Staff. (Illus.). ix, 160p. (J). (ps-12). 1998. pap. 24.99 (1-891613-00-6) Everett Sports.

***Our Goal Is Gold: The Official 1998 U. S. A. Hockey Team Publication: The Pictorial Profile of the U. S. A. Hockey Team.** Ed. by Michael Puccini. (Illus.). 200p. 1999. reprint ed. text 25.00 (0-7881-6606-9) DIANE Pub.

Our God & His People in the Old Testament: Students Workbook. Paul H. Treick. 292p. (YA). (gr. 8-12). 1998. pap., wbk. ed. write for info. (1-57579-115-3) Pine Hill Pr.

Our God & His People in the Old Testament: Teachers Manual. Paul H. Treick. (Illus.). 348p. 1998. pap., teacher ed. write for info. (1-57579-116-1) Pine Hill Pr.

Our God Has No Favourites: A Liberation Theology of the Eucharist. Anne Primavesi & Jennifer Henderson. 112p. 1994. pap. 20.00 (0-86012-170-4, Pub. by Srch Pr) St Mut.

***Our God Is an Awesome God.** Ed. by Kelly Petre & Dede Petre. (Daily Power Ser.: Vol. 11). 153p. 1999. pap. 7.99 (1-57782-122-X) Discipleshp.

Our god Is Awesome see Nuestro Dios Es Maravilloso: Encuentrese Cara a Cara Con el Poder y la Gloria de Neustro Dios

Our God Is Awesome: Encountering the Greatness of Our God. Tony Evans. 250p. 18.99 (0-8024-6187-5, 239) Moody.

Our God is in Heaven & on Earth see Bog Nash na Njbesi i na zjemli

Our God Is with Us. 1996. pap. 1.35 (0-8341-9502-X, AG-1016) Lillenas.

***Our God Is Wonderful.** William MacDonald. 154p. 1999. pap. 7.99 (1-882701-60-7, Gospel Folio Pr) Uplook Min.

Our God Reigns. 256p. 1995. otabind 17.95 (0-7935-3833-5, 00311695) H Leonard.

Our God Reigns, Vol. 153. 112p. 1995. per. 10.95 (0-7935-4399-1, 00100004) H Leonard.

Our God Reigns: An Inductive Approach to the Book of Revelation. Earl W. Morey. 401p. (Orig.). 1992. pap. 18.95 (0-9634717-0-8) A Minis VA.

Our Gods Are Not Born: A Book of American Short Stories. Charles R. Walker. LC 71-130076. (Short Story Index Reprint Ser.). 1977. 19.95 (0-8369-3657-4) Ayer.

Our Golda: The Story of Golda Meir. David A. Adler. (Women of Our Time Ser.). (Illus.). 64p. (J). (gr. 2-6). 1986. pap. 4.99 (0-14-032104-7, PuffinBks) Peng Put Young Read.

Our Golda, the Story of Golda Meir. David A. Adler. (Women of Our Time Ser.). (J). 1986. 9.70 (0-606-01704-6, Pub. by Turtleback) Demco.

Our Golden California - Student Workbook. Juanita Houston. (Illus.). (J). (gr. 4-6). 1991. pap., student ed. 15.95 (0-88280-097-3); pap., student ed. 20.95 (0-88280-098-1) ETC Pubns.

Our Golden Wedding (For the 50th Anniversary) Scrapbook Kit: Preserving the Precious. Jeanne English. 50p. 1994. 10.95 (1-885425-02-3) Restorat Source.

Our Good Community: A Book of Hope. Ed. by David Harrison. (Illus.). 160p. 1997. pap. 10.00 (0-9660130-0-X) Writers Hall.

Our Good Provider: Delighting in God's Gifts. Lin Johnson. (Knowing God Ser.). 64p. 1994. 5.99 (0-310-48321-2) Zondervan.

Our Good Teachers: What the Real Experts Are Saying about Education. Ellen R. McCormick. 96p. 1995. pap. 8.95 (0-9629972-5-0) Meredith VA.

Our Gospel Message. Oscar Vouga. 32p. 1967. reprint ed. pap. 1.99 (1-56722-047-9) Word Aflame.

Our Government: What It Does & How It Does It. Jesse Macy. (Notable American Authors Ser.). 1999. reprint ed. lib. bdg. 125.00 (0-7812-3909-5) Rprt Serv.

Our Government & the Arts: A Perspective from the Inside. Livingston L. Biddle. LC 88-6168. 554p. 1988. 19.95 (0-915400-67-7, ACA Bks) Am for the Arts.

Our Governors' Mansions. Cathy Keating et al. LC 97-3677. (Illus.). 376p. 1997. 60.00 (0-8109-3688-7, Pub. by Abrams) Time Warner.

***Our Gracie Aunt.** Jacqueline Woodson. LC 00-39721. 2001. write for info. (0-7868-0620-6) Hyperion.

Our Grandmothers: Loving Portraits by 74 Granddaughters. Ed. by Linda Sunshine. 168p. 1998. 29.95 (0-941807-13-4) Stewart Tabori & Chang.

Our Granny. Margaret Wild. LC 93-11950. (Illus.). 32p. (J). (ps-3). 1998. pap. 5.95 (0-395-88395-4) HM.

Our Granny. Margaret Wild. LC 93-11950. (Illus.). 32p. (J). (ps-2). 1994. 14.95 (0-395-67023-3) Ticknor & Flds Bks Yng Read.

Our Great Commission. Cornelius R. Stam. 142p. 1975. 11.00 (1-893874-10-9); pap. 7.50 (1-893874-23-0) Berean Bibl Soc.

Our Great Heritage, Vol. 1. Ed. by Lyle W. Lange. LC 90-63693. 608p. 1991. 36.99 (0-8100-0371-6, 15N0481) Northwest Pub.

Our Great Heritage, Vol. 2. Ed. by Lyle W. Lange. LC 90-63693. 640p. 1991. 36.99 (0-8100-0378-3, 15N0482) Northwest Pub.

Our Great Heritage, Vol. 3. Ed. by Lyle W. Lange. LC 90-63693. 776p. 1991. 38.99 (0-8100-0379-1, 15N0483) Northwest Pub.

Our Great Seal - Symbols of Our Heritage & Our Destiny. E. Raymond Capt. LC 79-53862. 96p. (Orig.). 1979. pap. 5.00 (0-934666-00-8) Artisan Pubs.

Our Great Solicitor: Josiah C. Wedgwood & the Jews. Joshua B. Stein. LC 91-51006. (Illus.). 176p. 1992. 32.50 (0-945636-40-7) Susquehanna U Pr.

Our Great Spring Victory: An Account of the Liberation of South Vietnam. Van Tien Dung. Tr. by John Speagens. LC 76-58106. 275p. 1977. 25.00 (0-85345-409-4, Pub. by Monthly Rev) NYU Pr.

Our Great West. Julian Ralph. LC 75-126250. (Select Bibliographies Reprint Ser.). 1977. 30.95 (0-8369-5477-7) Ayer.

Our Greatest Gift: A Meditation on Dying & Caring. Henri J. M. Nouwen. LC 93-34310. 144p. 1995. pap. 11.00 (0-06-066355-3, Pub. by Harper SF) HarpC.

Our Greatest Hope. George C. Bowman. (Illus.). 120p. (Orig.). 1987. pap. 3.95 (0-932807-24-0) Overmountain Pr.

Our Greek & Latin Roots. James Morwood & Mark Warman. Ed. by Ed Phinney. (Awareness of Language Ser.). (Illus.). 56p. (C). 1990. pap. text 9.95 (0-521-37841-9) Cambridge U Pr.

Our Green Family Cherokee Ancestors & Some of Their Descendants. fac. ed. Gregath Publishing Company Staff. (Illus.). ix, 168p. 1996. lib. bdg. 45.00 (0-944619-07-X) Gregath Pub Co.

***Our Grounds for Hope: Enduring Words of Comfort & Assurance.** Fulton J. Shern. LC 99-75980. 96p. 2000. reprint ed. pap. 7.95 (1-878718-56-8, Resurrection Pr) Catholic Bk Pub.

Our Growing Years - Accompaniment, 2 vols. Ed. by Robert J. Batastini & James R. Sydnor. 624p. 1998. spiral bd. 49.50 (1-57999-018-5, G-4750A) GIA Pubns.

Our Growing Years - Full Music Edition: A Hymnal. Ed. by Robert J. Batastini & James R. Sydnor. 400p. 1998. 16.00 (1-57999-032-0, G-4750C) GIA Pubns.

Our Growing Years - Pew Edition: A Hymnal. Ed. by Robert J. Batastini & James Rawlings Sydnor. 377p. 1998. text 24.00 (1-57999-017-7, G-4750) GIA Pubns.

Our Guardian Angel. George Brundage. (Illus.). 16p. (J). 1994. bds. 2.75 (0-89942-845-2, 845/22) Catholic Bk Pub.

***Our Guest Book.** Ed. by Rae D. Wakelin. (Illus.). 40p. 2000. 15.00 (1-892953-10-2, BK-GUEST) Talus Corp.

Our Guys: The Glen Ridge Rape & the Secret Life of the Perfect Suburb. Bernard Lefkowitz. LC 94-48276. (Men & Masculinity Ser.). (Illus.). 454p. 1997. 29.95 (0-520-20596-0, Pub. by U CA Pr) Cal Prin Full Svc.

Our Guys: The Glen Ridge Rape & the Secret Life of the Perfect Suburb. Bernard Lefkowitz. LC 98-5131. 1998. pap. 15.00 (0-375-70269-5) Vin Bks.

Our Hands Are Stained with Blood. Michael L. Brown. 266p. (Orig.). 1992. pap. 10.99 (1-56043-068-0) Destiny Image.

Our Hands Are Tied: Legal Tensions & Medical Ethics. Marshall B. Kapp. LC 97-38581. 192p. 1998. 55.00 (0-86569-276-9, Auburn Hse) Greenwood.

Our Haunted House. (Trick or Treat Tales Ser.). (Illus.). 24p. (J). (gr. 1-4). 1996. pap. write for info. (1-56144-049-3, Honey Bear Bks) Modern Pub NYC.

Our Haunted Planet. rev. ed. John Keel. LC 99-34184. 224p. 1999. pap. 14.95 (1-880090-16-3) Galde Pr.

***Our Haunting Good-Byes: The Journey from Grief to Life.** Eileen Dunn. 104p. 2000. pap. 9.95 (1-885003-61-7, Pub. by R D Reed Pubs) Midpt Trade.

Our Hawaii: What We Tell Friends To Do In Our Islands see How to Get Lost & Found in Our Hawaii

Our Health, Our Lives: A Revolutionary Approach to Total Health Care for Women. Eileen Hoffman. Ed. by Julie Rubenstein. 448p. 1996. reprint ed. per. 16.00 (0-671-88086-1, PB Trade Paper) PB.

Our Healthier Nation: A Contract for Health, Command Paper 3852. (Command Papers (All) Ser.: No. 81011068). 1998. pap. 25.00 (0-10-138522-6, HM85226, Pub. by Statnry Office) Bernan Associates.

Our Hearts Are Restless. Gilbert Kilpatrick. (C). 1946. pap. 4.00 (0-87574-032-4) Pendle Hill.

Our Hearts Are Restless: Meditations on Learning to Live. Howard A. Redmond. LC 96-53401. 96p. (Orig.). 1997. pap. 10.95 (1-55612-859-2, LI1859) Sheed & Ward WI.

Our Hearts Are Restless: The Prayer of St. Augustine. Francis J. Sheed. 96p. 1984. 4.95 (0-8164-2127-7) Harper SF.

Our Hearts Fell to the Ground. Calloway. 226p. 1996. pap. text 11.95 (0-312-13354-5) St Martin.

Our Hearts Fell to the Ground: Plains Indian Views of How the West was Lost. Ed. by Colin G. Calloway. 1997. pap. text 21.15 (0-312-19123-5) St Martin.

Our Hearts Fell to the Ground: Plains Indians Views of How the West Was Lost. Ed. & Intro. by Colin G. Calloway. (Bedford Series in History & Culture). 224p. 1996. text 39.95 (0-312-16050-X) St Martin.

Our Heart's True Home: Modern Women Find Fulfillment in the Ancient Christian Faith. Ed. by Virginia H. Nieuwsma. LC 96-26042. (Orig.). 1996. pap. 12.95 (1-888212-02-0) Conciliar Pr.

Our Hearts Were Young & Gay. Cornelia Otis Skinner. Ed. by Jean Kerr. 1974. pap. 5.50 (0-87129-247-5, O24) Dramatic Pub.

An Asterisk (*) at the beginning of an entry indicates that the title is appearing for the first time.

Our Hearts Were Young & Gay. Cornelia Otis Skinner & Emily Kimbrough. 1942. 6.95 (*0-396-02401-7*, G P Putnam) Peng Put Young Read.

Our Hearts Were Young & Gay. Cornelia Otis Skinner. (American Autobiography Ser.). 247p. 1995. reprint ed. lib. bdg. 79.00 (*0-7812-8640-9*) Rprt Serv.

Our Heavenly Father, 1. Ignatius. (Faith & Life Ser.). 1995. pap. 24.95 (*0-89870-502-9*) Ignatius Pr.

Our Heavenly Father: Activity Book. Daria M. Sockey. (Faith & Life Ser.: Bk. 1). (Illus.). 127p. (J). (gr. 1). 1987. pap. text 6.50 (*0-89870-092-2*) Ignatius Pr.

Our Heavenly Father Has No Equals: Unitarianism, Trinitarianism & the Doctrine of Doubt. Donald R. Snedeker. LC 97-34853. 422p. 1998. 79.95 (*1-57309-201-0*); pap. 59.95 (*1-57309-200-2*) Intl Scholars.

***Our Heavenly Home.** E. X. Heatherley. Ed. by James Michael Plake & Jennifer Plake. 150p. 2000. pap. 9.95 (*0-929488-97-0*) Balcony Pub Inc.

Our Heavenly Inheritance. Ruth Stewart. 4.99 (*1-56632-022-4*); pap. 2.99 (*1-56632-023-2*) Revival Lit.

Our Heavenly Mother. Lawrence Lovasik. LC 97-221214. (St. Joseph Board Bks.). (Illus.). 32p. (J). (ps-1). 1997. bds. 5.95 (*0-89942-272-1*, 272/22) Catholic Bk Pub.

Our Heilman Family, 1666-1991. Karl J. Heilman & James E. Raudabaugh. (Illus.). 700p. 1992. 55.00 (*0-9628193-0-1*) Heilman & Raudabaugh.

Our Heritage: The Bible. 2nd ed. W. Pascoe Goard. 48p. 1989. pap. 4.00 (*0-934666-34-2*) Artisan Pubs.

Our Heritage: The Past in the Present of African-American & African Existence. Tsenay Serequeberhan. LC 99-48901. 112p. 2000. pap. 17.95 (*0-8476-8921-2*); text 59.95 (*0-8476-8920-4*) Rowman.

Our Heritage & Common Life: Essays Honoring Frank Eiji Sugeno, Frederic & Alma R. Duncalf Professor of Church History, the Episcopal Theological Seminary of Southwest, Austin, Texas. Ed. by William S. Adams & Michael H. Floyd. LC 94-9588. 194p. (C). 1994. lib. bdg. 42.00 (*0-8191-9520-0*) U Pr of Amer.

Our Heritage, & Other Addresses. Herbert A. Bruce. LC 68-54334. (Essay Index Reprint Ser.). 1977. reprint ed. 23.95 (*0-8369-0259-9*) Ayer.

Our Heritage & Our Home. J. William Harris. LC 91-78277. 89p. 1992. pap. 7.95 (*0-87921-083-4*) Attic Pr.

Our Heritage & Our Hope: A History of Pullen Memorial Baptist Church 1884-1984. Roger H. Crook. LC 84-62984. (Illus.). 252p. 1985. 10.00 (*0-9614485-0-4*) Pullen Mem Baptist.

Our Heroes. Chaim Walder. LC 99-186583. 1998. 19.95 (*0-87306-866-1*) Feldheim.

Our High Calling. J. Sidlow Baxter. LC 93-13810. 208p. 1993. pap. 10.99 (*0-8254-2171-3*) Kregel.

Our Highland Heritage. Clara M. Beach. (Illus.). 391p. 29.00 (*0-9617450-0-2*) Highland Twnship.

Our Hills & Valleys: A History of the Helix-Spring Valley Region. Thomas J. Adema. LC 93-36144. (Illus.). 196p. (Orig.). 1993. pap. 14.95 (*0-918740-15-0*) San Diego Hist.

Our Hispanic Pilgrimage. Virgilio P. Elizondo & Angela Erevia. (Illus.). 77p. 1980. write for info. (*0-614-04875-3*) Mex Am Cult.

Our Historic Boundary Waters. Duane R. Lund. 1980. pap. 8.95 (*0-934860-13-0*) Adventure Pubns.

Our Historic Upper Mississippi. Duane R. Lund. 96p. 1991. pap. 8.95 (*0-934860-73-4*) Adventure Pubns.

Our Holiday in Africa. William W. Wheeler. 1977. 36.95 (*0-8369-9196-6*, 9065) Ayer.

Our Holidays in Poetry. Compiled by Mildred R. Harrington & Josephine H. Thomas. LC 29-26163. 479p. 1929. 30.00 (*0-8242-0039-X*) Wilson.

Our Home see Under the Microscope

Our Home. Hole. 1997. 10.95 (*0-7459-3880-9*, Pub. by Lion Pubng) Trafalgar.

Our Home. Alan Trustman. 1997. pap. text 14.95 (*0-9661829-0-1*) Fisher Isl.

Our Home in Heaven. Marilyn J. Wright. Ed. by Gordon Lindsay. 0.95 (*0-89985-252-1*) Christ for the Nations.

Our Home in the Ozarks. 2nd ed. Fay Noe. 1970. pap. 5.50 (*0-9600208-5-3*) Noe.

Our Home on the Hill: USMC Women's Reserve, Henderson Hall, 1943-1946. Nona J. Johnson. (Illus.). v, 175p. (Orig.). 1996. pap. 16.95 (*0-9653074-0-9*) Eagle Riv.

Our Home or Native Land? What Government's Aboriginal Policy Is Doing to Canada. Melvin H. Smith. 304p. 1996. pap. 19.95 (*0-7737-5821-6*) Stoddart Publ.

Our Home Place. Wanda M. Edgerton. (Illus.). 1977. pap. 5.50 (*0-686-22841-3*) Pine Hill Pr.

Our Home Too. Schim Schimmel. (Illus.). 295p. 69.00 (*0-9650972-0-X*) Art Impress.

Our Home, Too. Schim Schimmel. (Illus.). 295p. 1993. 95.00 (*1-885320-01-9*) Collect Edit.

Our Home Too. 2nd ed. Schim Schimmel. (Illus.). 295p. 69.00 (*0-9650972-1-8*) Art Impress.

Our Homestead Story: The First Years. Stephen B. Castleberry & Susie L. Castleberry. 210p. 1996. pap. 7.50 (*1-891907-02-6*) Castleberry.

Our Honeymoon: A Journal of Romantic Memories. Bruce A. Moulton. 1994. 7.95 (*0-9633573-1-X*) Lakeland Color.

Our Honeymoon: A Record Book of Our Getaway. 1997. 19.99 (*1-57977-108-4*) Havoc Pub.

Our Honeymoon: Photo Memory Album. 1997. 15.99 (*1-57977-211-0*) Havoc Pub.

Our Hope for the Future. David R. Rambo. (Christian Living Ser.). 1996. pap. 1.59 (*0-87509-670-0*) Chr Pubns.

Our Hope for Years to Come: The Search for Spiritual Sanctuary. Micah Marty & Martin E. Marty. 112p. 1995. pap. 15.99 (*0-8066-2836-7*, 9-2836) Augsburg Fortress.

Our Hope in Christ see Nuestra Esperanza en Cristo

Our Hope in Christ. rev. ed. Navigators Staff. (Design for Discipleship Ser.: Bk. 7). 48p. 1980. pap. 4.00 (*0-89109-042-8*) NavPress.

Our Hopes - Our Dreams: A Vision for America. Gary Bauer. (Orig.). 1996. mass mkt. 3.99 (*1-56179-433-3*) Focus Family.

Our House. N. M. Bodecker. (J). Date not set. 12.95 (*0-689-50375-X*) McElderry Bks.

Our House. Barbara Konig. Tr. by Roslyn Theobald. LC 97-47238. 180p. 1998. 26.95 (*0-8101-1512-3*, Hydra Bks) Northwestern U Pr.

Our House. Paul Rogers & Emma Rogers. LC 92-53015. (Illus.). 40p. (J). (ps up). 1993. 14.95 (*1-56402-134-3*) Candlewick Pr.

Our House. Curt Smith. LC 98-54350. (Illus.). 320p. 1999. 30.00 (*0-8092-2664-2*, 266420, Mstrs Pr) NTC Contemp Pub Co.

Our House: The Stories of Levittown. Pam Conrad. LC 94-42126. (Illus.). 80p. (J). (gr. 3-7). 1995. 14.95 (*0-590-46523-6*, Scholastic Hardcover) Scholastic Inc.

Our House Divided: Seven Japanese American Families in World War II. Tomi K. Knaefler. LC 91-19279. (Illus.). 144p. 1991. pap. 14.95 (*0-8248-1767-2*) UH Pr.

Our House Had a Mouse. Denise Worthington. (Illus.). 8p. (J). (gr. k-1). 1993. pap. 3.75 (*1-880612-29-1*) Seedling Pubns.

Our House in the Last World. Oscar Hijuelos. LC 82-15092. 236p. 1991. reprint ed. 18.95 (*0-89255-069-4*); reprint ed. pap. 12.00 (*0-89255-165-8*) Persea Bks.

Our Huckleberry Friend. Bob Bach. 1987. pap. 14.95 (*0-8184-0450-7*, L Stuart) Carol Pub Group.

Our Huckleberry Friend: The Life, Times & Lyrics of Johnny Mercer. Bob Bach & Ginger Mercer. 256p. 1982. 24.95 (*0-8184-0331-4*) Carol Pub Group.

Our Human Body from Science Source. AIT Staff. Ed. by Mindy Grewar. 32p. (Orig.). (YA). (gr. 7-12). 1992. text 7.95 (*0-7842-0604-X*) Agency Instr Tech.

Our Human Spirit see Nuestro Espiritu Humano

Our Human Spirit. Witness Lee. 82p. 1984. per. 4.50 (*0-87083-124-0*, 07-013-001) Living Stream Ministry.

Our Human Truths. Ferdinand C. Schiller. LC 75-3348. reprint ed. 57.50 (*0-404-59347-X*) AMS Pr.

Our Hundred Days in Europe. Oliver W. Holmes. (Notable American Authors Ser.). 1992. reprint ed. lib. bdg. 75.00 (*0-7812-3171-X*) Rprt Serv.

Our Hundred Days in Europe: The Writings of Oliver Wendell Holmes. Oliver W. Holmes. (American Biography Ser.). 301p. 1991. reprint ed. lib. bdg. 79.00 (*0-7812-8190-3*) Rprt Serv.

***Our Husband.** Stephanie Bond. 2000. mass mkt. 6.50 (*0-312-97565-1*) St Martin.

Our Idea of God. Thomas V. Morris. LC 90-19145. 216p. (C). 1991. text 15.00 (*0-268-01504-X*) U of Notre Dame Pr.

Our Idea of God: An Introduction to Philosophical Theology. Thomas V. Morris. 192p. 1998. pap. 21.95 (*1-57383-101-8*, Regent Coll Pub) Regent College.

Our Identities: Multicultural Readings for Writers, A Step-by-Step Approach. Alan Kaufman. 385p. (C). 1994. pap. text, per. 35.95 (*0-8403-8459-9*) Kendall-Hunt.

Our Immortality. Milton Ward. (Illus.). (Orig.). 1997. 15.00 (*0-614-30686-8*) Optimus Bks.

Our Indian Wards. George W. Manypenny. LC 68-54844. (American Scene Ser.). 1972. reprint ed. lib. bdg. 35.00 (*0-306-71140-0*) Da Capo.

Our Industrious Robots: A Guide to What Robots Can Do & How They Work. Michael A. Salant. LC 84-90027. (Illus.). 128p. (YA). (gr. 6 up). 17.95 (*0-9609288-3-9*); pap. 12.95 (*0-9609288-2-0*) M A Salant.

Our Inheritance: A Collection of Sermons & Addresses for All the Sabbaths & Festivals. Isaiah Raffalovich. 272p. 32.50 (*0-87559-146-9*) Shalom.

Our Inheritance in the Great Pyramid. Piazzi Smyth. (African Studies). reprint ed. 50.00 (*0-938818-94-5*) ECA Assoc.

Our Inheritance in the Great Pyramid. Piazzi Smyth. LC 77-5284. (Illus.). 672p. 1980. reprint ed. lib. bdg. 50.00 (*0-8334-0720-1*, Spir Sci Lib) Garber Comm.

Our Inner Conflicts: A Constructive Theory of Neurosis. Karen Horney. 256p. 1992. pap. 12.95 (*0-393-30940-1*) Norton.

Our Intimate Relationships: Marriage & the Family. 2nd ed. Ollie Pocs. (Illus.). 577p. (C). 1994. pap. text 28.95 (*0-87563-465-6*) Stipes.

Our Invisible Supply Pt. 1: How to Obtain. Frances L. Warner. 168p. 1996. reprint ed. spiral bd. 13.00 (*0-7873-1069-7*) Hlth Research.

Our Inviting Eastern Parklands. National Geographic Society Staff. LC 94-19638. 200p. 1994. 16.00 (*0-87044-978-8*) Natl Geog.

Our Inviting Eastern Parklands: From Acadia to the Everglades. 200p. 1998. pap. 15.00 (*0-7922-7354-0*) Natl Geog.

Our Irish Theatre: A Chapter of Autobiography. Isabella Augusta Gregory. 279p. 1972. 50.00 (*0-900675-28-4*, Pub. by Smyth) Dufour.

Our Iron Roads: Their History, Construction & Administration, Vol. 1: History of Construction. F. S. Williams. 272p. 1984. 49.00 (*0-905418-88-3*, Pub. by Gresham Bks) St Mut.

Our Iron Roads: Their History, Construction & Administration, Vol. 11: Operation & Administration. F. S. Williams. 272p. 1984. 49.00 (*0-7855-7050-0*, Pub. by Gresham Bks) St Mut.

Our Iron Roads Vol. 2: Operation & Administration. F. S. Williams. 272p. 1984. 45.00 (*0-905418-87-5*, Pub. by Gresham Bks) St Mut.

Our Island Jamaica. Morrissey. Date not set. pap. text. write for info. (*0-582-05602-0*, Pub. by Addison-Wesley) Longman.

Our Italian Fellow Citizens in Their Old Homes & Their New. Francis E. Clark. LC 74-17923. (Italian American Experience Ser.). (Illus.). 260p. 1975. reprint ed. 21.95 (*0-405-06396-2*) Ayer.

Our Italian Surnames. Joseph G. Fucilla. 299p. 1998. reprint ed. 28.50 (*0-8063-1187-8*, 2082) Genealog Pub.

Our Italy. Charles D. Warner. (Notable American Authors Ser.). 1999. reprint ed. lib. bdg. 125.00 (*0-7812-9904-7*) Rprt Serv.

Our Jerusalem. Yaffa Ganz. (Illus.). (J). (gr. k-2). 1979. pap. 4.95 (*0-87441-308-7*) Behrman.

Our Jerusalem: An American Family in the Holy City, 1881-1949. Bertha H. Vester. Ed. by Moshe Davis. LC 77-70752. (America & the Holy Land Ser.). 1977. reprint ed. lib. bdg. 33.95 (*0-405-10296-8*) Ayer.

Our Jesuit Life. Ed. by Jesuit General Curia Staff. Tr. by G. E. Ganss et al from LAT. (Jesuit Primary Sources in English Translation Ser.: No. 8). xvi, 124p. 1990. 6.50 (*0-912422-98-X*) Inst Jesuit.

Our Jewish Friends. rev. ed. Louis Goldberg. LC 76-56773. 155p. 1983. pap. text 8.99 (*0-87213-239-0*) Loizeaux.

Our John Willie. Catherine Cookson. LC 73-22687. 224p. 1974. 6.95 (*0-672-51897-X*) Macmillan.

***Our John Willie.** Catherine Cookson. 2000. 17.95 (*0-385-40132-9*, Pub. by Transworld Publishers Ltd) Trafalgar.

Our Journey: Diary of a Caregiver. Kenneth J. Vogt. 64p. 1992. pap. 5.99 (*0-8341-1433-X*) Beacon Hill.

Our Journey Home. Jean Vanier. Tr. by Maggie Parham. LC 96-49053. 220p. (Orig.). 1997. pap. 15.00 (*1-57075-117-X*) Orbis Bks.

Our Journey Home Vol. 1: A Guide for Conscious Ascension. Sage Oh'hne. (Illus.). 184p. (Orig.). 1996. pap. 16.95 (*0-9643360-0-6*) New Earth WI.

Our Journey Home Vol. 2: A Guide for Conscious Ascension. Sage Oh'hne. (Illus.). 360p. (Orig.). 1996. pap. 16.95 (*0-9643360-7-3*) New Earth WI.

Our Journey Home Vol. III: A Guide for Conscious Ascension. Sage. LC 96-213603. 258p. 1997. pap. write for info. (*0-9645194-5-3*, Pub. by TrHse Pr) New Leaf Dist.

Our Journey of Brotherhood: Sigma Phi Epsilon's First Hundred Years. David Eskes. Ed. by Rodney Nelson. 160p. 1999. 40.00 (*0-929690-46-X*) Herit Pubs AZ.

Our Journey to an Ownership Culture: Insights from the ESOP Community. ESOP Association Staff. Ed. by Dawn K. Brohawn. LC 97-3364. 256p. 1997. 35.00 (*0-8108-3229-1*) Scarecrow.

Our Journey with God: With Passport Instructions. Elizabeth Austin. 80p. (Orig.). 1997. pap. 4.99 (*0-9655514-1-5*, Inspir Wrd Pub) Inspiring Word.

Our Journey with Jesus: Discipleship in Luke-Acts. Dennis M. Sweetland. (Good News Studies: Vol. 23). 250p. (C). 1990. pap. 17.95 (*0-8146-5688-9*) Liturgical Pr.

Our Journeys Through Life. Ruth D. Hadfield. LC 86-17331. 1988. pap. 13.95 (*0-87949-255-4*) Ashley Bks.

Our Joyce: From Outcast to Icon. Joseph Kelly. LC 97-10877. (Literary Modernism Ser.). 304p. 1998. 39.95 (*0-292-74331-9*) U of Tex Pr.

Our Joyce: Growing up in Bristol. large type ed. Joyce Storey. 22.95 (*1-85695-185-5*, Pub. by ISIS Lrg Prnt) Transaction Pubs.

Our Jubilee Is Death. Leo Bruce. (Carolus Deene Mystery Ser.). 189p. 1986. pap. 5.95 (*0-89733-229-6*) Academy Chi Pubs.

Our Jungle Road to Tokyo. Robert L. Eichelberger. (Battery Classics Ser.: No. 5). (Illus.). 346p. 1989. reprint ed. 32.50 (*0-89839-132-6*) Battery Pr.

Our Jungle Road to Tokyo. Robert L. Eichelberger. 1983. reprint ed. 27.95 (*0-89201-100-9*) Zenger Pub.

Our Kate. Catherine Cookson. LC 74-161241. 1971. 5.95 (*0-672-51618-7*, Bobbs) Macmillan.

***Our Kate.** Catherine Cookson. (J). 2000. pap. 10.95 (*0-552-14093-7*, Pub. by Transworld Publishers Ltd) Trafalgar.

Our Kentucky: A Study of the Bluegrass State. James C. Klotter. LC 91-48220. 360p. (J). 1992. 29.00 (*0-8131-1783-6*, F451) U Pr of Ky.

***Our Kentucky: A Study of the Bluegrass State.** 2nd rev. ed. James C. Klotter. LC 99-47987. (Illus.). 360p. 2000. text 32.50 (*0-8131-2145-0*) U Pr of Ky.

***Our Kid.** large type ed. Billy Hopkins. 592p. 2000. write for info. (*0-7505-1460-4*, Pub. by Mgna Lrg Print) Ulverscroft.

Our Kind: Who We Are, Where We Came from, & Where We Are Going. Marvin Harris. LC 88-45514. 560p. 1990. reprint ed. pap. 17.00 (*0-06-091990-6*, Perennial) HarperTrade.

***Our Kind of Guys The United States & the Indonesian Military.** Allan Nairn. 1999. 20.00 (*1-85984-735-8*, Pub. by Verso) Norton.

Our Kind of People: Inside America's Black Upper Class. Lawrence Otis Graham. LC 98-34046. (Illus.). 432p. 1999. 25.00 (*0-06-018352-7*, G Carr Bks) HarpC.

***Our Kind of People: Inside America's Black Upper Class.** Lawrence Otis Graham. 448p. 2000. pap. 14.00 (*0-06-098438-4*, Perennial) HarperTrade.

Our Kingdom Come No. 342: The Counter-Reformation, the Republic of Dubrovnik, & the Liberation of the Balkan Slavs. Zdenko Zlator. 464p. 1993. text 65.50 (*0-88033-239-5*, 342, Pub. by East Eur Monographs) Col U Pr.

Our Kingdom Stands on Brittle Glass: Papers from Mental Health Education & Practice for Chicanos & the Mexican American Community: a State of the Art Workshop April 1-3, 1981, San Antonio, Texas. Ed. by Guadalupe Gibson. LC 82-22532. 178p. reprint ed. pap. 55.20 (*0-7837-5363-2*, 204512600005) Bks Demand.

Our Knowledge of God: Essays on Natural & Philosophical Theology. Ed. by Kelly J. Clark. (Studies in Philosophy & Religion). 240p. (C). 1992. lib. bdg. 152.50 (*0-7923-1485-9*, Pub. by Kluwer Academic) Kluwer Academic.

Our Knowledge of Right & Wrong. Harrison. 408p. 1994. 83.95 (*0-7512-0311-4*) Ashgate Pub Co.

Our Knowledge of the External World: As a Field for Scientific Method in Philosophy. Bertrand Russell. LC 93-16365. 256p. (C). 1993. reprint ed. pap. 18.99 (*0-415-09605-7*, B0417) Routledge.

Our Knowledge of the Growth of Knowledge: Popper or Wittgenstein? Peter Munz. (International Library of Philosophy). 341p. 1985. 42.50 (*0-7102-0460-4*, Routledge Thoemms) Routledge.

Our Knowledge of Universals. Richard I. Aaron. (Studies in Philosophy: No. 40). 1975. lib. bdg. 29.95 (*0-8383-0108-8*) M S G Haskell Hse.

Our Labeled Children: What Every Parent & Teacher Needs to Know about Learning Disabilities. Robert J. Sternberg & Elena L. Grigorenko. 304p. 1999. text 25.00 (*0-7382-0185-5*, Pub. by Perseus Pubng) HarpC.

***Our Labeled Children: What Every Parent & Teacher Needs to Know about Learning Disabilities.** Robert J. Sternberg & Elena Grigorenko. 304p. 2000. reprint ed. pap. text 16.00 (*0-7382-0365-3*, Pub. by Perseus Pubng) HarpC.

Our Ladies of Darkness: Feminine Daemonology in Male Gothic Fiction. Joseph Andriano. 192p. (C). 1993. 35.00 (*0-271-00870-9*) Pa St U Pr.

***Our Lady: An Erotic Thriller Novel.** Dale Gershwin. 1999. pap. 14.00 (*0-88962-692-8*) Mosaic.

Our Lady: The Mother of Jesus in Christian Faith & Devotion. Norman Pittenger. 1996. pap. text 16.00 (*0-334-02627-X*) TPI PA.

Our Lady, an Angel & Sister Agnes. Craig Driscoll. 48p. 1994. pap. 3.00 (*1-890137-32-4*) One Hund-One Fnd.

Our Lady at Fatima: Prophecies of Tragedy or Hope? 3rd ed. Antonio A. Borelli et al. Ed. by Edward Parrot. (Illus.). 104p. (C). 1994. pap. 7.95 (*1-877905-28-3*) Am Soc Defense TFP.

Our Lady at Fatima: Prophecies of Tragedy or Hope for America & the World? Antonio C. Machado et al. LC 85-70673. (Illus.). 128p. (Orig.). (J). (gr. 8). 1986. pap. 7.95 (*1-877905-10-0*) Am Soc Defense TFP.

Our Lady at Garabandal. Judith M. Albright. LC 92-75070. (Illus.). 100p. 1992. pap. 5.95 (*1-880033-04-6*) Queenship Pub.

Our Lady Czestochowa. Regina Press Staff. 1994. pap. 25.00 (*0-88271-433-3*) Regina Pr.

Our Lady in the Liturgy. J. D. Crichton. LC 97-13583. 1997. pap. 9.95 (*0-8146-2493-6*) Liturgical Pr.

Our Lady Lourdes. Regina Press Staff. 1994. pap. 25.00 (*0-88271-431-7*) Regina Pr.

***Our Lady of All Nations Who Once Was Mary.** Peter Klos. LC 97-75825. 113p. 1998. pap. 4.95 (*1-57918-049-3*, 3593) Queenship Pub.

Our Lady of Argentina. Rene Laurentin. 1993. pap. text 29.00 (*0-85597-538-5*) St Mut.

Our Lady of Babylon: A Novel. John Rechy. 352p. 1996. 23.45 (*1-55970-335-0*, Pub. by Arcade Pub Inc) Time Warner.

Our Lady of Banneux. Mary F. Windeatt. (Catholic Story Coloring Bks.). (Illus.). 32p. (J). (gr. 1-5). 1991. reprint ed. pap., student ed. 4.50 (*0-89555-364-3*) TAN Bks Pubs.

Our Lady of Beauraing. Mary F. Windeatt. (Catholic Story Coloring Bks.). (Illus.). 32p. (J). (gr. 1-5). 1988. reprint ed. pap., student ed. 4.50 (*0-89555-363-5*) TAN Bks Pubs.

Our Lady of Betania. 29p. 1993. pap. 3.00 (*1-890137-26-X*) One Hund-One Fnd.

Our Lady of Class Struggle: The Cult of the Virgin Mary in Haiti. Terry Rey. LC 98-31306. 400p. 1998. 79.95 (*0-86543-694-0*); pap. 21.95 (*0-86543-695-9*) Africa World.

Our Lady of Darkness. Fritz Leiber. 1993. reprint ed. lib. bdg. 18.95 (*0-89968-436-X*, Lghtyr Pr) Buccaneer Bks.

***Our Lady of Emmitsburg.** Dominic Forker. LC 00-130482. 100p. 2000. pap. 9.95 (*1-57918-127-9*, 3811) Queenship Pub.

Our Lady of Europe. Jeremy Hooker. LC 98-206531. 128p. 1997. pap. 19.95 (*1-900564-15-7*, Pub. by Enitha Pr) Dufour.

Our Lady of Fatima. Lawrence G. Lovasik. (Saint Joseph Picture Bks.). (Illus.). 1985. pap. 1.25 (*0-89942-387-6*, 387-00) Catholic Bk Pub.

Our Lady of Fatima. William T. Walsh. 240p. 1954. pap. 10.95 (*0-385-02869-5*, D1, Image Bks) Doubleday.

Our Lady of Fatima. Mary F. Windeatt. (Catholic Story Coloring Bks.). (Illus.). 32p. (J). (gr. 1-5). 1993. reprint ed. pap., student ed. 4.50 (*0-89555-357-0*) TAN Bks Pubs.

Our Lady of Fatima's Peace Plan from Heaven. 32p. 1983. reprint ed. pap. 0.75 (*0-89555-217-5*) TAN Bks Pubs.

***Our Lady of Good Success: Prophecies for Our Days.** Marian Therese Horvat. 65p. 1999. pap. 4.95 (*0-9672166-1-3*) Trad in Action.

Our Lady of Guadalupe. 1996. bond lthr. 59.95 (*1-55665-737-4*) Fireside Catholic Bibles.

Our Lady of Guadalupe. Lawrence G. Lovasik. (Saint Joseph Picture Bks.). (Illus.). 1985. pap. 1.25 (*0-89942-390-6*, 390-00) Catholic Bk Pub.

An Asterisk (*) at the beginning of an entry indicates that the title is appearing for the first time.

Our Lady of Guadalupe. Regina Press Staff. 1994. pap. text 25.00 (*0-88271-435-X*) Regina Pr.
Our Lady of Guadalupe. Francisco Serrano & Eugenia Guzman. (SPA.). 12p. (J). 1998. 16.95 (*0-88899-340-4*, Pub. by Grndwd Bks) Publishers Group.
Our Lady of Guadalupe. Francisco Serrano & Eugenia Guzman. (Illus.). 12p. (J). 1998. 16.95 (*0-88899-335-8*, Pub. by Grndwd Bks) Publishers Group.
Our Lady of Guadalupe. Mary F. Windeatt. (Catholic Story Coloring Bks.). (Illus.). 32p. (J). (gr. 1-5). 1993. reprint ed. pap., student ed. 4.50 (*0-89555-359-7*) TAN Bks Pubs.
Our Lady of Guadalupe: Faith & Empowerment among Mexican-American Women. Jeanette Rodriguez. LC 93-31267. (Illus.). 248p. (Orig.). (C). 1994. pap. 15.95 (*0-292-77062-6*); text 35.00 (*0-292-77061-8*) U of Tex Pr.
Our Lady of Guadalupe: The Origins & Sources of a Mexican National Symbol, 1531-1797. Stafford Poole. 325p. 1996. pap. 19.95 (*0-8165-1623-5*) U of Ariz Pr.
Our Lady of Guadalupe Vol. 1: Blessed Mother of the Americas. Anthony J. DelPopolo, Sr. (Illus.). 350p. (Orig.). 1996. pap. 18.95 (*0-9619531-0-1*) Cavalier Pub Hse.
Our Lady of Guadalupe & the Conquest of Darkness. Warren H. Carroll. 123p. (Orig.). 1983. pap. 6.95 (*0-931888-12-3*) Christendom Pr.
Our Lady of Guadalupe, the Last Gospel: The Miracle & Theology of the Holy Tilma. James D. Holloway, Jr. (Illus.). 410p. (Orig.). 1991. pap. 25.00 (*1-880432-00-5*); audio 60.00 (*1-880432-01-3*) Holy Cross.
Our Lady of Knock. Mary F. Windeatt. (Catholic Story Coloring Bks.). (Illus.). 32p. (J). (gr. 1-5). 1992. reprint ed. pap., student ed. 4.50 (*0-89555-362-7*) TAN Bks Pubs.
Our Lady of la Salette. Mary F. Windeatt. (Catholic Story Coloring Bks.). (Illus.). 32p. (J). (gr. 1-5). 1991. reprint ed. pap., student ed. 4.50 (*0-89555-361-9*) TAN Bks Pubs.
Our Lady of Lourdes. Lawrence G. Lovasik. (Saint Joseph Picture Bks.). (Illus.). (J). 1985. pap. 1.25 (*0-89942-391-4*, 391-00) Catholic Bk Pub.
Our Lady of Lourdes. Mary F. Windeatt. (Catholic Story Coloring Bks.). (Illus.). 32p. (J). (gr. 1-5). 1993. reprint ed. pap., student ed. 4.50 (*0-89555-358-9*) TAN Bks Pubs.
Our Lady of Mercy Hymnal. Mary A. Donnelly. LC 91-40804. 108p. 1992. 50.00 (*0-8201-1461-8*) Schol Facsimiles.
Our Lady of Mt. Carmel. Regina Press Staff. 1994. pap. 25.00 (*0-88271-425-2*) Regina Pr.
Our Lady of Mt. Carmel. Regina Press Staff. 1995. pap. 25.00 (*0-88271-434-1*) Regina Pr.
Our Lady of Pellevoisin. Mary F. Windeatt. (Catholic Story Coloring Bks.). (Illus.). 32p. (J). (gr. 1-5). 1992. reprint ed. pap., student ed. 4.50 (*0-89555-366-X*) TAN Bks Pubs.
Our Lady of Perpetual Emotion: A Journal for Feelings. Ellen Edith. 128p. Date not set. pap. 9.95 (*0-89087-862-5*) Celestial Arts.
Our Lady of Perpetual Help. Regina Press Staff. 1994. pap. 25.00 (*0-88271-398-1*) Regina Pr.
Our Lady of Perpetual Help. Regina Press Staff. 1994. pap. 25.00 (*0-88271-444-9*) Regina Pr.
Our Lady of Pontmain. Mary F. Windeatt. (Catholic Story Coloring Bks.). (Illus.). 32p. (J). (gr. 1-5). 1992. reprint ed. pap., student ed. 4.50 (*0-89555-365-1*) TAN Bks Pubs.
Our Lady of Sligo. Sebastian Barry. 1998. pap. 5.25 (*0-8222-1690-6*) Dramatists Play.
Our Lady of Soufanieh: And Other Phenomena. Antoine Mansour & Claire Mansour. 101p. 1991. pap. 8.00 (*1-890137-24-3*) One Hund-One Fnd.
Our Lady of the America's: The Messages of the Blessed Virgin Mary As Received by Estela Ruiz of South Phoenix, AZ. Estela Ruiz. 224p. 1994. pap. 9.95 (*1-891903-16-0*) St Andrew Prodns.
Our Lady of the Exile: Diasporic Religion at a Cuban Catholic Shrine in Miami. Thomas A. Tweed. LC 96-51082. (Religion in America Ser.). (Illus.). 240p. 1997. text 39.95 (*0-19-510529-X*) OUP.
Our Lady of the Flowers. Jean Genet. Tr. by Bernard Frechtman from FRE. LC 87-414. 320p. 1987. pap. 13.50 (*0-8021-3013-5*, Grove) Grove-Atltic.
Our Lady of the Freedoms. abr. ed. Norman Corwin. 1998. pap. 12.00 incl. audio (*0-671-58218-6*, 892889) S&S Audio.
Our Lady of the Miraculous Medal. Mary F. Windeatt. (Catholic Story Coloring Bks.). (Illus.). 32p. (J). (gr. 1-5). 1992. reprint ed. pap., student ed. 4.50 (*0-89555-360-0*) TAN Bks Pubs.
***Our Lady of the New Age: The Visions of Mary & God's Test.** Cathy A. Chandler. 111p. 1999. pap. write for info. (*0-9675588-0-8*) C Chandler.
Our Lady of the Pickpockets. Dilys Rose. 1995. pap. 6.99 (*0-7493-2118-0*) Buttrwrth-Heinemann.
Our Lady of the Serpents. Petrie Harbouri. 1999. 23.95 (*1-58234-031-5*) Bloomsbury Pubg.
Our Lady of the Snows: Sarah Bernhardt in Canada. Ramon Hathorn. (Currents in Comparative Romance Languages & Literatures Ser.: Vol. 38). X, 327p. (C). 1996. text 56.95 (*0-8204-2899-X*) P Lang Pubng.
Our Lady of the Tortilla. Luis Santeiro. 1991. pap. 5.25 (*0-8222-0869-5*) Dramatists Play.
***Our Lady of Victorian Feminism: The Madonna in the Work of Anna Jameson, Margaret Fuller & George Eliot.** Kimberly VanEsveld Adams. (Illus.). 352p. (C). 2000. text 59.95 (*0-8214-1361-9*); pap. text 24.95 (*0-8214-1362-7*) Ohio U Pr.
Our Lady of Vladamir. Regina Press Staff. 1994. pap. 25.00 (*0-88271-436-8*) Regina Pr.
Our Lady Says: Let Holy Mass Be Your Life. Albert J. Shamon. LC 89-60721. 72p. 1989. pap. 2.00 (*0-9618840-9-6*) CMJ Marian Pubs.
Our Lady Says: Love People. Albert J. Shamon. LC 90-64203. 80p. 1990. pap. 3.50 (*1-877678-14-7*) CMJ Marian Pubs.
Our Lady Says: Monthly Confession - The Remedy for the West. Albert J. Shamon. LC 89-62254. 80p. 1989. pap. 2.00 (*1-877678-04-X*) Queenship Pub.
Our Lady Says: Pray the Creed. Albert J. Shamon. LC 90-62091. 80p. 1990. pap. 2.00 (*1-877678-11-2*) CMJ Marian Pubs.
Our Lady Teaches about Prayer at Medjugorje. Albert J. Shamon. LC 88-60967. 64p. 1988. pap. 2.00 (*0-9618840-3-7*) CMJ Marian Pubs.
Our Lady Teaches about Sacramentals & Blessed Objects. Albert J. Shamon. LC 92-61267. 72p. 1992. pap. 2.00 (*1-877678-22-8*) CMJ Marian Pubs.
Our Lady's Book: Apparitions of Mary. Lauren Ford. LC 97-70810. 1997. pap. text 12.95 (*0-89870-637-8*) Ignatius Pr.
***Our Lady's Feasts.** Mary Jean Dorcy. (Illus.). 102p. (YA). (gr. 6). 1999. reprint ed. 8.00 (*1-892875-04-7*, 3009) New Hope Publicatns.
Our Lady's Mount: Memoirs of Rev. Dr. David W. Shaum. David W. Shaum. (Illus.). 100p. (Orig.). 1993. pap. 10.00 (*0-9635915-1-7*) D W Shaum.
Our Lady's Slave: The Story of St. Louis Mary Grignion de Montfort see St. Louis de Montfort: The Story of Our Lady's Slave
Our Lady's Vow of Virginity. Arthur B. Calkins. (Queen of Apostles Ser.: Vol. XVI). 16p. 1993. 0.65 (*1-56036-077-1*, 49747) AMI Pr.
Our Land - Our Time. Conlin. 1991. text 67.25 (*0-03-030542-X*) Holt R&W.
Our Land - Ourselves: American Indian Contemporary Artists. Paul Brach et al. Ed. by Deborah Ward et al. LC 90-71736. (Illus.). 78p. (Orig.). 1990. pap. 18.00 (*0-910763-05-4*) U Albany Art Mus.
***Our Land & Land Policy.** Henry George. Ed. by Kenneth C. Wenzer. LC 99-49018. (Illus.). 370p. 1999. pap. 22.95 (*0-87013-522-8*) Mich St U Pr.
Our Land & Land Policy. Henry George. (Notable American Authors Ser.). 1992. reprint ed. lib. bdg. 75.00 (*0-7812-2913-8*) Rprt Serv.
Our Land Is Our Life: Land Rights - Past, Present, & Future. Galarrwuy Yunupingu. LC 97-166767. 276p. 1997. pap. 32.95 (*0-7022-2958-X*, Pub. by Univ Queensland Pr) Intl Spec Bk.
Our Land of Israel. Chaya M. Burstein. (Illus.). (J). 1995. pap. 12.00 (*0-8074-0527-2*, 127272) UAHC.
Our Land of Israel. Chaya M. Burstein & Sondra Leiman. (Illus.). (J). (gr. 4). 1996. pap., teacher ed. 15.00 (*0-8074-0533-7*, 208037) UAHC.
***Our Land, Ourselves: Readings on People & Places.** Peter Forbes. 240p. 1999. pap. 16.95 (*0-9672806-0-5*, Pub. by The Tr for Public Land) Chelsea Green Pub.
Our Land Through Israeli Eyes: An Answer to News Distortions. Haim Gershoni. 336p. 1994. pap. 8.95 (*965-229-080-7*, Pub. by Gefen Pub Hse) Gefen Bks.
Our Land Till We Die. 2nd rev. ed. Jan Crichett. (Illus.). 112p. 1992. pap. 30.00 (*0-949823-24-4*, Pub. by Deakin Univ) St Mut.
Our Land Was a Forest: An Ainu Memoir. Kayano Shingeru. Tr. by Kyoko Selden. (Transitions Series: Asia & the Pacific). 192p. (C). 1994. pap. 24.00 (*0-8133-1880-7*, Pub. by Westview) HarpC.
Our Landed Heritage: The Public Domain, 1776-1970. Roy M. Robbins. LC 75-3569. (Illus.). 517p. reprint ed. 160.30 (*0-8357-9712-0*, 201911600010) Bks Demand.
Our Landed Heritage: The Public Domain, 1776-1970 2nd ed. Roy M. Robbins. LC 75-3569. xii, 503p. 1976. write for info. (*0-8032-0866-9*) U of Nebr Pr.
Our Landlady. L. Frank Baum. Ed. & Anno. by Nancy T. Koupal. LC 95-32094. (Illus.). xii, 287p. 1996. pap. 16.95 (*0-8032-6156-X*, Bison Books) U of Nebr Pr.
Our Landlady. annot. ed. L. Frank Baum. Ed. & Anno. by Nancy T. Koupal. LC 95-32094. (Illus.). xii, 287p. 1996. text 45.00 (*0-8032-1221-6*) U of Nebr Pr.
Our Lands: New Strategies for Protecting the West: Blueprints for Action. (Illus.). 147p. (Orig.). (C). 1995. pap. text 35.00 (*0-7881-1910-9*) DIANE Pub.
Our Language. Simeon Potter. 1990. pap. 13.95 (*0-14-013494-8*, Pub. by Pnguin Bks Ltd) Trafalgar.
Our Last Backpack: A Memoir. Daniel Doan. LC 93-15766. (Illus.). 224p. (Orig.). 1993. pap. 14.00 (*0-88150-273-1*, Pub. by Countryman) Norton.
***Our Last Best Shot: Guiding Our Children Through Early Adolescence.** Laura Sessions Stepp. LC 00-27974. 352p. 2000. 25.95 (*1-57322-160-0*, Riverhead Books) Putnam Pub Group.
Our Last Chance see Naufragio: 66 Dias a la Deriva
Our Last Chance: Sixty-Six Deadly Days Adrift. William A. Butler. LC 92-81605. (Illus.). 312p. 1992. 22.50 (*0-9632519-0-2*); pap. 14.50 (*0-9632519-2-9*) Exmart Assocs.
Our Last First Poets: Vision & History in Contemporary American Poetry. Cary Nelson. LC 81-5082. 239p. reprint ed. pap. 74.10 (*0-608-13447-3*, 202278300029) Bks Demand.
Our Last First Poets: Vision & History in Contemporary American Poetry. Cary Nelson. LC 81-5082. 240p. 1984. reprint ed. pap. text 11.95 (*0-252-01140-6*) U of Ill Pr.
Our Last Hope in Creation. Mohammed Hossain. 48p. 1999. pap. 10.00 (*0-8059-4624-1*) Dorrance.
Our Latin Heritage, Bk. 1. Hines. 1981. text 54.00 (*0-15-389465-2*) Holt R&W.
Our Latin Heritage, Bk. 2. Hines. 1981. text 56.50 (*0-15-389468-7*) Holt R&W.
Our Latin Heritage, Bk. 3. Lillian M. Hines. 1967. text 57.50 (*0-15-389515-2*) Holt R&W.
Our Latter-Day Hymns: The Stories & the Messages. Karen L. Davidson. LC 88-1067. ix, 486p. 1988. 21.95 (*0-87579-137-9*) Deseret Bk.
Our Lawless Police. Ernest J. Hopkins. LC 74-168829. (Civil Liberties in American History Ser.). 379p. 1971. reprint ed. lib. bdg. 45.00 (*0-306-70213-4*) Da Capo.
Our Legacy... Baldy View Entrepreneurs: Twenty-Five Profiles. Marie A. Boyd & Richard H. Barker. (Citrus Roots... Our Legacy Ser.: Vol. III). (Illus.). 1999. pap. 15.00 (*0-9669508-3-6*) Upland Public.
Our Legacy of Faith: A Brief History of the Reorganized Church of Jesus Christ of Latter Day Saints. Paul M. Edwards. 360p. (YA). 1991. pap. 10.00 (*0-8309-0594-4*) Herald Pub Hse.
Our Legal System. Katie Eyles. (Thematic Unit Ser.). (Illus.). 80p. (J). 1997. pap., teacher ed. 9.95 (*1-57690-060-6*, TCM2060) Tchr Create Mat.
Our Legal System & How It Operates. Burke Shartel. LC 73-173666. (American Constitutional & Legal History Ser). 628p. 1972. reprint ed. lib. bdg. 65.00 (*0-306-70411-0*) Da Capo.
Our Legal System & How It Operates. Burke Shartel. (Michigan Legal Publications). xxvii, 629p. 1986. reprint ed. lib. bdg. 55.00 (*0-89941-490-7*, 304170) W S Hein.
Our Liability Predicament: The Practical & Psychological Flaws of the American Tort System. J. T. Johnson. LC 97-1477. 238p. 1997. 59.50 (*0-7618-0702-0*); pap. 29.50 (*0-7618-0703-9*) U Pr of Amer.
Our Liberal Movement in Theology: Chiefly As Shown in Recollections of the History of Unitarianism in New England. 3rd ed. Joseph H. Allen. LC 73-38432. (Religion in America, Ser. 2). 230p. 1972. reprint ed. 23.95 (*0-405-04053-9*) Ayer.
***Our Life.** Nee Watchman. 1998. pap. 2.00 (*0-7363-0134-8*) Living Stream Ministry.
Our Life after Death. A. Chambers. 1972. 59.95 (*0-8490-0784-4*) Gordon Pr.
Our Life after Death: The Teaching of the Bible Concerning the Unseen World. Arthur Chambers. 239p. 1996. reprint ed. spiral bd. 16.50 (*0-7873-0162-0*) Hlth Research.
Our Life in Christ. Concordia Staff. (Our Life in Christ Adult Bible Study Ser.). 1997. pap. 5.50 (*0-570-09729-0*, 20-3080) Concordia.
Our Life in Christ: Adult Bible Studies. (Our Life in Christ Adult Bible Study Ser.). 104p. 1997. pap. 4.99 (*0-570-09728-2*, 20-3079) Concordia.
Our Life in Poetry: Selected Essays & Reviews. M. L. Rosenthal. 550p. 1990. 47.50 (*0-89255-149-6*) Persea Bks.
Our Life with Jesus, 3. Ignatius. (Faith & Life Ser.). 1995. pap. 24.95 (*0-89870-504-5*) Ignatius Pr.
Our Limits Transgressed: Environmental Political Thought in America. Bob P. Taylor. LC 92-10525. (American Political Thought Ser.). 200p. (Orig.). (C). 1992. 25.00 (*0-7006-0542-8*) U Pr of KS.
Our Limits Transgressed: Environmental Political Thought in America. Bob P. Taylor. LC 92-10525. (American Political Thought Ser.). 186p. (Orig.). (C). 1995. pap. 14.95 (*0-7006-0747-1*) U Pr of KS.

Our Little Flower Girl: A Child Has Her First Experience Participating in a Wedding. Charlotte E. Thomas. LC 92-72538. (Illus.). 32p. (J). (ps-3). 1992. lib. bdg. 19.95 (0-9633607-0-1) Golden Rings.
OUR LITTLE FLOWER GIRL is a delightful story book written specifically to help little girls prepare to participate in a wedding. In easy to read prose, written to be understood by young girls aged 4 to 8, it tells the story of Mandy, as she prepares to be in her Aunt Melody's wedding. The story follows Mandy from the day of the big announcement through the last dance of the reception. She learns about all the things she will be expected to do, & all the nice things she will experience. The story is gently written, yet covers all the facets of a traditional wedding. Following the conclusion of the story, there is a place to put a picture from the wedding & a page for the wedding party to sign, creating a keepsake that will be treasured for years to come. The book is 32 pages long, hardcover, full color & gift boxed. The book may be ordered directly from the publisher, Golden Rings Publishing Co., for $19.95 plus S&H, using MC/Visa/Discover/AmEx. Call 1-800-433-6173 or fax 856-596-7391. ***Publisher Paid Annotation.***

Our Little Secret. Edwina Dae. 254p. mass mkt. 4.99 (*1-55197-183-6*) Picasso Publ.
Our Liturgy: Your Guide to the Basics. Ed. by Nancy Benvenga. LC 89-92734. (RVC Liturgical Ser.). 64p. (Orig.). 1990. pap. 4.25 (*0-9623410-1-0*, Resurrection Pr) Catholic Bk Pub.
Our Lives: Canada since 1945. Alvin Finkel. LC 98-119286. (Illus.). 423p. 1997. 34.95 (*1-55028-550-5*, Pub. by J Lorimer); pap. 19.95 (*1-55028-551-3*, Pub. by J Lorimer) Formac Dist Ltd.
Our Lives: Lesbian Personal Writings. Frances Rooney. 280p. (Orig.). 1991. pap. 14.95 (*0-929005-21-X*, Pub. by Sec Story Pr) LPC InBook.
Our Lives Are Testimony. Marilyn Waring. 200p. 1996. pap. 24.95 (*1-86940-133-6*, Pub. by Auckland Univ) Paul & Co Pubs.
Our Lives Before the Law: Constructing a Feminist Jurisprudence Judith A. Baer. LC 98-55309. 1999. 55.00 (*0-691-03316-1*, Pub. by Princeton U Pr) Cal Prin Full Svc.
***Our Lives Before the Law: Constructing a Feminist Jurisprudence.** Judith A. Baer. LC 98-55309. 272p. 1999. 18.95 (*0-691-01945-2*, Pub. by Princeton U Pr) Cal Prin Full Svc.
Our Lives, Our Stories. Hildebrand. (College ESL Ser.). 220p. (J). 1995. mass mkt. 27.95 (*0-8384-4678-7*) Heinle & Heinle.
Our Lives, Our Stories. Hildebrand. (College ESL Ser.). (J). 1996. mass mkt., teacher ed. 10.95 (*0-8384-4679-5*) Heinle & Heinle.
Our Lives Were Meant to Be Shared. Paula Finn. (Illus.). 40p. 1995. 6.95 (*0-8378-9857-9*) Gibson.
***Our Lives Were Meant to Be Shared: Kim Anderson Collection.** Kim Anderson. (Illus.). 2000. 8.99 (*0-7667-6654-3*) Gibson.
Our Living Constitution - Then & Now. Jerry Aten. (Illus.). 168p. (YA). (gr. 5 up). 1986. student ed. 13.99 (*0-86653-386-9*, GA 1000) Good Apple.
Our Living Forests. Allan Fowler. 1999. lib. bdg. 4.95 (*0-516-26481-8*) Childrens.
Our Living Forests. Allan Fowler. LC 97-31669. (Rookie Read-About Science Ser.). 32p. (J). (gr. 1-2). 1999. 19.00 (*0-516-20811-X*) Childrens.
Our Living Heritage. Michael Joslin. (Illus.). 1998. pap. 19.95 (*1-57072-079-7*) Overmountain Pr.
Our Living History. Reader's Digest Editors. LC 96-30610. (Explore America Ser.). 1996. write for info. (*0-89577-945-5*) RD Assn.
Our Living History. Ed. by Reader's Digest Editors. LC 96-30610. (Explore America Ser.). 1996. write for info. (*0-89577-903-X*) RD Assn.
Our Living Oceans: The First Annual Report on the Status of U. S. Living Marine Resources. (Illus.). 123p. (Orig.). (C). 1992. pap. text 27.95 (*1-56806-062-9*) DIANE Pub.
Our Living Resources, 2 vols. 1997. lib. bdg. 600.95 (*0-8490-6170-9*) Gordon Pr.
Our Living Resources, 2 vols., Set. 1996. lib. bdg. 640.95 (*0-8490-6375-2*) Gordon Pr.
Our Living Resources: Report to the Nation on the Distribution, Abundance & Health of United States Plants, Animals & Ecosystems. Edward T. LaRoe. 542p. 1995. boxed set 51.00 (*0-16-061698-0*) USGPO.
Our Living Tradition: Seven Canadians. Ed. by Claude T. Bissell. LC 58-526. (Canadian University Paperbooks Ser.: No. 5). 159p. reprint ed. pap. 49.30 (*0-8357-4151-6*, 203692500007) Bks Demand.
Our Longhorn Council: The First Seventy-Five Years. Carl King, Jr. (Illus.). 175p. (Orig.). 1995. pap. 24.95 (*0-9649932-0-1*) Longhorn Coun.
Our Looks/Our Lives: Sex, Beauty, Power, & the Need to Be Seen. Nancy Friday. 848p. 1999. mass mkt. 7.99 (*0-06-109794-2*) HarpC.
Our Loons Are Always Laughing. Newton F. Tolman. reprint ed. lib. bdg. 20.95 (*0-89190-951-6*, Rivercity Pr) Amereon Ltd.
Our Lord Prays for His Own: Thoughts on John 17. Marcus Rainsford. LC 85-8095. 480p. 1985. pap. 17.99 (*0-8254-3617-6*, Kregel Class) Kregel.
Our Lord's Parables. Robert C. McQuilkin. 1980. pap. 5.95 (*0-310-41541-1*) Zondervan.
***Our Love Is Here to Stay: Inspirational Stories of Lasting Love.** David Kopp et al. LC 99-44131. 64p. 2000. 15.99 (*0-7369-0135-3*) Harvest Hse.
***Our Love Is Too Good to Feel So Bad: The 10 Prescriptions to Heal Your Relationship.** Mira Kirshenbaum. LC 97-36407. 336p. 1999. pap. 12.50 (*0-380-79577-9*, Avon Bks) Morrow Avon.
Our Love Story. Iris Howse & Nick Howse. (Illus.). 144p. (Orig.). 1996. mass mkt. 24.95 (*0-9656171-0-6*) In-House Prods.
Our Loving Father: Feeling God's Embrace. Jack Kuhatschek. (Knowing God Ser.). 64p. 1994. 5.99 (*0-310-48291-7*) Zondervan.
Our Loving God. Carine Mackinzie. 1997. 12.99 (*1-85792-294-8*) Christian Focus.
Our Loving God: A "Sun & Shield" Thomas B. Warren. 1963. 11.00 (*0-934916-38-1*) Natl Christian Pr.
Our Loving Grandparents. Kathy Fannoun. 20p. (J). Date not set. 4.50 (*1-884187-30-7*) AMICA Pub Hse.
Our Loving Grandparents. unabridged ed. Kathy Fannoun. Ed. by Mahlaqa Patel. (Islamic Akhlaq Ser.). (Illus.). 20p. (J). (ps-k). 1992. mass mkt. 4.00 (*1-56316-318-7*) Iqra Intl Ed Fdtn.
Our Lusty Forefathers: Being Diverse Chronicles of the Fervors, Frolics, Fights, Festivities, & Failings of Our American Ancestors. Fairfax D. Downey. LC 74-179725. (Biography Index Reprint Ser). (Illus.). 1977. reprint ed. 23.95 (*0-8369-8093-X*) Ayer.
Our Magnificent Earth. Rand McNally Staff. pap. 53.95 (*0-528-83088-0*) Rand McNally.
Our Mammoth. Adrian Mitchell. (Illus.). (J). (ps-3). 1987. 11.95 (*0-15-258838-8*) Harcourt.
Our Mammoth Goes to School. Priscilla Lamont. LC 86-26939. (Illus.). 32p. (J). (ps-3). 1988. 11.95 (*0-15-258837-X*, Harcourt Child Bks) Harcourt.
Our Man in Belize: A Memoir. Richard T. Conroy. LC 97-14778. 352p. 1997. 27.50 (*0-312-16959-0*, Thomas Dunne) St Martin.
Our Man in Havana. Graham Greene. 220p. Date not set. 21.95 (*0-8488-2284-6*) Amereon Ltd.
Our Man in Havana. Graham Greene. (Twentieth-Century Classics Ser.). 224p. 1992. pap. 18.99 (*0-14-018493-7*, Penguin Classics) Viking Penguin.
Our Man in Moscow: A Diplomat's Reflections on the Soviet Union. R. A. Ford. 368p. 1989. 35.00 (*0-8020-5805-1*); pap. text 18.95 (*0-8020-7367-0*) U of Toronto Pr.

An Asterisk (*) at the beginning of an entry indicates that the title is appearing for the first time.

***Our Man in Vienna.** Timothy Richard Conroy. 2000. text 24.95 (*0-312-26493-3*) St Martin.

***Our Man in Washington.** Roy Hoopes. 384p. 2000. text 24.95 (*0-312-86849-9*) St Martin.

Our Man Is Inside. Diego Asencio & Nancy Asencio. 288p. 1983. 17.00 (*0-316-05294-9*) Little.

Our Man Omar Vol. XXVIII: Complete Plays 28. Manuel Pereiras Garcia. 56p. 1998. pap. 4.95 (*1-885901-78-X*) Presbyters Peartree.

Our Man on the Hill: A British Diplomat Remembers. William M. Drower. LC 93-29492. 163p. (Orig.). reprint ed. pap. 50.60 (*0-608-20123-5*, 207139500011) Bks Demand.

Our Man Sam: Making the Most Out of Life with Muscular Dystrophy. Susan C. Bayley. 112p. 1998. pap. 9.95 (*0-9667440-0-4*) S Bayle.

Our Manifold Nature. Sarah Grand. LC 75-103513. (Short Story Index Reprint Ser.). 1977. 19.95 (*0-8369-3255-2*) Ayer.

***Our Marching Band.** Lloyd Moss. LC 99-37284. (Illus.). (J). 2001. write for info. (*0-399-23335-0*) Putnam Pub Group.

Our Marching Civilization. Warren D. Allen. LC 77-25408. (Music Reprint Ser.). 1978. reprint ed. lib. bdg. 23.50 (*0-306-77568-9*) Da Capo.

***Our Marriage: An Anniversary Keepsake Book.** Susan Waggoner. (Illus.). 112p. 2000. 19.95 (*1-55670-978-1*) Stewart Tabori & Chang.

***Our Martens: F. F. Martens, International Lawyer & Architecht of Peace.** V. V. Pustogarov & William Elliott Butler. LC 00-28721. 2000. write for info. (*1-898029-50-4*) Kluwer Academic.

Our Maryland. rev. ed. Jane Eagen & Jeanne McGinnis. (Illus.). 288p. (J). (gr. 4). 1997. 23.95 (*0-87905-233-3*) Gibbs Smith Pub.

Our Maryland Heritage, Vol. 11. William N. Hurley, Jr. LC 98-199388. 156p. 1998. pap. 17.50 (*0-7884-0923-9*, H883) Heritage Bk.

Our Maryland Heritage Bk. 1: The Fry Families. William N. Hurley, Jr. LC 97-182570. xii, 321p. 1997. pap. 23.00 (*0-7884-0625-6*, H872) Heritage Bk.

Our Maryland Heritage Bk. 5: The King Families. William N. Hurley, Jr. xii, 548p. 1997. pap. 36.00 (*0-7884-0716-3*, H876) Heritage Bk.

Our Maryland Heritage Bk. 9: The Purdum Families. William N. Hurley, Jr. 298p. 1998. pap. 23.50 (*0-7884-0863-1*, H881) Heritage Bk.

***Our Maryland Heritage Bk. 16: The White Families.** William Neal Hurley, Jr. (Illus.). 316p. 1999. pap. 28.00 (*0-7884-1230-2*, H855) Heritage Bk.

***Our Maryland Heritage Bk. 17: The Mullinix Families.** William Neal Hurley, Jr. 188p. 2000. pap. 19.50 (*0-7884-1377-5*, 1377) Heritage Bk.

***Our Maryland Heritage Bk. 18: The Young Families.** William Neal Hurley, Jr. 1999. pap. 21.00 (*0-7884-1410-0*, H886) Heritage Bk.

Our Maryland Heritage Vol. 6: The Burdette Families. William N. Hurley, Jr. 302p. 1998. pap. 24.00 (*0-7884-0837-2*, H864) Heritage Bk.

Our Maryland Heritage Vol. 7: The Soper Families. William N. Hurley, Jr. 179p. 1998. pap. 18.00 (*0-7884-0787-2*, H879) Heritage Bk.

Our Maryland Heritage Vol. 8: The Brandenburg Families. William N. Hurley, Jr. LC 98-147124. 274p. 1998. pap. 22.00 (*0-7884-0842-9*, H880) Heritage Bk.

Our Maryland Heritage Vol. 13: The Miles Family. William N. Hurley, Jr. (Illus.). 315p. 1999. pap. 28.50 (*0-7884-1146-2*, H884) Heritage Bk.

Our Maryland Heritage Vol. 14: The Lewis Family. William N. Hurley, Jr. 440p. 1999. pap. 36.00 (*0-7884-1188-8*, H870) Heritage Bk.

***Our Maryland Heritage Vol. 15: The Warfield Families.** William N. Harley, Jr. 201p. 1999. pap. 21.50 (*0-7884-1211-6*, H873) Heritage Bk.

Our Maryland Heritage - The Fulks Families, Bk. 3. William N. Hurley, Jr. LC 97-222720. viii, 167p. 1997. pap. text 16.50 (*0-7884-0699-X*, H875) Heritage Bk.

Our Maryland Heritage Book Four: The Watkins Families. William N. Huney, Jr. viii, 261p. 1997. pap. 22.00 (*0-7884-0752-X*, H878) Heritage Bk.

Our Master & His Message, the Master As I Saw Him, Kali the Mother, Lectures & Articles see Complete Works of Sister Nivedita

Our Master Plan. Dara Wier. LC 97-76753. (Poetry Ser.). 80p. 1999. 24.95 (*0-88748-293-7*, Pub. by Carnegie-Mellon); pap. 12.95 (*0-88748-294-5*) Carnegie-Mellon.

Our Master's Prayers: A Brief Story of Jesus' Life Based on His Prayers. Betty Quigley. (Illus.). 160p. (YA). 1991. 15.95 (*0-9626735-1-X*); pap. 8.95 (*0-9626735-3-6*) Rabeth Pub Co.

Our Masters the Rebels see Fighting for Defeat: Union Military Failure in the East, 1861-1865

Our Masters the Rebels: A Speculation on Union Military Failure in the East, 1861-1865. Michael C. Adams. LC 78-17107. 270p. reprint ed. pap. 83.70 (*0-7837-2213-3*, 205730300004) Bks Demand.

Our Master's Voice: Advertising. James Rorty. LC 75-39272. (Getting & Spending: The Consumer's Dilemma Ser.). 1976. reprint ed. 33.95 (*0-405-08044-1*) Ayer.

Our Masters' Voices: The Language & Body-Language of Politics. M. Atkinson. 224p. (C). 1984. pap. 17.99 (*0-415-01875-7*) Routledge.

Our Masters' Voices: The Language & Body-Language of Politics. Max Atkinson. (Illus.). 176p. 1984. 25.00 (*0-416-37690-8*, NO. 9265); pap. 14.95 (*0-416-37700-9*, NO. 9085) Routledge.

Our Mc Connell Family of Ohio & West Virginia. Marcia Croye. (Illus.). 352p. 1993. 60.00 (*0-910973-05-9*) Arrowhead AZ.

Our Meals: Making a Home for Family & Friends. Heather Watts & Jock Soto. 256p. 1998. pap. 15.00 (*1-57322-700-5*, Riverhd Trade) Berkley Pub.

Our Mecca Is Harlem: Clarence 13X (Allah) & the Five Percent. Ed. by Prince-A-Cuba. (Illus.). 69p. (Orig.). 1995. reprint ed. pap. 6.95 (*1-56411-076-1*, YBBG0081) Untd Bros & Sis.

Our Mediation Notebook. 3rd rev. ed. David W. Johnson & Roger T. Johnson. (Illus.). 112p. 1995. pap. text 7.50 (*0-939603-24-1*) Interaction Bk Co.

Our Medical Future: Breakthroughs in Health & Longevity by the Year 2000 & Beyond. Jeffrey A. Fisher. Ed. by Julie Rubenstein. LC 93-19867. Orig. Title: RX 2000. 272p. 1993. reprint ed. pap. 10.00 (*0-671-73845-3*) S&S Trade.

Our Menomonee Falls: (A Compilation of Recollections from Residents, Past & Present, of Menomonee Falls, Wisconsin) unabridged ed. Helen S. Strehlow. (Illus.). 100p. 1998. 7.50 (*0-9641418-1-7*) H S Strehlow.

Our Merciful Judge: Trusting God's Fairness. Marshall Shelley. (Knowing God Ser.). 64p. 1994. 5.99 (*0-310-48351-4*) Zondervan.

Our Michigan: Ethnic Tales & Recipes. Carole Eberly. (Illus.). 192p. (Orig.). 1979. pap. 8.95 (*0-932296-03-3*) Eberly Pr.

Our Michigan Adventure. David B. McConnell. Ed. by Stella M. McConnell. LC 98-155043. (Illus.). 282p. (J). (gr. 3-4). 1998. 30.95 (*0-910726-35-3*, 35-3) Hillsdale Educ.

Our Minerva: The Men & Politics of the University of London 1836-1858. F. M. Willson. (Illus.). 224p. (C). 1995. text 90.00 (*0-485-11479-8*, Pub. by Athlone Pr) Humanities.

Our Minnesota. enl. rev. ed. Fran Blacklock. (Illus.). 144p. 2000. 24.95 (*0-89658-221-3*) Voyageur Pr.

Our Minnesota. 3rd rev. ed. Photos by Les Blacklock et al. LC 92-28228. (Illus.). 144p. 1992. pap. 16.95 (*0-89658-258-2*) Voyageur Pr.

***Our Miracle Baby: Memories & Milestones in the Intensive Care Nursery.** Cheryl A. Bender. (Illus.). 112p. 2000. 32.95 (*0-9673025-2-8*) Wyatt-MacKenzie Pubg.

***Our Miracle Baby Parent Journal.** Cheryl A. Bender. (Illus.). 80p. 2000. 14.95 (*0-9673025-3-6*) Wyatt-MacKenzie Pubg.

Our Miraculous World. Paul A. Bartz & Bible Science Association Editors. LC 86-82927. v, 97 p. 1987. write for info. (*0-8403-4236-5*) Kendall-Hunt.

Our Miserable Life. William Steig. 1990. pap. 7.95 (*0-374-52216-2*) FS&G.

Our Miss Brooks - Musical. R. J. Mann. 182p. 1962. pap. 5.95 (*0-87129-708-6*, O03) Dramatic Pub.

Our Miss Brooks - Straight. rev. ed. R. J. Mann. 1978. pap. 5.95 (*0-87129-253-X*, O25) Dramatic Pub.

Our Miss Brooks & the Christmas Carol. R. J. Mann. 1954. pap. 3.50 (*0-87129-209-2*, O26) Dramatic Pub.

Our Mission of Love. (Image of God Ser.). (J). (gr. 5). 1996. pap. text 10.95 (*0-89870-334-4*) Ignatius Pr.

***Our Mission Past for Kids.** (J). 2000. pap. 10.95 (*1-878079-25-5*) Arts Pubns.

Our Molecular Nature: The Body's Motors, Machines & Messages. David S. Goodsell. LC 95-46846. (Copernicus Bks.). (Illus.). 183p. 1996. 25.00 (*0-387-94498-2*) Spr-Verlag.

Our Money. Margie Burton et al. Ed. by Alison Adams. (Early Connections Ser.). 16p. (J). (gr. k-2). 1999. pap. 4.50 (*1-58344-076-3*) Benchmark Educ.

Our Money. Karen B. Spies. LC 91-43231. (I Know America Ser.). (Illus.). 48p. (J). (gr. 2-4). 1992. pap. 8.95 (*1-56294-815-6*) Millbrook Pr.

Our Money, Ourselves: Redesigning Your Relationship with Money. C. Diane Ealy & Kay Lesh. LC 98-25714. 208p. 1998. pap. 25.95 (*0-8144-7999-5*) AMACOM.

***Our Monica, Ourselves: The Clinton Affair & the National Interest.** Ed. by Lauren Berlant & Lisa Duggan. 2001. 55.00 (*0-8147-9865-9*); pap. 18.95 (*0-8147-9864-0*) NYU Pr.

***Our Monongalia: A History of African Americans in Monongalia County, WV.** Connie P. Rice. (Illus.). 272p. 1998. 29.95 (*0-929915-26-7*) Headline Bks.

Our Moonlight Revels: "A Midsummer Night's Dream" in the Theatre. Gary J. Williams. LC 97-21764. (Studies in Theatre History & Culture). (Illus.). 378p. 1997. text 39.95 (*0-87745-592-9*) U of Iowa Pr.

Our Moral Life in Christ: A Basic Course in Moral Theology. Ed. by Aurelio Fernandez & James Socias. 384p. (YA). (gr. 11-12). 1998. pap. text 19.95 (*1-890177-05-9*) Midwest Theol.

Our Moral Nature. James McCosh. LC 75-3260. reprint ed. 32.50 (*0-404-59247-3*) AMS Pr.

Our Morality & the Moral Question: From the Medical Side. Lionel S. Beale. LC 73-20615. (Sex, Marriage & Society Ser.). 208p. 1974. reprint ed. 21.95 (*0-405-05793-8*) Ayer.

Our More Perfect Union: From Eighteen-Century Principles to Twentieth-Century Practice. Arthur N. Holcombs. LC 50-9371. 477p. reprint ed. pap. 147.90 (*0-608-30057-8*, 201950600013) Bks Demand.

Our Most Dear Friend: An Illustrated Bhagavad-Gita for Children. Jean Griesser. LC 95-46070. (Illus.). 32p. (J). (gr. 1-6). 1996. 14.95 (*1-887089-04-7*) Torchlght Pub.

***Our Most Noble Victory: Poems on the Vietnam Experience.** V. K. Inman. 24p. 2000. pap., boxed set 12.00 incl. audio (*0-913551-02-3*) Arbuta Hse.

Our Most Requested Recipes from Richmond Hill. John Babb. 48p. 1995. pap. write for info. (*1-887756-05-1*) Richmnd Hill.

Our Mother Blooming. Jim Bodeen. (Illus.). 24p. (Orig.). 1986. pap. 5.00 (*0-911287-09-4*) Blue Begonia.

Our Mother-Tempers. Marion J. Levy, Jr. 1989. 48.00 (*0-520-06422-4*, Pub. by U CA Pr) Cal Prin Full Svc.

Our Mothers. Alan Bott & Irene Clephane. LC 73-81813. (Illus.). 1972. 27.95 (*0-405-08293-2*, Pub. by Blom Pubns) Ayer.

Our Mothers: Portraits by 72 Women Photographers. Ed. by Viviane Esders. LC 95-40779. (Illus.). 160p. 1996. 29.95 (*1-55670-442-9*) Stewart Tabori & Chang.

Our Mother's Family. Allen D. Peterson. LC 98-92382. 114p. 1998. pap. 20.00 (*0-9646503-1-2*) A D Peterson.

Our Mothers' Land: Chapters in Welsh Women's, 1830-1939. John. (Illus.). 219p. 1998. pap. 25.00 (*0-7083-1129-6*, Pub. by Univ Wales Pr) Paul & Co Pubs.

Our Mothers' Land: Chapters in Welsh Women's, 1830-1939. Ed. by Angela V. John. (Illus.). 219p. 1998. 50.00 (*0-7083-1120-2*, Pub. by Univ Wales Pr) Paul & Co Pubs.

Our Mothers, Our Selves: Writers & Poets Celebrating Motherhood. Ed. by Karen J. Donnelly & J. B. Bernstein. LC 95-36903. 280p. 1996. 19.95 (*0-89789-445-6*, Bergin & Garvey) Greenwood.

Our Mothers' Spirits: Great Writers on the Death of Mothers & the Grief of Men. Bob Blauner. (Illus.). 352p. 1999. pap. 12.00 (*0-06-098731-6*, ReganBks) HarperTrade.

Our Mountain State Heritage: West Virginia Stories of the People. Ed. by Pam Kasey & Rae J. Sielen. LC 98-66051. (Illus.). 200p. 1998. pap. 18.00 (*0-9652699-2-2*) Populore Pub.

Our Movie Heritage. Tom McGreevey & Joanne L. Yeck. LC 97-3737. (Illus.). 208p. (C). 1997. 45.00 (*0-8135-2431-8*) Rutgers U Pr.

Our Movie Made Children. Henry J. Forman. LC 72-124028. (Literature of Cinema Ser.). 1970. reprint ed. 19.95 (*0-405-01646-8*) Ayer.

Our Mr. Wrenn. Sinclair Lewis. (Collected Works of Sinclair Lewis). 254p. 1988. reprint ed. lib. bdg. 88.00 (*1-58201-674-7*) Classic Bks.

Our Musical Past, 2 cass. 16p. (YA). pap. 16.95 incl. audio (*0-88432-403-6*, S11020) Audio-Forum.

***Our Mutts, Vol. 5.** Patrick McDonnell. (Illus.). 2000. pap. 9.95 (*0-7407-0456-7*); pap. 59.70 (*0-7407-1285-3*) Andrews & McMeel.

Our Mutual Friend see Oxford Illustrated Dickens

Our Mutual Friend. Charles Dickens. 1994. mass mkt. 6.95 (*0-553-85016-4*) Bantam.

Our Mutual Friend. Charles Dickens. 1994. 20.00 (*0-679-42028-2*) Everymns Lib.

Our Mutual Friend. Charles Dickens. LC 92-50212. 824p. 1992. 19.00 (*0-679-60022-1*) Modern Lib NY.

Our Mutual Friend. Charles Dickens. Ed. & Intro. by Adrian Poole. 928p. 1998. pap. 10.95 (*0-14-043497-6*) Viking Penguin.

***Our Mutual Friend.** Charles Dickens. (Classics Library). 1998. pap. 3.95 (*1-85326-194-7*, 1947WW, Pub. by Wrdsworth Edits) NTC Contemp Pub Co.

Our Mutual Friend. Charles Dickens. 900p. 1990. reprint ed. lib. bdg. 49.95 (*0-89966-683-3*) Buccaneer Bks.

Our Mutual Friend. Charles Dickens. Ed. & Intro. by Michael Cotsell. (Oxford World's Classics Ser.). 878p. 1998. reprint ed. pap. 9.95 (*0-19-283523-8*) OUP.

Our Mysterious Ocean. Peter Riley. LC 97-74769. (Windows on Science Ser.). (Illus.). 14p. (J). (gr. 4-6). 1998. 12.99 (*1-57584-058-8*) Rdrs Digest.

Our Mysterious Panics, 1830-1930: A Story of Events & the Men Involved. Charles A. Collman. LC 68-28621. 310p. 1968. reprint ed. lib. bdg. 69.50 (*0-8371-0050-X*, COMP, Greenwood Pr) Greenwood.

Our Name Is Melancholy: The Complete Books of Azrael. Leilah Wendell. LC 92-60090. (Illus.). 375p. (Orig.). 1992. pap. 17.95 (*0-944087-04-3*) Westgate Pr.

Our Nation under God. Michael J. McHugh. 1996. teacher ed. 4.00 (*1-930092-88-1*) Christian Liberty.

Our Nation under God. Michael J. McHugh. (Illus.). 154p. (J). (gr. 2-3). 1996. pap. text 7.95 (*1-930092-87-3*, CLP79920) Christian Liberty.

Our Nation under God: Test Booklet. Michael J. McHugh. 1996. 1.95 (*1-930092-89-X*) Christian Liberty.

Our National Anthem. Stephanie St. Pierre. LC 91-38891. (I Know America Ser.). (Illus.). 48p. (J). (gr. 2-4). 1992. pap. 8.95 (*1-878841-89-0*); lib. bdg. 20.90 (*1-56294-106-2*) Millbrook Pr.

Our National Anthem. Stephanie. (I Know America Ser.). 1992. 14.15 (*0-606-06646-2*, Pub. by Turtleback) Demco.

Our National Capital. Richard Steins. (I Know America Ser.). (Illus.). 48p. (J). (gr. 2-4). 1994. lib. bdg. 20.90 (*1-56294-439-8*) Millbrook Pr.

Our National Centennial Jubilee. Frederick Saunders. 1988. reprint ed. lib. bdg. 75.00 (*0-7812-0385-6*) Rprt Serv.

Our National Heritage Vol. 1: Essays in American History Before 1865. 2nd ed. Bowman & Campbell. 352p. 1993. per. 19.95 (*0-8403-8221-9*) Kendall-Hunt.

Our National Holidays. Karen B. Spies. LC 91-38894. (I Know America Ser.). (Illus.). 48p. (J). (gr. 2-4). 1992. pap. 5.95 (*1-878841-88-2*) Millbrook Pr.

Our National Holidays. Karen Bornemann Spies. (I Know America Ser.). 1992. 11.15 (*0-606-06647-0*, Pub. by Turtleback) Demco.

Our National Monuments. Eleanor Ayer. LC 91-43230. (I Know America Ser.). (Illus.). 48p. (J). (gr. 2-4). 1992. pap. 8.95 (*1-56294-816-4*); lib. bdg. 20.90 (*1-56294-078-3*) Millbrook Pr.

Our National Monuments. Eleanor H. Ayer. LC 91-43230. (I Know America Ser.). 1992. 14.15 (*0-606-06648-9*, Pub. by Turtleback) Demco.

Our National Park Policy: A Critical History. John Ise. Ed. by Stuart Bruchey. LC 78-53548. (Development of Public Land Law in the U. S. Ser.). 1979. reprint ed. lib. bdg. 53.95 (*0-405-11377-3*) Ayer.

Our National Park System: Caring for America's Greatest Natural & Historic Treasures. Dwight F. Rettie. LC 94-22632. 320p. 1995. 34.95 (*0-252-02148-7*) U of Ill Pr.

Our National Park System: Caring for America's Greatest Natural & Historic Treasures. Dwight F. Rettie. (Illus.). 320p. 1996. 21.95 (*0-252-06558-1*) U of Ill Pr.

Our National Parks. John Muir. LC 01-26282. Date not set. 10.00 (*0-403-00194-3*) Scholarly.

Our National Parks. John Muir. LC 90-45254. (John Muir Library). (Illus.). 296p. 1991. pap. 10.00 (*0-87156-626-5*, Pub. by Sierra) Random.

Our National Parks. Michael Weber. (I Know America Ser.). (Illus.). 48p. (J). (gr. 2-4). 1994. lib. bdg. 21.90 (*1-56294-438-X*) Millbrook Pr.

Our National Parks. Michael Weber. (I Know America Ser.). (Illus.). 48p. (J). (gr. 2-4). 1995. pap. 5.95 (*1-56294-680-3*) Millbrook Pr.

Our National Parks. Michael Weber. LC 93-35014. (I Know America Ser.). (J). 1994. 11.15 (*0-606-09724-4*, Pub. by Turtleback) Demco.

Our National Parks. John Muir. LC 70-120568. reprint ed. 22.50 (*0-404-04516-2*) AMS Pr.

Our National Parks. John Muir. 1988. reprint ed. lib. bdg. 49.00 (*0-7812-0771-1*) Rprt Serv.

Our National Parks. John Muir. LC 80-53957. 394p. 1981. reprint ed. 29.50 (*0-299-08590-2*); reprint ed. pap. 16.95 (*0-299-08594-5*) U of Wis Pr.

Our National Parks. rev. ed. Reader's Digest Editors. (Illus.). 352p. 1997. 30.00 (*0-89577-941-2*, Pub. by RD Assn) Penguin Putnam.

Our National Parks & the Search for Sustainability. Bob R. O'Brien. LC 98-9011. 248p. 1999. 40.00 (*0-292-76049-3*); pap. 19.95 (*0-292-76050-7*) U of Tex Pr.

Our National Symbols. Linda C. Johnson. LC 91-38893. (I Know America Ser.). (Illus.). 48p. (J). (gr. 2-4). 1992. pap. 9.95 (*1-878841-87-4*); lib. bdg. 20.90 (*1-56294-108-9*) Millbrook Pr.

Our National Symbols. Linda Carlson Johnson. LC 91-38893. (I Know America Ser.). 1992. 14.15 (*0-606-06649-7*, Pub. by Turtleback) Demco.

Our National Tapestry. Steven C. Levi. 1986. 2.00 (*0-932593-06-2*) Black Bear.

***Our Nation's Archive: The History of the United States in Documents.** Eric A. Bruun & Jay Crosby. LC 99-29451. 1999. 29.98 (*1-57912-067-9*) Blck Dog & Leventhal.

Our Nation's Capital in 3-D. Photos by Rick Sammon & Susan Sammon. (Illus.). 28p. (J). (gr. 1-6). 1995. 9.95 (*0-916200-15-9*) US Capitol Hist.

Our Nation's Capitol. D. C. Russell. LC 97-113690. 64p. (J). 1997. pap. 11.95 (*0-590-59929-1*) Scholastic Inc.

Our Nation's Crisis & How to Solve It: Main Political Resolution, Communist Party Twentieth National Convention. Communist Party Convention Staff. 96p. 1972. pap. 0.65 (*0-87898-087-3*) New Outlook.

Our Nation's Garden. Claire Murray. 1999. 10.95 (*0-8362-8743-6*) Andrews & McMeel.

Our Nation's Housing in 1993. Timothy S. Grail. 32p. 1995. pap. 3.75 (*0-16-061056-7*) USGPO.

Our Nation's Kids: Is Something Wrong? NIF Staff. 28p. 1997. pap. 2.15 (*0-7872-3917-8*) Kendall-Hunt.

Our Nation's Kids: Is Something Wrong? abr. ed. NIF Staff. 24p. 1997. 2.25 (*0-7872-3918-6*) Kendall-Hunt.

Our Nation's Travel: 1995 NPTS Early Results Report. 34p. pap. text 10.00 (*0-9999016-3-X*) DIANE Pub.

Our Nation's Water Resources: Policies & Politics. Ben Moreell & Herbert C. Hoover. LC 72-2857. (Use & Abuse of America's Natural Resources Ser.). 290p. 1972. reprint ed. 23.95 (*0-405-04521-2*) Ayer.

Our Native American Heritage. Ed. by Reader's Digest Editors. LC 96-907. (Explore America Ser.). 1996. write for info. (*0-89577-867-X*) RD Assn.

Our Natural History: The Lessons of Lewis & Clark. Daniel B. Botkin. 320p. 1996. reprint ed. pap. 14.00 (*0-399-52242-5*, Perigee Bks) Berkley Pub.

Our Natural Homes: Exploring Terrestrial Biomes of North & South America. Sneed B. Collard, III. LC 95-23978. (Illus.). 32p. (J). (gr. k-5). 1996. pap. 6.95 (*0-88106-928-0*) Charlesbridge Pub.

Our Natural Homes: Exploring Terrestrial Biomes of North & South America. Sneed B. Collard, III. LC 95-23978. (Illus.). 32p. (J). (ps-3). 1996. 16.95 (*0-88106-929-9*) Charlesbridge Pub.

Our Natural Knowledge of God: A Prospect for Natural Theology after Kant & Barth. Ned Wisnefske. LC 89-39719. 176p. (C). 1991. text 51.95 (*0-8204-1232-5*) P Lang Pubng.

Our Natural Resources: Environmental Conservation. John Tomikel. (Illus.). 160p. (Orig.). 1995. pap. text 24.95 (*0-910042-74-8*) Allegheny.

Our Nature. Bil Gilbert. LC 85-20891. 275p. 1986. reprint ed. pap. 85.30 (*0-608-03492-4*, 206420700008) Bks Demand.

Our Naval Heroes: Told in One Syllable Words, Vol. 4. Josephine Pollard. (Illus.). 256p. (J). 1998. reprint ed. 15.00 (*1-889128-45-7*) Mantle Ministries.

Our Naval War with France. Gardner W. Allen. (BCL1 - U. S. History Ser.). 323p. 1992. reprint ed. lib. bdg. 89.00 (*0-7812-6139-2*) Rprt Serv.

Our Need for Others & Its Roots in Infancy. Josephine Klein. 480p. (C). 1987. pap. 27.99 (*0-415-05879-1*) Routledge.

Our Need for Others & Its Roots in Infancy. Josephine Klein. 350p. 1987. 55.00 (*0-422-61410-6*, A0811, Pub. by Tavistock); pap. 15.95 (*0-422-61420-3*, A0815, Pub. by Tavistock) Routldge.

Our Neighbor Is a Strange, Strange Man. Tres Seymour. LC 98-12016. (Illus.). 32p. (J). (gr. k-4). 1999. lib. bdg. 16.99 (*0-531-33107-5*) Orchard Bks Watts.

O

Our Neighbor Is a Strange, Strange Man. Tres Seymour. LC 98-12016. (Illus.). 32p. (YA). (gr. k-4). 1999. 15.95 (*0-531-30107-9*) Orchard Bks Watts.
Our Neighbors in Space. Bob De Weese. Ed. by Marilyn Evans. (Science Ser.). (Illus.). 31p. (J). (gr. 4-6). Date not set. pap., wbk. ed. 3.50 (*1-58610-124-2*) Learn Horizon.
Our Neighbors in Space. DeWeese. (Illus.). 32p. (J). (gr. 4-6). 1997. pap., teacher ed. 2.95 (*1-55799-519-2*, 4121) Evan-Moor Edu Pubs.
Our Nell: A Scrapbook Biography of Nellie McClung. Candace Savage. (Illus.). 253p. 1979. mass mkt. 5.95 (*0-88780-134-X*, Pub. by Formac Publ Co) Formac Dist Ltd.
Our New Age: Words for the People. Christopher. LC 77-72309. (Illus.). (Orig.). 1977. pap. 2.95 (*0-916940-01-2*) World Light.
Our New Alaska. Charles Hallock. LC 76-125745. (American Environmental Studies). 1974. reprint ed. 17.95 (*0-405-02670-6*) Ayer.
Our New Baby. Beth Atchison. Ed. by Laura Ring. LC 98-61294. (Happy Day Bks.). (Illus.). 24p. (J). (ps-2). 1999. pap. 1.99 (*0-7847-0894-0*, 04267) Standard Pub.
Our New Baby. Jen Green. LC 98-16958. (How Do I Feel About... Ser.). (Illus.). 24p. (J). (gr. k-4). 1998. lib. bdg. 19.90 (*0-7613-0871-7*, Copper Beech Bks) Millbrook Pr.
Our New Baby. Wendy C. Lewison. (All Aboard Bks.). (Illus.). 32p. (Orig.). (J). (ps-3). 1996. pap. 2.95 (*0-448-41147-4*, G & D) Peng Put Young Read.
Our New Baby. Wendy Cheyette Lewison. (All Aboard Bks.). (Orig.). (J). 1996. 8.15 (*0-606-11714-8*, Pub. by Turtleback) Demco.
Our New Baby. Stephanie Longfoot & Gill Davies. (Now I Am Big Ser.). (Illus.). 24p. (J). (ps-1). 1996. 3.49 (*1-85854-367-3*) Brimax Bks.
*__Our New Baby.__ Dee Shulman. (Cuddly Board Bks.). (Illus.). 10p. (J). (ps-k). 2000. bds. 6.95 (*0-439-12913-3*, Cartwheel) Scholastic Inc.
Our New Baby, Level 1. Sue Kueffner. LC 98-49564. (Fisher-Price All-Star Readers Ser.). (Illus.). 32p. (J). (gr. k-3). 1999. mass mkt. 3.99 (*1-57584-292-0*) Rdrs Digest.
Our New Baby Needs Help: A Coloring Book for Families Whose New Baby Has Problems. Gail Klayman. 1996. 3.95 (*1-56123-075-8*) Centering Corp.
Our New Clothes: Acquisitions of the 1990s. Richard Martin & Metropolitan Museum of Art (New York, N. Y.) Staff. LC 99-14145. 80p. 1999. pap. 29.95 (*0-8109-6540-2*, Pub. by Abrams) Time Warner.
Our New Identity in Christ. Kirk Eland. 10p. (Orig.). 1992. pap. 0.50 (*0-914271-32-6*) Mnstry Pubns.
Our New Masters. Thomas Wright. LC 69-20019. (Reprints of Economic Classics Ser.). viii, 392p. 1969. reprint ed. 49.50 (*0-678-00482-X*) Kelley.
*__Our New Mummy.__ large type ed. Jennifer Taylor. 288p. 2000. 25.99 (*0-263-16181-1*, Pub. by Mills & Boon) Ulverscroft.
Our New National Security Strategy: America Promises to Come Back. James J. Tritten. LC 92-9125. 208p. 1992. 57.95 (*0-275-94357-7*, C4357, Praeger Pubs) Greenwood.
Our New Puppy. Isabelle Harper. LC 95-26168. (Illus.). 32p. (J). (ps-3). 1996. 14.95 (*0-590-56926-0*, Blue Sky Press) Scholastic Inc.
Our New West: Records of Travel Between the Mississippi & the Pacific Ocean. Samuel Bowles. LC 72-9429. (Far Western Frontier Ser.). (Illus.). 528p. 1973. reprint ed. 35.95 (*0-405-04960-9*) Ayer.
Our New West: Records of Travel Between the Mississippi River & the Pacific Ocean. Samuel Bowles. (Illus.). 526p. 1990. reprint ed. pap. 31.50 (*1-55613-354-5*) Heritage Bk.
Our NHS: Celebration of 50 Years. Ed. by G. Macpherson. (Illus.). 227p. 1998. text 36.00 (*0-7279-1279-8*, Pub. by BMJ Pub) Login Brothers Bk Co.
Our Nig: Sketches from the Life of a Free Black. Harriet E. Wilson. Ed. by Henry Louis Gates, Jr. LC 82-49197. 168p. 1983. 10.95 (*0-685-06645-2*) Vin Bks.
Our Nig: Sketches from the Life of a Free Black. Harriet E. Wilson. Ed. by Henry Louis Gates, Jr. LC 82-49197. 168p. 1983. pap. 12.00 (*0-394-71558-6*) Vin Bks.
Our Nine Tribunes. Louis Lusky. LC 92-28482. 232p. 1993. 55.00 (*0-275-94463-8*, C4463, Praeger Pubs) Greenwood.
Our Noble Blood: The Civil War Letters of Gen. Regis de Trobriand. Ed. by William B. Styple. Tr. by Nathalie Chartrain from FRE. (Illus.). 265p. 1997. 27.95 (*1-883926-10-6*) Belle Grv Pub.
Our Noise: A Novel. Jeff Gomez. 384p. (Orig.). 1995. per. 12.00 (*0-684-80099-3*, Scribner Pap Fic) S&S Trade Pap.
Our Non-veg Cow & Other Stories. Mahasveta Debi & Paramita Banerjee. LC 98-903268. x, 115 p. 1998. write for info. (*81-7046-145-6*) Seagull Bks.
Our Nordic Race: History of the White Race. Richard K. Hoskins. (Illus.). 76p. 1994. pap. 5.00 (*1-881867-00-5*) Virginia Pub.
Our North American World Heritage. Mark Swadling. 1997. 39.95 (*1-57769-004-4*) Wrld Heritage.
Our North American World Heritage: Our Land, Our Legacy. Mark Swadling. 1996. 39.95 (*0-646-22644-4*) Wrld Heritage.
Our North American World Heritage: Our Land, Our Legacy. limited ed. Mark Swadling. 304p. 1996. 125.00 (*0-646-22709-2*) Wrld Heritage.
Our Nuclear Heritage. James Sherry. (New American Poetry Ser.: No. 9). 264p. (Orig.). 1991. pap. 10.95 (*1-55713-126-0*) Sun & Moon CA.
*__Our Ocean Future: Themes & Issues Concerning the Nation[0012]s Stake in the Oceans.__ Ed. & Frwd. by D. James Baker. 57p. 2000. reprint ed. pap. text 20.00 (*0-7881-8873-9*) DIANE Pub.
Our Ocean Home. Robert L. Nelson. LC 96-46822. (Illus.). 48p. (Orig.). (J). (ps-1). 1997. 11.95 (*1-55971-596-0*, NorthWord Pr) Creat Pub Intl.
Our Oceans. (C). 1997. write for info. (*0-02-371043-8*, Macmillan Coll); write for info. (*0-02-371044-6*, Macmillan Coll); write for info. (*0-02-371045-4*, Macmillan Coll); write for info. (*0-02-371046-2*, Macmillan Coll) P-H.
Our Oceans. Lipps. (C). 1997. teacher ed. write for info. (*0-02-371042-X*, Macmillan Coll) P-H.
Our Oceans. Jere H. Lipps. (C). 1997. 61.00 (*0-02-371041-1*, Macmillan Coll) P-H.
Our Oceans: Experiments & Activities in Marine Science. Paul Fleisher. LC 95-1962. (Illus.). 80p. (J). (gr. 4-6). 1995. lib. bdg. 25.90 (*1-56294-575-0*) Millbrook Pr.
Our Old Fashioned Country Diary for 1986. Linda C. Franklin. (Old Fashioned Keepbook Ser.). (Illus.). 144p. 1982. 12.00 (*0-934504-51-2*) Michel Pub Co.
Our Old Home. Nathaniel Hawthorne. Ed. by William Charvat et al. LC 75-92336. (Centenary Edition of the Works of Nathaniel Hawthorne: Vol. 5). (Illus.). 497p. 1970. text 70.00 (*0-8142-0002-8*) Ohio St U Pr.
Our Old Home. Nathaniel Hawthorne. (Notable American Authors Ser.). 1992. reprint ed. lib. bdg. 75.00 (*0-7812-3048-9*) Rprt Serv.
Our Old House. Susan Vizurraga. LC 96-44215. (Illus.). 32p. (J). (ps-2). 1995. 15.95 (*0-8050-3911-2*) H Holt & Co.
Our Old House-Our New Home: A Practical Real Estate Purchasing Guide for Active Adults Planning for Retirement. Jared A. March. LC 98-92058. 275p. 1998. pap. 12.95 (*0-931673-11-9*) J March Pub Grp.
Our 125th Regiment Illinois Volunteer Infantry: Attention Batallion! Robert M. Rogers. (Illus.). 226p. 1999. reprint ed. lib. bdg. 35.00 (*0-8328-9813-9*) Higginson Bk Co.
Our Only Hope Is Humor: Some Public Poems. Ed. by Robert McGovern & Richard Snyder. 88p. (C). 1972. pap. 5.00 (*0-912592-13-3*) Ashland Poetry.
*__Our Only May Amelia.__ Jennifer L. Holm. LC 98-47504. 272p. (J). (gr. 5-9). 2000. mass mkt. 4.95 (*0-06-440856-6*) HarpC.
*__Our Only May Amelia.__ Jennifer L. Holm. LC 98-47504. (Illus.). 272p. (YA). (gr. 4 up). 1999. 15.95 (*0-06-027822-6*) HarpC Child Bks.
Our Only May Amelia. Jennifer L. Holm. LC 98-47504. (Illus.). 272p. (YA). (gr. 5-9). 1999. lib. bdg. 15.89 (*0-06-028354-8*) HarpC Child Bks.
Our Only Star & Compass: Locke & the Struggle for Political Rationality. Peter C. Myers. LC 98-36862. 288p. 1998. 23.95 (*0-8476-9099-7*); pap. 63.00 (*0-8476-9098-9*) Rowman.
Our Ordered Lives Confess: Three Nineteenth Century Missionaries in East Shantung. Irwin T. Hyatt, Jr. (Studies in American-East Asian Relations: No. 8). 252p. 1976. 36.50 (*0-674-64735-1*) HUP.
Our Organization. Brian O'Connell. 1987. pap. 12.95 (*0-8027-1006-9*) Walker & Co.
Our Oriental Heritage. Will Durant. (Story of Civilization Ser.). (Illus.). 1052p. 1993. 17.98 (*1-56731-012-5*, MJF Bks) Fine Comms.
Our Origin & Destiny: An Evolutionary Perspective on the New Millennium. Kathy L. Callahan. LC 96-44801. 312p. 1997. pap. 14.95 (*0-87604-368-6*, 478) ARE Pr.
Our Other Voices: Nine Poets Speaking. Ed. by John Wheatcroft. LC 89-46403. (Illus.). 224p. 1991. 38.50 (*0-8387-5196-2*) Bucknell U Pr.
Our Overloaded Economy: Inflation, Unemployment, & the Crisis in American Capitalism. Wallace C. Peterson. LC 81-51288. 256p. reprint ed. pap. 79.40 (*0-608-18131-5*, 203278500081) Bks Demand.
*__Our Own.__ Trish Maskew. 1999. 23.95 (*0-9669701-2-8*) Snowcap.
Our Own Agendas: Autobiographical Essays by Women Associated with McGill University. Ed. by Margaret Gillett & Ann Beer. LC 96-138281. (Illus.). 320p. 1995. pap. 22.95 (*0-7735-1340-X*, Pub. by McG-Queens Univ Pr) CUP Services.
Our Own Agendas: Autobiographical Essays by Women Associated with McGill University. Ed. by Margaret Gillett & Ann Beer. LC 96-138281. (Illus.). 320p. 1995. 65.00 (*0-7735-1339-6*, Pub. by McG-Queens Univ Pr) CUP Services.
Our Own Backyard: The United States in Central America, 1977-1992. William M. LeoGrande. LC 97-18198. 790p. 1998. 45.00 (*0-8078-2395-3*) U of NC Pr.
*__Our Own Backyard: The United States in Central America, 1977-1992.__ William M. LeoGrande. LC 97-18198. 790p. 2000. pap. 24.95 (*0-8078-4857-3*) U of NC Pr.
Our Own Bad Black Woman Words. Ed. by Sharon L. Goodman. 52p. 1989. pap. 5.00 (*0-935369-20-1*) In Tradition Pub.
Our Own Clues: Poets of the Lake Z. 2nd ed. Assef Al-Jundi et al. 96p. (C). 1993. pap. text 8.50 (*0-9639676-0-6*) Our Lady Lake.
Our Own Country. Priscilla L. McQueen. (Basic Readers Ser.). 1970. teacher ed. 3.25 (*0-685-36212-4*); student ed. 2.30 (*0-685-36213-2*) McQueen.
*__Our Own Devices.__ Ewan Morris. (New Directions in Irish History Ser.). (Illus.). 240p. 2000. 45.00 (*0-7165-2663-8*, Pub. by Irish Acad Pr) Intl Spec Bk.
Our Own God. George D. Watson. 1992. reprint ed. pap. 12.99 (*0-88019-285-2*) Schmul Pub Co.
Our Own Kind. Edward McSorley. LC 76-6357. (Irish Americans Ser.). 1976. reprint ed. 26.95 (*0-405-09350-0*) Ayer.
Our Own Language: An Irish Initiative. Gabrielle Maguire. (Multilingual Matters Ser.: No. 66). 262p. 1991. 99.00 (*1-85359-096-7*, Pub. by Multilingual Matters); pap. 34.95 (*1-85359-095-9*, Pub. by Multilingual Matters) Taylor & Francis.
Our Own Metaphor: A Personal Account of a Conference on the Effects of Conscious Purpose on Human Adaptation. Mary C. Bateson. LC 91-561. (Illus.). 366p. (C). 1991. pap. text 16.95 (*1-56098-070-2*) Smithsonian.
Our Own Religion in Ancient Persia. Lawrence H. Mills. LC 74-21262. reprint ed. 62.50 (*0-404-12811-4*) AMS Pr.
Our Own Snug Fireside: Images of the New England Home, 1760-1860. Jane C. Nylander. (Illus.). 330p. 1994. pap. 20.00 (*0-300-05953-1*) Yale U Pr.
Our Own Sweet Sounds: A Celebration of Popular Music in Arkansas. Robert Cochran. LC 96-30210. 1996. pap. 16.00 (*1-55728-443-1*) U of Ark Pr.
Our Own Sweet Sounds: A Celebration of Popular Music in Arkansas. Robert Cochran. LC 96-30210. 120p. 1996. 30.00 (*1-55728-442-3*) U of Ark Pr.
Our Own Sweet Time. Laurie O'Brien. 54p. 1996. pap. 10.00 (*0-944206-04-2*) W FL Lit Fed.
Our Own Time: A History of American Labor & the Working Day, 23. David R. Roediger & Philip S. Foner. LC 87-29543. (Contributions in Labor Studies: No. 23). 392p. 1989. 65.00 (*0-313-26062-1*, ROO/, Greenwood Pr) Greenwood.
Our Own Vine & Fig Tree: The Persistence of the Mother Bethel Family. Carolyn S. Beck. LC 88-35114. (Immigrant Communities & Ethnic Minorities in the U. S. & Canada Ser.: No. 36). 1989. 57.50 (*0-404-19446-X*) AMS Pr.
Our Own Worst Enemy. William J. Lederer. LC 68-13847. 1968. 4.95 (*0-393-05357-1*) Norton.
Our Own Years. Alice Lake. 244p. (C). 1982. reprint ed. 8.95 (*0-86683-667-5*) Harper SF.
Our Pagan Christmas. 2nd ed. R. J. Condon. (Illus.). 20p. 1989. reprint ed. 3.00 (*0-910309-60-4*, 5064) Am Atheist.
Our Parade. Suzanne Burke. Ed. by Alton Jordan. (I Can Eat an Elephant Ser.). (Illus.). (J). (gr. k-3). 1984. 7.95 (*0-89868-017-4*, Read Res); pap. 3.95 (*0-89868-050-6*, Read Res) ARO Pub.
Our Paradise: A GI's War Diary. Enrest Norquist. LC 88-61934. (Illus.). 385p. 1989. 19.95 (*0-9606240-9-0*) Pearl-Win.
Our Parents' Lives: Jewish Assimilation in Everyday Life. Neil M. Cowan & Ruth S. Cowan. LC 96-19113. (Illus.). 330p. (Orig.). 1996. pap. text 16.95 (*0-8135-2296-X*) Rutgers U Pr.
Our Paris: Sketches from Memory. Edmund White. (Illus.). 128p. 1995. 22.00 (*0-679-44166-2*) Knopf.
Our Parish Church. (Saint Joseph Picture Bks.). (Illus.). 1985. pap. 1.25 (*0-89942-499-6*, 499-00) Catholic Bk Pub.
Our Part of the River. Gerald Harrison. LC 95-70305. 198p. 1995. 9.95 (*0-9647958-6-8*) Sapphire Crescent Pubng.
Our Passion for Justice. Carter Heyward. LC 84-4936. 288p. (Orig.). 1984. pap. 14.95 (*0-8298-0705-5*) Pilgrim OH.
Our Passionate Journey: The Exciting Chronicles of Two Ordinary People. Bob Frazier & Doris Frazier. Ed. by David Enlow & Don Williams. 294p. (Orig.). 1994. pap. write for info. (*1-885729-05-7*) Toccoa Falls.
Our Past Preserved: A History of American Library Preservation, 1876-1910. Barbara B. Higginbotham. 346p. (C). 1998. text 20.00 (*0-7881-5292-0*) DIANE Pub.
Our Patchwork Planet. Helen R. Sattler. LC 90-32623. (Illus.). 48p. (J). (gr. 2 up). 1995. 16.00 (*0-688-09312-4*) Lothrop.
*__Our Peaceable Kingdom: The Photographs of John Drysdale.__ Compiled & Intro. by Margaret Regan. (Illus.). 112p. 2000. 19.95 (*0-312-26588-3*) St Martin.
Our Peaceful Classroom. Aline D. Wolf. LC 91-90027. (Illus.). 64p. (Orig.). 1991. pap. 12.95 (*0-939195-04-6*) Parent-Child Pr.
Our Peculiar Security: The Written Constitution & Limited Government. Ed. by Eugene W. Hickok et al. LC 92-27487. (Studies in American Constitutionalism). 240p. (C). 1993. pap. text 26.95 (*0-8476-7794-X*) Rowman.
Our Peculiar Security: The Written Constitution & Limited Government. Ed. by Eugene W. Hickok et al. LC 92-27487. (Studies in American Constitutionalism). 240p. (C). 1995. lib. bdg. 65.00 (*0-8476-7793-1*) Rowman.
*__Our Pen Is Time: A Pre Civil War Diary.__ Emma Finley. (Holly Springs Trilogy Ser.). 130p. 1999. pap. 12.95 (*0-9648638-6-3*) T Berryhill.
Our Pennsylvania Heritage. William A. Cornell & Millard Altland. LC 78-50430. (J). (gr. 7-12). 1997. 24.50 (*0-931992-21-4*) Penns Valley.
Our Pentecostal Heritage: Reclaiming the Priority of the Holy Spirit. John A. Sims. vii, 192p. 1995. pap. 9.99 (*0-87148-673-3*) Pathway Pr.
Our People: History of the Jews, Vol. 1. Jacob Isaacs. (Illus.). 176p. Date not set. reprint ed. 12.00 (*0-8266-0221-5*) Kehot Pubn Soc.
Our People: History of the Jews, Vol. 2. Jacob Isaacs. (Illus.). 296p. Date not set. reprint ed. 12.00 (*0-8266-0222-3*) Kehot Pubn Soc.
Our People: History of the Jews, Vol. 3. Jacob Isaacs. (Illus.). 254p. Date not set. reprint ed. 12.00 (*0-8266-0223-1*) Kehot Pubn Soc.
Our People: History of the Jews, Vol. 4. Jacob Isaacs. (Illus.). 212p. Date not set. reprint ed. 12.00 (*0-8266-0224-X*) Kehot Pubn Soc.
Our People: History of the Jews, Vol. 5. Jacob Isaacs. (Illus.). 224p. Date not set. reprint ed. 12.00 (*0-8266-0225-8*) Kehot Pubn Soc.
Our People: History of the Jews, Vol. 6. Jacob Isaacs. (Illus.). 276p. Date not set. reprint ed. 10.00 (*0-8266-0226-6*) Kehot Pubn Soc.
Our People: The Amish & Mennonites in Ohio. rev. ed. Levi Miller. LC 91-76519. (Illus.). 64p. 1992. pap. 4.99 (*0-8361-3582-2*) Herald Pr.
Our People, Our Resources: Supporting Rural Communities in Participatory Action Research on Population Dynamics & the Local Environment. Thomas George Barton & International Union of Conservation of Nature & Natural Resources Staff. LC 98-121789. xv, 259 p. 1997. write for info. (*2-8317-0389-1*) IEEE Standards.
Our Perfect Example: Following God's Ways. Phyllis Bennett. (Knowing God Ser.). 64p. 1994. 5.99 (*0-310-48331-X*) Zondervan.
Our Perfect Youth. Craig Moodie. LC 99-208336. 184p. 1998. pap. write for info. (*0-9665640-0-6*) Water Front Pr.
Our Perfecting World: Zarathushtra's Way of Life. Maneckji N. Dhalla. LC 74-21257. reprint ed. 55.00 (*0-404-12807-6*) AMS Pr.
*__Our Personal War: World War II, A Story of Love & Terror.__ Jan Tickner. LC 99-29492. 1999. write for info. (*1-57168-343-7*) Sunbelt Media.
Our Pets. (Sense of History Ser.). Date not set. pap. text. write for info. (*0-582-04021-3*, Pub. by Addison-Wesley) Longman.
Our Pets Have a Story to Tell. Cindy Fischer. LC 98-96387. (Illus.). 80p. 1998. pap. 7.95 (*0-9665889-1-6*) B G B Pubns.
Our Phil, & Other Stories. Katherine F. Dana. LC 74-113653. (Short Story Index Reprint Ser.). 1977. 17.95 (*0-8369-3382-6*) Ayer.
Our Philippine Problem. Henry P. Willis. LC 71-111748. (American Imperialism: Viewpoints of United States Foreign Policy, 1898-1941 Ser.). 1970. reprint ed. 25.95 (*0-405-02053-8*) Ayer.
Our Philosophical Heritage. Andrew Schoedinger. 484p. (C). 1996. pap. text, per. 53.95 (*0-7872-2913-X*) Kendall-Hunt.
*__Our Philosophical Heritage.__ 2nd ed. Andrew Shoedinger. 490p. (C). 1998. per. 55.95 (*0-7872-5575-0*, 41557501) Kendall-Hunt.
Our Philosophy. Muhammad B. As-Sadr. Tr. by Shams Inati. 480p. 1988. text 57.50 (*0-7103-0179-0*) Routledge.
Our Photograph Album. Nancy Cogan Akmon. (Illus.). 22p. 1998. 19.95 (*1-884807-36-4*) Blushing Rose.
Our Pioneers & Patriots. Philip J. Furlong. LC 96-61306. (Illus.). 505p. (J). (gr. 5-8). 1997. reprint ed. pap. text 21.00 (*0-89555-592-1*, 1396) TAN Bks Pubs.
Our Pioneers & Patriots - Answer Key. Maureen K. McDevitt. LC 96-61306. 90p. (J). (gr. 5-8). 1997. pap., student ed. 10.00 (*0-89555-606-5*, 1529) TAN Bks Pubs.
*__Our Place in God's World: The Biblical Idea of Office.__ rev. ed. Paul G. Schrotenboer. Ed. by Jerry S. Herbert. 48p. 1999. pap. 8.00 (*0-9652730-4-0*) Coal Christian Coll.
Our Places. Parker Towle. LC 98-12966. 1998. pap. 7.00 (*0-916897-31-1*) Andrew Mtn Pr.
Our Plague: A Film from New York. James Chapman. LC 92-73394. 302p. (Orig.). (C). 1993. pap. 10.00 (*1-879193-00-0*) Fugue State.
Our Planet. Scott Steedman. LC 96-27734. (Worldwise Ser.). (Illus.). (J). 1997. lib. bdg. 23.00 (*0-531-14439-9*) Watts.
Our Planet. Scott Steedman. LC 96-27734. (Worldwise Ser.). (Illus.). (J). 1998. pap. 7.00 (*0-531-15316-9*) Watts.
Our Planet: Earth - Book & Soft Globe. Lisa Feder-Feitel & Peter Spacek. (Illus.). (J). 1996. 14.99 (*0-590-73481-4*) Scholastic Inc.
Our Planet: Earth: Window on the Universe. Robert Estalella. (Illus.). 32p. (gr. 4-8). 1994. 12.95 (*0-8120-6368-6*) Barron.
Our Planet Earth see Planet Earth
Our Planet Earth. Christian Grenier. LC 98-74448. (Megascope Ser.). (Illus.). 64p. (J). (gr. 5 up). 1999. 6.95 (*0-7641-5181-9*) Barron.
Our Planet Earth. Claire Llewellyn. LC 97-12561. (Scholastic First Encyclopedia Ser.). (Illus.). 80p. (J). (gr. k-3). 1997. pap. 14.95 (*0-590-87929-4*, Scholastic Ref) Scholastic Inc.
Our Planet Earth see Isaac Asimov's New Library of the Universe
Our Planet, His Creation. Ed. by Alan Bond & Jill Bond. (Kids Write Ser.). (Illus.). 112p. (Orig.). (J). (gr. k-12). 1992. pap. 5.00 (*0-9631992-2-6*) Bonding Place.
Our Planet, Our Health: Report of the WHO Commission on Health & Environment. WHO Staff. (CHI, FRE & SPA.). xxxii, 282p. 1992. pap. text 45.00 (*92-4-156148-3*, 1150375) World Health.
Our Planet, Our Health: Report of the WHO Commission on Health & Environment: Report of the Panel on Energy. x, 155p. 1992. pap. text 13.50 (*0-614-08027-4*, 1932029) World Health.
Our Planet, Our Health: Report of the WHO Commission on Health & Environment: Report of the Panel on Food & Agriculture. x, 191p. 1992. pap. text 13.50 (*0-614-08028-2*, 1931029) World Health.
Our Planet, Our Health: Report of the WHO Commission on Health & Environment: Report of the Panel on Industry. xi, 191p. 1992. pap. text 13.50 (*0-614-08029-0*, 1934029) World Health.
Our Planet, Our Health: Report of the WHO Commission on Health & Environment: Report of the Panel on Urbanization. vii, 160p. 1992. pap. text 13.50 (*0-614-08030-4*, 1933029) World Health.
Our Planet, Our Home: A Gaia Learning Material. Philip S. Gang. 60p. 1989. teacher ed. 50.00 (*91-970957-5-3*) Dagaz Pr.

O

Our Playhouse. Greg Mitchell. LC 92-21451. (Voyages Ser.). (Illus.). (J). 1993. 3.75 (*0-383-03647-X*) SRA McGraw.

Our Police: A History of the Cincinnati Police Force, from the Earliest Period Until the Present Day. Ed. by George M. Roe. LC 77-156024. reprint ed. 72.50 (*0-404-09125-3*) AMS Pr.

Our Police Protectors: History of the New York Police. 3rd ed. Augustine Costello & Theodore N. Ferdinand. LC 79-129324. (Criminology, Law Enforcement, & Social Problems Ser.: No. 127). (Illus.). 653p. 1972. reprint ed. lib. bdg. 50.00 (*0-87585-127-4*) Patterson Smith.

Our Politics, Our Selves? Liberalism, Identity & Harm. Peter Digeser. LC 94-23387. 296p. 1995. text 39.50 (*0-691-03716-7*, Pub. by Princeton U Pr) Cal Prin Full Svc.

Our Polliwogs see Renacuajos

Our Polliwogs. Claire Livesey. (Books for Young Learners). (Illus.). 12p. (J). (gr. k-2). 1999. pap. text 5.00 (*1-57274-276-3*) R Owen Pubs.

Our Population: The Changing Face of America. Charles B. Nam. LC 87-21601. 1988. pap. 5.95 (*0-8027-6754-0*) Walker & Co.

Our Population: Thinking About. Charles Nam. lib. bdg. 28.90 (*0-8027-6753-2*) Walker & Co.

Our Portion of Manna. Jacob G. Schneider. (Illus.). 173p. (Orig.). 1983. pap. 7.95 (*0-9613335-0-2*) J G Schneider.

Our Position. Isaac Errett. (General Tracts Ser.). 1969. pap. 0.75 (*0-7847-0174-1*, 03261) Standard Pub.

Our Positions. Corrado Costa. Tr. by Paul Vangelisti from ITA. 1975. 2.50 (*0-88031-021-9*) Invisible-Red Hill.

Our Positively Golden Years Vol. 1: Reflections on Aging. large type ed. Rita J. Putnam. (Illus.). 200p. (Orig.). Date not set. pap. write for info. (*1-886909-04-0*) Dynam Comm.

Our Postal System. Eileen Lucas. LC 98-23316. (I Know America Ser.). 48p. (J). (gr. 2-4). 1999. lib. bdg. 20.90 (*0-7613-0966-7*, Copper Beech Bks) Millbrook Pr.

Our Power As Women: Wisdom & Strategies of Highly Successful Women. Helene Lerner-Robbins. 200p. (Orig.). 1996. pap. 11.95 (*0-943233-91-7*) Conari Press.

Our Power to Predict: Revolutionary New Tools for Predicting Our Economy & the Future of Business. Harry S. Dent, Jr. LC 90-1572. 128p. (Orig.). 1990. pap. write for info. (*0-938545-06-X*) Jennings & Keefe.

Our Powerful Helper: Relying on God's Strength. Marshall Shelley. (Knowing God Ser.). 64p. 1994. 5.99 (*0-310-48341-7*) Zondervan.

***Our Practices, Our Selves or, What It Means to Be Human.** Todd May. LC 00-32367. 2001. write for info. (*0-271-02086-5*) Pa St U Pr.

Our Prairie Home: A Picture Album. Brooke Goffstein. LC 87-30795. (Charlotte Zolotow Bk.). (Illus.). 32p. (J). (ps up). 1988. 12.95 (*0-06-022290-5*) HarpC Child Bks.

Our Prayers Are in This Place: Centuries of Pecos Pueblo Identity. Frances Levine. LC 98-58039. 1999. 39.95 (*0-8263-2044-9*) U of NM Pr.

Our Precarious Habitat. 2nd rev. ed. Melvin A. Benarde. (Illus.). 384p. (C). 1973. pap. text 10.50 (*0-393-09372-7*) Norton.

Our Precarious Habitat. 2nd rev. ed. Melvin A. Benarde. (Illus.). 384p. 1973. 8.25 (*0-393-06360-7*) Norton.

Our Precarious Habitat: Fifteen Years Later. Melvin A. Benarde. LC 88-29158. 656p. 1989. 54.95 (*0-471-61750-4*) Wiley.

Our Precious Metal: African Labour in South Africa's Gold Industry, 1970-1990. Wilmot G. James. LC 91-28479. 204p. 1992. text 10.95 (*0-253-33092-0*) Ind U Pr.

***Our Preposterous Use of Literature: Emerson & the Nature of Reading.** T. S. McMillin. LC 99-6662. 2000. 32.50 (*0-252-02538-5*) U of Ill Pr.

Our Present Discontents. William R. Inge. LC 72-1343. (Essay Index Reprint Ser.). 1977. reprint ed. 23.95 (*0-8369-2846-6*) Ayer.

Our Presidency. Karen B. Spies. LC 94-7437. (I Know America Ser.). (Illus.). 48p. (J). (gr. 2-4). 1994. lib. bdg. 21.90 (*1-56294-444-4*) Millbrook Pr.

Our Presidency. Karen B. Spies. (I Know America Ser.). (Illus.). 48p. (J). (gr. 2-4). 1996. pap. 8.95 (*0-7613-0093-7*) Millbrook Pr.

Our Presidency. Karen Bornemann Spies. LC 94-7437. (I Know America Ser.). (J). 1994. 14.15 (*0-606-09725-2*, Pub. by Turtleback) Demco.

Our President: Bill Clinton. Shelly Bedik. 32p. (J). (gr. k-3). 1993. pap. 2.50 (*0-590-47126-0*) Scholastic Inc.

Our Presidents. (J). 1988. pap. 4.95 (*0-88388-140-3*) Bellerophon Bks.

Our Presidents. Ideals Publications Editors. (Illus.). 80p. 1994. 9.95 (*0-8249-1127-X*) Ideals.

Our Presidents: From George Washington to Ronald Reagan. rev. ed. Richard Armour. LC 82-23762. (Illus.). 96p. 1983. 9.95 (*0-88007-133-8*); pap. 5.95 (*0-88007-134-6*) Woodbridge Pr.

Our Presidents Vol. 1: Their Lives & Stories. Nancy Skarmeas. (United States & Its Flag Ser.: No. 2). (Illus.). 80p. (J). (gr. 4-8). 1998. lib. bdg. 16.95 (*1-56674-223-4*) Forest Hse.

Our Presidents & How We Make Them. Alexander K. McClure. LC 79-130559. (Select Bibliographies Reprint Ser.). 1977. reprint ed. 28.95 (*0-8369-5532-3*) Ayer.

Our Presidents & the White House. Illus. by TNT Stone & Associates & Petertil Design Partners. (Powertools for Kids Ser.: No. 14). 4p. (J). (gr. 2-5). 1998. pap., wbk. ed. 4.95 (*1-58220-013-0*, 32504, PowerTools for Kids) Navigator.

Our Press Gang: or a Complete Exposition of the Corruptions & Crimes of the American Newspapers. Lambert A. Wilmer. LC 73-125723. (American Journalists Ser.). 1971. reprint ed. 29.95 (*0-405-01706-5*) Ayer.

Our Priceless Heritage: Pennsylvania State Parks, 1893-1993. Dan Cupper. (Illus.). 90p. 1993. pap. 12.95 (*0-89271-056-X*, 0916) Pa Hist & Mus.

Our Pride: Pointe Coupee. Bernard Curet. Ed. by Doug Woolfolk. (Illus.). 112p. 1981. 20.00 (*0-86518-020-2*) Moran Pub Corp.

Our Priests: Who They Are & What They Do. Daniel E. Pilarczyk. LC 81-85454. (Illus.). 48p. (Orig.). (YA). 1995. pap. 1.50 (*0-87973-661-5*, 661) Our Sunday Visitor.

Our Principal Kissed a Pig. Dakos. (J). 2000. 17.00 (*0-689-81117-9*) S&S Childrens.

***Our Private CIA: A Study in Parapsychology.** James C. Brewer. 192p. 2000. pap. 11.95 (*1-891929-53-4*) Four Seasons.

Our Private Lives: Journals, Notebooks & Diaries. Daniel Halpern. LC 97-28772. 1998. pap. 17.00 (*0-88001-584-5*, Ecco Press) HarperTrade.

Our Profession: Present Status & Future Directions. Ed. by Thomas H. Geno. 1980. pap. 10.95 (*0-915432-80-3*) NE Conf Teach Foreign.

Our Promised Land. Ed. by Bob Hall. (Southern Exposure Ser.). (Illus.). 225p. (C). 1974. pap. 3.50 (*0-943810-03-5*) Inst Southern Studies.

Our Prophet Vol. 1: Life in Makkah. 4th ed. Abidullah Ghazi & Tasneema Ghazi. 43p. (J). (gr. 1-3). 1988. reprint ed. text 6.00 (*1-56316-150-8*) Iqra Intl Ed Fdtn.

Our Prophet Vol. 2: Life in Madinah. Abidullah Ghazi & Tasneema Ghazi. 32p. (J). (gr. 1-3). 1991. text 6.00 (*1-56316-152-4*) Iqra Intl Ed Fdtn.

Our Prophet Workbook Vol. 1: Life in Makkah. 4th ed. Bushra Y. Ghazi & Tasneema Ghazi. 28p. (J). (gr. 1-3). 1988. reprint ed. pap. 4.00 (*1-56316-151-6*) Iqra Intl Ed Fdtn.

Our Prophet Workbook Vol. 2: Life in Madinah. 4th ed. Bushra Y. Ghazi. 12p. (J). (gr. 1-3). 1988. reprint ed. pap. 4.00 (*1-56316-153-2*) Iqra Intl Ed Fdtn.

Our Proud Past, Vol. I. rev. ed. Gail J. McCormick. 186p. 1993. 18.95 (*0-9635889-1-5*) G McCormick Pub.

Our Psychic Sense: A Clairvoyant & a Psychiatrist Explain How it Develops. Phoebe D. Bendit & Laurence J. Bendit. LC 67-7911. 1967. pap. 5.75 (*0-8356-0034-3*, Quest) Theos Pub Hse.

***Our Public Schools: A Pearl of Great Price.** Frank Schneider. 167p. 2000. pap. 12.95 (*1-887650-19-9*, Pub. by Factor Pr) BookWorld.

Our Pumpkin see Nuestra Calabaza

Our Pumpkin, Vol. 3711. Renee Keeler. (Emergent Reader Bks.). (Illus.). 8p. (J). (gr. k-2). 1995. pap. 1.75 (*1-57471-002-8*) Creat Teach Pr.

Our Pumpkin, Vol. 3768. Renee Keeler. (Emergent Reader Big Bks.). (Illus.). 8p. (J). (gr. k-2). 1996. pap. 8.98 (*1-57471-106-7*) Creat Teach Pr.

Our Puppies Are Growing. Carolyn Otto. LC 97-27697. (Let's-Read-&-Find-Out Science Ser.). (Illus.). 32p. (J). (ps-1). 1998. 15.95 (*0-06-027271-6*); lib. bdg. 15.89 (*0-06-027272-4*) HarpC.

Our Puppies Are Growing. Carolyn Otto. (Let's Read-&-Find-Out Science Ser.). (J). 1998. 10.15 (*0-606-13684-3*, Pub. by Turtleback) Demco.

Our Puppies Are Growing. Crolyn Otto. LC 97-27697. (Let's-Read-&-Find-Out Science Ser.). (Illus.). 32p. (J). (ps-1). 1998. pap. 4.95 (*0-06-445169-0*) HarpC.

Our Puppy's Baby Book: Pink for Girl Dogs. Robert Pilgrim. (Illus.). 32p. 1961. per. 11.95 (*0-87605-773-3*) Howell Bks.

Our Puppy's Baby Book (BLUE) Blue for Boy Dogs. Robert Pilgrim. (Illus.). 32p. 1961. per. 11.95 (*0-87605-772-5*) Howell Bks.

Our Purpose Is to Serve: The First Century of the North Dakota Agricultural Experiment Station. David B. Danbom. LC 89-63044. (Illus.). 225p. 1990. 24.00 (*0-911042-38-5*) NDSU Inst Reg.

Our Quaker Ancestors: Finding Them in Quaker Records. Ellen Berry & David Berry. 136p. 1996. reprint ed. 19.95 (*0-8063-1190-8*, 483) Genealog Pub.

Our Quaker Friends of Ye Olden Time. J. P. Bell. (Illus.). viii, 287p. 1997. reprint ed. pap. 23.50 (*0-7884-0723-6*, B148) Heritage Bk.

Our Quaker Heritage. Kenneth H. Southall. (Illus.). 82p. (C). 1989. (*0-85245-109-1*); pap. (*0-85245-110-5*) Friends Bk Centre.

Our Rabbis Taught - Tanu Rabbanan: Essays in Commemoration of the Centennial of the Central Conference of American Rabbis. Ed. by Joseph B. Glaser. 155p. 1990. 17.50 (*0-88123-012-X*) Central Conf.

Our Race Problems. Henry F. Suksdorf. LC 77-89433. (Black Heritage Library Collection). 1977. 18.95 (*0-8369-8662-8*) Ayer.

Our Racist Legacy: Will the Church Resolve the Conflict? Ivan A. Beals. LC 96-85046. (Church & the World Ser.: Vol. 9). 350p. (Orig.). 1996. pap. 21.95 (*0-940121-36-0*, P307) Cross Cultural Pubns.

Our Radiant World. David W. Lillie. (Illus.). 240p. 1987. pap. 13.95 (*0-8306-2851-7*) McGraw-Hill Prof.

Our Radiant World. David W. Lillie. LC 86-15344. 238p. 1986. reprint ed. pap. 73.80 (*0-608-00048-5*, 206081400006) Bks Demand.

Our Rainforests & the Issues. E. Morris & T. Sadler. (Illus.). 54p. (J). (gr. 6-11). 1992. pap. 16.95 (*0-643-05141-4*, Pub. by CSIRO) Accents Pubns.

***Our Raspberry Jam.** Illus. by David F. Marx & Paul Michalak. LC 99-88534. (Rookie Readers Ser.). (J). 2000. 18.00 (*0-516-22174-4*) Childrens.

***Our Readers' Book of Helpful Hints: Over 100 Useful Tips for Horsefolks.** Half Halt Press Staff. (Illus.). 64p. 1999. pap. 5.95 (*0-939481-55-3*) Half Halt Pr.

Our Red Brothers & the Peace Policy of President Ulysses S. Grant. Lawrie Tatum. LC 77-88093. 388p. 1970. reprint ed. pap. 120.30 (*0-608-03467-3*, 206417500008) Bks Demand.

Our Reformed Church Service Book. G. Van Rongen. LC 95-31942. 250p. (Orig.). 1995. pap. 13.90 (*0-921100-52-3*) Inhtce Pubns.

Our Rejected Children. Albert Deutsch. LC 74-1680. (Children & Youth Ser.: Vol. 29). 316p. 1974. reprint ed. 25.95 (*0-405-05958-2*) Ayer.

Our Relay Race: A Compilation of Selected Articles & Speeches. Joy Cherian. LC 96-41458. 192p. 1996. lib. bdg. 36.50 (*0-7618-0531-1*) U Pr of Amer.

Our Religion Is Islam Coloring Book. unabridged ed. Labiba Hassan & Tasneema Ghazi. (Illus.). 92p. (J). (ps-k). 1995. pap. 6.00 (*1-56316-059-5*) Iqra Intl Ed Fdtn.

Our Religions: The Seven World Religions Introduced by Preeminent Scholars from Each Tradition. Ed. by Arvind Sharma. LC 92-56128. 560p. 1994. pap. 21.00 (*0-06-067700-7*, Pub. by Harper SF) HarpC.

Our Responses to a Deadly Virus: The Group-Analytic Approach. Angela Molnos. 220p. 1990. pap. text 15.00 (*0-946439-80-X*, Pub. by H Karnac Bks Ltd) Other Pr LLC.

Our Restless Earth: The Geologic Regions of Tennessee. Edward T. Luther. LC 77-21433. (Tennessee Three Star Ser.). (Illus.). 106p. 1977. pap. 7.00 (*0-87049-230-6*) U of Tenn Pr.

Our Revelationary Age. Helen T. Otto. Ed. by Gene Myers & Jim Meyers. 576p. 1993. text 39.95 (*1-884332-08-0*); pap. text 29.95 (*1-884332-09-9*) Netwrk Pr TX.

Our Revelationary Age: The Prophecies for WWIII & the Year 2000. Helen T. Otto. LC 94-60322. 526p. (Orig.). 1994. 34.00 (*0-9639553-0-6*); pap. 20.00 (*0-9639553-1-4*) Verenikia Pr.

Our Revolution. Victor S. Yarros. 1975. 75.00 (*0-8490-0785-2*) Gordon Pr.

Our Revolutionary Forefathers: The Letters of Francois, Marquis De Barbe-Marbois During His Residence in the United States As Secretary of the French Legation 1779-1785. Francois Barbe-Marbois. LC 71-99659. (Select Bibliographies Reprint Ser.). 1977. 25.95 (*0-8369-5088-7*) Ayer.

Our Riches in Christ: Discovering the Believer's Inheritance in Ephesians. Ray C. Stedman. LC 98-7250. 416p. (Orig.). 1998. pap. 14.99 (*1-57293-033-0*) Discovery Hse Pubs.

Our Right to Drugs: The Case for a Free Market. Thomas Szasz. LC 91-30378. 232p. 1992. 24.95 (*0-275-94216-3*, C4216, Praeger Pubs) Greenwood.

Our Right to Drugs: The Case for a Free Market. Thomas Szasz. LC 95-46515. 229p. (C). 1996. pap. 19.95 (*0-8156-0333-9*, SZORP) Syracuse U Pr.

Our Rightful Share: The Afro-Cuban Struggle for Equality, 1886-1912. Aline Helg. LC 94-27196. (Illus.). 375p. 1995. pap. text 19.95 (*0-8078-4494-2*); lib. bdg. 45.00 (*0-8078-2184-5*) U of NC Pr.

Our Rights: Civil Liberties in the U. S. rev. ed. Reginald Wilson. (Think Ser.). 160p. (YA). (gr. 7 up). 1993. pap. 9.95 (*0-8027-7371-0*); lib. bdg. 15.85 (*0-8027-8127-6*) Walker & Co.

Our Rival, the Rascal: A Faithful Portrayal of the Conflict Between the Criminals of This Age & the Defenders of Society, the Police. Benjamin P. Eldridge & William B. Watts. LC 79-172578. (Criminology, Law Enforcement, & Social Problems Ser.: No. 166). (Illus.). 1973. reprint ed. 25.00 (*0-87585-166-5*) Patterson Smith.

***Our Rock Who Art in Heaven, Hallowed Be Thy Name.** Jacqueline Brook. (Illus.). 592p. 1999. per. 18.00 (*0-9676656-0-4*) Sinclair Pr.

Our Rocky Mountain Homestead. Douglas Furgitt & Roxane Christensen. (Illus.). 208p. 1993. pap. 11.95 (*0-9617159-2-8*) Willow Pr.

Our Roots Grow Deeper Than We Know: Pennsylvania Writers/Pennsylvania Life. Ed. by Lee Gutkind. LC 85-40338. 306p. 1985. reprint ed. pap. 94.90 (*0-608-00906-7*, 206170000010) Bks Demand.

Our Roots of Faith, Vol. 1. Paul E. Corn. LC 99-94768. xiv, 255p. 1999. pap. 14.00 (*0-9672208-0-7*, 47671) Key Projects.

Our Sacred Gifts: An Ojibwe Perspective in the Preparation of Parenthood; An Ojibwe Perspective on Embryo & Fetal Development; An Ojibwe Perspective on Infant Development; An Ojibwe Perspective on Toddlerhood, 4 vols., Set. Phyllis W. Grough. 1990. 75.00 (*1-881949-02-8*) MN Ind Wom Res.

Our Sacred Honor. Morton L. Kurland. Ed. by Ruth C. Rosen. (Flipside Fiction Ser.). 196p. (YA). (gr. 7-12). 1987. lib. bdg. 12.95 (*0-8239-0692-2*) Rosen Group.

Our Sacred Honor: Words of Advice from the Founders in Stories, Letters, Poems & Speeches. William J. Bennett. LC 97-33047. (Illus.). 384p. 1997. 24.50 (*0-684-84138-X*) S&S Trade.

Our Sacred Honor: Words of Advice from the Founders in Stories, Letters, Poems, & Speeches. Ed. by William J. Bennett. LC 97-29467. (Illus.). 320p. 1997. 14.99 (*0-8054-0153-9*) Broadman.

***Our Sacred Honor: Words of Advice from the Founders in Stories, Letters, Poems & Speeches.** Ed. by William J. Bennett. 430p. 2000. reprint ed. text 25.00 (*0-7881-6487-2*) DIANE Pub.

Our Sacred Identity: The Book of American Indian Names & Their Meanings. Ed. by Montez DeCarlo & Teresa Cunningham. (Illus.). 95p. (Orig.). (YA). (gr. 10 up). 1995. pap. 12.95 (*0-9648416-0-6*) Nat Exper.

Our Sacred Texts: Discovering the Jewish Classics. Ellen Singer. LC 92-16438. (J). (gr. 4-6). 1992. pap. 10.00 (*0-8074-0479-9*, 123936) UAHC.

Our Sacred Texts: Discovering the Jewish Classics. Ellen Singer. LC 92-16438. (J). (gr. 4-6). 1992. pap., teacher ed. 5.00 (*0-8074-0481-0*, 208031) UAHC.

Our Sages Showed the Way, Vol. 1. Yocheved Segal. Tr. by Esther Falk. (Jewish Youth Classics Ser.). (ENG.). 13.95 (*0-87306-289-2*) Feldheim.

Our Sages Showed the Way, Vol. 2. Yocheved Segal. Tr. by Esther Falk from HEB. (Jewish Youth Classics Ser.). (Illus.). 192p. 1982. text 13.95 (*0-87306-260-4*) Feldheim.

Our Sages Showed the Way, Vol. 3. Yocheved Segal. (Jewish Youth Classics Ser.). 13.95 (*0-87306-374-0*) Feldheim.

Our Sages Showed the Way, Vol. 4. Yocheved Segal. (Jewish Youth Classics Ser.). (J). (gr. 4-7). 1988. 13.95 (*0-87306-452-6*) Feldheim.

Our Saints among Us: 400 Years of New Mexican Devotional Art. Barbe Awalt & Paul Rhetts. LC 97-71662.Tr. of Nuestros Santos entre Nosotros. (Illus.). 120p. 1997. 59.95 (*0-9641542-2-6*); pap. 44.95 (*0-9641542-8-5*) LPD Pr.

Our Satellite: The Moon. Robert Estalella. LC 93-19897. (Window on the Universe Ser.).Tr. of Nuestro Satelite - la Luna. (Illus.). 32p. (J). (gr. 4-8). 1994. 12.95 (*0-8120-6369-4*) Barron.

Our Satellite, the Moon. Robert Estalella. LC 93-19879. (Window on the Universe Ser.). 1994. 12.15 (*0-606-06651-9*, Pub. by Turtleback) Demco.

Our Savior Is Born. Dan Carr. 24p. (J). (gr. 1 up). 1984. 8.99 (*0-570-04092-2*, 56-1460) Concordia.

Our Savior's Lutheran History, 1867-1992. Ardis B. Folstad. LC 57-9745. (Illus.). 46p. (Orig.). 1993. pap. write for info. (*0-9618318-1-2*) Folstad & Co.

***Our Saviour & His Love for Us.** Reginald Garrigou-Lagrange. Tr. by A. Bouchard from FRE. LC 98-61397. Orig. Title: Le Sauveur et Son Amour pour Nous. 398p. 1999. reprint ed. pap. 18.50 (*0-89555-635-9*, 1575) TAN Bks Pubs.

Our Saviour Has Arrived. Elijah Muhammad. 238p. 1996. reprint ed. pap. 9.95 (*1-884855-17-2*) Secretarius.

Our Saviour Has Arrived. Elijah Muhammad. 226p. 1990. reprint ed. pap. 11.95 (*1-56411-021-4*) Untd Bros & Sis.

Our Scene. Wilma Kaufman. 1998. mass mkt. 6.95 (*1-56333-682-0*) Masquerade.

Our Schools: What Happened? How to Fix Them. Stella Crawford & Phillip L. Vandivier. 236p. 1998. pap. 26.50 (*1-57502-693-7*, PO1958) Morris Pubng.

Our Schools - Frontline for the Twenty-First Century: What Our Schools Must Become. Mary B. Lane. Ed. by Quentin Baker. LC 98-84765. (Illus.). 140p. 1998. pap. 11.95 (*0-9663364-0-2*) Q Trips.

Our Scientific Heritage: An A-Z of Great Britain & Ireland. Trevor I. Williams. LC 97-140817. (Illus.). 256p. 1996. 38.95 (*0-7509-0820-3*, Pub. by Sutton Pub Ltd) Intl Pubs Mktg.

Our Seabed Frontier: Challenges & Choices. National Research Council Staff. 150p. 1989. pap. text 17.00 (*0-309-04126-0*) Natl Acad Pr.

Our Search for Happiness: An Invitation to Understand the Church of Jesus Christ of Latter-Day Saints. M. Russell Ballard. LC 93-29353. 124p. 1993. 11.95 (*0-87579-804-7*) Deseret Bk.

Our Search for Happiness: An Invitation to Understand the Church of Jesus Christ of Latter-Day Saints. M. Russell Ballard. LC 93-29353. 124p. 1995. pap. 6.95 (*0-87579-917-5*) Deseret Bk.

Our Search for Yesterday. Ginger McLaughlin. 180p. 1984. pap. 8.95 (*0-89697-154-6*) Intl Univ Pr.

Our Seas. Anne I. Rockwell. LC 98-27797. (J). 2001. 20.01 (*0-15-202023-3*) Harcourt.

Our Secret Feelings: Activities for Children of Alcoholics in Support Groups. Deborah S. Molchan. 58p. (Orig.). 1989. pap. 10.95 (*1-55691-020-7*, 207) Learning Pubns.

Our Secret Little War. 87p. 1991. 15.00 (*0-944426-47-6*) ASP & RS.

Our Secret Love. Miranda Harry. (Love Stories Ser.). 192p. (YA). (gr. 7-12). 1998. mass mkt. 3.99 (*0-553-48592-X*) BDD Bks Young Read.

Our Secrets. Chuck Weiler. 208p. 1998. mass mkt. 6.99 (*0-9665386-0-9*) Ours.

Our Secret's Out: Stories. Darrell Spencer. 176p. 1993. 24.95 (*0-8262-0927-0*) U of Mo Pr.

Our Selves: New Poems. William Bronk. LC 94-22917. 108p. 1994. pap. 10.95 (*1-883689-14-7*); lib. bdg. 30.95 (*1-883689-15-5*) Talisman Hse.

Our Selves, Our Souls & Bodies: Sexuality & the Household of God. Ed. by Charles C. Hefling. LC 96-8069. 213p. 1996. pap. 12.95 (*1-56101-122-3*) Cowley Pubns.

***Our Sense of The Real: Aesthetic Experience & Arendtian Politics.** Kimberly Curtis. LC 99-31256. 1999. pap. text 16.95 (*0-8014-8640-8*) Cornell U Pr.

Our Separate Darkness. Sy Kahn. 1968. 10.00 (*0-686-20735-1*) Sydon.

Our Separate Days. Sharyn McCrumb & Mona W. Helper. LC 89-10584. (Illus.). 114p. (Orig.). 1989. reprint ed. pap. 9.95 (*0-926487-01-9*) Rowan Mtn Pr.

Our Seven Principles in Story & Verse: A Collection for Children & Adults. Kenneth W. Collier. LC 97-161440. 120p. 1997. pap. 12.00 (*1-55896-353-7*, Skinner Hse Bks) Unitarian Univ.

Our Seventeen Years. Patricia Wellingham-Jones. 28p. (Orig.). 1996. pap. 3.50 (*0-939221-11-X*) Wellingham-Jones.

Our Sexuality. Crooks. (Adaptable Courseware Ser.). 1997. 36.25 (*0-534-49830-2*) Brooks-Cole.

Our Sexuality. 5th ed. Robert Crooks. (Health Sciences Ser.). 1993. text 41.00 (*0-534-33939-5*) Brooks-Cole.

Our Sexuality. 5th ed. Robert Crooks & Karla Baur. LC 92-23485. (C). 1993. text 49.50 (*0-8053-0212-3*) Benjamin-Cummings.

Our Sexuality. 6th ed. Robert Crooks. (Health Sciences Ser.). 1995. pap., student ed. 18.25 (*0-534-32096-1*) Brooks-Cole.

Our Sexuality. 6th ed. Robert Crooks & Karla Baur. LC 95-31922. 680p. 1995. pap. 47.50 (*0-534-32094-5*) Brooks-Cole.

O

Our Sexuality. 6th ed. Robert Crooks & Karla Baur. 1995. pap., teacher ed. write for info. (*0-534-34044-X*) Brooks-Cole.

Our Sexuality. 7th ed. Crooks. (Psychology Ser.). 1998. pap. 29.95 (*0-534-36237-0*); pap., student ed. 20.50 (*0-534-35988-4*) Brooks-Cole.

Our Sexuality. 7th ed. Crooks. LC 98-26371. (Health Sciences Ser.). (C). 1998. pap. 46.00 (*0-534-35467-X*) Brooks-Cole.

Our Sexuality. 7th ed. Crooks & Baur. (Psychology Ser.). 1999. pap. text 31.00 (*0-534-76789-3*) Wadsworth Pub.

***Our Sexuality.** 8th ed. Crooks & Baur. (Psychology Ser.). 2001. 52.00 (*0-534-57978-7*) Wadsworth Pub.

Our Sexuality: Study Guide. 5th ed. Robert Crooks. (Health Sciences Ser.). 1993. pap., student ed. 17.95 (*0-534-33943-3*) Brooks-Cole.

Our Sexuality: Test Items. 6th ed. Robert Crooks & Karla Baur. 1995. pap. write for info. (*0-534-32097-X*) Brooks-Cole.

Our Sexuality with InfoTrac. 7th ed. Crooks. (Psychology Ser.). 1998. pap. 46.75 incl. cd-rom (*0-534-36335-0*) Brooks-Cole.

***Our Sexy God.** deluxe ed. Ed. by Jon Ford. 80p. 2001. pap. 19.95 (*0-9700165-4-9*) Twin Rivers NC.

Our Share of Night. Nancy Fuchs. 183p. 1999. pap. 18.00 (*0-06-251285-4*) Harper SF.

Our Share of Night, Our Share of Morning see Parenting As a Spiritual Journey: Deepening Ordinary & Extraordinary Events into Sacred Occasions

Our Share of Night, Our Share of Morning: Parenting As a Spiritual Journey. Nancy Fuchs. 1996. 18.00 (*0-614-95740-0*) Harper SF.

Our Share of Time. Yves Navarre. Tr. by Dominic Di Bernardi & Noelle Domke from FRE. LC 86-72136. Orig. Title: Le Temps Uoulu. 240p. 1988. reprint ed. pap. 12.50 (*0-916583-28-7*) Dalkey Arch.

Our Short Story Writers. Blanche C. Williams. 384p. 1977. 22.95 (*0-8369-1164-4*) Ayer.

***Our Singing Country: Folk Songs & Ballads.** J. Lomax & A. Lomax. (J). 2000. pap. 14.95 (*0-486-41089-7*) Dover.

Our Singing Strength: An Outline of American Poetry (1620-1930) Alfred Kreymborg. LC 78-64040. (Des Imagistes: Literature of the Imagist Movement Ser.). reprint ed. 45.00 (*0-404-17123-0*) AMS Pr.

Our Singing Strength: An Outline of American Poetry (1620-1930) Alfred Kreymborg. (BCL1-PS American Literature Ser.). 643p. 1992. reprint ed. lib. bdg. 109.00 (*0-7812-6628-9*) Rprt Serv.

Our Singular Strengths: Meditations for Librarians. Michael Gorman. LC 97-34547. 196p. 1997. 20.00 (*0-8389-0724-5*) ALA.

Our Sister Editors: Sarah J. Hale & the Tradition of Nineteenth-Century American Women Editors. Patricia Okker. LC 94-15269. (Illus.). 280p. 1995. 40.00 (*0-8203-1686-5*) U of Ga Pr.

Our Sister Killjoy. Ama Ata Aidoo. LC 78-64625. 1979. 9.95 (*0-88357-064-5*); pap. 4.95 (*0-88357-065-3*) NOK Pubs.

Our Sister Killjoy: Longman African Writers. Ama Ata Aidoo. 134p. (C). 1997. pap. 14.86 (*0-582-30845-3*) Longman.

Our Sisters' Land: The Changing Identity of Women in Wales. Ed. by Jane Aaron et al. (Illus.). 312p. 1994. pap. 24.95 (*0-7083-1247-0*, Pub. by Univ Wales Pr) Paul & Co Pubs.

Our Sisters' Promised Land: Women, Politics, & Israeli-Palestinian Coexistence. Ayala H. Emmett. LC 96-9949. 288p. (C). 1996. text 37.50 (*0-472-10733-X*, 10733) U of Mich Pr.

Our Sixth-Grade Sugar Babies. Eve Bunting. LC 90-5487. (Trophy Bk.). 160p. (J). (gr. 4-7). 1992. pap. 4.95 (*0-06-440390-4*, HarpTrophy) HarpC Child Bks.

Our Sixth-Grade Sugar Babies. Eve Bunting. (J). 1992. 10.05 (*0-606-06150-9*, Pub. by Turtleback) Demco.

Our 6 Grade Sugar Baby. Eve Bunting. LC 90-5487. 160p. (J). (gr. 4-6). 1990. lib. bdg. 13.89 (*0-397-32452-9*) HarpC Child Bks.

Our Slavic Fellow Citizens. Emily G. Balch. LC 69-18758. (American Immigration Collection. Series 1). (Illus.). 1969. reprint ed. 29.95 (*0-405-00506-7*) Ayer.

***Our Snowbear Scrapbook.** Elizabeth Thalhimer. (Illus.). 60p. 2000. write for info. (*0-87517-111-7*) Dietz.

Our Snowman. M. Brooke Goffstein. LC 85-45836. (Charlotte Zolotow Bk.). (Illus.). 32p. (J). (ps up). 1986. 12.95 (*0-06-022152-6*) HarpC Child Bks.

Our Social & Sexual Revolution: Major Issues for a New Century. 3rd rev. ed. John R. W. Stott. 256p. 1999. pap. 14.99 (*0-8010-6113-X*) Baker Bks.

Our Social Heritage. Graham Wallas. LC 73-37916. (Select Bibliographies Reprint Ser.). 1977. reprint ed. 23.95 (*0-8369-6753-4*) Ayer.

Our Social World. 2nd ed. Donelson S. Forsyth. LC 94-11001. 1994. pap. 63.95 (*0-534-24516-1*) Brooks-Cole.

Our Social World: An Introduction to Sociology. Ed. by Jeanne H. Ballantine. (C). 1998. text. write for info. (*0-321-01179-1*) Addson-Wesley Educ.

Our Soils & Their Management. 6th ed. Roy L. Donahue et al. LC 82-82462. 608p. 1990. 56.25 (*0-8134-2848-3*); teacher ed. 14.95 (*0-8134-2890-4*) Interstate.

Our Solar System. (Jump Ser.). 36p. (J). (gr. 2-7). pap. write for info. (*1-882210-23-9*) Action Pub.

Our Solar System. 1997. 4.95 (*1-55708-578-1*, MCR758) McDonald Pub Co.

***Our Solar System, 6 vols.** Incl. Comets & Meteors. (Illus.). 48p. (J). (gr. 2-6). 2000. lib. bdg. 22.60 (*1-929298-63-3*, Pub. by Thameside Pr); Earth & Moon. (Illus.). 48p. (J). (gr. 2-6). 2000. lib. bdg. 22.60 (*1-929298-64-1*, Pub. by Thameside Pr); Far Planets. (Illus.). 48p. (J). (gr. 2-6). 2000. lib. bdg. 22.60 (*1-929298-65-X*, Pub. by Thameside Pr); Giant Planets. (Illus.). 48p. (J). (gr. 2-6). 2000. lib. bdg. 22.60 (*1-929298-66-8*, Pub. by Thameside Pr); Near Planets. (Illus.). 48p. (J). (gr. 2-6). 2000. lib. bdg. 22.60 (*1-929298-67-6*, Pub. by Thameside Pr); Sun. (Illus.). 48p. (J). (gr. 2-6). 2000. lib. bdg. 22.60 (*1-929298-68-4*, Pub. by Thameside Pr); (Illus.). 48p. (J). (gr. 2-6). 2000. Set lib. bdg. 135.60 (*1-929298-69-2*, Pub. by Thameside Pr) Smart Apple.

Our Solar System. Amanda Davis. LC 96-53488. (Exploring Space Ser.). (Illus.). 24p. (J). (gr. k-4). 1997. lib. bdg. 18.00 (*0-8239-5060-3*, PowerKids) Rosen Group.

Our Solar System. Fred Justus. (Science Ser.). 24p. (gr. 7). 1979. student ed. 5.00 (*0-8209-0145-8*, S-7) ESP.

Our Solar System. Jon Kirkwood. LC 98-29356. (Look into Space Ser.). 40p. (J). (gr. 4 up). 1998. lib. bdg. 22.90 (*0-7613-0864-4*, Copper Beech Bks) Millbrook Pr.

Our Solar System. Grace Maccarone. LC 95-36015. (Hello Reader! Ser.: Level 1). (Illus.). (J). 1997. pap. 3.50 (*0-590-73879-8*) Scholastic Inc.

Our Solar System. Moore & Jepson. (Illus.). 32p. (J). (gr. 2-3). 1996. pap., teacher ed. 2.95 (*1-55799-510-9*, 4112) Evan-Moor Edu Pubs.

Our Solar System. Jo Ellen Moore. Ed. by Marilyn Evans. (Science Ser.). (Illus.). 33p. (J). (gr. 2-3). Date not set. pap., wbk. ed. 3.50 (*1-58610-119-6*) Learn Horizon.

Our Solar System. Simon Seymour. LC 91-36665. (Illus.). 64p. (J). (gr. k). 1992. 20.00 (*0-688-09992-0*, Wm Morrow) Morrow Avon.

Our Solar System. Seymour Simon. LC 91-36665. (Illus.). 64p. (J). (gr. k). 1992. 19.93 (*0-688-09993-9*, Wm Morrow) Morrow Avon.

Our Solar System. rev. ed. Peter Riley et al. LC 98-65328. (Windows on Science Ser.). (Illus.). 16p. (J). (gr. 4-6). 1998. 12.99 (*1-57584-244-0*, Pub. by Rdrs Digest) Random.

Our Solar System: Easy Readers Science. Cindy Barden. (Easy Readers Ser.). 16p. (J). (ps-1). 1997. pap. 2.49 (*1-57690-280-3*) Tchr Create Mat.

Our Solar System & It's Planets. Ed. by Phyllis Pitluga. (Powertools for Kids Ser.: No. 12). (Illus.). 4p. (J). (gr. 3-7). 1998. pap., wbk. ed. 4.95 (*1-58220-011-4*, 32502, PowerTools for Kids) Navigator.

Our Sometime Sister. Norah Labiner. LC 97-43268. 452p. 1998. 21.95 (*1-56689-072-1*) Coffee Hse.

***Our Sometime Sister.** Norah Labiner. 442p. 2000. pap. 15.95 (*1-56689-095-0*) Coffee Hse.

Our Song, Our Toil: The Story of American Slavery As Told by Slaves. Ed. by Michele Stepto. LC 93-8323. (Illus.). 96p. (J). (gr. 4-6). 1994. lib. bdg. 25.90 (*1-56294-401-0*) Millbrook Pr.

Our Song Shall Rise to Thee. Contrib. by Carol Foss. 68p. 1992. 15.99 (*0-8341-9318-3*, MB-640) Lillenas.

***Our Sons Were Labeled Behavior Disordered: Here Are the Stories of Our Lives.** Joy-Ruth Mickelson. LC 99-58211. 224p. 2000. 48.00 (*1-891928-06-6*); pap. 23.95 (*1-891928-05-8*) Educ Intl Pr.

Our Souls to Keep: Black/ White Relations in America. George Henderson. LC 98-29811. 269p. 1999. pap. 19.95 (*1-877864-65-X*) Intercult Pr.

Our Southern Heritage: A Collection of Recipes from the Friends & Family of the Heritage School. Heritage School Staff. Ed. by Linda Mitchell & Leigh Kingman. (Illus.). 416p. 1994. 15.95 (*0-9641692-0-7*) Heritage Schl.

Our Southern Highlanders. Horace Kephart. LC 76-18903. (Illus.). 530p. 1976. reprint ed. pap. 16.95 (*0-87049-203-9*) U of Tenn Pr.

Our Southern Zion: A History of Calvanism in the South Carolina Low Country, 1690-1990. Erskine Clarke. LC 95-8150. (FRE & LAT., Illus.). 448p. (C). 1996. text 44.95 (*0-8173-0757-5*) U of Ala Pr.

Our Space Program. Carmen Bredeson. LC 98-21693. (I Know America Ser.). (Illus.). 48p. (J). (gr. 2-4). 1999. 20.90 (*0-7613-0952-7*, Copper Beech Bks) Millbrook Pr.

***Our Space Program.** Carmen Bredeson. (I Know America Ser.). (Illus.). 48p. (J). (gr. 2-4). 2000. pap. text 8.95 (*0-7613-1349-4*, Copper Beech Bks) Millbrook Pr.

***Our Space Program.** Carmen Bredeson. (I Know America Ser.). (Illus.). (J). 2000. 14.40 (*0-606-18292-6*) Turtleback.

Our Spark of Hope. Kevin Peterson. 168p. (Orig.). 1989. 18.00 (*0-944996-05-1*); pap. text 9.95 (*0-944996-04-3*) Carlsons.

Our Special Artist: Alfred R. Waud's Civil War. Frederic E. Ray. (Illus.). 192p. 1994. 22.95 (*0-8117-1194-3*) Stackpole.

Our Special Blend: A Cookbook. Easter Seal Auxiliary of Eastern Fairfield County. Ed. by Louise C. Thoman. LC 83-73727. (Illus.). 461p. 1984. 13.95 (*0-9613209-0-7*) Easter Rehabilitation Inc.

Our Special Dad: An Interactive Storybook about Mental Illness. Tootsie Sobkiewicz. (Illus.). 25p. (Orig.). (J). (gr. 1-6). 1996. pap. text 7.50 (*0-9644085-1-1*) Chldrn Mentally Ill.

Our Special Mom: An Interactive Storybook about Mental Illness. Tootsie Sobkiewicz. (Illus.). 25p. (Orig.). (J). (gr. 1-6). 1994. pap. text 7.50 (*0-9644085-0-3*) Chldrn Mentally Ill.

Our Spiritual Connection. James T. Greene & Martha Barham. LC 94-69486. 104p. (Orig.). 1995. pap. 7.95 (*0-87516-677-6*) DeVorss.

Our Spiritual Resources Vol. 4: The Life of Spirit. Robert R. Leichtman & Carl Japikse. (Illus.). 216p. (Orig.). 1997. pap. 10.95 (*0-89804-135-X*) Ariel GA.

Our Spiritual Wake-Up Calls. Harold Klemp. LC 97-30917. 244p. 1998. 14.00 (*1-57043-135-3*) Eckankar.

Our Square & the People in It. Samuel H. Adams. LC 78-106241. (Short Story Index Reprint Ser.). 1977. 25.95 (*0-8369-3277-3*) Ayer.

Our Stagflation Malaise: Halting Inflation & Unemployment. Sidney Weintraub. LC 80-39658. 214p. 1981. 49.95 (*0-89930-005-7*, WCA/, Quorum Bks) Greenwood.

Our Star: The Sun. Robert Estalella. LC 93-18067. (Window on the Universe Ser.). (Illus.). 32p. (J). (gr. 4-7). 1993. 12.95 (*0-8120-6370-8*) Barron.

Our Star: The Sun. Robert Estalella. (Window on the Universe Ser.). 1993. 12.15 (*0-606-05967-9*, Pub. by Turtleback) Demco.

Our Stars. Anne Rockwell. LC 97-49518. (Illus.). 24p. (J). 1999. 13.00 (*0-15-201868-9*) Harcourt.

Our Stars of Destiny. Faith Javane. LC 89-50409. 256p. 1989. pap. 14.95 (*0-914918-92-3*, Whitford) Schiffer.

***Our State Fair: Iowa's Blue Ribbon Story.** Mary Kay Shanley. LC 00-9331. (Illus.). 2000. write for info. (*1-888223-17-0*) Sigler Print.

Our State of Mind: Racial Planning & the Stolen Generations. Quentin Beresford & Paul Omaji. 296p. 1998. pap. 19.95 (*1-86368-235-X*, Pub. by Fremantle Arts) Intl Spec Bk.

Our Statue of Liberty. (Illus.). (J). (ps-2). 1991. pap. 5.10 (*0-8136-5960-4*); lib. bdg. 7.95 (*0-8136-5202-2*) Modern Curr.

Our Stolen Future. Theo Colburn et al. LC 97-159794. 1997. pap. 13.95 (*0-452-27414-1*, Plume) Dutton Plume.

Our Storehouse of Missouri Place Names. Robert L. Ramsay. LC 73-79512. 160p. 1973. pap. 10.95 (*0-8262-0586-0*) U of Mo Pr.

Our Stories: A Fiction Workshop for Young Authors. Compiled by Marion Dane Bauer. 208p. (J). (gr. 5). 1996. pap. 6.95 (*0-395-81599-1*) HM.

Our Stories: A Fiction Workshop for Young Authors. Marion Dane Bauer. 208p. (YA). 1996. 14.95 (*0-395-81598-3*, Pub. by Ticknor & Fields) HM.

Our Stories of Miscarriage: Healing with Words. Rachel Faldet & Karen Fitton. LC 96-35348. 224p. 1997. pap. 13.95 (*1-57749-033-9*) Fairview Press.

Our Stories, Our Lives. Alexandra J. McClanahan. (Illus.). 243p. (Orig.). 1986. pap. 15.95 (*0-938227-01-7*) CIRI Found.

***Our Story: A Grandparent's Record Book.** Reader's Digest Association Staff. 2000. pap. 24.95 (*0-7621-0303-5*, Pub. by RD Assn) Penguin Putnam.

Our Story According to St. Mark. William Hazzard Barnwell. 288p. (Orig.). (C). 1982. 9.95 (*0-86683-634-9*) Harper SF.

Our Story of Atlantis. W. P. Phelon. 242p. 1972. 9.95 (*0-932785-36-0*) Philos Pub.

***Our Strange New Land: Elizabeth's Diary, Jamestown, Virginia, 1609.** Patricia Hermes. LC 99-56356. (My America Ser.). (Illus.). 112p. (J). (gr. 2-5). 2000. 8.95 (*0-439-11208-7*) Scholastic Inc.

Our Struggle. Sutan Sjahrir. LC 77-2791. (Cornell University, Modern Indonesia Project, Monograph Ser.). 43p. reprint ed. pap. 30.00 (*0-608-16503-4*, 202722600054) Bks Demand.

Our Struggle for the Fourteenth Colony: Canada & the American Revolution, 2 vols. Justin Smith. LC 74-12272. (Era of the American Revolution Ser.). 1273p. 1974. reprint ed. lib. bdg. 115.00 (*0-306-70633-4*) Da Capo.

Our Stuff - A Literary Sampler: An Approach to Creative Writing from the Classroom. Ed. by Mary A. Luetkemeyer. (Illus.). 113p. 1998. 12.95 (*1-882935-33-0*) Westphalia.

***Our Sufficiency in Christ.** (RUS.). 288p. 2000. pap. write for info. (*1-56773-004-3*) Slavic Gospel.

Our Sufficiency in Christ. John MacArthur. LC 98-20910. 1998. 12.99 (*1-58134-013-3*) Crossway Bks.

Our Summer in Alaska, 1917. Huberta Swensen. (Illus.). 52p. (Orig.). 1991. pap. 5.95 (*0-945284-02-0*) Lynn Canal Pub.

Our Sun Will Rise. Amelia B. House. (Illus.). 72p. (Orig.). 1989. 8.00 (*0-89410-642-2*, Three Contnts) L Rienner.

Our Sunday Visitors Christmas Memories. Our Sunday Visitor Staff. LC 97-67611. 104p. 1997. pap. text 5.95 (*0-87973-919-3*) Our Sunday Visitor.

Our Sunday Visitor's Encyclopedia of Saints. Margaret Matthew et al. LC 97-69277. (Illus.). 800p. 1998. 39.95 (*0-87973-588-0*) Our Sunday Visitor.

***Our Sunday Visitor's Family Guide to Movies & Videos.** Ed. by Henry Herx. 912p. 1999. pap. 29.95 (*0-87973-369-1*) Our Sunday Visitor.

Our Sunday Visitor's Popular Bible Study Series, 7 bks. Alfred McBride. Incl. Director's Guide. 24p. 1992. pap. 1.95 (*0-87973-353-5*); Human Face of Jesus: Luke. LC 91-62164. 216p. 1992. pap. 5.95 (*0-87973-358-6*); Second Coming of Jesus: Meditation & Commentary on the Book of Revelation. LC 92-61979. 180p. (Orig.). 1993. pap. 5.95 (*0-87973-526-0*, 526); 35.95 (*0-87973-959-2*) Our Sunday Visitor.

***Our Sunday Visitor's Treasury of Catholic Stories.** Ed. & Compiled by Gerald M. Castello. LC 99-70510. 400p. 1999. 24.95 (*0-87973-947-9*) Our Sunday Visitor.

***Our Sunday Visitor's 2000 Catholic Almanac.** Matthew Bunson. LC 73-641001. 608p. 1999. pap. 28.95 (*0-87973-905-3*) Our Sunday Visitor.

***Our Sunday Visitor's 2000 Catholic Almanac.** Matthew Burson. LC 73-641001. 608p. 1999. 23.95 (*0-87973-904-5*) Our Sunday Visitor.

***Our Sunday Visitor's 2001 Catholic Almanac.** Ed. by Matthew Bunson. 608p. 2000. 28.95 (*0-87973-907-X*); pap. 23.95 (*0-87973-906-1*) Our Sunday Visitor.

Our Supreme Court. Meish Goldish. LC 94-7640. (I Know America Ser.). (Illus.). 48p. (J). (gr. 2-4). 1994. lib. bdg. 20.90 (*1-56294-445-2*) Millbrook Pr.

***Our Syndromes, Ourselves.** Cathy Hamilton. LC 99-44000. 2000. pap. 9.95 (*0-7407-0665-9*) Andrews & McMeel.

Our Task. Hans U. Von Balthasar. LC 94-75999. 220p. (Orig.). 1994. pap. 14.95 (*0-89870-515-0*) Ignatius Pr.

Our Tea Party. Kirsten Hall. LC 95-51385. (My First Hello Reader Ser.). (Illus.). 32p. (J). (ps-1). 1997. 3.99 (*0-590-68996-7*) Scholastic Inc.

Our Tea Party. Kirsten Hall. (My First Hello Reader! Ser.). 1997. 9.19 (*0-606-11715-6*, Pub. by Turtleback) Demco.

Our Teacher's Having a Baby. Eve Bunting. (Illus.). 32p. (J). (ps-3). 1992. 15.00 (*0-395-60470-2*, Clarion Bks) HM.

Our Teacher's in a Wheelchair. Mary E. Powers. Ed. by Kathleen Tucker. LC 86-1623. (Albert Whitman Concept Bks.). (Illus.). 32p. (J). (ps-3). 1986. lib. bdg. 13.95 (*0-8075-6240-8*) A Whitman.

Our Team! Insights from the Publicly Owned Scranton/Wilkes-Barre Red Barons. James J. Keeler. LC 99-14469. 1999. write for info. (*0-7618-1367-5*) U Pr of Amer.

Our Teen-Age Boys & Girls. Lester D. Crow & Alice Crow. LC 68-58783. (Essay Index Reprint Ser.). 1977. 21.95 (*0-8369-1030-3*) Ayer.

Our Tejano Heroes: Outstanding Mexican-Americans. Sammye Munson. Ed. by Edwin M. Eakin. (Illus.). 96p. (J). (gr. 5-6). 1989. 12.95 (*0-89015-691-3*) Sunbelt Media.

Our Tellings: Interior Salish Stories from the Nlha7kapmx People. Darwin Hanna. (Illus.). 217p. 1995. pap. 25.95 (*0-7748-0523-4*) U of Wash Pr.

***Our Texas Heritage: Traditions & Recipes.** Dorothy McConachie. (Illus.). 250p. 2000. pap. 18.95 (*1-55622-785-X*, Rep of TX Pr) Wordware Pub.

***Our Thanksgiving.** Kimberly Weinberger. LC 99-31426. (My First Hello Reader Ser.). (Illus.). 32p. (J). (ps-1). 1999. 3.99 (*0-439-09908-0*) Scholastic Inc.

Our Theatre Today. Ed. by Herschel L. Bricker. LC 79-128213. (Essay Index Reprint Ser.). 1977. 35.95 (*0-8369-1823-1*) Ayer.

Our 30 Year Old Friendship & Legacy: Letters from Louise Bogan, to Midwestern Mildred Weston Poems from the 'Twenties to the 'Nineties. Mildred Weston et al. LC 97-17329. 176p. 1997. 25.00 (*0-910055-39-4*) East Wash Univ.

Our Thought for the Day: The Best of Professor Joel Lerner's Lifetime Collection of Quotes. Joel Lerner. 366p. 1995. pap., spiral bd. 6.50 (*1-56245-182-0*) Great Quotations.

Our Thousand Year Old Bodies: Selected Poems, 1956-1976. Frederic Will. LC 79-9383. 112p. 1980. pap. 10.95 (*0-87023-284-3*); lib. bdg. 18.50 (*0-87023-283-5*) U of Mass Pr.

Our Threatened Climate. Wilfrid Bach. 1983. text 135.00 (*90-277-1680-3*) Kluwer Academic.

Our Threatened Inheritance. deluxe ed. 1984. 29.95 (*0-87044-536-7*) Natl Geog.

***Our Time: Embracing the 21st Century & a New Millennium.** Melvyn N. Klein. 1999. 27.95 (*0-9675800-0-5*) Woolford.

Our Time Has Come. Charles Allums. Ed. by Betty Allums. LC 89-91703. 85p. (Orig.). 1989. pap. 9.00 (*0-685-39071-3*) BA Cross Ctrl.

Our Time Has Come: A Delegate's Diary of Jesse Jackson's 1984 Presidential Campaign. Lucius J. Barker. LC 87-24357. 256p. 1988. 21.95 (*0-252-01426-X*) U of Ill Pr.

Our Time Has Come: African Christian Women Address the Issues of Today. Ed. by Judy Mbugua. LC 94-41369. (World Evangelical Fellowship Ser.). 154p. 1995. pap. 10.99 (*0-8010-2018-2*) Baker Bks.

Our Time under God Is Now. Woodie W. White. LC 93-9810. 96p. 1993. 13.95 (*0-687-29776-1*) Abingdon.

Our Times. 4th ed. Robert Atwan. 1995. pap. text, teacher ed. 22.00 (*0-312-11701-9*); pap. text, teacher ed. 5.00 (*0-312-11705-1*) St Martin.

Our Times. 5th ed. Robert Atwan. LC 97-74955. 544p. 1998. pap. text 35.95 (*0-312-14931-X*); pap. text 5.00 (*0-312-15262-0*); pap. text 23.00 (*0-312-15263-9*) St Martin.

Our Times: America at the Birth of the 20th Century. Mark Sullivan. Ed. by Dan Rather. LC 95-30055. (Illus.). 600p. 1995. 40.00 (*0-684-81573-7*) S&S Trade.

Our Times: The United States, 1900-1925, 6 vols., Set. Mark Sullivan. (History - United States Ser.). 1992. reprint ed. lib. bdg. write for info. (*0-7812-6215-1*) Rprt Serv.

Our Times Pocket Style. 4th ed. Atwan. 1996. pap. text 27.45 (*0-312-14968-9*) St Martin.

Our Todays & Yesterdays: A Story of Brunswick, Ga., & the Coastal Islands. rev. ed. Margaret D. Cate. (Illus.). 302p. 1997. lib. bdg. 36.00 (*0-8328-7063-3*) Higginson Bk Co.

***Our Toilets Are Not for Customers: Who Are the Customers? How to Drive Customers Away.** Floyd Coates. 192p. 2000. pap. 12.95 (*0-9678624-0-X*) Wing & Prayer IN.

***Our Tomorrows Never Came.** Etunia Bauer Katz. (Illus.). xxix, 144p. 2000. 25.00 (*0-8232-2031-1*); pap. 17.95 (*0-8232-2032-X*) Fordham.

Our Torment & Survival of World War II Germany. Ruth M. Violette. LC 98-65631. 240p. 1998. 21.95 (*1-57197-109-2*) Pentland Pr.

***Our Town.** (YA). 1999. 9.95 (*1-56137-625-6*) Novel Units.

***Our Town.** Gloria Levine. 44p. (YA). 1999. 11.95 (*1-56137-626-4*) Novel Units.

Our Town. Thornton Wilder. (Barron's Book Notes Ser.). 1985. pap. 3.95 (*0-8120-3533-X*) Barron.

Our Town: A Play in Three Acts. Thornton Wilder. LC 98-30096. 128p. 1998. pap. 8.00 (*0-06-092984-7*) HarpC.

Our Town: A Play in Three Acts. Thornton Wilder. 1985. 11.10 (*0-606-01194-3*, Pub. by Turtleback) Demco.

Our Town: A Unit Plan. Mary B. Collins. 146p. 1994. teacher ed., ring bd. 26.95 (*1-58337-010-2*) Teachers Pet Pubns.

An Asterisk (*) at the beginning of an entry indicates that the title is appearing for the first time.

Our Town: Activities for Helping Children Learn & Care about Their Community. Elizabeth McKinnon. Ed. by Brenda M. Harrison & Kathleen Cubley. LC 92-80995. (Learning & Caring About Ser.). (Illus.). 80p. (Orig.). (J). (ps). 1994. 8.95 (*0-911019-54-5*, WPH 1203) Totline Pubns.

Our Town: An American Play. Donald Haberman. (Masterwork Studies). 136p. (C). 1989. 25.95 (*0-8057-8054-8*, Twyne); pap. 13.95 (*0-8057-8048-3*, Twyne) Mac Lib Ref.

Our Town: Aperture, Issue 127. Aperture Staff. 1992. pap. 27.95 (*0-89381-521-7*) Aperture.

Our Town: Discover Ketchikan. Compiled by June Allen. (Illus.). 100p. 1998. pap. 4.95 (*0-9634438-1-X*) Hist Ketchikan.

Our Town: Images & Stories from the Museum of the City of New York. Contrib. by Hilton Als et al. LC 97-20742. (Illus.). 224p. 1997. 39.95 (*0-8109-3698-4*, Pub. by Abrams) Time Warner.

Our Town: Images & Stories from the Museum of the City of New York. Hilton Als & Museum of the City of New York Staff. LC 97-20742. 1997. pap. write for info. (*0-910961-09-3*) Abrams.

Our Town: Race, Housing, & the Soul of Suburbia. David L. Kirp et al. 267p. 1997. pap. 18.00 (*0-8135-2456-3*) Rutgers U Pr.

Our Town: Race, Housing, & the Soul of Suburbia. David L. Kirp et al. (Illus.). 267p. 1997. 29.95 (*0-8135-2253-6*) Rutgers U Pr.

Our Town: Reproducible Teaching Unit. rev. ed. James Scott. 29p. (YA). (gr. 7-12). 1996. teacher ed., ring bd. 29.50 (*1-58049-025-5*, TU36/U) Prestwick Hse.

Our Town: Seasons in the San Joaquin. Gardner Wheeler. LC 96-61703. (Illus.). 168p. (Orig.). 1997. pap. write for info. (*0-9655785-7-7*) Tule River.

Our Town by Thornton Wilder: Curriculum Unit. Center for Learning Network Staff. (Drama Ser.). 84p. 1991. reprint ed. spiral bd. 18.95 (*1-56077-172-0*) Ctr Learning.

Our Town, Mesa, Arizona: The Story of Mesa. 6th rev. ed. Our Town Revision Committee Staff. (Illus.). 208p. 1991. 24.95 (*0-9629563-0-9*) Mesa Pub Schl.

Our Town, 1993: A Daily Record of the Twenty Remaining Days of the Bush Administration & the First 100 Days of the Clinton Administration. David H. Li. LC 93-92769. 144p. (Orig.). 1993. pap. 10.00 (*0-9637852-0-6*) Premier MD.

Our Town Notes. MaryEllen Snodgrass. (Cliffs Notes Ser.). 56p. 1965. pap. 4.95 (*0-8220-0967-6*, Cliff) IDG Bks.

Our Town on Stage: The Original Promptbook in Fascimile. Intro. by Jeanne T. Newlin. (Barry & Mary Bingham Series in the Harvard Theatre Collection: No. 1). (Illus.). 96p. 1989. 29.95 (*0-674-64760-2*) HUP.

***Our Town on the Plains: J. J. Pennell's Photographs of Junction City, Kansas, 1893-1922.** James R. Shortridge & Joseph Judd Pennell. LC 00-38224. (Illus.). 2000. 29.95 (*0-7006-1043-X*) U Pr of KS.

Our Town Remembered. Regi Klein. (Illus.). 1992. pap. 9.95 (*0-9631989-0-4*) Designs Grace.

Our Town, 1749-1865: Likenesses of This Place & Its People Taken from Life. LC 56-9988. (Illus.). 114p. (Orig.). 1956. pap. write for info. (*0-614-29584-X*) Alexandria Assn.

Our Toxic World: Who Is Looking after Our Kids?: A Guide for Parents to Protect Their Children from Environmental Chemicals & Other Toxic Substances. Harold Buttram & Richard Piccola. LC 96-86207. 200p. (Orig.). 1996. pap. 14.95 (*0-9653616-0-8*) Foresight Am Fnd.

Our Toys. (Sense of History Ser.). Date not set. pap. text. write for info. (*0-582-04023-X*, Pub. by Addison-Wesley) Longman.

***Our Treasures: A Celebration of Mexican Heritage: Nuestros Tesoros: una Celebracion de la Herencia Mexicana de Nebraska.** Ralph F. Grajeda et al. LC 98-66432. 78 p. 1998. write for info. (*0-933307-14-4*) Nebraska Hist.

Our Tribe: A Baseball Memoir. Terry Pluto. LC 99-22125. 272p. 1999. 24.50 (*0-684-84505-9*) S&S Trade.

***Our Tribe: Queer Folks, God, Jesus & the Bible (Millennium Edition)** Nancy Wilson. LC 95-12266. 160p. 2000. pap. 14.00 (*1-886360-10-3*) Alamo Sq Pr.

Our Trip to Mesa Verde, 1922. Ruth Miller. LC 97-193038. (Illus.). 52p. (Orig.). 1997. pap. 6.95 (*1-890437-04-2*) Western Reflections.

Our Tuneful Heritage: American Musical Instruments from the Metropolitan Museum of Art. Laurence Libin. LC 94-42019. 103p. 1998. pap. 19.95 (*0-8425-2325-1*, Pub. by Brigham) U Ch Pr.

Our Turn: Women Who Triumph. Christopher Hayes. 1994. pap. 12.00 (*0-671-74006-7*) PB.

***Our Turn, Our Time: Women Truly Coming of Age.** Ed. by Cynthia Black. LC 00-28920. 272p. 2000. pap. 14.95 (*1-58270-029-X*) Beyond Words Pub.

Our Turn, Whitey. Raymond Marchese. Ed. by Gwen Costa. LC 91-22351. (Orig.). 1992. pap. 13.95 (*0-87949-316-X*) Ashley Bks.

Our Twelve Senses: How Wealthy Senses Refresh the Soul. Albert Soesman. Tr. by Jakob M. Cornelis from DUT. (Social Ecology Ser.). 176p. 1998. reprint ed. pap. 19.95 (*1-869890-75-2*, Pub. by Hawthorn Press) Anthroposophic.

***Our Twentieth Century Headlines: 100 Memorable Front Pages from Charleston's Newspapers.** Ed. by Barbara Williams. (Illus.). 104p. 1999. pap. 14.95 (*1-929647-01-8*) Evening Post.

Our Twentieth Century's Greatest Poems. John T. Campbell. 700p. 1982. 59.95 (*0-910147-00-0*) World Poetry Pr.

Our 24 Family Ways Coloring Book. Clay Clarkson. (Illus.). 28p. (J). (gr. 1-8). 1999. 3.95 (*1-888692-07-3*) Whole Heart.

***Our Twisted Hero.** Yi Mun-Yol. 2001. 21.95 (*0-7868-6670-5*, Pub. by Hyperion) Time Warner.

Our Two Ocean Voyages: The Orient & the Mediterranean. Ira Lunan-Ferguson. LC 68-31071. 319p. 1968. 9.95 (*0-685-03131-4*) Lunan-Ferguson.

Our Two Universes!! An Introduction to the Superchessmen of Spacetime (and a new proto bible for the astronautical age, or light summer reading for cosmology buffs) William H. Spears, Jr. LC 93-92679. 110p. (Orig.). 1994. pap. 12.95 (*0-9600106-4-5*) Spears.

Our Ultimate Fate. Meade Frierson, III. 128p. (Orig.). Date not set. pap. write for info. (*0-9639544-9-0*) A F A B.

Our Uncertain Universe. James Jespersen. (J). 1995. 15.95 (*0-689-31763-8*) Atheneum Yung Read.

Our Union County Families. Winnie P. McDonald & Bonnie H. Peters. (Illus.). 420p. 1993. lib. bdg. 50.00 (*0-9636662-0-7*) Peters McDonald.

Our Unitarian Heritage: An Introduction to the History of the Unitarian Movement. Earl M. Wilbur. LC 83-45635. reprint ed. 49.50 (*0-404-19877-5*) AMS Pr.

Our United States. Roger E. Kranich & Eileen L. Corcoran. (Illus.). 314p. (J). (gr. 4-5). 1989. pap. text, teacher ed. 11.95 (*0-88323-247-2*, 311) Pendergrass Pub.

Our United States: Reading Level 4-5. 1993. teacher ed. 5.99 (*1-56256-121-9*); wbk. ed. 7.99 (*1-56256-120-0*) Peoples Pub Grp.

Our United States Geography. Beverly Vaillancourt. 1993. 17.99 (*1-56256-119-7*) Peoples Pub Grp.

Our Universities Are Turning Us into the Ignorant Country. Ian Lowe. 1995. pap. 9.95 (*0-86840-126-9*, Pub. by New South Wales Univ Pr) Intl Spec Bk.

Our Unmet Needs: God Has an Answer for Us. Charles F. Stanley. 1999. audio 15.99 (*0-7852-7475-8*) Nelson.

Our Urban Future: New Paradigms for Equity & Sustainability. Akhtar A. Badshah. (Illus.). 256p. 1996. pap. 22.50 (*1-85649-406-3*, Pub. by Zed Books) St Martin.

Our Urgent Need - Spirit & Life. Witness Lee. 37p. 1988. pap. 3.50 (*0-87083-394-4*, 07-014-001) Living Stream Ministry.

Our Valley, Eden Valley, Wyoming. Ora E. Wright & Lenora S. Wright. (Illus.). 290p. (Orig.). 1987. pap. 15.00 (*0-9615936-0-1*) Gann Pub.

Our Valley: Happy & Cadron Valleys, Faulkner Co., Arkansas. Cornelia H. Weir. (Illus.). 178p. 1993. 24.95 (*1-56869-020-7*); pap. 19.95 (*1-56869-021-5*) Oldbuck Pr.

Our Values: Stories & Wisdom. Dale Evans Rogers & Carole C. Carlson. (Illus.). 160p. 1999. mass mkt. 5.99 (*0-8007-8671-8*, Spire) Revell.

Our Vampires, Ourselves. Nina Auerbach. LC 95-1044. 216p. 1995. pap. text 22.00 (*0-226-03201-9*) U Ch Pr.

Our Vampires, Ourselves. Nina Auerbach. 1997. pap. 12.95 (*0-226-03202-7*); pap. 12.95 (*0-614-27423-0*) U Ch Pr.

Our Vanishing Privacy: And What You Can Do to Protect Yours. Robert Ellis Smith. 1999. pap. 12.95 (*1-893626-01-6*) Breakout Prods Inc.

***Our Vanishing Relative.** H. D. Rijksen & E. Meijard. LC 99-27055. 1999. write for info. (*0-7923-5754-X*) Kluwer Academic.

Our Vanishing Wildlife: Its Extermination & Preservation. William T. Hornaday. LC 77-125748. (American Environmental Studies). 1974. reprint ed. 26.95 (*0-405-02674-9*) Ayer.

Our Very Own Rocket. Judy Mullican. (HBL Big Bks.). (Illus.). 8p. (J). (ps-k). 1994. pap. text 10.95 (*1-57332-010-2*) HighReach Lrning.

Our Victory over Death: Resurrection? Ed. by Marie-Emile Boismard. Tr. by Madeleine Beaumont from ENG. LC 98-29486. 168p. 1999. pap. 16.95 (*0-8146-2458-8*) Liturgical Pr.

***Our Vietnam: The War 1954-1975.** A. J. Langguth. (Illus.). 784p. 2000. 34.50 (*0-684-81202-9*) Simon & Schuster.

Our Village. large type ed. Mary R. Mitford. (Isis Clear Type Classic Ser.). 170p. 1992. 23.95 (*1-85089-489-2*, Pub. by ISIS Lrg Prnt) Transaction Pubs.

Our Village, 1824. Mary R. Mitford. LC 95-41976. (Revolution & Romanticism, 1789-1834 Ser.). 1996. 55.00 (*1-85477-185-X*) Continuum.

***Our Vine of Sharing Recipes.** Ed. by Donald Noiseux. (Illus.). 175p. 1999. spiral bd. 15.00 (*1-929486-04-9*) SonRises Bk Pubg.

Our Violent Earth. Nancy Watson et al. LC 80-8797. (Books for World Explorers Series 3: No. 2). (Illus.). 104p. (J). (gr. 3-8). 1982. 8.95 (*0-87044-383-6*); lib. bdg. 12.50 (*0-87044-388-7*) Natl Geog.

Our Vision & Values: Women Shaping the 21st Century. Frances C. Hutner. LC 93-11863. 232p. 1994. pap. 19.95 (*0-275-94932-X*, HQ1426, Praeger Pubs) Greenwood.

Our Vision & Values: Women Shaping the 21st Century. Ed. by Frances C. Hutner. LC 93-11863. 232p. 1994. 65.00 (*0-275-94032-2*, Praeger Pubs) Greenwood.

Our Voices: Essays in Culture, Ethnicity, & Communication. 2nd ed. Ed. by Alberto Gonzalez et al. LC 96-22550. 220p. (C). 1997. pap. text. write for info. (*0-935732-73-X*) Roxbury Pub Co.

Our Voices: Essays in Culture, Ethnicity & Communication. 3rd ed. Ed. by Alberto Gonzalez et al. LC 99-37121. 220p. (C). 2000. pap. text. write for info. (*1-891487-35-3*) Roxbury Pub Co.

***Our Voices: Psychology of Women.** Rider. LC 99-28656. (Psychology Ser.). 544p. 1999. pap. 46.95 (*0-534-34681-2*) Wadsworth Pub.

Our Voices Our Lives: Stories of Women from Central America & the Caribbean. Margaret Randall. 200p. 1995. text 29.95 (*1-56751-047-7*); pap. text 12.95 (*1-56751-046-9*) Common Courage.

***Our Voices, Our Town: A History of New London, New Hampshire, 1950-2000.** Ann Page Stecker. LC 00-32807. 2000. write for info. (*0-615-11590-X*) R E Reiner.

***Our Voices, Our Visions.** John Meyer. (Teenink Ser.). (YA). 2000. pap. 12.95 (*1-55874-816-4*) Health Comm.

Our Voices, Ourselves: Women Writing for the French Theatre. Celita Lamar. LC 90-21539. (Currents in Romance Languages & Literature Ser.: Vol. 5). XIV, 213p. (C). 1991. text 37.00 (*0-8204-1499-9*) P Lang Pubng.

Our Vulnerable Youth: The Financial Literacy of American 12th Graders. Lewis Mandell. LC 98-67337. 117p. 1998. pap. 14.95 (*0-9666010-0-9*) JumpStart Coalition.

***Our Walk, Vol. 6.** T. D. Jakes. (Six Pillars for the Believer Ser.: Vol. 6). 1999. pap. text 14.99 (*1-57778-112-0*) Albury Pub.

Our War: How the British Commonwealth Fought the Second World War. Christopher Somerville. (Illus.). 400p. 1998. 50.00 (*0-297-81668-3*, Pub. by Weidenfeld & Nicolson) Trafalgar.

Our War Nurses: The History of the Royal Australian Nursing Corps, 1902-1988. Rupert Goodman. 294p. (C). 1990. 120.00 (*0-86439-040-8*, Pub. by Boolarong Pubns) St Mut.

Our War Was Different: Marine Combined Action Platoons in Vietnam. Al Hemingway. LC 93-31408. (Illus.). 200p. 1994. 29.95 (*1-55750-355-9*) Naval Inst Pr.

***Our Warfare.** T. D. Jakes. (Six Pillars for the Believer Ser.: Vol. 2). 1999. pap. text 14.99 (*1-57778-108-2*) Albury Pub.

Our Washington: A Comprehensive Album of the Nation's Capital in Words & Pictures. Federal Writers' Project, Washington, D.C. LC 73-3602. (American Guide Ser.). reprint ed. 12.00 (*0-404-57906-X*) AMS Pr.

Our Way: Based on the Song "A Time That Was" Ed Shirak, Jr. Ed. by Mary A. Villanella et al. LC 95-94090. (Illus.). 150p. (Orig.). 1995. 21.95 (*0-9645933-0-0*); lib. bdg. 21.95 (*0-9645933-1-9*) Lepores Pub.

Our Way of Life: CVQ Customer Valued Quality. Gerald M. Czarnecki. 46p. 1995. pap. write for info. (*0-9648538-3-3*) UNC Inc.

Our Way of Making Prayer see Living Tradition of Yupik Mask: Agayuliyararput, Our Way of Making Prayer

Our Way of Proceeding. William A. Barry. LC 97-73844. (Series IV: Vol. 19). vii, 190p. 1997. pap. 12.95 (*1-880810-30-1*) Inst Jesuit.

***Our Wealth.** T. D. Jakes. (Six Pillars for the Believer Ser.: Vol. 1). 160p. 1999. pap. text 14.99 (*1-57778-107-4*) Albury Pub.

Our Wedding. 1997. 12.95 (*0-88271-554-2*) Regina Pr.

***Our Wedding.** Doney. 1999. 16.95 (*0-7459-4057-9*, Pub. by Lion Pubng) Trafalgar.

***Our Wedding.** Havoc Publishing Staff. 1999. 18.00 (*1-57977-888-7*); pap. 8.00 (*0-7416-1124-4*); pap. text 20.00 (*1-57977-158-0*) Havoc Pub.

***Our Wedding.** Havoc Publishing Staff. 1999. 18.00 (*1-57977-852-6*); 8.00 (*1-57977-665-5*) Havoc Pub.

Our Wedding. Playskool Staff. (J). 1999. pap. 9.99 (*0-525-45782-8*) NAL.

***Our Wedding, Vol. 4.** T. D. Jakes. (Six Pillars for the Believer Ser.: Vol. 4). 1998. pap. text 14.99 (*1-57778-110-4*) Albury Pub.

Our Wedding: A Journal. (Illus.). 96p. 1994. 19.95 (*0-00-255446-1*) Collins SF.

***Our Wedding: Keepsake Box & Photo Album with Other.** 1999. boxed set 18.00 (*1-57977-733-3*) Havoc Pub.

Our Wedding: A Keepsake Album see Recuerdos de Nuestra Boda

Our Wedding Anniversary Memory Book. (Illus.). 24p. 1997. reprint ed. 29.99 (*1-892953-00-5*) Talus Corp.

Our Wedding Day. Four Seasons Staff. 80p. 1999. 19.95 (*1-85645-122-4*, Pub. by Four Seasons Publishing Ltd) ACCESS Pubs Network.

***Our Wedding Guests.** Peggy Sneller. 2000. 18.99 (*1-56245-398-X*) Great Quotations.

Our Wedding Journal. Mary Engelbreit. (Illus.). 104p. (Orig.). 1996. spiral bd. 14.95 (*0-8362-4643-8*) Andrews & McMeel.

Our Wedding Memories. Janet Anastasio & Peter Gouck. 1992. 18.50 (*1-55850-120-7*) Adams Media.

***Our Wedding Memory Book.** Peggy Sneller. 2000. 24.99 (*1-56245-397-1*) Great Quotations.

Our Wedding Record Book. 1995. 10.95 (*0-7459-3367-X*, Pub. by Lion Pubng) Trafalgar.

***Our Wedding/Honeymoon.** Havoc Publishing Staff. 1999. 9.00 (*0-7416-1011-6*); 18.00 (*0-7416-1800-1*) Havoc Pub.

Our Weird Wonderful Ancestors: Soap-Opera Stories of Life & Loves in 1776. Donald Walton. (Illus.). 352p. 1998. 24.95 (*0-9662625-4-9*) Archer & Williams.

Our Welsh Heritage. 5th ed. Islyn Thomas. 100p. 1992. pap. 6.00 (*0-9639408-0-5*) Natl Welsh-Amer.

Our Western World's Greatest Poems. Ed. by John T. Campbell. 450p. 1983. 69.95 (*0-317-03222-4*); text 69.95 (*0-685-42659-9*) World Poetry Pr.

Our Wet World. Sneed B. Collard, III. LC 97-11873. (Illus.). 32p. (J). (ps-3). 1998. pap. 6.95 (*0-88106-268-5*) Charlesbridge Pub.

Our Wet World. Sneed B. Collard, III. LC 97-11873. (Illus.). 32p. (J). (gr. 8-12). 1998. 16.95 (*0-88106-267-7*) Charlesbridge Pub.

Our Whole Country (with J. W. Barber) Henry Howe. (Notable American Authors Ser.). 1992. reprint ed. lib. bdg. 75.00 (*0-7812-3207-4*) Rprt Serv.

Our Wild Harvest: Sowing, Reaping, Cooking, Eating. Rolf A. Pederson. Ed. by Nancy Carlson. (Illus.). 174p. (Orig.). 1982. pap. 9.95 (*0-910579-00-8*) Rolfs Gall.

Our Wild Indians: Thirty Three Years' Personal Experience Among the Red Men of the Great West. Richard I. Dodge. (Select Bibliographies Reprint Ser.). 1977. 60.95 (*0-8369-5230-8*) Ayer.

Our Wild Indians: Thirty Three Years Personal Experience Among the Red Men of the Great West. Richard I. Dodge. 657p. 1978. reprint ed. 39.95 (*0-87928-089-1*) Corner Hse.

Our Wilderness: How the People of New York Found, Changed, & Preserved the Adirondacks. Michael Steinberg. Ed. by Neal S. Burdick. LC 91-16550. (Illus.). 112p. (J). (gr. 4 up). 1994. pap. 9.95 (*0-935272-57-7*) ADK Mtn Club.

Our Wildest Dreams: Women Entrepreneurs Making Money, Having Fun, Doing Good. Joline Godfrey. LC 92-54854. (Illus.). 272p. 1993. pap. 13.00 (*0-88730-633-0*, HarpBusn) HarpInfo.

Our Wildest Dreams: Women Making Money, Having Fun, Doing Good. Joline Godfrey. LC 92-54854. 224p. 1992. 20.00 (*0-88730-545-8*, HarpBusn) HarpInfo.

Our Wisconsin River - Border to Border. Joe Glickman. (Illus.). 112p. 1997. 34.95 (*0-9655081-0-2*) Pamacheyon Pub.

Our Wise Counselor: Seeking God's Guidance. Phyllis Bennett. (Knowing God Ser.). 64p. 1994. 5.99 (*0-310-48311-5*) Zondervan.

Our Wish. Ralph Da Costa Nunez & Jenna Mandel. (Illus.). 23p. (J). (ps-k). 1997. pap. 4.95 (*0-9641784-1-9*) Homes Homeless.

Our Wish Activity Book. Ralph D. Nunez. (Illus.). 12p. (J). (ps-3). 1998. wbk. ed. 1.95 (*0-9641784-3-5*) Homes Homeless.

Our Wish to Kill: The Murder in All Our Hearts. Herbert S. Strean & Lucy Freeman. 256p. 1993. mass mkt. 4.99 (*0-380-71846-4*, Avon Bks) Morrow Avon.

Our Women. Arnold Bennett. LC 74-17107. (Collected Works of Arnold Bennett: Vol. 62). 1977. reprint ed. 25.95 (*0-518-19143-5*) Ayer.

***Our Women in the War: A Series of Papers Written by Southern Ladies - South Carolina News & Courier.** Compiled by William McKinnon. 401p. 1998. write for info. (*1-882194-47-0*) TN Valley Pub.

Our Wonderful Bible. R. K. Campbell. 417p. pap. 10.50 (*0-88172-010-0*) Believers Bkshelf.

Our Wonderful Earth see Nuestra Fantastica Tierra

Our Wonderful Earth. Nicola Baxter. (Launch Pad Library). (Illus.). 32p. (J). (gr. k-4). 1997. 11.95 (*0-915741-77-6*) C D Stampley Ent.

Our Wonderful World. (High Q Activity Bks.). (Illus.). 48p. (J). (gr. k-2). 1998. pap. 3.99 (*0-7681-0020-8*, McClanahan Book) Learn Horizon.

Our Wonderful World: Solutions for Math & Science. N. Beakes et al. (J). (gr. 5-9). 1987. 16.95 (*1-881431-08-8*, 1308) AIMS Educ Fnd.

***Our Word Is Our Weapon: Selected Writings.** Subcomandante Insurgente Marcos. Ed. by Juana Ponce de Leon. 416p. 2000. 27.95 (*1-58322-036-4*, Pub. by Seven Stories) Publishers Group.

Our Words - Our Ways: Reading & Writing in North Carolina. 2nd ed. Ed. by Sally Buckner. LC 95-68954. (Illus.). 748p. (J). (gr. 8). 1995. boxed set 40.00 (*0-89089-696-8*) Carolina Acad Pr.

Our Work, Our Lives, Our Words. Ed. by Leonore Davidoff & Belinda Westover. LC 86-14046. 240p. 1986. pap. 23.00 (*0-389-20656-3*, N8214) B&N Imports.

***Our Workmanship, Vol. 5.** T. D. Jakes. (Six Pillars for the Believer Ser.: Vol. 5). 160p. 1999. pap. text 14.99 (*1-57778-111-2*) Albury Pub.

Our World. J. Tyler et al. (World Geography Ser.). (Illus.). 96p. (J). (gr. 3-6). 1993. pap. text 12.95 (*0-7460-1845-2*, Usborne) EDC.

***Our World: An In-Depth Guide to Countries Around the World.** Martyn J Bramwell. (J). 1999. 16.99 (*1-84100-262-3*) Quadrillion Pubng.

Our World: Environmental Awareness. Gayle Bittinger. Ed. by Elizabeth McKinnon. LC 89-52145. (Learning & Caring About Ser.). (Illus.). 80p. (J). (ps-1). 1990. pap. 8.95 (*0-911019-30-8*, WPH 1201) Totline Pubns.

***Our World: Picture Atlas for Very Young Explorers.** 32p. (gr. k-3). 2000. per. 17.95 (*0-7922-7576-4*) Natl Geog.

Our World: The Path Towards Global Survival. Ed. by Hans-Wolff Graf. 258p. 1995. pap. text 39.00 (*2-88449-200-3*) Gordon & Breach.

Our World Belongs to God: A Contemporary Testimony. rev. ed. Contemporary Testimony Committee of the Christian. 92p. 1987. pap. text, student ed. 3.75 (*0-930265-31-9*) CRC Pubns.

Our World Belongs to God: A Contemporary Testimony. rev. ed. Contemporary Testimony Committee of the Christian. 92p. 1988. pap. text 1.95 (*1-56212-672-5*) CRC Pubns.

Our World, God's World. Ed. by Henry R. Rust. 71p. 1991. pap. 8.95 (*1-877871-12-5*, 3541) Ed Ministries.

Our World, in Chinese. John Kiang. Tr. by Shao-ping Tang. (CHI.). 126p. 1994. pap. 7.95 (*0-916301-06-0*) One World Pub.

***Our World in Transition: Making Sense of a Changing World.** Diarmuid O'Murchu. 160p. 2000. pap. 16.95 (*0-8245-1862-4*, Pub. by Crossroad NY) Natl Bk Netwk.

Our World Is Us - Inside Out. Iris O. Kendall. (Illus.). 64p. (Orig.). 1995. pap. 10.95 (*0-9640866-6-2*) EastWest Inst.

Our World of Circles. William Kalanta. (Illus.). 16p. (J). (gr. 1-3). 1997. 5.95 (*1-56550-047-4*) Vis Bks Intl.

Our World of Wonders. Sterling W. Sill. LC 86-81780. 96p. 1986. 9.98 (*0-88290-287-3*) Horizon Utah.

Our World: or The Slave-Holder's Daughter. LC 78-152927. (Black Heritage Library Collection). 1977. 33.95 (*0-8369-8771-3*) Ayer.

Our World Series, 10 bks., Set. (Illus.). 480p. (J). (gr. 5-8). 1991. lib. bdg. 129.50 (*0-382-09599-5*) Silver Burdett Pr.

Our Worlds: The Magnetism & Thrill of Planetary Exploration. Ed. by S. Alan Stern. (Illus.). 192p. 1998. pap. 19.95 (*0-521-64440-2*) Cambridge U Pr.

O

Our Worlds: The Magnetism & Thrill of Planetary Exploration. Ed. by S. Alan Stern. (Illus.). 192p. 1999. 54.95 (*0-521-63164-5*) Cambridge U Pr.

Our World's Best Loved Poems. John T. Campbell. 608p. 1983. 69.95 (*0-910147-03-5*) World Poetry Pr.

Our World's Heritage. Ed. by Carol B. Lutyk. LC 87-17174. 312p. 1987. 21.95 (*0-87044-696-7*); text 21.95 (*0-87044-698-3*); lib. bdg. 23.95 (*0-87044-697-5*) Natl Geog.

***Our Worship, Vol. 3.** T. D. Jakes. (Six Pillars for the Believer Ser.: Vol. 3). 160p. 1999. pap. text 14.99 (*1-57778-109-0*) Albury Pub.

Our Worst Suspicions. John Birtwhistle. 64p. 1985. pap. 13.95 (*0-85646-131-8*, Pub. by Anvil Press) Dufour.

Our Wyoming Heritage: As Seen Through the Eyes of the Young. Sagebruch Elementary School Scholars Staff. LC 90-721. (Illus.). 156p. (Orig.). 1990. pap. 7.95 (*0-932707-20-3*) Achievement Pr.

Our Yankee Heritage. Carleton Beals. LC 73-111814. (Essay Index Reprint Ser.). 1977. 23.95 (*0-8369-1593-3*) Ayer.

Our Yard Is Full of Birds. Anne Rockwell. LC 90-30436. (Illus.). 32p. (J). (ps-2). 1992. lib. bdg. 14.00 (*0-02-777273-X*, Mac Bks Young Read) S&S Childrens.

***Our Year with God: A Child's Introduction to Catholic Holy Days & the Liturgical Year.** Natalie Kadela. (Illus.). 152p. (J). (gr. 3-7). 2000. pap. 14.95 (*0-8198-5436-0*) Pauline Bks.

Our Yesterdays: The History of the Actuarial Profession in North America, 1809-1979. E. J. Moorhead. LC 89-31624. 1989. text 60.00 (*0-938959-08-5*) Soc Actuaries.

Our Yosemite National Park. John Muir. Ed. by William R. Jones. (Illus.). 96p. (Orig.). 1980. reprint ed. pap. 3.95 (*0-89646-061-4*) Vistabooks.

Ouragan - Portus Potter Was Loose! Robert Munsch. (Droles D'Histories Ser.). (FRE., Illus.). 24p. (J). (ps up). 1993. pap. 6.95 (*2-89021-206-8*, Pub. by La Courte Ech) Firefly Bks Ltd.

Our'an: A Modern English Version. Tr. by Majid Fakhry. LC 97-175101. 1998. pap. 16.95 (*1-85964-086-9*) LPC InBook.

Ouranos (Cinabrio-Verb-Maria) Jorge L. Morales. (Poetry Ser.). 133p. 1991. 50.00 (*0-317-05416-3*); pap. 40.00 (*0-317-05417-1*) Instit Nacional.

***Ouranos Theorema: The Ancient Search for the Confines of the Universe.** Alberto Buffo. LC 99-75570. (Illus.). 346p. 2000. 32.95 (*0-9675538-0-6*) Bovolo.

Ouray. Jack L. Benham. (Illus.). 64p. (Orig.). 1976. pap. 3.95 (*0-941026-01-9*) Bear Creek Pub.

Ouray: A Quick History: Including the Mines of Ouray County. P. David Smith. (Illus.). 96p. 1996. pap. 7.95 (*1-890437-11-5*) Western Reflections.

Ouray-Chief of the Utes. P. David Smith. Ed. by Jack Swanson. (Illus.). 222p. (Orig.). 1986. pap. 12.95 (*0-9608764-4-8*) Wayfinder Pr.

Ouray Hiking Guide: Favorite Hiking Trails of Ouray, Colorado. Kelvin B. Kent. 1993. pap. 11.95 (*0-943727-15-4*) Wayfinder Pr.

Ouregano. Paule Constant. (FRE.). 256p. 1985. pap. 11.95 (*0-7859-2006-4*, 2070376230) Fr & Eur.

Ourika. De Duras. Ed. by Little. (Exeter French Texts Ser.: Vol. 84). (FRE.). 109p. Date not set. pap. text 19.95 (*0-85989-394-4*, Pub. by Univ Exeter Pr) Northwestern U Pr.

Ourika: An English Translation. Claire De Duras. Tr. & Frwd. by John Fowles. (MLA Texts & Translations Ser.: No. 3b). xxxiii, 47p. (Orig.). 1994. pap. 5.95 (*0-87352-780-1*, P003P) Modern Lang.

Ourika: Madame de Duras. rev. ed. Madame De Duras. Ed. by Roger Little. 160p. 1998. pap. 23.95 (*0-85989-573-4*, Pub. by Univ Exeter Pr) Northwestern U Pr.

Ourika: The Original French Text. Claire De Duras. Ed. & Intro. by Joan DeJean. Intro. by Margaret Waller. (MLA Texts & Translations Ser.: No. 3a). (FRE.). xxviii, 45p. (Orig.). 1994. pap. 5.95 (*0-87352-779-8*, Q003P) Modern Lang.

Ours: Poetry in Words & Brush Strokes. Sue Hu. (Illus.). 99p. (Orig.). 1989. pap. 5.95 (*0-9623736-0-5*) WE Enterprises.

Ours by Right: Women's Rights as Human Rights. Ed. by Joanna Kerr. LC 93-24661. 192p. (C). 1993. text 62.50 (*1-85649-227-3*, Pub. by Zed Books); text 22.50 (*1-85649-228-1*, Pub. by Zed Books) St Martin.

Ours Once More: Folklore, Ideology & the Making of Modern Greece. Michael Herzfeld. 197p. (Orig.). 1987. pap. 10.00 (*0-918618-32-0*) Pella Pub.

Ours the Journey: Study Guide to Churches in Solidarity with Women. Barbara A. Horner-Ibler. (Orig.). 1992. pap. 5.95 (*0-377-00243-7*) Friendship Pr.

Ours to Keep: A Guide for Building a Community Assessment Strategy for Child Protection. Pamela Day et al. 256p. 1998. pap. text 18.95 (*0-87868-702-5*, 7025, CWLA Pr) Child Welfare.

Ours, Yours, Mine: Mutuality & the Emergence of the Separate Self. Anni Bergman. LC 98-21039. 1998. 45.00 (*1-56821-374-3*) Aronson.

Ourselves. B. North. Date not set. 5.99 (*1-871676-04-5*, Pub. by Christian Focus) Spring Arbor Dist.

Ourselves - Then & Now: A Collection of Personal Essays. unabridged ed. Academy for Learning in Retirement Members. Ed. by Marianne G. Finnegan. (Illus.). 288p. 1997. pap. 12.95 (*0-9659629-0-3*) Third Age Pr.

Ourselves Alone. Anne Devlin. 1999. pap. 5.25 (*0-8222-1672-8*) Dramatists Play.

Ourselves Alone. 2nd ed. Anne Devlin. 192p. 1986. pap. 9.95 (*0-571-14457-8*) Faber & Faber.

Ourselves Alone: Women's Emigration from Ireland, 1885-1920. Janet A. Nolan. LC 89-35145. 152p. 1989. text 20.00 (*0-8131-1684-8*) U Pr of Ky.

Ourselves Among Others. 4th ed. Verburg. 2000. pap. text 35.95 (*0-312-20764-6*) St Martin.

***Ourselves & Others: Perspectives on Morality from East & West.** Ed. by Jehanne Anabtawi. 512p. 2000. pap. text 43.95 (*1-889119-51-2*) Seven Bridges.

Ourselves & Others: The Development of a Greek Macedonian Cultural Identity since 1912. Ed. by Peter A. Mackridge & Eleni Yannakakis. LC 96-35258. 224p. 1997. 49.50 (*1-85973-133-3*, Pub. by Berg Pubs); pap. 19.50 (*1-85973-138-4*, Pub. by Berg Pubs) NYU Pr.

Ourselves As Students: Multicultural Voices in the Classroom. Broad Minds Collective Staff. LC 96-15621. 176p. (C). 1996. 34.95 (*0-8093-2087-8*) S Ill U Pr.

Ourselves As Students: Multicultural Voices in the Classroom. Ed. & Compiled by Broad Minds Collective Staff. LC 96-15621. 176p. (C). 1996. pap. 16.95 (*0-8093-2088-6*) S Ill U Pr.

Ourselves, Inc. Leo R. Ward. LC 79-128327. (Essay Index Reprint Ser.). 1977. 20.95 (*0-8369-2208-5*) Ayer.

Ourson Qui Voulait une Juliette. Jasmine Dube & Leanne Franson. (*2-89021-302-1*) La Courte Ech.

Ousamne Sow: Sculptures. Jean L. Pivin. (Illus.). 184p. 1996. 69.95 (*2-909571-14-9*, Pub. by Revue Noire) Dist Art Pubs.

Ousmane Sembene: Dialogues with Critics & Writers. Ed. by Samba Gadjigo et al. LC 93-8910. 136p. 1993. pap. 13.95 (*0-87023-889-2*) U of Mass Pr.

Out: A Novel. Ronald Sukenick. LC 72-96165. 295p. 1996. 18.95 (*0-9626530-3-9*) In Pr CO.

Out! The Vermont Secession Book. Frank Bryan & Bill Mares. LC 87-62288. (Illus.). 176p. (Orig.). 1987. pap. 8.95 (*0-933050-52-6*) New Eng Pr VT.

Out after Dark. Hugh Leonard. 192p. 1991. 24.95 (*0-233-98474-7*, Pub. by Andre Deutsch) Trafalgar.

Out after Dark: A Novel. Kai Maristed. LC 92-34341. 328p. 1993. 22.00 (*1-877946-30-3*) Permanent Pr.

Out & About. Kari Daniels & Connie Schaper. (Illus.). 166p. (J). (ps-12). 1998. spiral bd. 29.00 (*1-884135-37-4*) Mayer-Johnson.

Out & About. Dorling Kindersley Staff. (Treasure Hunt Board Bks.). (Illus.). 10p. (J). (ps-k). 1996. 4.95 (*0-7894-0626-8*) DK Pub Inc.

***Out & about.** Golden Books Staff. (Poky & Friends Ser.). (Illus.). 70p. (J). (ps-3). 2000. pap. 2.99 (*0-307-25738-X*) Gldn Bks Pub Co.

Out & About. Pati M. Gross. Ed. by Carol Marger. LC 97-92397. (Adventures in the Roo World - Young Roo Ser.: No. 3). (Illus.). 24p. (Orig.). (J). (ps-1). 1997. pap. 4.95 (*0-9652579-3-2*) Roo Publns.

Out & About: A Travel & Transport Guide. Richard Armitage & John Taylor. (C). 1989. 30.00 (*0-86242-092-X*, Pub. by Age Concern Eng) St Mut.

***Out & About: Poems from Hollywood.** Mark Dunster. 11p. 1999. pap. 5.00 (*0-89642-739-0*) Linden Pubs.

***Out & about Campus: Personal Accounts by Lesbian, Gay, Bisexual & Transgendered College Students.** unabridged ed. Ed. by Kim Howard & Annie Stevens. LC 99-59703. 320p. 2000. pap. 12.95 (*1-55583-480-9*, Pub. by Alyson Pubns) Consort Bk Sales.

Out & about Gay Travel Guide: U. S. A. Resorts & Warm Weather Vacations: Essential Information for Gay & Lesbian Travelers. Billy Kolber-Stuart & David Alport. LC 96-24613. (Out & About Gay Travel Guides Ser.). 384p. (J). 1997. pap. 14.45 (*0-7868-8177-1*, Pub. by Hyperion) Little.

Out & about in New Mexico. rev. ed. John Feinberg et al. (Out & About Ser.). (Illus.). 132p. 1988. pap. 7.95 (*0-923280-00-6*) HHR.

Out & About in Washington, DC: The Insider's Guide. Jeff Brauer & Veronica Wiles. LC 99-203430. (Illus.). 95p. 1999. pap. 7.95 (*0-9643789-2-2*) On Your Own.

Out & about Portland with Kids: The Ultimate Guide for Fun & Learning. Elizabeth H. DeSimone. 240p. (Orig.). 1997. pap. 12.95 (*0-9614626-7-1*) NW Parent Pub.

Out & about Seattle with Kids. Ann Bergman & Coleen Carroll. (Illus.). 213p. 1993. pap. 12.95 (*0-9614626-3-9*) NW Parent Pub.

Out & About Seattle with Kids: The Ultimate Family Guide for Fun & Learning. 2nd ed. Ann Bergman. 1998. pap. text 14.95 (*0-9614626-9-8*) NW Parent Pub.

Out & about with Jesse Bear. Carlstrom. 1996. 14.95 (*0-02-717274-0*) Macmillan.

Out Are the Lights. Richard Laymon. 224p. (Orig.). 1983. mass mkt. 2.75 (*0-446-90519-4*, Pub. by Warner Bks) Little.

Out at Home: The Glenn Burke Story. Glenn Burke & Erik Sherman. Ed. by Michael Sherman. 128p. (Orig.). 1995. pap. 14.95 (*0-9648158-0-X*) Excel Pubng.

Out at Home: Triumph & Tragedy in the Life of Milt Pappas. Milt Pappas et al. 350p. 2000. 28.00 (*0-939995-30-1*) Angel Pr WI.

Out at the Old Ball Game: A Novel. Bernie Bookbinder. LC 94-37578. 278p. 1995. 21.95 (*1-882593-09-X*) Bridge Wrks.

***Out at Work: Building a Gay-Labor Alliance.** Ed. by Kitty Krupat & Patrick McCreery. 2001. pap. 19.95 (*0-8166-3741-5*) U of Minn Pr.

Out Behind the Barn. B. Carlson. (Illus.). 137p. 1996. pap. 9.95 (*1-57166-054-2*) Quixote Pr IA.

Out Behind the Barn: A Celebration of Iowa's Sesquicentennial 1996. B. Carlson. (Illus.). 137p. 1996. pap. 9.95 (*1-57166-055-0*) Quixote Pr IA.

Out Facts: What You Need to Know about Gay & Lesbian Culture. Ed. by David Groff. 1997. 16.95 (*0-614-28232-2*) Universe.

Out Facts: What You Need to Know about Gay & Lesbian Culture. Ed. by David Groff. (Illus.). 112p. 1997. 16.95 (*0-7893-0083-4*, Pub. by Universe) St Martin.

Out Far, in Deep: Short Fiction. Alvin Handelman. LC 89-62209. Vol. 39. 110p. 1990. pap. 7.95 (*0-89823-113-2*) New Rivers Pr.

Out-Finessing the Geese. Dennis Hunt. Ed. & Illus. by Teresa Marrone. 144p. (Orig.). 1996. pap. 19.95 (*0-9653908-2-9*) D Hunt Huntg.

Out for Blood. John Peyton Cooke. 320p. 1991. pap. 3.95 (*0-380-75927-6*, Avon Bks) Morrow Avon.

Out for Business. Horatio Alger, Jr. (Works of Horatio Alger Jr.). 1989. reprint ed. lib. bdg. 79.00 (*0-685-27566-3*) Rprt Serv.

Out for Good: The Adventures of Panda & Koala. Thierry Dedieu. LC 98-17234. (Illus.). 32p. (J). (ps-3). 1999. 8.95 (*0-385-32634-3*) Doubleday.

***Out for Good: The Struggle to Build a Gay Rights Movement in America.** Dudley Clendinen & Adam Nagourney. LC 99-12523. (Illus.). 704p. 1999. 29.50 (*0-684-81091-3*) Simon & Schuster.

Out for Life. John D. Anderson & Ann T. Edwards. LC 96-784. (Illus.). iv, 182p. (Orig.). 1996. pap. 14.00 (*0-86663-208-5*) Ide Hse.

Out for Office: Campaigning in the Gay '90s. Ed. by Kathleen DeBold. LC 93-80847. 305p. 1994. pap. text 12.95 (*1-883665-01-9*) Gay & Lesbian.

Out for Revenge. Brent Rowley. LC 98-29766. (J). 1998. 11.95 (*1-57734-312-3*) Covenant Comms.

Out for the Count: A Counting Adventure. (Illus.). (J). 1991. pap. text 9.99 (*0-7112-0665-1*) F Lincoln.

Out from Behind the Eight-Ball: A History of Project Echo. Ed. by Donald C. Elder. (AAS History Ser.: Vol. 16). (Illus.). 176p. 1995. 50.00 (*0-87703-387-0*, Am Astronaut Soc); pap. 30.00 (*0-87703-388-9*, Am Astronaut Soc) Univelt Inc.

Out from Darkness. rev. ed. Ben Alexander. (Illus.). 224p. (Orig.). 1992. pap. 9.95 (*0-9634071-0-4*) Miranda Pr.

Out from Las Vegas. Florine Lawlor. LC 99-27088. (Illus.). 288p. 1999. mass mkt. 16.95 (*0-9647530-4-9*) Spotted Dog CA.

Out from Madness. Janet V. Allen. (Illus.). 133p. (Orig.). 1993. pap. 10.00 (*1-885193-04-1*) Good Samaritan.

***Out from Nassau.** Fia B. Scheyer. 272p. 2000. pap. 14.00 (*0-9660325-4-3*) Trillium Bks.

Out from the Heart. James Allen. 54p. 1992. pap. 6.00 (*0-89540-228-9*, SB-228) Sun Pub.

Out from the Inside: The Use of Creativity in Relationships. Larry R. Decker. LC 84-90461. 1985. 10.95 (*0-87212-186-0*) Libra.

***Out from the Ordinary: Sermons for Sundays after Pentecost, First Third.** Gary L. Carver. LC 99-32556. (First Lessons Ser.). 90p. 1999. pap. 9.25 (*0-7880-1382-3*) CSS OH.

Out from the Shadows: Essays on Contemporary Austrian Women Writers & Filmmakers. Ed. by Margarete Lamb-Faffelberger. LC 96-9842. (Studies in Austrian Literature, Culture, & Thought). 306p. 1997. 36.95 (*1-57241-037-X*) Ariadne CA.

***Out from the Shadows: The Life of John J. Harden.** Bob Burke. Ed. by Kenny Franks & Gini Moore Campbell. LC 98-67123. (Oklahoma Trackmaker Ser.). 224p. 1998. 16.95 (*1-885596-09-X*) OK Heritage.

Out from the Shadows: The U. S. & the Third World since 1945. Edwin Clausen et al. 200p. (C). 1999. pap. 39.00 (*0-8133-0816-X*); pap. text 14.95 (*0-8133-0817-8*) Westview.

Out from the Trees: Poems of the 60s. Dan Woodward. 60p. 1992. 12.95 (*1-882935-00-4*) Westphalia.

Out from This Place. Joyce Hansen. 1988. 9.60 (*0-606-00682-6*, Pub. by Turtleback) Demco.

Out from This Place. Joyce Hansen. 1988. 13.95 (*0-8027-6816-4*) Walker & Co.

Out from this Place. Joyce Hansen. LC 88-5594. 144p. (J). (gr. 4-7). 1992. mass mkt. 4.50 (*0-380-71409-4*, Avon Bks) Morrow Avon.

Out from Under: Texts by Women Performance Artists. Ed. by Lenora Champagne. LC 90-11257. 224p. 1990. reprint ed. pap. 12.95 (*1-55936-009-7*) Theatre Comm.

Out from under the Artist's Brush: A Lacanian Approach to Painting & Naturalism. Julie A. Molnar. LC 91-3967. (American University Studies, II, Romance Language & Literature: Vol. 176). XV, 173p. (C). 1994. text 43.95 (*0-8204-1642-8*) P Lang Pubng.

Out from Underdevelopment Revisited: Changing Global Structures & the Remaking of the Third World. James H. Mittelman & Mustapha K. Pasha. LC 96-28753. (International Political Economy Ser.). 256p. 1997. text 55.00 (*0-312-16466-1*) St Martin.

***Out Front.** Patrick McCreery. 150p. 2000. pap. 12.00 (*0-8223-6476-X*) Duke.

Out Front: Contemporary Gay & Lesbian Plays. Ed. by Don Shewey. LC 88-1257. 564p. 1988. pap. 14.95 (*0-8021-3025-9*, Grove) Grove-Atltic.

Out Front - The Cladie Bailey Story: The Cladie Bailey Story. Wendell Trogdon. (Illus.). 144p. (Orig.). 1994. pap. 9.50 (*0-9642371-0-5*) Backroads Pr.

Out Front Leadership: Discovering, Developing, & Delivering Your Potential. Joe Reynolds. 1993. 19.95 (*0-9636391-0-2*) Mott & Carlisle.

Out Harmsen's Way. Gianfranco Pagnucci. 62p. (Orig.). 1991. pap. 7.00 (*1-878660-10-1*) Fireweed WI.

Out Here. Alan Wearne. LC 87-73045. 64p. (Orig.). 1988. pap. 12.95 (*0-906427-72-X*, Pub. by Bloodaxe Bks) Dufour.

***Out Here by Ourselves: The Stories of Young People Whose Mothers Have AIDS.** Diane Duggan. LC 00-35376. (Children of Poverty Ser.). 2000. write for info. (*0-8153-3621-7*) Garland.

Out Here on Soap Creek: An Autobiography. Inez M. Faber. LC 81-23682. (Illus.). 194p. pap. 60.20 (*0-608-15595-0*, 202966700062) Bks Demand.

Out in All Directions: A Treasury of Gay & Lesbian America. Ed. by Lynn Witt et al. 656p. 1997. mass mkt. 16.99 (*0-446-67237-8*, Pub. by Warner Bks) Little.

Out in Culture: Gay, Lesbian, & Queer Essays on Popular Culture. Ed. by Corey K. Creekmur & Alexander Doty. LC 94-29810. (Series Q). (Illus.). 568p. 1995. text 64.95 (*0-8223-1532-7*); pap. text 22.95 (*0-8223-1541-6*) Duke.

Out in Force: Sexual Orientation & the Military. Ed. by Jared B. Jobe et al. LC 96-20110. 320p. 1996. pap. 18.95 (*0-226-40048-4*); lib. bdg. 65.00 (*0-226-40047-6*) U Ch Pr.

Out in Front: Effective Supervision in the Workplace. (Illus.). 228p. 1990. pap. 33.95 (*0-87912-180-7*, 15151-0000) Natl Safety Coun.

Out in Space. Melvin Berger. Ed. by Susan Evento. (Early Science Big Bks.). (Illus.). 16p. (Orig.). (J). (ps-2). 1995. pap. 16.95 (*1-56784-102-3*) Newbridge Educ.

Out in Space: Mini Book. Melvin Berger. Ed. by Susan Evento. (Early Science Big Bks.). (Illus.). 16p. (Orig.). (J). (ps-2). 1995. pap. 3.95 (*1-56784-127-9*) Newbridge Educ.

Out in Space Theme Pack. Melvin Berger. Ed. by Susan Evento. (Macmillan Early Science Big Bks.). (Illus.). (J). (ps-2). 1995. pap. 49.95 (*1-56784-184-8*) Newbridge Educ.

***Out in the Blue - Letters from Arabia 1937-1940: A Young American Geologist Explores the Deserts of Early Saudi Arabia.** Thomas C. Barger. LC 00-90642. (Illus.). xvi, 304p. 2000. 34.95 (*0-9701157-3-3*, Selwa) T V T.

Out in the Cold. Lynn Kirby. LC 98-5571. (Winning Edge Ser.). (J). (gr. 5-9). 1998. 5.99 (*0-8499-5836-9*) Tommy Nelson.

Out in the Cold: Academic Boycotts & the Isolation of South Africa. Lorraine J. Haricombe & F. W. Lancaster. 158p. 1995. 29.50 (*0-87815-067-6*) Info Resources.

***Out in the Dark: Poetry of the First World War in Context & with Basic Notes.** Ed. by David Roberts. (Illus.). 192p. 1998. pap. 20.00 (*0-9528969-1-5*, Pub. by Saxon Bks) Trans-Atl Phila.

Out in the Dark & Daylight. Aileen Fisher. LC 78-22492. (Illus.). 176p. (J). (gr. k-5). 1980. 11.95 (*0-06-021902-5*) HarpC Child Bks.

Out in the Field: Reflections of Lesbian & Gay Anthropolgists. Ed. by Ellen Lewin & William L. Leap. LC 95-32456. 312p. 1996. 16.95 (*0-252-06518-2*); text 39.95 (*0-252-02219-X*) U of Ill Pr.

Out in the Garden: Month by Month Advice for a Cape Cod Garden. Martha Hughes. LC 98-212422. (Illus.). 242p. 1998. pap. 12.95 (*1-57502-832-8*, PO2292) Morris Pubng.

Out in the Midday Shade: Memoirs of an African Hunter, 1949-1968. limited ed. William York. 275p. 1999. 70.00 (*1-57157-094-2*) Safari Pr.

Out! In the Name of Jesus. A. L. Gill. 1987. pap. 2.95 (*0-941975-00-2*) Powerhouse.

Out in the Open. Geoffrey Dutton. 1995. 39.95 (*0-7022-2681-5*, Pub. by Univ Queensland Pr) Intl Spec Bk.

Out in the Open. Cathal O. Searcaigh. Tr. by Frank Sewell from IRI. LC 97-164212. 244p. 24.95 (*1-900693-74-7*, Pub. by Clo Iar-Chonnachta) Dufour.

***Out in the Open.** Cathal O. Searcaigh. (ENG & IRI.). 2000. reprint ed. pap. 14.95 (*1-902420-21-7*, Pub. by Clo Iar-Chonnachta) Dufour.

Out in the Open: Life on the Street. Bob Ballantyne. LC 96-910691. (Illus.). 96p. 1997. pap. 15.95 (*1-55145-099-2*) NStone Publ.

Out in the Open: Poems. Margaret Gibson. LC 88-22053. 55p. 1989. pap. 11.95 (*0-8071-1519-3*) La State U Pr.

Out in the Open: The Complete Male Pelvis. R. Louis Schultz. LC 99-16525. (Illus.). 150p. 1999. pap. 14.95 (*1-55643-321-2*) North Atlantic.

Out in the Open? The School Records Debate. Lucy Hodges. (Chameleon Education Ser.). 144p. (Orig.). 1981. 9.95 (*0-906495-57-1*); pap. 4.95 (*0-906495-58-X*) Writers & Readers.

***Out in the South.** Ed. by Carlos L. Dews & Carolyn Leste Law. 256p. 2001. 69.50 (*1-56639-813-4*); pap. 22.95 (*1-56639-814-2*) Temple U Pr.

Out in the Sun. (Key Words Readers Ser.: B Series, No. 641-5b). (Illus.). (J). (ps-5). write for info. (*0-317-04014-6*, Ladybrd) Penguin Putnam.

***Out in the World: A Community Living Skills Manual.** 2nd ed. Rachel P. Johnson & Rose M. Orichowski. Ed. by Cindy Drolet & C. Gilles-Brown. 277p. 1999. pap. text 52.50 (*1-883315-44-1*, 8507) Imaginart Intl.

Out in the World: International Lesbian Organizing. Shelley Anderson. LC 91-22999. 56p. 1991. pap. 4.95 (*1-56341-005-2*) Firebrand Bks.

Out in the World: Selected Letters of Jane Bowles, 1935-1970. Jane Bowles. Ed. by Millicent Dillon. LC 84-24470. (Illus.). 321p. 1990. reprint ed. 25.00 (*0-87685-626-1*); reprint ed. pap. 15.00 (*0-87685-625-3*) Black Sparrow.

Out into the End of Time. Mark E. Johnston. LC 98-30722. 84p. 1998. pap. 14.95 (*0-7734-3088-1*, Mellen Poetry Pr) E Mellen.

Out-Island Doctor. Evans W. Cottman. 1999. lib. bdg. 23.95 (*1-56723-200-0*) Yestermorrow.

Out Island Doctor. Evans W. Cottman & Wyatt Blassingame. LC 63-8607. 264p. 1988. pap. 8.95 (*0-913428-18-3*) Landfall Pr.

Out Law Justice. K. Randall Ball. 272p. 1997. pap. text. write for info. (*0-9651605-1-3*) Five Ball.

***Out Looking In: Early Modern Polish Art, 1890-1918** Jan Cavanaugh. LC 99-35618. 403p. 2000. 60.00 (*0-520-21190-1*) U CA Pr.

Out Loud: A Collection of New Songs by Women. Ed. by Lockhart et al. LC 77-86751. (Illus.). 1979. pap. text 7.50 (*0-930712-00-5*) Inkworks.

Out Many Brief, Vol. 2. 2nd ed. John Mack Faragher & Buhle. 1998. pap. text, student ed. 19.33 (*0-13-921982-X*) S&S Trade.

An Asterisk (*) at the beginning of an entry indicates that the title is appearing for the first time.

Out Now! A Participant's Account of the Movement in the United States Against the Vietnam War. Fred Halstead. LC 78-59265. (Illus.). 759p. (C). 1978. reprint ed. lib. bdg. 70.00 (*0-913460-47-8*) Pathfinder NY.

Out Now! A Participant's Account of the Movement in the United States Against the Vietnam War. 2nd ed. Fred Halstead. LC 78-59265. (Illus.). 759p. (C). 1991. reprint ed. pap. 30.95 (*0-937091-12-X*) Pathfinder NY.

Out o' Luck. Thorne Smith. 17.95 (*0-8488-1174-7*) Amereon Ltd.

Out of a Dead End into the Unknown: Notes on Gorbachev's Perestroika. Vladimir K. Yegorov. Tr. by David Floyd from GER. LC 93-24701.Tr. of Aus der Sackgasse in die Ungewissheit. (Illus.). 159p. 1993. pap. 14.95 (*0-86715-267-2*) Edition Q.

Out of a Kantian Chrysalis? A Maritainian Critique of Fr. Marechal, Vol. 182. Ronald McCamy. LC 97-10691. (American University Studies: No. V). XV, 180p. (C). 1998. pap. text 24.95 (*0-8204-3722-0*) P Lang Pubng.

Out of a Whirlpool. large type ed. Alan Sillitoe. (Mainstream Ser.). 136p. 1988. reprint ed. 18.95 (*1-85089-224-5*, Pub. by ISIS Lrg Prnt) Transaction Pubs.

Out of a Wilderness. Georgia Detering. 91p. 1989. reprint ed. pap. 10.00 (*0-685-30402-7*) Fernwood Pr.

Out of Absence. Carol Dragone. Ed. by M. Hettich & Colleen Ahern. 25p. 1978. 1.50 (*0-686-38057-6*) MoonsQuilt Pr.

Out of Actions: Between Performance & the Object, 1949-1979. Ed. by Paul Schimmel & Russell Ferguson. LC 97-62054. (Illus.). 368p. 1998. pap. 45.00 (*0-500-28050-9*, Pub. by Thames Hudson) Norton.

Out of Actions: Between Performance & the Object, 1949-1979. Paul Schimmel et al. LC 97-48382. 1998. write for info. (*0-914357-56-5*) Los Angeles Mus Contemp.

Out of Afghanistan: The Inside Story of the Soviet Withdrawal. Diego Cordovez & Selig S. Harrison. (Illus.). 450p. Date not set. 35.00 (*0-614-19494-6*) OUP.

Out of Africa. Isak Dinesen. LC 92-50213. 420p. 1992. 16.50 (*0-679-60021-3*) Modern Lib NY.

Out of Africa. Isak Dinesen. 1993. reprint ed. lib. bdg. 18.95 (*0-89968-444-0*, Lghtyr Pr) Buccaneer Bks.

Out of Africa: I Thought Christianity Was a White Man's Religion until I Met Christ. Derek Grier. (Orig.). pap. 7.95 (*0-9632116-9-2*) Ham Pub Co.

Out of Africa: I Thought Christianity Was a White Man's Religion until I Met Christ. large type ed. Derek Grier. 112p. (Orig.). 1996. pap. 7.95 (*0-9632169-2-9*) Ham Pub Co.

Out of Africa & Shadows on the Grass. Isak Dinesen. LC 89-40144. (Vintage International Ser.). 512p. 1989. pap. 13.00 (*0-679-72475-3*) Vin Bks.

Out of Africa Piano Selections. J. Barry. 24p. 1986. pap. 7.95 (*0-7935-2385-0*, 00123603) H Leonard.

Out of America. Susan Schmidt. 224p. 1994. pap. 12.99 (*1-85242-256-4*) Serpents Tail.

***Out of America: A Black Man Confronts Africa.** Keith B. Richburg. LC 97-47710. 272p. (C). 1998. pap. 13.00 (*0-15-600583-2*) Harcourt.

Out of Anger with Love: Poems Collection. William D. Albright. 1993. pap. 9.95 (*0-9637935-0-0*) Davis Comm Grp.

Out of Area or Out of Reach? European Military Support for Operations in Southwest Asia. John E. Peters & Howard Deshong. LC 95-44672. 148p. (Orig.). 1995. pap. text 15.00 (*0-8330-2329-2*, MR-629-OSD) Rand Corp.

Out of Ashes. Keith Phillips. (Illus.). 196p. (Orig.). 1996. 12.00 (*0-9655553-0-5*) World Impact.

Out of Ashes. Helen W. Quintela. LC 91-10447. 160p. 1991. pap. 8.99 (*0-8361-3554-7*) Herald Pr.

***Out of Assa - Heart of the Congo: Medical Adventures in Central Africa.** Glenn W. Gelhoed. Ed. & Photos by Kurt E. Johnson. LC 99-74543. (Illus.). 350p. (Orig.). 1999. pap. 15.95 (*0-9669305-0-9*) Three Hawks.

Out of Awareness: A Psychological & Spiritual Exploration of War & Peace. Andrew B. Schmookler. (New Age Ser.). 352p. 1988. 21.95 (*0-685-18350-5*) Bantam.

Out of Babylon. Richard Grossinger. LC 96-50152. (Illus.). 500p. (Orig.). 1997. pap. 18.95 (*1-883319-57-9*) Frog Ltd CA.

Out of Barbed Wire: Into a Nazi Death March. Marie Kramer. LC 95-90109. (Illus.). 147p. (Orig.). 1995. pap. 9.50 (*0-9637525-2-9*) M Kramer.

Out of Battle. 2nd ed. Silkin. LC 97-52925. 380p. 1998. text 59.95 (*0-312-21404-9*) St Martin.

Out of Battle: The Poetry of the Great War. Jon Silkin. 384p. 1987. pap. 13.95 (*0-7102-1222-4*, 12224, Routledge Thoemms) Routledge.

Out of Betrayal: Breaking Free of Exploitive Relationships. Patrick Carnes. 250p. 1996. pap. 11.95 (*1-55874-393-6*, 3936) Health Comm.

Out of Body. Tom Baum. LC 96-52646. 1997. text 22.95 (*0-312-15620-0*) St Martin.

Out of Body. Tom Baum. 256p. 1998. mass mkt. 5.99 (*0-312-96735-7*, Pub. by Tor Bks) St Martin.

Out-of-Body Adventures. Rick Stack. 144p. (Orig.). 1988. pap. 12.95 (*0-8092-4560-4*, 456040, Contemporary Bks) NTC Contemp Pub Co.

Out of Body & Mind. Veronica Jean. LC 92-34343. 166p. 1993. pap. 16.00 (*1-877946-51-6*) Permanent Pr.

Out-of-Body Experiences. Janet L. Mitchell. LC 81-8145. 140p. 1981. lib. bdg. 28.50 (*0-89950-031-5*) McFarland & Co.

Out-of-Body Experiences. Lazar Puhalo. 32p. Date not set. pap. 4.00 (*1-879038-64-1*, 9034) Synaxis Pr.

Out of Body Experiences: How to Have Them & What to Expect. Bob Peterson. LC 97-176652. 224p. 1997. pap. 11.95 (*1-57174-057-0*) Hampton Roads Pub Co.

Out of Body, into Mind: A Novel of Suspense. Stephen H. Martin. 252p. (Orig.). 1995. pap. 14.95 (*0-9646601-6-4*) Oaklea Pr.

Out of Bondage. Linda Lovelace & Mike McGrady. 1986. 14.95 (*0-8184-0386-1*) Carol Pub Group.

Out of Bondage. Arnold Perrin. (Illus.). 52p. 1983. pap. 4.95 (*0-939736-45-4*) Wings ME.

***Out of Bounds.** Mandy Dickinson. (Orig.). 1999. mass mkt. 6.95 (*0-352-33431-2*) London Brdge.

Out of Bounds. Hank Herman. (Super Hoops Ser.: No. 13). (Illus.). 96p. (J). (gr. 4-6). 1997. pap. 3.50 (*0-553-48476-1*, Skylark BDD) BDD Bks Young Read.

Out of Bounds. Hank Herman. (Super Hoops Ser.: No. 13). (J). (gr. 4-6). 1997. 8.60 (*0-606-11943-4*, Pub. by Turtleback) Demco.

Out of Bounds. Carolyn Keene. (Nancy Drew Files: No. 45). 160p. (J). (gr. 7-12). 1991. per. 3.50 (*0-671-73911-5*, Archway) PB.

Out of Bounds. Carolyn Keene. (Nancy Drew Files: No. 45). (YA). (gr. 6 up). 1990. 8.60 (*0-606-04500-7*, Pub. by Turtleback) Demco.

Out of Bounds. Ted Kowalski. (C). 1994. pap. text. write for info. (*0-8013-1354-6*) Longman.

Out of Bounds. Elizabeth Sullam. xii, 116p. 1990. 23.50 (*0-916379-40-X*) Scripta.

Out of Bounds: An Anecdotal History of Notre Dame Football. Bonifer & Weaver. LC 78-60060. (Illus.). 1978. 15.00 (*0-87832-043-1*) Piper.

Out of Bounds: Contemporary Long Island Photographs. Ann Chwatsky. (Illus.). 30p. 1989. pap. 5.00 (*0-933793-11-1*) Guild Hall.

Out of Bounds: Male Writers & Gender(ed) Criticism. Ed. by Laura Claridge & Elizabeth Langland. LC 90-35674. 360p. 1990. 42.50 (*0-87023-734-9*); pap. 19.95 (*0-87023-735-7*) U of Mass Pr.

Out of Bounds: New Work by Eight Southeast Artists. Julia A. Fenton & Annette M. Carlozzi. Ed. by Kathy L. Maschke. (Illus.). 64p. (Orig.). 1996. pap. 20.00 (*0-9650938-0-8*) Nexus Contemp.

Out of Bounds: Poems. Harry Mathews. (Burning Deck Poetry Chapbooks Ser.). 44p. 1989. pap. 5.00 (*0-930901-61-4*) Burning Deck.

Out of Bounds: Sexual Exploitation in Counselling & Therapy. Janice Russell. (Illus.). 160p. (C). 1993. text 69.95 (*0-8039-8533-9*); pap. text 22.95 (*0-8039-8534-7*) Sage.

Out of Bounds: Sports, Media & the Politics of Identity. Aaron Baker & Todd Boyd. LC 96-19729. 1997. 39.95 (*0-253-33228-1*); pap. 17.95 (*0-253-21095-X*) Ind U Pr.

Out of Bounds: Women, Sport & Sexuality. Helen Lenskyj. 180p. reprint ed. pap. 10.95 (*0-88961-105-X*, Pub. by Womens Pr) LPC InBook.

Out of Canaan. Mary S. Hammond. 112p. 1993. pap. 9.95 (*0-393-30939-8*) Norton.

Out of Chaos! 2nd ed. Sanjay Jasuja. (Illus.). 176p. (Orig.). 1995. pap. 19.95 (*0-9647153-0-9*) Esteem Hse.

Out of Chaos: Refounding Religious Congregations. Gerald A. Arbuckle. LC 88-11969. 208p. 1988. pap. 12.95 (*0-8091-3004-1*) Paulist Pr.

Out of China: Culture & Traditions. Evelyn Lip. LC 93-23966. (Illus.). 1993. 29.90 (*0-685-65618-7*) Addison-Wesley.

Out of Circulation: Miss. Jo Dereske. LC 97-93011. (Miss Zukas Ser.). 212p. 1997. mass mkt. 5.99 (*0-380-78244-8*, Avon Bks) Morrow Avon.

Out of Conflict: From War to Peace in Africa. Ed. by Gunnar M. Sorbo & Peter Vale. LC 98-132697. 202p. 1997. 23.95 (*91-7106-413-3*, Pub. by Nordic Africa) Transaction Pubs.

Out of Context: Historical Reference & the Representation of Reality in Borges. Daniel Balderston. LC 92-23417. 231p. 1993. text 49.95 (*0-8223-1289-1*); pap. text 18.95 (*0-8223-1316-2*) Duke.

Out of Control. R. Ambrose. mass mkt. 6.95 (*0-7472-5168-1*) Headline Bk Pub.

***Out of Control.** Carolanne Foley. 180p. 1999. pap. 6.99 (*1-893108-23-6*) Neighbrhd Pr Pubng.

Out of Control. Judy Jackson. (Scarlet Ser.). (Orig.). 1997. mass mkt. 3.99 (*1-85487-963-4*, Pub. by Scarlet Bks) London Brdge.

Out of Control. Carolyn Keene. (Nancy Drew & Hardy Boys Super Mystery Ser.: No. 31). (YA). (gr. 6 up). 1997. pap. 3.99 (*0-671-53748-2*, Archway) PB.

Out of Control. Carolyn Keene. (Nancy Drew & Hardy Boys Super Mystery Ser.: No. 31). (YA). (gr. 6 up). 1997. 9.09 (*0-606-11668-0*, Pub. by Turtleback) Demco.

Out of Control. Elizabeth Levy. (Gymnasts Ser.: No. 12). 112p. (J). (gr. 4-7). 1990. pap. 2.75 (*0-590-42824-1*) Scholastic Inc.

Out of Control. G. Gordon Liddy. 352p. 1991. mass mkt. 5.99 (*0-312-92428-3*) St Martin.

Out of Control. Mark Lowry. 208p. 1997. pap. 10.99 (*0-8499-4049-4*) Word Pub.

Out of Control. Norma F. Mazer. LC 92-32516. 224p. (YA). (gr. 7 up). 1993. 16.00 (*0-688-10208-5*, Wm Morrow) Morrow Avon.

Out of Control. Norma F. Mazer. LC 92-32516. 224p. (YA). (gr. 7 up). 1994. mass mkt. 4.99 (*0-380-71347-0*, Avon Bks) Morrow Avon.

Out of Control. Norma Fox Mazer. LC 92-32516. 1993. 9.60 (*0-606-06652-7*, Pub. by Turtleback) Demco.

Out of Control. Bruce W. Sanford. 1996. 20.00 (*0-02-927721-3*) Free Pr.

Out of Control. Candace Schuler. 1997. per. 3.50 (*0-373-25748-1*, 1-25748-4) Harlequin Bks.

Out of Control. Kate William. (Sweet Valley High Ser.: No. 35). (YA). (gr. 7 up). 1987. 8.60 (*0-606-03283-5*, Pub. by Turtleback) Demco.

Out of Control: British Foreign Policy & the Union of Democratic Control, 1914-1918. Sally Harris. LC 96-207924. 300p. 1996. 25.00 (*0-85958-645-6*, Pub. by Univ of Hull Pr) Paul & Co Pubs.

Out of Control: Family Therapy & Domestic Disorder. Jaber F. Gubrium. (Library of Social Research: Vol. 189). 272p. (C). 1992. text 59.95 (*0-8039-4632-5*); pap. text 26.00 (*0-8039-4633-3*) Sage.

***Out of Control: Gambling & Other Impulse Control Disorders.** Linda N. Bayer. (Encyclopedia of Psychological Disorders Ser.). 2000. write for info. (*0-7910-5313-X*) Chelsea Hse.

Out of Control: Global Turmoil on the Eve of the Twenty-First Century. Zbigniew K. Brzezinski. Ed. by Robert Stewart. 240p. 1993. text 21.00 (*0-684-19630-1*, Scribners Ref) Mac Lib Ref.

Out of Control: Militia Abuses in the Philippines. Lawyers Committee for Human Rights Staff. 149p. (Orig.). 1990. pap. 8.00 (*0-934143-37-4*) Lawyers Comm Human.

Out of Control: The Addictive Behavioral Personality. Moses Calhoun. (Illus.). 250p. 1993. 29.95 (*0-9638949-0-0*) Winning Artist.

Out of Control: The New Biology of Machines, Social Systems, & the Economic World. Kevin Kelly. 528p. 1995. pap. 18.00 (*0-201-48340-8*) Addison-Wesley.

Out of Control: Who's Watching Our Child Protection Agencies. Brenda Scott. LC 94-76353. 208p. 1994. pap. 10.99 (*1-56384-069-3*) Huntington Hse.

Out of Control - A Winning Combination, 2 bks. in 1. Lori Copeland. 368p. 1994. mass mkt. 4.99 (*0-505-51951-8*, Love Spell) Dorchester Pub Co.

Out of Control & Loving It! Giving God Complete Control of Your Life. Lisa Bevere. LC 96-83756. 1996. pap. 12.99 (*0-88419-436-1*) Creation House.

Out of Control Room: A Hilarious Look at TV Production. Martin S. Dick. LC 87-90747. 103p. (Orig.). 1988. pap. 9.24 (*0-9618502-0-5*) Sugma Press.

Out of Court: How to Protect Your Business from Litigation. John F. Landrum. 160p. 1992. pap. 14.95 (*0-9633730-9-9*) Headwaters LA.

Out of Crisis: A Project for European Recovery. Ed. by Stuart Holland. (Forum for International Political & Social Economy Ser.). 199p. 1983. 42.50 (*0-85124-372-X*, Pub. by Spkesman) Coronet Bks.

Out of Dallas: Fourteen Stories. Dallas County Community College District Staff. Ed. by Jane R. Wood et al. LC 88-38942. (Illus.). 208p. 1989. pap. 12.95 (*0-929398-03-3*) UNTX Pr.

***Out of Danger.** Beverly Barton. 2000. mass mkt. 4.50 (*0-373-82240-5*, 1-82240-2) Harlequin Bks.

Out of Danger. James Fenton. LC 93-40178. 1994. 23.00 (*0-374-22831-0*) FS&G.

Out of Danger. James Fenton. 112p. 1995. pap. 10.00 (*0-374-52437-8*, Noonday) FS&G.

Out of Darkness. Geraldine C. Little. LC 92-32571. 110p. (C). 1993. lib. bdg. 32.00 (*0-8191-8907-3*) U Pr of Amer.

Out of Darkness. Ramela Martin. 1989. write for info. (*0-916431-28-2*) Zoryan Ins.

Out of Darkness. Keith C. Terry & Maurice R. Tanner. LC 95-32730. 1995. pap. 13.95 (*1-55503-866-2*, 01112082) Covenant Comms.

Out of Darkness. Janelle Wade. 238p. (Orig.). 1993. pap. 10.99 (*1-56043-756-1*, Treasure Hse) Destiny Image.

***Out of Darkness: Collected Writings on Depression, Despair & Melancholy.** J. M. McDonell. LC 00-33954. 2000. write for info. (*1-893224-15-5*, New Millenn Pr) New Millenn Enter.

Out of Darkness: Growing up with the Christian Brothers. Ivor A. Knight. 1998. pap. 16.95 (*1-86368-207-4*, Pub. by Fremantle Arts) Intl Spec Bk.

Out of Darkness: Ramela's Story. James Martin & Ramela Martin. LC 97-71582. (Illus.). 224p. (Orig.). 1997. pap. 16.95 (*1-882897-12-9*) Lost Coast.

Out of Darkness: The Controversy over Satanism & Ritual Abuse. David K. Sakheim & Susan E. Devine. LC 97-25722. 1997. pap. 22.95 (*0-7879-3954-4*) Jossey-Bass.

Out of Darkness: The Story of Louis Braille. Russell Freedman. LC 95-52533. (Illus.). 81p. (YA). (gr. 5 up). 1997. 16.00 (*0-395-77516-7*, Clarion Bks) HM.

***Out of Darkness: The Story of Louis Braille.** Russell Freedman. (Illus.). 88p. (J). (gr. 3-7). 1999. pap. 7.95 (*0-395-96888-7*, Clarion Bks) HM.

Out of Darkness: The Story of Louis Braille. Russell Freedman. (YA). (gr. 5 up). 1997. 15.95 (*0-614-28670-0*, Dutton Child) Peng Put Young Read.

Out of Darkness into the Light. Laurie Wallace. 161p. (Orig.). (C). 1995. pap. 14.95 (*0-9647002-0-4*) Brockton Pubng.

Out of Darkness into the Light: A Journey of Inner Healing. Gerald G. Jampolsky. 272p. 1990. pap. 13.95 (*0-553-34791-8*) Bantam.

Out of Death Came Life. Barbara Monroe. 15.95 (*0-9700876-0-8*) J&M Pubng NC.

Out of Debt. Robert Steinback. 120p. 1989. pap. 6.95 (*1-55850-994-1*) Adams Media.

Out of Debt, Out of Danger: An Analysis of the Federal Reserve System. Jerry Voorhis. 1991. lib. bdg. 79.95 (*0-8490-5179-7*) Gordon Pr.

Out of Despite see Por Despecho

Out of Discontent: Visions of the Contemporary University. Craig R. Eisendrath et al. (Illus.). 181p. 1973. 18.95 (*0-87073-155-6*) Schenkman Bks Inc.

Out-of-Doors in the Holy Land: Impressions of Travel in Body & Spirit. Henry Van Dyke. Ed. by Moshe Davis. LC 77-70751. (America & the Holy Land Ser.). (Illus.). 1977. reprint ed. lib. bdg. 29.95 (*0-405-10297-6*) Ayer.

Out of Dr. Bill's Black Bag: From Northern Wisconsin . . . a Country Doctor Looks Back (1941-1991) William B. Bauer. LC 94-94225. 315p. (Orig.). 1994. pap. text 19.95 (*0-9640154-1-2*) Brother Bills.

Out of Eastern Europe: Private Photography. John P. Jacob & Lynn Zelevansky. LC 86-63520. (Illus.). 56p. (Orig.). 1987. pap. 7.50 (*0-938437-17-8*) MIT List Visual Arts.

Out of Eden. Frankie Paino. LC 97-65398. (Poetry Ser.: Vol. LIV). 90p. (Orig.). 1997. pap. 12.00 (*1-880834-33-2*) Cleveland St Univ Poetry Ctr.

Out of Eden. Kathleen Sage. 352p. 1996. mass mkt. 5.99 (*0-515-11875-3*, Jove) Berkley Pub.

Out of Eden. Dana Self. (Illus.). 32p. 1997. pap. 12.00 (*1-891246-02-X*) Kemper Mus.

Out of Eden. large type ed. Kate Lehrer. (Niagara Large Print Ser.). 548p. 1997. 29.50 (*0-7089-5869-9*) Ulverscroft.

Out of Eden: Essays on Modern Art. W. S. Di Piero. LC 90-48336. (Illus.). 269p. 1991. 45.00 (*0-520-07065-8*, Pub. by U CA Pr); pap. 16.95 (*0-520-08432-2*, Pub. by U CA Pr) Cal Prin Full Svc.

Out of Eden: Reading, Rhetoric, & Ideology in Genesis 2-3. Beverly J. Stratton. LC 96-115083. (Journal for the Study of the Old Testament Supplement Ser.: Vol. 208). 292p. 1996. 85.00 (*1-85075-575-2*, Pub. by Sheffield Acad) CUP Services.

***Out of Egypt.** Ahmed Osman. 1998. 35.00 (*0-7126-7962-6*, Pub. by Random) Trafalgar.

***Out of Egypt.** Ahmed Osman. 1999. mass mkt. 13.95 (*0-09-927765-4*, Pub. by Random) Trafalgar.

Out of Egypt: A Memoir. Andre Aciman. LC 95-34143. 1996. pap. 14.00 (*1-57322-534-7*, Riverhd Trade) Berkley Pub.

Out of Egypt: A Prophetic Call to the End-Time Church. Chuck Crismier. 288p. 1999. pap. 15.99 (*1-57921-196-8*, Pub. by WinePress Pub) BookWorld.

***Out of Egypt: Inspriation for Conquering Life's Strongholds.** Gwen Shamblin. 208p. 2000. 16.99 (*0-7852-6849-9*) Nelson.

Out of Egypt: Scenes & Arguments of an Autobiography. Ihab Hassan. LC 85-30379. (Crosscurrents-Modern Critiques, Third Ser.). 128p. 1986. text 21.95 (*0-8093-1296-4*) S Ill U Pr.

***Out of Egypt into Canaan: Lessons in Spiritual Geography.** Martin Wells Knapp. (Illus.). 2000. pap. write for info. (*0-88019-412-X*) Schmul Pub Co.

Out of Egypt, Out of Bondage. Vernelle B. Allen. 80p. 1995. pap. write for info. (*1-885984-07-3*) Wings of Healing.

Out of Eldridge Street. Harold F. Swiss. Ed. by Vivian Vican. 516p. 1998. pap. 14.95 (*0-7392-0040-2*, PO2809) Morris Pubng.

Out of Equilibrium. Mario Amendola & Jean-Luc Gaffard. (Illus.). 296p. 1998. text 65.00 (*0-19-829380-1*) OUP.

Out of Every Tribe & Nation. Justo L. Gonzalez. 224p. (Orig.). 1992. pap. 12.95 (*0-687-29860-1*) Abingdon.

Out of Everywhere: Linguistically Innovative Poetry by Women in North America & the U. K. Ed. by Maggie O'Sullivan. 254p. 1996. 15.00 (*1-874400-08-3*, Pub. by Reality St Edits) SPD-Small Pr Dist.

Out-of-Field Teaching & Educational Equality. Richard M. Ingersoll. 70p. 1996. pap. 4.00 (*0-16-048833-8*) USGPO.

Out of Focus. Alf MacLochlainn. LC 85-72481. 64p. 1985. 20.00 (*0-916583-12-0*); pap. 7.95 (*0-916583-13-9*) Dalkey Arch.

Out of Focus: Network Television & the American Economy. Burton Y. Pines & Timothy W. Lamer. LC 93-46426. 384p. 1994. 24.00 (*0-89526-490-0*) Regnery Pub.

Out of Focus: Writings on Women & the Media. Ed. by Kath Davies et al. 256p. pap. 11.95 (*0-7043-4059-3*, Pub. by Womens Press) Trafalgar.

Out of Galileo No. 49: The Science of Waters 1628-1718. C. S. Maffioli. xx, 509p. 1994. 63.00 (*90-5235-071-X*, Pub. by Erasmus Pub) Balogh.

Out of Gas on Lovers Leap. Mark St. Germain. 1985. pap. 5.25 (*0-8222-0870-9*) Dramatists Play.

Out of Gloucester. James B. Connolly. LC 70-94712. (Short Story Index Reprint Ser.). 1977. 20.95 (*0-8369-3091-6*) Ayer.

Out of Grimsby. Alf May. 161p. (C). 1989. text 42.00 (*0-902662-86-4*, Pub. by R K Pubns); pap. text 21.00 (*0-902662-87-2*, Pub. by R K Pubns) St Mut.

Out of Harm's Way: Creating a Safe World for Our Children. Gelles. 1994. 24.95 (*0-02-911603-1*) S&S Trade.

Out of Harm's Way: The Extraordinary True Story of One Woman's Lifelong Devotion to Animals. Terri Crisp. 416p. 1997. per. 14.00 (*0-671-52278-7*) PB.

Out of Hearing: Representing Children in Court. J. M. Masson & Maureen Winn-Oakley. LC 98-35141. (Series in Child Protection & Policy). 190p. 1999. pap. 67.50 (*0-471-98642-9*) Wiley.

Out of Heart. MacDonald Carey. Ed. by Andrew Adler & Roger Adler. 1979. 5.95 (*0-916844-04-8*) Turtle Pr.

Out of Hell: An Adult Child of an Alcoholic-Dysfunctional Family Recovery Saga. Joe S. 294p. (Orig.). 1991. pap. 5.50 (*1-880998-00-9*) State Art OH.

Out of Hell Again. Joe S. (Illus.). 167p. (Orig.). 1991. pap. 8.95 (*1-880998-01-7*) State Art OH.

***Out of Her Mind: Women Writing on Madness.** Ed. by Rebecca Shannonhouse. LC 99-42208. 224p. 1999. 21.95 (*0-679-60330-1*) Modern Lib NY.

***Out of Hiding.** Catherine Farnes. LC 99-88171. 176p. (J). 2000. 6.49 (*1-57924-329-0*) Bob Jones Univ.

. . . Out of His Ashes. C. Bharti. (C). 1994. text 14.00 (*81-241-0193-0*, Pub. by Har-Anand Pubns) S Asia.

Out of History. Cairns Craig. 1996. 24.00 (*0-7486-6082-8*, Pub. by Polygon) Subterranean Co.

Out of History's Junk Jar. Judith Chalmer. LC 95-31079. 100p. 1995. pap. 12.50 (*1-56809-017-X*) Time Being Bks.

Out of History's Junk Jar: Poems of a Mixed Inheritance. Judith Chalmer. LC 95-31079. 100p. 1995. 18.95 (*1-56809-016-1*) Time Being Bks.

Out of Hock. Harry S. Dahlstrom. (Illus.). 50p. (Orig.). 1994. pap. 3.99 (*0-940712-54-7*) Dahlstrom & Co.

O

Out-of-Hospital Transfusion Therapy. Ed. by Joy L. Fridey et al. (Illus.). 110p. (C). 1994. text 20.00 (*1-56395-029-4*) Am Assn Blood.

Out of Hungary. George Nivrith. 1999. pap. text 11.95 (*1-57558-033-0*) Hearthstone OK.

***Out of Hungary: A Memoir.** George Neuvirth. 10p. 2000. pap. 9.95 (*1-891429-07-8*) Armadillo Pubng.

Out of India. Jamila Gavin. (Illus.). 96p. 1998. 19.95 (*1-85793-963-8*, Pub. by Pavilion Bks Ltd) Trafalgar.

Out of India: Image of the West in Hindi Literature. Danuta Stasik. LC 94-906521. (C). 1995. 14.00 (*81-7304-050-8*, Pub. by Manohar) S Asia.

***Out of India: Selected Stories.** Ruth Prawer Jhabvala. LC 99-46035. 288p. 1999. pap. text 14.00 (*1-58243-052-7*, Pub. by Counterpt DC) HarpC.

Out of Indochina! Freedom for Angela Davis! Our Goals for 1971 & How to Win Them. Gus Hall. 1971. pap. 0.85 (*0-87898-075-X*) New Outlook.

Out of Inferno: Strindberg's Reawakening As an Artist. Carlson. LC 95-35409. (McLellan Bks.). (Illus.). 412p. (C). 1996. pap. 24.95 (*0-295-97564-4*) U of Wash Pr.

Out of Ireland: The Story of Irish Emigration to America. Kerby Miller & Paul Wagner. (Illus.). 132p. 1997. 29.95 (*1-57098-179-5*); pap. 19.95 (*1-57098-180-9*) Roberts Rinehart.

Out of Isak Dinesen in Africa: Karen Blixen's Untold Story. 2nd rev. ed. Linda Donelson. LC 98-72165. (Illus.). 440p. 1998. pap. 19.95 (*0-9643893-9-8*, SAN 298-6043) Coulsong List.

Out of Isak Dinesen in Africa: Karen Blixen's Untold Story. 2nd rev. ed. Frwd. by Don Mowatt. LC 98-72165. (Illus.). 440p. 1998. 35.00 (*0-9643893-8-X*, SAN 298-6043) Coulsong List.

***Out of Its Mind.** Hobson. 2000. pap. 25.00 (*0-7382-0251-7*, Pub. by Perseus Pubng) HarpC.

Out of Jackie's Smoke House. Jackie Reynolds. (Illus.). 110p. (Orig.). 1996. pap. 19.95 (*0-9657632-1-8*, 76653-46873) Out Back Ranch.

Out of Kentucky Kitchens. Marion Flexner. LC 89-16651. (Illus.). 320p. 1989. 22.00 (*0-8131-1712-7*) U Pr of Ky.

***Out of Kenya: Kenyan Running Secret.** Karanja Kimani & Kibai Mwangi Gikuyu. LC 98-90451. 144p. 1999. pap. 15.00 (*0-9657641-1-7*) Wambui Pub.

Out of Land: New & Selected Poems. Lawrence Sail. 159p. 1992. pap. 19.95 (*1-85224-183-7*, Pub. by Bloodaxe Bks) Dufour.

Out of Left Field: Over 1,134 Newly Discovered Amazing Baseball Records. Jeffrey Lyons & Douglas B. Lyons. 1998. pap. 12.00 (*0-8129-2993-4*) Random.

***Out of Left Field 2.** Jeffrey Lyons. 2000. pap. write for info. (*0-8129-3315-X*, Times Bks) Crown Pub Group.

Out of Line. D'Emilio. 1997. 24.95 (*0-02-907355-3*) Free Pr.

Out of Line. Demilio. 2001. 24.95 (*0-684-82780-8*) Free Pr.

Out of Line. Laban Hill. LC 98-84827. (X Games Extreme Mysteries). 96p. (J). (gr. 3-7). 1998. pap. 3.95 (*0-7868-1264-8*, Pub. by Hyperion) Time Warner.

***Out of Line: Drawings by Illinois Artists.** John Brunetti. (Illus.). 32p. 2000. pap. 15.00 (*0-938903-29-2*) Cty of Chicago.

Out of Line: History, Psychoanalysis, & Montage in H. D.'s Long Poems. Susan Edmunds. LC 94-13823. xii, 244p. 1995. 35.00 (*0-8047-2370-2*) Stanford U Pr.

Out of Line: Homeric Composition Beyond the Hexameter. Matthew Clark. LC 97-35673. (Greek Studies). 224p. 1997. 61.00 (*0-8476-8697-3*); pap. 24.95 (*0-8476-8698-1*) Rowman.

Out of Line: The Story of British New Dance. Judith Mackrell. (Illus.). 160p. (Orig.). 1992. pap. 17.95 (*1-85273-038-2*, Pub. by Dance Bks) Princeton Bk Co.

Out of Little Coins, Big Fortunes Grow. 4th rev. ed. Don Bale, Jr. 1980. pap. 5.00 (*0-912070-08-0*) Bale Bks.

Out of Loneliness. limited ed. Fritz W. Faiss. (Illus.). 71p. 1972. pap. 10.00 (*0-916678-06-7*) Green Hut.

Out of Love. Victoria Clayton. LC 98-14839. 384p. 1998. text 25.95 (*0-312-18645-2*) St Martin.

***Out of Many.** 3rd ed. 2000. write for info. (*0-13-018704-6*) P-H.

Out of Many: A History of the American People. John Mack Faragher et al. LC 93-11738. 1152p. (C). 1993. text 78.00 (*0-13-556599-5*) P-H.

Out of Many: A History of the American People. 2nd abr. ed. John Mack Faragher. LC 98-5458. 616p. 1998. pap. text 40.00 (*0-13-841495-5*) P-H.

Out of Many: A History of the American People. 3rd ed. John Mack Faragher et al. 557p. (C). 1999. pap. text 57.33 (*0-13-949752-8*, Pub. by P-H) S&S Trade.

Out of Many: A History of the American People, Vol. 1. 2nd abr. ed. John Mack Faragher & Buhle. 328p. 1998. pap. text 31.60 (*0-13-841479-3*) P-H.

Out of Many: A History of the American People, Vol. 1. 3rd ed. John Mack Faragher. 559p. (C). 1999. pap. text 57.33 (*0-13-949306-9*, Pub. by P-H) S&S Trade.

***Out of Many: A History of the American People, Vol. C.** 3rd ed. John Mack Faragher et al. 429p. (C). 1999. pap. text 48.67 (*0-13-010033-1*) P-H.

***Out of Many: A History of the American People, Vol. A.** 3rd ed. John Mack Faragher et al. 463p. (C). 1999. pap. text 48.67 (*0-13-010031-5*) P-H.

***Out of Many: A History of the American People, Vol. B.** 3rd ed. John Mack Faragher et al. 302p. (C). 1999. pap. text 48.67 (*0-13-010032-3*) P-H.

Out of Many: A History of the American People - Brief Edition. 2nd ed. John Mack Faragher et al. 352p. 1998. pap. text 31.60 (*0-13-841487-4*) P-H.

Out of Many: A History of the American People - Brief Edition. 2nd ed. John Mack Faragher et al. 1998. pap. text, student ed. 19.33 (*0-13-921975-7*) P-H.

Out of Many: A History of the American People Combined. 3rd ed. John Mack Faragher. LC 98-34110. 1038p. (C). 1999. 75.33 (*0-13-949760-9*, Pub. by P-H) S&S Trade.

***Out of Many: Brief Edition, 1.** 3rd ed. John M. Faragher & Mari Jo Buthle. 408p. 2000. pap. 33.33 (*0-13-017702-4*) P-H.

***Out of Many: Brief Edition Combined.** 3rd ed. John M. Faragher & Mari Jo Buhle. 720p. 2000. pap. 46.67 (*0-13-017704-0*) P-H.

***Out of Many: History American People Combined.** 3rd ed. 1999. write for info. (*0-13-999657-5*, Prentice Hall) P-H.

***Out of Many: History American People Combined.** 3rd ed. 1999. write for info. (*0-13-999616-8*, Prentice Hall) P-H.

***Out of Many: History of American People** 3rd ed. Vol. 2. 79p. (C). 1999. write for info. (*0-13-016554-9*) S&S Trade.

***Out of Many Vol. 1: The History of American People.** 3rd ed. 2000. write for info. (*0-13-032257-1*) P-H.

***Out of Many Vol. 2: The History of American People.** 3rd ed. 2000. write for info. (*0-13-032259-8*) P-H.

Out of Many Brief Vol. 1. Neumeyer. 1995. pap. text, student ed. 19.33 (*0-13-564808-4*) P-H.

Out of Many Waters. Jacqueline D. Greene. (American History Series for Young People). (J). (gr. 5 up). 1988. 16.95 (*0-8027-6811-3*) Walker & Co.

Out of Many Waters. Jacqueline D. Greene. 208p. (J). (gr. 5 up). 1993. pap. 8.95 (*0-8027-7401-6*) Walker & Co.

Out of Many Waters. Jacqueline Dembar Greene. 1988. 14.05 (*0-606-08840-7*, Pub. by Turtleback) Demco.

Out of Margin: Feminist Economics Today. Ed. by Edith Kulper et al. LC 95-1524. 320p. (C). 1995. pap. 29.99 (*0-415-12575-8*) Routledge.

Out of Me see Composing Myself: A Journey Through Postpartum Depression

Out of Me Went 43 Demons. Antoinette Cannaday. 170p. (Orig.). 1994. pap. 6.95 (*0-89228-111-1*) Impact Christian.

Out of Mighty Waters: Sermons by African American Disciples. Ed. by Darryl M. Trimiew. 176p. (Orig.). 1994. pap. 12.99 (*0-8272-2708-6*) Chalice Pr.

Out of Mulberry Street. Jacob A. Riis. LC 74-104550. 279p. reprint ed. lib. bdg. 29.75 (*0-8398-1758-4*) Irvington.

Out of My Class. John Boyd. LC 85-20016. 192 p. 1985. write for info. (*0-85640-337-7*) Blckstaff Pr.

Out of My Head. S. Jowitt. mass mkt. 13.95 (*0-340-68055-5*, Pub. by Hodder & Stought Ltd) Trafalgar.

Out of My Head. Susannah Jowitt. 320p. 1996. text 35.00 (*0-340-68054-7*, Pub. by Hodder & Stought Ltd) Trafalgar.

Out of My Head: An Experience of Neurosurgery. Viv Martin. 162p. 1997. pap. 22.50 (*1-85776-179-0*, Pub. by Book Guild Ltd) Trans-Atl Phila.

Out of My Heart. Marjorie K. Hazen. 1997. pap. write for info. (*1-57553-738-9*) Watermrk Pr.

Out of My Later Years. Albert Einstein. 288p. 1995. reprint ed. pap. 10.95 (*0-8065-0357-2*, Citadel Pr) Carol Pub Group.

Out of My Later Years. Albert Einstein. LC 70-89016. 282p. 1971. reprint ed. lib. bdg. 59.75 (*0-8371-2086-1*, EILY, Greenwood Pr) Greenwood.

Out of My League. Everett Owens. (Love Stories Super Edition Ser.). 208p. (YA). (gr. 7-12). 1998. mass mkt. 4.50 (*0-553-48594-6*) BDD Bks Young Read.

Out of My League. George Plimpton. 160p. 1993. pap. 10.95 (*1-55821-238-8*) Lyons Pr.

Out of My Life & Thought. Albert Schweitzer. Tr. by A. B. Lemke. 1995. 24.95 (*0-8050-1467-5*) H Holt & Co.

Out of My Life & Thought. Albert Schweitzer. LC 98-28166. 292p. 1998. pap. 15.95 (*0-8018-6097-0*) Johns Hopkins.

Out of My Mind. Gloria Healy. 50p. (Orig.). 1997. pap. text 5.00 (*1-880764-09-1*) Northwind NJ.

***Out of My Mind.** Karen M. Weihs. Ed. by Tish Lynn. (Illus.). 80p. 1999. pap. 19.95 (*1-886699-20-8*) Five Corners.

Out of My Mind: A Painted Journal. Kristin N. Tinker. LC 97-7730. (Illus.). 232p. 1997. 35.00 (*0-8109-3691-7*, Pub. by Abrams) Time Warner.

***Out of My Mind: Musings of a Maineiac.** Thomas R. Poole. 96p. 1999. pap. 5.95 (*0-7392-0353-3*, PO3538) Morris Pubng.

***Out of My Mind: The Discovery of Saunders-Vixen.** Richard Bach. 112p. 2000. pap. 12.95 (*0-385-33490-7*, Delta Trade) Dell.

Out of My Mind: The Discovery of Saunders-Vixen. Richard Bach. LC 99-22728. (Illus.). 112p. 1999. 18.00 (*0-688-17296-2*, Wm Morrow) Morrow Avon.

Out of My Mind: Triple Axles, Sperm Tests, & Neutrinos. Jonathan Dobrer. Ed. by Susan L. Wells. 92p. (Orig.). 1995. pap. 8.95 (*0-9621390-1-7*) DAnca-Wells.

Out of Nigeria: Witness to a Giant's Toils. J. L. Brandler. (Illus.). 384p. 1994. text 39.50 (*1-85043-732-7*) St Martin.

Out of Nippon. (Torg Ser.). 4.95 (*0-87431-345-7*, 20607) West End Games.

Out of Noah's Ark: Animals in Ancient Art from the Leo Mildenberg Collection. Ed. by Patricia E. Mottahedeh.Tr. of Aus Noahs Arche. (Illus.). 196p. 1997. text 35.00 (*3-8053-2347-6*) P Zabern.

Out of Nova Scotia Gardens: Delicious, Nutritious Vegetable Recipes. Marie Nightindale. (Illus.). 196p. 1998. 16.95 (*1-55109-218-2*) Nimbus Publ.

***Out of Nowhere.** Keith Botsford. 2000. write for info. (*1-902881-24-9*, Pub. by Toby Pr Ltd); pap. 15.95 (*1-902881-25-7*, Pub. by Toby Pr Ltd) Toby Pr.

Out of Nowhere. Roger Granelli. 240p. 1996. pap. 16.95 (*1-85411-120-5*, Pub. by Seren Bks) Dufour.

Out of Nowhere. William Marshall. 1989. mass mkt. 3.95 (*0-445-40842-1*, Mysterious Paperbk) Warner Bks.

Out of Nowhere. Doris Mortman. LC 97-75385. 480p. 1998. text 23.95 (*1-57566-301-5*, Knsington) Kensgtn Pub Corp.

Out of Nowhere, 1. Doris Mortman. 544p. 1999. mass mkt. 6.99 (*0-8217-6253-2*) Kensgtn Pub Corp.

Out of Nowhere. Ouida Sebestyen. LC 93-37759. 192p. (YA). (gr. 6 up). 1994. 16.95 (*0-531-06839-0*); lib. bdg. 17.99 (*0-531-08689-5*) Orchard Bks Watts.

Out of Nowhere. Ouida Sebestyen. 183p. (YA). (gr. 6 up). 1995. pap. 4.99 (*0-14-037640-2*, PuffinBks) Peng Put Young Read.

Out of Nowhere. Patricia Wilson. (Romance Ser.). 1994. per. 2.99 (*0-373-03298-6*, 1-03298-6) Harlequin Bks.

Out of Nowhere. large type ed. Patricia Wilson. 1993. reprint ed. lib. bdg. 18.95 (*0-263-13203-X*) Mac Lib Ref.

Out of Nowhere: A Novel. Ouida Sebestyen. 1995. 9.09 (*0-606-08584-X*, Pub. by Turtleback) Demco.

***Out of Nowhere: Disaster & Tourism in the White Mountains.** Eric Purchase. LC 98-28897. (Illus.). xiii, 192p. 1999. write for info. (*0-8018-6013-X*) Johns Hopkins.

Out of One, Many Africas: Reconstructing the Study & Meaning of Africa. William G. Martin & Michael O. West. LC 98-58006. 240p. 1999. pap. 19.95 (*0-252-06780-0*) U of Ill Pr.

Out of One, Many Africas: Reconstructing the Study & Meaning of Africa. William G. Martin. LC 98-58006. 1999. 44.95 (*0-252-02471-0*) U of Ill Pr.

Out of Order. Bonnie Macdougal. LC 99-13477. 1999. 24.50 (*0-345-43444-7*) Ballantine Pub Grp.

***Out of Order.** Bonnie MacDougal. 2000. mass mkt. 6.99 (*0-345-43445-5*) Ballantine Pub Grp.

Out of Order. Thomas E. Patterson. 320p. 1994. pap. 12.00 (*0-679-75510-1*) Vin Bks.

Out of Order. Phoebe Atwood Taylor. (Asey Mayo Cape Cod Mystery Ser.). 280p. 1988. reprint ed. pap. 6.95 (*0-88150-105-0*, Foul Play) Norton.

Out of Order: Affirmative Action & the Crisis of Doctrinaire Liberalism. Nicholas Capaldi. LC 84-43181. 211p. 1985. 30.95 (*0-87975-279-3*) Prometheus Bks.

Out of Order: Arrogance, Corruption & Incompetence on the Bench. Max Boot. LC 97-52791. 272p. 1998. 25.00 (*0-465-05432-3*, Pub. by Basic) HarpC.

Out of Order: Arrogance, Corruption & Incompetence on the Bench. Max Boot. 272p. 1999. pap. 12.00 (*0-465-05375-0*, Pub. by Basic) HarpC.

Out of Order: Clinical Work & Unconscious Process. Martin Stanton. 140p. 1999. pap. 17.95 (*1-892746-18-2*, 46182) Other Pr LLC.

Out of Order: Homosexuality in the Bible & the Ancient Near East. Donald J. Wold. LC 98-22499. 240p. 1999. pap. text 17.99 (*0-8010-2114-6*) Baker Bks.

Out of Order: The Very Unofficial Vermont State House Archives. Bill Mares & Frank Bryan. LC 91-66745. (Illus.). 128p. 1991. pap. 9.95 (*0-933050-88-7*) New Eng Pr VT.

Out of Order, Out of Sight, 2 vols. Adrian Piper. Incl. Vol. 1. Selected Writings in Meta-Art 1968-1992. LC 95-24490. (Illus.). 320p. 1996. 50.00 (*0-262-16155-9*); Vol. 2. Selected Writings in Art Criticism 1967-1992. (Illus.). 320p. 1996. 50.00 (*0-262-16156-7*); 1996. 90.00 (*0-262-16163-X*) MIT Pr.

Out of Order, Out of Sight: Selected Writings, Vol. 1. Adrian Piper. (Illus.). 1999. pap. text 25.00 (*0-262-66152-7*) MIT Pr.

Out of Order, Out of Sight: Selected Writings, Vol. 2. Adrian Piper. (Illus.). 1999. pap. text 25.00 (*0-262-66153-5*) MIT Pr.

Out of Order, Out of Sight: Selected Writings, Vols. 1 & 2. Adrian Piper. (Illus.). 1999. pap. text 45.00 (*0-262-66154-3*) MIT Pr.

Out of Our Kitchen Closets: San Francisco Gay Jewish Cooking. Congregation Shalar Zahav Staff. LC 87-71707. (Illus.). 224p. (Orig.). 1987. pap. 12.95 (*0-9619242-0-9*) Cong Shaar Zahav.

Out of Our League & onto Your Table, Vol. 1. Junior Service League of Shawnee, Oklahoma Staff. 198p. 1993. 16.95 (*0-9645368-1-1*); disk 16.95 (*0-9645368-2-X*) Jr Srvc Leag.

Out of Our League, Too: Appetizers. Junior League of Greensboro Staff. (Illus.). 112p. 1986. pap. 5.95 (*0-9605788-2-X*) J League Greensboro.

Out of Our Lives. John T. O'Connor Writers Workshop Staff. LC 96-61778. 1996. pap. 10.00 (*1-882194-24-1*) TN Valley Pub.

Out of Our Lives: A Selection of Contemporary Black Fiction. Ed. by Quandra P. Stadler. LC 74-7092. 324p. 1981. pap. 12.95 (*0-88258-095-7*) Howard U Pr.

Out of Our Minds: Anti-Intellectualism & Talent Development in American Schooling. Aimee Howley et al. LC 94-44979. (Education & Psychology of the Gifted Ser.: Vol. 9). 1995. pap. 24.95 (*0-8077-3416-0*) Tchrs Coll.

Out of Our Minds: Anti-Intellectualism & Talent Development in American Schooling. Edwina D. Pendarvis et al. LC 94-44979. (Education & Psychology of the Gifted Ser.: Vol. 9). 288p. (C). 1995. text 50.00 (*0-8077-3417-9*) Tchrs Coll.

Out of Our Minds: How to Cope with the Everyday Problems of the Mentally Ill - a Guide for the Patient & Their Families. Sascha Garson. LC 85-46048. 284p. 1986. pap. 22.95 (*0-87975-320-X*) Prometheus Bks.

Out of Our Minds: "London in the Sixties. Sex, Drugs & Rock 'n' Roll, Politics & Pop" George O'Brien. 184p. 1995. pap. 15.95 (*0-85640-541-8*, Pub. by Blackstaff Pr) Dufour.

***Out of Our Minds: Reason & Madness in the Exploration of Central Africa.** Johannes Fabian. LC 99-88221. 400p. 2000. 50.00 (*0-520-22122-2*, Pub. by U CA Pr); pap. 19.95 (*0-520-22123-0*, Pub. by U CA Pr) Cal Prin Full Svc.

Out of Our Past: The Forces That Shaped Modern America. 3rd ed. Carl N. Degler. LC 83-48021. 672p. 1983. pap. 18.00 (*0-06-131985-6*, TB1985, Torch) HarpC.

Out of Our People's Past: Sources for the Study of Jewish History. Walter Ackerman. 1978. 7.50 (*0-8381-0221-2*) USCJE.

***Out of Paris: Days Out & Weekend Breaks Around the French Capital.** Vivienne Menkes-Ivry. (Passport's Regional Ser.). (Illus.). 256p. 2000. pap. 18.95 (*0-658-00062-4*, 000624) NTC Contemp Pub Co.

Out of Phaze. Piers Anthony. 488p. 1989. mass mkt. 6.50 (*0-441-64465-1*) Ace Bks.

Out of Place: A Memoir. Edward W. Said. LC 99-31106. (Illus.). 304p. 1999. 26.95 (*0-394-58739-1*) Knopf.

***Out of Place: A Memoir.** Edward W. Said. 336p. 2000. reprint ed. pap. 14.00 (*0-679-73067-2*) Knopf.

Out of Place: Englishness, Empire & the Locations of Identity. Ian Baucom. LC 98-25219. 1999. pap. 18.95 (*0-691-00403-X*, Pub. by Princeton U Pr) Cal Prin Full Svc.

Out of Place: Englishness, Empire & the Locations of Identity. Ian Baucom. LC 98-25219. 1999. 55.00 (*0-691-01666-6*, Pub. by Princeton U Pr) Cal Prin Full Svc.

Out of Place: Homeless Mobilizations, Subcities, & Contested Landscapes. Talmadge Wright. LC 96-48447. (SUNY Series, Interruptions). (Illus.). 408p. (C). 1997. text 59.50 (*0-7914-3369-2*); pap. text 19.95 (*0-7914-3370-6*) State U NY Pr.

Out of Place: Restoring Identity to the Regional Landscape. Michael Hough. (Illus.). 239p. (C). 1992. reprint ed. pap. 20.00 (*0-300-05223-5*) Yale U Pr.

Out of Place: Stories & Poems. Ed. by Ven Begamudre & Judith Krause. 216p. 1990. pap. 12.95 (*1-55050-019-8*, Pub. by Coteau) Genl Dist Srvs.

***Out of Poverty: And into Something More Comfortable.** John G. Stackhouse, Jr. 366p. 2000. write for info. (*0-679-31025-8*) Random.

Out of Practice. large type ed. Lynne Collins. 304p. 1998. pap. 17.99 (*0-7089-5358-1*, Linford) Ulverscroft.

Out of Prison. Mary A. Denison. LC 74-164558. (American Fiction Reprint Ser.). 1977. reprint ed. 29.95 (*0-8369-7034-9*) Ayer.

Out of Reach. Andrew Swarbrick. 224p. 1997. pap. 18.95 (*0-312-17452-7*) St Martin.

Out of Revolution: Autobiography of Western Man. Eugen Rosenstock-Huessy. LC 93-24321. 820p. 1993. 39.95 (*0-85496-400-2*) Argo Bks.

Out of Revolution: Autobiography of Western Man. rev. ed. Eugen Rosenstock-Huessy. LC 70-103631. (Illus.). 795p. 1993. pap. 24.95 (*0-912148-05-5*) Argo Bks.

Out of Revolution: Autobiography of Western Man see Velikie Revoliutsii: Avtobiografiia Zapadnogo Cheloveka

Out of River's Mist: The Collected Works of Martin Mcmurtrey Martin McMurtrey & W. Patrick Cunningham. LC 98-84755. xiv, 313p. 1998. write for info. (*1-890549-03-7*) Alpha Pub Grp.

Out of Ruby's Treasure Chest. Ruby Vaughan et al. (Illus.). 32p. (Orig.). (J). 1993. pap. 5.95 (*1-881617-11-4*) Teapot Tales.

***Out of Russia: A Gift of Scene Designs from Robert L. B. Tobin.** LC 99-70374. 24 p. 1999. write for info. (*0-916677-44-3*) M K McNay Art.

Out of Russian Orbit: Hungary Gravitates to the West, 382. Andrew Felkay. LC 96-50210. (Contributions in Political Science Ser.: Vol. 382). 160p. 1997. 62.95 (*0-313-29602-2*, Greenwood Pr) Greenwood.

Out of School: Modern Perspectives in Truancy & School Refusal. Ed. by Lionel A. Hersov & Ian Berg. LC 79-41725. (Wiley Series on Studies in Child Psychiatry). (Illus.). 391p. reprint ed. pap. 121.30 (*0-608-17345-2*, 202980200065) Bks Demand.

Out of Season. Humphrey Brown. LC 97-73439. 200p. 1997. 15.00 (*1-879418-83-5*) Audenreed Pr.

Out of Season. Steven F. Havill. LC 99-33893. 304p. 1999. text 23.95 (*0-312-24414-2*) St Martin.

Out of Season: Work by & about Young People Who Died. Ed. by Paula Trachtman & Edward Butscher. 284p. 1993. 15.00 (*0-943959-03-9*) Amagansett Pr.

Out of Shape Beats No Shape at All. Jim Davis. (Little Bks.). (Illus.). 80p. 1996. 4.95 (*0-8362-0935-4*) Andrews & McMeel.

Out of Sheer Rage: Wrestling with D. H. Lawrence. Geoff Dyer. LC 97-33053. 256p. 1998. 23.00 (*0-86547-533-4*) N Point Pr.

***Out of Sheer Rage: Wrestling with D. H. Lawrence.** Geoff Dyer. 256p. 1999. pap. 13.00 (*0-86547-540-7*) N Point Pr.

Out of Sight. Joe Bollard. (Illus.). 176p. 1998. pap. 12.95 (*0-86327-623-7*, Pub. by Wolfhound Press) Irish Amer Bk.

Out of Sight. Elmore Leonard. 352p. 1997. mass mkt. 6.99 (*0-440-21442-4*) Dell.

Out of Sight. Elmore Leonard. 304p. 1998. pap. 9.95 (*0-385-33291-2*, 892924Q, Delta Trade) Dell.

Out of Sight. large type ed. Elmore Leonard. LC 96-44356. 1996. 26.95 (*1-56895-385-2*) Wheeler Pub.

Out of Sight! From Quarks to Living Cells. Sven Kullander & Borje Larsson. (Illus.). 292p. (C). 1994. 32.95 (*0-521-35044-1*) Cambridge U Pr.

Out of Sight: International Edition. Elmore Leonard. 1997. mass mkt. 6.50 (*0-440-29553-X*) Dell.

***Out of Sight: Pictures of Hidden Worlds.** Seymour Simon. LC 00-25684. (Illus.). 2000. pap. write for info. (*1-58717-012-4*) SeaStar.

An Asterisk (*) at the beginning of an entry indicates that the title is appearing for the first time.

*Out of Sight: Pictures of Hidden Worlds.** Seymour Simon. (Illus.). (J). 2000. 15.95 (*1-58717-011-6*) SeaStar.

***Out of Sight--Out of Mind? A Report on Anti-Homeless Laws, Litigation & Alternatives in 50 U. S. Cities.** Kelly Cunningham. 90p. 1999. pap. text 25.00 (*0-7881-8276-5*) DIANE Pub.

Out of Sight, Out of Mind. Chester Aaron. LC 84-48356. 192p. (J). (gr. 6-9). 1985. lib. bdg. 11.89 (*0-397-32101-5*) HarpC Child Bks.

Out of Sight! Out of Mind! Claude LaPointe. LC 94-38165. (Illus.). 32p. (J). (gr. 1-5). 1995. 20.00 (*0-15-200956-6*, Creat Educ) Creative Co.

Out of Sight, Out of Mind: Homeless Children & Families in Small-Town America. Yvonne Vissing. (Illus.). 288p. 1996. pap. 18.00 (*0-8131-0872-1*) U Pr of Ky.

Out of Sight, Out of Mind: Invisible Maniac. Paul Nelson. (Illus.). 44p. (Orig.). 1997. pap. 5.00 (*1-890051-03-9*) It Plays in Peoria.

Out of Silence: An Autistic Boy's Journey into Language & Communication. Russell Martin. LC 93-28434. 1995. 22.50 (*0-8050-1998-7*) H Holt & Co.

Out of Silence: An Autistic Boy's Journey into Language & Communication. Russell Martin. 320p. 1995. pap. 12.95 (*0-14-024701-7*, Penguin Bks) Viking Penguin.

Out of Silence: Emerging Themes in Asian American Churches. Fumitaka Matsuoka. LC 94-33659. 152p. (Orig.). 1995. pap. 11.95 (*0-8298-1025-0*) Pilgrim OH.

Out of Silence: Selected Poems. Muriel Rukeyser. Ed. by Kate Daniels. 192p. 1992. 28.00 (*0-916384-11-X*, TriQuart) Northwestern U Pr.

Out of Silence: Selected Poems. Muriel Rukeyser. Ed. by Kate Daniels. 192p. 1994. pap. 14.95 (*0-8101-5015-8*) Northwestern U Pr.

Out of Site: A Social Criticism of Architecture. Ed. by Diane Ghirardo. LC 90-48948. (Illus.). 256p. (Orig.). (C). 1991. pap. 16.95 (*0-941920-19-4*) Bay Pr.

Out of Slavery: Abolition & after, 1833-1983. Ed. by Jack Hayward. (Legacies of West Indian Slavery Ser.). 224p. 1986. 49.50 (*0-7146-3260-0*, Pub. by F Cass Pubs) Intl Spec Bk.

Out of Small Beginnings: An Economic History of Harvard College in the Puritan Period, 1636-1712. Margery S. Foster. LC 62-13266. (Illus.). 259p. 1962. 22.00 (*0-674-64800-5*) Belknap Pr.

Out of Solitude: Three Meditations on the Christian Life. Henri J. M. Nouwen. (Illus.). 64p. 1974. pap. 6.95 (*0-87793-072-4*) Ave Maria.

Out of Soundings. Henry M. Tomlinson. LC 70-128322. (Essay Index Reprint Ser.). 1977. 21.95 (*0-8369-1854-1*) Ayer.

Out of Step: An Autobiography. Frank Chodorov. 1962. 6.95 (*0-8159-6408-0*) Devin.

Out of Step: The Family, American Society, & the Christian Gospel. Wayne G. Boulton. 106p. (Orig.). (C). 1992. pap. 16.00 (*0-8191-8502-7*); lib. bdg. 34.00 (*0-8191-8501-9*) U Pr of Amer.

***Out of Stone: Armenia & Artsakh.** Robert Kurkjian & Matthew Karanian. LC 99-93883. (Illus.). 184p. 1999. 49.95 (*0-9672120-0-6*) Stone Garden.

Out-of-Sync Child: Recognizing & Coping with Sensory Integration Dysfunction. Carol S. Kranowitz. LC 97-14601. 352p. 1998. pap. 14.00 (*0-399-52386-3*) Berkley Pub.

***Out of the Air & onto the Ground: The Clarence Davids Story.** Clarence Davids, Sr. LC 99-63451. 160p. 1999. pap. 10.99 (*1-57921-188-7*) WinePress Pub.

Out of the Angel's Hand. Leonard D. McGann. LC 93-90560. 204p. 1993. pap. 5.95 (*0-9636783-0-2*) Bell Pub NC.

Out of the Ark: Stories from the World's Religions. Anita Ganeri. LC 95-7269. (Illus.). 104p. (J). (gr. 3-7). 1996. 18.00 (*0-15-200943-4*) Harcourt.

Out of the Ashes. large type ed. Maisie Mosco. (Charnwood Library). 1991. 27.99 (*0-7089-8559-9*, Charnwood) Ulverscroft.

Out of the Ashes, No. 1. William W. Johnstone. 480p. 1996. mass mkt. 4.99 (*0-7860-0289-1*, Pinncle Kensgtn) Kensgtn Pub Corp.

Out of the Ashes: A Handbook for Starting Over. Patrick J. McDonald & Claudette M. McDonald. LC 96-44805. 144p. (Orig.). 1997. pap. 7.95 (*0-8091-3695-3*) Paulist Pr.

Out of the Ashes: An Abuser's Story of Hope & Restoration. Carl Bishop. LC 96-68496. 231p. 1996. pap. 10.95 (*1-880451-18-2*) Rainbows End.

Out of the Ashes: Burned Churches & the Community of Faith. Ed. by Norman A. Hjelm. LC 98-127835. 1997. pap. 9.99 (*0-7852-1390-2*) Nelson.

Out of the Ashes: Help for People Who Have Stopped Smoking. Peter Holmes & Peggy Holmes. LC 92-72161. 288p. 1992. pap. 10.95 (*0-925190-57-8*) Fairview Press.

***Out of the Ashes: The Resurrection of Saddam Hussein.** Andrew Cockburn. 336p. 2000. pap. 14.00 (*0-06-092983-9*, Perennial) HarperTrade.

***Out of the Ashes: The Resurrection of Saddam Hussein.** Andrew Cockburn & Patrick Cockburn. LC 98-53879. 336p. 1999. 26.00 (*0-06-019266-6*) HarpC.

***Out of the Ashes, Into the Wind.** Laura Burroughs-Saha. 2001. pap. 8.00 (*0-8059-5029-X*) Dorrance.

Out of the Ashes of Casa Blanca. rev. ed. Ben-o'ni. (Illus.). 182p. 1995. text 49.00 (*1-887042-00-8*) Four Wings.

Out of the Attic. Douglas S. Johnson. LC 98-67223. 96p. 1999. pap. 14.95 (*1-892668-04-1*) Prospect Pr.

***Out of the Back Forty.** Roland P. Richards. (Illus.). 366p. 1999. pap. 28.95 (*0-937816-42-6*) Tech Data.

Out of the Background: Readings on Canadian Native History. 2nd ed. Ed. by Robin Fisher & Kenneth Coates. 1996. write for info. (*0-7730-5533-9*) Addison-Wesley.

Out of the Bag. Judith Martin & Paper Bag Players Staff. LC 94-46006. (Illus.). 48p. (J). (gr. 1-5). 1997. pap. 13.45 (*0-7868-1061-0*, Pub. by Hyprn Ppbks) Little.

Out of the Bag: The Paper Boy Players Book of Plays. Judith Martin. LC 94-46006. (Illus.). 48p. (J). 1997. lib. bdg. 16.89 (*0-7868-2148-5*, Pub. by Hyprn Child) Little.

Out of the Banks of Pine Island Bayou. Ed. by Joan Howard & Angie Walker. (Illus.). (Orig.). 1997. pap. 14.85 (*0-9656943-0-5*) FBC Bevil Oaks.

Out of the Barrio: Toward a New Politics of Hispanic Assimilation. Linda Chavez. LC 91-70060. 224p. 1992. pap. 13.50 (*0-465-05431-5*, Pub. by Basic) HarpC.

Out of the Basement: Improving the Image of Organizations' Mail Centers. Martha Guyer. 41p. 1994. text 15.00 (*0-9642061-0-2*) IPMA.

Out of the Bishop's Closet: A Call to Heal Ourselves, Each Other & Our World. 2nd ed. Antonio A. Feliz. 1992. reprint ed. pap. 12.95 (*0-9624751-7-3*) Alamo Sq Pr.

***Out of the Black Patch: The Autobiography of Effie Marquess Carmack, Folk Musician, Artist, & Writer.** Ed. by Noel A. Carmack & Karen Lynn Davidson. LC 99-6901. (Life Writings of Frontier Women Ser.: Vol. 4). (Illus.). 380p. 1999. 29.95 (*0-87421-279-0*) Utah St U Pr.

Out of the Blackout. Robert Barnard. 188p. 1995. reprint ed. pap. 6.00 (*0-88150-327-4*, Foul Play) Norton.

Out of the Blue. Elizabeth Baxandall & Doris Ilingworth. 64p. (C). 1988. pap. 35.00 (*0-7212-0703-0*, Pub. by Regency Pr GBR) St Mut.

Out of the Blue. Nancy Berzinec. 36p. (Orig.). 1988. pap. 3.25 (*0-940844-28-1*) Wellspring.

Out of the Blue. Sarah Ellis. LC 94-78090. 144p. (YA). (gr. 5-9). 1995. pap. 15.00 (*0-689-80025-8*) McElderry Bks.

Out of the Blue. Sarah Ellis. LC 96-23205. (J). 1996. 9.09 (*0-606-10278-7*, Pub. by Turtleback) Demco.

Out of the Blue. Bartie Jones. (Illus.). 62p. (Orig.). 1980. pap. 3.00 (*0-9618702-1-4*) Barth Pub.

Out of the Blue. Laura L. Leffers. 4.80 (*0-9671113-5-8*) Electric Umb OR.

***Out of the Blue.** Sally Mandel. LC 99-42026. 304p. 2000. 23.00 (*0-345-42890-0*, Ballantine Epiphany) Ballantine Pub Grp.

Out of the Blue. Helen M. Martin. (Orig.). 1996. pap. write for info. (*1-57553-357-X*) Watermrk Pr.

***Out of the Blue.** Jill Shalvis. (Temptation Ser.: Bk. 804). 2000. mass mkt. 3.99 (*0-373-25904-2*, 1-25904-3) Harlequin Bks.

Out of the Blue. Janice Sims. (Arabesque Ser.). 256p. 1998. mass mkt. 4.99 (*0-7860-0596-3*, Pinncle Kensgtn) Kensgtn Pub Corp.

Out of the Blue. Lauraine Snelling. LC 96-35652. (High Hurdles Ser.: No. 4). 176p. (YA). (gr. 6-9). 1996. pap. 5.99 (*1-55661-508-6*) Bethany Hse.

Out of the Blue. Elise Title. 299p. 1994. per. 4.99 (*1-55166-016-4*, Mira Bks) Harlequin Bks.

Out of the Blue. Chester Woodward. LC 75-90697. (Essay Index Reprint Ser.). 1977. 20.95 (*0-8369-1239-X*) Ayer.

***Out of the Blue.** large type ed. Sally Mandel. LC 00-27767. 478p. 2000. 26.95 (*0-7862-2551-3*) Thorndike Pr.

Out of the Blue: A Pilot with the Chindits. large type ed. Terence O'Brien. (Non-Fiction Ser.). 480p. 1985. 11.50 (*0-7089-1392-X*) Ulverscroft.

Out of the Blue: Delight Comes into Our Lives. Mark Victor Hansen et al. 336p. 1997. pap. 11.95 (*0-06-092838-7*, Perennial) HarperTrade.

Out of the Blue: Depression & Human Nature. David B. Cohen. 368p. 1995. pap. 13.95 (*0-393-31299-2*, Norton Paperbks) Norton.

Out of the Blue: Modern-Day Miracles & Extraordinary Coincidences. Glennyce S. Eckersley. 164p. 1998. pap. 13.95 (*0-7126-7165-X*, Pub. by Rider) Trafalgar.

***Out of the Blue: One Woman's Story of Stroke, Love, & Survival.** Bonnie Sherr Klein. Orig. Title: Slow Dance: A Story of Stroke, Love, & Disability. 320p. 2000. pap. 15.95 (*1-885171-45-5*) Wldcat Canyon.

Out of the Blue: Russia's Hidden Gay Literature - An Anthology. Ed. by Kevin Moss. (Illus.). 416p. 1996. 50.00 (*0-940567-19-9*); pap. 19.95 (*0-940567-20-2*) Gay Sunshine.

Out of the Blue: Wild Cards & Other Big Future Surprises. John L. Petersen. Ed. by Ellen Crockett et al. (Orig.). (C). 1997. pap. 13.95 (*0-9659027-2-2*) Arlington Inst.

Out of the Blue: Wild Cards & Other Big Future Surprises. John L. Petersen. LC 99-47088. (Orig.). 2000. pap. 16.95 (*1-56833-135-5*) Madison Bks UPA.

Out of the Blues: A Recovery Guide for People with Depression. large type ed. LC 98-3758. (Illus.). 24p. 1998. pap. write for info. (*0-939838-47-8*) Pritchett & Hull.

Out of the Blues: Strategies That Work to Get You Through the Down Times. Jay Cleve. 368p. 1996. reprint ed. mass mkt. 6.99 (*0-425-15252-9*) Berkley Pub.

Out-of-the-Body Experiences. Robert Crookall. 224p. 1992. pap. 7.95 (*0-8065-1383-7*, Citadel Pr) Carol Pub Group.

Out-of-the-Body Travel. Stanley Plumly. LC 76-46174. (American Poetry Ser.: No. 10). 1977. pap. 4.95 (*0-912946-36-9*, Ecco Press) HarperTrade.

Out of the Box. Anne T. Perkins. (Big Books - Mini Bks.). (Illus.). 16p. (J). (ps-k). 1994. 12.00 (*1-884204-13-9*) Teach Nxt Door.

***Out of the Box: The Reinvention of Art: 1965-1975.** Carter Ratcliff. (Illus.). 224p. 2000. pap. 19.95 (*1-58115-073-3*, Pub. by Allworth Pr) Watsn-Guptill.

Out of the Box for Life. Warren Berland. 240p. 2000. pap. 13.00 (*0-06-093051-9*) HarpC.

Out of the Box for Life: (Being Free Is Just a Choice) Warren Berland. LC 98-31562. 240p. 1999. 23.95 (*0-06-019100-7*) HarpC.

Out-of-the-Box Leadership: Transforming the 21st Century Army & Other Top Performing Organizations. James G. Hunt & Leonard Wong. LC 98-54598. (Monographs in Leadership & Management: Vol. 1). 1999. 78.50 (*0-7623-0548-7*) Jai Pr.

Out of the Briars. Alexander H. Newton. LC 72-89385. (Black Heritage Library Collection). 1977. 17.95 (*0-8369-8637-7*) Ayer.

Out of the Bulrushes: A Tale of Romanian Adoptions. Mona McElderry. 184p. (Orig.). 1995. pap. 16.95 (*0-9641573-1-4*) Sisu Pr.

Out of the Catskills & Just Beyond: Literary & Visual Works by Catskills Writers & Artists. Bertha Rogers. (Illus.). 384p. (Orig.). 1997. pap. 24.95 (*0-9646844-6-2*) Bright Hill.

Out of the Cellar: A Poetry Anthology. Ed. by Judith Askew & Nona Nimnicht. 72p. (Orig.). (C). 1990. pap. 4.95 (*0-933022-03-4*) DAurora Pr.

Out of the Channel: The Exxon Valdez Oil Spill in Prince William Sound. 2nd ed. John Keeble. LC 98-54435. 1999. write for info. (*0-910055-54-8*) East Wash Univ.

Out of the Channel: The Exxon Valdez Oil Spill in Prince William Sound, 10th Anniversary Edition. 10th anniversary ed. John Keeble. LC 98-54435. 21p. 1999. pap. text 14.00 (*0-910055-53-X*, Pub. by East Wash Univ) U of Wash Pr.

Out of the Cloister: A Study of Organizational Dilemmas. Helen R. Ebaugh. 177p. 1977. text 12.50 (*0-292-76007-8*) U of Tex Pr.

Out of the Closet & Nothing to Wear. Leslea Newman. LC 97-1369. 232p. (Orig.). 1997. pap. 10.95 (*1-55583-415-9*) Alyson Pubns.

Out of the Closet & off the Wall: An Illustrated History of the Coat Hanger. William H. Weber & Judith M. Weber. (Illus.). 128p. (Orig.). 1984. pap. 5.95 (*0-914171-01-1*) Ronin Pub.

***Out of the Closet into God's Arms.** unabridged ed. Sylvia D. Huerta. 2000. pap. write for info. (*0-9701916-0-X*) Fathers Seed.

"Out of the Closet" One Death's Deliverance: In the Footsteps of Diogene. Jean-Elie Gilles. Tr. by Nancy D. Nelson from FRE. LC 95-236431.Tr. of Sur Les Pas De Diogene. (Illus.). 1995. pap. 14.95 (*0-9672904-2-2*) Jenair Pr.

Out of the Closets: The Sociology of Homosexual Liberation. Laud Humphreys. 192p. 1972. pap. 2.45 (*0-13-645317-1*, Spectrum IN) Macmillan Gen Ref.

Out of the Closets: Voices of Gay Liberation. 2nd anniversary ed. Ed. by Karla Jay & Allen Young. (C). 1992. pap. text 18.50 (*0-8147-4183-5*) NYU Pr.

Out of the Closets: Voices of Gay Liberation. 20th anniversary ed. Ed. by Karla Jay & Allen Young. (C). 1992. text 45.00 (*0-8147-4182-7*) NYU Pr.

Out of The Cocoon, 1. Simon Walker. LC 97-67132. 1997. pap. text 9.95 (*0-9657855-0-5*) N E Novelty.

Out of the Corner of My Eye: Living with Vision Loss in Later Life. large type ed. Nicolette P. Ringgold. LC 91-3352. 120p. 1991. pap. 23.95 (*0-89128-193-2*) Am Foun Blind.

Out of the Crackerbarrel: 150 Years of Recipes & Remembrances. Dennis D. Picard. Ed. by Gail Nano. 108p. 1998. pap. write for info. (*1-57502-879-4*, PO2395) Morris Pubng.

***Out of the Cradle.** John Kenrick Ellis. 309p. 1999. pap. write for info. (*0-7541-0797-3*, Pub. by Minerva Pr) Unity Dist.

Out of the Cradle: Exploring the Frontiers Beyond Earth. William K. Hartmann et al. LC 84-40316. (Illus.). 192p. (Orig.). 1984. pap. 11.95 (*0-89480-770-6*, 770) Workman Pub.

Out of the Crate: One Hundred & Twenty-Five Down-to-Earth Anecdotes - Humorous, Wise & Otherwise. Crate H. Jones. 1987. reprint ed. pap. 9.95 (*0-913029-16-5*) Stevens Bk Pr.

Out of the Crater: Chronicles of a Volcanologist. Richard V. Fisher. LC 98-17838. 179 p. 1999. 24.95 (*0-691-00226-6*, Pub. by Princeton U Pr) Cal Prin Full Svc.

***Out of the Crater: Chronicles of a Volcanologist.** Richard V. Fisher. (Illus.). 170p. 2000. pap. 14.95 (*0-691-07017-2*) Princeton U Pr.

Out of the Crisis. W. Edwards Deming. (Illus.). 507p. (C). 1986. 29.50 (*0-911379-01-0*) MIT Ctr Adv Educ.

***Out of the Crisis.** W. Edwards Deming. (Illus.). 507p. (C). 2000. pap. 22.95 (*0-262-54115-7*) MIT Pr.

Out of the Crucible. Marian Wells. LC 88-21121. (Treasure Quest Ser.: Vol. 2). 32p. (Orig.). 1988. pap. 8.99 (*1-55661-037-8*) Bethany Hse.

Out of the Crucible: Black Steel Workers in Western Pennsylvania, 1875-1980. Dennis C. Dickerson. LC 85-30450. (SUNY Series in Afro-American Studies). 323p. (C). 1986. text 21.50 (*0-88706-305-5*); pap. text 21.50 (*0-88706-306-3*) State U NY Pr.

Out of the Cults & into the Church: Understanding & Encouraging the Ex-Cultist. Janis Hutchinson. LC 94-11837. 224p. 1994. pap. 11.99 (*0-8254-2885-8*) Kregel.

Out of the Dark. Kathleen Aldrich. LC 94-48662. 106p. (J). 1995. pap. 6.49 (*0-89084-799-1*, 086942) Bob Jones Univ.

Out of the Dark. Dolores Bos. LC 97-221992. (Illus.). 152p. (Orig.). (J). (gr. 6-11). 1997. mass mkt. 5.99 (*0-87508-720-5*, 720) Chr Lit.

Out of the Dark. Justine Davis. (Intimate Moments Ser.). 1995. per. 3.75 (*0-373-07638-X*, 1-07638-9) Silhouette.

Out of the Dark. Welwyn W. Katz. 192p. (J). (gr. 4-8). 1996. pap. 6.95 (*0-88899-262-9*) Publishers Group.

Out of the Dark. Welwyn W. Katz. 192p. (J). (gr. 6-9). 1996. 16.00 (*0-689-80947-6*) S&S Bks Yung.

Out of the Dark. Patrick Modiano. Tr. by Jordan Stump from FRE. LC 98-13100. Orig. Title: Du Plus Loin de L'Oubli. 139p. 1998. text 45.00 (*0-8032-3196-2*) U of Nebr Pr.

Out of the Dark. Betty R. Wright. LC 93-48025. 128p. (J). (gr. 4-7). 1995. 13.95 (*0-590-43598-1*) Scholastic Inc.

***Out of the Dark Vol. I: Origins.** Robert W. Chambers. Ed. by Hugh Lamb. xii, 170p. 1998. 38.50 (*1-899562-41-9*) Ash-Tree.

***Out of the Dark Vol. II: Diversions.** Robert W. Chambers. Ed. by Hugh Lamb. xiv, 206p. 1999. 39.50 (*1-899562-74-5*) Ash-Tree.

***Out of the Darkness.** iv, 365p. 1999. pap. 14.00 (*0-9657992-1-2*) Maryann MG.

Out of the Darkness. Lynn Erickson. LC 95-6957. (Showcase Ser.). 299p. 1995. per. 3.50 (*0-373-70626-X*, 1-70626-6) Harlequin Bks.

Out of the Darkness. Susan Kelly. 352p. 1994. mass mkt. 4.50 (*0-8217-4620-0*, Zebra Kensgtn) Kensgtn Pub Corp.

Out of the Darkness. R. E. Patterson. Ed. by Donna Schwartz. (Illus.). (Orig.). Date not set. pap. 8.00 (*0-9669837-0-X*) Gotcha Pubns.

Out of the Darkness. Compiled by Maryann M. Garlasco. 25p. (Orig.). 1997. reprint ed. pap. 4.99 (*0-9657992-0-4*) Maryann MG.

Out of the Darkness. John W. Grant. LC 79-39085. (Black Heritage Library Collection). 1977. reprint ed. 22.95 (*0-8369-9023-4*) Ayer.

Out of the Darkness: Contemporary Perspectives on Family Violence. Ed. by Glenda K. Kantor & Jana Jasinski. LC 97-21053. 320p. 1997. 58.00 (*0-7619-0775-0*); pap. 27.50 (*0-7619-0776-9*) Sage.

Out of the Darkness: Coping with Disability. Robert Lovering. 148p. (Orig.). 1993. pap. 7.95 (*0-614-05342-0*) ARCS Inc.

Out of the Darkness: The Mystery & Majesty of God's Creation. Cody Carlson. (Illus.). 216p. 1998. 50.00 (*1-888237-13-9*) Baxter Pr.

***Out of the Darkness: The Story of Blacks Moving North: 1890-1940.** James Haskins & Kathleen Benson. LC 99-19882. (Great Journeys Ser.). 112p. (YA). (gr. 5-9). 2000. 31.36 (*0-7614-0970-X*, Benchmark NY) Marshall Cavendish.

Out of the Darkness: The Story of Mary Ellen Wilson. Eric A. Shelman & Stephen Lazoritz. LC 98-89460. (Illus.). 344p. (Orig.). 1999. pap. 16.95 (*0-9669400-0-8*, 9669400-0-8) Dolphin Moon.

Out of the Depths. Joseph Hayyim Brenner. 101p. 1992. text. write for info. (*0-8133-8446-X*) Westview.

Out of the Depths. John Newton. LC 80-85340. (Illus.). 160p. 1991. pap. 9.99 (*0-8254-3317-7*, Kregel Class) Kregel.

Out of the Depths. Walter W. Wade. 1.25 (*0-687-06169-5*) Abingdon.

Out of the Depths. large type ed. Leonard Holton. 1990. pap. 16.99 (*0-7089-6955-0*, Linford) Ulverscroft.

Out of the Depths. Marcus Lehman. Tr. by Nissan Mindel from GER. (Illus.). 108p. (YA). reprint ed. 11.00 (*0-8266-0336-X*, Merkos LInyonei Chinuch) Kehot Pubn Soc.

Out of the Depths: Restoring Fellowship with God. D. Martyn Lloyd-Jones. LC 94-33867. 112p. 1995. pap. 8.99 (*0-89107-838-X*) Crossway Bks.

Out of the Depths: The Experiences of Mi'kmaw Children at the Indian Residential School in Shubenacadie, Nova Scotia. Isabelle Knockwood. (Illus.). 160p. (Orig.). 1993. pap. 14.00 (*0-9694180-5-1*, Pub. by Roseway Publ) Nimbus Publ.

Out of the Depths: The Life-Story of Henry F. Milan. 2nd ed. Clarence W. Hall. LC 88-60426. 192p. 1988. reprint ed. 14.95 (*0-9605642-1-7*) Messengers Hope.

Out of the Depths: The Psalms Speak for Us Today. expanded rev. ed. Bernhard W. Anderson. LC 83-19801. 254p. (C). 1983. pap. 19.95 (*0-664-24504-8*) Westminster John Knox.

***Out of the Depths: The Psalms Speak for Us Today.** 3rd rev. expanded ed. Bernhard W. Anderson. (Illus.). 264p. 2000. pap. 24.95 (*0-664-25832-8*, Pub. by Westminster John Knox) Presbyterian Pub.

Out of the Depths Have I Cried: Thoughts on Incarnational Theology in the Eastern Christian Experience. Philip Saliba & Joseph J. Allen. Ed. by Metropolitan Staff. LC 79-18611. (Illus.). (Orig.). 1995. reprint ed. pap. 9.95 (*0-916586-32-4*) Holy Cross Orthodox.

Out of the Depths I Call to You: A Book of Prayers for the Married Jewish Woman. Ed. & Tr. by Nina B. Cardin. LC 91-15950. 148p. 1995. reprint ed. pap. text 25.00 (*1-56821-411-1*) Aronson.

***Out of the Depths of Hell: A Soldier's Story of Life & Death in Japanese Hands.** John McEwan. 1999. write for info. (*0-85052-668-X*) Pen & Sword Bks Ltd.

Out of the Depths of My Heart I Cried! 52p. (Orig.). 1996. pap. 8.95 (*0-9660541-0-5*) GMW Ents.

Out of the Depths or Triumph of Cross: African-American Women Writers, 1910-1940 by Plummer. Plummer. LC 97-16844. 1997. 30.00 (*0-7838-1425-9*, Hall Reference) Macmillan.

Out of the Depts (De Profundis) A Collection of Articles on the Russian Revolution. Ed. by Peter B. Struve. Tr. by William F. Woehrlin. LC 86-22052. xxix, 254p. (C). 1986. pap. 27.50 (*1-884445-16-0*) C Schlacks Pub.

***Out of the Desert.** John E. Blundell. 1999. 25.00 (*1-56311-536-0*) Turner Pub KY.

Out of the Doll's House: The Story of Women in the Twentieth Century. Angela Holdsworth. (Illus.). 208p. 1991. pap. 17.95 (*0-563-20631-4*, BBC-Parkwest) Parkwest Pubns.

O

An Asterisk (*) at the beginning of an entry indicates that the title is appearing for the first time.

Out of the Dump: Writings & Photographs by Children from Guatemala. Ed. by Kristine L. Franklin & Nancy McGirr. LC 95-9806. (Illus.). 56p. (J). (gr. 3 up). 1996. 19.00 (*0-688-13923-X*) Lothrop.

Out of the Dump: Writings & Photographs by Children of Guatemala. Ed. by Kristine L. Franklin & Nancy McGirr. LC 95-9806. (Illus.). (J). (gr. 4-7). 1996. lib. bdg. 18.93 (*0-688-13924-8*) Lothrop.

***Out of the Dust.** 1999. 9.95 (*1-58130-589-3*) Novel Units.

***Out of the Dust.** 1999. 11.95 (*1-58130-590-7*) Novel Units.

Out of the Dust. Karen Hesse. 240p. (YA). (gr. 5 up). pap. 4.99 (*0-8072-1526-0*) Listening Lib.

Out of the Dust. Karen Hesse. LC 96-40344. 227p. (J). (gr. 4-7). 1997. 15.95 (*0-590-36080-9*) Scholastic Inc.

***Out of the Dust: Literature Guide.** Karen Hesse. (Illus.). 16p. (J). (gr. 4-13). 2000. pap. 4.99 (*0-439-13112-X*) Scholastic Inc.

***Out of the Dust: Literature Unit.** Teacher Created Materials Staff & Sarah Kartchner Clark. Ed. by Barbara Wally. (Illus.). 48p. 1999. pap., teacher ed. 7.95 (*1-57690-623-X*, TCM2623) Tchr Create Mat.

Out of the Dustbin: Sentimental Musings on Art & Music in Seattle from 1936 to 1992. Hans Lehmann & Thelma Lehmann. 112p. 1992. pap. 12.95 (*0-9635567-0-3*) H Lehmann.

Out of the Earth. Louis Bromfield. 305p. reprint ed. lib. bdg. 24.95 (*0-88411-541-0*) Amereon Ltd.

Out of the Earth: A Heritage Farm Coast Cookbook. Kerry D. Romaniello. Ed. by Marsha McCabe & Joseph D. Thomas. (Illus.). 176p. 1999. 39.95 (*0-932027-40-7*) Spinner Pubns.

Out of the Earth: Civilization & the Life of the Soil. Daniel J. Hillel. LC 92-10461. (C). 1992. 17.95 (*0-520-08080-7*, Pub. by U CA Pr) Cal Prin Full Svc.

Out of the Earth, into the Fire: A Course in Ceramic Materials for the Studio Potter. Mimi Obstler. Ed. by Robina Simpson. LC 95-31026. (Illus.). 1996. 62.00 (*1-57498-001-7*, G021); pap. 52.00 (*1-57498-008-4*, G022) Am Ceramic.

Out of the East. Lafcadio Hearn. LC 72-4161. (Select Bibliographies Reprint Ser.). 1977. reprint ed. 23.95 (*0-8369-6883-2*) Ayer.

Out of the East: Transitions & Tradition in Asia. Hiroji Kubota. LC 96-44073. (Illus.). 204p. 1998. 60.00 (*0-393-04088-7*) Norton.

***Out of the Everywhere: Tales for the New World.** Jan Andrews. (Illus.). 80p. (J). (ps-3). 2000. 19.95 (*0-88899-402-8*) Grndwd Bks.

Out of the Fiery Furnace: The Impact of Metals on the History of Mankind. Robert Raymond. LC 86-2367. (Illus.). 1986. pap. 10.00 (*0-271-00441-X*) Pa St U Pr.

***Out of the Fire Mist.** R. Christopherson. 184p. 2000. mass mkt. 9.95 (*0-914597-03-5*) Pubs West AZ.

Out of the Flames. Lyn Dalebout. 270p. (Orig.). 1996. pap. 15.00 (*0-9655247-0-1*) Blue Bison Pr.

Out of the Fog. John M. Kelley. 180p. (Orig.). 1992. pap. 8.40 (*0-8309-0615-0*) Herald Pub Hse.

Out of the Fog: Treatment Options & Coping Strategies for Adult Attention Deficit Disorder. Kevin Murphy & Suzanne LeVert. 320p. (J). 1995. pap. 13.45 (*0-7868-8087-2*, Pub. by Hyperion) Time Warner.

Out of the Forties. Nicholas Lemann. 152p. 1998. pap. 24.95 (*1-56098-772-3*) Smithsonian.

Out of the Fringe. Cardad Svich. LC 99-44193. (Illus.). 400p. 1999. pap. 17.95 (*1-55936-171-9*, Pub. by Theatre Comm) Consort Bk Sales.

Out of the Frying Pan: Reflections of a Japanese American. Bill Hosokawa. LC 98-26215. 184p. 1998. 32.50 (*0-87081-500-8*); pap. 19.95 (*0-87081-513-X*) Univ Pr Colo.

Out of the Frying Pan: Seven Women Who Changed the Course on Postwar Cookery (In Britain) Hazel Castell & Kathleen Griffin. (Illus.). 183p. 1998. text 22.00 (*0-7881-5755-8*) DIANE Pub.

Out of the Frying Pan, onto the Freeway: A Cookbook for Soccer Moms (And Dads) & Other Working Cooks. Eileen Lafferty. LC 84-72116. (Illus.). 346p. (Orig.). Date not set. pap. 12.00 (*0-9613994-0-6*) Bird Hand Pub.

Out of the Fury. rev. ed. Edith S. Weigand. (Illus.). 227p. (Orig.). 1987. 6.95 (*1-882675-03-7*) Chosen People.

Out of the Gang. Keith E. Greenberg. (In My Shoes Ser.). (Illus.). 40p. (J). (gr. 4-8). 1992. lib. bdg. 19.93 (*0-8225-2553-4*, Lerner Publctns) Lerner Pub.

Out of the Garden: A Collection of Poetry. Craig J. Paulo. 52p. 1998. pap. 6.25 (*0-9664204-0-3*) Cath Colleg.

Out of the Garden: Toys, TV, & Children's Culture in the Age of Marketing. Stephen Kline. (C). 1995. pap. 22.00 (*1-85984-059-0*, Pub. by Verso) Norton.

Out of the Garden: William Faulkner & Southern Culture. Joel Williamson. LC 92-22780. 544p. (C). 1993. 35.00 (*0-19-507404-1*) OUP.

Out of the Garden: Women Writers on the Bible. Ed. by Christina Buchmann & Celina Spiegel. 368p. 1995. pap. 12.95 (*0-449-91017-2*) Fawcett.

Out of the Ghetto. Joe Jacobs. (Illus.). 320p. (Orig.). 1993. pap. 19.95 (*0-948984-18-X*, Pub. by Phoenix Pr) AK Pr Dist.

***Out of the Ghetto.** Jack Klajman & Ed Klajman. (Library of Holocaust Testimonies). (Illus.). 288p. 2000. pap. 19.50 (*0-85303-389-7*, Pub. by M Vallentine & Co) Intl Spec Bk.

Out of the Ghetto: A Path to Socialist Rewards. Mike Prior & Dave Purdy. 193p. 1979. pap. 19.95 (*0-85124-260-X*, Pub. by Spkesman) Coronet Bks.

Out of the Ghetto: The Catholic Community in Modern Scotland. Raymond Boyle & Peter S. Lynch. 200p. 1998. pap. 45.00 (*0-85976-487-7*, Pub. by J Donald) St Mut.

Out of the Ghetto: The Social Background of Jewish Emancipation, 1770-1870. Jacob Katz. LC 98-25601. (Modern Jewish History Ser.). 1998. pap. 18.95 (*0-8156-0532-3*) Syracuse U Pr.

***Out of the Girls' Room & into the Night.** Thisbe Nissen. LC 00-38991. 208p. 2000. pap. 12.00 (*0-385-72053-X*, Anchor NY) Doubleday.

Out of the Girls' Room & into the Night. Thisbe Nissen. LC 99-16672. (John Simmons Short Fiction Award Ser.). 250p. 1999. pap. 19.95 (*0-87745-691-7*) U of Iowa Pr.

Out of the Golden Cage. Lois A. Overton. LC 98-94831. (Illus.). 1999. pap. 12.00 (*0-9661040-1-3*) Cedar Tr Pr.

Out of the Grave. Robert Noyola. 1997. 10.00 (*0-9656116-0-4*) Stonegate Pr.

Out of the Heart. Ed. by John W. Chadwick & Annie H. Chadwick. LC 70-86795. (Granger Index Reprint Ser.). 1977. 19.95 (*0-8369-6072-6*) Ayer.

Out of the Hood: And into God's Purpose. Carlos Reid. LC 99-231698. 154p. 1997. pap. 8.99 (*1-884369-68-5*, EBED Pubns) McDougal Pubng.

Out of the House of Bondage. Kelly Miller. LC 69-18554. (American Negro: His History & Literature. Series 2). 1969. reprint ed. 11.95 (*0-405-01882-7*) Ayer.

Out of the House of Bondage: Runaways, Resistance & Marronage in Africa & the New World. Ed. by Gad Heuman. 224p. 1986. 49.50 (*0-7146-3287-2*, Pub. by F Cass Pubs) Intl Spec Bk.

Out of the House of Life. Chelsea Quinn Yarbro. 464p. 1994. pap. 14.95 (*0-312-89026-5*) Orb NYC.

Out of the Howling Storm: The New Chinese Poetry. Ed. by Tony Barnstone. LC 92-56899. (Wesleyan Poetry Ser.). 179p. 1993. pap. 14.95 (*0-8195-1210-9*, Wesleyan Univ Pr); text 30.00 (*0-8195-2207-4*, Wesleyan Univ Pr) U Pr of New Eng.

Out of the Hurly-Burly: or Life in an Odd Corner. Charles H. Clark. LC 70-158228. (Illus.). reprint ed. 47.50 (*0-404-00295-1*) AMS Pr.

Out of the Inferno: Poles Remember the Holocaust. Ed. by Richard C. Lukas. LC 89-5646. 224p. 1989. 27.50 (*0-8131-1692-9*) U Pr of Ky.

Out of the Jungle: A Survival Guide with Compass. Constance H. Foster. (Illus.). 50p. (Orig.). (YA). 1994. pap. 5.95 (*0-9639070-1-8*) ebooksonthe.

Out of the Jungle: The Way of Dynamic Harmlessness. 5th rev. ed. H. Jay Dinshah. (Ahimsa Bks.). (Illus.). 96p. (Orig.). 1995. pap. 7.95 (*0-942401-14-X*) Am Vegan Soc.

Out of the Kumbla: Womanist Perspectives on Caribbean Literature. Ed. by Carole B. Davis & Elaine Fido. LC 88-70199. 450p. 1989. 49.95 (*0-86543-042-X*); pap. 15.95 (*0-86543-043-8*) Africa World.

Out of the Labyrinth: Selected Poems. Charles H. Ford. 144p. (Orig.). 1990. pap. 6.95 (*0-87286-251-8*) City Lights.

Out of the Lecture Hall & into the Classroom: 1992-93 Colleges Graduates & Elementary/Secondary School Teaching, with An Essay on Undergraduate Academic Experiences. Robin R. Henke. 136p. 1996. pap. 11.00 (*0-16-048768-4*) USGPO.

Out of the Locker Room of the Male Soul: Men Seeking the Heart of God. Steve Masterson & George McPeek. LC 97-191580. 386p. 1997. pap. 12.99 (*0-88965-136-1*, Pub. by Horizon Books) Chr Pubns.

Out of the Loud Hound of Darkness: A Dictionarrative. Karen E. Gordon. LC 98-6739. 210p. 1998. 23.00 (*0-375-40198-9*) Random.

Out of the Luminous Silence: Spirit in Dreams. Elisabeth C. Loher. (Illus.). 80p. 1994. 12.95 (*0-9641910-1-6*) Blue Gate Pub.

Out of the Madness: From the Projects to a Life of Hope. Jerrold Ladd. 208p. 1996. reprint ed. mass mkt. 10.99 (*0-446-67105-3*, Pub. by Warner Bks) Little.

Out of the Miry Clay. Bradley B. Williams. (Orig.). (YA). 1989. pap. 5.95 (*0-9620486-0-7*) B B Williams.

Out of the Mist. Lauraine Snelling. (Golden Filly Ser.: No. 7). 16p. (YA). (gr. 7-10). 1993. pap. 5.99 (*1-55661-338-5*) Bethany Hse.

***Out of the Mist: Demystifying & Understanding Other Cultures to Improve International Business.** Marvin E. Paymer. 1999. 48.95 (*1-881907-09-0*) Two Bytes Pub.

Out of the Mist: The Foundation of Modern Pathology & Medicine During the Nineteenth Century. Harold M. Malkin. (Illus.). 422p. 1993. pap. text 35.00 (*0-9637689-1-3*) Vesalius Bks.

Out of the Mist: The Foundation of Modern Pathology & Medicine During the Nineteenth Century. Harold M. Malkin. (Illus.). 422p. 1995. reprint ed. 80.00 (*0-9637689-0-5*) Vesalius Bks.

***Out of the Mist: Treasures of the Nuu-Chah-Nulth Chiefs.** Martha Black. (Illus.). 112p. 2000. pap. 35.00 (*0-7718-9547-X*) BC Archives.

Out of the Mists of Time: Who Wrote the Bible & Why. Milton L. Forbes. LC 91-91561. 125p. (YA). (gr. 12). 1992. pap. 4.95 (*0-9623700-2-9*) Mtntop Bks.

Out of the Mold: Independent Voices Breaking Out of the Mold. LC 97-201505. 214p. 1997. pap. 10.00 (*1-879556-27-8*) ABA.

Out of the Moral Maze see Escapa del Laberinto Moral

Out of the Moral Maze: Workbook for College Students (Leader's Guide Included) Josh McDowell. 176p. (C). 1995. pap., teacher ed., wbk. ed. 11.95 (*0-8054-9832-X*, 7800-07) Broadman.

Out of the Mouth of Babes: Earliest Stages in Language Learning. D. L. Olmsted. LC 70-17001. (Janua Linguarum, Ser. Minor: No. 117). (Illus.). 260p. (Orig.). 1971. pap. text 44.65 (*90-279-1892-9*) Mouton.

***Out of the Mouths of Babes: Quips, Quotes & Unforgettable Women's Wit.** Autumn Stephens. LC 00-9528. 2000. write for info. (*1-57324-558-5*) Conari Press.

Out of the Mouths of Babes: The Infant Formula Controversy. Fred D. Miller. 98p. 1983. pap. 16.95 (*0-912051-01-9*) Transaction Pubs.

Out of the Mouths of Babes: The Unforgettable Things Children Say. Ed. by Helen Lynas. (Illus.). 112p. 1998. pap. 15.95 (*0-233-99101-8*, Pub. by Andre Deutsch) Trafalgar.

Out of the Mouths of Babes & Dudes. John Bytheway. LC 97-14590. 96p. 1997. 5.95 (*1-57345-241-6*) Deseret Bk.

Out of the Mouths of Gentiles: Biblical Ingredients for an Inclusive Theology. Charles E. Link. 84p. (Orig.). 1995. pap. 7.25 (*0-7880-0619-3*) CSS OH.

Out of the Mouths of Mathematicians: A Quotation Book for Philomaths. Rosemary Schmalz. LC 93-79040. (MAA Spectrum Ser.). 304p. (Orig.). 1993. pap. text 34.95 (*0-88385-509-7*, OMMA) Math Assn.

Out of the Mouths of Slaves. Carole Marsh. (Our Black Heritage Ser.). (J). (gr. 3-12). 1994. pap. 19.95 (*1-55609-311-X*); lib. bdg. 29.95 (*1-55609-312-8*); disk 29.95 (*1-55609-313-6*) Gallopade Intl.

Out of the Mouths of Slaves: African-American Language & Educational Malpractice. John Baugh. LC 98-28384. 200p. 1999. 25.00 (*0-292-70872-6*); pap. 12.95 (*0-292-70873-4*) U of Tex Pr.

Out of the Nest. P. M. Malone. (Deep Woods Trilogy Ser.: Bk. I). (Illus.). 198p. (Orig.). (J). (gr. 1-8). 1991. pap. text 11.95 (*0-9631957-0-0*) Raspberry Hill.

***Out of the Nest, Cuckoo 2000.** Fauntleroy et al. (Illus.). 258p. 1999. 20.00 (*1-882296-06-0*) Houston Gourmet.

Out of the Night. L. Walker Arnold. 384p. 1987. 15.95 (*0-931117-08-9*) Univ Pub.

Out of the Night. Esther B. Corderman. 340p. 1994. pap. 12.95 (*0-87012-519-2*) McClain.
Set in the Appalachian mountains in the early 1900s, OUT OF THE NIGHT is a vivid portrayal of the many facets of passion exploding within one high-spirited young woman & the people who make up her world. It is not only the story of the woman's turmoil; it touches upon the growing pains of a nation in crisis. The author has skillfully recaptured some revealing realities of a bygone era. *Publisher Paid Annotation.*

Out of the Night. Penny Jordan. (Presents Ser.: No. 427). 1992. per. 2.79 (*0-373-11427-3*) Harlequin Bks.

Out of the Night. Lola M. Schaefer. LC 94-3330. (Illus.). 32p. (J). (ps-2). 1995. 14.95 (*1-879085-91-7*, Whispering Coyote) Charlesbridge Pub.

Out of the Night. Lola M. Schaefer. 1999. pap. 6.95 (*1-58089-023-7*, Whispering Coyote) Charlesbridge Pub.

Out of the Night: A Story of Tragedy & Hope from a Survivor of the 1959 Montana - Yellowstone Earthquake. Irene B. Dunn. 128p. 1998. 10.95 (*1-879628-16-3*, Plaudit Pr) Keokee ID.

Out of the Night: The Spiritual Journey of Vietnam Veterans. rev. ed. William P. Mahedy. 256p. 1996. pap. 16.95 (*1-884189-00-8*, 101) StressCare Pr.

Out of the Night: Writings from Death Row. Ed. by Marie M. Roberts & Benjamin Zephaniah. (Illus.). 192p. 1994. 45.00 (*1-873797-10-9*, Pub. by New Clarion); pap. 17.95 (*1-873797-09-5*, Pub. by New Clarion) Paul & Co Pubs.

Out of the Night & into the Dream: A Thematic Study of the Fiction of J. G. Ballard, 47. Gregory Stephenson. LC 91-21167. (Contributions to the Study of Science Fiction & Fantasy Ser.: No. 47). 200p. 1991. 52.95 (*0-313-27922-5*, SKH, Greenwood Pr) Greenwood.

Out of the Night & into the Light. Cynthia A. Esters. 37p. (Orig.). 1995. pap. 2.95 (*1-879366-93-2*) Hearthstone OK.

***Out of the Night That Covers Me.** Pat Cunnigham Devoto. 368p. 2001. 23.95 (*0-446-52751-3*) Warner Bks.

Out of the Nightmare: Recovery from Depression & Suicidal Pain. David L. Conroy. LC 90-63398. 364p. (Orig.). 1991. reprint ed. pap. 12.95 (*1-879204-00-2*) New Liberty Pubns.

Out of the Noosphere: Adventure, Sports, Travel & the Environment - The Best of Outside Magazine. Compiled by Outside Magazine Editors. 480p. 1998. per. 15.00 (*0-684-85233-0*, Fireside) S&S Trade Pap.

Out of the North. Ronald Johnson. LC 91-7935. 139p. 1991. 16.95 (*0-917635-10-8*); pap. 8.95 (*0-917635-11-6*) Plover Pr.

Out of the North: Contemporary Art from Denmark & Sweden. Text by Daniel Bernbaum & Frederikke Hansen. (Illus.). 144p. 1999. pap. 30.00 (*3-89322-509-9*) Edition Cantz.

Out of the North: The Subarctic Collection of the Haffenreffer Museum of Anthropology, Brown University. Barbara A. Hail & Kate C. Duncan. LC 89-80594. (Studies in Anthropology & Material Culture: Vol. V). (Illus.). 301p. (C). 1989. pap. 25.00 (*0-912089-07-5*) Haffenreffer Mus Anthro.

Out of the Nursery, into the Night. Kathleen Hague. LC 86-14270. (Illus.). 32p. (J). (ps-2). 1995. 13.95 (*0-8050-0088-7*, Bks Young Read) H Holt & Co.

Out of the Ocean. Debra Frasier. LC 96-5274. (Illus.). 40p. (J). (ps-3). 1998. lib. bdg. 16.00 (*0-15-258849-3*) Harcourt.

Out of the Old Earth. Harold Heslop. (Illus.). 270p. 1994. pap. 19.95 (*1-85224-153-5*, Pub. by Bloodaxe Bks) Dufour.

Out of the Old Earth. Harold Heslop. (Illus.). 270p. 1995. 45.00 (*1-85224-152-7*, Pub. by Bloodaxe Bks) Dufour.

Out of the Ordinary. Annie Dalton. LC 89-39787. 256p. (YA). (gr. 7 up). 1990. 14.95 (*0-06-021424-4*) HarpC Child Bks.

Out of the Ordinary. Annie Dalton. LC 89-39787. (Trophy Keypoint Bk.). 256p. (YA). (gr. 7 up). 1992. pap. 3.95 (*0-06-447081-4*, HarpTrophy) HarpC Child Bks.

***Out of the Ordinary.** Noelle Howey. LC 00-25493. (Illus.). 240p. 2000. pap. 13.95 (*0-312-24489-4*) St Martin.

Out of the Ordinary. Robert K. Johnson. 68p. (Orig.). 1994. pap. 8.00 (*0-9637523-1-6*) Impatiens Pr.

***Out of the Ordinary.** Steve Terrill. 2000. 12.99 (*0-89221-494-5*) New Leaf.

Out of the Ordinary: A Digest on Disability. Robert Lovering. LC 85-71798. 260148p. (Orig.). 1985. 14.95 (*0-9615213-0-9*) ARCS Inc.

Out of the Ordinary: Folklore & the Supernatural. Ed. by Barbara Walker. 1995. 34.95 (*0-87421-191-3*); pap. 19.95 (*0-87421-196-4*) Utah St U Pr.

***Out of the Ordinary: Prayers, Poems & Reflections for Every Season.** Joyce Rupp. LC 99-52395. 256p. 2000. pap. 13.95 (*0-87793-920-9*) Ave Maria.

Out of the Ordinary: Recipes from the Hingham Historical Society. Hingham Historical Society Staff. LC 98-70445. (Illus.). 160p. 1998. 16.95 (*0-9661892-0-5*) Hingham MA.

Out of the Ordinary Series 1: Awareness of God in the Everyday Life. Peter Verity. LC 98-11998. 128p. 1998. reprint ed. pap. 8.95 (*0-7648-0213-5*) Liguori Pubns.

Out of the Ozarks. William Childress. LC 87-4609. 200p. 1987. 11.95 (*0-8093-1365-0*) S Ill U Pr.

***Out of the Park: The Top 10 Book of Screwball Players, Lucky Bounces & Other Baseball Oddities.** Floyd Connor. LC 99-86476. 2000. pap. 12.95 (*1-57488-229-5*) Brasseys.

Out of the Past. Jean Curtis. (Rainbow Romances Ser.: No. 884). 160p. 1994. 14.95 (*0-7090-4936-6*) Parkwest Pubns.

Out of the Past. Christine M. Fraser. 224p. 1998. 24.00 (*0-7278-5275-2*) Severn Hse.

Out of the Past. large type ed. Margaret A. Carr. (Linford Mystery Library). 302p. 1989. pap. 16.99 (*0-7089-6640-3*, Linford) Ulverscroft.

Out of the Past. large type ed. Jean Curtis. (Linford Romance Library). 272p. 1995. pap. 16.99 (*0-7089-7717-0*, Linford) Ulverscroft.

***Out of the Past.** large type ed. Christine M. Fraser. 320p. 1999. 31.99 (*0-7505-1161-3*, Pub. by Mgna Lrg Print) Ulverscroft.

Out of the Past: A Miss Silver Mystery. Patricia Wentworth. 21.95 (*0-89190-922-2*) Amereon Ltd.

***Out of the Past: Adventures in Film Noir.** Barry Gifford. Orig. Title: Devil Thumbs a Ride. 208p. 2001. reprint ed. pap. 16.00 (*1-57806-290-X*) U Pr of Miss.

Out of the Past Amish Traditon & Faith. Mary Ann McDonald. 1998. pap. text 12.98 (*1-880908-45-X*) Todtri Prods.

Out of the Past: An Introduction to Archaeology. David L. Webster et al. LC 92-15099. 626p. (C). 1993. pap. text 58.00 (*1-55934-153-X*, 1153) Mayfield Pub.

Out of the Past: An Introduction to Archaeology Student Study Guide. David L. Webster et al. (C). 1993. pap. text, student ed. 19.95 (*1-55934-213-7*, 1213) Mayfield Pub.

Out of the Past: Selected Poems, 1961-1986 - Jim Burns. Jim Burns. (Illus.). 92p. (C). 1988. pap. 40.00 (*0-947612-27-0*, Pub. by Rivelin Grapheme Pr) St Mut.

Out of the Past Faculty Guide/Instructor's Manual: An Introduction to Archaeology. David L. Webster et al. ix, 142p. (C). 1993. pap. text, teacher ed. write for info. (*1-55934-217-X*, 1217) Mayfield Pub.

Out of the Past of Greece & Rome. Michael I. Rostovtzeff. LC 63-18047. (Illus.). 1960. 30.00 (*0-8196-0126-8*) Biblo.

Out of the Picture. Created by Francine Pascal. (Sweet Valley University Ser.: No. 33). 240p. (Orig.). (YA). (gr. 7 up). 1997. mass mkt. 3.99 (*0-553-57057-9*) BDD Bks Young Read.

Out of the Pit! Overcoming the Self-Sabotage of Depression & Anxiety. Susan F. Tackett. (Illus.). 208p. Date not set. per. 12.00 (*0-9674266-0-X*) S F Tackett.

Out of the Poverty Trap: A Conservative Strategy for Welfare Reform. Stuart Butler & Anna Kondratas. LC 87-14640. 275p. 1987. text 35.00 (*0-02-905061-8*) Free Pr.

Out of the Question & a Counterfeit Presentment: Plays. William Dean Howells. (Notable American Authors Ser.). 1992. reprint ed. lib. bdg. 75.00 (*0-7812-3270-8*) Rprt Serv.

Out of the Rain. Ed. by Malcolm Garcia & Vincent de Paul Ozanam Shelter Staff. LC 87-28888. 112p. 1988. pap. 9.95 (*0-89407-141-6*) Strawberry Hill.

Out of the Rain. Gleyn Maxwell. 128p. 1993. pap. 16.95 (*1-85224-193-4*) Dufour.

Out of the Red. George G. Siposs. 339p. mass mkt. 5.99 (*1-896329-62-4*) Picasso Publ.

Out of the Red & into the Black: A Credit & Collections Guide for Radio. 74p. 1992. pap. 40.00 (*0-89324-154-7*, 3545) Natl Assn Broadcasters.

***Out of the Red Shadow.** Anne de Graaf. LC 99-6418. (Hidden Harvest Ser.: Vol. 3). 352p. 1999. pap. 10.99 (*1-55661-620-1*) Bethany Hse.

Out of the Red Shadows: Anti-Semitism in Stalin's Russia. Gennadi V. Kostyrchenko. LC 94-39151. (Illus.). 333p. (C). 1995. 24.95 (*0-87975-930-5*) Prometheus Bks.

***Out of the Revolution: The Development of Africana Studies.** Delores P. Aldridge & Carlene Young. LC 99-87501. 2000. write for info. (*0-7391-0111-0*) Lxngtn Bks.

Out of the River Mist. 3rd ed. C. Raymond Clar. (Illus.). 135p. 1984. pap. 7.00 (*0-9613635-0-9*) C R Clar.

Out of the Rough. rev. ed. Joseph T. Shaw. (Illus.). 237p. 1992. reprint ed. 28.00 (*0-940889-36-6*) Classics Golf.

Out of the Rough: An Intimate Portrait of Laura Baugh & Her Sobering Journey. Laura Baugh. LC 99-28337. 256p. 1999. 22.95 (*1-55853-755-4*) Rutledge Hill Pr.

Out of the Rough: Meditations for Golfers. James Dyet. LC 96-6444. 160p. 1996. 12.99 (*0-7852-7659-9*) Nelson.

O

***Out of the Ruins.** William Johnson. (Poetry Ser.). 65p. 2000. pap. 10.00 (*1-881090-31-0*, Pub. by Confluence Pr) Midpt Trade.

Out of the Saddle: Native American Horsemanship. GaWaNi Pony Boy. LC 98-36080. (Illus.). 96p. (J). (gr. 3-6). 1998. 17.95 (*1-889540-37-4*) Bowtie Press.

Out of the Saltbox: The Savour of Old Vermont. Ruth M. Simpson. LC 88-17791. (Illus.). 280p. 1990. reprint ed. pap. 12.95 (*0-87797-157-9*) Larlin Corp.

***Out of the Saltshaker: Evangelism As a Way of Life.** Rebecca Manley Pippert. 1999. pap. 7.99 (*0-8308-2234-8*) InterVarsity.

Out of the Saltshaker: Evangelism As a Way of Life. Rebecca M. Pippert. LC 79-1995. 192p. 1979. reprint ed. pap. 10.99 (*0-87784-735-5*, 735) InterVarsity.

***Out of the Saltshaker: Evangelism As a Way of Life (Anniversary Edition)** 20th ed. Rebecca Manley Pippert. LC 99-30885. 1999. 16.99 (*0-8308-2233-X*) InterVarsity.

***Out of the Saltshaker: Evangelism As a Way of Life, 20th Anniversary Edition.** 20th ed. Rebecca Manley Pippert. LC 99-30885. 1999. pap. 11.99 (*0-8308-2220-8*) InterVarsity.

***Out of the Sand Creek Massacre.** Nellie O. Jackson. 2000. 25.00 (*0-7388-0740-0*); pap. 18.00 (*0-7388-0741-9*) Xlibris Corp.

Out of the Shadow: A Russian Jewish Girlhood on the Lower East Side. Rose Cohen. (Documents in American Social History Ser.). (Illus.). 336p. 1995. text 39.95 (*0-8014-3156-5*); pap. text 15.95 (*0-8014-8268-2*) Cornell U Pr.

Out of the Shadow: Artists of the Warhol Circle, Then & Now. Debra M. Miller. 100p. 1996. pap. 20.00 (*1-887421-01-7*) Univ Gall U of DE.

Out of the Shadow of Antiquity: The Politics of Technological Change in Prussia, 1809-1848. Eric D. Brose. 312p. 1992. text 49.50 (*0-691-05685-4*, Pub. by Princeton U Pr) Cal Prin Full Svc.

***Out of the Shadow of Famine: Evolving Food Markets & Food Policy in Bangladesh.** Raisuddin Ahmed. 2000. pap. 35.00 (*0-8018-6476-3*) Johns Hopkins.

***Out of the Shadow of Famine: Evolving Food Markets & Food Policy in Bangladesh.** Raisuddin Ahmed et al. LC 99-41406. 344p. 2000. write for info. (*0-8018-6333-3*) Johns Hopkins.

Out of the Shadows. Daisy C. Fernandez. (Orig.). 1997. pap. write for info. (*1-57553-465-7*) Watermrk Pr.

***Out of the Shadows.** Sue Hines. LC 99-94489. 160p. (YA). (gr. 7-12). 2000. mass mkt. 6.99 (*0-380-81192-8*, Avon Bks) Morrow Avon.

***Out of the Shadows.** Kay Hooper. 2000. mass mkt. 6.50 (*0-553-57695-X*) Bantam.

Out of the Shadows. Susan Evans McCloud. LC 98-74083. 1998. 16.95 (*1-57008-571-4*) Bookcraft Inc.

***Out of the Shadows** Scottie Pippen. 2001. mass mkt. write for info. (*0-7868-8982-9*) Disney Pr.

***Out of the Shadows.** Scottie Pippen. 256p. 2000. 22.95 (*0-7868-6618-7*, Pub. by Disney Pr) Time Warner.

***Out of the Shadows.** Elsa Stockton. 2000. pap. write for info. (*1-58235-084-1*) Watermrk Pr.

***Out of the Shadows.** Titia Sutherland. 2000. pap. 9.95 (*0-552-99529-0*, Pub. by Transworld Publishers Ltd) Trafalgar.

Out of the Shadows: A Photographic Portrait of Jewish Life in Central Europe Since the Holocaust. Edward Serotta. (Illus.). 256p. 1991. text 49.95 (*1-55972-088-3*, Birch Ln Pr) Carol Pub Group.

Out of the Shadows: Birthfathers' Stories. Mary M. Mason. (Illus.). 270p. (Orig.). 1995. pap. 14.95 (*0-9646259-1-1*) O J Howard Pub.

Out of the Shadows: Canada in the Second World War. W. A. Douglas & Brereton Greenhous. 1977. 18.95 (*0-19-540257-X*) OUP.

Out of the Shadows: Confronting America's Mental Illness Crisis. E. Fuller Torrey. LC 96-7716. 256p. 1996. 27.95 (*0-471-16161-6*) Wiley.

Out of the Shadows: Confronting America's Mental Illness Crisis. 2nd ed. E. Fuller Torrey. 256p. 1998. pap. 16.95 (*0-471-24532-1*) Wiley.

Out of the Shadows: Contemporary German Feminism. Silke Beinssen-Hesse & Catherine Rigby. LC 97-187653. (Interpretations Ser.). 160p. 1996. pap. 14.95 (*0-522-84592-4*, Pub. by Melbourne Univ Pr) Paul & Co Pubs.

Out of the Shadows: Defeating Disabilities. Robert Petty et al. (Illus.). 149p. (Orig.). 1992. pap. text 8.50 (*0-9632731-0-8*) Delano Pr.

Out of the Shadows: The Communities of Population in Resistance in Guatemala. (Illus.). 27p. 1993. pap. 3.50 (*0-918346-13-4*) EPICA.

***Out of the Shadows: The First African Indigenous Women's Conference.** Ed. by Angeline Van Achterberg. 288p. 1999. pap. 25.00 (*90-5727-026-9*, Pub. by Intl Bks) Paul & Co Pubs.

Out of the Shadows: Understanding Sexual Addiction. 2nd ed. Patrick Carnes. Orig. Title: Sexual Addiction. 182p. 1992. pap. 14.95 (*1-56838-055-0*) Hazelden.

***Out of the Shadows: What the TRC Achieved.** Ed. by Truth & Reconciliation Commission Staff. (Illus.). 300p. 1999. pap. 29.50 (*0-333-78082-5*, Pub. by Macmillan) Trans-Atl Phila.

Out of the Shadows: Women & Politics in the French Revolution, 1789-95. Shirley Elson-Roessler. LC 94-40970. (Studies in Modern European History: Vol. 14). 275p. 1998. pap. 34.95 (*0-8204-4012-4*, DC158) P Lang Pubng.

Out of the Shadows: Women, Resistance & Politics in South America. Jo Fisher. 228p. (Orig.). (C). 1993. pap. text 19.00 (*0-85345-873-1*, Pub. by Monthly Rev) NYU Pr.

Out of the Shadows, Emotions & the Enneagram see Emotions & the Enneagram: Working Through Your Shadow Life Script

***Out of the Shadows Into Reality: Philosophical Exposition of John Newman's Grammar of Assent.** Edward Joseph Alam. 200p. 2000. pap. 7.00 (*0-9634349-6-9*, Pub. by Notre Dame Univ) Platform Intl.

Out of the Shelter. David Lodge. 272p. 1989. pap. 12.95 (*0-14-012279-6*, Penguin Bks) Viking Penguin.

Out of the Silence. Ralph Butler. 142p. 1978. pap. 6.50 (*0-7050-0059-1*) Attic Pr.

Out of the Silence. Patrick F. Mahony. 1985. 20.00 (*0-941694-17-8*) Inst Study Man.

Out of the Silence: A Personal Testimony of God's Healing Power. Duane Miller. LC 96-36852. 1997. pap. 12.99 (*0-7852-7407-3*) Nelson.

Out of the Silence: A Study of a Religious Community for Women: The Community of the Holy Name. Lynne Strahan. (Illus.). 316p. 1989. 39.95 (*0-19-554898-1*) OUP.

Out of the Silent Planet. C. S. Lewis. 1980. 14.95 (*0-02-570790-6*) Macmillan.

Out of the Silent Planet. C. S. Lewis. LC 96-10402. 160p. 1996. per. 6.95 (*0-684-82380-2*) S&S Trade.

Out of the Silent Planet. C. S. Lewis. LC 96-30110. 160p. 1996. 21.50 (*0-684-83364-6*) S&S Trade.

Out of the Silent Planet. C. S. Lewis. 1965. 12.05 (*0-606-01214-1*, Pub. by Turtleback) Demco.

Out of the Silent Planet. C. S. Lewis. 1998. lib. bdg. 20.95 (*1-56723-071-7*) Yestermorrow.

Out of the Silent Planet. large type ed. C. S. Lewis. 234p. 1998. 23.95 (*0-7838-0411-3*) Mac Lib Ref.

Out of the Silent Planet. C. S. Lewis. 1991. reprint ed. lib. bdg. 21.95 (*1-56849-039-9*) Buccaneer Bks.

Out of the Silent Planet. C. S. Lewis. 174p. 1990. reprint ed. 45.00 (*0-02-570795-7*, Hudson Rvr Edtn) S&S Trade.

Out of the Silent Planet Study Guide. Andrew Clausen. 38p. (YA). (gr. 9-12). 1993. student ed., ring bd. 14.99 (*1-58609-156-5*) Progeny Pr WI.

Out of the Sixties: Storytelling & the Vietnam Generation. David Wyatt. LC 93-18179. (Cambridge Studies in American Literature & Culture: No. 66). 242p. (C). 1993. pap. text 18.95 (*0-521-44689-9*) Cambridge U Pr.

Out of the Sixties: Storytelling & the Vietnam Generation. David Wyatt. LC 93-18179. (Cambridge Studies in American Literature & Culture: No. 66). 242p. (C). 1993. text 69.95 (*0-521-44151-X*) Cambridge U Pr.

Out of the Slave Coast. Matthew Uzukwu. LC 96-90823. 175p. (Orig.). 1996. pap. 10.00 (*0-9637326-3-3*) Feli Pub.

Out of the Smoke Filled Room: A History of Michigan Politics. Neil Staebler. 1991. pap. 14.50 (*0-911586-41-5*) Wahr.

Out of the Soil. Irene Armstrong. Ed. by Doreen Hanners. 130p. 1998. pap. 10.95 (*0-9661337-1-4*) Son-Kin.

Out of the Spider's Web: Love Triumphs. Carroll Peaden. 180p. 1998. pap. 10.95 (*1-57502-852-2*, PO2337) Morris Pubng.

Out of the Storm. Catherine George. (Romance Ser.). 1993. per. 2.89 (*0-373-03261-7*, 1-03261-4) Harlequin Bks.

Out of the Storm. Grace Livingston Hill. Date not set. 23.95 (*0-8488-2330-3*) Amereon Ltd.

Out of the Storm. Grace Livingston Hill. 1990. pap. 5.00 (*0-7451-1282-X*, Pub. by Chivers N Amer) Chivers N Amer.

Out of the Storm. Michael Thorpe. 64p. 1984. 6.95 (*0-920806-62-7*, Pub. by Penumbra Pr) U of Toronto Pr.

Out of the Storm. Patricia Willis. LC 94-2133. 192p. (J). (gr. 4-8). 1995. 15.00 (*0-395-68708-X*, Clarion Bks) HM.

Out of the Storm. Patricia Willis. 192p. (J). 1996. pap. 3.99 (*0-380-72695-5*, Avon Bks) Morrow Avon.

Out of the Storm. large type ed. Grace Livingston Hill. (Nightingale Ser.). 245p. 1990. pap. 13.95 (*0-8161-4990-9*, G K Hall Lrg Type) Mac Lib Ref.

Out of the Storm: The End of the Civil War, April-June 1865. Noah A. Trudeau. LC 93-34683. (Illus.). 496p. (C). 1995. pap. 19.95 (*0-8071-2033-2*) La State U Pr.

Out of the Sun. Robert Goddard. LC 96-44331. 1997. 25.00 (*0-8050-5109-0*) H Holt & Co.

Out of the Sun. Robert Goddard. 352p. 1998. pap. 13.00 (*0-8050-5836-2*, Owl) H Holt & Co.

Out of the Sun. large type ed. Robert Goddard. (Charnwood Large Print Ser.). 496p. 1997. 27.99 (*0-7089-8967-5*) Ulverscroft.

Out of the Tiger's Mouth. C. Chao. Date not set. pap. 6.99 (*1-871676-59-2*, Pub. by Christian Focus) Spring Arbor Dist.

Out of the Trap. Ed. by Mark Watts. LC 86-70112. 160p. (Orig.). 1985. pap. 10.95 (*0-89708-147-1*, 86-070112) And Bks.

Out of the Treasure: The Parables in the Gospel of Matthew. Jan Lambrecht. (Louvain Theological & Pastoral Monographs). 296p. (Orig.). (C). 1992. pap. 25.00 (*0-8028-0662-7*) Eerdmans.

***Out of the Twilight: Fathers of Gay Men Speak.** Andrew R. Gottlieb. LC 99-55438. 284p. (C). 2000. 39.95 (*0-7890-0614-6*); pap. 19.95 (*1-56023-951-4*) Haworth Pr.

Out of the Valley of Darkness. Mary-Etta Hinkle. 104p. (Orig.). 1992. pap. 6.95 (*0-89228-022-0*) Impact Christian.

Out of the Volcano: Portraits of Contemporary Mexican Artists. Margaret Sayers Peden. LC 91-52842. (Illus.). 264p. (C). 1991. pap. 34.95 (*1-56098-061-3*) Smithsonian.

***Out of the Vortex Finding Order in Merger & Acquisition Chaos.** American Compensation Association Staff. (Building Blocks Ser.). (Illus.). 1998. pap. 39.95 (*1-57963-062-6*) Am Compensation.

Out of the Wailing. Stephen C. Wright. 40p. 1992. pap. 8.00 (*1-879025-05-1*) Christopher-Burghardt.

Out of the West. Jane Archer. 1996. mass mkt. 5.99 (*0-671-53710-5*) PB.

Out of the Whirlind: A Novel. M. T. Kelly. LC 96-111872. 208p. 1996. pap. 14.95 (*0-7737-5822-4*) Stoddart Publ.

Out of the Whirlwind. Gilbert Morris. LC 93-35507. (Appomattox Saga Ser.: No. 5). (Illus.). 316p. 1994. pap. 8.99 (*0-8423-1658-2*) Tyndale Hse.

Out of the Whirlwind: A Reader of Holocaust Literature. 2nd rev. ed. Ed. by Albert H. Friedlander & Aron Hirt-Manheimer. LC 98-49236. (Illus.). 608p. 1999. pap. 16.95 (*0-8074-0703-8*, 959068) UAHC.

***Out of the Whirlwind: First Lesson Sermons for Sundays after Pentecost (Last Third), Cycle B.** John A. Stroman. LC 99-32555. 70p. 1999. pap. 7.75 (*0-7880-1388-2*) CSS OH.

Out of the Whirlwind: Illustrations to the Book of Job. Illus. by Roger Wagner. 52p. 1997. reprint ed. pap. 16.99 (*1-900507-58-7*, Pub. by Solway) OM Literature.

Out of the Whirlwind: Three Decades of Arts Commentary. Dore Ashton. Ed. & Frwd. by Donald Kuspit. LC 87-5018. (Contemporary American Art Critics Ser.: No. 8). 546p. reprint ed. 169.30 (*0-8357-1741-0*, 207068900004) Bks Demand.

Out of the Wilderness. Debra Vanasse. LC 98-22692. 176p. (YA). (gr. 5-9). 1999. 15.00 (*0-395-91421-3*, Clarion Bks) HM.

Out of the Wilderness. Jane D. Chaplin. LC 74-38644. (Black Heritage Library Collection). 1977. reprint ed. 22.95 (*0-8369-9002-1*) Ayer.

Out of the Wilderness: Douglas Clyde Macintosh's Journeys Through the Grounds & Claims. Preston Warren. (American University Studies: Philosophy: Ser. V, Vol. 51). XVI, 284p. (C). 1989. text 39.50 (*0-8204-0777-1*) P Lang Pubng.

Out of the Wilderness: The Brethren & Two Centuries of Life in Central Pennsylvania. Earl C. Kaylor. (Illus.). 384p. 1981. 12.50 (*0-8453-4716-0*, Cornwall Bks) Assoc Univ Prs.

Out of the Wilderness: The Civil War Memoir of Corporal Norton C. Shepard, 146th New York Volunteer Infantry. Norton C. Shepard. Ed. by Raymond W. Smith. LC 98-44362. 37p. 1998. pap. 10.95 (*1-892059-00-2*) Edmonston Publ.

Out of the Wilderness: The Life of Abraham Lincoln. William Hanchett. LC 93-39609. (Illus.). 128p. (C). 1994. 10.95 (*0-252-06400-3*); text 21.50 (*0-252-02111-8*) U of Ill Pr.

Out of the Woodpile: Black Characters in Crime & Detective Fiction, 27. Frankie Y. Bailey. LC 90-45804. (Contributions to the Study of Popular Culture Ser.: No. 27). 208p. 1991. 55.00 (*0-313-26671-9*, BOW, Greenwood Pr) Greenwood.

Out of the Woods. Thomas Bolt. LC 88-30313. 80p. (C). 1989. 18.00 (*0-300-04469-0*) Yale U Pr.

Out of the Woods: Essays in Environmental History. Ed. by Char Miller & Hal Rothman. LC 97-4747. 368p. 1997. pap. 22.95 (*0-8229-5631-4*); text 50.00 (*0-8229-3982-7*) U of Pittsburgh Pr.

Out of the Woods: Stories. Chris Offutt. LC 98-43041. 192p. 1999. 21.00 (*0-684-82556-2*) S&S Trade.

***Out of the Woods: Stories.** Chris Offutt. 176p. 2000. per. 11.00 (*0-684-85376-0*) S&S Trade.

Out of the Woods: The Origins of the Literary Fairy Tale in Italy & France. Ed. by Nancy Canepa. (Illus.). 448p. 1997. 39.95 (*0-8143-2687-0*) Wayne St U Pr.

Out of the Words of Birds. Marvin D. Goldfarb & Deanna Condino. Ed. by Phyllis Weprin. 60p. (J). (gr. 1-6). 1998. pap. text 20.00 (*0-9662884-0-8*) Menasha Pr.

Out of Their Faces & into Their Shoes: How to Understand Spiritually Lost People & Give Them Help. John Kramp. 1997. pap. 11.99 (*0-8054-6350-X*) Broadman.

Out of Their League. large type ed. David Meggyesy. 385p. 1999. 27.95 (*1-56000-482-7*) Transaction Pubs.

Out of Their Minds. Carol Matas & Perry Nodelman. LC 97-41277. (Illus.). 192p. (J). (gr. 5-9). 1998. 16.00 (*0-689-81946-3*) S&S Bks Yung.

Out of Their Minds: The Lives & Discoveries of 15 Great Computer Scientists. Dennis E. Shasha & Cathy Lazere. (Illus.). 296p. 1995. 23.00 (*0-387-97992-1*) Spr-Verlag.

Out of Their Minds: The Lives & Discoveries of 15 Great Computer Scientists. Dennis Shasha & Cathy Lazere. LC 98-16911. (Illus.). 296p. 1997. pap. 18.00 (*0-387-98269-8*) Spr-Verlag.

Out of These Roots. Agnes E. Meyer. Ed. by Annette K. Baxter. LC 79-8801. (Signal Lives Ser.). (Illus.). 1980. reprint ed. lib. bdg. 46.95 (*0-405-12848-7*) Ayer.

Out of Thin Air: A History of Air Products & Chemicals, Inc., 1940-1990. Andrew J. Butrica. LC 90-39618. 344p. 1990. 75.00 (*0-275-93765-8*, C3765, Praeger Pubs) Greenwood.

Out of Thin Air: A Satire on Owls & Ozone, Beef & Biodiversity, Grains & Global Warming. Alex Jack. 112p. 1993. pap. 7.95 (*0-9628528-7-2*) One Peaceful World.

Out of Third Reich: Refugee Historians in Postwar Britian. Alter. 250p. 1998. text 59.50 (*1-86064-189-X*, Pub. by I B T) St Martin.

Out of This Furnace. Thomas Bell. LC 76-6657. (Illus.). 424p. (C). 1976. reprint ed. pap. 14.95 (*0-8229-5273-4*) U of Pittsburgh Pr.

Out of This Furnace: Fiftieth Anniversary Edition. Thomas Bell. LC 91-50105. (Social & Labor History Ser.). (Illus.). 424p. (C). 1991. text 29.95 (*0-8229-3690-9*) U of Pittsburgh Pr.

Out of This Kitchen: A History of the Ethnic Groups & Their Foods in the Steel Valley. 2nd ed. Publassist Staff. (Illus.). 186p. 1998. lib. bdg. 15.00 (*0-9638745-0-0*, TX-3-619-596) Publassist.

Out of This Nettle, Danger. Harold W. Dodds. LC 78-99631. (Essay Index Reprint Ser.). 1977. 17.95 (*0-8369-1406-6*) Ayer.

Out of This World. Penny King & Clare Roundhill. LC 96-53245. (Making Pictures Ser.). (J). 1998. (*1-57572-193-7*) Rigby Educ.

Out of This World. Carole Stott. LC 98-5691. (Illus.). 24p. (J). (gr. 2-3). 1998. 11.99 (*0-7636-0372-4*) Candlewick Pr.

Out of This World. Carole Stott. LC 98-5691. (Illus.). 24p. (J). (gr. 3-6). 1998. pap. 4.99 (*0-7636-0646-4*) Candlewick Pr.

Out of This World. Graham Swift. 207p. 1993. pap. 11.00 (*0-679-74032-5*) McKay.

***Out of This World.** Graham Swift. 1999. 4.50 (*0-671-67309-2*) S&S Trade.

Out of This World. rev. ed. Arthur J. Wiebe et al. (J). (gr. 4-8). 1994. 16.95 (*1-881431-43-6*, 1310) AIMS Educ Fnd.

Out of This World: A Guide to the Retreat Houses of Great Britain. George Target. 1985. 35.00 (*0-900873-67-1*, Pub. by Bishopsgate Pr Ltd) St Mut.

Out of This World: A Guide to the Retreat Houses of Great Britain. George Target. 1985. pap. 30.00 (*0-900873-73-6*, Pub. by Bishopsgate Pr) St Mut.

Out of this World: A Journey of Healing. Mary Swander. 288p. 1996. pap. 11.95 (*0-14-024170-1*, Penguin Bks) Viking Penguin.

Out of This World: An Exhibition of Fantastic Landscapes from the Renaissance to the Present: March 20-April 30, 1964, Fine Arts Gallery, University of St. Thomas. Jermayne MacAgy & Etienne Sourian. (Illus.). 1964. pap. 5.00 (*0-914412-23-X*, Inst Arts Catalogues) Menil Found.

Out of This World: Canadian Science Fiction & Fantasy Literature. Compiled by Andrea Paradis. LC 95-195635. (Illus.). 264p. 1995. pap. 19.95 (*1-55082-150-4*, Pub. by Quarry Pr) LPC InBook.

Out of This World: Handbook of Ghosts, Spirits, Alien Sightings & Psychic Phenomena. Robert McKinney. (Illus.). 1985. pap. 4.95 (*0-913290-67-X*) Camaro Pub.

Out of This World: Poems. Joseph Somoza. LC 89-85832. 96p. (Orig.). 1990. pap. 8.95 (*0-938317-11-3*) Cinco Puntos.

Out of This World: The Natural History of Milton Acorn. Chris Gudgeon. LC 97-118627. (Illus.). 240p. 1996. 23.95 (*1-55152-030-3*, Pub. by Arsenal Pulp) LPC InBook.

Out-of-This-World Marriage: (Spellbound) Maggie B. Shayne. (Intimate Moments Ser.). 1995. per. 3.75 (*0-373-07633-9*, 1-07633-0) Silhouette.

***Out of This World Ohio Coloring Book.** Carole Marsh. (Ohio Experience! Ser.). (Illus.). (J). (gr. k-5). 2000. pap. 3.95 (*0-7933-9474-0*) Gallopade Intl.

***Out of This World Oklahoma Coloring Book.** Carole Marsh. (Oklahoma Experience! Ser.). (Illus.). (J). (gr. k-5). 2000. pap. 3.95 (*0-7933-9599-2*) Gallopade Intl.

***Out of Time.** Lynn Abbey. 2000. mass mkt. 5.99 (*0-441-00751-1*) Ace Bks.

Out of Time. Chris Archer. (Mindwarp Ser.: No. 9). 144p. (YA). (gr. 4-7). 1998. pap. 3.99 (*0-671-02169-9*, Minstrel Bks) PB.

Out of Time. James C. Bull. (Illus.). 83p. 1999. pap. 15.00 (*0-9669299-0-X*) Wolff Pub Works.

Out of Time. Caroline B. Cooney. 1996. pap. 10.95 (*0-385-21933-4*) Delacorte.

Out of Time. Caroline B. Cooney. LC 95-22186. (Romantic Time Travel Ser.: No. 2). 224p. (YA). (gr. 7-12). 1997. mass mkt. 4.99 (*0-440-21933-7*) Dell.

Out of Time. Caroline B. Cooney. LC 95-22186. 1997. 9.60 (*0-606-11716-4*, Pub. by Turtleback) Demco.

Out of Time. 2nd ed. Paula Martinac. LC 90-36973. (Djuna Bks.). 224p. 1999. reprint ed. pap. 12.95 (*1-58005-020-4*) Seal Pr WA.

Out of Time: A Casey Jones Mystery. Katy Munger. LC 97-94934. (Casey Jones Mystery Ser.). 256p. 1998. mass mkt. 5.99 (*0-380-79138-2*, Avon Bks) Morrow Avon.

***Out of Time: Designs for the 20th-Century Future.** Norman Brosterman. (Illus.). 96p. 2000. pap. 19.95 (*0-8109-2939-2*, Pub. by Abrams) Time Warner.

Out of Time: History & Evolution in Anthropological Discourse. 2nd ed. Nicholas Thomas. LC 96-13807. 176p. 1996. pap. text 18.95 (*0-472-08377-5*, 08377) U of Mich Pr.

Out of Time: Imp. Version R. E. M. (Piano-Vocal-Guitar Ser.). 72p. 1994. otabind 2.16 (*0-7935-2833-X*, 00353167) H Leonard.

Out of Time: Imp. Version with Notes & Tablature. 64p. 1994. otabind. write for info. (*0-7935-2835-6*, 00694907) H Leonard.

Out of Time: Why English Football Isn't Working. Alex Fynn & Lynton Guest. 355p. 1999. reprint ed. text 25.00 (*0-7881-6128-8*) DIANE Pub.

Out of Time & Place: Amazing Accounts That Challenge Our View of Human History. Ed. & Compiled by Terry O'Neill. LC 98-33309. (Illus.). 272p. 1999. 9.95 (*1-56718-261-5*) Llewellyn Pubns.

Out of Torch: I Shot My Congressman. Ed. by Rosaline Don & John B. Fonyam. 1992. 19.95 (*0-910253-40-4*) Backwards & Backwards.

Out of Touch: When Parents & Children Lose Contact after Divorce. Geoffrey L. Greif. 256p. 1997. 25.00 (*0-19-509535-9*) OUP.

Out of Town. large type ed. Jack Hargreaves. (Illus.). 256p. 1992. 27.99 (*0-7089-2576-6*) Ulverscroft.

Out-of-Town Retailing, 1991. Ed. by Euromonitor Staff. 200p. 1991. pap. 895.00 (*0-86338-495-1*, Pub. by Euromonitor PLC) Gale.

Out of Tune: David Helfgott & the Myth of Shine. Margaret Helfgott & Tom Gross. LC 97-32316. 294p. 1998. 24.00 (*0-446-52383-6*, Pub. by Warner Bks) Little.

O

Out of Tune: David Helfgott & the Myth of Shine. Margaret Helfgott & Tom Gross. 1999. pap. write for info. (0-446-67516-4) Warner Bks.

Out of Tune: Listening to the First Amendment. John Frohnmayer. LC 95-12267. (Illus.). 150p. (Orig.). 1995. pap. 16.95 (1-55591-932-4) Fulcrum Pub.

Out of Utopia: Toward a Reorientation of Sociological Analysis. Ralf Dahrendorf. (Reprint Series in Social Sciences). (C). 1993. reprint ed. pap. text 5.00 (0-8290-2719-X, S-58) Irvington.

Out of Wedlock: A Study of the Problems of the Unmarried Mother & Her Child. Leontine Young. LC 78-16486. 261p. 1978. reprint ed. lib. bdg. 59.75 (0-313-20604-X, YOWE, Greenwood Pr) Greenwood.

Out-of-Wedlock Births: The United States in Comparative Perspective. Mark Abrahamson. LC 97-43954. 184p. 1998. 55.00 (0-275-95662-8, Praeger Pubs); pap. 18.95 (0-275-95665-2, Praeger Pubs) Greenwood.

Out of What Began: A History of Irish Poetry in English. Gregory A. Schirmer. LC 98-8409. 368p. 1998. 35.00 (0-8014-3498-X) Cornell U Pr.

Out of Women's Experience: Creating Relational Leadership. Helen B. Regan & Gwen H. Brooks. LC 95-12698. (Illus.). 136p. 1995. 45.95 (0-8039-6233-9) Corwin Pr.

Out of Work. John Law. (Radical Fiction Ser.). 304p. 1990. reprint ed. lib. bdg. 25.00 (0-929587-39-1) I R Dee.

Out of Work: A Study of Unemployment. Frances A. Kellor. LC 71-137172. (Poverty U. S. A. Historical Record Ser.). 1978. reprint ed. 41.95 (0-405-03111-4) Ayer.

Out of Work: Unemployment & Government in Twentieth-Century America. Richard K. Vedder. LC 97-12516. 1997. pap. text 19.50 (0-8147-8792-4) NYU Pr.

Out of Yesterday. F. R. Smith. 212p. 1986. pap. 40.00 (0-7223-2014-0, Pub. by A H S Ltd) St Mut.

Out of Yesterday. F. R. Smith. 212p. 1987. pap. 35.00 (0-7855-1994-7, Pub. by A H S Ltd) St Mut.

Out of Yesterday. large type ed. Eva Burfield. 320p. 1987. 27.99 (0-7089-1622-8) Ulverscroft.

Out of Your Mind - The Only Place to Be! Debbie Shapiro & Eddie Shapiro. 224p. 1992. pap. 12.95 (1-85230-306-9, Pub. by Element MA) Penguin Putnam.

Out on a Cloud I. Claudette Clerin. 1997. pap. 56.95 (1-57553-536-X) Watermrk Pr.

***Out on a Farm.** Joyce Di Maggio. (Illus.). 24p. (J). (ps-1). 1999. pap. 5.00 (1-928970-10-9) GWR Pr.

Out on a Limb. Sue Limb. LC 99-487841. 224p. 1999. 25.00 (0-7278-2292-6, Pub. by Severn Hse) Chivers N Amer.

Out on a Limb. Louise Baker. (American Autobiography Ser.). 213p. 1995. reprint ed. lib. bdg. 79.00 (0-7812-8446-5) Rprt Serv.

Out on a Limb: The Story of Zacchaeus. Marilyn Lashbrook. (Me Too Bks.). (Illus.). 30p. (J). 1996. 8.95 (0-87973-868-5) Our Sunday Visitor.

Out on a Limb: The Story of Zacchaeus. Marilyn Lashbrook. (J). (ps-2). 1998. pap. 5.95 (0-933657-73-0) Rainbow Studies.

Out on a Loom: 15 Patterns & Instructions for Loom Bead Weaving. (Illus.). 32p. 1999. pap. 19.95 (0-9670964-0-5, Pub. by Minoa) Helby Import.

Out on Fraternity Row: Personal Accounts of Being Gay in a College Fraternity. Ed. by Shane Windmeyer & Pamela W. Freeman. LC 98-8371. 336p. (Orig.). 1998. pap. 12.95 (1-55583-409-4, Alyson Bks) Alyson Pubns.

Out on Main Street: And Other Stories. Shani Mootoo. 128p. 1993. pap. 12.95 (0-88974-052-6, Pub. by Press Gang Pubs) LPC InBook.

Out on My Own. Gil Gibson et al. 96p. 1985. 7.95 (0-941162-03-6) D Gibson.

***Out on Stage: Lesbian & Gay Theater in the Twentieth Century.** Alan Sinfield. LC 99-28103. 394p. 1999. 29.95 (0-300-08102-2) Yale U Pr.

***Out on the Balcony for 365 Days.** Michael Anthony Lobevero. LC 00-190167. (Balcony Ser.: Bk. 1). 402p. 2000. 25.00 (0-7388-1597-7); pap. 18.00 (0-7388-1598-5) Xlibris Corp.

Out on the Cutting Edge. Lawrence Block. (Matthew Scudder Mystery Ser.). 256p. 1990. reprint ed. mass mkt. 5.99 (0-380-70993-7, Avon Bks) Morrow Avon.

Out on the Edge. Ninian Dunnett. 1999. pap. 15.00 (0-86241-777-5) Interlink Pub.

Out on the Edge: A Wake up Call for Church Leaders on the Edge of the Media Reformation. Michael Slaughter. LC 98-5913. 160p. 1998. pap. 19.95 incl. cd-rom (0-687-05453-2) Abingdon.

Out on the Ice in the Middle of the Bay. Peter Cumming. (Illus.). 32p. (J). (ps-3). 1993. pap. 6.95 (1-55037-277-7, Pub. by Annick); lib. bdg. 15.95 (1-55037-276-9, Pub. by Annick) Firefly Bks Ltd.

Out on the Porch: An Evocation in Words & Pictures. Ed. by Clifton Dowell. (Illus.). 128p. 1992. 17.95 (0-945575-93-9) Algonquin Bks.

Out on the Rim. 1990. mass mkt. 4.95 (0-445-77298-0, Pub. by Warner Bks) Little.

Out on the Rim. Ross Thomas. LC 87-42697. 320p. 1987. 17.95 (0-89296-212-7, Pub. by Mysterious Pr) Little.

Out on the Shoals: Twenty Years of Photography on the Isles of Shoals. Peter E. Randall. (Illus.). 64p. 1995. pap. 16.50 (0-914339-52-4, Pub. by P E Randall Pub) U Pr of New Eng.

Out on the Winds: Poles & Danes in Lincoln County, Minnesota, 1880-1905. John Radzilowski. (Illus.). 128p. 1992. pap. 11.95 (0-9614119-4-5) Crossings Pr.

Out on Your Own. Robert Moskowitz. 216p. 1997. ring bd. 21.95 (0-9624415-3-8) Key Pubns Woodland Hills.

Out Our Back Door: 24 Driving Tours from Coos Bay Area. Tom Baake. LC 97-90390. (Illus.). 144p. (Orig.). 1997. pap. 9.95 (0-9658012-0-9) Westways Pr.

Out, Out, Out. Martha Alexander. LC 68-15251. (Illus.). (J). (gr. k-3). 1968. lib. bdg. 6.95 (0-685-01457-6, Dial Yng Read) Peng Put Young Read.

***Out-Patient Rehabilitation in Chronic Obstructive Pulmonary Disease.** Thierry Troosters. (Acta Biomedica Lovaniensia Ser.: No. 203). (Illus.). 156p. 1999. pap. 36.50 (90-6186-982-X, Pub. by Leuven Univ) Coronet Bks.

Out-Posts - Avant-Postes. Caroline Baynard & Jack David. 254p. (C). 1978. pap. text 12.00 (1-55022-039-X, Pub. by ECW) Genl Dist Srvs.

Out-Posts/Avant-Postes. Caroline Baynard & Jack David. 254p. (C). 1978. text 20.00 (1-55022-040-3, Pub. by ECW) Genl Dist Srvs.

Out Rage: Dykes & Bis Resist Homophobia. Ed. by Mona Oikawa et al. 286p. pap. 12.95 (0-88961-188-2, Pub. by Womens Pr) LPC InBook.

Out-Smarting Your Karma: And Other Preordained Conditions. Barry Neil Kaufman. LC 95-67841. (Illus.). 141p. (Orig.). 1996. pap. 9.95 (1-887254-04-8) Epic Century.

Out Sounds: The Gay & Lesbian Music Alternative. Will Grega & Randy Jones. (Illus.). 128p. (Orig.). 1996. pap. 12.00 (0-9639871-7-8) Pop Front.

Out Takes: Essays on Queer Theory & Film. Ellis Hanson. LC 98-37161. (Series Q). 1999. write for info. (0-8223-2309-5); pap. 19.95 (0-8223-2342-7) Duke.

***Out the in Door: New Techniques in Lucid Dreaming.** Michael J. Szul. LC 99-91464. 128p. 2000. pap. 11.95 (0-9675883-0-8) Midknight Club.

Out There. Stephen Schwartz. LC 96-187386. (Illus.). 48p. (J). 1996. 9.70 (0-7868-6224-6, Pub. by Hyperion) Time Warner.

Out There. Howard Blum. Ed. by Julie Rubenstein. 352p. 1991. reprint ed. mass mkt. 6.99 (0-671-66261-9, Pocket Star Bks) PB.

Out There: A Satiric Anthology on the American Biker. Mark Bradley. (Illus.). 1996. pap. 19.95 (0-9650916-0-0) AG Pubng.

Out There: Marginalization & Contemporary Cultures. 4th ed. Contrib. by Joell Hooks et al. LC 90-5562. (Documentary Sources in Contemporary Art: Vol. 4). (Illus.). 447p. 1992. reprint ed. pap. 19.95 (0-262-56064-X) New Mus Contemp Art.

Out There: Stories of Private Desires, Horror & the After Life. Perry Brass. Ed. by Tom Laine. LC 94-70482. 192p. (Orig.). 1994. pap. 10.95 (0-9627123-4-5) Belhue Pr.

Out There in Space: Poems by Aileen Fisher. Aileen Fisher. LC 99-63741. (Illus.). 32p. Date not set. write for info. (1-56397-802-4, Wordsong) Boyds Mills Pr.

Out to Canaan. Jan Karon. (Mitford Ser.). 21.95 (1-57490-257-1) T T Beeler.

Out to Canaan. Jan Karon. LC 97-5867. (Mitford Years Ser.: Vol. 4). (Illus.). 352p. 1997. 23.95 (0-670-87485-X) Viking Penguin.

Out to Canaan. Jan Karon. LC 97-5867. (Mitford Years Ser.: Vol. 4). 342p. 1998. pap. 12.95 (0-14-026568-6) Viking Penguin.

Out to Canaan. large type ed. Jan Karon. LC 97-20642. (Mitford Years Ser.: Vol. 4). (Illus.). 412p. 1997. lib. bdg. 26.95 (1-57490-104-4, Beeler LP Bks) T T Beeler.

Out to Dry: Riddles about Deserts. June Swanson. LC 93-26294. (You Must Be Joking! Riddle Bks.). (Illus.). 32p. (J). (gr. 1-4). 1994. lib. bdg. 14.60 (0-8225-2343-4, Lerner Publctns) Lerner Pub.

***Out to Eat: Melbourne.** Carolyn Papworth. (Out to Eat Guides). (Illus.). 248p. 1999. pap. 12.95 (1-86450-040-9) Lonely Planet.

Out to Eat: Sydney. Kath Kenny. (Out to Eat Guides). (Illus.). 248p. 1999. pap. 12.95 (1-86450-060-3) Lonely Planet.

***Out to Eat London.** Ryan Ver Berkmoes. (Illus.). 320p. 2000. pap. 12.95 (1-86450-083-2) Lonely Planet.

***Out to Eat San Francisco.** Kim Zetter. (Out to Eat Guides). (Illus.). 288p. 2000. pap. 12.99 (1-86450-084-0) Lonely Planet.

Out to Gumball Pond, Vol. 2918. Margaret Allen. Ed. by Joel Kupperstein. (Dr. Maggie's Phonics Readers Ser.). (Illus.). 16p. (J). 1999. pap. 2.99 (1-57471-593-3) Creat Teach Pr.

Out! To Lead. Gideon Farebee, Jr. Ed. by Lynne E. Lewis. LC 93-73649. 193p. (Orig.). 1994. pap. 10.95 (1-885487-01-0) Brownell & Carroll.

Out to Lunch. Peggy P. Anderson. LC 97-30836. 32p. (J). (ps-1). 1998. 14.00 (0-395-89826-9) HM.

Out to Pastor: The Autobiography of Thomas S. Goslin II. Thomas S. Goslin & Carnegie S. Callian. LC 98-42988. (Illus.). 208p. 1999. pap. 12.95 (0-932727-04-2) Hope Pub Hse.

Out to Pasture: But Not over the Hill. Effie Leland Wilder. LC 94-48008. (Illus.). 177p. 1995. 14.95 (1-56145-101-0) Peachtree Pubs.

Out to Pasture: But Not over the Hill. Effie L. Wilder. 1996. audio 15.95 (1-56145-136-3) Peachtree Pubs.

Out to Play: The Middle Years of Childhood. Alasdair Roberts. 175p. 1980. text 13.00 (0-08-025719-4, Pergamon Pr); pap. text 13.00 (0-08-025718-6, Pergamon Pr) Elsevier.

Out to the Ball Game with Tom Wolfe. Douglas Congdon-Martin. LC 92-63110. (Illus.). 64p. (Orig.). 1993. pap. 12.95 (0-88740-497-9) Schiffer.

Out to the Edge. Ben Weinberg. Ed. by B. Holmes. LC 92-62941. 200p. (YA). (gr. 6-10). 1993. pap. 8.95 (0-932433-47-2) Windswept Hse.

Out to Win. Micki Nesbit. (Illus.). 78p. (Orig.). Date not set. pap. 7.99 (0-9659759-0-8) Nat Tech Inst.

Out to Work: A History of Wage-Earning Women in the United States. Jane Brettle. 1999. 3.98 (1-57717-102-0) Todtri Prods.

Out to Work: A History of Wage-Earning Women in the United States. Alice Kessler-Harris. (Illus.). 416p. 1983. pap. text 15.95 (0-19-503353-1) OUP.

Out Visiting & Back Home: Russian Stories on Aging. Ed. & Tr. by Thomas H. Hoisington from RUS. LC 97-48552. 250p. 1998. 26.95 (0-8101-1470-4, Hydra Bks) Northwestern U Pr.

Out Walking. John Welch. 88p. 1984. pap. 14.95 (0-85646-116-4, Pub. by Anvil Press) Dufour.

***Out Walking: Reflections on Our Place in the Natural World.** John Leax. LC 99-58138. 144p. 2000. pap. 14.99 (0-8010-1197-3) Baker Bks.

***Out Walking: Reflections on Our Place in the Natural World.** John Leax. 176p. (gr. 13 up). 2000. pap. 13.99 (0-8010-6175-X, Ravens Ridge) Baker Bks.

Out West. Fred G. Leebron. LC 97-25492. 256p. 1997. pap. 12.00 (0-15-600546-8) Harcourt.

***Out West: A Journey Through Lewis & Clark's America.** Dayton Duncan. (Illus.). 464p. 2000. reprint ed. pap. 18.95 (0-8032-6626-X, Bison Books) U of Nebr Pr.

Out West: An American Journey. Dayton Duncan. (Illus.). 448p. 1988. pap. 13.95 (0-14-008362-6, Penguin Bks) Viking Penguin.

***Out with a Passion: A United Methodist Pastor's Quest for Authenticity.** Richard T. Rossiter. LC 99-60588. 128p. 1999. pap. 11.95 (1-886360-07-3) Alamo Sq Pr.

Out with It: Gay & Straight Teens Write about Homosexuality. Youth Communication Staff. Ed. by Al Desetta et al. (Illus.). viii, 115p. 1996. 8.00 (0-9661256-0-6) P Fell Cartoons.

Out with the Bondwoman: What, When, How, & Why? Nettie M. Hart. 108p. Date not set. pap. write for info. (1-886096-01-5) Priceless Prnting.

Out with the Kansas Hillbillies. Dorothy Kelley. Ed. by Linda Kelley. (Illus.). x, 292p. 1999. pap. 12.95 (0-9668009-0-7, 1) Wheat Field.

Out with the Stars. James Purdy. 192p. 1993. pap. 9.95 (0-87286-284-4) City Lights.

Out with the Stars. James Purdy. 192p. 1993. 30.00 (0-7206-0861-9, Pub. by P Owen Ltd) Dufour.

Outage: A Journey into Electric City. rev. ed. Bruce Powe. LC 94-42171. 1995. text 21.00 (0-88001-418-0) HarpC.

***Outback.** Aaron Fletcher. 448p. 2000. pap. 5.50 (0-8439-4686-5, Leisure Bks) Dorchester Pub Co.

Outback Australia. Jane Taylor. 1999. 49.95 (1-86436-323-1) New Holland.

***Outback Australia: A Guide to the Northern Territory & Kimberly.** 4th ed. Malcolm Gordon. (Illus.). 2000. pap. 19.95 (1-86315-112-5) Little Hills.

Outback by Escort. Pam Brown. 290p. 1994. pap. 16.95 (0-9641728-2-8) Custom Services.

Outback Ghettos: Aboriginal Institutionalisation & Survival. Peggy Brock. LC 93-16329. (Studies in Australian History). (Illus.). 256p. (C). 1993. pap. write for info. (0-521-44708-9) Cambridge U Pr.

Outback Ghettos: Aboriginal Institutionalisation & Survival. Peggy Brock. LC 93-16329. (Studies in Australian History). (Illus.). 190p. (C). 1993. text 59.95 (0-521-43435-1) Cambridge U Pr.

Outback Heat. Emma Darcy. (Australians Ser.). 1998. per. 4.50 (0-373-82573-0) Harlequin Bks.

Outback Heat. large type ed. Emma Darcy. 1999. 21.95 (0-263-15845-4, G K Hall & Co) Mac Lib Ref.

***Outback Husband.** Jessica Hart. 2000. per. 3.50 (0-373-15840-8) Harlequin Bks.

***Outback Husband.** Jessica Hart. (Romance Ser.). 2000. mass mkt. 3.50 (0-373-03594-2) Harlequin Bks.

Outback Legacy. Aaron Fletcher. 448p. 1996. mass mkt. 5.99 (0-8439-3961-3) Dorchester Pub Co.

Outback Man. Miranda Lee. (Presents Ser.). 1993. per. 2.99 (0-373-11562-8, 1-11562-5) Harlequin Bks.

***Outback Mistress.** Lindsay Armstrong. (Presents Ser.). 2000. mass mkt. 3.99 (0-373-12124-5, 1-12124-3) Harlequin Bks.

***Outback Mistress.** large type ed. Lindsay Armstrong. 1999. 25.99 (0-263-16053-X, Pub. by Mills & Boon) Ulverscroft.

Outback Nights. Emilie Richards. (Here Come the Grooms Ser.: No. 29). 1996. per. 3.99 (0-373-30129-4, 1-30129-0) Harlequin Bks.

Outback Outfitters, Incorporated Family Camping Guide. Thomas Anderson. (Illus.). 126p. 1998. per. 10.00 (0-9663759-0-4) Outback.

Outback Rambling. Richard Symanski. LC 89-20675. 197p. 1990. pap. 61.10 (0-608-05639-1, 206609300006) Bks Demand.

Outback Runaway. large type ed. Dorothy Cork. (Linford Romance Library). 327p. 1984. pap. 16.99 (0-7089-6045-6, Linford) Ulverscroft.

Outback Station. Aaron Fletcher. 480p. 1996. mass mkt. 5.99 (0-8439-3962-1) Dorchester Pub Co.

***Outback Station.** Aaron Fletcher. 480p. 2000. mass mkt. 5.99 (0-8439-4730-6, Leisure Bks) Dorchester Pub Co.

***Outback Wife & Mother: Daddy Boom.** Barbara Hannay. (Romance Ser.: No. 3578). 1999. per. 3.50 (0-373-03578-0, 1-03578-1) Harlequin Bks.

***Outback Wife & Mother: Daddy Boom.** large type ed. Barbara Hannay. (Larger Print Ser.: No. 424). 1999. per. 3.50 (0-373-15824-6, 1-15824-5) Harlequin Bks.

Outback Woman. large type ed. Sally Blake. (Magna Large Print Ser.). 1994. 27.99 (0-7505-0647-4, Pub. by Mgna Lrg Print) Ulverscroft.

Outbelieving Existence: The Measured Motion of James Dickey. Gordon Van Ness. LC 92-17370. (LCENG Ser.). xii, 150p. 1992. 55.00 (1-879751-27-5) Camden Hse.

Outboard Boater's Handbook: Advanced Seamanship & Practical Skills. David R. Getchell. (Illus.). 288p. 1994. pap. 21.95 (0-87742-409-8) Intl Marine.

Outboard Boater's Handbook: Advanced Seamanship & Practical Skills. David R. Getchell. 288p. 1994. pap. 21.95 (0-07-023053-6) McGraw.

Outboard Engines: Troubleshooting, Maintenance, & Repair. annuals Ed Sherman. LC 96-6562. (Illus.). 132p. 1997. 21.95 (0-07-057856-7) McGraw.

Outboard Motor Flat Rate Manual. 10th ed. Intertec Publishing Staff. 96p. 1991. pap. 26.95 (0-87288-451-1, OF-10) Intertec Pub.

Outboard Motor Manual: A Guide to Choosing, Using & Maintaining Your Engine. Keith Henderson. (Illus.). 186p. 1994. pap. 29.95 (0-7136-3424-3) Sheridan.

Outboard Motor Service Manual, Vol. 1. LC 91-77479. 600p. 1992. pap. 26.95 (0-87288-464-3, OS1-11) Intertec Pub.

Outboard Motor Service Manual, Vol. 2. LC 91-77343. 720p. 1992. pap. 26.95 (0-87288-465-1, OS2-11) Intertec Pub.

Outboard Service Guide. Lawrence Corcoran. Ed. by Lynn Corcoran. 1977. pap. text 3.25 (0-686-24789-2) L Corcoran.

***Outboard Troubleshooter.** White. (Illus.). 93p. 2000. pap. 16.95 (1-898660-23-9, Pub. by Fernhurst Bks) Motorbooks Intl.

Outbound. (Voyage Through the Universe Ser.). (Illus.). 144p. 1989. lib. bdg. 24.60 (0-8094-6876-X) Time-Life.

Outbound: An Explorer's Guide. TSR Inc. Staff. (Adventure Ser.). 1999. 16.95 (0-7869-1339-8, Pub. by TSR Inc) Random.

Outbound Journeys in Pennsylvania: A Guide to Natural Places for Individual & Group Outings. Marcia Bonta. LC 86-43283. (Illus.). 216p. 1987. pap. 14.95 (0-271-00606-4) Pa St U Pr.

Outbound Telephone Selling: A Management Manual. Patricia M. Cochrane. LC 99-24996. 200p. 1999. 74.95 (0-566-08089-3, Pub. by Ashgate Pub) Ashgate Pub Co.

Outbreak. Robin Cook. 400p. 1988. mass mkt. 6.99 (0-425-10687-X) Berkley Pub.

Outbreak. Robin Cook. 1988. 12.09 (0-606-00934-5, Pub. by Turtleback) Demco.

Outbreak. Robert DeMaria. Date not set. 22.95 (0-8488-2423-7) Amereon Ltd.

Outbreak. Robin Loon. 400p. (Orig.). 1996. pap. text 6.99 (0-425-15396-7) Berkley Pub.

Outbreak! Russell G. Wright. (Event-Based Science Ser.). (YA). (gr. 5-8). 1998. 8.95 (0-201-49744-1); 21.95 incl. VHS (0-201-49746-8) Seymour Pubns.

***Outbreak: Disease Detectives at Work.** Mark P. Friedlander, Jr. LC 99-38334. (Discovery! Ser.). (Illus.). 128p. (YA). (gr. 5 up). 2000. 23.93 (0-8225-2860-6, Lerner Publctns) Lerner Pub.

***Outbreak Alert: Responding to the Increasing Threat of Infectious Diseases.** Jason Eberhart-Phillips. Orig. Title: Plagues on the Doorstep. 232p. 2000. pap. 15.95 (1-57224-201-9) New Harbinger.

Outbreak of Rebellion. John G. Nicolay. (Illus.). 246p. 1995. pap. 12.95 (0-306-80657-6) Da Capo.

Outbreak of the First World War. 3rd ed. Brian Tierney et al. (C). 1976. pap. text 9.50 (0-07-553615-3) McGraw.

Outbreak of the First World War: Strategic Planning, Crisis Decision Making, & Deterrence Failure. John H. Maurer. LC 95-22012. (Studies in Diplomacy & Strategic Thought). 168p. 1995. 55.00 (0-275-94998-2, Praeger Pubs) Greenwood.

Outbreak of the First World War: 1914 in Perspective. D. Stevenson. LC 96-34264. (Studies in European History). 96p. 1997. pap. 11.95 (0-312-16539-0) St Martin.

Outbreak of the Irish Rebellion of 1641. M. Perceval-Maxwell. 408p. 1994. 60.00 (0-7735-1157-1, Pub. by McG-Queens Univ Pr) CUP Services.

Outbreak of the Peloponnesian War. Donald Kagan. LC 69-18212. (Illus.). 438p. 1969. text 49.95 (0-8014-0501-7) Cornell U Pr.

Outbreak of the Peloponnesian War. Donald Kagan. LC 69-18212. (Illus.). 438p. 1989. pap. text 18.95 (0-8014-9556-3) Cornell U Pr.

***Outbreak of War Vol. 1: September 1939-January 1940.** Ed. by John A. Hammerton. (Second World War). (Illus.). 680p. 2000. 35.00 (1-58279-100-7) Trident Pr Intl.

Outbreak of World War I: Causes & Responsibilities. 5th ed. Ed. by Holger H. Herwig. LC 90-80529. (Problems in European Civilization Ser.). 138p. (C). 1991. pap. text 16.76 (0-669-21359-4) HM Trade Div.

Outbreak of World War I: Causes & Responsibilities. 6th ed. Holger H. Herwig. 192p. (C). 1996. pap. text 16.76 (0-669-41692-4) HM Trade Div.

Outburst: A Todd Mills Mystery. R. D. Zimmerman. (Illus.). 304p. 1999. pap. 11.95 (0-385-31923-1) Delacorte.

Outburst: A Todd Mills Mystery. R. D. Zimmerman. LC 98-18711. 304p. 1998. 21.95 (0-385-32375-1) Dell.

Outbursts in Academe: Multiculturalism & Other Sources of Conflicts. Kathleen Dixon. LC 98-29882. (Crosscurrents Ser.). 1998. pap. text 22.00 (0-86709-477-X) Heinemann.

Outcast. Beverly Barton. 1995. per. 3.50 (0-373-07614-2, 1-07614-0) Silhouette.

Outcast. Patricia Bernard. 304p. (YA). (gr. 7-12). 1998. pap. 7.95 (0-7322-5768-9) HarpC.

Outcast. Emily Carmichael. 368p. (Orig.). 1995. mass mkt. 5.99 (0-446-36411-8, Pub. by Warner Bks) Little.

Outcast. Joel Durham. LC 99-62822. (Illus.). 229p. 1999. pap. 19.99 (0-7615-2209-3) Prima Pub.

***Outcast.** Jose Latour. LC 99-70482. 220p. 1999. pap. 13.95 (1-888451-07-6, AKB04, Pub. by Akashic Bks) SPD-Small Pr Dist.

Outcast. Created by Francine Pascal. (Sweet Valley High Ser.: No. 41). (YA). (gr. 7 up). 1987. mass mkt. 3.95 (0-553-16797-9) BDD Bks Young Read.

O

An Asterisk (*) at the beginning of an entry indicates that the title is appearing for the first time.

Outcast. Rosemary Sutcliff. LC 94-46355. (Illus.). 240p. (J). (gr. 7 up). 1995. pap. 5.95 (*0-374-45673-9*, Sunburst Bks) FS&G.

Outcast. Rosemary Sutcliff. LC 94-46355. (J). 1995. 11.05 (*0-606-09726-0*, Pub. by Turtleback) Demco.

Outcast. Stuart Thorogood. 150p. 1999. pap. 12.95 (*0-85449-282-8*) LPC InBook.

Outcast. Rosalyn West. (Men of Pride County Ser.). 384p. 1998. mass mkt. 5.99 (*0-380-79579-5*, Avon Bks) Morrow Avon.

Outcast. Anna F. Wierauch. 1975. 17.95 (*0-405-07376-3*, 14530) Ayer.

Outcast. Kate William. (Sweet Valley High Ser.: No. 41). (YA). (gr. 7 up). 1987. 8.05 (*0-606-03633-4*, Pub. by Turtleback) Demco.

Outcast No. 2: Time Master. Louise Cooper. 1992. mass mkt. 4.99 (*0-8125-1973-6*, Pub. by Tor Bks) St Martin.

***Outcast Brigade.** Jason Elder. 176p. 2000. pap. 3.99 (*0-8439-4699-7*, Leisure Bks) Dorchester Pub Co.

Outcast Cape Town. John Western. LC 96-8462. (Illus.). 380p. (C). 1997. pap. 17.95 (*0-520-20737-8*, Pub. by U CA Pr) Cal Prin Full Svc.

Outcast Cape Town. John Western. LC 81-14640. 391p. 1981. reprint ed. pap. 121.30 (*0-608-00796-X*, 205934500010) Bks Demand.

Outcast of Redwall. Brian Jacques. (Redwall Ser.: Vol. 8). (Illus.). 367p. (J). (gr. 4-7). 1997. mass mkt. 5.99 (*0-441-00416-4*) Ace Bks.

Outcast of Redwall. Brian Jacques. (Redwall Ser.). (Illus.). 360p. (J). (gr. 4-8). 1996. 21.99 (*0-399-22914-0*, Philomel) Peng Put Young Read.

Outcast of Redwall. Brian Jacques. (Redwall Ser.). (J). (gr. 4-8). 1997. 12.15 (*0-606-13011-X*, Pub. by Turtleback) Demco.

Outcast of the Islands. Joseph Conrad. (Airmont Classics Ser.). (YA). (gr. 9 up). 1966. mass mkt. 1.50 (*0-8049-0113-9*, CL-113) Airmont.

Outcast of the Islands. Joseph Conrad. 1976. 17.95 (*0-8488-1273-5*) Amereon Ltd.

***Outcast of the Islands.** Joseph Conrad. (Oxford World's Classics Ser.). (Illus.). 448p. 1999. pap. 7.95 (*0-19-283840-7*) OUP.

Outcast of the Islands. Joseph Conrad. 384p. 1996. pap. 7.95 (*0-460-87773-9*, Everyman's Classic Lib) Tuttle Pubng.

Outcast of the Islands. large type ed. Joseph Conrad. LC 97-16032. 320p. 1997. text 24.95 (*1-56000-533-5*) Transaction Pubs.

Outcast Red: The P-47 in the South Pacific. William B. Rogers. 320p. (Orig.). 1987. pap. 9.95 (*0-89896-260-9*) Larksdale.

Outcast Woman. Lucy Gordon. (Special Edition Ser.: No. 749). 1992. per. 3.39 (*0-373-09749-2*, 5-09749-8) Harlequin Bks.

Outcaste: Jewish Life in Southern Iran. Ed. by L. Loeb. (Library of Anthropology). xxvi, 328p. 1977. text 117.00 (*0-677-04530-1*) Gordon & Breach.

***Outcasts.** large type ed. James O. Lowes. 224p. 1999. pap. 18.99 (*0-7089-5540-1*, Linford) Ulverscroft.

Outcasts: Signs of Otherness in Northern European Art of the Late Middle Ages, 2 vols., Vol. Set. Ruth Mellinkoff. (California Studies in the History of Art: No. 32). 1994. 225.00 (*0-520-07815-2*, Pub. by U CA Pr) Cal Prin Full Svc.

Outcasts: The Image of Journalists in Contemporary Film. Howard Good. LC 88-7688. (Illus.). 195p. 1989. 28.50 (*0-8108-2162-1*) Scarecrow.

Outcasts & Other Stories. Maxim Gorky. LC 75-113664. (Short Story Index Reprint Ser.). 1977. 20.95 (*0-8369-3393-1*) Ayer.

Outcasts from Eden: Ideas of Landscape in British Poetry since 1945. Edward Picot. LC 96-224899. 322p. 1997. 39.95 (*0-85323-531-7*, Pub. by Liverpool Univ Pr); pap. 24.95 (*0-85323-541-4*, Pub. by Liverpool Univ Pr) Intl Spec Bk.

Outcasts from Evolution: Scientific Attitudes of Racial Inferiority, 1859-1900. John S. Haller, Jr. LC 94-48231. 248p. (C). 1995. pap. 15.95 (*0-8093-1982-9*) S Ill U Pr.

Outcasts in Their Own Land: Mexican Industrial Workers, 1906-1911. Rodney D. Anderson. LC 74-28896. (Origins of Modern Mexico Ser.). (Illus.). 407p. 1976. 35.00 (*0-87580-054-8*) N Ill U Pr.

***Outcasts of Picture Rocks: A Western Story.** Cherry Wilson. LC 99-14742. 1999. 19.95 (*0-7862-1902-5*) Mac Lib Ref.

Outcasts of Poker Flat. Bret Harte. 58p. (YA). (gr. 10 up). 1968. pap. 3.50 (*0-87129-547-4*, O27) Dramatic Pub.

Outcasts of Poker Flat. Bret Harte. (Jamestown Classics Ser.). 1995. pap., teacher ed. 7.32 (*0-89061-053-3*, Jamestwn Pub) NTC Contemp Pub Co.

Outcasts of Poker Flat. Bret Harte. (Jamestown Classics Ser.). (J). 1995. pap., student ed. 5.99 (*0-89061-052-5*, Jamestwn Pub) NTC Contemp Pub Co.

Outcasts of Poker Flat & the Luck of Roaring Camp. rev. ed. Bret Harte. Ed. by Robert J. Dixson. (American Classics Ser.: Bk. 5). (gr. 9 up). 1987. audio 55.00 (*0-685-38996-0*, 58225) Prentice ESL.

Outcasts of Poker Flats. Bret Harte. (J). 1997. pap. 2.95 (*0-8167-0461-9*) Troll Communs.

***Outcasts of Poker Flats.** Bret Harte. 1999. 9.30 (*0-606-12469-1*) Turtleback.

Outcasts of Poker Flats, The Luck of Roaring Camp: And Other Sketches. Bret Harte. 1976. reprint ed. lib. bdg. 20.95 (*0-88411-592-5*) Amereon Ltd.

Outcasts on Main Street: The Report of the Federal Task Force on Homelessness & Severe Mental Illness. (Illus.). 107p. (Orig.). 1993. pap. text 30.00 (*0-7881-0073-4*) DIANE Pub.

***(Out)Classed Women: Contemporary Chicana Writers on Inequitable Gendered Power Relations, 184.** Phillipa Kafka. LC 00-23948. (Contributions in Women's Studies: Vol. 184). 208p. 2000. 50.00 (*0-313-31123-4*, GM1123, Greenwood Pr) Greenwood.

Outcome after Head, Neck, & Spinal Trauma: A Medico-Legal Guide. Ed. by Robert Macfarlane & David Hardy. 456p. 1997. text 135.00 (*0-7506-2178-8*) Buttrwrth-Heinemann.

Outcome & Innovation in Psychological Treatment of Schizophrenia. Til Wykes et al. LC 97-18366. 304p. 1999. pap. 37.50 (*0-471-97842-6*) Wiley.

Outcome Assessment in Residential Treatment. Ed. by Steven I. Pfeiffer. LC 96-20075. (Residential Treatment for Children & Youth Ser.: Vol. 13, No. 4). 99p. (C). 1996. 39.95 (*1-56024-839-4*) Haworth Pr.

Outcome Based Budgeting: Connecting Budget Development, Allocation & Outcomes. Thomas Anderes. 1995. 10.00 (*0-614-13553-2*) SHEEO.

Outcome Based Education. Bruno Manno. (Issue Paper #3-96 Ser.). 30p. 1996. pap. write for info. (*1-57655-147-4*) Independ Inst.

Outcome-Based Education: Critical Issues & Answers. William G. Spady. 224p. 1995. 22.75 (*0-614-25101-X*, 021-0488) Am Assn Sch Admin.

Outcome-Based Education: Developing Programs Through Strategic Planning. Floyd Boschee & Mark A. Baron. LC 93-61024. 150p. 1996. pap. text 24.95 (*1-56676-083-6*) Scarecrow.

Outcome Based Education: Miracle Cure or Plague? Bruno V. Manno. (Illus.). 24p. (Orig.). 1995. pap. 5.00 (*0-9647703-1-8*, S95-06) Mackinac Ctr Public Pol.

Outcome-Based Evaluation. Robert L. Schalock. (Illus.). 260p. 1995. 39.50 (*0-306-45051-8*, Kluwer Plenum) Kluwer Academic.

Outcome-Based Quality Improvement in Long-Term Care. Marilyn Rantz et al. LC 98-35896. 320p. 1998. ring bd. 129.00 (*0-8342-1147-5*, 11475) Aspen Pub.

Outcome Concept Systems: A Guide to the Measurement of Patient Outcomes. 2nd rev. ed. Alexis A. Wilson & Mary Hartnett. LC 95-62349. 58p. 1996. text 125.00 (*0-9633599-2-4*) Wilson & Assocs.

Outcome Equity in Education. Ed. by Robert Berne et al. LC 94-31096. (Yearbook of the American Education Finance Association Ser.: Vol. 15). (Illus.). 288p. 1994. 54.95 (*0-8039-6160-X*) Corwin Pr.

Outcome Funding: A New Approach to Targeted Grantmaking. 2nd ed. Harold S. Williams et al. 226p. 1993. pap. 21.00 (*0-9629798-2-1*) Rensselaerville Inst.

Outcome Funding: A New Approach to Targeted Grantmaking. 3rd rev. ed. Harold S. Williams et al. LC 91-62146. 1996. pap. 21.00 (*0-9629798-5-6*) Rensselaerville Inst.

At all of its levels, a primary function of government is to give out money. Government "funds" many groups to carry out public purposes. This book presents a new approach which shifts funding to investment. It replaces the traditional "Request for proposal" process with a sharp focus on key investor questions: "What are we buying?" & "What is the probability we will get it?" OUTCOME FUNDING asks grant-seekers to define their customers, their product, & their performance target. The long proposal becomes a short plan as government (as well as foundations & other donors) seek to make their money work as hard as do their people. A key gain to grant-seekers; they no longer have to write one long document to get money & another to spend it. The framework presented has been tested in a number of states & local governments throughout the US. Authors are Harold S. Williams, President of The Rensselaerville Institute, Arthur Y. Webb, Chief Executive Officer of the Village Centers of Care & William J. Phillips, Director of the Innovation Group at The Rensselaerville Institute. *Publisher Paid Annotation.*

Outcome Initiatives in Child Welfare. Amy Gordon. 1999. pap. text 14.95 (*0-87868-901-X*) Child Welfare.

Outcome Management: Achieving Outcomes for People with Disabilities. Art Dykstra. Ed. by Alex Lubertozzi. (Illus.). 162p. 1995. 27.50 (*1-57654-000-6*) High Tide Pr.

Outcome Management: Achieving Outcomes for People with Disabilities. Art Dykstra. (Illus.). 162p. 1996. reprint ed. 27.50 (*0-9653744-0-8*) High Tide Pr.

Outcome Management: Redesigning Your Business Systems to Achieve Your Vision. C. Dan McArthur & Larry Womack. LC 95-5100. 242p. 1995. 24.95 (*0-527-76292-X*) Productivity Inc.

Outcome Management & Program Evaluation Made Easy: A Toolkit for Occupational Therapy Practitioners. Stephen Forer. 150p. (Orig.). 1996. pap. text 48.00 (*1-56900-038-7*, 1146) Am Occup Therapy.

Outcome Measurements in Cardiovascular Medicine. Kenneth J. Tuman. 191p. 68.00 (*0-7817-2223-3*) Lppncott W & W.

Outcome Measures for Child Welfare Services: Theory & Applications. Stephen Magura & Beth Silverman Moses. 252p. 1986. pap. 34.95 (*0-87868-224-4*) Child Welfare.

Outcome Measures for Health Education & Other Health Care Interventions. John Lynch et al. 168p. (C). 1996. 38.00 (*0-7619-0066-7*); pap. 16.95 (*0-7619-0067-5*) Sage.

Outcome Measures in Home Care: Research, Vol. I. Ed. by Lynn T. Rinke & Alexis A. Wilson. 250p. (Orig.). 1987. pap. 22.95 (*0-88737-378-X*) Natl League Nurse.

Outcome Measures in Trauma. Ed. by P. B. Pynsent et al. LC 94-9397. (Illus.). 280p. 1994. text 95.00 (*0-7506-1653-9*) Buttrwrth-Heinemann.

Outcome of Severe Damage to the Central Nervous System. CIBA Foundation Staff. LC 76-361019. (CIBA Foundation Symposium: New Ser.: No. 34). 364p. reprint ed. pap. 112.90 (*0-608-13977-7*, 202216200024) Bks Demand.

Outcome of the Civil War, 1863-65. James K. Hosmer. (Notable American Authors Ser.). 1992. reprint ed. lib. bdg. 75.00 (*0-7812-3182-5*) Rprt Serv.

***Outcome of the Critically Ill: Medicine, Surgery & Trauma.** R. B. Vukmir. (Illus.). 208p. 2000. text 44.00 (*1-85070-903-3*) Prthnon Pub.

Outcome of the European Programe on Emissions, Fuels, & Engine Technologies. 1996. 38.00 (*1-56091-861-6*, SP-1204) Soc Auto Engineers.

Outcome of the Uruguay Round: An Initial Assessment Supporting Papers to the Trade & Development Report. LC 97-207617. 247p. 45.00 (*92-1-112362-3*, E.94.II.D.28) UN.

Outcome Oriented Rehabilitation: Principles, Strategies & Tools for Effective Program Management. Pat K. Landrum et al. 340p. 1995. 57.00 (*0-8342-0665-X*) Aspen Pub.

Outcome Oriented Therapeutic Massage. Carla-Krystin Andrade & Paul Clifford. 400p. pap. text 34.95 (*0-7817-1743-4*) Lppncott W & W.

Outcome Standards in Home Health Vol. III: State of the Art. 72p. 1987. 16.95 (*0-88737-389-5*) Natl League Nurse.

***Outcomes: A Different Approach to Motivation.** 30p. 1999. write for info. (*1-930414-02-1*) L I M R A Intl.

Outcomes: NVQs & the Emerging Model of Education & Training. Gilbert Jessup. 224p. 1991. 75.00 (*1-85000-972-4*, Falmer Pr); pap. 34.95 (*1-85000-973-2*, Falmer Pr) Taylor & Francis.

Outcomes: Poems from Hollywood. Mark Dunster. 11p. 1998. pap. write for info. (*0-89642-606-8*) Linden Pubs.

***Outcomes & Incomes: How to Evaluate, Improve & Market Your Psychotherapy Practice by Measuring Outcomes.** Paul W. Clement. LC 99-28874. (Clinician's Toolbox Ser.). 244p. 1999. otabind 50.00 incl. cd-rom (*1-57230-486-3*) Guilford Pubns.

Outcomes & Measures in Family Literacy Programs. Susan P. McShane. Ed. by Andrew E. Hayes. 73p. (Orig.). 1996. pap. text 15.00 (*1-884458-01-7*) Natl Ctr Fmly Lit.

***Outcomes & Technology Assessment in Nuclear Medicine.** Leslee Shaw & Frank J. Papatheofanis. LC 99-16296. 112p. 1999. pap. write for info. (*0-932004-71-7*, Pub. by Soc Nuclear Med) Matthews Medical Bk Co.

Outcomes Assessment at Kean College of New Jersey: Academic Programs' Procedures & Models. Ed. by Michael E. Knight et al. 200p. (Orig.). (C). 1991. lib. bdg. 48.00 (*0-8191-8364-4*) U Pr of Amer.

Outcomes Assessment in Clinical Practice. Ed. by Lloyd I. Sederer & Barbara Dickey. LC 95-4785. (Illus.). 384p. 1996. write for info. (*0-683-07630-2*) Lppncott W & W.

Outcomes Based Education: An Introduction for Teachers, Administrator, Parents & Patrons. Tom Contine. 59p. 1993. teacher ed. 25.00 (*1-878276-33-6*) Educ Systs Assocs Inc.

Outcomes Comm Care for Serv U. S. A Social Services Perspective. H. Qureshi. LC 95-49669. 192p. 1996. pap. 34.95 (*0-335-19668-3*) OpUniv Pr.

Outcomes Curriculum for Gifted Students: Differential Strategies for Elementary & Secondary Levels. Patricia A. Gabriel et al. 62p. 1995. pap. text 16.00 (*0-910609-30-6*) Gifted Educ Pr.

Outcomes Effectiveness of Physical Therapy: An Annotated Bibliography. 551p. 1995. ring bd. 59.95 (*0-912452-94-3*, P-106) Am Phys Therapy Assn.

Outcomes Evaluation in Children's Services: A Guide for Mental Health, Child Welfare, Juvenile Justice, & Special Education Specialists. Ed. by Anne M. Christner. 150p. 1997. 75.00 (*1-884937-49-7*) Manisses Communs.

Outcomes for Children & Youth with Emotional & Behavioral Disorders & Their Families: Programs & Evaluation Best Practices. Albert J. Duchnowski. Ed. by Michael H. Epstein & Krista Kutash. LC 97-21294. 1998. 44.00 (*0-89079-750-1*) PRO-ED.

Outcomes in Neurological & Neurosurgical Disorders. Ed. by Michael Swash. (Illus.). 628p. (C). 1998. text 135.00 (*0-521-44327-X*) Cambridge U Pr.

Outcomes in Path-Based Collaborative Practice. Suzanne S. Blancett & Dominick L. Flarey. 400p. 1998. pap. 99.00 (*0-8342-1048-7*, 10487) Aspen Pub.

Outcomes in Process: Setting Standards for Language Use. Roseanne Y. DeFabio. LC 93-42432. 211p. (C). 1994. pap. text 20.00 (*0-86709-341-2*, 0341, Pub. by Boynton Cook Pubs) Heinemann.

Outcomes into Clinical Practice. Ed. by Tony Delamothe. 169p. (Orig.). 1994. pap. text 35.00 (*0-7279-0888-X*, Pub. by BMJ Pub) Login Brothers Bk Co.

Outcomes, Learning & the Curriculum: Implications for NVQs & Other Qualifications. Ed. by John Burke. LC 94-24819. 274p. 1994. 95.00 (*0-7507-0288-5*, Falmer Pr); pap. 27.95 (*0-7507-0289-3*, Falmer Pr) Taylor & Francis.

***Outcomes Management: Applications to Clinical Practice.** Anne W. Wojner. (Illus.). 350p. 1999. write for info. (*1-55664-411-6*) Mosby Inc.

Outcomes Management: Using Data for Decision Making. Patrice L. Spath et al. (Illus.). 105p. 1995. 30.00 (*1-929955-03-0*) Brown Spath.

Outcomes Management Resource Guide. Eric D. Joseph. 61p. (Orig.). 1995. pap. text 30.00 (*0-916499-63-4*) Care Educ Grp.

Outcomes Mandate: Case Management in Healthcare Today. Cohen & Vivien DeBack. LC 98-37881. 432p. 1998. text 42.95 (*0-323-00277-3*) Mosby Inc.

Outcomes Measurement in the Human Services: Cross-Cutting Issues & Methods. Ed. by Edward J. Mullen & Jennifer L. Magnabosco. LC 97-7824. 360p. (Orig.). (C). 1997. pap. text 36.95 (*0-87101-275-8*, 2758) Natl Assn Soc Wkrs.

Outcomes of a Group Career Planning Process. Garrett McAuliffe. 1988. 3.00 (*0-318-40010-3*, OC 126) Ctr Educ Trng Employ.

Outcomes of a Study Excursion. James A. Fraser. LC 75-176785. (Columbia University. Teachers College. Contributions to Education Ser.: No. 778). reprint ed. 37.50 (*0-404-55778-3*) AMS Pr.

Outcomes of Community Care for Users & Carers: A Social Services Perspective. Andrew Nocon & Hazel Qureshi. LC 95-49669. 192p. 1996. 108.95 (*0-335-19669-1*) OpUniv Pr.

Outcomes of Effective Management Practice. Ed. by Kathleen Kelly. (Series on Nursing Administration: Vol. 8). (Illus.). 265p. 1996. 39.95 (*0-8039-7175-3*) Sage.

Outcomes Research Resource Guide, 97-98: A Survey of Current Activities. Ed. by American Medical Association. 1998. pap. 49.95 (*0-89970-907-9*) AMA.

Outcrop Quiz. John B. Wright. (Illus.). 64p. (C). 1986. pap. text 12.95 (*0-04-550041-X*) Routledge.

Outcrop Study of the Lower Green River Formation for Reservoir Characterization & Hydrocarbon Production Enhancement in the Altamont-Bluebell Field, Uinta Basin, Utah. Ann Garner & T. H. Morris. (Miscellaneous Publication of the Utah Geological Survey Ser.: Vol. 96-2). (Illus.). 61p. (Orig.). 1996. pap. 6.00 (*1-55791-384-6*, MP96-2) Utah Geological Survey.

Outcroppings from Navajoland: Poems. Donald Levering. LC 83-73475. 72p. 1985. 5.00 (*0-912586-52-4*) Dine College Pr.

Outcry. Harold Schechter. 1997. per. 6.50 (*0-671-73217-X*) PB.

Outcry see Works of Henry James Jr.: Collected Works

Outcry from the Inferno, Atomic Bomb Tanka Anthology. Ed. & Tr. by Jiro Nakano from JPN. LC 95-23262. (Bamboo Ridge Ser.: Nos. 67-68). 104p. 1995. pap. 10.00 (*0-910043-38-8*) Bamboo Ridge Pr.

Outcry in the Barrio. Freddie Garcia & Ninfa Garcia.Tr. of Clamor en El Barrio. (SPA.). 224p. (Orig.). 1988. reprint ed. pap. 3.50 (*0-9619319-0-6*) F Garcia Ministries.

***Outdogs, Undercasts, & Other Superzeroes: A Collection.** Robert Putis. 142p. 1999. pap. 15.00 (*0-9669874-1-1*, 002) Maple Leaf.

Outdoor Action Games for Elementary Children: Active Games & Academic Activities for Fun & Fitness. David R. Foster & James L. Overholt. LC 93-34562. (Illus.). 240p. (C). 1994. pap. text 27.95 (*0-13-009895-7*, Parker Publishing Co) P-H.

***Outdoor Activities.** 2nd rev. ed. Christine Dillon. (My First Report Ser.). (Illus.). 56p. (J). 1999. ring bd. 5.95 (*1-57896-050-9*, 2573, Hewitt Homeschl Res) Hewitt Res Fnd.

***Outdoor Activities For Kids.** 1999. pap. text 16.95 (*1-85967-915-3*, Pub. by Anness Pub) Random.

Outdoor Adventure Activities for School & Recreation Programs. Paul Darst & George Armstrong. (Illus.). 307p. (C). 1991. reprint ed. pap. text 23.95 (*0-88133-583-5*) Waveland Pr.

Outdoor Adventure & Self Concept: A Research Analysis. Alan W. Ewert. 42p. 1983. pap. 7.00 (*0-943272-17-3*) Inst Recreation Res.

Outdoor Adventure Handbook. Hugh McManners. 64p. (J). (gr. 3-7). 1996. 16.95 (*0-7894-1035-4*) DK Pub Inc.

Outdoor Adventures with Kids. Mary M. McConnell. LC 95-44971. 230p. 1996. pap. 12.95 (*0-87833-849-7*) Taylor Pub.

Outdoor Advertising. Billy Mason. 1976. pap. 5.00 (*0-942140-07-9*) Kelso.

Outdoor Affairs: Picnics & Barbecues. Richard Cawley. LC 93-39689. (Creative Cook Ser.). 64p. 1994. 16.95 (*1-56426-657-5*) Cole Group.

Outdoor Amusement Industry. William F. Mangels. lib. bdg. 20.95 (*0-8488-2002-9*) Amereon Ltd.

Outdoor & Location Portrait Photography. Jeff Smith. (Illus.). 112p. 1999. pap. 29.95 (*0-936262-80-X*) Amherst Media.

***Outdoor & Survival Skills for Nature Photographers.** Ralph LaPlant & Amy Sharpe. (Illus.). 80p. 2000. pap. 17.95 (*1-58428-017-4*) Amherst Media.

Outdoor & Trail Guide to the Wichita Mountains of Southwest Oklahoma. 6th expanded rev. ed. Edward C. Ellenbrook. LC 83-140822. (Illus.). 148p. 1998. pap. 9.95 (*0-941634-01-9*) In Valley Wichitas.

Outdoor Athlete: Total Training for Outdoor Performance. Steve Ilg. LC 87-13626. (Illus.). 270p. (Orig.). 1987. pap. 14.95 (*0-917895-17-7*) Johnson Bks.

Outdoor Brickwork. Penny Swift & Janek Szymanowski. (Step-by-Step Ser.). (Illus.). 96p. 1998. pap. 15.95 (*1-85368-091-5*, Pub. by New5 Holland) Sterling.

Outdoor Careers: Exploring Occupations in Outdoor Fields. Ellen Shenk. LC 92-17530. 224p. 1992. pap. 16.95 (*0-8117-2542-1*) Stackpole.

***Outdoor Careers: Exploring Occupations in Outdoor Fields.** 2nd ed. Ellen Shenk. LC 99-47776. 224p. 2000. 16.95 (*0-8117-2873-0*) Stackpole.

Outdoor Careers Guide. Gene R. Hawes & Douglass L. Brownstone. LC 82-15725. 139p. reprint ed. pap. 43.10 (*0-8357-3498-6*, 203975800013) Bks Demand.

***Outdoor Celebrities Cookbook.** Bill Cooper. (Illus.). 270p. 1999. 21.95 (*0-9672035-0-3*) Dry Creek Pr.

O

An Asterisk (*) at the beginning of an entry indicates that the title is appearing for the first time.

Outdoor Companion: The Mary Engelbreit Look & How to Get It. Mary Engelbreit. LC 95-40322. (Mary Engelbreit Look & How to Get It Ser.). (Illus.). 136p. 1996. 24.95 (*0-8362-1085-9*) Andrews & McMeel.

Outdoor Cookbook. Jim McKinley. (Illus.). 210p. 1996. ring bd. 24.95 (*0-9639134-2-5*) Peak Media.

Outdoor Cooking. John P. Carroll. Ed. by Chuck Williams. LC 96-24078. (Williams-Sonoma Kitchen Library). (Illus.). 108p. (J). (gr. 11). 1999. 18.95 (*0-7835-0320-2*) Time-Life.

Outdoor Cooking: From Backyard to Backpack. Louise DeWald. 176p. 1991. 13.95 (*0-916179-32-X*) Ariz Hwy.

***Outdoor Decor.** Provo Craft Designers Staff. (Illus.). 22p. 1999. write for info. (*1-58050-086-2*) Provo Craft.

Outdoor Decor: Decorative Projects for the Porch, Patio & Yard. Home Decorating Institute Staff. LC 95-20876. (Arts & Crafts for Home Decorating Ser.). (Illus.). 128p. 1996. 18.95 (*0-86573-385-6*); pap. 16.95 (*0-86573-386-4*) Creat Pub Intl.

Outdoor Decorative Products in Canada: A Strategic Entry Report, 1997. Compiled by Icon Group International Staff. (Country Industry Report). (Illus.). 128p. 1999. ring bd. 1280.00 incl. audio compact disk (*0-7418-0221-X*) Icon Grp.

Outdoor Development for Managers. 2nd ed. John Bank. LC 93-48694. 192p. 1994. 74.95 (*0-566-07395-1*, Pub. by Gower) Ashgate Pub Co.

Outdoor Dutch Oven Cookbook. Sheila Mills. LC 97-6193. 170p. 1997. pap. 16.95 (*0-07-043023-3*) McGraw.

Outdoor Education: Theory & Practice. Nicholas P. Gair. (Issues in Education Ser.). 1997. pap. 29.95 (*0-304-33944-X*) Continuum.

Outdoor Emergency Care: Comprehensive First Aid for Nonurban Settings. 2nd ed. Warren D. Bowman. Ed. by Rebecca W. Ayers. LC 93-84167. (Illus.). 546p. 1993. pap. 30.00 (*0-929752-01-5*) Natl Ski Patrol.

Outdoor Entertaining: Picnics, Parties, & Portable Feasts. Elizabeth Sahatjian. (Illus.). 240p. 1991. 19.98 (*0-89660-017-3*, Artabras) Abbeville Pr.

Outdoor Family Fun Guide: A Complete Camping, Hiking, Canoeing, Nature Watching, Mountain Biking, Skiing, Climbing, & General Fun Book for Kids (And Their Parents) Michael Hodgson. LC 98-9822. (Illus.). 192p. 1998. pap. 14.95 (*0-07-029184-5*) Intl Marine.

Outdoor Family Guide to Acadia National Park. Lisa G. Evans. LC 97-19040. 224p. 1997. pap. 14.95 (*0-89886-528-X*) Mountaineers.

Outdoor Family Guide to Rocky Mountain National Park. 2nd ed. Lisa G. Evans. LC 97-43535. (Outdoor Family Guide Ser.). (Illus.). 224p. 1998. pap. 14.95 (*0-89886-546-8*) Mountaineers.

Outdoor Family Guide to the Southwest's Four Corners. Tom Wharton & Gayen Wharton. LC 95-23138. (Illus.). 224p. 1995. pap. 14.95 (*0-89886-407-0*) Mountaineers.

Outdoor Family Guide to Washington's National Parks & Monuments: Mount Rainier, Mount St. Helens, North Cascades, the Olympics. Vicky Spring & Tom Kirkendall. LC 98-11790. (Outdoor Family Guide Ser.). 224p. 1998. pap. 16.95 (*0-89886-552-2*) Mountaineers.

Outdoor Family Guide to Yellowstone & Grand Teton National Parks. Lisa G. Evans. LC 95-51254. 224p. 1996. pap. text 14.95 (*0-89886-428-3*) Mountaineers.

***Outdoor Feasts.** Hugo Arnold. (Illus.). 160p. 1999. 29.95 (*1-85626-284-7*, Pub. by Cathie Kyle) Trafalgar.

Outdoor First-Aid: A Field Guide to Recognition & Treatment of Outdoor Injuries & Illnesses. Robert J. Koester. LC 91-72633. (Illus.). 104p. 1992. spiral bd. 13.95 (*1-879471-14-0*) DBS Prodns.

Outdoor First-Aid: A Field Guide to Recognition & Treatment of Outdoor Injuries & Illnesses. 2nd ed. Robert J. Koester. (Illus.). 136p. 1997. 23.95 (*1-879471-26-4*) DBS Prodns.

Outdoor First-Aid: A Field Guide to Recognition & Treatment of Outdoor Injuries & Illnesses. 2nd ed. Robert J. Koester. (Illus.). 136p. 1999. pap. 9.95 (*1-879471-27-2*) DBS Prodns.

Outdoor First-Aid: A Field Guide to Recognition & Treatment of Outdoor Injuries & Illnesses, Waterproof. 2nd ed. Robert J. Koester. (Illus.). 136p. 1999. pap. 13.95 (*1-879471-28-0*) DBS Prodns.

Outdoor First-Aid: Instructor's Manual. Robert J. Koester. 260p. (Orig.). 1996. pap. text, teacher ed. 60.00 (*1-879471-23-X*) DBS Prodns.

Outdoor Fun. Owl Magazine Editors & Chicadee Magazine Editors. (Illus.). 32p. (J). (gr. 2 up). 1996. pap. 7.95 (*0-920775-37-3*, Pub. by Greey dePencier) Firefly Bks Ltd.

Outdoor Fun: Great Things to Make & Do on Sunny Days. Diane Cherkerzian. LC 92-74583. (Illus.). 32p. (J). (gr. 2-7). 1993. pap. 3.95 (*1-56397-162-3*) Boyds Mills Pr.

Outdoor Furniture see Art of Woodworking Series

Outdoor Games. Frederick Alderson. (Junior Reference Ser.). (Illus.). 64p. (J). (gr. 6 up). 1980. 14.95 (*0-7136-2031-5*) Dufour.

Outdoor Games. David Buskin. (Illus.). (J). (gr. k-4). 1966. lib. bdg. 13.95 (*0-87460-090-1*) Lion Bks.

Outdoor Grill for Fin & Fowl. 2nd rev. ed. Sherri Eldridge & Robert Groves. (Illus.). 32p. 1997. pap. 2.95 (*1-886862-19-2*, MN GRL) Harv Hill ME.

***Outdoor Guide to the Big South Fork: National River & Recreation Area.** 2nd ed. Russ Manning. LC 00-9435. (Illus.). 240p. 2000. pap. 16.95 (*0-89886-639-1*) Mountaineers.

Outdoor Insights: What a Dad Can Teach a Child in God's Great Outdoors. Steve Chapman. LC 98-45820. 156p. 1999. pap. 8.99 (*0-7369-0059-4*) Harvest Hse.

***Outdoor Insulators.** R. S. Gorur et al. (Illus.). 268p. 1999. text 195.00 (*0-9677611-0-7*) R S Gorur.

Outdoor Journal: Adventures & Reflections: A Personal Memoir. rev. ed. Jimmy Carter. LC 94-5845. 320p. 1994. reprint ed. pap. 22.00 (*1-55728-354-0*) U of Ark Pr.

Outdoor Journal-Book. Richard P. Nadeau. 48p. 1994. pap. text 4.95 (*1-881857-02-6*) Moose Riv Trading.

***Outdoor Knots.** 2nd ed. Cliff Jacobson. LC 98-49873. (Illus.). 64p. 1999. pap. text 7.95 (*0-7627-0428-4*) Globe Pequot.

Outdoor Leadership: Technique, Common Sense, & Self-Confidence. John Graham. LC 97-1379. (Illus.). 192p. (Orig.). 1997. pap. 16.95 (*0-89886-502-6*) Mountaineers.

***Outdoor Life: 100 Years in Pictures.** Cowles Creative Publishing Staff et al. LC 97-49710. 224p. 1998. 34.95 (*0-86573-075-X*) Creat Pub Intl.

Outdoor Life Deer Hunter's Encyclopedia. J. Madson. 1985. 49.95 (*0-943822-53-X*) Times Mir Mag Bk Div.

***Outdoor Life Hunting Big Game in North America: Outdoor Life's Experts Reveal Their Secrets.** Outdoor Life Staff. (Outdoor Life Ser.). (Illus.). 224p. 2000. pap. 14.95 (*0-86573-123-3*) Creat Pub Intl.

Outdoor Life in the Menominee Forest. Sylvester Norick. 154p. 1979. 3.95 (*0-8199-0767-7*, Frncscn Herld) Franciscan Pr.

Outdoor Lifetime: Six Decades in a Writer's Life. Byron W. Dalrymple. 1994. 24.95 (*0-8329-0508-9*, Winchester Pr) New Win Pub.

Outdoor Lighting Pattern Book. Lighting Research Center Staff. (Illus.). 208p. 1996. 59.95 (*0-07-037188-1*) McGraw.

Outdoor Lighting Systems. Richard K. Miller & Marcia E. Rupnow. LC 89-85436. (Survey on Technology & Markets Ser.: No. 128). 50p. 1991. pap. text 200.00 (*1-55865-151-9*) Future Tech Surveys.

Outdoor Living Skills Instructor's Manual. 97p. 1997. teacher ed., spiral bd. 21.95 (*0-87603-155-6*) Am Camping.

Outdoor Moments with God. W. Phillip Keller. LC 92-17859. 192p. 1994. pap. 10.99 (*0-8254-2996-X*) Kregel.

Outdoor Optics. Leif J. Robinson. (Illus.). 160p. 1990. pap. 13.95 (*1-55821-065-2*) Lyons Pr.

Outdoor Pastimes of an American Hunter. Theodore Roosevelt. LC 70-25762. (American Environmental Studies). 1971. reprint ed. 31.95 (*0-405-02687-0*) Ayer.

Outdoor Pastimes of an American Hunter. Theodore Roosevelt. LC 90-9884. (Classics of American Sport Ser.). (Illus.). 480p. 1990. reprint ed. pap. 18.95 (*0-8117-3033-6*) Stackpole.

Outdoor Photographer's Bible. H. Lea Lawrence & Aubrey Watson. LC 96-21940. (Illus.). 160p. 1997. pap. 12.00 (*0-385-48220-5*, Main St Bks) Doubleday.

Outdoor Photography: 101 Tips & Hints. Heather Angel. LC 98-125195. (Magic Lantern Guides Ser.). (Illus.). 176p. (C). 1998. pap. 19.95 (*1-883403-41-3*, H 156, Silver Pixel Pr) Saunders Photo.

Outdoor Pig Production. Keith Thornton. (Illus.). 224p. 1988. 29.95 (*0-85236-178-5*, Pub. by Farming Pr) Diamond Farm Bk.

Outdoor Play for Infants & Toddlers. Suzanne Winter. (Bright Ideas Ser.). (Illus.). 30p. (Orig.). 1995. pap. 4.00 (*0-942388-17-8*) So Early Chldhood Assn.

Outdoor Play in the Early Years: Management & Innovation. Helen Bilton. 1998. 24.95 (*1-85346-519-4*) Taylor & Francis.

Outdoor Pony. Susan McBane. (Threshold Picture Guides Ser.). (Illus.). 24p. 1992. pap. 12.00 (*1-872082-30-0*, Pub. by Kenilworth Pr) Half Halt Pr.

Outdoor Potted Bulb. Rob Proctor. LC 93-6664. (Illus.). 128p. 1993. 20.00 (*0-671-87034-3*) S&S Trade.

***Outdoor Power Equipment.** Webster. (C). 2000. pap., lab manual ed. 12.00 (*0-7668-1392-4*) Thomson Learn.

Outdoor Power Equipment. Jay Webster. (C). 2000. pap. 43.95 (*0-7668-1391-6*) Thomson Learn.

Outdoor Power Equipment Basic Four Stroke Test Study Guide. William A. Schuster. 52p. 1993. pap. 10.50 (*0-8273-6031-2*) Delmar.

Outdoor Power Equipment Compact Diesel Test Study Guide. William A. Schuster. 61p. 1995. pap. text 10.00 (*0-8273-6936-0*) Delmar.

Outdoor Projects for Children. Gerri Jenny. (J). 1992. pap. 10.95 (*1-878767-55-0*) Murdoch Bks.

Outdoor Projects for the Country Home. Peter Badger. LC 92-45742. 1993. pap. 14.95 (*0-8306-4399-0*) McGraw-Hill Prof.

Outdoor Projects 1-2-3. Ed. by Ben Allen. LC 97-71598. (Illus.). 480p. 1998. 34.95 (*0-696-20673-0*, Home Depot) Meredith Bks.

Outdoor Projects 1-2-3: Latino Edition. Home Depot Staff. (Home Depot 1-2-3 Ser.). (ENG & SPA., Illus.). 480p. 1998. text 34.95 (*0-696-20884-9*, Home Depot) Meredith Bks.

Outdoor Recreation. Hilmi Ibrahim & Kathleen A. Cordes. 432p. (C). 1992. text. write for info. (*0-697-13152-1*) Brown & Benchmark.

Outdoor Recreation. 2nd ed. Ibrahim & Cordes. 2001. 29.74 (*0-697-25880-7*, WCB McGr Hill) McGraw-H Hghr Educ.

Outdoor Recreation: United States National Parks, Forests & Public Lands. Charles I. Zinser. LC 94-38100. 898p. 1995. 140.00 (*0-471-05373-2*) Wiley.

Outdoor Recreation & Public Policy. Ed. by John D. Hutcheson et al. (Orig.). 1987. pap. 15.00 (*0-918592-97-6*) Pol Studies.

Outdoor Recreation & the Urban Environment. Stephen Williams. LC 94-36920. 224p. (C). 1995. pap. 18.99 (*0-415-09633-2*, C0389) Thomson Learn.

Outdoor Recreation & the Urban Environment. Stephen Williams. LC 94-36920. 224p. (C). (gr. 13). 1995. pap. 71.95 (*0-415-09632-4*, C0388) Thomson Learn.

Outdoor Recreation Areas. rev. ed. Time-Life Books Editors. (Home Repair & Improvement Ser.). (Illus.). 128p. 1989. reprint ed. 14.60 (*0-8094-7354-2*); reprint ed. pap. write for info. (*0-8094-7357-7*); reprint ed. text. write for info. (*0-8094-7356-9*); reprint ed. lib. bdg. 20.60 (*0-8094-7355-0*) Time-Life.

Outdoor Recreation Checklists. Don Brundige & Sharron Brundige. LC 96-95421. (Illus.). 422p. 1998. pap. 14.95 (*0-9619151-9-6*) BD Enterprises.

Outdoor Recreation in America. 5th ed. Clayne R. Jensen. LC 95-2202. (Illus.). 288p. 1995. text 39.00 (*0-87322-496-5*, BJEN0496) Human Kinetics.

Outdoor Recreation in American Life. Ken Cordell. LC 98-83130. (Illus.). 400p. 1999. pap. 49.95 (*1-57167-246-X*) Sagamore Pub.

Outdoor Recreation in Economic Development. Deen Boe. (New Alliances for Rural America Ser.). (Orig.). 1988. pap. text 6.00 (*1-55877-021-6*) Natl Governor.

***Outdoor Recreation in Southern New Hampshire: From Hiking Trails to Parks & Playgrounds.** Sharon Enright. Ed. by Kris Eichstaedt. LC 99-62851. (Illus.). 108p. 1999. pap. 10.95 (*0-9671884-1-5*) Skyline NH.

Outdoor Recreation Legislation & Its Effectiveness. Andrew G. Truxal. LC 68-58630. (Columbia University. Studies in the Social Sciences: No. 311). reprint ed. 21.00 (*0-404-51311-5*) AMS Pr.

Outdoor Recreation Management. J. J. Pigram & John Jenkins. LC 98-48278. 1999. 100.00 (*0-415-15999-7*) Routledge.

Outdoor Recreation Management Theory & Application. 3rd ed. Alan Jubenville & Ben W. Twight. LC 93-85328. (Illus.). 329p. (C). 1993. text 34.95 (*0-910251-61-4*) Venture Pub PA.

Outdoor Recreation Policy: Pleasure & Preservation, 263. John D. Hutcheson, Jr. et al. LC 90-36580. (Contributions in Political Science Ser.: No. 263). 312p. 1990. 57.95 (*0-313-27522-X*, HUO, Greenwood Pr) Greenwood.

Outdoor Recreation Safety. School & Community Safety Society of America Staff. Ed. by Neil J. Dougherty. LC 97-38948. (Illus.). 312p. 1998. text 35.00 (*0-87322-944-4*, BDOU0944) Human Kinetics.

Outdoor Rooms: Designs for Porches, Terraces, Decks, Gazebos. Julie D. Taylor. (Illus.). 160p. 1999. 35.00 (*1-56496-423-X*) Rockport Pubs.

Outdoor Safety. Nancy Loewen. LC 95-25905. (Safety Sense Ser.). (Illus.). 24p. (J). (gr. k-4). 1996. lib. bdg. 18.50 (*1-56766-256-0*) Childs World.

Outdoor Science. Anita Ganeri. LC 93-13125. (Science Questions & Answers Ser.). (Illus.). 48p. (J). (gr. 5 up). 1993. lib. bdg. 13.95 (*0-87518-579-7*, Dillon Silver Burdett) Silver Burdett Pr.

Outdoor Science Adventures. Melvin Berger. 112p. (J). (gr. 4-7). 1994. pap. 2.95 (*0-590-46855-3*) Scholastic Inc.

Outdoor Science Education in Orange County, California: A Comprehensive Directory of Facilities & Programs. Jennifer A. Rigby. 35p. 1992. 7.95 (*1-881150-00-3*) Acorn Grp.

Outdoor Science Projects for Young People. George Barr. Orig. Title: Young Scientist Takes a Walk: Guide to Outdoor Observations. (Illus.). 160p. (J). 1998. reprint ed. pap. 3.95 (*0-486-26855-1*) Dover.

Outdoor Science Series, 4 bks., Set. Rose Wyler. (Illus.). 64p. (J). (gr. k-2). 1989. pap. 19.80 (*0-382-24536-9*, Julian Messner) Silver Burdett Pr.

Outdoor Sculpture in Ljubljana. Spelca Copic et al. Tr. by Gerda Fras. LC 95-123496. 186 p. 1991. write for info. (*86-341-0672-1*) Drazvna Zaloba.

Outdoor Sculpture in Milwaukee: A Cultural & Historical Guidebook. Diane M. Buck & Virginia A. Palmer. LC 94-39585. (Illus.). 240p. 1995. pap. 20.00 (*0-87020-276-6*, OUSC) State Hist Soc Wis.

Outdoor Space. M. J. Vroom. (Illus.). 208p. 1995. 49.95 (*90-6868-048-X*, Pub. by Thoth Pubs) Bks Nippan.

Outdoor Sports Photography Book. 1982. spiral bd. 11.95 (*0-89037-231-4*) Anderson World.

***Outdoor Stonework: 16 Easy-to-Build Projects for Your Yard & Garden.** Alan Bridgewater & Gill Bridgewater. 96p. 2001. pap. 17.95 (*1-58017-333-0*) Storey Bks.

Outdoor Structures. (Home Repair & Improvement Ser.). (Illus.). 136p. 1978. lib. bdg. 20.60 (*0-8094-2403-7*) Time-Life.

Outdoor Structures. (Home Repair & Improvement Ser.). (Illus.). 136p. 1978. 14.60 (*0-8094-2402-9*) Time-Life.

Outdoor Structures. Reader's Digest Editors. (Woodworking Ser.). 124p. 1999. pap. 14.95 (*0-7621-0158-X*, Pub. by RD Assn) Penguin Putnam.

Outdoor Structures. Time-Life Books Editors. LC 96-18706. (Home Repair & Improvement Ser.). (Illus.). 128p. (gr. 11). 1999. spiral bd. 14.95 (*0-7835-3903-7*) Time-Life.

Outdoor Style. Penny Swift. (Illus.). 208p. 1998. 24.95 (*1-85368-250-0*, Pub. by New5 Holland) Sterling.

Outdoor Style: The Complete Book of Garden Design & Outdoor. Penny Swift & Janet Szymanowski. LC 96-162921. (Illus.). 208p. 1996. 39.95 (*1-86825-237-X*, Pub. by New5 Holland) Sterling.

Outdoor Survival Handbook: A Guide to the Resources & Material Available in the Wild & How to Use Them for Food, Shelter, Warmth, & Navigation. Raymond Mears. LC 93-9683. (Illus.). 240p. (Orig.). 1993. pap. 14.95 (*0-312-09359-4*) St Martin.

Outdoor Survival Skills. Larry D. Olsen. 1990. pap. 5.99 (*0-671-72298-0*) S&S Trade.

Outdoor Survival Skills. rev. ed. Larry D. Olsen. (Illus.). 1988. pap. 9.95 (*0-960234-2-0*) Salmon Falls Pub.

Outdoor Survival Skills. 6th rev. ed. Larry D. Olsen. LC 97-20442. (Illus.). 272p. 1997. pap. 14.95 (*1-55652-323-8*) Chicago Review.

Outdoor Survival Training for Alaska's Youth: Instructor's Manual. Dolly Garza. (Sea Grant Education Publication: No. 16). (Illus.). 108p. (Orig.). 1993. pap., teacher ed. 8.00 (*1-56612-013-6*) AK Sea Grant CP.

Outdoor Tables & Tales: Recipes & Food Memories from America's Top Outdoor Writers. Southeast Out Press Writers Assoc. Staff. Ed. by Robert H. Neill & Ellen Rolfes. (Illus.). 228p. 1992. spiral bd. 15.95 (*1-879958-02-3*, Tradery) Wimmer Cos.

Outdoor Things. Illus. by Ethel Gold. (Picture Bks.: No. S8817-3). (J). (ps). pap. 3.95 (*0-7214-5142-X*, Ladybrd) Penguin Putnam.

Outdoor Training for Employee Effectiveness. Mark Tuson. 208p. 1993. pap. 125.00 (*0-85292-549-2*, Pub. by IPM Hse) St Mut.

Outdoor Traveler's Guide: Australia. Garry Ellis & Sharon Cohen. LC 87-33586. (Illus.). 400p. 1988. pap. 25.00 (*1-55670-019-9*) Stewart Tabori & Chang.

Outdoor Traveler's Guide to Canada. David Dunbar. LC 90-48520. (Outdoor Traveler's Guides Ser.). (Illus.). 400p. (Orig.). 1991. pap. 12.50 (*1-55670-169-1*) Stewart Tabori & Chang.

Outdoor Traveler's Guide to the Alps. Marcia Lieberman. LC 91-3146. (Illus.). 360p. 1991. pap. 12.50 (*1-55670-177-2*) Stewart Tabori & Chang.

***Outdoor Water Features: 16 Easy-to-Build Projects for Your Yard.** Alan Bridgewater & Gill Bridgewater. 96p. 2001. pap. 17.95 (*1-58017-334-9*) Storey Bks.

Outdoor Wok Cuisine: Traditional Chinese Recipes Adapted for Outdoor Cooking. Brenda Kulibert. LC 90-85218. (Illus.). 128p. (Orig.). 1992. pap. 8.95 (*0-9623430-6-4*) Explorers Guide Pub.

Outdoor Wok Cuisine: Traditional Chinese Recipes Adapted for Outdoor Cooking. 2nd ed. Brenda Kulibert. (Illus.). 150p. (Orig.). 1998. pap. 9.95 (*1-879432-20-X*) Explorers Guide Pub.

Outdoor Wood Furnishing: 35 Easy Projects for Your Yard. Creative Publishing International Staff. LC 98-49168. (Black & Decker Outdoor Home Ser.). (Illus.). 160p. 1998. pap. text 16.95 (*0-86573-633-2*) Creat Pub Intl.

Outdoor Wood Works: With Complete Plans for Ten Projects. Tina Skinner. LC 97-40473. 160p. 1998. 19.95 (*0-7643-0446-1*) Schiffer.

Outdoor Woodwork. Mike Lawrence. (Step-by-Step Ser.). (Illus.). 96p. 1998. pap. 15.95 (*1-85368-225-X*, Pub. by New5 Holland) Sterling.

Outdoor World of the Sacramento Region: A Local Field Guide. rev. ed. Ed. by Jo Smith. (Illus.). 214p. (Orig.). 1993. pap. 9.95 (*1-887815-03-1*) Amer River Nat Hist.

Outdoor Writers Association of America Outdoor Style Manual. Outdoor Writers Association of America Staff. Ed. by Jack Brown et al. LC 91-61065. 88p. (Orig.). 1991. pap. 10.00 (*0-944973-00-0*) Outdoor Writ.

Outdoor Writers Association of America Outdoor Style Manual. rev. ed. Ed. by Carol J. Kersavage. LC 91-61065. 99p. (Orig.). 1995. pap. 10.00 (*0-944973-01-9*) Outdoor Writ.

Outdoor Yarns & Outright Lies. Gene Hill & Steve Smith. LC 83-8159. (Illus.). 184p. 1983. 19.95 (*0-8117-0698-2*) Stackpole.

***Outdoors.** (Baby's World (Antique Collector's Club) Ser.). (Illus.). (J). (ps). 1999. bds. 6.99 (*0-7112-1124-8*) F Lincoln.

Outdoors Alaska Directory: Hunting. David M. Johnson. 1997. pap. text 9.95 (*0-9656355-0-3*) Outdoors Am Commns.

***Outdoors Almanac.** Len McDougall. LC 99-28384. (Illus.). 208p. 1999. pap. 16.95 (*1-58080-035-1*) Burford Bks.

Outdoors Austin: A Sierra Club Guide. 3rd ed. Ed. by Nancy Fuentes. LC 94-66625. (Illus.). 208p. (C). 1996. pap. 12.95 (*0-89096-693-1*) Tex A&M Univ Pr.

Outdoors Cooking. 1947. 12.95 (*0-405-10073-6*, 13373) Ayer.

Outdoors in Arizona: A Guide to Hiking & Backpacking. 5th ed. John Annerino et al. (Illus.). 136p. 2000. pap. 10.95 (*0-916179-50-8*) Ariz Hwy.

Outdoors Just for Kids. Mark Henckel. (Illus.). 128p. (Orig.). (J). (gr. 1-8). 1992. spiral bd. 8.95 (*0-9627618-3-4*) Billings Gazette.

Outer Banks. Anthony Bailey. LC 98-49043. (Chapel Hill Book Ser.). 288p. 1999. pap. 16.95 (*0-8078-4820-4*) U of NC Pr.

Outer Banks. Patrick D. Crosland. LC 81-132857. (Illus.). 52p. (Orig.). 1981. pap. 6.95 (*0-936478-05-5*) Interpretive Pubns.

Outer Banks. Anne Rivers Siddons. LC 90-56370. 576p. 1992. mass mkt. 6.99 (*0-06-109973-2*, Harp PBks) HarpC.

Outer Banks. Bill Yenne. (Illus.). 48p. 1998. pap. 14.95 (*0-7627-0384-9*) Globe Pequot.

Outer Banks. large type ed. Anne Rivers Siddons. 654p. 1992. reprint ed. lib. bdg. 21.95 (*1-56054-282-9*) Thorndike Pr.

Outer Banks: An Artist's Sketchbook. Susan B. Fecho. (Illus.). 40p. 1993. pap. 8.50 (*1-884824-02-1*) Tryon Pubng.

Outer Banks: From a Flying Machine. Martin Conway. LC 89-60752. (Illus.). 46p. 1989. pap. write for info. (*0-938634-09-7*) Carabelle.

Outer Banks & Other Poems. 2nd ed. W. D. Ehrhart. 52p. 1985. pap. 7.00 (*0-938566-28-8*) Adastra Pr.

***Outer Banks Architecture: An Anthology of Outposts, Lodges & Cottages.** Marimar McNaughton. (Illus.). 130p. 2000. pap. 14.95 (*0-89587-192-0*) Blair.

Outer Banks Cuisine. 32p. 1995. 5.00 (*0-9638258-9-5*) Bicast.

Outer Banks Marketplace, Inc. Simulation. Date not set. teacher ed. write for info. (*0-02-814561-5*) Glencoe.

An Asterisk (*) at the beginning of an entry indicates that the title is appearing for the first time.

Outer Banks Mysteries & Seaside Stories. Charles H. Whedbee. LC 78-58535. 141p. 1980. 12.95 (0-89587-006-1) Blair.

***Outer Banks, North Carolina.** John Hairr. (Images of America Ser.). (Illus.). 128p. 1999. pap. 18.99 (0-7385-0169-7) Arcadia Publng.

Outer Banks, North Carolina Vol. 1: Memories. Mary A. Haggerty. (Illus.). 128p. 1996. 16.95 (0-9651200-0-7) Northlight Studio.

Outer Banks of North Carolina, 1584-1958. David Stick. (Illus.). xv, 352p. (C). 1990. reprint ed. 27.50 (0-8078-0746-X); reprint ed. pap. 14.95 (0-8078-4277-X) U of NC Pr.

***Outer Banks Pocket Companion.** Mary E. Riddle & Catherine Kozak. (Insiders' Guide Travel Ser.). (Illus.). 160p. 1998. pap. 6.95 (1-57380-099-6, The Insiders Guide) Falcon Pub Inc.

Outer Banks Reader. Ed. & Selected by David Stick. LC 97-40791. 336p. 1998. pap. 17.95 (0-8078-4726-7) U of NC Pr.

Outer Banks Reader. Ed. by David Stick. LC 97-40791. 336p. 1998. 32.50 (0-8078-2420-8) U of NC Pr.

Outer Banks Story. Judy J. Preston. (Illus.). 117p. (Orig.). (J). (gr. 5 up). 1985. pap. 4.25 (0-9613824-0-6) Seabright.

Outer Banks Tales to Remember. Charles H. Whedbee. LC 86-3593. 133p. 1985. 12.95 (0-89587-044-4) Blair.

Outer Bay. Michael A. Rigsby. (Illus.). 24p. 1996. pap. 4.95 (1-878244-12-4) Monterey Bay Aquarium.

Outer Buoy. large type ed. Jan De Hartog. (Ulverscroft Large Print Ser.). 480p. 1997. 27.99 (0-7089-3771-3) Ulverscroft.

Outer Circle: Women in the Scientific Community. Ed. by Harriet Zuckerman et al. LC 92-83816. (Illus.). 351p. 1992. reprint ed. pap. 108.90 (0-608-07857-3, 205404000011) Bks Demand.

Outer Coast. Richard Batman. LC 85-7613. (Illus.). 400p. 1985. 18.95 (0-15-170450-3) Harcourt.

Outer Dark. Cormac McCarthy. 1994. 24.00 (0-8446-6749-8) Peter Smith.

Outer Dark. Cormac McCarthy. LC 92-50588. 1993. pap. 12.00 (0-679-72873-2) Vin Bks.

Outer Darkness: The Lost Earth. James Axler. (Outlanders Ser.: No. 10). 1999. mass mkt. 5.99 (0-373-63823-X, 1-63823-8, Wrldwide Lib) Harlequin Bks.

Outer Galaxy. Ed. by Leo Blitz & F. J. Lockman. (Lecture Notes in Physics Ser.: Vol. 306). ix, 291p. 1988. 42.95 (0-387-19484-3) Spr-Verlag.

Outer Game of Trading: Modeling the Trading Strategies of Today's Market Wizards. Robert Koppel. 225p. 1994. text 37.50 (1-55738-598-X, Irwn Prfssnl) McGraw-Hill Prof.

Outer Hebrides: The Last 14,000 Years. Ed. by David D. Gilbertson et al. (Search Ser.: No. 2). 300p. 1996. 75.00 (1-85075-613-9, Pub. by Sheffield Acad) CUP Services.

Outer Hebrides Handbook & Guide. 143p. 1995. pap. 39.95 (0-9511003-5-1, Pub. by Kittiwake Pr) St Mut.

Outer Hebrides Handbook & Guide. Kittiwake Press Staff. 96p. 1992. pap. 29.00 (0-9511003-3-5, Pub. by Kittiwake Pr) St Mut.

Outer Lands: A Natural History Guide to Cape Cod, Martha's Vineyard, Nantucket, Block Island, & Long Island. Dorothy Sterling. (Illus.). 216p. 1992. pap. 16.95 (0-393-06441-7) Norton.

Outer Limits, 11. John Peel. 1999. mass mkt. 3.99 (0-8125-7568-7, Pub. by Tor Bks) St Martin.

Outer Limits, Vol. 1. Howard Hendrix. LC 96-67914. (Illus.). 256p. 1996. per. 12.00 (0-7615-0619-5) Prima Pub.

Outer Limits, Vol. 2. Richard Lupoff. LC 96-67914. (Illus.). 224p. 1997. pap. 12.00 (0-7615-0620-9) Prima Pub.

Outer Limits, Vol. 3. Richard Lupoff. LC 96-67914. 272p. 1997. pap. 12.00 (0-7615-0621-7) Prima Pub.

Outer Limits: Armageddon Dreams. Kevin J. Anderson. 224p. Date not set. pap. 12.95 (1-58185-700-4) Quadrillion Media.

Outer Limits: The Nightmare. John Peel. (The Outer Limits Ser.). 1998. mass mkt. 3.99 (0-8125-7565-2, Pub. by Tor Bks) St Martin.

Outer Limits Innocent. John Peel. (Outer Limits Ser.: No. 6). (J). 1998. pap. text 3.99 (0-8125-6455-3, Pub. by Tor Bks) St Martin.

Outer Limits 2, Vol. 1. John Peel. 1997. pap. text 3.99 (0-8125-9064-3, Pub. by Tor Bks) St Martin.

Outer Path: Finding My Way in Tibet. Jim Reynolds. Ed. by Kathleen Hallam. LC 91-21086. (Illus.). 184p. (Orig.). 1992. pap. 10.95 (0-933271-06-9) Fair Oaks CA.

Outer Planets: Proceedings of Symposium 4 & Part of the Topical Meeting of the COSPAR Interdisciplinary Scientific Commission C (Meeting C2) of the COSPAR 27th Plenary Meeting Held in Espoo, Finland, 18-29 July, 1988. Ed. by T. V. Johnson & S. K. Atreya. (Advances in Space Research Ser.: Vol. 10). (Illus.). 250p. 1989. pap. 95.75 (0-08-040156-2, Pergamon Pr) Elsevier.

Outer Planets & Their Cycles: The Astrology of the Collective. 2nd ed. Liz Greene. (Illus.). 182p. 1996. reprint ed. pap. 13.95 (0-916360-60-1) CRCS Pubns CA.

Outer Reaches of Life. John R. Postgate. LC 93-11579. (Illus.). 288p. (C). 1994. text 25.95 (0-521-44010-6) Cambridge U Pr.

Outer Reaches of Life. John R. Postgate. (Canto Book Ser.). (Illus.). 290p. (C). 1995. pap. 12.95 (0-521-55873-5) Cambridge U Pr.

Outer Search/Inner Journey: An Orphan & Adoptee's Quest. Peter F. Dodds. LC 96-97016. 280p. (Orig.). 1997. pap. 15.00 (1-889702-24-2) Aphrodite WA.

***Outer Shell: Skin.** Sarah Angliss. (Human Machine Ser.). (Illus.). 32p. (J). 1999. lib. bdg. 15.95 (1-929298-21-8, Pub. by Thameside Pr) Smart Apple.

Outer Solar System, 17th Annual AAS Meeting, Jun. 28-30, 1971, Seattle, WA: Proceedings of the Annual Meeting, 17th, Seattle, 1971, 2 pts., Pt. 2. Ed. by Juris Vagners. LC 57-43769. (Advances in the Astronautical Sciences Ser.: Vol. 29). 740p. 1971. 45.00 (0-87703-060-X, Am Astronaut Soc) Univelt Inc.

Outer Space, 12 vols. LC 97-49010. (Illus.). (YA). 1998. lib. bdg. 285.00 (0-7172-9179-0) Grolier Educ.

Outer Space. Roger Cleeve. Ed. by Jane Steltenpohl. LC 89-29194. (Science up Close Ser.). (Illus.). 32p. (J). (gr. 3-5). 1990. pap. 4.95 (0-671-68631-3, Julian Messner); lib. bdg. 10.98 (0-671-68628-3, Julian Messner) Silver Burdett Pr.

Outer Space. Bob De Weese. (Science Mini-Unit Intermediate Ser.). (Illus.). 16p. (J). (gr. 3-6). 1994. pap. text 5.95 (1-55799-303-3, EMC 843) Evan-Moor Edu Pubs.

***Outer Space.** Ed. by McGraw-Hill Book Company Staff. (Fact Finders Ser.). (Illus.). (J). 2000. pap. 9.95 (1-57768-764-7) MG-Hill OH.

Outer Space. Smithmark Staff. (CD ROM Factfinders Ser.). (Illus.). 32p. 1997. 14.98 (0-7651-9346-9) Smithmark.

Outer Space. rev. ed. Ed. by Lincoln P. Bloomfield. LC 68-27433. 1968. reprint ed. pap. 2.50 (0-317-02959-2, 64511) Am Assembly.

Outer Space: A New Dimension of the Arms Race. Ed. by Bhupendra Jasani. 424p. 1982. 63.00 (0-85066-231-1) Taylor & Francis.

Outer Space: A Source of Conflict or Co-Operation? 270p. 35.00 (92-808-0759-5, E.91.III.A.9) UN.

Outer Space: Myths, Name Meanings, Calendars from the Emergence of History to the Present Day. Gertrude Jobes & James Jobes. LC 64-11783. 479p. 1980. reprint ed. lib. bdg. 52.00 (0-8108-0108-6) Scarecrow.

Outer Space: Problems of Law & Policy. 2nd ed. Glenn H. Reynolds. 464p. 1998. pap. 40.00 (0-8133-6680-1, Pub. by Westview) HarpC.

Outer Space: Prospects for Man & Society. rev. ed. American Assembly Staff. Ed. by Lincoln P. Bloomfield. LC 72-3391. (Essay Index Reprint Ser.). 1977. reprint ed. 19.95 (0-8369-2886-5) Ayer.

Outer Space: Wacky Words. Greg Lee. LC 92-43965. (Little Jokester Ser.). 24p. (J). (gr. k-4). 1993. lib. bdg. 10.95 (0-86593-267-0) Rourke Corp.

Outer Space: Wacky Words. Greg Lee. LC 92-43965. (Little Jokester Ser.). (J). (gr. 3 up). 1993. 9.50 (0-685-66292-6) Rourke Corp.

Outer Space Adventures. Alba Arboleda et al. (BrainBooster Ser.). (Illus.). 32p. (J). (gr. 3 up). 1986. 6.95 (0-88679-462-5) Educ Insights.

Outer Space & All That Junk. Mel Gilden. LC 88-37110. (Illus.). 176p. (J). (gr. 5-9). 1989. 12.95 (0-397-32306-9); lib. bdg. 12.89 (0-397-32307-7) HarpC Child Bks.

Outer Space & Legal Liability. Morris D. Forkosch. 1982. lib. bdg. 101.00 (90-247-2582-8) Kluwer Academic.

Outer Space Frequency Directory. Anthony R. Curtis. 80p. 1994. pap. 17.95 (0-936653-49-3) Tiare Pubns.

Outer Space Mystery. Created by Gertrude Chandler Warner. LC 96-106163. (Boxcar Children Ser.: No. 59). (J). (gr. 2-5). 1997. pap. 3.95 (0-8075-6287-4); lib. bdg. 13.95 (0-8075-6286-6) A Whitman.

Outer Space Mystery. Created by Gertrude Chandler Warner. (Boxcar Children Ser.: No. 59). (J). (gr. 2-5). 1997. 9.05 (0-606-11162-X, Pub. by Turtleback) Demco.

Outer Space Prospects for Man & Society. American Assembly Staff. Ed. by Lincoln P. Bloomfield. LC 62-9281. (Illus.). 220p. reprint ed. pap. 68.20 (0-608-18392-X, 202986400066) Bks Demand.

Outer Space Tracing Fun Book. Joan Berger. 32p. (J). (ps-3). 1992. pap. 1.95 (0-590-45133-2) Scholastic Inc.

Outerbridge. Elaine Dines-Cox. (Illus.). 252p. 1999. 39.99 (3-8228-6618-0) Taschen Amer.

Outerbridge Reach. Robert Stone. 416p. 1998. pap. 13.00 (0-395-93894-5) HM.

Outerbridge Reach. large type ed. Robert Stone. 711p. 1993. lib. bdg. 15.95 (1-56054-929-7) Thorndike Pr.

Outercourse: The Be-Dazzling Voyage. Mary Daly. 478p. 1993. pap. 12.00 (0-7043-4372-X, Pub. by Womens Press) Trafalgar.

Outermost Dream: Literary Sketches. William Maxwell. LC 97-70220. (Graywolf Rediscovery Ser.). 240p. 1997. pap. 12.95 (1-55597-264-0) Graywolf.

Outermost House. Henry Beston. 10.00 (0-614-30536-5) NAVH.

Outermost House: A Year of Life on the Great Beach of Cape Cod. Henry Beston. 256p. 1995. pap. 9.95 (0-8050-1966-9, Owl) H Holt & Co.

Outermost Island: An Oral History of San Salvador, the Bahamas. Virginia White. 70p. (Orig.). 1987. pap. text 8.00 (0-935909-19-2) Bahamian.

Outerspace, Innerspace: The Start of a Personal Journey. Robert Roberta. LC 97-181120. (Illus.). 184p. (Orig.). 1996. pap. 12.95 (0-9654252-5-8) Pearly Everlast.

Outerspace Jokes & Riddles Book. Jeffrey S. Nelson. (Jokes & Riddles Bks.). (Illus.). 24p. (J). (gr. 3 up). 1988. pap. 1.95 (1-56288-343-7) Checkerboard.

Outfielder. H. R. Coursen. LC 91-38244. (Illus.). 270p. 1993. 19.95 (0-918606-10-1) Heidelberg Graph.

***Outfit.** Richard Stark. LC 98-6631. 224p. 1998. mass mkt. 12.00 (0-446-67467-2, Pub. by Warner Bks) Little.

Outfit. Richard Stark. LC 80-26554. 142p. 1981. reprint ed. 25.00 (0-89366-149-X) Ultramarine Pub.

Outfitting, Vol. I. Ed. by Practical Sailor Staff. (Practical Sailor Library). (Illus.). 1995. pap. 14.95 (1-879620-32-4) Belvoir Pubns.

Outfitting & Organizing Your Boat: For a Day, a Week or a Lifetime. Michael L. Frankel. Ed. by Robert Lollo & John P. Kaufman. LC 98-71300. (Illus.). 174p. 1998. spiral bd. 24.95 (1-892216-06-X) Bristol Fash.

Outfitting Your Canoe. Charlie Walbridge. (Nuts-N-Bolts Guides Ser.). 32p. 1995. pap. 4.95 (0-89732-177-4) Menasha Ridge.

***Outfitting Your Home Business for Much Less.** Walter Zooi et al. LC 99-55460. 288p. 2000. pap. 18.95 (0-8144-7993-6) AMACOM.

Outfitting Your Van for Camping. W. L. Anderson & S. W. Anderson. (Illus.). 300p. 1988. 9.95 (0-940452-01-4) Marduk Manumit.

Outflying Philosophy. Robert Sencourt. LC 68-6262. (Studies in Comparative Literature: No. 35). 1969. reprint ed. lib. bdg. 75.00 (0-8383-0679-9) M S G Haskell Hse.

***Outfoxed.** Rita Mae Brown. LC 99-44243. 384p. 2000. 24.00 (0-345-42818-8) Ballantine Pub Grp.

***Outfoxed.** large type ed. Rita Mae Brown. LC 99-86684. 2000. 26.95 (1-56895-844-7) Wheeler Pub.

***Outfoxing Coyote: Poems.** Carolyn Dunn. Ed. by Paula Gunn Allen. (Paula Gunn Allen American Indian Poets Ser.: No. 1). 90p. 2000. pap. 13.95 (1-928708-08-0) That Painted Horse.

Outgrowing the Ingrown Church. C. John Miller. 176p. 1986. pap. 12.99 (0-310-28411-2, 12815P) Zondervan.

Outgrowing the Pain. Eliana Gil. 96p. (Orig.). 1988. pap. 9.95 (0-440-50006-0, Dell Trade Pbks) Dell.

Outhouse Book: Readin' That's Probably Not Ready for Indoor Plumbing. Wayne Allred. (Illus.). 101p. 1997. pap. 5.95 (1-885027-07-9) Willow T Bks.

Outhouse by Any Other Name. Thomas Harding. LC 99-43679. 96p. 1999. pap. 7.95 (0-87483-578-X) August Hse.

Outhouse Humor. Billy E. Wheeler. LC 87-31666. (Illus.). 112p. (Orig.). 1988. pap. 7.95 (0-87483-058-3) August Hse.

Outhouse Revisited. Don Harron. (Illus.). 96p. 1996. text 19.95 (1-55209-062-0) Firefly Bks Ltd.

Outhouses. 1998. 12.95 (1-55209-683-1) Firefly Bks Ltd.

Outhouses. Illus. by Londie G. Padelsky et al.-LC 98-39588. 112p. 1998. pap. 25.95 (1-56313-927-8) BrownTrout Pubs Inc.

Outhouses: Postcard Book. BrownTrout Publishers Incorporated, Staff. (Illus.). 1997. pap. 7.95 (1-56313-932-4) BrownTrout Pubs Inc.

***Outhouses by Famous Architects.** Steve Schaecher. LC 99-57034. 2000. 17.95 (0-7649-1260-7) Pomegranate Calif.

Outhouses of Alaska. Harry M. Walker. LC 95-52938. (Illus.). 64p. 1996. 14.95 (0-945397-41-0) Epicenter Pr.

Outhouses of the East. Sherman Hines. (Illus.). 72p. 1991. 14.95 (0-920852-03-3) Nimbus Publ.

***Outhouses of the West.** Photos by Sherman Hines. (Illus.). 72p. 2000. 19.95 (1-55209-523-1) Firefly Bks Ltd.

Outils et Signes: Perspectives Actuelles de la Theorie de Vygotski. Ed. by Christiane Moro et al. (Exploration Ser.). (FRE., Illus.). vi, 221p. 1997. 36.95 (3-906757-88-9, Pub. by P Lang) P Lang Pubng.

Outing: An Original Chintzland Prenatal Storybook. Sandra M. Rome. LC 98-96653. (Illus.). iii, 18p. (J). 1998. pap. write for info. (0-9668895-0-9) Chintzland.

Outing: Playscript. Arnold Rabin. 53p. (YA). 1992. pap. 6.00 (0-87602-303-0) Anchorage.

Outing: Shattering the Conspiracy of Silence. Warren Johansson. 1994. pap. 19.95 (1-56023-041-X, Harrington Park) Haworth Pr.

Outing: Shattering the Conspiracy of Silence. Warren Johansson & William Percy. LC 93-17368. 322p. 1994. lib. bdg. 49.95 (1-56024-419-4) Haworth Pr.

Outing Goethe & His Age. Ed. by Alice A. Kuzniar. LC 95-36492. 342p. 1996. 49.50 (0-8047-2614-0); pap. 17.95 (0-8047-2615-9) Stanford U Pr.

Outing Yourself. Michelangelo Signorile. 208p. 1996. per. 11.00 (0-684-82617-8) S&S Trade Pap.

Outland. Mary H. Austin. (Collected Works of Mary Hunter Austin). 306p. 1998. reprint ed. lib. bdg. 98.00 (1-58201-528-7) Classic Bks.

Outland Strip. Ben Sloane. (Horn Ser.: No. 3). 1991. per. 4.50 (0-373-64003-X) Harlequin Bks.

Outlander. Diana Gabaldon. 640p. 1991. 25.95 (0-385-30230-4) Delacorte.

Outlander. Diana Gabaldon. 864p. 1992. mass mkt. 7.99 (0-440-21256-1) Dell.

Outlander. Diana Gabaldon. 640p. 1998. pap. 13.95 (0-385-31995-9) Doubleday.

Outlander. Jane Rule. LC 80-84221. (Illus.). 224p. (Orig.). 1981. pap. 8.95 (0-930044-17-7) Naiad Pr.

Outlanders. David B. Coe. 640p. 1999. mass mkt. 6.99 (0-8125-7113-4, Pub. by Tor Bks) St Martin.

Outlanders, 6. pap. 14.95 (1-56971-423-1, Pub. by Dark Horse Comics) Penguin Putnam.

***Outlanders, 7.** 1999. pap. 14.95 (1-56971-424-X, Pub. by Dark Horse Comics) Penguin Putnam.

***Outlanders, 8.** 2000. pap. 14.95 (1-56971-425-8, Pub. by Dark Horse Comics) Penguin Putnam.

Outlanders, Bk. 4. Johji Manabe. (Illus.). 168p. 1995. pap. 12.95 (1-56971-069-4) Dark Horse Comics.

Outlanders, Vol. 3. Johji Manabe. (Illus.). 160p. 1994. pap. 13.95 (1-56971-011-2) Dark Horse Comics.

Outlanders, Vol. 5. Johji Manabe. (Illus.). 1998. pap. 14.95 (1-56971-275-1) Dark Horse Comics.

Outlanders: Hellbound Fury. James Axler. (Outlanders Ser.: No. 8). 1999. mass mkt. 5.99 (0-373-63821-3, 1-63821-2, Wrldwide Lib) Harlequin Bks.

Outlanders: LonTobyn Chronicle. David B. Coe. LC 98-23672. 416p. 1998. 26.95 (0-312-86447-7, Pub. by Tor Bks) St Martin.

***Outlandish: Writing Between Exile & Diaspora.** Nico Israel. LC 99-86062. 277p. 2000. 45.00 (0-8047-3073-3) Stanford U Pr.

Outlandish Companion. Diana Gabaldon. LC 99-22969. 608p. 1999. 24.95 (0-385-32413-8) Delacorte.

***Outlandish Knight.** Richard Adams. 256p. 2000. 26.00 (0-7278-5496-8, Pub. by Severn Hse) Chivers N Amer.

Outlands: Journeys to the Outer Edges of Cape Cod. Robert Finch. LC 85-45972. 160p. 1986. 16.95 (0-87923-619-1) Godine.

Outlaw see Three Plays

Outlaw. Susan L. Crose. 1995. mass mkt. 5.99 (0-671-88534-0) PB.

Outlaw. Susan Johnson. 448p. 1993. mass mkt. 5.99 (0-553-29955-7) Bantam.

Outlaw. Nicole Jordan. 384p. (Orig.). 1996. mass mkt. 5.50 (0-380-77832-7, Avon Bks) Morrow Avon.

Outlaw. Elizabeth Lowell. 256p. 1994. per. 4.99 (1-55166-006-7, 1-66066-7, Mira Bks) Harlequin Bks.

Outlaw. Elizabeth Lowell. 1998. mass mkt. 5.99 (1-55166-559-X, Mira Bks) Harlequin Bks.

***Outlaw.** Elizabeth Lowell. 2000. 6.99 (1-55166-619-7, 1-66573-6, Mira Bks) Harlequin Bks.

Outlaw. Elizabeth Lowell. 1994. mass mkt. 4.50 (0-373-48304-X, 5-48304-5) Silhouette.

Outlaw. Lisa Plumley. 320p. 1999. mass mkt. 4.99 (0-8217-6120-X) Kensgtn Pub Corp.

Outlaw. Joann Ross. (Temptation Ser.). 1996. per. 3.50 (0-373-25685-X, 1-25685-8) Harlequin Bks.

Outlaw. Georges Simenon. Tr. by Howard Curtis. 1987. 15.95 (0-15-170509-7) Harcourt.

Outlaw. Millie M. Wicklund. LC 79-84612. 40p. 1979. 10.00 (0-930012-12-7); pap. 3.00 (0-930012-11-9) J Mudfoot.

Outlaw. John Wright. 12p. (Orig.). 1996. pap. 5.00 (1-887289-20-8) Rodent Pr.

Outlaw. large type ed. Frank Gruber. (Linford Western Library). 384p. 1994. pap. 16.99 (0-7089-7494-5, Linford) Ulverscroft.

Outlaw. large type ed. Frank Scarman. (Linford Western Library Ser.). 240p. 1997. pap. 16.99 (0-7089-5153-8) Ulverscroft.

Outlaw & the City Slicker. Debbi Rawlins. LC 96-2469. (American Romance Ser.). 249p. 1996. per. 3.75 (0-373-16622-2, 1-16622-2) Harlequin Bks.

Outlaw Ballads, Legends & Lore. Wayne Erbsen. 68p. (Orig.). 1998. pap. 10.95 (0-7866-2609-7, 96471); pap. 20.95 incl. audio (0-7866-4085-5, 96471P); pap. 25.95 incl. audio compact disk (0-7866-4086-3, 96471CDD) Mel Bay.

Outlaw Ballads, Legends & Lore. Wayne Erbsen. (Illus.). 64p. (Orig.). 1996. pap. 5.95 (1-883206-16-2, NGB-500) Native Ground.

***Outlaw Bible of American Poetry.** Ed. by Alan Kaufman. 685p. 1999. 34.95 (1-56025-236-7, Thunders Mouth) Avalon NY.

Outlaw Bible of American Poetry. Ed. by Alan Kaufman & S. A. Griffin. LC 99-18930. (Illus.). 685p. 1999. pap. 24.95 (1-56025-227-8, Thunders Mouth) Avalon NY.

***Outlaw Bride.** Sandra Chastain. 2000. mass mkt. 5.99 (0-553-58047-7) Bantam.

Outlaw Bride. Katherine Compton. 400p. (Orig.). 1991. mass mkt. 4.50 (0-380-76411-3, Avon Bks) Morrow Avon.

***Outlaw Bride: The Texas Brand.** Maggie Shayne. (Intimate Moments Ser.). 1999. mass mkt. 4.25 (0-373-07967-2) Silhouette.

Outlaw Brides. Elaine Coffman & Ruth Langan. 1996. per. 5.99 (0-373-83315-6, 1-83315-1) Harlequin Bks.

***Outlaw Bunch.** large type ed. Logan Stuart. 304p. 2000. pap. 20.99 (1-85389-988-7, Dales) Ulverscroft.

***Outlaw Class.** Charles Lewis. 2001. write for info. (0-380-97682-X, Wm Morrow) Morrow Avon.

Outlaw Cook. John Thorne. 384p. 1994. pap. 14.00 (0-86547-479-6) N Point Pr.

Outlaw Cook. John Thorne & Matt L. Thorne. 1992. 25.00 (0-374-22836-1) FS&G.

Outlaw Culture: Resisting Representations. Bell Hooks. LC 94-27403. 272p. (C). (gr. 13). 1994. pap. 17.99 (0-415-90811-6, B2857) Routledge.

Outlaw Deputy. Peter Field. 176p. 1989. pap. 2.95 (0-380-70711-X, Avon Bks) Morrow Avon.

Outlaw Gulch. Ramsey Montgomery. (Choose Your Own Adventure Ser.: No. 125). (J). (gr. 4-8). 1992. 8.60 (0-606-00596-X, Pub. by Turtleback) Demco.

Outlaw Gunner. Harry M. Walsh. LC 71-180856. (Illus.). 190p. 1971. 22.50 (0-87033-162-0, Tidewtr Pubs) Cornell Maritime.

Outlaw Heart. Suzannah Davis. 352p. 1989. pap. 3.95 (0-380-75672-2, Avon Bks) Morrow Avon.

Outlaw Heart. Samantha James. 384p. (Orig.). 1993. mass mkt. 4.50 (0-380-76936-0, Avon Bks) Morrow Avon.

Outlaw Heart. Quinn Wilder. (Romance Ser.: No. 191). 1992. per. 2.89 (0-373-03191-2, 1-03191-3) Harlequin Bks.

Outlaw Hearts. 1987. mass mkt. 3.95 (0-446-73449-7, Pub. by Warner Bks) Little.

***Outlaw Hearts.** Rebecca Brandewyne. 512p. (Orig.). 2000. pap. 5.99 (0-505-52360-4, Love Spell) Dorchester Pub Co.

***Outlaw in My Heart: A User's Manuel.** Stephen Gaskin. (Illus.). 192p. 2000. pap. 12.95 (0-940159-64-3) Camino Bks.

Outlaw in Paradise. Patricia Gaffney. 17.47 (0-7862-1492-9) Five Star.

Outlaw in Paradise. large type ed. Patricia Gaffney. LC 98-14667. (Large Print Book Ser.). 1998. pap. 22.95 (1-56895-544-8, Wheeler) Wheeler Pub.

Outlaw in the Hills: A Writer's Year. Michael Wilcox. (Illus.). 182p. (C). 1991. pap. 29.95 (0-413-64910-5, A0567, Methuen Drama) Methn.

Outlaw James Copeland & the Champion-Belted Empress. Jeanne Lebow. LC 90-36868. (Contemporary Poetry Ser.). 72p. 1991. pap. 14.95 (0-8203-1281-9) U of Ga Pr.

Outlaw Jesse James: Outlaw Hearts. Cindy Gerard. 1999. per. 3.75 (0-373-76198-8, Harlequin) Harlequin Bks.

O

An Asterisk (*) at the beginning of an entry indicates that the title is appearing for the first time.

Outlaw Justice. Doyle Trent. 256p. 1995. mass mkt. 3.99 (*0-8217-4822-X*, Pinncle Kensgtn) Kensgtn Pub Corp.

Outlaw Kingdom. Matt Braun. 1996. mass mkt. 5.99 (*0-312-95618-5*, Pub. by Tor Bks) St Martin.

Outlaw Legend: A Cultural Tradition in Britain, America & Australia. Graham Seal. (Illus.). 264p. (C). 1996. text 59.95 (*0-521-55317-2*); pap. text 19.95 (*0-521-55740-2*) Cambridge U Pr.

Outlaw Love. Judith Stacy. (Debut Author Ser.). 1997. per. 4.99 (*0-373-28960-X*, 1-28960-2) Harlequin Bks.

***Outlaw Machine.** Brock Yates. LC 00-20018. (Illus.). 288p. 2000. pap. 14.95 (*0-7679-0516-4*) Broadway BDD.

Outlaw Machine: Harley Davidson & the Search for the American Soul. Brock Yates. (Illus.). 272p. (YA). (gr. 8). 1999. 24.00 (*0-316-96718-1*) Little.

***Outlaw Mountain.** J. A. Jance. 384p. 2000. mass mkt. 6.99 (*0-380-79248-6*, Avon Bks) Morrow Avon.

Outlaw Mountain: A Joanna Brady Mystery. J. A. Jance. LC 99-20841. 384p. 1999. 24.00 (*0-380-97500-9*, Avon Bks) Morrow Avon.

Outlaw of Buffalo Flat. Max Brand. 160p. Date not set. 18.95 (*0-8488-2215-3*) Amereon Ltd.

Outlaw of Gor see Gor Promotion

Outlaw of Gor. John Norman. (Gor Ser.). 1997. reprint ed. mass mkt. 6.95 (*1-56333-487-9*, Masquerade SF) Masquerade.

Outlaw of the Lowest Planet. Jack Micheline. (Orig.). pap. 5.00 (*0-929730-47-X*) Zeitgeist Pr.

Outlaw of Torn. Edgar Rice Burroughs. 256p. 22.95 (*0-8488-1256-5*) Amereon Ltd.

Outlaw of Torn. Edgar Rice Burroughs. 1976. reprint ed. lib. bdg. 10.55 (*0-89966-042-8*) Buccaneer Bks.

Outlaw Red. James A. Kjelgaard. (J). 1981. 9.60 (*0-606-01109-9*, Pub. by Turtleback) Demco.

Outlaw Red. Jim Kjelgaard. 192p. (J). 1984. pap. 4.99 (*0-553-15686-1*) Bantam.

***Outlaw Redeemer.** Max Brand. LC 00-23523. 207p. 2000. 30.00 (*0-7862-2106-2*, Five Star MI) Mac Lib Ref.

Outlaw Robin Hood. Moses Goldberg. (J). 1967. 6.00 (*0-87602-168-2*) Anchorage.

Outlaw Roundup. large type ed. Bradford Scott. (Linford Western Library). 304p. 1994. pap. 16.99 (*0-7089-7500-3*, Linford) Ulverscroft.

***Outlaw School.** Rebecca Ore. 320p. 2000. pap. 13.50 (*0-380-79250-8*, Avon Bks) Morrow Avon.

Outlaw Sprint Car Racer. John Gerber. LC 98-145922. (Illus.). 256p. 1997. 22.50 (*0-9627653-9-2*) Witness Prods.

Outlaw Tales: Legends, Myths, & Folklore from America's Middle Border. Ed. by Judy D. Young & Richard Young. 224p. 1992. pap. 10.95 (*0-87483-195-4*) August Hse.

Outlaw Tales of Montana. Gary A. Wilson. LC 95-61348. (Illus.). 240p. (Orig.). 1995. pap. 16.95 (*0-9632240-0-X*) High-Line Bks.

Outlaw Thanksgiving. Emily Arnold McCully. LC 97-29553. (Illus.). (J). (gr. k-3). 1998. 15.99 (*0-8037-2197-8*, Dial Yng Read) Peng Put Young Read.

***Outlaw Thanksgiving.** Emily Arnold McCully. (Illus.). 40p. (J). (gr. k-3). 2000. pap. 6.99 (*0-14-056768-2*, PuffinBks) Peng Put Young Read.

***Outlaw Town.** Luke Adams. (Apache Law Ser.: Vol. 3). 176p. 2000. mass mkt. 3.99 (*0-8439-4732-2*, Leisure Bks) Dorchester Pub Co.

***Outlaw Trail.** Jason Manning. 240p. 2000. mass mkt. 5.99 (*0-312-97569-4*) St Martin.

Outlaw Trail: A History of Butch Cassidy & His Wild Bunch. Charles Kelly. LC 95-50396. (Illus.). xxiii, 398p. 1996. pap. 15.00 (*0-8032-7778-4*, Bison Books) U of Nebr Pr.

***Outlaw Trail: Butch Cassidy & the Wild Bunch.** Charles Kelly. 374p. 1999. reprint ed. 7.98 (*1-56852-242-8*) W S Konecky Assocs.

Outlaw Valley. large type ed. Evan Evans, pseud. LC 92-18522. (Nightingale Ser.). 344p. 1992. pap. 14.95 (*0-8161-5601-8*, G K Hall Lrg Type) Mac Lib Ref.

Outlaw Valley. Max Brand. Date not set. reprint ed. lib. bdg. 22.95 (*0-89190-205-8*, Am Repr) Amereon Ltd.

Outlaw Viking. Sandra Hill. 448p. (Orig.). 1998. mass mkt. 5.50 (*0-505-52273-X*, Love Spell) Dorchester Pub Co.

Outlaw Visions. Ed. by Tony Cohan & Gordon Beam. LC 77-80089. (Illus.). 1977. 11.00 (*0-918226-05-8*); pap. 9.95 (*0-918226-04-X*) Acrobat.

***Outlaw Voices.** Arthur Winfield Knight. 40p. 2000. pap. 4.95 (*0-9647373-7-X*) Marimbo Commun.

Outlaw Wife. Ana Seymour. 1997. per. 4.99 (*0-373-28977-4*, 1-28977-6) Harlequin Bks.

Outlaw with a Star. David Austin. 256p. 1999. 5.99 (*0-425-16817-4*) Berkley Pub.

Outlaw Women. J. R. Roberts. (Gunsmith Ser.: No. 134). 192p. (Orig.). 1993. mass mkt. 3.99 (*0-515-11045-0*, Jove) Berkley Pub.

Outlaw Years: The History of the Land Pirates of the Natchez Trace. Robert M. Coates. LC 85-31811. (Illus.). 360p. reprint ed. pap. 111.60 (*0-608-20014-X*, 207129000010) Bks Demand.

Outlawed! B. J. Daniels. LC 96-3685. (Intrigue Ser.). 251p. 1996. per. 3.50 (*0-373-22353-6*, 1-22353-6) Harlequin Bks.

Outlawed. large type ed. Ray Hogan. LC 96-30309. 1996. 21.95 (*0-7838-1908-0*, G K Hall Lrg Type) Mac Lib Ref.

Outlawed Party: Social Democracy in Germany, 1878-1890. Vernon L. Lidtke. LC 66-14311. 388p. reprint ed. 120.30 (*0-8357-9506-3*, 201148000078) Bks Demand.

Outlawing the Spoils: A History of the Civil Service Movement, 1865-1883. Ari A. Hoogenboom. LC 82-11507. 306p. 1982. reprint ed. lib. bdg. 65.00 (*0-313-22821-3*, HOOS, Greenwood Pr) Greenwood.

Outlawry of War: A Constructive Policy for World Peace. Charles C. Morrison. LC 71-147607. (Library of War & Peace; Kellogg Pact & the Outlawry of War). 1972. lib. bdg. 46.00 (*0-8240-0367-5*) Garland.

***Outlawry of War: A Series of Lectures Delivered Before the Academy of International Law at the Hague & in the Institut Universitaire de Hautes Etudes Internationales at Geneva.** Hans Wehberg. LC 99-44893. 2000. write for info. (*1-57588-576-X*) W S Hein.

Outlaws. Charles L. Convis. (True Tales of the Old West Ser.: Vol. 11). ii, 62p. 1999. pap. 7.95 (*1-892156-01-6*, Pub. by Pioneer Pr NV) Sunbelt Pubns.

Outlaws. Tim Green. 1997. mass mkt. 5.99 (*0-614-27747-7*, Harp PBks) HarpC.

Outlaws. Tim Green. 496p. 1999. mass mkt. 6.99 (*0-446-60635-9*, Pub. by Warner Bks) Little.

Outlaws. George V. Higgins. 1988. mass mkt. 4.95 (*0-8217-3194-7*, Zebra Kensgtn) Kensgtn Pub Corp.

***Outlaws.** Wayne D. Overholser. LC 00-23521. 208p. 2000. 30.00 (*0-7862-2102-X*) Mac Lib Ref.

Outlaws. Paul Thomas. LC 96-52430. (Rebels with a Cause Ser.). (Illus.). 48p. (J). 1998. lib. bdg. 24.97 (*0-8172-4658-4*) Raintree Steck-V.

Outlaws. Kenneth Ulyatt. LC 77-10127. (Illus.). 128p. (J). (gr. 4-8). 1978. 11.95 (*0-397-31773-5*) HarpC Child Bks.

Outlaws. large type ed. 2001. 30.00 (*0-7862-2124-0*) Mac Lib Ref.

Outlaws. Ernst Von Salomon. Tr. by I. F. Morrow from GER. (History of Political Violence Ser.). 1985. reprint ed. lib. bdg. 60.00 (*0-527-41202-3*) Periodicals Srv.

***Outlaws: Rafe.** Connie Mason. (Outlaws Ser.). 400p. 2000. mass mkt. 5.99 (*0-8439-4702-0*, Leisure Bks) Dorchester Pub Co.

Outlaws: The Illustrated History of the James-Younger Gang. Marley Brant. LC 95-46715. (Illus.). 220p. 1997. 29.95 (*1-880216-36-1*, Elliott Clark) Black Belt Communs.

Outlaws: The Official Strategy Guide. Rick Barba. LC 96-70481. 264p. 1997. pap., per. 19.99 (*0-7615-0939-9*) Prima Pub.

Outlaws: The Search for Butch & Sundance. Eamonn P. O'Neill. (Illus.). 256p. 1998. 29.95 (*1-85158-931-7*, Pub. by Mainstream Pubng) Trafalgar.

Outlaws All. Max Brand. 272p. 1998. reprint ed. mass mkt. 4.50 (*0-8439-4398-X*, Leisure Bks) Dorchester Pub Co.

Outlaws All: A Western Trio. large type ed. Max Brand. LC 95-47325. (West-Hall Ser.). 362p. 1997. lib. bdg. 22.95 (*0-7838-1575-1*, G K Hall Lrg Type) Mac Lib Ref.

Outlaws All: A Western Trio. large type ed. Max Brand. (Five-Star Western Ser.). 1996. 16.95 (*0-7862-0592-X*) Thorndike Pr.

Outlaws & Blues Queens, Tricksters & Gods: The Melting Pot of Myth, Legend & Folklore in America. David Leeming & Jake Page. LC 97-48607. (Illus.). 240p. 1999. 25.00 (*0-19-511783-2*) OUP.

Outlaws & Gunfighters of the Old West. Phillip W. Steele. LC 98-2613. 124p. 1998. pap. 8.95 (*1-56554-137-5*) Pelican.

Outlaws & Heroes, 3 bks. in 1. John Johnston et al. 1995. per. 4.99 (*0-373-83311-3*) Harlequin Bks.

***Outlaws & Lawmen of the American West.** M. A. Macpherson. 232p. 2000. pap. 10.95 (*1-55105-164-8*) Lone Pine.

Outlaws & Lawmen of the Wild West Series, 10 bks., Set. Carl R. Green & William R. Sanford. (Illus.). (J). (gr. 4-10). 1992. lib. bdg. 150.50 (*0-89490-391-8*) Enslow Pubs.

***Outlaws & Lawmen of Western Canada.** (Illus.). 1998. pap. text. write for info. (*0-919214-52-5*, Heritage Hse) Cottage Pr MA.

***Outlaws & Lawmen of Western Canada, Vol. 1.** Heritage House, Inc. Staff. (Illus.). 128p. 1999. reprint ed. pap. 9.95 (*1-895811-79-1*) Heritage Hse.

Outlaws & Lawmen of Western Canada, Vol. 2. (Illus.). 128p. 1996. reprint ed. pap. 10.95 (*0-919214-54-1*) Heritage Hse.

Outlaws & Lawmen of Western Canada, Vol. 3. (Illus.). 160p. 1994. reprint ed. pap. 11.95 (*0-919214-88-6*) Heritage Hse.

Outlaws & Lovers. Kathleen Korbel et al. 1996. per. 5.99 (*0-373-20126-5*, 1-20126-8) Harlequin Bks.

Outlaws & Outcasts. Compiled by Jerry Silverman. (Traditional Black Music Ser.). (Illus.). 72p. (YA). (gr. 5 up). 1995. lib. bdg. 15.95 (*0-7910-1835-0*) Chelsea Hse.

***Outlaw's Bride.** Liz Ireland. (Historical Ser.: No. 498). 2000. per. 4.99 (*0-373-29098-5*, 1-29098-0, Harlequin) Harlequin Bks.

Outlaw's Bride. Joan Johnston. 416p. 1993. mass mkt. 6.99 (*0-440-21278-2*) Dell.

Outlaw's Code. Max Brand. 210p. Date not set. reprint ed. lib. bdg. 20.95 (*0-89190-206-6*, Am Repr) Amereon Ltd.

Outlaw's Fortune. W. W. Lee. LC 92-44495. 154p. 1993. 19.95 (*0-8027-1270-3*) Walker & Co.

Outlaws, Heroes & Jokers of the Old Southwest. Peter R. Odens. (Illus.). 77p. 1975. reprint ed. pap. 5.00 (*0-9609484-6-5*) P R Odens.

Outlaws in Petticoats. Ann Ruff. (Women of the West Ser.). 1995. pap. 12.95 (*1-55622-315-3*, Rep of TX Pr) Wordware Pub.

Outlaws in the Big Thicket. Wanda A. Landrey. 128p. 1979. pap. 12.95 (*0-89015-144-X*) Sunbelt Media.

Outlaw's Lady. Bobbi Smith. 400p. 1998. mass mkt. 5.99 (*0-8439-4383-1*, Leisure Bks) Dorchester Pub Co.

Outlaw's Lady. Scotney St. James. 384p. 1996. mass mkt. 4.99 (*0-8217-5319-3*) Kensgtn Pub Corp.

***Outlaws, Mobsters & Crooks, 3 vols.** LC 98-14861. 495p. (J). 1998. text 84.00 (*0-7876-2803-4*, 00158547, UXL) Gale.

Outlaws, Mobsters & Crooks: From the Old West to the Internet. Marie J. Macnee & Jane Hoehner. LC 98-14861. (J). 1998. 84.00 (*0-7876-2806-9*, UXL) Gale.

Outlaws, Mobsters & Crooks: From the Old West to the Internet. Marie J. MacNee & Janes Hoehner. LC 98-14861. (J). 1998. 84.00 (*0-7876-2804-2*, UXL); pap. 84.00 (*0-7876-2805-0*, UXL) Gale.

Outlaws of Cave-in-Rock. Otto A. Rothert. LC 70-140371. (Select Bibliographies Reprint Ser.). 1977. 22.95 (*0-8369-5614-1*) Ayer.

Outlaws of Cave-in-Rock. Otto A. Rothert. (Shawnee Classics Ser.). (C). 1995. pap. 12.95 (*0-8093-2034-7*) S Ill U Pr.

Outlaws of Country. Friedman-Fairfax & Sony Music Staff. (CD Ser.). 1995. pap. 16.98 incl. audio compact disk (*1-56799-128-9*, Friedman-Fairfax) M Friedman Pub Grp Inc.

***Outlaws of Medieval Legend.** Maurice Keen. (Illus.). 280p. 2000. pap. 17.95 (*0-415-23900-1*) Routledge.

***Outlaws of Medieval Legend.** Maurice Keen. (Illus.). 280p. 2000. 65.00 (*0-415-23650-9*) Routledge.

Outlaws of Medieval Legend. Maurice H. Keen. 258p. (C). 1987. pap. 15.95 (*0-7102-1203-8*, Routledge Thoemms) Routledge.

Outlaws of Mesquite: Frontier Stories. Louis L'Amour. 240p. 1990. mass mkt. 4.50 (*0-553-28714-1*) Bantam.

Outlaws of Mesquite: Frontier Stories. Louis L'Amour. 1990. 9.09 (*0-606-04997-5*, Pub. by Turtleback) Demco.

Outlaws of New Mexico: A Guide. Peter Hertzog. LC 83-18301. 48p. (Orig.). 1984. pap. 4.95 (*0-86534-039-0*) Sunstone Pr.

Outlaws of Ravenhurst. M. Imelda Wallace, Sr. (Illus.). (J). (gr. 6-10). 1950. 12.95 (*0-910334-25-0*); pap. 5.95 (*0-910334-26-9*) Neumann Pr.

Outlaws of Ravenhurst. M. Imelda Wallace. (Illus.). 232p. (YA). (gr. 5 up). 1996. reprint ed. 19.00 (*0-911845-32-1*) Neumann Pr.

Outlaws of Sherwood. Robin Mckinley. 1989. mass mkt. 5.99 (*0-441-64451-1*) Ace Bks.

Outlaws of Sherwood. Robin Mckinley. LC 88-45227. 256p. (J). (ps-3). 1988. 17.00 (*0-688-07178-3*, Grenwillow Bks) HarpC Child Bks.

***Outlaws of the Canadian West.** M. A. Macpherson. 232p. 1999. pap. 11.95 (*1-55105-166-4*) Lone Pine.

Outlaws of the Marsh, 3 vols. Shi Nai'an & Lo Kuan-Chung. 1650p. 1993. pap. 39.95 (*7-119-01662-8*, Pub. by Foreign Lang) China Bks.

Outlaws of the Marsh. abr. ed. Shi Nai'an & Lo Kuan-Chung. Tr. by Sidney Shapiro. 458p. 1991. pap. 19.99 (*962-07-1067-3*, Pub. by Commercial Pr) Cheng & Tsui.

Outlaws of the Old West. C. W. Breihan. 22.95 (*0-8488-0223-3*) Amereon Ltd.

***Outlaws of the Pacific Northwest.** Bill Gulick. Ed. by Wayne Cornell. LC 99-57972. (Illus.). 216p. 2000. pap. 18.95 (*0-87004-396-X*, 0396X0) Caxton.

Outlaws of the Purple Cow & Other Stories. Lester Goran. LC 99-13044. 358p. 1999. pap. 35.00 (*0-87338-639-6*) Kent St U Pr.

***Outlaws of the Sea: 3000 Years of Piracy.** Konemann Inc. Staff. (Illus.). 2000. pap. 19.95 (*3-8290-4850-5*) Konemann.

Outlaws on Horseback: The History of the Organized Bands of Bank & Train Robbers Who Terrorized the Prairie Towns of Missouri, Kansas, Indian Territory, & Oklahoma for Half a Century. Harry S. Drago. LC 97-32634. (Illus.). xxix, 328p. 1998. pap. 15.00 (*0-8032-6612-X*, Bison Books) U of Nebr Pr.

Outlaws on Parnassus. Margaret Kennedy. LC 73-121484. (Essay Index Reprint Ser.). 1977. 20.95 (*0-8369-1968-8*) Ayer.

Outlaws, Renegades & Saints: Diary of a Mixed-Up Halfbreed. Tiffany Midge. 1996. pap. 12.95 (*0-912678-93-3*) Greenfld Rev Lit.

Outlaw's Tale. Margaret Frazer. 224p. (Orig.). 1995. mass mkt. 5.99 (*0-425-15119-0*) Berkley Pub.

Outlaws Three. Peter Field. LC 77-2903. (Powder Valley Western Ser.). 322p. (J). 1977. write for info. (*0-89340-072-6*) Chivers N Amer.

Outlaw's Wife: Outlaw Hearts. Cindy Gerard. (Desire Ser.: No. 1175). 1998. per. 3.75 (*0-373-76175-9*, 1-76175-8) Harlequin Bks.

Outlaw's Woman. large type ed. Bret Rey. (Linford Western Library Ser.). 208p. 1997. pap. 16.99 (*0-7089-5152-X*) Ulverscroft.

Outlearning the Wolves: Surviving & Thriving in a Learning Organization. 2nd ed. David Hutchens. LC 97-53299. (Illus.). 68p. 1998. pap. 19.95 (*1-883823-24-2*, FT004) Pegasus Comm.

***Outlet Bound: Guide to the Nations Best Outlets.** 10th rev. ed. Randy Marks. (Illus.). 200p. 1999. pap. 9.95 (*0-9631319-9-0*) Outlet Mktg.

Outlet Boxes & Fittings for Use in Hazardous (Classified) Locations, UL 886. 10th ed. (C). 1994. pap. text 135.00 (*1-55989-522-5*) Underwrtrs Labs.

Outlet Report. Elysa Lazar. 1992. pap. 9.95 (*1-881642-01-1*) Lazar Comms.

Outlet Shopper: A Guide to Factory Outlet Shopping in Pennsylvania, Maryland, Virginia & the District of Columbia. 2nd ed. Carolyn V. Benson. Ed. by Nancy C. Modrak. (Illus.). 192p. 1990. pap. 9.95 (*0-915168-20-0*) Wash Bk Trad.

Outlets: Poems from Hollywood. Mark Dunster. 11p. 1998. pap. 5.00 (*0-89642-504-5*) Linden Pubs.

Outliers in Statistical Data. 3rd ed. Vic Barnett & Toby Lewis. 604p. 1994. 195.00 (*0-471-93094-6*) Wiley.

Outline Alphabets: One Hundred Complete Fonts. Dan X. Solo. 104p. 1988. pap. 8.95 (*0-486-25824-6*) Dover.

Outline & Annotated Bibliography of Chinese Philosophy. Wing-Tsit Chan. 1961. 14.95 (*0-88710-055-4*) Yale Far Eastern Pubns.

Outline & General Principles of the History of Life: University of California Syllabus Series, Vol. 213. William D. Matthew. Ed. by Stephen Jay Gould. LC 79-8335. (History of Paleontology Ser.). (Illus.). 1980. reprint ed. lib. bdg. 24.95 (*0-405-12719-7*) Ayer.

Outline & Manual of Logic. rev. ed. Joseph McLaughlin. 165p. (C). 1994. pap. 15.00 (*0-87462-401-0*) Marquette.

Outline & Syllabus for Music Theory. Ed. by John W. Verrall. iv, 30p. (Orig.). (C). 1965. pap. 4.95 (*0-87015-132-0*) Pacific Bks.

Outline Constitutional Law. America's Bar Review Staff. (C). 1995. pap. text 12.95 (*1-879563-21-5*) Lexicon CA.

Outline Contracts. America's Bar Review Staff. (C). 1995. pap. text 12.95 (*1-879563-22-3*) Lexicon CA.

Outline Criminal Law. America's Bar Review Staff. (C). 1995. pap. text 9.95 (*1-879563-23-1*) Lexicon CA.

Outline Criminal Procedure. America's Bar Review Staff. (C). 1995. pap. text 9.95 (*1-879563-24-X*) Lexicon CA.

Outline Dialectic, 2 vols., Vol.2. Thomas T. Sekine. LC 97-11879. 1997. text 130.00 (*0-312-17558-2*) St Martin.

Outline Dictionary of Maya Glyphs. William Gates. LC 77-92481. (Illus.). 204p. 1978. reprint ed. pap. 7.95 (*0-486-23618-8*) Dover.

Outline Evidence. America's Bar Review Staff. (C). 1995. pap. text 12.95 (*1-879563-25-8*) Lexicon CA.

Outline for a Metaphysics of Mind. Canyn L. Whals. (Illus.). 147p. (Orig.). (C). 1991. pap. text 12.00 (*0-9629846-0-4*) Walsh Pub NY.

Outline for Economic Evaluation of Steam Valley Preservation. Benjamin H. Stevens & Robert E. Coughlin. (Discussion Papers: No. 10). 1966. pap. 10.00 (*1-55869-088-3*) Regional Sci Res Inst.

Outline for Methods in Search for Legal Authorities. 16p. write for info. (*0-318-59781-0*) West Pub.

Outline for Online Ready Reference Services: Occasional Paper, No. 3. Ed. by Susan J. Beck. (C). 1989. pap. text 12.00 (*0-8389-7317-5*) ALA.

Outline for the Study of Calculus, Vol. 2. 6th ed. Leithold & Minnick. 400p. (C). 1997. pap. 33.00 (*0-06-044547-5*) Addison-Wesley.

***Outline for the Study of Primitive Peoples in North, Central, & South America.** Paul Honigsheim. (LC History-America-E). 1999. reprint ed. lib. bdg. 69.00 (*0-7812-4260-6*) Rprt Serv.

Outline Guide to Chinese Herbal Patent Medicines in Pill Form - with Sample Pictures of the Boxes: An Introduction to Chinese Herbal Medicines. 2nd ed. Margaret A. Naeser. LC 90-80264. (Illus.). 372p. (Orig.). 1990. pap. 34.95 (*0-9625651-1-3*) Boston Chinese Med.

Outline Guide to Shakespeare. Paul Kaufman. 1972. 59.95 (*0-8490-0786-0*) Gordon Pr.

Outline History - American Jazz. David Sharp et al. 160p. (C). 1996. pap. text, spiral bd. 43.95 (*0-7872-0407-2*) Kendall-Hunt.

Outline History of American Drama. 2nd ed. Walter J. Meserve. 416p. 1996. reprint ed. pap. 19.95 (*0-937657-18-2*) Feedbk Theabks & Prospero.

Outline History of American Jazz. 2nd ed. David E. Sharp et al. LC 98-150882. 172p. 1997. per. 69.95 (*0-7872-2790-0*, 41279001) Kendall-Hunt.

Outline History of an Expedition to California: Containing the Fate of the Get All You Can Mining Association. Peter Browning. LC 99-19022. (Illus.). 48p. 1999. reprint ed. 8.95 (*0-944220-09-6*) Great West Bks.

Outline History of Greek Religion. Lewis R. Farnell. 160p. (Orig.). 1986. pap. 15.00 (*0-89005-025-2*) Ares.

Outline History of Hong Kong. Liu Shuyong. 290p. 1997. pap. 14.95 (*7-119-01946-5*, Pub. by Foreign Lang) China Bks.

Outline History of Japanese Drama. Frank A. Lombard. LC 68-717. (Studies in Drama: No. 39). 1969. reprint ed. lib. bdg. 75.00 (*0-8383-0585-7*) M S G Haskell Hse.

Outline History of Rock & Roll. Randall Snyder. 84p. (C). 1996. spiral bd. 21.95 (*0-7872-2178-3*) Kendall-Hunt.

Outline History of Rock & Roll. 2nd ed. Randall Snyder. 112p. (C). 1997. per. 38.95 (*0-7872-4294-2*, 41429401) Kendall-Hunt.

Outline History of Spanish American Literature. 4th ed. John E. Englekirk et al. 1981. pap. text 15.95 (*0-89197-326-5*) Irvington.

Outline History of the Fine Arts. Benson J. Lossing. (Notable American Authors Ser.). 1999. reprint ed. lib. bdg. 125.00 (*0-7812-3857-9*) Rprt Serv.

Outline History of the Glen Canyon Region, 1776-1922. C. Gregory Crampton. (Glen Canyon Ser.: No. 9). reprint ed. 32.50 (*0-404-60642-3*) AMS Pr.

Outline History of the Greek Language. Procope S. Costas. LC 97-177918. 143p. 1997. pap. 20.00 (*0-89005-259-X*) Ares.

Outline History of the Japanese Drama. Frank A. Lombard. (Illus.). 356p. (C). 1996. reprint ed. text 65.00 (*0-7007-0265-2*, Pub. by Curzon Pr Ltd) UH Pr.

Outline History of Western Music. 8th ed. Milo Wold et al. 320p. (C). 1993. per. write for info. (*0-697-12504-1*) Brown & Benchmark.

Outline History West Music. 9th ed. Wold. LC 96-79545. 1997. 25.74 (*0-697-34056-2*, McGrw-H College) McGrw-H Hghr Educ.

Outline Maps - The U. S. 1998. 4.95 (*1-55708-208-1*, MCR657) McDonald Pub Co.

Outline Maps - The World. 1993. 4.95 (*1-55708-209-X*, MCR658) McDonald Pub Co.

Outline Maps on File. Facts on File Staff. (Illus.). 276p. 1997. pap. 165.00 (*0-8160-3476-1*) Facts on File.

Outline of a Jungian Aesthetics. Morris H. Philipson. LC 63-15299. 224p. reprint ed. pap. 69.50 (*0-608-11192-9*, 200688400060) Bks Demand.

Outline of a Labor Cost System in an Average Clothing Factory. 11p. 1954. 5.00 (*0-318-19659-X*) Clothing Mfrs.

O

An Asterisk (*) at the beginning of an entry indicates that the title is appearing for the first time.

Outline of a New Philosophy. Daniel Greenberg. 463p. (Orig.). 1974. pap. 30.00 (*1-888947-17-9*) Sudbury Valley.

Outline of a Nominalist Theory of Propositions: An Essay in the Theory of Meaning & in the Philosophy of Logic. Paul Gochet. Tr. by Margareth Jackson & Anthony Dale from FRE. (Synthese Library: No. 98). 217p. 1980. text 126.50 (*90-277-1031-7*, D Reidel) Kluwer Academic.

Outline of a Phenomenology of Right. Alexandre Kojeve. Tr. by Bryan-Paul Frost et al. 600p. 2000. 50.00 (*0-8476-8922-0*) Rowman.

Outline of a Semantic Theory of Kernel Sentences. Emanuel Vasiliu. (Janua Linguarum, Ser. Major: No. 71). 219p. 1972. text 66.15 (*90-279-2240-3*) Mouton.

Outline of a Theory of Practice. Pierre Bourdieu. LC 76-11073. (Cambridge Studies in Social & Cultural Anthropology: No. 16). (Illus.). 224p. 1977. pap. text 21.95 (*0-521-29164-X*) Cambridge U Pr.

Outline of Administrative Responsibilities in a Hebrew Day School. 1997. pap. 1.00 (*0-914131-47-8*, C250) Torah Umesorah.

Outline of American Government: The Continuing Experiment. Barbara Hinckley. (Illus.). 288p. 1981. pap. 24.85 (*0-13-645200-0*) P-H.

Outline of an Anarchistic Theory of Knowledge. 1991. lib. bdg. 77.95 (*0-8490-4650-5*) Gordon Pr.

Outline of an Anglican Life: Lessons in the Faith & Practice of the Anglican Church. 3rd ed. Louis R. Tarsitano. 1994. pap. 9.95 (*0-9644227-0-0*) Inscription Pub.

Outline of Ancient Greek Coins. Zander Klawans. (Illus.). 210p. 1982. reprint ed. pap. 15.00 (*0-915262-70-3*) S J Durst.

Outline of Ancient History to A. D. 180. Mary A. Hamilton & Alfred W. Blunt. LC 85-21883. (Illus.). 193p. 1986. reprint ed. lib. bdg. 59.75 (*0-8371-7627-1*, HAOA, Greenwood Pr) Greenwood.

***Outline of Anglo-Saxon Law.** Harry F. Barrell. 84p. 1999. reprint ed. 30.00 (*1-56169-545-9*) Gaunt.

Outline of Animal Development. Richard Davenport. LC 78-62548. (Life Sciences Ser.). (Illus.). 1979. text. write for info. (*0-201-01814-4*) Addison-Wesley.

Outline of Arabic Contributions to Medicine. Amin Khairallah. 1946. 12.00 (*0-86685-345-6*) Intl Bk Ctr.

Outline of at Anatomy, with Reference to the Human. abr. ed. Stephen G. Gilbert. LC 99-14036. (Illus.). 96p. 2000. pap. text 10.00 (*0-295-97818-X*) U of Wash Pr.

Outline of Austrian Constitutional Law. Kurt Heller. 70p. 1989. 45.50 (*90-6544-404-1*) Kluwer Law Intl.

Outline of Basic Verb Inflections of Oklahoma Cherokee. Charles D. Van Tuyl. 79p. (Orig.). (C). 1994. pap. text 12.00 (*0-940392-07-0*) Indian U Pr OK.

Outline of Bible History & Major Christian Movements. Michael L. Wilson. 1974. pap. 4.95 (*0-88027-014-4*) Firm Foun Pub.

Outline of Booth's Chart of the Ages. R. P. Daniel. pap. 3.25 (*0-88172-018-6*) Believers Bkshelf.

Outline of Buddhism. William Stoddart. 140p. 2000. pap. 11.95 (*0-9629984-4-3*, Pub. by Foun Trad Studies) Kazi Pubns.

Outline of Business Management. J. P. Bose. (C). 1989. 35.00 (*0-89771-435-0*, Pub. by Current Dist) St Mut.

Outline of Chinese Acupuncture. Academy of Traditional Chinese Medicine, Shanghai. 305p. 17.50 (*0-317-31550-1*) Chans Corp.

Outline of Christian Worship. Gordon S. Wakefield. 256p. 1998. 47.95 (*0-567-08610-0*, Pub. by T & T Clark) Bks Intl VA.

Outline of Classical Chinese Grammar. Edwin G. Pulleyblank. LC 95-173932. 206p. 1996. pap. 36.95 (*0-7748-0541-2*, PL1101, Pub. by UBC Pr) U of Wash Pr.

Outline of Classical Origins: Rome. Thomas J. Corcoran. (Illus.). 77p. 5.75 (*0-939507-10-2*, B305) Amer Classical.

Outline of Clinical Diagnosis. Brian J. Prout & John G. Cooper. 264p. 1987. pap. text 39.00 (*0-7506-2106-0*) Buttrwrth-Heinemann.

Outline of Clinical Diagnosis. 2nd ed. Brian J. Prout & J. G. Cooper. (Illus.). 280p. 1987. pap. 18.00 (*0-318-35047-5*) Mosby Inc.

Outline of Clinical Diagnosis in the Horse. Date not set. pap. 59.95 (*0-8464-4164-0*) Beekman Pubs.

Outline of Clinical Diagnosis in the Horse. 2nd ed. P. J. Pinsent & C. J. Fuller. LC 96-52363. (Illus.). 202p. 1997. pap. 41.95 (*0-632-04136-8*) Blackwell Sci.

Outline of Confucianism. Don Y. Lee. LC 85-80477. 113p. (C). 1984. 29.50 (*0-939758-10-5*) Eastern Pr.

Outline of Confucianism. rev. ed. Don Y. Lee. LC 85-80477. (C). 1988. 33.50 (*0-939758-16-4*) Eastern Pr.

Outline of Contemporary American & British Literature. Max J. Herzberg. 1972. 59.95 (*0-8490-0787-9*) Gordon Pr.

Outline of Contemporary Drama. Thomas H. Dickinson. LC 70-88059. 1969. reprint ed. 32.00 (*0-8196-0249-3*) Biblo.

Outline of Contract Law in Australia. 2nd ed. J. W. Carter. LC 94-169166. 328p. 1994. pap. 54.00 (*0-409-30278-3*, Austral, MICHIE) LEXIS Pub.

Outline of Copyright Law. Richard C. De Wolf. xxiv, 330p. 1986. reprint ed. 42.50 (*0-8377-2030-3*, Rothman) W S Hein.

Outline of CTRON. Ed. by TRON Association Staff. (Original CTRON Specification Ser.: Vol. 1). xii, 208p. (gr. 12). 1988. pap. 65.00 (*4-274-07471-4*, Pub. by IOS Pr) IOS Press.

***Outline of Cultural Anthropology.** 174p. (C). 2000. per. 29.95 (*0-7872-7275-2*) Kendall-Hunt.

Outline of Cultural Anthropology. 2nd ed. (C). 1986. write for info. (*0-8087-5911-6*) Pearson Custom.

Outline of Cultural Materials. 5th rev. ed. George P. Murdock et al. LC 81-83836. (HRAF Manuals Ser.). 273p. 1982. pap. 25.00 (*0-87536-654-6*) HRAFP.

Outline of Dahomean Religious Belief. Melville Jean Herskovits & Frances S. Herskovits. LC 34-5259. (American Anthropological Association Memoirs Ser.). 1933. 25.00 (*0-527-00540-1*) Periodicals Srv.

Outline of Employment Law. N. L. Wallace-Bruce. 320p. 1994. pap. 59.00 (*0-409-30892-7*, Austral, MICHIE) LEXIS Pub.

Outline of English Literature. 2nd ed. Ed. by Pat Rogers. LC 98-17245. (Illus.). 528p. 1998. pap. 15.95 (*0-19-288078-0*) OUP.

Outline of English Literature. 2nd ed. Thornley & Roberts. 1985. pap. text. write for info. (*0-582-74917-4*, Pub. by Addison-Wesley) Longman.

Outline of Equity & Trusts. 2nd ed. M. Evans. 506p. 1993. pap. 66.00 (*0-409-30381-X*, Austral, MICHIE) LEXIS Pub.

Outline of Equity & Trusts. 3rd ed. M. Evans. 506p. 1996. pap. write for info. (*0-409-31138-3*, MICHIE) LEXIS Pub.

Outline of Esoteric Science. Rudolf Steiner. Tr. by Catherine Creeger from GER. LC 97-37188. (Classics in Anthroposophy). 436p. 1997. pap. 19.95 (*0-88010-409-0*, 1898) Anthroposophic.

Outline of European History: From 1789 to 1989. Ed. by Sergio Romano. Tr. by Lynn Gunzberg from ITA. LC 98-27407.Tr. of Disegno Della Storia D'Europa pal 1789 al 1989. 192p. (C). 1998. 39.95 (*1-57181-076-5*) Berghahn Bks.

Outline of Foreign Policy for the United States. Edgar E. Foster. 1949. 14.00 (*0-912314-02-8*); pap. 5.80 (*0-912314-01-X*) Academy Santa Clara.

Outline of Forensic Dentistry. Ed. by James A. Cottone & S. Miles Standish. LC 81-24081. 179p. reprint ed. pap. 55.50 (*0-608-15905-0*, 203084000071) Bks Demand.

Outline of Fractures. 10th ed. John C. Adams & David L. Hamblen. (Illus.). 302p. 1992. pap. text 49.95 (*0-443-04371-X*) Church.

Outline of Fractures, Including Joint Injuries. 11th ed. John C. Adams & David L. Hamblen. LC 98-32447. 1999. write for info. (*0-443-06027-4*) Church.

Outline of French Grammar with Vocabularies. rev. ed. Henry B. Richardson. (FRE.). 1950. text 15.50 (*0-89197-327-3*) Irvington.

Outline of Hawaiian Physical Therapeutics. E. S. Handy et al. (BMB Ser.: No. 126). 1974. reprint ed. 25.00 (*0-527-02232-2*) Periodicals Srv.

Outline of Hindi Grammar. R. C. McGregor. (ENG & HIN.). 1991. 29.95 (*0-8288-8467-6*, F29977) Fr & Eur.

Outline of Hindi Grammar: With Exercises. 3rd ed. R. S. McGregor. (Illus.). 336p. 1995. pap. text 29.95 (*0-19-870008-3*) OUP.

Outline of Hindi Grammar: With Exercises. 3rd ed. R. S. McGregor. (Illus.). 320p. 1996. pap. 49.95 incl. audio (*0-19-870009-1*); text 70.00 (*0-19-870007-5*) OUP.

Outline of Hinduism. F. H. Smith. 1972. 59.95 (*0-8490-0788-7*) Gordon Pr.

Outline of Hinduism. William Stoddart. (Illus.). 128p. (Orig.). 1993. pap. 10.95 (*0-9629984-1-9*) Foun Trad Studies.

Outline of History, 4 vols. H. G. Wells. 1920. reprint ed. 250.00 (*0-403-03082-X*) Somerset Pub.

Outline of History of Saiva Philosophy. K. C. Pandey. Ed. by R. C. Dwivedi. 278p. 1986. 14.95 (*0-317-60575-5*, Pub. by Motilal Bnarsidass) S Asia.

Outline of History of Saiva Philosophy. Kanti C. Pandey. Ed. by R. C. Dwivedi. 300p. 1986. reprint ed. 20.00 (*81-208-0091-5*, Pub. by Motilal Bnarsidass) S Asia.

Outline of Indian Culture. A. S. Ray. 112p. 1978. 8.95 (*0-318-36962-1*) Asia Bk Corp.

Outline of Indian Philosophy. J. N. Sinha. (C). 1989. 35.00 (*0-89771-449-0*, Pub. by Current Dist) St Mut.

Outline of Indian Philosophy. A. K. Warder. 261p. 1971. 11.95 (*0-318-37027-1*) Asia Bk Corp.

Outline of Indian Philosophy. A. K. Warder. 262p. 1986. 15.95 (*81-208-0083-4*, Pub. by Motilal Bnarsidass) S Asia.

Outline of J. R. Kantor's Psychological Linguistics. Sidney W. Bijou & Patrick M. Ghezzi. 79p. (C). 1994. student ed. 12.95 (*1-878978-11-X*) Context Pr.

Outline of Japanese Economic History, 1603-1940: Major Works & Research Findings. Ed. by Mikio Sumiya & Koji Taira. LC 79-670232. 386p. reprint ed. pap. 119.70 (*0-7837-6270-4*, 204598200010) Bks Demand.

Outline of Jungian Aesthetics. Morris H. Philipson. 1991. pap. 18.95 (*0-938434-88-8*) Sigo Pr.

Outline of Law & Procedure in Representation Cases, 2 vols. 1997. lib. bdg. 605.95 (*0-8490-7688-9*) Gordon Pr.

***Outline of Law & Procedure in Representation Cases.** John E. Higgins. 507p. 1998. per. 34.00 (*0-16-061842-8*) USGPO.

***Outline of Law & Procedure in Representation Cases.** John E. Higgins. 384p. 2000. ring bd. 43.00 (*0-16-050195-4*) USGPO.

Outline of Law & Procedure in Representation Cases: (Basic Manual) December 1992, & Supplement February 1994. Contrib. by National Labor Relations Board Staff. 521p. 1994. ring bd. 25.00 (*0-16-043141-7*) USGPO.

Outline of Madhva Philosophy. K. Narain. 241p. 1986. 39.95 (*0-318-37015-8*) Asia Bk Corp.

Outline of Manx Language & Literature. Adrian Pilgrim. 1985. pap. 9.95 (*0-89979-064-X*) British Am Bks.

Outline of Mathematical Logic: Fundamental Results & Notions Explained with All Details. A. Grzegorczyk. LC 72-97956. (Synthese Library: No. 70). 606p. 1974. text 206.50 (*90-277-0359-0*, D Reidel); pap. text 86.00 (*90-277-0447-3*) Kluwer Academic.

Outline of Medical Imaging, 2 vols., Set. Louis Kreel & Anna Thornton. (Illus.). 1276p. 1995. 435.00 (*0-7506-0219-8*) Buttrwrth-Heinemann.

Outline of Middle English Grammar. Margaret M. Roseborough. LC 70-109833. 112p. 1970. reprint ed. lib. bdg. 35.00 (*0-8371-4324-1*, ROMI, Greenwood Pr) Greenwood.

Outline of Mineralogy & Geology: Intended for the Use of Those Who May Desire to Become Acquainted with the Elements of Those Sciences. William R. Phillips. Ed. by Claude C. Albritton, Jr. LC 77-6536. (History of Geology Ser.). (Illus.). 1978. reprint ed. lib. bdg. 19.95 (*0-405-10456-1*) Ayer.

***Outline of My Lover: A Novel.** Douglas A. Martin. 166p. 2000. pap. 12.00 (*1-887128-47-6*) Soft Skull Pr.

Outline of Neurology. Christopher D. Ward. (John Wright Outline Ser.). (Illus.). 208p. 2000. pap. text. write for info. (*0-7506-1407-2*) Buttrwrth-Heinemann.

Outline of New Developments since the Writing of HUD Housing Programs: Tenants Rights, 1985 Supplement. National Housing Law Project Staff. 42p. 1987. pap. 4.50 (*0-685-23181-X*, 41,125) NCLS Inc.

Outline of 19th Century. Lorenz E. Eitner. LC 92-21788. 720p. 1992. pap. 40.00 (*0-06-430223-7*, Perennial) HarperTrade.

Outline of Occult Science (1922) Rudolf Steiner. 400p. 1998. reprint ed. pap. 24.95 (*0-7661-0163-0*) Kessinger Pub.

***Outline of Opthalmology.** Roger L. Coakes & Patrick Holmes Sellors. (Illus.). 192p. 2000. pap. 40.00 (*0-7506-4460-5*) Buttrwrth-Heinemann.

Outline of Orthopaedics. 10th ed. John C. Adams. LC 85-14924. (Illus.). 514p. reprint ed. pap. 159.40 (*0-8357-4655-0*, 203758700008) Bks Demand.

Outline of Orthopaedics. 12th ed. John C. Adams & David L. Hamblen. LC 95-6579. 1995. text 28.95 (*0-443-05149-6*) Church.

***Outline of Peridontics.** B. M. Manson & J. D. Eley. (Illus.). 405p. 1999. pap. text 60.00 (*0-7236-1070-3*) Buttrwrth-Heinemann.

Outline of Periodontics. 3rd ed. J. D. Manson & B. M. Eley. LC 95-7449. 320p. 1995. pap. text 60.00 (*0-7236-1018-5*) Buttrwrth-Heinemann.

Outline of Phanerozoic Biogeography. A. Hallam. (Oxford Biogeography Ser.: No. 10). (Illus.). 256p. (C). 1995. text 82.00 (*0-19-854061-2*); pap. text 37.95 (*0-19-854060-4*) OUP.

Outline of Philosophy. Bertrand Russell. 264p. (C). 1996. 60.00 (*0-415-14030-7*); pap. 17.99 (*0-415-14117-6*) Routledge.

Outline of Projective Geometry. Lynn E. Garner. 220p. 1981. 53.25 (*0-444-00423-8*) P-H.

Outline of Prophesy. Roger P. Daniel. 54p. (Orig.). 1990. pap. 3.95 (*0-88172-151-4*) Believers Bkshelf.

Outline of Psychoanalysis. rev. ed. Sigmund Freud. Ed. & Tr. by James Strachey. 1989. reprint ed. pap. 7.95 (*0-393-00151-2*) Norton.

Outline of Psychology. Edward B. Titchener. 370p. 100.00 (*1-85506-685-8*) Thoemmes Pr.

Outline of Psychotherapy for Medical Students & Practitioners. Harold Maxwell. 107p. 1986. text 27.50 (*0-7236-0849-0*) Buttrwrth-Heinemann.

Outline of Roman Law. John S. Muirhead. LC 97-74173. 199p. 1997. reprint ed. 66.00 (*1-56169-323-5*, 14644) Gaunt.

Outline of Sanity: A Biography of G. K. Chesterton. Alzina S. Dale. LC 82-11452. 376p. reprint ed. pap. 116.60 (*0-608-17707-5*, 203006300067) Bks Demand.

Outline of Scientific Writing: For Researchers with English As a Foreign Language. Jen Tsi Yang. Ed. by Janet N. Yang. LC 95-44681. 200p. 1995. 24.00 (*981-02-2466-4*) World Scientific Pub.

Outline of Set Theory. J. M. Henle. (Problem Books in Mathematics). (Illus.). 130p. 1986. 49.95 (*0-387-96368-5*) Spr-Verlag.

Outline of Sexology. 112p. (Orig.). (C). 1993. pap. 29.95 (*0-9635611-0-3*) Am Board Sex.

Outline of Statistical Methods for Use in the Textile Industry. 9th ed. A. Brearley & T. Cox. 1980. 60.00 (*0-7855-1020-6*) St Mut.

Outline of Statistical Methods for Use in the Textile Industry. 9th ed. Wira Staff. (C). 1980. 125.00 (*0-900820-00-4*, Pub. by British Textile Tech) St Mut.

Outline of Statutory Provisions Controlling Purchasing for North Carolina Local Governments. rev. ed. Warren J. Wicker & Frayda S. Bluestein. 15p. (C). 1996. pap. text 8.00 (*1-56011-285-9*) Institute Government.

Outline of Strategy. William C. Waddell. 150p. 1986. pap. 19.95 (*0-912841-22-2*) Planning Forum.

Outline of Stratificational Grammar. Sydney M. Lamb & Leonard E. Newell. LC 66-28562. (Illus.). 115p. reprint ed. pap. 35.70 (*0-7837-6331-X*, 204604400010) Bks Demand.

Outline of Succession. K. Mackie & M. Burton. LC 95-135572. 300p. 1994. pap. write for info. (*0-409-30491-3*, MICHIE) LEXIS Pub.

Outline of Swine Diseases: A Handbook. Ross P. Cowart. LC 95-22163. 152p. 1995. pap. text 24.95 (*0-8138-2899-6*) Iowa St U Pr.

Outline of the Activity of Listening. 3rd ed. Franklin H. Ernst, Jr. 1973. pap. 3.95 (*0-916944-09-3*) Addressoset.

Outline of the Bible: Book by Book. Benson Y. Landis. (Illus.). 192p. (Orig.). 1994. pap. 14.00 (*0-06-463263-6*, EH 263, Harper Ref) HarpC.

Outline of the Bible: Why the Religious Right Can't Call Itself Christian. Herb Doylesmith. LC 95-79025. 100p. (Orig.). 1995. pap. 18.95 (*0-9647891-5-9*) A Denburn Pubng.

Outline of the Book of Concord. Lyle W. Lange. LC 94-67906. 136p. 1994. 19.99 (*0-8100-0538-7*, 15N2047) Northwest Pub.

Outline of the Book of Nehemiah. H. Smith. pap. 4.95 (*0-88172-125-5*) Believers Bkshelf.

Outline of the Dialectic of Capital, Vol. I. Thomas T. Sekine. LC 97-11879. 196p. 1997. text 65.00 (*0-312-17559-0*) St Martin.

Outline of the Documentary History of the Zuni Tribe: Somatological Observations of Indians of the Southwest. Adolph F. Bandelier & Herman F. Ten Kate. LC 76-21219. (Journal of American Ethnology & Archaeology: Vol. 3). reprint ed. 47.50 (*0-404-58043-2*) AMS Pr.

Outline of the Grammar of the Dialect of West Somerset . . . Frederic T. Elworthy. (English Dialect Society Publications: No. 19). 1974. reprint ed. pap. 25.00 (*0-8115-0449-2*) Periodicals Srv.

Outline of the History of Christian Literature. George Hurst. 1977. lib. bdg. 69.95 (*0-8490-2395-5*) Gordon Pr.

Outline of the History of Economic Thought. Ernesto Screpanti & Stefano Zamagni. Tr. by David Field. (Illus.). 452p. 1995. pap. text 24.00 (*0-19-877455-9*) OUP.

Outline of the History of Music. Karl Nef. (Music Book Index Ser.). 400p. 1992. reprint ed. lib. bdg. 89.00 (*0-7812-9483-5*) Rprt Serv.

Outline of the History of Phytopathology. Herbert H. Whetzel. Ed. by Frank N. Egerton, 3rd. LC 77-74256. (History of Ecology Ser.). 1978. reprint ed. lib. bdg. 17.95 (*0-405-10425-1*) Ayer.

Outline of the History of the Arctic & Boreal Biota During the Quaternary Period. Eric Hulten. (Illus.). 1972. reprint ed. 56.00 (*3-7682-0006-X*) Lubrecht & Cramer.

Outline of the History of the Flaming Gorge Area. William M. Purdy. (Upper Colorado Ser.: No. 1). reprint ed. 20.00 (*0-404-60637-7*) AMS Pr.

Outline of the Law of Agency. 3rd ed. Basil S. Markesinis & R. J. Munday. 338p. 1992. pap. 32.00 (*0-406-00145-6*, UK, MICHIE) LEXIS Pub.

Outline of the Law of Contract. 4th ed. Guenter H. Treitel. 1989. pap. 39.00 (*0-406-66849-3*, UK, MICHIE) LEXIS Pub.

Outline of the Law of Partnership. Stephen Graw. LC 95-178119. 150p. 1994. text 30.00 (*0-455-21269-4*, Pub. by LawBk Co) Gaunt.

Outline of the Phonology & Morphology of Old Provencal. Charles H. Grandgent. LC 72-1627. reprint ed. 37.50 (*0-404-08348-X*) AMS Pr.

Outline of the Powers & Duties of Justices of the Peace in Queensland. 7th ed. T. R. Hartigan & F. N. Albietz. xxiv, 245p. 1987. pap. 32.00 (*0-455-20751-8*, Pub. by LawBk Co) Gaunt.

Outline of the Rise & Progress of Freemasonry in Louisiana. James Scot. 134p. 1995. reprint ed. pap. 21.00 (*1-887560-00-9*) M Poll Pub.

Outline of the Science of Political Economy (1836) With Appendices. Nassau W. Senior. LC 65-16991. (Reprints of Economic Classics Ser.). xii, 249p. 1965. reprint ed. 35.00 (*0-678-00077-8*) Kelley.

Outline of the Structure of Shila. Joseph R. Applegate. LC 58-13941. viii, 71p. (C). 1971. reprint ed. pap. 3.00 (*0-87950-252-5*) Spoken Lang Serv.

Outline of the Structure of the Pipe Organ. William H. Clarke. (Illus.). 1977. reprint ed. pap. text 18.00 (*0-913746-09-6*) Organ Lit.

Outline of the System of Education at New Lanark. Robert D. Owen. (Notable American Authors Ser.). 1999. reprint ed. lib. bdg. 125.00 (*0-7812-4680-6*) Rprt Serv.

Outline of Theatre Law. Milton C. Jacobs. LC 72-5454. xii, 148p. 1972. reprint ed. lib. bdg. 59.50 (*0-8371-6436-2*, JATL, Greenwood Pr) Greenwood.

Outline of Theosophy. Charles W. Leadbeater. 1994. pap. 6.50 (*81-7059-073-6*) Theos Pub Hse.

Outline of Theosophy (1915) C. W. Leadbeater. 100p. 1996. reprint ed. pap. 14.95 (*1-56459-940-X*) Kessinger Pub.

Outline of Torts. D. G. Gardiner. 440p. 1992. pap. 66.00 (*0-409-30308-9*, Austral, MICHIE) LEXIS Pub.

Outline of Torts. 2nd ed. D. G. Gardiner. 400p. 1996. pap. write for info. (*0-409-31023-9*, MICHIE) LEXIS Pub.

Outline of Trade Practices & Consumer Protection Law. 2nd ed. A. Hurley & G. Wiffen. 344p. 1994. pap. 58.00 (*0-409-30850-1*, Austral, MICHIE) LEXIS Pub.

Outline of Transportation - Related Requirements for Compliance with the Clean Air Act Amendments of 1990. Amy Stephenson & George B. Dresser. (Illus.). 64p. (C). 1998. pap. text 20.00 (*0-7881-4940-7*) DIANE Pub.

Outline of World Cultures. 6th rev. ed. George P. Murdock. LC 83-80510. (HRAF Manuals Ser.). 259p. 1983. pap. 25.00 (*0-87536-664-3*) HRAFP.

Outline of World History: For Boys & Girls. H. C. Knapp-Fisher. (J). 25.00 (*0-8196-2798-4*) Biblo.

Outline Property. America's Bar Review Staff. (C). 1995. pap. text 12.95 (*1-879563-26-6*) Lexicon CA.

Outline Sociological Theory. Lawrence Sneden. 136p. (C). 1995. pap. text, per. 23.95 (*0-7872-0976-7*, 41097601) Kendall-Hunt.

Outline Student Calculus, Vol. 3. 6th ed. Leithold & Minnick. (C). 1997. pap. 31.00 (*0-06-044548-3*) Addison-Wesley.

Outline Studies in Acts. Robert Lee. LC 87-3083. 128p. 1987. reprint ed. pap. 5.99 (*0-8254-3141-7*) Kregel.

Outline Studies in Christian Doctrine. George P. Pardington. 370p. 1926. pap. 11.99 (*0-87509-116-4*) Chr Pubns.

Outline Studies in Galatians. Robert Lee. LC 87-3096. 128p. 1987. reprint ed. pap. 5.99 (*0-8254-3143-3*) Kregel.

Outline Studies in John. Robert Lee. LC 87-3623. 144p. 1987. reprint ed. pap. 5.99 (*0-8254-3140-9*) Kregel.

O

Outline Studies in Luke. W. Griffith Thomas. LC 84-784. 406p. (C). 1984. reprint ed. pap. 12.99 (*0-8254-3821-7*, Kregel Class) Kregel.

Outline Studies in Romans. Robert Lee. LC 87-3094. 112p. 1987. reprint ed. pap. 5.99 (*0-8254-3142-5*) Kregel.

Outline Studies of the Tabernacle. Ada R. Habershon. LC 73-85298. 64p. 1974. pap. 5.99 (*0-8254-2820-3*, Kregel Class) Kregel.

Outline Study of Law. 2nd ed. Isaac F. Russell. LC 97-28836. xii, 280p. 1997. reprint ed. 45.00 (*0-8377-2584-4*, Rothman) W S Hein.

Outline Talks for Teens see Bosquejos de Sermones Para la Juventud

Outline Talks for Teens. Charles R. Wood. LC 83-25543. (Easy-to-Use Sermon Outline Ser.). 64p. 1984. pap. 4.99 (*0-8254-4024-6*) Kregel.

Outline to Accompany Atkins. Beran. (C). 1990. 12.00 (*0-7167-2116-3*) W H Freeman.

Outline Torts. America's Bar Review Staff. (C). 1995. pap. text 9.95 (*1-879563-27-4*) Lexicon CA.

Outlined Bible. Robert Lee. 1982. mass mkt. 14.99 (*0-310-44821-2*, 10465P) Zondervan.

Outlines. Hopkins. Date not set. pap. text. write for info. (*0-582-01664-9*, Pub. by Addison-Wesley) Longman.

Outlines. Carol Montgomery. (Illus.). 32p. 1990. 35.00 (*0-934714-21-5*); pap. 3.00 (*0-934714-20-7*) Swamp Pr.

Outlines American History, 1. 3rd ed. A. C. Wotherspoon. 1998. pap. 25.00 (*0-07-230067-1*) McGraw.

Outlines & Stitches: A Guide to Design. Pat Earnshaw. (Illus.). 106p. (C). 1992. 65.00 (*0-9513891-4-9*, Pub. by Gorse) Lacis Pubns.

Outlines for Commitment: From Herzl to Balfour & Wilson. Aaron Klieman. LC 90-13805. (American Zionism Ser.: Vol. 2). 424p. 1991. reprint ed. text 55.00 (*0-8240-7350-9*) Garland.

Outlines for Evangelism see Bosquejos para Evangelizar

Outlines for Study Groups. Theorectical Studies Committee. write for info. (*0-318-61183-X*) Natl Lawyers Guild.

Outlines in Irish History: Eight Hundred Years of Struggle. Seamus P. Metress. LC 95-67850. 180p. (Orig.). 1995. pap. 8.95 (*0-9651836-0-2*) Connolly Bks.

Outlines in Local Color. Brander Matthews. LC 76-98584. (Short Story Index Reprint Ser.). 1977. 20.95 (*0-8369-3158-0*) Ayer.

Outlines in Pathology. John H. Sinard. Ed. by Bill Schmitt. 256p. 1996. pap. text 44.00 (*0-7216-6341-9*, W B Saunders Co) Harcrt Hlth Sci Grp.

Outlines in Roman History. William C. Morey. 1972. 59.95 (*0-8490-0789-5*) Gordon Pr.

Outlines of a Course of Lectures on History. Andrew D. White. (Notable American Authors Ser.). 1999. reprint ed. lib. bdg. 125.00 (*0-7812-9931-4*) Rprt Serv.

Outlines of a Critical Theory of Ethics. John Dewey. LC 71-92299. 253p. 1969. reprint ed. lib. bdg. 35.00 (*0-8371-2707-6*, DETE, Greenwood Pr) Greenwood.

Outlines of a Cultural Strategy. Taha J. Alwani. LC 95-195124. (Occasional Papers: No. 1). 32p. 1989. pap. 4.00 (*0-912463-58-9*) IIIT VA.

Outlines of a Philosophy of Art. Robin George Collingwood. 1988. reprint ed. lib. bdg. 49.00 (*0-7812-0127-6*) Rprt Serv.

Outlines of a Philosophy of Art. Robin George Collingwood. LC 25-26891. 104p. 1925. reprint ed. 39.00 (*0-403-07231-X*) Somerset Pub.

Outlines of a Philosophy of Art, 1925. R. G. Collingwood. (Key Texts Ser.). 110p. 1996. reprint ed. pap. 15.00 (*1-85506-316-6*) Bks Intl VA.

Outlines of a System of Political Economy. Thomas Joplin. LC 68-30530. (Reprints of Economic Classics Ser.). xxii, 463p. 1970. reprint ed. 57.50 (*0-678-00590-7*) Kelley.

Outlines of a Theory of the Light Sense. Ewald Hering. Tr. by Leo M. Hurvich & Dorothea Jameson. LC 64-11130. 349p. reprint ed. pap. 108.20 (*0-7837-2273-7*, 205736100004) Bks Demand.

Outlines of Aesthetics. Rudolf Hermann Lotze. 1973. 59.95 (*0-8490-0790-9*) Gordon Pr.

Outlines of Buddhism: A Historical Sketch. C. Rhys Davids. LC 78-72412. reprint ed. 18.50 (*0-404-17276-8*) AMS Pr.

Outlines of Buddhism: A Historical Sketch. Caroline A. Davids. 126p. 1934. reprint ed. text 22.00 (*0-685-13700-7*) Coronet Bks.

Outlines of Chinese Art. John C. Ferguson. LC 70-37879. (Select Bibliographies Reprint Ser.). 1977. 23.95 (*0-8369-6716-X*) Ayer.

Outlines of Chinese Symbolism & Art Motives. C. A. Williams. LC 76-40397. (Illus.). 472p. 1976. pap. 10.95 (*0-486-23372-3*) Dover.

Outlines of Classification & Special Morphology of Plants. K. Goebel. 515p. 1984. pap. 175.00 (*0-7855-0384-6*, Pub. by Intl Bks & Periodicals) St Mut.

Outlines of Cosmic Philosophy. John Fiske. (Notable American Authors Ser.). 1992. reprint ed. lib. bdg. 75.00 (*0-7812-2841-7*) Rprt Serv.

Outlines of Criminal Procedure. R. V. Kelkar. 692p. 1984. 225.00 (*0-7855-1326-4*) St Mut.

Outlines of Economic History in the 19th Century. G. Dropper. 1977. lib. bdg. 59.95 (*0-8490-2396-3*) Gordon Pr.

Outlines of Economic Theory. Herbert J. Davenport. LC 67-29500. (Reprints of Economic Classics Ser.). xxi, 381p. 1968. reprint ed. 45.00 (*0-678-00389-0*) Kelley.

Outlines of English Law. S. B. Marsh & J. Soulsby. 304p. 1982. write for info. (*0-07-084655-3*) McGraw.

Outlines of Entomology. 7th ed. R. G. Davies. (Illus.). 350p. (gr. 13). 1988. pap. text 46.95 (*0-412-26680-6*) Chapman & Hall.

Outlines of Historical Jurisprudence, 2 vols. Paul Vinogradoff. LC 74-177869. reprint ed. 34.50 (*0-404-06784-0*) AMS Pr.

Outlines of Historical Jurisprudence, 2 vols., Set. Paul Vinogradoff. LC 94-75663. 768p. 1994. reprint ed. 185.00 (*1-56169-085-6*) Gaunt.

Outlines of Historical Jurisprudence, 1920, 2 vols. Paul Vinogradoff. LC 98-42298. 428, x, 315p. 1999. reprint ed. 150.00 (*1-886363-64-1*) Lawbk Exchange.

Outlines of History of the Territory of Dakota: And Emigrant's Guide to the Free Lands of the Northwest. James S. Foster. LC 77-165632. (Select Bibliographies Reprint Ser.). 1977. reprint ed. 16.95 (*0-8369-5939-6*) Ayer.

Outlines of Imperfect & Disordered Mental Action. Thomas C. Upham. LC 73-2426. (Mental Illness & Social Policy; the American Experience Ser.). 1973. reprint ed. 28.95 (*0-405-05235-9*) Ayer.

Outlines of Indian Philology, ISSP Vol. 1, No. 2. John Beams. 50p. 1974. reprint ed. 10.00 (*0-88065-053-2*) Scholarly Pubns.

Outlines of Indian Philosophy. M. Hiriyanna. (C). 1994. reprint ed. pap. 15.00 (*81-208-1086-4*, Pub. by Motilal Bnarsidass) S Asia.

Outlines of Law. Edwin E. Bryant. vi, 415p. 1987. reprint ed. 45.00 (*0-8377-1945-3*, Rothman) W S Hein.

Outlines of Literature, English & American. Truman Backus. 1972. 250.00 (*0-8490-0791-7*) Gordon Pr.

Outlines of Medieval History. 2nd ed. Charles W. Previte-Orton. LC 64-25837. 1916. 30.00 (*0-8196-0147-0*) Biblo.

Outlines of Modern Chinese Law. William S. Hung. LC 76-20212. (Studies in Chinese Government & Law). 317p. 1976. reprint ed. lib. bdg. 69.50 (*0-313-26978-5*, U6978, Greenwood Pr) Greenwood.

Outlines of Modern Geography on a New Plan. Charles A. Goodrich. (Notable American Authors Ser.). 1992. reprint ed. lib. bdg. 75.00 (*0-7812-2931-6*) Rprt Serv.

Outlines of Muhammadan Law. 4th ed. Asaf A. Fyzee. (Illus.). 544p. 1993. text 24.00 (*0-19-560375-3*) OUP.

Outlines of Muhammadan Law. 4th ed. Ed. by Asaf A. Fyzee. (Illus.). 540p. 1999. pap. text 19.95 (*0-19-564814-5*) OUP.

Outlines of Musical Bibliography: A Catalogue of Early Music & Musical Works Printed or Otherwise Produced in the British Isles. Andrew Deakin. 112p. reprint ed. lib. bdg. 48.50 (*3-487-05925-8*) G Olms Pubs.

Outlines of Ornament in the Leading Styles see Designs & Patterns from Historic Ornament

Outlines of Our Warm Bodies. Pat Jasper. 85p. 1990. pap. 7.95 (*0-86492-120-9*, Pub. by Goose Ln Edits) Genl Dist Srvs.

Outlines of Paint Technology. 3rd ed. W. M. Morgans. 503p. 1990. 275.00 (*0-470-21654-9*) Wiley.

Outlines of Polish History. Roman Dyboski. LC 78-24236. 285p. 1979. reprint ed. lib. bdg. 65.00 (*0-313-20831-X*, DYOP, Greenwood Pr) Greenwood.

Outlines of Political Economy. John McVickar. LC 64-22240. (Reprints of Economic Classics Ser.). vi, 242p. 1965. reprint ed. 45.00 (*0-678-00118-9*) Kelley.

Outlines of Psychology. Harald Hoffding. 381p. 100.00 (*1-85506-670-X*) Thoemmes Pr.

Outlines of Psychology. Oswald Kulpe. 480p. 120.00 (*1-85506-682-3*) Thoemmes Pr.

Outlines of Psychology. Rudolf Hermann Lotze. 173p. 55.00 (*1-85506-668-8*) Thoemmes Pr.

Outlines of Psychology. Wilhelm M. Wundt. 364p. 100.00 (*1-85506-686-6*) Thoemmes Pr.

Outlines of Psychology. Rudolf Hermann Lotze. LC 73-2974. (Classics in Psychology Ser.). 1978. reprint ed. 16.95 (*0-405-05147-6*) Ayer.

Outlines of Psychology. Wilhelm M. Wundt. 1897. reprint ed. 39.00 (*0-403-00038-6*) Scholarly.

Outlines of Psychology, 6. Rudolf Hermann Lotze. Tr. by George T. Ladd from GER. LC 77-72191. (Contributions to the History of Psychology Ser.: Vol. 6, Pt. A, Orientations). 454p. 1977. reprint ed. lib. bdg. 79.50 (*0-313-26930-0*, U6930, Greenwood Pr) Greenwood.

Outlines of Psychology: An Elementary Treatise, with Some Practical Applications. Josiah Royce. LC 75-3334. reprint ed. 41.50 (*0-404-59337-2*) AMS Pr.

Outlines of Psychology: Based Upon the Results of Experimental Investigation. Oswald Kulpe. LC 73-2970. (Classics in Psychology Ser.). 1977. reprint ed. 31.95 (*0-405-05142-5*) Ayer.

Outlines of Pyrrhonism. Sextus Empiricus. Tr. by R. G. Bury. LC 89-64198. (Great Books in Philosophy). 283p. (C). 1990. reprint ed. pap. 8.95 (*0-87975-597-0*) Prometheus Bks.

Outlines of Roman Law: Comprising Its Historical Growth & General Principles. 4th ed. William C. Morey. xiii, 433p. 1985. reprint ed. 45.00 (*0-8377-0851-6*, Rothman) W S Hein.

Outlines of Roman Law: Consisting Chiefly of an Analysis & Summary of the Institutes. T. Whitcombe Greene. LC 93-79696. 252p. 1994. reprint ed. 60.00 (*1-56169-054-6*) Gaunt.

Outlines of Romantic Theology: With Which Is Reprinted, Religion & Love in Dante: the Theology of Romantic Love. Charles Williams. Ed. by Alice M. Hadfield. LC 90-40135. 127p. 1990. reprint ed. pap. 39.40 (*0-7837-8097-4*, 204785100008) Bks Demand.

Outlines of Russian Culture: The Origins of Ideology. Paul N. Miliukov. Tr. by Joseph L. Wieczynski from RUS. LC 74-81632. (Russian Ser.: Vol. 19, Pt. 1). 1974. 24.50 (*0-87569-056-4*) Academic Intl.

Outlines of Scepticism. Sextus Empiricus. Ed. by Julia Annas & Jonathan Barnes. 267p. (C). 1994. pap. text 18.95 (*0-521-31206-X*) Cambridge U Pr.

Outlines of Shakespeare's Plays. rev. ed. Homer A. Watt et al. LC 57-8496. 240p. (Orig.). (C). 1971. pap. 13.00 (*0-06-460025-4*, CO 25) HarpC.

Outlines of Sociology. Ludwig Gumplowicz. Tr. by Frederick W. Moore. LC 74-25755. (European Sociology Ser.). 234p. 1975. reprint ed. 24.95 (*0-405-06509-4*) Ayer.

Outlines of Sociology. Ludwig Gumplowicz. LC 78-62687. (Social Science Classics Ser.). 336p. 1980. reprint ed. 39.95 (*0-87855-309-6*); reprint ed. pap. text 24.95 (*0-87855-693-1*) Transaction Pubs.

Outlines of the Anthropology of the Timor Archipelago. Hendricus J. Bijlmer. LC 77-87480. (Illus.). reprint ed. 48.00 (*0-404-16697-0*) AMS Pr.

Outlines of the Catholic Faith see Katolikus Hit Elemei

Outlines of the Chief Camp Diseases of the United States Armies. Joseph Woodward. (American Civil War Medical Ser.: No. 11). 364p. 1991. reprint ed. 65.00 (*0-930405-43-9*) Norman SF.

Outlines of the Geography of Plants: Native Country, the Culture, & the Uses of the Principal Cultivated Plants on Which the Prosperity of Nations Is Based. Franz J. Meyen, 3rd. Ed. by Frank N. Egerton. LC 77-74239. (History of Ecology Ser.). 1978. reprint ed. lib. bdg. 39.95 (*0-405-10408-1*) Ayer.

Outlines of the Geology of England & Wales: General Principles of That Science, & Comparative Views of the Structure of Foreign Countries. W. D. Conybeare & William R. Phillips. Ed. by Claude C. Albritton, Jr. LC 77-6516. (History of Geology Ser.). 1978. reprint ed. lib. bdg. 41.95 (*0-405-10438-3*) Ayer.

Outlines of the History of Botany. Robert J. Harvey-Gibson. Ed. by I. Bernard Cohen. LC 80-2128. (Development of Science Ser.). (Illus.). 1981. lib. bdg. 27.95 (*0-405-13877-6*) Ayer.

Outlines of the History of English & American Law. William F. Walsh. xiv, 533p. 1995. reprint ed. 57.50 (*0-8377-2778-2*, Rothman) W S Hein.

Outlines of the History of Ethics. Henry Sidgwick. LC 88-10986. (HPC Classics Ser.). 312p. (C). 1988. reprint ed. pap. 7.95 (*0-87220-060-4*); reprint ed. lib. bdg. 24.95 (*0-87220-061-2*) Hackett Pub.

Outlines of the History of Ethics, 1886. Henry Sidgwick. (Key Texts Ser.). 310p. 1996. reprint ed. pap. 19.95 (*1-85506-220-8*) Bks Intl VA.

Outlines of the History of Greek Philosophy. Eduard Zeller. 352p. 1980. reprint ed. text 8.95 (*0-486-23920-9*) Dover.

Outlines of the History of Greek Philosophy. rev. ed. Eduard Zeller. Tr. by L. P. Palmer. (Key Texts Ser.). 340p. 1998. pap. 22.00 (*1-85506-545-2*) Thoemmes Pr.

Outlines of the History of the English Language. Ernest Classen. LC 79-95091. 283p. 1970. reprint ed. lib. bdg. 65.00 (*0-8371-2547-2*, CLEL, Greenwood Pr) Greenwood.

Outlines of the Life of Shakespeare, 2 vols. James O. Halliwell-Phillips. 1973. 200.00 (*0-8490-0793-3*) Gordon Pr.

Outlines of the Life of Shakespeare. James O. Halliwell-Phillipps. LC 17-10828. reprint ed. 67.50 (*0-404-03084-X*) AMS Pr.

Outlines of the Literary History of Colonial Pennsylvania. M. Katherine Jackson. LC 71-170835. reprint ed. 35.00 (*0-404-03542-6*) AMS Pr.

Outlines of the Philosophy of Aristotle. 4th ed. Compiled by Edwin S. Wallace. LC 75-13300. (History of Ideas in Ancient Greece Ser.). 1976. reprint ed. 12.95 (*0-405-07343-7*) Ayer.

Outlines of the Science of Jurisprudence: An Introduction to the Systematic Study of Law. Ed. & Tr. by W. Hastie. (GER.). xliv, 282p. 1982. reprint ed. 39.00 (*0-8377-0642-4*, Rothman) W S Hein.

Outlines of Theology. A. A. Hodge. 1983. 27.99 (*0-85151-160-0*) Banner of Truth.

Outlines of Tudor & Stuart Plays, 1497-1642. Karl J. Holznecht. 1988. reprint ed. lib. bdg. 99.00 (*0-7812-0061-X*) Rprt Serv.

Outlines of Tudor & Stuart Plays, 1497-1642. Karl J. Holznecht. reprint ed. 69.00 (*0-403-04196-1*) Somerset Pub.

Outlines of Zuni Creation Myths. Frank H. Cushing. LC 74-7947. reprint ed. 42.50 (*0-404-11834-8*) AMS Pr.

Outlines on the Holy Spirit. Croft M. Pentz. (Sermon Outline Ser.). 64p. 1978. pap. 4.99 (*0-8010-7029-5*) Baker Bks.

Outlines on the New Testament. C. W. Keiningham. (Sermon Outline Ser.). 64p. 1989. pap. 4.99 (*0-8010-5279-3*) Baker Bks.

Outlines on the Parables of Jesus. Croft M. Pentz. (Sermon Outline Ser.). 48p. 1980. pap. 4.99 (*0-8010-7055-4*) Baker Bks.

***Outlines on the Science of Jurisprudence: An Introduction to the Systematic Study of Law.** W. Hastie. xliv, 282p. 2000. reprint ed. 98.00 (*1-56169-603-X*) Gaunt.

Outlining Goes Electronic. Jonathan Price. LC 98-51776. (ATTW Contemporary Studies in Technical Communications). 1999. pap. write for info. (*1-56750-379-9*) Ablx Pub.

***Outlining Goes Electronic.** Jonathan Price. LC 98-51776. (ATTW Contemporary Studies in Technical Communications). 1999. 63.50 (*1-56750-378-0*) Ablx Pub.

Outlive Your Enemies. Terry Sanford. LC 95-46575. 157p. 1996. 23.95 (*1-56072-289-4*); pap. 17.45 (*1-56072-278-9*, Nova Kroshka Bks) Nova Sci Pubs.

Outliving the Self: Generativity & the Interpretation of Lives. John N. Kotre. LC 84-47950. 295p. reprint ed. pap. 91.50 (*0-608-06073-9*, 206640500008) Bks Demand.

***Outlook: The Complete Reference 2000.** C. Michael Woodward. (Complete Reference Ser.). (Illus.). 2000. pap. 39.99 (*0-07-212436-9*) McGraw.

Outlook & Insight. 4th ed. Paul A. Eschholz. 1994. pap. text, teacher ed. 5.00 (*0-312-10111-2*) St Martin.

Outlook Annoyances. Woody Leonhard et al. Ed. by Ron Petrusha. (Illus.). 400p. 1998. pap. 24.95 (*1-56592-384-7*) OReilly & Assocs.

Outlook Express - Win 95/NT. (Quick Study Computer Ser.). 4p. pap. 2.95 (*1-57222-279-4*) Barcharts.

Outlook for American Prose. Joseph W. Beach. LC 68-22901. (Essay Index Reprint Ser.). 1977. 20.95 (*0-8369-0179-7*) Ayer.

Outlook for American Prose. Joseph W. Beach. (BCL1-PS American Literature Ser.). 284p. 1992. reprint ed. lib. bdg. 79.00 (*0-7812-6635-1*); reprint ed. lib. bdg. 79.00 (*0-7812-6639-4*) Rprt Serv.

Outlook for Commercial Aircraft, 1991-2010. (Illus.). 61p. (Orig.). (C). 1992. pap. text 30.00 (*0-941375-97-8*) DIANE Pub.

Outlook for Commercial Supersonic & Hypersonic Transport Aircraft. (Transportation Research Circular Ser.: No. 333). 91p. 1988. 7.00 (*0-685-38573-6*) Transport Res Bd.

Outlook for Fiber in Business & Residential Applications International. 1996. pap. 1995.00 (*1-56851-135-3*, IGIC48) Info Gatekeepers.

Outlook for International Bank Lending. Capital Movements & the Growth of International Indebtedness Study Group Staff. (Report Ser.). 51p. 1981. pap. 10.00 (*1-56708-054-5*) Grp of Thirty.

Outlook for Japanese & German Future Technology: Comparing Technology Forecast Survey. K. Cuhls & Takeo Kuwahara. (Technology, Innovation, & Policy Ser: Vol. 1). 238p. 1994. 68.95 (*3-7908-0800-8*) Spr-Verlag.

Outlook for Literature. Ashley H. Thorndike. (Essay Index Reprint Ser.). 1977. 18.95 (*0-8369-1235-7*) Ayer.

Outlook for Managed Care, 1998: The National Picture. Efrem Sigel & Jondavid Klipp. 100p. 1997. 895.00 (*0-9662321-0-0*) Corp Res Grp.

Outlook for Mineral Commodities. R. H. Carnegie. (Report Ser.). 39p. 1986. pap. 10.00 (*1-56708-068-5*) Grp of Thirty.

Outlook for Mining Equipment. L. Levine. 308p. 1997. 1995.00 (*0-945235-55-0*) Lead Edge Reports.

Outlook for New Developments in the Machine Tool Industry. E. F. DuBrul. (Technical Papers: Vol. P74). (Illus.). 7p. 1930. pap. text 30.00 (*1-55589-151-9*) AGMA.

Outlook for Oil & Gas to 2010. (Illus.). 118p. (Orig.). (C). 1992. pap. text 40.00 (*0-941375-55-2*) DIANE Pub.

Outlook for State Spending & Revenues in the Late '80's. Billy Hamilton. Ed. by Steve Pejovich & Henry Dethloff. (Series on Public Issues: No. 19). 14p. 1985. pap. 2.00 (*0-86599-055-7*) PERC.

Outlook for Television. Orrin E. Dunlap, Jr. 1977. 23.95 (*0-405-03564-0*, 11231) Ayer.

***Outlook for the California Economy: Summer, 1999.** Stephen Levy. 60p. 1999. 75.00 (*1-878316-39-7*) CCSCE.

Outlook for the Forest & Forest Products Sector of the U. S. S. R. 105p. 32.00 (*92-1-116459-1*, E.89.II.E.24) UN.

Outlook for United States Agricultural Exports. Government Printing Office Staff. pap. 8.00 (*0-16-009389-9*, Agriculture Dept) USGPO.

Outlook for U.S.-China Relations Following the 1997-1998 Summits: Chinese & American Perspectives on Security, Trade & Cultural Exchange. Ed. by Peter Koehn & Joseph T. Cheng. (Illus.). 428p. (C). text 44.50 (*962-201-881-5*, Pub. by Chinese Univ) U of Mich Pr.

Outlook for Water: Quality, Quantity, & National Growth. Nathaniel Wollman & Gilbert W. Bonem. LC 75-149243. 286p. 1971. 30.00 (*0-8018-1260-7*) Resources Future.

***Outlook 98.** ENI Publishing Ltd. Staff. (Pasaporte Ser.). 2000. pap. text 15.95 (*2-7460-0103-9*); pap. text 7.95 (*2-7460-0109-8*) ENI Publng.

Outlook 98: Byte by Bite. Glenda L. Friesen. (Byte by Bite Ser.). 65p. 1998. pap. 10.00 (*1-891412-12-4*) Training Solut.

Outlook 98 Fast & Easy. Donna Payne & Payne Consulting Group. LC 97-76319. (Fast & Easy Ser.). 336p. 2000. pap. 16.99 (*0-7615-1405-8*) Prima Pub.

***Outlook 98 Introduction.** Computer Confidence Staff. (Illus.). xviii, 160p. 1998. spiral bd. 29.95 incl. disk (*1-57533-088-1*, 9811) Comput Confidence.

***Outlook 98 Introduction.** deluxe ed. Computer Confidence Staff. (Illus.). xviii, 160p. 1998. pap. 25.95 (*1-57533-126-8*) Comput Confidence.

Outlook 98 Made Easy: The Basics & Beyond. Martin S. Matthews. LC 98-216395. (Made Easy Ser.). 608p. 1998. pap. 24.99 (*0-07-882525-3*) Osborne-McGraw.

Outlook 97: Byte by Bite. Glenda Friesen. (Byte by Bite Ser.). (Illus.). iv, 36p. 1997. pap. 10.00 (*1-891412-08-6*) Training Solut.

Outlook, '97: Just the Basics. D D C Publishing Staff. (One-Day Course Ser.). 1997. pap. text 22.00 incl. cd-rom (*1-56243-528-0*, DC-11) DDC Pub.

Outlook 97 - Customizing (MOUG Version) Ed. by Ron Pronk. (Illus.). 134p. 1997. pap. write for info. (*1-58264-098-X*) ActiveEd.

Outlook, '97 Essentials. Rob Tidrow. LC 97-65610. (Illus.). 160p. 1997. 22.99 (*1-57576-803-8*) Sams.

Outlook 97 Expert Test Preparation. Ed. by Ron Pronk. (Illus.). 120p. 1997. pap. 20.00 (*1-58264-028-9*, 146) ActiveEd.

Outlook, '97 One Step at a Time. Trudi Reisner. LC 97-76682. (New Tutorial Ser.). 350p. 1997. pap. 29.99 (*0-7645-3128-X*) IDG Bks.

Outlook on Ohio. Ed. by William O. Reichert & Steven O. Ludd. (Orig.). 1983. pap. 13.50 (*0-940390-04-3*) Comwealth Bks NJ.

Outlook on Our Inner Western Way. William Gray. (Illus.). 160p. 1980. pap. 6.95 (*0-87728-493-8*) Weiser.

Outlook on Space Law over the Next 30 Years. Lafferranderie. 1997. 195.00 (*90-411-0405-4*) Kluwer Law Intl.

Outlook on Space Law over the Next 30 Years: Essays Published for the 30th Anniversary of the Space Treaty. Ed. by Gabriel Lafferranderie & Daphne Crowther. LC 97-12996. 1997. lib. bdg. 195.00 (*90-411-0402-X*) Kluwer Academic.

Outlook Two Thousand. 1991. lib. bdg. 250.00 (*0-8490-4948-2*) Gordon Pr.

***Outlook 2000.** 192p. 1999. 39.99 (*1-58076-102-X*) P-H.

***Outlook 2000.** ENI Publishing Staff. (Straight to the Point Ser.). 2000. pap. 7.95 (*2-7460-0792-4*) ENI Publng.

***Outlook 2000: Byte by Bite.** Glenda Friesen. (Byte by Bite Ser.). 71p. 1999. pap. 10.00 (*1-891412-21-3*) Training Solut.

***Outlook 2000: Integration.** Niit. 2000. 8.00 (*0-619-01418-0*) Course Tech.

Outlook 2000 Expert. Ed. by Course Technology Incorporated Staff. (C). 1999. 15.00 (*0-619-00128-3*) Course Tech.

Outlook 2000 Fast & Easy. Lisa Wagner. LC 98-68393. (Fast & Easy Ser.). (Illus.). 374p. 1999. pap. 16.99 (*0-7615-1927-0*, Prima Tech) Prima Pub.

***Outlook 2000 for Windows: Visual QuickStart Guide.** Michael J. Young. (Illus.). 288p. 1999. pap. text 17.99 (*0-201-69952-4*) Peachpit Pr.

***Outlook 2000 in a Nutshell.** Tom Syroid & Bo Leuf. Ed. by Troy Mott. (Illus.). 550p. 2000. pap. 24.95 (*1-56592-704-4*) OReilly & Assocs.

***Outlook 2000 Intermediate.** Ed. by Ron Pronk. (Illus.). 2000p. 1999. pap. 20.00i (*1-58264-094-7*) ActiveEd.

***Outlook 2000 Introduction.** rev. ed. Dawnette Wilkinson. Ed. by Holly Freeman et al. (Illus.). 244p. 2000. pap. 20.00 (*1-58264-112-9*) ActiveEd.

Outlook 2000 VBA Programmer's Reference. Dwayne Gifford. 400p. 1999. pap. 24.99 (*1-86100-253-X*) Wrox Pr Inc.

***Outlook 2000.** ENI Publishing Ltd. Staff. (On Your Side Ser.). 2000. pap. 15.95 (*2-7460-0796-7*) ENI Publng.

***Outlook 2000.** ENI Publishing Ltd. Staff. (Pasaporte Ser.). 2000. pap. 15.95 (*2-7460-0959-5*); pap. 7.95 (*2-7460-0960-9*) ENI Publng.

***Outlook 2000.** ENI Publishing Ltd. Staff. (Finding Your Way Ser.). (Illus.). 2000. pap. 12.95 (*2-7460-0974-9*) ENI Publng.

Outlook 2000 Developer's Handbook. Tom Howe. 1999. pap. 49.99 (*0-7821-2475-5*) Sybex.

Outlook 2000 Essentials. 192p. (C). 1999. pap. text 22.99 (*1-58076-087-2*) Cisco Press.

Outlook 97: Day 2. DDC Publishing Staff. (One-Day Course Ser.). 1998. pap. text 22.00 (*1-56243-582-5*, DC32) DDC Pub.

Outlook 97 - Win 95/NT. (Quick Study Computer Ser.). 4p. pap. 3.95 (*1-57222-214-X*) Barcharts.

Outlook 97 Essentials. 145p. 1997. teacher ed., spiral bd. 49.99 (*1-57576-813-5*) Que Educ & Trng.

Outlook 97 Introduction. Computer Confidence Staff. (Illus.). xviii, 140p. 1997. spiral bd. 29.00 incl. disk (*1-57533-066-0*, 07945) Comput Confidence.

Outlook 98 - Win 95/NT. (Quick Study Computer Ser.). 4p. pap. 3.95 (*1-57222-289-1*) Barcharts.

Outlook 98 Answers! Kathy Ivens. (Answers! Ser.). 1998. pap. text 24.99 (*0-07-211851-2*) Osborne-McGraw.

Outlook 98 Visual Reference Basics. DDC Publishing Staff. 1999. pap. 17.00 (*1-56243-690-2*) DDC Pub.

Outlooks. 4th ed. Eschholz. 1998. pap. text 32.05 (*0-312-19803-5*) St Martin.

Outlooks. 5th ed. Eschholz. 1995. pap. write for info. (*0-312-18373-9*) St Martin.

Outlooks: Environmental Literacy Readings. Michael McKinney & Robert Schoch. LC 98-139749. (Earth Science Ser.). 288p. 1997. pap. 15.00 (*0-7637-0658-2*) Jones & Bartlett.

Outlooks: Lesbian & Gay Sexualities & Visual Culture. Ed. by Peter Horne & Reina Lewis. LC 95-38745. (Illus.). 208p. (C). 1996. 75.00 (*0-415-12467-0*) Routledge.

Outlooks: Lesbian & Gay Sexualities & Visual Culture. Ed. by Peter Horne & Reina Lewis. LC 95-38745. (Illus.). 208p. (C). 1996. pap. 22.99 (*0-415-12468-9*) Routledge.

Outlooks & Insights. Z. Leff. 1993. 15.99 (*0-89906-531-7*) Mesorah Pubns.

Outlooks & Insights. Z. Leff. 1993. 18.99 (*0-89906-530-9*) Mesorah Pubns.

Outlooks & Insights: A Reader for College Writers. 4th ed. Alfred F. Rosa & Paul A. Eschholz. 656p. (C). 1994. pap. 38.95 (*0-312-10110-4*) St Martin.

Outlooks from the New Standpoint. Ernest Belfort Bax. (Essay Index Reprint Ser.). 1977. 20.95 (*0-8369-2742-7*) Ayer.

Outlying Districts. Anselm Hollo. LC 90-35355. 112p. (Orig.). 1990. pap. 8.95 (*0-918273-76-5*) Coffee Hse.

Outmaneuver the Bureaucrats: Make Them Say "Yes", 1. Lynella Grant. 1999. pap. write for info. (*1-888739-53-3*) Off the Page.

Outnation: A Search for the Soul of Japan. Jonathan Rauch. LC 91-37946. (Illus.). 182p. 1992. 18.95 (*0-87584-320-4*) Harvard Busn.

Outnation: Searching the Soul of Japan. Rauch. 200p. 1992. 22.50 (*0-07-103370-X*) McGraw.

Outnumbered - Exploding the Myth of 144,000. Russell Warren. 1986. pap. 5.95 (*1-883858-15-1*) Witness CA.

Outpacing the Pros. Blitzer. 2000. 30.00 (*0-07-135586-3*) McGraw.

Outpatient & Primary Care Medicine, 2001 Edition: Current Clinical Strategies. rev. ed. Paul D. Chan. 195p. 1999. pap. 12.95 (*1-881528-89-8*) Current Clin Strat.

Outpatient Anesthesia. Ed. by Paul F. White. LC 90-1556. (Illus.). 536p. reprint ed. pap. 166.20 (*0-7837-6228-3*, 204594200010) Bks Demand.

Outpatient Antimicrobial Therapy: Recent Advances. Klein et al. 185p. 1989. 22.50 (*0-945986-12-2*) Health Care NJ.

Outpatient Care Handbook. 2nd rev. ed. Peter A. Glassman et al. LC 98-41940. 350p. 1999. pap. text 39.00 (*1-56053-260-2*) Hanley & Belfus.

Outpatient Case Management: Strategies for a New Reality. Ed. by Michelle R. Donovan & Theodore A. Matson. LC 94-9597. 298p. 1994. pap. write for info. (*1-55648-119-5*, 027100) AHPI.

Outpatient Coloproctology. Dodi & Spencer. (Illus.). 842p. 1996. text 250.00 (*88-299-1161-5*, Pub. by Piccin Nuova) Gordon & Breach.

Outpatient Gynecologic Surgery. A. Jefferson Penfield. LC 96-49541. (Illus.). 304p. 1997. 69.00 (*0-683-30176-4*) Lppncott W & W.

Outpatient Invasive Radiologic Procedures: Diagnostic & Therapeutic. Dublin. 1989. text 65.00 (*0-7216-1532-5*, W B Saunders Co) Harcrt Hlth Sci Grp.

Outpatient Management of HIV Infection. 2nd rev. ed. Joseph R. Masci. (Illus.). 448p. (C). (gr. 13). 1996. spiral bd. 39.95 (*0-8151-6144-1*, 25691) Mosby Inc.

Outpatient Management of Pediatric Infectious Disease. Jerome O. Klein et al. 400p. 1996. write for info. (*0-683-04650-0*) Lppncott W & W.

Outpatient Medicine. fac. ed. Ed. by Louis M. Aledort et al. LC 78-51280. (Illus.). 335p. pap. 103.90 (*0-7837-7182-7*, 204711700005) Bks Demand.

Outpatient Medicine. 2nd ed. Stephen D. Fihn. LC 96-46544. 1997. pap. text 49.00 (*0-7216-6257-9*, W B Saunders Co) Harcrt Hlth Sci Grp.

***Outpatient Medicine: 2001 Edition.** rev. ed. Paul D. Chan & Michael Safani. (Current Clinical Strategies Ser.). 110p. 2000. pap. 28.95 incl. cd-rom (*1-881528-90-1*) Current Clin Strat.

Outpatient Medicine, 1997: Current Clinical Strategies. Paul D. Chan & Michael Safani. 110p. 1997. pap. 12.75 (*1-881528-29-4*) Current Clin Strat.

Outpatient Medicine Recall. John P. Franko & Steven A. Meixel. LC 97-34982. (Illus.). 352p. 1997. pap. 28.00 (*0-683-18018-5*) Lppncott W & W.

Outpatient Parenteral Antimicrobial Therapy: Current Status: Proceedings of an Opat Advisory Board Meeting, May 16-18, 1996, Chicago, Illinois. Alan Tice & Scientific American Medicine (Firm) Staff. LC 97-2577. 1997. write for info. (*0-89454-028-9*) Scientific Am Inc.

Outpatient Physical Therapy Policy & Procedure Manual. JoAnne Whipple. 1993. 110.00 (*1-879575-29-9*) Acad Med Sys.

Outpatient Psychiatry. 2nd ed. Aaron Lazare. (Illus.). 752p. 1988. lib. bdg. 79.00 (*0-683-04851-1*) Lppncott W & W.

Outpatient Services: Designing, Organizing & Managing Outpatient Resources. Duane C. Abbey. LC 97-41392. 250p. 1996. pap. text 60.00 (*0-7863-1085-5*, Irwn Prfssnl) McGraw-Hill Prof.

Outpatient Surgery. 3rd ed. George J. Hill. (Illus.). 600p. 1988. text 105.00 (*0-7216-2104-X*, W B Saunders Co) Harcrt Hlth Sci Grp.

Outpatient Treatment of Child Molesters. Stan Friedman. Ed. by Harold H. Smith, Jr. LC 90-50824. (Practitioner's Resource Ser.). 64p. 1991. pap. 15.45 (*0-943158-65-6*, OTCBP) Pro Resource.

Outpatient Urologic Surgery. Keith W. Kaye. Ed. by Judith G. Bronson. LC 84-4411. 328p. reprint ed. pap. 101.70 (*0-7837-2720-8*, 204310000006) Bks Demand.

Outpatient Utilization Profile. 1994. write for info. (*1-880678-60-8*) HCIA.

Outpatient Utilization Profile. 1995. write for info. (*1-57372-000-3*) HCIA.

***Outperform the Dow: Using Options, Futures & Portfolio Strategies to Beat the Market.** Gunter Meissner & Randall Folsom. (Trading Advantage Ser.). 224p. 2000. 39.95 (*0-471-39311-8*) Wiley.

Outperforming the Market: Everyone's Guide to High-Profit, Low-Risk Investing. John F. Merrill. LC 98-13950. (Illus.). 280p. 1998. 27.95 (*0-07-041979-5*) McGraw.

Outperforming Wall Street: Stock Market Profits Through Patience. Daniel A. Seiver. (Illus.). 192p. 1987. 23.95 (*0-13-645235-3*) P-H.

Outplacement: A Guide to Management & Delivery. Ed. by Max Eggert. 128p. (C). 1992. pap. 50.00 (*0-85292-468-2*, Pub. by IPM Hse) St Mut.

Outplacement of Older Psychiatric Patients into the Community. Robert D. Narkiewicz. LC 91-37479. (Studies on the Elderly in America). 96p. 1992. text 20.00 (*0-8153-0520-6*) Garland.

Outpost. Date not set. mass mkt. write for info. (*0-345-43523-0*, Del Rey) Ballantine Pub Grp.

Outpost. Scott Mackay. LC 97-36367. 352p. 1998. text 24.95 (*0-312-86467-1*) St Martin.

***Outpost.** Scott Mackay. 352p. 1999. pap. 14.95 (*0-312-86842-1*, Pub. by Tor Bks) St Martin.

***Outpost.** Howard Swindle. 272p. 2000. mass mkt. 5.99 (*0-312-97054-4*, St Martins Paperbacks) St Martin.

Outpost! large type ed. Dana Fuller Ross. LC 93-8890. (Wagons West Ser.: Vol. 3). 1993. lib. bdg. 23.95 (*0-8161-5516-X*, G K Hall Lrg Type) Mac Lib Ref.

Outpost. Jane G. Austin. (Works of Jane (Goodin) Austin). 1989. reprint ed. lib. bdg. 79.00 (*0-7812-1823-3*) Rprt Serv.

***Outpost: John McLoughlin & the Far Northwest.** Dorothy Morrison. LC 98-3162. (Illus.). 1998. 35.00 (*0-87595-267-4*) Oregon Hist.

Outpost! Wagons West. Dana Fuller Ross. (Frontier Trilogy Ser.: No. 3). 464p. 1993. mass mkt. 6.50 (*0-553-29400-8*) Bantam.

Outpost Berlin: The History of the American Military Forces in Berlin, 1945-1994. Henrik Bering. LC 95-11172. (Illus.). 200p. 1995. pap. 16.95 (*1-883695-07-4*) Edition Q.

Outpost in the North Atlantic: Marines in the Defense of Iceland. James A. Donovan. (Illus.). 33p. 1996. reprint ed. pap. text 20.00 (*0-7881-3524-4*) DIANE Pub.

Outpost of Hellenism: The Emergence of Heraclea on the Black Sea. Stanley M. Burstein. LC 74-620189. (University of California Publications: Classical Studies: Vol. 14). 164p. reprint ed. pap. 50.90 (*0-608-18654-6*, 202126800021) Bks Demand.

Outpost of the Sioux Wars: A History of Fort Robinson. Frank N. Schubert. LC 94-45252. (Illus.). xii, 250p. 1995. pap. 12.95 (*0-8032-9226-0*, Bison Books) U of Nebr Pr.

Outpost Official Strategy Guide. Bruce Balfour. LC 93-87075. (Illus.). 300p. 1994. pap. 19.95 (*1-55958-508-0*) Prima Pub.

Outpost on Apollo's Moon. Eric Burgess. (Illus.). 288p. (C). 1993. 44.00 (*0-231-07666-5*) Col U Pr.

***Outpost War: The U. S. Marine Corps in Korea, 1952.** Lee Ballenger. LC 99-86415. 2000. 24.95 (*1-57488-241-4*) Brasseys.

Outposter. Gordon Rupert Dickson. 256p. 1992. mass mkt. 4.99 (*0-671-72140-2*) Baen Bks.

Outposts: A Catalog of Rare & Disturbing Information. Russ Kirk. (Illus.). 264p. 1995. pap. 18.95 (*0-7867-0202-8*) Carroll & Graf.

Outposts & Allies: U. S. Army Logistics in the Cold War, 1945-1953. James A. Huston. LC 86-43218. (Illus.). 1988. 44.50 (*0-941664-84-8*) Susquehanna U Pr.

Outposts & Allies: U. S. Army Logistics in the Cold War, 1945-1953. James A. Huston. 349p. (C). 1998. reprint ed. text 50.00 (*0-7881-7137-2*) DIANE Pub.

Outposts of Civilization. Henning. text 35.00 (*0-8147-3605-X*) NYU Pr.

Outposts of Empire: Korea, Vietnam, & the Origins of the Cold War in Asia, 1949-1954. Steven H. Lee. 320p. 1996. pap. text 19.95 (*0-7735-1420-1*, Pub. by McG-Queens Univ Pr) CUP Services.

Outposts of Empire: Korea, Vietnam & the Origins of the Cold War in Asia, 1949-1954. Steven H. Lee. LC 97-135057. 312p. 1995. 55.00 (*0-7735-1326-4*, Pub. by McG-Queens Univ Pr) CUP Services.

Outposts of the Forgotten: Socially Terminal People in Slum Hotels & Single Room Occupancy Tenements. Harvey A. Siegal. LC 76-1777. 220p. 1978. 39.95 (*0-87855-141-7*) Transaction Pubs.

***Outposts of the Spirit.** William Justice. 320p. 2000. pap. 12.95 (*1-57174-157-7*) Hampton Roads Pub Co.

Outposts on the Gulf: Saint George Island & Apalachicola from Early Exploration to World War II. William W. Rogers. LC 85-17802. (Illus.). 312p. 1987. 34.95 (*0-8130-0832-8*) U Press Fla.

Outpouring. Elwood McQuaid. LC 85-29866. 1990. pap. 8.95 (*0-915540-49-5*) Frnds Israel.

Outpouring of the Soul. Nachman of Breslov & Nathan of Breslov. Tr. by Aryeh Kaplan from HEB.Tr. of Hishtap'kuth HaNefesh. 96p. (Orig.). 1980. reprint ed. pap. 4.00 (*0-930213-14-9*) Breslov Res Inst.

Outpouring of the Spirit. Kenneth Copeland. 1993. mass mkt. 30.00 incl. audio (*0-88114-288-3*) K Copeland Pubns.

Outpouring of the Spirit: The Result of Prayer. Kenneth Copeland. 20p. 1983. mass mkt. 3.95 (*0-88114-297-2*) K Copeland Pubns.

Outpourings: Moments of Reflection. rev. ed. Lenore Turkeltaub. LC 87-83183. (Illus.). 72p. 1988. pap. 7.95 (*0-9614768-6-9*) Lenjalin Pubns.

Output & Employment Fluctuations. Ed. by K. F. Zimmermann. (Studies in Empirical Economics). (Illus.). 272p. 1994. 89.00 (*0-387-91478-1*) Spr-Verlag.

Output & Performance Measurement in Government: The State of the Art. Ed. by Martin Cave et al. 160p. 1990. 49.95 (*1-85302-521-6*) Taylor & Francis.

Output & Productivity in the Electric & Gas Utilities, 1899-1942. Jacob M. Gould. (General Ser.: No. 47). 207p. 1946. reprint ed. 53.90 (*0-87014-046-9*) Natl Bur Econ Res.

Output Decline in Eastern Europe: Unavoidable, External Influence or Homemade? Ed. by Robert Holzman et al. LC 94-44976. (International Studies in Economics & Econometrics: Vol. 34). 396p. (C). 1995. lib. bdg. 132.50 (*0-7923-3285-7*) Kluwer Academic.

Output, Employment, & Productivity in the United States after 1800. Ed. by Dorothy S. Brady. (Studies in Income & Wealth: No. 30). 674p. 1966. reprint ed. 160.00 (*0-87014-186-4*) Natl Bur Econ Res.

Output, Input & Productivity Measurement. Conference on Research in Income & Wealth. LC 60-12234. (National Bureau of Economic Research. Studies in International Economic Relations: Vol. 25). 516p. reprint ed. pap. 160.00 (*0-608-14417-7*, 205170200006) Bks Demand.

Output, Input & Productivity Measurement. Conference on Research In Income And Wealth. (Studies in Income & Wealth: No. 25). 516p. 1961. reprint ed. 129.00 (*0-87014-181-3*) Natl Bur Econ Res.

Output Measurement in the Service Sectors. Zvi Griliches et al. LC 92-17561. (Studies in Income & Wealth: Vol. 56). (Illus.). 572p. 1992. lib. bdg. 82.50 (*0-226-30885-5*) U Ch Pr.

Output Measurements for Medical Ultrasound. Ed. by R. C Preston. (Illus.). xvi, 180p. 1991. 117.95 (*0-387-19692-7*) Spr-Verlag.

Output Measures for Children's Services in Wisconsin Public Libraries. Douglas L. Zweizig et al. 44p. 1989. pap. 5.00 (*0-936442-13-1*) U Wis Sch Lib.

Output Measures for Public Libraries: A Manual on Standardized Procedures. 2nd ed. Nancy A. Van House et al. LC 87-11479. 144p. 1987. pap. text 25.00 (*0-8389-3340-8*) ALA.

Output Measures for Public Library Service to Children. Virginia A. Walter. LC 91-44354. (Illus.). 129p. (C). 1992. pap. text 25.00 (*0-8389-3404-8*) ALA.

Output Measures for School Library Media Programs. Frances B. Bradburn. LC 98-45557. 125p. 1999. pap. 49.95 (*1-55570-326-7*) Neal-Schuman.

Output of Manufacturing Industries, 1899-1937. Solomon Fabricant. LC 75-19712. (National Bureau of Economic Research Ser.). (Illus.). 1975. reprint ed. 57.95 (*0-405-07592-8*) Ayer.

Output of Manufacturing Industries, 1899-1937. Solomon Fabricant & Julius Shiskin. (General Ser.: No. 39). 708p. 1940. reprint ed. 160.00 (*0-87014-038-8*) Natl Bur Econ Res.

Output Oriented Manager. Reddin. 400p. 1989. 78.95 (*0-566-02711-9*) Ashgate Pub Co.

Output Oriented Organization. Reddin. 272p. 1989. 78.95 (*0-566-02710-0*) Ashgate Pub Co.

Output, Productivity & Externalities: The Case of Banking. R. J. Colwell & E. P. Davis. LC 93-5002. (Bank of England, Economics Division: Vol. 3). (Illus.). 38p. 1992. reprint ed. pap. 30.00 (*0-608-07934-0*, 206790700012) Bks Demand.

Output Regulation of Uncertain Nonlinear Systems. Ed. by Christopher I. Byrnes et al. LC 97-5748. (Systems & Control Ser.). 120p. 1997. 36.50 (*0-8176-3997-7*) Birkhauser.

Output Regulation of Uncertain Nonlinear Systems. Christopher I. Byrnes et al. LC 97-5748. (Systems & Control Ser.). 136p. 1997. write for info. (*3-7643-3997-7*) Birkhauser.

***Output-Related Funding in Vocational Education & Training: A Discussion Paper & Case Studies.** Alan Felstead et al. LC 98-234483. 64p. 1998. write for info. (*92-828-4388-2*, Pub. by Comm Europ Commun) Bernan Associates.

Outrace the Dawn: Collected Poems, 1925-1989. Francis S. Hewitt. LC 93-35946. 1993. write for info. (*0-911057-03-X*) Belvedere Pr.

Outrage. Lucille Iverson. 1974. pap. 2.50 (*0-912786-31-0*) Know Inc.

Outrage: A Novel of Beirut. Dale Dye. 1988. 17.95 (*0-316-20010-7*) Little.

Outrage! A Tale of Legal Thievery in Minnesota. Garry De Young. 1989. pap. 3.00 (*0-936128-18-6*) De Young Pr.

Outrage! An Oral History. Ian Lucas. 256p. 1999. pap. text 21.50 (*0-304-33358-1*) Continuum.

Outrage! An Oral History. Ian Lucas. 256p. 1999. 55.00 (*0-304-33357-3*) Continuum.

Outrage: The Five Reasons Why O. J. Simpson Got Away. Vincent T. Bugliosi. 528p. 1997. mass mkt. 7.50 (*0-440-22382-2*, Island Bks) Dell.

Outrage: The Five Reasons Why O.J. Simpson Got Away with Murder. Vincent T. Bugliosi. 320p. 1996. 25.00 (*0-393-04050-X*) Norton.

Outrage & Hope: A Bishop's Reflections in Times of Change & Challenge. Frederick H. Borsch. LC 96-10961. 280p. (Orig.). 1996. pap. 15.00 (*1-56338-170-2*) TPI PA.

Outrage & Insight: Modern French Writers & the 'Fait Divers' David H. Walker. Ed. by John E. Flower. (French Studies). 288p. 1995. 55.00 (*0-85496-780-X*) Berg Pubs.

Outrage at Blanco. Bill Crider. 1998. mass mkt. 5.99 (*0-440-23454-9*) Dell.

Outrage at Lincheng: China Enters the Twentieth Century. Michael J. Nozinski. LC 89-80780. (Illus.). 243p. 1990. 19.95 (*0-944435-07-6*) Glenbridge Pub.

***Outrage in Orlando.** Susan Murray & Robert Davies. 192p. 2000. pap. 5.99 (*1-55207-023-9*) R Davies Pub.

Outraged Conscience: Seekers of Justice for Nazi War Criminals in America. Rochelle G. Saidel. LC 84-15. 250p. (C). 1985. text 49.50 (*0-87395-897-7*); pap. text 16.95 (*0-87395-898-5*) State U NY Pr.

Outrageous! Charles Barkley & Roy S. Johnson. 376p. 1993. mass mkt. 5.99 (*0-380-72101-5*, Avon Bks) Morrow Avon.

Outrageous. Christina Dodd. 384p. 1994. mass mkt. 3.99 (*0-06-108151-5*, Harp PBks) HarpC.

Outrageous. Lori Foster. (Blaze Ser.). 1997. per. 3.50 (*0-373-25729-5*, 1-25729-4) Harlequin Bks.

***Outrageous.** Kathryn Hockett. (Historical Romance Ser.). 2000. mass mkt. 5.99 (*0-8217-6455-1*, Zebra Kensgtn) Kensgtn Pub Corp.

***Outrageous.** Norah-Jean Perkin. 1999. 6.99 (*1-57343-018-8*) LionHearted.

Outrageous: The Photographs. Ed. by US Magazine Editorial Staff. LC 98-229766. (Illus.). 144p. 1999. text 29.95 (*0-312-19284-3*) St Martin.

Outrageous!! Unforgettable Service . . . Guilt-Free Selling. T. Scott Gross. LC 98-5611. 304p. 1998. pap. 19.95 (*0-8144-7986-3*) AMACOM.

Outrageous Acts & Everyday Rebellions. Gloria Steinem. LC 95-31711. 1995. pap. 12.95 (*0-8050-4202-4*, Owl) H Holt & Co.

Outrageous & Scandalous Satire. John H. Braccio. (Illus.). 246p. 1993. pap. 10.00 (*0-9637854-0-0*) Reg Psychol.

Outrageous Antics of Tadwag: The Little Satyr Who Distured the Smugness of the Universe. Illus. by Hunter B. Shirley et al. (Tadwag Ser.). 127p. (Orig.). pap. 5.00 (*0-929026-69-1*) Twnty-First Century Bks.

Outrageous... At Any Age: Personal Coaching Yourself! Ted Borgeas. 105p. 1999. 15.95 (*0-9666110-4-7*) Age-Trott.

Outrageous Atlas: A Guide to North America's Strangest Places. Richard A. Rogers & Laurine Rogers. (Illus.). 160p. 1993. pap. 9.95 (*0-8065-1445-0*, Citadel Pr) Carol Pub Group.

O

Outrageous, Bodacious Boliver Boggs! Jo Harper. LC 95-6029. (Illus.). 32p. (J). (ps-3). 1996. per. 15.00 (*0-689-80504-7*) S&S Bks Yung.

Outrageous Chinese: A Guide to Chinese Street Language. James J. Wang. Ed. by Greg Jones. LC 95-124646. (CHI & ENG., Illus.). 124p. 1994. pap. 9.95 (*0-8351-2532-7*) China Bks.

Outrageous Clip Art for Youth Ministry: Wild, Read-to-Use Cartoons. Illus. by Rand Kruback. 131p. 1988. pap. 16.99 (*0-931529-39-5*) Group Pub.

Outrageous Dates. Youth Specialties. 1998. pap. 6.00 (*0-310-67949-4*) HarpC.

Outrageous! Education Practices: Truth about Our Education System. A. A. Axiom. LC 89-91065. 96p. (Orig.). 1989. pap. 15.95 (*0-922958-09-2*) H W Parker.

Outrageous Educational Proposal. unabridged ed. S. Gianinazzi. 1998. pap. 14.95 (*1-893336-01-8*) B Newton.

Outrageous Exposures. large type ed. John Penn. (Mystery Ser.). 1991. 27.99 (*0-7089-2350-X*) Ulverscroft.

Outrageous Fortune. Patricia Wentworth. 22.95 (*0-8488-1219-0*) Amereon Ltd.

Outrageous Fortune. Patricia Wentworth. 240p. 1990. mass mkt. 3.95 (*0-446-35910-6*, Pub. by Warner Bks) Little.

Outrageous Grace: Finding a Forever Friendship with God. Dwight K. Nelson. LC 98-25929. 1998. 1.99 (*0-8163-1679-1*) Pacific Pr Pub Assn.

Outrageous Idea: Natural Prayer: A Powerful Answer to America's Prayer Dilemma. Patty Jo Cornish. (Illus.). 108p. 14.95 (*0-9613717-1-4*) Hilltop Hse.

Outrageous Idea of Christian Scholarship. George M. Marsden. (Illus.). 152p. 1997. 25.00 (*0-19-510565-6*) OUP.

Outrageous Idea of Christian Scholarship. George M. Marsden. (Illus.). 160p. 1998. reprint ed. pap. 11.95 (*0-19-512290-9*) OUP.

Outrageous Japanese: Slang, Curses, & Epithets. Jack Seward. (JPN.). 156p. (Orig.). 1992. pap. 7.95 (*0-8048-1694-8*) Tuttle Pubng.

Outrageous Jerry Springer. MARKHAM-SMITHAN. 256p. 1999. 26.00 (*1-85782-331-1*, Pub. by Blake Publng) Seven Hills Bk.

Outrageous Joy. Barbara Johnson et al. LC 98-55904. 1999. 15.99 (*0-310-22648-1*) Zondervan.

Outrageous Macintosh Filters. David D. Busch. LC 95-10900. 1995. pap. 39.95 (*1-55828-429-X*, MIS Pr) IDG Bks.

Outrageous One Act Plays. Miguel Pinero. LC 86-71600. 160p. 1986. pap. 9.50 (*0-934770-68-9*, Pub. by Arte Publico) Empire Pub Srvs.

Outrageous Origin. Jim Davis. (Garfield's Pet Force Ser.: Vol. 1). (J). (gr. 3-7). 1998. pap. text 3.99 (*0-590-05908-4*) Scholastic Inc.

Outrageous Outdoor Games. Bob Gregson. LC 83-62564. (J). (gr. k-12). 1984. pap. 15.99 (*0-8224-5099-2*) Fearon Teacher Aids.

Outrageous Party Games. unabridged ed. Brian L. Pellham & Allison Kent. Ed. by Sally Neary. (Illus.). 128p. 1998. pap. 8.95 (*0-9649678-2-0*) Kheper Pubg.

Outrageous PC F/X: Tools & Techniques for Outrageous Graphic Effects. David D. Busch. 428p. 1994. pap. 34.95 incl. cd-rom (*1-55828-394-3*, MIS Pr) IDG Bks.

O

Outrageous Practices: How Gender Bias Threatens Women's Health. Leslie Laurence & Beth Weinhouse. LC 97-12096. xxi, 434p. (Orig.). 1997. pap. 18.95 (*0-8135-2448-2*) Rutgers U Pr.

Outrageous Practices: The Alarming Truth about How Medicine Mistreats Women. Leslie Laurence & Beth Weinhouse. 434p. 1998. text 22.00 (*0-7881-5948-8*) DIANE Pub.

Outrageous Proposal. April Kihlstrom. (Signet Regency Romance Ser.). 224p. 1998. mass mkt. 4.99 (*0-451-19594-9*, Sig) NAL.

Outrageous Proposal. Miranda Lee. LC 95-7050. (Presents Ser.). 188p. 1995. per. 3.25 (*0-373-11737-X*, 1-11737-3) Harlequin Bks.

***Outrageous Pursuit of Hope: Prophetic Dreams for the Twenty-First Century.** Mary C. Grey. 2001. pap. 14.95 (*0-8245-1882-9*) Crossroad NY.

Outrageous Questions: Legacy of Bronson Alcott & America's One-Room Schools. Laurie James. LC 93-77360. (Illus.). 104p. (Orig.). 1994. pap. 10.95 (*0-944382-05-3*); text 16.95 (*0-944382-06-1*) Golden Heritage Pr.

Outrageous RI. Christina Dood. 384p. 1999. mass mkt. 3.99 (*0-06-108562-6*) HarpC.

***Outrageous Seas: Shipwreck & Survival in the Waters off Newfoundland, 1583-1893.** Ed. by Rainer K. Baehre. (Illus.). 152p. 1999. pap. 22.95 (*0-88629-319-7*) McG-Queens Univ Pr.

***Outrageous Seas: Shipwreck & Survival in the Waters off Newfoundland, 1583-1893.** Kathleen Rainer. Ed. by Rainer K. Baehre. (Illus.). 152p. 1999. text. write for info. (*0-88629-358-8*, Pub. by McG-Queens Univ Pr) CUP Services.

Outrageous Temp Stories. Leslie Buterin. 57p. 1998. pap. 7.00 (*0-9658697-1-7*) Lead Edge.

Outrageous 3-D Big Bugs. Ian Boyd. LC 98-125650. (Illus.). 24p. (J). (ps-3). 1998. pap. 4.95 (*0-8167-4354-1*) Troll Communs.

Outrageous 3-D Dangerous Creatures. Jan Boyd. LC 98-120099. (Illus.). (J). (ps-3). 1997. pap. 4.95 (*0-8167-4355-X*) Troll Communs.

Outrageous 3-D Deadly Hunters. Ian Boyd. (Illus.). 24p. (J). (ps-3). 1999. pap. 4.95 (*0-8167-4960-4*) Troll Communs.

Outrageous Truth about My Cat Einstein. Carol Kopec. LC 98-119389. 155p. (J). (gr. 3-6). 1998. pap. 9.99 (*0-88092-404-7*, 4047) Royal Fireworks.

Outrageous Women of Ancient Times. Vicki Leon. LC 97-10836. (Outrageous Women Ser.). 128p. (YA). (gr. 5-9). 1997. pap. 12.95 (*0-471-17006-2*) Wiley.

Outrageous Women of Ancient Times. Vicki Leon. LC 97-30307. (Outrageous Women Ser.). 128p. (J). (gr. 4-7). 1998. pap. 12.95 (*0-471-17004-6*) Wiley.

***Outrageous Women of Colonial America.** Mary Rodd Furbee. 2001. pap. 12.95 (*0-471-38299-X*) Wiley.

***Outrageous Women of the Renaissance.** Vicki Leon. LC 98-30357. (Outrageous Women Ser.). (Illus.). 128p. (YA). (gr. 5-12). 1999. pap. text 12.95 (*0-471-29684-8*) Wiley.

Outrageous 3-D Outer Space. Ian Boyd. (Illus.). 24p. (J). (ps-3). 1998. pap. 4.95 (*0-8167-4959-0*) Troll Communs.

Outrageously Alice. Phyllis Reynolds Naylor. LC 96-7744. (Alice Ser.). 144p. (YA). (gr. 4-8). 1998. per. 3.99 (*0-689-80596-9*) Aladdin.

Outrageously Alice. Phyllis Reynolds Naylor. LC 96-7744. (Alice Ser.). 144p. (YA). (gr. 5-8). 1997. 15.00 (*0-689-80354-0*) Atheneum Yung Read.

Outrageously Gross Jokes XXVI. Julius Alvin. 160p. 1997. mass mkt. 4.99 (*0-8217-5784-9*, Zebra Kensgtn) Kensgtn Pub Corp.

Outrageously Offensive Jokes, No. 4. Maude Thickett. 128p. (Orig.). 1991. pap. 3.50 (*0-671-74254-X*) PB.

Outrageously Offensive Jokes III. Maude Thickett. 1990. pap. 3.50 (*0-671-73031-2*, PB Trade Paper) PB.

Outre-Mer: Essays. Henry Wadsworth Longfellow. (Notable American Authors Ser.). 1999. reprint ed. lib. bdg. 125.00 (*0-7812-3821-8*) Rprt Serv.

Outreach: Sharing Good News. Gary Wilde. LC 97-173705. (Encouragers for Men Ser.). 64p. 1997. pap. text 3.99 (*1-56476-616-0*, Victor Bks) Chariot Victor.

Outreach: Sharing the Real Gospel with the World. Navigators Staff. (Foundations for Christian Living Ser.). 1997. pap. text 6.00 (*1-57683-012-8*) NavPress.

Outreach - Proceedings: Symposium Organised by the Pompidou Group & the World Health Organization - Bergen, 22-24 February, 1993. 1994. 18.00 (*92-871-2601-1*, Pub. by Council of Europe) Manhattan Pub Co.

Outreach & the Changing Reform Jewish Community: Creating an Agenda for Our Future, a Program Guide. 140 p. 1994. pap. 10.00 (*0-8074-0444-6*, 280054) UAHC.

Outreach, '89: APLIC Proceedings of the 22nd Annual Conference. Ed. by Jane Vanderlin & William Barrows. 65p. (Orig.). 1990. pap. text 16.00 (*0-933438-16-8*) APLIC Intl.

Outreach in Counseling: Applying the Growth & Prevention Model in Schools & Colleges. David J. Drum & Howard E. Figler. LC 77-8091. 242p. 1976. reprint ed. pap. 8.50 (*0-910328-11-0*) Sulzburger & Graham Pub.

Outreach Promises: God's Encouragement for Sharing Your Faith. Philip M. Bickel. LC 98-91364. (Illus.). 112p. 1998. pap. 8.95 (*0-9663765-0-1*) Roll Coaster.

Outreach-Risk Reduction Strategies for Changing HIV-Related Risk Behaviors among Injection Drug Users. (Illus.). 77p. (Orig.). (C). 1995. pap. text 20.00 (*0-7881-2175-8*) DIANE Pub.

Outreach Skits for Youth Ministry. Ed. by Amy Simpson. LC 98-39392. 128p. (YA). 1998. per. 16.99 (*0-7644-2100-X*, Vital Ministry) Group Pub.

***Outreach Spanish.** William C. Harvey. 288p. 2000. pap. 8.95 (*0-7641-1324-0*) Barron.

Outreach to the Aging Blind: Some Strategies for Community Action. Irving R. Dickman. LC 77-155406. 174p. reprint ed. pap. 54.00 (*0-7837-0133-0*, 204042100016) Bks Demand.

Outreach to the Rural Disadvantaged: Issues & Strategies for the 21st Century. Ed. by Ntam Baharanyi et al. LC 90-71907. 267p. (Orig.). (C). 1990. pap. text. write for info. (*0-9625021-1-1*) Tuskegee U CAENS.

Outreach with the Elderly: Community Education, Assessment, & Therapy. Robert Knight. 320p. (C). 1990. pap. text 19.00 (*0-8147-4607-1*) NYU Pr.

Outreach Work with Drug Users: Principles & Practice. 1996. 15.00 (*92-871-3110-4*, Pub. by Council of Europe) Manhattan Pub Co.

Outreach Worker. Jack Rudman. (Career Examination Ser.: C-3559). 1994. pap. 23.95 (*0-8373-3559-0*) Nat Learn.

Outremer. Nabil Saleh. 208p. 1999. pap. 13.95 (*0-7043-8103-6*, Pub. by Quartet) Interlink Pub.

***Outriders of Hell.** large type ed. Lee F. Gregson. 240p. 1999. pap. 20.99 (*1-85389-893-7*) Ulverscroft.

Outrigger Canoes of Bali & Madura, Indonesia. Adrian Horridge. (Illus.). 94p. 1987. 19.50 (*0-930897-20-X*, SP77) Bishop Mus.

Outright Freud. Frederick C. Crews. LC 98-11418. 301p. 1998. 24.95 (*0-670-87221-0*) Viking Penguin.

***Outrunning Your Shadow: Caring for Dying Parents.** Fred Hill. 2000. pap. 12.99 (*0-9673667-0-4*) VanMeter Pubg.

Out's Gay & Lesbian Guide to the Web. James Fitch & Out Magazine Staff. LC 98-160785. (Lycos Insites Ser.). 284p. 1997. 29.99 (*0-7897-1059-5*, Lycos Pr) Que.

Outside. Todd Baron. 72p. (Orig.). (C). 1994. pap. 9.95 (*0-939691-11-6*) Avenue B.

Outside. Joseph S. Bonsall. LC 98-13303. (Molly the Cat Book Ser.). (Illus.). (J). 1998. 14.95 (*1-57102-130-2*, Ideals Child) Hambleton-Hill.

Outside Academe: New Ways of Working in the Humanities. Ed. by Marjorie Lightman & Howard Negrin. LC 81-13463. 74p. 1982. pap. text 12.00 (*0-86656-132-3*) Haworth Pr.

***Outside Adventure Travel: Mountain Biking.** Rob Story. 224p. 2000. reprint ed. pap. 21.00 (*0-393-32071-5*) Norton.

***Outside Adventure Travel: Sea Kayaking.** Jonathan Hanson. 224p. 2000. pap. 21.00 (*0-393-32070-7*) Norton.

***Outside Adventure Travel: Trekking.** David Noland. 224p. 2000. reprint ed. pap. 21.00 (*0-393-32072-3*) Norton.

Outside Agency. Conor Daly. LC 96-79079. 320p. 1997. 18.95 (*1-57566-162-4*, Knsington) Kensgtn Pub Corp.

Outside Agency. Conor Daly. 288p. 1998. mass mkt. 5.99 (*1-57566-319-8*) Kensgtn Pub Corp.

***Outside Agitator: Jon Daniels & the Civil Rights Movement in Alabama.** Charles W. Eagles. 2000. pap. 24.95 (*0-8173-1069-X*) U of Ala Pr.

Outside & Inside Alligators. Sandra Markle. LC 97-39804. (Illus.). 40p. (J). (gr. 3-6). 1998. 16.00 (*0-689-81457-7*) Atheneum Yung Read.

Outside & Inside Bats. Sandra Markle. LC 96-48291. (Illus.). 40p. (J). (gr. 1-5). 1997. 16.00 (*0-689-81165-9*) S&S Childrens.

Outside & Inside Big Cats. (J). 2002. 16.00 (*0-689-82299-5*) Atheneum Yung Read.

Outside & Inside Birds. Sandra Markle. LC 93-38910. (Illus.). 40p. (J). (ps-3). 1994. mass mkt. 15.95 (*0-02-762312-2*, Mac Bks Young Read) S&S Childrens.

Outside & Inside Dinosaurs. Sandra Markle. LC 99-45808. (J). (gr. k-3). 2001. 16.00 (*0-689-82300-2*) Atheneum Yung Read.

Outside & Inside Kangaroos. Sandra Markle. LC 98-45354. 40p. (J). (gr. 3-6). 1999. 16.00 (*0-689-81456-9*) Atheneum Yung Read.

Outside & Inside Rats. (J). 2000. 16.00 (*0-689-82301-0*) Atheneum Yung Read.

Outside & Inside Sharks. Sandra Markle. LC 95-30245. (Illus.). 40p. (J). (ps-3). 1996. 16.00 (*0-689-80348-6*) Atheneum Yung Read.

Outside & Inside Sharks. Sandra Markle. LC 95-30245. (Illus.). 40p. (ps-3). 1999. pap. 5.99 (*0-689-82683-4*, 076714005990) S&S Childrens.

Outside & Inside Snakes. Sandra Markle. LC 94-20647. 40p. (J). 1998. mass mkt. 5.99 (*0-689-81998-6*) Aladdin.

Outside & Inside Snakes. Sandra Markle. LC 94-20647. (Illus.). 40p. (J). (ps-3). 1995. lib. bdg. 17.00 (*0-02-762315-7*) Atheneum Yung Read.

***Outside & Inside Snakes.** Sandra Markle. (Illus.). (J). 1999. pap. 13.40 (*0-613-08505-1*) Econo-Clad Bks.

Outside & Inside Snakes. Sandra Markle. (Outside & Inside Ser.). 1998. 11.19 (*0-606-13691-6*, Pub. by Turtleback) Demco.

***Outside & Inside Spiders.** Sandra Markle. LC 92-22643. (Illus.). 40p. (J). (ps-3). 1999. mass mkt. 5.99 (*0-689-83120-X*) Aladdin.

Outside & Inside Spiders. Sandra Markle. LC 93-22643. (Illus.). 40p. (J). (ps-3). 1994. lib. bdg. 17.00 (*0-02-762314-9*) Atheneum Yung Read.

Outside & Inside You. Sandra Markle. (Illus.). (J). 1996. pap. 4.95 (*0-689-71896-9*) Aladdin.

Outside & Inside You. Sandra Markle. LC 90-37791. (Illus.). 40p. (J). (ps-3). 1991. 14.95 (*0-02-762311-4*) Atheneum Yung Read.

Outside & Other Reflections. Tony Kinton. LC 91-93127. 200p. 1991. 15.95 (*0-9631038-0-6*) T Kinton.

Outside Architecture: Outdoor Rooms Designed by Architects. Susan Zevon. (Illus.). 192p. 1999. 50.00 (*1-56496-460-4*) Rockport Pubs.

Outside Belongings. Elspeth Probyn. LC 95-26496. 181p. (C). 1996. 80.00 (*0-415-91583-X*); pap. 21.99 (*0-415-91584-8*) Routledge.

Outside Brother's Check - Up. 2nd ed. Dave Ray. LC 99-176502. (Illus.). 166 p. 1998. pap., wbk. ed. 14.95 (*1-57326-026-6*) Core Ministries.

Outside Chance. unabridged ed. Louisa Dixon. 420p. 1999. 24.95 (*1-885478-63-1*, Pub. by Genesis Press) BookWorld.

Outside Chicago: Richardsons' Trail Traveler. Christopher Collier. Ed. by John Johnson. (Illus.). 50p. (Orig.). (C). 1996. spiral bd. 15.95 (*0-932647-17-0*) Rchrdsns Pubng.

Outside Child. Nina Bawden. 1994. 9.09 (*0-606-05968-7*, Pub. by Turtleback) Demco.

Outside Cuba - Fuera de Cuba: Contemporary Cuban Visual Artists. Ed. by Ileana Fuentes-Perez et al. (Illus.). 368p. (C). 1989. text 59.95 (*0-935501-13-4*) Transaction Pubs.

Outside Demands & Pressures on the Public Schools. James F. Waller. LC 73-177665. (Columbia University. Teachers College. Contributions to Education Ser.: No. 542). v, 151p. 1972. reprint ed. 37.50 (*0-404-55542-X*) AMS Pr.

Outside Directors in the Family Owned Business: Why, When, Who & How. Leon A. Danco. LC 81-12931. 1995. reprint ed. 29.95 (*0-9603614-3-X*) Ctr Family Busn.

Outside Doctor on Call: The Life-Story of Dr. Ezra & Frances DeVol. Betty M. Hockett. LC 92-71948. (Illus.). 80p. (J). (gr. 3-8). 1992. pap. 5.00 (*0-943701-20-1*) George Fox Pr.

Outside Dog. Charlotte Pomerantz. (I Can Read Bks.). (Illus.). 64p. (J). (gr. k-3). 1996. pap. 8.95 incl. audio (*0-694-70050-9*) HarpC.

Outside Dog. Charlotte Pomerantz. (I Can Read Bks.). (Illus.). 64p. (J). (gr. 2-4). 1993. lib. bdg. 15.89 (*0-06-024783-5*) HarpC Child Bks.

Outside Dog. Charlotte Pomerantz. (I Can Read Bks.). (Illus.). 64p. (J). (gr. 2-4). 1995. pap. 3.95 (*0-06-444187-3*, HarpTrophy) HarpC Child Bks.

Outside Dog. Charlotte Pomerantz. (I Can Read Bks.). (J). (gr. 2-4). 1995. 9.40 (*0-606-07983-1*) Turtleback.

Outside Dog: A Study Guide. Duncan Searl. Ed. by J. Friedland & R. Kessler. (Novel-Ties Ser.). (J). (gr. 1-3). 1996. pap. text 15.95 (*1-56982-603-X*) Lrn Links.

Outside Eden. John C. Squire. LC 74-150562. (Short Story Index Reprint Ser.). 1977. reprint ed. 19.95 (*0-8369-3860-7*) Ayer.

Outside History: Selected Poems. Eavan Boland. 160p. 1991. pap. 10.95 (*0-393-30822-7*) Norton.

Outside Humanity: A Study of Kafka's Fiction. Ramon G. Mendoza. 310p. (Orig.). (C). 1986. pap. text 26.00 (*0-8191-5516-0*) U Pr of Amer.

***Outside-In.** Sheila Lockhead. 1999. pap. 21.00 (*1-85072-121-1*, Pub. by W Sessions) St Mut.

Outside In. George Nelson. 63p. (Orig.). (YA). (gr. 5-12). 1994. pap. 4.00 (*1-57514-119-1*, 1075) Encore Perform Pub.

Outside In. Clare Smallman & Edwina Riddell. (Illus.). 32p. (J). (ps-2). 1986. 14.95 (*0-8120-5760-0*) Barron.

Outside In. University of Minnesota, Geometry Center Staff. 1994. per. 44.00 incl. VHS (*1-56881-046-6*) AK Peters.

Outside In. Karen R. Young. (J). Date not set. lib. bdg. 15.89 (*0-06-029368-3*, Grenwillow Bks) HarpC Child Bks.

***Outside In.** Karen Romano Young. (J). 2001. 15.95 (*0-688-17363-2*, Greenwillow Bks) HarpC Child Bks.

Outside In: A Cameron Andrews Mystery. Nanisi B. D'Arnuk. LC 96-18719. 200p. (Orig.). 1996. pap. 10.95 (*0-934678-75-8*) New Victoria Pubs.

Outside In: Minorities & the Transformation of American Education. Paula S. Fass. 336p. 1991. reprint ed. pap. text 24.95 (*0-19-507135-2*) OUP.

Outside in the Teaching Machine. Gayatri Chakravorty Spivak. 350p. (C). (gr. 13). 1993. pap. 24.99 (*0-415-90489-7*, A6382) Routledge.

Outside-In Universe: A Case for Ether & Rotating Spiral Structures. Richard L. Vansandt. LC 97-73849. (Illus.). 93p. (Orig.). 1997. pap. 9.95 (*0-9646898-9-8*) Leathers Pub.

Outside Inn. George E. Lyon. LC 90-14285. (Illus.). 32p. (J). (ps-1). 1997. pap. 6.95 (*0-531-07086-7*) Orchard Bks Watts.

Outside, Inside. Carolyn Crimi. LC 93-46897. (Illus.). 40p. (J). (ps-2). 1995. 15.00 (*0-671-88688-6*) S&S Bks Yung.

Outside Inside. Kathleen Fain. LC 97-22570. (J). 1999. bds. 5.95 (*0-8118-1981-7*) Chronicle Bks.

Outside, Inside: A Fresh Look at Tzniut. Gila Manolson. 100p. 1997. pap. 11.95 (*1-56871-123-9*, Pub. by Targum Pr) Feldheim.

Outside Inside Poems. Arnold Adoff. LC 94-25179. (Illus.). 36p. (J). (gr. 1-5). 1995. pap. 5.00 (*0-15-200224-3*, Voyager Bks) Harcourt.

Outside Inside Poems. Arnold Adoff. (J). 1995. 10.20 (*0-606-07984-X*) Turtleback.

Outside Insights. Gordon S. Jackson. LC 97-192194. 1998. pap. text 20.00 (*0-7981-3689-8*) Human & Rousseau.

Outside Lies Magic: Regaining History & Awareness in Everyday Places. John R. Stilgoe. LC 98-3790. 187p. 1998. 21.00 (*0-8027-1340-8*) Walker & Co.

Outside Lies Magic: Regaining History & Awareness in Everyday Places. John R. Stilgoe. 187p. 1999. pap. 10.95 (*0-8027-7563-2*) Walker & Co.

Outside Literature. Tony Bennett. 320p. (C). 1990. pap. 24.99 (*0-415-01094-2*, A4848) Routledge.

Outside Lobbying: Public Opinion & Interest Group Strategies. Ken Kollman. LC 97-39536. 216p. 1998. text 49.50 (*0-691-01740-9*, Pub. by Princeton U Pr); pap. text 17.95 (*0-691-01741-7*, Pub. by Princeton U Pr) Cal Prin Full Svc.

Outside Looking In. James L. Collier. 144p. 1990. pap. 2.95 (*0-380-70961-9*, Avon Bks) Morrow Avon.

***Outside Looking In.** Rowntree. 2000. 25.95 (*0-385-40564-2*, Pub. by Transworld Publishers Ltd) Trafalgar.

Outside Looking In. K. Rowntree. 292p. 1996. pap. 10.95 (*0-552-99606-8*) Bantam.

Outside Looking In: An African Perspective on American Pluralistic Society. Kofi K. Apraku. LC 94-12349. 144p. 1996. 47.95 (*0-275-94207-4*, Praeger Pubs) Greenwood.

Outside Looking In: The Near-Death Experience. Rosemary S. Bahr. (Illus.). 180p. (Orig.). (C). 1992. pap. text 35.00 (*1-881604-00-4*) Scopcraeft.

***Outside Looking in: When Someone You Love Is in Therapy.** Patrice Moulton & Linda Harper. LC 99-24827. 160p. 1999. 20.00 (*1-884444-57-1*) Safer Soc.

Exposure: 20 Years of Photographing the World. Ed. by Outside Magazine Staff. LC 98-125204. (Illus.). 128p. 1997. 40.00 (*1-56579-242-4*) Westcliffe Pubs.

Outside Magazine's Guide to the Pacific Northwest: The Pacific Northwest. Karl Samson. (Frommer's Travel Guides Ser.). (Illus.). 496p. 1997. 18.95 (*0-02-861160-8*) Prntice Hall Bks.

***Outside Magazine's the Ascent Calendar 2000: Legendary Climbs of the Twentieth Century.** David Roberts. (Illus.). 28p. 1999. 9.95 (*1-56512-228-3*, 72228) Algonquin Bks.

Outside Man. Richard North Patterson. 320p. 1982. mass mkt. 6.99 (*0-345-30020-3*) Ballantine Pub Grp.

Outside Man. Richard North Patterson. 1997. pap. 12.00 (*0-345-41815-8*) Ballantine Pub Grp.

***Outside Man.** large type ed. Richard North Patterson. LC 00-39870. 2000. write for info. (*1-56895-907-9*) Wheeler Pub.

***Outside Modernism.** Lynne Hapgood. LC 99-87394. 2000. text 55.00 (*0-312-23202-0*) St Martin.

***Outside Money: Soft Money & Issue Advocacy in the 1998 Congressional Elections.** Ed. by David B. Magleby. LC 99-49349. 192p. 2000. 55.00 (*0-7425-0042-X*); pap. 19.95 (*0-7425-0043-8*) Rowman.

Outside Moscow: Power, Politics & Budgetary Policy in the Soviet Republics. Donna L. Bahry. LC 87-8020. (Illus.). 224p. 1987. text 50.00 (*0-231-06290-7*) Col U Pr.

Outside My Window. Robert D. Darby. 118p. (Orig.). 1996. pap. 5.95 (*1-57502-291-5*, PO1001) Morris Pubng.

***Outside My Window Series, 4 bks.** Ernestine Giesecke. 24p. 1999. 79.68 (*1-57572-685-8*) Heinemann Lib.

***Outside of a Dog: The Essential Groucho.** Ed. by Stephan Kanfer. LC 99-58519. 288p. 2000. pap. 12.00 (*0-375-70213-X*) Vin Bks.

Outside over There. Maurice Sendak. LC 79-2682. (Ursula Nordstrom Bk.). (Illus.). 40p. (J). (gr. k up). 1981. lib. bdg. 19.89 (*0-06-025524-2*) HarpC Child Bks.

An Asterisk (*) at the beginning of an entry indicates that the title is appearing for the first time.

Outside over There. Maurice Sendak. LC 79-2680. (J). 1981. 14.15 (*0-606-03980-5*, Pub. by Turtleback) Demco.
Outside Over There. Maurice Sendak. LC 79-2682. (Ursula Nordstrom Bk.). (Illus.). 40p. (J). (gr. k up). 1981. 20.00 (*0-06-025523-4*) HarpC Child Bks.
Outside Over There. Maurice Sendak. LC 79-2682. (Trophy Picture Bk.). (Illus.). 40p. (J). (ps-3). 1989. pap. 8.95 (*0-06-443185-1*, HarpTrophy) HarpC Child Bks.
Outside Passage: Memoir of an Alaskan Childhood. Julia Scully. LC CT275.S397A3 1999. 1999. pap. 12.95 (*0-375-75240-4*) Modern Lib NY.
Outside Person: An American Corporation Wife Experiences an Alien Culture (Japan) Lois L. Horn. LC 89-83664. (Illus.). 325p. (Orig.). 1989. pap. 12.95 (*0-9622672-0-1*) Konami Pr.
Outside Plant. rev. ed. Frank E. Lee. LC 73-85629. (ABC of the Telephone Ser.: Vol. 4). (Illus.). 128p. (C). 1987. spiral bd. 19.95 (*1-56016-056-X*) ABC TeleTraining.
Outside Plant Communications Cables, Specifying Metric Wire Sizes. rev. ed. 1990. 36.00 (*0-614-18713-3*, S-77-528-1983) Insulated Cable.
Outside Play & Learning Book: Activities for Young Children. Karen Miller. Ed. by Kathleen Charner. LC 88-82595. (Illus.). 253p. (Orig.). 1989. pap. 14.95 (*0-87659-117-9*) Gryphon Hse.
Outside Providence. Peter Farrelly. LC 98-15443. 208p. 1998. pap. 12.95 (*0-385-49058-5*) Doubleday.
***Outside Robins Sing: Selected Haiku by Paul O. Williams.** Paul O. Williams. Ed. by Jeremy Coulter. 48p. 1999. 12.00 (*0-913719-98-6*) Brooks Books.
Outside Shooter. Thomas J. Dygard. (J). 1987. 10.09 (*0-606-04767-0*, Pub. by Turtleback) Demco.
Outside Shot. Walter Dean Myers. (J). 1987. 9.09 (*0-606-03069-7*, Pub. by Turtleback) Demco.
Outside Shot. Walter Dean Myers. 192p. (YA). (gr. k-12). 1986. reprint ed. mass mkt. 4.50 (*0-440-96784-8*, LLL BDD) BDD Bks Young Read.
Outside Stories. Eliot Weinberger. LC 92-9869. 160p. (Orig.). 1992. pap. 10.95 (*0-8112-1221-1*, NDP751, Pub. by New Directions) Norton.
Outside the Arch: Kohut & Five Modern Writers. Catharine Rising. LC 99-20581. 128p. 1999. 33.00 (*0-7618-1385-3*) U Pr of Amer.
Outside the Badge. Mitchell Grobeson. LC 95-90394. 2000. pap. 14.95 (*0-533-11559-0*) Vantage.
Outside the Box: A Book about Life. William McKelvey. (Illus.). 110p. (Orig.). 1997. pap. 10.95 (*0-9633719-1-6*) Eclipse Pub.
Outside the Box: An Unusual Guide for Business Owners. large type ed. Angelita Moreno-Jones. (Orig.). 1997. pap. 14.95 (*0-9637441-5-1*) Kehori.
Outside the Box: How to Beat Your Competitions' Brains Out. Gary D. Zeume. (Illus.). 300p. (Orig.). 1996. pap. 19.95 (*0-9643563-0-9*) Securities Pr.
Outside the Bungalow: America's Arts & Crafts Garden. Paul Duchscherer. LC 99-70250. (Illus.). 192p. 1999. 32.95 (*0-670-88355-7*) Viking Penguin.
Outside the Camp. R. K. Campbell. 16p. pap. 0.30 (*0-88172-157-3*) Believers Bkshelf.
Outside the Dog Museum. Jonathan Carroll. 336p. 1993. mass mkt. 5.99 (*0-553-56164-2*) Bantam.
Outside the Dog Museum. Jonathan Carroll. 256p. 1992. 20.00 (*0-385-41973-2*) Doubleday.
Outside the Door Activity Book, Unit 3. (Networks Ser.). 1991. pap. 2.10 (*0-88106-721-0*, N134) Charlesbridge Pub.
Outside the Door Activity Book (EV), Unit 3. (Networks Ser.). 1991. pap. 3.90 (*0-88106-720-2*) Charlesbridge Pub.
Outside the Door Anthology, Unit 3. (Networks Ser.). 1991. pap. 4.95 (*0-88106-718-0*, N131) Charlesbridge Pub.
Outside the Dream: Child Poverty in America. Stephen Shames. (Illus.). 96p. 1991. 37.95 (*0-89381-468-7*) Aperture.
Outside the Fold: Conversion, Modernity & Belief. Gauri Viswanathan. LC 97-34908. 328p. 1998. text 55.00 (*0-691-05898-9*, Pub. by Princeton U Pr); pap. text 16.95 (*0-691-05899-7*, Pub. by Princeton U Pr) Cal Prin Full Svc.
Outside the Fold, Outside the Frame. Anita Skeen. LC 99-6068. 1999. 17.95 (*0-87013-512-0*) Mich St U Pr.
Outside the Frame: Performance & the Object. Robyn Brentano & Olivia Georgia. Ed. by Kathleen Mills. (Illus.). 80p. 1994. pap. text 24.95 (*1-880353-06-7*) Cleveland Ctr.
Outside the Gates of the World: Selected Short Stories. Thomas Hardy. Ed. by John Bayley & Jan Jedrzejewski. 288p. 1996. pap. 6.95 (*0-460-87574-4*, Everyman's Classic Lib) Tuttle Pubng.
Outside the Hat. Gary Barwin. 114p. 1998. pap. 19.95 (*1-55245-030-9*, Pub. by Coach Hse Bks) SPD-Small Pr Dist.
Outside the House of Baal. Emyr Humphreys. 380p. 1996. pap. 16.95 (*1-85411-102-7*, Pub. by Seren Bks) Dufour.
Outside the Human Aquarium: Masters of Science Fiction. 2nd ed. M. L. Ford & Brian M. Stableford. LC 95-9971. (Popular Writers of Today Ser.: Vol. 32). 152p. 1995. pap. 19.00 (*0-89370-457-1*) Millefleurs.
Outside the Ivory Tower: A Guide for Academics Considering Alternative Careers. Margaret Newhouse. 164p. (Orig.). 1993. pap. 13.00 (*0-943747-08-2*) Harvard OCS.
Outside the Kremlin. Margo Solod. Ed. by Roy Zarucchi. (Chapbook Ser.). (Illus.). 32p. 1996. boxed set 7.95 (*1-879205-69-6*) Nightshade Pr.
Outside the Law. Robert J. Conley. (Illus.). (J). 1995. mass mkt. 4.99 (*0-671-89867-1*) PB.
Outside the Law. Robert Kammen. 160p. 1995. mass mkt. 4.50 (*0-8217-5078-X*, Zebra Kensgtn) Kensgtn Pub Corp.
Outside the Law: A Thief's Primer. Bruce Jackson. LC 79-186713. 243p. 1972. reprint ed. pap. 21.95 (*0-87855-531-5*) Transaction Pubs.
Outside the Law: Narratives on Justice in America. Ed. by Susan R. Shreve & Porter Shreve. LC 96-47163. 196p. 1998. pap. 12.50 (*0-8070-4407-5*) Beacon Pr.
Outside the Lines. R. M. Davis. 1990. write for info. (*0-9617714-3-7*) Cow Hill Pr.
Outside the Lines. Joe S. (Illus.). 69p. student ed. 10.95 (*1-880998-03-3*) State Art OH.
Outside the Lines: African-Americans & the Integration of the National Football League. Charles K. Ross. LC 99-6581. 2000. text 35.00 (*0-8147-7495-4*) NYU Pr.
Outside the Lines: Issues in Interdisciplinary Research. Ed. by Liora Salter & Alison Hearn. LC 97-190867. 216p. 1997. 60.00 (*0-7735-1438-4*, Pub. by McG-Queens Univ Pr) CUP Services.
Outside the Lines: Paintings by Alexandra Nechita. Alexandra Nechita. LC 95-82242. (Illus.). 100p. 1996. 29.95 (*1-56352-454-6*) Longstreet.
Outside the Lines but on the Page: Perspectives on Writing in an Individualized, Writing-Intensive Baccalaureate Degree Program. Sally Nereson. Ed. by Lillian Bridwell-Bowles & Mark Olson. (Technical Reports: No. 8). 38p. (Orig.). (C). 1994. pap. 3.50 (*1-881221-14-8*) U Minn Ctr Interdis.
Outside the Magic Circle: The Autobiography of Virginia Foster Durr. Ed. by Hollinger F. Barnard. LC 84-2556. (Illus.). 384p. 1990. pap. 19.95 (*0-8173-0517-3*) U of Ala Pr.
Outside the Market No Salvation? Ed. by Mieth Dietmar & Marciano Vidal. LC 97-203360. (Concilium Ser.). 150p. 1997. pap. 15.00 (*1-57075-127-7*) Orbis Bks.
Outside the Pale: Cultural Exclusion, Gender Difference, & the Victorian Woman Writer. Elsie B. Michie. LC 93-2458. (Reading Women Writing Ser.). 208p. 1993. pap. text 14.95 (*0-8014-8085-X*) Cornell U Pr.
Outside the Pale: The Architecture of Fay Jones. Ed. by Mark Christ. LC 98-46529. (Illus.). 112p. 1999. pap. 18.00 (*1-55728-543-8*) U of Ark Pr.
Outside the Rules. large type ed. Linda Hughes. LC 93-14357. 331p. (Orig.). 1993. reprint ed. lib. bdg. 15.95 (*0-7862-0010-3*) Thorndike Pr.
Outside the School of Theology. Teri Zipf. LC 97-60378. 82p. (Orig.). 1997. pap. 10.00 (*0-9644440-4-6*) Tsunami.
Outside the Southern Myth. Noel Polk. LC 96-50045. 1997. 45.00 (*0-87805-979-2*); pap. 17.00 (*0-87805-980-6*) U Pr of Miss.
Outside the Subject. Emmanuel Levinas. LC 92-83918. 128p. (C). 1993. 35.00 (*0-8047-2197-1*); pap. 12.95 (*0-8047-2199-8*) Stanford U Pr.
Outside the Wall: The Life of a Prisoner's Wife. Lourdes Santiago. LC 92-41731. 250p. 1993. pap. 14.95 (*0-8135-1987-X*); text 40.00 (*0-8135-1986-1*) Rutgers U Pr.
Outside the Walls of the Asylum: On Care in the Community in Modern Britain & Ireland. Peter Bartlett & David Wright. LC 98-54264. 260p. 1999. 90.00 (*0-485-11541-7*, Pub. by Athlone Pr); pap. 33.95 (*0-485-12147-6*, Pub. by Athlone Pr) Transaction Pubs.
Outside the Window. Alana Sherman. Ed. by Lorraine DeGennaro. 16p. (Orig.). 1990. pap. 3.95 (*0-939689-09-X*) Alms Hse Pr.
Outside Wisconsin: Richardsons' Trail Traveler, 2 vols. Christopher Collier & Margaret Wells. LC 97-219120. (Illus.). (Orig.). 1997. pap., spiral bd. 15.95 (*0-932647-18-9*) Rchrdsns Pubng.
Outsider. Barbara Delinsky. 1997. per. 5.50 (*1-55166-287-6*, 1-66287-3, Mira Bks) Harlequin Bks.
***Outsider.** Barbara Delinsky. LC 00-30291. 2000. write for info. (*0-7862-2617-X*) Thorndike Pr.
Outsider. Howe. (J). 2001. 16.00 (*0-689-81459-3*) Atheneum Yung Read.
Outsider. Melinda Metz. (Rosewell High Ser.: No. 1). 170p. (YA). (gr. 7-12). 1998. mass mkt. 1.99 (*0-671-02374-8*, Archway) PB.
***Outsider.** Melinda Metz. (Rosewell High Ser.: No. 1). (YA). (gr. 7-12). 1999. per. 5.99 (*0-671-77466-2*, Pocket Books) PB.
Outsider. Penelope Williamson. 560p. 1997. mass mkt. 6.50 (*0-446-60477-1*, Pub. by Warner Bks) Little.
Outsider. Richard Wright. (Perennial Library). (Illus.). (J). 1989. 14.10 (*0-606-04291-1*, Pub. by Turtleback) Demco.
Outsider. Colin Wilson. 282p. 1990. reprint ed. lib. bdg. 22.95 (*0-89966-670-1*) Buccaneer Bks.
Outsider. Colin Wilson. LC 79-84901. 336p. 1987. reprint ed. pap. 12.95 (*0-87477-206-0*, Tarcher Putnam) Putnam Pub Group.
Outsider. Richard Wright. LC 88-45970. 672p. 1993. reprint ed. pap. 9.00 (*0-06-081248-6*, P 976, Perennial) HarperTrade.
Outsider: A Journey into My Father's Struggle with Madness. Nathaniel Lachenmeyer. 288p. 2000. 24.00 (*0-7679-0190-8*) Broadway BDD.
***Outsider: Prejudice & Politics in Italy.** Paul M. Sniderman et al. LC 99-89723. (Illus.). 216p. 2000. 29.95 (*0-691-04839-8*, Pub. by Princeton U Pr) Cal Prin Full Svc.
Outsider & Other Stories. Bess S. Aldrich. 20.95 (*0-8488-0161-X*) Amereon Ltd.
Outsider Art. Ferrier. 1998. pap. 27.50 (*2-87939-150-4*) Stewart Tabori & Chang.
Outsider Art: An Exploration of Chicago Collections. Barbara Freeman. (Illus.). 44p. (Orig.). 1997. pap. 18.00 (*0-938903-22-5*) Cty of Chicago.
Outsider Art: Contesting Boundaries in Contemporary Culture. Ed. by Vera L. Zolberg & Joni M. Cherbo. LC 96-52184. (Cultural Social Studies). (Illus.). 236p. (C). 1997. text 59.95 (*0-521-58111-7*); pap. text 22.95 (*0-521-58921-5*) Cambridge U Pr.
***Outsider Art: Spontaneous Alternatives.** Colin Rhodes. LC 99-65579. (World of Art Ser.). (Illus.). 224p. 2000. pap. 14.95 (*0-500-20334-2*, Pub. by Thames Hudson) Norton.
Outsider Art of the South. Kathy Moses. LC 98-43877. (Illus.). 240p. 1999. 59.95 (*0-7643-0729-0*) Schiffer.
Outsider at the Heart of Things: Essays by R. P. Blackmur. Ed. & Intro. by James T. Jones. LC 88-17401. 304p. 1989. text 29.95 (*0-252-01579-7*) U of Ill Pr.
Outsider Features: American Independent Films of the 1980s, 52. Richard K. Ferncase. LC 95-52798. (Contributions to the Study of Popular Culture Ser.: Vol. 52). 176p. 1996. 55.00 (*0-313-27607-2*, Greenwood Pr) Greenwood.
Outsider in Amsterdam. Janwillem Van de Wetering. LC 76-378559. ix, 245p. 1976. write for info. (*0-434-85920-6*) Buttrwrth-Heinemann.
Outsider in Amsterdam. Janwillem Van de Wetering. LC 75-12579. (Soho Crime Ser.). 304p. 1994. pap. 12.00 (*1-56947-017-0*) Soho Press.
Outsider in the House: A Political Autobiography. Bernie Sanders & Huck Gutman. 256p. 1998. pap. 15.00 (*1-85984-177-5*, Pub. by Verso) Norton.
Outsider in the House: A Political Autobiography. Bernie Saunders & Huck Gutman. LC 97-24753. 1997. 25.00 (*1-85984-871-0*, Pub. by Verso) Norton.
Outsiders. 32p. (YA). 1998. 9.95 (*1-56137-362-1*, NU3621) Novel Units.
Outsiders. Adult Ya Reco Young. 1979. 13.20 (*0-394-77997-5*) Random.
Outsiders. Howard S. Becker. 224p. 1997. 14.95 (*0-684-83635-1*) Free Pr.
***Outsiders.** Cliffs Notes Staff. (Cliffs Notes Ser.). 80p. 2000. pap. 4.99 (*0-7645-8559-2*) IDG Bks.
Outsiders. S. E. Hinton. 1990. pap. 5.50 (*0-87129-277-7*, O41) Dramatic Pub.
Outsiders. S. E. Hinton. 156p. (YA). (gr. 7 up). pap. 5.99 (*0-8072-1430-2*) Listening Lib.
Outsiders. S. E. Hinton. 192p. (YA). (gr. 7 up). 1967. 16.99 (*0-670-53257-6*, Viking Child) Peng Put Young Read.
Outsiders. S. E. Hinton. (J). 1997. 10.09 (*0-606-12150-1*, Pub. by Turtleback) Demco.
Outsiders. S. E. Hinton. LC 67-13606. (Illus.). 192p. (YA). (gr. 7-12). 1997. pap. 5.99 (*0-14-038572-X*) Viking Penguin.
***Outsiders.** S. E. Hinton. 1999. pap. 13.50 (*0-88103-039-2*) Econo-Clad Bks.
***Outsiders.** Todd Howard. LC 00-9238. (Understanding Great Literature Ser.). (Illus.). (J). 2001. write for info. (*1-56006-702-0*) Lucent Bks.
Outsiders. M. McCoy Smith. Date not set. 4.99 (*1-871676-52-5*, Pub. by Christian Focus) Spring Arbor Dist.
***Outsiders.** Anne Troy. 36p. (YA). 1999. 11.95 (*1-56137-406-7*) Novel Units.
Outsiders: A History of European Minorities. Panikos Panayi. LC 98-35351. 1998. 35.00 (*1-85285-179-1*) Hambledon Press.
Outsiders: A Literature Unit. Patty Carratello & John Carratello. (Literature Unit Ser.). (Illus.). 48p. (J). Date not set. student ed. 7.95 (*1-55734-406-X*, TCM406) Tchr Create Mat.
Outsiders: A Student Response Journal. rev. ed. James Scott. 15p. (YA). (gr. 7-12). 1998. ring bd. 19.95 (*1-58049-750-0*, RJ03R) Prestwick Hse.
Outsiders: A Study in Life & Letters. Hans Mayer. Tr. by Denis Sweet. 422p. 1982. 49.50 (*0-262-13175-7*) MIT Pr.
Outsiders: A Unit Plan. Mary B. Collins. 152p. 1994. teacher ed., ring bd. 26.95 (*1-58337-020-X*) Teachers Pet Pubns.
Outsiders: American Short Stories for Students of English as a Second Language. Jean Mullen. (Illus.). 256p. (C). 1984. pap. text 31.80 (*0-13-645366-X*) P-H.
Outsiders: Class, Gender & Nation. Dorothy Thompson. 200p. (C). 1993. pap. 19.00 (*0-86091-650-2*, B0529, Pub. by Verso) Norton.
Outsiders: Class, Gender & Nation. Dorothy Thompson. 200p. (C). (gr. 13). 1993. 60.00 (*0-86091-490-9*, B0525, Pub. by Verso) Norton.
Outsiders: Fifteen Funny Gay Stories. Sherwin Carlquist. 224p. 1996. 12.00 (*0-9648861-1-1*) Pinecone Press.
Outsiders: Poems about Rebels, Exiles, & Renegades. Ed. by Laure-Anne Bosselaar. LC 98-32217. 282p. 1999. pap. 16.95 (*1-57131-409-1*) Milkweed Ed.
Outsiders: Poets of Contemporary Ireland. Frank L. Kersnowski. LC 74-21131. 210p. reprint ed. pap. 65.10 (*0-608-14213-1*, 202157000022) Bks Demand.
Outsiders: Reproducible Teaching Unit. rev. ed. James Scott. 29p. (YA). (gr. 7-12). 1995. teacher ed., ring bd. 29.50 (*1-58049-026-3*, TU37/U) Prestwick Hse.
Outsiders: Studies in the Sociology of Deviance. Howard S. Becker. LC 63-8413. 1966. pap. 14.95 (*0-02-902140-5*) Free Pr.
Outsiders - Study Guide. Marcia Tretler. Ed. by Joyce Friedland & Rikki Kessler. (Novel-Ties Ser.). (J). (gr. 6-8). 1993. pap. text 15.95 (*0-88122-030-2*) Lrn Links.
Outsiders & Durango Street: Curriculum Unit. S. E. Hinton & Frank Bonham. (Novel Ser.). 92p. (YA). (gr. 7). 1994. spiral bd. 18.95 (*1-56077-311-1*) Ctr Learning.
Outsiders & Insiders: Perspectives of Third World Culture in British & Post-Colonial Fiction. Michael Harris. LC 91-28482. (Studies of World Literature in English: Vol. 1). 203p. (C). 1992. text 45.95 (*0-8204-1668-1*) P Lang Pubng.
Outsiders & Openness in the Presidential Nominating System. Andrew E. Busch. LC 96-45916. (Policy & Institutional Studies). 248p. 1997. pap. 19.95 (*0-8229-5627-6*); text 45.00 (*0-8229-3976-2*) U of Pittsburgh Pr.
Outsiders & Others: Stories of Outcasts, Rebels, & Seekers by American Teen Writers. Ed. by Kathryn Kulpa & R. James Stahl. LC 95-23611. (American Teen Writer Ser.). (Illus.). 144p. (YA). 1996. pap. 9.95 (*1-886427-05-4*) Merlyns Pen.
Outsiders in a Hearing World: A Sociology of Deafness. Paul C. Higgins. LC 80-12150. (Sociological Observations Ser.: Vol. 10). (Illus.). 205p. 1980. pap. 21.95 (*0-8039-1422-9*) Sage.
Outsiders in the Clubhouse: The World of Women's Professional Golf. Todd W. Crosset. LC 94-27916. (SUNY Series on Sport, Culture, & Social Relations). 276p. (C). 1995. pap. text 21.95 (*0-7914-2490-1*) State U NY Pr.
Outsiders in the Greek Cities of the Fourth Century. Paul McKechnie. 320p. 1989. 45.00 (*0-415-00340-7*) Routledge.
Outsiders in the Lands of Islam: Mamluks, Mongols & Eunuchs. David Ayalon. (Collected Studies: No. CS269). 328p. (C). 1988. reprint ed. lib. bdg. 109.95 (*0-86078-217-4*, Pub. by Variorum) Ashgate Pub Co.
Outsiders in 19th-Century Press History: Multicultural Perspectives. Ed. by Frankie Hutton & Barbara S. Reed. LC 95-30628. 251p. (C). 1995. pap. 19.95 (*0-87972-688-1*) Bowling Green Univ Popular Press.
Outsiders Looking In: A Communication Perspective on the Hill/Thomas Hearings. Ed. by Paul Siegel & Susan J. Drucker. (Communication Ser.). (Illus.). 352p. (Orig.). (C). 1996. text 69.50 (*1-57273-018-8*); pap. text 27.50 (*1-57273-019-6*) Hampton Pr NJ.
Outsiders Looking In: How to Keep from Going Crazy When Someone You Love Goes to Jail. Toni D. Weymouth & Maria Telesco. 352p. 1998. pap. 19.95 (*1-891261-40-1*) Olinc Pub.
***Outsider's Redemption.** Joanna Wayne. (Intrigue Ser.). 2000. mass mkt. 4.25 (*0-373-22593-8*, 1225937) Harlequin Bks.
***Outsiders' Response to European Integration.** Seev Hirsch. LC 98-106682. 1999. 35.00 (*87-16-13233-5*) Mksgaard.
***Outsiders Together: Virginia & Leonard Woolf.** Natania Rosenfeld. LC 99-53742. 2000. 37.50 (*0-691-05884-9*, Pub. by Princeton U Pr) Cal Prin Full Svc.
Outsiders 2: William Oxley. Ed. by James Hogg. 123p. pap. write for info. (*3-7052-0209-X*, Pub. by Poetry Salzburg) Intl Spec Bk.
Outskirts Includes: The King & Me & Tomorrow Today. Hanif Kureishi. 96p. (Orig.). 1984. pap. 9.95 (*0-7145-3971-6*) Riverrun NY.
Outskirts of Bethlehem: A Collection of Selected Poetry. Shawna Maggard. 110p. 1997. pap. write for info. (*1-57502-558-2*, PO1616) Morris Pubng.
Outskirts of Hell. Charles R. Goodman. 288p. 1986. mass mkt. 3.25 (*0-87067-831-0*, BH831) Holloway.
***Outskirts of Paris.** Michelin Staff. 1999. 8.95 (*2-06-010125-5*) Michelin.
Outsmart Crime: 200 Creative Strategies for Baffling the Criminal Mind. Al Ward & Douglas P. Shadel. (Illus.). 256p. (Orig.). 1995. pap. text 12.95 (*0-87877-198-0*) Newcastle Pub.
***Outsmart Your Allergies: Understanding & Identifying the Symptoms, Triggers & Solutions to Your Allergy Problems.** Art Ulene. 288p. 1999. pap. 10.95 (*1-58333-003-8*, Avery) Penguin Putnam.
Outsmarting Diabetes: A Breakthrough Approach for Reducing the Effects of Insulin-Dependent Diabetes. Richard Beaser. 256p. 1994. pap. 14.95 (*0-471-34694-2*) Wiley.
Outsmarting Diabetes: A Breakthrough Approach for Reducing the Effects of Insulin-Dependent Diabetes. Richard S. Beaser. LC 94-11324. 256p. 1994. pap. 14.95 (*1-56561-051-2*) Wiley.
Outsmarting Female Fatigue. Debra Waterhouse. 256p. 2000. 22.95 (*0-7868-6538-5*, Pub. by Hyprn Ppbks) Little.
Outsmarting Female Fatigue. Debra Waterhouse. 256p. 2001. 12.95 (*0-7868-8457-6*, Pub. by Hyprn Ppbks) Little.
***Outsmarting Goliath: How to Achieve Equal Footing with Companies That Are Bigger, Richer, Older & Better Known.** Debra Koontz Traverso. LC 99-54588. 250p. 2000. 19.95 (*1-57660-031-9*, Pub. by Bloomberg NJ) Norton.
Outsmarting IQ: The Emerging Science of Learnable Intelligence. David Perkins. 1995. 25.00 (*0-02-925212-1*) Free Pr.
Outsmarting Managed Care: A Doctor Shares His Insider's Secret to Getting What You Want. Bruce A. Barron. LC 99-31033. 304p. 1999. pap. 15.00 (*0-8129-2981-0*, Times Bks) Crown Pub Group.
Outsmarting Stress. Richard Koole. LC 92-23983. 184p. 1993. pap. 10.99 (*0-8254-3044-5*) Kregel.
Outsmarting the Competition: Practical Approaches to Finding & Using Competitive Information. John J. McGonagle, Jr. & Carolyn M. Vella. LC 92-46122. 1993. 25.00 (*0-07-707755-5*) McGraw.
***Outsmarting the Female Fat Cell: The First Weight-Control Program Designed Specifically for Women.** Debra Waterhouse. LC 93-20498. 256p. 1999. mass mkt. 12.99 (*0-446-67580-6*, Pub. by Warner Bks) Little.
Outsmarting the Female Fat Cell: The First Weight-Control Program Designed Specifically for Women. Debra Waterhouse. 256p. 1994. reprint ed. mass mkt. 5.99 (*0-446-60129-2*, Pub. by Warner Bks) Little.
Outsmarting the Midlife Fat Cell: Winning Weight Control Strategies for Women over 35 to Stay Fit Through Menopause. Debra Waterhouse. LC 97-46937. (Illus.). 270p. (J). 1998. 22.45 (*0-7868-6284-X*, Pub. by Hyperion) Time Warner.

O

Outsmarting the Midlife Fat Cell: Winning Weight Control Strategies for Women over 35 to Stay Fit Through Menopause. Debra Waterhouse. LC 97-46937. (Illus.). 288p. 1999. reprint ed. pap. 12.95 (*0-7868-8412-6*, Pub. by Hyperion) Time Warner.

*__Outsmarting the Post-Pregnancy Fat Cell.__ Debra Waterhouse. 256p. 2001. pap. 12.95 (*0-7868-8456-8*, Pub. by Hyperion) Time Warner.

Outsmarting the Post-Pregnancy Fat Cell. Debra Waterhouse. 256p. 2002. 22.95 (*0-7868-6537-7*, Pub. by Hyperion) Time Warner.

Outsmarting Wall Street: A Profit Proven System for Picking Stocks & Timing the Market. 3rd ed. Daniel Alan Seiver. 225p. 1994. text 29.95 (*1-55738-583-1*, Irwn Prfssnl) McGraw-Hill Prof.

Outsource IT: The Legal Contract. Rachel Burnett. LC 97-47695. 175p. 1998. 96.95 (*0-566-07698-5*, Pub. by Gower) Ashgate Pub Co.

Outsourced: The Employee Handbook: 12 New Rules for Running Your Career in an Interconnected World. Price Pritchett. 56p. (Orig.). 1997. pap. 5.95 (*0-944002-68-4*) Pritchett Assocs.

Outsourcing. International Facility Management Association Staf. (IFMA Research Reports: No. 10). (Illus.). 34p. (Orig.). 1993. pap. 100.00 (*1-883176-04-2*, 146005) Intl Facility Mgmt Assn.

Outsourcing. Mike Johnson. LC 97-7489. (In Brief Ser.). 1997. pap. 29.95 (*0-7506-2876-6*) Buttrwrth-Heinemann.

Outsourcing. N. Dean Meyer. 106p. (Orig.). 1999. pap. 8.95 (*1-892606-04-6*) NDMA Pubng.

Outsourcing promises tantalizing benefits: cost savings, improved responsibilities & fewer distractions. Unfortunately, those claims don't hold up under the harsh test of reality. The ugly truth is that outsourcing is often the last resort for executives frustrated with staff departments. But does it make sense to get rid of management headaches by eliminating an entire department? This book offers practical guidelines that answer the fundamental questions: When is outsourcing appropriate & when is it just throwing too much money at the problem?
Publisher Paid Annotation.

Outsourcing: A CEO's Perspective. Oakie D. Williams. LC 98-5000. 224p. 1998. 39.95 (*1-57444-216-3*, SL2163) St Lucie Pr.

Outsourcing: A Guide to . . . Selecting the Correct Business Unit . . . Negotiating the Contract . . . Maintaining Control of the Business. Steven M. Bragg. LC 98-9842. 384p. 1998. pap. 64.95 (*0-471-25268-9*) Wiley.

Outsourcing: A Guide to . . . Selecting the Correct Business Unit . . . Negotiating the Contract . . . Maintaining Control of the Business, 1. Steven M. Bragg. LC 98-9842. 384p. 1998. 115.00 (*0-471-24728-6*) Wiley.

Outsourcing: Implications for Supply Management. Lisa Ellram & Arnold Maltz. LC 98-130255. 139p. (Orig.). 1997. pap. text 20.00 (*0-945968-26-4*) Ctr Advanced Purchasing.

*__Outsourcing: Solutions for the New Utility.__ L. Dennis Smith et al. 198p. 1999. spiral bd. 495.00 (*1-891790-23-4*) Chartwell Inc.

Outsourcing: Would It Benefit Your Organization's Mail Center? Lewis C. Smith. 40p. 1995. text 17.50 (*0-9642061-1-0*) IPMA.

Outsourcing Cataloging, Authority Work, & Physical Processing: A Checklist of Considerations. Marie A. Kascus & Dawn Hale. 40p. (Orig.). 1995. pap. text, per. 15.00 (*0-8389-3449-8*) ALA.

Outsourcing Dilemma: What's Best for Internal Auditing. Larry E. Rittenberg & Institute of Internal Auditors Research Foundation. Ed. by Lee A. Campbell. LC 97-216324. (Illus.). 155p. 1997. pap. 95.00 (*0-89413-384-5*) Inst Inter Aud.

Outsourcing Document Conversion & Indexing Services. James Fruscione. 148p. 1995. per. 59.00 (*0-89258-297-9*, R019) Assn Inform & Image Mgmt.

Outsourcing, Downsizing & Reengineering. Albert J. Marcella. Ed. by Lee A. Campbell. LC 95-189683. 352p. 1995. pap. 50.00 (*0-89413-331-4*, A890) Inst Inter Aud.

Outsourcing Human Resources Functions: Strategies for Providing Enhanced HR Services at Lower Cost. Mary F. Cook. LC 98-26302. 350p. 1998. 107.95 (*0-8144-0419-7*) AMACOM.

Outsourcing in Health Care: The Administrator's Guide. Jo Surpin & Gerri Weidman. LC 98-47917. 1999. 32.00 (*1-55648-251-5*) AHPI.

Outsourcing in Metropolitan Libraries. George D'Elia. Ed. & Illus. by Urban Libraries Council Staff. (Frequent Fast Facts Survey Ser.). 304p. 1999. pap. 45.00 (*1-885251-22-X*) Urban Libraries.

Outsourcing Info Systems. Kathy Ripin. 1997. pap. 28.95 (*0-201-63457-0*) Addison-Wesley.

Outsourcing Library Operations in Academic Libraries: An Overview of Issues & Outcomes. Claire-Lise Benaud & Sever Bordeianu. LC 98-17118. 215p. 1998. 40.00 (*1-56308-509-7*) Libs Unl.

Outsourcing Library Technical Services: A How-to-Do-It Manual for Librarians. Arnold Hirshon & Barbara A. Winters. LC 96-3402. (How-to-Do-It Manuals Ser.). 200p. 1996. pap. 55.00 (*1-55570-221-X*); disk 72.00 (*1-55570-273-2*) Neal-Schuman.

Outsourcing Library Technical Services Operations: Practices in Academic, Public, & Special Libraries. Association for Library Collections & Technical Services, American Library Association. Ed. by Karen A. Wilson & Marylou Colver. LC 97-22901. 239p. 1997. 38.00 (*0-8389-0703-2*) ALA.

Outsourcing Manual of Management. Robert White & Barry James. 318p. 1996. 113.95 (*0-566-07834-1*, Pub. by Gower) Ashgate Pub Co.

Outsourcing of DoD Commercial Activities: Impacts on Civil Service. Albert A. Robbert et al. LC 97-27520. (Illus.). 137p. 1997. pap. 15.00 (*0-8330-2521-X*, MR-866-OSD) Rand Corp.

*__Outsourcing R & D Toolkit.__ Peter A. Sammons. 240p. 2000. ring bd. 262.95 (*0-566-08314-0*, Pub. by Gower) Ashgate Pub Co.

Outsourcing Security Services: The Modern Strategy. John Stees. LC 98-21893. 164p. 1998. 34.95 (*0-7506-7023-1*, Newnes) Buttrwrth-Heinemann.

Outsourcing Solutions: Workforce Strategies That Improve Profitability. Carleen Nelson-Nesvig. LC 97-67219. 160p. (Orig.). 1997. pap. 12.95 (*1-890394-01-7*) Rhodes & Easton.

Outsourcing State & Local Government Services: Decision-Making Strategies & Management Methods. John A. O'Looney. LC 98-18502. 256p. 1998. 59.95 (*1-56720-169-5*, Quorum Bks) Greenwood.

Outsourcing to Industrial Sales RE for Manufacturers & Distributors. Hank Lavin. (Illus.). 40p. 1998. 14.95 (*0-941890-07-4*, B9) Lavin Assocs.

*__Outsourcing Training & Education.__ Garry J. DeRose. LC 99-72435. 247p. 1999. pap. 27.95 (*1-56286-112-3*) Am Soc Train & Devel.

Outsourcing Trends in the Customer Support Industry. Char LaBounty. Ed. by Patrick Bultema et al. (Illus.). 70p. (Orig.). pap. write for info. (*1-57125-017-4*) Help Desk Inst.

*__Outspeak: Narrating Identities That Matter.__ Sean P. O'Connell. LC 99-86459. (C). 2000. pap. text 18.95 (*0-7914-4738-3*) State U NY Pr.

*__Outspeak: Narrating Identities That Matter.__ Sean P. O'Connell. LC 99-86459. (C). 2000. text 57.50 (*0-7914-4737-5*) State U NY Pr.

Outspeaks: A Rhapsody. Albert Saijo. (Bamboo Ridge Ser.: Vol. 71). 199p. 1997. pap. 12.00 (*0-910043-50-7*) Bamboo Ridge Pr.

Outspoken: Keith Howes' Gay News Interviews 1976-1983. Keith Howes. Date not set. pap. 16.95 (*0-304-33397-2*, Pub. by Cassell) LPC InBook.

OutSpoken: Role Models from the Lesbian & Gay Community. Michael T. Ford. LC 97-40576. 240p. (YA). (gr. 7 up). 1998. mass mkt. 4.95 (*0-688-14897-2*, Wm Morrow) Morrow Avon.

OutSpoken: Role Models from the Lesbian & Gay Community. Michael T. Ford. LC 97-40576. 240p. (J). (gr. 7-12). 1998. 16.00 (*0-688-14896-4*, Wm Morrow) Morrow Avon.

Outspoken Essays. William R. Inge. LC 75-156664. (First Ser.). 1977. reprint ed. 23.95 (*0-8369-2404-5*); reprint ed. 23.95 (*0-8369-2405-3*) Ayer.

Outspoken Essays on Music. Camille Saint-Saens. Tr. by Fred Rothwell. LC 71-84335. (Essay Index Reprint Ser.). 1977. 18.95 (*0-8369-1105-9*) Ayer.

Outspoken Essays on Music. Camille Saint-Saens. Tr. by Fred Rothwell. LC 79-100835. 186p. 1970. reprint ed. lib. bdg. 49.50 (*0-8371-4010-2*, SAES, Greenwood Pr) Greenwood.

Outspoken Essays on Music. Camille Saint-Saens. 186p. 1990. reprint ed. lib. bdg. 59.00 (*0-7812-9004-X*) Rprt Serv.

Outstanding Achievement. Ed. by Case & Lawrence. (Illus.). 144p. 1997. text 49.95 (*1-885206-49-6*) Cader Pubng.

Outstanding African Americans of Congress. Shirley Washington. LC 98-61369. (Outstanding Members of Congress Ser.). (Illus.). 88p. (YA). (gr. 7-12). 1998. pap. 5.95 (*0-916200-23-X*) US Capitol Hist.

Outstanding African Americans Series, 12 bks. Incl. Great African Americans in Business. Pat Rediger. LC 95-24879. (Illus.). 64p. (YA). (gr. 4-11). 1995. pap. 8.95 (*0-86505-817-2*); Great African Americans in Business. Pat Rediger. LC 95-24879. (Illus.). 64p. (YA). (gr. 4-11). 1995. lib. bdg. 21.28 (*0-86505-803-2*); Great African Americans in Civil Rights. Pat Rediger. LC 95-24881. (Illus.). 64p. (YA). (gr. 4-11). 1995. pap. 8.95 (*0-86505-812-1*); Great African Americans in Civil Rights. Pat Rediger. LC 95-24881. (Illus.). 64p. (YA). (gr. 4-11). 1995. lib. bdg. 21.28 (*0-86505-798-2*); Great African Americans in Entertainment. Pat Rediger. LC 95-37451. (Illus.). 64p. (YA). (gr. 4-11). 1995. pap. 8.95 (*0-86505-813-X*); Great African Americans in Entertainment. Pat Rediger. (Illus.). 64p. (YA). (gr. 4-10). 1995. lib. bdg. 21.28 (*0-86505-799-0*); Great African Americans in Film. Janice Parker. LC 96-46677. (Illus.). 64p. (YA). (gr. 4-10). 1997. pap. 8.95 (*0-86505-822-9*); Great African Americans in Film. Janice Parker. LC 96-46677. (Illus.). 64p. (YA). (gr. 4-10). 1997. lib. bdg. 21.28 (*0-86505-808-3*); Great African Americans in Government. Karen Dudley. LC 96-35446. (Illus.). 64p. (YA). (gr. 4-11). 1997. pap. 8.95 (*0-86505-820-2*); Great African Americans in Government. Karen Dudley. LC 96-35446. (Illus.). 64p. (YA). (gr. 4-10). 1997. lib. bdg. 21.28 (*0-86505-806-7*); Great African Americans in History. Carlotta Hacker. LC 96-38690. (Illus.). 64p. (YA). (gr. 4-7). 1997. pap. 8.95 (*0-86505-819-9*); Great African Americans in History. Carlotta Hacker. LC 96-38690. (Illus.). 64p. (YA). (gr. 4-10). 1997. lib. bdg. 21.28 (*0-86505-805-9*); Great African Americans in Jazz. Carlotta Hacker. LC 96-41844. (Illus.). 64p. (YA). (gr. 4-11). 1997. pap. 8.95 (*0-86505-818-0*); Great African Americans in Jazz. Carlotta Hacker. LC 96-41844. (Illus.). 64p. (YA). (gr. 4-10). 1997. lib. bdg. 21.28 (*0-86505-804-0*); Great African Americans in Literature. Pat Rediger. (Illus.). 64p. (YA). (gr. 4-10). 1995. pap. 8.95 (*0-86505-816-4*); Great African Americans in Literature. Pat Rediger. (Illus.). 64p. (YA). (gr. 4-10). 1995. lib. bdg. 21.28 (*0-86505-802-4*); Great African Americans in Music. Pat Rediger. (Illus.). 64p. (YA). (gr. 4-10). 1995. pap. 8.95 (*0-86505-814-8*); Great African Americans in Music. Pat Rediger. (Illus.). 64p. (YA). (gr. 4-10). 1995. lib. bdg. 21.28 (*0-86505-800-8*); Great African Americans in Sports. Pat Rediger. LC 95-24880. (Illus.). 64p. (YA). (gr. 4-11). 1995. pap. 8.95 (*0-86505-815-6*); Great African Americans in Sports. Pat Rediger. (Illus.). 64p. (YA). (gr. 4-10). 1995. lib. bdg. 21.28 (*0-86505-801-6*); Great African Americans in the Arts. Carlotta Hacker. LC 96-46676. (Illus.). 64p. (YA). (gr. 4-11). 1997. pap. 8.95 (*0-86505-821-0*); Great African Americans in the Arts. Carlotta Hacker. LC 96-46676. (Illus.). 64p. (YA). (gr. 4-10). 1997. lib. bdg. 21.28 (*0-86505-807-5*); Great African Americans in the Olympics. Shaun Hunter. LC 96-46148. (Illus.). 64p. (YA). (gr. 4-10). 1997. pap. 8.95 (*0-86505-823-7*); Great African Americans in the Olympics. Shaun Hunter. LC 96-46148. (Illus.). 64p. (YA). (gr. 4-10). 1997. lib. bdg. 21.28 (*0-86505-809-1*); (Illus.). (J). Set pap. 107.40 (*0-86505-825-3*); Set lib. bdg. 21.28 (*0-86505-811-3*) Crabtree Pub Co.

Outstanding American Statesmen: Lectures by William Henry Harbaugh, Arthur S. Link, Frank Freidel, Alfred I. Chandler, Jr. Ed. by Russell H. Lucas. LC 70-118577. 61p. 1970. reprint ed. pap. 30.00 (*0-608-05342-2*, 206504700012) Bks Demand.

*__Outstanding Art.__ Lillian Coppock. (Illus.). 2000. pap. 15.95 (*0-947882-30-8*) Belair Pubns Ltd.

Outstanding Art Ideas for Kids, 4-6. Troll Books Staff. 96p. 1999. pap. text 12.95 (*0-8167-2596-9*) Troll Communs.

Outstanding Athletes of Congress. Doris R. Corbett. (Outstanding Members of Congress Ser.). (Illus.). 80p. (Orig.). (YA). (gr. 7-12). 1997. pap. 4.95 (*0-916200-21-3*) US Capitol Hist.

*__Outstanding Bar & Restaurant Designs.__ Antique Collectors Club Staff. (Illus.). 1998. pap. 24.95 (*2-7450-0011-X*) Telleri Edit.

Outstanding Black Sermons. Ed. by J. Alfred Smith. LC 76-2084. 96p. 1976. pap. 12.00 (*0-8170-0664-8*) Judson.

Outstanding Black Sermons, Vol. 2. Ed. by Walter B. Hoard. 1978. pap. 12.00 (*0-8170-0832-2*) Judson.

Outstanding Black Sermons, Vol. 3. Ed. by Milton E. Owens, Jr. 80p. 1982. pap. 12.00 (*0-8170-0973-6*) Judson.

Outstanding Blues & Jazz Compositions: Beginners - Intermediate Level, Vol. I. Andrew D. Gordon. 53p. 1990. 19.95 incl. audio (*1-882146-01-8*); 24.95 incl. disk (*1-882146-02-6*) A D G Prods.

Outstanding Blues & Jazz Compositions: Intermediate - Advanced Level, Vol. I. Andrew D. Gordon. 66p. 1990. 19.95 incl. audio (*1-882146-06-9*) A D G Prods.

Outstanding Blues & Jazz Compositions, Vol. I: Intermediate - Advanced Level, Vol. I. Andrew D. Gordon. 66p. 1990. 24.95 incl. disk (*1-882146-07-7*) A D G Prods.

Outstanding Books for Children & Young People: The LA Guide to Carnegie/Greenaway Medal. Keith Barker. 135p. 1998. pap. 35.00 (*1-85604-287-1*, LAP2871, Pub. by Library Association) Bernan Associates.

Outstanding Books for the College Bound: Choices for a Generation. Young Adult Library Services Association Staff. LC 96-5086. 200p. (YA). 1996. pap. 25.00 (*0-8389-3456-0*) ALA.

Outstanding Child Care with a Professional Nanny. Alexandra Allison. 38p. (Orig.). pap. 29.99 (*1-878235-24-9*) Taylor Pub MI.

Outstanding Customer Service: Implementing the Best Ideas from Around the World. Colin G. Armistead & Graham Clark. LC 93-29974. 300p. 1993. 25.00 (*1-55623-629-8*, Irwn Prfssnl) McGraw-Hill Prof.

Outstanding Customer Service: The Key to Customer Loyalty. David E. Deviney. Ed. by Karen Massetti Miller. LC 98-72664. (How-to Book Ser.). 103p. 1998. pap. 12.95 (*1-884926-95-9*) Amer Media.

Outstanding Hotel Designs. Olivier Boissiere. (Illus.). 160p. 24.95 (*2-7450-0031-4*) Telleri Edit.

Outstanding in His Field. Steven Rottgers. LC 95-68405. (Illus.). 27p. (Orig.). 1995. pap. 8.95 (*1-882792-10-6*) Proctor Pubns.

Outstanding in His Field: Perspectives on American Agricultural History in Honor of Wayne D. Rasmussen. Ed. by Frederick V. Carstensen et al. LC 92-45889. (Henry A. Wallace Series on Agricultural History & Rural Studies). (Illus.). 176p. (C). 1993. text 44.95 (*0-8138-0739-5*) Iowa St U Pr.

Outstanding International Press Reporting: From the Consequences of World War I to the End of World War II, 1928-1945, 3 vols., Vol. 1. Ed. by Heinz-Dietrich Fischer. LC 83-18962. (Illus.). liii, 368p. 1984. 115.40 (*3-11-008918-1*) De Gruyter.

Outstanding International Press Reporting: Pulitzer Prize Winning Articles in Foreign Correspondence, Vol. 4. Ed. by Heinz-Dietrich Fischer. (Illus.). xlviii, 332p. (C). 1991. lib. bdg. 152.35 (*3-11-012539-0*, 171-91) De Gruyter.

Outstanding International Press Reporting: Pulitzer Prize Winning Articles in Foreign Correspondence, 1946-1962: From the End of World War II to the Various Stations of the Cold War, Vol. 2. Ed. by Heinz-Dietrich Fischer. (Illus.). lxviii, 304p. 1985. 115.40 (*3-11-009824-5*) De Gruyter.

Outstanding International Press Reporting: Pulitzer Prize Winning Articles in Foreign Correspondence, 1963-1977: From the Escalation of the Vietnam War to the East Asian Refugee Problems, Vol. 3. Ed. by Heinz-Dietrich Fischer. (Illus.). xxvi, 309p. 1986. lib. bdg. 103.10 (*3-11-009842-3*) De Gruyter.

Outstanding Jazz Keyboard - Organ Solos. Andrew D. Gordon. 92p. 1997. write for info. (*1-882146-56-5*) ADG Prods.

Outstanding Jazz Saxophone Solos. Frank Villafranca. Ed. by Andrew D. Gordon. 57p. 1998. pap. 19.95 incl. audio compact disk (*1-882146-63-8*) A D G Prods.

Outstanding Lives: Profiles of Lesbians & Gay Men. Ed. by Christa Brelin & Michael J. Tyrkus. LC 97-11522. (Illus.). 454p. 1997. 24.95 (*1-57859-008-6*) Visible Ink Pr.

Outstanding Medicaid Eligibility Workers at Community & Migrant Health Centers. Tim M. Henderson. Ed. by Karen Glass. 49p. (Orig.). 1992. pap. text 15.00 (*1-55877-151-4*) Natl Governor.

Outstanding Oceans. Annalisa Suid. (Super-Duper Science Ser.). (Illus.). 80p. (Orig.). (J). (gr. 1-3). 1996. pap. 9.95 (*1-878279-91-2*, MM2020) Monday Morning Bks.

Outstanding Oregon Recipes. Daniela Mahoney. (Illus.). 120p. 1992. reprint ed. spiral bd. 6.95 (*0-941016-87-0*) Penfield.

Outstanding Public & Private Elementary Schools in the United States. Pref. by Richard W. Hostrop. LC 88-16236. 448p. 1989. pap. 19.95 (*0-88280-121-X*) ETC Pubns.

Outstanding Scenic Geological Features of Pennsylvania, Pt. 2. Alan R. Geyer & William H. Bolles. (Environmental Geology Reports: No. 7, Pt. 2). (Illus.). 270p. (Orig.). 1987. pap. 4.60 (*0-8182-0080-4*) Commonweal PA.

Outstanding School Administrators: Their Keys to Success. Frederick C. Wendel et al. LC 95-23208. 192p. 1995. 55.00 (*0-275-94822-6*, Praeger Pubs) Greenwood.

*__Outstanding Shop Designs.__ (Illus.). 160p. 1998. 24.95 (*2-7450-0016-0*) Telleri Edit.

*__Outstanding Short Stories.__ Lv. 5. (C). 2000. 7.00 (*0-582-41933-6*) Addison-Wesley.

Outstanding Similar & Identical Events in the Life of the Lord Jesus Christ. (Walk with Jesus Ser.). 20p. 1987. pap. 5.00 (*1-57277-204-2*) Script Rsch.

*__Outstanding Stage Monologs & Scenes from the 90s: Professional Auditions for Student Actors.__ Ed. by Steven H. Gale & Ted Zapel. 200p. (YA). 2000. pap. 14.95 (*1-56608-058-4*) Meriwether Pub.

Outstanding Stories by General Authorities. Compiled by Leon R. Hartshorn. pap. 13.95 (*1-55517-381-0*) CFI Dist.

Outstanding Women Athletes: Who They Are & How They Influenced Sports in America. 2nd ed. Janet Woolum. LC 98-17076. (Illus.). 412p. (YA). (gr. 5 up). 1998. text 54.95 (*1-57356-120-7*) Oryx Pr.

Outstanding Women Members of Congress. Shirley A. Washington. LC 95-61450. (Outstanding Members of Congress Ser.). (Illus.). 72p. (Orig.). (YA). (gr. 7-12). 1995. pap. 4.95 (*0-916200-13-2*) US Capitol Hist.

Outstanding Young Men of America, Vol. 1. 1997. 109.95 (*0-9651664-0-6*) Recognition Progs.

Outstanding Young Women of America. 1996. 109.95 (*0-9651664-1-4*) Recognition Progs.

Outstandingly His: The Life Story of Paul & Mary Williams (Uncle Paul & Aunt Mary) Lorene Moothart. (Orig.). 1993. pap. 7.95 (*1-885729-02-2*) Toccoa Falls.

Outstaring Nature's Eye: The Fiction of John McGahern. Denis Sampson. LC 92-25058. 267p. 1993. 34.95 (*0-8132-0766-5*) Cath U Pr.

*__Outtakes.__ Dan Patrick. LC 99-57923. (Illus.). 160p. 2000. pap. 12.95 (*0-7868-8539-4*, Pub. by Hyperion) Time Warner.

Outtakes: Devotions for Girls. Bill Sanders. LC 88-18283. 180p. (YA). (gr. 9-12). 1988. pap. 9.99 (*0-8007-5284-8*) Revell.

Outward. David Gordon. 73p. 1991. pap. 11.95 (*0-943373-14-X*) Natl Poet Foun.

Outward & Visible Signs. Julia M. Gibert. 1987. write for info. (*0-318-61905-9*) Viking Penguin.

Outward Angel. Alanna Knight. 224p. 1996. 19.00 (*0-7278-4483-0*) Severn Hse.

Outward Appearances: Dressing State & Society in Indonesia. Ed. by Henk S. Nordholt. LC 98-120168. (Proceedings Ser.: Vol. 4). (Illus.). 378p. 1998. pap. 37.00 (*90-6718-118-8*, Pub. by KITLV Pr) Cellar.

Outward Bound. James Patrick Hogan. LC 98-43789. (Jupiter Ser.: No. 6). 220p. 1999. 22.95 (*0-312-86243-1*, Pub. by Tor Bks) St Martin.

*__Outward Bound.__ James Patrick Hogan. 224p. 2000. mass mkt. 5.99 (*0-8125-7191-6*, Pub. by Tor Bks) St Martin.

Outward Bound. Sutton Vane. (Illus.). 1952. 4.95 (*0-87140-829-5*, Pub. by Liveright) Norton.

*__Outward Bound: American Art at the Brink of the Twenty-First Century.__ Nancy Matthews & Eric Gibson. LC 99-62969. (Illus.). 100p. 1999. pap. 25.00 (*0-9661013-1-6*) Meridian Int Ctr.

Outward Bound: Relocation & Community Care for People with Learning Difficulties. Tim Booth et al. 192p. 1990. 113.00 (*0-335-15431-X*); pap. 40.95 (*0-335-15430-1*) OpUniv Pr.

Outward Bound Canoeing Handbook. Paul Landry & Mattie McNair. (Illus.). 144p. 1992. pap. 12.95 (*1-55821-149-7*) Lyons Pr.

Outward Bound EarthBook. Ed. by Larry Crenshaw. (Illus.). 128p. 1995. pap. 14.95 (*0-89732-195-2*) Menasha Ridge.

Outward Bound Map & Compass Handbook. 2nd rev. ed. Glenn Randall. LC 98-18603. (Illus.). 128p. 1998. pap. 10.95 (*1-55821-747-9*) Lyons Pr.

*__Outward Bound Staying Warm in the Outdoors Handbook.__ Glenn Randall. 2000. 14.95 (*1-58574-089-6*) Lyons Pr.

Outward Bound, the Inward Odyssey. Mark Zelinski. Ed. by Gary Schaeffer. LC 91-71043. (Illus.). 204p. 1991. 39.95 (*0-941831-64-7*) Beyond Words Pub.

Outward Bound Wilderness First-Aid Handbook. Jeffrey Isaac. LC 97-43329. 1998. pap. 14.95 (*1-55821-682-0*) Lyons Pr.

O

***Outward Bound Wilderness Survival Handbook.** Len McDougall. (Illus.). 2001. pap. 14.95 (*1-58574-159-0*) Lyons Pr.

Outward Dreams: Black Inventors & Their Inventions. Jim Haskins. 128p. (J). (gr. 7). 1991. 13.95 (*0-8027-6993-4*); lib. bdg. 14.85 (*0-8027-6994-2*) Walker & Co.

Outward Leg. Tristan Jones. LC 98-230591. 286p. 1998. reprint ed. pap. 14.95 (*1-57409-061-5*) Sheridan.

Outward Show: Music for Shakespeare on the London Stage, 1660-1830, 27. Randy L. Neighbarger. LC 92-5423. (Contributions to the Study of Music & Dance Ser.: No. 27). 340p. 1992. 59.95 (*0-313-27805-9*, NML, Greenwood Pr) Greenwood.

Outward Side. James Colton. 1995. mass mkt. 6.95 (*1-56333-304-X*, Hard Candy) Masquerade.

Outward Sign & Inward Grace: The Place of Sacraments in Wesleyan Spirituality. Robert L. Staples. 304p. 1991. kivar 21.99 (*0-8341-1378-3*) Beacon Hill.

Outward Signs: The Language of Christian Symbolism for Artists & Designers. Edward N. West. (Illus.). 256p. (Orig.). 1992. reprint ed. pap. 14.95 (*0-8027-7364-8*) Walker & Co.

Outward Signs: The Language of Christian Symbols. Edward N. West. (Illus.). 288p. 1989. 30.00 (*0-8027-1073-5*) Walker & Co.

***Outwitting Bears.** Gary Brown. 2001. pap. 14.95 (*1-58574-160-4*) Lyons Pr.

***Outwitting Critters.** Bill Adler, Jr. 1998. pap. 12.95 (*0-676-57281-2*) Random.

Outwitting Critters: A Humane Guide for Confronting Devious Animals & Winning. Bill Adler, Jr. LC 96-2750. 272p. 1997. pap. 12.95 (*1-55821-523-9*) Lyons Pr.

***Outwitting Deer.** Bill Adler, Jr. LC 99-33059. (Illus.). 1999. pap. 14.95 (*1-55821-629-4*) Lyons Pr.

Outwitting Hitler, Surviving Stalin: The Story of Arthur Spindler. Arthur Spindler. 192p. 1997. pap. 19.95 (*0-86840-496-9*, Pub. by New South Wales Univ Pr) Intl Spec Bk.

***Outwitting Mice.** Bill Adler, Jr. (Illus.). 224p. 2000. 14.95 (*1-58574-004-7*) Lyons Pr.

Outwitting Mother Nature: Why & How to Use Diet Pills. Ernest D. Swersky. LC 97-170399. 149p. 1997. pap. 14.95 (*0-9656544-0-0*) E D Swersky.

Outwitting Squirrels. rev. ed. Storey Publishing Staff. 1997. pap. 11.95 (*0-676-57118-2*) Random.

Outwitting Squirrels: 101 Cunning Stratagems to Reduce Dramatically the Egregious Misappropriation of Seed from Your Birdfeeder by Squirrels. 2nd ed. Bill Adler, Jr. LC 88-20283. (Illus.). 188p. 1996. pap. 11.95 (*1-55652-302-5*) Chicago Review.

Outwitting the Devil: Jack Tales from Wise County, Virginia. Ed. by Charles L. Perdue, Jr. LC 87-71657. (New Deal & Folk Culture Ser.). (Illus.). 129p. 1987. pap. 10.95 (*0-941270-42-4*) Ancient City Pr.

Outwitting the Gestapo. Lucie Aubrac. Tr. by Betsy Wing & Konrad Bieber. LC 92-26861. (Illus.). xxiii, 241p. 1993. pap. 12.00 (*0-8032-5923-9*, Bison Books) U of Nebr Pr.

Outwitting the Gestapo. large type ed. Lucie Aubrac. Tr. by Konrad Bieber & Betsy Wing from GER. LC 93-30906. 408p. 1993. lib. bdg. 17.95 (*0-7862-0039-1*) Thorndike Pr.

Outwitting the Hun: My Escape from a German Prison Camp. Pat A. O'Brien. (American Biography Ser.). 283p. 1991. reprint ed. lib. bdg. 69.00 (*0-7812-8301-9*) Rprt Serv.

***Outwitting the Neighbors: A Practical & Entertaining Guide to Achieving Peaceful Coexistence with Your Neighbors.** Bill Adler, Jr. 2000. pap. 14.95 (*1-58574-161-2*) Lyons Pr.

Outwitting the State Vol. 7: Political Anthropology. Ed. by Peter Skalnick. 172p. 1989. text 34.95 (*0-88738-274-6*) Transaction Pubs.

Outwitting the Tiger: A Chinese Legend. Margaret Mooney. LC 93-26261. (Illus.). (J). 1994. 4.25 (*0-383-03776-X*) SRA McGraw.

***Outwitting Ticks.** Susan C. Hauser. (Illus.). 2000. pap. 14.95 (*1-58574-021-7*) Lyons Pr.

Outwitting Toddlers. Ed. by Bill Adler, Jr. & Peggy Robin. (Illus.). 192p. (Orig.). 1993. pap. 12.95 (*1-56565-032-8*) Lowell Hse.

Outwitting Your Alcoholic: Exploring & Escaping from the Strange World of Alcoholism. Kenneth Lucas. LC 98-17877. 1998. pap. 14.00 (*1-882883-38-1*) Idyll Arbor.

Outworld. McRobbie. (Clipper Fiction Ser.). 1994. pap. text. write for info. (*0-582-80266-0*, Pub. by Addison-Wesley) Longman.

Outwrite: Lesbianism & Popular Culture. Griffin. LC 93-2991. 204p. (C). 49.95 (*0-7453-0687-X*, Pub. by Pluto GBR); pap. 15.95 (*0-7453-0688-8*, Pub. by Pluto GBR) Stylus Pub VA.

Ouverture en Bemol. Plantu. (FRE.). 174p. 1991. pap. 15.95 (*0-7859-4365-X*, 2070383857) Fr & Eur.

Ouvertures Text with List Cass. Siskin. 1997. 74.00 (*0-03-097171-3*) Harcourt Coll Pubs.

Ouvrage Didie a la Memoire Du Professor Henry Germain (1903-1989) Avec la Collaboration de Michel Coste. Ed. by Michel Ricard. (Illus.). 265p. 1990. 150.00 (*3-87429-322-X*, Pub. by Koeltz Sci Bks) Lubrecht & Cramer.

OV-10 Bronco in Action. Jim Mesko. (Aircraft in Action Ser.). (Illus.). 50p. 1995. pap. 9.95 (*0-89747-340-X*) Squad Sig Pubns.

Ova-Dose: Australian Women & the New Reproductive Technology. (Illus.). 144p. (Orig.). 1992. pap. text 16.95 (*1-86373-056-7*, Pub. by Allen & Unwin Pty) Paul & Co Pubs.

Oval Hour. Kathleen Peirce. LC 98-44842. (Iowa Poetry Prize Ser.). 86p. 1999. pap. 10.95 (*0-87745-664-X*) U of Iowa Pr.

Oval Stained Glass Pattern Book: 60 Full Page Designs. Connie C. Eaton. (Stained Glass Ser.). (Illus.). 64p. 1983. pap. 6.95 (*0-486-24519-5*) Dover.

***Ovals.** Jennifer S. Burke. (Welcome Bks.). (Illus.). (J). 2000. 13.50 (*0-516-23076-X*) Childrens.

***Ovals.** Jennifer S. Burke. (City Shapes Ser.). (Illus.). 24p. (J). (ps-2). 2000. pap. 4.95 (*0-516-23001-8*) Childrens.

Ovals. George Tysh. 52p. 1985. pap. 4.95 (*0-932597-02-5*) In Camera.

Ovarialkarzinom. Ed. by A. Pfleiderer. (Journal: Onkologie: Vol. 7, Suppl. 2). 70p. 1984. pap. 17.50 (*3-8055-3922-3*) S Karger.

***Ovarian & Fallopian Tube Cancer.** John J. Kavanagh et al. (Illus.). 1998. 95.00 (*0-632-04432-2*) Blackwell Sci.

***Ovarian Apoptosis.** Ed. by Benjamin K. Tsang. (Biological Signals & Receptors Ser.: Vol. 9, No. 2 (2000)). (Illus.). 56p. 2000. pap. 25.25 (*3-8055-7090-2*) S Karger.

Ovarian Autoimmunity: Clinical & Experimental Data. Ed. by Roy Moncayo & Helga E. Moncayo. LC 94-42131. (Neuroscience Intelligence Unit Ser.). 120p. 1995. text 69.00 (*1-57059-219-5*) Landes Bioscience.

Ovarian Cancer. 1997. lib. bdg. 250.95 (*0-8490-8155-6*) Gordon Pr.

Ovarian Cancer. Ed. by David S. Alberts & Earl A. Surwit. (Cancer Treatment & Research Ser.). 1985. text 153.00 (*0-89838-676-4*) Kluwer Academic.

***Ovarian Cancer.** Robert F. Ozols. (ACS Atlas of Clinical Oncology Ser.). 300p. 2000. boxed set 89.95 incl. cd-rom (*1-55009-096-8*) DEKR.

Ovarian Cancer. Stephen C. Rubin. text. write for info. (*0-7817-2408-2*) Lppncott W & W.

Ovarian Cancer, Bk. 4. Ed. by Frank Sharp et al. (Illus.). 344p. 1996. text 79.00 (*0-412-72370-0*, Pub. by E A) OUP.

Ovarian Cancer: A Bibliography. 1995. lib. bdg. 250.95 (*0-8490-6707-3*) Gordon Pr.

Ovarian Cancer: Controversies in Management. David M. Gershenson & William P. McGuire. LC 97-34798. (Illus.). 464p. 1997. text 75.00 (*0-443-07804-1*) Church.

Ovarian Cancer: Methods & Protocols. Ed. by John M. S. Bartlett. (Methods in Molecular Medicine Ser.: Vol. 39). (Illus.). 839p. 2000. 149.50 (*0-89603-583-2*) Humana.

Ovarian Cancer: Proceedings of the International Symposium on Ovarian Cancer, 24-25 September 1979, Birmingham. Ed. by C. E. Newman et al. LC 80-40166. (Illus.). 249p. 1980. 50.00 (*0-08-025532-9*, Pergamon Pr) Elsevier.

Ovarian Carcinoma: Etiology, Diagnosis & Treatments. 3rd ed. H. R. Barber. (Illus.). 424p. 1992. 119.00 (*0-387-97824-0*) Spr-Verlag.

Ovarian Cell Interactions: Genes to Physiology. Ed. by Aaron J. Hsueh & D. W. Schomberg. (Serono Symposia Ser.). (Illus.). 176p. 1993. 119.00 (*0-387-94052-9*) Spr-Verlag.

Ovarian Disorders: Pathology, Diganosis & Management. A. Altcheck & L. Deligdisch. (Illus.). 512p. 1996. 119.95 (*0-89640-263-0*) Igaku-Shoin.

Ovarian Endocrinopathies: Proceedings of the Eighth Reinier de Graaf Symposium, Amsterdam, the Netherlands, September 2-4, 1993. Ed. by R. Schats et al. LC 94-8351. 288p. 1994. 65.00 (*1-85070-540-2*) Prthnon Pub.

Ovarian Tumors. Luther W. Brady et al. (Oncologic Ser.: Vol. 20). (Illus.). 232p. 1984. pap. 120.00 (*0-08-027472-2*, Pergamon Pr) Elsevier.

Ovary. Ed. by Eli Y. Adashi & Peter C. Leung. LC 93-1668. (Comprehensive Endocrinology Ser.). 704p. 1993. text 165.00 (*0-7817-0079-5*) Lppncott W & W.

Ovary. fac. ed. Ed. by Giovan B. Serra. LC 77-77961. (Comprehensive Endocrinology Ser.). (Illus.). 446p. pap. 138.30 (*0-7837-7186-X*, 204711300005) Bks Demand.

Ovary, 2 vols. 2nd ed. Incl. Vol. 1. Bituminous Materials Vol. 1: General Aspects. 1977. text 103.50 (*0-12-782601-7*); 1977. write for info. (*0-318-50322-0*) Acad Pr.

Ovary: Regulation, Dysfunction & Treatment. Ed. by M. Filicori & Carlo Flamigni. LC 96-20246. (International Congress Ser.: No. 1106). 450p. 1996. 189.50 (*0-444-82284-4*) Elsevier.

Ovary of Eve. Pinot-Correia. (Illus.). 396p. 1998. pap. 17.50 (*0-226-66954-8*) U Ch Pr.

Ovary of Eve: Egg & Sperm & Preformation. Clara Pinto-Correia. LC 97-14011. 396p. 1997. 29.95 (*0-226-66952-1*) U Ch Pr.

Ovations. Incl. Barry Bonds. Michael E. Goodman. LC 93-49767. (Illus.). 32p. (YA). (gr. 3 up). 1998. lib. bdg. 21.30 (*0-88682-694-2*, Creat Educ); Grant Hill. Michael E. Goodman. LC 96-46220. (Illus.). 32p. (YA). (gr. 3 up). 1998. lib. bdg. 21.30 (*0-88682-831-7*, Creat Educ); Hillary Rodham Clinton. Nancy Loewen. LC 93-50795. (Illus.). 32p. (YA). (gr. 3 up). 1998. lib. bdg. 21.30 (*0-88682-636-5*, Creat Educ); Jeff Gordon. Julie Bach. LC 97-41467. (Illus.). 32p. (YA). (gr. 3 up). 1998. lib. bdg. 21.30 (*0-88682-939-9*, Creat Educ); Monica Seles. Michael E. Goodman. LC 93-49768. (Illus.). 32p. (YA). (gr. 3 up). 1998. lib. bdg. 21.30 (*0-88682-699-3*, Creat Educ); Shaquille O'Neal. Michael E. Goodman. LC 93-49103. (Illus.). 32p. (YA). (gr. 3 up). 1998. lib. bdg. 21.30 (*0-88682-633-0*, Creat Educ); Spike Lee. Ferguson Chapman. LC 93-49821. (Illus.). 32p. (YA). (gr. 3 up). 1998. lib. bdg. 21.30 (*0-88682-697-7*, Creat Educ); Whoopi Goldberg. Andy DeBoer. LC 93-50691. (Illus.). 32p. (YA). (gr. 3 up). 1998. lib. bdg. 21.30 (*0-88682-696-9*, Creat Educ); (YA). (gr. 3 up). 59.80 (*0-88682-693-4*, Creat Educ) Creative Co.

Ovations, 12 bks. rev. ed. (J). 2000. lib. bdg. 255.60 (*0-88682-937-2*, Creat Educ) Creative Co.

Ovations Series, 2 vols. Incl. Jeff Gordon. Julie Bach. (Illus.). 32p. (J). 2000. pap. 10.60 (*0-89812-025-X*, Creative Paperbks); Shaquille O'Neal. Michael E. Goodman. (Illus.). 32p. (J). 2000. pap. 10.60 (*0-89812-026-8*, Creative Paperbks); (Illus.). 32p. (J). Set pap. 21.20 (*0-89812-010-1*, Creative Paperbks) Creative Co.

Ove Arup & Partners. Boyd-Whyte. text. write for info. (*0-471-48948-4*) Wiley.

Ove Arup & Partners: Engineering the Built Environment. Degenhard Sommer et al. (Illus.). 120p. 1994. pap. 48.00 (*3-7643-2954-8*, Pub. by Birkhauser) Princeton Arch.

Oveja Lanuda: Big Book. Lada J. Kratky. (Que Maravilla! Ser.). (SPA., Illus.). 16p. (Orig.). (J). (gr. 1-3). 1992. pap. text 29.95 (*1-56334-029-1*) Hampton-Brown.

Oveja Lanuda: Small Book. Lada J. Kratky. (Que Maravilla! Ser.). (SPA., Illus.). 16p. (Orig.). (J). (gr. 1-3). 1992. pap. text 6.00 (*1-56334-043-7*) Hampton-Brown.

Oveja Perdida. Bishop & Tim Dowley. (Libros de Carton).Tr. of Lost Sheep. (SPA.). (J). 1991. bds. 2.99 (*1-56063-224-0*, 490390) Editorial Unilit.

Oveja Perdida. Tim Dowley. (Serie Libros de Carton - Board Bks.).Tr. of Lost Sheep. (SPA.). 8p. (J). 1991. bds. write for info. (*0-614-27090-1*) Editorial Unilit.

***Oveja Perdida.** Tracy Harrast. (SPA.). 2000. 6.99 (*0-8297-2220-3*) Vida Pubs.

Oveja Perdida Es Hallada - The Lost Sheep. Gordon Stowell. (Serie Pescaditos - Little Fish Ser.). (SPA.). 24p. (J). 1991. write for info. (*1-56063-135-X*) Editorial Unilit.

Oveja Perdida y Otras Historias. Mig Holder. (SPA., Illus.). 20p. 1995. pap. 5.99 (*0-8254-1322-2*, Edit Portavoz) Kregel.

***Ovejas.** Peter Brady. Ed. by Isabel Schon. Tr. by Martin Luis Guzman Ferrer. (Animales de La Granja Ser.). (Illus.). 24p. 1999. 15.93 (*1-56065-790-1*, Bridgestone Bks) Capstone Pr.

Ovejas. Capstone Press Staff. (J). 1998. 14.00 (*0-516-21373-3*) Childrens.

Ovejas. Lynn M. Stone. (Animales de Granja Ser.).Tr. of Sheep. 24p. (J). (gr. k-4). 1991. lib. bdg. 14.60 (*0-86592-915-7*) Rourke Enter.

Oven & Rotisserie Roasting. David DiResta & Joanne Foran. LC 97-195760. (Illus.). 176p. (Orig.). 1997. pap. 8.95 (*1-55867-167-6*, Nitty Gritty Ckbks) Bristol Pub Ent CA.

***Oven-Baked Vegetarian Dishes.** Gabriele Redden. LC 99-86988. 2000. 14.95 (*0-7641-1279-1*) Barron.

Oven Dishes see Atbak Alforn

Oven Heated by the Baker: On Fire for the Lord! Linda L. Allen. 110p. 1998. pap. 11.95 (*1-892878-00-3*) You Deserve It.

Oven Lane. Michael Coady. 74p. 1992. pap. 12.95 (*1-85235-020-2*) Dufour.

Oven Mitts to Die For & How to Make Them. Diane Wallis. (Illus.). 104p. 1999. pap. 14.95 (*1-55192-174-X*) Raincoast Bk.

Ovenless Cookies - 118 of 'Em. Ed. by Louise Surland. (Illus.). 36p. 1987. pap. 4.25 (*0-938592-06-8*) Harriets Kitchen.

Over a Century of Leadership: South Dakota Territorial & State Governors. Lynwood E. Oyos. LC 87-71833. (Illus.). 250p. 1987. 9.95 (*0-931170-34-6*) Ctr Western Studies.

Over a Century of Leadership: South Dakota Territorial & State Governors. deluxe ed. Lynwood E. Oyos. LC 87-71833. (Illus.). 250p. 1987. 25.00 (*0-931170-35-4*) Ctr Western Studies.

Over a Century of Moving to the Drum: Salish Indian Celebrations on the Flathead Indian Reservation. Johnny Arlee. Ed. by Robert Bigart. LC 99-52175. (Illus.). 104p. 1998. pap. 14.95 (*0-917298-57-8*) MT Hist Soc.

Over Achievers: Business Clusters That Work: Prospects for Regional Development. Stuart Rosenfeld. 52p. (Orig.). 1996. pap. 7.00 (*0-9636927-3-9*) Reg Tech Strat.

Over America. Andrei Codrescu et al. (Wings over America Ser.). (Illus.). 128p. 1995. 35.00 (*1-887451-06-4*) Weldon Owen.

Over an Angel's Shoulder: One Soul's Journey Through Time. Bonnie A. Gilchrist. LC 95-4330. (Illus.). 580p. (Orig.). 1995. pap. 16.95 (*1-56825-023-1*) Rainbow Books.

Over & Back: The History of Ferryboats in New York Harbor. Brian J. Cudahy. LC 89-84357. (Illus.). 472p. 1990. 39.95 (*0-8232-1245-9*) Fordham.

***Over & Out, 1.** large type ed. Michael Francis Gilbert. LC 99-36650. 300p. 1999. pap. 21.95 (*0-7838-8736-1*, G K Hall Lrg Type) Mac Lib Ref.

Over & Out: Poems from Hollywood. Mark Dunster. 11p. 1999. pap. 5.00 (*0-89642-665-3*) Linden Pubs.

Over & Over. Charlotte Zolotow. LC 56-8149. (Charlotte Zolotow Bk.). (Illus.). 32p. (J). (ps-3). 1957. lib. bdg. 15.89 (*0-06-026956-1*) HarpC Child Bks.

Over & Over. Charlotte Zolotow. LC 56-8149. (Trophy Picture Bk.). (Illus.). 32p. (J). (ps-3). 1995. pap. 4.95 (*0-06-443415-X*, HarpTrophy) HarpC Child Bks.

Over & Over. Charlotte Zolotow. (J). 1987. 10.15 (*0-606-08431-2*, Pub. by Turtleback) Demco.

Over & Over Again. Gengzhe Chang & Thomas Sederberg. LC 97-74344. (New Mathematical Library). (Illus.). 325p. 1997. pap. text 31.50 (*0-88385-641-7*) Math Assn.

***Over & over Again.** Fabio Herrera. LC 00-100845. 112p. 2000. 16.95 (*1-58244-059-X*) Rutledge Bks.

Over & over Again: Understanding Obsessive-Compulsive Disorder. rev. ed. Fugen A. Neziroglu & Jose A. Yaryura-Tobia. LC 97-12122. 240p. 1997. pap. 17.95 (*0-7879-0876-2*) Jossey-Bass.

Over Back. Beverly Major. LC 91-19696. (Illus.). 32p. (J). (gr. k-4). 1993. 15.00 (*0-06-020286-6*); lib. bdg. 14.89 (*0-06-020287-4*) HarpC Child Bks.

Over Boston. David K. Gleason. LC 85-16633. (Illus.). x, 134p. 1985. 49.95 (*0-8071-1283-6*) La State U Pr.

Over by the Caves. Jennifer Stone. 64p. (Orig.). 1977. pap. 9.95 (*0-917658-07-8*) BPW & P.

Over by the River. William Maxwell. LC 76-30608. 256p. 1984. pap. 10.95 (*0-87923-541-1*) Godine.

Over California. Kevin Starr & Laurie Wertz. Ed. by Jane Fraser. (Wings over America Ser.). (Illus.). 256p. 1995. reprint ed. pap. 35.00 (*1-887451-02-1*) Weldon Owen.

Over Coming Speech Fright. Dwyer. (C). 1997. pap. text 26.75 (*0-15-505328-0*) Harcourt Coll Pubs.

Over-Constrained Systems. Michael Jampel et al. LC 96-28300. (Lecture Notes in Computer Science Ser.: Vol. 110). 1996. 56.00 (*3-540-61479-6*) Spr-Verlag.

Over Counter Drug Book. Michael Brodin. LC 99-195314. 1998. mass mkt. 6.99 (*0-671-01380-7*) S&S Trade.

Over DeSoto's Bones. 2nd ed. W. Conger Beasley, Jr. Ed. by Orvis C. Burmaster. LC 78-74299. (Ahsahta Press Modern & Contemporary Poets of the West Ser.). 72p. 1979. pap. 6.95 (*0-916272-11-7*) Ahsahta Pr.

***Over Earth & Ocean: The Archers of Ttolderodden & Gracemere.** Lorna McDonald. 412p. 2000. pap. 39.95 (*0-7022-3145-2*, Pub. by Univ Queensland Pr) Intl Spec Bk.

Over Easy. Les Edgerton. 2000. 23.00 (*0-375-50212-2*) Random.

Over 88 Tips & Ideas to Supercharge Your Exhibit Sales. Steve Miller & Charmel Bowden. 100p. (Orig.). 1996. pap. 11.95 (*0-9655412-0-7*) Hikelly Prod.

Over Europe. Jan Morris. Ed. by Mary-Dawn Earley & Jane Frasier. (Illus.). 288p. 1995. reprint ed. 45.00 (*1-887451-00-5*) Wldon Owen Ref.

Over Exposed: Essays on Contemporary Photography. Ed. by Carol Squiers. 1998. pap. 18.95 (*1-56584-522-6*, Pub. by New Press NY) Norton.

Over 50's Jokes. Bill Stott. Ed. by Helen Exley & Samantha Armstrong. (Joke Bks.). (Illus.). 60p. 1994. 8.50 (*1-85015-522-4*) Exley Giftbooks.

Over 55: A Handbook on Health. Theodore G. Duncan. 668p. 1982. 99.95 (*0-89859-726-9*) L Erlbaum Assocs.

Over Fifty Five Financial Management Guide 1992. C. Colburn Hardy. (C). 1991. 91.50 (*0-13-646977-9*, Macmillan Coll) P-H.

Over-Fifty Insurance Survival Guide: How to Know What You Need, Get What You Want & Avoid Rip-offs. Cynthia Davidson. 1994. pap. 16.95 (*1-56343-070-3*) Silver Lake.

Over Fifty Years Ago: In Europe During World War II. Philip Steele. (History Detectives Ser.). (Illus.). 32p. (YA). (gr. 6 up). 1993. lib. bdg. 20.00 (*0-02-786886-9*, Mac Bks Young Read) S&S Childrens.

Over Fifty Years of Caring: A History of Rainier School & Mental Retardation. Howard D. Baumgart. LC 96-95407. (Illus.). vi, 432p. 1997. pap. 25.00 (*0-9629616-3-9*) Magden Assocs.

Over Florida. Mark Derr. Ed. by Jane Fraser & Ruth Jacobson. (Wings over America Ser.). (Illus.). 256p. 1995. reprint ed. pap. 35.00 (*1-887451-04-8*) Weldon Owen.

Over Forties Jokes. Bill Stott. Ed. by Helen Exley & Samantha Armstrong. (Joke Bks.). (Illus.). 60p. 1992. 8.50 (*1-85015-351-5*) Exley Giftbooks.

Over Forty & Fit: The Baby Boomer's Common Sense Guide for Staying Lean, Muscular, & Healthy. David Devon. LC 94-96747. (Illus.). 120p. (Orig.). 1995. pap. 9.99 (*0-9644558-0-3*) Grunt.

Over Forty & Looking for Work? A Guide for the Unemployed, Underemployed, & Unhappily Employed. Rebecca J. Anthony & Gerald Roe. 180p. 1990. pap. 7.95 (*1-55850-870-8*) Adams Media.

Over Forty at Last. Susanna Kubelka. 1982. 12.95 (*0-02-567150-2*) Macmillan.

Over Forty Dinners in under Thirty Minutes: Recipe Book & Meal Planner. Monica J. Busch. Ed. by Harold Ashe & Suzanne Ashe. LC 90-85201. (Illus.). 80p. 1990. ring bd. 18.95 (*0-9627669-0-9*) Ashford Pr IL.

Over Forty MPH. Daniel F. Conroy. LC 90-32393. 1991. pap. 13.95 (*0-87949-342-9*) Ashley Bks.

Over Four Hundred & Fifty Years Ago: In the New World. Philip Sauvain. LC 93-2649. (History Detectives Ser.). (Illus.). 32p. (YA). (gr. 6 up). 1993. lib. bdg. 13.95 (*0-02-726327-4*, New Dscvry Bks) Silver Burdett Pr.

Over-Fulfilled Expectations: A Life & an Era in Rural America. Harold F. Breimyer. LC 90-46633. (Henry A. Wallace Series on Agricultural History & Rural Studies). (Illus.). 316p. 1991. text 49.95 (*0-8138-0856-1*) Iowa St U Pr.

***Over Half a Century of Michigan Pharmacology, 1942-2001.** Ed. by E. F. Domino. (Illus.). 500p. 2001. 50.00 (*0-916182-12-6*) NPP Bks.

Over Hawaii. Steven Goldsberry. Ed. by Jane Fraser & Laurie Wertz. (Wings over America Ser.). (Illus.). 256p. 1995. pap. 35.00 (*1-887451-03-X*) Weldon Owen.

***Over Hawaii.** Steven Goldsberry & Reg Morrison. 256p. 1998. 19.98 (*1-887451-18-8*) Weldon Owen Ref.

***Over Hawaii.** LC 99-88294. (Little Guides Ser.). (Illus.). 320p. 2000. reprint ed. pap. 14.95 (*1-875137-77-7*) Weldon Owen.

Over Her Dead Body: Configurations of Femininity, Death & the Aesthetic. Elisabeth Bronfen. (Illus.). 450p. (C). (gr. 13). 1992. pap. 20.99 (*0-415-90661-X*, A7646) Routledge.

Over Her Dead Body: The Construction of Male Subjectivity in Onetti. Judy Maloof. LC 93-44115. (American University Studies, Series XXII: Vol. 24). 189p. (C). 1995. text 41.95 (*0-8204-2450-1*) P Lang Pubng.

An Asterisk (*) at the beginning of an entry indicates that the title is appearing for the first time.

Over Here. Raymond Seitz. LC 98-185266. 1999. 35.00 (*0-297-81598-9*, Pub. by Weidenfeld & Nicolson) Trafalgar.

Over Here. Edgar A. Guest. 192p. 1980. reprint ed. lib. bdg. 18.95 (*0-89968-192-1*, Lghtyr Pr) Buccaneer Bks.

Over Here: Criticizing America, 1968-1989. Thomas R. Edwards. 200p. (C). 1991. pap. 15.95 (*0-8135-1710-9*); text 40.00 (*0-8135-1709-5*) Rutgers U Pr.

Over Here: Modernism, the First Exile, 1914-1919. Ed. by Kermit S. Champa. LC 89-50243. (Illus.). 225p. 1989. pap. 20.00 (*0-933519-17-6*) D W Bell Gallery.

Over Here: The First World War & American Society. David M. Kennedy. 416p. 1982. reprint ed. pap. text 15.95 (*0-19-503209-8*) OUP.

Over Here, over There. Maxene Andrews & Bill Gilbert. (Illus.). 288p. 1993. 22.95 (*0-8217-4117-9*, Zebra Kensgtn) Kensgtn Pub Corp.

Over Here, over There. Maxene Andrews & Bill Gilbert. 288p. 1994. pap. 12.95 (*0-8217-4645-6*, Zebra Kensgtn) Kensgtn Pub Corp.

Over Here, over There: The Andrews Sisters & the USO Stars in World War II. large type ed. Maxene Andrews & Bill Gilbert. LC 93-33463. 1994. lib. bdg. 18.95 (*0-7862-0094-4*) Thorndike Pr.

Over Here Zebra. Tony Potter. (J). 1998. 7.95 (*1-902553-05-5*) Grimond.

Over Home. Jeannette Kinyon. LC 92-71059. 244p. (J). (gr. 4-8). 1992. 24.95 (*1-880531-01-1*); pap. 13.95 (*1-880531-02-X*) East Eagle.

Over Hong Kong. Photos by Magnus Bartlett & Kasyan Bartlett. (Illus.). 160p. 1998. 34.95 (*962-217-506-6*) Tuttle Pubng.

***Over in the Grasslands.** Anna Wilson. (Illus.). 32p. (J). (ps-1). 2000. 14.95 (*0-316-93910-2*) Little.

Over in the Meadow. Illus. by Cathy Beylon. (Baby Shaped Board Bks.). 28p. (J). (ps). 1990. 2.95 (*0-02-689484-X*) Checkerboard.

Over in the Meadow. Jane Cabrera. LC 99-22683. 32p. (J). 2000. 16.95 (*0-8234-1490-6*) Holiday.

Over in the Meadow. Galdone. (J). 1998. pap. 5.95 (*0-87628-986-3*) Ctr Appl Res.

Over in the Meadow. Illus. & Adapted by Paul Galdone. LC 88-18349. 32p. (J). (ps-1). 1989. pap. 5.95 (*0-671-67837-X*) S&S Bks Yung.

Over in the Meadow. Ezra Jack Keats. LC 98-47037. (Illus.). 32p. (ps-3). 1999. pap. 5.99 (*0-14-056508-6*, PuffinBks) Peng Put Young Read.

Over in the Meadow. Ezra Jack Keats. (Illus.). 32p. (YA). (ps-3). 1992. 19.95 (*0-590-72809-1*) Scholastic Inc.

Over in the Meadow. Ezra Jack Keats. LC 98-47037. (Illus.). 32p. (gr. k-3). 1999. 15.99 (*0-670-88344-1*) Viking Penguin.

Over in the Meadow. John M. Langstaff. LC 57-8587. (Illus.). 32p. (J). (ps-3). 1992. pap. 19.95 (*0-15-258853-1*) Harcourt.

Over in the Meadow. Feodor Rojankovsky & John M. Langstaff. LC 57-8587. (Illus.). 32p. (J). (ps-3). 1957. 16.00 (*0-15-258854-X*, Harcourt Child Bks) Harcourt.

***Over in the Meadow.** Louise Voce. (Illus.). 32p. (J). (ps-2). 2000. pap. 19.99 (*0-7636-1285-5*, Pub. by Candlewick Pr) Penguin Putnam.

Over in the Meadow. Olive A. Wadsworth. (Illus.). 32p. (J). (ps-3). 1985. 4.99 (*0-590-44848-X*) Scholastic Inc.

Over in the Meadow. Feodor Rojankovsky & John M. Langstaff. LC 57-8587. (Illus.). 32p. (J). (ps-3). 1973. reprint ed. pap. 7.00 (*0-15-670500-1*, Voyager Bks) Harcourt.

Over in the Meadow: A Book of Colors & Counting. Illus. by Doug Bowles. 8p. (J). 1999. 9.99 (*1-58476-001-X*) Innovative Kids.

Over in the Meadow: A Counting-Out Rhyme. Mary M. Rae. (Picture Puffin Ser.). (Illus.). 32p. (J). (ps). 1986. pap. 3.95 (*0-685-14199-3*, Penguin Bks) Viking Penguin.

Over in the Meadow: An Old Nursery Counting Rhyme. Paul Galdone. (J). 1989. 11.15 (*0-606-04292-X*, Pub. by Turtleback) Demco.

Over in the Meadow: Level Three, Blue. Louise Voce. LC 98-21294. (Reading Together Ser.). (Illus.). 32p. (J). 1999. pap. write for info. (*0-7636-0852-1*) Candlewick Pr.

Over in the Meadow Big Book: Black & White Nellie Edge I Can Read & Sing Big Book. Illus. by Sheila Somerville. (J). (ps-2). 1988. pap. text 20.00 (*0-922053-09-X*) N Edge Res.

Over Indonesia: Aerial Views of the Archipelago. 1998. text 39.95 (*981-3018-84-4*) Arch Pr.

Over Indulgence. Charles Kemp. 112p. 1998. pap. 10.00 (*0-8059-4345-5*) Dorrance.

Over Is Not Up! Dale Smith. LC 95-76028. (It's a Bitsie Book Ser.). (Illus.). 32p. (J). 1995. 14.95 (*1-886864-00-4*) Goldn Anchor Pr.

Over Jordan. Norma Johnston. LC 99-21938. 192p. (J). (gr. 4-7). 1999. 15.00 (*0-380-97635-8*, Avon Bks) Morrow Avon.

Over Land & Sea: Memoir of an Austrian Rear Admiral's Life in Europe & Africa, 1857-1909. Ludwig Ritter Von Hohnel. Ed. by Ronald E. Coons & Pascal J. Imperato. LC 99-45080. (Illus.). 384p. 2000. 40.00 (*0-8419-1390-0*) Holmes & Meier.

Over Lincoln's Shoulder: The Committee on the Conduct of the War. Bruce Tap. LC 97-36525. (Modern War Studies). 344p. 1997. 39.95 (*0-7006-0871-0*) U Pr of KS.

Over Miami. David K. Gleason. LC 90-5859. (Illus.). 134p. 1990. 49.95 (*0-8071-1635-1*) La State U Pr.

Over My Dead Body. Anthony Fingleton & Michael Sutton. LC 98-177800. 1998. pap. 5.25 (*0-8222-1601-9*) Dramatists Play.

Over My Dead Body. Rex Stout. 20.95 (*0-89190-341-0*) Amereon Ltd.

Over My Dead Body. Rex Stout. (Crime Line Ser.). 272p. 1993. mass mkt. 5.50 (*0-553-23116-2*) Bantam.

Over My Dead Body: A Preterist View of the Fourth Gospel. L. Michael Hall. 300p. (Orig.). 1997. pap. 20.00 (*1-890001-13-9*) Empowerment Tech.

Over My Dead Body! The Story of Hillside Cemetery, Silverton, Colorado. 2nd abr. ed. Freda C. Peterson. LC 96-76377. Orig. Title: The Story of Hillside Cemetery Burials 1872-1988. 154p. 1996. pap. 11.95 (*0-927562-20-0*) Levite Apache.

Over My Head: A Doctor's Account of Head Injury from the Inside Looking Out. Claudia L. Osborn. LC 97-40542. 256p. 1998. 21.95 (*0-8362-5419-8*) Andrews & McMeel.

Over My Head: A Doctor's Account of Head Injury from the Inside Looking Out. Claudia L. Osborn. LC 97-67529. iv, 240p. 1997. pap. 18.95 (*0-9658750-0-8*) Peripatetic Pub.

***Over My Head: A Doctor's Own Story of Head Injury from the Inside Looking Out.** Claudia L. Osborn. 2000. pap. 12.95 (*0-7407-0598-9*) Andrews & McMeel.

Over My Head There's Trouble in the Air. Henry Hardee. write for info. (*1-884978-09-6*) Black Boys Dream.

Over My Shoulder: A Collection of Warmth. Jack Campbell. 110p. 1991. pap. text 9.95 (*0-942761-10-3*) JONopher Pub.

Over My Shoulder: Reflections on a Science Fiction Era. Lloyd A. Eshbach. 1983. 20.00 (*1-880418-11-8*) D M Grant.

Over New England. Neal R. Peirce. Ed. by Jane Fraser & Laurie Wertz. (Wings over America Ser.). (Illus.). 256p. 1995. reprint ed. pap. 35.00 (*1-887451-05-6*) Weldon Owen.

Over New Orleans. David K. Gleason. (Illus.). 134p. 1985. 49.95 (*0-8071-1288-7*) La State U Pr.

Over 900 Years Ago: With the Vikings. Hazel M. Martell. LC 93-2647. (History Detectives Ser.). (Illus.). 32p. (YA). (gr. 6 up). 1993. lib. bdg. 13.95 (*0-02-726325-8*, New Dscvry Bks) Silver Burdett Pr.

Over Nine Waves: A Book of Irish Legends. Ed. by Marie Heaney. 256p. 1995. pap. 12.95 (*0-571-17518-X*) Faber & Faber.

Over 90 of the Best Ultimate Country. rev. ed. 48p. 1995. otabind 19.95 (*0-7935-4280-4*, 00310036) H Leonard.

Over on the Dry Side. Louis L'Amour. 192p. 1985. mass mkt. 4.50 (*0-553-25321-2*) Bantam.

Over on the Lonesome Side. James A. Ritchie. 192p. 1991. 19.95 (*0-8027-4118-5*) Walker & Co.

***Over 150 Astonishing Beauty Tips.** Chrissie Painell. (Illus.). 128p. 2000. 9.95 (*1-85868-978-3*, Pub. by Carlton Bks Ltd) Natl Bk Netwk.

***Over 150 Essential Jigs, Aids & Devices for Today's Woodworker.** V. J. Taylor. LC 99-231780. (Illus.). 192p. 1999. 24.95 (*0-7153-0686-3*, Pub. by D & C Pub) Sterling.

Over One Hundred One Inexpensive Ways to Entertain Children (Traditional Crafts & Games) Juanita M. Ferrey. LC 88-71491. (Illus.). 143p. (Orig.). 1988. per. 11.95 (*0-939339-01-3*, 662-4685) AFCOM Pub.

Over One Hundred One Uses for a Dead Husband. Larry-Wolfe Horwitz. 1990. pap. 6.95 (*0-9624895-0-6*) L W Horwitz.

***Over 100 Traits of Truly Horrible People.** Mort Todd. (Illus.). 128p. 2000. pap. 12.95 (*0-942154-44-4*, 444) Radius Pr.

***Over 100 Truly Astonishing Sex Tips.** Lisa Sussman. (Illus.). 144p. 2000. 9.95 (*1-85868-865-5*, Pub. by Carlton Bks Ltd) Natl Bk Netwk.

Over One Hundred Ways to Make Money with Your Personal Computer. William J. Flippo. LC 92-82880. 288p. (Orig.). 1993. pap. 21.95 (*0-9634754-0-1*) Newpo Prods.

Over One Hundred Ways to Use Your Bumper Crop of Zucchine. Jo Hagney. Ed. by Gregory W. Frazier. 130p. (Orig.). 1993. pap. 14.95 (*0-935151-33-8*) Arrowstar Pub.

Over Our Heads: A Local Look at Global Climate. John C. Ryan. Ed. by Ellen W. Chu. LC 97-76494. (New Report: No. 6). (Illus.). 80p. 1997. pap. 9.95 (*1-886093-06-7*) NW Environ Watch.

Over Our Way. rev. ed. D'Costa. LC 95-122360. 1995. pap. text. write for info. (*0-582-22580-9*, Pub. by Addison-Wesley) Longman.

Over Periscope Pond: Letters from Two American Girls in Paris, October 1916-January 1918. Esther S. Root. (American Biography Ser.). 295p. 1991. reprint ed. lib. bdg. 69.00 (*0-7812-8328-0*) Rprt Serv.

Over-Pin Measurement Tolerances for Various AGMA Classes of Fine-Pitch Gears. G. W. Michalec. (Technical Papers: Vol. P239.04). (Illus.). 20p. 1957. pap. text 30.00 (*1-55589-301-5*) AGMA.

Over Prairie Trails. Frederick Philip Grove. 168p. 1996. pap. text 5.95 (*0-7710-9964-9*) McCland & Stewart.

***Over-scheduled.** Alvin Rosenfeld. 2000. pap. write for info. (*0-312-26339-2*, St Martin Griffin) St Martin.

Over Sea, under Stone. Susan Cooper. LC 66-11199. (Dark is Rising Sequence Ser.). (Illus.). 252p. (YA). (gr. 5 up). 1966. 17.00 (*0-15-259034-X*, Harcourt Child Bks) Harcourt.

Over Sea, under Stone. Susan Cooper. (Dark Is Rising Sequence Ser.). (J). 1989. 9.05 (*0-606-04293-8*, Pub. by Turtleback) Demco.

Over Sea, under Stone. Susan Cooper. LC 88-37690. (Dark is Rising Sequence Ser.). 243p. (J). (gr. 4-7). 1989. reprint ed. pap. 3.95 (*0-02-042785-9*) Harcourt.

Over Seas: A Spirited Guide for Enduring International Flights. John B. Gordon. (Illus.). 148p. (Orig.). 1991. pap. 8.95 (*1-880213-04-4*) Creat Alliance.

Over-Sensitivity. Jalal Toufic. LC 96-8582. (Sun & Moon Classics Ser.: No. 119). 220p. (Orig.). 1996. pap. 13.95 (*1-55713-270-4*) Sun & Moon CA.

***Over 75 Good Ideas for Promoting Your Book.** Patricia L. Fry. 60p. 2000. pap. 6.50 (*0-9612642-5-X*) Matilija Pr.

Over Six Thousand Years Ago: In the Stone Age. Hazel M. Martell. LC 91-39458. (History Detectives Ser.). (Illus.). 32p. (YA). (gr. 6 up). 1992. lib. bdg. 20.00 (*0-02-762429-3*, Mac Bks Young Read) S&S Childrens.

Over Sixteen Hundred Years Ago in the Roman Empire. Philip Sauvain. LC 91-43328. (History Detectives Ser.). (Illus.). 32p. (YA). (gr. 6 up). 1992. lib. bdg. 20.00 (*0-02-781083-6*, Mac Bks Young Read) S&S Childrens.

***Over 60s' Jokes.** Ed. by Helen Exley & Claire Lipscomb. (Joke Bks.). (Illus.). 64p. 1998. 8.50 (*1-86187-020-5*) Exley Pubns Ltd.

Over Sixty-Five Million Years Ago: Before the Dinosaurs Died. Richard Moody. LC 91-44774. (History Detectives Ser.). (Illus.). 32p. (YA). (gr. 6 up). 1992. lib. bdg. 20.00 (*0-02-767270-0*, Mac Bks Young Read) S&S Childrens.

Over the Andes to Hell. Ramsay Thorne. (Renegade Ser.: No. 8). 192p. (Orig.). 1982. mass mkt. 2.25 (*0-446-30781-5*, Pub. by Warner Bks) Little.

Over the Applegate Trail to Oregon in 1846 - The Pringle Diary & Other Pertinences: Genealogy (Pringle) by Anne Billeter. Bert Webber. LC 96-23359. (Illus.). 1996. pap. 13.95 (*0-936738-81-2*) Webb Research.

Over the Balkans & South Russia, 1917-19. H. A. Jones. 210p. pap. 19.95 (*0-947898-62-X*, 5570) Stackpole.

Over the Battlefronts: Amazing Air Action of World War One. Peter Kilduff. (Illus.). 256p. 1996. 29.95 (*1-85409-265-0*, Pub. by Arms & Armour) Sterling.

Over the Beach: The Air War in Vietnam. Zalin Grant. 1989. mass mkt. 5.99 (*0-671-69650-5*) PB.

Over the Bent World. Ed. by Mary Louise. LC 73-105031. (Essay Index Reprint Ser.). 1977. 44.95 (*0-8369-1676-X*) Ayer.

***Over the Bent World: Poems & Images from Gerard Manley Hopkins.** David Porter. 175p. 1999. reprint ed. text 30.00 (*1-900507-77-3*, Pub. by Solway) OM Literature.

Over the Border. William Winter. (Notable American Authors Ser.). 1999. reprint ed. lib. bdg. 125.00 (*0-7812-7757-4*) Rprt Serv.

Over the Brink. Irving A. Greenfield. 1990. mass mkt. 3.95 (*0-8217-3123-8*, Zebra Kensgtn) Kensgtn Pub Corp.

Over the Chihuahua & Santa Fe Trails, 1847-1848: George Rutledge Gibson's Journal. George R. Gibson. Ed. by Robert W. Frazer. LC 81-52054. 123p. reprint ed. pap. 38.20 (*0-608-15777-5*, 203100200073) Bks Demand.

Over the Cliff & Other Stories: Prepared to Accompany the Bible Answer Card "Our Words" Vivian D. Gunderson. 1974. pap. 3.25 (*0-915374-13-7*, 13-7) Rapids Christian.

Over-the-Counter Derivatives Products: A Guide to Business & Legal Risk Management & Documentation. Robert M. Mclaughlin. LC 98-9513. 480p. 1998. 75.00 (*0-7863-1078-2*, Irwn Prfssnl) McGraw-Hill Prof.

Over-the-Counter Doctor. Charles B. Inlander. LC 97-16161. (Illus.). 352p. 1997. pap. 14.95 (*0-8362-3581-9*, Cader Bks) Andrews & McMeel.

Over-the-Counter-Doctor. People's Medical Society Staff. (Illus.). 352p. (Orig.). 1997. pap. 14.95 (*0-614-30550-0*, Cader Bks) Andrews & McMeel.

***Over-the-counter-drugs in Hong Kong: A Strategic Entry Report, 1999.** Compiled by Icon Group International. (Illus.). 121p. 1999. ring bd. 1210.00 incl. audio compact disk (*0-7418-1769-1*) Icon Grp.

Over-the-Counter Pharmaceutical Formulations. David B. Braun. LC 94-2511. (Illus.). 443p. 1994. 129.00 (*0-8155-1347-X*) Noyes.

Over-the-Counter Pharmaceuticals in the European Union, No. R212. 1995. 1250.00 (*0-85058-830-8*) Economist Intell.

Over-the-Counter Pharmaceuticals in United Kingdom: A Strategic Entry Report, 1998. Compiled by Icon Group International Staff. (Country Industry Report). (Illus.). 100p. 1999. ring bd. 1000.00 incl. audio compact disk (*0-7418-0465-4*) Icon Grp.

Over-the-Counter Securities Markets. 4th ed. Julian G. Buckley, Jr. & Leo M. Loll. (Illus.). 480p. 1986. 33.95 (*0-13-647172-2*) P-H.

Over the Counter Trading. Nenner & Nyif. 1998. text. write for info. (*0-7352-0047-5*) P-H.

Over the Dead Line: Or Tracked by Bloodhounds, Giving the Author's Personal Experience During Eleven Months that He was Confined...As a (Confederate) Prisoner of War...; with Numerous & Varied Incidents & Anecdotes of His Prison Life. S. M. Dufour. (Illus.). 283p. 1997. reprint ed. lib. bdg. 39.00 (*0-8328-6495-1*) Higginson Bk Co.

Over the Door: The Ornamental Stonework of New York. Photos by John Yang. LC 97-102560. (Illus.). 192p. 1995. 19.95 (*1-56898-057-4*) Princeton Arch.

Over the Earth I Come: The Great Sioux Uprising of 1862. Duane Schultz. (Illus.). 320p. 1993. pap. 12.95 (*0-312-09360-8*) St Martin.

Over the Earth I Come: The Great Sioux Uprising of 1862. large type ed. Duane Schultz. (General Non-Fiction Ser.). 640p. 1993. 27.99 (*0-7089-2942-7*) Ulverscroft.

Over the Edge. Bill G. Cox. LC 97-210558. 320p. 1997. mass mkt. 5.99 (*0-7860-0430-4*, Pinncle Kensgtn) Kensgtn Pub Corp.

Over the Edge. Hal Friedman. LC 98-8825. 320p. 1998. 24.00 (*0-06-018265-2*) HarpC.

Over the Edge. Hal Friedman. 398p. 1999. mass mkt. 6.99 (*0-06-109367-X*) HarpC.

Over the Edge. Carolyn Keene. (Nancy Drew Files: No. 36). (YA). (gr. 6 up). 1991. per. 3.50 (*0-671-74656-1*, Archway) PB.

Over the Edge. Carolyn Keene. (Nancy Drew Files: No. 36). (YA). (gr. 6 up). 1989. 8.60 (*0-606-04294-6*, Pub. by Turtleback) Demco.

Over the Edge. Jonathan Kellerman. 433p. 1993. mass mkt. 6.99 (*0-451-17801-7*, Sig) NAL.

Over the Edge, Vol. 9. Patricia H. Rushford. LC 97-4713. (Jennie McGrady Mystery Ser.). 16p. (J). (gr. 7). 1997. mass mkt. 4.99 (*1-55661-562-0*) Bethany Hse.

Over the Edge: A Melissa Craig Mystery. Betty Rowlands. LC 92-40543. 252p. 1993. 19.95 (*0-8027-3228-3*) Walker & Co.

Over the Edge: A Mystery Novel. Robert C. Jackson. 320p. 1999. pap. 14.95 (*0-89407-130-0*) Strawberry Hill.

Over the Edge: An Odyssey in Extreme Sports. Michael Bane. 256p. 1998. pap. text 12.95 (*0-02-862280-4*) Macmillan.

***Over the Edge: An Odyssey in Extreme Sports.** Michael Bane. LC 00-35175. 243p. 2000. pap. 19.95 (*0-89997-265-9*) Wilderness Pr.

Over the Edge: Remapping Western Experience. Valerie J. Matsumoto & Blake Allmendinger. LC 97-39311. 1998. 48.00 (*0-520-21148-0*, Pub. by U CA Pr); pap. 19.95 (*0-520-21149-9*, Pub. by U CA Pr) Cal Prin Full Svc.

Over the Edge: The Growth of Homelessness in the 1980s. Martha R. Burt. LC 91-18000. (Illus.). 278p. 1992. reprint ed. 45.00 (*0-87154-177-7*) Russell Sage.

Over the Edge: The Growth of Homelessness in the 1980s. Martha R. Burt. 278p. 1993. reprint ed. pap. 16.95 (*0-87154-178-5*) Russell Sage.

Over the Edge: The Role-Playing Game of Surreal Danger. 2nd rev. ed. Jonathan Tweet & Robin D. Laws. Ed. by John Nephew. (Over the Edge Ser.). (Illus.). 240p. (Orig.). 1997. pap. 25.00 (*1-887801-52-9*) Trident MN.

***Over the Edge: Thrilling Real-Life Adventures in the Grand Canyon.** Larry Vardiman. LC 99-66476. 160p. 1999. pap. 9.99 (*0-89051-323-6*) Master Bks.

Over the Edge: Youth Devotional. Kenneth Copeland & Gloria Copeland. 1998. pap. 14.99 (*1-57794-138-1*) Harrison Hse.

Over the Edge Flying with the Polar Heros. K. C. Tessendorf. LC 97-34768. (Illus.). 128p. (J). (gr. 3-7). 1998. 17.00 (*0-689-31804-9*) Atheneum Yung Read.

***Over The Edge Planner.** Harrison House Publishing Staff. 1999. pap. 9.99 (*1-57794-193-4*) Harrison Hse.

***Over the Edge Xtreme Planner for Students.** Kenneth Copeland. 2000. pap. 9.99 (*1-57794-290-6*) Harrison Hse.

Over the Falls: A Child's Guide to Chagrin Falls. David H. Cockley. (Illus.). 24p. (Orig.). (J). (gr. 1-6). 1981. pap. 2.25 (*0-940900-00-9*) Aschley Pr.

Over the Fence: A Neighbor's Memories of Elvis. Sara Erwin. (Illus.). 72p. (Orig.). 1997. pap. 10.00 (*0-9659265-0-8*) S Erwin.

Over the Footlights. Collier-Thomas. 1996. pap. 14.95 (*0-8050-4406-X*); text 25.00 (*0-8050-4405-1*) St Martin.

Over the Front: The Complete Record of Fighter Aces & Units of United States & French Air Services, 1914-1918. Norman Franks & Frank Bailey. (Above the Trenches Ser.). (Illus.). 250p. 1992. 49.95 (*0-948817-54-2*, Pub. by Grub St) Seven Hills Bk.

Over the Gate. Read. Date not set. lib. bdg. 21.95 (*0-8488-1695-1*) Amereon Ltd.

Over the Gate. large type ed. Miss Read. LC 96-5402. (Illus.). 1996. 25.95 (*0-7838-1656-1*, G K Hall Lrg Type) Mac Lib Ref.

Over the Graves of Horses. Michael Delp. LC 88-11963. (Great Lakes Bks.). 86p. 1989. 21.95 (*0-8143-2044-9*); pap. 11.95 (*0-8143-2045-7*) Wayne St U Pr.

Over the Great Navajo Trail. Carl Eickemeyer. LC 74-7965. (Illus.). reprint ed. 41.50 (*0-404-11853-4*) AMS Pr.

Over the Green Hill: A German Jewish Memior, Germany 1913-1943. Lotte Strauss. LC 99-33711. (Illus.). 190p. 1999. 25.00 (*0-8232-1919-4*, Pub. by Fordham) BookMasters.

Over the Green Hills. Rachel Isadora. LC 91-12761. 32p. (J). (ps-3). 1992. 16.00 (*0-688-10509-2*, Grenwillow Bks) HarpC Child Bks.

Over the Hedge. Michael Fry. LC 96-84001. (Illus.). 128p. (Orig.). 1996. pap. 9.95 (*0-8362-2122-2*) Andrews & McMeel.

Over the Hedge 3, Vol. 3. Michael Fry & T. Lewis. LC 97-71632. (Illus.). 128p. (Orig.). 1997. pap. 9.95 (*0-8362-3731-5*) Andrews & McMeel.

Over the Hedge 2. Michael Fry & T. Lewis. LC 96-79241. 128p. 1997. pap. text 9.95 (*0-8362-2696-8*) Andrews & McMeel.

Over the Hill. Ed. by Patrick Caton. 80p. 1997. spiral bd. 7.95 (*1-56245-289-4*) Great Quotations.

Over the Hill? Grampa Gray. 48p. (Orig.). 1996. pap. 7.50 (*1-885631-20-0*, 20-0) G F Hutchison.

Over the Hill. Herbert Kavet. (Illus.). 64p. 1997. pap. 5.95 (*1-889647-25-X*) Boston Am.

Over the Hill: Is the Church over the Hill, Buried & Dead? or ... Is the Kingdom of God at Hand? David Yaniv. Ed. by Chuck Dean. 80p. (Orig.). 1993. pap. 8.95 (*0-9622413-3-4*) WinePress Pub.

Over the Hill - Deal with It! Jan B. King. Ed. by Cliff Carle. (Illus.). 128p. 1997. pap. 6.95 (*1-57644-022-2*) CCC Pubns.

Over the Hill & on a Roll: Laugh Lines for the Better Half of Life. Bob Phillips. LC 99-224098. 250p. 1999, mass mkt. 4.99 (*0-7369-0002-0*) Harvest Hse.

Over-the-Hill at 60 . . . & Picking up Speed. large type ed. E. L. Stephenson. Ed. & Illus. by Jan Cooper. 132p. (Orig.). 1996. pap. 9.00 (*0-9654107-0-6*) My Office Pubng.

Over the Hill Game Book. Courtney Cooke. 32p. 1997. 3.95 (*0-671-57604-6*) S&S Trade.

An Asterisk (*) at the beginning of an entry indicates that the title is appearing for the first time.

***Over the Hill in Hungary.** Virginia P. White. LC 98-48597. 1998. write for info. (*1-56072-631-8*, Nova Kroshka Bks) Nova Sci Pubs.

Over the Hill Test: How Far over the Hill Are You? Ed. by Patrick Caton. 80p. 1997. spiral bd. 7.95 (*1-56245-288-6*) Great Quotations.

***Over the Hill Twice: A Bio-Narrative of Paul McCorkle.** Andrew Offenburger. Ed. by Denise M. Godwin. xi, 176p. 2000. write for info. (*0-9678576-0-0*); pap. write for info. (*0-9678576-1-9*) S & T Pubng.

Over the Hills & Far Away. write for info. (*0-9702281-5-5*) T Mooney.

Over the Hills & Far Away. Lucille J. Thomas. 222p. 1992. 19.95 (*0-87770-505-4*) Ye Galleon.

Over the Hills & Far Away: A Book of Nursery Rhymes. Ed. & Illus. by Alan Marks. LC 94-10263. 104p. (J). (ps-1). 1994. 19.95 (*1-55858-285-1*, Pub. by North-South Bks NYC) Chronicle Bks.

***Over the Hills & Far Away: More Stories from Southern Illinois.** Norma Jacke Tucker. Ed. by Joyce Leacy Brown. LC 99-66634. (Illus.). 132p. 1999. pap. 10.95 (*0-9674173-1-7*) Good Read Pr.

Over the Hills to Georgian Bay: The Ottawa, Arnprior & Parry Sound Railway. Niall MacKay. LC 97-154681. (Illus.). 136p. 1995. pap. text 15.95 (*0-919783-06-6*, Pub. by Boston Mills) Genl Dist Srvs.

Over the Himalaya. Koichiro Ohmori. (Illus.). 108p. 1994. 29.95 (*0-938567-37-3*) Mountaineers.

Over The Horizon. Hollins. LC 99-20567. 268p. 1999. pap. 60.95 (*0-471-98717-4*) Wiley.

Over-the-Horizon Radar. Andrei A. Kolosov. LC 87-19318. (Artech House Radar Library). 296p. 1987. reprint ed. pap. 91.80 (*0-608-01414-1*, 206217700002) Bks Demand.

Over the Interstate Lines of the Mind. Bob Zark. 62p. 1995. pap. 7.95 (*1-886496-02-1*) Panic Button Priest.

Over the Ivy Walls: The Educational Mobility of Low-Income Chicanos. Patricia Gandara. LC 94-38546. (SUNY Series, the Social Context of Education). 151p. (C). 1995. pap. text 18.95 (*0-7914-2610-6*) State U NY Pr.

Over the Ivy Walls: The Educational Mobility of Low-Income Chicanos. Patricia Gandara. LC 94-38546. (SUNY Series, the Social Context of Education). 151p. (C). 1995. text 50.50 (*0-7914-2609-2*) State U NY Pr.

Over the Joshua Slope. Lyman Hafen. LC 93-30712. 160p. (J). (gr. 4-8). 1994. mass mkt. 14.95 (*0-02-741100-1*, Bradbury S&S) S&S Childrens.

Over the Line: A Stevie Houston Mystery. Tracey Richardson. LC 97-52740. 240p. (Orig.). 1998. pap. 11.95 (*1-56280-202-X*) Naiad Pr.

Over the Line: North Korea's Negotiating Strategy. Chuck Downs. 340p. 1999. pap. 19.95 (*0-8447-4029-2*, Pub. by Am Enterprise) Pub Resources Inc.

Over the Lip of the World: Among the Storytellers of Madagascar. Colleen J. McElroy. LC 99-14595. (Illus.). 350p. 1999. 24.95 (*0-295-97824-4*) U of Wash Pr.

Over the Marble Mountain. Barbara Beveridge. LC 92-27097. (Illus.). (J). (gr. 4 up). 1993. 2.50 (*0-383-03589-9*) SRA McGraw.

Over the Misty Blue Hills: The Story of Cocke County, Tennessee. Ruth W. O'Dell. 436p. 1982. reprint ed. 37.50 (*0-89308-276-7*, TN 53) Southern Hist Pr.

Over the Misty Mountains. Gilbert Morris & Aaron McCarver. LC 96-45907. (Spirit of Appalachia Ser.). 352p. 1997. pap. 10.99 (*1-55661-885-9*) Bethany Hse.

Over the Moon. Rachel Vail. LC 97-21964. (Illus.). 32p. (J). (ps-2). 1998. 15.95 (*0-531-30068-4*); lib. bdg. 16.99 (*0-531-33068-0*) Orchard Bks Watts.

Over the Moon: An Adoption Tale. Karen Katz. LC 96-37554. (Illus.). 32p. (J). 1997. 15.95 (*0-8050-5013-2*, Bks Young Read) H Holt & Co.

***Over the Moon! Best-Loved Nursery Rhymes.** David Melling. (Illus.). 24p. (J). (ps-3). 2000. 14.99 (*0-525-46498-0*, Dutton Child) Peng Put Young Read.

Over the Moon Bear. Jasmine Brook. (Illus.). 12p. (J). 1998. 7.95 (*0-7641-5071-5*) Barron.

Over the Mountain. Gregory L. Lucente. LC 97-145523. 229p. (Orig.). 1996. pap. 12.95 (*0-9653968-0-0*) G Lucente.

Over the Mountain. large type ed. Maryanne Kerr. (Ulverscroft Large Print Ser.). 464p. 1997. 27.99 (*0-7089-3811-6*) Ulverscroft.

Over the Mountain. Ruthven Todd. Ed. by R. Reginald & Douglas Melville. LC 77-84270. (Lost Race & Adult Fantasy Ser.). 1978. reprint ed. lib. bdg. 26.95 (*0-405-11010-3*) Ayer.

Over the Mountain Men: Their Early Court Records in Southwest Virginia. Anne L. Worrell. LC 63-495. 69p. 1996. reprint ed. pap. 7.50 (*0-8063-0671-8*, 6500) Genealog Pub.

Over the Mountains of the Moon: An American Novel. Mary Ramstetter. LC 94-93954. 458p. (Orig.). 1998. reprint ed. pap. 14.00 (*0-9643283-0-5*) C Lazy Three.

Over the Next Hill: RVing Seniors in North America. Dorothy A. Counts & David R. Counts. 240p. 1996. pap. 16.95 (*1-55111-116-0*) Broadview Pr.

Over the Pacific: Japanese Space Policy into the Twenty-First Century. Joan Johnson-Freese. 200p. (C). 1993. per. 47.95 (*0-8403-8623-0*) Kendall-Hunt.

Over the Plum Pudding. John K. Bangs. LC 70-86136. (Short Story Index Reprint Ser.). 1977. 20.95 (*0-8369-3040-1*) Ayer.

Over the Rainbow. Christopher Carrie. (Crayola Coloring Storybks.). (Illus.). 32p. (Orig.). (J). (ps). 1990. 1.99 (*0-86696-239-5*) Binney & Smith.

Over the Rainbow. Marjorie Eatock. 480p. 1993. mass mkt. 4.50 (*0-8217-4032-6*, Zebra Kensgtn) Kensgtn Pub Corp.

Over the Rainbow. E.Y. Harburg. (Illus.). 32p. 15.95 (*0-06-028949-X*) HarpC.

Over The Rainbow. E.Y. Harburg. (Illus.). 32p. 5.95 (*0-06-443677-2*) HarpC.

***Over the Rainbow.** Maxfield Parrish & E. Y. Harburg. LC 00-27015. (Illus.). 32p. 2000. 17.95 (*0-941807-38-X*) Welcome Enterprises.

Over the Rainbow. large type ed. Marjorie Eatock. LC 94-1764. 445p. 1994. lib. bdg. 18.95 (*0-7862-0206-8*) Thorndike Pr.

Over the Rainbow: Money, Class & Homophobia. Field. 1995. 44.95 (*0-7453-0825-2*, Pub. by Pluto GBR); pap. 16.95 (*0-7453-0826-0*, Pub. by Pluto GBR) Stylus Pub VA.

Over the Rainbow: The Wizard of Oz As a Secular Myth of America. Paul Nathanson. LC 90-10163. (McGill Studies in the History of Religions). (Illus.). 432p. (C). 1991. pap. text 21.95 (*0-7914-0710-1*) State U NY Pr.

Over the Rainbow: The Wizard of Oz As a Secular Myth of America. Paul Nathanson. LC 90-10163. (McGill Studies in the History of Religions). (Illus.). 432p. (C). 1992. text 64.50 (*0-7914-0709-8*) State U NY Pr.

Over the Rhine: The Last Days of War in Europe. Brian S. Jewell. (C). 1991. 39.00 (*0-946771-70-7*, Pub. by Spellmnt Pubs) St Mut.

***Over the Rim: The Parley P. Pratt Exploring Expedition to Southern Utah, 1849-50.** Ed. by William B. Smart & Donna T. Smart. LC 99-6764. (Illus.). 230p. 1999. 37.95 (*0-87421-282-0*); pap. 19.95 (*0-87421-281-2*) Utah St U Pr.

Over the River & Through the Wood. Lydia Maria Child. LC 96-2012. (Illus.). 32p. (J). (ps-3). 1995. 15.95 (*0-8050-3825-6*, B Martin BYR) H Holt & Co.

Over the River & Through the Wood. Lydia Maria Child. 32p. (J). (gr. k-3). 1999. 6.95 (*0-8050-6311-0*) H Holt & Co.

Over the River & Through the Wood. Lydia Maria Child. Ed. by ALC Staff. LC 88-4712. (Illus.). 32p. (J). (ps up). 1992. mass mkt. 4.95 (*0-688-11839-9*, Wm Morrow) Morrow Avon.

Over the River & Through the Wood. Lydia Maria Child. LC 93-16614. (Illus.). 32p. (J). (gr. k-3). 1993. lib. bdg. 14.88 (*1-55858-211-8*, Pub. by North-South Bks NYC) Chronicle Bks.

Over the River & Through the Wood. Lydia Maria Child. LC 93-16614. (Illus.). 32p. (J). (gr. k-3). 1998. pap. 6.95 (*1-55858-959-7*, Pub. by North-South Bks NYC) Chronicle Bks.

Over the River & Through the Wood. Lydia Maria Child. (Reading Rainbow Bks.). (J). 1992. 9.15 (*0-606-01367-9*, Pub. by Turtleback) Demco.

Over the River & Through the Wood. Lydia Maria Child. (Blue Ribbon Bks.). (Illus.). 32p. (J). (gr. k-3). 1987. reprint ed. pap. 3.95 (*0-590-41190-X*, Blue Ribbon Bks) Scholastic Inc.

Over the River & Through the Wood: Big Book Edition. Lydia Maria Child. Ed. by Amy Cohn. LC 88-4712. (Illus.). 32p. (J). (ps-3). 1992. pap. 18.95 (*0-688-13632-X*, Wm Morrow) Morrow Avon.

Over the River & Through the Woods. Joe DiPietro. pap. 5.95 (*0-8222-1712-0*) Dramatists Play.

Over the River & Through the Woods. Mary Engelbreit. LC 95-123626. (Illus.). 32p. 1994. 6.95 (*0-8362-4622-5*) Andrews & McMeel.

Over the River & Through the Woods. Illus. by John Steven Gurney. 32p. (J). (ps-2). 1992. pap. 2.99 (*0-590-45258-4*, Cartwheel) Scholastic Inc.

Over the River & Through the Woods: The Best Short Fiction of Clifford D. Simak. Clifford Simak. 217p. 1996. 25.00 (*0-9648320-2-X*); lthr. 40.00 (*0-9648320-3-8*) Tachyon Pubns.

Over the River & Through the Woods Board Book. Lynne Cravath. (Illus.). 12p. (J). (ps up). 1998. 6.95 (*0-694-01218-1*) HarpC.

Over-the-Road Driver's Training Manual. Richard Rower. 170p. 1999. spiral bd. 32.50 (*0-9653817-3-0*) Mellwood Pub.

Over the Roofs of the World. Thomas R. Peters, Jr. Ed. by Darrin Daniel. (Spike Ser.: No. 7). (Illus.). 80p. 2000. pap. 7.95 (*1-885089-04-X*, Pub. by Cityful Pr) SPD-Small Pr Dist.

Over the Sea to Sky. Robert Hutchinson. LC 97-25778. (Illus.). 96p. (J). 1997. write for info. (*1-56313-907-3*) BrownTrout Pubs Inc.

***Over the Side Mickey: A First Hand Account of the 1997 Newfoundland Seal Hunt.** Michael J. Dwyer. (Illus.). 148p. 1999. pap. 14.95 (*1-55109-253-0*) Nimbus Publ.

Over the Steamy Swamp. Paul Geraghty. LC 88-21319. (Illus.). 32p. (J). (ps-1). 1989. 13.95 (*0-15-200561-7*, Gulliver Bks) Harcourt.

Over the Steamy Swamp. Paul Geraghty. LC 88-21319. (Illus.). 32p. (C). (ps-1). 1995. pap. 6.00 (*0-15-200226-X*, Gulliver Bks) Harcourt.

Over the Steamy Swamp. Paul Geraghty. (J). 1989. 10.15 (*0-606-07985-8*) Turtleback.

Over the Teacup. Catherine D. Cattell. 98p. (Orig.). 1983. pap. 4.50 (*0-913342-41-6*) Barclay Pr.

Over the Teacups. deluxe ed. Oliver W. Holmes. 400p. 1968. reprint ed. 39.00 (*0-403-02466-8*) Scholarly.

Over the Teacups. Oliver W. Holmes. (Notable American Authors Ser.). 1992. reprint ed. lib. bdg. 75.00 (*0-7812-3160-4*) Rprt Serv.

Over the Threshold. Daniels. LC 98-47351. 272p. 1999. pap. 19.99 (*0-415-91805-7*) Routledge.

Over the Threshold: Intimate Violence in Early America. Ed. by Christine Daniels & Michael V. Kennedy. LC 98-47351. 272p. 1999. 75.00 (*0-415-91804-9*) Routledge.

Over the Top see Mas Alla de la Cumbre

Over the Top. Barbara J. Crane. (Crane Reading System-English Ser.). (Illus.). (gr. k-2). 1977. pap. text 5.15 (*0-89075-100-5*) Bilingual Ed Serv.

Over the Top. Zig Ziglar. LC 97-27090. 1997. 19.99 (*0-7852-7119-8*) Nelson.

Over the Top: A Bridge to Academic & Critical Thinking Skills. Ed. by Prentice-Hall Staff. (C). 2000. pap. 28.00 (*0-13-021608-9*) S&S Trade.

Over the Top: Advance Two Hand Tapping for the Guitar. Dave Celentano. 50p. 1994. pap. 17.95 incl. audio compact disk (*0-931759-82-X*) Centerstream Pub.

Over the Top: The True Story of Guns & Roses. Mark Putterford. (Illus.). 192p. 1997. pap. 16.95 (*0-7119-5222-1*, OP 47793) Omnibus NY.

Over the Top: Veterans of the First World War. Turner Publishing Company Staff. LC 93-60962. (Illus.). 200p. 1993. 24.95 (*1-56311-108-X*) Turner Pub KY.

Over the Top & on the Side: The Ultimate Book of Sauces, Salsas, Dips, Dressings, Relishes, Raitas & Marinades. Silvana Franco & Shirley Gill. (Illus.). 192p. 1997. pap. 16.95 (*1-85967-485-2*, Lorenz Bks) Anness Pub.

***Over the Top of the World.** Will Steger & Jon Bowermaster. (Illus.). 64p. (gr. 3-7). 1999. pap. 5.99 (*0-590-84861-5*) Scholastic Inc.

Over the Top of the World: Explorer Will Steger's Trek Across the Arctic. Will Steger & Jon Bowermaster. LC 96-6913. (Illus.). 63p. (J). 1997. 17.95 (*0-590-84860-7*) Scholastic Inc.

Over the Top with Jim. Hugh Lunn. 278p. 1998. reprint ed. pap. 16.95 (*0-7022-2255-0*, Pub. by Univ Queensland Pr) Intl Spec Bk.

***Over the Top with Jim.** 2nd ed. Hugh Lunn. 356p. 1999. pap. 16.95 (*0-7022-3138-X*, Pub. by Univ Queensland Pr) Intl Spec Bk.

***Over the Top with the Tartan Army: Active Service, 1992-97.** Andrew McArthur. 2000. pap. 14.94 (*0-946487-45-6*) Luath Pr Ltd.

***Over the Wall.** John H. Ritter. LC 99-49911. (Illus.). 320p. (YA). (gr. 5-9). 2000. 17.99 (*0-399-23489-6*, Philomel) Peng Put Young Read.

Over the Wall: Protecting Religious Expression in the Public Square. Frank Guliuzza, III. LC 99-41434. (C). 2000. pap. text 20.95 (*0-7914-4450-3*) State U NY Pr.

Over the Wall: Protecting Religious Expression in the Public Square. Frank Guliuzza, III. LC 99-41434. (C). 2000. text 62.50 (*0-7914-4449-X*) State U NY Pr.

***Over the Wall: The Men Behind the 1934 Death House Escape.** Patrick M. McConal. LC 99-54607. 2000. write for info. (*1-57168-365-8*, Eakin Pr) Sunbelt Media.

Over the Wall: The Story of Paul's Escape in a Basket. Patricia L. Nederveld. LC 98-15638. (God Loves Me Ser.). (Illus.). 24p. (J). (ps). 1998. pap. 2.45 (*1-56212-318-1*, 1105-0149) CRC Pubns.

Over the Water. Maude Casey. 88p. (J). 1995. write for info. (*0-8050-3276-2*) H Holt & Co.

Over the Water. Maude Casey. 1996. 10.09 (*0-606-08841-5*, Pub. by Turtleback) Demco.

***Over the Waves.** Marianne Olson. LC 99-64152. (Illus.). iv, 147p. (YA). (gr. 4 up). 1999. pap. 9.95 (*0-9673497-0-2*) Rafter Five Pr.

Over the Wine Dark Sea. H.N. Turtletaub. text. write for info. (*0-312-87660-2*) St Martin.

Over the Wire & on TV: CBS & UPI in Campaign '80. Michael J. Robinson et al. LC 81-66977. 350p. 1983. 17.50 (*0-87154-722-8*) Russell Sage.

Over the World. Henry Howe. (Notable American Authors Ser.). 1992. reprint ed. lib. bdg. 75.00 (*0-7812-3210-4*) Rprt Serv.

Over Their Dead Bodies see Epitaphs to Remember: Remarkable Inscriptions from New England Gravestones

Over There. (Collected Works of Arnold Bennett: Vol. 63). 1977. reprint ed. 22.95 (*0-518-19144-3*, 19144) Ayer.

Over There. unabridged ed. Kyle Jarrard. LC 96-46642. 1997. 21.00 (*1-880909-53-7*) Baskerville.

Over There: A Marine in the Great War. Carl A. Brannen. LC 95-43731. (C. A. Brannen Ser.: No. 1). (Illus.). 192p. 1996. 24.95 (*0-89096-690-7*) Tex A&M Univ Pr.

Over There: A Marine in the Great War. Carl Andrew Brannen. (C. A. Brannen Ser.: No. 1). 1997. pap. 15.95 (*0-89096-791-1*) Tex A&M Univ Pr.

Over There: European Reactions to Americans in World War I. Ed. by Robert C. Walton. LC 72-174163. (Primary Sources in American History Ser.). (C). 1971. pap. text 7.95 (*0-88295-791-0*) Harlan Davidson.

Over There! The American Soldier in World War I. Jonathan Gawne. LC 99-22458. (G.I. Ser.). (Illus.). 84p. 1999. 19.95 (*0-7910-5371-7*) Chelsea Hse.

Over There! The American Soldier in World War I. Jonathan Gawne. LC 96-49842. (G. I.: Vol. 7). (Illus.). 80p. 1997. pap. 12.95 (*1-85367-268-8*) Stackpole.

Over There: The Story of America's First Great Overseas Crusade. rev. ed. Frank Freidel. 270p. 1990. 49.95 (*0-87722-718-7*) Temple U Pr.

Over There: The United States in the Great War, 1917-18. Byron Farwell. LC 98-35705. (Illus.). 320p. 1999. 27.95 (*0-393-04698-2*) Norton.

***Over There: The United States in the Great War, 1917-1918.** Byron Farwell. 352p. 2000. pap. 15.95 (*0-393-32028-6*) Norton.

Over These Steps. Harvey Sletten. LC 79-89330. 1980. 7.00 (*0-87212-098-8*) Libra.

***Over 30s' Jokes.** Stuart Macfarlane & Linda MacFarlane. Ed. by Helen Exley. (Joke Bks.). (Illus.). 64p. 1999. 8.50 (*1-86187-123-6*) Exley Giftbooks.

Over This Soil: An Anthology of World Farm Poems. Ed. by Catherine Webster. LC 97-33444. 184p. 1998. pap. 12.95 (*0-87745-617-8*); text 24.95 (*0-87745-616-X*) U of Iowa Pr.

Over Three Hundred Anxious Gift Catalogs, Vol. 1. James Lewis. 96p. 1987. pap. 5.00 (*0-9617322-6-1*) Flat Surface.

Over 300 Successful Business Letters for All Occasions. Alan Bond. LC 97-33521. 224p. 1998. pap. 14.95 (*0-7641-0322-9*) Barron.

Over Three Thousand Years Ago: In Ancient Egypt. Philip Sauvain. (History Detectives Ser.). (Illus.). 32p. (YA). (gr. 6 up). 1993. lib. bdg. 20.00 (*0-02-781084-4*, Mac Bks Young Read) S&S Childrens.

Over to Candleford. large type ed. Flora Thompson. 1978. 27.99 (*0-7089-0231-6*) Ulverscroft.

Over to You. Roald Dahl. LC 74-158082. 160p. 1990. pap. 10.95 (*0-14-003574-5*, Penguin Bks) Viking Penguin.

Over to You: An Exchange of Poems. Dave Widup & Stellasue Lee. 58p. (Orig.). 1991. pap. 8.95 (*0-941017-23-0*) Bombshelter Pr.

Over to You, Aggers. Jonathan Agnew. (Illus.). 224p. 1998. 40.00 (*0-575-06454-4*, Pub. by V Gollancz) Trafalgar.

***Over Tumbled Graves.** Jess Walter. 2000. 23.00 (*0-06-039386-6*); pap. 13.00 (*0-06-098867-3*) HarpC.

***Over 200 Proven Ways & Places to Pick up Girls by an Average Looking Guy.** 2nd rev. ed. Steve Pell. LC 99-229485. 1999. pap. 19.95 (*0-9668698-0-X*) S A Pell.

Over-Under. Catherine Matthias. LC 83-21005. (Rookie Readers Ser.). (Illus.). 32p. (J). (ps-2). 1984. pap. 4.95 (*0-516-42048-8*) Childrens.

Over, Under & Through. Tana Hoban. LC 72-81055. (Illus.). 32p. (J). (ps-2). 1973. lib. bdg. 16.00 (*0-02-744820-7*, Mac Bks Young Read) S&S Childrens.

Over under in the Garden: A Botanical Alphabet. Pat Schories. (Illus.). 32p. (J). (gr. k-2). 1996. 16.00 (*0-374-35677-7*) FS&G.

Over under Sideways Down. Gordon Skene. 240p. 1999. 24.95 (*0-947993-79-7*, Pub. by Mlvrn Pubg Co) Brit Bk Co Inc.

Over Washington. Murray Morgan. Ed. by Beverley Barnes & Lesley Dow. (Wings over America Ser.). (Illus.). 256p. 1995. reprint ed. 45.00 (*1-887451-07-2*); reprint ed. pap. 35.00 (*1-887451-01-3*) Weldon Owen.

Over West: Selected Writings of Frederick Eckman, with Commentaries & Appreciations. Frederick Eckman. Ed. by Linda Wagner-Martin & David Adams. LC 99-26529. 280p. 1999. pap. 15.95 (*0-943373-58-1*) Natl Poet Foun.

Over What Hill? Notes from the Pasture. large type ed. Effie Leland Wilder. LC 96-16513. (Illus.). 180p. 1996. 14.95 (*1-56145-131-2*) Peachtree Pubs.

Over 10 Childrens. Assorted. (J). 1995. per. 1.25 (*0-671-31438-6*) Simon & Schuster.

Overactive Child. Ed. by Eric A. Taylor. (Clinics in Developmental Medicine Ser.: No. 97). (Illus.). 269p. (C). 1991. text 49.95 (*0-521-41216-1*, Pub. by Mc Keith Pr) Cambridge U Pr.

Overall Collection: Songs by Linda Book. Linda Book. (Illus.). 87p. (J). (gr. k-6). 1994. spiral bd. 14.00 (*0-9626294-1-3*) Words & Muse Prodns.

Overall Direction Vol. 1: A Guide to Getting Where You Want to Go & Being Who You Want to Be. E. Perry Good. LC 96-68955. (Illus.). 222p. (Orig.). 1996. pap. 18.00 (*0-944337-33-3*, 333) New View Pubns.

Overall Economic Perspective to the Year 2000. 224p. 1988. pap. 48.00 (*92-1-116416-8*, 88.II.E.4) UN.

Overall Evaluations of Carcinogenicity - An Updating of IARC Monographs Volumes 1-42: Evaluation of Carcinogenic Risks to Human. (IARC Monographs). 434p. 1988. text, suppl. ed. 72.00 (*92-832-1411-0*) World Health.

Overall Morphology Pattern see Central Nervous System of Vertebrates: A General Survey of Its Comparative Anatomy with an Introduction to Pertinent Fundamental Biologic & Logical Concepts

Overall Program Plan: National Customs Automation Program. 1997. lib. bdg. 250.95 (*0-8490-8108-4*) Gordon Pr.

Overall Program Plan: National Customs Automation Program. Government Printing Office Staff. 270p. 1995. per. 18.00 (*0-16-048081-7*) USGPO.

Overall Socio-Economic Perspectives of the World Economy to the Year 2000. 262p. 19.95 (*92-1-109117-9*, E.90.II.C.2) UN.

Overall Work Program for the San Francisco Bay Area, 1993-1997. 200p. 1992. 12.00 (*0-318-22677-4*) Assn Bay Area.

Overboard. Chip Dunham. (Illus.). 128p. (Orig.). 1991. pap. 8.95 (*0-8362-1880-9*) Andrews & McMeel.

Overboard. Jessica Pierce. 144p. 1999. mass mkt. 3.50 (*0-8217-5121-2*) NAL.

***Overboard! A Provocative History of the U. S. S. J. P. Kennedy, Jr. (DD850)** Claire D. Branand. 184p. 1999. 29.95 (*0-9675160-0-5*) Skye Pubng Co.

Overbooked in Arizona. Samuel H. Gottlieb. LC 93-33521. (Illus.). 112p. 1994. pap. 9.95 (*0-9639966-0-6*) Camelback Gallery.

Overbooked in Arizona. Samuel H. Gottlieb. LC 93-33521. (Illus.). 112p. 1995. 20.00 (*0-9639966-1-4*) Camelback Gallery.

Overburdened Economy: Uncovering the Causes of Chronic Unemployment, Inflation, & National Decline. Lloyd J. Dumas. 256p. 1986. pap. 14.95 (*0-520-06169-1*, Pub. by U CA Pr) Cal Prin Full Svc.

Overburian Characters, to Which Is Added, a Wife. Thomas Overbury. Ed. by W. J. Paylor. LC 75-41207. reprint ed. 32.50 (*0-404-14580-9*) AMS Pr.

Overbury Mystery: A Chronicle of Fact & Drama of the Law. Edward A. Parry. LC 71-174850. 1972. reprint ed. 22.95 (*0-405-08835-3*) Ayer.

Overcentralization in Economic Administration: A Critical Analysis Based on Experience in Hungarian Light Industry. Janos Kornai. Tr. by John Knapp. (Illus.). 280p. 1994. reprint ed. text 49.95 (*0-19-828758-5*) OUP.

Overcharges: How to Prevent or Collect. Karl Emerson. 145p. 1985. text 21.50 (*0-9615741-0-0*) Persepolis Pr.

Overcharges: How to Prevent or Collect see How to Reduce Your Freight Costs: Shippers' Guide to Trucking Services

Overcoat see Six Great Modern Short Novels

O

An Asterisk (*) at the beginning of an entry indicates that the title is appearing for the first time.

Overcoat. Nikolai Vasilevich Gogol. 1995. 3.50 (0-87129-568-7, O20) Dramatic Pub.

Overcoat & Other Short Stories. Nikolai Vasilevich Gogol. (Thrift Editions Ser.). 112p. (Orig.). 1992. pap. 1.50 (0-486-27057-2) Dover.

Overcoat & Other Tales of Good. Nikolai Vasilevich Gogol. 1976. 23.95 (0-8488-1014-7) Amereon Ltd.

Overcoat & Other Tales of Good & Evil. Nikolai Vasilevich Gogol. Tr. & Intro. by David Magarshack. LC 79-17318. 1979. reprint ed. lib. bdg. 20.00 (0-8376-0442-7) Bentley Pubs.

Overcoat, Nose, Nevsky . . . unabridged ed. Nikolai Vasilevich Gogol. (World Classic Literature Ser.). (RUS.). pap. 6.95 (2-87714-260-4, Pub. by Bookking Intl) Distribks Inc.

Overcome: A Black Passover. Peter W. Bramble. LC 89-81167. (Illus.). 203p. (Orig.). 1989. pap. 14.95 (0-935132-17-1) C H Fairfax.

Overcome Addictions. Bruce Goldberg. 1992. 12.00 incl. audio (1-885577-41-9) B Goldberg.

***Overcome by Modernity: History, Culture & Community in Interwar Japan.** Harry D. Harootunian. LC 00-22857. 400p. 2000. 35.00 (0-691-00650-4, Pub. by Princeton U Pr) Cal Prin Full Svc.

Overcome by the Spirit. Francis MacNutt. LC 90-44727. 192p. (gr. 10). 1990. pap. 11.99 (0-8007-9170-3) Chosen Bks.

Overcome Neck & Back Pain. Kit Laughlin. (Illus.). 208p. 1998. pap. 15.00 (0-684-85252-7, Fireside) S&S Trade Pap.

Overcome Procrastination. Bruce Goldberg. 1994. 12.00 incl. audio (1-885577-71-0) B Goldberg.

Overcome Shyness from Inside & Succeed in Life: New Approach to Shyness Control Without Medication or Boring Treatment. Antun Murakovic. (ENG & JPN.). 200p. (Orig.). 1989. pap. write for info. (0-929602-01-3) Mura Pub Co.

***Overcome, Succeed & Prosper: The 5 Attitudes for Success to Enable Individuals or Families.** Lenell Geter. 2000. 22.00 (0-9678783-0-6) Marzina Pubng Grp.

Overcome Your Foreign Accent & Speak English with Confidence. Jeffrey E. Bedell. 1987. pap. 7.00 (0-916014-51-7) Am Spch Imprvmnt.

Overcome Your Foreign Accent & Speak English with Confidence. rev. ed. Jeffrey E. Bedell. 32p. 1987. 129.95 incl. audio (0-916014-50-9) Am Spch Imprvmnt.

Overcomer. Lora Allison. 96p. (Orig.). 1993. pap. 8.99 (1-56043-098-2) Destiny Image.

Overcomers. Witness Lee. 109p. 1992. per. 6.25 (0-87083-674-9, 08-037-001) Living Stream Ministry.

Overcomers. George E. Vanderman. LC 91-37998. 96p. 1992. pap. 4.99 (0-8163-1083-1) Pacific Pr Pub Assn.

Overcomers Are Coming Forth! Lora Allison. 90p. (Orig.). 1991. pap. 5.95 (0-9631284-1-8) Celebrat Minist.

Overcomer's Handbook: A Practical Guide to Victory in Christ. rev. ed. Mary Fear. Date not set. pap. 16.00 (0-9670856-0-8) Overcomers NE.

Overcomers Outreach: A Bridge to Recovery. Bob Bartosch & Pauline Bartosch. 276p. 1994. 16.00 (0-9643136-0-X) Meister Pr.

Overcomers, the see **Vencedores**

Overcoming. Steven P. Kaelin. 1997. pap. text 6.95 (0-9650754-0-0) Kaelin Bks.

Overcoming: Applying God's Power Where You Need It Most. Bill Hybels. (Interactions). 80p. 1998. pap., student ed. 5.99 (0-310-22445-4) Zondervan.

Overcoming Learning & Behaviour Difficulties: Partnership with Pupils. Ed. by Kevin Jones & Tony Charlton. 272p. (C). 1996. 75.00 (0-415-11866-2); pap. 22.99 (0-415-11867-0) Routledge.

Overcoming Acne: The How & Why of Healthy Skin Care. Alvin Silverstein et al. LC 89-13748. (Illus.). 112p. (YA). (gr. 7 up). 1990. 16.00 (0-688-08344-7, Wm Morrow) Morrow Avon.

***Overcoming Addiction: A Common Sense Approach.** abr. ed. Michael Hardiman. LC 99-57493. 128p. 2000. pap. 10.95 (1-58091-013-0, Pub. by Crossing Pr) Publishers Group.

***Overcoming Addiction: Positive Steps for Breaking Free of Addiction & Building Self-Esteem.** Corinne Sweet. 308p. 2000. pap. 14.95 (0-7499-2015-7, Pub. by Piatkus Bks) London Brdge.

Overcoming Addiction Without a Twelve Step Conviction. Oliver Rhodes. Ed. by Nick Tradas. LC 98-96213. (Illus.). 330p. (Orig.). 1997. pap., mass mkt. 19.95 (0-9658665-0-5, 001) Corp Hlth.

***Overcoming Addictions.** Lisa J. Roberts et al. LC 99-13341. 240p. 1999. pap. 25.00 (0-393-70299-5) Norton.

Overcoming Addictions: The Spiritual Solution. Deepak Chopra. LC 97-168267. 1997. 17.50 (0-609-60034-6) Harmony Bks.

Overcoming Addictions: The Spiritual Solution. Deepak Chopra. LC 97-50046. 144p. 1998. pap. 12.00 (0-609-80195-3) Three Rivers Pr.

Overcoming Adversity, 6 bks. Incl. Abraham Lincoln: U. S. President. Thomas Bracken. LC 97-48305. (Illus.). 128p. (YA). (gr. 5 up). 1999. lib. bdg. 19.95 (0-7910-4704-0); Bill Clinton: U. S. President. Michael Kelly. LC 98-13775. (Illus.). 128p. (YA). (gr. 5 up). 1999. lib. bdg. 19.95 (0-7910-4700-8); James Earl Jones: Actor. Judy Hasday. LC 97-31919. (Illus.). 128p. (YA). (gr. 5 up). 1999. lib. bdg. 19.95 (0-7910-4702-4); Roseanne: Entertainer. Ann Gaines. LC 97-48508. (Illus.). 128p. (YA). (gr. 5 up). 1999. lib. bdg. 19.95 (0-7910-4706-7); Tim Allen. John Wukovits. LC 98-13039. (Illus.). 112p. (YA). (gr. 6 up). 1998. lib. bdg. 19.95 (0-7910-4696-6); William Penn: Pennsylvania's Founder. Rebecca Stefoff. LC 97-23998. (Illus.). 128p. (YA). (gr. 5 up). 1999. lib. bdg. 19.95 (0-7910-4873-X); 139.65 (0-7910-4694-X) Chelsea Hse.

Overcoming Adversity. (Illus.). 112-128p. (gr. 5). pap. 129.35 (0-7910-4695-8) Chelsea Hse.

Overcoming Adversity, No. 5. Charles Stanley. 24p. 1995. pap. 2.50 (1-56476-434-6, 6-3434, Victor Bks) Chariot Victor.

Overcoming Agricultural Pollution of Water: The Challenge of Integrating Agricultural & Environmental Policies in the European Community. Susanne M. Scheirling. LC 94-23669. (Technical Papers: No. 269). 100p. 1995. pap. 22.00 (0-8213-3118-3, 13118) World Bank.

Overcoming AIDS: Case Histories of Those Who Conquered AIDS. 1992. lib. bdg. 79.95 (0-8490-8799-6) Gordon Pr.

Overcoming AIDS with Natural Medicine. Stephen C. Byrnes. LC 97-92719. (Illus.). ix, 224p. 1997. pap. 19.95 (1-891530-04-6) Centaur Bks.

Overcoming Alcoholism. Walter E. Kloss. 32p. (Orig.). 1985. pap. 0.89 (0-8280-0252-5) Review & Herald.

Overcoming All Obstacles: The Women of the Academie Julian. Ed. by Gabriel P. Weisberg & Jane R. Becker. LC 99-25673. (Illus.). 170p. 1999. text 65.00 (0-8135-2755-4) Rutgers U Pr.

Overcoming All Obstacles: The Women of the Academie Julian. Gabriel P. Weisberg et al. LC 99-25673. 170p. 1999. pap. 35.00 (0-8135-2756-2) Rutgers U Pr.

Overcoming Ambivalence: Mobilizing Motivation to End an Addiction. Bernie Schailehn. 100p. 1992. pap. text 11.95 (1-883050-00-6) Zealous Heart.

Overcoming America's Infrastructure Deficit. S. Jay Levy & Walter M. Caclette. (Public Policy Brief Highlights Ser.: No. 40A). (Illus.). 6p. 1998. pap. write for info. (0-941276-48-1) J Levy.

Overcoming America's Infrastructure Deficit: A Fiscally Responsible Plan for Public Capitol Investment. S. Jay Levy & Walter M. Cadette. (Public Policy Brief Ser.: No. 40). (Illus.). 28p. 1998. pap. write for info. (0-941276-47-3) J Levy.

Overcoming Anxiety: A Primer for Better Life Management. Lynn Fossum. Ed. by Michael G. Crisp. LC 89-82051. (Fifty-Minute Ser.). (Illus.). 76p. (Orig.). 1990. pap. 10.95 (1-56052-029-9) Crisp Pubns.

Overcoming Anxiety: From Short-Time Fixes to Long-Term Recovery. Reneau Peuifoy. LC 96-29376. 192p. (Orig.). 1997. pap. 12.95 (0-8050-4789-1, Owl) H Holt & Co.

Overcoming Anxiety at Work. Vincent Miskell & Jane R. Miskell. LC 93-12077. 128p. 1993. pap. 10.95 (1-55623-869-X, Irwn Prfssnl) McGraw-Hill Prof.

***Overcoming, Anxiety, Panic & Depression: New Ways to Regain Your Confidence.** James Gardner & Art Bell. 224p. 1999. pap. 14.99 (1-56414-435-6) Career Pr Inc.

Overcoming Anxiety, Panic, Phobias Through a Support Group see You Have Choices: Recovering from Anxiety, Panic & Phobia

Overcoming Arthritis. Unofficial Panel of Experts Staff et al. (Unofficial Guides). (Illus.). 354p. 1999. pap. 15.95 (0-02-862714-8, Pub. by Macmillan) S&S Trade.

Overcoming Arthritis & Other Rheumatic Diseases. Max Warmbrand. LC 75-13348. 220p. 1975. 15.00 (0-8159-6311-4) Devin.

Overcoming Barriers: Lifeline Seismic Improvement Programs. Craig E. Taylor et al. LC 98-40664. (Technical Council on Lifeline Earthquake Engineering Monographs: No. 13). 292p. 1998. 39.00 (0-7844-0399-6) Am Soc Civil Eng.

Overcoming Barriers in Family Life & Sex Education from African Perspective, 2 vols., 1. Michael E. Akpan & Juliana M. Akpan. LC 93-71701. (Illus.). 114p. (Orig.). 1993. pap. 13.95 (0-9634998-2-3) Ebewos Afr-Am.

Overcoming Barriers in Family Life & Sex Education from African Perspective, 2 vols., 2. Michael E. Akpan & Juliana M. Akpan. LC 93-71701. (Illus.). 114p. (Orig.). 1993. pap. 15.00 (0-9634998-5-8) Ebewos Afr-Am.

Overcoming Barriers to Church Growth. Steve Clapp. 128p. 1995. pap. 14.00 (0-9637206-3-5) LifeQuest IN.

***Overcoming Barriers to Collaborative Research: Report of a Workshop.** 60p. 1999. pap. 18.00 (0-309-06784-7) Natl Acad Pr.

Overcoming Barriers to Construction: Social, Economic, Environmental & Political. Patricia J. Lancaster. (Civil Engineering - Advisors Ser.). 1999. 69.95 (0-8493-7486-3, 7486) CRC Pr.

Overcoming Barriers to Education Restructuring: A Call for System Literacy. Grady McGonagill. 40p. 1993. pap. 2.50 (0-87652-194-4) Am Assn Sch Admin.

Overcoming Binge Eating. Christopher G. Fairburn. 247p. 1995. lib. bdg. 15.95 (0-89862-179-8); lib. bdg. 36.95 (0-89862-961-6, 2961) Guilford Pubns.

Overcoming Bladder Disorders: Compassionate, Authoritative, Medical & Self-Help Solutions. Rebecca Chalker & Kristene E. Whitmore. LC 89-45789. 352p. 1991. pap. 14.00 (0-06-092083-1, Perennial) HarperTrade.

Overcoming Burnout Naturally. VINZENZ MANSMANN. LC 99-36726. 1999. pap. text 11.95 (0-8069-2029-7) Sterling.

Overcoming by the Blood: Of the Lamb & by the Word of Your Testimony. Kevin Orr. 50p. (Orig.). 1996. pap. write for info. (1-57502-149-8) Morris Pubng.

Overcoming Candida: The Ultimate Cookery Guide. Xandria Williams. LC 98-18620. 128p. 1998. pap. 9.95 (1-86204-172-5, Pub. by Element MA) Penguin Putnam.

Overcoming Career Barriers: Cognitive & Emotional Reactions & Effective Coping Strategies. Manuel London. LC 97-22282. (Management Ser.). 300p. 1997. write for info. (0-8058-2579-7); pap. write for info. (0-8058-2580-0) L Erlbaum Assocs.

Overcoming Challenges. Compiled by John Cook. LC 97-31315. (Pocket Positives Ser.). 256p. 1997. pap. 8.95 (1-57749-061-4) Fairview Press.

***Overcoming Child Abuse: A Window on a World Problem.** Ed. by Michael Freeman. LC 99-30102. (Issues in Law & Society Ser.). 375p. 1999. text 99.95 (1-85521-982-4, Pub. by Ashgate Pub); pap. text 30.95 (1-85521-986-7, Pub. by Ashgate Pub) Ashgate Pub Co.

Overcoming Childhood Misfortune: Children Who Beat the Odds. Warren A. Rhodes & Kim Hoey. LC 93-19611. 168p. 1993. 52.95 (0-275-94081-0, Praeger Pubs) Greenwood.

***Overcoming Childhood Trauma: A Self-Help Guide Using Cognitive Behavioral Techniques.** Helen Kennerley. LC 00-38678. 2000. pap. write for info. (0-8147-4753-1) NYU Pr.

Overcoming Chronic Fatigue. Susan M. Lark. (Good Health Guide Ser.). (Orig.). 1996. pap. 3.95 (0-87983-716-0, Keats Publng) NTC Contemp Pub Co.

Overcoming Co-Dependency Through the Elimination of Human Relations: The Mildly Depressed Person's Guide to Daily Living. Mona Lovejoy & Sunny Knight. (Illus.). xx, 96p. 1995. pap. 5.95 (0-9650821-0-5, Halfway Hse) Lazarus Trust.

***Overcoming Crisis in Leadership: Indian Army.** K. Kuldip. LC 98-906906. 1998. 142.50 (81-7049-096-0, Pub. by Manas Pubns) S Asia.

Overcoming Dating Anxiety: A Self-Help Approach. Kandee S. Grossman & J. Regis McNamara. LC 90-50765. 96p. (Orig.). 1991. pap. 8.95 (0-933701-52-7) Westport Pubs.

Overcoming Dead Ends. Nancy E. Carlberg. 320p. (Orig.). 1991. pap. 20.00 (0-944878-10-5) Carlberg Pr.

Overcoming Deficits of Aging: A Behavioral Approach. Roger L. Patterson. (Applied Clinical Psychology Ser.). 306p. 1982. 55.00 (0-306-40947-X, Plenum Trade) Perseus Pubng.

Overcoming Depression. Concordia Publishing Staff. LC 96-173141. (Master's Touch Bible Study Ser.). 1996. pap. 4.50 (0-570-09550-6, 20-2591) Concordia.

Overcoming Depression. Paul Gilbert. LC 98-24978. 336p. 1999. pap. 13.95 (0-19-512688-2) OUP.

Overcoming Depression. Paul A. Hauck. LC 72-13416. 140p. 1973. pap. 16.95 (0-664-24969-8) Westminster John Knox.

Overcoming Depression. Dennis Leonard. 1991. pap. 4.95 (1-880809-01-X) D Leonard Pubns.

Overcoming Depression. Richard K. Mower. LC 85-29228. 1994. pap. 6.95 (0-87579-946-9) Deseret Bk.

Overcoming Depression. 3rd ed. Demitri Papolos. 1998. 4.62 (0-06-093177-9) HarpC.

Overcoming Depression. 3rd ed. Janice Papolos. LC 96-33534. (Illus.). 432p. 1997. reprint ed. pap. 15.00 (0-06-092782-8, Perennial) HarperTrade.

***Overcoming Depression: A Cognitive Therapy Approach for Taming the Depression Beast, Client Work.** Mark Gilson. 128p. 2000. pap. 25.00 (0-12-784455-4) Acad Pr.

Overcoming Depression: A Self-Help Workbook. Katherine Benziger. 60p. (Orig.). (YA). 1992. pap. text 15.00 (1-880931-02-8) KBA Pub.

***Overcoming Depression: Get Rid of Depression Using This Practical Two-Part Programme.** Dean Juniper. 144p. 2000. pap. 14.95 (1-85703-600-X, Pub. by How To Bks) Midpt Trade.

***Overcoming Depression: Therapist Protocol.** Gary Emery. 128p. 1999. pap. 19.95 (1-57224-160-8) New Harbinger.

Overcoming Depression & Manic Depression (Bipolar Depression) the Non Drug Approach. Paul A. Wider. 169p. 1993. pap. text 18.95 (0-9649151-0-3) Wider Pubs.

Overcoming Depressive Living Syndrome: How to Enjoy Life, Not Just Endure It. Earnie Larsen & Cara A. Macken. LC 95-46964. 208p. (Orig.). 1996. pap. 13.95 (0-89243-868-1, Liguori Triumph) Liguori Pubns.

Overcoming Difficulties - Primary Level: Using Multicultural Literature. Linda B. Hill. (Illus.). 144p. (Orig.). (J). (gr. 3-6). 1999. reprint ed. pap. text 15.00 (0-7881-6012-5) DIANE Pub.

Overcoming Discouragement. Chris Harvey. 79p. 1994. pap. 7.00 (1-886357-02-1) C Harvey Minist.

Overcoming Discouragement. Elbert Willis. 1976. 2.00 (0-89858-000-5) Fill the Gap.

Overcoming Divorce. Arnetha Williams. 72p. (Orig.). 1995. pap. 5.00 (1-885857-17-9) Four Wnds Pubng.

Overcoming Dog Problems: Practical Guidelines, Remedies & Treatments. 2nd rev. ed. Silvia Hartmann-Kent. LC 99-29606. (Illus.). 1999. reprint ed. pap. 19.95 (1-888994-15-0) Howln Moon.

Overcoming Doubt. Elbert Willis. 28p. 1997. pap. 2.00 (0-614-31155-1) Fill the Gap.

Overcoming Doubt, Fear & Procrastination: Identifying the Symptoms, Overcoming the Obstacles. Barbara W. Sykes. 248p. 1996. pap. 24.95 (0-9632857-7-7) Collins Pubns.

Overcoming Doubt, Fear & Procrastination: Identifying the Symptoms, Overcoming the Obstacles. Barbara W. Sykes. 64p. 1998. pap., wbk. ed. 9.95 (0-9632857-8-5) Collins Pubns.

Overcoming Dysfunction. Karen Westbrooks. 1994. pap. 4.50 (0-570-09363-5, 20-2701) Concordia.

Overcoming Dyslexia: A Practical Handbook for the Classroom. Hilary Broomfield & Margaret Combley. LC 97-138107. 238p. 1996. pap. 49.95 (1-56593-836-4, 1634) Thomson Learn.

Overcoming Dyslexia in Children, Adolescents, & Adults. 2nd ed. Dale R. Jordan. LC 95-37940. 367p. (C). 1996. pap. text 34.00 (0-89079-642-4, 7669) PRO-ED.

Overcoming Eating Disorders: A Cognitive-Behavioral Treatment for Bulimai Nervosa & Binge-Eati. W. Stewart Agras. 1999. pap. text 37.50 (0-12-785054-6) Acad Pr.

***Overcoming Eating Disorders Client Workbook: A Cognitive-Behavioral Treatment for Bulimia Nervosa.** W Stewart Agras. 1999. pap. text, wbk. ed. 43.50 (0-12-785055-4) Acad Pr.

Overcoming Economic Crisis in Developing Countries: Policies for Recovery & Development. Ed. by Machiko Nissanke & Adrian Hewitt. 288p. 1994. 59.00 (1-85567-152-2, Pub. by P P Pubs) Cassell & Continuum.

Overcoming Evil with Good: The Impact of a Life Well-Lived. Joseph M. Stowell. LC 95-172399. pap. 4.99 (0-8024-4699-X, 239) Moody.

Overcoming Exclusion Through Adult Learning. Ian Nash & John Walshe. 180p. 1999. pap. 29.00 (92-64-17026-X, 96 1999 03 1 P, Pub. by Org for Econ) OECD.

Overcoming Failure at School. OECD Staff. 100p. 1998. pap. 25.00 (92-64-16151-1, 9198041P) OECD.

***Overcoming Fatal Attractions & Other Titanic Love Affairs: Stop the Maddness!** Michael Eaton. 250p. 2000. pap. 14.99 (0-9672439-0-4) Issach Pubns.

Overcoming Fear. Walt Croom. 170p. 1999. pap. 7.95 (0-7392-0149-2, PO3090) Morris Pubng.

Overcoming Fear. Denise Fragipane. (Discernment Ser.). 52p. 1996. pap. text 3.50 (1-886296-04-9, DF1-003) Arrow Publications.

Overcoming Fear: Reaching for Your Dreams & Knowing Peace of Mind. Dale R. Olen. (Illus.). 212p. (Orig.). 1992. pap. 5.95 (1-56583-010-5) JODA.

Overcoming Fear & Discouragement. Kay Arthur et al. LC 99-21976. (International Inductive Study Ser.). 156p. 1999. 5.99 (1-56507-702-4) Harvest Hse.

Overcoming Fear of Fat. Ed. by Laura S. Brown & Esther D. Rothblum. LC 89-19860. (Women & Therapy Ser.: Vol. 8, No. 3). 99p. 1994. pap. text 9.95 (0-918393-71-X, Harrington Park) Haworth Pr.

Overcoming Fear of Riding. Theresa Jordan & Robyn Hold. (Illus.). 200p. 1996. 29.95 (0-914327-54-2) Breakthrgh NY.

Overcoming Fears: Creating Safety for You & Your World. Amy E. Dean. Ed. by Dan Olmos. LC 93-39153. 380p. 1994. pap. 18.00 (1-56170-079-7, 155) Hay House.

Overcoming Food Allergies: You Don't Have to Live with It. Gwynne H. Davies. 128p. 1997. pap. text 9.99 (1-85398-088-9, Pub. by Ashgrove Pr) Words Distrib.

Overcoming Frustration & Anger. Paul A. Hauck. LC 73-20285. 142p. 1974. pap. 16.95 (0-664-24983-3) Westminster John Knox.

***Overcoming Generalized Anxiety Disorder: Client Manual.** John White. (Best Practices for Therapy Ser.). 128p. 1999. pap. 11.95 (1-57224-145-4, Pub. by New Harbinger) Publishers Group.

***Overcoming Generalized Anxiety Disorder: Therapist Protocol.** John White. (Best Practices for Therapy Ser.). 105p. 1999. pap. 19.95 (1-57224-144-6, Pub. by New Harbinger) Publishers Group.

Overcoming Giants of the Heart: Experiencing Freedom from Inner Wounds That Imprison Us. Kenneth Hepner. LC 98-61040. 288p. (C). 1998. pap. 14.95 (1-57921-141-0, Pub. by WinePress Pub) BookWorld.

Overcoming Heterosexism & Homophobia: Strategies That Work. James T. Sears & Walter L. Williams. LC 96-50483. (Between Men - Between Women Ser.). 1997. 52.00 (0-231-10422-7); pap. 19.50 (0-231-10423-5) Col U Pr.

***Overcoming High-Tech Anxiety: Thriving in a Wired World.** Beverly Goldberg. LC 99-6309. 208p. 1999. 26.00 (0-7879-1022-8) Jossey-Bass.

Overcoming Hindrances to Receiving the Baptism in the Holy Spirit. John Osteen. 56p. 1987. mass mkt. 2.00 (0-912631-37-6) J O Pubns.

Overcoming HIV Infection: Myths of HIV Testing & Test Results, the History of AIDS, Treatments for HIV Infection. 1991. lib. bdg. 79.95 (0-8490-5138-X) Gordon Pr.

Overcoming Human Poverty. Ed. by United Nations Development Programme, New York Staff. 92p. 1998. 15.00 (92-1-126105-8) UN.

Overcoming Hurts & Anger. Dwight L. Carlson. LC 80-83852. 1981. pap. 7.99 (0-89081-277-2) Harvest Hse.

***Overcoming Hurts & Anger: Freedom from Negative Emotions.** rev. expanded ed. Dwight Carlson. LC 99-57244. 200p. 2000. pap. 8.99 (0-7369-0196-5) Harvest Hse.

Overcoming Hypertension. Kenneth H. Cooper. 464p. 1991. mass mkt. 6.99 (0-553-28937-3) Bantam.

Overcoming Impotence: Doctor's Guide to Regaining Sexual Vitality. 2nd ed. Steven Morganstern. (C). 1994. pap. 15.95 (0-13-146978-9) P-H.

***Overcoming Incontinence: A Straightforward Guide to Your Options.** Mary Dierich & Felicia Froe. LC 99-36372. 120p. 2000. pap. 14.95 (0-471-34795-7) Wiley.

Overcoming Indecisiveness. Theodore I. Rubin. 208p. 1986. mass mkt. 4.99 (0-380-69977-X, Avon Bks) Morrow Avon.

Overcoming Indifference: 10 Key Challenges in Today's Changing World. Ed. by Klaus Schwab. LC 94-24536. 372p. (C). 1994. text 55.00 (0-8147-8008-3) NYU Pr.

Overcoming Indifference: 10 Key Challenges in Today's Changing World. Ed. by Klaus Schwab. 372p. (C). 1995. pap. text 20.00 (0-8147-8036-9) NYU Pr.

Overcoming Infertility. Robert Jansen. 474p. 1998. pap. 16.95 (0-7167-3302-1) W H Freeman.

Overcoming Infertility: A Compassionate Resource for Getting Pregnant. Robert Jansen. 1997. text 24.95 (0-7167-3055-3) W H Freeman.

Overcoming Infertility: 12 Couples Share Their Success Stories. Herbert A. Goldfarb. 252p. 1995. pap. 14.95 (0-471-55706-4) Wiley.

Overcoming Infertility Naturally. Karen Bradstreet. 1994. pap. 12.95 (0-913923-86-9) Woodland UT.

O

An Asterisk (*) at the beginning of an entry indicates that the title is appearing for the first time.

***Overcoming Institutional Constraints to Implementing Macroeconomic Policies.** Economic & Social Commission for Asia & the Pacific Staff. (Least Developed Countries Ser.: No.1). 162p. 1998. 27.00 (*92-1-119825-9*) UN.

Overcoming Intestinal Disorders. Deepak Chopra. 1995. pap. 11.00 (*0-517-88492-5*) Random Hse Value.

Overcoming Isolation: Information & Transportation Networks in Development Strategies for Peripheral Areas. Ed. by David F. Batten et al. LC 95-30839. (Advances in Spatial Science Ser.). (Illus.). viii, 272p. 1995. 112.00 (*3-540-59423-X*) Spr-Verlag.

***Overcoming Jealousy.** Wendy Dryden. 1999. pap. text. write for info. (*0-85969-765-7*, Pub. by Sheldon Pr); pap. text 10.95 (*0-85969-756-8*) Sheldon Pr.

Overcoming Jealousy & Possessiveness. Paul A. Hauck. LC 81-3040. 140p. 1981. pap. 15.95 (*0-664-24374-6*) Westminster John Knox.

Overcoming Jet Lag. Charles F. Ehret & Lynne Waller. 160p. (Orig.). 1987. pap. 10.95 (*0-425-09936-9*) Berkley Pub.

Overcoming Job Burnout: How to Renew Enthusiasm for Work. 2nd ed. Beverly A. Potter. (Illus.). 224p. 1998. pap. 14.95 (*1-57951-000-0*) Ronin Pub.

Overcoming Law. Richard A. Posner. LC 94-12753. 608p. 1995. text 42.50 (*0-674-64925-7*, POSOVE) HUP.

Overcoming Law. Richard A. Posner. 608p. 1996. pap. 17.95 (*0-674-64926-5*) HUP.

Overcoming Legal Uncertainties about Use of Solar Energy Systems. American Bar Foundation Staff et al. LC 77-95217. (American Bar Foundation Publications). viii, 80p. 1978. pap. 20.00 (*0-910058-89-X*, 305000) W S Hein.

Overcoming Life. W. E. Lee. 191p. 1997. per. 8.75 (*1-57593-909-6*, 07-061-002) Living Stream Ministry.

Overcoming Life. Dwight Lyman Moody. LC 95-177069. (Classics Ser.). mass mkt. 4.99 (*0-8024-5445-3*, 391) Moody.

Overcoming Life: The Basis for the Normal Christian Life. Watchman Nee. 180p. 1997. 18.00 (*1-57593-817-0*, 07-061-901) Living Stream Ministry.

Overcoming Life on a Small Planet: Heaven Style Living for Earthlings. Ron McGatlin. Orig. Title: Kingdom Freedom I. (Illus.). 166p. 1996. pap. 12.95 (*0-9654546-0-6*) Basileia Pub.

Overcoming Life's Challenges. Samuel Chiel. LC 94-10837. 1994. 20.00 (*0-88125-240-9*) Ktav.

Overcoming Life's Challenges: Biblical Answers for Life's Difficulties. Roger W. Skepple. (Illus.). 137p. 1997. pap. text 15.00 (*0-9660562-1-3*) Eden Bk Pr.

***Overcoming Life's Difficulties.** Peter Jeffery. 1999. pap. text 8.99 (*0-85234-434-1*) Evangelical Pr.

Overcoming Life's Toughest Problems: Finding God's Peace & Strength. Ed Hindson. LC 98-31334. 200p. 1999. pap. 9.99 (*0-7369-0009-8*) Harvest Hse.

***Overcoming Loneliness.** W. Leslie Carter et al. 224p. 2000. mass mkt. 7.99 (*0-8007-8689-0*, Spire) Revell.

Overcoming Loneliness in Everyday Life. Jacqueline Olds et al. 256p. 1996. 19.95 (*1-55972-343-2*, Birch Ln Pr) Carol Pub Group.

Overcoming Loss: A Healing Guide. Rita Freedman. (Pocket Gift Editions Ser.). (Illus.). 64p. 1998. 4.95 (*0-88088-094-5*) Peter Pauper.

***Overcoming Macular Degeneration: A Guide to Seeing Beyond the Clouds.** Yale Solomon. LC 99-49520. 272p. 2000. pap. 12.50 (*0-380-80589-8*, Avon Bks) Morrow Avon.

***Overcoming Male Infertility: Understanding Its Causes & Treatments.** Leslie R. Schover & Anthony J. Thomas, Jr. LC 99-51353. (Illus.). 290p. 1999. pap. 16.95 (*0-471-24471-6*) Wiley.

Overcoming Math Anxiety. Sheila Tobias. LC 93-3648. 1994. 23.00 (*0-393-03577-8*) Norton.

Overcoming Math Anxiety. expanded rev. ed. Sheila Tobias. 272p. 1995. pap. 12.95 (*0-393-31307-7*, Norton Paperbks) Norton.

Overcoming Math Anxiety. 2nd ed. Randy Davidson. LC 99-38594. 144p. (C). 1999. pap. text 23.00 (*0-321-06918-8*) Addison-Wesley.

Overcoming Migraine: A Comphrehensive Guide to Treatment & Prevention by a Survivor. enl. rev. ed. Betsy Wyckoff. LC 93-35705. 1993. pap. 10.95 (*0-88268-163-X*) Station Hill Pr.

Overcoming Migraine: A Comprehensive Guide to Treatment & Prevention by a Survivor. Betsy Wyckoff. (Illus.). 112p. 1991. pap. 9.95 (*0-88268-126-5*); text 21.95 (*0-88268-110-9*) Station Hill Pr.

Overcoming Missionary Stress. Marjory F. Foyle. 1987. pap. 12.95 (*0-9617751-0-6*) Evangel Missions.

Overcoming Modern Confusion: Consistency & Choice. Adolfo Critto. LC 99-18632. 352p. 1999. pap. 34.50 (*0-7618-1361-6*) U Pr of Amer.

Overcoming National Barriers to International Waste Trade: A New Perspective on the Transnational Movement of Hazardous & Radioactive Wastes. Elli Louka. (International Environmental Law & Policy Ser.). 240p. (C). 1994. lib. bdg. 92.00 (*0-7923-2850-7*) Kluwer Academic.

Overcoming Nervous Breakdown. Tony Lake. 107p. 1989. reprint ed. pap. 7.95 (*1-878290-01-0*) Intl Hlth MD.

Overcoming Objections. Red Point Publishing Staff. 1997. pap. text 3.95 (*0-9658795-3-4*) Red Pt Publ.

Overcoming Objections: The Definitive Objection-Handling Methods for the Call Center Environment. Kathy Sisk. LC 94-60302. vi, 96p. 1994. write for info. (*0-936840-16-1*) Tech Marketing.

Overcoming Objections in Inbound & Outbound Call Center Applications. Kathy Sisk. Ed. by Technology Marketing Corp. Staff. 100p. 1994. write for info. (*0-936840-13-7*) Tech Marketing.

Overcoming Obsessive-Compulsive Disorder - Client Manual. Gail S. Steketee. LC 98-67412. (Best Practices Ser.). 72p. 1999. pap. 11.95 (*1-57224-129-2*) New Harbinger.

Overcoming Obsessive-Compulsive Disorder - Therapist Protocol. Gail S. Steketee. LC 98-67411. (Best Practices Ser.). 144p. 1999. pap. 24.95 (*1-57224-128-4*) New Harbinger.

***Overcoming Obstacles: A Program for Success: High School Level, 16 vols.** (YA). (gr. 9-12). 1999. pap. text. write for info. (*1-929393-13-X*) Community for Ed.

***Overcoming Obstacles: A Program for Success: Middle School Level, 13 vols.** (YA). (gr. 6-9). 1999. pap. text 11.50 (*1-929393-00-8*) Community for Ed.

Overcoming Obstacles: Barriers to Success. Tim Downs. (Life Skills Ser.). (Illus.). 4p. (C). 1996. teacher ed., ring bd. 1.25 (*1-57334-018-9*, 742-101t); student ed., ring bd. 3.25 (*1-57334-017-0*, 742-101s) WSN Pr.

Overcoming Obstacles in Environmental Policymaking: Creating Partnerships Through Mediation. John K. Gamman. LC 94-2262. (SUNY Series in International Environmental Policy & Theory). 250p. (C). 1994. text 57.50 (*0-7914-2207-0*); pap. text 19.95 (*0-7914-2208-9*) State U NY Pr.

Overcoming Obstacles to Institutional Development. 68p. pap. 9.00 (*92-1-104369-7*, 91.II.A.11) UN.

Overcoming Opposition: How to Succeed in Doing the Will of God. Lisa Comes. 28p. 1990. mass mkt. 1.50 (*0-912631-40-6*) J O Pubns.

Overcoming Opposition: How to Succeed in Doing the Will of God see Venciendo la Oposicion: Como Triunfar para Hacer la Voluntad de Dios

Overcoming Organizational Defenses. Chris Argyris. 180p. 1990. 70.00 (*0-205-12338-4*, H23385) Allyn.

Overcoming Our Obsessions: A Spiritual Journey. Phillip Ferranti. 1979. pap. 12.95 (*0-88280-069-8*) ETC Pubns.

Overcoming Overeating. Janae R. Hirschmann. 1998. mass mkt. 6.99 (*0-449-00382-5*, Crest) Fawcett.

Overcoming Overeating. Jane R. Hirschmann & Carol H. Hunter. 1989. pap. 11.00 (*0-449-90407-5*, Columbine) Fawcett.

Overcoming Overeating. 2nd ed. Rick Guyton. 178p. (C). 1992. pap. text 24.80 (*0-536-58157-6*) Pearson Custom.

Overcoming Overspending: A Winning Plan for Spenders & Their Partners. Olivia Mellan. 216p. 1997. reprint ed. pap. 12.95 (*0-8027-7495-4*) Walker & Co.

Overcoming Overspending: A Winning Plan for Spenders & Their Spouse. Olivia Mellan & Sherry Christie. 216p. 1995. 20.95 (*0-8027-1309-2*) Walker & Co.

Overcoming Panic & Fear: Risk & Crisis Communications. Barry McLoughlin. (Communicate with Power 2000 Ser.). 140p. 1998. reprint ed. spiral bd. 20.00 (*1-886712-09-3*) McLoughlin MultiMed.

Overcoming Panic, Anxiety, & Phobias: New Strategies to Free Yourself from Worry & Fear. Shirley Babior & Carol Goldman. LC 95-42389. 176p. (Orig.). 1995. pap. 12.95 (*1-57025-072-3*) Whole Person.

Overcoming Panic Disorder. Lorna Weinstock & Eleanor Gilman. LC 97-42182. 288p. 1998. pap. 14.95 (*0-8092-3102-6*, 310260, Contemporary Bks) NTC Contemp Pub Co.

Overcoming Panic Disorder & Agoraphobia: Client Manual. Elke Zuercher-White. (Best Practices). 88p. 1999. pap. 11.95 (*1-57224-147-0*, Pub. by New Harbinger) Publishers Group.

Overcoming Panic Disorder & Agoraphobia: Therapist Protocol. Elke Zuercher-White. (Best Practices). 290p. 1999. pap. 24.95 (*1-57224-146-2*, Pub. by New Harbinger) Publishers Group.

Overcoming Paralysis: Into the Water & Out of the Wheelchair. Igor Burdenko & Scott Biehler. LC 99-20886. (Illus.). 241p. 1999. pap. text 14.95 (*0-89529-883-X*, Avery) Penguin Putnam.

***Overcoming Parasites: What You Need to Know.** Ann L. Gittleman. 48p. 1999. pap. 3.95 (*0-89529-983-6*, Avery) Penguin Putnam.

Overcoming Pastoral Pitfalls. Kurt Brink. LC 97-176583. 1997. pap. 13.00 (*0-570-04969-5*, 12-3319) Concordia.

Overcoming Perfectionism, the Superhuman Syndrome. Ann W. Smith. 1990. pap. 8.95 (*1-55874-111-9*) Health Comm.

Overcoming Post-Traumatic Stress Disorder: Client Manual. Larry Smyth. (Best Practices). 95p. 1998. pap. 11.95 (*1-57224-163-2*, Pub. by New Harbinger) Publishers Group.

Overcoming Post-Traumatic Stress Disorder: Therapist Protocol. Larry Smyth. (Best Practices). 190p. 1999. pap. 24.95 (*1-57224-162-4*, Pub. by New Harbinger) Publishers Group.

Overcoming Postpartum Depression: A Doctor's Own Story. Lois V. Nightingale. 128p. 1998. pap. 10.95 (*1-889755-26-5*) Nightngale Rose.

Overcoming Postpartum Depression & Anxiety. Linda Sebastian. LC 98-16262. (Illus.). 152p. 1998. pap. 12.95 (*1-886039-34-8*) Addicus Bks.

***Overcoming Procrastination.** Windy Dryden. 2000. pap. 9.95 (*0-85969-815-7*) Sheldon Pr.

Overcoming Procrastination. Albert Ellis & William J. Knaus. LC 76-26333. 1972. pap. 7.95 (*0-917476-04-2*) A Ellis Institute.

Overcoming Procrastination. Albert Ellis & William J. Knaus. 1979. mass mkt. 5.99 (*0-451-15931-4*, Sig) NAL.

***Overcoming Procrastination.** Duane Vander Klok. 64p. 1999. write for info. (*1-890900-30-3*) Insight Intl.

Overcoming Racism. Rick Joyner. (Combating Spiritual Strongholds Ser.). 60p. 1996. pap. 3.00 (*1-878327-45-3*, RJI-012) Morning NC.

Overcoming Racism & Sexism. Ed. by Linda A. Bell & David Blumenfeld. 276p. (C). 1995. pap. text 25.95 (*0-8476-8031-2*); lib. bdg. 66.00 (*0-8476-8030-4*) Rowman.

Overcoming Rejection. Frank Hammond. 96p. (Orig.). 1987. pap. 5.95 (*0-89228-105-7*) Impact Christian.

Overcoming Relationship Addiction: A Workshop for Women Who Love Too Much. Kathryn Apgar. LC 90-39462. (Workshop Models for Family Life Education Ser.). 94p. 1991. pap. 15.95 (*0-87304-239-5*) Manticore Pubs.

Overcoming Repetitive Motion Injuries the Rossiter Way. Richard H. Rossiter & Sue MacDonald. LC 98-68749. 256p. 1999. pap. 15.95 (*1-57224-134-9*) New Harbinger.

Overcoming Resistance: A Practical Guide to Producing Change in the Workplace. Jerald M. Jellison. 208p. 1993. 19.00 (*0-671-74949-8*) S&S Trade.

Overcoming Resistance: Rational-Emotive Therapy with Difficult Clients. Albert Ellis. 240p. 1985. 38.95 (*0-8261-4910-3*) Springer Pub.

Overcoming Resistance: Success in Counseling Men. George A. Harris. LC 95-35032. 156p. 1995. pap. 21.00 (*1-56991-032-4*) Am Correctional.

***Overcoming Resistance: Video Workshop Manual.** Rise VanFleet. v, 26p. 1999. pap. 6.50 (*1-930557-03-5*) Play Therapy Pr.

Overcoming Resistance to Self-Direction. Ed. by Roger Hiemstra & Ralph G. Brockett. LC 85-644750. (New Directions for Adult & Continuing Education Ser.: No. ACE 64). 110p. (Orig.). 1994. pap. 22.00 (*0-7879-9981-4*) Jossey-Bass.

Overcoming Rheumatism & Arthritis. James G. Speight. 109p. 1984. pap. 7.95 (*0-85207-166-3*, Pub. by C W Daniel) Natl Bk Netwk.

Overcoming Rheumatism & Arthritis. Phyllis Speight. 88p. (Orig.). pap. 8.95 (*0-8464-4265-5*) Beekman Pubs.

Overcoming Satanic Obstacles. Harvey L. Hester, Jr. Ed. by Tanya C. Stokes. (Orig.). 1990. pap. 2.00 (*0-9627849-1-5*) Temperance Pub Hse.

Overcoming Sexual Immorality. expanded rev. ed. Bill Rudge. 42p. 2000. pap. 2.00 (*1-889809-13-6*) Liv Truth.

Overcoming Sexual Performance Problems: A Self-Help Guide for Men. Lynn W. Aurich. (Illus.). 173p. 1997. pap. 39.95 incl. audio (*0-9659482-0-X*) New Hope Publns.

Overcoming Shyness. M. Blaine Smith. LC 93-36043. 228p. (Orig.). 1993. pap. 11.99 (*0-8308-1630-5*, 1630) InterVarsity.

Overcoming Shyness & Social Phobia: A Step-by-Step Guide. Ronald M. Rapee. LC 97-27509. 144p. 1998. pap. 25.00 (*0-7657-0120-0*) Aronson.

Overcoming Sin & Enjoying God. Danny Bond. Ed. by Chuck Smith. (Calvary Basics Ser.). 83p. 1996. pap. 3.50 (*0-936728-69-8*) Word for Today.

***Overcoming Sleep Disorders: A Natural Approach.** Brenda O'Hanlon. LC 00-30709. 2000. pap. 10.95 (*1-58091-014-9*) Crossing Pr.

***Overcoming Soft Additions.** Judith Sewell Wright. 2000. write for info. (*0-9661401-7-6*) Except Liv Pr.

Overcoming Specific Phobia - Therapist Protocol: A Hierarchy & Exposure-Based Protocol for the Treatment of All Specific Phobias. Edmund J. Bourne. LC 98-66708. (Best Practices Ser.). 90p. 1998. pap. 19.95 (*1-57224-114-4*) New Harbinger.

Overcoming Specific Phobias - Client Manual: A Hierarchy & Exposure-Based Protocol for the Treatment of All Specific Phobias. Edmund J. Bourne. (Best Practices Ser.). 60p. 1998. pap. 9.95 (*1-57224-115-2*) New Harbinger.

***Overcoming Spiritual Barriers in Japan: Identifying Strongholds & Redemptive Gifts.** Keith E. Webb. LC 99-90496. 57p. 1999. pap. 4.50 (*0-9665658-0-0*) NxtChrch Rescs.

Overcoming Stage Fright in Every Day Life. Joyce Ashley. 176p. 1997. pap. 12.00 (*0-609-80097-3*) Random Hse Value.

Overcoming Stress: Everything You Ever Need to Know! Ed. by Horace W. Batson & Gary Batson. 100p. (Orig.). 1987. pap. 9.95 (*0-938503-00-6*) Welstar Pubns.

***Overcoming Stress in the Workplace.** Carol Berman. 260p. 2000. 29.95 (*0-8290-5212-7*) Ardent Media.

Overcoming Stress in the Workplace. Carol Berman. 275p. Date not set. write for info. (*0-8290-2634-7*) Irvington.

Overcoming Strife--The AIDS Virus of the Spirit. Billy J. Daugherty. 32p. (Orig.). 1993. pap. 0.50 (*1-56267-084-0*) Victory Ctr OK.

Overcoming Student Failure: Changing Motives & Incentives for Learning. Martin V. Covington & Karen Manheimteel. LC 95-39473. (Psychology in Classroom Ser.). 131p. (Orig.). 1996. pap. text, teacher ed. 17.95 (*1-55798-343-7*) Am Psychol.

Overcoming Tension & Strain, 5 vols. J. Oswald Sanders. 1987. pap. 3.75 (*9971-972-12-3*) OMF Bks.

Overcoming that "After-Camp Spiritual Dive" Paul Parmer. 10p. (YA). (gr. 3 up). Date not set. pap. write for info. (*1-884838-17-0*) Walterick Pubs.

Overcoming the Accuser. Rick Joyner. (Combating Spiritual Strongholds Ser.). 61p. 1996. pap. 3.00 (*1-878327-47-X*, RJI-011) Morning NC.

Overcoming the Adversary see Venciendo al Adversario

Overcoming the Adversary. Mark I. Bubeck. pap. 9.99 (*0-8024-0333-6*, 241) Moody.

Overcoming the Dark Side of Leadership: The Paradox of Personal Dysfunction. Gary L. McIntosh & Samuel D. Rima, Sr. LC 97-22265. 240p. 1998. pap. 12.99 (*0-8010-9047-4*) Baker Bks.

***Overcoming the Demons.** Cloteal J. Monroe. LC 99-93939. 2000. pap. 9.95 (*0-533-13201-0*) Vantage.

Overcoming the Diet Dilemma. Neva Coyle. LC 91-24062. 192p. (Orig.). 1991. pap. 8.99 (*1-55661-232-X*) Bethany Hse.

Overcoming the Enemy: Discover God's Plan for Winning Spiritual Battles. Charles Stanley. LC 97-222139. (The In Touch Study Ser.). 120p. 1997. pap. 7.99 (*0-7852-7277-1*) Nelson.

Overcoming the Fear of Success. Martha Friedman. 208p. 1986. mass mkt. 7.95 (*0-446-38381-3*, Pub. by Warner Bks) Little.

Overcoming the Giants in Your Land. Reginald Klimionok. 168p. 1993. pap. 10.99 (*1-56043-750-2*, Treasure Hse) Destiny Image.

Overcoming the Giants in Your Life. Bill Rudge. 73p. 1999. pap. 6.00 (*1-889809-08-X*) Liv Truth.

Overcoming the Invisible Crime: A Tricultural Autobiography. Yinka Vidal. 352p. 1993. pap. 19.99 (*0-9640818-0-6*) Lara Pubns.

Overcoming the Language Barrier: Problems of Interdisciplinary Dialogue. Ed. by Robert Flower et al. 120p. 1998. pap. 25.00 (*0-9633272-1-6*) Temple U Frontier Sci.

Overcoming the Legacy of Overeating: How to Change Your Negative Eating Patterns. rev. ed. Nan K. Fuchs. 288p. 1996. pap. 16.00 (*1-56565-453-6*) Lowell Hse.

Overcoming the Legacy of Overeating: How Your Mother Influenced Your Eating Patterns & How You Can Change Them. Nan K. Fuchs. Orig. Title: My Mother Made Me Do It. 240p. 1990. reprint ed. pap. 9.95 (*0-929923-27-8*) Lowell Hse.

Overcoming the Legacy of Overeatings: How to Change Your Negative Eating Patterns. 3rd ed. Nan Kathryn Fuchs. LC 99-41599. 288p. 1999. pap. 16.95 (*0-7373-0255-0*, 02550W) NTC Contemp Pub Co.

Overcoming the Myth of Self-Worth: Reason & Fallacy in What You Say to Yourself. Richard L. Franklin. (Illus.). 226p. (Orig.). 1994. pap. 12.95 (*0-9639387-0-3*) R L Franklin.

Overcoming the Odds, 12 bks. (J). (gr. 3-7). 1997. 203.76 (*0-8172-4132-9*) Raintree Steck-V.

Overcoming the Odds: High Risk Children from Birth to Adulthood. Emmy E. Werner & Ruth S. Smith. LC 91-23415. (Illus.). 304p. 1992. text 47.50 (*0-8014-2584-0*); pap. text 17.95 (*0-8014-8018-3*) Cornell U Pr.

Overcoming the Pain of Inflammatory Arthritis: The Pain-Free Promise of Pantothenic Acid. Phyllis Eisenstein. 1999. mass mkt. 6.95 (*0-89529-902-X*, Avery) Penguin Putnam.

Overcoming the Pain of Inflammatory Arthritis: The Pain-Free Promise of Pantothenic Acid. Phyllis Eisenstein & Samuel M. Scheiner. 192p. Date not set. pap. 11.95 (*0-89529-810-4*, Avery) Penguin Putnam.

Overcoming the Polish Crisis. Jozef Kaleta. (WVSS on the Soviet Union & Eastern Europe Ser.). (C). 1996. pap. text 36.00 (*0-8133-7882-6*) Westview.

Overcoming the Power of the Occult. Terry A. Modica. LC 96-61570. 1997. pap. 9.50 (*1-880033-24-0*) Queenship Pub.

Overcoming the Rating Game: Beyond Self-Love - Beyond Self-Esteem. Paul A. Hauck. 112p. (Orig.). 1992. pap. 16.95 (*0-664-25310-5*) Westminster John Knox.

Overcoming the Recurring Nightmare of Schizophrenia. 2nd ed. Jeanette Keil. 21p. reprint ed. pap. 2.95 (*0-9616230-0-4*) K&A Pubns.

Overcoming the Religious Spirit. Rick Joyner. (Combating Spiritual Strongholds Ser.). 62p. 1996. pap. 3.00 (*1-878327-44-5*, RJI-013) Morning NC.

Overcoming the Seven Devils That Ruin Success. James Dillehay. LC 93-94313. 72p. (Orig.). 1994. pap. 6.95 (*0-9629923-1-3*) Warm Snow.

Overcoming the Spirit of Poverty. Rick Joyner. (Combating Spiritual Strongholds Ser.). 78p. 1996. pap. 3.00 (*1-878327-55-0*, RJI-017) Morning NC.

Overcoming the Storms of Life. Billy J. Daugherty. 32p. 1991. pap. 0.50 (*1-56267-006-9*) Victory Ctr OK.

Overcoming Tradition & Modernity: The Search for Islamic Authenticity. Robert D. Lee. LC 97-7391. 224p. (C). 1997. pap. text 23.00 (*0-8133-2798-9*, Pub. by Westview) HarpC.

***Overcoming Underachieving: A Simple Plan to Boost Your Kids' Grades & Their Homework Blahs.** Ruth Allen Peters. LC 00-24990. 256p. 2000. 12.95 (*0-7679-0458-3*) Broadway BDD.

Overcoming Underachieving: An Action Guide to Helping Your Child Succeed in School. Sam Goldstein & Nancy Mather. LC 97-38519. (Illus.). 312p. 1998. pap. 16.95 (*0-471-17032-1*) Wiley.

Overcoming Unintentional Racism in Counseling & Therapy: A Practitioner's Guide to International Action. Charles R. Ridley. (Multicultural Aspects of Counseling Ser.: Vol. 5). 120p. 1994. 42.00 (*0-8039-4869-7*); pap. 18.95 (*0-8039-4870-0*) Sage.

Overcoming Welfare: Expecting More from the Poor & from Ourselves. James L. Payne. LC 98-5360. 288p. 1998. 26.50 (*0-465-06924-X*, Pub. by Basic) HarpC.

Overcoming Witchcraft. Rick Joyner. (Combating Spiritual Strongholds Ser.). 77p. 1996. pap. 3.00 (*1-878327-46-1*, RJI-014) Morning NC.

Overcoming World Hunger. Ed. by Clifford M. Hardin. LC 69-15333. 1969. 4.95 (*0-317-02960-6*, 64697) Am Assembly.

Overcoming Worries, Fears, & Anxieties: A Guide to Recovery. Helen Kennerley. LC 96-16032. 170p. (C). 1997. pap. 14.95 (*0-8147-4690-X*) NYU Pr.

Overcoming Worries, Fears, & Anxieties: A Guide to Recovery. Helen Kennerley. LC 96-16032. 170p. (C). 1997. text 37.50 (*0-8147-4689-6*) NYU Pr.

Overcoming Worry. Elbert Willis. 1976. 2.00 (*0-89858-001-3*) Fill the Gap.

Overcoming Worry & Fear. Paul A. Hauck. LC 74-20629. 112p. 1975. pap. 16.95 (*0-664-24811-X*) Westminster John Knox.

Overcoming Writing Blocks. Karin Mack & Eric Skjei. 1980. 10.00 (*0-685-02301-X*); pap. 6.95 (*0-685-02302-8*) HM.

Overcoming Your Barriers. Gerald W. Piaget & Barbara Binkley. 236p. 1985. 14.95 (*0-8290-0438-6*) Irvington.

O

Overcoming Your Barriers: A Guide to Personal Reprogramming. Gerald W. Piaget & Barbara M. Binkley. 14.95 (0-88282-005-2) New Horizon NJ.
Overcoming Your Fear of Public Speaking. Michael T. Motley. (C). 1994. pap. text 18.25 (0-07-043521-9) McGraw.
Overcoming Your Fear of the Dentist. Jane Stewart. 50p. (Orig.). 1994. pap. 8.95 (1-886174-23-7) Awakenings Pr.
Overcoming Your Fear of the Dentist: A Dental Office Program Guide to Controlling Dental Anxiety. 2nd ed. Leonard G. Horowitz. (Freedom from Ser.). 20p. 1987. 19.95 incl. audio (0-9609386-2-1) Tetrahedron.
Overcoming Your Strengths: 8 Reasons Why Successful People Fail. Lois Frankel. 1997. 25.00 (0-614-19856-9) Harmony Bks.
Overcrowded World? Population, Resources & the Environment. Ed. by Philip Sarre & John Blunden. (Shape of the World Ser.). 288p. (C). 1996. pap. text 24.95 (0-19-874189-8) OUP.
Overcrowded World? Population, Resources & the Environment. Ed. by Philip Sarre & John Blunden. (Shape of the World Ser.: Bk. 3). 288p. 1996. text 57.95 (0-19-874188-X) OUP.
Overcurrent & Overtemperature Protectors for Radio- & Television-Type Appliances, UL 1416. 6th ed. (C). 1999. pap. text 95.00 (1-55989-685-X) Underwrtrs Labs.
Overcurrents & Undercurrents - All about GFCLs: Electrical Safety Advances Through Electronics. Earl W. Roberts. (Illus.). ix, 145p. 1996. pap. 15.00 (0-9674323-0-8) Reptec.
Overdentures Made Easy: A Guide to Implant & Root Supported Prostheses. Harold W. Preiskel. 240p. 1996. text 98.00 (1-85097-039-4) Quint Pub Co.
Overdentures on Oral Implants. Ed. by E. Scherers. 173p. (Orig.). 1991. pap. 52.50 (90-6186-433-X, Pub. by Leuven Univ) Coronet Bks.
Overdrive: Bill Gates & the Race to Control Cyberspace. James Wallace. LC 97-4464. 320p. 1997. 24.95 (0-471-18041-6) Wiley.
Overdrive: Bill Gates & the Race to Control Cyberspace. James Wallace. 307p. 1998. pap. 14.95 (0-471-29106-4) Wiley.
Overdrive: Managing in Crisis Filled Times. Michael Silva & Terry McGann. 272p. 1995. 29.95 (0-471-51549-3) Wiley.
Overdue. Richie Tankersley Cusick. (J). 1995. 9.09 (0-606-07986-6, Pub. by Turtleback) Demco.
Overdue. Richie T. Cusizk. Ed. by Lisa Clancey. 256p. (YA). (gr. 7 up). 1995. mass mkt. 3.99 (0-671-88743-2, Archway) PB.
Overdue Notice: Poems from the Library. David Drake. LC 94-33632. 126p. 1995. pap. 21.95 (0-7864-0052-8) McFarland & Co.
Overeaters: Eating Styles & Personality. Jonathan K. Wise & Susan K. Wise. LC 79-719. 224p. 1979. 35.95 (0-87705-405-3, Kluwer Acad Hman Sci); pap. 19.95 (0-89885-233-1, Kluwer Acad Hman Sci) Kluwer Academic.
Overeaters Anonymous. LC 80-50589. 204p. 1980. pap. 3.50 (0-9609898-1-1) Overeaters Anym.
Overeating: A Dialogue: An Application of the Principles of "A Course in Miracles" 2nd ed. Kenneth Wapnick. LC 95-51650. 70p. 1999. pap. 5.00 (0-933291-11-6) Foun Miracles.
***Overeducated Worker? The Economics of Skill Utilization.** Ed. by Lex Borghans & Andries De Grip. LC 99-87189. 288p. 2000. 90.00 (1-84064-155-X) E Elgar.
Overeducation in the U. S. Labor Market. Russell W. Rumberger. LC 80-24648. 148p. 1981. 57.95 (0-275-90715-5, C0715, Praeger Pubs) Greenwood.
Overengineering in Building Services: An International Comparison of Design & Installation Methods. BSRIA Staff & C. J. Parsloe. 82p. 1995. pap. 120.00 (0-86022-423-6, Pub. by Build Servs Info Assn) St Mut.
Overexposed: U. S. Banks Confront the Third World Debt Crisis. Raul M. Madrid. 260p. 1990. pap. 35.00 (0-931035-50-3) IRRC Inc DC.
Overexposure: Health Hazards in Photography. 2nd ed. Susan D. Shaw & Monona Rossol. 320p. 1991. pap. 18.95 (0-9607118-6-4) Allworth Pr.
Overexpression & Knockout of Cytokines in Transgenic Mice. Ed. by Chaim O. Jacob. (Illus.). 191p. 1994. text 69.00 (0-12-378450-6) Acad Pr.
Overextended & Undernourished: A Self-Care Handbook for People in Helping Roles. Dennis Portnoy. LC 95-53695. 60p. (Orig.). 1996. pap. 7.00 (1-56246-115-X, 3279, HazeldenJohnson Inst) Hazelden.
***Overfight... The Tales of Telucan.** John Thomas. LC 99-62373. 344p. 2000. pap. 12.95 (1-56167-540-7) Am Literary Pr.
Overflight. Charles Neider. 235p. 1986. 15.95 (0-88282-026-5) New Horizon NJ.
Overflow. Hope Taylor-McGriff. LC 93-72710. 120p. (Orig.). 1993. pap. 6.95 (0-9638672-0-2) Bryant & Dillon.
Overflowing with Love. Carol Crook. 29p. (YA). (gr. 7 up). 1989. pap. 2.50 (0-939399-06-7) Bks of Truth.
Overflowing with the Holy Spirit. Pat Harrison. LC 98-206498. 1998. pap. text 10.99 (1-57794-128-4) Harrison Hse.
Overflowings: Love & Friendship. rev. ed. Lenore Turkeltaub. LC 87-83184. (Illus.). 72p. 1988. pap. 7.95 (0-9614768-5-0) Lenjalin Pubns.
Overglazes on Glass. Hugh Giese & Adrienne Cocalas. LC 86-62428. 52p. (Orig.). 1986. pap. text 3.98 (0-916809-06-4) Scott Pubns MI.
Overgroups of Sylow Subgroups in Sporadic Groups. M. Aschbacher. LC 86-1040. (Memoirs of the AMS Ser.: Vol. 60/343). 235p. 1986. pap. 29.00 (0-8218-2344-2, MEMO/60/343) Am Math.
Overgrown Path. Robert Holman. (Royal Court Writers Ser.). 64p. (C). 1988. pap. 5.95 (0-413-59760-1, A0203) Heinemann.
Overgrown with Love. Scott Ely. LC 93-16392. 168p. 1993. pap. 16.00 (1-55728-298-6) U of Ark Pr.
Overhaul No. 5. J. Steven Kidd & John Czajkowski. 1994. teacher ed. write for info. (0-8151-5174-8) Mosby Inc.
Overhead. Jack M. Bickham. (Brad Smith Ser.: No. 3). 352p. 1993. mass mkt. 4.50 (0-8125-1194-8) Tor Bks.
Overhead: What It Is & How It Works. Jack F. Fultz. (Illus.). 160p. 1984. reprint ed. lib. bdg. 40.50 (0-8191-4407-X) U Pr of Amer.
Overhead & Underfoot. rev. ed. Arthur J. Wiebe et al. (J). (gr. 3-5). 1994. 16.95 (1-881431-52-5, 1206) AIMS Educ Fnd.
Overhead Color Counters. 1995. write for info. (0-201-48078-6) Addison-Wesley.
Overhead Cost. Innes. 1998. pap. 19.95 (1-86152-445-5) Thomson Learn.
Overhead Cost. John Innes & Falconer Mitchell. (Advanced Management Accounting & Finance Ser.). (Illus.). 160p. 1993. pap. text 19.95 (0-12-372140-7) Acad Pr.
Overhead Graphics for Psychology II. Darrell Franken. 150p. 1994. (0-934957-68-1) Wellness Pubns.
Overhead in London Snack Bars. Susan Catherine. (Overheard Ser.: No. 6). (Illus.). 64p. (Orig.). 1987. pap. 2.50 (0-944617-06-9) Cherry Stone Pr.
Overhead Projection. Jerry D. Sparks. Ed. by James E. Duane. LC 80-21334. (Instructional Media Library: Vol. 10). (Illus.). 112p. 1981. 27.95 (0-87778-170-2) Educ Tech Pubns.
***Overhead Projection for I Want to Tell You about the Benefits of Living by Optimum Christian Lifestyles.** Darrell Franken. 322p. 1999. (0-934957-73-8) Wellness Pubns.
Overhead Projector Games. Ed Dunlop. Ed. by Karen Brewer. (Illus.). 48p. (J). (gr. 1-6). 1996. teacher ed. 10.99 (0-7847-0506-2, 03509) Standard Pub.
Overhead Transparencies:Economics Of Money, Banking, & Financial Markets. 5th ed. Mishkin. 1p. 1997. pap. text 266.67 (0-321-01755-2) Addison-Wesley.
Overhead Trolley Chain Conveyors No. 601: CEMA 601-1995. 32p. 1995. pap. 20.00 (1-891171-13-5) Conveyor Equip Mfrs.
Overheard. Stacy Aumonier. LC 72-3289. (Short Story Index Reprint Ser.). 1977. reprint ed. 20.95 (0-8369-4142-X) Ayer.
Overheard at America's Lunch Counters, No. 7. Susan Catherine. (Overheard Ser.). (Illus.). 64p. (Orig.). 1987. pap. 2.50 (0-944617-07-7) Cherry Stone Pr.
Overheard at the Country Cafe. Ed. by Mike Beno. LC 98-67163. 178p. 1998. 15.99 (0-89821-238-3) Reiman Pubns.
Overheard at the Square Dance. Ed. by Gordon Goss & Valerie Thornton. 1989. pap. 5.96 (0-8065-1120-6, Citadel Pr) Carol Pub Group.
Overheard in Seattle Donut Shops. Susan Catherine. (Overheard Ser.: No. 8). (Illus.). 64p. (Orig.). 1988. pap. 2.98 (0-944617-08-5) Cherry Stone Pr.
***Overhearing Film Dialogue.** Sarah Kozloff. LC 99-46452. 332p. 2000. pap. 18.95 (0-520-22138-9) U CA Pr.
Overheating Protection for Motors, UL 2111. (C). 1997. 156.00 (0-7629-0166-7) Underwrtrs Labs.
Overjoyed: 60 Devotions. Marilyn Meberg et al. LC 98-11682. 208p. 1999. 14.99 (0-310-22653-8) Zondervan.
Overkill. Alane Ferguson. 176p. (J). (gr. 5 up). 1994. mass mkt. 3.99 (0-380-72167-8, Avon Bks) Morrow Avon.
Overkill. Alane Ferguson. LC 92-11426. 192p. (YA). (gr. 7 up). 1992. lib. bdg. 14.95 (0-02-734523-8, Bradbury S&S) S&S Childrens.
Overkill. Robert Romano. 246p. 1997. pap. 9.95 (1-57502-627-9, P01785) Morris Pubng.
Overkill: Weapons of the Nuclear Age. John Cox. LC 77-27663. (Illus.). (YA). (gr. 7 up). 1978. lib. bdg. 12.89 (0-690-03857-7) HarpC Child Bks.
Overkill - The Years of Decay. Ed. by Mark Phillips. (Play-It-Like-It-Is Guitar Ser.). pap. 19.95 (0-89524-553-1); pap. 14.95 (0-89524-597-3) Cherry Lane.
Overkill of Cost Measurement. Ansari. 56p. 1999. pap. 5.00 (0-256-26394-9) McGraw.
Overlake School Cookbook. 3rd ed. Overlake School Staff. Ed. by Bonnie S. Mickelson. LC 89-63118. (Illus.). 190p. 1984. 11.95 (0-9612946-0-4) Overlake Schl.
Overlake School Cookbook: The Little Blue Book of Great Recipes. rev. ed. Ed. by Bonnie S. Mickelson. (Illus.). 182p. 1993. reprint ed. 13.95 (0-9622412-6-1) Pickle Point.
Overland. Keats Jaynes. LC 98-66903. 100p. 1999. pap. 12.95 (0-9649531-3-7) Newcomb Pub.
Overland see Collected Works of John W. De Forest
Overland. John W. De Forest. (Collected Works of John W. De Forest). 1988. reprint ed. lib. bdg. 59.00 (0-7812-1156-5) Rprt Serv.
Overland: The California Emigrant Trail of 1841-1870. Greg MacGregor. LC 95-32470. (Illus.). 168p. (C). 1996. 75.00 (0-8263-1703-0); pap. 24.95 (0-8263-1704-9) U of NM Pr.
Overland Escape. Lee Roddy. LC 88-63471. (American Adventure Ser.: No. 1). 176p. (J). (gr. 3-8). 1989. pap. 5.99 (1-55661-026-2) Bethany Hse.
Overland from Canada to British Columbia: By Mr. Thomas McMicking of Queenston, Canada West. Ed. by Joanne Leduc. (Pioneers of British Columbia Ser.). (Illus.). 169p. 1981. pap. 15.95 (0-7748-0393-2) U of Wash Pr.
Overland in 1846: Diaries & Letters of the California-Oregon Trail, 2 vols., 1. Ed. by Dale L. Morgan. LC 93-8247. (Illus.). 475p. 1993. text 50.00 (0-8032-3176-8) U of Nebr Pr.
Overland in 1846: Diaries & Letters of the California-Oregon Trail, 2 vols., 2. Ed. by Dale L. Morgan. LC 93-8247. (Illus.). vii, 368p. 1993. text 50.00 (0-8032-3177-6) U of Nebr Pr.
Overland in 1846: Diaries & Letters of the California-Oregon Trail, 2 vols., Vol. 1. Ed. by Dale L. Morgan. LC 93-8247. (Illus.). 475p. 1993. pap. 19.95 (0-8032-8200-1, Bison Books) U of Nebr Pr.
Overland in 1846: Diaries & Letters of the California-Oregon Trail, 2 vols., Vol. 2. Ed. by Dale L. Morgan. LC 93-8247. (Illus.). vii, 368p. 1993. pap. 14.95 (0-8032-8201-X, Bison Books) U of Nebr Pr.
Overland Journal of Amos Piatt Josselyn. Ed. by William T. Barrett, II. 129p. 1978. 12.50 (0-685-02326-5) Holmes.
Overland Journey: From New York to San Francisco in the Summer of 1859. Horace Greeley. (American Biography Ser.). 326p. 1991. reprint ed. lib. bdg. 79.00 (0-7812-8154-7) Rprt Serv.
Overland Journey from New York to San Francisco in the Summer of 1859. Horace Greeley. LC 99-11171. (Illus.). xviii, 386p. 1999. pap. 15.00 (0-8032-7079-8, Bison Books) U of Nebr Pr.
Overland Journey from New York to San Francisco in the Summer of 1859. Horace Greeley. (BCL1 - United States Local History Ser.). 386p. 1991. reprint ed. text 89.00 (0-7812-6325-5) Rprt Serv.
Overland Journey to California. James Bennett. 90p. 1986. 14.95 (0-87770-391-4) Ye Galleon.
Overland Journey to California, from the Pages of a Pioneer's Diary. Hermann B. Scharmann. LC 73-99670. (Select Bibliographies Reprint Ser.). 1977. 19.95 (0-8369-5099-2) Ayer.
***Overland Kid: A Western Trio.** Max Brand. LC 99-55131. 2000. 30.00 (0-7862-1846-0) Mac Lib Ref.
Overland Kid: A Western Trio. large type ed. 2001. 30.00 (0-7862-1853-3) Mac Lib Ref.
Overland Mail, 1849-1869. LeRoy R. Hafen. LC 73-90099. reprint ed. 49.50 (0-404-03022-X) AMS Pr.
Overland Migrations. David Lavender. LC 79-607769. (Official National Park Handbook Ser.: No. 105). 1980. pap. 7.50 (0-912627-02-6) Natl Park Serv.
Overland Migrations: Settlers to Oregon, California & Utah. 1997. lib. bdg. 250.99 (0-8490-6146-6) Gordon Pr.
Overland Migrations: Settlers to Oregon, California & Utah. David Lavender. 111p. 1980. pap. 221.00 (0-16-003439-6); per. 7.50 (0-16-003502-3) USGPO.
Overland Models: The First Ten Years. Brian T. Marsh. (Illus.). 1987. spiral bd. 39.00 (0-9617955-1-4, OMI 2013) Overland Models.
Overland Models: The First Ten Years. limited ed. Brian T. Marsh. (Illus.). 1987. 57.00 (0-9617955-0-6, OMI 2014) Overland Models.
Overland Passages: A Guide to Overland Documents in the Oregon Historical Society. Ed. by Kris White & Mary-Catherine Cuthill. 125p. 1993. pap. 15.00 (0-87595-242-9) Oregon Hist.
Overland Route: Union Pacific. Krause & Grenard. (Hobby Bks.: No. C60). 1988. pap. 15.95 (0-911868-60-7) Carstens Pubns.
Overland Stage to California: Personal Reminiscences & Authentic History of the Great Overland Stage Line & Pony Express. Frank A. Root & William E. Connelly. (Illus.). xvii, 630p. 1989. reprint ed. lib. bdg. 64.00 (0-8328-1428-8) Higginson Bk Co.
Overland Through Asia: Pictures of Siberian, Chinese & Tartar Life, Travels & Adventures in Kamchatka, Siberia, China, Mongolia, Chinese Tartary & European Russia. Thomas W. Knox. LC 78-115553. (Russia Observed Ser., No. 1). 1970. reprint ed. 35.95 (0-405-03039-8) Ayer.
***Overland Through Southern Africa.** Willie Oliver. 1998. pap. text 29.95 (1-86872-105-1) Struik Pubs.
Overland to California, 1849. William Johnston. (American Autobiography Ser.). 272p. 1995. reprint ed. lib. bdg. 79.00 (0-7812-8568-2) Rprt Serv.
Overland to California in 1859: A Guide for Wagon Train Travelers. Louis M. Bloch, Jr. LC 83-71506. (Illus.). 64p. (J). (gr. 3-6). 1990. pap. 12.95 (0-914276-04-2) Bloch & Co OH.
Overland to India, 2 vols., Set. Sven A. Hedin. LC 68-55193. 1969. lib. bdg. 85.00 (0-8371-3894-9, HEOI, Greenwood Pr) Greenwood.
Overland to India, 2 vols., Vol. 1. Sven A. Hedin. LC 68-55193. 1969. lib. bdg. 49.50 (0-8371-0469-6, HEOA, Greenwood Pr) Greenwood.
Overland to India, 2 vols., Vol. 2. Sven A. Hedin. LC 68-55193. 1969. lib. bdg. 49.50 (0-8371-0814-4, HEOB, Greenwood Pr) Greenwood.
Overland to Oregon. Edward H. Lenox. LC 93-13113. Orig. Title: Overland to Oregon in the Tracks of Lewis & Clarke. 1993. 15.95 (0-87770-520-8) Ye Galleon.
Overland to Oregon in the Tracks of Lewis & Clarke see Overland to Oregon
Overland to Starvation Cove: With the Inuit in Search of Franklin, 1878-1880. Heinrich Klutschak. Ed. & Tr. by William Barr. (Illus.). 261p. 1987. 30.00 (0-8020-5762-4) U of Toronto Pr.
Overland to Starvation Cove: With the Inuit in Search of Franklin, 1878-1880. 11th ed. Heinrich Klutschak. (Illus.). 281p. 1993. pap. 24.95 (0-8020-7397-2) U of Toronto Pr.
Overland Trail. James Monaghan. LC 73-107726. (Essay Index Reprint Ser.). 1977. 30.95 (0-8369-1999-8) Ayer.
Overland Trail. large type ed. Jenny Felix. 268p. 1995. pap. 18.99 (1-85389-565-2, Dales) Ulverscroft.
Overland Trip to the Grand Canyon: Northern Arizona As Powell Saw It in 1870. John Wesley Powell. LC 77-29657. (Wild & Woolly West Ser.: No. 28). (Illus.). 40p. 1974. pap. 4.00 (0-910584-84-2) Filter.
Overland with Kit Carson: A Narrative of the Old Spanish Trail in '48. George D. Brewerton. LC 93-10688. (Illus.). xxiii, 301p. (C). 1993. pap. 12.95 (0-8032-6113-6, Bison Books) U of Nebr Pr.
Overland with Mark Twain: James B. Pond's Photographs & Journal of the North American Lecture Tour of 1895. Ed. by Alan Gribben. 112p. 1992. 29.00 (1-880817-00-4) EC Ctr Mark T Stu.
Overlander Songbook. Ron Edwards. 1990. pap. 16.95 (0-7022-2287-9, Pub. by Univ Queensland Pr) Intl Spec Bk.
Overlap Determinant Method in the Theory of Pericyclic Reactions. R. Ponec. (Lecture Notes in Chemistry Ser.: Vol. 65). (Illus.). 126p. 1995. 41.95 (3-540-59189-3) Spr-Verlag.
Overlap Determinant Method in the Theory of Pericyclic Reactivity. R. Ponec. LC 95-12985. (Lecture Notes in Chemistry Ser.: Vol. 65). 1995. write for info. (0-387-59189-3) Spr-Verlag.
Overlapping of Attainments in Certain Sixth, Seventh & Eighth Grades. Paul J. Kruse. LC 78-176941. (Columbia University. Teachers College. Contributions to Education Ser.: No. 92). reprint ed. 37.50 (0-404-55092-4) AMS Pr.
Overlapping Structures As a Model of Money: An Analytical Review. Bruno Schonfelder. LC 92-12919. (Microeconomic Studies). (Illus.). x, 242p. 1992. 107.95 (0-387-55274-X) Spr-Verlag.
Overlay: Contemporary Art & the Art of Prehistory. Lucy Lippard. 296p. 1995. pap. 20.00 (1-56584-238-3, Pub. by New Press NY) Norton.
Overlay of Random & Order: Selected Poems by Jan Dunbar. Jan Dunbar. LC 97-67160. 128p. 1997. pap. 11.95 (1-889087-02-5) P S A Pr.
Overlay, Overlay: How to Bet Horses Like a Pro. Bill Heller. 228p. (Orig.). 1990. pap. 9.95 (0-933893-86-8) Bonus Books.
Overline: SEW NEWS Presents Sew Much Better: The Secrets to Sewing Better, Faster & Easier. Ed. by Peggy Bendel. (Illus.). 208p. (C). 1989. 19.95 (0-9621148-1-2) PRMDIA Spcl Intrst.
Overload. Linda Howard. (Summer Sizzlers Ser.). 1993. mass mkt. 4.99 (0-373-48255-8, 5-48255-9) Silhouette.
Overload: Attention Deficit Disorder & the Addictive Brain. Dave Miller & Kenneth Blum. 224p. 1995. pap. 10.95 (0-8362-0460-3) Andrews & McMeel.
Overload & Boredom: Essays on the Quality of Life in the Information Society, 57. Orrin E. Klapp. LC 85-17532. (Contributions in Sociology Ser.: No. 57). (Illus.). 174p. 1986. 49.95 (0-313-25001-4, KLO, Greenwood Pr) Greenwood.
***Overload, Fatigue, Performance Incompetence & Regeneration.** Manfred Lehmann et al. LC 99-15839. (Illus.). 1999. write for info. (0-306-46106-4, Kluwer Plenum) Kluwer Academic.
***Overload Syndrome: Learning to Live Within Your Limits.** 1999. pap. 12.00 (1-57683-131-0) NavPress.
Overload Syndrome: Learning to Live Within Your Limits. Richard A. Swenson. LC 98-17030. 1998. 18.00 (1-57683-067-5) NavPress.
Overloaded Ark. Gerald Durrell. (Illus.). 238p. 1987. pap. 14.95 (0-571-05371-8) Faber & Faber.
Overlook Film Encyclopedia: Horror. Ed. by Phil Hardy. 496p. 1995. pap. 40.00 (0-87951-624-0, Pub. by Overlook Pr) Penguin Putnam.
Overlook Film Encyclopedia: Horror. Tom Milne & Paul Willemen. Ed. by Phil Hardy. LC 93-23387. (Illus.). 496p. 1994. 65.00 (0-87951-518-X, Pub. by Overlook Pr) Penguin Putnam.
Overlook Film Encyclopedia: Science Fiction. Ed. by Phil Hardy. LC 93-24440. (Illus.). 478p. 1994. 65.00 (0-87951-516-3, Pub. by Overlook Pr) Penguin Putnam.
Overlook Film Encyclopedia: Science Fiction. Ed. by Phil Hardy. 478p. 1995. pap. 40.00 (0-87951-626-7, Pub. by Overlook Pr) Penguin Putnam.
Overlook Film Encyclopedia: The Gangster Film. Ed. by Phil Hardy. LC 98-16620. (Illus.). 416p. 1998. 65.00 (0-87951-881-2, Pub. by Overlook Pr) Penguin Putnam.
***Overlook Film Encyclopedia: The Gangster Film.** Ed. by Phil Hardy. (Illus.). 416p. 2000. pap. 45.00 (0-87951-899-5, Pub. by Overlook Pr) Penguin Putnam.
Overlook Film Encyclopedia: The Western. Ed. by Phil Hardy. LC 93-24439. (Overlook Film Encyclopedia Ser.). (Illus.). 416p. 1994. 65.00 (0-87951-517-1, Pub. by Overlook Pr) Penguin Putnam.
Overlook Film Encyclopedia: The Western. Ed. by Phil Hardy. 416p. 1995. pap. 40.00 (0-87951-625-9, Pub. by Overlook Pr) Penguin Putnam.
Overlook Guide to Growing Rare & Exotic Plants. Raymond Foster. LC 83-22057. (Overlook Gardening Ser.). Orig. Title: The Gardener's Guide to Rare, Exotic & Difficult Plants. (Illus.). 216p. 1985. 18.95 (0-87951-968-1, Pub. by Overlook Pr) Penguin Putnam.
Overlook Guide to Winter Gardens. Sonia Kinahan. LC 85-10680. (Overlook Gardening Ser.). (Illus.). 160p. 1985. 24.95 (0-87951-235-0, Pub. by Overlook Pr) Penguin Putnam.
Overlook Illustrated Dictionary of Nautical Terms. Graham Blackburn. LC 80-39640. (Illus.). 368p. 1981. 35.00 (0-87951-124-9, Pub. by Overlook Pr) Penguin Putnam.
Overlook Illustrated Dictionary of Nautical Terms. Graham Blackburn. LC 80-39640. (Illus.). 368p. 1984. pap. 15.95 (0-87951-950-9, Pub. by Overlook Pr) Penguin Putnam.
Overlook Martial Arts Dictionary. Emil Farkas & John Corcoran. LC 81-47415. (Illus.). 320p. 1985. reprint ed. pap. 13.95 (0-87951-996-7, Pub. by Overlook Pr) Penguin Putnam.
Overlook Martial Arts Handbook. David Mitchell. LC 87-22087. (Illus.). 192p. 1988. 17.95 (0-87951-285-7, Pub. by Overlook Pr) Penguin Books.

O

An Asterisk (*) at the beginning of an entry indicates that the title is appearing for the first time.

Overlook Martial Arts Handbook. David Mitchell. (Illus.). 192p. 1997. pap. 13.95 (*0-87951-759-X*, Pub. by Overlook Pr) Penguin Putnam.

Overlook Martial Arts Reader. Ed. by Randy F. Nelson. 356p. 1989. 19.95 (*0-87951-347-0*, Pub. by Overlook Pr) Penguin Putnam.

Overlook Martial Arts Reader: Classic Writings on Philosophy & Technique. Ed. by Randy F. Nelson. 356p. 1992. reprint ed. pap. 15.95 (*0-87951-459-0*, Pub. by Overlook Pr) Penguin Putnam.

Overlook Treasury of Federal Antiques. George Michael. 1988. pap. 19.95 (*0-87951-268-7*, Pub. by Overlook Pr) Penguin Putnam.

Overlooked Christianity. Gene Edwards. LC 97-190975. 1997. 14.95 (*0-940232-58-8*) Seedsowers.

Overlooked in America: The Success & Failure of Federal Land Management. Robert G. Ketchum. (Illus.). 120p. 1991. 53.00 (*0-89381-466-0*) Aperture.

Overlooked Law of Nature: A New Concept in Kinetics Analysis. Ralph W. Lai. (Illus.). 210p. (C). 1991. 45.00 (*0-9628526-1-9*) Toshi Co.

Overlooking Nazareth: The Ethnography of Exclusion in a Mixed Town in Galilee, Vol. 105. Dan Rabinowitz. LC 96-11922. (Cambridge Studies in Social & Cultural Anthropology: No. 105). (Illus.). 236p. 1997. text 59.95 (*0-521-56361-5*); pap. text 20.95 (*0-521-56495-6*) Cambridge U Pr.

Overlooking Stoneybrook. Carol M. McLernon. 80p. (J). (gr. 6-9). 1998. pap. 8.00 (*1-57502-864-6*, PO2356) Morris Pubng.

Overlord. Jerry Ahern. (Survivalist Ser.: No. 15). 224p. 1987. mass mkt. 2.50 (*0-8217-2070-8*, Zebra Kensgtn) Kensgtn Pub Corp.

Overlord. Thomas Bianchini. 92p. (Orig.). 1983. pap. 5.00 (*0-9612286-0-1*) Whitewater.

Overlord: D-Day & the Battle for Normandy. Max Hastings. 368p. 1985. pap. 13.00 (*0-671-55435-2*) S&S Trade.

Overlord: Pete Quesada & the Triumph of Tactical Air Power in World War II. Thomas Hughes. 1995. 27.50 (*0-02-915351-4*) Free Pr.

Overlord: The Triumph of Light, 1944-1945, Vol. 3, Bks. 7-9. Nicholas Hagger. Vol. 3. 224p. 1997. pap. 24.95 (*1-86204-016-8*, Pub. by Element MA) Penguin Putnam.

Overlord: The Triumph of Light, 1944-1945, Vol. 4, Bks.10-12. Nicholas Hagger. Vol. 4. 224p. 1997. pap. 24.95 (*1-86204-017-6*, Pub. by Element MA) Penguin Putnam.

Overlord: The Triumph of Light, 1944-1945, Vol. 11, Bks. 3-6. Nicholas Hagger. Vol. 3. 256p. 1996. pap. 39.95 (*1-85230-787-0*, Pub. by Element MA) Penguin Putnam.

Overlord Vol. 1, Bks. 1-2: An Epic Poem. Nicholas Hagger. 1995. pap. 19.95 (*1-85230-649-1*, Pub. by Element MA) Penguin Putnam.

Overlords. David Davidson. LC 98-92924. (Illus.). 256p. 1998. pap. 14.95 (*0-9664135-0-4*) Daves Tree.

Overlords & Olympians. William G. Allen. 182p. 1996. reprint ed. spiral bd. 21.50 (*0-7873-0029-2*) Hlth Research.

Overlord's Eagles: Operations of the United States Army Air Forces in the Invasion of Normandy in World War II. John J. Sullivan. LC 97-1650. (Illus.). 223p. 1997. boxed set 45.00 (*0-7864-0212-1*) McFarland & Co.

Overlords of Atlantis & the Great Pyramid. Brad Steiger. 204p. 1989. 15.00 (*0-938294-63-6*) Inner Light.

Overloving Parent: Making Love Work for You & Your Child. Beverly B. Runyon. 160p. 1992. pap. 10.95 (*0-87833-803-9*) Taylor Pub.

Overly on Electronic Evidence in California Michael R. Overly. LC 98-55952. (Expert Ser.). 1999. write for info. (*0-314-23371-7*) West Pub.

***Overman.** Upton Sinclair. (Collected Works of Upton Sinclair). 90p. 1999. reprint ed. lib. bdg. 88.00 (*1-58201-829-4*) Classic Bks.

Overmind. Bill Coffin. (Illus.). (Orig.). (YA). (gr. 10 up). 1995. pap. 9.99 (*0-88092-141-2*); lib. bdg. 23.00 (*0-88092-142-0*) Royal Fireworks.

***Overmountain Men.** Cameron Judd. (Illus.). 448p. 2000. pap. 16.95 (*1-58182-097-6*, Cumberland Hearthside) Cumberland Hse.

Overmountain Men. Pat Alderman. (Illus.). 308p. 1970. reprint ed. 22.95 (*0-932807-15-1*); reprint ed. pap. 17.95 (*0-932807-16-X*) Overmountain Pr.

Overnight. R. L. Stine, pseud. (Fear Street Ser.: No. 16). (YA). (gr. 7 up). 1991. mass mkt. 3.99 (*0-671-74650-2*, Archway) PB.

Overnight. R. L. Stine, pseud. (Fear Street Ser.: No. 16). (YA). (gr. 7 up). 1989. 9.09 (*0-606-02169-8*, Pub. by Turtleback) Demco.

Overnight Alibi. Marilyn Pappano. 1998. per. 4.25 (*0-373-07848-X*, 1-07848-4) Silhouette.

Overnight Consultant. Marsha D. Lewin. LC 95-17526. 234p. 1995. 55.00 (*0-471-11944-X*); pap. 19.95 (*0-471-11945-8*) Wiley.

Overnight Father. Debbi Rawlins. (American Romance Ser.). 1999. per. 3.99 (*0-373-16790-3*, 1-16790-7) Harlequin Bks.

Overnight Float: A Mystery. Claire Munnings et al. 288p. 2000. 23.95 (*0-393-03849-1*) Norton.

Overnight Groom: Oops! Still Married! Elizabeth Sinclair. 1999. per. 3.99 (*0-373-16787-3*, 1-16787-3) Harlequin Bks.

Overnight Heiress. Modean Moon. 1998. per. 3.75 (*0-373-76150-3*, 1-76150-1) Silhouette.

Overnight in the Guest House of the Mystic: Poems. Dick Allen. LC 83-25620. 59p. 1984. reprint ed. pap. 30.00 (*0-608-00860-5*, 206165100010) Bks Demand.

Overnight or Short Stay at Religious Houses Around the World. rev. ed. Ed. by James J. Hughes. (Illus.). 154p. 1996. per. 19.95 (*0-9632427-2-5*) Hugen Pr.

Overnight Resume. 2nd rev. ed. Donald Asher. LC 98-54145. 154p. 1999. pap. 14.95 (*1-58008-041-3*) Ten Speed Pr.

Overnight Sensation: The Story of the Raspberries. 2nd ed. Ken Sharp. LC 93-86391. (Illus.). 350p. 1998. reprint ed. pap. 30.00 (*0-9662081-1-0*) Poptastic.

Overnight Wife. Mollie Molay. 1997. per. 3.75 (*0-373-16703-2*, 1-16703-0) Harlequin Bks.

Overpacking Disease, Telling Your Child about Nordstrom & Other Adulthood Traumas. Doug Hurd. 303p. (Orig.). 1997. pap. 13.50 (*0-9658630-2-6*) QBS Publ.

Overpaid, Oversexed, & over Here: The American GI in World War II Britain. Juliet Gardiner. (Illus.). 224p. 1992. 19.95 (*1-55859-408-6*) Abbeville Pr.

Overpayments of Veterans Administration Benefits. Keith D. Snyder. 236p. (Orig.). 1985. 20.00 (*0-941077-11-X*, 39,980) NCLS Inc.

Overpopulation. Rebecca Stefoff. (Earth at Risk Ser.). (Illus.). 128p. (YA). (gr. 5 up). 1992. lib. bdg. 19.95 (*0-7910-1581-5*) Chelsea Hse.

Overpopulation. limited ed. Thomas R. Crowe. (Illus.). (Orig.). 1995. pap. 1.00 (*0-614-10111-5*, 13) New Native Pr.

Overpopulation: Crisis or Challenge? Nathan Aaseng. LC 90-13121. (Science, Technology & Society Ser.). (Illus.). 160p. (YA). (gr. 9-12). 1991. lib. bdg. 24.00 (*0-531-11006-0*) Watts.

Overpopulation Myth. Thomas R. Saving. Ed. by Svetozar Pejovich & Henry Dethloff. (Series on Public Issues: No. 4). (Illus.). 16p. (Orig.). 1983. pap. 2.00 (*0-86599-013-1*) PERC.

Overpopulation of Cats & Dogs: Causes, Effects, & Prevention. New York State Humane Association Staff. Ed. by Marjorie Anchel. LC 90-82350. xx, 260p. 1990. 25.00 (*0-8232-1296-3*) Fordham.

Overproduction & Crises. J. Karl Rodbertus. Tr. by Julia Franklin. LC 69-18027. (Reprints of Economic Classics Ser.). 140p. 1969. reprint ed. 29.50 (*0-678-00497-8*) Kelley.

Overproduction Trap in United States Agriculture: A Study of Resource Allocation from World War I to the Late 1960s. Ed. by Glenn L. Johnson & Leroy Quance. LC 72-186509. 232p. reprint ed. pap. 72.00 (*0-608-12537-7*, 202380200034) Bks Demand.

Overprotection: The Error of Dedicated Parents see Sobreproteccion: La Error de los Padres

Overreached on All Sides: The Freedmen's Bureau Administrators in Texas, 1865-1868. William L. Richter. LC 91-15364. 448p. 1991. 49.50 (*0-89096-473-4*) Tex A&M Univ Pr.

Overreaching in Paradise: United States Policy in Palau since 1945. Sue R. Roff. LC 90-3608. (Illus.). xii, 244p. (Orig.). (C). 1991. pap. 27.50 (*0-938737-22-8*) Denali Press.

Overregularization in Language Acquisition. Gary F. Marcus et al. 188p. 1992. pap. text 15.00 (*0-226-50456-5*) U Ch Pr.

Overriding a CICA Stay. Timothy J. Saviano. (Monograph 2d Ser.: Vol. 3). 42p. (Orig.). 1995. pap., per. 25.00 (*0-935165-38-X*) GWU Gov Contracts.

Overruled. Isabella Alden. (Grace Livingston Hill Ser.: Vol. 19). 1997. pap. 5.99 (*0-8423-3195-6*) Tyndale Hse.

Overruled. George Bernard Shaw. 50p. (Orig.). 1992. pap. 6.00 (*0-88734-248-5*) Players Pr.

Overruled by Love (Delta Justice) M. J. Rodgers. (Delta Justice Ser.). 1998. per. 4.50 (*0-373-82567-6*, 1-82567-8) Harlequin Bks.

Oversampling Delta-Sigma Data Converters: Theory, Design, & Simulation. Ed. by James C. Candy & Gabor C. Temes. LC 91-19110. (Illus.). 512p. 1991. text 79.95 (*0-87942-285-8*, PC0274-1) Inst Electrical.

Overseas Acquisitions & Mergers: Combining for Profits Abroad. Duane Hall. LC 86-8204. 194p. 1986. 49.95 (*0-275-92111-5*, C2111, Praeger Pubs) Greenwood.

Overseas Aid Motivations: The Economics of Australia's Bilateral Aid. Rukmani Gounder. LC 95-79848. 272p. 1995. 67.95 (*1-85972-075-7*, Pub. by Avebry) Ashgate Pub Co.

Overseas Americans. Harlan Cleveland et al. Ed. by Stuart Bruchey. LC 80-558. (Multinational Corporations Ser.). 1981. reprint ed. lib. bdg. 36.95 (*0-405-13354-5*) Ayer.

Overseas Assignment: A Professional's Guide for Working in Developing Countries. C. N. Weller, Jr. LC 95-10763. 1995. 35.00 (*0-87814-436-6*) PennWell Bks.

Overseas Business Activities: The International Conference on Business History, 9. Ed. by Akio Okochi & Tadakatsu Inoue. 296p. 1984. 42.50 (*0-86008-325-X*, Pub. by U of Tokyo) Col U Pr.

Overseas Chinese: Ethnicity in National Context. L. K. Hsu. Ed. by Francis L. Hsu & Hendrick Serrie. LC 98-18865. 248p. (C). 1998. 42.50 (*0-7618-1163-X*) U Pr of Amer.

Overseas Chinese & the 1911 Revolution. Yen Ching Hwang. (East Asian Historical Monographs). 1977. 27.50 (*0-19-580311-6*) OUP.

Overseas Chinese Business Networks in Asia. Contrib. by East Asia Analytical Unit Staff. 362p. 1995. 39.95 (*0-642-22960-0*, Pub. by AGPS Pr) Intl Spec Bk.

***Overseas Chinese Entrepreneurship & Capitalist Development in Southeast Asia.** Annabelle Gambe. LC 00-27820. 2000. write for info. (*0-312-23496-1*) St Martin.

Overseas Clinical Elective: A Survival Guide for Healthcare Workers. Renee Adomat. LC 96-25101. 176p. (Orig.). 1996. pap. text 29.95 (*0-632-04102-1*) Blackwell Sci.

Overseas Contracts - Conception to Completion. (Conference Proceedings Ser.). 104p. 1980. 30.00 (*0-7277-0099-5*, Pub. by T Telford) RCH.

Overseas Direct Investment - MA 4, 1996. Orig. Title: Overseas Transactions. 1998. 110.00 (*0-11-536358-0*, HM63580, Pub. by Statnry Office) Bernan Associates.

***Overseas Employment Opportunities for Educators: Department of Defense Dependents Schools.** Ed. by Barry Leonard. (Illus.). 44p. 1999. pap. text 20.00 (*0-7881-8075-4*) DIANE Pub.

Overseas Information Service of the United States Government. Charles A. Thomson. LC 72-4681. (International Propaganda & Communications Ser.). 397p. 1972. reprint ed. 24.95 (*0-405-04765-7*) Ayer.

Overseas Investments, Capital Gains & the Balance of Payments. Cliff Pratten. (Research Monographs: No. 48). 121p. (Orig.). (C). 1992. pap. 22.50 (*0-255-36303-6*, Pub. by Inst Economic Affairs) Coronet Bks.

Overseas Manufacturing Investment & the Balance of Payments. G. Hufbauer & F. W. Adler. Ed. by Stuart Bruchey & Eleanor Bruchey. LC 76-5047. (American Business Abroad Ser.). 1976. reprint ed. 19.95 (*0-405-09311-X*) Ayer.

Overseas Migration from East-Central & Southeastern Europe, 1880-1940. Julianna Puskas & Akademiai Kiado Staff. (Studia Historica Academiae Scientiarum Hungaricae Ser.: No. 191). 246p. (C). 1990. 78.00 (*963-05-4992-1*, Pub. by Akade Kiado) St Mut.

***Overseas Mission on Biomaterials to Japan '98.** W. Bonfield. 88p. 1998. pap. 70.00 (*1-86125-067-3*) Institute of Management Consultants.

Overseas Presence: Issues Involved in Reducing the Impact of the U. S. Military Presence on Okinawa. Reginald L. Fun. Ed. by Carol R. Schuster. (Illus.). 62p. 1999. text 20.00 (*0-7881-7943-8*) DIANE Pub.

Overseas Presence: More Data & Analysis Needed to Determine Whether Cost-Effective Alternatives Exist. Sharon L. Pickup. (Illus.). 56p. (C). 1997. pap. text 25.00 (*0-7881-4738-2*) DIANE Pub.

Overseas Presence: Staffing at U. S. Diplomatic Posts. (Illus.). 70p. (Orig.). (C). 1995. pap. text 25.00 (*0-7881-1672-X*) DIANE Pub.

Overseas Private Investment Corporation: A Critical Analysis. U. S. Congress, House of Representatives Staff. Ed. by Stuart Bruchey & Eleanor Bruchey. LC 76-5055. (American Business Abroad Ser.). (Illus.). 1976. reprint ed. 19.95 (*0-405-09313-6*) Ayer.

Overseas Private Investment Corporation: A Study in Political Risk. Alan C. Brennglass. LC 83-9566. 291p. 1983. 55.00 (*0-275-90952-2*, C0952, Praeger Pubs) Greenwood.

Overseas Projects - Crucial Problems. Institution of Civil Engineers Staff. 72p. 1988. 32.00 (*0-7277-1350-7*, Pub. by T Telford) RCH.

Overseas Research: A Practical Guide. Christopher B. Barrett & Jeffrey W. Cason. LC 96-48307. 168p. 1997. text 35.00 (*0-8018-5513-6*); pap. text 12.95 (*0-8018-5514-4*) Johns Hopkins.

Overseas Students in Higher Education: Issues in Teaching & Learning. Ed. by David Mcnamara & Robert Harris. (Illus.). 240p. (C). 1997. 75.00 (*0-415-13199-5*) Routledge.

Overseas Students in Higher Education: Issues in Teaching & Learning. Ed. by David McNamara & Robert Harris. (Illus.). 240p. (C). 1997. pap. 22.99 (*0-415-13200-2*) Routledge.

Overseas Summer Jobs 1998: Your Complete Guide to Thousands of Summer Employment Opportunities Abroad. 28th ed. (Vacation Work's Ser.). 256p. 1997. pap. 16.95 (*1-85458-194-5*) Petersons.

Overseas Summer Jobs, 1999. 29th rev. ed. 256p. Date not set. pap. 16.95 (*1-85458-220-8*, Pub. by Vac Wrk Pubns) Petersons.

Overseas Summer Jobs, 1997. Petersons. (Orig.). 1997. pap. write for info. (*1-8545-153-8*) Intl School Servs.

Overseas Summer Jobs, 1997. 28th ed. 256p. 1997. pap. 15.95 (*0-614-22851-4*) Petersons.

***Overseas Summer Jobs 2000.** 31st ed. Peterson's Guides Staff. 256-528p. 1999. pap. write for info. (*1-85458-229-1*, Pub. by Vac Wrk Pubns) Petersons.

Overseas Trade & Traders: Essays on the Commercial, Financial & Political Challenges of British Atlantic Merchants, 1600-1775. Jacob Price. LC 96-26142. (Collected Studies: No. CS554). 320p. 1996. 98.95 (*0-86078-591-2*, Pub. by Variorum) Ashgate Pub Co.

***Overseas Trade Statistics: United Kingdom Trade with Countries Outside the European Community.** HM Customs & Excise, Tariff & Statistical Office. (Illus.). 1000p. 1999. 1800.00 (*0-11-781967-0*, Pub. by Statnry Office) Balogh.

Overseas Transactions see Overseas Direct Investment - MA 4, 1996

Overseer: A Novel. Jonathan Rabb. LC 97-44624. 400p. 1998. 24.00 (*0-609-60253-5*, Crown) Crown Pub Group.

Overseer: A Novel. Jonathan Rabb. 1999. reprint ed. mass mkt. 6.99 (*0-515-12558-X*, Jove) Berkley Pub.

***Overselling of Population Ageing: Apocalyptic Demography, Intergenerational Challenges, & Social Policy.** Ed. by Ellen Gee & Gloria Gutman. (Studies on Canadian Population). 192p. 2000. pap. 19.95 (*0-19-541465-9*) OUP.

Oversexed Office. (Kake Ser.: No. 26). 1997. pap. 11.00 (*1-879055-13-9*) Tom Finland.

Overshadowed. Sutton E. Griggs. LC 71-144621. reprint ed. 29.50 (*0-404-00166-1*) AMS Pr.

Overshadowed. Sutton E. Griggs. LC 79-161261. (Black Heritage Library Collection). 1977. reprint ed. 25.95 (*0-8369-8820-5*) Ayer.

Overshadower: For Brett, Death Is Only the Beginning . . . Sylvia Groves. 224p. 1997. pap. text 18.95 (*1-85398-085-4*, Pub. by Ashgrove Pr) Words Distrib.

Overshoot. Mona Clee. 1998. mass mkt. 5.99 (*0-441-00509-8*) Ace Bks.

Overshoot: The Ecological Basis of Revolutionary Change. William R. Catton, Jr. LC 80-13443. 320p. 1980. text 29.95 (*0-252-00818-9*) U of Ill Pr.

Overshoot: The Ecological Basis of Revolutionary Change. William R. Catton, Jr. LC 80-13443. 320p. 1982. pap. text 16.95 (*0-252-00988-6*) U of Ill Pr.

Overshooting in the Foreign Exchange Market. Richard M. Levich. (Occasional Paper Ser.: Vol. 5). 38p. 1981. pap. 7.00 (*1-56708-004-9*) Grp of Thirty.

Oversight & Accountability of the U. S. Intelligence Agencies: An Evaluation. American Bar Association. Working Group on Intelli & American Bar Association. Standing Committee on La. LC 86-132506. iii, 119p. 1985. pap. 5.00 (*0-89707-213-8*, 355-0010) Amer Bar Assn.

Oversight Hearing on Arctic Snow Geese: Hearing before the Subcommittee on Fisheries Conservation, Wildlife, & Oceans of the Committee on Resources, House of Representatives, One Hundred Fifth Congress, Second Session, April 23, 1998, Washington, D.C. United States Staff. LC 98-183100. iii, 60 p. 1998. write for info. (*0-16-057016-6*) USGPO.

Oversight Hearing on Forest Service Law Enforcement: Hearing Before the Subcommittee on Forest & Forest Health of the Committee on Resources, House of Representatives, One Hundred Fifth Congress, Second Session, June 23, 1998, Washington, Dc. LC 98-212627. iii, 39 p. 1998. write for info. (*0-16-057353-X*) USGPO.

***Oversight Hearing on Gettysburg National Military Park General Management Plan & Provised Visitors Center: Congressional Hearing.** Ed. by James V. Hansen. (Illus.). 223p. 2000. pap. text 30.00 (*0-7567-0099-X*) DIANE Pub.

Oversight Hearing on Outer Continental Shelf Oil & Gas Leasing: Oversight Hearing Before the Subcommittee on Energy & Mineral Resources of the Committee on Resources, House of Representatives, 105th Congress, 2nd Session, May 14, 1998, Washington, D. C. USGPO Staff. LC 98-194372. iii, 49 p. 1998. pap. write for info. (*0-16-057134-0*) USGPO.

Oversight Hearing on Pfiesteria & Its Impact on Our Fishery Resources: Oversight Hearing Before the Subcommittee on Fisheries Conservation, Wildlife, & Oceans of the Committee on Resources, House of Representatives, One Hundred Fifth Congress, First Session, October 9, 1997, Washington, DC. United States. LC 98-160873. iii, 206 p. 1998. write for info. (*0-16-056245-7*) USGPO.

Oversight Hearing on Salton Sea Stabilization & Water Quality Improvement: Oversight Hearing Before the Subcommittee on Water & Power Resources of the Committee on Resources, House of Representatives, 105th Congress, First Session, October 3, 1997, Palm Desert, California. LC 98-160931. iii, 112p. 1998. write for info. (*0-16-056198-1*) USGPO.

***Oversight Hearing on the Future Water Needs of California under Calfed, Calfed Financing, the Monitoring & Performance Standards of Calfed & Calfed Public Participation: Oversight Hearing Before the Subcommittee on Water & Power of the Committee on Resources, House of Representatives, One Hundred Fifth Congress, Second Session, May 12, 1998, Washington, DC.** USGPO Staff. LC 98-190677. iii, 335 p. 1998. write for info. (*0-16-057088-3*) USGPO.

Oversight Hearing on the President's Fiscal Year 1999 Budget Request for Agencies: Oversight Hearing Before the Subcommittee on Energy & Mineral Resources of the Committee on Resources, House of Representatives, 105th Congress, Second Session ... February 26, 1998, Washington, D. C. LC 98-160415. iii, 89p. 1998. write for info. (*0-16-056427-1*) USGPO.

Oversight Hearing on the Reintroduction of the Grizzly Bear in the Public Domain National Forests: Oversight Hearing Before the Subcommittee on Forest & Forest Health of the Committee on Resources, House of Representatives, 105th Congress, 1st Session, June 12, 1997--Washington, D. C. USGPO Staff. LC 98-138999. iii, 208p. 1997. pap. write for info. (*0-16-055862-X*) USGPO.

Oversight Hearing on the Water Management Implications of the 1997/98 El Nidno: Oversight Hearing Before the Subcommittee on Water & Power of the Committee on Resources, House of Representatives, One Hundred Fifth Congress, First Session, October 30, 1997, Washington, D.C. United States Staff. LC 98-160862. iii, 81 p. 1998. write for info. (*0-16-056216-3*) USGPO.

***Oversight Hearing on U. S. Forest Service Strategic Plan under the Government Performance & Results Act: Hearing Before the Subcommittee on Forest & Forest Health of the Committee on Resources, House of Representatives, 105th Congress, 1st Session, July 31, 1997, Washington, D. C.** USGPO Staff. LC 98-142563. iii, 126p. 1998. pap. write for info. (*0-16-056102-7*) USGPO.

Oversight Hearings on Clinton-Gore Administration's Forest Service Roadless Area Moratorium: Oversight Hearings Before the Subcommittee on Forest & Forest Health of the Committee on Resources, House of Representatives, 105th Congress, Second Session, February 25 & March 17, 1998, Washington, D. C. LC 98-167727. iv, 359p. 1998. write for info. (*0-16-056435-2*) USGPO.

***Oversight Investigation of the Death of Esequiel Hernandez, Jr: A Report of Chairman Lamar Smith to the Subcommittee on Immigration & Claims of the Committee on the Judiciary, House of Representatives, 150th Congress.** USGPO Staff. LC 99-173922. iii, 270 p. 1998. write for info. (*0-16-057719-5*) USGPO.

O

Oversight of Defense Surplus Equipment & the Activities of the Defense Reutilization & Marketing Service: Hearing Before the Subcommittee on Government Management, Information & Technology of the Committee on Government Reform & Oversight, House of Representatives, 105th Congress, 1st Session, September 12, 1997. USGPO Staff. LC 98-176383. iv, 162p. 1998. pap. write for info. (*0-16-056483-2*) USGPO.

Oversight of District of Columbia Cash Status, Operating Deficit & Private Financial Market Access: Hearing Before the Subcommittee on the District of Columbia of the Committee on Government Reform & Oversight, House of Representatives, One Hundred Fourth Congress, Second Session, July 19, 1996. United States Government. LC 98-147320. iii, 103 p. 1997. write for info. (*0-16-055874-3*) USGPO.

Oversight of District of Columbia Metropolitan Police Department & the Booz-Allen Mou: Hearing Before the Subcommittee on the District of Columbia of the Committee on Government Reform & Oversight, House of Representatives, 105th Congress, First Session, September 26, 1997. LC 98-167889. iii, 130p. 1998. write for info. (*0-16-056475-1*) USGPO.

Oversight of Federal Drug Interdiction Efforts in Mexico: Review of a Rising National Security Threat : Hearing Before the Subcommittee on National Security, International Affairs & Criminal Justice of the Committee on Government Reform & Oversight, House of Representatives, One Hundred Fourth Congress, Second Session, June 12, 1996. United States Government. LC 98-133864. iii, 101 p. 1997. 5.00 (*0-16-055740-2*) USGPO.

Oversight of Gas's Government Performance & Results Act Strategic Plan: Hearing Before the Subcommittee on Government Management, Information & Technology of the Committee on Government Reform & Oversight, House of Representatives, 105th Congress, First Session, October 8, 1997. LC 98-175815. iii, 32p. 1998. write for info. (*0-16-056592-8*) USGPO.

Oversight of Metropolitan Statistical Areas: Hearing Before the Subcommittee on Government Management, Information & Technology of the Committee on Government Reform & Oversight, House of Representatives, One Hundred Fifth Congress, First Session, July 29, 1997. USGPO Staff. LC 98-160042. iii, 110 p. 1998. write for info. (*0-16-056217-1*) USGPO.

Oversight of NIH & FDA: Bioethics & The Adequacy Of Informed Consent : Hearing Before The Subcommittee On Human Resources of The Committee On Government Reform & Oversight, House of Representatives, One Hundred Fifth Congress, First Session, May 8, 1997. United States Government. LC 98-147308. iii, 228 p. 1997. 11.00 (*0-16-055827-1*) USGPO.

Oversight of Omb's GPRA Strategic Plan: Hearing Before the Subcommittee on Government Management, Information & Technology of the Committee on Government Reform & Oversight, House of Representatives, 105th Congress, First Session, October 6, 1997. LC 98-175819. iii, 106p. 1998. write for info. (*0-16-056551-0*) USGPO.

Oversight of Performance Based Organizations: Hearing Before the Subcommittee on Government Management, Information & Technology of the Committee on Government Reform & Oversight, House of Representatives, One Hundred Fifth Congress, First Session, July 8, 1997. United States Government. LC 98-158607. iii, 236 p. 1998. write for info. (*0-16-056215-5*) USGPO.

Oversight of Statistical Proposals: Hearing Before the Subcommittee on Government Management, Information &Technology of the Committee on Government Reform & Oversight, House of Representatives, One Hundred Fifth Congress, First Session, July 29, 1997. United States Government. LC 98-155992. iii, 76 p. 1998. write for info. (*0-16-056336-4*) USGPO.

Oversight of the Administrative Procedures & Examination of Antislamming Laws: Hearing Before the Subcommittee on Administrative Oversight & the Courts of the Committee on the Judiciary, United States Senate, 105th Congress, First Session ... November 3, 1997. LC 98-207586. (S. Hrg. Ser.). iii, 101p. 1998. write for info. (*0-16-057199-5*) USGPO.

Oversight of the Administrative Process for Disposing on Government Surplus Parts & Equipment: Hearing Before the Subcommittee of Administrative Oversight & the Courts of the Committee on the Judiciary, United States Senate, One Hundred Fifth Congress, First Session . . . July 8, 1997. United States Government. LC 98-114894. (S. Hrg. Ser.). iii, 69 p. 1997. write for info. (*0-16-055781-X*) USGPO.

Oversight of the Antitrust Division: Hearing Before the Subcommittee on Antitrust, Business Rights & Competition of the Committee on the Judiciary, United States Senate, One Hundred Fifth Congress, Second Session . . . February 26, 1998. USGPO Staff. LC 98-190694. (S. Hrg. Ser.). iii, 31 p. 1998. write for info. (*0-16-057163-4*) USGPO.

Oversight of the Department of Education & the National Institute of Mental Health: Current Approaches to Attention Deficit/Hyperactivity Disorders : Hearing Before the Subcommittee on Human Resources & Intergovernmental Relations of the Committee on Government Reform & Oversight, House of Representatives, One Hundred Fourth Congress, Second Session, July 16, 1996. USGPO Staff. LC 98-159935. iii, 180 p. 1997. write for info. (*0-16-055847-6*) USGPO.

Oversight of the Department of Labor's Efforts Against Labor Racketeering: Hearing Before the Subcommittee on Human Resources & Intergovernmental Relations of the Committee on Government Reform & Oversight, House of Representatives, One Hundred Fourth Congress, Second Session, July 11, 1996. United States Government. LC 98-133509. iii, 169 p. 1997. write for info. (*0-16-055942-1*) USGPO.

Oversight of the Disability Appeals Process: Hearing Before the Subcommittee on Social Security of the Committee on Ways & Means, House of Representatives, One Hundred Fifth Congress, First Session, April 24, 1997. United States. LC 98-160504. iii, 147p. 1998. write for info. (*0-16-056200-7*) USGPO.

***Oversight of the Federal Election Commission.** LC 99-170787. iii, 232 p. 1998. write for info. (*0-16-057501-X*) USGPO.

Oversight of the Fiscal Year 1999 Budget for the Forest Service, House of Representatives, One Hundred Fifth Congress, Second Session, May 7, 1998. USGPO Staff. LC 98-207723. iii, 155 p. 1998. write for info. (*0-16-057221-5*) USGPO.

Oversight of the General Services Administration: Hearing Before the Subcommittee on Government Management, Information & Technology of the Committee on Government Reform & Oversight, House of Representatives, 104th Congress, 2nd Session, May 10, 1996. USGPO Staff. LC 98-106879. iii, 117p. 1997. write for info. (*0-16-055472-1*) USGPO.

Oversight of the Implementation of the Clinger-Cohen Act: Hearing Before the Subcommittee on Government Management, Information &Technology of the Committee on Government Reform & Oversight, House of Representatives, One Hundred Fifth Congress, First Session, October 27, 1997. USGPO Staff. LC 98-207767. iii, 163 p. 1998. write for info. (*0-16-057127-8*) USGPO.

Oversight of the Implementation of the Vacancies Act: Hearing Before the Committee on Governmental Affairs, United States Senate, One Hundred Fifth Congress, Second Session, On S. 1764 ... March 18, 1998. USGPO Staff. LC 98-190603. iii, 193 p. 1998. write for info. (*0-16-057060-3*) USGPO.

Oversight of the Management Practices of the U. S. Customs Service: Hearing Before the Subcommittee on Government Management, Information & Technology of the Committee on Government Reform & Oversight, House of Representatives, 105th Congress, 1st Session, October 16, 1997. USGPO Staff. LC 98-192041. iii, 102p. 1998. pap. write for info. (*0-16-057050-6*) USGPO.

Oversight of the National Bankruptcy Review Commission Report: Hearing Before the Subcommittee on Administrative Oversight & the Courts of the Committee on the Judiciary, United States Senate, One Hundred Fifth Congress, First Session . . . October 21, 1997. United States Government. LC 98-139332. (S. Hrg. Ser.). iii, 135 p. 1997. write for info. (*0-16-055822-0*) USGPO.

Oversight of the National Labor Relations Board: Hearing Before the Subcommittee on Human Resources of the Committee on Government Reform & Oversight, House of Representatives, One Hundred Fifth Congress, First Session, July 24, 1997. United States. LC 98-158291. iii, 264p. 1998. write for info. (*0-16-056309-7*) USGPO.

Oversight of the National Organ Procurement & Transplantation Network: Hearing Before the Subcommittee on Human Resources of the Committee on Government Reform & Oversight, House of Representatives, 105th Congress, 2nd Session, April 8, 1998. USGPO Staff. LC 98-212891. iii, 277p. 1998. pap. write for info. (*0-16-057241-X*) USGPO.

Oversight of the Occupational Safety & Health Administration: Hearing Before the Subcommittee on Public Health & Safety of the Committee on Labor & Human Resources, United States Senate, One Hundred Fifth Congress, First Session . . . July 10, 1997. USGPO Staff. LC 98-106729. (S. Hrg. Ser.). iii, 112 p. 1997. write for info. (*0-16-055382-2*) USGPO.

Oversight of the Post-FTS 2000 Telecommunications Contract: Hearing Before the Subcommittee on Government Management, Information & Technology of the Committee on Government Reform & Oversight, House of Representatives, 105th Congress, 1st Session, April 30, 1997. USGPO Staff. LC 98-132549. iii, 39 p. 1997. write for info. (*0-16-055700-3*) USGPO.

***Oversight of the U. S. Customs Service.** LC 98-211752. iii, 102 p. 1998. write for info. (*0-16-057341-6*) USGPO.

***Oversight of the U. S. Role in the International Maritime Organization: Hearing Before the Subcommittee on Coast Guard & Maritime Transportation of the Committee on Transportation & Infrastructure, House of Representatives, 105th Congress, 2nd Session, June 25, 1998.** USGPO Staff. LC 99-184808. iv, 428p. 1998. pap. write for info. (*0-16-057729-2*) USGPO.

Oversight of the U.S. Postal Service: Inspector General of the U.S. Postal Service, Governors of the U.S. Postal Service : Hearing Before the Subcommittee on the Postal Service of the Committee on Government Reform & Oversight, House of Representatives, One Hundred Fifth Congress, First Session, March 19, 1997. United States Government. LC 98-108174. iii, 125 p. 1997. write for info. (*0-16-055635-X*) USGPO.

Oversight of U. S. Regional Counterdrug Efforts : Hearing Before the Subcommittee on National Security, International Affairs & Criminal Justice of the Committee on Government Reform & Oversight, House of Representatives, One Hundred Fourth Congress, Second Session, March 12, 1998. USGPO Staff. LC 98-212821. iii, 114 p. 1998. write for info. (*0-16-057304-1*) USGPO.

***Oversight of U. S. Trade Policy with Japan: Hearing Before the Committee on Governmental Affairs, U. S. Senate, 1991.** Ed. by Carl Levin. 283p. (C). 2000. reprint ed. pap. text 40.00 (*0-7881-7270-0*) DIANE Pub.

***Oversight of United States/Mexico Drug Cooperation.** LC 99-170784. v, 180 p. 1998. write for info. (*0-16-057547-8*) USGPO.

Oversight of Va's Vocational Rehabilitation: Hearing before the Subcommittee on Benefits of the Committee on Veterans' Affairs, House of Representatives, One Hundred Fifth Congress, Second Session, February 4, 1998. United States Staff. LC 98-212896. iii, 102p. 1998. write for info. (*0-16-057191-X*) USGPO.

***Oversight Review of the Treasury Department's Inspector General: Congressional Hearings.** Ed. by Susan Collins. 1736p. (C). 2000. reprint ed. pap. text 95.00 (*0-7881-8683-3*) DIANE Pub.

Oversize Color Images Project, 1994-1995: A Report to the Commission on Preservation & Access. Janet Gertz. 24p. 1995. pap. 10.00 (*1-887334-42-4*) Coun Lib & Info.

Oversize of Wormgear Hobs. A. H. Candee & A. Zamis. (Technical Papers: Vol. P129.09). (Illus.). 12p. 1953. pap. text 30.00 (*1-55589-156-X*) AGMA.

Oversized Air Handling Plant. J. R. J. Brittain. 1997. pap. 40.00 (*0-86022-463-5*, Pub. by Build Servs Info Assn) St Mut.

Oversized Cooling & Pumping Plant. J. R. J. Brittain. 1997. pap. 40.00 (*0-86022-464-3*, Pub. by Build Servs Info Assn) St Mut.

Oversized Heating Plant. J. R. J. Brittain. 1997. pap. 40.00 (*0-86022-469-4*, Pub. by Build Servs Info Assn) St Mut.

Oversocialized Conception of Man. Dennis H. Wrong. LC 98-28944. 330p. 1999. pap. 24.95 (*0-7658-0445-X*) Transaction Pubs.

Oversocialized Conception of Man in Modern Sociology. Dennis H. Wrong. (Reprint Series in Social Sciences). (C). 1993. reprint ed. pap. text 5.00 (*0-8290-2717-3*, S-653) Irvington.

Oversoul Seven Trilogy: The Education of Oversoul Seven; The Further Education of Oversoul Seven; Oversoul Seven & the Museum of Time. Jane Roberts. 560p. 1995. pap. 19.95 (*1-878424-17-3*) Amber-Allen Pub.

Overspent American: Upscaling, Downshifting, & the New Consumer. Juliet B. Schor. LC 97-42493. 256p. 1998. 25.00 (*0-465-06056-0*, Pub. by Basic) HarpC.

Overspent American: When Buying Becomes You. Juliet B. Schor. 1997. pap. write for info. (*0-465-06057-9*) Basic.

Overspent American: Why We Want What We Don't Need. Juliet Schor. LC 98-52011. (Illus.). 272p. 1999. pap. 13.00 (*0-06-097758-2*) HarpC.

Overstory Zero: Life in the Timber Country. Robert L. Heilman. 224p. 1996. pap. 14.95 (*1-57061-084-3*) Sasquatch Bks.

Overstory Zero: Real Life in the Timber Country of Oregon. Robert L. Heilman. LC 95-12199. 224p. 1995. 21.95 (*1-57061-037-1*) Sasquatch Bks.

Overstreet Comic Book Companion: Identification & Price Guide. 6th ed. Robert M. Overstreet. (Confident Collector Ser.). (Illus.). 608p. 1992. mass mkt. 6.00 (*0-380-76911-5*, Avon Bks) Morrow Avon.

Overstreet Comic Book Grading Guide. Robert M. Overstreet & Gary Carter. 320p. (Orig.). 1992. pap. 12.00 (*0-380-76910-7*, Avon Bks) Morrow Avon.

***Overstreet Comic Book Price Guide.** Robert M. Overstreet. 2000. pap. 15.00 (*0-380-77307-4*) Morrow Avon.

Overstreet Comic Book Price Guide. 22nd ed. Robert M. Overstreet. 544p. 1992. pap. 15.00 (*0-380-76912-3*, Avon Bks) Morrow Avon.

Overstreet Comic Book Price Guide. 23rd ed. Robert M. Overstreet. 760p. 1993. pap. 15.00 (*0-380-77220-5*, Avon Bks) Morrow Avon.

Overstreet Comic Book Price Guide. 25th ed. Robert M. Overstreet. (Illus.). 816p. 1995. pap. 17.00 (*0-380-78210-3*, Avon Bks) Morrow Avon.

Overstreet Comic Book Price Guide. 27th ed. Robert M. Overstreet. 896p. 1997. pap. 18.00 (*0-380-79463-2*, Avon Bks) Morrow Avon.

Overstreet Comic Book Price Guide. 28th ed. Robert M. Overstreet. 960p. 1998. pap. 18.00 (*0-380-80075-6*, Avon Bks) Morrow Avon.

***Overstreet Comic Book Price Guide.** 30th rev. ed. Robert M. Overstreet. (Illus.). 992p. 2000. pap. 22.00 (*0-06-095734-4*) HarpC.

Overstreet Comic Book Price Guide, Vol. 26. 26th rev. ed. Robert M. Overstreet. (Illus.). 832p. 1996. pap. 17.00 (*0-380-78778-4*, Avon Bks) Morrow Avon.

Overstreet Comic Book Price Guide: 29th Edition Collectibles. 29th ed. Robert M. Overstreet. (Illus.). 1008p. 1999. pap. 20.00 (*0-380-80780-7*, Avon Bks) Morrow Avon.

Overstreet Comic Book Price Guide Companion. 7th ed. Robert M. Overstreet. 464p. 1995. pap. 6.00 (*0-380-78229-4*, Avon Bks) Morrow Avon.

Overstreet Comic Price Guide. 24th ed. Robert M. Overstreet. 1994. pap. 15.00 (*0-380-77854-8*, Avon Bks) Morrow Avon.

Overstreet Comics & Cards Price Guide. Robert M. Overstreet. 464p. (Orig.). 1993. mass mkt. 6.00 (*0-380-77310-4*, Avon Bks) Morrow Avon.

Overstreet Indian Arrowheads: Identification & Price Guide. 3rd ed. Robert M. Overstreet & Howard Peake. xvi, 784p. (Orig.). 1993. pap. 20.00 (*0-380-77186-1*, Avon Bks) Morrow Avon.

Overstreet Indian Arrowheads: Identification & Price Guide. 4th ed. Robert M. Overstreet & Howard Peake. (Illus.). 816p. (Orig.). 1995. pap. 20.00 (*0-380-78211-1*, Avon Bks) Morrow Avon.

***Overstreet Indian Arrowheads Identification & Price Guide.** 6th ed. Robert M. Overstreet. (Confident Collector Ser.). (Illus.). 972p. (Orig.). 1999. pap. 24.00 (*0-380-80781-5*, Avon Bks) Morrow Avon.

Overstreet's New Wine Guide: Celebrating the New Wave in Winemaking. Dennis Overstreet & David Gibbons. LC 99-13373. 272p. 1999. 40.00 (*0-517-70784-5*) C Potter.

***Overstreet's New Wine Guide: Celebrating the New Wave in Winemaking.** Overstreet Editors et al. 272p. 1999. pap. 27.50 (*0-609-80518-5*) Crown.

Overtapped Oasis: Reform or Revolution for Western Water. Marc P. Reisner & Sarah F. Bates. LC 89-24459. (Illus.). 197p. (C). 1990. pap. 19.95 (*0-933280-75-0*); text 38.00 (*0-933280-76-9*) Island Pr.

Overtaxed! Your Guide to Honest Property Tax Reductions by Understanding & Effectively Protesting Your Assessment. Ed C. Tomlinson. 168p. 1991. pap. 8.95 (*0-9626776-3-9*) Diamond Pubns.

Overthrow of Allende & the Politics of Chile, 1964-1976. Paul E. Sigmund. LC 77-7181. (Pitt Latin American Ser.). 341p. 1977. reprint ed. pap. 105.80 (*0-608-07703-8*, 206779300010) Bks Demand.

Overthrow of Colonial Slavery, 1776-1848. Robin Blackburn. 576p. (C). 1989. pap. 25.00 (*0-86091-901-3*, Pub. by Verso) Norton.

Overthrow of the Phlogiston Theory: The Chemical Revolution of 1775-1789. James B. Conant. LC 50-8087. (Harvard Case Histories in Experimental Science Ser.: No. 2). 61p. reprint ed. pap. 30.00 (*0-608-10216-4*, 201768100007) Bks Demand.

Overtime. Don Clerkin. 104p. 1993. 6.95 (*0-9627494-5-1*) D Clerkin.

Overtime. Philip Whalen. Ed. by Michael Rothenberg. LC 98-48926. (Penguin Poets Ser.). 311p. 1999. pap. 16.95 (*0-14-058918-X*) Viking Penguin.

Overtime: A Modern Sequel to The Merchant of Venice. A. R. Gurney. LC 98-115329. 1996. pap. 5.25 (*0-8222-1540-3*) Dramatists Play.

Overtime: Ten Years of Punching Out with the Mill Hunk Herald (1977-87) Mill Hunk Herald Editors. 208p. (Orig.). 1990. pap. 12.95 (*0-931122-55-4*) West End.

Overtime: The Jazz Photographs of Milt Hinton. Milt Hinton et al. (Illus.). 160p. (Orig.). 1996. pap. 34.95 (*0-7649-0017-X*) Pomegranate Calif.

Overton County, Tennessee: Genealogical Records. Edythe R. Whitley. LC 79-50040. 97p. 1997. reprint ed. pap. 12.00 (*0-8063-0841-9*) Clearfield Co.

Overton, TN. Ronald Dishman. (Illus.). 575p. 1992. text 70.00 (*0-88107-210-9*) Curtis Media.

Overtones: A Book of Temperaments. James G. Huneker. LC 74-121479. (Essay Index Reprint Ser.). 1977. 23.95 (*0-8369-1711-1*) Ayer.

Overtones & Undertones: Reading Film Music. Royal S. Brown. LC 93-46924. 1994. pap. 24.95 (*0-520-08544-2*, Pub. by U CA Pr) Cal Prin Full Svc.

Overtons - 700 Years: With Allied Familes from England to Virginia, Kentucky & Texas. Nan O. West. LC 91-65569. (Illus.). xxii, 552p. 1997. 55.00 (*0-9633463-2-6*) N O West.

Overtraining in Sport. Ed. by Richard B. Kreider et al. LC 97-31205. (Illus.). 416p. 1997. text 45.00 (*0-88011-563-7*, BKRE0563) Human Kinetics.

Overture. Clamp. (Illus.). 184p. 1997. pap. text 15.95 (*1-56931-189-7*, Viz Comics) Viz Commns Inc.

***Overture.** James Loy. 1999. pap. 39.95 (*1-892465-32-9*) G Gallery.

Overture & Finale: Rodgers & Hammerstein & the Creation of Their Two Greatest Hits. Max Wilk. (Illus.). 192p. 1999. pap. text 16.95 (*0-8230-8820-0*) Watson-Guptill.

Overture for Beginners. R. F. Delderfield. LC 74-553890. (Illus.). 224 p. 1970. write for info. (*0-340-10628-X*) St Martin.

Overture in Venice. large type ed. Hester Rowan. 320p. 1985. 27.99 (*0-7089-1353-9*) Ulverscroft.

Overture to Death. Ngaio Marsh. (Dead Letter Mysteries Ser.). 1998. mass mkt. 5.99 (*0-312-96425-0*) St Martin.

Overture to Death. Ngaio Marsh. 1976. reprint ed. lib. bdg. 24.95 (*0-88411-492-9*) Amereon Ltd.

Overture to Death see Ngaio Marsh

Overtures. Mark Dunster. 20p. (Orig.). (YA). (gr. 9-12). 1996. pap. 5.00 (*0-89642-328-X*) Linden Pubs.

Overtures. 2nd ed. Siskin. (C). 1998. pap. text, teacher ed. 26.75 (*0-03-025111-7*) Harcourt Coll Pubs.

Overtures: Cours Intermediaire de Franciais. 2nd ed. H. Jay Siskin et al. 848p. (C). 1997. text 51.50 (*0-03-020079-2*, Pub. by Harcourt Coll Pubs) Harcourt.

Overtures & Preludes in Full. Richard Wagner. 288p. 1996. 16.95 (*0-486-29201-0*) Dover.

***Overturned Chariot: The Autobiography of Phan-Boi-Chau.** Phan Boi Chau. Tr. by Nicholas Wickenden & Vinh Sinh from VIE. LC 97-19313. (SHAPS Library of Translations). (Illus.). 288p. 1999. text 28.00 (*0-8248-1875-X*) UH Pr.

Overuse Injuries of the Musculoskeletal System. Ivan Bojanic & Marko M. Pecina. LC 93-8061. 384p. 1993. boxed set 136.95 (*0-8493-4492-1*, RD97) CRC Pr.

Overview. National Research Council Staff. (Space Science in the Twenty-First Century Series: Imperatives for the Decades 1995 to 2015). 108p. 1988. pap. text 14.95 (*0-309-03838-3*) Natl Acad Pr.

Overview. 2nd ed. Charles D. Yates. LC 94-141160. 284p. 1994. pap. text 36.00 (*0-536-58506-7*) Pearson Custom.

Overview: Introduction to Ten Body Systems. Competence Assurance Systems Staff. (Illus.). 1985. pap. text 70.00 (*0-89147-070-0*) CAS.

An Asterisk (*) at the beginning of an entry indicates that the title is appearing for the first time.

Overview: National Surveys of Kazakhstan & Kyrgyzstan, November, 1995. Steven Wagner et al. (Illus.). ii, 90p. 1996. pap. 11.00 (*1-879720-02-7*) Intl Fndt Elect.

Overview: Overview. Khan. Date not set. pap. 8.95 (*0-7453-1027-3*, Pub. by Pluto GBR) Stylus Pub VA.

Overview: Russia National Survey, September, 1995. Gary Ferguson. (Illus.). 94p. 1996. pap. text 11.00 (*1-879720-03-5*) Intl Fndt Elect.

Overview Vol. 1: Complete Plays 1. Manuel P. Garcia. 128p. 1998. 4.95 (*1-885901-51-8*, Liberts) Presbyters Peartree.

Overview & Comparison of Demand Assignment Multiple Access (DAMA) Concepts for Satellite Communications Networks. Phillip M. Feldman. LC 96-23899. (Illus.). 129p. 1996. pap. text 13.00 (*0-8330-2421-3*, MR-762-AF) Rand Corp.

Overview & Compilation of United States Trade Statutes, June 25, 1997. Government Printing Office Staff. 1100p. 1997. per. 48.00 (*0-16-055194-3*) USGPO.

Overview & Compilation of United States Trade Statutes & Economic Data. 1992. lib. bdg. 555.85 (*0-8490-5547-4*) Gordon Pr.

Overview & Economic Analysis of Property & Criminal Law. Ed. by Jenny B. Wahl. LC 98-48288. (Law & Economics Ser.: Vol. 1). 376p. 1998. reprint ed. 80.00 (*0-8153-3085-5*) Garland.

Overview & Strategies of Ephemeroptera & Plecoptera. Ed. by J. Alba-Tercedor & A. Sanchez-Ortega. xiv, 588p. 1991. 95.00 (*1-877743-08-9*) Sandhill Crane.

Overview & Update of ITS System Developments: 1996 International Congress & Exposition. (Special Publications). 48p. 1996. pap. 31.00 (*1-56091-773-3*, SP-1143) Soc Auto Engineers.

Overview Effect: Space Exploration & Human Evolution. 2nd ed. Frank White. LC 98-23507. xxii, 314p. 1998. write for info. (*1-56347-260-0*) AIAA.

Overview of Addiction Treatment Effectiveness. Mim J. Landry. (Illus.). 116p. (Orig.). (C). 1996. pap. text 35.00 (*0-7881-3656-9*) DIANE Pub.

Overview of Affirmative Action: Hearing Before the Committee on the Judiciary, U. S. Senate. Ed. by Hank Brown. 137p. (C). 1998. pap. text 35.00 (*0-7881-4956-3*) DIANE Pub.

Overview of Anesthesia for Nurses. Linda B. Chitwood. LC 94-60203. 81p. (Orig.). (C). 1992. pap. text 19.95 (*1-878025-40-6*) Western Schls.

Overview of Arbitration in California Managed Health Care Plans, Vol. 5. Marcus Nieto. 13p. 1997. pap. write for info. (*1-58703-072-1*, CRB Note 4) CA St Libry.

Overview of Automotive Industry in Argentina: A Strategic Entry Report, 1997. Compiled by Icon Group International Staff. (Country Industry Report). (Illus.). 140p. 1999. ring bd. 1400.00 incl. audio compact disk (*0-7418-0121-3*) Icon Grp.

Overview of Cardiac Surgery for the Cardiologist. Ed. by Richard T. Lee et al. LC 93-3832. 1993. 64.00 (*0-387-94066-9*) Spr-Verlag.

Overview of Cardiac Surgery for the Cardiologist. Richard T. Lee et al. (Illus.). 190p. 1993. write for info. (*3-540-94066-9*) Spr-Verlag.

Overview of Charter Schools: Hearing of the Committee on Labor & Human Resources, United States Senate, 105th Congress, Second Session ... March 31, 1998. LC 98-192015. (S. Hrg. Ser.). iii, 101p. 1998. write for info. (*0-16-057045-X*) USGPO.

Overview of Computers in the Building Service Industry. A. Michie & J. Wix. (C). 1983. 80.00 (*0-86022-106-7*, Pub. by Build Servs Info Assn) St Mut.

Overview of Down Syndrome. rev. ed. Siegfried M. Pueschel. 26p. 1986. pap. 4.00 (*0-318-22870-X*, 10-6) Arc of the US.

Overview of East-West Relations see Trilateral Commission Task Force Reports

Overview of East-West Relations: A Report to the Trilateral Commission. Richard Lowenthal et al. (Triangle Papers: No. 15). 1978. 6.00 (*0-930503-42-2*) Trilateral Comm.

Overview of Entitlement Programs, 6 vols., Set. 1995. lib. bdg. 2995.95 (*0-8490-7547-5*) Gordon Pr.

Overview of European Technology in Computers, Telecommunications, & Electronics. 1992. lib. bdg. 248.95 (*0-8490-5570-9*) Gordon Pr.

Overview of Exploration Geophysics in China, 1988. Ed. by Jingxiang Zhao & Stanley H. Ward. (Geophysical References Ser.: No. 3). 550p. 1989. text 38.00 (*0-931830-80-X*, 162A) Soc Expl Geophys.

Overview of Food & Beverage Operations Skillbook. Educational Foundation of the National Restaurant. (Management Skills Program Ser.). 60p. (Orig.). 1992. pap. 10.95 (*0-915452-47-2*) Educ Found.

Overview of Global Real Estate Finance. 1989. 10.00 (*0-935988-37-8*) Todd Pub.

Overview of Global Real Estate Finance. M. A. Hines. 18p. (Orig.). 1995. pap. 25.00 (*0-614-23690-8*) Todd Pub.

Overview of How Companies Are Granting Stock Options. Ryan Weeden et al. (Illus.). 48p. 1999. pap. 15.00 (*0-926902-49-0*) NCEO.

***Overview of Information Warfare: Principles & Practice.** Frederic H. Levien. (Overview Summary Ser.). (Illus.). 32p. 1999. pap. 8.00 (*1-885897-11-1*) Lynx Pubng.

Overview of Intellectual Property: An Original Anthology. American Intellectual Property Law Association Sta. LC 76-43205. (Illus.). 1977. reprint ed. lib. bdg. 26.95 (*0-405-09876-6*) Ayer.

Overview of Leonardo's Career & Projects until c. 1500. Ed. by Claire Farago. LC 99-32158. (Leonardo Da Vinci Ser.: Vol. 2). (Illus.). 528p. 1999. reprint ed. text 100.00 (*0-8153-2934-2*) Garland.

***Overview of Logging in Cameroon.** Global Forest Watch Staff. 56p. 2000. pap. 20.00 (*1-56973-437-2*) World Resources Inst.

Overview of New York City's Fiscal Crisis. Roger Dunstan. 10p. 1995. pap. write for info. (*1-58703-033-0*) CA St Libry.

Overview of NIH Programs: Hearing Before the Subcommittee on Health & Environment of the Committee on Commerce, House of Representatives, 105th Congress, 1st Session, September 30, 1997. USGPO Staff. LC 98-115008. iii, 56 p. 1997. pap. write for info. (*0-16-055721-6*) USGPO.

Overview of Nuclear Legislation in Central & Eastern Europe & in the NIS. NEA Staff. LC 98-144342. 132p. 1998. pap. 25.00 (*92-64-16018-3*, 66 98 05 1 P, Pub. by Org for Econ) OECD.

Overview of Ocular Disorders. Nancy Gwin. (Basic Bookshelf for Eyecare Professionals Ser.). (Illus.). 112p. 1998. pap. 30.00 (*1-55642-336-5*, 63365) SLACK Inc.

***Overview of Ocular Surgery & Surgical Counseling.** Kim Pickett. LC 98-46244. (Basic Bookshelf for Eyecare Professionals Ser.). 128p. 1999. pap. 30.00 (*1-55642-332-2*, 63322) SLACK Inc.

Overview of Precast Prestressed Segmental Bridges. (PCI Journal Reprints Ser.). 32p. 1985. pap. 16.00 (*0-318-19773-1*, JR202) P-PCI.

Overview of Regional History: Classroom Resources for Secondary Schools. Ed. by Catherine H. Sunshine & Deborah Menkart. LC 91-62719. (Caribbean Connections Ser.). (Illus.). 180p. (Orig.). 1991. pap. 16.00 (*1-878554-06-9*) Netwrk of Educ.

Overview of Russian Cases. Galina McLaws. LC 95-61381. (Texts Ser.). (RUS.). 96p. (Orig.). (C). 1996. pap. 12.95 (*0-941051-33-1*) Focus Pub-R Pullins.

Overview of Sociological Research in Hungary. Tamas Szecsko. 212p. (C). 1978. pap. 50.00 (*963-05-1728-0*, Pub. by Akade Kiado) St Mut.

Overview of Solutions to Breastfeeding & Sucking Problems. Susan M. Maher. 32p. 1988. pap. 6.50 (*0-912500-31-X*) La Leche.

Overview of Stability & Transition in External Aerodynamics. R. A. Henkes & J. L. Van Ingen. (Series 01 - Aerodynamics: No. 12). (Illus.). 44p. 1998. pap. 14.95 (*90-407-1575-0*, Pub. by Delft U Pr) Coronet Bks.

Overview of State & Federal Law on Sexual Harassment. 32p. (Orig.). (C). 1993. pap. text 25.00 (*0-7881-0000-9*) DIANE Pub.

Overview of the Alaska Highway Gas Pipeline: The World's Largest Project. 136p. 1978. pap. 12.00 (*0-87262-130-8*) Am Soc Civil Eng.

Overview of the Buddhadharma. Sheng-Yen Lu. Tr. by Janny Chow from CHI. LC 97-11942. 1997. pap. write for info. (*1-881493-06-7*) Purple Lotus Soc.

Overview of the Cultural Resources of the Western Mojave Desert. E. Gary Stickel & Lois J. Weinman-Roberts. (Illus.). 358p. (C). 1980. reprint ed. pap. text 37.50 (*1-55567-393-7*) Coyote Press.

Overview of the Educational System of Albania, Vol. 93A. Ann M. Koenig. (ECE Presents Ser.). (Illus.). 46p. (Orig.). (C). 1993. pap. 15.00 (*1-883971-02-0*) Educ Credential.

Overview of the Esselen Indians of Central Monterey County, California. fac. ed. G. S. Breschini & Trudy Haversat. (Illus.). 43p. (C). 1994. reprint ed. pap. text 4.69 (*1-55567-514-X*) Coyote Press.

Overview of the Esteem Builders' Complete Program. Michele Borba. 1994. pap. 44.95 (*1-880396-00-9*, JP9600-9) Jalmar Pr.

Overview of the Experiences of the ILIR Manpower Laboratory: The Development of a Model Approach to the Retrieval, Dissemination, & Utilization of Information on Manpower Operations. Louis A. Ferman & John C. Erfurt. 1973. ring bd. 5.00 (*0-87736-332-3*) U of Mich Inst Labor.

Overview of the Food Industry. 1991. lib. bdg. 79.95 (*0-8490-4626-2*) Gordon Pr.

Overview of the Hospitality Industry. Educational Foundation of the National Restaurant. 81p. (Orig.). 1993. pap., student ed. write for info. (*0-915452-08-1*) Educ Found.

Overview of the Housing & Community Development Act of 1992. Housing Assistance Council Staff. 21p. 1995. 4.00 (*1-58064-080-X*) Housing Assist.

Overview of the Indigent Health Care System in Texas. Don Brown & Andrew Cohen. (Working Paper Ser.: No. 67). 76p. 1992. pap. 5.50 (*0-89940-549-5*) LBJ Sch Pub Aff.

Overview of the Machine Vision Industry in Europe. 165p. 595.00 (*0-317-65599-X*) TBC Inc.

***Overview of the Markets: Debt & Equity Markets.** 2000. pap. 120.00 (*0-85297-452-3*, Pub. by Chartered Bank) St Mut.

Overview of the Massachusetts Economic Policy Analysis (MEPA) Model & Its Use from 1977 Through 1980. B. H. Stevens et al. (Discussion Papers: No. 118). 1980. pap. 10.00 (*1-55869-089-1*) Regional Sci Res Inst.

Overview of the New Age Movement. William A. Reck. LC 95-74802. 96p. 1995. pap. 4.50 (*1-877678-38-4*) Queenship Pub.

Overview of the Third Text Retrieval Conference (TREC-3) Ed. by D. K. Harmon. (Illus.). 583p. (Orig.). 1996. pap. text 75.00 (*0-7881-2945-7*) DIANE Pub.

Overview of the Total Army Design & Cost System. Robert L. Petruschell et al. LC 93-19192. 1993. pap. 13.00 (*0-8330-1371-8*, MR-195-A) Rand Corp.

Overview of Trade Flows of Energy-Using Products Between APEC Member Economies. Karen Holmes. 127p. 1998. pap. write for info. (*0-9669083-0-9*) Export Coun.

Overview of Turbulence Models for External Aerodynamics. R. A. Henkes. (Series 01 - Aerodynamics: No. 13). (Illus.). 35p. 1998. pap. 14.95 (*90-407-1576-9*, Pub. by Delft U Pr) Coronet Bks.

***Overview of U. S. Policy Toward South America & the President's Upcoming Trip to the Region: Hearing Before the Subcommittee on the Western Hemisphere of the Committee on International Relations, House of Representatives, 105th Congress, 1st Session, October 8, 1997.** USGPO Staff. LC 98-144055. iii, 62 p. 1998. pap. write for info. (*0-16-056039-X*) USGPO.

Overview of United States Export Controls. L. J. Kutten & B. Murphy. 172p. 1989. pap. 47.00 (*90-6544-396-7*) Kluwer Law Intl.

Overview of U.s. Policy Toward Mexico & Canada: Hearing Before the Subcommittee on the Western Hemisphere of the Committee on International Relations, House of Representatives, One Hundred Fifth Congress, First Session, September 17, 1997. LC 98-161377. iii, 95 p. 1998. write for info. (*0-16-055985-5*) USGPO.

Overview of Vocational & Applied Technology Education. John L. Scott & Michelle Sarkees-Wircenski. (Illus.). 258p. 1996. text 38.96 (*0-8269-4014-5*) Am Technical.

Overview of Welsh Poetry Before the Norman Conquest. Carol L. Wood. LC 95-43021. (Welsh Studies: Vol. 11). 132p. 1995. text 69.95 (*0-7734-8859-6*) E Mellen.

Overview of Western Civilization: A Guide, Vol. I. William F. Ricketson & Jean C. Ricketson. 196p. (Orig.). (C). 1984. pap. text 22.00 (*0-8191-3968-8*) U Pr of Amer.

Overview of World Elasmorbranch Fisheries. FAO Staff. 125p. 1994. 15.00 (*92-5-103566-0*, F35660, Pub. by FAO) Bernan Associates.

Overview of Writing Assessment: Theory, Research, & Practice. Willa Wolcott & Sue M. Legg. LC 98-17197. 207p. 1998. pap. 25.95 (*0-8141-3490-4*) NCTE.

***Overview on NIH Programs: Congressional Hearing.** Ed. by Michael Bilirakis. 56p. (C). 1999. reprint ed. pap. text 20.00 (*0-7881-8301-X*) DIANE Pub.

Overviews: Poems from Hollywood. Mark Dunster. 11p. 1999. pap. 5.00 (*0-89642-634-3*) Linden Pubs.

Overviews & Perspectives on the Food Stamp Program: Report. United States General Accounting Office Staff. viii, 79p. write for info. (*0-318-60231-8*) US GAO.

Overvoltage Protection Components Markets, Trends & Forecasts, 1995-2000. Dennis M. Zogbi. 301p. (Orig.). 1995. pap. 1800.00 (*0-929717-30-9*) Paumanok Pubns.

Overweight? It's All in Your Mind. John D. Hutto. LC 86-72988. (Illus.). (Orig.). 1987. pap. 5.00 (*0-940879-00-X*) All Amer Pr.

***Overweight Child: Promoting Fitness & Self-Esteem.** Teresa Pitman & Miriam Kaufman. (Issues in Parenting Ser.). 192p. 2000. pap. 14.95 (*1-55209-474-X*) Firefly Bks Ltd.

Overweight Teenagers: Don't Bear the Burden Alone. Michael D. LeBow. (Illus.). 270p. (C). 1995. 23.95 (*0-306-45047-X*, Plenum Trade) Perseus Pubng.

Overwhelmed. Nancy K. Schlossberg. 154p. 1994. pap. 13.95 (*0-02-927896-1*) Jossey-Bass.

Overwhelmed: Coping with Life's Ups & Downs. Nancy K. Schlossberg. LC 89-31459. 176p. 1999. reprint ed. pap. 16.95 (*0-7391-0031-9*) Lxngtn Bks.

Overwhelmed Person's Guide to Time Management. Ronnie Eisenberg. LC 96-36208. 1997. pap. 12.95 (*0-452-27682-9*, Plume) Dutton Plume.

Overwhelming, Overpowering, Overshadowing. Bill Panko & Margaret Panko. (Illus.). 100p. (Orig.). Date not set. pap. 9.95 (*1-885342-11-X*) Creative Ways.

Overwhelming Question: A Study of the Poetry of T. S. Eliot. Balachandra Rajan. LC 75-32519. 161p. reprint ed. pap. 50.00 (*0-608-15420-2*, 202934600060) Bks Demand.

Ovid. Sara Mack. LC 87-37157. 180p. (C). 1988. pap. 15.00 (*0-300-04295-7*) Yale U Pr.

Ovid: Amores I. Ed. by J. Barsby. (Bristol Latin Texts Ser.). (LAT.). 192p. 1991. reprint ed. 20.95 (*0-906515-45-9*, Pub. by Brist Class Pr) Focus Pub-R Pullins.

Ovid: Amores, Metamorohoses Selections, Vols. I-IV. Ed. by D. E. Hill. 1985. 49.00 (*0-86516-092-9*) Bolchazy-Carducci.

Ovid: Amores, Metamorphoses Selection (Teacher Edition) Charbra A. Jestin & Phyllis B. Katz. 1999. pap., teacher ed. 20.00 (*0-86516-427-4*) Bolchazy-Carducci.

Ovid: Amores, Metamorphoses Selections (Student Edition) Charbra A. Jestin & Phyllis B. Katz. 1999. pap., student ed. 15.00 (*0-86516-414-2*) Bolchazy-Carducci.

Ovid: Heroides, Vols. XVI-XXI. E. J. Kenney. (Cambridge Greek & Latin Classics Ser.). 283p. 1996. text 64.95 (*0-521-46072-7*) Cambridge U Pr.

Ovid: Heroides, Vols. XVI-XXI. E. J. Kenney. (Greek & Latin Classics Ser.). 283p. (C). 1996. pap. text 22.95 (*0-521-46623-7*) Cambridge U Pr.

Ovid: Metamorphoses I, Vol. I. Ed. by A. G. Lee. (Bristol Latin Texts Ser.). (LAT.). 168p. 1992. pap. 20.95 (*0-86292-144-9*, Pub. by Brist Class Pr) Focus Pub-R Pullins.

Ovid: Metamorphoses III, Vol. III. Ed. by A. R. Henderson. (Bristol Latin Texts Ser.). (LAT.). 143p. 1979. 20.95 (*0-906515-02-5*, Pub. by Brist Class Pr) Focus Pub-R Pullins.

Ovid: Metamorphoses XI, Vol. XI. Ed. by G. Murphy. (Bristol Latin Texts Ser.). (LAT.). 144p. 1979. reprint ed. 20.95 (*0-906515-40-8*, Pub. by Brist Class Pr) Focus Pub-R Pullins.

***Ovid: Metamorphosis IX-XII.** Ed. & Tr. by D. E. Hill from LAT. (Classical Texts Ser.). 240p. 1999. text 59.95 (*0-85668-645-X*, Pub. by Aris & Phillips); pap. text 28.00 (*0-85668-646-8*, Pub. by Aris & Phillips) David Brown.

Ovid: The Art of Love & Remedies for Love. Ovid. Tr. by Jack Shapiro. LC 66-22893. (Orig.). 1967. pap. 7.95 (*0-934810-09-5*) Carissimi Laurida.

Ovid I-IV: Metamorphoses. Ovid. Ed. by D. E. Hill. (Classical Texts Ser.). 1985. 59.99 (*0-85668-256-X*, Pub. by Aris & Phillips) David Brown.

Ovid I-IV: Metomorphoses. Ovid. Ed. by D. E. Hill. (Classical Texts Ser.). 1985. pap. 28.00 (*0-85668-257-8*, Pub. by Aris & Phillips) David Brown.

Ovid II: Amores. Ovid. Ed. by Joan Booth Booth. (Classical Texts Ser.). 1991. 59.99 (*0-85668-174-1*, Pub. by Aris & Phillips); pap. 28.00 (*0-85668-175-X*, Pub. by Aris & Phillips) David Brown.

Ovid V-VIII: Metamorphoses. Ovid. Ed. by D. E. Hill. (Classical Texts Ser.). 1992. pap. 28.00 (*0-85668-395-7*, Pub. by Aris & Phillips) David Brown.

Ovid V-VIII: Metamorphoses. Ovid. Ed. by D. E. Hill. (Classical Texts Ser.). 1992. 59.99 (*0-85668-394-9*, Pub. by Aris & Phillips) David Brown.

Ovid - Metamorphoses, Bk. 1. Ed. by A. G. Lee. 1985. 14.00 (*0-86516-040-6*) Bolchazy-Carducci.

Ovid - Werk Und Wirkung: Festgabe Fur Michael Von Albrecht Zum 65. Geburtstag. Werner Schubert. 1220p. 1999. 142.95 (*3-631-49607-9*) P Lang Pubng.

Ovid & Medieval Schooling. Ralph J. Hexter. (Munchener Beitrage zur Mediavistik und Renaissance-Forschung Ser.: Bd. 38). (GER.). xiv, 336p. 1986. 98.00 (*3-615-00168-0*, Pub. by Weidmann) Lubrecht & Cramer.

Ovid & the Canterbury Tales. Richard L. Hoffman. LC 67-17174. 231p. reprint ed. 71.70 (*0-8357-9748-1*, 205174800005) Bks Demand.

Ovid & the Elizabethans. Frederick S. Boas. (Studies in Shakespeare: No. 24). 1970. reprint ed. pap. 19.95 (*0-8383-0008-1*) M S G Haskell Hse.

Ovid & the Fasti: An Historical Study. Geraldine Herbert-Brown. (Oxford Classical Monographs). 262p. 1994. text 49.95 (*0-19-814935-2*) OUP.

Ovid & the Renascence in Spain. Rudolph Schevill. (Textos y Estudios Clasicos De las Literaturas Hispanicas Ser.). 268p. 1971. reprint ed. lib. bdg. 53.50 (*3-487-04029-8*) G Olms Pubs.

***Ovid, Aratus & Agustus: Astronomy in Ovid's Fasti.** Emma Gee. (Cambridge Classical Studies). (Illus.). 235p. (C). 2000. 54.95 (*0-521-65187-5*) Cambridge U Pr.

Ovid Ars Amatoria, Bk. 1. Elizabeth Block. (Latin Commentaries Ser.). 83p. (Orig.). (C). 1984. pap. text 6.00 (*0-929524-45-4*) Bryn Mawr Commentaries.

Ovid Fasti, Vol. II. John F. Miller. (Latin Commentaries Ser.). 102p. (Orig.). (C). 1985. pap. text 7.00 (*0-929524-46-2*) Bryn Mawr Commentaries.

Ovid Fasti, Vol. V. Betty R. Nagle. (Latin Commentaries Ser.). 96p. (Orig.). (C). 1996. pap. text 6.00 (*0-929524-86-1*) Bryn Mawr Commentaries.

***Ovid in Love.** Guy Lee. (Illus.). 208p. 2000. 17.95 (*0-312-26891-2*, Thomas Dunne) St Martin.

Ovid-Poems. (Everyman's Library). 1998. mass mkt. 3.50 (*0-460-87942-1*, Everyman's Classic Lib) Tuttle Pubng.

Ovid with Love: Selection from the Ars Amatoria, Books I & II. Ed. by Paul Murgatroyd. 228p. 1982. pap. text 16.00 (*0-86516-015-5*) Bolchazy-Carducci.

O

Ovidii, Nasonis: Fastorum Libri Sex. Ed. by Alton et al. (LAT.). 1997. pap. 29.95 (*3-8154-1568-3*, T1568, Pub. by B G Teubner) U of Mich Pr.

Ovidii, Nasonis: Metamorphoses. Ed. by Anderson. 1996. pap. 29.95 (*3-8154-1565-9*, T1565, Pub. by B G Teubner) U of Mich Pr.

Ovidii, Nasonis: Ponto Libri Quattuor. Ed. by Richmond. (LAT.). 1990. 32.50 (*3-322-00669-7*, T1566, Pub. by B G Teubner) U of Mich Pr.

Ovidii, Nasonis: Tristia. Ed. by Hall. (LAT.). 1995. 64.50 (*3-8154-1567-5*, T1567, Pub. by B G Teubner) U of Mich Pr.

Ovidius und Sein Verhaltnis Zu Den Vorgangern und Gleichzeitigen Romischen Dichtern. Anton Zingerle. xii, 342p. 1967. reprint ed. write for info. (*0-318-71250-4*) G Olms Pubs.

Ovid's Amores. Ovid & Guy Lee. LC 68-135400. vii, 202 p. 1968. write for info. (*0-7195-1796-6*) John Murray.

Ovid's Art of Love, 3 vols. Ovid. Tr. by John Dryden et al. LC 73-161789. (Augustan Translators Ser.). reprint ed. 49.50 (*0-404-54127-5*) AMS Pr.

Ovid's Causes: Cosmogony & Aetiology in the Metamorphoses. K. Sara Myers. 224p. 1994. text 47.50 (*0-472-10459-4*, 10459) U of Mich Pr.

Ovid's Fasti: Roman Holidays. Betty R. Nagle. LC 94-21660. Orig. Title: Fasti. (ENG.). 224p. 1995. pap. 8.95 (*0-253-20933-1*) Ind U Pr.

Ovid's Fasti: Roman Holidays. Ovid. Tr. & Notes by Betty R. Nagle. LC 94-21660. Orig. Title: Fasti. (ENG.). 224p. 1995. 25.00 (*0-253-33967-7*) Ind U Pr.

Ovid's Heroines: A Verse Translation of the Heroides. Tr. by Daryl Hine. 176p. (C). 1991. 40.00 (*0-300-05093-3*) Yale U Pr.

Ovid's Literary Loves: Influence & Innovation in the "Amores" Barbara W. Boyd. LC 97-24003. 264p. (C). 1997. text 42.50 (*0-472-10759-3*, 10759) U of Mich Pr.

Ovid's Metamorphoses. Tr. by Charles Boer from LAT. LC 89-4223. (Dunquin Ser.: No. 17). ix, 342p. (Orig.). 1989. pap. 22.00 (*0-88214-217-8*) Spring Pubns.

Ovid's Metamorphoses, Bks. 1-5. Ed. & Comment by William S. Anderson. LC 96-11064. 584p. 1997. text 49.95 (*0-8061-2845-3*) U of Okla Pr.

Ovid's Metamorphoses, Bks. 6-10. Ed. by William S. Anderson. LC 74-160488. (American Philological Association Ser.: Vol. 2). 540p. 1972. pap. 19.95 (*0-8061-1456-8*) U of Okla Pr.

Ovid's Metamorphoses: An Index to the 1632 Commentary of George Sandys. Christopher Grose. LC 81-51359. (Humana Civilitas Ser.: Vol. 7). 154p. 1981. 36.00 (*0-89003-074-X*); pap. 26.00 (*0-89003-073-1*) Undena Pubns.

Ovid's Metamorphoses: Books 1-5, Bks. 1-5. Ed. & Comment by William S. Anderson. LC 96-11064. (Illus.). 584p. 1998. pap. 21.95 (*0-8061-2894-1*) U of Okla Pr.

Ovid's Metamorphoses: Prolegomena to a Revision of Hugo Magnus' Edit. F. W. Lenz. iv, 104p. 1967. write for info. (*3-296-14180-4*) G Olms Pubs.

Ovid's Metamorphoses: Susanna's Selections. large type unabridged ed. Ovid. (Illus.). 216p. (Orig.). 1997. pap. 15.00 (*0-9612018-9-4*) B RUGGED.

***Ovid's Metamorphoses: The Arthur Golding Translation, of 1567.** Arthur Golding et al. Ed. by John Frederick Nims. LC 99-39904. 465p. 2000. reprint ed. pap. 22.95 (*0-9664913-1-9*, Pub. by Paul Dry Bks) IPG Chicago.

Ovid's Metamorphoses in Fifteen Books. Ovid & H. Dryden. Tr. by Joan Dryden et al. LC 70-158323. (Augustan Translators Ser.). reprint ed. 105.00 (*0-404-54128-3*) AMS Pr.

Ovid's Metamorphosis Englished, Mythologized, & Represented in Figures. George Sandys. Ed. by Karl K. Hulley & Stanley T. Vandersall. LC 66-13402. 745p. 1970. reprint ed. pap. 200.00 (*0-608-02785-5*, 206385200007) Bks Demand.

Ovid's Poetry of Exile. Tr. by David R. Slavitt from LAT. LC 89-45495. 240p. 1989. pap. 13.95 (*0-8018-3916-5*) Johns Hopkins.

Ovid's Toyshop of the Heart: Epistulae Heroidum. Florence Verducci. LC 84-42906. 320p. 1985. text 59.50 (*0-691-06638-8*, Pub. by Princeton U Pr) Cal Prin Full Svc.

Ovid's Toyshop of the Heart: Epistulae Heroidum. Florence Verducci. LC 84-42906. 320p. 1985. reprint ed. pap. 99.20 (*0-608-04644-2*, 206533100003) Bks Demand.

Ovimbundu of Angola. Frederick H. Rawson-Field Museum Ethnological Expedition to West Africa 1929-30. 2nd ed. Wilfrid D. Hambly. LC 34-41556. (Field Museum of Natural History Anthropological Ser.: Vol. 21, No. 2). (Illus.). 360p. 1934. reprint ed. pap. 111.60 (*0-608-02705-7*, 206337000004) Bks Demand.

Oviraptor. Janet Riehecky. (Libros Sobre Dinosaurios! Ser.). (SPA., Illus.). 32p. (J). (gr. k-4). 1994. lib. bdg. 21.36 (*1-56766-146-7*) Childs World.

Oviraptor, Set IV. David White. (Dinosaur Library: Set V). (Illus.). 24p. (J). 1984. lib. bdg. 18.60 (*0-86592-528-3*) Rourke Enter.

Ovis: North American Wild Sheep. Guy Tillett. (Illus.). 74p. 1997. pap. 15.95 (*0-9528607-2-4*, Pub. by Bear Print) Mountain Pr.

Ovitz: The Inside Story of Hollywood's Most Controversial Power Broker. Robert Slater. LC 97-13046. 1997. write for info. (*0-7863-1011-1*, Irwn Prfssnl) McGraw-Hill Prof.

Ovnis. Aurora Ecchevarria. 1998. pap. 4.50 (*84-01-54045-3*) Lectorum Pubns.

Ovnis: Cual Es la Verdad? Cesar V. Manzanares.Tr. of UFO: What Is the Truth?. (SPA.). 63p. 1991. pap. 3.99 (*1-56063-178-3*, 490264) Editorial Unilit.

Ovnis Vol. 1: Conciencia, Energia y Realidad. Ed. by Judi P. Zion. Tr. by Juan M. Castro. (SPA.). 229p. (Orig.). 1994. pap. 14.00 (*0-9627267-2-9*) Sin Limites.

Ovnis y la Agenda de Extraterrestres. Larson.Tr. of UFOs & the Alien Agenda. (SPA.). 1997. 9.99 (*0-88113-497-X*, B001-497X) Caribe Betania.

Ovo-Implantation, Human Gonadotropines & Prolactin: Proceedings of the International Seminar on Reproductive Physiology & Sexual Endocrinology, 2nd, Brussels, 1968. International Seminar on Reproductive Physiology &. Ed. by P. O. Hubinont et al. (Illus.). 1970. 57.50 (*3-8055-0959-6*) S Karger.

Ovocie Ducha. Vladimir Uhri. (SLO.). 53p. (Orig.). 1995. pap. 2.00 (*1-56983-016-9*) New Creat WI.

Ovulation & Its Disorders. Ed. by W. M. Thompson et al. (Studies in Fertility & Sterility). 1984. lib. bdg. 114.50 (*0-85200-811-2*) Kluwer Academic.

Ovulation Induction. Ed. by R. L. Collins & Herbert J. Buchsbaum. (Clinical Perspectives in Obstetrics & Gynecology Ser.). (Illus.). 184p. 1990. 89.00 (*0-387-97351-6*) Spr-Verlag.

Ovulation Induction. Ed. by Machelle M. Seibel & Richard E. Blackwell. LC 93-41785. 288p. 1994. text 82.00 (*0-7817-0161-9*) Lppncott W & W.

Ovulation Induction Update '98. Ed. by M. Filicori & C. Flamigni. (Illus.). 246p. 1998. 68.00 (*1-85070-025-7*) Prthnon Pub.

Ovulation Method: Natural Family Planning. John Billings. 40p. 1973. pap. 9.95 (*0-8146-1011-0*) Liturgical Pr.

Ovulation Method Charting Booklet. 3rd rev. ed. Suzannah C. Doyle. (Illus.). 124p. 1991. pap. 10.00 (*0-9628284-0-8*) FA Services.

Ovulation Method of Natural Family Planning: A User Friendly Manual. Twin Cities Natural Family Planning Center, Inc. S. LC 86-50298. (Illus.). 130p. 1986. pap. 14.95 (*0-9616827-0-1*) TCNFPC.

Ovulation Method of Natural Family Planning: An Introductory Booklet for New Users. rev. ed. Thomas W. Hilgers. LC 92-81747. (Illus.). 1993. pap. text 4.80 (*0-9626485-2-3*) Pope Paul Sixth.

Ovulation, Methods for Its Prediction & Detection. Ed. by S. L. Jeffcoate. LC 83-6885. (Current Topics in Reproductive Endocrinology Ser.: No. 3). (Illus.). 136p. reprint ed. pap. 42.20 (*0-8357-8637-4*, 203506100092) Bks Demand.

Owain Glyndewr, Prince of Wales Ian Skidmore. LC 79-309733. 195p. 1978. write for info. (*0-7154-0472-5*) C Davies Pubs.

Owain Glyndwr: Prince of Wales. Ian Skidmore. (Illus.). 195p. 1996. pap. 29.95 (*0-8464-4873-4*) Beekman Pubs.

Owe No Man: Scriptural Principles of Good Stewardship & Divine Providence. Ann R. Colton & Jonathan Murro. LC 86-70153. (Illus.). 374p. 1986. 21.95 (*0-917189-05-1*) A R Colton Fnd.

Owed to an Honorable Ex. Shirlock St. Haughey. 200p. 1996. pap. text 12.95 (*0-9647976-0-7*) Southrn Poetry.

Owed to Milwaukee: Mr. Mike's Personal Poems for the Masses, the Misses & the Mouses. Michael G. Corenthal. (Illus.). 56p. 1992. 20.00 (*0-9617673-4-0*) Yester Memories.

Owen. Kevin Henkes. LC 92-30084. 32p. (J). (ps-3). 1993. 15.89 (*0-688-11450-4*, Grenwillow Bks) HarpC Child Bks.

Owen. Kevin Henkes. LC 92-30084. 32p. (J). (ps up). 1993. 15.95 (*0-688-11449-0*, Grenwillow Bks) HarpC Child Bks.

Owen. Kevin Henkes. 1997. 11.95 (*84-241-3363-3*) Lectorum Pubns.

Owen Barfield & the Origin of Language. Owen Barfield. 1979. pap. 2.50 (*0-916786-42-0*, Saint George Pubns) R Steiner Col.

Owen Bus Studnts Internet W/I. Glenn Owen. 160p. (C). 1996. pap. text 19.96 (*0-395-76714-8*) HM.

Owen Co. KY - Stray Books, Vol. 1 & 2: Animals, 1819-1864. rev. ed. Carrie Eldridge. (Illus.). 87p. 1997. spiral bd. 15.00i (*1-928979-25-4*) C Eldridge.

Owen D. Young & American Enterprise: A Biography. Everett N. Case & Josephine Y. Case. LC 80-83945. (Illus.). 992p. (C). 1986. 25.00 (*0-87923-360-5*) Godine.

Owen Foote, Frontiersman. Stephanie Greene. LC 98-44843. (Illus.). 96p. (J). (gr. 1-3). 1999. 14.00 (*0-395-61578-X*) HM.

***Owen Foote, Money Man.** Stephanie Greene. (Illus.). 96p. (ps-3). 2000. 14.00 (*0-618-02369-0*, Clarion Bks) HM.

Owen Foote, Second Grade Strongman. Stephanie Greene. LC 95-11693. (Illus.). 81p. (J). (gr. 1-3). 1996. 15.00 (*0-395-72098-2*, Clarion Bks) HM.

Owen Foote, Soccer Star. Stephanie Greene. LC 97-16592. (Illus.). 96p. (YA). (ps-4). 1998. 14.00 (*0-395-86143-8*, Clarion Bks) HM.

Owen Glyndwr. Arthur G. Bradley. LC 73-14435. (Heroes of the Nations Ser.). xvii, 357 p. 1978. reprint ed. 47.50 (*0-404-58253-2*) AMS Pr.

Owen Lattimore & the "Loss" of China. Robert P. Newman. 685p. 1992. 45.00 (*0-520-07388-6*, Pub. by U CA Pr) Cal Prin Full Svc.

Owen Wingrave see Works of Henry James Jr.: Collected Works

Owen Wister: Chronicler of the West, Gentleman of the East. Darwin Payne. LC 85-1989. (Illus.). 392p. 1985. lib. bdg. 24.95 (*0-87074-205-1*) SMU Press.

Owen Wister's Medicine Bow. Tryntje V. Seymour. (Illus.). 96p. 1981. 37.50 (*0-915998-12-2*) Lime Rock Pr.

Owenism & the Working Class, 1821-1834. LC 72-2535. (British Labour Struggles Before 1850 Ser.). 1974. 24.95 (*0-405-04428-3*) Ayer.

Owen's Defense. Bill Wall. 65p. (Orig.). 1986. pap. 6.00 (*0-931462-50-9*) Chess Ent.

***Owens River Gorge Climbs.** 9th rev. ed. Martyn Lewis. (Eastern Sierra Climbing Guides Ser.: Vol. 1). (Illus.). 134p. 2000. pap. 19.00 (*0-9676116-2-8*) Maximus Pr.

Owen's Touch: Try to Remember. Lee Magner. 1998. per. 4.25 (*0-373-07891-9*, 1-07891-4) Silhouette.

Owens Valley: Guide to Independence & Lone Pine. Helen Hoffman. LC 84-80666. (Illus.). 80p. (Orig.). 1984. 4.95 (*0-9613329-0-5*) High Sierra.

Owens Valley & the Los Angeles Controversy: Owens Valley As I Knew It. Richard C. Wood. 1973. pap. 5.95 (*0-86575-124-2*) Commun Print.

***Owens Valley Controversy & A. A. Brierly: The Untold Story.** Robert Pearce. Ed. by Sheila Reiter. LC 99-30722. (Illus.). 112p. 1999. pap. 10.95 (*1-886225-37-0*) Dageforde Pub.

Owl see Living Things - Group 3

***Owl.** Pam Adams. 1999. pap. text 1.99 (*0-85953-862-1*) Childs Play.

Owl. Mary Ling. LC 92-52811. (See How They Grow Ser.). (Illus.). 16p. (J). (ps-1). 1992. 19.95 (*1-56458-115-2*) DK Pub Inc.

Owl. Kenneth Meadows. LC 97-42267. (Little Earth Medicine Library). 64p. 1998. 8.95 (*0-7894-2880-6*) DK Pub Inc.

Owl - On - Bou - Gh. Robert Grenier. 1998. 120.00 (*0-942996-31-3*) Post Apollo Pr.

Owl & Mrs. Wren: Correct Behavior. Kou L. Lee. (ENG & LAO.). 36p. (Orig.). (J). 1995. pap. text 10.95 (*0-9645686-1-6*) NKL Multicult Educ.

Owl & the Goose on the Grave. John Hawkes. (Sun & Moon Classics Ser.: No. 67). 232p. (Orig.). 1995. pap. 12.95 (*1-55713-194-5*) Sun & Moon CA.

Owl & the Nightingale. Ed. by J. H. Grattan & G. F. Sykes. (Early English Text Society Extra Ser.: No. 119). 1996. reprint ed. 27.00 (*0-85991-717-7*, Pub. by EETS) Boydell & Brewer.

Owl & the Nightingale. Ed. by J. H. Grattan & G. F. Sykes. (EETS, ES Ser.: No. 119). 1974. reprint ed. 35.00 (*0-527-00322-0*) Periodicals Srv.

Owl & the Nightingale. Ed. by John E. Wells. LC 74-144437. (Belles Lettres Ser. Section II: No. 2). reprint ed. 39.50 (*0-404-53612-3*) AMS Pr.

Owl & the Nightingale: Facsimile of Jesus College Oxford MS. 29 & British Museum MS. Cotton Caligula Aix. fac. ed. Ed. by N. R. Ker. (EETS Original Ser.: No. 251). 1963. 30.00 (*0-19-722251-X*, Pub. by EETS) Boydell & Brewer.

Owl & the Nightingale: Sources, Date, Author. Kathryn Huganir. 1970. reprint ed. lib. bdg. 75.00 (*0-8383-0572-5*) M S G Haskell Hse.

Owl & the Nightingale - Cleanness - St. Erkenwald. rev. ed. Intro. by Brian Stone. 272p. 1988. pap. 6.95 (*0-317-66032-2*, Penguin Bks) Viking Penguin.

Owl & the Pussy Cat. Edward Lear. LC 95-83849. (Illus.). 32p. (J). (ps-2). 1996. 13.00 (*0-689-81032-6*) S&S Childrens.

Owl & the Pussy-Cat, & Other Nonsense Poems. Edward Lear. LC 95-13076. (Illus.). 64p. (J). (gr. k-3). 1995. 18.95 (*1-55858-467-6*, Pub. by North-South Bks NYC) Chronicle Bks.

Owl & the Pussycat. Jan Brett & Edward Lear. (Illus.). 32p. (J). (ps-3). 1991. 15.95 (*0-399-21925-0*, G P Putnam) Peng Put Young Read.

Owl & the Pussycat. Edward Lear. (Illus.). (J). (ps-2). Date not set. 13.00 (*0-614-19209-9*) Atheneum Yung Read.

Owl & the Pussycat. Edward Lear. LC 97-2131. (Illus.). 32p. (J). (ps-3). 1997. pap. 5.99 (*0-7636-0336-8*) Candlewick Pr.

Owl & the Pussycat. Edward Lear. 32p. (J). (ps-1). 1989. pap. 6.95 (*0-89919-854-6*, Clarion Bks) HM.

Owl & the Pussycat. Edward Lear. (Illus.). 16p. (J). (ps-2). 1993. 12.95 (*0-8249-8571-0*, Ideals Child) Hambleton-Hill.

Owl & the Pussycat. Edward Lear. LC 86-46115. (Poetry Pop-Up Bk.). (Illus.). 14p. (J). (ps-3). 1987. 6.95 (*0-694-00193-7*) HarpC Child Bks.

Owl & the Pussycat. Edward Lear. LC 92-52640. (Michael di Capua Bks.). (Illus.). 32p. (J). (gr. k up). 1998. lib. bdg. 15.89 (*0-06-205011-7*) HarpC Child Bks.

Owl & the Pussycat. Edward Lear. LC 92-52640. (Michael di Capua Bks.). (Illus.). 32p. (J). (gr. k up). 1998. 15.95 (*0-06-205010-9*) HarpC Child Bks.

Owl & the Pussycat. Edward Lear. LC 90-32244. (Illus.). 32p. (J). (ps-3). 1996. pap. 6.99 (*0-698-11367-5*, PapStar) Peng Put Young Read.

Owl & the Pussycat. Edward Lear. LC 97-196479. (Illus.). 32p. 1997. bds. 7.95 (*0-399-23193-5*, G P Putnam) Peng Put Young Read.

Owl & the Pussycat. Edward Lear & Lewis Carroll. (Illus.). 64p. (J). write for info. (*0-19-276102-1*) OUP.

Owl & the Pussycat. Mortimer. (Illus.). 32p. (J). (ps-4). Date not set. 15.95 (*0-06-027228-7*); lib. bdg. 15.89 (*0-06-027229-5*) HarpC.

Owl & the Pussycat. Duke of Valderano. 346p. Date not set. 15.95 (*0-7541-0627-6*) Communs Plus.

Owl & the Pussycats. large type ed. Stella Whitelaw. 304p. 1995. 27.99 (*0-7089-3361-0*) Ulverscroft.

Owl & the Tuba. James H. Lehman. LC 91-73880. (Illus.). 32p. (J). 1991. 13.95 (*1-878925-02-4*) Brotherstone Pubs.

***Owl & the Woodpecker.** Brian Wildsmith. (Illus.). 32p. 2000. pap. 8.95 (*0-19-272403-7*) OUP.

Owl & Three Pussycats. Alice Provensen. 1981. 8.99 (*0-224-01821-3*) Random.

Owl Answers see Kuntu Drama

Owl at Dawn: A Sequel to Hegel's Phenomenology of Spirit. Andrew Cutrofello. LC 94-24303. (SUNY Series in Radical Social & Political Theory). 196p. (C). 1995. text 57.50 (*0-7914-2583-5*); pap. text 18.95 (*0-7914-2584-3*) State U NY Pr.

Owl at Home. Arnold Lobel. (I Can Read Bks.). (Illus.). 64p. (J). (gr. 1-3). 1975. lib. bdg. 15.89 (*0-06-023949-2*) HarpC Child Bks.

Owl at Home. Arnold Lobel. LC 74-2630. (I Can Read Bks.). (Illus.). 64p. (J). (gr. 1-3). 1982. pap. 3.95 (*0-06-444034-6*, HarpTrophy) HarpC Child Bks.

Owl at Home. Arnold Lobel. (I Can Read Bks.). (J). (gr. 1-3). 1982. 8.95 (*0-606-01963-4*, Pub. by Turtleback) Demco.

Owl at Home. abr. ed. Arnold Lobel. (I Can Read Bks.). (Illus.). 64p. (J). (gr. 1-3). 1990. 8.95 incl. audio (*1-55994-240-1*, TBC 2401) HarpC.

Owl Babies. Martin Waddell. LC 91-58750. (Illus.). 32p. (J). (ps-2). 1992. 15.99 (*1-56402-101-7*) Candlewick Pr.

***Owl Babies.** Martin Waddell. (Illus.). 32p. (J). (ps-2). 2000. pap. 19.99 (*0-7636-1283-9*, Pub. by Candlewick Pr) Penguin Putnam.

Owl Babies. Martin Waddell. (CHI & ENG.). (J). write for info. (*1-85430-343-0*, 93441, Pub. by MAGI1 UK); write for info. (*1-85430-348-1*, 93442, Pub. by MAGI1 UK) Midpt Trade.

Owl Babies. Martin Waddell. (BEN.). (J). 1995. write for info. (*1-85430-342-2*, Pub. by MAGI1 UK); write for info. (*1-85430-344-9*, Pub. by MAGI1 UK); write for info. (*1-85430-345-7*, Pub. by MAGI1 UK); write for info. (*1-85430-346-5*, Pub. by MAGI1 UK); write for info. (*1-85430-347-3*, Pub. by MAGI1 UK) Midpt Trade.

Owl Babies Board Book. Martin Waddell. LC 91-58750. (Illus.). 22p. (J). (ps up). 1996. reprint ed. 6.99 (*1-56402-965-4*) Candlewick Pr.

Owl Creek. James W. Brazzil. LC 88-92061. (Illus.). 144p. 1988. 12.50 (*0-9620993-0-9*) J W Brazzil.

Owl Editorial Style Guide: The Writer's Helper. Jeanne B. Ewing. 435p. (Orig.). 1989. reprint ed. pap. 45.95 (*1-884690-11-4*) Owl Press.

Owl Eyes. Frieda Gates. (J). (gr. 4-7). 1994. 15.00 (*0-688-12472-0*) Lothrop.

Owl Feather for Emily. Gerrie Human. LC 91-26734. (Illus.). 32p. (Orig.). (J). (ps-2). 1992. pap. 4.95 (*0-931093-77-5*) Red Hen Pr.

Owl Hoots Again: A Memoir. Cornelius V. Whitney. LC 88-2217. 154p. (Orig.). 1988. pap. 10.95 (*0-86534-123-0*) Sunstone Pr.

Owl in Love. Patrice Kindl. LC 92-26952. 208p. (YA). 1993. 15.00 (*0-395-66162-5*) HM.

Owl in Love. Patrice Kindl. 208p. (J). (gr. 7 up). 1994. pap. 4.99 (*0-14-037129-X*, PuffinBks) Peng Put Young Read.

Owl in Love. Patrice Kindl. LC 94-15028. 1994. 9.60 (*0-606-06653-5*, Pub. by Turtleback) Demco.

***Owl in Love, Class Set.** unabridged ed. Patrice Kindl. (J). 1998. boxed set 102.80 incl. audio (*0-7887-2562-9*, 46732) Recorded Bks.

***Owl in Love, Homework Set.** unabridged ed. Patrice Kindl. (J). 1998. 49.75 incl. audio (*0-7887-2106-2*, 40701) Recorded Bks.

Owl in Monument Canyon: And Other Stories from Indian Country. H. Jackson Clark. (Illus.). 192p. 1993. 24.95 (*0-87480-438-8*); pap. 14.95 (*0-87480-439-6*) U of Utah Pr.

Owl in the Cedar Tree. N. Scott Momaday. LC 91-41866. (Illus.). 117p. (J). 1992. reprint ed. pap. 9.95 (*0-8032-8184-6*) U of Nebr Pr.

Owl in the Mask of the Dreamer. John Haines. 320p. 1993. 25.00 (*1-55597-184-9*) Graywolf.

Owl in the Mask of the Dreamer. John Haines. LC 96-75793. 320p. 1996. pap. 14.95 (*1-55597-246-2*) Graywolf.

***Owl in the Office, Vol. 11.** Ben Baglio. (Animal Ark Ser.: No. 11). (Illus.). 192p. (J). (gr. 3-6). 1999. pap. text 3.99 (*0-439-08416-4*) Scholastic Inc.

Owl Light. M. Pearson. 1996. mass mkt. 8.95 (*0-340-65572-0*, Pub. by Hodder & Stought Ltd) Trafalgar.

Owl Magic for Kids see Animal Magic for Kids

Owl Moon. Jane Yolen. LC 87-2300. (Illus.). 32p. (J). (ps-3). 1987. 16.99 (*0-399-21457-7*, Philomel) Peng Put Young Read.

Owl of Minerva. James Laughlin. LC 86-73198. 96p. (Orig.). 1987. 15.00 (*1-55659-005-9*); pap. 9.00 (*1-55659-004-0*) Copper Canyon.

Owl on Every Post. Sanora Babb. LC 94-15110. 240p. 1994. pap. 10.95 (*0-8263-1531-3*) U of NM Pr.

Owl on the Teapot. Joan Grant. (Illus.). 138p. text 28.95 (*0-905483-87-1*, Pub. by Whittet Bks) Diamond Farm Bk.

Owl Pen. Kenneth M. Wells. LC 97-163805. 296p. 1996. pap. text 15.95 (*0-7737-5746-5*, Pub. by Boston Mills) Genl Dist Srvs.

Owl Sacred Pack of the Fox Indians. Truman Michelson. (Bureau of American Ethnology Bulletins Ser.). 83p. 1995. lib. bdg. 79.00 (*0-7812-4072-7*) Rprt Serv.

Owl Sandwiches. rev. ed. John B. Keane. 128p. 1993. pap. 11.95 (*0-86322-075-4*, Pub. by Brandon Bk Pubs) Irish Bks Media.

Owl Service. Alan Garner. LC 79-10140. 156p. 1979. 7.95 (*0-529-05520-1*) Collins SF.

Owl Service. Alan Garner. LC 98-56268. 240p. 1999. pap. 6.00 (*0-15-201798-4*, Voyager Bks) Harcourt.

Owl-Spirit Dwelling. Tess Gallagher. (Illus.). Date not set. write for info. (*0-932264-07-7*); pap. 15.00 (*0-932264-01-8*) Trask Hse Bks.

Owl Story. Greg Evans. (Blue Bananas Ser.). (Illus.). (J). 1997. pap. 4.99 (*0-7497-2633-4*) Dell.

Owl, the Elephant, & the Other Side of the Mountain: An Academic Odyssey. Virgil Lagomarcino. LC 96-222834. (Illus.). 186p. 1997. pap. text 14.95 (*0-8138-2877-5*) Iowa St U Pr.

***Owl, the Raven & the Dove: The Religious Meaning of the Grimms' Magic Fairy Tales.** G. Ronald Murphy. (Illus.). 224p. 2000. 25.00 (*0-19-513607-1*) OUP.

Owl Too Many. large type ed. Charlotte MacLeod. (General Ser.). 355p. 1991. lib. bdg. 20.95 (*0-8161-5235-7*, G K Hall Lrg Type) Mac Lib Ref.

Owl Was a Baker's Daughter. Marion Woodman. (Illus.). 214p. 1995. pap. 16.00 (*0-919123-03-1*, Pub. by Inner City Bks) BookWorld.

Owl Who Became the Moon. Jonathan London. LC 92-14699. (J). 1996. 11.19 (*0-606-11717-2*, Pub. by Turtleback) Demco.

Owl Who Couldn't Give A Hoot. Don Conroy et al. (Illus.). 80p. (J). (gr. 1-4). 1995. pap. 8.95 (*0-86278-370-4*) Dufour.

Owlet Moths of Ohio (Order Lepidoptera Family Noctuidae) Roy W. Rings et al. LC 91-62768. (Bulletin New Ser.: Vol. 9, No. 2). (Illus.). 200p. 1992. pap. text 20.00 (*0-86727-110-8*) Ohio Bio Survey.

Owlflight. Mercedes Lackey & Larry Dixon. LC 98-103995. (Darian's Tale Ser.: Vol. 1). 304p. 1997. 21.95 (*0-88677-754-2*, Pub. by DAW Bks) Penguin Putnam.

Owlflight. Mercedes Lackey & Larry Dixon. (Darian's Tale Ser.: Vol. 1). (Illus.). 342p. 1998. pap. 6.99 (*0-88677-804-2*, Pub. by DAW Bks) Penguin Putnam.

***Owlhoot Nights.** large type ed. Vic J. Hanson. 224p. 1999. pap. 20.99 (*1-85389-913-5*, Dales) Ulverscroft.

Owlhoot Trail. large type ed. Cliff Farrell. LC 96-53967. (Sagebrush Large Print Westerns Ser.). 1997. lib. bdg. 17.95 (*1-57490-056-0*) T T Beeler.

***Owlknight.** Mercedes Lackey. 2000. mass mkt. 6.99 (*0-88677-916-2*, Pub. by DAW Bks) Penguin Putnam.

Owlknight. Mercedes Lackey & Larry Dixon. (Darian's Tale Ser.: Vol. 3). 326p. 1999. 24.95 (*0-88677-851-4*, Pub. by DAW Bks) Penguin Putnam.

Owls see Zoobooks

Owls see North American Wildlife Series

Owls see Animals Series

Owls see Welcome to the World of Animals

Owls see Lechuzas

Owls. (Curious Creatures Ser.). 1997. pap. 8.95 (*0-7609-0118-X*) Curriculum MA.

Owls. 1998. 12.95 (*1-55209-681-5*) Firefly Bks Ltd.

Owls. Timothy Biel & Quality Productions Staff. (Zoobooks Ser.). (Illus.). 24p. (J). (gr. 1-6). 1997. 13.95 (*1-888153-44-X*) Wildlife Educ.

Owls. Fern G. Brown. Ed. by Mary Perrotta. LC 90-13093. (First Bks.). (Illus.). 64p. (J). (gr. 4-6). 1991. lib. bdg. 22.00 (*0-531-20008-6*) Watts.

O

Owls. Michael George. LC 97-28749. (Nature Books Ser.). (Illus.). 32p. (J). (gr. 2-6). 1998. lib. bdg. 22.79 (*1-56766-481-4*) Childs World.

Owls. Keith Graham. LC 98-205518. (Illus.). 48p. (Orig.). (YA). 1997. pap. 9.95 (*1-900455-23-4*, Pub. by Colin Baxter Ltd) Voyageur Pr.

***Owls.** Deborah Kops. LC 99-56071. (Illus.). 24p. (J). (gr. 3-5). 2000. lib. bdg. 16.95 (*1-56711-274-9*) Blackbirch.

Owls. Chris Mead. (Illus.). 128p. text 19.95 (*0-905483-59-6*, Pub. by Whittet Bks) Diamond Farm Bk.

Owls. John Sparks & Tony Soper. (Illus.). 240p. 1996. pap. 19.95 (*0-7153-0423-2*, Pub. by D & C Pub) Sterling.

Owls. Lynn M. Stone. (Illus.). 24p. (J). (gr. k-4). 1989. lib. bdg. 14.60 (*0-86592-326-4*) Rourke Enter.

Owls. Wildlife Education, Ltd. Staff & Quality Productions Staff. (Illus.). 20p. (Orig.). (YA). (gr. 5 up). 1997. pap. 2.75 (*0-937934-32-1*) Wildlife Educ.

Owls. rev. ed. Connie Toops. LC 97-24189. Orig. Title: Enchanting Owl. (Illus.). 128p. 1998. pap. 19.95 (*0-89658-140-3*) Voyageur Pr.

Owls: A Guide to the Owls of the World. Konig Claus et al. LC 99-60571. (Illus.). 320p. 1999. 50.00 (*0-300-07920-6*) Yale U Pr.

Owls A Portrait of the Animal World, 1. Paul Sterry. 1998. pap. text 10.98 (*1-880908-31-X*) Todtri Prods.

Owls: A Wildlife Handbook. Kim Long. LC 98-2578. (Nature Ser.: Vol. 4). (Illus.). 192p. 1998. pap. 15.95 (*1-55566-200-5*) Johnson Bks.

Owls: An Ornithologists Guide. Ron Freethy. (Illus.). 130p. 1990. 34.95 (*0-85219-042-5*, Pub. by Bishopsgte Pr) Intl Spec Bk.

Owls: Ghosts of the Forest. Photos by Tim Fitzharris. (Illus.). 23p. 1999. pap. 9.95 (*1-55209-417-0*) Firefly Bks Ltd.

Owls: On Silent Wings. Ann Cooper. LC 94-65092. (Wonder Ser.). (Illus.). 64p. (Orig.). (J). 1994. pap. 7.95 (*1-879373-78-5*) Roberts Rinehart.

Owls: The Silent Fliers. R. D. Lawrence. (Illus.). 176p. 1997. 29.95 (*1-55209-146-5*) Firefly Bks Ltd.

***Owls: Thematic Unit.** Fran Van Vorst. Ed. by Janet Hale. (Illus.). 80p. (J). 1999. pap., teacher ed. 9.95 (*1-57690-375-3*, TCM2375) Tchr Create Mat.

Owls: Whoo Are They? Kila Jarvis & Denver W. Holt. LC 96-3174. (Illus.). 64p. (J). (gr. 1 up). 1996. pap. 12.00 (*0-87842-336-2*) Mountain Pr.

***Owls & Other Birds of Prey.** Mary E. Reid & World Book, Inc. Staff. LC 00-21634. (Animals of the World Ser.). (Illus.). 64p. (J). (gr. 1-4). 2000. write for info. (*0-7166-1203-8*) World Bk.

Owls & Pussycats: Nonsense Verse. Edward Lear & Lewis Carroll. LC 93-2714. (Illus.). 64p. (J). (gr. 2 up). 1993. 16.95 (*0-87226-366-5*, 63665B, P Bedrick Books) NTC Contemp Pub Co.

Owls & Their Homes. Deborah C. Gibson. LC 98-15375. (Animal Habitats Ser.). (Illus.). 24p. (J). (gr. 2-4). 1999. lib. bdg. 18.60 (*0-8239-5308-4*, PowerKids) Rosen Group.

***Owls Aren't Wise & Bats Aren't Blind: A Naturalist Debunks Our Favorite Fallacies about Wildlife.** Warner Shedd. LC 99-58301. (Illus.). 304p. 2000. 23.00 (*0-609-60529-1*, NAT037000) Harmony Bks.

Owls Bay in Babylon. Charles Black. (American Dust Ser.: No. 13). 90p. 1980. 7.95 (*0-913218-92-8*); pap. 2.95 (*0-913218-91-X*) Dustbooks.

Owls by Day & Night. Hamilton A. Tyler. LC 78-778. (Illus.). 208p. 1978. pap. 10.95 (*0-87961-064-6*) Naturegraph.

Owls, Caves & Fossils: Predation, Preservation & Accumulation of Small Mammal Bones in Caves, with An Analysis of the Ple. Peter Andrews. LC 90-33933. (Illus.). 240p. 1990. 47.95 (*0-226-02037-1*) U Ch Pr.

Owls Do Cry. Janet Frame. LC 79-28167. 211p. 1982. pap. 11.95 (*0-8076-0956-0*) Braziller.

***Owl's Eyes & Seeking a Spirit: Kootenai Indian Stories.** Howard Kallowat & Confederated Salish & Kootenai Tribes of the Flathead Reservation Staff. LC 99-41884. (Illus.). 32p. 1999. pap. 5.95 (*0-917298-66-7*) MT Hist Soc.

Owls Fly! Kees Moerbeek Pop-Up Book. Kees Moerbeek & McClanahan Book Co., Inc. Staff. LC 96-136731. (Illus.). 8p. (J). (ps-k). 1996. bds. 5.99 (*1-56293-860-6*, McClanahan Book) Learn Horizon.

Owls for Kids. Neal D. Niemuth. LC 95-6694. (Wildlife for Kids Ser.). (Illus.). 48p. (Orig.). (J). (gr. 3-7). 1995. pap. 6.95 (*1-55971-475-1*, NorthWord Pr) Creat Pub Intl.

***Owls in the Family.** 1999. 9.95 (*1-56137-199-8*) Novel Units.

***Owls in the Family.** 1999. 11.95 (*1-56137-707-4*) Novel Units.

Owls in the Family. Farley Mowat. 1976. 21.95 (*0-89190-820-X*) Amereon Ltd.

Owls in the Family. Farley Mowat. 96p. (J). 1996. pap. 4.50 (*0-440-41361-3*) BDD Bks Young Read.

Owls in the Family. Farley Mowat. (J). 1996. 9.19 (*0-606-02220-1*, Pub. by Turtleback) Demco.

Owls in the Family. rev. ed. Mowat. 1989. pap. 6.99 (*0-7710-6693-7*) McCland & Stewart.

Owl's Journey: Four Centuries of an American County. Maura D. Shaw. LC 94-68193. (Illus.). 165p. (J). (gr. 3-7). 1994. 15.95 (*1-885482-01-9*) Shawangunk Pr.

Owl's Landscape. Jon Veinberg. LC 87-14247. 96p. (C). 1987. pap. 10.95 (*0-8265-1229-1*) Vanderbilt U Pr.

Owls Number School. Pam Adams. LC 90-48662. 24p. (J). 1989. 9.99 (*0-85953-166-X*) Childs Play.

Owls of Europe. Heimo Mikkola. LC 83-71804. (Illus.). 400p. 1983. 40.00 (*0-931130-10-7*) Harrell Bks.

Owls of Old Forests of the World. Bruce G. Marcot. (Illus.). 64p. (C). 1998. pap. text 20.00 (*0-7881-7348-0*) DIANE Pub.

Owls of Southern Africa. Ed. by Alan Kemp. (Illus.). 176p. (C). 1988. 410.00 (*0-7855-4043-1*) St Mut.

Owls of the World. John A. Burton. 1990. 19.98 (*0-88486-022-1*) Arrowood Pr.

Owls of the World. Rob Hume. 1998. 17.99 (*1-85585-352-3*, Pub. by Collins & Br) Trafalgar.

Owls, Owls - Fantastical Fowls. Krystyna Weinstein. 1985. 14.95 (*0-318-59600-8*) S&S Trade.

Owl's Secret. Louise Gallop. (Illus.). 36p. (J). 1993. pap. 8.95 (*0-934007-21-7*) Paws Four Pub.

Owl's Secret. Louise Gallop. (Illus.). 36p. (J). (gr. k-6). 1993. 15.95 (*0-934007-22-5*) Paws Four Pub.

Owl's Secret. Louise Gallop. 1993. 14.15 (*0-606-10280-9*, Pub. by Turtleback) Demco.

Owl's Song. Janet C. Hale. 144p. (YA). (gr. 7 up). 1976. pap. 2.50 (*0-380-00605-7*, 60212-1, Avon Bks) Morrow Avon.

Owl's Song. Janet C. Hale. LC 97-38236. 153p. (J). 1998. pap. 12.95 (*0-8263-1861-4*) U of NM Pr.

Owl's Tale. Elaine Anderson. 32p. (J). (ps-3). 1994. 8.99 (*0-904748-69-3*) Review & Herald.

***Owls, the Silent Hunters.** Sara Swan Miller & Steve Savage. LC 99-42008. (Animals in Order Ser.). (Illus.). 2000. 23.00 (*0-531-11595-X*) Watts.

Owls to Athens: Essays on Classical Culture Presented to Sir Kenneth Dover. Ed. by Elizabeth M. Craik. (Illus.). 430p. 1990. text 98.00 (*0-19-814478-4*) OUP.

Owl's World. Disney Enterprises, Inc. Staff. (Disney's "Out & about with Pooh" Library: Vol. 18). (Illus.). 44p. (J). (gr. 1-6). 1996. 3.49 (*1-885222-72-6*) Advance Pubs.

Owlsight. Mercedes Lackey & Larry Dixon. LC 99-188017. (Darian's Tale Ser.: Vol. 2). (Illus.). 389p. 1998. 24.95 (*0-88677-802-6*, Pub. by DAW Bks) Penguin Putnam.

Owlsight. Mercedes Lackey & Larry Dixon. (Darian's Tale Ser.: Vol. 2). 450p. 1999. mass mkt. 6.99 (*0-88677-803-4*, Pub. by DAW Bks) Penguin Putnam.

Owly. Mike Thaler. LC 81-47727. (Illus.). 32p. (J). (ps-3). 1982. 12.95 (*0-06-026151-X*) HarpC Child Bks.

Owly. Mike Thaler. LC 98-10682. (Illus.). 32p. (J). (ps-1). 1998. reprint ed. pap. 5.95 (*0-8027-7545-4*) Walker & Co.

Own-Children Method of Fertility Estimation. Lee-Jay Cho et al. 188p. 1986. text 25.00 (*0-86638-082-5*) EW Ctr HI.

Own Court Book of Tennis. James J. Davis. 1987. pap. write for info. (*0-318-62750-7*) Davis Turner Pub.

Own It & Keep It: How to Reduce Your Taxes, Preserve Your Assets, & Protect Your Survivors. Theodore E. Hughes & David Klein. LC 94-42399. (Illus.). 192p. 1995. 19.95 (*0-8160-3279-3*) Facts on File.

Own or Other Culture. Judith Okely. LC 95-25985. 256p. (C). 1996. 90.00 (*0-415-11512-4*); pap. 25.99 (*0-415-11513-2*) Routledge.

Own Worst Enemies: Local Charity Unmasked. Marvin L. Peebles. 300p. 1984. ring bd. 32.50 (*0-939020-50-5*) MLP Ent.

Own Your Own: The No-Cash Down Business Guide. Arnold S. Goldstein. LC 82-22973. 208p. 1983. pap. 6.95 (*0-13-647479-9*) P-H.

Own Your Own Body. Stan Malstrom. LC 76-58968. 414p. 1980. reprint ed. pap. 5.95 (*0-87983-215-0*, Keats Publng) NTC Contemp Pub Co.

Own Your Own Cable System. Bruce D. Jacobs et al. 41p. 1983. 19.50 (*0-918943-00-0*) Natl Con Coopera Bank.

Own Your Own Franchise: Everything You Need to Know about the 160 Best Opportunities in America. Ray Bard & Sheila Henderson. 1987. pap. 22.95 (*0-201-11438-0*) Addison-Wesley.

Owner-Builder & the Code. Kern et al. 192p. pap. 20.00 (*0-686-31223-6*) Owner-Builder.

Owner-Builder Book: How You Can Save More Than $100,000 in the Construction of Your Custom Home. Mark A. Smith & Elaine M. Smith. Ed. by Carolyn Tice. LC 97-94742. (Illus.). 252p. 1998. pap. 29.95 (*0-9661428-0-2*) Consensus Gp.

***Owner-Builder Book: How You Save More Than $100,000 in the Construction of Your Custom Home.** 2nd rev. expanded ed. Mark A. Smith & Elaine M. Smith. LC 99-91684. (Illus.). xix, 314p. 2000. pap. 24.95 (*0-9661428-3-7*, Pub. by Consensus Gp) Partners Pubs Grp.

Owner-Built Home. Ken Kern. 375p. spiral bd. 20.00 (*0-686-31220-1*) Owner-Builder.

Owner-Built Home Revisited. Ken Kern. (Illus.). spiral bd. 20.00 (*0-317-66213-9*) Owner-Builder.

Owner-Built Homestead. Barbara Kern & Ken Kern. 400p. pap. 20.00 (*0-686-31219-8*) Owner-Builder.

Owner Built Pole Frame House. Ken Kern. (Illus.). spiral bd. 20.00 (*0-684-16767-0*) Owner-Builder.

Owner Financing. Wade B. Cook. 1997. reprint ed. pap. 5.95 (*0-910019-05-3*) Lghthse Pub Gp.

Owner of the House. Latifa Zayyat. Tr. by Sophie Bennett. 208p. 1998. pap. 12.00 (*0-7043-8043-9*, Pub. by Quartet) Interlink Pub.

Owner Operator Management System: How to Start & Manage a Trucking Business. 3rd rev. ed. Lew Grill. Orig. Title: Interstate Drivers - Independent Operator Training Series. 200p. 1996. ring bd. 47.95 (*1-881912-13-2*) Atlantic Pac Res.

Owner Operator Management Training Series: Independent Study Program for Going into the Trucking Business, Includes Jumpstart, Truckforms, Dictionary, & Principals of Business. Lewis J. Grill. (Illus.). 288p. (C). 1995. ring bd. 44.95 (*1-881812-11-1*) IDEALAB.

Owner Unknown: The Workbook: Your Guide to Real Estate Treasure Hunting. Jay D. Segel. LC 90-86039. 129p. wbk. ed. 17.95 (*0-8063-1295-5*, 5290) Clearfield Co.

Owner Will Carry: How to Take Back a Mortgage Without Being Taken. Bill Broadbent & George Rosenberg. Orig. Title: Sell Your Property Fast. 176p. 1993. pap. 25.00 (*0-9637838-0-7*) Whos Who Creat.

Owner's & Builder's Guide to Low-Cost & Efficient Shelter. 1992. lib. bdg. 375.00 (*0-8490-8887-9*) Gordon Pr.

Owners & Contractors Protective Liability. Ed. by Diana Kowatch. 57p. 1996. 19.95 (*1-56461-168-X*) Rough Notes.

Owner's & Manager's Guide to Condominium Management. rev. ed. LC 83-81899. (Illus.). 341p. 1984. 62.95 (*0-912104-61-9*, 812) Inst Real Estate.

Owners & Neighbours in Roman Law. Alan Rodger. (C). 1972. text 12.00 (*0-19-825309-5*) OUP.

Owners & Occupiers: Changes in Rural Society in South-West Scotland Before 1914. R. H. Campbell. (Aberdeen University Press Bks.). 192p. 1991. text 29.90 (*0-08-041218-1*, Pub. by Aberdeen U Pr) Macmillan.

Owners & Officers of Private Companies, 1991, 2 vols. 91st ed. Ed. by William Wade. 2350p. 1991. 260.00 (*1-879784-10-6*) Taft Group.

Owners & Officers of Private Companies, 1992, 2 vols. 92nd ed. Ed. by Scott. 1992. 260.00 (*1-879784-49-1*, 600359) Taft Group.

Owners & Officers of Private Companies, 1993, 2 vols. 93rd ed. Ed. by Mark W. Scott. 2902p. 1992. 270.00 (*1-879784-65-3*, 600423) Taft Group.

Owners & Officers of Private Companies, 1994, 2 Vols. 94th ed. Ed. by Scott. (Illus.). 1100p. 1993. 320.00 (*1-879784-91-2*) Fund Raising.

Owners & Officers of Private Companies, 1995, 2 vols. 95th ed. Ed. by Debbie Tracey. 3000p. 1994. 320.00 (*1-879784-94-7*) Taft Group.

Owners & Officers of Private Companies 1997. Mark W. Scott. write for info. (*1-56995-052-0*); 280.00 (*1-56995-051-2*) Taft Group.

Owners & Officers of Private Companies 1997, Vol. 2. Mark W. Scott. write for info. (*1-56995-053-9*) Taft Group.

Owner's Guide: The Dalmation. Patti Strand & Rod Strand. (Owner's Guide to a Happy, Healthy Pet Ser.). (Illus.). 160p. 1995. 12.95 (*0-87605-384-3*) Howell Bks.

***Owner's Guide to Business Succession Planning.** Stephen P. Clifford. Ed. by Alex Teodosio. (Illus.). 64p. 1999. pap. 14.95 (*0-933522-25-8*, Pub. by Kent Popular) OEOC.

Owner's Guide to Cat Health. Lowell Ackerman. (Illus.). 208p. 1996. 34.95 (*0-7938-0595-3*, TS251) TFH Pubns.

Owner's Guide to Dog Behavior. Ed. by Lowell Ackerman. (Illus.). 288p. 1996. 29.95 (*0-7938-2094-4*, TS252) TFH Pubns.

***Owner's Guide to Fatherhood: A Lighthearted Look at the Days of a Dad.** Chris Ewing. 224p. 2000. 12.99 (*1-57748-682-X*) Barbour Pub.

***Owner's Guide to Happy, Healthy Fish.** Gregory Skomal. LC 98-51715. (Howell Book House's Owner's Guide to a Happy Healthy Pet Ser.). (Illus.). 126p. 1999. 12.95 (*1-58245-032-3*) Howell Bks.

Owner's Guide to Parenting Teenagers: A Step-by-Step, Solution-Focused Approach to Raising Adolescents Without Losing Your Mind. Pat J. Baxter & Cynthia D. Naff. LC 96-136286. 212p. (Orig.). 1996. pap. 14.95 (*0-9650651-0-3*) Real Life Pr.

***Owner's Guide to Selling your Property: Step-by-Step Method for Selling Your Property Yourself.** unabridged ed. Ronald W. Ewart. (Illus.). 120p. 2000. pap. text 13.95 (*0-9679818-1-6*) Tri-Tron Global.

Owner's Guide to Successful Restaurant & Retail Business. Anthony Ramsey. 175p. (Orig.). 1997. pap. 17.95 (*0-9646898-3-9*) Silent Comn.

Owner's Guide to the Body. Roger Golten. (Illus.). 192p. 1999. pap. 19.95 (*0-7225-3737-9*) Thorsons PA.

Owner's Guide to the Construction Process. Philip J. Millage & Deno Rousopoulos. 96p. 1999. pap. 12.95 (*0-9669315-0-5*) Educ Media.

Owner's Guide to the Garden Pond. Roseanne Conrad. LC 97-45784. 128p. 1998. pap. 12.95 (*0-87605-447-5*) Howell Bks.

Owner's Manual. Yogi Bhajan. Ed. & Illus. by Hari J. Khalsa. 50p. 1995. pap. 14.95 (*0-9639847-0-5*) KRI.

Owner's Manual: A Fast, Fun, & Easy Way to Knowing & Understanding Your Lover. Linda B. Ford & Beth M. Goodman. (Orig.). 1993. pap. 7.95 (*0-9634919-1-1*) Ford Grp.

Owners Manual: A Fast, Fun & Easy Way to Knowing & Understanding Your Lover. Linda Ford & Beth Goodman. 50p. (Orig.). 1992. pap. 9.95 (*0-9634919-0-3*) Ford Grp.

Owner's Manual: A Parent's Guide & Medical Record for a Child's First Two Years. James A. Waler. LC 98-93107. 115p. 1998. pap. 13.95 (*0-9664486-0-X*) Concpt Prodns.

Owner's Manual: For Becoming a Successful Human Being. P. A. Alexander. 138p. 1996. per. 16.95 (*0-7872-2225-9*) Kendall-Hunt.

Owner's Manual for New Business Ventures: How to Uncover a Legitimate Business Opportunity & Start Smart...a Reference Guide. Terry R. Dull. Ed. by Kim Donaldson. LC 93-83994. (Illus.). 160p. (Orig.). 1993. pap. text 19.95 (*1-883416-00-0*) Nat Home Ofc.

***Owner's Manual for Personality at Work.** 288p. 2000. 19.95 (*1-885167-45-8*) Bard Press.

***Owner's Manual for the Brain: Everyday Applications from Mind-Brain Research.** 2nd ed. Pierce J Howard. LC 99-41862. 736p. 1999. pap. 24.95 (*1-885167-41-5*, Pub. by Bard Press) Natl Bk Netwk.

***Owner's Manual for the Brain: Everyday Applications from Mind-Brain Research.** 2nd ed. Pierce J. Howard. 736p. 2000. 34.95 (*1-885167-38-5*, Pub. by Bard Press) Natl Bk Netwk.

Owner's Manual for the Human Body: Kundalini Yoga As Taught by Yogi Bhajan. Yogi Bhajan. (Illus.). iv, 49p. (Orig.). 1997. reprint ed. spiral bd. write for info. (*0-9639991-0-9*) KRI.

Owner's Manual for the Unfinished Soul. Calvin Miller. LC 96-37642. 176p. 1997. 15.99 (*0-87788-554-0*, H Shaw Pubs) Waterbrook Pr.

***Owner's Manual No One Gave You! A Manual for Basic Human Operation & Accelerated Performance.** James Fortin. 224p. 1999. pap. 14.95 (*0-9668311-0-1*) Performance Mastery.

Owner's Manuai to the Soul: A Modern Guide to Spirituality from the Most Ancient Jewish Torah Sources. Nehemiah Blavin. LC 99-23299. 2000. 30.00 (*0-7657-6107-6*) Aronson.

***Owners of Nuclear Power Plants.** R. L. Reid. 82p. 2000. pap. 8.00 (*0-16-059183-X*) USGPO.

Owner's Pictorial Guide for the Care & Understanding of the Bally Slot Machine. Robert N. Geddes. Ed. & Illus. by Daniel R. Mead. LC 90-91665. (Owner's Pictorial Guide Ser.). 236p. (Orig.). 1994. pap. 44.95 (*0-934422-05-2*, BKS130440) Mead Pub Corp.

Owner's Pictorial Guide for the Care & Understanding of the Jennings Bell Slot Machine. Robert N. Geddes & Daniel R. Mead. (Illus.). 163p. (Orig.). 1980. pap. 31.95 (*0-934422-18-4*) Mead Pub Corp.

Owner's Pictorial Guide for the Care & Understanding of the Mills Bell Slot Machine. 3rd ed. Robert N. Geddes & Daniel R. Mead. LC 79-88432. (Owner's Pictorial Guide Ser.). (Illus.). 208p. 1995. pap. 39.95 (*0-934422-00-1*, 130220) Mead Pub Corp.

Owner's Pictorial Guide for the Care & Understanding of the Pace Bell Slot Machine. Deborah L. Mead & Daniel R. Mead. LC 82-73747. (Owner's Pictorial Guide Ser.). (Illus.). 142p. 1983. pap. 29.95 (*0-934422-03-6*, 100285) Mead Pub Corp.

Owner's Pictorial Guide for the Care & Understanding of the Watling Bell Slot Machine. Robert N. Geddes & Daniel R. Mead. (Illus.). 148p. (Orig.). 1981. pap. 29.95 (*0-934422-04-4*, 130330) Mead Pub Corp.

Owner's Toolbox on Equity Incentives: Includes CD-ROM, Guidebook & Sample Legal Plan Documents. Foundation for Enterprise Development Staff & Kauffman Center for Entrepreneurial Leadership. 300p. 1998. 249.00 (*0-9664077-0-9*) Found Enter Dev.

Owners vs. Players: Baseball & Collective Bargaining. James B. Dworkin. LC 81-3472. 320p. 1981. 29.95 (*0-86569-072-3*, Auburn Hse) Greenwood.

Ownership: Early Christian Teaching. Charles Avila. LC 83-8330. 240p. (Orig.). reprint ed. pap. 74.40 (*0-7837-5525-2*, 204529500005) Bks Demand.

Ownership: Strategic Coroprate Governance in the New Economy. Carlsson. text 37.00 (*0-471-63219-8*) Wiley.

Ownership & Control: What's at Stake in the Corporate Governance Debates? Margaret M. Blair. 384p. 1995. 44.95 (*0-8157-0948-X*); pap. 19.95 (*0-8157-0947-1*) Brookings.

Ownership & Development: A Comparison of Domestic & Foreign Firms in Colombian Manufacturing. Brian F. Wallace. LC 86-33255. (Monographs in International Studies; Latin America Ser.: No. 12). 186p. 1987. reprint ed. pap. 57.70 (*0-7837-9600-5*, 206035700005) Bks Demand.

Ownership & Management of Fishery Research Vessels. FAO Staff. 55p. 1984. 12.00 (*92-5-101374-8*, F2619, Pub. by FAO) Bernan Associates.

Ownership & Performance in Electric Utilities: The International Evidence on Privatization & Efficiency. Michael Pollitt. (Oxford Institute for Energy Studies). (Illus.). 256p. 1996. text 98.00 (*0-19-730015-4*) OUP.

Ownership & Productivity of Marine Fishery Resources: An Essay on the Resolution of Conflict in the Use of the Ocean Pastures. Elmer A. Keen. LC 88-794. (Illus.). xii, 122p. (Orig.). 1988. pap. 14.95 (*0-939923-05-X*) M & W Pub Co.

Ownership, Control, & the Future of Housing Policy, 316. Ed. by R. Allen Hays. LC 92-35553. (Contributions in Political Science Ser.: No. 316). 288p. 1993. 65.00 (*0-313-28846-1*, GM8846, Greenwood Pr) Greenwood.

Ownership in Islam. Ayatullah Beheshti. Tr. by Ali R. Afghari. 80p. (Orig.). 1989. pap. text 5.60 (*1-871031-28-1*) Abjad Bk.

Ownership Income of Management. Wilbur G. Lewellen. (Fiscal Studies Ser.: No. 14). 220p. 1971. reprint ed. 57.20 (*0-87014-222-4*) Natl Bur Econ Res.

Ownership of Enterprise. Henry Hansmann. (Illus.). 384p. 1996. 39.95 (*0-674-64970-2*) Belknap Pr.

***Ownership of Enterprise.** Henry Hansmann. 2000. pap. text 22.95 (*0-674-00171-0*) HUP.

Ownership of Jobs: A Comparative Study. Frederic Meyers. (Monograph & Research Ser.: No. 11). 114p. 1964. 5.00 (*0-89215-012-2*) U Cal LA Indus Rel.

Ownership of Rights in Audiovisual Productions: A Comparative Study. Marjut Salokannel. LC 97-16315. 400p. 1997. 225.00 (*90-411-0415-1*) Kluwer Law Intl.

Ownership of Tax-Exempt Securities, 1913-1953. George E. Lent. (Occasional Papers: No. 47). 150p. 1955. reprint ed. 39.00 (*0-87014-361-1*) Natl Bur Econ Res.

Ownership of the Human Body: Philosophical Considerations on the Use of the Human Body & Its Parts in Healthcare. H. Ten Have et al. LC 98-26395. (Philosophy & Medicine Ser.). 1998. 120.00 (*0-7923-5150-9*) Kluwer Academic.

Ownership Solution: Toward a Shared Capitalism for the Twenty-First Century. Jeffrey Gates. LC 97-43298. 432p. 1998. 27.50 (*0-201-32808-9*) Addison-Wesley.

Ownership Solution Tpb: Toward a Shared Capitalism for the Twenty-First Century. Jeff Gates. 416p. 1999. pap. text 16.00 (*0-7382-0131-6*, Pub. by Perseus Pubng) HarpC.

***Owning a No-Cash down Business Made E-Z.** Goldstein. 224p. 2000. pap. 17.95 (*1-56382-455-8*) E-Z Legal.

***Owning a Piece of the Minors.** Jerry Klinkowitz. LC 98-21616. (Writing Baseball Ser.). 177p. 1999. 24.95 (*0-8093-2194-7*) S Ill U Pr.

An Asterisk (*) at the beginning of an entry indicates that the title is appearing for the first time.

Owning a Racehorse. Diane Harvey. 100p. 1990. pap. 40.00 (*0-85131-466-X*, Pub. by J A Allen) St Mut.

Owning & Operating a Service Business. Charles L. Martin. LC 95-74739. (Small Business & Entrepreneurship Ser.). 203p. (Orig.). 1996. pap. 15.95 (*1-56052-362-X*) Crisp Pubns.

Owning It: Zen & the Art of Facing Life. Perle Besserman. LC 97-5153. 192p. 1997. 18.00 (*1-56836-177-7*) Kodansha.

Owning It All. William Kittredge. LC 87-80011. 182p. (Orig.). 1987. pap. 12.00 (*0-915308-96-7*) Graywolf.

Owning Jolene. Shelby Hearon. 1990. mass mkt. 4.95 (*0-446-35944-0*) Warner Bks.

Owning Natural Resources: Mining "Tax Gold" (Depletion Allowances) When Extracting from the Earth's Crust. Holmes F. Crouch. Ed. by Irma J. Crouch. LC 98-70249. (Series 400 Tax Guides: Vol. 402). (Illus.). 224p. 1998. pap. 19.95 (*0-944817-54-8*) Allyear Tax.

***Owning, Raising & Training a German Shepherd Dog.** (Complete Idiot's Guide Ser.). 352p. 1999. write for info. (*1-58245-044-7*) S&S Trade.

Owning, Raising & Training a Jack Russell Terrier. Deborah Britt-Hay. LC 99-10109. (Illus.). 302p. 1999. pap. text. write for info. (*1-58245-042-0*) Macmillan Gen Ref.

Owning, Raising & Training a Rottweiler. Richard G. Beauchamp. LC 99-62691. (Complete Idiot's Guides (Lifestyle) Ser.). (Illus.). 284p. 1999. pap. write for info. (*1-58245-041-2*) Macmillan Gen Ref.

Owning Scientific & Technical Information: Ethical Issues. Ed. by Vivian Weil & John W. Snapper. 520p. (C). 1989. text 40.00 (*0-8135-1454-1*); pap. text 20.00 (*0-8135-1455-X*) Rutgers U Pr.

Owning the Dream: Triumph & Hope in the Projects. Ed. by Flagg Taylor & A. Lawrence Chickering. LC 96-7846. 1996. 19.95 (*1-55815-293-8*) ICS Pr.

Owning the Future: Staking Claims on the Knowledge Frontier. Seth Shulman. LC 98-39653. 224p. 1999. 25.00 (*0-395-84175-5*) HM.

Owning the Right Cat. Phil Maggitti. 1993. 29.95 (*1-56465-111-8*, 16003) Tetra Pr.

Owning the Right Dog. Phil Maggitti. 1993. 29.95 (*1-56465-110-X*, 16001) Tetra Pr.

Owning Your Numbers: An Introduction to Budgeting for Special Libraries. Alice S. Warner. 1992. student ed. 85.00 (*0-87111-387-2*) SLA.

Owning Your Own Shadow: Understanding the Dark Side of the Psyche. Robert A. Johnson. LC 90-56468. 128p. 1993. reprint ed. pap. 11.00 (*0-06-250754-0*, Pub. by Harper SF) HarpC.

Owning Your Territory: How the Top Salespeople Make It to the Top. John Sterner. 168p. 1993. pap. 12.95 (*0-9635371-0-5*); audio 49.95 (*0-9635371-1-3*) Human Res MI.

Owsley County, Kentucky, 1880 Annotated Census. Margaret M. Hayes. 218p. (Orig.). 1994. pap. text 31.00 (*0-7884-0047-9*) Heritage Bk.

Owsley County, Kentucky, 1880 Annotated Census. 2nd rev. ed. Margaret M. Hayes. LC 96-214019. 220p. (Orig.). 1996. pap. 35.00 (*0-7884-0514-4*, H097) Heritage Bk.

Owyhee Trails: The West's Forgotten Corner. Mike Hanley & Ellis Lucia. LC 76-140118. (Illus.). 1973. pap. 14.95 (*0-87004-281-5*) Caxton.

Owzan va Mizan: Weights & Balance. Shah Maghsoud Sadegh Angha. (PER.). 157p. 1975. 110.00 (*0-7812-0738-X*) MTO Printing & Pubn Ctr.

Ox. Piers Anthony. 1976. pap. 3.95 (*0-380-00461-5*, Avon Bks) Morrow Avon.

Ox. Jay Brothers. LC 74-17683. 240p. 1975. 7.95 (*0-672-52076-1*, Bobbs) Macmillan.

Ox. Kwok Man-Ho. LC 93-48006. (Chinese Horoscopes Library). (Illus.). 42p. 1994. 8.95 (*1-56458-600-6*) DK Pub Inc.

Ox Against the Storm: A Biography of Tanaka Shozo-Japan's Conservationist Pioneer. Kenneth Strong. 250p. 1985. 65.00 (*0-904404-20-X*, Pub. by P Norbury Pubns Ltd) St Mut.

Ox Against the Storm: A Biography of Tanaka Shozo: Japan's Conservationist Pioneer. Kenneth Strong. (Illus.). 234p. (C). 1996. pap. text 20.00 (*1-873410-14-X*, Pub. by Curzon Pr Ltd) UH Pr.

Ox-Bow Incident. Walter V. Clark. 1990. 17.50 (*0-8446-0060-1*) Peter Smith.

Ox-Bow Incident. Walter Van Tilburg Clark. 1960. 11.05 (*0-606-01219-2*, Pub. by Turtleback) Demco.

Ox-Bow Incident. Walter Van Tilburg Clark. reprint ed. lib. bdg. 24.95 (*0-88411-135-0*) Amereon Ltd.

Ox-Bow Incident Notes. Clyde Burkholder. (Cliffs Notes Ser.). 56p. 1974. pap. 4.95 (*0-8220-0971-4*, Cliff) IDG Bks.

***Ox-Cart Man.** (J). 1999. 9.95 (*1-56137-457-1*) Novel Units.

Ox-Cart Man. Donald Hall. LC 79-14466. (Illus.). (J). (gr. k-3). 1979. 16.99 (*0-670-53328-9*, Viking Child) Peng Put Young Read.

Ox-Cart Man. Donald Hall. LC 83-8008. (Illus.). 40p. (J). (ps-3). 1983. pap. 5.99 (*0-14-050441-9*, PuffinBks) Peng Put Young Read.

Ox-Cart Man. Donald Hall. (Picture Puffin Ser.). (Illus.). (J). 1983. 11.19 (*0-606-02886-2*, Pub. by Turtleback) Demco.

Ox-Cart Man. unabridged ed. Donald Hall. (J). (gr. k-3). 1984. pap. 15.95 incl. audio (*0-941078-40-X*) Live Oak Media.

Ox-Cart Man. unabridged ed. Donald Hall. Tr. by Barbara Cooney. (J). (gr. k-3). 1984. 24.95 incl. audio (*0-941078-42-6*) Live Oak Media.

Ox-Cart Man, 4 bks., Set. unabridged ed. Donald Hall. Tr. by Barbara Cooney. (J). (gr. k-3). 1984. pap., teacher ed. 31.95 incl. audio (*0-941078-41-8*) Live Oak Media.

Ox-Cart Man: A Study Guide. G. Christopher. Ed. by J. Friedland & R. Kessler. (Little Novel-Ties Ser.). (J). (gr. k-2). 1997. pap. text 14.95 (*0-7675-0170-5*) Lrn Links.

Ox-Cart Man Study Guide. Rebecca Gilleland. 28p. (J). (gr. 1-3). 1993. student ed., ring bd. 9.99 (*1-58609-117-4*) Progeny Pr WI.

Ox in the Ditch: Bible Interpretation As the Fundation of Christian Ethics. Kerry Duke. LC 93-24149. 1993. 6.95 (*0-929540-16-6*) Pub Designs.

Ox in the Ditch: Nine Southern Stories of the Forties. Tom Adams. 200p. 1995. pap. 12.95 (*0-9648638-1-2*) T Berryhill.

Ox of the Wonderful Horns: And Other African Folktales. Ashley Bryan. LC 75-154749. (Illus.). 48p. (J). (gr. k-4). 1993. 14.95 (*0-689-31799-9*) Atheneum Yung Read.

Ox on the Roof. James Harding. LC 84-19879. (Music Reprint Ser.). 261p. 1986. reprint ed. 25.00 (*0-306-76256-0*) Da Capo.

Ox Tale. Yvonne Reynolds. LC 98-96220. (Illus.). 24p. (J). (gr. 2-5). 1998. pap. write for info. (*0-9650824-1-5*) Lolot Pr.

Ox, the Ass, the Oyster. 2nd ed. Ed. by Marie Einspruch & Henry Einspruch. 91p. 1975. pap. 3.99 (*1-880226-11-1*) M J Pubs.

Oxalis: A Story of Renewal. Keith G. Davis. (Illus.). 64p. 1998. pap. 16.95 (*0-9647751-2-3*) Clayton Paige Pubng.

Oxazoles, Vol. 45. I. J. Turchi. LC 85-12478. (Chemistry of Heterocyclic Compounds, a Series of Monographs: Vol. 45). 1064p. 1986. 689.00 (*0-471-86958-9*) Wiley.

***Oxbow Deed.** large type ed. D. B. Newton. LC 00-39531. 2000. write for info. (*0-7838-9093-1*, G K Hall Lrg Type) Mac Lib Ref.

Oxboy. Anne Mazer. 112p. (YA). (gr. 10 up). 1999. reprint ed. pap. 6.95 (*0-89255-240-9*) Persea Bks.

Oxcart Catholicism on Fifth Avenue: The Impact of the Puerto Rican Migration upon the Archdiocese of New York. Ana M. Diaz-Stevens. LC 92-53747. (Studies in American Catholicism: Vol. 12). (C). 1993. text 40.50 (*0-268-01509-0*) U of Notre Dame Pr.

Oxcart Catholicism on Fifth Avenue: The Impact of the Puerto Rican Migration upon the Archdiocese of New York. Ana M. Diaz-Stevens. LC 92-53747. (Notre Dame Studies in American Catholicism: Vol. 12). (C). 1995. reprint ed. pap. text 15.00 (*0-268-01510-4*) U of Notre Dame Pr.

Oxcart Trail see Krause Trio

Oxenbury Boxed Set 4 Baby Board Books. Helen Oxenbury. (J). 1996. 8.99 (*0-689-80608-6*) S&S Bks Yung.

Oxfam Emergency Water Supplies Manuals, Set. Oxfam Staff. (C). 1995. pap. 47.50 (*0-85598-239-X*, Pub. by Oxfam Pub) Stylus Pub VA.

Oxfam Emergency Well Digging Manuals. Oxfam Staff. (C). 1995. pap. 47.50 (*0-85598-238-1*, Pub. by Oxfam Pub) Stylus Pub VA.

Oxfam 50: Our World in Photographs. (Illus.). 144p. 1992. pap. 12.99 (*1-85585-113-X*, Pub. by Oxfam Pub) Stylus Pub VA.

Oxfam Handbook of Development & Relief, 3 vols., Set. Deborah Eade et al. LC 96-137960. (Information & Reference Ser.). 1200p. (C). 1995. boxed set 39.95 (*0-85598-274-8*, Pub. by Oxfam Pub) Stylus Pub VA.

Oxfam Handbook of Development & Relief, Vol. 1. Deborah Eade et al. LC 96-137960. (Information & Reference Ser.). 1272p. (C). 1995. 79.95 (*0-85598-273-X*, Pub. by Oxfam Pub) Stylus Pub VA.

Oxfam Handbook Resource Directory. Oxfam Staff. LC 96-155609. 216p. 1996. pap. 15.00 (*0-85598-309-4*, Pub. by Oxfam Pub) Stylus Pub VA.

Oxfam Poverty Report: Information & Reference. Kevin Watkins. LC 96-139918. (Information & Reference Ser.). (Illus.). 240p. (C). 1995. pap. 15.95 (*0-85598-318-3*, Pub. by Oxfam Pub) Stylus Pub VA.

Oxfam Vegetarian Cookbook. Compiled by Rose Elliot. (Illus.). 192p. 8.99 (*0-09-175437-2*, Pub. by Oxfam Pub) Stylus Pub VA.

Oxfam Vegetarian Cooking for Children. Ed. by Rose Elliot. (Illus.). 192p. 1995. pap. 8.99 (*0-09-180816-2*, Pub. by Oxfam Pub) Stylus Pub VA.

Oxford. Andrew Duncan. (Illus.). (C). 1989. 25.00 (*1-85368-055-9*, Pub. by New5 Holland) St Mut.

Oxford. Insight Guides Staff. (Insight Guides). 1998. pap. text 7.95 (*0-88729-552-5*) Langenscheidt.

Oxford. Insight Guides Staff. (Insight Guides). 1998. pap. text 21.95 (*0-88729-734-X*) Langenschiedt.

Oxford. 3rd ed. Jan Morris. (Illus.). 304p. 1988. pap. 13.95 (*0-19-282065-6*) OUP.

Oxford: A Cultural & Literary Companion. David Horan. LC 99-38631. (Cities of the Imagination Ser.). 256p. 1999. pap. 15.00 (*1-56656-348-8*) Interlink Pub.

Oxford: An Architectural Guide. Peter Howard & Helena Webster. 320p. 1998. pap. 12.95 (*1-899858-47-4*) Watsn-Guptill.

Oxford: An Architectural Guide. Geoffrey Tyack. LC 98-159750. (Illus.). 384p. 1998. text 65.00 (*0-19-817419-5*) OUP.

Oxford: An Architectural Guide. Geoffrey Tyack. (Illus.). 384p. 1998. reprint ed. pap. 21.50 (*0-19-817423-3*) OUP.

Oxford: Words & Watercolors. Ed. by Elaine Wilson. (Illus.). 112p. 1985. 25.00 (*0-85683-090-9*, Pub. by Shepheard-Walwyn Pubs) Paul & Co Pubs.

Oxford A to Z of Word Games. Tony Augarde. (Illus.). 270p. 1996. pap. 9.95 (*0-19-866231-9*) OUP.

Oxford Activity Books for Children, Bk. 1. Christopher Clark. (Illus.). 32p. 1984. pap. text 5.95 (*0-19-421830-9*) OUP.

Oxford Activity Books for Children, Bk. 2. Christopher Clark. (Illus.). 32p. 1984. pap. text 5.95 (*0-19-421831-7*) OUP.

Oxford Activity Books for Children, Bk. 3. Christopher Clark. (Illus.). 32p. 1984. pap. text 5.95 (*0-19-421832-5*) OUP.

Oxford Activity Books for Children, Bk. 4. Christopher Clark. (Illus.). 32p. 1985. pap. text 5.95 (*0-19-421833-3*) OUP.

Oxford Activity Books for Children, Bk. 5. Christopher Clark. (Illus.). 32p. 1985. pap. text 5.95 (*0-19-421834-1*) OUP.

Oxford Activity Books for Children, Bk. 6. Christopher Clark. (Illus.). 32p. 1985. pap. text 5.95 (*0-19-421835-X*) OUP.

Oxford Activity Books for Children: Card Pack A, Bks. 1-3. Christopher Clark. (Illus.). 1987. 7.95 (*0-19-421851-1*) OUP.

Oxford Advanced Learner's Dictionary. 4th deluxe ed. A. S. Hornby. Ed. by A. P. Cowie. (Illus.). 1598p. 1991. 28.95 (*0-19-431296-8*) OUP.

Oxford Advanced Learner's Dictionary. 5th ed. A. S. Hornby. (Illus.). 1,438p. 1995. pap. 24.95 (*0-19-431180-5*) OUP.

Oxford Advanced Learner's Dictionary. 5th ed. A. S. Hornby. Ed. by Jonathan Crowther. (Illus.). 1,438p. 1995. text 26.95 (*0-19-431421-9*) OUP.

Oxford Advanced Learner's Dictionary: Of Current English. 5th ed. A. S. Hornby. Ed. by Jonathan Crowther & Michael Ashby. (Illus.). 1428p. 1995. pap. 21.95 (*0-19-431422-7*) OUP.

Oxford Advanced Learner's Encyclopedic Dictionary. Ed. by Jonathan Crowther et al. (Illus.). 1,120p. 1995. pap. text 23.95 (*0-19-431310-7*) OUP.

Oxford Advanced Learner's English-Chinese Dictionary. 4th rev. ed. Ed. by A. S. Hornsby. (CHI & ENG., Illus.). 1910p. 1995. pap. 14.95 (*0-19-585603-1*) OUP.

***Oxford Albanian-English Dictionary.** Leonard D. Newmark. (ALB & ENG.). 1056p. 2000. pap. 27.50 (*0-19-860322-3*) OUP.

Oxford Amer.dictionary. Ed. by Stuart Bergflexner et al. 832p. 1980. pap. 12.50 (*0-380-51052-9*, Avon Bks) Morrow Avon.

Oxford Amer.dictionary. Ed. by Stuart Bergflexner et al. 832p. 1982. mass mkt. 4.99 (*0-380-60772-7*, Avon Bks) Morrow Avon.

Oxford American Children's Encyclopedia, 9 vols. LC 97-40343. (Illus.). 1712p. (J). 1999. 300.00 (*0-19-511081-1*) OUP.

Oxford American Desk Dictionary. Ed. by Frank Abate. (Illus.). 816p. 1998. 12.95 (*0-19-512673-4*) OUP.

Oxford American Desk Thesaurus. Ed. by Christine A. Lindberg. 528p. 1998. 12.95 (*0-19-512674-2*) OUP.

Oxford American Dictionary. Compiled by Eugene H. Ehrlich et al. 832p. (C). 1980. 19.95 (*0-19-502795-7*) OUP.

Oxford American Dictionary & Language Guide. Ed. by Frank Abate. (Illus.). 1306p. 1999. 35.00 (*0-19-513449-4*) OUP.

Oxford American Dictionary of Current English. Ed. by Frank Abate. LC 99-39972. (Illus.). 1008p. 1999. 17.95 (*0-19-513374-9*) OUP.

Oxford American Thesaurus of Current English. Ed. by Christine A. Lindberg. LC 99-31092. 863p. 1999. 17.95 (*0-19-513375-7*) OUP.

Oxford American Wordpower Dictionary. Ruth Urbom. LC 98-22115. (Illus.). 800p. 1998. pap. text 12.95 (*0-19-431319-0*) OUP.

***Oxford Anagram Finder.** 526p. 1999. pap. 11.95 (*0-19-860221-9*) OUP.

Oxford & Cambridge. 5th ed. Tyack. 256p. 1999. pap. 19.95 (*0-393-31934-2*) Norton.

Oxford & Cambridge Magazine Vol. 1, Nos. 1-12: Conducted by Members of the Two Universities. Ed. by William Fulford & William Morris. reprint ed. 65.00 (*0-404-19566-0*) AMS Pr.

Oxford & Empire: The Last Lost Cause? Richard Symonds. (Illus.). 408p. 1993. pap. 28.00 (*0-19-820300-4*) OUP.

Oxford & the Pre-Raphaelites. John Whitely. (Illus.). 80p. 1989. text 19.95 (*1-85444-042-X*, 946, Pub. by Ashmolean Mus) A Schwartz & Co.

Oxford & the Pre-Raphaelites. John Whitely. (Illus.). 80p. 1989. pap. 12.95 (*0-907849-94-6*, 946-P, Pub. by Ashmolean Mus) A Schwartz & Co.

Oxford & Working Class Education. Ed. by Sylvia Harrop. 270p. (C). 1987. 60.00 (*0-7855-2390-1*, Pub. by Univ Nottingham) St Mut.

Oxford & Working Class Education: Nineteen Hundred Eight Report Reprinted with Inductory Essays. Ed. by Sylvia Harrop. (C). 1987. 60.00 (*1-85041-018-6*, Pub. by Univ Nottingham) St Mut.

Oxford Anthology of Contemporary Chinese Drama. Ed. by Martha P. Cheung & Jane Lai. LC 97-5298. (Illus.). 900p. 1997. text 105.00 (*0-19-586880-3*) OUP.

Oxford Anthology of English Literature. Incl. Vol. 1. Middle Ages Through the Eighteenth Century. Ed. by Frank Kermode. (Illus.). 2406p. 1973. pap. text 43.95 (*0-19-501657-2*); Vol. 2. 1800 to the Present. Frank Kermode. (Illus.). 2,270p. 1973. pap. text 43.95 (*0-19-501658-0*); (Illus.). 1973. write for info. (*0-318-54869-0*) OUP.

Oxford Anthology of English Poetry Vol. I: Spenser to Crabbe. Ed. by John Wain. 684p. 1991. pap. 17.95 (*0-19-282797-9*) OUP.

Oxford Anthology of English Poetry Vol. II: Blake to Heaney. Ed. by John Wain. 790p. 1991. pap. 17.95 (*0-19-282798-7*) OUP.

Oxford Anthology of Indian Wildlife Hunting & Shooting, 1. Ed. by Mahesh Rangarajan. 456p. 2000. 19.95 (*0-19-564592-8*) OUP.

Oxford Anthology of Indian Wildlife Watching & Conserving, 2. Ed. by Mahesh Rangarajan. 320p. 2000. 19.95 (*0-19-564593-6*) OUP.

Oxford Anthology of Modern Indian Poetry. Ed. by Vinay Dharwadker & A. K. Ramanujan. 286p. 1995. text 19.95 (*0-19-562865-9*) OUP.

Oxford Anthology of Modern Indian Poetry. Ed. by Vinay Dharwadker & A. K. Ramanujan. 286p. 1998. pap. 12.95 (*0-19-563917-0*) OUP.

***Oxford Anthology of Raj Stories.** Ed. by Saros Cowasjee. LC 98-909291. 360p. 1999. text 29.95 (*0-19-564279-1*) OUP.

Oxford Anthology of Shakespeare. William Shakespeare. 416p. 1990. reprint ed. pap. 11.95 (*0-19-282240-3*) OUP.

Oxford Apostles: A Character Study of the Oxford Movement. Geoffrey C. Faber. LC 75-30022. reprint ed. 72.50 (*0-404-14027-0*) AMS Pr.

Oxford Bible Atlas. 3rd ed. Ed. by Herbert G. May. (Illus.). 144p. 1985. 30.00 (*0-19-143452-3*); pap. 21.95 (*0-19-143451-5*) OUP.

Oxford Blood: A Jemima Shore Mystery. Antonia Fraser. LC 85-15265. (Jemima Shore Mysteries Ser.). 224p. 1998. pap. 10.00 (*0-393-31824-9*, Norton Paperbks) Norton.

Oxford, Bodleian Library, Ms. Lat. liturg b. 5. Ed. by David Hiley. (Veroffentlichungen Mittelalterlicher Musikhandschriften-Publications of Mediaeval Manuscripts: Vol. 20). (ENG & LAT.). xix, 274p. 1995. lib. bdg. 300.00 (*0-931902-93-2*) Inst Mediaeval Mus.

Oxford, Bodleian Library, MS.Canon.Misc. 213. fac. ed. Ed. by Margaret Bent. (Late Medieval & Early Renaissance Music in Facsimile Ser.). (Illus.). 376p. 1995. lib. bdg. 175.00 (*0-226-23706-0*) U Ch Pr.

Oxford, Bodleian Library, MSS Music School E 376-381. Ed. by Howard Brown et al. (Renaissance Music in Facsimile Ser.: Vol. 15). 1456p. 1986. text 70.00 (*0-8240-1464-2*) Garland.

Oxford Book of Adventure Stories. Ed. by Joseph Bristow. 436p. 1995. 35.00 (*0-19-214214-3*) OUP.

Oxford Book of Aging: Reflections on the Journey of Life. Thomas R. Cole & Mary C. Winkler. 432p. 1994. 30.00 (*0-19-507369-X*) OUP.

Oxford Book of America Light Verse. Ed. by William Harmon. 590p. 1979. text 39.95 (*0-19-502509-1*) OUP.

Oxford Book of American Detective Stories. Ed. by Tony Hillerman & Rosemary Herbert. 704p. (C). 1996. 35.00 (*0-19-508581-7*) OUP.

Oxford Book of American Detective Stories. Ed. by Tony Hillerman & Rosemary Herbert. 704p. 1997. reprint ed. pap. 15.95 (*0-19-511792-1*) OUP.

Oxford Book of American Short Stories. Ed. by Joyce Carol Oates. 784p. 1992. 40.00 (*0-19-507065-8*) OUP.

Oxford Book of American Short Stories. Ed. by Joyce Carol Oates. 784p. 1994. reprint ed. pap. 18.95 (*0-19-509262-7*) OUP.

Oxford Book of American Verse. Francis O. Matthiessen. 1188p. (YA). (gr. 9 up). 1950. text 49.95 (*0-19-500049-8*) OUP.

Oxford Book of Animal Poems. Ed. by Michael Harrison & Christopher Stuart-Clark. (Illus.). 160p. (YA). (gr. 5 up). 1997. pap. 12.95 (*0-19-276148-X*) OUP.

Oxford Book of Animal Stories. Selected by Dennis Pepper. LC 94-234038. (Illus.). 320p. (YA). (gr. 4 up). 1994. 25.00 (*0-19-278134-0*) OUP.

Oxford Book of Animal Stories. Ed. by Dennis Pepper. (Illus.). 304p. (YA). (gr. 5-9). 1999. pap. 12.95 (*0-19-278160-X*) OUP.

Oxford Book of Aphorisms. Compiled by John Gross. 400p. 1987. pap. 14.95 (*0-19-282015-X*) OUP.

Oxford Book of Australian Essays. Ed. by Imre Salusineszky. (Oxford Books of Prose). 304p. 1998. text 39.95 (*0-19-553739-4*) OUP.

Oxford Book of Australian Ghost Stories. Ken Gelder. 312p. (C). 1996. 39.95 (*0-19-553560-X*) OUP.

Oxford Book of Australian Letters. Brenda Niall & John Thompson. LC 98-198961. 336p. 1999. 35.00 (*0-19-553985-0*) OUP.

Oxford Book of Australian Religious Verse. Kevin Hart. 296p. (C). 1996. 39.95 (*0-19-553498-0*) OUP.

Oxford Book of Australian Short Stories. Ed. by Michael Wilding. 368p. 1995. 35.00 (*0-19-553610-X*) OUP.

Oxford Book of Australian Travel Writing. Ed. by Roslyn Pesman et al. LC 97-108823. 352p. 1997. 49.95 (*0-19-553640-1*) OUP.

Oxford Book of Australian Women's Verse. Susan Lever. 282p. (C). 1996. pap. text 29.95 (*0-19-553505-7*) OUP.

Oxford Book of Ballads, 2 vols in 1. Ed. by Arthur Quiller-Couch. 800p. reprint ed. 55.00 (*0-403-08625-6*) Somerset Pub.

Oxford Book of Board Games. David Parlett. LC 99-229056. (Illus.). 400p. 1999. 45.00 (*0-19-212998-8*) OUP.

Oxford Book of British Bird Names. W. B. Lockwood. 184p. 1984. 18.95 (*0-19-214155-4*) OUP.

Oxford Book of Caribbean Short Stories. Ed. by Stewart Brown & John Wickham. LC 98-29731. 512p. 1999. pap. 18.95 (*0-19-283241-7*) OUP.

Oxford Book of Carols: Music Edition, with Notes. Ed. by Percy Dearmer et al. 478p. 1985. pap. 23.95 (*0-19-353315-4*) OUP.

Oxford Book of Children's Verse. Ed. by Iona Opie & Peter Opie. (Illus.). 440p. (J). 1995. reprint ed. pap. 15.95 (*0-19-282349-3*) OUP.

Oxford Book of Children's Verse in America. Ed. by Donald Hall. LC 84-20755. (Illus.). 319p. (J). 1985. text 35.00 (*0-19-503539-9*) OUP.

Oxford Book of Children's Verse in America. Ed. by Donald Hall. 368p. (J). (gr. 3 up). 1990. reprint ed. pap. 15.95 (*0-19-506761-4*) OUP.

Oxford Book of Christmas Poems. Ed. by Michael Harrison & Christopher Stuart-Clark. (Illus.). 160p. (YA). 1999. pap. 12.95 (*0-19-276214-1*) OUP.

Oxford Book of Christmas Stories. Ed. by Dennis Pepper. (Illus.). 224p. (YA). 1999. pap. 12.95 (*0-19-278161-8*) OUP.

An Asterisk (*) at the beginning of an entry indicates that the title is appearing for the first time.

*__Oxford Book of Classical Verse.__ Ed. by Adrian Poole & Jeremy Maule. (Oxford Books of Verse). 656p. 2000. pap. 18.95 (0-19-282528-3) OUP.

Oxford Book of Comic Verses. Ed. by John Gross. 546p. 1996. pap. 14.95 (0-19-283207-7) OUP.

Oxford Book of Creatures. Ed. by Fleur Adcock & Jacqueline Simms. 400p. (C). 1996. 30.00 (0-19-214226-7) OUP.

*__Oxford Book of Days.__ Bonnie J. Blackburn & Leofranc Holford-Strevens. 640p. 2000. 18.95 (0-19-866260-2) OUP.

Oxford Book of Death. Ed. by D. J. Enright. 368p. 1983. 30.00 (0-19-214129-5) OUP.

*__Oxford Book of Detective Stories.__ Ed. by Patricia Craig. LC 99-45926. 587p. 2000. pap. 18.95 (0-19-288067-5) OUP.

Oxford Book of Detective Stories. Ed. by Tony Hillerman & Rosemary Herbert. 1996. 25.00 (0-614-96759-7) OUP.

Oxford Book of English Detective Stories. Ed. by Patricia Craig. 576p. 1990. 35.00 (0-19-214187-2) OUP.

Oxford Book of English Detective Stories. Ed. by Patricia Craig. 576p. 1992. pap. 14.95 (0-19-282968-8) OUP.

Oxford Book of English Ghost Stories. Ed. by R. A. Gilbert. 524p. 1989. reprint ed. pap. 14.95 (0-19-282666-2) OUP.

Oxford Book of English Love Stories. Ed. by John Sutherland. 464p. (C). 1996. 30.00 (0-19-214237-2) OUP.

Oxford Book of English Love Stories. Ed. by John Sutherland. 464p. 1997. reprint ed. pap. 15.95 (0-19-283268-9) OUP.

Oxford Book of English Madrigals. Ed. by Philip Ledger. 408p. 1979. pap. text 17.95 (0-19-343664-7) OUP.

Oxford Book of English Mystical Verse. Ed. by D. H. Nicholson & A. H. Lee. LC 96-43195. 648p. 1997. pap. 24.95 (1-889051-16-0) Acrpls Bks CO.

Oxford Book of English Mystical Verse. Ed. by D. H. Nicholson & A. H. Lee. LC 96-43195. 648p. 1997. reprint ed. 39.95 (1-889051-02-0, I Lvl) Acrpls Bks CO.

Oxford Book of English Short Stories. Ed. by A. S. Byatt. (Oxford Books of Prose). 470p. 1998. 30.00 (0-19-214238-0) OUP.

*__Oxford Book of English Short Stories.__ A. S. Byatt. 2000. pap. 18.95 (0-19-288111-6) OUP.

Oxford Book of English Verse. Christopher Ricks. LC 99-20831. 750p. 1999. 39.95 (0-19-214182-1) OUP.

Oxford Book of Essays. Ed. by John Gross. 704p. 1999. pap. 19.95 (0-19-288106-X) OUP.

Oxford Book of Fantasy Stories. Ed. by Tom Shippey. 528p. 1994. 30.00 (0-19-214216-X) OUP.

Oxford Book of Fantasy Stories. Selected by Tom Shippey. 522p. 1995. pap. 15.95 (0-19-282398-1) OUP.

Oxford Book of French-Canadian. Ed. by Richard Teleky. (Illus.). 286p. 1984. pap. text 16.95 (0-19-540298-7) OUP.

Oxford Book of French Chansons. Ed. by Frank Dobbins. 322p. 1987. pap. text 19.95 (0-19-343539-X) OUP.

Oxford Book of Gothic Tales. Ed. by Chris Baldick. LC 92-41146. 566p. 1993. pap. 15.95 (0-19-283117-8) OUP.

Oxford Book of Hebrew Short Stories. Ed. by Glenda Abramson. 422p. 1996. 35.00 (0-19-214206-2) OUP.

Oxford Book of Hebrew Short Stories. Ed. by Glenda Abramson. 422p. 1997. reprint ed. pap. 15.95 (0-19-288039-X) OUP.

Oxford Book of Historical Stories. Ed. by Michael Cox & Jack Adrian. 464p. 1995. 35.00 (0-19-214219-4) OUP.

Oxford Book of Humorous Prose. Ed. by Frank Muir. 1,196p. 1992. pap. 18.95 (0-19-282959-9) OUP.

Oxford Book of Ireland. Ed. by Patricia Craig. (Illus.). 530p. 1998. 35.00 (0-19-214261-5) OUP.

Oxford Book of Ireland. Ed. by Patricia Craig. (Oxford Books of Verse Ser.). (Illus.). 536p. 1999. pap. 17.95 (0-19-288112-4) OUP.

Oxford Book of Irish Short Stories. Ed. by William Trevor. 586p. 1989. 35.00 (0-19-214180-5) OUP.

Oxford Book of Irish Short Stories. Ed. by William Trevor. 584p. 1991. reprint ed. pap. 14.95 (0-19-282845-2, 12351) OUP.

Oxford Book of Italian Madrigals. Ed. by Alec Harman. 332p. 1983. pap. text 19.95 (0-19-343647-7) OUP.

Oxford Book of Japanese Short Stories. Ed. & Intro. by Theodore Goossen. 484p. 1997. pap. 19.95 (0-19-283304-9) OUP.

Oxford Book of Jewish Stories. Ed. by Ilan Stavans. LC 98-16631. 512p. 1998. 30.00 (0-19-511019-6) OUP.

Oxford Book of Latin American Essays. Ed. by Ilan Stavans. LC 97-10976. 528p. 1997. 35.00 (0-19-509234-1) OUP.

Oxford Book of Latin American Short Stories. Ed. by Roberto G. Echevarria. LC 97-5395. 496p. 1997. 35.00 (0-19-509590-1) OUP.

Oxford Book of Latin American Short Stories. Roberto Gonzalez Echevarria. 496p. 1999. pap. 19.95 (0-19-513085-5) OUP.

Oxford Book of Legal Anecdotes. Ed. by Michael F. Gilbert. LC 85-13857. 350p. 1989. reprint ed. pap. 14.95 (0-19-282112-1) OUP.

Oxford Book of Letters. Ed. by Frank Kermode & Anita Kermode. LC 94-36412. (Illus.). 584p. 1995. text 35.00 (0-19-214188-0) OUP.

Oxford Book of Letters. Ed. by Frank Kermode & Anita Kermode. LC 96-16939. (Illus.). 584p. 1996. reprint ed. pap. 16.95 (0-19-282522-4) OUP.

Oxford Book of Local Verses. Ed. by John Holloway. (Oxford Books of Verse). 352p. 1987. 35.00 (0-19-214149-X) OUP.

Oxford Book of London. Ed. by Paul Bailey. 400p. 1996. 30.00 (0-19-214192-9) OUP.

Oxford Book of Marriage. Ed. by Helge Rubenstein. 400p. 1990. 35.00 (0-19-214150-3) OUP.

Oxford Book of Medieval Latin Verse. Ed. by Frederick J. Raby. 1959. 59.00 (0-19-812119-9) OUP.

Oxford Book of Memory. James McConkey. 1996. 30.00 (0-614-96853-4) OUP.

Oxford Book of Military Anecdotes. Ed. by Max Hastings. LC 85-5014. 524p. 1986. pap. 14.95 (0-19-520528-6) OUP.

Oxford Book of Modern Australian Verse. Ed. by Peter Porter. 310p. 1999. pap. 29.95 (0-19-550706-1) OUP.

Oxford Book of Modern Fairy Tales. Ed. by Alison Lurie. 480p. 1994. reprint ed. pap. 14.95 (0-19-282385-X) OUP.

Oxford Book of Modern Women's Stories. Ed. by Patricia Craig. 544p. 1994. 30.00 (0-19-214232-1) OUP.

Oxford Book of Modern Women's Stories. Ed. by Patricia Craig. 538p. 1995. pap. 13.95 (0-19-283204-2) OUP.

Oxford Book of Nature Writing. Richard Mabey. 272p. 1995. pap. 15.00 (0-19-282519-4) OUP.

Oxford Book of Nature Writing. Ed. by Richard Mabey. 272p. 1995. 30.00 (0-19-214172-4) OUP.

Oxford Book of New Zealand Short Stories. Selected by Vincent O'Sullivan. 464p. 1994. pap. text 19.95 (0-19-558291-8) OUP.

Oxford Book of Prayer. Ed. by George Appleton. (Illus.). 416p. 1985. 35.00 (0-19-213222-9) OUP.

Oxford Book of Prayer. Ed. by George Appleton. (Illus.). 416p. 1989. pap. 14.95 (0-19-282108-3) OUP.

Oxford Book of Royal Anecdotes. Ed. by Elizabeth Longford. (Illus.). 572p. 1989. 27.50 (0-19-214153-8) OUP.

Oxford Book of Satirical Verse. Ed. by Geoffrey Grigson. LC 94-30212. 1983. pap. 12.95 (0-19-281425-7) OUP.

Oxford Book of Scary Tales. Ed. by Dennis Pepper. (J). Date not set. 14.95 (0-614-19310-9) OUP.

Oxford Book of Science Fiction Stories. Ed. by Tom Shippey. 614p. 1993. pap. 15.95 (0-19-283167-4) OUP.

Oxford Book of Scottish Short Stories. Ed. by Douglas Dunn. 504p. 1996. reprint ed. pap. 15.95 (0-19-282521-6) OUP.

Oxford Book of Sea Stories. Ed. by Tony Tanner. 428p. 1995. pap. 16.95 (0-19-282415-5) OUP.

Oxford Book of Short Poems. Ed. by Patrick J. Kavanagh & James Michie. 352p. 1987. pap. 14.95 (0-19-282073-7) OUP.

Oxford Book of Short Poems. Ed. by James Michie & Patrick J. Kavanagh. 1986. pap. 9.95 (0-685-10547-4) OUP.

Oxford Book of Short Stories. Selected by V. S. Pritchett. 576p. 1981. text 35.00 (0-19-214116-3) OUP.

Oxford Book of Short Stories. Ed. by V. S. Pritchett. 558p. 1988. pap. 15.95 (0-19-282113-X) OUP.

*__Oxford Book of Sonnets.__ Ed. by John Fuller. 352p. 2000. 20.00 (0-19-214267-4) OUP.

Oxford Book of Spy Stories. Ed. by Michael Cox. 376p. (C). 1996. 30.00 (0-19-214242-9) OUP.

Oxford Book of Spy Stories. Ed. by Michael Cox. 376p. 1997. reprint ed. pap. 14.95 (0-19-283267-0) OUP.

*__Oxford Book of Stories by Canadian Women in English.__ Ed. by Rosemary Sullivan. 500p. 2000. 24.95 (0-19-541426-8) OUP.

Oxford Book of Story Poems. Michael Harrison & Christopher Stuart-Clark. (Illus.). 176p. (YA). (gr. 3 up). 1990. 25.00 (0-19-276087-4) OUP.

Oxford Book of Story Poems. Michael Harrison & Christopher Stuart-Clark. LC 96-166418. (Illus.). 176p. (YA). (gr. 3 up). 1996. pap. 14.95 (0-19-276103-X) OUP.

Oxford Book of Story Poems. Ed. by Michael Harrison & Christopher Stuart-Clark. (Illus.). 176p. (J). 2000. pap. 14.95 (0-19-276212-5) OUP.

Oxford Book of the American South: Testimony, Memory & Fiction. Ed. by Edward L. Ayers & Bradley C. Mittendorf. LC 96-45135. 608p. 1997. 30.00 (0-19-508522-1) OUP.

Oxford Book of the American South: Testimony, Memory, & Fiction. Ed. by Edward L. Ayers & Bradley C. Mittendorf. 608p. 1998. reprint ed. pap. 19.95 (0-19-512493-6) OUP.

Oxford Book of the Sea. Ed. by Jonathan Raban. LC 92-41179. 542p. (Orig.). 1993. pap. 16.95 (0-19-283148-8) OUP.

Oxford Book of Travel Stories. Patricia Craig. 458p. 1996. 35.00 (0-19-214253-4) OUP.

Oxford Book of Travel Stories. Ed. by Patricia Craig. 458p. 1997. pap. 14.95 (0-19-288031-4) OUP.

Oxford Book of Tudor Anthems. Christopher Morris. (Illus.). 360p. 1978. pap. 17.95 (0-19-353325-1) OUP.

Oxford Book of Twentieth Century English Verse. Ed. by Philip Larkin. 692p. 1973. 35.00 (0-19-812137-7) OUP.

Oxford Book of Twentieth-Century Ghost Stories. Michael Cox. 446p. 1997. pap. 12.95 (0-19-288038-1) OUP.

Oxford Book of War Poetry. Ed. by Jon Stallworthy. 352p. 1984. 30.00 (0-19-214125-2) OUP.

Oxford Book of Wild Flowers: Pocket Edition. S. Ary. (Illus.). 240p. 1976. pap. 9.95 (0-19-910013-6) OUP.

*__Oxford Book of Women's Writing in the United States.__ Ed. by Linda Wagner-Martin & Cathy N. Davidson. 596p. 1999. pap. 18.95 (0-19-513245-9) OUP.

Oxford Book Of Work. Keith Thomas. LC 98-36795. 656p. 1999. 35.00 (0-19-214217-8) OUP.

Oxford Business English: Grammar & Practice. Michael Duckworth. (Illus.). 224p. 1996. pap. text 12.95 (0-19-457068-1) OUP.

Oxford Business English Skills: Effective Presentations. Jeremy Comfort. (Illus.). 48p. 1996. pap. text, teacher ed. 7.50 (0-19-457089-4) OUP.

*__Oxford Cartoon-Strip German Vocabulary Builder.__ Ed. by Neil Morris & Roswitha Morris. (Illus.). 80p. 2000. pap. 11.95 (0-19-860305-3) OUP.

Oxford Chekhov. Anton Chekhov. Ed. by Ronald Hingley. Incl. Vol. 1. Short Plays. 222p. 1968. 65.00 (0-19-211349-6); Vol. 8. Stories, 1895-1897. Tr. by Ronald Hingley. 340p. 1965. text 65.00 (0-19-211340-2); write for info. (0-318-54870-4) OUP.

Oxford Children's Book of Famous People. Oxford University Press Staff. LC 99-461930. (Illus.). 384p. (J). (gr. 4-7). 1999. 37.50 (0-19-521517-6) OUP.

Oxford Children's Book of Famous People. 2nd ed. LC 99-461930. (Illus.). 384p. (YA). 2000. pap. 19.95 (0-19-521518-4) OUP.

Oxford Children's Book of Science. Charles Taylor & Stephen Pople. (Illus.). 192p. (J). write for info. (0-19-910036-5) OUP.

Oxford Children's Book of Science. Charles Taylor & Stephen Pople. (J). 1996. 29.95 (0-614-15686-6) OUP.

Oxford Children's Book of Science: Basic Principles of Science-Explained in Everyday Language. Charles Taylor & Stephen Pople. (Illus.). 192p. (J). (gr. 5-9). 1996. 30.00 (0-19-521165-0) OUP.

Oxford Children's Book of Science: Basic Principles of Science-Explained in Everyday Language. Charles Taylor & Stephen Pople. (Illus.). 192p. (YA). 1999. pap. 16.95 (0-19-521535-4) OUP.

*__Oxford Children's Book of the 20th Century.__ Stewart Ross. LC 98-31233. (Illus.). 48p. (J). 1999. text 18.95 (0-19-521488-9) OUP.

Oxford Children's Dictionary. 3rd ed. Ed. by Alan Spooner. LC 93-17585. (Illus.). (J). 1993. 7.99 (0-19-861297-4) OUP.

Oxford Children's Encyclopedia. Ed. by Mary Worrall. (Illus.). 1641p. (J). (gr. 3-8). 1993. 200.00 (0-19-910136-1) OUP.

*__Oxford Children's History of the World.__ Neil Grant. (Illus.). 192p. (J). 2000. text 25.95 (0-19-910500-6) OUP.

Oxford Children's Picture Dictionary. L. A. Hill & C. Innes. (ENG & ITA., Illus.). 56p. 1996. pap. text 9.95 (0-19-431266-6); pap. text 9.95 (0-19-431263-1) OUP.

Oxford Children's Science Library, 3 vols., Set. Ed. by Oxford University Press Staff. (Illus.). 160p. (J). (gr. 3-9). 1995. 120.00 (0-19-521142-1) OUP.

*__Oxford Choral Classics: Christmas Motets.__ 128p. 1999. 10.95 (0-19-343704-X) OUP.

Oxford Choral Classics: European Sacred Music. Ed. by John Rutter. (Oxford Choral Classics). 360p. 1996. pap. 15.95 (0-19-343695-7) OUP.

Oxford Choral Classics: Opera Choruses. Ed. by John Rutter & Clifford Bartlett. 384p. 1995. pap. 15.95 (0-19-343693-0) OUP.

Oxford Choral Classics: Opera Choruses. Ed. by John Rutter & Clifford Bartlett. (Oxford Choral Classics Ser.). (C). 1995. pap. 16.50 incl. audio (0-19-343699-X); 27.95 (0-19-343700-7) OUP.

Oxford Christmas Storybook. Dennis Pepper. (Illus.). 166p. (J). (gr. 1-5). 1998. reprint ed. pap. 12.95 (0-19-278136-7) OUP.

Oxford Classical Dictionary. 3rd ed. Ed. by Simon Hornblower & Antony Spawforth. LC 96-5352. 1,696p. 1996. 99.95 (0-19-866172-X) OUP.

*__Oxford Classical Dictionary.__ 3rd ed. Ed. by Simon & Antony. 1640p. 2000. 150.00 incl. cd-rom (0-19-521693-8) OUP.

Oxford Collection of the Drawings of Roger de Gagnieres & the Royal Tombs of Saint-Denis. Elizabeth A. Brown. LC 87-72867. (Transactions Ser.: Vol. 78, Pt. 5). (Illus.). (C). 1988. pap. 12.00 (0-87169-785-8, T785-BRE) Am Philos.

*__Oxford College Italian Dictionary.__ Debora Mazza & Lexus (Firm). LC 98-49987. 380p. 2000. pap. 11.95 (0-19-860282-0) OUP.

*__Oxford College Spanish Dictionary.__ 2nd ed. Ed. by Carol Styles Carvajal & Jane Horwood. LC 98-49985. (SPA.). 1024p. 2000. pap. 9.95 (0-19-860281-2) OUP.

Oxford Color Dictionary. rev. ed. Maurice Waite. 800p. 1998. pap. 8.95 (0-19-860202-2) OUP.

Oxford Color Dictionary & Thesaurus. Ed. by Sara Hawker. 608p. 1996. pap. 8.95 (0-19-860038-0) OUP.

Oxford Color French Dictionary: French-English, English-French; Francais-Anglais, Anglais-Francais. rev. ed. Annette Rieck. 576p. 1998. pap. 7.95 (0-19-860190-5) OUP.

Oxford Color German Dictionary: German-English, English-German; Deutsch-Englisch, Englisch-Deutsch. rev. ed. Compiled by Gunhild Prowe & Jill Schneider. 528p. 1998. pap. 8.95 (0-19-860189-1) OUP.

Oxford Color Italian Dictionary. 2nd rev. ed. Ed. by Debora Mazza. 512p. 1999. pap. 9.95 (0-19-860251-0) OUP.

*__Oxford Color Portuguese Dictionary.__ John Whitlam & Lia Correia Raitt. 464p. 2000. pap. text 9.95 (0-19-860273-1) OUP.

Oxford Color Russian Dictionary. Compiled by Della Thompson. LC 97-38609. 528p. 1998. pap. 8.95 (0-19-860212-X) OUP.

Oxford Color Spanish Dictionary: Spanish-English, English-Spanish; Espanol-Ingles, Ingles-Espanol. 2nd rev. ed. Compiled by Christine Lea. 528p. 1998. pap. 7.95 (0-19-860214-6) OUP.

Oxford Color Thesaurus. 2nd rev. ed. Compiled by Alan Spooner. 592p. 1998. pap. 8.95 (0-19-860196-4) OUP.

Oxford Colour Spelling Dictionary. 2nd ed. Maurice Waite. 638p. 1996. pap. 11.95 (0-19-860030-5) OUP.

Oxford Compact Chinese Dictionary. 2nd ed. Compiled by Commercial Press, Beijing Staff. 1176p. 1999. pap. 13.95 (0-19-591151-2) OUP.

*__Oxford Compact English-Chinese Chinese-English Dictionary.__ 1376p. 2000. 25.00 (0-19-591918-1) OUP.

Oxford Companion to African-American Literature. Ed. by William L. Andrews et al. LC 96-41565. 896p. 1997. 55.00 (0-19-506510-7) OUP.

Oxford Companion to American History. Thomas H. Johnson. 912p. (YA). (gr. 9 up). 1966. 65.00 (0-19-500597-X) OUP.

Oxford Companion to American Literature. 6th ed. James D. Hart. Ed. by Phillip Leininger. 800p. 1995. 60.00 (0-19-506548-4) OUP.

Oxford Companion to American Military History. Ed. by John Whiteclay Chambers. LC 99-21181. (Illus.). 960p. 2000. 60.00 (0-19-507198-0) OUP.

Oxford Companion to Archaeology. Ed. by Brian M. Fagan. (Illus.). 864p. 1996. 65.00 (0-19-507618-4) OUP.

Oxford Companion to Art. Ed. by Harold Osborne. (Illus.). 1,290p. 1970. 60.00 (0-19-866107-X) OUP.

Oxford Companion to Australian Children's Literature. Stella Lees & Pamela Macintyre. (Illus.). 494p. 1994. text 49.95 (0-19-553284-8) OUP.

*__Oxford Companion to Australian Film.__ Ed. by Brian McFarlane et al. (Illus.). 608p. 2000. text 65.00 (0-19-553797-1) OUP.

Oxford Companion to Australian Folklore. Ed. by Gwenda B. Davey & Graham Seal. (Illus.). 398p. 1993. text 55.00 (0-19-553057-8) OUP.

Oxford Companion to Australian History. Ed. by Graeme Davidson et al. (Illus.). 800p. 1999. 75.00 (0-19-553597-9) OUP.

Oxford Companion to Australian Jazz. Bruce Johnson. 336p. 1988. 55.00 (0-19-554791-8) OUP.

Oxford Companion to Australian Literature. William H. Wilde et al. 772p. 1991. reprint ed. pap. 29.95 (0-19-553273-2) OUP.

Oxford Companion to Australian Literature. 2nd ed. Joy Hooton & William H. Wilde. 844p. 1995. text 85.00 (0-19-553381-X) OUP.

Oxford Companion to Australian Military History. Ed. by Peter Dennis et al. (Illus.). 714p. 1996. 75.00 (0-19-553227-9) OUP.

Oxford Companion to Australian Music. Ed. by Warren Bebbington. (Illus.). 704p. 1998. text 75.00 (0-19-553432-8) OUP.

Oxford Companion to Australian Sport. Ed. by Wray Vamplew et al. (Illus.). 440p. 1993. 45.00 (0-19-553287-2) OUP.

Oxford Companion to British History. Ed. by John Cannon. LC 97-27598. (Illus.). 1,056p. (C). 1997. 60.00 (0-19-866176-2) OUP.

Oxford Companion to British Railway History: From 1603 to the 1990s. Jack Simmons. (Illus.). 607p. 1999. pap. 35.00 (0-19-866238-6) OUP.

Oxford Companion to Canadian Literature. 2nd ed. Ed. by Eugene Benson & William Toye. LC PR9180.2.O94 1997. 1168p. 1998. 65.00 (0-19-541167-6) OUP.

Oxford Companion to Canadian Theater. Ed. by Eugene Benson & L. W. Conolly. (Illus.). 680p. 1990. 59.00 (0-19-540672-9) OUP.

Oxford Companion to Chess. 2nd ed. David Hooper & Kenneth Whyld. (Illus.). 492p. 1996. reprint ed. pap. 22.50 (0-19-280049-3) OUP.

Oxford Companion to Children's Literature. Humphrey Carpenter & Mari Prichard. (J). write for info. (0-318-59415-3) HM.

Oxford Companion to Children's Literature. Humphrey Carpenter & Mari Prichard. (Illus.). 600p. 1999. pap. 24.95 (0-19-860228-6) OUP.

Oxford Companion to Christian Art & Architecture. Peter Murray & Linda Murray. (Illus.). 608p. 1996. 60.00 (0-19-866165-7) OUP.

Oxford Companion to Christian Art & Architecture. Peter Murray & Linda Murray. (Illus.). 624p. 1998. reprint ed. pap. 26.50 (0-19-860216-2) OUP.

*__Oxford Companion to Christian Thought.__ Ed. by Adrian Hastings et al. 688p. 2000. 55.00 (0-19-860024-0) OUP.

Oxford Companion to Classical Civilization. Ed. by Simon Hornblower & Simon Spawforth. LC 99-191129. (Illus.). 828p. 1999. 55.00 (0-19-860165-4) OUP.

Oxford Companion to Classical Literature. 2nd ed. Margaret Howatson. (Illus.). 640p. 1989. 60.00 (0-19-866121-5) OUP.

Oxford Companion to Crime & Mystery Writing. Ed. by Rosemary Herbert. LC 99-21182. (Illus.). 535p. 1999. 49.95 (0-19-507239-1) OUP.

*__Oxford Companion to English Literature.__ 5th ed. Margaret Drabble. LC 99-204339. 1,166p. 1999. 60.00 (0-19-866233-5) OUP.

*__Oxford Companion to English Literature.__ 6th ed. Ed. by Margaret Drabble. 1216p. 2000. 55.00 (0-19-866244-0) OUP.

*__Oxford Companion to Fairy Tales.__ Ed. by Jack Zipes. (Illus.). 601p. 2000. 49.95 (0-19-860115-8) OUP.

Oxford Companion to Food. Alan Davidson. (Illus.). 908p. 1999. 60.00 (0-19-211579-0) OUP.

Oxford Companion to German Literature. 3rd ed. Henry Garland & Mary Garland. LC 96-53309. (Illus.). 966p. 1997. text 80.00 (0-19-815896-3) OUP.

Oxford Companion to Irish History. Ed. by S. J. Connolly. LC 98-150895. (Illus.). 636p. (YA). 1998. 49.95 (0-19-211695-9) OUP.

Oxford Companion to Irish History. Ed. by S. J. Connolly. (Illus.). 636p. 1999. pap. 19.95 (0-19-866240-8) OUP.

Oxford Companion to Irish Literature. Ed. by Robert Welch & Bruce Stewart. LC 95-44943. (Illus.). 640p. (C). 1996. 55.00 (0-19-866158-4, Clarendon Pr) OUP.

Oxford Companion to Local & Family History. David Hey. 528p. 1996. pap. 27.00 (0-19-860215-4) OUP.

Oxford Companion to Music. 10th ed. Percy A. Scholes. Ed. by John O. Ward. (Illus.). 1,250p. 1970. 60.00 (0-19-311306-6) OUP.

Oxford Companion to Musical Instruments. Anthony Baines. LC 92-8635. (Illus.). 416p. 1992. 55.00 (0-19-311334-1) OUP.

Oxford Companion to New Zealand Literature. Ed. by Roger Robinson & Nelson Wattie. LC 99-200843. 624p. 1999. 72.00 (0-19-558348-5) OUP.

O

An Asterisk (*) at the beginning of an entry indicates that the title is appearing for the first time.

***Oxford Companion to New Zealand Military History.** Ed. by Ian McGibbon. (Illus.). 720p. 2000. text 75.00 (*0-19-558376-0*) OUP.

Oxford Companion to Philosophy. Ed. by Ted Honderich. (Illus.). 1,030p. 1995. 55.00 (*0-19-866132-0*) OUP.

Oxford Companion to Politics of the World. Ed. by Joel Krieger et al. LC 92-25043. (Illus.). 1088p. 1993. 60.00 (*0-19-505934-4*) OUP.

Oxford Companion to Popular Music. Peter Gammond. 748p. 1991. 55.00 (*0-19-311323-6*, 12284) OUP.

Oxford Companion to Ships & the Sea. Ed. by Peter K. Kemp. (Oxford Paperback Reference Ser.). (Illus.). 978p. 1994, pap. 29.95 (*0-19-282084-2*) OUP.

Oxford Companion to the American Theater. 2nd ed. Gerald Bordman. 752p. 1992. 65.00 (*0-19-507246-4*, 11857) OUP.

Oxford Companion to the Bible. Ed. by Bruce M. Metzger & Michael D. Coogan. (Illus.). 932p. (C). 1993. 60.00 (*0-19-504645-5*) OUP.

Oxford Companion to the Bible. Ed. by Bruce M. Metzger & Michael David Coogan. (Illus.). 1998. 45.00 (*0-19-511267-9*) OUP.

Oxford Companion to the Bible: Window's Version. Ed. by Bruce M. Metzger & Michael David Coogan. (Illus.). 1996. 45.00 (*0-19-511266-0*) OUP.

Oxford Companion to the English Language. Thomas McArthur. (Illus.). 1216p. 1992. 55.00 (*0-19-214183-X*) OUP.

Oxford Companion to the Mind. Ed. by Richard L. Gregory & O. L. Zangwill. (Illus.). 874p. 1987. 60.00 (*0-19-866124-X*) OUP.

Oxford Companion to the Mind. Ed. by Richard L. Gregory. LC 98-22974. (Illus.). 874p. 1999. reprint ed. pap. 26.50 (*0-19-860224-3*) OUP.

Oxford Companion to the Romantic Age: British Culture, 1776-1832. Iain McCalman. (Illus.). 800p. 1999. text 150.00 (*0-19-812297-7*) OUP.

Oxford Companion to the Second World War. I. C. Dear. (Illus.). 1268p. 2000. 65.00 (*0-19-214168-6*) OUP.

Oxford Companion to the Supreme Court of the United States. Kermit L. Hall. Ed. by James W. Ely, Jr. et al. (Illus.). 1066p. 1992. 60.00 (*0-19-505835-6*) OUP.

Oxford Companion to the Theatre. 4th ed. Ed. by Phyllis Hartnoll. (Illus.). 640p. 1983. 65.00 (*0-19-211546-4*) OUP.

***Oxford Companion to the Wines of North America.** Ed. by Bruce Cass & Jancis Robinson. 320p. 2000. 45.00 (*0-19-860114-X*) OUP.

Oxford Companion to the Year: An Exploration of Calendar Customs & Time Reckoning. Bonnie J. Blackburn & Leofranc Blackburn. (Illus.). 957p. 2000. 49.95 (*0-19-214231-3*) OUP.

Oxford Companion to Twentieth-Century Literature in English. Ed. by Jenny Stringer. 772p. (C). 1996. 55.00 (*0-19-212271-1*) OUP.

Oxford Companion to Wine. Jancis Robinson. (Illus.). 1,102p. 1994. 60.00 (*0-19-866159-2*) OUP.

Oxford Companion to Wine. 2nd ed. Jancis Robinson. (Illus.). 848p. 1999. 65.00 (*0-19-866236-X*) OUP.

Oxford Companion to Women's Writing in the United States. Ed. by Cathy N. Davidson & Linda Wagner-Martin. 1056p. 1995. 60.00 (*0-19-506608-1*) OUP.

Oxford Companion to Women's Writing in the United States. Ed. by Cathy N. Davidson & Linda Wagner-Martin. 1021p. 1999. reprint ed. text 45.00 (*0-7881-6143-1*) DIANE Pub.

Oxford Composer: J.S. Bach. Malcolm Boyd. LC 98-19587. (Oxford Composer Companion Ser.). (Illus.). 656p. 1999. 49.95 (*0-19-866208-4*) OUP.

Oxford Concise Italian Dictionary. 3rd ed. Ed. by Giuseppe Ragazzini et al. (Illus.). 1,248p. 1998. 27.95 (*0-19-860243-X*) OUP.

Oxford Conspirators: A History of the Oxford Movement 1833-45. Marvin R. O'Connell. 478p. (C). 1991. reprint ed. pap. text 38.00 (*0-8191-8074-2*) U Pr of Amer.

Oxford County, Maine: A Guide to Its Historic Architecture. Randall H. Bennett. LC 84-62624. (Illus.). xxiv, 564p. (Orig.). 1987. pap. 18.00 (*0-9614460-0-5*) Oxford Co Hist.

Oxford Desk Dictionary & Thesaurus: American Edition. Ed. by Frank Abate. 992p. 1997. 16.95 (*0-19-511214-8*) OUP.

Oxford Diaries of Arthur Hugh Clough. Arthur H. Clough. Ed. by Anthony Kenny. (Illus.). 350p. 1990. text 95.00 (*0-19-811739-6*) OUP.

Oxford Dictionary & Thesaurus: American Edition. Ed. by Frank Abate. LC 96-14847. 1856p. 1996. 35.00 (*0-19-509949-4*) OUP.

Oxford Dictionary & Usage Guide to the English Language. Ed. by Maurice Waite et al. 630p. 1996. reprint ed. pap. 10.95 (*0-19-861325-3*) OUP.

***Oxford Dictionary for Writers & Editors.** 2nd ed. Ed. by R. M. Ritter. 480p. 2000. 24.95 (*0-19-866239-4*) OUP.

Oxford Dictionary of American Legal Quotations. Fred R. Shapiro. 600p. 1993. 55.00 (*0-19-505859-3*) OUP.

Oxford Dictionary of American Usage & Style. Bryan A. Garner. 384p. 2000. pap. 16.95 (*0-19-513508-3*) OUP.

***Oxford Dictionary of American Usage & Style.** Oxford University Press Staff. (Essential Resource Library). 2000. mass mkt. 5.99 (*0-425-17598-7*) Berkley Pub.

Oxford Dictionary of Art. Ed. by Ian Chilvers et al. (Paperback Reference Ser.). 558p. 1994. reprint ed. pap. 19.95 (*0-19-280022-1*) OUP.

Oxford Dictionary of Art. 2nd rev. ed. Ed. by Ian Chilvers et al. LC 97-200771. (Illus.). 660p. (C). 1997. 49.95 (*0-19-860084-4*) OUP.

***Oxford Dictionary of Biochemistry & Molecular Biology.** rev. ed. Ed. by A. D. Smith. (Illus.). 672p. 2000. 65.00 (*0-19-850673-2*) OUP.

Oxford Dictionary of British Bird Names. rev. ed. W. B. Lockwood. (OxfordPaperback Reference Ser.). 192p. 1993. pap. 16.95 (*0-19-866196-7*) OUP.

Oxford Dictionary of Business English for Learners of English. Ed. by Allene Tuck. 496p. 1993. pap. text 14.95 (*0-19-431440-5*) OUP.

Oxford Dictionary of Byzantium, 3 vols., Set. Ed. by Alexander P. Kazhdan. (Illus.). 2366p. 1991. text 350.00 (*0-19-504652-8*) OUP.

Oxford Dictionary of Computing for Learners of English. Sandra Pyne. 400p. 1996. pap. text 13.95 (*0-19-431441-3*) OUP.

Oxford Dictionary of Current English. 2nd rev. ed. Ed. by Della Thompson. 1,104p. 1998. pap. 8.95 (*0-19-860233-2*) OUP.

***Oxford Dictionary of Dance.** Debra Craine & Judith Mackrell. (Illus.). 512p. 2000. 39.95 (*0-19-860106-9*) OUP.

Oxford Dictionary of English Etymology. Ed. by Charles T. Onions et al. 1,042p. 1966. 65.00 (*0-19-861112-9*) OUP.

Oxford Dictionary of English Grammar. Ed. by Slyvia Chalker & Edmund Weiner. LC 98-11436. (Oxford Paperback Reference Ser.). (Illus.). 464p. (Orig.). 1998. pap. 12.95 (*0-19-280087-6*) OUP.

Oxford Dictionary of English Grammar. Ed. by Edmund S. Weiner & Sylvia Chalker. (Illus.). 460p. (Orig.). (C). 1996. pap. 15.95 (*0-19-861314-8*) OUP.

Oxford Dictionary of Foreign Words & Phrases. Ed. by Jennifer Speake. LC 96-49006. 528p. 1997. 35.00 (*0-19-863159-6*) OUP.

***Oxford Dictionary of Foreign Words & Phrases.** Jennifer Speake. (Oxford Paperback Reference Ser.). 528p. 2000. pap. 11.95 (*0-19-280112-0*) OUP.

Oxford Dictionary of Foreign Words & Phrases. Ed. by Jennifer Speake. 528p. 1998. reprint ed. pap. 11.95 (*0-19-860236-7*) OUP.

Oxford Dictionary of Humorous Quotations. Ed. by Ned Sherrin. 543p. (YA). 1995. 45.00 (*0-19-214244-5*) OUP.

Oxford Dictionary of Humorous Quotations. Ed. by Ned Sherrin. (Oxford Paperback Reference Ser.). 568p. 1996. reprint ed. pap. 14.95 (*0-19-280045-0*) OUP.

***Oxford Dictionary of Idioms.** Jennifer Speake. LC 98-49758. 1999. write for info. (*0-19-860170-0*) OUP.

***Oxford Dictionary of Idioms.** Ed. by Jennifer Speake. (Oxford Paperback Reference). 400p. 2000. pap. 14.95 (*0-19-280111-2*) OUP.

Oxford Dictionary of Literary Quotations. Ed. by Peter Kemp. LC 97-10181. 498p. 1998. 40.00 (*0-19-860056-9*) OUP.

Oxford Dictionary of Literary Quotations. Ed. by Peter Kemp. (Oxford Paperback Reference Bks). 512p. 2000. pap. 15.95 (*0-19-280090-6*) OUP.

Oxford Dictionary of Local & Family History. David Hey. 304p. 1997. pap. 9.95 (*0-19-860080-1*) OUP.

Oxford Dictionary of Modern Greek. rev. ed. Ed. by Julian T. Pring. (GEC.). 592p. 1995. pap. 15.95 (*0-19-864197-4*) OUP.

Oxford Dictionary of Modern Quotations. Ed. by A. J. Augarde. 384p. 1991. 45.00 (*0-19-866141-X*, 12288) OUP.

Oxford Dictionary of Modern Quotations. Ed. by Tony Augarde. 542p. 1993. pap. 14.95 (*0-19-283086-4*) OUP.

Oxford Dictionary of Modern Slang. Ed. by John Simpson & John Ayto. 308p. 1994. reprint ed. pap. 11.95 (*0-19-280007-8*) OUP.

Oxford Dictionary of Music. 2nd expanded rev. ed. Michael Kennedy. Ed. by Joyce Bourne. (Illus.). 1,002p. 1995. 49.95 (*0-19-869162-9*) OUP.

Oxford Dictionary of New Words. 2nd ed. Ed. by Elizabeth Knowles & Julia Elliott. LC 97-16257. 368p. (C). 1997. 35.00 (*0-19-863152-9*) OUP.

Oxford Dictionary of New Words. 2nd ed. Ed. by Elizabeth Knowles & Julia Elliot. LC 98-14521. 368p. 1999. reprint ed. pap. 13.95 (*0-19-860235-9*) OUP.

Oxford Dictionary of Nursery Rhymes. 2nd ed. Ed. by Iona Opie & Peter Opie. (Illus.). 588p. (J). 1998. 49.95 (*0-19-860088-7*) OUP.

Oxford Dictionary of Opera. John Warrack & Ewan West. 800p. 1992. 55.00 (*0-19-869164-5*) OUP.

***Oxford Dictionary of People & Places.** Ed. by Frank A. Abate. (Illus.). 896p. 2000. 27.50 (*0-19-513872-4*) OUP.

Oxford Dictionary of Philosophy. Simon Blackburn. (Illus.). 416p. 1994. 49.95 (*0-19-211694-0*) OUP.

Oxford Dictionary of Philosophy. Simon Blackburn. (Oxford Paperback Reference Ser.). (Illus.). 428p. 1996. pap. 14.95 (*0-19-283134-8*) OUP.

***Oxford Dictionary of Phrase & Fable.** Ed. by Elizabeth Knowles. 1184p. 2000. 39.95 (*0-19-860219-7*) OUP.

Oxford Dictionary of Phrase, Proverb & Quotation. Ed. by Elizabeth Knowles. LC 97-8800. 712p. 1997. 45.00 (*0-19-866229-7*) OUP.

Oxford Dictionary of Political Quotations. Ed. by Antony Jay. LC 96-11425. 528p. 1997. 35.00 (*0-19-863158-8*) OUP.

Oxford Dictionary of Popes. J. N. Kelly. LC 85-15599. (Oxford Paperback Reference Ser.). 368p. 1989. reprint ed. pap. 14.95 (*0-19-282085-0*) OUP.

Oxford Dictionary of Quotations. 4th deluxe ed. Ed. by Angela Partington. 1078p. 1993. 90.00 (*0-19-866202-5*) OUP.

Oxford Dictionary of Quotations. 4th rev. ed. Ed. by Angela Partington. 1104p. 1996. 45.00 (*0-19-860058-5*) OUP.

Oxford Dictionary of Quotations, 5 vols. 5th ed. Ed. by Elizabeth Knowles. LC 99-12096. 1,152p. 1999. 40.00 (*0-19-860173-5*) OUP.

Oxford Dictionary of Saints. 4th ed. David H. Farmer. LC 97-12837. (Oxford Paperback Reference). 570p. 1998. pap. 15.95 (*0-19-280058-2*) OUP.

Oxford Dictionary of Slang. John Ayto. LC 99-201836. 480p. 1999. 35.00 (*0-19-863157-X*) OUP.

***Oxford Dictionary of Slang.** Ed. by John Ayto. 2000. pap. 13.95 (*0-19-280104-X*) OUP.

Oxford Dictionary of Spanish & Hispanic Literature: Diccionario Oxford de Literatura Espanola e Hispanoamericana. Philip Ward. (SPA.). 864p. 1984. 75.00 (*0-8288-1579-8*, S6303) Fr & Eur.

Oxford Dictionary of Sports Science & Medicine. 2nd ed. Michael Kent. LC 97-41377. (Illus.). 582p. 1998. text 39.95 (*0-19-262845-3*) OUP.

Oxford Dictionary of the Christian Church. 3rd ed. Ed. by F. L. Cross & E. A. Livingstone. LC 97-165294. 1,824p. (C). 1997. text 125.00 (*0-19-211655-X*) OUP.

Oxford Dictionary of the Jewish Religion. Ed. by Geoffrey Wigoder & Raphael J. Werblowsky. LC 96-45517. 792p. 1997. 95.00 (*0-19-508605-8*) OUP.

Oxford Dictionary of the World. Ed. by David Munro. LC 95-22546. (Illus.). 698p. 1996. 39.95 (*0-19-866184-3*) OUP.

Oxford Dictionary of the World. Ed. by David Munro. (Illus.). 704p. 1997. reprint ed. pap. 16.95 (*0-19-860060-7*) OUP.

***Oxford Dictionary of Thematic Quotations.** Ed. by Susan Ratcliffe. 576p. 2000. 24.95 (*0-19-860218-9*) OUP.

Oxford Dictionary of Twentieth Century Quotations. Elizabeth Knowles. LC 98-17511. 496p. 1999. 30.00 (*0-19-860103-4*) OUP.

Oxford Dictionary of World Religions. John Bowker. 1,135p. pap. write for info. (*0-19-866242-4*) OUP.

Oxford Dictionary of World Religions. Ed. by John Bowker. LC 97-166787. 1,124p. 1997. 60.00 (*0-19-213965-7*) OUP.

Oxford Dictionnaire de l'Antiquite Mythologie, Litterature, Civilisation, French Edition. Margaret C. Howatson. (FRE.). 1993. pap. 59.95 (*0-7859-7810-0*, 2221068009) Fr & Eur.

***Oxford-Duden College German Dictionary: English-German, German-English.** Dudenredaktion (Bibliographisches Institut) & Oxford University Press. Dictionary Dept. German Section. Ed. by Michael Clark & Olaf Thyen. LC 98-49986. 960p. 2000. pap. 11.95 (*0-19-860280-4*) OUP.

Oxford Duden German & Spanish Dictionary: Oxford Duden Bildworterbuch Deutsch und Spanisch. Manuel Alvar Ezquerra. (GER & SPA.). 860p. 1985. 75.00 (*0-8288-0347-1*, F19220) Fr & Eur.

Oxford-Duden German Desk Dictionary. rev. ed. Ed. by Michael Clark & Olaf Thyen. LC 97-193253. 864p. 1997. 14.95 (*0-19-860147-6*) OUP.

***Oxford-Duden German Dictionary.** 2nd ed. Michael Clark. 1,728p. 1999. 45.00 (*0-19-860248-0*) OUP.

***Oxford-Duden German Dictionary.** 2nd ed. Ed. by Michael Clark & Olaf Thyen. (Illus.). 1,728p. 1999. 45.00 (*0-19-860226-X*) OUP.

Oxford-Duden German Minidictionary. 2nd rev. ed. Gunhild Prowe. Ed. by Jill Schneider. 710p. 1999. vinyl bd. 6.50 (*0-19-860252-9*) OUP.

***Oxford-Duden Pictorial Chinese & English Dictionary.** Keys Publishing Company. LC 98-17680. 1998. write for info. (*0-19-860192-1*) OUP.

Oxford-Duden Pictorial English & Chinese Dictionary: Simplified Character. (Illus.). 854p. 1995. pap. 21.95 (*0-19-582785-6*) OUP.

Oxford-Duden Pictorial English Dictionary. 2nd ed. (Illus.). 812p. 1995. pap. 18.95 (*0-19-861311-3*) OUP.

Oxford-Duden Pictorial French & English Dictionary. 2nd ed. (FRE & ENG., Illus.). 880p. (C). 1996. 49.95 (*0-19-864537-6*); pap. 21.95 (*0-19-864538-4*) OUP.

Oxford-Duden Pictorial German & English Dictionary. 2nd rev. ed. (ENG & GER., Illus.). 872p. 1995. pap. 21.95 (*0-19-864502-3*) OUP.

Oxford-Duden Pictorial Italian & English Dictionary. (ITA & ENG.). 872p. 1995. pap. 19.95 (*0-19-864517-1*) OUP.

Oxford-Duden Pictorial Japanese & English Dictionary. (JPN., Illus.). 864p. 1997. pap. 21.95 (*0-19-860119-0*) OUP.

Oxford-Duden Pictorial Portuguese & English Dictionary. (ENG & POR., Illus.). 950p. 1993. pap. 22.50 (*0-19-864182-6*) OUP.

Oxford-Duden Pictorial Spanish & English Dictionary. 2nd ed. Oxford University Press Staff. (SPA & ENG., Illus.). 884p. 1995. pap. 21.95 (*0-19-864515-5*) OUP.

Oxford-Duden Pictorial Thai & English Dictionary. (THA & ENG., Illus.). 810p. (C). 1997. pap. 25.00 (*0-19-860014-3*) OUP.

Oxford Easy Anthem Book. 192p. 1962. pap. 12.95 (*0-19-353321-9*) OUP.

***Oxford Easy French Grammar.** Pierre Cousin & Wendy Lee. 128p. 2000. pap. 7.95 (*0-19-860341-X*) OUP.

***Oxford Easy German Grammar.** 128p. 2000. pap. 7.95 (*0-19-860342-8*) OUP.

***Oxford Easy Spanish Grammar.** Pierre Cousin & Wendy Lee. 128p. 2000. pap. 7.95 (*0-19-860343-6*) OUP.

Oxford Economics in the Late Nineteenth Century. Alon Kadish. (Oxford Historical Monographs). 1982. 55.00 (*0-19-821886-9*) OUP.

Oxford Elementary Learner's Dictionary. 2nd ed. Ed. by Angela Crawley. (Illus.). 430p. (J). 1994. pap. text 13.95 (*0-19-431275-5*) OUP.

Oxford Encyclopaedia of European Community Law & Institutional Law, Vol. I. Akos G. Toth. 648p. 1991. text 180.00 (*0-19-825589-6*) OUP.

***Oxford Encyclopedia of Ancient Egypt.** Donald B. Redford. LC 99-54801. 2000. write for info. (*0-19-513821-X*); write for info. (*0-19-513822-8*); write for info. (*0-19-513823-6*) OUP.

***Oxford Encyclopedia of Ancient Egypt, 3 vols.** Ed. by Donald B. Redford. LC 99-54801. (Illus.). 1632p. 2000. text 450.00 (*0-19-510234-7*) OUP.

Oxford Encyclopedia of Archaeology in the Near East, 5 vols., Set, Vols. 1-4. Ed. by Eric M. Meyers. LC 96-17152. (Illus.). 2608p. 1996. text 595.00 (*0-19-506512-3*) OUP.

Oxford Encyclopedia of European Community Law, Vol. II. Akos G. Toth. 680p. 2000. 135.00 (*0-19-825600-0*) OUP.

***Oxford Encyclopedia of Global Change.** Ed. by Andrew S. Goudie. LC 99-215457. (Illus.). 1999. write for info. (*0-19-510825-6*) OUP.

***Oxford Encyclopedia of Mesoamerican Cultures, 3vols., Set.** Ed. by David Carrasco. (Illus.). 1344p. 2000. text 395.00 (*0-19-510815-9*) OUP.

Oxford Encyclopedia of the Modern Islamic World, 4 vols., Set. Ed. by John L. Esposito. (Illus.). 1877p. 1995. text 465.00 (*0-19-506613-8*) OUP.

Oxford Encyclopedia of the Reformation, 4 vols., Set. Ed. by Hans J. Hillerbrand. (Illus.). 2016p. 1996. text 495.00 (*0-19-506493-3*) OUP.

Oxford Encyclopedic Dictionary of Music: French Edition, 2 vols., Set. Denis Arnold. (FRE.). 2400p. 1988. pap. 95.00 (*0-8288-7288-0*, 2221900243) Fr & Eur.

Oxford Encyclopedic English Dictionary. Ed. by Joyce M. Hawkins & Robert A. Allen. (Illus.). 1824p. 1991. 35.00 (*0-19-861248-6*) OUP.

Oxford Encyclopedic English Dictionary. 2nd ed. Judith M. Pearsall & William R. Trumble. 1804p. 1995. 35.00 (*0-19-521158-8*) OUP.

Oxford English see Needed Words

Oxford English & Spanish Computer Dictionary: Diccionario Oxford de Informatica. 2nd ed. Mendizabal. (ENG & SPA.). 450p. 1986. 125.00 (*0-8288-0256-4*, S8231) Fr & Eur.

Oxford English-Arabic Dictionary of Current Usage. Ed. by N. S. Doniach. (ARA & ENG.). 1,406p. 1972. text 95.00 (*0-19-864312-8*) OUP.

Oxford English Computing. P. Charles Brown & Keith Boeckner. (Illus.). 212p. 1993. pap. text, student ed. 12.95 (*0-19-457387-7*) OUP.

Oxford English Dictionary, 2 vols., Set. 2nd ed. J. A. Simpson & Edmund S. Weiner. 21,728p. 1989. text 3000.00 (*0-19-861186-2*) OUP.

Oxford English Dictionary: Additions, 2 vols., 1. Ed. by John A. Simpson & Edmund S. Weiner. LC 92-47491. 352p. 1994. 45.00 (*0-19-861292-3*) OUP.

Oxford English Dictionary: Additions, 2 vols., 2. Ed. by John A. Simpson & Edmund S. Weiner. LC 92-47491. 352p. 1994. 45.00 (*0-19-861299-0*) OUP.

Oxford English Dictionary Additions Series, Vol. 3. Ed. by Michael Proffitt. 418p. (C). 1997. 55.00 (*0-19-860027-5*) OUP.

Oxford English Dictionary & the State of the Language. Robert W. Burchfield & Hans Aarsleff. LC 88-600085. 56p. 1988. 3.95 (*0-8444-0602-3*) Lib Congress.

Oxford English Electronics. Eric Glendinning & John McEwan. (Illus.). 208p. 1993. pap. text, student ed. 12.95 (*0-19-457384-2*) OUP.

Oxford English for Computing: Answer Book. P. Charles Brown & Keith Boeckner. (Illus.). 64p. 1993. pap. text 6.95 (*0-19-457388-5*) OUP.

Oxford English for Electrical & Mechanical Engineering: Answer Book with Teaching Notes. Eric H. Glendinning. (Illus.). 46p. 1995. pap. text, teacher ed. 6.95 (*0-19-457393-1*) OUP.

Oxford English for Electrical & Mechanical Engineering: Student Book. Eric H. Glendinning. (Illus.). 190p. 1995. pap. text, student ed. 12.95 (*0-19-457392-3*) OUP.

Oxford English for Electronics: Answer Book with Teaching Notes. Eric Glendinning. 48p. 1993. pap. text 6.95 (*0-19-457385-0*) OUP.

Oxford English Grammar. Sidney Greenbaum. (Illus.). 668p. (C). 1996. 39.95 (*0-19-861250-8*) OUP.

Oxford English-Hebrew Dictionary. Ed. by N. Doniach & A. Kahane. 1,114p. 1998. reprint ed. pap. 22.50 (*0-19-860172-7*) OUP.

Oxford English-Marathi Dictionary. Ramesh V. Dhongde. 823p. (C). 1998. text 9.95 (*0-19-564244-9*) OUP.

Oxford English Minidictionary. 5th ed. Ed. by Lucinda Coventry & Martin Nixon. LC PE1628.O868 1999. 632p. 1999. pap. 6.95 (*0-19-860255-3*) OUP.

Oxford ESL Dictionary: For Students of American English. A. S. Hornby. (Illus.). 752p. (YA). (gr. 7-12). 1991. pap. text 12.50 (*0-19-431403-0*) OUP.

***Oxford Essays in Jurisprudence.** Ed. by Jeremy Horder. 296p. 2000. text 74.00 (*0-19-826858-0*) OUP.

Oxford Essays in Jurisprudence, Third Series. John M. Eekelaar & John S. Bell. 274p. 1987. text 69.00 (*0-19-825507-1*) OUP.

Oxford Essays in Medieval History. Herbert E. Salter. (Essay Index Reprint Ser.). 274p. 1982. reprint ed. lib. bdg. 17.00 (*0-8290-0834-9*) Irvington.

Oxford Essays in Medievial History Presented to Herbert Edward Salter. Herbert E. Salter. (Essay Index Reprint Ser.). 1977. 23.95 (*0-8369-0760-4*) Ayer.

Oxford Essential Biographical Dictionary: American Edition. 436p. 1999. mass mkt. 5.99 (*0-425-16993-6*) Berkley Pub.

Oxford Essential Dictionary. Oxford University Press Staff. (Illus.). 810p. 1998. mass mkt. 6.99 (*0-425-16420-9*) Berkley Pub.

Oxford Essential Dictionary of Foreign Terms i n English: The World's Most Trusted Dictionaries. Press Boulevard Company Staff. 1999. mass mkt. 5.99 (*0-425-16995-2*) Berkley Pub.

Oxford Essential Geographical Dictionary: The World's Most Trusted Dictionaries. Press Boulevard Company Staff. 1999. mass mkt. 5.99 (*0-425-16994-4*) Berkley Pub.

***Oxford Essential Guide for Puzzle Solvers.** Oxford University Press Staff. (Essential Resource Library). 2000. mass mkt. 5.99 (*0-425-17599-5*) Berkley Pub.

An Asterisk (*) at the beginning of an entry indicates that the title is appearing for the first time.

***Oxford Essential Guide to the U. S. Government.** Oxford University Press Staff. (Essential Resource Library). 2000. mass mkt. 6.99 (*0-425-17615-0*) Berkley Pub.

***Oxford Essential Guide to Writing.** Oxford University Press Staff. (Essential Resource Library). 2000. mass mkt. 5.99 (*0-425-17640-1*) Berkley Pub.

Oxford Essential Spelling Dictionary: American Edition. Oxford University Press Staff. 433p. 1998. mass mkt. 5.99 (*0-425-16388-1*) Berkley Pub.

Oxford Essential Thesaurus. Oxford University Press Staff. 1998. mass mkt. 6.99 (*0-425-16421-7*) Berkley Pub.

Oxford Exit. Veronica Stallwood. LC 94-28815. 192p. 1995. 19.50 (*0-684-19729-4*) S&S Trade.

Oxford 50th Anniversary Book of the United Nations. Charles Patterson. (Illus.). 240p. (YA). (gr. 7 up). 1995. 40.00 (*0-19-508280-X*) OUP.

***Oxford Figures: A History of Mathematics at Oxford.** Ed. by John Fauvel et al. LC 99-27797. (Illus.). 304p. 2000. text 60.00 (*0-19-852309-2*) OUP.

Oxford First Ancient History. Roy Burrell. (Rebuilding the Past Ser.). (Illus.). 320p. (J). (gr. 4-8). 1994. bds. 37.95 (*0-19-521058-1*) OUP.

Oxford First Ancient History. Roy Burrell. (Rebuilding the Past Ser.). (Illus.). 320p. (J). (gr. 4-8). 1997. reprint ed. pap. 22.95 (*0-19-521373-4*) OUP.

***Oxford First Book of Animals.** Barbara Taylor. (Illus.). 48p. (YA). 2000. 18.95 (*0-19-521687-3*) OUP.

***Oxford First Book of Art.** Gillian Wolfe. (Illus.). 48p. (J). (gr. k-4). 1999. 18.95 (*0-19-521556-7*) OUP.

***Oxford First Book of Space.** Andrew Langley. (Illus.). 48p. (YA). 2000. 18.95 (*0-19-521686-5*) OUP.

Oxford First Companion to Composers & Their Music. Kenneth McLeish & Valerie McLeish. (Illus.). 192p. 1982. pap. text 13.95 (*0-19-321438-5*) OUP.

Oxford First Companion to Instruments & Orchestras. Kenneth McLeish & Valerie McLeish. (Illus.). 192p. 1982. pap. text 13.95 (*0-19-321435-0*) OUP.

Oxford First Companion to Music Round the World. Kenneth McLeish & Valerie McLeish. (Illus.). 192p. 1982. pap. text 13.95 (*0-19-321434-2*) OUP.

Oxford First Companion to the Story of Music. Kenneth McLeish & Valerie McLeish. (Illus.). 192p. 1982. pap. text 13.95 (*0-19-321437-7*) OUP.

Oxford Food: An Anthology. Ursula Aylmer & Carolyn McCrum. (Illus.). 218p. 1996. 37.50 (*1-85444-063-2*, 0632, Pub. by Ashmolean Mus); pap. 25.00 (*1-85444-058-6*, 0586, Pub. by Ashmolean Mus) A Schwartz & Co.

Oxford Frederick Douglass Reader. Frederick Douglass. Ed. & Intro. by William L. Andrews. 384p. (C). 1996. pap. text 27.95 (*0-19-509118-3*) OUP.

***Oxford French Cartoon-Strip Vocabulary Builder.** Marie-Helene Correard. (ENG & FRE., Illus.). 80p. 2000. pap. 11.95 (*0-19-860267-7*) OUP.

Oxford French Dictionary: French-English, English-French. Michael Janes & Dora Carpenter. 560p. 1997. mass mkt. 4.99 (*0-425-16010-6*) Berkley Pub.

Oxford French Minidictionary. 2nd ed. Michael Janes & Dora Carpenter. LC 97-191055. 704p. 1997. pap. 5.95 (*0-19-860140-9*) OUP.

Oxford French Minidictionary. 3rd ed. Ed. by Michael Janes et al. 640p. 1999. pap. 6.50 (*0-19-860245-6*) OUP.

***Oxford French Workpack.** Valerie Grundy. (FRE.). 128p. 2000. pap. 7.95 (*0-19-860335-5*) OUP.

Oxford Gardens. Pevensey Pr. Staff. (C). 1987. text 60.00 (*0-907115-27-6*, Pub. by Pevensey) St Mut.

Oxford German Dictionary: German-English, English-German. Ed. by Jill Schneider. LC 98-160396. (ENG & GER.). 576p. 1974. mass mkt. 4.99 (*0-425-16011-4*) Berkley Pub.

***Oxford German Workpack.** Ed. by Valerie Grundy. 128p. 2000. pap. 7.95 (*0-19-860336-3*) OUP.

***Oxford Girl.** Presley Abbot. 176p. 2000. mass mkt. 7.95 (*1-56201-173-1*, Pub. by Blue Moon Bks) Publishers Group.

Oxford Global Science Library, 4 vols. Oxford Staff. 1995. 149.95 (*0-19-521147-2*) OUP.

Oxford Goldsmiths Before 1800. Ann N. Hansen. LC 96-85528. (Illus.). 165p. 1996. 40.00 (*0-9613491-3-1*) At The Sign.

***Oxford Greek Dictionary.** Oxford University Press Staff. (Essential Resource Library). (GRE & ENG.). 2000. mass mkt. 5.99 (*0-425-17600-2*) Berkley Pub.

Oxford Greek Minidictionary. Ed. by Niki Watts. 662p. 1998. pap. 7.95 (*0-19-864147-8*) OUP.

Oxford Group & Alcoholics Anonymous: A Design for Living That Works. 2nd rev. ed. B., Dick. LC 98-91226. (History of Early A. A.'s Spiritual Roots & Successes Ser.: Vol. 4). Orig. Title: Design for Living: The Oxford Group's Contribution to Early A. A.. 432p. 1998. per. 17.95 (*1-885803-19-2*, 951) Paradise Res Inc.

Oxford Guide to British Women Writers. Joanne Shattock. LC 92-47232. 502p. (C). 1993. 35.00 (*0-19-214176-7*) OUP.

Oxford Guide to Contemporary World Literature. John Sturrock. 502p. 1997. pap. 19.95 (*0-19-283318-9*) OUP.

Oxford Guide to Contemporary Writing. Ed. by John Sturrock. 502p. 1996. 40.00 (*0-19-818262-7*) OUP.

Oxford Guide to English Usage. 2nd ed. Edmund S. Weiner & Andrew Delahunty. (Paperback Reference Ser.). 318p. 1995. pap. 8.95 (*0-19-280024-8*) OUP.

Oxford Guide to Family History. David Hey. LC 92-18524. (Illus.). 256p. 1993. 39.95 (*0-19-869177-7*) OUP.

Oxford Guide to Film Studies. Ed. by John Hill et al. LC 97-44590. (Illus.). 646p. (C). 1998. pap. text 41.95 (*0-19-871124-7*) OUP.

Oxford Guide to Heraldry. Thomas Woodcock & John M. Robinson. LC 95-40007. (Illus.). 288p. 1990. pap. 24.95 (*0-19-285224-8*) OUP.

Oxford Guide to Library Research. Thomas Mann. (Illus.). 336p. 1998. 35.00 (*0-19-512312-3*); pap. 14.95 (*0-19-512313-1*) OUP.

***Oxford Guide to Literature in English Translation.** Ed. by Peter France. 680p. 2000. text 99.00 (*0-19-818359-3*) OUP.

***Oxford Guide to the Mind.** Ed. by Geoffrey Underwood. (Illus.). 416p. 2000. pap. 19.95 (*0-19-860083-6*) OUP.

***Oxford Guide to the United States Government.** Richard M. Pious & Donald A. Ritchie. Ed. by John J. Patrick. 640p. 2001. 35.00 (*0-19-514273-X*) OUP.

Oxford Guide to United States Supreme Court Decisions. Ed. by Kermit L. Hall. LC 98-8747. 448p. 1999. 35.00 (*0-19-511883-9*) OUP.

***Oxford Guide to United States Supreme Court Decisions.** Ed. by Kermit L. Hall. 448p. 2000. pap. 17.95 (*0-19-513924-0*) OUP.

Oxford Guide to Word Games. Tony Augarde. LC 76-352512. (Illus.). 256p. 1986. pap. 7.95 (*0-19-282005-2*) OUP.

Oxford Guide to Writing. Thomas S. Kane. Ed. by Nancy Sommers. (Illus.). 1983. teacher ed. write for info. (*0-19-503297-7*) OUP.

Oxford Guides to Chaucer: The Canterbury Tales. 2nd ed. Helen Cooper. (Oxford Guides to Chaucer Ser.). 452p. (C). 1996. pap. text 26.00 (*0-19-871155-7*) OUP.

Oxford Guides to Chaucer: Troilus & Criseyde. Barry Windeatt. (Illus.). 428p. 1995. pap. text 24.95 (*0-19-811194-0*) OUP.

***Oxford-Hachette College French Dictionary.** 2nd ed. Ed. by Marie-Helene Correard. LC 98-49988. 800p. 2000. pap. 11.95 (*0-19-860279-0*) OUP.

Oxford-Hachette Concise French/English/French Dictionnaire. Oxford. (ENG & FRE.). 1997. 59.95 (*0-320-00427-9*) Fr & Eur.

Oxford-Hachette Dictionary French-English--English-French. M-H. Correard & Valerie Grundy. (ENG & FRE.). 1943p. 1994. pap. 95.00 (*0-7859-8896-3*) Fr & Eur.

Oxford-Hachette French Desk Dictionary. Ed. by Marie-Helene Correard. LC 98-118884. (FRE.). 800p. 1997. 16.95 (*0-19-860149-2*) OUP.

Oxford-Hachette French Dictionary. 2nd ed. Marie-Helene Correard. LC 98-104077. (FRE.). 2,008p. 1997. 45.00 (*0-19-860068-2*) OUP.

Oxford Hanbook of Criminology. 2nd ed. Ed. by Mike Maguire et al, LC 97-35701. (Illus.). 1,292p. 1998. pap. text 45.00 (*0-19-876485-5*) OUP.

Oxford Handbook in Dental Patient Care. Crispian Scully. LC 98-9869. (Illus.). 456p. 1998. pap. 37.95 (*0-19-262915-8*) OUP.

Oxford Handbook of Accident & Emergency Medicine. Jonathan Wyatt et al. LC 98-4298. (Illus.). 800p. 1999. pap. 39.50 (*0-19-262751-1*) OUP.

Oxford Handbook of Acute Medicine. Punit s. Ramrakha & Kevin P. Moore. LC 97-26292. (Illus.). 892p. 1998. pap. 34.50 (*0-19-262682-5*) OUP.

Oxford Handbook of Clinical & Operative Surgery. G. McLatchie. (Illus.). 1990. pap. 32.50 (*0-19-261710-9*) OUP.

***Oxford Handbook of Clinical Dentistry.** 3rd ed. David A. Mitchell & Laura Mitchell. LC 98-42398. (Illus.). 824p. 1999. pap. 39.95 (*0-19-262963-8*) OUP.

Oxford Handbook of Clinical Haematology. Drew Provan. LC 98-28128. 640p. 1998. pap. 39.95 (*0-19-262903-4*) OUP.

Oxford Handbook of Clinical Immunology. Gavin Spickett. LC RC582.S66 1999. 736p. 1999. pap. 34.50 (*0-19-262721-X*) OUP.

Oxford Handbook of Clinical Medicine. Ed. by David E. Thaler et al. LC 98-49082. (Illus.). 864p. 1999. pap. 29.95 (*0-19-512572-X*) OUP.

Oxford Handbook of Clinical Medicine. 4th ed. Tony Hope et al. LC 99-187742. (Illus.). 848p. 1998. pap. 34.50 (*0-19-262783-X*) OUP.

Oxford Handbook of Clinical Specialties. 5th ed. J. A. Collier et al. (Illus.). 864p. 1999. pap. 32.50 (*0-19-262943-3*) OUP.

Oxford Handbook of Criminology. Ed. by Mike Maguire et al. LC 93-49443. (Illus.). 1,274p. 1994. pap. text 25.00 (*0-19-876241-0*, Clarendon Pr) OUP.

Oxford Handbook of Criminology. 2nd ed. Ed. by Mike Maguire et al. LC 97-35701. 1296p. 1997. text 140.00 (*0-19-826297-3*) OUP.

Oxford Handbook of Critical Care. Mervyn Singer & Andrew Webb. (Illus.). 560p. 1996. pap. 29.50 (*0-19-262542-X*) OUP.

***Oxford Handbook of Economic Geography.** Ed. by Gordon L. Clark et al. (Illus.). 760p. 2000. text 98.00 (*0-19-823410-4*) OUP.

***Oxford Handbook of Memory.** Ed. by Endel Tulving & Fergus M. Craik. LC 99-27533. (Illus.). 688p. 2000. text 65.00 (*0-19-512265-8*) OUP.

Oxford Handbook of Nucleic Acid Structure. Ed. by Stephen Neidle. LC 98-34431. (Illus.). 680p. 1999. text 140.00 (*0-19-850038-6*) OUP.

***Oxford Handbook of Oncology.** James Cassidy & D. Bissett. (Illus.). 2000. pap. text 29.95 (*0-19-263035-0*) OUP.

Oxford Handbook of Operative Surgery. Ed. by G. McLatchie & David J. Leaper. (Illus.). 734p. 1996. pap. 34.50 (*0-19-262097-5*) OUP.

Oxford Handbook of Patients' Welfare: A Doctor's Guide. Adam Sandell. LC 98-8016. 294p. 1999. pap. 39.95 (*0-19-262957-3*) OUP.

Oxford Handbook of Sports Medicine. Ed. by Eugene Sherry & Stephen Wilson. LC 98-11503. (Illus.). 958p. 1998. pap. 34.50 (*0-19-262890-9*) OUP.

Oxford Handbook of Tropical Medicine. Michael Eddleston & Stephen Pierini. LC 98-50045. (Illus.). 666p. 1999. pap. 39.95 (*0-19-262772-4*) OUP.

Oxford Harrap Standard German-English Dictionary, 3 vols. Ed. by Trevor Jones. Incl. Vol. 3. L-R. 1978. 84.00 (*0-19-864131-1*); write for info. (*0-318-54871-2*) OUP.

Oxford Harriet Beecher Stowe Reader. Harriet Beecher Stowe. Ed. by Joan D. Hedrick. (Illus.). 576p. (C). 1998. pap. text 31.95 (*0-19-509117-5*) OUP.

Oxford Hebrew-English-Hebrew Dictionary. (HEB & ENG.). pap. 18.50 (*965-307-027-4*) Shalom.

Oxford Hebrew-English-Russian Dictionary. (HEB, ENG & RUS.). pap. 29.50 (*965-307-026-6*) Shalom.

Oxford, Hebron & Minot Register, 1906 (Town Histories & Directories) Compiled by Mitchell & Davis. 142p. 1997. reprint ed. pap. 22.00 (*0-8328-5886-2*) Higginson Bk Co.

Oxford Hills. Jack Barnes & Diane Barnes. (Images of America Ser.). 1995. pap. 16.99 (*0-7524-0060-6*) Arcadia Publng.

Oxford Hindi-English Dictionary. Ed. by R. S. McGregor. (HIN.). 1,104p. 1997. reprint ed. pap. text 25.00 (*0-19-864339-X*) OUP.

Oxford History of Australia: Aboriginal Australia, Vol. 1. Ed. by Tim Murray. (Illus.). 360p. Date not set. 39.00 (*0-19-554609-1*) OUP.

Oxford History of Australia: 1860 -1990. Glad, Confident Morning, Vol. 3. Ed. by Beverley Kingston. (Illus.). 384p. 1989. text 49.95 (*0-19-554611-3*) OUP.

Oxford History of Australia: 1901 - 1942, the Succeeding Age, 5 vols., Vol. 4. Ed. by Stuart F. MacIntyre. LC 87-107443. (Illus.). 420p. 1987. text 45.00 (*0-19-554612-1*) OUP.

Oxford History of Australia, 1860-1900 Vol. 3: Glad, Confident Morning. Ed. by Beverley Kingston. (Illus.). 384p. (C). 1993. reprint ed. pap. 21.00 (*0-19-553519-7*, 612) OUP.

Oxford History of Australia, 1942-1988 Vol. 5: The Middle Way. Geoffrey Bolton. (Illus.). 52p. (C). 1993. reprint ed. pap. 21.00 (*0-19-553520-0*) OUP.

Oxford History of Australia Vol. 5: 1942 - 1988: The Middle Way. Ed. by Geoffrey Bolton. (Illus.). 360p. 1990. text 45.00 (*0-19-554613-X*) OUP.

Oxford History of Australia, 1901-1942 Vol. 4: The Succeeding Age. Stuart Macintyre. (Illus.). 420p. 1993. reprint ed. pap. text 21.00 (*0-19-553518-9*) OUP.

Oxford History of Australia, 1770-1860 Vol. 2: Possessions. Jan Kociumbas. (Illus.). 424p. 1995. pap. 29.95 (*0-19-553744-0*) OUP.

Oxford History of Britain. 2nd rev. ed. Ed. by Kenneth O. Morgan. LC 98-30644. (Illus.). 772p. 1999. pap. 18.95 (*0-19-285349-X*) OUP.

Oxford History of Britain Vol. 1: Roman & Anglo-Saxon Britain. Peter Salway & John Blair. Ed. by Kenneth O. Morgan. (Illus.). 160p. 1992. pap. 12.95 (*0-19-285263-9*) OUP.

Oxford History of Christianity. Ed. by John McManners. (Illus.). 778p. 1994. pap. text 16.95 (*0-19-285291-4*) OUP.

Oxford History of Classical Art. Ed. by John Boardman. LC 96-38850. (Illus.). 416p. 1997. reprint ed. pap. 24.95 (*0-19-285337-6*) OUP.

Oxford History of English Music: c. 1715 to the Present Day, Vol. 2. John Caldwell, pseud. (Illus.). 648p. 1999. text 135.00 (*0-19-816288-X*) OUP.

Oxford History of English Music Vol. 1: From the Beginnings to c. 1715. John Caldwell, pseud. (Oxford History of English Music Ser.). (Illus.). 708p. 1992. text 105.00 (*0-19-816129-8*) OUP.

Oxford History of Greece & the Hellenistic World. Ed. by John Boardman et al. (Illus.). 528p. 1991. pap. text 16.95 (*0-19-285247-7*) OUP.

Oxford History of Hungarian Literature: From Earliest Times to the Present. Lorant Czigany. LC 83-3997. 582p. 1984. 79.00 (*0-19-815781-9*) OUP.

Oxford History of India. 4th ed. Vincent Arthur Smith. Ed. by Percival Spear. (Illus.). 964p. 1981. text 14.95 (*0-19-561297-3*) OUP.

Oxford History of Ireland. Ed. by Roy Foster. (Illus.). 360p. 1992. pap. 15.95 (*0-19-285271-X*) OUP.

Oxford History of Islam. Ed. by John L. Esposito. LC 99-13219. (Illus.). 768p. 2000. 549.95 (*0-19-510799-3*) OUP.

Oxford History of Medieval Europe. George Holmes. (Illus.). 410p. 1992. pap. text 14.95 (*0-19-285272-8*) OUP.

***Oxford History of Mexico.** Ed. by Michael C. Meyer & William H. Beezley. LC 99-56044. (Illus.). 768p. 2000. write for info. (*0-19-511228-8*) OUP.

***Oxford History of Modern Europe.** Ed. by T. C. W. Blanning. 400p. 2000. pap. 16.95 (*0-19-285371-6*) OUP.

Oxford History of Modern India, 1740-1975. 2nd ed. Percival Spear. (Illus.). 482p. 1979. pap. text 13.95 (*0-19-561076-8*) OUP.

***Oxford History of Modern War.** Ed. by Charles Townshend. 384p. 2000. pap. 15.95 (*0-19-285373-2*) OUP.

Oxford History of Music, 8 vols. 1990. reprint ed. lib. bdg. 560.00 (*0-7812-9023-6*) Rprt Serv.

Oxford History of Music, 8 vols. 2nd rev. ed. Incl. Polyphonic Period II, 1400-1600. 2nd ed. H. E. Wooldridge. 1973. 37.50 Symphony & Drama, 1850-1900. H. C. Colles. 1973. 37.50 (*0-8154-0475-1*); 1973. reprint ed. write for info. (*0-318-51444-3*) Cooper Sq.

Oxford History of New Zealand. 2nd ed. Ed. by Geoffrey W. Rice. (Illus.). 774p. 1993. pap. text 45.00 (*0-19-558257-8*) OUP.

Oxford History of New Zealand Literature. Ed. by Terry Sturm. 768p. 1991. text 65.00 (*0-19-558211-X*) OUP.

Oxford History of New Zealand Literature in English. Ed. by Terry Sturm. 768p. 1993. reprint ed. pap. 38.00 (*0-19-558240-3*) OUP.

Oxford History of Opera. Ed. by Roger Parker. (Illus.). 400p. 1996. reprint ed. pap. 15.95 (*0-19-284028-2*) OUP.

Oxford History of the American People: Prehistory to 1789, Vol. 1. Samuel Eliot Morison. (Illus.). 422p. 1994. pap. 15.95 (*0-452-01130-2*, Mer) NAL.

Oxford History of the American People: 1789 Through the Reconstruction, Vol. II. Samuel Eliot Morison. (Illus.). 540p. 1994. pap. 15.95 (*0-452-01131-0*, Mer) NAL.

Oxford History of the American People: 1869 Through the Death of John F. Kennedy, Vol. III. Samuel Eliot Morison. (Illus.). 520p. 1994. pap. 15.95 (*0-452-01132-9*, Mer) NAL.

Oxford History of the American West. Ed. by Clyde A. Milner et al. (Illus.). 904p. 1996. reprint ed. pap. 27.50 (*0-19-511212-1*) OUP.

Oxford History of the Biblical World. Michael D. Coogan. (Illus.). 672p. 1999. 49.95 (*0-19-508707-0*) OUP.

Oxford History of the British Army. Ed. by David Chandler & Ian F. Beckett. LC 96-13051. (Illus.). 492p. 1997. pap. 16.95 (*0-19-285333-3*) OUP.

***Oxford History of the British Empire: Historiography, Vol. 5.** Ed. by Robin Winks & Roger Louis. (Oxford History of the British Empire Ser.: Vol. V). 760p. 1999. 49.95 (*0-19-820566-X*) OUP.

Oxford History of the British Empire: The Eighteenth Century, Vol. 2. Ed. by P. J. Marshall & Alaine Low. (Illus.). 662p. 1998. 45.00 (*0-19-820563-5*) OUP.

Oxford History of the British Empire: The Nineteenth Century, Vol. III. Andrew Porter. (Oxford History of the British Empire Ser.). (Illus.). 796p. 1999. 45.00 (*0-19-820565-1*) OUP.

Oxford History of the British Empire: The Origins of Empire: British Overseas Enterprise to the Close of the Seventeenth Century, Vol. 1. Ed. by Nicholas Canny. (Illus.). 554p. 1998. 45.00 (*0-19-820562-7*) OUP.

Oxford History of the British Empire Vol. 4: The Twentieth Century. Ed. by Judith M. Brown & Roger Louis. (Oxford History of the British Empire Ser.: Vol. IV). (Illus.). 800p. 1999. 45.00 (*0-19-820564-3*) OUP.

Oxford History of the Classical World. Ed. by John Boardman et al. (Illus.). 892p. 1986. 60.00 (*0-19-872112-9*) OUP.

Oxford History of the Classical World: Greece & the Hellenistic World, Vol. 1. Ed. by John Boardman. (Illus.). 454p. 1988. pap. text 22.50 (*0-19-282165-2*) OUP.

Oxford History of the Classical World: The Roman World, Vol. 2. Ed. by John Boardman. (Illus.). 466p. 1988. pap. text 22.50 (*0-19-282166-0*) OUP.

Oxford History of the French Revolution. William Doyle. (Illus.). 480p. 1989. 40.00 (*0-19-822781-7*) OUP.

Oxford History of the French Revolution. William Doyle. (Illus.). 478p. 1990. reprint ed. pap. text 15.95 (*0-19-285221-3*) OUP.

Oxford History of the Prison: The Practice of Punishment in Western Society. Ed. by Norval Morris & David J. Rothman. (Illus.). 512p. 1995. 49.95 (*0-19-506153-5*) OUP.

Oxford History of the Prison: The Practice of Punishment in Western Society. Ed. by Norval Morris & David J. Rothman. (Illus.). 448p. 1997. pap. 19.95 (*0-19-511814-6*) OUP.

Oxford History of the Roman World. Ed. by John Boardman et al. (Illus.). 526p. 1991. pap. text 16.95 (*0-19-285248-5*) OUP.

***Oxford History of the Twentieth Century.** Ed. by Michael Howard & W. Roger Louis. (Illus.). 540p. 2000. pap. 22.50 (*0-19-285370-8*) OUP.

Oxford History of the Twentieth Century. W. Roger Louis. Ed. by Michael Howard. LC 98-12861. (Illus.). 540p. 1998. 39.95 (*0-19-820428-0*) OUP.

***Oxford History of Western Art.** Ed. by Martin Kemp. (Illus.). 648p. 2000. 60.00 (*0-19-860012-7*) OUP.

Oxford History of Western Philosophy. Ed. by Anthony Kenny. LC 94-9858. (Illus.). 420p. 1994. 49.95 (*0-19-824278-6*) OUP.

***Oxford History of Western Philosophy.** Anthony Kenny. 416p. 2000. pap. 15.95 (*0-19-289329-7*) OUP.

Oxford History of World Cinema. Ed. by Geoffrey Nowell-Smith. (Illus.). 846p. 1996. 55.00 (*0-19-811257-2*) OUP.

Oxford History of World Cinema. Ed. by Geoffrey Nowell-Smith. (Illus.). 846p. 1999. reprint ed. pap. 27.50 (*0-19-874242-8*) OUP.

Oxford Illustrated Book of American Children's Poems. Ed. by Donald Hall. LC 99-34419. (Illus.). 96p. (J). (gr. 2-6). 1999. 22.95 (*0-19-512373-5*) OUP.

***Oxford Illustrated Companion to Medicine.** Ed. by Stephen Lock et al. (Illus.). 1024p. 2001. 60.00 (*0-19-262950-6*) OUP.

Oxford Illustrated Dickens, 21 vols., Set. Incl. Adventures of Oliver Twist. Illus. by George Cruickshank. 446p. 1987. 15.95 (*0-19-254505-1*); American Notes & Pictures from Italy. Illus. by Marcus Stone. 454p. 1987. 17.95 (*0-19-254519-1*); Barnaby Rudge: A Tale of the Riots of 'Eighty. Charles Dickens. (Illus.). 660p. 1987. 17.95 (*0-19-254513-2*); Bleak House. Charles Dickens. (Illus.). 908p. 1987. 17.95 (*0-19-254503-5*); Christmas Books. Intro. by Eleanor Farjeon. (Illus.). 413p. 1987. 15.95 (*0-19-254514-0*); Christmas Stories. Charles Dickens. (Illus.). 772p. 1987. 16.95 (*0-19-254517-5*); Dealings with the Firm of Dombey, & Son, Wholesale, Retail, & for Exploration. Charles Dickens. (Illus.). 904p. 1987. 18.95 (*0-19-254507-8*); Hard Times for These Times. Illus. by F. Walker & Maurice Greiffenhagen. 322p. 1987. 16.95 (*0-19-254515-9*); Life & Adventures of Martin Chuzzlewit. Charles Dickens. (Illus.). 864p. 1987. 18.95 (*0-19-254509-4*); Life & Adventures of Nicholas Nickleby. Charles Dickens. (Illus.). 864p. 1987. 18.95 (*0-19-254508-6*); Little

O

Dorrit. Charles Dickens. (Illus.). 858p. 1987. 17.95 (*0-19-254512-4*); Master Humphrey's Clock & a Child's History of England. Charles Dickens. (Illus.). 544p. 1987. 17.95 (*0-19-254520-5*); Mystery of Edwin Drood. Illus. by Luke Fildes & Charles Collins. 294p. 1987. 16.95 (*0-19-254516-7*); Old Curiosity Shop. Charles Dickens. (Illus.). 574p. 1987. 16.95 (*0-19-254506-X*); Our Mutual Friend. Illus. by Marcus Stone. 850p. 1987. 17.95 (*0-19-254510-8*); Personal History of David Copperfield. Charles Dickens. (Illus.). 896p. 1987. 17.95 (*0-19-254502-7*); Posthumous Papers of the Pickwick Club. Charles Dickens. (Illus.). 826p. 1987. 17.95 (*0-19-254501-9*); Sketches by Boz: Illustrative of Every-Day Life & Every-Day People. Illus. by George Cruickshank. 708p. 1987. 18.95 (*0-19-254518-3*); Uncommercial Traveller, & Reprinted Pieces. Charles Dickens. (Illus.). 776p. 1987. 18.95 (*0-19-254521-3*); (Illus.). (J). 1987. 375.00 (*0-19-254522-1*) OUP.

Oxford Illustrated Dictionary. (GER., Illus.). 1000p. 1998. write for info. (*3-283-00366-1*) G Olms Pubs.

Oxford Illustrated Dictionary of Australian History. Jan Bassett. (Illus.). 316p. (C). 1993. 49.95 (*0-19-553243-0*) OUP.

Oxford Illustrated Dictionary of Australian History. Jan Bassett. (Illus.). 310p. 1998. reprint ed. pap. text 24.00 (*0-19-554083-2*) OUP.

Oxford Illustrated Encyclopedia: Complete Set (Volumes 1-9), 9 vols., Set. Ed. by Harry Judge. (Illus.). 3300p. 1993. 265.00 (*0-19-869223-4*) OUP.

Oxford Illustrated Encyclopedia: World History: From Earliest Times to 1800, Vol. 3. Ed. by Harry Judge. (Illus.). 400p. 1988. 49.95 (*0-19-869135-1*) OUP.

Oxford Illustrated Encyclopedia: World History from Earliest Times to 1800 & World History from 1800 to the Present Day, 2 vols., Set, Vols. III & IV. Ed. by Harry Judge & Robert Blake. (Illus.). 800p. 1988. 95.00 (*0-19-869161-0*) OUP.

Oxford Illustrated Encyclopedia Vol. 4: World History from 1800 to the Present Day. Ed. by Lord Blake. (Illus.). 400p. 1988. 49.95 (*0-19-869136-X*) OUP.

Oxford Illustrated Encyclopedia Vol. 7: Peoples & Cultures. Ed. by Richard Hoggart. (Illus.). 400p. 1992. 49.95 (*0-19-869139-4*) OUP.

Oxford Illustrated Encyclopedia Vol. 9: Index & Ready Reference, Vol. 8. Ed. by Harry Judge. 272p. 1993. 22.95 (*0-19-869174-2*) OUP.

Oxford Illustrated History of Ancient Egypt. Ed. by Ian Shaw. (Oxford Illustrated Histories Ser.). (Illus.). 640p. 2000. 40.00 (*0-19-815034-2*) OUP.

Oxford Illustrated History of Britain. Ed. by Kenneth O. Morgan. LC 83-21990. (Illus.). 654p. 1984. 49.95 (*0-19-822684-5*) OUP.

Oxford Illustrated History of Britain. Ed. by Kenneth O. Morgan. LC 83-21990. (Illus.). 654p. 1986. pap. 26.50 (*0-19-285174-8*) OUP.

***Oxford Illustrated History of Britain.** Ed. by Kenneth O. Morgan. (Illus.). 672p. 2001. pap. 24.95 (*0-19-289326-2*) OUP.

Oxford Illustrated History of Christianity. Ed. by John McManners. (Oxford Illustrated Histories Ser.). (Illus.). 736p. 1990. 55.00 (*0-19-822928-3*) OUP.

Oxford Illustrated History of Christianity. Ed. by John McManners. (Oxford Illustrated Histories Ser.). (Illus.). 736p. 1992. pap. 27.50 (*0-19-285259-0*) OUP.

Oxford Illustrated History of Classical Art. Ed. by John Boardman. LC 93-6835. (Illus.). 416p. 1993. 55.00 (*0-19-814386-9*) OUP.

Oxford Illustrated History of England. Ed. by Nigel Saul. (Illus.). 320p. 1997. 49.95 (*0-19-820502-3*) OUP.

Oxford Illustrated History of English Literature. Ed. by Pat Rogers. (Illus.). 544p. 1990. reprint ed. pap. 24.95 (*0-19-282728-6*) OUP.

Oxford Illustrated History of Ireland. Ed. by R. F. Foster. (Oxford Illustrated Histories Ser.). (Illus.). 398p. 1989. 49.95 (*0-19-822970-4*) OUP.

Oxford Illustrated History of Ireland. Ed. by R. F. Foster. (Oxford Illustrated Histories Ser.). (Illus.). 398p. 1991. reprint ed. pap. 23.50 (*0-19-285245-0*) OUP.

Oxford Illustrated History of Italy. Ed. by George Holmes. LC 98-100006. (Oxford Illustrated Histories Ser.). (Illus.). 400p. (C). 1997. 45.00 (*0-19-820527-9*) OUP.

Oxford Illustrated History of Medieval Europe. Ed. by George Holmes. (Illus.). 414p. 1988. reprint ed. 49.95 (*0-19-820073-0*) OUP.

Oxford Illustrated History of Medieval Europe. Ed. by George Holmes. (Illus.). 414p. 1990. reprint ed. pap. 24.95 (*0-19-285220-5*) OUP.

Oxford Illustrated History of Modern Europe. Ed. by Timothy C. W. Blanning. (Oxford Illustrated Histories Ser.). (Illus.). 372p. (C). 1996. 49.95 (*0-19-820374-8*) OUP.

Oxford Illustrated History of Modern Europe. Ed. by T. C. Blanning. LC 98-10536. (Illus.). 372p. 1998. reprint ed. pap. 22.50 (*0-19-285348-1*) OUP.

Oxford Illustrated History of Modern War. Ed. by Jeremy Black et al. (Illus.). 366p. 1997. 49.95 (*0-19-820427-2*) OUP.

Oxford Illustrated History of New Zealand. 2nd ed. Keith Sinclair. (Illus.). 416p. 1998. pap. text 34.00 (*0-19-558381-7*) OUP.

Oxford Illustrated History of Opera. Ed. by Roger Parker. (Illus.). 556p. 1995. 49.95 (*0-19-816282-0*) OUP.

Oxford Illustrated History of Roman Britain. Peter Salway. (Illus.). 576p. 1993. 55.00 (*0-19-822984-4*) OUP.

Oxford Illustrated History of the British Army. Ed. by David Chandler & Ian F. Beckett. (Illustrated Histories Ser.). (Illus.). 510p. 1994. 49.95 (*0-19-869178-5*) OUP.

Oxford Illustrated History of the British Monarchy. John Cannon & Ralph Griffiths. (Illus.). 744p. 1988. 55.00 (*0-19-822786-8*) OUP.

Oxford Illustrated History of the Crusades. Ed. by Jonathan Riley-Smith. (Oxford Illustrated Histories Ser.). (Illus.). 448p. (C). 1995. 49.95 (*0-19-820435-3*) OUP.

Oxford Illustrated History of the Crusades. Ed. by Jonathan Riley-Smith. LC 96-39343. (Illus.). 448p. 1997. pap. 24.95 (*0-19-285294-9*) OUP.

***Oxford Illustrated History of the First World War.** Ed. by Hew Strachan. (Oxford Illustrated Histories Ser.). (Illus.). 368p. 2000. pap. 22.50 (*0-19-289325-4*) OUP.

Oxford Illustrated History of the Monarchy. John Cannon & Ralph Griffiths. LC 97-39075. (Oxford Paperback Reference Ser.). (Illus.). 738p. 1998. reprint ed. pap. 26.50 (*0-19-288073-X*) OUP.

Oxford Illustrated History of the Vikings. Ed. by Peter Sawyer. LC 97-16649. (Illus.). 316p. 1997. 49.95 (*0-19-820526-0*) OUP.

Oxford Illustrated History of the Vikings. Ed. by Peter Sawyer. (Oxford Illustrated Histories Ser.). (Illus.). 344p. 2000. pap. 22.50 (*0-19-285365-1*) OUP.

Oxford Illustrated History of Theatre. Ed. by John R. Brown. (Oxford Illustrated Histories Ser.). (Illus.). 616p. (YA). 1995. 55.00 (*0-19-212997-X*) OUP.

Oxford Illustrated History of Theatre. John R. Brown. LC 97-30250. (Oxford Illustrated Histories). (Illus.). 590p. 1997. reprint ed. pap. 25.00 (*0-19-288062-4*) OUP.

Oxford Illustrated History of Tudor & Stuart Britain. Stuart Britain. Ed. by John Morrill. (Oxford Illustrated Histories Ser.). (Illus.). 464p. 1996. 49.95 (*0-19-820325-X*) OUP.

Oxford Illustrated History of Tudor & Stuart Britain. John Morrill. (Illus.). 1996. 39.95 (*0-614-96822-4*) OUP.

***Oxford Illustrated History of Tudor & Stuart Britain.** Ed. by John Morrill. (Oxford Illustrated Histories Ser.). (Illus.). 536p. 2001. pap. 26.50 (*0-19-289327-0*) OUP.

Oxford Illustrated History of Western Philosophy. Ed. by Anthony Kenny. (Illus.). 420p. 1997. pap. 22.50 (*0-19-285335-X*) OUP.

Oxford Illustrated Jane Austen, 6 vols. 3rd ed. Jane Austen. Ed. by R. W. Chapman. Incl. Vol. I. Sense & Sensibility. 3rd ed. (Illus.). 446p. 1988. reprint ed. 20.00 (*0-19-254701-1*); Vol. III. Mansfield Park. 3rd ed. (Illus.). 580p. 1988. reprint ed. 20.00 (*0-19-254703-8*); Vol. IV. Emma. 3rd ed. (Illus.). 536p. 1988. reprint ed. 20.00 (*0-19-254704-6*); Vol. V. Northanger Abbey. 3rd ed. (Illus.). 624p. 1988. reprint ed. 20.00 (*0-19-254705-4*); Vol. VI. Minor Works. (Illus.). 504p. 1988. reprint ed. 20.00 (*0-19-254706-2*); (Illus.). 3,184p. 1988. 120.00 (*0-19-254707-0*) OUP.

Oxford Illustrated Old Testament: With Drawings by Contemporary Artists, 5 vols. Incl. Vol 1. Pentateuch. 1968. Vol 2. History Books. 1968. Vol 3. Poetical Books. 1968. Vol 4. Prophets. 1969. Vol 5. Apocrypha. 1969. 1969. 75.00 (*0-19-519661-9*) OUP.

Oxford Illustrated Prehistory of Europe. Ed. by Barry Cunliffe. (Illus.). 544p. 1994. 49.95 (*0-19-814385-0*) OUP.

Oxford in English Literature: The Making, & Undoing, of "The English Athens" John Dougill. LC 98-8954. (Illus.). 400p. 1998. 34.50 (*0-472-10784-4*, 10784) U of Mich Pr.

Oxford in Fiction: An Annotated Bibliography. Judy Batson. LC 88-34700. 219p. 1989. text 10.00 (*0-8240-7036-4*) Garland.

Oxford in North America: The Art of Biography, No. 8. Ed. by Eva Klimas. 40p. 1993. write for info. (*1-883718-03-1*) Oxford U Dev.

Oxford in North America No. 10: The Refugee Crisis - the Migration of Peoples. Ed. by Eva Klimas. 45p. (Orig.). 1994. write for info. (*1-883718-05-8*) Oxford U Dev.

Oxford in North America Vol. 7: "An Early Look at the First 100 Days of the Clinton Administration" Ed. by Eva Klimas. 45p. 1993. write for info. (*1-883718-02-3*) Oxford U Dev.

Oxford India Anthology of Twelve Modern Indian Poets. Arvind K. Mehrotra. 200p. 1993. pap. 10.95 (*0-19-562867-5*) OUP.

Oxford India Companion to the "Indian Mutiny" of 1857. Ed. by P. J. Taylor. (Illus.). 452p. (C). 1996. text 55.00 (*0-19-563863-8*) OUP.

Oxford Introduction to Language Study: Pragmatics. George Yule. 150p. 1996. pap. text 11.95 (*0-19-437207-3*) OUP.

Oxford Introductions to Language Study: Linguistics. H. G. Widdowson. (Illus.). 148p. 1996. pap. text 11.95 (*0-19-437206-5*) OUP.

Oxford Irish Minidictionary. Ed. by Valerie Grundy & Breandan O'Croinin. 686p. 1999. pap. 6.50 (*0-19-860227-8*) OUP.

Oxford Irish Quotations. Ed. by Bernard O'Donoghue. LC 98-39813. 336p. 1999. pap. 7.95 (*0-19-860239-1*) OUP.

Oxford Italian Desk Dictionary. Ed. by Deborah Mazza et al. LC 98-116332. (ENG & ITA.). 390p. (C). 1997. 15.95 (*0-19-860158-1*) OUP.

Oxford Italian Dictionary: Italian-English, English-Italian. Ed. by Debora Mazza. LC 98-194788. (ENG & ITA.). 512p. 1997. mass mkt. 4.99 (*0-425-16012-2*) Berkley Pub.

Oxford Italian Minidictionary. 2nd rev. ed. Ed. by Oxford University Press Staff. 630p. 1999. vinyl bd. 6.50 (*0-19-860253-7*) OUP.

Oxford Junior Dictionary. 3rd ed. Rosemary Sansome & Dee Reid. 256p. (J). 1995. 11.95 (*0-19-910304-6*) OUP.

Oxford Junior Thesaurus. Alan Spooner. 302p. (J). 1995. (*0-19-910306-2*) OUP.

Oxford Large Print Dictionary. 2nd ed. Ed. by Elaine Pollard & Helen Liebeck. 952p. 1996. 39.95 (*0-19-861322-9*) OUP.

Oxford Latin Course. 2nd ed. Maurice G. Balme & James Morwood. (Illus.). 64p. (C). 1996. pap. text, teacher ed. 15.95 (*0-19-912230-X*) OUP.

Oxford Latin Course, Pt. I. 2nd ed. Maurice G. Balme & James Morwood. LC 96-209131. (Illus.). 157p. (C). 1996. pap. text 21.95 (*0-19-521203-7*) OUP.

Oxford Latin Course, Pt. I. 2nd ed. Maurice G. Balme & James H. Morwood. LC 97-201005. (Illus.). 102p. 1997. pap. text, teacher ed. 15.95 (*0-19-912232-6*) OUP.

Oxford Latin Course, Pt. II. 2nd ed. Maurice G. Balme & James Morwood. (Illus.). 176p. (C). 1996. pap. text 21.95 (*0-19-521205-3*) OUP.

Oxford Latin Course, Pt. III. Maurice G. Balme & James Morwood. (Illus.). 256p. (C). 1988. pap. text 20.95 (*0-19-912092-7*) OUP.

Oxford Latin Course, Pt. III. 2nd ed. Maurice G. Balme & James Morwood. LC 96-209131. (Illus.). 224p. (C). 1997. pap. text 23.95 (*0-19-521207-X*) OUP.

***Oxford Latin Course Cassette II: Recordings for Part III & the Reade.** Maurice Balme & James Morwood. (Oxford Latin Course Ser.). (C). 1999. audio 19.95 (*0-19-840562-6*) OUP.

Oxford Latin Course Pt. 2, Pt. II. 2nd ed. Maurice G. Balme & James H. Morwood. (Illus.). 76p. 1997. pap. text, teacher ed. 15.95 (*0-19-912231-8*) OUP.

Oxford Latin Dictionary. Ed. by P. G. Glare. 2,150p. 1983. text 275.00 (*0-19-864224-5*) OUP.

Oxford Latin Dictionary. Ed. by James Morwood. 704p. 1998. pap. 6.95 (*0-19-860139-5*) OUP.

Oxford Latin Liturgical D 20. Ed. by Luther Dittmer. (Veroffentlichungen Mittelalterlicher Musikhandschriften - Publications of Mediaeval Musical Manuscripts Ser.: Vol. 6). (ENG & GER.). 1961. pap. 32.00 (*0-912024-06-2*) Inst Mediaeval Mus.

Oxford Latin Reader, Pt. IV. 2nd ed. Maurice Balme & James Morwood. LC 97-189694. (Oxford Latin Course Ser.). (Illus.). 256p. (C). 1997. pap. text 22.95 (*0-19-521209-6*); pap. text, teacher ed. 15.95 (*0-19-912233-4*) OUP.

Oxford Learner's Pocket Dictionary. 2nd ed. 496p. 1991. pap. text 7.95 (*0-19-431282-8*) OUP.

Oxford Learner's Pocket Dictionary: English-Greek, Greek-English. Fiona Sibbald. (ENG & GRE.). 528p. 1993. pap. text 7.95 (*0-19-431279-8*) OUP.

***Oxford Lectern Bible.** 1200p. 1998. 450.00 (*0-19-107010-6*) OUP.

***Oxford Lectern Bible.** 1200p. 1998. 450.00 (*0-19-107009-2*) OUP.

Oxford Lecture: And Other Discourses. Frederick Pollock. LC 76-39718. (Essay Index Reprint Ser.). 1977. reprint ed. 20.95 (*0-8369-2780-X*) Ayer.

Oxford Lectures. Frederick Pollock. Ed. by Roy M. Mersky & J. Myron Jacobstein. LC 74-114033. (Classics in Legal History Reprint Ser.: Vol. 4). 303p. 1970. reprint ed. lib. bdg. 43.50 (*0-89941-003-0*, 301200) W S Hein.

Oxford Lectures on Classical Subjects, 1909-1920. (Essay Index Reprint Ser.). 1977. 23.95 (*0-8369-0761-2*) Ayer.

Oxford Lectures on History, 1904-1923, 10 Vols in One. LC 67-22107. (Essay Index Reprint Ser.). 1977. 26.95 (*0-8369-1334-5*) Ayer.

Oxford Lectures on Literature, 1907-1920. (Essay Index Reprint Ser.). 1977. 23.95 (*0-8369-0762-0*) Ayer.

Oxford Lectures on Philosophy, 1910-1923, 8 Vols. LC 67-22108. (Essay Index Reprint Ser.). 1977. 26.95 (*0-8369-1335-3*) Ayer.

Oxford Lectures on Poetry. Ernest De Selincourt. LC 67-23202. (Essay Index Reprint Ser.). 1977. 19.95 (*0-8369-0371-4*) Ayer.

Oxford Lectures on Poetry. A. C. Bradley. ix, 395p. 1986. reprint ed. pap. 29.95 (*0-935005-35-8*); reprint ed. lib. bdg. 46.95 (*0-935005-16-1*) Lincoln-Rembrandt.

Oxford Lectures on University Studies, 1906-1921, 12 Vols. LC 67-22110. (Essay Index Reprint Ser.). 1977. 26.95 (*0-8369-1336-1*) Ayer.

Oxford Literary Guide to Australia. Ed. by Peter Pierce. (Illus.). 360p. 1988. text 62.00 (*0-19-554592-3*) OUP.

Oxford Literary Guide to Australia. 2nd ed. Ed. by Peter Pierce. (Illus.). 516p. 1993. reprint ed. pap. text 35.00 (*0-19-553447-6*) OUP.

Oxford Literary History of Australia. Ed. by Bruce Bennett & Jennifer Strauss. LC 98-193279. 496p. 1999. 45.00 (*0-19-553737-8*) OUP.

Oxford Love Quotations. Ed. by Susan Ratcliffe. LC 98-39812. 336p. 1999. pap. 7.95 (*0-19-860240-5*) OUP.

Oxford Manuscripts, Pt. I. Ed. by Elise B. Jorgens. (English Song 1600-1675 Ser.). 472p. 1987. text 30.00 (*0-8240-8236-2*) Garland.

Oxford Manuscripts, Pt. II. Ed. by Elise B. Jorgens. (English Song 1600-1675 Ser.). 504p. 1987. text 30.00 (*0-8240-8237-0*) Garland.

Oxford Mark Twain, 29 vols. Mark Twain, pseud. Ed. by Shelley F. Fishkin. (Illus.). 14176p. 1997. 495.00 (*0-19-511345-4*) OUP.

Oxford Mark Twain: Chapters from My Autobiography (1906-1907) Ed. by Shelley F. Fishkin. LC 96-15218. (Illus.). 368p. 1996. 16.95 (*0-19-510156-1*) OUP.

Oxford Mark Twain: How to Tell a Story & Other Essays (1897) Ed. by Shelly F. Fishkin. (Illus.). 336p. 1996. 22.00 (*0-19-510149-9*) OUP.

Oxford Mark Twain: The Adventures of Tom Sawyer (1876) Ed. by Shelly F. Fishkin. (Illus.). 368p. 1996. 16.95 (*0-19-510136-7*) OUP.

Oxford Mark Twain: The American Claimant (1892) Shelley F. Fishkin. (Illus.). 368p. 1996. 22.00 (*0-19-510143-X*) OUP.

Oxford Mark Twain: The Celebrated Jumping Frog of Calaveras County, & Other Sketches (1867) Shelley F. Fishkin. LC 96-12305. (Illus.). 288p. 1996. 16.95 (*0-19-510131-6*) OUP.

Oxford Mark Twain: The Diaries of Adam & Eve (1904, 1906) Shelley F. Fishkin. (Illus.). 304p. 1996. 22.00 (*0-19-510152-9*) OUP.

Oxford Mark Twain: The Prince & the Pauper: A Tale for Young People of All Ages (1881) Shelley F. Fishkin. (Illus.). 496p. 1996. 16.95 (*0-19-510138-3*) OUP.

Oxford Mark Twain: The Tragedy of Pudd'nhead Wilson & the Comedy Those Extraordinary Twins (1894) Ed. by Shelley F. Fishkin. (Illus.). 512p. 1996. 16.95 (*0-19-510147-2*) OUP.

Oxford Mark Twain: The 1,000,000 Pound Bank-Note & Other New Stories (1893) Ed. by Shelley F. Fishkin. (Illus.). 352p. 1997. text 28.00 (*0-19-511413-2*) OUP.

Oxford Mark Twain: 1601 & Is Shakespeare Dead? (1882, 1909) Ed. by Shelly F. Fishkin. (Illus.). 256p. 1996. 22.00 (*0-19-510160-X*) OUP.

Oxford Mark Twain 29-vol., Set. Mark Twain, pseud. Ed. by Shelley Fisher Fishkin. (The Oxford Mark Twain Ser.). (Illus.). 14176p. 1997. 1250.00 (*0-19-511446-9*) OUP.

Oxford Medical Companion. Ed. by John Walton et al. (Illus.). 1,062p. 1994. 65.00 (*0-19-262355-9*) OUP.

Oxford Minireference Dictionary & Thesaurus. Ed. by Sara Hawker. 752p. 1998. pap. 6.95 (*0-19-860183-2*) OUP.

Oxford Minireference French Usage. Ed. by Richard Wakely & Henri Bejoint. 230p. 1996. pap. 6.95 (*0-19-860041-0*) OUP.

Oxford Minireference French Usage. Ed. by Richard Wakely & Henri Bejoint. 230p. 1997. pap. 7.95 (*0-19-864334-9*) OUP.

Oxford Minireference Spanish Grammar. Ed. by John Butt. (Minireference Ser.). (SPA.). 364p. 1996. pap. 5.95 (*0-19-864521-X*) OUP.

Oxford Minireference Thesaurus. 2nd ed. Ed. by Lucinda Coventry & Martin Nixon. LC 98-51864. 640p. 1999. pap. 7.95 (*0-19-860256-1*) OUP.

Oxford Mourning: A Kate Ivory Mystery. large type ed. Veronica Stallwood. 448p. 31.50 (*0-7089-3710-1*) Ulverscroft.

Oxford Movement: A Revision Eighteen Thirty-Three to Nineteen Eighty-Three. J. Griffin. 1985. 20.00 (*0-7855-2133-X*, Pub. by Pentland Pr) St Mut.

Oxford Movement & Its Leaders: A Bibliography of Secondary & Lesser Primary Sources. Lawrence N. Crumb. LC 88-10217. (American Theological Library Association Monograph: No. 24). 736p. 1988. 70.00 (*0-8108-2141-9*) Scarecrow.

Oxford Movement & Its Leaders: A Bibliography of Secondary & Lesser Primary Sources. Lawrence N. Crumb. LC 93-16025. (American Theological Library Association Monograph: No. 24). 320p. 1993. suppl. ed. 47.50 (*0-8108-2700-X*) Scarecrow.

Oxford Movement in America. Clarence A. Walworth. LC 77-150436. (Monographs: No. 30). (Illus.). 1974. reprint ed. 12.00 (*0-930060-10-5*) US Cath Hist.

Oxford Movement in Context: Anglican High Churchmanship, 1760-1857. Peter B. Nockles. 359p. 1997. pap. text 24.95 (*0-521-58719-0*) Cambridge U Pr.

Oxford Museum: Oxford, 1855-60 Deane & Woodward. Trevor Garnham. (Architecture in Detail Ser.). (Illus.). 60p. (C). 1993. pap. 29.95 (*0-7148-2769-X*, Pub. by Phaidon Press) Phaidon Pr.

Oxford New Spanish Dictionary: The World's Most Trusted Dictionaries. Press Boulevard Company Staff. 1999. mass mkt. 5.99 (*0-425-17090-X*) Berkley Pub.

***Oxford New Testament.** 1998. 12.99 (*0-19-107015-7*); 17.99 (*0-19-107016-5*) OUP.

Oxford Observed: Town & Gown. Peter Snow. (Illus.). 256p. 1993. pap. 24.95 (*0-7195-5144-7*, Pub. by John Murray) Trafalgar.

Oxford Pamphlets, Leaflets & Circulars of Charles Lutwidge Dodgson. Charles Lutwidge Dodgson. Ed. by Edward Wakeling. (Pamphlets of Lewis Carroll Ser.: Vol. 1). (C). 1993. text 70.00 (*0-8139-1250-4*) U Pr of Va.

Oxford Paperback Dictionary. 4th rev. ed. Elaine Pollard. Ed. by Helen Liebeck. LC 93-43215. 960p. (C). 1994. pap. 4.99 (*0-19-280012-4*) OUP.

***Oxford Paperback Encyclopedia.** (Illus.). 1504p. 1998. pap. 21.95 (*0-19-280082-5*) OUP.

Oxford Paperback French Dictionary & Grammar. William Rowlinson et al. (FRE.). 806p. 1995. pap. 13.95 (*0-19-864529-5*) OUP.

Oxford Paperback German Dictionary & Grammar. William Rowlinson et al. (GER.). 862p. 1995. pap. 13.95 (*0-19-864530-9*) OUP.

Oxford Paperback Greek Dictionary. Ed. by Niki Watts. LC 96-17297. (GRE.). 480p. (C). 1998. pap. 8.95 (*0-19-864542-2*) OUP.

Oxford Paperback Spanish Dictionary & Grammar. Ed. by Christine Lea et al. LC 98-112179. (SPA.). 864p. 1997. pap. 13.95 (*0-19-860079-8*) OUP.

Oxford Paperback Thesaurus. Betty Kirkpatrick. 920p. (C). 1994. pap. (*0-19-282841-X*) OUP.

Oxford Papers, Studies in British Paper History. Peter Bower. (Studies in British Paper History: Vol. 1). (Illus.). 108p. 1996. pap. 29.95 (*0-9525757-0-1*) Oak Knoll.

***Oxford Physics in the 13th Century, 1250-1270: Motion, Infinity, Place & Time.** Cecilia Trifogli. (Studien und Texte Zur Geistesgeschichte des Mittelalters). 304p. 2000. 95.00 (*90-04-11657-5*) Brill Academic Pubs.

***Oxford Picture Dictionary.** Norma Shapiro & Jayme Adelson-Goldstein. LC 97-50610. (Illus.). 1998. 13.50 (*0-19-435189-0*) OUP.

***Oxford Picture Dictionary.** Norma Shapiro & Jayme Adelson-Goldstein. LC 98-10946. 1998. 13.50 (*0-19-435190-4*) OUP.

***Oxford Picture Dictionary.** Norma Shapiro & Jayme Adelson-Goldstein. LC 97-50624. 1998. 13.50 (*0-19-435203-X*) OUP.

***Oxford Picture Dictionary.** Norma Shapiro & Jayme Adelson-Goldstein. LC 98-10728. (Illus.). 1998. pap. 13.50 (*0-19-435193-9*) OUP.

***Oxford Picture Dictionary.** Norma Shapiro & Jayme Adelson-Goldstein. LC 98-9378. 1999. 13.50 (*0-19-435194-7*) OUP.

An Asterisk (*) at the beginning of an entry indicates that the title is appearing for the first time.

***Oxford Picture Dictionary.** Norma Shapiro & Jayme Adelson-Goldstein. LC 98-10708. 1999. write for info. (*0-19-436197-7*) OUP.

***Oxford Picture Dictionary.** Norma Shapiro & Jayme Adelson-Goldstein. LC 98-55453. 2000. write for info. (*0-19-436281-7*) OUP.

***Oxford Picture Dictionary.** Norma Shapiro et al. LC 98-4984. 1999. 13.50 (*0-19-435195-5*) OUP.

Oxford Picture Dictionary: English - Spanish Edition. 2nd ed. Norman Shapiro. LC 97-43652. (Illus.). 238p. 1998. pap. text 13.50 (*0-19-435188-2*) OUP.

***Oxford Picture Dictionary: English-Korean Edition.** Norman Shapiro. LC 98-10947. (Illus.). 240p. 1998. text 13.50 (*0-19-435191-2*) OUP.

Oxford Picture Dictionary: English/Russian Edition. Norman Shapiro. LC 98-10026. (Illus.). 240p. 1998. pap. text 13.50 (*0-19-435192-0*) OUP.

Oxford Picture Dictionary: Monolingual Edition. Norman Shapiro. LC 97-21963. (Illus.). 1998. pap. text 13.50 (*0-19-470059-3*) OUP.

***Oxford Picture Dictionary for Kids.** Joan Ross Keyes. (Illus.). 146p. 1998. pap. 10.95 (*0-19-434997-7*) OUP.

***Oxford Picture Dictionary for Kids.** Joan Ross Keyes. (Illus.). 288p. 1998. text, teacher ed. 19.95 (*0-19-434998-5*) OUP.

***Oxford Picture Dictionary for Kids.** Joan Ross Keyes. (Illus.). (J). 1998. 10.95 (*0-19-436662-6*) OUP.

Oxford Picture Dictionary for Kids: Monolingual Edition. Joan R. Keyes. (Illus.). 144p. 1998. text 17.95 (*0-19-434996-9*) OUP.

***Oxford Picture Dictionary for the Content Areas.** Dorothy Kauffman & Gary Apple. LC 98-36196. 2000. 12.95 (*0-19-434338-3*); 18.95 (*0-19-434336-7*) OUP.

Oxford Picture Dictionary of American English. E. C. Parnwell. (Illus.). 1988. pap. write for info. (*0-318-54877-1*) OUP.

***Oxford Pocket Bible.** 1200p. 1998. 19.99 (*0-19-107039-4*); 21.99 (*0-19-107046-7*) OUP.

***Oxford Pocket Bible.** PCKT OXF. 1200p. 1998. pap. 39.99 (*0-19-528209-4*); pap. 44.99 (*0-19-528210-8*); pap. 44.99 (*0-19-528211-6*) OUP.

***Oxford Pocket Bible.** Oxford University Press Staff. 1998. bond lthr. 44.99 (*0-19-528207-8*) OUP.

***Oxford Pocket Bible.** Oxford University Staff. 1998. 49.99 (*0-19-528214-0*); bond lthr. 44.99 (*0-19-528206-X*) OUP.

***Oxford Pocket Bible: Berkshire Leather.** Oxford University Staff. 1998. lthr. 49.99 (*0-19-528215-9*) OUP.

***Oxford Pocket Bible: Bonded Leather.** PCKT OXF. 1200p. 1998. pap. 39.99 (*0-19-528208-6*) OUP.

Oxford Pocket Bible: Bonded Leather. Pckt Staff. 1472p. 1998. 39.99 (*0-19-528202-7*) OUP.

Oxford Pocket English Grammar. A. J. Thompson & A. V. Martinet. (Illus.). 320p. 1990. pap. text 10.95 (*0-19-431301-8*) OUP.

***Oxford Pocket Irish Dictionary.** 640p. 2000. pap. 14.95 (*0-19-860254-5*) OUP.

***Oxford Pocket Latin Set, 2.** M. Moorewood. 1999. 36.80 (*0-19-521505-2*) OUP.

Oxford Poems of Hugh Primus & the Arundel Lyrics. Hugh Primus. Ed. by C. J. McDonough. (LAT.). x, 134p. pap. text 7.43 (*0-88844-465-6*) Brill Academic Pubs.

Oxford Poetry by Richard Eedes & George Peele. Ed. by Dana F. Sutton. LC 95-21074. (Renaissance Imagination Ser.). 260p. 1995. text 79.00 (*0-8153-2161-9*) Garland.

***Oxford Portraits in Science.** Owen Gingerich. (Oxford Portraits in Science Ser.). (Illus.). 1999. lib. bdg. 273.00 (*0-19-521541-9*) OUP.

Oxford Portuguese Dictionary. Oxford University Press Staff. (POR.). 1998. mass mkt. 4.99 (*0-425-16389-X*) Berkley Pub.

Oxford Portuguese Minidictionary. Compiled by John Whitlam & Lia C. Raitt. 656p. 1998. pap. 6.95 (*0-19-860143-3*) OUP.

Oxford Practice Grammar: With Key. John Eastwood. (Illus.). 334p. 1993. pap. text 12.95 (*0-19-431352-2*) OUP.

Oxford Practice Grammar: Without Key. John Eastwood. (Illus.). 302p. 1993. pap. text 10.95 (*0-19-431353-0*) OUP.

Oxford Progressive English Readers: Emma. 2nd ed. Jane Austen. (Illus.). 62p. 1993. pap. text 5.95 (*0-19-585270-2*) OUP.

Oxford Progressive English Readers: 3700 Headwords Far from the Madding Crowd. Thomas Hardy. (Illus.). 110p. 1995. pap. text 5.95 (*0-19-586317-8*) OUP.

Oxford Provencal Chansonnier. W. P. Shepard. (Elliott Monographs: Vol. 21). 1927. 35.00 (*0-527-02624-7*) Periodicals Srv.

***Oxford Pulpit Bible.** 1376p. 1999. 190.00 (*0-19-528221-3*); 200.00 (*0-19-528222-1*); 190.00 (*0-19-528223-X*); 200.00 (*0-19-528224-8*); 59.99 (*0-19-528237-X*); 69.99 (*0-19-528238-8*); 59.99 (*0-19-528239-6*); 69.99 (*0-19-528240-X*); 59.99 (*0-19-528241-8*); 69.99 (*0-19-528242-6*); 90.00 (*0-19-528243-4*); 100.00 (*0-19-528244-2*); 90.00 (*0-19-528245-0*); 100.00 (*0-19-528246-9*) OUP.

***Oxford Puzzle Solver.** 352p. 1999. pap. 9.95 (*0-19-860222-7*) OUP.

***Oxford Quick Reference Spelling Dictionary.** Maurice Waite. 320p. 1998. pap. 6.95 (*0-19-860168-9*) OUP.

***Oxford Reader's Companion to Conrad.** Ed. by Owen Knowles & Gene M. Moore. (Illus.). 386p. 2000. 49.95 (*0-19-866214-9*) OUP.

***Oxford Reader's Companion to Dickens.** Paul Schlicke. LC 99-230991. (Oxford Readers Ser.). (Illus.). 672p. (YA). 1999. 49.95 (*0-19-866213-0*) OUP.

***Oxford Reader's Companion to Dickens.** Ed. by Paul Schlicke. (Illus.). 640p. 2000. pap. 15.95 (*0-19-866253-X*) OUP.

***Oxford Reader's Companion to George Eliot.** Ed. by John Rignall. (Illus.). 672p. 2000. 55.00 (*0-19-860099-2*) OUP.

***Oxford Reader's Companion to Hardy.** Ed. by Norman Page. (Illus.). 448p. 2000. 49.95 (*0-19-860074-7*) OUP.

Oxford Reader's Companion to Trollope. R. C. Terry. (Illus.). 672p. 1999. 49.95 (*0-19-866210-6*) OUP.

Oxford Readings in Aristophanes. Ed. by Erich Segal. 356p. (C). 1996. text 70.00 (*0-19-872156-0*); pap. text 18.95 (*0-19-872157-9*) OUP.

Oxford Readings in Greek Tragedy. Ed. by Erich Segal. 464p. 1989. pap. text 29.95 (*0-19-872110-2*) OUP.

Oxford Readings in the Greek Novel. Simon Swain. LC 98-45077. 424p. 1999. text 62.00 (*0-19-872189-7*) OUP.

Oxford Readings in the Roman Novel. S. J. Harrison. LC 98-40793. 378p. 1999. pap. text 24.95 (*0-19-872174-9*) OUP.

***Oxford Readings in the Roman Novel.** Ed. by S.J. Harrison. LC 98-40793. 378p. 1999. text 62.00 (*0-19-872173-0*) OUP.

Oxford Readings in Vergil's Aeneid. Ed. by S. J. Harrison. 488p. 1990. pap. text 38.00 (*0-19-814388-5*) OUP.

Oxford Reference Bible. Oxford Reference Staff. 1578p. 1997. 85.00 (*0-19-111603-3*) OUP.

Oxford Reformers. Frederic Seebohm. LC 70-147115. reprint ed. 37.50 (*0-404-05696-2*) AMS Pr.

Oxford Regional Economic Atlases: The United States & Canada. 2nd ed. Ed. by John D. Chapman et al. (Illus.). 176p. 1975. pap. text 25.00 (*0-19-894308-3*) OUP.

***Oxford Reverse Dictionary.** Compiled by David Edmonds. LC 99-21464. 416p. 2000. pap. 15.95 (*0-19-860176-X*) OUP.

Oxford Reviews in Reproductive Biology, Vol. 16. Ed. by Henry M. Charlton. (Illus.). 344p. 1994. text 89.00 (*0-19-262426-1*) OUP.

Oxford Reviews of Reproductive Biology, Vol. 3. Ed. by C. A. Finn. (Illus.). 1325p. 1981. text 85.00 (*0-19-857536-X*) OUP.

Oxford Reviews of Reproductive Biology, Vol. 13. Ed. by S. R. Milligan. (Illus.). 328p. 1991. 89.00 (*0-19-857761-3*) OUP.

Oxford Reviews of Reproductive Biology, Vol. 14. Ed. by S. R. Milligan. (Illus.). 384p. 1992. text 110.00 (*0-19-262241-2*) OUP.

Oxford Reviews of Reproductive Biology, Vol. 15. Ed. by S. R. Milligan. (Illus.). 384p. 1993. 79.00 (*0-19-262346-X*) OUP.

Oxford Reviews of Reproductive Biology, Vol. 17. Ed. by Henry M. Charlton. (Illus.). 302p. 1995. text 125.00 (*0-19-262629-9*) OUP.

Oxford Russian Desk Dictionary. Ed. by Colin Howlett. 638p. 1997. 19.95 (*0-19-860162-X*) OUP.

***Oxford Russian Dictionary.** 2nd ed. Ed. by Marcus Wheeler et al. 1320p. 2000. 60.00 (*0-19-860160-3*) OUP.

Oxford Russian Dictionary. 2nd rev. ed. Ed. by Marcus Wheeler et al. LC 98-157754. 1,358p. 1998. 55.00 (*0-19-860153-0*) OUP.

Oxford Russian Dictionary: Russian-English, English-Russian. Ed. by Jessie Coulson et al. (ENG & RUS.). 1360p. (C). 1994. 55.00 (*0-19-864189-3*) OUP.

Oxford Russian Dictionary: Russian-English, English-Russian. Della Thompson. LC 98-132068. (ENG & RUS.). 512p. 1997. mass mkt. 4.99 (*0-425-16013-0*) Berkley Pub.

Oxford Russian-English Dictionary. Marcus Wheeler. 913p. 1993. 49.95 (*0-7859-9076-3*) Fr & Eur.

Oxford Russian-English Dictionary. 2nd ed. Ed. by Boris O. Unbegaun & Marcus Wheeler. 944p. 1992. pap. 29.95 (*0-19-864193-1*) OUP.

Oxford Russian Minidictionary. Ed. by Della Thompson. LC 97-210037. 704p. 1997. pap. 6.95 (*0-19-860142-5*) OUP.

Oxford S-A-B Song Book, 2 vols., 1. Ed. by Reginald Jacques. (J). (gr. 7-9). 1951. 6.95 (*0-19-330511-9*) OUP.

Oxford S-A-B Song Book, 2 vols., 2. Ed. by Reginald Jacques. (J). (gr. 7-9). 1951. 6.95 (*0-19-330513-5*) OUP.

Oxford School A-Z of English. John Ayto. 320p. (J). Date not set. write for info. (*0-19-910308-9*) OUP.

Oxford Scottish Song Book. Ed. by Cedric T. Davie & George McVicar. 1969. 12.00 (*0-19-330270-5*); pap. 12.00 (*0-19-330271-3*); pap. 3.50 (*0-19-330272-1*) OUP.

Oxford Shakespeare: Titus Andronocus. William Shakespeare. (Oxford World's Classics Ser.). (Illus.). 236p. 1998. pap. 7.95 (*0-19-283610-2*) OUP.

***Oxford Shakespeare The History Of King Lear: (the 1608 Quarto)** William Shakespeare. Ed. by Stanley Wells. (Illus.). 300p. 2000. text 85.00 (*0-19-818290-2*) OUP.

Oxford Shakespeare Histories. William Shakespeare. Ed. by Stanley Wells et al. (Oxford Shakespeare Ser.). (Illus.). 496p. 1994. pap. 11.95 (*0-19-818272-4*) OUP.

Oxford Slavonic Papers. Ed. by J. L. Fennell. (New Ser.: Vol. 16). 188p. 1985. text 45.00 (*0-19-815659-6*) OUP.

***Oxford Slavonic Papers.** Ed. by C. M. MacRobert et al. (Illus.). 161p. 1999. text 65.00 (*0-19-815966-8*) OUP.

Oxford Slavonic Papers, Vol. 12. Ed. by John L. Fennell et al. (New Ser.). 1980. 39.00 (*0-19-815654-5*) OUP.

Oxford Slavonic Papers, Vol. 14. Ed. by J. L. Fennell et al. (New Ser.). 160p. 1982. text 37.50 (*0-19-815657-X*) OUP.

Oxford Slavonic Papers, Vol. 15. Ed. by J. L. Fennell et al. (New Ser.). 174p. 1983. text 39.50 (*0-19-815658-8*) OUP.

Oxford Slavonic Papers, Vol. 17. Ed. by J. L. Fennell et al. (New Ser.). 114p. 1986. text 45.00 (*0-19-815661-8*) OUP.

Oxford Slavonic Papers, Vol. 18. Ed. by J. L. Fennell et al. (New Ser.). (Illus.). 156p. 1986. text 42.00 (*0-19-815663-4*) OUP.

Oxford Slavonic Papers, Vol. 19. J. L. Fennell et al. (New Ser.). 180p. 1987. text 55.00 (*0-19-815665-0*) OUP.

Oxford Slavonic Papers, Vol. 20. Ed. by I. P. Foote et al. (New Ser.). (Illus.). 166p. 1988. text 60.00 (*0-19-961044-4*) OUP.

Oxford Slavonic Papers, Vol. 22. Ed. by I. P. Foote et al. (New Ser.). (Illus.). 188p. 1990. 65.00 (*0-19-815668-5*) OUP.

Oxford Slavonic Papers, Vol. 23. Ed. by I. P. Foote et al. (Illus.). 112p. 1991. 59.00 (*0-19-815167-5*, 12220) OUP.

Oxford Slavonic Papers, Vol. 24. I. P. Foote et al. Ed. by G. S. Smith & Gerald C. Stone. (Illus.). 150p. 1992. text 75.00 (*0-19-815669-3*) OUP.

Oxford Slavonic Papers, Vol. 28. 28th ed. Ed. by C. M. MacRobert et al. LC Vol. 28. (New Ser.). (Illus.). 143p. (C). 1996. text 65.00 (*0-19-815916-1*) OUP.

Oxford Slavonic Papers, Vol. 29. Ed. by C. M. MacRobert et al. (New Ser.). (Illus.). 136p. 1997. text 65.00 (*0-19-815673-1*) OUP.

Oxford Slavonic Papers, Vol. 30. Ed. by G. S. Smith et al. (Oxford Studies in Physics). (Illus.). 126p. (C). 1998. text 65.00 (*0-19-815954-4*) OUP.

Oxford Slavonic Papers, Vol.11. Ed. by R. Auty et al. (New Ser.). (Illus.). 1979. 32.00 (*0-19-815653-7*) OUP.

***Oxford Slavonic Papers, New Series.** Ed. by C. M. MacRobert & G. S. Smith. 136p. 2000. text 60.00 (*0-19-815990-0*) OUP.

Oxford Slavonic Papers, New Series, Vol. XXV. Ed. by C. M. MacRobert et al. (New Ser.). (Illus.). 176p. 1993. text 75.00 (*0-19-815670-7*) OUP.

Oxford Slavonic Papers, New Series, Vol. XXVI (1993) Ed. by C. M. MacRobert et al. (New Ser.). (Illus.). 108p. 1994. text 65.00 (*0-19-815671-5*) OUP.

Oxford Slavonic Papers, 1994 Vol. XXVII. Ed. by G. S. Stone et al. (New Ser.: Vol. 10). (Illus.). 180p. 1995. text 55.00 (*0-19-815672-3*) OUP.

***Oxford Spanish Cartoon-Strip Vocabulary Builder.** Monica Tamariz. Orig. Title: '. (ENG & SPA., Illus.). 80p. 2000. pap. 11.95 (*0-19-860288-X*) OUP.

Oxford Spanish Desk Dictionary. Ed. by Carol S. Carvajal & Jane Horwood. (SPA.). 992p. (C). 1997. 14.95 (*0-19-521352-1*) OUP.

Oxford Spanish Dictionary. Ed. by Carol Styles Carvajal & Jane Horwood. (SPA.). 1504p. 1996. 25.00 (*0-19-864523-6*) OUP.

Oxford Spanish Dictionary: Spanish-English, English-Spanish. Christine Lea. (ENG & SPA.). 512p. 1997. mass mkt. 4.99 (*0-425-16009-2*) Berkley Pub.

***Oxford Spanish Dictionary: Spanish-English/English-Spanish.** 2nd ed. Ed. by Jane Horwood & Carol Styles Carvajal. 1856p. 1999. 45.00 (*0-19-860070-4*) OUP.

Oxford Spanish Minidictionary. 2nd ed. Ed. by Carol S. Carvajal et al. LC 98-49688. 640p. 1999. pap. 6.50 (*0-19-860231-6*) OUP.

***Oxford Spanish Workpack.** Valerie Grundy. 128p. 2000. pap. 7.95 (*0-19-860337-1*) OUP.

Oxford Stamp, & Other Essays. Frank Aydelotte. LC 67-26712. (Essay Index Reprint Ser.). 1977. 19.95 (*0-8369-0166-5*) Ayer.

Oxford Starter French Dictionary. Ed. by Marie H. Correard & Mary O'Neill. LC 97-24384. 416p. 1997. pap. 8.95 (*0-19-864527-9*) OUP.

Oxford Starter German Dictionary. Ed. by Neil Morris & Roswitha Morris. LC 96-43637. 376p. 1997. pap. 8.95 (*0-19-860033-X*) OUP.

Oxford Starter Italian Dictionary. Ed. by Colin McIntosh. 320p. 1999. pap. 9.95 (*0-19-860257-X*) OUP.

Oxford Starter Russian Dictionary. Ed. by Della Thompson. LC 97-17712. 320p. 1997. pap. 9.95 (*0-19-860032-1*) OUP.

Oxford Starter Spanish Dictionary. Ed. by Jane Horwood et al. LC 96-45309. 376p. 1997. pap. 8.95 (*0-19-860035-6*) OUP.

Oxford Student's Dictionary for Hebrew Speakers. A. S. Hornby. (ENG & HEB.). 824p. 1986. 29.95 (*0-8288-1208-X*, M 15630) Fr & Eur.

Oxford Student's Dictionary of American English. 2nd ed. A. S. Hornby. Ed. by Dolores Harris & William A. Stewart. (Illus.). 1986. 15.95 (*0-317-57090-0*) OUP.

Oxford Student's Dictionary of Current English. A. S. Hornby & Ch. Ruse. 748p. (C). 1990. 35.00 (*963-05-5651-0*, Pub. by Akade Kiado) St Mut.

***Oxford Studies in Ancient Philosophy, Vol. XVIII.** Ed. by David Sedley. 256p. 2000. text 60.00 (*0-19-825081-9*) OUP.

***Oxford Studies in Ancient Philosophy, Vol. XVIII.** Ed. by David Sedley. 256p. 2000. pap. text 35.00 (*0-19-825082-7*) OUP.

Oxford Studies in Ancient Philosophy: Supplementary Volume, 1988. Ed. by Julia Annas & Robert H. Grimm. 240p. 1989. text 75.00 (*0-19-824476-2*) OUP.

Oxford Studies in Ancient Philosophy Vol. III: 1985, Vol. I. Ed. by Julia Annas. 310p. 1986. pap. 29.95 (*0-19-824910-1*) OUP.

Oxford Studies in Ancient Philosophy Vol. V: 1987, Vol. V. Ed. by Julia Annas. 272p. 1988. pap. text 39.95 (*0-19-824457-6*) OUP.

Oxford Studies in Ancient Philosophy Vol. VI: 1988, Vol. V. Ed. by Julia Annas. 290p. 1989. pap. text 39.95 (*0-19-824835-0*) OUP.

Oxford Studies in Ancient Philosophy Vol. VII: 1989, Vol. V. Ed. by Julia Annas. 268p. 1990. text 80.00 (*0-19-824242-5*); pap. text 39.95 (*0-19-824241-7*) OUP.

Oxford Studies in Ancient Philosophy Vol. VIII: 1990, Vol. V. Ed. by Julia Annas. 310p. 1991. text 80.00 (*0-19-824286-7*); pap. text 39.95 (*0-19-824285-9*) OUP.

Oxford Studies in Ancient Philosophy Vol. IX: 1991, Vol. I. Julia Annas. 224p. 1992. pap. 49.95 (*0-19-823991-2*) OUP.

Oxford Studies in Ancient Philosophy Vol. X: 1992, Vol. X. Ed. by Julia Annas. 304p. 1993. text 80.00 (*0-19-824047-3*) OUP.

Oxford Studies in Ancient Philosophy, 1993, Vol. XI. Ed. by C. C. W. Taylor. (Illus.). 276p. 1994. text 65.00 (*0-19-824095-3*) OUP.

Oxford Studies in Ancient Philosophy, 1994, Vol. XII. Ed. by C. C. W. Taylor. (Illus.). 280p. 1995. text 59.00 (*0-19-823527-5*) OUP.

Oxford Studies in Ancient Philosophy, 1995, Vol. XIII. Ed. by C. C. W. Taylor. (Illus.). 304p. 1996. text 65.00 (*0-19-825000-2*) OUP.

Oxford Studies in Ancient Philosophy, 1996, Vol. XIV. Ed. by C. C. W. Taylor. (Illus.). 322p. 1997. text 68.00 (*0-19-823670-0*) OUP.

Oxford Studies in Ancient Philosophy, 1997, Vol. 15. Ed. by C. C. Taylor. 304p. 1998. text 68.00 (*0-19-823760-X*) OUP.

***Oxford Studies in Ancient Philosophy 1999, Vol. XVII.** Ed. by David Sedley. 376p. 1999. text 60.00 (*0-19-825019-3*) OUP.

***Oxford Studies in Ancient Philosophy 1998, Vol. XVI, 1998.** Ed. by C. C. Taylor. 368p. 1999. text 65.00 (*0-19-823815-0*) OUP.

Oxford Supplementary Skills: Elementary Reading. Ed. by Alan Maley. (Illus.). 64p. 1992. pap. text 6.95 (*0-19-453400-6*) OUP.

Oxford Supplementary Skills: Elementary Writing. Alan Maley. (Illus.). 64p. 1992. pap. text 6.95 (*0-19-453404-9*) OUP.

Oxford Supplementary Skills: Upper-Intermediate Reading. Alan Maley. (Illus.). 96p. 1992. pap. text 6.95 (*0-19-453402-2*) OUP.

Oxford Supplementary Skills: Upper-Intermediate Writing. Ed. by Alan Maley. (Illus.). 96p. 1992. pap. text 6.95 (*0-19-453406-5*) OUP.

Oxford Surveys in Evolutionary Biology, Vol. 2: 1985. Ed. by Richard Dawkins & Mark Ridley. (Illus.). 232p. 1986. 59.00 (*0-19-854174-0*) OUP.

Oxford Surveys in Evolutionary Biology, Vol. 3: 1986. Richard Dawkins & Mark Ridley. (Illus.). 256p. 1987. 65.00 (*0-19-854199-6*) OUP.

Oxford Surveys in Evolutionary Biology, Vol. 4: 1987. Ed. by Paul H. Harvey & Linda Partridge. (Illus.). 256p. 1988. text 65.00 (*0-19-854230-5*) OUP.

Oxford Surveys in Evolutionary Biology, Vol. 5: 1988. Ed. by Paul H. Harvey & Linda Partridge. (Illus.). 272p. 1989. text 79.00 (*0-19-854236-4*) OUP.

Oxford Surveys in Evolutionary Biology, Vol. 6: 1989. Ed. by Paul H. Harvey & Linda Partridge. (Illus.). 264p. 1990. text 69.00 (*0-19-854252-6*) OUP.

Oxford Surveys in Evolutionary Biology, 1991, Vol. 8. Ed. by Douglas J. Futuyma & Janis Antonovics. (Illus.). 416p. 1992. text 90.00 (*0-19-507623-0*) OUP.

Oxford Surveys in Information Technology, Vol. 3, 1986. Ed. by Peter I. Zorkoczy. (Illus.). 324p. 1987. 69.00 (*0-19-859018-0*) OUP.

Oxford Surveys of Plant Molecular & Cell Biology, Vol. 3: 1986. Ed. by B. J. Miflin. (Illus.). 482p. (Orig.). 1987. pap. 48.00 (*0-19-854202-X*) OUP.

Oxford Surveys of Plant Molecular & Cell Biology, Vol. 4: 1987. Ed. by B. J. Miflin & H. F. Miflin. (Illus.). 376p. (Orig.). 1988. pap. 48.00 (*0-19-854233-X*) OUP.

Oxford Surveys of Plant Molecular & Cell Biology, Vol. 5: 1988. Ed. by B. J. Miflin. (Illus.). 224p. (Orig.). 1989. pap. 48.00 (*0-19-854238-0*) OUP.

Oxford Surveys of Plant Molecular & Cell Biology, 1989, Vol. 6. Ed. by B. J. Miflin. (Illus.). 322p. 1990. pap. 48.00 (*0-19-857735-4*) OUP.

Oxford Surveys of Plant Molecular Biology, Vol. 7. B. J. Miflin. (Illus.). 342p. 1991. pap. 55.00 (*0-19-857750-8*) OUP.

Oxford Surveys on Eukaryotic Genes, Vol. 7. Ed. by Norman Maclean. (Illus.). 184p. 1991. 75.00 (*0-19-854256-9*) OUP.

Oxford Surveys on Eukaryotic Genes, 1987, Vol. 4. Ed. by Norman Maclean. (Illus.). 216p. 1988. 49.95 (*0-19-854231-3*) OUP.

Oxford System of Decimal Classification for Forestry. CABI Staff. (Illus.). 118p. (Orig.). 1954. pap. text 35.00 (*0-85198-372-3*) OUP.

***Oxford Textbook of Clinical Hepatology.** 2nd ed. J. Bircher. LC 98-30555. (Illus.). 1999. write for info. (*0-19-263039-3*); write for info. (*0-19-263040-7*) OUP.

Oxford Textbook Of Clinical Hepatology, 2 vols. 2nd ed. Ed. by Johannes Bircher et al. LC 98-30555. (Illus.). 2392p. 1999. text 350.00 (*0-19-262515-2*) OUP.

Oxford Textbook of Clinical Hepatology, 2 vols., Set. Ed. by N. McIntyre et al. 1772p. 1992. 295.00 (*0-19-261968-3*) OUP.

Oxford Textbook of Clinical Nephrology, 3 vols. 2nd ed. Alex M. Davison et al. LC 98-121868. (Illus.). 3,166p. 1997. text 495.00 (*0-19-262413-X*) OUP.

***Oxford Textbook of Clinical Nephrology.** 2nd ed. Alex M. Davison et al. 1998. text 275.00 (*0-19-268581-3*) OUP.

Oxford Textbook of Critical Care. Ed. by Andrew Webb et al. LC 98-34573. (Illus.). 1,458p. 1999. text 198.50 (*0-19-262737-6*) OUP.

Oxford Textbook of Functional Anatomy, Vol. 1. 2nd rev. ed. Pamela C. MacKinnon & John B. Morris. LC 92-48317. (Oxford Medical Publications). (Illus.). 174p. (C). 1994. pap. text 24.95 (*0-19-262195-5*) OUP.

Oxford Textbook of Functional Anatomy Vol. 2: Thorax & Abdomen. Pamela C. MacKinnon & John B. Morris. (Illus.). 150p. 1988. pap. text 27.95 (*0-19-261518-1*) OUP.

Oxford Textbook of Functional Anatomy Vol. 3: Head & Neck, Vol. 2. rev. ed. Pamela C. Mackinnon & John F. Morris. (Illus.). 162p. 1991. pap. text 35.00 (*0-19-261519-X*) OUP.

Oxford Textbook of Geriatric Medicine. Ed. by J. Grimley Evans & T. Franklin Williams. LC 92-8669. (Illus.). 776p. 1992. text 135.00 (*0-19-261590-4*) OUP.

An Asterisk (*) at the beginning of an entry indicates that the title is appearing for the first time.

***Oxford Textbook of Geriatric Medicine.** 2nd ed. Ed. by John Grimley Evans et al. (Illus.). 1280p. 2000. text 198.00 (*0-19-262830-5*) OUP.

Oxford Textbook of Medicine, 3 vols. 3rd ed. David A. Warrell & D. J. Weatherall. (Illus.). 5,024p. (C). 1996. text 299.00 (*0-19-262140-8*) OUP.

Oxford Textbook of Oncology, 2 vols., Set. Ed. by Michael Peckham et al. (Illus.). 1995. text 275.00 (*0-19-261685-4*) OUP.

Oxford Textbook of Ophthalmology, 2 vols., Set. Ed. by David L. Easty & John M. Sparrow. (Illus.). 1,396p. 1999. text 295.00 (*0-19-262557-8*) OUP.

***Oxford Textbook of Palliative Medicine.** 2nd ed. Ed. by Derek Doyle et al. (Illus.). 1,309p. 1999. pap. text 95.00 (*0-19-263057-1*) OUP.

Oxford textbook of Palliative Medicine. 2nd ed. Ed. by Derek Doyle et al. LC 97-34659. (Illus.). 1,308p. 1997. text 139.50 (*0-19-262566-7*) OUP.

Oxford Textbook of Pathology, 3 vols., Vol. 2, Pt. 3. Ed. by Nicholas A. Wright et al. Incl. Pathology of Systems., **2 bks.** Ed. by James O'D. McGee & Peter G. Isaacson. (Illus.). 1995. pap. Principles of Pathology. Ed. by James D. McGee & Peter G. Issacson. 1995. pap. 2628p. 1995. 245.00 (*0-19-521136-7*) OUP.

Oxford Textbook of Pathology Vol. 1: General Principles of Pathology, Vol. 1. Ed. by James O. McGee et al. (Illus.). 918p. 1992. pap. text 85.00 (*0-19-261972-1*) OUP.

Oxford Textbook of Pathology Vol. 2: Pathology of Systems, 2 bks., Vol. 2, Pts. 1 & 2. Ed. by James O. McGee et al. (Illus.). 1992. pap. text 160.00 (*0-19-261974-8*) OUP.

Oxford Textbook of Psychiatry. 3rd ed. Michael G. Gelder et al. (Illus.). 956p. (C). 1996. pap. text 65.00 (*0-19-262501-2*) OUP.

Oxford Textbook of Psychiatry. 3rd ed. Michael G. Gelder et al. (Illus.). 956p. (C). 1996. text 115.00 (*0-19-262500-4*) OUP.

Oxford Textbook of Psychopathology. Ed. by Theodore Millon & Paul H. Blaney. LC 98-49669. (Oxford Textbooks in Clinical Psychology Ser.). (Illus.). 744p. 1999. text 85.00 (*0-19-510307-6*) OUP.

Oxford Textbook of Public Health, 3 vols., Set. 3rd ed. Ed. by James McEwen et al. (Illus.). 1,646p. 1997. text 475.00 (*0-19-262553-5*) OUP.

Oxford Textbook of Rheumatology, 2 vols. 2nd ed. Ed. by Peter J. Maddison et al. LC 98-149774. (Illus.). 1998. text 375.00 (*0-19-262697-3*) OUP.

Oxford Textbook of Rheumatology, 1. Ed. by P. J. Maddison et al. LC 92-48994. (Illus.). 240p. 1996. text (*0-19-262432-6*) OUP.

Oxford Textbook of Rheumatology, 2. Ed. by P. J. Maddison et al. LC 92-48994. 1993. write for info. (*0-19-262343-5*) OUP.

Oxford Textbook of Sports Medicine. 2nd ed. Ed. by Mark Harries et al. LC 98-16976. (Illus.). 984p. 1998. text 115.00 (*0-19-262717-1*) OUP.

***Oxford Textbook of Sports Medicine.** 2nd ed. Ed. by Mark Harries et al. (Illus.). 960p. 2000. pap. text 98.50 (*0-19-263236-1*) OUP.

Oxford Textbook of Surgery. Ed. by Peter J. Morris & Ronald A. Malt. (Illus.). cd-rom 300.00 (*0-614-19712-0*, OP916195WE) OUP.

Oxford Textbook of Surgery. Ed. by Peter J. Morris & Ronald A. Malt. (Illus.). 1994. text 225.00 (*0-19-261800-8*) OUP.

Oxford Thackeray, 17 vols., Set. William Makepeace Thackeray. (BCL1-PR English Literature Ser.). 1992. reprint ed. lib. bdg. 1275.00 (*0-7812-7701-9*) Rprt Serv.

Oxford Thesaurus: American Edition. Ed. by Laurence Urdang. 1024p. 1992. 25.00 (*0-19-507354-1*) OUP.

Oxford to Zimbabwe: A Life's Recall. Andrew Hunt. 1995. pap. 14.95 (*0-9517695-5-3*, Pub. by New Cherwell) Intl Spec Bk.

Oxford Tragedy. J. C. Masterman. (Black Dagger Crime Ser.). 192p. 1997. 19.50 (*0-7451-8707-2*, Black Dagger) Chivers N Amer.

***Oxford Treasures Then & Now.** Douglas Hanks, Jr. (Illus.). 204p. 1999. write for info. (*0-9624156-6-9*); pap. write for info. (*0-9624156-5-0*) Creekside Pubs.

Oxford Treasury of Children's Poems. Ed. by Michael Harrison & Christopher Stuart-Clark. (Illus.). 176p. (YA). 1999. pap. 12.95 (*0-19-276202-8*) OUP.

Oxford Treasury of Children's Stories. Ed. by Michael Harrison & Christopher Stuart-Clark. (Illus.). 176p. (J). (gr. 1 up). 1997. pap. 12.95 (*0-19-278112-X*) OUP.

***Oxford Treasury of Christmas Poems.** Michael Harrison & Stuart-Clark, Christopher. LC 99-36900. 96p. (YA). 2000. 25.00 (*0-19-276224-9*) OUP.

Oxford Treasury of Classic Poems. Ed. by Michael Harrison. (J). (gr. 4 up). Date not set. 25.00 (*0-614-19308-7*) OUP.

Oxford Treasury of Classic Poems. Michael Harrison & Christopher Stuart-Clark. (Illus.). 160p. 1998. pap. 15.95 (*0-19-276187-0*) OUP.

Oxford Treasury of Time Poems. Ed. by Michael Harrison & Christopher Stuart-Clark. LC 98-5382. (Illus.). 158p. (YA). (gr. 4 up). 1999. 25.00 (*0-19-276175-7*) OUP.

***Oxford Treasury of Time Poems.** Ed. by Michael Harrison & Christopher Stuart-Clark. (Illus.). 160p. (YA). 2000. pap. 14.95 (*0-19-276236-2*) OUP.

Oxford Treasury of World Stories. Retold by Michael Harrison & Christopher Stuart-Clark. LC 98-5385. (Illus.). 144p. (J). (gr. 2-7). 1999. 25.00 (*0-19-278144-8*) OUP.

***Oxford Treasury of World Stories.** Michael Harrison & Christopher Stuart-Clark. (Illus.). 144p. (YA). 2001. pap. 16.95 (*0-19-278181-2*) OUP.

Oxford Treatise & Disputation on the Eucharist. Ed. & Tr. by Joseph C. McLelland. (Sixteenth Century Essays & Studies: Vol. 7). text 45.00 (*0-943549-89-2*) Truman St Univ.

Oxford Union Murals. John Christian. LC 79-23664. (Chicago Visual Library: CVL 33). (Illus.). 84p. 1981. lib. bdg. 29.00 (*0-226-68922-0*) U Ch Pr.

Oxford University Papers on India, Vol. 1, Pt. 1. Ed. by N. J. Allen et al. (Illus.). 160p. 1987. 19.95 (*0-19-561860-2*) OUP.

Oxford University Press: An Informal History. Peter Sutcliffe. (Illus.). 304p. 1978. 24.95 (*0-19-951084-9*) OUP.

Oxford University's Old Mortality Society: A Study in Victorian Romanticism. Gerald Monsman. LC 98-22818. 140p. 1998. text 69.95 (*0-7734-8362-4*) E Mellen.

Oxford W. E. B. Du Bois Reader. Ed. by Eric J. Sundquist. 688p. (C). 1996. pap. text 26.95 (*0-19-509178-7*) OUP.

Oxford Word Challenge. Tony Augarde. LC 98-3224. 160p. 1999. pap. 8.95 (*0-19-860113-1*) OUP.

Oxford Wordpower Dictionary. Ed. by Sally Wehmeier. (Illus.). 760p. 1993. pap. text 12.95 (*0-19-431138-4*) OUP.

Oxford Writers' Dictionary. R. E. Allen. 448p. 1990. pap. 11.95 (*0-19-282669-7*) OUP.

Oxford Years: Letters of Willmore Kendall to His Father. Willmore Kendall. Ed. by Yvona K. Mason. LC 93-77795. 527p. 1993. pap. 14.95 (*1-882926-02-1*) ISI Books.

Oxford's Own: The Men & Machines of No. XV Squadron Royal Flying Corps. Martyn R. Ford-Jones & Valerie A. Ford-Jones. (Illus.). 376p. 1999. 59.95 (*0-7643-0954-4*) Schiffer.

Oxfordshire. John Steane. (Illus.). 224p. 1997. pap. 19.95 (*0-7126-6199-9*, Pub. by Pimlico) Trafalgar.

Oxfordshire & Oxford. Marilyn Yurdan. (Country Guide Ser.: Vol. 20). (Illus.). 80p. write for info. (*0-85263-935-X*, Pub. by Shire Pubns) Lubrecht & Cramer.

Oxfordshire Village Book. Nigel Hammond. 192p. 1987. 50.00 (*0-905392-22-1*) St Mut.

Oxfordshire Words (Supplement) see English Dialect Society Publications, No. 32: Original Glossaries XXIII-XXVII

Oxherding Tale. Charles Johnson. 224p. 1995. pap. 12.95 (*0-452-27503-2*, Plume) Dutton Plume.

Oxidant Air Pollution Impacts in the Montane Forests of Southern California: The San Bernardino Mountain Case Study. Ed. by P. Miller & J. R. McBride. LC 98-11498. (Ecological Studies: Vol. 134). (Illus.). 464p. 1998. 139.00 (*0-387-98493-3*) Spr-Verlag.

Oxidants, Antioxidants & Disease Prevention. LC 96-109460. (Concise Monographs). (Illus.). 24p. 1995. pap. 12.50 (*0-944398-52-9*, 398529) ILSI.

Oxidants, Antioxidants & Free Radicals. Steven I. Baskin & Harry Salem. LC 97-13108. 450p. 1997. boxed set 135.00 (*1-56032-644-1*) Hemisp Pub.

Oxidation. Ron Marson. (Task Cards Ser.: No. 11). (Illus.). 48p. 1995. teacher ed. 8.00 (*0-941008-81-9*) Tops Learning.

Oxidation. Ed. by Robert L. Augustine. LC 69-18430. (Techniques & Applications in Organic Synthesis Ser.: Vol. 1). 378p. 1969. reprint ed. pap. 117.20 (*0-608-02233-0*, 204107200001) Bks Demand.

Oxidation, Vol. 2. Robert L. Augustine & David J. Trecker. LC 69-18430. (Techniques & Applications in Organic Synthesis Ser.). (Illus.). 216p. reprint ed. pap. 67.00 (*0-7837-0758-4*, 204107200002) Bks Demand.

Oxidation, Vol. 7. S. V. Ley. 1992. 445.00 (*0-08-040598-3*, Pergamon Pr) Elsevier.

Oxidation & Corrosion of Intermetallic Alloys. Ed. by Gerhard Welsch & Pramod D. Desai. LC 96-13481. 430p. 1996. 169.00 (*0-931682-60-6*, 6498) Purdue U Pubns.

Oxidation & Phosphorylation see Methods in Enzymology

Oxidation & Reduction in Inorganic & Analytical Chemistry: A Programmed Introduction. Alan Vincent. LC 84-29096. 93p. reprint ed. pap. 30.00 (*0-7837-4406-4*, 204414900012) Bks Demand.

Oxidation Inhibition in Organic Materials, Vol. I. Ed. by Jan Pospisil & Peter P. Klemchuk. 384p. 1989. lib. bdg. 395.00 (*0-8493-4767-X*, TP156) CRC Pr.

Oxidation Inhibition in Organic Materials, Vol. II. Ed. by Jan Pospisil & Peter P. Klemchuk. 400p. 1989. lib. bdg. 395.00 (*0-8493-4768-8*, TP156) CRC Pr.

Oxidation Inhibition in Organic Materials, Vols. I-II. Ed. by Jan Pospisil & Peter P. Klemchuk. 1989. 311.00 (*0-685-74180-X*) CRC Pr.

Oxidation of Cyclohexane. I. Berezin & E. Denisiv. LC 66-12651. 1966. 140.00 (*0-08-011378-8*, Pub. by Pergamon Repr) Franklin.

Oxidation of High-Temperature Intermetallics: Proceedings of the Workshop on the Oxidation of High-Temperature Intermetallics, Held in Cleveland, Ohio, September 22-23, 1988. Workshop on the Oxidation of High-Temperature Inte. Ed. by Toni Grobstein & Joseph Doychak. LC 88-62445. (Illus.). 303p. reprint ed. pap. 94.00 (*0-7837-6066-3*, 205251200008) Bks Demand.

Oxidation of Intermetallics. H. J. Grabke. Ed. by Michael Schutze. 366p. 1998. 260.00 (*3-527-29509-7*) Wiley.

Oxidation of Metals. Karl Hauffe. LC 63-17648. 464p. reprint ed. pap. 143.90 (*0-608-10844-8*, 205197900027) Bks Demand.

Oxidation of Metals & Alloys. 2nd ed. Oswald Kubaschewski & B. E. Hopkins. LC QD0171.K8. 331p. reprint ed. pap. 102.70 (*0-608-18014-9*, 205631400057) Bks Demand.

Oxidation of Metals & Alloys: Papers Presented at a Seminar of the American Society for Metals, October 17 & 18, 1970. LC 72-182305. 283p. reprint ed. pap. 87.80 (*0-608-10157-5*, 205091500094) Bks Demand.

Oxidation of Metals & Associated Mass Transport: Proceedings of a Symposium Sponsored Jointly by the Metallurgical Society of AIME & the MSD-ASM Atomic Transport Activity Held at the TMS-AIME Fall Meeting in Orlando, Florida, October, 6-7, 1986 & Dedicated to the Memory of Norman L. Peterson. Norman L. Peterson Memorial Symposium on Oxidation. Ed. by M. A. Dayananda et al. LC 87-14192. 353p. reprint ed. pap. 109.50 (*0-7837-2208-7*, 205245800004) Bks Demand.

Oxidation of Organic Compounds: Proceedings, 3 vols., 1. International Oxidation Symposium (1967: San Franc. LC 68-31614. (Advances in Chemistry Ser.: Nos. 75-77). (Illus.). 382p. 1968. reprint ed. pap. 118.50 (*0-608-08453-0*, 205219900001) Bks Demand.

Oxidation of Organic Compounds: Proceedings, 3 vols., 2. International Oxidation Symposium (1967: San Franc. LC 68-31614. (Advances in Chemistry Ser.: Nos. 75-77). (Illus.). 448p. 1968. reprint ed. pap. 138.90 (*0-608-08454-9*, 205219900002) Bks Demand.

Oxidation of Organic Compounds: Proceedings, 3 vols., 3. International Oxidation Symposium (1967: San Franc. LC 68-31614. (Advances in Chemistry Ser.: Nos. 75-77). (Illus.). 320p. 1968. reprint ed. pap. 99.20 (*0-608-08455-7*, 205219900003) Bks Demand.

Oxidation of Oxygen & Related Chemistry: The Selected Papers of Neil Bartlett. 500p. 1998. lib. bdg. 55.00 (*981-02-2775-2*) World Scientific Pub.

Oxidation of Stressed Polymers. A. A. Popov et al. xiii, 335p. 1991. text 427.00 (*2-88124-735-0*) Gordon & Breach.

Oxidation of Sulfide Minerals in Benefication Processes. A. Abramov & V. M. Avdohin. 336p. 1997. text 81.00 (*90-5699-570-7*) Gordon & Breach.

***Oxidation-Reduction Reactions.** 5th ed. James M. Postma et al. 2000. pap. text, lab manual ed. 1.95 (*0-7167-9448-9*) W H Freeman.

Oxidation Technologies for Water & Wastewater Treatment: Selected Proceedings of the International Conference on Oxidation Technologies for Water & Wastewater Treatment, Held in Clausthal-zellerfeld, Germany, 12-15 May 1996. Ed. by A. Vogelpohl & S. U. Geissen. 362p. 1997. pap. write for info. (*0-08-043098-8*) Elsevier.

Oxidation/Diffusion Overview. TEEX Staff. (Illus.). vii, 69p. 1997. spiral bd. 39.95 (*1-58257-006-X*, 8126B) TX Eng Extsn Servs.

Oxidations & Reduction in Organic Synthesis. Timothy Donohoe. (Oxford Chemistry Primers Ser.: No. 6). (Illus.). 96p. (C). 2000. pap. text 9.95 (*0-19-855664-0*) OUP.

Oxidations in Organic Chemistry. Ed. by Milos Hudlicky. (ACS Monograph: No. 186). 336p. 1990. pap. 49.95 (*0-8412-1781-5*) Am Chemical.

Oxidations in Organic Chemistry. 2nd ed. Ed. by Milos Hudlicky. (ACS Monograph: No. 186). 433p. 1990. text 95.00 (*0-8412-1780-7*, Pub. by Am Chemical) OUP.

Oxidative Balance: How to Lead the Antioxidant Lifestyle. David A. Leaf & Peter A. Glassman. LC 99-51361. (Illus.). 174p. 2000. pap. 14.95 (*0-917634-01-2*) EMIS.

Oxidative Behavior of Materials by Thermal Analytical Techniques. Ed. by Alan T. Riga & Gerald H. Patterson. LC 97-39992. (STP Ser.: Vol. STP1326). (Illus.). 247p. 1997. 69.00 (*0-8031-2483-X*, STP1326) ASTM.

Oxidative Coupling of Phenols. Ed. by William I. Taylor & Alan R. Battersby. LC 67-21702. (Organic Substances of Natural Origin Ser.: Vol. 1). (Illus.). 401p. reprint ed. pap. 124.40 (*0-608-30240-6*, 201769000001) Bks Demand.

Oxidative Damage & Related Enzymes, Vol. 2. G. Rotilio. (Life Chemistry Reports). x, 436p. 1984. pap. text 225.00 (*3-7186-0221-0*) Gordon & Breach.

Oxidative Injury in Dermatopathology. J. Fuchs. (Illus.). 360p. 1992. 208.00 (*0-387-54355-4*) Spr-Verlag.

Oxidative Stress. Ed. by Helmut Sies. 1985. text 104.00 (*0-12-642760-7*) Acad Pr.

Oxidative Stress: Oxidants & Antioxidants. Ed. by Helmut Sies. (Illus.). 507p. (C). 1991. text 104.00 (*0-12-642762-3*) Acad Pr.

Oxidative Stress & Aging. Ed. by R. G. Cutler et al. LC 95-105254. (Molecular & Cell Biology Updates Ser.). 1995. write for info. (*3-7643-5039-3*, Pub. by Birkhauser) Princeton Arch.

Oxidative Stress & Aging. R. G. Cutler et al. Ed. by Lester Packer. LC 95-105254. (Molecular & Cell Biology Updates Ser.: Vol. 12). 396p. 1995. 149.00 (*0-8176-5039-3*, Pub. by Birkhauser) Princeton Arch.

Oxidative Stress & Signal Transduction. Ed. by Enrique Cadenas & Henry Jay Forman. LC 96-47089. (Illus.). 576p. 1997. write for info. (*0-412-07681-0*) Kluwer Academic.

Oxidative Stress & the Molecular Biology of Antioxidant Defenses. Ed. by John G. Scandalios. LC 96-92949. (Mongraphs: Vol. 34). (Illus.). 992p. (C). 1996. text 155.00 (*0-87969-502-1*) Cold Spring Harbor.

Oxidative Stress, Cell Activation & Viral Infection. Ed. by C. Pasquier et al. LC 93-44396. (Molecular & Cell Biology Updates Ser.). (Illus.). 376p. 1993. 99.00 (*0-8176-2941-6*) Birkhauser.

Oxidative Stress in Cancer, AIDS & Neurodegenerative Diseases. Ed. by Luc Montagnier & C. Pasquier. LC 97-41304. (Oxidative Stress & Disease Ser.). (Illus.). 578p. 1997. text 195.00 (*0-8247-9862-7*) Dekker.

Oxidative Stress in Dermatology. Ed. by Jurgen Fuchs & Lester Packer. (Basic & Clinical Dermatology Ser.: Vol. 8). (Illus.). 560p. 1993. text 250.00 (*0-8247-9049-9*) Dekker.

Oxidative Stress in Male Infertility. Ed. by Falk R. Ochsendorf & Jurgen Fuchs. 1995. 129.95 (*0-8493-4798-X*, 4798) CRC Pr.

Oxidative Stress in Neuronal Death. Irene Ceballos-Picot. LC 97-19204. (Medical Intelligence Unit Ser.). 196p. 1997. 99.00 (*1-57059-454-6*) Landes Bioscience.

Oxidative Stress in Skeletal Muscle. A. Z. Reznick. LC 98-6332. (Molecular & Cell Biology Updates Ser.). 1998. 140.00 (*0-8176-5820-3*) Birkhauser.

Oxidative Stress in Skeletal Muscle. Ed. by A. Z. Reznick et al. LC 98-6332. (Molecular & Cell Biology Updates Ser.). 500p. 1998. 140.00 (*3-7643-5820-3*) Birkhauser.

Oxidative Stress, Lipoproteins & Cardiovascular Dysfunction. Ed. by K. R. Bruckdorfer & Catherine A. Rice-Evans. (Portland Press Research Monographs: Vol. 6). 184p. (C). 1995. text 102.00 (*1-85578-045-3*, Pub. by Portland Pr Ltd) Ashgate Pub Co.

***Oxidative/Energy Metabolism in Neurodegenerative Disorders.** Ed. by John P. Blass & Fletcher H. McDowell. 1999. write for info. (*1-57331-209-6*) NY Acad Sci.

Oxide Dispersion Strengthening: Proceedings of a Symposium, Bolton Landing, New York, June 27-29, 1966. Ed. by George S. Ansell et al. LC 67-26577. (Metallurgical Society Conference Ser.: Vol. 47). 922p. reprint ed. pap. 200.00 (*0-608-11366-2*, 200153500079) Bks Demand.

Oxide-Electrolyte Interfaces: Proceedings of Symposium Papers Held at the 142nd Meeting of the Society. Robert S. Alwitt. LC 73-75171. 310p. reprint ed. pap. 96.10 (*0-608-10058-7*, 205182000008) Bks Demand.

Oxide Films on Metals & Alloys VII. K. R. Hebert & G. E. Thompson. (Proceedings Ser.: Vol. 94-25). 328p. 1995. pap. 46.00 (*1-56677-084-X*) Electrochem Soc.

Oxide Minerals: Petrologic & Magnetic Significance. Ed. by D. H. Lindsley. (Reviews in Mineralogy Ser.: Vol. 25). 509p. 1991. per. 28.00 (*0-939950-30-8*) Mineralogical Soc.

Oxide Semiconductors. Z. M. Jarzebski. LC 73-6971. 304p. 1973. 129.00 (*0-08-016968-6*, Pub. by Pergamon Repr) Franklin.

Oxides: Phase Transitions, Non Stoichiometry, Superconductors. Ed. by C. Boulesteix. (Key Engineering Materials Ser.: Vols. 155-156). (Illus.). 476p. (C). 1998. text 172.00 (*0-87849-798-6*, Pub. by Trans T Pub) Enfield Pubs NH.

Oxides & Oxide Films. Ed. by John W. Diggle. LC 72-83120. (Anodic Behavior of Metals & Semiconductors Ser.: Vol. 1). 560p. reprint ed. 173.60 (*0-8357-9090-8*, 205508200001) Bks Demand.

Oxides & Oxide Films, 2 vols., Vol. 2. Ed. by John W. Diggle et al. LC 72-83120. (Anodic Behavior of Metals & Semiconductors Ser.). (Illus.). 416p. 1973. reprint ed. pap. 129.00 (*0-7837-0699-5*, 204103200002) Bks Demand.

Oxides & Oxide Films, Vol. 3. Ed. by John W. Diggle & Ashok K. Vijh. LC 72-83120. (Anodic Behavior of Metals & Semiconductors Ser.). (Illus.). 351p. 1976. reprint ed. pap. 108.90 (*0-7837-4208-8*, 204103200003) Bks Demand.

Oxides & Oxide Films, 2 vols., Vol. 4. Ed. by John W. Diggle et al. LC 72-83120. (Anodic Behavior of Metals & Semiconductors Ser.). (Illus.). 295p. 1976. reprint ed. pap. 91.50 (*0-7837-0700-2*, 204103200004) Bks Demand.

Oxides & Oxide Films, Vol. 5. Ed. by John W. Diggle & Ashok K. Vijh. LC 72-83120. (Anodic Behavior of Metals & Semiconductors Ser.). (Illus.). 201p. 1977. reprint ed. pap. 62.40 (*0-7837-4209-6*, 204103200005) Bks Demand.

Oxides & Oxide Films, Vol. 6. Ed. by John W. Diggle & Ashok K. Vijh. LC 72-83120. (Anodic Behavior of Metals & Semiconductors Ser.). (Illus.). 359p. 1981. reprint ed. pap. 111.30 (*0-7837-4210-X*, 204103200006) Bks Demand.

Oxides of Nitrogen. (Environmental Health Criteria Ser.: No. 4). 79p. 1977. pap. text 12.00 (*92-4-154064-8*, 1160004) World Health.

Oxides of Nitrogen. A. S. Young. (Solubility Data Ser.). 1981. 130.00 (*0-08-023960-9*, Pergamon Pr) Elsevier.

Oxides of Nitrogen: A Critical Survey. Watson House. 150p. 1974. 5.00 (*0-318-12667-2*, M30574) Am Gas Assn.

Oxidized Virgin. Gordon Walmsley. LC 85-72266. (Illus.). 80p. (Orig.). (C). 1986. pap. 9.95 (*0-912543-01-9*) Bridgehead Pr.

Oxidizing & Bleaching Agents. Contrib. by George Innes. 144p. 1996. 2750.00 (*1-56965-048-9*, C-196) BCC.

***Oxidizing Methoxybenzyl Alcohol to Methoxybenzaldehyde Using Phase-Transfer Catalysis.** Joseph W. LeFevre. Ed. by Joe Jeffers. (Modular Laboratory in Chemistry Ser.). 16p. (C). 1999. pap. text 1.75 (*0-87540-725-0*, SYNT 725-0) Chem Educ Res.

Oxidoreduction at the Plasma Membrane Vol. 1: Relation to Growth & Transport: Animals. Frederick L. Crane et al. 328p. 1990. lib. bdg. 230.00 (*0-8493-6937-1*, QP602) CRC Pr.

Oxidoreduction at the Plasma Membrane Vol. 2: Relation to Growth & Transport: Plants. Frederick L. Crane et al. 264p. 1991. lib. bdg. 225.00 (*0-8493-6938-X*, QP602) CRC Pr.

Oximetry Equipment & Supplies. (Market Research Reports: No. 311). 151p. 1993. 795.00 (*0-317-05018-4*) Theta Corp.

Oxopetra Elegies. Odysseus Elytis. Tr. by David Connelly. (Greek Poetry Archives Ser.). 100p. 1997. text 36.00 (*3-7186-5871-2*, Harwood Acad Pubs); pap. text 12.00 (*3-7186-5881-X*, Harwood Acad Pubs) Gordon & Breach.

***Oxord Readings in the Greek Novel.** Simon Swain. LC 98-45077. 424p. 1999. pap. text 24.95 (*0-19-872188-9*) OUP.

Oxorn-Foote Human Labor & Birth. 5th ed. Harry Oxorn. (Illus.). 918p. (C). 1998. pap. text 55.00 (*0-8385-7665-6*, A7665-1, Apple Lange Med) McGraw.

Oxota: A Short Russian Novel. Lyn Hejinian. 1991. pap. 15.00 (*0-935724-44-3*) Figures.

Oxota: A Short Russian Novel. deluxe ed. Lyn Hejinian. 1991. pap. 25.00 (*0-935724-48-6*) Figures.

Oxridge Woman. Leialoha A. Perkins. (ENG, FRE & HAW.). (Orig.). 1998. pap. 28.00 (*1-892174-02-2*) Kamalu uluolele.

Oxter English Dictionary: Uncommon Words Used by Uncommonly Good Writers. George S. Saussy. LC 84-13789. 291p. reprint ed. pap. 90.30 (*0-608-16044-X*, 203317100084) Bks Demand.

Oxy. Mike Gellerman. (Welding Ser.). (C). 2000. pap., lab manual ed. 12.95 (*0-8273-7626-X*) Delmar.

Oxy-Acetylene Gas Welding & Related Studies see Welding Craft Practice

Oxy-Acetylene Welding. 1987. 65.00 (*0-85083-039-7*) St Mut.

Oxy-Fuel Gas Torches, UL 123. 10th ed. (C). 1999. pap. text 95.00 (*1-55989-916-6*) Underwrtrs Labs.

Oxyacetylene Safety (Reference Card) Tel-A-Train, Inc. Staff. 1979. student ed. 0.15 (*1-56355-214-0*) Tel-A-Train.

Oxyacetylene Weldor's Handbook. 7th ed. Ted B. Jefferson. (Monticello Bks.). 320p. 1972. 7.50 (*0-686-12005-1*) Jefferson Pubns.

Oxycal vs. Arthritis. Michael A. Cox. 171p. (Orig.). 1984. pap. 5.95 (*0-942078-07-1*) R Tanner Assocs Inc.

Oxychirotidae. John B. Heppner. (Lepidopterorum Catalogus Ser.: Vol. 8: Fasc. 62). (Illus.). 8p. (Orig.). 1997. pap. text 4.50 (*0-945417-58-6*) Sci Pubs.

Oxycise! How Anyone Can Get Rid of Fat Forever in Only 15 Minutes a Day. (Illus.). 144p. 1997. pap. write for info. (*1-890320-01-3*) Oxycise Intl.

Oxycise! Chart Your Success. 80p. 1997. pap. write for info. (*1-890320-03-X*) Oxycise Intl.

Oxycise! Fuel for Success. 72p. 1997. pap. write for info. (*1-890320-02-1*) Oxycise Intl.

***Oxyfuel.** (Boilermaking Lev 1 Ser.). 2000. per. 12.00 (*0-13-031333-5*) P-H.

Oxyfuel Gas Welding. Kevin E. Bowditch & Mark A. Bowditch. LC 98-44626. (Illus.). 130p. (YA). (gr. 9-12). 1999. text 17.20 (*1-56637-508-8*) Goodheart.

Oxygen. Jean F. Blashfield. LC 98-4508. (Sparks of Life Ser.). (J). 1999. 27.12 (*0-8172-5037-9*) Raintree Steck-V.

Oxygen. Ed. by K. Maiprie De Reuck. 1991. 61.00 (*0-632-01476-8*) CRC Pr.

Oxygen. John Farndon. LC 97-52236. (Elements Ser.). 32p. (J). (gr. 3-5). 1999. lib. bdg. 22.79 (*0-7614-0879-7*, Benchmark NY) Marshall Cavendish.

Oxygen: Basis of the Regulation of Vital Functions in the Fetus. Ed. by W. Kunzel & M. Kirschbaum. LC 92-20354. (Illus.). 190p. 1992. 129.00 (*0-387-55413-0*) Spr-Verlag.

***Oxygen: Nature's Most Important Dietary Supplement.** Stephen R. Krauss. 342p. 1999. pap. 21.95 (*0-7392-0115-8*, PO3015) Morris Pubng.

***Oxygen: New Poets from Wales.** Ed. by Amy Wack & Grahame Davis. 2000. pap. 25.95 (*1-85411-284-8*, Pub. by Seren Bks) Dufour.

Oxygen: Walter Desalting. Planck, Max, Society for the Advancement of Scienc et al. (Gmelin Handbuch der Anorganischen Chemie Ser.). (Illus.). 339p. 1974. 565.00 (*0-387-93280-1*) Spr-Verlag.

Oxygen Administration. National Safety Council Staff. LC 94-215136. 60p. 1994. pap. 15.00 (*0-86720-983-6*); pap., teacher ed. 15.00 (*0-86720-986-0*) Jones & Bartlett.

Oxygen Administration Teaching Package. National Safety Council Staff. (Emergency Care Ser.). 1994. 395.00 (*0-86720-925-9*) Jones & Bartlett.

Oxygen & Life, No. 39. Royal Society of Chemistry Staff. 1989. 30.00 (*0-85186-825-8*) CRC Pr.

Oxygen & Living Processes: An Interdisciplinary Approach. Ed. by Daniel L. Gilbert. (Topics in Environmental Physiology & Medicine Ser.). (Illus.). 401p. 1981. 137.00 (*0-387-90554-5*) Spr-Verlag.

Oxygen & Ozone. Battino. (Solubility Data Ser.). 1981. 130.00 (*0-08-023952-8*, Pergamon Pr) Elsevier.

Oxygen & the Conversion of Future Feedstocks, No. 48. Royal Society of Chemistry Staff. 1988. 48.00 (*0-85186-915-7*) CRC Pr.

Oxygen Application to Chloride Leaching of Complex Sulfide Ores. KuoTung Chou. (MIRL Reports: No. 77). (Illus.). 27p. (Orig.). (C). 1988. pap. 4.00 (*0-911043-04-7*) UAKF Min Ind Res Lab.

Oxygen, Carbon, Hydrogen, & Nitrogen in Crystalline Silicon, Vol. 59. Ed. by J. W. Corbett et al. (Materials Research Society Symposium Proceedings Ser.). 1986. text 17.50 (*0-931837-24-3*) Materials Res.

Oxygen Chemistry. Donald T. Sawyer. (International Series of Monographs on Chemistry). (Illus.). 240p. 1991. text 50.00 (*0-19-505798-8*) OUP.

Oxygen Complexes & Oxygen Activation by Transition Metals. Ed. by Arthur E. Martell & Donald T. Sawyer. LC 87-32170. (Illus.). 352p. 1988. 95.00 (*0-306-42789-3*, Plenum Trade) Perseus Pubng.

Oxygen Content of Air-Saturated Fresh Waters, & Aids in Calculating Percentage Saturation. C. H. Mortimer. (International Association of Theoretical & Applied Limnology, Communications Ser.: No. 6). (Illus.). 20p. 1956. pap. 15.00 (*3-510-52006-8*, Pub. by E Schweizerbartsche) Balogh.

Oxygen Content of Air-Saturated Fresh Waters over Ranges of Temperature & Atmospheric Pressure of Limnological Interest. C. H. Mortimer. (International Association of Theoretical & Applied Limnology, Communications Ser.: No. 22). (Illus.). 23p. 1981. pap. 15.00 (*3-510-52022-X*, Pub. by E Schweizerbartsche) Balogh.

Oxygen Delignification Symposium, 1984 Notes. Technical Association of the Pulp & Paper Industry. LC TS1176.6.B6. 159p. reprint ed. pap. 49.30 (*0-608-12995-X*, 202477400038) Bks Demand.

Oxygen Delignification Symposium, 1990: Sheraton Centre Hotel, Toronto, Ontario, October 17-19. Technical Association of the Pulp & Paper Industry. LC TS1176.6.B6. (TAPPI Notes Ser.). 169p. reprint ed. pap. 52.40 (*0-8357-3463-3*, 203972500013) Bks Demand.

Oxygen Disorder Effects in High Tc Superconductors. Ed. by J. L. Moran-Lopez & I. K. Schuller. (Illus.). 228p. 1990. 75.00 (*0-306-43409-1*, Plenum Trade) Perseus Pubng.

Oxygen Dynamics in Chesapeake Bay: A Synthesis of Recent Research. Ed. by David E. Smith et al. LC 91-68257. 234p. (C). 1992. text 24.95 (*0-943676-50-9*) MD Sea Grant Col.

Oxygen Effects on Radiation-Induced Inactive Macro., Vol. 10, No. 1. Eidus. 40p. 1997. pap. text 20.00 (*3-7186-5828-3*, Harwood Acad Pubs) Gordon & Breach.

Oxygen Electrochemistry. Ed. by R. R. Adzic et al. LC 95-61599. (Proceedings Ser.: Vol. 95-26). (Illus.). 246p. 1996. 42.00 (*1-56677-121-8*) Electrochem Soc.

Oxygen-Enhanced Combustion. Charles E. Baukal. LC 97-46803. 384p. 1998. boxed set 79.95 (*0-8493-1695-2*) CRC Pr.

Oxygen Equipment. 1995. lib. bdg. 257.95 (*0-8490-6601-8*) Gordon Pr.

Oxygen-Free Museum Cases. Ed. by Shin Maekawa. LC 98-15964. (Research in Conservation Ser.). (Illus.). 100p. 1998. pap. 30.00 (*0-89236-529-3*, Pub. by J P Getty Trust) OUP.

Oxygen Free Radicals & Scavengers in the Natural Science. Ed. by G. Mozsik et al. 356p. 1993. pap. 295.00 (*963-05-6589-7*, Pub. by Akade Kiado) St Mut.

Oxygen Free Radicals & Tissue Damage. Symposium on Oxygen Free Radicals & Tissue Damage. LC 79-11805. (Ciba Foundation Symposium: New Ser.: No. 65). 389p. reprint ed. pap. 120.60 (*0-608-16209-4*, 201464900093) Bks Demand.

Oxygen-Free Radicals in Shock. Ed. by G. P. Novelli. (Illus.). xii, 248p. 1986. 139.25 (*3-8055-4233-X*) S Karger.

Oxygen Free Radicals in Tissue Damage. Ed. by Merrill Tarr & Fred Samson. LC 92-49815. x, 295p. 1992. 109.00 (*0-8176-3609-9*) Birkhauser.

Oxygen, Gene Expression, & Cellular Function, Vol. 105. Donald Massaro & Linda B. Clerch. LC 97-11362. (Lung Biology in Health & Disease Ser.). (Illus.). 512p. 1997. text 199.00 (*0-8247-0062-7*) Dekker.

Oxygen Healing Therapies see Terapias de Oxigeno

Oxygen Healing Therapies: For Optimum Health & Vitality. expanded rev. ed. Nathaniel Altman. LC 98-23505. 296p. 1998. pap. 14.95 (*0-89281-793-3*, Heal Arts VT) Inner Tradit.

Oxygen Homeostasis & Its Dynamics. Ed. by Yuzuru Ishimura et al. LC 97-41378. (Keio University Symposia for Life Science & Medicine Ser.). (Illus.). xxii, 622p. 1998. 260.00 (*4-431-70202-4*) Spr-Verlag.

Oxygen in Catalysis. Ed. by Adam Bielanski & Jerzy Haber. (Chemical Industries Ser.: Vol. 43). (Illus.). 488p. 1990. text 195.00 (*0-8247-8320-4*) Dekker.

Oxygen in the Metal & Gaseous Fuel Industries, No. 32. Royal Society of Chemistry Staff. 1989. 28.00 (*0-85186-138-5*) CRC Pr.

***Oxygen Ion & Mixed Conductors & Their Technological Applications: Proceedings from the NATO International Scientific Exchange Programmes Advanced Study Institute, Erice, Sicily, Italy, 15-30 July, 1997.** NATO International Scientific Exchange Programmes Advanced Study Institute Staff et al. LC 00-26058. (NATO Science Ser.). 2000. write for info. (*0-7923-6253-5*) Kluwer Academic.

Oxygen Keeps You Alive. Franklyn M. Branley. LC 73-139093. (Let's-Read-&-Find-Out Science Bks.). (Illus.). (J). (gr. k-3). 1971. 11.95 (*0-690-60702-4*) HarpC Child Bks.

Oxygen Man. Steve Yarbrough. LC 98-41951. 280p. 1999. 20.00 (*1-878448-85-4*) MacMurray & Beck.

***Oxygen Man: A Novel.** Steve Yarborough. 2000. pap. 12.00 (*0-7432-0165-5*, Scribner Pap Fic) S&S Trade Pap.

Oxygen Multistep Therapy. Von Ardenne. 65.00 (*0-86577-377-7*) Thieme Med Pubs.

Oxygen Multistep Therapy: Physiological & Technical Foundations. Manfred Von Ardenne. Tr. by Paula Kirby & Winfried Kruger from GER. (Illus.). (C). 1997. text 79.00 (*3-13-743501-3*, Pub. by G Thieme) Thieme Med Pubs.

Oxygen Radicals: Systemic Events & Disease Processes. Ed. by D. K. Das & Walter B. Essman. (Illus.). xii, 196p. 1990. 151.50 (*3-8055-5049-9*) S Karger.

Oxygen Radicals & the Disease Process. Ed. by Craig E. Thomas & Balaraman Kalyanaraman. 296p. 1998. text 39.00 (*90-5702-226-5*, Harwood Acad Pubs); pap. text 14.00 (*90-5702-227-3*, Harwood Acad Pubs) Gordon & Breach.

Oxygen Radicals in Biological Systems. Sidney P. Colowick & Nathan O. Kaplan. (Methods in Enzymology Ser.: Vol. 105). 1984. text 188.00 (*0-12-182005-X*) Acad Pr.

Oxygen Radicals in Biological Systems, Pt. C. Ed. by Lester Packer et al. (Methods in Enzymology Ser.: Vol. 233). (Illus.). 711p. 1994. text 115.00 (*0-12-182134-X*) Acad Pr.

Oxygen Radicals in Biological Systems, Pt. D. Ed. by Lester Packer. (Methods in Enzymology Ser.: Vol. 234). 704p. 1994. text 115.00 (*0-12-182135-8*) Acad Pr.

Oxygen Radicals in Biological Systems Pt. B: Oxygen Radicals & Antioxidants. Ed. by Lester Packer et al. (Methods in Enzymology Ser.: Vol. 186). 855p. 1990. text 142.00 (*0-12-182087-4*) Acad Pr.

Oxygen Radicals in Biology & Medicine. Ed. by Michael G. Simic et al. (Basic Life Sciences Ser.: Vol. 49). (Illus.). 1068p. 1988. 175.00 (*0-306-43021-5*, Plenum Trade) Perseus Pubng.

Oxygen Radicals in Chemistry & Biology: Proceedings - Third International Conference. Ed. by Wolf Bors et al. LC 84-1691. xix, 1029p. 1984. 192.35 (*3-11-009704-4*) De Gruyter.

Oxygen Radicals in the Pathophysiology of Heart Disease. Ed. by Pawan K. Singal. (Developments in Cardiovascular Medicine Ser.). (C). 1988. text 150.00 (*0-89838-375-7*) Kluwer Academic.

Oxygen Regulation of Ion Channels & Gene Expression. Ed. by Jose Lopez-Barneo & E. Kenneth Weir. LC 97-50337. (Illus.). 288p. 1998. 120.00 (*0-87993-694-0*) Futura Pub.

Oxygen Responses, Reactivities, & Measurements in Biosystems. Satya N. Mukhopadhyay & Dipak K. Das. LC 94-6561. 224p. 1994. lib. bdg. 179.00 (*0-8493-4730-0*) CRC Pr.

Oxygen Sensors. USG/NTIS Staff. 1996. 85.00 (*0-614-18496-7*, 135P35) Info Gatekeepers.

Oxygen-Seventeen & Silicon-Twenty-Nine. J. P. Kintzinger & H. Marsmann. (NMR-Basic Principles & Progress Ser.: Vol. 17). (Illus.). 235p. 1981. 79.95 (*0-387-10414-3*) Spr-Verlag.

Oxygen Status of Arterial Blood. Ed. by R. Zander & F. O. Mertzlufft. (Illus.). xii, 294p. 1991. 68.75 (*3-8055-5280-7*) S Karger.

Oxygen Stress & Tissue Damage. Ed. by J. Feher et al. LC 95-109779. 172p. 1994. pap. 210.00 (*963-05-6657-5*, Pub. by Akade Kiado) St Mut.

Oxygen Therapeutics - Current Technologies, Trends & Market Opportunities. 2nd rev. ed. Pamela Bassett. Ed. by Susan C. DiClemente. (Illus.). 775p. 1997. spiral bd. 3950.00 (*1-57936-050-5*, 939) IBC USA.

Oxygen Therapies. Ed McCabe. 142p. 12.00 incl. audio (*1-879323-08-7*) Sound Horizons AV.

Oxygen Therapies: A New Way of Approaching Disease. Ed McCabe. (Energy Publications Alternatives). (Illus.). 224p. (Orig.). (C). 1988. pap. 12.00 (*0-9620527-0-1*) Energy Pubns.

***Oxygen Therapy.** Lonny J. Ashworth. (CPG Mentor - Patient Cases in Respiratory Care Ser.: Unit 2). 1998. write for info. (*0-8151-2278-0*) Mosby Inc.

Oxygen Transfer from Atmosphere to Tissues. Ed. by N. C. Gonzalez & M. R. Fedde. LC 88-2531. (Advances in Experimental Medicine & Biology Ser.: Vol. 227). (Illus.). 374p. 1988. 95.00 (*0-306-42825-3*, Plenum Trade) Perseus Pubng.

Oxygen Transport in Biological Systems: Modelling of Pathways from Environment to Cell. Ed. by S. Eggington & H. F. Ross. (Society for Experimental Biology Seminar Ser.: No. 51). (Illus.). 310p. (C). 1993. text 115.00 (*0-521-41488-1*) Cambridge U Pr.

Oxygen Transport in the Critically Ill Patient: Munster (FRG), 11-12 May, 1990. Ed. by M. Wendt et al. (Anaesthesiologie & Intensivmedizin Ser.). (Illus.). 240p. 1990. 33.95 (*0-387-52498-3*) Spr-Verlag.

Oxygen Transport to Tissue. Ed. by A. G. Hudetz & Duane F. Bruley. (Advances in Experimental Medicine & Biology Ser.: 454). (Illus.). 706p. (C). 1998. text 195.00 (*0-306-46043-2*, Kluwer Plenum) Kluwer Academic.

Oxygen Transport to Tissue, No. VIII. Ed. by Ian S. Longmuir. LC 86-15125. (Advances in Experimental Medicine & Biology Ser.: Vol. 200). 670p. 1986. 125.00 (*0-306-42379-0*, Plenum Trade) Perseus Pubng.

Oxygen Transport to Tissue, No. IX. Ed. by I. A. Silver & A. Silver. LC 87-3329. (Advances in Experimental Medicine & Biology Ser.). (Illus.). 414p. 1987. 89.50 (*0-306-42597-1*, Plenum Trade) Perseus Pubng.

Oxygen Transport to Tissue, No. X. Ed. by M. Mochizuki et al. LC 87-32879. (Advances in Experimental Medicine & Biology Ser.: Vol. 222). (Illus.). 784p. 1988. 145.00 (*0-306-42795-8*, Plenum Trade) Perseus Pubng.

Oxygen Transport to Tissue, No. XI. Ed. by K. Rakusan et al. (Advances in Experimental Medicine & Biology Ser.: Vol. 247). (Illus.). 812p. 1989. 165.00 (*0-306-43156-4*, Plenum Trade) Perseus Pubng.

Oxygen Transport to Tissue, No. XII. Ed. by J. Piiper et al. LC 90-7835. (Advances in Experimental Medicine & Biology Ser.: Vol. 277). (Illus.). 930p. 1990. 175.00 (*0-306-43682-5*, Plenum Trade) Perseus Pubng.

Oxygen Transport to Tissue, Vol. 18. Ed. by Edwin M. Nemoto & Joseph C. LaManna. LC 97-4326. (Advances in Experimental Medicine & Biology Ser.: Vol. 411). (Illus.). 624p. (C). 1997. text 159.50 (*0-306-45516-1*, Kluwer Plenum) Kluwer Academic.

Oxygen Transport to Tissue, Vol. 115. Ed. by W. Erdmann & Duane F. Bruley. (Advances in Experimental Medicine & Biology Ser.: Vol. 317). (Illus.). 940p. (C). 1992. text 222.00 (*0-306-44232-9*, Kluwer Plenum) Kluwer Academic.

Oxygen Transport to Tissue: Proceedings of the 24th Annual Meeting of the International Society Held in Dundee, Scotland, August 19-23, 1996, Vol. 428. Ed. by David K. Harrison & David T. Delpy. LC 97-31219. (Advances in Experimental Medicine & Biology Ser.: Vol. XIX). (Illus.). 736p. 1998. 210.00 (*0-306-45711-3*, Kluwer Plenum) Kluwer Academic.

Oxygen Transport to Tissue 17: Proceedings of the 22nd Annual Meeting of the International Society on Oxygen Transport to Tissue Held in Istanbul, Turkey, August 22-26, 1994. Ed. by C. Ince et al. LC 95-50023. (Advances in Experimental Medicine & Biology Ser.: Vol. 388). 654p. 1996. 149.50 (*0-306-45200-6*, Kluwer Plenum) Kluwer Academic.

Oxygen Transport to Tissue XVI, No. XVI. Ed. by Michael C. Hogan et al. LC 94-44823. (Advances in Experimental Medicine & Biology Ser.: Vol. 361). (Illus.). 672p. (C). 1995. text 155.00 (*0-306-44827-0*, Kluwer Plenum) Kluwer Academic.

Oxygen Transport to Tissue. Ed. by T. K. Goldstick et al. (Advances in Experimental Medicine & Biology Ser.: Vol. 316). (Illus.). 504p. (C). 1992. text 174.00 (*0-306-44342-2*, Kluwer Plenum) Kluwer Academic.

***Oxygen Transport to Tissue XXI.** Andras Eke & David T. Delpy. LC 99-40549. (Advances in Experimental Medicine & Biology Ser.). 1999. write for info. (*0-306-46281-8*, Kluwer Plenum) Kluwer Academic.

Oxygen Transport to Tissue, Vol. 15. P. Vaupel et al. (Advances in Experimental Medicine & Biology Ser.: Vol. 345). (Illus.). 976p. (C). 1994. text 185.00 (*0-306-44632-4*, Kluwer Plenum) Kluwer Academic.

Oxygenases & Model Systems. Ed. by Takuzo Funabiki. LC 96-35768. (Catalysis by Metal Complexes Ser.). 408p. (C). 1996. text 217.50 (*0-7923-4240-2*) Kluwer Academic.

Oxygenates As Fuel Additives: Clean Coal Technology; CNG, LNG, & LPG Use As Alternative Fuels; Trace Element Geochemistry of Coal & Related Fuels; Thermal Decomposition & Gasification Mechanisms; General Papers; Preprints of Papers Presented at the 207th ACS National Meeting, San Diego, CA, March 13-17, 1994. American Chemical Society, Division of Fuel Chemis. LC TP0315.. (Preprints of Papers: Vol. 39, No. 2). 374p. reprint ed. pap. 116.00 (*0-7837-6800-1*, 204663200003) Bks Demand.

Oxygenates by Homologation or CO Hydrogenation with Metal Complexes. Ed. by Giuseppe Braca. LC 93-23650. (CMCO - Catalysis by Metal Complexes Ser.). 240p. (C). 1994. text 142.00 (*0-7923-2628-8*) Kluwer Academic.

***Oxygenates in Water: Critical Information & Research Needs.** J. Micheal Davis. 65p. 2000. reprint ed. pap. text 20.00 (*0-7567-0070-1*) DIANE Pub.

***Oxygenation.** Sheldon. (Nursing Concepts Ser.). 2000. 22.95 (*1-889325-55-4*, Pub. by Fence Crk Pubng) Blackwell Sci.

Oxygenic Photosynthesis: The Light Reactions. Ed. by Donald Ort. (Advances in Photosynthesis Ser.). 696p. (C). 1996. pap. text 147.00 (*0-7923-3684-4*) Kluwer Academic.

Oxygenic Photosynthesis: The Light Reactions. Charles F. Yocum. Ed. by Donald Ort. LC 96-9020. (Advances in Photosynthesis Ser.). 696p. (C). 1996. lib. bdg. 280.00 (*0-7923-3683-6*) Kluwer Academic.

***Oxygen/Nitrogen Radicals & Cellular Injury.** Ed. by Kenneth B. Adler et al. (Illus.). 141p. (C). 2000. reprint ed. pap. text 30.00 (*0-7881-8538-1*) DIANE Pub.

Oxymoron Vol. I: Chance. Ed. by Patricia Hagood & Edward Binkowski. (Illus.). 216p. (Orig.). 1997. pap. 53.70 (*0-9653852-0-5*) Oxymoron Media.

Oxymoron Vol. 2: The Fringe. 2nd ed. Ed. by Edward Binkowski. (Illus.). 200p. 1998. pap. 49.95 (*0-9653852-1-3*) Oxymoron Media.

Oxyoke. large type ed. Frank Bosworth. (Lythway Ser.). 160p. 1991. 19.95 (*0-7451-1250-1*, G K Hall Lrg Type) Mac Lib Ref.

Oxytenidae. Vitor O. Becker. Ed. by J. B. Heppner. (Lepidopterorum Catalogus Ser.: Vol. 19: Fasc. 115). (Illus.). 10p. 2000. pap. text 4.50 (*0-945417-69-1*) Sci Pubs.

Oxytocin. Pleasant Gehman. 160p. 1999. pap. 13.00 (*1-888277-09-2*, Pub. by Incommcdo San Diego) Consort Bk Sales.

Oxytocin: Cellular & Molecular Approaches in Medicine & Research. Ed. by Richard Ivell & John A. Russell. (Advances in Experimental Medicine & Biology Ser.: Vol. 395). (Illus.). 692p. (C). 1996. text 174.00 (*0-306-45290-1*, Kluwer Plenum) Kluwer Academic.

Oxytocin in Maternal, Sexual, & Social Behaviors, Vol. 652. Ed. by Cort A. Pedersen et al. 492p. 1992. 125.00 (*0-89766-699-2*) NY Acad Sci.

Oxywrite Revealed (3.5) Herbert L. Tyson. 1991. 24.95 (*0-8306-6749-0*) McGraw-Hill Prof.

Oy. Jerry Cooper. 24p. (Orig.). 1996. pap. 3.95 (*1-889419-16-8*) J Cooper.

***Oy, Gevalt! Book of Yiddish Wit & Wisdom.** Living Language Staff. (Living Language Ser.). 2000. 4.95 (*0-609-60616-6*) Liv Lang.

***Oy, Joy!** Lucy Frank. LC 98-54299. 288p. (YA). (gr. 6-9). 1999. 16.95 (*0-7894-2538-6*) DK Pub Inc.

Oy of Sex: Jewish Women Write Erotica. Ed. by Marcy Sheiner. LC 99-11003. 200p. 1999. pap. 14.95 (*1-57344-083-3*) Cleis Pr.

Oy Vey the - Things They Say: A Book of Jewish Wit. Andrews & McMeel Staff. (Illus.). 80p. 1994. 4.95 (*0-8362-3096-5*) Andrews & McMeel.

Oya: Ifa & the Spirit of the Wind. Fa'lokum Fatunmbi. 32p. 1994. pap. 4.95 (*0-942272-34-X*) Original Pubns.

Oyer & Allied Families: Their History & Genealogy. Phyllis S. Oyer. (Illus.). 400p. 1988. 30.00 (*0-9620297-0-X*) P S Oyer.

***Oyl.** Denise Duhamel & Maureen Seaton. 40p. 2000. pap. 8.00 (*1-888219-16-5*) Pearl Edit.

Oyo: An Ohio River Anthology, 3 vols. Ed. by Don Wallis. (Illus.). 540p. (C). pap. 25.00 (*0-685-71984-7*) Oyo Pr.

Oyo: An Ohio River Anthology, Vol. I: Movement & Place. Ed. by Don Wallis. (Illus.). 180p. (C). pap. 10.00 (*0-685-71981-2*) Oyo Pr.

Oyo: An Ohio River Anthology, Vol. II: River Journeys. Ed. by Don Wallis. (Illus.). 180p. (C). pap. 10.00 (*0-685-71982-0*) Oyo Pr.

Oyo: An Ohio River Anthology, Vol. III: River Lives. Ed. by Don Wallis. (Illus.). 180p. (C). pap. 10.00 (*0-685-71983-9*) Oyo Pr.

Oyo Empire, c. 1600-c. 1836: A West African Imperialism in the Era of the Atlantic. Robin Law. (Modern Revivals in History Ser.). 354p. 1992. 63.95 (*0-7512-0006-9*, Pub. by Gregg Revivals) Ashgate Pub Co.

Oyster. Janette Turner Hospital. 408p. 1999. pap. 14.00 (*0-393-31936-9*) Norton.

Oyster. William K. Brooks. (Maryland Paperback Bookshelf Ser.). (Illus.). 230p. (C). 1996. reprint ed. pap. 14.95 (*0-8018-5391-5*) Johns Hopkins.

O

Oyster, No. 6. 1996. mass mkt. 13.95 (*0-340-66695-1*) Hodder & Stought Ltd.

Oyster: A Novel. Janette T. Hospital. LC 97-34071. 392p. 1998. 25.95 (*0-393-04618-4*) Norton.

Oyster & the Eagle: Selected Aphorisms & Parables of Multatuli. Ed. & Tr. by E. M. Beekman from DUT. LC 73-93171. 124p. 1974. lib. bdg. 20.00 (*0-87023-123-5*) U of Mass Pr.

Oyster Cans. Vivian Karsnitz & James Karsnitz. LC 93-85226. (Illus.). 160p. 1993. pap. 29.95 (*0-88740-462-6*) Schiffer.

***Oyster Catchers.** Iris Gower. (J). 2000. pap. 8.95 (*0-552-13688-3*, Pub. by Transworld Publishers Ltd) Trafalgar.

Oyster Cookery. 2nd ed. Sharon Montoya-Welsh & Marjorie Speare-Yerxa. (Illus.). 168p. 1984. reprint ed. pap. 9.95 (*0-9613895-0-8*) Shoalwater Kitch.

Oyster Cookery: Sixty Recipes. Joe Daniels. (Illus.). 64p. (Orig.). 1988. pap. 3.95 (*0-940828-18-9*) D Youra Studios.

Oyster Creek Icebreak. Shirley Warren. 32p. (Orig.). 1989. pap. 4.95 (*1-877801-00-3*) Still Waters.

Oyster Moon. Margaret Meacham. LC 96-15057. (Illus.). 112p. (J). (gr. 4-8). 1996. pap. 9.95 (*0-87033-459-X*, Tidewtr Pubs) Cornell Maritime.

Oyster Pirates. Jim Walker. LC 96-25283. (Wells Fargo Trail Ser.: Bk. 6). 336p. 1996. pap. 8.99 (*1-55661-701-1*) Bethany Hse.

Oyster Plates. Vivian Karsnitz & James Karsnitz. LC 93-85227. (Illus.). 160p. 1993. pap. 29.95 (*0-88740-529-0*) Schiffer.

***Oyster Recipes of St. Mary's County, Maryland.** Ann Loher & Alech Loker. (Illus.). 97p. 1999. mass mkt. 8.00 (*1-928874-00-2*) Solitude Pr.

Oyster Redux. expanded ed. James Jennings. 432p. 1996. mass mkt. 6.95 (*0-7867-0390-3*) Carroll & Graf.

Oyster Wars & Public Trust: Property, Law & Ecology in New Jersey History. McCay. LC 97-33776. 304p. 1998. 45.00 (*0-8165-1804-1*) U of Ariz Pr.

Oyster Wars of Chesapeake Bay. John R. Wennersten. LC 81-5810. (Illus.). 159p. 1981. 14.95 (*0-87033-263-5*, Tidewtr Pubs) Cornell Maritime.

Oysterback Spoken Here. Helen Chappell. LC 98-16063. (Illus.). 208p. 1998. pap. 14.95 (*1-891521-01-2*) Woodholme Hse.

Oysterback Tales. Helen Chappell. LC 93-37407. 1994. 19.95 (*0-8018-4815-6*) Johns Hopkins.

Oystercatcher. Desmond Nethersole-Thompson. (Natural History Ser.: No. 28). (Illus.). 24p. 1989. pap. 5.25 (*0-85263-949-X*, Pub. by Shire Pubns) Parkwest Pubns.

Oystercatcher: From Individuals to Populations. Ed. by John D. Goss-Custard. (Oxford Ornithology Ser.). (Illus.). 452p. 1996. text 115.00 (*0-19-854647-5*) OUP.

Oystering from New York to Boston. John M. Kochiss. LC 74-5965. (American Maritime Library: No. 7). (Illus.). 273p. reprint ed. pap. 84.70 (*0-7837-6146-5*, 204415500009) Bks Demand.

Oysters. John DeMers & Andrew Jaeger. 96p. 1999. pap. 5.95 (*0-89087-869-2*) Celestial Arts.

***Oysters: A Culinary Celebration.** rev. ed. Joan Reardon. LC 99-35886. (Illus.). 256p. 2000. 25.00 (*1-55821-944-7*) Lyons Pr.

Oysters: A True Delicacy. Shirly Line. (Illus.). 64p. 1995. 12.95 (*0-02-860376-1*) Macmillan.

Oyster's Last Stand. Robert N. Feinstein. LC 94-6558. (Illus.). 96p. (Orig.). 1994. pap. 10.00 (*0-914061-44-5*) Orchises Pr.

Oysters of Locmariaquer. Eleanor Clark. LC 77-82670. (Illus.). 1978. pap. 3.95 (*0-226-10763-9*, P752) U Ch Pr.

Oyvind Fahlstrom. Pontus Hulten et al. LC 82-60794. (Illus.). 120p. 1982. pap. 9.00 (*0-89207-035-8*) S R Guggenheim.

Oz. L. Frank Baum & Patrick Shanahan. 53p. 1996. pap. 5.50 (*0-87129-713-2*, O55) Dramatic Pub.

***Oz.** Cathy Beylon. (Little Activity Bks.). (Illus.). (J). 1998. pap. 1.00 (*0-486-40045-X*) Dover.

Oz: A Gathering of Heroes. Stu Kerr & Ralph Griffith. (Illus.). 160p. (Orig.). 1996. pap. 14.95 (*0-941613-88-7*, Caliber Comics) Stabur Pr.

Oz: Mayhem in Munchkinland. Stu Kerr & Ralph Griffith. (Illus.). 176p. (Orig.). 1995. pap. 14.95 (*0-941613-73-9*, Caliber Comics) Stabur Pr.

Oz: The Hundredth Anniversary Celebration. Peter Glassman. LC 99-87236. 64p. (J). 2000. 24.95 (*0-688-15915-X*, Wm Morrow) Morrow Avon.

***Oz: 100th Anniversary Celebration.** Glassman. 2000. lib. bdg. 19.89 (*0-06-029219-9*) HarpC.

Oz No. 4: Dorothy & Wizard in Oz. L. Frank Baum. 240p. 1986. mass mkt. 4.99 (*0-345-34168-6*, Del Rey) Ballantine Pub Grp.

Oz No. 8: Tik Tok of Oz. L. Frank Baum. 272p. 1985. mass mkt. 4.99 (*0-345-33435-3*, Del Rey) Ballantine Pub Grp.

Oz No. 10: Rinkitink in Oz. L. Frank Baum. 304p. 1985. mass mkt. 5.99 (*0-345-33317-9*, Del Rey) Ballantine Pub Grp.

Oz No. 11: Lost Princess of Oz. L. Frank Baum. 304p. 1985. mass mkt. 4.99 (*0-345-33367-5*, Del Rey) Ballantine Pub Grp.

Oz & Beyond: The Fantasy World of L. Frank Baum. Michael O. Riley. LC 97-276. (Illus.). xiii, 286p. 1998. 29.95 (*0-7006-0832-X*) U Pr of KS.

***Oz & Beyond: The Fantasy World of L. Frank Baum.** Michael O. Riley. LC 97-276. (Illus.). 302p. 1998. pap. 15.95 (*0-7006-0933-4*) U Pr of KS.

***Oz Before the Rainbow: L. Frank Baum's "The Wizard of Oz" on Stage & Screen for 1939.** Mark Evan Swartz. (Illus.). 288p. 2000. 34.95 (*0-8018-6477-1*) Johns Hopkins.

***Oz Box Set.** L. Frank Baum. 272p. (J). 2000. pap., boxed set 19.50 (*0-06-440947-3*, HarpTrophy) HarpC Child Bks.

Oz Clarke's Encyclopedia of Wine: An Illustrated A-to-Z Guide to Wines of the World. Oz Clarke. LC 93-17939. (Illus.). 1994. 35.00 (*0-671-79295-4*) S&S Trade.

***Oz Clarke's Introducing Wine.** Oz Clarke. 144p. 2000. 20.00 (*0-15-100642-3*) Harcourt.

Oz Clarke's New Encyclopedia of Wine. Oz Clarke. LC 99-33068. 416p. 1999. 40.00 (*0-15-100565-6*, Harvest Bks) Harcourt.

Oz Clarke's Pocket Wine Guide, 1999. Oz Clarke. (Illus.). 304p. (C). 1998. 12.00 (*0-15-100430-7*) Harcourt.

***Oz Clarke's Pocket Wine Guide 2001.** rev. ed. Oz Clarke. (Illus.). 320p. 2000. 13.00 (*0-15-100634-2*) Harcourt.

Oz Clarke's Pocket Wine Guide 2000. Oz Clarke. 320p. 1999. 12.00 (*0-15-100571-0*, Harvest Bks) Harcourt.

Oz Clarke's Wine Advisor, 1995: An Opinionated A-Z Guide to Wines by the World's Most Readable Wine Writer. Oz Clarke. 288p. 1994. pap. 12.00 (*0-671-88252-X*, Fireside) S&S Trade Pap.

Oz Clarke's Wine Advisor 1999. Oz Clarke. (C). 1998. pap. 12.00 (*0-15-600628-6*) Harcourt.

Oz Clarke's Wine Atlas: Wines & Wine Regions of the World. Oz Clarke. (Illus.). 320p. (gr. 8). 1995. 60.00 (*0-316-14697-8*) Little.

Oz Clarke's Wine Handbook, 1993. LC 92-30116. 1993. pap. 10.00 (*0-671-79361-6*, Fireside) S&S Trade Pap.

Oz Clark's Encyclopedia of World Wines. Contrib. by Oz Clark. LC 93-1948. 1994. 22.50 (*0-671-79294-6*) S&S Trade.

Oz Light. Mike Kalibabky. Ed. by Mary A. Centa. (Illus.). 52p. 1997. pap. text 4.95 (*0-9640212-2-6*) Moonlight MN.

***Oz Principle.** 1998. 14.00 (*0-13-018304-0*) P-H.

Oz Principle: Getting Results Through Individual & Organizational Accountability. Roger Connors et al. 320p. 1998. pap. text 14.00 (*0-7352-0043-2*) PH Pr.

Oz Principle: What the Management Wizards Can't or Won't Tell You about Getting Results. Connors & Hickman. (C). 1995. 12.95 (*0-13-254301-X*) P-H.

Oz Principle: What the Management Wizards Can't or Won't Tell You about Getting Results. Roger Connors et al. 304p. (C). 1994. text 22.95 (*0-13-032129-X*) P-H.

Oz-Story, No. 1. L. Frank Baum. Ed. by David Maxine. (Illus.). 128p. (Orig.). (J). (gr. 2-5). 1995. pap. 14.95 (*0-9644988-1-2*) Hungry Tiger.

Oz-Story, No. 2. L. Frank Baum & Eloise J. McGraw. Ed. by David Maxine. (Illus.). 128p. (Orig.). (J). (gr. 2-6). 1996. pap. 14.95 (*0-9644988-2-0*) Hungry Tiger.

Oz-Story, Vol. 3. L. Frank Baum & Rachel C. Payes. Ed. & Illus. by David Maxine. Illus. by Eric Shanower. 128p. (Orig.). (J). (gr. 2-6). 1997. pap. 14.95 (*0-9644988-4-7*) Hungry Tiger.

***Oz-Story, Vol. 4.** L. Frank Baum et al. Ed. by David Maxine. (Illus.). 128p. (Orig.). (J). (gr. 3-7). 1998. pap. 14.95 (*0-9644988-7-1*) Hungry Tiger.

***Oz-Story 5.** L. Frank Baum & W. W. Denslow. Ed. by David Maxine. (Oz Ser.: No. 5). (Illus.). 128p. (J). (gr. 3-7). 1999. pap. 14.95 (*1-929527-00-4*) Hungry Tiger.

Oz Toy Book, Vol. 2. Eric Shanower. (Illus.). 14p. (Orig.). (J). (gr. 2-6). 1994. pap. 8.00 (*0-9644988-0-4*) Hungry Tiger.

Ozark Almanac. A. E. Lucas. 1986. pap. 8.00 (*0-8309-0443-3*) Independence Pr.

Ozark Baptizings, Hangings, & Other Diversions: Theatrical Folkways of Rural Missouri, 1885-1910. Robert K. Gilmore. LC 83-40324. (Illus.). 296p. 1990. pap. 13.95 (*0-8061-2270-6*) U of Okla Pr.

Ozark Christian College. Lynn Gardner. 360p. 19.99 (*0-89900-590-X*) College Pr Pub.

Ozark Clan of Elkhead Creek: Early Life in Northwest Colorado. 2nd rev. ed. Irby H. Miller. LC 96-61963. (Illus.). 336p. 1997. pap. 15.95 (*0-9655961-0-9*) Yellow Cat.

Ozark Country. W. K. Mcneil. LC 95-14859. (Folklife in the South Ser.). (Illus.). 180p. 1995. pap. 16.95 (*0-87805-729-3*); text 40.00 (*0-87805-728-5*) U Pr of Miss.

Ozark Flats. Bob Williams. (Illus.). (Orig.). 1983. 12.95 (*0-911506-16-0*) Thueson.

Ozark Folksong. Waldenbooks Publishing Company Staff. (Illus.). pap. 14.95 (*0-681-28841-8*) Waldenbooks Co Inc.

Ozark Ghost Stories. Richard Young & Judy D. Young. 174p. (Orig.). (J). (gr. 5 up). 1993. pap. 9.95 incl. audio (*0-87483-211-X*) August Hse.

Ozark Ghost Stories. Richard Young & Judy D. Young. (American Storytelling Ser.). (Illus.). 176p. (Orig.). 1995. pap. 12.95 (*0-87483-410-4*) August Hse.

Ozark Heritage, Vol. 3: Dent County Missouri Area Cemeteries & Families. Ken Fiebelman & Deloris G. Wood. LC 94-70114. (Illus.). 624p. 1994. 65.00 (*0-9640325-0-3*) Lost Generation.

Ozark Hideaways: Twenty-Seven Day Trips for Hiking & Fishing. 2nd ed. Louis C. White. LC 98-7613. (Illus.). 256p. 1998. pap. 19.95 (*0-8262-1196-8*) U of Mo Pr.

Ozark Highlands Trail Guide. 4th ed. Tim Ernst. (Illus.). 136p. 1998. pap. 16.95 (*1-882906-39-X*) CLOUDLAND.

***Ozark Hillbilly CEO: An Autobiography.** Joe McNabb. LC 99-71335. 384p. 1999. pap. 39.95 (*0-9672491-3-9*) WRDSWRTH.

Ozark Magic & Folklore. Vance Randolph. Orig. Title: Ozark Superstition. 367p. 1947. pap. 7.95 (*0-486-21181-9*) Dover.

Ozark Meandering. James Bogan. 91p. 1999. pap. 12.00 (*0-944048-13-7*) Timberline Missouri.

Ozark Mountain Area Retirement & Relocation Guide. large type ed. (Retirement & Relocation Guides Ser.). (Illus.). 350p. Date not set. pap. 24.95 (*1-56559-139-9*) HGI-Over Fifty.

Ozark Mountain Girl. Wilma G. Harryman. (Illus.). 267p. 1995. 23.95 (*0-9651141-0-4*); pap. 12.95 (*0-9651141-1-2*) Ozark Mtn Girl.

Ozark Mountain Humor. W. K. McNeil. 240p. 1989. pap. 8.95 (*0-87483-086-9*) August Hse.

Ozark National Scenic Riverways. Eunice A. Pennington & D. D. Pennington. (Illus.). 80p. (Orig.). 1967. 3.00 (*0-685-09252-6*); pap. 1.00 (*0-685-09253-4*) Pennington.

Ozark, Ozark: A Hillside Reader. Ed. by Miller Williams. LC 80-26242. 208p. 1984. pap. 17.95 (*0-8262-0472-4*) U of Mo Pr.

Ozark Parson. Ida B. Bontrager. 1978. pap. 5.50 (*0-87813-512-X*) Christian Light.

Ozark Remedies. Fern Angus. (Ozark Ser.: No. 3). (Illus.). 64p. (Orig.). 1995. pap. 3.50 (*0-9637913-3-8*) Angus Pubns.

Ozark Reservoir Papers: Archeology in West-Central Arkansas 1965-1970. Michael P. Hoffman et al. (Illus.). 145p. 1977. pap. 4.00 (*1-56349-020-X*, RS10) AR Archaeol.

Ozark Sketches: A Family Chronicle. LaNell Compton. LC 90-83321. 1991. 10.95 (*0-8158-0463-6*) Chris Mass.

Ozark Story Poems. Diane T. Denarski. LC 93-9915. 84p. 1993. pap. 7.95 (*0-935304-30-4*) August Hse.

Ozark Superstition see Ozark Magic & Folklore

Ozark Superstitions. Fern Angus. (Illus.). 37p. 1993. pap. 3.00 (*0-9637913-2-X*) Angus Pubns.

Ozark Tall Tales: Collected from the Oral Tradition. Richard Young & Judy D. Young. LC 89-35858. 215p. 1989. pap. 12.95 (*0-87483-099-0*) August Hse.

***Ozark Trilogy.** Suzette Haden Elgin. LC 99-51760. 520p. 2000. pap. 30.00 (*1-55728-592-6*) U of Ark Pr.

Ozark Trout Tales: A Fishing Guide for the White River System. Steve Wright. (Illus.). 200p. (Orig.). 1994. pap. 24.95 (*0-9638832-9-1*) White Riv Chronicle.

Ozark Vernacular Houses: A Study of Rural Homeplaces in the Arkansas Ozarks, 1830-1930. Jean Sizemore. (Illus.). 264p. 1994. text 34.00 (*1-55728-310-9*) U of Ark Pr.

Ozark Whitewater: A Paddler's Guide to the Mountain Streams of Arkansas & Missouri. Tom Kennon. (Illus.). 300p. 1989. pap. 12.95 (*0-89732-065-4*) Menasha Ridge.

Ozark Wildflowers: A Field Guide. Don R. Kurz. LC 98-33997. (Illus.). 272p. 1999. pap. 19.95 (*1-56044-730-3*) Falcon Pub Inc.

Ozark Writers on Writing: Essays on Creativity. Ed. by L. Pate. LC 95-71608. 151p. (Orig.). 1996. pap. 12.95 (*0-9630829-4-9*) Seven Oaks Pub.

Ozarks: The People, the Mountains, the Magic. Photos & Text by George O. Miller. LC 95-36141. (Illus.). 96p. 1996. pap. 4.95 (*0-89658-281-7*) Voyageur Pr.

Ozarks Impressions: A Journey Through the Seasons. Robert E. Gustafson. (Illus.). 80p. (Orig.). 1995. pap. 12.95 (*0-9645834-0-2*) Lancelot Pub.

Ozarks Outdoors: A Guide for Fishermen, Hunters, & Tourists. Milton D. Rafferty. LC 85-40478. (Illus.). 408p. 1988. 29.95 (*0-8061-1554-8*); pap. 19.95 (*0-8061-2088-6*) U of Okla Pr.

Ozark's Seasons of the Heart. Marvin A. Matthews. LC 99-173716. (Illus.). 288p. 1998. pap. 22.95 (*0-938041-34-7*) Arc Pr AR.

Ozette Woodworking Technology. fac. ed. Paul F. Gleeson. (Washington State University, Lab. of Archaeology & History Project Reports: No. 3). (Illus.). 238p. (C). 1980. reprint ed. pap. text 25.00 (*1-55567-507-7*) Coyote Press.

Ozhivi Pokoinika (To Wake the Dead) Roman (A Novel) Alexander Romadanov. LC 90-86134. (RUS., Illus.). 240p. (Orig.). 1991. pap. text 15.00 (*0-911971-63-7*) Effect Pub.

Ozidi Saga. Ed. by John P. Clark. 1979. 59.00 (*0-19-575558-8*) OUP.

Ozidi Saga. Clarke. 436p. 1991. pap. 24.95 (*0-88258-108-2*) Howard U Pr.

Ozma of Oz. L. Frank Baum. 1996. 22.95 (*0-8488-0706-5*) Amereon Ltd.

Ozma of Oz. L. Frank Baum. LC 88-63291. (Books of Wonder). (Illus.). 288p. (J). (gr. 2 up). 1989. 21.95 (*0-688-06632-1*, Wm Morrow) Morrow Avon.

Ozma of Oz. L. Frank Baum. (Juveniles Ser.). (Illus.). 288p. (J). (gr. 2 up). 1985. reprint ed. pap. 6.95 (*0-486-24779-1*) Dover.

Ozma of Oz: A Tale of Time. Susan L. Zeder. (J). (gr. 4 up). 1981. 6.50 (*0-87602-233-6*) Anchorage.

Ozma of Oz No. 3. L. Frank Baum. LC 77-89301. 264p. (Orig.). (J). 1986. mass mkt. 4.99 (*0-345-33589-9*, Del Rey) Ballantine Pub Grp.

Oznayim L'Torah Vol. V: Insights in the Torah Devarim. Z. Sorotzkin. 1994. 20.99 (*0-89906-532-5*); pap. 17.99 (*0-89906-533-3*) Mesorah Pubns.

Oznayim L'Torah, Vol. I: Insights in the Torah: Bereishis. Z. Sorotzken. 1991. 20.99 (*0-89906-540-6*); pap. 17.99 (*0-89906-541-4*) Mesorah Pubns.

Oznayim L'Torah, Vol. II: Insights in the Torah: Shemos. Z. Sorotzken. 1992. 20.99 (*0-89906-538-4*); pap. 17.99 (*0-89906-539-2*) Mesorah Pubns.

Oznayim L'Torah, Vol. III: Insights in the Torah: Vayikra. Z. Sorotzken. 1993. 20.99 (*0-89906-536-8*); pap. 17.99 (*0-89906-537-6*) Mesorah Pubns.

Oznayim L'Torah, Vol. IV: Insights in the Torah Bamidear. Z. Sorotzkin. 1994. 20.99 (*0-89906-534-1*); pap. 17.99 (*0-89906-535-X*) Mesorah Pubns.

Ozonation for Drinking Water Treatment: Proceedings of the PAG Conference, Pasadena, California, U. S. A., 1992. 400p. 1992. 70.00 (*0-685-56836-9*) Pan Am Intl Ozone.

Ozonation Systems & Drinking Water Treatment. 1989. 30.00 (*0-685-38311-3*) Pan Am Intl Ozone.

Ozone. Don Nardo. LC 91-6275. (Overview Ser.). (Illus.). 112p. (YA). (gr. 5-8). 1991. lib. bdg. 22.45 (*1-56006-101-4*) Lucent Bks.

Ozone: Analytical Aspects & Odor Control. Ed. by Rip G. Rice & Myron E. Browning. LC 76-17611. (Illus.). 1976. text 25.00 (*0-918650-09-7*) Pan Am Intl Ozone.

Ozone: The Eternal Purifier of the Earth & Cleanser of All Living Beings. H. E. Sartori. 356p. 1994. text 69.00 (*0-614-07402-9*) Life Sci Fnd.

Ozone Alert. John Wood. (Artists' Books Ser.). (Illus.). 32p. (Orig.). 1996. pap. 10.00 (*0-89822-118-8*) Visual Studies.

Ozone & Biological Treatment for DBP Control & Biological Stability. (Illus.). 276p. 1994. pap. 120.00 (*0-89867-752-1*, 90649) Am Water Wks Assn.

***Ozone & Climate Change: A Beginner's Guide.** Stephen J. Reid. 220p. 2000. text 45.00 (*90-5699-232-5*, G & B Science); pap. text 23.00 (*90-5699-233-3*, G & B Science) Gordon & Breach.

Ozone & Other Photochemical Oxidants. Assembly of Life Sciences (U. S.) Committee on Med. LC 77-1293. (Illus.). 729p. reprint ed. pap. 200.00 (*0-8357-6646-2*, 203531300094) Bks Demand.

Ozone & Ozone-Peroxide Disinfection of Giardia & Viruses. (Illus.). 148p. 1992. pap. 42.00 (*0-89867-621-5*, 90605) Am Water Wks Assn.

Ozone & Particulate Matter Research Act of 1997. Ed. by James M. Inhofe. 149p. (C). 1999. pap. text 35.00 (*0-7881-7854-7*) DIANE Pub.

Ozone As an Aid to Coagulation & Filtration. (Illus.). 152p. 1993. pap. 56.00 (*0-89867-695-9*, 90643) Am Water Wks Assn.

Ozone Chemistry & Technology: This Book Presents Sixty Papers Constituting the Proceedings of the International Ozone Conference Held in Chicago, November 1956. International Ozone Conference (1956: Chicago) Sta. LC 59-3922. (Advances in Chemistry Ser.: Vol. 21). (Illus.). 473p. 1959. reprint ed. pap. 146.70 (*0-608-06898-5*, 206710600009) Bks Demand.

Ozone Chlorine-Dioxide Oxidation Products of Organic Materials. Ed. by Rip G. Rice & Joseph A. Cotruvo. LC 78-53924. (Illus.). 1978. text 50.00 (*0-918650-02-X*) Pan Am Intl Ozone.

Ozone Crisis: The Fifteen Year Evolution of a Sudden Global Emergency. Sharon Roan. 270p. 1990. pap. 9.95 (*0-471-52823-4*) Wiley.

Ozone Depletion & Aquatic Ecosystems. Donat P. Hader. (Environmental Intelligence Unit Ser.). 224p. 1997. 89.00 (*1-57059-427-9*, 0-12-312945-1) Landes Bioscience.

Ozone Depletion & Health. Ed. by R. Russell Jones & T. M. Wigley. LC 89-16614. 302p. 1989. text 375.00 (*0-471-92316-8*) Wiley.

Ozone Depletion, Greenhouse Gases, & Climate Change: Proceedings of a Joint Symposium. fac. ed. National Research Council, Board on Atmospheric Sc. LC 88-31544. (Illus.). 136p. 1989. pap. 38.80 (*0-7837-7565-2*, 2036997) Bks Demand.

Ozone Depletion, Greenhouse Gases, & Climate Change: Proceedings of a Joint Symposium by the Board of Atmospheric Sciences & Climate & the Committee on Global Change. National Research Council Staff. LC 88-31544. (Illus.). 136p. reprint ed. pap. 42.20 (*0-8357-4215-6*, 203699700003) Bks Demand.

Ozone Dilemma: A Reference Handbook. David E. Newton. LC 95-18722. (Contemporary World Issues Ser.). 196p. (YA). (gr. 9 up). 1995. lib. bdg. 45.00 (*0-87436-719-0*) ABC-CLIO.

Ozone Diplomacy: New Directions in Safeguarding the Planet. Richard E. Benedick. LC 90-20879. (Illus.). 320p. 1991. 35.00 (*0-674-65000-X*, BENOZO); pap. text 17.95 (*0-674-65001-8*, BENOZX) HUP.

Ozone Diplomacy: New Directions in Safeguarding the Planet. Richard E. Benedick. LC 97-26498. 512p. 1998. 39.95 (*0-674-65002-6*); pap. 18.95 (*0-674-65003-4*) HUP.

Ozone Discourse: Science & Politics in Global Environmental Cooperation. Karen Litfin. LC 94-8867. (New Directions in World Politics Ser.). (Illus.). 296p. 1994. 52.50 (*0-231-08136-7*) Col U Pr.

Ozone Discourses: Science & Politics in Global Environmental Cooperation. Karen Litfin. Ed. by Helen V. Milner & John G. Ruggie. (New Directions in World Politics Ser.). 296p. 1995. pap. 19.50 (*0-231-08137-5*) Col U Pr.

Ozone Disinfection in Municipal Water & Wastewater. Richard K. Miller et al. (Market Research Survey Ser.: No. 279). 50p. 1996. 200.00 (*1-55865-300-7*) Future Tech Surveys.

Ozone Disinfection of Giardia & Cryptosporidium. (Illus.). 84p. 1994. pap. 57.00 (*0-89867-762-9*, 90661) Am Water Wks Assn.

Ozone for Drinking Water Treatment - Oxidation-Disinfection-Biofiltration: Proceedings Cambridge MA Conference, November 12-15, 1995. 1995. 75.00 (*0-614-96187-4*) Pan Am Intl Ozone.

Ozone Hole. Alex Edmonds. LC 96-38756. (Closer Look at...Ser.). (Illus.). 32p. (J). (gr. 4-7). 1997. lib. bdg. 19.90 (*0-7613-0572-6*, Copper Beech Bks) Millbrook Pr.

Ozone Hole Sally Morgan. LC 98-51696. (Earth Watch Ser.). 1999. 20.25 (*0-531-14569-7*) Watts.

Ozone Hole. Darlene R. Stille. LC 90-20843. (New True Books Ser.). (Illus.). 48p. (J). (ps-3). 1991. lib. bdg. 21.00 (*0-516-01117-0*) Childrens.

Ozone in the Americas: Proceedings of Toronto Conference. 1991. 65.00 (*0-685-51582-6*) Pan Am Intl Ozone.

Ozone in the Atmosphere: Proceedings of Quadrennial Ozone Symposium, 1988. Ed. by R. D. Bojkov & P. Fabian. LC 89-77829. (Illus.). 822p. 1990. 87.00 (*0-937194-15-8*) A Deepak Pub.

Ozone in Water & Wastewater Treatment: Proceedings of the Eleventh Ozone World Congress, 2 vols. 1993. 130.00 (*0-685-70333-9*) Pan Am Intl Ozone.

Ozone in Water Treatment. Bruno Langlais & David R. Reckhow. 592p. 1991. boxed set 99.95 (*0-87371-474-1*, L474) Lewis Pubs.

An Asterisk (*) at the beginning of an entry indicates that the title is appearing for the first time.

Ozone Layer. Patricia Armentrout. LC 96-2883. (Earthly Oddities Ser.). 1996. lib. bdg. 17.27 (*1-57103-156-1*) Rourke Pr.

*__Ozone Layer.__ Rhonda Lucas Donald. LC 00-38412. (True Bks.). (Illus.). (J). 2001. write for info. (*0-516-22195-7*) Childrens.

Ozone Layer. Marshall Fisher. (Earth at Risk Ser.). (Illus.). 128p. (YA). (gr. 5 up). 1992. lib. bdg. 19.95 (*0-7910-1576-9*) Chelsea Hse.

Ozone Layer Chlorofluorocarbons & Building Services. BSRIA Staff. 1988. 35.00 incl. audio (*0-86022-225-X*, Pub. by Build Servs Info Assn) St Mut.

Ozone Layer Dictionary. Ed. by Denis Rivard. (FRE.). 493p. (Orig.). 1993. pap. 36.95 (*0-660-58897-8*, Pub. by Canadian Govt Pub) Accents Pubns.

Ozone Layer Protection: Country Incremental Costs. Ed. by Kenneth King & Mohan Munasinghe. 122p. 1995. pap. 22.00 (*0-8213-3133-7*, 13133) World Bank.

Ozone Measuring Instruments of the Stratosphere. William B. Grant. LC 89-63231. 438p. (Orig.). 1989. pap. 77.00 (*1-55752-042-9*) Optical Soc.

O!!Zone 98 - International Visual Poetry. Harry Burrus. (Illus.). 1998. pap. 25.00 (*1-884185-15-0*) O Zone.

O!!Zone 97 (International Visual Poetry) International Visual Poets Staff. (Illus.). 83p. 1997. pap. 25.00 (*1-884185-14-2*) O Zone.

Ozone Project. 1995. 15.00 (*92-871-2536-8*, Pub. by Council of Europe) Manhattan Pub Co.

Ozone Protection in the United States: Elements of Success. Ed. by Elizabeth Cook. 130p. 1996. pap. 20.00 (*1-56973-088-1*) World Resources Inst.

Ozone Reactions with Organic Compounds: A Symposium Sponsored by the Division of Petroleum Chemistry at the 161st Meeting of the American Chemical Society, Los Angeles, California, March 29-30, 1971. Philip S. Bailey. LC 72-88560. (American Chemical Society Advances in Chemistry Ser.: Vol. 112). 141p. reprint ed. pap. 43.80 (*0-608-12444-3*, 202423700036) Bks Demand.

Ozone Reality Check: Dispelling the Myths about the Ozone Depletion. Friends of the Earth. 23p. (Orig.). 1995. pap. 5.00 (*0-913890-90-1*) Friends of Earth.

Ozone Risk Communication & Management. Ed. by Edward J. Calabrese et al. (Illus.). 216p. 1990. lib. bdg. 95.00 (*0-87371-130-0*, L130) Lewis Pubs.

Ozone World Congress, 6th: Proceedings. 1985. 45.00 (*0-317-07466-0*) Pan Am Intl Ozone.

O!!Zone 99-00. limited ed. International Visual Poetry Staff. 25.00 (*1-884185-16-9*) O Zone.

Ozonization Manual for Water & Wastewater Treatment. Ed. by Willy J. Masschelein. LC 81-21986. (Illus.). 346p. reprint ed. pap. 107.30 (*0-8357-6650-0*, 203531900094) Bks Demand.

Ozoplaning with the Wizard of Oz. Ruth P. Thompson. (Illus.). 256p. (J). (gr. 3 up). 1996. pap. 12.95 (*0-929605-57-8*) Books of Wonder.

Ozu: His Life & Films. Donald Richie. (Illus.). 1974. pap. 16.95 (*0-520-03277-2*, Pub. by U CA Pr) Cal Prin Full Svc.

Ozu & the Poetics of Cinema. David Bordwell. (Illus.). 384p. 1988. pap. text 39.50 (*0-691-00822-1*, Pub. by Princeton U Pr) Cal Prin Full Svc.

Ozuma in L. A. Richard Hertz. LC 93-80168. (Illus.). 199p. (Orig.). 1995. pap. 12.95 (*0-9640165-0-8*) Minneola Pr.

Ozumacin Chinantec Texts Vol. 2: Folklore Texts in Mexican Indian Languages. Compiled by Nadine Rupp & James E. Rupp. LC 93-86273. (Language Data, Amerindian Ser.: No. 11). 96p. 1994. pap. 12.50 (*0-88312-624-9*) S I L Intl.

Ozu's "Tokyo Story" Ed. by David Desser. LC 96-46113. (Cambridge Film Handbooks Ser.). (Illus.). 208p. (C). 1997. text 49.95 (*0-521-48204-6*); pap. text 13.95 (*0-521-48435-9*) Cambridge U Pr.

*__Ozy & Millie.__ David C. Simpson. (Illus.). 151p. 2000. pap. 12.95 (*1-929462-11-5*) Plan Nine Publ.

Ozzie: An Odyssey of Love. Anne Hudson & Neil Daniels. LC 83-81305. (Illus.). 72p. (Orig.). (J). (gr. 1-6). 1983. pap. 3.95 (*0-940258-10-2*) Kripalu Pubns.

Ozzie on His Own. Johanna Hurwitz. LC 94-20111. (Illus.). 128p. (J). (gr. 2 up). 1995. 15.00 (*0-688-13742-3*, Wm Morrow) Morrow Avon.

Ozzmosis. Composed by Ozzy Osbourne. 88p. 1996. otabind 22.95 (*0-7935-6371-2*) H Leonard.

Ozzy Osbourne: No More Tears with Notes & Tablature. 96p. 1992. per. 19.95 (*0-7935-1507-6*, 00694830) H Leonard.

Ozzy Ozbourne - Randy Rhoads Tribute: Guitar - Vocal. Ed. by Mark Phillips & Wolf Marshall. (Illus.). 127p. (Orig.). 1990. pap. text 22.95 (*0-89524-347-4*, Pub. by Cherry Lane) H Leonard.

Ozzy Ozbourne Songbook: Guitar - Vocal. Ed. by Milton Okun. (Illus.). 175p. (Orig.). 1990. pap. text 24.95 (*0-89524-237-0*, Pub. by Cherry Lane) H Leonard.

P

p see Gas Lighting

P see Tohi Vagahau Niue: Niue Language Dictionary

P . . . Respecteus, Morts Sans Sepulture. Jean-Paul Sartre. (Folio Ser.: No. 868). (FRE.). pap. 8.95 (*2-07-036868-8*) Schoenhof.

P. A. T. H. Wellness Manual. Eric R. Braverman. (Illus.). 363p. 1993. pap. 25.00 (*0-9638869-0-8*) Pubns for Achieving.

P-Acid Analysis: Proceedings of the International Conference Held in Trento, Italy, May 29-June 2, 1989. Ed. by F. Baldassari et al. (Lecture Notes in Mathematics Ser.: Vol. 1454). v, 382p. 1991. 59.95 (*0-387-53477-6*) Spr-Verlag.

P-Acid Valued Distributions in Mathematical Physics. Andrei Khrennikov. (Mathematics & Its Applications Ser.). 280p. (C). 1994. text 166.50 (*0-7923-3172-9*) Kluwer Academic.

P-Adic Analysis. Neal Koblitz. (London Mathematical Society Lecture Note Ser.: No. 46). 150p. 1980. pap. text 30.95 (*0-521-28060-5*) Cambridge U Pr.

P-Adic Analysis & Mathematical Physics. V. S. Vladimirov et al. (Series on Soviet & East European Mathematics: No. 10). 340p. 1994. text 86.00 (*981-02-0880-4*) World Scientific Pub.

P-Adic Functional Analysis. Ed. by Jose M. Bayod et al. (Lecture Notes in Pure & Applied Mathematics Ser.: Vol. 137). (Illus.). 236p. 1991. pap. text 135.00 (*0-8247-8660-2*) Dekker.

*__P-Adic Functional Analysis: Proceedings of the Fifth International Conference.__ J. Kqakol et al. LC 99-35164. (Lecture Notes in Pure & Applied Mathematics). 1999. write for info. (*0-8247-8254-2*) Dekker.

P-Adic Functional Analysis: Proceedings of the Fourth International Conference. Wilhelmus H. Schikhof et al. LC 97-13115. (Lecture Notes in Pure & Applied Mathematics Ser.). (Illus.). 416p. 1997. pap. text 175.00 (*0-8247-0038-4*) Dekker.

*__P-Adic L-Functions of P-Adic Representations.__ Bernadette Perrin-Riou. LC 99-56550. (SMF Texts & Monographs: Vol. 3). 150p. 2000. 49.00 (*0-8218-1946-1*) Am Math.

P-Adic Methods & Their Applications. Ed. by Andrew J. Baker & Roger J. Plymen. (Illus.). 206p. 1992. text 65.00 (*0-19-853594-5*) OUP.

P-Adic Methods in Number Theory & Algebraic Geometry. Ed. by Alan Adolphson et al. LC 92-20147. (Contemporary Mathematics Ser.: Vol. 133). 241p. 1992. pap. 39.00 (*0-8218-5145-4*, CONM/133) Am Math.

P-Adic Monodromy & the Birch & Swinnerton-Dyer Conjecture, Vol. 165. Ed. by Barry Mazur & Glenn Stevens. LC 94-10073. 315p. 1994. 34.00 (*0-8218-5180-2*, CONM/165C) Am Math.

P-adic Numbers: An Introduction. Fernando Q. Gouvea. LC 93-25593. (Universitext Ser.). 1993. 42.95 (*0-387-56844-1*) Spr-Verlag.

P-adic Numbers: An Introduction. Fernando Q. Gouvea. (Illus.). vi, 282p. 1993. pap. write for info. (*3-540-56844-1*) Spr-Verlag.

P-adic Numbers: An Introduction. 2nd ed. Fernando Q. Gouvea. LC 97-14730. (Universitext Ser.). vi, 298p. 1997. pap. 39.95 (*3-540-62911-4*) Spr-Verlag.

P-Adic Numbers, P-Adic Analysis & Zeta Functions. 2nd ed. Neal Koblitz. (Graduate Tests in Mathematics Ser.: Vol. 58). (Illus.). 288p. 1996. 49.95 (*0-387-96017-1*) Spr-Verlag.

P & H Chemical Hazards of the Workplace. 4th ed. Gloria J. Hathaway et al. LC 96-18126. (Industrial Health & Safety Ser.). 720p. 1996. text 104.95 (*0-442-02050-3*, VNR) Wiley.

P & I Clubs: Law & Practice. 2nd ed. Steven J. Hazelwood. LC 95-195036. 377p. 1994. 145.00 (*1-85044-521-4*) LLP.

P & I Clubs: The Law & Practice. 2nd ed. Steven J. Hazelwood. 1994. 145.00 (*1-85044-230-4*) LLP.

P & L IBM. 1988. 149.95 (*0-13-647058-0*) P-H.

P-Automorphisms of Finite P-Groups. E. I. Khukhro. LC 97-28654. (London Mathematical Society Lecture Note Ser.: Vol. 246). (Illus.). 222p. (C). 1998. pap. text 39.95 (*0-521-59717-X*) Cambridge U Pr.

P. B. Bear Read-Alongs. Lee Davis. Incl. What Does P. B. Bear Choose? LC 97-14044. (J). (ps). 1997. (*0-7894-2223-9*); What Is P. B. Bear Doing? LC 97-14042. (J). (ps). 1997. (*0-7894-2224-7*); Where Is P. B. Bear? LC 97-14177. (Illus.). (J). (ps). 1997. pap. (*0-7894-2222-0*); 29.95 (*0-614-31313-9*) DK Pub Inc.

P. B. Bear's Bedtime Book. (P. B. Bear Ser.). (Illus.). 32p. (J). (ps). 1998. 12.95 (*0-7894-2870-9*) DK Pub Inc.

P. B. Bear's Big Board Book. LC 97-32446. 12p. (J). (ps). 1998. bds. 7.95 (*0-7894-2858-X*) DK Pub Inc.

P. B. Bear's Treasure Hunt. Lee Davis. LC 95-5466. (Illus.). 32p. (J). (ps-1). 1995. 12.95 (*0-7894-0214-9*, 5-70627) DK Pub Inc.

P. B. Bear's Wonderful Word Book. (Illus.). 24p. (J). (ps). 1998. 17.95 (*0-7894-3109-2*) DK Pub Inc.

P. Bear's New Year's Party: A Counting Book. Paul Owen Lewis. 1999. pap. text 6.95 (*1-883672-99-6*) Tricycle Pr.

P. Bear's New Year's Party: A Counting Book. Paul Owen Lewis. (J). 1999. 13.95 (*1-58246-002-7*) Tricycle Pr.

P-Boat Pilot: With a Patrol Squadron in the Battle of the Atlantic. Robert L. Carlisle. LC 92-33211. (Illus.). 158p. (Orig.). 1993. pap. 9.95 (*1-56474-046-3*) Fithian Pr.

"P" Book: Phonological Awareness: A Critical Factor in Dyslexia. Joseph Torgesen. (Orton Emeritus Ser.). 1995. 5.00 (*0-89214-009-7*) Intl Dyslexia.

P. Buckley Moss: Painting the Joy of the Soul. Peter M. Rippe. Ed. by Becky Johnston. (Illus.). 168p. 1997. 50.00 (*0-9646870-9-7*) Landauer Bks IA.

P. Buckley Moss, The People's Artist: An Autobiography. P. Buckley Moss. Ed. by Malcolm Henderson et al. (Illus.). 103p. 1989. lib. bdg. 12.00 (*0-9626627-1-2*) Shenandoah Pub.

*__P C Interfacing & Data Acquisition Techniques for Measurement.__ James. 2000. 56.95 (*0-7506-4624-1*) Buttrwrth-Heinemann.

*__P-ChIPS (Parent Version of ChIPS) Report Forms for P-ChIPS.__ Elizabeth B. Weller et al. 1999. pap. 19.95 (*0-88048-399-7*) Am Psychiatric.

*__P-ChIPS (Parent Version of ChIPS) Scoring Forms for P-ChIPS.__ Elizabeth B. Weller et al. 1999. pap. 24.95 (*0-88048-396-2*) Am Psychiatric.

P. D. James. Richard B. Gidez. (Twayne English Authors Ser.: No. 430). 184p. (C). 1986. 22.95 (*0-8057-6924-2*, Twyne) Mac Lib Ref.

P. D. R. Yemen: Outpost of Socialist Development in Arabia. Helen Lackner. 219p. 1985. 30.00 (*0-685-13333-8*) Evergreen Dist.

P. Demarchelier. Photos by Patrick Demarchelier. (Illus.). 144p. 1998. pap. 35.00 (*0-8212-2514-6*, Pub. by Bulfinch Pr) Little.

*__P. E. A. C. E.__ Guy Holmes. LC 00-38750. 320p. 2000. pap. write for info. (*0-684-87079-7*) Simon & Schuster.

P. E. Curriculum Guide. John Ortwerth & Mel J. Nicks. (Illus.). 160p. 1984. student ed. 12.99 (*0-86653-262-5*, GA 599) Good Apple.

P. E. in Elementary School. 9th ed. Kirchner & Fishburne. 1994. teacher ed. 12.18 (*0-697-15249-9*) McGraw.

P. E. O. Cook Book: Souvenir Edition. Ed. by David E. Schoonover. LC 91-40585. (Iowa Szathmary Culinary Arts Ser.). (Illus.). 232p. 1992. reprint ed. pap. 15.95 (*0-87745-370-5*) U of Iowa Pr.

P. E. PreExam (Electrical) A Guide to Professional Engineering Examination (Electrical) A. R. Seth. (Illus.). 405p. (Orig.). 1995. pap. 49.00 (*0-9643571-1-9*) SDR Pubns.

P. E. R. S. U. A. D. E. Communication Strategies That Move People to Action. Marlene Caroselli. Ed. by Kelly Scanlon. LC 96-67386. 177p. (Orig.). 1996. pap. 15.95 (*1-57294-053-0*, 13-0019) SkillPath Pubns.

P. E. T. - Parent Effectiveness Training. Thomas Gordon. 1975. pap. 13.95 (*0-452-26461-8*, Plume) Dutton Plume.

P. E. T. in Action: Parent Effectiveness Training. Thomas Gordon. 1996. pap. 10.95 (*0-399-51372-8*, Perigee Bks) Berkley Pub.

P. E. T. (Parent Effectiveness Training) Thomas Gordon. 14.95 (*0-317-63115-2*) McKay.

P. E. T. Parent Effectivenss Training. Thomas Gordon. 14.95 (*0-317-62733-3*) McKay.

P. E. Teacher's Skill Activities Program: Success Oriented Sports Experiences for Grades K-8. F. Turner & Susan L. Turner. (Illus.). 272p. (C). 1989. pap. text 28.95 (*0-13-669987-1*) P-H.

P Factor: The Personality Jumpstart Advantage. Jeffrey L. Magee. Ed. by Nancey Spaith. 250p. 1993. pap. 19.95 (*0-9641240-0-9*) J Magee Intl.

P-51D Mustang Pilot Manual. (Illus.). 104p. 1997. reprint ed. spiral bd. 13.95 (*1-891570-06-4*) Boomerang.

P-51 Mustang. Larry Davis. (Aircraft Specials Ser.). (Illus.). 64p. 1995. pap. text 11.95 (*0-89747-350-7*) Squad Sig Pubns.

P-51 Mustang. Robert F. Dorr. LC 95-6118. (Warbird History Ser.). (Illus.). 128p. 1995. pap. 19.95 (*0-7603-0002-X*) MBI Pubg.

P-51 Mustang. Michael O'Leary. (Color Classics Ser.). (Illus.). 128p. 1997. pap. 10.95 (*1-85532-714-7*, Pub. by Osprey) Stackpole.

P-51 Mustang. 2nd rev. ed. P-51 Mustang Pilots Association Staff. LC 87-51161. (Illus.). 192p. 1987. 49.95 (*1-56311-080-6*) Turner Pub KY.

North American P-51 Mustang: A Photo Chronicle. Larry Davis. LC 92-81714. (Illus.). 112p. 1992. pap. 19.95 (*0-88740-411-1*) Schiffer.

P-51 Mustang: Nose Art Gallery. John Campbell & Donna Campbell. LC 93-37242. (Illus.). 96p. 1994. pap. text 7.98 (*0-87938-782-3*) MBI Pubg.

P-51 Mustang Vol. 51: In Detail & Scale Part 2. Bert Kinzey. LC 98-113853. 72p. 1997. pap. 14.95 (*1-888974-03-6*) Squad Sig Pubns.

P-51 Mustang Flight Manual. (Illus.). 122p. 1992. reprint ed. 13.95 (*0-9605900-7-2*) Boomerang.

P-51 Mustang in Action. (Aircraft in Action Ser.). (Illus.). 58p. 1984. pap. 9.95 (*0-89747-114-8*, 1045) Squad Sig Pubns.

P-51D Walk Around. Larry Davis. (Walk Around Ser.: No. 7). (Illus.). 80p. (Orig.). 1996. pap. 14.95 (*0-89747-360-4*, 5507) Squad Sig Pubns.

P-47 Pilot: Scared, Bored, & Deadly. Jack B. Pitts. (Illus.). xviii, 250p. 1997. pap. 13.95 (*0-9656793-0-6*) Pitts Enterprises.

P-47 Pilots: The Fighter-Bomber Boys. Tom Glenn. LC 98-14352. (Illus.). 160p. 1998. pap. 19.95 (*0-7603-0548-X*) MBI Pubg.

P-47 Thunderbolt. Ernest McDowell. LC 99-189653. (Illus.). 64p. 1998. pap. 9.95 (*0-89747-393-0*, 6076) Squad Sig Pubns.

P-47 Thunderbolt Aces of He ETO/MTO. Jerry Scutts. (Aircraft of the Aces Ser.: No. 24). (Illus.). 96p. 1998. pap. 16.95 (*1-85532-729-5*, Pub. by Ospry) Motorbooks Intl.

P-47 Thunderbolt in Action. Larry Davis. (Aircraft in Action Ser.). 50p. 1985. pap. 9.95 (*0-89747-161-X*, 1067) Squad Sig Pubns.

P-47 Thunderbolt in Detail & Scale. Bert Kinzey. LC 98-232323. (Illus.). 80p. 1998. pap. 14.95 (*1-888974-07-9*, 8254) Squad Sig Pubns.

P-47 Thunderbolt Walk Around. Lou Drendel. LC 97-178717. (Walk Around Ser.: No. 11). (Illus.). 80p. (Orig.). 1997. pap. 14.95 (*0-89747-375-2*, 5511) Squad Sig Pubns.

P-40 Warhawk. Frederick Johnsen. LC 98-23724. (Warbird History Ser.). (Illus.). 128p. 1998. pap. 19.95 (*0-7603-0253-7*) MBI Pubg.

P-40 Warhawk. Warhawk Pilots Association Staff. LC 90-71733. (Illus.). 88p. 1991. 34.95 (*1-56311-018-0*) Turner Pub KY.

*__P-40 Warhawk Pt. 1: In Detail.__ Bert Kinzey. 80p. 1999. pap. 14.95 (*1-888974-14-1*) Squad Sig Pubns.

*__P-40 Warhawk Pt. 2: In Detail, Vol. 62.__ Bert Kinzey. 80p. 1999. pap. 14.95 (*1-888974-15-X*) Squad Sig Pubns.

*__P-40 Warhawk Aces of the CBI.__ Carl Molesworth. (Aircraft of the Aces Ser.: Vol. 35). (Illus.). 96p. 2000. pap. 17.95 (*1-84176-079-X*, 130585AE, Pub. by Ospry) Motorbooks Intl.

P-40 Warhawk Walk Around. Lou Drendel. (Walk Around Ser.: No. 8). (Illus.). 80p. (Orig.). 1996. pap. 14.95 (*0-89747-361-2*, 5508) Squad Sig Pubns.

P-450 & Chemical Carcinogenesis. Ed. by Yusaku Tagashira & Tsuneo Omura. (GANN Monographs on Cancer Research: No. 30). 190p. 1985. 79.50 (*0-306-42123-2*, Plenum Trade) Perseus Pubng.

*__P450Guide - Pocket Reference to Enzymatic Drug Metabolism: Year 2000 Edition.__ Frederick M. Brown & Pamela S. Griffiths. 36p. (C). 1999. pap. 4.95 (*0-9700084-0-6*) PFourFiveZeroguide.

P-Functions & Boolean Matrix Factorization: A Unified Approach for Wired, Programmed & Microprogrammed Implementations of Discrete Algorithms. A. Thayse. (Lecture Notes in Computer Science Ser.: Vol. 175). xii, 248p. 1984. 33.00 (*0-387-13358-5*) Spr-Verlag.

P. G. P. 6. 0 Platform-Independent Source Code, 8 vols. 3726p. 1998. spiral bd. 38.00 (*1-58368-002-0*) Network Assocs.

P. G. P. 6. 0 MacIntosh-Specific Source Code, 8 vols. 3446p. 1998. spiral bd. 38.00 (*1-58368-000-4*) Network Assocs.

P. G. P. 6. 0 Platform-Independent Documentation: P. G. P. Installation Guide, an Introduction to Cryptography, & Administration Guide. 186p. 1998. spiral bd. 38.00 (*1-58368-005-5*) Network Assocs.

P. G. P. 6. 0 Windows-Specific Documentation. 346p. 1998. spiral bd. 38.00 (*1-58368-004-7*) Network Assocs.

P. G. P. 6. 0 Windows-Specific Source Code, 9 vols. 4104p. 1998. spiral bd. 38.00 (*1-58368-001-2*) Network Assocs.

P. G. T. Beauregard: Napoleon in Gray. T. Harry Williams. LC 55-7362. (Southern Biography Ser.). (Illus.). 346p. (C). 1995. pap. 17.95 (*0-8071-1974-1*) La State U Pr.

P. G. Wodehouse: A Comprehensive Bibliography & Checklist. Ed. by Eileen McIlvaine et al. (Illus.). 489p. (Orig.). 1991. lib. bdg. 135.00 (*0-87008-125-X*) JAS Heineman.

P. G. Wodehouse: A Comprehensive Bibliography & Checklist. Eileen McIlvaine et al. (Wodehouse Monographs: No. 2). (Illus.). 544p. (Orig.). 1995. 135.00 (*0-87008-101-2*) JAS Heineman.

P. G. Wodehouse: Five Complete Novels. P. G. Wodehouse. (Avenel Readers Library). 688p. 1995. 11.99 (*0-517-40538-5*) Random Hse Value.

P. G. Wodehouse Checklist. Ed. by J. Clauss. 12.95 (*0-89190-843-9*) Amereon Ltd.

P. H. C.'s Lessons in Magic: Eighteen Sixty-Five to Eighteen Sixty-Eight. Henry Hatton & Marjie Buffum. LC 79-52207. (Illus.). write for info. (*0-934542-01-5*) Abracadabra Pr.

P. H. Emerson: The Fight for Photography As Fine Art. Nancy Newhall. LC 74-76911. (Monographs). (Illus.). 266p. 76.00 (*0-89381-383-4*) Aperture.

P-H Executive Action Report. ring bd. write for info. (*0-318-57385-7*) P-H.

*__P H R F Handicaps Book - 2000.__ 2000. 25.00 (*1-882502-79-5*) US Sail Assn.

P

rock. Visions of a sea of shells dazzle his senses & he imagines that he is a prince claiming each shell for a castle in his kingdom, only to discover that the shells are occupied. By turtles no less! When P. Hermit comes to his senses he realizes that he must get back to his tidepool to find the home of his dreams. After all, only in his natural habitat can he search for a new shell. P. HERMIT CLAIMS A CASTLE encourages children to face change with a spirit of adventure as the tides of life ebb & flow & create new pools of experience. And bedtime story lovers can snuggle into their beds when George Ulrich's animated Hermit snuggles inside a new home that suits him just fine & "drifts off to sleep." To order: Images Press, tel: 650-948-8251, FAX: 650-941-6114. E-mail: Bugsmom2@aol.com. Also available for booksellers & libraries through Baker & Taylor, Ingram Books & Quality Books, Inc. & on the internet through amazon.com. ***Publisher Paid Annotation.***

P-I-C-K-L-E-S for Parents. Patricia T. Kienzle. (Illus.). 52p. 1997. pap. 4.95 (*1-890798-09-6*) P T Kienzle.

P. I. School: How to Become a Private Detective. Wayne Harrison. (Illus.). 1991. pap. 14.00 (*0-87364-637-1*) Paladin Pr.

***P. I. Webworks: Secrets of How to Develop, Design & Market Your Web Site.** Ralph D. Thomas. 1999. pap. 35.00 (*1-891247-35-2*) Thomas Investigative.

***P. I. Who Loved Her.** Tori Carrington. (Temptation Ser.: Vol. 776). 2000. per. 3.99 (*0-373-25876-3*) Harlequin Bks.

***P Is for. . .** Sue Grafton. 2000. 27.00 (*0-8050-5956-3*) H Holt & Co.

P Is for Pioneers: An Alphabet Book for LDS Children. Melanie Z. Carmack. LC 97-92940. (Illus.). 32p. (J). 1997. 14.95 (*0-9656612-0-2*) Buffalo Bks.

P. J. & Puppy. Cathryn Falwell. (Illus.). (J). 1997. 8.95 (*0-614-28668-9*, Clarion Bks) HM.

P. J. & Puppy. Cathryn Falwell. LC 96-8252. (Illus.). 32p. (J). (ps). 1997. 8.95 (*0-395-56918-4*, Clarion Bks) HM.

P. J. Funnybunny & His Very Cool Birthday Party. Marilyn Sadler. (J). 1996. pap. 3.25 (*0-679-87788-6*) Random.

P. J. Funnybunny Camps Out. Marilyn Sadler. LC 92-6156. (Step into Reading Ser.: A Step 1 Book). (Illus.). 32p. (J). (ps-1). 1994. pap. 3.99 (*0-679-83269-6*, Pub. by Random Bks Yng Read) Random.

P. J. Funnybunny Camps Out. Marilyn Sadler. LC 92-6156. (Step into Reading Ser.: A Step 1 Book). (Illus.). 32p. (J). (ps-3). 1994. lib. bdg. 11.99 (*0-679-93269-0*, Pub. by Random Bks Yng Read) Random.

P. J. Proudhon: A Chronology. V. Munoz. Tr. by W. Scott Johnson. (Libertarian & Anarchist Chronology Ser.). 1979. lib. bdg. 59.95 (*0-8490-3038-2*) Gordon Pr.

***P. K. Life in a Methodist Parsonage.** John Reed Bumgarner. LC 99-93768. 2000. pap. 10.95 (*0-533-13149-9*) Vantage.

P. K. Page & Her Works. John Orange. (Canadian Author Studies). 53p. (C). 1989. pap. text 9.95 (*1-55022-011-X*, Pub. by ECW) Genl Dist Srvs.

P. L. Travers. Patricia Demers. (Twayne's English Authors Ser.). 160p. 1991. 22.95 (*0-8057-7005-4*, TEAS 483, Twyne) Mac Lib Ref.

P. L. 94-142: Impact on the Schools. Roberta Weiner. LC 85-73365. 362p. (Orig.). (C). 1985. 18.00 (*0-937925-01-2*, IOTS) Capitol VA.

P. L. 94-142-The Idea Handbook. Daniel J. Lobmire & Dennis K. Flattre. (SPA.). 129p. 1995. 39.95 (*0-9648200-1-3*) Talking Textbks.

P. L. 94-142-The Idea Handbook. Daniel S. Lobmire & Dennis K. Flattre. 129p. 1995. 39.95 (*0-9648200-0-5*) Talking Textbks.

P-M Analysis: An Advanced Step in TPM Implementation. Kunio Shirose et al. (Illus.). 198p. 1995. 65.00 (*1-56327-035-8*) Productivity Inc.

P-M in Aerospace & Defense Technologies, Vol. 1. Compiled by F. H. Froes. LC 90-6680. (Illus.). 224p. 1990. pap. 40.00 (*0-918404-96-7*) Metal Powder.

P-M in Aerospace & Defense Technologies, 1991. Compiled by F. H. Froes. LC 91-19049. (Illus.). 424p. 1991. pap. 50.00 (*1-878954-06-7*) Metal Powder.

P-M in Aerospace, Defense & Demanding Applications, 1993. Ed. by F. H. Froes. LC 93-7184. (Illus.). 402p. 1993. pap. 125.00 (*1-878954-31-8*) Metal Powder.

P-M in Government Products: Nineteen Seventy-One Conference Proceedings of the Tutorial Seminar Two Potentials for P-M in Military & Other Government Products. Tutorial Seminar on P-M in Ordnance Staff. LC 78-102208. (Progress in Powder Metallurgy Ser.: Vol. 27, Pt. 2). 134p. reprint ed. pap. 41.60 (*0-8357-6989-5*, 205707300009) Bks Demand.

P-M in Ordnance: 1971 Conference Proceedings of the P-M in Ordnance Seminar. Tutorial Seminar on P-M in Ordnance Staff. LC 78-102207. (Progress in Powder Metallurgy Ser.: Vol. 27, Pt. 1). 173p. reprint ed. pap. 53.70 (*0-8357-6988-7*, 205707200009) Bks Demand.

P-M Steels, Vol. 5. 560p. 1992. 125.00 (*1-878954-24-5*) Metal Powder.

***P. Meera Khan Dedication Issue.** Ed. by H. P. Klinger & P. L. Pearson. (Cytogenetics & Cell Genetics Ser.: Vol. 86, No. 2). (Illus.). 78p. 1999. pap. 25.25 (*3-8055-6989-0*) S Karger.

P. Michigan Koenen: Michigan Texts Published in Honor of Ludwig Koenen. Ed. by Cornelia E. Romer & Traianos Gagos. (Studia Amstelodamensia ad Epigraphicam, Ius Antiquum et Papyrologictam Pertinentia: Vol. XXXVI). (ENG & GER., Illus.). 440p. 1996. lib. bdg. 227.00 (*90-5063-127-4*, Pub. by Gieben) J Benjamins Pubng Co.

P. N. K. 1999. SPG Inc. Staff & Calvin P. Kline. 37p. 1999. pap. 3.95 (*0-614-04795-1*) Sneaky Pete.

P. O. P. S. Polishing Our People Skills. Katherine Byrlat & Tim Nay. 79p. (Orig.). 1990. pap. 15.00 (*1-877592-18-8*) GSH&MC.

P. O. P. S. Principles of Pop Singing. Jodi Lyons & Lanelle Stevenson. 320p. 1990. spiral bd. 32.00 incl. audio (*0-02-871971-9*, Schirmer Books) Mac Lib Ref.

P. O. P. Works. AG Publishers Editors. (Illus.). 216p. 1994. 69.95 (*4-87246-303-X*, Pub. by AG Pubs) Bks Nippan.

P. O. R. N. Rae Wilder. 200p. write for info. (*0-318-69932-X*) Longitude & Lat.

P. O. V.'s Living Large: The Guy's Guide to Getting Ahead, Getting It Right & Getting It Often. Randall Lane. LC 98-21260. 384p. 1998. pap. 20.00 (*0-06-273521-7*) HarpC.

P. O. W. in the Pacific: Memoirs of an American Doctor in World War II. William N. Donovan. Ed. by Josephine Donovan. LC 97-48354. (Illus.). 176p. 1998. 22.95 (*0-8420-2725-4*) Scholarly Res Inc.

P-100 Plebe Summer Sailing Study Guide. 3rd ed. Taylor. 112p. 1997. spiral bd. 6.00 (*0-7872-3708-6*) Kendall-Hunt.

P. Ovidi Nasonis Metamorphoseon: Ovid's Metamorphoses, 15 bks., Set. Ovid. lib. bdg. write for info. (*0-318-50866-4*) Ayer.

P. Ovidi Nasonis Metamorphoseon Liber I. Ovid. Ed. by A. G. Lee. LC 78-67140. 170p. reprint ed. pap. 48.50 (*0-608-13034-6*, 2024505) Bks Demand.

P. P. Bliss Songwriter. 2nd ed. William Guest. (Illus.). 162p. 1997. pap. 9.99 (*1-84030-008-6*) Emerald House Group Inc.

P. P. Ewald & His Dynamical Theory of X-Ray Diffraction. Ed. by D. W. Cruickshank et al. LC 92-9876. (International Union of Crystallography Monographs on Crystallography: No. 2). (Illus.). 172p. (C). 1992. text 69.00 (*0-19-855379-X*) OUP.

P. Papini Stati Thebaidos Libri XII: Recensuit et Cum Apparatu Critico et Exegetico Instruxit D. E. Hill. D. E. Hill. (Mnemosyne Ser.: Supplements, 79). 428p. 1996. reprint ed. 128.00 (*90-04-10584-0*) Brill Academic Pubs.

P. Papinius Statius: Thebaid: A Commentary on Book Three. H. Snijder. 284p. 1968. 88.00 (*0-685-38353-9*, Pub. by AM Hakkert) BookLink Distributors.

P Phosphorus: Suppl. Vol. C: Mononuclear Compounds with Hydrogen, Pt. 1. Ed. by Gmelin Institute for Inorganic Chemistry of the Ma. (Gmelin Handbook of Inorganic & Organometallic Chemistry Ser.). (Illus.). xvi, 326p. 1993. 1410.00 (*0-387-93680-7*) Spr-Verlag.

P Phosphorus Pt. C, Section 5a: The Compounds: Cyclic Phosphorus-Nitrogen Compounds. Three-, Four-, & Five-Membered Ring Systems. 8th ed. (Gmelin Ser.). (Illus.). xiv, 238p. 1996. suppl. ed. 1041.00 (*3-540-93736-6*) Spr-Verlag.

P-Prolog: A Parallel Logic Programming Language. Rong Yang. (Series in Computer Science: Vol. 9). 152p. (C). 1988. text 49.00 (*9971-5-0508-8*) World Scientific Pub.

***P. R. Crisis Bible: How to Take Charge of the Media When All Hell Breaks Loose.** Robin Cohn. LC 00-40232. 2000. write for info. (*0-312-25230-7*) St Martin.

P. R. E. P. Guide: To the Real Estate Licensing Exams. Leslie K. Purvis. (Orig.). 1995. pap. text 24.95 (*0-9638207-4-5*) Purvis Real Est.

P. R. O. B. E., No. 3. Philip Baxter. pap. write for info. (*0-06-100519-3*, Harp PBks) HarpC.

P. S. Jack Wohl. (Illus.). 64p. 1993. pap. 4.95 (*0-8431-3570-0*, Price Stern) Peng Put Young Read.

P. S. A Memoir. Pierre Salinger. 320p. 1996. pap. 14.95 (*0-312-15187-X*) St Martin.

P. S. A Memoir. Pierre Salinger. (Illus.). 304p. 1999. reprint ed. text 25.00 (*0-7881-6220-9*) DIANE Pub.

P. S. The Autobiography of Paul Simon. Paul Simon. LC 98-74186. (Illus.). 401p. 1998. 24.95 (*1-56625-112-5*) Bonus Books.

P. S., a Memoir. Pierre Salinger. LC 95-30777. (Illus.). 304p. 1995. text 24.95 (*0-312-13578-5*) St Martin.

P. S. Friends Forever. Devra Newberger Speregen. Ed. by Lisa Clancy. (Full House Stephanie Ser.). 144p. (J). (gr. 4-6). 1995. per. 3.99 (*0-671-89861-2*, Minstrel Bks) PB.

P. S. God Loves You! limited ed. Connie Witter. 160p. 1997. 12.99 (*1-56292-191-6*) Honor Bks OK.

P. S. God Loves You! Words of Grace & Encouragement from God's Heart to Yours. Connie Witter. 160p. 1995. pap. 6.99 (*1-56292-198-3*) Honor Bks OK.

P. S. I. Guide for Bearings: Prefix-Suffix Identification Guide for Bearings. S. H. Friedman. 1997. pap. 125.00 (*0-916966-50-X*) Interchange.

P. S. I Love You. H. Jackson Brown, Jr. 160p. 1999. lthr. 16.95 (*1-55853-753-8*) Rutledge Hill Pr.

P. S. I Love You. Barbara Conklin. (J). 1988. mass mkt. 3.95 (*0-553-19550-6*) BDD Bks Young Read.

P. S. I Love You. Valerie Parv. LC 95-6885. (Romance Ser.). 189p. 1995. per. 2.99 (*0-373-03366-4*, 1-03366-1) Harlequin Bks.

P. S. I Love You. large type ed. Valerie Parv. (Harlequin Romance Ser.). 1995. 19.95 (*0-263-14239-6*) Thorndike Pr.

P. S. I Love You. 2nd ed. H. Jackson Brown. LC 90-8309. (Illus.). 160p. 1990. reprint ed. pap. 6.95 (*1-55853-071-1*) Rutledge Hill Pr.

P. S. I Love You. 2nd ed. H. Jackson Brown. LC 90-8309. 160p. 1991. reprint ed. 12.95 (*1-55853-108-4*) Rutledge Hill Pr.

P. S. I Love You: Baby Collection. Lynda S. Milligan & Nancy J. Smith. Ed. by Sharon Holmes. (Illus.). 80p. (Orig.). 1990. pap. 16.95 (*0-9622477-2-3*) Pssblts Denver.

P. S. Longer Letter Later. Paula Danziger & Ann M. Martin. 234p. (J). (gr. 3-7). 1999. pap. 4.99 (*0-590-21311-3*) Scholastic Inc.

P. S. Longer Letter Later: A Novel in Letters. Paula Danziger & Ann M. Martin. LC 97-19120. 234p. (J). (gr. 5-8). 1998. 15.95 (*0-590-21310-5*) Scholastic Inc.

P. S. Longer Letter Later: A Novel in Letters. Paula Danziger & Ann M. Martin. 240p. (J). (gr. 3-5). pap. 4.99 (*0-8072-1537-6*) Listening Lib.

***P. S. Love You Madly.** Bethany Campbell. (Superromance Ser.). 2000. mass mkt. 4.50 (*0-373-70931-5*, 1-70931-0) Harlequin Bks.

P. S. Roadtripper: Electronic Field Trips for Public Speakers. E. Sam Cox. 128p. (C). 1998. per. 19.95 (*0-7872-5420-7*, 41542001) Kendall-Hunt.

P. S. We Love You, Vol. 1. Ellen Rendle. (Illus.). xi, 75p. 1993. 24.95 (*0-9657328-4-3*, 104) Cedar Tree Bks.

P. S. What Do You Think of the Market. James L. Fraser. LC 66-29458. (Orig.). 1966. reprint ed. pap. 11.00 (*0-87034-023-9*) Fraser Pub Co.

***P. S. Wish You Were Here.** Mary-Kate Olsen & Ashley Olsen. (Two of a Kind Ser.: no. 11). 112p. (J). (gr. 3-7). 2000. mass mkt. 4.25 (*0-06-106581-1*) HarpC.

P. S. Write Soon! All about Letters. Intro. by William F. Bolger. LC 82-600641. (Illus.). 64p. (Orig.). (J). (gr. 4-8). 1982. pap. 2.50 (*0-8141-3796-2*, 37962) USPS.

P. S. Your Cat Is Dead. James Kirkwood. 224p. 1986. mass mkt. 4.99 (*0-446-34597-0*, Pub. by Warner Bks) Little.

P-61 Black Widow in Action. Larry Davis. (Aircraft in Action Ser.: Vol. 106). (Illus.). 50p. 2000. reprint ed. pap. 9.95 (*0-89747-248-9*, 1106) Squad Sig Pubns.

P-61 Black Widow Units of World War 2. Warren Thompson. (Illus.). 96p. 1998. pap. 16.95 (*1-85532-725-2*, Pub. by Osprey) Motorbooks Intl.

P. T. Barnum. David K. Wright. LC 96-20369. (First Biographies Ser.). (Illus.). 32p. (J). 1997. lib. bdg. 21.40 (*0-8172-4456-5*) Raintree Steck-V.

P. T. Barnum. David K. Wright. LC 96-20369. 32p. (J). (gr. 1-6). 1997. pap. text 5.95 (*0-8172-6887-1*) Raintree Steck-V.

P. T. Barnum: The Greatest Showman on Earth: A Biography of P. T. Barnum. Ann Tompert. LC 87-13600. (People in Focus Ser.). (Illus.). 120p. (YA). (gr. 6 up). 1988. lib. bdg. 13.95 (*0-87518-370-0*, Dillon Silver Burdett) Silver Burdett Pr.

P. T. Barnum: The Legend & the Man. Arthur H. Saxon. (Illus.). 437p. 1989. 41.00 (*0-231-05686-9*) Col U Pr.

P. T. Barnum: The Legend & the Man. Arthur H. Saxon. 437p. 1995. pap. 19.50 (*0-231-05687-7*) Col U Pr.

P. T. Barnum: The World's Greatest Showman. Alice Fleming. 128p. (J). (gr. 4-7). 1993. 14.95 (*0-8027-8234-5*); lib. bdg. 15.85 (*0-8027-8235-3*) Walker & Co.

P. T. Forsyth: The Man, the Preacher's Theologian & Prophet for the Twentieth Century. Donald G. Miller et al. (Pittsburgh Theological Monographs: No. 36). 1981. pap. 15.00 (*0-915138-48-4*) Pickwick.

P. T. Forsyth Bibliograph & Index, 27. Robert Benedetto. LC 92-46527. (Bibliographies & Indexes in Religious Studies: No. 27). 192p. 1993. lib. bdg. 69.50 (*0-313-28753-8*, GR8753, Greenwood Pr) Greenwood.

P-38 Lightning. Larry Davis. (Aircraft in Action Ser.). (Illus.). 50p. 1990. pap. 9.95 (*0-89747-255-1*, 1109) Squad Sig Pubns.

P-38 Lightning. 2nd ed. Turner Publishing Company Staff. LC 89-50039. (Illus.). 216p. 1992. 49.95 (*1-56311-030-X*) Turner Pub KY.

P-38 Lightning in Detail & Scale, Pt. 1. Bert Kinzey. LC 99-218212. (Illus.). 80p. 1998. pap. 14.95 (*1-888974-10-9*, 8257) Squad Sig Pubns.

P-38 Lightning in Detail & Scale, Pt. 2. Bert Kinzey. (Illus.). 80p. 1998. pap. 14.95 (*1-888974-11-7*, 8258) Squad Sig Pubns.

P-38 Lightning in World War II Color. Jeffery L. Ethell. LC 93-48650. (Enthusiast Color Ser.). (Illus.). 96p. 1994. pap. 13.95 (*0-87938-868-4*) MBI Pubg.

P-35 "Mini" in Action. Larry Davis. (Mini in Action Ser.). (Illus.). 50p. 1994. pap. 5.95 (*0-89747-321-3*) Squad Sig Pubns.

***P-39 Airacobra Aces of World War 2.** John Stanaway. (Aircraft of the Aces Ser.: Vol. 36). (Illus.). 96p. 2000. pap. 17.95 (*1-84176-204-0*, 130733AE, Pub. by Osprey) Motorbooks Intl.

***P-39 Airacobra in Detail.** Bert Kinzey. 80p. 1999. pap. 14.95 (*1-888974-16-8*) Squad Sig Pubns.

P-12 - F-4B in Action. Larry Davis. (Aircraft in Action Ser.). (Illus.). 50p. 1994. pap. 9.95 (*0-89747-309-4*) Squad Sig Pubns.

P-26 "Mini" in Action. Larry Davis. (Mini in Action Ser.). (Illus.). 50p. 1994. pap. 5.95 (*0-89747-322-1*) Squad Sig Pubns.

P. U. R. Guide: Principles of Public Utilities Operations & Management. (Illus.). 560p. 1999. pap. 350.00 (*0-910325-40-5*) Public Util.

***P. U. R. Guide: Principles of Public Utilities Operations & Management.** Ed. by Lori M. Rodgers. (Illus.). 560p. 1999. pap. 350.00i (*0-910325-76-6*) Public Util.

P. Vergilius Maro Aeneis Buch VI, Eklart von Eduard Norden. Virgil. LC 75-41282. reprint ed. 82.50 (*0-404-14727-5*) AMS Pr.

P. Virgili Maronis Aeneidos, Liber Sextus: With Commentary. Virgil. (Illus.). 316p. 1986. pap. text 24.95 (*0-19-872128-5*) OUP.

P. W. Liveaboard Cat. Bob Kingett. (Illus.). 48p. 1988. pap. 5.95 (*0-9621316-0-1*) Catalina Creations.

P. W. Liveaboard Cat. Robert P. Kingett. (Illus.). 48p. (Orig.). (J). 1988. pap. write for info. (*0-318-64027-9*) Catalina Creations.

PA Cavalcade. Federal Writers' Project Staff & Writers Program-WPA Staff. (American Guide Ser.). 1989. reprint ed. lib. bdg. 79.00 (*0-7812-1062-3*, 1062) Rprt Serv.

Pa Chin & His Writings: Chinese Youth Between the Two Revolutions. Olga Lang. LC 67-17314. (Harvard East Asian Ser.: No. 28). 418p. 1967. reprint ed. pap. 129.60 (*0-7837-4115-4*, 205793800011) Bks Demand.

PA Dutch Humor. 83.40 (*1-56148-283-8*) Good Bks PA.

PA Dutch Jokes, Vol. 1. Gary Gates. (Illus.). 96p. 1998. pap. 6.95 (*1-56148-245-5*) Good Bks PA.

PA Dutch Jokes, Vol. 2. Gary Gates. (Illus.). 96p. 1998. pap. 6.95 (*1-56148-246-3*) Good Bks PA.

PA Employee Handbook Forms Kit. James O. Castagnera & John Ryan. 1997. ring bd. 89.50 incl. disk (*1-887024-76-X*) Bisel Co.

Pa Grape's Shapes. Phil Vischer. LC 97-27852. (Vegucational Ser.). (Illus.). 32p. (J). (ps-2). 1997. pap. 8.99 (*0-8499-1507-4*) Tommy Nelson.

Pa-Kua: Eight-Trigram Boxing. Robert W. Smith & Allen Pittman. (Illus.). 96p. 1990. pap. 10.95 (*0-8048-1618-2*) Tuttle Pubng.

PA Labor & Employment Law Forms Kit. James O. Castagnera. 1997. ring bd. 89.50 incl. disk (*1-887024-75-1*) Bisel Co.

Pa Lia's First Day. Edwards. LC 98-28567. 50p. (J). (gr. 1-3). 1999. 14.00 (*0-15-201974-X*, Harcourt Child Bks) Harcourt.

Pa. Public Utility Commission: January 1996 to December 1996, Vol. 86. Michael Arnzen. Ed. by Shirley Leming. 681p. Date not set. write for info. (*0-8182-0235-1*) Commonweal PA.

Pa. Public Utility Commission Decisions July 1995 to December 1995, Vol. 85. Pa. Public Utility Commission Staff. Ed. by Shirley Leming. 719p. 1995. 235.62 (*0-8182-0219-X*) Commonweal PA.

PA-RISC 2.0 Architecture. Gerry Kane. 496p. (C). 1995. pap. text 30.80 (*0-13-182734-0*) P-H.

PA-38 Tomahawk: A Pilot's Guide. Jeremy M. Pratt. LC 95-15209. (Pilot's Guide Ser.). 1995. pap. 14.95 (*1-56027-216-3*, ASA-PG-PA-38) ASA Inc.

PA-28 Cherokee: A Pilot's Guide. Jeremy M. Pratt. LC 95-15210. (Pilot's Guide Ser.). 1995. pap. 14.95 (*1-56027-215-5*, ASA-PG-PA-28C) ASA Inc.

PA-28 Warrior: A Pilot's Guide. Jeremy M. Pratt. (Pilot's Guide Ser.). 1995. pap. 14.95 (*1-56027-214-7*, ASA-PG-PA-28W) ASA Inc.

Paa Veien til Smeltepotten see On the Way to the Melting Pot: A Novel

Pa'ahana! Illus. by 'Umi Kahalio'umi & Kahanano'eau Morita. (HAW.). (J). (ps-k). 1992. 6.95 (*1-58191-043-6*) Aha Punana Leo.

Paasch's Illustrated Marine Dictionary: An Authentic Document of the Age of Steam & Sail. Henry Paasch. LC 97-201662. Orig. Title: From Keel to Truck. (Illus.). 408p. 1997. reprint ed. 25.00 (*1-55821-650-2*) Lyons Pr.

Pablo - Paul. Gordon Stowell. (Serie Pescaditos - Little Fish Ser.). (SPA.). 16p. (J). 1989. write for info. (*0-945792-96-4*) Editorial Unilit.

Pablo & Fernande: Portrait of Picasso As a Young Man: an Interpretive Biography. Norman Mailer. LC 93-2332. 1994. 40.00 (*0-385-47272-2*, N A Talese) Doubleday.

Pablo & Pimienta (Pablo y Pimienta) Ruth M. Covault. LC 94-25445. (ENG & SPA., Illus.). 32p. (J). (gr. 1-3). 1994. lib. bdg. 14.95 (*0-87358-588-7*, Rising Moon Bks) Northland AZ.

Pablo & Pimienta (Pablo y Pimienta) Ruth M. Covault. (ENG & SPA., Illus.). 32p. (J). (gr. 1-3). 1998. pap. 7.95 (*0-87358-708-1*, Rising Moon Bks) Northland AZ.

Pablo Casals. rev. ed. Lillian Littlehales. LC 72-97385. 232p. 1970. reprint ed. lib. bdg. 49.50 (*0-8371-3010-7*, LIPC, Greenwood Pr) Greenwood.

Pablo Casals: Cellist for the World. David Goodnough. LC 96-47792. (Hispanic Biographies Ser.). 128p. (YA). (gr. 6 up). 1997. lib. bdg. 20.95 (*0-89490-889-8*) Enslow Pubs.

Pablo Casals: Spanish Cellist & Conductor. Hedda Garza & Robert Green. (Hispanics of Achievement Ser.). (Illus.). 120p. (YA). (gr. 5 up). 1993. lib. bdg. 19.95 (*0-7910-1237-9*) Chelsea Hse.

Pablo Casals: Spanish Cellist & Conductor. Hedda Garza & Robert Green. (Hispanics of Achievement Ser.). (Illus.). 120p. (YA). (gr. 5 up). 1993. pap. 8.95 (*0-7910-1264-6*) Chelsea Hse.

Pablo Casals in Puerto Rico. Arturo O. Quintana. (Puerto Rico Ser.). 1979. lib. bdg. 59.95 (*0-8490-2981-3*) Gordon Pr.

Pablo Neruda. Luis Poirot. 1990. pap. 25.00 (*0-393-30643-7*) Norton.

Pablo Neruda: All Poets the Poet. Salvatore Bizzarro. LC 78-24437. 204p. 1979. lib. bdg. 21.00 (*0-8108-1189-8*) Scarecrow.

Pablo Neruda: Chilean Poet & Diplomat. Joseph Roman. (Hispanics of Achievement Ser.). (Illus.). 120p. (YA). (gr. 5 up). 1992. lib. bdg. 19.95 (*0-7910-1248-4*) Chelsea Hse.

Pablo Neruda: Fifty Odes. Pablo Neruda. Ed. & Tr. by George D. Schade. iv, 349p. (C). 1996. 35.00 (*0-924047-13-5*); pap. 17.00 (*0-924047-14-3*) Host Pubns.

Pablo Neruda: Nobel Prize-Winning Poet. David Goodnough. LC 97-32888. (Hispanic Biographies Ser.). (Illus.). 128p. (YA). (gr. 6 up). 1998. lib. bdg. 20.95 (*0-7660-1042-2*) Enslow Pubs.

Pablo Neruda: Selected Poems. Pablo Neruda. Ed. by Nathaniel Tarn. Tr. by Anthony Kerrigan. 508p. 1990. pap. 15.95 (*0-395-54418-1*) HM.

Pablo Neruda & Nicanor Parra Face to Face: A Bilingual & Critical Edition of Their Speeches on the Occasion of Neruda's Appointment to the Faculty of the

P

University of Chile. Pablo Neruda & Nicanor Parra. Tr. by Marlene Gottlieb. LC 97-2196. (Hispanic Literature Ser.: Vol. 36). 120p. 1997. text 59.95 (0-7734-8673-9) E Mellen.

Pablo Neruda Reading His Poetry: Neruda,&Pablo. abr. ed. Pablo Neruda. (SPA.). 1995. audio 12.00 (0-694-51710-0, CPN 1215) HarperAudio.

Pablo Picasso. 5.95 (1-57717-141-1) Todtri Prods.

***Pablo Picasso.** Abrams Staff. (Illus.). 1999. 12.95 (0-8109-5820-1, Pub. by Abrams) Time Warner.

Pablo Picasso. John Beardsley. (Illus.). 92p. (J). 1991. 19.95 (0-8109-3713-1, Pub. by Abrams) Time Warner.

Pablo Picasso. Ibi Lepscky. LC 83-347. (Famous People Ser.). (Illus.). 24p. (J). (gr. k-3). 1984. 9.95 (0-8120-5511-X) Barron.

Pablo Picasso. Ibi Lepscky. (Famous People Ser.). (Illus.). 28p. (J). (gr. k-3). 1992. pap. 5.95 (0-8120-1450-2) Barron.

Pablo Picasso. Linda Lowery. LC 99-21965. (On My Own Biographies Ser.). 48p. (J). (gr. 2-4). 1999. pap. 5.95 (1-57505-370-5, Carolrhoda) Lerner Pub.

Pablo Picasso. Linda Lowery. LC 99-21965. (On My Own Bks.). (Illus.). 48p. (J). (gr. 1-3). 1999. 19.93 (1-57505-331-4) Lerner Pub.

Pablo Picasso. Matthew Meadows. (Art for Young People Ser.). (Illus.). 32p. (J). 1996. 14.95 (0-8069-6160-0) Sterling.

Pablo Picasso. Carl Rollyson. LC 92-44757. (Arts Ser.). 112p. (YA). 1993. lib. bdg. 25.27 (0-86625-488-9) Rourke Pubns.

Pablo Picasso. Ingrid Schaffner. 1999. 12.95 (0-8362-1934-1) Andrews & McMeel.

Pablo Picasso. John W. Selfridge. (Hispanos Notables Ser.). (SPA., Illus.). 120p. (YA). (gr. 5 up). 1994. pap. 8.95 (0-7910-3111-X); lib. bdg. 19.95 (0-7910-3101-2) Chelsea Hse.

Pablo Picasso. Clarice Swisher. LC 94-8475. (Importance of... Biographies Ser.). (Illus.). 112p. (J). (gr. 5-8). 1995. lib. bdg. 22.45 (1-56006-062-X) Lucent Bks.

Pablo Picasso. I. F. Walther. 1994. pap. 9.99 (3-8228-9635-7) Taschen Amer.

***Pablo Picasso: A Modern Master.** Richard Leslie. (Illus.). 1998. 16.98 (1-880908-73-5) Todtri Prods.

Pablo Picasso: A Vision. David F. Setford. 55p. (Orig.). 1994. 19.95 (0-943411-25-4) Norton Gal Art.

Pablo Picasso: Academic & Anti-Academic (1895-1900) Josep P. Fabre. Ed. by Charles A. Riley, 2nd. Tr. by Amy Gore. (Illus.). 147p. 1996. 25.00 (1-887054-00-6) Yoshii Gallery.

Pablo Picasso: Buffon's Natural History, Rare Proofs. Barry Walker. LC 98-155844. (Illus.). 44p. 1998. pap. write for info. (0-9653006-1-7, 713-523-4300) G Wurzer Gall.

Pablo Picasso: Catalogue of the Printed Graphic Work 1904-1972, 3 Vols. George Bloch. 911p. 1979. 600.00 (1-55660-173-5) A Wofsy Fine Arts.

Pablo Picasso: Catalogue of the Printed Graphic Work 1904-1972, 4 vols., Set. George Bloch. 911p. 1979. 795.00 (1-55660-044-5) A Wofsy Fine Arts.

***Pablo Picasso: Genius! The Artist & the Process.** Patricia MacDonald. (Illus.). 128p. (YA). (gr. 7-9). 1999. text 20.00 (0-7881-6842-8) DIANE Pub.

***Pablo Picasso: Human Form in the 20th Century.** Roland Doschka. (Illus.). 2000. 65.00 (3-7913-2350-4) Prestel Pub NY.

Pablo Picasso: Postcard Book. (Illus.). 18p. 1993. pap. 8.95 (3-7913-1314-2, Pub. by Prestel) te Neues.

Pablo Picasso: Spanish Painter. John W. Selfridge. LC 93-19205. (Hispanics of Achievement Ser.). (Illus.). 120p. (YA). (gr. 5 up). 1993. lib. bdg. 19.95 (0-7910-1777-X) Chelsea Hse.

***Pablo Picasso: The Appeal of Surface.** Pablo Picasso. (Illus.). 2000. pap. 45.00 (3-7757-0858-8) Gerd Hatje.

***Pablo Picasso: The Communist Years.** Gertje R. Utley. (Illus.). 288p. 2000. 55.00 (0-300-08251-7) Yale U Pr.

***Pablo Picasso: The Lithographs.** Henri Deschamps & Erich Franz. (Illus.). 2000. 85.00 (3-7757-0981-9, A20411, Pub. by Gerd Hatje) Dist Art Pubs.

***Pablo Picasso: The Sculptures.** Text by Werner Spies. (Illus.). 400p. 2000. 75.00 (3-7757-0909-6, A20401, Pub. by Gerd Hatje) Dist Art Pubs.

Pablo Picasso Dessins. Jean Bouret. (FRE., Illus.). 1950. lib. bdg. 95.00 (0-8288-3976-X) Fr & Eur.

Pablo Picasso on the Path to Sculpture: The Paris & Dinard Sketchbooks of 1928 from the Marina Picasso Collection. Werner Spies et al. (Illus.). 168p. 1995. text 70.00 (3-7913-1611-7, Pub. by Prestel) te Neues.

Pablo Picasso I, 6 vols. Ed. by TASHCEN VERLAG BENEDIKT. 1996. pap. 11.99 (3-8228-8769-2) Benedikt Taschen.

Pablo Recuerda: La Fiesta del Dia de los Muertos (Pablo Remembers) Jorge A. Diaz. (SPA.). 48p. (YA). (gr. 4-7). 1993. 16.00 (0-688-12894-7) Lothrop.

Pablo Remembers: The Fiesta of the Day of the Dead. George Ancona. LC 92-22819. (Illus.). (J). (gr. 4 up). 1993. 16.00 (0-688-11249-8); lib. bdg. 15.93 (0-688-11250-1) Lothrop.

Pablo y su Elefante. 2nd ed. Elvira Menendez. (Punto Infantil Ser.).Tr. of Paul & his Elephant. (SPA.). 1991. 10.60 (0-606-05529-0) Turtleback.

Pablo y Sus Amigos. Penny Frank & Eric Ford. (Historias de la Biblia Ser.).Tr. of Paul & Friends. (SPA.). (J). 1989. 1.50 (0-945792-58-1, 490351); pap. write for info. (0-614-27091-X) Editorial Unilit.

Pablo's Petunias. Prieto. LC 72-190269. (Illus.). 32p. (J). (gr. 3-5). 1972. lib. bdg. 9.95 (0-87783-058-4) Oddo.

Pablo's Petunias. deluxe ed. Prieto. LC 72-190269. (Illus.). 32p. (J). (gr. 3-5). 1972. pap. 3.94 (0-87783-102-5) Oddo.

Pablo's Tree. Pat Mora. LC 92-27145. (Illus.). 32p. (J). (ps-1). 1994. mass mkt. 16.00 (0-02-767401-0, Mac Bks Young Read) S&S Childrens.

Pabulum Pig: The Yule Swine. Terry L. Blacke & Debra Rider. LC 91-68193. (Illus.). 41p. (J). (gr. 4). 1992. pap. 7.98 (0-9630718-2-3) New Dawn NY.

PAC Directory: A Complete Guide to Political Action Committees. Ed. by Marvin I. Weinberger & Doug Greevy. LC 82-11480. 1536p. 1982. text 240.00 (0-88410-856-2, HarpBusn) HarpInfo.

***Pac Man World.** 20th anniversary ed. Prima. LC 99-67319. (Illus.). 80p. 1999. pap. 12.99 (0-7615-2631-5) Prima Pub.

PAC Power: Inside the World of Political Action Committees. Larry J. Sabato. LC 84-6068. 280p. 1985. pap. 8.95 (0-393-30257-1) Norton.

Pac-Rim Sourcebook. Chris Pasquarette. (Illus.). 160p. 1994. 12.00 (0-937279-46-3, CP3311) Talsorian.

Pacaa Nova: Clash of Cultures on the Brazilian Frontier. Bernard Von Graeve. (Illus.). 168p. (C). 1989. pap. text 14.95 (0-921149-36-0) Broadview Pr.

Pacatnamu Papers, Vol. I. Ed. by Guillermo A. Cock & Christopher B. Donnan. LC 86-61112. (Illus.). 192p. (Orig.). (C). 1986. text 40.00 (0-930741-14-5); pap. text 22.00 (0-930741-11-0) UCLA Fowler Mus.

Pacatnamu Papers: The Moche Occupation, Vol. 2. Christopher B. Donnan & Guillermo A. Cock. (ENG & SPA., Illus.). 300p. (Orig.). 1997. 50.00 (0-930741-56-0); pap. 29.00 (0-930741-57-9) UCLA Fowler Mus.

Pacatus: Panegyric to the Emperor Theodosius. Tr. & Intro. by C. E. Nixon. (Translated Texts for Historians Ser.). 128p. (Orig.). 1992. reprint ed. pap. text 15.95 (0-85323-076-5, Pub. by Liverpool Univ Pr) U of Pa Pr.

Pacatus, a Trade-Mark from Antiquity: History of Art & Industry from Rome, Pompeii to the Present. Joseph Domjan & Evelyn A. Domjan. Ed. by Jane Emig. LC 78-73444. (Illus.). 1979. 20.00 (0-933652-13-5) Domjan Studio.

Paccar: The Pursuit of Quality. 3rd ed. Alex Groner. LC 98-31629. 1998. write for info. (0-935503-24-2) Document Bk.

Pace-A Program for Acquiring Competence in Entrepreneurship. rev. ed. 166p. 1983. 120.00 (0-318-15525-7, RD240) Ctr Educ Trng Employ.

Pace Family Recipe Round-Up: 100 Easy Recipes from Pace Picante Sauce. Campbell Soup Company Staff & Time-Life Books Editors. LC 96-28262. (Illus.). 112p. (gr. 11). 1999. 14.95 (0-7835-4861-3) Time-Life.

Pace Family, 1607-1750. Freda R. Turner & Eleanor P. Terrell. 244p. 1993. 25.00 (0-9628557-8-2) Genlgcl Socs Henry & Clayton.

Pace-Forward: Policy Analytic & Computational Environment for Dutch Freight Transport. Manuel J. Carrillo et al. LC 96-37007. 72p. 1996. pap. 13.00 (0-8330-2457-4, MR-732/EAC/VW) Rand Corp.

Pace Panini: Towards a Word-Based Theory of Morphology. Rajendra Singh et al. LC 96-47415. (American University Studies XIII: Vol. 34). XIV, 149p. (C). 1997. text 35.95 (0-8204-3355-1) P Lang Pubng.

***Pace Society of America, Bulletins.** Freda Reid Turner. LC 98-60478. (Illus.). 502p. 1999. 35.00 (1-883793-31-9) Wolfe Pubng.

PACE Study Manual. Ed. by France Whiteside. (Orig.). 1996. pap. 55.00 (0-9623567-4-3) Natl Fed Para.

PACE System: An Expert Consulting System for Nursing. S. Evans. (Computers & Medicine Ser.). (Illus.). 167p. 1996. 49.00 (0-387-94731-0) Spr-Verlag.

Pace That Kills. Edgar E. Saltus. LC 79-93535. reprint ed. 37.50 (0-404-05508-7) AMS Pr.

Pace University Software Exercises. 274p. (C). 1995. text 27.60 (0-536-58920-8) Pearson Custom.

Pace University Software Exercises. 2nd ed. 292p. (C). 1996. text 24.20 (0-536-59611-5) Pearson Custom.

***Pacem in Terris: A Love Story.** Frederick Franck. LC 00-25446. (Illus.). 128p. 2000. pap. 18.00 (1-930337-02-7) Codhill Pr.

Pacemaker Activity & Intercellular Communication. Ed. by Jan D. Huizinga. LC 94-28589. (Electronic Engineering Systems Ser.). 368p. 1995. boxed set 224.95 (0-8493-7669-6) CRC Pr.

Pacemaker Activity & Intercellular Communication, 2 vols., Set. Marvin Thompson. LC 87-18375. (Calcium Binding Proteins Ser.). 1988. 186.00 (0-8493-4857-9, QP552, CRC Reprint) Franklin.

Pacemaker Clinic of the 90's: Essentials in Brady-Pacing. Ed. by N. M. Van Hemel et al. LC 95-23889. (Developments in Cardiovascular Medicine Ser.: Vol. 175). 276p. 1995. text 95.50 (0-7923-3688-7) Kluwer Academic.

Pacemaker Emergency Intervention System. AAMI Staff. (Illus.). 8p. (Orig.). 1993. pap. 62.00 (1-57020-009-2, PAC49-209) Assn Adv Med Instrn.

Pacemaker Interpretation for Nurses. Carol J. Wallace. LC 95-69076. (Illus.). 1995. pap. 19.95 (0-9627246-6-1) Power NY.

Pacemaker Primer. Julie Ann Purcell. write for info. (0-7817-1900-3) Lppncott W & W.

Pacemakers: Patient Care, Troubleshooting, Rhythm Analysis. Karen S. Kesten & Colleen K. Norton. 215p. (Orig.). 1985. pap. text 17.00 (0-932491-22-7) Res Appl Inc.

Pacer Power: The 1994 Wonder Season of the Indiana Pacers. Steve Mannheimer. LC 94-77613. 210p. 1994. pap. 9.95 (1-878208-48-9) Guild Pr IN.

Pacer Story Writing Cards. 1981. 73.95 (0-89075-084-X) Bilingual Ed Serv.

Paces de los Reyes y Judia de Toledo. Lope de Vega. (SPA.). 166p. 1971. 7.95 (0-8288-7173-6, S9076) Fr & Eur.

Pacesetter: The Untold Story of Carl G. Fisher. Jerry M. Fisher. LC 97-51403. 440p. 1998. 22.95 (1-882897-21-8) Lost Coast.

Pacesetters: Setting the Standard, Not Following the Trend. Benny Perez. LC 97-100155. 176p. 1996. pap. 10.00 (1-883893-69-0, Pub. by WinePress Pub) BookWorld.

Pachacamac. Max Uhle. (University Museum Monographs: No. 62). (Illus.). 155p. (C). 1991. reprint ed. text 25.00 (0-924171-09-X) U Museum Pubns.

Pachamama's Children see Journey to Machu Picchu: Spiritual Wisdom from the Andes

Pachanga Deliciosa see Delicious Hullabaloo

Pacheco's Art of Ybor City. Ferdie Pacheco. LC 97-11190. (Illus.). 112p. 1997. 39.95 (0-8130-1517-0) U Press Fla.

Pachelbel's Canon: Arranged for Harp Solo, Harp Duet & Harp & Flute or Violin. Sylvia Woods. 26p. 1986. pap. 8.95 (0-936661-00-3) Woods Mus Bks.

Pachelbel's Canon in D & 19 Movie Themes. Ed. by Carol Cuellar. 80p. (Orig.). 1995. pap. 12.95 (0-89724-251-3, VF1753A) Wrner Bros.

Pachinko Woman. Henry Mynton. LC 99-18700. 400p. 1999. 25.00 (0-688-16170-7, Wm Morrow) Morrow Avon.

Pachomian Koinonia I: The Life of St. Pachomius. Tr. by Armand Veilleux. (Cistercian Studies: No. 45). (GRE.). 524p. 1981. pap. 14.95 (0-87907-945-2) Cistercian Pubns.

Pachomian Koinonia III. Instructions, Letters & Other Writings, No. 47. Tr. by Armand Veilleux from COP. (Cistercian Studies). 322p. 1983. pap. 14.95 (0-87907-947-9) Cistercian Pubns.

Pachomian Koinonia II: Chronicles & Rules. Tr. by Armand Veilleux. (Cistercian Studies: No. 46). 239p. 1981. pap. 14.95 (0-87907-946-0) Cistercian Pubns.

***Pachomius: The Making of a Community in Fourth-Century Egypt, Vol. 6.** Philip Rousseau. 250p. 1999. pap. 19.95 (0-520-21959-7, Pub. by U CA Pr) Cal Prin Full Svc.

Pachycephalosaurus. (Microfaxc Ser.). (J). 1997. pap. text 0.99 (0-7894-2119-4) DK Pub Inc.

Pachycephalosaurus. Janet Riehecky. (Dinosaurs Bks.). (Illus.). 32p. (J). (gr. k-4). 1991. lib. bdg. 21.36 (0-89565-632-9) Childs World.

Pachyderms. Danny Budy. 176p. mass mkt. 4.99 (1-55197-130-5) Picasso Publ.

***Pachypodium (Apocynaceae) Taxonomy, Habitats & Cultivation.** S. H. Rapanarivo et al. (Illus.). 128p. (C). 1999. text 48.50 (90-5410-485-6, Pub. by A A Balkema) Ashgate Pub Co.

Paciente Ingles. Michael Ondaatje. 1998. pap. 6.95 (84-01-46329-7) Lectorum Pubns.

Pacific. Maggie Nelson. 55p. 1997. pap. 8.00 (1-887128-98-0) Soft Skull Pr.

Pacific: A Forecast. Percy T. Etherton & Hubert H. Tiltman. LC 74-111754. (American Imperialism: Viewpoints of United States Foreign Policy, 1898-1941 Ser.). 1970. reprint ed. 23.95 (0-405-02016-3) Ayer.

Pacific: California, Hawaii. Thomas G. Aylesworth & Virginia L. Aylesworth. LC 94-45822. (Discovering America Ser.). 88p. (J). (gr. 4 up). 1995. pap. 8.95 (0-7910-3425-9) Chelsea Hse.

Pacific: California, Hawaii. Thomas G. Aylesworth & Virginia L. Aylesworth. LC 94-45822. (Discovering America Ser.). (Illus.). 88p. (J). (gr. 4 up). 1995. lib. bdg. 19.95 (0-7910-3407-0) Chelsea Hse.

Pacific: Hawaii & Alaska. Steve Barth & Kim Heacox. LC 94-29730. (Guides to Natural America Ser.). (Illus.). 1995. 19.95 (0-89599-044-X) Smithsonian Bks.

Pacific: Peace, Security & the Nuclear Issue. Ed. by Ranini Walker & William Sutherland. LC 88-17225. (UNU Studies in Peace & Regional Security). (Illus.). 272p. (C). 1988. pap. 17.50 (0-86232-815-2, Pub. by Zed Books); text 49.95 (0-86232-814-4, Pub. by Zed Books) St Martin.

Pacific: Yesterday & the Day Before That. Harold S. Jacoby. LC 89-33490. (Illus.). xvi, 199p. (Orig.). 1989. pap. 12.50 (0-933994-09-5) Comstock Bon.

Pacific Alliance: United States Foreign Economic Policy & Japanese Trade Recovery, 1947-1955. William S. Borden. LC 83-14541. 336p. 1984. text 28.95 (0-299-09550-9) U of Wis Pr.

Pacific Answers Western Hegemony. Wassmann. LC 98-150948. 1997. 57.50 (1-85973-154-6, Pub. by Berg Pubs) NYU Pr.

Pacific Answers Western Hegemony. Jurg Wassmann. LC 98-150948. 1997. pap. 22.50 (1-85973-159-7, Pub. by Berg Pubs) NYU Pr.

Pacific Appointment: Two Lives That Met at Pearl Harbor. Alec C. Boatman. (Illus.). 128p. (Orig.). 1996. pap. 9.95 (1-56474-155-9) Fithian Pr.

Pacific Arcadia: Images of California, 1600-1915. Claire Perry. LC 98-3382. (Illus.). 256p. 1999. 40.00 (0-19-510936-8); pap. 25.00 (0-19-510937-6) OUP.

Pacific Asia. David W. Smith. (Introductions to Development Ser.). (Illus.). 192p. (C). 1991. pap. 16.99 (0-415-06985-8, A6509) Routledge.

Pacific-Asia & the Future of the World-System, 142. Ed. by Ravi A. Palat. LC 92-18384. (Contributions in Economics & Economic History Ser.: No. 142). 224p. 1993. 65.00 (0-313-28401-6, PPG, Greenwood Pr) Greenwood.

Pacific Asia in the Global System: An Introduction. Peter Preston. LC 97-43338. 269p. 1998. 62.95 (0-631-20237-4); pap. 29.95 (0-631-20238-2) Blackwell Pubs.

Pacific Asia in the 21st Century: Geographical & Developmental Perspectives. Ed. by Yue-man Yeung. 358p. (C). 1997. 34.50 (962-201-599-9, Pub. by Chinese Univ) U of Mich Pr.

Pacific Asian American Ministry in a Time of Shifting Paradigms: The Example of Asian American Conflict Management. Alban Institute Action Research Team on Conflict Management. pap. 7.50 (1-56699-163-3, OD117) Alban Inst.

Pacific Asian Art. 5p. 1991. teacher ed. 30.00 (1-56290-026-9, 6012) Crystal.

Pacific-Asian Issues: American & Chinese Views. Ed. by Robert A. Scalapino & Chen Qimao. LC 86-81320. (Research Papers & Policy: No. 17). viii, 289p. 1986. pap. 20.00 (0-912966-86-6) IEAS.

Pacific Atoll Populations. Ed. by Vern Carroll. LC 75-1264. (Association for Social Anthropology in Oceania Monographs: No. 3). (Illus.). 554p. reprint ed. pap. 171.80 (0-8357-8531-9, 203483300091) Bks Demand.

Pacific Banking, 1859-1959: East Meets West. Ed. by Olive Checkland et al. LC 94-27000. 1994. text 75.00 (0-312-12386-8) St Martin.

Pacific Basin. (Proceedings of the Academy of Political Science Ser.: Vol. 36, No. 1). 1986. pap. 12.95 (0-614-04171-6) Acad Poli Sci.

Pacific Basin: Korea, Southeast Asia, the Philippines, Thailand, Indonesia, Australia, & the Pacific Islands. 1995. lib. bdg. 252.95 (0-8490-6762-6) Gordon Pr.

Pacific Basin & Oceania. Gerald W. Fry & Rufino Mauricio. LC 88-150904. (World Bibliographical Ser.: No. 70). 508p. 1987. lib. bdg. 55.00 (1-85109-015-0) ABC-CLIO.

Pacific Basin Capital Markets Research. S. C. Rhee & R. P. Chang. 592p. 1990. 127.50 (0-444-88459-9) Elsevier.

Pacific-Basin Capital Markets Research, Vol. 2. Ed. by Rhee S. Ghon & R. P. Chang. 700p. 1991. 127.50 (0-444-88665-6, North Holland) Elsevier.

Pacific-Basin Capital Markets Research, Vol. III. S. G. Rhee & R. P. Chang. 506p. 1992. 127.50 (0-444-89288-5, North Holland) Elsevier.

Pacific Basin Developing Countries: Prospects for the Future. fac. ed. Marcus Noland. LC 90-25083. 248p. 1990. reprint ed. pap. 76.90 (0-7837-8295-0, 204907700009) Bks Demand.

Pacific Basin Industries in Distress. Ed. by Hugh T. Patrick. 560p. 1991. text 67.00 (0-231-07570-7) Col U Pr.

Pacific Basin Nuclear Conference, 9th, 1994: Nuclear Energy, Science & Technology, Pacific Partnership, 2 vols., Set. Intro. by Neil R. McDonald. (National Conference Publication Ser.: No. 94-6). (Illus.). 1087p. (Orig.). 1994. pap. 105.50 (0-85825-602-9, Pub. by Inst Engrs Aust-EA Bks) Accents Pubns.

Pacific Basin since 1945. Roger C. Thompson. LC 93-44480. (Post War World Ser.). (C). 1995. text 79.50 (0-582-02128-6, Pub. by Addison-Wesley) Longman.

Pacific Basketmakers: A Living Tradition. Ed. by Suzi Jones. (Illus.). 80p. 1983. pap. text 9.00 (0-8248-0916-5) UH Pr.

Pacific Boating Almanac, 1998: Northern California & the Delta. Griffes. 1998. pap. text 19.95 (1-57785-051-3, 10298) ProStar Pubns.

Pacific Boating Almanac, Cruising Guide: Pacific Northwest & Alaska. Peter L. Griffes. 1999. pap. text 29.95 (1-57785-007-6) ProStar Pubns.

Pacific Boating Almanac, 1998: Southern California & Mexico. Griffes. 1998. pap. text 19.95 (1-57785-050-5, 10198) ProStar Pubns.

Pacific Boating Almanac, 1998 Vol. 1: Pacific Northwest. Griffes. 1998. pap. text 19.95 (1-57785-052-1, 10398) ProStar Pubns.

Pacific Boating Almanac's Cruising Guides: Channel Islands. Peter L. Griffes. 288p. (Orig.). 1999. 24.95 (1-57785-015-7, PB205, Pac Boating) ProStar Pubns.

Pacific Bridges: The New Immigration from Asia & the Pacific Islands. Ed. by James T. Fawcett & Benjamin V. Cariño. LC 86-26402. (Immigration Theory & Policy Ser.). 489p. (C). 1987. pap. 14.50 (0-934733-09-0) CMS.

Pacific Campaign: The U. S.-Japanese Naval War, 1941-1945. Dan Van der Vat. (Illus.). 432p. 1992. pap. 15.00 (0-671-79217-2, Touchstone) S&S Trade Pap.

Pacific Centuries: Pacific & Pacific Rim Economic History since the 16th Century. Dennis O. Flynn et al. LC 98-11844. 240p. (C). 1999. 85.00 (0-415-18431-2) Routledge.

Pacific Century. 2nd ed. Pauletta Otis. LC 98-32337. 128p. 1998. pap., student ed. 15.00 (0-8133-3605-8, Pub. by Westview) HarpC.

Pacific Century: Economic & Political Consequences of Asian-Pacific Dynamism. Staffan B. Linder. 168p. 1986. 27.50 (0-8047-1294-8); pap. 11.95 (0-8047-1305-7) Stanford U Pr.

Pacific Century: The Emergence of Modern Pacific Asia. 2nd ed. Mark Borthwick. LC 97-42756. 600p. (C). 1998. pap. text 40.00 (0-8133-3471-3, Pub. by Westview) HarpC.

Pacific Challenge in International Business. Ed. by W. Chan Kim & Philip K. Y. Young. LC 87-5008. (Research for Business Education Ser.: No. 72). 350p. reprint ed. pap. 108.50 (0-8357-1620-1, 207034800088) Bks Demand.

Pacific Charter: Our Destiny in Asia. Hallett Abend. LC 72-4478. (Essay Index Reprint Ser.). 1977. reprint ed. 20.95 (0-8369-2932-2) Ayer.

Pacific Coast. Bayard H. McConnaughey & Evelyn McConnaughey. Ed. by Charles Elliott. LC 84-48673. (Audubon Society Nature Guides Ser.). (Illus.). 633p. 1985. pap. 19.95 (0-394-73130-1) Knopf.

***Pacific Coast.** Maria Mudd-Ruth. LC 00-20008. (Ecosystems of North America Ser.). (Illus.). (YA). 2001. 27.07 (0-7614-0935-1, Benchmark NY) Marshall Cavendish.

***Pacific Coast.** Photos by Thea Schrack. (Illus.). 1999. pap. 11.95 (0-8118-2002-5) Chronicle Bks.

Pacific Coast. Rick Steber. (Tales of the Wild West Ser.: Vol. 2). (Illus.). 60p. 1987. pap. 4.95 (0-945134-02-9); lib. bdg. 14.95 (0-945134-80-0) Bonanza Pub.

Pacific Coast: America's Scenic Western Shoreline Steven L. Walker. LC 95-70820. 95p. 1995. write for info. (1-879924-22-6) Camelback Design.

P

Pacific Coast Adventures. Fraser Bridges & Donald Stone. LC 95-17208. (Illus.). 400p. 1995. pap. 16.95 (*0-7615-0135-5*) Prima Pub.

Pacific Coast Adventures: The Driver's Guide. Fraser Bridges. 1991. pap. 12.95 (*0-9694136-3-7*) Amer Traveler.

Pacific Coast Adventures: The Driver's Guide. 2nd enl. rev. ed. Fraser Bridges. (Fraser Bridges Driver's Guide Ser.). (Illus.). 352p. 1993. pap. 14.95 (*1-883470-00-5*) Amer Traveler.

Pacific Coast Berry Finder: A Manual for Identifying Native Plants with Fleshy Fruits, Vol. 1. Glenn Keator. (Illus.). 62p. 1978. pap. 3.00 (*0-912550-02-3*) Nature Study.

Pacific Coast Bird Finder: A Manual for Identifying 61 Common Birds of Pacific Coast, Vol. 1. Roger J. Lederer. (Illus.). 62p. 1977. pap. 3.00 (*0-912550-04-X*) Nature Study.

Pacific Coast Crabs & Shrimps. Gregory C. Jensen. Ed. by Mary K. Wicksten & Ken Hashagen. LC 94-39292. (Illus.). 96p. 1995. pap. 21.95 (*0-930118-20-0*, 30J) Sea Chall.

Pacific Coast Current Tables of North America & Asia. (N. O. A. A. Tide & Tidal Current Tables, 1999 Ser.). (Illus.). 1998. 14.95 (*1-57785-063-7*, 81399PCC) ProStar Pubns.

Pacific Coast Fern Finder, Vol. 1. Glenn Keator & Ruth M. Heady. (Illus.). 62p. 1981. pap. 3.00 (*0-912550-13-9*) Nature Study.

Pacific Coast Fish: A Guide to Marine Fish of the Pacific Coast of North America. Ron Russo. (Illus.). 112p. 1990. pap. 5.75 (*0-912550-19-8*) Nature Study.

Pacific Coast Fishes. Roger Tory Peterson. (Peterson Field Guides Ser.). (Illus.). 1999. pap. 19.00 (*0-618-00212-X*) HM.

***Pacific Coast Highway.** Tom Snyder. LC 00-27325. 160p. 2000. pap. 12.95 (*0-312-26370-8*) St Martin.

Pacific Coast Highway. Alice Starmore. (Illus.). 112p. 1997. pap. text 18.95 (*0-9625586-7-2*) Unicorn Bks & Crafts.

Pacific Coast Inshore Fishes. 3rd rev. ed. Daniel W. Gotshall. LC 89-27672. (Illus.). 96p. 1989. pap. 18.95 (*0-930118-16-2*, 1G) Sea Chall.

Pacific Coast League: A Statistical History, 1903-1957. Dennis Snelling. LC 94-43242. 406p. 1995. pap. 29.50 (*0-7864-0045-5*) McFarland & Co.

Pacific Coast League, 1903-1988. Bill O'Neal. Ed. by Melissa Roberts. (Illus.). 356p. 1990. 21.95 (*0-89015-776-6*) Sunbelt Media.

Pacific Coast Lighthouses: Postcard Book. Ed. by BrownTrout Publishing Company Staff. (Illus.). 1997. pap. 7.95 (*1-56313-931-6*) BrownTrout Pubs Inc.

Pacific Coast Mammals: A Guide to Mammals of the Pacific Coast States, Their Tracks, Skulls & Other Signs. Ron Russo & Pam Olhausen. (Illus.). 96p. 1987. pap. 4.25 (*0-912550-16-3*) Nature Study.

Pacific Coast Nudibranchs: A Guide to the Opisthobranchs Alaska to Baja California. 2nd rev. ed. David W. Behrens. Ed. by Ken Hashagen. LC 91-13522. (Illus.). 107p. 1991. pap. 25.95 (*0-930118-17-0*, 2B) Sea Chall.

***Pacific Coast of North America & Asia.** (Tidal Current Tables 2000 Ser.). 1999. pap. 13.95 (*0-07-135330-5*) McGraw-Hill Prof.

Pacific Coast of North America & Asia. (N. O. A. A. Tidal Current Tables, 1998 Ser.). (Illus.). Date not set. 13.95 (*1-57785-024-6*, 81398) ProStar Pubns.

Pacific Coast of North America & Asia. National Oceanic & Atmospher Staff. (Tide Tables 1999 Ser.). 1998. pap. text 13.95 (*0-07-047188-6*) Intl Marine.

Pacific Coast Pelagic Invertebrates: A Guide to the Common Gelatinous Animals. David Wrobel & Claudia E. Mills. Ed. by Hans Bertsch. LC 97-42060. (Illus.). 112p. (C). 1997. pap. 16.95 (*0-930118-23-5*, 220W) Sea Chall.

Pacific Coast Petroleum Directory. 11th rev. ed. Ed. by Paula Jepperson. 300p. 1994. pap. 67.00 (*0-912553-47-2*) Hart Pubns.

Pacific Coast Petroleum Directory. 12th rev. ed. Ed. by Paula Jepperson. 250p. 1995. pap. text 69.00 (*0-912553-54-5*) Hart Pubns.

Pacific Coast Railway: Central California's Premier Narrow Gauge. Kenneth E. Wescott & Curtis H. Johnson. Ed. by Benchmark Ltd. Staff. LC 98-31171. (Illus.). 296p. 1998. 49.95 (*0-9615467-4-3*) Benchmark Ltd.

Pacific Coast Seafaring: Photographic Collection, 1850's to 1950's. Wayne Bonnett. (Illus.). 218p. 1988. 55.00 (*0-915269-07-4*) Windgate Pr.

Pacific Coast Squadrons Pt. 2: Colors & Markings. Bert Kinzey. (A-7 Corsair II Aero Ser.). 1990. pap. 12.95 (*0-8306-8539-1*) McGraw-Hill Prof.

Pacific Coast Tree Finder: A Manual for Identifying Pacific Coast Trees, Vol. 1. Tom Watts. (Illus.). 62p. 1973. pap. 3.00 (*0-912550-06-6*) Nature Study.

Pacific Coastal Wildlife Region, Vol. 1. 2nd rev. ed. Charles Yocom & Raymond Dasmann. (Illus.). 120p. 1965. pap. 7.95 (*0-911010-04-1*) Naturegraph.

Pacific Community. E. Gough Whitlam. (Council on East Asian Studies Ser.). 136p. (C). 1981. 22.50 (*0-674-65070-0*) HUP.

Pacific Conference on Gravitation & Cosmology: February 1-6, 1996, Sheraton Walker-Hill, Seoul, Korea. Pacific Conference on Gravitation & Cosmology Staff et al. LC 98-45010. 348p. 1999. 78.00 (*981-02-3698-0*) World Scientific Pub.

Pacific Cooperation & Development. Ed. by George Kozmetsky et al. LC 88-15272. 235p. 1988. 59.95 (*0-275-93095-5*, C3095, Praeger Pubs) Greenwood.

Pacific Cooperation from the Japanese & the German Viewpoint. Ed. by Herbert Hax et al. (Illus.). 192p. 1990. 44.00 (*0-387-51694-8*) Spr-Verlag.

Pacific Counterblow: The 11th Bombardment Group & the 67th Fighter Squadron in the Battle for Guadalcanal, An Interim Report. 56p. 1993. pap. 3.00 (*0-16-038130-4*) USGPO.

***Pacific Crest Trail: A Hiker's Companion.** Karen Berger & Daniel R. Smith. (Illus.). 2000. pap. 18.95 (*0-88150-431-9*, Pub. by Countryman) Norton.

Pacific Crest Trail Vol. 1: California, Vol. 1: California. 5th rev. ed. Schaffer et al. LC 95-9325. (Illus.). 480p. (Orig.). 1995. pap. 24.95 (*0-89997-178-4*) Wilderness Pr.

***Pacific Crest Trail Vol. 2: Oregon & Washington.** 2nd rev. ed. Jeffrey P. Schaffer. Vol. 2. 336p. 2000. pap. 24.95 (*0-89997-268-3*) Wilderness Pr.

Pacific Crossing. Gary Soto. LC 91-46909. 144p. (J). (gr. 3-7). 1992. 15.95 (*0-15-259187-7*, Harcourt Child Bks); pap. 8.00 (*0-15-259188-5*) Harcourt.

Pacific Crossing Guide. RCC Pilotage Foundation Staff. Ed. by Michael Pocock. (Illus.). 224p. 1997. 59.50 (*1-57409-036-4*) Sheridan.

Pacific Crossings: A Philippine Cookbook. Lily G. O'Boyle. LC 93-12794. (Illus.). 192p. 1994. 35.00 (*0-944863-25-6*) Acacia Corp.

Pacific Designs. Rebbeca Jewell. LC 98-183360. (British Museum Pattern Bks.). 27 p. 1998. write for info. (*0-7141-8076-9*) BRI5.

***Pacific Destiny.** Dale L. Walker. LC 00-27676. 320p. 2000. 24.95 (*0-312-86933-9*, Pub. by Forge NYC) St Martin.

Pacific Destiny. large type ed. Dana Fuller Ross. LC 94-25460. 507p. 1994. lib. bdg. 23.95 (*0-8161-7466-0*, G K Hall Lrg Type) Mac Lib Ref.

Pacific Destiny. Richard S. Elegant. 544p. 1991. reprint ed. pap. 12.95 (*0-380-71462-0*, Avon Bks) Morrow Avon.

Pacific Dreams: Currents of Surrealism & Fantasy in California Art, 1934-1957. Susan Ehrlich. (Illus.). 208p. 1995. pap. 35.00 (*0-614-07751-6*) U of Wash Pr.

Pacific Dreams: Currents of Surrealism & Fantasy in Early California Art, 1934-1957. Ed. by Susan Ehrlich. LC 94-48299. (Illus.). 208p. 1995. pap. 29.95 (*0-943739-18-7*) F S Wight Art.

Pacific Dynamism & the International Economic System. Ed. by C. Fred Bergsten. LC 92-37824. (Illus.). 402p. (Orig.). (C). 1993. pap. text 25.00 (*0-88132-196-6*) Inst Intl Eco.

Pacific Economic Development Report, 1995. Pacific Economic Cooperation Council Staff. Ed. by E. Mark Borthwick. (Illus.). 192p. (Orig.). 1994. pap. text. write for info. (*1-886418-00-4*) US Natl Committee.

Pacific Economic Outlook, 1998-1999. 10th ed. Contrib. by Lawrence B. Krause. (Illus.). 80p. 1998. pap. 29.00 (*1-892325-00-4*) Asia Found.

Pacific Economic Relations in the 1990s: Conflict or Cooperation? Ed. by Richard Higgott et al. LC 93-17999. 392p. (Orig.). 1993. pap. text 25.00 (*1-55587-433-9*) L Rienner.

Pacific Economy Growth & External Stability. Ed. by Mohamed Ariff. 372p. 1991. 44.95 (*1-86373-036-2*, Pub. by Allen & Unwin Pty); pap. 29.95 (*1-86373-035-4*, Pub. by Allen & Unwin Pty) Paul & Co Pubs.

Pacific Edge. Kim Stanley Robinson. 336p. 1995. pap. 13.95 (*0-312-89038-9*, Pub. by Tor Bks) St Martin.

Pacific Edge: Contemporary Architecture on the Pacific Rim. Peter Zellner. LC 98-65885. (Illus.). 224p. 1998. 60.00 (*0-8478-2116-1*, Pub. by Rizzoli Intl) St Martin.

Pacific Electric in Color, Vol. 1. P. A. Copeland. LC 97-73625. (Illus.). 128p. 1997. 49.95 (*1-878887-88-2*) Morning NJ.

***Pacific Electric in Color, Vol. 2.** P. A. Copeland. (Illus.). 128p. 1999. 54.95 (*1-58248-024-9*) Morning NJ.

Pacific Electric Stations. Ed. by John Heller. (Illus.). 250p. 1998. 30.00 (*0-9664304-0-9*) Elctrc Rlwy Hist.

Pacific Empire. G. Miki Hayden. LC 97-68452. (Illus.). 197p. 1997. pap. 12.95 (*0-9657929-1-9*) JONA Bks.

***Pacific Empires.** Ed. by Alan Frost & Jane Samson. 346p. 1999. text 75.00 (*0-7748-0757-1*, Pub. by U BC Pr) Raincoast Bk.

***Pacific Empires: Essays in Honour of Glyndwr Williams.** Glyndwr Williams et al. Ed. by Alan Frost & Jane D. Samson. 334p. 1999. pap. 27.95 (*0-7748-0758-X*, Pub. by U BC Pr) Raincoast Bk.

Pacific Encounters: Recollections & Humor. Marshall Green. (Illus.). 224p. (Orig.). 1997. pap. 15.00 (*1-885965-02-8*) Dacor Pr.

Pacific Energy Outlook: Strategies & Policy Imperatives to 2010. Ed. by Fereidun Fesharaki & Allen L. Clark. LC 95-10496. (Occasional Papers: Vol. 1). 1995. pap. write for info. (*0-86638-173-2*) EW Ctr HI.

Pacific Equatorial Countercurrent. T. Robert Kendall. LC 71-125496. (Illus.). 82p. 1970. 16.00 (*0-914704-01-X*) ICER Pr.

Pacific Estrangement: Japanese & American Expansion, 1897-1911. Akira Iriye. LC 72-79307. (Studies in American-East Asian Relations: No. 2). (Illus.). 304p. 1972. 26.50 (*0-674-65075-1*) HUP.

Pacific Far East: Endangered American Strategic Position. Robert J. Hanks. LC 81-84807. (Special Reports). 75p. 1981. 11.95 (*0-89549-036-6*) Inst Foreign Policy Anal.

Pacific Fast Mail: Twenty Five Years of Fine Models. Phil Kohl & Ruth Kohl. Ed. by Pacific Fast Mail Staff. 100p. 1979. pap. 8.95 (*0-915713-03-9*) Pac Fast Mail.

Pacific Fish: An Educational Coloring Book. Spizzirri Publishing Co. Staff. Ed. by Linda Spizzirri. (Illus.). 32p. (J). (gr. 1-8). 1989. pap. 1.99 (*0-86545-136-2*) Spizzirri.

Pacific Fishing Almanac, 1999: Northern California - The Delta. 1998. pap. 24.95 (*1-57785-054-8*, 20299, Lghthse Pr) ProStar Pubns.

Pacific Fishing Almanac, 1999: Pacific Northwest. 1998. pap. 24.95 (*1-57785-055-6*, 20399, Lghthse Pr) ProStar Pubns.

Pacific Fishing Almanac, 1999: Southern California. Peter L. Griffes. 1998. 24.95 (*1-57785-053-X*, 20199) ProStar Pubns.

Pacific Flavors: Oriental Recipes for a Contemporary Kitchen. Hugh Carpenter. LC 87-26775. (Illus.). 272p. 1988. 40.00 (*1-55670-020-2*) Stewart Tabori & Chang.

Pacific Flavors: Oriental Recipes for a Contemporary Kitchen. Hugh Carpenter. LC 87-26775. (Illus.). 272p. 1993. pap. 23.50 (*1-55670-333-3*) Stewart Tabori & Chang.

Pacific Fresh: Great Recipes from the West Coast. Maryana Vollstedt. LC 94-13124. 320p. 1995. pap. 12.95 (*0-8118-0391-0*) Chronicle Bks.

***Pacific Game Fishing.** S. Kip Farrington. (Blue Water Classics Ser.). 368p. 2000. lthr. 65.00 (*1-56416-145-5*) Derrydale Pr.

Pacific Gardener. 10th ed. A. R. Willis. (Illus.). 160p. 1994. pap. 9.95 (*0-88826-047-4*) Whitecap Bks.

***Pacific Gateway: An Illustrated History of the Port of Oakland.** Woodruff Minor. (Illus.). viii, 192p. (C). 2000. pap. 24.95 (*0-9678617-0-5*) Port of Oakland.

Pacific General. Michael Knight. LC 97-68839. 272p. 1997. per. 16.99 (*0-7615-1073-7*) Prima Pub.

Pacific Glory: Airlines of the Great Ocean. Freddy Bullock. LC 99-27102. (Illus.). 112p. 1999. pap. 24.95 (*0-7603-0700-8*, 128433AP) MBI Pubg.

Pacific Graphics '97 Conference. LC 97-75144. 400p. 1997. pap. 125.00 (*0-8186-8028-8*) IEEE Comp Soc.

Pacific Graveyard. 4th rev. ed. James A. Gibbs. LC 64-21182. (Illus.). 296p. 1993. pap. 14.95 (*0-8323-0481-6*) Binford Mort.

Pacific Graveyard Shipwreck Chart. rev. ed. James A. Gibbs. LC 64-21182. (Illus.). 1991. 3.50 (*0-8323-0492-1*) Binford Mort.

***Pacific Grilling: Recipes for the Fire from Baja California to the Pacific NW.** Denis Kelly. (Illus.). 272p. 2000. pap. 18.95 (*1-57061-175-0*) Sasquatch Bks.

Pacific Growth & Financial Interdependence. Ed. by Augustine Tan & Basant Kapur. (Illus.). 384p. 1986. text 44.95 (*0-86861-904-3*, Pub. by Allen & Unwin Pty); pap. text 24.95 (*0-86861-912-4*, Pub. by Allen & Unwin Pty) Paul & Co Pubs.

Pacific Halibut: The Resource of the Fishery. F. Heward Bell. LC 80-29218. (Illus.). 279p. 1981. pap. 19.95 (*0-88240-141-6*, Alaska NW Bks) Gr Arts Ctr Pub.

***Pacific Heat.** Anne Mather. 1999. per. 3.75 (*0-373-12019-2*, 1-12019-5, Harlequin) Harlequin Bks.

Pacific Heat. Anne Mather. 1999. 21.95 (*0-263-15986-8*, G K Hall & Co) Mac Lib Ref.

***Pacific Heights West.** (San Francisco On the Level Ser.: Vol. 5). (Illus.). 20p. 2000. pap. 3.95 (*0-9679270-5-6*) On the Level.

Pacific Highway Boo-Blooz. Mudrooroo. 1996. pap. 16.95 (*0-7022-2834-6*, Pub. by Univ Queensland Pr) Intl Spec Bk.

Pacific History: Papers from the 8th Pacific History Association Conference. Intro. by Donald H. Rubinstein. (Illus.). vi, 476p. (Orig.). (C). 1992. pap. 12.00 (*1-878453-14-9*) Univ Guam MAR Ctr.

Pacific Horizons, the Exploration of the Pacific Before Captain Cook. Christopher Lloyd. LC 75-41177. reprint ed. 37.50 (*0-404-14710-0*) AMS Pr.

Pacific Horticulture Book of Western Gardening. Ed. by George Waters & Nora Harlow. (Illus.). 312p. 1990. 50.00 (*0-87923-763-5*) Godine.

***Pacific Images: Views From Captain Cook's Third Voyage.** Ed. by Eleanor C. Nordyke. (Illus.). 176p. 1999. text 45.00 (*0-945048-04-1*) UH Pr.

Pacific in the Nineteen Nineties: Economic & Strategic Change. Ed. by Janos Radvanyi. 166p. (C). 1990. pap. text 22.50 (*0-8191-7901-9*); lib. bdg. 47.50 (*0-8191-7900-0*) U Pr of Amer.

Pacific International Conference on Aerospace Science & Technology, 2nd, 1995 & Australian Aeronautical Conference, 6th, 1995. Contrib. by W. J. Belton. (National Conference Proceedings 95 Ser.: Vol. 1). (Illus.). 982p. 1995. pap. 91.50 (*0-85825-624-X*, Pub. by Inst Engrs Aust-EA Bks) Accents Pubns.

Pacific Intertidal Life: A Guide to Organisms of Rocky Reefs & Tide Pools from Alaska to Baja California, Vol. 1. Ron Russo & Pam Olhausen. (Illus.). 1981. pap. 3.00 (*0-912550-10-4*) Nature Study.

Pacific Island. Herbert Ypma. LC 95-72932. (Illus.). 160p. 1996. pap. 27.50 (*1-55670-479-8*) Stewart Tabori & Chang.

Pacific Island Battlegrounds of World War II: Then & Now. Earl Hinz. Ed. by Bud Bendix. (Illus.). 128p. 1995. pap. 19.95 (*1-880188-94-5*); lib. bdg. 29.95 (*1-57306-008-9*) Bess Pr.

Pacific Island Countries: Selected Issues in Development Policy & Subregional Co-Operation in the 1990s. 117p. pap. 17.50 (*92-1-119262-5*) UN.

Pacific Island Economies: Building a Resilient Economic Base for the Twenty-First Century. LC 95-48482. (World Bank Country Study). 166p. 1996. pap. 22.00 (*0-8213-3554-5*, 13554) World Bank.

Pacific Island Legends: Tales from Micronesia, Melanesia, Polynesia & Australia. Bo Flood et al. (Illus.). 48p. 1999. pap., teacher ed. 14.95 (*1-57306-103-4*) Bess Pr.

***Pacific Island Legends: Tales from Micronesia, Melanesia, Polynesia & Australia.** Bo Flood et al. (Illus.). 280p. (J). (gr. 4-9). 1999. pap. 14.95 (*1-57306-078-X*) Bess Pr.

Pacific Island Odyssey: Whistling Past the Foxholes. Carl R. Thien. LC 94-60913. (Illus.). 128p. 1995. pap. 10.95 (*1-885240-01-5*) Wanpela Bks.

Pacific Island Studies: A Survey of the Literature, 7. Ed. by Miles M. Jackson et al. LC 86-343. (Bibliographies & Indexes in Sociology Ser.: No. 7). 256p. 1986. lib. bdg. 65.00 (*0-313-23528-7*, JIP/, Greenwood Pr) Greenwood.

***Pacific Island Style.** Glenn Jowitt & Peter Shaw. LC 99-65178. (Illus.). 192p. 2000. 40.00 (*0-500-23772-7*, Pub. by Thames Hudson) Norton.

Pacific Island Theses & Dissertations: A Bibliography. Coppell & Susan Stratigos. (Australian National University Press Ser.). 1996. pap. write for info. (*0-08-032989-6*, Pergamon Pr) Elsevier.

Pacific Islander Americans: An Annotated Bibliography in the Social Sciences. Paul R. Spickard et al. (Institute for Polynesian Studies Monographs: No. 7). 102p. (Orig.). (C). 1995. pap. text 14.00 (*0-939154-54-4*) Inst Polynesian.

Pacific Islands. Kenneth Carpenter. LC 95-22632. (OIES Country Guide Ser.). 1996. 20.00 (*0-929851-56-0*) Am Assn Coll Registrars.

Pacific Islands. Katherine Kristen. LC 95-26299. (Portrait of America Library). 48p. (J). (gr. 4-8). 1996. pap. 5.95 (*0-8114-7479-8*) Raintree Steck-V.

Pacific Islands. Katherine Kristen. (Portrait of America Library). 48p. (J). (gr. 3-6). 1996. lib. bdg. 22.83 (*0-8114-7398-8*) Raintree Steck-V.

Pacific Islands. 3rd ed. Douglas L. Oliver. LC 88-38668. (Illus.). 336p. (C). 1989. pap. text 18.00 (*0-8248-1233-6*) UH Pr.

***Pacific Islands: An Encyclopedia.** Brij V. Lal & Kate Fortune. LC 99-34571. 2000. 100.00 incl. cd-rom (*0-8248-2265-X*) UH Pr.

Pacific Islands: Environment & Society. Ed. by Moshe Rapaport. (Illus.). 480p. (C). 1999. pap. text 39.95 (*1-57306-042-9*) Bess Pr.

Pacific Islands: Politics, Economics, & International Relations. Teo I. Fairbairn et al. LC 91-13100. 184p. (C). 1991. pap. text 17.00 (*0-86638-140-6*) EW Ctr HI.

Pacific Islands Cook Book. Monica Bayley. (Illus.). (Orig.). 1977. pap. 2.50 (*0-915696-05-3*) Determined Prods.

Pacific Islands under Japanese Mandate. Tadao Yanaihara. LC 75-41304. (Institute of Pacific Relations Ser.). 1977. reprint ed. 47.50 (*0-404-14636-8*) AMS Pr.

Pacific Lane. Russell L. Swigart. 176p. (Orig.). 1996. pap. 9.95 (*1-56474-181-8*) Fithian Pr.

Pacific Language Connections. Tadasu Tokumaru. (JPN.). 150p. (Orig.). 1989. pap. write for info. (*0-9625279-0-4*) Tokumaru Pr.

Pacific Languages: An Introduction. John Lynch. LC 97-24552. xix, 359p. 1998. pap. text 35.00 (*0-8248-1898-9*) UH Pr.

Pacific Latin America in Prehistory: The Evolution of Archaic & Formative Cultures. Ed. by Michael Blake. LC 98-43834. (Illus.). 234p. 1999. pap. text 50.00 (*0-87422-166-8*) Wash St U Pr.

Pacific Law Bibliography. 2nd ed. Jacqueline C. Elliott. Date not set. 65.00 (*1-875192-03-4*) W S Hein.

Pacific Law Journal: 1970-1995/96, 27 vols. 1921. 1207.50 (*0-8377-9129-4*, Rothman) W S Hein.

Pacific Law Journal: 1970-1995/96, Vols. 1-24. 1970. mic. film 1207.00 (*0-318-57454-3*) W S Hein.

Pacific Light. Jay Dunitz. Ed. by Peter Levitt. (Illus.). 112p. 1989. 95.00 (*0-941831-23-X*) Beyond Words Pub.

Pacific Light Cooking. Ruth Law. 1998. 27.50 (*1-55611-519-9*, Pub. by D I Fine) Penguin Putnam.

Pacific Magic. large type ed. Ivy Preston. (Romance Ser.). 320p. 1987. 27.99 (*0-7089-1690-2*) Ulverscroft.

Pacific Microphone. William J. Dunn. LC 88-12193. (Military History Ser.: No. 8). (Illus.). 416p. 1988. 24.95 (*0-89096-339-8*) Tex A&M Univ Pr.

Pacific Nations & Territories. Reilly Ridgell. 1995. pap., teacher ed. 9.95 (*1-57306-003-8*) Bess Pr.

Pacific Nations & Territories. Reilly Ridgell. LC 88-70787. (Illus.). 112p. 1995. pap., student ed. 8.95 (*1-57306-002-X*) Bess Pr.

Pacific Nations & Territories. 3rd ed. Reilly Ridgell. (Illus.). 184p. 1995. pap. 34.95 (*1-57306-006-2*) Bess Pr.

Pacific Nations & Territories. 3rd rev. ed. Reilly Ridgell. LC 88-70787. (Illus.). 176p. 1995. 44.95 (*1-57306-001-1*) Bess Pr.

Pacific Neighbors: The Islands of Micronesia, Melanesia, & Polynesia. Betty Dunford & Reilly Ridgell. (Illus.). 192p. (J). (gr. 4-9). 1996. text 44.95 (*1-57306-022-4*) Bess Pr.

Pacific Neogene: Environment, Evolution, & Events. Ed. by Ryuichi Tsuchi & J. C. Ingle. 250p. 1993. text 94.50 (*0-86008-491-4*, Pub. by U of Tokyo) Col U Pr.

Pacific Neogene Datum Planes: Contributions to Biostratigraphy & Chronology. Ed. by Nobuo Ikebe & Ryuichi Tsuchi. 283p. 1984. 97.50 (*0-86008-354-3*, Pub. by U of Tokyo) Col U Pr.

Pacific Neogene Datum Planes: Contributions to Biostratigraphy & Chronology. Ed. by Nobuo Ikebe & Ryuichi Tsuchi. LC 84-238889. 298p. 1984. reprint ed. pap. 92.40 (*0-608-01216-5*, 206190500001) Bks Demand.

Pacific Nightmare: How Japan Starts World War III - a Future History. Simon Winchester. LC 92-16509. 256p. 1992. 18.95 (*1-55972-136-7*, Birch Ln Pr) Carol Pub Group.

Pacific North Coast, '90: Southeast Alaska, Washington, Oregon, British Columbia. 320p. 1990. 12.95 (*0-685-31376-X*) McKay.

Pacific North West. Fodors Staff. (Bed & Breakfasts & Country Inns Ser.). 1999. pap. 19.00 (*0-679-00178-6*) Fodors Travel.

Pacific Northeast Asia in Prehistory: Hunter-Fisher-Gatherers, Farmers, & Sociopolitical Elites. Ed. by C. Melvin Aikens & Song N. Rhee. LC 92-26733. 236p. 1993. pap. 40.00 (*0-87422-092-0*) Wash St U Pr.

Pacific Northwest. (Bed & Breakfast Ser.). (Illus.). 128p. 1991. pap. 15.00 (*0-13-068438-4*, P-H Travel) Prntice Hall Bks.

***Pacific Northwest.** Jean Galton & Time-Life Books Staff. LC 00-24944. (Williams-Sonoma New American Cooking Ser.). (Illus.). 144p. 2000. 22.95 (*0-7370-2045-8*) Time-Life Educ.

An Asterisk (*) at the beginning of an entry indicates that the title is appearing for the first time.

Pacific Northwest. John McKinney. LC 97-2645. (Great Walks of North America Ser.). 1997. pap. 14.95 (0-8050-4420-5, Owl) H Holt & Co.

Pacific Northwest. Edward W. Nuffield. 288p. (Orig.). 1990. pap. 16.95 (0-88839-236-2) Hancock House.

Pacific Northwest. 3rd ed. Insight Guides Staff. (Insight Guides). 1998. pap. text 22.95 (0-88729-735-8) Langenscheidt.

***Pacific Northwest.** 13th ed. Ed. by Fodors Travel Publications, Inc. Staff. 512p. 2000. pap. 17.50 (0-679-00373-8) Fodors Travel.

Pacific Northwest: An Index to People & Places in Books. Joseph G. Drazan. LC 79-16683. 176p. 1979. 20.00 (0-8108-1234-7) Scarecrow.

Pacific Northwest: An Interpretive History. enl. rev. ed. Carlos A. Schwantes. LC 95-31650. (Illus.). xxiii, 570p. 1996. pap. 27.50 (0-8032-9228-7, Bison Books); text 60.00 (0-8032-4225-5) U of Nebr Pr.

Pacific Northwest: Essays in Honor of James W. Scott. Ed. by Howard J. Critchfield. 280p. (C). 1993. text 26.00 (0-930216-06-7); pap. text 16.00 (0-930216-05-9) West Wash Univ.

Pacific Northwest: Geographical Perspectives. James Ashbaugh. LC 97-72001. 440p. (C). 1997. per. 50.00 (0-7872-3606-3) Kendall-Hunt.

Pacific Northwest: Geographical Perspectives, Preliminary Edition. James Ashbaugh. 436p. (C). 1994. per. 40.95 (0-8403-9347-4) Kendall-Hunt.

Pacific Northwest: Insight Guide. Insight Publishing Staff. Ed. by Junie Freeburg & Diana Ackland. write for info. (0-318-59689-X) S&S Trade.

Pacific Northwest: Land of Light & Water. Photos by Art Wolfe. LC 98-6129. (Illus.). 160p. 1998. 35.00 (1-57061-150-5); pap. 24.95 (1-57061-160-2) Sasquatch Bks.

***Pacific Northwest: Natures Adventures in Parks, Preserves, Forests, Wildlife Refuges, Wilderness Areas.** LC 99-85986. (National Geographic Guide to America's Outdoors). 288p. 2000. per. 24.00 (0-7922-7740-6, Pub. by Natl Geog) S&S Trade.

Pacific Northwest: Oregon & Washington Territory. Northern Pacific Railroad Staff. (Shorey Historical Ser.). 32p. 1975. reprint ed. pap. 10.00 (0-8466-0229-6) Shoreys Bkstore.

Pacific Northwest: Past, Present & Future. Dale Lambert. (Illus.). 480p. (YA). (gr. 8-12). 1986. teacher ed. 7.95 (0-685-10071-5); teacher ed. 2.95 (0-939688-18-2); student ed. 3.95 (0-939688-17-4); text 19.95 (0-939688-14-X); 9.95 (0-939688-16-6) Directed Media.

Pacific Northwest: The Rough Guide. Tim Jepson & Phil Lee. (Illus.). 572p. 1994. pap. 16.95 (1-85828-092-3, Penguin Bks) Viking Penguin.

Pacific Northwest, a Photographic Tour. C. Highsmith & Landphair. LC 98-35691. 1999. 14.99 (0-517-20401-0) Random Hse Value.

Pacific Northwest Agricultural Insect & Plant Disease Study Manual. Hugh W. Homan & Russell W. Clausen. 56p. (C). 1998. pap. text, student ed. 20.00 (0-7881-4898-2) DIANE Pub.

Pacific Northwest Americana. 3rd rev. ed. Charles W. Smith. Ed. by Isabel Mayhew. 392p. 1951. pap. 20.00 (0-8323-0352-6) Binford Mort.

Pacific Northwest Americana Supplement, 1949-1974. Ed. by Richard E. Moore & Nadine H. Purcell. LC 81-65510. 372p. 1981. pap. 20.00 (0-8323-0389-5) Binford Mort.

Pacific Northwest & Beyond: Essays in Honor of Howard J. Critchfield. Scott. (Occasional Papers: No. 14). 1986. pap. 6.95 (0-318-23332-0) WWU CPNS.

***Pacific Northwest & British Columbia.** Santo Criscuolo. (Ski & Snowboard America Ser.). (Illus.). 2000. pap. 17.95 (0-7627-0844-1) Globe Pequot.

Pacific Northwest & California see Gale Encyclopedia of Native American Tribes

Pacific Northwest Bell Office Building. (PCI Journal Reprints Ser.). 12p. 1984. pap. 12.00 (0-318-19805-3, JR296) P-PCI.

Pacific Northwest Berry Book: A Complete Guide to Finding, Harvesting & Preparing Wild Berries & Fruits in the Pacific Northwest. Bob Krumm & James Krumm. LC 98-3819. 1998. pap. 11.95 (1-56044-681-1) Falcon Pub Inc.

Pacific Northwest Bookfinder: A Directory of Used Bookshops & Bookdealers in Alaska, British Columbia, Idaho, Oregon & Washington. 6th rev. ed. Ed. by Sheryl Rasmussen. (Illus.). 80p. (Orig.). 1996. 5.50 (0-9652864-0-1) Antiquarian Direct.

Pacific Northwest Cenozoic Biostratigraphy. Ed. by John M. Armentrout. LC 80-82937. (Geological Society of America, Special Paper: No. 184). (Illus.). 178p. reprint ed. pap. 55.20 (0-8357-6841-4, 203552900095) Bks Demand.

Pacific Northwest Coast. Sandra G. Garrett. LC 94-9098. (American Food Library). 48p. (J). (gr. 3-6). 1994. lib. bdg. 22.60 (0-86625-513-3) Rourke Pubns.

Pacific Northwest Coast: Living with the Shores of Oregon & Washington. Paul D. Komar. LC 97-23870. (Living with the Shore Ser.). (Illus.). 248p. 1998. pap. 18.95 (0-8223-2020-7); lib. bdg. 54.95 (0-8223-2010-X) Duke.

Pacific Northwest Cooking Secrets. Kathleen D. Fish. LC 96-83612. (Illus.). 288p. 1996. pap. text 15.95 (1-883214-07-6) Bon Vivant Pr.

Pacific Northwest Gardener's Book of Lists. Jan McNeilan & Ray McNeilan. LC 96-52183. (Illus.). 208p. (Orig.). 1997. pap. 17.95 (0-87833-956-6) Taylor Pub.

Pacific Northwest Gateway: A Historical & Contemporary Portrait of Portland International Airport. Harry A. Lenhart, Jr. LC 97-66363. (Illus.). 120p. 1997. 34.95 (1-882933-15-X) Cherbo Pub Grp.

Pacific Northwest GPS Companion: Includes Idaho, Oregon, Washington. Ed. by Clayton Wendt. 398p. 1998. pap. 13.95 (1-891759-10-8, 50247) Wendt Cos Inc.

Pacific Northwest in World War II. Ed. by Carlos A. Schwantes. (Illus.). 88p. 1986. pap. text 15.00 (0-89745-089-2) Sunflower U Pr.

Pacific Northwest Lighthouses: Oregon, Washington, Alaska & British Columbia. Bruce Roberts & Ray Jones. LC 99-26351. (Lighthouse Ser.). (Illus.). 112p. 1999. 29.95 (0-7910-5490-X) Chelsea Hse.

Pacific Northwest Lighthouses: Oregon, Washington & British Columbia. rev. ed. Ray Jones. LC 97-16544. (Lighthouse Ser.). (Illus.). 96p. 1997. pap. 19.95 (0-7627-0082-3) Globe Pequot.

Pacific Northwest, Oregon, Washington, & Alaska. Bob Devine & Phil Schofield. LC 97-5864. (Driving Guides to America Ser.). 1997. 45.00 (0-7922-3429-4) Natl Geog.

Pacific Northwest Palate: Four Seasons of Great Cooking. Susan Bradley. 1989. 22.07 (0-201-51764-7) Addison-Wesley.

***Pacific Northwest Plant Locator, 2000-2001.** Susan Narizny & Susan Hill. 350p. 2000. pap. 19.95 (0-9674907-1-5) Black-Eyed.

***Pacific Northwest Plant Locator, 1999-2000.** Susan Narizny & Susan Hill. 280p. 1999. pap. 19.99 (0-9674907-0-7) Black-Eyed.

Pacific Northwest Railroads of McGee & Nixon. 2nd ed. Richard Green. (Illus.). 280p. 1998. reprint ed. 59.95 (0-915370-07-7, 509-9) NW Short Line.

Pacific Northwest Region Vegetation & Inventory Monitoring System. Timothy A. Max et al. (Illus.). 28p. 1997. reprint ed. pap. 4.00 (0-89904-569-3, Bear Meadows Resrch Grp) Crumb Elbow Pub.

Pacific Northwest Road Atlas. Susan Farewell. (Road Atlas Ser.). (Illus.). 64p. 1992. pap. 5.95 (0-13-932237-X, H M Gousha) Prntice Hall Bks.

Pacific Northwest Road Atlas. 2nd ed. H. M. Gousha. LC 96-675521. 1995. 7.95 (0-671-53599-4) S&S Trade.

Pacific Northwest Road Atlas: 1999 Edition. Thomas Bros. Maps Staff. (Illus.). 456p. 1998. pap. 24.95 (1-58174-035-2) Thomas Bros Maps.

***Pacific Northwest Road Atlas & Drivers Guide, Oregon, Washington, Southwestern British Columbia & Western Idaho: 2000 Edition.** (Illus.). 384p. 1999. pap. 24.95 (1-58174-204-5) Thomas Bros Maps.

Pacific Northwest Salmon Cookbook. Curt Smitch et al. 180p. (Orig.). 1985. pap. 9.95 (0-9614579-0-2) Northwest Res.

Pacific Northwest Scholarship Guide: Finding Money for College. 6th rev. ed. Ed. by Douglas J. Breithaupt. 205p. (Orig.). 1996. pap. text 29.95 (1-880344-06-8) Col Plan Netwk.

Pacific Northwest Scholarship Guide: Finding Money for College. 7th ed. Douglas J. Breithaupt. 220p. (Orig.). (YA). (gr. 7-12). 1998. pap. 29.95 (1-880344-09-2) Col Plan Netwk.

Pacific Northwest Seafood. Linda Sollars & Pascha Scott. 36p. (Orig.). 1991. pap. 3.25 (0-940844-41-9) Wellspring.

Pacific Northwest Seafood Cookery. Jones Staff. (Illus.). 176p. 1981. pap. 7.95 (0-939936-01-1) Jones Pub.

Pacific Northwest Trail Cook Book: Trail Cook's Favorite Recipes. John T. Wolcott & Roberta O. Wolcott. (Illus.). 80p. (Orig.). 1991. pap. text 7.95 (0-931435-04-8) Features NW.

Pacific Northwest Tribes Missions Collection of the Oregon Province Archives of The Society of Jesus. Jesuits Staff & Robert C. Carriker. LC 87-4682. 34 p. 1987. 20.00 (0-8420-3038-7) Scholarly Res Inc.

Pacific Northwest Women, 1815-1925: Lives, Memories, & Writings. Ed. by Jean M. Ward & Elaine A. Maveety. LC 95-17850. 352p. 1995. text 29.95 (0-87071-387-6) Oreg St U Pr.

Pacific Northwest Women, 1815-1925: Lives, Memories, & Writings. Ed. by Jean M. Ward & Elaine A. Maveety. LC 95-17850. (Illus.). 352p. 1997. reprint ed. pap. 17.95 (0-87071-393-0) Oreg St U Pr.

Pacific Northwest Writers Conference Story. Loralie Cecotti. (Illus.). 60p. (Orig.). 1983. pap. 6.95 (0-933992-27-0) Coffee Break.

Pacific Northwestern Spiritual Poetry. Charles Potts et al. 384p. 1998. pap. 20.00 (0-9644440-5-4) Tsunami.

Pacific Ocean. Ed. by V. S. Gorshkov. 340p. 1976. 740.75 (0-08-021144-5, Pergamon Pr) Elsevier.

Pacific Ocean. David Lambert. LC 96-28228. (Seas & Oceans Ser.). (Illus.). 48p. (J). 1997. lib. bdg. 24.26 (0-8172-4507-3) Raintree Steck-V.

Pacific Ocean. John F. Prevost. LC 98-12069. (Oceans & Seas Ser.). (J). 2000. lib. bdg. 19.92 (1-57765-093-X) ABDO Pub Co.

Pacific Ocean. Felix Riesenberg. LC 79-128300. (Essay Index Reprint Ser.). 1977. 23.95 (0-8369-2125-9) Ayer.

Pacific Ocean. Leighton Taylor. LC 98-17329. (Life in the Sea Ser.). (Illus.). 48p. (J). (gr. 5-7). 1998. lib. bdg. 17.95 (1-56711-243-9) Blackbirch.

***Pacific Ocean: The Deepest Ocean.** Aileen Weintraub. LC 00-39166. (Great Record Breakers in Nature Ser.). (Illus.). (J). 2000. write for info. (0-8239-5639-3, PowerKids) Rosen Group.

Pacific Ocean Boundary Problems: Status & Solutions. Douglas M. Johnston & Mark J. Valencia. (C). 1991. lib. bdg. 100.50 (0-7923-0862-X) Kluwer Academic.

Pacific Odyssey: History of the U. S. S. Steele During WWII. 2nd ed. F. W. Bates. Ed. by Walbrook Swank. LC 98-44055. 92p. 1998. reprint ed. pap. 9.95 (1-57249-145-0, Burd St Pr) White Mane Pub.

Pacific Overtures. John Weidman & Stephen Sondheim. LC 90-29041. 144p. 1991. 17.95 (1-55936-025-9); pap. 8.95 (1-55936-026-7) Theatre Comm.

Pacific Particle Physics Phenomenology. M. Drees. (High Energy Physics Conference Proceedings Ser.). 1998. 78.00 (981-02-3623-9) World Scientific Pub.

Pacific Partners: Canada & the United States. Charles Doran et al. (Institute for Foreign Policy Anaylsis Ser.). 143p. 1994. pap. 11.95 (0-02-881076-7) Brasseys.

Pacific Partners: The Japanese Presence in Canadian Business, Society, & Culture. Carin Holroyd & Ken Coates. LC 96-168144. 186p. 34.95 (1-55028-493-2, Pub. by J Lorimer); pap. 19.95 (1-55028-492-4, Pub. by J Lorimer) Formac Dist Ltd.

Pacific Partnerships for Health: Charting a New Course. Ed. by Jill C. Feasley & Robert S. Lawrence. LC 98-134880. 1998. pap. text 31.00 (0-309-05948-8) Natl Acad Pr.

Pacific Passage. Thomas J. Watson, Jr. (Illus.). 180p. 1993. 39.95 (0-913372-68-4) Mystic Seaport.

Pacific Passage: The Study of American-East Asian Relations on the Eve of the Twenty-First Century. Ed. by Warren I. Cohen. LC 95-44851. 352p. 1996. 44.50 (0-231-10406-5) Col U Pr.

Pacific Passage: The Study of American-East Asian Relations on the Eve of the Twenty First Century. Ed. by Warren I. Cohen. LC 95-44851. 352p. 1996. pap. 20.00 (0-231-10407-3) Col U Pr.

Pacific Passions Cookbook: Celebrating the Cuisine of the Pacific Northwest. Karen Barnaby. (Illus.). 224p. 1995. pap. 16.95 (1-55110-380-X) Whitecap Bks.

Pacific People & Change. Max Quanchi. (Pacific in the Twentieth Century Ser.). (Illus.). 110p. (C). 1991. pap. text 19.95 (0-521-37627-0) Cambridge U Pr.

Pacific People & Place. Stephanie Fahey & Stephen Duggan. LC 93-26526. (Pacific in the Twentieth Century Ser.). (C). 1994. pap. 16.95 (0-521-37626-2) Cambridge U Pr.

Pacific People & Society. Martin Peake. (Pacific in the Twentieth Century Ser.). (Illus.). 122p. (C). 1991. pap. text 19.95 (0-521-37628-9) Cambridge U Pr.

***Pacific People & Their Food.** Ed. by A. B. Blakeney & L. O'Brian. (Illus.). 225p. 1998. 79.00 (1-891127-03-9) Am Assn Cereal Chem.

Pacific People Sing Out Strong. Ed. by William L. Coop. LC 81-22211. (Illus.). 99p. 1982. reprint ed. pap. 30.70 (0-608-01656-X, 206230800002) Bks Demand.

***Pacific Pioneers: Japanese Journeys to Hawaii & America, 1850-80.** John E. Van Sant. LC 99-6829. (Asian American Experience Ser.). 2000. 37.50 (0-252-02560-1) U of Ill Pr.

Pacific Plainsong, Vols. I-XIII. Pref. by Peter Michelson. LC 77-95077. (Illus.). 1978. pap. 4.95 (0-89681-000-3) Brillig Works.

Pacific Plant Areas, Vol. 5. Ed. by M. M. Van Balgooy. (Illus.). 260p. 1993. pap. 31.00 (90-71236-18-8, Pub. by Rijksherbarium) Balogh.

Pacific Prelude: A Journey to Samoa & Australasia, 1929. Margery Perham. LC 88-70563. 272p. 1988. 40.00 (0-7206-0683-7, Pub. by P Owen Ltd) Dufour.

Pacific Railways & Nationalism in the Canadian American Northwest, 1845-1873. Leonard B. Irwin. LC 69-10107. 246p. 1969. reprint ed. lib. bdg. 69.50 (0-8371-0495-5, IRPR, Greenwood Pr) Greenwood.

Pacific Raincoast: Environment & Culture of an American Eden, 1778-1900. Robert Bunting. LC 96-9655. (Development of Western Resources Ser.). 256p. 1996. 29.95 (0-7006-0805-2) U Pr of KS.

Pacific Region: Challenges to Policy & Theory. Ed. by Peter A. Gourevitch. (Annals Ser.: Vol. 505). 1989. 26.00 (0-8039-3580-3); pap. 17.00 (0-8039-3581-1) Sage.

Pacific Research Centres. 525p. 1989. text 310.00 (0-582-05287-4) Longman.

***Pacific Rim.** Elaine Pascoe. LC 98-28556. 128p. (YA). (gr. 7 up). 1999. 24.90 (0-7613-3015-1) TFC Bks NY.

Pacific Rim, Vol. 1. Jennifer Reselbach & Clay Hathorn. Ed. by Jennifer Haupt. Tr. by WA Academy of Languages Staff from ENG. LC 93-61377. (JPN., Illus.). 160p. 1994. text 49.95 (0-9634100-1-6) Wyndham Pubns.

Pacific Rim, Vol. 2. Jennifer Reselbach & Clay Hathorn. Ed. by Jennifer Haupt. Tr. by WA Academy of Languages Staff. LC 93-61377. (Illus.). 160p. 1994. text 49.95 (0-9634100-2-4) Wyndham Pubns.

Pacific Rim Cities in the World Economy Vol. 2: Comparative Urban & Community Research. Ed. by Michael P. Smith. 196p. 1989. pap. 21.95 (0-88738-735-7) Transaction Pubs.

Pacific Rim Design: Works of Fifteen Pacific Rim Graphic Designers. Wei Yew. (Illus.). 224p. 1991. 60.00 (0-9694432-4-2, Pub. by Quon Edns) Bks Nippan.

Pacific Rim Development: Integration & Globalisation in the Asia-Pacific Economy. Peter J. Rimmer. LC 97-158825. 240p. 1997. pap. 24.95 (1-86373-978-5, Pub. by Allen & Unwin Pty) Paul & Co Pubs.

Pacific Rim Discovery Student Resource Guide. Cranny & Gerrod. (HA - Social Studies Ser.). 1995. mass mkt. 41.95 (0-538-66135-6) S-W Pub.

Pacific Rim Energy Demand & Capital Requirements in the 1990s. Thomas R. McHale. 20p. 1992. pap. 10.00 (0-918714-32-X) Intl Res Ctr Energy.

Pacific Rim Explorer: The Outdoor Guide. Bruce Obee. (Illus.). 200p. 1994. pap. 14.95 (0-920620-77-9) Whitecap Bks.

Pacific Rim Fly Fishing: The Unrepentant Predator. Jim Repine. (Illus.). 64p. 1995. pap. 9.95 (1-57188-025-9) F Amato Pubns.

Pacific Rim Forestry - Bridging the World. (Convention Proceedings, 1991 Ser.). 606p. (Orig.). 1991. pap. 42.00 (0-939970-47-3, SAF 91-05) Soc Am Foresters.

Pacific Rim Region: A World Marketplace Approach Through Trade & Investment. Charles Dangler. 178p. 1992. 21.95 (0-8191-8629-5) Madison Bks UPA.

Pacific Rim Tourism. Ed. by Martin Oppermann. LC 97-34916. (A CAB International Publication). 288p. 1998. text 65.00 (0-85199-221-8) OUP.

Pacific Rim TransTech Conference Vol. II: International Ties, Management Systems, Propulsion Technology, Strategic Highway Research Program, ASCE 3rd International Conference, July 25-28. Ed. by Christ T. Hendrickson & Kumares C. Sinha. LC 93-5096. (Rise into the Future Ser.: Vol. 2). 576p. 1993. 38.00 (0-87262-972-4) Am Soc Civil Eng.

Pacific Rising: The Emergence of a New World Culture. Simon Winchester. (Illus.). 496p. (C). 1998. text 25.00 (0-7881-5591-1) DIANE Pub.

Pacific Salmon. Buffy Childerhose. pap. text 27.75 (0-88894-342-3) Sierra.

Pacific Salmon: From Alaska to California. A. M. Kosh. Ed. by Angela Tripp. (Illus.). 32p. (Orig.). 1994. pap. 10.95 (1-880352-28-1) Albion Pub.

Pacific Salmon: From Egg to Exit. Gordon Bell. (Illus.). 128p. (Orig.). 1996. pap. 12.95 (0-88839-379-2) Hancock House.

Pacific Salmon: Life Histories. L. Margolis & C. Guoot. (Illus.). 608p. 1991. text 95.00 (0-7748-0359-2) U of Wash Pr.

Pacific Salmon & Their Ecosystems: Status & Future Options. Robert J. Naiman et al. LC 96-38439. (Illus.). 512p. 1997. write for info. (0-412-98691-4) Kluwer Academic.

Pacific Salmon Fisheries: A Study of Irrational Conservation. James A. Crutchfield & Giulio Pontecorvo. LC 72-75180. (Resources for the Future Ser.). (Illus.). 220p. 1969. 19.95 (0-8018-1025-6) Johns Hopkins.

Pacific Shore Fishing. Michael R. Sakamoto. LC 84-16372. (Illus.). 272p. 1985. pap. 12.95 (0-8248-0892-4, Kolowalu Bk) UH Pr.

***Pacific Siege, 1 vol., Vol. 8.** Keith Douglas. (Seal Team Seven Ser.). 1999. mass mkt. 5.99 (0-425-16941-3) Berkley Pub.

Pacific Square-Riggers: Pictorial History of the Great Windships of Yesteryear. enl. rev. ed. Jim Gibbs. LC 87-61703. (Illus.). 224p. 1987. pap. 19.95 (0-88740-106-6) Schiffer.

Pacific States. William B. Logan et al. LC 96-40544. (Smithsonian Guides to Historic America Ser.). 496p. 1998. pap. 19.95 (1-55670-638-3) Stewart Tabori & Chang.

Pacific States Region: Grades 4-6. Ruth Emmel & Lynn Smith. (Illus.). 64p. 1997. pap., teacher ed. 6.95 (1-889369-15-2, TI0043) Teaching Ink.

Pacific Steamers. Will Lawson. (C). 1987. 96.00 (0-85174-245-9) St Mut.

Pacific Street. large type ed. Cecelia Holland. 430p. 1992. reprint ed. lib. bdg. 18.95 (1-56054-434-1) Thorndike Pr.

Pacific Strike. Lawrence Cortesi. (World at War Ser.). (Orig.). 1982. mass mkt. 2.95 (0-8217-1041-9, Zebra Kensgtn) Kensgtn Pub Corp.

Pacific Strike Playtesters' Guide. Tuesday Frase & Rob Irving. (Illus.). 96p. (Orig.). 1994. pap. 14.95 (0-929373-17-0) Origin Syst.

Pacific Symposium on Biocomputing, '96. 776p. 1995. 65.00 (981-02-2578-4) World Scientific Pub.

Pacific Tales. Louis Becke. LC 70-98561. (Short Story Index Reprint Ser.). 1977. 21.95 (0-8369-3135-1) Ayer.

Pacific Tales. Louis Becke. (Pacific Basin Ser.). 1998. pap. 31.00 (0-7103-0254-1, Pub. by Kegan Paul Intl) Col U Pr.

Pacific Theater see World War II at Sea: A Bibliography of Sources in English

Pacific Theater: Island Representations of World War II. Ed. by Geoffrey M. White & Lamont Lindstrom. LC 89-4862. (Pacific Islands Monographs: No. 8). (Illus.). 448p. 1989. text 38.00 (0-8248-1146-1) UH Pr.

***Pacific Troller: Life on the Northwest Fishing Grounds.** Francis E. Caldwell. LC 99-34. (Illus.). 152p. 1999. pap. 16.00 (1-55212-283-2) Trafford Pub.

Pacific Tunas & Billfishes: Atlas of Commercial Catches. FAO Staff. (Illus.). 82p. 1997. 96.00 (92-5-103901-1, F39011, Pub. by FAO) Bernan Associates.

Pacific Turning Point: The Solomons Campaign, 1942-1943. Charles W. Koburger. LC 95-5314. 192p. 1995. 52.95 (0-275-95236-3, Praeger Pubs) Greenwood.

Pacific 2010: Urbanisation in Polynesia John Connell & John P. Lea. LC 97-120511. (Pacific Policy Papers). viii, 161 p. 1995. write for info. (0-7315-1954-X) ANU Res Sch.

Pacific 2010: Urbanisation in Polynesia. P. A. McGavin & Australian National University Staff. LC 98-197170. (Pacific Policy Papers). viii, 84p. 1997. write for info. (0-7315-2364-4) ANU Res Sch.

Pacific Vortex. Clive Cussler. 288p. 1984. mass mkt. 7.99 (0-553-27632-8) Bantam.

Pacific Wanderer. Earl R. Hinz. Ed. by Julius M. Wilensky. LC 91-65015. (Illus.). 304p. 1991. pap. 22.95 (0-918752-13-2) Wescott Cove.

Pacific War. John Costello. LC 82-15054. 800p. 1982. pap. 18.95 (0-688-01620-0, Quil) HarperTrade.

Pacific War: Japan vs. the Allies, 130. Alan J. Levine. LC 94-39948. 216p. 1995. 55.00 (0-275-95102-2, Praeger Pubs) Greenwood.

Pacific War & Peace: Americans of Japanese Ancestry in Military Intelligence, 1941 to 1952. Ed. by Clifford Uyeda & Barry Saiki. 95p. 1992. pap. 10.00 (1-881506-02-9) Natl Japnse Am HS.

Pacific War Atlas. David Smurthwaite. (Illus.). 144p. 1995. 26.95 (0-8160-3285-8); pap. text 15.95 (0-8160-3286-6) Facts on File.

Pacific War Atlas, 1941-1945. David Smurthwaite. (Illus.). 132p. 1999. reprint ed. pap. text 20.00 (0-7881-6141-5) DIANE Pub.

P

An Asterisk (*) at the beginning of an entry indicates that the title is appearing for the first time.

Pacific War Dairy, Illustrated. abr. ed. James J. Fahey. Ed. by James J. Von Hardesty. LC 93-41536. (Illus.). 248p. 1994. pap. 29.95 (*0-295-97304-8*) U of Wash Pr.

Pacific War Diary. large type ed. James J. Fahey. 1993. 110.95 (*0-7838-1114-4*, G K Hall Lrg Type) Mac Lib Ref.

Pacific War Diary, 1942-1945. James J. Fahey. LC 92-21716. (Illus.). 426p. 1992. pap. 14.00 (*0-395-64022-9*) HM.

Pacific War Diary, 1942-1945. large type ed. James J. Fahey. LC 93-6723. 648p. 1993. lib. bdg. 22.95 (*1-56054-684-0*) Thorndike Pr.

Pacific War Encyclopedia, 2 vols. James F. Dunnigan & Albert A. Nofi. LC 97-15634. (Illus.). 800p. 1998. 125.00 (*0-8160-3439-7*, Checkmark) Facts on File.

***Pacific War Encyclopedia.** James F. Dunnigan & Albert A. Nofi. (Illus.). 800p. 2000. pap. 24.95 (*0-8160-4393-0*, Checkmark) Facts on File.

Pacific War, 1931-1945: A Critical Perspective on Japan's Role in World War II. Saburo Ienaga. Tr. by Frank Baldwin. LC 77-88768. 1979. pap. 14.00 (*0-394-73496-3*) Pantheon.

Pacific War Remembered: An Oral History Collection. John T. Mason, Jr. LC 86-5438. (Illus.). 373p. 1986. text 45.00 (*0-87021-522-1*) Naval Inst Pr.

Pacific War Revisited. Ed. by Gunter Bischof & Robert L. Dupont. LC 97-5178. (Eisenhower Center Studies on War & Peace). (Illus.). 200p. 1997. text 25.00 (*0-8071-2156-8*) La State U Pr.

***Pacific Warbird: Coming of Age in World War II.** Bob Hamilton. LC 99-89469. 1999. 25.00 (*0-7388-0289-1*); pap. 18.00 (*0-7388-0290-5*) Xlibris Corp.

Pacific Way: A Memoir. Ratu S. Mara. LC 96-25815. (Illus.). 298p. 1997. pap. text 15.00 (*0-8248-1893-8*) UH Pr.

Pacific Way: Regional Cooperation in the South Pacific. Michael Haas. LC 88-27515. (Illus.). 205p. 1989. 57.95 (*0-275-93121-8*, C3121, Praeger Pubs) Greenwood.

Pacific West. Jill C. Wheeler. LC 94-18504. (America, This Land Is Your Land Ser.). (J). 1994. lib. bdg. 15.98 (*1-56239-299-9*) ABDO Pub Co.

Pacific Whiting: Harvesting, Processing, Marketing, & Quality Assurance. Ed. by Gilbert Sylvia & Michael T. Morrissey. 1992. pap. text 10.00 (*1-881826-07-4*) OR Sea Grant.

Pacific Windows: Collected Poems of Roy K. Kiyooka. Roy K. Kiyooka. Ed. by Roy Miki. LC 98-138917. 320p. 1997. pap. 26.95 (*0-88922-378-5*, Pub. by Talonbks) Genl Dist Srvs.

Pacific World Directory. Intro. by Francisco T. Uludong. 365p. (Orig.). (C). 1988. pap. 50.00 (*0-318-23883-7*) Pac Info Bank.

Pacifica Radio: The Rise of an Alternative Network. Matthew Lasar. LC 98-19096. (American Subjects Ser.). (Illus.). 304p. 1999. 49.95 (*1-56639-660-3*) Temple U Pr.

***Pacifica Radio: The Rise of an Alternative Network.** rev. ed. Matthew Lasar. (American Subjects Ser.). (Illus.). 320p. 2000. pap. 19.95 (*1-56639-777-4*) Temple U Pr.

Pacification. Tran Dinh Tho. 219p. 1989. reprint ed. pap. 24.00 (*0-923135-07-3*) Dalley Bk Service.

Pacification: The American Struggle for Vietnam's Hearts & Minds. Richard A. Hunt. (C). 1998. pap. text 32.00 (*0-8133-3459-4*, Pub. by Westview) HarpC.

Pacification of Central America: Political Change in the Isthmus, 1987-1993. James Dunkerley. LC 93-46843. 180p. (C). 1994. pap. 19.00 (*0-86091-648-0*, Pub. by Verso) Norton.

Pacification of Melanesia. Ed. by Margaret Rodman & Matthew Cooper. LC 83-14551. (ASAO Monographs: No. 7). 246p. (C). 1983. reprint ed. lib. bdg. 52.00 (*0-8191-3404-X*) U Pr of Amer.

Pacification of the Psyche Training Manual. Oscar Ichazo. 81p. 1986. ring bd. 25.00 (*0-916554-11-2*) Arica Inst Pr.

Pacificorp & the Energy Group PLC: A Report on the Proposed Acquisition Monopolies & Mergers Commission Report, Command Paper 3816. (Command Papers (All) Ser.: No. 81011068). 1998. 40.00 (*0-10-138162-X*, HM8162X, Pub. by Statnry Office) Bernan Associates.

Pacifier Days: A Fond Farewell, Vol. 5. Stan Berenstain & Jan Berenstain. LC 98-73132. (Berenstain Bears Baby Board Books Ser.). (Illus.). 14p. (J). (ps). 1999. pap. 4.99 (*0-679-89336-9*) Random.

Pacifism & Citizenship: Can They Coexist? Ed. by Kenneth M. Jensen & Kimber M. Schraub. LC 91-7307. 1991. pap. text 10.95 (*1-878379-11-9*) US Inst Peace.

Pacifism & Revolution, 1916-18: The No-Conscription Fellowship: Pacifism & Revolution 1916-18, Vol. 14. Louis Greenspan et al. LC 95-6523. 720p. (C). (gr. 13). 1995. 190.00 (*0-415-09410-0*, C0233) Routledge.

Pacifism & the Jews: Studies of 20th Century Jewish Pacifists. Evelyn Wilcock. LC 94-165835. (Conflict & Peacemaking Ser.). 248p. (Orig.). 1994. pap. 16.95 (*1-869890-48-5*, Pub. by Hawthorn Press) Anthroposophic.

Pacifism As Pathology: Reflections on the Role of Armed Struggle in North America. Ryan Churchill & Ward Churchill. LC 99-160610. 170p. 1999. pap. 9.95 (*1-894037-07-3*) Arbeiter Ring.

Pacifism in Britain, 1914-1945: The Defining of a Faith. Martin Ceadel. (Oxford Historical Monographs). 1980. 55.00 (*0-19-821882-6*) OUP.

Pacifism in Europe to 1914. Peter Brock. LC 75-166362. (History of Pacifism Ser.: Vol. 1). 556p. 1972. reprint ed. pap. 175.50 (*0-7837-9305-7*, 206004500004) Bks Demand.

Pacifism in the Modern World. Ed. by Devere Allen. LC 72-137526. (Peace Movement in America Ser.). xvii, 278p. 1972. reprint ed. lib. bdg. 35.95 (*0-89198-053-9*) Ozer.

Pacifism in the Social Ethics of Walter George Muelder: With His Social Ethics. Michael D. Blackwell. LC 94-37006. 472p. 1995. text 109.95 (*0-7734-2283-8*) E Mellen.

Pacifism in the Twentieth Century: A Survey from Antiquity to the Outset of the Twentieth Century. Peter Brock & Nigel Young. LC 99-201765. 452p. 1999. pap. 29.95 (*0-8156-8125-9*) Syracuse U Pr.

Pacifist. Donald Wetzel. LC 85-63552. 208p. 1986. 22.00 (*0-932966-70-5*) Permanent Pr.

Pacifist Impulse in Historical Perspective. Ed. by Harvey L. Dyck. 448p. 1996. text 70.00 (*0-8020-0777-5*) U of Toronto Pr.

Pacifist in Trouble. William R. Inge. LC 75-152176. (Essay Index Reprint Ser.). 1977. 21.95 (*0-8369-2192-5*) Ayer.

Pacifist Option: The Moral Argument Against War in Eastern Orthodox Theology. Alexander F. Webster. LC 97-49358. 620p. 1998. 54.95 (*1-57309-244-4*) Intl Scholars.

Pacifist Option: The Moral Argument Against War in Eastern Orthodox Theology. Alexander F. C. Webster. LC 97-49358. 620p. 1999. pap. 31.50 (*1-57309-243-6*) Intl Scholars.

Pacifist Program. Richard B. Gregg. (C). 1983. pap. 4.00 (*0-87574-005-7*) Pendle Hill.

***Pacifists in Action: The Experience of the Friends Ambulance Unit in the Second World War.** Lyn Smith. LC 99-488460. (Illus.). 464p. 1999. pap. 53.00 (*1-85072-215-3*, Pub. by W Sessions) St Mut.

Pacifist's Progress: Norman Thomas & the Decline of American Socialism. Bernard K. Johnpoll. LC 87-8655. 344p. 1987. reprint ed. lib. bdg. 67.50 (*0-313-25895-3*, JBPP, Greenwood Pr) Greenwood.

Pacifying the Plains: General Alfred Terry & the Decline of the Sioux, 1866-1890, 17. John W. Bailey. LC 78-19300. (Contributions in Military History Ser.: No. 17). 236p. 1979. 59.95 (*0-313-20625-2*, BAT/, Greenwood Pr) Greenwood.

Pacing Mustang. rev. ed. Ernest Thompson Seton. (Illus.). 72p. (YA). (gr. 3-8). 1991. pap. 10.95 (*0-9623072-5-4*) S Ink WA.

Pacing the Moon. Joanne M. Riley. LC 85-4159. 72p. 1985. pap. 5.95 (*0-941608-04-2*) Chantry Pr.

Pacing the World: Construction in the Sculpture of David Rabinowitch. Whitney Davis et al. LC 96-30954. (Illus.). 310p. 1996. 50.00 (*0-916724-93-X*, Pub. by Harvard Art Mus); pap. 35.00 (*0-916724-91-3*, Pub. by Harvard Art Mus) HUP.

Pacing Yourself: Steps to Help Save Your Energy. Diane Christy & Carol A. Sarafconn. (Illus.). 128p. (Orig.). 1990. pap. 10.95 (*0-915708-31-0*) Cheever Pub.

Pacioli 2000 User Manual. Jose Hurtado. Ed. by Steve Beyer. (Illus.). (Orig.). 1990. write for info. (*0-929978-70-6*) M-USA Busn Systs.

Pack a Picnic, Vol. 4145. Kimberlee Graves. (Science Ser.). (Illus.). 16p. (J). (gr. k-1). 1997. pap. 2.75 (*1-57471-308-6*, 4145) Creat Teach Pr.

Pack, Band & Colony: The World of Social Animals. Judith Kohl & Herbert R. Kohl. LC 82-20951. (Illus.). 128p. (YA). (gr. 6 up). 1983. 13.95 (*0-374-35694-7*) FS&G.

Pack Goat. John Mionczynski. LC 92-16298. (Illus.). 147p. 1992. pap. 15.95 (*0-87108-828-2*) Pruett.

Pack It Up Vol. 1: A Book for the Contemporary Traveler. 3rd rev. ed. Anne McAlpin. LC 90-82758. (Illus.). 89p. (Orig.). 1996. pap. 7.95 (*0-9627263-0-3*) Flying Cloud.

Pack Lightly Sleep Naked: The Handbook to Make Travel Easier, Safer, & Sexier. (Illus.). 127p. 1996. pap. 11.95 (*0-9641477-3-4*, 682825Q) Rebecca Entpses.

Pack My Bag: A Self Portrait. Henry Green, pseud. LC 92-39386. 256p. 1993. 18.95 (*0-8112-1234-3*, Pub. by New Directions) Norton.

Pack of Autolycus or Strange & Terrible News of Ghosts: Broadside Ballads of the Years 1624-1693. Ed. by Hyder E. Rollins. LC 27-4308. (Illus.). 287p. 1969. 17.50 (*0-674-65125-1*) HUP.

Pack of Cards: Stories. Penelope Lively. 336p. 1999. reprint ed. pap. 13.00 (*0-8021-3624-9*, Grove) Grove-Atltic.

Pack of Liars. large type ed. Anne Fine. (Illus.). (J). 1998. pap. 16.95 (*0-7540-6023-3*, Galaxy Child Lrg Print) Chivers N Amer.

Pack of Lies. Barbara Davoll. (Christopher Churchmouse Classics Ser.). (Illus.). 24p. (J). (ps-2). 1989. 8.99 (*0-89693-497-7*, 6-1497, Victor Bks) Chariot Victor.

Pack of Lies. Barbara Davoll & Dennis Hockerman. (Christopher Churchmouse Ser.). (Illus.). 24p. (J). (ps-2). 1989. 11.99 incl. audio (*0-89693-030-0*, 3-1202, Victor Bks) Chariot Victor.

Pack of Lies. large type ed. Geraldine McCaughrean. 320p. (J). (gr. 3 up). 1990. 16.95 (*0-7451-1154-8*, G K Hall Lrg Type) Mac Lib Ref.

Pack of Lies: A Trilogy. Gilbert Sorrentino. LC 96-51793. 580p. (Orig.). 1997. reprint ed. pap. 14.95 (*1-56478-154-2*) Dalkey Arch.

Pack of Lies: Towards a Sociology of Lying. J. A. Barnes. LC 93-23455. (Themes in the Social Sciences Ser.). 214p. (C). 1994. pap. text 19.95 (*0-521-45978-8*) Cambridge U Pr.

Pack of Ragamuffins: A Grimm's Fairy Tale. Illus. by Carla Grillis. 24p. (J). 1997. 14.95 (*0-86315-232-5*, 2061, Pub. by Floris Bks) Anthroposophic.

***Pack of Thieves.** Richard Chesnoff. 2001. reprint ed. pap. 14.00 (*0-385-72064-5*, Anchor NY) Doubleday.

Pack of Thieves: How Hitler & Europe Plundered the Jews & Committed the Greatest Theft in History. Richard Z. Chesnoff. LC 99-33257. 320p. 1999. 27.50 (*0-385-48763-0*) Doubleday.

Pack of Two: The Intricate Bond Between Dogs & the People Who Love Them. Caroline Knapp. LC 98-4152. 272p. 1998. 21.95 (*0-385-31698-4*, Dial Pr) Dell.

***Pack of Two: The Intricate Bond Between Dogs & the People Who Love Them.** large type ed. Caroline Knapp. LC 98-46085. 1999. 27.95 (*0-7862-1726-X*) Thorndike Pr.

Pack of Two: The Intricate Bond Between People & Dogs. Caroline Knapp. 272p. 1999. pap. 12.95 (*0-385-31701-8*) Broadway BDD.

Pack of Wolves. Vasil Bykau. Tr. by Lynn Solotaroff from RUS. LC 80-2456. 192p. (YA). (gr. 7 up). 1981. 11.74 (*0-690-04114-4*); lib. bdg. 12.89 (*0-690-04115-2*) HarpC Child Bks.

Pack 1 - The Medieval World. Bea Stimpson et al. (First Quest Ser.). (Illus.). 112p. (J). (gr. 6-9). 1998. pap. 22.50 (*0-7487-3585-2*, Pub. by S Thornes Pubs) Trans-Atl Phila.

Pack Pride: An Illustrated History of North Carolina State Basketball. Douglas Herakovich. Ed. by Frank Weedon & Stuart Coman. (Illus.). 140p. 1994. 39.95 (*0-9646026-0-1*) Yesterdays Future.

Pack Rats Day & Other Poems. Jack Prelutsky. 1974. pap. 8.50 (*0-02-775050-7*) Macmillan.

Pack the Skillet: American Pioneer Cooking. Patricia B. Mitchell. 36p. 1997. pap. 4.00 (*0-925117-84-6*) Mitchells.

Pack Train & Transit Through Joseph's Domain. Ernest M. Foster. 77p. 1987. 14.95 (*0-87770-419-8*) Ye Galleon.

Pack Trip. Bonnie Bryant. (Saddle Club Ser.: No. 18). 144p. (J). (gr. 4-7). 1991. pap. 3.99 (*0-553-15928-3*) Bantam.

Pack Trip. Bonnie Bryant. (Saddle Club Ser.: No. 18). (J). (gr. 4-6). 1991. 9.09 (*0-606-00683-4*, Pub. by Turtleback) Demco.

Pack up My Backpack for a Critter County Fieldtrip: Children's Activity Book. Paula Bussard. Ed. by Judy Gillespie & Cathy Walker. (Nineteen Ninety-Six 50-Day Spiritual Adventure Ser.). (Illus.). 64p. (Orig.). (J). (gr. k-2). 1995. pap., wbk. ed. 6.00 (*1-879050-74-9*) Chapel of Air.

Pack up Your Gloomees in a Great Big Box: Then Sit on the Lid & Laugh! Barbara Johnson. 1993. pap. 10.99 (*0-8499-3364-1*) Word Pub.

Pack up Your Gloomees in a Great Big Box: Then Sit on the Lid & Laugh! Barbara Johnson. 1994. mass mkt. 4.99 (*0-8499-5071-6*) Word Pub.

Pack up Your Gloomees in a Great Big Box, Then Sit on the Lid & Laugh! see Guarda Tus Tristezas en una Caja Grande, Sientate Encimas y Rie!

Pack up Your Troubles. Maxie Dunnam. LC 92-42037. (Protestant Pulpit Exchange Ser.). 1993. pap. 8.95 (*0-687-09755-X*) Abingdon.

Pack up Your Troubles: 25 Years of Northern Ireland Cartoons. Illus. by Martyn Turner. 128p. 1996. pap. 14.95 (*0-85640-569-8*, Pub. by Blackstaff Pr) Dufour.

Pack Your Bag, Jesus Is Coming. McAllis. 1993. pap. 8.95 (*0-923417-42-7*) Shepherd Minst.

Pack Your Own Parachute: How to Survive Mergers, Takeovers, & Other Corporate Disasters. Paul Hirsch. LC 87-14388. 1987. pap. 9.57 (*0-201-12205-7*) Addison-Wesley.

Pack Your Own Parachute: The Three Secrets to Being Successful No Matter Who You Work For. Barbara A. Rudnicki. LC 96-92863. (Illus.). xx, 100p. (Orig.). 1996. pap. 11.95 (*1-890013-00-5*) Sebastian Prods.

Package see Set 11

Package & Label Design. Rockport Publishers Editors. (Motif Design Ser.). (Illus.). 160p. 1997. 44.99 incl. cd-rom (*1-56496-354-3*) Rockport Pubs.

Package & Label Design. Compiled by Rockport Publishers Editors. (Illus.). 1997. cd-rom 34.99 (*1-56496-403-5*) Rockport Pubs.

***Package & Label Design.** Ed. by Rockport Publishing Staff. (Illus.). 2000. pap. 19.99 (*1-56496-682-8*) Rockport Pubs.

Package & Label Design No. 2. Rockport Publishers Staff. 192p. 1999. 40.00 (*1-56496-567-8*) Rockport Pubs.

***Package Based Communications: Designing Packaging to Communicate with the Customer.** Robert Hamlin. 256p. 2001. 74.95 (*0-7506-4684-5*) Buttrwrth-Heinemann.

Package Design: JPDA Members Works Today, 1996, JPDA No. 6. Japan Package Design Society Staff. (Illus.). 360p. 1996. 89.95 (*4-89737-240-2*, Pub. by Rikuyo-Sha) Bks Nippan.

Package Design & Brand Identity: 38 Case Studies of Strategic Imagery for the Marketplace. Coleman et al. LC 94-230304. (Illus.). 160p. 1993. 34.95 (*1-56496-041-2*, 30533) Rockport Pubs.

Package Design in Japan, No. 6. Japan Package Design Association Staff. (Illus.). 280p. 1995. 115.00 (*4-89737-221-6*, Pub. by Rikuyo-Sha) Bks Nippan.

Package Design in Japan, Vol. 7. Ed. by Japan Package Design Assoc. Staff. (Illus.). 288p. 1997. 89.95 (*4-89737-261-5*, Pub. by PIE Bks) Bks Nippan.

***Package Design in Japan, Vol. 8.** Ed. by Japan Package Design Assoc. Staff. (Illus.). 296p. 1999. 95.00 (*4-89737-330-1*, Pub. by Rikuyo-Sha) Bks Nippan.

Package Design JPDA, 1997. Ed. by Japan Package Design Assoc. Staff. (Illus.). 288p. pap. 89.95 (*4-89737-303-4*, Pub. by Rikuyo-Sha) Bks Nippan.

Package Dyeing. Ed. by Wira Staff. 1984. 60.00 (*0-7855-1028-1*) St Mut.

Package Electrical Modeling, Thermal Modeling & Processing for GAAS Wireless Applications. Dean L. Monthei. LC 98-46068. (Electronic Packaging & Interconnects Ser.). xi, 234 p. 1999. write for info. (*0-7923-8364-8*) Kluwer Academic.

Package Evaluation: A Practical Guide to Selecting Application & Systems Software. Richard Sharland. 248p. 1991. text 72.95 (*1-85628-819-6*, Pub. by Avebury Technical) Ashgate Pub Co.

Package Holiday. Jules Verne. lib. bdg. 22.95 (*0-8488-2075-4*) Amereon Ltd.

Package Holiday. Jules Verne. 190p. 1977. 17.95 (*0-8464-1118-0*) Beekman Pubs.

Package in Hyperspace. Janet Asimov. (Illus.). (J). (gr. 4-7). 1988. 13.95 (*0-8027-6822-9*); lib. bdg. 14.85 (*0-8027-6823-7*) Walker & Co.

Package of Eight Recommended Books. (Nineteen Ninety-Eight Fifty-Day Spiritual Adventure Ser.). Date not set. 99.00 incl. VHS (*1-57849-068-5*) Mainstay Church.

Package Printing. Nelson R. Eldred. LC 92-30588. (Illus.). 532p. 1993. 99.50 (*0-9616302-5-6*, 630256) Jelmar Pub.

***Package X: Reference Copies of Federal Tax Forms & Instructions, 1999, Vol. 1.** 448p. 1999. per. 69.00 (*0-16-059162-7*) USGPO.

Packaged Air Conditioning. Bernard J. Hough. (Illus.). 112p. 1993. pap. text 34.95 (*0-7506-0920-6*) Buttrwrth-Heinemann.

***Packaged Air Conditioning Units in Saudi Arabia: A Strategic Entry Report, 1996.** Compiled by Icon Group International Staff. (Country Industry Report). (Illus.). 131p. 1999. ring bd. 1310.00 incl. audio compact disk (*0-7418-0599-5*) Icon Grp.

Packaged Cogeneration Systems. Richard K. Miller & Marcia E. Rupnow. LC 90-83915. (Survey on Technology & Markets Ser.: No. 108). 50p. 1991. pap. text 200.00 (*1-55865-131-4*) Future Tech Surveys.

***Packaged Educational Software in Australia: A Strategic Entry Report, 1995.** Compiled by Icon Group International Staff. (Illus.). 132p. 1999. ring bd. 1320.00 incl. audio compact disk (*0-7418-1545-1*) Icon Grp.

Packaged Japaneseness: Weddings, Business & Brides. Ofra Goldstein-Gidoni. LC 96-49251. (ConsumAsian Ser.). 1997. text 38.00 (*0-8248-1954-3*); pap. text 22.95 (*0-8248-1955-1*) UH Pr.

Packaged Repair Guides for Service Departments in Equipment Dealerships: Parts & Labor Are Included with Detailed Breakdowns. James P. Beal. Ed. by Lenore A. Beal. 65p. 1988. wbk. ed. 500.00 (*0-9634476-5-3*) Taking Care Of Busn.

Packaged Software in France: A Strategic Entry Report, 1997. Compiled by Icon Group International Staff. (Illus.). 136p. 1999. ring bd. 1360.00 incl. audio compact disk (*0-7418-0800-5*) Icon Grp.

Packaged Software in Germany: A Strategic Entry Report, 1996. Compiled by Icon Group International Staff. (Illus.). 99p. 1999. ring bd. 990.00 incl. audio compact disk (*0-7418-1149-9*) Icon Grp.

***Packaged Software in Taiwan: A Strategic Entry Report, 1999.** Compiled by Icon Group International. (Illus.). 117p. 1999. ring bd. 1170.00 incl. audio compact disk (*0-7418-1763-2*) Icon Grp.

Packages see BiB Television Programming Source Books, 1997-98

Packages & Groups: Multiplication & Division. Karen Economopoulos et al. Ed. by Priscilla C. Samii et al. LC 94-214862. (Investigations in Number, Data, & Space Ser.). (Illus.). 107p. (Orig.). 1994. pap., teacher ed. 22.95 (*0-86651-816-9*, DS21254) Seymour Pubns.

Packages for Transportation & Storage of Radioactive Materials. Ed. by R. W. Carlson. (PVP Ser.: Vol. 254). 116p. 1993. 40.00 (*0-7918-0981-1*, H00813) ASME.

Packaging. 379p. 1996. pap. 21.95 (*1-55512-254-X*) McGraw.

Packaging: Food Cycle Technology Source Books. UNIFEM Staff. 48p. (Orig.). 1996. pap. 15.50 (*1-85339-334-7*) Stylus Pub VA.

Packaging: Specifications, Purchasing, & Quality Control. 4th ed. Edmund A. Leonard. (Packaging & Converting Technology Ser.: Vol. 7). (Illus.). 304p. 1996. text 95.00 (*0-8247-9755-8*) Dekker.

Packaging & Environmental Issues. Ed. by Edward L. Rzepecki. (Illus.). (C). 1991. pap. text 65.00 (*0-9624229-4-0*) St Thomas Tech.

Packaging & Solid Waste Management. 5th ed. Laura H. Nelson & Deb Starkey. Ed. by Judith Thorman. 1996. pap. 5.00 (*1-55516-510-9*, 4656) Natl Conf State Legis.

Packaging & the Environment. Christine V. Johnson. Ed. by Katarina Stenstedt. (Real-World Mathematics Through Science Ser.). 90p. (Orig.). (YA). (gr. 6-8). 1994. pap. 18.95 (*0-201-86124-0*) Supplementary Div.

Packaging & the Environment. Susan E. Selke. LC 89-52136. 194p. 1990. 29.95 (*0-87762-595-6*) Technomic.

Packaging & the Environment: Alternatives, Trends & Solutions. rev. ed. Susan E. Selke. LC 94-61891. 250p. 1994. text 39.95 (*1-56676-104-2*) Technomic.

Packaging As an Effective Marketing Tool. Bill Stewart. 208p. 1995. 94.95 (*1-85802-099-9*, 020999) Technomic.

Packaging Challenges for the 80s: Regional Technical Conference, April 4-5, 1984, Cleveland, Ohio. Society of Plastics Engineers Staff. LC TA0455.P5. 177p. reprint ed. pap. 54.90 (*0-608-12924-0*, 202473000038) Bks Demand.

Packaging Design. Howard Milton. (Issues in Design Ser.). (Illus.). 104p. (C). 1991. pap. 29.95 (*0-85072-280-2*, Pub. by Design Council Bks) Ashgate Pub Co.

Packaging Design. Rotovision S. A. Staff. (Illus.). 160p. 1996. pap. text 35.00 (*0-8230-6502-2*) Watsn-Guptill.

***Packaging Design: Dutch Design, 2000 - 2001.** Ed. by Association of Dutch Design Staff. 80p. 2000. 29.95 (*90-72007-62-X*, Pub. by Bis NLD) Gingko Press.

***Packaging Design 8.** Ed. by B. Martin Pedersen. (Illus.). 256p. 2000. 70.00 (*1-888001-87-9*, Pub. by Graphis US) Watsn-Guptill.

Packaging Design Strategy. Bill Stewart. 199p. 1994. 84.95 (*1-85802-064-6*, 020646) Technomic.

Packaging Designer's Book of Patterns. Laszlo Roth & George Wybenga. (Illus.). 496p. 1991. pap. 46.95 (*0-442-00524-5*, VNR) Wiley.

***Packaging Designer's Book of Patterns.** rev. ed. Laszlo Roth & George L. Wybenga. 608p. 2000. pap. 54.95 (*0-471-38504-2*) Wiley.

An Asterisk (*) at the beginning of an entry indicates that the title is appearing for the first time.

Packaging Designer's Book of Patterns. 2nd ed. Laszlo Roth & George L. Wybenga. 496p. 1991. pap. 54.95 (*0-471-28411-4*, VNR) Wiley.

***Packaging Development Process: A Guide for Engineers & Project Managers.** Kristine DeMaria. LC 99-67777. 112p. 1999. pap. text 59.95 (*1-56676-801-2*) Technomic.

Packaging Drugs & Pharmaceuticals. Wilmer Jenkins & Kenton R. Osborn. LC 93-60377. 365p. 1993. 99.95 (*1-56676-014-3*) Technomic.

Packaging Equipment & Machinery in Thailand: A Strategic Entry Report, 1997. Compiled by Icon Group International Staff. (Illus.). 143p. 1999. ring bd. 1430.00 incl. audio compact disk (*0-7418-0881-1*) Icon Grp.

***Packaging Equipment in Egypt: A Strategic Entry Report, 1997.** Compiled by Icon Group International Staff. (Country Industry Report). (Illus.). 157p. 1999. ring bd. 1570.00 incl. audio compact disk (*0-7418-0288-0*) Icon Grp.

***Packaging Equipment in Peru: A Strategic Entry Report, 1998.** Compiled by Icon Group International Staff. (Illus.). 148p. 1999. ring bd. 1480.00 incl. audio compact disk (*0-7418-1535-4*) Icon Grp.

***Packaging Equipment in Sweden: A Strategic Entry Report, 1996.** Compiled by Icon Group International Staff. (Illus.). 97p. 1999. ring bd. 970.00 incl. audio compact disk (*0-7418-1233-9*) Icon Grp.

Packaging Equipment in Turkey: A Strategic Entry Report, 1997. Compiled by Icon Group International Staff. (Illus.). 161p. 1999. ring bd. 1610.00 incl. audio compact disk (*0-7418-0843-9*) Icon Grp.

Packaging Equipment Market in Russia: A Strategic Entry Report, 1998. Compiled by Icon Group International Staff. (Country Industry Report). (Illus.). 182p. 1999. ring bd. 1820.00 incl. audio compact disk (*0-7418-0201-5*) Icon Grp.

Packaging Foods with Plastics. William Jenkins & James Harrington. LC 90-71793. 342p. 1991. 49.95 (*0-87762-790-8*) Technomic.

***Packaging for Food Processing in India: A Strategic Entry Report, 1995.** Compiled by Icon Group International Staff. (Illus.). 194p. 1999. ring bd. 1940.00 incl. audio compact disk (*0-7418-1582-6*) Icon Grp.

***Packaging Forensics--Package Failure in the Courts.** Walter Stern. 240p. 2000. 65.00 (*0-913875-78-3*, 5783-N) Lawyers & Judges.

***Packaging in the Environment.** Geoffrey M. Levy. 273p. 1998. 140.00 (*0-8342-1347-8*) Aspen Pub.

Packaging in the Medical & Pharmaceutical Industries: Market Demands Specialized Products. 210p. 1992. 1495.00 (*1-56753-025-7*) Frost & Sullivan.

Packaging in Today's Society. Robert J. Kelsey. LC 89-50117. 149p. 1989. pap. 36.95 (*0-87762-605-7*) Technomic.

***Packaging Law Europe.** Patricia M. Bailey. LC 99-72611. (Ashgate Studies in Environmental Policy & Practice). 156p. 1999. text 61.95 (*1-85972-282-2*, Pub. by Avebry) Ashgate Pub Co.

***Packaging Machinery & Equipment in Argentina: A Strategic Entry Report, 1996.** Compiled by Icon Group International Staff. (Illus.). 153p. 1999. ring bd. 1530.00 incl. audio compact disk (*0-7418-1360-2*) Icon Grp.

***Packaging Machinery & Materials in Japan: A Strategic Entry Report, 1999.** Compiled by Icon Group International. (Illus.). 157p. 1999. ring bd. 1570.00 incl. audio compact disk (*0-7418-1856-6*) Icon Grp.

***Packaging Machinery for Food Processing in India: A Strategic Entry Report, 1999.** Compiled by Icon Group International. (Illus.). 194p. 1999. ring bd. 1940.00 incl. audio compact disk (*0-7418-1698-9*) Icon Grp.

Packaging Machinery in Chile: A Strategic Entry Report, 1997. Compiled by Icon Group International Staff. (Country Industry Report). (Illus.). 123p. 1999. ring bd. 1230.00 incl. audio compact disk (*0-7418-0202-3*) Icon Grp.

***Packaging Machinery in Colombia: A Strategic Entry Report, 1996.** Compiled by Icon Group International Staff. (Illus.). 184p. 1999. ring bd. 1840.00 incl. audio compact disk (*0-7418-1361-0*) Icon Grp.

Packaging Machinery Systems. H. Hughes. (Packaging & Converting Technology Ser.). Date not set. write for info. (*0-8247-0053-8*) Dekker.

Packaging Market in Netherlands: A Strategic Entry Report, 1998. Compiled by Icon Group International Staff. (Country Industry Report). (Illus.). 124p. 1999. ring bd. 1240.00 incl. audio compact disk (*0-7418-0528-6*) Icon Grp.

Packaging matters: Around the World Video Tape. Institute of Packaging Professionals Staff. (C). 1993. VHS 7.00 (*1-930268-13-0*) Packaging Prof.

Packaging of Australia: Politics & Culture Wars. Gregory Melleuish. LC 98-198373. 143p. 1997. pap. 24.95 (*0-86840-584-1*, Pub. by New South Wales Univ Pr) Intl Spec Bk.

Packaging of Electronic Systems: A Mechanical Engineering Approach. J. W. Dally. (C). 1989. text 73.00 (*0-07-015214-4*) McGraw.

Packaging of Healthcare Devices & Products Vol. IV: Fourth Annual Conference, Chicago, IL, November 17-18, 1994. 181p. 1994. ring bd. 59.95 (*1-56676-249-9*, 762499) Technomic.

Packaging of Healthcare Devices & Products Vol. V: Fifth Annual Healthpack Conference, Northbrook, IL, November 2-3, 1995. 142p. 1995. ring bd. 99.95 (*1-56676-401-7*, 764017) Technomic.

Packaging of Power Semiconductor Devices. C. A. Neugebauer et al. (Electrocomponent Science Monographs: Vol. 7). viii, 86p. 1986. text 75.00 (*2-88124-135-2*) Gordon & Breach.

***Packaging, Policy & the Environment.** Levy. LC 99-51890. 448p. 1999. 135.00 (*0-8342-1718-X*, 1718X) Aspen Pub.

Packaging Politics: Political Communications in Britain's Media Democracy. Bob Franklin. LC 94-2892. 272p. 1995. pap. text 19.95 (*0-340-55596-3*, B3558, Pub. by E A) OUP.

Packaging Prototypes. Edward Denison. 1999. pap. 35.00 (*2-88046-389-0*, Rotovision) Watsn-Guptill.

***Packaging Sector in Poland: A Strategic Entry Report, 1998.** Compiled by Icon Group International Staff. (Country Industry Report). (Illus.). 190p. 1999. ring bd. 1900.00 incl. audio compact disk (*0-7418-0289-9*) Icon Grp.

Packaging Sourcebook, 1998: North American Edition. Ed. by Holly Mogil. 1328p. 1998. pap. 375.00 (*1-888576-21-9*) North Am Pub Co.

Packaging Sourcebook 2000. 5th ed. Ed. by Lisa A. Denshuick. 1999. pap. 349.00 (*1-888576-58-8*) North Am Pub Co.

Packaging Strategy: Meeting the Challenge of Changing Times. Arthur W. Harckham. LC 88-50947. 180p. 1989. 69.95 (*0-87762-586-7*) Technomic.

Packaging Strategy: Winning the Consumer. Mona Doyle. LC 96-60500. 185p. 1996. text 39.95 (*1-56676-298-7*) Technomic.

Packaging the New South. (Illus.). 112p. 1978. pap. 3.00 (*0-943810-23-X*) Southern Exposure.

Packaging the Presidency: A History & Criticism of Presidential Campaign Advertising. 3rd ed. Kathleen H. Jamieson. (Illus.). 598p. 1996. pap. text 18.95 (*0-19-508942-1*) OUP.

Packaging Trends in World Semiconductor IC Markets: SMT, TAB & MCM Forge Ahead in the 1990s. 216p. 1992. 1495.00 (*1-56753-005-2*) Frost & Sullivan.

Packaging User's Handbook. Frank A. Paine. 1991. text 139.95 (*0-442-30283-5*) Chapman & Hall.

Packaging with Plastics. Ed. by Paul F. Bruins. LC 72-78922. x, 212p. 1974. text 249.00 (*0-677-12200-4*) Gordon & Breach.

Packard. Dennis Adler. LC 98-8468. (Illus.). 156p. 1998. 39.95 (*0-7603-0482-3*) MBI Pubg.

Packard. 5th ed. George Damann et al. LC 96-14073. (Illus.). 448p. 1996. 44.95 (*0-7603-0104-2*, Crestline Pub) MBI Pubg.

Packard: The Complete Story. Michael G. Scott. (Illus.). 208p. (Orig.). 1985. 24.95 (*0-8306-2108-3*, 2108) McGraw-Hill Prof.

Packard Motor Cars 1946-1958 Photo Archive: Photographs from the Detroit Public Library's National Automotive History Collection. Ed. by Mark A. Patrick. LC 95-82099. (Photo Archive Ser.). (Illus.). 128p. 1996. pap. 29.95 (*1-882256-45-X*) Iconografix.

Packard Motor Cars 1935-1942 Photo Archive: Photographs from the Detroit Public Library's National Automotive History Collection. Ed. by Mark A. Patrick. LC 95-82098. (Photo Archive Ser.). (Illus.). 128p. 1996. pap. 29.95 (*1-882256-44-1*) Iconografix.

Packard the Pride. deluxe ed. J. M. Fenster. LC 89-84. (Illus.). 208p. 1989. 225.00 (*0-685-28294-5*, 3-AQ-0056) Auto Quarterly.

Packards at Speed. unabridged ed. Robert J. Neal. LC 95-78246. (Illus.). 352p. 1995. 65.00 (*0-9647483-0-4*) Aero-Marine Hist Pubng.

Packe of Spanish Lyes, Sent Abroard in the World. LC 77-38224. (English Experience Ser.: No. 487). 1972. reprint ed. 20.00 (*90-221-0487-7*) Walter J Johnson.

Packed Distillation Columns. Ed. by Equipment Testing Procedures Committee Staff. 54p. 1991. pap. text 65.00 (*0-8169-0498-7*, E-28) Am Inst Chem Eng.

Packed Towers: In Processing & Environmental Technology. Reinhard Billet. LC 94-45292. 383p. 1995. 250.00 (*3-527-28616-0*, Wiley-VCH) Wiley.

Packer. Jack Rudman. (Career Examination Ser.: C-1647). 1994. reprint ed. pap. 19.95 (*0-8373-1647-2*) Nat Learn.

Packer Chronicles Vol. 1: Waiting for the Pack to Come Back... Lyle Lahey. Ed. by Carol H. Lahey. LC 97-94198. (Illus.). 224p. 1997. pap. 14.95 (*0-9659774-0-4*) Green Bay News.

***Packer Fan(atic) Handbook.** Daniel Edelstein. (Illus.). 84p. 1999. pap. 9.95 (*1-878569-63-5*) Badger Bks Inc.

Packer Hall of Faith. Steve Rose. (Leap of Faith Ser.). 1998. pap. text 14.95 (*0-9666819-0-8*) Winners Success Netwrk.

Packer Legends in Facts: Stats, Rosters, Team History & Complete Team Photos of the Green Bay Packers, 1919-1993. 75th rev. ed. Eric Goska. LC 98-130251. (Illus.). x, 388p. 1993. write for info. (*0-937816-35-3*) Tech Data.

Packer Legends in Facts: 75th Year in NFL Anniversary Edition. Eric Goska. LC 98-130252. (Illus.). 416p. 1995. pap. 29.95 (*0-937816-37-X*) Tech Data.

Packer Tapes: My Thirty-Two Years with the Green Bay Packers. Domenic Gentile & Gary D'Amato. LC 95-23837. (Illus.). 176p. 1995. pap. 12.95 (*1-879483-28-9*) Prairie Oak Pr.

***Packer Way.** Ron Wolf & Paul Attner. 288p. 1999. pap. 14.95 (*0-312-24320-0*) St Martin.

Packer Way: Nine Stepping Stones to Building a Winning Organization. Ron Wolf & Paul Attner. LC 98-8576. 260p. 1998. 23.95 (*0-312-19312-2*) St Martin.

Packers. Steve Cameron. 1996. pap. text 23.95 (*0-87833-133-6*) Taylor Pub.

Packers vs. Bears. Glenn Swain. (Illus.). 408p. (Orig.). 1996. pap. 19.95 (*0-912880-08-2*) Charles Pub.

Packet. Mark Dunster. 18p. (Orig.). (YA). (gr. 9-12). 1996. pap. 5.00 (*0-89642-335-2*) Linden Pubs.

***Packet: A Collection of Patterns, Articles & Essays...** Mark Tully. (Illus.). 48p. 1998. pap. 9.95 (*1-893832-00-7*) Ballind.

Packet: Speed, More Speed & Applications. Ed. by Rich Roznoy. LC 97-180549. 1997. pap. 15.00 (*0-87259-605-2*) Am Radio.

Packet Communication. Robert Metcalfe. Ed. by Peter H. Salus. LC 96-204442. (Computer Classics Revisited Ser.). 224p. 1996. 39.95 (*1-57398-033-1*) Annabooks.

Packet Communications. Fraidoon Mazda. (Telecommunication Ser.). (Illus.). 254p. 1996. pap. text 32.95 (*0-240-51455-6*, Focal) Buttrwrth-Heinemann.

Packet for Classroom Teachers about Alternatives to Violence. Ed. by Danene M. Bender. (Illus.). 108p. 1996. pap. text, teacher ed. 9.95 (*0-9619819-5-4*) Peace Grows.

Packet Guide Clinical Exam. Epstein. 1997. 16.95 (*0-7234-2577-9*) Mosby Inc.

Packet Made Easy. Buck Rogers. (Illus.). 72p. 1992. pap. 9.95 (*1-891237-15-2*, MFJ-32) MFJ Ent.

Packet of Rhymes: Scottish & English Nursery Rhymes. deluxe limited ed. Illus. by Joyce Alexander. (J). 1989. pap. 15.00 (*0-937686-12-3*) Turtles Quill.

Packet Radio for BEMS Communications: An Investigation & Demonstration. M. K. White & A. K. Bromley. 1990. 120.00 (*0-86022-262-4*, Pub. by Build Servs Info Assn) St Mut.

Packet Radio Handbook. Jonathan L. Mayo. (Illus.). 224p. 1987. pap. 14.95 (*0-8306-2722-7*, NO. 2722) McGraw-Hill Prof.

Packet Radio Handbook. 2nd ed. Jonathan L. Mayo. (Illus.). 240p. 1989. pap. 16.95 (*0-8306-3222-0*) McGraw-Hill Prof.

Packet Radio, What? Why? How? Articles & Information on General Packet Radio Topics. Ed. by Greg Jones. 132p. 1996. pap. 12.00 (*0-9644707-0-5*) Tucson Amat Pack Rad.

Packet Switching. 2nd ed. Roy D. Rosner. 1989. text. write for info. (*0-442-31803-0*, VNR) Wiley.

Packet Switching: Tomorrow's Communications Today. Roy D. Rosner. (Illus.). 371p. 1982. text 79.95 (*0-534-97965-3*, VNR) Wiley.

Packet Switching Evolution from Narrowband to Broadband ISDN. Michel Smouts. (Telecommunications Library). 213p. 1992. text 65.00 (*0-89006-542-X*) Artech Hse.

Packet Video: Modeling & Signal Processing. Naohisa Ohta. LC 93-38080. 207p. 1994. 79.00 (*0-89006-519-5*) Artech Hse.

***Packet Video Communications over ATM Networks.** K. R. Rao & Z. S. Bojkovic. LC 99-44156. (Illus.). 420p. 1999. 65.00 (*0-13-011518-5*) P-H.

Packetradio Operators Handbook. Buck Rogers. (Illus.). 121p. (Orig.). 1992. pap. 12.95 (*1-891237-09-8*, MFJ-3036) MFJ Ent.

Packets & Protocols. (Illus.). 90p. (Orig.). (C). 1994. pap. text 30.00 (*0-7881-1424-7*) DIANE Pub.

Packhorse Librarians. Kathi Appelt. (J). 16.95 (*0-06-029135-4*, Wm Morrow); lib. bdg. 16.89 (*0-06-029244-X*, Wm Morrow) Morrow Avon.

Packing & Filling Problems - Student's Manual: Molding Materials & Process Troubleshooting, Module Four, Lesson 4. (Illus.). 1997. pap., student ed. write for info. (*1-58677-037-3*) Polymer Train.

Packing Book: Secrets of the Carry-On Traveler. 3rd rev. ed. Judith Gilford. LC 98-204143. (Illus.). 237p. 1998. pap. 8.95 (*1-58008-021-9*) Ten Speed Pr.

Packing by the Book: How to Pack - What to Pack. R. J. Nyks. Ed. by R. Barns & E. Krijgsman. (Illus.). 250p. 1997. pap. 17.95 (*0-9657337-0-X*) Inside Info.

Packing Effects on the Part - Student's Manual Pt. I: Controlling Pressures, Lesson 3. (Illus.). 1997. pap., student ed. write for info. (*1-58677-054-3*) Polymer Train.

Packing for a Picnic. Lorraine Long & Mary Lou Roberts. (Illus.). 32p. (J). (ps-1). 1998. pap. 3.99 (*1-893919-03-X*, 004, Sing Read Ad) Peri Pk Ed Prodn.

Packing for Heaven. Debra Delp. Ed. by Suzanne W. Zoglio. (Illus.). 32p. (Orig.). (J). (ps-k). 1991. pap. text 8.95 (*0-941668-03-7*) Tower Hill Pr.

Packing for the Big Trip: Enhancing Your Life Through Awareness of Death. Charlie Walton. Ed. by Eugene D. Wheeler. LC 96-45354. 112p. (Orig.). 1997. pap. 9.95 (*0-934793-63-8*) Pathfinder CA.

Packing Fraction: And other Tales of Science & Imagination. Ed. by Julie E. Czerneda. (Illus.). 128p. (YA). (gr. 7-10). 1998. pap. 4.95 (*1-895579-89-9*) Trifolium Inc.

Packing Heat. Karina Moore. (Black Lace Ser.). 1999. mass mkt. 6.95 (*0-352-33356-1*) Virgin Bks.

Packing Industry. Institute of American Meat Packers Staff & School of Commerce & Administration of the Univers. LC 75-22796. (America in Two Centuries Ser.). (Illus.). 1976. reprint ed. 33.95 (*0-405-07667-3*) Ayer.

Packing Iron: Gunleather of the Frontier West. Richard C. Rattenbury. Ed. by Janet Begley. LC 93-17019. (Illus.). 218p. 1993. 45.00 (*0-939549-08-5*) ZON Intl Pub.

Packing It In. David Rees. 160p. (Orig.). 1992. pap. 13.95 (*1-873741-07-3*, Pub. by Millvres Bks) LPC InBook.

Packing of Particles. K. Bagnal et al. (Handbook of Powder Technology Ser.: 6). 150p. 1979. pap. 116.50 (*0-444-41041-4*) Elsevier.

Packing up for Paradise: Selected Poems, 1946-1996. James Broughton. Ed. by Jim Cory. LC 97-41887. 331p. 1997. 27.50 (*1-57423-053-0*); pap. 16.00 (*1-57423-052-2*) Black Sparrow.

Packing up for Paradise: Selected Poems, 1946-1996. limited ed. James Broughton. Ed. by Jim Cory. LC 97-41887. 331p. 1997. 35.00 (*1-57423-054-9*) Black Sparrow.

***Packing up the Past.** Sebastian Junyent. Ed. by Phyllis Zattin. Tr. by Ana Mengual from SPA. LC 99-71173. (Contemporary Spanish Plays Ser.: Vol.. 18).Tr. of Hay que Deshacer la Casa. (Illus.). 64p. (C). 2000. pap. 8.00 (*1-888463-10-4*) Estreno.

***Packinghouse Daughter: A Memoir.** Cheri Register. LC 00-40214. 2000. pap. write for info. (*0-87351-392-4*) Minn Hist.

Packinghouse Worker's Fight for Justice: The Mark Curtis Story. Naomi Craine. (FRE.). 83p. pap. 6.00 (*0-87348-817-2*) Pathfinder NY.

Packinghouse Worker's Fight for Justice: The Mark Curtis Story. Naomi Craine. (Illus.). 83p. 1996. pap. 6.00 (*0-87348-844-X*) Pathfinder NY.

Packings & Stationary Phases in Chromatographic Techniques. Klaus K. Unger. (Chromatographic Science Ser.: Vol. 47). (Illus.). 840p. 1989. text 255.00 (*0-8247-7940-1*) Dekker.

Packrat Middens: The Last 40,000 Years of Biotic Change. Ed. by Julio L. Betancourt et al. LC 89-38454. 469p. 1990. 67.50 (*0-8165-1115-2*) U of Ariz Pr.

Paclitaxel in Cancer Treatment, No. 8. Ed. by William P. McGuire & Erick K. Rowinsky. LC 95-2352. (Basic & Clinical Oncology Ser.: Vol. 8). (Illus.). 368p. 1995. text 145.00 (*0-8247-9307-2*) Dekker.

Paco & Ana Learn to Share see Paco y Ana Aprenden A Compartir

Paco & Ana Learn to Trust God see Paco y Ana Aprenden A Confiar en Dios

Paco de Lucia: A New Tradition for the Flamenco Guitar. Paco Sevilla. LC 95-92225. 202p. (Orig.). 1995. pap. 19.95 (*0-9646374-0-5*) Sevilla Pr.

Paco de Lucia & Family: The Master Plan. D. E. Pohren. 1995. pap. 11.95 (*0-933224-62-1*, 1140) Bold Strummer Ltd.

Paco Hacia el Paraiso: Dichos de Muhammad el Enviado de Dios. 2nd rev. ed. Ed. by M. M. Alazami. Tr. by Ahmad M. Safi from ARA. LC 94-5296. (SPA.). 304p. (Orig.). 1995. pap. 6.95 (*0-915957-18-3*) amana pubns.

Paco Pumpkin. James Haas. Ed. by Mary C. Kendzia. (Illus.). 32p. (Orig.). (J). 1992. pap. 4.95 (*0-89622-529-1*) Twenty-Third.

Paco y Ana Aprenden A Compartir. Carol Martinez. (Paco y Ana Aprenden Serie).Tr. of Paco & Ana Learn to Share. (SPA., Illus.). 34p. (J). 1996. pap. text 2.50 (*0-311-38593-1*, Edit Mundo) Casa Bautista.

Paco y Ana Aprenden A Confiar en Dios. Carol Martinez. (Paco y Ana Aprenden Serie).Tr. of Paco & Ana Learn to Trust God. (SPA., Illus.). 32p. (J). 1996. pap. text 2.50 (*0-311-38594-X*, Edit Mundo) Casa Bautista.

Paco y Ana Aprenden Acerca de la Amabilidad: Frankie & Ann Learn about Kindness. Carol Martinez. (Paco y Ana Aprenden Ser.). (SPA., Illus.). 32p. (Orig.). (J). (gr. 2-4). 1988. pap. 2.50 (*0-311-38590-7*, Edit Mundo) Casa Bautista.

Paco y Ana Aprenden Acerca de la Amistad: Frankie & Ann Learn about Friendship. Carol Martinez. (Paco y Ana Aprenden Ser.). (SPA., Illus.). (Orig.). (J). (gr. 2-4). 1988. pap. 2.50 (*0-311-38589-3*, Edit Mundo) Casa Bautista.

Paco y Ana Aprenden Acerca de la Honradez: Frankie & Ann Learn about Honesty. Carol Martinez. (Paco y Ana Aprenden Ser.). (SPA., Illus.). 32p. (Orig.). (J). (gr. 2-4). 1988. pap. 2.50 (*0-311-38587-7*, Edit Mundo) Casa Bautista.

Paco y Ana Aprenden Acerca de la Obediencia: Frankie & Ann Learn about Obedience. Carol Martinez. (Paco y Ana Aprenden Ser.). (SPA., Illus.). 32p. (Orig.). (J). (gr. 2-4). 1988. pap. 2.50 (*0-311-38588-5*, Edit Mundo) Casa Bautista.

Paco Y Ana Aprenen Atener Dominio Propio. Carol Martinez. (Paco y Ana Aprenden Ser.).Tr. of Frankie & Ann Learn Self Control. (SPA., Illus.). 32p. (J). 1995. pap. 2.50 (*0-311-38591-5*, Edit Mundo) Casa Bautista.

Paco Yana Aprenden Atener Valor. Carol Martinez. (Paco y Ana Aprenden Ser.).Tr. of Frankie & ann Learn to Have Courage. (SPA., Illus.). 32p. (J). 1995. 2.50 (*0-311-38592-3*, Edit Mundo) Casa Bautista.

PACOMS '96: Proceedings of the 4th Pacific-Asia Offshore Mechanics Symposium, 1996. Ed. by Sae K. Oh. (Illus.). 325p. 1996. pap. 60.00 (*1-880653-27-3*) ISOPE.

Paco's Garden see Huerto de Paco

Paco's Garden. Lois Podoshen. (Books for Young Learners). (Illus.). 12p. (J). (gr. k-2). 1999. pap. text 5.00 (*1-57274-235-6*) R Owen Pubs.

Pacovska's Art Pack, Vol. 1. Kveta Pacovska. (J). 1996. pap. text 5.99 (*1-55858-533-8*, Pub. by North-South Bks NYC) Chronicle Bks.

***PACS: A Guide to the Filmless Revolution.** Keith J. Dreyer et al. (Illus.). 500p. 1999. 79.95 (*1-929987-05-6*) Login Brothers Bk Co.

PACS: Basics Principles & Applications. H. K. Huang. LC 98-23684. 519p. 1998. pap. 98.50 (*0-471-25393-6*, Wiley-Liss) Wiley.

PACS: Picture Archiving & Communication Systems in Biomedical Imaging. H. K. Huang. 489p. 1996. 179.00 (*0-471-18607-4*) Wiley.

PACs Americana. 1248p. 1991. 250.00 (*0-685-48872-1*) Sunshine Serv.

PACs Americana: The Directory of Political Action Committees & Their Interests. 2nd ed. Ed. by Edward Roeder. 1986. 250.00 (*0-942236-01-7*) Sunshine Serv.

***PACS Design & Evaluation.** Ed. by G. James Blaine & Steven C. Horii. 460p. 1999. pap. text 111.00 (*0-8194-3134-6*) SPIE.

Pact: A Love Story. Jodi Picoult. LC 97-36432. 384p. 1998. 24.00 (*0-688-15812-9*, Wm Morrow) Morrow Avon.

***Pact: A Love Story.** Jodi Picoult. LC 97-36432. 400p. 1999. reprint ed. pap. 13.00 (*0-688-17052-8*, Wm Morrow) Morrow Avon.

***Pact: A Novel.** Walter J. Roers. 151p. 2000. pap. 21.95 (*0-89823-204-X*) New Rivers Pr.

Pact: My Friendship with Isak Dinesen. Thorkild Bjornvig. Tr. by Ingvar Schousboe & William J. Smith from DAN. LC 83-9335. 183p. 1983. pap. 56.80 (*0-7837-8513-5*, 204932200011) Bks Demand.

PACT: Positive Adolescent Choices Training: A Model for Violence Prevention Groups with African American Youth. W. Rodney Hammond & Betty R. Yung. LC 94-74959. 142p. (Orig.). 1995. pap. text 17.95 (*0-87822-359-2*, 4805) Res Press.

***Pact at Star's Crossing.** Darrell Pruett. LC 00-24222. 224p. 1999. pap. 13.95 (*0-87714-503-2*) Denlingers.

PACT, 95: Working Conference on Parallel Architectures & Compilation Techniques. 324p. 1995. pap. text 46.00 (*0-89791-745-6*, 417951) Assn Compu Machinery.

Pact with Bruno. David O'Neal. 248p. 1998. pap. 6.50 (*0-9660851-1-6*) Pac Coast Pr.

Pactane Sunt Servanda? Reiner Osswald. Ed. by Hans Hattenbauer. (Rechtshistorische Reihe Ser.: Vol. 175). XXI, 473p. 1998. pap. 67.95 (*3-631-32043-4*) P Lang Pubng.

Pacto Con El Diablo. Jack Higgins. 1998. pap. text 9.95 (*84-08-02722-0*) Planeta.

Pacto de Gracia. William Hendriksen. (SPA.). 81p. pap. 3.25 (*1-55883-084-7*, 6704-4510C) Libros Desafio.

Pacto de Holcroft. Robert Ludlum. Orig. Title: Holcroft Covenant. 1999. 11.95 (*84-01-49929-1*) Plaza.

Pacto Muy Especial (A Very Special Agreement) Sandra Field. (Bianca Ser.). (SPA.). 1998. per. 3.50 (*0-373-33443-5*, 1-33443-2) Harlequin Bks.

Pactolus Prime. Albion W. Tourgee. LC 68-57555. (Muckrakers Ser.). 359p. reprint ed. lib. bdg. 52.00 (*0-8398-1969-2*) Irvington.

Pacts & Treaties Series, 4 vols. Susan Gold. Incl. Arms Control. LC 96-50311. (Illus.). 128p. (J). (gr. 5-8). 1997. lib. bdg. 21.40 (*0-8050-4812-X*); Human Rights. LC 96-40952. (Illus.). 128p. (J). (gr. 5-8). 1997. lib. bdg. 21.40 (*0-8050-4811-1*); Indian Treaties. LC 96-47621. (Illus.). 128p. (J). (gr. 5-8). 1997. lib. bdg. 21.40 (*0-8050-4813-8*); Land Pacts. LC 96-44967. (Illus.). 128p. (J). (gr. 5-8). 1995. lib. bdg. 21.40 (*0-8050-4810-3*); 57.54 (*0-8050-4814-6*) TFC Bks NY.

Pacts with the Devil: A Chronicle of Sex, Blasphemy & Liberation. 2nd ed. S. Jason Black & Christopher S. Hyatt. (Illus.). 256p. (Orig.). 1993. pap. 14.95 (*1-56184-058-0*) New Falcon Pubns.

PACU Manual. Andrew Rosenberg. 300,p. 1998. text 49.00 (*0-397-58791-0*) Lppncott W & W.

PACU Policy & Procedure Guideline Manual: Policy & Procedure Guideline Manual. Diane I. Howery. 148p. 1994. spiral bd. 105.00 (*1-879575-08-6*) Acad Med Sys.

***Pad.** Collins. 402p. 2000. 120.00 (*0-471-87736-0*) Wiley.

***Pad: The Guide to Ultra-Living.** Matt Maranian. LC 99-40880. (Illus.). 208p. 2000. 24.95 (*0-8118-2653-8*) Chronicle Bks.

***Pad Process Guide; The Pad Process Toolbox; Performance, Analysis & Development, 2 vols., Set.** Carlene Reinhart. (Illus.). 106p. 1999. pap. 125.00 (*0-9672850-1-1*) Manta Press.

Pada Index & Reverse Pada Index to Early Jain Canons: The Ayaranga, Suyagada, Uttarajjhaya, Dasaveyaliya & Isibhasiyaim. Compiled by Moriichi Yamazaki & Yumi Ousaka. 538p. 1996. pap. 30.00 (*4-333-01763-7*, Pub. by Kosei Pub Co) Tuttle Pubng.

Padaeng Chronicle & the Jengtung State Chronicle Translated. Sao Saimong Mangrai. LC 80-67342. (Michigan Papers on South & Southeast Asia: No. 19). (Illus.). xxiv, 301p. (C). 1981. 19.95 (*0-89148-020-X*) Ctr S&SE Asian.

***Padagogik - Politik - Asthetik: Paradigmenwechsel Um '68.** Axel Jansa. (GER.). 290p. 1999. 49.00 (*3-631-33088-X*) P Lang Pubng.

Padagogische Aspekte der Vormundschaftsarbeit Mit Erwachsenen. Petra Hulshoff. vi, 306p. 1989. write for info. (*3-487-09245-X*) G Olms Pubs.

Padagogische Fallstudien. Karl Binneberg. (GER., Illus.). 272p. 1997. 45.95 (*3-631-32368-9*) P Lang Pubng.

Padagogische Grenzganger in Europa. Elmar Lechner. 451p. 1997. 76.95 (*3-631-30798-5*) P Lang Pubng.

***Padagogische Professionalisierung Im Bundesheer: Dokumentation und Reflexion Des Padak-Sonderstudienganges Wehrpadagogisches Management.** Rudolf Egger & Heinz Florian. (GER.). 216p. 1999. 37.95 (*3-631-34713-8*) P Lang Pubng.

Padagogische Schriften: Mit Einer Einfuhrung Herausgegeben von Phillip S. McKnight. Johann K. Wezel. (GER., Illus.). 246p. 1996. 44.95 (*3-631-47890-9*) P Lang Pubng.

P

Padarr Citybook. (Bloodshadows Ser.). 18.00 (*0-87431-385-6*, 33004) West End Games.

Padataditaka of Syamilaka, Pt. 1. Ed. by G. H. Schokker & P. J. Worsley. LC 67-84054. 1975. lib. bdg. 135.00 (*90-277-0690-5*) Kluwer Academic.

Padataditaka of Syamilaka, Pt. 2. Ed. by G. H. Schokker & P. J. Worsley. LC 67-84054. 1975. lib. bdg. 135.00 (*90-277-0425-2*) Kluwer Academic.

Paddies. J. Patrick Mulrooney. LC 97-78449. 260p. 1999. pap. 16.50 (*0-88739-206-7*) Creat Arts Bk.

Paddies. Patrick Mulrooney. LC 97-78449. 260p. 1999. 24.50 (*0-88739-194-X*) Creat Arts Bk.

Paddington, 5 vols., Set. Michael Bond. 1992. boxed set 16.25 (*0-440-36042-0*) Dell.

Paddington Abroad, 001. Michael Bond. LC 72-2753. (Paddington Ser.). (Illus.). 128p. (J). (gr. 2-5). 1973. 16.00 (*0-395-14331-4*) HM.

Paddington at Large see Hilarious Adventures of Paddington

Paddington at Large. rev. ed. Michael Bond. LC 63-14525. (Paddington Ser.). (Illus.). 144p. (J). (gr. 2-5). 1998. 15.00 (*0-395-91294-6*) HM.

Paddington at the Seashore. Michael Bond. (Illus.). 28p. (J). (ps). 1992. 3.95 (*0-694-00397-2*) HarpC Child Bks.

Paddington at Work see Hilarious Adventures of Paddington

Paddington at Work, 001. Michael Bond. LC 67-20372. (Paddington Ser.). (Illus.). 128p. (J). (gr. 2-5). 1967. 15.00 (*0-395-06637-9*) HM.

Paddington Bear. rev. ed. Michael Bond. LC 97-74636. (Illus.). 40p. (J). (ps-3). 1998. 13.95 (*0-06-027854-4*) HarpC.

Paddington Bear: A Lift-the-Flap Rebus Book. Michael Bond. (Illus.). 16p. (J). (ps-3). 1995. 11.95 (*0-694-00838-9*, HarpFestival) HarpC Child Bks.

Paddington Bear: My Scrapbook. Michael Bond. (Illus.). 20p. (J). (ps-3). 1999. 12.95 (*0-694-00886-9*, HarpFestival) HarpC Child Bks.

Paddington Bear all Day. Michael Bond. LC 98-163045. (Illus.). 7p. (J). (ps up). 1998. 5.95 (*0-694-00893-1*) HarpC Child Bks.

Paddington Bear & the Busy Bee Carnival. Michael Bond. LC 97-71019. (Illus.). 40p. (J). (ps-3). 1998. 12.95 (*0-06-027765-3*) HarpC Child Bks.

***Paddington Bear & the Busy Bee Carnival.** Michael Bond. LC 97-71019. (Paddington Bear Ser.). (Illus.). 40p. (J). (ps-3). 2000. pap. 5.95 (*0-06-443658-6*, HarpTrophy) HarpC Child Bks.

Paddington Bear & the Christmas Surprise. Michael Bond. LC 96-14362. (Illus.). 40p. (J). (ps-3). 1997. 11.95 (*0-694-00897-4*, HarpFestival); 12.95 (*0-06-027766-1*) HarpC Child Bks.

Paddington Bear & the Christmas Surprise. Michael Bond. LC 96-14362. (Illus.). 32p. (J). (ps-3). 1999. pap. 5.95 (*0-06-443595-4*) HarpC Child Bks.

Paddington Bear at the Circus. Michael Bond. LC 99-64789. (Illus.). 40p. (J). (ps-3). 2000. 12.95 (*0-06-028213-4*) HarpC Child Bks.

Paddington Bear Board Book & Rattle. Michael Bond. (Illus.). 14p. (J). (ps up). 1999. 15.95 (*0-694-00887-7*, HarpFestival) HarpC Child Bks.

Paddington Bear Goes to Market. Michael Bond. LC 98-163046. (Illus.). 7p. (J). (ps up). 1998. 5.95 (*0-694-00891-5*) HarpC Child Bks.

***Paddington Dressing Up.** Michael Bond. 12p. (J). (ps-2). 1999. 4.95 (*0-694-00425-1*, HarpFestival) HarpC Child Bks.

Paddington en Apuros - Paddington Marches On. Michael Bond. 1996. pap. text 7.50 (*84-279-3702-4*) Lectorum Pubns.

Paddington Goes to Town, 001. Michael Bond. LC 68-28043. (Paddington Ser.). (Illus.). 128p. (J). (gr. 2-5). 1977. 15.00 (*0-395-06635-2*) HM.

Paddington Helps Out see Hilarious Adventures of Paddington

Paddington Helps Out. rev. ed. Michael Bond. (Paddington Ser.). (Illus.). 144p. (J). (gr. 2-5). 1999. 15.00 (*0-395-96037-1*) HM.

Paddington in the Kitchen. Michael Bond. (Illus.). 28p. (J). (ps). 1992. 3.95 (*0-694-00396-4*) HarpC Child Bks.

Paddington Marches On, 001. Michael Bond. (Paddington Ser.). (Illus.). 128p. (J). (gr. 2-5). 1965. 15.00 (*0-395-06642-5*) HM.

Paddington Meets the Queen. Michael Bond. LC 92-24938. (Illus.). 32p. (J). (ps-3). 1993. 3.95 (*0-694-00460-X*, HarpFestival) HarpC Child Bks.

Paddington on Stage, Michael Bond & Alfred Bradley. LC 76-62497. (Paddington Ser.). (Illus.). 112p. (J). (gr. 2-5). 1977. 15.00 (*0-395-25155-9*) HM.

***Paddington on Top.** rev. ed. Michael Bond. (Paddington Ser.). (Illus.). (J). (gr. 2-5). 2000. pap. 15.00 (*0-618-07041-9*) HM.

Paddington Rides On! Michael Bond. LC 92-24937. (Illus.). 32p. (J). (ps-3). 1993. 3.95 (*0-694-00461-8*, HarpFestival) HarpC Child Bks.

Paddington Takes the Test. Michael Bond. (Illus.). 128p. (J). (gr. 3-6). 1980. 15.00 (*0-395-29519-X*) HM.

***Paddington Takes to TV.** Michael Bond. (Paddington Ser.). (Illus.). 144p. (J). (gr. 2-5). 2000. 15.00 (*0-395-91370-5*) HM.

***Paddington Treasury.** Michael Bond. (Illus.). 416p. (J). (gr. 3-6). 1999. 29.95 (*0-395-90507-9*) HM.

Paddington's: Paddington's One Hundred Twenty Three. Michael Bond. LC 94-116492. (J). 1996. 10.19 (*0-606-09728-7*, Pub. by Turtleback) Demco.

Paddington's ABC. Michael Bond. (Illus.). 32p. (J). 1996. pap. 4.99 (*0-14-055763-6*, PuffinBks) Peng Put Young Read.

Paddington's ABC. Michael Bond. LC 94-122871. (J). 1996. 10.19 (*0-606-09729-5*, Pub. by Turtleback) Demco.

Paddington's Colors. Michael Bond. (Illus.). 32p. (J). 1996. pap. 4.99 (*0-14-055764-4*, PuffinBks) Peng Put Young Read.

Paddington's Colors. Michael Bond. LC 93-129083. (J). 1996. 10.19 (*0-606-09730-9*, Pub. by Turtleback) Demco.

Paddington's First Word Book. Michael Bond. 32p. (J). 1998. pap. 5.99 (*0-14-056326-1*, PuffinBks) Peng Put Young Read.

Paddington's First Word Book. Michael Bond. 1998. 11.19 (*0-606-13692-4*, Pub. by Turtleback) Demco.

Paddington's Opposites. Michael Bond. (Illus.). 32p. (J). (ps-3). 1991. 11.99 (*0-670-84105-6*, Viking Child) Peng Put Young Read.

Paddington's Opposites. Michael Bond. (Illus.). 32p. (J). 1996. pap. 4.99 (*0-14-055765-2*, PuffinBks) Peng Put Young Read.

Paddington's Opposites. Michael Bond. LC 93-104753. (J). 1996. 10.19 (*0-606-09731-7*, Pub. by Turtleback) Demco.

Paddington's Storybook, 001. Michael Bond. (Illus.). 160p. (J). (gr. 1-5). 1984. 23.00 (*0-395-36667-4*) HM.

Paddington's 1 2 3. Michael Bond. (Illus.). 32p. (J). (ps-3). 1991. 11.99 (*0-670-84103-X*, Viking Child) Peng Put Young Read.

Paddington's 1 2 3. Michael Bond. (Illus.). 32p. (J). 1996. pap. 4.99 (*0-14-055762-8*, PuffinBks) Peng Put Young Read.

Paddiwak & Cozy. Berlie Doherty. 1999. pap. 4.99 (*0-14-055271-5*) NAL.

***Paddiwak & Cozy.** Berlie Doherty. LC 98-46168. (Illus.). 32p. (J). (ps-1). 1999. 14.95 (*0-531-30180-X*) Orchard Books.

Paddle America: A Guide to Trips & Outfitters in all 50 States. Nick Shears. LC 91-75664. (Illus.). 324p. 1992. pap. 12.95 (*0-9622806-5-8*) Starfish Pr.

Paddle America: A Guide to Trips & Outfitters in All 50 States. 3rd enl. rev. ed. David Shears & Nick Shears. LC 95-72415. (Illus.). 364p. 1996. pap. 15.95 (*0-9622806-7-4*) Starfish Pr.

***Paddle Indiana.** 399p. 2000. 22.95 (*0-9672922-0-4*) J L Waters & Co.

Paddle Routes of the Inland Northwest: 50 Flatwater & Whitewater Trips for Canoe & Kayak. Rich Landers & Dan Hansen. LC 97-45681. (Illus.). 272p. 1998. pap. 14.95 (*0-89886-556-5*) Mountaineers.

***Paddle Routes of Western Washington: 50 Flatwater Trips for Canoe & Kayak.** 2nd ed. Verne Huser. LC 99-50878. (Illus.). 240p. 2000. pap. 16.95 (*0-89886-630-8*) Mountaineers.

Paddle Routes of Western Washington: 50 Flatwater Trips for Canoes & Kayaks. Verne Huser. LC 89-49132. (Illus.). 240p. (Orig.). 1990. pap. 14.95 (*0-89886-231-0*) Mountaineers.

***Paddle Sports.** Beth Geiger. LC 00-24909. (Discovery Travel Adventures Ser.). (Illus.). 224p. 2000. pap. 19.95 (*1-56331-930-6*) Discovery Channel.

Paddle to Perfection!, 3 pts. Mark B. Solomon & Gary B. Solomon. Incl. Paddle to Perfection! Getting off the Ground! (Illus.). 112p. (Orig.). 1994. pap. 14.95 (*1-883085-04-7*, 90120); 39.95 (*1-883085-07-1*, 90140) Aquatics Unltd.

Paddle to Perfection!: Getting off the Ground! see Paddle to Perfection!

Paddle to Perfection - Toolbox: Getting off the Ground! Mark B. Solomon. Ed. by Gary B. Solomon. (Getting off the Ground! Instructional Watersport Ser.). 1995. pap. 11.95 (*1-883085-06-3*) Aquatics Unltd.

Paddle to the Amazon: The Ultimate 12,000-Mile Canoe Adventure. Don Starkell. (Illus.). 316p. 1994. pap. 14.95 (*0-7710-8256-8*) McCland & Stewart.

Paddle to the Arctic. Don Starkell. (Illus.). 304p. 1996. 24.95 (*0-7710-8239-8*) McCland & Stewart.

Paddle to the Arctic. Don Starkell. (Illus.). 304p. 1997. mass mkt. 6.99 (*0-7710-8248-7*) McCland & Stewart.

***Paddle to the Arctic: The Incredible Story of a Kayak Quest Across the Roof of the World.** Don Starkell. (Douglas Gibson Bks.). (Illus.). 320p. 2001. pap. 15.95 (*0-7710-8265-7*) McCland & Stewart.

Paddle to the Arctic: The Incredible Story of a Kayak Quest Across the Roof of the World. Don Starkell. 1996. text 24.95 (*0-07-061037-1*) McGraw.

Paddle to the Sea. C. S. Holling. 1980. 14.15 (*0-606-12471-3*, Pub. by Turtleback) Demco.

Paddle-to-the-Sea, 001. Holling C. Holling. (Illus.). 64p. (J). (gr. 4-6). 1941. 20.00 (*0-395-15082-5*) HM.

Paddle-to-the-Sea, 001. Holling C. Holling. (Illus.). 64p. (J). (gr. 4-7). 1980. pap. 10.00 (*0-395-29203-4*) HM.

Paddle Warships: The Earliest Steam Powered Fighting Ships, 1815-1850. D. K. Brown. (Conway's Ship Type Ser.). (Illus.). 128p. 1995. 41.95 (*0-85177-616-7*) Naval Inst Pr.

Paddle Whispers. Douglas Wood. LC 92-61330. (Illus.). 192p. (Orig.). 1993. pap. 12.95 (*0-938586-73-4*) Pfeifer-Hamilton.

Paddle Your Own Canoe. Gary McGuffin & Joanie McGuffin. (Illus.). 240p. 1999. 29.95 (*1-55046-214-8*, Pub. by Boston Mills) Genl Dist Srvs.

Paddler's Guide to Eastern North Carolina. Bob Benner & Tom McCloud. LC 86-31091. (Illus.). 272p. 1987. pap. 15.95 (*0-89732-041-7*) Menasha Ridge.

***Paddler's Guide to Everglades National Park.** Johnny Molloy. LC 00-25638. (Illus.). 224p. (YA). 2000. pap. 16.95 (*0-8130-1787-4*) U Press Fla.

Paddlers Guide to Northern Georgia. Bob Sehlinger & Don Otey. (Illus.). 312p. 1993. pap. 15.95 (*0-89732-134-0*) Menasha Ridge.

Paddler's Guide to Quetico Provincial Park. Robert Beymer. LC 85-80675. 168p. (Orig.). 1985. pap. 7.95 (*0-933287-00-3*) Fisher Co.

Paddler's Guide to Southern Georgia. Bob Sehlinger & Don Otey. LC 84-115744. (Illus.). 200p. 1980. pap. 16.95 (*0-89732-135-9*) Menasha Ridge.

Paddler's Journal & Companion. Stackpole Books Staff. 1997. pap. 19.95 (*0-8117-1207-9*) Stackpole.

Paddler's Planner. Ed. by Patricia J. Bell. 200p. (Orig.). 1989. pap. 7.95 (*0-9618227-3-2*) Cats-paw MN.

Paddles! The Foibles & Finesse of One World War II Landing Signal Officer. John A. Harper. (Illus.). 300p. 1996. 24.95 (*0-7643-0077-6*) Schiffer.

Paddles Flashing in the Sun. Walter Rand. (Illus.). 314p. (Orig.). 1995. pap. 22.95 (*0-9649728-0-8*) Pathfndr CT.

Paddles on the Yukon: 1,800 Miles in a Canoe on the Wildest River in North America. Carl T. Taylor. Ed. & Photos by Kendrick B. Taylor. LC 98-91499. (Illus.). 160p. 1998. pap. 15.95 (*0-9664709-0-7*) Mountain Empire.

Paddletail the Beaver & His Neighbors. Neil W. Northey. (Illus.). 182p. 1998. pap. 6.95 (*1-881545-84-9*) Angelas Bkshelf.

Paddlewheel Inboard. C. Bradford Mitchell. LC 83-50816. (Illus.). 66p. 1984. pap. 12.00 (*0-913423-06-8*) Steamship Hist Soc.

Paddlewheelers of Alaska & the Yukon: 100th Anniversary Collection. Graham Wilson. (Illus.). 1999. pap. 9.95 (*0-9681955-5-5*, Pub. by WCBI) Gr Arts Ctr Pub.

***Paddling Cape Cod: A Coastal Explorer's Guide.** Shirley Bull & Fred Bull. LC 99-87152. 2000. pap. 16.95 (*0-88150-441-6*, Pub. by Countryman) Norton.

***Paddling Coastal Massachusetts: From the North Shore to Cape Cod.** Lisa Gollin Evans. (Illus.). 224p. 1999. pap. 14.95 (*1-878239-84-8*, Pub. by AMC Books) Globe Pequot.

Paddling Hawaii. rev. ed. Audrey Sutherland. LC 97-48610. (Illus.). 248p. 1998. pap. 16.95 (*0-8248-2041-X*) UH Pr.

***Paddling Her Own Canoe: The Times & Texts of E. Pauline Johnson.** Carole Gerson. (Illus.). 400p. 2000. pap. text 24.95 (*0-8020-8024-3*) U of Toronto Pr.

***Paddling Illinois: 64 Great Trips by Canoe & Kayak.** Mike Svob. Ed. by Judith Ettenhofer. LC 99-69918. (Illus.). 160p. 2000. pap. 18.95 (*0-915024-77-2*) Trails Media.

Paddling Minnesota. Greg Breining. LC 99-14402. (Illus.). 240p. 1999. pap. 14.95 (*1-56044-690-0*) Falcon Pub Inc.

Paddling Montana. Hank Fischer & Carol Fischer. LC 99-18249. (Illus.). 156p. 1999. pap. 12.95 (*1-56044-589-0*) Falcon Pub Inc.

Paddling My Own Canoe. Audrey Sutherland. LC 78-16374. (Illus.). 1978. pap. 7.95 (*0-8248-0699-9*, Kolowalu Bk) UH Pr.

Paddling Northern Wisconsin: 82 Great Trips by Canoe & Kayak. Mike Svob. Ed. by Elizabeth McBride. LC 98-60596. (Illus.). 184p. 1998. pap. 18.95 (*0-915024-65-9*) Trails Media.

Paddling Okeefenokee National Wildlife Refuge. David O'Neill & Elizabeth O'Neill. LC 98-42199. (Illus.). 120p. 1998. pap. 12.95 (*1-56044-613-7*) Falcon Pub Inc.

Paddling Oregon. Robb Keller. LC 98-23764. (Illus.). 470p. 1997. pap. 19.95 (*1-56044-533-5*) Falcon Pub Inc.

Paddling South Carolina: A Guide to Palmetto State River Trails. Gene Able & Jack Horan. 135p. 1990. reprint ed. 12.50 (*0-87844-101-8*) Sandlapper Pub Co.

Paddling the Payette: A Complete Flat-Water & Whitewater Guide to the Payette River Basin. Stephen Stuebner. (Illus.). 224p. (Orig.). 1995. pap. 16.95 (*0-9644343-1-8*) Boise Front.

Paddling Yellowstone & Grand Teton National Parks. Don Nelson. (Illus.). 128p. 1999. pap. 10.95 (*1-56044-627-7*) Falcon Pub Inc.

Paddock Shift: Changing Views on Grassland Farming. Allan Nation. LC 97-12623. 192p. (Orig.). 1997. pap. text 25.95 (*0-9632460-5-4*) Green Park.

Paddy. R. D. Lawrence. LC 99-158602. (Illus.). 240p. 1998. reprint ed. pap. 14.95 (*1-55821-573-5*, 15735) Lyons Pr.

Paddy Clarke Ha Ha Ha. Roddy Doyle. 288p. 1995. pap. 12.95 (*0-14-023390-3*, Penguin Bks) Viking Penguin.

Paddy Clarke Ha Ha Ha. large type ed. Roddy Doyle. LC 94-8218. 1994. 23.95 (*1-56895-070-5*) Wheeler Pub.

Paddy Finn's Children. Terry Glover. 106p. (C). 1989. text 45.00 (*1-872795-35-8*, Pub. by Pentland Pr) St Mut.

Paddy Irrigation & Water Management in Southeast Asia. E. B. Rice. (Operations & Evaluation Studies). 84p. 1997. pap. 22.00 (*0-8213-3914-1*, 13914) World Bank.

***Paddy Madigan: An Irish Idyll.** Herbert A. Kenny. 248p. 1999. 21.95 (*0-938864-24-6*) Ipswich Pr.

Paddy Paws & Friends Presents Christmas. Karen Chase. (Illus.). 60p. Date not set. pap. 9.95 (*1-57377-052-3*, 01988402248) Easl Pubns.

Paddy Reilly Songbook. Paddy Reilly. (Illus.). 64p. 1989. pap. 14.95 (*0-7119-1825-2*, AM74733) Music Sales.

Paddy Soils: Proceedings. 800p. 1982. 94.95 (*0-387-10900-5*) Spr-Verlag.

Paddy Soils in Tropical Asia: Their Material Nature & Fertility. Keizaburo Kawaguchi. LC 77-21463. (Monographs of the Center for Southeast Asian Studies, Kyoto University: No. 10). (Illus.). 274p. 1977. reprint ed. pap. 78.10 (*0-608-04386-9*, 2065167) Bks Demand.

Paddy the Cope: An Irish Life. Patrick Gallagher. 1942. 12.00 (*0-8159-6500-1*) Devin.

Paddy under Water. John S. Goodall. LC 83-71901. (Illus.). 32p. (J). 1984. 12.95 (*0-689-50297-4*) McElderry Bks.

Paddy's Lament: Ireland, 1846-1847; Prelude to Hatred. Thomas Gallagher. 372p. (C). 1987. pap. 15.00 (*0-15-670700-4*, Harvest Bks) Harcourt.

***Paddy's O'Possum's Prayer Book.** Lois Keffer. LC 98-235729. (Illus.). 20p. (J). (ps-3). 1998. 9.99 (*1-57673-379-3*) Zondervan.

Pade Approximants. 2nd ed. George A. Baker, Jr. & Peter Graves-Morris. (Encyclopedia of Mathematics & Its Applications Ser.: No. 59). (Illus.). 762p. (C). 1996. text 120.00 (*0-521-45007-1*) Cambridge U Pr.

Pade Approximants for Operators: Theory & Applications. Annie Cuyt. (Lecture Notes in Mathematics Ser.: Vol. 1065). ix, 138p. 1984. 29.95 (*0-387-13342-9*) Spr-Verlag.

Pade Approximation & Its Applications: Bad Honnef, 1983. Ed. by H. W. Werner & H. J. Buenger. (Lecture Notes in Mathematics Ser.: Vol. 1071). (ENG & FRE.). vi, 264p. 1984. 39.95 (*0-387-13364-X*) Spr-Verlag.

Pade-Typed Approximation & General Orthogonal Polynomials. C. Brezinski. (International Series of Numerical Mathematics: No. 50). 250p. 1980. 84.00 (*0-8176-1100-2*) Birkhauser.

Padeia Proposal. Adler. 1998. pap. 8.00 (*0-684-84188-6*) S&S Trade.

***Paden City Catalogue Reprints of the 1920s & 1930s.** 224p. 2000. pap. 24.95 (*1-57080-074-X*) Antique Pubns.

Paderborn, Universitat: Die Matrikel der Universitat Paderborn, 1614-1844. Ed. by Joseph Freisen. (Alumni of German Universities Ser.). 1990. reprint ed. 100.00 (*0-8115-3804-4*) Periodicals Srv.

Paderewski: The Story of a Modern Immortal. Charles J. Phillips. LC 77-17399. (Music Reprint Ser.). (Illus.). 1978. reprint ed. lib. bdg. 55.00 (*0-306-77534-4*) Da Capo.

Paderewski As I Knew Him: From the Diary of Aniela Strakacz. Aniela Strakacz. LC 49-11799. (Illus.). 352p. reprint ed. pap. 109.20 (*0-608-10831-6*, 205066700089) Bks Demand.

An Asterisk (*) at the beginning of an entry indicates that the title is appearing for the first time.

Paderewski Memoirs. Jan I. Paderewski & Mary Lawton. LC 80-21323. (Music Ser.). 1980. reprint ed. 45.00 (*0-306-76046-0*) Da Capo.

Padfield: Criminal Law. Nicola Padfield. (Butterworths Core Text Ser.). 1997. pap. write for info. (*0-406-03310-2*, PCL, MICHIE) LEXIS Pub.

PADI Deep Diver Manual. (Illus.). 70p. pap. text 12.95 (*1-878663-13-5*) PADI.

PADI Divemaster Manual. 2nd ed. Alex Brylske. Ed. by Tonya Palazzi & Mary E. Beveridge. (Illus.). 224p. (C). 1990. reprint ed. pap. text 19.75 (*1-878663-07-0*) PADI.

Padju Epat: The Ma'anyan of Indonesian Borneo. Alfred B. Hudson. Ed. by Louise S. Spindler & George D. Spindler. (Case Studies in Cultural Anthropology). 144p. 1982. reprint ed. pap. text 8.95 (*0-8290-0315-0*) Irvington.

Padlock Collector: Illustrations & Prices of 2800 Padlocks of the Past 100 Years. 6th ed. Franklin M. Arnall. LC 96-84415. (Illus.). 284p. 1996. pap. 21.95 (*0-914638-05-X*) Collctr Clrmnt.

Padlock Collector: 100 Years of Padlocks. 5th ed. Franklin M. Arnall. LC 87-72771. (Illus.). 190p. 1988. pap. 14.95 (*0-914638-04-1*) Collctr Clrmnt.

Padlock Your Heart. large type ed. Anne Saunders. (Linford Romance Library). 384p. 1997. pap. 16.99 (*0-7089-5081-7*, Linford) Ulverscroft.

Padlocks, Keen Kutter & Simmons. Alvin Sellens. (Illus.). 1995. pap. 10.00 (*0-9612068-5-3*) Sellens.

Padma, Girl of India & Other Works. Natalie McKelvy. Ed. by Charles McKelvy. 456p. 1998. pap. 8.00 (*0-944771-22-X*) Dunery Pr.

Padma Purana, Pt. III. Ed. by N. A. Deshpande. (Ancient Puranas Ser.). 1990. 26.00 (*81-208-0624-7*, Pub. by Motilal Bnarsidass) S Asia.

Padma Purana, Pt. 8. N. A. Deshpande. (C). 1991. 26.00 (*81-208-0807-X*, Pub. by Motilal Bnarsidass) S Asia.

Padma Purana, Vol. 40, Pt. II. Ed. & Tr. by N. A. Deshpande. (Ancient Indian Tradition & Mythology Ser.). 1989. 26.00 (*81-208-0583-6*, Pub. by Motilal Bnarsidass) S Asia.

Padma Purana Pt. 9: Ancient Indian Tradition & Mythology, Vol. 47. N. A. Deshpande. (C). 1991. 26.00 (*81-208-0881-9*, Pub. by Motilal Bnarsidass) S Asia.

Padma Purana (AITM 43) Vol. 5: Ancient Indian Tradition & Mythology. Tr. by N. A. Deshpande. 1990. 26.00 (*81-208-0701-4*, Pub. by Motilal Bnarsidass) S Asia.

Padmanabha's Kanhadada: India's Greatest Patriotic Saga of Medieval Times. Tr. by V. S. Bhatnagar. (C). 1991. 27.50 (*81-85179-54-9*, Pub. by Aditya Prakashan) S Asia.

Padmasambhava & Buddhism in Tibet. Ed. by Tarthang Tulku. (Crystal Mirror Ser.: Vol. IV). (Illus.). 294p. 1975. pap. 12.95 (*0-913546-11-9*) Dharma Pub.

Padmavati. Prem Prasad. (Illus.). 28p. (Orig.). (C). 1994. pap. text 5.00 (*1-878173-37-5*) Birnham Wood.

Padok-Retrievaltest. Christa Womser-Hacker. (Sprache und Computer Ser.: Vol. 10). (GER.). xii, 181p. 1989. write for info. (*3-487-09214-X*) G Olms Pubs.

Padraic Pearse: Rogha Danta - Selected Poems. Padraic H. Pearse. 80p. (Orig.). 1993. reprint ed. pap. 9.95 (*1-874597-50-2*, Pub. by New Island Books) Irish Bks Media.

Padre Ama a Sus Hijas. T. D. Jakes.Tr. of Daddy Loves His Girls. (SPA.). 1997. pap. 8.99 (*0-88419-514-7*) Creation House.

Padre Amoroso - The Loving Father. (SPA.). 30p. (J). 1995. write for info. (*1-56063-885-0*) Editorial Unilit.

***Padre de Su Hija (The Father of Her Child) The Mother of His Child.** Sandra Field. (Bianca Ser.: No. 194). (SPA.). 2000. per. 3.50 (*0-373-33544-X*, 1-33544-7) Silhouette.

***Padre de Verdad (The Real Father) Let's Have a Baby!** Christy Lockhart. (Deseo Ser.: No. 187). (SPA.). 156p. 1999. per. 3.50 (*0-373-35317-0*, 1-35317-6) Harlequin Bks.

Padre Inesperado (The Unexpected Father) Kathryn Ross. (Bianca Ser.). (SPA.). 1998. per. 3.50 (*0-373-33444-3*, 1-33444-0) Harlequin Bks.

Padre Island National Seashore. Joseph E. Brown. Ed. by T. J. Priehs. LC 90-60725. (Illus.). 64p. (Orig.). 1991. pap. 8.95 (*0-911408-90-8*) SW Pks Mnmts.

Padre Island National Seashore--A Guide to the Geology, Natural Environments, & History of a Texas Barrier Island. B. R. Weise & W. A. White. (Guidebook Ser.: GB 17). (Illus.). 94p. 1980. pap. 5.00 (*0-686-31762-9*) Bur Econ Geology.

Padre Island National Seashore, Texas. (Illus.). 1996. 8.99 (*1-56695-047-3*) Trails Illustrated.

Padre Juan Luis: Hacedor de Maravillas en America. Jeffrey J. Moynihan. (SPA.). 64p. 1997. pap. 2.95 (*1-57918-046-9*, 3531S) Queenship Pub.

Padre Kino's Favorite Meatloaf & Other Recipes from Baja Arizona. LC 91-66595. (Illus.). 235p. 1991. pap. 9.95 (*0-9648339-0-5*) Comm Food Bank.

Padre Martinez & Bishop Lamy. 3rd ed. Ray J. De Aragon. LC 78-70565. (History Ser.). (Illus.). (C). 1978. pap. 7.95 (*0-932906-00-1*) Pan-Am Publishing Co.

Padre Miguel Hidalgo: Father of Mexican Independence. Hubert J. Miller. 77p. (Orig.). 1986. pap. text 5.00 (*0-938738-05-4*) U TX Pan Am Pr.

***Padre Millonario.** Leanne Banks. (Harlequin Deseo Ser.: Vol. 157).Tr. of Millionaire Dad. (SPA.). 156p. 1999. per. 3.50 (*0-373-35287-5*, 1-35287-1) Harlequin Bks.

Padre Mio me abbandono a Te see Summoned by Love

Padre Nuestro. E. Reeves.Tr. of Lord's Prayer. (SPA.). (J). 1.89 (*0-7899-0480-2*, 498667) Editorial Unilit.

Padre Nuestro Que Te Escondes en el Cielo: De San Anton Al Bronx. Armando Pacheco-Matos. Ed. by Bomexi Iztaccihuatl. (SPA.). 70p. 1990. mass mkt. 6.99 (*1-929183-01-1*) Edit Fundacion.

Padre Pio see City on a Mountain - Padre Pio

***Padre Pio.** Fabrizio Contessa. Tr. by Edmund C. Lane from ITA. LC 99-35027. (Illus.). xii, 80p. 1999. pap. 6.95 (*0-8189-0826-2*) Alba.

Padre Pio. 2nd rev. expanded ed. C. Bernard Ruffin. LC 81-81525. (Illus.). 444p. (Orig.). 1991. pap. 13.95 (*0-87973-673-9*, 673) Our Sunday Visitor.

Padre Pio: His Life & Mission. Mary F. Ingoldsby. 191p. 1988. reprint ed. pap. 10.95 (*0-905092-64-3*, Pub. by Veritas Pubns) St Mut.

***Padre Pio: In My Own Words.** Anthony Chiffolo. (Illus.). 128p. 2000. 13.95 (*0-7648-0657-2*) Liguori Pubns.

***Padre Pio: Man of Hope.** Renzo Allegri. LC 99-59678. 240p. 2000. pap. 10.99 (*1-56955-138-3*, Charis) Servant.

Padre Pio: The Pierced Priest: A Biography. Jim Gallagher. (Illus.). 240p. 1996. pap. 13.00 (*0-00-627881-7*, Pub. by HarpC) Harper SF.

Padre Pio: The Stigmatist. Charles M. Carty. (Illus.). 1994. reprint ed. pap. 15.00 (*0-89555-054-7*, 115) TAN Bks Pubs.

***Padre Pio: The Wonder Worker.** Francis Mary. 1999. pap. 12.95 (*0-89870-770-6*) Ignatius Pr.

Padre Pio - Stigmatist. Carty. pap. 15.00 (*0-89555-355-4*, 0115) TAN Bks Pubs.

Padre Pio Profile. John A. Schug. LC 87-16664. 163p. (Orig.). 1987. pap. 9.95 (*0-932506-56-9*) St Bedes Pubns.

***Padre Que Yo Quiero Ser.** Josh McDowell. Tr. by Josie de Smith.Tr. of Father Connection. (SPA.). 176p. 1998. pap. text 10.99 (*0-311-46157-3*, Edit Mundo) Casa Bautista.

Padre Soltero (A Single Husband) Jennifer Greene. (SPA.). 1999. mass mkt. 3.50 (*0-373-35272-7*, 1-35272-3) Harlequin Bks.

***Padre to the Papagos: Father Bonaventura Oblasser.** Regis Rohder. (Illus.). 73p. 1999. reprint ed. pap. text 14.00 (*0-7881-6180-6*) DIANE Pub.

Padre Varela: Pensador, Sacerdote, Patriota. fac. ed. Roberto Esquenazi-Mayo. LC 90-40425. (SPA.). 103p. 1990. reprint ed. pap. 32.00 (*0-7837-7777-9*, 204753200007) Bks Demand.

***Padres.** Matt Silverman. (Total Baseball Companions Ser.). 96p. 2000. mass mkt. 2.50 (*1-892129-79-5*) Total Sprts.

Padres de Tiempo Completo. Patrica Galaz. 1997. pap. text 7.98 (*970-643-079-2*) Selector.

Padres E Hijos. Ivan S. Turguieniev. Tr. by Victor Andresco. (Nueva Austral Ser.: Vol. 130). (SPA.). 1991. pap. text 24.95 (*84-239-1930-7*) Elliots Bks.

Padres Eficaces con Entrenamiento Sistematico. Don Dinkmeyer & Gary D. McKay. (SPA.). 1981. teacher ed. 45.95 (*0-913476-87-0*, 5461) Am Guidance.

Padres in No Man's Land: Canadian Chaplains & the Great War. Duff Crerar. LC 95-181165. (McGill-Queen's Studies in the History of Religion Ser.: No. 16). (Illus.). 440p. 1995. 55.00 (*0-7735-1230-6*, Pub. by McG-Queens Univ Pr) CUP Services.

Padres Que Sufren. John White.Tr. of Parents in Pain. (SPA.). 55p. 1991. write for info. (*1-56063-090-6*) Editorial Unilit.

Padres Solteros: Una Jornada en el Desierto. Robert Barnes, Jr. Orig. Title: Wilderness Journey. (SPA.). 61p. 1991. pap. 4.99 (*1-56063-094-9*, 498418) Editorial Unilit.

Padres Son Maestros. Ruth Bowdoin. Tr. by Carmen E. Diaz Zayas. (Metodo Bowdoin Ser.). (Illus.). 320p. 1992. 30.00 (*0-915741-32-6*) C D Stampley Ent.

Padres Son Maestros, 10 vols. Ruth Bowdoin. Tr. by Ana Wier from ENG. (Metodo Bowdoin Ser.: Vol. I). (SPA., Illus.). 48p. 1978. pap. text. write for info. (*1-55997-060-X*) Websters Intl.

Padroes de Vida see Patterns for Living: Through the Old Testament

PADS, 94: 8th Workshop on Parallel & Distributed Simulation. 204p. 1994. pap. text 30.00 (*0-89791-664-6*, 577940) Assn Compu Machinery.

PADS, 97: 11th Workshop on Parallel & Distributed Simulation. 1997. pap. 32.00 (*0-89791-913-0*, 577970) Assn Compu Machinery.

PADS, 96: Workshop on Parallel & Distributed Simulation. 224p. 1996. pap. text 32.00 (*0-89791-824-X*, 577960) Assn Compu Machinery.

Padua & the Tudors: English Students in Italy, 1485-1603. Jonathan Woolfson. LC 99-483164. (Illus.). 320p. 1998. text 60.00 (*0-8020-0946-8*) U of Toronto Pr.

Padua in the 1450s: Marco Zoppo & His Contemporaries. Hugo Chapman et al. LC 98-183279. 80p. 1998. write for info. (*0-7141-2616-0*) British Mus Pr.

Padua under the Carrara, 1318-1405. Benjamin G. Kohl. LC 97-30172. (Illus.). 472p. 1998. text 45.00 (*0-8018-5703-1*) Johns Hopkins.

Paduans, Medals by Giovanni Cavino. Richard H. Lawrence. (Illus.). 1980. pap. 5.00 (*0-916710-74-2*) Obol Intl.

Padyacudamani of Buddhaghosacarya. Buddhaghosa. LC 78-72387. reprint ed. 32.50 (*0-404-17248-2*) AMS Pr.

Padyavand, Vol. I. Ed. by Amnon Netzer. LC 95-37762. (Judeo-Iranian & Jewish Studies Ser.). (Illus.). 470p. 1995. lib. bdg. 35.00 (*1-56859-036-9*) Mazda Pubs.

Padyavand, Vol. II. Ed. by Amnon Netzer. (Judeo-Iranian & Jewish Studies Ser.: Vol. 1). (Illus.). 682p. 1998. lib. bdg. 40.00 (*1-56859-063-6*) Mazda Pubs.

***Padyavand, Vol. III.** Ed. by Amnon Netzer. (Judeo-Iranian & Jewish Studies Ser.). 420p. 2000. 40.00 (*1-56859-127-6*) Mazda Pubs.

Paean for Survival. Scott Keyes. 8p. 1992. pap. 3.00 (*0-9633179-2-X*) D Scott Pubs.

Paeans & Laments. 2nd ed. Lucy Maroulleti. (ENG & GRE., Illus.). 48p. (Orig.). 1996. reprint ed. pap. 6.50 (*1-888447-01-X*) Vsns Two-Thousand.

***Paediatric Anaesthesia.** Ed. by Edward Sumner & David Hatch. (An Arnold Publication). (Illus.). 592p. 2000. text 98.50 (*0-340-71942-7*) OUP.

***Paediatric Anaesthesia & Critical Care in the District Hospital.** N. S. Norton & Jane M. Peutrell. (Illus.). 226p. 2000. pap. text 50.00 (*0-7506-4302-1*) Buttrwrth-Heinemann.

Paediatric & Adolescent Gynecology. Ed. by A. S. Garden. LC 97-3430. (Illus.). 448p. 1998. text 65.00 (*0-340-60764-5*, Pub. by E A) OUP.

Paediatric Audiology: Zero to Five Years. 2nd ed. Barry McCormick. 458p. 1993. 55.00 (*1-56593-239-0*, 0558) Singular Publishing.

Paediatric Cardiac Arrhythmias. Ed. by Christopher Wren & Ronald W. Campbell. (Illus.). 384p. 1996. text 125.00 (*0-19-262295-1*) OUP.

Paediatric Chemical Pathology. B. E. Clayton. 176p. 1980. pap. 24.95 (*0-632-00564-5*) Blackwell Sci.

Paediatric Cholestasis: Novel Approaches to Treatment: Proceedings of the 63rd Falk Symposium Held in Titisee-Black Forest, Germany, October 9-10, 1992. Falk Symposium Staff. Ed. by M. Lentze & J. Reichen. LC 92-15070. 384p. (C). 1992. text 164.00 (*0-7923-8977-8*) Kluwer Academic.

Paediatric Clinical Examination. 2nd ed. Denis Gill & Niall O'Brien. LC 92-49185. (Illus.). 224p. 1993. pap. text 26.95 (*0-443-04725-1*) Church.

Paediatric Dentistry. Richard Welbury. LC 96-44038. (Illus.). 412p. 1997. pap. text 68.95 (*0-19-262630-2*) OUP.

Paediatric Dentistry. Richard Welbury. (Illus.). 412p. 1997. text 135.00 (*0-19-262631-0*) OUP.

Paediatric Endocrinology in Clinical Practice. A. Aynsley-Green. 1984. text 147.50 (*0-85200-864-3*) Kluwer Academic.

Paediatric Epilepsy Syndromes & Their Surgical Treatment. Tuxhom. 894p. 149.00 (*0-86196-536-1*, Pub. by J Libbey Med) Bks Intl VA.

***Paediatric Exercise Science & Medicine.** Ed. by Neil Armstrong & Willem Van Mechelen. (Illus.). 480p. 2000. text 129.50 (*0-19-262977-8*) OUP.

Paediatric Gastroenterology. Ed. by J. Navarro & J. Schmitz. Tr. by Brian Barefoot. (Illus.). 572p. 1992. 165.00 (*0-19-261771-0*) OUP.

Paediatric Gastroenterology, No. 2. 2nd ed. Anderson. (gr. 13). 1989. 145.00 (*0-86793-176-0*) Mosby Inc.

Paediatric History & Examination. Ian A. Laing & Neil McIntosh. (Illus.). 95p. 1994. text 15.95 (*0-7020-1809-0*, Pub. by W B Saunders) Saunders.

Paediatric Infectious Diseases in Arab Countries. Ed. by Abdelaziz Y. Elzouki. LC 86-9258. (Wiley-Medical Publication). 307p. reprint ed. pap. 95.20 (*0-7837-3236-8*, 204325500007) Bks Demand.

Paediatric Intensive Care. Ed. by Neil S. Morton. (Illus.). 310p. 1997. text 65.00 (*0-19-262511-X*) OUP.

***Paediatric Intensive Care Nursing.** Carol Williams & Julie Asquith. LC 99-33459. 2000. text. write for info. (*0-443-05528-9*) Church.

Paediatric MCQ Revision for MRCP & MRCPCH. Jane Lucas & James Nicholson. 192p. 1997. pap. text 32.00 (*0-7506-3014-0*, Newnes) Buttrwrth-Heinemann.

Paediatric MCQs for Postgraduate Exams, Vol. 1. Simon Attard et al. 848p. 1996. pap. text 37.50 (*0-7506-2769-7*) Buttrwrth-Heinemann.

Paediatric MCQs for Postgraduate Exams, Vol. 2. Simon Attard-Montalto et al. LC 96-197400. 112p. 1996. pap. text 37.50 (*0-7506-2845-6*, Focal) Buttrwrth-Heinemann.

Paediatric Neoplasia: An Atlas & Text. S. Variend. LC 93-20356. (Current Histopathology Ser.: Vol. 22). 128p. (C). 1993. text 209.50 (*0-7923-8900-X*) Kluwer Academic.

Paediatric Nephrology: A Research Update. Ed. by D. Boda & S. Turi. (Contributions to Nephrology Ser.: Vol. 67). (Illus.). x, 238p. 1988. 29.75 (*3-8055-4689-0*) S Karger.

Paediatric Nephrourology: Progress in Research & Practice. Ed. by Hilary M. Hoey & Prem Puri. LC 89-24891. (Illus.). 110p. 1990. reprint ed. pap. 34.10 (*0-608-01645-4*, 206223000002) Bks Demand.

Paediatric Neurosurgery. Ed. by M. Choux et al. (Illus.). 700p. (C). 1999. text 250.00 (*0-443-05630-7*) Church.

Paediatric Oncology. Ed. by W. Duncan. (Recent Results in Cancer Research Ser.: Vol. 88). (Illus.). 170p. 1983. 76.00 (*0-387-12349-0*) Spr-Verlag.

Paediatric Oncology: Acute Nursing Care, 1. Margaret Evans. 17p. 1998. pap. text 37.95 (*1-86156-047-8*) Singular Publishing.

Paediatric Oncology: Clinical Practice & Controversies. Ed. by P. N. Plowman & C. R. Pinkerton. (Illus.). 672p. 1992. 132.95 (*0-442-31595-3*) Chapman & Hall.

Paediatric Ophthalmology. 2nd ed. David Conrad Taylor. LC 96-24809. (Illus.). 1216p. 1997. text 299.95 (*0-86542-831-X*) Blackwell Sci.

Paediatric Orthopaedics & Fractures, 2 vols., Set. 3rd ed. W. J. Sharrard. (Illus.). 1752p. 1992. 299.95 (*0-632-03457-2*) Blackwell Sci.

Paediatric Osteology: New Developments in Diagnostics & Therapy: Proceedings of the First International Workshop on Paediatric Osteology, Cologne, Germany, 5-7 October 1995. Ed. by Eckhard Schonau. LC 96-6146. (International Congress Ser.: No. 1105). 316p. 1996. text 182.25 (*0-444-82277-1*, Excerpta Medica) Elsevier.

Paediatric Osteology: Prevention of Osteoporosis - A Paediatric Task?: Proceedings of the 2nd International Workshop on Paediatric Osteology, Cologne, October 3-5, 1997. Eckhardshop Sch Onau & V. Matkovic. LC 98-4052. (International Congress Ser.). 1998. write for info. (*0-444-82840-0*) Elsevier.

Paediatric Pathology. Ed. by C. L. Berry. (Illus.). 710p. 1985. 115.00 (*0-387-10507-7*) Spr-Verlag.

Paediatric Pathology. 2nd ed. Ed. by C. L. Berry. (Illus.). 750p. 1989. 266.00 (*0-387-19536-X*) Spr-Verlag.

Paediatric Pathology. 3rd ed. Ed. by Colin L. Berry. LC 95-33587. 960p. 1995. 214.00 (*3-540-19936-5*) Spr-Verlag.

Paediatric Perspectives on Epilepsy: A Symposium Held at the Grand Hotel, Eastbourne, December 1984, Vol. 198. Ed. by Euan Ross. LC 85-12009. 176p. 1985. 340.00 (*0-471-90817-7*) Wiley.

Paediatric Problems in General Practice. 3rd ed. Michael Modell et al. (Oxford General Practice Ser.: No. 36). (Illus.). 352p. 1996. pap. text 49.95 (*0-19-262512-8*) OUP.

Paediatric Research: Proceedings of the WHO Scientific Group, Geneva, 1967. WHO Staff. (Technical Reports: No. 400). 1968. pap. text 3.00 (*92-4-120400-1*, 1100400) World Health.

Paediatric Respiratory Disease. Ed. by M. H. Goetz & O. B. Stur. (Progress in Respiratory Research Ser.: Vol. 17). (Illus.). x, 306p. 1982. 152.00 (*3-8055-2658-X*) S Karger.

Paediatric Respiratory Physiology & Clinical Aspects of Paediatric Pneumology. Ed. by R. Kraemer. (Modern Problems in Pediatrics Ser.: Vol. 21). (Illus.). xii, 248p. 1982. pap. 143.50 (*3-8055-3505-8*) S Karger.

Paediatric Rheumatology Update. Barbara M. Ansell & Patricia H. White. Ed. by Patricia Woo et al. (Illus.). 222p. 1990. 65.00 (*0-19-261860-1*) OUP.

Paediatric Surgery. John D. Atwell. LC 98-12130. (An Arnold Publication). (Illus.). 864p. 1998. text 250.00 (*0-340-58608-7*) OUP.

Paediatric Surgical Pathology. Gray. 1995. text 139.00 (*0-443-04122-9*, W B Saunders Co) Harcrt Hlth Sci Grp.

Paediatric Thoracic Surgery. Ed. by N. A. Myers & T. A. Angerpointner. (Progress in Pediatric Surgery Ser.: Vol. 27). (Illus.). 272p. 1991. 185.00 (*0-387-52525-4*) Spr-Verlag.

Paediatric Vade Mecum. 13th ed. Jack Insley. LC 97-178973. (Arnold Publication). (Illus.). 450p. 1997. pap. text 24.95 (*0-340-60158-2*) OUP.

***Paediatrics.** S. Attard-Montalto & V. Saha. LC 99-36782. (Illus.). 200p. 1998. pap. write for info. (*0-443-05516-5*) Church.

Paediatrics. A. Evans & C. McCarthy. (Management of Common Diseases in Family Practice Ser.). 1986. text 73.50 (*0-85200-759-0*) Kluwer Academic.

Paediatrics. 2nd ed. Thomas. (C). 1998. pap. text 16.95 (*0-443-05880-6*, W B Saunders Co) Harcrt Hlth Sci Grp.

Paediatrics: Key Questions Answered. Jonathan Round. LC 98-41105. (Key Questions Answered Ser.). 308p. 1999. pap. text 29.95 (*0-19-262904-2*) OUP.

Paediatrics: Understanding Child Health. Ed. by Tony Waterston et al. LC 97-218843. (Oxford Core Texts Ser.). (Illus.). 432p. (C). 1997. text 95.00 (*0-19-262564-0*) OUP.

Paediatrics & Blood Transfusion. Smith C. Sibinga. 1982. text 94.00 (*90-247-2619-0*) Kluwer Academic.

***Paediatrics & Child Health.** Malcolm I. Levene & Mary C. J. Rudolf. LC 98-24257. (Illus.). 10p. 1999. pap. 54.95 (*0-86542-957-X*) Blackwell Sci.

Paediatrics Revision. Kwei C. Chin & Michael J. Tarlow. (Illus.). 180p. 1989. pap. text 26.00 (*0-443-03274-2*) Church.

Paediatrische Infektionskrankheiten IV. Ed. by U. B. Schaad. (Paediatrische Fortbildungskurse fuer die Praxis Ser.: Vol. 59). (Illus.). xii, 188p. 1985. pap. 34.00 (*3-8055-3954-1*) S Karger.

Paediatrische Infektionskrankheiten III. Ed. by U. B. Schaad. (Paediatrische Fortbildungskurse fuer die Praxis Ser.: Vol. 58). (Illus.). xvi, 132p. 1983. pap. 42.75 (*3-8055-3680-1*) S Karger.

Paedophiles & Sexual Offences Against Children. D. Howitt. 1995. pap. text 61.00 (*0-471-95591-4*) Wiley.

Paedophilia: Policy & Prevention. Ed. by Marianne James. LC 98-201095. (Research & Public Policy Ser.: Vol. 12). 85p. 1999. pap. 75.00 (*0-642-24047-7*, Pub. by Aust Inst Criminology) St Mut.

***Paekpom Ilchi: The Autobiography of Kim Ku.** Tr. by Jongsook Lee. (Illus.). 464p. 2000. 62.50 (*0-7618-1685-2*) U Pr of Amer.

Paella! Spectacular Rice Dishes from Spain. Penelope Casas. LC 98-34727. (Illus.). 226p. 1999. 30.00 (*0-8050-5623-8*) H Holt & Co.

Paella Perfect! Casas. Date not set. pap. 15.95 (*0-8050-5624-6*, Owl) H Holt & Co.

Paeonien: Pfingstrosen. Reinhilde Frank.Tr. of Peonies. (GER., Illus.). 152p. 1999. 20.00 (*3-8001-6639-9*, Pub. by Eugen Ulmer) Balogh.

Paese: A Portrait of a Village. Paul Strand. Tr. by Marguerite Shore. LC 96-80073. (Illus.). 106p. 1997. 60.00 (*0-89381-700-7*) Aperture.

Paese Fortunato see Oh Lucky Country

Paestum. Old Vicarage Publications Staff. (C). 1982. pap. text 60.00 (*0-7855-3135-1*, Pub. by Old Vicarage) St Mut.

Paestum: Greeks & Romans in Southern Italy. John G. Pedley. LC 89-51868. (New Aspects of Antiquity Ser.). (Illus.). 184p. 1990. 35.00 (*0-500-39027-4*, Pub. by Thames Hudson) Norton.

PAF Help Guide. Diane M. Anderson. 89p. pap. 14.95 (*1-877677-86-8*) Herit Quest.

Pagalami: Ethnopsychiatric Knowledge in Bengal. Deborah P. Bhattacharyya. (Foreign & Comparative Studies Program, South Asian Ser.: No. 11). (Orig.). (C). 1986. pap. 13.00 (*0-915984-89-X*) Syracuse U Foreign Comp.

Pagan. Lyubomir Nikolov. Tr. by Roland Flint & Viara Tcholakova from BUL. LC 92-70687. (Poetry Ser.). 48p. (Orig.). 1992. pap. 11.95 (*0-88748-146-9*) Carnegie-Mellon.

Pagan - Christian Conflict over Miracle in the Second Century. Harold Remus. LC 83-6729. (Patristic Monograph: No. 10). xiii, 371p. 1983. pap. 11.00 (*0-915646-09-9*) N Amer Patristic Soc.

P

An Asterisk (*) at the beginning of an entry indicates that the title is appearing for the first time.

Pagan - Ultima VIII: Ultimate Strategy Guide. Joe Hutsko. LC 94-66630. (Illus.). 256p. 1994. pap. 19.95 (*1-55958-594-3*) Prima Pub.

Pagan & Christian Creeds. Edward Carpenter. 1972. 59.95 (*0-8490-0794-1*) Gordon Pr.

Pagan & Christian Creeds: Their Origin & Meaning. Edward Carpenter. 319p. 1996. reprint ed. spiral bd. 18.50 (*0-7873-0147-7*) Hlth Research.

Pagan & Christian Creeds: Their Origin & Meaning. Edward Carpenter. 318p. 1992. reprint ed. pap. 24.95 (*1-56459-211-1*) Kessinger Pub.

Pagan & Christian in an Age of Anxiety: Some Aspects of Religious Experience from Marcus Aurelius to Constantine. Eric R. Dodds. 160p. (C). 1991. pap. text 18.95 (*0-521-38599-7*) Cambridge U Pr.

Pagan & Christian Rome. Rodolfo Lanciani. LC 67-23856. (Illus.). 1972. reprint ed. 39.95 (*0-405-08728-4*, Pub. by Blom Pubns) Ayer.

***Pagan Babies.** Elmore Leonard. 224p. 2000. 24.95 (*0-385-33392-7*) Delacorte.

***Pagan Babies.** large type ed. Elmore Leonard. 2000. 24.95 (*0-375-43086-5*) Random Hse Lrg Prnt.

Pagan Background of Early Christianity. W. R. Holiday. 334p. 1988. reprint ed. spiral bd. 38.00 (*0-7873-0416-6*) Hlth Research.

Pagan Book of Days: Celebrating Festivals & Sacred Days Through the Millenium. Nigel Pennick. (Illus.). 160p. 1992. pap. 9.95 (*0-89281-369-5*) Inner Tradit.

***Pagan Book of Halloween: A Complete Guide to the Magick, Incantations, Recipes, Spells & Lore.** Gerina Dunwich. (Illus.). 224p. 2000. pap. 11.00 (*0-14-019616-1*) Penguin Putnam.

Pagan Book of Living & Dying: Practical Rituals, Prayers, Blessings & Meditations on Crossing Over. M. Macha Nightmare et al. LC 97-26317. (Illus.). 384p. 1997. pap. 18.00 (*0-06-251516-0*, Pub. by Harper SF) HarpC.

Pagan Celtic Britain. Anne Ross. 1996. pap. text 17.95 (*0-89733-435-3*) Academy Chi Pubs.

Pagan Celtic Ireland: The Enigma of the Irish Iron Age. Barry Raftery. LC 93-61274. (Illus.). 240p. 1998. pap. 29.95 (*0-500-27983-7*, Pub. by Thames Hudson) Norton.

Pagan Celts. Anne Ross. (Illus.). 250p. 1998. pap. 26.95 (*0-8464-4923-4*) Beekman Pubs.

Pagan Celts. Anne Ross. (Illus.). 224p. pap. 17.95 (*1-871083-61-3*, Pub. by J Jones Pub) Dufour.

***Pagan City & Christian Capital: Rome in the Fourth Century.** John Curran. LC 99-36418. (Oxford Classical Monographs). (Illus.). 300p. 2000. text 80.00 (*0-19-815278-7*) OUP.

Pagan Delights. 1999. mass mkt. 7.95 (*0-7867-0643-0*) Carroll & Graf.

Pagan Desires. Veronica Ashley. 352p. 1997. mass mkt. 4.99 (*0-8217-5764-4*, Zebra Kensgtn) Kensgtn Pub Corp.

Pagan Divinities & Their Worship As Depicted in the Work of St. Augustine. Mary Madden. 1972. 59.95 (*0-8490-0796-8*) Gordon Pr.

Pagan Family: Handing the Old Ways Down. Ceisiwr Serith. LC 93-48689. 264p. 1994. pap. 12.95 (*0-87542-210-1*) Llewellyn Pubns.

Pagan Feasts: Seasonal Food for the Eight Festivals. A. Franklin & S. Phillips. (Orig.). 1997. pap. 31.95 (*1-86163-009-3*, Pub. by Capall Bann Pubng) Holmes Pub.

Pagan Fires. large type ed. Lyn Granville. (Linford Romance Library). 400p. 1997. pap. 16.99 (*0-7089-5186-4*) Ulverscroft.

***Pagan Fleshworks: The Alchemy of Body Modification.** Maureen Mercury. LC 00-35700. 2000. pap. 19.95 (*0-89281-809-3*) Inner Tradit.

Pagan Grace: Dionysos, Hermes & Goddess Memory in Daily Life. Ginette Paris. Tr. by Joanna Mott from FRE. LC 89-26330. 152p. (Orig.). 1990. pap. 16.00 (*0-88214-342-5*) Spring Pubns.

Pagan Herbal: Herbs of Welsh Witchcraft. Rhuddlwm Gawr. LC 85-73746. (Illus.). 140p. 1989. 14.95 (*0-931760-36-4*, CP 10113); pap. 10.95 (*0-931760-13-5*) Camelot GA.

Pagan Kennedys Living. Pagan Kennedy. LC 97-9635. 1997. pap. 14.95 (*0-312-15621-9*) St Martin.

Pagan Land. large type ed. Thomas Marriott. 688p. 1983. 27.99 (*0-7089-8124-0*, Charnwood) Ulverscroft.

Pagan Logic & the Number Line Illusion. unabridged ed. Vance Cornell. (Illus.). 96p. 1998. pap. 5.95 (*1-882190-15-7*) Polar Bear ME.

Pagan Love Songs. Gavin G. Dillard. LC 87-71217. (Illus.). 94p. (Orig.). (C). 1987. pap. 7.95 (*0-944050-00-X*) Bhakti.

Pagan Meditations: Aphrodite, Hestia, Artemis. Ginette Paris. Tr. by Gwendolyn Moore from FRE. LC 86-6675. 204p. (Orig.). (C). 1986. pap. 19.00 (*0-88214-330-1*) Spring Pubns.

Pagan Middle Ages. Ed. by Ludo J. Milis. LC 98-40431. 168p. 1998. 55.00 (*0-85115-638-X*, Boydell Pr) Boydell & Brewer.

***Pagan Monotheism in Late Antiquity.** Ed. by Polymnia Athanassiadi & Michael Frede. LC 98-37019. (Illus.). 220p. 1999. text 70.00 (*0-19-815252-3*) OUP.

Pagan Operetta. Carl Hancock Rux. LC 98-13535. 140p. 1998. pap. 14.95 (*0-9639585-8-5*) Fly By Night.

Pagan Origins of the Christ Myth. John G. Jackson. 32p. 1988. 6.00 (*0-910309-53-1*, 5204) Am Atheist.

Pagan Papers. Kenneth Grahame. LC 72-3427. (Essay Index Reprint Ser.). 1977. reprint ed. 18.95 (*0-8369-2903-9*) Ayer.

***Pagan Parenting: Spiritual, Magical & Emotional Development of the Child.** Kristin Madden. 2000. pap. 14.95 (*1-56718-492-8*) Llewellyn Pubns.

Pagan Path. Janet Farrar et al. LC 95-205366. (Illus.). 224p. (Orig.). 1995. pap. 14.95 (*0-919345-40-9*) Phoenix WA.

***Pagan Patterns & Designs.** Elizabeth Fegley. (Illus.). 100p. 2000. spiral bd. write for info. (*1-890846-01-5*) Rowan Pr.

Pagan Priests: Religion & Power in the Ancient World. Ed. by Mary Beard & John North. LC 89-42954. 240p. 1989. text 47.50 (*0-8014-2401-1*) Cornell U Pr.

Pagan Prophet, William Morris. Charlotte H. Oberg. LC 77-4730. 199p. reprint ed. pap. 61.70 (*0-8357-3281-9*, 203950400013) Bks Demand.

Pagan Rabbi & Other Stories. Cynthia Ozick. (Library of Modern Jewish Literature). 228p. 1995. pap. 16.95 (*0-8156-0351-7*) Syracuse U Pr.

Pagan Races of the Malay Peninsula, 2 vols., Set. Walter W. Skeat & Charles O. Blagden. (Illus.). 1966. 75.00 (*0-7146-2027-0*, Pub. by F Cass Pubs) Intl Spec Bk.

Pagan Religions of the Ancient British Isles: Their Nature & Legacy. Ronald Hutton. (Illus.). 416p. (C). 1994. pap. text 27.95 (*0-631-18946-7*) Blackwell Pubs.

Pagan Resurrection Myths & the Resurrection of Jesus: A Christian Perspective. Leon McKenzie. 164p. (C). 1997. 21.95 (*1-880404-13-3*, Sthrn Academic) Bkwrights.

Pagan Rites of Passage. Lee Schrhodinger. LC 98-219240. 151 p. 1998. write for info. (*0-9664718-0-6*) Certain Publ.

Pagan Rites of Passage. 2nd ed. Pauline Campanelli. LC 97-53320. (Illus.). 288p. 1999. pap. 14.95 (*1-56718-111-2*) Llewellyn Pubns.

Pagan Ritual & Myth in Russian Magic Tales: A Study of Patterns. Marjorie Yovino-Young. LC 93-24800. (Illus.). 140p. 1993. text 69.95 (*0-7734-9307-7*) E Mellen.

Pagan Shore: Ireland in the Age of King Arthur. John Carnahan et al. Ed. by Sam Shirley. (Pendragon Roleplaying Ser.). (Illus.). 125p. 1994. pap. 18.95 (*1-56882-016-X*, 2713) Chaosium.

Pagan Soul. 208p. (Orig.). 8.95 (*0-8464-4266-3*) Beekman Pubs.

Pagan Spain. Richard Wright. LC 94-48234. 320p. 1995. pap. 12.00 (*0-06-092565-5*, Perennial) HarperTrade.

Pagan Summer. David Beasley. LC 96-900672. 256p. 1998. pap. 10.95 (*0-915317-07-9*, Pub. by Davus Pub) U of Toronto Pr.

Pagan Temptation. Thomas S. Molnar. LC 87-8898. 205p. (Orig.). reprint ed. pap. 63.60 (*0-7837-0519-0*, 204084300018) Bks Demand.

Pagan Traditions of the Holidays. David Ingraham. 38p. (Orig.). 1993. pap. 2.95 (*1-879366-42-8*) Hearthstone OK.

Pagan Tribes of Borneo, 2 vols., Set. Charles Hose & William McDougall. (Asia Handbook Reprints Ser.). (Illus.). 940p. 1993. reprint ed. text 140.00 (*0-19-588592-9*) OUP.

Pagan Virtue: An Essay in Ethics. John Casey. 254p. 1991. reprint ed. pap. text 26.00 (*0-19-824003-1*) OUP.

Pagan Wall. David Arnason. LC 92-246771. 304p. (Orig.). 1992. pap. 16.95 (*0-88922-312-2*, Pub. by Talonbks) Genl Dist Srvs.

Pagan Ways: Finding Your Spirituality in Nature. Gwydion O'Hara. LC 97-22994. (Illus.). 208p. (Orig.). 1999. pap. 7.95 (*1-56718-341-7*) Llewellyn Pubns.

Paganini. John Sugden. (Illustrated Lives of the Great Composers Ser.). (Illus.). 168p. 1996. 17.95 (*0-7119-0264-X*, OP 42506) Omnibus NY.

Paganini: Caprice No. 24 for Electric Classical Guitar. M. Paganini. 32p. 1993. pap. 17.95 (*0-7935-2335-4*, 00699381) H Leonard.

Paganini of Genoa. Lillian Day. 318p. 1990. reprint ed. lib. bdg. 79.00 (*0-7812-9101-1*) Rprt Serv.

Paganini, the Romantic Virtuoso. Jeffrey Pulver. (Music Book Index Ser.). 328p. 1992. reprint ed. lib. bdg. 89.00 (*0-7812-9470-3*) Rprt Serv.

Paganini 1887-1891. Ed. by H. Robert Cohen. (Repertoire International de la Presse Musicale Ser.). (ITA.). 310p. 1993. lib. bdg. 145.00 (*0-8357-2260-0*) UMI.

Paganism: A Beginner's Guide. Teresa Vidgen-Moorey. (Beginners Ser.). (Illus.). 96p. 1996. pap. 11.95 (*0-340-67013-4*, Pub. by Hodder & Stought Ltd) Trafalgar.

Paganism & Christianity, 100-425 C.E. A Sourcebook. Ed. by Ramsay MacMullen & Eugene N. Lane. LC 92-3069. 224p. (Orig.). 1992. pap. 20.00 (*0-8006-2647-8*, 1-2647, Fortress Pr) Augsburg Fortress.

Paganism in Arthurian Romance. John Darrah. LC 97-23497. 320p. 1997. pap. 35.00 (*0-85991-426-7*, DS Brewer) Boydell & Brewer.

Paganism in Our Christianity. Arthur Weigall. 1974. 250.00 (*0-87968-149-7*) Gordon Pr.

Paganism in Roumanian Folklore. Marcu Beza. LC 74-173102. (Illus.). 172p. 1972. reprint ed. lib. bdg. 17.95 (*0-405-08267-3*, Pub. by Blom Pubns) Ayer.

Paganism in the Roman Empire. Ramsay MacMullen. LC 80-54222. 384p. 1983. pap. 16.00 (*0-300-02984-5*) Yale U Pr.

Pagans. Arlo Bates. LC 70-104411. 275p. reprint ed. lib. bdg. 32.00 (*0-8398-0153-X*) Irvington.

Pagans. Arlo Bates. (C). 1986. reprint ed. pap. text 7.95 (*0-8290-1860-3*) Irvington.

Pagans & Christians: The Interplay Between Christian Latin & Traditional Germanic Cultures in Early Medieval Europe. Ed. by L. A. Houwen et al. (Mediaevalia Groningana Ser.: No. XVI). 212p. 1995. pap. 52.00 (*90-6980-076-4*, Pub. by Egbert Forsten) Hod1der & Stoughton.

***Pagans & Christians: The Personal Spiritual Experience.** Gus DiZerega. 2001. pap. 14.95 (*1-56718-228-3*) Llewellyn Pubns.

***Pagans & Christians in Late Antiquity: A Sourcebook.** A. D. Lee. LC 00-21697. 2000. pap. write for info. (*0-415-13893-0*) Routledge.

Pagans, Christians & Jews. rev. ed. David C. Riede & J. Wayne Baker. LC 73-166489. v, 149p. 1974. write for info. (*0-8403-0440-4*) Kendall-Hunt.

***Pagan's Crusade.** Catherine Jinnks. LC 99-50746. (Starmaker Books Ser.). 156p. (J). (gr. 6-9). 2000. pap. 5.50 (*0-88489-506-8*) St Marys.

Pagan's Father. Michael Arditti. LC 96-12308. 436p. 1996. 24.00 (*1-56947-062-0*) Soho Press.

Pagan's Father. Michael Arditti. 416p. 2000. pap. 14.00 (*1-56947-183-5*) Soho Press.

Pagans in My Blood. John Magor. 120p. 1992. pap. 14.95 (*0-88839-291-5*) Hancock House.

Pagans of North Borneo. Owen Rutter. (Illus.). 298p. 1986. 32.50 (*0-19-582627-2*) OUP.

Pagans of North Borneo. Owen Rutter. LC 77-87003. (Illus.). reprint ed. 37.50 (*0-404-16776-4*) AMS Pr.

Page. Mark Dunster. 30p. (Orig.). 1990. pap. 5.00 (*0-89642-181-3*) Linden Pubs.

Page. Tamora Pierce. LC 99-89894. (Protector of the Small Ser.: No. 2). 240p. (J). (gr. 5-9). 2000. 16.00 (*0-679-88915-9*, Pub. by Random Bks Yng Read) Random.

Page. Tamora Pierce. LC 99-89894. (Protector of the Small Ser.: No. 2). (Illus.). 240p. (J). (gr. 5-9). 2000. lib. bdg. 17.99 (*0-679-98915-3*, Pub. by Random Bks Yng Read) Random.

Page: Genealogical Registers of Ancestors & Descendants of Lemuel Page & Polly Paige, Peter Joslin & Sarah Kidder, with Brief Accounts of Them & Their Ancestors. Luke J. Page. (Illus.). 155p. 1994. reprint ed. pap. 25.00 (*0-685-75322-0*); reprint ed. lib. bdg. 35.00 (*0-685-75321-2*) Higginson Bk Co.

Page: Genealogy of the Page Family in Virginia, Also a Condensed Account of the Nelson, Walker, Pendleton & Randolph Families with References to Other Distinguished Families in Virginia. 2nd ed. Richard C. Page. (Illus.). 275p. 1993. reprint ed. pap. 45.00 (*0-8328-3093-3*); reprint ed. lib. bdg. 55.00 (*0-8328-3092-5*) Higginson Bk Co.

Page: Plays One. Louise Page. (Methuen World Dramatists Ser.). 324p. (Orig.). (C). 1990. pap. 13.95 (*0-413-64500-2*, A0498, Methuen Drama) Methn.

Page: The Family of John Page of Haverhill, Massachusetts: A Comprehensive Genealogy from 1614 to 1977. Lynn Case & Page Sanderson. (Illus.). 250p. 1991. reprint ed. pap. 37.50 (*0-8328-1936-0*); reprint ed. lib. bdg. 47.50 (*0-8328-1935-2*) Higginson Bk Co.

Page: Wisconsin Page Pioneers & Kinfolk. Turner & Sayre. (Illus.). 485p. 1991. reprint ed. pap. 74.50 (*0-8328-1827-5*); reprint ed. lib. bdg. 84.50 (*0-8328-1826-7*) Higginson Bk Co.

Page a Day Pursuits. Ed. by Scholastic, Inc. Staff. 1993. pap. 15.95 (*0-590-49024-9*) Scholastic Inc.

Page a Minute Memory Book. Harry Lorayne. LC 96-223854. 1996. pap. 10.00 (*0-345-41014-9*) Ballantine Pub Grp.

Page As a Stage Set: Storyboard Pictures Books. Amy E. Spaulding. LC 94-12276. 1995. 41.50 (*0-8108-2892-8*) Scarecrow.

Page, Carolina Pages: A Compilation of Genealogical Information on Page Families in the Carolinas Beginning in 1521 to Present Time. Robert E. Page, III. (Illus.). 293p. 1992. pap. 45.00 (*0-8328-2701-0*); lib. bdg. 55.00 (*0-8328-2700-2*) Higginson Bk Co.

Page County, Virginia Marriage Bonds, 1831-1850. John Vogt & T. William Kethley, Jr. (Illus.). 74 p. (Orig.). 1983. pap. 7.95 (*0-935931-11-2*) Iberian Pub.

Page d'Amour. Emile Zola. (Coll. Diamant). 14.95 (*0-685-23947-0*) Fr & Eur.

Page d'Amour. Emile Zola. (FRE.). 404p. 1989. pap. 10.95 (*0-7859-1378-5*, 2070381870) Fr & Eur.

***Page Design.** Ed. by Lynn Haller. (Creative Edge Ser.). (Illus.). 144p. 2000. pap. 21.99 (*1-58180-064-9*, North Lght Bks) F & W Pubns Inc.

Page Disgracie: The Text As Confession. Mary L. Gude. LC 78-21281. (Romance Monographs: No. 33). 169p. 1979. 24.00 (*84-499-2554-1*) Romance.

Page et le Petit Ecran: Culture et Televison: Le Cas d'Apostrophes. Gisele Holtzer. (Sciences pour la Communication Ser.: Vol. 47). (FRE.). 7212p. 1996. 35.95 (*3-906754-36-7*, Pub. by P Lang) P Lang Pubng.

Page Layout. Robin B. McAllister. (C). 1997. pap. 12.95 (*0-8273-7920-X*) Delmar.

***Page Layout.** Roger Walton. (Illus.). 144p. 2000. 35.00 (*0-688-17989-4*) HarpC.

Page of History in Relief, 1944-1946. Eryl Hall-Williams. 1999. pap. 21.00 (*1-85072-124-6*, Pub. by W Sessions) St Mut.

***Page of the Duke of Savoy.** Alexandre Dumas. 252p. 2000. pap. 9.95 (*0-594-03021-8*) Eightn Hundrd.

Page on Wills: Bowe-Parker Revision, 8 vols. William J. Bowe et al. 7732p. 1983. text. write for info. (*0-87084-682-5*) Anderson Pub Co.

Page on Wills: 1998 Supplement, 8 vols. Jeffery A. Schoenbleum. 1997. pap. write for info. (*0-614-30940-9*) Anderson Pub Co.

Page One. New York Times Staff. 1992. 17.98 (*0-88365-809-7*) Galahad Bks.

Page One. Cabral Vasquez. 365p. 1996. 24.95 (*1-57087-192-2*) Prof Pr NC.

***Page One.** rev. ed. New York Times Staff. 416p. 2000. 24.99 (*1-57866-088-2*) Galahad Bks.

Page One: Major Events As Presented in the New York Times, 1920-1981. Herbert J. Cohen. 19.95 (*0-405-14350-8*, 19818) Ayer.

Page One: Major Events, Nineteen Twenty to Nineteen Seventy-Eight, As Presented in the New York Times. 1980. 18.95 (*0-405-11751-5*) Ayer.

Page One: Major Events, 1920-1976, As Presented in the New York Times. (Illus.). 292p. 1976. 18.95 (*0-405-06645-7*) Arno Press.

Page One: Major Events, 1922-1980 as Presented in the New York Times. Herbert J. Cohen. 1980. 19.95 (*0-405-13698-6*) Ayer.

Page One: The Front Page History of World War II. New York Times Staff. LC 96-77431. 192p. 1996. 19.98 (*0-88365-962-X*) Galahad Bks.

Page One: The New York Times, 1995. New York Times Staff. 1995. 24.98 (*0-88365-906-9*) Galahad Bks.

Page One: The New York Times, 1997 Edition. New York Times Staff. (Illus.). 400p. 1997. 24.99 (*1-57866-006-8*) Galahad Bks.

Page One: 1994 Edition Major Events 1920-1994 As Presented in the New York Times. New York Times Staff. 1994. 19.98 (*0-88365-884-4*) Galahad Bks.

Page One: The New York Times: Major Events 1900-1998 as Presented in The New York Times, 1998 Edition. New York Times Staff. 1998. 24.99 (*1-57866-032-7*) Galahad Bks.

Page Plus 3 for You. Richard Hunt. (Orig.). 1996. pap. 34.95 (*1-898307-41-5*, Pub. by Capall Bann Pubng) Holmes Pub.

Page Street. Mark J. Boskovich. Ed. by Vicki Werkley. LC 93-71592. (Illus.). 272p. (Orig.). 1993. pap. 9.95 (*0-9635958-0-6*) Abalone Pub.

Page to Screen: Taking Literacy into the Electronic Era. Ed. by Ilana Snyder. 240p. 1997. pap. 29.95 (*1-86448-435-7*, Pub. by Allen & Unwin Pty) Paul & Co Pubs.

Page to Screen: Taking Literacy into the Electronic Era. Ilana Snyder. LC 97-28483. (Illus.). 260p. (C). 1997. 75.00 (*0-415-17464-3*); pap. 24.99 (*0-415-17465-1*) Routledge.

Page Turner. David Leavitt. LC 97-44864. 192p. 1998. 24.00 (*0-395-75285-X*) HM.

Page Turner. David Leavitt. 192p. 1999. pap. 12.00 (*0-395-95787-7*, Mariner Bks) HM.

Page-Turner. David Shapiro. 57p. 1973. 4.95 (*0-87140-575-X*, Pub. by Liveright) Norton.

Page-Turner. David Shapiro. 1973. pap. 2.50 (*0-87140-287-4*, Pub. by Liveright) Norton.

***Pageant.** Albert Evans et al. LC 98-222978. (Musical Library). 61p. 1998. write for info. (*0-573-69655-1*) French.

Pageant. Trevor Winkfield. LC 97-28596. (Art Profile Ser.: Vol. 4). 40p. 1997. pap. text 19.95 (*1-889097-12-8*) Hard Pr MA.

Pageant-Master of the Republic. David L. Dowd. LC 72-75507. (Select Bibliographies Reprint Ser.). 1977. 24.95 (*0-8369-5005-4*) Ayer.

***Pageant of a Woman.** Josee Andrei. (Illus.). 146p. 2000. pap. 30.00 (*1-892453-05-3*) AMP Pr.

Pageant of Art. Vienna I. Curtiss. LC 77-280. (Illus.). 1979. 27.50 (*0-9602742-2-7*) Collectors Choice.

Pageant of Dickens. W. Walter Crotch. LC 72-3293. (Studies in Dickens: No. 52). 1972. reprint ed. lib. bdg. 75.00 (*0-8383-1502-X*) M S G Haskell Hse.

Pageant of English Actors. Donald Brook. LC 71-38315. (Biography Index Reprint Ser.). 1977. reprint ed. 20.95 (*0-8369-8116-2*) Ayer.

Pageant of Ibero-American Civilization: An Introduction to Its Cultural History. Rafael E. Tarrago. LC 95-10931. (Illus.). 138p. (C). 1995. 34.00 (*0-8191-9972-9*) U Pr of Amer.

Pageant of Indian Culture, 2 vols., Set. A. K. Bhattacharyya. (C). 1995. 225.00 (*0-317-99886-2*, Pub. by Abhinav) S Asia.

Pageant of Its Time: Edward Dorn's "Slinger" & the Sixties. James Elmborg. LC 96-17601. (Studies in Modern Poetry: Vol. 6). XII, 143p. (C). 1998. text 38.95 (*0-8204-3320-9*) P Lang Pubng.

Pageant of Letters. Alfred Noyes. LC 68-22935. (Essay Index Reprint Ser.). 1977. reprint ed. 23.95 (*0-8369-0749-3*) Ayer.

Pageant of Manuscript Books from the 13th to the 19th Centuries - Les Fastes du Livre Manuscrit du XIIIe au XIX e Siecle. Sandra Hindman. (ENG & FRE.). 168p. 1993. pap. text. write for info. (*0-9634255-1-X*) Les Enluminures.

Pageant of Old Scandinavia. Ed. by Henry G. Leach. LC 68-57061. (Granger Index Reprint Ser.). 1977. 21.95 (*0-8369-6025-4*) Ayer.

Pageant of Transport Through the Ages. W. H. Boulton. 1976. lib. bdg. 344.95 (*0-8490-2398-X*) Gordon Pr.

Pageant of Transport Through the Ages. William H. Boulton. LC 77-81514. (Illus.). 245p. 1972. 24.95 (*0-405-08296-7*, Pub. by Blom Pubns) Ayer.

Pageantry of the English Language. 2nd rev. ed. W. D. Snively. LC 83-80274. (Illus.). 80p. 1983. reprint ed. pap. text 9.95 (*0-930982-03-7*) U of Evansville Pr.

Pageantry on the Shakespearean Stage. Alice V. Griffin. (Orig.). 1951. pap. 15.95 (*0-8084-0239-0*) NCUP.

Pageants. Houghton Mifflin Company Staff. (Reading Ser.). (J). 1988. pap., teacher ed., suppl. ed. 9.20 (*0-395-45595-2*); pap., teacher ed., wbk. ed. 21.36 (*0-395-45571-5*); pap., wbk. ed. 17.84 (*0-395-45556-1*) HM.

Pageants. Houghton Mifflin Company Staff. (Reading Ser.). (J). 1988. pap., teacher ed. 87.00 (*0-395-43703-2*) HM.

Pageants of Despair. Dennis Hamley. LC 74-10841. 180p. (J). (gr. 7-10). 1974. 26.95 (*0-87599-205-6*) S G Phillips.

PageMaker: Graphic Design with Pagemaker Macintosh Version 5.0. Bill Parsons. LC 93-37661. 337p. 1993. pap. 31.95 (*0-8273-5751-6*) Delmar.

PageMaker: Start to Finish. Jon M. Duff. 528p. 1991. pap. 38.95 (*0-8273-4480-5*) Delmar.

PageMaker Companion 5. Robin Williams et al. 969p. 46.00 (*0-614-25532-5*, 00PO44631) Print Indus Am.

PageMaker 5 for the Mac for Dummies. Galen Gruman. LC 94-77186. 384p. 1994. pap. 19.95 (*1-56884-178-7*) IDG Bks.

P

An Asterisk (*) at the beginning of an entry indicates that the title is appearing for the first time.

PageMaker 5 for Windows: A Self-Teaching Guide. Kim Baker & Sunny Baker. 304p. 1993. pap. 22.95 (*0-471-58953-5*) Wiley.

PageMaker 5 for Windows: Everything You Need to Know. William B. Sanders. LC 93-16253. 1993. pap. 19.95 (*1-55958-337-1*) Prima Pub.

PageMaker 5 for Windows for Dummies. Deke McClelland. LC 94-77746. 416p. 1994. pap. 19.95 (*1-56884-160-4*) IDG Bks.

PageMaker 5 Mac & IBM. DDC Publishing Staff. LC 94-171352. 1994. spiral bd. 12.00 (*1-56243-134-X*, PM18) DDC Pub.

PageMaker 5.0. Douglas M. Finney. 230p. 1995. spiral bd. 29.95 incl. 3.5 hd (*1-56435-034-7*) Finney Lrng Systs.

PageMaker 5.0: Basics & Beyond. M. G. Detienne. (Illus.). 97p. pap. text 29.00 (*1-887580-05-0*) Tec Trek.

PageMaker 5.0 Expert Techniques (Macintosh Edition) Michael J. Nolan. (Illus.). 208p. 1993. 34.95 (*1-56830-017-4*) Hayden.

PageMaker 5.0 for the Macintosh: Techniques & Applications. Jay Cosnett. 1995. pap. 29.95 incl. disk (*1-55828-286-6*, MIS Pr) IDG Bks.

PageMaker 5.0 for Windows & Macintosh: Quick Course. William R. Pasewark. (Quicktorial Ser.). 1996. mass mkt. 22.95 (*0-538-71505-7*) S-W Pub.

PageMaker 5.0 for Windows by Example. Webster & Associates Staff. LC 93-17388. 1995. pap. 29.95 incl. disk (*1-55851-297-7*, M&T Bks) IDG Bks.

PageMaker 5.0 for Windows Complete Scripting Guide. G. Keith Gurganus. 1994. 61.00 (*0-07-025238-6*) McGraw.

PageMaker 5.0 Windows Introduction. Computer Confidence Staff. (Illus.). 160p. 1995. spiral bd. 29.95 incl. disk (*1-57533-003-2*) Comput Confidence.

PageMaker 5.0: A Professional Approach. Deborah A. Hinkle. LC 94-5261. 1995. write for info. (*0-02-802230-0*) Glencoe.

PageMaker for the Macintosh. Robert Krumm. LC 88-12945. 1988. 19.95 (*0-943518-96-2*, MIS Pr) IDG Bks.

PageMaker 4 for MAC Concepts & Applications Desktop. Moore & Arntson. (DF - Computer Applications Ser.). (C). mass mkt. 34.95 (*0-538-70609-0*) S-W Pub.

PageMaker 4.0 for Windows: From Installation to Output. William B. Sanders. 352p. (Orig.). 1991. pap. 19.95 (*1-55958-093-3*) Prima Pub.

PageMaker 4.0 Macintosh Version: Concepts & Applications for the Desktop Publisher. Carolyn Taylor. (C). 1992. pap. 47.95 (*0-538-70611-2*) S-W Pub.

PageMaker 4.0 (PC) Douglas M. Finney. 225p. 1991. student ed., spiral bd. 29.95 incl. disk (*1-56435-013-4*) Finney Lrng Systs.

PageMaker 4.2 for the Macintosh: Everything You Need to Know. William B. Sanders. (Illus.). 288p. (Orig.). 1992. pap. 19.95 (*1-55958-239-1*) Prima Pub.

***Pagemaker Plus-illustrated.** TBD. (Illustrated Ser.). 2001. write for info. (*0-619-01768-6*) Course Tech.

PageMaker Production Techniques. Gary Poyssick. (Illus.). 320p. (Orig.). 1995. pap. text 30.00 (*1-56830-170-7*, Alpha Ref) Macmillan Gen Ref.

PageMaker 6: Training on CD. Quay2 Multimedia Staff. 1996. pap. 69.95 incl. cd-rom (*0-201-88410-0*) Peachpit Pr.

PageMaker 6 for Windows & Macintosh Quicktorial. William R. Pasewark. (DF - Computer Applications Ser.). 1996. pap. text, mass mkt. 21.95 incl. disk (*0-538-71640-1*) S-W Pub.

Pagemaker 6.5 for Windows for Dummies. 3rd ed. Elizabeth A. McClelland. LC 97-70370. 408p. 1997. pap. 19.99 (*0-7645-0126-7*) IDG Bks.

PageMaker 6.5 for Macintosh: Visual QuickStart Guide. Ted Alspach. LC 97-222189. 304p. (C). 1997. pap. text 18.95 (*0-201-69649-5*, Pub. by Peachpit Pr) Addison-Wesley.

PageMaker 6.5 for Macintosh & Windows. David D. Busch. LC 97-104. (Teach Yourself Ser.). 448p. 1997. pap. text 29.95 (*1-55828-539-3*, MIS Pr) IDG Bks.

PageMaker 6.5 for Windows: Visual QuickStart Guide. Ted Alspach. LC 97-226315. 304p. (C). 1997. pap. text 18.95 (*0-201-69650-9*, Pub. by Peachpit Pr) Addison-Wesley.

PageMaker 6.5 for Windows 95 Bible. Nigel French. LC 97-73912. 600p. 1997. pap. 39.99 (*0-7645-4034-3*) IDG Bks.

***Pagemaker 6.5 Plus for Windows: Visual Quickstart Guide.** 2nd ed. Ted Alspach. LC 99-461830. 320p. (C). 1999. pap. text 18.99 (*0-201-35460-8*) Peachpit Pr.

PageMaker 6.0 for Windows. Boyd & Fraser Staff. (STAR Ser.). 1996. pap. 12.95 (*0-7895-0348-4*) Course Tech.

PageMaker 3 Solutions. Lee Noel, Jr. (Illus.). (Orig.). 1989. pap. 18.95 (*0-929307-06-2*) GP Pubns.

PageMaker Workshop. 2nd rev. ed. Steven Kosek & Joy Kuhnen. LC 96-68973. (Illus.). 320p. (C). 1996. pap. text 65.00 (*1-57576-445-8*) Que Educ & Trng.

PageMaker "X" by Example: Macintosh Edition. Tony Webster & David Webster. 550p. (Orig.). 1995. pap. 29.95 incl. disk (*1-55851-292-6*, M&T Bks) IDG Bks.

Pagemaker 6.5: Design & Applications. L. Louise Van Osdol. LC 97-42025. 1997. write for info. (*1-56118-801-8*); write for info. (*1-56118-802-6*); 34.95 (*1-56118-805-0*) Paradigm MN.

Pagemaker 6.5 - Win 95/NT. (Quick Study Computer Ser.). 4p. pap. 3.95 (*1-57222-268-9*) Barcharts.

PageMaker 6.5 Complete. Shamms Mortier. LC 96-78099. 928p. 1997. 45.00 (*1-56830-331-9*) Hayden.

Pagemaster. Adapted by Carol A. Hanshaw. (Comes to Life Bks.). 16p. (J). (ps-2). 1994. write for info. (*1-883366-41-0*) YES Ent.

Pagemaster. Todd Strasser. 128p. (YA). 1994. pap. 3.50 (*0-590-20243-X*) Scholastic Inc.

PageMill: Training on CD. Multimedia Quay2 Staff. 1996. pap. text 49.95 (*0-201-88616-2*) Peachpit Pr.

***PageMill 3 for Macintosh & Windows: Visual QuickStart Guide.** Maria Langer. (Visual QuickStart Guide Ser.). 304p. (C). 1998. pap. text 17.99 (*0-201-35443-8*, Pub. by Peachpit Pr) Addison-Wesley.

PageMill 2 for Macintosh: Visual QuickStart Guide. Maria Langer. LC 97-127589. (Illus.). 256p. (C). 1996. pap. text 16.95 (*0-201-69402-6*) Peachpit Pr.

Pagenstecher-Lekythoi. Rolf Hurschmann. (Jahrbuch des Deutschen Archaeologischen Instituts Ser.: Vol. 29). (GER., Illus.). xi, 81p. (Orig.). (C). 1997. pap. text 83.00 (*3-11-014861-7*) De Gruyter.

Pageplus for Windows 3.1 Made Simple. Sinclair. 160p. Date not set. pap. text 19.95 (*0-7506-2312-8*) Buttrwrth-Heinemann.

***Pager (Beeper) Manual.** unabridged ed. John J. Williams. (Illus.). 23p. 1998. pap. 29.00 (*0-934274-76-2*) Consumertronics.

Pager Handbook for the Radio Amateur. Philip N. Anderson. 124p. 1996. pap. 14.95 (*1-887736-08-5*) Xtal Set Soc.

Pages: Innovative Book Making Techniques. Linda F. Kenzle. LC 97-74245. (Illus.). 128p. 1998. pap. 19.95 (*0-87341-547-7*) Krause Pubns.

***Pages: New Poems & Cuttings.** John Matthias. LC 99-32582. 160p. 2000. 28.95 (*0-8040-1019-6*); pap. 14.95 (*0-8040-1020-X*) Ohio U Pr.

Pages & Pictures from Forgotten Children's Books. Andrew W. Tuer et al. 1973. 44.95 (*0-8490-0797-6*) Gordon Pr.

Pages Choisies. (FRE.). (C). 1996. pap. 6.99 (*0-8442-1031-5*, VF1031-5) NTC Contemp Pub Co.

Pages Choisies. Antoine de Saint-Exupery. (FRE.). pap. 8.50 (*0-685-37085-2*) Fr & Eur.

Pages Complementaires. Nouveau. Ed. by Pakenham. (Exeter French Texts Ser.: Vol. 49). (FRE.). 144p. Date not set. pap. text 19.95 (*0-85989-178-X*, Pub. by Univ Exeter Pr) Northwestern U Pr.

Pages de Prose. Paul Claudel. (FRE.). 428p. 1944. 14.95 (*0-7859-1119-7*, 2070215091) Fr & Eur.

Page's Drift: R. S. Thomas at Eighty. Ed. by E. Wynn Thomas. 232p. 1993. 45.00 (*1-85411-093-4*, Pub. by Seren Bks) Dufour.

Page's Drift: R. S. Thomas at Eighty. Ed. by E. Wynn Thomas. 232p. 1993. pap. 19.95 (*1-85411-100-0*, Pub. by Seren Bks) Dufour.

Pages from a Charred Notebook. Eisman. write for info. (*0-88125-677-3*) Ktav.

Pages from a Child's Documentary. Kesa Thomas. LC 79-67480. (Illus.). 1979. pap. 9.95 (*0-917986-06-7*) NFS Pr.

Pages from a Journal. Joyce Butler. LC 76-685. (Illus.). 171p. 1976. 11.95 (*0-89080-006-5*) Rosemary Hse.

Pages from a Journal, with Other Papers. William H. White. (BCL1-PR English Literature Ser.). 343p. 1992. reprint ed. lib. bdg. 89.00 (*0-7812-7577-6*) Rprt Serv.

Pages from a Musician's Life. Fritz Busch. Tr. by Marjorie Strachey. LC 71-106715. (Illus.). 223p. 1971. reprint ed. lib. bdg. 59.50 (*0-8371-3445-5*, BUML, Greenwood Pr) Greenwood.

Pages from a Palo Alto Editor's Scrapbook. Ward Winslow. LC 94-90135. (Illus.). 224p. (Orig.). 1994. pap. 11.09 (*0-9641432-5-9*) Ward Winslow.

Pages from a Scrapbook of Immigrants. Morton Marcus. LC 88-30234. 144p. (Orig.). (YA). (gr. 10-12). 1988. pap. 8.95 (*0-918273-47-1*) Coffee Hse.

Pages from a Vice-Chancellor's Diary. Iqbal Narain. 1990. 21.50 (*81-7001-080-2*, Pub. by Chanakya) S Asia.

Pages from a Worker's Life. William Z. Foster. LC 72-130864. (Illus.). 1970. reprint ed. pap. 3.25 (*0-7178-0149-7*) Intl Pubs Co.

Pages from an Old Volume of Life. Oliver W. Holmes. (Notable American Authors Ser.). 1992. reprint ed. lib. bdg. 75.00 (*0-7812-3159-0*) Rprt Serv.

Pages from Hopi History. Harry C. James. LC 73-86451. 258p. 1974. pap. 15.95 (*0-8165-0500-4*) U of Ariz Pr.

Pages from My Life's Book see Paginas del Libro de Mi Vida

Pages from Russian Fiction: Russian Reader with Explanatory Notes. Ed. by N. A. Eremina. 352p. 1989. pap. text 8.95 (*0-8285-4901-X*) Firebird NY.

***Pages from the Book of the Sun: New & Selected Poems.** Niyi Osundare. LC 00-33217. 2000. pap. write for info. (*0-86543-868-4*) Africa World.

Pages from the Harlem Renaissance: A Chronicle of Performance. Anthony Hill. (Studies in African & African-American Culture: Vol. 6). XII, 185p. (C). 1996. pap. text 29.95 (*0-8204-2864-7*) P Lang Pubng.

Pages from the Mages: Forgotten Realms Accessory. Ed Greenwood. 1995. 15.00 (*0-7869-0183-7*, Pub. by TSR Inc) Random.

Pages from the Past. Herbert A. Fisher. LC 75-90638. (Essay Index Reprint Ser.). 1977. 20.95 (*0-8369-1260-8*) Ayer.

Pages from the Past: A Pictorial History of Fort Jefferson. Albert C. Manucy. (Illus.). 32p. 1999. pap. 7.95 (*0-945142-06-4*) FL Natl Parks.

Pages from the Past: Thirty Years of Victorian Life in the Beverley Guardian. Paul Hesp & Peter Robinson. (C). 1989. text 40.00 (*0-948929-05-7*) St Mut.

Pages Glued Apart. Fern E. Winklepleck-Stuefen. Ed. by Janet Leih. (Illus.). 104p. (Orig.). 1990. pap. 10.00 (*1-877649-11-2*) Tesseract SD.

Pages in History: The Art of Aminah Robinson. Dennison W. Griffith. Ed. by Norma J. Roberts. (Illus.). 65p. (Orig.). 1990. pap. 8.95 (*0-918881-24-2*) Columbus Mus Art.

Pages in Waiting. James Milne. LC 74-93357. (Essay Index Reprint Ser.). 1977. 20.95 (*0-8369-1308-6*) Ayer.

***Pages of Day & Night.** A. Adonis. 2001. pap. 15.95 (*0-8101-6081-1*) Northwestern U Pr.

Pages of Day & Night. Ali Ahmed Sa'id Adonis. Tr. by Samuel Hazo from ARA. LC 93-79810. 144p. 1994. 22.95 (*0-910395-96-9*) Marlboro Pr.

Pages of Glory: Georgia's Documentary Heritage. Josephine Hart Brandon. LC 98-75550. (Illus.). 189p. 1998. 15.00 (*1-881682-06-4*) GA Hist Soc.

Pages of Italian Photography, 1900-1998. Text by Patrick C. Coffield. (Illus.). 216p. 1999. pap. 35.00 (*88-8158-177-9*, Pub. by Charta) Dist Art Pubs.

Pages of Music. Tony Johnston. (Illus.). 32p. (J). (gr. k-3). 1988. lib. bdg. 13.95 (*0-399-21436-4*, G P Putnam) Peng Put Young Read.

***Pages of My Mind.** 2nd rev. ed. Dana D. Hanes. (Illus.). 88p. 1999. per. 11.95 (*0-9660447-1-1*) Syntax Pubng.

***Pages of My Mind, Vol. 2.** 2nd rev. ed. Dana D. Hanes. (Illus.). 88p. 1999. per. 11.95 (*0-9660447-2-X*) Syntax Pubng.

***Pages of My Mind, Vol. 3.** 2nd rev. ed. Dana D. Hanes. (Illus.). 88p. 1999. per. 11.95 (*0-9660447-3-8*) Syntax Pubng.

***Pages of My Mind: Cool, Calm, Collected.** 2nd ed. Dana Hawes. LC 99-97545. (Illus.). 180p. 2000. pap. 19.95 (*0-9660447-4-6*) Syntax Pubng.

Pages of Pain. Troy Denning. 1998. pap. 5.99 (*0-7869-0825-4*) TSR Inc.

Pages of Pain. TSR Inc. Staff. 1998. pap. 5.99 (*0-7869-0671-5*, Pub. by TSR Inc) Random.

Pages of Stone: Geology of Western National Parks & Monuments: Grand Canyon & the Plateau Country, Vol. 4. Halka Chronic. LC 82-422. (Illus.). 182p. (Orig.). 1988. pap. 16.95 (*0-89886-155-1*) Mountaineers.

***Pages of Time.** Murdic H. Jones. 206p. 1999. pap. 12.95 (*0-7392-0379-7*, PO3595) Morris Pubng.

Pages of Time: Memoirs of a Southern Sportsman. S. Lloyd Newberry. (Illus.). 350p. 1996. 24.95 (*0-9650388-0-7*) Spartina Pubng.

Pages of Time, 1984. Paul W. Bates. (Illus.). 24p. (Orig.). 1993. pap. 4.95 (*1-56046-084-9*) Interact Pubs.

Pages of Time, 1918. Paul W. Bates. (Illus.). 24p. (Orig.). 1993. pap. 4.95 (*1-56046-018-0*) Interact Pubs.

Pages of Time, 1980. Paul W. Bates. (Illus.). 24p. (Orig.). 1993. pap. 4.95 (*1-56046-080-6*) Interact Pubs.

Pages of Time, 1988. Paul W. Bates. (Illus.). 24p. (Orig.). 1993. pap. 4.95 (*1-56046-088-1*) Interact Pubs.

Pages of Time, 1985. Paul W. Bates. (Illus.). 24p. (Orig.). 1993. pap. 4.95 (*1-56046-085-7*) Interact Pubs.

Pages of Time, 1989. Paul W. Bates. (Illus.). 24p. (Orig.). 1993. pap. 4.95 (*1-56046-089-X*) Interact Pubs.

Pages of Time, 1981. Paul W. Bates. (Illus.). 24p. (Orig.). 1993. pap. 4.95 (*1-56046-081-4*) Interact Pubs.

Pages of Time, 1987. Paul W. Bates. (Illus.). 24p. (Orig.). 1993. pap. 4.95 (*1-56046-087-3*) Interact Pubs.

Pages of Time, 1986. Paul W. Bates. (Illus.). 24p. (Orig.). 1993. pap. 4.95 (*1-56046-086-5*) Interact Pubs.

Pages of Time, 1983. Paul W. Bates. (Illus.). 24p. (Orig.). 1993. pap. 4.95 (*1-56046-083-0*) Interact Pubs.

Pages of Time, 1982. Paul W. Bates. (Illus.). 24p. (Orig.). 1993. pap. 4.95 (*1-56046-082-2*) Interact Pubs.

Pages of Time, 1911. Paul W. Bates. (Illus.). 24p. (Orig.). 1993. pap. 4.95 (*1-56046-311-2*) Interact Pubs.

Pages of Time, 1915. Paul W. Bates. (Illus.). 24p. (Orig.). 1993. pap. 4.95 (*1-56046-015-6*) Interact Pubs.

Pages of Time, 1950. Paul W. Bates. (Illus.). 24p. (Orig.). 1989. pap. 4.95 (*1-56046-050-4*) Interact Pubs.

Pages of Time, 1958. Paul W. Bates. (Illus.). 24p. (Orig.). 1989. pap. 4.95 (*1-56046-058-X*) Interact Pubs.

Pages of Time, 1955. Paul W. Bates. (Illus.). 24p. (Orig.). 1989. pap. 4.95 (*1-56046-055-5*) Interact Pubs.

Pages of Time, 1954. Paul W. Bates. (Illus.). 24p. (Orig.). 1989. pap. 4.95 (*1-56046-054-7*) Interact Pubs.

Pages of Time, 1959. Paul W. Bates. (Illus.). 24p. (Orig.). 1989. pap. 4.95 (*1-56046-059-8*) Interact Pubs.

Pages of Time, 1951. Paul W. Bates. (Illus.). 24p. (Orig.). 1989. pap. 4.95 (*1-56046-051-2*) Interact Pubs.

Pages of Time, 1957. Paul W. Bates. (Illus.). 24p. (Orig.). 1989. pap. 4.95 (*1-56046-057-1*) Interact Pubs.

Pages of Time, 1956. Paul W. Bates. (Illus.). 24p. (Orig.). 1989. pap. 4.95 (*1-56046-056-3*) Interact Pubs.

Pages of Time, 1953. Paul W. Bates. (Illus.). 24p. (Orig.). 1989. pap. 4.95 (*1-56046-053-9*) Interact Pubs.

Pages of Time, 1952. Paul W. Bates. (Illus.). 24p. (Orig.). 1989. pap. 4.95 (*1-56046-052-0*) Interact Pubs.

Pages of Time, 1940. Paul W. Bates. (Illus.). 24p. (Orig.). 1989. pap. 4.95 (*1-56046-040-7*) Interact Pubs.

Pages of Time, 1948. Paul W. Bates. (Illus.). 24p. (Orig.). 1989. pap. 4.95 (*1-56046-048-2*) Interact Pubs.

Pages of Time, 1945. Paul W. Bates. (Illus.). 24p. (Orig.). 1989. pap. 4.95 (*1-56046-045-8*) Interact Pubs.

Pages of Time, 1944. Paul W. Bates. (Illus.). 24p. (Orig.). 1989. pap. 4.95 (*1-56046-044-X*) Interact Pubs.

Pages of Time, 1949. Paul W. Bates. (Illus.). 24p. (Orig.). 1989. pap. 4.95 (*1-56046-049-0*) Interact Pubs.

Pages of Time, 1941. Paul W. Bates. (Illus.). 24p. (Orig.). 1989. pap. 4.95 (*1-56046-041-5*) Interact Pubs.

Pages of Time, 1947. Paul W. Bates. (Illus.). 24p. (Orig.). 1989. pap. 4.95 (*1-56046-047-4*) Interact Pubs.

Pages of Time, 1946. Paul W. Bates. (Illus.). 24p. (Orig.). 1989. pap. 4.95 (*1-56046-046-6*) Interact Pubs.

Pages of Time, 1943. Paul W. Bates. (Illus.). 24p. (Orig.). 1989. pap. 4.95 (*1-56046-043-1*) Interact Pubs.

Pages of Time, 1942. Paul W. Bates. (Illus.). 24p. (Orig.). 1989. pap. 4.95 (*1-56046-042-3*) Interact Pubs.

Pages of Time, 1914. Paul W. Bates. (Illus.). 24p. (Orig.). 1993. pap. 4.95 (*1-56046-014-8*) Interact Pubs.

Pages of Time, 1919. Paul W. Bates. (Illus.). 24p. (Orig.). 1993. pap. 4.95 (*1-56046-019-9*) Interact Pubs.

Pages of Time, 1990. Paul W. Bates. (Illus.). 24p. (Orig.). 1993. pap. 4.95 (*1-56046-090-3*) Interact Pubs.

Pages of Time, 1991. Paul W. Bates. (Illus.). 24p. (Orig.). 1993. pap. 4.95 (*1-56046-091-1*) Interact Pubs.

Pages of Time, 1992. Paul W. Bates. (Illus.). 24p. (Orig.). 1993. pap. 4.95 (*1-56046-092-X*) Interact Pubs.

Pages of Time, 1917. Paul W. Bates. (Illus.). 24p. (Orig.). 1993. pap. 4.95 (*1-56046-017-2*) Interact Pubs.

Pages of Time, 1970. Paul W. Bates. (Illus.). 24p. (Orig.). 1993. pap. 4.95 (*1-56046-070-9*) Interact Pubs.

Pages of Time, 1978. Paul W. Bates. (Illus.). 24p. (Orig.). 1993. pap. 4.95 (*1-56046-078-4*) Interact Pubs.

Pages of Time, 1975. Paul W. Bates. (Illus.). 24p. (Orig.). 1993. pap. 4.95 (*1-56046-075-X*) Interact Pubs.

Pages of Time, 1974. Paul W. Bates. (Illus.). 24p. (Orig.). 1993. pap. 4.95 (*1-56046-074-1*) Interact Pubs.

Pages of Time, 1979. Paul W. Bates. (Illus.). 24p. (Orig.). 1993. pap. 4.95 (*1-56046-079-2*) Interact Pubs.

Pages of Time, 1971. Paul W. Bates. (Illus.). 24p. (Orig.). 1993. pap. 4.95 (*1-56046-071-7*) Interact Pubs.

Pages of Time, 1977. Paul W. Bates. (Illus.). 24p. (Orig.). 1993. pap. 4.95 (*1-56046-077-6*) Interact Pubs.

Pages of Time, 1976. Paul W. Bates. (Illus.). 24p. (Orig.). 1993. pap. 4.95 (*1-56046-076-8*) Interact Pubs.

Pages of Time, 1973. Paul W. Bates. (Illus.). 24p. (Orig.). 1993. pap. 4.95 (*1-56046-073-3*) Interact Pubs.

Pages of Time, 1972. Paul W. Bates. (Illus.). 24p. (Orig.). 1993. pap. 4.95 (*1-56046-072-5*) Interact Pubs.

Pages of Time, 1916. Paul W. Bates. (Illus.). 24p. (Orig.). 1993. pap. 4.95 (*1-56046-016-4*) Interact Pubs.

Pages of Time, 1960. Paul W. Bates. (Illus.). 24p. (Orig.). 1989. pap. 4.95 (*1-56046-060-1*) Interact Pubs.

Pages of Time, 1968. Paul W. Bates. (Illus.). 24p. (Orig.). 1989. pap. 4.95 (*1-56046-068-7*) Interact Pubs.

Pages of Time, 1965. Paul W. Bates. (Illus.). 24p. (Orig.). 1989. pap. 4.95 (*1-56046-065-2*) Interact Pubs.

Pages of Time, 1964. Paul W. Bates. (Illus.). 24p. (Orig.). 1989. pap. 4.95 (*1-56046-064-4*) Interact Pubs.

Pages of Time, 1969. Paul W. Bates. (Illus.). 24p. (Orig.). 1989. pap. 4.95 (*1-56046-069-5*) Interact Pubs.

Pages of Time, 1961. Paul W. Bates. (Illus.). 24p. (Orig.). 1989. pap. 4.95 (*1-56046-061-X*) Interact Pubs.

Pages of Time, 1967. Paul W. Bates. (Illus.). 24p. (Orig.). 1989. pap. 4.95 (*1-56046-067-9*) Interact Pubs.

Pages of Time, 1966. Paul W. Bates. (Illus.). 24p. (Orig.). 1989. pap. 4.95 (*1-56046-066-0*) Interact Pubs.

Pages of Time, 1963. Paul W. Bates. (Illus.). 24p. (Orig.). 1989. pap. 4.95 (*1-56046-063-6*) Interact Pubs.

Pages of Time, 1962. Paul W. Bates. (Illus.). 24p. (Orig.). 1989. pap. 4.95 (*1-56046-062-8*) Interact Pubs.

Pages of Time, 1910. Paul W. Bates. (Illus.). 24p. (Orig.). 1993. pap. 4.95 (*1-56046-310-4*) Interact Pubs.

Pages of Time, 1913. Paul W. Bates. (Illus.). 24p. (Orig.). 1993. pap. 4.95 (*1-56046-013-X*) Interact Pubs.

Pages of Time, 1930. Paul W. Bates. (Illus.). 24p. (Orig.). 1989. pap. 4.95 (*1-56046-030-X*) Interact Pubs.

Pages of Time, 1938. Paul W. Bates. (Illus.). 24p. (Orig.). 1989. pap. 4.95 (*1-56046-038-5*) Interact Pubs.

Pages of Time, 1935. Paul W. Bates. (Illus.). 24p. (Orig.). 1989. pap. 4.95 (*1-56046-035-0*) Interact Pubs.

Pages of Time, 1934. Paul W. Bates. (Illus.). 24p. (Orig.). 1989. pap. 4.95 (*1-56046-034-2*) Interact Pubs.

Pages of Time, 1939. Paul W. Bates. (Illus.). 24p. (Orig.). 1989. pap. 4.95 (*1-56046-039-3*) Interact Pubs.

Pages of Time, 1931. Paul W. Bates. (Illus.). 24p. (Orig.). 1989. pap. 4.95 (*1-56046-031-8*) Interact Pubs.

Pages of Time, 1937. Paul W. Bates. (Illus.). 24p. (Orig.). 1989. pap. 4.95 (*1-56046-037-7*) Interact Pubs.

Pages of Time, 1936. Paul W. Bates. (Illus.). 24p. (Orig.). 1989. pap. 4.95 (*1-56046-036-9*) Interact Pubs.

Pages of Time, 1933. Paul W. Bates. (Illus.). 24p. (Orig.). 1989. pap. 4.95 (*1-56046-033-4*) Interact Pubs.

Pages of Time, 1932. Paul W. Bates. (Illus.). 24p. (Orig.). 1989. pap. 4.95 (*1-56046-032-6*) Interact Pubs.

Pages of Time, 1912. Paul W. Bates. (Illus.). 24p. (Orig.). 1993. pap. 4.95 (*1-56046-312-0*) Interact Pubs.

Pages of Time, 1920. Paul W. Bates. (Illus.). 24p. (Orig.). 1989. pap. 4.95 (*1-56046-020-2*) Interact Pubs.

Pages of Time, 1928. Paul W. Bates. (Illus.). 24p. (Orig.). 1989. pap. 4.95 (*1-56046-028-8*) Interact Pubs.

Pages of Time, 1925. Paul W. Bates. (Illus.). 24p. (Orig.). 1989. pap. 4.95 (*1-56046-025-3*) Interact Pubs.

Pages of Time, 1924. Paul W. Bates. (Illus.). 24p. (Orig.). 1989. pap. 4.95 (*1-56046-024-5*) Interact Pubs.

Pages of Time, 1929. Paul W. Bates. (Illus.). 24p. (Orig.). 1989. pap. 4.95 (*1-56046-029-6*) Interact Pubs.

Pages of Time, 1921. Paul W. Bates. (Illus.). 24p. (Orig.). 1989. pap. 4.95 (*1-56046-021-0*) Interact Pubs.

Pages of Time, 1927. Paul W. Bates. (Illus.). 24p. (Orig.). 1989. pap. 4.95 (*1-56046-027-X*) Interact Pubs.

Pages of Time, 1926. Paul W. Bates. (Illus.). 24p. (Orig.). 1989. pap. 4.95 (*1-56046-026-1*) Interact Pubs.

Pages of Time, 1923. Paul W. Bates. (Illus.). 24p. (Orig.). 1989. pap. 4.95 (*1-56046-023-7*) Interact Pubs.

Pages of Time, 1922. Paul W. Bates. (Illus.). 24p. (Orig.). 1989. pap. 4.95 (*1-56046-022-9*) Interact Pubs.

Pages of Time Series: A Nostalgia News Report, Set. 1989. write for info. (*1-56046-099-7*) Interact Pubs.

Pages off the Doctor's Pad. Harold C. Klein. LC 93-79811. 104p. 1994. pap. 9.95 (*1-879653-07-9*) Lakeside Pr.

Page's Ohio Revised Code Annotated, 36 vols., annot. ed. Anderson Publishing Company Staff. 1997. 1100.00 (*0-87084-950-6*) Anderson Pub Co.

***Page's Ohio Revised Code Annotated: Annual General Index.** rev. ed. 730p. 1998. 59.00 (*1-58360-038-8*) Anderson Pub Co.

Page's Ohio Revised Code Annotated, General Index. rev. annot. ed. pap. 59.00 (*1-58360-303-4*) Anderson Pub Co.

Pages Passed from Hand to Hand: Stories from the Hidden Tradition of Homosexual Literature from the Eighteenth Century to the Great War. Ed. by David Leavitt & Mark Mitchell. LC 97-25631. 576p. 1998. 30.00 (*0-395-83706-5*, Mariner Bks); pap. 18.00 (*0-395-83705-7*, Mariner Bks) HM.

P

An Asterisk (*) at the beginning of an entry indicates that the title is appearing for the first time.

***Pages Paysages: In the Meantime.** Marc Claramunt. (Illus.). 192p. 2000. pap. 42.00 (*3-7643-6322-3*) Birkhauser.

Page's Pencilsharpener. Meredith B. Olson. LC 97-94520. (Illus.). 64p. (J). (gr. 3-4). 1998. 11.95 (*0-9657061-7-6*) Glenhaven.

Pages sur Crist. Blaise Pascal & Ivan Gobry. (FRE.). 128p. 1963. pap. 10.95 (*0-7859-5390-6*) Fr & Eur.

Paget's Disease of the Bone: Assessment & Management. R. C. Hamdy. 216p. 1981. 69.50 (*0-275-91344-9*, C1344, Praeger Pubs) Greenwood.

Paget's Law of Banking. 10th ed. Mark Hapgood. 1989. boxed set 247.00 (*0-406-33353-X*, U.K., MICHIE) LEXIS Pub.

Paget's Law of Banking. 11th ed. Mark Hapgood. 1996. write for info. (*0-406-02598-3*, PLOB11, MICHIE) LEXIS Pub.

Paginas Cubanas I. Hortensia R. Del Vizo. LC 97-80043. (Coleccion Cuba y sus Jueces). (SPA.). 143p. 1998. pap. 12.00 (*0-89729-848-9*) Ediciones.

Paginas de Mi Vida: Poesias y Pensamientos. Malvina A. Godoy. LC 91-75910. (Coleccion Espejo de Paciencia). (SPA.). 127p. (Orig.). 1992. pap. 12.00 (*0-89729-622-2*) Ediciones.

Paginas del Libro de Mi Vida. D. S. Prince.Tr. of Pages from My Life's Book. (SPA.). 3.99 (*0-7899-0115-3*, 550082) Editorial Unilit.

Paginas Escogidas. Camilo Jose Cela. Ed. by Dario Villanueva. (Nueva Austral Ser.: Vol. 229). (SPA.). 1991. pap. text 24.95 (*84-239-7229-1*) Elliots Bks.

Paginas Ingeniosas para la Escuela Dominical. Haystead.Tr. of Sunday School Smart Pages. (SPA.). 270p. 1995. 14.99 (*0-7899-0024-6*, 498577) Editorial Unilit.

Paginas Sueltas. Lydia Cabrera. LC 94-71015. (Coleccion del Chichereku). (SPA., Illus.). 579p. (Orig.). 1994. pap. 29.00 (*0-89729-733-4*) Ediciones.

***Paging Equipment in Chile: A Strategic Entry Report, 1996.** Compiled by Icon Group International Staff. (Illus.). 111p. 1999. ring bd. 1110.00 incl. audio compact disk (*0-7418-1472-2*) Icon Grp.

***Paging Technology Handbook.** Neil Boucher. 327p. 1998. 104.95 (*0-471-29775-5*) Wiley.

Pagliacci in Full Score. Ruggiero Leoncavallo. 304p. 1993. text 16.95 (*0-486-27363-6*) Dover.

Pagliacci Libretto. Ruggiero Leoncavallo. (ENG & ITA.). 32p. 1986. pap. 4.95 (*0-7935-2616-7*, 50340300) H Leonard.

Pagne Noir. Bernard B. Dadie. (FRE.). 160p. 1970. pap. 14.95 (*0-7859-3453-7*) Fr & Eur.

Pagoda. Patricia Powell. LC 99-26980. 256p. 1999. pap. 12.00 (*0-15-600829-7*, Harvest Bks) Harcourt.

Pagoda. Patricia Powell. LC 98-14568. 256p. 1998. 23.00 (*0-679-45489-6*) Knopf.

Pagoda-Skyline Drive: An Illustrated History of Reading's Mountaintop Landmarks. Connie Crupi. Ed. by Charles J. Adams. Date not set. pap. 5.95 (*1-887762-05-1*) His Soc Brks Cnty.

Pagoda Tree. large type ed. Berkely Mather. 576p. 1982. 27.99 (*0-7089-0892-6*) Ulverscroft.

Pagodas, Gods & Spirits of Vietnam. Ann H. Unger. Ed. by Walter Unger. LC 97-60321. (Illus.). 208p. 1997. 50.00 (*0-500-01803-0*, Pub. by Thames Hudson) Norton.

Pagoo, 001. Holling C. Holling. (Illus.). 88p. (J). (gr. 3-9). 1957. 20.00 (*0-395-06826-6*) HM.

Pagoo. Holling C. Holling. (Illus.). 96p. (J). (gr. 4-6). 1990. pap. 10.00 (*0-395-53964-1*) HM.

PAH in Work Atmospheres: Occurrence & Determination. Alf Bjorseth & G. Becher. LC 85-30731. 184p. 1986. 106.00 (*0-8493-6064-1*, CRC Reprint) Franklin.

Pahari Styles of Indian Murals. S. D. Charak & Anita Billawaria. LC 98-915504. 1998. 115.00 (*81-7017-356-6*, Pub. by Abhinav Pubns) S Asia.

Pahlavi Texts, 5 vols, Set. E. W. West. 1974. lib. bdg. 1500.00 (*0-87968-566-2*) Krishna Pr.

Pahokee, Vol. V. Ann O. Rust. LC 92-97012. (Floridians Ser.). 275p. 1992. 17.50 (*0-9620556-8-9*); pap. 12.95 (*0-9620556-9-7*) Amaro Bks.

PAHO/WHO Inter-Regional Conference on the Postgraduate Preparation of Health Workers for Health Education. (Technical Report Ser.: No. 278). 48p. 1964. pap. text 5.00 (*92-4-120278-5*) World Health.

Pahrump: A Valley Waiting to Become a City. Robert D. McCracken. (Illus.). 96p. (Orig.). 1996. pap. 12.95 (*1-878138-53-7*) Nye Cty Pr.

PAHs & Related Compounds: Biology. Ed. by A. H. Neilson & O. Hutzinger. (Handbook of Environmental Chemistry Ser.: Vol. 3, Pt. J). (Illus.). 400p. 1997. 198.00 (*3-540-63422-3*) Spr-Verlag.

PAHs & Related Compounds: Chemistry. Ed. by A. N. Neilson & O. Hutzinger. (Handbook of Environmental Chemistry Ser.: Vol. 3, Pt. I). (Illus.). 326p. 1997. 198.00 (*3-540-62394-9*) Spr-Verlag.

Pahsimeroi - Land Beyond Words, Poems & Drawings. 2nd ed. Edson Fichter. (Illus.). 48p. 1995, pap. 12.00 (*0-937179-02-7*) Blue Scarab.

Pai Ka Leo. Aha Punana Leo Curriculum Development Committee. (HAW., Illus.). 34p. (J). (ps-6). 1989. pap. 14.95 incl. audio (*1-880188-62-7*, Pub. by Bess Pr) Aha Punana Leo.

Pai Ka Leo. Punana Leo. (Illus.). 40p. (J). (ps-6). 1989. pap. 14.95 (*0-935848-63-0*) Bess Pr.

***Pai Lum Tao: Way of the White Dragon.** Glenn Wilson. 180p. 2000. pap. 14.95 (*0-86568-179-1*) Unique Pubns.

Paian: Studien zur Geschichte Einer Gattung. Lutz Kappel. (Untersuchungen zur Antiken Literatur und Geschichte Ser.: No. 37). (GER.). xxvi, 428p. (C). 1992. lib. bdg. 175.40 (*3-11-012967-1*) De Gruyter.

Paid & Loving Eyes. Jonathan Gash. 307p. 1994. pap. 5.99 (*0-14-023557-4*, Penguin Bks) Viking Penguin.

Paid & Loving Eyes. large type ed. Jonathan Gash. 1994. 25.99 (*0-7089-3164-2*) Ulverscroft.

***Paid Family Leave: At What Cost.** Anita U. Hahiangadi. LC 00-101903. 101p. 2000. 20.00 (*0-916559-61-0*, 2079) EPF.

Paid for the Privilege: Hearing the Voices of Autism. Dan Reed. 163p. (Orig.). 1996. pap. 16.00 (*1-886928-06-1*) DRI Pr.

***Paid in Full.** D. C. Brod. LC 00-30847. (Standard Print Mystery Ser.). 2000. write for info. (*0-7862-2673-0*) Five Star.

Paid in Full. Annie M. Smithson. 1990. pap. 12.95 (*0-85342-953-7*) Dufour.

Paid in Full: War Memories of a German Lieutenant. unabridged ed. Edwin K. Mahlo. Ed. by Eric Poersch. (Memories...Ser.: Vol. 1). (Illus.). 225p. 1995. 24.95 (*0-9655013-0-2*) Condor Literary.

Paid to Kill: True Stories of Today's Contract Killers. Frank Jones. (Illus.). 352p. 1996. mass mkt. 11.95 (*0-7472-4480-4*, Pub. by Headline Bk Pub) Trafalgar.

Paid to Kill: True Stories of Today's Contract Killers. large type ed. Frank Jones. (Large Print Ser.). (Illus.). 528p. 1996. 27.99 (*0-7089-3652-0*) Ulverscroft.

***Paideia: Philosophy/Phenomenology of Life Inspiring Education of Our Times.** Anna-Teresa Tymieniecka. LC 00-39122. (Analecta Husserliana Ser.). (ENG & SPA.). 2000. write for info. (*0-7923-6319-1*) Kluwer Academic.

***Paideia Agonistes: The Lost Soul of Modern Education.** John E. Grote. 332p. 2000. pap. 32.50 (*0-7618-1726-3*) U Pr of Amer.

Paideia Classroom: Teaching for Understanding. Terry Roberts & Laura Billings. LC 98-29063. 170p. 1999. pap. 26.95 (*1-883001-60-9*) Eye On Educ.

***Paideia of God: And Other Essays on Education.** Douglas Wilson. 160p. 1999. pap. 10.00 (*1-885767-59-5*) Canon Pr ID.

Paideia, the Ideals of Greek Culture: In Search of the Divine Centre, Vol. II. 2nd ed. Werner W. Jaeger. Tr. by Gilbert Highet. 460p. 1986. pap. text 24.95 (*0-19-504047-3*) OUP.

Paideia, the Ideals of Greek Culture: The Conflict of Cultural ideas in the Age of Plato, Vol. III. Werner W. Jaeger. Tr. by Gilbert Highet. 384p. 1986. pap. text 24.95 (*0-19-504048-1*) OUP.

Paideia, the Ideals of Greek Culture Vol. I: Archaic Greece - The Mind of Athens. 2nd ed. Werner W. Jaeger. Tr. by Gilbert Highet. 544p. 1986. pap. text 24.95 (*0-19-500425-6*) OUP.

Paige. Judy Baer. (Springsong Bks.). 16p. (YA). (gr. 7-10). 1995. mass mkt. 4.99 (*1-55661-585-X*) Bethany Hse.

Paik Video. Edith Decker. Tr. by Marie-Genvieve Iselin et al from GER. LC 97-42066. (Illus.). 242p. (Orig.). 1996. pap. 18.95 (*1-886449-35-X*, P935X) Barrytown Ltd.

Pail of Air. Fritz Leiber. 1976. reprint ed. lib. bdg. 20.95 (*0-88411-933-5*) Amereon Ltd.

Pail of Nails. Harriet M. Savitz & K. Michael Syring. LC 88-7653. (Illus.). (J). (gr. 3 up). 1990. 3.29 (*0-687-29974-8*) Abingdon.

Pain. Ed. by J. Brihaye et al. (Acta Neurochirugica - Supplementum Ser.: No. 38). (Illus.). 200p. 1987. 180.00 (*0-387-81990-8*) Spr-Verlag.

***Pain.** Kazanowski. (Nursing Concepts Ser.). 2000. 22.95 (*1-889325-56-2*, Pub. by Fence Crk Pubng) Blackwell Sci.

Pain. Dan Middleman. (Illus.). 226p. 1998. pap. 17.50 (*0-911521-52-6*) Tafnews.

***Pain.** Richard Thomas. LC 99-29962. (Alternative Answers to... Ser.). 2000. 22.95 (*0-7621-0245-4*, Pub. by RD Assn) Penguin Putnam.

Pain. Ed. by John J. Bonica. LC 79-5214. (Association for Research in Nervous & Mental Disease Research Publications: No. 58). (Illus.). 419p. 1980. reprint ed. pap. 129.90 (*0-608-00598-3*, 206118500007) Bks Demand.

Pain. Ed. by John L. Echternach. LC 86-28385. (Clinics in Physical Therapy Ser.: No. 12). (Illus.). 326p. reprint ed. pap. 101.10 (*0-7837-6810-9*, 204664200003) Bks Demand.

Pain: A Handbook for Nurses. 2nd ed. Beatrice Sofaer. LC 92-49745. 1992. 35.00 (*1-56593-045-2*, 0293) Thomson Learn.

Pain: A Sourcebook for Nurses & Other Professionals. Ada K. Jacox. 1977. text 22.50 (*0-316-45590-3*, Little Brwn Med Div) Lppncott W & W.

Pain: A Spike-Interval Coded Message in the Brain. Raimond Emmers. LC 81-12044. 144p. 1981. reprint ed. pap. 44.70 (*0-608-00345-X*, 206106100007) Bks Demand.

Pain: Cause, Effect, Evaluation, 6 vols., Set. John P. Adams et al. (Illus.). 1987. 295.00 (*0-87473-463-0*, 62000-10, MICHIE) LEXIS Pub.

Pain: Clinical Manual. 2nd ed. Margo McCaffery & Christine Pasero. (Illus.). 814p. 1999. text 39.95 (*0-8151-5609-X*, 29563) Mosby Inc.

Pain: Its Modes & Functions. Frederik J. Buytendijk. Tr. by Eda O'Shiel. LC 72-12494. 189p. 1973. reprint ed. lib. bdg. 55.00 (*0-8371-6741-8*, BUPM, Greenwood Pr) Greenwood.

Pain: Its Nature & Management. Veronica Thomas. 1997. pap. text 36.95 (*0-7020-2293-4*, Pub. by W B Saunders) Saunders.

***Pain: Learning to Live Without It.** David Corey. (Illus.). 211p. 1999. reprint ed. pap. text 14.00 (*0-7881-6796-0*) DIANE Pub.

Pain: Making Life Liveable. Dana S. DeBoskey. (Illus.). 80p. (Orig.). 1995. pap. 12.50 (*1-882855-36-1*) HDI Pubs.

Pain: Meaning & Management. Ed. by W. Lynn Smith et al. (Illus.). 182p. 1980. text 22.50 (*0-88331-170-4*) R B Luce.

Pain: Mechanisms & Management. Rene Cailliet. LC 93-9422. (Pain Ser.). (Illus.). 299p. (C). 1993. pap. text 24.95 (*0-8036-1635-X*) Davis Co.

Pain: Mechanisms & Management. Howard L. Fields. (Illus.). 354p. 1987. text 50.00 (*0-07-020701-1*) McGraw-Hill HPD.

Pain: Mechanisms & Management. 2nd ed. Howard L. Fields. 450p. 1999. text 50.00 (*0-07-020748-8*) McGraw.

Pain: Principles, Practice & Patients. 3rd ed. Beatrice Sofaer. (Illus.). 144p. 1998. pap. 36.50 (*0-7487-3329-9*, Pub. by S Thornes Pubs) Trans-Atl Phila.

Pain: Scientific Basis & Clin. Cousins. 2000. text. write for info. (*0-7216-6220-X*, W B Saunders Co) Harcrt Hlth Sci Grp.

Pain: The Gift Nobody Wants. Grace R. MacMullen. (Joyful Living Ser.). 1986. pap. 2.50 (*0-912623-00-4*) Joyful Woman.

Pain: The Gift Nobody Wants. Paul Brand & Philip Yancey. 352p. 1999. reprint ed. text 22.00 (*0-7881-6372-8*) DIANE Pub.

***Pain: The Science of Suffering.** Patrick Wall. LC 00-23889. 192p. 2000. 24.95 (*0-231-12006-0*) Col U Pr.

***Pain: The Science of Suffering.** Patrick Wall. LC 00-23889. (Maps of the Mind Ser.). 2000. write for info. (*0-231-12007-9*) Col U Pr.

Pain: Theory, Research & Intervention. Sandra Horn & Marcus Munafo. LC 96-29576. (Health Psychology Ser.). 152p. 1997. 94.00 (*0-335-19689-6*); pap. 29.95 (*0-335-19688-8*) OpUniv Pr.

***Pain: What Psychiatrists Need to Know.** Ed. by Mary Jane Massie. (Review of Psychiatry Ser.: Vol. 19, No. 2). 224p. 2000. pap. 28.50 (*0-88048-173-0*) Am Psychiatric.

Pain Acute & Chronic. 2nd ed. Edward A. Shipton. LC 99-36443. 246p. 1999. pap. text 49.95 (*0-340-64612-8*, Pub. by E A) OUP.

Pain, Analgesia, & Addiction: The Pharmacologic Treatment of Pain. Barry Stimmel. LC 82-21608. 326p. 1983. reprint ed. pap. 101.10 (*0-608-04703-1*, 206542400004) Bks Demand.

Pain & Anxiety Control for the Conscious Dental Patient. John Meechan. (Illus.). 396p. 1998. text (*0-19-262849-6*) OUP.

Pain & Anxiety Control for the Conscious Dental Patient. John G. Meechan et al. LC 97-34665. (Illus.). 396p. 1998. pap. text 69.50 (*0-19-262848-8*) OUP.

Pain & Anxiety Control in Dentistry. Dionne. 2000. text. write for info. (*0-7216-7278-7*, W B Saunders Co) Harcrt Hlth Sci Grp.

Pain & Behavioral Medicine: A Cognitive-Behavioral Perspective. Dennis C. Turk et al. LC 82-11695. (Clinical Psychology & Psychotherapy Ser.). 452p. 1987. pap. text 30.00 (*0-89862-917-9*) Guilford Pubns.

Pain & Central Nervous System Disease: The Central Pain Syndromes. Bristol-Myers Squibb Symposium on Pain Research St. Ed. by Kenneth L. Casey. LC 91-10602. (Bristol-Myers Squibb Symposium on Pain Research Ser.). (Illus.). 304p. 1991. reprint ed. pap. 94.30 (*0-608-07240-0*, 206746500009) Bks Demand.

Pain & Disability: Clinical, Behavioral, & Public Policy Perspective. Institute of Medicine Staff. Ed. by Marian Osterweis et al. LC 87-11232. 318p. reprint ed. pap. 98.60 (*0-7837-2777-1*, 204316800006) Bks Demand.

Pain & Grace. Annemarie Schimmel. 320p. 1996. 69.00 (*0-614-21326-6*, 936) Kazi Pubns.

***Pain & Grace: A Journey Through Vietnam.** deluxe ed. Jim Gensheimer et al. (Illus.). 128p. (C). 2000. 29.95 (*0-9653207-4-X*) San Jose Mercury.

Pain & Its Conquest. H. B. Gibson. 224p. 1982. 30.00 (*0-7206-0595-4*) Dufour.

Pain & Its Ending: The Four Noble Truths in the Theravada Buddhist Canon. Carol Anderson. (Critical Studies in Buddhism: Vol. 10). 288p. 1999. text 55.00 (*0-7007-1065-5*, Pub. by Curzon Pr Ltd) UH Pr.

Pain & Its Relief. Nancy Knight. LC 83-19483. (Illus.). 84p. 1988. reprint ed. pap. 5.50 (*0-685-44184-9*) Natl Mus Am.

Pain & Its Relief: An Exhibition at the National Museum of American History. Nancy Knight. (Illus.). 84p. (Orig.). 1983. pap. 5.50 (*0-929847-01-6*) Natl Mus Am.

Pain & Its Relief Without Addiction: Clinical Issues in the Use of Opioids & Other Analgesics. 2nd ed. Barry Stimmel. LC 96-8993. (Illus.). 420p. 1997. pap. 24.95 (*0-7890-0126-8*, Hawrth Medical) Haworth Pr.

Pain & Its Relief Without Addiction: Clinical Issues in the Use of Opioids & Other Analgesics. 2nd ed. Barry Stimmel. LC 96-8993. (Illus.). 420p. (C). 1997. 49.95 (*1-56024-906-4*, Hawrth Medical) Haworth Pr.

Pain & Joy in Intimate Relationships. Mavis Klein. 272p. 1993. 24.95 (*0-7145-2943-5*) M Boyars Pubs.

Pain & Joy of Love. Keith E. Renninson. 100p. 1995. pap. 15.00 (*0-9648551-4-3*) Namaste Pub.

Pain & Kampo: The Use of Japanese Herbal Medicine in Management of Pain. Ed. by T. Oyama & G. Smith. LC 93-47603. 1994. write for info. (*4-431-70135-4*); write for info. (*3-540-70135-4*); write for info. (*0-387-70135-4*) Spr-Verlag.

Pain & Neurogenic Inflammation. Susan D. Brain & P. K. Moore. (Progress in Inflammation Research Ser.). 330p. 1999. (*3-7643-5875-0*) Birkhauser.

Pain & Neurogenic Inflammation. Susan D. Brain & P. K. Moore. LC 98-54474. (Progress in Inflammation Research Ser.). 1999. write for info. (*0-8176-5875-0*) Birkhauser.

Pain & Passion: A Psychoanalyst Explores the World of S & M. R. J. Stoller. (Illus.). 316p. (C). 1991. 24.95 (*0-306-43770-8*, Plenum Trade) Perseus Pubng.

Pain & Pleasure: A Study of Bodily Feelings. Thomas Szasz. 368p. 1988. reprint ed. pap. 19.95 (*0-8156-0230-8*) Syracuse U Pr.

Pain & Polemic: Anti-Judaism in the Gospels. George M. Smiga. LC 92-28044. (Stimulus Bks.). 240p. 1993. pap. 9.95 (*0-8091-3355-5*) Paulist Pr.

Pain & Possibility. Gabriele L. Rico. 288p. 1991. pap. 16.95 (*0-87477-571-X*, Tarcher Putnam) Putnam Pub Group.

Pain & Praise: The Book of Psalms. Mariann Martin. (Generation Why: Vol. 2:5). 36p. (YA). (gr. 9-12). 1997. pap. 14.95 (*0-87303-270-5*) Faith & Life.

Pain & Pride of Being Bir Hospital (Research & Evaluation of the Services) B. K. Suvedi. (C). 1992. 45.00 (*0-7855-0207-6*, Pub. by Ratna Pustak Bhandar) St Mut.

Pain & Suffering. William K. Livingston. LC 98-40341. (Illus.). 268p. 1998. 48.00 (*0-931092-24-8*) Intl Assn Study Pain.

Pain & Suffering, 4 vols., Vols. 4, 4a, 4b & 4c. Loring F. Chapman. (Courtroom Medicine Ser.). 1967. ring bd. 830.00 (*0-8205-1242-7*) Bender.

Pain & Survival: Human Rights Violations & Mental Health. Ed. by Nils J. Lavik. 244p. 1994. 33.00 (*82-00-21907-0*) Scandnvan Univ Pr.

Pain & the Great One. Judy Blume. (Illus.). 32p. (J). (ps-3). 1985. pap. 6.99 (*0-440-40967-5*) Dell.

Pain & the Great One. Judy Blume. 28p. (J). (gr. k-3). pap. 5.99 (*0-8072-1265-2*) Listening Lib.

Pain & the Great One. Judy Blume. LC 84-11009. (Illus.). 32p. (J). (gr. k-3). 1984. 16.00 (*0-02-711100-8*, Bradbury S&S) S&S Childrens.

Pain & the Great One. Judy Blume. 1984. 11.19 (*0-606-00365-7*, Pub. by Turtleback) Demco.

Pain & the Promise: The Struggle for Civil Rights in Tallahassee, Florida. Glenda A. Rabby. LC 98-44087. (Illus.). 330p. 1999. 40.00 (*0-8203-2051-X*) U of Ga Pr.

Pain & Touch. 2nd ed. Ed. by Lawrence Kruger. LC 96-22523. (Handbook of Perception & Cognition Ser.). (Illus.). 394p. 1996. text 69.95 (*0-12-426910-9*) Acad Pr.

Pain, Anesthesia & Analgesia in Common Laboratory Animals. 1995. lib. bdg. 250.95 (*0-8490-7587-4*) Gordon Pr.

Pain Anniversaire a Villard d'Arene en Oisans. M. Maget. 237p. 1989. pap. text 51.00 (*2-88124-263-4*) Gordon & Breach.

Pain As Human Experience: An Anthropological Perspective. Mary-Jo D. Good. 1992. pap. 16.95 (*0-520-07512-9*, Pub. by U CA Pr) Cal Prin Full Svc.

Pain Behind the Mask: Overcoming Masculine Depression. John Lynch & Christopher T. Kilmartin. LC 98-45944. (Illus.). 226p. 1999. pap. 19.95 (*0-7890-0558-1*); lib. bdg. 39.95 (*0-7890-0557-3*) Haworth Pr.

***Pain Buster: A Doctor's 4-Step Program to Conquer Chronic Pain.** John Stamatos. 2001. text 15.00 (*0-8050-6347-1*) H Holt & Co.

***Pain Buster: Doctor's 4-Step Program to Conquer Chronic Pain.** John Stamatos. 2000. text 24.00 (*0-8050-6346-3*) H Holt & Co.

Pain Clinic. Ed. by Sampson Lipton et al. LC 89-10878. (Advances in Pain Research & Therapy Ser.: Vol. 13). (Illus.). 435p. 1990. reprint ed. pap. 134.90 (*0-608-05865-3*, 205983200007) Bks Demand.

Pain Clinic No. I: Proceedings of the 1st International Symposium, Delft, the Netherlands, 1984, Vol. 1. Ed. by W. Erdmann et al. 378p. 1985. 87.50 (*90-6764-039-5*, Pub. by VSP) Coronet Bks.

Pain Clinic No. II: Proceedings of the 2nd International Symposium, Lille, France, 1986, Vol. 2. Ed. by P. Scherpereel et al. 356p. 1987. 105.00 (*90-6764-096-4*, Pub. by VSP) Coronet Bks.

Pain Clinic No. IV: Proceedings of the 4th International Symposium, Kyoto, Japan, 1990, No. 4. Ed. by M. Hyodo et al. 368p. 1992. 125.00 (*90-6764-147-2*, Pub. by VSP) Coronet Bks.

Pain Clinic Manual. Stephen E. Abram et al. (Illus.). 458p. 1990. pap. text 52.00 (*0-397-50936-7*) Lppncott W & W.

Pain Clinic Manual. Ed. by Simon J. Dolin et al. LC 95-43195. 320p. 1996. text 75.00 (*0-7506-2036-6*) Buttrwrth-Heinemann.

Pain Control after Surgery: A Practical Guide. 1995. lib. bdg. 250.95 (*0-8490-6806-1*) Gordon Pr.

Pain Control with Transcutaneous Electrical Neuro Stimulation (TENS) Robert A. Ersek. LC 78-50175. 280p. 1981. 23.75 (*0-87527-168-5*) Green.

Pain Cure: The Proven Medical Program That Helps End Your Chronic Pain. Dharma S. Khalsa & Cameron Stauth. LC 98-36540. (Illus.). 432p. 1999. 25.00 (*0-446-52305-4*, Pub. by Warner Bks) Little.

***Pain Cure: The Proven Medical Program That Helps End Your Chronic Pain.** Dharma Singh Khalsa & Cameron Stauth. 432p. 2000. mass mkt. 14.95 (*0-446-67586-5*) Warner Bks.

Pain de l'Exil. Marc A. Christophe. LC 88-80261. (FRE.). 95p. (Orig.). 1988. pap. 10.95 (*0-945306-00-8*) W F Garnett.

Pain de Menage see Oeuvres

Pain des Reves. Louis Guilloux. (FRE.). 496p. 1983. pap. 11.95 (*0-7859-2387-X*, 2070369099) Fr & Eur.

Pain, Distress, & the Newborn Baby. Margaret Sparshot. 224p. (Orig.). 1996. pap. text 34.95 (*0-632-04077-7*) Blackwell Sci.

Pain Erasure: The Bonnie Prudden Way. Bonnie Prudden. 1985. pap. 12.00 (*0-345-33102-8*) Ballantine Pub Grp.

Pain Free: A Revolutionary Method for Stopping Chronic Pain. Pete Egoscue & Roger Gittines. LC 97-31745. 320p. 1998. 23.95 (*0-553-10630-9*) Bantam.

Pain Free: A Revolutionary Method for Stopping Chronic Pain. Pete Egoscue & Roger Gittines. 320p. 2000. pap. 13.95 (*0-553-37988-7*) Bantam.

Pain Free: A Self-Help Guide & Program Description for Becoming Pain Free Again. Peter Migaly. (Illus.). 100p. (Orig.). Date not set. pap. 15.95 (*0-9647363-2-2*) P Migaly.

An Asterisk (*) at the beginning of an entry indicates that the title is appearing for the first time.

Pain Free: The Definitive Guide to Healing Arthritis, Low-Back Pain, & Sports Injuries Through Nutrition & Supplements. Luke Bucci. LC 94-47120. 276p. 1995. 24.95 (*1-56530-161-7*) Summit TX.

Pain-Free Arthritis. Dvera Berson & Sander Roy. (Illus.). 130p. 1982. 23.50 (*0-9609608-0-5*) S & J Books.

Pain Free at Your Computer: Guided Relaxations to Reduce the Painful Effects of Computer Use. Scott Donkin. (Illus.). 12p. 1996. 9.95 incl. audio (*1-55961-347-5*, BP7507) Relaxtn Co.

Pain Free at Your PC. Pete Egoscue & Roger Gittines. LC 99-26664. 208p. 1999. pap. 10.95 (*0-553-38052-4*) Bantam.

Pain Free Childbirth: Your Right. Janice A. Duseau. 16p. (Orig.). 1989. pap. write for info. (*0-318-65841-0*) Word Power Pub.

***Pain-Free Magnet Therapy: Discover How Magnets Can Work to Help Relieve Your Arthritis, Sports Injuries, Fibromyalgia & Much More.** Lara Owen. LC 00-26820. 240p. 2000. pap. text 14.95 (*0-7615-2086-4*) Prima Pub.

Pain-Free Tryptophan Diet. Robert L. Polfack et al. 256p. 1987. 16.45 (*0-446-51317-2*); mass mkt. 3.95 (*0-446-34359-5*, Pub. by Warner Bks) Little.

Pain-Free Typing Technique: Simple Solutions to Prevent Repetitive Strain Injuries from a Concert Pianist. Howard Richman. (Illus.). 12p. 1999. pap. 4.95 (*1-882060-80-6*) Sound Feelings.

Pain Game. C. Norman Shealy. LC 75-28770. 156p. 1995. pap. 6.95 (*0-89087-157-4*) Celestial Arts.

Pain in Animals. A. Iggo. 1988. 35.00 (*0-7855-1114-8*) St Mut.

***Pain in Childbearing.** Margaret Yerby. LC 99-34395. 2000. text. write for info. (*0-7020-2299-3*) Bahai.

Pain in Childbearing & Its Control. Rosemary Mander. LC 98-15544. xii, 252p. 1998. pap. 29.95 (*0-632-04097-1*) Blackwell Sci.

Pain in Children: Nature, Assessment & Treatment. Patricia A. McGrath. LC 89-11009. 466p. 1989. lib. bdg. 52.00 (*0-89862-390-1*) Guilford Pubns.

Pain in Infants, Children & Adolescents. Neil L. Schechter et al. LC 92-15865. (Illus.). 720p. 1993. 99.00 (*0-683-07588-8*) Lppncott W & W.

Pain in Neonates. Ed. by K. J. S. Anand & Patrick J. McGrath. LC 92-48284. (Pain Research & Clinical Management Ser.: Vol. 5). 356p. 1993. 239.50 (*0-444-81226-1*) Elsevier.

Pain in Neonates. Ed. by K. J. S. Anand & Patrick J. McGrath. (Pain Research & Clinical Management Ser.: Vol. 5). 356p. 1995. pap. 92.00 (*0-444-82238-0*) Elsevier.

***Pain in Neonates.** 2nd rev. enl. ed. K. J. S. Anand et al. LC 99-53891. (Pain Research & Clinical Management Ser.). 1999. write for info. (*0-444-50349-8*) Elsevier.

Pain in Shoulder & Arm: An Integrated View. Ed. by J. M. Greep et al. (Developments in Surgery Ser.: No. 1). 306p. 1979. text 141.50 (*90-247-2146-6*) Kluwer Academic.

Pain in the Cancer Patient. Ed. by M. Zimmermann et al. (Recent Results in Cancer Research Ser.: Vol. 89). (Illus.). 230p. 1983. 83.00 (*0-387-12347-4*) Spr-Verlag.

Pain in the Critically Ill: Assessment & Management. Kathleen A. Puntillo. 276p. 1991. text 52.00 (*0-8342-0222-0*, 20222) Aspen Pub.

Pain in the Elderly. Ed. by Betty R. Ferrell & Bruce A. Ferrell. LC 96-28282. (Illus.). 152p. 1996. pap. 25.00 (*0-931092-15-9*) Intl Assn Study Pain.

Pain in the Neck: The Latest Information on Causes, Therapies Prevention. Arthur Winter & Ruth Winter. Ed. by Craig Winter. LC 97-90874. (Illus.). 96p. 1997. pap. 11.95 (*0-9659599-0-2*) WiseGuide Pub.

Pain-Its Neurosurgical Management: Part I: Procedures on Primary Afferent Neurons. (Progress in Neurological Surgery Ser.: Vol. 7). 1977. 166.50 (*3-8055-2317-3*) S Karger.

Pain-Its Neurosurgical Management Pt. II: Central Procedures. Ed. by H. Krayenbuehl et al. (Progress in Neurological Surgery Ser.: Vol. 8). 1977. 164.50 (*3-8055-2414-5*) S Karger.

***Pain Journal.** Bob Flanagan. (Native Agents Ser.). 205p. 2000. pap. 11.95 (*1-58435-002-4*, Pub. by Semiotexte) MIT Pr.

Pain Management. Rebholz. (Professional Reference - Nursing Ser.). 1998. student ed. 31.50 (*0-8273-7382-1*) Delmar.

***Pain Management.** Rosenberg. (C). 1999. text 120.00 (*0-7020-2285-3*, Pub. by Harcourt Coll Pubs) Harcourt.

***Pain Management.** C. C. Spanswick & C. J. Main. (Illus.). 304p. 1998. text. write for info. (*0-443-05683-8*) Church.

Pain Management, 2 vols. Ed. by Richard Weiner. (Illus.). 1994. lib. bdg. 195.00 (*1-57444-045-4*) St Lucie Pr.

Pain Management: A Comprehensive Review. P. Prithvi Raj. (Illus.). 592p. (C). (gr. 13). 1995. pap. text 64.95 (*0-8016-7998-2*, 07998) Mosby Inc.

Pain Management: Assessment & Treatment of Chronic & Acute Syndromes. Ed. by Wen-Hsien Wu. 397p. 1986. 45.95 (*0-89885-265-X*, Kluwer Acad Hman Sci) Kluwer Academic.

Pain Management: Expiring Patents Open OTC Markets. Market Intelligence Staff. 332p. 1993. 1995.00 (*1-56753-488-0*) Frost & Sullivan.

Pain Management: Nursing Perspective. Judith H. Watt-Watson & Marilee I. Donovan. (Illus.). 558p. (gr. 13). 1992. spiral bd. 35.95 (*1-55664-251-2*) Mosby Inc.

Pain Management: PreTest Self-Assessment & Review. Ed. by Cynthia Kahn. (PreTest Specialty Level Ser.). (Illus.). 224p. 1996. pap. text 45.00 (*0-07-052079-8*) McGraw-Hill HPD.

Pain Management: Principles. Christine Miaskowski. 1999. text 65.00 (*0-7216-6040-1*, W B Saunders Co) Harcrt Hlth Sci Grp.

Pain Management: Theory & Practice. Ed. by Russell K. Portenoy & Ronald M. Kanner. LC 95-52200. (Contemporary Neurology Ser.: No. 48). (Illus.). 384p. 1996. text 99.00 (*0-8036-0171-9*) OUP.

Pain Management Vol. 1: A Practical Guide for Clinicians. 5th ed. Ed. by Richard S. Weiner. LC 95-39061. 514p. 1997. lib. bdg. 97.50 (*1-57444-201-5*) St Lucie Pr.

Pain Management & Anesthesiology. Ed. by Michael A. Ashburn et al. LC 98-9867. (Developments in Critical Care Medicine & Anesthesiology Ser.). 324p. 1998. 148.00 (*0-7923-4995-4*) Kluwer Academic.

Pain Management by Physical Therapy. 2nd ed. Ed. by Peter E. Wells et al. (Illus.). 326p. 1994. text 52.50 (*0-7506-0569-3*) Buttrwrth-Heinemann.

Pain Management for Health Professionals. P. O'Hara. (Illus.). 192p. (Orig.). 1996. pap. 39.95 (*1-56593-436-9*, 1105) Singular Publishing.

Pain Management for the Practicing Physician. Gordon A. Irving & Mark S. Wallace. LC 96-35129. 1996. pap. text 53.00 (*0-443-07913-7*) Church.

***Pain Management for the Small Animal Practitioner.** William J. Tranquilli et al. (Made Easy Ser.). (Illus.). 130p. 2000. pap. 65.00 incl. cd-rom (*1-893441-16-4*); spiral bd. 49.00 incl. cd-rom (*1-893441-20-2*) Teton New.

Pain Management Handbook. Evelyn Salerno & Joyce S. Willens. LC 95-43752. (Illus.). 544p. (C). (gr. 13). 1996. spiral bd. 34.95 (*0-8151-7924-3*, 26181) Mosby Inc.

Pain Management Handbook: A Concise Guide to Diagnosis & Treatment. Ed. by M. Eric Gershwin & Maurice E. Hamilton. LC 98-5986. (Current Clinical Practice Ser.). 390p. 1998. 79.50 (*0-89603-423-2*) Humana.

Pain Management in Cardiothoracic Surgery. Ed. by Glenn P. Gravlee et al. LC 92-48508. (Society of Cardiovascular Anesthesiologists Monograph Ser.). (Illus.). 236p. 1993. reprint ed. pap. 73.20 (*0-608-05857-2*, 205982400007) Bks Demand.

Pain Management in the Cancer Patient. 1994. lib. bdg. 260.95 (*0-8490-8526-8*) Gordon Pr.

Pain Management of AIDS Patients. Ed. by Thomas Janisse. (Current Management of Pain Ser.). (C). 1991. text 106.50 (*0-7923-1056-X*) Kluwer Academic.

***Pain Management of HIV AIDS Patients.** Nedeljkovic. (Illus.). 304p. 2000. pap. text 65.00 (*0-7506-7167-X*) Buttrwrth-Heinemann.

Pain Management Patient Education Manuel. annuals Aspen Reference Group Staff. Date not set. ring bd., suppl. ed. 179.00 (*0-8342-0634-X*, S168) Aspen Pub.

Pain Management Practice Guide for Clinicians. 5th ed. Richard S. Weiner. 616p. 1997. lib. bdg. 97.50 (*1-57444-200-7*) St Lucie Pr.

Pain Management Psychotherapy: A Practical Guide. Bruce N. Eimer & Arthur M. Freeman. LC 97-15702. 528p. 1998. 69.50 (*0-471-15708-2*) Wiley.

Pain Management Secrets. Ed. by Ronald M. Kanner. LC 96-49764. (Secrets Ser.). (Illus.). 350p. (Orig.). 1997. pap. text 38.00 (*1-56053-160-6*) Hanley & Belfus.

Pain Management Techniques for Older Adults. Sue V. Saxon. 114p. 1991. pap. 19.95 (*0-398-06414-8*) C C Thomas.

Pain Management Techniques for Older Adults. Sue V. Saxon. 114p. (C). 1991. text 31.95 (*0-398-05734-6*) C C Thomas.

Pain Measurement & Assessment. fac. ed. Ed. by Ronald Melzack. LC 82-40296. (Illus.). 311p. pap. 96.50 (*0-7837-7506-7*, 204700000005) Bks Demand.

Pain Mechanisms & Management. Ed. by J. C. Wells & Clifford Woolf. (British Medical Bulletin Ser.: Vol. 47, 3). (Illus.). 264p. 1992. text 62.00 (*0-443-04491-0*) Church.

Pain, My Companion. I. Howat. Date not set. 6.99 (*1-871676-42-8*, Pub. by Christian Focus) Spring Arbor Dist.

***Pain 1999--An Updated Review: Refresher Course Syllabus: LASP Refresher Courses on Pain Management Held in Conjunction with the 9th World Congress on Pain, August 22-27, 1999, Vienna, Austria.** IASP Refresher Courses on Pain Management Staff & IASP Scientific Program Committee. Ed. by Mitchell B. Max. LC 99-32277. 600p. 1999. pap. 35.00 (*0-931092-32-9*) Intl Assn Study Pain.

Pain of Being Human. rev. ed. Eugene Kennedy. LC 97-29515. 180p. 1997. pap. 14.95 (*0-8245-1682-6*) Crossroad NY.

Pain of Betrayal. large type ed. Stella Ross. (Linford Romance Library). 272p. 1994. pap. 16.99 (*0-7089-7555-0*) Ulverscroft.

Pain of Christ & the Sorrow of God. Gerald Vann. LC 93-38395. 94p. 1993. pap. 4.95 (*0-8189-0689-8*) Alba.

Pain of Innocence. Lorene Wingard. LC 96-42247. 1997. write for info. (*1-56763-297-1*); pap. write for info. (*1-56763-298-X*) Ozark Pub.

Pain of Premature Parents: A Psychological Guide for Coping. Michael T. Hynan & Lauren Leslie-Hynan. 106p. (Orig.). 1987. pap. text 16.00 (*0-8191-5809-7*); lib. bdg. 34.00 (*0-8191-5808-9*) U Pr of Amer.

Pain of the Macho: And Other Plays. unabridged ed. Rick Najera. Ed. by William-Alan Landes. LC 96-39820. 152p. 1997. pap. 13.00 (*1-55885-190-9*, Pub. by Arte Publico) Empire Pub Srvs.

Pain on Their Faces: Testimonies on the Paper Mill Strike, Jay, Maine, 1987-1988. Jay-Livermore Falls Working Class History Project. Ed. by Peter Kellman. LC 98-25624. (Illus.). 108p. 1998. pap. 11.95 (*0-945257-96-1*) Apex Pr.

Pain, Pain, Go Away. William J. Faber & Morton Walker. (Illus.). 352p. 1990. pap. 14.95 (*0-923891-17-X*, M5) Ishi Pr Intl.

Pain, Perplexity & Promotion: A Prophetic Interpretation of the Book of Job. Bob Sorge. LC 99-30852. 160p. 1999. pap. 12.00 (*0-9621185-6-7*) Oasis Hse.

Pain, Pleasure & Aesthetics. Henry R. Marshall. LC 75-3281. reprint ed. 29.50 (*0-404-59269-4*) AMS Pr.

Pain, Pleasure, & American Childbirth: From the Twilight Sleep to the Read Method, 1914-1960, 13. Margarete Sandelowski. LC 83-18510. (Contributions in Medical History Ser.: No. 13). (Illus.). 152p. 1984. 39.95 (*0-313-24076-0*, SFC/) Greenwood.

***Pain Procedure in Clinical Practice.** 2nd rev. ed. Ed. by Ted A. Lennard. LC 99-42857. (Illus.). 350p. (C). 2000. text 75.00 (*1-56053-367-6*, Pub. by Harcourt Coll Pubs) Harcourt.

Pain Relief: How to Say No to Acute, Chronic & Cancer Pain. Jane Cowles. 416p. 1994. 22.95 (*0-942361-77-6*) MasterMedia Pub.

Pain Relief - The L.A. Pain Clinic Guide. 2nd ed. Gary S. Zaboly. 150p. 1997. pap. 10.00 (*0-9650767-1-7*) St-of-the-Art Tech.

Pain Relief Breakthrough: The Power of Magnets to Relieve Backaches, Arthritis, Menstrual Cramps, Carpal Tunnel Syndrome, Sports Injuries, & More. Julian Whitaker & Brenda Adderly. LC 97-76355. 224p. 1998. 22.95 (*0-316-60193-4*) Little.

Pain Relief Breakthrough: The Power of Magnets to Relieve Backaches, Arthritis, Menstrual Cramps, Carpal Tunnel Syndrome, Sports Injuries, & More. Julian Whitaker & Brenda Adderly. 224p. 1999. pap. 12.95 (*0-452-28088-5*) NAL.

Pain Relief Handbook. C. Wells. 1996. pap. 19.95 (*0-09-181371-9*, Pub. by Random) Trafalgar.

Pain Relief Handbook: Self-Help Methods for Managing Pain. Chris Wells & Graham Nown. (Illus.). 216p. 1998. pap. 14.95 (*1-55209-243-7*) Firefly Bks Ltd.

Pain Relief in Anesthesia in Obstetrics. Andre Van Zundert. 1995. text 126.00 (*0-443-04474-0*) Church.

Pain Relief in Far Advanced Cancer. Robert G. Twycross. 1994. pap. text 73.00 (*0-443-04119-9*) Church.

Pain Relief in Labour. Contrib. by Robin Russell et al. 252p. 1997. pap. 43.00 (*0-7279-1009-4*, Pub. by BMJ Pub) Login Brothers Bk Co.

Pain Relief in Labour. 5th ed. Donald D. Moir. LC 85-11702. (Illus.). 196p. 1985. pap. text. write for info. (*0-443-03389-7*) Church.

Pain Relievers, Diet Pills & Other Over-the-Counter Drugs. Ed. by Steven L. Jaffe. LC 99-20186. (Illus.). 80p. (J). (gr. 4-8). 1999. lib. bdg. 19.95 (*0-7910-5203-6*) Chelsea Hse.

Pain Remedies. Philip Goldberg. Ed. by Prevention Magazine Editors. 384p. 1998. reprint ed. mass mkt. 5.99 (*0-440-22655-4*) Dell.

Pain Remedies: Over 1,000 Quick & Easy Pain Remedies from Little Ouches to Big Aches. Philip Goldberg & Prevention Magazine Editors. 320p. 1998. 27.95 (*0-87596-545-8*) Rodale Pr Inc.

Pain Remedies over 1,000 Quick & Easy Pain Remedies from Little Ouches to Big Aches. Philip Goldberg & Prevention Magazine Health Books Staff. LC 97-8239. 352p. 1997. text 27.95 (*0-87596-285-8*) Rodale Pr Inc.

Pain Seeking Understanding: Suffering, Medicine & Faith. Ed. by Margaret E. Mohrmann & Mark J. Hanson. LC 99-34494. 224p. 1999. pap. 19.95 (*0-8298-1354-3*) Pilgrim OH.

Pain Sourcebook. Ed. by Allan Cook. LC 97-37833. (Health Reference Ser.: Vol. 32). 1997. lib. bdg. 78.00 (*0-7808-0213-6*) Omnigraphics Inc.

Pain Specialist's Approach to the Headache Patient. Seymour Diamond. LC 93-13888. 162p. 1993. 27.50 (*0-8236-3930-4*) Intl Univs Pr.

***Pain Surgery, 2 vols., Set.** Kim J. Burchiel. (Illus.). 864p. 2000. 179.00 (*0-86577-912-0*) Thieme Med Pubs.

Pain System. W. D. Willis. (Pain & Headache Ser.: Vol. 8). (Illus.). x, 346p. 1985. 125.25 (*3-8055-3930-4*) S Karger.

Pain to Peace: Your Deepest Pain Is Your Greatest Source of Peace. David C. Jones. 1997. audio 11.95 (*1-878400-06-1*) Dolphin Pub.

Pain to Peace: Your Deepest Pain Is Your Greatest Source of Peace. David C. Jones. 175p. 1997. pap. text 11.95 (*1-878400-03-7*) Dolphin Pub.

Pain to Peace, a Journey. Mary L. Noack. LC 96-85569. 1996. mass mkt., spiral bd. 12.95 (*1-889131-00-8*) CasAnanda.

Pain Treatment Centers at a Crossroads: A Practical & Conceptual Reappraisal. Ed. by Mitchell J. Cohen & James N. Campbell. LC 96-12622. (Progress in Pain Research & Management Ser.: Vol. 7). (Illus.). 352p. 1996. 39.00 (*0-931092-14-0*) Intl Assn Study Pain.

***Pain Tree: And Other Teenage Angst-Ridden Poems.** Ed. & Illus. by Esther Pearl Watson. 64p. (YA). 2000. 16.00 (*0-618-01558-2*) HM.

Pain vs. Man. Ed. by Federigo Sicuteri et al. LC 91-27914. (Advances in Pain Research & Therapy Ser.: Vol. 20). 320p. 1992. reprint ed. pap. 99.20 (*0-608-04741-4*, 206546200004) Bks Demand.

Paine. David F. Hawke. 528p. 1992. pap. 14.95 (*0-393-30919-3*) Norton.

Paine: Ancestors & Descendants of David Paine & Abigail Shepard of Ludlow, MA, 1463-1913. Compiled by C. P. Ohler. (Illus.). 252p. 1993. reprint ed. pap. 39.50 (*0-8328-3731-8*); reprint ed. lib. bdg. 49.50 (*0-8328-3730-X*) Higginson Bk Co.

***Paine: Political Writings.** 2nd ed. Thomas Paine. Ed. by Bruce Kuklick. (Cambridge Studies in Comparative Politics). 300p. (C). 2000. text 47.95 (*0-521-66088-2*); pap. text 14.95 (*0-521-66799-2*) Cambridge U Pr.

Paine Ancestry: The Family of Robert Treat Paine, Signer of the Declaration of Independence, Including Maternal Lines. S. C. Paine. Ed. by Charles H. Pope. 336p. 1989. reprint ed. pap. 50.50 (*0-8328-0927-6*); reprint ed. lib. bdg. 58.50 (*0-8328-0926-8*) Higginson Bk Co.

Paine Family Records: A Journal of Genealogical & Biographical Information Respecting the American Family of Payne, Paine, Payn, Etc., 2 vols. in 1. Ed. by H. O. Paine. (Illus.). 522p. 1989. reprint ed. pap. 78.00 (*0-8328-0929-2*); reprint ed. lib. bdg. 86.00 (*0-8328-0928-4*) Higginson Bk Co.

Paine, Scripture, & Authority: The Age of Reason As Religious & Political Ideal. Edward H. Davidson & William J. Scheick. LC 92-55135. 1994. 29.50 (*0-934223-29-7*) Lehigh Univ Pr.

Painesdale, Michigan: Old & New. (Copper Country Local History Ser.: Vol. 23). (Illus.). 116p. 1983. 3.00 (*0-942363-22-1*) C J Monette.

Painful Cervical Trauma: Diagnosis & Rehabilitative Treatment of Neuromusculoskeletal Injuries. John R. Satterthwaite & C. David Tollison. (Illus.). 512p. 1992. 83.00 (*0-683-08337-6*) Lppncott W & W.

Painful Choices: Research & Essays on Health Care. David Mechanic. 320p. 1989. 39.95 (*0-88738-258-4*) Transaction Pubs.

***Painful Decisions, Positive Results: United Way & Community Chest, 1915-2000.** Richard N. Aft & Daniel J. Ransohoff. (Illus.). 272p. (Orig.). 2000. pap. 20.00 (*0-9676382-0-8*) Comm Chest & Council.

***Painful Demise of Eurocentrism: An Afrocentric Response to Critics** Molefi K. Asante. LC 99-20777. 1999. 19.95 (*0-86543-743-2*) Africa World.

Painful Field: The Psychiatric Dimension of Modern War, 75. Richard A. Gabriel. LC 87-31789. (Contributions in Military Studies Ser.: No. 75). 207p. 1988. 55.00 (*0-313-24718-8*, GBP/, Greenwood Pr) Greenwood.

Painful Inheritance: Health & the New Generation of Fatherless Families. Ronald J. Angel & Jacqueline L. Angel. LC 93-18788. (Life Course Studies). (Illus.). 288p. (Orig.). (C). 1994. pap. 19.95 (*0-299-13964-6*); lib. bdg. 55.00 (*0-299-13960-3*) U of Wis Pr.

***Painful News I Have to Write: Letters & Diaries of Four Hite Brothers of Page County in the Service of the Confederacy.** Ed. & Compiled by Harlan R. Jessup. LC 99-209691. (Army of Northern Virginia Ser.: Vol. 10). (Illus.). 204p. 1999. 25.00 (*0-935523-72-3*) Butternut & Blue.

Painful Partings: Divorce & Its Aftermath. Lita L. Schwartz & Florence W. Kaslow. LC 96-19118. (Couples & Family Dynamics & Treatment Ser.). 310p. 1997. 59.95 (*0-471-11009-4*) Wiley.

Painful Passages: Working with Children with Learning Disabilities. Elizabeth Dane. LC 90-6463. 221p. 1990. 24.95 (*0-87101-175-1*) Natl Assn Soc Wkrs.

Painful People & How to Deal with Them. Jo Dunn. 1998. pap. 13.95 (*0-7322-5737-9*) HarpC.

Painful Pleasures. Illus. by Francis Heuber. 283p. 1995. 34.95 (*1-897767-03-X*, Pub. by Delectus Bks) Xclusiv Distrib.

Painful Prescription: Rationing Hospital Care. Henry J. Aaron & William B. Schwartz. LC 83-45962. (Studies in Social Economics). 161p. 1984. 29.95 (*0-8157-0034-2*); pap. 11.95 (*0-8157-0033-4*) Brookings.

Painful Questions: Facing Struggles with Faith. Gary L. Watts. LC 99-22002. 240p. 1999. pap. 12.99 (*0-8361-9121-8*) Herald Pr.

Painful Season & a Stubborn Hope: The Odyssey of an Eritrean Woman in Prison. Abeba Tesfagiorgis. LC 92-14196. 200p. 1992. 39.95 (*0-932415-83-0*); pap. 12.95 (*0-932415-84-9*) Red Sea Pr.

Painfully Clear: The Parables of Jesus. Andrew Parker. (Biblical Seminar Ser.: No. 37). 166p. 1996. pap. 19.95 (*1-85075-771-2*, Pub. by Sheffield Acad) CUP Services.

***Painfully Rich: J. Paul Getty & His Heirs.** John Pearson. (Illus.). 349p. 2000. reprint ed. text 30.00 (*0-7881-6919-X*) DIANE Pub.

***Painitings of Our Lives.** Grace Schulman. 72p. 2001. 22.00 (*0-618-08622-6*) HM.

Painless Afrikaans. G. Holloway. 120p. 1991. reprint ed. pap. 15.00 (*0-7021-0596-1*) IBD Ltd.

Painless Algebra. Lynette Long. LC 98-18911. (Illus.). 224p. (J). 1998. pap. 8.95 (*0-7641-0676-7*) Barron.

Painless American History Curt Lader. LC 98-50020. (Painless... Ser.). 1999. 8.95 (*0-7641-0620-1*) Barron.

Painless Astrology: A Simple & Fun Guide to Natal Chart Interpretation. rev. ed. Paul V. Beyerl. (Illus.). 200p. 1996. pap. write for info. (*0-9655687-0-9*) Hermits Grove.

Painless Fractions. Alyece Cummings. LC 98-23068. (Illus.). 224p. (J). 1998. pap. 8.95 (*0-7641-0445-4*) Barron.

Painless Grammar. Rebecca Elliott. LC 97-7370. (Illus.). 264p. 1997. pap. 8.95 (*0-8120-9781-5*) Barron.

Painless Guide to a Healthy Back. Ilan Horowitz. Tr. by Karen Gold from HEB. LC 93-11225. (Illus.). 93p. 1993. reprint ed. pap. 12.95 (*1-55643-168-6*) North Atlantic.

Painless Ingebretsen, The Rock & Roll Dentist. Al Blair. 4p. 1988. pap. 3.95 (*0-930366-28-X*) Northcountry Pub.

Painless Mandolin Melodies. Wayne Erbsen. (Illus.). 30p. 1985. pap. 12.95 (*1-883206-13-8*, NGE-021) Native Ground.

Painless Parker: A Dental Renegade's Fight to Make Advertising "Ethical" Arden G. Christen & Peter M. Pronych. (Illus.). 492p. 1995. pap. 24.95 (*1-885873-01-8*) Dental Tobacco.

Painless Path to Proper Punctuation: or Who Killed Albert the Crook? Ed. by Stan Malotte. (Illus.). 161p. 1998. reprint ed. pap. text 9.00 (*0-7881-5191-6*) DIANE Pub.

P

An Asterisk (*) at the beginning of an entry indicates that the title is appearing for the first time.

Painless Perfect Grammar: The National Grammar Hotline's Most Frequently Asked Questions. 3rd rev. ed. Michael Strumpf & Auriel Douglas. Orig. Title: Painless Perfect Grammar, Tips from the Grammar Hotline. 144p. 1996. reprint ed. pap. 12.95 (*0-942208-43-9*) Bandanna Bks.

Painless Perfect Grammar, Tips from the Grammar Hotline see Painless Perfect Grammar: The National Grammar Hotline's Most Frequently Asked Questions

Painless Police Report Writing: An English Guide for Criminal Justice Professionals. Barbara Frazee & Joseph N. Davis. 144p. 1992. pap. text 41.00 (*0-13-647629-5*) P-H.

Painless Public Speaking. 4th ed. Sharon Bower. (Illus.). 227p. 1990. reprint ed. pap. 20.00 (*0-9665262-0-1*) Confi Train.

Painless Public Speaking: A Work Text Approach. Abne M. Eisenberg & Teri K. Gamble. 272p. (C). 1991. reprint ed. pap. text 28.50 (*0-8191-8147-1*) U Pr of Amer.

Painless Publishing. Daniel Morris. (Illus.). 60p. (C). 1988. write for info. (*0-318-62977-1*) Osage Pr.

Painless Research Projects. Rebecca S. Elliott & James Elliott. LC 97-48597. 288p. (YA). 1998. pap. 8.95 (*0-7641-0297-4*) Barron.

Painless Science Projects. Faith Hickman Brynie. LC 98-4169. 224p. (J). 1998. pap. 8.95 (*0-7641-0595-7*) Barron.

Painless Spelling. Mary E. Podhaizer. LC 98-18313. (Illus.). 224p. 1998. pap. 8.95 (*0-7641-0567-1*) Barron.

Painless Windows, a Handbook for SAS Users. Jodie Gilmore. 336p. (C). 1997. pap. 32.95 (*1-58025-054-8*, BR55769) SAS Publ.

***Painless Windows 3.1: A Beginner's Handbook for SAS Users.** Jodie Gilmore. 304p. 1998. pap. 38.95 (*1-58025-358-X*, BR56514) SAS Publ.

Painless Windows 3.1: A Beginner's Handbook for SAS(R) Users. LC 97-148013. 304p. (C). 1998. pap. 32.95 (*1-55544-878-X*, BR55505) SAS Publ.

***Painless Word Problems.** Marcie F. Abramson. LC 00-31248. 2001. write for info. (*0-7641-1533-2*) Barron.

Painleve Property: One Century Later. Ed. by R. Conte. LC 99-16039. (CRM Series in Mathematical Physics). (Illus.). 600p. 1999. 98.00 (*0-387-98888-2*) Spr-Verlag.

Painleve Transcendents: Their Asymptotics & Physical Applications. Ed. by D. Levi & P. Winternitz. LC 96-5775. (NATO ASI Ser.: Vol. 278). (Illus.). 472p. (C). 1992. text 162.00 (*0-306-44050-4*, Kluwer Plenum) Kluwer Academic.

Pains & Pleasures of Parenthood. Lib U. Griffin. Ed. by Joe Johnson. 168p. (Orig.). 1993. pap. 10.00 (*0-9636705-0-6*) Bedlam Pr.

***Pains of April.** Frank T. Hollon. 101p. 1999. 17.95 (*0-9643727-3-8*) Over the Transom.

Pains of Glass: The Story of the Passion from King's College Chapel, Cambridge. Wendy Becket & George Pattison. (Illus.). 48p. 1996. 12.95 (*0-563-37170-6*, BBC-Parkwest) Parkwest Pubns.

Painswick Line see Henry Cecil Reprint Series

Paint. (Jump Ser.). (Illus.). 36p. (J). (gr. 2-6). pap. write for info. (*1-882210-32-8*) Action Pub.

Paint. (Five-Minute Art Ideas Ser.). (Illus.). 24p. (J). (ps up). 1995. pap. 6.95 (*1-57102-036-5*, Ideals Child) Hambleton-Hill.

***Paint.** Ivan Bulloch & Diana James. (Let's Ser.). (Illus.). (J). 2000. pap. 4.95 (*1-58728-030-2*) Two Can Pub.

Paint. Jann Haworth. LC 95-60781. (Fun to Do Ser.). 32p. (J). (gr. 2 up). 1995. lib. bdg. 15.95 (*1-887238-04-2*) Fitzgerald.

Paint! Kim Solga. (Art & Activities for Kids Ser.). (Illus.). 48p. (J). (gr. 1-6). 1991. 11.99 (*0-89134-383-0*, 30338, North Lght Bks) F & W Pubns Inc.

***Paint.** rev. ed. Ivan Bulloch. (Let's Ser.). (Illus.). (J). 2000. 9.95 (*1-58728-026-4*) Two Can Pub.

Paint: Choosing, Mixing & Decorating with Water-Based Paints. John Sutcliffe. 1995. 45.00 (*0-8050-4739-5*) H Holt & Co.

Paint: Colors, Techniques, Inspiration. Mary Engelbreit. LC 99-41051. (Illus.). 112p. 1999. 16.95 (*0-7407-0029-4*) Andrews & McMeel.

Paint - Country Living. Hearst Books Staff. LC 97-51934. 1998. 30.00 (*0-688-15099-3*, Wm Morrow) Morrow Avon.

***Paint & Surface Coatings: Theory & Practice.** 2nd ed. R. Lambourne & T.A. Strivens. 950p. 1999. 285.00 (*1-884207-73-1*) William Andrew.

***Paint a Poem.** Moira Andrew. (Kids' Stuff Ser.). (J). 1999. pap. text 15.95 (*0-947882-44-8*) Belair Pubns Ltd.

Paint a Victorian Holiday. Lisa Notch. (Illus.). 1994. pap. 6.95 (*1-883675-01-4*, 101) J Shaw Studio.

Paint a Victorian Memory, Vol. 1. Lisa Notch. (Illus.). 1992. pap. 5.95 (*0-941284-91-3*, 91) J Shaw Studio.

Paint Adventures! Kathy Savage-Hubbard & Rose C. Speicher. (Art & Activities for Kids Ser.). (Illus.). 48p. (J). 1993. 11.99 (*0-89134-508-6*, 30524, North Lght Bks) F & W Pubns Inc.

***Paint Along with Jerry Yarnell.** Jerry Yarnell. (Illus.). 128p. 2000. pap. 19.99 (*1-58180-036-3*, North Lght Bks) F & W Pubns Inc.

Paint Along with Nancy Kominsky: Still Lifes. Nancy Kominsky. (Illus.). (Orig.). 1981. mass mkt. 7.95 (*0-446-87792-1*, Pub. by Warner Bks) Little.

Paint & Body Handbook. rev. ed. Don Taylor & Larry Hofer. LC 93-48885. (Illus.). 144p. (Orig.). 1994. pap. 17.95 (*1-55788-082-4*, HP Books) Berkley Pub.

Paint & Coating Testing Manual. 14th rev. ed. Ed. by Joseph V. Koleske. LC 95-10632. (Manual Ser.: Vol. 17). Orig. Title: Paint Testing Manual. 1995. 220.00 (*0-8031-2060-5*, MNL17) ASTM.

Paint & Coatings for Corrosion Protection. J. Baghdachi. (Materials Engineering Ser.). (Illus.). Date not set. text. write for info. (*0-8247-0065-1*) Dekker.

Paint & Color. Jessica E. Hirschman. LC 96-9759. (For Your Home Ser.). 72p. 1996. pap. 12.95 (*1-56799-329-X*, Friedman-Fairfax) M Friedman Pub Grp Inc.

Paint & Painting;The Colors, the Techniques, the Surfaces. (Voyages of Discovery Ser.). (Illus.). 48p. (J). (gr. 4-6). 1994. 19.95 (*0-590-47636-X*) Scholastic Inc.

Paint & Paper: Pleasures of Home. Harry Levinson. (Illus.). 128p. 1998. pap. 14.95 (*0-304-35090-7*) Continuum.

Paint & Patches: Painting on Fabric with Pigments. Vicki L. Johnson. LC 95-38143. 144p. 1995. 18.95 (*0-89145-856-5*, 4515, Am Quilters Soc) Collector Bks.

Paint & Purpose: A Study of Technique over Four Centuries of British Art. Ed. by Stephen Hackney et al. (Illus.). 256p. 1998. pap. 45.00 (*1-85437-248-3*, Pub. by Tate Gallery) U of Wash Pr.

Paint & Repair. Harry Levinson. (Pleasures of Home Ser.). (Illus.). 128p. 1997. 21.95 (*0-304-34628-4*, Pub. by Cassell) Sterling.

Paint & Surface Coatings: Theory & Practice. 2nd ed. Ed. by R. Lambourne & T. A. Strivens. 950p. 1999. boxed set 225.00 (*1-85573-348-X*, Pub. by Woodhead Pubng) Am Educ Systs.

Paint & Wallpaper. (Home Repair & Improvement Ser.). (Illus.). 136p. 1976. 14.60 (*0-8094-2354-5*); lib. bdg. 20.60 (*0-8094-2355-3*) Time-Life.

Paint & Wallpaper. Time-Life Books Editors. LC 95-30729. (Home Repair & Improvement Ser.). (Illus.). 128p. (gr. 11). 1999. spiral bd. 14.95 (*0-7835-3896-0*) Time-Life.

Paint Around Your Collar. Meldra Johnson & Fay Moore-Sines. (Illus.). 24p. (Orig.). 1987. pap. 5.95 (*0-941284-44-1*) J Shaw Studio.

Paint Box, Vol. 1. Vienna Paint Staff. 1996. 60.00 (*1-56496-282-2*) Rockport Pubs.

Paint Box: A Colorful Romance. Debbie Tomassi. LC 98-13419. (Illus.). 64p. 1999. 12.95 (*0-8212-2482-4*, Pub. by Bulfinch Pr) Little.

Paint Box Ideas - Full of Animals, Vol. 37. Susan Scheewe Brown. (Illus.). 100p. (Orig.). (C). 1998. pap. 12.95 (*1-56770-450-6*) S Scheewe Pubns.

Paint Box of Ideas, Vol. 34. Susan S. Brown. (Illus.). 109p. 1998. pap. 12.95 (*1-56770-430-1*) S Scheewe Pubns.

Paint Box of Ideas - Watercolor & Acrylic, Vol. 35. Susan Scheewe Brown. (Illus.). 100p. (Orig.). (C). 1998. pap. 12.95 (*1-56770-442-5*) S Scheewe Pubns.

Paint Box of Ideas "Welcomes", Vol. 36. Susan Scheewe Brown. (Illus.). 100p. 1998. pap. 12.95 (*1-56770-445-X*) S Scheewe Pubns.

Paint Brush Kid. Robert C. Bulla. LC 97-51153. 1998. lib. bdg. 11.99 (*0-679-99282-0*, Pub. by Random Bks Yng Read) Random.

Paint Brush Kid. Robert C. Bulla. (J). 1998. pap. 3.99 (*0-679-89282-6*, Pub. by Random Bks Yng Read) Random.

Paint by Numbers. Barbara Mellin. 16p. 1996. pap. 20.00 (*0-201-48999-6*) Addison-Wesley.

Paint by Pattern Gardens. Jillybean J. Fitzhenry et al. (Illus.). 60p. 1998. pap. 10.95 (*1-57377-045-0*, 019884-22343) Easl Pubns.

Paint by Pattern Pets. Jill Fitzhenry. 1997. pap. text 10.95 (*1-57377-006-X*) Easl Pubns.

Paint Cans. Paul Donovan. 256p. 1992. pap. 11.95 (*0-921586-18-3*, Pub. by New Star Bks) Genl Dist Srvs.

Paint-Coatings Dictionary. Ed. by Federation of Societies for Coatings Technology, D. 632p. 1995. boxed set 135.00 (*0-686-95495-5*) Fed Soc Coat Tech.

Paint Contracting & Estimating Made Easy: An Instructive Manual on How to Become A More Successful Painting Contractor & Estimator. LC 98-124942. (Illus.). 1997. pap. 34.95 (*0-9659313-0-7*) Hignell & Hignell.

Paint Contractor's Complete Handbook. Dennis D. Gleason. (Illus.). 520p. 1998. 85.95 (*0-07-063368-1*); pap. 47.95 (*0-07-063367-3*) McGraw-Hill Prof.

Paint Contractor's Manual. Dave Matis & Jobe H. Toole. LC 84-29315. (Illus.). 224p. 1985. pap. 26.00 (*0-910460-46-9*) Craftsman.

Paint Craft. Editors at Eaglemoss. (Illus.). 144p. 1995. pap. 16.95 (*0-89134-650-3*, North Lght Bks) F & W Pubns Inc.

Paint Effects. Lindsey Durrant. 1999. pap. 11.95 (*0-85532-875-4*) Srch Pr.

Paint Effects. Jo Finnis. 1995. 7.98 (*0-7858-0122-7*) Bk Sales Inc.

Paint Effects. Maggie Philo. (The Inspirations Ser.). (Illus.). 96p. 1998. 12.95 (*1-85967-602-2*, Lorenz Bks) Anness Pub.

Paint Finishes. Charles Hemming. (Illus.). 144p. 1989. 12.98 (*0-89009-909-X*) Bk Sales Inc.

Paint Flow & Pigment Dispersion: A Rheological Approach to Coating & Ink Technology. 2nd ed. Temple C. Patton. LC 78-10774. 656p. 1979. 245.00 (*0-471-03272-7*, Wiley-Interscience) Wiley.

Paint Fun. R. Gibson & R. Gee. (You & Your Child Ser.). (Illus.). 32p. (J). (ps-2). 1992. pap. 5.95 (*0-7460-1085-0*) EDC.

Paint Fun. R. Gibson & R. Gee. (You & Your Child Ser.). (Illus.). 32p. (J). (ps-2). 1999. lib. bdg. 14.95 (*0-88110-285-7*) EDC.

***Paint Group: Hirschl & Adler Galleries, 21 East 70th Street, New York, New York.** Hirschl & Adler Galleries. LC 99-71885. (Illus.). 1999. write for info. (*0-915057-61-1*) Hirschl & Adler Gall.

Paint Handbook. Ed. by Guy E. Weismantel. (Illus.). 752p. 1981. 89.95 (*0-07-069061-8*) McGraw.

Paint Her Face Dead. Jane Johnston. 224p. 1988. reprint ed. spiral bd. 3.50 (*0-373-26013-X*) Harlequin Bks.

***Paint Ideas & Decorating Techniques.** Better Homes & Gardens. LC 99-75939. (Better Homes & Gardens Ser.). (Illus.). 160p. 2000. pap. 19.95 (*0-696-21032-0*) Meredith Bks.

Paint in America: The Colors of Historic Buildings. Ed. by Roger W. Moss. 320p. 1995. pap. 19.95 (*0-471-14411-8*) Wiley.

Paint in America: The Colors of Historic Buildings. Ed. by Roger W. Moss. LC 96-18763. (Illus.). 320p. 1995. 39.95 (*0-471-14410-X*) Wiley.

Paint It Today. H. D., pseud. Ed. & Intro. by Cassandra Laity. (Cutting Edge: Lesbian Life & Literature Ser.). 160p. (C). 1992. text 45.00 (*0-8147-3487-1*); pap. text 16.00 (*0-8147-3488-X*) NYU Pr.

Paint Lick Idyll & Other Poems. Harry Brown. Ed. by Patricia Schultz. LC 89-33520. (Poetry Ser.: Vol. 1). 72p. 1989. pap. 12.95 (*0-88946-886-9*) E Mellen.

Paint Manufacturing Industry: Guides to Pollution Prevention. (Illus.). 67p. (Orig.). (C). 1993. pap. text 25.00 (*1-56806-666-X*) DIANE Pub.

Paint Me a Picture--Make Me a Poem. Norbert Blei. (Illus.). 108p. 1987. pap. 5.95 (*0-933180-97-7*) Spoon Riv Poetry.

Paint Me Rainbows. Fern Michaels. 256p. 1994. per. 4.99 (*1-55166-003-2*, 1-66003-4, Mira Bks) Harlequin Bks.

Paint Me Rainbows. Fern Michaels. 2000. mass mkt. 5.99 (*0-373-48398-8*, 1-48398-1) Harlequin Bks.

Paint Me Rainbows. Fern Michaels. 1994. mass mkt. 4.50 (*0-373-48316-3*, 5-48316-9) Silhouette.

Paint Now, Learn Later. Guy R. Williams. (Illus.). 12.95 (*0-87523-158-6*) Emerson.

Paint Radiant Realism in Watercolor, Ink & Colored Pencil. Sueellen Ross. LC 99-21136. (Illus.). 128p. 1999. 27.99 (*0-89134-900-6*, 31424, North Lght Bks) F & W Pubns Inc.

Paint Recipes. Jocasta Innes. (Around the House Ser.). (Illus.). 96p. 1997. 12.95 (*0-8212-2451-4*, Pub. by Bulfinch Pr) Little.

Paint Recipes: A Step-By-Step Guide to Colors & Finishes for the Home. Liz Wagstaff. (Illus.). 192p. 1996. pap. 19.95 (*0-8118-1173-5*) Chronicle Bks.

***Paint Recipes & Paint Effects.** Sacha Cohen. (Practical Encyclopedia of ... Ser.). 1999. 35.00 (*0-7548-0199-3*, Lorenz Bks) Anness Pub.

***Paint Recipes for Surfaces: Over 40 Instant Wall & Floor Transformations.** Stewart Walton. (Illus.). 2000. pap. 12.95 (*0-7548-0309-0*, Lorenz Bks) Anness Pub.

Paint Shop Pro 5 for Windows: Visual QuickStart Guide. Ben Sawyer & Joann Meyer. LC 99-165376. (Visual QuickStart Guide Ser.). 304p. (C). 1998. pap. text 16.95 (*0-201-35362-8*, Pub. by Peachpit Pr) Addison-Wesley.

***Paint Shop Pro for Dummies.** David Kay. (For Dummies Ser.). (Illus.). 384p. 2000. pap. 24.99 (*0-7645-0693-5*) IDG Bks.

Paint Shop Pro Power! Lorin R. Davis. 416p. 1999. pap. 39.99 (*0-9662889-2-0*) Muska Lipman.

***Paint Shop Pro Solutions: Create, Edit & Prepare Your Graphics.** Lori J. Davis. (Solutions Ser.). (Illus.). 288p. 2000. pap. 29.95 (*1-929685-09-2*, Pub. by Muska Lipman) IPG Chicago.

Paint Shop Pro Web Techniques. T. Michael Clark. LC 97-6578. 350p. 1997. 44.99 (*1-56205-756-1*) New Riders Pub.

***Paint Shop Pro 6 Visual Insight.** Ramona Pruitt. LC 99-49157. 1999. pap. text 29.99 (*1-57610-525-3*) Coriolis Grp.

Paint Spirit. Audrey Pavia. LC 97-32167. (Spirit of the Horse Ser.). (Illus.). 64p. 1998. pap. 16.95 (*1-889540-21-8*) Bowtie Press.

Paint Techniques for Home Decorating: Walls, Furniture & Floors. Plaid. LC 97-35572. (Plaid Enterprises Ser.). (Illus.). 128p. 1998. 27.95 (*0-8069-0551-4*) Sterling.

Paint Techniques for Home Decorating: Walls, Furniture & Floors. Plaid. 1999. pap. text 14.95 (*0-8069-7783-3*) Sterling.

Paint Testing Manual see Paint & Coating Testing Manual

Paint Testing Manual: Physical & Chemical Examination of Paints, Varnishes, Lacquers & Colors. 13th ed. American Society for Testing & Materials Staff. Ed. by G. G. Sward. LC 75-186850. (ASTM Special Technical Publication: No. 500). 612p. reprint ed. pap. 189.80 (*0-608-12023-5*, 202283500030) Bks Demand.

***Paint the Sea in Oils Using Special Effects.** E. John Robinson. Ed. by Terri Dodd. (Illus.). 128p. 1999. write for info. (*1-929834-00-4*) Intl Artist Pubg.

***Paint the Sea in Oils Using Special Effects.** E. John Robinson. (Illus.). 2000. 24.99 (*1-929834-04-7*) Intl Artist Pubg.

Paint with Pittard: 13 New Paintings with Lynne Pittard in Four Stages & Full Color. Lynne Pittard. (Illus.). 72p. (Orig.). 1985. pap. 14.95 (*0-943295-06-8*) Graphics Plus FL.

Paint with Pittard III: 12 New Paintings by Lynne Pittard in Four Stages & Full Color. Lynne Pittard. (Illus.). 72p. (Orig.). 1989. pap. 14.95 (*0-943295-10-6*) Graphics Plus FL.

Paint with the Watercolor Masters: A Step-by-Step Guide to Materials & Techniques. Jonathan Stephenson. (Illus.). 160p. 1998. pap. text 24.95 (*0-8230-3447-X*) Watsn-Guptill.

Paint Without Brushes. Liz Wilmes & Dick Wilmes. (Illus.). 128p. (Orig.). 1993. pap. 12.95 (*0-943452-15-5*) Building Blocks.

Paint Works: Fast Cars. (Works Ser.). (Illus.). 32p. (J). (gr. 3 up). 1997. 16.95 (*1-56010-236-5*, QK12) W Foster Pub.

Paint Works: Favorite Pets. (Works Ser.). (Illus.). 32p. (J). (gr. 3 up). 1997. 16.95 (*1-56010-234-9*, QK10) W Foster Pub.

Paint Works: Horses & Ponies. (Works Ser.). (Illus.). 32p. (YA). (gr. 3 up). 1997. 16.95 (*1-56010-235-7*, QK11) W Foster Pub.

Paint Works: Tractors & Trucks. (Works Ser.). (Illus.). 32p. (J). (gr. 3 up). 1997. 16.95 (*1-56010-233-0*, QK09) W Foster Pub.

Paint Your Face & Other Poems. Jenny Keller. Ed. by Marquetta Herring. (Illus.). 22p. (C). 1986. pap. 3.50 (*0-942186-01-X*) Paperbacks Plus.

Paint Your Feelings Starting Today: Anastasia's Basic of Painting I. Anastasia Cole. LC 89-80074. (Illus.). 116p. (C). 1989. student ed. 15.95 (*0-9622944-0-3*) Anastasias Art.

Paint Your Home: Skills, Techniques, & Tricks of the Trade for Professional Looking Interior Painting. Francis Donegan. LC 96-46950. 1997. 18.95 (*0-89577-838-6*, Pub. by RD Assn) Penguin Putnam.

Paint Your House with Powdered Milk: And Hundreds More Offbeat Uses for Brand-Name Products. Joey Green. LC 96-5424. (Illus.). 192p. (J). 1996. pap. 7.70 (*0-7868-8208-5*, Pub. by Hyperion) Time Warner.

Paint Your Own Rainbow: Upbeat Mottos for the Young in Heart. Annette Bradshaw & Gwyn Franson. 1983. 5.98 (*0-88290-237-7*) Horizon Utah.

Paint Your Own T-Shirts: Including 20 Iron-On Transfers. Monika Neubacher-Fesser & Dieter Kohner. (Illus.). 96p. 1996. pap. 19.95 (*0-85532-811-8*, 8118, Pub. by Srch Pr) A Schwartz & Co.

Paint Your Wagon. (Vocal Score Ser.). 264p. 1981. per. 45.00 (*0-88188-043-4*, 00312311) H Leonard.

Paint Your Wagon: Vocal Selections. Ed. by Michael Lefferts. (Illus.). 44p. (Orig.). (C). 1981. pap. 8.95 (*0-88188-103-1*, 00312310) H Leonard.

Paintball! Strategies & Tactics. Bill Barnes. LC 93-4012. (Illus.). 176p. 1993. pap. 12.95 (*0-914457-52-7*) Mustang Pub.

Paintball: The Wizard's Way: Authoritative Book on Paintball Equipment, Strategy, & Tactics. Ronald E. Elbe. LC 94-19169. (Illus.). 160p. (Orig.). (C). 1994. pap. 16.95 (*0-941540-21-9*, 3010) Blacksmith Corp.

***Paintball Legend Logbook.** 2nd ed. Glenn Murray. (Illus.). ii, 75p. 1999. 79.95 (*1-58527-011-3*) Legend Pubns NY.

Paintball Warrior. Jessica Pierce. (Spider's Child Ser.: Vol. 4). 144p. 1999. mass mkt. 3.50 (*0-8217-4917-X*, Zebra Kensgtn) Kensgtn Pub Corp.

***Paintbox, No. 2.** Andreas Fitzner. (Illus.). 312p. 2000. 65.00 (*3-7913-2363-6*) Prestel Pub NY.

***Paintbox No. 1.** Ed. by Andreas Fitzner & Albert Winkler. (Illus.). 272p. 2000. pap. 29.95 (*3-7913-2410-1*) Prestel.

Paintbox Penguins, A Book about Colors. Marcia Leonard. LC 89-4979. (Illus.). 24p. (J). (gr. k-2). 1990. lib. bdg. 14.50 (*0-8167-1716-8*) Troll Communs.

Paintbox Penguins, A Book about Colors. Marcia Leonard. LC 89-4979. (Illus.). 24p. (J). (gr. k-2). 1997. pap. 2.50 (*0-8167-1717-6*) Troll Communs.

Paintbox Penguins, A Book about Colors. Marcia Leonard. 1999. pap. text 16.95 (*0-8167-2657-4*) Troll Communs.

Paintbox Summer. Betty Cavanna. 212p. (J). 1981. reprint ed. lib. bdg. 27.95 (*0-89966-357-5*); reprint ed. lib. bdg. 16.95 (*0-89967-031-8*, Harmony Rain) Buccaneer Bks.

Paintbrush in Paris: The Artistic Adventures of an American Cat in Paris. Jill Butler. LC 94-6228. (Illus.). 96p. 1994. 9.95 (*1-56305-524-4*, 3524) Workman Pub.

***Paintco Vi Marketing Simulation for Marketing By Evans,berman & Wellington.** 2nd ed. 70p. 1999. teacher ed. write for info. (*0-13-017346-0*) P-H.

Paintcrafts. Gillian Souter. LC 97-4044. 160p. 1997. pap. 20.00 (*0-609-80035-3*) Random Hse Value.

Painted & Printed Fabrics: The History of the Manufactory at Jouy & Other Ateliers in France, 1760-1815 by Henri Clouzot: Notes on the History of Cotton Printing Especially in England & America by Frances Morris. Henri Clouzot & Frances Morris. LC 70-168418. (Metropolitan Museum of Art Publications in Reprint). (Illus.). 222p. 1974. reprint ed. 34.95 (*0-405-02256-5*) Ayer.

Painted Architecture & Polychrome Monumental Sculpture in Mesoamerica. Ed. by Elizabeth H. Boone. LC 85-4514. (Illus.). 201p. 1985. 24.00 (*0-88402-142-4*) Dumbarton Oaks.

Painted Bird. Jerzy N. Kosinski. LC 95-19520. 256p. 1995. pap. 12.00 (*0-8021-3422-X*, Grove) Grove-Atltic.

***Painted Bird.** Jerzy N. Kosinski. LC 99-39919. 270p. 1999. pap. 24.95 (*0-7658-0655-X*) Transaction Pubs.

Painted Bird. large type ed. Jerzy N. Kosinski. 320p. 1999. 24.95 (*1-56000-485-1*) Transaction Pubs.

Painted Birdhouses. Plaid. LC 98-14776. (Illus.). 128p. 1998. 24.95 (*0-8069-1345-2*, Chapelle) Sterling.

Painted Birdhouses. Plaid. 1999. 14.95 (*0-8069-1877-2*) Sterling.

Painted Blessings, Vol. 11. Chris Thornton. 66p. 1995. pap. 10.50 (*1-56770-323-2*) S Scheewe Pubns.

Painted Bodies: By 45 Artists. Photos by Roberto Edwards. LC 97-158829. (Illus.). 364p. 1996. 85.00 (*0-7892-0268-9*) Abbeville Pr.

***Painted by the Sun.** Elizabeth Grayson. 2000. mass mkt. 5.99 (*0-553-58013-2*) Bantam.

Painted Canoe. Anthony Winkler. LC 88-28738. vi, 302p. 1989. pap. 13.95 (*0-226-90206-4*) U Ch Pr.

***Painted Ceramics: Colour & Imagery on Clay.** Brenda Pegrum. (Illus.). 160p. 2000. 50.00 (*1-86126-236-1*, Pub. by Cro1wood) Trafalgar.

Painted Ceramics of the Western Mound at Awatovi. Watson Smith. LC 79-102785. (Peabody Museum Papers: Vol. 38). (Illus.). 658p. 1971. pap. 22.00 (*0-87365-114-6*) Peabody Harvard.

***Painted Chairs: 20 Fresh & Fun Projects.** Jennifer R. Ferguson & Judy Skinner. (Illus.). 96p. 2001. pap. 21.95 (*1-56477-340-X*) Martingale & Co.

Painted Chamber at Westminster. Paul Binski. (Illus.). 256p. 1986. pap. 32.50 (*0-500-99044-1*, Pub. by Soc Antiquaries) David Brown.

An Asterisk (*) at the beginning of an entry indicates that the title is appearing for the first time.

Painted Cherub, Bk. 3. Penny Ives. (Illus.). 12p. (J). (ps-3). 1995. 4.95 (*0-689-80334-6*) Aladdin.

Painted Churches of Romania: A Visitor's Impressions. John Fletcher & Isabel Wyatt. (Illus.). 52p. 1971. 19.95 (*0-88010-062-1*, Pub. by R Steiner Pr) Anthroposophic.

Painted Comanche Tree. Kent Conwell. LC 97-94023. 192p. 1997. 18.95 (*0-8034-9261-8*, Avalon Bks) Bouregy.

Painted Cougar. Elizabeth M. Hopkins. LC 78-306189. 32p. 1980. reprint ed. pap. 9.95 (*0-88922-125-1*, Pub. by Talonbks) Genl Dist Srvs.

***Painted Crafts Made Easy.** Susan Penny. (Illus.). 64p. 2000. 12.95 (*0-7153-0976-5*) D & C Pub.

Painted Crucifixes in Croatia. Grgo Gamulin. 133p. 1983. 30.00 (*0-918660-35-1*) Ragusan Pr.

Painted Delight: Indian Paintings from Philadelphia Collections. Stella Kramrisch. LC 85-31013. (Illus.). 196p. (Orig.). 1986. pap. 22.00 (*0-87633-064-2*) Phila Mus Art.

Painted Deocration on the Floors of Bronze Age Structures on Crete & the Greek Mainland. Ethel S. Hirsch. (Studies in Mediterranean Archaeology: Vol. LIII). (Illus.). 63p. (Orig.). 1977. pap. 39.50 (*91-85058-76-9*, Pub. by P Astroms) Coronet Bks.

Painted Desert: A Novel. Frederick Barthelme. 1997. pap. 11.95 (*0-14-024214-7*) Viking Penguin.

Painted Desert: A Novel. Frederick Barthelme. 288p. 1999. pap. 20.95 (*0-670-85840-4*) Viking Penguin.

Painted Desert: Land of Light & Shadow. Rose Houk. (Illus.). 48p. (Orig.). (C). 1990. pap. 7.95 (*0-945695-03-9*) Petrified Forest Mus Assn.

Painted Desert, Green Shade: Essays on Contemporary Writers for Children & Young Adults. David Rees. LC 83-12996. 211p. 1984. pap. 13.95 (*0-87675-286-5*) Horn Bk.

Painted Designs Etc. Cy DeCosse Incorporated Staff. LC 96-26995. (Creative Touches Ser.). (Illus.). 64p. 1996. pap. 9.95 (*0-86573-999-4*) Creat Pub Intl.

Painted Devil. Michael Bedard. LC 92-35637. 224p. (J). (gr. 5-9). 1994. 15.95 (*0-689-31827-8*) Atheneum Yung Read.

Painted Devil. large type ed. John Welcome. 1990. 27.99 (*0-7089-2264-3*) Ulverscroft.

Painted Dial Clocks. Brian Loomes. (Illus.). 350p. 1995. 59.50 (*1-85149-183-X*) Antique Collect.

Painted Diaries: A Mother & Daughter's Experience Through Alzheimers. Kim H. Zabbia. (Illus.). 224p. 1996. 24.95 (*1-57749-007-X*) Fairview Press.

***Painted Dreams.** Karen L. Williams. LC 97-32920. (Illus.). 40p. (J). (gr. k-2). 1998. 15.89 (*0-688-13902-7*, Wm Morrow) Morrow Avon.

Painted Dreams. Karen L. Williams. LC 97-32920. (Illus.). 40p. (J). (gr. k-3). 1998. 16.00 (*0-688-13901-9*, Wm Morrow) Morrow Avon.

Painted Dreams: Native American Rock Art. Thor Conway. LC 93-19666. (Illus.). 1996. 29.95 (*1-55971-213-9*, NorthWord Pr) Creat Pub Intl.

Painted Eggs: Using Dyes, Watercolors, Gouache, Pencils & Inks. Heidi Haupt-Battaglia. (Illus.). 64p. 1994. pap. 16.95 (*0-85532-672-7*, 672-7, Pub. by Srch Pr) A Schwartz & Co.

Painted Enamels of Limoges. Susan L. Caroselli. LC 92-85528. (Illus.). 208p. 1993. 50.00 (*0-500-97406-3*, Pub. by Thames Hudson) Norton.

Painted Enamels of Limoges in the Walters Art Gallery: A Picture Book. (Illus.). 1968. pap. 1.50 (*0-911886-14-1*) Walters Art.

Painted Face. large type ed. Jean Stubbs. (Large Print Ser.). 464p. 1996. 27.99 (*0-7089-3640-7*) Ulverscroft.

Painted Faces on the Renaissance Stage: The Moral Significance of Face-Painting Conventions. Annette Drew-Bear. LC 92-54668. (C). 1994. 29.50 (*0-8387-5230-6*) Bucknell U Pr.

Painted Fans of Japan: 15 Noh Drama Masterpieces. Reiko Chiba. LC 62-20775. (Illus.). 42p. 1962. 29.95 (*0-8048-0468-0*) Tuttle Pubng.

Painted Field. Robin Robertson. LC 97-27711. 108p. (C). 1998. 22.00 (*0-15-100366-1*) Harcourt.

Painted Field. Robin Robertson. LC 97-27711. 89p. (C). 1999. pap. 13.00 (*0-15-600647-2*) Harcourt.

Painted Finishes for Walls & Furniture. Susan Driggers. LC 97-51565. (Illus.). 128p. 1998. 24.95 (*0-8069-9441-X*) Sterling.

***Painted Finishes for Walls & Furniture: Easy Techniques for Great New Looks.** Susan Goans Driggers. (Illus.). 128p. 1999. pap. 14.95 (*0-8069-9416-9*) Sterling.

Painted Furniture. Pamela Innes. (Weekend Decorator Ser.). (Illus.). 96p. (Orig.). 1996. pap. 14.95 (*1-85410-427-6*, Pub. by Aurum Pr) London Brdge.

Painted Furniture. Richard Wiles. (Quick & Easy Ser.). (Illus.). 96p. 1997. pap. text 14.95 (*0-7063-7681-1*, Pub. by WrLock) Sterling.

Painted Furniture: Making Ordinary Furniture Extrordinary with Paint, Pattern & Color. Katrin Cargill. LC 98-75319. 128p. (gr. 8). 1999. 27.50 (*0-8212-2541-3*) Little.

Painted Furniture: Simple Techniques for Fresh, New Looks. Diane M. Weaver. (Illus.). 160p. 1996. pap. 17.95 (*0-8069-0840-8*) Sterling.

Painted Furniture Inspired by Masters: In the Studio with a Dozen Artists. Lisa Skolnik. (Illus.). 144p. 1999. pap. 24.99 (*1-56496-455-8*, Quarry Bks) Rockport Pubs.

Painted Furniture Sourcebook. Annie Sloan. LC 98-65886. (Illus.). 160p. 1998. 29.95 (*0-8478-2120-X*, Pub. by Rizzoli Intl) St Martin.

Painted Garden. Ed. by Kimberly Gorton. 1998. 69.95 (*1-57553-613-7*) Watermrk Pr.

***Painted Garden: A Year in Words & Watercolors.** Mary Woodin. 1999. 17.95 (*0-7624-0408-6*) Running Pr.

***Painted Garden: Designs for Folk Art & Tole Painting.** Kate Coombe. (Milner Craft Ser.). (Illus.). 2000. pap. 16.95 (*1-86351-236-5*) Sally Milner.

Painted Girl. large type ed. Nara Lake. 1995. 27.99 (*0-7089-3275-4*) Ulverscroft.

Painted Hallway. Nancy-Lou Patterson. 208p. 1992. pap. write for info. (*0-88984-142-X*) Porcup Quill.

Painted Horse. Bonnie Bryant. (Saddle Club Ser.: No. 75). 144p. (J). (gr. 4-6). 1998. pap. 3.99 (*0-553-48625-X*, Skylark BDD) BDD Bks Young Read.

Painted Horse. Katharine Kincaid. (Zebra Bks.). 384p. 1998. mass mkt. 4.99 (*0-8217-6042-4*, Zebra Kensgtn) Kensgtn Pub Corp.

Painted House: Over 100 Original Designs for Mural & Trompe L'Oeil Decoration. Graham Rust. (Illus.). 188p. 1997. pap. 29.95 (*0-8212-2454-9*, Pub. by Bulfinch Pr) Little.

Painted House: Painted Finished for Walls & Floor. Debbie Travis. 1997. 29.95 (*0-609-60155-5*) C Potter.

Painted House: Quick & Easy Painted Finishes for Walls, Floors, & Surfaces. Debbie Travis & Barbara Dingle. LC 96-37440. 1997. pap. 25.00 (*0-517-88840-8*) C Potter.

Painted Illusions. Home Decorating Institute Staff. LC 96-15853. (Arts & Crafts for Home Decorating Ser.). (Illus.). 128p. 1996. 18.95 (*0-86573-402-X*); pap. 16.95 (*0-86573-403-8*) Creat Pub Intl.

Painted Images. Melvin Lars. Ed. by Sweettie A. Johnson. LC 94-12045. (Illus.). 125p. (Orig.). (YA). (gr. 9 up). 1996. pap. 12.00 (*0-9638218-4-9*) M Lars.

Painted in Blood, Remember Wyoming: America's First Civil War. Jay L. Glickman. (Illus.). 300p. Date not set. 30.00 (*1-879915-15-4*); pap. 16.00 (*1-879915-16-2*) Affil Writers America.

Painted Jars. Conny Hubbard. (Illus.). 72p. 1999. pap. 10.50 (*1-56770-454-9*) S Scheewe Pubns.

***Painted Kitchen: Over 60 Quick & Easy Ways to Transform Your Kitchen Cupboards.** Henny Donovan. (Illus.). 128p. 2000. 29.95 (*1-55209-455-3*) Firefly Bks Ltd.

***Painted Kitchen: Over 60 Quick & Easy Ways to Transform Your Kitchen Cupboards.** Henny Donovan. (Illus.). 128p. 2000. pap. 19.95 (*1-55209-501-0*) Firefly Bks Ltd.

Painted Lace & Other Pieces, 1914-1937, Vol. Five Of Unpubli. Gertrude Stein. LC 77-103665. (Select Bibliographies Reprint Ser.). 1980. 30.95 (*0-8369-5165-4*) Ayer.

Painted Ladies. James N. Harvey. 1992. mass mkt. 5.99 (*0-312-92895-5*) St Martin.

Painted Ladies: Butterflies of North America. Millie Miller & Cyndi Nelson. (Illus.). (Orig.). 1993. pap. 5.95 (*1-55566-103-3*) Johnson Bks.

Painted Ladies: Modern Military Aircraft Nose Art & Unusual Markings. Randy Walker. LC 91-67900. (Illus.). 128p. 1992. pap. 24.95 (*0-88740-392-1*) Schiffer.

Painted Ladies Revisited: San Francisco's Resplendent Victorians Inside & Out. Elizabeth Pomada & Michael Larsen. (Illus.). 144p. 1989. pap. 24.95 (*0-525-48508-2*, Dutt) Dutton Plume.

Painted Lady. Donna Baker. 224p. 25.00 (*0-7278-5512-3*) Severn Hse.

Painted Lady. Lucinda Baker. LC 98-96335. 192p. 1998. lib. bdg. 18.95 (*0-8034-9315-0*, Avalon Bks) Bouregy.

Painted Lady. large type ed. Harriet Crawley. 480p. 1996. 27.99 (*0-7089-3513-3*) Ulverscroft.

***Painted Lady.** large type ed. Delia Ellis. 320p. 1999. 31.99 (*0-7089-4070-6*, Linford) Ulverscroft.

***Painted Lady Butterflies: Life Cycles.** Donna Schaffer. LC 98-53026. (Life Cycles Ser.). (Illus.). 24p. (J). 1999. 15.93 (*0-7368-0211-8*, Bridgestone Bks) Capstone Pr.

Painted Light: California Impressionist Paintings from the Gardena High School - Los Angeles Unified School District Collection. Jean Stern. Ed. by Pamela Hammond. LC 98-70213. (Illus.). 60p. 1998. 40.00 (*0-9662490-1-1*); pap. 25.00 (*0-9662490-0-3*) Cal St U Dom.

Painted Light: Poems. M. L. Harvey. LC 92-45618. 64p. 1993. pap. 14.95 (*0-7734-0027-3*, Mellen Poetry Pr) E Mellen.

Painted Lives. large type ed. Charlotte Vale Allen. (General Ser.). 470p. 1991. lib. bdg. 20.95 (*0-8161-5180-6*, G K Hall Lrg Type) Mac Lib Ref.

***Painted Lives.** Charlotte Vale Allen. 266p. 1999. reprint ed. pap. 20.00 (*1-892738-33-3*) Isld Nation.

Painted Love: Prostitution in French Art of the Impressionist Era. Hollis Clayson. (Illus.). 232p. 1992. 55.00 (*0-300-04730-4*) Yale U Pr.

Painted Meadow Stencils: Cornflowers & Daisies. Jocasta Innes & Stewart Walton. (Illus.). 8p. 1997. pap. 16.95 (*0-356-20635-1*) Trafalgar.

Painted Moon. Karin Kallmaker. LC 94-16242. 272p. 1994. pap. 11.95 (*1-56280-075-2*) Naiad Pr.

Painted Page: Italian Renaissance Book Illumination 1450-1550. Compiled by Jonathan J. Alexander et al. (Illus.). 198p. 1994. 85.00 (*3-7913-1385-1*, Pub. by Prestel) te Neues.

***Painted Panorama.** Bernard Comment. Tr. by Anne-Marie Glasheen. LC 99-88310. (Illus.). 272p. 2000. 65.00 (*0-8109-4365-4*, Pub. by Abrams) Time Warner.

Painted Paragraphs. Donald Newlove. 88p. 1995. pap. 9.95 (*0-8050-2591-X*) H Holt & Co.

Painted Paragraphs: Inspired Description for Writers & Readers. Donald Newlove. 192p. 1995. 14.95 (*0-8050-2978-8*) H Holt & Co.

Painted Photograph, 1839-1914: Origins, Techniques, Aspirations. Heinz K. Henisch & Bridget A. Henisch. 242p. 1996. 80.00 (*0-271-01507-1*) Pa St U Pr.

***Painted Pieces in a Weekend.** Julie Collins. 2000. pap. 14.95 (*1-58290-022-1*, Pub. by Jrny Editions) Tuttle Pubng.

Painted Ponies: American Carousel Art. William Manns et al. Ed. by Dru Riley. LC 86-51050. (Illus.). 256p. 1986. 40.00 (*0-939549-01-8*) ZON Intl Pub.

Painted Ponies: American Carousel Art, 1. Jeffrey L. Zon International Publishing Staff. 1999. 10.95 (*0-939549-20-4*) ZON Intl Pub.

***Painted Pots.** Plaid Enterprises Staff. (Illus.). 128p. 1999. pap. 14.95 (*0-8069-8201-2*, Chapelle) Sterling.

***Painted Pots: Over 20 Inspirational Projects for the Home & Garden.** Simona Hill. (Illus.). 64p. 2000. 11.95 (*0-7548-0460-7*, Lorenz Bks) Anness Pub.

Painted Prayers: The Book of Hours in Medieval & Renaissance Art. Roger S. Wieck. LC 96-36927. (Illus.). 144p. 1997. 35.00 (*0-8076-1418-1*) Braziller.

Painted Prayers: The Book of Hours in Medieval & Renaissance Art. Roger S. Wieck. LC 96-36927. (Illus.). 144p. 1999. pap. 25.00 (*0-8076-1419-X*, Pub. by Braziller) Norton.

***Painted Prayers: The Book of Hours in Medieval & Renaissance Art.** Roger S. Wieck. (Illus.). 1999. pap. 25.00 (*0-8076-1457-2*) Braziller.

Painted Queen. Olga Hesky. 1962. 12.95 (*0-8392-1083-3*) Astor-Honor.

Painted Rock of California. Myron F. Angel. Ed. by Lachlan P. MacDonald. LC 79-26494. (Illus.). 128p. 1979. reprint ed. pap. 5.95 (*0-914598-14-7*) Bear Flag Bks.

Painted Rock Reservoir Project Phase I: Preliminary Survey & Recommendations. Lynn S. Teague & Anne R. Baldwin. (Archaeological Ser.: Vol. 126). (Illus.). 69p. 1978. pap. 5.95 (*1-889747-65-3*) Ariz St Mus.

Painted Rocks. Ruth Alter. (Illus.). 35p. (Orig.). (J). (gr. 3-8). 1996. pap. 8.95 (*0-9653725-0-2*) San Dieguito Riv.

***Painted Rocks.** Klutz Editors. (Illus.). 64p. (J). 2000. 14.95 (*1-57054-529-4*) Klutz.

***Painted Room.** Inger Christensen. Tr. by Denise Newman. (Illus.). 96p. 2000. pap. text 18.00 (*1-86046-593-5*) Harvill Press.

Painted Room: Ideas for Creative Interior Decoration. Kerry Skinner. (Illus.). 144p. 1999. 27.95 (*0-7153-0840-8*, Pub. by D & C Pub) Sterling.

Painted Scene, & Other Stories of the Theater. Henry K. Webster. LC 79-152962. (Short Story Index Reprint Ser.). (Illus.). 1977. reprint ed. 25.95 (*0-8369-3877-1*) Ayer.

Painted Scenery. Charles E. Dunbar. 200p. (Orig.). 1994. pap. 7.95 (*0-9640309-0-X*) C E D Prods.

Painted Scrolls of Asia: Hindu Buddhist & Lamaistic. Shiv K. Sharma. (Illus.). x, 116p. 1994. 32.00 (*81-7076-057-7*, Pub. by Intellect Pub Hse) Nataraj Bks.

Painted Shadows. Niel Jean-Baptiste. Tr. by James Kirkup from FRE. 288p. 1991. 19.95 (*0-7043-2785-6*, Pub. by Quartet) Interlink Pub.

Painted Shadows. Richard Le Gallienne. LC 77-94738. (Short Story Index Reprint Ser.). 1977. 21.95 (*0-8369-3118-1*) Ayer.

Painted Signboards of Russia: Tradition & the Avant-Garde. A. V. Povelikhina & E. F. Kovtun. 1990. write for info. (*0-8109-3754-9*) Abrams.

Painted Sketch: American Impressions from Nature, 1830-1880. Eleanor J. Harvey. Ed. by Fronia Simpson. LC 98-2960. (Illus.). 304p. 1998. pap. 35.00 (*0-936227-24-9*) Dallas Mus.

Painted Sketch: American Impressions from Nature, 1830-1880. Eleanor Jones Harvey. LC 98-2960. (Illus.). 304p. 1998. 49.50 (*0-8109-6364-7*, Pub. by Abrams) Time Warner.

Painted Smiles, Vol. 1. Tracia Ward-Rainey. LC 97-73836. 136p. 1997. pap. 12.00 (*0-9659118-0-2*) Akili Publ.

Painted Sounds of Romarc Bearden. Gail Gelburd & Richard Long. (Illus.). 64p. (Orig.). 1994. pap. write for info. (*1-890789-03-8*) Coun for Creat Proj.

Painted Spider. Kathryn Williamson. 346p. pap. 13.75 (*0-9663285-1-5*) Coyote Pr FL.

Painted Steel: The Late Work of David Smith. William Rubin. (Illus.). 60p. 1998. pap. 30.00 (*1-880154-23-4*) Gagosian Gallery.

Painted, Tainted, Sainted: Four Plays. Sky Gilbert. LC 97-122470. 280p. 1997. text 19.95 (*0-88754-550-5*) Theatre Comm.

Painted Towns of Shekhawati: A Mapin Guide to India. Ilay Cooper. LC 96-146445. (Illus.). 230p. 1994. pap. 17.50 (*81-85822-17-4*, Pub. by Mapin Pubng) Antique Collect.

Painted Truth: An Alix Thorssen Mystery. Lise McClendon. 1996. per. 4.99 (*0-373-26222-1*, 1-26222-9, Wrldwide Lib) Harlequin Bks.

Painted Truth: An Alix Thorssen Mystery. Lise McClendon. LC 95-34117. 252p. 1995. 22.95 (*0-8027-3271-2*) Walker & Co.

Painted Turtle: Woman with Guitar. Clarence Major. (Sun & Moon Classics Ser.: No. 73). 64p. 1996. pap. 11.95 (*1-55713-085-X*) Sun & Moon CA.

***Painted Veil.** 1999. (*0-7351-0194-9*) Replica Bks.

***Painted Veil.** W. Somerset Maugham. 290p. 1999. 27.95 (*0-7351-0173-6*) Replica Bks.

Painted Veil. W. Somerset Maugham. 256p. 1992. pap. 12.95 (*0-14-018599-2*, Penguin Classics) Viking Penguin.

Painted Veil. large type ed. W. Somerset Maugham. 1974. 27.99 (*0-85456-255-9*) Ulverscroft.

Painted Wood History & Conservation: Proceedings of a Symposium at Williamsburg, Virginia, November 1994. Valerie Dorge & F. Carey Howlett. LC 97-36527. (Symposium Proceedings). 576p. 1998. pap. 75.00 (*0-89236-501-3*, Pub. by J P Getty Trust) OUP.

Painted Wood Projects in the Pennsylvania Folk Art Style. Alan Bridgewater & Gill Bridgewater. LC 95-14927. (Illus.). 144p. 1995. 27.95 (*0-8069-0508-5*) Sterling.

Painted Wood Projects in the Pennsylvania Folk Art Style. Alan Bridgewater & Gill Bridgewater. (Illus.). 144p. 1997. pap. 14.95 (*0-8069-0509-3*) Sterling.

Painted Woodcraft. Stewart Walton & Sally Stewart. (Illus.). 128p. 1997. 27.95 (*0-8069-9582-3*, 707902) Sterling.

Painted Woodcraft. Stewart Walton & Sally Walton. (Illus.). 128p. 1998. 14.95 (*0-8069-9583-1*) Sterling.

Painted Wooden Furniture. Cate Withacy. LC 97-73022. (Illus.). 128p. 1997. pap. 19.95 (*0-87341-539-6*, PWF) Krause Pubns.

Painted Wooden Sculptures in Norway, 1100-1250. Martin Blindheim. 160p. 1998. text 43.00 (*82-00-37681-8*) Scandnvan Univ Pr.

Painted Word. Tom Wolfe. 112p. 1999. pap. 12.95 (*0-553-38065-6*) Bantam.

Painted Word. Tom Wolfe. (Illus.). 128p. 1975. 18.95 (*0-374-22878-7*) FS&G.

Painted Word: British History Painting, 1750-1830. Ed. by Peter Cannon-Brookes. (Illus.). 140p. (C). 1991. 75.00 (*0-85115-290-2*) Boydell & Brewer.

***Painted Word: Samuel Beckett's Dialogue with Art.** Lois Oppenheim. LC 99-50634. (Theater Ser.). (Illus.). 248p. 2000. text 49.50 (*0-472-11117-5*, 11117) U of Mich Pr.

Painted Words. Valerie Robillard & Els Jongeneel. 200p. 1997. pap. 27.50 (*90-5383-523-7*, Pub. by VU Univ Pr) Paul & Co Pubs.

Painted Zoo. (J). 14.95 (*1-57054-425-5*) Klutz.

Painter. Peter Catalanotto. LC 94-48808. (Illus.). 32p. (J). (ps-2). 1996. 15.95 (*0-531-09465-0*); lib. bdg. 16.99 (*0-531-08765-4*) Orchard Bks Watts.

Painter. Peter Catalanotto. LC 94-48808. (Illus.). 32p. (J). (ps-2). 1999. pap. 5.95 (*0-531-07116-2*) Orchard Bks Watts.

Painter. Jack Rudman. (Career Examination Ser.: C-570). 1994. pap. 23.95 (*0-8373-0570-5*) Nat Learn.

Painter & Poet. Chauncey B. Tinker. LC 73-80402. (Essay Index Reprint Ser.). 1977. 24.95 (*0-8369-1052-4*) Ayer.

Painter & Poet in Ancient Greece: Iconography & the Literary Arts. Eva C. Keuls. LC 97-152609. (Illus.). 373p. (C). 1997. text 115.00 (*3-519-07636-5*) B G Teubner.

Painter Bela Kadar: Modernist & Romantic. Melanie Fisher. (Illus.). 104p. 1998. pap. 27.00 (*0-8059-4497-4*) Dorrance.

Painter Depicted: Painters As a Subject in Painting. Michael Levey. (Illus.). 1982. 10.95 (*0-500-55013-1*, Pub. by Thames Hudson) Norton.

Painter 5: Visual Quickstart Guide. Elaine Weinmann. (C). 1997. pap. text. write for info. (*0-201-69693-2*) Addison-Wesley.

Painter 5: Visual Quickstart Guide. Elaine Weinmann. (C). 1998. pap. text. write for info. (*0-202-69669-3*) Addison-Wesley.

Painter 5 Wow! Book. 3rd ed. Cher Threinen-Pendarvis. LC 98-148549. 288p. 1997. pap. text 44.95 (*0-201-69651-7*) Peachpit Pr.

Painter, Gilder & Varnisher's Companion, Containing Rules & Regulations in Every Thing, Relating to the Arts of Painting, Gilding, Varnishing & Glass-Staining... Ed. by Henry C. Baird. (Illus.). 216p. 1995. reprint ed. lib. bdg. 35.00 (*0-8328-4498-5*) Higginson Bk Co.

Painter in Glass. Ed. by Alison Lloyd. 74p. 1993. pap. 37.95 (*0-8464-4680-4*) Beekman Pubs.

Painter in Glass. Ed. by Alison Lloyd. 74p. 1993. pap. 38.00 (*0-86383-976-2*, Pub. by Gomer Pr) St Mut.

Painter Knight. Fiona Patton. 544p. 1998. mass mkt. 6.99 (*0-88677-780-1*, Pub. by DAW Bks) Penguin Putnam.

Painter Meets Computer: What Computers Are & How They Can Help Your Business. Lynn H. Fife. Ed. by Lafferty & Assoc. Staff. (Illus.). 120p. (Orig.). 1994. pap. 24.95 (*1-882947-15-0*) Evergreen Tech.

Painter of Dishonour. Pedro Calderon de la Barca. Tr. by David Johnston & Laurence Boswell. 128p. (Orig.). 1996. pap. 12.95 (*0-948230-88-6*, Pub. by Absolute Classics) Theatre Comm.

Painter of His Dishonour. Pedro Calderon de la Barca. (Hispanic Classics Ser.). 1991. pap. 25.00 (*0-85668-347-7*, Pub. by Aris & Phillips) David Brown.

Painter of His Dishonour. Pedro Calderon de la Barca. (Hispanic Classics Ser.). 1991. 59.95 (*0-85668-346-9*, Pub. by Aris & Phillips) David Brown.

Painter of Modern Life & Other Essays. Charles Baudelaire. Ed. by Jonathan Mayne. (Illus.). 298p. 1988. 13.95 (*0-306-80279-1*) Da Capo.

Painter of Modern Life & Other Essays. rev. ed. Charles Baudelaire. Ed. & Tr. by Jonathan Mayne. (Arts & Letters Ser.). (Illus.). 264p. (C). 1995. pap. 14.95 (*0-7148-3365-7*) Chronicle Bks.

Painter of Our Time. John Berger. 1996. pap. 12.00 (*0-679-73723-5*) Vin Bks.

Painter of Our Time. John Berger. 192p. 1981. 11.95 (*0-904613-12-7*); pap. 4.95 (*0-904613-13-5*) Writers & Readers.

***Painter 6 F/X & Design.** Sherry London. LC 00-21571. (Illus.). 335p. 2000. pap. text. write for info. (*1-57610-611-X*) Coriolis Grp.

***Painter 6 Wow! Book.** 4th ed. Cher Threinen-Pendarvis. (Illus.). 368p. 2000. pap. 49.99 incl. cd-rom (*0-201-35449-7*) Peachpit Pr.

Painter Speaks: Artists Discuss Their Experiences & Careers, 2. Ed. by Joan Jeffri. LC 92-46395. (Contributions to the Study of Art & Architecture Ser.: No. 2). 264p. 1993. 59.95 (*0-313-28915-8*, GM8915, Greenwood Pr) Greenwood.

Painter to Painter, Vol. 5. Donna Bell. (Illus.). 98p. 1992. pap. 10.50 (*1-56770-263-5*) S Scheewe Pubns.

Painter Who Loved Chickens. Oliver Dunrea. LC 94-27562. (Illus.). 32p. (J). (ps-3). 1995. 15.00 (*0-374-35729-3*) FS&G.

Painter Who Loved Chickens. Olivier Dunrea. LC 94-4243. (J). (gr. 2 up). 1995. text 14.95 (*0-02-733209-8*, Mac Bks Young Read) S&S Childrens.

Painter Who Loved Chickens. Olivier Dunrea. (Illus.). 32p. (gr. k-3). 1998. pap. text 5.95 (*0-374-45708-5*) FS&G.

P

Painter Who Loved Chickens. Olivier Dunrea. 1998. 11.15 (*0-606-13693-2*, Pub. by Turtleback) Demco.

Painter 6 in Depth, 1. Sherry London. 1999. pap. text 49.99 (*1-57610-381-1*) Coriolis Grp.

Painterly Abstraction in Modernist American Poetry: Infinite Incantations of Ourselves. Charles Altieri. (Cambridge Studies in American Literature & Culture: No. 37). 537p. (C). 1990. text 80.00 (*0-521-33085-8*) Cambridge U Pr.

Painterly Abstraction in Modernist American Poetry: The Contemporaneity of Modernism. Ed. by Charles Altieri. LC 94-30713. (Literature & Philosophy Ser.). (Illus.). 544p. 1995. pap. 22.50 (*0-271-01419-9*) Pa St U Pr.

Painterly Figure. Klaus Kertess & Trudy C. Kramer. LC 83-61884. (Illus.). 78p. (Orig.). (C). 1983. pap. 8.00 (*0-943526-08-6*) Parrish Art.

Painterly Photography: Awakening the Artist Within. 2nd ed. Elizabeth Murray. LC 92-62862. (Illus.). 88p. 1997. boxed set 19.95 (*1-56640-601-3*, A653) Pomegranate Calif.

Painters. Paul Binski. (Medieval Craftsmen Ser.). (Illus.). 72p. 1991. pap. text 19.95 (*0-8020-6918-5*) U of Toronto Pr.

Painters. Laura Conlon. LC 94-11602. (Performers Discovery Library). (J). 1994. lib. bdg. 14.60 (*1-57103-065-4*) Rourke Pr.

Painters & Personality: A Collector's View of Modern Art. Sam A. Lewisohn. LC 70-152188. (Essay Index Reprint Ser.). 1977. reprint ed. 42.95 (*0-8369-2238-7*) Ayer.

Painters & Politics: The European Avant-Garde & Society, 1900-1925. Theda Shapiro. LC 75-20954. 341p. 1981. lib. bdg. 29.95 (*0-444-99012-7*, SPN/) Greenwood.

Painters & Politics in the People's Republic of China, 1949-1979. Julia F. Andrews. LC 93-38071. 480p. 1994. 65.00 (*0-520-07981-7*, Pub. by U CA Pr) Cal Prin Full Svc.

Painters & Public Life in Eighteenth-Century Paris. Thomas E. Crow. LC 85-5375. 292p. 1987. reprint ed. pap. 27.50 (*0-300-03764-3*, Y-670) Yale U Pr.

Painters & Sculptors. Kenyon Cox. LC 70-105006. (Essay Index Reprint Ser.). 1977. 23.95 (*0-8369-1458-9*) Ayer.

***Painters & the American West: The Anschutz Collection.** Joan C. Troccoli & Sarah Anschutz Hunt. (Illus.). 300p. 2000. 45.00 (*0-300-08722-5*) Yale U Pr.

Painter's Daughter: The Story of Sandro Botticelli & Alessandra Lippi. Carolyn Street LaFond. LC 99-22016. (Illus.). 432p. 2000. 35.00 (*0-913720-78-X*) Beil.

Painter's Eye: Notes & Essays on the Pictorial Arts. Henry James. LC 89-40258. 312p. (C). 1989. reprint ed. pap. text 17.95 (*0-299-12284-0*) U of Wis Pr.

Painter's Garden. Jane Dillon. 63p. 1996. pap. 10.50 (*1-56770-354-2*) S Scheewe Pubns.

Painter's Garden. Alexandra Leaf. 1998. write for info. (*0-609-60040-0*) C Potter.

Painters Garden, No. 3. Jane Dillon. (Illus.). 80p. 1999. pap. 10.50 (*1-56770-458-1*) S Scheewe Pubns.

Painter's Garden: Cultivating the Creative Life. 2nd ed. Ed. & Photos by Christine Walker. (Illus.). 144p. 1997. 18.95 (*0-9700217-0-4*) Compozarts.

Painter's Guide to Color. Stephen Quiller. LC 99-26870. (Illus.). 144p. 1999. pap. 24.95 (*0-8230-3913-7*) Watsn-Guptill.

Painter's Guide to the Catskills of Rip Van Winkle: The Magic Places. Judith O. Kate. LC 96-8207. (Illus.). 160p. 1997. 35.00 (*0-925168-51-3*) North Country.

Painter's Handbook. Mark D. Gottsegen. LC 93-14996. (Illus.). 320p. (Orig.). 1993. pap. 29.95 (*0-8230-3003-2*) Watsn-Guptill.

Painter's Handbook. William McElroy. 320p. (Orig.). 1987. pap. 21.25 (*0-934041-28-8*) Craftsman.

Painter's Handbook: Experiencing Color Between Darkness & Light. Lois Schroff. (Illus.). 61p. (Orig.). 1985. pap. text 9.00 (*0-9615740-0-3*) Newlight Bks.

***Painters Have More Fun Than People.** Doug Morrell. (Illus.). 211p. 1999. 14.95 (*1-891029-48-7*) Henderson Pub.

***Painter's House: Balthus at the Grand Chalet.** Kishin Shinoyama. (Illus.). 88p. 2000. 25.00 (*3-8238-5472-0*) te Neues.

***Painters in Paris, 1895-1950.** William S. Lieberman. 144p. 2000. 45.00 (*0-8109-6548-8*, Pub. by Abrams) Time Warner.

Painter's Kitchen: Recipes from the Kitchen of Georgia O'Keeffe. rev. ed. Margaret Wood. LC 91-60329. (Illus.). 128p. 1997. pap. 14.95 (*1-878610-61-9*) Red Crane Bks.

Painter's Manual of Dionysius of Fourna. Ed. & Tr. by Paul Hetherington from GRE. 128p. 1990. reprint ed. per. 12.95 (*1-879038-00-5*) Oakwood Pubns.

Painter's Methods & Materials. Arthur P. Laurie. (Illus.). 250p. 1967. reprint ed. pap. 8.95 (*0-486-21868-6*) Dover.

Painter's Object. Ed. by Myfanwy Evans. LC 73-109022. (Contemporary Art Ser.). (Illus.). 1970. reprint ed. 15.95 (*0-405-00742-6*) Ayer.

Painters of a New Century: The Eight & American Art. Elizabeth Milroy & Gwendolyn Owens. (Illus.). 256p. 1991. pap. 29.95 (*0-944110-08-8*) Milwauk Art Mus.

***Painters of Alaska, Vol. 27, No. 3.** Kessler Woodward. (Illus.). 96p. 2000. pap. 21.95 (*1-56661-051-6*) Alaska Geog Soc.

Painters of Cape Ann, 1840-1940: One Hundred Years in Gloucester & Rockport. Lisa N. Peters & Karen Quinn. (Illus.). 16p. 1996. pap. 12.00 (*0-945936-12-5*) Spanierman Gallery.

***Painters of Provence.** Philippe Cros. (Illus.). 2000. 45.00 (*2-08-013686-0*, Pub. by Flammarion) Abbeville Pr.

Painters of the Ashcan School: The Immortal Eight. Bernard B. Perlman. (Illus.). 224p. 1990. pap. 12.95 (*0-486-25747-9*) Dover.

Painters of the Caves. Patricia Lauber. (Illus.). 48p. (YA). (gr. 3 up). 1998. 17.95 (*0-7922-7095-9*, Pub. by Natl Geog) Publishers Group.

Painters of the Golden Age: A Biographical Dictionary of Seventeenth-Century European Painting. Adelheid M. Gealt. LC 92-40223. 800p. 1993. lib. bdg. 145.00 (*0-313-24310-7*, GBB, Greenwood Pr) Greenwood.

Painters of the Great Lakes Scene: Highlights from the Collection of Great Lakes Regional Painting. Michael D. Hall & Jacqueline C. Shinners. LC 96-225844. (Illus.). 32p. (Orig.). 1996. pap. write for info. (*0-9636721-2-6*) Dennos Mus.

Painters of the Great Ming: The Imperial Court & the Zhe School. Richard M. Barnhart. LC 92-43258. 1993. 65.00 (*0-936227-11-7*); pap. 35.00 (*0-936227-12-5*) Dallas Mus.

Painters of the Pahari Schools. Ed. by Vishwa Chandler & Roy C. Craven. LC 98-902737. 1998. 59.00 (*81-85026-41-6*) Art Media Resources.

Painters of the Sea. David Cordingly. (Illus.). 1980. pap. 20.00 (*0-85331-425-X*) Eastview.

Painters of the Wagilag Sisters Story, 1937-1997. Ed. by Wally Caruana & Nigel Lendon. LC 97-62503. (Illus.). 300p. 1998. pap. 34.95 (*0-500-97468-3*, Pub. by Thames Hudson) Norton.

Painters on Painting. Eric Protter. LC 97-34498. (Illus.). 312p. pap. 8.95 (*0-486-29941-4*) Dover.

Painters, Paintings & Books: An Essay on Indo-Persian Technical Literature 12-19th Centuries. Yves Porter. (C). 1994. text 28.00 (*81-85425-95-7*, Pub. by Manohar) S Asia.

Painter's Paradise: Artists & the California Landscape: Essays. William H. Gerdts et al. LC 96-28426. 1996. write for info. (*0-89951-093-0*) Santa Barb Mus Art.

***Painters, Patrons & Identity: Essays in Native American Art to Honor J. J. Brody.** Joyce M. Szabo & J. J. Brody. LC 00-9017. 2001. pap. write for info. (*0-8263-2025-2*) U of NM Pr.

***Painter's Poet: Stephane Mallarme & His Impressionist Circle.** Jane M. Roos et al. (Illus.). 135p. 1999. pap. 20.00 (*1-885998-17-1*) Hunter College.

Painter's Potpourri. Ed. by Julie Vosberg. (Illus.). 44p. (Orig.). (YA). (gr. 12). 1994. pap. write for info. (*0-943883-31-8*) Natl Soc of Tole.

Painter's Practice: How Artists Lived & Worked in Traditional China. James Cahill. (Bampton Lectures in America). (Illus.). 208p. 1995. pap. 26.50 (*0-231-08181-2*) Col U Pr.

Painter's Practice in Renaissance Tuscany. Anabel Thomas. (Illus.). 418p. 1997. pap. text 25.95 (*0-521-55563-9*) Cambridge U Pr.

Painter's Psalm: The Mural from Walter Anderson's Cottage. rev. ed. Redding S. Sugg, Jr. LC 92-1355. (Illus.). 96p. 1992. 25.00 (*0-87805-560-6*) U Pr of Miss.

Painter's Quest: Art As a Way of Revelation. Peter Rogers. (Orig.). 1994. pap. 17.95 (*1-879041-22-7*) Sigo Pr.

Painter's Wild Workshop: Expand Your Creativity: Inspiration from 4 Master Artists. Lynn L. Loscutoff. (Illus.). 144p. 1998. 29.99 (*1-56496-434-5*, Quarry Bks) Rockport Pubs.

Painter's Workshop. W. G. Constable. (Illus.). 148p. 1979. reprint ed. pap. 6.95 (*0-486-23836-9*) Dover.

Painting. Mike Bathum. (Portfolio of Illustrated Four-Step Art Projects Ser.). (Illus.). 72p. 1983. pap. text 12.95 (*0-87628-326-1*) Ctr Appl Res.

Painting. Jeff Beneke. Ed. by David W. Toht. (Easy-Step Ser.). (Illus.). 64p. (Orig.). 1998. pap. 6.95 (*0-89721-342-4*, 05989, Ortho Bks) Meredith Bks.

Painting. Jane Bower. LC 98-122237. (Arts & Crafts Skills Ser.). 32p. (J). 1998. 20.00 (*0-516-20457-2*) Childrens.

Painting. Boy Scouts of America. (Illus.). 32p. (YA). (gr. 6-12). 1983. pap. 2.90 (*0-8395-3372-1*, 33372) BSA.

Painting. Illus. by Jonathan Clark. LC 99-181873. (Easy-Step Ser.). 64p. (Orig.). 1998. pap. 4.95 (*0-8069-7057-X*) Sterling.

Painting. P. Foster. (Hobby Guides Ser.). (Illus.). 32p. (J). (gr. 5 up). 1981. pap. 6.95 (*0-86020-546-0*) EDC.

Painting. P. Foster. (Hobby Guides Ser.). (Illus.). 32p. (J). (gr. 5 up). 1999. lib. bdg. 14.95 (*0-88110-026-9*) EDC.

Painting. Shirley Glubok. LC 93-8319. (Great Lives Ser.). (Illus.). 256p. (J). (gr. 4-6). 1994. 24.95 (*0-684-19052-4*) Scribner.

***Painting.** Sally Laity et al. 352p. 1999. pap. 4.97 (*1-57748-640-4*) Barbour Pub.

Painting. Andrew Pekarik. LC 92-52987. (Behind the Scenes Ser.). (Illus.). 64p. (J). (gr. 3-7). 1992. 18.95 (*1-56282-296-9*, Pub. by Hyprn Child); lib. bdg. 18.89 (*1-56282-297-7*, Pub. by Hyprn Child) Little.

Painting. Andrew Pekarik. LC 92-52987. (Behind the Scenes Ser.). (Illus.). 64p. (J). (gr. 3-7). 1995. pap. 8.70 (*0-7868-1031-9*, Pub. by Hyprn Ppbks) Little.

Painting. Lori V. Schue. (ArtWorks for Kids Ser.: Vol. 2). (Illus.). 48p. (J). (gr. 1-6). 1995. pap. text, teacher ed. 9.95 (*1-55799-363-7*, EMC 292) Evan-Moor Edu Pubs.

Painting. Sue Stocks. LC 93-44582. (First Arts & Crafts Ser.). (Illus.). 32p. (J). (gr. 1-6). 1994. lib. bdg. 21.40 (*1-56847-162-9*) Raintree Steck-V.

Painting: Behind the Scenes. Andrew Pekarik. (J). 1992. 14.15 (*0-606-07987-4*) Turtleback.

Painting: Commercial & Residential, Level 1. rev. ed. NCCER Staff. 392p. (C). 1997. pap. text 50.00 (*0-13-771239-1*) P-H.

Painting: Commercial & Residential, Level One, Level 1. NCCER Staff. 460p. (C). 1997. teacher ed., ring bd. 50.00 (*0-13-772922-7*) P-H.

Painting: Commercial & Residential, Level One, Level 1. rev. ed. NCCER Staff. 404p. (C). 1997. ring bd. 50.00 (*0-13-772914-6*) P-H.

Painting: Commercial & Residential Level One: Perfect Bound Without Core, Level 1. NCCER Staff. 442p. (C). 1997. pap. text, teacher ed. 50.00 (*0-13-771288-X*) P-H.

Painting: Level Two, Level 2. rev. ed. NCCER Staff. 532p. (C). 1997. student ed., ring bd. 80.00 (*0-13-772930-8*, Prentice Hall) P-H.

Painting: Royal Academy of Arts-A Young Artist's Guide. Elizabeth Waters & Annie Harris. LC 93-3576. (Young Artists Ser.). (Illus.). 40p. (J). (gr. 3-6). 1993. 14.95 (*1-56458-348-1*) DK Pub Inc.

Painting a Place in America: Jewish Artists in New York, 1900-1945. Ed. by Norman L. Kleeblatt & Susan Chevlowe. LC 91-582. (Illus.). 208p. 1991. 41.95 (*0-253-33121-8*) Ind U Pr.

Painting a Poem: Mary Baker Eddy & James F. Gilman Illustrate Christ & Christmas. Illus. by James F. Gilman. 243p. 1997. 27.95 (*0-87510-370-7*, G61212) Writings of Mary Baker.

***Painting... A Quest Toward Xtraordinary.** Judi Betts & Charlotte Huntley. LC 99-95214. (Illus.). 1999. write for info. (*0-9616679-3-1*) Aquarelle Pr.

Painting Acrylics. Vicki Lord. LC 96-241. (First Steps Ser.). (Illus.). 128p. 1996. pap. 18.99 (*0-89134-668-6*, North Lght Bks) F & W Pubns Inc.

***Painting after Pollock: Structures of Influence.** Jeanne Siegel. (Illus.). 240p. 1999. text 39.95 (*90-5701-292-8*, Verlag Kunst); pap. text 24.95 (*90-5701-302-9*, Verlag Kunst) Gordon & Breach.

***Painting Amazing Web Images with MetaCreations Painter.** David D. Busch. 350p. 1999. pap. 45.95 incl. cd-rom (*0-12-147617-0*) Morgan Kaufmann.

Painting American Folk Art. Andy Jones. LC 99-46330. 112p. 1999. pap. text 14.95 (*0-8230-1278-6*) Watsn-Guptill.

Painting Ancient & Medieval Warriors with Mike Davidson. Mike Davidson. LC 98-86530. (Illus.). 64p. (Orig.). 1999. pap. 14.95 (*0-7643-0648-0*) Schiffer.

Painting & Calligraphy in the "Wu-tsa-tsu" Conservative Aesthetics in Seventeenth Century China. Sewall J. Oertling, III. LC 97-2840. (Michigan Monographs in Chinese Studies: No. 68). 1997. text 50.00 (*0-89264-098-7*) Ctr Chinese Studies.

Painting & Coloring Dinosaurs see Draw, Model & Paint

Painting & Decorating. Fulcher. LC 98-55554. 1998. pap. text 29.95 (*0-632-04159-5*) Blackwell Sci.

Painting & Decorating. Elizabeth Gundrey. (Orig.). 1989. pap. 29.95 (*0-8464-1036-2*) Beekman Pubs.

Painting & Decorating. 3rd ed. A. Fulcher et al. (Illus.). 288p. (C). 1989. pap. text 28.95 (*0-632-02368-6*) Blackwell Sci.

Painting & Decorating: A Guide for Houseowner & Decorator. J. H. Goodier. LC TT0305.G6. 160p. reprint ed. pap. 49.60 (*0-608-13227-6*, 202526500043) Bks Demand.

Painting & Decorating: Skills & Techniques for Success. E. Keith Blankenbaker. LC 98-51813. (Illus.). 2000. 39.96 (*1-56637-506-1*) Goodheart.

Painting & Decorating Birdhouses. Dorothy Egan. LC 96-30348. (Illus.). 128p. 1997. pap. 23.99 (*0-89134-737-2*, North Lght Bks) F & W Pubns Inc.

Painting & Decorating Boxes. Phillip C. Myer. LC 96-50004. (Creative Finishes Ser.). (Illus.). 112p. 1997. pap. 23.99 (*0-89134-768-2*, North Lght Bks) F & W Pubns Inc.

Painting & Decorating Cabinets & Chests. Phillip C. Myer. LC 98-19914. (Creative Finishes Ser.). (Illus.). 112p. 1998. pap. 23.99 (*0-89134-804-2*, North Lght Bks) F & W Pubns Inc.

Painting & Decorating Frames. Phillip C. Myer. LC 97-53121. (Creative Finishes Ser.). (Illus.). 112p. 1998. pap. 23.99 (*0-89134-803-4*, North Lght Bks) F & W Pubns Inc.

Painting & Decorating Furniture. Sheila McGraw. (Illus.). 304p. 1997. 40.00 (*1-55209-137-6*) Firefly Bks Ltd.

Painting & Decorating Furniture. Sheila McGraw. (Illus.). 304p. 1997. reprint ed. pap. 29.95 (*1-55209-380-8*) Firefly Bks Ltd.

Painting & Decorating Tables. Phillip C. Myer. LC 97-3071. (Creative Finishes Ser.). (Illus.). 112p. 1997. pap. 23.99 (*0-89134-769-0*, North Lght Bks) F & W Pubns Inc.

Painting & Drawing. Judy Martin. (First Guide Ser.). (Illus.). 96p. (J). (gr. 3-6). 1993. pap. 9.95 (*1-56294-709-5*); lib. bdg. 23.90 (*1-56294-203-4*) Millbrook Pr.

Painting & Drawing Horses. Jennifer Bell. 1995. pap. 35.00 (*0-85131-637-9*, Pub. by J A Allen) Trafalgar.

Painting & Experience in Fifteenth-Century Italy: A Primer in the Social History of Pictorial Style. 2nd ed. Michael Baxandall. (Illus.). 190p. 1988. pap. text 13.95 (*0-19-282144-X*) OUP.

Painting & Finishing Models. Ian Peacock. (Illus.). 160p. (Orig.). 1987. pap. text 19.95 (*0-85242-912-6*, Pub. by Nexus Special Interests) Trans-Atl Phila.

Painting & History During the French Restoration: Abandoned by the Past. Beth S. Wright. (Illus.). 292p. (C). 1997. text 70.00 (*0-521-57203-7*) Cambridge U Pr.

Painting & Illumination in Early Renaissance Florence, 1300-1450. Laurence B. Kanter et al. LC 94-29418. (Illus.). 400p. 1994. pap. 29.95 (*0-87099-726-2*); pap. text 60.00 (*0-8109-6488-0*) Metro Mus Art.

***Painting & Patronage in Cologne 1300-1500.** Brigitte Corley. (Illus.). 300p. 1999. text 98.00 (*1-872501-51-6*, Pub. by Harvey Miller) Gordon & Breach.

Painting & Performance: Chinese Picture Recitation & Its Indian Genesis. Victor H. Mair. (Illus.). 302p. 1997. pap. text 19.00 (*0-8248-1915-2*) UH Pr.

Painting & Poetry: Forms, Mataphor & the Language of Literature. Franklin R. Rogers. LC 83-46175. (Illus.). 248p. 1986. 42.50 (*0-8387-5077-X*) Bucknell U Pr.

Painting & Politics of George Caleb Bingham. Nancy Rash. (Illus.). 304p. (C). 1991. 42.50 (*0-300-04731-2*) Yale U Pr.

Painting & Private Life in Eleventh-Century China: Mountain Villa by Li Gonglin. Robert E. Harrist & Kung-Lin Li. LC 97-22344. 256p. 1998. text 65.00 (*0-691-01609-7*, Pub. by Princeton U Pr) Cal Prin Full Svc.

Painting & Sculpture from Antiquity to Nineteen Forty-Two. Steven A. Nash & Albright-Knox Art Gallery Staff. LC 77-79651. (Illus.). 1979. pap. 25.00 (*0-914782-17-7*) Buffalo Fine-Albrght-Knox.

Painting & Sculpture in Europe: 1780-1880. Fritz Novotny. (Pelican History of Art Ser.). (Illus.). 483p. (C). 1988. reprint ed. pap. 25.00 (*0-300-05321-5*) Yale U Pr.

Painting & Sculpture in Europe: 1880-1940. 4th ed. George H. Hamilton. LC 94-119000. (Illus.). 610p. (C). 1989. pap. 27.50 (*0-300-05649-4*) Yale U Pr.

Painting & Sculpture in France, 1700-1789. Michael Levey. LC 92-32503. (Pelican History of Art Ser.). (Illus.). 304p. (C). 1993. 60.00 (*0-300-05344-4*) Yale U Pr.

Painting & Sculpture in France, 1700-1789. Michael Levey. 1995. pap. 30.00 (*0-300-06494-2*) Yale U Pr.

Painting & Sculpture in Germany & the Netherlands, 1500-1600. Gert Von Der Osten & Horst Vey. (Pelican History of Art Ser.). (Illus.). 295p. (C). 1979. reprint ed. 55.00 (*0-300-05311-8*) Yale U Pr.

Painting & Sculpture in the Museum of Modern Art: Catalog of the Collection, 1987. rev. ed. Ed. by Alicia Legg & Mary B. Smalley. 136p. 1989. pap. 12.50 (*0-87070-572-5*) Mus of Modern Art.

Painting & Sculpture in the Museum of Modern Art, 1929-1967. Alfred H. Barr. LC 68-54923. (Illus.). 1977. 40.00 (*0-87070-540-7*) Mus of Modern Art.

Painting & System. Marcelin Pleynet. Tr. by Sima N. Godfrey from FRE. LC 84-209. (Illus.). 168p. (C). 1994. 17.50 (*0-226-67093-7*) U Ch Pr.

Painting & The Journal of Eugene Delacroix. Michelle Hannoosh. LC 94-25302. (Nineteenth-Century Art, Culture, & Society Ser.). 312p. 1995. text 39.50 (*0-691-04394-9*, Pub. by Princeton U Pr) Cal Prin Full Svc.

Painting & the Market in Early Modern Antwerp. Elizabeth A. Honig. LC 98-3629. (Illus.). 336p. 1998. 45.00 (*0-300-07239-2*) Yale U Pr.

Painting & the Politics of Culture: New Essays on British Art, 1700-1850. Ed. by John Barrell. (Illus.). 320p. 1992. 85.00 (*0-19-817392-X*) OUP.

Painting & Wallpapering. Robert C. Yeager. Ed. by Sally W. Smith. LC 82-63123. (Illus.). 96p. (Orig.). 1983. pap. 9.95 (*0-89721-015-8*, Ortho Bks) Meredith Bks.

Painting & Wallpapering. rev. ed. Sharon M. Ross. Ed. by Robert J. Beckstrom. LC 94-69599. (Illus.). 96p. 1995. pap. 9.95 (*0-89721-259-2*, 05970B, Ortho Bks) Meredith Bks.

***Painting & Wallpapering for Dummies.** Gene Hamilton & Katie Hamilton. LC 99-62841. (For Dummies Ser.). (Illus.). 264p. 1999. pap. 16.99 (*0-7645-5150-7*) IDG Bks.

Painting & Weathering Railroad Models. Jeffrey Wilson. Ed. by Kent Johnson. (Illus.). 80p. 1995. per. 14.95 (*0-89024-215-1*, 12142) Kalmbach.

Painting Animals. Andy Jones. LC 99-57310. 112p. 1999. pap. 14.95 (*0-8230-1279-4*) Watsn-Guptill.

Painting Animals in Watercolour. Sally Michel. (Illus.). 128p. pap. 22.50 (*0-85532-648-4*, 648-4, Pub. by Srch Pr) A Schwartz & Co.

***Painting As a Language.** Robertson. (C). 1999. pap. text 54.50 (*0-15-505600-X*, Pub. by Harcourt Coll Pubs) Harcourt.

Painting As a Model. Yve-Alain Bois. (Illus.). 357p. (C). 1993. pap. text 25.00 (*0-262-52180-6*) MIT Pr.

Painting As An Art. Richard Wollheim. (Illus.). 384p. (Orig.). 1987. pap. text 35.00 (*0-691-01892-8*, Pub. by Princeton U Pr) Cal Prin Full Svc.

Painting at Northwestern: Conger, Paschke, Valerio. Dennis Adrian et al. (Illus.). 64p. (Orig.). (C). 1986. 30.00 (*0-941680-04-5*); pap. 15.00 (*0-941680-03-7*) M&L Block.

Painting Baby Animal Treasures. Peggy Harris. LC 98-48509. (Illus.). 128p. 1999. pap. 22.99 (*0-89134-909-X*, North Lght Bks) F & W Pubns Inc.

Painting Baby Animals. Sadako Mano. (How to Draw & Paint Ser.). (Illus.). 32p. 1989. pap. 6.95 (*0-929261-86-0*, HT189) W Foster Pub.

Painting Baby Animals with Peggy Harris. Peggy Harris. LC 96-1778. (Illus.). 128p. 1996. pap. 21.99 (*0-89134-719-4*, North Lght Bks) F & W Pubns Inc.

Painting Ballerina. Gloria M. Buono. (Illus.). 80p. (J). (gr. 3 up). 1999. pap. 12.95 (*0-9669818-0-4*) AabaGlo.

Painting Beautiful Watercolors from Photographs. Jan Kunz. LC 97-27742. (Illus.). 128p. 1998. 27.99 (*0-89134-791-7*, North Lght Bks) F & W Pubns Inc.

Painting Better Landscapes. Margaret Kessler. (Illus.). 160p. 1992. reprint ed. pap. 22.50 (*0-8230-3576-X*, Watson-Guptill Bks) Watsn-Guptill.

***Painting Birds & Animal.** Patricia Monahan. 1999. 14.99 (*0-7858-1144-3*) Book Sales.

Painting Birds Step by Step. Bart Rulon. LC 95-35786. (Illus.). 144p. 1996. 28.99 (*0-89134-632-5*, North Lght Bks) F & W Pubns Inc.

***Painting Blooms & Blossoms.** Judy Deptula & Lynne Deptula. LC 99-16726. (Illus.). 128p. 2000. pap. 24.99 (*0-89134-989-8*, 31460, North Lght Bks) F & W Pubns Inc.

Painting by Numbers: Komar & Melamid's Scientific Guide to Art. Vitaly Komar & Alexander Melamid. Ed. by JoAnn Wypijewski. LC 97-75189. (Illus.). 224p. 1997. 50.00 (*0-374-22880-9*) FS&G.

An Asterisk (*) at the beginning of an entry indicates that the title is appearing for the first time.

Painting by Numbers: Komar & Melamid's Scientific Guide to Art. Vitaly Komar et al. LC 98-28904. (Illus.). 205p. 1999. pap. 24.95 (*0-520-21861-2*, Pub. by U CA Pr) Cal Prin Full Svc.

Painting Cats in Watercolour. Sally Michel. (Leisure Arts Ser.: No. 26). (Illus.). 32p. pap. 4.95 (*0-85532-558-5*, 558-5, Pub. by Srch Pr) A Schwartz & Co.

Painting Ceramics: Easy Projects & Stylish Designs in a Weekend. Moira Neal & Lynda Howarth. LC 98-34767. (Weekend Crafter Ser.). (Illus.). 80p. 1999. pap. 14.95 (*1-57990-090-9*) Lark Books.

Painting Ceramics: How to Paint & Stencil Already Made Ceramic Pieces - 12 Projects. Lesley Harle & Simon Willis. 96p. 1995. pap. 14.95 (*0-8050-2383-6*, Owl) H Holt & Co.

Painting China. Phyllis Imhof. (Craft Library). 32p. pap. 4.95 (*0-85532-583-6*, 583-6, Pub. by Srch Pr) A Schwartz & Co.

Painting China & Porcelain. Sheila Southwell. (Illus.). 128p. 1995. 27.95 (*0-7153-0283-3*, Pub. by D & C Pub) Sterling.

Painting China & Porcelain. Sheila Southwell. (Illus.). 128p. 1998. pap. 17.95 (*0-7153-0723-1*, Pub. by D & C Pub) Sterling.

Painting China for Pleasure & Profit. Ruth Little. (Illus.). 290p. 1962. 20.00 (*0-9624294-1-4*) R Little.

Painting Civil War Figures. Photos & Text by Jeffrey B. Snyder. LC 95-24293. (Illus.). 64p. (Orig.). 1995. pap. 14.95 (*0-88740-884-2*) Schiffer.

Painting Clay Pot-Pourii, Vol. 3. Max Terry. 72p. 1994. pap. 10.50 (*1-56770-310-0*) S Scheewe Pubns.

***Painting Close-Focus Flowers in Watercolor.** Ann Pember. LC 00-20370. (Illus.). 128p. 2000. 27.99 (*0-89134-947-2*) F & W Pubns Inc.

Painting Collection of Lana Jean Israel. Alfred Israel. LC 89-91940. (Illus.). 58p. 1989. pap. 500.00 (*0-9623405-1-0*) L Israel.

Painting Collections of the Courtauld Institute of Art. Courtauld Institute of Art, London Staff & Philip Troutman. LC 78-13168. 128p. 1995. lib. bdg. 96.00 (*0-226-68904-2*, CVL 24) U Ch Pr.

Painting Color. Sara Doherty & Betty L. Schlemm. (Best of Watercolor Ser.). (Illus.). 144p. 1998. 24.99 (*1-56496-349-7*, Quarry Bks) Rockport Pubs.

Painting Composition. Betty L. Schlemm & Sara M. Doherty. (Best of Watercolor Ser.). (Illus.). 144p. 1997. 24.99 (*1-56496-370-5*, Quarry Bks) Rockport Pubs.

***Painting Country Cottages & Gardens.** Diane Trierweiler. LC 99-89907. (Illus.). 128p. 2000. pap. 23.99 (*0-89134-996-0*, North Lght Bks) F & W Pubns Inc.

Painting Cowboys & the Old West by Robert Hagan. Robert Hagan. Ed. by Terri Dodd. (Illus.). 118p. 1996. 29.95 (*0-9586816-3-5*, Pub. by Intl Art Servs) W Thomas Gallery.

Painting Day. Fay Johnston. LC 93-112. (Illus.). (J). 1994. write for info. (*0-383-03706-9*) SRA McGraw.

Painting Decorative Heirlooms with DeLane Lange. DeLane Lange. LC 98-45644. (Illus.). 128p. 1999. pap. 23.99 (*0-89134-869-7*, North Lght Bks) F & W Pubns Inc.

Painting Detail in Watercolour. Richard Bolton. (Leisure Arts Ser.: No. 9). (Illus.). 32p. pap. 4.95 (*0-85532-440-6*, 440-6, Pub. by Srch Pr) A Schwartz & Co.

Painting Dreams: Minnie Evans, Visionary Artist. Mary E. Lyons. LC 95-3994. (Illus.). 48p. (J). (gr. 3-7). 1995. 14.95 (*0-395-72032-X*) HM.

Painting Duck Decoys: Twenty-Four Full-Color Plates & Complete Instructions. Anthony Hillman. (Woodworking Ser.). 52p. 1985. pap. 5.95 (*0-486-24810-0*) Dover.

Painting Dynamic Watercolors: Capturing the Spontaneity of Nature. DOMENIC DISTEFANO. Ed. by Herbert Rogoff. (Illus.). 128p. 1999. 27.99 (*0-929552-15-6*, 31508) Art Instr Assocs.

Painting Eggs. Mouseworks. (J). 1998. 3.98 (*1-57082-777-X*, Pub. by Mouse Works) Little.

Painting Essentials. Cowles Creative Publishing Staff. (Black & Decker Quick Steps Ser.). (Illus.). 80p. (Orig.). 1996. pap. 9.95 (*0-86573-655-3*) Creat Pub Intl.

***Painting European Folk Art.** Andy B. Jones. (Illus.). 112p. 2000. pap. 14.95 (*0-8230-1283-2*) Watsn-Guptill.

Painting Expressive Pastel Portraits. Paul Leveille. LC 98-6131. (Illus.). 128p. 1998. 27.99 (*0-89134-815-8*, North Lght Bks) F & W Pubns Inc.

Painting Expressive Portraits in Oil. Paul Leveille. LC 96-37071. (Illus.). 128p. 1997. 27.99 (*0-89134-726-7*, North Lght Bks) F & W Pubns Inc.

Painting Fabric. Marion Elliot. 88p. 1995. pap. write for info. (*0-8050-3324-6*) H Holt & Co.

***Painting Fabric.** Marion Elliot. (Contemporary Crafts Ser.). (Illus.). 96p. 1999. pap. text 14.95 (*1-85368-629-8*) New5 Holland.

Painting Fabrics: Over 20 Decorative Projects for the Home. Susie Stokoe. (Inspirations Ser.). 1999. 12.95 (*0-7548-0186-1*, Lorenz Bks) Anness Pub.

Painting Faces. Suzanne Haldane. (J). 1995. 10.19 (*0-606-07988-2*) Turtleback.

Painting Fantasy Flowers. Georgia Bartlett. 100p. 1989. pap. text 7.50 (*1-56770-215-5*) S Scheewe Pubns.

***Painting Faux Finishes with the Color Shaper Wide: A Creative Guide for Faux Finish Painters,** Paula DeSimone. 2000. pap. text 29.99 (*1-56496-634-8*) Rockport Pubs.

***Painting Faux Finishes with the Color Shaper Wide: A Creative Guide for Faux Finish Painters,** Paula DeSimone. (Illus.). 96p. 2000. pap. text 16.99 (*1-56496-635-6*) Rockport Pubs.

***Painting Figures & Animals with Confidence.** Margaret Evans. (Illus.). 2000. 24.95 (*0-7153-0921-8*) D & C Pub.

Painting Figures & Portraits in Watercolor: Basic Techniques & Exercise Series. Jose M. Parramon. LC 98-38267. (Basic Techniques & Exercises). (Illus.). 96p. 1999. pap. 18.95 (*0-8230-5130-7*) Watsn-Guptill.

Painting Floor Cloths: 20 Canvas Rugs to Stamp, Stencil, Sponge & Spatter in a Weekend. Kathy Cooper. Ed. by Deborah Morgenthal. LC 99-25458. (Illus.). 80p. 1999. pap. 14.95 (*1-57990-134-4*) Lark Books.

Painting Floorcloths. Plaid Enterprises Staff. LC 99-21383. (Illus.). 128p. 1999. 24.95 (*0-8069-6521-5*) Sterling.

Painting Flowers. Elizabeth Leonard. (Illus.). 144p. 1991. pap. 18.95 (*0-8230-3630-8*) Watsn-Guptill.

Painting Flowers & Gardens. Alison Hoblin. LC 97-191395. (Illus.). 128p. 1997. 24.95 (*0-7153-0349-X*, Pub. by D & C Pub) Sterling.

***Painting Flowers from A to Z.** Sherry C. Nelson. LC 99-55967. (Illus.). 144p. 2000. pap. 24.99 (*0-89134-938-3*, North Lght Bks) F & W Pubns Inc.

Painting Flowers in Acrylic. Wendy Jelbert. (Leisure Art Ser.: Vol. 37). (Illus.). 32p. 1990. pap. 4.95 (*0-85532-649-2*, 649-2, Pub. by Srch Pr) A Schwartz & Co.

Painting Flowers in Watercolor with Louise Jackson. Louise Jackson. LC 96-46678. (Illus.). 128p. 1997. pap. 23.99 (*0-89134-764-X*, North Lght Bks) F & W Pubns Inc.

Painting Flowers in Watercolour. Sarah J. Coleridge. (Leisure Arts Ser.: No. 6). (Illus.). 32p. pap. 4.95 (*0-85532-405-8*, 405-8, Pub. by Srch Pr) A Schwartz & Co.

Painting Flowers in Watercolour. Simmons. LC 96-41745. (Illus.). 128p. (Orig.). reprint ed. pap. 14.95 (*0-486-29508-7*) Dover.

Painting Flowers on Rocks. Lin Wellford. (Illus.). 128p. 1999. pap. 21.99 (*0-89134-945-6*, 31373, North Lght Bks) F & W Pubns Inc.

Painting Flowers on Silk. Lydie Ottlelart. 64p. pap. 14.95 (*0-85532-706-5*, 706-5, Pub. by Srch Pr) A Schwartz & Co.

***Painting Flowers on Silk.** Mandy Southan. (Illus.). 2000. pap. 17.95 (*0-85532-901-7*) Srch Pr.

Painting Flowers the Van Wyk Way. Helen Van Wyk. Ed. by Herbert Rogoff. (Illus.). 120p. 1985. pap. text 23.75 (*0-929552-02-4*) Art Instr Assocs.

Painting Flowers the Van Wyk Way. 2nd rev. ed. Helen Van Wyk. Ed. by Herbert Rogoff. (Illus.). 128p. 1997. 29.99 (*0-929552-12-1*) Art Instr Assocs.

Painting Flowers with Augie. Augie Reis. 48p. 1984. pap. text 6.50 (*1-56770-152-3*) S Scheewe Pubns.

Painting Flowers with Watercolors. Ed. by Parramon Ediciones Team Staff. Tr. by Barron's Educational Editors. LC 94-46433.Tr. of Fores a la Acuarela. (ENG & SPA., Illus.). 64p. 1995. 12.95 (*0-8120-9292-9*) Barron.

Painting Folk Art Flowers with Enid Hoessinger. Enid J. H. Hoessinger. LC 98-41457. (Illus.). 144p. 1999. pap. 22.99 (*0-89134-889-1*, 31360, North Lght Bks) F & W Pubns Inc.

Painting for Calligraphers. Marie Angel. LC 83-24981. (Illus.). 128p. (C). 1984. 27.50 (*0-87951-969-X*, Pub. by Overlook Pr) Penguin Putnam.

Painting for Calligraphers. Marie Angel. (Illus.). 128p. 1997. 35.00 (*0-87951-804-9*, Pub. by Overlook Pr) Penguin Putnam.

Painting for Freedom. H. V. O'Brien & Gaynell O'Brien. LC 87-50148. (Illus.). 160p. 1987. 12.95 (*0-9618480-0-6*) Times Pub TX.

Painting for Money: The Visual Arts & the Public Sphere in Eighteenth-Century England. David H. Solkin. LC 92-53965. (Illus.). 320p. (C). 1993. 75.00 (*0-300-05741-5*) Yale U Pr.

Painting for Money: The Visual Arts & the Public Sphere in Eighteenth-Century England. David H. Solkin. (Illus.). 312p. 1996. pap. 30.00 (*0-300-06720-8*) Yale U Pr.

Painting French Dolls with China Painting Techniques. Neva W. Garnett. (Illus.). 96p. 1985. pap. 12.95 (*0-87588-245-5*, 2915) Hobby Hse.

Painting Fresh Florals in Watercolor. Arleta Pech. LC 97-38979. (Illus.). 128p. 1998. 27.99 (*0-89134-814-X*, North Lght Bks) F & W Pubns Inc.

Painting from the Source: Awakening the Artist's Soul in Everyone. Aviva Gold & Elena Oumano. LC 97-50342. (Illus.). 240p. 1998. pap. 16.00 (*0-06-095272-5*) HarpC.

***Painting Function: Making It Real.** Saul Ostrow. (Illus.). 24p. 2000. pap. 3.00 (*0-9667008-2-1*) SPACES.

Painting Furniture: A Practical Guide. Rosie Fisher. 1994. pap. 17.95 (*0-316-28388-6*) Little.

Painting Furniture: How to Create Your Own Beautiful, Unique Pieces of Furniture - 12 Projects. Jaclynn Fischman. 1995. pap. 15.95 (*0-8050-3585-0*) H Holt & Co.

Painting Garden Birds with Sherry C. Nelson. Sherry C. Nelson. LC 97-36341. (Illus.). 128p. 1998. pap. 24.99 (*0-89134-771-2*, North Lght Bks) F & W Pubns Inc.

Painting Gardens. Norman Battershill. LC 94-27793. (Illus.). 128p. 1995. pap. text 12.95 (*0-486-28401-8*) Dover.

Painting Glass in a Weekend see Weekend Crafter - Painting Glass: Stylish Designs & Practical Projects to Paint in a Weekend

***Painting Glass with the Color Shaper: A Creative Guide for Decorating Glass.** Paula DeSimone. (Illus.). 2000. pap. 17.00 (*1-56496-713-1*) Rockport Pubs.

Painting Gorilla. Michael Rex. LC 96-44209. (Illus.). 32p. (J). 1997. 15.95 (*0-8050-5020-5*, Bks Young Read) H Holt & Co.

Painting Great Pictures from Photographs. Hazel Harrison. (Illus.). 128p. 1999. 24.95 (*0-8069-6821-4*) Sterling.

Painting Greeting Cards for Fun & Profit. Jeanette Robertson. LC 99-19203. (Illus.). 128p. 1999. pap. 23.99 (*0-89134-907-3*, 31444, North Lght Bks) F & W Pubns Inc.

Painting Greeting Cards in Watercolor. Jacqueline Penney. LC 96-36396. (Illus.). 128p. 1997. pap. 22.99 (*0-89134-715-1*, North Lght Bks) F & W Pubns Inc.

***Painting Heads & Faces.** Pat Clarke. LC 99-43575. (First Steps Ser.). (Illus.). 128p. 2000. pap. 18.99 (*0-89134-856-5*, North Lght Bks) F & W Pubns Inc.

Painting Historic Interiors. Sara B. Chase. 14p. 1992. pap. 1.00 (*0-16-061649-2*) USGPO.

Painting Horizons: Jane Freilicher, Albert York, April Gornik. Klaus Kertess. LC 89-61177. (Illus.). 48p. 1989. pap. 15.00 (*0-943526-19-1*) Parrish Art.

Painting Horses in Oil. Cindy Larimore. (How to Draw & Paint Ser.). (Illus.). 32p. (Orig.). 1990. pap. 6.95 (*1-56010-065-6*, HT-228) W Foster Pub.

Painting Houses, Cottages & Towns on Rocks. Lin Wellford. (Illus.). 128p. 1996. pap. 21.99 (*0-89134-720-8*, North Lght Bks) F & W Pubns Inc.

Painting Illustrated in Three Dialogues. William Aglionby. (Printed Sources of Western Art Ser.). 418p. 1981. reprint ed. boxed set 60.00 (*0-915346-50-8*) A Wofsy Fine Arts.

Painting in Acrylics. Gordon Davies. (Illus.). 128p. 1990. pap. 22.50 (*0-85532-684-0*, 684-0, Pub. by Srch Pr) A Schwartz & Co.

Painting in Britain: 1530-1790. 5th ed. Ellis K. Waterhouse. (Pelican History of Art Ser.). (Illus.). 387p. (C). 1993. 50.00 (*0-300-05832-2*); pap. 25.00 (*0-300-05833-0*) Yale U Pr.

Painting in Bruges at the Close of the Middle Ages: Studies in Society & Visual Culture. Jean C. Wilson. LC 96-31024. 1998. 65.00 (*0-271-01653-1*) Pa St U Pr.

Painting in Canada: A History. 2nd ed. J. Russell Harper. (Illus.). 1977. pap. 22.95 (*0-8020-6307-1*) U of Toronto Pr.

Painting in Eighteenth-Century Venice. 3rd ed. Michael Levey. LC 94-17558. 267p. 1994. pap. 22.50 (*0-300-06057-2*) Yale U Pr.

Painting in Four Mediums: Oil, Watercolor, Acrylic, Pastel. William Palluth. (How to Draw & Paint Ser.). (Illus.). 32p. (Orig.). 1990. pap. 6.95 (*1-56010-055-9*, HT226) W Foster Pub.

Painting in Gouache. Oliver Grard & Eric Millan. (Leisure Arts Ser.: No. 30). (Illus.). 32p. pap. 4.95 (*0-85532-586-0*, 586-0, Pub. by Srch Pr) A Schwartz & Co.

Painting in Italy: 1500-1600. 3rd ed. Sydney J. Freedberg. LC 93-237078. (Illus.). 767p. (C). 1971. pap. 30.00 (*0-300-05587-0*) Yale U Pr.

Painting in Oils. Ed. by Michael Bowers. (Illus.). 128p. pap. 22.50 (*0-85532-703-0*, 703-0, Pub. by Srch Pr) A Schwartz & Co.

Painting in Oils. William Palluth. (Artist's Library). (Illus.). 64p. (Orig.). 1989. pap. 7.95 (*0-929261-01-1*, AL01) W Foster Pub.

Painting in Oils Without Turpentine: An Art Calendar Guide. Stanley Sporny. Ed. by Drew Steis. (Environmentally Safe Methods & Materials Ser.). 29p. 1999. pap. 9.95 (*0-945388-17-9*) Art Calendar.

***Painting in Renaissance Italy.** Filippo Pedrocco & Simonetta Nava. (Illus.). 312p. 2000. 60.00 (*0-8478-2255-9*, Pub. by Rizzoli Intl) St Martin.

Painting in Renaissance Venice. Peter Humfrey. (Illus.). 328p. 1997. pap. 20.00 (*0-300-06715-1*) Yale U Pr.

Painting in Sixteenth-Century Venice: Titian, Veronese, Tintoretto. rev. ed. David Rosand. LC 96-50388. (Illus.). 352p. (C). 1997. pap. text 24.95 (*0-521-56568-5*) Cambridge U Pr.

Painting in South Africa. Esme Berman. 500p. 1999. 20.95 (*1-86812-479-7*) Menasha Ridge.

Painting in Spain. Tomlinson. (C). 1997. pap. text 13.53 (*0-13-610940-3*) P-H.

Painting in Spain, 1500-1700. Jonathan Brown. LC 98-23228. (Yale University Press Pelican History of Art Ser.). (Illus.). 342p. 1998. 75.00 (*0-300-06472-1*) Yale U Pr.

Painting in Spain, 1500-1700. Jonathan Brown. LC 98-23228. (Yale University Press Pelican History of Art Ser.). (Illus.). 342p. 1999. pap. 35.00 (*0-300-06474-8*) Yale U Pr.

Painting in Spain in the Age of Enlightenment: Goya & His Contemporaries. Ed. by Suzanne L. Stratton. (Illus.). 350p. 1997. pap. 50.00 (*0-295-97603-9*) U of Wash Pr.

Painting in Spain, 1650-1700. Nina A. Mallory et al. Ed. by June Guicherneau. (Illus.). 182p. (C). 1982. text 55.00 (*0-691-03992-5*, Pub. by Princeton U Pr) Cal Prin Full Svc.

Painting in Spain, 1650-1700: From North American Collections with an Historical Essay by J. H. Elliott. Edward J. Sullivan & Nina A. Mallory. LC 81-47953. 202p. 1982. reprint ed. pap. 62.70 (*0-7837-9290-5*, 206002900004) Bks Demand.

Painting in the Age of Giotto: A Historical Reevaluation. Hayden B. Maginnis. LC 96-11306. 1997. 55.00 (*0-271-01599-3*) Pa St U Pr.

Painting in the Musee d'Orsay. Genevieve Lacambre et al. (Illus.). 160p. 1987. text 30.00 (*0-85667-228-9*) Scala Books.

Painting in the Netherlands: Fifteenth & Sixteenth Centuries. E. G. Troche. LC 79-91701. (Illus.). 1980. 50.00 (*0-87817-271-8*) Hacker.

Painting in the North: Alaskan Art in the Anchorage Museum of History & Art. Kesler E. Woodward. LC 93-21556. (Illus.). 172p. 1993. pap. 24.95 (*0-295-97320-X*) U of Wash Pr.

Painting in the Pantry with Jackie. Jackie Shaw. (Illus.). 32p. (Orig.). 1982. pap. 5.50 (*0-941284-15-8*) J Shaw Studio.

Painting in the People's Republic of China: The Politics of Style. Arnold Chang. (Special Studies on China & East Asia). 1980. 19.00 (*0-89158-676-8*) Westview.

Painting in Vienna at the Turn of the Century. Ilona Sarmany-Parsons. 136p. 1999. 25.00 (*963-13-3384-1*, Pub. by Corvina Bks) St Mut.

Painting in Watercolor. Kate Gwynn. 176p. 1997. 14.98 (*0-7858-0737-3*) Bk Sales Inc.

Painting in Watercolors, Markers, Acrylics, & Gouache. Jose M. Parramon. LC 93-6203. (Complete Course on Painting & Drawing Ser.). (Illus.). 128p. 1994. pap. 16.95 (*0-8120-1926-1*) Barron.

Painting in Watercolours. Ed. by Yvonne Deutch. (Illus.). 128p. pap. 22.50 (*0-85532-704-9*, 704-9, Pub. by Srch Pr) A Schwartz & Co.

***Painting Indiana: Portraits of Indiana's 92 Counties.** Anne Bryan Carter. LC 99-48558. (Illus.). 216p. 2000. 39.95 (*0-253-33692-9*) Ind U Pr.

Painting Inspector. Jack Rudman. (Career Examination Ser.: C-1778). 1994. pap. 27.95 (*0-8373-1778-9*) Nat Learn.

***Painting Landscapes & Atmsphere.** Jose Maria Parramon. (Illus.). 64p. 2000. pap. 11.95 (*84-95323-34-6*) Lema Pubns.

Painting Landscapes & Still Lifes in Watercolor: Basic Techniques & Exercises Series. Jose M. Parramon. LC 98-30026. 96p. 1999. pap. 18.95 (*0-8230-5129-3*) Watsn-Guptill.

***Painting Landscapes from Your Imagination.** Tony Simbert. (Illus.). 2000. pap. 24.99 (*1-929834-02-0*) Intl Artist Pubg.

Painting Landscapes in Acrylics. Wendy Clouse. (Leisure Arts Ser.: No. 29). (Illus.). 32p. pap. 4.95 (*0-85532-579-8*, 579-8, Pub. by Srch Pr) A Schwartz & Co.

Painting Landscapes in Oil. Ed. by Parramon Ediciones Team Staff. LC 94-49011. (Easy Painting & Drawing Ser.). (Illus.). 64p. 1995. 12.95 (*0-8120-9291-0*) Barron.

Painting Landscapes in Oils. Norman Battershill. (Leisure Arts Ser.: No. 3). (Illus.). 32p. pap. 4.95 (*0-85532-402-3*, 402-3, Pub. by Srch Pr) A Schwartz & Co.

Painting Landscapes in Watercolors. David S. Cuevas. LC 95-37534. (Easy Painting & Drawing Ser.). 64p. 1996. 12.95 (*0-8120-9399-2*) Barron.

Painting, Language & Modernity. Michael Phillipson. 256p. 1985. pap. 35.00 (*0-7102-0480-9*, Routledge Thoemms) Routledge.

Painting Level One. National Center for Construction Staff. 404p. (C). 1997. teacher ed., ring bd. 80.00 (*0-13-909342-7*) P-H.

Painting Level Two, Level 2. rev. ed. NCCER Staff. 524p. (C). 1997. teacher ed., ring bd. 80.00 (*0-13-772948-0*, Prentice Hall) P-H.

Painting Level Two, Level 2. rev. ed. NCCER Staff. 516p. (C). 1997. pap. text, student ed. 80.00 (*0-13-771296-0*, Prentice Hall) P-H.

Painting Level Two, Level 2. rev. ed. NCCER Staff. 508p. (C). 1997. pap. text, teacher ed. 80.00 (*0-13-771304-5*, Prentice Hall) P-H.

***Painting Level 3.** rev. ed. NCCER Staff. 1998. pap. text, teacher ed. 80.00 (*0-13-949066-3*, Prentice Hall); pap. text, student ed. 80.00 (*0-13-949041-8*, Prentice Hall); teacher ed., ring bd. 80.00 (*0-13-949058-2*, Prentice Hall); teacher ed., ring bd. 80.00 (*0-13-949074-4*, Prentice Hall) P-H.

Painting Light & Shadow. Betty L. Schlemm & Sara M. Doherty. (Best of Watercolor Ser.). (Illus.). 144p. 1997. 24.99 (*1-56496-348-9*, Quarry Bks) Rockport Pubs.

Painting Light & Shadow in Watercolor. William B. Lawrence. LC 94-21078. (Illus.). 144p. 1995. 27.99 (*0-89134-577-9*, North Lght Bks) F & W Pubns Inc.

Painting Literature: Dostoevsky, Kafka, Pirandello, & Garcia Marquez in Living Color. Constance A. Pedoto. 122p. (C). 1993. lib. bdg. 32.50 (*0-8191-9099-3*) U Pr of Amer.

***Painting Luscious Fruit.** Elizabeth Hayes. LC 00-22016. (Illus.). 2000. pap. write for info. (*1-58180-083-5*, North Lght Bks) F & W Pubns Inc.

Painting Machines: Industrial Image & Process in Contemporary Art. Caroline Jones. LC 96-84502. (Illus.). 64p. (C). 1997. pap. 20.00 (*1-881450-07-4*) Boston U Art.

Painting Masterpieces: Recreating 30 Works by Famous Artists. Ed. by Mark Churchill. LC 98-48460. (Illus.). 160p. 1998. pap. 17.95 (*0-8069-3768-8*) Sterling.

Painting Materials: A Short Encyclopedia. Rutherford J. Gettens & George L. Stout. (Illus.). 333p. 1965. pap. 8.95 (*0-486-21597-0*) Dover.

Painting Miniature Military Figures. Mike Davidson. LC 94-66368. (Illus.). 80p. (Orig.). 1994. pap. 14.95 (*0-88740-625-4*) Schiffer.

Painting Miniatures in Acrylic. Cyril Turner. (Illus.). 32p. 1990. pap. 4.95 (*0-85532-650-6*, 650-6, Pub. by Srch Pr) A Schwartz & Co.

Painting Moments: Art, AIDS & Nick Palazzo. Ed. by Mary Melfi. LC 97-72805. 150p. 1998. pap. 18.00 (*1-55071-067-2*) Guernica Editions.

Painting More Animals on Rocks. Lin Wellford. LC 97-17887. (Illus.). 128p. 1998. pap. 21.99 (*0-89134-800-X*, North Lght Bks) F & W Pubns Inc.

Painting Murals. Patricia Seligman. (Illus.). 168p. 1988. 29.99 (*0-89134-265-6*, 30081, North Lght Bks) F & W Pubns Inc.

Painting Myself In. Nina Mariette. LC 98-167675. (Illus.). 1997. pap. 19.95 (*1-877133-16-7*, Pub. by Univ Otago Pr) Intl Spec Bk.

Painting Napoleonic Miniatures. Mike Davidson. (Illus.). 80p. 1996. pap. 16.95 (*0-7643-0129-2*) Schiffer.

Painting Nature in Pen & Ink with Watercolor. Claudia Nice. LC 98-12672. (Illus.). 128p. 1998. 27.99 (*0-89134-813-1*, North Lght Bks) F & W Pubns Inc.

P

Painting Nature's Wonders. Jeff Kinzie & Sharon Kinzie. LC 88-60022. 52p. 1988. pap. text 8.95 (*0-916809-21-8*) Scott Pubns MI.

***Painting Nightscapes with Artificial Light.** Jose Maria Parramon. (Illus.). 64p. 2000. pap. 11.95 (*84-95323-36-2*) Lema Pubns.

Painting of Eugene Delacroix: A Critical Catalogue, Vols. 1 & 2: 1816-1831. Ed. by Lee Johnson. (Illus.). 1981. text 295.00 (*0-19-817314-8*) OUP.

Painting of Modern Life: Paris in the Art of Manet & His Followers. rev. ed. T. J. Clark. LC 99-29643. (Illus.). 1999. pap. 24.95 (*0-691-00903-1*, Pub. by Princeton U Pr) Cal Prin Full Svc.

Painting of Plastics. Rose Ann Ryntz. (Illus.). 32p. 1994. pap. 30.00 (*0-934010-36-6*) Fed Soc Coat Tech.

***Painting of Sand.** L. Luis Lopez. LC 00-132305. vi, 56p. 2000. pap. 8.00 (*0-9679844-1-6*) Farolito Pr.

Painting of T'Ang Yin. Ann D. Clapp. (Illus.). 320p. 1991. 57.50 (*0-226-10699-3*) U Ch Pr.

Painting of the Baroque. Andreas Prater & Hermann Bauer. (Epochs & Styles Ser.). (Illus.). 159p. 1997. pap. 14.99 (*3-8228-8253-4*) Taschen Amer.

***Painting of the Gothic Era.** Robert Suckale. 1999. 14.99 (*3-8228-6525-7*) Taschen Amer.

Painting of the High Renaissance in Rome & Florence, 2 vols. 3rd rev. ed. Sydney J. Freedberg. LC 84-82388. (Illus.). 1158p. 1985. reprint ed. lib. bdg. 120.00 (*0-87817-301-3*) Hacker.

Painting of the Late Renaissance in Rome & Florence, I Vol. I: From the High Renaissance to Mannerism, 1520-1570. rev. ed. Hermann Voss. Tr. & Rev. by Suzanne Pelzel. (Illus.). 288p. 1997. 125.00 (*1-55660-186-7*) A Wofsy Fine Arts.

Painting of the Late Renaissance in Rome & Florence, II Vol. II: The Diffusion & Transformation of Mannerism, 1570-1600. rev. ed. Hermann Voss. Tr. & Rev. by Suzanne Pelzel. (Illus.). 298p. 1997. 125.00 (*1-55660-259-6*) A Wofsy Fine Arts.

Painting of the Life of St. Francis in Assisi, with Notes on the Arena Chapel. Leonetto Tintori & Millard Meiss. LC 62-10308. 222p. reprint ed. pap. 68.90 (*0-608-11068-X*, 205084200061) Bks Demand.

Painting of the Romantic Era. Norbert Wolf. 1999. pap. 14.99 (*3-8228-7061-7*) Taschen Amer.

Painting of the Romantic Era. Norbert Wolf. (Epochs & Styles Ser.: Vol. 3). (Illus.). 160p. 1999. pap. 14.99 (*3-8228-8254-2*) Taschen Amer.

Painting Oils. Louise DeMore. LC 96-247. (First Steps Ser.). (Illus.). 128p. 1996. pap. 18.99 (*0-89134-676-7*, North Lght Bks) F & W Pubns Inc.

***Painting on Ceramics.** Kate Byrne. (Illus.). 2000. 24.95 (*1-57145-669-4*, Laurel Glen Pub) Advantage Pubs.

***Painting on Ceramics.** Kate Byrne et al. LC 00-32249. (Illus.). 2000. write for info. (*1-57145-670-8*, Laurel Glen Pub) Advantage Pubs.

***Painting on Glass: Contemporary Designs, Simple Techniques.** Paige Gilchrist. LC 99-49867. (Illus.). 128p. 2000. 27.95 (*1-57990-155-7*, Pub. by Lark Books) Sterling.

***Painting on Light: Drawings & Stained Glass in the Age of Dhurer & Holbein.** Barbara Butts et al. LC 99-59416. (Illus.). 328p. 2000. 125.00 (*0-89236-578-1*, J P Getty Museum) J P Getty Trust.

Painting on Porcelain: Composition & Technique. Dony Alexier. (French Art & Craft Books). (Illus.). 80p. pap. 19.95 (*2-84415-001-2*, Pub. by Ulisse Editions) Penton Overseas.

Painting on Porcelain: Oriental Designs. Annick Perret. (Illus.). 96p. (Orig.). 1995. pap. 22.50 (*0-85532-786-3*, 786-3, Pub. by Srch Pr) A Schwartz & Co.

Painting on Porcelain: Traditional & Contemporary Design. Annick Perret. (Illus.). 96p. (Orig.). (YA). 1994. pap. 22.50 (*0-85532-766-9*, 766-9, Pub. by Srch Pr) A Schwartz & Co.

Painting on Silk: Images of Africa. Zarza. (Illus.). 64p. (Orig.). pap. 22.95 (*0-85532-742-1*, 742-1, Pub. by Srch Pr) A Schwartz & Co.

Painting on Stones. Genevieve Ploquin. (Illus.). 48p. 1998. pap. text 11.95 (*0-85532-864-9*, Pub. by Srch Pr) A Schwartz & Co.

Painting on Sugar, 1. 1999. 8.95 (*1-85391-196-8*, Pub. by Merehurst Ltd) Tuttle Pubng.

Painting on the Left: Diego Rivera, Radical Politics & San Francisco's Public Murals. Anthony W. Lee. LC 98-18740. 1999. 50.00 (*0-520-21133-2*, Pub. by U CA Pr) Cal Prin Full Svc.

***Painting on the Left: Diego Rivera, Radical Politics & San Francisco's Public Murals.** Anthony W. Lee. 290p. 1999. pap. 24.95 (*0-520-21977-5*, Pub. by U CA Pr) Cal Prin Full Svc.

Painting on the Macintosh: A Non-Artist's Guide to Superpaint, Pixelpaint, Painter, & Many More. rev. ed. Deke McClelland. (Desktop Publishing Library). 1993. pap. 25.00 (*1-55623-910-6*, Irwn Prfssnl) McGraw-Hill Prof.

Painting on the Page: Interartistic Approaches to Modern Hispanic Texts. Rosemary G. Feal & Carlos Feal. LC 94-38023. (SUNY Series in Latin American & Iberian Thought & Culture). 341p. (C). 1995. text 59.50 (*0-7914-2603-3*); pap. text 19.95 (*0-7914-2604-1*) State U NY Pr.

Painting on the PC: A Non-Artist's Guide to Popular Painting Programs. rev. ed. Deke McClelland. 1993. pap. 25.00 (*1-55623-912-2*, Irwn Prfssnl) McGraw-Hill Prof.

Painting Our Way to a Better Future: An Art-Coloring Book of Contemporary Career Options for Women. 2nd ed. Ed. by Mary Baird & Donna Larrivee-Cohen. (Illus.). 56p. (Orig.). (J). (gr. k-9). 1997. pap. 6.95 (*0-9627833-0-7*) Hard Hatted Women.

Painting Out of Sorrow. Claudine Bing. LC 98-43468. (Illus.). 88p. 1999. 19.95 (*1-883280-12-5*) Font & Ctr Pr.

Painting Paradise: The Art of Ting Shao Kuang. Ann B. Wicks. (Illus.). 84p. 1998. 89.95 (*0-8351-2637-4*); pap. 44.95 (*0-8351-2638-2*) China Bks.

Painting People in Watercolor: A Design Approach. Alex Powers. (Illus.). 144p. 1997. pap. text 19.95 (*0-8230-3868-8*) Watsn-Guptill.

***Painting Pets on Rocks.** Lin Wellford. LC 00-35507. (Illus.). 128p. 2000. pap. 22.99 (*1-58180-032-0*, North Lght Bks) F & W Pubns Inc.

Painting Pets with Watercolors. Tr. by Barron's Educational Editors. LC 94-46432. (Easy Painting & Drawing Ser.).Tr. of Animales Domesticos a la Acuarela. (ENG & SPA., Illus.). 64p. 1995. 12.95 (*0-8120-9293-7*) Barron.

Painting Place: The Life & Work of David B. Milne. David P. Silcox. (Illus.). 464p. 1996. text 65.00 (*0-8020-4095-0*) U of Toronto Pr.

Painting Plant Portraits: A Step-by-Step Guide. Keith R. West. LC 96-28308. (Illus.). 112p. 1997. pap. 19.95 (*0-88192-372-9*) Timber.

Painting Popular Bird Carvings. Anthony Hillman. 40p. 1990. pap. 5.95 (*0-486-26248-0*) Dover.

Painting Popular Duck Decoys. Anthony Hillman. (Illus.). 40p. 1989. pap. 5.95 (*0-486-26100-X*) Dover.

Painting Porcelain the Meissen Way. Uwe Geissler. LC 97-19519. 1997. pap. 24.95 (*0-7643-0280-9*) Schiffer.

Painting Portraits. rev. ed. Everett R. Kinstler. Ed. by Susan E. Meyer. (Illus.). 144p. 1987. 29.95 (*0-8230-3822-X*) Watsn-Guptill.

Painting Portraits: Families Groups & Systems. (Conference Proceedings Ser.). 141p. (Orig.). 1989. pap. 15.00 (*1-882147-07-3*) Am Art Therapy.

Painting Portraits, Nudes & Clothed Figures. Jan DeRuth. (Illus.). 143p. 1999. reprint ed. text 22.00 (*0-7881-6383-3*) DIANE Pub.

***Painting Portraits of Homes in Pen, Ink & Watercolor.** Helen J. Haberstroh. (Illus.). 128p. 2000. pap. 24.99 (*0-89134-954-5*, North Lght Bks) F & W Pubns Inc.

Painting, Power & Patronage: The Rise of the Professional Artist in Renaissance Italy. Bram Kempers. LC 95-159908. (Illus.). 416p. 1995. pap. 14.95 (*0-14-012488-8*, Penguin Bks) Viking Penguin.

Painting Rainbows with Broken Crayons: 101 Prayers for Teachers, Parents & Other Caretakers. Bernadette M. Snyder. LC 94-79361. (Illus.). 152p. 1995. pap. 6.95 (*0-87793-547-5*) Ave Maria.

Painting Realistic Flowers in Acrylic. Arlene Beck. LC 97-17884. (Illus.). 128p. 1998. pap. 24.99 (*0-89134-776-3*, North Lght Bks) F & W Pubns Inc.

Painting Realistic Watercolor Textures. Michael P. Rocco. (Illus.). 128p. 1996. 27.99 (*0-89134-659-7*, North Lght Bks) F & W Pubns Inc.

Painting Reasons on the Mirror. Frances Langeher. (Illus.). (Orig.). 1989. pap. text 6.50 (*0-9623824-0-X*) Broken Mirrors Pr.

***Painting Religion in Public: John Singer Sargent's Triumph of Religion at the Boston Public Library.** Sally M. Promey. LC 99-12158. (Illus.). 376p. 1999. 45.00 (*0-691-01565-1*, Pub. by Princeton U Pr) Cal Prin Full Svc.

***Painting Revolution: Kandinsky, Malevich & the Russian Avant Garde.** Illus. by John Bowlt. 212p. 2000. pap. write for info. (*0-9678451-0-6*) Fndt for Intl Arts.

Painting Roses with Deanne Fortnam, MDA. Deanne Fortnam. LC 97-35460. (Illus.). 128p. 1998. pap. 23.99 (*0-89134-793-3*) F & W Pubns Inc.

Painting Sea & Sky in Watercolour. Leslie Worth. (Leisure Arts Ser.: No. 8). (Illus.). 32p. pap. 4.95 (*0-85532-407-4*, 407-4, Pub. by Srch Pr) A Schwartz & Co.

Painting Seascapes in Oils. Miguel Ferron. LC 95-31108. (Easy Painting & Drawing Ser.). (Illus.). 62p. 1996. 12.95 (*0-8120-9401-8*) Barron.

Painting Shapes & Edges: Give Depth, Clarity & Form to Your Artwork. Hazel Harrison. (Illus.). 128p. 1996. 27.99 (*0-89134-735-6*, North Lght Bks) F & W Pubns Inc.

Painting Ships, Shores & the Sea. Rachel Wolf. LC 97-14318. (Illus.). 144p. 1998. 28.99 (*0-89134-787-9*, North Lght Bks) F & W Pubns Inc.

Painting Shorebird Decoys. Anthony Hillman. (Illus.). 40p. 1987. pap. 5.95 (*0-486-25349-X*) Dover.

Painting Songbird Carvings: Sixteen Full-Color Plates & Complete Instructions. Anthony Hillman. (Illus.). 40p. (Orig.). 1988. pap. 6.95 (*0-486-25580-8*) Dover.

***Painting Spectacular Light Effects in Watercolor.** Paul C. Jackson. LC 99-26717. (Illus.). 144p. 2000. 29.99 (*0-89134-916-2*, North Lght Bks) F & W Pubns Inc.

Painting, Staining & Finishing. Tom Philbin. LC 96-49071. (Illus.). 317p. 1997. 49.95 (*0-07-049730-3*); pap. 29.95 (*0-07-049731-1*) McGraw.

Painting Still Lifes in Oils. Olive De Puig. LC 95-37550. (Easy Painting & Drawing Ser.). (Illus.). 62p. 1996. 12.95 (*0-8120-9402-6*) Barron.

Painting Styles Mix Media Painting Techniques. Phillip C. Myer. (Designer Ser.). (Illus.). 32p. 1986. pap. 8.95 (*0-917121-15-5*, 50-102) M F Weber Co.

Painting Sumptuous Vegetables, Fruits & Flowers in Oil. Joe A. Arnett. LC 97-22334. (Illus.). 128p. 1998. 27.99 (*0-89134-770-4*, North Lght Bks) F & W Pubns Inc.

Painting Sunlit Still Lifes in Watercolor. Liz Donovan. LC 96-49205. (Illus.). 144p. 1997. 28.99 (*0-89134-732-1*, North Lght Bks) F & W Pubns Inc.

Painting Sunsets with the Angels. Vann Wesson. LC 96-90014. (Illus.). 36p. (J). (ps-4). 1996. 15.95 (*1-887754-04-0*) Orion Media.

Painting Techniques & Faux Finishes. Hennings & Niven. 128p. 1999. pap. text 16.95 (*0-86573-182-9*) Creat Pub Intl.

Painting Texas History to 1900. Sam D. Ratcliffe. LC 92-9752. (American Studies). (Illus.). 190p. 1992. 29.95 (*0-292-78113-X*) U of Tex Pr.

Painting Texture. Betty L. Schlemm & Sara M. Doherty. (Best of Watercolor Ser.). (Illus.). 144p. 1998. 24.99 (*1-56496-369-1*, Quarry Bks) Rockport Pubs.

***Painting Texture & Volume.** Jose Maria Parramon. (Illus.). 64p. 2000. pap. 11.95 (*84-95323-35-4*) Lema Pubns.

Painting Textured Carvings. Pearl E. Carpenter. (Illus.). 42p. (Orig.). 1991. student ed., spiral bd. 13.95 (*0-9614021-1-3*) Shades Mother Nat.

Painting Textures in Acrylics. Wendy Jelbert. (Leisure Arts Ser.: No. 35). (Illus.). 32p. pap. 4.95 (*0-85532-639-5*, 639-5, Pub. by Srch Pr) A Schwartz & Co.

Painting the American Heartland in Watercolor. Diane Phalen. LC 96-29887. (Illus.). 128p. 1997. pap. 23.99 (*0-89134-747-X*, North Lght Bks) F & W Pubns Inc.

Painting the Black. Carl Deuker. LC 96-23763. 256p. (YA). (gr. 6 up). 1997. 14.95 (*0-395-82848-1*) HM.

Painting the Black. Carl Deuker. 256p. (YA). (gr. 7 up). 1999. mass mkt. 4.50 (*0-380-73104-5*, Avon Bks) Morrow Avon.

Painting the Black. Carol Deuker. (YA). (gr. 7 up). 1997. 14.95 (*0-614-28826-6*) HM.

Painting the Country: Contemporary Art from the Kimberley Region, Western Australia. John E. Stanton. pap. 17.95 (*0-85564-289-0*, Pub. by Univ of West Aust Pr) Intl Spec Bk.

Painting the Cows: Twenty Years of Wildlife Conservation in California & the West. T. A. Roberts. LC 98-14508. 176p. 1998. pap. 14.95 (*1-880284-29-4*) J Daniel.

***Painting the Dakota: Seth Eastman at Fort Snelling.** Marybeth Lorbiecki & Seth Eastman. LC 00-40161. 2000. write for info. (*1-890434-32-9*) Afton Hist Soc.

Painting the Darkness. Robert Goddard. Ed. by Julie Rubenstein. 592p. 1991. reprint ed. mass mkt. 5.95 (*0-671-64948-5*) PB.

Painting the Drama of Wildlife Step by Step. Terry Isaac. LC 97-49068. (Illus.). 144p. 1998. 29.99 (*0-89134-812-3*, North Lght Bks) F & W Pubns Inc.

Painting the Dream: The Visionary Art of Navajo Painter David Chethlahe Paladin. David C. Paladin. LC 92-20099. (Illus.). 96p. (Orig.). 1992. pap. 24.95 (*0-89281-440-3*, Park St Pr) Inner Tradit.

Painting the Eastern Shore: A Guide to Chesapeake & Delaware Places & How to Capture Them in Watercolors. James D. Iams. LC 99-19001. (Illus.). 105p. 1999. 32.95 (*0-8018-6232-9*) Johns Hopkins.

Painting the Effects of Weather. Patricia Seligman. (Illus.). 144p. 1992. 27.99 (*0-89134-486-1*, 30442, North Lght Bks) F & W Pubns Inc.

***Painting the Faces of Wildlife Step-by-Step.** Kalon Baughan & Brook McClintic Baughan. LC 99-56287. (Illus.). 128p. 2000. 28.99 (*0-89134-962-6*, North Lght Bks) F & W Pubns Inc.

Painting the Figure in Pastels. David S. Cuevas. (Easy Painting & Drawing Ser.). (Illus.). 64p. 1996. 12.95 (*0-8120-9398-4*) Barron.

Painting the Fire. Jonathan Sherwood. LC 92-76022. (Illus.). 40p. (J). (gr. k-4). 1993. 14.95 (*1-56844-001-4*) Enchante Pub.

Painting the Fire: Anger. 2nd rev. ed. Jonathan Sherwood. Ed. by Gudrun Hoy & Bobi Martin. LC 92-76022. (Emotional Literacy Ser.). (Illus.). 40p. (J). (gr. k-5). 1996. 14.95 (*1-56844-101-0*) Enchante Pub.

Painting the Four Seasons: Atmospheric Landscapes in Watercolour: Four Well-Known Artists Interpret the Seasons. Wendy Jelbert et al. (Illus.). 144p. 1994. 27.50 (*0-85532-780-4*, 780-4, Pub. by Srch Pr) A Schwartz & Co.

***Painting the Heavens.** Eileen Reeves. 320p. 1999. pap. 24.95 (*0-691-00976-7*, Pub. by Princeton U Pr) Cal Prin Full Svc.

Painting the Heavens: Art & Science in the Age of Galileo. Eileen Reeves. LC 96-51631. 320p. 1997. text 45.00 (*0-691-04398-1*, Pub. by Princeton U Pr) Cal Prin Full Svc.

***Painting the House: Poems** Bibhu Padhi. LC 99-934542. 79p. 1999. write for info. (*81-250-1543-4*, Pub. by Orient Longman Ltd) S Asia.

Painting the Impressionist Landscape: Lessons in Interpreting Light & Color. Lois Griffel. LC 93-45313. (Illus.). 144p. 1994. 29.95 (*0-8230-3643-X*) Watsn-Guptill.

***Painting the Interior: Body, Self & Place in Nineteenth-Century Culture.** Susan Sidlauskas. LC 99-50140. (Illus.). 256p. 2000. write for info. (*0-521-77024-6*) Cambridge U Pr.

***Painting the Landscape in Pastel.** Albert Handell & Anita Louise West. (Illus.). 128p. 2000. pap. 21.95 (*0-8230-3912-9*) Watsn-Guptill.

Painting the Many Moods of Light. Rachel Rubin Wolf. LC 98-37194. (Illus.). 144p. 1999. 28.99 (*0-89134-879-4*, North Lght Bks) F & W Pubns Inc.

Painting the Map Red: Canada & the South African War, 1899-1902. Carman Miller. (Illus.). 542p. 1998. pap. 29.95 (*0-7735-1750-2*, Pub. by McG-Queens Univ Pr) CUP Services.

Painting the Map Red: Canada & the South African War, 1899-1902. Carman Miller. 592p. 1993. 49.95 (*0-7735-0913-5*) U of Toronto Pr.

Painting the Map Red Vol. 2: Canada & the South African War, 1899-1902. Carmen Miller. (Illus.). 557p. 1999. pap. 25.50 (*0-86980-939-3*) Univ Natal Pr.

Painting the Maya Universe: Royal Ceramics of the Classic Period. Dorie Reents-Budet. LC 93-29587. (Illus.). 402p. 1994. pap. text 42.95 (*0-8223-1438-X*) Duke.

Painting the Musical City: Jazz & Cultural Identity in American Art, 1910-1940. Donna M. Cassidy. LC 96-44169. (Illus.). 240p. 1997. text 45.00 (*1-56098-677-8*) Smithsonian.

Painting the Ontario Landscape: A Practical Guide to Working in Watercolour on Location. Jane Champagne. (Illus.). 192p. (Orig.). 1991. pap. 19.95 (*0-8020-6761-1*) U of Toronto Pr.

Painting the Orient. Genevieve Lacambre. (Art & Architecture Ser.). (Illus.). 360p. 1999. 39.95 (*3-89508-892-7*, 520587) Konemann.

Painting the Pink Roses Black. Gerard Smyth. (C). 1986. pap. 15.00 (*0-948268-10-7*, Pub. by Dedalus) St Mut.

Painting the Screen. Richard P. Braden. LC 94-17677. (Hands-on Windows Programming Ser.: Bk. 3). 160p. (Orig.). 1994. pap. 15.95 (*1-55622-434-6*) Wordware Pub.

Painting the Secret World of Nature. Illus. by Sylvia Frattini et al. 144p. 1990. pap. 22.50 (*0-85532-645-X*, 645-X, Pub. by Srch Pr) A Schwartz & Co.

Painting the Sky: Writing Poetry with Children. Shelley Tucker. 136p. (Orig.). (J). (gr. 3-6). 1995. pap. 12.95 (*0-673-36211-6*, GoodYrBooks) Addson-Wesley Educ.

Painting the Soul: Icons, Death Masks & Shrouds. Robin Cormack. (Essays in Art & Culture Ser.). (Illus.). 248p. 1997. pap. 24.95 (*1-86189-001-X*, Pub. by Reaktion Bks) Consort Bk Sales.

Painting the Spirit of Nature. Maxine Masterfield. (Illus.). 144p. 1996. pap. text 24.95 (*0-8230-3867-X*) Watsn-Guptill.

Painting the Town: A History of Art in Saugatuck & Douglas. Saugatuck-Douglas Historical Society Members. (Illus.). 64p. (Orig.). 1997. pap. 15.00 (*0-9657042-9-7*) Saugatuck-Douglas.

***Painting the Town: Cityscapes of New York, Paintings from the Museum of the City of New York.** Jan Seidler Ramirez et al. LC 99-54934. (Illus.). 320p. 2000. 45.00 (*0-300-08199-5*) Yale U Pr.

Painting the Towns: Murals of California. Robin J. Dunitz & James Prigoff. (Illus.). 304p. 1997. pap. 29.95 (*0-9632862-4-2*) RJD Ent.

Painting the Towns: Murals of California. unabridged ed. Robin J. Dunitz & James Prigoff. (Illus.). 304p. 1997. 49.95 (*0-9632862-5-0*) RJD Ent.

***Painting the Two White Lines: A Life Changing Look at the Commands of Christ.** Mark S. Schaufler. 220p. 2000. pap. 8.00 (*1-886904-38-3*) MST Minist.

Painting the Warmth of the Sun: St. Ives Artists, 1939-1975. Tom Cross. LC 97-66455. 1997. 49.95 (*0-7188-2941-7*, Lutterworth-Parkwest) Parkwest Pubns.

Painting the Warmth of the Sun: St. Ives Artists, 1939-1975. Tom Cross. (Illus.). 208p. 1997. pap. 32.95 (*0-7188-2942-5*, Lutterworth-Parkwest) Parkwest Pubns.

Painting the Wind: A Story of Vincent van Gogh. Michelle V. Dionetti. LC 95-5301. (Illus.). 32p. (J). (gr. k-3). 1996. 15.95 (*0-316-18602-3*) Little.

***Painting the Word: Christian Pictures & Their Meanings.** John Drury. LC 99-25840. (Illus.). 201p. 1999. 25.00 (*0-300-07777-7*) Yale U Pr.

***Painting Tiny Treasures.** Cindi Gordon. LC 00-35497. (Illus.). 128p. 2000. pap. write for info. (*0-89134-992-8*, North Lght Bks) F & W Pubns Inc.

Painting Vibrant Children's Portraits. Roberta C. Clark. (Illus.). 144p. 1997. pap. 22.99 (*0-89134-781-X*, North Lght Bks) F & W Pubns Inc.

Painting, Wallpapering & Stenciling. Robert W. Wood. (All Thumbs Guide Ser.). 144p. 1992. pap. 9.95 (*0-8306-2547-X*) McGraw-Hill Prof.

Painting Water: Watercolor Basics. Michael B. Edwards. (Illus.). 128p. 1996. pap. 19.95 (*0-7153-0363-5*, Pub. by D & C Pub) Sterling.

Painting Watercolor Florals That Glow. Jan Kunz. (Illus.). 144p. 1993. 27.99 (*0-89134-473-X*, 30512, North Lght Bks) F & W Pubns Inc.

Painting Watercolor Portraits. Al Stine. LC 96-25746. (Illus.). 128p. 1997. 27.99 (*0-89134-641-4*, North Lght Bks) F & W Pubns Inc.

Painting Watercolor Portraits That Glow. Jan Kunz. (Illus.). 160p. 1999. pap. 23.99 (*0-89134-934-0*, North Lght Bks) F & W Pubns Inc.

Painting Watercolors. Cathy Johnson. LC 95-6084. (First Steps Ser.). (Illus.). 128p. 1995. pap. 18.99 (*0-89134-616-3*, North Lght Bks) F & W Pubns Inc.

Painting Watercolors on Location with Tom Hill. Tom Hill. LC 95-51802. (Illus.). 128p. 1996. 27.99 (*0-89134-634-1*, North Lght Bks) F & W Pubns Inc.

Painting Waterfowl with J. D. Sprankle. Curtis J. Badger. (Illus.). 256p. 1998. pap. 34.95 (*0-8117-2893-5*) Stackpole.

Painting Waterfowl with J. D. Sprankle: Step-by-Step Full-Color Instruction for 13 Projects. J. D. Sprankle & Curtis J. Badger. LC 91-6820. (Illus.). 240p. 1991. 59.95 (*0-8117-1884-0*) Stackpole.

***Painting Weathered Buildings in Pen, Ink & Watercolor.** Claudia Nice. LC 99-45766. (Illus.). 144p. 2000. 28.99 (*0-89134-917-0*, North Lght Bks) F & W Pubns Inc.

Painting What You Want to See. Charles Reid. (Illus.). 144p. 1987. pap. 18.95 (*0-8230-3879-3*) Watsn-Guptill.

Painting Wild Geese. Beebe Hopper. Ed. by Jean Brubaker & Mary Cohen. (Martin F. Weber Fine Arts Library). (Illus.). 72p. (Orig.). 1987. pap. 14.95 (*0-917121-16-3*, 40-105) M F Weber Co.

Painting Wildflowers in Watercolour. Benjamin Perkins. (Leisure Arts Ser.: No. 28). (Illus.). 32p. pap. 4.95 (*0-85532-560-7*, 560-7, Pub. by Srch Pr) A Schwartz & Co.

Painting Wildlife Textures Step by Step. Rod Lawrence. LC 96-46457. (Illus.). 144p. 1997. 29.99 (*0-89134-669-4*, North Lght Bks) F & W Pubns Inc.

Painting with a Comet's Tail: The Touch of the Landscape Architect on the Blue Ridge Parkway. Harley E. Jolley. LC 85-11115. 50p. (Orig.). 1987. pap. 6.95 (*0-913239-48-8*) Appalach Consortium.

***Painting With Acrylics.** Wendy Jelbert. 2000. pap. text 10.95 (*0-85532-840-1*) Srch Pr.

An Asterisk (*) at the beginning of an entry indicates that the title is appearing for the first time.

***Painting with Acrylics.** Jenny Rodwell. 1999. 14.99 (*0-7858-1143-5*) Book Sales.

***Painting with Air: A Blopens Craft Package.** Joanne Oppenheim. (Illus.). 32p. (J). (gr. 2-5). 1999. per. 17.95 (*0-689-82528-5*) Litle Simon.

***Painting with Annigoni: Florence, 1958-68.** Dawn Cookson. (Illus.). 128p. 2000. pap. 35.00 (*0-906290-37-6*, Pub. by Unicorn Pr Lon) Boydell & Brewer.

Painting with Children. Brunhild Muller. 48p. 1990. pap. 8.95 (*0-86315-048-9*, 1192, Pub. by Floris Bks) Anthroposophic.

Painting with Computers: The Step by Step Guide & Showcase. Mario H. Chakkour. (Illus.). 144p. 1995. 29.99 (*1-56496-212-1*) Rockport Pubs.

Painting with Computers: The Step-by-Step Guide & Showcase. Mario H. Chakkour. (Illus.). 144p. 29.99 (*1-56496-284-9*) Rockport Pubs.

***Painting with Face Paints.** Paige Henson. LC 99-28554. (How to Paint & Draw Ser.). (Illus.). 32p. (J). (gr. 3-5). 1999. lib. bdg. 18.45 (*1-57103-314-9*) Rourke Pr.

Painting with Ilona. Ilona R. Smithkin. LC 83-80765. (Illus.). 80p. (Orig.). 1983. pap. 12.95 (*0-943274-02-8*) SC Ed Comm Inc.

Painting with Light. John Alton. LC 93-41275. 1994. 60.00 (*0-520-08630-9*, Pub. by U CA Pr); pap. 24.95 (*0-520-08949-9*, Pub. by U CA Pr) Cal Prin Full Svc.

Painting with Light. F. William Sunderman, Sr. (Illus.). 128p. 1993. 44.95 (*0-9632927-1-4*) Inst Clin Sci.

Painting with Light: A Centennial History of the Judson Studios. Jane Apostol. LC 97-73289. xii, 138p. 1997. write for info. (*0-914421-20-4*) Hist Soc So CA.

***Painting With Oils.** Noel Gregory. 2000. pap. text 10.95 (*0-85532-900-9*) Srch Pr.

Painting with O'Keeffe. John Poling. LC 99-10127. (Illus.). 184p. 1999. 24.95 (*0-89672-381-X*) Tex Tech Univ Pr.

***Painting With Pastels.** Peter Coombs. 2000. pap. text 10.95 (*0-85532-899-1*) Srch Pr.

Painting with Pastels. Leslie B. DeMille. (Artist's Library). (Illus.). 64p. (Orig.). 1989. pap. 7.95 (*0-929261-08-9*, AL08) W Foster Pub.

Painting with Pastels. Peter D. Johnson. (Illus.). 128p. 1992. pap. 22.50 (*0-85532-740-5*, 740-5, Pub. by Srch Pr) A Schwartz & Co.

Painting with Pastels. Aubrey Phillips. LC 94-9024. (Illus.). 126p. 1994. pap. text 12.95 (*0-486-28159-0*) Dover.

Painting with Paulson. Buck Paulson. 947p. 1996. pap. 11.95 (*1-56770-343-7*) S Scheewe Pubns.

Painting with Pixels: How to Draw with Your Computer. Glen Wilkins. (Illus.). 128p. 1999. pap. text 19.95 (*0-8069-6824-9*) Sterling.

***Painting with Tempera.** Paige Henson. LC 99-30658. (How to Paint & Draw Ser.). 32p. (J). (gr. 1-3). 1999. lib. bdg. 18.45 (*1-57103-311-4*) Rourke Pr.

Painting with Water-Soluble Colored Pencils. Gary Greene. LC 98-49177. (Illus.). 128p. 1999. 27.99 (*0-89134-884-0*, 31378, North Lght Bks) F & W Pubns Inc.

***Painting with Water-Soluble Oils.** Sean Dye. (Illus.). 144p. 2001. pap. 28.99 (*1-58180-033-9*, North Lght Bks) F & W Pubns Inc.

***Painting with Watercolors.** Paige Henson. LC 99-30659. (How to Paint & Draw Ser.). 32p. 1999. lib. bdg. write for info. (*1-57103-312-2*) Rourke Pr.

Painting with Watercolors, Oils, & Acrylics: Practical Handbook. Lorenz Books Staff. 1999. pap. text 9.95 (*0-7548-0004-0*, Lorenz Bks) Anness Pub.

***Painting With Watercolour.** Wendy Tait. 2000. pap. text 10.95 (*0-85532-903-3*) Srch Pr.

***Painting With Watercolours.** Frank E. Halliday. 2000. pap. text 10.95 (*0-85532-898-3*) Srch Pr.

Painting with Words. Sheila Kadra & Patricia Smith. (J). 1987. pap. text 12.90 (*0-88334-195-6*, 76160) Longman.

Painting Without a Brush. David Ferry. 1991. 17.98 (*1-55521-719-2*) Bk Sales Inc.

Painting Without Fainting: How the Pros Do It Fast, Easy & No Mess. Don A. Aslett. 1994. pap. 4.95 (*0-937750-09-3*) Marsh Creek Pr.

Painting Women: Victorian Women Artists. Deborah Cherry. LC 92-36713. (Illus.). 240p. (C). (gr. 13). 1993. pap. 25.99 (*0-415-06053-2*, B0717) Routledge.

Painting World War II Minatures. Mike Davidson. LC 97-80075. (Illus.). 80p. 1997. pap. 16.95 (*0-7643-0371-6*) Schiffer.

***Painting Zero Degree.** Carlos Basualdo & Ellen Tepfer. (Illus.). 84p. 2000. pap. 19.95 (*0-916365-57-3*, Pub. by Ind Curators) Dist Art Pubs.

Paintings. George Alpert. (Illus.). 85p. 1987. 50.00 (*0-941737-00-4*) Paradise Hse.

Paintings. Stan Rice. LC 97-73826. 1997. 35.00 (*0-375-40026-5*) Knopf.

Paintings. Tr. by Jennifer Riggs. LC 94-49433. (First Discovery Book).Tr. of Tableaux. (ENG & FRE., Illus.). 28p. (J). (ps-2). 1996. 11.95 (*0-590-55201-5*, Cartwheel) Scholastic Inc.

Paintings: American, British, Dutch, Flemish & German see Frick Collection: An Illustrated Catalogue

Paintings: Mike Hascall, Michael Knutson, Dyan Rey. Matthew Kangas. (Illus.). 1983. pap. 2.00 (*0-914435-09-4*) Marylhurst Art.

Paintings - Genuine, Fraud, Fake: Modern Methods of Examining Paintings. R. H. Marinjnissen. (Illus.). 415p. 1987. lib. bdg. 65.00 (*0-313-25874-0*, MPF/, Greenwood Pr) Greenwood.

Paintings & Drawings. Sue Coe et al. LC 84-27734. (Illus.). 164p. 1985. 34.50 (*0-8108-1782-9*) Scarecrow.

Paintings & Drawings, Lana Jean Israel. Lana Israel. LC 89-91455. (Illus.). 68p. 1989. 500.00 (*0-9623405-0-2*) L Israel.

Paintings & Miniatures at the Historical Society of Pennsylvania. Ed. by Nicholas B. Wainwright. 352p. 1974. 20.00 (*0-910732-08-6*) Pa Hist Soc.

Paintings & Sculpture at The Union League of Philadelphia. Maxwell Whiteman. LC 78-65751. (Illus.). 1978. 17.50 (*0-915810-03-4*); pap. 12.50 (*0-915810-04-2*) Union League PA.

Paintings & Sculpture from Central Pennsylvania Collectors: Exhibition Catalogue. Olga K. Preisner. (Illus.). 80p. 1984. pap. 4.50 (*0-911209-30-1*) Palmer Mus Art.

Paintings & Sketches. Charles M. Russell. (Illus.). (Orig.). pap. write for info. (*1-56944-041-7*) Terrell Missouri.

Paintings & Textiles of the Bass Museum of Art: Selections from the Collection. Margarita A. Russell. LC 90-82402. (Illus.). 176p. 1991. 40.00 (*1-880511-02-9*); pap. 25.00 (*1-880511-03-7*) Bass Museum.

Paintings & Varnishing. Peter H. Spectre. (Wooden Boat Ser.). (Illus.). 146p. 1995. pap. 22.95 (*0-937822-33-7*) WoodenBoat Pubns.

Paintings by G. P. A. Healy. Robert J. Evans. (Handbook of Collections: No. 2). (Illus.). 26p. 1974. pap. 0.75 (*0-89792-056-2*) Ill St Museum.

Paintings by Laurie Housemann-Whitehawk: Winnebago Woman Artist. Martha Kennedy & Laurie Housemann-Whitehawk. (Great Plains Art Ser.: No. 3). (Illus.). 32p. 1993. pap. text 5.00 (*0-938932-06-3*) U Nebr CFGPS.

Paintings by Masami Teraoka. James T. Ulak & Alexandra Munroe. (Illus.). 112p. 1996. pap. 29.95 (*0-8348-0352-6*) Weatherhill.

Paintings by Natan Nuchi: 8 Jewish Artists from the Pacifics Northwest. Ori Z. Soltes. LC 96-139650. (Illus.). (Orig.). 1995. pap. text. write for info. (*1-881456-24-2*) B B K Natl Jew Mus.

Paintings from Central India. R. A. Agarwala. (C). 1987. 75.00 (*0-8364-2183-3*, Pub. by Agam) S Asia.

Paintings from Europe & the Americas in the Philadelphia Museum of Art: A Concise Catalogue. Ed. by Philadelphia Museum of Art Staff. LC 94-23570. (Illus.). 548p. 1994. pap. 30.00 (*0-87633-093-6*) Phila Mus Art.

Paintings from Europe & the Americas in the Philadelphia Museum of Art: A Concise Catalogue. Ed. by Philadelphia Museum of Art Staff. LC 94-23570. (Illus.). 548p. (C). 1994. 99.95 (*0-8122-7964-6*) Phila Mus Art.

Paintings from India. Linda Leach. LC 99-214280. (The Nasser D. Khanlili Collection of Islamic Art: No. VIII). (Illus.). 260p. 1999. text 280.00 (*0-19-727629-6*) OUP.

Paintings from the C. R. Smith Collection. Ed. by Nicolai Cikovsky & William Robinson. (Illus.). 1970. pap. 5.00 (*0-87959-030-0*) U of Tex H Ransom Ctr.

Paintings from the Frick Collection. Bernice Davidson et al. (Illus.). 146p. 1991. 49.50 (*0-8109-3710-7*, Pub. by Abrams) Time Warner.

Paintings in German Museums: Catalog of Works on Exhibition in the Federal Republic of Germany, 12 vols. 2nd enl. rev. ed. Hans R. Schweers. 5500p. 1995. 2695.00 (*3-598-10927-X*) K G Saur Verlag.

Paintings in Taxicabs: Characteristics of Certain Art Consumers. Richard Lyons. LC 64-64377. 160p. 1965. pap. 3.00 (*0-911042-09-1*) NDSU Inst Reg.

Paintings in the Hermitage. Colin Eisler. (Illus.). 686p. 1995. 65.00 (*1-55670-419-4*) Stewart Tabori & Chang.

Paintings in the Louvre. Lawrence Gowing. LC 87-10221. (Illus.). 688p. 1994. 59.95 (*1-55670-007-5*) Stewart Tabori & Chang.

Paintings in the Musee d'Orsay. Robert Rosenblum. LC 89-11338. (Illus.). 686p. 1989. 65.00 (*1-55670-099-7*) Stewart Tabori & Chang.

***Paintings in the National Gallery, London.** William L. Barcham et al. (Illus.). 608p. 2000. 135.00 (*0-8212-2695-9*) Bulfinch Pr.

Paintings in the Royal Collection. Christopher Lloyd. LC 99-70868. (Royal Collection). (Illus.). 320p. 1999. pap. 18.95 (*0-500-97480-2*, Pub. by Thames Hudson) Norton.

Paintings in the Uffizi & Pitti Galleries Vol. 1. Mina Gregori et al. LC 94-72364. (Illus.). 648p. 1994. 135.00 (*0-8212-2084-5*, Pub. by Bulfinch Pr) Little.

Paintings in the Vatican. Carlo Pietrange. LC 96-86159. (Illus.). 608p. 1996. 135.00 (*0-8212-2316-X*, Pub. by Bulfinch Pr) Little.

Paintings of Benjamin West. Helmut Von Erffa et al. LC 85-22500. (Illus.). 600p. 1986. 110.00 (*0-300-03355-9*) Yale U Pr.

Paintings of California. Arnold Skolnick. LC 97-14015. 128p. 1997. 35.00 (*0-520-21252-5*, Pub. by U CA Pr); pap. 17.95 (*0-520-21184-7*, Pub. by U CA Pr) Cal Prin Full Svc.

Paintings of Carel Fabritius: Complete Edition with a Catalogue Raisonne. Christopher Brown. LC 80-69741. (Illus.). 168p. 1981. text 105.00 (*0-8014-1394-X*) Cornell U Pr.

Paintings of Charles Burchfield North by Midwest. Nannette V. Maciejunes et al. Ed. by Diana Murphy. LC 96-33433. (Illus.). 278p. 1997. 60.00 (*0-8109-3148-6*, Pub. by Abrams) Time Warner.

Paintings of David Jones. Nicolete Gray. (Illus.). 184p. (C). 1989. 80.00 (*0-85331-519-1*, Pub. by Lund Humphries) Antique Collect.

Paintings of Eduard Steichen. Anne C. DePietro. Ed. by Alayne Shoenfeld. LC 85-80519. (Illus.). 48p. (Orig.). 1985. pap. text 8.95 (*1-879195-00-3*) Heckscher Mus.

Paintings of Edward Hopper. Gail Levin. 125.00 (*0-393-04996-5*) Norton.

Paintings of Eugene Delacroix: A Critical Catalogue, 1832-1863, Vols. III & IV. Lee Johnson. (Illus.). 1987. text 300.00 (*0-19-817378-4*) OUP.

Paintings of F. Grayson Sayre, 1879-1939. Ray Redfern & Barbara S. Harmon. (Illus.). 76p. 1986. pap. 35.00 (*0-939370-06-9*) DeRus Fine Art.

Paintings of George Caleb Bingham: A Catalogue Raisonne. E. Maurice Bloch. LC 85-29013. (Illus.). 328p. 1986. text 64.00 (*0-8262-0461-9*) U of Mo Pr.

***Paintings of Gerrit Dou.** Ed. by Arthur K. Wheelock, Jr. (Illus.). 160p. 2000. 55.00 (*0-300-08369-6*) Yale U Pr.

Paintings of J. M. W. Turner. rev. ed. Martin Butlin & Evelyn Joll. LC 84-40182. (Studies in British Art). (Illus.). 944p. 1984. 325.00 (*0-300-03276-5*) Yale U Pr.

Paintings of James McNeill Whistler, 2 vols. Hamish Miles et al. LC 80-5214. (Studies in British Art). (Illus.). 567p. 1980. 275.00 (*0-300-02384-7*) Yale U Pr.

Paintings of James-Paul Brown. Illus. by James-Paul Brown. LC 98-8804. 240p. 1998. 55.00 (*0-88496-434-5*) Capra Pr.

Paintings of Japanese Beauties in the Meiji Period. Toshio Miyago. (Arts Collection Ser.: Vol. 39). (Illus.). 256p. 1997. pap. 14.95 (*4-7636-1539-4*, Pub. by Kyoto Shoin) Bks Nippan.

Paintings of Jason Berger, Vol. 1. Lois Katz. (Illus.). 312p. 1998. 65.00 (*0-9659024-0-4*) Kikaku Amer.

Paintings of Maine. Ed. by Arnold Skolnick. LC 96-1977. (Illus.). 128p. 1996. reprint ed. pap. 19.95 (*0-89272-379-3*) Down East.

Paintings of Mama & Papa. Mary C. Hudson. LC 94-570592. (Illus.). 1993. pap. 5.95 (*0-9627745-2-9*) M C Hudson.

Paintings of Manuel Ocampo, Virgin Destroyer. Jennifer Bloom. 96p. 1996. pap. 30.00 (*0-945367-17-1*) Hardy Marks Pubns.

Paintings of Markey. Elizabeth Sozanski. LC 90-60694. (Illus.). 60p. (Orig.). 1990. pap. text 19.95 (*0-9626171-0-5*) Renais Art Gallery.

Paintings of Michael Booth, the Reservation. Michael G. Booth. 1996. pap. text 25.00 (*1-888236-13-2*) Art Wise.

Paintings of New England. Carl Little. Ed. by Arnold Skolnick. (Illus.). 128p. 1996. 30.00 (*0-89272-384-X*) Down East.

Paintings of Paul Cezanne: A Catalogue Raisonne, 2 vols. John Rewald et al. LC 96-10853. (Illus.). 880p. 1996. boxed set 400.00 (*0-8109-4044-2*, Pub. by Abrams) Time Warner.

Paintings of Samuel Edmund Oppenheim. John H. Sanden & Norman J. Miller. LC 94-73957. (Illus.). 80p. 1994. 35.00 (*0-9643447-0-X*) E W Oppenheim.

Paintings of Siva in Indian Art, 2 vols., Set. Chitralekha Singh. 1990. 700.00 (*81-85067-53-8*, Pub. by Sundeep Prak) S Asia.

Paintings of Steven Campbell: The Story So Far. Duncan Macmillan. (Illus.). 120p. 1994. 35.00 (*1-85158-546-X*, Pub. by Mainstream Pubng) Trafalgar.

Paintings of Sylvia Plimack Mangold. Cheryl A. Brutvan. LC 93-41205. 1994. 35.00 (*0-914782-90-8*) Buffalo Fine-Albrght-Knox.

Paintings of the American West from the Eiteljorg Museum Postcards. Ed. by Eiteljorg Museum Staff. (Illus.). (J). 1994. pap. 4.95 (*0-486-27819-0*) Dover.

Paintings of the Babur Nama. M. S. Randhawa. 139p. 1983. 80.00 (*0-318-36345-3*) Asia Bk Corp.

Paintings of the Lotus Sutra. Willa J. Tanabe. (Illus.). 340p. 1988. 65.00 (*0-8348-0217-1*) Weatherhill.

Paintings of the Ming & Qing Dynasties from the Guangzhou Art Gallery. Ed. by Xie Wenyong. (CHI & ENG., Illus.). 1986. 87.50 (*962-7101-07-9*) Coronet Bks.

Paintings of the Ming Dynasty from the Palace Museum. Ed. by Shan Guoqiang. (CHI & ENG., Illus.). 284p. 1988. 87.50 (*962-7101-12-5*) Coronet Bks.

Paintings of the Prado. Jose R. Buendia et al. (Illus.). 656p. 1995. 135.00 (*0-8212-2235-X*, Pub. by Bulfinch Pr) Little.

Paintings of the Sea: A 2,000-Year Voyage. Miles Unger. (Illus.). 176p. 1998. 22.95 (*1-885440-36-7*) First Glance.

Paintings of the Willem van de Veldes. M. S. Robinson. (Illus.). 1136p. 1990. 395.00 (*0-85667-389-7*, Pub. by P Wilson) Hoovers TX.

Paintings of Thomas Gainsborough. Malcolm Cormack. (Illus.). 198p. (C). 1993. pap. text 24.95 (*0-521-38887-2*) Cambridge U Pr.

Paintings of XuGu & Qi Baishi. Jung Y. Tsao. 448p. 1993. 100.00 (*0-295-97340-4*) Far East Fine Arts.

Paintings on Glass: Studies in Romanesque & Gothic Monumental Art. Madeline H. Caviness. LC 97-843. (Variourm Collected Studies: Vol. 573). (Illus.). 304p. 1997. 175.95 (*0-86078-638-2*, Pub. by Ashgate Pub) Ashgate Pub Co.

Paintings on the Move: Heinrich Heine & the Visual Arts. Ed. by Susanne Zantop. LC 88-19087. (Illus.). 220p. 1989. reprint ed. pap. 68.20 (*0-7837-8905-X*, 204961600001) Bks Demand.

Paintings That Changed the World: From Lascaux to Picasso. Klaus Reichold & Bernhard Graf. LC 98-231241. (Illus.). 192p. 1998. 29.95 (*3-7913-1983-3*) te Neues.

Paintings Ulla Wachtmeister. Ed. & Illus. by Ulla L. Wachtmeister. LC 95-128868. 84p. 1994. pap. 25.00 (*0-9643093-0-0*) U Wachtmeister.

Paints & Coatings for Space. Frank L. Bouquet. (Illus.). 150p. (Orig.). 1993. 100.00 (*1-56216-173-3*); pap. 70.00 (*1-56216-174-1*) Systems Co.

Paints & Coatings for Space. 2nd ed. Frank L. Bouquet. (Illus.). 160p. (Orig.). 1994. 110.00 (*1-56216-217-9*); pap. 80.00 (*1-56216-218-7*) Systems Co.

Paints & Coatings Industry. C. Broyles. 450p. 1995. pap. 1495.00 (*0-318-04170-7*) Busn Trend.

Paints & Pintos see Great American Horses

Paints & Protective Coatings. 1991. lib. bdg. 73.00 (*0-8490-4118-X*) Gordon Pr.

Paints & Protective Coatings. 1995. lib. bdg. 255.95 (*0-8490-6640-9*) Gordon Pr.

Paints & Specialized Coatings in India: A Strategic Entry Report, 1996. Compiled by Icon Group International Staff. (Illus.). 188p. 1999. ring bd. 1880.00 incl. audio compact disk (*0-7418-0730-0*) Icon Grp.

Paints & Varnishes in Poland: A Strategic Entry Report, 1997. Compiled by Icon Group International Staff. (Illus.). 186p. 1999. ring bd. 1860.00 incl. audio compact disk (*0-7418-0855-2*) Icon Grp.

***Paints, Coatings & Solvents.** 2nd ed. Ed. by Dieter Stoye. LC 98-228265. 420p. 1998. 195.00 (*3-527-28863-5*) Wiley.

***Paints, Inks, Varnishes, Resins in Turkey: A Strategic Entry Report, 1996.** Compiled by Icon Group International Staff. (Illus.). 140p. 1999. ring bd. 1400.00 incl. audio compact disk (*0-7418-1273-8*) Icon Grp.

***Paints, Pigments & Varnishes in Canada: A Strategic Entry Report, 1998.** Compiled by Icon Group International Staff. (Country Industry Report). (Illus.). 138p. 1999. ring bd. 1380.00 incl. audio compact disk (*0-7418-0497-2*) Icon Grp.

Paintspitter: Paintings & Constructions by Robert Warrens. Robert M. Doty. LC 89-43674. (Illus.). 44p. (Orig.). 1990. pap. 14.95 (*0-89494-031-7*) New Orleans Mus Art.

Pair Correlations in Many-Fermion Systems. Ed. by Vladimir Z. Kresin. LC 98-5056. (Illus.). 306p. (C). 1998. text 110.00 (*0-306-45823-3*, Kluwer Plenum) Kluwer Academic.

Pair for the Queen. Barbara Comfort. LC 97-34473. (Tish McWhinny Mystery Ser.: Vol. 5). 192p. 1998. 22.00 (*0-393-04627-3*) Norton.

Pair for the Queen. Barbara Comfort. 1999. pap. 7.95 (*0-393-31913-X*) Norton.

***Pair for the Queen.** large type ed. Barbara Comfort. LC 99-50319. 335p. 1999. 26.95 (*0-7862-2297-2*) Thorndike Pr.

Pair of Blankets: "War-Time History in Letters to the Young People of the South" William H. Stewart. 274p. 1990. reprint ed. 30.00 (*0-916107-80-9*) Broadfoot.

Pair of Blue Eyes. Thomas Hardy. Ed. & Intro. by Alan Manford. (Oxford World's Classics Ser.). (Illus.). 428p. 1998. pap. 7.95 (*0-19-283482-7*) OUP.

Pair of Blue Eyes. Thomas Hardy. Ed. & Intro. by Pamela Dalziel. LC 99-162076. 448p. 1998. pap. 8.95 (*0-14-043529-8*) Viking Penguin.

Pair of Blue Eyes. Thomas Hardy. (Classics Library). 1998. pap. 3.95 (*1-85326-277-3*, 2773WW, Pub. by Wrdsworth Edits) NTC Contemp Pub Co.

Pair of Hearts. Myra Rowe. 400p. (Orig.). 1989. mass mkt. 3.95 (*0-446-34841-4*, Pub. by Warner Bks) Little.

Pair of Madcaps. John T. Trowbridge. (Notable American Authors). 1999. reprint ed. lib. bdg. 125.00 (*0-7812-9814-8*) Rprt Serv.

Pair of Patient Lovers. William Dean Howells. LC 78-125219. (Short Story Index Reprint Ser.). 1977. 23.95 (*0-8369-3585-8*) Ayer.

Pair of Protoceratops. Bernard Most. LC 96-26358. (Illus.). 36p. (J). (ps-3). 1998. 11.00 (*0-15-201443-8*) Harcourt.

Pair of Red Sneakers. Lisa Lawston. LC 98-10481. (Illus.). 32p. (J). (ps-2). 1998. 15.95 (*0-531-30104-4*); lib. bdg. 16.99 (*0-531-33104-0*) Orchard Bks Watts.

Pair of Silk Stockings & Other Stories. Kate Chopin. LC 96-20049. (Thrift Editions Ser.). 64p. 1998. reprint ed. pap. text 1.00 (*0-486-29264-9*) Dover.

Pair of Socks. Stuart J. Murphy. LC 95-19618. (MathStart Ser.). (Illus.). 40p. (J). (ps-3). 1996. lib. bdg. 15.89 (*0-06-025880-2*) HarpC Child Bks.

Pair of Socks. Stuart J. Murphy. LC 95-19618. (MathStart Ser.: Level 1). (Illus.). 40p. (J). (ps up). 1996. 14.95 (*0-06-025879-9*); pap. 4.95 (*0-06-446703-1*, HarpTrophy) HarpC Child Bks.

Pair of Socks. Stuart J. Murphy. (Mathstart Ser.). 1996. 10.15 (*0-606-09596-9*, Pub. by Turtleback) Demco.

Paired Maths Handbook: Parental Involvement & Peer Tutoring in Mathematics. Keith Topping. 1998. pap. 25.95 (*1-85346-497-X*, Pub. by David Fulton) Taylor & Francis.

Paired Pulse Stimulation of the Heart. Ed. by Paul F. Cranefield & Brian F. Hoffman. (Illus.). 224p. 1968. 7.50 (*0-87470-009-4*) Rockefeller.

Paired Reading, Spelling & Writing: The Handbook for Teachers & Parents. Keith J. Topping. LC 94-45161. (Cassell Practical Handbooks Ser.). 208p. 1995. pap. 24.95 (*0-304-32942-8*) Continuum.

Paired Science Handbook: Parental Involvement & Peer Tutoring in Science. Keith Topping. LC 98-148937. vii, 88p. 1998. pap. 23.95 (*1-85346-500-3*, Pub. by David Fulton) Taylor & Francis.

Paired Writing Handbook. Cameron & Walker. 1994. pap. text. write for info. (*0-582-86075-X*, Pub. by Addison-Wesley) Longman.

Pairing. George R. Bach & Ronald M. Deutsch. 1976. mass mkt. 4.95 (*0-380-00394-5*, Avon Bks) Morrow Avon.

Pairing Food with Wine. Robert Hoffman. 118p. 1999. pap. 8.95 (*1-893718-01-8*) Hoffman CA.

***Pairing Wine & Food: A Handbook for All Cuisines.** Linda Johnson-Bell. LC 99-32432. (Illus.). 208p. 2000. pap. 16.95 (*1-58080-037-8*) Burford Bks.

Pairpoint Lamps. Edward Malakoff & Sheila Malakoff. LC 90-63190. (Illus.). 160p. 1990. 95.00 (*0-88740-281-X*) Schiffer.

Pairpoint Manufacturing Company: 1894 Catalogue Reprint. Intro. by Louis O. St. Aubin, Jr. (Illus.). 200p. 1997. pap. 24.95 (*1-57080-028-6*) Antique Pubns.

Pairs: New Poems. Phillip Booth. LC 94-3899. (Poets Ser.). 96p. 1994. pap. 12.95 (*0-14-058724-1*, Penguin Classics) Viking Penguin.

PAIS Bulletin, 1989, Vol. 75. Ed. by Gwen Sloan. 1350p. 1989. lib. bdg. 245.00 (*1-877874-00-0*) Pub Aff Info.

PAIS Bulletin, 1990: Oct. 1989 Through Sept. 1990, Vol. 76. Ed. by Gwen Sloan. 1300p. 1990. 245.00 (*1-877874-03-5*) Pub Aff Info.

P

An Asterisk (*) at the beginning of an entry indicates that the title is appearing for the first time.

PAIS Bulletin, 1990: October Through December, 1990, Vol. 77. Ed. by Gwen Sloan. 547p. 1990. 75.00 (*1-877874-04-3*) Pub Aff Info.

Pais de Cuatro Pisos. Jose L. Gonzalez. LC 80-67414. (Nave y el Puerto Ser.). 150p. 1980. reprint ed. pap. 7.75 (*0-940238-32-2*) Ediciones Huracan.

Pais de la Jauja (Fantasy Land) Kasparavicius. (SPA.). 28p. (J). (gr. 1-3). 1994. 12.99 (*968-16-4501-4*, Pub. by Fondo) Continental Bk.

Pais de un Solo Hombre (Land of One Man) Vol. 1: El Mexico de Santa Anna (Santa Anna's Mexico) Enrique G. Pedrero. (SPA., Illus.). 690p. 1993. 49.99 (*968-16-3962-6*, Pub. by Fondo) Continental Bk.

PAIS Foreign Language Index, 1990, Vol. 20. Ed. by Alice Picon. 660p. 1990. lib. bdg. 495.00 (*1-877874-05-1*) Pub Aff Info.

PAIS International in Print: Author Index, Vol. 9. Ed. by Catherine Korvin. 450.00 (*1-877874-23-X*) Pub Aff Info.

PAIS International in Print: Subject Index, 2 vols., Vol. 8. Ed. by Catherine Korvin. 300p. 1999. 450.00 (*1-877874-20-5*) Pub Aff Info.

PAIS International in Print: Subject Index, Vol. 9. Ed. by Catherine Korvin. 500.00 (*1-877874-22-1*) Pub Aff Info.

PAIS International in Print: Subject Index & Author Index, 2 vols., Vol. 8. Ed. by Catherine Korvin. 1800p. 1999. 500.00 (*1-877874-19-1*) Pub Aff Info.

PAIS International in Print Vol. 4: Author Index: January-December, 1994. Ed. by Gwen Sloan. 1995. 50.00 (*1-877874-10-8*) Pub Aff Info.

PAIS International in Print Vol. 4: Subject Index: January-December, 1994. Ed. by Gwen Sloan. 1995. 325.00 (*1-877874-11-6*) Pub Aff Info.

PAIS International in Print Vol. 5: Author Index: January-December, 1995. Ed. by Gwen Sloan. 1996. 50.00 (*1-877874-12-4*) Pub Aff Info.

PAIS International in Print Vol. 5: Subject Index: January-December, 1995. Ed. by Gwen Sloan. 1996. 325.00 (*1-877874-13-2*) Pub Aff Info.

PAIS International in Print Vol. 6: Author Index: January-December, 1996. Ed. by Gwen Sloan. (C). 1997. 50.00 (*1-877874-16-7*) Pub Aff Info.

PAIS International in Print Vol. 6: Subject Index: January-December, 1996. Ed. by Gwen Sloan. (C). 1997. 325.00 (*1-877874-15-9*) Pub Aff Info.

PAIS International in Print Vol. 7: Author Index: January-December, 1997. Ed. by Catherine Korvin. 300p. 1998. 50.00 (*1-877874-18-3*) Pub Aff Info.

PAIS International in Print Vol. 7: Subject Index: January-December, 1997. Ed. by Catherine Korvin. 1700p. 1998. 325.00 (*1-877874-17-5*) Pub Aff Info.

PAIS International in Print, 1991, Vol. 1. Ed. by Gwen Sloan. 2062p. 1991. 300.00 (*1-877874-06-X*) Pub Aff Info.

PAIS International in Print, 1992, Vol. 2. Ed. by Gwen Sloan. 1987p. 1992. 300.00 (*1-877874-09-4*) Pub Aff Info.

Paisajes Despues de la Batalla. Juan Goytisolo. (SPA.). 199p. 1982. 12.00 (*84-85859-54-5*, 2008) Ediciones Norte.

Paisajes Despues de la Batalla. Juan Goytisolo. Ed. by Andres Sanchez Robayna. (Nueva Austral Ser.: Vol. 218). (SPA.). 1991. pap. text 17.95 (*84-239-7218-6*) Elliots Bks.

Paisajes y Recuerdos - Snapshots & Recollections. Andrew Debicki & Teresa Rozo. Tr. by Pat Harpstrite & David M. Moorhouse. (ENG & SPA.). 188p. (Orig.). 1994. pap. 15.95 (*1-886480-00-1*) Edici Latidos.

Paisajes y Semblanzas. Jose M. Areilza. (Nueva Austral Ser.: No. 64). (SPA.). 1991. pap. text 29.95 (*84-239-1856-4*) Elliots Bks.

Paisano: Nuevo Mexico: Vida y Dilema. Benedicto Cuesta. 1976. pap. 4.95 (*0-913270-59-8*) Sunstone Pr.

Paisanos: A Folklore Miscellany. Ed. by Francis Abernethy. 1978. 15.00 (*0-88426-054-2*) Encino Pr.

Paisanos: A Folklore Miscellany. Ed. by F. E. Abernethy. (Texas Folklore Society Publications: No. 41). (Illus.). 180p. 1978. reprint ed. 16.95 (*1-57441-059-8*) UNTX Pr.

Paisanos: Spanish Settlers on the Northern Frontier of New Spain. Oakah L. Jones, Jr. LC 96-17090. (Illus.). 368p. 1996. pap. text 21.95 (*0-8061-2885-2*) U of Okla Pr.

Paises Balticos. Pascal Lorot. (Breviarios Ser.). (SPA.). pap. 6.99 (*968-16-4957-5*, Pub. by Fondo) Continental Bk.

Paisius Ligarides. Harry T. Hiondes. LC 70-187634. (Twayne's World Authors Ser.). 169p. (C). 1972. text 20.95 (*0-8290-1743-7*) Irvington.

Paisley. Suzanne C. Crowley. Ed. by Miriam D. Irwin. (Illus.). 48p. 1990. 28.00 (*0-88014-082-8*) Mosaic Pr OH.

Paisley. Ed Moloney & Andy Pollak. (Illus.). 464p. 1986. pap. 13.95 (*0-905169-75-1*, Pub. by Poolbeg Pr) Dufour.

Paisley: A Visual Survey of Pattern & Color Variations. Tina Skinner. LC 98-84042. 112p. 1998. pap. 24.95 (*0-7643-0546-8*) Schiffer.

Paisley Designs: 44 Original Plates. Gregory Mirow. (Illus.). 48p. 1989. pap. 4.50 (*0-486-25987-0*) Dover.

Paisley Girl. Fran Gordon. LC 99-33989. 224p. 1999. text 22.95 (*0-312-20352-7*) St Martin.

***Paisley Girl.** Fran Gordon. 2000. pap. 13.95 (*0-312-26371-6*) St Martin.

Paisley Goes with Nothing: A Man's Guide to Style. Hal Rubenstein. 240p. 1997. pap. 11.95 (*0-385-48393-7*, Main St Bks) Doubleday.

Paisley Poets: A Critical Reappraisal of Their Work & Reputation. Stuart James & Gordon Mccrae. 90p. 1993. pap. 13.95 (*0-904391-05-1*, Pub. by Wilfion Bks) Dufour.

Paisleys & Other Textile Designs from India. K. Prakash. LC 93-39105. (Illus.). 160p. 1994. pap. 8.95 (*0-486-27959-6*) Dover.

Paita - Outpost of Empire: The Impact of the New England Whaling Fleet on the Socioeconomic Development of Northern Peru, 1932-1865. William L. Lofstrom. (Illus.). 232p. 1996. pap. 24.95 (*0-913372-74-9*) Mystic Seaport.

Paite: A Transborder Tribe of India & Burma. H. Kamkhenthang. (C). 1988. 34.00 (*81-7099-070-X*, Pub. by Mittal Pubs Dist) S Asia.

Paiute. Sessions S. Wheeler. LC 86-11238. 249p. 1986. reprint ed. pap. 71.00 (*0-608-01263-7*, 2062012) Bks Demand.

Paiute ATV Trail, UT. rev. ed. Ed. by Trails Illustrated Staff. (Illus.). 1994. 8.99 (*0-925873-82-9*) Trails Illustrated.

Paiute, Prospector, Pioneer. Thomas C. Fletcher. LC 87-70794. (Illus.). 123p. (Orig.). 1987. pap. 9.50 (*0-932347-03-7*) Artemisia Pr.

Paivi. Kathleen Appleby. (Illus.). 12p. 1999. pap. 15.00 (*0-9672237-0-9*, 1022) V A Pubg.

PAIVI BEE For the Light Bos. Kathleen Appleby. (Illus.). 10p. 1999. ring bd. 35.00 (*0-9672237-1-7*, 1023) V A Pubg.

Paix - Nouvelle Methode, Nouvelle Lumiere see Peace: New Method, New Light

Paix Chez les Betes. Sidonie-Gabrielle Colette. 1984. pap. 28.95 (*0-7859-5237-3*) Fr & Eur.

Paix Chez Soi. Georges Courteline. 40p. 1966. 8.95 (*0-7859-0694-0*, F97610) Fr & Eur.

Paix de l'Europe c. 1700. William Penn. 1999. pap. 21.00 (*1-85072-016-9*, Pub. by W Sessions) St Mut.

Paix de l'Europe circa 1700. Sessions, William Ltd., Staff. (C). 1990. 55.00 (*0-7855-5094-1*, Pub. by W Sessions) St Mut.

Paix de l'Europe circa 1700: William Penn's Famous Essay on the Peace of Europe. Sessions, William Ltd., Staff. (C). 1988. 55.00 (*0-7855-6665-1*, Pub. by W Sessions) St Mut.

Paix des Profondeurs. Aldous Huxley. (FRE.). 634p. 1978. pap. 13.95 (*0-7859-2408-6*, 2070370542) Fr & Eur.

Paix et l'Enseignement Pacifiste: Lecons Professees a l'Ecole des Hautes Etudes Sociales see Voices of French Pacifism

Paix et Liberte, ou le Budget Republicain. Frederic Bastiat. LC 72-147492. (Library of War & Peace; the Political Economy of War). 1972. lib. bdg. 46.00 (*0-8240-0286-5*) Garland.

Pajama Party. LC 97-32447. (P. B. Bear Ser.). (Illus.). 24p. (J). (ps). 1998. 6.95 (*0-7894-3107-6*) DK Pub Inc.

Pajama Party. Amy Hest. LC 93-11721. 1994. 10.15 (*0-606-06654-3*, Pub. by Turtleback) Demco.

Pajama Party. Joan Holub. (All Aboard Reading Ser.). (Illus.). 32p. (J). (ps-1). 1998. mass mkt. 3.99 (*0-448-41739-1*, G & D) Peng Put Young Read.

Pajama Party. Anne C. Martens. 1983. pap. 3.50 (*0-87129-289-0*, P12) Dramatic Pub.

Pajama Party. Amy Hest. LC 91-13676. (Illus.). 48p. (J). (gr. 2 up). 1994. reprint ed. pap. 4.95 (*0-688-12949-8*, Wm Morrow) Morrow Avon.

Pajama Party, Level 2. Joan Holub. LC 97-39734. (All Aboard Reading Ser.). (Illus.). 32p. (J). 1998. lib. bdg. 13.89 (*0-448-41867-3*, G & D) Peng Put Young Read.

***Pajama Sam.** G. Amaral. (Illus.). 112p. (J). (ps-2). 2000. pap. 2.99 (*1-57064-949-9*, 73116, Humongous Bks) Lyrick Pub.

***Pajama Sam Mission to the Moon.** Illus. by N. S. Greenfield. LC 00-100702. 24p. (J). (ps-2). 2000. pap. 3.99 (*1-57064-950-2*, 73117, Humongous Bks) Lyrick Pub.

***Pajama Sam Out to Lunch!** Biz Magoo. LC 00-105052. (Humongous Ser.). (Illus.). (J). (ps-1). 2001. 5.99 (*1-58668-065-X*) Lyrick Studios.

***Pajama Sam the Magic Hat Tree.** Illus. by N. S. Greenfield. LC 00-100703. 14p. (J). (ps). 2000. 7.99 (*1-57064-951-0*, Humongous Bks) Lyrick Pub.

***Pajama Sam What's Different?** Linda Dowdy. LC 00-105050. (Humongous Ser.). (Illus.). 32p. (J). (ps-1). 2001. 3.99 (*1-58668-064-1*) Lyrick Studios.

***Pajama Sam's Amazing TV Adventure!** Biz Magoo. LC 00-105049. (Humongous Ser.). (Illus.). 24p. (J). (ps-1). 2001. 3.99 (*1-58668-062-5*) Lyrick Studios.

***Pajama Time!** Sandra Boynton. (Boynton on Board Ser.). (Illus.). 24p. (J). (ps). 2000. 6.95 (*0-7611-1975-2*) Workman Pub.

Pajamas. Livingston Taylor & Maggie Taylor. LC 87-8589. (Illus.). 32p. (J). (ps-3). 1988. 13.95 (*0-15-200564-1*, Gulliver Bks) Harcourt.

Pajamas Don't Matter: or What Your Baby Really Needs. Trish Gribben. LC 79-90081. (Creative Parenting & Adventures of Squib Ser.). (Illus.). 52p. (C). 1980. pap. 5.95 (*0-915190-21-4*, JP9021-4) Jalmar Pr.

Pajarito Castano. Nicolas P. Diez-Arguelles. LC 90-86231. 188p. 1991. 15.00 (*0-89729-594-3*) Ediciones.

Pajarito Emilio. Charles M. Schulz. (Peanuts Ser.). (SPA.). 64p. (J). 1971. 4.95 (*0-8288-4510-7*) Fr & Eur.

Pajaritos. Clarita Kohen. (Laredo Children's Bilingual Library). (Illus.). 24p. (Orig.). (J). (gr. k-3). 1993. lib. bdg. 7.50 (*1-56492-104-2*) Laredo.

Pajaro Cu. Dorothy S. Bishop et al.Tr. of Cu Bird. (ENG & SPA., Illus.). 64p. (J). 1995. pap. 6.95 (*0-8442-7163-2*, 71632, Natl Textbk Co) NTC Contemp Pub Co.

Pajaro Cu (The Cu Bird) Marjorie E. Herrmann. (Bilingual Ser.). (ENG & SPA.). (J). 1978. 10.15 (*0-606-01266-4*, Pub. by Turtleback) Demco.

Pajaro del Alma (The Bird of the Soul) Mijal Snunit. Tr. by Flaminia C. Tuval & Carmen A. Garcia. (SPA.). 24p. (J). (gr. 1-3). 1993. 12.99 (*968-16-4059-4*, Pub. by Fondo) Continental Bk.

***Pajaro Que Limpia el Mundo.** Victor D. Montejo. (MYN & SPA.). 169p. 2000. pap. 12.95 (*1-886502-29-3*) Yax Te Found.

Pajaros. Susan Kuchella. (SPA.). (J). 1997. pap. 3.50 (*0-8167-3716-9*) Troll Communs.

Pajaros de Puerto Rico. Ana V. Vidal & Laura Sarraga Toro. (SPA.). 36p. 1995. pap. write for info. (*0-929441-73-7*) Pubns Puertorriquenas.

Pak: American Urban & Regional Experience. Efren Padilla. 390p. (C). 1996. 61.95 (*0-7872-2874-5*) Kendall-Hunt.

***Pak: Anybody's Guide to Total Fitness.** 6th ed. 120p. (C). 2000. per. 24.95 (*0-7872-7126-8*) Kendall-Hunt.

Pak: Biosphere 2000: Protecting Our Global Environment. 2nd ed. Kaufman & Franz. 720p. 1997. pap. text 78.95 (*0-7872-3898-8*, 41389801) Kendall-Hunt.

Pak: Class Justice Essays. Jack Curtin. 272p. (C). 1995. 31.19 (*0-7872-1302-0*) Kendall-Hunt.

***Pak: Critical Thinking Through Debate.** Corcoran et al. 368p. (C). 1999. pap. text 52.95 (*0-7872-5569-6*, 41556902) Kendall-Hunt.

Pak: Equity & the Underclass in Criminal Justice. John Curtin. 226p. (C). 1997. pap. text 39.95 (*0-7872-3404-4*, 41340401) Kendall-Hunt.

Pak: Ethnicity & Psychology. Kenneth Monteiro. 96p. (C). 1995. pap., student ed., per. write for info. (*0-7872-0470-6*); pap., per. write for info. (*0-7872-0425-0*) Kendall-Hunt.

***Pak: Game Plan.** 80p. (C). 2000. pap. 65.95 (*0-7872-6693-0*) Kendall-Hunt.

Pak: Interactive Reading Manual for College Students. Daly et al. 166p. (C). 1998. pap. text 36.95 (*0-7872-4647-6*, 41464701) Kendall-Hunt.

Pak: Journeys & Destinations. 3rd ed. Center for Gifted Education Staff. (C). 1998. 65.95 (*0-7872-5166-6*) Kendall-Hunt.

Pak: Mathematics for Business. Lawrence Clar & James Hart. 752p. (C). 1995. 58.95 (*0-7872-0820-5*) Kendall-Hunt.

Pak: Mathematics for Business & Personal Finance. 2nd ed. Lawrence Clar. 792p. (C). 1997. 65.95 (*0-7872-4233-0*) Kendall-Hunt.

Pak: Men, Media, & Masculinity. Edward LaFrance. 48p. (C). 1995. student ed. write for info. (*0-7872-1769-7*); pap., per. write for info. (*0-7872-1577-5*); 41.93 (*0-7872-1770-0*) Kendall-Hunt.

Pak: Military Modern Japan. Andrew Hanami. 228p. (C). 1995. 32.50 (*0-7872-1334-9*) Kendall-Hunt.

Pak: Mind Your Logic. Donald Gregory. 230p. (C). 1998. pap. text 54.95 (*0-7872-1946-0*, 41194601) Kendall-Hunt.

Pak: Multicultural Women: Health, Disability & Rehabilitation. Anita Leal-Idrogo et al. 446p. (C). 1996. pap. text, student ed., wbk. ed. 66.95 (*0-7872-1998-3*, 41199801) Kendall-Hunt.

Pak: Pragmatics of California Government. Francis G. Navarrette. 288p. (C). 1995. pap. text 30.95 (*0-7872-1344-6*, 41134401) Kendall-Hunt.

Pak: Pragmatics of Government. Francis G. Navarrette. 416p. (C). 1995. pap. text 38.95 (*0-7872-1294-6*, 41129401) Kendall-Hunt.

Pak: Presentational Speaking. George McLemore. 320p. (C). 1996. 34.95 (*0-7872-0024-7*) Kendall-Hunt.

Pak: Questions of Value. Donald Viney. 338p. (C). 1998. pap. text 40.95 (*0-7872-1699-2*, 41169901) Kendall-Hunt.

Pak: Racial & Ethnic Families in America. 3rd ed. Juan Gonzales. 404p. (C). 1998. pap. text 48.95 (*0-7872-2764-1*, 41276401) Kendall-Hunt.

Pak: Racial & Ethnic Groups in America. Juan Gonzales. 452p. (C). 1998. pap. text 52.95 (*0-7872-1745-X*, 41174501) Kendall-Hunt.

Pak: Racial & Ethnic Groups in America. 3rd ed. Juan L. Gonzales. 576p. (C). 1996. 38.95 (*0-7872-2329-8*) Kendall-Hunt.

Pak: Readings in Art History. Maria Cheremeteff. 346p. (C). 1998. pap. text 60.95 (*0-7872-4437-6*, 41443701) Kendall-Hunt.

Pak: Readings in World Music. James Chopyak. 272p. (C). 1995. pap. text 17.95 (*0-7872-1338-1*, 41133801) Kendall-Hunt.

Pak: Reforming Juvenile Justice: Reasons & Strategies. Macallair-Schiraldi. 314p. (C). 1997. pap. text 63.95 (*0-7872-4550-X*, 41455001) Kendall-Hunt.

Pak: Science Experiments by the Hundreds. Julia Cothron et al. 224p. 1996. teacher ed. 26.95 (*0-7872-2140-6*) Kendall-Hunt.

Pak: Security. John Chuvala, 3rd. (C). 1995. pap. text 44.95 (*0-7872-1584-8*, 41158401) Kendall-Hunt.

Pak: Sex & Relationships: An Anthology. John Elia. 424p. (C). 1999. pap. text 34.95 (*0-7872-5603-X*, 41560301) Kendall-Hunt.

Pak: Small Business Management. Peter Churchill. 400p. (C). 1995. 56.95 (*0-7872-0449-8*) Kendall-Hunt.

Pak: Sound. Vinay Shrivastava. 352p. (C). 1995. 45.95 (*0-7872-1571-6*) Kendall-Hunt.

Pak: Spanish B-25 Booklets. Jerry Johns. 1998. pap. text 24.95 (*0-7872-5593-9*, 41559301) Kendall-Hunt.

Pak: Spanish Kit B. Jerry Johns. 1998. boxed set 49.95 (*0-7872-3744-2*) Kendall-Hunt.

Pak: Spanish Reading Inventory Performance Booklet Form A. Jerry L. Johns. 12p. 1997. 22.95 (*0-7872-4475-9*) Kendall-Hunt.

Pak: Speaking for Results. Stephen Nielsen. 336p. (C). 1996. 39.95 (*0-7872-2161-9*) Kendall-Hunt.

Pak: Textbook of Psychology. Don Donderi. 112p. (C). 1995. pap., per. write for info. (*0-7872-1102-8*) Kendall-Hunt.

Pak: Textbook of Psychology. 4th ed. Don Donderi. LC 96-132348. 464p. (C). 1995. pap., per. write for info. (*0-7872-1101-X*) Kendall-Hunt.

Pak: The Creative Mind. William Cleveland. 516p. 1997. pap. text 87.95 (*0-7872-3264-5*, 41326401) Kendall-Hunt.

Pak: The Dynamics of California Government & Politics. Richard Harvey. 474p. (C). 1996. 36.95 (*0-7872-1855-3*) Kendall-Hunt.

Pak: The New Filipino Story. Efren Padilla. 336p. (C). 1997. pap. text 58.95 (*0-7872-4565-8*, 41456501) Kendall-Hunt.

***Pak: The Student Teaching Experience.** 2nd ed. Billie Enz. 176, 174p. (C). 2000. per. 34.95 (*0-7872-7260-4*) Kendall-Hunt.

Pak: Threads of Change in 19th Century Literature. Center for Gifted Education Staff. 900p. (C). 1998. boxed set 65.95 (*0-7872-5346-4*, 41534601) Kendall-Hunt.

Pak: Urban Education Reader 300B. Stephanie Evans. 128p. (C). 1997. boxed set 45.95 (*0-7872-3725-6*) Kendall-Hunt.

Pak: Urban Education Reader 414. Stephanie Evans. 176p. (C). 1997. boxed set 54.95 (*0-7872-3727-2*) Kendall-Hunt.

Pak: Using American Law Books. 4th ed. Alfred Lewis. 304p. (C). 1995. pap. text 39.95 (*0-7872-0734-9*, 41073401) Kendall-Hunt.

Pak: War, Peace & Power in the Post Cold War Era. Andrew Hanami. 516p. (C). 1997. pap. text 101.95 (*0-7872-3788-4*, 41378801) Kendall-Hunt.

Pak: Wave 1 Anthem Connecticut. AGS Staff. 1997. 8.47 (*0-7872-4577-1*) Kendall-Hunt.

Pak: Wave 1 HMSA Hawaii. AGS Staff. 1997. 8.47 (*0-7872-4589-5*) Kendall-Hunt.

Pak: Women, Culture & Society. 2nd ed. Blancero & Marron. 544p. (C). 1998. pap. text 42.95 (*0-7872-5385-5*, 41538501) Kendall-Hunt.

Pak in Indonesia. Alain Chenneviere. Tr. by Lisa Davidson. LC 95-31072. (My Future Ser.). 1996. lib. bdg. 22.60 (*0-8225-2826-6*, Lerner Publctns) Lerner Pub.

Pak Mei Kung Fu. Un Ho Bun. 96p. 1996. pap. 17.95 (*0-901764-19-1*, 93327) P H Crompton.

Pakistan see Fiesta 2!

Pakistan. 1996. 21.95 (*0-614-97032-6*) NTC Contemp Pub Co.

Pakistan. Elspeth Clayton. LC 95-26779. (Worldfocus Ser.). (J). 1998. 18.50 (*1-57572-077-9*) Heinemann Lib.

Pakistan. Guidebook Company Staff. (Illus.). pap. 9.95 (*962-217-107-9*) China Guides.

Pakistan. Insight Guides Staff. (Insight Guides). 1998. pap. text 21.95 (*0-88729-736-6*) Langenscheidt.

Pakistan. Eaniqa Khan & Rob Unwin. LC 97-3015. (Country Insights Ser.). (J). 1998. lib. bdg. 24.96 (*0-8172-4793-9*) Raintree Steck-V.

Pakistan. Mano Rumalshah. (Focus On Ser.). (Illus.). 32p. (YA). (gr. 7-10). 1991. write for info. (*0-237-60193-1*) EVN1 UK.

Pakistan. Isobel Shaw. (Asian Guides Ser.). (Illus.). 232p. 1992. pap. 12.95 (*0-8442-9918-9*, Passprt Bks) NTC Contemp Pub Co.

Pakistan. U. S. Government Staff. (Country Studies). 1996. 22.00 (*1-57980-053-X*, UPAKIS) Claitors.

Pakistan. U. S. Government Staff. (Country Studies). 1996. 22.00 (*0-614-30835-6*, UPAKIS) Claitors.

Pakistan. annot. ed. Ed. by David Conrad Taylor. LC 90-154424. (World Bibliographical Ser.: No. 10). 290p. 1990. lib. bdg. 70.00 (*1-85109-081-9*) ABC-CLIO.

Pakistan see Cultures of the World - Group 7

Pakistan. 2nd ed. LC 97-930857. (Illus.). 1997. write for info. (*0-19-577838-3*) OUP.

Pakistan. 3rd ed. Burki. LC 98-55927. 272p. 2000. pap. 26.00 (*0-8133-3621-X*, Pub. by Westview) HarpC.

Pakistan: A Country Study. Ed. by Peter R. Blood. LC 95-17247. (Area Handbook Ser.). 1995. 22.00 (*0-8444-0834-4*, 008020013773) Lib Congress.

Pakistan: A Country Study. 6th ed. Ed. by Peter R. Blood. (Illus.). 398p. 1996. reprint ed. text 45.00 (*0-7881-3631-3*) DIANE Pub.

***Pakistan: A Country Study Guide.** Global Investment & Business Center, Inc. Staff. (World Country Study Guides Library: Vol. 130). (Illus.). 350p. 2000. pap. 59.00 (*0-7397-2428-2*) Intl Business Pubns.

Pakistan: A Cultural Unity. S. F. Faizi. 195p. 1985. 12.95 (*1-56744-350-8*) Kazi Pubns.

***Pakistan: A Withering State?** Sreedhar. LC 99-932831. (Illus.). 1999. 34.00 (*81-87412-00-3*, Pub. by Wordsmiths) S Asia.

Pakistan: An Islamic Treasure. Jabeen Yusufali. (Discovering Our Heritage Ser.). (Illus.). 128p. (YA). (gr. 5 up). 1990. lib. bdg. 14.95 (*0-87518-433-2*, Dillon Silver Burdett) Silver Burdett Pr.

Pakistan: Contemporary Forms of Slavery. Human Rights Watch Asia Staff. 96p. (Orig.). 1995. pap. 7.00 (*1-56432-154-1*) Hum Rts Watch.

Pakistan: Human Rights after Martial Law: Report of a Mission. International Commission of Jurists. LC 89-103631. 158p. reprint ed. pap. 49.00 (*0-7837-6980-6*, 204679200004) Bks Demand.

Pakistan: In Search of Modernization. Attar Chand. (C). 1992. 48.00 (*81-7041-559-4*, Pub. by Anmol) S Asia.

Pakistan: Islam, Politics, & National Solidarity. Anwar H. Syed. LC 82-12366. 203p. 1982. 55.00 (*0-275-90913-1*, C0913, Praeger Pubs) Greenwood.

Pakistan: Islamic Nation in Crisis. Ali N. Memon. LC 97-18601. 1996. pap. 16.95 (*0-915957-66-3*) amana pubns.

Pakistan: Its Ideology & Foreign Policy. Aris Hussain. 188p. 1966. 27.50 (*0-7146-2015-7*, Pub. by F Cass Pubs) Intl Spec Bk.

Pakistan: Its People, Its Society, Its Culture. Donald N. Wilber. LC 64-8647. (Survey of World Cultures Ser.: No. 13). 503p. reprint ed. pap. 156.00 (*0-608-11684-X*, 202175000023) Bks Demand.

Pakistan: Its Politics & Bureaucracy. Mustafa Chowdhury. xi, 244p. 1988. text 30.00 (*81-7045-025-X*, Pub. by Assoc Pub Hse) Advent Bks Div.

Pakistan: Major World Nations. John C. Caldwell. LC 99-11827. (Illus.). 144p. 1999. 19.95 (*0-7910-5392-X*) Chelsea Hse.

Pakistan: Meeting the Challenge. Peter Stewart & Jenny Sturgis. (Illus.). 200p. 1996. 170.00 (*1-85564-396-0*, Pub. by Euromoney) Am Educ Systs.

Pakistan: Political & Economic History since 1947. Omar Noman. 238p. 1996. pap. 15.95 (*0-614-21497-1*, 940); pap. 15.95 (*0-614-21696-6*, 940) Kazi Pubns.

Pakistan: Political & Economic History Since 1947. Omar Noman. 285p. 1990. pap. 15.95 (*0-7103-0389-0*, A4718) Routledge.

Pakistan: Political Economy of a Developing State. Pandav Nayak. 1988. 48.50 (*81-7050-049-4*, Pub. by Patriot Pubs) S Asia.

***Pakistan: Political Roots & Development 1947-1999.** Safdar Mahmood. 500p. 2000. text 24.95 (*0-19-579373-0*) OUP.

***Pakistan: The Barren Years; The Viewpoint Editorials & Columns of Mazhar Ali Khan 1975-1992.** Ali Mazhar Khan. LC 99-200365. 769p. 1999. text 26.00 (*0-19-579004-9*) OUP.

Pakistan: The Continuing Search for Nationhood. 2nd rev. ed. Shahid J. Burki. (Nations of Contemporary Asia Ser.). 243p. (C). 1991. pap. 21.50 (*0-8133-8101-0*) Westview.

Pakistan: The Development of Its Laws & Constitution, Volume 8. Alan Gledhill. LC 80-20180. (British Commonwealth, the Development of Its Laws & Constitutions Ser.: Vol. 8). 263p. 1980. reprint ed. lib. bdg. 65.00 (*0-313-20842-5*, GLPA) Greenwood.

***Pakistan: The Economy of an Elitist State.** Ishrat Husain. LC 99-210405. 468p. 1999. text 29.95 (*0-19-579014-6*) OUP.

Pakistan: The First Twelve Years: The Pakistan Times Editorials of Mazhar Ali Khan. Mazhar A. Khan. 784p. (C). 1996. 52.00 (*0-19-577676-3*) OUP.

Pakistan: The Formative Phase, 1857-1948. Khalid B. Sayeed. 350p. 1994. pap. text 16.95 (*0-19-577114-1*) OUP.

Pakistan: The India Factor. Rajendra Sareen. 615p. 1984. 37.95 (*0-317-38651-4*, Pub. by Allied Pubs) Asia Bk Corp.

Pakistan: The Long View. William J. Barnds et al. Ed. by Lawrence Ziring. LC 76-4320. (Duke University Center for Commonwealth & Comparative Studies Publication: No. 43). 503p. reprint ed. pap. 156.00 (*0-608-12778-7*, 202347700033) Bks Demand.

Pakistan: The Modern Nations in Historical Perspective. Singhat Damodar. 214p. 1972. 9.95 (*0-13-648469-7*) Asia Bk Corp.

Pakistan: The Problem of India. Shukatullah Ansari. 1997. 20.00 (*81-7169-426-8*, Commonwealth) S Asia.

Pakistan: The Social Sciences' Perspective. Ed. by Akbar S. Ahmed. (Illus.). 310p. 1990. text 21.00 (*0-19-577388-8*) OUP.

Pakistan: Tradition & Change. Khavar Mumtaz & Yameema Mithra. (Oxfam Country Profiles Ser.). (Illus.). 64p. 1996. pap. 9.95 (*0-85598-336-1*, Pub. by Oxfam Pub) Stylus Pub VA.

Pakistan: Zia & After . . . Anthony Hyman et al. (C). 1989. 17.50 (*81-7017-253-5*, Pub. by Abhinav) S Asia.

Pakistan: Zia to Benazir. V. T. Joshi. (C). 1995. 22.50 (*81-220-0390-7*, Pub. by Konark Pubs) S Asia.

Pakistan - A Country Study Guide: Basic Information for Research & Pleasure. Global Investment Center, USA Staff. (World Country Study Guide Library: Vol. 130). (Illus.). 350p. 1999. pap. 59.00 (*0-7397-1527-5*) Intl Business Pubns.

Pakistan - The India Factor. Rajendra Sareen. 615p. 1984. 37.95 (*0-318-37252-5*) Asia Bk Corp.

Pakistan-American Institute of Science & Technology (PAISTECH), University of Maryland, Proceedings. Abdus Salam. Ed. by M. Yameen Zubairi. 1984. write for info. (*0-930895-03-7*) Byron Daven Pubs.

Pakistan & Bangladesh: Political Culture & Political Parties. Mokhdum E. Mushrafi. (C). 1992. 54.00 (*81-85565-17-1*, Pub. by Uppal Pub Hse) S Asia.

Pakistan & the Bomb: Public Opinion & Nuclear Options. Ed. by David Cortright & Samina Ahmed. LC 97-3802. (Studies on International Peace). 1998. pap. 20.00 (*0-268-03818-X*) U of Notre Dame Pr.

***Pakistan Army 1998.** annuals 2nd ed. Stephen P. Cohen. LC 98-930868. (Oxford Pakistan Paperbacks Ser.). (Illus.). 210p. 1999. pap. text 12.95 (*0-19-577948-7*) OUP.

PAKISTAN Business & Investment Opportunities Yearbook-98: Business, Investment, Export-Import. Contrib. by Russian Information & Business Center, Inc. Staff. (Business & Investment Opportunity Library-98). (Illus.). 350p. 1998. pap. 99.00 (*1-57751-979-5*) Intl Business Pubns.

***Pakistan Business Intelligence Report, 190 vols.** Global Investment & Business Center, Inc. Staff. (World Business Intelligence Library: Vol. 130). (Illus.). 350p. 2000. pap. 99.95 (*0-7397-2628-5*) Intl Business Pubns.

***Pakistan Business Law Handbook.** Global Investment & Business Center, Inc. Staff. (Global Business Law Handbooks Library: Vol. 130). (Illus.). 2000. pap. 99.95 (*0-7397-2028-7*) Intl Business Pubns.

***Pakistan Business Opportunity Yearbook.** Global Investment & Business Center, Inc. Staff. (Global Business Opportunity Yearbooks Library: Vol. 130). (Illus.). 2000. pap. 99.95 (*0-7397-2228-X*) Intl Business Pubns.

***Pakistan Business Opportunity Yearbook: Export-Import, Investment & Business Opportunities.** International Business Publications, U. S. A. Staff & Global Investment Center, U. S. A. Staff. (Global Business Opportunity Yearbooks Library: Vol. 130). (Illus.). 350p. 1999. pap. 99.95 (*0-7397-1328-0*) Intl Business Pubns.

Pakistan-China Relations. P. L. Bhola. 304p. 1986. 37.50 (*0-8364-1865-4*, Pub. by Manohar) S Asia.

Pakistan Cinema: 1947-1997. Mushtaq Gazdar. LC 97-930889. (The Jubilee Ser.). (Illus.). 368p. 1998. text 75.00 (*0-19-577817-0*) OUP.

***Pakistan Country Review 2000.** Robert C. Kelly et al. (Illus.). 60p. 1999. pap. 39.95 (*1-58310-554-9*) CountryWatch.

Pakistan Development. Date not set. pap. 31.00 (*0-674-65200-2*) HUP.

Pakistan Divided. Safdar Mahmood. 1993. 35.00 (*1-56744-178-5*) Kazi Pubns.

Pakistan, Energy Planning in a Strategic Vortex. Charles K. Ebinger. LC 80-8767. 168p. reprint ed. pap. 52.10 (*0-608-18250-8*, 205669800081) Bks Demand.

***Pakistan Export-Import & Business Directory: Ultimate Directory for Conducting Export-Import Operations in the Country. Largest Exporters & Importers, Strategic Government & Business Contacts, Selected Export-Import Regulations & More.** International Business Publications, USA Staff & Global Investment Center, USA Staff. (World Export-Import & Business Library: 24). (Illus.). 250p. 2000. pap. 99.95 (*0-7397-3381-8*) Intl Business Pubns.

Pakistan, 50 Years of Independence. Ed. by Verinder Grover. (C). 1997. 175.00 (*81-7100-926-3*, Pub. by Deep & Deep Pubns) S Asia.

***Pakistan Foreign Policy & Government Guide.** Contrib. by Global Investment & Business Center, Inc. Staff. (World Foreign Policy & Government Library: Vol. 125). (Illus.). 350p. 1999. pap. 99.00 (*0-7397-3623-X*) Intl Business Pubns.

***Pakistan Foreign Policy & Government Guide.** Global Investment & Business Center, Inc. Staff. (World Foreign Policy & Government Library: Vol. 125). (Illus.). 350p. 2000. 99.95 (*0-7397-3828-3*) Intl Business Pubns.

Pakistan from Jinnah to Sharif. M. K. Akbar. LC 97-904082. vi, 360p. 1997. 45.00 (*81-7099-656-2*, Pub. by Mittal Pubs Dist) Nataraj Bks.

***Pakistan Government & Business Contacts Handbook: Strategic Government & Business Contacts for Conducting Succesful Business, Export-Import & Investment Activity.** International Business Publications, USA Staff & Global Investment Center, USA Staff. (World Export-Import & Business Library: 108). (Illus.). 250p. 2000. pap. 99.95 (*0-7397-6097-1*) Intl Business Pubns.

Pakistan Handbook. David Winter & Ivan Mannheim. (Illus.). 576p. 1996. 21.95 (*0-8442-4903-3*, Passprt Bks) NTC Contemp Pub Co.

***Pakistan in Perspective, 1947-1997.** Ed. by Rafi Raza. LC 97-930910. (The Jubilee Ser.). 354p. 1998. 35.00 (*0-19-577842-1*) OUP.

Pakistan in Pictures. Ed. by Lerner Publications, Department of Geography Staff. (Visual Geography Ser.). (Illus.). 64p. (YA). (gr. 5 up). 1989. lib. bdg. 19.95 (*0-8225-1850-3*, Lerner Publctns) Lerner Pub.

Pakistan in the Bush Years: Foreign Aid & Foreign Influence. Terrence L. Deibel. (Pew Case Studies in International Affairs). 50p. (C). 1994. pap. text 3.50 (*1-56927-365-0*, GU Schl Foreign) Geo U Inst Dplmcy.

Pakistan in the Twentieth Century: A Political History. Lawrence Ziring. (The Jubilee Ser.). 658p. 1998. text 38.00 (*0-19-577816-2*) OUP.

***Pakistan in the Twentieth Century: A Political History.** Lawrence Ziring. 658p. 2000. pap. 19.95 (*0-19-579276-9*) OUP.

***Pakistan Investment & Business Guide.** Global Investment & Business Center, Inc. Staff. (Global Investment & Business Guide Library: Vol. 130). (Illus.). 2000. pap. 99.95 (*0-7397-1828-2*) Intl Business Pubns.

Pakistan Investment & Business Guide: Economy, Export-Import, Business & Investment Climate, Business Contacts. Contrib. by Russian Information & Business Center, Inc. Staff. (Russia, NIS & Emerging Markets Investment & Business Library-98). (Illus.). 350p. 1998. pap. 99.00 (*1-57751-874-8*) Intl Business Pubns.

***Pakistan Investment & Business Guide: Export-Import, Investment & Business Opportunities.** International Business Publications, USA Staff & Global Investment Center, USA Staff. (World Investment & Business Guide Library-99: Vol. 130). (Illus.). 350p. 1999. pap. 99.95 (*0-7397-0325-0*) Intl Business Pubns.

Pakistan, Islam & Economics: Failure of Modernity. Izzud-Din Pal. LC 99-921971. 220p. 1999. text 19.95 (*0-19-579068-5*) OUP.

Pakistan Issue. Jung N. Yar. 1985. 29.95 (*0-318-37273-8*) Asia Bk Corp.

***Pakistan Leadership Challenges Leadership Faced by Pakistan.** Jahan Dad Khan. LC 99-921716. (Illus.). 305p. 1999. text 29.95 (*0-19-577990-8*) OUP.

Pakistan Literature & Society. Fahmida A. Riaz. 1986. 14.00 (*81-7050-021-4*, Pub. by Abhinav) S Asia.

Pakistan, 1997. Craig Baxter & Charles H. Kennedy. LC 97-50622. 200p. 1998. 65.00 (*0-8133-2975-2*, Pub. by Westview) HarpC.

Pakistan or Partition of India. Bhimrao R. Ambedkar. LC 77-179171. (South & Southeast Asia Studies). reprint ed. 41.00 (*0-404-54801-6*) AMS Pr.

Pakistan Papers. Mani S. Aiyar. (C). 1995. pap. 11.00 (*81-7476-007-5*, Pub. by UBS Pubs) S Asia.

Pakistan Party-Politics Pressure Groups & Minorities. Attar Chand. (C). 1991. 25.00 (*81-7169-145-5*, Pub. by Commonwealth) S Asia.

Pakistan Society: Islam, Ethnicity & Leadership in South Asia. Akbar S. Ahmed. 300p. 1987. 25.00 (*0-19-577350-0*) OUP.

Pakistan Society: Islam, Ethnicity & Leadership in South Asia. Ed. by Akbar Ahmed. (Oxford Pakistan Paperbacks Ser.). (Illus.). 272p. 1997. reprint ed. pap. text 23.00 (*0-19-577837-5*) OUP.

Pakistan Society & Politics. Panda U. Nayak. 1985. 22.50 (*0-8364-1348-2*, Pub. by S Asia Pubs) S Asia.

Pakistan Today. M. K. Akbar. 237p. 1998. 26.00 (*81-7099-700-3*, Pub. by Mittal Pubs Dist) Nataraj Bks.

Pakistan Transition to Democracy: Joint Study of Indian & Pakistani Scholars. Ed. by Kalim Bahadur & Uma Singh. (C). 1989. 32.50 (*81-7050-100-8*, Pub. by Patriot Pubs) S Asia.

***Pakistan 2000.** Ed. by Charles H. Kennedy & Craig Baxter. 208p. 2000. 60.00 (*0-7391-0168-4*) Lxngtn Bks.

***Pakistan 2010: Realizing Pakistan's Full Potential.** Asian Development Bank Staff. 1000p. 2000. 30.00 (*971-561-243-1*, Pub. by Asian Devel Bank) Paul & Co Pubs.

Pakistan-U. S. Relations: Social, Political & Economic Factors. Ed. by Noor A. Husain & Leo E. Rose. LC 88-80208. (Research Papers & Policy: No. 22). 322p. (Orig.). 1988. pap. 17.00 (*1-55729-003-2*) IEAS.

Pakistan under Bhutto's Leadership. S. N. Kaushik. 362p. 1985. 39.95 (*0-318-37257-6*) Asia Bk Corp.

***Pakistan Under Musharraf.** Mohan. 2000. 34.00 (*81-7341-138-7*, Pub. by Chanakya) S Asia.

Pakistani Economy: Economic Growth & Structural Reform. Robert E. Looney. LC 96-37731. 216p. 1997. 65.00 (*0-275-94737-8*, Praeger Pubs) Greenwood.

Pakistani Folk Tales: Toon Toony Pie & Other Stories. Ashoaf Siddiqui & Marilyn Lerch. (Library of Folklore). (Illus.). 158p. (J). (gr. 1-2). 1998. 9.95 (*0-7818-0703-4*) Hippocrene Bks.

Pakistani Short Stories. Ed. by Waqas A. Khwaja. (C). 1992. text 15.00 (*81-85674-45-0*, Pub. by UBS Pubs Dist) S Asia.

Pakistani Twins. Denis J. Shaw. (Twins Ser.). (Illus.). (J). (gr. 6-9). 1965. 12.95 (*0-8023-1094-X*) Dufour.

***Pakistani Voter, Electoral Politics & Voting Behaviour in the Punjab.** Andrew Wilder. LC 99-921972. (Illus.). 1999. write for info. (*0-19-579072-3*) OUP.

Pakistani Women: A Socioeconomic & Demographic Profile. Ed. by Nasra M. Shah. xliii, 412p. 1986. 12.00 (*0-86638-053-1*); pap. 9.00 (*0-685-30417-5*) EW Ctr HI.

Pakistanis in Michigan: A Study of Third Culture & Acculturation. Iftikhar H. Malik. LC 88-84006. (Immigrant Communities & Ethnic Minorities in the U. S. & Canada Ser.: No. 59). 1989. 42.50 (*0-404-19469-9*) AMS Pr.

***Pakistan's Criminal Folly in Kashmir: The Drama of Accession & Rescue of Ladakh.** M. L. Chibber. LC 98-901168. (Illus.). 247p. 1998. 30.00 (*81-7049-095-2*, Pub. by Manas Pubns) S Asia.

Pakistan's Democracy at Work. K. K. Bhardwaj. 1998. write for info. (*81-207-2014-8*) Sterling Pubs.

Pakistan's Development Priorities: Choices for the Future. Ed. by Robert LaPorte, Jr. & Shahid J. Burki. (UGC Series in Economics). (Illus.). 1985. pap. 18.95 (*0-19-577333-0*) OUP.

Pakistan's Economic Development. B. N. Bhatia. 282p. 1979. 24.95 (*0-318-37251-7*) Asia Bk Corp.

Pakistan's Economic Development: Freedom to Bondage (1948-1988) B. M. Bhatia. 332p. 1990. text 35.00 (*81-220-0155-6*, Pub. by Konark Pubs Pvt Ltd) Advent Bks Div.

Pakistan's Economy at the Crossroads: Past Policies & Present Imperatives. Parvez Hasan. LC 98-930643. 386p. 1998. 19.95 (*0-19-577939-8*) OUP.

Pakistan's Islamic Bomb. D. K. Patil. 150p. 1979. 14.95 (*0-7069-0911-9*) Asia Bk Corp.

Pakistan's Nuclear Development. Kapur Ashok. 272p. 1987. 49.50 (*0-7099-3101-8*, Pub. by C Helm) Routldge.

Pakistan's Nuclear Policy. Savita Pande. (C). 1991. 14.00 (*81-7018-657-9*, Pub. by BR Pub) S Asia.

Pakistan's Politics: The Zia Years. Mushahid Hussain. (Orig.). 1991. pap. text 20.00 (*81-220-0217-X*, Pub. by Konark Pubs Pvt Ltd) Advent Bks Div.

Pakistan's Public Agricultural Enterprises: Inefficiencies, Market Distortions, & Proposals for Reform. Rashid Faruqee et al. (World Bank Discussion Papers: Vol. 305). 78p. 1995. pap. 22.00 (*0-8213-3459-X*) World Bank.

Pakistan's Quest for Food Security. Asmi Raza. (C). 1993. 18.50 incl. cd-rom (*81-7024-550-8*, Pub. by Ashish Pub Hse) S Asia.

Pakistan's Security under Zia, 1977-1988. Robert G. Wirsing. 230p. 1991. text 49.95 (*0-312-06067-X*) St Martin.

Pakistan's Thrust in the Muslim World: India As a Factor: A Study of RCD. Surendra Chopra. (C). 1992. 20.00 (*81-7100-408-3*, Pub. by Deep & Deep Pubns) S Asia.

Pakistan's Trade with Eastern Bloc Countries. Michael Kidron. LC 77-176397. (Special Studies in International Economics & Development). 1972. 32.50 (*0-89197-875-5*) Irvington.

***Pakistan's Upstream Petroleum Laws & Related Legislation.** Sohaid Qadar. 211p. 2000. pap. 210.00 (*0-89069-012-X*) Barrows Co.

Pakkins' Land: Paul's Adventure. Gary Shipman & Rhoda Shipman. (Illus.). 1997. pap. 9.95 (*0-941613-97-6*, Caliber Comics) Stabur Pr.

Pakkins' Land: Paul's Adventure, One. Gary Shipman. Ed. by Rhoda Shipman. (Pakkins' Land). (Illus.). 160p. (J). 1997. pap. 15.95 (*0-9700241-0-X*) Pakkins.

Paks: Parents-&-Kids Science: 24 Activities for Kids & Adults to Share. Danny L. McKenzie. 64p. (J). (gr. 1-3). 1996. 8.99 (*0-86653-865-8*, FE3865) Fearon Teacher Aids.

***Paktong 1680-1820: The Chinese Alloy in Europe, 1680-1820.** KEITH PINN. 204p. 1999. 89.50 (*1-85149-324-7*) Antique Collect.

Pakua. R. W. Smith. pap. 10.95 (*0-685-22068-0*) Wehman.

Pal: Readings in Criminology. Judson Landis & Thomas Kando. 240p. (C). 1995. 24.95 (*0-7872-1372-1*); student ed. write for info. (*0-7872-1097-8*); pap., per. write for info. (*0-7872-1096-X*) Kendall-Hunt.

Pal Agreement. Dale H. Klooster. (BB - Record Keeping I Ser.: Vol. 1). 1992. 216.95 (*0-538-40227-X*) S-W Pub.

Pal & Sal. R. A. Herman. LC 97-27174. (All Aboard Reading Ser.). (Illus.). 32p. (J). 1998. 3.99 (*0-448-41716-2*, G & D) Peng Put Young Read.

Pal for Martin. Christiane Renauld. (Child's World Library). (Illus.). 32p. (J). (gr. k-5). 1992. lib. bdg. 18.50 (*0-89565-756-2*) Childs World.

Pal for Pat. (Fisher-Price Phonics Storybks. Ser.: Vol. 6). (Illus.). (J). 1998. pap. write for info. (*0-7666-0174-9*, Honey Bear Bks) Modern Pub NYC.

Pal Hall's Hawaiian Horses Donkeys & Mules Coloring Book. Illus. by Pat Hall. 24p. (J). (ps-3). 1996. pap. 3.95 (*0-9633493-4-1*) Pacific Greetings.

Pal Joey: Vocal Score. Ed. by Michael Lefferts. (Vocal Score Ser.). 184p. (Orig.). (C). 1981. per. 45.00 (*0-88188-044-2*, 00312314) H Leonard.

Pal Joey: Vocal Selections. Ed. by Michael Lefferts. (Illus.). 32p. (Orig.). (C). 1981. pap. 8.95 (*0-88188-104-X*, 00312313) H Leonard.

PAL (Preliminary Achievement Level) Book 1: Giving Information & Socializing. Edwin T. Cornelius, Jr. (New Technology English Ser.: Vol. 1). (Illus.). 148p. 1984. text 8.95 (*0-89209-105-3*); pap. text 6.25 (*0-89209-400-1*) Pace Grp Intl.

PAL (Preliminary Achievement Level) Book 1: Giving Information & Socializing, 6 cass., Set. Edwin T. Cornelius, Jr. (New Technology English Ser.: Vol. 1). (Illus.). 148p. 1984. audio 25.00 (*0-89209-107-X*) Pace Grp Intl.

PAL (Preliminary Achievement Level) Book 2: Taking an Active Role in Conversations. Edwin T. Cornelius, Jr. (New Technology English Ser.: Vol. 2). (Illus.). 151p. 1984. text 8.95 (*0-89209-106-1*); pap. text 6.25 (*0-89209-401-X*) Pace Grp Intl.

PAL (Preliminary Achievement Level) Book 2: Taking an Active Role in Conversations, 6 cass., Set. Edwin T. Cornelius, Jr. (New Technology English Ser.: Vol. 2). (Illus.). 151p. 1984. audio 25.00 (*0-89209-108-8*) Pace Grp Intl.

Pal the Pony. A. Herman. LC 95-30265. (All Aboard Reading Ser.: Level 1). (Illus.). 32p. (J). (ps-1). 1996. pap. write for info. (*0-448-41257-8*, G & D) Peng Put Young Read.

Pala d'Oro: Photographs by Nineteenth-Century Travellers. Italo Zannier. (Tesoro di San Marco Ser.). (Illus.). 1996. 55.00 (*88-86502-01-X*, Pub. by Canal & Stamperia) Antique Collect.

Palabas: Essays on Philippine Theater History. Doreen G. Fernandez. LC 96-946102. 274p. 1997. pap. text 30.00 (*971-550-188-5*, Pub. by Ateneo de Manila Univ Pr) UH Pr.

Palabra. Zulu LaSarre. LC 93-199226. (Colecciom Luz Ser.). (SPA., Illus.). 76p. 1991. pap. 12.50 (*0-9634009-0-8*) Luz Bilingual.

Palabra de Dios 1999. Ed. by Miguel Arias. (SPA.). 1998. pap. 7.00 (*1-56854-220-8*, SAHW99) Liturgy Tr Pubns.

***Palabra de Honor.** Marion Dane Bauer. (SPA.). 1998. pap. 8.50 (*84-279-3234-0*) Noguer Edit.

Palabra del Sol. Ed. by Colombian Cultural Concil Staff. (Poesia Ser.: Vol. 3). (SPA.). 75p. 1996. pap. 7.00 (*1-889111-00-7*) Colombian Cultural.

***Palabra, el Mombre, la Sangre.** Joyce Meyer. (SPA.). 1999. pap. 8.99 (*958-9269-66-4*) Spanish Hse Distributors.

Palabra Nueva: Cuentos Chicanos II. Sergio D. Elizondo et al. (SPA.). 135p. (Orig.). (C). 1987. pap. 12.00 (*0-9615403-2-X*) Dos Pasos Ed.

Palabra Nueva: Poesia Chicana. Ed. by Ricardo Aguilar et al. (SPA.). (Orig.). pap. text 9.00 (*0-9615403-0-3*) Dos Pasos Ed.

Palabra por Palabra: Spanish Vocabulary Organizer. Daniel Aaron. (Efficient Language Ser.). (SPA., Illus.). 68p. (Orig.). 1994. pap. 39.95 incl. disk (*1-884677-01-0*) Salix.

Palabra Santa para el Avivamiento Matutino: Colosenses. Witness Lee.Tr. of The/Holy Word for Morning Revival:Colossians. (SPA.). 71p. 1991. pap. 4.75 (*0-87083-574-2*, 13-029-002) Living Stream Ministry.

Palabra Santa para el Avivamiento Matutino: Cronicas, Esdras, Nehemias, Esther. Witness Lee.Tr. of Holy Word For Morning Revival: Chronicles, Ezra, Nehemiah, Esther. (SPA.). 43p. 2001. pap. 4.25 (*0-87083-850-4*, 13-051-002) Living Stream Ministry.

Palabra Santa para el Avivamiento Matutino: Daniel y Zacarias. Witness Lee.Tr. of The/Holy Word for Morning Revival: Daniel & Zechariah. (SPA.). 87p. 1991. pap. 5.25 (*0-87083-611-0*, 13-030-002) Living Stream Ministry.

Palabra Santa para el Avivamiento Matutino: Efesios, 2 vols. Witness Lee.Tr. of The/Holy Word for Morning Revival:Ephesians. (SPA.). 173p. 1990. pap. 10.50 (*0-87083-557-2*, 13024002) Living Stream Ministry.

Palabra Santa para el Avivamiento Matutino: Filipenses. Witness Lee.Tr. of The/Holy Word for Morning Revival: Philippians. (SPA.). 85p. 1991. pap. 5.25 (*0-87083-569-6*, 13-028-002) Living Stream Ministry.

Palabra Santa para el Avivamiento Matutino: Galatas. Witness Lee.Tr. of The/Holy Word for Morning Revival: Galatians. (SPA.). 99p. 1990. pap. 5.50 (*0-87083-540-8*, 13-023-002) Living Stream Ministry.

Palabra Santa para el Avivamiento Matutino: Hebreos, 4. Witness Lee.Tr. of The/Holy Word for Morning Revival: Hebrews. (SPA.). 287p. 1993. pap. 14.25 (*0-87083-675-7*, 13037002) Living Stream Ministry.

P

Palabra Santa para el Avivamiento Matutino: Isaias. Witness Lee.Tr. of The/Holy Word for Morning Revival: Isaiah. (SPA.). 71p. 1991. pap. 4.25 (*0-87083-566-1*, 13-026-002) Living Stream Ministry.

Palabra Santa para el Avivamiento Matutino: Jacobo. Witness Lee.Tr. of The/Holy Word for Morning Revival: James. (SPA.). 74p. 1993. pap. 4.75 (*0-87083-744-3*, 13-045-002) Living Stream Ministry.

Palabra Santa para el Avivamiento Matutino: Jeremias y Lamentaciones. Witness Lee.Tr. of The/Holy Word for Morning Revival: Jeremiah & Lamentations. (SPA.). 71p. 1992. pap. 4.75 (*0-87083-638-2*, 13-033-002) Living Stream Ministry.

Palabra Santa para el Avivamiento Matutino: Job. Witness Lee.Tr. of The/Holy Word for Morning Revival: Job. (SPA.). 57p. 1993. pap. 4.75 (*0-87083-696-X*, 13-041-002) Living Stream Ministry.

Palabra Santa para el Avivamiento Matutino: Josue, Jueces y Ruth. Witness Lee.Tr. of The/Holy Word for Morning Revival: Joshua, Judges, & Ruth. (SPA.). 75p. 1993. pap. 5.00 (*0-87083-731-1*, 13-042-002) Living Stream Ministry.

Palabra Santa para el Avivamiento Matutino: Profetas Menores. Witness Lee.Tr. of The/Holy Word for Morning Revival: Minor Prophets. (SPA.). 71p. 1992. pap. 4.75 (*0-87083-665-X*, 13-036-002) Living Stream Ministry.

Palabra Santa Para El Avivamiento Matutino: Proverbios, Eclesiastes, Cantar De Los Cantares. Witness Lee.Tr. of The/Holy Word for Morning Revival: Proverbs, Ecclesiastes, Song of Songs. (SPA.). 61p. 1995. pap. 4.25 (*0-87083-903-9*, 13-053-002) Living Stream Ministry.

Palabra Santa para el Avivamiento Matutino: Romamos, 3 vols. Witness Lee.Tr. of The/Holy Word for Morning Revival: Romans 1:1--5:11. (SPA.). 217p. 1990. pap. 14.25 (*0-87083-484-3*, 13006002) Living Stream Ministry.

Palabra Santa para el Avivamiento Matutino: Tesalonicenses. Witness Lee.Tr. of The/Holy Word for Morning Revival: Thessalonians. (SPA.). 87p. 1991. pap. 5.25 (*0-87083-615-3*, 13-031-002) Living Stream Ministry.

Palabra Santa para el Avivamiento Matutino: Tito y Filemon. Witness Lee.Tr. of The/Holy Word for Morning Revival: Titus & Philemon. (SPA.). 57p. 1992. pap. 4.25 (*0-87083-645-5*, 13-035-002) Living Stream Ministry.

Palabra Santa para el Avivamiento Matutino: 1 Corintios, 3 vols. Witness Lee.Tr. of Holy Word for Morning Revival: 1 Corinthians. (SPA.). 219p. 1990. pap. 14.25 (*0-87083-505-X*, 13020002) Living Stream Ministry.

Palabra Santa para el Avivamiento Matutino: 1 Juan, 2. Witness Lee.Tr. of The/Holy Word for Morning Revival:1 John. (SPA.). 117p. 1995. pap. 8.50 (*0-87083-867-9*, 13049002) Living Stream Ministry.

Palabra Santa para el Avivamiento Matutino: 1 Pedro, 2. Witness Lee.Tr. of The/Holy Word for Morning Revival:1 Peter. (SPA.). 115p. 1994. pap. 8.50 (*0-87083-800-8*, 13047002) Living Stream Ministry.

Palabra Santa para el Avivamiento Matutino: 1 Timoteo. Witness Lee.Tr. of The/Holy Word for Morning Revival: 1 Timothy. (SPA.). 76p. 1991. pap. 4.75 (*0-87083-630-7*, 13-032-002) Living Stream Ministry.

Palabra Santa para el Avivamiento Matutino: 1 y 2 Reyes. Witness Lee.Tr. of The/Holy Word for Morning Revival: 1 & 2 Kings. (SPA.). 71p. 1994. pap. 4.75 (*0-87083-789-3*, 13-048-002) Living Stream Ministry.

Palabra Santa para el Avivamiento Matutino: 1 y 2 Samuel. Witness Lee.Tr. of The/Holy Word for Morning Revival: 1 & 2 Samuel. (SPA.). 71p. 1994. pap. 4.75 (*0-87083-747-8*, 13-044-002) Living Stream Ministry.

Palabra Santa para el Avivamiento Matutino: 2 Corintios, 2. Witness Lee.Tr. of The/Holy Word for Morning Revival: 2 Corinthians. (SPA.). 143p. 1990. pap. 9.50 (*0-87083-534-3*, 13021002) Living Stream Ministry.

Palabra Santa para el Avivamiento Matutino: 2 Juan, 3 Juan, Judas. Witness Lee.Tr. of The/Holy Word for Morning Revival: 2 John, 3 John, Jude. (SPA.). 47p. 1995. pap. 4.25 (*0-87083-906-3*, 13-054-002) Living Stream Ministry.

Palabra Santa para el Avivamiento Matutino: 2 Pedro, Vol. 2. Witness Lee.Tr. of HOLY WORD FOR MORNING REVIVAL, THE: 2 PETER. (SPA.). 60p. 1994. pap. 4.50 (*0-87083-821-0*, 13-050-002) Living Stream Ministry.

Palabra Santa para el Avivamiento Matutino: 2 Timoteo. Witness Lee.Tr. of The/Holy Word for Morning Revival: 2 Timothy. (SPA.). 57p. 1992. pap. 4.25 (*0-87083-640-4*, 13-034-002) Living Stream Ministry.

Palabra Santa Para El Avivamiento Matutino Cuerpo De Cristo: Constitucion Y La Edificacion Del Cuerpo De Cristo... Witness Lee.Tr. of The/Holy Word for Morning Revival: Constitution & Building up of the Body of Christ . . .. (SPA.). 79p. 1992. pap. 5.00 (*0-87083-694-3*, 13-043-002) Living Stream Ministry.

Palabra Total. Mercedes Tomas. (SPA.). 1994. pap. 9.95 (*0-89729-757-1*) Ediciones.

***Palabras.** Alma Flor Ada. (SPA., Illus.). 1999. pap. text 4.95 (*1-58105-404-1*) Santillana.

Palabras. Kenneth E. Hagin.Tr. of Words. (SPA.). 1983. pap. 1.00 (*0-89276-157-1*) Faith Lib Pubns.

Palabras de Aliento. (Serie Palabras de... - Words of...Ser.).Tr. of Words of Encouragement. (SPA.). 46p. 1986. pap. 1.99 (*0-8423-6291-6*, 497511) Editorial Unilit.

Palabras de Amistad. (Palabras de...Ser.).Tr. of Words of Friendship. (SPA.). 1986. 1.99 (*0-8423-6292-4*, 497512); pap. write for info. (*0-614-27093-6*) Editorial Unilit.

Palabras de Amor. (Serie Palabras de... - Words of...Ser.).Tr. of Words of Love. (SPA.). 48p. 1985. pap. 1.99 (*0-8423-6191-X*, 497500) Editorial Unilit.

Palabras de Consuelo. (Palabras de...Ser.).Tr. of Words of Comfort. (SPA.). 1986. 1.99 (*0-8423-6293-2*, 497513); pap. write for info. (*0-614-27092-8*) Editorial Unilit.

Palabras de Dios Confirmada. Jose Zapico.Tr. of Word of God Confirmed. (SPA.). 159p. 6.99 (*1-56063-456-1*, 550126) Editorial Unilit.

Palabras de Esperanza. (Palabras de...Ser.).Tr. of Words of Hope. (SPA.). 1985. 1.99 (*0-318-72878-8*, 497507); pap. write for info. (*0-8423-6285-1*) Editorial Unilit.

Palabras de Fe. (Serie Palabras de... - Words of...Ser.).Tr. of Words of Faith. (SPA.). 43p. 1985. pap. 1.99 (*0-8423-6189-8*, 497502) Editorial Unilit.

Palabras de Gozo. (Palabras de...Ser.).Tr. of Words of Joy. (SPA.). 1985. 1.99 (*0-318-72879-6*, 497504); pap. write for info. (*0-614-27094-4*) Editorial Unilit.

Palabras de Gratitud. (Serie Palabras de... - Words of...Ser.).Tr. of Words of Thanks. (SPA.). 43p. 1983. pap. 1.99 (*0-8423-6294-0*, 497514) Editorial Unilit.

Palabras de los Padres y Su Asombroso Poder. Norman Wright.Tr. of Power of a Parent's Words. (SPA.). 222p. 1991. pap. 7.99 (*1-56063-705-6*, 498432) Editorial Unilit.

Palabras de Paciencia. (Palabras de...Ser.).Tr. of Words of Patience. (SPA.). 1986. 1.99 (*0-8423-6296-7*, 497516); pap. write for info. (*0-614-27095-2*) Editorial Unilit.

Palabras de Paz. (Serie Palabras de... - Words of...Ser.).Tr. of Words of Peace. (SPA.). 48p. 1985. pap. 1.99 (*0-8423-6286-X*, 497508) Editorial Unilit.

Palabras de Piedra (Words of Stone) Kevin Henkes. (SPA.). (J). (gr. 5). 1996. pap. text 8.95 (*84-241-5948-9*) Lectorum Pubns.

Palabras de Promesa. (Serie Palabras de... - Words of...Ser.).Tr. of Words of Promise. (SPA.). 48p. 1985. pap. 1.99 (*0-8423-6190-1*, 497506) Editorial Unilit.

Palabras de Renovacion. (Serie Palabras de... - Words of...Ser.).Tr. of Words of Renewal. (SPA.). 48p. 1988. pap. 1.99 (*0-8423-6295-9*, 497515) Editorial Unilit.

Palabras de Siqueiros (Words of Siqueiros) Compiled by Raquel Tibol. (SPA.). 537p. 1996. pap. 29.99 (*968-16-4922-2*, Pub. by Fondo) Continental Bk.

***Palabras de Vida de Dios.** Vida Publishers Staff. (SPA.). 1999. 9.97 (*0-8297-2301-3*) Vida Pubs.

Palabras Del Desierto. Elizabeth A. Hellier. (SPA., Illus.). iv, 52p. 1998. spiral bd. 7.00 (*0-9654727-4-4*, 26) Izzybo Prods.

Palabras en el Tiempo. Francisco L. Mora. (Aqui y Ahora Ser.). 103p. 1997. pap. 6.95 (*0-8477-0290-1*) U of PR Pr.

Palabras en la Arena. Gaston Baquero. Ed. by Rosario Hiriart. (SPA.). 102p. (Orig.). 1997. pap. 15.00 (*1-887175-03-2*) ECV NY.

Palabras Griegas Del Nuevo Testamento: New Testament Words. William Barclay. Tr. by Javier-Jose Marin. 220p. 1976. reprint ed. pap. 10.50 (*0-311-42052-4*) Casa Bautista.

Palabras Mas Que Comunes: Ensayos Sobre el Teatro de Jose Triana. Kirsten F. Nigro. LC 93-85373. (SPA.). 112p. 1994. pap. 32.00 (*0-89295-073-0*) Society Sp & Sp-Am.

Palabras Mayas: Sq'anej Maya' Gaspar P. Gonzalez. (MYN & SPA.). 93p. 1998. pap. 12.95 (*1-886502-19-6*) Yax Te Found.

Palabras Que Se Ganan a los Ninos. 2nd ed. Ruth Bowdoin. (Bowdoin Method I Ser.). Orig. Title: Words That Win Children. (SPA., Illus.). 36p. 1991. reprint ed. pap. write for info. (*1-55997-063-4*) Websters Intl.

Palabras Sabias para los Ninos (Wise Words for Little People) K. Taylor. (SPA.). 9.99 (*0-685-74971-1*, 490363) Editorial Unilit.

Palabras Son Palabras. Maria Vaquero. (SPA.). 632p. 1997. pap. text 15.95 (*1-56328-121-X*) Edit Plaza Mayor.

Palabras (Words) Noemi Escandell. Tr. by Joan Dargan. (ENG & SPA.). 108p. (Orig.). 1986. pap. 8.00 (*0-917129-03-2*) SLUSA.

Palabras y Cantos de Jesus. Christopher C. Walker et al. (Illus.). 64p. (J). (ps-6). 1996. 15.95 (*0-915531-47-X*) OR Catholic.

Palabras y Cantos de Jesus Activity/Coloring Book. Christopher Walker & Paule Freeburg. Tr. by Mariano Fuertes. (Illus.). 25p. (J). 1996. pap. 1.50 (*0-915531-49-6*) OR Catholic.

***Palace.** Lisa St. Aubin DeTeran. 2000. pap. 13.00 (*0-06-095653-4*, Ecco Press) HarperTrade.

Palace. Wieslaw Mysliwski. Tr. by Ursula Phillips from POL. 208p. 1991. 32.00 (*0-7206-0790-6*, Pub. by P Owen Ltd) Dufour.

Palace. Lisa St. Aubin de Teran. LC 98-30251. 272p. 1990. 23.95 (*0-88001-662-0*) HarpC.

Palace: A Personal History of the Brisbane Dental Hospital, 1941-1991. Colin Wilson. LC 92-191869. xvi, 236p. 1992. write for info. (*0-86776-448-1*) U of Queensland.

Palace & Gardens of Fronteira: 17th & 18th Century Portuguese Style. J. Cassiano Neves & Nicolas Safieha. (Garden Ser.). (POR., Illus.). 142p. 1996. 50.00 (*0-935748-98-9*) M T Train.

Palace & Gardens of Queluz. Ines Ferro. (Illus.). 96p. 1998. 30.00 (*1-85759-174-7*) Scala Books.

Palace & Politics in Prewar Japan. David A. Titus. LC 74-6109. (Columbia University East Asian Institute Occasional Papers). 372p. reprint ed. pap. 115.40 (*0-608-30414-X*, 201539100093) Bks Demand.

Palace Architecture see **Ancient Chinese Architecture**

Palace Beautiful. Albert E. Sims. 1993. pap. 2.50 (*0-87813-956-7*) Christian Light.

Palace Beautiful & Other Poems. Robert H. Newell. (Notable American Authors Ser.). 1999. reprint ed. lib. bdg. 125.00 (*0-7812-4630-X*) Rprt Serv.

Palace City Prince. Arlene James. (Romance Ser.: No. 866). 1992. per. 2.69 (*0-373-08866-3*, 5-08866-1) Silhouette.

Palace Corbie, No. 5. Ed. by Wayne Edwards. 232p. 1994. pap. 10.95 (*1-888283-02-5*) Merrimack Bks.

Palace Corbie, No. 6. Ed. by Wayne Edwards. 224p. 1995. pap. 9.95 (*1-888283-03-3*) Merrimack Bks.

Palace Corbie, Vol. 8. Ed. by Wayne Edwards. 285p. 1999. pap. 15.95 (*1-888283-08-4*) Merrimack Bks.

Palace Corbie Seven: The Piano Player Has No Fingers. Ed. by John Marshall & Wayne Edwards. 330p. 1996. pap. 12.95 (*1-888283-06-8*) Merrimack Bks.

Palace for the Antichrist. Joseph Chambers. LC 96-69688. 296p. 1996. pap. 11.95 (*0-89221-333-7*) New Leaf.

Palace Gates: Parables for the Days of Awe. Ed. by Shalom M. Wallach. LC 94-33005. Orig. Title: Shaare Armon. 1994. 18.95 (*0-87306-694-4*) Feldheim.

Palace Gates: Under Seige in Hue City: TET January 1968. Richard L. Brown. LC 95-67279. (Illus.). 240p. 1995. 24.95 (*0-88740-745-5*) Schiffer.

Palace Gates Haggadah. Tr. by Avraham Sutton. 1995. pap. 10.95 (*0-87306-703-7*) Feldheim.

Palace Guard. Charlotte MacLeod. 176p. 1982. mass mkt. 3.99 (*0-380-59857-4*, Avon Bks) Morrow Avon.

Palace Home Inspections, Inc. Vol. 1: Home Inspection Reporting System. large type ed. Palace Home Inspections, Inc. Staff. (Illus.). i, 45p. 1997. spiral bd. 29.95 (*0-9661124-0-7*, 001) Palace Home.

Palace of Cards. Peter Thomson. (Illus.). 32p. (J). (gr. 1-3). 1995. 19.95 (*0-370-31863-3*, Pub. by Bodley Head) Trafalgar.

Palace of Charles V in Granada. Earl E. Rosenthal. LC 85-3366. (Illus.). 401p. 1985. reprint ed. pap. 124.40 (*0-608-07164-1*, 206738900009) Bks Demand.

Palace of Desire. Naguib Mahfouz. (Cairo Trilogy Ser.: 2). 432p. 1991. pap. 12.95 (*0-385-26468-2*, Anchor NY) Doubleday.

Palace of Desire. Naguib Mahfouz. 432p. 1992. pap. 8.95 (*0-385-40208-2*) Doubleday.

Palace of Dreams. Ismail Kadare. Tr. by Jusuf Vrioni & Barbara Bray. LC 97-29724. 208p. 1998. pap. 12.45 (*1-55970-416-0*, Pub. by Arcade Pub Inc) Time Warner.

Palace of Earth. Sonya Dorman. Ed. by Constance Hunting. 60p. 1984. pap. 5.95 (*0-913006-31-9*) Puckerbrush.

Palace of Justice: A Colombian Tragedy. Ana Carrigan. LC 93-8704. (Illus.). 303p. 1993. 22.95 (*0-941423-82-4*) FWEW.

Palace of King Soul. Yaphet Kotto & Paramahansa Yogananda. (Illus.). 35p. (J). (ps-6). Date not set. 9.95 (*0-9655950-0-5*) Cauldwell-Bissell.

Palace of Nestor at Pylos in Western Messenia: Acropolis & Lower Town; Tholoi, Grave Circle, & Chamber Tombs; Discoveries Outside the Citadel, Vol. III. Ed. by Carl W. Blegen et al. LC 65-17131. (Illus.). 364p. reprint ed. pap. 112.90 (*0-608-11403-0*, 201303200083) Bks Demand.

Palace of Pleasure, 4 vols. William M. Painter. Ed. by Hamish Miles. LC 30-20341. reprint ed. 240.00 (*0-404-04880-3*) AMS Pr.

Palace of Pleasure, 3 vols. 4th ed. Notes by Marvin Spevak. cvii, 1224p. 1968. reprint ed. write for info. (*0-318-71604-6*) G Olms Pubs.

Palace of Pleasure: Elizabethan Versions of Italian & French Novels from Boccaccio, Bandello, Cinthio, Straparola, Queen Margaret of Navarre & Others, 3 vols., Set. 4th ed. Contrib. by Marvin Spevak. (Anglistica & Americana Ser.: No. 3). 1968. reprint ed. 219.70 (*0-685-66499-6*, 05101931) G Olms Pubs.

Palace of Secrets: Beroalde de Verville & Renaissance Conception of Knowledge. Neil Kenny. (Illus.). 318p. 1991. text 80.00 (*0-19-815862-9*) OUP.

Palace of Stars. Patricia Lakin. LC 92-36796. (Illus.). 32p. (J). (ps up). 1993. 14.00 (*0-688-11176-9*, Wm Morrow) Morrow Avon.

***Palace of Tears: A Reverie.** Alev Lytle Croutier. LC 00-27921. 2000. write for info. (*0-385-33488-5*) Davies Grp.

***Palace of the Peacock.** Wilson Harris. 1998. pap. 13.95 (*0-571-19323-4*) Faber & Faber.

Palace of the Silver Princess. Jean Wells. 1981. 5.50 (*0-394-51837-3*) Random.

Palace of the Sun: The Louvre of Louis the Fourteenth. Robert W. Berger. (Illus.). 336p. (C). 1993. 75.00 (*0-271-00847-4*) Pa St U Pr.

Palace of the White Skunks. Reinaldo Arenas. Tr. by Andrew Hurley. 368p. 1993. pap. 12.50 (*0-14-009792-9*, Penguin Bks) Viking Penguin.

Palace of Time: The Proof of God & Immortality. K. R. Macdonald. (Illus.). 106p. 1999. pap. 15.00 (*0-9670022-0-6*) Rain Bks.

Palace of Versailles. James Barter. LC 98-15262. (Building History Ser.). (YA). (gr. 7 up). 1998. 23.70 (*1-56006-433-1*) Lucent Bks.

Palace of Wasted Footsteps: Stories. Cary C. Holladay. LC 98-22318. 224p. 1998. pap. 17.95 (*0-8262-1186-0*) U of Mo Pr.

Palace of Water. James Magorian. LC 90-81003. (Illus.). 16p. (J). (gr. 2-5). 1990. pap. 3.00 (*0-930674-33-2*) Black Oak.

Palace School of Muhammad the Conqueror. Barnett Miller. LC 73-6291. (Middle East Ser.). 1973. reprint ed. 20.95 (*0-405-05349-5*) Ayer.

***Palace Sculptures of Abomey: History Told on Walls.** Francesca Pique et al. LC 99-31042. (Conservation & Cultural Heritage Ser.). (Illus.). 120p. 1999. pap. 24.95 (*0-89236-569-2*, Pub. by J P Getty Trust) OUP.

Palace Thief. large type ed. Ethan Canin. 261p. 1994. lib. bdg. 22.95 (*0-8161-7468-7*, G K Hall Lrg Type) Mac Lib Ref.

Palace Thief: Stories. Ethan Canin. LC 94-45087. 1994. pap. 11.00 (*0-312-11930-5*) St Martin.

Palace Walk. Naguib Mahfouz. (Cairo Trilogy Ser.: 1). 512p. 1990. pap. 14.00 (*0-385-26466-6*, Anchor NY) Doubleday.

Palace Walk U. K. 512p. 1990. pap. 7.99 (*0-385-40092-6*, Anchor NY) Doubleday.

***Palaces.** Laura Brooks. 1999. 10.95 (*1-57717-146-2*) Todtri Prods.

Palaces. David Ross. LC 98-20535. (Great Architecture Ser.). (Illus.). 120p. 1998. 16.98 (*1-56799-472-5*, MetroBooks) M Friedman Pub Grp Inc.

Palaces & Forts of the Hawaiian Kingdom: From Thatch to American Florentine. Walter F. Judd. LC 73-91595. (Illus.). 176p. 1975. 17.95 (*0-87015-216-5*) Pacific Bks.

Palaces & Large Residences of the Hellenistic Age. Bonnie L. Kutbay. LC 98-40471. (Studies in Classics: Vol. 8). xi, 193p. 1998. text 89.95 (*0-7734-8244-X*) E Mellen.

Palaces of Bangkok: Royal Residences of the Chakri Dynasty. Naengnoi Suksri. (Illus.). 368p. 1997. 80.00 (*974-8225-01-1*, Pub. by River Books) Weatherhill.

Palaces of Crete. rev. ed. James W. Graham. LC 85-43376. (Illus.). 349p. 1987. reprint ed. pap. 108.20 (*0-7837-8170-9*, 204787500008) Bks Demand.

***Palaces of Florence.** Patrizia Fabbri. (Illus.). 2000. pap. text 9.95 (*88-7743-214-4*) Arsenale Editrice.

Palaces of Florence. Francesco Gurrieri & Patrizia Fabbri. LC 96-18491. (Illus.). 312p. 1996. 85.00 (*0-8478-1965-5*, Pub. by Rizzoli Intl) St Martin.

***Palaces of Goa: Models & Types of Indo-Portuguese Architecture.** Helder Carita. 224p. 1999. 60.00 (*1-900826-10-0*, Pub. by M T Train) Antique Collect.

Palaces of Leningrad. Victor Kennett. (C). 1990. 210.00 (*0-7855-4486-0*, Pub. by Collets) St Mut.

Palaces of Minoan Crete. Gerald Cadogan. (Illus.). 168p. 1980. pap. 12.95 (*0-416-73160-0*, 2878) Routledge.

Palaces of Prague. Jiri Pesek & Zdenek Hojda. LC 94-24176. (Illus.). 216p. 1995. text 65.00 (*0-86565-958-3*) Vendome.

Palaces of Rome. Claudio Rendina & Massimo Listor. (Art & Architecture Ser.). (Illus.). 400p. 1999. 39.95 (*3-8290-1348-5*, 520774) Konemann.

Palaces of Rome. Caroline Vincenti. (Illus.). 312p. 1997. text 95.00 (*0-8478-2056-4*) St Martin.

Palaces of Seoul. Edward B. Adams. 1979. pap. 4.50 (*0-89860-027-8*) Eastview.

Palaces of Sicily. Gioachino L. Tomasi & Angheli Zalapi. (Illus.). 312p. 2000. 95.00 (*0-8478-2126-9*, Pub. by Rizzoli Intl) St Martin.

Palaces of the Gods: Khmer Art & Architecture in Thailand. Smitthi Siribhadra & Elizabeth Moore. (Illus.). 352p. 1998. 80.00 (*1-872727-15-8*) Weatherhill.

Palaces That Went to Sea. John T. Gibbons. (Illus.). 252p. 1989. write for info. (*0-318-66582-4*) Nereus Pub.

Palaces under the Sea: A Guide to Understanding the Coral Reef Environment. Joe Strykowski & Rena M. Bonem. LC 92-62290. (Illus.). 280p. 1993. 24.95 (*1-882533-00-3*) Star Thrower.

Palacio de los Gritos. Jose Corrales. (SPA.). 34p. 1993. pap. text 2.95 (*1-885901-00-3*) Presbyters Peartree.

Palacios de Espana. J. A. Sanchez Trigueros. (SPA., Illus.). 360p. 1993. 295.00 (*84-239-5296-7*) Elliots Bks.

Palacios de Roma. (Arte & Arquitectura Ser.). (Illus.). 400p. 1999. 39.95 (*3-8290-1710-3*, 540774) Konemann.

Paladin. C. J. Cherryh. 400p. (Orig.). 1988. mass mkt. 4.99 (*0-671-65417-9*) Baen Bks.

***Paladin.** Peter S. Sadler. 272p. 2000. 39.95 (*0-19-551304-5*) OUP.

Paladin in Hell. Monte Cook. 1998. 0.13 (*0-7869-1210-3*, Pub. by TSR Inc) Random.

Paladin Zero Six: A Desert Storm Memoir by a 101st Airborne Attack Helicopter Company Commander. Rafael J. Garcia, Jr. LC 94-11435. (Illus.). 176p. 1994. pap. 25.00 (*0-89950-979-7*) McFarland & Co.

Paladino. Arturo Schwartz. 1996. pap. 55.00 (*88-8158-058-6*, Pub. by Charta) Dist Art Pubs.

Paladins. James M. Ward & David Wise. (Double Diamond Triangle Saga Ser.). 1998. pap. 2.99 (*0-7869-0865-3*, Pub. by TSR Inc) Random.

Paladins: A Novel. Timothy J. Stoner. 352p. 1998. pap. 12.95 (*1-58169-002-9*, TS101, Third Stry Window) Genesis Comm Inc.

Paladins: Comedie Lyrique, Vol. 44. Jean-Phillipe Rameau. Ed. by R. Peter Wolf. LC 85-753846. (French Opera in the 17th & 18th Centuries Ser.: No. 3). (Illus.). 402p. 1987. lib. bdg. 94.00 (*0-918728-63-0*) Pendragon NY.

Paladin's Woman. Beverly Barton. (Intimate Moments Ser.). 1993. mass mkt. 3.50 (*0-373-07515-4*, 5-07515-5) Silhouette.

Palaeohistoria, Vol. 29. 269p. 1989. 162.00 (*90-6191-882-0*, Pub. by A A Balkema) Ashgate Pub Co.

Palaeohistoria, Vol. 31. 306p. 1991. 135.00 (*90-5410-111-3*, Pub. by A A Balkema) Ashgate Pub Co.

Palaeoecology of Africa, 1975-77, Vol. 11. E. M. Van Zinderen Bakker & J. A. Coetzee. 245p. (C). 1979. text 90.00 (*90-6191-037-4*, Pub. by A A Balkema) Ashgate Pub Co.

Palaeoanthropology & Palaeolithic Archaeology in the People's Republic of China. Ed. by John W. Olsen & Wu Rukang. 1985. text 55.00 (*0-12-601720-4*) Acad Pr.

Palaeobiogeography of China. Ed. by Yi Quiz Apogee Training & Development Staff. (Biogeography Ser.: No. 8). (Illus.). 384p. 1994. text 125.00 (*0-19-854671-8*) OUP.

Palaeobiology: A Synthesis. Ed. by Derek E. Briggs & Peter R. Crowther. (Illus.). 608p. 1992. pap. 85.00 (*0-632-03311-8*) Blackwell Sci.

Palaeobiology of Conodonts. Richard J. Aldridge. LC 86-211414. (British Micropalaeontological Society Ser.). 264p. 1987. text 74.95 (*0-470-20788-4*) P-H.

Palaeobiology of Trace Fossils. Donovan. 1994. text 177.00 (*0-471-94843-8*) Wiley.

Palaeobiology of Trace Fossils. Ed. by Stephen K. Donovan. LC 93-43120. 320p. (C). 1994. 49.00 (*0-8018-4851-2*) Johns Hopkins.

***Palaeobiology II.** D. E. G. Briggs & Peter R. Crowther. LC 00-31211. 2001. write for info. (*0-632-05147-7*) Blackwell Sci.

An Asterisk (*) at the beginning of an entry indicates that the title is appearing for the first time.

Palaeobotanical-Palaeoecological Studies of Tropical High Andean Peatbog Sections (Cordillera Oriental, Colombia) Peter Kuhry. (Dissertationes Botanicae Ser.: Band 116). (Illus.). 241p. 1988. pap. 83.00 (*3-443-64028-1*, Pub. by Gebruder Borntraeger) Balogh.

Palaeoclimatic Research. A. Ghazi. 1983. text 126.50 (*90-277-1676-5*) Kluwer Academic.

Palaeoclimatology & Palaeoceanography from Laminated Sediments. Ed. by A. E. Kemp. (Geological Society Special Publication Ser.: No. 116). (Illus.). 272p. 1996. 108.00 (*1-897799-67-5*, 345, Pub. by Geol Soc Pub Hse) AAPG.

Palaeodiet in the Aegean. Ed. by Sarah J. Vaughan & William D. Coulson. (Wiener Laboratory Monographs: Vol. I). (Illus.). 121p. 1999. pap. 54.00 (*1-900188-53-8*, Pub. by Oxbow Bks) David Brown.

Palaeoecological Events During the Last 15,000 Years: Regional Synthesis of Palaeoecological Studies in Lakes & Mires in Europe. Bjorn E. Berglund et al. 784p. 1996. 300.00 (*0-471-95840-9*, VS00) Wiley.

Palaeoecology of Africa, Vol. 13. E. M. Van Zinderen Bakker & J. A. Coetzee. 290p. (C). 1981. text 90.00 (*90-6191-203-2*, Pub. by A A Balkema) Ashgate Pub Co.

Palaeoecology of Africa, Vol. 14. E. M. Van Zinderen Bakker & J. A. Coetzee. 186p. (C). 1982. text 90.00 (*90-6191-204-0*, Pub. by A A Balkema) Ashgate Pub Co.

Palaeoecology of Africa, Vol. 16. E. M. Van Zinderen Bakker & J. A. Coetzee. 488p. (C). 1984. text 90.00 (*90-6191-510-4*, Pub. by A A Balkema) Ashgate Pub Co.

Palaeoecology of Africa, Vol. 18. Ed. by K. Heine. 486p. (C). 1987. text 90.00 (*90-6191-689-5*, Pub. by A A Balkema) Ashgate Pub Co.

Palaeoecology of Africa, Vol. 20. Ed. by K. Heine. (Illus.). 215p. (C). 1990. text 90.00 (*90-6191-880-4*, Pub. by A A Balkema) Ashgate Pub Co.

Palaeoecology of Africa, Vol. 24. Heine. 243p. 1997. 90.00 (*90-5410-660-3*) Ashgate Pub Co.

Palaeoecology of Africa, Vol. 24. Ed. by K. Heine. (Illus.). 220p. (C). 1997. text 85.00 (*90-5410-662-X*, Pub. by A A Balkema) Ashgate Pub Co.

***Palaeoecology of Africa, Vol. 26.** Ed. by Klaus Heine. (Illus.). 274p. 1999. 90.00 (*90-5410-476-7*, Pub. by A A Balkema) Ashgate Pub Co.

Palaeoecology of Africa, Vol.6. E. M. Van Zinderen Bakker. 312p. 1972. 90.00 (*0-86961-034-1*) Ashgate Pub Co.

Palaeoecology of Africa, Vol.7. E. M. Van Zinderen Bakker. 222p. 1972. 90.00 (*0-86961-035-X*) Ashgate Pub Co.

Palaeoecology of Africa, Vol.9. E. M. Van Zinderen Bakker. 231p. 1976. 90.00 (*0-86961-082-1*) Ashgate Pub Co.

Palaeoecology of Africa: African Society for Quaternary Research, Proceedings of the 7th Biennial Conference Held at the University of Stellenbosch, 29 March - 3 April 1985, Vol. 17. E. M. Van Zinderen Bakker & J. A. Coetzee. 272p. (C). 1986. text 90.00 (*90-6191-625-9*, Pub. by A A Balkema) Ashgate Pub Co.

Palaeoecology of Africa: Proceedings of the Scientific Committee on Antarctic Research Conference on Quaternary Studies, Canberra 9-12 August 1972, Vol.8. Ed. by E. M. Van Zinderen Bakker & J. A. Coetzee. 208p. 1973. 90.00 (*0-86961-032-5*) Ashgate Pub Co.

Palaeoecology of Africa: Sahara & Surrounding Seas: Sediments & Climatic Changes (Proceedings of an International Symposium, Mainz, 1-4 April 1979), Vol. 12. Ed. by Michael Sarnthein et al. 416p. (C). 1980. text 90.00 (*90-6191-050-1*, Pub. by A A Balkema) Ashgate Pub Co.

Palaeoecology of Africa: Southern African Society for Quaternary Research, Proceedings of the Biennial Conference, Pretoria, 6th ,26-29 May 1981, Vol.15. Ed. by J. C. Vogel et al. 235p. (C). 1982. text 90.00 (*90-6191-257-1*, Pub. by A A Balkema) Ashgate Pub Co.

Palaeoecology of Africa Vol. 19: Proceedings of the VIIIth Biennial Conference, Bloemfontein, 20-24 March, 1987. Ed. by J. A. Coetzee & E. M. Van Zinderen Bakker. (Illus.). 414p. (C). 1989. text 90.00 (*90-6191-834-0*, Pub. by A A Balkema) Ashgate Pub Co.

Palaeoecology of Africa Vol. 21: Proceedings of the IXth Biennial Conference Held at the University of Durban, 1-4 February 1989. Ed. by K. Heine & R. R. Maud. (Illus.). 328p. (C). 1990. text 90.00 (*90-6191-997-5*, Pub. by A A Balkema) Ashgate Pub Co.

Palaeoecology of Africa & the Surrounding Islands Vol. 25: Conference on Desert Margin Changes in Africa; Implications for Water, Carbon & Mankind IGCP-349/IGCP-404/INQUA. Ed. by K. Heine. (FRE & ENG.). 328p. (C). 1999. text 90.00 (*90-5410-451-1*, Pub. by A A Balkema) Ashgate Pub Co.

Palaeoecology of Africa, 1975-77 Vol. 10. Ed. by E. M. Van Zinderen Bakker & J. A. Coetzee. 200p. (C). 1978. text 90.00 (*90-6191-028-5*, Pub. by A A Balkema) Ashgate Pub Co.

Palaeoecology of Africa 22: Proceedings of the First Symposium of African Palynology, Rabat, 15-21 May 1989. Ed. by K. Heine. (Illus.). 299p. (C). 1991. text 90.00 (*90-5410-110-5*, Pub. by A A Balkema) Ashgate Pub Co.

Palaeoecology of Africa 23. K. Heine. (Illus.). 180p. (C). 1993. text 90.00 (*90-5410-154-7*, Pub. by A A Balkema) Ashgate Pub Co.

Palaeoekologische und Palaeolimnologische Studie des Rotsees Bei Luzern: Pollen-, Grossrest-, Diatomeen- und Sedimentanalytische Untersuchungen. Andre Lotter. (Dissertationes Botanicae Ser.: Band 124). (GER., Illus.). 187p. 1988. 65.00 (*3-443-64036-2*, Pub. by Gebruder Borntraeger) Balogh.

Palaeoethnobotanische Untersuchungen an Mittelalterlichen und Frueneuzeitlichen Pflanzenresten Aus Braunschweig. Maren Hellwig. (Dissertationes Botanicae Ser.: Band 156). (GER., Illus.). iv, 216p. 1990. pap. 65.00 (*3-443-64068-0*, Pub. by Gebruder Borntraeger) Balogh.

Palaeoethnobotany: Plants & Ancient Man in Kashmir. Farooq A. Lone. (C). 1993. text 42.00 (*81-204-0717-2*, Pub. by Oxford IBH) S Asia.

Palaeoethnobotany: Plants & Ancient Man in Kashmir. Farooq A. Lone et al. (Illus.). 288p. (C). 1993. text 82.00 (*90-6191-944-4*, Pub. by A A Balkema) Ashgate Pub Co.

Palaeoflora of Southern Africa: Prodromus of South African Megafloras, Devonia to Lower Cretaceous. John M. Anderson & Heidi M. Anderson. 424p. 1985. text 214.00 (*90-6191-575-9*, Pub. by A A Balkema) Ashgate Pub Co.

Palaeoflora of Southern Africa - Molteno Formation (Triassic) Fruits & Seeds; Spores & Pollen Grains, Vol. 4, Pts. 5 & 6. John M. Anderson & Heidi M. Anderson. (C). Date not set. text 150.00 (*90-6191-286-5*, Pub. by A A Balkema) Ashgate Pub Co.

Palaeoflora of Southern Africa - Molteno Formation (Triassic) Gymnosperms, Vol. 2, Pt. 3. John M. Anderson & Heidi M. Anderson. (C). 1988. text 150.00 (*90-6191-284-9*, Pub. by A A Balkema) Ashgate Pub Co.

Palaeoflora of Southern Africa - Molteno Formation (Triassic) Introduction; Dicroidium, Vol. 1 Pts. 1 & 2. John M. Anderson & Heidi M. Anderson. (Illus.). 240p. 1983. text 150.00 (*90-6191-283-0*, Pub. by A A Balkema) Ashgate Pub Co.

Palaeoflora of Southern Africa - Molteno Formation (Triassic) Localities & Communities; General Synthesis, Vol. 6 Pts. 9 & 10. John M. Anderson & Heidi M. Anderson. (C). Date not set. text 150.00 (*90-6191-288-1*, Pub. by A A Balkema) Ashgate Pub Co.

Palaeoflora of Southern Africa - Molteno Formation (Triassic) Non-Gymnosperms, Vol. 3, Pt. 4. John M. Anderson & Heidi M. Anderson. (C). 1991. text 150.00 (*90-6191-285-7*, Pub. by A A Balkema) Ashgate Pub Co.

Palaeoflora of Southern Africa - Molteno Formation (Triassic) Wood; Fauna, Vol. 5 Pts. 7 & 8. John M. Anderson & Heidi M. Anderson. (C). 1993. text 150.00 (*90-6191-287-3*, Pub. by A A Balkema) Ashgate Pub Co.

Palaeogeographie des Siluriums in Nord-, Mittel- und Westeuropa. Roland Walter. (Geotektonische Forschungen Ser.: Vol. 41). (GER.). ii, 180p. 1972. 52.00 (*3-510-50007-5*, Pub. by E Schweizerbartsche) Balogh.

Palaeographia Latina, 6 pts. in 1. Wallace M. Lindsay. (St. Andrews University Publications: Nos. 14, 16, 19, 20, 23, 28). 456p. 1989. reprint ed. 128.70 (*3-487-05308-X*) G Olms Pubs.

Palaeographic Guide for Spanish Manuscripts, Fifteenth-Seventeenth Centuries: Roman Numerals see Philological & Documentary Studies

Palaeogreographic-Palaeotectonic Atlas of North-Eastern Africa, Arabia & Adjacent Areas: Late Neoproterozoic to Holocene. Ed. by H. Schandelmeier & P. O. Reynolds. (Illus.). 180p. (C). 1997. text 168.00 (*90-5410-659-X*, Pub. by A A Balkema) Ashgate Pub Co.

Palaeohistoria: Acta et Communicationes Institui Bio-Archaeologici Universitatis Groninganae, Vol. 27 (1985) 320p. 1987. text 135.00 (*90-6191-781-6*, Pub. by A A Balkema) Ashgate Pub Co.

Palaeohistoria: Acta et Communicationes Instituti Bio-Archaeologici Universitatis Groninganae, Vol. 23. (Site of Hamburg Tradition Ser.). 199p. (C). 1994. text 135.00 (*90-6191-520-1*, Pub. by A A Balkema) Ashgate Pub Co.

Palaeohistoria: VL32 Acta et Communicationes Bio-Archaeologici Universitates Groninganae. (Illus.). 344p. (C). 1993. text 135.00 (*90-5410-136-9*, Pub. by A A Balkema) Ashgate Pub Co.

Palaeohistoria Vol. 28: Acta et Communicationes Instituti Bio-Archaeologici Universitatis Groninganae. 160p. (C). 1988. text 135.00 (*90-6191-832-4*, Pub. by A A Balkema) Ashgate Pub Co.

Palaeohistoria Vols. 37/38: Acta et Communicationes Instituti Bio-Archaeologici Universitatis Groninganae. (Illus.). 542p. (C). 1997. text 135.00 (*90-5410-652-2*, Pub. by A A Balkema) Ashgate Pub Co.

Palaeohistoria, 1984: Acta et Communicationes Instituti Bio-Archaeologici Universitatis Groninganae, Vol. 26. 229p. 1986. text 135.00 (*90-6191-626-7*, Pub. by A A Balkema) Ashgate Pub Co.

Palaeohistoria, 1982: Acta et Communicationes Instituti Bio-Archaeologici Universitatis Groninganae, Vol. 24. 296p. 1984. text 135.00 (*90-6191-527-9*, Pub. by A A Balkema) Ashgate Pub Co.

Palaeohistoria, No. 30: Acta & Communicationes Instituti Bio-Archaeologici Universitatis Groninganae. 150p. (C). 1990. text 125.00 (*90-6191-151-6*, Pub. by A A Balkema) Ashgate Pub Co.

Palaeohistoria 33-34, (1991-1992) Acta et Communicationes Instituti Bio-Archaeologici Universitatis Grononganae. (Illus.). 344p. (C). 1994. text 125.00 (*90-5410-188-1*, Pub. by A A Balkema) Ashgate Pub Co.

Palaeohydrology & Environmental Change. G. Benito et al. LC 98-7027. 368p. 1998. 165.00 (*0-471-98465-5*) Wiley.

Palaeolimnologische und Vegetationsgeschichtliche Untersuchungen an Sedimenten Aus Fuschlsee und Chiemsee (Salzburg und Bayern) Ricarda Voigt. (Dissertationes Botanicae Ser.: Band 270). (GER., Illus.). xvi, 303p. 1996. 83.00 (*3-443-64182-2*, Pub. by Gebruder Borntraeger) Balogh.

Palaeolithic Societies of Europe. Clive Gamble. LC 98-38087. (Cambridge World Archaeology Ser.). (Illus.). 400p. (C). 1999. 85.00 (*0-521-65105-0*); pap. 37.95 (*0-521-65872-1*) Cambridge U Pr.

Palaeomagnetic Applications in Hydrocarbon Exploration & Production. Ed. by P. Turner & A. Turner. (Geological Society Special Publication Ser.: No. 98). 312p. 1995. 108.00 (*1-897799-42-X*, 341, Pub. by Geol Soc Pub Hse) AAPG.

Palaeomagnetic Database. J. D. Piper. LC 87-34995. 304p. 1991. 360.00 (*0-471-93255-8*) Wiley.

Palaeomagnetism & Diagenesis in Sediments. Ed. by D. H. Tarling & P. Turner. (Geological Society Special Publication Ser.: No. 151). 224p. 1999. 112.00 (*1-86239-028-2*, Pub. by Geol Soc Pub Hse) AAPG.

Palaeomagnetism & Tectonics of the Mediterranean Region. Ed. by A. Morris & Donald H. Tarling. (Geological Society Special Publication: Series 105). (Illus.). vi, 432p. 1996. 110.00 (*1-897799-55-1*, 269, Pub. by Geol Soc Pub Hse) AAPG.

Palaeontographica Americana: A New Jellyfish (Kirklandia Texana Caster) from the Lower Cretaceous of Texas, No. 18. Kenneth E. Caster. 1945. 3.00 (*0-87710-319-4*) Paleo Res.

Palaeontographica Americana: Vol. 2, 7 pts. Incl. Devonian Brevicones of New York & Adjacent Areas No. 9. R. H. Flower. (Illus.). 84p. 1938. pap. 2.00 (*0-87710-310-0*); Individual Variations in the Rugose Coral Species Heliophyllum halli No. 6. E. Wells & H. J. Wells. 22p. 1937. pap. 2.00 (*0-87710-307-0*); No. 7. Turrid Illustrations, Mainly Claibornian. G. D. Harris. (Illus.). 122p. 1937. pap. 2.00 (*0-87710-308-9*); No. 8. Neocene Spondyli from the Southern United States & Tropical America. K. V. Palmer. 18p. 1938. pap. 2.00 (*0-87710-309-7*); No. 10. Study of the Pseudorthoceratidae. R. H. Flower. (Illus.). 214p. 1939. pap. 2.00 (*0-87710-311-9*); No. 11. Notes on Giant Fasciolarias. Burnett Smith. 10p. 1940. 1.00 (*0-87710-312-7*); No. 12. Titusvillidae, Paleozoic & Recent Branching Hexactinellida. Kenneth E. Caster. 52p. 1941. 2.00 (*0-87710-313-5*); 30.00 (*0-87710-354-2*) Paleo Res.

Palaeontographica Americana: Vol. 3, 13 pts. Incl. No. 20. Some Species of Platystrophia from the Trenton of Ontario & Quebec. G. Winston Sinclair. 1946. 2.00 (*0-87710-321-6*); No. 22. Two Marine Quaternary Localities. Burnett Smith. 16p. 1948. 1.00 (*0-87710-323-2*); No. 23. Studies of Carboniferous Crinoids: Oklahoma & Nebraska. 40p. 2.00 (*0-87710-324-0*); No. 24. Stereotoceras & the Brevicoceratidae. R. H. Flower. 36p. 1950. 2.00 (*0-87710-325-9*); 35.00 (*0-87710-355-0*) Paleo Res.

Palaeontographica Americana: Vol. 4, 8 pts. Incl. No. 29. Dalmanellidae of the Cincinnatian. Donald D. Hall. 38p. 1962. pap. 4.00 (*0-87710-330-5*); No. 30. Pelecypod Genus Byssonychia As It Occurs in the Cincinnatian at Cincinnati, Ohio. John Pojeta, Jr. 49p. 1962. pap. 5.00 (*0-87710-331-3*); 35.00 (*0-87710-356-9*) Paleo Res.

Palaeontographica Americana: Vol. 5, 4 pts. Incl. No. 34. Upper Tertiary Arcacea of the Mid-Atlantic Coastal Plain. S. O. Bird. 62p. 1965. pap. 5.00 (*0-87710-335-6*); No. 35. Dimyarian Pelecypods of the Mississippian Marshall Sandstone of Michigan. Egbert G. Driscoll. 65p. 1965. pap. 5.00 (*0-87710-336-4*); 50.00 (*0-87710-357-7*) Paleo Res.

Palaeontographica Americana: Vol. 6, 4 pts. Incl. No. 38. Lycopsid Stems & Roots & Sphenopsid Fructifications & Stems from the Upper Freeport Coal of Southeastern Ohio. Maxine L. Abbott. (Illus.). 50p. 1968. pap. 5.00 (*0-87710-339-9*); No. 39. Cenozoic Evolution of the Alticostate Venericards in Gulf & East Coastal North America. William G. Heaslip. (Illus.). 85p. 1968. pap. 6.50 (*0-87710-340-2*); 40.00 (*0-87710-358-5*) Paleo Res.

Palaeontographica Americana: Vol. 7, 5 pts. Incl. No. 42. Torreites Sanchezi (Douville) from Jamaica. Peter Jung. 13p. 1970. pap. 2.00 (*0-87710-343-7*); No. 43. Cancellariid Radula & Its Interpretation. A. A. Olsson. 11p. 1970. pap. 2.00 (*0-87710-344-5*); No. 44. Ontogeny & Sexual Dimorphism of Lower Paleozoic Trilobita. Chung-Hung Hu. (Illus.). 134p. 1971. pap. 15.00 (*0-87710-345-3*); No. 45. Rudists of Jamaica. L. J. Chubb. (Illus.). 100p. 1971. pap. 9.00 (*0-87710-346-1*); No. 46. Crinoids from the Girardeau Limestone. J. C. Brower. (Illus.). 240p. 1973. pap. 20.00 (*0-87710-347-X*); 45.00 (*0-87710-359-3*) Paleo Res.

Palaeontographica Americana: Vol. 8, 5 pts. Incl. No. 47. Revision of the Family Seraphsidae (Gastropoda: Strombacea) Peter Jung. (Illus.). 72p. 1974. pap. 6.00 (*0-87710-348-8*); No. 48. Anatomy & Morphology of Psilophyton Dawsoni, sp. n., from the Late Lower Devonian of Quebec (Gaspe) & Ontario, Canada. H. P. Banks & S. M. LeClercq. (Illus.). 55p. 1975. pap. 5.00 (*0-87710-349-6*); No. 49. Comparative Morphology & Shell History of the Ordovician Strophomenacea (Brachiopoda) J. K. Pope. (Illus.). 86p. 1976. pap. 10.00 (*0-87710-350-X*); No. 50. Evolution & Classification of Cenozoic North American & European Lucinidae (Mollusca, Bivalvia) Sara Bretsky. (Illus.). 118p. 1976. pap. 18.00 (*0-87710-351-8*); No. 51. Morphology & Anatomy of Aneurophyton: A Progymnosperm from the Late Devonian of New York. B. S. Serlin & H. P. Banks. (Illus.). 16p. 1978. pap. 4.00 (*0-87710-352-6*); 40.00 (*0-87710-360-7*) Paleo Res.

Palaeontographica Americana: Vol. 9, 2 pts. Incl. Triarthrus Eatoni (Trilobita) Vol. 53: Anatomy of Its Exoskeletal, Skeletomuscular, & Digestive Systems. J. L. Cisne. 48p. 1981. 15.00 (*0-87710-383-6*); No. 52. Lower Bajocian (Jurassic) Cephalopod Faunas from Western Canada, & Proposed Assemblage Zones for the Lower Bajocian of North America. R. L. Hall & G. E. Westermann. 93p. 1980. 18.00 (*0-87710-353-4*); 32.50 (*0-87710-386-0*) Paleo Res.

Palaeontographica Americana No. 57: Revised Taxonomic Procedures & Paleoecological Applications for Some North American Mississippian Fenestellidae & Polyporidae (Bryozoa) E. M. Snyder. 275p. 1991. 60.00 (*0-87710-419-0*) Paleo Res.

Palaeontographica Americana Vol. 54: Recent Advances in the Paleobiology & Geology of the Cnidaria. (Illus.). 558p. 1984. 60.00 (*0-87710-399-2*) Paleo Res.

Palaeontographica Americana Vol. 55: A Restudy of the Fossil Scorpionida of the World. E. N. Kjellesvig-Waering. 287p. 1986. 55.00 (*0-87710-401-8*) Paleo Res.

Palaeontographica Americana Vol. 56: Late Ordovician Sponges from the Malongulli Formation of Central New South Wales, Australia. Keith J. Rigby & Barry D. Webby. 147p. 1988. 50.00 (*0-87710-410-7*) Paleo Res.

Palaeontologia Cathayana, Vol. 5. Ed. by Y. C. Lu. 334p. 1990. 118.95 (*0-387-52145-3*) Spr-Verlag.

Palaeontologia Cathayana, Vol. 6. Ed. by Nanjing Institute of Geology & Palaeontology, Acad. 454p. 1996. 80.00 (*7-03-002816-3*, Pub. by Sci Pr) Lubrecht & Cramer.

Palaeontology. James Scott. 160p. 1986. 55.00 (*0-89771-000-2*) St Mut.

Palaeontology: Proceedings of the 27th International Geological Congress, Vol. 2. International Geological Congress Staff. 230p. 1984. lib. bdg. 87.00 (*90-6764-011-5*, Pub. by VSP) Coronet Bks.

Palaeontology & Historical Geology see Proceedings of the 30th International Geological Congress

Palaeooekologie, Palaeobotanik und Stratigraphie des Jungquartaers Im Nordmitteleuropaeischen Tiefland: Unter Besonderer Beruecksichtigung Des Elbe-Saale-Gebietes. Thomas Litt. (Dissertationes Botanicae Ser.: Band 227). (Illus.). ii, 1855p. 1994. pap. 65.00 (*3-443-64139-3*, Pub. by Gebruder Borntraeger) Balogh.

Palaeopathology of Aboriginal Australians: Health & Disease Across a Hunter-Gatherer Continent. Stephen Webb. (Illus.). 336p. (C). 1995. text 69.95 (*0-521-46044-1*) Cambridge U Pr.

Palaeopathology of Danish Skeletons: A Comparative Study of Demography, Disease, & Injury. Pia Bennike. (Illus.). 272p. (Orig.). 1985. pap. text 58.50 (*87-500-2571-6*) Coronet Bks.

Palaeoserology: Blood Typing with Fluorescent Antibody Method. I. A. Lengyel. 240p. (C). 1975. 60.00 (*963-05-0355-7*, Pub. by Akade Kiado) St Mut.

Palaeosurfaces: Recognition, Reconstruction & Palaeoenvironmental Interpretation. Ed. by M. Widdowson. (Geological Society Special Publication Ser.: No. 120). vi, 300p. 1997. 107.00 (*1-897799-57-8*, 361, Pub. by Geol Soc Pub Hse) AAPG.

Palaeoweathering, Palaeosurfaces & Related Continental Deposits. Medard Thiry & Regine Simon-Coincon. LC 98-43514. (Special Publications of the International Association of Sedimentologists: No. 27). (Illus.). 1999. pap. 110.00 (*0-632-05311-9*) Blackwell Sci.

Palaeozoic Vertebrate Biostratigraphy & Biogeography. Ed. by John A. Long. LC 93-11551. 383p. 1994. reprint ed. pap. text 42.50 (*0-8018-4779-6*) Johns Hopkins.

Palaeozoikum in den Kordilleren Nordchiles. Christoph Breitkreuz. (Geotektonische Forschungen Ser.: Vol. 70). (GER.). ii, 88p. 1986. 52.00 (*3-510-50036-9*, Pub. by E Schweizerbartsche) Balogh.

Palaestinawissenschaft in Deutschland: Das Gustaf-Dalman-Institut Greifswald 1920-1995. Ed. by Christof Hardmeier & Thomas Neumann. (GER.). xii, 71p. (C). 1995. pap. text 36.95 (*3-11-015026-3*) De Gruyter.

Palais des Machines: Paris 1889 Charles-Louis-Ferdinand Dutert. Stuart Durant & Angus Low. LC 95-150965. (Architecture in Detail Ser.). (Illus.). 60p. (C). 1994. pap. 29.95 (*0-7148-2930-7*, Pub. by Phaidon Press) Phaidon Pr.

Palais, Maisons et Autres Edifices Modernes Dessines a Rome. Charles Percier & Pierre F. Fontaine. 1980. reprint ed. write for info. (*3-487-06920-2*) G Olms Pubs.

Palais-Royal. Richard Sennett. 1994. pap. 11.95 (*0-393-31251-8*) Norton.

Palampam Day. David Gershator & Phillis Gershator. LC 96-54899. (Illus.). 32p. (J). (gr. k-3). 1997. 15.95 (*0-7614-5002-5*) Marshall Cavendish.

Palancas. Capstone Press Staff. Price not set. (*1-56065-793-6*) Capstone Pr.

Palancas. Capstone Press Staff. (J). 1998. 14.00 (*0-516-21382-2*) Childrens.

Palanpur: The Economy of an Indian Village. C. J. Bliss & N. H. Stern. (Illus.). 352p. 1982. text 39.95 (*0-19-828419-5*) OUP.

Palanthas. Steven Brown. 96p. 1998. 11.95 (*0-7869-1199-9*, Pub. by TSR Inc) Random.

Palaobiologie und Stammeschichte: Paleobiology & Phylogeny. Othenio Abel. Ed. by Stephen Jay Gould. LC 79-8320. (History of Paleontology Ser.). (GER., Illus.). 1980. reprint ed. lib. bdg. 44.95 (*0-405-12701-4*) Ayer.

Palaographie, 1981. Gabriel Silagi. (Munchener Beitrage zur Mediavistik und Renaissance-Forschung Ser.: Bd. 32). (GER.). xii, 270p. 1982. 80.00 (*3-615-00163-X*) G Olms Pubs.

Palas of Sri Kavi Karna, 4 vols., Set. Ed. by Kapila Vatsyayan. (Kalamulasasatra Ser.). (C). 1991. 120.00 (*81-208-0958-0*, Pub. by Motilal Bnarsidass) S Asia.

Palastina - Erez Israel. Wolf Kaiser. (Wissenschaftliche Abhandlungen des Salomon Ludwig Steinheim-Instituts Fur Deutsch-Judische Geschichte Ser.: Vol. 2). (GER.). 584p. 1992. write for info. (*3-487-09529-7*) G Olms Pubs.

Palastina-Jahrbuch des Deutschen Evangelischen Instituts Fur Altertumswissenschaft des Heiligen Landes Zu Jerusalem. Ed. by Gustav Dalman & Albrecht Alt. lvi, 4361p. 1975. reprint ed. write for info. (*3-487-05514-7*) G Olms Pubs.

Palatable Pantries & Lavish Larders. Rhonda Mircovich. LC 92-30475. (Illus.). 208p. 1993. pap. 14.95 (*0-942963-33-4*) Distinctive Pub.

Palatin Joseph's Schriften. S. Domanovszky & F. Glatz. 804p. (C). 1991. 216.00 (*963-05-4831-3*, Pub. by Akade Kiado) St Mut.

P

Palatinate-a Full Declaration of the Faith & Ceremonies Professed in the Dominions of Prince Fredericke, 5. Prince Elector Palatine. Tr. by J. Rolte. LC 79-84129. (English Experience Ser.: No. 947). 208p. 1979. reprint ed. lib. bdg. 20.00 (*90-221-0947-X*) Walter J Johnson.

Palatine. Old Vicarage Publications Staff. 94p. (C). 1982. pap. text 34.00 (*0-7855-3132-7*, Pub. by Old Vicarage) St Mut.

***Palatine.** Palatine Historical Society Staff. (Images of America Ser.). 128p. 1999. pap. 18.99 (*0-7385-0149-2*) Arcadia Publng.

Palatine Church Visitations, 1609: Deanery of Kusel. Tr. by Ricardo W. Staudt. LC 80-68128. 136p. 1998. reprint ed. pap. 18.00 (*0-8063-0908-3*) Clearfield Co.

Palatine Familes of Ireland. 2nd ed. Hank Z. Jones. LC 90-61260. 194p. 1990. 37.50 (*0-929539-09-5*, 1109) Picton Pr.

Palatine Families of New York: A Study of the German Immigrants Who Arrived in Colonial New York in 1710, 2 vols. Henry Z. Jones, Jr. LC 84-81704. (Illus.). 1374p. 1995. 89.50 (*0-9613888-2-X*, 1113) Picton Pr.

Palatine Roots: The 1710 German Settlement in New York As Experienced by Johann Peter Wagner. Nancy W. Dixon. 352p. 1994. 49.50 (*0-89725-175-X*, 1521) Picton Pr.

Palatine Ship: Ghost Ship of Block Island. Robert W. Carlson. 60p. 1994. pap. 7.95 (*1-886066-00-0*) Ctr Archaeoastronomy.

Palatine Transcripts (Series) Baptism & Marriage Records from Early New York State Churches. Arthur C. Kelly. LC F129.R4R4. 1968. lib. bdg. write for info. (*1-56012-000-2*) Kinship Rhinebeck.

Palatines, Liberty & Property: German Lutherans in Colonial British America. A. G. Roeber. LC 92-25647. (Early America Ser.). 448p. 1993. text 52.00 (*0-8018-4459-2*) Johns Hopkins.

Palatines, Liberty, & Property: German Lutherans in Colonial British America. A. G. Roeber. (Early America). 448p. 1998. reprint ed. pap. text 18.95 (*0-8018-5968-9*) Johns Hopkins.

Palatines of Olde Ulster. Benjamin M. Brink. 80p. (Orig.). 1996. pap. 9.95 (*0-910746-20-6*) Hope Farm.

Palatka. Ann O. Rust. LC 89-84402. (Floridians Ser.). 235p. (Orig.). 1989. pap. 12.95 (*0-9620556-1-1*) Amaro Bks.

Palatka, Vol. II. Ann O. Rust. LC 89-84402. (Floridians Ser.: Vol. 2). 231p. (Orig.). 1994. pap. text 17.50 (*1-883203-00-7*) Amaro Bks.

Palatkwapi Trail. James Byrkit. (Plateau Ser.: Vol. 59, No. 1). 32p. 1988. pap. 4.95 (*0-685-72095-0*) Mus Northern Ariz.

Palau. 3rd rev. ed. Nancy Barbour. Ed. by Elaine DeMan. (Illus.). 175p. 2000. pap. 24.95 (*0-9626344-2-5*) Full Court CA.

Palau: A Challenge to the Rule of Law in Micronesia: Report of a Mission by William J. Butler, Esq., The Hon. George C. Edwards, The Hon. Michael D. Kirby, C.M.G. Pref. by Andres A. Mawdsley. 58p. (Orig.). (C). 1988. pap. text 5.00 (*0-916265-04-8*) Am Assn Intl Comm Jurists.

***Palau: A Country Study Guide.** Global Investment & Business Center, Inc. Staff. (World Country Study Guides Library: Vol. 131). (Illus.). 350p. 2000. pap. 59.00 (*0-7397-2429-0*) Intl Business Pubns.

Palau: Portrait of Paradise. Mandy T. Etpison. Ed. by Jenna Cobb. (ENG & JPN., Illus.). 250p. (Orig.). 1993. write for info. (*0-9637875-0-0*); pap. write for info. (*0-9637875-1-9*) Neco Marine.

Palau - A Country Study Guide: Basic Information for Research & Pleasure. Global Investment Center, USA Staff. (World Country Study Guide Library: Vol. 131). (Illus.). 350p. 1999. pap. 59.00 (*0-7397-1528-3*) Intl Business Pubns.

Palau, Belau: Your Future in Tourism: PATA Task Force Study. Ian Oelrichs & Pacific Asia Travel Association Staff. LC 94-112128. xi, 86 p. 1993. 35.00 (*1-882866-00-2*) Pac Asia Trvl.

***Palau Business Intelligence Report, 190 vols.** Global Investment & Business Center, Inc. Staff. (World Business Intelligence Library: Vol. 131). (Illus.). 350p. 2000. pap. 99.95 (*0-7397-2629-3*) Intl Business Pubns.

***Palau Business Law Handbook.** Global Investment & Business Center, Inc. Staff. (Global Business Law Handbooks Library: Vol. 131). (Illus.). 2000. pap. 99.95 (*0-7397-2029-5*) Intl Business Pubns.

***Palau Business Opportunity Yearbook.** Global Investment & Business Center, Inc. Staff. (Global Business Opportunity Yearbooks Library: Vol. 131). (Illus.). 2000. pap. 99.95 (*0-7397-2229-8*) Intl Business Pubns.

***Palau Business Opportunity Yearbook: Export-Import, Investment & Business Opportunities.** International Business Publications, U. S. A. Staff & Global Investment Center, U. S. A. Staff. (Global Business Opportunity Yearbooks Library: Vol. 131). (Illus.). 350p. 1999. pap. 99.95 (*0-7397-1329-9*) Intl Business Pubns.

***Palau Country Review 2000.** Robert C. Kelly et al. (Illus.). 60p. 1999. pap. 39.95 (*1-58310-555-7*) CountryWatch.

***Palau Foreign Policy & Government Guide.** Global Investment & Business Center, Inc. Staff. (World Foreign Policy & Government Library: Vol. 190). (Illus.). 350p. 2000. 99.95 (*0-7397-3829-1*) Intl Business Pubns.

***Palau Investment & Business Guide.** Global Investment & Business Center, Inc. Staff. (Global Investment & Business Guide Library: Vol. 131). (Illus.). 2000. pap. 99.95 (*0-7397-1829-0*) Intl Business Pubns.

***Palau Investment & Business Guide: Export-Import, Investment & Business Opportunities.** International Business Publications, USA Staff & Global Investment Center, USA Staff. (World Investment & Business Guide Library-99: Vol. 131). (Illus.). 350p. 1999. pap. 99.95 (*0-7397-0326-9*) Intl Business Pubns.

Palauan Social Structure. DeVerne R. Smith. LC 81-19987. 368p. 1983. reprint ed. pap. 114.10 (*0-7837-5684-4*, 205911200005) Bks Demand.

Palaver: West Indian Poems. Althea Romeo-Mark. 1978. pap. 1.50 (*0-917402-10-3*) Downtown Poets.

Palaver: 3 Dramatic Discussion Starters. Wole Soyinka. LC PN6120.A4P3. 39p. reprint ed. pap. 30.00 (*0-7837-1954-X*, 204217100001) Bks Demand.

Palawan at the Crossroads: Development & the Environment on a Philippine Frontier. Ed. by James F. Eder & Janet O. Fernandez. LC 96-946519. 184p. 1997. pap. text 17.00 (*971-550-210-5*, Pub. by Ateneo de Manila Univ Pr) UH Pr.

Palazzi & Villas of Rome. Caroline Vincenti Montanaro. 191p. 1999. pap. 9.95 (*88-7743-202-0*) Arsenale Editrice.

Palazzi di Genova, 2 vols in 1. Peter Paul Rubens. LC 68-21226. (Illus.). 1972. reprint ed. 66.95 (*0-405-08901-5*) Ayer.

Palazzo. Jan Smith. 256p. (Orig.). 1997. mass mkt. 5.95 (*0-352-33156-9*, Pub. by BLA4) London Brdge.

Palazzo Bricherasio. Companino. (Illus.). 48p. 1997. pap. 12.95 (*88-435-5484-0*, Pub. by Art Bks Intl) Partners Pubs Grp.

Palazzo da Festa in Vicenza. Erik Forssman. Tr. by Catherine Enggass from ITA. LC 75-20027. (Corpus Palladianum Ser.: Vol. 8). (Illus.). 186p. 1980. lib. bdg. 56.00 (*0-271-01202-1*) Pa St U Pr.

Palazzo Vecchio: Guide to the Building, the Apartments & the Collections. Ugo Muccini. (Illus.). 128p. 1992. 19.95 (*0-8161-0611-8*, G K Hall & Co) Mac Lib Ref.

Palazzo Vecchio, 1298-1532: Government, Architecture, & Imagery in the Civic Palace of the Florentine Republic. Nicoli Rubinstein. (Oxford-Warburg Studies). (Illus.). 172p. 1995. text 89.00 (*0-19-920602-3*) OUP.

***Palbykin: My Life as a Don.** Donald J. Palbykin. (Illus.). ix, 436p. 2000. 29.95 (*0-9679577-0-2*); pap. 17.95 (*0-9679577-1-0*) Pal Pubng.

***Palchalbel: Canon in D.** Ed. by Peter Pickow. (Concert Performer Ser.). 4p. 1999. pap. text 6.95 incl. cd-rom (*0-8256-1751-0*, AM949840) Music Sales.

Pale As Real Ladies: Poems for Pauline Johnson. Joan Crate. 76p. 1989. pap. 11.95 (*0-919626-43-2*, Pub. by Brick Bks) Genl Dist Srvs.

***Pale as the Moon.** Donna Campbell. LC 99-32229. (Carolina Young People Ser.). (Illus.). 104p. (J). (gr. 4-8). 1999. pap. 10.95 (*1-928556-02-7*) Coastal NC.

***Pale Bird, Spouting Fire.** Susan Yuzna. LC 00-41153. (Poetry Ser.). 2000. write for info. (*1-884836-63-1*) U Akron Pr.

Pale Blue Dot: A Vision of the Human Future in Space. Carl Sagan. 384p. 1997. pap. 12.95 (*0-345-37659-5*) Ballantine Pub Grp.

Pale Blue Dot: A Vision of the Human Future in Space. Carl Sagan. LC 94-28121. 1994. 35.00 (*0-679-43841-6*) Random.

Pale Blue Dot: A Vision of the Human Future in Space. Carl Sagan. (Illus.). 432p. 1995. pap. 25.00 (*0-679-76486-0*) Random.

Pale Cast of Thought: Hesitation & Decision in the Renaissance Epic. James L. Shulman. LC 97-33581. 200p. 1998. 35.00 (*0-87413-635-0*) U Delaware Pr.

Pale Comparison. Kenneth Von Gunden. 272p. (Orig.). 1994. mass mkt. 4.99 (*0-441-00064-9*) Ace Bks.

Pale Fire. Vladimir Nabokov. 1992. 17.00 (*0-679-41077-5*) McKay.

Pale Fire: A Novel. Vladimir Nabokov. (International Ser.). 1989. pap. 13.00 (*0-679-72342-0*) Vin Bks.

Pale Gray for Guilt. John D. MacDonald. 1996. mass mkt. 5.99 (*0-449-22460-0*) Fawcett.

Pale Gray for Guilt. John D. MacDonald. 1997. mass mkt. 5.99 (*0-449-45721-4*) Fawcett.

Pale Green, Light Orange: A Portrait of Bourgois Ireland, 1930-1950. Niall Rudd. LC 94-184818. 168p. 1994. pap. 18.95 (*1-874675-21-X*) Dufour.

Pale Hecates Team: Examination of the Beliefs on Witchcraft & Magic Among Shakespeare's Contemporaries & His Immediate Succesors. Katherine M. Briggs. Ed. by Richard M. Dorson. LC 77-70582. (International Folklore Ser.). (Illus.). 1977. lib. bdg. 26.95 (*0-405-10083-3*) Ayer.

Pale Horse. Agatha Christie. LC 00-1941. 256p. 1992. mass mkt. 5.99 (*0-06-100377-8*, Harp PBks) HarpC.

Pale Horse. Agatha Christie. 1992. 11.09 (*0-606-12472-1*, Pub. by Turtleback) Demco.

Pale Horse. Joe Penhall. 1996. pap. 9.95 (*0-413-70410-6*, Methuen Drama) Methn.

Pale Horse. large type ed. Agatha Christie. 1987. 16.95 (*0-7089-1739-9*) Ulverscroft.

Pale Horse, Pale Rider: Three Short Novels. Katherine Anne Porter. 1990. 17.00 (*0-15-170755-3*) Harcourt.

Pale Kings & Princes. abr. ed. Robert B. Parker. 1988. 14.95 incl. audio (*0-671-66073-X*) S&S Audio.

Pale Kings & Princes. Robert B. Parker. 320p. 1988. reprint ed. mass mkt. 6.99 (*0-440-20004-0*) Dell.

Pale Moon: Selected Poems. Harvey Hirsch. LC 98-93510. 144p. 1998. 12.50 (*0-929613-01-5*, 100PM) Cbblstn Pr.

Pale Moon of Morning. Liam Lynch. LC 95-231231. 218p. 1998. pap. 11.95 (*0-86327-310-6*, Pub. by Wolfhound Press) Irish Amer Bk.

Pale Moon Rider. Marsha Canham. 384p. 1998. mass mkt. 6.50 (*0-440-22259-1*) Dell.

Pale of Words: Reflections on the Humanities & Performance. James A. Winn. LC 98-5743. 160p. 1998. 20.00 (*0-300-07412-3*) Yale U Pr.

Pale Orchid. large type ed. Anne Mather. (Magna Romance Ser.). 1992. 11.95 (*0-7505-0226-6*, Pub. by Mgna Lrg Print) Ulverscroft.

Pale Phoenix. Kathryn Reiss. LC 93-32299. (J). (gr. 5 up). 1994. pap. 3.95 (*0-15-200031-3*) Harcourt.

Pale Phoenix. Kathryn Reiss. LC 93-32299. 256p. (YA). (gr. 7 up). 1994. 10.95 (*0-15-200030-5*) Harcourt.

Pale Phoenix. Kathryn Reiss. (J). 1997. pap. 4.99 (*0-590-48405-2*, Point) Scholastic Inc.

Pale Phoenix. Kathryn Reiss. 1997. 10.09 (*0-606-13012-8*, Pub. by Turtleback) Demco.

Pale Pink. Phyllis Galembo. (Artists' Books Ser.). (Illus.). 24p. (Orig.). 1983. pap. 6.00 (*0-89822-033-5*) Visual Studies.

Pale Rainbow: Gaelic Folksongs with English Translations. Brian O'Rourke. 96p. 1989. 25.00 (*0-7165-2425-2*, Pub. by Irish Acad Pr) Intl Spec Bk.

Pale Ramon. Rane Arroyo. LC 98-7789. 96p. 1998. pap. 13.00 (*0-944072-94-1*) Zoland Bks.

Pale Rider. Myrna Temte. 1997. per. 3.99 (*0-373-24124-0*, 1-24124-9) Silhouette.

Pale Star. Don Coldsmith. LC 85-16032. 1986. 12.95 (*0-385-23227-6*) Doubleday.

***Pale Truth: A Novel.** Daniel Alef. LC 00-9450. 2000. write for info. (*0-9700174-1-3*) Maxit Pubng.

***Pale View of Hills.** large type ed. Kazuo Ishiguro. 1999. 21.95 (*0-7862-2172-0*) Thorndike Pr.

Pale View of the Hills. Kazuo Ishiguro. LC 90-50178. 192p. 1990. pap. 11.00 (*0-679-72267-X*) Vin Bks.

Paleantologisches Woerterbuch. 3rd ed. Ulrich Lehmann. (GER.). 739p. 1985. pap. 45.00 (*0-8288-5506-4*, M7577) Fr & Eur.

Paleface. Wyndham Lewis. 1973. lib. bdg. 250.00 (*0-87968-018-0*) Gordon Pr.

Paleface. Wyndham Lewis. LC 73-95438. (English Biography Ser.: No. 31). 1970. reprint ed. lib. bdg. 75.00 (*0-8383-0990-9*) M S G Haskell Hse.

Paleface, the Philosophy of the Melting Pot. Wyndham Lewis. 1971. reprint ed. 39.00 (*0-403-01073-X*) Scholarly.

Palenque, 1926-1945. 2nd ed. Ed. by Roberto Garcia. 463p. 1991. pap. 18.00 (*968-6487-93-X*, IN032) UPLAAP.

***Paleo.** Yvonne Navarro. (Buffy the Vampire Slayer Ser.: Vol. 11). 272p. (gr. 8-12). 2000. 6.99 (*0-7434-0034-8*) PB.

Paleo-Indian. University of Minnesota Staff. 256p. 1995. pap. text, per. 35.00 (*0-7872-1349-7*) Kendall-Hunt.

Paleo-Indian Settlement Pattern in the Hudson & Delaware River Drainages. Leonard Eisenberg. (Occasional Publications in Northeastern Anthropology: No. 4). (Illus.). viii, 159p. 6.00 (*0-318-22321-X*) F Pierce College.

Paleo-Indian Settlement Pattern in the Hudson & Delaware River Drainages. Leonard Eisenberg. (Occasional Publications in Northeastern Anthropology: No. 4). 1978. 6.00 (*0-318-19883-5*) Fund Anthrop.

Paleo-Indian Site in Eastern Pennsylvania: An Early Hunting Culture. John Witthoft & Richard M. Gramly. 40p. (C). 1987. reprint ed. pap. 4.95 (*0-9615462-1-2*) Persimmon NY.

Paleoalterites & Paleosols: Imprints of Terrestrial Processes in Sedimentary Rocks. Robert Meyer. (Illus.). 162p. (C). 1997. text 94.00 (*90-5410-724-3*, Pub. by A A Balkema) Ashgate Pub Co.

Paleoanthropology. 2nd ed. Milford H. Wolpoff. (C). 1994. pap. text. write for info. (*0-07-071679-X*) McGraw.

Paleoanthropology. 2nd ed. Milford H. Wolpoff. LC 97-7536. 936p. (C). 1998. 97.50 (*0-07-071676-5*) McGraw.

Paleoanthropology: Morphology, & Paleoecology. Ed. by Russell H. Tuttle. (World Anthropology Ser.). (Illus.). xvi, 454p. 1975. 62.30 (*90-279-7699-6*) Mouton.

Paleoanthropology Annual, 1990, Vol. 1. Ed. by Eric Delson et al. LC 10-594124. 304p. 1992. text 20.00 (*0-8153-0069-7*, H1428) Garland.

***Paleobiogeography: Using Fossils to Study Global Change, Plate Techtonics & Evolution.** Bruce S. Lieberman. LC 99-55322. (Topics in Geobiology Ser.). 1999. write for info. (*0-306-46277-X*, Kluwer Plenum) Kluwer Academic.

Paleobiological Study of the Late Triassic Bivalve Honotis from Japan. Hisao Ando. (Illus.). 148p. 1987. 44.50 (*0-86008-416-7*, Pub. by U of Tokyo) Col U Pr.

***Paleobiology & Paleoenvironments of Escene Rocks: McMurdo Sound East Antarctica.** Ed. by Jeffrey D. Stillwell & Rodney M. Feldmann. (Antarctic Research Ser.: Vol. 76). 372p. 2000. 80.00 (*0-87590-947-7*) Am Geophysical.

Paleobiology of Climactichnites, an Enigmatic Late Cambrian Fossil. Ellis L. Yochelson & Mikhail A. Fedonkin. LC 92-43329. (Smithsonian Contributions to Paleobiology Ser.: No. 74). (Illus.). 78p. reprint ed. pap. 30.00 (*0-7837-5165-6*, 204489400004) Bks Demand.

Paleobiology of North American Hyaenodon (Mammalia Creodonta) J. S. Mellett. Ed. by F. S. Szalay. (Contributions to Vertebrate Evolution Ser.: Vol. 1). 1976. 65.25 (*3-8055-2379-3*) S Karger.

Paleobiology of the Black Mingo Group (Paleocene) of South Carolina, U. S. A. Albert E. Sanders. LC 98-24663. (Transactions of the American Philosophical Society Ser.: Vol. 88, Pt.4). 1999. pap. 25.00 (*0-87169-884-6*) Am Philos.

Paleobiology of the Dinosaurs. Ed. by James O. Farlow. LC 89-16937. (Geological Society of America, Special Paper: No. 238). (Illus.). 106p. 1989. reprint ed. pap. 32.90 (*0-608-00228-3*, 206073000006) Bks Demand.

Paleobotany, 2 vols., Vol. 1. Edith L. Taylor. 1984. text 78.95 (*0-442-28291-5*, VNR) Wiley.

Paleobotany: Plants of the Past, Their Evolution, Paleoenvironment & Environment in Exploration of Fossil Fuels. rev. ed. S. N. Agashe. 350p. 1996. pap. 39.00 (*1-886106-72-X*) Science Pubs.

Paleobotany & the Evolution of Plants. 2nd ed. Wilson N. Stewart & Gar W. Rothwell. LC 96-3380. (Illus.). 535p. (C). 1993. text 57.95 (*0-521-38294-7*) Cambridge U Pr.

Paleobotany, Paleoecology, & Evolution, 2 vols., Set. Ed. by Karl J. Niklas. LC 81-1838. 1981. 95.00 (*0-275-90691-4*, C06910, Praeger Pubs) Greenwood.

Paleobotany, Paleoecology, & Evolution, 2 vols., Vol. 1. Ed. by Karl J. Niklas. LC 81-1838. 1981. 69.50 (*0-275-90690-6*, C06901, Praeger Pubs) Greenwood.

Paleobotany, Paleoecology, & Evolution, 2 vols., Vol. 2. Ed. by Karl J. Niklas. LC 81-1838. 1981. 125.00 (*0-275-90689-2*, C06892, Praeger Pubs) Greenwood.

Paleoceanography. Thomas J. Schopf. LC 79-12546. (Illus.). 353p. 1980. 46.95 (*0-674-65215-0*) HUP.

Paleoceanography of the Mesozoic Alpine Tethys. Kenneth J. Hsu. LC 75-32124. (Geological Society of America, Special Paper: No. 170). 48p. reprint ed. pap. 30.00 (*0-608-17155-7*, 202736600055) Bks Demand.

Paleocene-Eocene Bathyal & Abyssal Foraminifera from the Atlantic Basin. R. C. Tjalsma & G. P. Lohmann. (Micropaleontology Special Publications: No. 4). 1982. 45.00 (*0-686-84256-1*) Am Mus Natl Hist.

Paleocene Stratigraphic Successions in the Northern Peninsular Ranges, Orange & Riverside Counties, California. Ed. by I. P. Colburn & P. C. Ramirez. 74p. 1995. 9.00 (*1-878861-72-7*) Pac Section SEPM.

Paleocene Stratigraphy, West Coast of North America. Ed. by Mark V. Filewicz & Richard L. Squires. (Illus.). 281p. (Orig.). 1988. pap. 18.00 (*1-878861-11-5*) Pac Section SEPM.

Paleoclimate Analysis & Modelling. Ed. by Alan D. Hecht. LC 84-22175. (Environmental Science & Technology Ser.). 461p. reprint ed. pap. 143.00 (*0-7837-2396-2*, 204008100006) Bks Demand.

Paleoclimate & Basin Evolution of Playa Systems. Ed. by Michael R. Rosen. LC 93-50091. (Special Papers: No. 289). 1994. pap. 33.75 (*0-8137-2289-6*) Geol Soc.

Paleoclimate & Evolution, with Emphasis on Human Origins. Ed. by Elisabeth S. Vrba et al. 547p. 1996. 95.00 (*0-300-06348-2*) Yale U Pr.

Paleoclimatology. Crowley & North. (Series on Geology & Geophysics: No. 18). (Illus.). 360p. 1996. pap. text 43.95 (*0-19-510533-8*) OUP.

Paleoclimatology. Thomas J. Crowley & Gerald R. North. (Illus.). 360p. (C). 1995. pap. 35.00 (*0-19-515338-3*) OUP.

Paleoclimatology: Reconstructing Climates of the Quaternary. 2nd ed. Raymond S. Bradley. (International Geophysics Ser.). 613p. 1999. text 69.95 (*0-12-124010-X*) Harcourt.

Paleoclimatology & Paleometeorology: Modern & Past Patterns of Global Atmospheric Transport. Ed. by Margaret Leinen & Michael Sarnthein. (C). 1989. text 373.50 (*0-7923-0341-5*) Kluwer Academic.

Paleocology of Volcanic Soils in the Columbian Central Cordillera (Parque Nacional Natural de los Nevados) Johannes Barwold. (Dissertationes Botanicae Ser.: Band 95). (Illus.). 212p. 1986. pap. 53.00 (*3-443-64007-9*, Pub. by Gebruder Borntraeger) Balogh.

Paleocommunities: A Case Study from the Silurian & Lower Devonian. Ed. by A. J. Boucot & J. D. Lawson. (World & Regional Geology Ser.: No. 6). (Illus.). 600p. (C). 1999. text 300.00 (*0-521-36398-5*) Cambridge U Pr.

***Paleoconservatives: New Voices of the Old Right.** Ed. by Joseph Scotchie. LC 99-17346. 4p. 1999. 29.95 (*1-56000-427-4*) Transaction Pubs.

Paleocurrents & Basin Analysis. 2nd ed. P. E. Potter & F. J. Pettijohn. LC 76-30293. (Illus.). 1977. 138.95 (*0-387-07952-1*) Spr-Verlag.

Paleoecologia y Arqueologia en la Frontera Norte de Mesoamerica: Un Analisis. Roy B. Brown. 134p. 1991. pap. 5.00 (*968-6487-61-1*, IN062) UPLAAP.

Paleoecology: Constructions, Sedimentology Diagenesis & Association of Fossils, Report 1976-78. Ed. by F. Westphal & A. Adolf Seilacher. (Neues Jahrb. fuer Geologie & Paleontologie Ser.: Vol. 157: 1-2). (ENG & GER., Illus.). 276p. 1978. pap. text 61.25 (*0-945345-32-1*) Lubrecht & Cramer.

Paleoecology & Archeology of an Acheulian Site at Caddington, England. Ed. by C. Garth Sampson. LC 67-5086. (Illus.). 168p. 1978. pap. 12.95 (*0-685-14427-5*) SMU Press.

Paleoecology & Microfloristics of Miocene Diatomites from the Otis Basin-Juntura Region of Harney & Malheur Counties, Oregon. S. L. Van Landingham. (Illus.). 1967. pap. 26.00 (*3-7682-5426-7*) Lubrecht & Cramer.

Paleoecology & Regional Paleoclimatic Implications of the Farmdalian Craigmile & Woodfordian Waubonsie Mammalian Local Faunas, Southwestern Iowa. R. Sanders Rhodes, II. (Reports of Investigations: No. 40). (Illus.). viii, 51p. (Orig.). 1984. pap. 5.00 (*0-89792-103-8*) Ill St Museum.

Paleoecology, Biostratigraphy, Paleoceanography & Taxonomy of Agglutinated Foraminifera. Ed. by Christoph Hemleben et al. (C). 1990. lib. bdg. 397.50 (*0-7923-1041-1*) Kluwer Academic.

Paleoecology Concepts & Applications. 2nd ed. James W. Dodd. LC 89-22502. 528p. 1990. 210.00 (*0-471-85711-4*) Wiley.

Paleoenvironmental & Tectonic Controls in Coal-Forming Basins of the United States. Ed. by Paul C. Lyons & Charles L. Rice. LC 86-25716. (Geological Society of America Ser.: Vol. 210). (Illus.). 213p. 1986. reprint ed. pap. 66.10 (*0-608-07737-2*, 206782500010) Bks Demand.

***Paleoenvironmental Reconstruction in Arid Lands.** Ed. by A. K. Singhvi & E. Derbyshire. (Illus.). 336p. 1999. 85.00 (*90-5410-710-3*, Pub. by A A Balkema) Ashgate Pub Co.

Paleoenvironments & Archaeology of the Trigo Mountains: Data Recovery in the Hart Mine & Cibola Quarry Areas, Yuma County, Arizona. Steven D. Shelley & Jeffrey H. Altschul. (Illus.). 153p. 1989. pap. text 20.00 (*0-317-01835-3*) Gray Lit Pr.

Paleoenvironments & Archaeology of the Trigo Mountains: Data Recovery in the Hart Mine & Cibola Quarry Areas, Yuma County, Arizona. Steven

P

An Asterisk (*) at the beginning of an entry indicates that the title is appearing for the first time.

D. Shelley & Jeffrey H. Altschul. (Statistical Research Technical Ser.: No. 15). (Illus.). 141p. 1989. reprint ed. spiral bd. 12.50 (*1-879442-13-2*) Stats Res.

Paleoepidemiological Studies on Great Basin Coprolites: Estimation of Dietary Fiber Intake & Evaluation of the Ingestion of Anthelmintic Plant Substances. Michael Kliks. LC GN0296.K55. (Illus.). 82p. reprint ed. pap. 30.00 (*0-7837-2613-9*, 204277700006) Bks Demand.

***Paleoethnobotany: A Handbook of Procedures.** 2nd ed. Deborah M. Pearsall. 700p. 2000. 89.95 (*0-12-548042-3*) Acad Pr.

Paleoethnobotany of the Kameda Peninsula Jomon. Gary W. Crawford. (Anthropological Papers Ser.: No. 73). (Illus.). 200p. 1983. pap. 8.00 (*0-932206-95-6*) U Mich Mus Anthro.

Paleogene Fossil Sporomorpha of the Bakony Mountains. M. Kedves. (Studia Biologica Hungarica Ser.: No. 21). 120p. (C). 1986. pap. 33.00 (*963-05-4066-5*, Pub. by Akade Kiado) St Mut.

Paleogeodynamics. L. P. Zonenshain et al. Tr. by Benjamin M. Page & L. A. Torchigina from ENG. LC 97-43346. 218p. 1997. 45.00 (*0-87590-873-X*) Am Geophysical.

Paleogeography & Petroleum Synthesis of Western Venezuela. E. Zambrano et al. (Illus.). 66p. (C). 1972. 140.00 (*2-7108-0194-9*, Pub. by Edits Technip) Enfield Pubs NH.

***Paleogeographic Evolution & Non-Glacial Eustacy: Northern South America.** Ed. by James L. Pindell & Charles Drake. (Special Publications: Vol. 58). (Illus.). 443p. 1998. 119.00 (*1-56576-041-7*) SEPM.

Paleogeographic Provinces & Provinciality. Ed. by Charles A. Ross. LC 74-193154. (Society of Economic Paleontologists & Mineralogists, Special Publication Ser.: No. 21). 243p. reprint ed. pap. 75.40 (*0-608-12951-8*, 202474300038) Bks Demand.

Paleogeography & Geological History of Greater Antilles. K. M. Khudoley & A. A. Meyerhoff. LC 77-129999. (Geological Society of America, Memoir Ser.: No. 129). 215p. reprint ed. pap. 66.70 (*0-608-13958-0*, 202502400041) Bks Demand.

Paleogeography, Paleoclimate, & Source Rocks. Ed. by A. Y. Huc. (Studies in Geology: No. 40). (Illus.). viii, 347p. 1995. pap. 89.00 (*0-89181-048-X*, 568) AAPG.

Paleognathous Birds from the Early Tertiary of the Northern Hemisphere. Peter Houde. (Publications of the Nuttall Ornithological Club: No. 22). (Illus.). 148p. (C). 1988. 25.00 (*1-877973-32-7*) Nuttall Ornith.

Paleographical Papers, 1907-1965, 2 vols. E. A. Lowe. Ed. by Ludwig Bieler. 1972. 69.00 (*0-19-818220-1*) OUP.

Paleography Collection, Vol. 2. large type ed. 1994. 220.00 (*0-7838-2217-0*, G K Hall Lrg Type) Mac Lib Ref.

Paleography of Greek Papyri. F. G. Kenyon. 160p. 1976. 20.00 (*0-89005-083-X*) Ares.

Paleohistoria: Acta et Communicationes Institui Bio-Archaeologici Universitatis Groninganae, Vol. 25 (1983) 224p. (C). 1986. text 135.00 (*90-6191-606-2*, Pub. by A A Balkema) Ashgate Pub Co.

Paleohistoria 35-36: Acta et Communicationes Instituti Bio-Archaeologici Universitatis Groninganae. (Illus.). 280p. (C). 1995. text 135.00 (*90-5410-611-5*, Pub. by A A Balkema) Ashgate Pub Co.

Paleohydrology & Sedimentology of Lake Missoula Flooding in Eastern Washington. Victor R. Baker. LC 72-89463. (Geological Society of America. Special Paper Ser.). vii, 79p. 1973. write for info. (*0-8137-2144-X*) Geol Soc.

Paleoindian & Early Archaic Southeast. Ed. by David G. Anderson & Kenneth E. Sassaman. LC 96-1902. (Illus.). 544p. (Orig.). (C). 1996. pap. text 29.95 (*0-8173-0835-0*) U of Ala Pr.

Paleoindian Geoarchaeology of the Southern High Plains. Vance T. Holliday. LC 96-25213. (Illus.). 312p. 1997. 50.00 (*0-292-73109-4*); pap. 24.95 (*0-292-73114-0*) U of Tex Pr.

Paleoindian Research in Virginia, a Synthesis. 2nd rev. ed. Ed. by J. Mark Wittkofski & Theodore R. Rinehart. (Cova Ser.: Vol. 19). 208p. 1994. pap. text 28.00 (*1-884626-24-6*) Archeolog Soc.

Paleokarst. Ed. by N. P. James & P. W. Choquette. (Illus.). xii, 420p. 1987. 115.95 (*0-387-96563-7*) Spr-Verlag.

Paleokarst: A Systematic & Regional Review. Ed. by P. Bosak et al. (Developments in Earth Surface Processes Ser.: No. 1). 726p. 1990. 295.00 (*0-444-98874-2*) Elsevier.

Paleokarst Related Hydrocarbon Reservoirs. Ed. by Richard D. Fritz et al. (Core Workshop Notes Ser.: No. 18). (Illus.). 281p. 1993. pap. 59.00 (*1-56576-004-2*) SEPM.

Paleolimnology. H. Loffler. (Developments in Hydrobiology Ser.). 1987. lib. bdg. 276.50 (*90-6193-624-1*) Kluwer Academic.

Paleolimnology & the Reconstruction of Ancient Environments. Ed. by Ronald B. Davis. (C). 1990. text 257.50 (*0-7923-0571-X*) Kluwer Academic.

Paleolimnology of European Maar Lakes. Ed. by Jorg F. Negendank & Bernd Zolitschka. LC 93-4663. (Lecture Notes in Earth Sciences Ser.: Vol. 49). 1993. 126.95 (*0-387-56570-1*) Spr-Verlag.

Paleolimnology of European Maar Lakes. Ed. by Jorg F. Negendank & Bernd Zolitschka. (Lecture Notes in Earth Sciences Ser.: Vol. 49). (Illus.). x, 514p. 1993. pap. write for info. (*3-540-56570-1*) Spr-Verlag.

Paleolithic Archaeology in Iran. Philip E. Smith. (American Institute of Iranian Stuides, Monograph: No. I). (Illus.). xiv, 111p. 1986. pap. text 15.00 (*0-934718-73-3*) U Museum Pubns.

Paleolithic Man & the Nile-Faiyum Divide, Vol. 1. Kenneth S. Sandford & W. J. Arkell. LC 30-8240. (Illus.). 77p. 1930. lib. bdg. 24.00 (*0-226-62104-9*, OIP10) U Ch Pr.

Paleolithic of Siberia: New Discoveries & Interpretations. A. P. Derevianko et al. Tr. by Inna P. Karucgeva from ENG. LC 97-4703. 416p. 1998. text 59.95 (*0-252-02052-9*) U of Ill Pr.

Paleolithic Prehistory of the Zagros-Taurus. Ed. by Deborah I. Olszewski & Harold L. Dibble. LC 93-12382. (University Museum Monographs: Vol. 83/V). xiii, 237p. (C). 1983. 50.00 (*0-924171-24-3*) U Museum Pubns.

Paleolithic Site of the Douara Cave & Palaeogeography of Palmyra Basin in Syria: The Paleolithic Site at Douara Cave in Syria, Part II. Ed. by Fuyuji Takai & Hisashi Suzuki. 1974. 40.00 (*0-86008-107-9*, Pub. by U of Tokyo) Col U Pr.

Paleolithic Site of the Douara Cave & Paleogeography of Palmyra Basin in Syria: A Synopsis of the Sparoid Fish Genus Lethrinus, with the Description of a New Species. Ed. by Torao Sato. 90p. 1978. 26.50 (*0-86008-207-5*, Pub. by U of Tokyo) Col U Pr.

Paleolithic Site of the Douara Cave & Paleogeography of Palmyra Basin in Syria: Stratigraphy & Paleogeography in the Late Quarternary, Part I. Ed. by Kazuro Hanihara & Yutaka Sakaguchi. 121p. 1978. 49.50 (*0-86008-209-1*, Pub. by U of Tokyo) Col U Pr.

Paleolithic Site of the Douara Cave & Paleogeography of Palmyra Basin in Syria: 1984 Excavations, Part IV. Ed. by Takeru Akazawa & Yutaka Sakaguchi. (Illus.). 276p. 1987. text 69.50 (*0-86008-415-9*, Pub. by U of Tokyo) Col U Pr.

Paleolithic Site of the Douara Cave & Paleogeography of the Palmyra Basin in Syria: Prehistoric Occurrences & Chronology in Palmyra Basin, Part II. Ed. by Kazuro Hanihara & Takeru Akazawa. 270p. 1979. 52.50 (*0-86008-246-6*, Pub. by U of Tokyo) Col U Pr.

Paleomagnetic Principles & Practice. Lisa Tauxe. LC 98-34667. (Modern Approaches in Geophysics Ser.). 1998. 135.00 (*0-7923-5258-0*) Kluwer Academic.

Paleomagnetic Rotations & Continental Deformation. Ed. by Catherine Kissel & Carlo Laj. (C). 1988. text 260.00 (*0-7923-0006-8*) Kluwer Academic.

***Paleomagnetism.** 2nd ed. Michael W. McElhinny. 400p. 1999. 69.95 (*0-12-483355-1*) Acad Pr.

Paleomagnetism: Magnetic Domains to Geologic Terranes. R. F. Butler. (Illus.). 336p. 1991. pap. 59.95 (*0-86542-070-X*) Blackwell Sci.

Paleomagnetism of the Atlantic, Tethys, & Iapetus Oceans. Rob Van der Voo. LC 92-575. (Illus.). 421p. (C). 1993. text 105.00 (*0-521-41941-7*) Cambridge U Pr.

Paleomagnetology. A. N. Khramov. (Illus.). 330p. 1987. 142.95 (*0-387-17360-9*) Spr-Verlag.

Paleonthology: The Record of Life. Colin W. Stearn et al. 464p. 1989. text 90.95 (*0-471-84528-0*) Wiley.

Paleontologi: A Biographical & Bibliographical Register of Paleontologists, Vol. 72. K. Lambrecht & W. A. Quenstedt. Ed. by Claude C. Albritton, Jr. LC 77-6526. (History of Geology Ser.). 1978. reprint ed. lib. bdg. 44.95 (*0-405-10445-6*) Ayer.

Paleontological Events: Stratigraphic, Ecological, & Evolutionary Implications. Ed. by Carlton E. Brett & Gordon C. Baird. LC 96-1558. (Illus.). 616p. 1996. 68.50 (*0-231-08250-9*) Col U Pr.

Paleontologist's Notebook. Susan S. Nash. (Illus.). 96p. 1995. pap. 9.00 (*1-880516-16-0*) Left Hand Bks.

Paleontology: Or, a Systematic Summary of Extinct Animals & Their Geological Relations. Richard Owen. Ed. by Stephen Jay Gould. LC 79-8342. (History of Paleontology Ser.). (Illus.). 1980. reprint ed. lib. bdg. 40.95 (*0-405-12732-4*) Ayer.

Paleontology in China, 1979: Selected Papers Presented at the 3rd General Assembly & 12th National Meeting of the Palaeontological Society of China, April 1979. Ed. by Curt Teichert et al. LC 81-19997. (Geological Society of America Ser.: Vol. 187). (Illus.). 272p. reprint ed. pap. 84.40 (*0-608-07722-4*, 206781000010) Bks Demand.

Paleontology of Invertebrates. R. Enay. Tr. by Thomas Reimer from FRE. LC 93-26800. 1993. 47.95 (*0-387-53891-7*); write for info. (*3-540-53891-7*) Spr-Verlag.

Paleontology of Vertebrates. Jean Chaline. (Illus.). 200p. 1990. 42.95 (*0-387-51755-3*) Spr-Verlag.

Paleontology of Vertebrates. Norman King. 510p. (C). 1998. per. 42.95 (*0-7872-4598-4*) Kendall-Hunt.

Paleonutrition: The Diet & Health of Prehistoric Americans. Ed. by Kristin D. Sobolik. LC 93-70265. (Center for Archaeological Investigations Occasional Paper Ser.: No. 22). (Illus.). xviii, 321p. (Orig.). 1994. pap. 30.00 (*0-88104-078-9*) Center Archaeol.

Paleopalynology. A. Traverse. 500p. (C). 1985. text 75.00 (*0-04-561001-0*); pap. text 44.95 (*0-04-561002-9*) Routledge.

Paleopathological & Paleoepidemiological: Study of Osseous Syphilis in Skulls of the Edo Period. Takao Suzuki. 50p. 1984. 34.50 (*0-86008-358-6*, Pub. by U of Tokyo) Col U Pr.

Paleopathology: An Introduction to the Study of Ancient Evidences of Disease. Roy L. Moodie. LC 75-23744. reprint ed. 74.50 (*0-404-13350-9*) AMS Pr.

Paleopathology: Disease in the Fossil Record. Bruce M. Rothschild & Larry Martin. 400p. 1992. 148.95 (*0-8493-8897-X*, R134) CRC Pr.

Paleoreconstruction of the Continents. M. W. McElhinny & D. A. Valencio. (Geodynamics Ser.: Vol. 2). 194p. 1981. 20.00 (*0-87590-511-0*) Am Geophysical.

Paleoseismic Analysis of the Wasatch Fault Zone at the Brigham City Trench Site, Brigham City, Utah & the Pole Patch Trench Site, Pleasant View, Utah. Stephen F. Personius. LC TN24.U8 A322. (Special Study Ser.: Vol. 76). (Illus.). 39p. 1991. pap. 6.00 (*1-55791-195-9*, SS-76) Utah Geological Survey.

Paleoseismic Investigation at Rock Canyon, Provo Segment, Wasatch Fault Zone, Utah County, Utah. William R. Lund & Bill D. Black. LC TN24.U8A315. (Special Study of the Utah Geological Survey Ser.: Vol. 93, No. 8). (Illus.). 21p. 1998. pap. 8.00 (*1-55791-613-6*, SS-93) Utah Geological Survey.

Paleoseismic Investigation on the Salt Lake City Segment of the Wasatch Fault Zone at the South Fork Dry Creek & Dry Gulch Sites, Salt Lake County, Utah. Bill D. Black et al. LC 97-103871. (Special Study of the Utah Geological Survey Ser.: Vol. 92). (Illus.). 22p. 1996. pap. 5.25 (*1-55791-399-4*, SS-92) Utah Geological Survey.

***Paleoseismic Studies in the Southeastern United States & New England.** R. Gelinas. 587p. 1998. per. 44.00 (*0-16-062949-7*) USGPO.

Paleoseismology. James P. McCalpin. (Illus.). 588p. (C). 1998. pap. text 49.95 (*0-12-481826-9*) Acad Pr.

Paleoseismology. Ed. by James P. McCalpin & Alan R. Nelson. (International Geophysics Ser.: Vol. 62). (Illus.). 588p. (C). 1996. text 89.95 (*0-12-481825-0*) Acad Pr.

Paleoshorelines & Prehistory: An Investigation of Method. Lucy L. Johnson & Melanie Stright. 256p. 1991. boxed set 79.95 (*0-8493-8855-4*, GN) CRC Pr.

Paleosols & Weathering Through Geologic Time: Principles & Applications. Ed. by Juergen Reinhardt & Wayne R. Sigleo. LC 87-35459. (Geological Society of America Ser.: Vol. 216). (Illus.). 193p. 1988. reprint ed. pap. 59.90 (*0-608-07742-9*, 206783000010) Bks Demand.

Paleostructures of Nigeria & Adjacent Countries. Hugo Buser. (Geotektonische Forschungen Ser.: Vol. 24). (GER.). ii, 90p. 1966. pap. 20.00 (*3-510-50915-3*, Pub. by E Schweizerbartsche) Balogh.

Paleotectonics & Sedimentation in the Rocky Mountain Region, United States. Ed. by James A. Peterson. LC 86-17467. (American Association of Petroleum Geologists. Memoir Ser.: No. 41). (Illus.). 703p. reprint ed. pap. 200.00 (*0-608-04228-5*, 206498500012) Bks Demand.

Paleotethysides in West Yunnan & Sichuan, China. Xu Xiaozu et al. 250p. 1999. 79.95 (*7-03-006749-5*, Pub. by Sci Pr) Lubrecht & Cramer.

Paleozoic & Early Mesozoic Paleogeographic Relations: Sierra Nevada, Klamath Mountains, & Related Terranes. Ed. by D. S. Harwood & M. M. Miller. (Special Papers: No. 255). (Illus.). 432p. 1991. pap. 31.00 (*0-8137-2255-1*) Geol Soc.

***Paleozoic & Triassic Paleography & Tectonics of Western Nevada & Northern California.** George E. Gehrels & M. J. Soreghan. LC 00-37199. (Special Papers). 2000. write for info. (*0-8137-2347-7*) Geol Soc.

Paleozoic Epibionts. R. R. Alexander. 116p. 1991. pap. text 108.00 (*3-7186-5130-0*, Harwood Acad Pubs) Gordon & Breach.

Paleozoic Life: An Educational Coloring Book. Spizzirri Publishing Co. Staff. Ed. by Linda Spizzirri. (Illus.). 32p. (J). (gr. 1-8). 1981. pap. 1.99 (*0-86545-024-2*) Spizzirri.

Paleozoic Paleogeography of the Western United States - II, 2 vols., 1. Ed. by John D. Cooper & Calvin H. Stevens. (Illus.). 872p. (Orig.). 1991. pap. write for info. (*1-878861-01-8*) Pac Section SEPM.

Paleozoic Paleogeography of the Western United States - II, 2 vols., 2. Ed. by John D. Cooper & Calvin H. Stevens. (Illus.). 872p. (Orig.). 1991. pap. write for info. (*1-878861-02-6*) Pac Section SEPM.

Paleozoic Paleogeography of the Western United States - II, 2 vols., Set. Ed. by John D. Cooper & Calvin H. Stevens. (Illus.). 872p. (Orig.). 1991. pap. 55.00 (*1-878861-03-4*) Pac Section SEPM.

Paleozoic Salt Bearing Formations of the World. M. A. Zharkov. (Illus.). 440p. 1984. 136.95 (*0-387-13133-7*) Spr-Verlag.

Paleozoic Sea-Level Changes in the Appalachian Basin, No. T354. Ed. by Dennison. (IGC Field Trip Guidebooks Ser.). 64p. 1989. 28.00 (*0-87590-672-9*) Am Geophysical.

Paleozoic Sequence Stratigraphy: Views from the North American Craton. Ed. by Brian J. Witzke et al. LC 96-2879. (Special Papers: No. 306). (Illus.). 1996. pap. 115.00 (*0-8137-2306-X*) Geol Soc.

Paleozoic Sequence Stratigraphy, Biostratigraphy, & Biogeography: Studies in Honor of J. Granville "Jess" Johnson. Ed. by Gilbert Klapper et al. LC 97-34722. (Special Paper Ser.: No. 319). (Illus.). 1997. pap. 108.00 (*0-8137-2321-3*) Geol Soc.

Paleozoic Shelf-to-Basin Transition in Owens Valley, California. Ed. by Calvin H. Stevens. (Illus.). 58p. (Orig.). 1991. pap. 10.00 (*1-878861-62-X*) Pac Section SEPM.

Paler Shade of White. Ed. by Ginny L. Ballor & Carrie Neumann. 40p. (Orig.). (C). 1996. pap. 3.00 (*1-882294-18-1*) Green Gate.

Palermo. Blinky Palermo. Ed. by Delano Greenidge & Erich Maas. LC 88-51594. (ENG & GER.). 160p. 1989. 60.00 (*0-929445-01-5*) D Greenidge Editions.

Palermo Stone & the Archaic Kings of Egypt. Patrick F. O'Mara. (Studies in the Structural Archaeology of Ancient Egypt: Vol. I). (Illus.). xvi, 208p. (Orig.). 1979. pap. 22.00 (*0-686-30249-4*) Paulette Pub.

Palestina. Suzanne T. Moore. 1983. 8.95 (*0-938758-13-6*) MTM Pub Co.

Palestine. M. Russell. 400p. 1985. 300.00 (*1-85077-053-0*, Pub. by Darf Pubs Ltd) St Mut.

Palestine, Bk. 1. Joe Sacco. 144p. 1994. pap. 16.95 (*1-56097-150-9*) Fantagraph Bks.

Palestine, Bk. 2. Joe Sacco. 144p. 1995. pap. 16.95 (*1-56097-300-5*) Fantagraph Bks.

***Palestine: A Country Study Guide, 110 vols.** International Business Publications, USA Staff & Global Investment Center, USA Staff. (World Country Study Guides Library Ser.: Vol. 217). (Illus.). 350p. 2000. pap. 69.95 (*0-7397-1040-0*) Intl Business Pubns.

Palestine: A Study of Jewish, Arab, & British Policies, 2 Vols, Set. Esco Foundation for Palestine, Inc. Staff. LC 47-2569. 1974. reprint ed. 210.00 (*0-527-27750-9*) Periodicals Srv.

Palestine: Continuing Dispossession. Glenn E. Perry et al. LC 85-20031. (AAUG Monographs: No. 21). 145p. (Orig.). 1986. pap. 10.00 (*0-937694-72-X*) Assn Arab-Amer U Grads.

Palestine: Mohammedan Holy Land. Ibn Al-Firkah & Ibrahim ibn Abd Al-Rahman. Ed. by Charles Matthews. LC 78-63568. (Yale Oriental Series: Researches: No. 24). reprint ed. 34.50 (*0-404-60324-6*) AMS Pr.

Palestine: Profile of an Occupation. Khamsin Collective Staff. LC 89-35868. (Khamsin Collective Ser.: Vol. 14). 192p. (C). 1989. pap. 17.50 (*0-86232-889-6*, Pub. by Zed Books); text 49.95 (*0-86232-888-8*, Pub. by Zed Books) St Martin.

Palestine: The Prize & Price of Zion. Kenneth Cragg. LC 98-109158. 224p. 1997. pap. 24.95 (*0-304-70075-4*) Continuum.

Palestine: The Suppression of an Idea. Muhammad Hallaj. (Occasional Papers: No. 8). 40p. 1983. pap. 2.00 (*0-937694-61-4*) Assn Arab-Amer U Grads.

Palestine - A Twice-Promised Land? The British, the Arabs, & Zionism, Vol. 1. Isaiah Friedman. LC 99-30396. 321p. 1999. 44.95 (*1-56000-391-X*) Transaction Pubs.

Palestine--Divided or United? The Case for a Bi-National Palestine Before the United Nations. M. Leon Reiner et al. LC 80-39531. 104p. 1983. reprint ed. lib. bdg. 59.75 (*0-8371-2617-7*, MAPA, Greenwood Pr) Greenwood.

Palestine & Israel: A Challenge to Justice. John Quigley. LC 89-39218. 345p. (Orig.). (C). 1990. text 54.95 (*0-8223-1011-2*); pap. text 22.95 (*0-8223-1023-6*) Duke.

Palestine & Israel: Conflict & Change. Ed. by Robert W. McGee. 1998. 25.00 (*1-892736-00-4*) Dumont Inst.

Palestine & Israel: The Uprising & Beyond. David McDowell. 1990. 40.00 (*0-520-06902-1*, Pub. by U CA Pr) Cal Prin Full Svc.

Palestine & Israel: The Uprising & Beyond. David McDowall. (Illus.). 335p. 1991. reprint ed. pap. 16.95 (*0-520-07653-2*, Pub. by U CA Pr) Cal Prin Full Svc.

Palestine & Israel in the 19th & 20th Centuries. Ed. by Elie Kedourie & Sylvia G. Haim. (Illus.). 286p. 1982. 49.50 (*0-7146-3121-3*, Pub. by F Cass Pubs) Intl Spec Bk.

Palestine & Jewish History: Criticism at the Borders of Ethnography. Jonathan Boyarin. LC 95-39566. 1996. pap. 19.95 (*0-8166-2765-7*); text 49.95 (*0-8166-2764-9*) U of Minn Pr.

Palestine & Roumania: A Description of the Holy Land & the Past & Present State of Roumania & the Roumanian Jews. Haym Z. Sneersohn. Ed. by Moshe Davis. LC 77-70745. (America & the Holy Land Ser.). 1977. reprint ed. lib. bdg. 19.95 (*0-405-10291-7*) Ayer.

Palestine & Saints in Caesar's Household. Adam C. Powell, Sr. 215p. 1998. reprint ed. pap. 35.95 (*1-58073-006-X*) BCP Bks.

Palestine & Saints in Caesar's Household. Adam C. Powell, Sr. 215p. 1998. reprint ed. pap. 35.95 (*0-933121-91-1*) Black Classic.

Palestine & the Arab-Israeli Conflict. 3rd ed. Charles D. Smith. 358p. 1995. pap. text 26.95 (*0-312-09649-6*) St Martin.

Palestine & the Arab-Israeli Conflict. 4th ed. Smith. pap. text 33.95 (*0-312-20828-6*) St Martin.

***Palestine & the Arab-Israeli Conflict.** 4th ed. Charles Smith. 2000. text 39.95 (*0-312-22756-6*) St Martin.

Palestine & the Arabs' Fight for Liberation. Fred Feldman & Georges Sayad. 62p. 1989. reprint ed. pap. 4.00 (*0-87348-547-5*) Pathfinder NY.

Palestine & the Bible. Ed. by Mohammad T. Mehdi. LC 71-114557. 1971. pap. 5.00 (*0-911026-06-1*) New World Press NY.

Palestine & the Egyptian National Identity. Ghada H. Talhami. LC 91-27807. 192p. 1992. 57.95 (*0-275-94124-8*, C4124, Praeger Pubs) Greenwood.

Palestine & the Great Powers, 1945-1948. Michael J. Cohen. LC 82-3858. 432p. reprint ed. pap. 134.00 (*0-8357-3428-5*, 203968600013) Bks Demand.

Palestine & the Jews: The Impending Crisis. Charles M. Evans. LC 88-63960. 89p. 1975. 10.00 (*0-937181-03-X*) Charlemarie.

Palestine & the Law: Guidelines for the Resolution of the Arab-Israel Conflict. Musa Mazzawi. LC 98-111964. 432p. 1997. 45.00 (*0-86372-222-9*, Pub. by Garnet-Ithaca) LPC InBook.

Palestine & the Palestinians. Samih K. Farsoun & Christina E. Zacharia. LC 97-21954. 400p. 1998. pap. text 22.00 (*0-8133-2773-3*, Pub. by Westview) HarpC.

Palestine & the United Nations: Prelude to Solution. Jacob Robinson. LC 71-147221. 269p. 1971. reprint ed. lib. bdg. 65.00 (*0-8371-5986-5*, ROPU, Greenwood Pr) Greenwood.

Palestine & Transjordan Administration Reports, 1918-1949, 16 vols. 11,500p. 1994. reprint ed. lib. bdg. 2995.00 (*1-85207-557-0*, Pub. by Archive Editions) N Ross.

Palestine at the Crossroads. Ernest Main. LC 71-180359. reprint ed. 42.50 (*0-404-56291-4*) AMS Pr.

Palestine Boundaries, 1833-1947, 4 vols., Set. Ed. by P. L. Toye. (Illus.). 2500p. (C). 1989. reprint ed. lib. bdg. 695.00 (*1-85207-175-3*, Pub. by Archive Editions) N Ross.

P

An Asterisk (*) at the beginning of an entry indicates that the title is appearing for the first time.

***Palestine Business & Investment Opportunities Yearbook: Investment, Export-Import & Other Business Opportunities & Contacts, 110 vols.** International Business Publications, USA Staff & Global Investment Center, USA Staff. (World Business Opportunities Library Ser.: Vol. 202). (Illus.). 350p. 2000. pap. 99.95 (*0-7397-1089-3*) Intl Business Pubns.

***Palestine Business Law Handbook: Basic Business Legislation & Regulations Affecting Business & Investment Activities.** International Business Publications, USA Staff & Global Investment Center, USA Staff. (World Law Handbooks Library: Vol. 202). (Illus.). 2000. pap. 99.95 (*0-7397-1090-7*) Intl Business Pubns.

Palestine Campaigns. Archibald P. Wavell. LC 72-7114. (Select Bibliographies Reprint Ser.). 1977. reprint ed. 37.95 (*0-8369-6957-X*) Ayer.

Palestine Conflict in the History of Modern Iraq: The Dynamics of Involvement, 1928-1948. Michael Eppel. LC 94-2031. 240p. 1994. 49.50 (*0-7146-4543-5*, Pub. by F Cass Pubs) Intl Spec Bk.

Palestine Dances! Folk Dances of Palestine: Music Book Index. Corinne Chochem. 63p. 1993. reprint ed. lib. bdg. 69.00 (*0-7812-9676-5*) Rprt Serv.

Palestine Diary. Chaim Chissin. 1976. 10.00 (*0-685-82598-1*) Herzl Pr.

Palestine Diary. Frederick H. Kisch. LC 73-180354. reprint ed. 31.45 (*0-404-56286-8*) AMS Pr.

Palestine Documents. Zafarul-Islam Khan. LC 98-903536. 894p. 1998. 30.00 (*81-7221-011-6*, Pub. by Pharos Media) M Ansari.

Palestine Economic Society Bulletin: Proceedings of the Bulletin of the Palestine Economic Society, Tel Aviv, Aug. 21 - Feb., 1934, 6 vols. in 5. Palestine Economic Society Bulletin Staff. reprint ed. write for info. (*0-404-56240-X*) AMS Pr.

***Palestine for the Muslims: The Ideology of Hamas.** Andrea Nusse. 204p. 1998. text 42.00 (*90-5702-333-4*, Harwood Acad Pubs); pap. text 22.00 (*90-5702-334-2*, Harwood Acad Pubs) Gordon & Breach.

***Palestine Government & Business Contacts Handbook: Strategic Government & Business Contacts for Conducting Succesful Business, Export-Import & Investment Activity.** International Business Publications, USA Staff & Global Investment Center, USA Staff. (World Export-Import & Business Library: 124). (Illus.). 250p. 2000. pap. 99.95 (*0-7397-6139-0*) Intl Business Pubns.

Palestine Immigration Policy under Sir Herbert Samuel: British, Zionist & Arab Attitudes. M. Mossek. 197p. 1978. 45.00 (*0-7146-3096-9*, Pub. by F Cass Pubs) Intl Spec Bk.

Palestine in Crisis. rev. ed. Graham Usher. 196p. (C). 1996. pap. 13.95 (*0-7453-0974-7*, Pub. by Pluto GBR) Stylus Pub VA.

Palestine in General History. T. H. Robinson et al. (British Academy, London, Schweich Lectures on Biblical Archaeology Series, 1930). 1974. reprint ed. pap. 25.00 (*0-8115-1268-1*) Periodicals Srv.

Palestine in Perspective: Politics, Human Rights & the West Bank. David H. Ott. 14.95 (*0-7043-2263-3*, Pub. by Quartet) Charles River Bks.

Palestine in Postwar United States & World Affairs, 2 vols. Aaron Klieman. Vol. 11. 792p. 1991. reprint ed. write for info. (*0-318-68399-7*); reprint ed. write for info. (*0-318-68400-4*) Garland.

Palestine in Postwar United States & World Affairs, 2 vols., Set. Aaron Klieman. LC 90-45877. (American Zionism Ser.: Vol. 11). 792p. 1991. reprint ed. text 80.00 (*0-8240-7359-2*) Garland.

Palestine in the Late Ottoman Period: Political, Social & Economic Transformation. David Kushner. xii, 434p. 1986. 112.50 (*90-04-07792-8*) Brill Academic Pubs.

Palestine in the Time of Jesus: Social Structures & Social Conflicts. K. C. Hanson. LC 98-18073. 1998. pap. text 21.00 (*0-8006-2808-X*, Fortress Pr) Augsburg Fortress.

Palestine in Transition: The Emergence of Ancient Israel. David N. Freedman & D. F. Graf. (Social World of Biblical Antiquity Ser.: No. 2). 108p. 1983. 28.50 (*0-907459-32-3*, Pub. by Sheffield Acad) CUP Services.

***Palestine Investment & Business Guide: Investment, Export-Import, Foreign Economic Assistance Projects, Contacts & More.** International Business Publications, USA Staff & Global Investment Center, USA Staff. (World Investment Guides Library Ser.: Vol. 207). (Illus.). 350p. 2000. pap. 99.95 (*0-7397-1088-5*) Intl Business Pubns.

Palestine Is, but Not in Jordan. Sheila Ryan & Muhammad Hallaj. (Information Papers: No. 24). 36p. (Orig.). 1983. pap. text 3.50 (*0-937694-60-6*) Assn Arab-Amer U Grads.

Palestine Is Coming: The Revival of Ancient Philistia. Kermit Zarley. 271p. (Orig.). 1990. pap. 12.95 (*0-929292-13-8*) Hannibal Bks.

***Palestine, Jerusalem - The Bradt Travel Guide.** Henry Stedman. (Illus.). 1999. pap. 18.95 (*1-84162-001-7*) Globe Pequot.

Palestine Jewry & the Arab Question, 1917-1925. Neil Caplan. 268p. 1978. 49.50 (*0-7146-3110-8*, Pub. by F Cass Pubs) Intl Spec Bk.

Palestine Mission: A Personal Record. Richard H. Crossman. Ed. by Moshe Davis. LC 77-70672. (America & the Holy Land Ser.). (Illus.). 1977. reprint ed. lib. bdg. 23.95 (*0-405-10240-2*) Ayer.

***Palestine Question.** 2000. 29.50 (*0-86356-932-3*) Saqi.

Palestine Question. Henry Cattan. 320p. 1987. lib. bdg. 57.50 (*0-7099-4860-3*, Pub. by C Helm) Routldge.

Palestine Question: A Select Bibliography. 370p. 25.00 (*92-1-100513-2*, E.93.I.17) UN.

Palestine Question: An Annotated Bibliography. Glenn E. Perry. (Bibliography Ser.: No. 6). 138p. (Orig.). 1990. pap. 6.95 (*0-937694-86-X*) Assn Arab-Amer U Grads.

Palestine Question in American History. American Jewish Historical Society Staff et al. Ed. by American Historical Association Staff. 1978. 17.95 (*0-405-11521-0*) Ayer.

Palestine Reborn. Walid Khalidi. 200p. 1992. text 65.00 (*1-85043-563-4*, Pub. by I B T); text 24.95 (*1-85043-559-6*, Pub. by I B T) St Martin.

Palestine, Still a Dilemma. Frank Sakran. LC 76-29879. 10.00 (*0-686-70283-2*) New World Press NY.

Palestine 30 A. D. You Are There. Colleen Britton. (Illus.). 73p. (Orig.). (J). (ps-6). 1987. pap. 12.95 (*0-940754-38-X*) Ed Ministries.

Palestine To-Day & To-Morrow: A Gentile's Survey of Zionism. John H. Holmes. Ed. by Moshe Davis. LC 77-70701. (America & the Holy Land Ser.). 1977. reprint ed. lib. bdg. 26.95 (*0-405-10253-4*) Ayer.

Palestine to Israel: From Mandate to Independence. Michael J. Cohen. 1987. 49.50 (*0-7146-3312-7*, Pub. by F Cass Pubs) Intl Spec Bk.

Palestine under the Moslems. Tr. by Guy Le Strange. LC 70-180356. reprint ed. 84.50 (*0-404-56288-4*) AMS Pr.

Palestine Yearbook International Law, No. 4. 1988. lib. bdg. 105.00 (*90-411-0341-4*) Kluwer Law Intl.

Palestine Yearbook International Law, No. 6. 1991. lib. bdg. 105.00 (*90-411-0343-0*) Kluwer Law Intl.

Palestine Yearbook International Law # 7 19, No. 7. 1996. lib. bdg. 105.00 (*90-411-0344-9*) Kluwer Law Intl.

***Palestine Yearbook of International Law, Vol. 10.** Ed. by Anis F. Kassim. 432p. 1999. text 190.00 (*90-411-1304-5*) Kluwer Law Intl.

***Palestine Yearbook of International Law Vol. IX: 1996-1997.** Ed. by Anis F. Kassim. 480p. 1998. 214.00 (*90-411-1009-7*) Kluwer Law Intl.

Palestine Yearbook of International Law, 1984. 1984. lib. bdg. 105.00 (*90-411-0338-4*) Kluwer Academic.

Palestine Yearbook of International Law, 1985. 1995. text 105.00 (*90-411-0339-2*) Kluwer Law Intl.

Palestine Yearbook of International Law, 1986. 1986. text 105.00 (*90-411-0340-6*) Kluwer Law Intl.

Palestine Yearbook of International Law, 1989. 1989. text 105.00 (*90-411-0342-2*) Kluwer Law Intl.

Palestine Yearbook of International Law, 1995, Vol. PYIL 8. Ed. by Anis F. Kassim. 1997. 228.00 (*90-411-0314-7*) Kluwer Law Intl.

Palestine/Israel: The Long Conflict. James Ciment. LC 96-48371. (Conflict & Crisis in the Post-Cold War World Ser.). 1997. 23.95 (*0-8160-3526-1*) Facts on File.

***Palestine's Children: Returning to Haifa & Other Stories.** Ghassan Kanafani. Tr. by Barbara Harlow & Karen E. Riley. LC 00-24783. 160p. 2000. pap. 13.95 (*0-89410-890-5*, Three Contnts) L Rienner.

***Palestine's Children: Returning to Haifa & Other Stories.** Ghassan Kanafani. Tr. by Barbara Harlow & Karen E. Riley. LC 00-24783. 160p. 2000. lib. bdg. 25.00 (*0-89410-865-4*, Three Contnts) L Rienner.

Palestinian Agenda for the West Bank & Gaza. Ed. by Emile A. Nakhleh. LC 80-15596. (AEI Studies: No. 277). 143p. reprint ed. pap. 44.40 (*0-8357-4520-1*, 203737900008) Bks Demand.

Palestinian Arab Cultural Nationalism, 1919-1960. Adnan Abu-Ghazaleh. 135p. (Orig.). (C). 1990. pap. 12.50 (*0-915597-75-6*) Amana Bks.

Palestinian Arab National Movement, 1929-1939 Vol. 2: From Riots to Rebellion. Yehoshua Porath. 414p. 1977. pap. 27.50 (*0-7146-4197-9*, Pub. by F Cass Pubs) Intl Spec Bk.

Palestinian Catastrophe. Michael Palumbo. 1990. pap. 11.95 (*0-7043-0099-0*, Pub. by Quartet) Interlink Pub.

Palestinian Citizens in an Ethnic Jewish State: Identities in Conflict. Nadim N. Rouhana. LC 96-51073. 312p. 1997. 32.00 (*0-300-06685-6*) Yale U Pr.

Palestinian Conflict: Identifying Propaganda Techniques. Neal Bernards. LC 90-37741. (Opposing Viewpoints Juniors Ser.). (Illus.). 36p. (J). (gr. 3-6). 1990. lib. bdg. 16.20 (*0-89908-602-0*) Greenhaven.

Palestinian Convenant & Its Meaning. Y. Harkabi. 159p. 1979. 45.00 (*0-85303-200-9*, Pub. by M Vallentine & Co); pap. 19.50 (*0-85303-206-8*, Pub. by M Vallentine & Co) Intl Spec Bk.

***Palestinian Democracy: An Appraisal of the Legislative Council.** David K. Schenker. LC 99-54846. (Policy Papers). 1999. pap. write for info. (*0-944029-34-5*) Wash Inst NEP.

Palestinian Dilemma: Nationalist Consciousness & University Education in Israel. Khalil Nakhleh. (Monographs: No. 10). 134p. (Orig.). 1979. pap. text 6.00 (*0-937694-04-5*) Assn Arab-Amer U Grads.

Palestinian Economy: Between Imposed Integration & Voluntary Separation. Arie Arnon et al. LC 97-26555. (Social, Economic & Political Studies of the Middle East & Asia: No. 60). (Illus.). 288p. 1997. 79.50 (*90-04-10538-7*) Brill Academic Pubs.

Palestinian Education: A Threat to Israel's Security? Jerusalem Media & Communication Centre Staff. (Information Papers: No. 26). 51p. (Orig.). 1989. pap. 5.00 (*0-937694-85-1*) Assn Arab-Amer U Grads.

Palestinian Entity, 1959-1974: Arab Politics & the PLO. Moshe Shemesh. LC 88-469. 1988. 57.50 (*0-7146-3281-3*, Pub. by F Cass Pubs) Intl Spec Bk.

Palestinian Entity, 1959-1974: Arab Politics & the PLO. 2nd rev. ed. Moshe Shemesh. LC 95-50679. 456p. (C). 1996. pap. 29.50 (*0-7146-4253-3*, Pub. by F Cass Pubs) Intl Spec Bk.

Palestinian Exodus, 1948-1998, 1. Ghada Karmi. 1999. 45.00 (*0-86372-244-X*) Garnet-Ithaca.

Palestinian External Trade under Israeli Occupation. 141p. 26.00 (*92-1-112276-7*, E.89.II.D.10) UN.

Palestinian Financial Sector under Israeli Occupation. 163p. 39.00 (*92-1-112273-2*, E.89.II.D.7) UN.

Palestinian Folk Costume. Jehan S. Rajab. 200p. 1988. lib. bdg. 65.00 (*0-7103-0283-5*) Routledge.

***Palestinian Hamas: Vision, Violence & Coexistence.** Shaul Mishal & Avraham Sela. LC DS119.76.M57 2000. 2000. 49.50 (*0-231-11674-8*); pap. 17.50 (*0-231-11675-6*) Col U Pr.

Palestinian Higher Education in the West Bank & the Gaza Strip: A Critical Assessment. Sami N. Anabtawi. 250p. 1987. text 45.00 (*0-7103-0119-7*) Routledge.

Palestinian Identities & Preferences: Israel's & Jerusalem's Arabs. Avaraham Ashkenasi. LC 91-16682. 208p. 1992. 57.95 (*0-275-93503-5*, C3503, Praeger Pubs) Greenwood.

Palestinian Identity. Rashid Khalidi. LC 96-45757. 304p. 1997. 42.00 (*0-231-10514-2*) Col U Pr.

***Palestinian Identity: The Construction of a Modern National Consciousness.** Rashid Khalidi. 305p. 1998. pap. 16.50 (*0-231-10515-0*) Col U Pr.

Palestinian Intifada. Edgar O'Ballance. LC 97-38060. 1998. text 59.95 (*0-312-21172-4*) St Martin.

Palestinian-Israeli Accord. Phyllis Corzine. LC 96-34886. (Overview Ser.). (Illus.). (YA). (gr. 4-12). 1996. lib. bdg. 22.45 (*1-56006-181-2*) Lucent Bks.

Palestinian-Israeli Peace Process & Turkey. Bulent Aras. LC 98-5134. 1998. 65.00 (*1-56072-549-4*) Nova Sci Pubs.

Palestinian Lawyers & Israeli Rule: Law & Disorder in the West Bank. George E. Bisharat. 263p. 1990. text 30.00 (*0-292-76513-4*) U of Tex Pr.

Palestinian Leadership on the West Bank: The Changing Role of the Arab Mayors under Jordan & Israel. Moshe Ma'oz. (Illus.). 232p. 1984. 49.50 (*0-7146-3234-1*, Pub. by F Cass Pubs) Intl Spec Bk.

Palestinian Liberation Organization: From Armed Struggle to the Declaration of Independence. Jamal R. Nassar. LC 90-44335. (Illus.). 256p. 1991. 59.95 (*0-275-93779-8*, C3779, Praeger Pubs) Greenwood.

Palestinian Liberation Organization: People, Power & Politics. Helena Cobban. (Cambridge Middle East Library: No. 5). (Illus.). 320p. 1985. pap. text 21.95 (*0-521-27216-5*) Cambridge U Pr.

Palestinian Messengers in America, 1849-79: A Record of Four Journeys. Baron W. Salo & Jennette M. Baron. Ed. by Moshe Davis. LC 77-70670. (America & the Holy Land Ser.). 1977. reprint ed. lib. bdg. 18.95 (*0-405-10226-7*) Ayer.

Palestinian Peasants & Ottoman Officials: Rural Administration around Sixteenth-Century Jerusalem. 219p. 1995. pap. text 25.95 (*0-521-47679-8*) Cambridge U Pr.

***Palestinian Perspectives.** Wolfgang Freund. (Controversies from the Promised Land Ser.: Vol. 1). (Illus.). xx, 207p. 1999. pap. 39.95 (*3-631-34307-8*) P Lang Pubng.

Palestinian Perspectives. Ed. by Wolfgang Freund. LC 99-23616. (Controversies from the Promised Land Ser.: Vol. 1). (Illus.). XX, 207p. 1999. pap. 39.95 (*0-8204-3648-8*) P Lang Pubng.

Palestinian Problem, Vol. 1. Ed. by Andrew C. Kimmens. (Reference Shelf Ser.). 256p. (C). 1989. pap. text 25.00 (*0-8242-0780-7*) Wilson.

Palestinian Refugee Negotiations: From Madrid to Oslo II. Salim Tamari. 1996. pap. 4.95 (*0-88728-265-2*) Inst Palestine.

Palestinian Refugees & the Peace Process. Elia T. Zureik. 1996. pap. 8.95 (*0-88728-266-0*) Inst Palestine.

Palestinian Self-Determination: A Study of the West Bank & Gaza Strip. Hassan B. Talal. (Illus.). 160p. (C). 1982. 14.95 (*0-7043-2312-5*, Pub. by Quartet) Charles River Bks.

Palestinian Self-Government (Autonomy) Its Past & Its Future. Harvey Sicherman. LC 91-32273. (Policy Papers: No. 27). 154p. 1991. pap. 8.00 (*0-944029-14-0*) Wash Inst NEP.

Palestinian Society & Politics. Joel S. Migdal et al. LC 79-84002. 308p. reprint ed. pap. 95.50 (*0-8357-2553-7*, 204024400015) Bks Demand.

Palestinian State: Implications for Security & American Policy. Ed. by James Colbert. 68p. 1999. pap. 10.00 (*0-9644523-6-7*) Jewish Inst Nat Secur.

Palestinian State: The Implications for Israel. Mark A. Heller. (Illus.). 208p. 1983. 29.00 (*0-674-65221-5*) HUP.

Palestinian State: The Implications for Israel. Mark A. Heller. (Illus.). 208p. 1984. pap. text 15.50 (*0-674-65222-3*) HUP.

Palestinian Teenage Refugees & Immigrants Speak Out. Nabil Marshood. LC 96-44197. (In Their Own Voices Ser.). (Illus.). 64p. (YA). (gr. 7-12). 1997. lib. bdg. 16.95 (*0-8239-2442-4*, D2442-4) Rosen Group.

Palestinian Uprising. Ed. by Samir Abed-Rabbo & Doris Safie. 435p. (Orig.). 1990. pap. 19.95 (*0-937694-87-8*) Assn Arab-Amer U Grads.

Palestinian Uprising: A War by Other Means. F. Robert Hunter. 280p. 1991. 35.00 (*0-520-07489-0*, Pub. by U CA Pr) Cal Prin Full Svc.

Palestinian Uprising: A War by Other Means. F. Robert Hunter. LC 92-41650. 280p. 1993. 17.95 (*0-520-08271-0*, Pub. by U CA Pr) Cal Prin Full Svc.

Palestinian Vocalised Piyyut Manuscripts in the Cambridge Genizah Collections. Ed. by Joseph Yahalom. (Cambridge Genizah Ser.: No. 7). (Illus.). 110p. 1997. text 115.00 (*0-521-58399-3*) Cambridge U Pr.

Palestinian Wedding: A Bilingual Anthology of Contemporary Palestinian Resistance Poetry. Ed. & Tr. by Abdelwahab M. Elmessiri from ARA. (ARA & ENG., Illus.). 249p. (C). 1982. 16.95 (*0-89410-095-5*, Three Contnts) L Rienner.

Palestinian Women: Identity & Experience. Ed. by Ebba Augustin. LC 93-5394. 256p. (C). 1993. text 22.50 (*1-85649-234-6*, Pub. by Zed Books) St Martin.

Palestinian Women of Gaza & the West Bank. Suha Sabbagh. LC 97-40148. 304p. 1998. 39.95 (*0-253-33377-6*); pap. 16.95 (*0-253-21174-3*) Ind U Pr.

Palestinians. Jonathan Dimbleby. 25.00 (*0-7043-2205-6*, Pub. by Quartet) Charles River Bks.

Palestinians: New Directions. Ed. by Michael C. Hudson. 262p. (Orig.). 1990. text 29.95 (*0-932568-18-1*) GU Ctr CAS.

Palestinians: New Directions. Intro. by Michael C. Hudson. 262p. (Orig.). 1990. pap. text 14.95 (*0-932568-19-X*) GU Ctr CAS.

Palestinians: The Making of a People. Baruch Kimmerling & Joel S. Migdal. xix, 396p. 1993. 32.95 (*0-02-917321-3*) Free Pr.

Palestinians: The Making of a People. Baruch Kimmerling & Joel S. Migdal. (Illus.). 416p. 1994. 19.50 (*0-674-65223-1*, KIMPAX) HUP.

Palestinians: The Road to Nationhood. David McDowall. 224p. pap. 19.95 (*1-873194-90-0*, Pub. by Minority Rts Pubns) Paul & Co Pubs.

Palestinians: The Road to Nationhood. David McDowall. (Illus.). 224p. 1995. 24.95 (*1-873194-70-6*, Pub. by Minority Rts Pubns) Paul & Co Pubs.

Palestinians & Israel. Yehoshafat Harkabi. 285p. 1974. boxed set 39.95 (*0-87855-172-7*) Transaction Pubs.

Palestinians & Israel: Role Play Peacegames. David W. Felder. (Illus.). 48p. 1996. pap. text 8.95 (*0-910959-54-4*, B&G 10E) Wellington Pr.

Palestinians & Israelis in the Theatre. Ed. by Dan Urian. (Contemporary Theatre Review Ser.). 228p. 1995. pap. text 25.00 (*3-7186-5709-0*, Harwood Acad Pubs) Gordon & Breach.

Palestinians & Their Society. Sarah Graham-Brown. (Illus.). 192p. 1981. 25.00 (*0-7043-2225-0*, Pub. by Quartet); pap. 14.95 (*0-7043-3343-0*, Pub. by Quartet) Charles River Bks.

Palestinians Between Israel & Jordan: Squaring the Triangle. Raphael Israeli. LC 90-24506. 216p. 1991. 55.00 (*0-275-93938-3*, C3938, Praeger Pubs) Greenwood.

Palestinians Between Terrorism & Statehood. Pinhas Inbari. LC 96-130065. 284p. 1996. 65.00 (*1-898723-20-6*, Pub. by Sussex Acad Pr) Intl Spec Bk.

Palestinians Between Terrorism & Statehood. Pinhas Inbari. LC 96-130065. 284p. 1997. pap. 29.95 (*1-898723-21-4*, Pub. by Sussex Acad Pr) Intl Spec Bk.

Palestinians in Perspective: Implications for Mideast Peace & U. S. Policy. Ed. by George E. Gruen. LC 82-71810. 112p. 1982. pap. 3.50 (*0-87495-042-2*) Am Jewish Comm.

Palestinians in the Arab World. Laurie A. Brand. 286p. 1991. pap. text 22.00 (*0-231-06723-2*) Col U Pr.

Palestinians in the Arab World: Institution Building & the Search for State. Laurie A. Brand. 286p. 1988. text 61.50 (*0-231-06722-4*) Col U Pr.

Palestinians in the Arab World: Institution Building & the Search for State. Laurie A. Brand. 286p. (C). 1998. pap. text 25.00 (*0-7881-5503-2*) DIANE Pub.

Palestinians, Refugees, & the Middle East Peace Process. Don Peretz. LC 93-37820. 1993. pap. text 12.95 (*1-878379-32-1*) US Inst Peace.

Palestinians under Israeli Rule. Ed. by Ian S. Lustick. LC 93-51256. (Arab-Israeli Relations Ser.: Vol. 9). 352p. 1994. reprint ed. text 20.00 (*0-8153-1589-9*) Garland.

Palestinians under Occupation: Prospects for the Future. Ed. by Peter F. Krogh & Mary C. McDavid. 121p. (Orig.). 1989. text 21.75 (*0-932568-16-5*); pap. text 9.75 (*0-932568-17-3*) GU Ctr CAS.

Palestra Historial: De Virtudes, y Exemplares Apostolicos. Francisco De Burgoa. (SPA.). 280p. 1997. 31.00 (*968-842-617-2*, UN043) UPLAAP.

Palestrina. Alberto Cametti. LC 74-24055. reprint ed. 44.50 (*0-404-12878-5*) AMS Pr.

Palestrina: A Research Guide. Guy A. Marco & Clara Marvin. (Composer Resource Manuals Ser.). 300p. 1998. text 45.00 (*0-8153-2351-4*) Garland.

Palestrina: An Index to the Casimiri, Kalmus & Haberl Editions. Compiled by Allison Hall. (Music Library Association Index & Bibliography Ser.: No. 22). 84p. 1980. pap. 15.00 (*0-914954-18-0*) Scarecrow.

Palestrina: Music Book Index. Henry Coates. 243p. 1993. reprint ed. lib. bdg. 79.00 (*0-7812-9613-7*) Rprt Serv.

Palette: Blending Literature, Language, & Culture: Readings for Intermediate German. Jillian S. Haeseler. LC 94-36016. 256p. (C). 1995. pap. 34.38 (*0-07-025427-3*) McGraw.

Palette & the Pen: Poems & Drawings. Nannette Hoffman. (Illus.). 43p. (Orig.). 1992. pap. 5.00 (*0-9623903-1-3*) Ellicott Pr.

Palette for Murder: A Murder, She Wrote Mystery. Jessica Fletcher. Vol. 6. 304p. 1996. mass mkt. 5.99 (*0-451-18820-9*, Sig) NAL.

***Palette in the Kitchen.** anniversary rev. ed. Compiled by C. Counter & Karl Tani. (Illus.). 64p. 1999. pap. 10.95 (*0-86534-283-0*) Sunstone Pr.

Palette of Light: California Paintings from the Irvine Museum. Jean Stern. LC 95-75366. 64p. (Orig.). 1995. pap. 15.00 (*0-9635468-4-8*) Irvine Mus.

Palette of Period Pigments. Linda Anfuso. 32p. 1995. pap. 3.00 (*1-57433-011-X*) Interset Pr.

Palette of Rocky Mountain Cuisine: Classic Recipes from the Historic Hotels of the Rocky Mountains. John Feinberg. 1994. pap. 12.95 (*0-923280-01-4*) HHR.

Palette Picker: Your Guide to Creative Color Combination. Mark Greenelsh. (Illus.). 1997. 27.99 incl. cd-rom (*1-56496-401-9*) Rockport Pubs.

Paleur et le Sang. Nicolas Brehal. (FRE.). 247p. 1988. pap. 11.95 (*0-7859-2101-X*, 2070380726) Fr & Eur.

Palezoic Paleogeography of the Western United States: Symposium, No. 1. Ed. by John H. Stewart et al. (Illus.). 502p. (Orig.). 1977. pap. 10.00 (*1-878861-59-X*) Pac Section SEPM.

Palgue 4-5-6 of Tae Kwon Do Hyung, Vol. 2. Kim P. Soo. Ed. by John Scura. LC 74-28711. (Illus.). 160p. 1975. reprint ed. pap. 15.95 (*0-89750-013-X*, 118) Ohara Pubns.

Palgue One, Two Three of Tae Kwon Do Hyung. K. P. Soo. 10.95 (*0-685-41910-X*) Wehman.

Palgue One, Two, Three of Tae Kwon Do Hyung. Kim Pyung Soo. Ed. by John Corcoran. LC 73-85437. (Korean Arts Ser.). (Illus.). 1973. pap. text 15.95 (*0-89750-008-3*, 113) Ohara Pubns.

Pali - English Dictionary. William Stede & Caroline A. Rhys-Davids. 753p. 1989. 95.00 (*0-8288-8479-X*) Fr & Eur.

Pali Buddhism. Ed. by Frank Hoffman & Deegalle Mahinda. (Curzon Studies in Asian Philosophy). 260p. (C). 1996. text 42.00 (*0-7007-0359-4*, Pub. by Curzon Pr Ltd) UH Pr.

Pali Buddhist Texts: An Introductory Reader & Grammar. Rune E. Johansson. 160p. 1998. reprint ed. pap. text 25.00 (*0-7007-1068-X*, Pub. by Curzon Pr Ltd) UH Pr.

Pali-English Dictionary. Hahotta M. Budd. (ENG & PLI.). 43.95 (*0-87557-056-9*) Saphrograph.

Pali-English Dictionary. T. W. Davids & William Stede. (C). 1993. text 56.00 (*81-208-1144-5*, Pub. by Motilal Bnarsidass) S Asia.

Pali-English Dictionary. T. W. Davids & William Stede. (C). 1925. 40.00 (*0-86013-059-2*, Pub. by Pali Text) Elsevier.

Pali-English Glossary of Buddhist Technical Terms. Bhikkhu Nanamoli. LC 94-904965. 176p. 1994. 9.60 (*955-24-0086-4*, Pub. by Buddhist Pub Soc) Vipassana Res Pubns.

Pali Grammar. Wilhelm Geiger. Ed. by K. R. Norman. Tr. by Batakrishna Ghosh from GER. 243p. (C). 1943. 27.00 (*0-86013-318-4*); pap. 14.00 (*0-86013-315-X*) Wisdom MA.

Pali Language & Literature, 2 vols. Kanai Lal Hazra. 823p. 1998. pap. 650.00 (*81-246-0004-X*, Pub. by Print Hse) St Mut.

Pali Literature of Burma. Mabel H. Bode. LC 77-87008. reprint ed. 37.50 (*0-404-16796-9*) AMS Pr.

Pali Metre. A. K. Warder. (C). 1967. 33.50 (*0-86013-061-4*, Pub. by Pali Text) Elsevier.

Pali Primer. Lily De Silva. 152p. 1995. pap. 5.95 (*81-7414-014-X*) Vipassana Res Pubns.

Pali Reader. Dines Anderson. 130p. 1985. reprint ed. 39.00 (*0-932051-66-9*) Rprt Serv.

Pali Reader & Pali Glossary, 2 vols. Dines Andersen. 1996. 54.00 (*81-206-1197-7*, Pub. by Asian Educ Servs) S Asia.

Pali Reader with Notes & Glossary. Dines Andersen. 1988. reprint ed. lib. bdg. 49.00 (*0-7812-0120-9*) Rprt Serv.

Pali Reader with Notes & Glossary. Dines Andersen. 1976. reprint ed. 49.00 (*0-403-05978-X*, Regency) Scholarly.

Pali Text Society Journal, Vol. 2. (C). 1978. reprint ed. 32.50 (*0-86013-200-5*, Pub. by Pali Text) Elsevier.

Pali Text Society Journal, Vol. 3. (C). 1978. reprint ed. 25.50 (*0-86013-201-3*, Pub. by Pali Text) Elsevier.

Pali Text Society Journal, Vol. 4. (C). 1978. reprint ed. 29.50 (*0-86013-202-1*, Pub. by Pali Text) Elsevier.

Pali Text society Journal, Vol. 5. (C). 1978. reprint ed. 36.00 (*0-86013-203-X*, Pub. by Pali Text) Elsevier.

Pali Text Society Journal, Vol. 6. (C). 1978. reprint ed. 45.00 (*0-86013-204-8*, Pub. by Pali Text) Elsevier.

Pali Text Society Journal, Vol. 7. (C). 1978. reprint ed. 37.00 (*0-86013-205-6*, Pub. by Pali Text) Elsevier.

Pali Text Society Journal, Vol. 8. (C). 1978. reprint ed. 19.00 (*0-86013-206-4*, Pub. by Pali Text) Elsevier.

Pali Text Society Journal, Vol. 9. (C). 1981. 35.50 (*0-86013-207-2*, Pub. by Pali Text) Elsevier.

Pali Text Society Journal, Vol. 10. (C). 1985. 35.50 (*0-86013-208-0*, Pub. by Pali Text) Elsevier.

Pali Text Society Journal, Vol. 11. (C). 1987. 35.50 (*0-86013-271-4*, Pub. by Pali Text) Elsevier.

Pali Text Society Journal, Vol. 12. (C). 1988. 35.50 (*0-86013-281-1*, Pub. by Pali Text) Elsevier.

Pali Text Society Journal, Vol. 13. 233p. (C). 1989. 35.50 (*0-86013-290-0*, Pub. by Pali Text) Elsevier.

Pali Text Society Journal, Vol. 14. 233p. (C). 1990. 35.50 (*0-86013-292-7*, Pub. by Pali Text) Elsevier.

Pali Text Society Journal, Vol. 15. 217p. (C). 1990. 35.50 (*0-86013-297-8*, Pub. by Pali Text) Elsevier.

Pali Text Society Journal, Vol. 16. Ed. by K. R. Norman. 185p. (C). 1992. 35.50 (*0-86013-304-4*) Wisdom MA.

Pali Text Society Journal, Vol. 17. Ed. by K. R. Norman. 224p. (C). 1992. 35.50 (*0-86013-305-2*) Wisdom MA.

Pali Text Society Journal, Vol. 18. Ed. by K. R. Norman. 185p. (C). 1993. 35.50 (*0-86013-307-9*) Wisdom MA.

Pali Text Society Journal, Vol. 19. Ed. by K. R. Norman. 224p. (C). 1993. 35.50 (*0-86013-309-5*) Wisdom MA.

Pali Text Society Journal, Vol. 20. Ed. by K. R. Norman. 240p. (C). 1994. 35.50 (*0-86013-314-1*) Wisdom MA.

Pali Text Society Journal, 1882-1884, Vol. 1. (C). 1978. reprint ed. 32.50 (*0-86013-199-8*, Pub. by Pali Text) Elsevier.

Pali Text Society Journal Index 1882-1927. P. D. Ratnatunga & S. S. Davidson. (C). 1973. pap. 16.00 (*0-86013-058-4*, Pub. by Pali Text) Elsevier.

***Pali Workbook: Pali Vocabulary from the 10-Day Vipassana Courses.** Ed. by Lynne Martineau. (Illus.). 159p. 2000. spiral bd., wbk. ed. 14.00 (*1-928706-04-5*) Vipassana Res Pubns.

Palice of Honour. Gawin Douglas. Ed. by John G. Kinnear. LC 70-144417. (Bannatyne Club, Edinburgh. Publications: No. 17). reprint ed. 31.50 (*0-404-52717-5*) AMS Pr.

Palimino Horses: Austria's Haflingers see Magnificent Horses of the World

Palimpsest. Ann Lovett. LC 90-70210. (Illus.). 48p. (Orig.). 1990. pap. 16.95 (*0-89822-064-5*) Visual Studies.

Palimpsest: A Memoir. Gore Vidal. (Illus.). 480p. 1996. pap. 13.95 (*0-14-026089-7*) Viking Penguin.

Palimpsest: Editorial Theory in the Humanities. Ed. by George Bornstein & Ralph G. Williams. LC 92-41139. (Editorial Theory & Literary Criticism Ser.). (Illus.). 328p. 1993. text 54.50 (*0-472-10371-7*, 10371) U of Mich Pr.

Palimpsestes: La Literature au Second Degre. Gerard Genette. (FRE.). 1992. pap. 22.95 (*0-7859-2734-4*) Fr & Eur.

Palimpsesto del Calco Aparente: Una Poetica del Barroco de Indias. Daniel Torres. LC 92-16156. (American University Studies: Latin American Literature: Ser. XXII, Vol. 16). 132p. (C). 1993. text 43.95 (*0-8204-1984-2*) P Lang Pubng.

Palimpsests: Literature in the Second Degree. Gerard Genette. Tr. by Channa Newman & Claude Doubinsky. LC 96-51576. (Stages Ser.). xvi, 491p. 1997. text 85.00 (*0-8032-2168-1*); pap. text 30.00 (*0-8032-7029-1*) U of Nebr Pr.

Palimsestos. Pedro X. Solis. (SPA.). 67p. (Orig.). 1996. pap. 6.00 (*1-888938-00-5*) Edit Decenio.

Palindor. D. R. Evans. LC 93-20220. (Illus.). 288p. (J). 1993. pap. 7.99 (*0-7814-0117-8*, Chariot Bks) Chariot Victor.

***Palindor.** D. R. Evans. 2000. pap. 18.00 (*0-7388-2165-9*) Xlibris Corp.

***Palindromania.** Jon Agee. 2002. text. write for info. (*0-374-35730-7*) FS&G.

Palindrome. Stuart Woods. 464p. 1991. mass mkt. 6.99 (*0-06-109936-8*, Harp PBks) HarpC.

***Palindrome.** Stuart Woods. LC 98-44851. 1998. 23.95 (*1-56895-688-6*) Wheeler Pub.

Palindrome Is a Pal Indeed. Eugene Lesser. 16p. (Orig.). 1991. pap. 5.00 (*0-912449-38-1*) Floating Island.

Palindromes & Anagrams. Howard W. Bergerson. 192p. (Orig.). 1973. pap. 5.95 (*0-486-20664-5*) Dover.

Palinuro of Mexico. Fernando Del Paso. Tr. by Elisabeth Plaister. LC 95-53205. 557p. 1996. pap. 14.95 (*1-56478-095-3*) Dalkey Arch.

Palinurus Suite. Mark McMorris. 47p. (Orig.). 1992. pap. 5.00 (*0-945926-37-5*) Paradigm RI.

Palinurus Suite. deluxe ed. Mark McMorris. (Orig.). 1992. pap. 12.00 (*0-945926-38-3*) Paradigm RI.

Palis of Honoure. Gavin Douglas. Ed. by David Parkinson. LC 92-32976. (Teams Middle English Text Ser.). 1992. pap. 8.00 (*1-879288-25-7*) Medieval Inst.

Palis of Honoure. Garvin Douglas. LC 77-6155. (English Experience Ser.: No. 89). 80p. 1969. reprint ed. 25.00 (*90-221-0089-8*) Walter J Johnson.

Palisade Amusement Park: A Century of Fond Memories. Vince Gargiulo. LC 95-14484. (Illus.). 200p. (C). 1995. 29.95 (*0-8135-2224-2*) Rutgers U Pr.

Palisades of the Hudson. Arthur C. Mack. (Illus.). 64p. 1982. reprint ed. pap. 6.95 (*0-915850-05-2*) Walking News Inc.

Palisades Project-Elyn Zimmerman: And Related Works, 1972-1981. Charles F. Stuckey. LC 81-84872. (Illus.). 48p. (Orig.). 1982. pap. 2.00 (*0-943651-16-6*) Hudson Riv.

Paliser Case. Edgar E. Saltus. LC 70-113269. reprint ed. 42.50 (*0-404-05543-5*) AMS Pr.

Palissy Ware: Nineteenth-Century French Ceramists from Avisseau to Renoleau. Marshall P. Katz & Robert Lehr. (Illus.). 220p. (C). 1996. text 120.00 (*0-485-11497-6*, Pub. by Athlone Pr) Humanities.

Palkhi: An Indian Pilgrimage. D. B. Mokashi. Tr. by Philip C. Engblom & Eleanor Zelliot. LC 86-30001. 291p. (C). 1987. pap. text 23.95 (*0-88706-462-0*) State U NY Pr.

***Palko the Piper.** Elek Benedek. (J). 1999. pap. text 21.00 (*963-13-4781-8*, Pub. by Corvina Bks) St Mut.

Palko the Piper. Benedekj Elek. (Granny's Storybooks Ser.). (J). 1989. pap. 25.00 (*963-13-3358-2*, Pub. by Corvina Bks) St Mut.

Palladas: Poems. 2nd ed. Tony Harrison. 48p. 1992. pap. 13.95 (*0-85646-127-X*, Pub. by Anvil Press) Dufour.

***Palladian Ideal.** Joseph Rykwert. (Illus.). 228p. 2000. 85.00 (*0-8478-2158-7*, Pub. by Rizzoli Intl) St Martin.

Palladian Landscape: Geographical Change & Its Cultural Representations in Sixteenth-Century Italy. Denis Cosgrove. LC 92-33774. (Illus.). 352p. (C). 1993. 65.00 (*0-271-00942-X*) Pa St U Pr.

***Palladian Style.** Steven Parissien. (Illus.). 2000. pap. 29.95 (*0-7148-4026-2*) Phaidon Pr.

Palladian Style. Steven Parissien. LC 95-128883. (Illus.). 240p. (C). 1994. text 55.00 (*0-7148-2921-8*, Pub. by Phaidon Press) Phaidon Pr.

Palladii. Ed. by Rodgers. (LAT.). 1975. 53.50 (*3-322-00214-4*, T1573, Pub. by B G Teubner) U of Mich Pr.

Palladio. James Ackerman. 1974. pap. 13.95 (*0-14-013500-6*, Viking) Viking Penguin.

Palladio. Taschen, Benedikt Staff. (Architecture & Design Ser.). (SPA.). Date not set. 24.99 (*3-8228-0223-9*) Taschen Amer.

Palladio. Manfred Wundram. 1994. pap. 24.99 (*3-8228-0271-9*) Taschen Amer.

Palladio & America: Selected Papers Presented to the Centro Internazionale di Studi de Architettura Andrea Palladio. Ed. by Christopher Weeks. Tr. by Robert De Lucca from ITA. LC 97-72904. (Illus.). 144p. (Orig.). 1997. pap. 25.00 (*0-932958-18-4*) Golden Coast.

Palladio & British Classicism, 1615-1815. Giles Worsley. LC 94-19211. 349p. 1995. 60.00 (*0-300-05896-9*) Yale U Pr.

***Palladio & Northern Europe.** Guido Beltramini et al. (Illus.). 176p. 1999. 45.00 (*88-8118-524-5*, Pub. by Skira IT) Abbeville Pr.

Palladio & Palladianism. Robert Tavernor. LC 90-70179. (World of Art Ser.). (Illus.). 224p. 1991. pap. 14.95 (*0-500-20242-7*, Pub. by Thames Hudson) Norton.

Palladio Guide. 2nd rev. ed. Caroline Constant. LC 93-23987. (Illus.). 160p. 1998. pap. 19.95 (*1-878271-85-7*) Princeton Arch.

Palladio's Architecture & Its Influence: A Photographic Guide. Joseph C. Farber & Henry H. Reed. (Illus.). 144p. 1980. pap. 9.95 (*0-486-23922-5*) Dover.

Palladis Tamia. Francis Meres. LC 39-10093. 192p. 1978. reprint ed. 50.00 (*0-8201-1188-0*) Schol Facsimiles.

Palladium Alloys. E. M. Savitskii et al. LC 69-76747. (Illus.). 215p. 1969. 37.00 (*0-911184-11-2*) Primary.

Palladium Catalyzed Oxidation of Hydrocarbons. Patrick Henry. (Catalysis by Metal Complexes Ser.). 1979. text 192.00 (*90-277-0986-6*) Kluwer Academic.

Palladium of Conscience. Philip Furneaux. LC 74-122161. (Civil Liberties in American History Ser.). 267p. 1974. reprint ed. lib. bdg. 35.00 (*0-306-71972-X*) Da Capo.

Palladium of Justice: Origins of Trial by Jury. Leonard W. Levy. 108p. 1999. 18.95 (*1-56663-259-5*, Pub. by I R Dee) Natl Bk Netwk.

***Palladium of Justice: Origins of Trial by Jury.** Leonard W. Levy. 128p. 2000. reprint ed. pap. 12.95 (*1-56663-313-3*, Pub. by I R Dee) Natl Bk Netwk.

Palladium. Poems. Alice Fulton. LC 85-31807. (National Poetry Ser.). 128p. 1987. 10.95 (*0-252-01280-1*) U of Ill Pr.

Palladium Reagents & Catalysts: Innovations in Organic Synthesis. Jiro Tsuji. 574p. 1997. pap. 125.00 (*0-471-97202-9*) Wiley.

Palladium RPG. 2nd rev. ed. Kevin Siembieda. Ed. by Alex Marciniszyn & Kevin Kirsten. (Illus.). 300p. (Orig.). (YA). (gr. 8 up). 1996. pap. 24.95 (*0-916211-91-6*, 450) Palladium Bks.

Palladius: Dialogue on the Life of St. John Chrysostom. Ed. by Robert T. Meyer. (Ancient Christian Writers Ser.: No. 45). 1985. 16.95 (*0-8091-0358-3*) Paulist Pr.

Palladius on Husbondrie. Rutilius T. Palladius. Ed. by Barton Lodge & S. J. Herrtage. (EETS, OS Ser.: No. 52, 72). 1974. reprint ed. 63.00 (*0-527-00047-7*) Periodicals Srv.

Palladius on Husbondrie, Englisht, Part. II. Ed. by S. J. Herrtage. Vol. 52 & 72. 1974. reprint ed. pap. write for info. (*0-318-59015-8*) Periodicals Srv.

Pallaksch, Pallaksch. Liliane Giraudon. Tr. by Julia Hine from FRE. (Sun & Moon Classics Ser.: No. 61). 128p. (Orig.). 1994. pap. 12.95 (*1-55713-191-0*) Sun & Moon CA.

Pallas. L. Neil Smith. 480p. 1995. 5.99 (*0-8125-0904-8*, Pub. by Tor Bks) St Martin.

Pallas Armata: or Militarie Instructions. Thomas Kellie. LC 72-209. (English Experience Ser.: No. 331). 130p. 1971. reprint ed. 45.00 (*90-221-0331-5*) Walter J Johnson.

Pallas Athena: Poseidon Hestia see Greek Mythology

Pallas Guide to Modern London No. 1: The City & East End. Clare Melhuish. (Illus.). 464p. (Orig.). 1995. pap. 23.95 (*1-873429-10-X*, Pub. by Pallas Athene) Cimino Pub Grp.

Pallbearer. David Lipsky. 200p. (Orig.). (J). 1996. pap. 9.70 (*0-7868-8184-4*, Pub. by Hyperion) Time Warner.

***Pallbearers Envying the One Who Rides.** Stephen Dobyns. LC 99-18492. 160p. 1999. pap. 15.95 (*0-14-058916-3*, Penguin Bks) Viking Penguin.

Palletizer Terms & Definitions. 5p. 1994. pap. 1.50 (*1-891171-17-8*) Conveyor Equip Mfrs.

Palli Giti, Pt. 3. Ahmad Nawaz. LC 98-71442. (BEN.). xiv, 100p. 1998. pap. 10.00 (*1-58225-141-X*) Ananta Prakashani.

Palliation in Malignant Disease. J. G. Mosley. (Illus.). 170p. 1988. text 60.00 (*0-443-03690-X*) Church.

Palliative & Terminal Care: Health Care Needs Assessment: The Epidemiologically Based Needs Assessment Reviews, Second Series. Andrew Stevens et al. LC 97-13354. 1997. write for info. (*1-85775-206-6*, Radcliffe Med Pr) Scovill Paterson.

Palliative Cancer Care: Policy Statement Based on the Recommendations of a WHO Consultation. 48p. 1989. pap. text 15.00 (*92-890-1059-2*) World Health.

Palliative Care: The Nurses's R. Lugton. LC 98-48825. (C). 1999. pap. text 29.95 (*0-443-05513-0*) Church.

***Palliative Care & Rehabilitation of Cancer Patients** Charles F. Von Gunten. LC 99-27955. (Cancer Treatment & Research Ser.). 1999. write for info. (*0-7923-8525-X*) Kluwer Academic.

Palliative Care Ethics: A Companion for All Specialties. 2nd ed. Fiona Randall & Robin S. Downie. LC 99-20410. 332p. 1999. pap. text 34.95 (*0-19-263068-7*) OUP.

Palliative Care for People with AIDS. 2nd ed. Ruth Sims & Veronica A. Moss. 170p. 1995. pap. 35.25 (*0-340-61371-8*, Pub. by E A) Routldge.

Palliative Care for People with AIDS. 2nd ed. Ruth Sims & Veronica A. Moss. 144p. 1994. pap. text 35.25 (*1-56593-359-1*, 0683) Singular Publishing.

Palliative Care for People with Cancer. 2nd ed. write for info. (*0-340-61391-2*, Pub. by E A) Routldge.

Palliative Care for People with Cancer. 2nd ed. Jenny Penson & Ronald A. Fisher. 336p. 1995. pap. text 38.25 (*1-56593-598-5*, 1224) Singular Publishing.

***Palliative Care in Amyotrophic Lateral Sclerosis: Motor Neurone Disease.** Ed. by David Oliver et al. (Illus.). 240p. 2001. text 79.50 (*0-19-263166-7*) OUP.

Palliative Care Patient & Family Couseling Manual. Aspen Reference Group Staff. 1996. 139.00 (*0-8342-0762-1*, S289) Aspen Pub.

Palliative Day Care. write for info. (*0-340-62521-X*, Pub. by E A) Routldge.

Palliative Day Care: Prevention, Harm Minimization, & Treatment. Ed. by Ronald A. Fisher & Pearl McDaid. (Illus.). 272p. (Orig.). 1996. pap. 38.25 (*1-56593-753-8*, 1464) Singular Publishing.

Palliative Medicine: A Case-Based Manual. Ed. by Neil MacDonald et al. (Illus.). 330p. 1998. pap. text 29.95 (*0-19-262657-4*) OUP.

Palliative Medicine: Problem Areas in Pain & Symptom Management. Ed. by G. W. Hanks. (Cancer Surveys Ser.: Vol. 21). 257p. 1995. 54.00 (*0-87969-435-1*) Cold Spring Harbor.

Palliative Medicine: Symptomatic & Supportive Care for Patients with Advanced Cancer & AIDS. 3rd ed. Roger Woodruff. LC 99-216273. 430p. 1999. pap. text 59.50 (*0-19-550647-2*) OUP.

Palliative Medicine Secrets. Suresh K. Joishy. LC 98-43418. (Secrets Ser.). (Illus.). 250p. 1998. pap. text 35.00 (*1-56053-304-8*) Hanley & Belfus.

Palliative Pain & Symptom Management for Children & Adolescents. Robert A. Milch. 29p. 1985. pap. 7.95 (*0-317-61842-3*) Child Hospice VA.

***Palliatives: Poems from Hollywood.** Mark Dunster. 11p. 1999. pap. 5.00 (*0-89642-951-2*) Linden Pubs.

Pallidotomy for the Treatment of Parkinson's Disease & Movement Disorders. Joachim K. Krauss & Robert G. Grossman. LC 98-19196. 400p. 1998. text 135.00 (*0-7817-1225-4*) Lppncott W & W.

***Palliser Expedition: An Account of John Palliser's British North American Exploring Expedition 1857-1860.** 2nd rev. ed. Irene M. Spry. (Western Canadian Classics). (Illus.). 315p. 1999. pap. 9.95 (*1-895618-52-5*) Fifth Hse Publ.

Palliser Novels, 6 vols., Set. Anthony Trollope. (Illus.). 4894p. 1991. 120.00 (*0-19-520901-X*) OUP.

Pallisers. Anthony Trollope. Date not set. lib. bdg. 26.95 (*0-8488-2169-6*) Amereon Ltd.

Palm: A Guide to Your Hidden Potential. Rita Robinson. 128p. 1988. pap. 10.95 (*0-87877-133-6*) Newcastle Pub.

Palm - Tree of Life: Biology, Utilization & Conservation. Ed. by Michael J. Balick. LC 87-36900. (Advances in Economic Botany Ser.: Vol. 6). (Illus.). 296p. (C). 1988. pap. text 45.70 (*0-89327-326-0*) NY Botanical.

Palm at the End of the Mind: Selected Poems & a Play. Holly Stevens. 415p. 1990. pap. 13.00 (*0-679-72445-1*) Vin Bks.

Palm Beach. Pat Booth. 1986. mass mkt. 5.99 (*0-345-33357-8*) Ballantine Pub Grp.

Palm Beach: The Novel. Richard G. Hughes. LC 83-63232. 1984. pap. 9.95 (*0-88100-037-X*) Natl Writ Pr.

Palm Beach - An Irreverent Guide. Jack Owen. (Illus.). 52p. (Orig.). 1986. pap. 6.95 (*0-938673-00-9*) Old Bk Shop Pubn.

Palm Beach Babylon. Weiss. 1997. mass mkt. 5.99 (*0-7860-0398-7*) Kensgtn Pub Corp.

Palm Beach Babylon: Sins, Scams, & Scandals. Murray Weiss & William Hoffman. (Illus.). 224p. 1992. 21.95 (*1-55972-141-3*, Birch Ln Pr) Carol Pub Group.

Palm Beach Community "Check-Up" Residents Respond to the Issues Facing Their County. Steve Farkas. 36p. (Orig.). 1995. pap. 10.00 (*1-889483-40-0*) Public Agenda.

Palm Beach County: In a Class by Itself. Donald Curl et al. (Illus.). 208p. 1997. 39.95 (*0-9647106-2-5*) Copperfld Pubns.

Palm Beach Facts & Fancies, Caprices & Curiosities: The Insider's Guide to the Passions, Possessions & Pleasures of the World's Richest Society. 5th rev. ed. James J. Sheeran. LC 89-90814. (Illus.). 416p. 1997. 19.95 (*0-9622977-9-8*) Palm Beach Soc.

Palm Beach Houses. Roberto Schezen & Shirley Johnson. LC 90-48659. (Illus.). 324p. 1991. 75.00 (*0-8478-1313-4*, Pub. by Rizzoli Intl) St Martin.

Palm Beach Map & entertainment Directory. James J. Sheeran. (Illus.). 1993. 2.95 (*1-893449-01-7*) Palm Beach Soc.

Palm Beach Panorama: Turn-of-Century PHotographs by E. W. Hazard. Sandra Barghini. (Illus.). 36p. (Orig.). 1996. pap. 10.00 (*0-9651333-0-3*) Flagler Mus.

***Palm Beach Power & Glory, Wit & Wisdom.** 6th ed. James J. Sheeran. LC 89-90814. (Illus.). 448p. 2000. pap. 22.95 (*1-893449-00-9*) Palm Beach Soc.

Palm Beach Prep No. 4: Screen Test. Elle Wolfe. (J). (gr. 4-7). 1990. pap. 2.95 (*0-8125-1062-3*, Pub. by Tor Bks) St Martin.

Palm Beach Prep No. 5: Troublemaker. Elle Wolfe. (J). (gr. 4-7). 1990. pap. 2.95 (*0-8125-1065-8*, Pub. by Tor Bks) St Martin.

Palm Beach Roots & Recipes. Charles D. Reese. (Illus.). 120p. (Orig.). 1991. reprint ed. pap. 12.95 (*0-9629266-0-4*) Palm Bch Roots.

Palm Beach Sketchbook. Agnes Ash. (Great Places Ser.). (Illus.). 144p. 1988. 32.00 (*0-923078-01-0*) Olendorf Graph.

Palm Beach Story. Roxanne Pulitzer. 288p. 1997. mass mkt. 5.99 (*1-57566-167-5*, Knsington) Kensgtn Pub Corp.

Palm Beach Story. John Pym. LC 98-215541. (Film Classics Ser.). (Illus.). 80p. 1998. pap. 10.95 (*0-85170-671-1*) Ind U Pr.

Palm Beach Wit & Wisdom: A Pastiche of Perceptions about the Social Mores & Customs, Treasures & Pleasures of Palm Beachers; & Some Glorious Guidelines for Making It Big with the World's Richest People. James J. Sheeran. LC 92-60865. (Illus.). 384p. 1992. 17.95 (*0-9622977-3-9*) Palm Beach Soc.

Palm Coast. Jim Martin. (Illus.). 96p. (Orig.). 1991. pap. 8.00 (*0-918949-10-6*) Martin Jim.

***Palm Computing.** Brown. (Bible Ser.). 816p. 2000. 39.99 (*0-7645-3408-4*) IDG Bks.

Palm Computing for Dummies. Mariva H. Aviram. (For Dummies). 224p. 2000. spiral bd. 12.99 (*0-7645-0580-7*) IDG Bks.

***Palm Computing for Dummies.** Bill Dyszel. 408p. 1999. pap. 24.99 incl. cd-rom (*0-7645-0581-5*) IDG Bks.

***Palm Database Programming: The Complete Developer's Guide.** Eric Giguere. LC 99-36711. 358p. 1999. pap. 49.99 incl. cd-rom (*0-471-35401-5*) Wiley.

P

***Palm Decoder.** Tre McCalmly. 144p. 1999. pap. text 19.95 (*0-7641-1186-8*) Barron.

Palm Desert: A Book by Rudy Vanderlans Based on Music & Lyrics by Van Dyke Parks. Rudy VanderLans et al. (Illus.). 96p. 1999. 24.95 (*0-9669409-0-3*) Emig.

Palm Fever. Carole Marsh. (Carole Marsh Short Story Ser.). (Illus.). (J). (gr. 4-12). 1994. 29.95 (*1-55609-185-0*); pap. 19.95 (*1-55609-237-7*) Gallopade Intl.

Palm for Mrs. Pollifax. Dorothy Gilman. 192p. 1985. mass mkt. 5.99 (*0-449-20864-8*, Crest) Fawcett.

Palm Leaf Patterns: A New Approach to Clothing Design. Margaret Fisher. LC 76-57189. (Illus.). 20p. 1977. pap. 5.95 (*0-915572-20-6*) Panjandrum.

Palm Leaves & Postcards: Material Culture & Its Representation in Colonial Ceylon. Jonathan S. Walters. Ed. by Ben Mitchell. 1995. 10.00 (*1-880269-14-7*) D H Sheehan.

Palm Ninety. Thomas J. Cox. 20p. 1993. vinyl bd. 7.45 (*1-879810-07-7*) Riverside FL.

Palm of My Heart: Poetry by African American Children. Ed. by Davida Adedjouma. LC 96-13426. (Illus.). 32p. (J). (ps up). 1996. 15.95 (*1-880000-41-5*) Lee & Low Bks.

Palm of My Heart: Poetry by African American Children. Ed. by Davida Adedjouma. LC 96-13426. (Illus.). 32p. (YA). (ps up). 1998. pap. 6.95 (*1-880000-76-8*) Lee & Low Bks.

Palm-of-the-Hand Stories. Yasunari Kawabata. Tr. by Lane Dunlop & J. Martin Holman from JPN. LC 87-82590. Orig. Title: Tenohira no Shosetsu. 240p. 1990. pap. 13.00 (*0-86547-412-5*) N Point Pr.

Palm Oil & Protest: An Economic History of the Ngwa Region, South-eastern Nigeria, 1800-1980. Susan M. Martin. (African Studies: No. 59). (Illus.). 224p. 1988. text 80.00 (*0-521-34376-3*) Cambridge U Pr.

***Palm Organizers.** 2nd ed. Jeff Carlson. (Visual QuickStart Guides Ser.). (Illus.). 304p. 2000. pap. text 16.99 (*0-201-70063-8*) Addison-Wesley.

***Palm OS Programming Bible: Featuring Palm VII.** Lonnon R. Foster. (Illus.). 800p. 2000. pap. text 39.99 (*0-7645-4676-7*) IDG Bks.

Palm OS Programming for Dummies. John Schettino. (For Dummies Ser.). 408p. 1999. pap. 24.99 incl. cd-rom (*0-7645-0563-7*) IDG Bks.

***Palm PCs with Windows CE.** John D. Ruley. (Mastering Ser.). 432p. 2000. pap. 29.99 (*0-7821-2651-0*) Sybex.

***Palm Pilot.** Antonin Dvorak. 2000. pap. 34.99 (*0-13-026113-0*) P-H.

Palm Probabilities & Stationary Queues. Francois L. Baccelli & P. Bremaud. (Lecture Notes in Statistics Ser.: Vol. 41). vii, 106p. 1987. 41.95 (*0-387-96514-9*) Spr-Verlag.

***Palm Programming.** Glenn Bachmann. (Illus.). 363p. 1999. pap. 29.99 incl. cd-rom (*0-672-31493-2*) Sams.

Palm Programming: Ground Up. Robert Mykland. 1999. write for info. (*0-07-212150-5*) McGraw.

***Palm Programming: The Developers Guide.** Neil Rhodes & Julie McKeehan. Ed. by Mark Stone. (Illus.). 457p. 1998. pap. 32.95 incl. cd-rom (*1-56592-525-4*) OReilly & Assocs.

***Palm Programming from the Ground Up.** Robert Mykland. (From the Ground Up Ser.). 608p. 1999. pap. 34.99 incl. cd-rom (*0-07-212152-1*) Osborne-McGraw.

***Palm Reading.** Dorling Kindersley Publishing Staff. (Secrets of... Ser.). (Illus.). 224p. 2000. pap. 9.95 (*0-7894-6777-1*) DK Pub Inc.

Palm Reading: For Fun, Health & Success. Joyce Andrews. 96p. 1991. pap. 6.95 (*0-9631450-0-2*) Drew Pubs.

***Palm Reading for Beginners: Find the Future in the Palm of Your Hand.** Richard Webster. LC 00-25070. (Illus.). 264p. 2000. pap. 9.95 (*1-56718-791-9*) Llewellyn Pubns.

Palm Reading for Fun & Profit: May I See Your Hand? Myrna L. Goldbaum. (Illus.). 60p. 1997. pap. 24.99 (*0-934172-03-X*) WIM Pubns.

Palm Reading for Fun & Profit: May I See Your Hand? Myrna L. Goldbaum. LC 96-39737. (Illus.). 60p. 1997. pap. 24.00 (*0-934172-48-X*) WIM Pubns.

Palm Readings: Stories from Southern California. Maria Escandon et al. Ed. by Eva L. Caram. (New Voices Ser.: Vol. 11). 144p. (Orig.). 1998. pap. 17.95 (*0-911051-02-3*) Plain View.

Palm Sago. Ruddle & Johnson. (Australian National University Press Ser.). 1996. pap. write for info. (*0-08-033013-4*, Pergamon Pr) Elsevier.

Palm Springs & Valley Cities Close Up: Palm Springs Close Up. 4th rev. ed. Jack Titus. Ed. by Barbara McClure. (Illus.). 158p. 1996. reprint ed. pap. 15.95 (*0-9654926-0-5*) J Titus.

Palm Springs Lifestyle Cookbook. Ris. 1996. 13.95 (*0-9656813-1-9*) Haricot Verts.

***Palm Springs Modern: Houses in the California Desert.** Adele Cygelman. LC 98-48811. (Illus.). 192p. 1999. 50.00 (*0-8478-2091-2*, Pub. by Rizzoli Intl) St Martin.

Palm Springs Nutritional Plan: A Thin Book about Fat. Irvin Caplin. Ed. by Jim Foote & Johnnie Foote. 150p. (Orig.). 1992. pap. 10.00 (*0-9628752-1-X*) Fifty-Six Palms.

Palm Springs Oasis: Photographic Portfolio of the Coachella Valley Region. Greg Lawson. LC 89-85067. (Pictorial Bks.). (Illus.). 1990. 19.95 (*0-916251-40-3*) Sunbelt Pubns.

Palm Springs Restaurants: A Guide to Restaurants & Menus of Palm Springs, Cathedral City, Rancho Mirage, Palm Desert, Indian Wells & La Quinta. Carol Fox & Rochelle D. Ventura. LC 94-94175. 388p. 1994. pap. text 14.95 (*0-9640629-6-8*) Excursions.

Palm Springs Safari: A Guide of Palm Springs, 1977-78. Fred Hartley & Glory Hartley. pap. 2.95 (*0-686-17555-7*) Hartley Ent.

Palm Sunday. Kurt Vonnegut, Jr. 320p. 1999. pap. 11.95 (*0-385-33426-5*) Dell.

Palm Sunday Parade. Martha McKown. 20p. (Orig.). 1995. pap. 4.50 (*0-7880-0322-4*) CSS OH.

Palm Therapy: Program Your Mind through Your Palms-A Major Breakthrough in Palmistry. Moshe Zwang et al. (Illus.). 730p. 1995. pap. 29.95 (*0-9645519-2-6*) Ult Mind Pub.

Palm III & PalmPilot: Visual QuickStart Guide. Jeff Carlson. LC 99-190536. (Visual QuickStart Guides Ser.). 264p. (C). 1998. pap. text 15.99 (*0-201-35390-3*, Pub. by Peachpit Pr) Addison-Wesley.

Palm Tree Bible: The Favorite Stories of God & His People from the Old Testament, Bk. 3. (Illus.). 64p. (J). 1996. pap. 9.99 (*1-885358-19-9*, DB46203) Rainbow CA.

Palm Tree Bible: The Favorite Stories of God & His People from the Old Testament, Bk. 4. (Illus.). 64p. (J). 1996. pap. 9.99 (*1-885358-20-2*, DB46204) Rainbow CA.

Palm Tree Bible: The Wonderful Stories of Jesus from the New Testament, Bk. 1. (Illus.). 64p. (J). (ps-7). 1996. pap. 9.99 (*1-885358-17-2*, Lgacy Pr) Rainbow CA.

Palm Tree Bible Vol. 2: The Wonderful Stories of Jesus from the New Testament. (Illus.). 64p. (J). (ps-7). 1996. pap. 9.99 (*1-885358-18-0*, Lgacy Pr) Rainbow CA.

Palm Tree Manhunt see Sugar Creek Gang Series

Palm Trees. Nancy Cote. LC 92-18938. (Illus.). 40p. (J). (ps-2). 1993. lib. bdg. 14.95 (*0-02-724760-0*, Four Winds Pr) S&S Childrens.

Palm Trees. Marcia S. Freeman. LC 98-7181. (Trees Ser.). (Illus.). 24p. (J). (ps-3). 1998. 13.25 (*0-7368-0094-8*, Pebble Bks) Capstone Pr.

Palm Trees. Marcia S. Freeman. (Trees (Capstone) Ser.). (J). 1998. 13.25 (*0-516-21506-X*) Childrens.

Palm-Wine Drinkard & His Dead Palm-Wine Tapster in the Dead's Town. Amos Tutuola. LC 78-104255. 130p. 1970. reprint ed. lib. bdg. 38.50 (*0-8371-4044-7*, TUPD, Greenwood Pr) Greenwood.

Palm-Wine Drinkard & My Life in the Bush of Ghosts. Amos Tutuola. LC 93-32520. 320p. 1988. pap. 13.50 (*0-8021-3363-0*, Grove) Grove-Atltic.

Palma Cathedral. Michael James Denham White. LC 98-39425. 51 p. 1998. 14.95 (*0-87081-516-4*) Univ Pr Colo.

Palma Vecchio. Philip Rylands. (Studies in the History of Art). (Illus.). 402p. (C). 1992. text 139.95 (*0-521-37332-8*) Cambridge U Pr.

Palmas Ya No Son Verdes: Analisis y Testimonios de la Tragedia Cubana. Juan E. Noya. LC 85-80134. (Coleccion Cuba y sus Jueces). (SPA., Illus.). 93p. (Orig.). 1985. pap. 9.95 (*0-89729-368-1*) Ediciones.

Palmate. Mark DeFoe. 40p. (Orig.). 1988. pap. 5.95 (*0-9620863-0-4*) Pringle Tree Pr.

Palmeiras no Brasil: Nativas e Exoticas. Harri Lorenzi et al. (POR., Illus.). 320p. 1997. 90.00 (*85-86714-03-8*, Pub. by Inst Plantarum) Balogh.

Palmen (Palms) 2nd rev. ed. W. Lotschert. (GER., Illus.). 159p. 1995. 58.00 (*3-8001-6532-5*, Pub. by Eugen Ulmer) Balogh.

Palmer: Editorial Cartoons from the Montgomery Advertiser. Jim Palmer. 160p. 1992. 9.95 (*1-882616-00-6*) Advertiser.

Palmer (& Trimble) Genealogical Record of the Descendants of John & Mary Palmer of Concord, PA. Also Includes Surnames Almond, Arment, Baker, & Others. Lyman L. Palmer. (Illus.). 725p. 1990. reprint ed. pap. 107.00 (*0-8328-1527-6*); reprint ed. lib. bdg. 115.00 (*0-8328-1526-8*) Higginson Bk Co.

Palmer Basketball: The Alden Skinner Story. Terry F. Holub. LC 89-61577. (Illus.). 250p. (Orig.). (C). 1989. pap. write for info. (*0-9623112-0-0*) Schaller Herald.

Palmer Buddhist. 1971. lib. bdg. 65.00 (*90-247-5061-X*) Kluwer Academic.

Palmer D'Amico Accounting for Canadian Colleges. Palmer. 1997. text. write for info. (*0-201-34634-6*) Addison-Wesley.

Palmer Families in America Vol. I: Lt. William Palmer of Yarmouth, Mass., & His Descendants of Greenwich, Ct. Horace W. Palmer. Ed. by Nellie M. Palmer. (Illus.). 889p. 1997. reprint ed. pap. 125.00 (*0-8328-9485-0*); reprint ed. lib. bdg. 135.00 (*0-8328-9484-2*) Higginson Bk Co.

Palmer-Hughes Accordion Course Lesson Book 2. Bill Palmer & Bill Hughes. 48p. 1952. pap. 7.50 (*0-7390-0366-6*, 204) Alfred Pub.

Palmer-Hughes Prep Accordian Course, Bk. 1A. Bill Palmer & Bill Hughes. 32p. 1952. 5.95 (*0-7390-0566-9*, 215) Alfred Pub.

Palmer Method: Stories. E. S. Goldman. 320p. (Orig.). 1995. pap. 14.95 (*1-880284-09-X*) J Daniel.

Palmer Method Cursive, Consumable. Fred D. King. (Palmer Method Easy to Teach Ser.). (Illus.). (J). (gr. 6). 1979. student ed. 3.96 (*0-914268-68-6*, 79-6C) A N Palmer.

Palmer Method Cursive, Consumable. Fred M. King. (Palmer Method Easy to Teach Ser.). (Illus.). 1979. student ed. 3.96 (*0-914268-66-X*, 79-5C) A N Palmer.

Palmer Method Cursive, Consumable. Fred M. King. (Palmer Method Easy to Teach Ser.). (Illus.). (J). (gr. 4). 1979. teacher ed. 5.60 (*0-914268-65-1*, 79-4CTE); student ed. 3.96 (*0-914268-64-3*, 79-4C) A N Palmer.

Palmer Method Cursive, Consumable. Fred M. King. (Palmer Method Easy to Teach Ser.). (Illus.). (J). (gr. 5). 1979. teacher ed. 5.60 (*0-914268-67-8*, 79-5CTE) A N Palmer.

Palmer Method Cursive, Consumable. Fred M. King. (Palmer Method Easy to Teach Ser.). (Illus.). (J). (gr. 6). 1979. teacher ed. 5.60 (*0-914268-69-4*, 79-6CTE) A N Palmer.

Palmer Method Cursive, Non-Consumable. Fred M. King. (Palmer Method Easy to Teach Ser.). 1979. teacher ed. 5.60 (*0-914268-79-1*, N79-4CTE); student ed. 4.24 (*0-914268-78-3*, N79-4C) A N Palmer.

Palmer Method Cursive, Non-Consumable. Fred M. King. (Palmer Method Easy to Teach Ser.). (Illus.). 1979. teacher ed. 5.60 (*0-914268-83-X*, N79-6CTE); teacher ed. 5.60 (*0-914268-81-3*, N79-5CTE); student ed. 4.24 (*0-914268-82-1*, N79-6C); student ed. 4.24 (*0-914268-80-5*, N79-5C) A N Palmer.

Palmer Method Cursive, Non-Consumable. Fred M. King. (Palmer Method Easy to Teach Ser.). (Illus.). (J). (gr. 7). 1979. teacher ed. 5.60 (*0-914268-85-6*, N79-SL1TE); student ed. 4.24 (*0-914268-84-8*, N79-SL1) A N Palmer.

Palmer Method Cursive, Non-Consumable. Fred M. King. (Palmer Method Easy to Teach Ser.). (Illus.). (J). (gr. 8). 1979. teacher ed. 5.60 (*0-914268-87-2*, N79-SL2TE); student ed. 4.24 (*0-914268-86-4*, N79-SL2) A N Palmer.

Palmer Method Manuscript, Consumable. Fred M. King. (Palmer Method Easy to Teach Ser.). (Illus.). (J). (gr. 1). 1979. teacher ed. 5.60 (*0-914268-57-0*, 79-1MTE); 3.96 (*0-914268-56-2*, 79-1M) A N Palmer.

Palmer Method Manuscript, Consumable. Fred M. King. (Palmer Method Easy to Teach Ser.). (Illus.). (gr. 2). 1979. teacher ed. 5.60 (*0-914268-59-7*, 79-2MTE); student ed. 3.96 (*0-914268-58-9*, 79-2M) A N Palmer.

Palmer Method Manuscript, Non-Consumable. Fred M. King. (Palmer Method Easy to Teach Ser.). (Illus.). (J). (gr. 1). 1979. teacher ed. 5.60 (*0-914268-71-6*, N79-1MTE); student ed. 4.24 (*0-914268-70-8*, N79-1M) A N Palmer.

Palmer Method Manuscript, Non-Consumable. Fred M. King. (Palmer Method Easy to Teach Ser.). (Illus.). (J). (gr. 2). 1979. teacher ed. 5.60 (*0-914268-73-2*, N79-2MTE); student ed. 4.24 (*0-914268-72-4*, N79-2M) A N Palmer.

Palmer Method Transition on Cursive, Consumable. (Palmer Method Easy to Teach Ser.). 1979. teacher ed. 5.60 (*0-914268-63-5*, 79-3TC TE); student ed. 3.96 (*0-914268-62-7*, 79-3TC) A N Palmer.

Palmer Method Transition on Cursive, Non-Consumable. Fred M. King. (Palmer Method Easy to Teach Ser.). (Illus.). (J). (gr. 3). 1979. teacher ed. 5.60 (*0-914268-77-5*, N79-3TC TE); student ed. 4.24 (*0-914268-76-7*, N79-3TC) A N Palmer.

Palmer Method Transition to Cursive, Consumable. Fred M. King. (Palmer Method Easy to Teach Ser.). (Illus.). (J). (gr. 2). 1979. teacher ed. 5.60 (*0-914268-61-9*, 79-2TCTE); student ed. 3.96 (*0-914268-60-0*, 79-2TC) A N Palmer.

Palmer Method Transition to Cursive, Non-Consumable. Fred M. King. (Palmer Method Easy to Teach Ser.). (Illus.). (J). (gr. 2). 1979. teacher ed. 5.60 (*0-914268-75-9*, N79-2TCTE); student ed. 4.24 (*0-914268-74-0*, N79-2TC) A N Palmer.

Palmer Method Writing Readiness, Consumable. Fred M. King. (Illus.). (J). (gr. k-1). 1979. student ed. 3.96 (*0-914268-55-4*, 79-WR) A N Palmer.

Palmer Museum of Art: A New Building by Charles W. Moore, FAIA, in Association with Arbonies King Vlock. Craig Zabel. Ed. by Mary A. Miles & Mary F. Linda. (Illus.). 40p. (Orig.). 1993. pap. text 5.00 (*0-911209-44-1*) Palmer Mus Art.

Palmer Museum of Art Twenty-Fifth Anniversary, 1972-1997. Frwd. by Jan K. Muhlert. (Illus.). 46p. 1997. pap. 5.00 (*0-911209-46-8*) Palmer Mus Art.

Palmer's Journal of Travels over the Rocky Mountains, 1845-46 see Early Western Travels, 1748-1846

Palmerston. Kenneth Bourne. (Illus.). 750p. 1982. write for info. (*0-318-54242-0*) Macmillan.

Palmerston & Africa: The Rio Nunez Affair, Competition, Diplomacy & Justice. Roderick Braithwaite. LC 96-60448. (Illus.). 256p. 1996. text 65.00 (*1-86064-109-1*) St Martin.

Palmerston, Metternich & the European System, 1830-1841. C. K. Webster. LC 74-34457. (Studies in Philosophy: No. 40). (C). 1972. reprint ed. lib. bdg. 49.95 (*0-8383-0135-5*) M S G Haskell Hse.

Palmerston Papers, Gladstone & Palmerston. Henry T. Palmerston. Ed. by Philip Guedalla. LC 73-157351. (Select Bibliographies Reprint Ser.). 1977. reprint ed. 28.95 (*0-8369-5812-8*) Ayer.

Palmerston's Foreign Policy, 1848. George J. Billy. LC 91-30737. (American University Studies: History: Ser. IX, Vols. 120). XV, 256p. (C). 1993. text 53.95 (*0-8204-1730-0*) P Lang Pubng.

Palmetto Country. Stetson Kennedy. 352p. 1989. pap. 17.95 (*0-8130-0959-6*) U Press Fla.

Palmetto Hospitality - Inn Style: A Recipe Guidebook to the Finest Inns in South Carolina. Tracy Winters & Phyllis Winters. LC 93-61906. (Illus.). 112p. (Orig.). 1994. pap. 10.00 (*1-883651-01-8*) Winters IN.

Palmetto Journal: Walks in the Natural Areas of South Carolina. Phillip Manning. LC 94-49584. (Illus.). 238p. (Orig.). 1995. pap. 13.95 (*0-89587-124-6*) Blair.

Palmetto Leaves. Harriet Beecher Stowe. LC 98-53476. 1999. pap. 12.95 (*0-8130-1693-2*) U Press Fla.

Palmetto State Glovebox Guide to BBQ: South Carolina. BBQ Digest Staff. LC 96-79806. 192p. (Orig.). 1997. pap. 12.95 (*1-56352-408-2*) Longstreet.

***Palmetto Women, South Carolina.** Ron Chepesiuk & Gina White Price. (Images of America Ser.). (Illus.). 128p. 1999. pap. 18.99 (*0-7385-0035-6*) Arcadia Publng.

Palmiers de L'Eldorado (The Palms of El Dorado) F. Kahn. (ENG & FRE., Illus.). 252p. 1997. pap. 59.00 (*2-7099-1359-3*, Pub. by LInstitut Francais) Balogh.

Pal'Mira (Palmyra) Mikhail Gershenzon. Ed. & Intro. by Vera Proskurina. (RUS.). 126p. 1997. 12.00 (*1-55779-099-X*) Hermitage Pubs.

Palmist Hand Journal. Cavallini & Company Staff. 1995. 16.00 (*1-57489-005-0*); 24.00 (*1-57489-006-9*) Cavallini.

Palmistry. Kristyna Arcarti. (For Beginners Ser.). (Illus.). 103p. 1995. pap. 11.95 (*0-340-59552-3*, Pub. by Headway) Trafalgar.

Palmistry. David V. Barrett. LC 95-11682. (Predictions Library). (Illus.). 56p. 1995. 8.95 (*0-7894-0311-0*, 6-70517) DK Pub Inc.

Palmistry. Ray Douglas. (Teach Yourself Ser.). 224p. 1998. pap. 11.95 (*0-8442-0278-9*, 02789, Teach Yrslf) NTC Contemp Pub Co.

Palmistry. New Holland Publishing Ltd. Staff. LC 99-176195. (Ancient Wisdom for the New Age Ser.). (Illus.). 72p. 1998. 9.95 (*1-85368-977-7*, Pub. by New5 Holland) Sterling.

***Palmistry.** Batia Shorek. (Illus.). 144p. 2000. pap. 14.95 (*965-494-121-X*) Astrolog Pub.

Palmistry: How to Chart the Lines of Your Life. Roz Levine. (Illus.). 128p. (Orig.). 1993. pap. 15.00 (*0-671-78501-X*, Fireside) S&S Trade Pap.

***Palmistry: How to Discover Success, Love & Happiness.** Sasha Fenton. 2000. pap. text 18.95 (*1-84222-002-0*) Carlton Bks Ltd.

Palmistry: The Whole View. 2nd rev. ed. Judith Hipskind. LC 83-80174. (Llewellyn's Inner Awareness Ser.). (Illus.). 248p. 1999. pap. 9.95 (*0-87542-306-X*) Llewellyn Pubns.

Palmistry & the Inner Self. Ray Douglas. (Illus.). 256p. 1995. pap. 12.95 (*0-7137-2520-6*, Pub. by Blandford Pr) Sterling.

Palmistry & the Inner Self. Douglas Ray. 1995. pap. 150.00 (*81-208-1350-2*, Pub. by Print Hse) St Mut.

Palmistry Box. Ann Fiery. (Illus.). 48p. 1998. 18.95 (*0-8118-1748-2*) Chronicle Bks.

Palmistry Encyclopedia. Rhoda Hamilton. (Illus.). 451p. 1996. pap. 23.95 (*0-9655382-0-6*) Rhoda.

Palmistry, How to Master It? A Gist of Indian & Western Systems of Hand Reading. Dayanand. (C). 1994. 10.00 (*81-7386-116-1*, Pub. by DK Pubs Ind) S Asia.

Palmistry Made Easy. J. S. Bright. 261p. 1983. 8.95 (*0-318-36393-3*) Asia Bk Corp.

Palmistry Made Easy. Fred Gettings. 1977. pap. 7.00 (*0-87980-114-X*) Wilshire.

Palmistry Made Practical. Elizabeth Daniels Squire. 1978. pap. 7.00 (*0-87980-115-8*) Wilshire.

Palmistry, Marriage & Family Welfare. M. Katakkar. (C). 1993. pap. 6.00 (*81-85674-42-6*, Pub. by UBS Pubs Dist) S Asia.

Palmistry Revealed. Paul Fenton-Smith. (Illus.). 192p. 1997. reprint ed. pap. 10.95 (*0-89346-843-6*) Heian Intl.

Palmistry Workbook. Nathaniel Altman. (Workbook Ser.). (Illus.). 160p. 1984. pap. 14.95 (*0-85030-352-4*) Sterling.

Palmist's Companion: A History & Bibliography of Palmistry. Andrew Fitzherbert. LC 92-5150. (Illus.). 244p. 1992. 29.00 (*0-8108-2524-4*) Scarecrow.

PalmPilot: The Ultimate Guide. David Pogue. (Illus.). 489p. 1998. pap. 29.95 incl. cd-rom (*1-56592-420-7*) OReilly & Assocs.

***PalmPilot: The Ultimate Guide.** 2nd ed. David Pogue. Ed. by Tim O'Reilly. (Illus.). 520p. 1999. pap. 29.95 incl. cd-rom (*1-56592-600-5*) OReilly & Assocs.

***PalmPilot! (And Palm Organizers) I Didn't Know You Could Do That...** 4th ed. Neil Salkind. 272p. 1999. pap. 19.99 incl. audio compact disk (*0-7821-2588-3*) Sybex.

PalmPilot Resource Kit. Glenn Brown. (Illus.). 208p. 1998. spiral bd. 29.99 incl. cd-rom (*0-7645-3219-7*) IDG Bks.

PalmPilot's Amazing Secrets. Mark Minasi. 1998. pap. text 24.99 (*0-7821-2247-7*) Sybex.

Palms. Martin Gibbons. 80p. 1993. 6.98 (*1-55521-837-7*) Bk Sales Inc.

Palms. Ed. by Wolfgang Hageney. (Express Art Ser.). (Illus.). 96p. (Orig.). 1993. pap. 11.95 (*88-7070-172-7*) Belvedere USA.

Palms. Charlie Smith. 72p. 1994. pap. 8.95 (*0-393-31096-5*) Norton.

Palms: An Action Plan for Their Conservation. Ed. by Dennis V. Johnson. LC 97-164259. (C). 1993. pap. text 27.00 (*2-8317-0352-2*, Pub. by IUCN) Island Pr.

Palms & Cycads of Thailand. Donald R. Hodel. LC 98-60613. 190 p. 1998. write for info. (*0-935868-98-4*) Allen Pr.

Palms & Pearls, or, Scenes in Ceylon Alan Walters. LC 98-905017. 317 p. 1997. write for info. (*81-206-1235-3*) Asian Educ Servs.

Palms for Human Needs in Asia: Palm Utilization & Conservation in India, Indonesia, Malaysia & the Philippines. Ed. by Dennis Johnson. (Illus.). 264p. (C). 1992. text 91.00 (*90-6191-181-8*, Pub. by A A Balkema) Ashgate Pub Co.

Palms for the Garden & Home. Jennifer Simpson. (C). 1989. 40.00 (*1-85368-039-7*, Pub. by New5 Holland) St Mut.

Palms in Forest Ecosystems of Amazonia. F. Kahn & J. J. Degranville. (Ecological Studies: Vol. 95). (Illus.). 240p. 1992. 158.95 (*0-387-54399-6*) Spr-Verlag.

Palms of British East India. W. Griffith. 182p. (C). 1978. text 750.00 (*0-89771-628-0*, Pub. by Intl Bk Distr) St Mut.

Palms of British East India. W. Griffith. 182p. 1978. reprint ed. 450.00 (*0-7855-3055-X*, Pub. by Intl Bk Distr) St Mut.

Palms of British India & Ceylon. E. Blatter. (C). 1978. text 500.00 (*0-89771-557-8*, Pub. by Intl Bk Distr) St Mut.

Palms of British India & Ceylon. E. Blatter. 600p. 1978. reprint ed. 300.00 (*0-7855-6637-6*, Pub. by Intl Bk Distr) St Mut.

Palms of Madagascar. John Dransfield & Henk Beentje. (Illus.). 520p. 1995. boxed set 99.00 (*0-947643-82-6*, Pub. by Royal Botnic Grdns) Balogh.

Palms of New Caledonia: Les Palmiers De Nouvelle-Caledonie. Donald R. Hodel & Jean-Christophe Pintaud. LC 98-60823. (Illus.). write for info. (*0-935868-99-2*) Allen Pr.

P

An Asterisk (*) at the beginning of an entry indicates that the title is appearing for the first time.

Palms of South Florida. rev. ed. George B. Stevenson. LC 95-49516. (Illus.). 251p. (C). 1996. pap. 19.95 (*0-8130-1441-7*) U Press Fla.

Palms of the Amazon. Andrew Henderson. (Illus.). 388p. 1995. text 120.00 (*0-19-508311-3*) OUP.

Palms Throughout the World. David L. Jones. LC 95-68615. (Illus.). 432p. 1995. 55.00 (*1-56098-616-6*) Smithsonian.

Palms, Wine & Witnesses: Public Spirit & Private Gain in an African Farming Community. David J. Parkin. (Illus.). 113p. (C). 1994. reprint ed. pap. text 10.50 (*0-88133-802-8*) Waveland Pr.

Palmway. Dennis Saleh. LC 75-42432. 46p. 1975. 3.50 (*0-87886-065-7*, Greenfld Rev Pr) Greenfld Rev Lit.

Palmyra & Its Empire: Zonobia's Revolt Against Rome. Richard Stoneman. 216p. 1995. pap. 24.95 (*0-472-08315-5*, 08315) U of Mich Pr.

Palmyra & Zenobia. W. Wright. 432p. 1987. 320.00 (*1-85077-155-3*, Pub. by Darf Pubs Ltd) St Mut.

Palmyrena: A Topographical Itinerary. Alois Musil. LC 77-87087. (American Geographical Society Oriental Explorations & Studies: No. 4). reprint ed. 55.00 (*0-404-60234-7*) AMS Pr.

Palmyrene Aramaic Texts. Delbert R. Hillers & Eleonora Cussini. LC 95-32142. (Publications of the Comprehensive Aramaic Lexicon Project). (Illus.). 458p. (C). 1996. text 65.00 (*0-8018-5278-1*) Johns Hopkins.

***Palmyrenes of Dura-Europos: A Study of Religious Interaction in Roman Syria.** Lucinda Dirven. LC 99-44510. (Religions in the Graeco-Roman World Ser.). 1999. write for info. (*90-04-11589-7*) Brill Academic Pubs.

Palo Alto: A Centennial History. Palo Alto Historical Association Staff & Ward Winslow. LC 93-85698. (Illus.). 352p. 1993. write for info. (*0-9638098-3-0*) Palo Alto Hist.

Palo Duro. Bruce H. Thorstad. Ed. by Doug Grad. 288p. (Orig.). 1993. mass mkt. 3.99 (*0-671-75905-1*) PB.

Palo Mayombe: Spirits, Rituals, Spells. Carlos Montenegro. (Illus.). 154p. 1997. pap. 9.95 (*0-942272-42-0*) Original Pubns.

Paloma. Douglas L. Heinsohn. LC 81-12683. 301p. 1987. 22.95 (*0-87949-213-9*) Ashley Bks.

Paloma. Rich Winograd. LC 97-67153. 170p. (Orig.). 1997. pap. 14.95 (*1-886036-21-7*) Passages Pbg.

***Paloma the Dove.** Patricia R. Herring. 25p. (J). (gr. 2-5). 1998. pap. 12.95 (*0-9616484-1-4*) Santos-Santos Pubns.

Palominas Pistolero & Smoke Wagon Kid. Nelson Nye. 1978. mass mkt. 1.95 (*0-89083-418-0*, Zebra Kensgtn) Kensgtn Pub Corp.

Palomino. Elizabeth Jolley. 260p. 1988. pap. 8.95 (*0-89255-136-4*) Persea Bks.

Palomino. Danielle Steel. 480p. 1982. mass mkt. 6.99 (*0-440-16753-1*) Dell.

Palomino. Elizabeth Jolley. 1998. reprint ed. pap. 16.95 (*0-7022-1948-7*, Pub. by Univ Queensland Pr) Intl Spec Bk.

Palomino Horse see Learning about Horses Series

Palomino Horse. Gail B. Stewart. (Illus.). 48p. (J). (gr. 3-7). 1995. 19.00 (*0-516-35299-7*) Childrens.

Palomino Horse. limited ed. Doreen M. Norton. (Illus.). 265p. 1996. reprint ed. 45.00 (*0-87505-419-6*) Borden.

Palomino Horses. Janet L. Gammie. LC 95-5448. (Horses Ser.). (Illus.). 24p. (J). (ps-4). 1995. lib. bdg. 13.98 (*1-56239-442-8*) ABDO Pub Co.

Palomino Stud. large type ed. Jeff Sadler. (Dales Large Print Ser.). 206p. 1997. pap. 18.99 (*1-85389-725-6*) Ulverscroft.

Palominos see Great American Horses

***Palomita.** large type ed. Lance Howard. 296p. 2000. pap. 18.99 (*0-7089-5665-3*, Linford) Ulverscroft.

Palookas of the Ozone. Joel Lewis. 1992. pap. 4.00 (*0-938979-38-8*) EG Bksellers.

Palos Verdes Peninsula: Time & the Terraced Land. Augusta Fink. LC 66-18957. (Illus.). 164p. 1987. pap. 10.95 (*0-934136-37-8*) Good Life.

Palouse Country: A Land & Its People. Richard Scheuerman. (Illus.). 137p. (Orig.). 1993. 34.00 (*0-9637310-1-7*); pap. 24.00 (*0-9637310-2-5*) Color Pr.

Palpable Elysium. Jonathan Williams. (Illus.). 24p. 1997. 3000.00 (*1-891472-11-9*) Dim Gray.

***Palpable Elysium.** Jonathan Williams. (Illus.). 2001. pap. 30.00 (*1-56792-149-3*) Godine.

Palpation Skills: Assessment & Diagnosis Through Touch. Leon Chaitow. LC 96-37078. 1996. pap. text 39.95 (*0-443-05320-0*) Church.

Palpitations & Arrhythmias: A Guide for Patients. Nora Goldschlanger. (Cardiology Ser.). 32p. 1997. pap. text 2.95 (*1-885274-50-5*) Health InfoNet Inc.

Pals: Tllc Activ Black. McCloskey et al. 80p. 1996. pap. text 39.69 (*0-201-85320-5*) Addison-Wesley.

PALS: Working with the Revised Passive Loss Rules. 56p. 1995. pap. 6.50 (*0-614-26803-6*, 12295BLS03) CCH INC.

***Pals & Pets, Vol. 2.** Florence M. Lindstrom. (Illus.). 28p. (J). (gr. k-1). 1998. pap. text 11.00 (*1-930092-28-8*, CLP29931) Christian Liberty.

PAL's in Profile. Joshua Goldstein. (Illus.). 98p. (Orig.). 1995. pap. 10.00 (*0-939715-24-4*) Ctr Politics.

Pals Plus Instructor's Guide. American Safety Video Publishers, Inc. Staff. 96p. 1993. teacher ed. 39.95 (*0-8016-7761-0*) Mosby Inc.

Pals, Potions, & Pixies: Family Songbook. Jo Harper. (Harper Voices Ser.: Vol. 2). (ENG & SPA., Illus.). 20p. (Orig.). (J). (gr. 1-5). 1988. pap. 8.00 incl. audio (*0-929932-01-3*) JCH Pr.

Palsgrave's Acolastus. Ed. by E. L. Carver. (EETS, OS Ser.: No. 202). 1974. reprint ed. 55.00 (*0-527-00202-X*) Periodicals Srv.

***Paltinis Diary.** Gabriel Liiceanu. (Library of Ideas). 250p. (C). 2000. 49.95 (*963-9116-88-2*); pap. 22.95 (*963-9116-89-0*) Ctrl Europ Univ.

Palucci Vendetta. large type ed. Genevieve Lyons. 625p. 1993. 27.99 (*0-7505-0510-9*, Pub. by Mgna Lrg Print) Ulverscroft.

Paludes. Andre Gide. (FRE.). 1973. pap. 10.95 (*0-8288-3684-1*, M3482) Fr & Eur.

Paludes. Andre Gide. (Folio Ser.: No. 436). 160p. 1973. 6.95 (*2-07-036436-4*) Schoenhof.

Palyno-Taxonomy of Selected Indian Liverworts. Asha Gupta & Ram Udar. Ed. by S. R. Gradstein. (Bryophytorum Bibliotheca: Vol. 29). (GER., Illus.). 202p. 1986. pap. 48.00 (*3-443-62003-5*, Pub. by Gebruder Borntraeger) Balogh.

Palynological Correlation of Major Pennsylvanian (Middle & Upper Carboniferous) Chronostratigraphic Boundaries in the Illinois & Other Coal Basins. Russel A. Peppers. (Memoir Ser.: No. 188). (Illus.). 1996. 55.00 (*0-8137-1188-6*) Geol Soc.

Palynological Study of the Liabeae (Asteraceae) Harold E. Robinson. LC 86-600032. (Smithsonian Contributions to Botany Ser.: No. 64). 54p. reprint ed. pap. 30.00 (*0-608-15314-1*, 202955200061) Bks Demand.

***Palynologische Untersuchungen Ueber die Holozaene Vegetations-, Klima und Siedlungsgeschichte in Hochasien (Nanga Parbat, Karakorum, Nianbaoyeze, Lhasa)** F. Schluetz. (Dissertationes Botanicae Ser.: Band 54). (GER., Illus.). 188p. 1999. 50.00 (*3-443-64227-6*, Pub. by Gebruder Borntraeger) Balogh.

***Palynologische Untersuchungen zur Vegetationsgeschichte des Weichsel-Spatglazial und Fruhholozan an Jahrlich Geschichteten Sedimenten des Meerfelder Maares (Eifel), Band 320.** Martina Stebich. (Illus.). 127p. 1999. 49.00 (*3-443-64232-2*, Pub. by Gebruder Borntraeger) Balogh.

Palynology. M. R. Saxena. 135p. 1993. text 23.00 (*81-204-0803-9*, Pub. by Oxford & IBH Pubng) Science Pubs.

Palynology in Oil Exploration: A Symposium. Ed. by Aureal T. Cross. LC 72-182534. (Society of Economic Paleontologists & Mineralogists, Special Publication Ser.: No. 11). 208p. reprint ed. pap. 64.50 (*0-608-12956-9*, 202473700038) Bks Demand.

Palynology of Arid Lands. Aharon Horowitz. LC 92-8579. 546p. 1992. 224.75 (*0-444-88277-4*) Elsevier.

Palynology of the Almond Formation, Rock Springs Uplift, Wyoming see Bulletins of American Paleontology: Vol. 64

Palynology und Palynofacies of the Upper Tertiary in Venezuela. Maria A. Lorente. (Dissertationes Botanicae Ser.: Band 99). (Illus.). ix, 225p. 1986. pap. 71.00 (*3-443-64011-7*, Pub. by Gebruder Borntraeger) Balogh.

Pam, Sam & Bam Cat. Joan Simko & Marjorie Cahell. (Illus.). 19p. (Orig.). 1993. pap. 7.95 (*1-885993-03-X*) East Meets West.

Pam Tillis. Ace Collins. LC 97-222716. 1997. mass mkt. 5.99 (*0-312-96404-8*, St Martins Paperbacks) St Martin.

Pamba & the Bink. Date not set. pap. 3.95 (*0-89868-153-7*) ARO Pub.

Pamba & the Bink. Bob Reese. (Illus.). (J). (gr. k-6). 1984. 9.95 (*0-89868-152-9*) ARO Pub.

Pamdemonium. Pamela Anderson Lee. (Illus.). 1997. 23.00 (*0-446-52269-4*) Warner Bks.

Pamdemonium. Pamela A. Lee & Todd Gold. 1998. mass mkt. 24.00 (*0-446-60668-5*, Warner Vision) Warner Bks.

Pamela. Judy Baer. (Springsong Ser.). 176p. (YA). (gr. 7-10). 1996. mass mkt. 4.99 (*1-55661-749-6*) Bethany Hse.

***Pamela.** Patrick Henden. 208p. 1999. mass mkt. 7.95 (*1-56201-137-5*, Pub. by Blue Moon Bks) Publishers Group.

Pamela, 001. Samuel Richardson. Ed. by T. C. Duncan-Eaves & B. D. Kimpel. LC 71-134860. (Orig.). (C). 1971. pap. 13.96 (*0-395-11152-8*, RivEd) HM.

Pamela. Samuel Richardson. 453p. (Orig.). 1991. pap. 7.95 (*0-460-87064-5*, Everyman's Classic Lib) Tuttle Pubng.

***Pamela.** large type ed. Mary Mackie. LC 99-49387. (General Ser.). 2000. pap. 22.95 (*0-7862-2308-1*) Thorndike Pr.

Pamela: A Novel. Pamela Lu. LC 99-230981. 98p. 1998. pap. 12.95 (*1-891190-04-0*, Pub. by Atelos) SPD-Small Pr Dist.

Pamela & the Revolution. Mary J. Prowense. Ed. by Molly Schatz. (Illus.). 130p. (J). (gr. 7 up). 1993. 12.95 (*0-9635107-2-X*) Marc Anthony.

Pamela Anderson Lee. Esme Hawes. LC 97-24535. (Superstars of Film Ser.). (Illus.). 48p. (YA). (gr. 5 up). 1999. lib. bdg. 15.95 (*0-7910-4647-8*) Chelsea Hse.

Pamela Camel. Bill Peet. (Illus.). 32p. (J). (gr. 4-8). 1986. pap. 7.95 (*0-395-41670-1*, Sandpiper) HM.

Pamela Censured: In a Letter to the Editor. Intro. by Charles Batten, Jr. LC 92-23719. (Augustan Reprints Ser.: No. 175). 1976. reprint ed. 14.50 (*0-404-70175-2*, PR3664) AMS Pr.

Pamela: or Virtue Rewarded. Samuel Richardson. Ed. by Petr Sabor. (English Library). 544p. 1981. pap. 7.95 (*0-14-043140-3*) Viking Penguin.

Pamela: or Virtue Rewarded see Complete Novels of Mr. Samuel Richardson

Pamela's First Musical. Wendy Wasserstein. LC 95-36133. (Illus.). 48p. (J). (gr. k-5). 1996. lib. bdg. 16.89 (*0-7868-2063-2*, Pub. by Hyprn Child) Little.

Pamela's First Musical. Wendy Wasserstein. LC 95-36133. (Illus.). 40p. (J). 1998. pap. 5.95 (*0-7868-1292-3*, Pub. by Hyprn Ppbks) Little.

Pamela's Palace. large type ed. Arlene J. Fitzgerald. 336p. 1995. 27.99 (*0-7089-3258-4*) Ulverscroft.

Pamela's Plan. Kate Noble. (Zoo Stories Ser.). (Illus.). 32p. (J). (ps-4). 15.95 (*0-9631798-4-5*) Salmon Run.

Pamiat' Teper' Mnogoe Razvorachivaet: Iz Literaturnogo Naslediia Kruchenykh. Aleksei Kruchenykh. Ed. by Nina Gourianova. (Modern Russian Literature & Culture: Vol. 41). (Illus.). 498p. (Orig.). (C). 1999. pap. text 40.00 (*1-57201-052-5*) Berkeley Slavic.

Pamjatniki Drevnej Russkoj Pis'mennosti. (Russkaja Istoriceskaja Biblioteca Ser.: Vol. XIII, No. 1). 872p. 1985. reprint ed. write for info. (*3-487-07707-8*) G Olms Pubs.

Pamlico County: A Brief History. Joe A. Mobley. (Illus.). xiv, 144p. (Orig.). 1991. pap. 10.00 (*0-86526-252-7*) NC Archives.

***Pammie Pigeon.** Dave Sargent. LC 99-89897. (Illus.). (J). 2000. pap. write for info. (*1-56763-452-4*) Ozark Pub.

Pampa Grande & the Mochica Culture. Izumi Shimada. LC 93-26108. 323p. 1994. 60.00 (*0-292-77674-8*) U of Tex Pr.

Pampangans: Colonial Society in A Philippine Province. John A. Larkin. LC 74-165232. (Illus.). 358p. reprint ed. pap. 111.00 (*0-7837-4814-0*, 204446100003) Bks Demand.

Pamper Your Partner. Penny Rich. 1990. per. 15.95 (*0-671-69526-6*) S&S Trade.

Pamper Your Pooch. Lorenz Staff. 1998. 11.95 (*1-85967-674-X*) Anness Pub.

***Pampered Cowboy.** Johnny D. Boggs. (Illus.). 250p. 2000. pap. 18.95 (*1-55622-782-5*, Rep of TX Pr) Wordware Pub.

Pamphlet, 1. Carol Ann Duffy. 1999. pap. text 11.95 (*0-85646-307-8*) Anvil Pub.

Pamphlet Against Anthologies. Laura R. Jackson & Robert Graves. LC 78-120220. reprint ed. 32.50 (*0-404-05332-7*) AMS Pr.

Pamphlet Against Anthologies. Laura Riding. (BCL1-PR English Literature Ser.). 192p. 1992. reprint ed. lib. bdg. 69.00 (*0-7812-7082-0*) Rprt Serv.

Pamphlet Architecture Vol. 21: Situation Normal. Paul Lewis et al. LC 98-39325. (Illus.). 80p. 1998. pap. 12.95 (*1-56898-154-6*) Princeton Arch.

Pamphlet Architecture 1-10. Ed. by Steven Holl & William Stout. LC 97-43563. 1998. 40.00 (*1-56898-126-0*) Princeton Arch.

Pamphlet Debate on the Union Between Great Britain & Ireland, 1797-1800. W. J. McCormack. 144p. 1996. 39.50 (*0-7165-2568-2*, Pub. by Irish Acad Pr) Intl Spec Bk.

Pamphlet for Spies: Invisible Inks, Codes & Ciphers. R. E. Brown. 1994. 10.00 (*1-885293-12-7*) Maldonado Pubng.

Pamphlet for Spies: The Field. R. E. Brown. 1994. 15.00 (*1-885293-13-5*) Maldonado Pubng.

Pamphlet Literature from Onitsha. B. Chinaka et al. (B. E. Ser.: No. 34). 1965. 75.00 (*0-8115-2985-1*) Periodicals Srv.

Pamphlet Wars: Prose in English Revolution. Ed. by James Holstun. 1992. text 29.50 (*0-7146-3458-1*, Pub. by F Cass Pubs) Intl Spec Bk.

***Pamphletaires Allemands et la France de Louis XIV.** Jean Schillinger. xi, 720p. 1999. 67.95 (*3-906762-30-0*) P Lang Pubng.

Pamphleteer, 29 vols., Set. 16500p. (C). (gr. 13). 1994. text, boxed set 6600.00 (*0-415-11563-9*, B4733) Routledge.

Pamphlets & Public Opinion: The Campaign for a Union of Orders in the Early French Revolution. Kenneth Margerison. LC 97-14474. 296p. 1997. 36.95 (*1-55753-109-9*) Purdue U Pr.

Pamphlets & the American Revolution. LC 76-41289. 872p. 1976. 100.00 (*0-8201-1280-1*) Schol Facsimiles.

***Pamphlets of Protest: An Anthology of Early African American Protest Literature, 1790-1860.** Ed. by Richard Newman et al. 320p. 2000. 45.00 (*0-415-92443-X*); pap. 22.99 (*0-415-92444-8*) Routledge.

Pamphlets of Thomas Robert Malthus, 1800-1817. Thomas Robert Malthus. LC 77-117389. (Reprints of Economic Classics Ser.). v, 320p. 1970. reprint ed. lib. bdg. 45.00 (*0-678-00646-6*) Kelley.

Pamphlets on American Business Abroad: An Original Anthology. Thwaite et al. Ed. by Stuart Bruchey & Eleanor Bruchey. LC 76-5053. (American Business Abroad Ser.). (Illus.). 1976. reprint ed. 34.95 (*0-405-09294-6*) Ayer.

Pamphlets on the Constitution of the United States. Paul L. Ford. LC 68-22228. (American History, Politics & Law Ser.). 1968. reprint ed. lib. bdg. 35.00 (*0-306-71144-3*) Da Capo.

***Pamphlets on the Constitution of the United States, Published During Its Discussion by the People, 1787-1788; 1888.** Paul L. Ford. LC 99-25089. 2000. 75.00 (*1-886363-95-1*) Lawbk Exchange.

Pamphlets, Periodicals & Songs of the French Revolutionary Era: In the Princeton University Library. Stephen Ferguson. LC 89-1588. 582p. 1989. text 10.00 (*0-8240-4110-0*) Garland.

Pamphlets Printed & Distributed by the Women's Anti-Suffrage Association of the Third Judicial District of the State of New York. 340p. 1990. reprint ed. 47.50 (*0-8377-2748-0*, Rothman) W S Hein.

Pam's Cruise Guide, 1993: How to Get the Most from Your Cruise Dollar. Pamela M. Sorensen. 264p. 1992. pap. text 12.95 (*0-9633661-0-6*) White Lamb.

Pam's Paradise Ranch: A Story of Hawaii. Armine Von Tempski. LC 92-24538. (Illus.). viii, 334p. (YA). 1992. reprint ed. pap. 14.95 (*0-918024-96-X*) Ox Bow.

Pamsy & Me. Pamela H. Wilson. (Orig.). (J). (gr. 3-6). 1997. pap. 6.95 (*0-533-12347-X*) Vantage.

Pamukkale. 96p. pap. text 12.95 (*88-8029-041-X*, Pub. by Bonechi) Eiron.

Pamunkey Indians of Virginia. Garland Pollard. (Bureau of American Ethnology Bulletins Ser.). 99p. 1995. lib. bdg. 89.00 (*0-7812-4017-4*) Rprt Serv.

Pamunkey Indians of Virginia. Garland Pollard. 1988. reprint ed. lib. bdg. 49.00 (*0-7812-0056-3*) Rprt Serv.

Pan: From Lieutenant Thomas Glahn's Papers. Knut Hamsun. Tr. by James W. McFarlane from NOR. 192p. (Orig.). 1956. pap. 10.00 (*0-374-50016-9*) FS&G.

Pan: From the Papers of Lieutenant Thomas Glahn. Knut Hamsun. Tr. by Sverre Lyngstad from ENG. LC 98-11351. (Twentieth-Century Classics Ser.). 224p. 1998. pap. 9.95 (*0-14-118067-6*) Viking Penguin.

Pan Africa: Across the Sahara in 1941 with Pan Am. Tom Culbert & Andy Dawson. Ed. by R. E. Davies. (Illus.). 184p. 1998. lib. bdg. 30.00 (*1-888962-12-7*) Paladwr Pr.

Pan-African Biography. Ed. by Robert A. Hill. 232p. 1987. pap. 25.00 (*0-918456-59-2*, Crossroads) African Studies Assn.

Pan-African Chronology: A Comprehensive Reference to the Black Quest for Freedom in Africa, the Americas, Europe & Asia, 1400-1865. Everett Jenkins, Jr. LC 95-8294. 448p. 1996. lib. bdg. 55.00 (*0-7864-0139-7*) McFarland & Co.

Pan-African Chronology II Vol. II: A Comprehensive Reference to the Black Quest for Freedom in Africa, the Americas, Europe & Asia, 1865-1915. Everett Jenkins, Jr. LC 97-34101. 582p. 1998. lib. bdg. 65.00 (*0-7864-0385-3*) McFarland & Co.

Pan-African Connection: From Slavery to Garvey & Beyond. Tony Martin. LC 82-19521. (New Marcus Garvey Library: No. 6). (Illus.). xii, 262p. (C). 1984. reprint ed. pap. text 12.95 (*0-912469-11-0*) Majority Pr.

Pan-African Education: The Last Stage of Educational Developments. John K. Marah. LC 88-1696. (Studies in African Education & Social Development: Vol. 2). 336p. 1989. lib. bdg. 99.95 (*0-88946-186-4*) E Mellen.

Pan-African Protest: West Africa & the Italo-Ethiopian Crisis, 1934-1941. S. K. Asante. LC 78-312713. (Legon History Ser.). 260p. reprint ed. pap. 80.60 (*0-608-13164-4*, 202523100043) Bks Demand.

Pan African Theology: Providence & the Legacies of the Ancestors. Josiah U. Young. LC 91-75600. 310p. 1992. 45.00 (*0-86543-276-7*); pap. 12.95 (*0-86543-277-5*) Africa World.

Pan-Africanism. P. Olisanwuche Esedebe. LC 82-18692. 271p. 1982. pap. 12.95 (*0-88258-125-2*) Howard U Pr.

Pan-Africanism. Michael W. Williams. (Magill Bibliographies Ser.). 142p. 1992. 42.00 (*0-8108-2794-8*) Scarecrow.

Pan-Africanism: A Short Political Guide. Colin Legum. LC 75-25492. (Illus.). 296p. 1976. reprint ed. lib. bdg. 35.00 (*0-8371-8420-7*, LEPA, Greenwood Pr) Greenwood.

Pan-Africanism: Politics, Economy, & Social Change in the Twenty-First Century. Ed. by Tajudeen Abdul-Raheem. LC 96-19795. 255p. (C). 1996. text 50.00 (*0-8147-0660-6*); pap. text 18.50 (*0-8147-0661-4*) NYU Pr.

***Pan-Africanism - Exploring the Contradiction: Politics, Identity & Development in Africa & the African Diaspora.** William B. Ackah. (Interdisciplinary Research Series in Ethnic, Gender & Class Relations). 138p. 1999. text 61.95 (*1-84014-375-4*, Pub. by Ashgate Pub) Ashgate Pub Co.

Pan-Africanism & East African Integration. Joseph S. Nye. LC 65-22063. 327p. reprint ed. pap. 101.40 (*0-7837-3845-5*, 204366700010) Bks Demand.

Pan-Africanism & Its Detractors: A Response to Harvard's Race-Effacing Universalists. Opoku Agyeman. LC 97-39566. 140p. 1997. text 69.95 (*0-7734-8432-9*) E Mellen.

Pan-Africanism for Beginners. Sid Lemelle. LC 91-50561. (Writers & Readers Documentary Comic Bks.). 176p. (Orig.). (C). 1992. pap. 9.95 (*0-86316-148-0*) Writers & Readers.

Pan Africanism in the African Diaspora: An Analysis of Modern Afrocentric Political Movements. Ronald W. Walters. LC 92-30256. (African American Life Ser.). 452p. (C). 1993. 39.95 (*0-8143-2184-4*) Wayne St U Pr.

Pan Africanism in the African Diaspora: An Analysis of Modern Afrocentric Political Movements. 2nd ed. Ronald W. Walters. (African American Life Ser.). 452p. 1997. reprint ed. pap. 19.95 (*0-8143-2185-2*) Wayne St U Pr.

Pan-Africanism Reconsidered. American Society of African Culture Staff. LC 76-3618. 376p. 1976. reprint ed. lib. bdg. 35.00 (*0-8371-8792-3*, ASPA, Greenwood Pr) Greenwood.

***Pan-Africanists.** Barrington Watson. LC 99-55236. (Illus.). 84p. 2000. pap. 16.95 (*0-86543-810-2*) Africa World.

***Pan Am.** Lynn M. Homan & Thomas Reilly. (Images of Aviation Ser.). (Illus.). 128p. 2000. pap. 18.99 (*0-7385-0552-8*) Arcadia Publng.

Pan Am: An Airline & Its Aircraft. R. E. Davies. (Great Airlines of the World Ser.). (Illus.). 96p. 1987. 25.00 (*0-9626483-2-9*) Paladwr Pr.

Pan Am: An Aviation Legend. Barnaby Conrad. 200p. 1999. 39.95 (*0-942627-55-5*) Woodford Pubng.

Pan Am: Gone but Not Forgotten. Desmond Fairbairn. Ed. by Marion Harris. LC 96-29500. (Illus.). 136p. 1997. pap. 23.00 (*0-933449-30-5*) Transport Trails.

Pan Am 103: The Lockerbie Coverup. William C. Chasey. (Illus.). 372p. (Orig.). 1995. pap. 17.95 (*0-9640104-1-0*) Bridger Hse.

***Pan Am 103: The Bombing, the Betrayals & a Bereaved Family's Search for Justice.** Susan Cohen. 2000. 21.95 (*0-451-20165-5*, Sig) NAL.

Pan Am Pioneer: A Manager's Memoir from Seaplane Clippers to Jumbo Jets. S. B. Kauffman. Ed. by George E. Hopkins. LC 95-37144. 242p. 1995. 29.95 (*0-89672-357-7*) Tex Tech Univ Pr.

Pan-American Dream: Do Latin America's Cultural Values Discourage True Partnership with the United States & Canada? Lawrence E. Harrison. 320p. (C). 1998. pap. text 29.00 (*0-8133-3470-5*, Pub. by Westview) HarpC.

P

Pan American Exposition, Buffalo. Thomas Leary & Elizabeth C. Sholes. (Images of America Ser.). (Illus.). 128p. 1998. pap. 16.99 *(0-7524-0981-6)* Arcadia Publng.

Pan American Health Organization: Origins & Evolution. N. Howard-Jones. (History of International Public Health Ser.). 20p. 1981. 7.00 *(92-4-156066-5)* World Health.

Pan-American Livestock Dictionary. 2nd rev. ed. M. Eta Trabing.Tr. of Diccionario Pan Americano de Ganadero. (ENG & SPA., Illus.). 428p. (Orig.). 1996. pap. text 50.00 *(0-9654073-0-6)* Cattleman.

Pan American Poems: An Anthology. Ed. by Agnes B. Poor. 1977. lib. bdg. 59.95 *(0-8490-2400-5)* Gordon Pr.

Pan American Visions: Woodrow Wilson in the Western Hemisphere, 1913-1921. Mark T. Gilderhus. LC 86-16024. 194p. 1986. 33.50 *(0-8165-0936-0)* U of Ariz Pr.

Pan-Americanism. R. Usher. 1976. lib. bdg. 59.95 *(0-8490-2402-1)* Gordon Pr.

Pan-Americanism: Its Beginnings. Joseph B. Lockey. LC 79-111723. (American Imperialism: Viewpoints of United States Foreign Policy, 1898-1941 Ser.). 1970. reprint ed. 28.95 *(0-405-02034-1)* Ayer.

Pan Americanism: Its Meaning & History. John E. Fagg. LC 81-17176. (Anvil Ser.). 218p. (C). 1982. pap. text 15.00 *(0-89874-258-7)* Krieger.

Pan-Americanism: The Idea & Movement, 1776-1991. 2nd ed. P. Olisanwuche Esedebe. LC 94-8375. 1994. pap. 17.95 *(0-88258-186-4)* Howard U Pr.

Pan-Americanism from Monroe to the Present: A View from the Other Side. rev. ed. Alonso A. Monteverde. Tr. by Asa Zatz. LC 68-13659. 192p. reprint ed. pap. 59.60 *(0-7837-3914-1,* 204376200010) Bks Demand.

Pan Am's First Lady: The Diary of Betty Stettinius Trippe. Ed. & Illus. by R. E. Davies. 322p. 1996. 30.00 *(1-888962-00-3)* Paladwr Pr.

Pan & the Nightmare. James Hillman & Wilhelm H. Roscher. 160p. 2000. pap. 17.50 *(0-88214-225-9,* Pub. by Spring Pubns) Continuum.

Pan Angling's International Fishing Escapes. Jim C. Chapralis & Paul Melchior. LC 98-65439. (Illus.). 192p. 1998. pap. 12.95 *(0-9618193-1-6)* PanAngling Pub.

***Pan-Arabism before Nasser: Egyptian Power Politics & the Palestine Question.** Michael Doran. LC 98-23001. (Studies in Middle Eastern History). 240p. 1999. text 35.00 *(0-19-512361-1)* OUP.

Pan Crossword Dictionary. 2nd rev. ed. Ed. by Mike Hutchinson. 512p. 1995. pap. 22.50 *(0-330-34125-1,* Pub. by Pan) Trans-Atl Phila.

Pan de los Muertos. 2nd ed. Enrique L. Ruiz. LC 88-80745. (Coleccion Clasicos Cubanos). (SPA., Illus.). 225p. 1988. reprint ed. pap. 12.00 *(0-89729-482-3)* Ediciones.

Pan-European Biological & Landscape Diversity Strategy. (Nature & Environment Ser.: No. 74). 1996. 15.00 *(92-871-3046-9,* Pub. by Council of Europe) Manhattan Pub Co.

Pan-European Conference on the Potential Long-Term Ecological Impact of Genetically Modified Organisms: Proceedings - Strasbourg, 24-26 November, 1993. (Environmental Encounters Ser.: No. 20). 1995. 25.00 *(92-871-2679-8,* Pub. by Council of Europe) Manhattan Pub Co.

Pan Flute Pocketbook. Kristopher Faubion. 32p. 1993. pap. 0.95 *(1-56222-550-2,* 94848) Mel Bay.

Pan Hobbs' Britian. Pam Hobbs. 272p. 1995. pap. 18.95 *(0-385-25517-9)* Doubleday.

Pan-Islam. George W. Bury. LC 80-1938. reprint ed. 30.00 *(0-404-18956-3)* AMS Pr.

***Pan-Islam in British Indian Politics.** M. Naeem Qureshi. LC 99-196668. (Social, Economic & Political Studies of the Middle East & Asia). 1999. write for info. *(90-04-11371-1)* Brill Academic Pubs.

Pan-Islamism: Indian Muslims, the Ottomans & Britain (1877-1924) Azmi Ozcan. LC 97-5470. (Ottoman Empire & Its Heritage Ser.: No. 12). 260p. 1997. 90.50 *(90-04-10632-4,* NLG 143) Brill Academic Pubs.

Pan Michael, an Historical Novel of Poland, the Ukraine, & Turkey. Henryk Sienkiewicz. Tr. by Jeremiah Curtin. LC 69-10155. (Illus.). 527p. 1969. reprint ed. lib. bdg. 69.50 *(0-8371-0227-8,* SIPM, Greenwood Pr) Greenwood.

Pan Nuestro de Cada Dia Danoslo Hoy: Espiritual-Simple-Educacional, una Guia Paso a Paso Para Hornear Pan. Tr. by Beatriz Herren & Emilio Garcia. (SPA., Illus.). 32p. 1993. 14.99 *(0-9635606-0-3)* P D Mayers.

Pan Pacific Conference of Rehabilitation International, 6th: Proceedings, Seoul, Korea, 1979. 550p. 15.00 *(0-686-94895-5)* Rehab Intl.

Pan, Pan, Gran Pan: Big Book. Ina Cumpiano. (Rimas y Risas Red Ser.). (SPA., Illus.). 16p. (Orig.). (J). (gr. k-3). 1990. pap. text 29.95 *(0-917837-52-5)* Hampton-Brown.

Pan, Pan, Gran Pan: Small Book. Ina Cumpiano. (Rimas y Risas Red Ser.). (SPA., Illus.). 16p. (Orig.). (J). (gr. k-3). 1992. pap. text 6.00 *(1-56334-085-2)* Hampton-Brown.

Pan Tadeus. Adam Mickiewicz. Tr. by Kenneth R. Mackenzie from POL. LC 93-195891. (Illus.). 598p. 1992. pap. 19.95 *(0-7818-0033-1)* Hippocrene Bks.

Pan, the Goat-God: His Myth in Modern Times. Patricia Merivale. LC 69-12729. (Harvard Studies in Comparative Literature: No. 30). 319p. reprint ed. pap. 98.90 *(0-608-17496-3,* 202999600067) Bks Demand.

Pan the Low Waters. Arnold F. Rothmeier. 219p. 1999. pap. 12.95 *(1-891929-25-9)* Four Seasons.

Pan the Man: Kids vs. Drugs in 2 Acts. Stephen A. Orton. 36p. (YA). (gr. 7-12). 1991. pap. 3.50 *(0-88680-355-1)* I E Clark.

Pan-Turkism: From Irredentism to Cooperation. 2nd rev. ed. Jacob M. Landau. LC 94-42974. 256p. 1995. pap. 14.95 *(0-253-20960-9)*; text 35.00 *(0-253-32869-1)* Ind U Pr.

Pan-Turkism & Islam in Russia. Serge A. Zenkovsky. LC 60-5399. (Russian Research Center Studies: No. 36). (Illus.). 348p. 1960. reprint ed. pap. 107.90 *(0-7837-4203-7,* 205905300012) Bks Demand.

Pan XIII - Particles & Nuclei: Procedings of the Thirteenth International Conference. Pascolini. 864p. 1994. text 162.00 *(981-02-1799-4)* World Scientific Pub.

Pan y Mermelada para Francisca. Russell Hoban.Tr. of Bread & Jam for Frances. (SPA.). 1995. 12.40 *(0-606-07989-0)* Turtleback.

Pana O'ahu: Sacred Stones, Sacred Land. Photos by Jan Becket & Joseph Singer. LC 98-31995. (Illus.). 232p. 1999. text 42.00 *(0-8248-1828-8,* Latitude Twenty) UH Pr.

Panache at Rose Hill. Barbara Duke. 1998. pap. text 14.95 *(0-9658397-0-2)* Panache Rose Hill.

Panache Litteraire. 2nd ed. Baker & Couvin. (C). 1989. pap. 30.95 *(0-8384-3658-7)* Heinle & Heinle.

Panache Litteraire. 3rd ed. Baker & Cauvin. (FRE.). 1994. pap. text 50.95 incl. audio *(0-8384-5533-6)* Heinle & Heinle.

Panache Litteraire 3e-student Tape. 3rd ed. Baker. (College French). (FRE.). (C). 1994. student ed., suppl. ed. 6.95 incl. audio *(0-8384-5512-3)* Heinle & Heinle.

Panache Litteraire 3e-student Text. 3rd ed. Baker. (College French). (FRE.). (C). 1994. mass mkt. 37.95 *(0-8384-4234-X)* Heinle & Heinle.

Panache Petitgris. Beatrix Potter. (FRE., Illus.). 60p. (J). 1990. 9.95 *(0-7859-3713-7)* Fr & Eur.

Panache Petitgris. Beatrix Potter. (Gallimard Ser.). (FRE.). 59p. (J). 1990. 10.95 *(2-07-056102-X)* Schoenhof.

Panache That Pays: The Young Professionals Guide - How to Outclass Your Competition. Maria Everding. Ed. by Jodi Everding. LC 96-95445. (Illus.). 134p. 1997. pap. 12.00 *(0-9617665-1-4)* GME Pub Co.

Panaflex User's Manual. 2nd ed. David W. Samuelson. (Illus.). 272p. 1996. pap. 29.95 *(0-240-80267-5,* Focal) Buttrwrth-Heinemann.

Panagia Houses at Mycenae. Ione M. Shear. (University Museum Monographs: Vol. 68). (Illus.). xx, 172p. 1987. text 80.00 *(0-934718-84-9)* U Museum Pubns.

Panait Musoiu: A Chronology. V. Munoz. (Libertarian & Anarchist Chronology Ser.). 1980. lib. bdg. 59.95 *(0-8490-3088-9)* Gordon Pr.

Panajachel: A Guatemalan Town in Thirty-Year Perspective. Robert E. Hishaw. LC 74-17838. (Pitt Latin American Ser.). 231p. reprint ed. pap. 71.70 *(0-7837-2141-2,* 204242700004) Bks Demand.

Panama see American Nations Past & Present

Panama see Enchantment of the World Series

Panama see Statements of the Laws of the OAS Member States in Matters Affecting Business

Pan/Ama. Nuala Archer. (Shot Works Ser.). 24p. 1992. pap. 3.00 *(0-87376-070-0)* Red Dust.

***Panama.** William Y. Boyd. LC 99-39375. 192p. 1999. 21.95 *(1-892123-15-0)* Capital VA.

Panama. Eleanor D. Langstaff. (World Bibliographical Ser.: No. 14). 184p. 1982. lib. bdg. 28.00 *(0-903450-26-7)* ABC-CLIO.

Panama, 2 vols. Forbes Lindsay. 1976. lib. bdg. 200.00 *(0-8490-2403-X)* Gordon Pr.

Panama. Thomas McGuane. 175p. 1995. pap. 11.00 *(0-679-75291-9)* Random.

Panama. Dana Meachen-Rau. LC 98-2812. (Geography Ser.). (J). 1999. 32.00 *(0-516-21189-7)* Childrens.

Panama. Dana Meachen Rau. (True Bks.). (Illus.). 48p. (gr. 2-4). 1999. lib. bdg. 6.95 *(0-516-26497-4)* Childrens.

Panama. Gordon L. Rottman. (Elite Ser.: No. 37). (Illus.). 64p. pap. 12.95 *(1-85532-156-4,* 9452, Pub. by Osprey) Stackpole.

Panama. large type ed. Eric Zencey. (Niagara Large Print Ser.). 514p. 1996. 29.50 *(0-7089-5833-8)* Ulverscroft.

Panama see Cultures of the World - Group 12

Panama, Vol. 14. 2nd rev. ed. Eleanor Langstaff. (World Bibliographical Ser.). 250p. 1997. lib. bdg. 79.00 *(1-85109-251-X)* ABC-CLIO.

***Panama: A Country Study Guide.** Global Investment & Business Center, Inc. Staff. (World Country Study Guides Library: Vol. 132). (Illus.). 350p. 2000. pap. 59.00 *(0-7397-2430-4)* Intl Business Pubns.

***Panama: A Novel.** Carlos Ledson Miller. 2000. 25.00 *(0-7388-0714-1)*; pap. 18.00 *(0-7388-0715-X)* Xlibris Corp.

Panama: A Novel. Eric Zencey. LC 95-19555. 384p. 1995. 24.00 *(0-374-22943-0)* FS&G.

Panama: A Novel. Eric Zencey. 400p. 1997. reprint ed. mass mkt. 6.99 *(0-425-15602-8)* Berkley Pub.

Panama: An Assessment. Ed. by Victor H. Krulak. 72p. (Orig.). 1990. pap. 9.00 *(0-913187-03-8)* U S Strat Inst.

Panama: Assault on Human Rights. (SPA.). 1988. 3.00 *(0-318-35547-7)* Amnesty Intl USA.

Panama: Latin America's Best Kept Secret. William Chislett. (Illus.). 200p. 1995. 170.00 *(1-85564-351-0,* Pub. by Euromoney) Am Educ Systs.

Panama: Made in the U. S. A. John Weeks. 80p. 1991. pap. 12.00 *(0-85345-816-2,* Pub. by Lat Am Bur) Monthly Rev.

Panama: Major World Nations. Tricia Haynes. LC 98-16070. (Major World Nations Ser.). (Illus.). 144p. (YA). (gr. 5 up). 1999. lib. bdg. 19.95 *(0-7910-4977-9)* Chelsea Hse.

Panama: The Failure of State Activism. Daniel L. Wisecarver. 40p. 1987. pap. 9.95 *(0-917616-89-8)* ICS Pr.

Panama: The Truth about the U. S. Invasion. Cindy Jaquith et al. 44p. 1990. reprint ed. pap. 5.00 *(0-87348-582-3)* Pathfinder NY.

Panama - A Country Study Guide: Basic Information for Research & Pleasure. Global Investment Center, USA Staff. (World Country Study Guide Library: Vol. 132). (Illus.). 350p. 1999. pap. 59.00 *(0-7397-1529-1)* Intl Business Pubns.

Panama - Assault on Human Rights. 1988. 3.00 *(0-685-23308-1)* Amnesty Intl USA.

Panama - Pacific International Exposition: Postal Markings. David Savadge. 110p. (C). 1997. pap. text 16.00 *(1-880065-21-5)* Machine Cancel Soc.

Panama & the Canal. W. Abbot. 1976. lib. bdg. 250.00 *(0-8490-2404-8)* Gordon Pr.

Panama & the United States: The Forced Alliance. Michael L. Conniff. LC 91-7319. (United States & the Americas Ser.). 208p. 1992. 40.00 *(0-8203-1359-9)*; pap. 20.00 *(0-8203-1360-2)* U of Ga Pr.

Panama & the United States - Divided by the Canal see Single Titles Series

Panama at the Crossroads: Economic Development & Political Change in the Twentieth Century. Andrew Zimbalist & John Weeks. LC 90-50923. 256p. 1991. pap. 17.95 *(0-520-07501-3,* Pub. by U CA Pr) Cal Prin Full Svc.

***Panama Business Intelligence Report, 190 vols.** Global Investment & Business Center, Inc. Staff. (World Business Intelligence Library: Vol. 132). (Illus.). 350p. 2000. pap. 99.95 *(0-7397-2630-7)* Intl Business Pubns.

***Panama Business Law Handbook.** Global Investment & Business Center, Inc. Staff. (Global Business Law Handbooks Library: Vol. 132). (Illus.). 2000. pap. 99.95 *(0-7397-2030-9)* Intl Business Pubns.

***Panama Business Opportunity Yearbook.** Global Investment & Business Center, Inc. Staff. (Global Business Opportunity Yearbooks Library: Vol. 132). (Illus.). 2000. pap. 99.95 *(0-7397-2230-1)* Intl Business Pubns.

Panama Canal. Tim McNeese. LC 96-45623. (Building History Ser.). (Illus.). (YA). (gr. 4-12). 1997. lib. bdg. 22.45 *(1-56006-425-0)* Lucent Bks.

***Panama Canal.** Jorge Eduardo Ritter. 2000. 65.00 *(958-9393-82-9)* Villegas Ed.

Panama Canal. Barbara G. Winkelman. LC 98-3493. (Cornerstones to Freedom Ser.). 32p. (J). (gr. 4-6). 1999. 20.00 *(0-516-21142-0)* Childrens.

Panama Canal. Barbara Gaines Winklemann. (Cornerstones to Freedom Ser.). (Illus.). 32p. (J). (gr. 4-6). 1999. pap. text 5.95 *(0-516-26460-5)* Childrens.

Panama Canal: A Study in International Law & Diplomacy. Harmodio Arias. LC 79-111707. (American Imperialism: Viewpoints of United States Foreign Policy, 1898-1941 Ser.). 1977. reprint ed. 18.95 *(0-405-02001-5)* Ayer.

Panama Canal: Heart of America's Security. Jon P. Speller. (Illus.). 176p. 1972. 12.95 *(0-8315-0119-7)* Speller.

Panama Canal: Its History, Activities & Organization. Darrell H. Smith. LC 72-3060. (Brookings Institution. Institute for Government Research. Service Monographs of the U. S. Government: No. 44). reprint ed. 55.00 *(0-404-57144-1)* AMS Pr.

Panama Canal: The Crisis in Historical Perspective. rev. ed. Walter LaFeber. (Illus.). 288p. 1990. pap. 13.95 *(0-19-506192-6)* OUP.

***Panama Canal: The Greatest Giveaway.** John Dorson. 2000. pap. 7.95 *(0-533-13285-1)* Vantage.

Panama Canal: The Story of How a Jungle Was Conquered & the World Made Smaller. Elizabeth Mann. LC 98-22457. (Wonders of the World Book Ser.). (Illus.). 48p. (YA). (gr. 4 up). 1998. 19.95 *(0-9650493-4-5,* Pub. by Mikaya Pr) Firefly Bks Ltd.

***Panama Canal & United States Interests: Congressional Hearing.** Ed. by Jesse Helms. 61p. 2000. reprint ed. pap. text 20.00 *(0-7881-8504-7)* DIANE Pub.

Panama Canal Controversy: U. S. Diplomacy & Defense Interests. Paul B. Ryan. LC 77-20643. (Publication Ser.: No. 187). (Illus.). 1978. pap. 2.78 *(0-8179-6872-5)* Hoover Inst Pr.

Panama Canal in American History. Ann Graham Gaines. LC 98-14477. (In American History Ser.). 128p. (YA). (gr. 5 up). 1999. lib. bdg. 20.95 *(0-7660-1216-6)* Enslow Pubs.

Panama Canal in American National Consciousness, 1870-1990. Alfred Richard. LC 90-3045. (Foreign Economic Policy of the United States Ser.). 378p. 1990. reprint ed. text 10.00 *(0-8240-7471-8)* Garland.

Panama Canal in Mortal Danger. Frank F. Farrar. 194p. (Orig.). 1996. pap. write for info. *(0-9637291-1-X)* Sextant Pr.

Panama Canal Negotiations. William M. Habeeb & I. William Zartman. (Pew Case Studies in International Affairs). 57p. (Orig.). (C). 1994. pap. text 3.50 *(1-56927-407-X)* Geo U Inst Dplmcy.

Panama Canal Review Alphabetical Index: Living in the Canal Zone, 1950 until 1981. Jeanne F. Stough. LC 92-80968. (Illus.). 55p. (Orig.). 1992. pap. 5.00 *(0-9632932-0-6)* LCS Pr TX.

***Panama Canal Transfer: Controversy at the Crossroads.** Susan Dudley Gold. LC 98-47196. 1999. 25.69 *(0-8172-5762-4)* Raintree Steck-V.

***Panama Country Review 2000.** Robert C. Kelly et al. (Illus.). 60p. 1999. pap. 39.95 *(1-58310-556-5)* CountryWatch.

***Panama Elecciones Generales, 2 de Mayo de 1999: Observacion Electoral IFES, Informe Final.** Nhelli Saleh. (FRE.). iv, 66p. 1999. pap. 9.00 *(1-879720-63-9)* Intl Fndt Elect.

***Panama Foreign Policy & Government Guide.** Contrib. by Global Investment & Business Center, Inc. Staff. (World Foreign Policy & Government Library: Vol. 126). (Illus.). 350p. 1999. pap. 99.00 *(0-7397-3624-8)* Intl Business Pubns.

***Panama Foreign Policy & Government Guide.** Global Investment & Business Center, Inc. Staff. (World Foreign Policy & Government Library: Vol. 126). (Illus.). 350p. 2000. 99.95 *(0-7397-3830-5)* Intl Business Pubns.

Panama Forest & Shore. Burton Gordon. (Illus.). (Orig.). 1983. 15.00 *(0-910286-88-4)* Boxwood.

***Panama General Elections: May 2, 1999 IFES Election Observation Final Report.** Nhelli Saleh. iv, 60p. 1999. pap. text 9.00 *(1-879720-52-3)* Intl Fndt Elect.

***Panama Government & Business Contacts Handbook: Strategic Government & Business Contacts for Conducting Succesful Business, Export-Import & Investment Activity, 110.** International Business Publications, USA Staff & Global Investment Center, USA Staff. (World Export-Import & Business Library: 134). (Illus.). 250p. 2000. pap. 99.95 *(0-7397-6149-8)* Intl Business Pubns.

Panama Guide: A Cruising Guide to the Isthmus of Panama. Nancy S. Zydler & Tom Zydler. LC 96-45096. (Illus.). 337p. 1996. pap. 39.95 *(0-9639566-3-9)* Seaworthy WI.

Panama Gunner. Ramsay Thorne. (Renegade Ser.: No. 6). 256p. (Orig.). 1983. mass mkt. 2.25 *(0-446-30829-3,* Pub. by Warner Bks) Little.

Panama Hat Trail: A Journey to South America. Tom Miller. LC 87-45913. (Departures Ser.). 272p. 1988. pap. 11.00 *(0-394-75774-2)* Vin Bks.

Panama in Pictures. Lerner Publications, Department of Geography Staff. (Visual Geography Ser.). (Illus.). 64p. (YA). (gr. 5 up). 1987. lib. bdg. 19.95 *(0-8225-1818-X,* Lerner Publctns) Lerner Pub.

Panama in Transition: Local Reactions to Development Policies. John Bort & Mary Helms. (Monographs in Anthropology: No. 6). (Illus.). v, 195p. 1983. pap. 9.50 *(0-913134-75-9)* Mus Anthro MO.

Panama Invaded: Imperial Occupation vs. Struggle for Sovereignty. Philip E. Wheaton. LC 92-80542. (Illus.). 204p. 1992. 32.95 *(0-932415-67-9)*; pap. 11.95 *(0-932415-68-7)* Red Sea Pr.

***Panama Investment & Business Guide.** Global Investment & Business Center, Inc. Staff. (Global Investment & Business Guide Library: Vol. 132). (Illus.). 2000. pap. 99.95 *(0-7397-1830-4)* Intl Business Pubns.

***Panama Investment & Business Guide: Export-Import, Investment & Business Opportunities.** International Business Publications, USA Staff & Global Investment Center, USA Staff. (World Investment & Business Guide Library-99: Vol. 132). (Illus.). 350p. 1999. pap. 99.95 *(0-7397-0327-7)* Intl Business Pubns.

Panama 'm Tombe (My Hat Fell off) Dale M. Foreman. 300p. (Orig.). 1986. pap. text 4.95 *(0-939688-19-0)* Directed Media.

Panama Money in Barbados, 1900-1920. Bonham C. Richardson. LC 85-6127. (Illus.). 308p. 1986. text 34.00 *(0-87049-477-5)* U of Tenn Pr.

Panama, 1987: Health Consequences of Police & Military Actions. Physicians for Human Rights Staff. 73p. 1988. pap. 6.00 *(0-614-14419-1)* Phy Human Rights.

Panama, the Canal, & the United States: A Guide to Issues & References. Thomas M. Leonard. LC 93-26255. (Guides to Contemporary Issues Ser.: No. 9). 1993. 21.95 *(0-941690-55-5)*; pap. 11.95 *(0-941690-56-3)* Regina Bks.

***Panama Traveler: From Rainforest Adventures to Canal Cruises.** David Dudenhoefer. (Illus.). 224p. (Orig.). 1999. pap. 13.95 *(0-942297-09-1)* Windham Bay.

Panamanian Business Law. Panamanian Business Law Staff. LC KZ0132.. 308p. reprint ed. pap. 95.50 *(0-7837-2409-8,* 204009400006) Bks Demand.

Panamanian Militarism: A Historical Interpretation. Carlos G. Mann. LC 95-40747. (Monographs in International Studies, Latin America Ser.: No. 25). (Illus.). 243p. (Orig.). (C). 1996. pap. text 23.00 *(0-89680-189-6)* Ohio U Pr.

Panamanian Politics: From Guarded Nation to National Guard. Steve C. Ropp. LC 81-17831. (Politics in Latin America, A Hoover Institution Ser.). 151p. 1982. 33.95 *(0-275-91817-3,* C1817, Praeger Pubs) Greenwood.

Panamanian Problem: How the Reagan & Bush Administration Dealt with the Noriega Regime. G. St. Malo & Godfrey Harris. 1993. 22.95 *(0-935047-17-4)* Americas Group.

Panamanian Problem: How the Reagan & Bush Administration Dealt with the Noriega Regime. G. St. Malo & Godfrey Harris. LC 88-71640. (Illus.). 384p. 1993. pap. 16.95 *(0-935047-08-5)* Americas Group.

Panama's Canal: What Will Happen after the United States Gives the Canal to Panama? Mark Falcoff. LC 98-14395. 125p. 1998. 29.95 *(0-8447-4030-6)*; pap. 14.95 *(0-8447-4031-4)* Am Enterprise.

Panama's Poor: Victims, Agents, & Historymakers. Gloria Rudolf. LC 99-13978. 1999. 49.95 *(0-8130-1680-0)* U Press Fla.

***Panamericana: On the Road Through Mexico & Central America.** Simon Calder. (Illus.). 2000. pap. 19.95 *(1-85458-234-8)* Vac Wrk Pubns.

Panandata Yantok at Daga: Filipino Stick & Dagger. Amante P. Marinas, Sr. (Illus.). 88p. 1988. pap. 18.00 *(0-87364-447-6)* Paladin Pr.

Panare: Tradition & Change on the Amazonian Frontier. Paul Henley. LC 81-40432. (Illus.). 320p. (C). 1982. 55.00 *(0-300-02504-1)* Yale U Pr.

Panarion of Epiphanius of Salamis, Bks. II-III. Tr. by F. Williams. (Coptic Gnostic Library). 744p. 1993. 249.00 *(90-04-09898-4,* NLG350) Brill Academic Pubs.

Panathenaia: Studies in Athenian Life & Thought in the Classical Age. Ed. by Anthony J. Podlecki & T. E. Gregory. 1979. 10.00 *(0-87291-126-8)* Coronado Pr.

P

An Asterisk (*) at the beginning of an entry indicates that the title is appearing for the first time.

Panatubiji' an Owens Valley Paiute. fac. ed. Julian H. Steward. (Smithsonian Institution, Bureau of American Ethnology, Anthropological Papers: No. 119). 14p. (C). 1938. reprint ed. pap. text 1.88 (*1-55567-795-9*) Coyote Press.

Panavia Tornado. Andy Evans. (Illus.). 200p. 1999. 52.95 (*1-86126-201-9*, 128164AE, Pub. by Crolwood) Motorbooks Intl.

Panbiogeography: Tracking the History of Life. Robin C. Craw et al. (Oxford Biogeography Ser.: No. 11). (Illus.). 240p. 1999. text 65.00 (*0-19-507441-6*) OUP.

Pancadasi. Swami Vidyaranya. Tr. by Swami Swahananda. 1967. pap. 10.95 (*81-7120-507-0*) Vedanta Pr.

Pancadasi: A Critical Study. Shakuntala Panjani. 1985. 29.95 (*0-318-37028-X*) Asia Bk Corp.

Pancahtantra of Vasubhaga: A Critical Study. 145p. 1987. 19.95 (*0-318-36922-2*) Asia Bk Corp.

Pancake Day: A Bring It-All-Together Book. Gina C. Erickson. (Illus.). 24p. (J). (gr. k-3). 1995. pap. text 3.95 (*0-8120-1055-8*) Barron.

Pancake Day: A Bring It All Together Book. Kelli C. Foster & Gina C. Erickson. (Get Ready...Get Set...Read! Ser.: Set 3). (Illus.). 32p. (J). (gr. k-2). 1996. lib. bdg. 11.95 (*1-56674-142-4*) Forest Hse.

Pancake Handbook. Stephen Siegelman et al. LC 93-46566. (Illus.). 138p. 1994. pap. 9.95 (*0-89815-593-2*) Ten Speed Pr.

Pancake Man & Friends: Stories That Raise the Spirit & Warm the Heart. Richard Speight. LC 91-46432. 144p. (Orig.). 1992. pap. 10.00 (*0-687-30006-1*) Dimen for Liv.

Pancake Memos: And Other Stories for Growing Christians. Ed Stewart. 96p. 1991. pap. 7.99 (*0-8341-1388-0*) Beacon Hill.

Pancake That Ran Away. Loek Koopmans. 26p. (J). (ps-1). pap. 12.95 (*0-86315-174-4*, 26312, Pub. by Floris Bks) Gryphon Hse.

Pancakes. Cullinan. 1994. text 13.90 (*0-15-302280-9*) Harcourt.

Pancakes: Recipes to Flip Over. Dorie Greenspan. LC 95-47353. 1996. 125.00 (*0-614-10076-3*, RBC-PK95, Wm Morrow) Morrow Avon.

Pancakes - Waffles: The Fine Art of Pancake, Waffle, Crepe & Blintz Cooking. Carol D. Brent. LC 73-122449. 1970. 5.95 (*0-88351-007-3*) Test Recipe.

Pancakes A to Z. Marie Simmons. Ed. by Rux Martin. LC 97-13767. (A to Z Cookbook Ser.). (Illus.). 96p. (Orig.). 1997. 15.00 (*1-57630-043-9*, Chapters Bks) HM.

Pancakes & Coffee: A Canoe Trek Through the Alaskan Wilderness. unabridged ed. Gary Myers. Ed. by Janice K. Marvin & Clyde R. Myers. 167p. 2000. pap. 8.95 (*0-9668176-1-3*, 1002) Myers Pubg.

Pancakes & More. Bob Cochrane. (Illus.). 179p. 1991. pap. 25.00 (*0-9662803-0-X*) R M Cochrane.

Pancakes & Other Recipes to Flip Over. Dorie Greenspan. 1997. pap. 15.00 (*0-688-14104-8*, Wm Morrow) Morrow Avon.

Pancakes & Waffles. Cara Hobday. 64p. 1995. 5.98 (*0-7858-0423-4*) Bk Sales Inc.

Pancakes, Crackers & Pizza: A Book of Shapes. Marjorie Eberts & Margaret Gisler. LC 84-7699. (Rookie Readers Ser.). (Illus.). 32p. (J). (ps-2). 1984. pap. 4.95 (*0-516-42063-1*) Childrens.

Pancakes, Crackers & Pizza: A Book of Shapes. Marjorie Eberts & Margaret Gisler. LC 84-7699. (Rookie Readers Ser.). (Illus.). 32p. (J). (ps-3). 1984. lib. bdg. 17.00 (*0-516-02063-3*) Childrens.

Pancakes for Breakfast. Tomie De Paola. LC 77-15523. (Illus.). 32p. (C). (ps-3). 1978. pap. 5.00 (*0-15-670768-3*, Voyager Bks) Harcourt.

Pancakes for Breakfast. Tomie De Paola. LC 77-15523. (Illus.). 32p. (J). (ps-3). 1978. 14.95 (*0-15-259455-8*, Harcourt Child Bks) Harcourt.

Pancakes for Breakfast. Tomie De Paola. (J). 1978. 10.20 (*0-606-02221-X*, Pub. by Turtleback) Demco.

***Pancakes for Breakfast.** Wendi J. Silvano. (Books for Young Learners). (Illus.). 12p. (J). (gr. k-2). 1999. pap. text 5.00 (*1-57274-277-1*, A2493) R Owen Pubs.

Pancakes, Pancakes! Eric Carle. LC 88-32438. (Illus.). 32p. (J). (ps-3). 1998. per. 5.99 (*0-689-82246-4*) Aladdin.

Pancakes, Pancakes! Eric Carle. 40p. (J). (ps-3). 1992. 5.95 (*0-590-44453-0*, Blue Ribbon Bks) Scholastic Inc.

Pancakes, Pancakes! Eric Carle. (Blue Ribbon Bks.). (J). 1990. 11.19 (*0-606-02825-0*, Pub. by Turtleback) Demco.

Pancakes, Pancakes! Eric Carle. LC 88-32438. (Illus.). 32p. (J). (ps up). 1991. reprint ed. 16.00 (*0-88708-120-7*, Picture Book Studio) S&S Childrens.

Pancakes, Pancakes! Mini Book. Eric Carle. LC 88-32438. (Illus.). 28p. (J). 1992. 4.95 (*0-88708-275-0*, Picture Book Studio) S&S Childrens.

Pancakramatippani of Munisribhadra: Introduction & Romanized Sanskrit Text. Ed. by Zhongxin Jiang & Toru Tomabechi. (Schweizer Asiatische Studien: Bd. 23). 105p. 1996. pap. 29.95 (*3-906756-20-3*, Pub. by P Lang) P Lang Pubng.

Pancaratra Samhitas & Early Vaisnava Theology. Mitsunori Matsubara. (C). 1995. 22.50 (*81-208-1221-2*, Pub. by Motilal Bnarsidass) S Asia.

Pancasila & the Search for Identity & Modernity in Indonesian Society: A Cultural & Ethical Analysis. Eka Darmaputera. x, 254p. (Orig.). 1988. pap. 72.00 (*90-04-08422-3*) Brill Academic Pubs.

Pancatantra. (Mongolia Society Special Papers: Issue II). 6.50 (*0-910980-22-5*) Mongolia.

Pancatantra: The Book of India's Folk Wisdom. Ed. & Tr. by Patrick Olivelle from SAN. LC 97-2843. (The World's Classics Ser.). 256p. 1998. pap. 11.95 (*0-19-283299-9*) OUP.

Pancatantra of Vishnusarman. M. R. Kale. 500p. 1986. reprint ed. 14.00 (*81-208-0219-5*, Pub. by Motilal Bnarsidass); reprint ed. pap. 10.50 (*81-208-0220-9*, Pub. by Motilal Bnarsidass) S Asia.

Pancha Buddha & Dance. M. M. Pradhan. 1996. pap. 22.00 (*0-7855-7470-0*, Pub. by Ratna Pustak Bhandar) St Mut.

***Pancha Ratna Kritis of Saint Thyagaraja.** Tara Balagopal. LC 98-900856. 1998. 438.00 (*81-85151-60-1*, Pub. by Harman Pub Hse) S Asia.

Panchadal. Ahmad Nawaz. LC 98-70824. (BEN.). xiv, 61p. 1998. pap. 10.00 (*1-58225-142-8*) Ananta Prakashani.

Panchadasigita: Gita-Texts Re-Arranged into Fifteen Chapters According to the Principles of Karma, Bhakti & Jnana Yogas with English Translations & Notes. Jatindra M. Chatterjee. LC 98-902472. 1998. 36.00 (*81-215-0773-1*, Pub. by M Manoharial) Coronet Bks.

***Panchakarma Treatment of Ayurveda.** T. L. Devaraj. 1998. 36.00 (*81-7030-591-8*, Pub. by Sri Satguru Pubns) S Asia.

Panchakrma Therapy in Ayurveda. Divakar Ojha & Ashok Kumar. 219p. 1979. pap. 18.95 (*0-89744-057-9*) Auromere.

Pancharamas in Medieval Andhradesa. M. Krishna Kumari. (C). 1989. 78.00 (*0-8364-2427-1*, Pub. by Agam Kala Prakashan) S Asia.

Panchatantra. J. Hertel. 1973. lib. bdg. 79.95 (*0-87968-523-9*) Krishna Pr.

Panchatantra. Tr. by Arthur W. Ryder. 1994. pap. text 15.00 (*0-226-73249-5*) U Ch Pr.

Panchatantra Reconstructed. Ed. by F. Edgerton. (American Oriental Ser.: Vol. 3). 1924. 32.00 (*0-527-02677-8*) Periodicals Srv.

Panchayat Raj, Rural Development & the Political Economy of Village India. Norman K. Nicholson. (Occasional Paper Ser.: No. 1). 61p. (Orig.). (C). 1973. pap. text 4.95 (*0-86731-014-6*) Cornell CIS RDC.

Panchayati Raj: An Annotated Resource Guide. N. B. Inamdar et al. (C). 1991. 28.50 (*81-7022-378-4*, Pub. by Concept) S Asia.

Panchayati Raj & the Decentralisation of Development Planning in West Bengal: A Case Study. Neil Webster. 1992. 12.00 (*81-7074-119-X*, Pub. by KP Bagchi) S Asia.

Panchayati Raj in India. M. G. Krishnan. (C). 1992. 19.00 (*81-7099-355-5*, Pub. by Mittal Pubs Dist) S Asia.

Panchayati Raj in India: Literature on Features Trends & Prospects. B. S. Tomar. (C). 1991. 45.00 (*0-685-50238-4*, Indian Biblio Bureau) S Asia.

Panchayati Raj in Jammu & Kashmir. Ed. by George Mathew. (C). 1990. text 23.00 (*81-7022-315-6*, Pub. by Concept) S Asia.

Panchikaranam. Shankara. pap. 2.50 (*0-87481-068-X*, Pub. by Advaita Ashrama) Vedanta Pr.

Pancho: The Biography of Florence Lowe Barnes. Barbara H. Schultz. LC 96-94354. 260p. 1996. pap. 14.95 (*0-9652181-0-4*, 001) Little Buttes.

Pancho & Black Jack. Frederic Bean. 1995. mass mkt. 5.50 (*0-671-88691-6*) PB.

Pancho & Lefty Ride Out. Conal Creedon. LC 96-157003. 98p. 1995. pap. 12.95 (*1-898256-06-3*) Dufour.

Pancho Diablo. Carlos Morton. LC 93-15620. 1993. pap. 5.00 (*0-88734-340-6*) Players Pr.

Pancho Montana: Un Viaje Inesperado. Francisco E. Rodriguez. (SPA., Illus.). 55p. (Orig.). (J). (gr. 4-6). 1996. pap. 7.95 (*1-887578-45-5*) SpanPr.

Pancho Villa. Bob Carroll. LC 95-11707. (Importance of Ser.). (Illus.). 112p. (YA). (gr. 5-12). 1996. lib. bdg. 22.45 (*1-56006-069-7*) Lucent Bks.

Pancho Villa. Steven O'Brian. (Hispanos Notables Ser.). (SPA., Illus.). 120p. (YA). (gr. 5 up). 1995. pap. 8.95 (*0-7910-3114-4*) Chelsea Hse.

Pancho Villa: Mexican Revolutionary. Steven O'Brien. LC 93-37890. (Hispanics of Achievement Ser.). (Illus.). 120p. (YA). (gr. 5 up). 1994. lib. bdg. 19.95 (*0-7910-1257-3*) Chelsea Hse.

Pancho Villa: Strong Man of the Revolution. Larry A. Harris. (Illus.). 130p. 1996. pap. 9.95 (*0-944383-31-9*) High-Lonesome.

Pancho Villa: The Mexican Centaur. Oren Arnold. LC 76-29143. 1979. 20.00 (*0-916620-06-9*) Portals Pr.

Pancho Villa: Un Intento de Semblanza (A Biographical Sketch) Marte R. Gomez. (SPA.). 88p. 1973. pap. 6.99 (*968-16-1183-7*, Pub. by Fondo) Continental Bk.

Pancho Villa & John Reed: Two Faces of Romantic Revolution. Jim Tuck. LC 84-8770. (Illus.). 262p. reprint ed. pap. 81.30 (*0-608-20016-6*, 207129200010) Bks Demand.

Pancho Villa, el Brazo Armado. Ernst Hoffen. (SPA.). (gr. 7 up). 1997. pap. text 6.98 (*968-403-827-5*) Selector.

Pancho Villa Sales & Marketing: The Twenty-First Century Bible. Glenn Van Warrebey. 200p. (Orig.). 1995. pap. 16.95 (*0-9642771-0-7*) G Van Warrebey.

Pancho Villa y Zapata. Victor Alba. LC 95-133981. (Memoria de La Historia Ser.). 1998. pap. 19.95 (*84-08-01176-6*) Planeta.

Pancho Villa's Revolution by Headlines. Mark Cronlund Anderson. LC 99-14135. (Illus.). 320p. 1999. 34.95 (*0-8061-3172-1*) U of Okla Pr.

Pancho's Pinata. Stefan Czernecki. LC 92-7325. 1994. 10.15 (*0-606-06655-1*, Pub. by Turtleback) Demco.

***Pancho's Pinata.** Stefan Czernecki & T. Rhodes. (SPA.). (J). 1999. pap. 15.49 (*0-7868-2189-2*, Pub. by Hyprn Child) Little.

Pancho's Pinata. Stefan Czernecki & Timothy Rhodes. LC 92-7235. (Illus.). 40p. (J). (ps-4). 1992. 14.95 (*1-56282-277-2*, Pub. by Hyprn Child); lib. bdg. 14.89 (*1-56282-278-0*, Pub. by Hyprn Child) Little.

Pancho's Pinata. Stefan Czernecki & Timothy Rhodes. LC 92-7235. (Illus.). 40p. (J). (ps-4). 1994. pap. 4.95 (*0-7868-1007-6*, Pub. by Hyprn Ppbks) Little.

Pancho's Pinata. large type ed. Stefan Czernecki & Timothy Rhodes. (Illus.). 40p. (J). (gr. k-4). 1992. write for info. (*0-920534-98-8*) Hyperion Pr.

Pancios of Galicia: A Pancio Family History. George E. Bell. Ed. by Jean P. Bell & Constance A. Ecker. (Illus.). 350p. (C). 1993. text. write for info. (*0-9623275-3-0*) Wayne Ridge.

Pancratia. Ed. by Edward Kaplan. (Illus.). 22p. 1987. 35.00 (*0-934714-01-0*); pap. 5.00 (*0-934714-02-9*) Swamp Pr.

Pancreas. Phillip P. Toskes. LC 97-5985. (Gastroenterology & Hepatology Ser.). 1998. text 135.00 (*0-443-07862-9*) Church.

***Pancreas, Vol. 2.** H. G. Beger et al. LC 97-7000. Vol. 2. (Illus.). 1664p. 1998. 499.95 (*0-86542-420-9*) Blackwell Sci.

Pancreas: A Text & Atlas. Banks. 1998. text. write for info. (*0-7216-6670-1*, W B Saunders Co) Harcrt Hlth Sci Grp.

Pancreas: Biology, Pathobiology, & Disease. 2nd ed. Ed. by Vay Liang W. Go et al. LC 92-48496. 1200p. 1993. text 278.00 (*0-88167-986-0*) Lppncott W & W.

Pancreas Transplantation. Ed. by Luis H. Toledo-Pereyra. (C). 1988. text 271.00 (*0-89838-369-2*) Kluwer Academic.

Pancreas Transplantation: Experimental & Clinical Studies. J. P. Squifflet. (Illus.). xvi, 188p. 1990. 128.00 (*3-8055-5102-9*) S Karger.

Pancreatic Cancer: Advances in Molecular Pathology, Diagnosis & Clinical Management. Ed. by Fazlul H. Sarkar & Michael C. Dugan. LC 98-22363. (Illus.). 200p. 1998. text 89.95 (*1-881299-12-0*, BioTechniques) Eaton Pub Co.

Pancreatic Cancer: Molecular & Clinical Advances. Ed. by John Neoptolemos et al. LC 95-35297. 360p. 1995. 150.00 (*0-86542-973-1*) Blackwell Sci.

Pancreatic Cancer: Pathogenesis, Diagnosis & Treatment. Ed. by Howard Reber. 360p. 1998. 125.00 (*0-89603-466-6*) Humana.

***Pancreatic Cancer Methods & Protocols.** Ed. by Paul Chiao et al. 375p. 2000. 99.50 (*0-89603-628-6*) Humana.

***Pancreatic Disease.** Vandam. 2001. text. write for info. (*0-7216-9149-8*, W B Saunders Co) Harcrt Hlth Sci Grp.

Pancreatic Disease: Progress & Prospects. Ed. by C. D. Johnson & C. W. Imrie. (Illus.). 392p. 1991. 129.00 (*0-387-19688-9*) Spr-Verlag.

Pancreatic Disease: State of the Art & Future Aspects of Research. Paul G. Lankisch. Ed. by E. P. DiMagno. LC 99-13105. (Illus.). xiii,270p. 1999. pap. 82.00 (*3-540-65357-0*) Spr-Verlag.

Pancreatic Disease: Towards the Year 2000 2nd ed. C. D. Johnson & C. W. Imrie. LC 98-17778. xviii, 468p. 1999. write for info. (*1-85233-037-6*) Spr-Verlag.

Pancreatic Diseases: New Horizons. Ed. by M. W. Buechler et al. (Journal Ser.: Vol. 11, No. 3-6, 1994). (Illus.). vi, 342p. 1995. pap. 146.25 (*3-8055-6191-1*) S Karger.

Pancreatic Enzymes in Health & Disease. Ed. by P. G. Lankisch. (Illus.). 224p. 1991. 100.00 (*0-387-53187-4*) Spr-Verlag.

Pancreatic Fistulas. Ed. by P. Pederzoli et al. LC 92-49618. 1992. 139.00 (*0-387-55338-X*) Spr-Verlag.

Pancreatic Growth & Regeneration. Nora Sarvetnick. (Tissue Engineering Intelligence Unit Ser.). 270p. 1997. 98.00 (*1-57059-500-3*) Landes Bioscience.

Pancreatic Growth & Regeneration. Ed. by Nora Sarvetnick. LC 97-41356. (Tissue Engineering Ser.). xiv, 250p. 1998. text 98.00 (*3-8055-6618-2*) S Karger.

Pancreatic Islet Cell Regeneration & Growth. A. I. Vinik. LC 92-49932. (Advances in Experimental Medicine & Biology Ser.: Vol. 321). (Illus.). 200p. (C). 1992. text 85.00 (*0-306-44259-0*, Kluwer Plenum) Kluwer Academic.

Pancreatic Transplantation. (C). 2001. 150.00 (*0-8385-8161-7*, Medical Exam) Appleton & Lange.

Pancreatic Transplantation. Ed. by C. C. Groth. 450p. 1988. text 142.00 (*0-7216-2637-8*, 791744, Grune & Strat) Harcrt Hlth Sci Grp.

Pancreatic Tumors in Children. G. Bennett Humphrey. 1982. text 191.50 (*90-247-2702-2*) Kluwer Academic.

Pancreatitis. P. G. Lankisch & Peter A. Banks. LC 97-21618. (Illus.). 504p. 1997. 109.00 (*3-540-61726-4*) Spr-Verlag.

Pancreatitis: Its Pathophysiology & Clinical Aspects. Ed. by Toshio Sato & Hidemi Yamauchi. LC 86-203452. (Japan Intractable Disease Research Foundation Publication Ser.: No. 24). 485p. 1985. reprint ed. pap. 150.40 (*0-608-01547-4*, 206195600001) Bks Demand.

Pancreatoduodenectomy. Ed. by F. Hanyu & K. Takasaki. LC 97-16186. (Illus.). xvi, 506p. 1997. 169.00 (*4-431-70194-X*) Spr-Verlag.

Panda. (Shaped Board Bks.). (Illus.). 12p. (J). (ps). 1998. bds. 3.95 (*0-7894-2929-2*) DK Pub Inc.

Panda. Judy Allen. (J). 1993. 10.19 (*0-606-07990-4*) Turtleback.

***Panda.** Michael Foreman. (Illus.). 64p. 1999. pap. 14.95 (*1-86205-290-5*, Pub. by Pavilion Bks Ltd) Trafalgar.

***Panda.** Michel Piquemal. LC 00-26186. (My Animal Library). (Illus.). (J). 2000. 6.95 (*0-7892-0664-1*) Abbeville Pr.

***Panda.** Rebecca Ward. (J). 1999. 3.99 (*1-84100-213-5*) Quadrillion Pubng.

Panda, Reading Level 3-4. Bob Propper. (World Animal Library). (Illus.). 28p. (J). (gr. 2-5). 1983. 12.50 (*0-685-58822-X*) Rourke Corp.

Panda: Wild about Bamboo. Valerie Tracqui & BIOS Agency Staff. LC 98-46101. (Animal Close-Ups Ser.). (Illus.). 27p. (ps-3). 1999. pap. 6.95 (*0-88106-737-7*) Charlesbridge Pub.

Panda & Monkey King Christmas - A Family's Year in China. Nelly M. Case & Stephen F. Ledoux. LC 97-72125. (Illus.). 200p. (Orig.). 1997. pap., spiral bd. 25.00 (*1-882508-10-6*) ABCs.

Panda Bear Goes Visiting. Liu Qian. (Illus.). 22p. (J). (gr. 3-4). 1982. 3.95 (*0-8351-1108-3*); pap. 3.95 (*0-8351-1139-3*) China Bks.

Panda Bear, Panda Bear. B. Martin. (J). 1995. 13.95 (*0-8050-1758-5*) H Holt & Co.

Panda Bears. Diana S. Helmer. LC 96-37697. (Bears of the World Ser.). (J). 1997. lib. bdg. 17.27 (*0-8239-5133-2*, PowerKids) Rosen Group.

Panda Bears. Stuart A. Kallen. LC 95-52342. (Bears Ser.). (J). 1997. lib. bdg. 13.98 (*1-56239-592-0*) ABDO Pub Co.

Panda Bear's Journey: A Heroic Tale of Heart & Home. Rio Alden. (Illus.). 32p. (Orig.). 1994. pap. 8.95 (*1-878321-09-9*, Compassion Pr) Compassion Bks.

Panda Big & Panda Small. Jane Cabrera. LC 98-28833. (Toddlers Storybook Ser.). 24p. (J). 1998. 9.95 (*0-7894-3485-7*) DK Pub Inc.

***Panda Big, Panda Small.** Jane Cobrera. LC 98-28833. (Toddlers Storybook Ser.). (Illus.). 24p. (J). (ps). 2000. pap. text 5.95 (*0-7894-5747-4*, D K Ink) DK Pub Inc.

Panda Climbs see Sierra Club's Growing up Books

Panda Magic for Kids see Animal Magic for Kids

***Panda-Monium in China.** Linda Lowery Keep. (Hannah & the Angels Ser.: No. 10). (J). (gr. 3-6). 2000. pap. 3.99 (*0-375-80258-4*, Pub. by Random Bks Yng Read) Random.

Panda One Investigates. large type ed. Peter N. Walker. (Linford Mystery Library). 1991. pap. 16.99 (*0-7089-7072-9*) Ulverscroft.

Panda Ore on Duty. large type ed. Peter N. Walker. 1990. pap. 16.99 (*0-7089-6895-3*, Linford) Ulverscroft.

Panda-Paper Dolls. Crystal Collins-Sterling. (J). 1989. pap. 2.95 (*0-486-25929-3*) Dover.

Panda-Sticker Paper Doll. Elizabeth King Brownd. (Illus.). (J). 1991. pap. text 1.00 (*0-486-26614-1*) Dover.

Panda Zoo. Norman A. Kirk. LC 82-22675. (Illus.). 96p. 1983. 20.00 (*0-911155-00-7*); pap. 10.00 (*0-911155-01-5*) West Boston.

Pandaemonium. Leslie Epstein. LC 96-53874. 384p. 1997. text 24.95 (*0-312-15622-7*) St Martin.

Pandaemonium. Leslie Epstein. 416p. 1998. pap. 14.95 (*0-312-18752-1*) St Martin.

Pandaemonium: Ethnicity in International Politics. Daniel P. Moynihan. LC 92-41370. 240p. 1993. 27.50 (*0-19-827787-3*) OUP.

Pandaemonium: Ethnicity in International Politics. Patrick Moynihan. 238p. 1994. reprint ed. pap. 8.95 (*0-19-827946-9*) OUP.

Pandaemonium, 1660-1886: The Coming of the Machine As Seen by Contemporary Observers. Humphrey Jennings. Ed. by Mary-Lou Jennings & Charles Madge. (Illus.). 376p. 1995. reprint ed. pap. 23.50 (*0-333-63837-9*, Pub. by Papermac) Trans-Atl Phila.

Pandamonium der Achtziger Jahre: Kurzprosa des Jahres, 1983. Jozef Modzelewski. LC 90-33820. (Studies in Modern German Literature: Vol. 37). (GER.). XIV, 313p. (C). 1990. text 66.95 (*0-8204-1226-0*) P Lang Pubng.

Pandary. Michael P. O'Connor. LC 89-11763. 47p. 1990. per. 8.95 (*0-934332-50-9*) LEpervier Pr.

Pandas see Books for Young Explorers

Pandas see Preschool Puppet Board Books

Pandas. Highlights for Children Editors. (Highlights Animal Bks.). (Illus.). 32p. (Orig.). (J). (gr. 2-5). 1993. pap. 3.95 (*1-56397-285-9*) Boyds Mills Pr.

Pandas. Kate Petty. (Baby Animals Ser.). 1992. 9.15 (*0-606-01607-4*, Pub. by Turtleback) Demco.

Pandas. Two Can Publishing Ltd. Staff. (Animal Bks.). (Illus.). 32p. (J). (gr. 2-7). 1991. pap. 2.95 (*0-87534-225-6*) Highlights.

Pandas. John Wexo. (Zoobooks Ser.). (Illus.). 20p. (J). (gr. 1-6). 1998. reprint ed. pap. 2.75 (*0-937934-18-6*) Wildlife Educ.

Pandas: A Portrait of the Animal World, 1. Jill Carvan. 1998. pap. text 10.98 (*1-880908-66-2*) Todtri Prods.

Pandas: USA Edition. Heather Angel. LC 97-42001. (WorldLife Library). (Illus.). 72p. (YA). (gr. 5 up). 1998. pap. 16.95 (*0-89658-364-3*) Voyageur Pr.

Panda's Birthday Surprise. Beverly S. Brown. (Illus.). 8p. (J). (gr. k-2). 1998. pap. 3.75 (*1-880612-80-1*) Seedling Pubns.

***Panda's Busy Day.** Laura Gates-Galvin. (Let's Go to the Zoo! Ser.: Vol. 1). (Illus.). 16p. (J). 1999. bds. 5.95 (*1-56899-794-9*) Soundprints.

Panda's Busy Day: Including Toy. Laura Gates-Galvin. (Let's Go to the Zoo! Ser.: Vol. 1). (Illus.). 16p. (J). 1999. bds. 9.95 (*1-56899-795-7*) Soundprints.

Pandas for Kids. Kathy Feeney. LC 96-46825. (Wildlife for Kids Ser.). (Illus.). 48p. (Orig.). (J). (gr. 3-7). 1997. pap. 6.95 (*1-55971-594-4*, NorthWord Pr) Creat Pub Intl.

Panda's New Toy. Joyce Dunbar. LC 98-14045. (Read Me Ser.). (Illus.). 24p. (J). (gr. k-2). 1999. 9.99 (*0-7636-0724-X*, Pub. by Candlewick Pr) Penguin Putnam.

Pandas of the World. Mitsuko Masui. Tr. by Diane T. Ooka. (Illus.). 32p. (J). (gr. k-2). 1989. 12.95 (*0-89346-314-0*) Heian Intl.

Panda's Surprise see All Day & Night Set

***Panda's Thumb.** Stephen Jay Gould. (C). 1999. pap. text 19.75 (*0-393-98202-5*) Norton.

Panda's Thumb: More Reflections in Natural History. Stephen Jay Gould. 352p. 1992. pap. 13.95 (*0-393-30819-7*) Norton.

Pandectes of the Law of Nations. William Fulbecke. LC 79-84109. (English Experience Ser.: No. 928). 192p. 1979. reprint ed. lib. bdg. 25.00 (*90-221-0928-3*) Walter J Johnson.

Pandeleteius of Venezuela & Colombia (Curculionidae: Brachyderinae: Tanymecini) Anne T. Howden. (Memoir Ser.: No. 24). (Illus.). 310p. 1976. 45.00 (*1-56665-022-4*) Assoc Pubs FL.

P

An Asterisk (*) at the beginning of an entry indicates that the title is appearing for the first time.

Pandelis Prevelakis & the Value of a Heritage. Andonis Decavelles. Ed. by Theofanis G. Stavrou. Tr. by Jean H. Woodhead from GRE. LC 81-81839. (Modern Greek History & Culture Ser.). 1981. 10.00 (0-935476-08-3) Nostos Bks.

Pandemic Influenza, 1700-1900: A Study in Historical Epidemiology. K. David Patterson. (Illus.). 128p. (C). 1987. 45.00 (0-8476-7512-2, R7512) Rowman.

Pandemic of Influenza, 1918-1919: The Urban Impact in the Western World. Ed. by Fred R. Van Hartesveldt. LC 92-35323. 212p. 1993. text 89.95 (0-7734-9195-3) E Mellen.

***Pandemonium.** (World Championship Wrestling - New World Order Coloring & Activity Bks.). (Illus.). 32p. 1999. pap. write for info. (0-7666-0422-5, Honey Bear Bks) Modern Pub NYC.

Pandemonium. Leslie Epstein. 1997. 24.95 (0-614-27910-0) St Martin.

***Pandemonium.** Ramiro Gomez. (SPA.). 208p. 1999. pap. write for info. (0-9675192-0-9) Gomez.

***Pandemonium: The Rise of Predatory Locales in the Postwar World.** Branden Hookway et al. (Illus.). 96p. 1999. pap. 24.95 (1-56898-191-0) Princeton Arch.

Pandemonium: Toward a Retro-Organization Theory. Gibson Burrell. 208p. 1996. 75.00 (0-8039-7776-X); pap. 26.95 (0-8039-7777-8) Sage.

***Pandita Ramabai Through Her Own Words.** Ed. by Meera Kosambi. (Illus.). 256p. 2000. text 18.95 (0-19-564754-8) OUP.

Panditaraja Jagannatha: The Renowned Sanskrit Poet of Medieval India. N. N. Sarma. LC 94-905534. (C). 1994. 28.00 (81-7099-393-8, Pub. by Motilal Bnarsidass) S Asia.

Pandolfini's Chess Complete: The Most Comprehensive Guide to the Game, from History to Strategy. Bruce Pandolfini. LC 92-16152. 352p. 1992. pap. 15.00 (0-671-70186-X, Fireside) S&S Trade Pap.

Pandolfini's Endgame Course. Bruce Pandolfini. (Illus.). 320p. 1988. pap. 11.00 (0-671-65688-0, Fireside) S&S Trade Pap.

Pandora see Oeuvres

Pandora. (Class. Garnier Ser.). write for info. Schoenhof.

Pandora. Anne Rice. (New Tales of the Vampires Ser.: Bk. 1). 1999. mass mkt. 6.99 (0-345-42238-4) Ballantine Pub Grp.

Pandora. Anne Rice. LC 97-49457. (New Tales of the Vampires Ser.: Bk. 1). 288p. 1998. 19.95 (0-375-40159-8) Random.

Pandora. large type ed. Anne Rice. LC 97-40717. (New Tales of the Vampires Ser.: Bk. 1). 288p. 1998. pap. 19.95 (0-375-70218-0) Random.

Pandora. limited ed. Anne Rice. (New Tales of the Vampires Ser.: Bk. 1). 356p. 1998. 150.00 (1-890885-02-9) B E Trice.

Pandora see Works of Henry James Jr.: Collected Works

Pandora: Women in Classical Greece. Ed. by E. D. Reeder. LC 95-60831. 400p. 1996. text 100.00 (0-691-01125-7, Pub. by Princeton U Pr) Cal Prin Full Svc.

Pandora: Women in Classical Greece. Ellen D. Reeder. (Illus.). 434p. 1995. pap. 35.00 (0-911886-41-9) Walters Art.

Pandora & Occam: On the Limits of Language & Literature. Horst Ruthrof. LC 91-26539. (Advances in Semiotics Ser.). (Illus.). 304p. 1992. text 14.95 (0-253-34995-8) Ind U Pr.

Pandora & the Magic Box: After Nathaniel Hawthorne. I. E. Clark. (Illus.). 20p. (J). (gr. 2 up). 1968. pap. 3.00 (0-88680-147-8) I E Clark.

Pandora & the Magic Box: Director's Script. I. E. Clark. (Illus.). 20p. (J). (gr. 2 up). 1968. pap. 7.50 (0-88680-148-6) I E Clark.

Pandora by Holly Hollander. Gene Wolfe. 208p. 1993. 8.95 (0-312-85298-3) Orb NYC.

Pandora Directive: A Tex Murphy Novel. Aaron Conners. 336p. 1995. mass mkt. 5.99 (0-7615-0068-5) Prima Pub.

Pandora Directive: The Official Strategy Guide. Rick Barba. LC 95-74690. 1996. pap. text 19.99 (0-7615-0373-0) Prima Pub.

Pandora Guide to Women Composers: Britain & the U. S., 1629-Present. Sophie Fuller. (Illus.). 368p. 1998. pap. text 22.00 (0-7881-5611-X) DIANE Pub.

Pandora Guide to Women Composers: Britian & the United States, 1629 to the Present. Sophie Fuller. (Illus.). 368p. 1995. pap. text 22.00 (0-04-440936-2) NYU Pr.

Pandora Principle, No. 49. Carolyn Clowes. (Star Trek Ser.). 288p. 1990. mass mkt. 4.99 (0-671-65815-8) PB.

Pandora Project. David Hodel. LC 96-31226. 1996. pap. 12.99 (0-7852-7625-4) Nelson.

***Pandora's Book of Sexual Fantasies: Open Your Mind to a New World of Sexual Adventures.** Suzie Hayman. 2000. pap. 18.95 (1-84222-034-9) Carlton Bks Ltd.

Pandora's Box. Marjorie Eccles. 160p. 1996. 20.00 (0-7278-4856-9) Severn Hse.

***Pandora's Box.** Kaiji Kawaguchi. (Eagle Ser.: Vol. 7). 2000. pap. 6.95 (1-56931-478-0) Viz Commns Inc.

Pandora's Box. Alice Thompson. LC 98-37076. 148p. 1999. 22.00 (0-88001-670-1) HarpC.

Pandora's Box. large type ed. Marjorie Eccles. (Magna Large Print Ser.). 273p. 1997. 27.99 (0-7505-1040-4) Ulverscroft.

Pandora's Box. Elizabeth Gage. Ed. by Julie Rubenstein. 872p. 1991. reprint ed. mass mkt. 6.99 (0-671-74327-9) PB.

Pandora's Box: An Anthology of Erotic Writing by Women. (Black Lace Ser.). 288p. (Orig.). 1996. mass mkt. 5.95 (0-352-33074-0, Pub. by Virgin Bks) London Brdge.

Pandora's Box: Feminism Confronts Reproductive Technology. Nancy Lublin. LC 97-26354. (New Feminist Perspectives Ser.). 208p. 1998. 60.00 (0-8476-8636-1); pap. 14.95 (0-8476-8637-X) Rowman.

***Pandora's Box: Open Your Mind to a New World of Sexual Adventure.** Suzie Hayman. (Illus.). 80p. 2000. boxed set 24.95 (1-85868-961-9, Pub. by Carlton Bks Ltd) Natl Bk Netwk.

Pandora's Box 3. Ed. by Kerri Sharp. (Black Lace Ser.). 1998. mass mkt. 6.95 (0-352-33274-3) BLA4.

Pandora's Box 2. Ed. by Kerri Sharpe. (Orig.). 1997. mass mkt. 5.95 (0-352-33151-8, Pub. by BLA4) London Brdge.

Pandora's Clock. John J. Nance. 1996. mass mkt. 6.99 (0-312-96034-4) St Martin.

Pandora's Clock. abr. ed. John J. Nance. 1995. write for info. incl. audio (0-7871-0534-1, Pub. by NewStar Media) Lndmrk Audiobks.

Pandora's Clock. large type ed. John J. Nance. 630p. 1996. 25.95 (0-7838-1577-8, G K Hall Lrg Type) Mac Lib Ref.

***Pandora's Game.** Christopher Andrews. LC 99-90687. 248p. 1999. 25.00 (0-7388-0484-3); pap. 18.00 (0-7388-0485-1) Xlibris Corp.

Pandora's Gift. Climo. (Illus.). 64p. (J). (gr. 3-4). 14.95 (0-06-028632-6) HarpC.

Pandora's Gift. Climo. 64p. (J). Date not set. pap. 3.95 (0-06-444271-3) HarpC Child Bks.

***Pandora's Gift.** Shirley Climo. 64p. (J). 2001. lib. bdg. 14.89 (0-06-028633-4) HarpC Child Bks.

Pandora's Hope: Essays on the Reality of Science Studies. Bruno Latour. LC 98-50061. 1999. 45.00 (0-674-65335-1); pap. 19.95 (0-674-65336-X) HUP.

***Pandora's Picnic Basket: The Potential & Hazards of Genetically Modified Foods.** Alan McHughen. (Illus.). 288p. 2000. 24.95 (0-19-850674-0) OUP.

Pandora's Poison: Chlorine, Health, & a New Environmental Strategy. Joe Thornton. LC 99-57011. (Illus.). 650p. 2000. 34.95 (0-262-20124-0) MIT Pr.

Pandora's Pride. May Gruber. 280p. (Orig.). 1985. pap. 8.95 (0-8184-0374-8, Citadel Pr) Carol Pub Group.

Pandora's Pulpit: Women in Ministry. Roger W. Sapp. 194p. (C). 1998. pap. 14.95 (0-9662085-0-1) All Nations Pubs.

***Pandora's Redoubt.** James Axler. (Deathlands Ser.: Bk. 50). 352p. 2000. per. 5.99 (0-373-62560-X, 1-62560-7, Wrldwide Lib) Harlequin Bks.

Pandora's Revenge. Pat Cook. 27p. (J). 1998. pap. 3.50 (0-87129-859-7, P64) Dramatic Pub.

Pandora's Shipyards. Bernard Steiner. 20p. Date not set. 20.00 (0-9647818-0-8); pap. 20.00 (0-9647818-2-4); text 20.00 (0-9647818-1-6); pap. text 20.00 (0-9647818-3-2) Steiner Pubng.

Pandy's Rainbow. Carol T. Plum. LC 90-64469. (I Am Special Story Bks.). (Illus.). 32p. (J). (gr. k-3). 1991. 6.95 (0-87973-008-0, 8); pap. 3.95 (0-87973-009-9, 9) Our Sunday Visitor.

Pane. Luis Gonzalez Palma. (Illus.). 112p. 1999. pap. 32.00 (88-8158-194-9, Pub. by Charta) Dist Art Pubs.

Pane e Lavoro: The Italian American Working Class. Ed. by George E. Pozzetta. 1978. 9.95 (0-934675-11-2) Am Italian.

***Paneb the Ardent.** Christian Jacq. (Stone of Light Ser.: No. 3). 2001. pap. 16.00 (0-7434-0348-7, PB Trade Paper) PB.

Panegyric. Guy Debord. Tr. by James Brook. LC 91-34269. 104p. (gr. 13). 1991. pap. 17.00 (0-86091-559-X, A6394, Pub. by Verso) Norton.

Panegyrici Latini: A Concordance to the Latin Panegyrics. Ed. by Tore Janson. (Alpha-Omega, Reihe A Ser.: Vol. XXXVII). (GER.). xii, 900p. 1979. 180.70 (3-487-06766-8) G Olms Pubs.

Panegyricus. (GER.). 500p. write for info. (0-318-70421-8) G Olms Pubs.

Panegyricus de Sexto Consulatu Honorii Augustii. Claudian. Ed. & Tr. by Michael Dewar. LC 96-1460. (ENG & LAT.). 490p. 1997. text 105.00 (0-19-814964-6, Clarendon Pr) OUP.

Panel Data Analysis. Ed. by Baldev Raj et al. (Studies in Empirical Economics). (Illus.). viii, 220p. 1992. 99.95 (0-387-91416-1) Spr-Verlag.

Panel Data & Labor Market Studies. Ed. by Geert Ridder et al. (Contributions to Economic Analysis Ser.: No. 192). 336p. 1990. 131.50 (0-444-88461-0, North Holland) Elsevier.

Panel Data & Labour Market Dynamics. Ed. by Peter Jensen et al. LC 93-34748. (Contributions to Economic Analysis Ser.: No. 222). 506p. 1993. 123.00 (0-444-81548-1, North Holland) Elsevier.

***Panel Data Econometrics: Future Directions: Papers in Honour of Professor Pietro Balestra.** Jayalakshmi Krishnakumar & Elvezio Ronchetti. LC 00-37171. 2000. write for info. (0-444-50237-8) Elsevier.

Panel Sawing Machinery. 1973. 39.00 (0-7855-1089-3) St Mut.

Panel Study of Income Dynamics: A User's Guide. Martha S. Hill. (Guides to Major Social Science Data Bases Ser.). 96p. (C). 1991. text 28.00 (0-8039-4609-0); pap. text 11.50 (0-8039-4230-3) Sage.

Panelboards, UL 67. 11th ed. (C). 1993. pap. text 290.00 (1-55989-579-9) Underwrtrs Labs.

Panels for Transportation Planning: Methods & Applications. Thomas F. Golob et al. LC 97-21872. (Transportation, Research, Economics & Policy Ser.). 1997. lib. bdg. 154.00 (0-7923-9966-8) Kluwer Academic.

Panels of the Seventh World Sanskrit Conference Vol. 3: The History of Sacred Places in India As Reflected in Traditional Literature. Ed. by J. Bronkhorst. 221p. 1990. 92.50 (90-04-09318-4) Brill Academic Pubs.

Panels of the Seventh World Sanskrit Conference Vol. 4: Sense & Syntax in Vedic; Vol. 5: Panini & the Veda, 2 vols. in 1. Ed. by Johannes Bronkhorst et al. LC 90-26169. (ENG & FRE.). 106; 74p. 1991. 88.00 (90-04-09356-7) Brill Academic Pubs.

Panels of the Seventh World Sanskrit Conference Vol. 6: Middle Indo Aryan & Jaina Studies, Sanskrit Outside India, Vol. 7. Ed. by Johannes Bronkhorst. 97; 66p. 1991. 72.00 (90-04-09426-1) Brill Academic Pubs.

Panels of the Seventh World Sanskrit Conference Vol. 8: Medical Literature from India, Sri Lanka & Tibet, Rules & Remedies in Classical Indian Law, Vol. 9. Ed. by Johannes Bronkhorst. 90p. 1991. 91.00 (90-04-09522-5) Brill Academic Pubs.

Panels of the Seventh World Sanskrit Conference Vol. 10: Indian Art & Archaeology. Ed. by Ellen M. Raven et al. LC 91-28801. (Illus.). 135p. 1991. 91.00 (90-04-09553-5) Brill Academic Pubs.

Panentheism in Hartshorne & Tillich Vol. 121: A Creative Synthesis. David Nikkel. (American University Studies: Series VII). VII, 229p. (C). 1996. text 42.95 (0-8204-1678-9) P Lang Pubng.

***Panes y los Peces (Loaves & Fishes)** Heather Amery. (Bible Tales Readers Ser.). (Illus.). 16p. (J). (ps up). 1999. 6.95 (0-7460-3650-7, Usborne) EDC.

Panetics & Dukkha: Integrated Study of the Infliction of Suffering & the Reduction of Infliction. R. G. Siu. LC 93-61385. 396p. 1994. pap. 25.00 (1-884437-02-8) Intl Soc Panetics.

Panetics Trilogy. R. G. Siu. 1994. pap. 75.00 (1-884437-00-1) Intl Soc Panetics.

Panfish. rev. ed. Dick Sternberg & Bill Ignizio. LC 95-51141. (Hunting & Fishing Library). (Illus.). 160p. 1996. 19.95 (0-86573-052-0) Creat Pub Intl.

***Panfish Identification.** Creative Publishing International Staff. (Fisherman's Pocket Guides Ser.). (Illus.). 2000. pap. 4.99 (0-86573-476-3) Creat Pub Intl.

Panfishing. Richard Martin et al. LC 91-60047. (Complete Angler's Library). 278p. 1991. write for info. (0-914697-37-4) N Amer Outdoor Grp.

Pangaea: Bk Ii Imperium Afire. Lisa Mason. 400p. 2000. mass mkt. 6.50 (0-553-58166-X) Bantam.

Pangaea Book I Bk. 1: Imperium Without End. Lisa Mason. 400p. 1999. mass mkt. 6.50 (0-553-57571-6) Bantam.

Pangasinan Dictionary. Richard A. Benton. LC 75-152456. (Hawaii University, Honolulu, Pacific & Asian Linguistics Institute Ser.). 329p. reprint ed. pap. 102.00 (0-608-11014-0, 2007975000068) Bks Demand.

Pangasinan, 1801-1900: The Beginnings of Modernization. Rosario M. Cortes. (Illus.). 191p. (Orig.). (C). 1991. pap. 17.50 (971-10-0426-7, Pub. by New Day Pub) Cellar.

Pangasinan, 1572-1800, Vol. I. Rosario M. Cortes. (Illus.). 189p. 1991. reprint ed. pap. 18.75 (971-10-0458-5, Pub. by New Day Pub) Cellar.

Pangasinan, 1901-1986: A Political, Socioeconomic & Cultural History. Rosario M. Cortes. (Illus.). 328p. (C). 1991. pap. 25.00 (971-10-0425-9, Pub. by New Day Pub) Cellar.

Pangasinan Reference Grammar. Richard A. Benton. Ed. by Howard P. McKaughan. LC 72-152458. (PALI Language Texts: Philippines Ser.). 286p. (C). reprint ed. 88.70 (0-8357-9826-7, 201721300004) Bks Demand.

Pangea: Paleoclimate, Tectonics, & Sedimentation During Accretion, Zenith & Breakup of a Supercontinent. G. D. Klein. (Special Papers: No. 288). 1994. pap. 54.38 (0-8137-2288-8) Geol Soc.

Pangeghtellghet (Visits to Siberia) Ed. by V. Kaneshiro. (ESK.). 71p. 1976. pap. 5.00 (0-933769-77-6) Alaska Native.

Panggung Semar: Aspects of Traditional Malay Theatre. Ghulam-Sarwar Yousof. (Illus.). 256p. 1995. 15.00 (983-888-012-4, Pub. by Delta Edits) Weatherhill.

Panglor. Jeffrey A. Carver. 1996. mass mkt. 5.99 (0-8125-5167-2, Pub. by Tor Bks) St Martin.

Pangs of Proximity: India & Sri Lanka's Ethnic Crisis. S. D. Muni. LC 93-12317. (Peace Research Institute, Oslo Ser.). (Illus.). 256p. (C). 1993. 33.50 (0-8039-9112-6) Sage.

***Pangs of the Messiah: The Troubled Birth of the Jewish State.** Martin Sicker. LC 99-28482. 280p. 2000. 55.00 (0-275-96638-0) Greenwood.

Pangu Mystical Qigong. Ou Wen Wei. (Illus.). 103p. 1999. pap. text 9.95 (1-892515-06-7) Multi-Media Commns.

Pangur Bawn the Cat: Ninth Century. Ed. & Tr. by Malachi McCormick. (Miniatures Ser.). 24p. 1991. pap. 7.00 (0-943984-48-3) Stone St Pr.

Panhandle Aspect of the Chaquaqua Plateau. Robert G. Campbell. (Graduate Studies: No. 11). (Illus.). 118p. (Orig.). 1976. pap. 5.00 (0-89672-021-7) Tex Tech Univ Pr.

Panhandle Cowboy. write for info. (0-9608612-3-8) Maverick Bks.

Panhandle Cowboy. John R. Erickson. LC 99-462455. (Western Life Ser.: Vol. 4). (Illus.). 207p. 1999. 24.95 (1-57441-064-4) UNTX Pr.

Panhandle Florida Retirement & Relocation Guide. large type ed. Maryann Zihala & Chris Stavreff. (Retirement & Relocation Guides Ser.). (Illus.). 350p. Date not set. pap. 24.95 (1-56559-120-8) HGI-Over Fifty.

Panhandle Gold. large type ed. Kent Conwell. 178p. 1992. reprint ed. lib. bdg. 14.95 (1-56054-571-2) Thorndike Pr.

Panhandle Pat's 50 Years: Recipes & Memories of Meyer's Chuck (Alaska) Pat Emel. (Illus.). 50p. 1995. pap. 10.00 (0-9622337-6-5) Perv Pub WA.

Panhandle Pilgrimage: Illustrated Tales Tracing History in the Texas Panhandle. 5th ed. Pauline D. Robertson & R. L. Robertson. LC 78-68222. (Illus.). 400p. 1989. 34.95 (0-942376-00-5) Paramount TX.

Panhandle Pistolero. large type ed. Ray Hogan. (Linford Western Library). 186p. 1989. pap. 16.99 (0-7089-6717-5, Linford) Ulverscroft.

Panhellenica: Essays in Ancient History. Ed. by Stanley M. Burstein & Louis Okin. 1980. 15.00 (0-87291-134-9) Coronado Pr.

Panic. Chris Curry. 1994. mass mkt. 4.99 (0-671-74947-1) PB.

Panic! UNIX System Crash Dump Analysis. Chris Drake & Kimberley Brown. 496p. (C). 1995. pap. 60.00 incl. cd-rom (0-13-149386-8) P-H.

***Panic & Agoraphobia Scale (PAS)** Borwin Bandelow. LC 99-71758. (Illus.). 88p. 1999. pap. 49.00 (0-88937-216-0) Hogrefe & Huber Pubs.

Panic & Anxiety Attacks: Warning of a Physical Problem. Glenn M. Alger. 159p. (Orig.). 1990. pap. text 7.95 (0-9626143-0-0) Glendor Bks.

Panic & Phobias. Ed. by I. Hand & H. U. Wittchen. (Illus.). 145p. 1986. 51.00 (0-387-16513-4) Spr-Verlag.

Panic Anxiety & Its Treatment: A Publication of the World Psychiatric Association. Ed. by Gerald L. Klerman et al. LC 93-16381. 162p. 1993. text 12.95 (0-88048-684-8, 8684) Am Psychiatric.

***Panic at EMU Flat, 8.** Robert Elmer. LC 99-6560. (Adventures Down Under Ser.). 160p. (J). (gr. 3-8). 1999. pap. text 5.99 (0-7642-2106-X) Bethany Hse.

Panic! At Fort Stevens: Japanese Navy Shells Fort Stevens, Oregon in World War-II: Documentary. Bert Webber. LC 95-14782. (Illus.). 94p. 1995. pap. 8.95 (0-936738-87-1) Webb Research.

Panic Attack, Anxiety & Phobia Solutions Handbook. Muriel K. Macfarlane. LC 95-60774. 336p. (Orig.). 1996. pap. 12.95 (1-887053-00-X) United Res CA.

***Panic Attack Recovery Book.** Shirley Swede. 2000. pap. 12.00 (0-451-20043-8, Sig) NAL.

Panic Attacks: A Natural Approach. 2nd rev. ed. Shirley Trickett. (Natural Approach Health Ser.). 156p. (Orig.). 1999. pap. 9.95 (1-56975-187-0) Ulysses Pr.

Panic Attacks & Phobias: Help! I Think I'm Dying. 2nd rev. ed. Abbot L. Granoff. LC 96-134157. (Illus.). 88p. (C). 1996. pap. 14.95 (0-938423-04-5) Mind Matters Pub.

***Panic Bird.** Myra Schneider. LC 99-195824. 1999. 18.95 (1-900564-21-1) Enitharmon Pr.

Panic Control after Surgery. 1995. lib. bdg. 250.75 (0-8490-7580-7) Gordon Pr.

Panic Disorder: A Critical Analysis. Richard J. McNally. LC 94-26243. 276p. 1994. lib. bdg. 38.00 (0-89862-263-8) Guilford Pubns.

Panic Disorder: Assessment & Treatment Through a Wide-Angle Lens. Frank M. Dattilio & Jesus A. Salas-Auvert. LC 99-27032. 2000. 38.50 (1-891944-35-5) Zeig Tucker.

Panic Disorder: The Facts. Stanley J. Rachman. Ed. by W. P. De Silva. LC 96-2511. (Facts Ser.). (Illus.). 108p. 1996. pap. 19.95 (0-19-262738-4) OUP.

Panic Disorder: The Great Pretender. H. M. Zal. LC 89-23176. (Illus.). 234p. (C). 1990. 22.95 (0-306-43297-8, Plen Insight) Perseus Pubng.

Panic Disorder: The Medical Point of View. 4th rev. ed. William D. Kerrode. Ed. by Anne Hill. (Illus.). 209p. 1997. pap. 17.95 (0-9631533-3-1) W Kernodle.

Panic Disorder: Theory, Research & Therapy. R. Baker. (Clinical Psychology Ser.). 364p. 1992. pap. 119.95 (0-471-93317-1) Wiley.

Panic Disorder & Agoraphobia: A Comprehensive Guide for the Practitioner. Ed. by John R. Walker et al. 704p. (C). 1991. text 71.95 (0-534-11286-2) Brooks-Cole.

***Panic Disorder & Agoraphobia: A Guide.** rev. ed. John H. Greist & James W. Jefferson. 69p. 1998. pap. 4.95 (1-890802-15-8) Madison Inst of Med.

Panic Disorder & Agoraphobia: A Guide. 2nd rev. ed. John H. Greist & James W. Jefferson. 58p. 1993. pap. 4.50 (1-890802-01-8) Madison Inst of Med.

Panic Disorder & Its Treatment. J. F. Rosenbaum & Mark H. Pollack. LC 98-4110. (Medical Psychiatry Ser.). (Illus.). 376p. 1998. text 99.75 (0-8247-0216-6) Dekker.

Panic Disorder in the Medical Setting. (Illus.). 135p. (Orig.). (C). 1994. pap. text 35.00 (0-7881-0528-0) DIANE Pub.

Panic Disorder in the Medical Setting. Wayne J. Katon. 145p. 1992. pap. 5.25 (0-16-036212-1) USGPO.

Panic Disorders: Causes & Cures. 1996. lib. bdg. 251.96 (0-8490-5911-9) Gordon Pr.

Panic Disorders in a Medical Setting. 1992. lib. bdg. 250.95 (0-8490-8902-6) Gordon Pr.

Panic Farm. Annie Kubler. 44p. (J). 1985. 4.99 (0-85953-258-5) Childs Play.

***Panic Free: Eliminate Anxiety/Panic Attacks Without Drugs & Take Control of Your Life.** rev. ed. Lynne Freeman. LC 98-9381. Orig. Title: Panic Free: Eliminate Anxiety Panic Attacks & Take Control of Your Life Without Drugs. 193p. 1999. pap. 13.95 (0-9668546-0-8, 299-7738) Arden Bks.

Panic Free: Eliminate Panic/Anxiety Attacks Without Drugs & Take Control of Your Life. unabridged ed. Lynne Freeman. Ed. by William Alan Landes & Bruce Fife. LC 97-51251. 192p. 1998. pap. 16.00 (0-941599-34-5, Pub. by Piccadilly Bks) Empire Pub Srvs.

Panic Free: Eliminate Anxiety Panic Attacks & Take Control of Your Life Without Drugs see Panic Free: Eliminate Anxiety/Panic Attacks Without Drugs & Take Control of Your Life

Panic Hardware, UL 305. 5th ed. (C). 1997. pap. text 95.00 (0-7629-0074-1) Underwrtrs Labs.

Panic in Box C. John Dickson Carr. 272p. 1987. mass mkt. 3.50 (0-88184-288-5) Carroll & Graf.

Panic in Paradise: Florida's Banking Crash of 1926. Raymond B. Vickers. LC 93-35974. 336p. (C). 1994. text 34.95 (0-8173-0723-0) U of Ala Pr.

***Panic in Puerto Vallarta: Quebec's Intelligentsia & the Fascist Temptation, 1939-1960.** K. Flanagan. LC 99-173068. 1998. pap. text 6.99 (1-55207-015-8) R Davies Multimed.

Panic in the Pantry: Facts & Fallacies about the Food You Buy. Elizabeth Whelan et al. LC 92-7986. 222p. (C). 1992. pap. 18.95 (0-87975-732-9) Prometheus Bks.

P

An Asterisk (*) at the beginning of an entry indicates that the title is appearing for the first time.

Panic in the Wild Waters. Lee Roddy. LC 95-10951. (Ladd Family Adventure Ser.: No. 12). (J). (gr. 3-7). 1995. pap. 5.99 (*1-56179-392-2*) Focus Family.

Panic Love, Vol. 1. Antonio D'Alfonso. 54p. 1993. pap. 8.00 (*0-920717-63-2*) Guernica Editions.

Panic No More: Your Guide to Overcome Panic Attacks. Jean Carlton. 288p. (Orig.). 1994. pap. 12.95 (*0-9639632-9-5*) Stonehorse.

Panic Now! The Y2K Millennium Bug Will Effect You! Philip Steinman. Ed. by Charles Bethancourt. 150p. 1998. mass mkt. 17.95 (*0-9665868-0-8*) Wisdom Pub Inc.

Panic of 1857. George W. Van Vleck. LC 77-182585. (Columbia University. Studies in the Social Sciences: No. 463). reprint ed. 20.00 (*0-404-51463-4*) AMS Pr.

Panic of 1837: Some Financial Problems of the Jacksonian Era. Reginald C. McGrane. 1993. pap. text 1.95 (*0-226-55858-4*, P202) U Ch Pr.

Panic of 1857 & the Coming of the Civil War. James L. Huston. LC 87-2705. 335p. 1987. pap. 103.90 (*0-7837-8524-0*, 204933300011) Bks Demand.

Panic on Gull Island. Franklin W. Dixon. (Hardy Boys Mystery Stories Ser.: No. 107). 160p. (J). (gr. 3-6). 1991. mass mkt. 3.99 (*0-671-69276-3*, Minstrel Bks) PB.

Panic on Gull Island. Franklin W. Dixon. (Hardy Boys Mystery Stories Ser.: No. 107). (J). (gr. 3-6). 1991. 9.09 (*0-606-04998-3*, Pub. by Turtleback) Demco.

***Panic Plan for the ACT 2001.** 2nd ed. 272p. 2000. pap. 9.95 (*0-7689-0504-4*) Petersons.

Panic Plan for the SAT. 3rd ed. Joan D. Carris. LC 98-8129. 224p. 1998. pap. text 9.95 (*1-56079-848-3*) Petersons.

***Panic Plan for the SAT 2001.** 4th ed. Joan Carris. 314p. 2000. pap. text 9.95 (*0-7689-0503-6*) Petersons.

Panic-Proof Investor: Lessons in Profitable Investing from a Market Wizard. 5th ed. Thomas Basso. 151p. 1994. pap. 14.95 (*0-471-03024-4*) Wiley.

***Panic Proof Parent: How to Create a Perfectly Safe Environment for Your Family.** Debra S. Holtzman. LC 99-38647. 256p. 2000. pap. 12.95 (*0-8092-2392-9*, 239290, Contemporary Bks) NTC Contemp Pub Co.

Panic Psychological Perspectives. Ed. by Jack D. Maser & Stanley J. Rachman. 392p. 1988. text 89.95 (*0-8058-0091-3*) L Erlbaum Assocs.

Panic Rules! Everything You Need to Know about the Global Economy. Robin Hahnel. LC 99-23928. 136p. 1999. 40.00 (*0-89608-610-0*, Pub. by South End Pr) Consort Bk Sales.

***Panic Rules! Everything You Need to Know about the Global Economy.** Robin Hahnel. LC 99-23928. 136p. 1999. pap. 12.00 (*0-89608-609-7*, Pub. by South End Pr) Consort Bk Sales.

***Panic Snap.** Laura Reese. LC 99-56344. 352p. 2000. text 24.95 (*0-312-24229-8*) St Martin.

***Panic Snap.** Laura Reese. 2001. pap. write for info. (*0-312-27275-8*, St Martin Griffin) St Martin.

Panic Stations. Judith Clarke. (YA). 1995. 11.95 (*0-7022-2696-3*, Pub. by Univ Queensland Pr) Intl Spec Bk.

PanicBuster: Learn to Conquer Panic Attacks & Agoraphobia. Bonnie Crandall. 67p. 1995. spiral bd., wbk. ed. 12.95 (*0-9663946-0-7*) Hatch Creek.

Panicking Ralph. James. Date not set. write for info. (*0-393-04762-8*) Norton.

Panico en el Campamento. R. L. Stine, pseud. (Escalofrios Ser.: No. 9).Tr. of Welcome to Camp Nightmare. (SPA., Illus.). 72p. (J). (gr. 3-7). 1997. pap. text 3.99 (*0-590-29963-8*) Scholastic Inc.

Panico En El Campemento. R. L. Stine, pseud. (Escalofrios Ser.: No. 9).Tr. of Welcome to Camp Nightmare. 1997. 9.09 (*0-606-11718-0*, Pub. by Turtleback) Demco.

Panico en la Discoteca, Level 3. Fernando Uria. (Leer en Espanol Ser.). (SPA.). (C). 1998. pap. 5.95 (*84-294-3431-3*) Santillana.

Panik - Ratgeber: Was Sie Schon Immer Ueber die Behandlung von Panikstoerungen Wissen Wollten. H. U. Wittchen et al. (GER., Illus.). viii, 70p. 1997. pap. 17.25 (*3-8055-6438-4*) S Karger.

Panini: A Survey of Research. George Cardona. (Trends in Linguistics, State-of-the-Art Reports: No. 6). 1976. pap. 80.80 (*90-279-3435-5*) Mouton.

Panini: His Description of Sanskrit: An Analytical Study of the Astadhyayi. Jag D. Singh. (C). 1991. text 34.00 (*0-685-50092-6*, Pub. by M Manoharial) S Asia.

Panini - History Work & Its Tradition Vol. 1: Background & Introduction. George Cardona. LC 98-909891. (C). 1997. 60.00 (*81-208-0419-8*, Pub. by Motilal Bnarsidass) S Asia.

Panini As a Linguist: Ideas & Patterns. Yajan V. Dahiya. (C). 1995. 62.00 (*81-86339-09-4*, Pub. by Eastern Bk Linkers) S Asia.

Panini, Bruschetta, Crostini: The Sandwich, Italian Style. Viana La Place. LC 93-39917. 144p. 1994. 23.00 (*0-688-11325-7*, Hearst) Hearst Commns.

Panini Re-Interpreted. Charu D. Shastri. 1990. 27.00 (*81-208-0627-1*, Pub. by Motilal Bnarsidass) S Asia.

Paninian Studies: Professor S. D. Joshi Felicitation Volume. Ed. by Madhav M. Deshpande & Saroja Bhate. LC 90-86276. (Michigan Papers on South & Southeast Asia: No. 37). 331p. 1991. 31.95 (*0-89148-064-1*); pap. 15.95 (*0-89148-065-X*) Ctr S&SE Asian.

***Panini's Grammatik, 2 pts.** Otto Bohtlingk. 480, 357p. 1998. pap. 500.00 (*81-208-1025-2*, Pub. by Motilal Bnarsidass) St Mut.

Panini's Metalanguage. Hartmut Scharfe. LC 71-167988. (American Philosophical Society, Memoirs Ser.: Vol. 89). 63p. reprint ed. pap. 30.00 (*0-608-13260-8*, 202513200042) Bks Demand.

Paniolo. Joseph Brennan. 1995. reprint ed. pap. 9.95 (*0-914916-39-4*) Ku Paa.

Paniqtuliutiq Kilitanik (How to Make Fish Strips) large type ed. Bessie Green. (ESK., Illus.). 12p. (J). (gr. k-3). 1999. pap. text 17.00 (*1-58084-120-1*) Lower Kuskokwim.

Panique au Cimetiere. Bertrand Gauthier. (Novels in the Roman Jeunesse Ser.). (FRE.). 96p. (J). (gr. 4-7). 1992. pap. 8.95 (*2-89021-169-X*, Pub. by La Courte Ech) Firefly Bks Ltd.

Panis Angelicus see O Lord Most Holy: Medium Voice & Piano in G

Panis Angelicus see O Lord Most Holy: High Voice & Piano in A

Panizzi Lectures: A History of Bookbinding as a Mirror of Society. Mirjam M. Foot. LC 99-183870. (Illus.). 144p. 1999. pap. write for info. (*0-7123-4597-3*, Pub. by B23tish Library) U of Toronto Pr.

Panj Sura: Collection of 5 Famous Prayers. 1994. 7.50 (*1-56744-180-7*) Kazi Pubns.

Panjabi Complete Course. Sue Tyon-Ward et al. (Teach Yourself Ser.). (PAN.). 288p. 1999. pap. 20.95 (*0-8442-0185-5*, 01855) NTC Contemp Pub Co.

Panjabi Language: A Descriptive Grammar. N. I. Tolstaya. (Languages of Asia & Africa Ser.). 88p. (Orig.). 1981. pap. 34.00 (*0-7100-0939-9*, Routledge Thoemms) Routledge.

Panjabi Manual & Grammar: A Guide to the Colloquial Panjabi. T. Grahame Bailey & T. Cummings. (C). 1994. reprint ed. text 22.00 (*81-206-0918-2*, Pub. by Asian Educ Servs) S Asia.

Panjandrum V: An Anthology of Poetry. Ed. by Dennis Koran. (Panjandrum Poetry Journal: No. 5). (Illus.). 1977. pap. 6.95 (*0-915572-15-X*) Panjandrum.

Panjandrum Number One. Ed. by Dennis Koran. (Illus.). 1972. pap. 12.00 (*0-915572-46-X*) Panjandrum.

Panjandrum Poetry Journal, No. 6-7. Ed. by Dennis Koran. (Illus.). 1978. pap. 6.95 (*0-915572-34-6*) Panjandrum.

Pankration: The Ultimate Game. Dyan Blacklock. LC 98-38559. 192p. (J). (gr. 5-9). 1999. lib. bdg. 15.95 (*0-8075-6323-4*) A Whitman.

Pankreas: Diagnostik, Therapie. Ed. by K. J. Paquet & W. A. Kozuschek. (Illus.). 584p. 1991. 178.50 (*3-8055-5545-8*) S Karger.

Pankreaserkrankungen. M. W. Buechler et al. (Illus.). x, 186p. 1996. 68.00 (*3-8055-6141-5*) S Karger.

Panmunjom: The Story of the Korean Military Armistice Negotiations. William H. Vatcher, Jr. LC 72-14001. (Illus.). 322p. 1973. reprint ed. lib. bdg. 35.00 (*0-8371-6743-4*, VAPA, Greenwood Pr) Greenwood.

Panna. Imre Hofbauer. (C). 1990. 45.00 (*0-7223-2470-7*, Pub. by A H S Ltd) St Mut.

Panna in Early Buddhism: Philosophy Analysis with Special Reference to the Visuddhimagga. Baidyanath Labh. (C). 1991. text 17.50 (*0-8364-2654-1*, Pub. by Manohar) S Asia.

Panna in Early Buddhism: With Special Reference to Visuddhimagga. Baidyanath Labh. xii, 163p. 1991. 14.00 (*0-685-62638-5*, Pub. by Eastern Bk Linkers) Nataraj Bks.

Panna Maria: An Image of Polish Texans. Joseph Jaworski. (Illus.). 96p. 1991. 24.95 (*0-945618-04-2*) Dorsoduro Pr.

Panna Nikt see Miss Nobody: A Novel

Panneaux a Base de Bois. (FRE.). 61p. 1993. 10.00 (*92-5-203438-2*, FF4382, Pub. by FAO) Bernan Associates.

Pannekoek & the Workers' Councils. Serge Bricianer. Tr. by Malachy Carroll from FRE. LC 78-50978. (C). 1978. 28.00 (*0-914386-17-4*) Telos Pr.

***Panning for Gold in the Kitchen Sink: Everyday Creative Writing.** Michael C. Smith & Suzanne Greenberg. LC 99-33424. 272p. 2000. pap. 14.95 (*0-658-00228-7*, 002287) NTC Contemp Pub Co.

Panning for Pleasure: An Alaska Cookbook. Winni R. Page. Ed. by Betsy Andrews et al. (Illus.). 262p. 1991. reprint ed. write for info. (*0-9621777-0-9*) W R Page.

Pannonhalma. Endre Racz. (Illus.). 95p. (C). 1989. 80.00 (*0-7855-5210-3*, Pub. by Collets) St Mut.

Pannonhalma. Endre Racz. (Illus.). 96p. 1999. 21.00 (*963-13-2868-6*, Pub. by Corvina Bks) St Mut.

Pannonian Basin: A Study in Basin Evolution. Ed. by Leigh H. Royden & Ferenc Horvath. LC 88-21095. (AAPG Memoir Ser.: Vol. 45). (Illus.). 463p. 1988. reprint ed. pap. 143.60 (*0-608-07374-1*, 206760200001) Bks Demand.

Pannonian Basin Maps: A Study in Basin Evolution. Ed. by Leigh H. Royden & Ferenc Horvath. LC 88-21095. (AAPG Memoir Ser.: Vol. 45). (Illus.). 81p. reprint ed. pap. 30.00 (*0-608-07375-X*, 206760200002) Bks Demand.

Pannychis: The Office of Christian Burial. Monks of New Skete. Tr. by Laurence Mancuso from GRE. (Liturgical Music Series II: Divine Services: Vol. I). 40p. 1987. pap. text 15.00 (*0-935129-08-1*) Monks of New Skete.

Panofsky & the Foundations of Art History. Michael A. Holly. LC 84-45143. 272p. (C). 1984. text 42.50 (*0-8014-1614-0*); pap. text 15.95 (*0-8014-9896-1*) Cornell U Pr.

Panola College: The First Half Century. Bill O'Neal. 200p. 1997. 16.95 (*1-57168-211-2*) Sunbelt Media.

Panola County, Texas Marriage Records, 1846-1912. Marsha Ivey. 175p. 1996. pap. text 25.00 (*1-57088-044-1*) J&W Ent.

Panoptic Federal Protest Package: How to Challenge Improprieties & Errors in the Procurement Process. Barry L. McVay. (Federal Contracting Ser.). 138p. 1997. ring bd. 39.95 (*0-912481-17-X*) Panoptic Ent.

Panoptic Federal Supply & Service Code Book. Barry L. McVay. (Panoptic Federal Contracting Ser.). 124p. (Orig.). 1997. pap. 24.95 (*0-912481-20-X*) Panoptic Ent.

Panorama. Williams. Date not set. pap. text. write for info. (*0-582-55358-X*, Pub. by Addison-Wesley) Longman.

Panorama: An Anthology of Modern Indian Short Stories. Ed. by Mulk Raj Anand & S. Balu Rao. (C). 1997. pap. write for info. (*81-207-1990-5*) Sterling Pubs.

Panorama: History of a Mass Medium. Stephan Oettermann. Tr. by Deborah L. Schneider. LC 96-30342. 1997. 37.50 (*0-942299-83-3*, Swerve Ed) Zone Bks.

Panorama Austria. Rand McNally Staff. pap. 19.95 (*0-528-91386-7*) Rand McNally.

Panorama Biblico. Ediciones Arrib Staff.Tr. of Panorama of the Bible. (SPA., Illus.). 1992. 14.99 (*0-685-74972-X*, 490471) Editorial Unilit.

Panorama Biblico de Espiral. Chirstliche.Tr. of Panorama of the Bible. (SPA., Illus.). 14.99 (*0-614-27096-0*, 490471) Editorial Unilit.

Panorama de la Biblia. Alfred Thompson Eade.Tr. of New Panorama Bible Study Course. (SPA.). 32p. 1972. reprint ed. pap. 7.50 (*0-311-03657-0*) Casa Bautista.

Panorama de la France: Intermediate. (FRE.). (C). pap., teacher ed. 35.95 (*0-8442-1483-3*, VF1483-3) NTC Contemp Pub Co.

Panorama de la Literatura Espanola. Nicholson Adams et al. (SPA.). (C). 1994. pap. text 21.95 (*0-942566-17-3*) LinguaText.

Panorama de la Nouvelle Litterature Francaise. G. Picon. (FRE.). 1988. pap. 24.95 (*0-7859-2939-8*) Fr & Eur.

Panorama de la Pegre. Blaise Cendrars. (FRE.). 1986. pap. 16.95 (*0-7859-3189-9*, 2264007605) Fr & Eur.

Panorama de la Poesie Haitienne. Carlos Saint-Louis & Maurice A. Lubin. (B. E. Ser.: No. 51). (FRE.). 1950. 65.00 (*0-8115-3002-7*) Periodicals Srv.

Panorama de la Poesie Haitienne: A Collection of Haitian Poetry from 1804-1950. 2nd ed. Intro. by Henock Vilsaint. 812p. (C). Date not set. pap. 39.95 (*1-881839-41-9*) Educa Vision.

Panorama de la Prensa. Juan Kattan-Ibarra. (SPA.). 160p. 1995. pap. 39.95 incl. audio (*0-8442-7304-X*, 7304X, Natl Textbk Co) NTC Contemp Pub Co.

Panorama de la Prensa: Temas Contemporaneos del Mundo Hispano. Juan Kattan-Ibarra. (SPA.). (C). pap., teacher ed. 8.40 (*0-8442-7155-1*, VS7155-1); pap., student ed. 23.95 (*0-8442-7154-3*, VS7154-3) NTC Contemp Pub Co.

Panorama de la Presse Parisienne: Histoire et Actualite, Genres et Langages. 2nd ed. Ed. by Ernst-Ulrich Grosse & Ernst Seibold. (Werkstruktur und Hintergrund Ser.: Vol. 3). (FRE., Illus.). 264p. 1996. 51.95 (*3-631-30648-2*) P Lang Pubng.

Panorama de las Americas. 8th ed. John A. Crow & George D. Crow. 308p. (C). 1996. pap. text 36.50 (*0-03-017528-3*, Pub. by Harcourt Coll Pubs) Harcourt.

Panorama de las Ideas en Latinoamerica see Pensamiento en America

Panorama del Antiguo Testamento. Paul N. Benware. (Comentario Biblico Portavoz Ser.). Orig. Title: Survey of the Old Testament (Everyman's Bible Commentary). (SPA.). 280p. 1994. pap. 8.99 (*0-8254-1060-6*, Edit Portavoz) Kregel.

Panorama del Antiguo Testamento: Mensaje, Forma y Trasfondo. W. S. LaSor et al. (SPA., Illus.). 688p. 32.00 (*1-55883-400-1*, 6791-0007C) Libros Desafio.

Panorama del Cuento Cubano. Berardo Valdes. 1976. pap. 10.00 (*0-89729-100-X*) Ediciones.

Panorama del Nuevo Testamento. Paul N. Benware. (Comentario Biblico Portavoz Ser.). Orig. Title: Survey of the New Testament (Everyman's Bible Commentary). (SPA.). 304p. 1993. pap. 8.99 (*0-8254-1061-4*, Edit Portavoz) Kregel.

Panorama del Periodismo Puertorriqueno. Jose A. Romeu. (UPREX, Communicacion Ser.: No. 67). 225p. 1985. pap. 6.00 (*0-8477-0067-4*) U of PR Pr.

***Panorama Histborico Forestal de Puerto Rico** rev. ed. Carlos Dominguez-Cristbobal. LC 99-35523. 2000. write for info. (*0-8477-0297-9*) U of PR Pr.

Panorama Historico de la Poesia en Lengua Castellana. Jesus Tome. LC 87-82693. (Huracan Academia Ser.). (SPA.). 336p. 1987. pap. 11.25 (*0-940238-94-2*) Ediciones Huracan.

Panorama Italiano. 4th ed. Charles Speroni & Carlo L. Golino. (ITA.). 276p. (C). 1980. pap. text 40.50 (*0-03-050601-8*, Pub. by Harcourt Coll Pubs) Harcourt.

Panorama Litteraire de l'Europe, 1833-1834. Thomas R. Palfrey. LC 73-128990. (Northwestern Humanities Ser.: No. 22). (FRE.). reprint ed. 29.50 (*0-404-50722-0*) AMS Pr.

Panorama Mysli Wspolczesnych. Geotan Picon. 713p. 1960. 9.00 (*0-940962-20-9*) Polish Inst Art & Sci.

Panorama of Brazilian Law. Ed. by Jacob Dolinger & Keith S. Rosenn. 522p. (C). 1991. 89.95 (*0-935501-37-1*, Pub. by U Miami N-S Ctr) L Rienner.

Panorama of Creation. Carl E. Baugh. (Illus.). 91p. 1992. pap. 7.95 (*1-879366-01-0*) Hearthstone OK.

Panorama of EU Industry, 1996/1997, 2 vols. Orig. Title: EC Industry. 1152p. 1997. 195.00 (*92-827-9301-X*, CO-57-96-000-EN, Pub. by Comm Europ Commun) Bernan Associates.

***Panorama of European Business, 1999.** Office for Official Publications of the European Communites. 552p. 2000. pap. 65.00 (*92-828-7638-1*, CA25-99-043-EN-C, Pub. by Comm Europ Commun) Balogh.

Panorama of Evil: Insights from the Behavioral Sciences, 10. Leonard W. Doob. LC 77-87964. (Contributions in Philosophy Ser.: No. 10). 186p. 1978. 45.00 (*0-313-20030-0*, DPE/, Greenwood Pr) Greenwood.

Panorama of Five Thousand Years: Korean History. 2nd rev. ed. Andrew C. Nahm. (Illus.). 123p. 1997. reprint ed. 27.95 (*0-930878-23-X*) Hollym Intl.

Panorama of Harmonic Analysis. Steven Krantz. (Carus Mathematical Monograph: No. 27). 220p. 1999. pap. text 39.95 (*0-88385-031-1*) Math Assn.

Panorama of Hell. Hideshi Hino. Tr. by Screaming Mad George & Charles Schneider from JPN. (Illus.). 200p. (Orig.). 1989. pap. 9.95 (*0-922233-00-4*) Blast Bks.

Panorama of Hungarian Peasant Painting: Folk Art in Village Life from the Painted Easter Egg to the Tulip Chest. Evelyn Domjan. Ed. by Lorry A. Skwerer. (Illus.). Date not set. pap. 20.00 (*0-933652-19-4*) Domjan Studio.

Panorama of Ideas in Latin America see Philosophical Thought in America

Panorama of Indian Buddhism: Selections from the Maha Bodhi Journal. Ed. by D. C. Ahir. LC 95-910357. (C). 1995. 42.00 (*81-7030-462-8*, Pub. by Sri Satguru Pubns) S Asia.

Panorama of Indian Culture. Prabha Chopra. (Illus.). 183p. 1983. 11.95 (*0-318-36986-9*) Asia Bk Corp.

Panorama of Indian Dances. U. S. Rao. (Raga Nrtya Ser.: No. 6). (C). 1993. 68.50 (*81-7030-330-3*) S Asia.

Panorama of Indian Diplomacy. N. M. Khilnani. 314p. 1981. 27.50 (*0-940500-74-4*) Asia Bk Corp.

Panorama of Jain Art. C. Sivaramurti. (C). 1984. 92.50 (*0-8364-2200-7*, Pub. by Motilal Bnarsidass) S Asia.

Panorama of Jaipur Paintings. Rita Pratap. LC 96-905211. 1996. 105.00 (*81-246-0068-6*, Pub. by DK Pubs Ind) S Asia.

Panorama of Judaism, 2 pts., Pt. 1. Ed. by Leo Jung. 275p. 1974. 14.95 (*0-900689-48-X*) Soncino Pr.

Panorama of Judaism, 2 pts., Pt. 2. Ed. by Leo Jung. 243p. 1974. 14.95 (*0-900689-49-8*) Soncino Pr.

Panorama of Northeast Alabama & Etowah County: Lookout Mountain Meets the Coosa. 2nd ed. Christine S. Puckett & Joe Barnes. (Illus.). 136p. (Orig.). (J). (gr. 4 up). 1992. reprint ed. pap. 8.95 (*0-9633116-0-3*) Starr Pub AL.

***Panorama of Paris: Selections from Tableau de Paris.** Louis-Sebastien Mercier. Ed. by Jeremy D. Popkin. LC 98-51840. 235p. 1999. 50.00 (*0-271-01930-1*) Pa St U Pr.

Panorama of Paris: Selections from Tableau de Paris. Louis-Sebastien Mercier. Ed. by Jeremy D. Popkin. 322p. 1999. pap. 17.00 (*0-271-01931-X*) Pa St U Pr.

Panorama of Prophecy. Lester Sumrall. 83p. (C). 1985. spiral bd. 12.00 (*0-937580-00-7*) Sumrall Pubng.

Panorama of Sanskrit Literature. Satyavrata. LC 98-917236. 292 p. 1998. write for info. (*81-86782-35-4*, Pub. by Publicat Schem) S Asia.

Panorama of Sikh Religion & Philosophy. S. C. Jain. 124p. (C). 1985. 19.95 (*0-317-66152-3*) Asia Bk Corp.

Panorama of Tapestry. Tr. by Converse of International School of Languages Staf. LC 86-71250. (ENG., Illus.). 40p. (Orig.). 1986. pap. 9.95 (*0-945858-00-0*) Am Tapestry Alliance.

Panorama of the Bible see Panorama Biblico

Panorama of the Bible see Panorama Biblico de Espiral

Panorama of the Hudson: Two Hundred Photos Showing Both Sides of the River from New York to Albany. W. G. Shear. 1977. lib. bdg. 200.00 (*0-8490-2405-6*) Gordon Pr.

***Panorama of the Renaissance.** (Illus.). 368p. 2000. 24.98 (*0-8109-8188-2*, Pub. by Abrams) Time Warner.

Panorama of the Renaissance. Margaret Aston. LC 96-15061. (Illus.). 368p. 1996. 45.00 (*0-8109-3704-2*, Pub. by Abrams) Time Warner.

Panorama of the World's Legal Systems, 3 vols., Set. John H. Wigmore. 1206p. 1992. reprint ed. 295.00 (*1-56169-003-1*) Gaunt.

Panorama of Theatre in India. Som Benegal. (Illus.). 1968. 69.50 (*0-614-01824-2*) Elliots Bks.

Panorama of Vesalius: A Lost Design from Titian's Studio. G. S. Cavanagh. (Illus.). 38p. 1996. 275.00 (*0-937543-54-3*) Sacrum Pr.

Panorama 1. Jean-Paul Valette & Rebecca M. Valette. (FRE.). 176p. (C). 1983. pap. text 19.60 (*0-669-05594-8*) McDougal-Littell.

Panorama Portavuz de Jerussalem. Robert Backouse. 32p. 1997. pap. text 8.99 (*0-8254-1052-5*) Kregel.

Panorama Social de America Latina, 1995 Edition. 186p. 1995. 25.00 (*92-1-321429-4*) UN.

Panorama Swiss. Rand McNally Staff. pap. 19.95 (*0-528-91385-9*) Rand McNally.

Panorama 2. Jean-Paul Valette & Rebecca M. Valette. (FRE.). 140p. (C). 1983. pap. 19.96 (*0-669-05345-7*) HM Trade Div.

Panoramas: Poems. Victor Hernandez Cruz. LC 97-16017. 175p. (Orig.). 1997. pap. 12.95 (*1-56689-066-7*) Coffee Hse.

Panoramas Literarios: Espana. Beverly M. Kienzle & Teresa Mendez-Faith. (SPA.). 416p. (C). 1997. pap. text 35.56 (*0-669-21804-9*) HM Trade Div.

Panoramas Literarios: Hispanoamerica. Teresa Mendez-Faith. (SPA.). 416p. (C). 1997. pap. text 35.56 (*0-669-21805-7*) HM Trade Div.

***Panoramas of England.** Photos by Adam Nicolson. (Illus.). 160p. 2000. pap. 17.95 (*1-85799-947-9*) Phoenix Hse.

Panoramas of English Villages. Quiney. 1993. 29.95 (*0-297-83126-7*, Pub. by Weidenfeld & Nicolson) Trafalgar.

***Panoramas of London.** Rowan Moore & Sampson Lloyd. (Illus.). 160p. 2000. pap. 17.95 (*1-85799-954-1*) Phoenix Hse.

Panoramas of Promise: Pacific Northwest Cities & Towns on Nineteenth-Century Lithographs. John W. Reps. LC 84-13164. (Illus.). 93p. 1984. 18.75 (*0-87422-016-5*); pap. 10.95 (*0-87422-017-3*) Wash St U Pr.

Panoramas of the Far East: Photographs by Lois Conner. Ed. by Constance Sullivan. (Photographers at Work Ser.). (Illus.). 60p. (Orig.). 1993. pap. 16.95 (*1-56098-331-0*) Smithsonian.

***Panoramas Overviews Vignettes Snapshots & Apocalypses Unveilings.** Herb Jahn. 206p. 1999. 19.95 (*0-9631951-9-0*) Exegeses.

Panoramic Colombia. Enrique Pulacio. LC 98-199846. 1998. 65.00 (*958-9393-38-1*) Villegas Ed.

P

Panoramic History of Agriculture in Puerto Rico. Juana G. Garcia. (Puerto Rico Ser.). 1979. lib. bdg. 59.95 (*0-8490-2982-1*) Gordon Pr.

Panoramic History of the Indian People. D. B. Vohra. (C). 1992. 47.50 (*81-215-0550-X*, Pub. by M Manoharial) Coronet Bks.

***Panoramic Journey Through Johannesburg & Surrounds.** 2000. 24.95 (*1-86872-469-7*, Pub. by Struik Pubs) BHB Intl.

***Panoramic Journey Through KwaZulu-Natal.** 2000. 24.95 (*1-86872-471-9*, Pub. by Struik Pubs) BHB Intl.

***Panoramic Journey Through Mpumalanga.** 2000. 24.95 (*1-86872-470-0*, Pub. by Struik Pubs) BHB Intl.

***Panoramic Journey Through the Garden Route.** 2000. 24.95 (*1-86872-394-1*, Pub. by Struik Pubs) BHB Intl.

Panoramic Maps of Cities in the United States & Canada. 1991. lib. bdg. 79.95 (*0-8490-4330-1*) Gordon Pr.

Panoramic Maps of Cities in the United States & Canada: A Checklist. 1995. lib. bdg. 252.99 (*0-8490-6766-9*) Gordon Pr.

Panoramic New York. Photos by Richard Berenholtz. LC 93-11114. (Illus.). 1993. text 35.00 (*0-86565-146-9*) Vendome.

Panoramic Photography. Joseph Meehan. LC 95-49226. (Illus.). 144p. 1996. pap. 27.50 (*0-8174-5347-4*, Amphoto) Watsn-Guptill.

Panoramic Views of St. Petersburg from 1716-1835. Larissa Salmina-Haskell. (Illus.). 32p. 1995. pap. 8.95 (*1-85444-046-2*, 0462, Pub. by Ashmolean Mus) A Schwartz & Co.

Panoramic World: A Global Adventure in 80 Astounding Images. Everen T. Brown. (Illus.). 88p. (Orig.). 1993. pap. 19.95 (*0-9636596-0-X*) E T Brown Spec.

***Panov Attack III: The Attack with 5...g6.** Eric Schiller. (Illus.). 168p. 1998. pap. 11.95 (*0-945470-67-3*) Chess Ent.

Panov Attack I. Eric Schiller. 99p. (Orig.). 1994. pap. 9.95 (*0-945470-43-6*) Chess Ent.

Panov Attack II. Eric Schiller. 127p. (Orig.). 1995. pap. 9.96 (*0-945470-47-9*) Chess Ent.

***Panriga: Tacarigua's Contribution to the Evolution of the Steelband Phenomenon in Trinidad & Tobago.** Kenrick P. Thomas. LC 99-74718. (Illus.). 192p. 2000. pap. 20.00 (*0-9641929-3-4*) Orig Wrld Pr.

Panruum Pilugungella. large type ed. Mary Tunuchuk & Abby Augustine. (ESK., Illus.). 8p. (J). (gr. k-3). 1997. pap. text 6.00 (*1-58084-010-8*) Lower Kuskokwim.

***Pan's Daughters.** Lois Hirshkowitz. Ed. by Jules Mann. (Illus.). 76p. 1998. pap. 12.00 (*1-879457-58-X*, Finders Keepers Pr) Norton Coker Pr.

Pan's Eyes. Joel Oppenheimer. LC 74-77760. (Haystack Bks.). 64p. 1974. pap. 3.50 (*0-685-46899-2*) Mulch Pr.

Pan's Garden: A Volume of Nature Stories. Algernon Blackwood. LC 74-157772. (Short Story Index Reprint Ser.). (Illus.). 1977. reprint ed. 30.95 (*0-8369-3884-4*) Ayer.

Pan's Travail: Environmental Problems of the Ancient Greeks & Romans. J. Donald Hughes. (Ancient Society & History Ser.). 288p. (C). 1996. reprint ed. pap. text 16.95 (*0-8018-5363-X*) Johns Hopkins.

Pansies. Scott D. Appell. LC 99-19215. 1999. text 15.00 (*1-56799-771-6*) M Friedman Pub Grp Inc.

Pansies & Roses. Bob Svoboda. 1997. pap. 56.95 (*1-57553-684-6*) Watermrk Pr.

Pansies, Violas & Violettas: The Complete Guide. Rodney Fuller. (Illus.). 240p. 1993. pap. 22.95 (*1-85223-748-1*, Pub. by Crolwood) Trafalgar.

Panslavism & National Identity in Russia & in the Balkans, 1830-1880: Images of the Self & Others. Jelena Milojkovic-Djuric. 177p. 1994. 30.50 (*0-88033-291-3*, 394, Pub. by East Eur Monographs) Col U Pr.

Panslavonic Folklore. Walter W. Strickland. LC 78-63227. (Folktale Ser.). 1980. reprint ed. 32.50 (*0-404-16166-9*) AMS Pr.

***Pansy Ann & Eva Stories.** Liz Wethington. Ed. by Noreen Wise. (Book-a-Day Collection). (Illus.). 48p. (YA). (ps up). 2000. pap. 6.95 (*1-58584-419-5*) Huckleberry CT.

Pansy Packrat. Dave Sargent & Pat Sargent. LC 97-27202. (Illus.). (J). 1998. write for info. (*1-56763-382-X*); pap. write for info. (*1-56763-383-8*) Ozark Pub.

Pansy Sonata. Kenneth Weyerhaeuser. (Illus.). 278p. 1994. pap. 14.95 (*0-943383-08-0*) FirstHand Ltd.

Pant Fitting Made Easy. Karen Howland. (Illus.). 32p. 1998. pap. 14.99 (*0-9648964-4-3*) Kensinger.

Panta 1: The Philosophical Basis of the New Testament. James A. Ketzel. 6p. 1996. 59.50 (*0-7618-0582-6*) U Pr of Amer.

Pantagleize see Ghelderode: Seven Plays

Pantagruel. Francois Rabelais. (FRE.). 1964. pap. 4.50 (*0-685-11475-9*, 1240) Fr & Eur.

Pantagruel. Francois Rabelais. Ed. by V. L. Saulnier. (FRE.). 448p. 1973. pap. 13.95 (*0-7859-4556-3*) Fr & Eur.

Pantagruel. Francois Rabelais. (Folio Ser.: No. 387). (FRE.). pap. 11.95 (*2-07-036387-2*) Schoenhof.

Pantagruel & les Sophistes: Contribution a l'Histoire de l'Humanisme Chretien au XVlieme Siecle. G. Defaux. (International Archives of the History of Ideas Ser.: No. 63). 258p. 1973. lib. bdg. 99.50 (*90-247-1566-0*) Kluwer Academic.

Pantagrueline Prognostication Pour l'An 1533: Avec les Almanachs pour les Ans 1533, 1535 et 1541. la Grande et Vraye Pronostication Nouvelle De 1544. Francois Rabelais. (FRE., Illus.). 180p. 1975. pap. 24.95 (*0-7859-5378-7*) Fr & Eur.

Pantaleon y las Visitadoras. 3rd ed. Mario Vargas Llosa. (SPA.). 309p. 1992. pap. 14.95 (*0-7859-0563-4*, 843223060X) Fr & Eur.

Pantalones Con Ajuste Perfecto. Cy DeCosse Inc., Staff. (Singer Sewing Reference Library). (SPA., Illus.). 128p. 1992. 17.95 (*0-86573-281-7*) Creat Pub Intl.

Pantaloon. J. M. Barrie. Ed. by William-Alan Landes. LC 93-19587. 1993. pap. 6.00 (*0-88734-316-3*) Players Pr.

Pantaloon. Kathryn Jackson. 32p. 1999. 9.95 (*0-307-10227-0*) Golden Bks Pub.

***Pantanal: Understanding & Protecting the World's Largest Wetland.** Ed. by Frederick A. Swarts. (Illus.). 336p. 2000. pap. 19.95 (*1-55778-791-3*) Paragon Hse.

Pantanal of Mato Grosso (Brazil) World's Largest Wetlands. Francis Dov Por. (Monographiae Biologicae). 120p. (C). 1995. text 92.50 (*0-7923-3481-7*) Kluwer Academic.

Pantanal of Pocon E: Biota & Ecology in the Northern Section of the World's Largest Pristine Wetland. Charles W. Heckman. LC 97-45514. (Monographiae Biologicae Ser.). 622p. 1998. lib. bdg. 285.00 (*0-7923-4863-X*) Kluwer Academic.

Pantarch: A Biography of Stephen Pearl Andrews. Madeleine B. Stern. LC 68-18386. 236p. reprint ed. pap. 73.20 (*0-7837-1242-1*, 204137900020) Bks Demand.

Panteleimon Kulish: A Sketch of His Life & Times. George S. Luckyj. (East European Monographs: No. 127). 229p. 1983. text 55.50 (*0-88033-016-3*, Pub. by East Eur Monographs) Col U Pr.

Pantera: Selections from "Far Beyond Driven" Ed. by Aaron Stang. (Authentic Tab Ser.). 76p. (Orig.). 1994. pap. 22.95 (*0-89724-273-4*, GF0650) Wrner Bros.

Pantera: The Great Southern Trendhill. Ed. by Aaron Stang. (Illus.). 96p. (Orig.). 1996. pap. text 22.95 (*1-57623-515-7*, PG9652) Wrner Bros.

Pantera - Selection from Two Albums. Ed. by Aaron Stang. 148p. (Orig.). 1994. pap. 24.95 (*0-89724-281-5*, GF0572) Wrner Bros.

Pantex Plant: Practices, Policy, & the Environmental Impact of the Final Assembly Point. rev. ed. Greg LeRoy. (Illus.). 35p. 1996. pap. text 4.00 (*0-945210-00-0*) Public Search.

***Panthans.** Olaf Caroe. 544p. 2000. text 110.00 (*0-7103-0682-2*) Col U Pr.

Panthee. A. Hardy. Ed. by P. Ford. (FRE.). 92p. (C). pap. 19.95 (*0-85989-164-X*, Pub. by Univ Exeter Pr) Northwestern U Pr.

Pantheism & Christianity, 1884. John Hunt. LC 78-102573. 405p. 1996. reprint ed. text 29.95 (*1-56459-569-2*) Kessinger Pub.

Pantheisticon: The Career of John Toland. Robert R. Evans. LC 90-41218. (American University Studies: History: Ser. IX, Vol. 98). X, 234p. (C). 1991. text 40.95 (*0-8204-1414-X*) P Lang Pubng.

Pantheon. William F. DeVault. Ed. by Jan Innes. (Illus.). 64p. 1997. pap. 10.00 (*0-9659576-0-8*, 5561) PanteraPress.

Pantheon: An Apotheosis. Richard S. Hoehler. LC 77-84798. (Illus.). 1977. pap. 10.00 (*0-930590-01-5*) R Hoehler Pub.

Pantheon: Design, Meaning & Progeny. William L. MacDonald. (Harvard Paperbacks Ser.). (Illus.). 160p. (C). 1976. pap. text 15.95 (*0-674-65346-7*) HUP.

Pantheon Great Jazz. Tom Piazza. 1991. pap. 14.95 (*0-679-40187-3*) McKay.

Pantheons of the Megaverse. C. J. Carella et al. Ed. by Alex Marciniszyn et al. (Rifts Conversion Bks.: No. 2). (Illus.). 208p. (Orig.). (YA). (gr. 8 up). 1994. pap. 20.95 (*0-916211-68-1*, 811) Palladium Bks.

***Panther.** Martin Booth. LC 00-28358. (Illus.). (J). 2001. write for info. (*0-689-82976-0*) McElderry Bks.

Panther. Uwe Feist & Bruce Culver. 270p. 1995. 75.00 (*0-9633824-4-6*) Ryton Pubns.

Panther: A Pictorial History of the Black Panthers & the Story Behind the Film. Mario Van Peebles et al. LC 95-7689. (Illus.). 192p. 1995. pap. 16.95 (*1-55704-227-6*, Pub. by Newmarket) Norton.

Panther: Panzerkampfwagen, No. 5. Horst Schubert. LC 91-60861. (Illus.). 48p. 1991. pap. 9.95 (*0-88740-314-X*) Schiffer.

***Panther: Shadow of the Swamp.** Jonathan London. LC 99-86437. (Illus.). 2000. 15.99 (*1-56402-623-X*) Candlewick Pr.

Panther & Its Variants, Vol. I. Walter J. Spielberger. Tr. by Don Cox from GER. LC 92-60360. (Spielberger German Armor Ser.). (Illus.). 288p. 1992. text 49.95 (*0-88740-397-2*) Schiffer.

Panther & the Hind: A Theological History of Angelicanism. Aidan Nichols. 208p. 1993. pap. text 24.95 (*0-567-29232-0*, Pub. by T & T Clark) Bks Intl VA.

Panther & the Lash. Langston Hughes. 128p. 1992. pap. 11.00 (*0-679-73659-X*) Vin Bks.

Panther Dream: A Story of the African Rainforest. Bob Weir & Wendy Weir. (J). 1993. 10.15 (*0-606-05969-5*, Pub. by Turtleback) Demco.

Panther Famiy. Horst Scheibert. LC 89-63356. (Illus.). 48p. 1989. pap. 9.95 (*0-88740-202-X*) Schiffer.

***Panther Girl.** Maity Schrecengost. LC 99-20002. (Illus.). 128p. (J). (gr. 3-5). 1999. pap. 5.95 (*0-929895-29-0*, Hoot Owl Bks) Maupin Hse.

Panther Glade. Helen Cavanagh. LC 92-23406. 160p. (J). (gr. 5-9). 1993. mass mkt. 16.00 (*0-671-75617-6*) S&S Bks Yung.

Panther in Action. (Armor in Action Ser.). (Illus.). 50p. 1984. pap. 9.95 (*0-89747-044-3*, 2011) Squad Sig Pubns.

Panther in the Basement. Amos Oz. Tr. by Nicholas De Lange from HEB. LC 97-20577. 160p. 1997. 21.00 (*0-15-100287-8*) Harcourt.

Panther in the Basement. Amos Oz. 160p. 1998. pap. 11.00 (*0-15-600630-8*, Harvest Bks) Harcourt.

Panther in the Sky. James A. Thom. 768p. 1990. mass mkt. 6.99 (*0-345-36638-7*) Ballantine Pub Grp.

***Panther Is a Black Cat: A Study in Depth of the Black Panther Party--Its Origins, Its Goals, Its Struggle for Survival.** Reginald Major. 308p. 2000. reprint ed. pap. write for info. (*1-58073-027-2*) BCP Bks.

Panther Medium Tank, 1943-45. Hilary Doyle & Tom Jentz. (New Vanguard Ser.: No. 21). (Illus.). 48p. 1996. pap. 12.95 (*1-85532-476-8*, Pub. by Ospry) Stackpole.

Panther Mystery. Created by Gertrude Chandler Warner. LC 98-19107. (Boxcar Children Ser.: No. 66). (Illus.). 128p. (J). (gr. 2-5). 1998. pap. 3.95 (*0-8075-6328-5*); lib. bdg. 13.95 (*0-8075-6327-7*) A Whitman.

Panther Passing Across: Poems by R. D. Baker. R. D. Baker. (Poetry Chapbook Ser.). (Illus.). 28p. (Orig.). 1995. pap. 4.00 (*1-887641-03-3*) Argonne Hotel Pr.

***Panther Tank.** Hughes. LC 00-26295. (Illus.). 96p. 2000. 17.95 (*0-7603-0841-1*, 129570AP, Pub. by MBI Pubg) Motorbooks Intl.

***Panther Tank.** Matthew Hughes & C. Mann. (Weapons of War Ser.: Vol. 4). 96p. 2000. 60.00 (*1-86227-072-4*, Pub. by Spellmnt Pubs) St Mut.

Panther Valley Tales. James Haldeman. Ed. by Sidney Moore. LC 99-179466. (Illus.). 165p. 1997. pap. 10.95 (*0-9643905-1-5*) E McKeever.

Panther Woman: Five Tales from the Cassette Recorder. Sarah Kirsch. Tr. & Intro. by Marion Faber. LC 89-30406. (European Women Writers Ser.). 128p. 1989. reprint ed. pap. 39.70 (*0-608-01858-9*, 206250800003) Bks Demand.

Panthers in the Skins of Men. Charles Nelson. 1989. pap. 9.95 (*0-8216-2006-1*, Univ Books) Carol Pub Group.

Panthers of the Coastal Plain. Charles R. Humphreys. LC 94-90596. (Illus.). 240p. (Orig.). 1994. pap. 19.95 (*0-9621623-1-0*) Fig Lf NC.

Panther's Prey. Doreen O. Malek. 432p. (Orig.). 1996. mass mkt. 5.99 (*0-8439-4015-8*) Dorchester Pub Co.

Panto Sphinx. Michael Henry. 62p. (Orig.). 1991. pap. 14.95 (*1-870612-46-9*, Pub. by Enitha Pr) Dufour.

Pantomime Book. Paul Harris. 224p. 1996. pap. 27.00 (*0-7206-1000-1*, Pub. by P Owen Ltd); pap. 27.00 (*0-7206-1013-3*, Pub. by P Owen Ltd) Dufour.

Pantomimes for Stage & Study. T. Earl Pardoe. LC 73-173118. 404p. 1972. reprint ed. 29.95 (*0-405-08833-7*, Pub. by Blom Pubns) Ayer.

Pantomimes 101. James W. Gousseff. 1974. pap. 9.95 (*0-87129-190-8*, P13) Dramatic Pub.

Pantone Black Colors & Effects. 1992. write for info. (*1-881509-16-8*) Pantone.

Pantone Book of Color. 1992. write for info. (*1-881509-29-X*) Pantone.

Pantone Color & Black Selector. 1992. write for info. (*1-881509-19-2*) Pantone.

Pantone Color Formula Guide 1000. 1992. write for info. (*1-881509-01-X*) Pantone.

Pantone Color Selector - Film. 1992. write for info. (*1-881509-17-6*) Pantone.

Pantone Color Selector - Foil. 1992. write for info. (*1-881509-18-4*) Pantone.

Pantone Color Selector 1000. 1992. write for info. (*1-881509-02-8*) Pantone.

Pantone Color Specifier 1000, Set, Vols. 1a &1B. 1992. write for info. (*1-881509-03-6*) Pantone.

Pantone Color Specifier 747XR. 1992. write for info. (*1-881509-21-4*) Pantone.

Pantone Color Tint Selector 1000. 1992. write for info. (*1-881509-04-4*) Pantone.

***Pantone Colors & Black: Duotone Guide for Adobe Photoshop.** Brady Peery. (Illus.). 300p. 1998. pap. 129.95 (*0-9651388-5-2*) PickerBook.

***Pantone Colors & Black Studio Edition: Duotone Guide for Adobe Photoshop.** Brady Peery. (Illus.). 300p. 1999. pap. 199.00 (*0-9651388-4-4*) PickerBook.

***Pantone Guide to Communicating with Color.** Leatrice Eiseman. (Illus.). 2000. pap. text 35.00 (*0-9666383-2-8*) Design Books.

Pantone Library of Color. 1992. write for info. (*1-881509-00-1*) Pantone.

Pantone Metallic Color Guide. 1992. write for info. (*1-881509-13-3*) Pantone.

Pantone Metallic Color Specifier. 1992. write for info. (*1-881509-14-1*) Pantone.

Pantone Metallic Integrated Process Color Selector. 1992. write for info. (*1-881509-15-X*) Pantone.

Pantone Pastel Color Formula Guide. 1992. write for info. (*1-881509-11-7*) Pantone.

Pantone Pastel Color Specifier. 1992. write for info. (*1-881509-12-5*) Pantone.

Pantone Process Color Imaging Guide 1000. 1992. write for info. (*1-881509-06-0*) Pantone.

Pantone Process Color Simulator 1000. 1992. write for info. (*1-881509-05-2*) Pantone.

Pantone Process Color System Guide: EURO Version. 1992. write for info. (*1-881509-09-5*) Pantone.

Pantone Process Color System Guide: SWOP Version. 1992. write for info. (*1-881509-07-9*) Pantone.

Pantone Process Color System Specifier: EURO Version. 1992. write for info. (*1-881509-10-9*) Pantone.

Pantone Process Color System Specifier: SWOP Version, Vols. 12A & 12B. 1992. write for info. (*1-881509-08-7*) Pantone.

Pantone Textile Color Guide. 1992. pap. write for info. (*1-881509-32-X*) Pantone.

Pantone Textile Color Selector. 1992. write for info. (*1-881509-31-1*) Pantone.

Pantone Textile Color Specifier. 1992. pap. write for info. (*1-881509-33-8*) Pantone.

Pantone Textile Color System. 1992. write for info. (*1-881509-30-3*); pap. write for info. (*1-881509-34-6*) Pantone.

Pantone Two Color Selector. 1992. write for info. (*1-881509-20-6*) Pantone.

Pantone Web Color Resource Kit. Hayden Development Team Staff. 1997. pap. 65.00 (*0-614-28472-4*, Hayden Sftwre) MCP SW Interactive.

***Pantry Cooking: Unlocking Your Pantry's Potential.** Cheryl F. Driggs. (Illus.). 160p. 2000. pap. 14.95 (*0-9658909-2-9*) CFD Pubns.

Pantry Print. Courage Books Staff. 160p. 1997. 5.98 (*0-7624-0222-9*, Courage) Running Pr.

***Pants.** Shelley Stenhouse. Ed. by David Baratier. 40p. 1999. pap. 6.00 (*1-886350-87-6*, Pub. by Pavement Saw) SPD-Small Pr Dist.

Pants down Sailor. (Kake Ser.: No. 18). 1997. pap. 11.00 (*1-879055-16-3*) Tom Finland.

Pants, Etc.! Draw Your Own Pant Pattern for a Custom Fit! Margaret E. Islander. 66p. 1991. spiral bd. 14.95 (*0-9629081-0-X*) Maring Pubns.

Pants, Etc! Draw Your Own Pants Pattern for a Custom Fit! rev. ed. Margaret E. Islander. (Illus.). 66p. 1991. 14.95 (*0-9629081-1-8*) Maring Pubns.

Pants Fitting: A Truly Make Sense Method. Margaret Komives. (Illus.). 13p. (Orig.). 1995. pap., ring bd. 6.95 (*1-878017-05-5*) Maggi K Ent.

Pants for Any Body. rev. ed. Pati Palmer & Susan Pletsch. LC 82-61290. (Illus.). 128p. (Orig.). 1982. pap. 8.95 (*0-935278-08-7*) Palmer-Pletsch.

***Pants with Pockets: And Other Tips on Managing an ADD/ADHD Child.** 2nd ed. Candi Matos & Chris Matos. Ed. by Ethel Maxam Crews & Patricia Richter. (SPA.). 138p. 1999. pap. 13.95 (*1-891990-02-0*) Herbal Way.

Pants with Pockets & Other Tips on Managing an ADD/ADHD Child. 2nd rev. ed. Candi Matos & Chris Matos. Ed. by Ethel Maxam Crews. (Illus.). x, 200p. 1998. reprint ed. pap. 13.95 (*1-891990-00-4*, 18891990004) Herbal Way.

Pantun Melayu. Ed. by Richard J. Wilkinson & Richard O. Winstedt. LC 77-87058. reprint ed. 32.50 (*0-404-16880-9*) AMS Pr.

Panuel & the Carousel. large type ed. Gerald B. Mirra. Ed. by Karen Bernardo. (Illus.). 32p. (J). (gr. 2-3). 1996. 6.95 (*0-9655486-0-0*) Signature Pub.

Panuelo de Seda. Alma F. Ada. (Cuentos con Alma Ser.). (SPA., Illus.). 24p. (J). 1993. 16.95 (*1-56492-105-0*) Laredo.

***Panza: The Legacy of a Collector : the Giuseppe Panza Di Biumo Collection at the Museum of Contemporary Art, Los Angeles.** Museum of Contemporary Art (Los Angeles, Calif.). Giuseppe Panza di Biumo Collection. LC 99-47687. 1999. write for info. (*0-914357-73-5*) Los Angeles Mus Contemp.

Panzer: A Pictorial Documentation. Horst Scheibert. LC 89-63369. (Illus.). 272p. 1989. 29.95 (*0-88740-207-0*) Schiffer.

***Panzer: The Illustrated History of Germany's Armored Forces in WWII.** S. Hart. LC 99-40954. (Illus.). 176p. 1999. 24.95 (*0-7603-0725-3*, 128796AP, Pub. by MBI Pubg) Motorbooks Intl.

Panzer Battles. F. W. Von Mellenthin. 1984. mass mkt. 6.95 (*0-345-32158-8*) Ballantine Pub Grp.

Panzer Called Iron Maiden. Dahk Knox. 325p. (C). 1994. 19.95 (*1-881116-07-7*, 040, Pub. by Black Forest Pr) Epic Bk Promo.

Panzer Colors: Markings of the German Army Panzer Forces 1939-45, Vol. 2. Bruce Culver. (Illus.). 96p. 1996. reprint ed. pap. 14.95 (*0-89747-069-9*, 6253) Squad Sig Pubns.

Panzer Commander: The Memoirs of Colonel Hans Von Luck. Hans Von Luck. 368p. 1991. mass mkt. 6.50 (*0-440-20802-5*) Dell.

Panzer Commander: The Memoirs of Colonel Hans Von Luck. Hans Von Luck. LC 88-39662. 301p. 1989. 39.95 (*0-275-93115-3*, C3115, Praeger Pubs) Greenwood.

Panzer Cops. Mamoru Oshii. (Hellhounds Ser.). (Illus.). 1997. pap. text 14.95 (*1-56971-256-5*) Dark Horse Comics.

Panzer Divisions. Martin Windrow. (Men-at-Arms Ser.: No. 24). (Illus.). 48p. pap. 12.95 (*0-85045-434-4*, 9001, Pub. by Osprey) Stackpole.

Panzer IV. Horst Scheibert. (Illus.). 48p. pap. 9.95 (*0-88740-677-7*) Schiffer.

***Panzer IV, Vol. 6081.** Kevin Hjermstad. (Illus.). 64p. 2000. pap. 9.95 (*0-89747-413-9*) Squad Sig Pubns.

Panzer IV & Its Variants, Vol. 3. Walter J. Spielberger. LC 93-84495. (Illus.). 168p. 1993. 29.95 (*0-88740-515-0*) Schiffer.

Panzer IV Family. Horst Scheibert. Tr. by Edward Force from GER. LC 91-62754. (Illus.). 48p. 1991. pap. 9.95 (*0-88740-359-X*) Schiffer.

Panzer IV (Lang) Horst Riebenstahl & Horst Scheibert. LC 96-213586. (Illus.). 48p. 1996. pap. 9.95 (*0-7643-0094-6*) Schiffer.

Panzer General: Official Strategy Guide. Ed Dille. 1995. pap. 19.95 (*1-55958-727-X*) Prima Pub.

***Panzer General 3D Assault Official Strategies & Secrets.** Mark H. Walker. 352p. 1999. pap. 19.99 (*0-7821-2681-2*) Sybex.

Panzer General 2: The Official Strategy Guide. Michael Knight. LC 97-69767. (Secrets of the Game Ser.). 288p. 1997. per. 19.99 (*0-7615-0105-3*) Prima Pub.

Panzer Grenadier - Grossdeutschland. Ronald Redmon & James Cuccarese. (Specials Ser.). (Illus.). 80p. 1993. pap. 14.95 (*0-89747-061-3*, 6009) Squad Sig Pubns.

Panzer-Grenadier, Motorcycle & Panzer Reconnaissance Units, 1935-1945: A History of the German Motorized Units, 1935-1945. Horst Scheibert. LC 90-62984. (Illus.). 176p. 1990. 29.95 (*0-88740-285-2*) Schiffer.

Panzer Kampfwagen IV. Thomas Jentz & Hilary Doyle. (Panzer Tracts Ser.). 60p. 1997. pap. 19.95 (*0-9648793-4-4*) Darlington Prods.

Panzer Leader. Heinz Guderian. (Great Commander Ser.). 524p. 1998. reprint ed. 30.00 (*1-56515-021-X*) Collect Reprints.

Panzer Leader. Heinz Guderian. Tr. by Constantine Fitzgibbon from GER. LC 95-43889. (GER., Illus.). 554p. 1996. reprint ed. pap. 17.95 (0-306-80689-4) Da Capo.

Panzer Leader. Heinz Guderian. LC 79-19897. 1981. reprint ed. 25.00 (0-89201-076-2) Zenger Pub.

***Panzer Legions: A Guide to the German Army Tank Divisions of World War II & Their Commanders.** Samuel W. Mitcham, Jr. 2000. lib. bdg. write for info. (0-313-31640-6, Greenwood Pr) Greenwood.

Panzer 35 (t) Horst Scheibert. (Illus.). 48p. pap. 9.95 (0-88740-678-5) Schiffer.

Panzer III. Horst Scheibert. (Illus.). 48p. pap. 9.95 (0-88740-676-9) Schiffer.

***Panzer Tracts No. 8 Sturmgeschutz: -S.Pak to Sturmmoerser.** Thomas Jentz. (Illus.). 60p. 2000. 19.95 (1-892848-04-X) Darlington Prods.

Panzer Truppen: The Complete Guide to the Creation & Combat Employment of Germany's Tank Force - 1943-1945/Formations - Organizations - Tactics Combat Reports - Unit Strengths - Statistics. Ed. by Thomas L. Jentz. (Illus.). 224p. 1996. 49.95 (0-7643-0080-6) Schiffer.

Panzer Truppen: The Complete Guide to the Creation & Combat Employment of Germany's Tank Force, 1933-1942. Thomas L. Jentz. (Illus.). 176p. (C). (gr. 13). 1996. 49.95 (0-88740-915-6) Schiffer.

Panzer II. Horst Scheibert. (Illus.). 48p. pap. 9.95 (0-88740-674-2) Schiffer.

Panzer II & Its Variants. Walter J. Spielberger. Tr. by Edward Force. LC 92-62386. (Spielberger German Armor Ser.: Vol. III). (Illus.). 168p. 1993. 29.95 (0-88740-448-0) Schiffer.

Panzerfaust & Other German Infantry Anti-Tank Weapons. Wolfgang Fleischer. (Illus.). 48p. pap. 9.95 (0-88740-672-6) Schiffer.

Panzergrenadiers in Action. Ronald Redmon. (Combat Troops in Action Ser.). (Illus.). 1995. pap. 9.95 (0-89747-096-6, 3005) Squad Sig Pubns.

Panzerjager. Horst Scheibert. LC 98-134350. 48p. 1998. pap. 9.95 (0-7643-0395-3) Schiffer.

***Panzerjager: Tank Hunter.** William B. Folkestad. LC 97-27305. (Illus.). 130p. 2000. pap. 12.95 (1-57249-182-5) White Mane Pub.

Panzerjager (Tank Hunter) Tank Hunter. William B. Folkestad. LC 97-27305. 119p. 1997. 24.95 (1-57249-074-8, Burd St Pr) White Mane Pub.

Panzerkampfwagen MAUS. Thomas L. Jentz. 60p. 1997. pap. 15.95 (0-9648793-2-8) Darlington Prods.

Panzerkampfwagen 38. Horst Scheibert. Tr. by Don Cox from GER. LC 97-219972. 48p. 1997. pap. 9.95 (0-7643-0298-1) Schiffer.

Panzerkorps Grossdeutschland: A Pictorial History. Helmuth Spaeter. Tr. by Edward Force from GER. LC 90-60468. (Illus.). 248p. 1990. 29.95 (0-88740-245-3) Schiffer.

Panzers Tiger I & II, Vols. I & II. Horst Scheibert. (Illus.). 48p. pap. 9.95 (0-88740-679-3) Schiffer.

Pao Zhi: An Introduction to Use of Processed Chinese Medicinals to Enhance Therapeutic Effects. Philippe Sionneau. Tr. by Bob Flaws. 350p. (Orig.). 1995. pap. 34.95 (0-936185-62-7) Blue Poppy Pr.

Paolino, Torna a Casa! Brigitte Weninger.Tr. of Where Have You Gone, Davy?. (ITA., Illus.). 32p. (J). (gr. k-3). 15.95 (88-8203-053-9, Pub. by North-South Bks NYC) Chronicle Bks.

Paolino, Tu Esageri ! Brigitte Weninger.Tr. of What Have You Done, Davy?. (ITA., Illus.). 32p. (J). (gr. k-3). 15.95 (88-8203-023-7, Pub. by North-South Bks NYC) Chronicle Bks.

Paolo Beni: A Biographical & Critical Study. P. B. Diffley. (Oxford Modern Languages & Literature Monographs). 206p. 1988. 69.00 (0-19-815855-6) OUP.

Paolo da Venezia. Michelangelo Muraro. LC 77-84667. (Illus.). 1970. 95.00 (0-271-00098-8) A Wofsy Fine Arts.

Paolo Giovio: The Historian & the Crisis of Sixteenth-Century Italy. T. Price Zimmermann. LC 95-4302. 400p. 1995. text 42.50 (0-691-04378-7, Pub. by Princeton U Pr) Cal Prin Full Svc.

Paolo Quagliati: Libro Primo de'Madrigali a Quattro Voci. Paolo Quagliati. Ed. by Judith Cohen. (Recent Researches in Music of the Baroque Era Ser.: Vol. RRB79). (Illus.). xxii, 110p. 1996. pap. 45.00 (0-89579-339-3) A-R Eds.

Paolo Quagliati: Recercate, et Canzone, Libro Primo a Quattro Voci, Rome, 1601. Ed. by Brian Mann. LC 94-1961. (Italian Instrumental Music of the Sixteenth & Early Seventeenth Centuries Ser.: Vol. 15). 168p. 1994. text 77.00 (0-8240-4514-9) Garland.

Paolo Rolli & the Italian Circle in London, 1715-1744. George E. Dorris. (Studies in Italian Literature: No. 2). (Orig.). 1967. pap. text 50.00 (0-89925-329-6) Mouton.

Paolo Tenorista in a New Fragment of the Italian Ars Nova. Nino Pirrotta. (Illus.). 83p. 1961. 22.50 (0-934082-07-3, M61-2053) Theodore Front.

Paolo Uccello. Franco Borsi & Stefano Borsi. LC 93-39788. (Illus.). 376p. 1994. 95.00 (0-8109-3919-3, Pub. by Abrams) Time Warner.

Paolo Uccello, Domenico Veneziano, Andrea del Castagno. Annarita Paolieri. Tr. by Lisa C. Pelletti from ITA. (Library of Great Masters). (Illus.). 80p. (Orig.). 1991. pap. 12.99 (1-878351-20-6) Riverside NY.

Paolozzi Portraits. Robin Gibson. (Illus.). 54p. 1989. pap. 14.95 (0-904017-87-7, Pub. by Natl Port Gall) Antique Collect.

Paon. Marcel Ayme. (Folio - Cadet Ser.: No. 87). (FRE., Illus.). (J). 1985. pap. 8.95 (2-07-031087-6) Schoenhof.

***Pap Bitter Ice.** Barbara Kent Lawrence. 2000. pap. write for info. (0-688-17777-8, Wm Morrow) Morrow Avon.

Pap Smear. 3rd ed. Mathilde E. Boon & Albert J. Suurmeijer. 384p. 1996. text 54.00 (3-7186-5857-7) Gordon & Breach.

Pap Smear: Translation in Japanese. 3rd ed. T. Tanaka & Tadashi Sugishita. (JPN.). 310p. 1998. text 90.00 (4-915929-04-3) Gordon & Breach.

Pap Test: The Procedure & Results. Mitchel S. Hoffman. Ed. by William Spellacy. (Women's Health Ser.). (Illus.). 24p. (Orig.). 1996. pap. 2.95 (1-885274-20-3) Health InfoNet Inc.

Pap War-h to Mak. 3rd rev. ed. James F. Dunnigan. LC 93-6568. 1993. pap. 16.00 (0-688-12157-8, Wm Morrow) Morrow Avon.

Papa! Philipe Corentin. LC 96-27138. (Illus.). 32p. (J). (ps-1). 1997. 13.95 (0-8118-1640-0) Chronicle Bks.

Papa: Can She Take It. Gary Sutton. 104p. 1999. pap. 4.95 (0-7392-0104-2, PO2995) Morris Pubng.

Papa: Hemingway in Key West. rev. ed. James McLendon. LC 88-81528. (Illus.). 240p. 1990. reprint ed. 24.95 (0-911607-08-0) Langley Pr Inc.

Papa: Hemingway in Key West. rev. ed. James McLendon. LC 88-81528. (Illus.). 240p. 1995. reprint ed. pap. 14.95 (0-911607-07-2) Langley Pr Inc.

Papa: The Legendary Lives of Ernest Hemingway, a Play in Two Acts. limited ed. John De Groot. Ed. by Tom Trusky. (Hemingway Western Studies). (Illus.). 112p. 1989. 75.00 (0-932129-07-2) Heming W Studies.

Papa! Turning Points, Level 3. Mario Papa. 1989. pap. text, wbk. ed. 8.00 (0-201-06322-0) Addison-Wesley.

Papa! Turning Points, Level 4. Mario Papa. 1989. pap. text, wbk. ed. 8.00 (0-201-06325-5) Addison-Wesley.

Papa a l'Essai. Heather MacAllister. (Horizon Ser.: Vol. 501). (FRE.). 1999. mass mkt. 3.50 (0-373-39501-9, 1-39501-1) Harlequin Bks.

Papa Alonzo Leatherby: A Collection of Tall Tales from the Best Storyteller in Carroll County. Marguerite W. Davol. LC 94-19372. (Illus.). 80p. (J). (gr. 3-7). 1995. per. 14.00 (0-689-80278-1) S&S Bks Yung.

Papa Alonzo Leatherby: The Best Storyteller in Carroll County. Marguerite W. Davol. LC 94-19372. (Illus.). (J). 14.00 (0-671-86580-3) S&S Bks Yung.

Papa & Me. Tadao Miyamoto. LC 94-1563. (J). (ps-3). 1994. lib. bdg. 19.95 (0-87614-843-7, Carolrhoda) Lerner Pub.

Papa Andrea's Sicilian Table: Recipes from a Sicilian Chef as Remembered by His Grandson. Vincent Schiavelli. LC 93-2517. (Illus.). 208p. 1993. 17.95 (1-55972-198-7, Birch Ln Pr) Carol Pub Group.

Papa Andrea's Sicilian Table: Recipes from a Sicilian Chef as Remembered by His Grandson. Vincent Schiavelli. (Illus.). 208p. 1995. pap. 12.95 (0-8065-1709-3, Citadel Pr) Carol Pub Group.

Papa au Grand Coeur. Cara Colter. (Horizon Ser.: No. 524). (FRE.). 1999. mass mkt. 3.99 (0-373-39524-8, 1-39524-3) Harlequin Bks.

Papa-Cause: The Friend of Santa Claus. John Solomon Sandridge. (J). (ps-4). 1998. pap. write for info. (0-9667336-0-6) Mus Liv History.

Papa, Charly Hat Gesagt... Wolf-Dietrich Zielinski. (Lehr-und Arbeitsbuch Ser.). (GER.). 112p. 17.50 incl. audio (3-468-49465-3) Langenscheidt.

Papa Coke: 65 Years Selling Coca-Cola. Sanders Rowland & Bob Terrell. LC 86-9526. (Illus.). 224p. 1986. 10.95 (0-914875-14-0) Bright Mtn Bks.

Papa Comble. Pamela Dalton. (Horizon Ser.: No. 484). (FRE.). 1998. 3.50 (0-373-39484-5, 1-39484-0) Harlequin Bks.

Papa, Cuentame un Cuento. Ramon Ferreira. LC 88-81505. (Coleccion Caniqui). (SPA.). 180p. (Orig.). 1989. pap. 12.00 (0-89729-494-7) Ediciones.

Papa Cuentanos Otro Cuento see Papa Tell Us Another Story

Papa dans L'Ame. Linda Varner. (Horizon Ser.: No. 500). (FRE.). 1999. mass mkt. 3.50 (0-373-39500-0, 1-39500-3) Harlequin Bks.

Papa de Arturo. Ginette Anfousse. (Coleccion Rosa Ser.). (SPA., Illus.). 60p. (J). (gr. 5 up). 1994. pap. 5.95 (958-07-0065-6) Firefly Bks Ltd.

Papa de David. Robert Munsch.Tr. of David's Father. (SPA., Illus.). 32p. (YA). (ps up). 1991. pap. 5.95 (1-55037-096-0, Pub. by Annick) Firefly Bks Ltd.

Papa de David. Robert Munsch. (Droles D'Histories Ser.).Tr. of David's Father. (FRE., Illus.). 24p. (J). (ps up). 1990. pap. 4.95 (2-89021-124-X, Pub. by La Courte Ech) Firefly Bks Ltd.

Papa de los Sonadores. Roberto V. Illa.Tr. of Pope of Dreamers. (ENG & SPA.). (Orig.). Date not set. pap. 15.00 (0-9660192-0-2) R V Illa.

Papa, el Consejero de la Familia. Dave Simmons.Tr. of Dad, the Family Counselor. (SPA.). 208p. 1996. 10.99 (0-88113-292-6, B022-2926) Caribe Betania.

Papa, el Entrenador de la Familia. Dave Simmons.Tr. of Dad, the Family Coach. (SPA.). 208p. 1996. 10.99 (0-88113-282-9, B022-2829) Caribe Betania.

Papa, el Mentor de la Familia. Dave Simmons.Tr. of Dad, the Family Mentor. (SPA.). 224p. 1996. 10.99 (0-88113-347-7, B022-3477) Caribe Betania.

Papa est Parti Maman Aussi. Remo Forlani. (FRE.). 305p. 1988. pap. 11.95 (0-7859-2550-3, 2070379140) Fr & Eur.

Papa Gambit vs. the French Defense: Beating the French. Mike Papa, Jr. (Illus.). 50p. (Orig.). 1991. pap. text 10.00 (0-9628959-0-3) Mich Pubns.

Papa Gatto: An Italian Fairy Tale. Ruth Sanderson. (J). 1995. write for info. (0-316-77107-4) Little.

Papa Gatto: An Italian Fairy Tale. Illus. & Retold by Ruth Sanderson. LC 94-16725. 32p. (J). (gr. k-3). 1995. 15.95 (0-316-77073-6) Little.

***Papa Gatto: An Italian Fairy Tale.** Ruth Sanderson. (Illus.). 32p. (J). (ps-3). 1999. pap. 5.95 (0-316-77112-0) Little.

Papa Hemingway. A. E. Hotchner. (Illus.). 304p. 1999. pap. 13.95 (0-7867-0592-2) Carroll & Graf.

***Papa, How Do You Know?** Dolores A. Newman. LC 99-91145. (Illus.). 32p. (J). 2000. pap. 9.95 (0-9676438-0-5) Sanctuary Pr MI.

***Papa, I Want to Be a Surgeon.** George Rawls. LC 99-73385. 140p. 1999. 22.95 (1-57860-032-4) Guild Pr IN.

Papa Jack: Cowman from the Wichitas. Paul McClung. LC 76-19071. 249p. reprint ed. 77.20 (0-8357-9738-4, 201623800002) Bks Demand.

Papa Jim Candle Book No. 6: Personal Use. James E. Sickafus. Ed. by Leticia M. Ayala. (Illus.). 90p. 1991. pap. 9.97 (1-878575-06-6) El Rey Pub.

Papa Jim Magical Herb Book: How to Use Herbs for Magical Purposes. Papa Jim, pseud. Ed. by Leticia M. Ayala. (Papa Jim Bks.: No. 1). (Illus.). 63p. 1985. pap. 3.95 (1-878575-00-7) El Rey Pub.

Papa Jim Magical Oil Book: How to Use Oils for Magical Purposes. Papa Jim, pseud. Ed. by Leticia M. Ayala. (Papa Jim Bks.: No. 2). (Illus.). 55p. 1989. pap. 3.95 (1-878575-01-5) El Rey Pub.

Papa Jim Medicinal Herbs: Commonly Used Herbs. Papa Jim, pseud. Ed. by Leticia M. Ayala. (Papa Jim Bks.: No. 4). (Illus.). 106p. 1990. pap. 3.95 (1-878575-03-1) El Rey Pub.

Papa Jim's Herbs for Illnesses: Herbs & Herbal Combinations. Papa Jim, pseud. Ed. by Leticia M. Ayala. (Papa Jim Bks.: No. 5). (Illus.). 78p. 1990. pap. 3.95 (1-878575-02-3) El Rey Pub.

Papa Jim's Spell Book: Rituals & Spells for Voodoo. Papa Jim, pseud. Ed. by Leticia M. Ayala. (Papa Jim Bks.: No. 3). (Illus.). 69p. 1989. pap. 3.95 (1-878575-04-X) El Rey Pub.

Papa La-Bas. John Dickson Carr & Brian M. Stableford. 288p. 1998. mass mkt. 4.95 (0-7867-0502-7) Carroll & Graf.

Papa Leonardo. Jeff Barth. (Still Waters Ser.). (Illus.). 60p. 1988. pap. 4.05 (0-7399-0142-7, 2343) Rod & Staff.

Papa Lucky's Shadow. Niki Daly. LC 91-24283. (Illus.). 32p. (J). (gr. k-3). 1999. per. 5.99 (0-689-82430-0) Aladdin.

Papa Lucky's Shadow. Niki Daly. LC 91-24283. (Illus.). 32p. (J). (ps-3). 1992. 16.00 (0-689-50541-8) McElderry Bks.

Papa, Mama Quiero Ir Al Cielo. Luis P. Palau. (Serie Cruzada - Crusade Ser.).Tr. of Mom, Dad, I Want to Go to Heaven. (SPA.). 27p. 1992. pap. 1.99 (1-56063-181-3, 498015) Editorial Unilit.

***Papa Married a Mormon.** (Illus.). 298p. 2000. reprint ed. pap. write for info. (0-914740-38-5) Western Epics.

***Papa Merveilleux.** Cara Colter. (Horizon Ser.: No. 540). (FRE.). 2000. mass mkt. 3.99 (0-373-39540-X, 1-39540-9, Harlequin French) Harlequin Bks.

Papa, Molly & the Great Prairie. Barbara Sobel. LC 87-81236. (J). (gr. 3-6). 1987. pap. 2.95 incl. audio (0-87386-044-6) Jan Prods.

Papa, My Father. Leo F. Buscaglia. 1989. 12.95 (1-55642-087-0) SLACK Inc.

***Papa New Guinea.** Bernan Press Staff & World Trade Organization Staff. (Trade Policy Review Ser.). 2000. 50.00 (0-89059-203-9) Bernan Pr.

Papa Noah Built an Ark. Carol Greene. LC 97-117446. (Read-n-Sing Bible Stories Ser.). (Illus.). 32p. (J). (ps-2). 1996. 6.99 (0-570-04809-5, 56-1824) Concordia.

Papa Ob Long: The Animals' Great Journey. Leroy Blankenship. LC 97-44248. (Illus.). 32p. (J). 1998. 12.99 (0-8499-5824-5) Tommy Nelson.

Papa Oso Vuelve a Casa. Else H. Minarik.Tr. of Father Bear Comes Home. 1981. 15.15 (0-606-10489-5, Pub. by Turtleback) Demco.

Papa Papa. Jean Marzollo. LC 99-69950. (Illus.). 14p. (J). (ps up). 2000. 5.95 (0-694-01246-7, HarpFestival) HarpC Child Bks.

Papa Par Interim. Emma Goldrick. (Azur Ser.). (FRE.). 1997. pap. 3.50 (0-373-34651-4, 1-34651-9) Harlequin Bks.

***Papa Penguin's Surprise.** (Illus.). (J). (gr. k-2). 2000. pap. 3.75 (1-58323-010-6) Seedling Pubns.

Papa Piccolo. (Key Concepts in Personal Development Ser.). 24p. (J). (gr. 1-4). 1992. pap., teacher ed. 16.95 (1-55942-030-8, 1033) Marsh Media.

Papa Piccolo. Carol Talley. LC 92-4319. (Key Concepts in Personal Development Ser.). (Illus.). 32p. (J). (gr. 1-4). 1992. 16.95 (1-55942-028-6, 7651) Marsh Media.

Papa Piccolo. Carol Talley & Itoko Maeno. (Key Concepts in Personal Development Ser.). 32p. (J). (gr. 1-4). 1992. teacher ed. 79.95 incl. VHS (1-55942-031-6, 9370) Marsh Media.

Papa Pit et Tim. Marcus Pfister.Tr. of Penguin Pete & Little Tim. (FRE., Illus.). 32p. (J). (gr. k-3). 1996. 15.95 (3-314-20830-8, Pub. by North-South Bks NYC) Chronicle Bks.

Papa Pit und Tim. Marcus Pfister.Tr. of Penguin Pete & Little Tim. (GER., Illus.). 32p. (J). (gr. k-3). 1996. 15.95 (3-314-00650-0, Pub. by North-South Bks NYC) Chronicle Bks.

Papa, Please Get the Moon for Me. Eric Carle. LC 91-14561. (Pixies Ser.). (Illus.). 28p. (J). (gr. k up). 1991. 5.95 (0-88708-177-0) S&S Childrens.

Papa, Please Get the Moon for Me. Eric Carle. LC 85-29785. (Illus.). 40p. (J). (ps up). 1991. 19.00 (0-88708-026-X, Picture Book Studio) S&S Childrens.

***Papa Please Get the Moon for Me.** Eric Carle. (Illus.). 32p. (J). (gr. k-3). 1999. pap. 9.99 (0-689-82959-0) Litle Simon.

Papa pour Cody. Leanna Wilson. (Horizon Ser.). 1999. mass mkt. 3.50 (0-373-39509-4, 1-39509-4) Harlequin Bks.

Papa pour Noel. Sally Carleen. (Horizon Ser.: Bk. 492). 1999. mass mkt. 3.50 (0-373-39492-6, 1-39492-3) Harlequin Bks.

Papa Raker's Dream: A Loving History of Good Shepherd. Richard W. Cowen. (Illus.). 318p. 1988. 15.00 (0-9620808-0-2) Good Shepherd.

Papa Retrouve. Patricia Knoll. (Horizon Ser.). 1999. mass mkt. 3.50 (0-373-39516-7, 1-39516-9) Harlequin Bks.

Papa, Reveille-Toi - 50 below Zero. Robert Munsch. (Droles D'Histories Ser.). (FRE., Illus.). 24p. (J). (ps up). 1987. pap. 6.95 (2-89021-071-5, Pub. by La Courte Ech) Firefly Bks Ltd.

***Papa Saves the Circus.** (Illus.). 40p. (J). 2001. 9.99 (0-7868-0716-4, Pub. by Disney Pr) Time Warner.

Papa Tell Us Another Story. Arturo Munoz Vasquez.Tr. of Papa Cuentanos Otro Cuento. (ENG & SPA., Illus.). 389p. (Orig.). (C). 1994. pap. 24.95 (0-927065-14-2) Marin Chula Vista.

Papa Tells Chita a Story. Elizabeth F. Howard. LC 93-1252. (Illus.). 32p. (J). (ps-2). 1998. pap. 5.99 (0-689-82220-0) Aladdin.

Papa Tells Chita a Story. Elizabeth F. Howard. LC 93-1252. (Illus.). 32p. (J). (ps-3). 1995. mass mkt. 15.00 (0-02-744623-9) S&S Bks Yung.

Papa Tembo. Eric Campbell. LC 97-45808. 288p. (J). (gr. 8 up). 1998. 16.00 (0-15-201727-5, Harcourt Child Bks) Harcourt.

Papa Topside: The Sealab Chronicles of Captain George F. Bond, USN. Ed. by Helen A. Siiteri. LC 92-33297. (Illus.). 270p. 1993. 28.95 (1-55750-795-3) Naval Inst Pr.

Papa, Tu Es Fu! William Saroyan. (FRE.). 1983. pap. 10.95 (0-7859-4180-0) Fr & Eur.

Papa Was a Preacher. Alyene Porter. 76p. 1954. pap. 5.50 (0-87129-681-0, P14) Dramatic Pub.

Papa Was a Promise Keeper. Rose G. Sims. (Illus.). (Orig.). 1995. pap. 10.95 (1-882415-02-7) New Life Church.

Papa Was a Riot. Andrew J. Ciulla. LC 83-61413. (Illus.). 212p. 1983. pap. 5.95 (0-913791-00-8) Rubicon Bks.

Papabile: The Man Who Would Be Pope. Michael J. Farrell. LC 97-40715. (Fiction Program Ser.). 192p. 1998. pap. 14.95 (0-8245-1730-X, Crsrd) Crossroad NY.

***Papacy.** James Akin. 80p. 2000. pap. 7.95 (1-888992-09-3) Catholic Answers.

Papacy. Bernhard Schimmelpfennig. Tr. by James Sievert from GER. 288p. 1992. text 73.50 (0-231-07514-6); pap. text 25.50 (0-231-07515-4) Col U Pr.

Papacy & Fascism: The Crisis of the 20th Century. Francis A. Ridley. LC 72-180422. (Studies in Fascism: Ideology & Practice). reprint ed. 45.00 (0-404-56156-X) AMS Pr.

Papacy & Law in the Gregorian Revolution: The Canaonistic Work of Anselm of Lucca. Kathleen Cushing. (Oxford Historical Monographs). 264p. 1998. text 74.00 (0-19-820724-7) OUP.

Papacy & the Church in the United States. Ed. by Bernard Cooke. 1989. pap. 10.95 (0-8091-3070-X) Paulist Pr.

Papacy & the Levant, 1204-1571 Vol. 1: The Thirteenth & Fourteenth Centuries. Kenneth M. Setton. LC 75-25476. (Memoirs Ser.: Vol. 114). 1976. 20.00 (0-87169-114-0, M114-SEK) Am Philos.

Papacy & the Levant, 1204-1571 Vol. 2. Joseph E. Harry. LC 68-789. (Studies in Poetry: No. 38). 1969. reprint ed. lib. bdg. 75.00 (0-8383-0567-9) M S G Haskell Hse.

Papacy & the Levant, 1204-1571: The Sixteenth Century, Vol. 3. Kenneth M. Setton. LC 75-25476. (Memoirs Ser.: Vol. 161). 1984. 25.00 (0-87169-161-2, M161-SEK) Am Philos.

Papacy & the Levant, 1204-1571: The Sixteenth Century, Vol. 4. Kenneth M. Setton. LC 75-25476. (Memoirs Ser.: Vol. 162). 1984. 25.00 (0-87169-162-0, M162-SEK) Am Philos.

Papacy & the Levant, 1204-1571 Vol. 2: The Fifteenth Century. Kenneth M. Setton. LC 75-25476. (Memoirs Ser.: Vol. 127). (Illus.). 1978. 25.00 (0-87169-127-2, M127-SEK) Am Philos.

Papacy & the People of God. Ed. by Gary MacEoin. LC 97-39381. 176p. (Orig.). 1998. pap. 15.00 (1-57075-178-1) Orbis Bks.

Papacy Confronts the Modern World. Frank J. Coppa. Date not set. pap. write for info. (1-57524-101-3) Krieger.

Papacy, Councils & Canon Law in the 11th-12th Centuries. Robert Somerville. (Collected Studies: No. CS312). 336p. 1990. text 115.95 (0-86078-260-3, Pub. by Variorum) Ashgate Pub Co.

Papacy, Scotland & Northern England, 1342-1378. A. D. Barrell. (Cambridge Studies in Medieval Life & Thought: No. 30). (Illus.). 317p. (C). 1995. text 59.95 (0-521-44182-X) Cambridge U Pr.

Papacy, 1073-1198: Continuity & Innovation. I. S. Robinson. (Cambridge Medieval Textbooks Ser.). 571p. (C). 1990. text 80.00 (0-521-26498-7); pap. text 27.95 (0-521-31922-6) Cambridge U Pr.

Papagayo: The Mischief Maker. Gerald McDermott. LC 91-4036. (Illus.). 32p. (J). (ps-3). 1992. pap. 8.00 (0-15-259464-7, Harcourt Child Bks) Harcourt.

Papagayo: The Mischief Maker. Gerald McDermott. LC 91-4036. (Illus.). 32p. (J). (ps-3). 1992. 16.95 (0-15-259465-5, Harcourt Child Bks) Harcourt.

Papagayo, the Mischief Maker. Gerald McDermott. (Voyager Bks.). 1992. 13.20 (0-606-01023-8, Pub. by Turtleback) Demco.

Papageien, Lebensweise, Art und Zucht. Wolfgang De Grahl. (GER., Illus.). 287p. 1985. lib. bdg. 35.00 (3-8001-7150-3, Pub. by Eugen Ulmer) Balogh.

Papageno: Emanuel Schikaneder: Man of the Theater in Mozart's Time. Kurt Honolka. Tr. by Jane M. Wilde. LC 89-17574. (Illus.). 236p. 1990. 21.95 (0-931340-21-7, Amadeus Pr) Timber.

Papago & Pima Indians of Arizona. Ruth M. Underhill. (Wild & Woolly West Ser.: No. 37). (Illus.). 64p. 1979. pap. 5.00 (0-910584-52-4) Filter.

Papago & Pima to English, English to Papago & Pima Dictionary. 2nd ed. Dean Saxton et al. Ed. by R. L. Cherry. LC 83-5098. (ENG.). 145p. (C). 1983. 24.95 (0-8165-0826-7) U of Ariz Pr.

P

Papago Calendar Record. Ruth M. Underhill. LC 76-43878. (Univ. of New Mexico Bulletin Anthropological Ser.: Vol. 2, No. 5). reprint ed. 29.50 (*0-404-15739-4*) AMS Pr.

Papago Grammar. Ofelia Zepeda. LC 82-17289. 190p. 1983. pap. 18.95 (*0-8165-0792-9*) U of Ariz Pr.

Papago Indian Pottery. Bernard L. Fontana et al. LC 84-45532. (American Ethnological Society Monographs: No. 37). 1988. reprint ed. 32.50 (*0-404-62936-9*) AMS Pr.

Papago Indian Religion. Ruth M. Underhill. LC 74-82363. (Columbia Univ. Contributions to Anthropology Ser.: Vol. 33). reprint ed. 37.50 (*0-404-50583-X*) AMS Pr.

Papago Indians of Arizona & Their Relatives the Pima. Ruth M. Underhill. LC 78-15079. (Indian Life & Customs: No. 3). 1977. reprint ed. 34.50 (*0-404-15736-X*) AMS Pr.

Papago Music. Frances Densmore. (Bureau of American Ethnology Bulletins Ser.). 229p. 1995. lib. bdg. 89.00 (*0-7812-4090-5*) Rprt Serv.

Papago Music. Frances Densmore. LC 72-1881. (Music Ser.). (Illus.). 276p. 1972. reprint ed. lib. bdg. 27.50 (*0-306-70509-5*) Da Capo.

Papago Nominal Stems. fac. ed. Juan Dolores. Ed. by Alden Mason. (University of California Publications in American Archaeology & Ethnology: Vol. 20: 2). 14p. (C). 1923. reprint ed. pap. text 1.88 (*1-55567-238-8*) Coyote Press.

Papago Traveler: The Memories of James McCarthy. James McCarthy. Ed. by John G. Westover. LC 85-14138. (Sun Tracks Ser.: Vol. 13). 200p. 1985. 24.95 (*0-8165-1810-6*) U of Ariz Pr.

Papago Verb Stems. fac. ed. Juan Dolores. (University of California Publications in American Archaeology & Ethnology: Vol. 10: 5). 23p. (C). 1913. reprint ed. pap. text 2.81 (*1-55567-191-8*) Coyote Press.

Papago Woman. Ruth M. Underhill. (Illus.). 98p. (C). 1985. reprint ed. pap. text 9.50 (*0-88133-042-6*) Waveland Pr.

Papaji: Interviews. Ed. by David Godman. 300p. 1993. pap. 15.00 (*0-9638022-0-8*) Avadhuta Fnd.

Papal Abdication in Later Medieval Thought. John R. Eastman. LC 89-37672. (Texts & Studies in Religion: Vol. 42). 180p. 1990. lib. bdg. 79.95 (*0-88946-831-1*) E Mellen.

Papal Coins. Allen G. Berman. (Illus.). 255p. 1991. 59.50 (*0-915018-43-8*) Attic Bks.

Papal Conspiracy Exposed & Protestantism Defended. Edward Beecher. LC 76-46066. (Anti-Movements in America Ser.). (Illus.). 1977. reprint ed. lib. bdg. 35.95 (*0-405-09940-1*) Ayer.

Papal Diplomacy in the Modern Age. Peter C. Kent & John F. Pollard. LC 93-23476. 304p. 1994. 59.95 (*0-275-94441-7*, Praeger Pubs) Greenwood.

***Papal Election in the Age of Transition, 1878-1922.** Francis A. Burkle-Young. 224p. 2000. 50.00 (*0-7391-0114-5*) Lxngtn Bks.

Papal Encyclicals, 1740-1981, 5 vols., Set. Ed. by Claudia Carlen. LC 81-84885. 1990. 495.00 (*0-87650-259-1*) Pierian.

Papal Enforcement of Some Medieval Marriage Laws. Charles E. Smith. LC 40-12564. 237p. reprint ed. pap. 73.50 (*0-608-13699-9*, 205531400013) Bks Demand.

Papal Genealogy: The Families & Descendants of the Popes. George L. Williams. LC 97-36093. 271p. 1998. lib. bdg. 52.50 (*0-7864-0315-2*) McFarland & Co.

***Papal Letters in the Early Middle Ages, Vol. 2.** Horst Fuhrmann. 2000. 39.95 (*0-8132-0919-6*) Cath U Pr.

Papal Monarchy: The Western Church from 1050 to 1250. Colin Morris. (Oxford History of the Christian Church Ser.). 690p. 1991. reprint ed. pap. text 39.95 (*0-19-826925-0*, 12306) OUP.

Papal Music & Musicians in Medieval & Renaissance Rome. Ed. by Richard Sherr. LC 97-2765. (Illus.). 368p. 1998. text 95.00 (*0-19-816417-3*) OUP.

Papal Numismatic History: The Emancipation of the Papal State. 2nd ed. Allen G. Berman. (Illus.). 165p. 1991. pap. 29.50 (*0-915018-44-6*) Attic Bks.

Papal Patronage & the Music of St. Peter's, 1380-1513. Christopher A. Reynolds. LC 94-5292. (Illus.). 410p. 1995. 65.00 (*0-520-08212-5*, Pub. by U CA Pr) Cal Prin Full Svc.

Papal Power. Henry T. Hudson. 1981. pap. 8.99 (*0-85234-269-1*, Pub. by Evangelical Pr) P & R Pubng.

Papal Primacy: Its Story from the Beginning to the Present. Klaus Schatz. 200p. (Orig.). 1996. pap. 19.95 (*0-8146-5522-X*, M Glazier) Liturgical Pr.

Papal Primacy & the Episcopate: Towards a Relational Understanding. Michael J. Buckley. LC 97-45932. 172p. 1998. pap. 12.95 (*0-8245-1745-8*, Herdr & Herdr) Crossroad NY.

Papal Pronouncements, a Guide, 1740-1978, 2 vols., Set. Ed. by Claudia Carlen. 1991. 195.00 (*0-87650-266-4*) Pierian.

Papal Pronouncements on Marriage & the Family: From Leo XIII to Pius XII, (1878-1954) Compiled by Alvin Werth & Clement S. Mihanovich. LC 82-6265. 189p. 1982. reprint ed. lib. bdg. 49.75 (*0-313-22521-4*, WEPA, Greenwood Pr) Greenwood.

Papal Reform & Canon Law in the 11th & 12th Centuries. Uta-Renate Blumenthal. LC 98-24267. (Variorum Collected Studies Ser.: Vol. 618). 360p. 1998. text 99.95 (*0-86078-695-1*, BX1178.B58, Pub. by Variorum) Ashgate Pub Co.

Papal Sin *see* **Buddhist Manifesto: The Papal Sin**

Papal Sin. Chris Eann. Ed. by Don Lee. 165p. 1995. 35.50 (*0-939758-31-8*) Eastern Pr.

Papal Sin: Structures of Deceit. Garry Wills. LC 99-54851. 304p. 2000. 25.00 (*0-385-49410-6*) Doubleday.

Papal State under Martin V. Peter Partner. 264p. 1958. 45.00 (*0-614-21816-0*, Pub. by British Schl Rome) David Brown.

Papal Supremacy & American Democracy. V. Norskov Olsen. LC 87-83037. 190p. (Orig.). 1988. pap. 10.95 (*0-944450-01-6*) La Sierra U Pr.

Papal Teaching on Private Property, 1891 to 1981. Matthew Habiger. LC 89-27956. 420p. (C). 1990. lib. bdg. 59.00 (*0-8191-7652-4*) U Pr of Amer.

Papal Thought on the State: Excerpts from Encyclicals & Other Writings of Recent Popes. Ed. by Gerard F. Yates. (Crofts Classics). 160p. 1958. pap. text 1.25 (*0-88295-064-9*) Harlan Davidson.

Papal Visit: John Paul II in Miami. Miami Herald Staff & Allison Owen. (SPA., Illus.). 112p. (Orig.). 1987. pap. 18.95 (*0-942084-67-5*) SeaSide Pub.

Papal Visit: John Paul II in Miami. Miami Herald Staff et al. (Illus.). 112p. (Orig.). 1987. pap. 18.95 (*0-942084-66-7*) SeaSide Pub.

Papal Visit: Pope John Paul II in Baltimore. Ed. by Archdiocese of Baltimore Staff. LC 95-71402. (Illus.). 128p. 1995. 39.95 (*1-885938-01-2*) Cathdrl Fndtn Pr.

Papal Whispers. Stephen Cartmell. 290p. 1998. 36.50 (*1-85776-335-1*, Pub. by Book Guild Ltd) Trans-Atl Phila.

Papal Wisdom: Words of Hope & Inspiration from Pope John Paul II. John Paul, II, pseud. 1997. pap. 8.95 (*0-452-27699-3*) Viking Penguin.

Papalote. Alma F. Ada. (Cuentos para Todo el Ano Ser.). (SPA., Illus.). 23p. (J). (gr. k-12). 1992. pap. 7.95 (*1-56014-227-8*) Santillana.

Papancasudani Majjhimanikayatthakatha of Buddhaghosacariya, 5 vols. in 4. Buddhaghosa. LC 78-72388. (Indian Life & Customs Ser.). reprint ed. write for info. (*0-404-17560-0*) AMS Pr.

Papanicolaou Technique: Approved Guideline, (1994) Kenneth D. McClatchy. 1994. 85.00 (*1-56238-238-1*, GP15-A) NCCLS.

Papa's Angels: A Christmas Story. Collin Wilcox Paxton & Gary Carden. LC 96-24238. (Illus.). 144p. 1996. 17.00 (*1-57731-004-7*) New Wrld Lib.

***Papa's Blues.** Javon Johnson. 104p. 2000. pap. 5.60 (*0-87129-978-X*, P89) Dramatic Pub.

Papa's Christmas Gift: Around the World on the Night Before Christmas. Cheryl Harness. LC 95-2579. (Illus.). 32p. (J). (gr. k-5). 1995. per. 15.00 (*0-689-80344-3*) S&S Childrens.

Papa's Cord: A Novel. Mary Pleshette Willis. LC 98-51914. 224p. 1999. 22.00 (*0-679-44696-6*, Pub. by Knopf Bks Yng Read) Random.

Papa's Daughter. Thyra F. Bjorn. 180p. 1992. reprint ed. 29.95 (*0-89966-882-8*) Buccaneer Bks.

Papas el Martes, Level 1. Dee Lillegard. (Let Me Read Ser.).Tr. of Potatoes on Tuesday. (SPA.). (J). 1996. 2.95 (*0-673-36327-9*, GoodYrBooks) Addson-Wesley Educ.

Papas' Greece. Tessa Papas. (Illus.). 96p. 1997. 49.95 (*0-9644651-1-6*) Chetwynd Stapylton.

***Papas' Instant Greek: How to Communicate in Greek as Quickly as You Can Twist Your Wrist!** 12th ed. William Papas. (GRE & ENG.). 1999. pap. text 12.95 (*0-9644651-2-4*) Chetwynd Stapylton.

Papa's Latkes. Jane Breskin Zalben. LC 93-37986. (Illus.). 32p. (J). (ps-2). 1995. 13.95 (*0-8050-4634-8*, B Martin BYR) H Holt & Co.

Papa's Latkes: Mini Book. Jane Breskin Zalben. (J). 1995. 5.95 (*0-8050-3099-9*) H Holt & Co.

Papa's Old Trunk. Mary K. Butler. LC 81-68812. (Illus.). (J). (gr. 6-12). 1981. 10.00 (*0-934530-03-3*) Buck Pub.

Papa's Panda. Nancy Willard. LC 78-31787. (Illus.). (J). (ps-2). 1979. 5.95 (*0-15-259462-0*, Harcourt Child Bks) Harcourt.

Papa's Place. Margaret Jensen. LC 97-29019. 160p. 1998. pap. 7.99 (*1-56507-798-9*) Harvest Hse.

Papas' Portland. Tessa Papas & Bill Papas. (Illus.). 96p. (Orig.). 1994. pap. 24.95 (*0-9644651-0-8*) Chetwynd Stapylton.

***Papa's Song.** Kate McMullan. LC 99-34556. (Illus.). 32p. (J). (ps-3). 2000. 15.00 (*0-374-35732-3*) FS&G.

Papa's Wife. Thyra F. Bjorn. 180p. 1992. reprint ed. lib. bdg. 33.95 (*0-89966-883-6*) Buccaneer Bks.

Papayanis Alphonse Merrheim. Sish. 1985. lib. bdg. 98.50 (*90-247-3224-7*, Pub. by M Nijhoff) Kluwer Academic.

Papazone Adventure Stories. Lew Wallace. LC 96-96055. 112p. (Orig.). (J). (gr. 1-6). 1996. pap. 5.95 (*1-889062-07-3*) Artel.

Papel del Lector en la Novela Mexicana Contemporanea: Jose Emilio Pacheco y Salvador Elizondo. Magda Graniela-Rodriguez. 1990. 46.50 (*0-916379-83-3*) Scripta.

Papel Mojado: Level C. Millas. text 8.95 (*0-88436-999-4*) EMC-Paradigm.

***Papeles De Pandora.** Rosario Ferre. LC 00-28977. (SPA.). 240p. 2000. pap. 13.00 (*0-375-72469-9*) Knopf.

Paper *see* **Craft Workshop Series**

Paper. (Jump Ser.). (Illus.). 36p. (J). (gr. 2-6). pap. write for info. (*1-882210-33-6*) Action Pub.

Paper. Barbara F. Backer. (Play & Learn Ser.). (Illus.). 48p. (J). (ps-k). 1998. pap. 3.95 (*1-57029-229-9*, W02309) Totline Pubns.

Paper. Erica Burt. (Craft Projects Ser.). (Illus.). 32p. (J). (gr. 2-6). 1990. lib. bdg. 11.95 (*0-685-46443-1*) Rourke Corp.

Paper. Gabrielle Falkiner. (Artisans Ser.). (Illus.). 144p. 1999. 19.95 (*0-8230-0304-3*) Watsn-Guptill.

Paper. Elizabeth S. Smith. LC 84-7271. (Inventions That Changed Our Lives Ser.). (Illus.). 64p. (J). (gr. 4 up). 1984. lib. bdg. 10.85 (*0-8027-6569-6*) Walker & Co.

Paper. Don Sparkman. 390p. 1998. pap. 16.95 (*1-892509-20-2*) Chambers Pubg Grp.

Paper. Illus. by Gerald Witcombmsia. (Butterfly Bks.). 32p. (J). (gr. 3-5). 1985. 9.95 (*0-86685-450-9*) Intl Bk Ctr.

Paper: An Engineered Stochastic Structure. M. Deng & C. T. J. Dodson. LC 94-17554. 308p. 1994. 69.00 (*0-89852-283-8*, 0101R238) TAPPI.

Paper: Building Great Designs with Paper. Lesa Sawahata. (Graphic Idea Resource Ser.). (Illus.). 96p. 1998. pap. 15.99 (*1-56496-514-7*) Rockport Pubs.

Paper: Making, Decorating & Designing. Beata Thackeray. (Illus.). 1998. pap. text 24.95 (*0-8230-3926-9*) Watsn-Guptill.

***Paper: Practical Papercraft in 30 Creative Projects.** Ed. by Lorenz Books Staff. (Illus.). 2000. 11.95 (*0-7548-0353-8*, Lorenz Bks) Anness Pub.

Paper Advertising Collectibles: Treasures from Almanacs to Window Signs. Robert Reed. (Illus.). 208p. 1998. pap. 24.95 (*0-930625-91-9*, Antique Trader) Krause Pubns.

Paper Aircraft. R. W. Simpson. (Illus.). 128p. Date not set. pap. 18.99 (*0-7524-1742-8*, Pub. by Tempus Pubng) Arcadia Publng.

Paper Airplane: The Thirtieth Issue. Ed. by Bradford Morrow. (Illus.). 385p. 1998. pap. 12.00 (*0-941964-46-9*) Conjunctions.

Paper Airplane Book. Seymour Simon. (J). (gr. 4-6). 1976. pap. 5.99 (*0-14-030925-X*, PuffinBks) Peng Put Young Read.

Paper Airplane Book. Seymour Simon. (J). 1976. 10.19 (*0-606-04271-7*, Pub. by Turtleback) Demco.

Paper Airplanes. Nick Robinson. 1991. 12.98 (*1-55521-724-9*) Bk Sales Inc.

Paper Airplanes: Models to Build & Fly. Emery J. Kelly. LC 96-10909. (Illus.). (YA). (gr. 5 up). 1996. lib. bdg. 23.93 (*0-8225-2401-5*, Lerner Publctns) Lerner Pub.

***Paper Airplanes: Models to Build & Fly.** Emery J. Kelly. (Illus.). (J). 2000. pap. 8.95 (*0-8225-9903-1*) Lerner Pub.

Paper Airplanes: 16 Models. (Illus.). 2000. pap. 7.95 (*3-8290-0447-8*) Konemann.

Paper Airplanes & Other Super Flyers. Neil Francis. (Kids Can Crafts Ser.). (Illus.). 40p. (J). 1996. 16.95 (*1-55074-328-7*) Kids Can Pr.

Paper Airplanes & Other Super Flyers. rev. ed. Neil Francis. (Kids Can Crafts Ser.). (Illus.). 40p. (J). 1996. pap. 5.95 (*1-55074-307-4*) Kids Can Pr.

Paper Airplanes from Around the World, Vol. 1. 4th enl. rev. ed. Ray Roberts. (Illus.). 260p. (YA). (gr. 6 up). 1995. reprint ed. 28.00 (*0-929995-00-7*) AIR Burbank.

Paper Airplanes in the Himalayas: Following the Unfinished Path Home. Paul A. Seaman. LC 97-66689. (The West & the Wider World Ser.: Vol. 13). 350p. (Orig.). 1997. pap. 19.95 (*0-940121-44-1*, P314) Cross Cultural Pubns.

Growing up in Pakistan as the son of United Methodist missionaries, this author has penned an unusual memoir. He revisits the years he spent at Murree Christian School in Pakistan, where he boarded for six months each year. With candor & deep insight he reflects on the legacy of such an upbringing. Like many "global nomads" Paul Seaman continued to struggle with a lost sense of belonging for as much as twenty years after returning to the United States. This book is an account of his search to discover a sense of "home." In an age of cultural alienation & transient loyalties, Seaman's story resonates with both urgency & comfort. There is clearly exposed the need to find & follow the emotional core that connects past experiences with present life. ***Publisher Paid Annotation.***

Paper & Books in Ancient Egypt. J. Cerny. 1985. reprint ed. pap. 5.00 (*0-89005-205-0*) Ares.

Paper & Carton Vocabulary: Vocabulaire des Papiers et des Cartons. Normand Cote. (ENG & FRE.). 77p. 1983. pap. 5.95 (*0-8288-1429-5*, M6650) Fr & Eur.

Paper & Composites from Agro-Based Resources. Roger M. Rowell et al. LC 96-8877. 384p. 1996. lib. bdg. 110.00 (*1-56670-235-6*) Lewis Pubs.

Paper & Fabric Mache: 100 Imaginative & Ingenious Projects to Make. Dawn Cusick. (Illus.). 128p. 1995. pap. 14.95 (*0-8069-0609-X*) Sterling.

Paper & Ink Relationships. Roger L. Williams. (C). 1986. 29.95 (*0-9618281-0-2*) Practical Print Mgmt.

Paper & Iron: Hamburg Business & German Politics in the Era of Inflation, 1897-1927. Niall Ferguson. (Illus.). 553p. (C). 1995. text 74.95 (*0-521-47016-1*) Cambridge U Pr.

***Paper & Paper Products in Russia: A Strategic Entry Report, 1995.** Compiled by Icon Group International Staff. (Illus.). 145p. 1999. ring bd. 1450.00 incl. audio compact disk (*0-7418-1621-0*) Icon Grp.

***Paper & Paperboard in Egypt: A Strategic Entry Report, 1999.** Compiled by Icon Group International. (Illus.). 165p. 1999. ring bd. 1650.00 incl. audio compact disk (*0-7418-1853-1*) Icon Grp.

***Paper & Paperboard in Hong Kong: A Strategic Entry Report, 1996.** Compiled by Icon Group International Staff. (Illus.). 139p. 1999. ring bd. 1390.00 incl. audio compact disk (*0-7418-1351-3*) Icon Grp.

***Paper & Paperboard in Mexico: A Strategic Entry Report, 1995.** Compiled by Icon Group International Staff. (Illus.). 131p. 1999. ring bd. 1310.00 incl. audio compact disk (*0-7418-1622-9*) Icon Grp.

Paper & Paperboards in India. Tirath Gupta & Nitin Shah. 96p. (C). 1987. 12.50 (*81-204-0243-X*, Pub. by Oxford IBH) S Asia.

***Paper & Pen.** Dorothy Sides. 2001. pap. 6.99 (*1-57532-300-1*) Press-Tige Pub.

Paper & Printing Dictionary German. W. Walenski. (GER.). 357p. 1993. 69.00 (*3-465-02619-5*, Pub. by Vittorio Kloster) IBD Ltd.

Paper & Printing Dictionary, German-English/English-German. W. Walenski. (ENG & GER.). 1993. 69.00 (*0-7859-9404-1*) Fr & Eur.

Paper & Scissors, Polygons & More. Linda Silvey. (Orig.). 1997. pap. text 18.95 (*1-57232-959-9*) Seymour Pubns.

Paper & Scissors, Polygons & More. rev. ed. Linda Silvey & Loretta Taylor. Ed. by Carol Zacny. (Paper & Scissors Polygons Ser.). (Illus.). 146p. (Orig.). (YA). 1996. pap. text 18.95 (*0-86651-959-9*, 21415) Seymour Pubns.

Paper & Scissors Truth Talks, No. 5. Arnold C. Westphal. (J). 1971. per. 4.95 (*0-915398-04-4*) Visual Evangels.

Paper & Thin Layer Chromatographic Analysis of Environmental Toxicants. M. E. Getz. LC 79-41719. (Heyden International Topics in Science Ser.). (Illus.). 175p. reprint ed. pap. 54.30 (*0-8357-3053-0*, 203931000012) Bks Demand.

Paper Animal Masks from Northwest Tribal Tales. Nancy L. Rudolph. LC 95-39222. (Illus.). 80p. (J). 1996. 19.95 (*0-8069-4383-1*) Sterling.

Paper Animals. Annabelle Curtis. (Illus.). 36p. (Orig.). 1994. pap. 6.95 (*0-906212-94-4*, Pub. by Tarquin Pubns) Parkwest Pubns.

Paper Animals. Michael LaFosse. (Make It with Paper Ser.). (Illus.). 72p. 1997. pap. 9.95 (*1-56010-385-X*, RPO1) W Foster Pub.

Paper Animals: 8 Step-by-Step Projects. Michael LaFosse. (Make It with Paper Ser.). (Illus.). 72p. 1997. pap. 19.99 (*1-56496-276-8*, Quarry Bks) Rockport Pubs.

Paper Anniversary. Joan Wickersham. Ed. by Jane Rosenman. 368p. 1995. pap. 12.00 (*0-671-89071-9*, WSP) PB.

***Paper Art: The Art of Sculpting with Paper.** Michael G. LaFosse. (Illus.). 144p. 1998. text. write for info. (*90-5703-132-9*, Harwood Acad Pubs) Gordon & Breach.

Paper Art: The Complete Guide to Papercraft Techniques. Diane V. Maurer-Mathison & Jennifer Philippoff. LC 97-28466. (Crafts Ser.). (Illus.). 144p. 1997. pap. 27.50 (*0-8230-3840-8*) Watsn-Guptill.

Paper Automata: Four Working Models to Cut Out & Glue together. Rob Ives. Date not set. pap. 11.95 (*1-899618-21-X*, Pub. by Tarquin Pubns) Parkwest Pubns.

Paper Bag Prince. Colin Thompson. (J). (gr. 1 up). 1997. reprint ed. pap. 5.99 (*0-614-28954-8*) Random Bks Yng Read.

***Paper Bag Princess.** (J). 1999. 9.95 (*1-56137-475-X*) Novel Units.

Paper Bag Princess. Robert Munsch. (Illus.). 32p. (J). (gr. k-3). 1980. pap. 5.95 (*0-920236-16-2*, Pub. by Annick); lib. bdg. 15.95 (*0-920236-82-0*, Pub. by Annick) Firefly Bks Ltd.

Paper Bag Princess. Robert Munsch. (Munsch for Kids Ser.). (J). 1980. 11.15 (*0-606-03290-8*, Pub. by Turtleback) Demco.

Paper Bag Princess. Robert Munsch. (Annikins Ser.: Vol. 1). (Illus.). 24p. (J). (ps-1). 1986. pap. 0.99 (*0-920236-25-1*, Pub. by Annick) Firefly Bks Ltd.

Paper Bag Princess. Colin Thompson. 1997. 12.19 (*0-606-11719-9*, Pub. by Turtleback) Demco.

Paper Bag Princess Doll & Book. Robert Munsch. (Illus.). 32p. (J). (ps-3). 1995. pap. 19.95 (*1-55037-392-7*, Pub. by Annick) Firefly Bks Ltd.

Paper Bag Puppets. Arden Druce. LC 97-37705. (School Library Media Ser.: No. 15). (Illus.). 224p. 1999. pap. 27.50 (*0-8108-3400-6*) Scarecrow.

Paper Bags. Joe Blades. 1989. pap. text 3.00 (*0-921411-14-6*) Genl Dist Srvs.

Paper Basics: Forestry, Manufacture, Selection, Purchasing, Mathematics & Metrics, Recycling. David Saltman. 250p. (C). 1991. reprint ed. lib. bdg. 29.50 (*0-89464-569-2*) Krieger.

Paper Bird. Robin Behn. LC 87-51682. 88p. 1988. 15.95 (*0-89672-164-7*); pap. 9.95 (*0-89672-163-9*) Tex Tech Univ Pr.

Paper Bird. Arcadio Lobato. LC 93-24469.Tr. of Papiervogel. (Illus.). (J). (ps-3). 1994. lib. bdg. 19.95 (*0-87614-817-8*, Carolrhoda) Lerner Pub.

Paper Birds That Fly. Norman Schmidt. LC 95-49194. (Illus.). 96p. (J). 1996. 19.95 (*1-895569-01-X*, Pub. by Sally Milner) Sterling.

Paper Birds That Fly. Norman Schmidt. (Illus.). 96p. (J). 1997. pap. 12.95 (*1-895569-11-7*, Pub. by Tamos Bks) Sterling.

Paper Birds That Fly Book & Kit. 1996. pap. 19.95 (*0-8069-9538-6*) Sterling.

Paper Black Feeling. Nikki Giovanni. LC 70-119846. 1971. pap. 10.00 (*0-688-25294-X*, Quil) HarperTrade.

Paper Boats. Hilary Tham. LC 86-50769. (Illus.). 119p. (C). 1987. pap. 12.95 (*0-89410-542-6*, Three Contnts) L Rienner.

***Paper Bodies: A Margaret Cavendish Reader.** Margaret C. Newcastle. Ed. by Sylvia L. Bowerbank & Sara Heller Mendelson. (Literary Texts Ser.). 340p. 2000. pap. 12.95 (*1-55111-173-X*) Broadview Pr.

Paper Book. Hannah Tofts. (J). 1990. pap. 11.95 (*0-671-70366-8*) S&S Trade.

Paper Book & Paper Maker. Shar Levine. LC 92-72021. (Illus.). 32p. (J). (gr. k-5). 1993. pap. 12.95 (*1-56282-235-7*, Pub. by Hyprn Child) Time Warner.

***Paper Book & Paper Maker: With Plastic Paper Maker.** Shar Levine et al. (Illus.). 56p. (J). (gr. 1-5). 1998. pap. 12.95 (*0-921051-75-1*) Somerville Hse.

Paper Boxes: 8 Step-by-Step Projects. Michael LaFosse. (Make It with Paper Ser.). (Illus.). 114p. 1997. pap. 19.99 (*1-56496-277-6*, Quarry Bks) Rockport Pubs.

Paper Boy. David Huddle. LC 78-23232. (Pitt Poetry Ser.). 69p. 1979. pap. 30.00 (*0-7837-8544-5*, 204935900011) Bks Demand.

Paper Boy. Stuart Keate. (Illus.). 238p. 1980. 15.95 (*0-7720-1300-4*) Genl Dist Srvs.

P

An Asterisk (*) at the beginning of an entry indicates that the title is appearing for the first time.

Paper Bridge: A Return to Budapest. Monica Porter. 256p. 1982. 17.95 (*0-7043-2296-X*, Pub. by Quartet) Charles River Bks.

***Paper Bridges: Selected Poems of Kadya Molodowsky.** Kadia Molodowsky. 1999. 49.95 (*0-8143-2846-6*) Wayne St U Pr.

Paper Bridges: Selected Poems of Kadya Molodowsky. Kadia Molodowsky & Kathryn Hellerstein. LC 98-15479. 1999. pap. 29.95 (*0-8143-2718-4*) Wayne St U Pr.

Paper Bullets: Print & Kingship under Charles II. Harold Weber. LC 95-14184. (Illus.). 304p. 1995. 39.95 (*0-8131-1929-4*) U Pr of Ky.

Paper Buyers Encyclopedia. 20th ed. Grade Finders Inc. Staff. Ed. by William A. Subers. LC 77-641850. (Illus.). 548p. 1997. pap. 90.00 (*0-929502-05-1*) Grade Finders.

Paper by Kids. rev. ed. Arnold E. Grummer. LC 79-22904. (Doing & Learning Bks.). (Illus.). 108p. (J). (gr. 2 up). 1980. 12.95 (*0-87518-191-0*) G Markim.

Paper Cable Ampacities at AEIC Temperatures. 1967. 40.00 (*0-614-18678-1*, P-48-426) Insulated Cable.

Paper Cage. Robin Skelton. 1982. pap. text 7.95 (*0-88982-030-9*, Pub. by Oolichan Bks) Genl Dist Srvs.

Paper Canoe: Guide to Theatre Anthropology. Eugenio Barba. Tr. by Richard Fowler. LC 94-7809. 224p. (C). 1995. pap. 22.99 (*0-415-11674-0*, B3202) Routledge.

Paper Capers: An Amazing Array of Games, Puzzles, & Tricks. Jack Botermans. LC 86-7596. (Illus.). 120p. 1995. pap. 16.95 (*0-8050-0139-5*, Owl) H Holt & Co.

Paper Card Book. Lisa Kerr. (Illus.). 108p. 1997. pap. 19.99 (*1-56496-327-6*, Quarry Bks) Rockport Pubs.

Paper Cards. Lisa Kerr. (Make It with Paper Ser.). (Illus.). 72p. 1997. pap. 9.95 (*1-56010-389-2*, RPO5) W Foster Pub.

Paper Chain. Claire Blake et al. LC 97-35088. (Illus.). 32p. (J). (gr. k-6). 1999. pap. 8.95 (*0-929173-28-7*) Health Press.

Paper Chain. Graham Molo. 380p. mass mkt. 4.99 (*1-896329-81-0*) Picasso Publ.

Paper Chains. Ed. by Klutz Editors. (Klutz Guides Ser.). (Illus.). (J). (gr. 2 up). 1998. pap. 4.95 (*1-57054-181-7*) Klutz.

Paper Chase. John J. Osborne, Jr. 21.95 (*0-8488-0185-7*) Amereon Ltd.

Paper Chase. Joseph Robinette & John J. Osborn, Jr. 1981. 5.50 (*0-87129-398-6*, P54) Dramatic Pub.

Paper Chase. Dianne Stewart. (Junior African Writers Ser.). (Illus.). 80p. (J). (gr. 3 up). 1992. pap. 3.88 (*0-7910-2904-2*) Chelsea Hse.

***Paper Chase.** large type ed. Bob Cook. 320p. 2000. 20.99 (*1-84137-040-1*, Pub. by Mgna Lrg Print) Ulverscroft.

Paper Chemistry. Ed. by J. C. Roberts. 288p. 1991. pap. 195.95 (*0-412-02511-6*, A4216, Chap & Hall NY) Chapman & Hall.

Paper Children. large type ed. Norma Levinson. 560p. 1988. 27.99 (*0-7089-1852-2*) Ulverscroft.

***Paper Chromatography.** 5th ed. James M. Postma et al. 2000. pap. text, lab manual ed. 1.95 (*0-7167-9447-0*) W H Freeman.

Paper City. E. Pease et al. 24p. (C). 1995. pap. 2.00 (*1-886845-02-6*) Penin Fine Arts.

Paper City. David R. Locke. LC 68-57539. (Muckrakers Ser.). 431p. reprint ed. lib. bdg. 42.00 (*0-8398-1166-7*) Irvington.

Paper City. David R. Locke. (Muckrakers Ser.). 431p. (C). 1986. reprint ed. pap. text 10.95 (*0-8290-1861-1*) Irvington.

***Paper Clay.** Rosette Gault. (Illus.). 128p. 1999. text. write for info. (*90-5703-871-4*, Pub. by Craftsman House) Gordon & Breach.

Paper Clay. Rosette Gault. LC 97-28057. (Ceramics Handbooks). (Illus.). 128p. (C). (gr. 13). 1998. pap. 24.95 (*0-8122-1642-3*) U of Pa Pr.

Paper Clay for Ceramic Sculptors: A Studio Companion. 2nd ed. Rosette Gault. LC 95-92133. (Illus.). 72p. (C). 1996. pap. text 19.95 (*0-9638793-0-8*) Clear Lght Pub.

Paper Clip Science: Simple & Fun Experiments. Steven W. Moje. LC 96-10993. (Illus.). 96p. (J). (gr. 3). 1996. 14.95 (*0-8069-4385-8*) Sterling.

Paper Clip Science: Simple & Fun Experiments. Steven W. Moje. (Illus.). 96p. (J). 1997. pap. 4.95 (*0-8069-4386-6*) Sterling.

Paper Clothes. Jan Bailey. Ed. by Sue L. Inman & Keller C. Freeman. (Poetry Ser.). 64p. (Orig.). 1995. pap. 10.00 (*0-9645778-0-1*) Emrys Pr.

Paper Coating Additives. Robert J. Kane. LC 95-7397. 140p. 1995. 74.00 (*0-89852-061-4*, 0102B060) TAPPI.

Paper Coating Additives: Descsription of Functional Properties. Technical Association of the Pulp & Paper Industry. Ed. by A. A. Adams. LC 90-24721. 75p. reprint ed. pap. 30.00 (*0-7837-1643-5*, 204193700024) Bks Demand.

Paper Coating Additives Test Procedures by Functional Profile: A Project of the Coating Binders Committee of Coating & Graphic Arts Division. Technical Association of the Pulp & Paper Industry. Ed. by R. W. B. Lewis. LC TS1109.T43. 112p. reprint ed. pap. 34.80 (*0-608-14045-7*, 202234600026) Bks Demand.

Paper Coating Pigments: A Project of the Coating Pigments Committee. Technical Association of the Pulp & Paper Industry. Ed. by Robert W. Hagemeyer. LC 76-13421. (TAPPI Monographs: No. 38). 236p. reprint ed. pap. 73.20 (*0-608-13595-X*, 202030600016) Bks Demand.

Paper Coating Trends: In the Worldwide Paper Industry. Ed. by Ken L. Patrick. (Illus.). 172p. 1991. pap. 58.00 (*0-87930-247-X*) Miller Freeman.

Paper Coins. Ray Beckman. LC 84-71865. (Illus.). 250p. (Orig.). 1985. pap. 9.95 (*0-9611240-3-2*) Basement Pr.

Paper Collage: Painted Pictures. Christine McKechnie. 80p. 1995. pap. 19.95 (*0-85532-784-7*, 784-7, Pub. by Srch Pr) A Schwartz & Co.

Paper Coming Age in Samo. annuals Margaret Mead. 1971. pap. 13.00 (*0-688-30974-7*, Quil) HarperTrade.

Paper Container Dictionary, English, Finnish, Russian, Swedish, French, Spanish: Paperi-Ja Kartonkisanakirja Englanti-Suomi-Ruotsi-Saksa-Ranska-Espanja. J. Laurila & A. Hattari. (ENG, FIN, FRE, GER & SPA.). 839p. 1986. 295.00 (*0-8288-0334-X*, F23020) Fr & Eur.

Paper Counties: The Illinois Experience, 1825-1867. Michael D. Sublett. LC 90-32617. (American University Studies: Geography: Ser. XXV). (Illus.). XIV, 254p. (C). 1990. text 51.95 (*0-8204-1249-X*) P Lang Pubng.

Paper Craft. Editors at Eaglemoss. (Illus.). 144p. 1993. pap. 16.99 (*0-89134-541-8*, 30530, North Lght Bks) F & W Pubns Inc.

***Paper Crafting Beautiful Boxes, Book Covers & Frames** Valeria Ferrari & Ersilia Fiorucci. LC 99-29387. 1999. 24.95 (*0-8069-9953-5*) Sterling.

Paper Crafts. Sharon Broutzas et al. (Drawing, Paper Folding & Craft Books for Children). (Illus.). 48p. (J). (gr. k-5). 1998. lib. bdg. 17.95 (*1-56674-229-3*) Forest Hse.

Paper Crafts. Jo Finnis. 1995. 7.98 (*0-7858-0121-9*) Bk Sales Inc.

Paper Crafts. Walter Foster. 1998. pap. text 6.88 (*1-56010-220-9*) W Foster Pub.

Paper Crafts. Moore. (Illus.). 80p. (J). (gr. 1-6). 1997. pap., teacher ed. 7.95 (*1-55799-623-7*, 723) Evan-Moor Edu Pubns.

Paper Crafts: 50 Extraordinary Gifts & Projects Step by Step. Gillian Souter. 160p. 1995. pap. 20.00 (*0-517-88484-4*) Random Hse Value.

Paper Crane. Molly Bang. LC 84-13546. (Illus.). 32p. (J). (ps-3). 1985. 16.00 (*0-688-04108-6*, Grenwillow Bks) HarpC Child Bks.

Paper Crane. Molly Bang. (J). 1985. 10.15 (*0-606-04295-4*, Pub. by Turtleback) Demco.

Paper Crane. Molly Bang. LC 84-13546. 32p. (J). (gr. k up). 1987. reprint ed. mass mkt. 5.95 (*0-688-07333-6*, Wm Morrow) Morrow Avon.

Paper Creations: Easy-to-Make Paperfolding Projects. Gay M. Gross. LC 96-51838. (Illus.). 128p. 1997. 12.98 (*1-56799-439-3*, Friedman-Fairfax) M Friedman Pub Grp Inc.

Paper Crown. Tom Hawkins. LC 88-23512. 79 p. 1989. 8.95 (*0-933532-70-9*) BkMk.

Paper Curtain: Employer Sanctions' Implementation, Impact, & Reform. Ed. by Michael Fix. LC 91-19906. (Illus.). 354p. 1991. pap. text 38.50 (*0-87766-550-8*) Urban Inst.

Paper Cut-Out Design Book. Ramona Jablonski. LC 76-2467. (Illus.). 112p. 1976. pap. 14.95 (*0-916144-04-6*) Stemmer Hse.

Paper Cuts: The American Political Scene from Bush to Newt. Dan Wasserman. 160p. 1995. pap. 14.95 (*1-56663-092-4*) I R Dee.

***Paper Cuts Vol. 149: Recovering the Paper Landscape.** Janet N. Abramovitz & Ashley T. Mattoon. Ed. by Jane Peterson. 80p. 1999. pap. 5.00 (*1-878071-51-3*) Worldwatch Inst.

Paper Cutting. Stewart Waltonn & Sally Walton. (New Craft Ser.). (Illus.). 96p. 1997. 15.95 (*1-85967-533-6*, Lorenz Bks) Anness Pub.

Paper Cutting Stories for Holidays & Special Events. Valerie Marsh. LC 94-26174. (Illus.). (J). 1994. pap. text 14.95 (*0-917846-42-7*, Alleyside) Highsmith Pr.

Paper Cutting Stories from A to Z. Valerie Marsh. (Illus.). 80p. 1992. pap. 14.95 (*0-913853-24-0*, 32535, Alleyside) Highsmith Pr.

Paper Dance: 55 Latino Poets. Ed. by Victor H. Cruz et al. 256p. (Orig.). 1995. pap. 13.95 (*0-89255-201-8*) Persea Bks.

***Paper Daughter.** large type unabridged ed. Elaine M. Mar. 2000. 26.95 (*0-7531-5789-6*, 157896, Pub. by ISIS Lrg Prnt) ISIS Pub.

Paper Daughter: A Memoir. M. Elaine Mar. LC 99-10589. 304p. 1999. 23.00 (*0-06-018293-8*) HarpC.

***Paper Daughter: A Memoir.** M. Elaine Mar. 304p. 2000. pap. 13.00 (*0-06-093052-7*, Perennial) HarperTrade.

***Paper Decorator: Original Paperwork for Stylish Interiors.** Kerry Skinner. (Illus.). 144p. 2000. pap. 24.95 (*0-8230-3932-3*) Watsn-Guptill.

Paper Designs. Jerome C. Brown. (Lake's Paper Crafts Ser.). (J). (gr. 1-6). 1982. pap. 6.99 (*0-8224-5193-X*) Fearon Teacher Aids.

Paper Dictionary. C. Katz. (ENG, FRE & GER.). 360p. 1997. pap. 105.00 (*0-320-02325-7*) Fr & Eur.

Paper Doll. Robert B. Parker. 288p. 1994. mass mkt. 6.99 (*0-425-14155-1*) Berkley Pub.

Paper Doll. large type ed. Robert B. Parker. LC 93-22854. 309p. 1993. lib. bdg. 22.95 (*0-7862-0003-0*) Thorndike Pr.

Paper Doll. large type ed. Robert B. Parker. LC 93-22854. 309p. 1994. lib. bdg. 14.95 (*0-7862-0004-9*) Thorndike Pr.

Paper Doll. large type ed. Jim Shepard. 416p. 1989. 27.99 (*0-7089-2049-7*) Ulverscroft.

Paper Doll - Gibson Girl. Tom Tierney. (J). 1985. pap. 4.95 (*0-486-24980-8*) Dover.

Paper Doll - Godey Fashion. S. Johnston. (J). 1977. pap. 4.95 (*0-486-23511-4*) Dover.

Paper Doll - Judy Garland. 81st ed. Tom Tierney. (J). 1983. pap. 4.95 (*0-486-24404-0*) Dover.

Paper Doll - Victorian Girls. Sue Shanaha. (Illus.). (J). (ps-3). 1998. pap. 4.50 (*0-486-29382-3*, 284295Q) Dover.

Paper Doll - Worth Fashion Review. Tom Tierney. (Illus.). (J). (ps-3). 1996. pap. 4.95 (*0-486-29396-3*, 309879Q) Dover.

Paper Doll Christmas: Holiday Fun for Creative Kids. Phyllis Amerikaner. Ed. by Clark Editorial & Design Staff. (Illus.). 56p. (J). (gr. k-7). 1998. pap. 9.95 (*0-88160-304-X*, LW373) Learning Wks.

Paper Doll Greeting Cards Activity Book. Peggy Jo Rosamond. (Illus.). 32p. (J). 1990. pap. 5.95 (*0-87588-327-3*) Hobby Hse.

Paper Doll Party. Phyllis Amerikaner. (Illus.). 56p. (Orig.). (J). (gr. 1-5). 1996. pap. 10.95 (*0-88160-291-4*, LW361) Learning Wks.

Paper Doll Portrait: Antique German Bisque Dolls. Peggy Jo Rosamond. (Illus.). 32p. 1990. pap. 5.95 (*0-87588-246-3*) Hobby Hse.

Paper Dolls & Paper Airplanes: Therapeutic Exercises for Sexually Traumatized Children. Liana Lowenstein et al. (Illus.). 478p. 1997. 39.95 (*1-55864-048-7*) Kidsrights.

Paper Dolls in the Style of Mucha. Charles Ventura. (Illus.). 32p. (ps up). 1990. pap. text 4.95 (*0-87588-359-1*) Hobby Hse.

Paper Door & Other Stories. Shiga Naoya. Tr. by Lane Dunlop. 192p. 1993. pap. 12.95 (*0-8048-1893-2*) Tuttle Pubng.

***Paper Door & Other Stories by Shiga Naoya.** Shiga Naoya. Tr. by Lane Dunlop. 192p. 2001. pap. text 14.50 (*0-231-12157-1*) Col U Pr.

Paper Doors: Japan from Scratch. Angus Waycott. 216p. 1995. 35.00 (*0-233-98886-6*, Pub. by Andre Deutsch) Trafalgar.

Paper Doves, Falling: Poems. Jamie A. Parsley. Ed. by James C. Smith, Jr. LC 91-38890. 48p. (Orig.). 1992. pap. 6.95 (*0-86534-172-9*) Sunstone Pr.

Paper Dragon. Marguerite W. Davol. LC 95-32166. (Illus.). 60p. (J). (gr. k-3). 1997. 17.00 (*0-689-31992-4*) Atheneum Yung Read.

Paper Dreams: The Art & Artists of Disney Storyboards. John Canemaker. LC 98-28884. (Illus.). 288p. 1999. text 60.00 (*0-7868-6307-2*, Pub. by Hyperion) Time Warner.

Paper Drums. Gene L. Williams, III. 180p. 1999. pap. 12.95 (*1-890440-07-8*) Honey Clouds.

Paper Dutchman & Slave, 2 plays. LeRoi Jones et al. LC 79-93084. 1971. pap. 8.95 (*0-688-21084-8*, Quil) HarperTrade.

Paper Dynasty. Theodore R. Gardner, II. LC 90-62330. 600p. 1991. 23.45 (*0-9627297-0-1*) A A Knoll Pubs.

Paper Economy. David T. Bazelon. LC 78-11587. 467p. 1979. reprint ed. lib. bdg. 79.50 (*0-313-21001-2*, BATP, Greenwood Pr) Greenwood.

Paper Engineering. Clive Gifford. (How to Make Ser.). (Illus.). 32p. (Orig.). (J). (gr. 3-7). 1997. pap. 6.95 (*0-7460-2327-8*, Usborne); lib. bdg. 14.95 (*0-88110-939-8*, Usborne) EDC.

Paper Engineering for Pop-Up Books & Cards. Mark Hiner. (Illus.). 72p. (Orig.). 1986. pap. 13.95 (*0-906212-49-9*, Pub. by Tarquin Pubns) Parkwest Pubns.

Paper Faces. Rachel Anderson. 88p. (J). (gr. 4-7). 1995. 14.95 (*0-8050-2527-8*, Bks Young Read) H Holt & Co.

Paper Finishing & Converting Conference, 1984: Proceedings. Technical Association of the Pulp & Paper Industry. LC TS1109.. 121p. reprint ed. pap. 37.60 (*0-608-16141-1*, 202478300038) Bks Demand.

Paper Fish. Annabelle Curtis. 1997. pap. 8.95 (*1-899618-20-1*, Pub. by Tarquin Pubns) Parkwest Pubns.

Paper Fish. Tina De Rosa. LC 96-19342. 176p. 1996. pap. 9.95 (*1-55861-145-2*); lib. bdg. 20.00 (*1-55861-146-0*) Feminist Pr.

Paper Flight: 48 Models Ready for Take-Off. Jack Botermans. Tr. by Deborah Ogle from DUT. LC 83-49043. 120p. 1995. pap. 16.95 (*0-8050-0500-5*, Owl) H Holt & Co.

Paper Flowers. R. Gibson. (How to Make Ser.). (Illus.). 32p. (J). (gr. 3-7). 1995. pap. 6.95 (*0-7460-2108-9*, Usborne); lib. bdg. 14.95 (*0-88110-717-4*, Usborne) EDC.

Paper Flowers. Michael G. LaFosse. (Make It with Paper Ser.). (Illus.). 72p. 1997. pap. 9.95 (*1-56010-387-6*, RPO3) W Foster Pub.

Paper Flowers: 8 Step-by-Step Projects. Michael LaFosse. (Make It with Paper Ser.). (Illus.). 72p. 1997. pap. 19.99 (*1-56496-275-X*, Quarry Bks) Rockport Pubs.

Paper Flying Machines. John Andrews. (Illus.). 36p. (Orig.). 1994. pap. 8.95 (*0-906212-93-6*, Pub. by Tarquin Pubns) Parkwest Pubns.

Paper Folding: A Fun & Effective Method for Learning Math. Robert Jones. 227p. 1995. pap. text 14.95 (*0-9648724-0-4*) LWCD.

***Paper Folding: A Fun & Effective Method for Learning Math.** Robert Jones. (Student Workbook Ser.). (Illus.). 80p. (J). (gr. 5-12). 1999. pap., student ed., wbk. ed. 5.00 (*0-9648724-1-2*) LWCD.

Paper Folding for the Mathematics Class. Donovan A. Johnson. (Illus.). 32p. (YA). (gr. 7-12). 1995. reprint ed. pap. 9.95 (*0-87353-412-3*) NCTM.

***Paper Forms & Political Piracy.** 3rd rev. ed. John Gila. 260p. 2000. pap. text 149.00 (*1-930420-00-5*) Due Process.

***Paper Forms & Political Piracy, 1999 Edition.** 2nd ed. John Gliha. 290p. 1999. pap. text 149.00 (*0-9671019-0-5*) Due Process.

Paper Forms Design Optimization for Electronic Image Management (EIM) ANSI/AIIM TR32-1994. Association for Information & Image Management Staff. 20p. 1993. pap. 45.00 (*0-89258-271-5*, TR32) Assn Inform & Image Mgmt.

Paper Frankenstein. Eve Wood. (Publications: Vol. 21, No. 1). 35p. 1998. pap. 5.00 (*1-892184-00-1*) Beyond Baroque.

Paper Ghetto: Karl Kraus & Anti-Semitism. John Theobald. 218p. 1996. pap. 42.95 (*3-631-49463-7*) P Lang Pubng.

Paper Ghetto: Karl Kraus & Anti-Semitism. John Theobald. 218p. 1996. pap. 42.95 (*0-8204-3201-6*) P Lang Pubng.

Paper Gifts & Jewelry. Florence Temko. LC 96-28132. (Paper Magic Ser.). (Illus.). 48p. (J). (gr. 3-6). 1997. pap. 7.95 (*0-7613-0182-8*); lib. bdg. 20.90 (*0-7613-0209-3*) Millbrook Pr.

***Paper Goods Market in Poland: A Strategic Entry Report, 1996.** Compiled by Icon Group International Staff. (Illus.). 193p. 1999. ring bd. 1930.00 incl. audio compact disk (*0-7418-1354-8*) Icon Grp.

Paper Grail. James P. Blaylock. 1992. mass mkt. 5.99 (*0-441-65127-5*) Ace Bks.

***Paper Graphics: The Power of Paper in Graphic Design.** Catharine Fishel. (Illus.). 192p. 1999. 40.00 (*1-56496-563-5*) Rockport Pubs.

Paper Hat Tricks Vol. 1: A Big Book of Hat Patterns Holidays, Careers, Characters, & Animals. Patt Newbold & Anne Diebel. (Illus.). 36p. (Orig.). 1988. pap. text 15.95 (*1-56422-999-8*, Paper Hat) Start Reading.

Paper Hat Tricks Vol. 2: A Big Book of Hat Patterns Farm, Ocean, & Insect Hats. Patt Newbold & Anne Diebel. (Illus.). 36p. (Orig.). 1990. pap. text 15.95 (*1-56422-998-X*, Paper Hat) Start Reading.

Paper Hat Tricks Vol. 3: A Big Book of Hat Patterns Zoo, Forest, & Dinosaur Hats. Anne Diebel & Patt Newbold. (Illus.). 39p. (Orig.). 1991. pap. text 15.95 (*1-56422-997-1*, Paper Hat) Start Reading.

Paper Hat Tricks Vol. 5: A Big Book of Hat Patterns, Circus, Sports, Fun Foods, & Safety First Hats. Patt Newbold & Anne Diebel. 39p. (J). (ps-5). 1992. pap. text 15.95 (*1-56422-995-5*, Paper Hat) Start Reading.

***Paper Head Last Lyrics.** Andrew Levy. 112p. 2000. pap. 11.95 (*0-937804-83-5*, Pub. by Segue NYC) SPD-Small Pr Dist.

***Paper in Germany: A Strategic Entry Report, 1995.** Compiled by Icon Group International Staff. (Illus.). 96p. 1999. ring bd. 960.00 incl. audio compact disk (*0-7418-1641-5*) Icon Grp.

***Paper in Harmony: A Collection of Origami Instrumentalists.** Marc Kirschenbaum. (Illus.). 150p. 2000. pap. 18.00 (*0-615-11281-1*) Fit To Print Pubng.

Paper in the Printing Processes: Proceedings of the 8th International Conference on Printing Res Inst, Aulanko, 1965. W. H. Banks. LC 67-13995. (Advances in Printing Science & Technology Ser.: Vol. 4). 1967. 201.00 (*0-08-012289-2*, Pub. by Pergamon Repr) Franklin.

Paper Industry in France: A Strategic Entry Report, 1997. Compiled by Icon Group International Staff. (Illus.). 124p. 1999. ring bd. 1240.00 incl. audio compact disk (*0-7418-0877-3*) Icon Grp.

Paper Industry in Japan: A Strategic Entry Report, 1997. Compiled by Icon Group International Staff. (Illus.). 167p. 1999. ring bd. 1670.00 incl. audio compact disk (*0-7418-0903-6*) Icon Grp.

***Paper Industry in Singapore: A Strategic Entry Report, 1996.** Compiled by Icon Group International Staff. (Illus.). 125p. 1999. ring bd. 1250.00 incl. audio compact disk (*0-7418-1352-1*) Icon Grp.

Paper Innovations: Handmade Paper & Handmade Objects of Cut, Folded & Molded Paper. LC 85-63043. (Illus.). 128p. 1985. pap. 25.00 (*0-914155-04-0*) Mingei Intl Mus.

Paper into Pots: And Other Fun Objects Using Hand-Made Recycled Paper & Papier-Mache Techniques. Gerry Copp. (Illus.). 48p. 1995. pap. 11.95 (*0-85532-772-3*, 772-3, Pub. by Srch Pr) A Schwartz & Co.

Paper Jacket. Paul Matthews. 1991. 13.50 (*1-879356-02-3*) Wolfe Pub Co.

Paper Jeweller: Imaginative Designs to Cut Out, Make & Wear. Lexi Strauss. 1995. pap. 7.95 (*1-899618-01-5*, Pub. by Tarquin Pubns) Parkwest Pubns.

Paper Jewelry. Florence Temko. (Origami Favorites Ser.). 1990. pap. 5.95 (*0-89346-324-8*) Heian Intl.

Paper Jewelry. Jessica Wrobel. (Make It with Paper Ser.). (Illus.). 72p. 1997. pap. 9.95 (*1-56010-390-6*, RPO6) W Foster Pub.

Paper Jewelry Book. Jessica Wrobel. (Illus.). 96p. 1998. pap. 19.99 (*1-56496-350-0*, Quarry Bks) Rockport Pubs.

***Paper Jewelry Collection.** Wendy Ramshaw & David Watkins. LC 00-101181. (Illus.). 40p. 2000. 25.95 (*0-500-51019-9*, Pub. by Thames Hudson) Norton.

Paper John. David Small. LC 86-45261. (Illus.). 32p. (J). (ps-3). 1987. 15.00 (*0-374-35738-2*) FS&G.

Paper John. David Small. 32p. (J). (ps up). 1989. reprint ed. pap. 5.95 (*0-374-45725-5*, Sunburst Bks) FS&G.

Paper John. unabridged ed. David Small. (Illus.). (J). (gr. k-4). 1998. 24.95 incl. audio (*0-87499-451-9*); pap. 15.95 incl. audio (*0-87499-450-0*) Live Oak Media.

***Paper John, 4 bks., Set.** David Small. (Illus.). (J). (gr. k-3). 1998. pap., teacher ed. 33.95 incl. audio (*0-87499-452-7*) Live Oak Media.

Paper Journey: Travels among the Village Papermakers of India & Nepal. limited ed. Nigel MacFarlane. (Illus.). 90p. 1993. 240.00 (*0-938768-45-X*) Oak Knoll.

Paper Kaleidoscopes. Kay Leonard. (Illus.). 40p. (J). (gr. k-12). 1989. pap. 6.95 (*0-9623455-0-4*) Eye Cue.

***Paper Liberals: Press & Politics in Restoration Spain, 73.** David Ortiz. LC 99-55208. (Contributions to the Study of World History Ser.: Vol. 73). 2000. write for info. (*0-313-31216-8*, Greenwood Pr) Greenwood.

Paper Lions. Maurice Smith. 1994. 18.00 (*0-7486-6187-5*, Pub. by Polygon) Subterranean Co.

Paper Loading Materials. Technical Association of the Pulp & Paper Industry et al. LC 58-1147. (TAPPI Monographs: No. 19). 140p. reprint ed. pap. 43.40 (*0-608-13733-2*, 202030100016) Bks Demand.

P

Paper Locksmith. Mark Hiner. (Illus.). (J). 1996. pap. 10.95 (1-899618-03-1, Pub. by Tarquin Pubns) Parkwest Pubns.

Paper Mache. Judy Balchin. LC 00-38889. (Step-by-Step Ser.). (Illus.). 2000. write for info. (1-57572-328-X) Heinemann Lib.

Paper Mache. Dana Craig. (Art for Children's Ser.). 96p. 1992. 12.98 (1-55521-773-7) Bk Sales Inc.

Paper Mache. DK Publishing Staff. (Fun Pax Activity Ser.). (J). 1998. pap. 4.95 (0-7894-3801-1) DK Pub Inc.

***Paper Mache Made Easy.** Susan Penny. 64p. 1999. 12.95 (0-7153-0932-3) Strlng Pub CA.

Paper Machine Clothing. Sabit Adanur. LC 97-60981. 375p. 1997. text 79.95 (1-56676-544-7) Technomic.

Paper Machine Clothing: A Literature Review. Dick Hoyland. (Pira Reviews of Pulp & Paper Technology Ser.). 66p. 1992. pap. 95.00 (0-902799-85-1, TS1120, Pub. by Pira Internatl) Bks Intl VA.

Paper Machine Drives: 1984 Seminar Notes. Technical Association of the Pulp & Paper Industry. LC TS1117.. 114p. reprint ed. pap. 35.40 (0-608-12033-2, 202279900030) Bks Demand.

Paper Machine Drives Seminar, 1986: Notes of Notes of TAPPI, Crown Plaza - Holiday Inn, Atlanta, GA., March 5-7, 1986. Technical Association of the Pulp & Paper Industry. LC TS1117.. 137p. pap. 42.50 (0-608-15250-1, 202917700059) Bks Demand.

Paper Machine Drives Short Course, 1991: Hyatt Regency Atlanta, Atlanta, GA, March 18-21. Technical Association of the Pulp & Paper Industry. LC TS1118.D7.P3. (TAPPI Notes Ser.). 261p. pap. 81.00 (0-7837-0263-9, 204057200017) Bks Demand.

Paper Machine Drives Short Course, 1992: Atlanta Hilton Hotel, Atlanta, GA, March 1-6. Technical Association of the Pulp & Paper Industry. LC TS1118.D7.P3. (TAPPI Notes Ser.). 255p. reprint ed. pap. 79.10 (0-7837-2055-6, 204233000004) Bks Demand.

Paper Machine Dynamic - Foundation Design. Paper Machine Dynamic - Foundation Design Comt. St. 82p. 1994. 45.00 (0-89852-284-6, 0101R239) TAPPI.

Paper Machine Operations. (Pulp & Paper Manufacture Ser.: Vol. 7). (Illus.). 692p. 1991. text 97.88 (1-895288-13-4) Pulp & Paper.

Paper Machine Rebuild Seminar, 1992: Westin Peachtree Plaza Hotel, Atlanta, GA, March 4-6. Technical Association of the Pulp & Paper Industry. LC TS1117.P43. (TAPPI Notes Ser.). 260p. reprint ed. pap. 80.60 (0-7837-2056-4, 204233100004) Bks Demand.

Paper Machine Series, Vol 2: The Working Piston Engine. Joel Moskowitz. 96p. 1986. pap. 79.50 (0-671-93855-X) S&S Trade.

Paper Machine Steam & Condensate Systems. 4th ed. Ed. by Robert D. Perrault. 40p. 1990. pap. 18.00 (0-89852-504-7, 0101R096) TAPPI.

Paper Machine Wet Press Manual. 3rd rev. ed. Ed. by P. Seifert. 184p. 1991. 73.00 (0-89852-056-8, 0102B042) TAPPI.

Paper Magic. Jane Gordon-Clark. LC 90-27836. (Illus.). 192p. 1992. reprint ed. pap. 24.00 (0-679-74263-8) Pantheon.

Paper Magic: Pop-Up Paper Craft. Masahiro Chatani. (Illus.). 92p. 1988. pap. 15.00 (0-87040-757-0) Japan Pubns USA.

Paper Magic: The Art of Origami. Katherine Gleason. (Illus.). 64p. (J). (gr. 3-7). 1998. pap. 5.95 (0-8167-4542-0) Troll Communs.

Paper Making: How to Create Original Effects with Paper, Including Watermarked, Embossed, & Marbled Papers - 13 Projects. Marion Elliot. 96p. 1995. pap. 15.95 (0-8050-3895-7, Owl) H Holt & Co.

Paper-Making Through Eighteen Centuries. Dard Hunter. 1993. reprint ed. lib. bdg. 89.00 (0-7812-5381-0) Rprt Serv.

***Paper Man.** Michael Frederick. 304p. 2000. 16.00 (1-893794-01-6) M Frederick.

Paper Man. Peter Wood. 192p. 1996. pap. write for info. (0-614-20083-0, Pub. by P Owen Ltd) Dufour.

Paper Mansions. James R. Padgett. LC 86-13628. (Illus.). 256p. 1986. 14.95 (0-914875-12-4) Bright Mtn Bks.

***Paper Marriage.** Bronwyn Williams. (Historical Ser.). 2000. mass mkt. 4.99 (0-373-29124-8, 1-29124-4) Harlequin Bks.

Paper Masks & Puppets for Stories, Songs & Plays. Ron L. Feller & Marsha Y. Feller. LC 85-72952. (Illus.). 104p. (Orig.). (J). (gr. 2-9). 1986. pap. 14.95 (0-9615873-0-X) Arts Factory.

Paper Matcher: A Directory of Paper Recycling Resources. 259p. (Orig.). 1993. pap. text 45.00 (1-56806-947-2) DIANE Pub.

Paper Medicine Man: John Gregory Bourke & His American West. Joseph C. Porter. LC 85-40943. (Illus.). 352p. 1989. pap. 17.95 (0-8061-2218-8) U of Okla Pr.

Paper Mills & a Nation's Capital. Robert E. Harrigan. (Illus.). 180p. (C). 1995. lib. bdg. 39.50 (0-7618-0033-6) U Pr of Amer.

Paper-Mills of Berne. J. T. Lindt. (Monumenta Chartae Papyraceae Ser.). (Illus.). 468p. (C). 1964. text 134.50 (90-5356-202-8, Pub. by Amsterdam U Pr) U of Mich Pr.

Paper, Mister? Downtown Dayton - 1935. Howard Redder. 205p. (Orig.). 1995. pap. 14.95 (0-9657401-0-2) H J Redder.

Paper Money. Ken Follett. 1987. mass mkt. 6.99 (0-451-16730-9) NAL.

Paper Money Bibliography. M. McKerchar. 1979. 15.00 (0-686-51600-1) S J Durst.

Paper Money Inflation in France see Fiat Money Inflation in France

Paper-Money Inflation in France. Andrew D. White. (Notable American Authors Ser.). 1999. reprint ed. lib. bdg. 125.00 (0-7812-9933-0) Rprt Serv.

Paper Money of Brazil. 2nd ed. Dale A. Seppa. (Illus.). 104p. 1975. pap. 5.00 (0-916710-21-1) Obol Intl.

Paper Money of the E. A. Wright Bank Note Company. C. Frederick Schwan. (Illus.). 36p. 1978. pap. 10.00 (0-931960-02-9) BNR Pr.

Paper Money of the United States. 14th rev. ed. Robert Friedberg. Ed. by Ira Friedberg & Arthur Friedberg. (Illus.). 304p. 1995. 24.50 (0-87184-514-8) Coin & Curr.

Paper Money of the United States: A Complete Guide with Valuations. 15th rev. ed. Arthur L. Friedberg et al. Ed. by Ira S. Friedberg. LC 86-70306. (Illus.). 336p. 1998. 35.00 (0-87184-515-6) Coin & Curr.

Paper Money of the United States: A Complete Illustrated Guide with Valuations. 7th ed. Robert Friedberg & Jack Friedberg. LC 72-80202. 327 p. 1972. write for info. (0-87184-507-5) Coin & Curr.

Paper Money of the United States: A Complete Illustrated Guide with Valuations. 8th ed. Robert Friedberg & Jack Friedberg. LC 74-20035. 327 p. 1975. write for info. (0-87184-508-3) Coin & Curr.

Paper Money of the United States: A Complete Illustrated Guide with Valuations. 9th ed. Robert Friedberg et al. LC 78-66813. 251 p. 1978. write for info. (0-87184-509-1) Coin & Curr.

Paper Moon. Patricia Rice. 382p. 1996. mass mkt. 5.99 (0-451-40652-4, Topaz) NAL.

Paper Museum: Writing about Painting, Mostly. Andrew Graham-Dixon. LC 97-2812. (Illus.). 400p. 1997. 35.00 (0-679-45520-5) Knopf.

Paper Napkin Poems. Leah Paransky. 62p. (Orig.). 1980. pap. 3.95 (0-931642-07-8) Lintel.

Paper Nights. Gilles Tibo. (Illus.). 32p. (J). (ps-1). 1992. pap. 5.95 (1-55037-224-6, Pub. by Annick); lib. bdg. 15.95 (1-55037-225-4, Pub. by Annick) Firefly Bks Ltd.

Paper Now: Bent, Molded & Manipulated. Jane Glaubinger. LC 86-20792. 76p. 1986. pap. 17.95 (0-910386-88-9) Cleveland Mus Art.

Paper Office: Forms, Guidelines & Resources. 2nd ed. Edward L. Zuckerman. LC 96-27737. 366p. 1997. pap. text 55.00 (1-57230-104-X, 0104) Guilford Pubns.

Paper Office: The Tools to Make Your Small Psychotherapy Practice Work Ethically, Legally, & Profitably. Edward Zukerman & Irvin P. Guyett. (Clinician's Toolbox Ser.). 252p. 1991. reprint ed. pap. text 39.95 incl. disk (0-9622281-3-3) Three Wishes.

Paper or Plastic. Michael W. Walsh. 36p. 1996. 3.00 (0-9653194-1-5) Future Tense.

Paper or Plastic? Energy, Environment, & Consumerism in Sweden & America. Rita J. Erickson. LC 96-54489. 192p. 1997. 55.00 (0-275-95766-7, Praeger Pubs) Greenwood.

Paper Palaces: The Rise of the Renaissance Architectural Treatise. Ed. by Vaughan Hart & Peter Hicks. LC 98-15257. (Illus.). 424p. 1998. 45.00 (0-300-07530-8) Yale U Pr.

Paper Pandas & Jumping Frogs. Florence Temko. LC 86-70960. (Illus.). 135p. (J). (gr. 3-6). 1986. pap. 12.95 (0-8351-1770-7) China Bks.

Paper, Paper Everywhere. Gail Gibbons. LC 82-3109. (Illus.). 32p. (J). (gr. 1-5). 1983. 10.95 (0-15-259488-4, Harcourt Child Bks) Harcourt.

Paper, Paper Everywhere. Gail Gibbons. LC 82-3109. (Illus.). 32p. 1997. pap. 5.00 (0-15-201491-8) Harcourt.

Paper, Paper Everywhere. Gail Gibbons. 1997. 10.65 (0-606-11720-2, Pub. by Turtleback) Demco.

Paper Party. Meish Goldish. (Whole-Language Big Bks.). 16p. (J). (ps-2). 1992. pap. 16.95 (1-56784-054-X) Newbridge Educ.

Paper, Pen & Think. Ed. by Scholastic, Inc. Staff. 1981. pap. 12.95 (0-590-49012-5, Scholastic Hardcover) Scholastic Inc.

Paper People. Annabelle Curtis. (Illus.). 32p. (Orig.). (J). (gr. 3-4). 1991. pap. 6.95 (0-906212-61-8, Pub. by Tarquin Pubns) Parkwest Pubns.

Paper Perfect: 25 Bright Ideas for Paper. LaBeena Ishaque. LC 98-34939. (Illus.). 112p. 1998. reprint ed. 22.95 (1-57990-076-3, Pub. by Lark Books) Random.

Paper Physics Fundamentals & Papermaking Practices Seminar, 1987: Notes of TAPPI, Paper Valley Hotel, Appleton, WI, February 25-26. Technical Association of the Pulp & Paper Industry. LC TS1080.P33. (Illus.). 184p. pap. 57.10 (0-608-18395-4, 202998600067) Bks Demand.

Paper Physics Fundamentals & Papermaking Practices Seminar, 1989: Paper Valley Hotel, Appleton, WI, Feb. 14-15. Technical Association of the Pulp & Paper Industry. LC TS1121.P35. (TAPPI Notes Ser.). (Illus.). 203p. pap. 63.00 (0-8357-6335-8, 203560800096) Bks Demand.

Paper Physics Fundamentals & Papermaking Practices Seminar, 1990: The Portland Marriott, Portland, OR, February 13-14. Technical Association of the Pulp & Paper Industry. LC TS1121.P35. (TAPPI Notes Ser.). (Illus.). 244p. reprint ed. pap. 75.70 (0-8357-3731-4, 203645700003) Bks Demand.

***Paper Piece a Merry Christmas.** Jodie Davis. LC 00-35510. (Illus.). 96p. 2000. pap. 24.95 (1-56477-296-9) Martingale & Co.

Paper Pieced A, B, C's & 1, 2, 3's. Shirley Liby. (Illus.). 70p. 1994. spiral bd. 14.95 (1-890952-10-9) S Liby Pubns.

Paper Pieced Cats & Dogs. Shirley Liby. LC 97-206912. (Illus.). 62p. 1997. spiral bd. 14.95 (1-890952-16-8) S Liby Pubns.

***Paper-Pieced Curves.** Jodie Davis. LC 99-87653. (Illus.). 80p. 2000. pap. 21.95 (1-56477-302-7, B432, Pub. by Martingale & Co) F & W Pubns Inc.

***Paper Pieced Down on the Farm.** Shirley Liby. (Illus.). 41p. 2000. spiral bd. 14.95 (1-890952-20-6, Pub. by S Liby Pubns) Hearts IN.

Paper Pieced Houses & Gardens. Shirley Liby. (Illus.). 44p. 1998. spiral bd. 14.95 (1-890952-18-4) S Liby Pubns.

Paper Pieced Little Landscapes. Shirley Liby. (Illus.). 54p. 1995. spiral bd. 14.95 (1-890952-11-7) S Liby Pubns.

Paper Pieced Sea & Shore. Shirley Liby. 49p. 1999. spiral bd. 14.95 (1-890952-19-2, Pub. by S Liby Pubns) Hearts IN.

Paper Piecing Old Favorites. Shirley Liby. LC 98-158292. (Illus.). 46p. 1998. spiral bd. 14.95 (1-890952-17-6) S Liby Pubns.

Paper Piecing Patterns. Shirley Liby. (Illus.). 82p. 1993. spiral bd. 14.95 (1-890952-07-9) S Liby Pubns.

Paper Piecing the Seasons: Foundation Piecing from Easy to Expert. Liz Schwartz & Stephen Seifert. (Illus.). 1998. pap. 24.95 (1-56477-248-9, B371, That Patchwrk Pl) Martingale & Co.

Paper Pile Quarterly Vol. V: April 1984-January 1985: Old Paper Collectibles, An Evolving Value Guide. Ed. by Ada Fitzsimmons. (Illus.). 96p. 1985. pap. 7.50 (0-915195-04-6) Paper Pile.

Paper Pile Quarterly Vol. VI: April 1985-January 1986: Old Paper Collectibles, an Evolving Value Guide. Ada Fitzsimmons. (Illus.). 130p. (Orig.). 1986. pap. 8.50 (0-915195-06-2) Paper Pile.

Paper Pilot. (Activity Fun Packs Ser.). (Illus.). (YA). (gr. 6 up). 1996. pap. 4.95 (0-7894-0764-7) DK Pub Inc.

Paper Planes Kid Kit. Iain Ashman. (Usborne Kid Kits Ser.). (Illus.). (J). (gr. 3 up). 1999. 9.95 (0-88110-882-0, Usborne) EDC.

Paper Plate Art. Ed. by Instructional Fair Staff. Date not set. pap. 8.95 (0-513-02104-3) Instruct Fair.

Paper Plate Arts & Crafts Activities: Week-by-Week Projects Using Paper Plates. Julie McKenzie & Thomas McKenzie. Ed. by Judy Mitchell. (Illus.). 112p. (Orig.). (J). (gr. k-3). 1996. pap., teacher ed. 10.95 (1-57310-039-0) Teachng & Lrning Co.

***Paper Plate Crafts: Creative Art Fun for 3- to 7-Year Olds.** Laura Check. (Little Hands Ser.). (Illus.). 144p. (J). (ps-2). 2000. pap. 12.95 (1-885593-43-0) Williamson Pub Co.

Paper Play see Homeplay: Joyful Learning for Children & Adults, Series I

Paper Pleasures: Five Centuries of Drawings & Watercolors. Charles R. Mack. 168p. (C). 1995. pap. 19.95 (1-57003-065-0) U of SC Pr.

Paper Plus: Unique Projects Using Handmade Paper. Nancy Worrell. LC 97-73032. (Illus.). 128p. 1997. pap. 18.95 (0-8019-8918-3, CHPP) Krause Pubns.

***Paper Pockets & Boxes.** Provo Craft Designers Staff. (Illus.). 32p. 1998. 7.99 (1-58050-061-7, 40-6196) Provo Craft.

Paper Politics: The Northern State Loan-Offices During the Confederation. John P. Kaminski. (Outstanding Studies in Early American History). 305p. 1989. reprint ed. 20.00 (0-8240-6185-3) Garland.

Paper Polyhedra in Colour: 15 Symmetrical Models to Cut Out & Glue Together. Gerald Jenkins & Magadalene Bear. (Illus.). (J). pap. 8.95 (1-899618-23-6, Pub. by Tarquin Pubns) Parkwest Pubns.

Paper Pop-Ups. Paul Jackson. (Make It with Paper Ser.). (Illus.). 96p. 1997. pap. 19.99 (1-56496-170-2, Quarry Bks) Rockport Pubs.

Paper Pop-Ups. Michael LaFosse. (Make It with Paper Ser.). (Illus.). 72p. 1997. pap. 9.95 (1-56010-386-8, RPO2) W Foster Pub.

Paper Pound of 1797-1812. 2nd ed. Ed. by Edwin Cannan. 72p. 1970. reprint ed. 35.00 (0-7146-1210-3, Pub. by F Cass Pubs) Intl Spec Bk.

Paper Pound of 1797-1812: The Bullion Report, 8th June, 1810. 2nd ed. Intro. by Edwin Cannan. LC 67-24748. (Reprints of Economic Classics Ser.). 1969. reprint ed. 35.00 (0-678-00536-2) Kelley.

Paper Presents: To Color, Cut Out & Glue Together. Peter Hyde. 1995. pap. 6.95 (1-899618-00-7, Pub. by Tarquin Pubns) Parkwest Pubns.

Paper Preservation: Current Issues & Recent Developments. Ed. by Philip Luner. LC 90-46550. 160p. reprint ed. pap. 49.60 (0-8357-2957-5, 203921900011) Bks Demand.

Paper Preservation-Conservation Techniques & Methodology. Dewayne J. Lener. (Illus.). 123p. 1988. pap. 19.95 (0-945433-04-2) Herit Quest.

Paper Preservation Symposium, 1988: Capital Hilton, Washington, DC, Oct., 19-21. Technical Association of the Pulp & Paper Industry. LC TS1080.. (TAPPI Proceedings Ser.). 227p. reprint ed. pap. 70.40 (0-8357-6248-3, 203466500090) Bks Demand.

Paper Princess. Elisa Kleven. LC 93-32612. (Illus.). (J). (ps-3). 1994. 15.99 (0-525-45231-1, Dutton Child) Peng Put Young Read.

Paper Princess. Elisa Kleven. 1998. 11.19 (0-606-13694-0, Pub. by Turtleback) Demco.

***Paper Processing Machinery in Saudi Arabia: A Strategic Entry Report, 1995.** Compiled by Icon Group International Staff. (Illus.). 129p. 1999. ring bd. 1290.00 incl. audio compact disk (0-7418-1623-7) Icon Grp.

Paper Protection - Human Rights Violation & the Mexican Criminal Justice System: A Report of the MLIHRC. MLIHRC Delegate Staff & Daniel Gerdtz. 65p. (Orig.). (C). 1990. pap. 7.00 (0-929293-07-X) MN Advocates.

Paper Purgatory. Michael Ambrose & Albert J. Manachino. (Illus.). 20p. (Orig.). 1990. pap. 2.50 (0-9634181-2-2) Argo Pr.

Paper Raincoat. Sonya Dorman. (Illus.). 60p. 1979. pap. 3.50 (0-913006-09-2) Puckerbrush.

Paper Recycling. Richard K. Miller & Marcia E. Rupnow. LC 90-83878. (Survey on Technology & Markets Ser.: No. 174). 50p. 1991. pap. text 200.00 (1-55865-198-5) Future Tech Surveys.

Paper Recycling: Strategies, Economics, & Technology. Ed. by Ken L. Patrick. (Illus.). 202p. (Orig.). 1991. pap. 49.00 (0-87930-231-3) Miller Freeman.

Paper Recycling Challenge: Stickies, Vol. 1. Mahendra R. Doshi & Jeffrey M. Dyers. 349p. 1997. (0-9657447-0-1) CA66.

Paper Recycling Challenge Vol. II: Deinking & Bleaching, 4 vols. Mahendra R. Doshi & Jeffrey M. Dyer. LC 97-213200. (Illus.). 320p. 1997. pap. write for info. (0-9657447-1-X) Doshi & Assocs.

***Paper Recycling Challenge Vol. III: Process Technology.** Mahendra R. Doshi & Jeffrey M. Dyer. LC 97-213200. (Illus.). 300p. 1998. pap. 105.00 (0-9657447-3-6) Doshi & Assocs.

***Paper Recycling Challenge Vol. IV: Process Control & Mensuration.** Mahendra R. Doshi & Jeffrey M. Dyer. (Illus.). 210p. 1999. pap. 75.00 (0-9657447-4-4) Doshi & Assocs.

***Paper Recycling Machinery in Canada: A Strategic Entry Report, 1998.** Compiled by Icon Group International Staff. (Country Industry Report). (Illus.). 135p. 1999. ring bd. 1350.00 incl. audio compact disk (0-7418-0550-2) Icon Grp.

***Paper Recycling Machinery in Mexico: A Strategic Entry Report, 1997.** Compiled by Icon Group International Staff. (Illus.). 142p. 1999. ring bd. 1420.00 incl. audio compact disk (0-7418-1075-1) Icon Grp.

Paper Requirements for Printing Performance Seminar, 1984 Notes. Technical Association of the Pulp & Paper Industry. LC TS1121.. 25p. reprint ed. pap. 30.00 (0-608-13000-1, 202477100038) Bks Demand.

***Paper Rose.** Diana Palmer. 1999. mass mkt. 5.99 (1-55166-539-5, Mira Bks) Harlequin Bks.

Paper Route Treasure. Marcia Hoehne. (J). (gr. 4-7). 1995. pap. 4.99 (0-7459-2801-3) Lion USA.

Paper Science Toys. E. Richard Churchill. LC 90-9891. (Illus.). 128p. (YA). (gr. 3-10). 1990. 14.95 (0-8069-5834-0) Sterling.

Paper, Scissors, Rock. Ann Decter. 192p. 1992. pap. 12.95 (0-88974-040-2, Pub. by Press Gang Pubs) LPC InBook.

Paper Sculpture: A Step-by-Step Guide. Kathleen Ziegler & Nick Greco. (Illus.). 152p. 1996. pap. 22.99 (1-56496-329-2) Rockport Pubs.

Paper Sculpture: A Step-by-Step Guide. Kathleen Zieler & Nick Greco. (Illus.). 152p. 1994. 29.99 (1-56496-034-X, 30510) Rockport Pubs.

Paper Sex & Temperment. Margaret Mead. 335p. 1971. pap. 12.95 (0-688-06016-1, Quil) HarperTrade.

***Paper Shadows: A Memoir of a Past Lost & Found.** Wayson Choy. 352p. 2000. 24.00 (0-312-26218-3, Picador USA) St Martin.

Paper Shapes. Meredith Thomas. LC 93-27994. (Voyages Ser.). (Illus.). (J). 1994. 4.25 (0-383-03767-0) SRA McGraw.

Paper Sheriff. large type ed. Luke Short. LC 91-34106. 282p. (Orig.). 1992. reprint ed. lib. bdg. 15.95 (1-56054-232-2) Thorndike Pr.

Paper Shield: Avoiding Confusion, Conflicts & Lawsuits. R. Dodge Woodson. LC 96-172756. 180p. 1995. 39.95 (1-56842-053-6) Marshall & Swift.

Paper Shoe Book. Horsey. 1995. pap. write for info. (0-517-88495-X) C Potter.

Paper Shredders: An Anthology of Surf Writing. Ed. by G. Murray Thomas & Gary Wright. LC 93-83925. (Illus.). 67p. (Orig.). 1994. reprint ed. pap. 8.00 (1-885021-00-3) Orange Ocean.

Paper Snake. Ray Johnson. LC 65-15545. (Illus.). 1965. 75.00 (0-89366-061-2) Ultramarine Pub.

Paper Soldiers: Illustrated History of Printed Paper Armies. Edward Ryan. LC 99-199545. (Illus.). 528p. 1995. 225.00 (0-904568-96-2, Pub. by Golden Age Edits) Pincushion Pr.

Paper Soldiers: The American Press & the Vietnam War. Clarence R. Wyatt. vi, 272p. 1994. pap. 14.95 (0-226-91795-9) U Ch Pr.

Paper Soldiers of American Revolution, Vol. 2. Bellerophon Staff. (J). (gr. 1-9). 1994. pap. text 3.95 (0-88388-038-5) Bellerophon Bks.

Paper Soldiers of the American Revolution, Vol. 1. Marko Zlatich. (J). (gr. 1-9). 1992. pap. 4.95 (0-88388-028-8) Bellerophon Bks.

Paper Soldiers of the Civil War. Alan Archambault. (Illus.). (J). (gr. 1-9). 1992. pap. 4.95 (0-88388-152-7) Bellerophon Bks.

***Paper Son: One Man's Story.** Tung Pok Chin & Winifred C. Chin. (Asian American History & Culture Ser.). (Illus.). 208p. 2000. 59.50 (1-56639-800-2); pap. 19.95 (1-56639-801-0) Temple U Pr.

Paper Stones: A History of Electoral Socialism. Adam Przeworski & John Sprague. LC 86-6984. (Illus.). vi, 230p. (C). 1986. 29.95 (0-226-68497-0) U Ch Pr.

Paper Stones: A History of Electoral Socialism. Adam Przeworski & John Sprague. LC 86-6984. (Illus.). vi, 224p. (C). 1994. pap. text 11.95 (0-226-68498-9) U Ch Pr.

Paper Stories. Jean Stangl. LC 84-60238. (J). (ps-3). 1984. pap. 11.99 (0-8224-5402-5) Fearon Teacher Aids.

Paper Structure & Properties. J. Anthony Bristow. Ed. by Peter Kolseth. (International Fiber Science & Technology Ser.: Vol. 8). (Illus.). 416p. 1986. text 235.00 (0-8247-7560-0) Dekker.

Paper Summaries of the 1995 ASNT Fall Conference. (Illus.). 204p. 1995. pap. 31.00 (1-57117-013-8, 1350) Am Soc Nondestructive.

Paper Summaries of the 1995 ASNT Spring Conference/Fourth Annual Research Symposium. (Illus.). 252p. (C). 1995. pap. 31.00 (1-57117-009-X, 1347) Am Soc Nondestructive.

Paper Tags & Cards. Florence Temko. LC 96-28133. (Paper Magic Ser.). (Illus.). 48p. (J). (gr. 3-6). 1997. lib. bdg. 20.90 (0-7613-0210-7) Millbrook Pr.

Paper Tangos. J. M. Taylor. LC 97-31240. (Public Planet Bks.). 136p. 1998. 39.95 (*0-8223-2175-0*) Duke.
Paper Tangos. Julie Taylor. LC 97-31240. (Public Planet Bks.). 136p. 1998. pap. 13.95 (*0-8223-2191-2*) Duke.
Paper Tearing Bible Talks, No. 4. Arnold C. Westphal. 1970. pap. 4.95 (*0-915398-03-6*) Visual Evangels.
Paper Tearing Evangels, No. 8. Arnold C. Westphal. 1975. per. 4.95 (*0-915398-07-9*) Visual Evangels.
Paper Tearing Gospel Illustrations, No. 3. Arnold C. Westphal. 1969. per. 4.95 (*0-915398-02-8*) Visual Evangels.
Paper Tearing Trick Talks, No. 1. Arnold C. Westphal. 1967. per. 4.95 (*0-915398-00-1*) Visual Evangels.
Paper Tears with a Gospel Message, No. 14. Arnold C. Westphal. LC 89-52045. 1990. per. 4.95 (*0-915398-28-1*) Visual Evangels.
Paper Television. Julia Vinograd. (Orig.). 1993. pap. 4.95 (*0-929730-45-3*) Zeitgeist Pr.
Paper Terms: Thesaurus for Use in Rare Book & Special Collections Cataloging. Association of College and Research Libraries, American Library Association. 52p. 1990. pap. text 9.00 (*0-8389-7427-9*) Assn Coll & Res Libs.
Paper Tiger. Tim Jessell. LC 95-39496. (J). 1997. 17.00 (*0-15-201312-1*) Harcourt.
Paper Tiger Guide to TV Repair. Paper Tiger Television Collective Staff. 32p. (Orig.). 1992. pap. 5.00 (*0-930495-19-5*) San Fran Art Inst.
Paper Tigers: The Latest, Greatest Newspaper Tycoons & How They Won the World. Nicholas Coleridge. LC 93-45736. 1994. 24.95 (*1-55972-215-0*, Birch Ln Pr) Carol Pub Group.
Paper Tigers & Minotaurs: The Politics of Venezuela's Economic Reforms. Moises Naim. LC 92-35295. 1992. 24.95 (*0-87003-025-6*); pap. 8.95 (*0-87003-026-4*) Carnegie Endow.
***Paper Tole Book.** large type ed. Dee Overduin. (Illus.). 94p. 1998. 23.95 (*0-9669185-0-9*) Tole Way.
Paper Towel Testing. rev. ed. Cary Sneider & Jacqueline Barber. Ed. by Lincoln Bergman & Kay Fairwell. (Great Explorations in Math & Science (GEMS) Ser.). (Illus.). 48p. (YA). (gr. 5-8). 1998. pap. 10.50 (*0-924886-11-0*, GEMS) Lawrence Science.
Paper Toy Making. Margaret W. Campbell. LC 75-2570. 96p. 1975. reprint ed. pap. 4.95 (*0-486-21662-4*) Dover.
***Paper Trail.** Barbara Snow Gilbert. LC 00-24231. 224p. (YA). (gr. 7-12). 2000. 16.95 (*1-886910-44-8*, Pub. by Front Str) Publishers Group.
Paper Trail: A Recollection of Writers. Dorothea Straus. LC 96-31207. 240p. 1997. 22.95 (*1-55921-195-4*) Moyer Bell.
Paper Trail: Essays. Michael Dorris. LC 93-41420. 384p. 1995. pap. 12.00 (*0-06-092593-0*, Perennial) HarperTrade.
Paper Trail: Personal & Financial Privacy in the Nineties. 2nd ed. M. L. Shannon. (Illus.). 193p. 1995. pap. text 25.97 (*1-884451-07-1*) Lysias Pr.
Paper Trail: The Guide for Protecting Your Ass(ets) Hugh M. Hyre. LC 98-93882. 104p. 1998. pap. 19.95 (*0-9668269-0-6*, PTS) Enoch Pr.
Paper Trail: The Real Estate Professional's Guide to Documented Liability Protection & Marketing Success. Oliver E. Frascona. LC 87-8904. (Real Law Bks.). 1990. pap. 35.00 (*0-941937-00-3*) Real Law Bks.
Paper Trail: The Real Estate Professional's Guide to Documented Liability Protection & Marketing Success. rev. ed. Oliver E. Frascona. LC 89-24349. (Risk Reduction Ser.). 204p. 1986. reprint ed. pap. 35.00 (*0-941937-01-1*) Real Law Bks.
Paper Trails: A Guide to Public Records in California. 2nd ed. Stephen Levine & Barbara Newcombe. 244p. (C). 1996. pap. 18.95 (*0-9621793-2-9*) CA News Pubs Assn.
Paper Trails: Prints, Drawings & Watercolors of the San Francisco School of Abstract Expressionism. Susan Landauer. LC 92-73567. (Illus.). (C). 1993. pap. 12.00 (*0-945952-00-7*) Mus Art Hist.
Paper Treasure. Anne Stephenson. 160p. (Orig.). (J). (gr. 3-6). 1991. pap. 4.95 (*0-7736-7336-9*) Stoddart Publ.
***Paper Trees.** Roy Sinclair. 373p. 1999. pap. 15.95 (*0-920576-78-8*) Caitlin Pr.
***Paper Trees: Genealogical Clip-Art.** Tony Matthews. LC 98-75467. 100p. 1999. pap. 14.95 (*0-8063-1607-1*) Genealog Pub.
Paper Tricks & Toys. E. Richard Churchill. LC 91-38789. 128p. (J). 1992. 16.95 (*0-8069-8416-3*) Sterling.
Paper Trip. Michael A. Lowe. (Illus.). 78p. 1999. pap. 12.99 (*0-9669687-1-9*) M A Lowe.
Paper Tube Zoo. Joy Evans & Jo E. Moore. (Illus.). 32p. (J). (gr. k-3). 1988. pap., teacher ed. 4.95 (*1-55799-139-1*, EMC 230) Evan-Moor Edu Pubs.
Paper Tubes & Bags. Leverne Kelvington Stroup. (Creative Factor Bible Activities for Church & Home Ser.). pap. 5.95 (*0-8272-9019-5*) Chalice Pr.
***Paper Universe.** (StarTrek Ser.). 192p. 2000. per. 13.95 (*0-671-04215-7*) PB.
Paper Wasp. Teresa Cader. LC 98-34132. 80p. 1998. 39.95 (*0-8101-5083-2*); pap. 14.95 (*0-8101-5084-0*) Northwestern U Pr.
Paper, Wasps & Packages: The Romantic Story of Paper & Its Influence on the Course of History. Alexander Weaver. 1977. lib. bdg. 59.95 (*0-8490-2407-2*) Gordon Pr.
Paper Wedding see Boda de Papel
Paper Weight. Lucy Kincaid. (You Can Make It Ser.). (Illus.). 24p. (J). 1997. 3.49 (*1-85854-543-9*) Brimax Bks.
Paper-Whites for Lady Jane. Louis D. Brodsky. LC 95-42905. 74p. 1995. pap. 12.50 (*1-877770-96-5*) Time Being Bks.
Paper-Whites for Lady Jane: Poems of a Midlife Love Affair. Louis D. Brodsky. LC 95-42905. 74p. 1995. 18.95 (*1-877770-95-7*) Time Being Bks.
Paper Wife. Linda Spalding. 248p. 1997. pap. 12.00 (*0-88001-524-1*) HarpC.
Paper Wife. Linda Spalding. 238p. 1996. reprint ed. text 23.00 (*0-88001-453-9*) HarpC.
Paper Wings: A Novel. Marly Swick. 288p. 1997. pap. 12.00 (*0-06-092837-9*, Perennial) HarperTrade.
Paper Women & the Men. Nikki Giovanni. LC 75-16237. 1979. pap. 9.00 (*0-688-07947-4*, Quil) HarperTrade.
Paperart: Sculpting with Paper. Michael LaFosse. (Illus.). 144p. 1998. 29.99 (*1-56496-378-0*, Quarry Bks) Rockport Pubs.
Paperback Books: Playscript. rev. ed. Mary Steelsmith. Ed. by William-Alan Landes. LC 96-21760. 55p. (Orig.). 1996. pap. 5.00 (*0-88734-306-6*) Players Pr.
Paperback Books for Young People: An Annotated Guide to Publishers & Distributors. 2nd ed. John T. Gillespie. LC 77-21627. 231p. reprint ed. pap. 71.70 (*0-608-12588-1*, 202395000034) Bks Demand.
Paperback Clinic: A Simplified Manual of Natural Therapeutics. Andrew Saul. 200p. 1994. 29.95 (*0-614-04558-4*) NY Chiro Coll.
Paperback Price Guide. 2nd ed. Kevin B. Hancer. (Illus.). 440p. 1982. pap. 9.95 (*0-517-54453-9*) Overstreet.
Paperback Romance. Karin Kallmaker. 256p. 1992. pap. 11.95 (*1-56280-019-1*) Naiad Pr.
Paperback Talk. Ray Walters. (Illus.). 350p. 1985. 19.95 (*0-89733-108-7*); pap. 11.00 (*0-89733-109-5*) Academy Chi Pubs.
Paperback Writers: The History of the Beatles in Print Bill Harry. LC 85-205165. 192 p. 1984. write for info. (*0-86369-021-1*) Virgin Bks.
Paperbag Princess see Princesa Vestida con una Bolsa de Papel
Paperbark: A Collection of Black Australian Writings. Ed. by Jack Davis et al. (Illus.). 369p. 1990. pap. 19.95 (*0-7022-2180-5*, Pub. by Univ Queensland Pr) Intl Spec Bk.
Paperbound Book in America: The History of Paperbacks & Their European Background. Frank L. Schick. LC 58-10097. 280p. reprint ed. pap. 86.80 (*0-608-11440-5*, 201397400088) Bks Demand.
Paperboy. Pete Dexter. 336p. 1996. pap. 12.95 (*0-385-31572-4*) Dell.
Paperboy. Isabelle Holland. LC 98-36880. 144p. (J). (gr. 3-7). 1999. 15.95 (*0-8234-1422-1*) Holiday.
Paperboy. Mary K. Kroeger & Louise Borden. LC 94-34246. (Illus.). 40p. (J). (gr. k-4). 1996. 16.95 (*0-395-64482-8*, Clarion Bks) HM.
Paperboy. Dav Pilkey. LC 95-30641. (Illus.). 32p. (J). (ps-5). 1996. 14.95 (*0-531-09506-1*); lib. bdg. 15.99 (*0-531-08856-1*) Orchard Bks Watts.
Paperboy. Dav Pilkey. LC 95-30641. (Illus.). 32p. (J). (ps-5). 1999. pap. 5.95 (*0-531-07139-1*) Orchard Bks Watts.
Paperboy. large type ed. Pete Dexter. LC 95-15715. (Large Print Bks.). 1995. pap. 22.95 (*1-56895-217-1*) Wheeler Pub.
***Paperboy: Essays, Short Stories, Profiles, Comments & Comic Pieces.** J. T. Knoll. Ed. by Linda Knoll. 182p. 1999. pap. 13.00 (*0-9670490-0-8*, 777) White Buf Pr.
Paperclip Conspiracy: The Hunt for Nazi Scientists. Tom Bower. 288p. 1988. 17.95 (*0-316-10399-3*) Little.
Papercraft. Meryl Doney. LC 96-35495. (World Crafts Ser.). 32p. (J). (gr. 4 up). 1998. lib. bdg. 21.00 (*0-531-14446-1*) Watts.
Papercraft. Lorenz. (Illus.). 19.98 (*0-7548-0332-5*, Pub. by Anness Pub) Random.
Papercraft: Making & Decorating Paper. Diane V. Maurer-Mathison & Jennifer Philippoff. LC 94-27976. (Illus.). 120p. 1995. 11.95 (*1-56799-151-3*, Friedman-Fairfax) M Friedman Pub Grp Inc.
Papercraft Projects with One Piece of Paper. Michael Grater. (Illus.). 112p. 1987. reprint ed. pap. 5.95 (*0-486-25504-2*) Dover.
Papercraft School. Clive Stevens. LC 96-11754. (Learn-As-You-Go Guides Ser.). (Illus.). 176p. 1996. 22.00 (*0-89577-873-4*, Pub. by RD Assn) Penguin Putnam.
Papercrafts. Meryl Doney. (World Crafts Ser.). (J). 1998. pap. 6.95 (*0-531-15330-4*) Watts.
***Papercrafts Around the World.** Phyllis Fiarotta. (Illus.). 2000. pap. 9.95 (*0-8069-4986-4*) Sterling.
Papercrafts Around the World. Phyllis Fiarotta & Noel Fiarotta. LC 95-44154. (Illus.). 96p. (J). 1996. 19.95 (*0-8069-3990-7*) Sterling.
Papercuts & Plenty: Studies in Classic Album Quilt Applique. Elly Sienkiewicz. LC 89-60479. (Baltimore Beauties & Beyond Ser.: Vol. III). (Illus.). 192p. 1995. pap. 27.95 (*0-914881-90-6*, 10108) C & T Pub.
Papercutting: An International Bibliography & Selected Guide to U. S. Collections. Martha Kreisel. LC 94-2516. (Illus.). 277p. 1994. 40.00 (*0-8108-2856-1*) Scarecrow.
Papered Rooms. Patricia Goodrich. Ed. by Shirley Warren. 28p. 1990. pap. 5.00 (*1-877801-10-0*) Still Waters.
Paperie: The Art of Writing & Wrapping with Paper. Bo Niles & Kate's Paperie Staff. LC 98-33664. (Illus.). 192p. 1999. 35.00 (*0-684-84423-0*) S&S Trade.
***Papering & Painting: The Essential Guide to Home Decorating.** Julian Cassell & Peter Parham. LC 99-89109. (Do-It-Yourself Factfile Ser.). (Illus.). 112p. (gr. 8). 2000. spiral bd. 12.95 (*0-7370-0310-3*) Time-Life.
Papering Projects Etc. Cy DeCosse Incorporated Staff. LC 96-28584. (Creative Touches Ser.). (Illus.). 64p. 1996. pap. 9.95 (*0-86573-877-7*) Creat Pub Intl.
Paperjack. Charles De Lint. (Illus.). 72p. 1992. boxed set 190.00 (*0-941826-21-X*) Cheap St.
Paperless Contracting: The EDI Revolution. John W. Davis. 177p. Date not set. ring bd. 99.00 (*1-56726-025-X*, B557) Mgmt Concepts.
Papermaker. Mark Richard. 1999. write for info. (*0-385-42569-4*) Doubleday.
***Papermakers.** Leonard Everett Fisher. (Colonial Craftsmen Ser.). (Illus.). (J). 2000. 21.36 (*0-7614-1147-X*, Benchmark NY) Marshall Cavendish.
***Papermaker's Companion: The Ultimate Guide to Making & Using Handmade Paper.** Helen Hiebert. (Illus.). 224p. 2000. pap. 18.95 (*1-58017-200-8*) Storey Bks.
Papermakers Conference, Chicago, April 11-13, 1988. Technical Association of the Pulp & Paper Industry. LC TS1080.. (TAPPI Proceedings Ser.). (Illus.). 407p. reprint ed. pap. 126.20 (*0-608-18427-6*, 203227300079) Bks Demand.
Papermakers Conference, 1984: Proceedings. Technical Association of the Pulp & Paper Industry. LC TS1080.P28. 265p. reprint ed. pap. 82.20 (*0-608-12038-3*, 202279300030) Bks Demand.
Papermakers Conference, 1987: Proceedings of TAPPI, Hyatt Regency, Atlanta, GA, April 6-8. Technical Association of the Pulp & Paper Industry. LC TS1080.. (Illus.). 352p. pap. 109.20 (*0-608-17483-1*, 202997800067) Bks Demand.
Papermakers Conference, 1985: Proceedings of TAPPI, Marriott Hotel, Denver, CO, April 15-17. Technical Association of the Pulp & Paper Industry. LC TS1080.. 349p. reprint ed. pap. 108.20 (*0-608-12812-0*, 202528800043) Bks Demand.
Papermakers Conference, 1986: Proceedings of TAPPI, Marriott Hotel, New Orleans, LA, April 14-16, 1986. Technical Association of the Pulp & Paper Industry. LC TS1080.. 343p. pap. 106.40 (*0-608-15254-4*, 202918000059) Bks Demand.
Papermakers Conference, 1989: Washington Hilton, Washington, DC, April 10-12. Technical Association of the Pulp & Paper Industry. LC TS1171.T43. (TAPPI Proceedings Ser.). (Illus.). 385p. reprint ed. pap. 119.40 (*0-8357-6336-6*, 203560900096) Bks Demand.
Papermakers Conference, 1995: Chicago Marriott Downtown, Chicago, IL, April 23-26, 1995. Technical Association of the Pulp & Paper Industry. LC TS1080.T3. (TAPPI Proceedings Ser.). (Illus.). 581p. reprint ed. pap. 180.20 (*0-608-09134-0*, 208246400007) Bks Demand.
Papermakers Conference, 1992: Opryland Hotel, Nashville, TN, April 5-8, Bk. 1. Technical Association of the Pulp & Paper Industry. LC TS1171.T43. (TAPPI Proceedings Ser.). 337p. reprint ed. pap. 104.50 (*0-7837-2440-3*, 204259200001) Bks Demand.
Papermakers Conference, 1992: Opryland Hotel, Nashville, TN, April 5-8, Bk. 2. Technical Association of the Pulp & Paper Industry. LC TS1171.T43. (TAPPI Proceedings Ser.). 279p. reprint ed. pap. 86.50 (*0-7837-2441-1*, 204259200002) Bks Demand.
Papermakers Conference, 1994: San Francisco Marriott, San Francisco, CA, April 24-27, Bk. 1. Technical Association of the Pulp & Paper Industry. LC TS1080.T3. (TAPPI Proceedings Ser.). (Illus.). 373p. 1994. reprint ed. pap. 115.70 (*0-608-05361-9*, 208241100001) Bks Demand.
Papermakers Conference, 1994: San Francisco Marriott, San Francisco, CA, April 24-27, Bk. 2. Technical Association of the Pulp & Paper Industry. LC TS1080.T3. (TAPPI Proceedings Ser.). (Illus.). 299p. 1994. reprint ed. pap. 92.70 (*0-608-05362-7*, 208241100002) Bks Demand.
Papermakers Conference, 1991: Westin Center, Seattle, WA, April 8-10. Technical Association of the Pulp & Paper Industry. LC 83-641085. (TAPPI Proceedings Ser.). 607p. pap. 188.20 (*0-7837-0253-1*, 204056300017) Bks Demand.
Papermakers Conference, 1990: Westin Peachtree Plaza, Atlanta, GA, April 23-25. Technical Association of the Pulp & Paper Industry. LC TS1171.T43. (TAPPI Proceedings Ser.). (Illus.). 425p. reprint ed. pap. 131.80 (*0-8357-4227-X*, 203701400002) Bks Demand.
Papermakers Conference, 1983: Marriott Marquis, Atlanta, Georgia, April 18-21, Bk. 1. Technical Associaton of the Pulp & Paper Industry. LC 83-641085. (TAPPI Proceedings Ser.). 355p. reprint ed. pap. 110.10 (*0-7837-5703-4*, 204502600001) Bks Demand.
Papermakers Conference, 1983: Marriott Marquis, Atlanta, Georgia, April 18-21, Bk. 2. Technical Associaton of the Pulp & Paper Industry. LC 83-641085. (TAPPI Proceedings Ser.). 329p. reprint ed. pap. 102.00 (*0-7837-5704-2*, 204502600002) Bks Demand.
Papermaking. Jules Heller. (Illus.). 216p. 1978. 29.95 (*0-8230-3895-5*) Watsn-Guptill.
Papermaking. Susie O'Reilly. LC 93-24397. (Arts & Crafts Ser.). (Illus.). 32p. (J). (gr. 1-6). 1994. lib. bdg. 21.40 (*1-56847-069-X*) Raintree Steck-V.
***Papermaking.** David Watson. LC 00-38307. (Step-by-Step Ser.). (Illus.). (YA). 2000. lib. bdg. write for info. (*1-57572-327-1*) Heinemann Lib.
***Papermaking.** David Watson. (Step-by-Step Children's Crafts Ser.). 32p. (J). 2000. pap. 8.95 (*0-85532-913-0*, Pub. by Srch Pr) Midpt Trade.
Papermaking. Dard Hunter. (Illus.). 672p. 1978. reprint ed. pap. 13.95 (*0-486-23619-6*) Dover.
Papermaking: How to Make Handmade Paper for Printmaking, Drawing, Painting, Relief & Cast Forms, Book Arts, & Mixed Media. Jules Heller. (Illus.). 216p. 1997. pap. 19.95 (*0-8230-3842-4*) Watsn-Guptill.
Papermaking: The New Crafts Collection. Elizabeth Couzins-Scott. (Illus.). 96p. 1999. 16.95 (*1-85967-892-0*) Anness Pub.
Papermaking Chemical Processing Aids Seminar, 1986: Notes of TAPPI, Marriott Hotel, New Orleans, LA, April 16-18, 1986. Technical Association of the Pulp & Paper Industry & W. R. Willets. LC TS1120.P36. 79p. pap. 30.00 (*0-608-18716-X*, 202918200059) Bks Demand.
Papermaking Fibers: A Photomicrographic Atlas. Ed. by Wilfred A. Cote. LC 80-131975. (Renewable Materials Institute Ser.: No. 1). (Illus.). 196p. reprint ed. pap. 60.80 (*0-8357-3122-7*, 203938300012) Bks Demand.
Papermaking Fillers. Kenoo Beazley. 1998. 100.00 (*1-85802-034-4*, Pub. by Pira Pub) Bks Intl VA.
Papermaking for Basketry & Other Crafts. L. Stearns. LC 92-15002. (Illus.). 160p. 1992. pap. 18.95 (*0-937274-62-3*) Lark Books.
Papermaking for Kids: Simple Steps to Handcrafted Paper. Beth Wilkinson. LC 97-6908. (Illus.). 48p. (YA). (gr. 2 up). 1997. pap. 10.95 (*0-87905-827-7*) Gibbs Smith Pub.
Papermaking for Kids, Simple Steps to Handcrafted Paper. Beth Wilkinson. 1997. 16.15 (*0-606-12788-7*, Pub. by Turtleback) Demco.
Papermaking in America. Norman B. Wilkinson. (Industry in America Ser.). (Illus.). 64p. 1975. pap. 3.50 (*0-914650-09-2*) Hagley Museum.
Papermaking in Britain, 1488-1988: A Short History. R. L. Hills. LC 88-3322. 192p. (C). 1988. text 35.00 (*0-485-11346-5*, Pub. by Athlone Pr) Humanities.
***Papermaking in Eighteenth-Century France: Management, Labor & Revolution at the Montgolfier Mill, 1761-1805.** Leonard N. Rosenband. LC 99-86391. 240p. 2000. 39.95 (*0-8018-6392-9*) Johns Hopkins.
Papermaking in the Classroom. Dard Hunter. (Illus.). 88p. 1991. reprint ed. 28.00 (*0-938768-24-7*) Oak Knoll.
Papermaking with Plants. Helen Hiebert. (Illus.). 1997. 24.95 (*0-15-801787-0*) Harcourt.
Papermaking with Plants: Creative Recipes & Projects Using Herbs, Flowers, Grasses, & Leaves. Helen Hiebert. LC 98-18735. (Illus.). 112p. 1998. pap. 24.95 (*1-58017-087-0*) Storey Bks.
Paperplay. R. Gibson. (You & Your Child Ser.). (Illus.). 32p. (J). (ps-2). 1990. pap. 5.95 (*0-7460-0466-4*, Usborne) EDC.
Paperplay. R. Gibson. (You & Your Child Ser.). (Illus.). 32p. (J). (ps-2). 1999. lib. bdg. 14.95 (*0-88110-422-1*, Usborne) EDC.
Paperplay Mini-Books. Incl. Vol. 1. Beauty of Irrelevant Music. Kenneth Gaburo. (Illus.). 22p. 1976. pap. 2.75 (*0-939044-01-3*); Vol. 2. C--Is. Kenneth Gaburo. 12p. 1976. pap. 2.75 (*0-939044-02-1*); Vol. 3. Murmur. Kenneth Gaburo. 8p. 1976. pap. 2.25 (*0-939044-03-X*); Vol. 4. Extraction. Kenneth Gaburo. (Illus.). 12p. 1976. pap. 2.25 (*0-939044-04-8*); Vol. 5. Musicology & Other Delights. Alan Skei. 8p. 1978. pap. 2.00 (*0-939044-15-3*); Vol. 6. Murmur. Kenneth Gaburo. 12p. 1976. pap. 2.75 (*0-939044-06-4*); Vol. 7. Language, a Magical Enterprise, the Body. Barry Casselman. (Illus.). 16p. 1978. pap. 2.50 (*0-939044-13-7*); Vol. 8. Literal Violence. Michel Pierssens. 16p. 1978. pap. 2.60 (*0-939044-14-5*); Vol. 9. Non-Scatological Set of Preliminary Remarks. Kenneth Gaburo. 12p. 1976. pap. 2.60 (*0-939044-05-6*); write for info. (*0-318-61023-X*) Lingua Pr.
Paperquake: A Puzzle. Kathryn Reiss. LC 97-33217. 264p. (J). (gr. 5-9). 1998. 17.00 (*0-15-201183-8*) Harcourt.
Papers Thomas Jefferson et al. LC 50-7486. 1950. write for info. (*0-691-01585-6*) Princeton U Pr.
Papers, 6 vols. Mirabeau B. Lamar. Ed. by Charles A. Gulick et al. LC 76-171643. reprint ed. 560.00 (*0-404-03820-4*) AMS Pr.
Papers - Experiences - Perspectives. A. Alan B. Pritsker. (QM - Quantitative Methods Ser.). (C). 1993. mass mkt. 57.00 (*0-89426-245-9*) S-W Pub.
Papers & Addresses. William P. Few. Ed. by Robert H. Woody. LC 68-20299. (Essay Index Reprint Ser.). 1977. reprint ed. 23.95 (*0-8369-0439-7*) Ayer.
Papers & Addresses of the Society of Colonial Wars in the State of Connecticut, Vol. 1. 1903. 3.00 (*0-940748-35-5*) Conn Hist Soc.
Papers & Correspondence of William Stanley Jevons Vol. 1: Biography & Personal Journal, Vol. 1. William S. Jevons. Ed. by R. D. Collison-Black. LC 72-77230. xiv, 243p. 1972. 45.00 (*0-678-07012-1*) Kelley.
Papers & Correspondence of William Stanley Jevons Vol. 2: Correspondence, 1850-1862, Vol. 2. William S. Jevons. Ed. by R. D. Collison-Black. LC 72-77230. xviii, 462p. 1973. 45.00 (*0-678-07011-3*) Kelley.
Papers & Correspondence of William Stanley Jevons Vol. 4: Correspondence, 1873-1878, Vol. 4. William S. Jevons. Ed. by R. D. Collison-Black. LC 72-77230. xxiii, 306p. 1977. 45.00 (*0-333-19977-4*) Kelley.
Papers & Correspondence of William Stanley Jevons Vol. 5: Correspondence, 1879-1882, Vol. 5. William S. Jevons. Ed. by R. D. Collison-Black. LC 72-77230. xvii, 202p. 1977. 45.00 (*0-333-19978-2*) Kelley.
Papers & Correspondence of William Stanley Jevons Vol. 6: Lectures on Political Economy 1875-76, Vol. 6. William S. Jevons. Ed. by R. D. Collison-Black. LC 72-77230. x, 140p. 1977. 45.00 (*0-333-10258-4*) Kelley.
Papers & Journals: A Selection. Soren Kierkegaard. LC 96-222622. 688p. 1996. pap. 13.95 (*0-14-044589-7*, Viking) Viking Penguin.
Papers & Proceedings of the Committee on the Police Problem, City of New York. New York State Chamber of Commerce Staff. LC 79-154581. (Police in America Ser.). 1971. reprint ed. 51.95 (*0-405-03364-8*) Ayer.
Papers & Proceedings of the Surgeon General's Conference on Agricultural Safety & Health. Ed. by Melvin L. Myers et al. (Illus.). 645p. (Orig.). (C). 1994. pap. text 75.00 (*0-7881-1225-2*) DIANE Pub.

P

An Asterisk (*) at the beginning of an entry indicates that the title is appearing for the first time.

Papers Concerning Robertson's Colony in Texas. Ed. by Malcolm D. McLean. Incl. Introductory Volume, Robert Leftwich's Mexico Diary & Letterbook, 1822-1824. (Illus.). 611p. 1986. lib. bdg. 35.00 (*0-932408-00-1*); Vol. I, 1788-1822, The Texas Association. (Illus.). lxxi, 567p. 1980. reprint ed. lib. bdg. 30.00 (*0-932408-01-X*); Vol. II, 1823 Through September, 1826, Leftwich's Grant. (Illus.). 687p. 1975. lib. bdg. 30.00 (*0-932408-02-8*); Vol. III, October, 1826, Through April, 1830, The Nashville Colony. (Illus.). 577p. 1976. lib. bdg. 30.00 (*0-932408-03-6*); Vol. IV, May Through October 10, 1830, Tenoxtitlan, Dream Capital of Texas. (Illus.). 627p. 1977. lib. bdg. 30.00 (*0-932408-04-4*); Vol. V, October 11, 1830, Through March 5, 1831, The Upper Colony. (Illus.). 628p. 1978. lib. bdg. 30.00 (*0-932408-05-2*); Vol. VI, March 6 Through December 5, 1831, The Campaigns Against the Tawakoni, Waco, Towash & Comanche Indians. (Illus.). 632p. 1979. lib. bdg. 30.00 (*0-932408-06-0*); Vol. VII, December 6, 1831, Through October, 1833, Those Eleven-League Grants. (Illus.). 664p. 1980. lib. bdg. 30.00 (*0-932408-07-9*); Vol. VIII, November, 1833, Through September, 1834, Robertson's Colony. (Illus.). 608p. 1981. lib. bdg. 30.00 (*0-932408-08-7*); Vol. X, March 21 Through July 25, 1835, The Ranger Rendezvous. (Illus.). 600p. 1983. lib. bdg. 30.00 (*0-932408-10-9*); Vol. XI, July 26 Through October 14, 1835, Nashville-on-the-Brazos. (Illus.). 666p. 1984. lib. bdg. 30.00 (*0-932408-11-7*); Vol. XII, October 15, 1835, Through January 14, 1836, the Municipality of Milam. (Illus.). 732p. 1985. lib. bdg. 35.00 (*0-932408-12-5*); Vol. XIII, January 15 Through March 17, 1936, The Convention at Washington-on-the-Brazos. (Illus.). 792p. 1987. lib. bdg. 35.00 (*0-932408-13-3*); Vol. XIV, March 18 Through July 22, 1836, The Battle of San Jacinto & the Fall of Fort Parker. (Illus.). 620p. 1988. lib. bdg. 35.00 (*0-932408-14-1*); Vol. XV, July 23, 1836, through August 9, 1837, The Gentleman from Milam. (Illus.). 613p. 1989. 35.00 (*0-932408-15-X*); Vol. XVI, August 10, 1837, through November, 1838, The Creation of Robertson County. (Illus.). 716p. 1990. 35.00 (*0-932408-16-8*); lib. bdg. write for info. (*0-318-68008-4*) UTA Pr.

Papers Concerning Robertson's Colony in Texas Vol. XVIII: August 11, 1840 Through March 4, 1842: The End of an Era. Ed. by Malcolm D. McLean. 411p. 1993. 35.00 (*0-932408-18-4*) UTA Pr.

***Papers Dedicated to C.T.C. Wall, 145.** Sylvain Cappell. (Annals of Mathematics Studies). 2000. pap. text 35.00 (*0-691-04938-6*, Pub. by Princeton U Pr) Cal Prin Full Svc.

Papers Dedicated to Egil Amundsen: On the Occasion of his 60th Birthday March 18, 1984. Ed. by A. O. Aasen et al. (Journal: European Surgical Research: Vol. 16, Supp. 2). (Illus.). iv, 172p. 1984. pap. 45.25 (*3-8055-3889-8*) S Karger.

Papers, Experiences, Perspectives. A. Alan B. Pritsker. 250p. 1990. 30.00 (*0-938974-03-3*, PR-1) Soc Computer Sim.

Papers, First, Second & Third Series, 3 Vols. Central Society Of Education London Staff. LC 74-5890. (Social History of Education Series 1). 1969. reprint ed. 150.00 (*0-678-08456-4*) Kelley.

Papers for Birth Dayes: Guide to the Fraktur Artists & Scriveners, 2 vols. 2nd ed. Corinne P. Earnest & Russell D. Earnest. (Illus.). 908p. (Orig.). 1997. pap. 89.50 (*1-879311-11-9*, TX 4-553-437) R D Earnest.

Papers for Printing: How to Choose the Right Paper at the Right Price for Any Printing Job. 2nd ed. Mark Beach. (Illus.). 108p. (Orig.). (C). 1991. pap. 39.50 (*0-943381-06-1*, 30280) Coast to Coast.

Papers for the First Interdisciplinary Conference on Netherlandic Studies: Held at the University of Maryland 11-13 June 1982. Ed. by William H. Fletcher. LC 85-9006. 248p. (Orig.). 1985. pap. text 29.00 (*0-8191-4708-7*); lib. bdg. 54.00 (*0-8191-4707-9*) U Pr of Amer.

Papers for the Millions: The New Journalism in Britain, 1850s to 1914, 13. Ed. by Joel H. Wiener. LC 88-25071. (Contributions to the Study of Mass Media & Communications Ser.: No. 13). 347p. 1988. 59.95 (*0-313-25939-9*, WNJ/, Greenwood Pr) Greenwood.

Papers for the V Congress of Southeast European Studies (Belgrade, September 1984) Ed. by Kot K. Shangriladze & Erica Townsend. 382p. 1984. pap. 24.95 (*0-89357-138-5*) Slavica.

P

Papers from a Conference on Thai Studies in Honor of William J. Gedney. Ed. by Robert J. Bickner et al. LC 84-45446. (Michigan Papers on South & Southeast Asia: No. 25). (Illus.). 265p. 1986. 31.95 (*0-89148-030-7*) Ctr S&SE Asian.

Papers from Eranos Yearbooks, 6 vols. Ed. by Joseph Campbell & R. F. C. Hull. Tr. by Ralph Manheim. Incl. Vol. 1. Spirit & Nature. (Illus.). 498p. 1982. pap. text 22.95 (*0-691-01841-3*, Pub. by Princeton U Pr); Vol. 2. Mysteries. 496p. 1955. pap. text 22.95 (*0-691-01823-5*, Pub. by Princeton U Pr); Vol. 3. Man & Time. (Illus.). 440p. 1957. pap. text 24.95 (*0-691-01857-X*, Pub. by Princeton U Pr); Vol. 4. Spirtual Disciplines. (Illus.). 528p. 1960. pap. text 22.95 (*0-691-01863-4*, Pub. by Princeton U Pr); Vol. 5. Man & Transformation. (Illus.). 413p. 1964. pap. text 22.95 (*0-691-01834-0*, Pub. by Princeton U Pr); (Bollingen Ser.: No. 30). 508p. 1969. Set pap. text 22.95 (*0-691-01842-1*, Pub. by Princeton U Pr) Cal Prin Full Svc.

Papers from the American Indian Languages Conferences Held at the University of California, Santa Cruz, July & August, 1991, Vol. 16. Ed. by J. E. Redden. (Occasional Papers on Linguistics: No. 16). (Illus.). 240p. (C). 1991. reprint ed. pap. text 25.63 (*1-55567-481-X*) Coyote Press.

Papers from the Fifth Annual Meeting of the Southeast Asian Linguistics Society, 1995. Ed. by Shobhana L. Chelliah & Willem J. De Reuse. (Illus.). xxi, 333p. (C). 1998. pap. 24.95 (*1-881044-17-3*) ASU Prog SE Asian.

Papers from the Fifth International Conference on English Historical Linguistics: Dedicated to the Memory of James Peter Thorne (1933-1988) Ed. by Sylvia Adamson et al. LC 90-681. (Current Issues in Linguistic Theory Ser.: Vol. 65). xxi, 583p. 1990. 112.00 (*90-272-3562-7*) J Benjamins Pubng Co.

Papers from the First Conference on the Uses of Phonology, Held at Southern Illinois University, Carbondale, Illinois. Ed. by Geoffrey S. Nathan & Margaret E. Winters. (Occasional Papers on Linguistics: No. 12). 126p. 1984. reprint ed. pap. text 13.75 (*1-55567-485-2*) Coyote Press.

Papers from the Fourth Annual Meeting of the Southeast Asian Linguistics Society, 1994. Ed. by Udom Warotamasikkhadit & Thanyarat Panakul. (Illus.). xiii, 250p. (C). 1998. pap. 19.95 (*1-881044-16-5*) ASU Prog SE Asian.

Papers from the Fourth International Conference on English Historical Linguistics, Amsterdam, April 10-13, 1985. Ed. by Roger Eaton et al. LC 85-22908. (Current Issues in Linguistic Theory Ser.: No. 41). xvii, 341p. 1985. 71.00 (*90-272-3531-7*) J Benjamins Pubng Co.

Papers from the Fourth International Conference on Historical Linguistics, Stanford, March 26-30, 1979. Ed. by Elizabeth C. Traugott et al. (Current Issues in Linguistic Theory Ser.: No. 14). x, 437p. 1980. 87.00 (*90-272-3501-5*) J Benjamins Pubng Co.

Papers from the Headmaster: Reflections on a World Fit for Children. Richard A. Hawley. LC 96-20349. 288p. 1996. 24.95 (*0-8397-6488-X*) Eriksson.

Papers from the International Conference on Music in Paris in the Eighteen Thirties (Smith College, April 1982) Sponsored by the National Endowment for the Humanities. Ed. by Peter Bloom. LC 87-2248. (Musical Life in Nineteenth-Century France Ser.: No. 4). (Illus.). 1987. lib. bdg. 62.00 (*0-918728-71-1*) Pendragon NY.

Papers from the International Workshop on Basic Aspects of Nonequilibrium Plasmas Interacting with Surfaces (Banpis '97) 26-27 January 1997, Nanki Seaside Lodge, Shirahama, Wakayama, Japan. United States Government et al. LC 97-75227. 1998. write for info. (*1-56396-769-3*) Am Inst Physics.

***Papers from the John F. Kennedy Assassination Records Collection at the National Archives.** Kermit L. Hall et al. LC 00-38160. 1999. write for info. (*1-55655-806-6*) U Pubns Amer.

Papers from the 1987 Hokan-Penutian Languages Workshop & Friends of Uto-Aztecan Workshop. Ed. by J. E. Redden. (Occasional Papers on Linguistics: No. 14). (Illus.). 89p. (C). 1988. reprint ed. pap. text 10.00 (*1-55567-483-6*) Coyote Press.

Papers from the 1983, 1984 & 1985 Hokan-Penutian Languages Conference. Ed. by J. E. Redden. (Occasional Papers of Linguistics: No. 13). 116p. (C). 1986. reprint ed. pap. text 13.13 (*1-55567-484-4*) Coyote Press.

Papers from the 1990 Hokan-Penutian Languages Workshop, Held at University of California, San Diego, June 22-23, 1990. Ed. by Margaret Langdon. (Occasional Papers on Linguistics: No. 15). 201p. 1990. reprint ed. pap. text 21.25 (*1-55567-482-8*) Coyote Press.

Papers from the Second Annual Meeting of the SE Asian Linguistics Society, 1992. Ed. by Karen L. Adams & Thomas J. Hudak. (Illus.). xiii, 440p. 1994. pap. text 24.95 (*1-881044-08-4*) ASU Prog SE Asian.

Papers from the Second Interdisciplinary Conference on Netherlandic Studies, Georgetown University 7-9 June, 1984. Ed. by William H. Fletcher. LC 86-28221. (Illus.). 168p. (Orig.). 1987. lib. bdg. 39.00 (*0-8191-6073-3*) U Pr of Amer.

Papers from the Second International Workshop on Japanese Syntax. Ed. by William J. Poser. LC 88-18763. 243p. 1989. 59.95 (*0-937073-39-3*); pap. 18.95 (*0-937073-38-5*) CSLI.

Papers from the Seventh International Conference on Historical Linguistics. Ed. by Anna G. Ramat et al. LC 87-8100. (Current Issues in Linguistic Theory Ser.: Vol. 48). xvi, 672p. (C). 1987. 139.00 (*90-272-3542-2*) J Benjamins Pubng Co.

Papers from the Third Annual Meeting of the Southeast Asian Linguistics Society (1993) Ed. by Mark Alves. 249p. (Orig.). 1995. pap. text 19.95 (*1-881044-12-2*) ASU Prog SE Asian.

Papers from the Third, Fourth & Sixth Navajo Studies Conferences. Ed. by June-el Piper. 1993. pap. 25.00 (*0-9639162-0-3*) Navajo Nation.

Papers from the Third International Conference on Historical Linguistics, Hamburg, August 22-26, 1977. Ed. by J. Peter Maher et al. (Current Issues in Linguistic Theory Ser.: No. 13). xvi, 434p. 1982. 81.00 (*90-272-3505-8*) J Benjamins Pubng Co.

Papers from the 3rd Scandinavian Symposium on Syntactic Variation. Ed. by Sven J. Jaconson. 180p. (Orig.). 1986. pap. text 37.50 (*91-22-00802-0*) Coronet Bks.

Papers from the 30th Regional Meeting of CLS, Vol. 1. Ed. by Katharine Beals et al. 457p. 1994. pap. 16.00 (*0-914203-45-2*) Chicago Ling.

Papers from the 31st Regional Meeting of CLS, Vol. 1. Ed. by Audra Dainora et al. 535p. 1995. pap. 16.00 (*0-614-16723-X*) Chicago Ling.

Papers from the 12th Regional Meeting of CLS, Vol. 1. Ed. by Salikoko S. Mufwene et al. 697p. 1976. pap. 7.00 (*0-614-16721-3*) Chicago Ling.

Papers from the 28th Regional Meeting of CLS, Vol. 1. Ed. by Costas P. Canakis et al. 566p. 1992. pap. 16.00 (*0-914203-39-8*) Chicago Ling.

Papers from the 25th Regional Meeting of CLS, Vol. 1. Ed. by Caroline Wiltshire et al. 496p. 1989. pap. 16.00 (*0-914203-32-0*) Chicago Ling.

Papers from the 29th Regional Meeting of CLS, Vol. 1. Ed. by Katharine Beals et al. 499p. 1993. pap. 16.00 (*0-914203-42-8*) Chicago Ling.

Papers from the 22nd Regional Meeting of CLS, Vol. 1. Ed. by Anne M. Farley et al. 360p. 1986. pap. 8.00 (*0-614-16722-1*) Chicago Ling.

Papers from the 27th Regional Meeting of CLS, Vol. 1. Ed. by Lise M. Dobrin et al. 491p. 1991. pap. 16.00 (*0-914203-37-1*) Chicago Ling.

Papers from the 26th Regional Meeting of CLS, Vol. 1. Ed. by Michael Ziolkowski et al. 467p. 1990. pap. 16.00 (*0-914203-35-5*) Chicago Ling.

Papers from the 1992 Hokan-Penutian Languages Conference & the J. P. Harrington Conference, Held at the University of California, Santa Barbara, & the Museum of Natural History, Santa Barbara, June 24-27, 1992, Vol. 17. Ed. by J. E. Redden. (Occasional Papers on Linguistics: No. 17). (Illus.). 149p. (C). 1992. reprint ed. pap. text 16.25 (*1-55567-480-1*) Coyote Press.

Papers from the 1993 International Conference on Scanning Tunneling Microscopy, 9-13 August, 1993, Kunlun Hotel, Beijing, China. International Conference on Scanning Tunneling Microscopy Staff et al. LC 94-71916. 1994. write for info. (*1-56396-362-0*) Am Inst Physics.

Papers from the 32nd Regional Meeting of the Chicago Linguistic Society Vol. 1: The Main Session. Ed. by Lise Dobrin et al. 1996. write for info. (*0-914203-50-9*) Chicago Ling.

Papers from the 32nd Regional Meeting of the Chicago Linguistic Society Vol. 2: The Parasession on Theory & Data in Linguistics. Ed. by Michelle AuCoin et al. 1996. write for info. (*0-914203-51-7*) Chicago Ling.

Papers from the 5th Nordic Conference on Bilingualism, 3 vols., 1. 1989. 59.00 (*1-85359-014-2*, Pub. by Multilingual Matters) Taylor & Francis.

Papers from the 5th Nordic Conference on Bilingualism, 3 vols., 2. 1989. 59.00 (*1-85359-015-0*, Pub. by Multilingual Matters) Taylor & Francis.

Papers from the 8th International Ocean Disposal Symposium 9-13 October 1989, Dubrovnik, Yugoslavia, Pt. I. I. W. Duedall. 127p. 1991. pap. text 355.00 (*2-88124-797-0*) Gordon & Breach.

Papers from Twenty-First Regional Meeting of C. L. S., Vol. I. Ed. by K. Peterson et al. 438p. (Orig.). 1985. pap. text 8.00 (*0-914203-23-1*) Chicago Ling.

Papers from Twenty-First Regional Meeting of C. L. S., Vol. 2: Parasession on Causatives & Agentivity. Ed. by K. Peterson et al. (Orig.). 1985. pap. text 8.00 (*0-914203-24-X*) Chicago Ling.

Papers Illustrative of the Political Condition of the Highlands of Scotland. Ed. by James M'Conechy. LC 75-175587. (Maitland Club, Glasgow. Publications: No. 64). reprint ed. 32.50 (*0-404-53071-0*) AMS Pr.

Papers in African Prehistory. Ed. by J. D. Fage & R. A. Oliver. LC 74-77286. (Illus.). 343p. reprint ed. pap. 97.80 (*0-608-17509-9*, 2030592) Bks Demand.

Papers in Algebra, Analysis & Statistics. Ed. by Rudolf Lidl. LC 82-1826. (Contemporary Mathematics Ser.: Vol. 9). 400p. 1982. pap. 35.00 (*0-8218-5009-1*, CONM/9) Am Math.

Papers in Boiotian Topography & History. John M. Fossey. 291p. 1990. pap. 57.00 (*90-5063-016-2*, Pub. by Gieben) J Benjamins Pubng Co.

Papers in Caribbean Anthropology. Compiled by Sidney W. Mintz. LC 74-123185. (Yale University Publications in Anthropology Reprints Ser.: Nos. 57-64). 252p. 1970. pap. 20.00 (*0-87536-524-8*) HRAFP.

Papers in Computational Linguistics. Ed. by Ferenc Papp & Gyorgy Szepe. (Janua Linguarum, Ser. Major: No. 91). 585p. 1977. text 147.70 (*90-279-3285-9*) Mouton.

Papers in Contrastive Linguistics. International Congress of Applied Linguistics Staf. Ed. by Gerhard Nickel. LC 78-149434. 131p. reprint ed. pap. 37.40 (*0-608-16502-6*, 2026350) Bks Demand.

Papers in Economic Prehistory: Studies. British Academy, Major Research Project in the Ear. Ed. by E. S. Higgs. LC 78-180019. 229p. reprint ed. pap. 65.30 (*0-608-16447-X*, 2026342) Bks Demand.

Papers in Ethics & Social Philosophy. David Lewis. (Studies in Philosophy). (Illus.). 304p. (C). 1999. 54.95 (*0-521-58249-0*); pap. 19.95 (*0-521-58786-7*) Cambridge U Pr.

Papers in Experimental Economics. Vernon L. Smith. (Illus.). 830p. (C). 1991. text 95.00 (*0-521-36456-6*) Cambridge U Pr.

Papers in General Linguistics. J. Kramsky. (Janua Linguarum, Series Minor: No. 209). 207p. (Orig.). 1976. pap. text 75.40 (*90-279-3131-3*) Mouton.

Papers in Greek Archaeology & History in Memory of Colin D. Gordon. Ed. by John Fossey. (McGill University Monographs in Classical Archaeology & History: No. 6). 170p. (C). 1987. 94.00 (*90-5063-010-3*, Pub. by Gieben) J Benjamins Pubng Co.

Papers in Hellenistic Philosophy. Jacques Brunschwig. (Illus.). 291p. (C). 1994. text 80.00 (*0-521-41712-0*) Cambridge U Pr.

Papers in Laboratory Phonology V: Language Acquisition & the Lexicon. Ed. by Michael Broe & Janet Pierrehumbert. (Papers in Laboratory Phonology). (Illus.). 408p. (C). 2000. 64.95 (*0-521-64363-5*) Cambridge U Pr.

Papers in Laboratory Phonology I: Between the Grammar & the Physics of Speech. Ed. by John A. Kingston & Mary E. Beckman. (Studies in Speech Science & Communication). (Illus.). 516p. (C). 1990. pap. text 36.95 (*0-521-36808-1*) Cambridge U Pr.

Papers in Laboratory Phonology I: Between the Grammar & the Physics of Speech. Ed. by John A. Kingston & Mary E. Beckman. (Studies in Speech Science & Communication). (Illus.). 516p. (C). 1991. text 99.95 (*0-521-36238-5*) Cambridge U Pr.

Papers in Laboratory Phonology II: Gesture, Segment, Prosody. Ed. by Gerard J. Docherty & D. Robert Ladd. 476p. (C). 1992. text 99.95 (*0-521-40127-5*) Cambridge U Pr.

Papers in Linguistics in Honor of Leon Dostert. Ed. by William M. Austin. (Janua Linguarum, Ser. Major: No. 25). 1967. text 83.85 (*90-279-0616-5*) Mouton.

Papers in Linguistics & Phonetics to the Memory of Pierre Delattre. Ed. by Albert Valdman. (Janua Linguarum, Ser. Major: No. 54). (Illus.). 513p. 1972. text 133.85 (*90-279-2310-8*) Mouton.

Papers in Mayan Linguistics. Ed. by Nora C. England. (Miscellaneous Publications in Anthropology Ser.: No. 6: Studies in Mayan Linguistics). v, 310p. 1978. pap. 15.00 (*0-913134-87-2*) Mus Anthro MO.

Papers in Metaphysics & Epistemology. David Lewis. LC 98-25689. (Studies in Philosophy). 288p. (C). 1999. text 64.95 (*0-521-58248-2*); pap. text 19.95 (*0-521-58787-5*) Cambridge U Pr.

Papers in Philosophical Logic, Vol. 1. David Lewis. LC 97-6656. (Studies in Philosophy). 272p. (C). 1997. text 54.95 (*0-521-58247-4*); pap. text 17.95 (*0-521-58788-3*) Cambridge U Pr.

Papers in Slavic Philology No. 1: In Honor of James Ferrell. Ed. by Benjamin A. Stolze. (Papers in Slavic Philology: No. 1). 326p. 1977. pap. 10.00 (*0-930042-24-7*) Mich Slavic Pubns.

Papers in Slavic Philology No. 2: To Honor Jernej Kopitar. Ed. by Rado L. Lencek & Henry R. Cooper, Jr. 1982. pap. 10.00 (*0-930042-46-8*) Mich Slavic Pubns.

Papers in Speech Communication: ASA Publications, 3 vols. Ed. by Raymond D. Kent et al. 1991. 95.00 (*0-685-67254-9*) Am Inst Physics.

Papers in Speech Communication: Speech Perception, 3 vols., Vol. 2. Ed. by Joanne L. Miller et al. LC 91-32651. 874p. 1991. text 46.00 (*0-88318-959-3*) Acoustical Soc Am.

Papers in Speech Communication: Speech Processing, 3 vols., Vol. 3. Ed. by Bishnu S. Atal et al. 672p. 1991. text 46.00 (*0-88318-960-7*) Acoustical Soc Am.

Papers in Speech Communication: Speech Production, 3 vols., Vol. 1. Ed. by Raymond D. Kent et al. LC 91-32651. 880p. 1991. text 46.00 (*0-88318-958-5*) Acoustical Soc Am.

Papers in the History of Linguistics: Proceedings of the Third International Conference on the History of the Language Sciences (ICHoLS III), Princeton, 19-23 August 1984. Ed. by Hans Aarsleff et al. LC 86-3528. (Studies in the History of Linguistics: Vol. 38). xxi, 680p. 1987. 177.00 (*90-272-4521-5*) J Benjamins Pubng Co.

Papers in Theoretical Linguistics. Niels Danielsen & Peter J. Maher. Ed. by Per Baerentzen. LC 91-39469. (Current Issues in Linguistic Theory Ser.: No. 23). xxii, 224p. 1992. 65.00 (*90-272-3509-0*) J Benjamins Pubng Co.

Papers in Vertebrate Paleontology Honoring Robert Warren Wilson. Ed. by Robert M. Mengel. LC 84-71697. (Special Publications: No. 9). (Illus.). 192p. (Orig.). 1984. pap. 25.00 (*0-935868-09-7*) Carnegie Mus.

Papers of a Pariah. Robert H. Benson. LC 67-23176. (Essay Index Reprint Ser.). 1977. 19.95 (*0-8369-0196-7*) Ayer.

Papers of A. Philip Randolph. A. Philip Randolph et al. LC 91-11920. (Black Studies Research Sources). 35p. 1990. write for info. (*1-55655-024-3*) U Pubns Amer.

Papers of "Adhesion '87" International Conference of the Plastics & Rubber Institute, England, September 1987: A Special Issue of the Journal Adhesion. Ed. by L. H. Sharpe. 204p. 1988. pap. text 835.00 (*2-88124-321-5*) Gordon & Breach.

Papers of Alexander Hamilton, 26 vols., Vol. 1-17. Alexander Hamilton. Ed. by Harold C. Syrett et al. Incl. Vol. 1. 1768-1778. LC 61-15593. 1961. text 127.50 (*0-231-08900-7*); Vol. 2. 1779-1781. LC 61-15593. 1961. text 127.50 (*0-231-08901-5*); Vol. 3. 1782-1786. LC 61-15593. 1962. text 127.50 (*0-231-08902-3*); Vol. 4. 1787-May, 1788. LC 61-15593. 1962. text 127.50 (*0-231-08903-1*); Vol. 5. June, 1788-November, 1789. LC 61-15593. 1962. text 127.50 (*0-231-08904-X*); Vol. 6. December, 1789-August, 1790. LC 61-15593. 1962. text 127.50 (*0-231-08905-8*); Vol. 7. September, 1790-January, 1971. LC 61-15593. 1963. text 127.50 (*0-231-08906-6*); Vol. 8. February, 1791-July, 1791. LC 61-15593. 1965. text 127.50 (*0-231-08907-4*); Vol. 9. August, 1791-September, 1791. LC 61-15593. 1965. text 127.50 (*0-231-08908-2*); Vol. 10. December, 1791-January, 1792. LC 61-15593. 1966. text 127.50 (*0-231-08909-0*); Vol. 11. February-June, 1792. LC 61-15593. 1966. text 127.50 (*0-231-08910-4*); Vol. 12. July-October, 1792. LC 61-15593. 1967. text 127.50 (*0-231-08911-2*); Vol. 13. November, 1792-February, 1793. LC 61-15593. 1967. text 127.50 (*0-231-08912-0*); Vol. 14. February-June, 1793. LC 61-15593. 1969. text 127.50 (*0-231-08913-9*); Vol. 15. June, 1793-January, 1794. LC 61-15593. 1969. text 127.50 (*0-231-08914-7*); Vol. 16. February 1794-July 1794. LC 61-15593. 1972. text 127.50 (*0-231-08915-5*); Vol. 17. August 1794-December 1794. LC 61-15593. 1972. text 127.50 (*0-231-08916-3*); LC 61-15593. 993.50 (*0-231-08202-9*) Col U Pr.

Papers of Alexander Hamilton, Vol. 23. Alexander Hamilton. Ed. by Harold C. Syrett. 624p. 1976. text 127.50 (*0-231-08922-8*) Col U Pr.

Papers of Alexander Hamilton, Vol. 24. Alexander Hamilton. Ed. by Harold C. Syrett. 664p. 1976. text 127.50 (*0-231-08923-6*) Col U Pr.

An Asterisk (*) at the beginning of an entry indicates that the title is appearing for the first time.

Papers of Alexander Hamilton, Vol. 25. Alexander Hamilton. Ed. by Harold C. Syrett. LC 61-15593. 1977. text 127.50 (*0-231-08924-4*) Col U Pr.

Papers of Alexander Hamilton: April 1797 to July 1798, Vol. 21. Alexander Hamilton. Ed. by Harold C. Syrett et al. 1974. text 127.50 (*0-231-08920-1*) Col U Pr.

Papers of Alexander Hamilton: August 1795 to December 1795, Vol. 19. Alexander Hamilton. Ed. by Harold C. Syrett et al. 640p. 1973. text 127.50 (*0-231-08918-X*) Col U Pr.

Papers of Alexander Hamilton: January 1795 to July 1795, Vol. 18. Alexander Hamilton. Ed. by Harold C. Syrett et al. 608p. 1973. text 127.50 (*0-231-08917-1*) Col U Pr.

Papers of Alexander Hamilton: January 1796 to 1797, Vol. 20. Alexander Hamilton. Ed. by Harold C. Syrett et al. 1974. text 127.50 (*0-231-08919-8*) Col U Pr.

Papers of Alexander Hamilton Vol. 27: Index. Alexander Hamilton. LC 61-15593. 1981. 70.00 (*0-685-01151-8*) Col U Pr.

Papers of Alexander Hamilton, July 1798 to March 1799 Vol. 22. Alexander Hamilton. Ed. by Harold C. Syrett et al. 640p. 1975. text 127.50 (*0-231-08921-X*) Col U Pr.

Papers of Alexander Hamilton, May 1802 to July 1804 Vol. 26, Vol. 26. Alexander Hamilton. 1979. text 127.50 (*0-231-08925-2*) Col U Pr.

Papers of Alfred Blalock, 2 Vols. Ed. by Mark M. Ravitch. (Illus.). 1966. 195.00 (*0-8018-0544-9*) Johns Hopkins.

Papers of Andrew Jackson: A Microfilm Supplement. Andrew Jackson et al. LC 86-14631. 39 p. 1986. write for info. (*0-8420-3000-X*) Scholarly Res Inc.

Papers of Andrew Jackson: Guide & Index to the Microfilm Editions. Ed. by Harold D. Moser et al. LC 86-33831. 343p. 1987. 50.00 (*0-8420-4007-2*) Scholarly Res Inc.

Papers of Andrew Jackson, 1804-1813, Vol. 2. Harold D. Moser et al. LC 79-15078. (Andrew Jackson Ser.). 664p. (C). 1985. 60.00 (*0-87049-441-4*) U of Tenn Pr.

Papers of Andrew Jackson, 1816-1820, Vol. 4. Ed. by Harold D. Moser et al. LC 79-15078. (Illus.). 676p. (C). 1993. text 60.00 (*0-87049-778-2*) U of Tenn Pr.

Papers of Andrew Jackson, 1821-1824: 1821-1824, Vol. 5. Ed. by Harold D. Moser et al. LC 79-15078. 664p. 1996. text 60.00 (*0-87049-897-5*) U of Tenn Pr.

Papers of Andrew Jackson, 1770-1803, Vol. 1. Ed. by Sam B. Smith & Harriet C. Owsley. LC 79-15078. (Illus.). 570p. 1980. 60.00 (*0-87049-219-5*) U of Tenn Pr.

Papers of Andrew Jackson, 1814-1815, Vol. 3. Ed. by Harold D. Moser et al. LC 79-15078. (Illus.). 648p. 1991. text 60.00 (*0-87049-650-6*) U of Tenn Pr.

Papers of Andrew Johnson, Vol. 7. Andrew Johnson. Ed. by Leroy P. Graf. LC 67-25733. (Papers of Andrew Johnson Ser.). (Illus.). 944p. 1986. text 60.00 (*0-87049-488-0*) U of Tenn Pr.

Papers of Andrew Johnson Vol. 15: Volume 15 September 1868 April 1869. Ed. by Paul H. Bergeron. LC 67-25733. (Illus.). 688p. 1998. text 60.00 (*1-57233-028-7*) U of Tenn Pr.

***Papers of Andrew Johnson Vol. 16: May 1896 - July 1875.** Ed. by Paul H. Bergeron. LC 67-25733. (Illus.). 840p. (C). 2000. text 60.00 (*1-57233-091-0*, Pub. by U of Tenn Pr) U Ch Pr.

Papers of Andrew Johnson, April-August 1868 Vol. 14. Ed. by Paul H. Bergeron. LC 67-25733. (Illus.). 624p. (C). 1997. text 60.00 (*0-87049-991-2*) U of Tenn Pr.

Papers of Andrew Johnson, August 1866-January 1867, Vol. 11. Ed. by Paul H. Bergeron. LC 67-25733. (Illus.). 800p. (C). 1994. text 60.00 (*0-87049-828-2*) U of Tenn Pr.

Papers of Andrew Johnson, 1852-1857, Vol. 2. Ed. by Andrew Johnson et al. LC 67-25733. (Illus.). 608p. 1970. 60.00 (*0-87049-098-2*) U of Tenn Pr.

Papers of Andrew Johnson, 1858-1860, Vol. 3. Ed. by Andrew Johnson et al. LC 67-25733. (Illus.). 796p. 1972. 60.00 (*0-87049-141-5*) U of Tenn Pr.

Papers of Andrew Johnson, 1861-1862, Vol. 5. Ed. by Andrew Johnson et al. LC 67-25733. 752p. 1979. text 60.00 (*0-87049-273-X*) U of Tenn Pr.

Papers of Andrew Johnson, 1862-1864, Vol. 6. Ed. by Andrew Johnson et al. LC 67-25733. 892p. 1983. 60.00 (*0-87049-346-9*) U of Tenn Pr.

Papers of Andrew Johnson, 1822-1851, Vol. 1. Ed. by Andrew Johnson et al. LC 67-25733. (Illus.). 752p. 1967. 60.00 (*0-87049-079-6*) U of Tenn Pr.

Papers of Andrew Johnson, February-August, 1867, Vol. 12. Ed. by Paul H. Bergeron. LC 67-25733. 592p. 1995. text 60.00 (*0-87049-896-7*) U of Tenn Pr.

Papers of Andrew Johnson, February-July, 1866, Vol. 10. Ed. by Paul H. Bergeron. LC 67-25733. (Illus.). 832p. 1992. text 60.00 (*0-87049-764-2*) U of Tenn Pr.

Papers of Andrew Johnson, May-August 1865, Vol. 8. Ed. by Paul H. Bergeron. LC 67-25733. (Papers of Andrew Johnson Ser.). 762p. 1990. text 60.00 (*0-87049-613-1*) U of Tenn Pr.

Papers of Andrew Johnson, September 1865-January 1866, Vol. 9. Ed. by Paul H. Bergeron. LC 67-25733. (Illus.). 712p. 1991. text 60.00 (*0-87049-689-1*) U of Tenn Pr.

Papers of Andrew Johnson, September 1867-March 1868, Vol. 13. Ed. by Paul H. Bergeron. LC 67-25733. 768p. (C). 1997. text 60.00 (*0-87049-946-7*) U of Tenn Pr.

Papers of Benjamin Franklin, 18 vols. Incl. Vol. 15. January 1, 1768 Through December 31, 1768. Ed. by William B. Willcox. LC 59-12697. (Illus.). 1972. 80.00 (*0-300-01469-4*); Vol. 16. Papers of Benjamin Franklin: January 1 1769 Through December 31, 1769. Ed. by William B. Willcox. LC 59-12697. (Illus.). 1982. 80.00 (*0-300-01570-4*); Vol. 3. January 1, 1745 Through June 30, 1750. Ed. by Leonard W. Labaree. LC 59-12697. (Illus.). xxv, 539p. 1961. 80.00 (*0-300-00652-7*); Vol. 4. July 1, 1750 Through June 30, 1753. Ed. by Leonard W. Labaree. LC 59-12697. (Illus.). xxviii, 572p. 1961. 80.00 (*0-300-00653-5*); Vol. 5. July 1, 1753 Through March 31, 1755. Ed. by Leonard W. Labaree. LC 59-12697. (Illus.). xxvi, 601p. 1962. 80.00 (*0-300-00654-3*); Vol. 6. April 1, 1755 Through September 24, 1756. Ed. by Leonard W. Labaree. LC 59-12697. (Illus.). xxix, 504p. 1963. 80.00 (*0-300-00655-1*); Vol. 7. October 1, 1756 Through March 31, 1758. Ed. by Leonard W. Lambaree. LC 59-12697. (Illus.). xxvi, 453p. 1963. 80.00 (*0-300-00657-8*); Vol. 8. April 1, 1758 Through December 31, 1759. Ed. by Leonard W. Labaree. LC 59-12697. (Illus.). xxiv, 514p. 1965. 80.00 (*0-300-00658-6*); 9. April 1, 1758 Through December 31, 1759. Ed. by Leonard W. Labaree. LC 59-12697. (Illus.). xxiv, 514p. 1965. pap. 16.00 (*0-300-06594-9*); Vol. 10. Januray 1, 1762 Through December 31, 1763. Ed. by Leonard W. Labaree. LC 59-12697. (Illus.). xxix, 459p. 1966. 80.00 (*0-300-00660-8*); Vol. 11. January 1, 1764 Through December 31, 1764. Ed. by Leonard W. Labaree. LC 59-12697. (Illus.). xxviii, 593p. 1967. 80.00 (*0-300-00661-6*); Vol. 12. January 1, 1765 Through December 31, 1765. Ed. by Leonard W. Labaree. LC 59-12697. (Illus.). 1968. 80.00 (*0-300-01073-7*); Vol. 12. January 1, 1765 Through December 31, 1765. Ed. by Leonard W. Labaree. LC 59-12697. (Illus.). 1968. (*0-300-11326-9*); Vol. 17. Benjamin Franklin. LC 59-12697. (Illus.). 1973. 80.00 (*0-300-01596-8*); Vol. 18. Benjamin Franklin. LC 59-12697. (Illus.). 30p. 1974. 80.00 (*0-300-01685-9*); Vol. 19. January 1, 1772 Through December 31, 1772. Benjamin Franklin. LC 59-12697. 1976. 80.00 (*0-300-01865-7*); Vol. 20. January 1, 1773 Through December 31, 1773. Benjamin Franklin. LC 59-12697. 1976. 80.00 (*0-300-01966-1*); Vol. 21. January 1, 1774 Through march 22, 1775. Benjamin Franklin. LC 59-12697. 1978. 80.00 (*0-300-02224-7*); LC 59-12697. write for info. (*0-318-56526-9*) Yale U Pr.

Papers of Benjamin Franklin, Vol. 1. Benjamin Franklin. Vol. 1. 1959. 80.00 (*0-300-00650-0*) Yale U Pr.

Papers of Benjamin Franklin, Vol. 2. Benjamin Franklin. Vol. 2. 1960. 80.00 (*0-300-00651-9*) Yale U Pr.

Papers of Benjamin Franklin, Vol. 9. Benjamin Franklin. Vol. 9. 1966. 80.00 (*0-300-00659-4*) Yale U Pr.

Papers of Benjamin Franklin, Vol. 13. Benjamin Franklin. Vol. 13. 1970. 80.00 (*0-300-01132-6*) Yale U Pr.

Papers of Benjamin Franklin, Vol. 25. Benjamin Franklin. Vol. 25. 1977. 80.00 (*0-300-03370-2*) Yale U Pr.

***Papers of Benjamin Franklin, Vol. 35.** Ed. by Barbara B. Oberg. (Illus.). 832p. 1999. 80.00 (*0-300-07841-2*) Yale U Pr.

Papers of Benjamin Franklin, Vol.#26. Benjamin Franklin. Ed. by William Wilcox. LC 59-12697. 848p. 1987. 80.00 (*0-300-03819-4*) Yale U Pr.

Papers of Benjamin Franklin: January 1 1769 Through December 31, 1769 see Papers of Benjamin Franklin

Papers of Benjamin Franklin: July 1 Through October 31, 1779, Vol. 30. Benjamin Franklin. Ed. by Barbara B. Oberg. Vol. 30. (Illus.). 784p. 1994. 80.00 (*0-300-05535-8*) Yale U Pr.

Papers of Benjamin Franklin: June 1 Through October 30, 1778, Vol. 27. Benjamin Franklin. (C). 1988. 80.00 (*0-300-04177-2*) Yale U Pr.

Papers of Benjamin Franklin: March 1 Through June 30, 1779, Vol. 29. Benjamin Franklin. Ed. by Barbara B. Oberg. Vol. 29. 928p. (C). 1992. 80.00 (*0-300-05188-3*) Yale U Pr.

Papers of Benjamin Franklin: May 1 Through September 30, 1777, Vol. 24. Benjamin Franklin. Ed. by William B. Willcox et al. LC 59-12697. Vol. 24. (Illus.). 672p. 1984. 80.00 (*0-300-03162-9*) Yale U Pr.

Papers of Benjamin Franklin: November 1, 1778 Through February 28, 1779, Vol. 28. Benjamin Franklin. Ed. by Barbara B. Oberg. Vol. 28. 984p. (C). 1991. 80.00 (*0-300-04673-1*) Yale U Pr.

Papers of Benjamin Franklin Vol. 31: November 1, 1779 Through February 29, 1780. Benjamin Franklin. LC 59-12697. 31p. (C). 1995. 80.00 (*0-300-06109-9*) Yale U Pr.

Papers of Benjamin Franklin Vol. 32: March 1 Through June 30, 1780. Ed. by Barbara B. Oberg. LC 59-12697. (Illus.). 800p. 1997. 80.00 (*0-300-06617-1*) Yale U Pr.

Papers of Benjamin Franklin Vol. 34: November 16, 1780, Through April 30, 1781. Ed. by Barbara B. Oberg et al. (Illus.). 720p. 1998. 80.00 (*0-300-07413-1*) Yale U Pr.

Papers of Benjamin Franklin, January 1767 to December 1767, Vol. 14. Benjamin Franklin. 1970. 80.00 (*0-300-01317-5*) Yale U Pr.

Papers of Benjamin Franklin, July 1 Through November 15, 1780 Vol. 33. Ed. by Barbara B. Oberg. LC 59-12697. Vol. 33. (Illus.). 672p. 1997. 85.00 (*0-300-07040-3*) Yale U Pr.

Papers of Benjamin Henry Latrobe: Series 2: The Architectural & Engineering Drawings; Vol. 2: The Architectural Drawings of Benjamin Henry Latrobe, Pts. 1 & 2. Jeffrey A. Cohen & Charles E. Brownell. (Illus.). 992p. 1995. 130.00 (*0-300-06100-5*) Yale U Pr.

Papers of Betty Gannett, 1929-1970: Guide to a Microfilm Edition. Ed. by Kent Gulley. 31p. 1976. pap. write for info. (*0-87020-161-1*) Chadwyck-Healey.

Papers of British Churchmen, 1780-1940. Royal Commission on Historical Manuscripts Staff. (Guides to Sources for British History Ser.: No. 6). 96p. 1987. 16.00 (*0-11-440212-4*, HM208, Pub. by Statnry Office) Balogh.

Papers of Calhoun Vol. 24: December 7, 1846-December 5, 1847. Ed. by Clyde N. Wilson et al. LC 59-10351. 800p. 1998. 59.95 (*1-57003-209-2*) U of SC Pr.

Papers of Captain Rufus Lincoln of Wareham, Mass. Ed. by Rufus Lincoln. LC 74-140872. (Eyewitness Accounts of the American Revolution Ser.). 1971. reprint ed. 23.95 (*0-405-01220-9*) Ayer.

***Papers of Carter G. Woodson & the Association for the Study of Negro Life & History, 1915-1950.** Jacqueline A. Goggin & Randolph Boehm. LC 99-16370. (Black Studies Research Sources). 1998. write for info. incl. mic. film (*1-55655-717-5*) U Pubns Amer.

Papers of Charles Willson Peale Vol. 2: The Artist as Museum Keeper 1791-1810. Charles W. Peale. Ed. by Lillian S. Miller. LC 87-10646. 1318p. 1988. 140.00 (*0-300-03422-9*) Yale U Pr.

Papers of Daniel Murray, 1881-1955: Guide to a Microfilm Edition. Ed. by Janet Wolff & Eleanor McKay. 16p. 1977. pap. write for info. (*0-87020-167-0*) Chadwyck-Healey.

Papers of Daniel Webster: General Index. Daniel Webster. Ed. by Alan R. Berolzheimer. LC 73-92705. 432p. 1989. text 50.00 (*0-87451-447-9*) U Pr of New Eng.

Papers of Daniel Webster: General Index. Daniel Webster. Ed. by Alan R. Berolzheimer. LC 73-92705. 432p. Date not set. reprint ed. pap. 134.00 (*0-608-20706-3*, 207180400002) Bks Demand.

Papers of Daniel Webster: Series 1, Correspondence, Vol. 1. Daniel Webster. Ed. by Charles M. Wiltse & Harold D. Moser. LC 73-92705. 544p. Date not set. reprint ed. pap. 168.70 (*0-608-20692-X*, 207180000001) Bks Demand.

Papers of Daniel Webster: Series 1, Correspondence, Vol. 2. Daniel Webster. Ed. by Charles M. Wiltse & Harold D. Moser. LC 73-92705. 587p. Date not set. reprint ed. pap. 182.00 (*0-608-20693-8*, 207180000002) Bks Demand.

Papers of Daniel Webster: Series 1, Correspondence, Vol. 3. Daniel Webster. Ed. by Charles M. Wiltse & Harold D. Moser. LC 73-92705. 573p. Date not set. reprint ed. pap. 177.70 (*0-608-20694-6*, 207180000003) Bks Demand.

Papers of Daniel Webster: Series 1, Correspondence, Vol. 4. Daniel Webster. Ed. by Charles M. Wiltse & Harold D. Moser. LC 73-92705. 588p. Date not set. reprint ed. pap. 182.30 (*0-608-20695-4*, 207180000004) Bks Demand.

Papers of Daniel Webster: Series 1, Correspondence, Vol. 5. Daniel Webster. Ed. by Charles M. Wiltse & Harold D. Moser. LC 73-92705. 618p. Date not set. reprint ed. pap. 191.60 (*0-608-20696-2*, 207180000005) Bks Demand.

Papers of Daniel Webster: Series 1, Correspondence, Vol. 6. Daniel Webster. Ed. by Charles M. Wiltse & Harold D. Moser. LC 73-92705. 564p. Date not set. reprint ed. pap. 174.90 (*0-608-20697-0*, 207180000006) Bks Demand.

Papers of Daniel Webster: Series 1, Correspondence, Vol. 7. Daniel Webster. Ed. by Charles M. Wiltse & Harold D. Moser. LC 73-92705. 730p. Date not set. reprint ed. pap. 200.00 (*0-608-20698-9*, 207180000007) Bks Demand.

Papers of Daniel Webster: Series 2, Legal Papers, Vol. 1. Daniel Webster. Ed. by Alfred S. Konefsky & Andrew J. King. LC 73-92705. 611p. Date not set. reprint ed. pap. 189.50 (*0-608-20699-7*, 207180100001) Bks Demand.

Papers of Daniel Webster: Series 2, Legal Papers, Vol. 3 Part 1. Daniel Webster. Ed. by Alfred S. Konefsky & Andrew J. King. LC 73-92705. 678p. Date not set. reprint ed. pap. 200.00 (*0-608-20700-4*, 207180100003) Bks Demand.

Papers of Daniel Webster: Series 3, Diplomatic Papers, Vol. 1. Daniel Webster. Ed. by Kenneth E. Shewmaker et al. LC 73-92705. 1008p. Date not set. reprint ed. pap. 200.00 (*0-608-20702-0*, 207180200001) Bks Demand.

Papers of Daniel Webster: Series 3, Diplomatic Papers, Vol. 2. Daniel Webster. Ed. by Kenneth E. Shewmaker et al. LC 73-92705. 856p. Date not set. reprint ed. pap. 200.00 (*0-608-20703-9*, 207180200002) Bks Demand.

Papers of Daniel Webster: Series 4, Speeches & Formal Writings, Vol. 1. Daniel Webster. Ed. by Charles M. Wiltse & Alan R. Berolzheimer. LC 73-92705. 662p. Date not set. reprint ed. pap. 200.00 (*0-608-20704-7*, 207180300001) Bks Demand.

Papers of Daniel Webster: Series 4, Speeches & Formal Writings, Vol. 2. Daniel Webster. Ed. by Charles M. Wiltse & Alan R. Berolzheimer. LC 73-92705. 720p. Date not set. reprint ed. pap. 200.00 (*0-608-20705-5*, 207180300002) Bks Demand.

Papers of David Settle Reid, Vol. 1, 1829-1852. Ed. by Lindley S. Butler. (Illus.). lxii, 495p. (C). 1993. 45.00 (*0-86526-249-7*) NC Archives.

Papers of David Settle Reid Vol. II: 1853-1913. Ed. by Lindley S. Butler. (Papers of David Settle Reid Ser.). (Illus.). xxv, 408p. (C). 1997. 35.00 (*0-86526-269-1*) NC Archives.

Papers of Dwight David Eisenhower: Columbia University, 2 vols., Set, Vols. X-XI. Ed. by Louis P. Galambos. LC 65-27672. 1664p. 1984. 125.00 (*0-8018-2720-5*) Johns Hopkins.

Papers of Dwight David Eisenhower: The Presidency: The Middle Way, 4 vols., Set. Ed. by Louis P. Galambos & Daun Van Ee. (Illus.). 3040p. 1996. text 195.00 (*0-8018-4752-4*) Johns Hopkins.

Papers of Dwight David Eisenhower: The War Years, 5 Vols, Set. Ed. by Alfred D. Chandler, Jr. LC 65-27672. (Illus.). 1970. 175.00 (*0-8018-1078-7*) Johns Hopkins.

Papers of Dwight David Eisenhower Vols. 6-9: Occupation, 1945; The Chief of Staff. Ed. by Louis P. Galambos. LC 65-27672. (Illus.). 2584p. 1978. text 150.00 (*0-8018-2061-8*) Johns Hopkins.

Papers of Dwight David Eisenhower Vols. 12 & 13: NATO & the Campaign of 1952, 2 vols., Set. Ed. by Louis P. Galambos. LC 65-27672. 1720p. 1989. text 125.00 (*0-8018-3726-X*) Johns Hopkins.

Papers of Eleanor Roosevelt, 1933-1945. Eleanor Roosevelt et al. LC 88-890656. (Research Collections in Women's Studies). 20 p. 1986. write for info. (*0-89093-925-X*) U Pubns Amer.

Papers of Elizabeth Cady Stanton & Susan B. Anthony: Guide & Index to the Microfilm Edition. Ed. by Patricia G. Holland et al. LC 92-22829. (Illus.). 230p. 1992. 50.00 (*0-8420-4077-3*) Scholarly Res Inc.

Papers of Francis Howard, Baron Howard of Effingham, 1643-1695. Pref. by Warren M. Billings. xxxvii, 473p. 1989. text 35.00 (*0-88490-165-3*) Library of VA.

Papers of Frederick Law Olmsted Vol. 1: Writings on Public Parks, Parkways, & Park Systems. Ed. by Charles E. Beveridge. LC 77-741. (Papers of Frederick Law Olmsted: Vol. 1). (Illus.). 744p. 1997. text 55.00 (*0-8018-5532-2*) Johns Hopkins.

Papers of Frederick Law Olmsted Vol. 3: Creating Central Park, 1857-1861. Charles E. Beveridge & David Schuyler. LC 82-4701. (Olsted Papers). (Illus.). 464p. 1983. text 55.00 (*0-8018-2751-5*) Johns Hopkins.

Papers of Frederick Law Olmsted Vol. 4: Defending the Union: The Civil War & the U. S. Sanitary Commission, 1861-1863. Ed. by Jane T. Censer. LC 85-24044. 770p. 1986. text 59.50 (*0-8018-3067-2*) Johns Hopkins.

Papers of Frederick Law Olmsted Vol. 5: The California Frontier, 1863-1865. Ed. by Victoria P. Ranney et al. LC 89-15315. (Illus.). 848p. 1990. text 55.00 (*0-8018-3885-1*) Johns Hopkins.

Papers of Frederick Law Olmsted Vol. 6: The Years of Olmsted, Vaux & Company, 1865-1874. Ed. by David Schuyler & Jane T. Censer. (Illus.). 704p. 1992. text 55.00 (*0-8018-4198-4*) Johns Hopkins.

Papers of General Lucius D. Clay: Germany, 1945-1949, Vol. 1. Lucius D. Clay. Ed. by Jean E. Smith. LC 73-16536. 570p. reprint ed. pap. 176.70 (*0-608-09959-7*, 205643700001) Bks Demand.

Papers of General Lucius D. Clay: Germany, 1945-1949, Vol. 2. Lucius D. Clay. Ed. by Jean E. Smith. LC 73-16536. 700p. reprint ed. pap. 200.00 (*0-608-09960-0*, 205643700002) Bks Demand.

Papers of General Nathanael Greene: 11 July-2 December 1781, Vol. 9. Nathanael Greene. (C). 1997. 90.00 (*0-8078-2310-4*) U of NC Pr.

***Papers of General Nathanael Greene Vol. IX: 7 April - 30 September 1782.** Ed. by Nathanael Greene et al. (Published for the Rhode Island Historical Society). (Illus.). 800p. 2000. 95.00 (*0-8078-2551-4*) U of NC Pr.

Papers of General Nathanael Greene Vol. X: 3 December, 1781-6 April, 1782. Nathanael Greene. Ed. by Dennis M. Conrad et al. (Illus.). 712p. 1998. 85.00 (*0-8078-2419-4*) U of NC Pr.

Papers of General Nathanael Greene, December 1766 to December 1776, Set, Vols. I-VIII. Ed. by Richard K. Showman & Dennis M. Conrad. 1976. 85.00 (*0-685-67666-8*) RI Hist Soc.

Papers of General Nathanael Greene, December 1766 to December 1776: December 1766 to December 1776, Vol. 1. Ed. by Richard K. Showman et al. LC 76-20441. lvi, 413p. 1976. 85.00 (*0-8078-1285-4*) RI Hist Soc.

Papers of General Nathanael Greene, December 1766 to December 1776: 1 January 1777-16 October 1778, Vol. 2. Ed. by Richard K. Showman et al. LC 76-20441. xxxix, 606p. 1976. 85.00 (*0-8078-1384-2*) RI Hist Soc.

Papers of General Nathanael Greene, December 1766 to December 1776: 1 June 1780-25 December 1780, Vol. 6. Ed. by Richard K. Showman & Dennis M. Conrad. LC 76-20441. (Illus.). 720p. (C). 1976. 85.00 (*0-8078-1993-X*) RI Hist Soc.

Papers of General Nathanael Greene, December 1766 to December 1776: 1 November 1779-31 May 1780, Vol. 5. Ed. by Richard K. Showman et al. LC 76-20441. (Illus.). xxviii, 668p. (C). 1976. 85.00 (*0-8078-1817-8*) RI Hist Soc.

Papers of General Nathanael Greene, December 1766 to December 1776: 11 May 1779-31 October 1779, Vol. 4. Ed. by Richard K. Showman et al. LC 76-20441. xxxviii, 614p. 1976. 85.00 (*0-8078-1668-X*) RI Hist Soc.

Papers of General Nathanael Greene, December 1766 to December 1776: 18 October 1778-10 May 1779, Vol. 3. Ed. by Richard K. Showman et al. LC 76-20441. xxxix, 543p. 1976. 85.00 (*0-8078-1557-8*) RI Hist Soc.

Papers of General Nathanael Greene, December 1766 to December 1776 Vol. VII: 26 December 1780-29 March 1781, Vol. 7. Ed. by Richard K. Showman & Dennis M. Conrad. LC 76-20441. (Illus.). xlii, 544p. (C). 1994. 85.00 (*0-8078-2094-6*) RI Hist Soc.

Papers of General Nathanael Greene, December 1766 to December 1776 Vol. VIII: 30 March-10 July 1781, Vol. 8. Ed. by Richard K. Showman et al. LC 76-20441. 624p. (C). 1976. 85.00 (*0-8078-2212-4*) RI Hist Soc.

Papers of George C. Marshall: Selected World War II Correspondence. George C. Marshall et al. LC 93-28320. (World War II Research Collections). 40 p. 1992. write for info. (*1-55655-455-9*) U Pubns Amer.

Papers of George Catlett Marshall Vol. 1: "The Soldierly Spirit", December 1880-June 1939. Ed. by Larry I. Bland & Fred L. Hadsel. LC 81-47593. (Illus.). 750p. 1981. text 55.00 (*0-8018-2552-0*) Johns Hopkins.

Papers of George Catlett Marshall Vol. 2: "We Cannot Delay" July 1, 1939 - December 6, 1941. Ed. by Larry I. Bland et al. LC 81-47593. 800p. 1986. text 55.00 (*0-8018-2553-9*) Johns Hopkins.

Papers of George Catlett Marshall Vol. 3: "The Right Man for the Job," December 3, 1941-May 31, 1943. George C. Marshall. Ed. by Larry I. Bland & Sharon R. Stevens. (Illus.). 800p. 1991. text 55.00 (*0-8018-2967-4*) Johns Hopkins.

Papers of George Catlett Marshall Vol. 4: "Aggressive & Determined Leadership" June 1, 1943-December 31, 1944. Ed. by Larry I. Bland & Sharon R. Stevens. (Illus.). 840p. 1996. text 55.00 (*0-8018-5368-0*) Johns Hopkins.

P

Papers of George Mason, 1725-1792, 3 vols., Vol. 1. George Mason. Ed. by Robert A. Rutland. LC 70-97016. 613p. reprint ed. pap. 190.10 (*0-7837-0318-X*, 204064000001) Bks Demand.

Papers of George Mason, 1725-1792, 3 vols., Vol. 2. George Mason. Ed. by Robert A. Rutland. LC 70-97016. 403p. reprint ed. pap. 125.00 (*0-7837-0319-8*, 204064000002) Bks Demand.

Papers of George Mason, 1725-1792, 3 vols., Vol. 3. George Mason. Ed. by Robert A. Rutland. LC 70-97016. 477p. reprint ed. pap. 147.90 (*0-7837-0320-1*, 204064000003) Bks Demand.

Papers of George Washington. Ed. by W. W. Abbot. (Revolutionary War Series, April-June 1776: Vol. 4). 1991. text 47.50 (*0-8139-1307-1*) U Pr of Va.

***Papers of George Washington.** Ed. by Philander D. Chase & Frank E. Grizzard, Jr. (Revolutionary War Ser.: Vol. 10). 768p. 2000. 67.50 (*0-8139-1901-0*) U Pr of Va.

Papers of George Washington. George Washington. Ed. by W. W. Abbot. LC 81-16307. (Colonial Ser.: Vol. 1). (Illus.). 1983. text 40.00 (*0-8139-0912-0*) U Pr of Va.

Papers of George Washington. George Washington. Ed. by W. W. Abbot. LC 81-16307. (Colonial Ser.: Vol. 2). (Illus.). 1983. text 40.00 (*0-8139-0923-6*) U Pr of Va.

Papers of George Washington. George Washington. Ed. by W. W. Abbot. LC 81-16307. (Colonial Ser.: Vol. 3). 488p. 1984. text 40.00 (*0-8139-1003-X*) U Pr of Va.

Papers of George Washington. George Washington. Ed. by W. W. Abbot. LC 81-16307. (Colonial Ser.: Vol. 4). 467p. 1984. text 40.00 (*0-8139-1006-4*) U Pr of Va.

Papers of George Washington. George Washington. Ed. by W. W. Abbot & Dorothy Twohig. LC 81-16307. (Presidential Series, April-May 1789: No. 2). 499p. 1987. text 37.50 (*0-8139-1105-2*) U Pr of Va.

Papers of George Washington. George Washington. Ed. by W. W. Abbot & Dorothy Twohig. LC 81-16307. (Presidential Series, September 1788-March 1789: No. 1). (Illus.). 477p. 1987. text 37.50 (*0-8139-1103-6*) U Pr of Va.

Papers of George Washington. George Washington. Ed. by W. W. Abbot. LC 81-16307. (Colonial Ser.: Vol. 6). 1988. text 42.00 (*0-8139-1145-1*) U Pr of Va.

Papers of George Washington. George Washington. (Presidential Ser.: Vol. 3). 1990. 42.50 (*0-8139-1210-5*) U Pr of Va.

***Papers of George Washington, Vol. 9.** Ed. by Philander D. Chase et al. Vol. 9. 672p. 2000. 62.50 (*0-8139-1922-3*) U Pr of Va.

***Papers of George Washington: April-December 1799.** Dorothy Twohig. LC 97-6770. (Retirement Ser.: Vol. 4). 603p. 1999. 55.00 (*0-8139-1855-3*) U Pr of Va.

Papers of George Washington: December 1790-March 1791. George Washington. Ed. by Jack D. Warren et al. (Presidential Ser.: Vol. 7). 768p. 1998. lib. bdg. 60.00 (*0-8139-1749-2*) U Pr of Va.

Papers of George Washington: February-December 1787. Ed. by W. W. Abbot. (Confederation Ser.: Vol. 5). 592p. 1997. lib. bdg. 47.50 (*0-8139-1672-0*) U Pr of Va.

Papers of George Washington: January - July 1784. Ed. by W. W. Abbot & Dorothy Twohig. (Confederation Ser.: Vol. 1). 600p. 1992. text 47.50 (*0-8139-1348-9*) U Pr of Va.

Papers of George Washington: January-June 1790. Ed. by Dorothy Twohig et al. (Presidential Ser.: Vol. 5). 656p. (C). 1996. pap. 47.50 (*0-8139-1619-4*) U Pr of Va.

Papers of George Washington: January-September 1788. Ed. by W. W. Abbot. (Confederation Ser.: Vol. 6). 608p. 1997. lib. bdg. 47.50 (*0-8139-1684-4*) U Pr of Va.

***Papers of George Washington: January-September, 1798.** George Washington. Ed. by W. W. Abbott et al. LC 97-6770. (Retirement Ser.: Vol. 2). 640p. 1998. lib. bdg. 55.00 (*0-8139-1762-X*) U Pr of Va.

Papers of George Washington: January 1761-June 1767. Ed. by W. W. Abbot & Dorothy Twohig. LC 81-16307. (Colonial Ser.: Vol. 7). 586p. 1990. text 45.00 (*0-8139-1236-9*) U Pr of Va.

Papers of George Washington: January 1772-March 1774. Ed. by W. W. Abbot & Dorothy Twohig. (Colonial Ser.: Vol. 9). 704p. 1994. text 55.00 (*0-8139-1465-5*) U Pr of Va.

Papers of George Washington: Journal of the Proceedings of the President 1793-1797. George Washington. Ed. by Dorothy Twohig. LC 80-17174. 393p. 1981. text 40.00 (*0-8139-0874-4*) U Pr of Va.

Papers of George Washington: July 1784 - May 1785. Ed. by W. W. Abbot & Dorothy Twohig. (Confederation Ser.: Vol. 2). 600p. 1992. text 47.50 (*0-8139-1349-7*) U Pr of Va.

Papers of George Washington: June-August 1776. Ed. by W. W. Abbot & Dorothy Twohig. (Revolutionary War Ser.: Vol. 5). 784p. 1993. text 67.50 (*0-8139-1447-7*) U Pr of Va.

Papers of George Washington: June-September 1775. George Washington. Ed. by W. W. Abbot. LC 81-16307. (Revolutionary War Ser.: No. 1). 460p. 1985. text 35.00 (*0-8139-1040-4*) U Pr of Va.

Papers of George Washington: March-December, 1797. George Washington. Ed. by W. W. Abbot. LC 97-6770. (Retirement Ser.: Vol. I). 608p. 1997. text 55.00 (*0-8139-1737-9*) U Pr of Va.

Papers of George Washington: March-June 1777. George Washington. Ed. by Dorothy Twohig & Philander D. Chase. (Revolutionary War Ser.: Vol. 9). 720p. 1999. text 60.00 (*0-8139-1825-1*) U Pr of Va.

Papers of George Washington: March-September 1791. George Washington. Ed. by Dorothy Twohig et al. (Presidential Ser.: Vol. 8). 632p. 1999. text 55.00 (*0-8139-1810-3*) U Pr of Va.

Papers of George Washington: October 1757-August 1758. George Washington. Ed. by W. W. Abbot. LC 81-16307. (Colonial Ser.: Vol. 5). 500p. 1988. text 40.00 (*0-8139-1144-3*) U Pr of Va.

Papers of George Washington: October 1776-January 1777. Ed. by Dorothy Twohig & Philander D. Chase. (Revolutionary War Ser.: Vol. 7). 640p. 1996. text 55.00 (*0-8139-1648-8*) U Pr of Va.

Papers of George Washington: Revolutionary War Series 2, September-December 1775. George Washington. Ed. by W. W. Abbot & Philander D. Chase. LC 81-16307. (Illus.). 628p. 1987. text 47.50 (*0-8139-1102-8*) U Pr of Va.

Papers of George Washington: Revolutionary War Series 3, January-March 1776. George Washington. Ed. by W. W. Abbot et al. LC 81-16307. 1250p. 1988. text 47.50 (*0-8139-1167-2*) U Pr of Va.

Papers of George Washington: September 1789 - January 1790. Ed. by W. W. Abbot & Dorothy Twohig. (Presidential Ser.: Vol. 4). 627p. (C). 1993. text 65.00 (*0-8139-1407-8*) U Pr of Va.

***Papers of George Washington: September 1798 - April 1799.** Ed. by Dorothy Twohig. LC 97-6770. (Retirement Ser.: Vol. 3). 524p. 1999. 55.00 (*0-8139-1838-3*) U Pr of Va.

Papers of George Washington: 13 August - 20 October 1776. Ed. by Philander D. Chase & Frank E. Grizzard, Jr. (Revolutionary War Ser.: Vol. 6). 680p. (C). text 47.50 (*0-8139-1538-4*) U Pr of Va.

Papers of George Washington Vol. 3: Confederation Series: May 1785-March 1786. Ed. by W. W. Abbot. 654p. (C). 1994. text 47.50 (*0-8139-1506-6*) U Pr of Va.

Papers of George Washington Vol. 10: March 1774-June 1775: Colonial Series. Ed. by Dorothy Twohig et al. 768p. (C). 1995. text 55.00 (*0-8139-1550-3*) U Pr of Va.

Papers of George Washington, Colonial Series Vol. 8: June 1767-December 1771. Ed. by W. W. Abbot. 654p. (C). 1993. text 47.50 (*0-8139-1362-4*) U Pr of Va.

Papers of George Washington Confederation Series Vol. 4: April 1786-January 1787. Dorothy Twohig. Ed. by W. W. Abbot. 688p. (C). 1995. text 47.50 (*0-8139-1560-0*) U Pr of Va.

Papers of George Washington Presidential Series Vol. 6: July-November 1790. Ed. by Mark A. Mastromarino. (Papers of George Washington). 800p. (C). 1996. text 57.50 (*0-8139-1637-2*) U Pr of Va.

Papers of George Wyatt. D. M. Loades. (Camden Fourth Ser.: No. 5). 200p. 27.00 (*0-901050-01-6*) David Brown.

Papers of Henry Bouquet: January 1 to August 31, 1759, Vol. 3. 686p. 1976. 30.00 (*0-911124-86-1*) Pa Hist & Mus.

Papers of Henry Bouquet: Sept 1, 1759 to August 31, 1760, Vol. 4. 759p. 1978. 30.00 (*0-911124-99-3*) Pa Hist & Mus.

Papers of Henry Bouquet: September 1, 1760 to October 31, 1761, Vol. 5. Louis M. Waddell. 875p. 1984. 45.00 (*0-89271-030-6*) Pa Hist & Mus.

Papers of Henry Bouquet Vol. VI: November 1761 - July 1765. Ed. by Louis M. Waddell. (Illus.). 898p. 1994. 65.00 (*0-89271-050-0*, 0713) Pa Hist & Mus.

Papers of Henry Clay, Vol. 2. Henry Clay. Ed. by James F. Hopkins & Mary W. M. Hargreaves. LC 59-13605. 951p. reprint ed. pap. 200.00 (*0-608-12716-7*, 202435900037) Bks Demand.

Papers of Henry Clay: Supplement, 1793-1852. Henry Clay. Ed. by Melba P. Hay. LC 59-13605. 400p. (C). 1992. text 60.00 (*0-8131-0061-5*) U Pr of Ky.

Papers of Henry Demarest Lloyd, 1840-1937: Guide to Microfilm Edition. Ed. by F. Gerald Ham. 28p. 1971. pap. write for info. (*0-89887-183-2*) Chadwyck-Healey.

Papers of Henry Laurens, Vol. XV. Ed. by David R. Chesnutt & C. James Taylor. 768p. 49.95 (*1-57003-307-2*) U of SC Pr.

Papers of Henry Laurens: July 7, 1778-December 9, 1778. Henry Laurens. Ed. by David R. Chesnutt et al. LC 67-29381. (Papers of Henry Laurens Ser.: Vol. 14). 700p. 1994. text 49.95 (*1-57003-030-8*) U of SC Pr.

Papers of Henry Laurens: Vol. X, December 12, 1774-January 4, 1776, Vol. X. Henry Laurens. Ed. by David R. Chesnutt et al. LC 67-29381. (Papers of Henry Laurens Ser.). 736p. 1985. text 49.95 (*0-87249-445-4*) U of SC Pr.

Papers of Henry Laurens: Vol. 1, September 11, 1746-October 31, 1755. Henry Laurens. Ed. by Philip M. Hamer & George C. Rogers. LC 67-29381. (Papers of Henry Laurens Ser.). (Illus.). xlii, 447p. 1968. text 49.95 (*0-87249-128-5*) U of SC Pr.

Papers of Henry Laurens: Vol. 2, November 1, 1755-December 31, 1758. Henry Laurens. Ed. by Philip M. Hamer & George C. Rogers, Jr. LC 67-29381. (Papers of Henry Laurens Ser.). (Illus.). xxviii, 608p. 1970. text 49.95 (*0-87249-141-2*) U of SC Pr.

Papers of Henry Laurens: Vol. 3, January 1, 1759-August 31, 1763. Henry Laurens. Ed. by Philip M. Hamer & George C. Rogers, Jr. LC 67-29381. (Papers of Henry Laurens Ser.). xxviii, 625p. 1972. text 49.95 (*0-87249-228-1*) U of SC Pr.

Papers of Henry Laurens: Vol. 5, September 1, 1765-July 31, 1768. Henry Laurens. Ed. by George C. Rogers, Jr. & David R. Chesnutt. LC 67-29381. xxxii, 872p. 1974. text 49.95 (*0-87249-331-8*) U of SC Pr.

Papers of Henry Laurens Vol. 6: August 1, 1768-July 31, 1769. Henry Laurens. Ed. by George C. Rogers, Jr. et al. LC 67-29381. (Illus.). xxvi, 685p. 1978. text 49.95 (*0-87249-356-3*) U of SC Pr.

Papers of Henry Laurens Vol. 7: August 1, 1769 to October 9, 1771. Henry Laurens. Ed. by George C. Rogers, Jr. et al. LC 67-29381. xxx, 656p. 1979. text 49.95 (*0-87249-372-5*) U of SC Pr.

Papers of Henry Laurens Vol. 8: October 10, 1771 to April 19, 1773. Henry Laurens. Ed. by George C. Rogers, Jr. LC 67-29381. xxiv, 784p. 1980. text 49.95 (*0-87249-385-7*) U of SC Pr.

Papers of Henry Laurens Vol. 9: April 19, 1773 to December 12, 1774. Henry Laurens. Ed. by George C. Rogers, Jr. & David R. Chesnutt. LC 67-29381. (Illus.). 734p. 1981. text 49.95 (*0-87249-399-7*) U of SC Pr.

Papers of Henry Laurens Vol. 11: January 6, 1776-November 1, 1777, Vol. XI. Henry Laurens. Ed. by David R. Chesnutt et al. LC 67-29381. (Papers of Henry Laurens Ser.: Vol. 11). 710p. 1988. text 49.95 (*0-87249-516-7*) U of SC Pr.

Papers of Henry Laurens Vol. 12: November 1, 1777-March 15, 1778. Henry Laurens. Ed. by David R. Chesnutt et al. LC 67-29381. (Papers of Henry Laurens Ser.: Vol. 12). 684p. 1990. text 49.95 (*0-87249-664-3*) U of SC Pr.

Papers of James C. H. Anderson. LC 97-35908. 1997. text. write for info. (*0-938959-50-6*) Soc Actuaries.

Papers of James Iredell, Vol. 2: 1778-1783. Ed. by Don Higginbotham. xxv, 508p. 1976. 20.00 (*0-86526-043-5*) NC Archives.

Papers of James Madison, 10 vols. James Madison. Ed. by William T. Hutchinson et al. Incl. March-December, 1781. Ed. by William H. Rachal. LC 62-9114. 381p. 1993. lib. bdg. 25.00 (*0-226-36295-7*); May 3, 1783-February 20, 1784. Ed. by William M. Rachal. LC 62-9114. 1971. lib. bdg. 35.00 (*0-226-36300-7*); May 27, 1787-March 3, 1788. Ed. by William H. Rachal. LC 62-9114. 1993. lib. bdg. 35.00 (*0-226-50107-8*); Vol. 8. March 10, 1784 - March 28, 1786. Ed. by William M. Rachal. LC 62-9114. 1992. lib. bdg. 30.00 (*0-226-50104-3*); Vol. 4. 1 January-31 July, 1782. Ed. by William M. Rachal. LC 62-9114. 486p. 1992. lib. bdg. 25.00 (*0-226-36296-5*); Vol. 5. 1 August-31 December 1782. Ed. by William M. Rachal. LC 62-9114. 1967. lib. bdg. 35.00 (*0-226-36297-3*); 1 January 1783-30 April, 1783. Ed. by William M. Rachal. LC 62-9114. 548p. 1969. lib. bdg. 35.00 (*0-226-36298-1*); LC 62-9114. (Illus.). write for info. (*0-318-56067-4*) U Ch Pr.

Papers of James Madison. James Madison et al. Ed. by Robert J. Brugger et al. LC 85-29516. (Secretary of State Series, 4 March-31 July 1801: Vol. 1). xxx, 526p. 1987. text 42.50 (*0-8139-1093-5*) U Pr of Va.

***Papers of James Madison, Vol. 5.** Ed. by David B. Mattern et al. Vol. 5. 704p. 2000. text 67.50 (*0-8139-1941-X*) U Pr of Va.

Papers of James Madison: August 1, 1801-February 28, 1802. James Madison. Ed. by Jeanne K. Cross et al. (Secretary of State Ser.: Vol. 2). 576p. (C). 1993. text 60.00 (*0-8139-1403-5*) U Pr of Va.

Papers of James Madison: March 1789 to January 1790. with a supplement 24 October 1775-24 January 1789. James Madison. Ed. by Robert A. Rutland & Charles F. Hobson. LC 62-9114. (Vol. 12). 498p. 1979. text 42.50 (*0-8139-0803-5*) U Pr of Va.

Papers of James Madison: 1 March-30 September 1809. James Madison. Ed. by Robert A. Rutland & Thomas A. Mason. LC 83-6953. (Presidential Ser.: Vol. 1). 414p. 1984. text 42.50 (*0-8139-0991-0*) U Pr of Va.

Papers of James Madison: 1 October 1809 - 2 November 1810. James Madison. Ed. by Jeanne K. Cross et al. (Presidential Ser.: Vol. 2). 681p. (C). 1992. text 55.00 (*0-8139-1345-4*) U Pr of Va.

Papers of James Madison: 8 October 1802 - 15 May 1803. James Madison. Ed. by Mary A. Hackett et al. (Secretary of State Ser.: Vol. 4). Date not set. 65.00 (*0-8139-1747-6*) U Pr of Va.

Papers of James Madison Vol. 3: 1 March 1802-6 October 1802: Secretary of State Series. James Madison. Ed. by David B. Mattern et al. 608p. (C). 1995. text 50.00 (*0-8139-1541-4*) U Pr of Va.

Papers of James Madison Vol. 11: 7 March 1788 to 1 March 1789. James Madison. Ed. by Robert A. Rutland & Charles F. Hobson. LC 62-9114. 471p. 1977. text 42.50 (*0-8139-0739-X*) U Pr of Va.

Papers of James Madison Vol. 16: 27 April 1795-27 March 1797. James Madison. Ed. by John C. Stagg et al. LC 62-9114. (Papers of James Madison). 576p. 1989. text 47.50 (*0-8139-1212-1*) U Pr of Va.

Papers of James Madison Vol. 17: 31 March 1797-3 March 1801, with a Supplement. James Madison. Ed. by J. C. Stagg et al. (Papers of James Madison). 656p. 1991. text 49.50 (*0-8139-1288-1*) U Pr of Va.

Papers of James Madison Presidential Series: 3 November 1810-4 November 1811. Ed. by Jeanne K. Cross et al. (Papers of James Madison). 648p. (C). 1996. text 55.00 (*0-8139-1632-1*) U Pr of Va.

Papers of Jefferson Davis: October 1863-August 1864, Vol. 10. Jefferson Davis. Ed. by Lynda L. Crist et al. (Illus.). 1000p. 1999. text 95.00 (*0-8071-2412-5*) La State U Pr.

Papers of Jefferson Davis, 1853-1855, Vol. 5. Jefferson Davis. Ed. by Lynda L. Crist & Mary S. Dix. LC 76-152704. (Illus.). xlii, 557p. 1985. text 75.00 (*0-8071-1240-2*) La State U Pr.

Papers of Jefferson Davis, 1856-1860, Vol. 6. Jefferson Davis. Ed. by Lynda L. Crist & Mary S. Dix. LC 76-152704. (Illus.). 840p. 1989. text 80.00 (*0-8071-1502-9*) La State U Pr.

Papers of Jefferson Davis, 1849-1852, Vol. 4. Jefferson Davis. Ed. by Lynda L. Crist. LC 76-152704. (Illus.). 472p. 1982. text 70.00 (*0-8071-1037-X*) La State U Pr.

Papers of Jefferson Davis, 1808-1840, Vol. 1. Jefferson Davis. Ed. by Haskell M. Monroe, Jr. & James T. McIntosh. LC 76-152704. (Illus.). xcii, 594p. 1971. text 80.00 (*0-8071-0943-6*) La State U Pr.

Papers of Jefferson Davis, 1861, Vol. 7. Jefferson Davis. Ed. by Lynda L. Crist & Mary S. Dix. LC 91-11198. (Illus.). 557p. 1991. text 75.00 (*0-8071-1726-9*) La State U Pr.

Papers of Jefferson Davis, 1862, Vol. 8. Jefferson Davis. Ed. by Lynda L. Crist et al. LC 95-152704. (Illus.). 720p. 1993. text 85.00 (*0-8071-1938-5*) La State U Pr.

Papers of Jefferson Davis, January-September 1863, Vol. 9. Jefferson Davis. Ed. by Lynda L. Crist et al. LC 91-11198. (Illus.). 552p. 1997. text 75.00 (*0-8071-2087-1*) La State U Pr.

Papers of Jefferson Davis, July 1846-December 1848, Vol. 3. Jefferson Davis. Ed. by James T. McIntosh. LC 76-152704. (Illus.). xxxiv, 598p. 1981. text 80.00 (*0-8071-0786-7*) La State U Pr.

Papers of Jefferson Davis, June 1841-July 1846, Vol. 2. Jefferson Davis. Ed. by James T. McIntosh. LC 76-152704. (Illus.). xlii, 806p. 1975. text 90.00 (*0-8071-0082-X*) La State U Pr.

Papers of John Adams: March 1780 - December 1780, 2 vols., Vols. 9 & 10. Gregg L. Lint. Ed. by Joanna M. Revelas et al. (Illus.). 1192p. 1996. 130.00 (*0-674-65445-5*) HUP.

Papers of John Adams Vols. 1 & 2: September 1755-April 1775. John Adams. Ed. by Robert J. Taylor et al. (Adams Papers: Series III). 876p. 1978. 107.00 (*0-674-65441-2*) Belknap Pr.

Papers of John Adams Vols. 3 & 4: May 1775-August 1776, 2 vols., Set. John Adams. Ed. by Robert J. Taylor et al. (Adams Papers: Series III). 1110p. 1979. 107.00 (*0-674-65442-0*) Belknap Pr.

Papers of John Adams Vols. 5 & 6: August 1776-July 1778, Set. John Adams. Ed. by Robert J. Taylor et al. (Adams Papers: Series III). (Illus.). 933p. (C). 1983. text 107.00 (*0-674-65443-9*) Belknap Pr.

Papers of John Adams Vols. 7 & 8: September 1778-February 1780, Set. Ed. by Gregg L. Lint & Robert J. Taylor. LC 77-4707. (Adams Papers: General Correspondence & Other Papers of the Adams Statesmen Ser.). (Illus.). 480p. 1989. 100.00 (*0-674-65444-7*) Belknap Pr.

Papers of John & Lugenia Burns Hope. Alton Hornsby et al. LC 85-893000. (Black Studies Research Sources). 21p. 1984. write for info. (*0-89093-696-X*) U Pubns Amer.

Papers of John C. Calhoun, Vol. 4, 1819-1820. John C. Calhoun. Ed. by W. Edwin Hemphill. LC 59-10351. xxii, 820p. 1969. text 59.95 (*0-87249-150-1*) U of SC Pr.

Papers of John C. Calhoun, Vol. 5, 1820-1821. John C. Calhoun. Ed. by Clyde N. Wilson et al. LC 59-10351. (Illus.). 791p. 1971. text 59.95 (*0-87249-210-9*) U of SC Pr.

Papers of John C. Calhoun, Vol. 7, 1822-1823. John C. Calhoun. Ed. by W. Edwin Hemphill. LC 59-10351. iiv, 663p. 1973. text 59.95 (*0-87249-288-5*) U of SC Pr.

Papers of John C. Calhoun, Vol. 15. John C. Calhoun. Ed. by Clyde N. Wilson. LC 59-10351. (Papers of John C. Calhoun Ser.). 902p. 1984. text 59.95 (*0-87249-418-7*) U of SC Pr.

Papers of John C. Calhoun Vol. 19: June 9 - September 30, 1844. John C. Calhoun. Ed. by Clyde N. Wilson. LC 59-10351. (Papers of John C. Calhoun Ser.). 966p. 1990. text 59.95 (*0-87249-677-5*) U of SC Pr.

Papers of John C. Calhoun Vol. 20: October-December, 1844. John C. Calhoun. Ed. by Clyde N. Wilson. LC 59-10351. 738p. 1991. text 59.95 (*0-87249-769-0*) U of SC Pr.

Papers of John C. Calhoun Vol. 21: January-June 1845. John C. Calhoun. Ed. by Clyde N. Wilson. LC 59-10351. 667p. 1993. text 59.95 (*0-87249-889-1*) U of SC Pr.

***Papers Of John C. Calhoun Vol. XXV: 1847-1848.** Ed. by Clyde N. Wilson et al. (Papers of John C. Calhoun Ser.: XXV). 768p. 1999. 59.95 (*1-57003-306-4*) U of SC Pr.

Papers of John C. Calhoun, 1843-1844, Vol. 17. John C. Calhoun. Ed. by Clyde N. Wilson. 988p. 1987. text 59.95 (*0-87249-483-7*) U of SC Pr.

Papers of John C. Calhoun, 1845-1846, 22 vols. , Vol. XXII. John C. Calhoun. Ed. by Clyde N. Wilson. LC 59-10351. 856p. 1995. text 59.95 (*1-57003-023-5*) U of SC Pr.

Papers of John C. Calhoun, 1846, Vol. XXIII. Ed. by Clyde N. Wilson. LC 59-10351. 780p. 1996. text 59.95 (*1-57003-104-5*) U of SC Pr.

Papers of John C. Calhoun, 1837-1839, Vol. 14. John C. Calhoun. Ed. by Clyde N. Wilson. LC 59-10351. (Illus.). 713p. 1981. text 59.95 (*0-87249-409-8*) U of SC Pr.

Papers of John D. Rockefeller, Sr. John D. Rockefeller et al. LC 92-23427. 66 p. 1991. write for info. (*1-55655-397-8*) U Pubns Amer.

Papers of John Foster Dulles & of Christian A. Herter, 1953-1961. John F. Dulles et al. LC 87-15979. (The Presidential Documents Ser.). 24p. 1986. write for info. (*0-89093-890-3*); write for info. (*0-89093-891-1*) U Pubns Amer.

Papers of John L. Lewis: Guide to a Microfilm Edition. Ed. by Eleanor M. Niermann. (Guides to Historical Resources Ser.). 12p. 1970. pap. 1.00 (*0-87020-182-4*) State Hist Soc Wis.

Papers of John L. Lewis, 1879-1969: Guide to a Microfilm Edition. Ed. by Eleanor McKay. 12p. 1970. pap. write for info. (*0-89887-182-4*) Chadwyck-Healey.

***Papers of John Marshall: Correspondence, Papers & Selected Judicial Opinions, January 1824 - April 1827.** Ed. by John Marshall & Charles F. Hobson. LC 74-9575. (Published for the Omohundro Institute of Early American History & Culture Ser.). (Illus.). 544p. 2000. 60.00 (*0-8078-2520-4*) U of NC Pr.

Papers of John Marshall: Correspondence, Papers, & Selected Judicial Opinions, 1807-1813. John Marshall. Ed. by Charles Hobson. LC 74-9575. (Institute of Early American History & Culture Ser.: Vol. 7). (Illus.). xxxviii, 446p. (C). 1993. 70.00 (*0-8078-2074-1*) U of NC Pr.

Papers of John Marshall Vol. I: Correspondence & Papers, November 10, 1775-June 23, 1788, & Account Book, September 1783-June 1788. John Marshall. Ed.

An Asterisk (*) at the beginning of an entry indicates that the title is appearing for the first time.

by Herbert A. Johnson et al. LC 74-9575. (Institute of Early American History & Culture Ser.). (Illus.). xlvi, 448p. 1974. 70.00 (*0-8078-1233-1*) U of NC Pr.

Papers of John Marshall Vol. II: Correspondence & Papers, July 1788-December 1795, & Account Book, July 1788-December 1795. John Marshall. Ed. by Charles T. Cullen & Herbert A. Johnson. LC 74-9575. (Institute of Early American History & Culture Ser.). xxxvi, 547p. 1977. 70.00 (*0-8078-1302-8*) U of NC Pr.

Papers of John Marshall Vol. III: Correspondence & Papers, January 1796-December 1798. John Marshall. Ed. by William C. Stinchcombe & Charles T. Cullen. LC 74-9575. (Institute of Early American History & Culture Ser.). (Illus.). xxix, 553p. 1979. 70.00 (*0-8078-1337-0*) U of NC Pr.

Papers of John Marshall Vol. IV: Correspondence & Papers, January 1799-October 1800. John Marshall. Ed. by Charles T. Cullen & Leslie Tobias. LC 74-9575. (Institute of Early American History & Culture Ser.). xxxii, 365p. 1984. 70.00 (*0-8078-1586-1*) U of NC Pr.

Papers of John Marshall Vol. V: Selected Law Cases, 1784-1800. John Marshall. Ed. by Charles F. Hobson et al. LC 74-9575. (Institute of Early American History & Culture Ser.). ixx, 583p. 1987. 70.00 (*0-8078-1746-5*) U of NC Pr.

Papers of John Marshall Vol. VI: Correspondence, Papers, & Selected Judicial Opinions, November 1800-March 1807. John Marshall. Ed. by Charles F. Hobson. LC 74-9575. (Institute of Early American History & Culture Ser.). (Illus.). xlvi, 568p. (C). 1990. 70.00 (*0-8078-1903-4*) U of NC Pr.

Papers of John Marshall Vol. VIII: Correspondence, Papers, & Selected Judicial Opinions. Ed. by Charles F. Hobson. LC 74-9575. (Published for the Institute of Early American History & Culture Ser.). (Illus.). 460p. (C). 1995. text 70.00 (*0-8078-2221-3*) U of NC Pr.

Papers of John Marshall Vol. IX: Correspondence, Papers, & Selected Judicial Opinions, January 1820-December 1823. John Marshall. Ed. by Charles F. Hobson. (Published for the Omohundro Institute of Early American History & Culture, Williamsburg, Virginia Ser.). (Illus.). 440p. 1998. 70.00 (*0-8078-2404-6*) U of NC Pr.

Papers of John Paul Jones: Guide to Microfilm Edition of the Papers of John Paul Jones, 1747-1792. 178p. 1986. lib. bdg. write for info. (*0-89887-049-6*) Chadwyck-Healey.

Papers of John Willis Ellis, 2 vols. Ed. by Noble J. Tolbert. Incl. Vol. 1, 1841-1859. civ, 341p. 1964. 15.00 (*0-86526-030-3*); Vol. 2, 1860-1861. iii, 576p. 1964. 15.00 (*0-86526-031-1*); (Illus.). write for info. (*0-318-54563-2*) NC Archives.

Papers of Joseph Vol. 1: The Albany Years, December 1797-October 1832. Ed. by Nathan Reingold. 496p. 1972. text 80.00 (*0-87474-123-8*, REP1) Smithsonian.

Papers of Joseph Henry Vol. 2: The Princeton Years, November 1832-December 1835. Ed. by Nathan Reingold. 564p. 1976. text 80.00 (*0-87474-164-5*, REP2) Smithsonian.

Papers of Joseph Henry Vol. 3: The Princeton Years, January 1836-December 1837. Ed. by Nathan Reingold. LC 72-2005. (Illus.). 585p. 1979. text 80.00 (*0-87474-174-2*, REP3) Smithsonian.

Papers of Joseph Henry Vol. 5: The Princeton Years, January 1841-December 1843. Ed. by Nathan Reingold. LC 72-2005. (Joseph Henry Papers). (Illus.). 500p. 1985. text 80.00 (*0-87474-793-7*, REP5) Smithsonian.

Papers of Joseph Henry Vol. 6: The Princeton Years, January 1844 - December 1846. Ed. by Marc Rothenberg. LC 72-2005. (Illus.). 592p. 1992. text 80.00 (*1-56098-112-1*) Smithsonian.

Papers of Joseph Henry Vol. 7: The Smithsonian Years, January 1847 - December 1849. Ed. by Marc Rothenberg. LC 72-2005. 704p. 1996. text 75.00 (*1-56098-533-X*) Smithsonian.

***Papers of Joseph Henry Vol. 8: The Smithsonian Years, January 1850-December 1853.** Ed. by Marc Rothenberg. (Illus.). 624p. 1998. 80.00 (*1-56098-891-6*) Smithsonian.

Papers of Joseph Smith Vol. 1: Autobiographical & Historical Writings. Ed. by Dean C. Jessee. LC 89-11720. (Illus.). xlix, 558p. 1989. 19.95 (*0-87579-199-9*) Deseret Bk.

Papers of Joseph Smith Vol. 2: Autobiographical & Historical Writings. Ed. by Dean C. Jessee. LC 89-11720. 642p. 1992. 21.95 (*0-87579-545-5*) Deseret Bk.

Papers of Leverett Saltonstall, 1816-1845, Vol. 1. Ed. by Robert E. Moody. LC 78-70086. (Collections of the Massachusetts Historical Society: Vol. 82). (Illus.). 1978. 50.00 (*0-934909-21-0*, Pub. by Mass Hist Soc) NE U Pr.

Papers of Leverett Saltonstall, 1816-1845, Vol. 2. Ed. by Robert E. Moody. LC 78-70086. (Collections of the Massachusetts Historical Society: Vol. 83). (Illus.). 1981. 50.00 (*0-934909-22-9*, Pub. by Mass Hist Soc) NE U Pr.

Papers of Leverett Saltonstall, 1816-1845, Vol. 3. Ed. by Robert E. Moody. LC 78-70086. (Collections of the Massachusetts Historical Society: Vol. 84). (Illus.). 1984. 50.00 (*0-934909-23-7*, Pub. by Mass Hist Soc) NE U Pr.

Papers of Leverett Saltonstall, 1816-1845, Vol. 4. Ed. by Robert E. Moody. LC 78-70086. (Collections of the Massachusetts Historical Society: Vol. 85). (Illus.). 1991. 50.00 (*0-934909-37-7*, Pub. by Mass Hist Soc) NE U Pr.

Papers of Leverett Saltonstall, 1816-1845, Vol. 5. Ed. by Robert E. Moody. (Collections of the Massachusetts Historical Society: Vol. 86). (Illus.). 1992. 50.00 (*0-934909-53-9*, Pub. by Mass Hist Soc) NE U Pr.

Papers of Lewis Morris. Lewis Morris. LC 73-117885. (Select Bibliographies Reprint Ser.). 1977. reprint ed. 25.95 (*0-8369-5338-X*) Ayer.

Papers of Lewis Morris, 1698-1730, Vol. 1. Ed. by Eugene R. Sheridan. LC 91-40946. xxxiii, 413p. 1991. 40.00 (*0-911020-23-3*) NJ Hist Soc.

Papers of Lewis Morris, 1731-1737, Vol. 2. unabridged ed. Ed. by Eugene R. Sheridan. LC 91-40946. xx, 326p. 1993. 40.00 (*0-911020-27-6*) NJ Hist Soc.

Papers of Lewis Morris, 1738-1746, Vol. 3. unabridged ed. Ed. by Eugene R. Sheridan. LC 91-40946. xx, 497p. 1993. 40.00 (*0-911020-28-4*) NJ Hist Soc.

Papers of Lieutenant Colonel Jose Enrique de la Pena: Selected Appendixes from His Diary, 1836-1839. Roger Borroel. (Illus.). 65p. (Orig.). 1997. pap. 11.99 (*0-9624727-2-7*) LaVillita Pubns.

Papers of Lieutenant Colonel Jose Enrique de la Pena Vol. II: The Last of the Appendixes from His Diary, 1836-1837. Roger Borroel. LC 97-60773. (Illus.). 109p. 1997. pap. 10.99 (*0-9624727-5-1*) LaVillita Pubns.

Papers of M. Carey Thomas in the Bryn Mawr College Archives: Reel Guide & Index to the Microfilm Collection. Lucy F. West. LC 81-23399. 359p. 1982. 300.00 (*0-89235-031-8*) Primary Srce Media.

Papers of Martin Luther King, Jr. Vol. 1: Called to Serve, January 1929-June 1951. Martin Luther King, Jr. Ed. by Clayborne Carson et al. LC 91-42336. (Illus.). 507p. 1992. 45.00 (*0-520-07950-7*, Pub. by U CA Pr) Cal Prin Full Svc.

Papers of Martin Luther King, Jr. Vol. 2: Rediscovering Precious Values, July 1951-November 1955. Martin Luther King, Jr. Ed. by Clayborne Carson et al. LC 91-42336. (Illus.). 800p. (C). 1994. 45.00 (*0-520-07951-5*, Pub. by U CA Pr) Cal Prin Full Svc.

Papers of Martin Luther King, Jr. Vol. 3: Birth of a New Age, December 1955-December 1956. Martin Luther King, Jr. Ed. by Clayborne Carson. LC 91-42336. (Illus.). 598p. 1997. 45.00 (*0-520-07952-3*, Pub. by U CA Pr) Cal Prin Full Svc.

***Papers of Martin Luther King, Jr. Symbol of the Movement, January 1957- December 1958, Vol. IV.** Martin Luther King, Jr. Ed. by Clayborne Carson. (Illus.). 696p. 2000. 50.00 (*0-520-22231-8*, Pub. by U CA Pr) Cal Prin Full Svc.

Papers of Mirabeau Buonaparte, 6 vols., Set. Lamar. 1993. reprint ed. lib. bdg. 450.00 (*0-7812-5941-X*) Rprt Serv.

Papers of Nathaniel P. Tallmadge: Guide to a Microfilm Edition. Ed. by Carolyn J. Mattern. 45p. 1973. pap. write for info. (*0-89887-185-9*) Chadwyck-Healey.

Papers of New England: Series 2, Legal Papers, Vol. 3 Part 2. Daniel Webster. Ed. by Alfred S. Konefsky. LC 73-92705. 462p. Date not set. reprint ed. pap. 143.30 (*0-608-20701-2*, 207180100004) Bks Demand.

Papers of Panton, Leslie & Company: A Guide to the Microfilm Collection. William S. Coker. 764p. 1987. lib. bdg. 425.00 (*0-89235-117-9*) Primary Srce Media.

Papers of Robert A. Taft, Vol. I: 1889-1938. Robert A. Taft. Ed. by Clarence E. Wunderlin. LC 97-6757. (Illus.). 752p. 1998. 60.00 (*0-87338-572-1*) Kent St U Pr.

Papers of Robert M. La Follette, 1876-1924: Guide to a Microfilm Edition. Ed. by F. Gerald Ham. 86p. 1972. pap. write for info. (*0-87020-121-2*) Chadwyck-Healey.

Papers of Robert Morris, 1781-1784. Robert Morris. Ed. by Mary Gallagher & Elizabeth Nuxoll. (Pittsburgh Series in Bibliography: Vol. 9). (Illus.). 1703p. 1999. text 90.00 (*0-8229-3999-1*) U of Pittsburgh Pr.

Papers of Robert Morris, 1781-1784, Vol. 8. Ed. by Elizabeth M. Nuxoll & Mary A. Gallagher. (Illus.). 1032p. 1996. text 100.00 (*0-8229-3886-3*) U of Pittsburgh Pr.

Papers of Robert Morris, 1781-1784, Vols. 1-9. Robert Morris. 1703p. 1999. text 460.00 (*0-8229-4088-4*) U of Pittsburgh Pr.

Papers of Robert Morris, 1781-1784 Vol. 1: February 7-July 31, 1781. Ed. by E. James Ferguson & John Catanzariti. LC 72-91107. (Robert Morris Papers). (Illus.). 504p. 1973. text 55.00 (*0-8229-3267-9*) U of Pittsburgh Pr.

Papers of Robert Morris, 1781-1784 Vol. 2: August-September 1781. Ed. by E. James Ferguson & John Catanzariti. LC 72-91107. (Robert Morris Papers). (Illus.). 440p. 1975. text 55.00 (*0-8229-3297-0*) U of Pittsburgh Pr.

Papers of Robert Morris, 1781-1784 Vol. 3: October 1, 1781-January 10, 1782. Ed. by E. James Ferguson & John Catanzariti. LC 72-91107. (Robert Morris Papers). (Illus.). 596p. 1977. text 55.00 (*0-8229-3324-1*) U of Pittsburgh Pr.

Papers of Robert Morris, 1781-1784 Vol. 4: January 11-April 15, 1782. Ed. by E. James Ferguson & John Catanzariti. LC 72-91107. (Robert Morris Papers). (Illus.). 720p. 1978. text 55.00 (*0-8229-3352-7*) U of Pittsburgh Pr.

Papers of Robert Morris, 1781-1784 Vol. 5: April 16-July 20, 1782. Ed. by E. James Ferguson & John Catanzariti. LC 72-91107. (Robert Morris Papers). (Illus.). 704p. 1980. text 55.00 (*0-8229-3420-5*) U of Pittsburgh Pr.

Papers of Robert Morris, 1781-1784 Vol. 6: July 22-October 31, 1782, Vol.6. John Catanzariti & E. James Ferguson. LC 72-91107. (Robert Morris Papers). (Illus.). 824p. 1984. text 55.00 (*0-8229-3485-X*) U of Pittsburgh Pr.

Papers of Robert Morris, 1781-1784 Vol. 7: November 1, 1782 - May 4, 1783. Ed. by John Catanzariti. LC 72-91107. (Illus.). 968p. (C). 1989. text 55.00 (*0-8229-3592-9*) U of Pittsburgh Pr.

Papers of Robert Redfield, 2 vols., 2. Robert Redfield. Ed. by Margaret P. Redfield. LC 62-10995. (Illus.). 301p. reprint ed. pap. 93.40 (*0-8357-6250-5*, 205681800002) Bks Demand.

Papers of Robert Redfield, 2 vols., Vol. 1: Human Nature & the Study of Society. Robert Redfield. Ed. by Margaret P. Redfield. LC 62-10995. (Illus.). 523p. reprint ed. pap. 162.20 (*0-8357-6249-1*, 205681800001) Bks Demand.

Papers of Robert Treat Paine, Vol. 1. Ed. by Stephen T. Riley & Edward W. Hanson. (Collections of the Massachusetts Historical Society Ser.: Vol. 87). 1992. 50.00 (*0-934909-30-X*, Pub. by Mass Hist Soc) NE U Pr.

Papers of Robert Treat Paine, Vol. 2. Ed. by Stephen T. Riley & Edward W. Hanson. (Collections of the Massachusetts Historical Society: Vol. 88). 1992. 50.00 (*0-934909-33-4*, Pub. by Mass Hist Soc) NE U Pr.

Papers of Sir William Johnson, 9 vols., Set. R. E. Day. 1993. reprint ed. lib. bdg. 675.00 (*0-7812-5171-0*) Rprt Serv.

Papers of Thaddeus Stevens, Vol. I. Ed. by Beverly W. Palmer & Holly B. Ochoa. LC 96-53675. 692p. 1997. text 37.50 (*0-8229-3972-X*) U of Pittsburgh Pr.

Papers of Thaddeus Stevens Vol. 2: April 1865-August 1868. Ed. by Beverly W. Palmer & Holly B. Ochoa. LC 96-53675. 547p. 1998. text 37.50 (*0-8229-4052-3*) U of Pittsburgh Pr.

Papers of the American Board of Commissioners for Foreign Affairs: Documents Administered by the Houghton Library of Harvard University. 435p. (C). 1994. 350.00 (*0-89235-162-4*) Primary Srce Media.

Papers of the American Slave Trade. Jay Coughtry et al. LC 97-46700. (Black Studies Research Sources). 1997. pap. text 3170.00 (*1-55655-650-0*); pap. text 4135.00 (*1-55655-651-9*) U Pubns Amer.

Papers of the Archaeological Institute of America, 6 vols., Set. Adolph F. Bandelier. (American Ser.). reprint ed. 177.00 (*0-404-19502-4*); reprint ed. 278.00 (*0-404-58050-5*) AMS Pr.

Papers of the British School at Rome, Vol. 28. annuals 32.50 (*0-614-21888-8*, Pub. by British Schl Rome) David Brown.

Papers of the British School at Rome, Vol. 29. annuals 32.50 (*0-614-21889-6*, Pub. by British Schl Rome) David Brown.

Papers of the British School at Rome, Vol. 30. annuals 32.50 (*0-614-21890-X*, Pub. by British Schl Rome) David Brown.

Papers of the British School at Rome, Vol. 33. annuals 32.50 (*0-614-21891-8*, Pub. by British Schl Rome) David Brown.

Papers of the British School at Rome, Vol. 34. annuals 32.50 (*0-614-21892-6*, Pub. by British Schl Rome) David Brown.

Papers of the British School at Rome, Vol. 35. annuals 32.50 (*0-614-21893-4*, Pub. by British Schl Rome) David Brown.

Papers of the British School at Rome, Vol. 36. annuals 32.50 (*0-614-21894-2*, Pub. by British Schl Rome) David Brown.

Papers of the British School at Rome, Vol. 37. annuals 32.50 (*0-614-21895-0*, Pub. by British Schl Rome) David Brown.

Papers of the British School at Rome, Vol. 38. annuals 32.50 (*0-614-21896-9*, Pub. by British Schl Rome) David Brown.

Papers of the British School at Rome, Vol. 39. annuals 32.50 (*0-614-21897-7*, Pub. by British Schl Rome) David Brown.

Papers of the British School at Rome, Vol. 40. annuals 32.50 (*0-614-21898-5*, Pub. by British Schl Rome) David Brown.

Papers of the British School at Rome, Vol. 41. annuals 32.50 (*0-614-21899-3*, Pub. by British Schl Rome) David Brown.

Papers of the British School at Rome, Vol. 42. annuals 32.50 (*0-614-21900-0*, Pub. by British Schl Rome) David Brown.

Papers of the British School at Rome, Vol. 43. annuals 32.50 (*0-614-21901-9*, Pub. by British Schl Rome) David Brown.

Papers of the British School at Rome, Vol. 44. annuals 32.50 (*0-614-21902-7*, Pub. by British Schl Rome) David Brown.

Papers of the British School at Rome, Vol. 45. annuals 32.50 (*0-614-21903-5*, Pub. by British Schl Rome) David Brown.

Papers of the British School at Rome, Vol. 46. annuals 32.50 (*0-614-21904-3*, Pub. by British Schl Rome) David Brown.

Papers of the British School at Rome, Vol. 47. annuals 32.50 (*0-614-21905-1*, Pub. by British Schl Rome) David Brown.

Papers of the British School at Rome, Vol. 48. annuals 32.50 (*0-614-21906-X*, Pub. by British Schl Rome) David Brown.

Papers of the British School at Rome, Vol. 49. annuals 32.50 (*0-614-21907-8*, Pub. by British Schl Rome) David Brown.

Papers of the British School at Rome, Vol. 50. annuals 32.50 (*0-614-21908-6*, Pub. by British Schl Rome) David Brown.

Papers of the British School at Rome, Vol. 51. annuals 32.50 (*0-614-21909-4*, Pub. by British Schl Rome) David Brown.

Papers of the British School at Rome, Vol. 52. annuals 32.50 (*0-614-21910-8*, Pub. by British Schl Rome) David Brown.

Papers of the British School at Rome, Vol. 53. annuals 32.50 (*0-614-21911-6*, Pub. by British Schl Rome) David Brown.

Papers of the British School at Rome, Vol. 54. annuals 32.50 (*0-614-21912-4*, Pub. by British Schl Rome) David Brown.

Papers of the British School at Rome, Vol. 55. annuals 32.50 (*0-614-21913-2*, Pub. by British Schl Rome) David Brown.

Papers of the British School at Rome, Vol. 58. annuals 37.50 (*0-614-21914-0*, Pub. by British Schl Rome) David Brown.

Papers of the British School at Rome, Vol. 59. annuals 48.00 (*0-614-21915-9*, Pub. by British Schl Rome) David Brown.

Papers of the British School at Rome, Vol. 60. annuals 52.00 (*0-614-21916-7*, Pub. by British Schl Rome) David Brown.

Papers of the British School at Rome, Vol. 61. annuals 55.00 (*0-614-21917-5*, Pub. by British Schl Rome) David Brown.

Papers of the British School at Rome, Vol. 62. annuals 1994. 55.00 (*0-614-21918-3*, Pub. by British Schl Rome) David Brown.

Papers of the Civil Rights Congress: Manuscript Collections from the Schomburg Ce. Civil Rights Congress (U.S.) et al. LC 89-24822. (Black Studies Research Sources). 125 p. 1989. write for info. (*1-55655-065-0*) U Pubns Amer.

Papers of the Congress of Racial Equality, 1941-1967: A Guide to the Microfilm Edition. 75p. 1980. pap. write for info. (*0-667-00622-2*) Chadwyck-Healey.

Papers of the Dictionary Society of North America. Incl. Pesticide Residues in Food, 1977 Evaluations. Ed. by Donald Hobar. LC 83-134228. 93p. 1982. 12.00: 1981. Ed. by Yeatman Anderson, III. LC 83-134228. 114p. 1983. 12.00 LC 83-134228. write for info. (*0-318-60125-7*) Dict Soc NA.

Papers of the Eighth International Conference on Liquefied Natural Gas: Los Angeles, U. S. A., June 15-19, 1986, 2 vols., Set. Ed. by Joseph R. Rensch. 768p. 1986. pap. 85.00 (*0-910091-59-5*) Inst Gas Tech.

Papers of the Fifth International Conference on Liquefied Natural Gas: Dusseldorf, Germany, August 29-September 1, 1977, 2 vols. 866p. 1977. pap. 43.00 (*0-910091-34-X*) Inst Gas Tech.

Papers of the Fourth International Conference on Liquefied Natural Gas: Algiers, Algeria, June 24-27, 1974. 850p. 1974. pap. 40.00 (*0-910091-33-1*) Inst Gas Tech.

Papers of the Henry Luce III Fellows in Theology, Vol. I. Ed. by Gary Gilbert. LC 96-27815. 266p. 1996. write for info. (*0-7885-0297-2*) Assn of Theol Schls.

Papers of the Henry Luce III Fellows in Theology, Vol. II. Ed. by Jonathan Strom. LC 96-27815. 176p. 1997. write for info. (*0-7885-0409-6*) Assn of Theol Schls.

Papers of the Henry Luce III Fellows in Theology, Vol. III. Ed. by Matthew Zyniewicz. LC 96-27815. 170p. 1998. write for info. (*0-7885-0531-9*) Assn of Theol Schls.

Papers of the Institute of Jewish Studies London, Vol. 1. Ed. by J. G. Weiss. LC 89-5496. (Brown Classics in Judaica Ser.). 234p. (C). 1989. reprint ed. lib. bdg. 41.00 (*0-8191-7276-6*) U Pr of Amer.

Papers of the International Workingmen's Association: Guide to a Microfilm Edition. Ed. by Carolyn J. Mattern. (Guides to Historical Resources Ser.). 132p. 1972. pap. 1.00 (*0-87020-151-4*) State Hist Soc Wis.

Papers of the International Workingmen's Association, 1868-1877: Guide to a Microfilm Edition. Ed. by Carolyn J. Mattern. 15p. 1972. pap. write for info. (*0-89887-181-6*) Chadwyck-Healey.

Papers of the League of Women Voters, 1918-1974. Susan Ware et al. LC 87-14773. (Research Collections in Women's Studies). 1985. 0.00 (*0-89093-795-8*) U Pubns Amer.

Papers of the Military Historical Society of Massachusetts, 15 vols., Set. Intro. by Bill Marvel. 1990. reprint ed. 500.00 (*0-916107-73-6*) Broadfoot.

Papers of the NAACP. John H. Bracey et al. LC 97-163130. (Black Studies Research Sources). 6 p. 1995. write for info. (*1-55655-544-X*) U Pubns Amer.

Papers of the NAACP. John H. Bracey et al. LC 97-42605. (Black Studies Research Sources Ser.). 1997. 2205.00 (*1-55655-654-3*) U Pubns Amer.

Papers of the NAACP. John H. Bracey et al. LC 98-13788. 1998. 1930.00 (*1-55655-655-1*) U Pubns Amer.

Papers of the Naacp. L. Lee Yanike et al. LC 87-10644. (Black Studies Research Sources). 1987. write for info. (*1-55655-542-3*) U Pubns Amer.

Papers of the National Negro Congress: Manuscript Collections from the Schomburg Center for Research in Black Culture, The New York Public Library. National Negro Congress (U.S.) et al. LC 91-11486. (Black Studies Research Sources). 94 p. 1988. write for info. (*1-55655-057-X*) U Pubns Amer.

Papers of the National War Labor Board, 1918-1919. Melvyn Dubofsky. LC 86-893393. (Research Collections on Labor Studies). 22 p. 1984. write for info. (*0-89093-711-7*) U Pubns Amer.

Papers of the Ninth International Conference on Liquefied Natural Gas: Nice, France, October 17-20, 1989, 2 vols., Set. 926p. 1989. pap. 100.00 (*0-910091-72-2*) Inst Gas Tech.

Papers of the Nixon White House. Paul Kesaris & University Publications of America Inc. LC 87-33984. (Research Collections in American Politics Ser.). 1987. write for info. (*1-55655-028-6*) U Pubns Amer.

Papers of the Order of the Indian Wars. Ed. by John M. Carroll. (Illus.). 1975. 27.50 (*0-88342-040-6*) Old Army.

Papers of the President's Science Advisory Committee, 1957-1961: Microfilmed from the Holdings of the Dwight D. Eisenhower Library. Robert Lester & Dwight D. Eisenhower Library. LC 91-486. (Science & Technology : Research Collections in U.S. Public Policy). 3 p. 1991. write for info. (*0-89093-979-9*) U Pubns Amer.

Papers of the Republican Party. Paul Kesaris et al. LC 87-10471. (Research Collections in American Politics Ser.). 51 p. 1987. write for info. (*0-89093-984-5*) U Pubns Amer.

P

Papers of the Seventh International Conference on Liquefied Natural Gas: Jakarta, Indonesia, May 15-19, 1983, 2 vols., Set. 908p. 1983. pap. 75.00 (0-910091-04-8) Inst Gas Tech.

Papers of the Sixth International Conference on Liquefied Natural Gas: Kyoto, Japan, April 7-10, 1980, 2 vols. 993p. 1980. pap. 60.00 (0-910091-35-8) Inst Gas Tech.

Papers of the Society of American Indians. John W. Larner et al. LC 86-24843. 10p. 1987. 10.00 (0-8420-4005-6) Scholarly Res Inc.

Papers of the St. Louis Fur Trade. William R. Swagerty et al. LC 92-33229. (Research Collections on the American West). 1991. write for info. (1-55655-411-7) U Pubns Amer.

Papers of the Tenth International Conference on Liquefied Natural Gas: Kuala Lumpur, Malaysia, May 25-28, 1992. xxii, 864p. 1992. pap. 100.00 (0-910091-86-2) Inst Gas Tech.

Papers of the Third Great Basin Archeological Conference. C. Hunt et al. (Publications of the Department of Anthropology, University of Utah: No. 26). (Illus.). 101p. (C). 1956. reprint ed. pap. text 11.25 (1-55567-476-3) Coyote Press.

Papers of the University Settlement Society of New York City: Guide to a Microfilm Edition. Ed. by Eleanor M. Niermann. (Guides to Historical Resources Ser.). 1972. pap. 1.00 (0-87020-183-2) State Hist Soc Wis.

Papers of the University Settlement Society of New York City, 1886-1945: Guide to a Microfilm Edition. Ed. by Eleanor M. Niermann. 15p. 1972. pap. write for info. (0-89887-187-5) Chadwyck-Healey.

Papers of the Women's Trade Union League & Its Principal Leaders. Ed. by Edward T. James et al. 319p. 1981. 225.00 (0-89235-026-1) Primary Srce Media.

Papers of the Yugoslav-American Seminar on Music. Ed. by Malcolm H. Brown. xii, 208p. 1970. pap. 9.95 (0-89357-006-0) Slavica.

Papers of Thomas A. Edison Vol. 2: From Workshop to Laboratory, June 1873-March 1876. Ed. by Robert A. Rosenberg et al. LC 88-9017. (Illus.). 776p. 1991. text 75.00 (0-8018-3101-6) Johns Hopkins.

Papers of Thomas A. Edison Vol. 3: Menlo Park: the Early Years April 1876-December 1877. Keith A. Nier. Ed. by Paul B. Israel et al. (Illus.). 752p. 1995. text 65.00 (0-8018-3102-4) Johns Hopkins.

Papers of Thomas A. Edison Vol. 4: The Wizard of Menlo Park, 1878. Thomas A. Edison. Ed. by Paul B. Israel et al. (Illus.). 808p. 1998. 75.00 (0-8018-5819-4) Johns Hopkins.

Papers of Thomas Jefferson, 60 vols. Thomas Jefferson. Incl. Vol. 1. 1760-1776. Ed. by J. P. Boyd. 744p. 1950. text 85.00 (0-691-04533-X, Pub. by Princeton U Pr); Vol. 2. 1777-1779. Ed. by J. P. Boyd. 696p. 1950. text 85.00 (0-691-04534-8, Pub. by Princeton U Pr); Vol. 3. 1779-1780. Ed. by J. P. Boyd. 712p. 1951. text 85.00 (0-691-04535-6, Pub. by Princeton U Pr); Vol. 4. 1780-1781. Ed. by J. P. Boyd. 744p. 1951. text 85.00 (0-691-04536-4, Pub. by Princeton U Pr); Vol. 5. 1781. Ed. by J. P. Boyd. 748p. 1951. text 85.00 (0-691-04537-2, Pub. by Princeton U Pr); Vol. 6. 1781-1784. Ed. by J. P. Boyd. 704p. 1952. text 85.00 (0-691-04538-0, Pub. by Princeton U Pr); Vol. 7. 1784-1785. Ed. by J. P. Boyd. 684p. 1953. text 85.00 (0-691-04539-9, Pub. by Princeton U Pr); Vol. 8. 1785. Ed. by J. P. Boyd. 724p. 1953. text 85.00 (0-691-04540-2, Pub. by Princeton U Pr); Vol. 9. 1785-1786. Ed. by J. P. Boyd. 704p. 1954. text 85.00 (0-691-04541-0, Pub. by Princeton U Pr); Vol. 10. 1786-1787. Ed. by J. P. Boyd. 688p. 1954. text 85.00 (0-691-04542-9, Pub. by Princeton U Pr); Vol. 11. 1787. Ed. by J. P. Boyd. 740p. 1955. text 85.00 (0-691-04543-7, Pub. by Princeton U Pr); Vol. 12. 1787-1788. Ed. by J. P. Boyd. 744p. 1955. text 85.00 (0-691-04544-5, Pub. by Princeton U Pr); Vol. 13. March to October 1788. Ed. by J. P. Boyd. 704p. 1956. text 85.00 (0-691-04545-3, Pub. by Princeton U Pr); Vol. 14. October 1788 to March 1789. Ed. by J. P. Boyd. 756p. 1958. text 85.00 (0-691-04546-1, Pub. by Princeton U Pr); Vol. 15. March to November 1789. Ed. by J. P. Boyd. 720p. 1958. text 85.00 (0-691-04547-X, Pub. by Princeton U Pr); Vol. 16. November 1789 to August 1790. Ed. by J. P. Boyd. 718p. 1961. text 85.00 (0-691-04548-8, Pub. by Princeton U Pr); Vol. 17. July to December 1790. Ed. by J. P. Boyd. 721p. 1965. text 85.00 (0-691-04549-6, Pub. by Princeton U Pr); Vol .18. November 1790 to January 1791. Ed. by J. P. Boyd. 730p. 1971. text 85.00 (0-691-04582-8, Pub. by Princeton U Pr); Vol. 19. January 24 to March 10, 1791. J. P. Boyd. 682p. 1974. text 85.00 (0-691-04583-6, Pub. by Princeton U Pr); Vol. 20. Ed. by J. P. Boyd. 792p. 1982. text 85.00 (0-691-04686-7, Pub. by Princeton U Pr); Vol. 21. Index, Vols. 1-20, 1760-1791. Ed. by Charles T. Cullen. LC 50-7486. 608p. 1982. text 85.00 (0-691-04687-5, Pub. by Princeton U Pr); 65.00 (0-691-04531-3) Princeton U Pr.

Papers of Thomas Jefferson, Vol. 26. Thomas Jefferson. 650p. (C). 1995. text 85.00 (0-691-04778-2, Pub. by Princeton U Pr) Cal Prin Full Svc.

Papers of Thomas Jefferson, Vol. 27. Thomas Jefferson. 856 pages inclup. (C). 1997. text 85.00 (0-691-04779-0, Pub. by Princeton U Pr) Cal Prin Full Svc.

Papers of Thomas Jefferson: 1 January-10 May 1793, Vol. 25. Thomas Jefferson. Ed. by John Catanzariti. (Illus.). 792p. (C). 1993. text 85.00 (0-691-04777-4, Pub. by Princeton U Pr) Cal Prin Full Svc.

Papers of Thomas Jefferson Vol. 22: 6 August-31 December 1791, Vol. 22. Charles T. Cullen. LC 50-7486. (Illus.). 556p. 1986. text 85.00 (0-691-04728-6, Pub. by Princeton U Pr) Cal Prin Full Svc.

Papers of Thomas Jefferson Vol. 23: January 1-May 31, 1792, Vol. 23. Thomas Jefferson. Ed. by Charles T. Cullen. (Illus.). 712p. (Orig.). 1986. text 85.00 (0-691-04739-1, Pub. by Princeton U Pr) Cal Prin Full Svc.

Papers of Thomas Jefferson Vol. 24: June 1-December 31, 1792, Vol. 24. Ed. by John Catanzariti. (Illus.). 928p. (Orig.). 1990. text 85.00 (0-691-04776-6, Pub. by Princeton U Pr) Cal Prin Full Svc.

Papers of Thomas Jordan Jarvis, Vol. 1, 1869-1882. Ed. by Wilfred B. Yearns. (Illus.). 1969. 15.00 (0-86526-045-1) NC Archives.

Papers of Thomas Ruffin, 4 vols. Thomas Ruffin. Ed. by J. G. Hamilton. LC 74-174788. reprint ed. 225.00 (0-404-04630-4) AMS Pr.

Papers of Tony Veitch. William McIlvanney. LC 82-18990. 256p. 1993. pap. 9.95 (0-15-670828-0) Harcourt.

Papers of Ulysses S. Grant: January 1-September 30, 1867. Ulysses S. Grant. Ed. by John Y. Simon et al. LC 67-10725. (Grant Papers: Vol. 17). 662p. (C). 1991. 65.00 (0-8093-1692-7) S Ill U Pr.

Papers of Ulysses S. Grant: October 1, 1867-June 30, 1868. Ulysses S. Grant. Ed. by John Y. Simon et al. LC 67-10725. (Grant Papers: Vol. 18). 688p. (C). 1991. 65.00 (0-8093-1693-5) S Ill U Pr.

Papers of Ulysses S. Grant Vol. 2: April to September, 1861. Ulysses S. Grant. Ed. by John Y. Simon. LC 67-10725. (Illus.). 437p. 1969. 65.00 (0-8093-0366-3) S Ill U Pr.

Papers of Ulysses S. Grant Vol. 3: October 1, 1861 to January 7, 1862. Ulysses S. Grant. Ed. by John Y. Simon. LC 67-10725. (Illus.). 513p. 1970. 65.00 (0-8093-0471-6) S Ill U Pr.

Papers of Ulysses S. Grant Vol. 4: January 8 to March 31, 1862. Ulysses S. Grant. Ed. by John Y. Simon & Roger D. Bridges. LC 67-10725. (Illus.). 558p. 1972. 65.00 (0-8093-0507-0) S Ill U Pr.

Papers of Ulysses S. Grant Vol. 5: April 1 to August 31, 1862. Ulysses S. Grant. Ed. by John Y. Simon & Thomas G. Alexander. LC 67-10725. (Illus.). 488p. 1974. 65.00 (0-8093-0636-0) S Ill U Pr.

Papers of Ulysses S. Grant Vol. 6: September 1 to December 8, 1862. Ulysses S. Grant. Ed. by John Y. Simon. LC 67-10725. (Illus.). 516p. 1977. 65.00 (0-8093-0694-8) S Ill U Pr.

Papers of Ulysses S. Grant Vol. 7: December 9, 1862 to March 31, 1863. Ulysses S. Grant. Ed. by John Y. Simon. LC 67-10725. (Illus.). 612p. 1979. 65.00 (0-8093-0880-0) S Ill U Pr.

Papers of Ulysses S. Grant Vol. 8: April 1 to July 6, 1863. Ulysses S. Grant. Ed. by John Y. Simon. LC 67-10725. (Illus.). 634p. 1979. 65.00 (0-8093-0884-3) S Ill U Pr.

Papers of Ulysses S. Grant Vol. 9: July 7-December 31, 1863. Ulysses S. Grant. Ed. by John Y. Simon. LC 67-10725. (Illus.). 724p. 1982. 65.00 (0-8093-0979-3) S Ill U Pr.

Papers of Ulysses S. Grant Vol. 10: January 1 - May 31, 1864. Ulysses S. Grant. Ed. by John Y. Simon. LC 67-10725. (Illus.). 644p. 1982. 65.00 (0-8093-0980-7) S Ill U Pr.

Papers of Ulysses S. Grant Vol. 11: June 1 - August 56, 1864. Ulysses S. Grant. Ed. by John Y. Simon. LC 67-10725. (Illus.). 512p. 1984. 65.00 (0-8093-1117-8) S Ill U Pr.

Papers of Ulysses S. Grant Vol. 12: August 16 - November 15, 1864. Ulysses S. Grant. Ed. by John Y. Simon. LC 67-10725. (Illus.). 525p. 1984. 65.00 (0-8093-1118-6) S Ill U Pr.

Papers of Ulysses S. Grant Vol. 13: November 16, 1864 - February 20, 1865. Ulysses S. Grant. Ed. by John Y. Simon & David L. Wilson. LC 67-10725. (Illus.). 512p. 1985. text 65.00 (0-8093-1197-6) S Ill U Pr.

Papers of Ulysses S. Grant Vol. 14: February 21 - April 30, 1865. Ulysses S. Grant. Ed. by John Y. Simon & David L. Wilson. LC 67-10725. (Illus.). 500p. 1985. text 65.00 (0-8093-1198-4) S Ill U Pr.

Papers of Ulysses S. Grant Vol. 15: May 1-December 31, 1865. Ulysses S. Grant. Ed. by John Y. Simon & David L. Wilson. LC 67-10725. (Illus.). 718p. 1988. text 65.00 (0-8093-1466-5) S Ill U Pr.

Papers of Ulysses S. Grant Vol. 19: July 1, 1868-October 31, 1869. Ed. by John Y. Simon. LC 67-10725. 608p. (C). 1995. 65.00 (0-8093-1964-0) S Ill U Pr.

Papers of Ulysses S. Grant Vol. 20: November 1, 1869-October 31, 1870. Ed. by John Y. Simon. LC 67-10725. 550p. (C). 1995. 65.00 (0-8093-1965-9) S Ill U Pr.

Papers of Ulysses S. Grant Vol. 21: November 1, 1870-May 31, 1871. John Y. Simon. 1998. 65.00 (0-8093-2197-1) S Ill U Pr.

Papers of Ulysses S. Grant Vol. 22: June 1, 1871-January 31, 1872. John Y. Simon. 1998. 65.00 (0-8093-2198-X) S Ill U Pr.

***Papers of Ulysses S. Grant Vol. 23: February 1-December 31, 1872.** Ed. by John Y. Simon et al. 560p. 2000. 65.00 (0-8093-2276-5) S Ill U Pr.

***Papers of Ulysses S. Grant, 1873, Vol. 24.** Ed. by John Y. Simon et al. 576p. 2000. 65.00 (0-8093-2277-3) S Ill U Pr.

Papers of Ulysses S. Grant, 1866, Vol. 16. Ulysses S. Grant. Ed. by John Y. Simon & David L. Wilson. LC 67-10725. (Illus.). 633p. 1988. text 65.00 (0-8093-1467-3) S Ill U Pr.

Papers of Ulysses S. Grant, 1837-1861, Vol. 1. Ulysses S. Grant. Ed. by John Y. Simon. LC 67-10725. (Illus.). 498p. 1967. 65.00 (0-8093-0248-9) S Ill U Pr.

Papers of Wade Hampton Frost, M.D. A Contribution to Epidemiological Method. Wade H. Frost. Ed. by Barbara G. Rosenkrantz & Kenneth F. Maxcy. LC 76-40635. (Public Health in America Ser.). (Illus.). 1977. reprint ed. lib. bdg. 51.95 (0-405-09826-X) Ayer.

Papers of Walter Clark, 2 vols., 1. Walter Clark. Ed. by Aubrey L. Brooks & Hugh T. Lefler. LC 48-6298. 643p. 1950. reprint ed. pap. 199.40 (0-7837-2068-8, 204234300001) Bks Demand.

Papers of Walter Clark, 2 vols., 2. Walter Clark. Ed. by Aubrey L. Brooks & Hugh T. Lefler. LC 48-6298. 634p. 1950. reprint ed. pap. 196.60 (0-7837-2069-6, 204234300002) Bks Demand.

Papers of Wilbur & Orville Wright, 2 vols., 1. Ed. by Marvin W. McFarland. LC 79-169428. (Literature & History of Aviation Ser.). 1979. reprint ed. 54.95 (0-405-03814-3) Ayer.

Papers of Wilbur & Orville Wright, 2 vols., Set. Ed. by Marvin W. McFarland. LC 79-169428. (Literature & History of Aviation Ser.). 1979. reprint ed. 160.00 (0-405-03771-6) Ayer.

Papers of Wilbur & Orville Wright, 2 vols., Vol. 2. Ed. by Marvin W. McFarland. LC 79-169428. (Literature & History of Aviation Ser.). 1979. reprint ed. 54.95 (0-405-03815-1) Ayer.

***Papers of Wilbur & Orville Wright, Including the Chanute-Wright Papers: 1899-1905, Vol. 1.** Marvin W. McFarland. (Illus.). 2000. 99.95 (0-07-136376-9) McGraw.

Papers of Will Rogers. Will Rogers. Ed. by Arthur F. Wertheim & Barbara Bair. LC 94-24165. (Illus.). 640p. 1996. 45.00 (0-8061-2745-7) U of Okla Pr.

Papers of William Alexander Graham, 8 vols. Incl. Vol. 1, 1825-1837. Ed. by J. G. Hamilton. xxiv, 555p. 1957. 15.00 (0-86526-035-4); Vol. 2, 1838-1844. Ed. by J. G. Hamilton. xviii, 552p. 1959. 15.00 (0-86526-036-2); Vol. 3, 1845-1850. Ed. by J. G. Hamilton. xvi, 541p. 1960. 15.00 (0-86526-037-0); Vol. 4, 1851-1856. Ed. by J. G. Hamilton. xxix, 701p. 1961. 15.00 (0-86526-038-9); Vol. 5, 1857-1863. Ed. by J. G. Hamilton & Max R. Williams. xxiii, 591p. 1973. 15.00 (0-86526-039-7); Vol. 6, 1864-1865. Ed. by Max R. Williams. xxiii, 514p. 1976. 16.00 (0-86526-040-0); Vol. 8, 1869-1875. Ed. by Max R. Williams & Mary R. Peacock. xxxiv, 576p. 1992. 45.00 (0-86526-245-4); write for info. (0-86526-034-6) NC Archives.

Papers of William H. Seward: Guide & Index to the Microfilm Collection. Ed. by Research Publications, Inc. Staff & Janice L. Budeit. 402p. 1983. 325.00 (0-89235-073-3) Primary Srce Media.

Papers of William Livingston, Vol. III. Ed. by Carl E. Prince. 576p. (C). 1986. text 50.00 (0-8135-1144-5) Rutgers U Pr.

Papers of William Livingston, Vol. IV. Ed. by Carl E. Prince & Mary L. Lustig. (Illus.). 590p. 1987. text 50.00 (0-8135-1213-1) Rutgers U Pr.

Papers of William Livingston: April 1783-1790, Vol. V. Ed. by Carl E. Prince et al. (Illus.). 683p. 1988. 75.00 (0-8135-1297-2) Rutgers U Pr.

Papers of William Livingston: Guide to the Microfilm Edition. Ed. by Mary L. Lustig et al. 205p. 1986. 20.00 (0-8357-0723-7) Univ Microfilms.

Papers of William Penn: Bibliography of the Publications of William Penn, Vol. V. Ed. by Edwin Bronner & David Fraser. LC 80-54052. (Illus.). 576p. 1986. 69.95 (0-8122-8019-9) U of Pa Pr.

Papers of William Penn, 1701-1718, Vol. IV. Ed. by Craig W. Horle et al. LC 80-54052. 840p. 1987. 79.95 (0-8122-8050-4) U of Pa Pr.

Papers of William Penn, 1685-1700, Vol. III. Ed. by Marianne S. Wokeck et al. LC 80-54052. 796p. 1987. 76.95 (0-8122-8029-6) U of Pa Pr.

Papers of William Thornton, 1781-1802, Vol. 1. Ed. by C. M. Harris & Daniel Preston. LC 94-18964. 720p. (C). 1995. text 60.00 (0-8139-1344-6) U Pr of Va.

Papers of Willie Person Mangum, 5 vols., Set. Ed. by Henry T. Shanks. Incl. Vol. 1, 1807-1832. xii, 613p. 1950. 15.00 (0-86526-050-8); Vol. 2, 1833-1838. xxi, 573p. 1952. 15.00 (0-86526-051-6); Vol. 3, 1839-1843. xxi, 521p. 1953. 15.00 (0-86526-052-4); Vol. 4, 1844-1846. xxviii, 579p. 1955. 15.00 (0-86526-053-2); Vol. 5, 1847-1894. xxxvii, 812p. 1956. 15.00 (0-86526-054-0); (Illus.). write for info. (0-86526-049-4) NC Archives.

Papers of Woodrow Wilson, 30 vols., Vols. 1-7. Incl. Vol. 10. 1896-1898. Woodrow Wilson. 632p. 1971. text 75.00 (0-691-04508-9, Pub. by Princeton U Pr); Vol. 13. Contents & Index, 1856-1900 Vols. 1-12. Woodrow Wilson. Ed. by A. S. Link. 352p. 1972. text 75.00 (0-691-04642-5, Pub. by Princeton U Pr); Vol. 50. Papers of Woodrow Wilson: The Complete Press Conferences, 1913-1919. Ed. by Arthur S. Link & Robert C. Hilderbrand. LC 66-10880. (Illus.). 688p. 1985. text 75.00 (0-691-04710-3, Pub. by Princeton U Pr); November 20, 1916 to January 23, 1917. Woodrow Wilson. Ed. by Arthur S. Link & John E. Little. LC 66-10880. (Illus.). 600p. 1982. text 75.00 (0-691-04690-5, Pub. by Princeton U Pr); Vol. 1. 1856-1880. Woodrow Wilson. Ed. by Arthur S. Link. 715p. 1966. text 75.00 (0-691-04550-X, Pub. by Princeton U Pr); Vol. 2. 1881-1884. Woodrow Wilson. Ed. by Arthur S. Link. 680p. 1967. text 75.00 (0-691-04551-8, Pub. by Princeton U Pr); Vol. 3. 1884-1885. Woodrow Wilson. Ed. by Arthur S. Link. 664p. 1967. text 75.00 (0-691-04552-6, Pub. by Princeton U Pr); Vol. 4. 1885. Woodrow Wilson. Ed. by Arthur S. Link. 776p. 1968. text 75.00 (0-691-04553-4, Pub. by Princeton U Pr); Vol. 5. 1885-1888. Woodrow Wilson. Ed. by Arthur S. Link. 812p. 1968. text 75.00 (0-691-04587-9, Pub. by Princeton U Pr); Vol. 6. 1888-1890. Woodrow Wilson. Ed. by Arthur S. Link. 752p. 1969. text 75.00 (0-691-04592-5, Pub. by Princeton U Pr); Vol. 7. 1890-1892. Woodrow Wilson. 688p. 1969. text 75.00 (0-691-04596-8, Pub. by Princeton U Pr); Vol. 8. 1892-1894. Woodrow Wilson. 736p. 1970. text 75.00 (0-691-04599-2, Pub. by Princeton U Pr); Vol. 9. 1894-1896. Woodrow Wilson. 630p. 1970. text 75.00 (0-691-04603-4, Pub. by Princeton U Pr); Vol. 11. 1898-1900. Woodrow Wilson. 630p. 1971. text 75.00 (0-691-04606-9, Pub. by Princeton U Pr); Vol. 12. 1900-1901. Woodrow Wilson. 536p. 1972. text 75.00 (0-691-04612-3, Pub. by Princeton U Pr); Vol. 14. 1901-1902. Woodrow Wilson. 608p. 1972. text 75.00 (0-691-04614-X, Pub. by Princeton U Pr); Vol. 15. 1903-1905. Woodrow Wilson. 632p. 1973. text 75.00 (0-691-04617-4, Pub. by Princeton U Pr); Vol. 16. 1905-1907. Woodrow Wilson. 624p. 1973. text 75.00 (0-691-04620-4, Pub. by Princeton U Pr); Vol. 17. 1907-1908. Woodrow Wilson. 669p. 1974. text 75.00 (0-691-04621-2, Pub. by Princeton U Pr); Vol. 18. 1908-1909. Woodrow Wilson. LC 66-10880. 692p. 1974. text 75.00 (0-691-04631-X, Pub. by Princeton U Pr); Vol. 19. 1909-1910. Woodrow Wilson. LC 66-10880. 807p. 1975. text 75.00 (0-691-04633-6, Pub. by Princeton U Pr); Vol. 20. January to July, 1910. Woodrow Wilson. LC 66-10880. 628p. 1975. text 75.00 (0-691-04635-2, Pub. by Princeton U Pr); Vol. 21. July to November, 1910. Woodrow Wilson. LC 66-10880. 664p. 1975. text 75.00 (0-691-04636-0, Pub. by Princeton U Pr); Vol. 22. 1911. Woodrow Wilson. LC 66-10880. 656p. 1976. text 75.00 (0-691-04638-7, Pub. by Princeton U Pr); Vol. 23. 1911-1912. Woodrow Wilson. LC 66-10880. 712p. 1977. text 75.00 (0-691-04643-3, Pub. by Princeton U Pr); Vol. 24. January to August, 1912. Woodrow Wilson. LC 66-10880. (Illus.). 640p. 1977. text 75.00 (0-691-04645-X, Pub. by Princeton U Pr); Vol. 25. August to November, 1912. Woodrow Wilson. LC 66-10880. (Illus.). 700p. 1978. text 75.00 (0-691-04650-6, Pub. by Princeton U Pr); Vol. 26. Contents & Index, Vols. 14-25, 1902-1912. Woodrow Wilson. Ed. by A. S. Link. LC 66-10880. 328p. 1980. text 75.00 (0-691-04664-6, Pub. by Princeton U Pr); Vol. 27. January to June, 1913. Woodrow Wilson. LC 66-10880. (Illus.). 632p. 1978. text 75.00 (0-691-04652-2, Pub. by Princeton U Pr); Vol. 28. 1913. Woodrow Wilson. LC 66-10880. (Illus.). 656p. 1978. text 75.00 (0-691-04653-0, Pub. by Princeton U Pr); Vol. 29. 1913-1914. Woodrow Wilson. LC 66-10880. 616p. 1979. text 75.00 (0-691-04659-X, Pub. by Princeton U Pr); Vol. 30. May to September, 1914. Woodrow Wilson. LC 66-10880. 552p. 1979. text 75.00 (0-691-04663-8, Pub. by Princeton U Pr); Vol. 31. September to December 1914. Woodrow Wilson. LC 66-10880. 616p. 1979. text 75.00 (0-691-04666-2, Pub. by Princeton U Pr); Vol. 32. January to April, 1915. Woodrow Wilson. LC 66-10880. 584p. 1980. text 75.00 (0-691-04667-0, Pub. by Princeton U Pr); Vol. 33. April to July, 1915. Woodrow Wilson. LC 66-10880. (Illus.). 600p. 1980. text 75.00 (0-691-04668-9, Pub. by Princeton U Pr); July to September, 1915. Woodrow Wilson. Ed. by David W. Hirst & John E. Little. LC 66-10880. (Illus.). 592p. 1980. text 75.00 (0-691-04673-5, Pub. by Princeton U Pr); January to May, 1916. Woodrow Wilson. Ed. by David W. Hirst & John E. Little. LC 66-10880. (Illus.). 650p. 1981. text 75.00 (0-691-04682-4, Pub. by Princeton U Pr); May 9 to August 7, 1916. Woodrow Wilson. Ed. by David W. Hirst & John E. Little. LC 66-10880. (Illus.). 650p. 1981. text 75.00 (0-691-04684-0, Pub. by Princeton U Pr); August 7 to November 19, 1916. Woodrow Wilson. Ed. by Arthur S. Link et al. LC 66-10880. (Illus.). 720p. 1982. text 75.00 (0-691-04689-1, Pub. by Princeton U Pr); Vol. 35. 1915-1916. Woodrow Wilson. Ed. by David W. Hirst & John E. Little. LC 66-10880. (Illus.). 568p. 1981. text 75.00 (0-691-04676-X, Pub. by Princeton U Pr); Woodrow Wilson. Ed. by Arthur S. Link et al. 608p. 1982. text 75.00 (0-691-04691-3, Pub. by Princeton U Pr); Vol. 42. Woodrow Wilson. Ed. by Arthur S. Link et al. 630p. 1982. text 75.00 (0-691-04692-1, Pub. by Princeton U Pr); June 25 to August 20, 1917. Woodrow Wilson. Ed. by Arthur S. Link. LC 66-10880. (Illus.). 552p. 1983. text 75.00 (0-691-04701-4, Pub. by Princeton U Pr); Vol. 44. August 21 to November 10, 1917. Woodrow Wilson. Ed. by Arthur S. Link et al. LC 66-10880. (Illus.). 568p. 1983. text 75.00 (0-691-04704-9, Pub. by Princeton U Pr); Vol. 45. November 11, 1917 to January 15, 1918. Woodrow Wilson. Ed. by Arthur S. Link. LC 66-10880. (Illus.). 625p. 1984. text 75.00 (0-691-04705-7, Pub. by Princeton U Pr); Vol. 46. January 16 to March 12, 1918. Woodrow Wilson. Ed. by Arthur S. Linl & David W. Hirst. LC 66-10880. 664p. 1984. text 75.00 (0-691-04706-5, Pub. by Princeton U Pr); March 13 to May 12, 1918. Woodrow Wilson. Ed. by Arthur S. Link. LC 66-10880. (Illus.). 632p. 1984. text 75.00 (0-691-04707-3, Pub. by Princeton U Pr); Content & Index to Vols. 27-38, 1913-1916. Ed. by Arthur S. Link et al. LC 66-10880. 300p. 1985. text 75.00 (0-691-04696-4, Pub. by Princeton U Pr); May 13 to July 17, 1918. Woodrow Wilson. Ed. by Arthur S. Link. LC 66-10880. (Illus.). 585p. 1985. text 75.00 (0-691-04708-1, Pub. by Princeton U Pr); July 18 to September 18, 1918. Woodrow Wilson. Ed. by Arthur S. Link. LC 66-10880. (Illus.). 665p. 1985. text 75.00 (0-691-04709-X, Pub. by Princeton U Pr); Vol. 68. April 8, 1922 - February 6, 1924. Ed. by Arthur S. Link. 656p. 1993. text 75.00 (0-691-04803-7, Pub. by Princeton U Pr); write for info. (0-318-55364-3) Princeton U Pr.

Papers of Woodrow Wilson: April 8, 1922-February 6, 1924, Vol. 69. Ed. by Arthur S. Link. 375p. 1993. text 75.00 (0-691-04812-6, Pub. by Princeton U Pr) Cal Prin Full Svc.

Papers of Woodrow Wilson: December 24, 1920-April 7, 1922, Vol. 67. Ed. by Arthur S. Link. (Illus.). 655p. 1993. text 75.00 (0-691-04799-5, Pub. by Princeton U Pr) Cal Prin Full Svc.

Papers of Woodrow Wilson: February 8-March 16, 1919, Vol. 55. Arthur S. Link et al. Ed. by David W. Hirst et al. (Illus.). 604p. 1986. text 75.00 (0-691-04737-5, Pub. by Princeton U Pr) Cal Prin Full Svc.

P

An Asterisk (*) at the beginning of an entry indicates that the title is appearing for the first time.

Papers of Woodrow Wilson: January 11-February 7, 1919, Vol. 54. Ed. by Arthur S. Link et al. (Illus.). 616p. 1986. text 75.00 (*0-691-04736-7*, Pub. by Princeton U Pr) Cal Prin Full Svc.

Papers of Woodrow Wilson: November 6, 1919 - February 27, 1920, Vol. 64. Ed. by Arthur S. Link et al. 565p. 1991. text 75.00 (*0-691-04791-X*, Pub. by Princeton U Pr) Cal Prin Full Svc.

Papers of Woodrow Wilson: November 9, 1918-January 11, 1919, Vol. 53. Ed. by Arthur S. Link & David W. Hirst. LC 66-10880. (Illus.). 736p. 1985. text 75.00 (*0-691-04731-6*, Pub. by Princeton U Pr) Cal Prin Full Svc.

Papers of Woodrow Wilson: September 14 to November 8, 1918, Vol. 51. Ed. by Arthur S. Link. LC 66-10880. (Illus.). 648p. 1985. text 75.00 (*0-691-04730-8*, Pub. by Princeton U Pr) Cal Prin Full Svc.

Papers of Woodrow Wilson: The Complete Press Conferences, 1913-1919 see Papers of Woodrow Wilson

Papers of Woodrow Wilson Vol. 52: Contents & Index, Vol. 40-49, 51. Ed. by Arthur S. Link et al. 240p. 1987. text 75.00 (*0-691-04744-8*, Pub. by Princeton U Pr) Cal Prin Full Svc.

Papers of Woodrow Wilson Vol. 56: March 17 - April 4, 1919. Ed. by Arthur S. Link et al. (Illus.). 696p. 1987. text 75.00 (*0-691-04742-1*, Pub. by Princeton U Pr) Cal Prin Full Svc.

Papers of Woodrow Wilson Vol. 57: April 5 - April 22, 1919. Arthur S. Link et al. Ed. by Frederick Aandahl. (Illus.). 704p. 1987. text 75.00 (*0-691-04743-X*, Pub. by Princeton U Pr) Cal Prin Full Svc.

Papers of Woodrow Wilson Vol. 58: April 23 to May 9, 1919. Ed. by Arthur S. Link et al. (Illus.). 696p. 1988. text 75.00 (*0-691-04748-0*, Pub. by Princeton U Pr) Cal Prin Full Svc.

Papers of Woodrow Wilson Vol. 59: May 10 - May 31, 1919. Ed. by Arthur S. Link et al. (Illus.). 744p. 1988. text 75.00 (*0-691-04754-5*, Pub. by Princeton U Pr) Cal Prin Full Svc.

Papers of Woodrow Wilson Vol. 60: June 1 - June 17, 1919. Ed. by Arthur S. Link. 752p. 1989. text 75.00 (*0-691-04762-6*, Pub. by Princeton U Pr) Cal Prin Full Svc.

Papers of Woodrow Wilson Vol. 61: June 18 - July 25, 1919. Ed. by Arthur S. Link. 620p. (C). 1989. text 75.00 (*0-691-04766-9*, Pub. by Princeton U Pr) Cal Prin Full Svc.

Papers of Woodrow Wilson Vol. 62: July 26-September 3, 1919. Ed. by Arthur S. Link. (Illus.). 688p. 1990. text 75.00 (*0-691-04767-7*, Pub. by Princeton U Pr) Cal Prin Full Svc.

Papers of Woodrow Wilson Vol. 63: September 4-November 5, 1919. Ed. by Arthur S. Link. (Illus.). 546p. 1990. text 75.00 (*0-691-04775-8*, Pub. by Princeton U Pr) Cal Prin Full Svc.

Papers of Woodrow Wilson Vol. 65: February 28-July 31, 1920. Ed. by Arthur S. Link. (Illus.). 673p. 1992. text 75.00 (*0-691-04792-8*, Pub. by Princeton U Pr) Cal Prin Full Svc.

Papers of Woodrow Wilson Vol. 66: August 2-December 23, 1920. Ed. by Arthur S. Link. (Illus.). 583p. 1992. text 75.00 (*0-691-04798-7*, Pub. by Princeton U Pr) Cal Prin Full Svc.

Papers of Zebulon Baird Vance, 1843-1862 Vol. 1. Ed. by Frontis W. Johnston. (Illus.). lxxiv, 475p. (C). 1963. 15.00 (*0-86526-071-0*) NC Archives.

Papers of Zebulon Baird Vance, 1863 Vol. 2. Ed. by Joe A. Mobley. LC 63-24722. (Papers of Zebulon Baird Vance). (Illus.). xxxix, 436p. (C). 1995. 35.00 (*0-86526-262-4*) NC Archives.

Papers of Zebulon Vance. Zebulon B. Vance et al. LC 87-29450. (Research Collections in American Politics Ser.). 39 p. 1987. write for info. (*0-89093-545-9*) U Pubns Amer.

Papers on African Literature: Given at the Seminar Series on African Art & Literature, Sheffield University, 1975. Ed. by Christopher Heywood. LC PL8010.P28. (Sheffield Papers on Literature & Society: 1). 135p. reprint ed. pap. 41.90 (*0-608-16176-4*, 202253800027) Bks Demand.

Papers on Agricultural Biotechnology. Ed. by Steven M. Gendel et al. (Studies in Technology & Social Change: No. 6). 160p. (Orig.). (C). 1988. pap. 12.00 (*0-945271-09-3*) ISU-CIKARD.

Papers on California Archaeology, Nos. 1-5. fac. ed. Sherburne F. Cook et al. (Reports of the University of California Archaeological Survey: No. 7). 25p. 1950. reprint ed. pap. 2.81 (*1-55567-333-3*) Coyote Press.

Papers on California Archaeology, Nos. 10-12. fac. ed. A. L. Koreber et al. (Reports of the University of California Archaeological Survey: No. 11). 40p. 1951. reprint ed. pap. 4.38 (*1-55567-335-X*) Coyote Press.

Papers on California Archaeology, Nos. 17-18. fac. ed. R. F. Heizer et al. (Reports of the University of California Archaeological Survey: No. 15). (Illus.). 48p. 1952. reprint ed. pap. 5.31 (*1-55567-337-6*) Coyote Press.

Papers on California Archaeology, Nos. 19-20. C. E. Meighan & R. J. Squier. (Reports of the University of California Archaeological Survey: No. 19). (Illus.). 58p. 1953. pap. 6.88 (*1-55567-340-6*) Coyote Press.

Papers on California Archaeology, Nos. 21-22. fac. ed. M. J. Harner & R. F. Heizer. (Reports of the University of California Archaeological Survey: No. 20). (Illus.). 46p. 1953. reprint ed. pap. 5.00 (*1-55567-341-4*) Coyote Press.

Papers on California Archaeology, Nos. 21-26. fac. ed. R. F. Heizer et al. (Reports of the University of California Archaeological Survey: No. 22). (Illus.). 46p. 1953. reprint ed. pap. 5.00 (*1-55567-342-2*) Coyote Press.

Papers on California Archaeology, Nos. 30-31. fac. ed. Clement W. Meighan & W. C. Gonsalves. (Reports of the University of California Archaeological Survey: No. 29). (Illus.). 56p. 1955. reprint ed. pap. 6.88 (*1-55567-347-3*) Coyote Press.

Papers on California Archaeology, Nos. 32-33. fac. ed. Clement W. Meighan & Martin A. Baumhoff. (Reports of the University of California Archaeological Survey: No. 30). 103p. 1955. reprint ed. pap. 11.56 (*1-55567-348-1*) Coyote Press.

Papers on California Archaeology, Nos. 34-36. fac. ed. Francis A. Riddell et al. (Reports of the University of California Archaeological Survey: No. 32). (Illus.). 48p. 1955. reprint ed. pap. 5.31 (*1-55567-350-3*) Coyote Press.

Papers on California Archaeology, Nos. 37-43. fac. ed. Martin A. Baumhoff et al. (Reports of the University of California Archaeological Survey: No. 33). (Illus.). 80p. 1956. reprint ed. pap. 9.06 (*1-55567-351-1*) Coyote Press.

Papers on California Archaeology, Nos. 44-46. fac. ed. Francis A. Riddell et al. (Reports of the University of California Archaeological Survey: No. 35). (Illus.). 69p. 1956. reprint ed. pap. 8.13 (*1-55567-353-8*) Coyote Press.

Papers on California Archaeology, Nos. 50-62. fac. ed. R. F. Heizer et al. (Reports of the University of California Archaeological Survey: No. 38). (Illus.). 64p. 1957. reprint ed. pap. 7.50 (*1-55567-355-4*) Coyote Press.

Papers on California Archaeology, Nos. 63-69. fac. ed. R. F. Heizer et al. (Reports of the University of California Archaeological Survey: No. 41). (Illus.). 54p. 1958. reprint ed. pap. 6.56 (*1-55567-358-9*) Coyote Press.

Papers on California Archaeology, Nos. 70-73. fac. ed. Byrne et al. (Reports of the University of California Archaeological Survey: No. 48). (Illus.). 120p. 1959. reprint ed. pap. 13.13 (*1-55567-365-1*) Coyote Press.

Papers on California Archaeology, Nos. 76-88. fac. ed. Jay C. Vonwerlhof et al. (Reports of the University of California Archaeological Survey: No. 50). (Illus.). 63p. 1960. reprint ed. pap. 7.50 (*1-55567-368-6*) Coyote Press.

Papers on California Archaeology: 27-29. Eugene Robinson et al. (University of California Archaeology Survey, Department of Anthropology Berkeley, CA Ser.: No. 28). (Illus.). 45p. (C). 1955. reprint ed. pap. text 5.00 (*1-55567-629-4*) Coyote Press.

Papers on California Ethnography. Heizer Kroeber et al. (University of California Archaeological Research Facility: No. 9). (Illus.). 164p. (C). 1970. reprint ed. pap. text 15.00 (*1-55567-589-1*) Coyote Press.

Papers on California Prehistory, No 8, Pt. 1. Gary S. Breschini et al. (Archives of California Prehistory Ser.: No. 8). (Illus.). 98p. (Orig.). 1986. pap. 9.69 (*1-55567-041-5*) Coyote Press.

Papers on California Prehistory, Vol. 22, Pt. 2. K. Dixon et al. (Archives of California Prehistory Ser.: Vol. 22). 118p. (Orig.). (C). 1988. pap. text 13.13 (*1-55567-058-X*) Coyote Press.

Papers on California Prehistory, Vol. 33, Pt. 3. Huddleston et al. (Archives of California Prehistory Ser.: Vol. 33). (Illus.). 94p. (Orig.). (C). 1991. pap. text 10.63 (*1-55567-073-3*) Coyote Press.

Papers on California Prehistory, Vol. 41, Pt. 4. E. B. Parkman et al. Ed. by G. S. Breschini & Trudy Haversat. (Archives of California Prehistory Ser.: Vol. 41). (Illus.). 136p. (Orig.). (C). 1995. pap. text 15.00 (*1-55567-109-8*) Coyote Press.

Papers on California Prehistory 5. Judith Porcasi et al. Ed. by Breschini & Haverrat. (Archives of California Prehistory Ser.: No. 45). (Illus.). 106p. (Orig.). (C). 1997. pap. text 11.88 (*1-55567-626-X*) Coyote Press.

Papers on Central California Prehistory. Gary S. Breschini & Trudy Haversat. (Archives of California Prehistory Ser.: No. 3). (Illus.). 90p. (Orig.). (C). 1984. pap. 10.31 (*1-55567-023-7*) Coyote Press.

Papers on Cephalopod Paleobiology & Phylogeny. K. Schmidt et al. (Neues Jahrb. fuer Geologie & Paleontologie Ser.: Vol. 165-3). (ENG & GER., Illus.). 181p. 1983. pap. text 95.00 (*0-945345-31-3*) Lubrecht & Cramer.

Papers on Fourth International Tanker Safety Conference. INTASAFCON 4 Staff & ICS Staff. 1979. 162.00 (*0-7855-1774-X*, Pub. by Witherby & Co) St Mut.

Papers on Fuchsian Functions. Jules Henri Poincare. Tr. by John C. Stillwell from FRE. (Illus.). iv, 483p. 1985. 79.95 (*0-387-96215-8*) Spr-Verlag.

Papers on General Topology & Applications: Eleventh Summer Conference at the University of Southern Maine. Ed. by Susan Andima. LC 96-51642. (Annals of the New York Academy of Sciences Ser.). 492p. 1997. pap. 110.00 (*1-57331-091-3*) NY Acad Sci.

Papers on General Topology & Applications: Eleventh Summer Conference at University of Southern Maine, Vol. 806. Ed. by Susan Andima et al. LC 96-51642. 492p. 1997. 110.00 (*1-57331-090-5*) NY Acad Sci.

Papers on General Topology & Applications: Seventh Conference at the University of Wisconsin. Ed. by Susan Andima et al. LC 93-48367. (Annals Ser.: Vol. 704). 367p. 1993. pap. 160.00 (*0-89766-720-4*) NY Acad Sci.

Papers on General Topology & Applications: Tenth Summer Conference at Amsterdam. Ed. by Eva Coplakova & Klaas Pieter Hart. LC 96-15559. (Annals of the New York Academy of Sciences Ser.). 1996. pap. 110.00 (*0-89766-964-9*) NY Acad Sci.

Papers on Great Basin Archaeology. fac. ed. Turner et al. (Reports of the University of California Archaeological Survey: No. 70). (Illus.). 161p. 1967. reprint ed. pap. 17.50 (*1-55567-386-4*) Coyote Press.

Papers on Great Basin Prehistory. fac. ed. R. F. Heizer et al. (Reports of the University of California Archaeological Survey: No. 71). (Illus.). 126p. 1968. reprint ed. pap. 13.75 (*1-55567-387-2*) Coyote Press.

Papers on Group Theory & Topology. M. Dehn. Tr. by John C. Stillwell. (Illus.). 400p. 1987. 69.95 (*0-387-96416-9*) Spr-Verlag.

Papers on Industrial Water & Industrial Waste. American Society for Testing & Materials Staff. LC 63-12705. (American Society for Testing & Materials Special Technical Publication Ser.: No. 337). 77p. reprint ed. pap. 30.00 (*0-608-10791-3*, 200014300025) Bks Demand.

Papers on Inter-Racial Problems. Ed. by G. Spiller. LC 70-93419. (Black Heritage Library Collection). 1977. 23.95 (*0-8369-8660-1*) Ayer.

Papers on Inter-Racial Problems Communicated to the First Universal Races Congress Held at the University of London, July 26-29, 1911. Ed. by G. Spiller. LC 70-94139. (American Negro: His History & Literature. Series 3). 1970. reprint ed. 23.95 (*0-405-01935-1*) Ayer.

Papers on International Environmental Negotiation, Vol. V. Ed. by William R. Moomaw et al. 220p. (Orig.). (C). 1995. pap. 20.00 (*1-880711-06-0*, Pon Bks) Prog Negot HLS.

Papers on Language Theory & History I: Creation & Tradition in Language. J. Peter Maher. (Current Issues in Linguistic Theory Ser.: No. 3). xx, 171p. 1979. 48.00 (*90-272-0904-9*) J Benjamins Pubng Co.

Papers on Linguistics & Child Language: Ruth Hirsch Weir Memorial Volume. Ed. by Vladimir Honsa & J. J. Hardman-De-Bautista. (Janua Linguarum, Series Major: No. 65). 1978. pap. text 83.85 (*90-279-7816-6*) Mouton.

Papers on Literature & Art, 2 pts. in 1. Margaret S. Ossoli. LC 76-144668. reprint ed. 49.50 (*0-404-04836-6*) AMS Pr.

Papers on Literature & Art. Sarah M. Ossoli. (BCL1-PS American Literature Ser.). 1992. reprint ed. lib. bdg. 99.00 (*0-7812-6816-8*) Rprt Serv.

Papers on Mediterranean Archaeology. Ed. by Marianne Maaskant-Kleibrink. (Caelcvlvs: Images of Ancient Latin Culture Ser.: Vol. I). 172p. 1993. pap. 40.00 (*0-685-68014-2*, Pub. by Egbert Forsten) Hod1der & Stoughton.

Papers on Merced County Prehistory. W. E. Pritchard et al. (Publications of the Department of Parks & Recreation: No. 21). (Illus.). 111p. (C). 1983. reprint ed. pap. text 3.15 (*1-55567-470-4*) Coyote Press.

Papers on Neogene Mollusks No. 19: Special Publication. A. A. Olsson. 163p. 1993. 16.00 (*0-87710-428-X*) Paleo Res.

Papers on Old Sacramento Archeology. Schulz, Hastings & Felton Staff et al. (Publications of the Department of Parks & Recreation: No. 19). (Illus.). 70p. (C). 1980. reprint ed. pap. text 3.15 (*1-55567-468-2*) Coyote Press.

Papers on Planning & Economic Management. Ely Devons & Alec Cairncross. LC 77-542200. vii, 278p. 1970. write for info. (*0-7190-0408-X*) Manchester Univ Pr.

Papers on Playmaking. Ed. by Brander Matthews. LC 75-111852. (Essay Index Reprint Ser.). 1977. 21.95 (*0-8369-1890-8*) Ayer.

Papers on Polymer Optical Fibers. 1995. 125.00 (*0-614-18417-7*) Info Gatekeepers.

Papers on Presidential Disability & the Twenty-Fifth Amendment. Kenneth Crispell et al. Ed. by Kenneth W. Thompson. 144p. 1997. 46.50 (*0-7618-0724-1*); pap. 26.50 (*0-7618-0725-X*) U Pr of Amer.

Papers on Presidential Disability & the Twenty-Fifth Amendment: By Medical, Historical, & Political Authorities, Vol. III. Ed. by Kenneth W. Thompson. 234p. 1996. pap. text 29.50 (*0-7618-0424-2*); lib. bdg. 49.00 (*0-7618-0423-4*) U Pr of Amer.

Papers on Presidential Disability & the Twenty-Fifth Amendment By Six Medical, Legal & Political Authorities. Ed. by Kenneth W. Thompson. (Orig.). (C). 1988. pap. text 23.00 (*0-8191-6921-8*) U Pr of Amer.

Papers on Presidential Disability & the Twenty-Fifth Amendment By Six Medical, Legal & Political Authorities. Ed. by Kenneth W. Thompson. (Orig.). (C). 1988. lib. bdg. 42.00 (*0-8191-6920-X*, Pub. by White Miller Center) U Pr of Amer.

Papers on Presidential Disability & the Twenty-Fifth Amendment, Vol. 2: By Six Medical, Legal, & Political Authorities. Ed. by Kenneth W. Thompson. (Papers on Presidential Disability & Foreign Policy). 164p. (C). 1991. pap. text 24.50 (*0-8191-8077-7*, Pub. by White Miller Center); lib. bdg. 41.50 (*0-8191-8076-9*, Pub. by White Miller Center) U Pr of Amer.

Papers on Probability, Statistics & Statistical Physics. 2nd ed. E. T. Jaynes. 458p. (C). 1989. pap. text 71.00 (*0-7923-0213-3*, D Reidel) Kluwer Academic.

Papers on Psychoanalytic Psychology. Heinz Hartmann et al. LC 64-18532. (Psychological Issues Monographs: No. 14, Vol. 4, No. 2). 206p. 1964. 40.50 (*0-8236-3980-0*) Intl Univs Pr.

Papers on Shelley, Wordsworth & Others. John A. Chapman. LC 67-23191. (Essay Index Reprint Ser.). 1977. 29.95 (*0-8369-0288-2*) Ayer.

Papers on Syntax. Zellig S. Harris. viii, 430p. 1981. lib. bdg. 146.00 (*90-277-1266-2*) Kluwer Academic.

Papers on Tai Languages, Linguistics, & Literatures (in Honor of Professor William J. Gedney) In Honor of Professor William J. Gedney on His 77th Birthday. Ed. by Carol Compton & John Hartmann. (Occasional Papers: No. 16). 302p. 1992. pap. 26.95 (*1-877979-16-3*) SE Asia.

Papers on the Amasis Painter & His World. LC 87-16902. (Illus.). 204p. 1987. pap. 35.00 (*0-89236-093-3*, Pub. by J P Getty Trust) OUP.

Papers on the Archaeology of Black Mesa, Arizona, Vol. II. Ed. by Stephen Plog & Shirley Powell. LC 75-32340. (Papers in Archaeology Ser.). (Illus.). 224p. 1984. 31.95 (*0-8093-1149-6*) S Ill U Pr.

Papers on the Archaeology of the Mojave Desert. Ed. by Mark Q. Sutton et al. (Archives of California Prehistory Ser.: No. 10). (Illus.). 156p. (Orig.). 1987. pap. 20.00 (*1-55567-043-1*) Coyote Press.

Papers on the Archaeology of the Mojave Desert, Vol. 32, Pt. 2. Joyce Nakamura et al. (Archives of California Prehistory Ser.: Vol. 32). (Illus.). 125p. (Orig.). (C). 1991. pap. text 13.75 (*1-55567-072-5*) Coyote Press.

Papers on the Archaeology of Western Great Basin. fac. ed. C. W. Clewlow, Jr. et al. (Reports of the University of California Archaeological Survey: No. 73). 245p. 1968. reprint ed. pap. 25.63 (*1-55567-389-9*) Coyote Press.

Papers on the Art of Anti-Administration. David J. Farmer. LC 98-9008. 1998. pap. write for info. (*1-57420-062-3*) Chatelaine.

Papers on the Constitution. 1997. lib. bdg. 251.95 (*0-8490-7753-2*) Gordon Pr.

Papers on the Development of Environmental Education Standards. rev. ed. Ed. by Deborah A. Simmons. 121p. (Orig.). 1995. pap. 8.00 (*1-884008-20-8*) NAAEE.

Papers on the Economy of Botswana. Ed. by Charles Harvey. (Studies in the Economics of Africa). 276p. (C). 1981. text 30.00 (*0-435-97199-9*, 97199) Heinemann.

Papers on the Ethnology & Archaeology of the Malay Peninsula. Ivor H. Evans. LC 76-44715. reprint ed. 49.50 (*0-404-15921-4*) AMS Pr.

Papers on the Great Pyramid. St. John V. Day. 127p. 1996. reprint ed. spiral bd. 12.00 (*0-7873-0260-0*) Hlth Research.

Papers on the Legal History of Government: Difficulties Fundamental & Artificial. Melville M. Bigelow. 256p. 1982. reprint ed. 35.00 (*0-8377-0326-3*, Rothman) W S Hein.

Papers on the Madrid Codex. Ed. by Victoria R. Bricker & Gabrielle Vail. LC 97-37003. (Publication Ser.: No. 64). 1997. write for info. (*0-939238-94-2*) Tulane MARI.

Papers on the Manding. Ed. by Carleton T. Hodge. LC 76-633893. (African Ser.: Vol. 3). (Orig.). 1971. pap. text 18.00 (*0-87750-158-0*) Res Inst Inner Asian Studies.

Papers on the Political Economy of Tanzania. K. S. Kim et al. (Studies in the Economics of Africa). 294p. 1995. text 40.00 (*0-435-97440-8*, 97440) Heinemann.

Papers on the Prehistoric Archaeology of Cranborne Chase. Ed. by John Barrett et al. (Oxbow Monographs in Archaeology: No. 11). (Illus.). 251p. 1991. pap. 42.00 (*0-946897-31-X*, Pub. by Oxbow Bks) David Brown.

Papers on Unified Field Theory. 3rd ed. James A. Green. LC 95-94997. (Field Physics Ser.). (Illus.). 355p. 1999. 51.00 (*1-890121-01-0*, 01-02-04) Grnwd Resch.

Papers on Welfare & Growth. Tibor Scitovsky. (Modern Revivals in Economics Ser.). 280p. (C). 1993. text 61.95 (*0-7512-0251-7*, Pub. by Gregg Revivals) Ashgate Pub Co.

Papers Papers. Richard F. Shepard. Date not set. write for info. (*0-614-96900-X*, Times Bks) Crown Pub Group.

Paper's Papers. deluxe ed. Richard F. Shepard. 1996. pap. write for info. (*0-8129-2863-6*, Times Bks) Crown Pub Group.

Paper's Papers: A Reporter's Journey Through the Archives of the New York Times. Richard F. Shepard. 1996. 30.00 (*0-614-96815-1*, Times Bks) Crown Pub Group.

Papers Please! Identity Documents, Permits & Authorizations of the Third Reich. Ray R. Cowdery & Josephine N. Cowdery. (Illus.). 144p. 1996. 29.95 (*0-910667-36-5*) USM.

Papers Presented at Enetworks Held in 1992, Paris, France. 1996. 145.00 (*0-614-18576-9*, E92NPR) Info Gatekeepers.

Papers Presented at the Technical Consultation on Reduction of Wastage in Fisheries Reports, Vol. 547. FAO Staff. (Fisheries Ser.). 338p. 1997. pap. 38.00 (*92-5-104030-3*, F40303, Pub. by FAO) Bernan Associates.

Papers Read at the Meeting of Grand Dragons Knights of the Ku Klux Klan, 1st, Asheville, North Carolina, July 1923. Ku Klux Klan Staff. Ed. by Gerald N. Grob. LC 76-46086. (Anti-Movements in America Ser.). 1977. reprint ed. lib. bdg. 24.95 (*0-405-09959-2*) Ayer.

Papers Relating to Political Economy: 1925 Edition, 3 vols., Set. Francis Y. Edgeworth. 1280p. 1996. reprint ed. 285.00 (*1-85506-188-0*) Bks Intl VA.

Papers Relating to the Early History of Maryland. Sebastian F. Streeter. LC 72-4224. (Select Bibliographies Reprint Ser.). 1977. reprint ed. 23.95 (*0-8369-6893-X*) Ayer.

Papers Relating to the First Dutch War, 1652-1654. 20.00 (*0-318-18643-8*) Welding Res Coun.

Papers Relating to the Spanish War, 1585-1587. Ed. by Julian S. Corbett. 420p. 1987. text 86.95 (*0-566-05565-1*, Pub. by Scolar Pr) Ashgate Pub Co.

Papers Relative to the Marriage of King James the Sixth of Scotland with the Princess Anna of Denmark. James T. Gibson Craig. LC 70-168143. (Bannatyne Club, Edinburgh. Publications: No. 26). reprint ed. 37.50 (*0-404-52732-9*) AMS Pr.

Papers Relative to the Regalia of Scotland. Ed. by William Bell. LC 71-39426. reprint ed. 42.50 (*0-404-52736-1*) AMS Pr.

Papers Relative to the Royal Guard of Scottish Archers in France. Ed. by Alexander Macdonald. LC 79-175588. (Maitland Club, Glasgow. Publications: No. 36). reprint ed. 27.50 (*0-404-53007-9*) AMS Pr.

Papers, 1771 to 1784, 2 vols. George R. Clark. Ed. by James A. James. LC 72-444. reprint ed. 215.00 (*0-404-01556-5*) AMS Pr.

P

An Asterisk (*) at the beginning of an entry indicates that the title is appearing for the first time.

Papers Toward Radical Metaphysics: Alchemy. Charles Ponce. 160p. (Orig.). 1984. pap. 8.95 (*0-938190-02-4*) North Atlantic.

Papers You Can't Afford to Lose see Safe-Deposit Box & Fireproof Safe Organizer Kit: Guide to Protecting Your Valuable Personal Records

Paperspace: Style As Ideology in Joyce's "Ulysses" Patrick McGee. LC 87-19074. 253p. 1988. reprint ed. pap. 78.50 (*0-608-02686-7*, 206333900004) Bks Demand.

Paperthick: Forms & Images in Cast Paper. Charles Hilger & John Vanco. (Illus.). 32p. 1988. 4.95 (*0-9616623-7-9*) Erie Art Mus.

Paperweight. Stephen Frey. pap. 13.95 (*0-7493-1397-8*, Pub. by Random) Trafalgar.

***Paperweight: Historicism, Art Nouveau, Art Deco.** Peter Von Brackel. (Illus.). 320p. 1999. 69.95 (*0-7643-1052-6*) Schiffer.

Paperweights. Sibylle Jangstorf. LC 91-67014. (Illus.). 224p. 1992. text 69.95 (*0-88740-375-1*) Schiffer.

Paperweights: The Collector's Guide to Selecting & Enjoying New & Antique Paperweights. Pat Reilly. 1999. pap. text 12.95 (*1-57715-075-9*) Knckerbocker.

***Paperweights from Great Britain.** John Simmonds. LC 99-57143. (Illus.). 192p. 2000. 39.95 (*0-7643-1074-7*) Schiffer.

Paperweights from the Corning Museum of Glass. 81st ed. 1987. pap. 3.50 (*0-486-25289-2*) Dover.

Paperweights of the Nineteenth & Twentieth Centuries. Paul Jokelson & Gerard Ingold. (Illus.). 144p. 1989. 60.00 (*0-9619547-1-X*) Papier Presse.

Paperweights of the World. 2nd rev. ed. Monika Flemming & Peter Pommerencke. (Illus.). 176p. 1998. 35.00 (*0-7643-0452-6*) Schiffer.

***Paperweights of the World.** 3rd ed. Monika Flemming & Peter Pommerencke. (Illus.). 176p. 2000. 35.00 (*0-7643-1079-8*) Schiffer.

***Paperwhite.** Nancy Elizabeth Wallace. LC 99-89178. (J). 2000. 14.00 (*0-618-04283-0*) HM.

Paperwork: The Potential of Paper in Graphic Design. Nancy Williams. (Illus.). 160p. 1995. pap. 29.95 (*0-7148-3461-0*, Pub. by Phaidon Press) Phaidon Pr.

Paperworks. Ed. by AG Publishers Editors. (Illus.). 224p. 1996. 69.95 (*4-900781-08-8*, Pub. by AG Pubs) Bks Nippan.

Paperwraps: A Collector's Guide to Paperbound Books. Linda F. Laugen. LC 97-92317. (Illus.). xii, 252p. 1999. pap. 17.95 (*0-9669296-0-8*) Shadowbend.

Papes. Adriano Bernareggi. (FRE., Illus.). 95p. 1940. lib. bdg. 8.95 (*0-8288-3998-0*) Fr & Eur.

Papesse Jean: (Pope Joan) Boureau. (Illus.). (C). text. write for info. (*0-472-09668-0*); pap. text. write for info. (*0-472-06668-4*) U of Mich Pr.

PapFor Conference, '92: Hotel Pribaltiskya, St. Petersburg, Russia, 20-23 September 1992. Technical Association of the Pulp & Paper Industry. LC TS1080.. (TAPPI Proceedings Ser.). (ENG & RUS.). 323p. 1992. reprint ed. pap. 100.20 (*0-7837-3747-5*, 200898300010) Bks Demand.

Paphiopedilum Grower's Manual. Lance A. Birk. (Illus.). 208p. 1984. 75.00 (*0-9612826-0-6*) Pisang Pr.

Paphnutius: Histories of the Monks of Upper Egypt & the Life of Onnophrius. Paphnutius Cephalas. Tr. & Intro. by Tim Vivian. LC 92-39032. (Cistercian Studies: No. 140). (COP & ENG.). (Orig.). 1993. 34.95 (*0-87907-440-X*); pap. 16.95 (*0-87907-540-6*) Cistercian Pubns.

Papiamentu Newspaper Reader. 1994. audio 19.00 (*0-931745-90-X*) Dunwoody Pr.

Papiamentu Newspaper Reader. Kate Howe & Roland De Cuba. LC 91-77057. xlvii, 200p. 1994. 46.00 (*0-931745-84-5*) Dunwoody Pr.

Papier de/Papers of Prudent L. Mercure: Histoire du Madawaska. Roger Paradis. 932p. 1998. 50.00 (*1-892079-00-3*) Madawaska Hist.

Papier Mache. (Jump Ser.). (Illus.). 36p. (J). (gr. 2-6). pap. write for info. (*1-882210-35-2*) Action Pub.

***Papier Mache.** Judy Balchin. (Step-by-Step Children's Crafts Ser.). 32p. (J). 2000. pap. 8.95 (*0-85532-912-2*, Pub. by Srch Pr) Midpt Trade.

Papier Mache. Marion Elliot. (The Inspirations Ser.). (Illus.). 96p. 1997. 12.95 (*1-85967-432-1*, Lorenz Bks) Anness Pub.

Papier Mache. Marion Elliot. (New Crafts Ser.). 1998. 15.95 (*1-85967-619-7*, Lorenz Bks) Anness Pub.

Papier-Mache. Marion Elliot. (Crafts for Children Ser.). (Illus.). 32p. (YA). (gr. 3 up). 1997. pap. 4.95 (*1-56010-213-6*, CC03) W Foster Pub.

Papier Mache. Ray Gibson. (How to Make Ser.). (Illus.). 32p. (J). (gr. 3-7). 1995. pap. 6.95 (*0-7460-2073-2*, Usborne); lib. bdg. 14.95 (*0-88110-777-8*, Usborne) EDC.

Papier Mache. Lone Halse. (Illus.). 68p. 1996. 18.95 (*1-870586-09-3*, D Porteous-Parkwest) Parkwest Pubns.

Papier Mache. Deri Robins. LC 92-41102. (Step-by-Step Ser.). (Illus.). 40p. (J). (gr. 3-7). 1993. pap. 7.95 (*1-85697-926-1*, Kingfisher) LKC.

Papier Mache. Deri Robins. LC 92-41102. (Step-by-Step Ser.). (Illus.). 40p. (J). (gr. 3-7). 1995. 13.90 (*1-85697-692-0*, Kingfisher) LKC.

***Papier-Mache.** unabridged ed. Renee F. Schwarz. (Kids Can Do It Ser.). (Illus.). 40p. (J). (gr. 3-7). 2000. pap. 5.95 (*1-55074-727-4*, Pub. by Kids Can Pr) Genl Dist Srvs.

***Papier-Mache.** unabridged ed. Renee F. Schwarz. (Kids Can Do It Ser.). (Illus.). 40p. (YA). (gr. 3-7). 2000. 12.95 (*1-55074-833-5*, Pub. by Kids Can Pr) Genl Dist Srvs.

***Papier-Mache: Fantastic Step-by-Step Creations from Papier-Mache.** Ed. by Lorenz Books Staff. (Illus.). 2000. 11.95 (*0-7548-0100-4*, Lorenz Bks) Anness Pub.

Papier Mache: Projects, Techniques, Pull-Out Designs. Juliet Bawden. (Illus.). 96p. 1998. 27.50 (*1-85029-682-0*, Pub. by Conran Octopus) Trafalgar.

Papier Mache: Projects, Techniques, Pull-Out Designs. Juliet Bawden. (Illus.). 96p. 1998. reprint ed. pap. 19.95 (*1-85029-973-0*) Conran Octopus.

Papier Mache for Kids. Sheila McGraw. (Illus.). 72p. (J). (gr. k-7). 1991. 17.95 (*0-920668-92-5*) Firefly Bks Ltd.

Papier Mache for Kids. Sheila McGraw. (Illus.). 72p. (J). (gr. 5-7). 1991. pap. 9.95 (*0-920668-93-3*) Firefly Bks Ltd.

Papier Mache Style: 100 Step-by-Step Designs for Bowls, Jewelry, Toys, Vases, Mirrors & Other Creations. Alec MacCormick. (Illus.). 128p. 1995. pap. 15.95 (*0-8019-8755-5*) Krause Pubns.

Papier-Mache Today. Sheila McGraw. (Illus.). 144p. (Orig.). 1990. pap. 19.95 (*0-920668-85-2*) Firefly Bks Ltd.

Papier Tue-Mouches. 3rd ed. Dashiell Hammett. (FRE.). 192p. 1987. pap. 195.00 (*0-7859-7541-1*, 2070378519) Fr & Eur.

Papiers des Assemblees de la Revolution aux Archives Nationales. Inventaire de la Serie C: Constituante, Legislative, Convention. A. Tuetey. (Societe de l'Histoire de la Revolution Francaise. Publications). 1990. reprint ed. 49.00 (*0-8115-0030-6*) Periodicals Srv.

Papiers D'Etat, 3 vols. Jean B. Teulet. LC 70-176146. (Bannatyne Club, Edinburgh. Publications: No. 107). reprint ed. 210.00 (*0-404-52870-8*) AMS Pr.

Papiers du Pickwick: Oliver Twist. Charles Dickens. (Pleiade Ser.). (FRE.). 1958. 99.50 (*0-8288-3430-X*, F79856) Fr & Eur.

Papiervogel see Paper Bird

Papilionatae, Caesalpinoideae, Mimosoideae. Tr. by Israel Program for Scientific Translations Staff from RUS. (Flora of the U. S. S. R. (Flora SSSR) Ser.: Vol. 11). (Illus.). xvii, 327p. 1985. reprint ed. 160.00 (*3-87429-231-2*, 018732, Pub. by Koeltz Sci Bks) Lubrecht & Cramer.

Papilionidae, Fasc. 95. J. B. Heppner. (Atlas of North American Lepidoptera Ser.). Date not set. pap. 18.95 (*0-945417-01-2*) Sci Pubs.

Papilionum Britanniae Icones. James Petiver. 1984. 95.00 (*0-7855-0668-3*) St Mut.

Papilloma Viruses & Human Cancer. Ed. by Herbert Pfister. 272p. 1990. lib. bdg. 229.00 (*0-8493-5860-4*, RC268) CRC Pr.

***Papillomavirus Infections in Human Pathology.** Kari J. Syrjanen. LC RC168.P15S97 1999. 630p. 2000. 360.00 (*0-471-97168-5*) Wiley.

Papillomaviruses. CIBA Foundation Staff. (CIBA Foundation Symposium Ser.: No. 120). 268p. 1986. 128.00 (*0-471-99837-0*) Wiley.

Papillomaviruses. Ed. by L. Gissmann. (Journal Ser.: Vol. 37, No. 3-4, 1994). (Illus.). 96p. 1994. pap. 78.25 (*3-8055-6096-6*) S Karger.

Papillomaviruses. Ed. by Bettie Steinberg et al. (Cancer Cells Ser.: No. 5). (Illus.). 480p. (Orig.). 1987. pap. text 80.00 (*0-87969-301-0*) Cold Spring Harbor.

Papillon. 20p. 1995. pap. 9.95 (*0-7935-5746-1*) H Leonard.

Papillon. Henri Charriere. 1994. pap. 12.95 (*84-01-49084-7*) Plaza.

***Papillon: An Owner's Guide to a Happy Healthy Pet.** Deborah Wood. (Illus.). 160p. 2000. 12.99 (*0-7645-6086-7*) IDG Bks.

Papillon: D Level. Henri Charriere. text 8.95 (*0-88436-997-8*) EMC-Paradigm.

Papillons: AKC Rank No. 51. D. Christian Gauss. (Illus.). 1997. pap. 9.95 (*0-7938-2320-X*, KW-175S) TFH Pubns.

Papillote Fish, Secrets of Papillote Cooking Vol. 5: No Mess Gourmet Cooking en Papillote. Gil Pique & Chantal Pique. (Illus.). 112p. 1994. text. write for info. (*0-9633688-5-0*) Papillote.

Papillote Meat, Secret of Papillote Cooking Vol. 2: No Mess Gourmet Cooking en Papillote. Gil Pique & Chantal Pique. (Illus.). 112p. 1994. text. write for info. (*0-9633688-4-2*) Papillote.

Papillote Poultry, Secret of Papillote Cooking Vol. 3: No Mess Gourmet Cooking en Papillote. Gil Pique & Chantal Pique. (Illus.). 112p. 1994. text. write for info. (*0-9633688-3-4*) Papillote.

Papillote Vegetable, Secret of Papillote Cooking Vol. 4: No Mess Gourmet Cooking en Papillote. Gil Pique & Chantal Pique. (Illus.). 112p. 1994. text. write for info. (*0-9633688-2-6*) Papillote.

Papillotes: Secret of Papillote Cooking. Gil Pique & Chantal Pique. (Illus.). 120p. 1993. reprint ed. pap. 15.00 (*0-9633688-1-8*) Papillote.

***Papiny Rqsskazy.** Ivan Klimin.Tr. of Father's Stories. (RUS., Illus.). 18p. 1999. text. write for info. (*0-9673753-2-0*) Gelany.

Papiros de Babel. Pedro L. Adorno. 526p. 1991. 23.85 (*0-8477-3237-1*) U of PR Pr.

Papists, Protestants & Puritans, 1559 - 1714. Diana Newton. LC 99-174433. (Perspectives in History Ser.). 96p. 1999. pap. 11.95 (*0-521-59845-1*) Cambridge U Pr.

Papita. Vita Sackville-West. 24.95 (*0-8488-1150-X*) Amereon Ltd.

***Papon Affair: Memory & Justice on Trial.** Ed. by Richard J. Golsan. LC 99-88535. 288p. 2000. 80.00 (*0-415-92364-6*) Routledge.

***Papon Affair: Memory & Justice on Trial.** Richard J. Golsan. LC 99-88535. 288p. 2000. pap. 24.99 (*0-415-92365-4*) Routledge.

Papovaviridae: The Polyomaviruses, Vol. 1. N. P. Salzman. LC 85-15160. (Viruses Ser.). (Illus.). 474p. (C). 1986. text 120.00 (*0-306-42308-1*, Kluwer Plenum) Kluwer Academic.

Papovaviridae Vol. 2: The Papillomaviruses. N. P. Salzman. LC 86-15160. (Viruses Ser.). (Illus.). 408p. (C). 1987. text 120.00 (*0-306-42452-5*, Kluwer Plenum) Kluwer Academic.

Papp. Kenneth Cameron. 1969. pap. 5.25 (*0-8222-0872-5*) Dramatists Play.

Pappa & Me. Barbara M. Wolff. (Illus.). 16p. (J). (ps-1). 1991. lib. bdg. 13.95 (*1-879567-11-3*, Valeria Bks) Wonder Well.

***Pappagallo Lined.** (Handstitched Tuscany Florals Ser.). 128p. 2000. 15.95 (*1-55156-154-9*) Paperblank.

Pappus of Alexandria: Book 7 of the Collection, 2 pts. Ed. by A. Jones. (Sources in the History of Mathematics & Physical Sciences Ser.: Vol. 8). (Illus.). 1985. 189.00 (*0-387-96257-3*) Spr-Verlag.

***Pappus of Alexandria & the Mathematics of Late Antiquity.** Serafina Cuomo. (Cambridge Classical Studies). (Illus.). 244p. (C). 2000. text 59.95 (*0-521-64211-6*) Cambridge U Pr.

Pappy: The Gentle Bear: A Coach Who Changed Football... And the Men Who Played It. Steve Cameron. LC 99-51514. (Illus.). 256p. 1999. 24.95 (*1-886110-80-8*, Pub. by Addax Pubng) Midpt Trade.

Pappy: The Life of John Ford. Dan Ford. LC 98-4344. (Illus.). 368p. 1998. reprint ed. pap. 15.95 (*0-306-80875-7*) Da Capo.

Paprika: In English. A. Somos. 302p. (C). 1984. 120.00 (*963-05-3299-9*, Pub. by Akade Kiado) St Mut.

***Paprika - Versions of Wisdom.** R. Lee Walker. 118p. (Orig.). 1999. pap. 13.00 (*1-881524-58-2*) Milligan Bks.

Paprus de Turin. E. Pleyte & F. Rossi. 253p. reprint ed. write for info. (*0-318-71390-X*) G Olms Pubs.

Pap's Place: A Two-Act Play about Family & Change. Paul McCusker. 1993. 8.99 (*0-685-72852-8*, MP-688); pap. 8.99 (*0-8341-9855-X*); pap. text 8.99 (*0-00-543972-8*) Lillenas.

Papst Paul III Als Alexander der Grosse: Das Freskenprogramm der Sala Paolina in der Engelsburg. Richard Harprath. (Beitraege zur Kunstgeschichte Ser.: No. 13). (C). 1978. 169.25 (*3-11-007020-0*) De Gruyter.

Papstlichen Legaten in England Bis Zur Beendigung der Legation Gualas, 1218. Helene Tillman. LC 80-2208. 1981. reprint ed. 29.50 (*0-404-18795-1*) AMS Pr.

Papua: The United States Army Campaigns of World War 2. Charles Anderson. 22p. 1992. pap. 1.00 (*0-16-035883-3*) USGPO.

Papua New Guinea see Enchantment of the World Series

Papua New Guinea see Cultures of the World - Group 16

***Papua New Guinea: A Country Study Guide.** Global Investment & Business Center, Inc. Staff. (World Country Study Guides Library: Vol. 133). (Illus.). 350p. 2000. pap. 59.00 (*0-7397-2431-2*) Intl Business Pubns.

Papua New Guinea: Struggle for Development. John Connell. LC 98-107783. (Routledge Studies in the Growth Economies of Asia Ser.). 368p. (C). 1997. 74.95 (*0-415-05401-X*) Routledge.

Papua New Guinea: Where She Invented Bow & Arrow. Nelleke Nix. (Illus.). 116p. 1996. 260.00 (*1-881067-06-8*); lib. bdg. 200.00 (*1-881067-07-6*) N Nelleke Studio.

Papua New Guinea - A Country Study Guide: Basic Information for Research & Pleasure. Global Investment Center, USA Staff. (World Country Study Guide Library: Vol. 133). (Illus.). 350p. 1999. pap. 59.00 (*0-7397-1530-5*) Intl Business Pubns.

***Papua New Guinea Business Intelligence Report, 190 vols.** Global Investment & Business Center, Inc. Staff. (World Business Intelligence Library: Vol. 133). (Illus.). 350p. 2000. pap. 99.95 (*0-7397-2631-5*) Intl Business Pubns.

***Papua New Guinea Business Law Handbook.** Global Investment & Business Center, Inc. Staff. (Global Business Law Handbooks Library: Vol. 133). (Illus.). 2000. pap. 99.95 (*0-7397-2031-7*) Intl Business Pubns.

***Papua New Guinea Business Opportunity Yearbook.** Global Investment & Business Center, Inc. Staff. (Global Business Opportunity Yearbooks Library: Vol. 133). (Illus.). 2000. pap. 99.95 (*0-7397-2231-X*) Intl Business Pubns.

***Papua New Guinea Business Opportunity Yearbook: Export-Import, Investment & Business Opportunities.** International Business Publications, U. S. A. Staff & Global Investment Center, U. S. A. Staff. (Global Business Opportunity Yearbooks Library: Vol. 133). (Illus.). 350p. 1999. pap. 99.95 (*0-7397-1331-0*) Intl Business Pubns.

***Papua New Guinea Country Review 2000.** Robert C. Kelly et al. (Illus.). 60p. 1999. pap. 39.95 (*1-58310-557-3*) CountryWatch.

***Papua New Guinea Foreign Policy & Government Guide.** Contrib. by Global Investment & Business Center, Inc. Staff. (World Foreign Policy & Government Library: Vol. 127). (Illus.). 350p. 1999. pap. 99.00 (*0-7397-3625-6*) Intl Business Pubns.

***Papua New Guinea Foreign Policy & Government Guide.** Global Investment & Business Center, Inc. Staff. (World Foreign Policy & Government Library: Vol. 127). (Illus.). 350p. 2000. 99.95 (*0-7397-3831-3*) Intl Business Pubns.

***Papua New Guinea Investment & Business Guide.** Global Investment & Business Center, Inc. Staff. (Global Investment & Business Guide Library: Vol. 133). (Illus.). 2000. pap. 99.95 (*0-7397-1831-2*) Intl Business Pubns.

***Papua New Guinea Investment & Business Guide: Export-Import, Investment & Business Opportunities.** International Business Publications, USA Staff & Global Investment Center, USA Staff. (World Investment & Business Guide Library-99: Vol. 133). (Illus.). 350p. 1999. pap. 99.95 (*0-7397-0328-5*) Intl Business Pubns.

Papua New Guinea (Pidgin) Phrasebook. John Hunter. (PAA.). 96p. 1986. pap. 2.95 (*0-908086-90-3*) Lonely Planet.

Papua New Guinea Sojourn: More Pleasures in Exile. E. A. Markham. LC 98-217141. 220p. 1998. 34.95 (*1-85754-328-9*, Pub. by Carcanet Pr) Paul & Co Pubs.

Papuan Borderlands: Huli, Duna, & Ipili Perspectives on the Papua New Guinea Highlands. Ed. by Aletta Biersack. LC 95-30130. 456p. 1995. text 65.00 (*0-472-10601-5*, 10601) U of Mich Pr.

Papuan Campaign: The Buna-Sanananda Operation: 16 Nov. 1942-23 Jan. 1943. (Illus.). 107p. 1997. reprint ed. pap. text 30.00 (*0-7881-3787-5*) DIANE Pub.

Papuan Campaign: The Buna-Sanananda Operation, 16 Nov. 1942-23 Jan. 1943. (Armed Forces in Action Ser.). (Illus.). 117p. 1990. reprint ed. per. 6.00 (*0-16-019217-X*, 008-029-00205-1) USGPO.

Papuan Campaign: The Buna-Sanananda Operation, 16 November 1942-2 January 1943. (Combat Arms Ser.: No. 20). (Illus.). 136p. 1989. reprint ed. 24.95 (*0-89839-138-5*) Battery Pr.

Papuan Epic. Keith Bushell. LC 75-35276. reprint ed. 32.50 (*0-404-14106-4*) AMS Pr.

Papuan Fairy Tales. Annie Ker. LC 78-67729. (Folktale Ser.). (Illus.). reprint ed. 28.00 (*0-404-16136-7*) AMS Pr.

Papyri, 3 vols. Incl. Vol. 1. Non-Literacy Papyri: Private Documents. Oppian. Tr. by A. S. Hunt. (ENG & GRE.). 14.50 (*0-674-99294-6*); Vol. 2. Non-Literary Papyri: Public Documents. A. S. Hunt & C. C. Edgar. (ENG & GRE.). 14.50 (*0-674-99312-8*); Vol. 3. Literary Papyri: Poetry. Papyri. (ENG & GRE.). 14.50 (*0-674-99397-7*); (Loeb Classical Library: Nos. 266, 282, 360). (ENG & GRE.). write for info. (*0-318-53132-1*) HUP.

Papyri aus Oberaegypten see Urkunden der Ptolemaeerzeit (Aeltere Funde)

Papyri aus Unteraegypten see Urkunden der Ptolemaeerzeit (Aeltere Funde)

Papyri Bodleianae I. R. P. Salomons. LC 97-134119. (Studia Amstelodamensia ad Epigraphicam, Ius Antiquum et Papyrologticam Pertinentia: Vol. XXXIV). (DUT & ENG., Illus.). 495p. 1996. lib. bdg. 227.00 (*90-5063-035-9*, Pub. by Gieben) J Benjamins Pubng Co.

Papyri, Ostraca, Parchments & Waxed Tablets in the Leiden Papyrological Institute. F. A. Hoogendijk & P. Van Minnen. LC 91-10686. (Papyrological Lugduno-Batava Ser.: No. 25). (Illus.). xii, 315p. 1991. 176.00 (*90-04-09339-7*) Brill Academic Pubs.

Papyrological Studies in Dionysiac Literature. Dana F. Sutton. LC 87-72088. (ENG & GRE.). 124p. 1987. pap. 15.00 (*0-86516-198-4*); text 30.00 (*0-86516-197-6*) Bolchazy-Carducci.

Papyros Ebers: Das Aelteste Buch Ueber Heilkunde. Tr. by H. Joachim from EGY. xx, 215p. (C). 1973. reprint ed. 106.95 (*3-11-004564-8*) De Gruyter.

Papyrus. Richard Parkinson & Stephen Quirke. (Egyptian Bookshelf Ser.). (Illus.). 100p. (Orig.). 1995. pap. 19.95 (*0-292-76563-0*) U of Tex Pr.

Papyrus Ani. fac. ed. Comment by E. Dondelinger. (Codices Selecti D Ser.: Vol. LXII). (GER., Illus.). 84p. 1978. 617.00 (*3-201-01048-0*, Pub. by Akademische Druck-und) Balogh.

Papyrus Companion Vol. 1: The Black Writer's Phrase Book. unabridged ed. Ginger Whitaker & Edwina Walker. 57p. (Orig.). 1995. pap. 8.95 (*1-886911-02-9*) Papyrus Literary.

Papyrus Eber: The First Medical Book in the World. Al I. Obaba. (Illus.). 167p. 1927. pap. text 22.00 (*0-916157-17-2*) African Islam Miss Pubns.

Papyrus Fragments of Sophocles: An Edition with Prolegomena & Commentary. Sophocles & Richard Carden. (Texte und Kommentare Ser.: Vol. 7). 261p. (C). 1974. 215.40 (*3-11-003833-1*) De Gruyter.

Papyrus, Tapa, Amate & Rice Paper: Papermaking in Africa, the Pacific, Latin America & Southeast Asia. 4th rev. ed. Lilian A. Bell. (Illus.). 146p. (C). 1992. pap. 24.00 (*0-9625076-4-4*) Liliaceae Pr.

Paqet GCA Standard 128-1995: Paper Quality EDI Transaction. Ed. by Alan Kotok et al. 48p. (Orig.). 1995. pap. 65.00 (*0-933505-33-7*) Graph Comm Assn.

Paquicefalosaurio (Pachycephalosaurus) Janet Riehecky. (Libros Sobre Dinosaurios! Ser.). (SPA., Illus.). 32p. (J). (gr. k-4). 1994. lib. bdg. 21.36 (*1-56766-129-7*) Childs World.

Par Avion. Jean-Jacques Sempe. (FRE.). 1992. pap. 12.95 (*0-7859-2931-2*) Fr & Eur.

Par Ce Demi-Clair Matin. Charles Peguy. pap. 5.95 (*0-685-37033-X*) Fr & Eur.

Par Choix: The Remarkable Life Story of Philippe. Thomas B. Murray. LC 93-24253. 192p. (Orig.). 1994. pap. 10.95 (*1-56474-069-2*) Fithian Pr.

***Par-Dela les Mensonges.** Susan Fox. 1999. mass mkt. 3.99 (*0-373-39535-3*) Silhouette.

***Par Excellence: A Celebration of Virginia Golf.** Jim Ducibella. (Illus.). 256p. 2000. 29.95 (*1-58261-103-3*) Sports Pub.

Par for the Course. John Runne. 1995. 13.95 (*0-87197-433-9*) Favorite Recipes.

***Par Four: A Jake Hines Mystery.** Elizabeth Gunn. 304p. 2000. mass mkt. 5.99 (*0-440-22636-8*) Dell.

Par Four: A Jake Hines Mystery. Elizabeth Gunn. (Jake Hines Mystery Ser.). 300p. 1999. pap. 22.95 (*0-8027-3324-7*) Walker & Co.

Par Hasard, Par Bonheur. B. J. James. (FRE.). 1998. mass mkt. 3.50 (*0-373-37477-1*, 1-37477-6) Harlequin Bks.

Par Ici: Echanges Intermediaires. Robert Ariew & Anne Nerenz. (FRE.). 448p. (C). 1993. pap. text 36.36 (*0-669-24885-1*); pap. text 34.36 (*0-669-24887-8*); pap. text, teacher ed. 2.66 (*0-669-24889-4*) HM Trade Div.

Par Ici: Echanges Intermediaires. annot. ed. Robert Ariew. (FRE.). (C). 1993. text, teacher ed. 51.16 incl. audio (*0-669-35189-X*) HM Trade Div.

Par Ici: Echanges Intermediaires. annot. ed. Robert Ariew & Anne Nerenz. (FRE.). 448p. (C). 1993. teacher ed. 39.56 incl. audio (*0-669-32597-X*) HM Trade Div.

An Asterisk (*) at the beginning of an entry indicates that the title is appearing for the first time.

Par Ici: Exchanges Intermediaires. Robert Ariew & Anne Nerenz. (FRE.). (C). 1993. 448p. audio 31.16 (*0-669-24890-8*); audio 7.16 (*0-669-32595-3*) HM Trade Div.

Par Ici: Lectures et Videos. Robert Ariew & Anne Nerenz. (FRE.). 224p. (C). 1995. pap. text 38.36 (*0-669-24888-6*) HM Trade Div.

Par Lagerkvist. Leif Sjoberg. LC 76-9052. (Columbia Essays on Modern Writers Ser.: No. 74). 1976. pap. text 12.00 (*0-231-03103-3*) Col U Pr.

Par Lagerkvist: A Critical Essay. Winston Weathers. LC 67-19326. (Contemporary Writers in Christian Perspective Ser.). 47p. reprint ed. pap. 30.00 (*0-608-30782-3*, 201291800083) Bks Demand.

Par les Champs et par les Greves. Gustave Flaubert. (Illus.). 1137.50 (*0-685-34906-3*) Fr & Eur.

Par les Yeux de Marcel Proust. Marcel Proust. Ed. by Muhlstein. (FRE.). 16.50 (*0-685-37070-4*) Fr & Eur.

Par Raison de Nombres: L'Art du Calcul et les Savoirs Scientifiques Medievaux. Guy Beaujouan. (Collected Studies: No. CS 344). 336p. 1991. text 119.95 (*0-86078-281-6*, Pub. by Variorum) Ashgate Pub Co.

Par 3 & Executive Course Directory. Ed. by National Golf Foundation Staff. 168p. 1999. pap. 99.00 (*1-57701-082-5*, 99GR115) Natl Golf.

***Par Trek: The Official Gold Calendar for the Year 2000.** Wall. (Illus.). 1999. 0.00 (*1-891715-22-4*) Pulse.

Para a Frente! An Intermediate Course in Portuguese. 2nd large type rev. ed. Larry D. King & Margarita Suner. (POR., Illus.). 326p. (C). 1991. pap. 37.95 (*0-942566-00-9*) LinguaText.

Para Alem Do Planejamonto Estrategico: Como Envolver Conselhos Diretores de Organizacoes Sem Fins Lucrativos em Acoes de Crescimento e Mudanca. Douglas C. Eadie.Tr. of Beyond Strategic Planning. (POR.). 23p. (Orig.). 1996. pap. write for info. (*0-925299-65-0*) Natl Ctr Nonprofit.

Para Alguien Especial. (Serie Pensamientos de Vida - Thoughts of Life Ser.: Vol. 2).Tr. of For Someone Special. (SPA.). 24p. 1985. pap. write for info. (*0-614-27100-2*) Editorial Unilit.

Para Atrapar un Foton. L. Virgilio Beltran. (Ciencia para Todos Ser.). (SPA.). pap. 6.99 (*968-16-3579-5*, Pub. by Fondo) Continental Bk.

Para Emergency Care Exam Review. 2nd ed. Cherry. LC 97-145945. 1997. pap. text 35.00 (*0-8359-5103-0*) P-H.

Para Empezar: Interacciones. David McAlpine et al. (C). 1995. pap., wbk. ed., lab manual ed. 32.19 (*0-07-044980-5*) McGraw.

Para Empezar: Interacciones & Exploracions. David McAlpine & Leon Book. 1995. pap. text, suppl. ed. write for info. (*0-07-044983-X*) McGraw.

Para empezar: Interacciones & Exploracions. David McAlpine & Leon Book. (C). 1995. student ed. 21.00 incl. audio (*0-07-911088-6*) McGraw.

Para Empezar: Interacciones & Exploracions. David McAlpine et al. (C). 1995. pap. text, teacher ed. 42.81 (*0-07-044979-1*) McGraw.

Para Empezar: Interacciones & Exploracions. David McAlpine et al. 1995. write for info. incl. audio (*0-07-911087-8*) McGraw.

Para Empezar - Interacciones: Beginning Spanish. David McAlpine et al. 432p. (C). 1995. 56.25 (*0-07-044978-3*) McGraw.

Para Estar Siempre Bien. Amy Thomas Harris. 1997. pap. text 10.98 (*968-419-553-2*) Grijalbo Edit.

Para Excitarlas, 39 Fantasias Sexuales. Aphrodite. 1997. pap. text 11.98 (*968-419-067-0*) Grijalbo Edit.

***Para Ganarle a Esos... !** Susan F. Tierno. Tr. by Ana M. Alvarado. (Think-Kids Book Collection).Tr. of That's a Though Team to Beat!. (SPA., Illus.). 16p. (J). (gr. 1-4). 2000. pap. 2.95 (*1-58237-055-9*) Creat Think.

Para Handy. Neil Munro. (Illus.). 432p. pap. 15.95 (*1-874744-02-5*, Pub. by Birlinn Ltd) Dufour.

Para la Esposa del Pastor, Con Amor. Orig. Title: For the Pastor's Wife, with Love. (SPA.). 128p. 1990. pap. 8.99 (*0-311-42082-6*) Casa Bautista.

Para la Salud: Health & the Hispanic Kitchen. Lilly B. Gardner. Ed. by Georgette J. Sodel. Tr. by Myrna Perkins. (ENG & SPA., Illus.). 268p. 1997. 25.00 (*0-9659500-0-X*) Precepts.

***Para la Vida: Kawsanapak.** FOIN Staff & FOISE Staff. (SPA.). 224p. 1999. write for info. (*92-806-3539-5*) U N I C E.

Para Leer al Pato Donald see How to Read Donald Duck: Imperialist Ideology in the Disney Comic

Para Llenar de Dias el Dia. Felix Cordova-Iturregui. LC 85-80201. (Flor del Agua Ser.). (SPA.). 56p. 1985. pap. 6.95 (*0-940238-80-2*) Ediciones Huracan.

Para Mama. (Serie Pensamientos de Vida - Thoughts of Life Ser.: Vol. 2).Tr. of For My Mother. (SPA.). 24p. 1985. pap. write for info. (*0-614-27097-9*) Editorial Unilit.

Para Matrimonios . . . Con Amor. David Hormachea.Tr. of To Marriage Couples...with Love. (SPA.). 225p. 1995. pap. write for info. (*0-614-27099-5*) Editorial Unilit.

Para Matrimonios con Amor. D. Hormachea.Tr. of To Married Couples with Love. 5.99 (*1-56063-563-0*, 498590) Editorial Unilit.

Para Matrimonios... Con Amor (To Married Couples... With Love) David Hormachea. (SPA.). 225p. 1995. write for info. (*0-614-24386-6*) Editorial Unilit.

Para Mi Amigo. Compiled by Nick Beilenson. (Petites Ser.).Tr. of For My Friend. (SPA., Illus.). 80p. 1998. text 4.95 (*0-88088-231-X*) Peter Pauper.

Para Mi Esposa. (Serie Pensamientos de Vida - Thoughts of Life Ser.: Vol. 2).Tr. of For My Wife. (SPA.). 24p. 1985. pap. write for info. (*0-614-27098-7*) Editorial Unilit.

Para Mi Esposo. (Serie Pensamientos de Vida - Thoughts of Life Ser.: Vol. 2).Tr. of For My Husband. (SPA.). 24p. 1985. pap. write for info. (*0-614-27102-9*) Editorial Unilit.

Para Mi Gaveta. Berta Montalvo. LC 88-84022. (Coleccion Espejo de Paciencia). (SPA.). 139p. (Orig.). 1990. pap. 12.00 (*0-89729-523-4*) Ediciones.

Para Mi Hijo. Ana L. Jaramillo. (SPA.). 90p. 1997. pap. 9.95 (*0-89729-822-5*) Ediciones.

Para Mi Maestro. Compiled by Suzanne S. Zenkel.Tr. of For My Teacher. (SPA., Illus.). 80p. 1998. text 4.95 (*0-88088-230-1*) Peter Pauper.

Para Mi Mejor Amiga. Kim Anderson. 1997. 7.95 (*987-9201-04-3*) Great Quotations.

Para Papa. (Serie Pensamientos de Vida - Thoughts of Life Ser.: Vol. 2).Tr. of For My Father. (SPA.). 24p. 1985. pap. write for info. (*0-614-27101-0*) Editorial Unilit.

Para-Professional Careers in Mental Hygiene. Jack Rudman. (Career Examination Ser.: C-3055). 1994. pap. 23.95 (*0-8373-3055-6*) Nat Learn.

Para Que el Amor No Se Apague. Gary Smalley.Tr. of Making Love Last Forever. (SPA.). 320p. 1996. 10.99 (*0-88113-416-3*, B008-4163) Caribe Betania.

Para Que el Mundo Sepa, No. 2. Raynard Vander Laan.Tr. of That the World May Know. (SPA.). 1996. pap., student ed. write for info. incl. VHS (*0-8297-2612-8*) Vida Pubs.

Para Que el Mundo Sepa, Vol. 10. Ray Van der Laan. (SPA.). 1998. pap. text 4.99 (*0-8297-2620-9*) Vida Pubs.

Para Que No Me Olvides. Marcela Serrano. 1997. pap. 19.95 (*968-19-0408-7*) Santillana.

Para Que Se Usa una Linea? see Homeplay: La Alegria de Aprender Entre Ninos y Adultos, Series I

Para Que Sirven los Sentidos?/How Do Your Senses Work? How Do Your Senses Work? Ed. by Alastair Smith. (Flip Flaps Ser.). (Illus.). 16p. (J). (ps up). 1999. 9.95 (*0-7460-3425-3*, Usborne) EDC.

Para Que Valga la Pena Escuchard (Your Words Can Make a Difference) Carole Mayhall. (Serie Realidades - Realities Ser.). (SPA.). 75p. 1994. write for info. (*1-56063-281-X*) Editorial Unilit.

Para que Vuestro Gozo Sea Colmado. Christophers. Tr. by Jose Casamada. (SPA.). 158p. 1986. pap. 4.00 (*0-317-46550-3*) Chrstphrs NY.

Para Siempre. Bob Reese. Tr. by Gloria Schaffer-Melendez. (Libro de Diaz Palabras Ser.). (SPA., Illus.). (J). (gr. k-3). 1994. pap. 3.95 (*0-89868-260-6*, Read Res); lib. bdg. 9.95 (*0-89868-259-2*, Read Res) ARO Pub.

Para Siempre Amor Mio. Eduardo Ferrer. (SPA.). 288p. 1995. 20.00 (*0-9648840-0-3*) E B Ferrer.

Para Ti: Un Regalo de Amor. (Serie Libros Nueva Vida - New Life Bks.).Tr. of For You: Gift of Love. (SPA.). 12p. 1986. pap. 1.00 (*0-8423-6460-9*, 490263) Editorial Unilit.

Para Todos Exemplos Morales, Humanos y Divinos. Juan Perez De Montalban. 592p. reprint ed. write for info. (*0-318-71628-3*) G Olms Pubs.

Para un Modelo de Historia del Teatro. Juan Villegas. LC 97-92979. (Ediciones de Gestos Ser.: Vol. 1). (SPA.). 236p. (Orig.). (C). 1997. pap. 22.50 (*0-9656914-0-3*) Gestos-Actas.

Para una Amiga Sincera. 1999. pap. text 3.95 (*968-406-749-6*) F Planeta.

Para una Lectura Americana del Barroco Mexicano: Sor Juana y Siguenza y Gongora. Rafael Catala. (SPA.). 200p. (Orig.). 1987. pap. text 8.95 (*0-910235-07-4*) Prisma Bks.

***Para una Vida Feliz.** J. Jordan. (SPA.). 48p. 1999. write for info. (*92-806-3536-0*) U N I C E.

Para Ver de Otra Manera: Desarrollo Personal y Servicio a los Demas a Traves de la Curacion de Actitudes. Susan S. Trout. Tr. by Carlos Rocha & Elsa St. John. LC 96-90761.Tr. of To See Differently: Personal Growth & Being of Service Through Attitudinal Healing. (SPA.). 280p. 1997. pap. 12.95 (*0-9625386-1-2*) Three Roses Pr.

Para Vivir en Paz. M. Rojas.Tr. of To Live in Peace. (SPA.). 52p. 22.29 (*0-7899-0222-2*, 496255) Editorial Unilit.

Para Worlds: Entanglements of Art & History. Donald Pearce. LC 88-43434. 304p. 1990. lib. bdg. 35.00 (*0-271-00667-6*) Pa St U Pr.

Parabellum: A Technical History of Swiss Lugers. Vittorio Bobba. (Illus.). 224p. 1996. 100.00 (*88-8068-052-8*) Safari Pr.

Parable about the Ancient Wisdom of Silence & Simplicity. Tori. (Grow in Light Ser.: Vol. 1). 128p. 1997. pap. 10.99 (*0-9661235-0-6*) Fiore.

***Parable & Prophecy: Unlocking the Bible's Mysteries.** Bill Donahue. (Bible 101 Ser.). 64p. 2000. pap. 4.99 (*0-8308-2066-3*) InterVarsity.

Parable & Story in Judaism & Christianity. Ed. by Clemens Thoma & Michael Wyschogrod. 1989. pap. 9.95 (*0-8091-3087-4*) Paulist Pr.

Parable of Fire. James Reiss. LC 94-68938. (Poetry Ser.). 58p. (C). 1996. 20.95 (*0-88748-238-4*); pap. 11.95 (*0-88748-239-2*) Carnegie-Mellon.

Parable of Hell. Philip J. King. (Heritage Ser.). 1995. pap. 1.59 (*0-87509-598-4*) Chr Pubns.

Parable of Joy. Michael Card. (Illus.). 288p. 1995. 19.99 (*0-7852-8229-7*, J Thoma Bks) Nelson.

Parable of Pa Diggle's Son. Bruce Porter. (Illus.). 40p. (Orig.). (J). (gr. 3 up). 1987. pap. 3.95 (*0-939925-11-7*) R C Law & Co.

Parable of Ten Preachers. Thomas H. Troeger. 144p. (Orig.). 1992. pap. 12.95 (*0-687-30030-4*) Abingdon.

Parable of the Blind. Gert Hofmann. Tr. by Christopher Middleton from GER. LC 85-24600.Tr. of Der/Blindensturz. 152p. 1989. pap. 7.95 (*0-88064-113-4*) Fromm Intl Pub.

Parable of the Bridesmaids. Helen Caswell. (Illus.). 24p. (J). (ps-3). 1992. 11.95 (*0-687-30022-3*) Abingdon.

Parable of the Cardinals & the Glass Wall. Vander Warner, Jr. LC 90-80646. (Illus.). 50p. (Orig.). 1990. 14.95 (*0-9625900-0-2*); pap. 5.95 (*0-9625900-1-0*) Grove Ave Baptist Ch.

Parable of the Dancing God. C. Baxter Kruger. (Illus.). 26p. 1995. pap. text. write for info. (*0-9645465-0-7*) Perichoresis.

Parable of the Lily. Liz C. Higgs. LC 96-44222. (Illus.). 32p. (J). (ps-2). 1997. 7.99 (*0-7852-7231-3*) Tommy Nelson.

Parable of the Lily, 1. Liz Curtis Higgs. 1999. write for info. (*0-8499-5891-1*) Tommy Nelson.

Parable of the Lost Coin. Helen Caswell. LC 92-33875. (Growing in Faith Library). (Illus.). 24p. (J). (gr. 1-3). 1993. pap. 5.95 (*0-687-30026-6*) Abingdon.

Parable of the Lost Sheep. Helen Caswell. LC 92-33876. (Growing in Faith Library). (Illus.). 24p. (Orig.). 1993. pap. 5.95 (*0-687-30027-4*) Abingdon.

Parable of the Sower. Octavia E. Butler. LC 93-8703. 352p. 1993. 19.95 (*1-888363-25-8*) Seven Stories.

Parable of the Sower. Helen Caswell. LC 90-23200. (J). (ps-3). 1991. 11.95 (*0-687-30020-7*) Abingdon.

Parable of the Sower. Octavia E. Butler. LC 99-46567. 336p. 2000. reprint ed. mass mkt. 13.95 (*0-446-67550-4*, Pub. by Warner Bks) Little.

Parable of the Sower. Octavia E. Butler & Cctavia E. Butler. 304p. 1995. reprint ed. mass mkt. 6.50 (*0-446-60197-7*, Pub. by Warner Bks) Little.

Parable of the Talents. Octavia E. Butler. LC 98-35863. 365p. 1998. 24.95 (*1-888363-81-9*) Seven Stories.

***Parable of the Talents.** Octavia E. Butler. LC 99-46566. 384p. 2000. mass mkt. 13.95 (*0-446-67578-4*, Pub. by Warner Bks) Little.

Parable of the Ten Virgins: Volume 2 of the Works, No. 2. Thomas Shepard. (Works of Thomas Shepard Ser.: Vol. 2). 635p. 1990. reprint ed. 35.00 (*1-877611-16-6*) Soli Deo Gloria.

Parable of the Tribes: The Problem of Power in Social Evolution. 2nd ed. Andrew B. Schmookler. LC 94-21492. 413p. (C). 1994. pap. text 24.95 (*0-7914-2420-0*) State U NY Pr.

Parable of the Vineyard. Helen Caswell. LC 90-23228. (J). (ps-3). 1991. 11.95 (*0-687-30021-5*) Abingdon.

Parable of the Wicked Tenants: An Inquiry into Parable Interpretation. Klyne Snodgrass. 150p. 1983. pap. 62.50 (*3-16-144610-0*, Pub. by JCB Mohr) Coronet Bks.

Parables. B. Boucher. 1989. pap. 21.00 (*0-86217-029-X*, Pub. by Veritas Pubns) St Mut.

***Parables.** James C. Christensen. LC 99-36919. (Illus.). 72p. 1999. 19.95 (*1-57345-558-X*, Shadow Mount) Deseret Bk.

Parables. Paul Johnson & Nicole Johnson. LC 98-56165. (SelectScripts Ser.: No. 3). 64p. 1999. pap. 14.99 (*0-8054-2025-8*) Broadman.

Parables. Roberta Letwenko & Edward Letwenko. (Jeremy the Bible Bookworm Ser.). (Illus.). 32p. (J). 3.95 (*0-614-22065-3*) Regina Pr.

Parables. Charles H. Spurgeon. (Spurgeon Collection: Vol. 4). 235p. 1998. pap. 9.99 (*1-889893-18-8*) Emerald House Group Inc.

***Parables.** rev. ed. John White. 1999. pap. 4.99 (*0-8308-3037-5*) InterVarsity.

Parables: A Theological Suspense Novel. Serendipity House Staff. (301 Depth Bible Study Ser.). 1998. pap. text 5.99 (*1-57494-106-2*) Serendipty Hse.

Parables: Biblical, Patristic & Liturgical Interpretation. Dmitri Royster. LC 96-36367. 1996. 8.95 (*0-88141-067-5*) St Vladimirs.

Parables: Jewish Tradition & Christian Interpretation. Brad H. Young. LC 98-17098. 352p. 1998. 24.95 (*1-56563-244-3*) Hendrickson MA.

***Parables: Stories Jesus Told.** Mary Hoffman. LC 99-87309. (Illus.). 32p. (J). (ps-3). 2000. 16.99 (*0-8037-2560-4*, Dial Yng Read) Peng Put Young Read.

Parables: The Arrows of God. Megan McKenna. LC 93-36627. 176p. (Orig.). 1994. pap. 12.00 (*0-88344-975-7*) Orbis Bks.

Parables: The Arrows of God. Megan McKenna. 192p. (Orig.). 1994. pap. 50.00 (*0-86012-237-9*, Pub. by Srch Pr) St Mut.

Parables: The Forgotten Message. Hendrik Van Tuyll. LC 92-61644. 112p. (Orig.). 1993. pap. 9.95 (*0-9634068-4-1*) Middle St Comms.

Parables: The Greatest Stories Ever Told. John White. (LifeGuide Bible Studies). (Orig.). 1988. pap., wbk. ed. 4.99 (*0-8308-1037-4*, 1037) InterVarsity.

Parables: Understanding What Jesus Meant. Gary Inrig. LC 91-2173. 192p. 1991. pap. 10.99 (*0-929239-39-3*) Discovery Hse Pubs.

***Parables: Wood Sculptures.** J. Christopher White. (Illus.). 128p. 2000. 34.95 (*1-56523-122-8*, Pub. by Fox Chapel Pub) IPG Chicago.

Parables & Fables: Exegesis, Textuality & Politics in Central Africa. V. Y. Mudimbe. LC 91-12498. (Illus.). 260p. (Orig.). (C). 1991. pap. 19.95 (*0-299-13064-9*); lib. bdg. 50.00 (*0-299-13060-6*) U of Wis Pr.

Parables & Fables for Modern Man. Peter Ribes. 184p. (C). 1990. text 60.00 (*0-85439-325-0*, Pub. by St Paul Pubns) St Mut.

Parables & Faxes. Gwyneth Lewis. 80p. 1995. pap. 15.95 (*1-85224-319-8*, Pub. by Bloodaxe Bks) Dufour.

***Parables & Miracles.** Enelle Eder. (Make It Take It Bible Crafts Ser.). (Illus.). (J). 2000. pap. 11.95 (*1-58411-007-4*) Rainbow CA.

Parables & Miracles: Blueprints for 30 Messages Built upon God's Word. C. Barry McCarty. (Sermon Starters Ser.). 64p. 1999. 5.99 (*0-7847-0933-5*, 23011) Standard Pub.

Parables & Other Allegories: The Work of Melvin Charney, 1975-1990. Ed. by Melvin Charney. (CCA Ser.). (Illus.). 216p. 1991. pap. text 34.95 (*0-262-53110-0*) MIT Pr.

Parables & Patter. Wild Goose Publications Staff. (C). 1990. 25.00 (*0-947988-33-5*, Pub. by Wild Goose Pubns) St Mut.

Parables & Presence: Forms of the New Testament Tradition. Robert W. Funk. LC 82-71827. 224p. (C). 1982. 15.95 (*0-944344-65-8*, 1-688) Polebridge Pr.

Parables As Poetic Fictions: The Creative Voice of Jesus. Charles W. Hedrick. LC 94-34579. 280p. (C). 1994. 24.95 (*0-913573-90-6*) Hendrickson MA.

Parables As Subversive Speech: Jesus As Pedagogue of the Oppressed. William R. Herzog, II. 272p. (Orig.). 1994. pap. 24.95 (*0-664-25355-5*) Westminster John Knox.

Parables by the Sea. Pamela Reeve. LC 77-6209. (Illus.). 46p. 1976. pap. text 7.99 (*0-930014-11-1*) Multnomah Pubs.

Parables Colorbook. A. Daniel Zook. (Bible Coloring Book Set Ser.). (Illus.). 48p. (J). (gr. 1-5). 1977. pap. 1.90 (*0-7399-0184-2*, 2913) Rod & Staff.

Parables for Children. Jane S. Bauld. (J). (ps-2). 1998. 8.95 (*1-880384-16-7*) Coldwater Pr.

Parables for Christmas. John Killinger. LC 85-9032. 80p. (Orig.). 1985. pap. 6.95 (*0-687-30061-4*) Abingdon.

Parables for Kids: Eight Contemporary Stories Based on Best-Loved Bible Parables. Danae Dobson & James Dobson. LC 98-33381. 1999. 14.99 (*0-8423-0637-4*) Tyndale Hse.

Parables for Little Kids. Glen Keane & Samii Taylor. LC 95-42468. (Illus.). 32p. (J). (ps). 1996. 7.99 (*0-7814-0258-1*) Chariot Victor.

Parables for Little People. Lawrence Castagnola. LC 86-60029. (Illus.). 104p. (J). (gr. 4 up). 1982. pap. 99.95 (*0-89390-034-6*) Resource Pubns.

Parables for Preachers: The Gospel of Mark - Year B. Barbara E. Reid. LC 99-28090. 1999. pap. text 11.95 (*0-8146-2551-7*) Liturgical Pr.

***Parables for Preachers Year C: The Gospel of Luke.** Barbara E. Reid. 144p. 2000. pap. 11.95 (*0-8146-2552-5*) Liturgical Pr.

Parables from the Back Side: Bible Stories with a Twist. J. Ellsworth Kalas. 144p. (Orig.). 1992. pap. 9.95 (*0-687-30062-2*) Abingdon.

Parables from the Past: The Prose Fiction of Chingiz Aitmatov. Joseph P. Mozur, Jr. (Russian & East European Studies). 212p. (C). 1994. pap. 22.95 (*0-8229-5531-8*); text 59.95 (*0-8229-3791-3*) U of Pittsburgh Pr.

Parables in Depth. George Drew. 55p. (Orig.). 1982. pap. 7.95 (*0-940754-18-5*) Ed Ministries.

Parables in Matthew's Gospel. R. K. Campbell. 1978. pap. 3.25 (*0-915374-42-0*, 42-0) Rapids Christian.

Parables in Midrash: Narrative & Exegesis in Rabbinic Literature. David Stern. 352p. (C). 1991. 42.50 (*0-674-65447-1*) HUP.

Parables in Midrash: Narrative & Exegesis in Rabbinic Literature. David Stern. 368p. 1994. pap. 19.50 (*0-674-65448-X*) HUP.

Parables in the Gospels. John Drury. 192p. 1989. pap. 9.95 (*0-8245-0947-1*) Crossroad NY.

Parables Jesus Told. Orig. Title: Bible Activities Book #10. 32p. (J). (ps-2). 1993. write for info. (*0-7814-0060-0*, Chariot Bks) Chariot Victor.

Parables Jesus Told. Ella K. Lindrall & Kent Puckett. (Tell-Me Stories Ser.). 160p. (J). (gr. 1-6). 1998. 18.99 (*0-8024-7116-1*) Moody.

Parables Jesus Told: Spot the Difference see Parabolas Jesus Conto: Localiza la Diferencia

Parables of a Country Parson: Heartwarming Stories of Christian Faith & Life. William E. Barton. Ed. by Garth Rosell & Stan Flewelling. 194p. 1998. pap. 12.95 (*1-56563-419-5*) Hendrickson MA.

Parables of Christ. E. X. Heatherley. 425p. 1997. 19.95 (*0-929488-98-9*) Balcony Pub Inc.

Parables of Christ. Leopold Fonck. 829p. 1997. reprint ed. 35.95 (*0-912141-47-6*) Roman Cath Bks.

Parables of Conversion: Lectionary Stories That Will Change Your Life. Lou Ruoff. LC 96-40258. 128p. (Orig.). 1997. pap. text 10.95 (*0-89390-403-1*) Resource Pubns.

Parables of Grace. Robert F. Capon. 1991. pap. 14.00 (*0-8028-0304-0*) Eerdmans.

***Parables of Hope: Inspiring Truths from People with Disabilities.** Allen J. Hoogewind. LC 97-35475. 160p. 1998. pap. 12.99 (*0-310-21624-9*) Zondervan.

Parables of Jesus. (Saint Joseph Picture Bks.). (Illus.). 1976. pap. 1.25 (*0-89942-291-8*, 291-00) Catholic Bk Pub.

Parables of Jesus. 22p. 1998. pap. 4.95 (*0-687-09548-4*) Abingdon.

Parables of Jesus. (Life of Jesus Pict-O-Graph Ser.). (J). 1981. 10.99 (*0-7847-1027-9*, 02227) Standard Pub.

Parables of Jesus. James M. Boice. pap. 10.99 (*0-8024-0163-5*, 243) Moody.

Parables of Jesus. Julianne Booth. (Arch Bks.). (Illus.). 24p. (J). (gr. k-4). 1982. pap. 1.99 (*0-570-06163-6*, 59-1309) Concordia.

Parables of Jesus. S. Parkes Cadman. 1999. 6.99 (*0-517-20546-7*) Random Hse Value.

Parables of Jesus. Tomie De Paola. (Illus.). 32p. (J). (ps-3). 1987. pap. 8.95 (*0-8234-1196-6*) Holiday.

Parables of Jesus. Tomie De Paola. LC 86-18323. (Illus.). 32p. (J). (ps up). 1987. lib. bdg. 16.95 (*0-8234-0636-9*) Holiday.

Parables of Jesus. Gladys Hunt. (Fisherman Bible Studyguide Ser.). 96p. (Orig.). 1986. pap. 15.99 (*0-87788-791-8*, H Shaw Pubs) Waterbrook Pr.

***Parables of Jesus.** Denis McBride. LC 99-25160. 1999. pap. 13.95 (*0-7648-0511-8*, Liguori Triumph) Liguori Pubns.

***Parables of Jesus.** Ellyn Sanna. (Young Reader's Christian Library). (Illus.). 224p. (J). 2000. pap. 1.39 (*1-57748-724-9*) Barbour Pub.

***Parables of Jesus.** Ed. by Michael E. Williams. (Storyteller's Companion to the Bible Ser.). 1999. 18.00 (*0-687-06126-1*) Abingdon.

P

Parables of Jesus. William Barclay. (William Barclay Library). 222p. 1999. reprint ed. pap. 15.00 (*0-664-25828-X*) Westminster John Knox.

Parables of Jesus. David Wenham. LC 89-36270. (Jesus Library). 192p. 1989. reprint ed. pap. 12.99 (*0-8308-1286-5*, 1286) InterVarsity.

Parables of Jesus. 2nd ed. Joachim Jeremias. LC 63-22114. (Illus.). 248p. (C). 1972. pap. text 20.00 (*0-02-360510-3*, Macmillan Coll) P-H.

Parables of Jesus, Vol. 2. Neil R. Lightfoot. LC 86-71089. (Way of Life Ser.). 95p. 1986. reprint ed. pap. 6.95 (*0-89112-179-X*) Abilene Christ U.

***Parables of Jesus: A Commentary.** Arland J. Hultgren. (Bible in Its World Ser.). 512p. 2000. 35.00 (*0-8028-4475-8*) Eerdmans.

Parables of Jesus: A History of Interpretation & Bibliography. Warren S. Kissinger. LC 78-23271. (American Theological Library Association Monograph: No. 4). 463p. 1979. lib. bdg. 50.00 (*0-8108-1186-3*) Scarecrow.

Parables of Jesus: Applications for Contemporary Life. Richard Gribble. 1998. pap. 14.50 (*0-7880-1200-2*) CSS OH.

Parables of Jesus: Applications for Contemporary Life, Cycle A. Richard Gribble. LC 98-5191. 1998. pap. 14.50 (*0-7880-1197-9*) CSS OH.

***Parables of Jesus: Applications for Contemporary Life, Cycle B.** Richard Gribble. LC 98-5191. 108p. 1999. pap. 10.50 (*0-7880-1355-6*) CSS OH.

***Parables of Jesus: Applications for Contemporary Life, Cycle C.** Richard Gribble. LC 98-5191. 278p. 2000. pap. 24.95 (*0-7880-1595-8*); disk 24.95 (*0-7880-1596-6*) CSS OH.

Parables of Jesus: In the Light of the Old Testament. Claus Westermann. Tr. by Friedmann Golka & Alastair Logan. 240p. 1998. pap. 25.95 (*0-567-29162-6*, Pub. by T & T Clark) Bks Intl VA.

***Parables of Jesus: Jesus Seminar Red Letter Edition.** Robert W. Funk et al. LC 88-25521. (Jesus Seminar Ser.). (Illus.). 128p. 1998. pap. 14.95 (*0-944344-07-0*) Polebridge Pr.

Parables of Jesus: Lessons in Life from the Master Teacher. Dwight J. Pentecost. LC 98-41466. 176p. 1998. pap. 9.99 (*0-8254-3458-0*) Kregel.

Parables of Jesus: New International Version Bible Scripture Quotes. LC 95-116481. (Teachings of Jesus Picture Bks.). (Illus.). 64p. 1994. 15.99 (*1-56476-256-4*, 6-3256, Victor Bks) Chariot Victor.

Parables of Jesus: Recovering the Art of Listening. Richard Q. Ford. LC 97-29607. 192p. 1997. pap. text 18.00 (*0-8006-2938-8*, 1-2938, Fortress Pr) Augsburg Fortress.

Parables of Jesus: The Master's Stories of Love & Grace. Lyndelle B. Chiomenti. LC 96-46582. 1997. pap. 2.97 (*0-8163-1376-8*) Pacific Pr Pub Assn.

Parables of Jesus: The Mustard Seed & Other Stories. Helen R. Caswell. (Illus.). 96p. (J). (ps-3). 1998. pap. 10.95 (*0-687-05606-3*) Abingdon.

Parables of Jesus (According to St. Luke) Harold N. Wendt. (Illus.). 76p. 1997. pap. text 9.50 (*1-891245-02-3*, 4440) Crossways Intl.

Parables of Jesus Christ. (Life & Teachings of Christ Ser.: Vol. 2). (SPA.). 1973. 3.95 (*0-89985-262-9*) Christ for the Nations.

Parables of Jesus Christ. Gordon Lindsay. (Life & Teachings of Christ Ser.: Vol. 1). (SPA.). 1973. 3.95 (*0-89985-261-0*) Christ for the Nations.

Parables of Jesus Christ, Vol. 1. Gordon Lindsay. (Life & Teachings of Christ Ser.). (SPA.). 3.95 (*0-89985-980-1*) Christ for the Nations.

Parables of Jesus Collection. Joachim Jeremias. 1985. pap. 13.50 (*0-684-16244-X*, Scribners Ref) Mac Lib Ref.

Parables of Jesus for Children. Savary. 1980. pap. 2.50 (*0-88271-161-X*) Regina Pr.

Parables of Judgement. Robert F. Capon. 1993. pap. 14.00 (*0-8028-0491-8*) Eerdmans.

Parables of Kierkegaard. Ed. by Thomas C. Oden. (Illus.). 212p. (C). 1989. pap. text 10.95 (*0-691-02053-1*, Pub. by Princeton U Pr) Cal Prin Full Svc.

P

Parables of Kryon. Lee Carroll. LC 96-24699. (Illus.). 160p. 1996. 17.00 (*1-56170-364-8*, 850) Hay House.

***Parables of Kryon.** Lee Carroll. 176p. 2000. reprint ed. pap. 10.95 (*1-56170-663-9*, 850T) Hay House.

Parables of Matthew. Daniel J. Davis. LC 98-74304. (Covenant Bible Studies). 120p. 1998. pap. 5.95 (*0-87178-013-5*, 8135) Brethren.

Parables of Matthew 13. Ken Blue. 51p. 1997. pap. 3.25 (*1-930452-02-0*) Local Church.

Parables of Our Lord & Savior Jesus Christ. John E. Millais. 1990. 12.50 (*0-8446-5225-3*) Peter Smith.

Parables of Possibility: The American Need for Beginnings. Terence Martin. LC 94-17486. 256p. 1995. 32.50 (*0-231-07050-0*) Col U Pr.

Parables of Sun Light: Observations on Psychology, the Arts & the Rest. Rudolf Arnheim. 379p. 1989. pap. 16.95 (*0-520-06536-0*, Pub. by U CA Pr) Cal Prin Full Svc.

Parables of the Barrio. Juan M. Flavier. 76p. 1989. 2.00 (*0-614-24866-3*) Intl Inst Rural.

Parables of the Barrio. Juan M. Flavier. 76p. 1991. 2.00 (*0-614-24867-1*) Intl Inst Rural.

Parables of the Baskets. Lorraine Otto. 84p. 1995. pap. 14.95 (*0-9648543-0-9*) L Otto.

Parables of the Forest. Pamela Reeve. Ed. by Larry R. Libby. LC 88-36472. (Illus.). 49p. (Orig.). 1989. pap. 7.99 (*0-88070-306-7*, Multnomah Bks) Multnomah Pubs.

Parables of the Good Shepherd: A Compilation of Parables Spoken by Jesus. Ed. & Intro. by Harlan D. Moore, Jr. LC 95-75970. (Illus.). 120p. (Orig.). 1996. pap. 8.95 (*1-887076-17-4*) Journey Bkshelf.

Parables of the Great Commission: A Daily Devotional for World Christians. Ruth A. Tucker. 384p. 1989. 12.98 (*0-310-51620-X*) Zondervan.

Parables of the Kingdom. G. Campbell Morgan. 221p. 1997. pap. 16.00 (*1-57910-089-9*) Wipf & Stock.

Parables of the Kingdom. Robert F. Capon. 176p. 1991. reprint ed. pap. 14.00 (*0-8028-0605-8*) Eerdmans.

Parables of the Lord Jesus Christ As Recorded in the Gospel of John & the First Chapter of Acts. (Walk with Jesus Ser.). 155p. 1988. pap. 25.00 (*1-57277-301-4*) Script Rsch.

Parables of the Lord Jesus Christ As Recorded in the Gospel of Luke. (Walk with Jesus Ser.). 157p. 1988. pap. 25.00 (*1-57277-228-X*) Script Rsch.

Parables of the Lord Jesus Christ As Recorded in the Gospel of Mark: The Servant of the Lord. (Walk with Jesus Ser.). 76p. 1988. pap. 15.00 (*1-57277-227-1*) Script Rsch.

Parables of the Lord Jesus Christ As Recorded in the Gospel of Matthew. (Walk with Jesus Ser.). 198p. 1988. pap. 30.00 (*1-57277-226-3*) Script Rsch.

Parables of the New Testament. unabridged ed. Sheryl Williams. (Illus.). 80p. (J). (gr. 2-6). 1997. pap. 5.95 (*0-89137-068-4*, 70684) Quality Pubns.

Parables of the Old Testament. Clarence E. Macartney. 160p. 1995. pap. 10.99 (*0-8254-3278-2*) Kregel.

Parables of the Windchimes. Margaret Gunnell. 9p. (Orig.). 1991. pap. 4.95 (*1-879877-02-3*) Moccasins Pr.

Parables on Stage. Jeannette Clift George. 1995. pap. 8.99 (*0-8341-9440-6*, MP-770) Nazarene.

Parables Related to the Kingdom of Heaven. (Walk with Jesus Ser.). 146p. 1989. pap. 25.00 (*1-57277-302-2*) Script Rsch.

Parables Related to the Kingdom of Hell. (Walk with Jesus Ser.). 59p. 1989. pap. 15.00 (*1-57277-303-0*) Script Rsch.

Parables Related to the Kingdoms of Heaven & Hell. (Walk with Jesus Ser.). 164p. 1989. pap. 25.00 (*1-57277-326-X*) Script Rsch.

Parables That Jesus Told. Rabbit. (J). pap. 19.95 (*0-689-80229-3*) Aladdin.

Parables That Jesus Told. Jason Root. LC 98-4428. (Illus.). 40p. (J). (ps-1). 1999. pap. 10.95 incl. audio (*0-689-82536-6*, Rabbit Ears) Litle Simon.

Parables Told by Jesus: Contemporary Approach. Wilfrid J. Harrington. LC 74-12395. 135p. (Orig.). 1974. pap. 4.95 (*0-8189-0296-5*) Alba.

***Parabola: Shorter Fictions - Including the Novella "Fata Morgana"** Joe Martin. 176p. 2000. pap. 13.00 (*1-878580-18-3*) Asylum Arts.

Parabola, a Rosicrucian Tale. Hinricus Madathanus. 50p. 1992. reprint ed. pap. 7.00 (*1-56459-035-6*) Kessinger Pub.

Parabolae Sancti Bernardi see Bernard of Clairvaux: Parables (Parabolae)

Parabolas de Identidad: Realida Interior y Estrategia Narrativa en Tres Novelistas de Postguerra. Bernardo A. Gonzalez. 28.00 (*0-916379-31-0*) Scripta.

Parabolas Jesus Conto: Localiza la Diferencia. A. Hudson.Tr. of Parables Jesus Told: Spot the Difference. (SPA.). (J). 1.89 (*1-56063-965-2*, 497756) Editorial Unilit.

Parabolic Anderson Problem & Intermittency. Rene A. Carmona & S. A. Molchanov. LC 93-48271. (Memoirs of the American Mathematical Society Ser.: No. 518). 125p. 1994. pap. 34.00 (*0-8218-2577-1*, MEMO/108/518) Am Math.

Parabolic Boundary Value Problems. S. D. Eidelman & N. V. Zhitarashu. Tr. by Gennady Pasechnik & Andrei Iacob. LC 98-4853. (Operator Theory, Advances & Applications Ser.). 1998. 152.00 (*0-8176-2972-6*) Birkhauser.

Parabolic Boundary Value Problems. S. D. Eidelman & N. V. Zhitarashu. Tr. by Gennady Pasechnik & Andrei Iacob from RUS. LC 98-4853. (Operator Theory Ser.: Vol. 101). 312p. 1998. 152.00 (*3-7643-2972-6*) Birkhauser.

***Parabolic Equation Methods for Electromagnetic Wave Propagation.** Mireille F. Levy. (IEE Electromagnetic Waves Ser.: No. 45). 350p. 2000. boxed set 85.00 (*0-85296-764-0*, Pub. by INSPEC Inc) Whitehurst & Clark.

Parabolic Equations on an Infinite Strip. N. A. Watson. (Pure & Applied Mathematics Ser.: Vol. 127). (Illus.). 312p. 1989. text 175.00 (*0-8247-7999-1*) Dekker.

Parabolic Subgroups of Algebraic Groups & Induction. D. Vella. LC 86-10942. (Memoirs Ser.: No. 62/347). 114p. 1986. pap. 25.00 (*0-8218-2348-5*, MEMO/62/347) Am Math.

Paracaidas, Paracaidas. Agatha A. Rodriguez. (Children's Storybook Ser.). (SPA., Illus.). 20p. (Orig.). (J). 1992. pap. 5.00 (*0-933196-05-9*) Bilingue Pubns.

Paracas Art & Architecture: Object & Context in South Coastal Peru. Ed. by Anne Paul. LC 91-16740. (Illus.). 455p. 1991. text 42.95 (*0-87745-327-6*) U of Iowa Pr.

Paracellular Pathway: Report of a Conference. Ed. by Stanley Bradley & Elizabeth F. Purcell. LC 82-81100. 390p. reprint ed. pap. 120.90 (*0-608-16367-8*, 202669500051) Bks Demand.

Paracelsian Lexicon. Arthur E. Waite & Franz Hartmann. Ed. by Patrick J. Smith. (Alchemical Studies Ser.: No. 10). 1998. pap. 8.95 (*1-55818-405-8*, Alchemical) Holmes Pub.

Paracelsus. Ralph Shirley. 1993. reprint ed. pap. 6.95 (*1-55818-243-8*) Holmes Pub.

Paracelsus. 2nd ed. W. Pagel. (Illus.). xii, 400p. 1982. 121.00 (*3-8055-3518-X*) S Karger.

Paracelsus: Essential Readings. 2nd ed. Tr. & Selected by Nicholas Goodrick-Clarke. (Illus.). 206p. 1999. pap. 14.95 (*1-55643-316-6*) North Atlantic.

Paracelsus: His Mystical & Medical Philosophy. Manly P. Hall. pap. 5.95 (*0-89314-808-3*) Philos Res.

Paracelsus: His Personality & Influence As Physician, Chemist & Reformer (1920) John M. Stillman. 190p. 1996. reprint ed. pap. 18.95 (*1-56459-529-3*) Kessinger Pub.

Paracelsus: Selected Writings. 2nd ed. Jolande Jacobi. (Bollingen Ser.: Vol. 28). (Illus.). 368p. 1958. pap. text 16.95 (*0-691-01876-6*, Pub. by Princeton U Pr) Cal Prin Full Svc.

Paracelsus: Speculative Theory & the Crisis of the Early Reformation. Andrew Weeks. LC 96-16616. (SUNY Series in Western Esoteric Traditions). 238p. (C). 1996. text 65.50 (*0-7914-3147-9*); pap. text 21.95 (*0-7914-3148-7*) State U NY Pr.

Paracelsus: The Man & His Reputation. Ole P. Grell. LC 98-25297. (Studies in the History of Christian Thought: Vol. 85). (Illus.). 272p. 1998. 103.00 (*90-04-11177-8*) Brill Academic Pubs.

Paracelsus Alchemical Catechism. Theophrastus P. Von Hohenheim. Tr. by A. E. Waite from LAT. 1983. reprint ed. pap. 4.95 (*0-916411-03-6*) Holmes Pub.

Paracelsus & Other One-Act Plays. Arthur Schnitzler. Tr. by G. J. Weinberger. LC 94-21539. (Studies in Austrian Literature, Culture, & Thought). 1995. pap. 22.95 (*0-929497-96-1*) Ariadne CA.

Paracelsus, His Methods of Healing. Douglas M. Baker. 1982. pap. 11.00 (*0-906006-72-4*, Pub. by Baker Pubns) New Leaf Dist.

Paracelsus, (Theophrast von Hohenheim), Samtliche Werke Bd. 1: Fruheste Schriften Ums Jahr 1520 Verfabt. Ed. by Karl Sudhoff & Wilhelm Matthieben. (GER.). lvi, 417p. 1966. reprint ed. 170.00 (*3-487-10082-7*) G Olms Pubs.

Paracelsus, (Theophrast von Hohenheim), Samtliche Werke Bd. 2: Fruhe Schriften zur Heilmittellehre (Arzneistoffe und Heilquellen) zur Begrundung der Tartarischen Lehre in der Pathologie, Samt Dem 6, 7 u 9. Ed. by Karl Sudhoff & Wilhelm Matthieben. (GER.). xxxii, 539p. 1966. reprint ed. 170.00 (*3-487-10083-5*) G Olms Pubs.

Paracelsus, (Theophrast von Hohenheim), Samtliche Werke Bd. 3: Drei Prinzipien, Spiritus Vitae, Mineralien, Cemente, Gradationen, Archidoxen und Zugehoriges, Vita Longa, Praeparationes, Brief an Erasmus, Macerscholien, Krankheitstypen Usw., Aus Dem Jahre 1526 und Anfang 1527. Ed. by Karl Sudhoff & Wilhelm Matthieben. (GER.). liii, 570p. 1966. reprint ed. 170.00 (*3-487-10084-3*) G Olms Pubs.

Paracelsus, (Theophrast von Hohenheim), Samtliche Werke Bd. 4: Vorlesungen des Sommers, 1527 zu Basel: De Gradibus, von Apostemen, Geschwaren, Offnen Schaden Etc., Vom Aderlass, Modus Pharmacandi, Aphorismen-Kommentar, de Urinis. Ed. by Karl Sudhoff & Wilhelm Matthieben. (GER.). xl, 676p. 1966. reprint ed. 170.00 (*3-487-10085-1*) G Olms Pubs.

Paracelsus, (Theophrast von Hohenheim), Samtliche Werke Bd. 5: Baseler Wintervorlesungen, 1527/28 Uber Tartarische Erkrankungen, Uber Spezielle Pathologie und Therapie "Paragraphen" Uber Wunden und Wundbehandlungen; Entwurfe zu Einer Polemisch Gehaltenen Chirurgie. Ed. by Karl Sudhoff & Wilhelm Matthieben. (GER.). xxi, 551p. 1966. reprint ed. 170.00 (*3-487-10086-X*) G Olms Pubs.

Paracelsus, (Theophrast von Hohenheim), Samtliche Werke Bd. 6: Aus Dem Jahre, 1528 (Kolmar Im Elsab) Ed. by Karl Sudhoff & Wilhelm Matthieben. (GER.). 498p. 1966. reprint ed. 170.00 (*3-487-10087-8*) G Olms Pubs.

Paracelsus, (Theophrast von Hohenheim), Samtliche Werke Bd. 7: Die Nurnberger Syphilisschriften und Andere Nurnberger Schrift Werke Aus Dem Jahre 1529. Ed. by Karl Sudhoff & Wilhelm Matthieben. (GER.). 552p. 1966. reprint ed. 170.00 (*3-487-10088-6*) G Olms Pubs.

Paracelsus, (Theophrast von Hohenheim), Samtliche Werke Bd. 8: Schriften Aus Dem Jahre, 1530, Geschrieben in der Oberpfalz, Regensburg, Bayern und Schwaben. Ed. by Karl Sudhoff & Wilhelm Matthieben. (GER.). 422p. 1966. reprint ed. 170.00 (*3-487-10089-4*) G Olms Pubs.

Paracelsus, (Theophrast von Hohenheim), Samtliche Werke Bd. 9: "Paramirisches" und Anderes Schriftwerk der Jahre, 1531-1535 Aus der Schweiz und Tirol. Ed. by Karl Sudhoff & Wilhelm Matthieben. (GER.). 706p. 1966. reprint ed. 170.00 (*3-487-10090-8*) G Olms Pubs.

Paracelsus, (Theophrast von Hohenheim), Samtliche Werke Bd. 10: Die Grobe Wundarznei und Anderes Schriftwerk des Jahres, 1536 Aus Schwaben und Bayern. Ed. by Karl Sudhoff & Wilhelm Matthieben. (GER.). xlviii, 688p. 1966. reprint ed. 170.00 (*3-487-10091-6*) G Olms Pubs.

Paracelsus, (Theophrast von Hohenheim), Samtliche Werke Bd. 11: Schriftwerk Aus Den Jahren, 1537-1541. Ed. by Karl Sudhoff & Wilhelm Matthieben. (GER.). xxxiv, 430p. 1966. reprint ed. 170.00 (*3-487-10092-4*) G Olms Pubs.

Paracelsus, (Theophrast von Hohenheim), Samtliche Werke Bd. 12: Astronomia Magna Oder die Ganze Philosophia Sagax der Groben und Kleinen Welt Samt Beiwerk. Ed. by Karl Sudhoff & Wilhelm Matthieben. (GER.). xix, 629p. 1966. reprint ed. 170.00 (*3-487-10093-2*) G Olms Pubs.

Paracelsus, (Theophrast von Hohenheim), Samtliche Werke Bd. 13: Schriften Unbestimmter Zeit zur Meteorologie, Kleineres. Ed. by Karl Sudhoff & Wilhelm Matthieben. (GER.). xvi, 570p. 1966. reprint ed. 170.00 (*3-487-10094-0*) G Olms Pubs.

Paracelsus, (Theophrast von Hohenheim), Samtliche Werke Bd. 14: Das Volumen Primum der Philosophia Magna. Ed. by Karl Sudhoff & Wilhelm Matthieben. (GER.). xxxv, 750p. 1966. reprint ed. 170.00 (*3-487-10095-9*) G Olms Pubs.

Paracetamol (Acetaminophen) A Critical Bibliographic Review. Laurie F. Prescott. 400p. 1996. 165.00 (*0-7484-0136-9*) Taylor & Francis.

Parachute Clown in the Rain Forest. Margaret Hardway. Ed. by Eloise Smith. (Illus.). 20p. (J). (ps-6). 1998. 7.00 (*0-9664035-1-7*) Mask Flight.

Parachute Games. Todd Strong & Dale LeFevre. LC 95-24027. (Illus.). 168p. (Orig.). 1995. pap. text 15.95 (*0-87322-793-X*, BSTR0793) Human Kinetics.

Parachute Infantry: An American Paratrooper's Memoir of D-Day & the Fall of the Third Reich. David K. Webster. (Illus.). 288p. 1997. pap. 12.95 (*0-8071-2222-X*) La State U Pr.

Parachute Jumping. 1997. lib. bdg. 251.95 (*0-8490-8157-2*) Gordon Pr.

Parachute Manual Vol. 1: A Technical Treatise on Aerodynamic Decelerators. 3rd rev. ed. Dan Poynter. LC 83-13350. (Illus.). 592p. 1991. pap. 49.95 (*0-915516-35-7*) Para Pub.

Parachute Manual Vol. 2: A Technical Treatise on Aerodynamic Decelerators. 4th rev. ed. Dan Poynter. LC 91-8828. 416p. 1991. pap. 49.95 (*0-915516-80-2*) Para Pub.

Parachute Movement Activities: A Complete Parachute Movement Program for Elementary Grades & Beyond. Ron French & Michael Horvat. Ed. by Frank Alexander. (Illus.). 82p. (Orig.). 1982. pap., teacher ed. 11.00 (*0-915256-13-4*) Front Row.

Parachute Play: For Indoor/Outdoor Fun. Liz Wilmes & Dick Wilmes. LC 85-71415. (Illus.). 96p. 1985. pap. 9.95 (*0-943452-03-1*) Building Blocks.

***Parachute Play: For Indoor/Outdoor Fun.** rev. expanded ed. Liz Wilmes. (Illus.). (J). 2000. pap. 12.95 (*0-943452-30-9*) Building Blocks.

Parachute Recovery Systems Design Manual. Theo W. Knacke. Ed. by Don Goodrich & J. D. Johnson. LC 91-43883. (Illus.). 512p. 1992. pap. 49.95 (*0-915516-85-3*) Para Pub.

Parachute Rigger Knowledge Test Guide, 1995. Government Printing Office Staff. 18p. 1995. pap. 2.00 (*0-16-048170-8*) USGPO.

Parachute Rigger Senior/Master Certification Guide. Government Printing Office Staff. 52p. 1988. pap. 1.75 (*0-16-005258-0*) USGPO.

Parachute Rigging Course: A Course of Study for the FAA Senior Rigging Certificate. 3rd rev. ed. Dan Poynter & Mark Schlatter. LC 94-4950. 90p. 1994. pap. 19.95 (*1-56860-005-4*) Para Pub.

Parachute Soldier. 2nd rev. ed. William H. Tucker. LC 95-78171. (Illus.). 166p. 1995. pap. 16.95 (*0-9647683-0-5*) Intl Airborne.

Parachute Soldiers's Post War Odyssey. William H. Tucker. Ed. by John Casella. (Illus.). 158p. (Orig.). 1996. pap. 14.95 (*0-9647683-1-3*) Intl Airborne.

Parachutes for Parents. 2nd ed. Bobbie Sandoz. LC 97-17006. 496p. 1997. pap. 14.95 (*0-8092-3025-9*, 302590, Contemporary Bks) NTC Contemp Pub Co.

Parachuting: Art of Freefall Relative Work. 2nd rev. ed. Pat Works & Jan Works. (Illus.). 240p. 1988. reprint ed. pap. text. write for info. (*0-9607814-5-5*) AeroGraphics.

***Parachuting: The Skydiver's Handbook.** 8th ed. Dan Poynter & Mike Turoff. (Illus.). 408p. 2000. pap. text 19.95 (*1-56860-062-3*) Para Pub.

***Parachuting Hamsters & Andy Russell.** David A. Adler. (Illus.). 144p. (YA). (gr. 4-7). 2000. 14.00 (*0-15-202185-X*, Harcourt Child Bks) Harcourt.

Parachuting I-E Course: A Program of Study to Prepare the Expert Parachutist for the USPA I/E Exam. 5th rev. ed. Dan Poynter. (Illus.). 60p. 1994. pap. 14.95 (*1-56860-004-6*) Para Pub.

Parachuting Manual with Log. 9th rev. ed. Dan Poynter. (Illus.). 24p. 1999. 2.95 (*1-56860-057-7*, PML-8) Para Pub.

***Parachuting Manual with Log for Accelerated FreeFall: With a Summary of the First Jump Course.** 4th rev. ed. Jan Meyer. LC 91-6811. (Illus.). 36p. 2000. pap. 3.95 (*1-56860-068-2*) Para Pub.

Parachuting Manual with Log for Round Canopies. 7th rev. ed. Dan Poynter. LC 76-14106. (Illus.). 24p. 1984. pap. 1.50 (*0-915516-11-X*) Para Pub.

Paraclete: An Essay on the Personality & Ministry of the Holy Ghost. Joseph Parker. 402p. 1997. pap. 32.00 (*1-57910-083-X*) Wipf & Stock.

Paracoccidioidomycosis. Franco. 448p. 1993. lib. bdg. 239.00 (*0-8493-4868-4*) CRC Pr.

Paraconsistent Logic: Essays on the Inconsistent. Ed. by Graham Priest et al. (Analytica Ser.). 704p. 1989. 265.00 (*3-88405-058-3*) Philosophia Pr.

Paracrine Control of the Development of Anterior Pituitary Cells in the Rat. D. Tilemans. No. 54. 124p. (Orig.). 1992. pap. 30.00 (*90-6186-515-8*, Pub. by Leuven Univ) Coronet Bks.

Paracriticisms: Seven Speculations of the Times. Ihab Hassan. LC 74-19108. 200p. (C). 1984. pap. text 12.50 (*0-252-01166-X*) U of Ill Pr.

***Parade.** Jason Robert Brown. 104p. 2000. otabind 17.95 (*0-634-01175-8*) H Leonard.

Parade. Donald Crews. LC 82-20927. (Illus.). 32p. (J). (gr. k-3). 1983. 16.00 (*0-688-01995-1*, Grenwillow Bks); lib. bdg. 15.93 (*0-688-01996-X*, Grenwillow Bks) HarpC Child Bks.

Parade. Donald Crews. LC 82-20927. (Illus.). (J). (ps-3). 1986. mass mkt. 4.95 (*0-688-06520-1*, Wm Morrow) Morrow Avon.

Parade. Caroljean Ellis. (Tales of Little Angels: Bk. 3). (Illus.). 40p. (Orig.). (J). (gr. k-4). 1996. pap. 8.95 (*1-889383-02-3*) Angel Publns NJ.

Parade. Rebera E. Foston & Cynthia E. Garnett. 96p. (Orig.). 1994. pap. 16.00 (*0-9641709-2-2*) Foston Adolescent.

Parade. Kitty Mendenhall. 70p. (Orig.). 1997. pap. 9.95 (*1-884754-29-5*) Potpourri Pubns.

Parade. Williams & Zanatta. 1997. pap. text, student ed. 9.87 (*0-673-19613-5*) Addson-Wesley Educ.

Parade: Poems from Hollywood. Mark Dunster. 11p. 1999. pap. 5.00 (*0-89642-626-2*) Linden Pubs.

Parade & Carnival Fun: A Dino-Mite Color & Activity Book. Lyricks Studios Staff. 80p. (J). 1998. pap. text 1.95 (*1-57064-312-1*) Lyrick Pub.

Parade & Other Works for Piano Four Hands. Erik Satie. 112p. 1999. text 11.95 (*0-486-40410-2*) Dover.

Parade at the Turn of the Millennium, Years 2000 Y2K-2001: Pittsburgh's Most Comprehenssive Historical Novel-Dialogue includes Race & Religion Problems in America. Helene Smith. LC 98-92336. 330p. 1999. ring bd. 29.95 (*0-945437-33-1*) MacDonald-Sward.

Parade Family Health Companion: A Reassuring Guide to Dealing with Life. Earl Ubell & Randi L. Gould. LC 96-42073. 496p. 1996. per. 20.00 (*0-7615-0307-2*) Prima Pub.

Parade Ground Soldiers: Military Uniforms & Headress, 1837-1910, in the Collections of the State Historical Society of Wisconsin. J. Phillip Langellier. LC 78-4681. 132p. 1978. pap. 5.00 (*0-87020-174-3*) State Hist Soc Wis.

Parade of Empty Boots. Charles A. Seltzer. 296p. 1975. reprint ed. lib. bdg. 23.95 (*0-88411-103-2*) Amereon Ltd.

Parade of Gumdrop Prose. Hunce Voelcker. (Illus.). 3.00 (*0-917996-04-6*) Panjandrum.

Parade of Stories see Child Horizons

Parade of the Anthony People. Anthony Saladino. 148p. (Orig.). 1995. pap. 6.50 (*0-9643465-0-8*) Creat Conspiracy.

Parade of the Dead: A U. S. Army Physician's Memoir of Imprisonment by the Japanese, 1942-1945. John R. Bumgarner. LC 95-6015. (Illus.). 222p. 1995. lib. bdg. 21.95 (*0-7864-0131-1*) McFarland & Co.

Parade Vocab Big Book 1. Herrera. 24p. 1997. 23.73 (*0-201-35719-4*) S&S Trade.

Parade Vocab Big Book 2. Herrera. 24p. 1997. 23.73 (*0-201-35710-0*) S&S Trade.

Parades. Houghton Mifflin Company Staff. (Reading Ser.). (J). 1988. pap., teacher ed., suppl. ed. 5.48 (*0-395-45586-3*); pap., teacher ed., wbk. ed. 16.88 (*0-395-45562-6*); pap., wbk. ed. 14.48 (*0-395-45547-2*) HM.

Parades. Houghton Mifflin Company Staff. (Reading Ser.). (J). 1988. pap., teacher ed. 66.88 (*0-395-43694-X*) HM.

Parades & Politics at Vichy: The French Officer Corps under Marshall Petain. Robert O. Paxton. LC 66-10557. 492p. reprint ed. pap. 152.60 (*0-608-30014-4*, 201057100069) Bks Demand.

Parades & Promenades: History of Antrim, N. H. Antrim History Commitee. LC 76-30841. (Illus.). 1977. 15.00 (*0-914016-39-3*) Phoenix Pub.

Parades & the Politics of the Street: Festive Culture in the Early American Republic. Simon P. Newman. LC 97-5392. (Early American Studies). (Illus.). 296p. 1997. text 39.95 (*0-8122-3399-9*) U of Pa Pr.

***Parades & the Politics of the Street: Festive Culture in the Early American Republic.** Simon P. Newman. 2000. pap. text 19.95 (*0-8122-1724-1*) U of Pa Pr.

Parade's End. Ford Madox Ford. LC 92-52922. 1992. 20.00 (*0-679-41728-1*) Everymns Lib.

Parade's Gone By. Kevin Brownlow. LC 75-17302. 1976. reprint ed. pap. 27.50 (*0-520-03068-0*, Pub. by U CA Pr) Cal Prin Full Svc.

Parades of the Wehrmacht: Berlin, 1934-1940. Horst Scheibert. Tr. by Edward Force from GER. LC 96-70670. (Illus.). 80p. 1997. 19.95 (*0-7643-0231-0*) Schiffer.

***Paradiddle Power: Increasing Your Technique on the Drumset with Paradiddles.** Ronald Spagnardi. 104p. 1999. spiral bd. 14.95 (*0-634-01047-6*) H Leonard.

Paradies im Widerspiel der Machte: Mythenlogik - eine Herausforderung fur die Theologie. Johannes Loh. 338p. 1998. 55.95 (*3-631-32173-2*) P Lang Pubng.

Paradigm Accounting: Computerized Payroll Procedures. David H. Weaver & Kristine Ellis. LC 93-25990. (Paradigm Accounting Ser.). (C). 1994. 15.95 (*1-56118-127-7*); 5.25 (*1-56118-138-2*); pap. text 21.95 (*1-56118-118-8*) Paradigm MN.

Paradigm Accounting: Computerized Systems. Rich Sathe & David H. Weaver. 1995. pap. text 21.95 (*1-56118-117-X*); pap. text, teacher ed. 5.25 (*1-56118-132-3*); pap. text, teacher ed. 8.00 (*1-56118-417-9*); pap. text, student ed. 10.00 (*1-56118-122-6*) Paradigm MN.

Paradigm & Paradox: Explorations into a Paradigmatic Theory of Meaning & Its Epistemological Background. Dirk Geeraerts. 407p. (Orig.). 1985. pap. 87.50 (*90-6186-173-X*, Pub. by Leuven Univ) Coronet Bks.

Paradigm & Parody: Images of Creativity in French Romanticism - Vigny, Hugo, Balzac, Gautier, Musset. Henry F. Majewski. LC 88-15419. 192p. 1989. text 35.00 (*0-8139-1177-X*) U Pr of Va.

Paradigm Change in Theology. Hans Kung. 1977. 64.95 (*0-567-09494-4*, Pub. by T & T Clark) Bks Intl VA.

Paradigm College Accounting. 4th ed. Robert L. Dansby & Burton S. Kaliski. LC 98-27081. 1999. text. write for info. (*0-7638-0160-7*) Paradigm MN.

Paradigm College Accounting: Annotated Instructor's Edition 1, 11. 3rd rev. ed. Robert Dansby. 59.95 (*0-7638-0037-6*) EMC-Paradigm.

Paradigm College Accounting: Annotated Instructor's Edition 1,29. 3rd ed. Robert L. Dansby et al. 79.95 (*0-7638-0036-8*) EMC-Paradigm.

Paradigm College Accounting: Annotated Instructor's Edition 1,29. 4th ed. Robert L. Dansby et al. 79.95 (*0-7638-0161-5*) EMC-Paradigm.

Paradigm College Accounting: Complete Text, Chapters 1,27. 3rd rev. ed. Robert L. Dansby et al. 962p. 49.75 (*0-7638-0033-3*) EMC-Paradigm.

Paradigm College Accounting: Solutions Manual 1,27. 3rd ed. 49.95 (*0-7638-0038-4*) EMC-Paradigm.

Paradigm College Accounting: Solutions Manual 1,29. Robert L. Dansby et al. 953p. 49.95 (*0-7638-0165-8*) EMC-Paradigm.

Paradigm College Accounting: Study Guide & Working Papers. 4th ed. Robert L. Dansby et al. 564p. 24.95 (*0-7638-0162-3*) EMC-Paradigm.

Paradigm College Accounting: Study Guide & Working Papers 1, 18. 4th ed. Robert L. Dansby et al. 747p. 24.95 (*0-7638-0163-1*) EMC-Paradigm.

Paradigm College Accounting: Study Guide & Working Papers, 19 ,29. Robert L. Dansby et al. 339p. 20.95 (*0-7638-0164-X*) EMC-Paradigm.

Paradigm College Accounting: Text, Chapters 1,11. Robert L. Dansby et al. 421p. 33.95 (*0-7638-0034-1*) EMC-Paradigm.

Paradigm College Accounting: Text, Chapters 1,12. 4th ed. Robert L. Dansby et al. 457p. 35.95 (*0-7638-0157-7*) EMC-Paradigm.

Paradigm College Accounting: Text, Charters 1, 18. Robert L. Dansby et al. 677p. 39.95 (*0-7638-0159-3*) EMC-Paradigm.

Paradigm College Accounting: Text 1, 12 & Study Guide. 4th ed. Robert L. Dansby et al. 54.95 (*0-7638-0274-3*) EMC-Paradigm.

Paradigm College Accounting: Text 1, 29 & Study Guide 1, 18. 4th ed. Robert L. Dansby et al. 73.90 (*0-7638-0276-X*) EMC-Paradigm.

Paradigm College Accounting: Text 1,18 & Study Guide 1, 18. 4th ed. Robert L. Dansby et al. 59.95 (*0-7638-0275-1*) EMC-Paradigm.

Paradigm Conspiracy: How Our Systems of Government, School, & Culture Violate Our Human Potential. Denise Breton & Christopher Largent. 325p. 1998. reprint ed. pap. 13.95 (*1-56838-208-1*) Hazelden.

Paradigm Cost Accounting: Principles & Applications. Robert L. Dansby & Michael D. Lawrence. LC 97-25595. 1997. text. write for info. (*0-7638-0075-9*) Paradigm MN.

***Paradigm Debates in Curriculum & Supervision: Modern & Postmodern Perspectives** Jeffrey Glanz & Linda S. Behar-Horenstein. LC 99-33207. 312p. 2000. 65.00 (*0-89789-624-6*, Bergin & Garvey) Greenwood.

Paradigm Dialog. Ed. by Egon G. Guba. 424p. (C). 1990. text 62.00 (*0-8039-3822-5*); pap. text 28.50 (*0-8039-3823-3*) Sage.

Paradigm Exchange: University of Minnesota Faculty & Students in Colloquium. Ed. by Rene Jara et al. 193p. (C). 1980. pap. text 6.95 (*0-9607884-0-9*) U of MN College Lib Arts.

Paradigm for Decentralized Process Modeling. Israel Ben-Shaul & Gail Kaiser. (International Series in Engineering & Computer Science, Natural Language Processing & Machine Translation: Secs. 337). 301p. (C). 1995. text 119.00 (*0-7923-9631-6*) Kluwer Academic.

Paradigm for Looking: Cross Cultural Research with Visual Media. Beryl L. Bellman & Bennetta Jules-Rosette. LC 77-15284. (Modern Sociology Ser.). (Illus.). 216p. 1977. text 73.25 (*0-89391-002-3*) Ablx Pub.

Paradigm for Management Information Systems. Philip Ein-Dor & Eli Segev. LC 81-1825. 287p. 1981. 65.00 (*0-275-90608-6*, C0608, Praeger Pubs) Greenwood.

Paradigm for Successful Utilization of Renewable Resources. David J. Sessa & Julious L. Willett. LC 98-7663. 295p. 1998. 105.00 (*0-935315-94-2*) Am Oil Chemists.

Paradigm Guide to English Essentials. Gregg Condon & Frank Andera. 60p. (C). 1991. teacher ed. 8.00 (*1-56118-037-8*); pap. text 10.95 (*1-56118-036-X*) Paradigm MN.

Paradigm Keyboarding: Sessions 1-30. 4th ed. William M. Mitchell. LC 97-44134. 1998. 32.44 (*0-7638-0123-2*); pap. 37.44 (*0-7638-0146-1*) Paradigm MN.

Paradigm Keyboarding & Applications: A Mastery Approach for Microcomputers & Typewriters. 3rd ed. William M. Mitchell et al. (C). 1990. pap. text 31.95 (*1-56118-160-9*) Paradigm MN.

Paradigm Keyboarding & Applications: A Mastery Approach for Microcomputers & Typewriters. 3rd ed. William M. Mitchell et al. (C). 1990. pap. text 18.00 (*1-56118-156-0*); 10.45 (*1-56118-159-5*) Paradigm MN.

Paradigm Keyboarding & Applications: A Mastery Approach for Microcomputers & Typewriters. 3rd ed. William Mitchell et al. (C). 1990. pap. text, teacher ed. 14.00 (*1-56118-151-X*) Paradigm MN.

Paradigm Keyboarding & Applications: A Mastery Approach for Microcomputers & Typewriters, Short Course. James LaBarre et al. (C). 1990. pap. text 23.95 (*1-56118-154-4*) Paradigm MN.

Paradigm Keyboarding & Applications: A Mastery Approach for Microcomputers & Typewriters, Short Course. William M. Mitchell et al. (C). 1990. pap. 9.95 (*1-56118-155-2*); 10.45 (*1-56118-158-7*) Paradigm MN.

Paradigm Keyboarding & Applications: Sessions 1-60. 4th ed. William M. Mitchell. LC 97-44133. 1998. write for info. (*0-7638-0147-X*) Paradigm MN.

Paradigm Keyboarding & Applications: A Mastery Approach for Microcomputers & Typewriters: Text with Student Disks, 3.5. 3rd ed. K. A. Mach & William Mitchell. text 29.95 incl. 3.5 hd (*1-56118-157-9*) EMC-Paradigm.

Paradigm Keyboarding Skills: A Mastery Approach for Microcomputers & Typewriters. William M. Mitchell et al. (C). 1990. pap. text 17.95 (*1-56118-150-1*) Paradigm MN.

Paradigm Keyboarding with WordPerfect: Version 5.1: Sessons 1-30. William M. Mitchell et al. LC 93-27499. 1994. pap. text 22.95 (*1-56118-508-6*) Paradigm MN.

Paradigm Lost: A Cultural & Systems Theoretical Critique of Political Economy. Kenneth M. Stokes. LC 94-23385. 440p. (gr. 13). 1995. text 93.95 (*1-56324-483-7*); pap. text 42.95 (*1-56324-484-5*) M E Sharpe.

Paradigm Lost: Reclaiming America's Educational Future. William G. Spady. Ed. by Ginger R. O'Neil. LC 97-74947. 1997. pap. 24.95 (*0-87652-232-0*, 236-001) Am Assn Sch Admin.

Paradigm Lost: The Linguistic Theory of Mikolaj Kruszewski. Joanna Radwanska Williams. LC 93-37183. (Studies in the History of the Language Sciences: No. 72). xii, 200p. 1994. 53.00 (*1-55619-608-3*) J Benjamins Pubng Co.

Paradigm Lost? Transitions & the Search for a New World Order. David Jablonsky. LC 94-38566. 144p. 1995. 55.00 (*0-275-95033-6*, Praeger Pubs) Greenwood.

Paradigm Maps. Alan C. Walter. Ed. by Beverly Miles. (Illus.). 37p. (Orig.). 1995. pap. text 29.97 (*1-57569-004-7*) Wisdom Pubng.

Paradigm Matrix & Its Effects on Future Prosperity & Human Events. Alan C. Walter. Ed. by Beverly Miles. (Illus.). 238p. (Orig.). 1995. pap. text 39.97 (*1-57569-002-0*) Wisdom Pubng.

Paradigm of Self-Organization: Current Trends in Self-Organization. Ed. by G. J. Dalenoort. (Studies in Cybernetics: Vol. 19). xii, 332p. 1989. pap. text 135.00 (*2-88124-709-1*) Gordon & Breach.

Paradigm of Self-Organization II. G. J. Dalenoort. (Studies in Cybernetics). 272p. 1994. pap. text 80.00 (*2-88124-976-0*) Gordon & Breach.

Paradigm Peachtree Accounting. Robert Dansby & Burton S. Kaliski. 192p. 16.95 (*0-7638-0200-X*) EMC-Paradigm.

***Paradigm Quest.** Jean Koberlein. 176p. 2000. pap. 10.95 (*1-58169-052-5*, Evergrn Pr AL) Genesis Comm Inc.

Paradigm QuickBooks Accounting. Robert L. Dansby et al. 192p. 16.95 (*0-7638-0202-6*) EMC-Paradigm.

Paradigm Reference Manual. Art Lyons & Patricia E. Seraydarian. 372p. (C). 1993. pap. text 16.95 (*1-56118-370-9*) Paradigm MN.

Paradigm Reference Manual. Art Lyons & Patricia E. Seraydarian. 372p. (C). 1994. pap. text, teacher ed. 8.00 (*1-56118-371-7*) Paradigm MN.

Paradigm Reference Manual: Workbook. Art Lyons et al. 256p. (C). 1994. student ed. 10.00 (*1-56118-372-5*) Paradigm MN.

Paradigm Shift. pap. 30.00 (*0-7657-6123-8*) Aronson.

Paradigm Shift: Teach the Universal Values. Robert L. Humphrey, J. D., & Associates Staff. LC 83-83386. (Illus.). 100p. 1984. pap. 7.95 (*0-915761-00-9*) Life Values Pr.

Paradigm Shift: The New Promise of Information Technology. Don Tapscott & Art Caston. 288p. 1993. 24.95 (*0-07-062857-2*) McGraw.

Paradigm Shift in the Church: How Natural Church Development Can Transform Theological Thinking. Christian Schwarz. 280p. 1999. 21.00 (*1-889638-05-6*) ChurchSmart.

Paradigm Skillbuilding: Keyboarding with Speed & Control. J. L. Mach et al. LC 97-52310. 1998. text 24.95 incl. cd-rom (*0-7638-0027-9*) Paradigm MN.

Paradigm Skillbuilding: Keyboarding with Speed & Control, Instructor's guide. J. L. Mach et al. 8.00 (*0-7638-0029-5*) EMC-Paradigm.

Paradigm Timed Writings. Jack Salem et al. 128p. 1992. pap. text, student ed. 16.95 (*1-56118-562-0*) Paradigm MN.

Paradigm Wars: Worldviews for a New Age. Mark B. Woodhouse. LC 95-50946. (Illus.). 632p. (Orig.). 1996. pap. 22.50 (*1-883319-42-0*) Frog Ltd CA.

Paradigmatic Grammar of Gikuyu. John M. Mugane. LC 96-38000. (Stanford Monographs in African Languages). 192p. (C). 1997. 36.95 (*1-57586-076-7*) CSLI.

Paradigmen: Facetten Einer Begriffskarriere. Michael Fischer & Paul Hoyningen-Huene. (Illus.). 309p. 1997. 51.95 (*3-631-32603-3*) P Lang Pubng.

Paradigmen der Moderne. Ed. by Helmut Bachmaier. LC 88-35224. (Viennese Heritage - Wiener Erbe Ser.: Vol. 3). (GER.). xxiii, 287p. (C). 1990. 89.00 (*90-272-3885-5*) J Benjamins Pubng Co.

Paradigms: Old & New. Jurgen Voigt. 1991. 7.95 (*0-942344-11-1*) Dakota Bks.

Paradigms: The Business of Discovering the Future. Joel A. Barker. LC 92-54950. Orig. Title: Future Edge. (Illus.). 256p. 1993. pap. 14.00 (*0-88730-647-0*, HarpBusn) HarpInfo.

Paradigms: The Economy of Inflection. Ed. by Frans Plank. LC 91-33626. (Empirical Approaches to Language Typology Ser.: No. 9). x, 317p. (C). 1991. lib. bdg. 136.95 (*3-11-012761-X*) Mouton.

Paradigms & Barriers: How Habits of Mind Govern Scientific Beliefs. Howard Margolis. LC 92-44650. (Illus.). 288p. (C). 1993. pap. text 15.95 (*0-226-50523-5*); lib. bdg. 40.00 (*0-226-50522-7*) U Ch Pr.

Paradigms & Conventions: Uncertainty, Decision Making, & Entrepreneurship. Young Back Choi. LC 92-39840. (Economics, Cognition, & Society Ser.). 200p. (C). 1993. text 54.50 (*0-472-10422-5*, 10422) U of Mich Pr.

Paradigms & Exercises in Syriac Grammar. 4th ed. Ed. by T. H. Robinson & L. H. Brockington. 176p. 1982. pap. text 21.00 (*0-19-815458-5*) OUP.

Paradigms & Paradoxes: The Philosophical Challenge of the Quantum Domain. Ed. by Robert G. Colodny. LC 79-158189. (University of Pittsburgh Series in the Philosophy of Science: No. 5). 466p. reprint ed. pap. 144.50 (*0-608-15648-5*, 203190100077) Bks Demand.

Paradigms & Paradoxes in the Life & Letters of Sigrid Undset. Margaret Dunn. LC 93-11754. 122p. (C). 1993. lib. bdg. 35.00 (*0-8191-9280-5*) U Pr of Amer.

Paradigms & Perspectives: Essays in Psychology. Hirsch L. Silverman. LC 97-25127. 208p. (C). 1997. 34.50 (*0-7618-0823-X*) U Pr of Amer.

Paradigms & Principal Parts for the Greek New Testament. Dale R. Bowne. LC 86-33989. 60p. (Orig.). (C). 1987. pap. text 14.00 (*0-8191-6099-7*) U Pr of Amer.

Paradigms & Programs. Amer. 96p. 1990. 15.95 (*0-02-897009-8*) Macmillan.

Paradigms & Promises: New Approaches to Educational Administration. William Foster. LC 86-18749. 218p. (Orig.). 1986. 36.95 (*0-87975-351-X*); pap. 23.95 (*0-87975-366-8*) Prometheus Bks.

Paradigms for Fast Parallel Approximability. J. Diaz et al. LC 96-51778. (Cambridge International Series in Parallel Computation). 166p. 1997. text 44.95 (*0-521-43170-0*) Cambridge U Pr.

***Paradigms for Health & Wellness.** 400p. (C). 1999. pap. text 34.20 (*0-536-02254-2*) Pearson Custom.

Paradigms for Language Theory & Other Essays. Jaakko Hintikka. LC 97-37727. (Jaakko Hintikka Selected Papers). 320p. 1998. text 147.00 (*0-7923-4780-3*) Kluwer Academic.

Paradigms in Behavior Therapy: Present & Promise. Ed. by Daniel B. Fishman et al. (Behavior Therapy & Behavioral Medicine Ser.). 392p. (C). 1988. 49.95 (*0-8261-5130-2*) Springer Pub.

Paradigms in Black Studies: Intellectual History, Cultural Meaning & Political Ideology. Ed. by Abdul Alkalimat. (Annual Theoretical Review in Afro-American Studies). 190p. (C). 1987. pap. 10.00 (*0-940103-03-6*); text 25.00 (*0-940103-02-8*) Twenty First Bks.

Paradigms in Economic Development: Classic Perspectives, Critiques & Reflections. Ed. by Rajani Kanth. LC 93-31934. 288p. (C). (gr. 13). 1994. text 77.95 (*1-56324-329-6*); pap. text 36.95 (*1-56324-330-X*) M E Sharpe.

Paradigms in Jewish Philosophy. Ed. by Raphael Jospe. LC 96-29952. 296p. 1997. 40.00 (*0-8386-3726-4*) Fairleigh Dickinson.

Paradigms in Medieval Thought Applications in Medieval Disciplines: A Symposium. Ed. by Nancy Van Deusen & Alvin E. Ford. LC 89-12866. (Medieval Studies: Vol. 3). 264p. 1990. lib. bdg. 89.95 (*0-88946-267-4*) E Mellen.

Paradigms in Passage: Patterns of Change in the Contemporary Study of Judaism. Jacob Neusner. (Studies in Judaism). 218p. (C). 1988. lib. bdg. 35.00 (*0-8191-6899-8*) U Pr of Amer.

Paradigms in Political Theory. 2nd ed. Ed. by Steven J. Gold. LC 92-40789. 236p. (C). 1993. text 44.95 (*0-8138-1283-6*) Iowa St U Pr.

Paradigms in Progress: Life Beyond Economics. rev. ed. Hazel Henderson. LC 91-37215. (Illus.). 304p. 1995. pap. 18.95 (*1-881052-74-5*) Berrett-Koehler.

Paradigms Lost. Ed. by Chester Hartman & Pedro Vilanova. 220p. (Orig.). (C). 1992. pap. 12.00 (*0-685-60303-2*) Inst Policy Stud.

Paradigms Lost: Online Oracles for the New Millennium. Gershon Siegel. 1995. pap. text 10.95 (*0-9644032-0-X*) Permnt Press.

Paradigms Lost: Tackling the Unanswered Mysteries of Modern Science. John L. Casti. 1990. pap. 14.00 (*0-380-71165-6*, Avon Bks) Morrow Avon.

Paradigms of Artificial Intelligence: A Methodological & Computational Analysis. Achim Hoffman. LC 98-19925. 1998. pap. 49.95 (*981-3083-97-2*, Pub. by Spr-Verlag) Spr-Verlag.

Paradigms of Artificial Intelligence Programming: Case Studies in Common LISP. Peter Norvig. LC 91-39187. 946p. 1992. pap. text 54.95 (*1-55860-191-0*, QA76.6) Morgan Kaufmann.

Paradigms of Clinical Social work. Ed. by Rachelle A. Dorfman. LC 88-2879. 464p. 1988. text 48.95 (*0-87630-512-5*) Brunner-Mazel.

Paradigms of Clinical Social Work, 2. Rachelle A. Dorfman. (Paradigms of Clinical Social Work Ser.). 1998. 48.95 (*0-87630-882-5*) Brunner-Mazel.

***Paradigms of Complexity: Fractals & Structures in the Sciences.** Ed. by Miroslav M. Novak. 400p. 2000. 98.00 (*981-02-4292-1*) World Scientific Pub.

Paradigms of Memory: The Occupation & Other Hi/stories in the Novels of Patrick Modiano. Ed. by Martin Guyot-Bender & William VanderWolk. LC 97-32336. (Currents in Comparative Romance Languages & Literatures Ser.: Vol. 64). VIII, 194p. (C). 1998. 44.95 (*0-8204-3864-2*) P Lang Pubng.

Paradigms of Personality. Jane Loevinger. (Psychology Ser.). (Illus.). 269p. (C). 1987. pap. text 24.95 (*0-7167-1840-5*) W H Freeman.

Paradigms of Social Change: Modernization Development. Wolf-Hagan Krauth. text 59.95 (*0-312-23394-9*) St Martin.

Paradigms of the Large-Scale Universe. V. G. Gurzadyan. 160p. 1994. text 61.00 (*2-88124-966-3*) Gordon & Breach.

Paradigms of the Past: The Story of Missouri Archaeology. Michael J. O'Brien. LC 95-36754. (Illus.). 592p. (C). 1995. pap. text 29.95 (*0-8262-1019-8*) U of Mo Pr.

***Paradigms Regained: A Further Exploration of the Mysteries of Modern Science.** John L. Casti. LC 99-45972. (Illus.). 256p. 2000. 25.00 (*0-688-16115-4*, Wm Morrow) Morrow Avon.

Paradigms Regained: Pluralism & the Practice of Criticism. James L. Battersby. LC 91-18260. 328p. (C). 1991. text 37.50 (*0-8122-3127-9*) U of Pa Pr.

P

An Asterisk (*) at the beginning of an entry indicates that the title is appearing for the first time.

Paradigms Regained: The Uses of Illuminative, Semiotic & Post-Modern Criticism As Modes of Inquiry in Educational Technology -- A Book of Readings. Ed. by Denis Hlynka & John C. Belland. LC 90-39819. 560p. (C). 1991. 49.95 (*0-87778-223-7*) Educ Tech Pubns.

Paradigms, Thought & Language. Ivana Markova. LC 81-22022. (Illus.). 241p. reprint ed. pap. 74.80 (*0-8357-3098-0*, 203935500012) Bks Demand.

Parading Through History: The Making of the Crow Nation in America, 1805-1935. Frederick E. Hoxie. (Studies in North American Indian History). (Illus.). 405p. (C). 1995. text 39.95 (*0-521-48057-4*) Cambridge U Pr.

Parading Through History: The Making of the Crow Nation in America, 1805-1935. Frederick E. Hoxie. 405p. 1997. pap. 17.95 (*0-521-48522-3*) Cambridge U Pr.

Parading with Piglets: A Playful ABC Pop-Up. Biruta A. Hansen. LC 95-71220. (Pop-Up Bks.). (Illus.). 7p. (J). (ps-1). 1996. 16.95 (*0-7922-2711-5*, Pub. by Natl Geog) S&S Trade.

Paradiplomacy in Action: The Foreign Relations of Subnational Governments. Ed. by Francisco Aldecoa & Michael Keating. LC 99-20579. 248p. 1999. pap. 26.50 (*0-7146-8018-4*, Pub. by F Cass Pubs) Intl Spec Bk.

*__Paradiplomacy in Action: The Foreign Relations of Subnational Governments.__ Ed. by Francisco Aldecoa & Michael Keating. LC 99-20579. 248p. 1999. 52.50 (*0-7146-4971-6*, Pub. by F Cass Pubs) Intl Spec Bk.

Paradis Artificiels. Charles Baudelaire. 1964. pap. 10.95 (*0-8288-9063-3*, LIV160) Fr & Eur.

Paradis Artificiels. Charles Baudelaire. (Folio Ser.: No. 964). (FRE.). pap. 8.95 (*2-07-036964-1*) Schoenhof.

Paradis Perdu Suivi de Cinquieme Colonne. Ernest Hemingway. (FRE.). 384p. 1972. pap. 11.95 (*0-7859-2274-1*, 2070361756) Fr & Eur.

Paradis Retrouve. Anthony Borgia. 180p. 1992. 19.95 (*2-920083-61-9*) Edns Roseau.

*__Paradisal Love: Johann Gottfried Herder & the Song of Songs.__ John D. Baildam. (Journal for the Study of the Old Testament Supplement Ser.: No. 298). 368p. 1999. 90.00 (*1-84127-022-9*, Pub. by Sheffield Acad) CUP Services.

Paradise, 1. Madeline Baker. 368p. 1999. mass mkt. 5.50 (*0-8439-4552-4*) Dorchester Pub Co.

Paradise. Caesarea Basil. 1994. pap. text 1.95 (*0-89981-068-3*) Eastern Orthodox.

Paradise. Elena Castedo. LC 89-25640. 336p. 1995. pap. 13.00 (*0-8021-3427-0*, Grove) Grove-Atltic.

Paradise. Phoebe Conn. 304p. 1995. mass mkt. 4.99 (*0-8217-5066-6*, Zebra Kensgtn) Kensgtn Pub Corp.

Paradise. Abdulrazak Gurnah. 256p. 1995. pap. 11.00 (*1-56584-163-8*, Pub. by New Press NY) Norton.

Paradise. Judith McNaught. Ed. by Linda Marrow. LC 91-12897. 720p. 1992. per. 7.99 (*0-671-77680-0*) PB.

Paradise. Toni Morrison. LC 97-80913. 318p. 1999. pap. 13.95 (*0-452-28039-7*, Plume) Dutton Plume.

Paradise. Toni Morrison. LC 97-80913. 320p. 1997. 25.00 (*0-679-43374-0*) Knopf.

Paradise. Ed. by Patrick Remy & Susanne Ricard-Konig. (Illus.). 224p. 1999. pap. 19.95 (*3-88243-640-9*, Pub. by Steidl) Dist Art Pubs.

Paradise. Mike Resnick. 1990. mass mkt. 4.99 (*0-8125-0716-9*) Tor Bks.

Paradise. large type enl. ed. Toni Morrison. LC 97-31896. 453p. 1997. pap. 25.00 (*0-375-70217-2*) Random.

Paradise: A Cultural Guide. Richard Harris. 200p. 1996. pap. 22.50 (*981-210-089-X*, Pub. by Times Academic) Intl Spec Bk.

Paradise: Class, Commuters, & Ethnicity in Rural Ontario. Stanley R. Barrett. (Anthropological Horizons Ser.: No. 5). 304p. (C). 1994. text 50.00 (*0-8020-0442-3*); pap. text 18.95 (*0-8020-7232-1*) U of Toronto Pr.

Paradise: Selected Poems. Elena Shvarts. Tr. by M. Molnar & C. Kelly from RUS. (ENG & RUS.). 144p. 1994. pap. 18.95 (*1-85224-249-3*, Pub. by Bloodaxe Bks) Dufour.

Paradise: Stories of a Changing Chesapeake. J. H. Hall. (Illus.). 130p. (Orig.). 1994. pap. 9.95 (*1-880902-07-9*) Rappahannock Pr.

Paradise - Abode of the Righteous Dead. Gordon Lindsay. 1967. 1.95 (*0-89985-085-5*) Christ for the Nations.

Paradise & Cash. David Bristol. LC 80-50064. (Series Five). 50p. 1980. pap. 7.00 (*0-931846-14-5*) Wash Writers Pub.

Paradise & Method: Poetry & Praxis. Bruce Andrews. (Avant-Garde & Modernism Studies). 296p. 1996. text 59.95 (*0-8101-1307-4*); pap. text 19.95 (*0-8101-1308-2*) Northwestern U Pr.

Paradise & More. Shirl Henke. 448p. 1991. pap. text, mass mkt. 4.99 (*0-8439-3170-1*) Dorchester Pub Co.

Paradise & More. Shirl Henke. 448p. 1997. mass mkt. 5.99 (*0-8439-4332-7*, Leisure Bks) Dorchester Pub Co.

Paradise & Paradigm: Key Symbols in Persian Christianity & the Baha'I Faith. Christopher Buck. LC 98-45882. 1p. (C). 1999. text 81.50 (*0-7914-4061-3*); pap. text 27.95 (*0-7914-4062-1*) State U NY Pr.

Paradise & Pestilence: Aspects of Provence. Suzanne, Duchess of St. Albans. LC 97-221653. 144p. 1998. 29.95 (*0-7206-1027-3*, Pub. by P Owen Ltd) Dufour.

*__Paradise Bank: The Mercantile Bank of India, 1893-1984.__ Edwin Green & Sara Kinsey. LC 99-16515. (Studies in Banking History). (Illus.). 242p. 1999. text 86.95 (*1-84014-685-0*, Pub. by Ashgate Pub) Ashgate Pub Co.

*__Paradise Bay.__ Victoria Alexander. 400p. 1999. mass mkt. 5.99 (*0-505-52350-7*, Love Spell) Dorchester Pub Co.

Paradise Burning: Adventures of a High Times Journalist. Chris Simunek. LC 98-22922. 192p. 1998. pap. 12.95 (*0-312-18753-X*) St Martin.

Paradise by Design. Kathryn Phillips. LC 97-18172. 265p. 1998. 25.00 (*0-86547-519-9*) N Point Pr.

Paradise by the River. V. Rossi. LC 99-172814. 1998. pap. text 11.95 (*0-88922-393-9*, Pub. by Talonbks) Genl Dist Srvs.

Paradise Called Pebble Beach. Ray A. March. Ed. by Sally Peters. 1992. 40.00 (*0-671-77722-X*) PB.

Paradise Called Texas. Janice J. Shefelman. (Illus.). 128p. (J). (gr. 4-5). 1983. 12.95 (*0-89015-409-0*); pap. 6.95 (*0-89015-506-2*) Sunbelt Media.

Paradise Called Texas. large type ed. Debra Frasier. 1993. 36.00 (*0-614-09850-5*, L-34108-00) Am Printing Hse.

Paradise Calls: Spellbinding Story of Hawaii's Evangelist Danny Yamashiro. Daniel K. Yamashiro. Ed. by Jean Tatami. Tr. by Kazuyo Kitaguchi. LC 97-198625. (Illus.). 145p. (Orig.). 1997. pap. 10.00 (*1-890312-00-2*) Jesus Christ.

Paradise Complex: An Exploration of the Forbidden. Douglas Lockhart. LC 96-41674. 368p. 1997. pap. 24.95 (*1-85230-809-5*, Pub. by Element MA) Penguin Putnam.

*__Paradise County.__ Karen Robards. 352p. 2000. 24.95 (*0-671-78645-8*, PB Hardcover) PB.

Paradise Court large type ed. Jenny Oldfield. LC 97-12886. 603 p. 1997. write for info. (*0-7540-2011-8*, Galaxy Child Lrg Print) Chivers N Amer.

Paradise Creek: A Love Story That Will Capture Your Heart. Brenton G. Yorgason. 167p. 1999. pap. 9.95 (*0-9659559-8-2*) Lghthse Pubs.

Paradise Dislocated: Morris, Politics, Art. Jeffrey Skoblow. LC 93-2748. (Victorian Literature & Culture Ser.). 224p. reprint ed. pap. 69.50 (*0-608-20048-4*, 207132000011) Bks Demand.

*__Paradise Divided: The Changes, the Challenges, the Choices.__ Paul Kelly. 304p. 2000. pap. 24.95 (*1-86508-291-0*, Pub. by Allen & Unwin Pty) Paul & Co Pubs.

*__Paradise Explained: A Reader's Road Map to the Novels of Toni Morrison.__ Ron David. 256p. 2000. pap. 14.95 (*0-375-70732-8*) Random Ref & Info.

Paradise Farm. Brenda S. Webster. LC 98-26875. 250p. (C). 1999. text 31.50 (*0-7914-4099-0*) State U NY Pr.

Paradise Farm. Brenda S. Webster. LC 98-26875. (C). 2000. pap. text 19.95 (*0-7914-4100-8*) State U NY Pr.

Paradise Fever: Growing up in the Shadow of the New Age. Ptolemy Tompkins. LC 97-23607. 288p. 1997. mass mkt. 23.00 (*0-380-97438-X*, Avon Bks) Morrow Avon.

Paradise Fever: Growing up in the Shadow of the New Age. Ptolemy Tompkins. 304p. 1998. pap. 12.50 (*0-380-79062-9*, Avon Bks) Morrow Avon.

Paradise for Sale. Carl N. McDaniel & John M. Gowdy. LC 99-12829. 208p. 2000. 45.00 (*0-520-21864-7*, Pub. by U CA Pr) Cal Prin Full Svc.

Paradise for Sale: Back to Sustainability. Carl N. McDaniel & John M. Gowdy. LC 99-12829. 208p. 2000. pap. 17.95 (*0-520-22229-6*, Pub. by U CA Pr) Cal Prin Full Svc.

Paradise for the Portuguese Queen: Poems. Benjamin Ivry. LC 97-25368. 80p. 1998. pap. 12.95 (*0-914061-69-0*) Orchises Pr.

Paradise Forks Rock Climbing. David Bloom. (Illus.). 50p. (Orig.). 1995. pap. 12.95 (*0-934641-98-6*) Falcon Pub Inc.

Paradise Found. Rebecca Cole. LC 99-24767. 2000. 35.00 (*0-609-60415-5*) C Potter.

Paradise Found: How to Live in North America's Best Climate for under 500 Dollars a Month. rev. ed. R. Emil Neuman. (Illus.). 176p. 1989. pap. 12.95 (*0-9614924-0-6*) United Res CA.

Paradise Found: Primitive Eden at the North Pole. W. F. Warren. 1991. lib. bdg. 78.95 (*0-8490-5034-0*) Gordon Pr.

Paradise Found: The Beautiful Retreats & Sanctuaries of California & the Southwest. Photos by Melba Levick. (Illus.). 132p. 1995. pap. 18.95 (*0-8118-0687-1*) Chronicle Bks.

Paradise Found: The Cradle of the Human Race at the North Pole. 11th ed. William F. Warren. 505p. 1996. reprint ed. spiral bd. 27.50 (*0-7873-0934-6*) Hlth Research.

Paradise Found: The Settlement of the Santa Catalina Mountains. Kathy Alexander. (Illus.). (Orig.). 1991. pap. write for info. (*0-9628832-0-4*) Skunkworks.

Paradise Found, & Lost: Odyssey in Chile. Eva Krutein. LC 94-70696. 241p. (Orig.). 1994. pap. 11.00 (*0-938513-16-8*) Amador Pubs.

Paradise Garden. A. Clifford. mass mkt. 6.95 (*0-7472-5069-3*, Pub. by Headline Bk Pub) Trafalgar.

Paradise Garden. Illus. by Colin Thompson. LC 97-28221. 32p. (J). 1998. 17.00 (*0-679-89076-9*) Knopf.

Paradise Garden: A Trip Through Howard Finster's Visionary World. Robert Peacock & Annibel Jenkins. LC 95-17481. (Illus.). 120p. 1996. 35.00 (*0-8118-1197-2*); pap. 22.95 (*0-8118-0941-2*) Chronicle Bks.

Paradise Garden Murals of Malinalco: Utopia & Empire in Sixteenth-Century Mexico. Jeanette F. Peterson. LC 92-7992. (Illus.). 246p. (C). 1993. text 40.00 (*0-292-72750-X*) U of Tex Pr.

Paradise, God's Guest of Tomorrow: A Mystical Visit to Purgatory & a Consideration of the Sabbatine Privilege. L. M. Dooley. 1986. 4.95 (*1-56036-002-X*, 40580) AMI Pr.

Paradise Hotel. Georges Feydeau. (Plays for Performance Ser.). 124p. 1990. pap. 7.95 (*0-929587-45-6*, Pub. by I R Dee); lib. bdg. 15.95 (*0-929587-48-0*, Pub. by I R Dee) Natl Bk Netwk.

*__Paradise Hotel.__ Richard Foreman. LC 99-87849. (Illus.). 256p. 2000. 29.95 (*1-58567-004-9*, Pub. by Overlook Pr); pap. 19.95 (*1-58567-015-4*, Pub. by Overlook Pr) Penguin Putnam.

Paradise in Mexico: Cuernavaca. E. De Davila. 1976. lib. bdg. 59.95 (*0-8490-2408-0*) Gordon Pr.

*__Paradise In Penang.__ large type ed. Barbara Cartland. LC 99-46305. 190p. 1999. 23.95 (*0-7838-8795-7*, G K Hall Lrg Type) Mac Lib Ref.

Paradise in the Palouse. Nancy M. Prevost. 35p. 1985. pap. 5.95 (*0-87770-365-5*) Ye Galleon.

Paradise Interpreted: Interpretations of Biblical Paradise in Judaism & Christianity. Gerard P. Luttikhuizen. LC 99-13596. 208p. 1999. 87.50 (*90-04-11331-2*) Brill Academic Pubs.

Paradise Is Full of Bugs. W. A. Corley. LC 97-5007. (Illus.). 173p. (Orig.). Date not set. 11.95 (*0-9656099-0-1*) Blue Heron Books.

Paradise Isle. large type ed. Jacqueline Hacsi. (Linford Romance Library). 320p. 1993. pap. 16.99 (*0-7089-7397-3*, Linford) Ulverscroft.

Paradise Job. Sally Spencer. 1999. 26.00 (*0-7278-5464-X*, Pub. by Severn Hse) Chivers N Amer.

Paradise Junction. large type ed. Phillip Finch. LC 93-21813. 549p. 1993. lib. bdg. 21.95 (*1-56054-708-1*) Thorndike Pr.

*__Paradise Lane.__ Hamilton. 2000. 27.95 (*0-593-03466-X*) Transworld Publishers Ltd.

*__Paradise Lane.__ Ruth Hamilton. 2000. pap. 10.95 (*0-552-14141-0*, Pub. by Transworld Publishers Ltd) Trafalgar.

Paradise Lost. E. Barbier et al. 1994. 32.00 (*1-85383-181-6*, Pub. by Escan Pubns) Island Pr.

Paradise Lost. Richard Bradford. (Open Guides to Literature Ser.). 112p. 1992. pap. 27.95 (*0-335-09982-3*) OpUniv Pr.

Paradise Lost. Ed. by Merritt Y. Hughes. 284p. (C). 1962. pap. text 37.80 (*0-02-358280-4*, Macmillan Coll) P-H.

Paradise Lost. John Milton. 1998. pap. text 14.95 (*1-55701-231-8*) BNI Pubns.

*__Paradise Lost, Vol. 1.__ John Milton. 1999. pap. 4.95 (*0-7910-4146-8*) Chehalem.

Paradise Lost. John Milton. Ed. by Roy Flannagan. LC 92-5970. (Illus.). 686p. (C). 1992. pap. 39.60 (*0-02-338235-X*, Macmillan Coll) P-H.

*__Paradise Lost.__ John Milton. (Penguin Classics Ser.). 375p. 2000. pap. 10.00 (*0-14-042426-1*, Penguin Bks) Viking Penguin.

Paradise Lost. Nancy Willard. 48p. 16.95 (*0-06-029035-8*); lib. bdg. 16.89 (*0-06-029036-6*) HarpC.

Paradise Lost. Zunder. LC 98-34392. 238p. 1999. text 55.00 (*0-312-21859-1*) St Martin.

Paradise Lost. large type ed. John Milton. 1997. pap. 19.95 (*1-55701-220-2*) BNI Pubns.

*__Paradise Lost.__ Don Blanding. (Illus.). 48p. 2000. reprint ed. pap. 5.95 (*0-912180-55-2*) Petroglyph.

Paradise Lost. John Milton. 395p. 1983. reprint ed. lib. bdg. 29.95 (*0-89966-457-1*) Buccaneer Bks.

Paradise Lost. John Milton. Ed. by Richard Bentley. (Anglistica & Americana Ser.: Vol. 175). 415p. 1976. reprint ed. lib. bdg. 115.00 (*3-487-06053-1*) G Olms Pubs.

Paradise Lost. 2nd ed. John Milton. Ed. by Alastair Fowler. LC 97-51835. (English Poets Ser.). 704p. (C). 1998. 98.25 (*0-582-21519-6*) Longman.

Paradise Lost, Bks. 1 & 2. John Milton. Ed. by John Broadbent. (Milton for Schools & Colleges Ser.). 160p. (gr. 11-12). 1972. pap. text 16.95 (*0-521-08298-6*) Cambridge U Pr.

Paradise Lost, Bks. 3 & 4. John Milton. Ed. by L. J. Potter & John Broadbent. LC 75-36681. (Milton for Schools & Colleges Ser.). 143p. 1976. pap. text 16.95 (*0-521-21150-6*) Cambridge U Pr.

Paradise Lost, Bks. 5 & 6. John Milton. Ed. by Robert Hodge & Isabel G. MacCaffrey. LC 75-8314. (Milton for Schools & Colleges Ser.). (Illus.). 167p. (C). 1975. pap. text 16.95 (*0-521-20796-7*) Cambridge U Pr.

Paradise Lost, Bks. 7 & 8. John Milton. Ed. by D. Aers & Mary Ann Radzinowics. LC 77-181884. (Milton for Schools & Colleges Ser.). 154p. 1974. pap. text 16.95 (*0-521-20457-7*) Cambridge U Pr.

Paradise Lost, Bks. 9 & 10. John Milton. Ed. by R. E. Houghton. 244p. 1970. pap. text 8.95 (*0-19-911001-8*) OUP.

Paradise Lost, Set. John Milton. Ed. by J. M. Evans. LC 72-87438. (Milton for Schools & Colleges Ser.). 208p. (C). 1973. pap. text 16.95 (*0-521-20067-9*) Cambridge U Pr.

Paradise Lost: A History of Game Preservation in East Africa. Thomas P. Ofcansky. (Illus.). 1997. 22.50 (*0-937058-29-7*) West Va U Pr.

Paradise Lost: A Prose Rendition. John Milton. Ed. by Robert Shepherd, Jr. (Illus.). 160p. 1984. 17.95 (*0-8164-0534-4*); 8.95 (*0-8164-2415-2*) Harper SF.

Paradise Lost: A Tercenenary Tribute. Ed. by Balachandra Rajan. LC 77-429833. 154p. reprint ed. pap. 47.80 (*0-608-12872-4*, 202365900033) Bks Demand.

Paradise Lost: An Annotated Bibliography. annot. ed. Paul J. Klemp. 264p. 1996. 39.50 (*0-8108-3152-X*) Scarecrow.

Paradise Lost: An Authoritative Text, Backgrounds & Sources, Criticism. 2nd ed. John Milton. Ed. by Scott Elledge. LC 92-9988. (Critical Editions Ser.). 688p. (C). 1993. pap. text 14.00 (*0-393-96293-8*) Norton.

Paradise Lost: California's Experience, America's Future. Peter Schrag. LC 97-30790. 344p. 1998. 25.00 (*1-56584-357-6*, Pub. by New Press NY) Norton.

*__Paradise Lost: California's Experience, America's Future.__ Peter Schrag. LC 98-43330. 347p. 1999. pap. 14.95 (*0-520-21898-1*, Pub. by U CA Pr) Cal Prin Full Svc.

Paradise Lost: Ideal & Tragic Epic. Francis C. Blessington. (Masterwork Studies: No. 12). 160p. 1988. 29.00 (*0-8057-7969-8*, Twayne) Mac Lib Ref.

Paradise Lost: Modern Library College Editions. John Milton. Ed. by William G. Madsen. 344p. (C). 1969. pap. 8.44 (*0-07-553668-4*, 30997) McGraw.

Paradise Lost: Reflections on the Struggle for Authenticity in the Middle East. C. A. Van Nieuwenhuijze. LC 96-45392. (Social, Economic & Political Studies of the Middle East: Vol. 56). 424p. 1997. 132.00 (*90-04-10672-3*) Brill Academic Pubs.

Paradise Lost: The Neo-Romantic Imagination In. David Mellor. (Illus.). 144p. (C). 1987. reprint ed. pap. 45.00 (*0-85331-532-9*, Pub. by Lund Humphries) Antique Collect.

Paradise Lost: The Novel. Joseph Lanzara. LC 93-87625. 255p. 1994. 24.95 (*0-9639621-4-0*) New Arts Lib.

Paradise Lost & Found. O. H. Spate. (Illus.). 410p. 1990. 51.00 (*0-08-034400-3*, Pergamon Pr) Elsevier.

Paradise Lost & Other Poems. J. Millon. 1961. mass mkt. 7.99 (*0-451-62826-8*) NAL.

Paradise Lost & Other Poems. John Milton. 1981. 12.09 (*0-606-03885-X*, Pub. by Turtleback) Demco.

Paradise Lost & Paradise Regained. John Milton. Ed. & Intro. by Christopher B. Ricks. (Signet Classics Ser.). 399p. 1975. mass mkt. 7.95 (*0-451-52474-8*, Sig Classics) NAL.

Paradise Lost & the Classical Epic. Francis C. Blessington. 1979. 19.95 (*0-7100-0160-6*, Routledge Thoemms) Routledge.

Paradise Lost & the Modern Reader. Thomas Wheeler. LC 73-76786. 144p. reprint ed. pap. 44.70 (*0-608-15804-6*, 203108100073) Bks Demand.

Paradise Lost & the Rise of the American Republic. Lydia D. Schulman. 256p. 1992. text 45.00 (*1-55553-125-3*) NE U Pr.

Paradise Lost & the Romantic Reader. Lucy Newlyn. LC 92-463. (Illus.). 308p. (C). 1993. text 65.00 (*0-19-811277-7*, Clarendon Pr) OUP.

Paradise Lost As Myth. Isabel G. MacCaffrey. LC 59-9282. 239p. reprint ed. pap. 74.10 (*0-7837-4169-3*, 205901800012) Bks Demand.

Paradise Lost in Short: Smith, Stillingfleet, & the Transformation of Epic. Kay G. Stevenson et al. LC 97-43455. (Illus.). 200p. 1998. 36.00 (*0-8386-3718-3*) Fairleigh Dickinson.

Paradise Lost Issue. (Review Ser.: No. 2). 136p. 1993. pap. 6.00 (*0-9641292-4-8*) Global Cty Pr.

Paradise Lost (Milton) Ruth Mitchell. (Barron's Book Notes Ser.). (C). 1984. pap. 2.50 (*0-8120-3435-X*) Barron.

Paradise Lost Notes. Roy C. Flannagan. (Cliffs Notes Ser.). 88p. 1963. pap. 4.95 (*0-8220-0977-3*, Cliff) IDG Bks.

Paradise Lost or Gained. Fernando Alegria. LC 91-11258. 240p. (Orig.). 1991. pap. 11.00 (*1-55885-037-6*) Arte Publico.

Paradise Lost, Paradise Regained! Diana G. Gallagher. (Secret World of Alex Mack Ser.: No. 34). (J). (gr. 3-6). 1998. pap. 4.50 (*0-671-02111-7*, Minstrel Bks) PB.

Paradise Man. Suzanne Simmons. 1997. mass mkt. 5.99 (*0-312-95633-9*) St Martin.

Paradise Mislaid: In Search of the Australian Tribe of Paraguay. Anne Whitehead. 635p. 1998. 35.00 (*0-7022-2651-3*, Pub. by Univ Queensland Pr) Intl Spec Bk.

Paradise Moon. Donna Anders. (Historical Ser.: No. 713). 1992. mass mkt. 3.99 (*0-373-28713-5*, 1-28713-5) Harlequin Bks.

Paradise Mountain. Thomas Anderson. 93p. (Orig.). (J). (gr. 4-6). 1995. pap. 9.99 (*0-88092-162-5*) Royal Fireworks.

Paradise Myth in Eighteenth-Century Russia: Utopian Patterns in Early Secular Russian Literature & Culture. Stephen L. Baehr. (Illus.). 330p. 1991. 42.50 (*0-8047-1533-5*) Stanford U Pr.

Paradise, New York: A Novel. Eileen Pollack. LC 98-33591. 288p. 2000. 49.50 (*1-56639-657-3*) Temple U Pr.

*__Paradise, New York: A Novel.__ Eileen Pollack. 288p. 2000. pap. 17.95 (*1-56639-789-8*) Temple U Pr.

Paradise News. David Lodge. 304p. 1993. pap. 12.95 (*0-14-016521-5*, Penguin Bks) Viking Penguin.

Paradise News. large type ed. David Lodge. LC 92-11067. 509p. 1992. reprint ed. 20.95 (*1-56054-450-3*) Thorndike Pr.

Paradise Now: Breaking the Trance. Charles Munn. LC 99-62035. 365p. 1999. 25.00 (*0-7388-0394-4*); pap. 15.00 (*0-7388-0395-2*) Xlibris Corp.

Paradise of Association: Popular Culture & Popular Organizations in the Paris Commune of 1871. Martin P. Johnson. 336p. (C). 1996. text 47.50 (*0-472-10724-0*, 10724) U of Mich Pr.

Paradise of Bombs. Scott R. Sanders. LC 92-30536. 176p. 1993. pap. 13.00 (*0-8070-6343-6*) Beacon Pr.

Paradise of Children: A Retelling of the Tale of Pandora's Box. Nathaniel Hawthorne. (J). (gr. 5-7). 1998. pap. 3.95 (*0-89979-113-1*) British Am Bks.

Paradise of Delights, 1620. John Sweetnam & Saint Benedict. LC 76-361687. (English Recusant Literature, 1558-1640 Ser.). 217 p. 1976. write for info. (*0-85967-279-4*) Scolar Pr.

Paradise of Forms: New & Selected Poems. Aaron Shurin. LC 99-20021. 142p. 1999. pap. 14.95 (*1-883689-81-3*, Pub. by Talisman Hse) SPD-Small Pr Dist.

Paradise of Forms: Selected Poems. Aaron Shurin. LC 99-20021. 136p. 1999. 32.95 (*1-883689-82-1*) Talisman Hse.

Paradise of Frolicsome Fools. Lonnie Bailey. 1999. pap. write for info. (*1-58235-036-1*) Watermrk Pr.

Paradise of Origamic Architecture. 2nd ed. Ed. by Masahiro Chatani & Keiko Nakawa. (Illus.). 76p. 1989. pap. 34.95 (*4-395-27018-2*, Pub. by Shokokusha) Bks Nippan.

Paradise of Poets. Jerome Rothenberg. LC 99-28856. 128p. 1999. pap. 14.95 (*0-8112-1427-3*, Pub. by New Directions) Norton.

An Asterisk (*) at the beginning of an entry indicates that the title is appearing for the first time.

Paradise of Snakes: An Archetypal Analysis of Conrad's Political Novels. Claire Rosenfield. LC 67-25522. 1994. lib. bdg. 12.50 (*0-226-72754-8*) U Ch Pr.

Paradise of the Blind. Duong T. Huong. 272p. 1994. pap. 18.99 (*0-14-023620-1*, Penguin Bks) Viking Penguin.

Paradise of the North: Alaska's Prince William Sound. Gloria J. Maschmeyer & John Wedin. (Illus.). 90p. 1995. pap. 19.95 (*0-936425-35-0*) Greatland Graphics.

Paradise of Women: Writings by Englishwomen of the Renaissance. Ed. by Betty S. Travitsky. 289p. 1989. pap. text 20.50 (*0-231-06885-9*) Col U Pr.

Paradise of Women: Writings by Englishwomen of the Renaissance, 22. Ed. by Betty S. Travitsky. LC 80-1705. (Contributions in Women's Studies: No. 22). 283p. 1981. 65.00 (*0-313-22177-4*, TPW/, Greenwood Pr) Greenwood.

Paradise on Earth. Jim Thorsell. 1997. 39.95 (*1-57769-001-X*) Wrld Heritage.

Paradise on Earth: Some Thoughts on European Images of Non-European Man. Henri Baudet. Tr. by Elizabeth Wentholt. LC 76-21632. 87p. 1977. reprint ed. lib. bdg. 55.00 (*0-8371-8973-X*, BAPOE, Greenwood Pr) Greenwood.

Paradise on Earth: The Gardens of Western Europe. Gabrielle Van Zuylen. Tr. by I. Mark Paris. LC 95-75671. (Discoveries Ser.). (Illus.). 176p. 1995. pap. 12.95 (*0-8109-2851-5*, Pub. by Abrams) Time Warner.

Paradise on Earth: The Natural World Heritage List. Mark Swadling. 336p. (YA). (gr. 9 up). 1995. 39.95 (*0-646-19397-X*) Wrld Heritage.

Paradise on Earth: The Natural World Heritage List. limited ed. Mark Swadling. 336p. (YA). (gr. 9 up). 1995. 120.00 (*0-646-19263-9*) Wrld Heritage.

***Paradise on the Plains.** Keith Cook. LC 98-75677. 258p. (Orig.). 1999. pap. 14.95 (*1-890622-61-3*) Leathers Pub.

Paradise on the Steppe. Joseph S. Height. 1989. reprint ed. 28.00 (*0-614-23867-6*) Am Hist Soc Ger.

Paradise on Your Doorstep: Brief Meditations on Revelation 3:20. Anthony M. Coniaris. LC 96-75549. 136p. 1996. pap. 10.95 (*1-880971-19-4*) Light&Life Pub Co MN.

***Paradise Outlaws: Remembering the Beats.** John Tytell. LC 99-18713. (Illus.). 240p. 1999. 24.00 (*0-688-16443-9*, Wm Morrow) Morrow Avon.

Paradise Overdose. Brian Antoni. 320p. 1994. 21.00 (*0-671-88426-3*) S&S Trade.

Paradise Overdose. Brian Antoni. LC 96-9581. 256p. 1997. reprint ed. pap. 12.00 (*0-8021-3487-4*, Grove) Grove-Atltic.

***Paradise Palace.** Peter Slater. 2000. pap. 9.99 (*1-902644-18-2*) Prowler Pr.

***Paradise Park.** Ed. by Karen Ingham. (Illus.). 2000. pap. 24.95 (*1-85411-281-3*, Pub. by Seren Bks) Dufour.

Paradise Paved: The Challenge of Growth in the New West. Raye C. Ringholz. LC 96-15764. (Illus.). 216p. 1996. pap. 14.95 (*0-87480-511-2*) U of Utah Pr.

Paradise, Piece by Piece. Molly Peacock. LC 97-49965. 384p. 1998. 23.95 (*1-57322-097-3*, Riverhead Books) Putnam Pub Group.

Paradise, Piece by Piece. Molly Peacock. 1999. reprint ed. pap. 14.00 (*1-57322-730-7*, Riverhd Trade) Berkley Pub.

Paradise Planters, the Story of Brook Farm. Katherine K. Burton. LC 72-2949. reprint ed. 52.50 (*0-404-10714-1*) AMS Pr.

Paradise Plume. Mary R. Stott. 258p. 1984. 8.95 (*0-89697-141-4*) Intl Univ Pr.

Paradise Postponed. John Mortimer. 384p. 1986. pap. 12.95 (*0-14-009864-X*, Penguin Bks) Viking Penguin.

Paradise Postponed. large type ed. Jane Converse. 1994. 27.99 (*0-7089-3183-9*) Ulverscroft.

Paradise Postponed: Essays on Research & Development in the South Pacific: Proceedings. Young Nations Conference, Sidney, 1976 Staff. Ed. by Alexander F. Mamak & Grant McCall. 1979. pap. text 21.00 (*0-08-023004-0*, Pergamon Pr) Elsevier.

Paradise Presented: Beautiful Gardens of Philadelphia & the Delaware Valley. Barbara Klaczynska. (Illus.). 80p. (Orig.). 1996. pap. 7.95 (*0-9653959-0-1*) Grdns Collaborative.

Paradise Preserves. Yvonne N. Armitage. LC 87-32710. (Illus.). 126p. (Orig.). 1988. pap. 7.95 (*0-916630-63-3*) Pr Pacifica.

Paradise Purchased, Paradise Promised. Brett White. LC 93-84205. 224p. (Orig.). 1993. pap. 14.95 (*1-880365-53-7*) Prof Pr NC.

Paradise Pursued: The Novels of Rose Macaulay. Alice Crawford. LC 94-30239. 1995. 36.50 (*0-8386-3573-3*) Fairleigh Dickinson.

***Paradise Reconsidered.** Justine Tally. (Toni Morrison's Histories & Truths Forecast Ser.: Vol. 3). 108p. 1999. pap. 19.95 (*3-8258-4204-5*, Pub. by CE24) Transaction Pubs.

Paradise Refunded: Winner of the 1998 Backwaters Prize. Kevin Griffith. Ed. by Greg Kosmicki. LC 99-200888. 84p. 1999. pap. write for info. (*0-7392-0081-X*, P02941) Morris Pubng.

Paradise Regained. Ed. by James Hogg. 217p. 1996. pap. 16.95 (*3-7052-0025-9*, Pub. by Poetry Salzburg) Intl Spec Bk.

Paradise Regained: A South African Steam Diary. Karl R. Zimmermann. (Illus.). 1979. pap. 5.95 (*0-931726-03-4*) Delford Pr.

Paradise Regained: Memoir of a Rebel. C. L. Sulzberger. LC 88-9719. 157p. 1988. 49.95 (*0-275-93076-9*, C3076, Praeger Pubs); pap. 19.95 (*0-275-93077-7*, B3077, Praeger Pubs) Greenwood.

Paradise Regained in the New Millennium. Gustav Schindler & Alice Shepherd Foundation Staff. LC 98-146916. 148p. 1997. pap. 12.95 (*1-85756-316-6*, Pub. by Janus Pubng) Paul & Co Pubs.

Paradise Remade: The Politics of Culture & History in Hawai'i. Elizabeth Buck. (Illus.). 256p. (C). 1994. pap. 22.95 (*1-56639-200-4*) Temple U Pr.

Paradise Resisted: Selected Poems 1978-1984. Tom Clark. LC 84-5524. 220p. 1984. pap. 10.00 (*0-87685-611-3*) Black Sparrow.

Paradise Resisted: Selected Poems 1978-1984, signed ed. deluxe ed. Tom Clark. LC 84-5524. 220p. 1984. 25.00 (*0-87685-613-X*) Black Sparrow.

Paradise Reviewed: An Interpretation of Gauguin's Polynesian Symbolism. Jehanne Teilhet-Fisk. Ed. by Stephen Foster. LC 82-4904. (Studies in the Fine Arts: The Avant-Garde: No. 31). 315p. reprint ed. pap. 97.70 (*0-8357-1900-6*, 207062400008) Bks Demand.

Paradise Road. David Giles & Martin Meader. LC 97-208355. 1997. pap. 12.95 (*0-312-17200-1*) St Martin.

Paradise Snare. A. C. Crispin. (Star Wars: No. 1). 336p. (YA). (gr. 5 up). 1997. mass mkt. 5.99 (*0-553-57415-9*, Spectra) Bantam.

Paradise Snare. A. C. Crispin. (Star Wars: No. 1). (YA). (gr. 5 up). 1997. 11.09 (*0-606-11896-9*, Pub. by Turtleback) Demco.

Paradise Theater: Styx. Ed. by Audrey Kleiner. 1981. 8.95 (*0-89898-068-2*) Almo Pubns.

Paradise to Prison: Studies in Genesis. John J. Davis. pap. 17.95 (*0-88469-050-4*) BMH Bks.

Paradise to Prison: Studies in Genesis. John J. Davis. 363p. 1998. reprint ed. pap. text 18.50 (*1-879215-35-7*) Sheffield WI.

Paradise Transformed: The Private Garden for the Twenty-First Century. Guy Cooper & Gordon Taylor. LC 96-24485. (Illus.). 224p. 1996. 50.00 (*1-885254-35-0*, Pub. by Monacelli Pr) Penguin Putnam.

Paradise Valley. Al Glover. 1975. pap. 5.00 (*0-685-73188-X*) Bellevue Pr.

Paradise Valley Days: A Photo Album Poetry Book. Detroit Black Writer's Guild Staff. Ed. by Herbert R. Metoyer & Debraha Watson. LC 97-78432. (Illus.). 120p. 1998. 35.00 (*1-888754-02-8*) Detroit Black.

Paradise Valley, Nevada: The People & Buildings of an American Place. Howard W. Marshall. LC 94-26968. (Illus.). 152p. 1995. 57.00 (*0-8165-1310-4*) U of Ariz Pr.

Paradise Vue. Kathryn H. Kidd. 205p. (Orig.). 1989. pap. 8.95 (*0-9624049-0-X*) Hatrack River.

Paradise War. Stephen R. Lawhead. (Song of Albion Ser.). 420p. 1992. pap. 11.95 (*0-7459-2242-2*) Lion USA.

Paradise War. Stephen R. Lawhead. (Song of Albion Ser.: Bk. 1). 432p. 1993. mass mkt. 5.99 (*0-380-71646-1*, Avon Bks) Morrow Avon.

Paradise War, 1. LC 97-44629. (Song of Albion Ser.). 1998. pap. 12.99 (*0-310-21792-X*) Zondervan.

Paradise Wild. Johanna Lindsey. 320p. 1981. mass mkt. 6.99 (*0-380-77651-0*, Avon Bks) Morrow Avon.

Paradise Wild. large type ed. Johanna Lindsey. LC 93-19644. 427p. 1993. 23.95 (*0-8161-5287-X*, G K Hall Lrg Type) Mac Lib Ref.

Paradise Wild. large type ed. Johanna Lindsey. LC 93-19644. 1994. lib. bdg. 17.95 (*0-8161-5288-8*, G K Hall Lrg Type) Mac Lib Ref.

Paradises Artificiels. Charles Baudelaire. (FRE.). 1977. pap. 10.95 (*0-7859-1857-4*, 2070369641) Fr & Eur.

Paradisi in Sole, Paradisus Terrestris, or a Garden of All Sorts of Pleasant Flowers Which Our English Ayre Will Permit. John Parkinson. LC 74-28880. (English Experience Ser.: No. 758). 1975. reprint ed. 145.00 (*90-221-0758-2*) Walter J Johnson.

Paradiso. Dante Alighieri. Tr. by John Ciardi from ITA. 1970. mass mkt. 6.99 (*0-451-62700-8*, Ment) NAL.

Paradiso. Dante Alighieri. 1993. 75.00 (*0-679-42821-6*) Random.

***Paradiso.** Jose Lezama Lima. Tr. by Gregory Rabassa from SPA. LC 99-35090. 478p. 1999. reprint ed. pap. 14.50 (*1-56478-228-X*, Pub. by Dalkey Arch) Chicago Distribution Ctr.

Paradiso: The Illuminations to Dante's Divine Comedy by Giovanni di Paolo. John W. Pope-Hennessy. LC 93-16598. (Illus.). 1993. 75.00 (*0-679-42739-2*) Random.

Paradiso y el Sistema Poelico de Lezama Lima. Margarita J. Fazzolari. (SPA.). 180p. 1979. pap. 12.50 (*0-685-13897-6*, 3025) Ediciones Norte.

Paradisus: Hawaiian Plant Watercolors by Geraldine King Tam. David Mabberley & James J. White. LC 98-75711. (Illus.). 152p. 1999. 49.95 (*0-937426-42-3*) Honolu Arts.

Paradoja de Maria: Como Pueden las Latinas Fortalecer Su Autoestima, Sin Abandonar Sus Tradiciones. Rosa M. Gil & Carmen I. Vazquez.Tr. of Maria Paradox: How Latinas Can Merge Old World Traditions with New World Self-Esteem. (ENG & SPA.). 289p. 1996. pap. 16.95 (*0-399-14172-3*, G P Putnam) Peng Put Young Read.

***Paradosis.** Edwin A. Abbott. 240p. 1999. pap. 22.00 (*1-57910-294-8*) Wipf & Stock.

Paradosis: Studies in Memory of Edwin A. Quain. Edwin A. Quain. LC 76-20905. 240p. reprint ed. pap. 74.40 (*0-7837-5617-8*, 204552060005) Bks Demand.

Paradosis & Survival: Three Chapters in the History of Epicurean Philosophy. Diskin Clay. LC 98-29087. 312p. 1998. text 47.50 (*0-472-10896-4*, 10896) U of Mich Pr.

Paradox. Don Cassel. (Source 1 Ser.). (C). 1993. pap. 9.33 (*0-13-834292-X*) P-H.

Paradox. Lynn Erickson. (Superromance Ser.). 1993. per. 3.39 (*0-373-70549-2*, 1-70549-0) Harlequin Bks.

Paradox: A Conversation of Life. Eugene Charles. 82p. (Orig.). 1995. pap. 9.95 (*0-9644217-0-4*) Charles Semin.

***Paradox: Introduction to a New Approach Towards Philosophical Investigation.** Tristam Lass. LC 99-70722. 64p. 1999. pap. 9.95 (*1-57197-182-3*) Pentland Pr.

Paradox - The Next Strategic Dimension: Using Conflict to Re-Energize Your Business. Jane McKenzie. LC 95-43633. 1996. write for info. (*0-07-709165-5*) McGraw.

Paradox & Counterparadox. Mara S. Palazzoli et al. Tr. by Elisabeth V. Burt from ITA. LC 84-45862. 208p. 1990. reprint ed. 45.00 (*0-87668-764-8*) Aronson.

Paradox & Identity in Theology. Robert T. Herbert. LC 78-20784. 200p. reprint ed. pap. 62.00 (*0-608-08096-9*, 206905500002) Bks Demand.

Paradox & Passion in Psychotherapy: An Existential Approach to Therapy & Counselling. Emmy Van Deurzen-Smith. LC 97-49908. 198p. 1998. 119.95 (*0-471-96191-4*) Wiley.

***Paradox & Passion in Psychotherapy: An Existential Approach to Therapy & Counselling.** Emmy Van Deurzen-Smith. LC 97-49908. 198p. 1998. pap. 42.50 (*0-471-97390-4*) Wiley.

Paradox & Process. Emmanuel Ghent. (RPBS Ser.). Date not set. write for info. (*0-88163-175-2*) Analytic Pr.

Paradox & Promise in Human Rights. fac. ed. Peggy Billings. LC 79-10325. (Illus.). 142p. (Orig.). 1979. pap. 44.10 (*0-7837-7706-X*, 204746500007) Bks Demand.

Paradox & Society: The Work of Bernard Mandeville. Louis Schneider. Ed. & Intro. by Jay Weinstein. 310p. 1986. 44.95 (*0-88738-112-X*) Transaction Pubs.

Paradox & the Family System. Camillo Loriedo & Gaspare Vella. LC 91-29684. 240p. 1992. text 35.95 (*0-87630-635-0*) Brunner-Mazel.

Paradox & Transformation: Toward a Theory of Change in Organization & Management. Ed. by Robert E. Quinn & Kim S. Cameron. 352p. 1988. text 29.95 (*0-88730-156-8*, HarpBusn) HarpInfo.

Paradox Box. Julian Rothenstein. 25.00 (*1-57062-512-3*, Pub. by Shambhala Pubns) Random.

Paradox, Dialectic & System: A Contemporary Reconstruction of the Hegelian Problematic. Howard P. Kainz. 144p. 1988. 28.50 (*0-271-00499-1*) Pa St U Pr.

Paradox 5 for Windows SmartStart. John Preston. LC 94-68909. 276p. 1995. 29.99 (*0-7897-0011-5*) Que.

Paradox 5 for Windows Power Program Secrets. Gregory B. Salcedo. 936p. 1995. pap. 44.95 (*1-56884-085-3*) IDG Bks.

Paradox 5 for Windows - New Perspectives Introductory, Incl. instr. resource kit, test bank, transparency. Roy Ageloff. (New Perspectives Ser.). (Illus.). 336p. (C). 1995. pap. 30.95 (*1-56527-538-1*) Course Tech.

Paradox 5 for Windows - New Perspectives Comprehensive, Incl. instr. resource kit, test bank, transparency. Roy Ageloff. (New Perspectives Ser.). (Illus.). 592p. 1995. pap. 42.95 (*1-56527-530-6*) Course Tech.

Paradox 5 for Windows - Illustrated, Incl. instr. resource kit, test bank, transparency. Jan Weingarten. (Illustrated Ser.). (Illus.). 208p. 1995. text, mass mkt. 20.95 incl. 3.5 ld (*1-56527-280-3*) Course Tech.

Paradox 5 for Windows: Standard Course. Nicholson. (DF - Computer Applications Ser.). (C). 1995. mass mkt. 34.95 (*0-538-71353-4*) S-W Pub.

Paradox 5 for Windows Essentials. Donna M. Matherly & O'Hara. 1995. teacher ed. 39.99 (*0-7897-0120-0*) Que.

Paradox 5.0 for Windows at a Glance. David B. McDaniel. (At a Glance Ser.). 136p. (Orig.). 1995. pap. 15.95 (*1-55622-456-7*) Wordware Pub.

Paradox 5.0 for Windows. Gary B. Shelly & T. Cashman. (Double Diamond Ser.). 184p. 1995. mass mkt. 22.95 (*0-7895-0334-4*) S-W Pub.

Paradox 5.0 for Windows. Rick Sullivan. (Computer Training Ser.). 180p. (C). 1995. spiral bd. 21.95 (*0-538-64151-7*) S-W Pub.

Paradox 5.0 for Windows: Quick Course. Sandra Cable. (Quick Course Ser.). 192p. 1995. mass mkt. 15.95 (*0-538-65038-9*) S-W Pub.

Paradox for Windows. Sullivan. (IN - Computer Training Ser.). 1998. pap. 18.95 (*0-538-66807-5*) S-W Pub.

Paradox for Windows: Advanced. 1993. teacher ed. 49.95 (*1-56877-113-4*) Catapult WA.

Paradox for Windows: Beginners. 1993. 29.95 (*1-56877-029-4*); teacher ed. 49.95 (*1-56877-030-8*) Catapult WA.

Paradox for Windows: Intermediate. 1993. 29.95 (*1-56877-117-7*); teacher ed. 49.95 (*1-56877-116-9*) Catapult WA.

Paradox for Windows (Advanced) Advanced. 1993. 29.95 (*1-56877-099-5*) Catapult WA.

Paradox for Windows at Work. Karen Watterson. 1992. pap. 24.95 (*0-201-60852-9*) Addison-Wesley.

Paradox for Windows Power Programming. 2nd ed. Que Development Group Staff. (Illus.). 550p. 1994. pap. 29.99 (*0-614-06068-0*) Que.

Paradox for Windows Programming. Valerie Schmeider. 1993. pap. 29.95 (*0-915391-72-4*) Slawson Comm.

Paradox for Windows Workshop. 1992. 44.95 (*1-56686-035-0*) Brady Pub.

Paradox 4 Programming Guide. Valerie Schmieder. Ed. by Lance A. Leventhal. LC 92-32255. (Lance A. Leventhal Microtrend Ser.). 500p. (Orig.). 1992. pap. 29.95 (*0-915391-62-7*) Slawson Comm.

Paradox 4.0 Application Development Instructor Guide, 2 pts. (Illus.). xvii, 214p. 1993. spiral bd. 29.00 (*0-7402-0043-7*, No. BLPDD40PIG) Accelerated Comput Train.

Paradox 4.5 for Windows. DDC Publishing Staff. LC 95-106438. 1993. spiral bd. 12.00 (*1-56243-122-6*, PW18) DDC Pub.

Paradox 4.5 for Windows. Sarah E. Hutchinson et al. (Advantage Series for Computer Education). 210p. (C). 1994. text 12.50 (*0-256-16467-3*, Irwn Prfssnl) McGraw-Hill Prof.

Paradox 4.0. Shelly Cashman. (C). 1994. text. write for info. (*0-318-70362-9*) S-W Pub.

Paradox 4.0. Sarah E. Hutchinson et al. LC 94-157205. 232p. (C). 1994. text 12.50 (*0-256-15775-8*, Irwn McGrw-H) McGrw-H Hghr Educ.

Paradox 4.0. Anna L. Slepecky. LC 93-2525. 1993. write for info. (*0-02-801090-6*) Glencoe.

Paradox 4.0, 1993: Production Software Guide. Martin. LC 93-71454. (C). 1993. pap. text 9.75 (*0-03-098358-4*) Harcourt Coll Pubs.

***Paradox in Oz.** Edward A. Einhorn. (Illus.). 240p. (J). (gr. 4-6). 2000. pap. 24.95 (*1-929527-01-2*) Hungry Tiger.

Paradox in the Religious Poetry of Zinaida Gippius. Olga Matich. bds. 40.00 (*3-7705-0653-7*) Adlers Foreign Bks.

Paradox Lost: Free Will & Political Liberty in American Culture, 1637-1760. Jon Pahl. (New Studies in American Intellectual & Cultural History). 224p. 1992. text 42.50 (*0-8018-4334-0*) Johns Hopkins.

Paradox Lost: Images of the Quantum. Philip R. Wallace. LC 95-49221. (Illus.). 166p. 1996. 29.95 (*0-387-94659-4*) Spr-Verlag.

Paradox of a Suffering God: On the Classical, Modern-Western & Third World Struggles to Harmonise the Incompatible Attributes of the Trinitarian God. Amuluche G. Nnamani. (Studies in the Intercultural History of Christianity: Vol. 95). 428p. 1995. pap. 69.95 (*3-631-49032-1*) P Lang Pubng.

Paradox of a Suffering God: On the Classical, Modern-Western & Third World Struggles to Harmonise the Incompatible Attributes of the Trinitarian God. Amuluche G. Nnamani. LC 95-40439. (Studien zur Interkulturellen Geschichte des Christentums, 0170-9240, Studies in the Intercultural History of Christianity: Bd. 95). 428p. 1995. pap. 69.95 (*0-8204-2935-X*) P Lang Pubng.

Paradox of Africa's Poverty. Tirfe Mammo. LC 97-46979. 321p. 1997. pap. 18.95 (*1-56902-049-3*) Red Sea Pr.

Paradox of Africa's Poverty: The Role of Indigenous Knowledge, Traditional Practices & Local Institutions - the Case of Ethiopia. Tirfe Mammo. LC 97-46979. 321p. 1997. 59.95 (*1-56902-048-5*) Red Sea Pr.

***Paradox of American Democracy: Elites, Special Interests & the Betrayal of the Public Trust.** John B. Judis. LC 99-16821. 320p. 2000. 26.00 (*0-679-43254-X*) Pantheon.

Paradox of Cause & Other Essays. John W. Miller. 1990. pap. 10.95 (*0-393-30731-X*) Norton.

Paradox of Change: American Women in the 20th Century. William H. Chafe. 272p. 1992. pap. text 11.95 (*0-19-504419-3*) OUP.

Paradox of Change: The Rise & Fall of Solidarity in Poland. William D. Perdue. LC 95-7551. 144p. 1995. 55.00 (*0-275-95295-9*, Praeger Pubs) Greenwood.

***Paradox of China's Post-Mao Reforms.** Merle Goldman. LC 98-43096. 1999. 55.00 (*0-674-65453-6*) HUP.

Paradox of China's Post-Mao Reforms Merle Goldman & Roderick MacFarquhar. LC 98-43096. (Contemporary China Ser.). 1999. 24.95 (*0-674-65454-4*) HUP.

Paradox of Christian Tragedy. Barbara J. Hunt. LC 82-50404. viii, 147p. 1985. 42.50 (*0-87875-251-X*) Whitston Pub.

Paradox of Consensualism in International Law. O. A. Elias & C. L. Lim. LC 97-42278. (Developments in International Law Ser.). 336p. 1998. 114.00 (*90-411-0516-6*) Kluwer Law Intl.

Paradox of Continental Production: National Investment Policies in North America. Barbara Jenkins. LC 92-52761. (Cornell Studies in Political Economy). (Illus.). 240p. 1993. text 37.50 (*0-8014-2676-6*) Cornell U Pr.

Paradox of Control: Crime & the Parolee. Patrick G. Jackson. LC 83-9516. 149p. 1983. 45.00 (*0-275-91016-4*, C1016, Praeger Pubs) Greenwood.

Paradox of Empowerment. Greene. 2000. 59.00 (*0-8133-9074-5*) Westview.

Paradox of George Orwell. Richard J. Voorhees. LC 61-62508. 128p. (Orig.). 1961. pap. 19.95 (*0-911198-80-6*) Purdue U Pr.

Paradox of Gissing. David Grylls. (C). 1986. text 49.95 (*0-04-800081-7*) Routledge.

Paradox of Human Existence: A Commentary on the Book of Jonah. Ze'ev H Lifshitz. LC 94-6287. 296p. 1995. pap. 30.00 (*1-56821-219-4*) Aronson.

Paradox of Hunger & Abundance. Eric Kashambuzi. LC 98-46881. 176p. 1999. 18.95 (*1-58141-007-7*) Rivercross Pub.

Paradox of Intention: Reaching the Goal by Giving up the Attempt to Reach It. Marvin C. Shaw. LC 87-29488. (Studies in Religion). 225p. 1988. pap. 13.95 (*1-55540-110-4*, 01 00 48) OUP.

Paradox of Jamestown, 1585-1700 see Drama of American History: Group 1

Paradox of Love in Chaucer's "Troilus" Xianjun Yuan. 192p. 1996. 69.95 (*7-301-02279-4*) Intl Scholars.

Paradox of Mass Politics: Knowledge & Opinion in the American Electorate. W. Russell Neuman. LC 86-288. (Illus.). 264p. 1986. pap. 18.50 (*0-674-65460-9*) HUP.

***Paradox of Meaning: Cultural Poetics & Critical Fictions.** John Moss. 224p. 1999. pap. 16.95 (*0-88801-230-6*) Turnstone Pr.

Paradox of Paradise: A Second Home Adventure. Richard A. Geudtner. LC 96-95022. (Illus.). 240p. (Orig.). 1996. pap. 16.95 (*0-942495-59-4*) Palmer Pubns Inc.

Paradox of Parties: Australian Political Parties in the 1990s. Ed. by Marian Simms. 216p. 1997. pap. 24.95 (*1-86448-051-3*, Pub. by Allen & Unwin Pty) Paul & Co Pubs.

Paradox of Peter the Great: Paradigms of Russian Historiography & Contemporary Reform in the Soviet Union. M. Aaron Talsky. (International Trends in Political Development Ser.). 100p. (Orig.). 1992. pap. text 15.95 (*1-56543-013-1*) Mt SA Coll Philos.

P

An Asterisk (*) at the beginning of an entry indicates that the title is appearing for the first time.

Paradox of Plenty: A Social History of Eating in Modern America. Harvey A. Levenstein. (Illus.). 368p. 1994. reprint ed. pap. 12.95 (*0-19-508918-9*) OUP.

***Paradox of Plenty: Hunger in a Bountiful World.** Douglas H. Boucher. LC 99-18244. 368p. 1999. pap. text 18.95 (*0-935028-71-4*) Inst Food & Develop.

Paradox of Plenty: Oil Booms & Petro-States. Terry L. Karl. LC 96-53044. (Studies in International Political Economy). 1997. 55.00 (*0-520-07168-9*, Pub. by U CA Pr); pap. 22.00 (*0-520-20772-6*, Pub. by U CA Pr) Cal Prin Full Svc.

Paradox of Political Philosophy: Socrates' Philosophic Trial. Jacob Howland. LC 97-41428. 354p. 1997. 71.50 (*0-8476-8975-1*); pap. 26.95 (*0-8476-8976-X*) Rowman.

Paradox of Poverty: A Reappraisal of Economic Development Policy. Paul Steidlmeier. LC 86-26589. 344p. 1987. text 34.95 (*0-88730-184-3*, HarpBusn) HarpInfo.

Paradox of Power: Voices of Warning & Reason in the Geosciences. Charles W. Welby & Monica E. Gowan. LC 98-9275. 1998. write for info. (*0-8137-4112-2*) Geol Soc.

Paradox of Power & Weakness: Levinas & an Alternative Paradigm for Psychology. George Kunz. LC 97-40917. (Series, Alternatives in Psychology). 224p. (C). 1998. text 59.50 (*0-7914-3889-9*); pap. text 19.95 (*0-7914-3890-2*) State U NY Pr.

Paradox of Power in a People's Republic of China Middle School. Martin Schoenhals. LC 92-38344. (Studies on Contemporary China). 226p. (gr. 13). 1993. pap. text 38.95 (*1-56324-189-7*, East Gate Bk) M E Sharpe.

Paradox of Power in a People's Republic of China Middle School. Martin Schoenhals. LC 92-38344. (Studies on Contemporary China). 226p. (C). (gr. 13). 1993. text 85.95 (*1-56324-188-9*, East Gate Bk) M E Sharpe.

Paradox of Preaching. Kring Allen. (Illus.). 104p. (Orig.). 1986. pap. 9.95 (*1-55630-018-2*) Brentwood Comm.

Paradox of Privacy: Epistolary Form in Clarissa. Christina M. Gillis. LC 83-14568. (University of Florida Humanities Monographs: No. 54). viii, 167p. (Orig.). 1984. pap. 19.95 (*0-8130-0761-5*) U Press Fla.

Paradox of Professionalism: Reform & Public Service in Urban America, 1900-1940, 119. Don S. Kirschner. LC 86-399. (Contributions in American History Ser.: No. 119). 208p. 1986. 49.95 (*0-313-25345-5*, KPX/, Greenwood Pr) Greenwood.

Paradox of Progress. James Willis. LC 94-46871. 1995. pap. 29.95 (*1-85775-063-2*, Radcliffe Med Pr) Scovill Paterson.

Paradox of Progress: Can Americans Regain Their Confidence in a Prosperous Future? Richard B. McKenzie. LC 96-23910. (Illus.). 256p. 1997. 27.50 (*0-19-510239-8*) OUP.

Paradox of Progressive Thought. David W. Noble. LC 58-8765. 282p. reprint ed. pap. 87.50 (*0-8357-8979-9*, 203327700085) Bks Demand.

Paradox of Religion. Willard L. Sperry. LC 77-27146. (Hibbert Lectures: 1927). reprint ed. 32.50 (*0-404-60424-2*) AMS Pr.

Paradox of Representation. David Lublin. 176p. 1999. pap. text 15.95 (*0-691-01010-2*, Pub. by Princeton U Pr) Cal Prin Full Svc.

Paradox of Representation: Racial Gerrymandering & Minority Interests in Congress. David Lublin. LC 96-45560. 174p. 1997. text 29.95 (*0-691-02669-6*, Pub. by Princeton U Pr) Cal Prin Full Svc.

Paradox of Revolution: Labor, the State, & Authoritarianism in Mexico. Kevin J. Middlebrook. LC 94-29470. 424p. 1995. text 59.95 (*0-8018-4922-5*) Johns Hopkins.

Paradox of Revolution: Labor, the State & Authoritarianism in Mexico. Kevin J. Middlebrook. LC 94-29470. 424p. 1995. pap. text 18.95 (*0-8018-5148-3*) Johns Hopkins.

Paradox of Salvation: Luke's Theology of the Cross. Peter Doble. (Society for New Testament Studies Monographs: No. 87). 286p. (C). 1996. text 64.95 (*0-521-55212-5*) Cambridge U Pr.

Paradox of Self-Amendment. Peter Suber. LC 89-13403. XXII, 500p. 1990. text 67.95 (*0-8204-1212-0*) P Lang Pubng.

Paradox of Self-Consciousness. Jose L. Bermudez. LC 97-40757. (Representation & Mind Ser.). (Illus.). 236p. 1998. 30.00 (*0-262-02441-1*, Bradford Bks) MIT Pr.

***Paradox of Self-Consciousness.** Jose Luis Bermudez. LC 97-40757. (Representation & Mind Ser.). (Illus.). 360p. 2000. reprint ed. pap. 18.00 (*0-262-52277-2*) MIT Pr.

Paradox of Self-Love: Christian Elements in George Eliot's Treatment of Egoism. Helena Granlund. (Stockholm Studies in English: No. LXXXIII). 186p. (Orig.). 1994. pap. 48.50 (*91-22-01618-X*) Coronet Bks.

Paradox of Sleep: The Story of Dreaming. Michel Jouvet. LC 98-50198. (Illus.). 184p. 1999. 25.00 (*0-262-10080-0*, Bradford Bks) MIT Pr.

***Paradox of Social Order: Linking Psychology & Sociology.** Pierre Moessinger. Tr. by Francesca Worrall & Stephan Scher. (Sociological Imagination & Structural Change Ser.). 256p. 1999. pap. text 24.95 (*0-202-30576-7*) Aldine de Gruyter.

***Paradox of Social Order: Linking Psychology & Sociology.** Pierre Moessinger. Tr. by Francesca Worrall & Stephen K. Scher. (Sociological Imagination & Structural Change Ser.). 256p. 1999. lib. bdg. 49.95 (*0-202-30575-9*) Aldine de Gruyter.

Paradox of Southern Progressivism, 1880-1930. William A. Link. LC 92-1328. (Fred W. Morrison Series in Southern Studies). (Illus.). xviii, 440p. (C). 1993. text 55.00 (*0-8078-2040-7*) U of NC Pr.

Paradox of Southern Progressivism, 1880-1930. William A. Link. LC 92-1328. (Illus.). 458p. (C). 1997. pap. 19.95 (*0-8078-4589-2*) U of NC Pr.

Paradox of Spontaneity. James T. Jones. 36p. 1994. pap. write for info. (*1-885887-00-0*) Elbow Pr.

Paradox of Subjectivity: The Self in the Transcendental Tradition. David Carr. LC 98-28135. 168p. 1999. text 35.00 (*0-19-512690-4*) OUP.

Paradox of Success: When Winning at Work Means Losing at Life: A Book of Renewal for Leaders. John R. O'Neill. 272p. 1994. pap. 13.95 (*0-87477-772-0*, Tarcher Putnam) Putnam Pub Group.

Paradox of the Cross in the Thought of St. Paul. Anthony Tyrrell Hanson. (JSNT Supplement Ser.: No. 17). 214p. 1987. pap. 23.75 (*1-85075-068-8*, Pub. by Sheffield Acad) CUP Services.

Paradox of the Cross in the Thought of St. Paul. Anthony Tyrrell Hanson. (JSNT Supplement Ser.: Vol. 17). 214p. 1987. 60.00 (*1-85075-069-6*, Pub. by Sheffield Acad) CUP Services.

Paradox of the Employee: Variants of a Social Theme in Modern Literature. Andrew Weeks. (Germanic Studies in America: Vol. 35). 160p. 1980. 29.00 (*3-261-04757-7*) P Lang Pubng.

Paradox of the Liar. Ed. by Robert L. Martin. (C). 1979. reprint ed. pap. text 13.00 (*0-917930-10-X*); reprint ed. lib. bdg. 27.00 (*0-917930-30-4*) Ridgeview.

Paradox of the Mexican State: Rereading Sovereignty from Independence to NAFTA. Julie A. Erfani. LC 94-31535. 238p. 1995. lib. bdg. 49.95 (*1-55587-418-5*) L Rienner.

Paradox of the Silicon Savior: Charting the Reformation of the High-Tech Super-State. Grant Venerable. 229p. (Orig.). (C). 1988. pap. 16.95 (*0-943425-00-X*) Ventek.

***Paradox of the Soul.** Richard S. Kuong. LC 00-40193. 2000. write for info. (*0-940706-81-4*) Management Advisory Pubns.

Paradox of Tragedy. David D. Raphael. LC 77-128293. (Essay Index Reprint Ser.). 1977. 18.95 (*0-8369-2021-X*) Ayer.

***Paradox Outpatient.** Bernie Schallehn. 2000. pap. 9.95 (*1-55279-028-2*) Picasso Publ.

Paradox Politics: People & Power in Idaho. LC 88-90516. (Illus.). 352p. (Orig.). (C). 1988. pap. 10.95 (*0-945648-15-4*) Ridenbaugh Pr.

Paradox pour windows, Mode d'Emploi. Henri Chene. 250p. 1993. pap. 32.95 (*0-7859-5643-3*, 2736110781) Fr & Eur.

Paradox Power for Windows. Karen Watterson. 1992. pap. 24.95 (*0-201-63234-9*) Addison-Wesley.

Paradox Principles: How High Performance Companies Manage Chaos Complexity & Condradiction to Achieve Superior Results. Price Waterhouse Change Integration Team Staff. LC 95-23346. 1995. 24.95 (*0-7863-0499-5*, Irwn Prfssnl) McGraw-Hill Prof.

Paradox Queries: A Developer's Reference. Dan Ehrmann. 1995. 39.95 incl. disk (*1-55851-311-6*, M&T Bks) IDG Bks.

Paradox, Rey. Y Nessi, Pio Baroja. Ed. by Jesus M. Lasagabaster. (Nueva Austral Ser.: No. 188). (SPA.). 1991. pap. text 24.95 (*84-239-1988-9*) Elliots Bks.

Paradox 7 for Windows 95: Illustrated Brief Edition. Meta Hirschl. (Illustrated Ser.). (Illus.). 96p. 1996. pap. 12.95 (*0-7600-3815-5*) Course Tech.

Paradox Smartstart, U. K. 1993. 25.99 (*1-57576-196-3*) Que.

***Paradox Trilogies, Vol. 1.** M. Jeersannidi Narasimhan. 1998. pap. write for info. (*0-7541-0509-1*, Pub. by Minerva Pr) Unity Dist.

Paradox Versions 1/4.5 for Windows - New Perspectives Introductory, Incl. instr. resource kit, test bank, transparency. Roy Ageloff. LC 95-224497. (New Perspectives Ser.). (Illus.). 312p. 1994. text. write for info. (*1-56527-083-5*) Course Tech.

Paradox 3.5 Einfuhrung und Leitfaden. Blasberg. (GER.). (C). 1991. text. write for info. (*0-201-55972-2*) Addison-Wesley.

Paradox 5 Essential. 1997. 16.99 (*0-7686-0091-X*) Quest Custom.

Paradox 5 Smart Start. 1997. 19.99 (*0-7686-0082-0*) Quest Custom.

Paradox 9 Power Programming. Brian Prestwood. 701p. 1999. pap. 39.99 (*0-07-211936-5*) McGraw.

Paradoxe Chez Blaise Pascal. Vlad Alexandrescu. (Sciences pour la Communication Ser.: Vol. 49). (FRE.). 262p. 1997. 43.95 (*3-906754-72-3*, Pub. by P Lang) P Lang Pubng.

Paradoxe sur le Comedien: Avec: Danaud, Jean-Claude. Un Ouvrage de Dames. Denis Diderot. (Illus.). 49p. 1977. 10.95 (*0-8288-9599-6*, F46850) Fr & Eur.

Paradoxe sur le Comedien: Paris, 1902. Denis Diderot. (FRE.). 125p. 1991. 10.95 (*0-7859-1073-5*, 2040192832) Fr & Eur.

Paradoxes. Jean Bodin. xiv, 128p. write for info. (*0-318-71322-5*) G Olms Pubs.

Paradoxes. John Hall. LC 56-6812. 128p. 1977. reprint ed. 50.00 (*0-8201-1233-X*) Schol Facsimiles.

Paradoxes. 2nd ed. R. M. Sainsbury. 175p. (C). 1995. pap. text 15.95 (*0-521-48347-6*) Cambridge U Pr.

Paradoxes, Ambiguity & Rationality. Ed. by Omar F. Hamouda & J. C. Rowley. (Foundations of Probability, Econometrics & Economic Games Ser.: Vol. 2). 520p. 1997. 180.00 (*1-85898-434-3*) E Elgar.

Paradoxes & Puzzles, Historical, Judicial & Literary. John Paget. LC 75-30035. reprint ed. 57.50 (*0-404-14037-8*) AMS Pr.

***Paradoxes d'Eros Ou l'Amour dans l'Oeuvre de Johann Christoph Gottsched.** Marie-Helene Queval. (Contacts Ser.: Vol. 48). xiii, 479p. 1999. 62.95 (*3-906763-63-3*, Pub. by P Lang) P Lang Pubng.

Paradoxes in Immunology. G. Hoffmann & J. Levy. LC 85-29070. 360p. 1986. 194.00 (*0-8493-5931-7*, CRC Reprint) Franklin.

Paradoxes in Probability Theory & Mathematical Statistics. Gabor J. Szekely. 1987. text 151.50 (*90-277-1899-7*) Kluwer Academic.

Paradoxes in the Modern Family. Milton R. Sapirstein. 152p. 1992. 21.95 (*0-89876-194-8*) Gardner Pr.

Paradoxes, Nouveaux Paradoxes see Paradoxes of Faith

Paradoxes of Belief & Strategic Rationality. Robert C. Koons. (Studies in Probability, Induction & Decision Theory). (Illus.). 188p. (C). 1992. text 74.95 (*0-521-41269-2*) Cambridge U Pr.

Paradoxes of Christian Faith & Life. Richard Holloway. LC 85-184171. (Christian Studies). ix, 144 p. 1984. 3.95 (*0-264-67005-1*) A R Mowbray.

Paradoxes of Civil Society: New Perspectives on Modern German & British History. Ed. by Frank Trentmann. LC 99-35022. 368p. 2000. 69.95 (*1-57181-142-7*) Berghahn Bks.

Paradoxes of Delusion: Wittgenstein, Schreber, & the Schizophrenic Mind. Louis A. Sass. 208p. 1993. text 35.00 (*0-8014-2210-8*) Cornell U Pr.

Paradoxes of Delusion: Wittgenstein, Schreber, & the Schizophrenic Mind. Louis A. Sass. LC 93-24931. 208p. 1995. pap. text 13.95 (*0-8014-9899-6*) Cornell U Pr.

Paradoxes of Democracy: Fragility, Continuity & Change. Shmuel N. Eisenstadt. LC 99-35073. (Woodrow Wilson Center Press Ser.). 160p. 1999. 29.95 (*0-8018-6309-0*) Johns Hopkins.

Paradoxes of Education in a Republic. Eva T. Brann. LC 78-10228. 1979. 12.95 (*0-226-07135-9*) U Ch Pr.

Paradoxes of Education in a Republic. Eva T. Brann. LC 78-10228. 178p. 1989. pap. text 13.50 (*0-226-07136-7*) U Ch Pr.

Paradoxes of Emotion & Fiction. Robert J. Yanal. LC 98-43075. 278p. 1999. 18.00 (*0-271-01894-1*) Pa St U Pr.

***Paradoxes of Emotion & Fiction.** Robert J. Yanal. LC 98-43075. 164p. 1999. 35.00 (*0-271-01893-3*) Pa St U Pr.

Paradoxes of European Foreign Policy. Jan Zielonka. LC 98-5118. 192p. 1998. 62.00 (*90-411-0571-9*) Kluwer Academic.

Paradoxes of Faith. Henri De Lubac. Tr. by Paule Simon et al. LC 86-62928. Orig. Title: Paradoxes, Nouveaux Paradoxes. (FRE.). 236p. (Orig.). 1986. pap. 11.95 (*0-89870-132-5*) Ignatius Pr.

Paradoxes of Fame: The Francis Scott Key Story. Sam Meyer. LC 95-60983. (Illus.). 144p. 1995. 15.95 (*1-885457-06-5*) Eastwind MD.

Paradoxes of Freedom. Sidney Hook. LC 87-61366. (Great Books in Philosophy). 174p. 1987. pap. 9.95 (*0-87975-410-9*) Prometheus Bks.

Paradoxes of Freedom: The Romantic Mystique of a Transcendence. Thomas McFarland. (Illus.). 158p. 1996. text 45.00 (*0-19-812181-4*) OUP.

Paradoxes of Gender. Judith Lorber. 1995. pap. 17.00 (*0-300-06497-7*) Yale U Pr.

***Paradoxes of Labour Reform: Chinese Labour Theory & Practice from Socialism to the Market.** Luigi Tomba. LC 00-34498. 2000. write for info. (*0-312-23853-3*) St Martin.

***Paradoxes of Leadership.** Charles R. Edmunson. 89p. 1999. pap. text 10.00 (*0-926902-53-9*) NCEO.

***Paradoxes of Legal Science.** Benjamin N. Cardozo. LC 00-24469. 2000. write for info. (*1-58477-097-X*) Lawbk Exchange.

Paradoxes of Legal Science. Benjamin N. Cardozo. LC 76-104241. 142p. 1970. reprint ed. lib. bdg. 38.50 (*0-8371-3263-0*, CALS, Greenwood Pr) Greenwood.

Paradoxes of Longevity. Ed. by Jean-Marie Robine et al. LC 99-10782. (Research & Perspectives in Longevity Ser.). vi, 128p. 1999. 95.00 (*3-540-65544-1*) Spr-Verlag.

Paradoxes of Love. Llewellyn Vaughan-Lee. LC 96-75080. 224p. (Orig.). 1996. pap. 12.95 (*0-9634574-6-2*) Golden Sufi Ctr.

Paradoxes of Mahathirism: An Intellectual Biography of Mahathir Mohamad. Khoo B. Teik. (Illus.). 408p. 1996. 39.95 (*967-65-3092-1*) OUP.

Paradoxes of Measures & Dimensions Originating in Felix Hausdorff's Ideas. Janusz Czyz. 300p. (C). 1994. text 109.00 (*981-02-0189-3*) World Scientific Pub.

Paradoxes of Mister Pond. G. K. Chesterton. xiii, 126p. 1990. pap. 5.95 (*0-486-26185-9*) Dover.

Paradoxes of Modernity: Culture & Conduct in the Theory of Max Weber. Wolfgang Schluchter. Tr. by Neil Solomon from GER. LC 95-16141. 398p. 1996. 49.50 (*0-8047-2455-5*) Stanford U Pr.

Paradoxes of Mr. Pond. G. K. Chesterton. 1998. lib. bdg. 15.95 (*1-56723-031-8*) Yestermorrow.

Paradoxes of Multiculturalism: Essays on Swedish Society. Carl-Ulrik Schieup & Aleksandra Alund. (Ethnic Relations Ser.). 250p. 1991. 56.95 (*1-85628-233-3*, Pub. by Avebry) Ashgate Pub Co.

Paradoxes of Order: Some Perspectives on the Fiction of V. S. Naipaul. Robert K. Morris. LC 74-23752. (Literary Frontiers Ser.). 112p. 1975. pap. 12.95 (*0-8262-0172-5*) U of Mo Pr.

Paradoxes of Paradise: Identity & Difference in the Song of Songs. Francis Landy. (Bible & Literature Ser.). 1983. pap. 10.95 (*0-907459-17-X*) Dove Bkslrs.

Paradoxes of Paradise: Identity & Difference in the Song of Songs. Francis Landy. (Bible & Literature Ser.: No. 7). 410p. 1983. 95.00 (*0-907459-16-1*, Pub. by Sheffield Acad) CUP Services.

Paradoxes of Peace: German Peace Movements since 1945. Alice H. Cooper. LC 94-48681. (Social History, Popular Culture, & Politics in Germany Ser.). 344p. (C). 1996. text 57.50 (*0-472-10624-4*, 10624) U of Mich Pr.

Paradoxes of Play: Proceedings of the 69th (i. e. 6th) Annual Meeting of the Association for the Anthropological Study of Play. Association for the Anthropological Study of Play,. Ed. by John W. Loy et al. LC 86-113483. (Illus.). 238p. 1982. reprint ed. pap. 73.80 (*0-608-07061-0*, 206726700009) Bks Demand.

Paradoxes of Police Work. Douglas A. Perez. LC 96-86235. 101p. (C). 1996. pap. 14.95 (*0-942728-72-6*) Copperhouse.

Paradoxes of Power: The Military Establishment in the Eighties. Adam Yarmolinsky & Gregory D. Foster. LC 82-48523. 160p. reprint ed. pap. 49.60 (*0-7837-3732-7*, 205791000009) Bks Demand.

Paradoxes of the American Presidency. Thomas E. Cronin & Michael A. Genovese. LC 97-29534. 448p. (C). 1998. pap. text 33.95 (*0-19-511693-3*) OUP.

Paradoxes of the American Presidency. Thomas E. Cronin & Michael A. Genovese. LC 97-29534. (Illus.). 448p. (C). 1998. 35.00 (*0-19-511692-5*) OUP.

Paradoxes of the Highest Science. Eliphas Levi. 172p. 1992. reprint ed. pap. 14.95 (*1-56459-020-8*) Kessinger Pub.

Paradoxes of the Highest Science. 2nd ed. Eliphas Levi. 172p. 1996. reprint ed. spiral bd. 16.50 (*0-7873-0555-3*) Hlth Research.

Paradoxes of the Highest Science: A New Translation. Eliphas Levi. Ed. & Tr. by Joseph Bouleur from FRE. 1996. pap. 8.95 (*1-55818-341-8*) Holmes Pub.

Paradoxes of Time in Saint Augustine. Roland J. Teske. (Aquinas Lectures: No. 60). (C). 1996. 15.00 (*0-87462-163-1*) Marquette.

Paradoxes of Traditional Chinese Literature: An Analysis of Literary Works from the Tang Dynasty to the Late Qing. Ed. by Eva Hung. LC 97-161338. 283p. (C). 1997. 34.50 (*962-201-594-8*, Pub. by Chinese Univ) U of Mich Pr.

Paradoxes of Zeno. J. A. Farris. (Avebury Series in Philosophy). 136p. 1996. text 64.95 (*1-85972-368-3*, Pub. by Avebry) Ashgate Pub Co.

***Paradoxia: A Predator's Diary.** Lydia Lynch. 1999. pap. text 13.95 (*1-84068-008-3*) Creation Books.

Paradoxia: A Predator's Story. Lydia Lynch. 160p. 1997. 16.95 (*1-871592-49-6*) Creation Books.

Paradoxic Mutations. Margot Lovejoy. 28p. 1993. pap. 28.00 (*0-9637531-1-8*) M Lovejoy.

Paradoxical Ascent to God: The Kabbalistic Theosophy of Habad Hasidism. Rachel Elior. Tr. by Jeffrey M. Green from HEB. LC 91-32060. (SUNY Series in Judaica: Hermeneutics, Mysticism, & Religion). 279p. (C). 1992. text 24.50 (*0-7914-1045-5*) State U NY Pr.

Paradoxical Breakthrough of Revelation: Interpreting the Devine-Human Interplay in Tillich's Work, 1913-1964. Uwe C. Scharf. 450p. 1998. 111.00 (*3-11-015577-X*) De Gruyter.

Paradoxical Community Vol. 6: The Emergence of a Social World in an Urban Renewal Setting. Haim Hazan. Ed. by Jaber F. Gubrium. (Contemporary Ethnographic Studies). 186p. 1990. 73.25 (*0-89232-963-7*) Jai Pr.

Paradoxical Effects of Social Behavior. Ed. by A. Diekmann & P. Mitter. (Illus.). xvi, 341p. 1986. 119.95 (*0-387-91285-1*) Spr-Verlag.

Paradoxical Feminism: The Novels of Rebecca West. Ann V. Norton. 112p. 1999. 74.95 (*1-57309-392-0*) Intl Scholars.

Paradoxical Psychotherapy: Theory & Practice with Individuals, Couples, & Families. Gerald R. Weeks & Luciano L'Abate. LC 81-17083. 288p. 1982. text 36.95 (*0-87630-289-4*) Brunner-Mazel.

Paradoxical Resolutions: American Fiction since James Joyce. Craig H. Werner. LC 81-11423. 248p. 1982. text 24.95 (*0-252-00931-2*) U of Ill Pr.

Paradoxical Self: Toward an Understanding of Our Contradictory Nature. Kirk J. Schneider. 248p. 1998. pap. 17.50 (*0-391-04066-9*) Humanities.

***Paradoxical Self: Toward an Understanding of Our Contradictory Nature.** Kirk J. Schneider. LC 99-45897. 1999. pap. write for info. (*1-57392-636-1*, Humanity Bks) Prometheus Bks.

Paradoxical Thinking: How to Profit from Your Contradictions. Jerry L. Fletcher & Kelle Olwyler. LC 97-16704. (Illus.). 200p. 1997. 24.95 (*1-881052-80-X*) Berrett-Koehler.

Paradoxical Vision: A Public Theology for the Twenty-First Century. Robert Benne. LC 94-18251. 256p. 1995. pap. 20.00 (*0-8006-2794-6*, 1-2794, Fortress Pr) Augsburg Fortress.

Paradoxie der Fiktionen: Literarische Venedig-Bilder, 1797-1984. Angelika Corbineau-Hoffmann. (Komparatistische Studien: No. 17). (GER.). x, 638p. (C). 1993. lib. bdg. 296.95 (*3-11-012937-X*) De Gruyter.

Paradoxisme: Un Nouveau Mouvement Litteraire. Florentin Smarandache. Ed. by Xiquan Publishing House Staff. (FRE., Illus.). 108p. (Orig.). 1992. pap. 9.85 (*1-879585-33-2*) Erhus Univ Pr.

Paradoxisme: Un Nouveau Movement Litteraire. Florentin Smarandache. LC 95-120926. (FRE., Illus.). 108p. reprint ed. pap. 33.50 (*0-608-10469-8*, 207108700008) Bks Demand.

Paradoxism's Main Roots. Florin Vasiliu. Ed. by R. Muller. Tr. by Rodica Stefanescu from ROM. LC 95-128986. 100p. 1993. pap. text 11.95 (*1-879585-36-7*) Erhus Univ Pr.

Paradoxist Distichs. Florentin Smarandache. (RUM.). 100p. 1998. pap. 9.95 (*1-879585-60-X*) Erhus Univ Pr.

Paradoxist Literary Movement. Constantin M. Popa. Ed. by R. Muiler & Xiquan Publishing House Staff. (RUM.). 60p. (Orig.). (C). 1992. pap. text 6.99 (*1-879585-29-4*) Erhus Univ Pr.

Paradoxist Poems. Florentin Smarandache. Ed. by R. Muller. (Illus.). 150p. (C). 1995. pap. 9.99 (*1-879585-41-3*) Erhus Univ Pr.

Paradoxist Writer. Ion Soare. Ed. by R. Muller. (Illus.). 100p. (C). 1995. pap. 9.99 (*1-879585-43-X*) Erhus Univ Pr.

An Asterisk (*) at the beginning of an entry indicates that the title is appearing for the first time.

Paraesthetics: Foucault, Lyotard, Derrida. David Carroll. 288p. 1987. 35.00 (*0-416-01721-5*, A0413) Routledge.

Paraesthetics: Foucault, Lyotard, Derrida. David Carroll. 288p. (C). 1987. pap. 19.99 (*0-415-90291-6*, A0417) Routledge.

Parafaith War. L. E. Modesitt, Jr. 1997. mass mkt. 6.99 (*0-8125-3894-3*, Pub. by Forge NYC) St Martin.

Paraflight Experience. John R. Carr. LC 91-90953. (Illus.). 165p. 1997. reprint ed. pap. 16.95 (*0-9629429-6-0*) Waltz Pub.

Paraganglia. P. Boeck. (Handbuch der Mikroskopischen Anatomie Des Menschen Ser.: Vol. 1-8). (Illus.). 400p. 1982. 228.00 (*0-387-10978-1*) Spr-Verlag.

Paraganglionic Chemoreceptor System: Physiology, Pathology, & Clinical Medicine. F. G. Zak & W. Lawson. (Illus.). 576p. 1982. 306.00 (*0-387-90621-5*) Spr-Verlag.

Paragliding: The Complete Guide. Noel Whittall. LC 97-38329. (Illus.). 200p. 1998. pap. 26.95 (*1-55821-661-8*) Lyons Pr.

***Paragliding: The Complete Guide.** rev. ed. Noel Whittall. (Illus.). 200p. 2000. pap. 26.95 (*1-58574-103-5*) Lyons Pr.

Paragliding Flight: Walking on Air. Dennis Pagen. (Illus.). 200p. 1990. pap. 19.95 (*0-936310-09-X*, Sport Aviation Pubns) Black Mntn.

Paragon. M. Sherman. (Lecture Notes in Computer Science Ser.: Vol. 189). xi, 364p. 1985. 49.00 (*0-387-15212-1*) Spr-Verlag.

Paragon House Spelling Dictionary. Paragon House Staff. 608p. 1994. pap. 12.95 (*1-56924-866-4*) Marlowe & Co.

Paragon of Human Perfection. H. A. Omar. 85p. 1984. 25.00 (*0-7212-0566-6*, Pub. by Regency Pr GBR) St Mut.

***Paragon of Zen House.** Xishan. Tr. by O'Hyun Park from CHI. LC 99-27940. (Asian Thought & Culture Ser.: Vol. 38). 198p. 2000. text 29.95 (*0-8204-4545-2*) P Lang Pubng.

Paragon Walk. Anne Perry. 1986. mass mkt. 5.99 (*0-449-45319-7*) Fawcett.

Paragon Walk. Anne Perry. 1986. mass mkt. 6.99 (*0-449-21168-1*) Fawcett.

***Paragon Walk.** large type ed. Anne Perry. LC 99-46443. 308p. 2000. lib. bdg. 27.95 (*1-58547-005-8*) Ctr Point Pubg.

Paragonah Canyon. deluxe limited ed. David Lee. 1991. 40.00 (*0-918116-52-X*) Brooding Heron Pr.

***Paragons.** Cliff Chandler. 250p. 2000. pap. 14.95 (*1-893196-03-8*) Brittney Pr.

Paragons of Chinese Courage: Ten Who Braved the Storm of the Cultural Revolution. Compiled by Guangming Daily Staff. 214p. (C). 1990. 42.00 (*1-86305-002-7*, Pub. by Pascoe Pub) St Mut.

Paragons of the Ordinary: The Biographical Literature of Mori Ogai. Marvin Marcus. LC 92-26583. (SHAPS Library of Asian Studies). 372p. 1992. text 45.00 (*0-8248-1450-9*) UH Pr.

Paragons of Virtue: Women & Domesticity in Seventeenth-Century Dutch Art. Wayne E. Franits. (Illus.). 295p. (C). 1995. pap. text 27.95 (*0-521-49875-9*) Cambridge U Pr.

Paragraph & Topic Sentence. rev. ed. Contrib. by Beth Bridgman. (Horizons Grammar Ser.). (Illus.). 24p. (J). (gr. 4-9). 1998. pap. 5.95 (*1-58086-072-9*, Usborne) EDC.

Paragraph Development. 2nd ed. Martin C. Arnaudet & Barrett. 208p. (C). 1990. pap. text 33.00 (*0-13-648502-2*) P-H.

Paragraph in Context. Ed. by Virginia M. Burke. LC 79-92274. (Composition & Rhetoric Ser.). (C). 1969. pap. write for info. (*0-672-60906-1*, CR20, Bobbs) Macmillan.

Paragraph Patterns. Barbara Auerbach & Beth Snyder. 147p. (C). 1983. pap. text 20.50 (*0-15-567983-X*) Harcourt Coll Pubs.

Paragraph Power: Communicating Ideas Through Paragraphs. George M. Rooks. (Illus.). 128p. (C). 1989. pap. text 31.40 (*0-13-648585-5*) P-H.

***Paragraph Power: Communicating Ideas Through Paragraphs.** 2nd ed. Rooks. LC 98-31833. 224p. 1998. pap. text 22.00 (*0-13-660754-3*) P-H.

Paragraph Practice: Writing the Paragraph & the Short Composition. 7th ed. Kathleen E. Sullivan. LC 93-14700. (Illus.). 256p. (C). 1993. pap. text 36.00 (*0-02-418351-2*, Macmillan Coll) P-H.

Paragraph Production. Linda Polon. (Study Skills Ser.). (Illus.). 48p. (J). (gr. 4-6). 1981. pap. 6.95 (*0-88160-039-3*, LW 224) Learning Wks.

Paragraph Strategies: A Basic Writing Guide. Mary S. Spangler & Rita R. Werner. Ed. by Leslie Taggart & Dawn Youngblood. LC 89-7454. 200p. (Orig.). (C). 1990. pap. text 17.50 (*0-03-029367-7*) Harcourt Coll Pubs.

Paragraph Structure Inference. Edward J. Crothers. LC 78-27307. 124p. 1979. text 73.25 (*0-89391-016-3*) Ablx Pub.

Para(graph) Trooper for MacArthur: From the Horse Cavalry to the USSMO. Joe Snyder. (Illus.). 229p. 1998. 17.95 (*1-890622-14-1*) Leathers Pub.

Paragraph Writing. Frank Chaplen. 1970. pap. 3.50 (*0-19-432708-6*) OUP.

Paragraph Writing. 2nd ed. Jo E. Moore & Leslie Tyron. (Illus.). 80p. (J). (gr. 2-4). 1997. pap. 7.95 (*1-55799-608-3*, EMC246) Evan-Moor Edu Pubs.

Paragraph Writing Simplified. John Ostrom & William Cook. LC 92-17962. (Simplified Ser.). 160p. (C). 1997. pap. text 14.66 (*0-06-501150-3*) Addson-Wesley Educ.

Paragraph Writing Skills see Ready-to-Use Writing Workshop Activities Kits

Paragraphs. Lindell Bruce. 80p. (C). 1994. pap. text 13.95 (*0-8403-9700-3*, 40970001) Kendall-Hunt.

Paragraphs & Essays, 7 vols. 7th ed. Brandon. (C). Date not set. 44.76 (*0-395-89801-3*) HM.

Paragraphs & Essays: With Multicultural Readings. 6th ed. Lee Brandon. 444p. (C). 1994. pap. text 37.96 (*0-669-29790-9*) HM Trade Div.

***Paragraphs 1999c: Globe Fearon English.** 45p. 1998. write for info. (*0-13-023244-0*) S&S Trade.

Paragraphs on Printing. Bruce Rogers. LC 79-50699. (Illus.). 198p. 1980. reprint ed. pap. 6.95 (*0-486-23817-2*) Dover.

Paragraphs on Translation. Peter Newmark. LC 92-42551. 1993. 69.00 (*1-85359-192-0*, Pub. by Multilingual Matters); pap. 24.95 (*1-85359-191-2*, Pub. by Multilingual Matters) Taylor & Francis.

Paraguas Amarillos: Los Poetas Latinos en New York. Ed. by Ivan Silen. (SPA.). 254p. 1983. pap. 14.00 (*0-910061-16-5*) Biling Rev-Pr.

Paraguay see American Nations Past & Present

Paraguay see Enchantment of the World Series

Paraguay see Statements of the Laws of the OAS Member States in Matters Affecting Business

Paraguay. R. Andrew Nickson. LC 88-143693. (World Bibliographical Ser.: No. 84). 240p. 1988. lib. bdg. 45.00 (*1-85109-028-2*) ABC-CLIO.

Paraguay. Rosa Q. Mesa. LC 73-180800. (Latin American Serial Documents Ser.: Vol. 9). 93p. 1973. reprint ed. pap. 30.00 (*0-8357-0077-1*, 201355100087) Bks Demand.

***Paraguay.** rev. ed. R. Andrew Nickson. (World Bibliographical Ser.: Vol. 84). 249p. 1999. 76.00 (*1-85109-320-6*) ABC-CLIO.

***Paraguay, 6 vols. , Set.** Leslie Jermyn. LC 99-27257. (Cultures of the World Ser.: Vol. 19). 128p. (YA). (gr. 5-9). 2000. lib. bdg. 35.64 (*0-7614-0979-3*) Marshall Cavendish.

Paraguay: A Country Study. Dennis M. Hanratty. 320p. 1990. boxed set 22.00 (*0-16-019101-7*) USGPO.

***Paraguay: A Country Study Guide.** Global Investment & Business Center, Inc. Staff. (World Country Study Guides Library: Vol. 134). (Illus.). 350p. 2000. pap. 59.00 (*0-7397-2432-0*) Intl Business Pubns.

Paraguay: A Riverside Nation. George Pendle. 1976. lib. bdg. 59.95 (*0-8490-2409-9*) Gordon Pr.

Paraguay: A Transition in Search of Democracy. (ENG & SPA.). 40p. 1990. 6.00 (*0-929513-17-7*) WOLA.

Paraguay: An Informal History. Harris G. Warren. LC 82-15519. (Illus.). 393p. 1982. reprint ed. lib. bdg. 75.00 (*0-313-23651-8*, WARP, Greenwood Pr) Greenwood.

Paraguay: International Donor Conference Final Report, December 6, 1995. Horacio Canepa et al. ii, 146p. 1996. pap. text 16.00 (*1-879720-24-8*) Intl Fndt Elect.

Paraguay: Its Cultural Heritage, Social Conditions & Educational Problems. Arthur E. Elliott. LC 70-176746. (Columbia University. Teachers College. Contributions to Education Ser.: No. 473). reprint ed. 37.50 (*0-404-55473-3*) AMS Pr.

Paraguay: Major World Nations. Marion Morrison. LC 99-13779. (Illus.). 144p. 1999. 19.95 (*0-7910-5393-8*) Chelsea Hse.

Paraguay: Pre-Election Technical Assessment, June 1995. Carina Perelli et al. ii, 194p. 1996. pap. text 21.00 (*1-879720-25-6*) Intl Fndt Elect.

Paraguay - A Country Study Guide: Basic Information for Research & Pleasure. Global Investment Center, USA Staff. (World Country Study Guide Library: Vol. 134). (Illus.). 350p. 1999. pap. 59.00 (*0-7397-1531-3*) Intl Business Pubns.

Paraguay, Brazil, & the Plate. Charles B. Mansfield. LC 79-128414. reprint ed. 55.00 (*0-404-04183-3*) AMS Pr.

***Paraguay Business Intelligence Report, 190 vols.** Global Investment & Business Center, Inc. Staff. (World Business Intelligence Library: Vol. 134). (Illus.). 350p. 2000. pap. 99.95 (*0-7397-2632-3*) Intl Business Pubns.

***Paraguay Business Law Handbook.** Global Investment & Business Center, Inc. Staff. (Global Business Law Handbooks Library: Vol. 134). (Illus.). 2000. pap. 99.95 (*0-7397-2032-5*) Intl Business Pubns.

***Paraguay Business Opportunity Yearbook.** Global Investment & Business Center, Inc. Staff. (Global Business Opportunity Yearbooks Library: Vol. 134). (Illus.). 2000. pap. 99.95 (*0-7397-2232-8*) Intl Business Pubns.

***Paraguay Business Opportunity Yearbook: Export-Import, Investment & Business Opportunities.** International Business Publications, U. S. A. Staff & Global Investment Center, U. S. A. Staff. (Global Business Opportunity Yearbooks Library: Vol. 134). (Illus.). 350p. 1999. pap. 99.95 (*0-7397-1332-9*) Intl Business Pubns.

***Paraguay Country Review 2000.** Robert C. Kelly et al. (Illus.). 60p. 1999. pap. 39.95 (*1-58310-558-1*) CountryWatch.

Paraguay, 1852 & 1968. Edward A. Hopkins et al. (Occasional Publication Ser.: No. 2). (Illus.). 64p. 1968. reprint ed. 10.00 (*0-318-12733-4*) Am Geographical.

***Paraguay Foreign Policy & Government Guide.** Contrib. by Global Investment & Business Center, Inc. Staff. (World Foreign Policy & Government Library: Vol. 128). (Illus.). 350p. 1999. pap. 99.00 (*0-7397-3626-4*) Intl Business Pubns.

***Paraguay Foreign Policy & Government Guide.** Global Investment & Business Center, Inc. Staff. (World Foreign Policy & Government Library: Vol. 128). (Illus.). 350p. 2000. 99.95 (*0-7397-3832-1*) Intl Business Pubns.

Paraguay in Pictures. Nathan A. Haverstock. (Visual Geography Ser.). (Illus.). 64p. (YA). (gr. 5 up). 1987. lib. bdg. 19.95 (*0-8225-1819-8*, Lerner Publctns) Lerner Pub.

***Paraguay Investment & Business Guide.** Global Investment & Business Center, Inc. Staff. (Global Investment & Business Guide Library: Vol. 134). (Illus.). 2000. pap. 99.95 (*0-7397-1832-0*) Intl Business Pubns.

***Paraguay Investment & Business Guide: Export-Import, Investment & Business Opportunities.** International Business Publications, USA Staff & Global Investment Center, USA Staff. (World Investment & Business Guide Library-99: Vol. 134). (Illus.). 350p. 1999. pap. 99.95 (*0-7397-0329-3*) Intl Business Pubns.

Paraguay, the Democratic Revolution: Why the Colorados. Prudewcio Mendez. (C). 1993. pap. text 2.00 (*0-9625497-0-3*) P Mendez.

Paraguay under Stroessner. Paul H. Lewis. LC 79-28554. 268p. reprint ed. pap. 83.10 (*0-8357-3896-5*, 203662800004) Bks Demand.

***Parahippocampal Region: Implications for Neurological & Psychiatric Diseases.** Helen E. Scharfman et al. LC 00-36153. 2000. write for info. (*1-57331-264-9*) NY Acad Sci.

***Para/Inquiry: Postmodern Religion & Cultue.** Victor E. Taylor. LC 99-20816. 136p. (C). 1999. text. write for info. (*0-415-18902-0*) Routledge.

Para/inquiry: Postmodern Religion & Culture Victor E. Taylor. LC 99-20816. 1999. pap. 22.99 (*0-415-18903-9*) Routledge.

Paraiso Bajo las Estrellas. Manuel C. Diaz. LC 95-61239. (Coleccion Caniqui). (SPA.). 91p. (Orig.). 1995. pap. 9.95 (*0-89729-783-0*) Ediciones.

Paraiso de Abuelita. Carmen S. Nodar. Ed. by Judith Mathews. Tr. by Teresa Mlawer. LC 92-3767. (SPA., Illus.). 32p. (J). (gr. k-3). 1992. text 14.95 (*0-8075-6346-3*) A Whitman.

Paraiso, Metamorfosis Y Memoria: La Influencia de Proust Y Kafka en la Obra de Mujica Lainez. Diana Garcia Simon. (Europaische Hochschulschriften Ibero-Romanische Sprachen und Literaturen Ser.). 226p. 39.95 (*3-631-32639-4*) P Lang Pubng.

Paraiso Perdido. Robyn Donald. (Bianca Ser.). 1996. per. 3.50 (*0-373-33363-3*, 1-33363-2) Harlequin Bks.

Paraisos Artificiales. Benigno S. Nieto. LC 97-80164. (Coleccion Caniqui). (SPA.). 496p. 1997. pap. 19.95 (*0-89729-854-3*) Ediciones.

Parajito Me Conto (A Little Bird Told Me) Ana M. Machado. (SPA.). 44p. (J). (gr. 3-4). 1992. pap. 5.99 (*968-16-3769-0*, Pub. by Fondo) Continental Bk.

Parakeet Girl. Marilyn Sadler. LC 95-9646. (Step into Reading Ser.: A Step 2 Book). (Illus.). 48p. (J). (gr. 1-4). 1997. pap. 3.99 (*0-679-87289-2*, Pub. by Random Bks Yng Read) Random.

Parakeet Girl. Marilyn Sadler. LC 95-9646. (Step into Reading Ser.: A Step 2 Book). (Illus.). (J). (gr. 1-4). 1997. lib. bdg. 11.99 (*0-679-97289-7*, Pub. by Random Bks Yng Read) Random.

Parakeet Girl. Marilyn Sadler. LC 95-9646. (Step into Reading Ser.: A Step 2 Book). (J). (gr. 1-3). 1997. 9.19 (*0-606-11721-0*, Pub. by Turtleback) Demco.

***Parakeet Handbook: Everything about the Purchase, Diet, Diseases & Behavior of Parakeets with a Special Chapter on Raising Parakeets.** 2nd ed. I. Birmelin & Annette Wolter. LC 99-41233. (Pet Handbks.). 144p. 2000. 9.95 (*0-7641-1018-7*) Barron.

Parakeets. Tina Hearne. (Responsible Pet Care Ser.). (Illus.). 32p. (J). (gr. 2-5). 1989. 11.95 (*0-685-58611-1*) Rourke Corp.

Parakeets. Earl Schneider & Matthew M. Vriends. (Illus.). 96p. 1984. reprint ed. 9.95 (*0-87666-749-3*, KW-036) TFH Pubns.

***Parakeets: A Complete Pet Owner's Manual.** Arthur Freud. LC 99-15227. 104p. 1999. pap. text 6.95 (*0-7641-1032-2*) Barron.

Parakeets (Budgerigars) Contrib. by David Lewis. (Junior Pet Care Ser.). (Illus.). 48p. (J). (gr. 2 up). 1999. lib. bdg. 14.95 (*0-7910-4909-4*) Chelsea Hse.

Parakeets Today. Elaine Radford. (Illus.). 64p. 1996. 12.95 (*0-7938-0106-0*, WW008) TFH Pubns.

Parakeets Today: A Complete & Up-to-Date Guide. Elaine Radford & American Society for the Prevention of Cruelty to. LC 97-3625. (Basic Domestic Pet Library). 76p. (J). (gr. 3 up). 1997. 19.95 (*0-7910-4615-X*) Chelsea Hse.

Parakrama Samudra Sri. F. Schiemer. 1983. 287.00 (*90-6193-763-9*, Pub. by Kluwer Academic) Kluwer Academic.

Paral (Program for the Analysis of Religion among Latinos) Series, 4 vols., Set. Ed. by Anthony M. Stevens & Gilbert R. Cadena. (Paral Studies). 1995. 95.00 (*0-929972-15-5*); pap. write for info. (*0-929972-16-3*) Bildner Ctr.

Paralanguage: A Linguistic & Interdisciplinary Approach to Interactive Speech & Sound. Fernando Poyatos. LC 92-42014. (Current Issues in Linguistic Theory Ser.: Vol. 92). xii, 478p. 1993. 125.00 (*1-55619-149-9*) J Benjamins Pubng Co.

Paralanguage & Kinesics: Nonverbal Communication with a Bibliography. Mary R. Key. LC 74-30217. 246p. 1975. 31.00 (*0-8108-0789-0*) Scarecrow.

Paralchimie: Avec: Architruc, l'Hypothese, Nuit. 2nd ed. Robert Pinget. (FRE.). 96p. 1990. pap. 17.95 (*0-7859-1520-6*, 2707313289) Fr & Eur.

Paralegal. Quinlan. LC 97-35254. (Careers Without College Ser.). (Illus.). 48p. (YA). (gr. 4-7). 1998. 19.00 (*1-56065-706-5*) Capstone Pr.

Paralegal. Kathryn A. Quinlan. (Careers Without College Ser.). (Illus.). 48p. (J). (gr. 3-7). 1998. 19.00 (*0-516-21285-0*) Childrens.

Paralegal. 3rd ed. William P. Statsky & Thomas L. Naps. Date not set. pap. text, student ed. write for info. (*0-314-71832-X*) West Pub.

Paralegal. 4th ed. William P. Statsky. 1992. pap. text, wbk. ed. 21.75 (*0-314-00678-8*) West Pub.

Paralegal: An Insider's Guide to One of the Fastest-Growing Careers. 3rd ed. Barbara Bernardo. LC 98-126339. (Peterson's Guides Ser.). 224p. 1997. pap. text 16.95 (*1-56079-894-7*) Petersons.

Paralegal: An Insider's Guide to One of the Fastest-Growing Occupations of the 1990s. 2nd ed. Barbara Bernardo. LC 92-45649. 224p. 1993. pap. 11.95 (*1-56079-242-6*) Petersons.

Paralegal Aide. Jack Rudman. (Career Examination Ser.: C-2245). 1994. pap. 27.95 (*0-8373-2245-6*) Nat Learn.

Paralegal Book of Letters, 1. Ed. by Wiley Law Publications Editorial Staff. 457p. 1998. pap. 72.00 (*0-471-04145-9*) Wiley.

Paralegal Career Starter. Learning Express Staff. LC 98-10846. (Career Starters Ser.). 1998. pap. 14.95 (*1-57685-098-6*) LrningExprss.

Paralegal Careers. Alice Fins. LC 98-17653. (Opportunities in... Ser.). 160p. 1998. 14.95 (*0-8442-6545-4*, 65454) NTC Contemp Pub Co.

Paralegal Careers. Alice Fins. LC 98-17653. (Opportunities in... Ser.). 160p. 1999. pap. 11.95 (*0-8442-6547-0*, 65470) NTC Contemp Pub Co.

Paralegal Careers. Schneeman. LC 99-53556. (Paralegal Ser.). 350p. (C). 2000. pap. 44.95 (*0-7668-0950-1*) Delmar.

Paralegal CTB, 1995. Delmar Staff. (Paralegal Ser.). 1996. 49.95 (*0-8273-7134-9*) Delmar.

Paralegal Discovery: Procedures & Forms, 1. 2nd ed. Pat Medina. 704p. 1994. boxed set 89.00 (*0-471-31076-X*) Wiley.

***Paralegal Discovery: Procedures & Forms.** 3rd ed. Pat Medina. 984p. 1999. boxed set 110.00 (*0-7355-1101-2*) Panel Pubs.

Paralegal Employment: Facts & Strategies for the 1990s. 2nd ed. William P. Statsky. Ed. by Hannan. LC 92-18131. 200p. (C). 1992. mass mkt. 23.75 (*0-314-01208-7*) West Pub.

Paralegal Ethics. Schneeman. LC 99-55790. (Paralegal Ser.). (C). 2000. pap. 35.95 (*0-7668-0949-8*) Delmar.

Paralegal Ethics & Regulation. 2nd ed. Statsky. (Paralegal). (C). 1993. pap. 72.00 (*0-314-01689-9*) Delmar.

Paralegal Ethics & Regulation. 2nd ed. William P. Statsky. Ed. by Hannan. LC 92-18128. 225p. (C). 1992. mass mkt. 30.25 (*0-314-01209-5*) West Pub.

Paralegal Guide to Automobile Accident Cases, 1. Jimmie W. Murvin. LC 95-23809. (Paralegal Litigation Library). 408p. 1995. boxed set 78.00 (*0-471-00656-4*) Wiley.

Paralegal Guide to Intellectual Property, 1. Valerie J. Atkinson. (Paralegal Law Library). 392p. 1994. boxed set 82.00 (*0-471-04303-6*) Wiley.

Paralegal Guide to Qualifed Pension Benefit Plans under ERISA, 1. Garrison Lee. LC 97-3367. 568p. 1998. pap. text 75.00 (*0-471-08664-9*) Wiley.

Paralegal Handbook. Hull. (Paralegal Ser.). (C). 1999. mass mkt. 24.50 (*0-7668-0772-X*) Delmar.

Paralegal Handbook Theory Practice & Materials. 464p. (C). 1990. text 72.00 (*0-536-57715-3*) Pearson Custom.

Paralegal Handbook Theory Practice & Materials. 464p. (C). 1990. pap. text 38.60 (*0-536-57716-1*) Pearson Custom.

Paralegal Internships Manual. 2nd ed. Charles P. Nemeth. 205p. (C). 1996. per. 34.95 (*0-929563-32-8*) Pearson Pubns.

***Paralegal Job: An Insider's Guide to the Fastest Growing Profession of the New.** 3rd ed. Wagner. 128p. 2000. pap. write for info. (*0-13-018832-8*) P-H.

Paralegal List - '93 Computer Test Bank. Michael P. Kearns. (Paralegal Ser.). 1993. pap. 52.00 (*0-8273-6244-7*) Delmar.

Paralegal List - Test Bank, 1994. Michael P. Kearns. (Paralegal Ser.). 1994. 49.95 (*0-8273-6245-5*) Delmar.

Paralegal Litigation: Forms & Procedures, 1. 2nd ed. Marcy Davis Fawcett Staff. 655p. 1995. boxed set 98.00 (*0-7355-1262-0*) Panel Pubs.

Paralegal Practice & Procedure: A Practical Guide for the Legal Assistant. 3rd ed. Deborah E. Larbalestrier. LC 94-28860. 576p. (C). 1994. pap. text 27.95 (*0-13-108564-6*) P-H.

Paralegal Primer. Scott A. Hatch. (Orig.). 1998. pap. text 19.00 (*0-8281-1314-9*) Forb Custom Pub.

Paralegal Primer. Scott A. Hatch & Lisa Z. Hatch. (Paralegal Certificate Course Ser.). (Illus.). 182p. (Orig.). 1997. pap. 19.00 (*0-9637248-0-0*) Ctr Legal Studies.

Paralegal Primer. 2nd rev. ed. Scott A. Hatch & Lisa Z. Hatch. (Illus.). 182p. (Orig.). 1997. pap. 19.00 (*0-9637248-1-9*) Ctr Legal Studies.

Paralegal Procedures & Practices. Scott A. Hatch & Lisa Z. Hatch. 175p. (C). 1993. pap. text 18.75 (*0-314-01348-2*) West Pub.

Paralegal Research. Hein. Date not set. pap. text, teacher ed. write for info. (*0-314-06970-4*) West Pub.

Paralegal Resource Manual, 2 vols., Vols. I-II. 2nd ed. Charles P. Nemeth. LC 94-71863. (Illus.). (C). 1994. pap. text 99.95 (*0-87084-612-4*) Anderson Pub Co.

***Paralegal Success: Going from Good to Great in the New Century.** Deborah Bogen. LC 99-12032. (Illus.). 320p. (C). 1999. pap. text 32.20 (*0-13-095193-5*) P-H.

Paralegal Today Essentials. Miller. Date not set. pap. text, teacher ed. write for info. (*0-314-06150-9*); pap. text, student ed. 13.75 (*0-314-06151-7*) West Pub.

Paralegal Trainer's Manual for Africa. Amy S. Tsanga & Olatokunbo Ige. LC KZ0400.. 104p. 1994. reprint ed. pap. 32.30 (*0-608-00493-6*, 206131200007) Bks Demand.

Paralegal Trial Handbook, 1. 2nd ed. Beverly K. Hutson. LC 95-7735. (Paralegal Law Library). 1350p. 1995. boxed set 78.00 (*0-471-12167-3*) Wiley.

P

An Asterisk (*) at the beginning of an entry indicates that the title is appearing for the first time.

Paralegals: Progress & Prospects of a Satellite Occupation, 2. Quintin Johnstone & Martin Wenglinsky. LC 85-9889. (Emerging Patterns of Work & Communications in an Information Age Ser.: No. 2). (Illus.). 257p. 1985. 59.95 (*0-313-24945-8*, JPG/) Greenwood.

Paralegal's Desk Reference: Up-to-the-Minute Information-Gathering Techniques for Today's Paralegal. Steve Albrecht. 224p. 1993. per. 12.95 (*0-671-84715-5*, Arc) IDG Bks.

Paralegal's Encyclopedic Dictionary. Valera Grapp. 1979. 29.50 (*0-13-648675-4*) P-H.

Paralegal's Guide to Administrative Law. William D. Haders. LC 93-72660. 315p. (C). 1993. pap. 29.95 (*0-87084-340-0*) Anderson Pub Co.

Paralegal's Guide to U. S. Government Jobs: How to Land a Job in 140 Law-Related Careers. 7th ed. Ed. by Richard L. Hermann et al. 140p. 1996. 19.95 (*0-929728-29-7*) Federal Reports Inc.

Paralegal's Handbook of Annotated Legal Forms, Clauses & Procedures. Deborah E. Larbalestrier. 384p. 1982. 39.50 (*0-13-648642-8*, Busn) P-H.

Paralegals in American Law: Introduction to Paralegalism. Angela Schneeman. LC 93-38409. 795p. (C). 1994. mass mkt. 52.25 (*0-8273-6078-9*) Delmar.

Paralegals In New York Law. Eric M. Gansberg. LC 93-50725. (Paralegal). 235p. (C). 1994. mass mkt. 38.95 (*0-8273-6322-2*) Delmar.

Paralegal's Introduction to Business Organizations. Lynn T. Slossberg. LC 96-78198. 688p. 1997. boxed set, wbk. ed. 44.00 (*1-56706-498-1*, 64981) Panel Pubs.

Paralegal's Introduction to Business Organizations, Incl. instr's. manual. Lynn T. Slossberg. 144p. 1997. pap. text, teacher ed. 18.95 (*1-56706-499-X*, 6499X) Panel Pubs.

Paralegal's Litigation Handbook. Carole A. Bruno. LC 79-19960. 544p. 1980. 45.00 (*0-87624-425-8*, Inst Busn Plan) P-H.

Paralegal's Litigation Handbook. 2nd ed. Carole A. Bruno. Ed. by Hannan. LC 92-40067. 600p. (C). 1993. mass mkt. 43.00 (*0-314-01177-3*) West Pub.

Paraleipomena Jeremiou. Ed. by Robert A. Kraft & Ann-Elizabeth Purintun. LC 72-88436. (Pseudepigrapha Ser.: No. 1). 53p. reprint ed. pap. 30.00 (*0-7837-5460-4*, 204522500005) Bks Demand.

Paralelismos Transatlanticos: Postcolonialismo y Narrativa Feminina en America Latina y Africa del Norte. Silvia Nagy-Zekmi. (SPA.). 140p. 1996. pap. 25.00 (*1-888135-02-6*) Ediciones Inti.

Paralipomena Grammaticae Graecae, 2 vols. in 1. Christian A. Lobeck. xii, 622p. 1967. reprint ed. write for info. (*0-318-70967-8*); reprint ed. write for info. (*0-318-72044-2*) G Olms Pubs.

Paralipomena Sophoclea. Lewis Campbell. xv, 287p. 1969. reprint ed. 95.00 (*0-685-66441-4*, 05102319) G Olms Pubs.

Parallax. Karen Chance. 1988. pap. 30.00 (*0-932526-17-9*) Nexus Pr.

***Parallax.** Steven Holl. (Illus.). 384p. 2000. pap. 40.00 (*1-56898-261-5*) Princeton Arch.

***Parallax: The Race to Measure the Cosmos.** Alan Hirshfeld. 2001. pap. text. write for info. (*0-7167-3711-6*) W H Freeman.

Parallax Red. James Axler. (Outlanders Ser.). 1998. per. 5.99 (*0-373-63818-3*, 1-63818-8, Wrldwide Lib) Harlequin Bks.

Parallax View. Loren Singer. LC 80-54848. 192p. 1981. reprint ed. pap. 16.00 (*0-933256-21-3*) Second Chance.

Parallax Visions: Making Sense of American-East Asian Relations at the End of the Century. Bruce Cumings. LC 98-32017. (Asia-Pacific Ser.). 288p. 1999. 27.95 (*0-8223-2276-5*) Duke.

***Parallel.** Lawerence Zaccaro. LC 99-65307. 192232p. 2000. pap. 11.95 (*1-56315-254-1*, Pub. by SterlingHse) Natl Bk Netwk.

Parallel Algorithm Derivation & Program Transformation. Ed. by Ralph Wachter et al. LC 93-1687. (International Series in Engineering & Computer Science, VLSI, Computer Architecture, & Digital Screen Processing). 248p. (C). 1993. text 115.50 (*0-7923-9362-7*) Kluwer Academic.

Parallel Algorithms: Third DIMACS Implementation Challenge, 1994. DIMACS (Group) Staff. Ed. by Sandeep N. Bhatt. LC 96-52111. (DIMACS Series in Discrete Mathematics & Theoretical Computer Science: Vol. 30). 162p. 1997. text 45.00 (*0-8218-0447-2*, DIMACS/30) Am Math.

Parallel Algorithms - 2nd Aizu International Symposium on Architecture Synthesis (PAS '97) LC 96-79898. 400p. 1997. 80.00 (*0-8186-7870-4*, PR07870) IEEE Comp Soc.

Parallel Algorithms & Architectures. M. Cosnard. LC 95-228378. 1995. pap. 49.95 (*1-85032-125-6*) Thomson Learn.

Parallel Algorithms & Architectures for DSP Applications. Ed. by Magdy A. Rayoumi. 304p. (C). 1991. text 117.00 (*0-7923-9209-4*) Kluwer Academic.

Parallel Algorithms & Matrix Computation. Jagdish J. Modi. (Oxford Applied Mathematics & Computing Science Ser.). (Illus.). 272p. 1989. pap. text 39.95 (*0-19-859670-7*) OUP.

Parallel Algorithms for Digital Image Processing, Computer Vision & Neural Networks. Ed. by Ioannis Pitas. LC 00-92. (Parallel Computing Ser.). 410p. 1993. 100.00 (*0-471-93566-2*) Wiley.

Parallel Algorithms for Irregular Problems: State of the Art. Ed. by Alfonso Ferreira & Jose D. P. Rolim. LC 95-30322. 352p. (C). 1995. text 158.50 (*0-7923-3623-2*) Kluwer Academic.

Parallel Algorithms for Irregularly Structured Problems: Second International Workshop, Lyon, France, September 4-6, 1995, Proceedings, Vol. X. Ed. by Afonso A. Ferreira & Jose D. P. Rolim. LC 95-37093. (Lecture Notes in Computer Science Ser.: Vol. 980). 409p. 1995. 68.00 (*3-540-60321-2*) Spr-Verlag.

Parallel Algorithms for Irregularly Structured Problems: Third International Workshop, Irregular 96, Santa Barbara, CA, U. S. A, August 19-21, 1996: Proceedings. Ed. by Afonso Ferreira. LC 96-9906. (Lecture Notes in Computer Science Ser.: Vol. 111). 358p. 1996. 62.00 (*3-540-61549-0*) Spr-Verlag.

Parallel Algorithms for Knapsack Type Problems. V. N. Aleksandrov & G. M. Megson. 280p. 1997. text 61.00 (*981-02-2120-7*) World Scientific Pub.

Parallel Algorithms for Machine Intelligence & Vision. Ed. by V. K. Kumar et al. (Symbolic Computation - Artificial Intelligence Ser.). (Illus.). xi, 433p. 1990. 79.95 (*0-387-97227-7*) Spr-Verlag.

Parallel Algorithms for Matrix Computations. Ed. by K. Gallivan et al. LC 90-22017. (Miscellaneous Bks.: No. 22). x, 197p. 1990. reprint ed. pap. 21.00 (*0-89871-260-2*) Soc Indus-Appl Math.

Parallel Algorithms for Optimal Control of Large Scale Linear Systems. Zoran Gajic & Xuemin Shen. LC 93-3304. 1993. 99.95 (*0-387-19825-3*) Spr-Verlag.

Parallel Algorithms for Regular Architectures: Meshes & Pyramids. Russ Miller & Quentin F. Stout. (Illus.). 336p. 1996. 42.00 (*0-262-13233-8*) MIT Pr.

Parallel Algorithms in Computational Science. D. W. Heermann & A. N. Burkitt. (Information Sciences Ser.: Vol. 24). (Illus.). xiii, 183p. 1991. 49.95 (*0-387-53418-0*) Spr-Verlag.

Parallel Algorithms on a Multiprocessor. Peter N. Oleinick. Ed. by Harold S. Stone. LC 82-4954. (Computer Science: Systems Programming Ser.: No. 4). 124p. 1982. reprint ed. pap. 38.50 (*0-8357-1327-X*, 207007900063) Bks Demand.

Parallel & Cluster Computing: Scalable Architecture & Programming. Kai Hwang & Zhiwei Xu. LC 97-41663. 710p. 1998. 92.00 (*0-07-031798-4*) McGraw-Hill Prof.

Parallel & Constraint Logic Programming: An Introduction to Logic, Parallelism & Constraints. Ioannis Vlahavas et al. LC 98-44241. (Series in Engineering & Computer Science). 1998. write for info. (*0-7923-8371-0*) Kluwer Academic.

Parallel & Distributed Computation: Numerical Methods. Dimitri P. Bertsekas & John N. Tsitsiklis. LC 97-70648. 730p. (C). 1997. pap. text 49.50 (*1-886529-01-9*) Athena Scientific.

Parallel & Distributed Computing: Theory & Practice; First Canada-France Conference, Montreal, Canada, May 19-21, 1994, Proceedings. Ed. by Michael Cosnard et al. LC 94-15892. (Lecture Notes in Computer Science Ser.: Vol. 805). 1994. write for info. (*0-387-58078-6*) Spr-Verlag.

Parallel & Distributed Computing & Systems. Ed. by K. Abdelrahman & E. Luque. LC 97-18498. (Illus.). 546p. 1996. pap. 152.00 (*0-88986-213-3*) Acta Pr.

Parallel & Distributed Computing Handbook. Ed. by Albert Y. Zomaya. LC 95-32594. (Computer Engineering Ser.). (Illus.). 1232p. 1995. 99.50 (*0-07-073020-2*) McGraw.

Parallel & Distributed Computing Systems (PDCS-94), 7th International Conference, October 6-8, 1994, Las Vegas, Nevada, U.S.A: Conference Proceedings Oct. 6-8, 1994, Las Vegas, Nevada. 850p. (C). 1994. write for info. (*1-880843-09-9*) Int Soc Comp App.

Parallel & Distributed Computing Systems (PDCS-97), 10th International Conference, October 1-3, 1997, New Orleans, Louisiana, U.S.A: Oct. 1-3, 1997, New Orleans, LA. Ed. by A. El-Amawy & S. Q. Zheng. LC 98-190481. 1997. write for info. (*1-880843-21-8*) Int Soc Comp App.

Parallel & Distributed Debugging Workshop, 1993. 114p. 1993. pap. text 16.00 (*0-89791-633-6*, 551932) Assn Compu Machinery.

Parallel & Distributed Information Systems. Ed. by Jeffrey F. Naughton & Gerhard Weikum. LC 97-44658. 116p. 1998. text 107.50 (*0-7923-8087-8*) Kluwer Academic.

Parallel & Distributed Methods for Image Processing II, Vol. 3452. Ed. by Hongchi Shi & Patrick C. Coffield. LC 99-159857. 1998. 59.00 (*0-8194-2907-4*) SPIE.

***Parallel & Distributed Methods for Image Processing III.** Ed. by Hongchi Shi & Patrick C. Coffield. 1999. pap. text 62.00 (*0-8194-3303-9*) SPIE.

Parallel & Distributed Methods for Imaging Processing. Ed. by Hongchi Shi & Patrick C. Coffield. LC 98-122068. 382p. 1997. 80.00 (*0-8194-2588-5*) SPIE.

Parallel & Distributed Processing. Ed. by J. Rolim et al. LC 99-25670. (Lecture Notes in Computer Science Ser.: Vol. 1586). xvii, 1443p. 1999. pap. 129.00 (*3-540-65831-9*) Spr-Verlag.

***Parallel & Distributed Processing: Proceedings of the LPDPS 2000 Workshops, Cancun, Mexico, May 1-5, 2000.** Ed. by Josbe D. P. Rolim. LC 00-38821. (Lecture Notes in Computer Science Ser.: Vol. 1800). 2000. pap. 110.00 (*3-540-67442-X*) Spr-Verlag.

Parallel & Distributed Processing: 10th International IPPS/SPDP'98 Workshops, Held in Conjunction with the 12th International Parallel Processing Symposium on Parallel & 9th Symposium on Parallel & Distributed Processing, Orlando, Florida, U. S. A., March 30-April 3, 1998, Vol. 138. Ed. by Jose D. P. Rolim et al. LC 98-18273. (Lecture Notes in Computer Science: Vol. 1388). xvii, 1168p. 1998. pap. 109.00 (*3-540-64359-1*) Spr-Verlag.

Parallel & Distributed Processing, 5th Euromicco Workshop (PDP '97) LC 10-666192. 520p. 1997. pap. 100.00 (*0-8186-7770-8*) IEEE Comp Soc.

Parallel & Distributed Processing for Computational Mechanics: Systems & Tools. Ed. by B. H. V. Topping. 320p. 1997. 264.00 (*1-874672-03-2*, Pub. by Civil-Comp) St Mut.

Parallel & Distributed Processing, 4th Euromicro Workshop on (PDP '96) LC 10-666192. 500p. 1996. pap. 100.00 (*0-8186-7376-1*) IEEE Comp Soc.

Parallel & Distributed Processing in Structural Engineering. Ed. by Hojjat Adeli. (Sessions Proceedings Ser.). 104p. 1988. 5.00 (*0-87262-640-7*) Am Soc Civil Eng.

Parallel & Distributed Real-Time Systems, 4th Workshop. LC 96-76269. 262p. 1996. pap. 50.00 (*0-8186-7515-2*) IEEE Comp Soc.

Parallel & Distributed Real-Time Systems, 5th International Workshop on (Wpdrts '97) LC 97-72685. 377p. 1997. pap. 125.00 (*0-8186-8096-2*) IEEE Comp Soc.

Parallel & Distributed Signal & Image Integration Problems: Proceedings of the Indo - U. S. Workshop. Ed. by Indo-U. S. Workshop on Parallel & Distributed Sign & Rabinder N. Madan. LC 95-14878. (Series on Advances in Mathematics for Applied Sciences). 480p. 1995. text 109.00 (*981-02-2148-7*) World Scientific Pub.

Parallel & Distributed Simulation: Proceedings of the 11th Workshop on Parallel & Distributed Simulation, Lockenhaus, Austria, 1997. LC 10-874097. 224p. 1997. pap. 110.00 (*0-8186-7964-6*) IEEE Comp Soc.

Parallel & Distributed Simulation (PADS, '98), 12th Workshop On. IEEE Staff. 200p. 1998. pap. 110.00 (*0-8186-8457-7*, PR8457, IEEE Inst Elec) IEEE Comp Soc.

***Parallel & Distributed Simulation Systems.** Richard M. Fujimoto. LC 99-25438. 300p. 1999. 79.95 (*0-471-18383-0*) Wiley.

Parallel & Distributed Systems: Proceedings: International Conference on Parallel & Distributed Systems (1998: Tainan, Taiwan, R. O. C.) 826p. 1998. pap. 130.00 (*0-8186-8603-0*) IEEE Comp Soc.

Parallel & Distributed Systems EURO-PDS '97. Ed. by E. Luque et al. LC 97-18562. (Illus.). 348p. 1997. pap. 105.00 (*0-88986-225-7*) Acta Pr.

Parallel & Distributed Systems, 1996 International Conference on (ICPADS '96) LC 96-177535. 350p. 1996. pap. 70.00 (*0-8186-7267-6*, PRO7267) IEEE Comp Soc.

***Parallel & Real-Time Systems: Proceedings of the 6th Australasian Conference on Parallel & Real-Time Systems, Melbourne, Australia, 29 November-1 December 1999.** Ed. by Wilson C. H. Cheng & A. S. M. Sajeev. LC 99-49592. 450p. 1999. 69.95 (*981-4021-59-8*) Spr-Verlag.

Parallel & Sequential Methods for Ordinary Differential Equations. Kevin Burrage. (Monographs on Numerical Analysis). (Illus.). 462p. 1995. text 110.00 (*0-19-853432-9*) OUP.

***Parallel Apocrypha.** 1999. 29.99 (*5-550-00797-5*) Nairi.

***Parallel Architectures, Algorithms, & Networks (I-SPAN'99) Proceedings: International Symposium on Parallel Architectrures, Algorithms, & Networks, I-SPAN'99 (4th: 1999: Perth/Fremantle, Australia)** 439p. 1999. 140.00 (*0-7695-0231-8*) IEEE Comp Soc.

Parallel Architectures, Algorithms & Networks, 1996 International Symposium: ISPAN, 96. LC 10-874089. 567p. 1996. pap. 100.00 (*0-8186-7460-1*) IEEE Comp Soc.

***Parallel Architectures & Compilation Techniques: Proceedings International Conference Newport Beach, California, 1999.** LC 99-66133. 321p. 1999. 125.00 (*0-7695-0425-6*) IEEE Comp Soc.

Parallel Architectures & Compilation Techniques: Proceedings of the IFIP WG10.3 Working Conference on Parallel Architectures & Compilation Techniques, PACT '94, Montreal, Canada, 24-26 August, 1994. Working Conference on Parallel Architectures & Com & Gabriel M. Silberman. Ed. by Michel Cosnard et al. LC 94-28408. (IFIP Transactions A: Computer Science & Technology Ser.). 374p. 1994. 133.50 (*0-444-81926-6*, North Holland) Elsevier.

Parallel Architectures & Compilation Techniques, 1996 Conference On: PACT, 96. LC 10-89795. 350p. 1996. pap. 70.00 (*0-8186-7632-9*) IEEE Comp Soc.

Parallel Architectures & Compilation Techniques, 1997 International Conference on (Pact '97) LC 10-89795. 320p. 1997. pap. 120.00 (*0-8186-8090-3*) IEEE Comp Soc.

Parallel Architectures & Neural Network: Third Italian Workshop, Vietri Sul Mare, Salerno, 15-18 May 1990. Ed. by E. R. Caianiello. 440p. (C). 1990. text 91.00 (*981-02-0308-X*) World Scientific Pub.

Parallel Architectures & Neural Networks: 1st Italian Workshop. Ed. by E. R. Caianiello. 212p. (C). 1989. text 77.00 (*9971-5-0905-9*) World Scientific Pub.

Parallel Architectures & Neural Networks: 2nd Italian Workshop. Ed. by E. R. Caianiello. 380p. (C). 1990. text 113.00 (*981-02-0146-X*) World Scientific Pub.

Parallel Architectures & Neural Networks: 4th Italian Workshop. Ed. by E. R. Caianiello. 350p. (C). 1991. text 89.00 (*981-02-0763-8*) World Scientific Pub.

Parallel Architectures & Parallel Algorithms for Integrated Vision Systems. Alok N. Choudhary & Janak H. Patel. (C). 1990. text 95.50 (*0-7923-9078-4*) Kluwer Academic.

Parallel Architectures & Their Efficient Use: First Heinz Nixdorf Symposium, Paderborn, Germany, November 11-13, 1992 Proceedings. Ed. by F. Meyer Auf der Heide et al. LC 93-29041. (Lecture Notes in Computer Science Ser.: Vol. 678). xii, 227p. 1993. 39.95 (*0-387-56731-3*) Spr-Verlag.

Parallel Architectures for Artificial Neural Networks: Paradigms & Implementations. N. Sundararajan & P. Saratchandran. LC 98-22934. 1998. 70.00 (*0-8186-8399-6*) IEEE Comp Soc.

Parallel Architectures for Data Knowledge-Based Systems. Ed. by L. L. Miller et al. LC 94-15104. 616p. 1994. 58.00 (*0-8186-6352-9*, BP06352) IEEE Comp Soc.

Parallel Array Processing. Paul G. Ducksbury. LC 86-2908. (Electrical & Electronic Engineering Ser.). 122p. 1986. text 44.95 (*0-470-20330-7*) P-H.

***Parallel Bars & Horizontal Bars.** Joanne Mattern. LC 99-27924. 48p. (J). 1999. lib. bdg. write for info. (*0-86593-570-X*) Rourke Corp.

***Parallel Bible.** 2000. 29.99 (*0-8297-2403-6*); 42.99 (*0-8297-2404-4*) Vida Pub.

***Parallel Bible.** 2000. 24.99 (*0-8297-2402-8*) Vida Pubs.

Parallel Bible: Updated Edition. 1728p. (J). 1999. 29.99 (*0-310-90215-0*) Zondervan.

Parallel Captures: Lord Jim & Lawrence of Arabia. J. N. Lockman. LC 98-145095. (Illus.). 44p. 1997. pap. 5.00 (*0-9648897-2-2*) Falcon Books.

Parallel Circuits. Bergwall. (Electronic Technology Ser.). 1991. 95.00 (*0-8273-4818-5*, VNR) Wiley.

Parallel Complexity of Linear System Solution. B. Codenotti & Mauro Leoncini. 228p. 1991. text 61.00 (*981-02-0502-3*); pap. text 36.00 (*981-02-0503-1*) World Scientific Pub.

Parallel Computation: Based on the Proceedings of a Conference on Parallel Computation. Ed. by A. E. Fincham & B. Ford. LC 93-31647. (Conference Series - The Institute of Mathematics & Its Applications). (Illus.). 384p. 1994. text 95.00 (*0-19-853680-1*, Clarendon Pr) OUP.

Parallel Computation: First International ACPC Conference, Salzburg, Austria, September 30-October 2, 1991, Proceedings. Ed. by H. P. Zima et al. LC 92-15346. (Lecture Notes in Computer Science Ser.: Vol. 591). ix, 451p. 1992. pap. 61.00 (*0-387-55437-8*) Spr-Verlag.

Parallel Computation: Models & Methods. Selim G. Akl. LC 96-42310. 608p. 1996. pap. 78.00 (*0-13-147034-5*) P-H.

Parallel Computation: Practical Implementation of Algorithms & Machines: XXX Macintosh CD-ROM. Ed. by Peter A. Gloor & Fillia Makedon. LC 93-42646. 1993. 79.95 (*0-387-14213-4*) Spr-Verlag.

Parallel Computation: Third International ACPC Conference with Special Emphasis on Parallel Databases & Parallel IO, Klagenfurt, Austria, September 1996: Proceedings. Boszormeny. LC 96-38442. (Lecture Notes in Computer Science Ser.: Vol. 1127). 235p. 1996. 43.00 (*3-540-61695-0*) Spr-Verlag.

Parallel Computation: 4th International ACPC Conference Including Special Tracks on Parallel Numerics (ParNum '99) & Parallel Computing in Image Processing, Video Processing, & Multimedia, Salzburg, Austria, February 16-18, 1999 : Proceedings. Ed. by Peter Zinterhof et al. LC 99-19969. (Lecture Notes in Computer Science Ser.: Vol. 1557). xv, 604p. 1999. pap. 91.00 (*3-540-65641-3*) Spr-Verlag.

Parallel Computation & Computers for Artificial Intelligence. Ed. by Janusz S. Kowalik. (C). 1987. text 125.00 (*0-89838-227-0*) Kluwer Academic.

***Parallel Computation in Image Processing.** Steven L. Tanimoto & Stephan Olariu. (International Series on Parallel Computation: Vol. 9). 320p. (C). 2000. text 49.95 (*0-521-77061-0*) Cambridge U Pr.

Parallel Computation Systems for Robotics: Algorithms & Architectures. Ed. by A. Fijany & A. Bejczy. LC 92-19670. (Series in Robotics & Automated Systems: Vol. 2). 300p. (C). 1994. pap. 36.00 (*981-02-0664-X*); text 98.00 (*981-02-0663-1*) World Scientific Pub.

Parallel Computational Fluid Dynamics: Algorithms & Results Using Advanced Computers: Proceedings of the Parallel CFD '96 Conference, Capri, Italy, May 20-23, 1996. P. D. Schiano. LC 97-295. 530p. 1997. 215.75 (*0-444-82327-1*) Elsevier.

Parallel Computational Fluid Dynamics: Development & Applications of Parallel Technology: Proceedings of the Parallel CFD'98 Conference, Hsinchu, Taiwan, May 11-14, 1998. Parallel CFD '98 Conference Staff & C. A. Lin. LC 99-26231. 548p. 1999. 175.00 (*0-444-82850-8*, North Holland) Elsevier.

Parallel Computational Fluid Dynamics: Implementations & Results. Horst D. Simon. (Scientific & Engineering Computation Ser.). (Illus.). 362p. 1992. 50.00 (*0-262-19326-4*) MIT Pr.

Parallel Computational Fluid Dynamics: New Algorithms & Applications: Proceedings of the Parallel CFD '94 Conference, Kyoto, Japan, 16-19 May 1994. Ed. by Nobuyuki Satofuka et al. LC 95-44406. 470p. 1995. 220.50 (*0-444-82317-4*) Elsevier.

Parallel Computational Fluid Dynamics, '92: Proceedings of the Conference on Parallel CFD '92 - Implementations & Results Using Parallel Computers, New Brunswick, NJ, 18-20 May, 1992. Ed. by R. B. Pelz et al. LC 93-16448. 438p. 1993. 177.25 (*0-444-89986-3*, North Holland) Elsevier.

Parallel Computational Fluid Dynamics '93: New Trends & Advances; Proceedings of the Parallel CFD Conference, Paris, France, May 10-12, 1993. Ed. by A. Ecer et al. LC 94-42676. 574p. 1994. 203.00 (*0-444-81999-1*) Elsevier.

Parallel Computational Fluid Dynamics '95: Implementations & Results Using Parallel Computers. Ed. by A. Ecer et al. 748p. 1996. 238.50 (*0-444-82322-0*, North Holland) Elsevier.

Parallel Computational Fluid Dynamics, '97: Recent Developments & Advances Using Parallel Computers - Proceedings of the Parallel CFD Conferences, Manchester, United Kingdom, 19-23 May 1997. Ed. by D. Emerson et al. 696p. 1998. 241.50 (*0-444-82849-4*, North Holland) Elsevier.

P

An Asterisk (*) at the beginning of an entry indicates that the title is appearing for the first time.

Parallel Computations: Paradigms & Applications. Albert Y. Zomaya. (Illus.). 544p. 1995. mass mkt. 74.95 (*1-85032-188-4*) ITCP.

Parallel Computations on Windows NT. Jenn-Ching Luo. LC 94-93901. 281p. (C). 1995. pap. 25.00 (*0-9644361-0-8*); pap. text 49.00 (*0-614-03971-1*) Paral Integ.

Parallel Computaton: Second International ACPC Conference, Gmundenn, Austria, October 4-6, 1993 Proceedings. Ed. by Jens Volkert. LC 93-21308. (Lecture Notes in Computer Science Ser.: Vol. 734). 1993. 44.95 (*0-387-57314-3*) Spr-Verlag.

Parallel Computer Architecture: A Hardware - Software Approach. Anoop Gupta et al. LC 98-28034. 1100p. (C). 1998. 89.95 (*1-55860-343-3*) Morgan Kaufmann.

Parallel Computer Architectures: Theory, Hardware, Software, Applications. Ed. by Arndt Bode & Mario D. Cin. LC 93-35538. (Lecture Notes in Computer Science Ser.: Vol. 732). 1993. 54.00 (*0-387-57307-0*) Spr-Verlag.

Parallel Computer Routing & Communication: Proceedings of the First International Workshop, PCRCW '94, Seattle, Washington, U. S. A., May 16-18, 1994. PCRCW '94 Staff. Ed. by Lawrence Snyder & Kevin Bolding. LC 94-33307. (Lecture Notes in Computer Science Ser.: 853). 1994. write for info. (*0-387-58429-3*) Spr-Verlag.

Parallel Computer Routing & Communication: Proceedings of the First International Workshop, PCRCW '94, Seattle, Washington, U. S. A., May 16-18, 1994. PCRCW '94 Staff. Ed. by Lawrence Snyder & Kevin Bolding. LC 94-33307. (Lecture Notes in Computer Science Ser.: 853). 1994. 50.95 (*3-540-58429-3*) Spr-Verlag.

Parallel Computer Routing & Communication: Second International Workshop, PCRCW '97, Atlanta, Georgia, U. S. A., June 26-27, 1997. Proceedings. Ed. by S. Yalamanchili et al. LC 98-24763. (Lecture Notes in Computer Science Ser.: Vol. 1417). xii, 309p. 1998. pap. 55.00 (*3-540-64571-3*) Spr-Verlag.

Parallel Computer Vision: Vis a Vis- A Virtual Image System. David Vernon & G. Sandini. LC 92-22081. 1992. 71.95 (*0-13-932716-9*, Pub. by Tavistock-E Horwood) Routldge.

Parallel Computers: Theory & Practice. Ed. by Thomas L. Casavant et al. LC 95-10090. (Reprint Collection). 432p. 1995. 58.00 (*0-8186-5162-8*, BP05162) IEEE Comp Soc.

Parallel Computers Two: Architecture, Programming & Algorithms. 2nd rev. ed. Roger W. Hockney & C. R. Jesshope. (Illus.). 644p. 1988. 282.00 (*0-85274-811-6*); pap. 51.00 (*0-85274-812-4*) IOP Pub.

Parallel Computing: An Introduction. Edward L. Lafferty et al. LC 93-866. (Illus.). 134p. 1993. 45.00 (*0-8155-1329-1*) Noyes.

***Parallel Computing: Fundamentals & Applications.** Ed. by E. H. D'Hollander et al. 850p. 2000. 138.00 (*1-86094-235-0*, Pub. by Imperial College) World Scientific Pub.

Parallel Computing: Fundamentals, Applications, & New Directions. E. D'Hollander. LC 98-20528. (Advances in Parallel Computing Ser.). 748p. 1998. 258.50 (*0-444-82882-6*) Elsevier.

Parallel Computing: Principles & Practice. T. J. Fountain. (Illus.). 358p. (C). 1995. text 44.95 (*0-521-45131-0*) Cambridge U Pr.

Parallel Computing: Techniques & Applications Using Networked Workstations & Parallel Computers. Barry Wilkinson. LC 98-27241. 431p. (C). 1998. pap. 55.00 (*0-13-671710-1*, Pub. by P-H) S&S Trade.

Parallel Computing: Technology & Practice. Gray & Nagdy. LC 94-79853. (Transputer & Ocean Engineering Ser.: Vol. 43). (gr. 12). 1994. 98.00 (*90-5199-196-7*) IOS Press.

Parallel Computing: The State-of-the-Art & Perspective: Proceedings of the International Conference ParCo95, Gent, Belgium, 19-22 September 1995. G. R. Joubert et al. Ed. by E. D'Hollander et al. LC 96-17143. (Advances in Parallel Computing Ser.: Vol. 11). 740p. 1996. 201.00 (*0-444-82490-1*) Elsevier.

Parallel Computing: Theory & Practice. 2nd ed. Quinn. 1993. 15.93 (*0-07-051295-7*) McGraw.

Parallel Computing: Theory & Practice. 2nd ed. Michael J. Quinn. LC 93-29813. (C). 1993. 93.13 (*0-07-051294-9*) McGraw.

Parallel Computing: Trade & Applications: Proceedings of the International Conference, ParCo93, Grenoble, France, 7-10 September 1993. International Conference, ParCo93, Staff. Ed. by F. J. Peters et al. (Advances in Parallel Computing Ser.). 744p. 1994. text 243.25 (*0-444-81841-3*, North Holland) Elsevier.

Parallel Computing & Applications (Transputers), '93. D. Arnold et al. LC 93-80962. (Transputer & Occam Engineering Ser.: Vol. 37). 392p. (YA). (gr. 12). 1992. 98.00 (*90-5199-149-5*, Pub. by IOS Pr) IOS Press.

Parallel Computing & Mathematical Optimization: Proceedings of the Workshop on Parallel Algorithms & Transputers for Optimization, Held at the University of Siegen, FRG, November 9, 1990. Ed. by M. Grauer et al. (Lecture Notes in Economics & Mathematical Systems Ser.: Vol. 367). (Illus.). v, 208p. 1991. pap. 35.00 (*0-387-54434-8*) Spr-Verlag.

Parallel Computing, from Theory to Sound Practice: Proceedings of the European Workshops on Parallel Computing, 23-24 March 1992, Barcelona, Spain. Ed. by Wouter Joosen & Elie Milgrom. LC 91-59038. (Transputer & Occam Engineering Ser.). 616p. (gr. 12). 1992. 125.00 (*90-5199-080-4*, Pub. by IOS Pr) IOS Press.

Parallel Computing in Computational Chemistry. Ed. by Timothy G. Mattson. LC 95-1232. (ACS Symposium Ser.: No. 592). (Illus.). 232p. 1995. text 78.00 (*0-8412-3166-4*, Pub. by Am Chemical) OUP.

Parallel Computing in Multiphase Flow Systems Simulations: 1994 International Mechanical Engineering Congress & Exposition, Chicago, Illinois - November 6-11, 1994. (FED Ser.: Vol. 199). 100p. 1994. 48.00 (*0-7918-1404-1*, G00899) ASME.

Parallel Computing in Optimization. Athanasios Migdalas et al. LC 97-14126. (Applied Optimization Ser.). 1997. lib. bdg. 260.00 (*0-7923-4583-5*) Kluwer Academic.

Parallel Computing in Science & Engineering. Ed. by R. Dierstein et al. (Lecture Notes in Computer Science Ser.: Vol. 295). vii, 180p. 1988. 30.00 (*0-387-18923-8*) Spr-Verlag.

Parallel Computing Methods, Algorithms & Applications. Ed. by D. J. Evans & C. Nodari Sutti. (Illus.). 320p. 1989. 40.00 (*0-85274-224-X*) IOP Pub.

Parallel Computing, 1988. Ed. by G. A. Van Zee et al. (Lecture Notes in Computer Science Ser.: Vol. 384). v, 135p. 1989. 27.00 (*0-387-51604-2*) Spr-Verlag.

Parallel Computing on Distributed Memory Multiprocessors. Ed. by Fusun Ozguner & Fikret Ercal. LC 92-43569. (NATO ASI Series F: Computer & Systems Sciences, Special Programme AET: Vol. 103). 1993. 94.95 (*0-387-56295-8*) Spr-Verlag.

Parallel Computing Structures & Algorithms for Logic Design Problems. Roy M. Matney, II & C. H. Roth, Jr. LC 72-133318. 124p. 1969. 19.00 (*0-403-04518-5*) Scholarly.

Parallel Computing Technologies. Nikolay Mirenkov. 450p. (C). 1991. text 118.00 (*981-02-0698-4*) World Scientific Pub.

Parallel Computing Technologies: Proceedings, 4th International Conference, PaCT-97, Yaroslavl, Russia, September 8-12, 1997. Conference on Parallel Computing Technologies Staf. Ed. by V. E. Malyshkin. LC 97-27823. (Lecture Notes in Computer Science Ser.: Vol. 1277). xiii, 455p. pap. 69.00 (*3-540-63371-5*) Spr-Verlag.

Parallel Computing Technologies: Third International Conference, PaCT-95, St. Petersburg, Russia, September 12-15, 1995, Proceedings, Vol. XII. Ed. by Victor Malyshkin et al. LC 95-36460. (Lecture Notes in Computer Science Ser.: Vol. 964). 497p. 1995. 81.00 (*3-540-60222-4*) Spr-Verlag.

***Parallel Computing Technologies: 5th International Conference, PaCT-99, St. Petersburg, Russia, September 6-10, 1999.** Ed. by V. E. Malyshkin et al. LC 99-41063. (Lecture Notes in Computer Science Ser.: Vol. 1662). xix, 510p. 1999. pap. 79.00 (*3-540-66363-0*) Spr-Verlag.

Parallel Computing Transputer Applications (I-II) Proceedings of the International Conference, PACTA 1992, September 21-25, 1992, Barcelona, Spain. Ed. by M. Valero et al. LC 92-53263. (Transputer & Occam Engineering Ser.: Vols. 28- 29). 1520p. (gr. 12). 1992. 195.00 (*90-5199-096-0*) IOS Press.

Parallel Computing Using Optical Interconnections. Keqin Li et al. LC 98-41635. (International Series in Engineering & Computer Science). 279p. 1998. write for info. (*0-7923-8296-X*) Kluwer Academic.

Parallel Computing Using the Prefix Problem. S. Lakshmivarahan & S. K. Dhall. (Illus.). 320p. 1994. text 80.00 (*0-19-508849-2*) OUP.

Parallel Computing Works! Mark Fox. Ed. by Roy D. Williams & Paul C. Messina. 977p. 1994. text 74.95 (*1-55860-253-4*) Morgan Kaufmann.

Parallel Convergence: National Strategies in Information Technology. Erik Arnold & Ken Guy. LC 86-16954. 228p. 1986. 49.95 (*0-89930-226-2*, ADC/, Quorum Bks) Greenwood.

Parallel Coupled Lines & Directional Couplers. Leo Young. LC 76-168946. (Illus.). 287p. reprint ed. pap. 89.00 (*0-608-10032-3*, 201210300080) Bks Demand.

Parallel Currency Markets in Developing Countries: Theory, Evidence, & Policy Implications. Pierre-Richard Agenor. LC 92-32099. (Essays in International Finance Ser.: No. 188). 40p. 1992. pap. 10.00 (*0-88165-095-1*) Princeton U Int Finan Econ.

Parallel Database Systems: Proceedings of PRISMA Workshop, Noordwijk, the Netherlands, September 24-26, 1990. Ed. by P. America. (Lecture Notes in Computer Science Ser.: Vol. 503). viii, 433p. 1991. 44.95 (*0-387-54132-2*) Spr-Verlag.

Parallel Database Techniques. Mahdi Abdelguerfi & Kam-Fai Wong. LC 97-51310. 1998. 40.00 (*0-8186-8398-8*) IEEE Comp Soc.

Parallel, Distributed & Multiagent Production Systems. Toru Ishida. LC 94-238713. (Lecture Notes in Computer Science, Vol. 878). 1994. 34.95 (*3-540-58698-9*) Spr-Verlag.

Parallel Distributed Processing: Explorations in the Microstructure of Cognition, 2 vols., Set. David E. Rumelhart et al. 1190p. 1987. pap. text 55.00 (*0-262-63112-1*, Bradford Bks) MIT Pr.

Parallel Distributed Processing: Explorations in the Microstructure of Cognition, Vol. 1: Foundations. PDP Research Group Staff et al. (Computational Models of Cognition & Perception Ser.). (Illus.). 567p. 1986. 65.00 (*0-262-18120-7*, Bradford Bks) MIT Pr.

Parallel Distributed Processing: Explorations in the Microstructure of Cognition, Vol. 1: Foundations. PDP Research Group Staff et al. (Computational Models of Cognition & Perception Ser.). (Illus.). 567p. 1987. pap. text 32.50 (*0-262-68053-X*, Bradford Bks) MIT Pr.

Parallel Distributed Processing: Explorations in the Microstructure of Cognition, Vol. 2: Psychological & Biological Models. David E. Rumelhart et al. Vol. 2. (Illus.). 623p. 1987. pap. text 33.00 (*0-262-63110-5*, Bradford Bks) MIT Pr.

Parallel Distributed Processing: Implications for Psychology & Neurobiology. Ed. by R. G. Morris. (Illus.). 352p. 1990. 75.00 (*0-19-852178-2*) OUP.

Parallel Evolution of Parallel Processors. G. Lerman & L. Rudolph. (Frontiers of Computer Science Ser.). (Illus.). 284p. (C). 1994. 75.00 (*0-306-44537-9*, Plenum Trade) Perseus Pubng.

Parallel Exchange Rates in Developing Countries. Kiguel. LC 96-34337. (Illus.). 400p. 1997. text 79.95 (*0-312-16558-7*) St Martin.

***Parallel Executation Models of Software Requirement Specification Languages.** Jeffrey J. Tsai & Bingren Li. 200p. 2000. 66.00 (*981-02-4096-1*) World Scientific Pub.

Parallel Execution of Logic Programs: ICLP '91 Pre-Conference Workshop Paris, June 24, 1991 Proceedings. Ed. by A. Beaumont et al. (Lecture Notes in Computer Science Ser.: Vol. 569). vii, 195p. 1991. 39.00 (*0-387-55038-0*) Spr-Verlag.

Parallel Execution of Parlog. A. Cheese. Ed. by G. Goos & J. Hartmanis. LC 92-16603. (Lecture Notes in Computer Science Ser.: Vol. 586). x, 184p. 1992. 36.95 (*0-387-55382-7*) Spr-Verlag.

Parallel Expeditions: Charles Darwin & the Art of John Steinbeck. Brian E. Railsback. 168p. 1995. lib. bdg. 24.95 (*0-89301-177-0*) U of Idaho Pr.

***Parallel 59.** Natalie Dallaire & Stephen Cole. (Doctor Who Ser.). 288p. 2000. mass mkt. 6.95 (*0-563-55590-4*, Pub. by BBC Bks) Genl Dist Srvs.

Parallel Finite Element Computations. B. H. V. Topping & A. I. Khan. 320p. 1996. pap. (*1-874672-00-8*) Saxe-Coburg.

Parallel Forces. Dewi Anggraeni. 197p. 1988. pap. 15.95 (*0-9587718-1-2*, Pub. by Indra Pub) Intl Spec Bk.

Parallel Genetic Algorithms: Theory & Applications. Ed. by Joachim Stender. LC 92-53268. (Frontiers in Artificial Intelligence & Applications Ser.: Vol. 14). 250p. (gr. 12). 1993. pap. 85.00 incl. disk (*90-5199-087-1*, Pub. by IOS Pr) IOS Press.

Parallel Government of Satara: A Phase of the Quit India Movement. A. B. Shinde. (C). 1990. 34.00 (*81-7023-138-8*, Pub. by Allied Pubs) S Asia.

Parallel Image Analysis: Second International Conference, ICPIA '92, Ube, Japan, December 1992: Proceedings. Ed. by Akira Nakamura et al. LC 92-39674. (Lecture Notes in Computer Science Ser.: Vol. 654). 1992. 52.95 (*0-387-56346-6*) Spr-Verlag.

Parallel Image Analysis: Theory & Applications. Ed. by Maurice Nivat et al. LC 96-141279. (Series in Machine Perception & Artificial Intelligence: Vol. 19). 280p. 1995. text 68.00 (*981-02-2476-1*, R-PB2947) World Scientific Pub.

Parallel Image Analysis: Tools & Models. Serge Miguet et al. LC 98-216411. (Series in Machine Perception & Artificial Intelligence: Vol. 31). 130p. 1998. 22.00 (*981-02-3458-9*) World Scientific Pub.

Parallel Image Analysis & Processing. P. S. Wang. (Series in Machine Perception & Artificial Intelligence). 236p. 1994. text 61.00 (*981-02-1866-4*) World Scientific Pub.

Parallel Image Analysis & Processings. S. P. Wang. (Series in Machine Perception & Artificial Intelligence). 1994. text 48.00 (*981-02-1882-6*) World Scientific Pub.

Parallel Image Processing. Maurice Nivat et al. (Series on Machine Perception). 268p. 1992. text 45.00 (*981-02-1120-1*) World Scientific Pub.

Parallel Implementations of Backpropagation Neural Networks on Transputers: A Study of Training Set Parallelism. Ed. by P. Saratchandran et al. LC 96-12119. (Progress in Neural Processing Ser.: Vol. 3). 220p. 1996. write for info. (*981-02-2654-3*) World Scientific Pub.

Parallel Importation in U. S. Trademark Law, 74. Timothy H. Hiebert. LC 93-14123. (Contributions in Legal Studies: No. 74). 192p. 1994. 62.95 (*0-313-28956-5*, GM8956, Greenwood Pr) Greenwood.

Parallel in the Heartland. Vivienne I. Bonnefil. LC 95-72009. (Illus.). 256p. (YA). (gr. 11-12). 1996. 21.95 (*1-56167-233-5*) Noble Hse MD.

***Parallel Interconnects: Proceedings of the International Conference, Anchorage, Alaska, 1999.** Ed. by Michael Haney. LC 99-66371. 240p. 1999. 115.00 (*0-7695-0440-X*) IEEE Comp Soc.

***Parallel Journeys.** Eleanor H. Ayer. (Illus.). 256p. (YA). (gr. 7). 2000. per. 5.99 (*0-689-83236-2*) Aladdin.

Parallel Journeys. Eleanor H. Ayer et al. LC 94-23277. (Illus.). 256p. (J). (gr. 7 up). 1995. 16.00 (*0-689-31830-8*) Atheneum Yung Read.

***Parallel Kinematic Machines: Theoretical Aspects & Industrial Requirements.** Ed. by C. R. Boer et al. LC 99-37640. (Advanced Manufacturing Ser.). (Illus.). 458p. 1999. pap. 119.00 (*1-85233-613-7*, Pub. by Spr-Verlag) Spr-Verlag.

Parallel King Lear, 1608-1623. William Shakespeare. 120p. 1988. 110.00 (*0-520-06476-3*, Pub. by U CA Pr) Cal Prin Full Svc.

Parallel Language & Compiler Research in Japan. Ed. by Lubomir Bic. 536p. (C). 1995. text 193.50 (*0-7923-9506-9*) Kluwer Academic.

Parallel Lines Never Meet. Richard Booth. LC 90-53077. (Orig.). 1990. pap. 6.00 (*0-88734-226-4*) Players Pr.

Parallel Lisp: Languages & Systems: U. S. - Japan Workshop of Parallel Lisp Sendai, Japan, June 5-8, 1989 Proceedings. Ed. by Takatoshi Ito et al. (Lecture Notes in Computer Science Ser.: Vol. 441). xii, 364p. 1990. 38.60 (*0-387-52782-6*) Spr-Verlag.

Parallel Lisp Systems. C. K. Yuen. (ITCP-UK Computer Science Ser.). (C). 1992. pap. 46.50 (*0-412-45560-9*) Thomson Learn.

Parallel Lisp Systems: A Study of Languages & Architectures. C. K. Yuen et al. LC 92-38834. (Parallel & Distributed Processing Ser.: Vol. 1). 1992. write for info. (*0-442-31568-6*) Chapman & Hall.

Parallel Lives, 11 vols. Incl. Vol. 1. Plutarch. 19.95 (*0-674-99052-8*); Vol. 2. Tr. by Beradotte Perrin. 19.95 (*0-674-99053-6*); Vol. 3. Tr. by Beradotte Perrin. 19.95 (*0-674-99072-2*); Vol. 4. Plutarch. 14.50 Vol. 5. Plutarch. 14.50 Vol. 6. Tr. by Beradotte Perrin. 19.95 (*0-674-99109-5*); Vol. 7. Tr. by Beradotte Perrin. 19.95 (*0-674-99110-9*); Vol. 8. Ed. by G. P. Goold. Tr. by Beradotte Perrin. 19.95 (*0-674-99111-7*); Vol. 9. Tr. by Beradotte Perrin. 19.95 (*0-674-99112-5*); Vol. 10. Tr. by Beradotte Perrin. 19.95 (*0-674-99113-3*); Vol. 11. Tr. by Beradotte Perrin. 19.95 (*0-674-99114-1*); (Loeb Classical Library: Nos. 46-47, 65, 80, 87, 98-103). write for info. (*0-318-53133-X*) HUP.

Parallel Lives. Kathy Najimy & Mo Gaffney. 1993. pap. 5.25 (*0-8222-1308-7*) Dramatists Play.

Parallel Lives: Five Victorian Marriages. Phyllis Rose. LC 84-40026. 336p. 1984. pap. 12.00 (*0-394-72580-8*) Vin Bks.

Parallel Lives: Judy Longley. Judy Longley. 32p. 1990. pap. 7.00 (*0-937669-37-7*) Owl Creek Pr.

Parallel Lives: Spanish & English Drama, 1580-1680. Ed. by Louise Fothergill-Payne & Peter Fothergill-Payne. LC 89-46404. (Illus.). 336p. 1991. 47.50 (*0-8387-5194-6*) Bucknell U Pr.

Parallel Lives of the Old & New Testaments. Clarence E. Macartney. LC 95-8799. 128p. 1995. pap. 9.99 (*0-8254-3280-4*) Kregel.

Parallel Logic Programming. Akikazu Takeuchi. LC 92-14589. (Series in Parallel Computing). 256p. 1992. 69.99 (*0-471-57801-0*) Wiley.

Parallel Logic Programming in Parlog: The Language & Its Implementation. Steve Gregory. 225p. (C). 1987. text 29.25 (*0-201-19241-1*) Addison-Wesley.

Parallel Machines: Parallel Machine Languages. Robert A. Iannucci. (C). 1990. text 103.50 (*0-7923-9101-2*) Kluwer Academic.

Parallel Models of Associative Memory. Ed. by Geoffrey E. Hinton & James A. Anderson. (Cognitive Science Ser.). 352p. 1989. pap. text 45.00 (*0-8058-0270-3*) L Erlbaum Assocs.

Parallel Models of Associative Memory. enl. ed. Ed. by Geoffrey E. Hinton & J. A. Anderson. 352p. 1989. text 79.95 (*0-8058-0269-X*) L Erlbaum Assocs.

Parallel Myths. J. F. Bierlein. 368p. 1994. pap. 14.00 (*0-345-38146-7*) Ballantine Pub Grp.

***Parallel Myths.** J. F. Bierlein. 1999. pap. 14.00 (*0-345-91529-1*) Ballantine Pub Grp.

Parallel Numerical Algorithms. Ahmed Sameh & V. Venkatakrishnan. Ed. by David E. Keyes. LC 96-38607. (ICASE - LaRC Interdisciplinary Series in Science & Engineering). 408p. (C). 1997. text 197.50 (*0-7923-4282-8*) Kluwer Academic.

***Parallel Numerical Computation with Applications** Tianruo Yang. LC 99-16566. (International Series in Engineering & Computer Science). 1999. write for info. (*0-7923-8588-8*) Kluwer Academic.

Parallel, Object-Oriented, & Active Knowledge Base Systems. Ed. by Ioannis Vlahavas & Nick Bassiliades. LC 97-49079. 168p. 1998. 118.00 (*0-7923-8117-3*) Kluwer Academic.

Parallel Optimization: Theory, Algorithms & Applications. Yair Censor & Stavros A. Zenios. LC 96-46988. (Numerical Mathematics & Scientific Computation Ser.). (Illus.). 576p. 1998. text 85.00 (*0-19-510062-X*) OUP.

Parallel Paths: Fiduciary Doctrine & the Crown-Native Relationship in Canada. Leonard I. Rotman. 336p. 1996. text 50.00 (*0-8020-0821-6*); pap. text 19.95 (*0-8020-7813-3*) U of Toronto Pr.

Parallel Pipeline Computer Architecture for Speech Processing. Vassilios J. Georgiou. LC 83-18133. (Computer Science: Computer Architecture & Design Ser.: No. 2). (Illus.). 122p. reprint ed. pap. 37.90 (*0-8357-1524-8*, 207038000088) Bks Demand.

Parallel Politics: Economic Policymaking in Japan & the United States. Ed. by Samuel Kernell. 390p. 1991. 39.95 (*0-8157-4892-2*); pap. 18.95 (*0-8157-4891-4*) Brookings.

Parallel Port Complete: Programming, Interfacing & Using the PC's Parallel Printer Port. Jan Axelson. LC 97-150463. (Illus.). 343p. (Orig.). 1997. pap. 39.95 (*0-9650819-1-5*) Lakeview Res.

Parallel Port Programming in Windows 95. Fred Bulback. 375p. 1998. 49.95 incl. cd-rom (*0-07-913662-1*) McGraw.

Parallel Port Programming Through Windows 95. Fred Bulback. 1998. pap. text 39.95 (*0-07-913661-3*) McGraw.

Parallel Problem Solving from Nature: Proceedings of First Workshop, PPSNI, Dortmund, FRG, October 1-3, 1990. Ed. by H. P. Schwefel & Reinhard Manner. (Lecture Notes in Computer Science Ser.: Vol. 496). xi, 485p. 1991. 47.95 (*0-387-54148-9*) Spr-Verlag.

Parallel Problem Solving from Nature - Evolutionary Computation: Proceedings of the International Conference on Evolutionary Computation, Held jointly with the Third Conference on Parallel Problem Solving from Nature, PPSN III, Jerusalem, Israel, October 9-14, 1994. Ed. by Y. Davidor et al. (Lecure Notes in Computer Science Ser.: Vol. 866). xv, 642p. 1994. 93.95 (*3-540-58484-6*) Spr-Verlag.

Parallel Problem Solving from Nature--PPSN IV: International Conference on Evolutionary Computation, the 4th Conference on Parallel Problem Solving from Nature, Berlin, Germany, September 22-26, 1996 - Proceedings, Vol. 114. Werner Ebeling. LC 96-35938. (Lecture Notes in Computer Science Ser.). xvii, 1050p. 1996. 149.00 (*3-540-61723-X*) Spr-Verlag.

Parallel Problem Solving from Nature-PPSN V: 5th International Conference, Amsterdam, the Netherlands, September, 1998, Vol. 149. Agoston Eiben. LC 98-41487. (Lecture Notes in Computer Science Ser.). 1998. pap. 115.00 (*3-540-65078-4*) Spr-Verlag.

P

Parallel Problem Solving from Nature, 2: Proceedings of the Second Conference on Parallel Problem Solving from Nature, Brussels, Belgium, 28-30 September, 1992. Ed. by Reinhard Manner & Bernard Manderick. LC 92-23499. 618p. 1992. 228.50 (*0-444-89730-5*, North Holland) Elsevier.

Parallel Processing. 115p. 425.00 (*0-317-65601-5*) TBC Inc.

Parallel Processing. Richard K. Miller & Terri C. Walker. LC 89-17155. 284p. 1989. pap. text 95.00 (*0-88173-101-3*) Fairmont Pr.

Parallel Processing. Richard K. Miller & Terri C. Walker. 200p. 1991. 285.00 (*0-89671-128-5*) SEAI Tech Pubns.

Parallel Processing: A Survey on Technology & Markets, No. 8. Richard K. Miller & Terri C. Walker. LC 88-80486. 32p. 1988. pap. text 200.00 (*1-55865-007-5*) Future Tech Surveys.

Parallel Processing: CONPAR 92 - VAPP V, Second Joint International Conference of Vector & Parallel Processing, Lyon, France, September 1992, Proceedings. Ed. by Yves Robert et al. LC 92-27828. (Lecture Notes in Computer Science Ser.: Vol. 634). xvii, 853p. 1992. 120.95 (*0-387-55895-0*) Spr-Verlag.

Parallel Processing: CONPAR 94-VAPP IV Proceedings of the Third Joint International Conference on Vector & Parallel Processing, Linz, Austria, September 1994, Vol. 854. Joint Conference on Vector & Parallel Processing. Ed. by Bruno Buchberger & Jens Volkert. LC 94-34411. 1994. 123.95 (*3-540-58430-7*) Spr-Verlag.

Parallel Processing: Principles & Practice. E. V. Krishnamurthy. (Illus.). 256p. (C). 1989. pap. text 35.00 (*0-201-17532-0*) Addison-Wesley.

***Parallel Processing: Proceedings International Conference Aizu-Wakamatsu City, Japan, 1999.** Ed. by Dhabaleswar K. Panda & Norio Shiratori. 561p. 1999. 145.00 (*0-7695-0350-0*) IEEE Comp Soc.

***Parallel Processing: Proceedings International Workshops Aizu-Wakamaatsu City, Japan, 1999.** Ed. by Dhabaleswar K. Panda & Makoto Takizawa. LC 99-64614. 644p. 1999. 155.00 (*0-7695-0353-5*) IEEE Comp Soc.

Parallel Processing: The Cm Experience. Edward F. Gehringer et al. LC 86-29119. 471p. 1987. reprint ed. pap. 146.10 (*0-608-00258-5*, AU0047000007) Bks Demand.

Parallel Processing Algorithms for GIS. Ed. by Richard G. Healey et al. LC 98-113409. 320p. 1996. pap. 39.95 (*0-7484-0509-7*, Pub. by Tay Francis Ltd) Taylor & Francis.

Parallel Processing Algorithms for GIS. Ed. by Richard G. Healey et al. LC 98-113409. 460p. 1997. 79.95 (*0-7484-0508-9*, Pub. by Tay Francis Ltd) Taylor & Francis.

Parallel Processing & Artificial Intelligence. Ed. by Mike Reeve & Steven E. Zenith. LC 89-16532. (Wiley Communicating Process Architecture Ser.). (Illus.). 307p. reprint ed. pap. 95.20 (*0-7837-6393-X*, 204610600010) Bks Demand.

Parallel Processing & Data Management. Patrick Valduriez. (C). 1990. mass mkt. 92.50 (*0-412-42800-8*) Chapman & Hall.

Parallel Processing & Data Management. Ed. by Patrick Valduriez. (UNICOM Applied Information Technology Ser.). 320p. 1992. 79.95 (*0-442-31580-5*) Chapman & Hall.

Parallel Processing & Medium-Scale Multiprocessors. Ed. by Arthur Wouk. LC 89-6435. (Proceedings in Applied Mathematics Ser.: No. 38). xii, 207p. 1989. pap. 35.50 (*0-89871-238-6*) Soc Indus-Appl Math.

***Parallel Processing & Parallel Algorithms: Theory & Computation.** Seyed H. Roosta. LC 99-13243. 550p. 1999. 69.95 (*0-387-98716-9*) Spr-Verlag.

Parallel Processing Applications for Jet Engine Control. H. A. Thompson. (Advances in Industrial Control Ser.). (Illus.). xxi, 268p. 1992. 76.95 (*0-387-19747-8*) Spr-Verlag.

Parallel Processing CONPAR 94-VAPP IV: Proceedings of the Third Joint International Conference on Vector & Parallel Processing, Linz, Austria, September 1994. Joint International Conference on Vector & Paralle. Ed. by Bruno Buchberger & Jens Volkert. LC 94-34411. (Lecture Notes in Computer Science Ser.: Vol. 854). 1994. write for info. (*0-387-58430-7*) Spr-Verlag.

Parallel Processing Developments: Wotug 19. Ed. by B. O'Neill. LC 96-7537. (Concurrent Systems Engineering Ser.: Vol. 47). 280p. (YA). (gr. 12). 1996. pap. 90.00 (*90-5199-261-0*, 261-0) IOS Press.

Parallel Processing for Artificial Intelligence. Ed. by L. N. Kanal et al. LC 94-15133. (Machine Intelligence & Pattern Recognition Ser.: Vol. 14-15). 444p. 1994. 188.50 (*0-444-81704-2*, North Holland); 158.75 (*0-444-81837-5*, North Holland) Elsevier.

Parallel Processing for Artificial Intelligence 3. Ed. by J. Geller et al. (Machine Intelligence & Pattern Recognition Ser.: No. 20). 356p. 1997. text 172.50 (*0-444-82486-3*, North Holland) Elsevier.

Parallel Processing for Scientific Computing. Ed. by Gary Rodrique. LC 88-62233. (Proceedings in Applied Mathematics Ser.: No. 35). xxix, 428p. 1988. pap. 50.50 (*0-89871-228-9*) Soc Indus-Appl Math.

Parallel Processing for Scientific Computing: Proceedings of the Fourth SIAM Conference. Ed. by Jack J. Dongarra et al. LC 90-10356. (Proceedings in Applied Mathematics Ser.: No. 44). xxii, 454p. 1990. pap. 52.50 (*0-89871-262-9*) Soc Indus-Appl Math.

Parallel Processing from Applications to Systems. Dan I. Moldovan. LC 92-44256. 567p. 1993. text 69.95 (*1-55860-254-2*) Morgan Kaufmann.

Parallel Processing in Computational Mechanics. Ed. by Hojjat Adeli. (New Generation Computing Ser.: Vol. 2). (Illus.). 376p. 1991. text 165.00 (*0-8247-8557-6*) Dekker.

Parallel Processing in Control: The Transputer & Other Architectures. Ed. by P. J. Fleming. (Control Engineering Ser.: No. 38). 244p. 1988. 87.00 (*0-86341-136-3*, CE038) INSPEC Inc.

Parallel Processing in Digital Control. D. Fabian Nocetti & Peter J. Fleming. Ed. by Michael J. Grimble & M. Johnson. LC 92-21882. (Advances in Industrial Control Ser.). (Illus.). xiv, 146p. 1992. 76.95 (*0-387-19728-1*) Spr-Verlag.

Parallel Processing in Engineering Applications: Proceedings of the First International Conference on Parallel Processing for Computational Mechanics, Southampton, 4-6 September 1990. Ed. by Robert A. Adey. 256p. 1990. 77.00 (*0-387-52962-4*) Spr-Verlag.

Parallel Processing in Structural Engineering. Hojjat Adeli & Osama Kamal. LC 92-42747. 1993. mass mkt. 104.95 (*1-85861-003-6*) Elsevier.

Parallel Processing in the Visual System: The Classification of Retinal Ganglion Cells & Its Impact on the Neurobiology of Vision. J. Stone. (Perspectives in Vision Research Ser.). (Illus.). 454p. (C). 1983. text 125.00 (*0-306-41220-9*, Kluwer Plenum) Kluwer Academic.

Parallel Processing, 1997 International Conference: Volume I: Architecture, Volume II: Algorithms & Applications, Volume III: Software, Volume IV: Workshop, 4 vols., Set. LC 01-903918. 600p. 1997. pap. 145.00 (*0-8186-8108-X*, PR08108) IEEE Comp Soc.

Parallel Processing of Discrete Optimization Problems: DIMACS Workshop, April 28-29, 1994. Ed. by Panos M. Pardalos et al. LC 95-10880. (DIMACS Series in Discrete Mathematics & Theoretical Computer Science: Vol. 22). 374p. 1995. text 89.00 (*0-8218-0240-2*, DIMACS/22) Am Math.

Parallel Processing of Discrete Problems. Ed. by P. M. Pardalos et al. LC 98-46021. (IMA Volumes in Mathematics & Its Applications Ser.: Vol. 106). (Illus.). 249p. 1999. 69.95 (*0-387-98664-2*) Spr-Verlag.

Parallel Processing Symposium, 11th International (IPPS '97) LC 10-637133. 900p. 1997. 180.00 (*0-8186-7792-9*, PR07792) IEEE Comp Soc.

Parallel Processing Symposium (IPPS, '98), 12th International. IEEE Staff. 900p. 1998. 180.00 (*0-8186-8403-8*, PR8403, IEEE Inst Elec) IEEE Comp Soc.

Parallel Processing Symposium, 10th International (IPPS '96) LC 10-637133. 900p. 1996. 180.00 (*0-8186-7255-2*, PRO7255) IEEE Comp Soc.

Parallel Processing Symposium, 10th International (IPPS '96) 1996. text, boxed set 60.00 incl. audio compact disk (*0-8186-7613-2*, SW07613) IEEE Comp Soc.

Parallel Processing Techniques for Simulation. Ed. by Madan G. Singh et al. (Applied Information Technology Ser.). 300p. 1986. 79.50 (*0-306-42409-6*, Plenum Trade) Perseus Pubng.

Parallel Processing with Communication. East. 224p. 1995. pap. 34.95 (*1-85728-239-6*, Pub. by UCL Pr Ltd) Taylor & Francis.

Parallel Processing, 1996 International Conference, 4 vols. Incl. Architecture. 1996. Software. 1996. pap. text Software. 1996. Not sold separately Vol. III. Algorithms. 1996. Vol. IV. Workshop. 1996. LC 01-903918. 936p. 1996. Set pap. 120.00 (*0-8186-7623-X*) IEEE Comp Soc.

Parallel Programming. Lou Baker & Bradley J. Smith. (Illus.). 352p. 1996. 55.00 (*0-07-912259-0*) McGraw.

Parallel Programming: A New Approach. Michael H. Coffin. 300p. (Orig.). 1992. 29.95 (*0-929306-13-9*) Silicon Pr.

Parallel Programming & Applications. (YA). (gr. 12). 1995. 105.00 (*90-5199-229-7*, 229-7) IOS Press.

Parallel Programming & Japan. (Concurrent Systems Engineering Ser.: No. 50). 348p. (gr. 12). 1997. pap. 73.00 (*90-5199-336-6*) IOS Press.

Parallel Programming Systems: Proceedings of the JSPS Seminar. Akinori Yonezawa & C. K. Yuen. 300p. 1993. text 95.00 (*981-02-1320-4*) World Scientific Pub.

Parallel Programming Using C++ Gregory V. Wilson. LC 96-12636. (Scientific & Engineering Computation Ser.). (Illus.). 760p. 1996. pap. text 47.50 (*0-262-73118-5*) MIT Pr.

Parallel Programming with MPI. Peter Pacheco. LC 96-39324. 419p. 1996. pap. text 47.95 (*1-55860-339-5*) Morgan Kaufmann.

Parallel Psychotherapy with Children & Parents. Barbara Piovano. LC 97-18427. 240p. 1998. 45.00 (*0-7657-0126-X*) Aronson.

***Parallel Robots.** J. P. Merlet. LC 00-38628. (Solid Mechanics & Its Applications Ser.). (Illus.). 2000. write for info. (*0-7923-6308-6*, Kluwer Plenum) Kluwer Academic.

Parallel Scientific Computing. Ed. by J. Dongarra & Jerry Wasniewski. LC 94-40217. (Lecture Notes in Computer Science Ser.: Vol. 879). 577p. 1994. 79.95 (*3-540-58712-8*) Spr-Verlag.

Parallel Scientific Computing: Proceedings of the First International Workshop, PARA '94, Lyngby, Denmark, June 20-23, 1994. First International Workshop Staff. Ed. by Jack Dongarra. LC 94-40217. (Lecture Notes in Computer Science Ser.: Vol. 879). 1994. write for info. (*0-387-58712-8*) Spr-Verlag.

Parallel Software Architecture. Thomas F. Duggan. LC 93-90692. 589p. 1993. lib. bdg. write for info. (*0-9642131-1-7*) Frndship Sftware.

Parallel Solution Methods in Computational Mechanics. Ed. by Manolis Papadrakakis. 520p. 1997. 230.00 (*0-471-95696-1*) Wiley.

Parallel Substitution Algorithm. S. Achasova et al. 232p. 1994. text 48.00 (*981-02-1777-3*) World Scientific Pub.

Parallel Supercomputing in Atmospheric Science. G. Hoffmann & T. Kauranne. 544p. 1993. text 109.00 (*981-02-1429-4*) World Scientific Pub.

Parallel Supercomputing in MIMD Architectures. R. Michael Hord. 432p. 1993. boxed set 115.95 (*0-8493-4417-4*, QA76) CRC Pr.

Parallel Supercomputing in SIMD Architectures. Ed. by R. Micheal Hord. 400p. (C). 1990. lib. bdg. 79.95 (*0-8493-4271-6*, QA76) CRC Pr.

Parallel Supercomputing in SIMD Architectures. Efrem G. Mallach. 404p. (C). 1990. text 51.50 (*0-07-413090-0*, Irwn McGrw-H) McGrw-H Hghr Educ.

Parallel Symbolic Computation Pasco, 1994: Proceedings of the First International Symposium. Howard V. Hong. LC 95-135937. (Lecture Notes Series on Computing). 448p. 1994. text 106.00 (*981-02-2040-5*) World Scientific Pub.

Parallel Symbolic Computing: Languages, Systems, & Applications; U. S. - Japan Workshop, Cambridge, MA, U. S. A., October 14-17, 1992 Proceedings. Ed. by Robert H. Halstead, Jr. & Takayasu Ito. LC 93-33440. (Lecture Notes in Computer Science Ser.: Vol. 748). 1993. 60.00 (*0-387-57396-8*) Spr-Verlag.

Parallel Symbolic Languages & Systems: International Workshop PSLS'95, Beaune, France, October 2-4, 1995: Proceedings. Ed. by Takatoshi Ito et al. LC 96-16992. (Lecture Notes in Computer Science Ser.: Vol. 1068). 361p. 1996. pap. 62.00 (*3-540-61143-6*) Spr-Verlag.

Parallel System Communications & Interconnections. Miro Kraetzl & D. Frank Hsu. 1999. 69.95 (*0-8493-3153-6*) CRC Pr.

Parallel Systems & Algorithms. LC 97-160082. 340p. 1997. 47.00 (*981-02-3044-3*) World Scientific Pub.

Parallel Systems in the Data Warehouse. MRJ Tech Solutions Staff. LC 97-34527. 416p. (C). 1997. 49.99 (*0-13-680604-X*) P-H.

Parallel Tables of Logarithms & Squares. rev. ed. C. K. Smoley. Ed. by E. R. Smoley & N. G. Smoley. 676p. 1989. lib. bdg. 52.00 (*0-911390-02-2*, QA) Smoley.

Parallel Teachings in Hinduism & Christianity. 2nd ed. George Wolfe. 20p. 1995. pap. 3.00 (*0-9656411-0-4*) Jomar Pr.

Parallel to the Shore. Michael Melcher. (Illus.). 19p. (Orig.). 1992. pap. 5.00 (*0-926935-68-2*) Runaway Spoon.

Parallel Tracks: The Railroad & Silent Cinema. Lynne Kirby. LC 96-26745. 344p. 1996. text 49.95 (*0-8223-1833-4*); pap. text 17.95 (*0-8223-1839-3*) Duke.

Parallel Universe. Nicola Baxter. LC 97-3613. (J). (gr. 4-6). 1997. lib. bdg. 24.00 (*0-531-14465-8*) Watts.

Parallel Universe. Nicola Baxter. (J). (gr. 7). 1997. pap. text 12.95 (*0-531-15867-5*) Watts.

Parallel Universes: The Search for Other Worlds. Fred A. Wolf. 352p. 1990. per. 12.00 (*0-671-69601-7*) S&S Trade Pap.

Parallel Utopias: Sea Ranch & Seaside; The Quest for Community. Richard Sexton et al. LC 94-41172. (Illus.). 168p. 1995. 50.00 (*0-8118-0547-6*) Chronicle Bks.

Parallel Views: Education & Access for Deaf People in France & the United States. French-American Foundation Staff. LC 94-13471. 276p. 1994. boxed set 45.00 (*1-56368-030-0*) Gallaudet Univ Pr.

Parallel Virtual Machine, EuroPVM '96: Third European PVM Conference, Munchen, Germany, October 7-9, 1996 Proceedings, Vol. 115. Arndt Bode. LC 96-43299. (Lecture Notes on Computer Science Ser.). xiv, 362p. 1996. 62.00 (*3-540-61779-5*) Spr-Verlag.

Parallel VLSI Neural System Design. David Zhang. LC 98-41790. 330p. 1999. pap. 39.00 (*981-3083-30-1*) Spr-Verlag.

Parallel Voices. Ed. by Matt Cohen & Andre Carpentier. 249p. 1993. pap. 18.95 (*1-55082-065-6*, Pub. by Quarry Pr) LPC InBook.

Parallel Voyages. Paul Blackburn. (Illus.). 136p. (Orig.). 1987. 50.00 (*0-933313-02-0*); 75.00 (*0-933313-08-X*); pap. 8.95 (*0-933313-03-9*) SUN Gemini Pr.

Parallel Worlds: An Anthropologist & a Writer Encounter Africa. Alma Gottlieb & Philip Graham. xii, 350p. 1994. pap. 17.00 (*0-226-30506-6*) U Ch Pr.

Parallele Datenverarbeitung Aktuel-TAT '94. R. Flieger & R. Grebe. (Transputer & Occam Engineering Ser.). 492p. (YA). (gr. 12). 1994. pap. 99.00 (*90-5199-195-9*) IOS Press.

Parallele de Plans des Plus Belles Salles de Spectacles d'Italie et de France. Gabriel P. Dumont. LC 68-17155. (FRE., Illus.). 1972. reprint ed. 43.95 (*0-405-08469-2*, Pub. by Blom Pubns) Ayer.

Parallele des Principaux Theatres Moderns de L'Europe, 2 vols., 1 bk. Clement Contant & Joseph De Filippi. LC 68-21209. (Illus.). 1972. reprint ed. 64.95 (*0-405-08376-9*) Ayer.

Parallelement. Paul M. Verlaine. (Illus.). 1800.00 (*0-685-37128-X*) Fr & Eur.

Paralleles. Allen & Foulet. 1995. text, student ed. 71.00 incl. audio (*0-13-337593-5*) P-H.

Paralleles. 2nd ed. Allen & Fouletier Smith. LC 99-42538. (FRE.). 544p. 1999. 58.00 (*0-13-608464-8*) S&S Trade.

Paralleles: Commuication et Culture. Wendy Allen & Nicole Foultier-Smith. (Illus.). 542p. (C). 1994. text 61.00 (*0-13-249889-8*) P-H.

Paralleles: Communication Et Culture. 2nd ed. (C). 2000. pap. text. write for info. (*0-13-026323-0*) P-H.

Paralleles Interactive MAC. Blyth & Kelton. (C). 1996. 66.67 (*0-13-242140-2*) P-H.

Parallelism & Implementation of Logic & Constraint Logic Programming. Ines de Castro Dutra et al. LC 99-23165. 379p. 1999. lib. bdg. 98.00 (*1-56072-673-3*) Nova Sci Pubs.

Parallelism & Programming in Classifier Systems. Stephanie Forrest. LC 90-41616. (Research Notes in Artificial Intelligence Ser.). 200p. 1990. pap. text 34.95 (*1-55860-107-4*) Morgan Kaufmann.

Parallelism in Production Systems. Anoop Gupta. LC 87-20428. (Research Notes in Artificial Intelligence Ser.). (Illus.). 224p. (Orig.). (C). 1988. pap. text 34.95 (*0-934613-55-9*) Morgan Kaufmann.

Parallelism in Two Disciplines: A Comparison of Auditing & Historical Method. Florence R. Sneed. Ed. by Richard P. Brief. LC 77-87304. (Development of Contemporary Accounting Thought Ser.). 1978. lib. bdg. 26.95 (*0-405-10943-1*) Ayer.

Parallelism, Learning, Evolution: Workshop on Evolutionary Models & Strategies, Neubiberg, Germany, March 10-11, 1989 Workshop on Parallel Processing: Logic, Organization & Technology - WOPPLOT 89, Wildbad Kreuth, Germany, July 24-28, 1989 Proceedings. Ed. by J. D. Becker et al. (Lecture Notes in Artificial Intelligence Ser.: Vol. 565). viii, 525p. 1991. 69.95 (*0-387-55027-5*) Spr-Verlag.

Parallelisms in the Literary Vision of Sin: Double-Readings of Natsume Soseki & Nathaniel Hawthorne, Akutagawa Ryunosuke & Ambrose Bierce, & Hagiwara Sakutaro & Stephen Crane. Tsutomo Takahashi. LC 92-40773. (Comparative Cultures & Literatures Ser.: Vol. 1). 1994. write for info. (*0-8204-2114-6*) P Lang Pubng.

Parallelities. Alan Dean Foster. LC 97-17938. 1998. 23.50 (*0-345-38373-7*) Ballantine Pub Grp.

Parallelities. Alan Dean Foster. 1998. mass mkt. 6.99 (*0-345-42461-1*, Del Rey) Ballantine Pub Grp.

Parallelization in Inference Systems: International Workshop, Dagstuhl Castle, Germany, December 17-18, 1990 Proceedings. Ed. by B. Fronhofer & G. Wrightson. LC 92-15381. (Lecture Notes in Computer Science Ser.: Vol. 590). viii, 372p. 1992. 57.95 (*0-387-55425-4*) Spr-Verlag.

***Parallels: Communication Et Culture.** 2nd ed. (C). 2000. 40.00 (*0-13-025989-6*) S&S Trade.

***Parallels: Communication Et Culture: Test Item File.** 2nd ed. 2000. 5.25 bd. write for info. (*0-13-095371-7*) P-H.

Parallels: The Soldiers' Knowledge & the Oral History of Contemporary Warfare. J. T. Hansen et al. (Communication & Social Order Ser.). (Illus.). 264p. 1992. pap. text 24.95 (*0-202-30392-6*); lib. bdg. 47.95 (*0-202-30391-8*) Aldine de Gruyter.

Parallels: 3 Artists - 47 Poets. Grace Glueck et al. LC 93-77571. (Books by Artists - Poets Ser.). (Illus.). 160p. (Orig.). 1993. pap. text 12.00 (*1-877675-14-8*) Midmarch Arts.

Parallels in Semitic Linguistics: The Development of Arabic La- & Related Semitic Particles. David Testen. LC 98-18946. (Studies in Semitic Languages & Linguistics). xii, 236p. 1998. 74.50 (*90-04-10973-0*) Brill Academic Pubs.

Paralogic Rhetoric: A Theory of Communicative Interaction. Thomas Kent. LC 92-19577. 232p. 1993. 34.50 (*0-8387-5250-0*) Bucknell U Pr.

Paralysin Cave: Impotence, Perception & Text in the Satyrica of Petronius. John M. McMahon. LC 97-40691. (Mnemosyne, Supplements Ser.: No. 176). (Illus.). 264p. 1998. 99.50 (*90-04-10825-4*) Brill Academic Pubs.

Paralytic Shellfish Poisoning. B. Halstead & E. Schantz. (WHO Offset Publications: No. 79). 60p. 1984. 6.00 (*92-4-170079-3*) World Health.

Paralyzing Fear: The Triumph over Polio in America. Jane S. Smith et al. (Illus.). 288p. 1998. 29.95 (*1-57500-070-9*, Pub. by TV Bks) HarpC.

Paramagnetic Ogranometallic Species in Activation-Selectivity: Catalysis. Ed. by Michel Chanon et al. (C). 1988. text 292.50 (*0-7923-0032-7*) Kluwer Academic.

Paramagnetism: Rediscovering Nature's Secret Force of Growth. Philip S. Callahan. LC 95-78655. (Illus.). 140p. 1995. pap. 15.00 (*0-911311-49-1*) Acres USA.

Paramahansa Yogananda: In Memoriam. Self-Realization Fellowship Editorial Staff. (Illus.). 127p. 1986. pap. 6.50 (*0-87612-170-9*) Self Realization.

Paramartha Katha Prasang: Spiritual Conversations with Swami Muktananda see Conversations with Swami Muktananda: The Early Years

Paramedic. American College of Emergency Physicians Staff. LC 97-21620. (Illus.). 896p. (gr. 13). 1997. text 49.95 (*0-8016-6361-X*, 06361) Mosby Inc.

Paramedic. Peter Canning. 1998. mass mkt. 6.99 (*0-8041-1614-8*) Ivy Books.

Paramedic: On the Front Lines of Medicine. Peter Canning. LC 97-7397. 320p. 1997. 24.00 (*0-449-91276-0*) Fawcett.

***Paramedic Care.** Bryan E. Bledsoe & Robert S. Porter. 2000. pap., teacher ed. 46.60 (*0-13-021631-3*) P-H.

***Paramedic Care: Patient.** Bryan E. Bledsoe & Robert S. Porter. 128p. 2000. wbk. ed. 31.33 (*0-13-021632-1*) P-H.

***Paramedic Careions Vol. 5: Principles & Practice.** Bryan Bledsoe & Robert Porter. 448p. 2000. 51.93 (*0-13-021599-6*) P-H.

Paramedic Computerized Student Review. 4th ed. (C). 1998. 25.60 (*0-8359-5378-5*) P-H.

Paramedic Emergency Care. Bruce R. Shade. 1993. teacher ed. 35.00 (*0-89303-981-0*) Mosby Inc.

Paramedic Emergency Care. 3rd ed. Bryan E. Bledsoe & Robert S. Porter. 1136p. 1996. 74.00 (*0-8359-4987-7*, Pub. by P-H) S&S Trade.

Paramedic Emergency Care. 4th ed. Bledsoe. 288p. 2000. 61.33 (*0-8359-5033-6*) P-H.

Paramedic Emergency Care: Instructor's Resource Manual. 3rd ed. Cherry. 1996. pap., teacher ed. 59.00 (*0-8359-5017-4*) P-H.

Paramedic Emergency Care: Trauma Emergencies. 4th ed. 448p. (C). 2001. 51.93 (*0-13-021613-5*) P-H.

P

An Asterisk (*) at the beginning of an entry indicates that the title is appearing for the first time.

Paramedic Exam Review. Marilyn W. Edwards. 1991. pap. 30.20 (*0-89303-805-9*) Mosby Inc.

Paramedic Examination Review Manual. David Edwards. 384p. 1991. pap. write for info. (*0-318-68269-9*) P-H.

Paramedic Field Care: A Complaint-Based Approach. American College of Emergency Physicians Staff. Ed. by Peter T. Pons & Debra Cason. 1997. wbk. ed. write for info. (*0-8016-6425-X*) Mosby Inc.

***Paramedic Field Care: A Complaint Based Approach.** American College of Emergency Physicians Staff. Ed. by Peter T. Pons & Debra Cason. 1998. teacher ed. write for info. (*0-8151-0088-4*) Mosby Inc.

Paramedic Licensing Exam. LearningExpress Staff. LC 98-26285. 256p. 1998. pap. 20.00 (*1-57685-148-6*) LrningExprss.

Paramedic Pocket Reference. 2nd ed. Bryan E. Bledsoe & Dwayne E. Clayden. LC 97-19809. 192p. 1997. pap. text 23.00 (*0-8359-5120-0*) P-H.

Paramedic Protocols. Ed. by Richard E. Westfal. LC 96-23226. (Illus.). 560p. 1996. text 26.95 (*0-07-069318-8*) McGraw-Hill HPD.

Paramedic Recertification Practice Exams. 208p. pap., per. 24.95 (*0-938329-76-6*) Info Guides.

Paramedic Recertification Study Guide. 208p. pap., per. 19.95 (*0-938329-78-2*) Info Guides.

Paramedic Refresher Course: A Case-Based Approach. Alice Dalton. (Illus.). 280p. (gr. 13). 1999. pap. text 19.95 (*0-8151-1729-9*, 30352) Mosby Inc.

Paramedic Review Guide. Gail Walraven. LC 88-2488. (C). 1988. pap. 23.60 (*0-89303-751-6*) Brady Pub.

Paramedic Review Manual. 3rd ed. Politis. 1992. pap. text 26.00 (*0-7216-5041-4*, W B Saunders Co) Harcrt Hlth Sci Grp.

Paramedic Skills & Equipment. Allison et al. (Illus.). 352p. 1991. 24.95 (*0-685-54092-8*) Mosby Inc.

Paramedic Skills Manual. 2nd ed. Charles L. Phillips. 256p. 1989. pap. write for info. (*0-318-65460-1*) P-H.

Paramedic Survival Handbook. Scott Martin. LC 99-226689. 300p. 1999. per. 35.95 (*1-56930-090-9*) Skidmore Roth Pub.

Paramedic Textbook with Pass Paramedic! Booklet. Sanders. (gr. 13). 1995. reprint ed. text 51.95 (*0-8151-7505-1*, 28790) Mosby Inc.

Paramedical Careers, 6 vols., Set. 98.00 (*0-685-23032-5*, CG360) Ready Ref Pr.

Paramedical Emergency Care. 3rd ed. Porter. LC 97-106333. 1996. pap., wbk. ed. 29.67 (*0-8359-5055-7*) P-H.

Paramente & Bucher der Christlichen Kirchen-Paraments Lituriques et livres des Eglises Chretiennes see Glossarium Artis, a Specialized & Systematic Dictionary

Parameter Estimation: Principles & Problems. Harold W. Sorenson. LC 80-19075. (Control & Systems Theory Ser.: Vol. 9). (Illus.). 398p. reprint ed. pap. 123.40 (*0-608-08992-3*, 206962700005) Bks Demand.

Parameter Estimation & Hypothesis Testing in Linear Models. K. R. Koch. (Illus.). xvii, 378p. 1988. 78.95 (*0-387-18840-1*) Spr-Verlag.

Parameter Estimation & Hypothesis Testing in Linear Models. 2nd enl. ed. K. R. Hock. LC 99-20521. (Illus.). xx, 321p. 1999. 84.95 (*3-540-65257-4*) Spr-Verlag.

Parameter Estimation & Hypothesis Testing in Spectral Analysis of Stationary Time Series. K. Dzhaparidze. Tr. by Samuel I. Kotz from DUT. (Series in Statistics). vi, 324p. 1985. 74.95 (*0-387-96141-0*) Spr-Verlag.

Parameter Estimation in Ecology: The Link Between Data & Models. O. Richter & D. Songdergath. LC 89-25070. 218p. 1990. 142.00 (*3-527-27954-7*, Wiley-VCH) Wiley.

Parameter Estimation in Reliability & Life Span Models. A. Clifford Cohen & Jones Whitten. (Statistics: Textbooks & Monographs: Vol. 96). (Illus.). 312p. 1988. text 135.00 (*0-8247-7980-0*) Dekker.

Parameter-Free Iterative Linear Solvers. Rudiger Weiss. 218p. 1996. pap. 94.95 (*3-527-40114-8*) Wiley.

Parameter Identification & Inverse Problems in Hydrology, Geology & Ecology. Paul Duchateau. Ed. by Johannes Gottlieb. LC 96-18938. (Water Science & Technology Library). 309p. (C). 1996. text 158.50 (*0-7923-4089-2*) Kluwer Academic.

Parameter of Aspect. Carlota S. Smith. (Studies in Linguistics & Philosophy). 480p. (C). 1991. lib. bdg. 188.50 (*0-7923-1136-1*) Kluwer Academic.

Parameter of Aspect. Carlota S. Smith. (Studies in Linguistics & Philosophy). 476p. (C). 1993. pap. text 73.50 (*0-7923-2496-X*) Kluwer Academic.

Parameter of Aspect. 2nd ed. 1997. pap. text 35.00 (*0-7923-4659-9*) Kluwer Academic.

Parameter of Aspect. 2nd ed. Carlota S. Smith. LC 97-23210. (Studies in Linguistics & Philosophy). 1997. lib. bdg. 175.00 (*0-7923-4657-2*) Kluwer Academic.

Parameter Sensitivity in Nonlinear Mechanics: Theory & Finite Element Computations. M. Kleiber. LC 96-40503. 422p. 1997. 150.00 (*0-471-96854-4*) Wiley.

Parameter Setting. Ed. by Tom Roeper & Edwin B. Williams. (C). 1986. pap. text 61.50 (*90-277-2316-8*) Kluwer Academic.

Parameter Setting. Ed. by Tom Roeper & Edwin B. Williams. (C). 1987. lib. bdg. 129.50 (*90-277-2315-X*) Kluwer Academic.

Parameter-Setting Model of L2 Acquisition. Suzanne Flynn. 1986. lib. bdg. 129.50 (*90-277-2374-5*) Kluwer Academic.

Parameterized Complexity. Rod Downey & M. F. Fellows. Ed. by D. Gries & F. Schneider. LC 97-22882. (Monographs in Computer Science). xv, 533p. 1999. 49.95 (*0-387-94883-X*) Spr-Verlag.

Parameters. 1980. 10.50 (*0-8176-0614-9*) Birkhauser.

Parameters: United States Army War College Quarterly. Government Printing Office Staff. 1984. per. 17.00 (*0-16-010324-X*) USGPO.

Parameters Affecting Stopping Sight Distance. (National Cooperative Highway Research Program Report Ser.: No. 270). 169p. 1984. 11.20 (*0-309-03711-5*, NR270) Transport Res Bd.

Parameters & Functional Heads: Essays in Comparative Syntax. Ed. by Adriana Belletti & Luigi Rizzi. (Studies in Comparative Syntax). 312p. 1996. text 65.00 (*0-19-508793-3*); pap. text 39.95 (*0-19-508794-1*) OUP.

***Parameters & Universals.** Richard S. Kayne. LC 99-38013. 336p. 2000. write for info. (*0-19-510236-3*); 65.00 (*0-19-510235-5*) OUP.

Parameters in Old French Syntax: Infinitival Complements. Elizabeth Pearce. (Studies in Natural Language & Linguistic Theory). 336p. (C). 1990. pap. text 65.50 (*0-7923-0433-0*); lib. bdg. 141.50 (*0-7923-0432-2*) Kluwer Academic.

Parameters of Archive Paradigm: Attidues of Near Years see Parametry Arkhivnykh Paradigm: Etjudy Blizhnikh Let

Parameters of British Naval Power, 1650-1850. Ed. by Michael Duffy. 170p. 1992. pap. text 23.95 (*0-85989-385-5*, Pub. by Univ Exeter Pr) Northwestern U Pr.

Parameters of Irish Literature in English. A. Norman Jeffares. (Princess Grace Irish Library Lecture: Vol. 1). 48p. 1987. pap. 8.95 (*0-86140-246-4*, Pub. by Smyth) Dufour.

Parameters of Morphosyntactic Change. Ed. by Ans VanKemenade & Nigel Vincent. LC 96-46074. 556p. 1997. text 74.95 (*0-521-58402-7*); pap. text 28.95 (*0-521-58643-7*) Cambridge U Pr.

Parameters of Postmodernism. Nicholas Zurbrugg. LC 92-20003. 128p. (C). 1993. 21.95 (*0-8093-1852-0*); pap. 14.95 (*0-8093-1887-3*) S Ill U Pr.

Parameters of Site for Certain Growth Components of Slash Pine (Pinus Elliottii Engelm) D. S. Jackson. LC SD0397.P55J3. (Duke University, School of Forestry Bulletin Ser.: No. 16). 126p. reprint ed. pap. 39.10 (*0-7837-6054-X*, 204586700008) Bks Demand.

***Parameters of Slavic Aspect.** Stephen M. Dickey. (Dissertations in Linguistics Ser.: Vol. 19). 225p. (C). 2000. text 59.95 (*1-57586-235-2*, Pub. by CSLI) Cambridge U Pr.

***Parameters of Slavic Aspect.** Stephen M. Dickey. (Dissertations in Linguistics Ser.: Vol. 192). 225p. (C). 2000. pap. 22.95 (*1-57586-236-0*, Pub. by CSLI) Cambridge U Pr.

Parameters of Slavic Morphosyntax. Steven Franks. (Studies in Comparative Syntax). (Illus.). 432p. 1995. text 85.00 (*0-19-508970-7*); pap. text 45.00 (*0-19-508971-5*) OUP.

Parametric Analysis of Static 2-Dimensional Riser Behavior. Michael M. Bernitsas et al. LC VM0605.. (University of Michigan, Dept. of Naval Architecture & Marine Engineering, Report Ser.: No. 287). 154p. reprint ed. pap. 47.80 (*0-608-12937-2*, 202468600038) Bks Demand.

Parametric & Feature-Based CAD/CAM: Concepts, Techniques, & Applications. Jami J. Shah & Martti Mantyla. LC 95-5673. 640p. 1995. 120.00 (*0-471-00214-3*) Wiley.

***Parametric Estimates by the Monte Carlo Method.** G. A. Mikhailov. 196p. 1999. 145.00 (*90-6764-297-5*, Pub. by VSP) Coronet Bks.

Parametric-Free Iterative Linear Solvers. R. Weiss. (Mathematical Research Ser.). 218p. 1996. pap. 120.75 (*3-05-501763-3*) Wiley.

Parametric Lie Group Actions on Global Generalised Solutions of Nonlinear PDES & a Solution to Hilbert's Fifth Problem. Elemer E. Rosinger. LC 98-34116. (Mathematics & Its Applications Ser.). 234p. 1998. 106.00 (*0-7923-5232-7*) Kluwer Academic.

Parametric Model for Syntactic Studies of a Textual Corpus: Demonstrated on the Hebrew of Deuteronomy 1-30, 2 vols. L. J. De Regt. (Studia Semitica Neerlandica: Vol. 24). (Illus.). ix, 138p. 1988. pap. text 32.00 (*90-232-2381-0*, Pub. by Van Gorcum) Eisenbrauns.

***Parametric Modeling with I-DEAS Master Series, No. 7.** Randy H. Shih. (Illus.). 280p. (C). 1999. pap. 49.95 (*1-58503-008-2*) Schroff Dev Corp.

***Parametric Modeling with Mechanical Desktop 4.** Randy Shih & Jack Zecher. (Illus.). 304p. 2000. pap. text 49.95 (*1-58503-013-9*, SDC Pubns) Schroff Dev Corp.

Parametric Normed Spaces & Normed Massives. K. K. Golovkin. LC 72-681. (Proceedings of the Steklov Institute of Mathematics Ser.: No. 106). 121p. 1972. pap. 55.00 (*0-8218-3006-6*, STEKLO/106) Am Math.

Parametric Optimization & Approximation. Ed. by F. Brosowski & F. Deutsch. (International Series of Numerical Mathematics: No. 72). 264p. 1985. 86.50 (*0-8176-1671-3*) Birkhauser.

Parametric Optimization & Related Topics II. Ed. by Jurgen Guddat et al. (Mathematical Research Ser.: Vol. 62). 175p. 1991. 36.00 (*3-05-501290-9*, Pub. by Akademie Verlag) Wiley.

Parametric Optimization & Related Topics IV: Proceedings of the International Conference on Parametric Optimization & Related Topics IV, Enschede (NL), June 6-9, 1995. Ed. by Jurgen Guddat et al. (Approximation & Optimization Ser.: Vol. 9). 382p. 1997. pap. 63.95 (*3-631-49769-5*) P Lang Pubng.

Parametric Optimization & Related Topics IV: Proceedings of the International Conference on Parametric Optimization & Related Topics IV, Enschede (NL), June 6-9, 1995. Ed. by Jurgen Guddat et al. (Approximation & Optimization Ser.: Vol. 9). 382p. 1997. pap. 63.95 (*0-8204-2984-8*) P Lang Pubng.

Parametric Processes see Progress in Quantum Electronics

Parametric Programming for CNC Machining & Turning Centers Answers. Mike Lynch. 67p. 1996. pap. text. write for info. (*1-930861-09-5*) C N C Con.

Parametric Programming for CNC Machining & Turning Centers Manual. Mike Lynch. (Illus.). 233p. 1996. pap. text. write for info. (*1-930861-07-9*) C N C Con.

Parametric Programming for CNC Machining & Turning Centers Workbook. Mike Lynch. (Illus.). 68p. 1996. pap. text. write for info. (*1-930861-08-7*) C N C Con.

Parametric Programming for Computer Numerical Control Machine Tools & Touch Probes: CNC's Best-Kept Secret. Mike Lynch. LC 96-70115. (Illus.). 433p. 1996. 83.00 (*0-87263-481-7*, 2544) SME.

Parametric Sensitivity in Chemical Systems. Arvind Varma et al. (Cambridge Series in Chemical Engineering). (Illus.). 300p. (C). 1998. text 64.95 (*0-521-62171-2*) Cambridge U Pr.

Parametric Statistical Inference. J. K. Lindsey. LC 97-109161. (Illus.). 508p. 1996. text 65.00 (*0-19-852359-9*) OUP.

Parametric Statistical Inference: Basic Theory & Modern Approaches. S. Zacks. LC 80-41715. (I.S. in Nonlinear Mathematics Series; Theory & Applications: Vol. 4). 400p. 1981. text 180.00 (*0-08-026468-9*, Pub. by Pergamon Repr) Franklin.

Parametric Statistical Theory. Johann Pfanzagl. LC 94-21850. xiii, 374p. 1994. text 89.95 (*3-11-014030-6*); pap. text 59.95 (*3-11-013863-8*) De Gruyter.

Parametric Study of English & Spanish. Karen Zogona. (C). 1988. text 153.00 (*1-55608-064-6*) Kluwer Academic.

Parametric Syntax: Case Studies in Semitic & Romance Languages. H. Borer. Ed. by Jan Koster & H. V. Riemsdyk. (Studies in Generative Grammar: No. 13). ix, 260p. 1984. pap. 57.70 (*90-6765-025-0*) Mouton.

***Parametrical Statistical Change Point Analysis.** Jie Chen & A. K. Gupta. 192p. 2000. 59.95 (*0-8176-4169-6*) Birkhauser.

Parametrization of Universal Grammar. Ed. by Gisbert Fanselow. LC 92-39961. (Linguistik Aktuell - Linguistics Today Ser.: No. 8). xvii, 232p. 1993. 59.00 (*1-55619-226-6*) J Benjamins Pubng Co.

Parametrizations in Control, Estimation, & Filtering Problems: Accuracy Aspects. Michel Gevers & Gang Li. LC 92-44290. (Communications & Control Engineering Ser.). 1993. 89.95 (*0-387-19821-0*) Spr-Verlag.

Parametrized Knot Theory. Stanley Ocken. LC 76-3641. (Memoirs Ser.: No. 5/170). 114p. 1976. pap. 22.00 (*0-8218-1870-8*, MEMO/5/170) Am Math.

Parametrized Measures & Variational Principles. P. Pedregal. LC 97-16343. 1997. write for info. (*0-8176-5697-9*) Birkhauser.

Parametrized Measures & Variational Principles. Pablo Pedregal. LC 97-16343. (Progress in Nonlinear Differential Equations & Their Applications Ser.). 1997. write for info. (*3-7643-5697-9*) Birkhauser.

Parametrized Relativistic Quantum Theory. John R. Fanchi. LC 93-22797. (Fundamental Theories of Physics Ser.: Vol. 56). 408p. (C). 1993. text 233.00 (*0-7923-2376-9*) Kluwer Academic.

Parametros Mensurables Para Perfilar el Desarrollo Del Nino de "Slow & Steady, Get Me Ready" El Libro de Instrucciones Que Crece Con el Nino. June R. Oberlander. Ed. by Clyde G. Oberlander. Tr. by Jose G. Roig from ENG. (SPA., Illus.). 8p. (Orig.). (J). (ps). 1994. pap. 3.95 (*0-9622322-6-2*) Bio-Alpha.

Parametry Arkhivnykh Paradigm: Etjudy Blizhnikh Let. Roman Sonynn. Ed. by Lubov Levin. LC 94-67243. (Biblioteka Bibliofila Ser.).Tr. of Parameters of Archive Paradigm: Attidues of Near Years. (RUS., Illus.). 48p. 1996. pap. 19.95 (*0-914265-52-0*) New Eng Pub MA.

Paramilitary. (Paranoia Ser.). 15.00 (*0-87431-167-5*, 12027) West End Games.

Paramiracles. Ted Lesley. Ed. by Stephen Minch. Tr. by Bill Palmer & Oliver Erens. (Illus.). 213p. 1994. 35.00 (*0-945296-12-6*) Hermetic Pr.

Paramo de Suenos. Ali Chumacero. (Fondo 2000 Ser.). (SPA.). pap. 2.99 (*968-16-5071-9*, Pub. by Fondo) Continental Bk.

Paramos: A Checklist of Plant Diversity, Geographical Distribution & Botanical Literature. Luteyn. LC 99-17171. (Memoirs of the New York Botanical Garden Ser.: Vol. 84). 14p. 1998. 64.00 (*0-89327-427-5*, MEM84) NY Botanical.

Paramount Banjos. reprint ed. 12.00 (*0-686-21420-X*) Mih.

Paramount Doctrines of Orthodoxy-the Tricompositeness of Man, Apology of A. Makrakis & the Trial of A. Makrakis. Apostolos Makrakis. Ed. by Orthodox Christian Educational Society Staff. Tr. by Denver Cummings. 904p. 1954. 19.95 (*0-938366-17-3*) Orthodox Chr.

Paramount in Paris: 300 Films Produced at the Joinville Studios, 1930-1933, with Credits & Biographies. Harry Waldman. LC 97-30059. 272p. 1998. 47.50 (*0-8108-3431-6*) Scarecrow.

Paramount, 1994. Kaplan. (Case; FB - Introduction to Finance Ser.). 1997. mass mkt. 3.75 (*0-538-85824-9*) S-W Pub.

Paramount 1993. Kaplan. (Case; FB - Introduction to Finance Ser.). 1997. mass mkt. 3.75 (*0-538-85823-0*) S-W Pub.

***Paramour.** Stacy Doris. 134p. 2000. pap. 9.00 (*1-928650-05-8*, Pub. by Krupskaya) SPD-Small Pr Dist.

Paramour. large type ed. Gerald Petievich. (General Ser.). 387p. 1992. 20.95 (*0-8161-5376-0*, G K Hall Lrg Type) Mac Lib Ref.

Paramus, Bergen County, New Jersey, Reformed Dutch Church Baptisms, 1740-1850: Together with Records from the Gravestones in the Church Yard & a List of Church Members. Ed. by Howard S. Randolph & Russell B. Rankin. Tr. by Dingman Versteeg. 224p. 1992. reprint ed. lib. bdg. 41.00 (*1-56012-124-6*, 120) Kinship Rhinebeck.

Paramyxoviruses. D. W. Kingsbury. (Viruses Ser.). (Illus.). 618p. (C). 1990. text 145.00 (*0-306-43553-5*, Kluwer Plenum) Kluwer Academic.

Parana: Social Boundaries in an Argentine City. Ruben E. Reina. LC 72-8265. (Latin American Monographs: No. 31). 446p. reprint ed. pap. 127.20 (*0-8357-7758-8*, 2036116) Bks Demand.

***Paranasal Sinuses of Higher Primates: Development, Function, & Evolution.** Ed. by Thomas Koppehl et al. LC 98-50232. 258p. 1999. 98.00 (*0-86715-359-8*) Quint Pub Co.

Paraneoplastic Syndromes. Ed. by Ursula Ruether et al. LC 97-46075. (Beitraege Zur Onkologie, Contributions to Oncology Ser.: Vol. 52, 1998). (Illus.). viii, 260p. 1998. 143.50 (*3-8055-6570-4*) S Karger.

Paraneurons. Ed. by T. Fujita et al. (Illus.). xii, 368p. 1988. 278.00 (*0-387-70026-9*) Spr-Verlag.

Parangon des Chansons (Premier Livre) (Lyons (1538)) & Le Parangon des Chansons. Second Livre Contenant XXXI Chansons (Lyons, 1540) Ed. by Jane A. Bernstein. LC 92-777218. (Sixteenth-Century Chanson Ser.: Vol. 24). 232p. 1993. text 88.00 (*0-8240-3123-7*) Garland.

Paranguaricutirimicuaro Que No Sabia Quien Era. Luis Gonzalez Palma. (SPA., Illus.). (gr. 3-5). 1998. pap. text 7.95 (*84-239-9027-3*) Espasa-Calpe.

Paranoia. 5th ed. 25.00 (*0-87431-171-3*, 12600) West End Games.

Paranoia: A Study in Diagnosis. Yehuda Fried & Joseph Agassi. (Boston Studies in the Philosophy of Science: No. 50). 227p. 1976. lib. bdg. 78.00 (*90-277-0704-9*) Kluwer Academic.

Paranoia: New Psychoanalytic Perspectives. Ed. by John M. Oldham & Stanley Bone. 166p. 1994. 27.50 (*0-8236-3985-1*) Intl Univs Pr.

Paranoia & Dirty Feet. Dan Daniels. 6.00 (*0-921884-14-1*) Genl Dist Srvs.

***Paranoia Factor.** Alan Peters. Ed. by Ann A. Hunter. (Illus.). 272p. 1999. 24.95 (*1-893846-51-2*) Loft Pr.

Paranoia Form Pack. (Paranoia Ser.). 6.00 (*0-87431-079-2*, 12006) West End Games.

Paranoia RPG, Set. 160p. 1990. boxed set 18.00 (*0-87431-018-0*) West End Games.

Paranoia Sourcebook. (Paranoia Ser.). 144p. 18.00 (*0-87431-163-2*, 12022) West End Games.

Paranoia, the Bomb & 1950s Science Fiction Films. Cyndy Hendershot. LC 99-26483. (Illus.). 173p. 1999. pap. 21.95 (*0-87972-800-0*) Bowling Green Univ Popular Press.

Paranoia Within Reason. Marcus. LC 99-188756. 1999. pap. text 25.00 (*0-226-50458-1*); lib. bdg. 75.00 (*0-226-50457-3*) U Ch Pr.

***Paranoid.** M. Wall. 1999. pap. text 19.95 (*1-85158-993-7*, Pub. by Mainstream Pubng) Trafalgar.

Paranoid: In & out of Prison. George B. Palermo & Edward M. Scott. LC 96-44157. (American Series in Behavioral Science & Law: No. 1093). 208p. 1997. text 49.95 (*0-398-06727-9*); pap. text 37.95 (*0-398-06728-7*) C C Thomas.

Paranoid Foothills. Peter B. Cloud. (Illus.). (Orig.). 1981. pap. 2.50 (*0-942396-29-4*) Blackberry ME.

Paranoid Style in American Politics. Richard Hofstadter. 352p. 1996. pap. 17.50 (*0-674-65461-7*) HUP.

Paranoid Style in American Politics: And Other Essays. Richard Hofstadter. LC 79-12579. 1994. pap. text 5.95 (*0-226-34817-2*, P840) U Ch Pr.

Paranoid Women Collect Their Thoughts: A Paranoia Annual Anthology. Ed. by Joan D'Arc. (Illus.). 155p. (Orig.). 1996. pap. 12.95 (*0-9653643-0-5*) Paranoia Pub.

Paranoid's Pocket Guide. Cameron Tuttle. LC 96-37545. 1997. 10.95 (*0-8118-1665-6*) Chronicle Bks.

Paranormal. Carlton. 240p. 78.95 (*0-7546-0170-6*) Ashgate Pub Co.

Paranormal. Anthony North. (Illus.). 272p. 1998. 16.95 (*0-7137-2715-2*, Pub. by Blandford Pr) Sterling.

Paranormal: A Guide to the Unexplained. Anthony North. (Illus.). 294p. 1996. 24.95 (*0-7137-2615-6*, Pub. by Blandford Pr) Sterling.

Paranormal: Mechanisms & Models, Pt. 2. Michael A. Persinger. LC 74-19227. 195p. 1974. 30.50 (*0-8422-5211-8*); pap. text 12.95 (*0-8422-0476-8*) Irvington.

Paranormal: The Patterns, Pt. 1. Michael A. Persinger. LC 74-19227. 248p. (C). 1974. 29.50 (*0-8422-5212-6*); pap. text 13.95 (*0-8422-0477-6*) Irvington.

***Paranormal Beliefs: A Sociological Introduction.** Erich Goode. 310p. 1999. pap. 17.95 (*1-57766-076-5*) Waveland Pr.

Paranormal Borderlands of Science. Ed. by Kendrick Frazier. LC 80-84403. (Science & the Paranormal Ser.). 469p. 1981. pap. 23.95 (*0-87975-148-7*) Prometheus Bks.

Paranormal Cookbook: Transcendental Recipes for Earthbound Souls. Bruce Schaffenberger. (Illus.). 110p. (Orig.). 1997. pap., spiral bd. 12.95 (*0-9637914-3-5*) Athanor Pr.

Paranormal Experience & Survival of Death. Carl B. Becker. LC 92-37751. (SUNY Series in Western Esoteric Traditions). 257p. (C). 1993. pap. text 23.95 (*0-7914-1476-0*) State U NY Pr.

Paranormal Foreknowledge: Problems & Perplexities. Jule Eisenbud. LC 81-2941. 312p. 1982. 45.95 (*0-89885-049-5*, Kluwer Acad Hman Sci) Kluwer Academic.

P

An Asterisk (*) at the beginning of an entry indicates that the title is appearing for the first time.

Paranormal Investigator's Handbook. Ed. by Valerie Hope & Maurice Townsend. LC 99-495084. (Illus.). 144p. 1999. pap. 14.95 (*1-85585-703-0*, Pub. by Collins & Br) Sterling.

Paranormal People: The Famous, the Infamous & the Supernatural. Paul Chambers. LC 98-170908. (Illus.). 232p. 1998. pap. 14.95 (*0-7137-2712-8*) Sterling.

Paranormal Perception of Color. Yvonne Duplessis. LC 75-19563. (Parapsychological Monographs: No. 16). 1975. pap. 8.00 (*0-912328-27-4*) Parapsych Foun.

***Paranormal Phenomena.** Patricia D. Netzley. LC 99-40473. (Overview Ser.). (Illus.). 128p. (YA). (gr. 6-9). 2000. lib. bdg. 23.70 (*1-56006-622-9*) Lucent Bks.

Paranormal Phenomena. Paul A. Winters. LC 96-49921. (Opposing Viewpoints Ser.). (Illus.). (YA). (gr. 5-12). 1997. pap. 16.20 (*1-56510-557-5*) Greenhaven.

Paranormal Phenomena. Paul A. Winters. LC 96-49921. (Opposing Viewpoints Ser.). (Illus.). (YA). (gr. 5-12). 1997. lib. bdg. 26.20 (*1-56510-558-3*) Greenhaven.

Paranormal Phenomena, Science, & Life after Death. C. J. Ducasse. LC 79-76282. (Parapsychological Monographs: No. 8). 1969. reprint ed. pap. 6.00 (*0-912328-12-6*) Parapsych Foun.

Paranormal Powers. Gary L. Blackwood. Ed. by Joyce Stanton. LC 97-48478. (Secrets of the Unexplained Ser.). (Illus.). 80p. (YA). (gr. 4-12). 1998. lib. bdg. 28.50 (*0-7614-0468-6*, Benchmark NY) Marshall Cavendish.

Paranormal Research. Ed. by Maurice L. Albertson et al. 1016p. (Orig.). (C). 1988. pap. text 35.00 (*0-317-91341-7*) Rocky Mtn Rsch Inst.

Paranormal Source Book: The Comprehensive Guide to Strange Phenomena Worldwide. Jenny Randles. (Illus.). 256p. 1997. pap. 14.95 (*0-7499-1411-4*, Pub. by Piatkus Bks) London Brdge.

***Paranormal Source Book: The Comprehensive Guide to Strange Phenomena Worldwide.** Jenny Randles. (Illus.). 1998. pap. 14.95 (*0-7499-1884-5*, Pub. by Piatkus Bks) London Brdge.

***Paranormal Sourcebook: A Comprehensive Guide to All Things Otherwordly.** Charles E. Sellier, Jr. & Joe Meier. LC 98-15023. 288p. 1999. 27.00 (*1-56565-961-9*, 09619W, Pub. by Lowell Hse) NTC Contemp Pub Co.

Paranormal Sourcebook: A Comprehensive Guide to All Things Otherworldly. Charles E. Sellier, Jr. & Joe Meier. (Roxbury Park Bks.). 304p. 2000. pap. 16.95 (*0-7373-0308-5*, 03085W, Pub. by Lowell Hse) NTC Contemp Pub Co.

Paranormal World of Paul McKenna. Paul McKenna. 192p. 1997. pap. 9.95 (*0-571-19245-9*) Faber & Faber.

Paranormal/CTV. (Paranoia Ser.). 18.00 (*0-87431-169-1*, 12028) West End Games.

Parapharyngeal Space: Diagnosist & Management of Commonly Encountered Entities. 3rd ed. Karen T. Pitman et al. LC RC280.P4P56 1998. (Self-Instructional Package Ser.). (Illus.). 67p. 1999. pap. text 25.00 (*1-56772-070-6*, 5506115) AAO-HNS.

Paraphase of an Imaginary Dialogue: The Poetics & Poetry of Pier Pasolini. Thomas E. Peterson. XVI, 356p. (C). 1994. text 48.95 (*0-8204-1529-4*) P Lang Pubng.

Paraphrase. Karlyn Kamm & Gerald Chastain, Jr. (Solar Reading - Flight One Ser.). (J). (gr. 3). disk 70.00 (*0-912899-12-3*) Lrning Multi-Systs.

Paraphrase. Karlyn Kamm & Gerald Chastain, Jr. (Solar Reading - Flight Two Ser.). (J). (gr. 5). 95.00 incl. disk (*0-912899-16-6*) Lrning Multi-Systs.

Paraphrase & Notes on the Epistles of St. Paul, 2 vols., Vol. 1. John Locke. Ed. by Arthur W. Wainright. (Clarendon Edition of the Works of John Locke Ser.). (Illus.). 496p. 1988. text 110.00 (*0-19-824801-6*) OUP.

Paraphrase & Notes on the Epistles of St. Paul, 2 vols., Vol. 2. John Locke. Ed. by Arthur W. Wainright. (Clarendon Edition of the Works of John Locke Ser.). (Illus.). 368p. 1988. text 89.00 (*0-19-824806-7*) OUP.

Paraphrase Grammars. R. M. Smaby. LC 76-13504. (Formal Linguistics Ser.: No. 2). 145p. 1970. text 121.50 (*90-277-0178-4*) Kluwer Academic.

Paraphrase of the Scriptures. C. Moeglin & J. L. Waldspurger. (Spectral Decomposition & Eisenstein Ser.: No. 113). (Illus.). 366p. (C). 1995. text 90.00 (*0-521-41893-3*) Cambridge U Pr.

Paraphrase on John. Desiderius Erasmus. Tr. & Anno. by Jane E. Phillips. (Collected Works of Erasmus: No. 46). 400p. 1991. text 85.00 (*0-8020-5859-0*) U of Toronto Pr.

Paraphrase on Mark. Desiderius Erasmus. Ed. & Tr. by Erika Rummel. (Collected Works of Erasmus: Vol. 49). 249p. 1988. text 50.00 (*0-8020-2631-1*) U of Toronto Pr.

Paraphrases on Romans & Galatians. Desiderius Erasmus. Ed. by Robert D. Sider. Tr. by John B. Payne et al. (Collected Works of Erasmus: Vol. 42). 232p. 1984. text 50.00 (*0-8020-2510-2*) U of Toronto Pr.

Parapolitics. Raghavan N. Iyer. (Illus.). 1986. pap. 21.75 (*0-685-08312-8*) Concord Grove.

Parapraxis in the Haizmann Case of Sigmund Freud. Gaston Vandendriessche. 1965. pap. 79.50 (*0-317-27533-X*) Elliots Bks.

Paraprofesionales en Salud Rural en Guatemala. Forrest D. Colburn. (Special Series on Paraprofessionals: No. 8). (SPA.). 55p. 1981. pap. text 6.45 (*0-86731-058-8*) Cornell CIS RDC.

Paraprofessional & the Professional Job Structure. Charlotte Mugnier. LC 80-12543. 163p. reprint ed. pap. 50.60 (*0-608-12589-X*, 202395100034) Bks Demand.

Paraprofessional in Home Health & Long-Term Care: Training Modules for Working with Older Adults. Ellen Cervantes et al. LC 95-11564. 272p. 1995. pap. text 30.00 (*1-878812-25-4*) Hlth Prof Pr.

Paraprofessionals: Training for the Classroom Leaders Guide. Carolyn S. Houk & Robert G. McKenzie. 1988. pap. text 49.95 (*0-88671-221-1*, 8301) Am Guidance.

Paraprofessionals: Training for the Classroom Teachers Handbook. Carolyn S. Houk & Robert G. McKenzie. 1988. teacher ed. 25.95 (*0-88671-223-8*, 8303) Am Guidance.

Paraprofessional's Guide to the Inclusive Classroom: Working As a Team. Mary B. Doyle. LC 97-14059. (Illus.). xiii, 146p. 1997. 23.95 (*1-55766-312-2*) P H Brookes.

Paraprofessional's Handbook for Working with Students Who Are Visually Impaired. Cyral Miller & Nancy Levack. LC 97-4158. 1997. write for info. (*1-880366-21-5*) TSBVI.

Paraprofessionals in Education. Kathy J. Skelton. LC 96-37460. 320p. (C). 1997. mass mkt. 34.95 (*0-8273-8182-4*) Delmar.

Paraprofessionals in Rural Development. Milton J. Esman et al. (Special Series on Paraprofessionals: No. 1). 149p. (Orig.). (C). 1980. pap. 9.05 (*0-86731-045-6*) Cornell CIS RDC.

Paraprofessionals in the Human Services. Ed. by Stanley Robin & Morton O. Wagenfeld. LC 80-18011. (Community Psychology Ser.: Vol. VI). 368p. 1981. 45.95 (*0-87705-490-8*, Kluwer Acad Hman Sci) Kluwer Academic.

Paraprofessionals in Village-Level Development in Sri Lanka: The Sarvodaya Shramadana Movement. Cynthia Moore. (Special Series on Paraprofessionals: No. 4). 64p. (Orig.). (C). 1981. pap. 6.85 (*0-86731-047-2*) Cornell CIS RDC.

Parapsychological Research with Children: An Annotated Bibliography. Athena A. Drewes & Sally A. Drucker. LC 91-39046. 245p. 1991. 29.00 (*0-8108-2514-7*) Scarecrow.

Parapsychology: A Concise History. John Beloff. 344p. 1997. pap. 18.95 (*0-312-17376-8*) St Martin.

Parapsychology: A Reading & Buying Guide to the Best Books in Print. 4th ed. Rhea A. White. (Bibliographies Ser.). (Orig.). 1990. pap. 18.00 (*0-944446-20-5*) EHE Network.

Parapsychology: New Sources of Information, 1973-1989. Rhea A. White. LC 90-21327. 713p. 1990. 71.00 (*0-8108-2385-3*) Scarecrow.

Parapsychology & Anthropology: Proceedings of the International Conference, Aug. 29-30, 1973. International Conference London Staff. Ed. by Allan Angoff & Diana Barth. LC 74-82959. 1973. 17.00 (*0-912328-24-X*) Parapsych Foun.

Parapsychology & Human Nature: Proceedings of an International Conference Held in Washington, D. C. November 1-2, 1986. Ed. by Betty Shapin & Lisette Coly. LC 89-61124. 211p. 1989. 20.00 (*0-912328-41-X*) Parapsych Foun.

Parapsychology & Self-Deception in Science. Ed. by R. A. McConnell. LC 81-90464. (Illus.). vii, 150p. 1983. pap. 7.00 (*0-9610232-2-8*) McConnell.

Parapsychology & Thanatology: Proceedings of the International Conference, Nov. 6-7, 1993. Parapsych Foundation Staff. LC 95-67318. 1995. 20.00 (*0-912328-46-0*) Parapsych Foun.

Parapsychology & the Experimental Method: Proceedings of an International Conference, New York, 1981. Ed. by Betty Shapin & Lisette Coly. LC 82-61144. 120p. (C). 1982. 16.00 (*0-912328-36-3*) Parapsych Foun.

Parapsychology & the Sciences: Proceedings of the International Conference, Aug. 23-25, 1972. International Conference, Amsterdam Staff. Ed. by Allan Angoff & Betty Shapin. LC 73-92492. 1974. 16.00 (*0-912328-23-1*) Parapsych Foun.

Parapsychology & the Unconscious. 2nd ed. Jule Eisenbud. (Illus.). 276p. 1984. pap. 16.95 (*1-55643-138-4*) North Atlantic.

Parapsychology for Parents: A Bibliography. 2nd ed. Rhea A. White. (Bibliographies Ser.). 36p. 1988. pap. 8.70 (*0-944446-06-X*) EHE Network.

Parapsychology for Teachers & Students: A Bibliographic Guide. 2nd ed. Rhea A. White. (Bibliographies Ser.). (Orig.). 1989. pap. 9.00 (*0-944446-13-2*) EHE Network.

Parapsychology from Duke to FRNM. J. B. Rhine et al. LC 65-28963. 121p. 1965. pap. 2.75 (*0-911106-00-6*) Parapsych Pr.

Parapsychology in Retrospect: My Search for the Unicorn. R. A. McConnell. LC 86-90590. (Illus.). 240p. (Orig.). 1987. pap. 15.00 (*0-9610232-4-4*) McConnell.

Parapsychology, New Age & the Occult - A Source Encyclopedia. Ed. by Cheryl K. Lacoff. 526p. 1994. 80.00 (*1-879583-01-1*); pap. 24.95 (*1-879583-00-3*) Ref Pr Intl.

Parapsychology, Philosophy, & Religious Concepts: Proceedings of an International Conference 1985. Ed. by Betty Shapin & Lisette Coly. LC 87-60201. (Annual International Conference Proceedings Ser.). 215p. 1987. 19.00 (*0-912328-40-1*) Parapsych Foun.

Parapsychology, Philosophy, & Spirituality: A Postmodern Exploration. David R. Griffin. LC 96-21472. (SUNY Series in Constructive Postmodern Thought). 339p. (C). 1997. text 59.50 (*0-7914-3315-3*); pap. text 19.95 (*0-7914-3316-1*) State U NY Pr.

Parapsychology Today: A Geographic View; Proceedings of the International Conference, 1971. International Conference, France Staff. Ed. by Allan Angoff & Betty Shapin. LC 72-94940. 1973. 16.00 (*0-912328-21-5*) Parapsych Foun.

Parapsychology's Second Century: Proceedings of An International Conference Held in London, England August 13-14, 1982. Ed. by Betty Shapin & Lisette Coly. LC 83-62083. (C). 1983. 18.00 (*0-912328-37-1*) Parapsych Foun.

Parapushkinistika. 3rd expanded ed. David Bayevsky. LC 98-38469. (RUS., Illus.). (Orig.). 1999. pap. 15.00 (*0-916201-23-6*) M I P Co.

Paraquat Health & Safety Guide. (Health & Safety Guides Ser.: No. 51). 36p. 1991. pap. text 5.00 (*92-4-151051-X*, 1860051) World Health.

Paraquat Poisoning: Mechanisms, Prevention, Treatment. Ed. by Chantal Bismuth & Alan H. Hall. LC 94-39917. (Drug & Chemical Toxicology Ser.: Vol. 10). (Illus.). 382p. 1995. reprint ed. pap. 118.50 (*0-608-05322-8*, 206586000010) Bks Demand.

Pararaton: A Study of the Southeast Asian Chronicle. I. Gusti Putu Phalgunadi. 1996. 52.00 (*81-85067-97-X*, Pub. by Sundeep Prak) S Asia.

Pararealities: The Nature of Our Fictions & How We Know Them. Floyd Merrell. (Purdue University Monographs in Romance Languages: No. 12). xii, 170p. 1983. 44.00 (*90-272-1722-X*) J Benjamins Pubng Co.

Paras: British Airborne Forces, 1940-1984. Greg Ferguson. (Elite Ser.: No. 1). (Illus.). 64p. pap. 12.95 (*0-85045-573-1*, 9400, Pub. by Ospry) Stackpole.

Paras: The Illustrated History of Britain's Airborne Forces. David Reynolds. LC 99-188000. (Illus.). 288p. 1998. 49.95 (*0-7509-1723-7*, Pub. by Sutton Pub Ltd) Intl Pubs Mktg.

Parasaurolophus. (Microfaxc Ser.). (J). 1997. pap. text 0.99 (*0-7894-2120-8*) DK Pub Inc.

Parasaurolophus. Janet Riehecky. (Dinosaurs Bks.). (Illus.). 32p. (J). (gr. k-4). 1991. lib. bdg. 21.36 (*0-89565-633-7*) Childs World.

Parasaurolophus. Janet Riehecky. (Libros Sobre Dinosaurios! Ser.). (SPA., Illus.). 32p. (J). (gr. k-4). 1994. lib. bdg. 21.36 (*1-56766-130-0*) Childs World.

Parasaurolophus (Cretaceous Period) see New Dinosaur Collection

***ParaScience Pack.** Uri Geller & Ron Van der Meer. 2000. 49.95 (*1-902413-53-9*, Pub. by Van der Meer) Abbeville Pr.

Parascript: Parasites & the Language of Evolution. Daniel R. Brooks & Deborah A. McLennan. LC 92-20822. (Series in Comparative Evolutionary Biology). (Illus.). 448p. (C). 1993. text 69.00 (*1-56098-215-2*); pap. text 25.00 (*1-56098-285-3*) Smithsonian.

Parasession on Clitics, Vol. 2. Ed. by Audra Dainora et al. 315p. 1995. pap. 16.00 (*0-914203-48-7*) Chicago Ling.

Parasession on Language in Context, Vol. 2. Ed. by Bradley Music et al. 300p. 1989. pap. 16.00 (*0-914203-33-9*) Chicago Ling.

Parasession on Negation, Vol. 2. Lise M. Dobrin. Ed. by Lynn Nichols et al. 373p. 1991. pap. 16.00 (*0-914203-38-X*) Chicago Ling.

Parasession on the Correspondence of Conceptual, Semantic & Grammatical Representations, Vol. 2. Ed. by Katharine Beals et al. 391p. 1993. pap. 16.00 (*0-914203-43-6*) Chicago Ling.

Parasession on the Cycle in Linguistic Theory, Vol. 2. Ed. by Jeannette M. Denton et al. 315p. 1992. pap. 16.00 (*0-914203-40-1*) Chicago Ling.

Parasession on the Syllable in Phonetics & Phonology, Vol. 2. Ed. by Michael Ziolkowski et al. 427p. 1990. pap. 16.00 (*0-914203-36-3*) Chicago Ling.

Parasession on Variation in Linguistic Theory, Vol. 2. Ed. by Katharine Beals et al. 349p. 1994. pap. 16.00 (*0-914203-46-0*) Chicago Ling.

***Parashah Plays: For Children of All Ages.** Richard J. Allen. LC 00-101923. 275p. (J). (gr. k-6). 2000. pap. 11.95 (*0-86705-047-0*) A R E Pub.

Parashat Hashavua: Genesis. Roberta Baum. (ENG & HEB.). 80p. Date not set. pap. text 5.95 (*0-87441-680-9*) Behrman.

Parasitaster: or The Fawn. John Marston. Ed. by David A. Blostein. LC 78-60170. (Revels Plays Ser.). 256p. reprint ed. pap. 79.40 (*0-608-06031-3*, 206636200008) Bks Demand.

Parasite. Ramsey Campbell. 352p. 1989. mass mkt. 4.95 (*0-8125-1668-0*) Tor Bks.

Parasite Antigens: Toward New Strategies for Vaccines. Ed. by Terry W. Pearson. LC 86-2141. (Receptors & Ligands in Intercellular Communication Ser.: No. 7). 427p. 1986. reprint ed. pap. 132.40 (*0-608-01332-3*, 206207500001) Bks Demand.

Parasite Antigens, Parasite Genes: A Laboratory Manual for Molecular Parasitology. R. M. Maizels et al. (Illus.). 234p. (C). 1992. spiral bd. 74.95 (*0-521-41927-1*) Cambridge U Pr.

Parasite Eve: Official Strategy Guide, 1. David Cassady. LC 98-73580. (Brady Games Strategy Guides Ser.). 1998. pap. text 14.99 (*1-56686-824-6*) Brady Pub.

Parasite Life Cycles. D. D. Despommier & W. Karapelou. (Illus.). 210p. 1987. 79.00 (*0-387-96486-X*) Spr-Verlag.

Parasite Menace: How to Prevent, Detect & Eradicate Parasites from Your Body. Skye Weintraub. 1998. pap. text 14.95 (*1-885670-88-5*) Woodland UT.

***Parasite Rex: Inside the Bizarre World of Nature's Most Dangerous Creatures.** Carl Zimmer. LC 00-37593. (Illus.). 320p. 2000. 25.50 (*0-684-85638-7*) Free Pr.

Parasite War. Timothy R. Sullivan. 256p. (Orig.). 1989. pap. 3.50 (*0-380-75550-5*, Avon Bks) Morrow Avon.

Parasites. Howard Facklam & Margery Facklam. (Invaders Ser.). (Illus.). 64p. (J). (gr. 5-8). 1995. lib. bdg. 18.90 (*0-8050-2858-7*) TFC Bks NY.

***Parasites.** Lisa Newman. LC 99-37373. (Crossing Press Pocket Ser.). 96p. 1999. pap. 6.95 (*1-58091-006-8*) Crossing Pr.

Parasites. Stanley Weinberger. 1998. pap. 11.95 (*0-9616184-8-5*) Healing Within Prods.

Parasites. Woodland Publishing, Inc. Staff. (The Woodland Health Ser.). 1997. pap. text 3.95 (*1-885670-89-3*) Woodland UT.

Parasites. Daphne Du Maurier. LC 72-184728. 320p. 1971. reprint ed. lib. bdg. 20.00 (*0-8376-0410-9*) Bentley Pubs.

Parasites: A Guide to Laboratory Procedures & Identification. Lawrence R. Ash & Thomas C. Orihel. LC 86-32179. (Illus.). 328p. 1987. text 15.00 (*0-89189-231-1*) Am Soc Clinical.

Parasites: An Epidemic in Disguise. Stanley Weinberger. 60p. 7.95 (*0-9616184-3-4*) Healing Within Prods.

Parasites: An Epidemic in Disguise. 2nd rev. ed. Stanley Weinberger. Ed. by Beth Kuper. (Illus.). 1993. pap. 7.95 (*0-9616184-5-0*) Healing Within Prods.

Parasites: Immunity & Pathology: The Consequences of Parasitic Infections in Mammals. Ed. by J. M. Behnke. 250p. 1990. 143.00 (*0-85066-499-3*) Taylor & Francis.

Parasites: The Enemy Within. Hanna Kroeger. 62p. (Orig.). 1991. pap. 5.00 (*1-883713-07-2*) Hanna Kroeger.

Parasites & Diseases of Wild Mammals in Florida. Donald J. Forrester. (Illus.). 479p. (C). 1992. 59.95 (*0-8130-1072-1*) U Press Fla.

Parasites & Pathogens of Insects, 2 vols., Set. Ed. by Beckage et al. (Illus.). 740p. 1993. 188.00 (*0-12-084440-0*) Acad Pr.

Parasites & Pathogens of Insects Vol. 1: Parasites. N. E. Beckage et al. (Illus.). 364p. 1993. text 100.00 (*0-12-084441-9*) Acad Pr.

Parasites & Pathogens of Insects Vol. 2: Pathogens. N. E. Beckage et al. (Illus.). 294p. 1993. text 100.00 (*0-12-084442-7*) Acad Pr.

Parasites & Skin Diseases. Peter Gray. 165p. 1995. pap. 75.00 (*0-85131-624-7*, Pub. by J A Allen) Trafalgar.

Parasites in Human Tissues. Lawrence R. Ash & Thomas C. Orihel. (Illus.). 300p. 1995. 165.00 (*0-89189-379-2*) Am Soc Clinical.

Parasites in Social Insects. Paul Schmid-Hempel. LC 98-10164. (Monographs in Behavior & Ecology). 392p. 1998. pap. text 35.00 (*0-691-05924-1*, Pub. by Princeton U Pr) Cal Prin Full Svc.

Parasites in Social Insects. Paul Schmid-Hempel. LC 98-10164. (Monographs in Behavior & Ecology). 392p. 1998. text 85.00 (*0-691-05923-3*, Pub. by Princeton U Pr) Cal Prin Full Svc.

Parasites in the Immunized Host: Mechanisms of Survival. CIBA Foundation Staff. LC 75-311586. (CIBA Foundation Symposium: New Ser.: No. 25). 288p. reprint ed. pap. 89.30 (*0-608-13984-X*, 202215400024) Bks Demand.

Parasites, Infections & Diseases of Fishes in Africa: An Update. Ilan Paperna. (CIFA Technical Papers: No. 31). (Illus.). 230p. 1996. pap. 27.00 (*92-5-103772-8*, F37728, Pub. by FAO) Bernan Associates.

Parasites of Laboratory Animals. Robert J. Flynn. LC 77-171165. (Illus.). 900p. reprint ed. pap. 200.00 (*0-608-15553-5*, 205638000062) Bks Demand.

Parasites of Man in Temperate Climates. Thomas W. Cameron. LC 43-17056. 227p. reprint ed. pap. 70.40 (*0-608-30219-8*, 201608200098) Bks Demand.

Parasites of North American Freshwater Fishes. 2nd ed. Glenn L. Hoffman. LC 98-49407. (Illus.). 548p. 1999. 85.00 (*0-8014-3409-2*, Comstock Pub) Cornell U Pr.

Parasitic & Infectious Diseases: Epidemiology & Ecology. Ed. by Marilyn E. Scott & Gary Smith. (Illus.). 398p. 1994. text 104.00 (*0-12-633325-4*) Acad Pr.

Parasitic & Related Diseases: Basic Mechanisms, Manifestations, & Control. Ed. by Thomas C. Cheng. LC 85-24447. (Comparative Pathobiology Ser.: Vol. 8). 176p. 1986. 65.00 (*0-306-42119-4*, Plenum Trade) Perseus Pubng.

Parasitic Birds & Their Hosts: Studies in Coevolution. Ed. by Stephen I. Rothstein & Scott K. Robinson. LC 97-18599. (Oxford Ornithology Ser.). (Illus.). 464p. 1998. text 150.00 (*0-19-509976-1*) OUP.

Parasitic Copepoda & Branchiura of Fishes, 2 pts., Set. Satyu Yamaguti. 1104p. 1985. pap. 350.00 (*0-7855-0385-4*, Pub. by Intl Bks & Periodicals) St Mut.

Parasitic Copepods from the Gulf of Mexico & Caribbean Sea Pt. 2: Part 2, Bomolochidae. Roger F. Cressey. LC 81-9055. (Smithsonian Contributions to Zoology Ser.: No. 389). 40p. reprint ed. pap. 30.00 (*0-608-14276-X*, 202219900024) Bks Demand.

Parasitic Copepods from the Gulf of Mexico & Caribbean Sea Pt. 3: Caligus. Roger F. Cressey. LC 81-9055. (Smithsonian Contributions to Zoology Ser.: No. 497). 57p. reprint ed. pap. 30.00 (*0-7837-0270-1*, 204057900003) Bks Demand.

Parasitic Diseases. M. B. Katz et al. (Illus.). 264p. 1986. 34.95 (*0-387-90689-4*) Spr-Verlag.

Parasitic Diseases. M. B. Katz et al. (Illus.). 301p. 1988. 61.00 (*0-387-96800-8*) Spr-Verlag.

Parasitic Diseases. 3rd ed. D. D. Despommier et al. (Illus.). 348p. 1994. 55.95 (*0-387-94223-8*) Spr-Verlag.

Parasitic Diseases: Immunology, Vol. 1. Ed. by John M. Mansfield. LC 81-9741. 335p. 1981. reprint ed. pap. 103.90 (*0-608-01299-8*, 206204500001) Bks Demand.

Parasitic Diseases: Treatment & Control. Ed. by Max J. Miller & Edgar J. Love. 352p. 1989. lib. bdg. 195.00 (*0-8493-4922-2*, RC119) CRC Pr.

Parasitic Diseases Vol. 2: Chemotherapy. Ed. by John M. Mansfield. LC 81-9741. 247p. 1981. reprint ed. pap. 76.60 (*0-608-01300-5*, 206204500002) Bks Demand.

Parasitic Diseases in Water Resources Development: The Need for Intersectoral Negotiation. J. M. Hunter et al. (ENG, FRE & SPA.). x, 152p. 1993. pap. text 35.00 (*92-4-156155-6*, 1150396) World Health.

Parasitic Diseases International Nomenclature of Diseases Vol. II: Infectious Diseases, 2. (International Nomenclature of Diseases Ser.: No. 4). 1987. pap. text 20.00 (*92-4-154222-5*) World Health.

***Parasitic Diseases of Wild Mammals.** Ed. by William Samuel et al. 720p. 2000. 94.95 (*0-8138-2978-X*) Iowa St U Pr.

Parasitic Diseases of Wild Mammals. Ed. by John W. Davis & Roy C. Anderson. LC 72-103854. (Illus.). 372p. reprint ed. pap. 115.40 (*0-608-17497-1*, 202999900067) Bks Demand.

An Asterisk (*) at the beginning of an entry indicates that the title is appearing for the first time.

Parasitic Disorders: Pathology, Diagnosis & Management. 2nd ed. Tsieh Sun. LC 98-10760. 431p. 1998. 150.00 (*0-683-30566-2*) Lppncott W & W.

Parasitic Fauna of Reservoir Fishes of the U. S. S. R. & Its Evolution. N. A. Izyumova. Tr. by B. R. Sharma from RUS. (Russian Translation Ser.: No. 61). 339p. (C). 1988. text 142.00 (*90-6191-906-1*, Pub. by A A Balkema) Ashgate Pub Co.

Parasitic Flowering Plants: Ecology & Management. J. Sauerborn. 127p. 1992. pap. 33.00 (*3-8236-1217-4*, Pub. by Backhuys Pubs) Balogh.

***Parasitic Gaps.** Ed. by Peter W. Culicover & Paul M. Postal. (Current Studies in Linguistics: No. 35). (Illus.). 496p. (C). 2001. 55.00 (*0-262-03284-8*) MIT Pr.

Parasitic Helminths & Zoonoses in Africa. Ed. by P. Craig & C. N. L. MacPherson. (Illus.). 308p. (C). 1990. text 82.00 (*0-04-445565-8*) Routledge.

Parasitic Infections. Ed. by James H. Leech et al. (Contemporary Issues in Infectious Diseases Ser.: Vol. 7). (Illus.). 364p. 1988. text 83.00 (*0-443-08561-7*) Church.

Parasitic Infections & the Immune System. Ed. by Felipe Kierszenbaum. (Illus.). 232p. 1993. text 63.00 (*0-12-406575-9*) Acad Pr.

Parasitic Infections in the Compromised Host. Peter D. Walzer & Robert M. Genta. (Infectious Disease & Therapy Ser.: Vol. 1). (Illus.). 552p. 1988. text 195.00 (*0-8247-7943-6*) Dekker.

Parasitic Infections of Domestic Animals: A Diagnostic Manual. Johannes Kaufmann. LC 95-39894. 423p. 1995. 69.50 (*0-8176-5115-2*) Birkhauser.

Parasitic Infections of Man & Animals: A Bibliography of Articles in Chinese Medical Periodicals, 1949-64. Lai-bing Kan. LC 66-6864. 134p. reprint ed. pap. 41.60 (*0-608-11114-7*, 202156000022) Bks Demand.

Parasitic Lung Diseases. Adel A. Mahmoud. LC 96-39908. (Lung Biology in Health & Disease Ser.: Vol. 101). (Illus.). 256p. 1997. text 145.00 (*0-8247-9722-1*) Dekker.

***Parasitic Nematodes: Molecular Biology, Biochemistry & Immunology.** Ed. by M. Kennedy & W. Harnett. (CABI Publishing Ser.). (Illus.). 448p. 2000. text. write for info. (*0-85199-423-7*) OUP.

Parasitic Nematodes - Antigens, Membranes & Genes. M. W. Kennedy. 250p. 1991. 110.00 (*0-85066-772-0*) Taylor & Francis.

Parasitic Nematodes of Freshwater Fishes of Europe. Frantisek Moravec. LC 93-215. 477p. (C). 1995. text 239.50 (*0-7923-2172-3*) Kluwer Academic.

Parasitic on Fishes. Keys & Notes for Identification of the Species: Keys & Notes for Identification of the Species. Z. Kabata. (Synopses of the British Fauna Ser.: No. 47). (Illus.). 272p. 1992. pap. 80.00 (*90-73348-16-1*, Pub. by Backhuys Pubs) Balogh.

Parasitic Protozoa. Julius P. Kreier & John R. Baker. LC 87-1486. (Illus.). 224p. 1987. text 75.00 (*0-04-591021-9*) Routledge.

Parasitic Protozoa. Julius P. Kreier & John R. Baker. LC 87-1486. (Illus.). 224p. 1989. pap. 64.95 (*0-04-591022-7*) Thomson Learn.

Parasitic Protozoa, 10 vols. 2nd ed. Kreier. 1995. 789.00 (*0-12-426010-1*) Acad Pr.

Parasitic Protozoa, Vol. 1. 2nd ed. Ed. by Julius P. Kreier & John R. Baker. (Illus.). 258p. (C). 1991. text 121.00 (*0-12-426011-X*) Acad Pr.

Parasitic Protozoa, Vol. 2. 2nd ed. Julius P. Kreier & John R. Baker. (Illus.). 323p. 1992. text 121.00 (*0-12-426012-8*) Acad Pr.

Parasitic Protozoa, Vol. 3. 2nd ed. Ed. by Julius P. Kreier & John R. Baker. (Illus.). 333p. 1993. text 121.00 (*0-12-426013-6*) Acad Pr.

Parasitic Protozoa, Vol. 4. 2nd ed. Ed. by Julius P. Kreier. Vol. 4. (Illus.). 323p. 1993. text 121.00 (*0-12-426014-4*) Acad Pr.

Parasitic Protozoa, Vol. 5. 2nd ed. Ed. by Julius P. Kreier. (Illus.). 343p. 1993. text 121.00 (*0-12-426015-2*) Acad Pr.

Parasitic Protozoa, Vol. 6. 2nd ed. Ed. by Julius P. Kreier. (Illus.). 385p. 1993. text 121.00 (*0-12-426016-0*) Acad Pr.

Parasitic Protozoa, Vol. 7. 2nd ed. Ed. by Julius P. Kreier. (Illus.). 314p. 1993. text 121.00 (*0-12-426017-9*) Acad Pr.

Parasitic Protozoa, Vol. 8. 2nd ed. Ed. by Julius P. Kreier. (Illus.). 328p. 1994. text 121.00 (*0-12-426018-7*) Acad Pr.

Parasitic Protozoa, Vol. 9. 2nd ed. Ed. by Julius P. Kreier. (Illus.). 216p. 1994. text 121.00 (*0-12-426019-5*) Acad Pr.

Parasitic Protozoa, Vol. 10. 2nd ed. Ed. by Julius P. Kreier. (Illus.). 430p. 1995. text 109.00 (*0-12-426020-9*) Acad Pr.

Parasitic Wasps. 2nd ed. Donald L. J. Quicke. LC 96-71731. (Illus.). 488p. 1997. write for info. (*0-412-58350-X*) Kluwer Academic.

Parasitic Wasps of the Subfamily Eupelminae - Classification & Revision of World Genera (Hymenoptera - Chalcidoidea - Eupelmidea) Gary A. Gibson. Ed. by Virendra K. Gupta. LC 95-38797. (Memoirs on Entomology, International Ser.: Volume 5, 1995). (Illus.). 428p. 1995. 65.00 (*1-56665-060-7*) Assoc Pubs FL.

Parasitic Weeds in Agriculture Striga. L. Musselman. LC 86-6139. 328p. 1986. 184.00 (*0-8493-6272-5*, CRC Reprint) Franklin.

Parasitic Weeds of the World. C. Parker & C. Riches. (Illus.). 304p. 1993. text 105.00 (*0-85198-873-3*) OUP.

Parasitic Worms. D. W. Crompton & S. M. Joyner. 208p. 1980. pap. 18.00 (*0-85109-830-4*) Taylor & Francis.

Parasitic Worms. Jim Flegg. (Natural History Ser.: No. 5). (Illus.). 24p. 1989. pap. 5.25 (*0-85263-761-6*, Pub. by Shire Pubns) Parkwest Pubns.

Parasitic Worms of Fish. Harford Williams & Arlene Jones. 650p. 1993. 200.00 (*0-85066-425-X*, Pub. by Tay Francis Ltd) Taylor & Francis.

Parasitic Zoonoses: Section C, 3 vols., Vol. I. Ed. by Arambulo. (CRC Handbook Series in Zoonoses). 400p. 1982. 208.00 (*0-8493-2916-7*, RC113, CRC Reprint) Franklin.

Parasitic Zoonoses: Section C, 3 vols., Vol. II. Ed. by Arambulo. (CRC Handbook Series in Zoonoses). 360p. 1982. 207.00 (*0-8493-2917-5*, CRC Reprint) Franklin.

Parasitic Zoonoses: Section C, 3 vols., Vol. III. Ed. by Arambulo. (CRC Handbook Series in Zoonoses). 384p. 1982. 195.00 (*0-8493-2918-3*, CRC Reprint) Franklin.

Parasitische Algen und Pilze Javas, 3 pts. in 1. M. Raciborski. 1973. reprint ed. 40.00 (*3-7682-0855-9*) Lubrecht & Cramer.

Parasitische Pilze an Gefaesspflanzen in Europe. W. Brandenburger. (Bibliotheca Mycologica Ser.: No. 37). (Illus.). 1248p. 1985. lib. bdg. 315.00 (*3-437-30433-X*) Lubrecht & Cramer.

Parasitism & Host Behaviour. Ed. by C. J. Barnard & J. M. Behnke. 220p. 1990. 142.00 (*0-85066-498-5*) Taylor & Francis.

Parasitism & Symbiology: An Introductory Text. Clark P. Read. LC 75-110390. 326p. reprint ed. 101.10 (*0-8357-9947-6*, 205513900008) Bks Demand.

***Parasitism & the Platyhelminths.** G. C. Kearn. LC 97-75126. 560p. 1998. write for info. (*0-412-80460-3*) Kluwer Academic.

***Parasitoid Population Biology.** Michael E. Hochberg. LC 00-20748. (Illus.). 320p. 2000. 75.00 (*0-691-04981-5*, Pub. by Princeton U Pr) Cal Prin Full Svc.

***Parasitoid Population Biology.** Michael E. Hochberg & Anthony R. Ives. LC 00-20748. (Illus.). 320p. 2000. pap. 24.95 (*0-691-04982-3*) Princeton U Pr.

Parasitoids: Behavioral & Evolutionary Ecology. H. C. Godfray. LC 93-13158. (Monographs in Behavior & Ecology). (Illus.). 520p. 1993. text 75.00 (*0-691-03325-0*, Pub. by Princeton U Pr) Cal Prin Full Svc.

Parasitology. Arthur Goven. 78p. (C). 1990. student ed. 21.20 (*1-56870-001-6*) RonJon Pub.

***Parasitology.** 2nd ed. Marquardt. 672p. 1999. 74.95 (*0-12-473275-5*) Acad Pr.

Parasitology: A Global Perspective. Ed. by K. S. Warren & J. Z. Bowers. (Illus.). 270p. 1983. 119.00 (*0-387-90840-4*) Spr-Verlag.

Parasitology for the 21st Century. M. Ziya Alkan. 1996. 104.25 (*0-85198-777-X*) C A B Intl.

Parasitology for the 21st Century: Keynote Papers from the VIII International Congress of Parasitology. Ed. by M. Ziya Alkan & M. Ali Izcel. (A CAB International Publication). (Illus.). 304p. 1996. text 105.00 (*0-85198-977-2*) OUP.

Parasitology in Focus. Ed. by H. Mehlhorn. (Illus.). 1040p. 1988. 288.00 (*0-387-17838-4*) Spr-Verlag.

Parasitology of Malaria: Proceedings of the WHO Scientific Group, Teheran, 1968. WHO Staff. (Technical Reports: No. 433). 70p. 1969. pap. text 5.00 (*92-4-120433-8*, 1100433) World Health.

Parasol. Anton Chekhov & Dunai. (Illus.). 96p. (Orig.). 1987. pap. text 5.95 (*0-318-22831-9*) Polyglot VA.

Parasol Dzieje Oddz, Dywersji Armii Krajowej. Piotr Stachiwicz. 708p. 1984. 50.00 (*0-614-25052-8*) Szwede Slavic.

***Parasol Tree Village.** Julia Lin. LC 99-67354. 176p. 2000. pap. 14.95 (*1-56167-569-5*, Five Star Spec Ed) Am Literary Pr.

Parasols of Fern: A Book about Wonder. Jack Perkins. LC 93-10874. (Illus.). 1993. 18.95 (*0-934745-17-X*) Acadia Pub Co.

Parastoo: Stories & Poems. Mehri Yafani. 120p. 1995. pap. 9.95 (*0-88961-211-0*) Womans Pr.

Parasuicide. Ed. by Norman Kreitman. LC 76-30355. 205p. reprint ed. pap. 63.60 (*0-608-17681-8*, 203039900069) Bks Demand.

***Parasyte, No. 2** Hitosi Iwaaki. Orig. Title: Kiseiju. (Illus.). 192p. (YA). (gr. 7). 1999. pap. 11.95 (*1-892213-07-9*, Mixx Manga) Mixx Enter Inc.

Parasyte, Vol. 1. Hitosi Iwaaki. Orig. Title: Kiseiju. (Illus.). 192p. (YA). (gr. 7 up). 1998. pap. 11.95 (*1-892213-02-8*, Mixx Special Edtns) Mixx Enter Inc.

Parasyte, Vol. 3. Hitosi Iwaaki. Orig. Title: Kiseiju. (Illus.). 192p. (YA). (gr. 7 up). 1999. pap. 11.95 (*1-892213-21-4*, Mixx Manga) Mixx Enter Inc.

***Parasyte, Vol. 4.** Hitosi Iwaaki. Orig. Title: Kiseiju. 2000. pap. 11.95 (*1-892213-44-3*) Mixx Enter Inc.

Parat Dictionary Library, Information Science: French/German/French. Saiedeh von Keitz. (FRE & GER.). 323p. 1994. 160.00 (*0-320-00560-7*) Fr & Eur.

Parat Dictionary of Artificial Intelligence & Neuronal Networks. Hans-Dieter Junge. (ENG & GER.). 238p. 1991. lib. bdg. 150.00 (*0-8288-3613-2*, F62550) Fr & Eur.

Parat Dictionary of Automotive Engineering: English-German, German-English. Hans-Dieter Junge. (ENG & GER.). 388p. 1991. 175.00 (*0-7859-6954-3*) Fr & Eur.

Parat Dictionary of Automotive Engineering: English-German, German-English. Hans-Dieter Junge & D. Lukhaup. (ENG & GER.). 395p. 1991. 125.00 (*3-527-28171-1*, Wiley-VCH) Wiley.

Parat Dictionary of Blasting Technology. B. Student-Bilharz. (ENG, FRE & GER.). 340p. 1987. 250.00 (*0-8288-0217-3*, F 22550) Fr & Eur.

Parat Dictionary of Ceramics & Earth: English-German, German-English. Bernd Pfannkuche. (ENG & GER.). 555p. 1993. 225.00 (*0-7859-6958-6*) Fr & Eur.

Parat Dictionary of Chemistry: English-German. Gerhard Wenske. (ENG & GER.). 1546p. 1992. 525.00 (*0-7859-6948-9*) Fr & Eur.

Parat Dictionary of Chemistry: German-English. Ed. by Hans-Dieter Junge & Gerhard Wenske. 2055p. 1993. 240.00 (*3-527-26429-9*, Wiley-VCH) Wiley.

Parat Dictionary of Chemistry: German-English. Gerhard Wenske. (ENG & GER.). 1600p. 1992. 525.00 (*0-7859-6949-7*) Fr & Eur.

Parat Dictionary of Ecology: English-German, German-English. Karl-Heinz Ohrbach. (ENG & GER.). 330p. 1991. 175.00 (*0-7859-6955-1*) Fr & Eur.

Parat Dictionary of Environmental Protection: English-German, German-English. Dieter Lukhaup. (ENG & GER.). 532p. 1992. 225.00 (*0-7859-6956-X*) Fr & Eur.

Parat Dictionary of Fluidics: English-German, German-English. Gunter Neubert. (ENG & GER.). 259p. 1993. 150.00 (*0-7859-6959-4*) Fr & Eur.

Parat Dictionary of Library & Information Science. Ed. by Saledah Von Keitz & Wolfgang Von Keitz. 527p. 1992. text 65.00 (*0-89573-945-3*, Wiley-VCH) Wiley.

Parat Dictionary of Machine Tools & Mechanical Engineering: English-German, German-English. Hans-Dieter Junge. (ENG & GER.). 551p. 1992. 195.00 (*0-7859-6953-5*) Fr & Eur.

Parat Dictionary of Measurement Engineering & Units. Hans-Dieter Junge. (ENG & GER.). 225p. 1991. lib. bdg. 175.00 (*0-8288-3612-4*, F114660) Fr & Eur.

Parat Dictionary of Plastics Technology. Hans-Dieter Junge. (ENG & GER.). 315p. 1987. 250.00 (*0-8288-0723-X*, F 22510) Fr & Eur.

Parat Dictionary of Washing. Gunter Jakobi & A. Loehr. 1992. 63.00 (*3-527-26983-5*, Wiley-VCH) Wiley.

Parat Dictionary of Washing: English-German. Ed. by Gunter Jakobi & Albrecht Lohr. LC 89-16494. 174p. 1989. 55.00 (*3-527-26982-7*, Wiley-VCH) Wiley.

Parat Dictionary of Washing: German & English. J. Gunter & Gunter Jakobi. (ENG & GER.). 170p. 1989. lib. bdg. 150.00 (*0-8288-3610-8*, F83110) Fr & Eur.

Parat Dictionary Plastics, Rubber Technology Vol. 1: German to English. 2nd ed. M. Welling. (ENG & GER.). 323p. 1994. 275.00 (*0-320-00573-9*) Fr & Eur.

Parat Dictionary Plastics, Rubber Technology Vol. 2: English to German. 2nd ed. M. Welling. (ENG & GER.). 193p. 1994. 275.00 (*0-320-00575-5*) Fr & Eur.

Parat Encyclopedia Dictionary Genetics: German/English/German. King & Stansfield. (ENG & GER.). 809p. 1990. 450.00 (*0-320-00610-7*) Fr & Eur.

Parat Index of Acronyms & Abbreviations in Electrical & Electronic Engineering. Ed. by Buro Scientia. LC 89-5638. 538p. 1989. 195.00 (*0-89573-812-0*, Wiley-VCH) Wiley.

Parat Index of Polymer Trade Names. 2nd ed. Ed. by FIZ Chemie Staff. 670p. 1992. text 190.00 (*1-56081-194-3*, Wiley-VCH); disk 275.00 (*1-56081-195-1*, Wiley-VCH) Wiley.

Parat Lexikon Chemische Technik. Ernst Hengeln. (GER.). 742p. 1988. 225.00 (*0-7859-8413-5*, 3527261214) Fr & Eur.

Parat Lexikon Elektrochemie. D. B. Hibbert. (GER.). 257p. 1987. 175.00 (*0-7859-8414-3*, 3527263535) Fr & Eur.

Parat Lexikon Elektronik. Albrecht Moschwitzer. (GER.). 1000p. 1993. 225.00 (*0-7859-8415-1*, 3527281533) Fr & Eur.

Parat Lexikon Folientechnik. Joachim Nentwig. (GER.). 550p. 1991. 165.00 (*0-7859-8417-8*, 3527281819) Fr & Eur.

Parat Lexikon Information und Kommunilation. Dennis Longley. (GER.). 637p. 1993. 195.00 (*0-7859-8683-9*, 352726843x) Fr & Eur.

Parat Pocket Dictionary of Laboratory Equipment. Hans-Dieter Junge. (ENG & GER.). 201p. 1987. pap. 85.00 (*0-8288-0169-X*, F 22490) Fr & Eur.

Parat Woerterbuch Bruchmechanik: English-German, German-English. Gunter Korzak. (ENG & GER.). 277p. 1989. 135.00 (*0-7859-6952-7*) Fr & Eur.

Parat Woerterbuch Chemie German-English Computer Version. Gerhard Wenske. (ENG & GER.). 1993. 495.00 (*3-527-29031-1*, 3527290311) Fr & Eur.

Parat Woerterbuch Kunstofftechnologie: German-English. Manfred S. Welling. (ENG & GER.). 220p. 1985. 225.00 (*0-7859-6950-0*) Fr & Eur.

Parat Woerterbuch Waschen: English-German-French-Italian. Gunter Jakobi. (ENG, FRE & GER.). 353p. 1992. 125.00 (*0-7859-6951-9*) Fr & Eur.

Parat Worterbuch Informationstechnologie. Hans-Dieter Junge. (ENG & GER.). 927p. 1989. lib. bdg. 295.00 (*0-8288-3617-5*, 3527264302) Fr & Eur.

Parat Worterbuch Informationstechnologie. Hans-Dieter Junge. (ENG & GER.). 686p. 1990. lib. bdg. 250.00 (*0-8288-3611-6*, 3527264205) Fr & Eur.

Paratabloids. Michael A. Arnzen. (Illus.). 45p. 1999. pap. write for info. (*1-893816-04-4*) Ozark Tri.

Paratexts: The Thresholds of Textuality. Gerard Genette. Tr. by Jane E. Lewin from FRE. LC 97-164762. (Literature, Culture, Theory Ser.: No. 20). 452p. (C). 1997. text 64.95 (*0-521-41350-8*); pap. text 23.95 (*0-521-42406-2*) Cambridge U Pr.

Paratextuality in Balzac's 'La Peau de Chagrin' - 'The Wild Ass's Skin' Jeri D. King. LC 92-12238. (Studies in French Literature: Vol. 11). (Illus.). 268p. 1992. lib. bdg. 89.95 (*0-7734-9507-X*) E Mellen.

Parathink: The Paranoia of Everyday Life. Steven Starker. LC 86-12485. 1986. 15.95 (*0-88282-022-2*) New Horizon NJ.

Parathink: The Paranoia of Everyday Life. Steven Starker. LC 86-12485. 1990. 9.95 (*0-88282-063-X*) New Horizon NJ.

Parathion Health & Safety Guide. (Health & Safety Guides Ser.: No. 74). 37p. 1992. pap. text 5.00 (*92-4-151074-9*, 1860074) World Health.

Parathyroid Glands: Ultrastructure, Secretion, & Function. Ed. by Pieter Gaillard et al. LC 65-17290. 365p. reprint ed. pap. 113.20 (*0-608-13377-9*, 202409200035) Bks Demand.

Parathyroid Hormone. Ed. by Robert A. Nissenson & M. W. Draper. (Journal: Mineral & Electrolyte Metabolism Ser.: Vol. 8, No. 3-4). (Illus.). vi, 124p. 1982. pap. 68.00 (*3-8055-3550-3*) S Karger.

Parathyroid Hormone: An Unexpected Bone Builder for Treating Osteoporosis. James F. Whitfield. LC 98-42194. (Medical Intelligence Unit Ser.: No. 6). 129p. 1998. 99.00 (*1-57059-556-9*) Landes Bioscience.

Parathyroid Hormone in Kidney Failure: Proceedings of the International Symposium, 1st, New York, May, 1979. International Symposium on Parathyroid in Uremia Staff. Ed. by M. M. Avran & Geoffrey M. Berlyne. (Contributions to Nephrology Ser.: Vol. 20). 1980. pap. 29.75 (*3-8055-0151-X*) S Karger.

Parathyroid Hormone-Related Protein: Normal Physiology & Its Role in Cancer. Bernard P. Halloran & Robert A. Nissenson. 224p. 1992. lib. bdg. 179.00 (*0-8493-4539-1*, QP572) CRC Pr.

Parathyroid Surgery. Ed. by M. Rothmund & S. A. Wells, Jr. (Progress in Surgery Ser.: Vol. 18). (Illus.). x, 250p. 1986. 154.00 (*3-8055-4217-8*) S Karger.

Parathyroids: Basic & Clinical Concepts. Ed. by John P. Bilezikian et al. LC 93-4126. (Illus.). 889p. 1994. reprint ed. pap. 200.00 (*0-608-07316-4*, 206754400009) Bks Demand.

Paratransit in America: Jitneys, Vans & Minibuses. Robert B. Cervero. LC 96-21246. 320p. 1997. 59.95 (*0-275-95725-X*, Praeger Pubs) Greenwood.

Paratrisika-Vivarana: The Secret of Tantric Mysticism. Abhinavagupta. Ed. by Bettina Baumer. Tr. by Jaideva Singh. (C). 1988. 31.00 (*81-208-0462-7*, Pub. by Motilal Bnarsidass); pap. 21.00 (*81-208-0472-4*, Pub. by Motilal Bnarsidass) S Asia.

Paratrooper: The Life of General James M. Gavin. T. Michael Booth et al. (Illus.). 494p. 1994. 27.50 (*0-671-73226-9*) S&S Trade.

Paratrooper! The Saga of the U. S. Army & Marine Parachute & Glider Combat Troops During World War II. Gerard M. Devlin. (Illus.). 736p. 1986. pap. 14.95 (*0-312-59652-9*) St Martin.

Paratroopers of the French Foreign Legion: From Vietnam to Bosnia. Howard R. Simpson, III. LC 96-50414. (Association of the U. S. Army Book Ser.). (Illus.). 208p. 1997. 26.95 (*1-57488-117-5*) Brasseys.

***Paratroopers of the French Foreign Legion: From Vietnam to Bosnia.** Howard R. Simpson. 1999. pap. 18.95 (*1-57488-226-0*) Brasseys.

***Paratuberculosis: Proceedings International Colloguium on Paratuberculosis, 6th, Melbourne, Australia, 1999.** Ed. by Elizabeth J. B. Manning & Michael T. Collins. LC 99-48113. 720p. 1999. 225.00 (*0-9633043-4-8*) Intl Assn Paratuber.

Paratwa. Christopher Hinz. (Paratwa Saga Ser.: Bk. 3). 416p. 1995. mass mkt. 5.99 (*0-8125-3093-4*, Pub. by Tor Bks) St Martin.

Paravents. Jean Genet. 288p. 1976. write for info. (*0-318-63574-7*) Fr & Eur.

Paravents. Jean Genet. (FRE.). 1981. pap. 10.95 (*0-8288-3676-0*, M11898); pap. 10.95 (*0-7859-2446-9*, 2070373096) Fr & Eur.

Paravents. Jean Genet. (Folio Ser.: No. 1309). (FRE.). 288p. 1976. pap. 8.95 (*2-07-037309-6*) Schoenhof.

Paraverbal Communication with Children: Not Through Words Alone. E. P. Heimlich & A. J. Mark. (Illus.). 250p. (C). 1990. 49.50 (*0-306-43624-8*, Plenum Trade) Perseus Pubng.

Parbajtorvivas see Epee Fencing: A Complete System

Parboiled Pastor: Musings on the Joys & Pressures of Parish Ministry. Steven L. McKinley. LC 98-9839. 1998. pap. text 11.99 (*0-8066-3633-5*, 9-3633, Augsburg) Augsburg Fortress.

ParBowling: The Challenge. Thomas C. Kouros. 394p. 1993. pap. text 19.95 (*0-9639136-0-3*) Pin-Count Enter.

Parc see Park

Parc. Phillipe Sollers. (FRE.). 160p. 1981. pap. 11.95 (*0-7859-1251-7*, 2020057387) Fr & Eur.

Parc aux Sortileges. Denis Cote. (Novels in the Roman Jeunesse Ser.). (FRE.). 96p. (J). (gr. 4-7). 1994. pap. 8.95 (*2-89021-210-6*, Pub. by La Courte Ech) Firefly Bks Ltd.

Parc National de Tal, Cote D'Ivoire: Synthese des Connaissances. Ed. by E. P. Riezebos et al. (Tropenbos Technical Ser.: No. 8). (Illus.). 322p. 1994. pap. 63.00 incl. disk (*90-5113-020-1*, Pub. by Backhuys Pubs) Balogh.

***Parcel Arrived Safely: Tied with String: My Autobiography.** Michael Crawford. (Illus.). 384p. 2000. 24.95 (*0-7126-8440-9*, Pub. by CEN3) Trafalgar.

***Parcel Based GIS.** Anne Vernez Moudon. 416p. 2000. text 79.95 (*0-471-37163-7*) Wiley.

***Parcel for Stanley.** Ian Whybrow. (J). 1999. pap. text 6.95 (*1-86233-082-4*) Levinson Bks.

Parcel for Stanley. Ian Whybrow. LC 99-228075. (Illus.). 32p. (J). (ps-3). 1998. 14.95 (*1-899607-53-6*) Sterling.

Parcel of Patterns. Jill Paton Walsh. LC 83-48143. 144p. (YA). 1992. pap. 3.95 (*0-374-45743-3*) FS&G.

Parcel of Patterns. Jill Paton Walsh. 137p. (YA). (gr. 7 up). pap. 3.95 (*0-8072-1485-X*) Listening Lib.

Parcel of Patterns. Jill Paton Walsh. 1995. 17.75 (*0-8446-6819-2*) Peter Smith.

Parcel of Patterns. Jill Paton Walsh. 1992. 9.05 (*0-606-02412-3*, Pub. by Turtleback) Demco.

Parceling Out Land in Baltimore, 1632-1796. Garrett Power. (Illus.). 56p. (Orig.). 1993. pap. 6.00 (*0-938420-37-2*) MD Hist.

Parcella, '88. Ed. by G. K. Wolf et al. (Lecture Notes in Computer Science Ser.: Vol. 342). vii, 380p. 1989. 43.00 (*0-387-50647-0*) Spr-Verlag.

P

An Asterisk (*) at the beginning of an entry indicates that the title is appearing for the first time.

***Parcells.** New York Daily News Editors. (Illus.). 304p. 2000. 22.95 (*1-58261-146-7*) Sports Pub.

***Parcells: A Biography.** Bill Gutman. (Illus.). 320p. 2000. 25.00 (*0-7867-0731-3*, Pub. by Carroll & Graf) Publishers Group.

Parchment Boat. Moya Cannon. LC 98-102742. 48p. 1998. 24.95 (*1-85235-202-7*, Pub. by Gallery Pr); pap. 14.95 (*1-85235-201-9*, Pub. by Gallery Pr) Dufour.

Parchment Craft. Janet Wilson. 80p. 1996. pap. 17.95 (*0-85532-796-0*, 960, Pub. by Srch Pr) A Schwartz & Co.

Parchment Craft: Over 15 Original Projets Plus Dozens of New Design Ideas. Martha Ospina. LC 98-41226. 80p. 1998. 18.95 (*1-57990-095-X*, Pub. by Lark Books) Random.

Parchment, Guns & Constitutional Order: Classical Liberalism, Public Choice & Constitutional Democracy. Richard E. Wagner. (Shaftesbury Papers: Vol. 3). 84p. 1993. pap. 13.00 (*1-85278-839-9*) E Elgar.

Parchment Peace: The United States Senate & the Washington Conference, 1921-1922. John C. Vinson. LC 84-6731. 259p. (C). 1984. reprint ed. lib. bdg. 65.00 (*0-313-24532-0*, VIPA, Greenwood Pr) Greenwood.

Parchment, Printing, & Hypermedia: Communication & World Order Transformation. Ronald J. Deibert. LC 97-15336. (New Directions in World Politics Ser.). (Illus.). 344p. 1997. pap. 19.50 (*0-231-10713-7*); lib. bdg. 52.00 (*0-231-10712-9*) Col U Pr.

Parchment, Quill & Verse, Vol. 1. Ed. by Jef Sturm. 300p. 1998. write for info. (*1-888680-27-X*) Poetry Guild.

Parchments of Gender: Deciphering the Body of Antiquity. Ed. by Maria Wyke. LC 98-8002. 304p. 1999. text 72.00 (*0-19-815080-6*) OUP.

Parcival. Friedrich De La Motte Fouque. Ed. by Christoph Lorenz. (Werke II. Abteilung: Bd. 6). 630p. 1997. 125.00 (*3-487-10329-X*) G Olms Pubs.

Parcours Linguistiques de Discours Specialises: Actes du Colloque en Sorbonne (Paris, Septembre 1992) 2nd ed. Ed. by Sophie Moirand et al. (Sciences pour la Communication Ser.: Vol. 41). (FRE.). 404p. 1995. 60.95 (*3-906751-28-7*, Pub. by P Lang) P Lang Pubng.

Parcourse de L'Ombre: Les Trois Indecidables. Bertrand St. Sernin. (FRE.). 200p. 1994. pap. text 31.00 (*2-88124-967-1*) Gordon & Breach.

Parda: A Study of Muslim Women's Life in Northern India, 8. Cora Vreede-de Stuers. LC 70-1402. (Samenlevingen Buiten Europa Non-European Societies Ser.: No. 8). (Illus.). 128p. 1981. reprint ed. lib. bdg. 59.50 (*0-313-22915-5*, VRPA) Greenwood.

Pardee Holler: An Easy Taylor Mystery. Roland Keller. (An Easy Taylor Mystery Ser.). 256p. (Orig.). 1996. pap. 8.95 (*0-9651928-0-6*) PKA Publns.

P'Ardee's Party. Paula M. Vance. LC 95-92156. (Illus.). 36p. (J). (gr. k-4). 1995. pap. 9.95 (*0-9646349-0-2*) Plan Research.

Pardes Rimonim: A Marriage Manual for the Jewish Family. rev. ed. Moshe D. Tendler. (Illus.). 160p. 1988. pap. 11.95 (*0-88125-144-5*) Ktav.

Pardner & Freddie: A Puppet Play. Courtaney Brooks. (Illus.). (J). (gr. k up). 1983. pap. text 2.50 (*0-941274-03-9*) Belnice Bks.

Pardners. Rex Ellingwood Beach. LC 74-101792. (Short Story Index Reprint Ser.). 1977. 20.95 (*0-8369-3180-7*) Ayer.

Pardners. Rex Ellingwood Beach. (Collected Works of Rex Ellingwood Beach). 278p. 1998. reprint ed. lib. bdg. 88.00 (*1-58201-538-4*) Classic Bks.

Pardners, Bks. 1 & 2. Stan Lynde. LC 90-84936. (Illus.). 88p. (J). (gr. 3 up). 1991. pap. 14.95 (*1-886370-14-1*) Cttnwd Pub.

Pardners: Three Stories on Friendship. Blaine M. Yorgason & Brenton Yorgason. (Illus.). 64p. (Orig.). (YA). (gr. 9 up). 1988. pap. 3.95 (*0-929985-05-2*) Jackman Pubng.

Pardo Expeditions, 1565-1566. C. D. Huneycutt & Roy Blalock, Jr. (Illus.). 100p. 1988. pap. 12.95 (*0-915153-31-9*) Gold Star Pr.

Pardon. James M. Grippando. 336p. 1995. mass mkt. 6.50 (*0-06-109286-X*, Harp PBks) HarpC.

Pardon: A Novel. large type ed. James M. Grippando. LC 94-40737. 1994. 24.95 (*1-56895-159-0*) Wheeler Pub.

Pardon? Said the Giraffe. Colin West. LC 85-45750. (Illus.). 24p. (J). (ps-2). 1986. lib. bdg. 11.89 (*0-397-32173-2*) HarpC Child Bks.

Pardon & Amnesty under Lincoln & Johnson: The Restoration of the Confederates to Their Rights & Privileges, 1861-1898. Jonathon T. Dorris. LC 77-5940. 459p. 1977. lib. bdg. 59.75 (*0-8371-9646-9*, Greenwood Pr) Greenwood.

Pardon Gentles All. Mary Nash Pollard. LC 96-94138. 200p. (Orig.). 1996. pap. 7.95 (*0-9652662-0-6*) Littlefish Ltd.

***Pardon Me, But Aren't You... ?** Daniel Lievanos. LC 99-96743. 2000. pap. 8.95 (*0-533-13344-0*) Vantage.

Pardon Me, but Your References Are Showing! 32 Proven & Fun Activities to Build Reference Skills for Grades 4-8. 2nd ed. Teddy Meister. LC 96-4320. 48p. 1996. pap. 12.95 (*0-917846-80-X*, Alleyside) Highsmith Pr.

Pardon Me, Do You Speak Computer? Jim Ciano. (Illus.). 120p. (Orig.). 1994. pap. 19.95 (*1-888672-04-8*) J Ciano Pubng.

Pardon Me, Your Manners Are Showing! Professional Etiquette, Protocol & Diplomacy. Bruce Gjovig. Ed. by Mae M. Blackmore. LC 92-90582. (Illus.). 72p. (Orig.). (C). 1992. pap. 10.00 (*0-9626855-1-8*) Ctr for Innov.

Pardon Me, You're Stepping on My Eyeball. Paul Zindel. 240p. (YA). (gr. 8-12). 1993. mass mkt. 4.50 (*0-553-26690-X*) Bantam.

Pardon Me, You're Stepping on My Eyeball! Paul Zindel. 1977. 9.09 (*0-606-01198-6*, Pub. by Turtleback) Demco.

Pardon My Allusion. Del Corey. (Illus.). 64p. (Orig.). 1997. pap. 10.00 (*1-56439-064-0*) Ridgeway.

Pardon My Backcast. Alan Pratt. LC 96-209893. (Illus.). 80p. 1996. pap. 6.95 (*1-57188-059-3*) F Amato Pubns.

Pardon My Dust . . . I'm Remodeling: Build Your Character, Experience Your Self-Esteem. Casey Chaney. Ed. by Lisa Haqq & Berdell Moffett. 128p. (Orig.). (C). 1990. pap. text 8.95 (*0-9626403-0-1*) Mocha Pub.

Pardon of St. Anne. William Palmer. 256p. 1997. pap. 17.95 (*0-224-04311-0*, Pub. by Jonathan Cape) Trafalgar.

Pardoner & the Friar. John Heywood. LC 70-133675. (Tudor Facsimile Texts. Old English Plays Ser.: No. 13). reprint ed. 59.50 (*0-404-53313-2*) AMS Pr.

Pardoner's Prologue. Geoffrey Chaucer. (Longman Critical Essays Ser.). Date not set. pap. text. write for info. (*0-582-06049-4*, Pub. by Addison-Wesley) Longman.

Pardoner's Prologue & Tale from the Canterbury Tales. 2nd ed. Geoffrey Chaucer. Ed. by J. Winny. (Selected Tales from Chaucer Ser.). 111p. (C). 1994. pap. text 10.95 (*0-521-46818-3*) Cambridge U Pr.

Pardoner's Wallet. Samuel M. Crothers. LC 78-39161. (Essay Index Reprint Ser.). 1977. reprint ed. 23.95 (*0-8369-2685-4*) Ayer.

Pardons: Justice, Mercy, & the Public Interest. Kathleen D. Moore. 288p. 1997. reprint ed. pap. 18.95 (*0-19-511394-2*) OUP.

Pardoxes of Group Life: Understanding Conflict, Paralysis, & Movement in Group Dynamics. Kenwyn K. Smith & David N. Berg. LC 97-25647. (Joint Publication of the Jossey-Bass Education Series & the Jossey-Bass Higher & Adult Education Ser.). 1997. 25.00 (*0-7879-3948-X*) Jossey-Bass.

***Pards.** Texas Bix Bender Staff. (Small Treasures Ser.: Vol. 4). (Illus.). 60p. 2000. 5.95 (*1-58685-000-8*) Gibbs Smith Pub.

Pare Lorentz & the Documentary Film. Robert L. Snyder. LC 93-22828. (Illus.). 248p. (C). 1993. reprint ed. pap. 15.95 (*0-87417-231-4*) U of Nev Pr.

Paredes Hablan - Talking Walls. Margy Burns Knight. Tr. by Clarita Kohen. (SPA., Illus.). 32p. 1992. pap. 8.95 (*0-88448-157-3*) Tilbury Hse.

Paredes Hablan/Talking Walls: Cuentan Mas Historias/The Stories Continue. Margy Burns Knight. Tr. by Clarita Kohen. (SPA.). (J). (gr. 3-8). 1996. 17.95 (*0-88448-166-2*); pap. 8.95 (*0-88448-167-0*) Tilbury Hse.

Paregentan (Thanksgiving) Hovhannes Toumanian. Ed. by Ohannes Hannessian. (ARM., Illus.). 12p. (J). 1985. pap. 3.50 (*1-58253-003-3*) Shirak.

Pareils a des Enfants. Marc Bernard. (FRE.). 1979. pap. 11.95 (*0-7859-1887-6*, 2070371034) Fr & Eur.

Pareja Abierta (Asking for Trouble) Miranda Lee. (Harlequin Bianca - Harlequin Presents Ser.: Vol. 360).Tr. of Asking for Trouble. (ENG & SPA.). 1996. per. 3.50 (*0-373-33360-9*) Harlequin Bks.

***Pareja de Tres.** Catherine George.Tr. of Couple of Three. (SPA.). 2000. per. 3.50 (*0-373-33547-4*) Harlequin Bks.

***Pareja Humana: Su Vida, Muerte y Estructura.** rev. ed. Jean G. Lemaine. 358p. 1999. pap. 8.99 (*968-16-2140-9*) Fondo CA.

Pareja Sensual. Ruth K. Westheimer. (SPA.). 1997. pap. 8.98 (*968-403-852-6*) Selector.

***Parent 98-99.** 208p. (C). 1998. text 7.00 (*0-536-01094-3*) Pearson Custom.

Parent - Child Learning Library: Communication. Educational Assessment Publishing Company Staff. (Illus.). 32p. (J). (ps). 1991. text 10.95 (*0-7854-0232-2*, 15126) Am Guidance.

Parent - Child Learning Library: Communication English Big Book. Educational Assessment Publishing Company Staff. (Illus.). 32p. (J). (gr. k-3). 1991. text 18.95 (*0-7854-0100-8*, 15127) Am Guidance.

Parent - Child Learning Library: Communication Spanish Big Book. Educational Assessment Publishing Company Staff. (SPA., Illus.). 32p. (J). (gr. k-3). 1991. text 18.95 (*0-7854-0101-6*, 15427) Am Guidance.

Parent - Child Learning Library: Communication Spanish Edition. Educational Assessment Publishing Company Staff. (SPA.). 32p. (J). (ps). 1991. text 10.95 (*0-7854-0180-6*, 15426) Am Guidance.

Parent - Child Learning Library: Courtesy. Educational Assessment Publishing Company Staff. (Illus.). 32p. (J). (ps). 1991. text 10.95 (*0-7854-0233-0*, 15131) Am Guidance.

Parent - Child Learning Library: Courtesy English Big Book. Educational Assessment Publishing Company Staff. (Illus.). 32p. (J). (gr. k-3). 1991. text 18.95 (*0-7854-0102-4*, 15132) Am Guidance.

Parent - Child Learning Library: Courtesy Spanish Big Book. Educational Assessment Publishing Company Staff. (SPA., Illus.). 32p. (J). (gr. k-3). 1991. text 18.95 (*0-7854-0103-2*, 15432) Am Guidance.

Parent - Child Learning Library: Courtesy Spanish Edition. Educational Assessment Publishing Company Staff. (SPA.). 32p. (J). 1991. text 10.95 (*0-7854-0181-4*, 15431) Am Guidance.

Parent - Child Learning Library: Drug Information. Educational Assessment Publishing Company Staff. (Illus.). 32p. (J). (gr. k-3). 1991. text 10.95 (*0-7854-0229-2*, 15111) Am Guidance.

Parent - Child Learning Library: Drug Information English Big Book. Educational Assessment Publishing Company Staff. (Illus.). 32p. (J). (gr. k-3). 1991. text 18.95 (*0-7854-0118-0*, 15112) Am Guidance.

Parent - Child Learning Library: Drug Information Spanish Big Book. Educational Assessment Publishing Company Staff. (SPA., Illus.). 32p. (J). (gr. k-3). 1991. text 18.95 (*0-7854-0119-9*, 15412) Am Guidance.

Parent - Child Learning Library: Drug Information Spanish Edition. Educational Assessment Publishing Company Staff. (SPA., Illus.). 32p. (J). (ps). 1991. text 10.95 (*0-7854-0176-8*, 15411) Am Guidance.

Parent - Child Learning Library: Health Relationships Spanish Big Book. Educational Assessment Publishing Company Staff. (SPA., Illus.). 32p. (J). (gr. k-3). 1991. text 18.95 (*0-7854-0121-0*, 15417) Am Guidance.

Parent - Child Learning Library: Healthy Relationships. Educational Assessment Publishing Company Staff. (Illus.). 32p. (J). (gr. k-3). 1991. text 10.95 (*0-7854-0230-6*, 15116) Am Guidance.

Parent - Child Learning Library: Healthy Relationships English Big Book. Educational Assessment Publishing Company Staff. (Illus.). 32p. (J). (gr. k-3). 1991. text 18.95 (*0-7854-0120-2*, 15117) Am Guidance.

Parent - Child Learning Library: Healthy Relationships Spanish Edition. Educational Assessment Publishing Company Staff. (SPA.). 32p. (J). (ps). 1991. text 10.95 (*0-7854-0177-6*, 15416) Am Guidance.

Parent - Child Learning Library: Honesty. Educational Assessment Publishing Company Staff. (Illus.). 32p. (J). (ps-k). 1991. text 10.95 (*0-7854-0227-6*, 15101) Am Guidance.

Parent - Child Learning Library: Honesty English Big Book. Educational Assessment Publishing Company Staff. (Illus.). 32p. (J). (gr. k-3). 1991. text 18.95 (*0-7854-0113-X*, 15102) Am Guidance.

Parent - Child Learning Library: Honesty Spanish Big Book. Educational Assessment Publishing Company Staff. (SPA., Illus.). 32p. (J). (gr. k-3). 1991. text 18.95 (*0-7854-0112-1*, 15402) Am Guidance.

Parent - Child Learning Library: Honesty Spanish Edition. Educational Assessment Publishing Company Staff. (SPA., Illus.). 32p. (J). (ps). 1991. text 10.95 (*0-7854-0179-2*, 15401) Am Guidance.

Parent - Child Learning Library: Responsibility. Educational Assessment Publishing Company Staff. (Illus.). 32p. (J). (gr. k-3). 1991. text 10.95 (*0-7854-0231-4*, 15121) Am Guidance.

Parent - Child Learning Library: Responsibility English Big Book. Educational Assessment Publishing Company Staff. (Illus.). 32p. (J). 1991. text 18.95 (*0-7854-0114-8*, 15122) Am Guidance.

Parent - Child Learning Library: Responsibility Spanish Edition. Educational Assessment Publishing Company Staff. (SPA.). 32p. (J). (ps). 1991. text 18.95 (*0-7854-0115-6*, 15422) Am Guidance.

Parent - Child Learning Library: Self-Esteem. Educational Assessment Publishing Company Staff. (Illus.). 40p. (J). 1991. text 10.95 (*0-7854-0228-4*, 15106) Am Guidance.

Parent - Child Learning Library: Self-Esteem English Big Book. Educational Assessment Publishing Company Staff. (Illus.). 40p. (J). (gr. k-3). 1991. text 18.95 (*0-7854-0116-4*, 15107) Am Guidance.

Parent - Child Learning Library: Self-Esteem Spanish Big Book. Educational Assessment Publishing Company Staff. (SPA., Illus.). 40p. (J). (gr. k-3). 1991. text 18.95 (*0-7854-0117-2*, 15407) Am Guidance.

Parent - Child Learning Library: Self-Esteem Spanish Edition. Educational Assessment Publishing Company Staff. (SPA.). 40p. (J). (ps). 1991. text 10.95 (*0-7854-0175-X*, 15406) Am Guidance.

Parent - Child Learning Library: Your Uniqueness. Educational Assessment Publishing Company Staff. (Illus.). 32p. (J). (ps-k). 1991. text 10.95 (*0-7854-0234-9*, 15136) Am Guidance.

Parent - Child Learning Library: Your Uniqueness English Big Book. Educational Assessment Publishing Company Staff. (Illus.). 32p. (J). (gr. k-3). 1991. text 18.95 (*0-7854-0104-0*, 15137) Am Guidance.

Parent - Child Learning Library: Your Uniqueness Spanish Big Book. Educational Assessment Publishing Company Staff. (SPA., Illus.). 32p. (J). (gr. k-3). 1991. text 18.95 (*0-7854-0105-9*, 15437) Am Guidance.

Parent - Child Learning Library: Your Uniqueness Spanish Edition. Educational Assessment Publishing Company Staff. (SPA.). 32p. (J). (ps). 1991. text 10.95 (*0-7854-0182-2*, 15436) Am Guidance.

Parent - Infant Communication: A Family-Centered Curriculum of Listening & Communication Skills Development for Children Birth - 4 Years of Age with Hearing Loss. 4th rev. ed. Valerie Schuyler & Jayne Sowers. 268p. 1998. ring bd. 55.00 (*1-883204-09-7*) Hearing & Speech.

Parent - Teen Breakthrough: The Relationship Approach. Mira Kirshenbaum & Charles Foster. 320p. (Orig.). 1991. pap. 13.95 (*0-452-26616-5*, Plume) Dutton Plume.

Parent Academy. Joseph Jones & Earl Jones. 20p. 1988. pap. 139.50 (*0-685-29118-9*) Academy Concepts.

Parent Activity Cards: Birth to Age 12 - The Marazon Classroom System. Renee A. Marazon. Ed. by David A. Marazon. 96p. 1997. pap. text. write for info. (*1-889114-05-7*) Maps for Life.

Parent Activity Cards: Birth to Age 12 - The Marazon Parent System. Renee A. Marazon. Ed. by David A. Marazon. 96p. 1997. pap. text. write for info. (*1-889114-08-1*) Maps for Life.

Parent Adolescent Communication. Florence Cherry. Ed. by Trudie Calvert. 76p. 1996. ring bd. 10.50 (*1-57753-088-8*, 321HDFS54) Corn Coop Ext.

Parent-Adolescent Relationships. Ed. by Brian K. Barber & Boyd C. Rollins. 254p. (Orig.). (C). 1989. pap. text 25.00 (*0-8191-7744-X*) U Pr of Amer.

Parent & Child. J. W. Byers. 60p. pap. 1.50 (*0-686-29132-8*) Faith Pub Hse.

Parent & Child. Ellyn Satter. Ed. by David Bull et al. (Illus.). 58p. 1985. pap. 2.50 (*0-933161-04-2*) Better H Prog.

Parent & Child: An International Collection of Literature, Philosophy, & Poetry Specially Selected for Book Discussion Groups by the Great Books Foundation. Ed. & Intro. by Great Bks. Foundation Staff. (Fiftieth Anniversary Ser.). 368p. (Orig.). 1997. pap. 14.95 (*1-880323-76-1*) Great Bks Found.

Parent & Child: Understanding the Generation Gap. James Deyo. (Illus.). (Orig.). 1994. pap. 4.00 (*0-9642851-0-X*) Deyo Prods.

Parent & Child Relations. John M. Carlevale. 256p. (C). 1991. pap. text 16.95 (*0-940139-23-5*) Consortium RI.

Parent & Child Relations. 2nd ed. John M. Carlevale. (Illus.). 292p. 1999. text 22.95 (*0-940139-49-9*) Consortium RI.

Parent & Community Involvement in Education. Barry Rutherford. LC 97-174276. 142p. 1997. pap. 11.00 (*0-16-048890-7*) USGPO.

***Parent & Educators' Drug Reference: A Guide to Common Medical Conditions & Drugs Used in School.** Alan P. Agins. 1999. pap. 34.95 (*1-55766-429-3*) P H Brookes.

Parent & Educators Title IX Team Project Workshop Kit: P. E. T. T. Project. Linda J. Carpenter & Vivian Acosta. 63p. 1995. ring bd., wbk. ed. 15.00 (*0-88314-803-X*, 303-10036) AAHPERD.

Parent & Teacher As Partners: Issues & Challenges. Robert E. Rockwell et al. LC 95-75403. 336p. (C). 1995. pap. text 35.00 (*0-15-500483-2*, Pub. by Harcourt Coll Pubs) Harcourt.

Parent & the Fatally Ill Child: A Demonstration of Parent Participation in a Hospital Pediatric Department. Maurice B. Hamovitch. 152p. 1964. 12.00 (*0-940876-01-9*) City Hope.

***Parent Articles about ADHD.** Clare B. Jones. 200p. 1999. pap. 49.00 (*0-12-784462-7*) Acad Pr.

Parent Articles for Early Intervention. Ed. by Marsha D. Klein. (Illus.). 220p. 1990. pap. text 57.00 (*0-7616-7549-3*) Commun Skill.

Parent Articles 1: Enhance Parent Involvement in Language Learning. Ed. by Margaret Schrader. (Illus.). 222p. 1987. pap. text 57.00 (*0-7616-7439-X*) Commun Skill.

***Parent as Mystic, Mystic as Parent.** David Spangler. 208p. 2000. pap. 12.00 (*1-57322-778-1*, Riverhd Trade) Berkley Pub.

Parent as Mystic, Mystic as Parent. David Spangler. LC 98-36005. 208p. 1998. 21.95 (*1-57322-106-6*, Riverhead Books) Putnam Pub Group.

Parent Book. Harold Bessell & Thomas Kelly. LC 77-71461. (Creative Parenting Ser.). (Illus.). (C). 1977. pap. 9.95 (*0-915190-15-X*, JP9015-X) Jalmar Pr.

Parent Care-Helper. Jonathan Silver. 27p. 1998. pap. 10.00 (*1-892870-00-2*) Best Years Inc.

Parent-Centered Early School: Highland Community School of Milwaukee. Michael R. Williams. Ed. by David Fetterman. LC 96-48330. (Studies in Education & Culture: Vol. 10). (Illus.). 224p. 1997. text 50.00 (*0-8153-2399-9*, SS1116) Garland.

Parent-Child Activities: Threes & Fours. 1978. 9.00 (*0-939418-18-5*) Ferguson-Florissant.

Parent Child & Adolescent: A Handbook for Family Interaction. Victor M. Uribe. LC 98-130282. (Illus.). 189p. 1997. pap. 18.00 (*1-886094-49-7*) Chicago Spectrum.

Parent-Child Connection: Your Guide to Baby & Child Behavior in the First Six Years. Arnold Rincover. 208p. 1990. per. 8.95 (*0-671-68164-8*) PB.

Parent-Child Development Program. Leland E. Pulley. 400p. 1999. 34.95 (*0-9611282-2-4*); pap. 29.95 (*0-9611282-3-2*) Stewardship Enters.

Parent-Child Game: The Proven Key to a Happier Family. Sue Jenner. 288p. 1999. 24.95 (*1-58234-038-2*) Bloomsbury Pubg.

Parent-Child Interaction & Developmental Disabilities: Theory, Research, & Intervention. Ed. by Kofi Marfo. LC 87-25908. 395p. 1988. 69.50 (*0-275-92835-7*, C2835, Praeger Pubs) Greenwood.

Parent-Child Interaction & Parent-Child Relations. Ed. by Marion Perlmutter. (Minnesota Symposia on Child Psychology Ser.: Vol. 17). 208p. 1984. text 39.95 (*0-89859-380-8*) L Erlbaum Assocs.

Parent-Child Interaction in Transition, 10. Ed. by George Kurian. LC 85-27208. (Contributions in Family Studies: No. 10). (Illus.). 416p. 1986. 69.50 (*0-313-25108-8*, KPA/, Greenwood Pr) Greenwood.

Parent-Child Interaction Therapy: A Step-by-Step Guide for Clinicians. Toni L. Hembree-Kigin & Cheryl B. McNeil. (Clinical Child Psychology Library). (Illus.). 184p. (C). 1995. 42.00 (*0-306-44976-5*, Kluwer Plenum); pap. 23.00 (*0-306-45024-0*, Kluwer Plenum) Kluwer Academic.

Parent-Child Manual on Daycare. Charlene M. Solomon. 1989. mass mkt. 5.95 (*0-8125-9468-1*, Pub. by Tor Bks) St Martin.

Parent-Child Manual on Latchkey Kids. Charlene M. Solomon. 1989. mass mkt. 5.95 (*0-8125-9466-5*, Pub. by Tor Bks) St Martin.

Parent-Child Play: Descriptions & Implications. Kevin MacDonald. LC 92-20562. (SUNY Series, Children's Play in Society). 389p. (C). 1993. pap. text 21.95 (*0-7914-1464-7*) State U NY Pr.

Parent-Child Play: Descriptions & Implications. Ed. by Kevin MacDonald. LC 92-20562. (SUNY Series, Children's Play in Society). 389p. (C). 1993. text 64.50 (*0-7914-1463-9*) State U NY Pr.

Parent-Child Relations: An Introduction to Parenting. 5th ed. Jerry J. Bigner. LC 96-40941. 600p. 1997. 65.00 (*0-13-602038-0*) P-H.

Parent-Child Relations: Contemporary Approaches & Issues. George W. Holden. 224p. 1995. pap. text. write for info. (*0-697-14576-X*) Brown & Benchmark.

Parent Child Relations Throughout Life. Ed. by Kathleen McCartney & Karl A. Pillemer. 304p. 1991. text 59.95 (*0-8058-0822-1*) L Erlbaum Assocs.

P

An Asterisk (*) at the beginning of an entry indicates that the title is appearing for the first time.

Parent-Child Retreats: Spiritual Experiences for Children Ages 3-6 & Their Parents. Maggie Pike et al. Ed. by Kathy Coffey & Dirk DeVries. LC 97-217782. (Illus.). 224p. 1997. pap. 14.95 (*1-889108-16-2*) Liv Good News.

Parent Child Retreats: Spiritual Experiences for Children Ages 7-10 & Their Parents. Mary A. Figlino et al. Ed. by Kathy Coffey et al. (Illus.). 216p. 1996. 14.95 (*1-889108-37-5*) Liv Good News.

Parent-Child Separation: Psychosocial Effects on Development. Faren R. Akins et al. LC 81-7304. 368p. 1981. 95.00 (*0-306-65196-3*, Kluwer Plenum) Kluwer Academic.

Parent-Child Socialization in Diverse Cultures. Ed. by Jaipaul L. Roopnarine et al. (Advances in Applied Developmental Psychology Ser.: Vol. 5). 336p. (C). 1992. text 73.25 (*0-89391-849-0*) Ablx Pub.

Parent Communication. Barbara Gruber. (Instant Idea Bks.). (Illus.). 64p. 1989. 7.95 (*0-86734-080-0*, FS-8318) Schaffer Pubns.

Parent Connection: A Health Resource for Parents of Teens. Susan Boe. Ed. by David Mackin. (Parent Connection for Total Health Ser.). (Illus.). 313p. 1997. spiral bd., wbk. ed. 11.95 (*0-9646843-5-7*) RiversEdge Pub.

Parent Contracts: Parent Contracts to Improve School Behaviors. Susan Smith. LC 96-79862. 32p. (Orig.). 1997. pap. 7.95 (*1-57543-021-5*) Mar Co Prods.

Parent Control of Schools: Denver Flunks the Chicago Test: Will CDM Mean 'Can't Do Much' or 'Consumers Demand More'? Edward L. Lederman. (Issue Papers: No. 6-91). 18p. 1991. pap. text 8.00 (*1-57655-039-7*) Independ Inst.

Parent Difference: Uniting School, Family, & Community. 2nd rev. ed. Kathy Barclay & Elizabeth Boone. LC 96-78398. (Illus.). 263p. 1996. pap. 32.95 (*1-57517-073-6*, 1467) SkyLght.

Parent Directory: Success by 6. United Way of Minneapolis Area Staff. 104p. 1996. pap. write for info. (*1-887418-01-6*) United Way MN.

Parent Education: A Survey of the Minnesota Program, Vol. 17. Edith Davis & Esther McGinnis. LC 76-141544. (University of Minnesota Institute of Child Welfare Monographs: No. 17). (Illus.). 153p. 1975. reprint ed. lib. bdg. 22.50 (*0-8371-5891-5*, CWDP) Greenwood.

Parent Education: Parents As Partners. Dorothy Knopper. (Professional Development Series, Current Themes in Gifted Education). 76p. 1997. reprint ed. pap. text 14.25 (*0-9638228-4-5*) Open Space Comn.

Parent Education: The Contributions of Ira J. Gordon. Patricia P. Olmsted et al. Ed. by Sylvia Sunderlin. LC 80-12211. (Illus.). 64p. (Orig.). 1980. 4.75 (*0-87173-094-4*) ACEI.

Parent Education & Elementary Counseling. Jackie Lamb & Wesley Lamb. LC 77-12942. (New Vistas in Counseling Ser.: Vol. V). 151p. 1978. 29.95 (*0-87705-318-9*, Kluwer Acad Hman Sci) Kluwer Academic.

Parent Education & Public Policy. Ed. by Ron Haskins et al. LC 83-12260. (Child & Family Policy Ser.: Vol. 3). 368p. 1983. text 73.25 (*0-89391-173-9*) Ablx Pub.

Parent Education As Early Childhood Intervention: Emerging Directions in Theory, Research & Practice. Ed. by Purdue University Staff et al. (Advances in Applied Developmental Psychology Ser.: Vol. 3). 256p. (C). 1988. text 73.25 (*0-89391-502-5*) Ablx Pub.

Parent Education for Early Childhood: Child-Rearing Concepts & Program Content for the Student & Practicing Professional. Christine Z. Cataldo. LC 86-14573. 288p. reprint ed. pap. 89.30 (*0-7837-6483-9*, 204651000001) Bks Demand.

***Parent Education Library, Set.** Irene D. H. Sasman. (Illus.). 1998. pap. 355.00 (*1-56831-584-8*) Lrning Connect.

***Parent Educator's Ready Reference.** 2nd ed. Dan J. McLaughlin. Ed. by Susan Beatty. 185p. (YA). (gr. 4-12). 1999. pap. 14.95 (*0-9660937-5-5*) CHEP.

Parent Educator's Ready Reference: A Quick Reference Guide to the Four Subject Areas for Parents & Students. Dan J. McLaughlin. Ed. by Susan Beatty. 185p. 1998. pap. 14.95 (*0-9660937-3-9*) CHEP.

***Parent Effectiveness Training: The Proven Program for Raising Responsible Children: 30th Anniversary Edition.** 30th anniversary ed. Thomas Gordon. 352p. 2000. pap. 15.00 (*0-609-80693-9*, Three Riv Pr) Crown Pub Group.

Parent Effectiveness Training: The Tested New Way to Raise Responsible Children. Thomas Gordon. LC 74-130756. 1970. 12.95 (*0-88326-039-5*, Wyden) McKay.

Parent Enabling Policies for Education. 21p. 1991. 10.00 (*1-55516-326-2*, 3116) Natl Conf State Legis.

Parent Enrichment Coordinator. (Career Examination Ser.: C-3676). pap. 39.95 (*0-8373-3676-7*) Nat Learn.

Parent Enrichment Trainer's Manual. rev. ed. Gary B. Wilson & T. Thomas McMurrain. LC 79-92342. (Illus.). 116p. (Orig.). 1987. pap. 14.95 (*0-89334-056-1*) Humanics Ltd.

Parent Guidance in the Nursery School. Margarete Ruben. LC 60-8066. 72p. 1970. reprint ed. 27.50 (*0-8236-4000-0*); reprint ed. pap. 24.95 (*0-8236-8180-7*, 24000) Intl Univs Pr.

Parent Guide to Study Skills. rev. ed. Herman Ohme. Ed. by Jean Ohme. (Illus.). 48p. 1989. pap. 5.00 (*0-936047-06-2*) CA Educ Plan.

Parent Guide to U. S. A. Junior Field Hockey. Rainer Martens. 52p. 1982. 4.00 (*0-317-01164-2*) US Field Hockey.

Parent-H to Survive. Lois F. Akner. 1994. pap. 12.00 (*0-688-13791-1*, Quil) HarperTrade.

Parent Handbook for Water Exploration. National Safety Council Staff. (Emergency Care Ser.). 16p. Date not set. pap. 2.50 (*0-86720-537-7*) Jones & Bartlett.

Parent Handouts. (Looking at Life Ser.). 42p. 1988. write for info. (*1-55672-033-5*) US HHS.

Parent in Control: Restore Order in Your Home & Create a Loving Relationship with Your Adolescent. Gregory Bodenhamer. LC 95-535. 192p. 1995. per. 10.00 (*0-684-80777-7*, Fireside) S&S Trade Pap.

Parent-Infant Habilitation: A Comprehensive Approach to Working with Hearing-Impaired Infants & Toddlers & Their Parents. Valerie Schuyler & Nancy Rushmer. LC 86-83118. (Illus.). 576p. (C). 1987. 40.00 (*0-9618297-2-9*) Hearing & Speech.

Parent-Infant Interaction. CIBA Foundation Staff. LC 77-676760. (CIBA Foundation Symposium: New Ser.: No. 33). 336p. reprint ed. pap. 104.20 (*0-608-10681-X*, 202216100024); reprint ed. pap. 95.80 (*0-608-30668-1*, 2022161) Bks Demand.

Parent-Infant Nursing Science: Paradigms, Phenomena, Methods. Lorraine O. Walker. LC 91-25136. (Illus.). 450p. 1991. 55.00 (*0-8036-9028-2*) Davis Co.

Parent-Infant Relationships. fac. ed. David R. Harvey. LC 86-4122. (Perinatal Practice Ser.: Vol. 4). 189p. 1987. reprint ed. pap. 58.60 (*0-7837-8267-5*, 204904800009) Bks Demand.

Parent Involvement Begins at Birth: How to Engage Parents of Children, Birth Through Age Five. Sally Goldberg. LC 96-42956. 222p. (C). 1997. pap. text 33.00 (*0-205-17415-9*) Allyn.

Parent Involvement Facilitator: Elementary Edition. 300p. 1997. ring bd. 49.95 (*0-914607-45-6*, 1721) Master Tchr.

Parent Involvement Facilitator: Secondary Edition. 200p. 1997. ring bd. 49.95 (*0-914607-46-4*, 1997) Master Tchr.

***Parent Involvement in Children's Education: Efforts by Public Elementary Schools.** Nancy Carey. LC 98-115864. 59p. 1998. pap. 5.00 (*0-16-049388-9*) USGPO.

Parent Involvement in Education: Your Child Can Achieve. Nancy Ridgley. (Illus.). 136p. 1997. pap. 16.00 (*0-8059-4113-4*) Dorrance.

Parent Involvement in the Public Schools: Proposals, Issues, Opportunities. Don Davies. 24p. 1985. pap. 5.95 (*1-56602-005-0*) Research Better.

Parent Involvement Resource Manual. Judith G. Dato. (Illus.). 211p. 1995. write for info. (*1-55997-177-0*) Websters Intl.

Parent Leadership Program Training Manual. Joan Blough et al. (Illus.). 151p. 1996. pap. 20.00 (*0-9642014-3-7*) Inst Fmly Ctr.

Parent Letters for Early Learning. Anthony D. Fredericks & Mary F. Brigham. (Illus.). 80p. (Orig.). 1988. pap. 8.95 (*0-673-38114-5*, GoodYrBooks) Addson-Wesley Educ.

Parent Letters for the Intermediate Grades, Vol. 3337. Learning Letter Staff. Ed. by Karen Hall. (Parent Letters Ser.: Vol. 2). (Illus.). 128p. 1997. pap. 12.98 (*1-57471-233-0*, 3337) Creat Teach Pr.

Parent Letters for the Primary Grades, Vol. 3336. Learning Letter Staff. Ed. by Joellyn T. Cicciarelli. (Parent Letters Ser.). (Illus.). 128p. 1997. pap. 12.98 (*1-57471-232-2*, 3336) Creat Teach Pr.

Parent Letters from Your Parish, Vols. 1-7. Beth B. McNamara et al. Incl. Parent Letters from Your Parish: Letters 1-3. 1994. 9.95 (*0-87973-816-2*); 1994. 16.95 (*0-87973-818-9*) Our Sunday Visitor.

Parent Letters from Your Parish: Letters 1-3 see Parent Letters from Your Parish

Parent Lifesaver: Practical Help for Everyday Childhood Problems. Todd Cartmell. LC 98-24536. (Illus.). 208p. (Orig.). (C). (gr. 13). 1998. pap. 11.99 (*0-8010-5826-0*) Baker Bks.

Parent Manual see Choices That Lead to Lifelong Success

Parent Meeting Models 1. rev. ed. Center for Learning Network Staff. (Parish Ministry Manuals Ser.). 108p. 1989. spiral bd. 15.95 (*1-56077-033-3*) Ctr Learning.

Parent Number for Shrink Wrapped Set of Manual Transmission & Transaxle Guides, 2 vols. pap. text. write for info. (*1-57932-003-1*) Chek-Chart.

Parent-Offspring Conflict & Its Resolution in the European Starling. E. Litovich & H. W. Power. (Ornithological Monographs: Vol. 47). (Illus.). 71p. 1992. 15.00 (*0-935868-58-5*) Am Ornithologists.

***Parent Partners: Workshops to Foster School/Home/Family Partnerships.** Jacqueline Barber. (Illus.). 2000. pap. 19.95 (*0-924886-54-4*, GEMS) Lawrence Science.

Parent Plan. Judith Arnold. 1994. mass mkt. 3.50 (*0-373-70581-6*, 1-70581-3) Harlequin Bks.

Parent Plan. Paula D. Riggs. (Thirty-Six Hours Ser.). 1998. per. 4.50 (*0-373-65016-7*, 1-65016-7) Harlequin Bks.

Parent Plot. Kate William. (Sweet Valley High Ser.: No. 67). (YA). (gr. 7 up). 1990. 8.60 (*0-606-04501-5*, Pub. by Turtleback) Demco.

Parent Points. Amy M. Burke. 44p. (J). 1996. pap. 9.99 (*0-89824-224-X*) Royal Fireworks.

Parent Police: The U. N. Wants Your Children. Ingrid Guzman. LC 95-75886. 48p. 1995. pap. 3.49 (*1-56384-096-0*) Huntington Hse.

Parent Power! A Common-Sense Approach to Parenting in the '90s & Beyond. John K. Rosemond. 358p. (Orig.). 1991. pap. 9.95 (*0-8362-2808-1*) Andrews & McMeel.

Parent Power: Preserving Your Identity Through Realistic Parenting. Bud Zukow & Margaret O. Ryan. LC 92-12853. (Illus.). 195p. (Orig.). 1992. pap. 12.95 (*0-9626184-5-4*, Bramble Bks) Bramble Co.

***Parent Power: 90 Winning Ways to Be Involved & Help Your Child Get the Most Out of School.** Roberta Kirshbaum & Robin Dellabough. LC 98-22591. 304p. (J). 1998. pap. 12.45 (*0-7868-8329-4*, Pub. by Hyperion) Time Warner.

***Parent Power - Child Power: The Win-Win Way to Rasie Your Child.** Helen DeRosis. 2000. pap. 14.95 (*1-57826-043-4*, Pub. by Hatherleigh) Norton.

Parent Programs in Reading: Guidelines for Success. Anthony D. Fredericks & David Conrad Taylor. LC 85-851. 85p. reprint ed. pap. 30.00 (*0-7837-5989-4*, 204579800008) Bks Demand.

Parent Project: A Workshop Approach to Parent Involvement. James Vopat. LC 94-20935. (Illus.). 248p. 1994. pap. text 23.00 (*1-57110-001-6*) Stenhse Pubs.

Parent Relations: Building an Active Partnership. Ed. by Roger Neugebauer. (Best of Exchange Ser.). 48p. (Orig.). (C). 1994. pap. 10.00 (*0-942702-13-1*) Child Care.

Parent Resource Guide for NOVA. rev. ed. Ed. by Karen Toussant. (Illus.). 96p. 1996. pap. 4.95 (*0-9640891-2-2*) Parent Res Guide.

Parent Resource Guide for Suburban Maryland - Washington D. C. 72p. 1995. 4.95 (*0-9640891-1-4*) Parent Res Guide.

Parent-School Collaboration: Feminist Organizational Structures & School Leadership. Mary E. Henry. LC 95-8928. (SUNY Series, the Social Context of Education). 229p. (C). 1996. pap. text 19.95 (*0-7914-2856-7*) State U NY Pr.

Parent Seminars. Center for Learning Network Staff. (Parish Ministry Manuals Ser.). 160p. 1985. spiral bd. 15.95 (*1-56077-034-1*) Ctr Learning.

Parent Shadowing. rev. ed. Carol A. Schroeder & Rose E. Schraufnagel. 81p. 1990. pap. text 9.95 (*0-318-69174-4*) W Bend HS.

Parent Soup A to Z Guide to Your New Baby. Kate Hanley. LC 97-50256. 288p. 1998. pap. 14.95 (*0-8092-2960-9*, 296090, Contemporary Bks) NTC Contemp Pub Co.

Parent Soup A-to-Z Guide to Your Toddler. Kate Hanley & Alan Greene. LC 98-35478. 288p. 1999. pap. 16.95 (*0-8092-2959-5*, 295950, Contemporary Bks) NTC Contemp Pub Co.

Parent Soup Baby Name Finder. Kate Hanley. LC 97-39946. 320p. 1999. pap. 15.95 (*0-8092-2961-7*, 296170, Contemporary Bks) NTC Contemp Pub Co.

Parent Source Resource Directory: 1997 Greater Boston Area, Vol. 5000. Ed. by Jim Hoyt et al. (Illus.). 502p. (Orig.). 1996. pap. 14.95 (*1-890153-03-6*) TMSI.

Parent Source Resource Directory: 1997 Greater Chicago Area, Vol. 5000. Ed. by Jim Hoyt et al. (Illus.). 505p. (Orig.). 1996. pap. 14.95 (*1-890153-00-1*) TMSI.

Parent Source Resource Directory: 1997 Greater Cincinnati Area, Vol. 5000. Ed. by Jim Hoyt et al. (Illus.). 430p. (Orig.). 1996. pap. 14.95 (*1-890153-01-X*) TMSI.

Parent Source Resource Directory: 1997 Greater Philadelphia Area, Vol. 5000. Ed. by Jim Hoyt et al. (Illus.). 485p. (Orig.). 1996. pap. 14.95 (*1-890153-02-8*) TMSI.

Parent Source Resource Directory: 1997 Minneapolis-St. Paul Area, Vol. 5000. Ed. by Jim Hoyt et al. (Illus.). 452p. (Orig.). 1996. pap. 14.95 (*1-890153-04-4*) TMSI.

Parent-Specific Adjustments for Assessment of Recumbent Length & Stature. Ed. by D. Thissen et al. (Monographs in Pediatrics: Vol. 13). (Illus.). x, 90p. 1981. pap. 57.50 (*3-8055-2594-X*) S Karger.

***Parent Stick.** Lynton Smith. LC 99-90735. 168p. 2000. pap. 9.95 (*0-9700939-0-X*) Parent Two Chld.

Parent-Student Instructional Grievance Committees: Helping to Professionalize Education. Don Stewart. (Chance for Instructional Excellence Ser.: Bk. 3). (Illus.). 422p. (Orig.). 1989. 19.45 (*0-913448-16-8*); pap. 14.45 (*0-913448-17-6*) SLATE Servs.

Parent Survival Manual: A Guide to Crisis Resolution in Autism & Related Developmental Disorders. Ed. by Eric Schopler. LC 95-23155. (Illus.). 240p. (C). 1995. pap. 35.00 (*0-306-44977-3*, Plenum Trade) Perseus Pubng.

Parent Survival Training. Marvin Silverman & David A. Lustig. 1988. pap. 15.00 (*0-87980-419-X*) Wilshire.

Parent System: Birth to Age 12. Renee A. Marazon. Ed. by David A. Marazon. 444p. 1997. boxed set 96.00 (*1-889114-07-3*) Maps for Life.

Parent Talk. Willard Abraham. LC 96-41025. (Illus.). 176p. (Orig.). 1996. pap. 14.95 (*1-57022-053-0*, ECS0530) ECS Lrn Systs.

Parent Talk. Thom Davenport. (YouthSearch: Small-Group Resources Ser.: Vol. 10). 64p. 1996. pap. 5.95 (*0-687-05532-6*) Abingdon.

Parent Talk: Words That Empower, Words That Wound. Chick Moorman. (Illus.). 200p. 1998. 24.95 (*0-9616046-4-6*) Prsnl Power Pr.

Parent, Teacher, Child: Working Together in Children's Learning. Dorothy Hamilton & Alex Griffiths. 192p. 1984. pap. 9.95 (*0-416-36730-5*, NO. 9170) Routledge.

Parent Teacher Conference: Facilitator Guide. 2nd rev. ed. Joe Hasenstab. (Illus.). 30p. 1993. pap. 185.00 incl. VHS (*1-892334-02-X*) Perf Lrn Systs.

Parent Teacher Conference: Participant. 2nd rev. ed. Joe Hasenstab. (Illus.). 30p. 1993. pap. 8.00 (*1-892334-03-8*) Perf Lrn Systs.

Parent-Teacher Conference Essentials: Idea Booklet & Pocket Folder Organizer. Karen Sevaly. (Illus.). 16p. 1997. pap., teacher ed., wbk. ed. 3.99 (*1-57882-013-8*, TF-1264) Teachers Friend Pubns.

Parent-Teacher Conferencing. Gerda Lawrence & Madeline C. Hunter. LC 95-12896. 112p. (Orig.). 1978. pap. text 19.95 (*0-8039-6327-0*) Corwin Pr.

Parent-Teacher Conferencing in Early Childhood Education. S. Dianne Lawler. 112p. 1991. pap. 11.95 (*0-8106-0356-X*) NEA.

Parent-Teacher Conferencing Skills Developer Kit. rev. ed. John F. Toker. 35p. (Orig.). 1989. 45.00 (*1-878276-38-7*) Educ Systs Assocs Inc.

Parent-Teacher Partnership: Practical Approaches to Meet Special Educational Needs. Mike Blamires et al. LC 97-202739. (Resource Materials for Teachers Ser.). 112p. 1997. pap. 24.95 (*1-85346-470-8*, Pub. by David Fulton) Taylor & Francis.

Parent Teacher Partnerships: Birth to Age 12 - The Marazon System. Renee A. Marazon. Ed. by David A. Marazon & Sylvia Phillips. (Illus.). 276p. (Orig.). 1995. pap. text 30.00 (*1-889114-02-2*) Maps for Life.

Parent-Teacher Resource Book. Gale Dredge. (Illus.). 200p. (Orig.). 1989. per. 14.95 (*0-685-28887-0*) Parent-Teacher.

Parent-Teen Communication: Toward the Prevention of Unintended Pregnancies. J. Jaccard & P. Dittus. (Recent Research in Psychology Ser.). ix, 118p. 1990. 71.95 (*0-387-97457-1*) Spr-Verlag.

Parent-Teen Manual for Learning to Drive. Warren P. Quensel. (Illus.). 96p. (Orig.). 1994. pap. 9.50 (*0-9636134-0-5*) Safety Ent.

Parent-Teen Relationships. Gail Daniels Hassett. Ed. by Thomas Zanzig. (Horizons Ser.: Level 1, Minicourse 4). (Illus.). 60p. (YA). (gr. 9). 1996. pap. text, student ed. 9.95 (*0-88489-349-9*) St Marys.

***Parent-Tested Ways to Grow Your Child's Confidence.** Silvana Clark. LC 00-24913. 160p. 2000. pap. write for info. (*0-88166-369-7*) Meadowbrook.

***Parent-Tested Ways to Grow Your Child's Confidence.** Silvana Clark. 160p. 2000. per. 8.00 (*0-671-31823-3*) S&S Trade.

Parent Time Curriculum Guide: A Learning Activities Guide for the PACE Family Literacy Program. Lina Cramer. 188p. 1991. ring bd. 35.00 (*1-885429-02-9*) Family Resource.

***Parent Toolkit for Success with Children.** T. Lee Burnham. 150p. 1999. 20.00 (*0-9676686-0-3*) Rocky Mtn Ctr.

Parent Training Today: A Social Necessity. Kerby T. Alvy. LC 94-70800. 377p. (Orig.). 1994. pap. 19.95 (*1-884984-06-1*) Ctr Improve Chld.

Parent Trap. Dallas Schulze et al. 1996. per. 5.99 (*0-373-20122-2*, 1-20122-7) Harlequin Bks.

Parent Traps: Understanding & Overcoming the Pitfalls That All Parents Face. Donna G. Corwin. LC 97-11912. 208p. 1997. pap. 11.95 (*0-312-16961-2*) St Martin.

Parent Traps: Understanding & Overcoming the Pitfalls That All Parents Face, Vol. 1. Donna G. Corwin. 1997. mass mkt. write for info. (*0-312-96166-9*) St Martin.

Parent Volunteer Program - San Antonio: School of the Future. 32p. pap. text 10.00 (*0-9999014-6-X*) DIANE Pub.

Parent Warrior. Karen S. Linamen. 204p. 1993. pap. 10.99 (*1-56476-127-4*, 6-3127, Victor Bks) Chariot Victor.

Parent Warrior: Protecting Your Children through Prayer. Linda Scalf Linamin. LC 98-31892. 224p. 1999. pap. 11.99 (*0-8007-5698-3*) Revell.

Parentage Testing Accreditation Requirements Manual. 2nd ed. Ed. by Richard H. Walker. 67p. (C). 1995. pap. text, lab manual ed. 30.00 (*1-56395-051-0*) Am Assn Blood.

Parental Alienation Syndrome: A Guide for Mental Health & Legal Professionals. 2nd rev. ed. Richard A. Gardner. LC 98-12941. 1998. pap. 35.00 (*0-933812-42-6*) Creative Therapeutics.

Parental & Psychopathology. Ed. by C. Perris et al. LC 94-11557. (Clinical Psychology Ser.). 360p. 1995. 250.00 (*0-471-94226-X*) Wiley.

Parental Authority: The Community & the Law. Julius Cohen et al. LC 80-153. (Illus.). 301p. 1980. reprint ed. lib. bdg. 38.50 (*0-313-22351-3*, COPR, Greenwood Pr) Greenwood.

Parental Behavior in Diverse Societies, No. 40. Ed. by Robert Le Vine et al. LC 85-644581. (New Directions for Child Development Ser.: No. CD 40). 1988. pap. 25.00 (*1-55542-915-7*) Jossey-Bass.

Parental Behavior of Rodents. Ed. by Robert W. Elwood. LC 82-8625. (Wiley-Interscience Publications). 306p. reprint ed. pap. 94.90 (*0-8357-6938-0*, 203799700009) Bks Demand.

Parental Belief Systems: The Psychological Consequences for Children. Ed. by Irving E. Sigel. LC 66-9640. (Illus.). 253p. reprint ed. pap. 78.50 (*0-8357-3119-7*, 203937700012) Bks Demand.

Parental Belief Systems: The Psychological Consequences for Children. 2nd rev. ed. Ed. by Irving E. Sigel et al. 480p. 1992. text 89.95 (*0-8058-0652-0*) L Erlbaum Assocs.

Parental Bereavement. Lieberman. Date not set. 29.95 (*0-465-05444-7*, Pub. by Basic) HarpC.

Parental Care in Mammals. Ed. by David J. Gubernick & Peter H. Klopfer. LC 80-36692. 478p. 1981. 85.00 (*0-306-40533-4*, Plenum Trade) Perseus Pubng.

Parental Choice & Education. Ed. by Mark Halstead. (Books for Teachers). 180p. 1994. pap. 34.00 (*0-7494-1058-2*) Taylor & Francis.

Parental Choice & Educational Policy. Michael Adler et al. (Edinburgh Education & Society Ser.). 228p. 1990. pap. 30.00 (*0-85224-656-0*, Pub. by Edinburgh U Pr) Col U Pr.

Parental Choice & School Ethos: From Theory to Practice. Rina Shapira & Peter W. Cookson. LC 97-15094. 400p. 1997. write for info. (*0-08-042777-4*) Elsevier.

Parental Concerns in College Student Mental Health. Ed. by Leighton C. Whitaker. LC 87-33625. (Journal of College Student Psychotherapy: Vol. 2, Nos. 1-2). (Illus.). 204p. 1988. pap. 3.95 (*0-86656-800-X*) Haworth Pr.

P

Parental Concerns in College Student Mental Health. Ed. by Leighton C. Whitaker. LC 87-33625. (Journal of College Student Psychotherapy: Vol. 2, Nos. 1-2). (Illus.). 204p. 1989. text 6.95 (*0-86656-720-8*) Haworth Pr.

Parental Descriptions of Child Personality: Developmental Antecedents of the Big Five? Ed. by Geldolph A. Kohnstamm et al. LC 97-32503. (Personality & Clinical Psychology Ser.). 200p. 1998. write for info. (*0-8058-2301-8*) L Erlbaum Assocs.

Parental Development. Ed. by Jack Demick et al. 296p. 1993. text 59.95 (*0-8058-1192-3*) L Erlbaum Assocs.

Parental Divorce. Debra Goldentyer. LC 94-32085. (Teen Hotline Ser.). (Illus.). 80p. (YA). (gr. 6 up). 1995. lib. bdg. 25.68 (*0-8114-3817-1*) Raintree Steck-V.

Parental Experience in Midlife. Ed. by Carol D. Ryff & Marsha M. Seltzer. LC 96-12012. (Illus.). 688p. 1996. 39.95 (*0-226-73251-7*) U Ch Pr.

Parental Figures & the Representation of God: A Psychological & Cross-Cultural Study. A. Vergote & A. Tamayo. 267p. (Orig.). 1980. pap. 47.50 (*90-6186-098-9*, Pub. by Leuven Univ) Coronet Bks.

Parental Grief: Solace & Resolution. Dennis Klass. (Death & Suicide Ser.). 248p. 1988. 31.95 (*0-8261-5930-3*) Springer Pub.

Parental Images. 2nd ed. M. Esther Harding. 256p. 1991. pap. 16.95 (*0-938434-62-4*) Sigo Pr.

Parental Income & College Opportunities. H. B. Goetsch. LC 72-176807. (Columbia University. Teachers College. Contributions to Education Ser.: No. 795). reprint ed. 37.50 (*0-404-55795-3*) AMS Pr.

***Parental Involvement: A Practical Guide for Collaboration & Teamwork for Students with Disabilities.** George R. Taylor. LC 00-23451. 2000. write for info. (*0-398-07072-5*) C C Thomas.

Parental Involvement & Peer Tutoring in Mathematics & Science. Keith Topping. LC 98-153257. 1998. pap. 23.95 (*1-85346-541-0*, Pub. by David Fulton) Taylor & Francis.

Parental Involvement & the Political Principle: Why the Existing Governance Structure of Schools Should Be Abolished. Seymour B. Sarason. LC 94-33600. (Education Ser.). 192p. 1995. text 29.95 (*0-7879-0054-0*) Jossey-Bass.

Parental Leave & Child Care: Setting a Research & Policy Agenda. Ed. by Janet S. Hyde & Marilyn J. Essex. (Women in the Political Economy Ser.). 448p. 1991. 59.95 (*0-87722-732-2*) Temple U Pr.

Parental Loss & Achievement. Marvin Eisenstadt et al. xiv, 338p. 1989. 52.50 (*0-8236-4111-2*) Intl Univs Pr.

Parental Loss of a Child. Ed. by Therese A. Rando. LC 86-61549. 570p. (Orig.). 1986. pap. text 22.95 (*0-87822-281-2*, 2812) Res Press.

Parental Participation in Children's Development & Education. Sheila Wolfendale. LC 82-11946. (Special Aspects of Education Ser.: Vol. 3). xvi, 214p. 1983. text 97.00 (*0-677-06060-2*); pap. text 69.00 (*0-677-06065-3*) Gordon & Breach.

Parental Perspectives in Cases of Suspected Child Abuse. Hedy Cleaver. 230p. 1995. pap. 45.00 (*0-11-321786-2*, HM17862, Pub. by Statnry Office) Bernan Associates.

Parental Presence: Reclaiming a Leadership Role in Bringing up Our Children. Haim Omer. LC 99-34352. 160p. 2000. pap. 19.95 (*1-891944-39-8*) Zeig Tucker.

Parental Priorities. Mulligan. LC 97-21621. 344p. 1997. pap. text 24.95 (*0-226-54840-6*); lib. bdg. 60.00 (*0-226-54839-2*) U Ch Pr.

Parental Psychiatric Disorder: Distressed Parents & Their Families. Ed. by Michael Gopfert et al. (Illus.). 382p. (C). 1996. text 125.00 (*0-521-45259-7*); pap. text 44.95 (*0-521-45892-7*) Cambridge U Pr.

Parental Rights: The Contemporary Assault on Traditional Liberties. Ed. by Stephen M. Krason & Robert J. D'Agostino. 208p. (Orig.). 1988. pap. 9.95 (*0-931888-31-X*) Christendom Pr.

Parental Skills for Parenting Children of Color. Ed. by Rose M. Duhon-Sells. LC 91-42619. (Illus.). 128p. 1992. lib. bdg. 59.95 (*0-7734-1655-2*) E Mellen.

Parental Survival. Walter E. Adams. 126p. (Orig.). 1984. pap. 6.95 (*0-937408-30-1*) GMI Pubns Inc.

Parental Unemployment. Ellen Wijnberg. LC 93-25154. (Teen Hotline Ser.). (Illus.). 80p. (J). (gr. 6-9). 1993. lib. bdg. 25.68 (*0-8114-3525-3*) Raintree Steck-V.

Parental Voice: Problems Faced by Parents of the Deaf-Blind, Severely & Profoundly Handicapped Child. Robert Holzberg & Sara Walsh-Rubin. LC 95-30790. 172p. 1995. pap. 28.95 (*0-398-06554-3*) C C Thomas.

Parental Voice: Problems Faced by Parents of the Deaf-Blind, Severely & Profoundly Handicapped Child. Robert Holzberg et al. LC 95-30790. 172p. (C). 1996. 39.95 (*0-398-06553-5*) C C Thomas.

Parentalk Guide to the Childhood Years. S. Chalker. 11.95 (*0-340-72168-5*, Pub. by Hodder & Stought Ltd) Trafalgar.

Parentator (Life of Increase Mather) Cotton Mather. (Notable American Authors Ser.). 1999. reprint ed. lib. bdg. 125.00 (*0-7812-3969-9*) Rprt Serv.

Parentazine: Tips for Parents, Vol. I. Ed. & Compiled by Dee Frances. Date not set. lib. bdg. 15.00 (*1-885519-20-6*) DDDD Pubns.

Parentcare Survival Guide: Helping Your Folks Through the Not-So-Golden Years. Enid Pritikin & Trudy Reece. 256p. 1993. pap. 8.95 (*0-8120-4975-6*) Barron.

Parent/Child & Preschool Aquatic Program Manual. YMCA of the U. S. A. Staff. LC 98-37501. (YMCA Swim Lessons Ser.). (Illus.). 208p. 1999. pap. write for info. (*0-7360-0053-4*) Human Kinetics.

***Parent/Child Game.** Sue Jenner. 288p. 2000. pap. 14.95 (*1-58234-091-9*) Bloomsbury Pubg.

Parente Spirituelle. F. Heritier-Auge & E. Copet-Rougier. (Ordres Sociaux Ser). 304p. 1996. pap. text 41.00 (*2-919875-03-5*) Gordon & Breach.

Parenteral & Enteral Nutrition. 2nd ed. Howard Silberman. (Illus.). 458p. (C). 1989. pap. text 85.00 (*0-8385-7727-X*, A7727-9, Apple Lange Med) McGraw.

Parenteral Quality Control: Sterility, Pyrogen, Particulate, & Package Integrity Testing. 2nd rev. ed. Michael J. Akers. LC 93-25667. (Advances in Parenteral Sciences Ser.: Vol. 5). (Illus.). 400p. 1993. text 130.00 (*0-8247-9088-X*) Dekker.

Parenterale Ernaehrung (Forschung und Praxis) Deutsch-Skandinavisches Symposium, Kopenhagen, 197. Ed. by N. Zoellner. (Beitraege zur Infusionstherapie und Klinische Ernaehrung Ser.: Band 1). (Illus.). 1978. pap. 15.00 (*3-8055-2963-5*) S Karger.

Parenterale Ernaehrung unter besonderer Beruecksichtigung der Fettzufuhr. Ed. by J. Eckart. (Beitraege zur Infusionstherapie und Klinische Ernaehrung Ser.: Vol. 13). (Illus.). 210p. 1986. 58.50 (*3-8055-4164-3*) S Karger.

Parentesis. Alicia Z. Galvan. Ed. by Angela De Hoyos.Tr. of Parenthesis. (SPA., Illus.). 86p. (Orig.). 1997. per. 10.00 (*0-913983-17-9*) M & A Edns.

Parenthese in Ovids Metamorphosen und Ihre Dichterische Funktion. Michael V. Albrecht. (Spudasmata Ser.: Vol. 7). (GER.). 233p. 1994. write for info. (*3-487-00907-2*) G Olms Pubs.

Parenthese in Ovids Metamorphosen und Ihre Dichterische Funktion. Michael Von Albrecht. (GER.). 233p. 1964. write for info. (*0-318-70613-X*) G Olms Pubs.

Parentheses of Blood. rev. ed. Sony L. Tansi. Ed. by Francoise Kourilsky. Tr. by Lorraine Alexander from FRE. 92p. (Orig.). 1996. pap. 10.95 (*0-913745-47-2*) Ubu Repertory.

Parenthesis see Parentesis

Parenthesis. Alicia Z. Galvan. (Illus.). 73p. (Orig.). 1994. pap. 10.00 (*0-9644836-0-2*) Galvart Pub.

Parenthesis in Eternity: Living the Mystical Life. Joel S. Goldsmith. LC 64-10368. 384p. 1986. pap. 18.00 (*0-06-063231-3*, PL 4125, Pub. by Harper SF) HarpC.

Parenthood. Bishops' Committee for Pastoral Research Staff & Practices National Conference of Catholic Bishops. (Marriage Is a Sacrament Ser.). 48p. (Orig.). (C). 1990. pap. 2.95 (*1-55586-352-3*) US Catholic.

Parenthood: Its Psychology & Psychopathology. Ed. by E. James Anthony & Therese Benedek. 648p. 1996. pap. 60.00 (*0-7657-0012-3*) Aronson.

Parenthood: Its Psychology & Psychopathology. Ed. by E. James Anthony & Therese Benedek. LC 75-112005. 650p. 1970. 33.00 (*0-316-04370-2*, Little Brwn Med Div) Lppncott W & W.

Parenthood: Rising to the Challenge of a Lifetime. Bill Hybels. (Interactions). 96p. 1996. pap., student ed. 5.99 (*0-310-20676-6*) Zondervan.

Parenthood: Who's Raising Whom? Strategies for Saving Your Sanity. Michael M. Thomson. Ed. by John Lauritsen. (Illus.). 200p. (Orig.). 1994. pap. 14.95 (*1-883980-00-3*) Yats Esool Prods.

***Parenthood by Proxy.** Laura C. Schlessinger. 288p. 2000. 24.00 (*0-06-019125-2*, Cliff Street) HarperTrade.

Parenthood Decision: Discovering Whether You Are Ready & Willing to Become a Parent. Beverly Engel. LC 98-13932. 256p. 1998. pap. 11.95 (*0-385-48980-3*) Doubleday.

***Parenthood in America: An Encyclopedia, 2 Vols.** Lawrence Balter. 2001. lib. bdg. 150.00 (*1-57607-213-4*) ABC-CLIO.

Parenthood in Modern Society: Legal & Social Issues for the Twenty-First Century. Ed. by John M. Eekelaar & Peter Sarcevic. LC 92-44993. 640p. (C). 1993. lib. bdg. 160.00 (*0-7923-2123-5*) Kluwer Academic.

Parenthood Is Your Greatest Achievement: An Interactive Family, Education & Genealogical Resource Book & Diary. Benjamin A. Benson. 140p. 1993. 12.95 (*0-9637122-0-9*) Partners Educ.

***Parenthood Lost: Healing the Pain after Miscarriage, Stillbirth & Infant Death.** Ed. by Michael R. Berman. LC 00-29257. 224p. 2000. 24.95 (*0-89789-614-9*, Bergin & Garvey) Greenwood.

Parenting. Ed. by Betty Garee. LC 89-85623. 90p. (Orig.). 1989. pap. 7.95 (*0-915708-26-4*) Cheever Pub.

Parenting. Hopson. 256p. (C). 2000. write for info. (*0-471-34569-5*) Wiley.

Parenting. Cheryl Reames. (Lifesearch Ser.). 64p. (Orig.). 1994. pap. 4.95 (*0-687-77868-9*) Abingdon.

Parenting. Serendipity House Staff. (Focus Ser.). 1994. pap. text 4.95 (*1-883419-96-4*) Serendipity Hse.

***Parenting.** Paula Spencer. (Illus.). 384p. 2000. pap. 16.00 (*0-345-41181-1*, Ballantine) Ballantine Pub Grp.

Parenting. 2nd ed. Jane B. Brooks. LC 97-20105. xvi, 345p. 1997. pap. text 26.95 (*1-55934-937-9*, 1937) Mayfield Pub.

***Parenting.** 3rd ed. Jane B. Brooks. LC 00-55044. 2000. write for info. (*0-7674-1797-6*) Mayfield Pub.

Parenting: A Curriculum for the Single Working Mother. Barbara L. Makris & Linda Davis-Debeuneure. 22p. 1983. pap. text 15.00 (*0-934966-10-9*) Wider Oppor Women.

Parenting: A Life Span Perspective. Carole A. Martin & Karen K. Colbert. LC 96-22890. 416p. (C). 1996. pap. 42.81 (*0-07-040768-1*) McGraw.

Parenting: A Practical Manual in Anticipatory Guidance. Shu Shum. LC 97-93933. 206p. 1997. pap. 9.95 (*0-9659408-0-2*) Amarillo Pediatric.

Parenting: A Skills Training Manual. Louise F. Guerney. LC 78-70674. (Illus.). 151p. (gr. 10-12). 1980. pap. 5.95 (*0-932990-00-2*) IDEALS PA.

Parenting: An Annotated Bibliography, 1965-1987. Sandra Feinberg et al. LC 94-13721. 814p. 1995. 102.50 (*0-8108-2664-X*) Scarecrow.

Parenting: An Ecological Perspective. Ed. by Tom Luster & Lynn Okagaki. 272p. 1993. pap. 29.95 (*0-8058-0857-4*); text 59.95 (*0-8058-0792-6*) L Erlbaum Assocs.

Parenting: Its Causes & Consequences. Ed. by L. Wladis Hoffman et al. 176p. 1982. text 29.95 (*0-89859-086-8*) L Erlbaum Assocs.

Parenting: Nurturing a Baby into a Well-Adjusted Teenager. Robert L. Berko. 72p. write for info. (*0-318-61889-3*) Consumer Ed Res.

Parenting: Rewards & Responsibilities: Teacher's Annotated Edition. 5th annot. ed. Hildebrand. 608p. 1999. teacher ed. 44.99 (*0-02-642957-8*) Glencoe.

Parenting: Roles, Styles & Outcomes. Nigel Barber. LC 98-7502. 159p. 1998. 34.00 (*1-56072-573-7*) Nova Sci Pubs.

Parenting: Successful Church Leaders Share Biblical Principles for Raising Kids in the Nineties. Hal Donaldson & Kenneth M. Dobsen. 280p. 1993. pap. 11.95 (*1-880689-02-2*) Onward Bks.

Parenting: The Early Years. Kay E. Marchand. LC 95-77707. (Spiritual Discovery Ser.). 96p. 1995. pap., teacher ed. 9.95 (*0-88243-206-0*); pap., student ed. 4.95 (*0-88243-106-4*) Gospel Pub.

***Parenting: What Really Counts?** Susan Golombok. LC 00-29096. 2000. pap. write for info. (*0-415-22716-X*) Routledge.

Parenting a Business. Donna L. Montgomery. LC 88-63423. (Illus.). (Orig.). 1989. pap. 14.95 (*0-938577-04-2*) St Johns Pub.

Parenting a Child with a Behavior Problem. Penny Paquette & Cheryl G. Tuttle. 216p. 1996. pap. 16.00 (*1-56565-477-3*) Lowell Hse.

Parenting a Child with a Behavior Problem. 2nd ed. Penny Paquette. LC 99-43084. 216p. 1999. pap. 16.95 (*0-7373-0256-9*, 02569W) NTC Contemp Pub Co.

Parenting a Child with a Learning Disability: A Practical, Empathetic Guide. Cheryl G. Tuttle & Penny Paquette. LC 93-1646. 204p. 1993. 22.95 (*1-56565-082-4*, Legcy) Lowell Hse.

Parenting a Child with AD/HD. Nancy S. Boyles & Darlene Contadino. 272p. 1996. 26.00 (*1-56565-446-3*) Lowell Hse.

Parenting a Child with Arthritis: A Practical, Empathetic Guide to Help You & Your Child Live with Arthritis. Earl J. Brewer, Jr. & Kathy C. Angel. 224p. 1992. 21.95 (*0-929923-55-3*) Lowell Hse.

Parenting a Child with Attention-Deficit Hyperactivity Disorder. Jane Hannah. LC 98-27891. ix, 139 p. 1999. 29.00 (*0-89079-791-9*) PRO-ED.

Parenting a Child with Attention Deficit/Hyperactivity Disorder. 2nd ed. Nancy S. Boyles. LC 99-34870. 304p. 1999. pap. 16.95 (*0-7373-0257-7*, 02577W) NTC Contemp Pub Co.

Parenting a Child with Diabetes. 2nd ed. Gloria Loring. LC 99-41048. 224p. 1999. pap. 14.95 (*0-7373-0301-8*, 03018W, Pub. by Lowell Hse) NTC Contemp Pub Co.

Parenting a Child with Traumatic Brain Injury. Barry K. Hughes. (Illus.). 111p. 1990. pap. 20.95 (*0-398-06156-4*) C C Thomas.

Parenting a Child with Traumatic Brain Injury. Barry K. Hughes. (Illus.). 111p. (C). 1990. text 31.95 (*0-398-05646-3*) C C Thomas.

Parenting a Diabetic Child: A Practical, Empathetic Guide to Help You & Your Child Live with Diabetes. Gloria Loring. 240p. 1991. 19.95 (*0-929923-33-2*) Lowell Hse.

***Parenting a New Church.** Dirk Hart. (Healthy Church Ser.). 24p. 2000. pap. 1.75 (*1-56212-557-5*, 216781) CRC Pubns.

Parenting a Path Through Childhood. Dotty T. Coplen. 1988. pap. 8.50 (*0-903540-61-4*, 20239, Pub. by Floris Bks) Gryphon Hse.

Parenting A to Z: Mom & Dad's Guide to Everything from Conception to College. 2nd rev. ed. David M. Brownstone & Irene M. Franck. LC 96-6311. Orig. Title: The Parent's Desk Reference. 736p. 1996. 32.50 (*0-06-271598-4*) HarpC.

***Parenting a Toddler.** Kristin Thoennes. (Skills for Teens Who Parent Ser.). 64p. (YA). (gr. 7-12). 2000. lib. bdg. 22.60 (*0-7368-0703-4*, LifeMatters Bks) Capstone Pr.

Parenting Across the Life Span: Biosocial Dimensions. Ed. by Jane B. Lancaster et al. (Evolutionary Foundations of Human Behavior Ser.). (Illus.). 486p. (C). 1987. lib. bdg. 59.95 (*0-202-30332-2*) Aldine de Gruyter.

Parenting Adolescents. Kevin Huggins. LC 89-62657. 272p. 1989. pap. 14.00 (*0-89109-697-3*) NavPress.

***Parenting after Divorce: Resolving Conflicts & Meeting Your Child's Needs.** Philip M. Stahl. 224p. 2000. pap. 15.95 (*1-886230-26-9*, Rebuilding Bks) Impact Pubs CA.

Parenting, an Heir Raising Experience: Raising Your Child with Confidence. Mary G. Peeples & Sam L. Peeples, Jr. Ed. by Betsy Lee. (Illus.). 190p. 1993. 17.00 (*0-9634836-1-7*) Sheep Shoppe.

***Parenting an Infant.** Kristin Thoennes. (Skills for Teens Who Parent Ser.). 64p. (YA). (gr. 7-12). 2000. lib. bdg. 22.60 (*0-7368-0702-0*, LifeMatters Bks) Capstone Pr.

Parenting an Only Child. Susan Newman. 256p. 1990. pap. 12.95 (*0-385-24964-0*) Doubleday.

Parenting & Child Care see Handbook of Infant Mental Health

Parenting & Children's Internalization of Values: A Handbook of Contemporary Theory. Joan E. Grusec & Leon Kuczynski. LC 97-1325. 439p. 1997. 99.00 (*0-471-12383-8*) Wiley.

Parenting & Family Values: A Cognitive-Behavioral MRT Workbook. Gregory L. Little & Kenneth D. Robinson. (Illus.). 75p. 1995. pap. 15.00 (*0-940829-15-0*) Eagle Wing Bks.

Parenting & Teaching Young Children. Verna Hildebrand. Ed. by Carol Newman. (Illus.). 432p. (gr. 10-12). 1981. text 30.04 (*0-07-028775-9*) McGraw.

Parenting & Teaching Young Children. 2nd ed. Verna Hildebrand. 448p. 1985. text 28.40 (*0-07-028778-3*) McGraw.

Parenting & the AD/HD Child: A New Approach. Eduardo Bustamante. Ed. by Carroll Robbins. LC 97-62018. 160p. 1997. pap. 12.95 (*0-9633007-4-1*) Whitcomb MA.

Parenting & the Power of Respect: Parenting Without Intimidation, Coercion or Force. Phillip L. Wright. (Illus.). 140p. 1999. pap. text 14.95 (*0-9669717-0-1*) Laser Print.

Parenting & You: A Guide for Parents with Seizure Disorders. Epilepsy Foundation of America Staff. 130p. 1994. pap. 12.95 (*0-916570-13-4*) Epilepsy Foundation of America.

Parenting As a Spiritual Journey: Deepening Ordinary & Extraordinary Events into Sacred Occasions. Nancy Fuchs-Kreimer. LC 98-35483. Orig. Title: Our Share of Night, Our Share of Morning. 224p. 1998. reprint ed. pap. 16.95 (*1-58023-016-4*) Jewish Lights.

***Parenting Begins Before Conception: A Guide to Preparing Body, Mind & Spirit for You & Your Future Child.** Carista Luminare-Rosen. LC 99-89235. (Illus.). 288p. 2000. pap. 16.95 (*0-89281-827-1*) Inner Tradit.

Parenting Behaviors That Promote School Success. Thomas J. Brown. LC 98-93068. 80p. 1998. pap. 9.95 (*1-891404-06-7*, BA016, B&A Pr) Brown & Assocs.

Parenting Behaviour & Children's Cognitive Development. Sara Meadows. (Essays in Developmental Psychology Ser.). 160p. 1996. pap. 19.95 (*0-86377-403-2*) Psychol Pr.

Parenting Breakdown. (SSRC-DHSS Studies in Deprivation & Disadvantage). 1988. text 72.95 (*0-566-05582-1*, Pub. by Avebry) Ashgate Pub Co.

Parenting Builds Leadership. Patty Wipfler. 2.00 (*1-885357-35-4*) Rational Isl.

Parenting by Heart: How to Connect with Your Kids in the Face of Too Much Advice, Too Many Pressures, & Never Enough Time. Ron Taffel & Melinda Blau. 1993. pap. 13.00 (*0-201-63226-8*) Addison-Wesley.

Parenting by the Book. 1999. write for info. (*0-7814-0108-9*, Victor Bks) Chariot Victor.

Parenting by the Spirit. Kathie Walters. Ed. & Intro. by David Walters. 55p. 1994. lib. bdg. 4.99 (*0-9629559-4-9*) Good News Min.

Parenting Challenge: Practical Answers to Childrearing Questions. rev. ed. Barbara K. Polland. LC 93-48937. 232p. (J). (ps-12). 1993. reprint ed. pap. 9.95 (*1-883672-08-2*) Tricycle Pr.

Parenting Challenge: Your Child's Behavior from 6-12. Arnold Rincover. Ed. by Sally Peters. 256p. (Orig.). 1991. pap. 9.00 (*0-671-68163-X*) PB.

Parenting Child Nursing-215. Ingeborg Grutzner. (C). 1995. pap. 11.61 (*1-56870-177-2*) RonJon Pub.

Parenting Children with Disabilities. Peggy M. Miezo. 1983. 49.75 (*0-8247-1090-8*) Phoenix Soc.

***Parenting Clues for the Clueless: God's Word in Your World.** Illus. by Elwood Smith. (Clues for the Clueless Ser.). 256p. 1999. pap. 8.99 (*1-57748-673-0*) Barbour Pub.

Parenting Companion: Meditations & Exercises for "Giving the Love That Heals" Harville Hendrix & Helen Hunt. 384p. (Orig.). 1999. pap. 14.00 (*0-671-86885-3*, PB Trade Paper) PB.

Parenting Cookbook: A Comprehensive Guide to Cooking, Eating, & Entertaining for Today's Families. Kathy Gunst. 432p. 1995. 27.50 (*0-8050-3783-7*) H Holt & Co.

Parenting Cookbook: Recipes for Raising Successful Children. Steven A. Szykula. LC 91-90938. 232p. (Orig.). 1991. pap. 19.95 (*0-9629370-0-2*) Family First.

Parenting Edge: Simple Guide to Effective Parenting. Dan Singer. Ed. by Strand & Ornelas. 1998. pap., wbk. ed. 12.95 (*0-944958-45-1*) Elfin Cove Pr.

***Parenting Education & Support: New Opportunities.** Sheila Wolfendale. (Home & School - A Working Alliance Ser.). 1999. pap. 27.95 (*1-85346-579-8*) David Fulton.

***Parenting Encyclopedia.** Caryl Waller Krueger. LC 00-38577. 2000. write for info. (*0-687-08927-1*) Abingdon.

Parenting for a Healthy Future. Dotty T. Coplen. 126p. 1995. 14.95 (*1-869890-53-1*, Pub. by Hawthorn Press) Anthroposophic.

Parenting for a Peaceful Home: Challenges & Solutions for Almost Perfect Parenting. Ed. by Louise K. Horvath. LC 97-36483. 160p. (Orig.). 1997. pap. 14.95 (*1-887969-04-7*) Cathedral PA.

Parenting for Dummies. Sandra H. Gookin. (For Dummies Ser.). 408p. 1995. pap. 16.99 (*1-56884-383-6*) IDG Bks.

Parenting for Dummies: A Reference for the Rest of Us. abr. ed. Sandy Gookin & Dan Gookin. (For Dummies Ser.). 1996. audio 12.00 (*0-694-51668-6*, CPN 10069) HarperAudio.

Parenting for Education. Vivian W. Owens. LC 89-80830. 112p. (Orig.). 1989. pap. 6.00 (*0-9623839-0-2*) Eschar Pubns.

Parenting for Prevention: Communicating - How to Confront Kids when They're Doing Wrong--How to Encourage Them when They're Doing Right. Johnson Institute Staff. LC 97-3375. 1997. 2.25 (*1-56246-137-0*, 3138, HazeldenJohnson Inst) Hazelden.

Parenting for Prevention: How to Enforce Consequences when Kids Violate Limits. Johnson Institute Staff. LC 97-3371. 1997. 2.25 (*1-56246-136-2*, 3136, HazeldenJohnson Inst) Hazelden.

Parenting for Prevention: How to Raise a Child to Say No to Alcohol - Drugs for Parents, Teachers, & Other Concerned Adults. rev. ed. David J. Wilmes. 244p. (Orig.). 1995. pap. text 15.00 (*0-935908-46-3*, 3195, HazeldenJohnson Inst) Hazelden.

Parenting for Prevention: How to Set Limits for Kids. Johnson Institute Staff. LC 97-3373. 1997. 2.25 (*1-56246-135-4*, 3144, HazeldenJohnson Inst) Hazelden.

Parenting for Prevention: How to Stop Enabling & Start Empowering Kids. Johnson Institute Staff. LC 97-3372. 1997. 2.25 (*1-56246-134-6*, 3142, HazeldenJohnson Inst) Hazelden.

Parenting for the First Time. Dale R. Olen. 195p. 1994. pap. 8.95 (*1-56583-015-6*) JODA.

Parenting for the New Millennium: Friendly Families Through the Power of Respect. Karen Ryce. Ed. by Suzanne Stasa. (Illus.). 210p. (Orig.). 1996. pap. 14.95 (*0-9651103-0-3*) HU Enterprises.

Parenting for the '90s. Philip Osborne. LC 89-2009. 314p. 1989. pap. 9.95 (*0-934672-73-3*) Good Bks PA.

Parenting from a Distance: Your Right & Responsibilities. Jan Walker. 178p. 1987. pap. 19.95 (*0-8134-2750-9*) Interstate.

Parenting from the Heart. Jack Pransky. Ed. by Martha Gagliardi. LC 97-92271. (Illus.). 160p. (Orig.). 1997. pap. 14.00 (*0-9659057-0-5*) NEHRI Pubns.

Parenting from the Heart Vol. 1: Selected Articles from Motherwear's Magazine for Nurturing Families. Ed. by Carolyn D. Mailler. LC 95-81645. (Illus.). 240p. (Orig.). 1996. pap. 14.95 (*0-9649867-0-1*) Motherwear.

***Parenting Guide to Pregnancy & Childbirth.** Paula Spencer. 1999. pap. 12.00 (*0-345-91507-0*) Ballantine Pub Grp.

Parenting Guide to Pregnancy & Childbirth. Paula Spencer. Ed. by Parenting Magazine Staff. LC 97-35736. 384p. 2000. pap. 16.00 (*0-345-41179-X*, Ballantine) Ballantine Pub Grp.

Parenting Guide to Pregnancy II. 1998. mass mkt. 0.00 (*0-345-43100-6*) Ballantine Pub Grp.

Parenting Guide to Your Baby's First Year. Parenting Magazine Editors & Anne Krueger. LC 98-21987. 384p. 2000. pap. 16.00 (*0-345-41180-3*, Ballantine) Ballantine Pub Grp.

Parenting Happy Healthy Children. Karen Olness. 1981. pap. 8.95 (*0-9602790-4-0*) Hlth Frontiers.

Parenting in a Contemporary Society. 4th ed. (C). 2000. text 53.00 (*0-205-29646-7*, Longwood Div) Allyn.

Parenting in a TV Age. J. Francis Davis et al. (Illus.). 1991. student ed. 21.95 (*1-879419-03-3*, W52/53) Ctr Media Values.

Parenting in Contemporary Society. 3rd ed. Tommie J. Hamner & Pauline H. Turner. LC 94-44703. 400p. 1995. pap. 64.00 (*0-205-16105-7*) Allyn.

Parenting in Contemporary Society. 3rd ed. Tommie J. Hamner & Pauline H. Turner. (C). 1995. pap., teacher ed. write for info. (*0-205-17637-2*, H7637-5) Allyn.

***Parenting in Contemporary Society.** 4th ed. 2000. write for info. (*0-205-33155-6*) Allyn.

***Parenting in Public: Family Shelter & Public Assistance.** Donna H. Friedman & Rosalind Clark. LC 99-87067. 2000. pap. 22.50 (*0-231-11105-3*) Col U Pr.

Parenting in Stepfamilies: Social Attitudes, Parental Perceptions & Parenting Behaviours in Hong Kong. Gladys Lan Tak Lam-Chang. LC 98-74644. (Social & Political Studies from Hong Kong). 9p. 1999. text 69.95 (*1-84014-969-8*, Pub. by Ashgate Pub) Ashgate Pub Co.

***Parenting in the Aftermath of Family Violence: Changing the Dynamics Between Parent & Child.** Christina Dalpiaz. Ed. by Yash Holbrook. 2000. pap. 14.95 (*0-9650669-1-6*) Chance.

Parenting in the Electronic Age: What Every Parent Needs to Know about Safe, Sensible, Purposeful Computing. Steve Bennett & Ruth Bennett. 1997. 22.00 (*0-679-44856-X*) Random.

Parenting in the Nineties. Susan Fadem. (Illus.). 138p. (Orig.). 1992. pap. 5.95 (*0-9631448-1-2*) VA Pub Corp.

Parenting in the Nineties: A Comprehensive Resource Guide for Austin Parents. 1990th ed. Ed. by Sandy Kemp. (Illus.). 180p. (Orig.). 1989. pap. write for info. (*0-9624402-0-5*) Cameron Pubns.

Parenting in the '90s: Where Have We Gone Wrong? Trevor Crabtree & Karen Crabtree. 286p. 1998. pap. 13.00 (*1-887827-04-8*) New Authors Pubns.

Parenting in the Pew: Guiding Your Children into the Joy of Worship. Robbie Castleman. LC 92-40659. 125p. (Orig.). 1993. pap. 8.99 (*0-8308-1627-5*, 1627) InterVarsity.

***Parenting Infants & Toddlers Without Going Nuts.** Maria M. Marinakis. Ed. & Photos by Jerry Metellus. 129p. 1999. pap. 14.95 (*0-9669558-0-3*) FourKid.

Parenting Isn't for Cowards see Tener Hijos No es para Cobardes

Parenting Isn't for Cowards see Criando a los Hijos Con Plena Confianza

Parenting Isn't for Cowards. rev. ed. James C. Dobson. 240p. 1997. pap. 12.99 (*0-8499-4014-1*) Word Pub.

Parenting Keys: Keys to Raising a Deaf Child. Virginia F. Frazier-Maiwald & Lenore M. Williams. LC 98-50393. (Parenting Keys Ser.). 208p. 1999. pap. 6.95 (*0-7641-0723-2*) Barron.

Parenting Lessons from God, the Perfect Parent. Joey A. Perry, Sr. 180p. (Orig.). 1997. pap. 11.95 (*0-9653365-5-7*) Albatross Pub.

Parenting Made Simple: An Operator's Manual. Novel Stokes & Cynthia Stokes. 1998. pap. 25.00 (*1-57502-872-7*, PO2372) Morris Pubng.

Parenting Matters. Joy W. Berry. Ed. by Annette Gouch. LC 90-26140. 250p. (Orig.). 1991. pap. 19.95 (*0-929635-05-1*) Cole Pub Co Inc.

***Parenting 911: How to Safeguard & Rescue Your 10 to 15 Year Old from Substance Abuse, Depression, Sexual Encounters, Violence, Failure in School, Danger on the Internet & Other Risky Situations.** Charlene C Giannetti & Margaret Sagarese. LC 99-18784. 304p. 1999. pap. 15.00 (*0-7679-0321-8*) Broadway BDD.

Parenting on Purpose see Criando con Proposito

***Parenting on the Go: Effective Discipline Strategies for the Busy, Devoted Parent.** L. Tobin. 192p. 2000. pap. 14.95 (*1-57025-206-8*) Whole Person.

Parenting on Your Own. Lynda Hunter. LC 97-30616. 336p. 1997. 14.99 (*0-310-21309-6*) Zondervan.

Parenting One Day at a Time: Using the Tools of Recovery to Become Better Parents & Raise Better Kids. Alex J. Packer. LC 98-48414. 290p. 1999. pap. 14.95 (*1-56838-323-1*, 1123) Hazelden.

Parenting 101: Because Kids Don't Come with Instructions. Melanie Bazarte. (Illus.). 438p. 1998. 27.95 (*0-9664365-0-4*) Dr Melanie.

Parenting 101. Lisa Phelan. 168p. (Orig.). 1995. pap. 5.95 (*1-56245-188-X*) Great Quotations.

Parenting Online. Melissa Wolf. LC 97-32784. 1998. pap. text 16.95 (*1-881025-47-0*) Equinox Pr.

***Parenting Our Daughters: For Parents & Other Caring Adults.** rev. ed. Judy Gordon. 200p. 1999. pap. text 19.95 (*1-929573-00-6*) Girls Count.

Parenting Our Daughters: For Parents & Other Caring Adults see Animando a Nuestras Hijas: Para Padres de Familia y Otros Adultos Interesados

Parenting Our Parents. 6th ed. Doug Manning. 14p. 1989. reprint ed. pap. 1.50 (*1-892785-08-0*) In-Sight Bks Inc.

Parenting Our Parents: Senior Care Options for Concerned Families. Brad Zweck. 32p. (Orig.). 1988. pap. 3.95 (*0-945485-07-7*) Comm Intervention.

***Parenting... Part Joy... Part Guerrilla Warfare: Celebrating the Delights & Challenges of Parenting.** Ed. by Hazelden Publishing Staff. 2000. pap. 8.00 (*1-56838-383-5*) Hazelden.

***Parenting Partners: How to Encourage Dads to Participate in the Daily Lives of Their Children.** Robert Frank. 288p. 2000. pap. 12.95 (*0-312-26754-1*) St Martin.

Parenting Playfully: Dancing the Developmental Ladder, Birth to Three. Tom Potter & Beatrice Parnes. (Illus.). 112p. (Orig.). 1995. pap. 12.95 (*0-9646045-0-7*) Parent Educ.

Parenting Postulates: Guidelines for Passage to Parenting Peace. Ulysses J. Hall. LC 97-97162. vii, 440p. 1997. pap. 24.95 (*1-891730-00-2*, N971001) W L S U.

Parenting Pre-School Children: How to Cope with Common Behavioral Problems. Paul Stallard. 144p. 1998. pap. 19.95 (*1-85703-266-7*, Pub. by How To Bks) Trans-Atl Phila.

Parenting Puzzle. Ramon Lewis & Susan Lewis. (C). 1989. pap. 60.00 (*0-86431-036-6*, Pub. by Aust Council Educ Res) St Mut.

Parenting, Schooling & Children's Behaviour: Interdisciplinary Approaches. Ed. by Ann Buchanan & Barbara Hudson. LC 98-73508. 218p. 1998. text 59.95 (*1-84014-556-0*, Pub. by Ashgate Pub) Ashgate Pub Co.

Parenting Skills: Workbook & Trainer's Manual. 2nd ed. Richard R. Abidin. LC 81-13314. 85p. 1982. student ed. 20.95 (*0-89885-118-1*, Kluwer Acad Hman Sci) Kluwer Academic.

***Parenting Skills for the New Millenium.** Lynne Marie Williams. 162p. 2000. pap. 12.00 (*1-881524-33-7*) Milligan Bks.

Parenting Skills Workshop Series: A Manual for Parent Educators. John Bailey et al. (Illus.). 108p. 1995. ring bd. 19.00 (*1-57753-004-7*, 321PSW) Corn Coop Ext.

***Parenting Smart: (Everything You Need to Know to Do It Right!)** Patrice A. Parsons & Patricia A. Parsons. LC 99-96130. (Illus.). 120p. 1999. pap. 20.00 (*0-9674412-0-X*) Parsons Printwrks.

Parenting too requires some training & practice. The SMART program is a "Two Generation Approach" to parenting, which means it empowers both parent(s) & child. "Parenting SMART" was written to help parents better understand themselves & a child's behavior - with the final focus being our "FORMULA" for decision making. However, this book is not just for parents. Anyone at any age with the ability to read this book will benefit by doing so (you don't have to be a parent). Adults as well as intelligent teenagers can find out by reading this book what their parents perhaps should have done for them & what they can do now for themselves or their children (if they have any). This book was written & is to be used by parents (or the reader) as a preventative measure. You will find quizzes, quotes, a short story & poetry all pertinent to parenting because we want you to enjoy learning the SMART program. http://www.ameritech.net/users/Parentingsmart/parentingsmart.html ***Publisher Paid Annotation.***

***Parenting, SportsMom Style: Real-Life Solutions for Surviving Youth Sports.** Laurel Phillips & Barbara Stahl. Ed. by Barb Meyer. (Illus.). 186p. 2000. pap. 16.95 (*0-9659445-5-7*, Pub. by Three Hund Seven Bks) BookWorld.

Parenting Streetwise Kids: Parents of Kids at Risk. (Family Growth Electives Ser.). 1995. pap., student ed. 24.99 (*0-7814-5137-X*, 21758) Cook.

***Parenting Survival Kit: How to Make It Through the Parenting Years with Your Family, Sanity & Wallet Intact.** Aleta Koman & Edward Myers. LC 99-51915. 2000. pap. 14.95 (*0-399-52580-7*, Perigee Bks) Berkley Pub.

Parenting Teenagers. Bob Myers. 152p. 1996. pap. 19.95 (*1-85302-366-3*, Pub. by Jessica Kingsley) Taylor & Francis.

Parenting Teenagers. rev. ed. Don Dinkmeyer. 180p. 1998. pap. 15.95 (*0-8129-3014-2*, Times Bks) Crown Pub Group.

Parenting Teenagers: Systematic Training for Effective Parenting of Teens Don C. Dinkmeyer. LC 98-231149. v, 154 p. 1998. write for info. (*0-7854-1468-1*) Am Guidance.

Parenting Teens with Love & Logic: Preparing Adolescents for Responsible Adulthood. Foster Cline & Jim Fay. LC 92-64090. 272p. 1992. 18.00 (*0-89109-695-7*) Pinon Press.

***Parenting the ADHD Child: Can't Do? Want Do?** David Pentecost. LC 99-43195. (Illus.). 1999. pap. 23.95 (*1-85302-811-8*) Jessica Kingsley.

Parenting the Adolescent. Carl E. Pickhardt. (Illus.). 200p. (Orig.). 1987. pap. 12.95 (*0-938934-16-3*) LCN.

***Parenting the Child Who Hurts: The First Steps.** Caroline Archer. LC 99-41636. 1999. pap. 19.95 (*1-85302-801-0*) Jessica Kingsley.

***Parenting the Child Who Hurts: The Next Steps, Vol. 2.** Caroline Archer. LC 99-41637. 1999. pap. 24.95 (*1-85302-802-9*) Jessica Kingsley.

Parenting the Elementary Child. Raymond T. Brock. (Spiritual Discovery Ser.). 128p. 1996. pap., teacher ed. 9.95 (*0-88243-209-5*); pap., student ed. 4.95 (*0-88243-109-9*) Gospel Pub.

Parenting the Enlightened Child: A Handbook for Revealing & Guiding the Spiritual Child. Alyce B. Soden. 1997. pap. text 11.95 (*1-57087-356-9*) Prof Pr NC.

Parenting the High-Need Child. Martha Sears & William M. Sears. LC 95-48381. (Illus.). 256p. 1996. pap. 12.95 (*0-316-77916-4*) Little.

Parenting the Overactive Child: Alternatives to Drug Therapy. Paul Lavin. LC 89-2613. (Illus.). 160p. (Orig.). (C). 1989. 21.95 (*0-8191-7297-9*); pap. 10.95 (*0-8191-7315-0*) Madison Bks UPA.

Parenting the Prodigal. S. Rutherford McDill. LC 96-22680. 120p. 1996. pap. 7.99 (*0-8361-9042-4*) Herald Pr.

Parenting the Strong-Willed Child: The Clinically Proven Program for Parents of Two- to Six-Year-Olds. Rex Forehand & Nicholas Long. (Illus.). 272p. 1996. pap. 14.95 (*0-8092-3265-0*, 326500, Contemporary Bks) NTC Contemp Pub Co.

***Parenting the Wild Child.** Miles McPherson. 192p. 2000. pap. 11.99 (*0-7642-2370-4*) Bethany Hse.

***Parenting Through Crisis: Helping Kids in Times of Loss, Grief & Change.** Barbara Coloroso. 288p. 2000. 24.00 (*0-06-019856-7*, HarpRes) HarpInfo.

Parenting Through Divorce . . . the Lasting Effects. Karen Todd & Nancy Barios. 244p. (Orig.). 1995. pap. 16.95 (*0-9649210-8-1*) Motivo Pubng.

***Parenting Tips for the Strung Out Mom & Dad - A Toolkit.** Ruthann Saphier. LC 00-102344. (Fridge Notes Ser.). (Illus.). 100p. 2000. pap. 10.00 (*0-9700280-0-8*) M R Enterprses.

Parenting to Inspire Values: Children Learn What They Live see Com Inculcar Valores a Sus Hijos: Los Ninos Aprenden Lo Que Viven

Parenting to Make a Difference: Your One- to Four-Year Old Child. Brenda Hussey-Gardner. (Illus.). (Orig.). 1992. pap. 12.95 (*0-89718-118-2*) VORT CA.

Parenting Today. Ailsa Drent. (C). 1990. teacher ed. 60.00 (*0-86431-074-9*, Pub. by Aust Council Educ Res); teacher ed. 90.00 (*0-86431-073-0*, Pub. by Aust Council Educ Res) St Mut.

***Parenting Today.** 2nd ed. Ailsa Drent. 100p. 2000. pap. 29.95 (*0-86431-334-9*, Pub. by Aust Council Educ Res) Stylus Pub VA.

Parenting Today: A Teaching Guide. Ed. by Margaret Torrie et al. LC 83-26513. (Contemporary Parenting Choices Ser.: Module 3). 256p. 1984. reprint ed. pap. 79.40 (*0-608-00085-X*, 206084900006) Bks Demand.

Parenting Today's Adolescent. Dennis Rainey et al. LC 98-29878. 320p. 1998. 19.99 (*0-7852-7084-1*) Nelson.

Parenting Together: Men & Women Sharing the Care of Their Children. Diane Ehrensaft. 350p. 1987. 29.95 (*0-02-909440-2*) Free Pr.

Parenting Together: Men & Women Sharing the Care of Their Children. Diane Ehrensaft. 288p. 1990. pap. text 15.95 (*0-252-06137-3*) U of Ill Pr.

Parenting Toward Solutions: Positive Techniques to Help Parnets Use the Skills They Already Have to Raise Responsible, Loving Kids. Linda Metcalf. LC 96-17949. 256p. 1996. text 27.95 (*0-13-269622-3*) P-H.

Parenting Toward Solutions: Positive Techniques to Help Parnets Use the Skills They Already Have to Raise Responsible, Loving Kids. Linda Metcalf. LC 96-26483. 256p. 1996. pap. text 19.95 (*0-13-269614-2*) P-H.

Parenting Tricks of the Trade: 1280 Hints for Your Child's First Ten Years. Kathleen Wall. LC 94-17576. (Illus.). 256p. 1994. pap. 14.95 (*1-55591-185-4*) Fulcrum Pub.

Parenting under Pressure: Mothers & Fathers with Learning Difficulties. Tim Booth & Wendy Booth. LC 94-230. 1994. pap. 31.95 (*0-335-19194-0*) OpUniv Pr.

Parenting What's It All About. David Heller & Elizabeth Heller. LC 95-69888. 160p. 1995. pap. 9.95 (*0-89221-291-8*) New Leaf.

Parenting with a Purpose: A Positive Approach for Raising Confident, Caring Youth. Dean Feldmeyer & Eugene C. Roehlkepartain. (Everyone's an Asset-Builder Ser.). 16p. 1998. pap. 3.95 (*1-57482-328-0*) Search Inst.

Parenting with C. A. R. E. Credibility, Assertiveness, Responsibility, Esteem-Building. Ray Nordine & Linda Vettrus. 128p. Date not set. pap. 9.95 (*1-929293-02-X*) Whole Child Institute.

Parenting with Ease: It Doesn't Have to Be Difficult. Elaine Lawrence-Wynn. 243p. 1996. pap. 14.95 (*0-9649665-0-6*) E Lawrence-Wynn.

Parenting with Grace, Vol. 2. Orley R. Herron. 80p. 1996. write for info. (*1-889555-05-3*) Stephen Aubry.

Parenting with Grace Catholic Parent Guide to Raising Almost Perfect Kids. Gregory K. Popcak et al. LC 99-75099. 240p. 1999. pap. 12.95 (*0-87973-730-1*) Our Sunday Visitor.

Parenting with Intimacy. David Ferguson & Vicki Warren. LC 96-145145. 390p. 1995. pap., wbk. ed. 14.99 (*1-56476-523-7*, 6-3523, Victor Bks) Chariot Victor.

Parenting with Intimacy. Teresa Ferguson & Vicki Warren. 244p. 1995. 10.99 (*1-56476-522-9*, 6-3522, Victor Bks) Chariot Victor.

Parenting with Love & Limits. Bruce S. Narramore. 312p. 1987. pap. 8.95 (*0-310-30541-1*, 11246P) Zondervan.

Parenting with Love & Logic: Teaching Children Responsibility. Foster W. Cline & Jim Fay. LC 92-60546. 229p. 1990. 18.00 (*0-89109-311-7*) Pinon Press.

Parenting with Pleasure. Doris M. Jones. 1992. pap. 13.95 (*0-9633378-0-7*) Fam Outreach.

Parenting with Prayer. Mary A. Kuharski. LC 93-83241. 180p. (Orig.). 1993. pap. 8.95 (*0-87973-553-8*, 553) Our Sunday Visitor.

Parenting with Purpose: Progressive Discipline in the Toddler Years. Lynda Madison. LC 98-19803. xiii, 235 p. 1998. pap. 12.95 (*0-8362-6768-0*) Andrews & McMeel.

Parenting with Respect & Peacefulness: The Most Difficult Job in the World. Louise A. Dietzel. LC 94-67445. 304p. 1995. pap. 10.95 (*0-914984-66-7*) Starburst.

Parenting with Truth. 2000. pap. 7.99 (*0-310-22571-X*) Zondervan.

Parenting with Truth: Parenting with Grace & Truth. Henry Cloud & John Townsend. LC 98-51434. 1999. 17.99 (*0-310-22569-8*) Zondervan.

Parenting Without God: Experience of a Humanist Mother. Jane W. Wilson. 76p. 1997. pap. 12.95 (*1-900219-11-5*, Pub. by Educ Heretics) Intl Spec Bk.

Parenting Without Guilt: The Predictable & Situational Misbehaviors of Childhood. G. Kenneth West. (Illus.). 290p. (C). 1986. 49.95 (*0-398-05267-0*) C C Thomas.

***Parenting Without Perfection.** David John Seel, Jr. 2000. pap. 12.00 (*1-57683-200-7*) NavPress.

Parenting Without Pressure: A Whole Family Approach To. Teresa A. Langston. LC 94-65638. 160p. 1994. pap. 14.00 (*0-89109-750-3*) Pinon Press.

Parenting Without Punishment: Making Problem Behavior Work for You. John Maag. LC 95-47277. 260p. (Orig.). 1996. pap. 17.95 (*0-914783-78-5*) Charles.

Parenting Young Children. rev. ed. Don Dinkmeyer & G. D. McKay. 1997. pap. 15.95 (*0-679-77797-0*) Random.

Parenting Young Children: Helpful Strategies Based on Systemic Training for Effective Parenting (Step) Don Dinkmeyer, Sr. et al. 1990. pap. 12.00 (*0-679-73220-9*) Random.

Parenting Young Children: Parent's Handbook. Don Dinkmeyer, Sr. et al. (Early Childhood STEP Ser.). 1989. pap. 14.95 (*0-88671-356-0*, 4302) Am Guidance.

Parenting Young Children: Systematic Training for Effective Parenting (step) of Children Under Six Don C. Dinkmeyer. LC 98-231175. v, 138p. 1997. write for info. (*0-7854-1189-5*) Am Guidance.

Parenting Your Adopted Child: A Complete & Loving Guide. Stephanie E. Siegel. 1989. 17.95 (*0-318-41490-2*) P-H.

Parenting Your Adopted Child: A Complete & Loving Guide. 2nd rev. ed. Stephanie E. Siegel. LC 97-91120. xviii, 242p. 1997. pap. 15.00 (*0-9660762-0-6*) SES Pub.

***Parenting Your Adult Child: How You Can Help Them Achieve Their Full Potential.** Ross Campbell & Gary Chapman. 1999. pap. 11.99 (*0-8024-7312-1*) Moody.

***Parenting Your Adult Child: How You Can Help Them Achieve Their Full Potential.** Ross Campbell & Gary Chapman. 1999. pap. 14.99 incl. audio (*0-8024-7389-X*) Moody.

Parenting Your Adult Child: How You Can Help Them Achieve Their Full Potential. Ross Campbell & Gary Chapman. LC 99-215576. 200p. 1999. pap. 11.99 (*1-881273-12-1*) Northfield Pub.

Parenting Your Aging Parents. Francine Moskowitz & Robert Moskowitz. LC 90-92272. 304p. 1991. 21.95 (*0-9624415-0-3*) Key Pubns Woodland Hills.

Parenting Your 1- to 4-Year-Old: Parent's Workbook. Michael H. Popkin et al. (Illus.). 96p. (Orig.). 1996. pap., wbk. ed. 12.95 (*1-880283-17-4*) Active Parenting.

Parenting Your Parents. Dorothy Gager. (Lifesearch Ser.). 64p. 1996. pap. 4.95 (*0-687-01498-0*) Abingdon.

***Parenting Your Parents.** Jane Powell Thomas. Ed. by Laurel Strand. LC 99-75762. 64p. 2000. pap. 9.95 (*0-944958-35-4*) Elfin Cove Pr.

Parenting Your Superstar: How to Help Your Child Balance Achievement & Happiness. Robert Rotella & Linda Bunker. (Illus.). 256p. 1998. pap. 14.95 (*1-57243-295-0*) Triumph Bks.

Parenting Your Teenager. David Elkind. 256p. 1994. reprint ed. pap. 10.00 (*0-345-38679-5*) Ballantine Pub Grp.

Parenting Your Teenager: Leader's Kit. rev. ed. Dale Baker & Thomas Baker. (SPA.). 55p. 1994. ring bd. 150.00 (*1-885903-02-2*) ParentingKids.

Parenting Your Teenager: Parent's Guide. rev. ed. Dale Baker & Thomas Baker. 83p. 1994. pap. 12.00 (*1-885903-00-6*, TX3882 835) ParentingKids.

Parenting Your Toddler: The Expert's Guide to the Tough & Tender Years. Patricia H. Shimm & Kate Ballen. LC 94-23148. (Illus.). 224p. 1995. pap. 12.00 (*0-201-62298-X*) Addison-Wesley.

***ParenTips: For Effective, Enjoyable Parenting.** Marilyn Heins. LC 99-74764. 272p. 1999. pap. 17.95 (*0-913951-06-4*) Develop Pubns.

P

Parentmaking: A Practical Handbook for Teaching Parent Classes about Babies & Toddlers. 2nd rev. ed. B. Annye Rothenberg et al. Ed. by Carol Whiteley. LC 95-3150. (Illus.). 495p. (Orig.). 1995. pap. text 35.95 (*0-9604620-2-3*) Banster Pr.

Parentmaking Educators Training Program: A Comprehensive Skills Development Course to Train Early Childhood Parent Educators (Birth to 5), 3 cass; set. B. Annye Rothenberg et al. LC 92-19352. (Illus.). 412p. (Orig.). 1993. pap. text 149.95 incl. VHS (*0-9604620-1-5*, HQ755.7.R665) Banster Pr.

Parent/Parent Biographical Dictionary. Laverne Galeener-Moore. 279p. (Orig.). 1995. pap. 22.50 (*0-7884-0341-9*) Heritage Bk.

Parents see People Series

Parents. (Cross Training Ser.: Vol. 2). 64p. (J). (gr. 7-9). 1994. pap. 29.95 incl. VHS (*1-57405-013-3*) CharismaLife Pub.

Parents. J. M. Parramon et al.Tr. of Los Padres. (Illus.). 32p. (J). (gr. 3-5). 1987. pap. 6.95 (*0-8120-3852-5*) Barron.

Parents. J. M. Parramon et al.Tr. of Los Padres. (SPA., Illus.). 32p. (J). (gr. 3-5). 1987. pap. 6.95 (*0-8120-3856-8*) Barron.

Parents. Gail Saunders-Smith. (J). 1998. 13.25 (*0-516-21239-7*) Childrens.

Parents. Ed. by Connie Steele. (Illus.). 84p. (Orig.). 1992. pap. 15.00 (*0-932706-20-7*) WSU Art Gallrs.

Parents: Help Your Preschooler Now! Andrea Brink. LC 97-65971. (Illus.). 91p. (Orig.). 1997. pap. 11.95 (*1-883122-09-0*) Pearce Pub.

Parents: Help Your Preschooler Now! Home Activities for Learning & Growing. rev. ed. Andrea Brink. (Illus.). 96p. (J). (ps). 1998. pap. 11.95 (*1-58112-898-3*) Dissertation.

Parents: The Astonishing Secret Benefits for Kids to Play Sports. P. D. Blainey. 220p. 1994. 27.00 (*0-9642277-0-3*) Cicero Better.

Parents - Passing the Torch of Faith. John M. Drescher. LC 97-13311. 94p. (Orig.). 1997. pap. 7.99 (*0-8361-9076-9*) Herald Pr.

Parents - Single Or Otherwise - Their Sex, Stress, Struggles & Survival: Index of New Information & Reference Research Bible. rev. ed. James L. Bunn. 191p. 1997. 47.50 (*0-7883-1610-9*); pap. 44.50 (*0-7883-1611-7*) ABBE Pubs Assn.

Parents, Adolescents & Their Faith. Raymond Bardy. 1989. pap. 22.00 (*0-86217-163-6*, Pub. by Veritas Pubns) St Mut.

Parents & Adolescents in Changing Families. Ed. by David H. Demo et al. (Families in Focus Ser.: Vol. 3). 280p. (Orig.). (C). 1995. pap. text 36.95 (*0-916174-51-4*) Natl Coun Family.

Parents & Adolescents Living Together: The Basics, Pt. 1. Gerald R. Patterson & Marion Forgatch. (Illus.). 286p. (Orig.). 1987. pap. 12.95 (*0-916154-16-5*) Castalia Pub.

Parents & Adolescents Living Together Pt. 2: Family Problem Solving. Gerald R. Patterson & Marion Forgatch. (Illus.). xiii, 299p. (Orig.). 1989. pap. 13.95 (*0-916154-12-2*) Castalia Pub.

Parents & Children: Build Your Child's Self-Esteem. Sue E. Willett. (Family Ser.). 374p. (Orig.). 1995. pap. 9.95 (*1-56383-052-3*, 9202) G & R Pub.

Parents & Children: God's Design for the Family. 96p. 1980. pap. 6.00 (*0-89109-029-0*) NavPress.

Parents & Children: Incomes in Two Generations. A. B. Atkinson et al. (DHSS Studies in Deprivation & Disadvantage: No. 10). 224p. 1983. text 78.95 (*0-435-82097-4*) Ashgate Pub Co.

Parents & Children Learn Together: Parent Cooperative Nursery Schools. 3rd ed. Katharine W. Taylor. LC 81-5825. 400p. 1981. pap. 21.95 (*0-8077-2638-9*) Tchrs Coll.

***Parents & Grandparents as Spiritual Guides: Nurturing Children of the Promise.** Betty S. Cloyd. Ed. by Karen Williams. 176p. 2000. pap. 13.00 (*0-8358-0923-4*) Upper Room Bks.

***Parents & Kids Talking about School Violence.** Val J. Peter. 2000. pap. 4.95 (*0-938510-74-6*) Boys Town Pr.

Parents & Other Strangers. Ann White & Deborah Grayson. LC 86-17215. 1987. 22.95 (*0-87949-271-6*) Ashley Bks.

Parents & Peers in Social Development: A Sullivan-Piaget Perspective. James Youniss. LC 79-25457. (Illus.). 320p. 1980. lib. bdg. 28.00 (*0-226-96484-1*) U Ch Pr.

Parents & Peers in Social Development: A Sullivan-Piaget Perspective. James Youniss. LC 79-25457. (Illus.). 320p. 1982. pap. text 11.95 (*0-226-96486-8*) U Ch Pr.

Parents & Schools: A Source Book. Angela L. Carrasquillo & Clement B. London. LC 92-6699. 256p. 1993. text 46.00 (*0-8153-0820-5*, SS775) Garland.

Parents & Schools: From Visitors to Partners. Ed. by Rebecca C. Burns. LC 93-31951. 1993. pap. write for info. (*0-8106-1856-7*) NEA.

Parents & Schools: The Contemporary Challenge. Ed. by Flora Macleod. 200p. 1989. 75.00 (*1-85000-498-6*, Falmer Pr); pap. 37.95 (*1-85000-499-4*, Falmer Pr) Taylor & Francis.

***Parents & Schools: The 150-Year Struggle for Control in American Education.** William W. Cutler, III. LC 99-88447. 296p. 2000. 25.00 (*0-226-13216-1*) U Ch Pr.

***Parent's & Student Athlete's Guide to Athletic Scholarships: Getting Money Without Being Taken for a Ride.** Dion Wheeler. LC 99-89752. 192p. 2000. pap. 14.95 (*0-8092-2443-7*, 244370, Contemporary Bks) NTC Contemp Pub Co.

Parents & Teachers. Jane Baskwill. 1993. pap. 8.95 (*0-590-73187-4*) Scholastic Inc.

Parents & Teachers: Helping Children Learn to Read & Write. Timothy V. Rasinski. LC 94-75766. (Illus.). 200p. (Orig.). (C). 1994. pap. text 37.00 (*0-15-501315-7*, Pub. by Harcourt Coll Pubs) Harcourt.

Parents & Teachers: Partners in Language Development. Audrey A. Simmons & Karen Glover-Rossi. (Centennial Celebration Ser.). 386p. (C). 1990. pap. text 27.95 (*0-88200-167-1*) Alexander Graham.

Parents & Teachers: Power & Participation. Carol Vincent. LC 95-26508. 224p. 1996. 79.95 (*0-7507-0517-5*, Falmer Pr); pap. 27.95 (*0-7507-0518-3*, Falmer Pr) Taylor & Francis.

Parents & Teachers As Discipline Shapers. Kevin J. Swick. 32p. 1985. pap. 5.95 (*0-8106-1694-7*) NEA.

Parents & Teachers Ask about Reading. Harold Newman. 115p. 1986. pap. text 15.00 (*0-9613577-1-1*) Prestige Educ.

Parents' & Teachers' Guide. Colleen Carroll. (How Artist See Ser.). 1996. teacher ed. 10.95 (*0-7892-0271-9*, Abbeville Kids) Abbeville Pr.

Parents' & Teachers' Guide to Bilingualism. Colin Baker. LC 94-49737. (Bilingual Education & Bilingualism Ser.: No. 5). 270p. 1995. 59.00 (*1-85359-265-X*, Pub. by Multilingual Matters) Taylor & Francis.

Parents' & Teachers' Guide to Bilingualism. Colin Baker & Ofelia Garcia. LC 94-49737. (Bilingual Education & Bilingualism Ser.: No. 5). 270p. 1995. pap. 19.95 (*1-85359-264-1*, Pub. by Multilingual Matters) Taylor & Francis.

***Parents' & Teachers' Guide to Bilingualism.** 2nd ed. Colin Baker. LC 99-28420. (Parents' & Teachers' Guides Ser.). 2000. pap. 15.95 (*1-85359-455-5*) Taylor & Francis.

Parents' & Teachers' Guide to Dyslexia. Trevor Payne & Elizabeth Turner. LC 98-27057. 260p. 1998. 44.95 (*1-85359-411-3*); pap. 15.95 (*1-85359-410-5*) Multilingual Matters.

Parents' & Teachers' Guide to Helping Young Children Learn: Creative Ideas from 35 Respected Experts. Ed. by Betty Farber. LC 97-6282. (Illus.). 364p. (Orig.). 1997. pap. text 24.95 (*1-881425-05-3*) Preschl Pubns.

Parent's & Teacher's Handbook on Identifying & Preventing Child Abuse: Warning Signs, Choosing a Day Care Center & Babysitters, Keeping Children Safe on the Internet. James A. Monteleone. LC 98-22804. (Illus.). 200p. 2000. pap. 18.95 (*1-878060-27-9*, 31141) GW Medical.

Parents & Teachers Together: Partnership in Primary & Nursery Education. Mary Stacey. (Innovations in Education Ser.). 160p. 1991. pap. 33.95 (*0-335-09435-X*) OpUniv Pr.

Parents & the Three R's for an Educated America: How to Help Your Child Succeed at School in Minutes a Day, Vol. 1 Primary Grades. M. G. Christopher. (Illus.). 139p. (Orig.). 1990. pap. 16.95 (*0-9624022-1-4*) Venture Bk Pubns.

Parents & the Three R's for an Educated America, Vol. 2: How to Help Your Child Succeed at School in Minutes a Day, Intermediate Grades. M. G. Christopher. (Illus.). 140p. (Orig.). 1992. pap. 16.95 (*0-9624022-0-6*) Venture Bk Pubns.

Parents & the Three R's for an Educated America, Vol. 2: How to Help Your Child Succeed at School in Minutes a Day, Intermediate Grades, Set. M. G. Christopher. (Illus.). 140p. (Orig.). 1992. pap. write for info. (*0-9624022-2-2*) Venture Bk Pubns.

Parents & Their Children. annuals Verdene Ryder. LC 98-48864. 544p. 2000. text 45.28 (*1-56637-517-7*) Goodheart.

Parents & Young Mentally Handicapped Children: A Review of Research Issues. Helen McConachie. 276p. 1986. text 29.95 (*0-914797-28-X*) Brookline Bks.

***Parents Answer Book.** Parents Magazine Editors. (Illus.). 896p. 2000. pap. 21.95 (*0-312-26372-4*, St Martin Griffin) St Martin.

Parents Answer Book. unabridged ed. Ann P. Murphy. Ed. by Parents Magazine Staff. LC 98-23766. (Illus.). 896p. 1998. text 35.00 (*0-307-44060-5*, Whitman Coin) St Martin.

Parent's Answer Book: Over 100 Most-Asked Questions about Your Child's Emotional Well-Being. Gerald Deskin & Greg Steckler. 224p. 1995. 22.95 (*0-925190-79-9*) Fairview Press.

Parent's Answer Book: Over 100 Most-Asked Questions about Your Child's Emotional Well-Being. Gerald Deskin & Greg Steckler. 224p. 1996. pap. 12.95 (*1-57749-005-3*) Fairview Press.

Parents Are Forever: A Parenting Handbook. Rachmiel Tobesman. 75p. 1997. 19.95 (*0-9677266-3-8*) Child Access Ctr MD.

Parents Are Forever: A Step-by-Step Guide to Becoming Successful Co-Parents after Divorce. Shirley Thomas. Ed. by Dorothy Rankin. LC 94-73653. 168p. 1995. pap. 13.95 (*0-9646378-2-0*) Springbd Pubns.

Parents Are Lifesavers: A Handbook for Parent Involvement in Schools. Carol S. Batey. LC 95-32513. 120p. 1996. 43.95 (*0-8039-6240-1*); pap. 18.95 (*0-8039-6241-X*) Corwin Pr.

Parents Are Teachers: A Child Management Program. Wesley C. Becker. LC 72-75091. (Illus.). 200p. (Orig.). 1971. pap. text 12.95 (*0-87822-019-4*, 0194) Res Press.

Parents Are Teachers Too: Enriching Your Child's First Six Years. Claudia Jones. Ed. by Susan Williamson. LC 87-37246. (Illus.). 192p. 1988. pap. 9.99 (*0-913589-35-7*) Williamson Pub Co.

Parents Aren't Perfect. Vernelle B. Allen. 110p. 1994. pap. write for info. (*1-885984-01-4*) Wings of Healing.

Parents Aren't Supposed to Like It: People & Trends in Popular Music. David P. Bianco. LC 97-34040. (J). 1997. write for info. (*0-7876-1732-6*, UXL) Gale.

Parents Aren't Supposed to Like It: People & Trends in Popular Music, 3 vols., Set. David P. Bianco. LC 97-34040. 672p. (YA). (gr. 7 up). 1997. text 69.00 (*0-7876-1731-8*, UXL) Gale.

Parents As Care Managers: The Experiences of Those Caring for Young Children with Cerebral Palsy. Gillian Bridge. LC 99-72593. 324p. 1999. text 69.95 (*1-84014-973-6*, Pub. by Ashgate Pub) Ashgate Pub Co.

Parents As Educators: Training Parents to Teach Their Children. Keith J. Topping. 341p. 1986. text 29.95 (*0-914797-29-8*); pap. text 17.95 (*0-914797-30-1*) Brookline Bks.

Parents As First Teachers (14-24 Months) 1984. 8.00 (*0-939418-78-9*) Ferguson-Florissant.

Parents As First Teachers (14-24 Months) 1985. 8.00 (*0-939418-53-3*) Ferguson-Florissant.

Parents As First Teachers (24-36 Months) 1985. pap. 9.50 (*0-939418-57-6*) Ferguson-Florissant.

Parents As First Teachers (0-14 Months) 1982. 9.50 (*0-939418-49-5*) Ferguson-Florissant.

Parents As Image-Makers. 1979. 1.00 (*0-939418-26-6*) Ferguson-Florissant.

***Parents as Mentors: A New Perspective on Parenting That Can Change Your Child's Life.** Sandra Burt & Linda Perlis. LC 98-33958. (Illus.). 272p. 2000. pap. 14.00 (*0-7615-1685-9*) Prima Pub.

Parents As Partners. 1976. 1.50 (*0-939418-37-1*) Ferguson-Florissant.

***Parents as Partners: Helping Your Child's Literacy & Language Development.** Education Department of Western Autralia. 44p. 1999. pap. text 6.00 (*0-325-00202-9*) Heinemann.

Parents As Partners in Education: Families & Schools Working Together. 5th ed. Eugenia Hepworth Berger. LC 99-18773. (Illus.). 563p. (C). 1999. pap. text 40.00 (*0-13-099654-8*) P-H.

Parents As Partners in Schooling. Caroline St. John-Brooks et al. LC 98-121320. 212p. 1997. pap. 30.00 (*92-64-15492-2*, 96-97-02-1, Pub. by Org for Econ) OECD.

Parents As Playmates: A Games Approach to the Preschool Years. Joan Millman & Polly Behrmann. LC 79-4547. 140p. 1979. pap. 18.95 (*0-87705-404-5*, Kluwer Acad Hman Sci) Kluwer Academic.

Parents As Reading Tutors. Steven F. Duvall et al. 28p. 1996. pap. 7.50 (*1-57035-054-X*, 81PARENT) Sopris.

Parents As Therapeutic Partners: Listening to Your Child's Play. Arthur Kraft & Garry Landreth. LC 97-20340. 280p. 1998. pap. 40.00 (*0-7657-0106-5*) Aronson.

Parents Assuring Student Success (PASS) Achievement Made Easy by Learning Together. John R. Ban. 141p. (Orig.). 1995. pap. text 23.95 (*1-879639-25-4*) Natl Educ Serv.

Parents at Last: Celebrating Adoption & the New Pathways to Parenthood. Cynthia Peck & Wendy Wilkinson. LC 98-15737. (Illus.). 160p. 1998. 27.50 (*0-609-60290-X*) C Potter.

Parent's Bar/Bas Mitzvah Guide: Everything You Need to Know about Planning Your Child's Special Day. rev. ed. Randi Reisfeld. (Illus.). 208p. 1997. 18.95 (*1-55972-417-X*, Birch Ln Pr) Carol Pub Group.

Parent's Bedside Companion: Inspiration for Parents of Young Children. Randolph K. Sanders. LC 92-4963. (Illus.). 160p. 1992. pap. 9.99 (*0-8361-3591-1*) Herald Pr.

Parents-Black Pearls. Eric V. Copage. LC 94-33073. (Illus.). 388p. 1995. pap. 10.00 (*0-688-13098-4*, Quil) HarperTrade.

Parent's Blood: A Biographical Novel. unabridged ed. Ginger Sage. (Illus.). xviii, 242p. 1996. pap. 20.00 (*0-9661929-0-7*) Ginger.

***Parent's Book about Bullying: Changing the Course of Your Child's Life.** William Voors. 120p. 2000. pap. 11.00 (*1-56838-517-X*) Hazelden.

Parent's Book about Divorce. Richard A. Gardner. 416p. 1982. mass mkt. 6.99 (*0-553-28632-3*) Bantam.

Parents Book about Divorce. 2nd ed. Richard A. Gardner. Ed. by Toni Burbank & Jay Howland. LC 91-21283. 394p. 1991. reprint ed. 22.00 (*0-933812-27-2*) Creative Therapeutics.

Parents Book for Raising a Healthy Child. Morris Wessel. (Orig.). 1999. mass mkt. 5.98 (*0-345-43642-3*) Ballantine Pub Grp.

***Parents Book for the Toddler Years.** Adrienne Popper. LC 86-90928. 1999. mass mkt. 5.98 (*0-345-43639-3*) Ballantine Pub Grp.

***Parents Book for Your Baby's First Year.** Maja Bernath. (Orig.). 1999. pap. 5.98 (*0-345-43638-5*, Ballantine) Ballantine Pub Grp.

***Parent's Book of Baby Names.** Kelly Martin. 1999. mass mkt. 5.98 (*0-345-43643-1*) Ballantine Pub Grp.

Parent's Book of Ballet: Answers to Critical Questions about the Care & Development of the Young Dancer. Angela Whitehill & William Noble. Ed. by Arthur L. Zapel. LC 88-13658. (Illus.). 192p. (Orig.). 1988. pap. 14.95 (*0-916260-52-6*, B121) Meriwether Pub.

Parents Book of Child Safety. David Laskin. (Parents Magazine Childcare Ser.). 320p. (Orig.). 1991. mass mkt. 4.99 (*0-345-35104-5*) Ballantine Pub Grp.

Parents Book of Discipline. Barbara Bjorklund & David Bjorklund. 1999. mass mkt. 5.98 (*0-345-43640-7*) Ballantine Pub Grp.

***Parents Book of Lists.** Parents Magazine Staff. 192p. 2000. pap. 12.95 (*0-312-26373-2*) St Martin.

***Parents Book of Toilet Teaching.** Joanna Cole. 126p. 1999. mass mkt. 5.98 (*0-345-43641-5*, Ballantine Epiphany) Ballantine Pub Grp.

Parents Can Be Different. Laura Numeroff. LC 99-22575. (J). (ps-3). 2000. 14.00 (*0-689-80552-7*) S&S Bks Yung.

Parents Can Teach Successfully: A Guide to Help Parents Teach Their Elementary-Age Children. AnnMae Johnson. LC 98-40706. (Illus.). 256p. 1998. pap. 14.95 (*1-880090-77-5*) Galde Pr.

Parents, Children, & Adolescents: Interactive Relationships & Development in Context. Anne-Marie Ambert. LC 96-24646. 398p. (C). 1997. 59.95 (*0-7890-6034-5*) Haworth Pr.

Parents, Children, & Adolescents: Interactive Relationships & Development in Context, Incl. instr's. manual. Anne-Marie Ambert. LC 96-24646. 398p. (C). 1997. pap. 24.95 (*0-7890-0181-0*) Haworth Pr.

Parents, Children & Communication: Frontiers of Theory & Research. Ed. by Thomas J. Socha & Glen Stamp. 385p. 1995. pap. 45.00 (*0-8058-1605-4*); text 89.95 (*0-8058-1604-6*) L Erlbaum Assocs.

Parents, Children & Sex. Ed. by John Robson. (Illus.). (Orig.). 1981. pap. 2.50 (*0-936098-31-7*) Intl Marriage.

Parents, Children & Social Workers: Working in Partnership under the Children Act 1989. Margaret Williams. LC 96-79372. (International Child Care Ser.). 186p. 1997. text 64.95 (*1-85972-531-7*, Pub. by Avebry) Ashgate Pub Co.

Parents, Children & the Facts of Life: A Text on Sex Education for Christian Parents & for Those Concerned with Helping Parents. Henry V. Sattler. LC 93-60170. 272p. 1993. reprint ed. pap. 9.00 (*0-89555-489-5*) TAN Bks Pubs.

Parents' Choice: A Sourcebook of the Very Best Products to Educate, Inform, & Entertain Children of All Ages. Diana H. Green. (Illus.). 208p. (Orig.). 1993. pap. 9.95 (*0-8362-8036-9*) Andrews & McMeel.

***Parent's Complete Guide to Charter Schools: Is it Right for My Child?** Frederick A. Birkett. (Illus.). 304p. 2000. pap. 16.00 (*0-7615-2516-5*) Prima Pub.

***Parent's Complete Guide to Ear Infections.** Alan R. Greene. LC 97-8335. (Illus.). 240p. 1999. mass mkt. 5.99 (*0-380-81047-6*, Avon Bks) Morrow Avon.

Parent's Complete Guide to Ear Infections. rev. ed. Alan R. Greene. LC 97-8335. 256p. 1997. pap. 14.95 (*1-882606-29-9*) Peoples Med Soc.

Parent's Complete Guide to Soccer. Joe Provey. LC 99-16818. 2000. pap. 14.95 (*0-7615-1697-2*) Prima Pub.

Parents Complete Guide to Youth Sports. 1989. 12.00 (*0-88314-394-1*) AAHPERD.

Parents' Complete Special Education Guide: Tips, Techniques & Materials for Helping Your... Roger Pierangelo & Robert Jacoby. 336p. (C). 1996. pap. text 27.95 (*0-87628-614-7*) P-H.

***Parent's Computer Companion: A Guide to Software & Online Resources.** Jason D. Baker. LC 99-32104. 144p. 1999. pap. 9.99 (*0-8010-6077-X*) Baker Bks.

Parent's Crash Course in Career Planning: Helping Your College Student Succeed. Marcia Harris & Sharon Jones. (Illus.). 192p. (Orig.). 1996. pap. 12.95 (*0-8442-4491-0*, 44910, VGM Career) NTC Contemp Pub Co.

Parents' Cultural Belief Systems: Their Origins, Expressions, & Consequences. Ed. by Sara Harkness & Charles M. Super. LC 95-36802. (Culture & Human Development Ser.). 558p. 1995. lib. bdg. 63.00 (*1-57230-031-0*, 0031) Guilford Pubns.

Parents' Day. Paul Goodman. LC 85-9218. (Illus.). 275p. 1985. reprint ed. pap. 12.50 (*0-87685-634-2*) Black Sparrow.

Parent's Desk Reference see Parenting A to Z: Mom & Dad's Guide to Everything from Conception to College

Parent's Diary: A Journal of the Life of Your Child. unabridged ed. Debra K. Traverso. (Illus.). xix, 230p. 1997. ring bd. 25.00 (*0-9663977-0-3*) D Traverso.

Parents Do Make a Difference: How to Raise Kids with Solid Character, Strong Minds, & Caring Hearts. Michele Borba. LC 98-58112. 272p. 1999. pap. text 18.00 (*0-7879-4605-2*) Jossey-Bass.

Parents Duties Childrens Debts. Dean. 196p. 1996. 58.95 (*1-85742-298-8*) Ashgate Pub Co.

Parents, Education & the State. Ed. by Cedric Cullingford. LC 96-85136. (Monitoring Change in Education Ser.). 196p. 1996. text 55.95 (*1-85742-338-0*, Pub. by Arena) Ashgate Pub Co.

***Parents' Education as Autism Therapists: Applied Behaviour Analysis in Context.** Micky Keenan. 1999. pap. text 22.95 (*1-85302-778-2*) Jessica Kingsley.

Parents, Expectant Parents, All Persons Concerned with Childcare see How to Raise Emotionally Healthy Children: Meeting the Five Critical Needs of Children - And Parents Too!

***Parent's Experienced Opinion on Medication Drugs & Hyperactive Children.** 2nd ed. 56p. 1999. pap. 9.95 (*1-877633-45-3*) Luthers.

Parents, Families, & the Stuttering Child. Lena Rustin. (Illus.). 130p. (Orig.). (C). 1991. pap. text 32.95 (*1-879105-16-0*, 0210) Thomson Learn.

Parents' Financial Survival Guide. rev. ed. Theodore E. Hughes & David Klein. LC 94-23873. (Illus.). 208p. 1995. pap. 14.95 (*0-8160-3278-5*) Facts on File.

Parents for Children, Children for Parents: The Adoption Alternative. Laraine M. Glidden. (Monographs of the American Association on Mental Retardation). 200p. (Orig.). (C). 1989. pap. 17.00 (*0-940898-20-9*) Am Assn Mental.

Parents Forever. Sidney Callahan. 228p. 1995. pap. 14.95 (*0-8245-1513-7*) Crossroad NY.

Parents from Space. George Bowering. 200p. (YA). (gr. 6 up). 1994. pap. 5.95 (*1-896184-00-6*) Roussan Pubs.

Parents from the 13th Dimension. R. L. Stine, pseud. (Ghosts of Fear Street Ser.: No. 27). (J). (gr. 4-7). 1984. per. 1.50 (*0-671-00857-9*) PB.

Parents from the 13th Dimension. R. L. Stine, pseud. (Ghosts of Fear Street Ser.: No. 27). (J). (gr. 4-7). 1997. 9.09 (*0-606-13423-9*, Pub. by Turtleback) Demco.

Parents, Gender, & Education Reform. Miriam E. David. LC 92-31272. (Family Life Ser.). 1993. pap. 22.95 (*0-7456-0637-7*) Blackwell Pubs.

P

An Asterisk (*) at the beginning of an entry indicates that the title is appearing for the first time.

Parents, God & the under Fives. St. Paul Publications Staff. (C). 1988. 50.00 (*0-85439-110-X*, Pub. by St Paul Pubns) St Mut.

Parents Grade Your Childs School: Evaluate & Control Your Childs School. Charles Horne. 80p. (Orig.). 1996. pap. 10.00 (*1-57502-106-4*) Morris Pubng.

Parents' Guide. Iqbal Ali. 30p. 1996. pap. 2.50 (*0-614-21521-8*, 944) Kazi Pubns.

Parents' Guide. Disney Enterprises, Inc. Staff. (Disney's "Storytime Treasures" Library: Vol. 19). (Illus.). 44p. 1997. 3.49 (*1-57973-015-9*) Advance Pubs.

Parent's Guide. Disney Enterprises, Inc. Staff. (Disney's "Out & about with Pooh" Library: Vol. 19). (Illus.). 44p. (J). (gr. 1-6). 1996. 3.49 (*1-885222-73-4*) Advance Pubs.

Parents' Guide see Walt Disney's Read & Grow Library

***Parent's Guide: English.** 2000. pap. text. write for info. (*0-8108-3819-2*) Scarecrow.

***Parent's Guide: Spanish.** 2000. pap. text. write for info. (*0-8108-3820-6*) Scarecrow.

Parents Guide: The Step Approach to Parenting Your Teens. Don Dinkmeyer, Sr. & Gary D. McKay. LC 82-74294. (Illus.). 192p. 1984. 10.95 (*0-394-72771-1*) Random.

Parent's Guide: When Young Children Visit the Nursing Home. Steven Ross. LC 95-23197. (Illus.). 64p. 1995. pap. 9.95 (*0-942963-60-1*) Distinctive Pub.

Parent's Guide - Studying Made Easy: A Practical Step-by-Step Guide for Parents, to Study Skills That Work. Barbara Keller & Ray Keller. Ed. by Pamella Hayes. (Illus.). 32p. (Orig.). 1993. pap. 6.95 (*1-881966-05-4*, 42C) Eagles MT.

***Parents Guide Best Family videos.** McCormick. 1999. pap., student ed. write for info. (*0-312-24575-0*) St Martin.

Parents' Guide for Helping Kids Become "A" Students. Anne Farrell et al. (Illus.). 128p. 1990. pap. 11.95 (*0-933025-21-1*) Blue Bird Pub.

Parent's Guide for Suicidal & Depressed Teens: Help for Recognizing if a Child Is in Crisis & What to Do about It. Kate Williams. LC 94-46390. 220p. (Orig.). pap. 11.95 (*1-56838-040-2*) Hazelden.

Parent's Guide 3-5. W. Vandyck. (J). (gr. 3-5). 1996. mass mkt. 5.95 (*0-340-67281-1*, Pub. by Hodder & Stought Ltd) Trafalgar.

Parent's Guide to . . . the World of Comic Books. S. A. Bennett. (World of Cartooning Ser.). (Illus.). 64p. 16.95 (*0-944099-23-8*) Comic Art.

Parents' Guide to Alternatives in Education. Ronald E. Koetzsch. LC 96-39064. 240p. 1997. pap. 17.00 (*1-57062-067-9*, Pub. by Shambhala Pubns) Random.

Parent's Guide to Anorexia & Bulimia: Understanding & Helping Self-Starvers & Binge - Purgers. Katherine Byrne. 88p. 1995. pap. 9.95 (*0-8050-1037-8*, Owl) H Holt & Co.

Parent's Guide to Asthma: How You Can Help Your Child Control Asthma at Home, School, & Play. Nancy J. Sander. (Illus.). 336p. 1994. pap. 13.95 (*0-452-27216-5*) NAL.

Parent's Guide to Attention Deficit Disorders. Stephen B. McCarney & Angela M. Bauer. 408p. 1995. pap. 20.00 (*1-878372-01-7*, 840) Hawthorne Educ Servs.

Parent's Guide to Autism. Charles Hart. Ed. by Claire Zion. LC 93-9438. 256p. (Orig.). 1993. per. 14.00 (*0-671-75099-2*) S&S Trade.

Parents Guide to Baby & Child Medical Care. rev. ed. Ed. by Terril H. Hart. LC 89-29066. (Illus.). 240p. 1991. pap. 8.00 (*0-88166-132-5*) Meadowbrook.

Parent's Guide to Better Nutrition for Tots to Teenagers. Emory W. Thurston. LC 76-10041. 1979. pap. 4.95 (*0-87983-194-4*, Keats Publng) NTC Contemp Pub Co.

Parent's Guide to Buying That First Horse: How-to Find the Ideal Horse for Your Family & Avoid Buying a Lemon! Bonnie Marlewski-Probert. Ed. by Kandee Haertel. (Illus.). 164p. (Orig.). 1995. pap. 16.95 (*0-9646181-0-9*) K&B Products.

Parent's Guide to Cambridge Schools, 1998 Edition. Nancy Walser. (Illus.). 192p. 1997. pap. 17.95 (*0-9655642-1-5*) Huron Village.

Parents' Guide to CFIDS: How to Be an Advocate for Your Child with Chronic Fatigue Immune Dysfunction Syndrome. David S. Bell et al. LC 98-21756. 162p. 1999. 39.95 (*0-7890-0631-6*, Hawrth Medical); pap. 17.95 (*0-7890-0711-8*, Hawrth Medical) Haworth Pr.

Parents' Guide to Child Raising. Glenn Austin et al. 384p. pap. 7.95 (*0-318-43151-3*) P-H.

Parents' Guide to Child Therapy. Richard Bush. LC 94-72054. 352p. 1994. pap. 40.00 (*1-56821-315-8*) Aronson.

Parent's Guide to Children's Educational Games. Ann Fusco & Joanne McGowan. (Orig.). 1996. pap. text 12.00 (*0-9607368-1-6*) Leprechaun Pr.

Parent's Guide to Children's Martial Arts: What's the Right Style for Your Child? Len Losik. Ed. by Sandra Losik. (Illus.). 110p. 1997. pap. 19.95 (*0-9661179-6-4*) SanLen Ent.

Parent's Guide to Cleft Lip & Palate. Sylvia Johnson et al. 137p. 1990. 16.95 (*0-8166-1491-1*) U of Minn Pr.

Parent's Guide to Coaching Football see Parent's Guide to Coaching Youth Football

Parent's Guide to Coaching Hockey. Richard Zulewski. (Betterway Coaching Kids Ser.). (Illus.). 176p. 1993. pap. 12.99 (*1-55870-308-X*, Betrwy Bks) F & W Pubns Inc.

Parent's Guide to Coaching Soccer. John P. McCarthy, Jr. (Betterway Coaching Kids Ser.). (Illus.). 136p. (Orig.). 1991. pap. 12.99 (*1-55870-144-3*, Betrwy Bks) F & W Pubns Inc.

Parent's Guide to Coaching Youth Football. 2nd rev. ed. John P. McCarthy, Jr. LC 95-14391. (Betterway Coaching Kids Ser.). Orig. Title: A Parent's Guide to Coaching Football. (Illus.). 176p. 1995. pap. 12.99 (*1-55870-395-0*, Betrwy Bks) F & W Pubns Inc.

Parent's Guide to College Entrance Exams: How You Can Help Your College-Bound Student Succeed. Jay Blumenthal & Andrea K. Blumenthal. LC 99-38552. 240p. 2000. pap. 14.95 (*1-57685-266-0*) LrningExprss.

***Parent's Guide to Computer Games: Dozens of Titles & Hundreds of Games.** Craig Wessel. 240p. 2000. pap. 14.99 (*0-9675127-4-3*, Pub. by Mars Pubng) IPG Chicago.

Parent's Guide to Cystic Fibrosis. Burton L. Shapiro & Ralph C. Heussner, Jr. (Guides to Birth & Childhood Disorders Ser.). (Illus.). 120p. 1991. 16.95 (*0-8166-1488-1*) U of Minn Pr.

Parents Guide to Disciplining Your Child. write for info. (*0-318-65154-8*) P-H.

Parent's Guide to Down Syndrome: Toward a Brighter Future. Ed. by Siegfried M. Pueschel. (Illus.). 336p. (C). 1990. pap. text 22.95 (*1-55766-060-3*, 0603) P H Brookes.

Parent's Guide to Early Childhood Education, 10 bks., Set. Diane T. Dodge & Joanna Phinney. (Illus.). 22p. (Orig.). (C). 1990. pap. text 22.50 (*0-9602892-5-9*) Tchng Strtgs.

Parent's Guide to Early Childhood Education, 10 bks., Set. Diane T. Dodge & Joanna Phinney. (CHI., Illus.). 22p. (Orig.). 1995. pap. text 22.50 (*1-879537-17-6*) Tchng Strtgs.

Parent's Guide to Eating Disorders: Prevention & Treatment of Anorexia Nervosa & Bulimia. Brett Valette. 208p. 1990. mass mkt. 4.50 (*0-380-70834-5*, Avon Bks) Morrow Avon.

Parent's Guide to Eating Disorders: Prevention & Treatment of Anorexia Nervosa & Bulimia. Brett Valette. 1988. 18.95 (*0-8027-1040-9*) Walker & Co.

Parents' Guide To Feeding Your Kids Right. Childres Television Workshop Staff. 1989. 19.95 (*0-13-649922-8*) P-H.

Parent's Guide to Financing Your Child's Life. Neale S. Godfrey. 1996. 25.00 (*0-614-15437-5*, HarpBusn) HarpInfo.

***Parent's Guide to 1st Grade: What Your Kids Are Being Taught-And How You Can Help Them Learn.** Peter W. Cookson. (Illus.). 2000. pap. text 14.95 (*1-57685-310-1*) LrningExprss.

Parents Guide to Football Safety. Glenn P. Joyner. 1978. pap. text 5.50 (*0-932800-01-7*) Ginseng Pr.

Parent's Guide to Giving Your Children a Great Education: A Handbook for Parents with School-Age Children. Antoinette M. Thomas. 1991. pap. text 9.95 (*0-9630525-0-0*) Tiffany Prods.

***Parent's Guide to Great Explorations in Math & Science (GEMS)** rev. ed. Jacqueline Barber et al. Ed. by Carl Babcock. (Great Explorations in Math & Science (GEMS) Ser.). (Illus.). 52p. 1999. pap., teacher ed. 10.50 (*0-924886-26-9*, GEMS) Lawrence Science.

Parent's Guide to Home Computers & Software. 1983. spiral bd. 6.95 (*0-317-12964-3*, Touchstone) S&S Trade Pap.

Parent's Guide to Horseback Riding. Jessica Jahiel. LC 99-18259. (Illus.). 208p. 1999. pap. 14.95 (*0-7373-0040-X*, 0040XW) NTC Contemp Pub Co.

Parent's Guide to Houston Private Schools. 3rd ed. Cecile F. McKenzie et al. 200p. 1994. 14.95 (*0-9642974-0-X*) McKenzie-Kurio.

Parent's Guide to Houston Private Schools. 4th ed. Ed. by Barbara Monroe & Billue Callier. (Illus.). iv, 102p. 1998. reprint ed. pap. 24.95 (*0-9665964-0-4*) Schls & Such.

Parent's Guide to Infant - Toddler Programs, 10 bks. Amy L. Dombro et al. (Illus.). 24p. 1998. pap. text 22.50 (*1-879537-32-X*) Tchng Strtgs.

Parent's Guide to Innovative Education: Working with Teachers, Schools, & Your Children for Real Learning. Anne W. Dodd. LC 91-51219. 288p. (Orig.). 1992. pap. 12.95 (*1-879360-16-0*) Noble Pr.

Parent's Guide to Kidney Disorders. Glenn H. Bock et al. LC 92-35697. (Guides to Birth & Childhood Disorders Ser.). (Illus.). 188p. (C). 1993. 18.95 (*0-8166-1745-7*) U of Minn Pr.

Parents' Guide to Kids' Sports. Lee R. Schreiber. 138p. 1998. pap. text 9.00 (*0-7881-5301-3*) DIANE Pub.

Parent's Guide to Learning Disabilities. Stephen B. McCarney & Angela M. Bauer. 200p. 1991. pap. 17.00 (*1-878372-05-X*) Hawthorne Educ Servs.

Parent's Guide to Learning Disabilities. Corinne Smith & Lisa Strick. LC 97-12469. 224p. 1997. 25.00 (*0-684-82738-7*) Free Pr.

Parent's Guide to Legal Violence: The Pawning of Our Children. Louise Wallace. LC 94-69170. (Visiting Mother Ser.: Vol. I). 64p. (Orig.). 1993. pap. 8.00 (*1-885800-00-2*) PineTree Pr.

Parent's Guide to Literacy for the 21st Century: Pre-K Through Grade 5. Janie Hydrick. LC 96-4576. (Illus.). 97p. 1996. pap. 11.95 (*0-8141-4688-0*) NCTE.

Parents' Guide to Martial Arts. Ruth M. Hunter & Debra M. Fritsch. LC 98-20902. (Illus.). 208p. 1998. pap. 14.95 (*1-880336-22-7*, PGMA) Turtle CT.

Parent's Guide to Medical Emergencies: First Aid for Your Child. Janet Zand et al. LC 97-7955. (Illus.). 196p. pap. 11.95 (*0-89529-736-1*, Avery) Penguin Putnam.

Parent's Guide to Middle Ear Infections. Dorinne S. Davis. Ed. by E. Patricia Birsner. LC 94-96116. (Illus.). 128p. (Orig.). 1994. pap. 24.95 (*0-9622326-2-9*) The Davis Ctr.

Parent's Guide to New York City's Best Public Elementary Schools. Clara Hemphill. LC 97-27420. 340p. 1997. pap. 24.00 (*1-56947-099-5*) Soho Press.

***Parent's Guide to Nintendo: Hundreds of Detailed Descriptions.** Craig Wessel. 192p. 2000. pap. 14.99 (*0-9675127-6-X*, Pub. by Mars Pubng) IPG Chicago.

Parent's Guide to Nutrition. Boston's Children's Hospital Staff et al. 1987. pap. write for info. (*0-318-61793-5*) Addison-Wesley.

Parents' Guide to Opus Dei. J. J. Garvey. LC 90-72030. 58p. (Orig.). 1991. pap. 7.95 (*0-9628502-0-9*) Sicut Dixit Pr.

Parents' Guide to Outdoor Adventure: A Trailside Guide. Alice Cary. LC 96-40320. (Illus.). 256p. 1997. pap. 18.95 (*0-393-31652-1*) Norton.

Parents Guide to Paying for College: Practical Strategies & Financial Guidelines for Covering College Costs. Gerald Krefetz. 160p. 1999. 14.95 (*0-87447-604-6*, 006046, Pub. by College Bd) H Holt & Co.

Parents' Guide to Personal Computers. Ed Porrazzo & Karen Odell. (Illus.). 1985. 19.95 (*0-13-649963-5*) P-H.

Parent's Guide to Piano Lessons. James W. Bastien. LC 76-21927. (Illus.). 1976. pap. 3.75 (*0-910842-05-1*, WP29) Kjos.

***Parent's Guide to Pitching.** Brad Woodall & Neil Caudle. x, 38p. 2000. pap. 10.00 (*0-9679589-0-3*) Raincreek Pubng Co.

***Parent's Guide to Playstation: Both Classic & PlayStation 2 Titles.** Craig Wessel. 240p. 2000. pap. 14.99 (*0-9675127-5-1*, Pub. by Mars Pubng) IPG Chicago.

Parent's Guide to Prayer. Anita E. Keire. LC 92-73106. (Illus.). 214p. (Orig.). 1992. pap. text 9.95 (*0-9633911-0-0*) Curr Dev Assocs.

***Parent's Guide to Protecting Your Children in Cyberspace: How to Make Sure Your Child Navigates Safely Through the Perilous World of the Internet.** Parry Aftab. (Illus.). 330p. 1999. pap. 12.95 (*0-07-135752-1*) McGraw.

Parent's Guide to Quality Schools: Taking Charge of Your Child's Education. James B. Lewellen. 1994. 12.95 (*0-533-10794-6*) Vantage.

Parents Guide to Raising a Gifted Child: Recognizing & Development of Your Child's Potential. James Alvino & Gifted Children Newsletter Staff. 1985. 21.95 (*0-316-03727-3*) Little.

Parent's Guide to Raising a Gifted Toddler: Recognizing & Developing the Potential of Your Child from Birth to Five Years. Gifted Children Monthly Editors & James Alvino. 1989. 19.95 (*0-316-03636-6*) Little.

***Parent's Guide to Raising Creative Kids: Practical Advice & Activity Ideas.** Evelyn Petersen. (Raising... Kids Ser.). (Illus.). 2000. pap. text 3.99 (*1-55254-165-7*) Brighter Vision.

Parents Guide to Raising Gifted Children. James & Editors of Alvino. 1999. pap. write for info. (*0-316-03728-1*) Little.

***Parent's Guide to Raising Happy Kids: Practical Advice & Activity Ideas.** Evelyn Petersen. (Raising... Kids Ser.). (Illus.). 2000. pap. text 3.99 (*1-55254-166-5*) Brighter Vision.

Parents' Guide To Raising Kids Who Love To Learn. Childres Television Workshop Staff. 1989. 19.95 (*0-13-650094-3*) P-H.

***Parent's Guide to Raising Responsible Kids.** Evelyn Petersen. (Raising... Kids Ser.). 2000. pap. text 3.99 (*1-55254-167-3*) Brighter Vision.

***Parent's Guide to Raising Thinking Kids.** Evelyn Petersen. 2000. pap. text 3.99 (*1-55254-168-1*) Brighter Vision.

Parent's Guide to Raising Twins. Elizabeth Friedrich & Cherry Rowland. (Illus.). 320p. 1990. pap. 12.95 (*0-312-03906-9*) St Martin.

Parent's Guide to School Selection: Alameda-Contra Costa County Edition. Nancy G. Gill. Ed. by Jane Ginsburg & Peggy Ginsburg. (Illus.). 200p. (Orig.). 1995. pap. 15.95 (*0-9613846-3-8*) Haskala Pr.

Parent's Guide to School Selection in San Mateo & Santa Clara County. 4th rev. ed. Nancy G. Gill. (Illus.). 216p. 1998. pap. 15.95 (*0-9613846-4-6*) Haskala Pr.

Parent's Guide to School Success: Helping Your Child to Success. Christine Samuels et al. 1997. pap. write for info. (*0-9648737-5-3*) Rekindlng Heart.

***Parent's Guide to Science Fairs.** John Barron. LC 99-38907. 160p. 1999. pap. 15.95 (*0-7373-0269-0*, 02690W) NTC Contemp Pub Co.

***Parent's Guide to 2nd Grade: What Your Kids Are Being Taught-And How You Can Help Them Learn.** Peter W. Cookson. (Illus.). 2000. pap. text 14.95 (*1-57685-311-X*) LrningExprss.

Parents' Guide to Sex Education. Mary A. Mayo. 208p. 1986. pap. 7.95 (*0-310-44581-7*, 11357P) Zondervan.

Parent's Guide to Soccer. Dan Woog. LC 98-50483. (Illus.). 160p. 1999. pap. 12.95 (*0-7373-0047-7*, 00477W) NTC Contemp Pub Co.

Parents' Guide to Special Needs Schooling: Early Intervention Years. Jeffrey A. Cantor & Ruth F. Cantor. LC 95-24262. 264p. 1995. 45.00 (*0-86569-243-2*, Auburn Hse) Greenwood.

Parent's Guide to Speech Correction - P. Karen Sheppard-Nene. (Illus.). 1998. spiral bd. 16.95 (*1-892563-02-9*, P) Alpha Spch & Lang.

Parent's Guide to Speech Correction - R. Karen Sheppard-Nene. (Illus.). 1998. spiral bd. 14.95 (*1-892563-00-2*, R) Alpha Spch & Lang.

Parent's Guide to Speech Correction - S. Karen Sheppard-Nene. (Illus.). 1998. spiral bd. 16.95 (*1-892563-01-0*, S) Alpha Spch & Lang.

Parent's Guide to Spina Bifida. Beth-Ann Bloom & Edward L. Selijeskog. LC 88-10784. (Guides to Birth & Childhood Disorders Ser.). (Illus.). 96p. 1988. 16.95 (*0-8166-1486-5*) U of Minn Pr.

Parent's Guide to Street Gangs. Felix Aguirre. (Illus.). 145p. (Orig.). (C). 1993. pap. 15.00 (*0-927065-09-6*) Marin Chula Vista.

Parent's Guide to String Instrument Study. Lorraine Fink. LC 77-79565. (Illus.). 1985. pap. 2.50 (*0-8497-5700-2*, WS3) Kjos.

Parents Guide to Successful Child Modeling. Fred Vanore. 1991. pap. text 24.95 (*0-9632501-0-8*) Vanore Prods.

Parents Guide to Surviving the College Admissions Process. Ellen Fitzpatrick-Pinkman. LC 96-41724. (Illus.). 128p. 1996. pap. text 9.95 (*0-8065-1825-1*, Citadel Pr) Carol Pub Group.

Parents Guide to Teachers of Gifted - Teachers Guide to Parents. Sandra Warren. 1990. pap. 14.99 (*0-89824-507-9*) Trillium Pr.

Parent's Guide to Teaching Children Mitzvot: A Halakhic Guide. Shmuel Singer. 14.95 (*0-88125-367-7*); pap. 11.95 (*0-88125-368-5*) Ktav.

Parents' Guide to Teaching Kids to Play. Chet Murphy. LC 81-85622. (Illus.). 144p. (Orig.). 1983. reprint ed. pap. 44.70 (*0-608-07106-4*, 206733300009) Bks Demand.

Parents' Guide to Teenage Pregnancy. Margaret Brownley. 36p. (Orig.). 1988. pap. 3.95 (*0-945485-05-0*) Comm Intervention.

Parent's Guide to Teenage Sexuality. Jay Gale. 256p. 1995. pap. 9.95 (*0-8050-1648-1*, Owl) H Holt & Co.

Parent's Guide to the Ausarian Resurrection Myth: How to Teach Yourself & Your Child Principles of Universal Religion. Mnata A. Ashbi. (Illus.). 64p. 1997. pap. 5.99 (*1-884564-30-5*) Cruzian Mystic.

Parents Guide to the Best Family Videos. McCormick. LC 99-23458. 288p. 1999. pap. 11.95 (*1-58238-054-6*, Whitman Coin) St Martin.

***Parent's Guide to the California STAR Program: Grades 3-4.** 64p. 2000. 6.95 (*0-7432-0178-7*) Free Pr.

Parents' Guide to the Delaware Valley. Cynthia S. Roberts. LC 88-15021. 270p. (Orig.). 1989. pap. 12.95 (*0-940159-04-X*) Camino Bks.

***Parents Guide to the Internet.** Government Printing Office Staff. 24p. 1998. pap. 12.00 (*0-16-049712-4*) USGPO.

Parents' Guide to the Internet: And How to Protect Your Children in Cyberspace. Parry Aftab. LC 97-61817. (Illus.). xxv, 328p. 1997. pap. 22.95 (*0-9660491-0-1*) SC Pr.

Parent's Guide to the Internet: Raising Your Family on the Information Superhighway. Travis West. (Illus.). x, 134p. (Orig.). 1997. pap. 14.95 (*0-9658266-3-5*) Sivart Pub.

***Parent's Guide to the ISATs for Grade 3.** 64p. 2000. 6.95 (*0-7432-0179-5*) Free Pr.

Parent's Guide to the Law. Wilkinson. 1998. pap. 12.00 (*0-15-600366-X*) Harcourt.

Parents' Guide to the Montessori Classroom. rev. ed. Aline D. Wolf. (Illus.). 64p. 1995. pap. 5.95 (*0-939195-15-1*) Parent-Child Pr.

***Parent's Guide to the North Carolina End-of-Grade Tests for Grades 4 & 5.** Kaplan Staff. 2000. write for info. (*0-7432-0495-6*) Kaplan.

Parent's Guide to the Social Studies. Daniel Roselle. 16p. 1974. pap. 1.25 (*0-87986-053-7*, 491-15274) Nat Coun Soc Studies.

***Parents' Guide to the Spiritual Growth of Children: Helping Your Child Develop a Personal Faith.** John T. Trent. (Heritage Builders Ser.). 512p. 2000. 29.95 (*1-56179-791-X*) Bethany Hse.

***Parent's Guide to the Teen Years: Raising Your 11- to 14-Year-Old in the Age of Chat Rooms & Naval Rings.** Susan Panzarine. LC HQ777.15.P36 2000. 256p. 2000. 24.95 (*0-8160-4032-X*, Checkmark); pap. 14.95 (*0-8160-4033-8*, Checkmark) Facts on File.

Parent's Guide to the Teenage Years. B. B. Williamson. 112p. 1998. pap. 11.95 (*0-9668603-0-6*) Winsome Bk.

Parents' Guide to Tokyo. Hartzenbusch. 1996. pap. 20.95 (*4-07-973004-7*) Shufu No.

Parent's Guide to Top 10 Dangers Teens Face. Stephen Arterburn. 332p. 1999. mass mkt. 5.99 (*1-56179-689-1*) Focus Family.

Parent's Guide to Understanding & Motivating Children. Amy Lew & Betty L. Bettner. 459p. 1996. pap. 5.00 (*0-9624841-8-0*) Connex Pr.

Parent's Guide to Understanding & Motivating Children. Amy Lew & Betty Lou Bettner. 78p. 2000. pap. 7.00 (*0-9624841-3-X*) Connex Pr.

Parent's Guide to Video & Audio Cassettes for Children. Andrea E. Cascardi. 1987. mass mkt. 7.95 (*0-446-38513-1*, Pub. by Warner Bks) Little.

Parents Guide to Video Games. Steven Schwartz. 256p. 1994. pap. 12.95 (*1-55958-474-2*) Prima Pub.

Parent's Guide to Video Games. 95th ed. David Sheff. 1994. pap. 10.00 (*0-679-75282-X*) Random.

Parent's Guide to Washington Public Schools. Anthony S. Bastian. 104p. (Orig.). 1991. pap. 5.95 (*0-9630022-3-6*) Bastian Bks.

Parent's Guide to Youth Soccer. Carolyn J. Mullins. LC 83-80731. (Illus.). 144p. 1983. reprint ed. pap. 44.70 (*0-608-07060-2*, 206726600009) Bks Demand.

Parent's Handbook. Don Dinkmeyer, Sr. 1982. pap. 9.95 (*0-394-71031-2*) Random.

Parents' Handbook. Chris E. Stout. LC 96-95357. 209p. (Orig.). 1997. pap. text 29.95 (*1-890056-06-5*, 1990-56065) Grayson Pub.

Parent's Handbook: Systematic Training for Effective Parenting Don C. Dinkmeyer & Gary D. McKay. LC 98-230528. v, 138 p. 1997. write for info. (*0-7854-1188-7*) Am Guidance.

Parents Handbook: Systematic Training for Effective Parenting. Don Dinkmeyer, Sr. & Gary D. McKay. 1989. pap. 12.95 (*0-318-42598-X*) Random.

Parent's Handbook: Systematic Training for Effective Parenting. rev. ed. Don Dinkmeyer & G. D. McKay. (Illus.). 138p. 1997. pap. 15.95 (*0-679-77798-9*) Random.

P

Parent's Handbook: Systematic Training for Effective Parenting (STEP) Don C. Dinkmeyer & Gary D. McKay. LC 81-20481. 120 P. :p. 1982. 6.95 (0-913476-77-3) Am Guidance.

Parent's Handbook of Child Development. Renee A. Marazon. Ed. by David A. Marazon et al. LC 98-205942. (Illus.). 338p. (Orig.). 1997. pap. 40.00 (1-889114-03-0, 2000) Maps for Life.

Parent's Handbook of Drug & Alcohol Prevention & Family Problem Solving. Telesis Corp. Staff. Tr. by Mary Ortega from ENG. 15p. (Orig.). 1985. 1.50 (1-56117-008-9) Telesis CA.

Parent's Handbook of Filial Play Therapy. Rise VanFleet. (Illus.). Date not set. pap. 15.00 (1-930557-06-X) Play Therapy Pr.

Parent's Helper: Who to Call on Health & Family Issues. Christine L. Williams & John J. Connolly. LC 95-70170. (Illus.). 409p. (Orig.). 1996. pap. 15.95 (1-883769-72-8) Castle Connolly Med.

Parent's Homework Dictionary. 2nd ed. Dan J. McLaughlin. 1998. pap. 15.95 (1-892565-10-2) Damand.

Parent's Homework Helper: 3rd Grade. 3rd ed. Ed. by Express Staff. pap. 14.95 (1-57685-226-1) Random.

Parent's Homework Helper: 4th Grade. 4th ed. Learning Express Staff. pap. 14.95 (1-57685-227-X) Random.

Parents Impacting Discipline & Heritage. Ed. by Fairy C. Hayes-Scott. (Illus.). 200p. 1998. pap. text 25.00 (1-889743-05-4) R Dean Pr.

Parents in a Pressure Cooker: A Guide to Responsible & Loving Parent-Child Relationships. rev. ed. Jane Bluestein & Lynn Collins. (Illus.). 181p. 1989. reprint ed. pap. 10.95 (0-935493-20-4, RRB 413) Modern Learn Pr.

Parents in a Pressure Cooker: Win-Win Classroom Teachers Workbook. Jane Bluestein. 60p. (Orig.). 1990. pap. 5.00 (0-935493-25-5, RRB415) Modern Learn Pr.

Parents in a Pressure Cooker, Parent Workbook: A Guide to Responsible & Loving Parent-Child Relationships. Jane Bluestein & Lynn Colling. Ed. by Linda Sklakal. 60p. 1990. pap. 5.00 (0-935493-24-7) Modern Learn Pr.

Parents in Contemporary America: A Sympathetic View. 4th ed. E. E. LeMasters & John D. Defrain. 304p. (C). 1983. pap. write for info. (0-534-10669-2) Wadsworth Pub.

Parents in Love: Reclaiming Intimacy after Your Child Is Born. Linda Salazar. LC 98-91210. 141p. 1998. pap. 11.95 (0-9662250-0-7) Kystar Pubg.

Parents in Pain see Padres Que Sufren

Parents in Pain. John White. LC 78-24760. 245p. (Orig.). 1979. pap. 12.99 (0-87784-582-4, 582) InterVarsity.

Parents in Positive Control: Learn Techniques to Free Your Child from the "Adult No" for Part of Each Day. E. Robbins Kimball. LC 87-91723. (Illus.). 208p. (Orig.). 1987. pap. text. write for info. (0-9619113-0-1) E R Kimball.

Parents in Prison: Addressing the Needs of Families. James Boudouris. LC 96-25772. 120p. 1996. pap. 22.95 (1-56991-050-2) Am Correctional.

Parents in Prison: Children in Crisis, an Issue Brief. Cynthia B. Seymour. LC 97-221753. 48p. 1997. pap. 6.95 (0-87868-697-5) Child Welfare.

Parents in the Pigpen, Pigs in the Tub. Amy Ehrlich. (Illus.). 40p. (J). (ps-3). 1997. pap. 5.99 (0-14-056297-4, PuffinBks) Peng Put Young Read.

Parents in the Pigpen, Pigs in the Tub. Amy Ehrlich. (J). 1997. 11.19 (0-606-13013-6, Pub. by Turtleback) Demco.

Parents Instruction Destruction Book. Lucy Benedict. 120p. 1993. pap. 6.95 (1-56850-034-3) Chicago Plays.

Parents Intensive Phonics Mini Manual. Charlotte F. Lockhart. LC 91-91750. 187p. (Orig.). 1991. pap. 34.00 (0-9605654-9-3) Char-L.

Parent's Introduction to Behavior Modification. Jim Wilson. Ed. by R. Wayne Gilpin. 51p. (Orig.). 1996. pap. 14.95 (1-885477-24-4) Fut Horizons.

Parents' Jobs & Children's Lives. Toby L. Parcel & Elizabeth G. Menaghan. (Sociology & Economics Ser.). 228p. 1994. pap. text 21.95 (0-202-30484-1); lib. bdg. 43.95 (0-202-30483-3) Aldine de Gruyter.

Parents, Kids & Character: 21 Strategies to Help Your Children Develop Good Character. Helen Legette. 172p. 1998. pap. 15.95 (1-892056-01-1) Character Dev.

Parents, Learning, & Whole Language Classrooms. Gerald R. Oglan & National Council of Teachers of English Staff. LC 97-31287. (Illus.). 96p. 1997. pap. 12.95 (0-8141-3495-5) NCTE.

Parent's Little Book of Lists: Do's & Dont's of Effective Parenting. Jane Bluestein. LC 97-29511. 200p. 1997. pap. 10.95 (1-55874-512-2) Health Comm.

Parent's Little Book of Wisdom. Buck Tilton & Melissa Gray. (Little Books of Wisdom Ser.). 160p. (Orig.). 1996. pap. 6.95 (1-57034-039-0) Globe Pequot.

***Parent's Little Book of Wisdom: Suggestions, Observations & Reminders for Parents to Read.** Buck Tilton. 2000. pap. 6.95 (0-7627-0873-5) Globe Pequot.

***Parents Make the Best Shrinks: What You Need to Know to Help Your Troubled Child.** Henry A. Paul. LC 00-25332. 256p. 2000. pap. 13.00 (0-440-50887-8) Dell.

Parents' Manual. MSA Women's Committee. 1990. pap. 4.00 (0-89259-093-9) Am Trust Pubns.

Parents' Manual: A Guide for Muslim Parents Living in North America. Women's Committe MSA. 150p. 1996. pap. 6.50 (0-614-21522-6, 945) Kazi Pubns.

Parents' Medical Manual. Glenn Austin et al. 426p. 11.95 (0-13-650317-9) P-H.

Parent's Meditation Book. Beattie. 1992. per. 7.95 (0-13-650565-1) P-H.

***Parents Need to Know.** Edmund F. Benson & Susan Benson. (Illus.). 1999. pap. text 2.95 (1-58614-094-9) Arise Found.

Parents' Night Fright. Elizabeth Levy. LC 97-14294. (Hello Reader! Ser.). (Illus.). (J). (gr. 2-4). 1998. 3.99 (0-590-60324-8) Scholastic Inc.

Parents' Night Fright, 6. Elizabeth Levy. (Invisible Inc. Ser.). 1998. 9.09 (0-606-13526-X, Pub. by Turtleback) Demco.

Parents' Nutrition Bible: A Guide to Raising Healthy Children. rev. ed. Earl R. Mindell. LC 91-71698. Orig. Title: The Vitamin Bible for Kids. 256p. 1991. pap. 9.00 (1-56170-018-5, 137) Hay House.

Parents of Oscar Wilde: Sir William & Lady Wilde. Terrence D. White. LC 79-8086. reprint ed. 31.00 (0-404-18394-8) AMS Pr.

Parents of the Homosexual see Coming Out As Parents: You & Your Homosexual Child

Parents of the Passion. William R. Grimbol. (Orig.). 1989. pap. 6.50 (1-55673-100-0, 9811) CSS OH.

Parents on Board: Leader's Guide: Building Academic Success Through Parent Involvement for Parents of 4 to 14 Year Olds. Michael H. Popkin et al. 111p. 1995. spiral bd. 24.95 (1-880283-14-X) Active Parenting.

Parents on Dyslexia. Van der Stoel. 1990. 69.00 (1-85359-077-0, Pub. by Multilingual Matters); pap. 24.95 (1-85359-076-2, Pub. by Multilingual Matters) Taylor & Francis.

Parents on the Run. Willard Beecher & Marguerite Beecher. LC 73-83773. 238p. 1983. reprint ed. pap. 6.95 (0-87516-522-2) DeVorss.

Parents on Your Side: A Comprehensive Parent Involvement Program for Teachers. Lee Canter. (Illus.). 300p. 1991. pap. 14.95 (0-939007-39-8) Canter & Assocs.

Parents on Your Side: Administrator Guide. Lee Canter. (Illus.). 310p. 1993. student ed. 69.95 (0-939007-51-7) Canter & Assocs.

Parents on Your Side: Resource Materials Workbook. Lee Canter. (Illus.). 128p. (Orig.). 1991. pap. 9.95 (0-939007-40-1) Canter & Assocs.

Parents Party Book. Parents Magazine Editors. LC 99-13235. 2000. pap. 12.95 (1-58238-039-2, Whitman Coin) St Martin.

Parents, Peers, & Pot II: Parents in Action. Marsha Manatt. 160p. (Orig.). 1996. reprint ed. pap. text 25.00 (0-7881-3091-9) DIANE Pub.

Parents' Perspective: Delinquency, Aggression & Mental Health. Paul Lerman. (Applied Social Problems & Intervention Ser.: Vol. 1). 248p. 1995. pap. text 20.00 (3-7186-0582-1, Harwood Acad Pubs) Gordon & Breach.

Parents' Perspective: Delinquency, Aggression & Mental Health. Paul Lerman & Kathleen J. Pottick. (Applied Social Problems & Intervention Ser.: Vol. 1). 248p. 1995. text 50.00 (3-7186-0581-3, Harwood Acad Pubs) Gordon & Breach.

Parent's Pipeline Guide: Plain Talk about Teens & Alcohol, Drugs, Sex, Eating Disorders & Depression. Sheila Fuller & Leigh Rudd. Ed. by Robert F. Fuller & Patty B. Walker. (Illus.). 175p. 1994. pap. 9.95 (0-9631049-1-8) Parents Pipeline.

***Parents' Pipeline Guide, Connecticut Edition: Plain Talk about Teens & Alcohol, Drugs, Sex, Eating Disorders & Depression.** Sheila Fuller & Leigh Rudd. Ed. by Robert Fuller. Orig. Title: The No-Nonsense Parents' Guide, Connecticut Edition. (Illus.). 180p. 2000. pap. 14.95 (0-9631049-2-6) Parents Pipeline.

Parents, Please Don't Sit on Your Kids: A Parent's Guide to Nonpunitive Discipline. Clare Cherry. 1985. pap. 13.99 (0-8224-5307-X) Fearon Teacher Aids.

Parents' Pocket Guide to Kids & Computers: Top 100 Kids' Software Titles/Top 100 Fun & Safe Internet Sites. Family Computer Workshop Staff. LC 98-96563. 196p. 1999. pap. 12.95 (0-9666456-3-4) Family Computer.

Parents Pony Books. Carolyn Henderson. 178p. 1990. pap. 45.00 (0-85131-495-3, Pub. by J A Allen) St Mut.

Parents, Pregnant Teens, & the Adoption Option: Help for Families. Jeanne W. Lindsay. LC 88-8359. 208p. (Orig.). 1988. pap. 8.95 (0-930934-28-8) Morning Glory.

Parents' Preschool Primer. Mary R. Craig. 34p. 1989. pap. 2.00 (0-923672-03-6) Hearth Pubns.

Parent's Preschooler Dictionary: Commonsense Solutions to Early Childhood Behavioral Problems. Elinor Verville. LC 94-36288. 288p. 1995. 24.50 (0-89603-293-0) Humana.

Parent's Primer: Seven Short Lessons in Child-Raising. Jon Merritt. 100p. 1991. pap. 8.95 (0-685-50035-7) Parent Res.

Parent's Primer: What You Need to Know about Your Child's Elementary School. Elizabeth Fideler. LC 87-16901. 402p. (C). 1988. pap. 22.95 (0-8290-1916-2); text 36.50 (0-8290-1915-4) Irvington.

Parents Programs: How to Create Lasting Ties. Ed. by Larry J. Weiss. 239p. 1989. 41.50 (0-89964-296-9, 24001) Coun Adv & Supp Ed.

Parent's Promise Pocketbook see Promesas para los Padres

Parent's Promise Pocketbook. Ed. by Susan Jahns. (Pocketpac Bks.). 96p. 1989. per. 2.99 (0-87788-642-3, H Shaw Pubs) Waterbrook Pr.

Parents' Public School Handbook: How to Make the Most Out of Your Child's Education, from Kindergarten Through Middle School. Kenneth Shore. 336p. 1994. per. 12.00 (0-671-79498-1, Fireside) S&S Trade Pap.

***Parent's Quick Reference to Baby's Health: Birth to Age 5.** Alia Y. Antoon & Denise M. Tompkins. 2000. pap. 18.95 (0-7373-0492-8, Pub. by Lowell Hse) NTC Contemp Pub Co.

Parents' Resource Almanac: Where to Write, Who to Call, What to Buy & How to Find Out Everything You Need to Know. Beth Defrancis. LC 94-15476. 1994. pap. 15.00 (1-55850-394-3) Adams Media.

Parent's Resource Guide to College. Osher-Kellogg. 192p. (C). 1998. per. 6.33 (0-7872-5066-X, 41506601) Kendall-Hunt.

Parent's School Action Guide: Making the Education System Work for Your Child. David Whale. LC 99-13439. 176p. 1999. lib. bdg. 26.00 (1-888105-36-4) Avisson Pr.

Parents Shape School Success. AnnMae Johnson. LC 97-37203. 128p. 1997. pap. 12.95 (1-880090-45-7) Galde Pr.

Parent's Solution to a Problem Child. Brad Burklow. (Illus.). 104p. 1995. pap. 11.95 (0-933025-38-6) Blue Bird Pub.

Parents Speak Out: Then & Now. 2nd ed. H. Rutherford Turnbull & Ann Turnbull. 304p. (C). 1990. pap. text 30.00 (0-675-20404-6, Merrill Coll) P-H.

Parents Stop! Don't Give up, There Is Hope. Elizabeth W. Brown. 96p. 1998. pap. 8.95 (0-89228-116-2) Impact Christian.

Parent's Survival Guide to Childhood Depression. Susan E. Dubuque. 85p. (Orig.). 1996. pap. 14.95 (1-882732-49-9) Childswork.

Parents Talking Television. Philip Simpson. 144p. 1987. pap. 12.95 (1-85178-033-5, Pub. by Comedia) Routldge.

***Parent's Tao Te Ching: Ancient Advice for Modern Parents.** William C. Martin. LC 98-54591. (Illus.). 128p. 1999. pap. 11.95 (1-56924-662-9, Pub. by Marlowe & Co) Publishers Group.

Parents-Teachers & African Children - A Triangle of Hope: Ebonics Vocabulary Enclosed. 200p. 1997. pap. 10.00 (1-56411-163-6) Untd Bros & Sis.

Parents, Teenagers & Sex. Ed. by John Robson. (Illus.). 40p. (Orig.). 1982. pap. 2.50 (0-936098-34-1) Intl Marriage.

Parents, Teens & Boundaries: How to Draw the Line. Jane Bluestein. 200p. 1993. pap. 8.95 (1-55874-279-4) Health Comm.

***Parents, Teens & Drugs.** Billy James Nolen. LC 99-91298. 168p. 2000. pap. 14.95 (1-56167-575-X) Am Literary Pr.

Parents Terribles see Indiscretions

Parents Terribles. Jean Cocteau. (FRE.). 192p. 1972. pap. 10.95 (0-8288-9125-7, F96680) Fr & Eur.

Parents Terribles. Jean Cocteau. (Folio Ser.: No. 149). (FRE.). pap. 6.95 (2-07-036149-7) Schoenhof.

Parents, Their Children & Schools. James S. Coleman. Ed. by Barbara Schneider. (C). 1996. pap. 27.00 (0-8133-3077-7, Pub. by Westview) HarpC.

***Parents, "They're Driving Me Crazy!"** Kate Havelin. LC 99-29807. (Perspectives on Relationships Ser.). (Illus.). 64p. (YA). (gr. 5-9). 1999. 22.60 (0-7368-0285-1) Capstone Pr.

***Parents, "They're Driving Me Crazy!"** Kate Havelin. LC 99-32713. 1999. 22.60 (0-7368-0295-9) Capt Andersons Rest.

***Parent's Toolshop: The Universal Blueprint for Building a Healthy Family.** 2nd ed. Jody J. Pawel. LC 99-65065. (Illus.). 450p. 2000. pap. 24.95 (0-9659119-4-2) Ambris Publ.

***Parent's Toolshop: The Universal Blueprint for Building a Healthy Family.** 2nd ed. Jody Johnston Pawel. 450p. 2000. pap. 24.95 (1-929643-34-9, Pub. by Ambris Publ) ACCESS Pubs Network.

Parent's Toolshop: The Universal Blueprint for Building a Healthy Family. 2nd unabridged ed. Jody Johnston Pawel. LC 97-92298. (Illus.). 448p. 1997. pap. 29.95 (0-9659119-3-4) Ambris Publ.

Parents: Growing Closer. (Cross Training Ser.: Vol. 4). 56p. (YA). (gr. 10-12). 1995. pap. 29.95 incl. VHS (1-57405-034-6) CharismaLife Pub.

Parents' Victory Kit. Lewis F. Shaffer. (Orig.). 1988. pap. write for info. (0-929389-03-4) Son Shine Ministries.

Parents Wanted! Ruth J. Dale. (Romance Ser.: No. 3557). 1999. per. 3.50 (0-373-03557-8, 1-03557-5, Harlequin) Harlequin Bks.

Parents Wanted! large type ed. Ruth J. Dale. (Larger Print Ser.: No. 403). 1999. per. 3.50 (0-373-15803-3, 1-15803-9, Harlequin) Harlequin Bks.

Parents Who Love Reading, Kids Who Don't. Mary Leonhardt. 1995. pap. 12.00 (0-517-88222-1, Crown) Crown Pub Group.

***Parents Who Love Too Much: Reclaiming the Respect of Our Children by Giving Them What They Need.** James Fogarty & Jane Nelson. 1999. 22.95 (0-7615-2142-9) Prima Pub.

Parents Who Teach: Stories from Home & from School. Pat Sikes. LC 97-179489. 160p. 1997. pap. 22.50 (0-304-33333-6) Continuum.

Parents Who Think Too Much. Anne Cassidy. LC 97-50127. 288p. 1998. pap. 12.95 (0-440-50812-6) Doubleday.

Parents Whose Parents Were Divorced. R. Thomas Berner. LC 91-6813. (Illus.). 164p. 1992. pap. 19.95 (1-56024-139-X); lib. bdg. 39.95 (1-56024-138-1) Haworth Pr.

Parents Work Is Never Done: Helping Children from 16-30 Grow Toward Psychological Well-Being. James Haines & Margery A. Neely. 280p. 1989. pap. 9.95 (0-88282-057-5) New Horizon NJ.

Parents Work Is Never Done: Helping Children from 16-30 Grow Toward Psychological Well-Being. James Haines & Margery A. Neely. 280p. 1989. 17.95 (0-88282-027-3) New Horizon NJ.

Pareto. Julien Freund. Ed. & Tr. by Simona Draghici from FRE. LC 87-11880. 234p. (Orig.). (C). 1988. pap. 9.95 (0-943045-00-2) Plutarch Pr OR.

Pareto Charts: Plain & Simple. Joiner Assocs., Inc. Staff. Ed. by Sue Reynard. (Illus.). 130p. (Orig.). 1995. pap., student ed. 19.95 (1-884731-04-X) Oriel Inc.

Parexel's Pharmaceutical R&D Statistical Sourcebook, 1996. Ed. by Mark Mathiew. 180p. 1996. 195.00 (1-882615-26-3) Parexel Intl.

Pareys Blumenbuch. Wildbluehende Pflanzen Deutschland und Nordwesteuropas (Parey's Flower Book. Wild Flowers of Germany & Northwestern Europe) expanded rev. ed. Richard Fitter et al. (Illus.). 336p. 1986. pap. 20.00 (3-8263-8181-5, Pub. by Blckwell Wissenschafts) Balogh.

Pareys Buch der Baeume. Nadel- und Laubbaeume in Europa Noerdlich des Mittelmeeres (Parey's Book of Trees. Conifer & Hardwood Trees in Europe North of the Mediterranean) 3rd rev. ed. Alan Mitchell et al. Tr. by Peter Schutt. (Illus.). 272p. 1997. pap. 25.00 (3-8263-8462-8, Pub. by Blckwell Wissenschafts) Balogh.

Pareys Buch der Pilze (Parey's Book of Mushroom) Marcel Bon. (Illus.). 362p. 1988. pap. 22.00 (3-8263-8169-6, Pub. by Blckwell Wissenschafts) Balogh.

Pareys Mittelmeerfuehrer. Pflanzen- und Tierwelt der Mittelmeer-Region (Parey's Guide to the Mediterranean Guide. Plants & Animals of the Mediterranean Region) Tegwyn Harris. Tr. by Joachim Haupt. (Illus.). 224p. 1982. 20.00 (3-8263-8154-8, Pub. by Blckwell Wissenschafts) Balogh.

Parfait Jogger. M. Weisenfeld & B. Burr. (FRE.). 235p. 1985. pap. text 23.00 (2-903928-17-7) Gordon & Breach.

Parfit Knight. Juliet Blyth. 1987. reprint ed. pap. 3.50 (0-317-64583-8) St Martin.

Parfois Grand, Parfois Petit - Big or Little. Kathy Stinson. (FRE., Illus.). 32p. (J). 1996. pap. 4.95 (1-55037-051-0, Pub. by Les Editions) Firefly Bks Ltd.

Parfum de Jasmin. Michel Deon. (FRE.). 243p. 1978. pap. 10.95 (0-7859-1878-7, 2070370550) Fr & Eur.

***Pargeting.** Tim Buxbaum. 1999. pap. 25.00 (0-7478-0414-1, Pub. by Shire Pubns) St Mut.

Pargiters: The Novel Essay Portion of "The Years" Virginia Woolf. Ed. by Mitchell A. Leaska. LC 77-2389. (Illus.). 167p. 1977. 25.00 (0-87104-268-1) NY Pub Lib.

Pari-Mutuel Examiner. Jack Rudman. (Career Examination Ser.: C-644). 1994. pap. 23.95 (0-8373-0644-2) Nat Learn.

Pari sur un Mariage. Kate Hoffmann. (Rouge Passion Ser.). (FRE.). 1997. pap. 3.50 (0-373-37431-3, 1-37431-3) Harlequin Bks.

Paria des Iles. Joseph Conrad. (FRE.). 1983. pap. 12.95 (0-7859-2224-5, 207037436X) Fr & Eur.

***Pariah.** Wendall Horne. LC 91-91370. 2000. 25.00 (0-7388-0748-6); pap. 18.00 (0-7388-0749-4) Xlibris Corp.

Pariah. Collin Wilcox. 1989. mass mkt. 4.95 (0-445-40790-5, Mysterious Paperbk) Warner Bks.

***Pariah.** Thomas Zigal. LC 99-32900. 320p. 1999. 21.95 (0-385-31930-4) Delacorte.

***Pariah.** Thomas Zigal. (Kurt Muller Mysteries Ser.). 336p. 2000. mass mkt. 5.99 (0-440-22443-8) Dell.

Pariah's Handbook. J. J. Maloney. LC 92-32968. 1992. write for info. (0-9617499-3-8) Woods Colt Pr.

Pariahs, Partners, Predators: German-Soviet Relations, 1922-1941. Aleksandr M. Nekrich. Tr. by Gregory L. Freeze from RUS. LC 96-29605. 308p. 1997. 37.00 (0-231-10676-9) Col U Pr.

Pariahs Stand Up! The Founding of the Liberal Feminist Movement in France, 1858-1889, 31. Patrick K. Bidelman. LC 81-4222. (Contributions in Women's Studies: No. 31). 285p. 1982. 49.95 (0-313-23006-4, BPU/, Greenwood Pr) Greenwood.

Parian Phenomenon: A Survey of Victorian Parian Porcelain Statuary & Busts. Paul Atterbury. (Illus.). 268p. 1989. 95.00 (0-903685-22-1, Pub. by R Dennis) Antique Collect.

Parian Poems. Gisele D'Ailly. (Illus.). 48p. 1995. 40.00 (0-930126-48-3) Typographeum.

Parian Ware. Dennis Barker. (Album Ser.: No. 142). (Illus.). 32p. 1998. pap. 6.25 (0-85263-737-3, Pub. by Shire Pubns) Parkwest Pubns.

Paricutin: The Volcano Born in a Mexican Cornfield. James F. Luhr & Tom Simkin. LC 93-77812. (Illus.). 456p. (Orig.). 1993. 50.00 (0-945005-14-8) Geoscience Pr.

Parid & Environs Red Guide. Michelin Staff. 1994. pap. 12.95 (0-7859-7174-2, 2060068495) Fr & Eur.

Parientes de los Dinosaurios. Janet Riehecky. (Libros Sobre Dinosaurios! Ser.). (SPA., Illus.). 32p. (J). (gr. k-4). 1994. lib. bdg. 21.36 (1-56766-125-4) Childs World.

Parietal Lobe Contributions to Orientation in 3-D Space. P. Thier & H. O. Karnath. LC 97-10326. (Experimental Brain Research Ser.). 1997. write for info. (3-540-62052-4) Spr-Verlag.

Parigi Cookbook. Andree Falls. 1992. pap. 16.95 (0-9632711-0-5) PARIGI.

Parikh Normal (Error) & Log-Normal (Error) Distributions Versus Incorrect First Discovery of Normal Law by De Moivre 1733, Laplace (1777), & Gauss (1816) Navinchandra T. Parikh. 140p. (C). 1996. pap. text 100.00 (0-9651959-0-2, SNPN-001) S N Publng.

Pariksamukham. Ed. by Sarat C. Ghoshal. xi, 210p. 1990. reprint ed. 55.00 (0-685-59965-5, Pub. by Today Tomorrow) Scholarly Pubns.

Pariksamukham: With Prameya-ratnamala by Anantavirya. Manikyanandi. Tr. by Sarat C. Ghoshal. LC 73-3845. (Sacred Books of the Jainas Ser.: No. 11). 1995. reprint ed. 57.50 (0-404-57711-3) AMS Pr.

Parilla: The Mexican Grill. Reed Hearon. LC 95-43475. (Illus.). 144p. 1996. pap. 19.95 (0-8118-1034-8) Chronicle Bks.

Parings. Edward Locke. 76p. (Orig.). 1995. pap. 7.00 (0-9646587-0-4) Harlequinade.

Paris see World Cities

Paris see Cities of the World

***Paris.** 208p. 2000. spiral bd. 16.95 (1-56251-332-X, Pub. by AAA) S&S Trade.

P

Paris. 1975. pap. 20.00 (*92-3-099909-1*, UM9091) Bernan Associates.

***Paris.** (DK Eyewitness City Maps Ser.). 1999. 7.95 (*0-7894-4858-0*) DK Pub Inc.

Paris. 7.95 (*0-318-52316-7*) Fr & Eur.

Paris. (Panorama Bks.). (FRE., Illus.). 3.95 (*0-685-11477-5*) Fr & Eur.

Paris. (Frommer's Irreverent Guides Ser.). 1996. pap. 12.95 (*0-614-12829-3*) Macmillan.

Paris. 496p. 1999. pap. 15.95 (*0-02-863095-5*) Macmillan.

Paris. (FRE.). 1999. 9.95 (*2-06-633201-1*) Michelin.

Paris. (Baedeker's Ser.). (Illus.). 1991. pap. 17.00 (*0-13-094798-9*, P-H Travel) Prntice Hall Bks.

Paris. Nathan Aaseng. LC 92-709. (Cities at War Ser.). (Illus.). 96p. (YA). (gr. 6 up). 1992. lib. bdg. 18.00 (*0-02-700010-9*, Mac Bks Young Read) S&S Childrens.

Paris. Photos by Eugene Atget. (Illus.). 80p. 1998. 19.95 (*3-8238-0363-8*) te Neues.

***Paris.** Gerald Bauer. 1998. pap. text 12.95 (*2-86656-117-1*) Scala Edit.

Paris. Alice Bialestowski & Ginette Sainderichin. 80p. 1999. text 18.95 (*0-7893-0379-5*) Universe.

Paris. Barbara-Ann Campbell. (Architecture Guides Ser.). (Illus.). 320p. 1998. pap. 5.95 (*3-89508-642-8*, 520200) Konemann.

Paris. G. W. Edwards. 1972. 59.95 (*0-8490-0799-2*) Gordon Pr.

Paris. Julian Green. Tr. by J. A. Underwood from FRE. (Illus.). 160p. (C). 1991. 21.95 (*0-7145-2927-3*) M Boyars Pubs.

Paris. Griffin Trade Paperbacks Publishing Staff. (Let's Go 2000 Ser.). (Illus.). 368p. 1999. pap. 16.99 (*0-312-24479-7*, St Martin Griffin) St Martin.

Paris. William Hart. (Illus.). 30p. (Orig.). 1996. pap. 7.50 (*0-944048-09-9*) Timberline Missouri.

Paris. Burton Holmes. Ed. by Arthur Meier Schlesinger, Jr. & Fred L. Isreal. LC 97-36085. (World 100 Years Ago Ser.). (Illus.). 144p. (YA). (gr. 5 up). 1999. lib. bdg. 29.95 (*0-7910-4662-1*) Chelsea Hse.

Paris. Ed. by Fred L. Israel & Arthur Meier Schlesinger, Jr. LC 97-36085. (World 100 Years Ago Ser.). (Illus.). 144p. (YA). (gr. 5 up). 1999. pap. 19.95 (*0-7910-4663-X*) Chelsea Hse.

***Paris.** James Kavanagh. (Pocket Traveller City Ser.). (Illus.). 2000. 5.95 (*1-58355-017-8*, Pub. by Waterford WA) Falcon Pub Inc.

***Paris.** Konemann Inc. Staff. (Illus.). 2000. 14.95 (*3-8290-4838-6*) Konemann.

Paris. Lisa Legarde. LC 93-6988. (Frommer's Walking Tours Ser.). 1993. pap. 12.00 (*0-671-79764-6*, P-H Travel) Prntice Hall Bks.

Paris. Michelin Staff. 1999. pap. text 9.95 (*2-06-661201-4*) Michelin.

Paris. National Geographic Society Staff. LC 99-11168. (National Geographic Traveler Ser.). (Illus.). 272p. 1999. per. 22.95 (*0-7922-7429-6*, Pub. by Natl Geog) S&S Trade.

Paris. Daniel Noin & Paul White. LC 97-206195. (World Cities Ser.). 302p. 1997. 110.00 (*0-471-94944-2*) Wiley.

Paris. NTC Publishing Group Staff. (Passport Essential Guide Ser.). 128p. 1998. pap. 8.95 (*0-8442-0133-2*, Passprt Bks) NTC Contemp Pub Co.

Paris. Ed. by James O'Reilly et al. (Travelers' Tales Guides Ser.). 417p. 1997. pap. 17.95 (*1-885211-10-4*) Trvlers Tale.

***Paris.** Judith Pasternak. LC 99-56402. (Timeless Places Ser.). (Illus.). 96p. 2000. 17.95 (*1-56799-926-3*, Friedman-Fairfax) M Friedman Pub Grp Inc.

Paris. Ed. by Pocket Books Staff. 1988. pap. 5.95 (*0-671-88279-1*) PB.

Paris. Milena E. Pozzoli. (Places & History Ser.). 1998. 24.95 (*1-55670-693-6*) Stewart Tabori & Chang.

***Paris.** Random House Value Publishing Staff. (Illus.). 128p. 2000. 12.99 (*0-517-16175-3*) Random Hse Value.

Paris. Melissa Shales. Ed. by Globetrotter Staff. (Globe Trotter Travel Guides Ser.). (Illus.). 128p. 1996. pap. 22.00 (*1-85368-423-6*, Pub. by New5 Holland) Globe Pequot.

Paris. R. Conrad Stein. (Cities of the World Ser.). 64p. (J). 1997. pap. 9.95 (*0-516-26073-1*) Childrens.

***Paris.** Teneues Publishing Company Staff. 1999. 10.95 (*3-8238-0558-4*) te Neues.

Paris. Alan Tillier. LC 92-53472. (Eyewitness Travel Guides Ser.). (Illus.). 432p. 1993. pap. 24.95 (*1-56458-185-3*) DK Pub Inc.

Paris. Ed. by Tripbuilder Staff. 1997. pap. 59.50 (*1-56621-116-6*) TripBuilder.

Paris. Emile Zola. Tr. by Ernest Alfred Vizetelly. LC 75-20446. 1981. lib. bdg. 250.00 (*0-87968-236-1*) Gordon Pr.

Paris. Emile Zola. Tr. by Ernest Alfred Vizetelly. LC 93-26292. (Pocket Classics Ser.). (Illus.). 488p. 1993. pap. 10.95 (*0-7509-0450-X*, Pub. by Sutton Pub Ltd) Intl Pubs Mktg.

Paris. Julian Green. Tr. by J. A. Underwood. (FRE & ENG., Illus.). 160p. 1999. reprint ed. pap. 13.95 (*0-7145-2928-1*, Pub. by M Boyars Pubs) LPC InBook.

Paris. Vivienne Menkes-Ivry. Ed. by Arthur Eperon. (Regional Guides of France Ser.). (Illus.). 248p. 1994. reprint ed. pap. text 16.95 (*0-8442-9942-1*, Passprt Bks) NTC Contemp Pub Co.

***Paris.** rev. ed. Let's Go Staff. (Let's Go 2001 Ser.). (Illus.). 368p. 2000. pap. 16.99 (*0-312-24686-2*, St Martin Griffin) St Martin.

Paris. 2nd ed. (Charming Small Hotel Guides Ser.). (Illus.). 160p. 1999. pap. 13.95 (*1-55650-868-9*) Hunter NJ.

***Paris.** 2nd ed. Ed. by Fodors Travel Publications, Inc. Staff. 2000. pap. 13.50 (*0-679-00385-1*) Fodors Travel.

Paris. 2nd ed. Insight Guides Staff. (Insight Guides). 1998. pap. text 7.95 (*0-88729-553-3*) Langenscheidt.

Paris. 2nd ed. Elizabeth Morris. LC 94-67813. (Illustrated Travel Guides from Thomas Cook Ser.). (Illus.). 192p. (Orig.). 1994. pap. 12.95 (*0-8442-9048-3*, Passprt Bks) NTC Contemp Pub Co.

***Paris.** 2nd ed. New Holland Publishing Staff. (Globetrotter Travel Guides Ser.). 2001. pap. 10.95 (*1-85974-066-9*); pap. 14.95 (*1-85974-483-4*) New5 Holland.

Paris. 2nd rev. ed. Elisabeth Morris. LC 99-179930. (Thomas Cook Travellers Ser.). 192p. 1996. write for info. (*0-7495-1353-5*, Pub. by Auto Assn Guides) Hunter NJ.

Paris. 3rd ed. Dana Facaros. 1999. text 16.95 (*1-86011-909-3*) Cadgn Bks.

Paris. 4th ed. Insight Guides Staff. (Insight Guides). 1998. pap. text 12.95 (*0-88729-925-3*) Langenschiedt.

Paris. 4th ed. Elisabeth Morris. (Passport's Illustrated Travel Guides from Thomas Cook Ser.). (Illus.). 192p. 1999. pap. 14.95 (*0-658-00034-9*, 000349, Passprt Bks) NTC Contemp Pub Co.

Paris. 5th ed. Insight Guides Staff. (Insight Guides). 1998. pap. text 21.95 (*0-88729-443-X*) Langenscheidt.

Paris. 7th ed. Penguin Books Staff. 352p. 1999. pap. 14.95 (*0-14-027451-0*) Viking Penguin.

Paris. 7th ed. Rough Guides Staff. 464p. 1999. pap. 14.95 (*1-85828-407-4*, Pub. by Rough Guides) Penguin Putnam.

Paris, Vol. 206. Compiled by Frances Chambers. LC 99-218231. (World Biographical Series). 142p. 1998. lib. bdg. 54.00 (*1-85109-271-4*) ABC-CLIO.

Paris: A Guide to Archival Sources for American Art History. Susan Grant. 175p. (Orig.). 1997. pap. write for info. (*1-880193-10-8*) Arch Am Art.

Paris: A Guide to the Principal Buildings. Renzo Salvadori. 1998. pap. 19.95 (*88-86502-80-X*, Pub. by Canal & Stamperia) Antique Collect.

***Paris: A Musical Gazetteer.** Nigel Simeone. LC 99-54362. (Illus.). 299p. 2000. 40.00 (*0-300-08053-0*); pap. 18.95 (*0-300-08054-9*) Yale U Pr.

Paris: A New Look. Reg Butler. (City Breaks Ser.). 96p. 1997. pap. 6.95 (*1-872876-49-8*, Pub. by Settle Pr) Assoc Pubs Grp.

***Paris: Alex & Dana.** Rachel Hawthorne. (Love Stories Ser.). (YA). (gr. 7-12). 2000. mass mkt. 4.50 (*0-553-49327-2*) Bantam.

Paris: An Architectural Guide. Heinfried Wischerman. (Illus.). 144p. (Orig.). 1996. pap. 17.95 (*88-7743-162-8*, Pub. by Arsenale Editrice) Antique Collect.

Paris: An Architectural History. Anthony Sutcliffe. LC 93-24. (Illus.). 232p. 1993. 47.00 (*0-300-05445-9*) Yale U Pr.

Paris: An Architectural History. Anthony Sutcliffe. LC 93-24. (Illus.). 288p. 1996. pap. 25.00 (*0-300-06886-7*) Yale U Pr.

Paris: An Illustrated Guide with Over 850 Drawings & Neighborhood Maps. Michel Poisson. Tr. by John Goodman from FRE. LC 98-42780. (Illus.). 464p. 1999. 39.95 (*0-8109-4355-7*, Pub. by Abrams) Time Warner.

Paris: Birthplace of the U. S. A. Daniel Jouve. 103p. 1995. 35.00 (*0-7859-9924-8*) Fr & Eur.

***Paris: Buildings & Monuments : An Illustrated Guide with Over 850 Drawings & Neighborhood Maps.** Michel Poisson. LC 98-42780. 144p. 2000. pap. 24.95 (*0-8109-2915-5*, Pub. by Abrams) Time Warner.

Paris: Capital of Europe: From the Revolution to the Belle Epoque. Johannes Willms. Tr. by Eveline L. Kanes from GER. 580p. 1996. text 40.00 (*0-8419-1245-9*) Holmes & Meier.

Paris: Center of Artistic Enlightenment. Ed. by George Mauner et al. (Papers in Art History: Vol. IV). (Illus.). 250p. (Orig.). 1988. pap. 22.00 (*0-915773-03-1*) Penn St Univ Dept Art Hist.

Paris: Contemporary Architecture. Andrea Gleiniger et al. LC 97-11552. (Illus.). 160p. 1997. 49.95 (*3-7913-1678-8*, Pub. by Prestel) te Neues.

Paris: Deluxe Gift Edition. DK Publishing Staff. (Eyewitness Travel Guides Ser.). 432p. 1999. pap. 40.00 (*0-7894-4977-3*, D K Ink) DK Pub Inc.

Paris: English Edition. Casa Bonechi. 64p. pap. text 11.95 (*88-7009-204-6*, Pub. by Bonechi) Eiron.

Paris: Its Sites, Monuments & History. Maria H. Lansdale. 1977. lib. bdg. 59.95 (*0-8490-2413-7*) Gordon Pr.

Paris: Nineteen Twenty-Eight to Nineteen Twenty-Nine. Ed. by Wolfgang Hageney. (ENG, FRE, GER, ITA & SPA., Illus.). 224p. 1986. 54.95 (*88-7070-069-0*) Belvedere USA.

Paris: Panorama. Marc Wiltz. (Illus.). 128p. 1999. 39.90 (*2-911589-28-9*, Pub. by Editions dIndochine) BHB Intl.

Paris: Passport's Illustrated Travel Guides. 3rd ed. Thomas Cook. LC 96-70699. (Illus.). 192p. 1996. pap. text 14.95 (*0-8442-4840-1*) NTC Contemp Pub Co.

Paris: Poems. Jim Barnes. LC 96-45831. 120p. 1997. 16.95 (*0-252-06622-7*) U of Ill Pr.

***Paris: Portrait of a City.** Matthew Weinreb. 240p. 1999. pap. 9.95 (*0-7148-3455-6*) Phaidon Pr.

Paris: Siege & Commune, 1870-1871. (Illus.). 1988. pap. 20.00 (*0-87959-107-2*) U of Tex H Ransom Ctr.

Paris: The Travel Notebook. Pascale Loiseau. 104p. 1997. 14.95 (*2-911141-03-2*, Pub. by Les Edtns Pascale) Assoc Pubs Grp.

Paris: Underground. pap. 16.95 (*0-528-94977-2*) Rand McNally.

Paris - 1961. Hans G. Reinshagen. (FRE & GER., Illus.). (C). 1996. 41.00 (*3-8170-2514-9*, Pub. by Knstvrlag Weingrtn) Intl Bk Import.

***Paris -The Collected Traveler: An Inspired Anthology & Travel Resource.** Barrie Kerper. LC 99-59313. 512p. 2000. pap. 16.00 (*0-609-80444-8*, Three Riv Pr) Crown Pub Group.

Paris Access. Richard S. Wurman. (Access Travel Guides Ser.). (Illus.). 183p. (Orig.). 1986. pap. 14.95 (*0-671-62577-2*, Access Trvl) HarpInfo.

***Paris Air Show.** Don Berliner. (Illus.). 156p. 2000. pap. 29.95 (*0-7603-0728-8*, 129830AP, Pub. by MBI Pubg) Motorbooks Intl.

Paris Alive, the Point of View of an American. Judith Clancy et al. Orig. Title: Paris Vivant. (ENG & FRE., Illus.). 72p. 1986. pap. 10.00 (*0-912184-06-X*) Synergistic Pr.

***Paris Along The Nile; Architecture In Cairo From The Belle Epoque.** Cynthia Myntti. 1999. 39.95 (*977-424-510-5*, Pub. by Am Univ Cairo Pr) Col U Pr.

Paris along the Seine. Gerald K. Geerlings. LC 87-34210. (Illus.). 160p. 1988. pap. 20.00 (*0-933444-47-8*) French Inst.

***Paris & Elsewhere.** R. Cobb. 1998. text 45.00 (*0-7195-5469-1*, Pub. by John Murray) Trafalgar.

***Paris & Elsewhere: Selected Writings.** Richard Cobb. Ed. & Intro. by David Gilmour. 288p. 1999. pap. 24.95 (*0-7195-5462-4*, Pub. by John Murray) Trafalgar.

***Paris & Environs Hotels & Restaurants: 2000 Edition.** 100th ed. Michelin Staff. (Red Guide Paris Ser.). (Illus.). 2000. pap. text. write for info. (*2-06-968049-5*) Michelin.

Paris & Other Poems, 1980-1997. Barbara M. Yarnold. LC 98-30723. 82p. 1998. pap. 14.95 (*0-7734-2851-8*, Mellen Poetry Pr) E Mellen.

Paris & Provence. Andre Gayot. (Illus.). 288p. 1998. pap. text 15.00 (*1-881066-39-8*) Gault Millau.

Paris & Rome: The Gallican Church & the Ultramontane Campaign 1848-1853. Austin Gough. 280p. 1986. 65.00 (*0-19-821977-6*) OUP.

Paris & the Anarchists: Aesthetes & Subversives During the Fin-de-si('e)cle. Alexander Varias. LC 96-30670. 224p. 1996. text 45.00 (*0-312-16061-5*) St Martin.

Paris & the Legacy of French Architectural Ceramics. Susan Tunick et al. (FRE & JPN., Illus.). 42p. 1997. pap. 20.00 (*0-9636061-3-1*) Frnds of TC.

Paris & the Nineteenth Century. Christopher Prendergast. (Writing the City Ser.). (Illus.). 296p. 1995. pap. text 28.95 (*0-631-19694-3*) Blackwell Pubs.

Paris & Vienne Translated from the French & Printed by William Caxton. Ed. by M. Leach. (EETS Original Ser.: No. 234). 1970. reprint ed. 30.00 (*0-19-722234-X*, Pub. by EETS) Boydell & Brewer.

Paris Anglophone: The Directory of English Speaking Paris. 4th ed. David Applefield. 1996. pap. 14.95 (*2-84096-046-X*, Pub. by Parigramme Edits) Midpt Trade.

Paris Apartment: Romantic Decor on a Flea-Market Budget. Claudia Strasser. (Illus.). 160p. 1997. 26.00 (*0-06-039169-3*, HarperStyle) HarpC.

Paris As Revolution: Writing in the Nineteenth-Century City. Priscilla P. Ferguson. LC 93-44374. (C). 1994. 45.00 (*0-520-08642-2*, Pub. by U CA Pr) Cal Prin Full Svc.

Paris As Revolution: Writing in the Nineteenth-Century City. Priscilla P. Ferguson. LC 93-44374. (Illus.). 1997. pap. 17.95 (*0-520-20887-0*, Pub. by U CA Pr) Cal Prin Full Svc.

Paris at Its Best. Robert S. Kane. 1986. pap. 9.95 (*0-8442-9563-9*, Passprt Bks) NTC Contemp Pub Co.

Paris at Night. (Panorama Bks.). (FRE., Illus.). 3.95 (*0-685-11478-3*) Fr & Eur.

Paris Atlas - 1900. Ed. by Larousse Staff. (FRE.). 310p. 1989. 150.00 (*0-7859-9839-X*) Fr & Eur.

Paris Atlas by Arrondissements. 6th ed. Michelin Staff. 1994. pap. 29.95 (*0-7859-9145-X*) Fr & Eur.

Paris Atlas by Arrondissements. 8th ed. Michelin Staff. 1997. per. 15.00 (*2-06-700015-2*, 015) Michelin.

Paris Atlas Par Arrondissements. 16th ed. Michelin Staff. 1999. pap. text 12.95 (*2-06-001601-0*) Jonathan Cape.

Paris Atlas with Metro & Regional. 13th ed. Michelin Staff. 1994. pap. write for info. (*0-7859-9129-8*) Fr & Eur.

Paris au Mois D'Aout. Rene Fallet. (FRE.). 224p. 1974. pap. 10.95 (*0-7859-2345-4*, 2070365964) Fr & Eur.

Paris au Vingtieme Siecle. Jules Verne. 1994. 49.95 (*0-7859-9875-6*) Fr & Eur.

Paris, B. N. Fonds Latin 35449 & London, B. L., Add. 36,881. Ed. by Bryan Gillingham. (Veroffentlichungen Mittelalterlicher Musikhandschriften - Publications of Mediaeval Musical Manuscripts Ser.: Vol. 16). (ENG, FRE & GER.). 112p. 1987. 60.00 (*0-931902-56-8*) Inst Mediaeval Mus.

Paris Babylon: The Story of the Paris Commune. Rupert Christiansen. 320p. 1996. pap. 13.95 (*0-14-012980-4*, Penguin Bks) Viking Penguin.

Paris, Bibliotheque Nationale, Fonds Latin 1139. Ed. by Bryan Gillingham. (Veroffentlichungen Mittelalterlicher Musikhandschriften - Publications of Mediaeval Musical Manuscripts Ser.: Vol. 14). (ENG, FRE & GER.). 450p. 1987. 110.00 (*0-931902-54-1*) Inst Mediaeval Mus.

Paris, Bibliotheque Nationale, Fonds Latin 3719. Ed. by Bryan Gillingham. (Veroffentlichungen Mittelalterlicher Musikhandschriften - Publications of Mediaeval Musical Manuscripts Ser.: Vol. 15). (ENG, FRE & GER.). 249p. 1987. 95.00 (*0-931902-55-X*) Inst Mediaeval Mus.

Paris, Bibliotheque Nationale, Fonds Latin 7211. Ed. by Alma C. Santosuosso. (Veroffentlichungen Mittelalterlicher Musikhandschriften - Publications of Mediaeval Musical Manuscripts Ser.: Vol. 18). 248p. 1991. 92.00 (*0-931902-68-1*) Inst Mediaeval Mus.

Paris Bistro Cooking. Linda Dannenberg. (Illus.). 160p. 1991. 35.00 (*0-517-57433-0*) C Potter.

Paris Book of Hours, Vol. 1. Csaba Csapodi. (Illus.). 1999. pap. 14.00 (*963-13-2397-8*, Pub. by Corvina Bks) St Mut.

Paris Book of Hours, Vol. 2. Csaba Csapodi. (Illus.). 1999. pap. 14.00 (*963-13-2398-6*, Pub. by Corvina Bks) St Mut.

***Paris Book Trade in the Middle Ages 1200-1500.** Richard Rouse & Mary Rouse. (Illus.). 800p. 1999. text 225.00 (*1-872501-41-9*, Pub. by Harvey Miller) Gordon & Breach.

Paris Boulangerie Cookbook. Linda Dannenberg. LC 93-36414. (Illus.). 160p. 1994. 35.00 (*0-517-59221-5*) Crown Pub Group.

Paris Bourse & French Finance with Reference to Organized Speculation in New York. William Parker. LC 20-18734. (Columbia University. Studies in the Social Sciences: No. 204). reprint ed. 20.00 (*0-404-51204-6*) AMS Pr.

Paris Cafe Cookbook: Rendezvous And Recipes From 50 Best Cafes. Daniel Young. LC 98-2840. (Illus.). 160p. 1998. 24.00 (*0-688-15330-5*, Wm Morrow) Morrow Avon.

Paris Cat. Leslie A. Baker. LC 97-42169. (Illus.). 32p. (J). (gr. k-3). 1999. 15.95 (*0-316-07309-1*) Little.

Paris City Councillors in the Sixteenth Century: The Politics of Patrimony. Barbara B. Diefendorf. LC 82-47591. 379p. 1983. reprint ed. pap. 117.50 (*0-7837-9330-8*, 206007100004) Bks Demand.

Paris Codex: Handbook for a Maya Priest. Bruce Love. LC 93-13028. (Illus.). 176p. (C). 1994. text 37.50 (*0-292-74674-1*) U of Tex Pr.

Paris Collection: French Doll Fashions & Accessories. Sylvia MacNeil. LC 92-203522. (Illus.). 192p. 1992. 29.95 (*0-87588-372-9*) Hobby Hse.

Paris Commune. Draper. 1971. pap. text 10.00 (*0-85345-219-9*, Pub. by Monthly Rev) NYU Pr.

***Paris Commune 1871.** Robert Tombs. LC 99-13460. (Turning Points in History Ser.). 244p. 1999. pap. 27.53 (*0-582-30903-4*) Longman.

***Paris Commune 1871.** Robert Tombs. LC 99-13460. (Turning Points in History Ser.). 256p. (C). 1999. 69.95 (*0-582-30915-8*) Longman.

Paris Confidential. 2nd ed. Warren Trabant & Jean Trabant. 160p. 1991. 12.95 (*0-945332-26-2*) Agora Inc MD.

***Paris Confidential 2000.** Anne-Cecile Sanchez. 160p. 2000. text 19.95 (*2-84323-189-2*, Pub. by Assouline) St Martin.

Paris Connection. Carolyn Keene & Franklin W. Dixon. (Nancy Drew & Hardy Boys Super Mystery Ser.: No. 6). 224p. (YA). (gr. 6 up). 1991. mass mkt. 3.99 (*0-671-74675-8*, Archway) PB.

Paris Connections: African American Artists in Paris. Ed. by Asake Bomani & Belvie Rooks. Tr. by Lydia Rand & Nellie Timmons. LC 92-50057. (ENG & FRE., Illus.). 96p. 1992. pap. 30.00 (*0-936609-25-7*) QED Ft Bragg.

Paris Connections: African & Caribbean Artists in Paris. Ed. by Asake Bomani & Belvie Rooks. Tr. by Lydia Rand. LC 92-5235. (ENG & FRE., Illus.). 64p. 1992. pap. 14.95 (*0-936609-26-5*) QED Ft Bragg.

Paris Conservatoire & the Contest Solos for Bassoon. Kristine K. Fletcher. LC 87-45442. 160p. 1988. 8.95 (*0-253-34215-5*) Ind U Pr.

Paris, Contemporary Architecture. Andrea Gleininger et al. LC 97-11552. 1997. write for info. (*3-7913-1655-9*, Pub. by Prestel) te Neues.

Paris Dances: Textual Choreographies in the Nineteenth Century French Novel. Sarah D. Cordova. (Illus.). 341p. 1998. 74.95 (*1-57309-335-1*) Intl Scholars.

Paris de L'Introuvable. (ENG & FRE.). 1996. 34.95 (*0-7859-9364-9*) Fr & Eur.

Paris Deluxe. Alexis Gregory. LC 97-11098. (Illus.). 240p. 1997. 65.00 (*0-8478-2061-0*, Pub. by Rizzoli Intl) St Martin.

Paris Diary & the New York Diary, 1951-1961. Ned Rorem. LC 97-46200. (Illus.). 431p. 1998. reprint ed. pap. 16.95 (*0-306-80838-2*) Da Capo.

Paris During the Commune. W. Gibson. LC 75-1245. (World History Ser.: No. 48). 1974. lib. bdg. 75.00 (*0-8383-1776-6*) M S G Haskell Hse.

Paris Eighty-Nine: Personal & Archetypal Dynamics in the Analytical Relationship. Mary A. Mattoon. LC 81-3357. 530p. 1995. 35.00 (*3-85630-529-7*); pap. 25.00 (*3-85630-524-6*) Continuum.

Paris Embassy of Sir Eric Phipps: Anglo-French Relations & Foreign Office, 1937-1939. John Herman. LC 98-29477. 276p. 1998. 75.00 (*1-902210-04-2*, Pub. by Sussex Acad Pr) Intl Spec Bk.

Paris Era Una Fiesta. Ernest Hemingway. 1998. pap. 6.95 (*84-322-3009-X*) Continental Bk.

Paris Est une Fete. Ernest Hemingway. (FRE.). 1973. pap. 10.95 (*0-7859-2323-3*, 2070364658) Fr & Eur.

Paris et Sa Banlieue: French Edition-Country & City Guides. (Green Guides). pap. 14.95 (*0-686-56409-X*) Fr & Eur.

Paris Fashion: A Cultural History. rev. ed. Valerie Steele. 320p. 1998. pap. 19.50 (*1-85973-973-3*, Pub. by Berg Pubs) NYU Pr.

Paris Fashions of the 1890's: A Picture Source Book with 450 Designs, Including 24 in Full Color. Ed. by Stella Blum. (Antiques Ser.). 88p. (Orig.). 1984. pap. 9.95 (*0-486-24534-9*) Dover.

Paris Fever. large type ed. Jane Gurney. (Linford Romance Library). 1991. pap. 16.99 (*0-7089-7050-8*) Ulverscroft.

Paris Flea Market. Herbert Ypma. (Illus.). 160p. 1996. pap. 27.50 (*1-55670-500-X*) Stewart Tabori & Chang.

***Paris for Families.** Larry Lain. 2000. pap. 15.00 (*1-56656-360-7*) Interlink Pub.

Paris for Free (or Extremely Cheap) Hundreds of Free & Inexpensive Things to Do in Paris. 2nd rev. ed. Mark Beffart. LC 96-49219. (Illus.). 192p. 1997. pap. 10.95 (*0-914457-87-X*) Mustang Pub.

Paris for Less. (For Less Compact Guides Ser.). 1999. pap. 9.95 (*1-901811-85-9*) IPG Chicago.

Paris for Less: The Total Guidebook. Christina Prostano. (For Less Guidebook Ser.). (Illus.). 288p. 1998. pap. 19.95 (*1-901811-15-8*, Pub. by Metropolis International) IPG Chicago.

Paris-Forfar. David Kinloch. 88p. (Orig.). 1994. 10.95 (*0-7486-6183-2*, Pub. by Polygon) Subterranean Co.

Paris France. Gertrude Stein. 128p. 1996. reprint ed. pap. 11.00 (*0-87140-160-6*, Pub. by Liveright) Norton.

P

Paris, France - Cooking with Betty Evans. Betty Evans. LC 87-61698. (Illus.). (Orig.). 1987. pap. 6.95 (*0-931104-20-3*) SunInk Pubn.

Paris from $60 a Day, 1997. Arthur Frommer. (Frommer's Dollar-A-Day Guides Ser.). 1997. pap. 14.95 (*0-02-861331-7*) Macmillan.

Paris Gourmet Guide. Jacques-Louis Delpal. LC 95-15364. (Illus.). 142p. 1995. text 29.95 (*0-86565-959-1*) Vendome.

Paris Green Guide. 2nd ed. Michelin Staff. 1996. pap. 19.95 (*0-7859-9147-6*) Fr & Eur.

Paris Green Guide: Europe. Ed. by Michelin Staff. (JPN.). 1991. per. 36.00 (*4-408-01301-3*, 9353) Michelin.

Paris Green Guide: France (Guides Regionaux) 4th ed. Ed. by Michelin Staff. (FRE.). 1997. per. 18.00 (*2-06-035204-5*, 352) Michelin.

Paris Green Guide: France (Regional Guides) 3rd ed. Ed. by Michelin Staff. (Illus.). 1996. per. 18.00 (*2-06-135503-X*, 1355) Michelin.

Paris Green Guide French Edition. Michelin Staff. (FRE.). 1996. pap. 19.95 (*0-7859-7216-1*, 2067003526) Fr & Eur.

Paris Guia Turistica, 1998. rev. ed. Berlitz Editors. (Pocket Guides Ser.). (SPA., Illus.). 144p. 1998. pap. 8.95 (*2-8315-6563-4*) Berlitz.

Paris Guide. 2nd rev. ed. Robert F. Howe & Diane Huntley. 288p. 1997. pap. 13.95 (*1-883323-66-5*) Open Rd Pub.

Paris (Hotel & Restaurant Guide), 1996. Michelin Staff. 1996. 11.95 (*0-7859-9905-1*) Fr & Eur.

Paris Hotel & Restaurant Guide 1998. Michelin. (ENG, FRE, GER & ITA.). 1998. 11.95 (*0-7859-9610-9*) Fr & Eur.

***Paris Hotels.** 2nd ed. Alastair Sawday Staff. Ed. by Anne Cooke-Yarborough. (Alastair Sawday's Special Places to Stay Ser.). (Illus.). 192p. 2000. pap. 14.95 (*0-7627-0724-0*) Globe Pequot.

***Paris Hotels.** 3rd ed. Ann Cooke-Yarborough. (Alastair Sawday's Special Places to Stay Ser.). (Illus.). 2001. pap. 14.95 (*0-7627-0773-9*) Globe Pequot.

Paris, Ile de France & the Loire Valley. Andre Gayot. LC 97-4451. (Illus.). 160p. 1997. pap. 15.00 (*1-881066-32-0*) Gault Millau.

***Paris in a Basket: Markets in Paris.** Konemann Inc. Staff. (Illus.). 352p. 2000. 19.95 (*3-8290-4624-3*) Konemann.

Paris in American Literature. Jean Meral. LC 88-33910. 296p. reprint ed. pap. 91.80 (*0-608-08616-9*, 206913900003) Bks Demand.

Paris in August. Adrian George. (Illus.). 119p. 1995. 55.00 (*0-7206-0937-2*, Pub. by P Owen Ltd) Dufour.

Paris in Color see Travel Guides in Color

***Paris In Despair.** Hollis Clayson. 1998. 60.00 (*0-226-10951-8*) U Ch Pr.

Paris in Japan: The Japanese Encounter with European Painting. Shuji Takashina & J. Thomas Rimer. LC 87-50582. (Illus.). 288p. (Orig.). 1987. pap. 20.00 (*0-936316-11-X*) Wash U Gallery.

***Paris in New York: French Jewish Artists in Private Collections.** Ed. by Susan Chevlowe. LC 00-131238. (Illus.). 64p. 2000. pap. 19.95 (*0-87334-079-5*) Jewish Mus NY.

Paris in Seventeen Eighty-Nine to Seventeen Ninety-Four, Farewell Letters of Victims of the Guillotine. John G. Alger. LC 78-113540. reprint ed. 57.50 (*0-404-00323-0*) AMS Pr.

Paris in Splendor, 2 vols., Set. E. A. Reynolds-Ball. 1976. lib. bdg. 200.00 (*0-8490-2412-9*) Gordon Pr.

Paris in the Cities. Goldstein Gallery Staff. (Illus.). 16p. (Orig.). 1986. pap. 3.00 (*0-939719-01-0*) UMN Goldstein Gall.

Paris in the 1890s. Jane Kinsman et al. LC 96-60302. (Illus.). 250p. (Orig.). 1997. pap. 24.95 (*0-500-97440-3*, Pub. by Thames Hudson) Norton.

Paris in the Fall. large type ed. Tamsin Hamilton. 496p. 1983. 11.50 (*0-7089-0972-8*) Ulverscroft.

***Paris in the Fifties.** Stanley Karnow. 2000. 26.50 (*0-8446-7125-8*) Peter Smith.

Paris in the 50's. Stanley Karnow. LC 97-18521. 368p. 1999. pap. 14.00 (*0-8129-3137-8*, Times Bks) Crown Pub Group.

Paris in the Twentieth Century. Jules Verne. Tr. by Richard Howard. LC 97-94115. (Illus.). 222p. 1997. pap. 11.95 (*0-345-42039-X*, Del Rey) Ballantine Pub Grp.

Paris in Your Pocket Guide. Michelin Staff. (In Your Pocket Guides Ser.). 1996. per. 9.95 (*2-06-630201-5*, 6302) Michelin.

Paris Inside Out: The Insider's Handbook to Life in Paris. 5th ed. David Applefield. LC 99-56913. 380p. 1999. pap. 19.95 (*0-7627-0594-9*) Globe Pequot.

Paris Insolite. Jean-Paul Clebert. (FRE.). 1972. pap. 10.95 (*0-7859-2198-2*, 207036285X) Fr & Eur.

Paris Interiors. Lisa Lovatt-Smith. 1995. 39.99 (*3-8228-8932-6*) Taschen Amer.

Paris Interview. Ron Churchill. 347p. 1994. 24.00 (*0-9642455-0-7*); pap. 13.00 (*0-9642455-8-2*) Ave A Pr.

Paris Is Fun: A Bilingual Guide. Lory Alder. 1969. 12.00 (*0-7207-0225-9*) Transatl Arts.

Paris la Belle. Jacques Prevert & P. Prevert. (FRE.). 5.95 (*0-686-54914-7*) Fr & Eur.

Paris Law Courts: Sketches of Men & Manners. Tr. by Gerald P. Moriarty from FRE. viii, 293p. 1999. reprint ed. 95.00 (*1-56169-496-7*) Gaunt.

Paris Law Courts: Sketches of Men & Manners. Tr. by Gerald P. Moriarty from FRE. (Illus.). viii, 293p. 1987. reprint ed. 42.50 (*0-8377-2434-1*, Rothman) W S Hein.

Paris Lights. Beverly Pabst. (Illus.). 40p. (Orig.). 1986. pap. 10.95 (*0-87663-504-4*, Pub. by Universe) St Martin.

Paris, Maine: The Second Hundred Years, 1893-1993. Paris, Maine Historical Society Staff. LC 94-66187. (Illus.). 1216p. 1994. 60.00 (*0-89725-165-2*, 1512, Penobscot Pr) Picton Pr.

Paris Mapguide. Michael Middleditch. 64p. 1995. pap. 8.95 (*0-14-046962-1*, Penguin Bks) Viking Penguin.

Paris Modern: The Swedish Ballet, 1920-1925. Nancy V. Baer. LC 95-61830. (Illus.). 168p. 1996. pap. 24.95 (*0-88401-081-3*) Fine Arts Mus.

Paris, Mon Amour. Jean-Claude Gautrand. (Illus.). 268p. 1999. 29.99 (*3-8228-7022-6*) Taschen Amer.

***Paris Never Leaves You.** Adreana Robbins. 2000. mass mkt. 6.99 (*0-8125-7078-2*) Forge NYC.

Paris Never Leaves You. 2nd ed. Adreana Robbins. LC 99-21743. 384p. 1999. 25.95 (*0-312-86755-7*, Pub. by Forge NYC) St Martin.

Paris Nights & Other Impressions of Places & People. Arnold Bennett. (Collected Works of Arnold Bennett: Vol. 64). (Illus.). 1977. reprint ed. 36.95 (*0-518-19145-1*, 19145) Ayer.

Paris, 1985. Georgia I. Hesse. Ed. by Robert C. Fisher. (Fisher Annotated Travel Guides Ser.). 128p. 1984. 8.95 (*0-8116-0020-3*) NAL.

Paris 1900: The "American School" at the Universal Exposition. Linda J. Docherty & Montclair Art Museum Staff. Ed. by Diane P. Fischer. LC 98-45276. (Illus.). 256p. (C). 1999. 50.00 (*0-8135-2640-X*); pap. 30.00 (*0-8135-2641-8*) Rutgers U Pr.

Paris 1900 Postcard Book. (Arts Collection Ser.: Vol. 67). (Illus.). 48p. pap. 14.95 (*4-7636-1567-X*, Pub. by Kyoto Shoin) Bks Nippan.

Paris, 1997. Egon Ronay Staff. (Travel Guides 1997 Ser.). (Illus.). 380p. (Orig.). 1997. pap. 14.95 (*1-898718-79-2*, Pub. by Ringpr Bks) Seven Hills Bk.

Paris, 1937: Worlds on Exhibition. James D. Herbert. LC 97-35973. (Illus.). 224p. 1998. text 39.95 (*0-8014-3494-7*) Cornell U Pr.

Paris, 1928. Ed. by Wolfgang Hageney. (ENG, FRE, GER, ITA & SPA., Illus.). 96p. 1986. pap. 26.95 (*88-7070-092-5*) Belvedere USA.

Paris, 1929. Ed. by Wolfgang Hageney. (ENG, FRE, GER, ITA & SPA., Illus.). 96p. 1986. pap. 26.95 (*88-7070-093-3*) Belvedere USA.

Paris 1921 see International Congress on the History of Art

Paris Noir. Tyler Stovall. 368p. 1998. pap. 15.00 (*0-395-90140-5*) HM.

Paris Noir: African Americans in the City of Light. Tyler Stovall. LC 96-24566. 288p. 1996. 24.95 (*0-395-68399-8*) HM.

Paris Northeast Map with Index. 11th ed. Michelin Staff. (Orig.). 1996. pap. 12.95 (*2-06-700020-9*, 20) Michelin.

Paris Northwest Map with Index. 11th ed. Michelin Staff. (Orig.). 1996. pap. 12.95 (*2-06-700018-7*, 18) Michelin.

Paris Notebook. C. W. Gusewelle. LC 85-18219. (Illus.). 228p. (Orig.). 1985. pap. 9.95 (*0-932845-01-0*) Lowell Pr.

Paris, Nouv. Acg. Frc. 13531. Ed. by Luther Dittmer. (Veroffentlichungen Mittelalterlicher Musikhandschriften - Publications of Mediaeval Musical Manuscripts Ser.: Vol. 4). (ENG & GER.). 1961. pap. 20.00 (*0-912024-04-6*) Inst Mediaeval Mus.

Paris of Henri IV: Architecture & Urbanism. Hilary Ballon. (Illus.). 304p. 1991. 48.00 (*0-262-02309-1*) MIT Pr.

Paris of Henri IV: Architecture & Urbanism. Hilary Ballon. (Illus.). 378p. 1994. pap. text 24.00 (*0-262-52197-0*) MIT Pr.

Paris of la Boheme. Contrib. & Intro. by Victor Koshkin-Youritzin. (Illus.). 22p. (Orig.). 1996. pap. 10.00 (*0-614-13527-3*) Okla City Art.

Paris of the Novelists. A. B. Maurice. 1972. 59.95 (*0-8490-0801-8*) Gordon Pr.

Paris on the March Thru the Heartland of California at 65 MPH. Pat'rick N. Pugh. (Illus.). (Orig.). pap. 7.95 (*1-883184-17-7*) PNP.

Paris Opera: An Encyclopedia of Operas, Ballets, Composers & Performers, Genesis & Glory, 1671-1715. Spire Pitou. LC 82-21140. 364p. 1983. lib. bdg. 59.95 (*0-313-21420-4*, PFO/, Greenwood Pr) Greenwood.

Paris Opera: An Encyclopedia of Operas, Ballets, Composers & Performers, Genesis & Glory, 1671-1715. Spire Pitou. LC 82-21140. 619p. 1985. lib. bdg. 115.00 (*0-313-24394-8*, POR/, Greenwood Pr) Greenwood.

Paris Opera: An Encyclopedia of Operas, Ballets, Composers & Performers, Genesis & Glory, 1671-1715. Spire Pitou. LC 87-21140. 1608p. 1990. lib. bdg. 185.00 (*0-313-26218-7*, PGH, Greenwood Pr) Greenwood.

Paris Opera: An Encyclopedia of Operas, Ballets, Composers, & Performers; Growth & Grandeur, 1815-1914; A-L, Vol. 1. Spire Pitou. LC 82-21140. 816p. 1990. lib. bdg. 185.00 (*0-313-27782-6*, PGH01, Greenwood Pr) Greenwood.

Paris Opera: An Encyclopedia of Operas, Ballets, Composers, & Performers; Growth & Grandeur, 1815-1914; A-L, Vol. 2. Spire Pitou. LC 82-21140. 768p. 1990. lib. bdg. 185.00 (*0-313-27783-4*, Greenwood Pr) Greenwood.

Paris Out of Hand: A Wayward Guide. Karen E. Gordon et al. LC 95-49308. 160p. 1996. 19.95 (*0-8118-0969-2*) Chronicle Bks.

Paris, Page a Page. Ed. by Pierre-Edmond Robert. (FRE.). 191p. 1992. pap. 16.95 (*2-278-04201-7*, Pub. by Edns Didier) Hatier Pub.

Paris par Arrondissement. 1995. pap. 24.95 (*0-7859-9041-0*) Fr & Eur.

Paris Pas Cher '97. Ann Riou. 874p. 1996. 24.95 (*0-7859-9363-0*) Fr & Eur.

***Paris Pas Cher 2000.** annuals Anne Riou. (FRE.). 1999. pap. 39.95 (*0-320-03688-X*) Fr & Eur.

Paris Peasant. Louis Aragon. Tr. by Simon W. Taylor from FRE. 224p. (Orig.). 1993. reprint ed. pap. 15.95 (*1-878972-10-3*) Exact Change.

Paris Pendant la Reaction Thermidorienne et sous le Directoire, 5 vols., Set. Francois V. Aulard. LC 70-161713. (Collection de documents relatifs a l'histoire de Paris pendant la Revolution francaise). reprint ed. 675.00 (*0-404-52570-9*) AMS Pr.

***Paris Pilgrims.** Clancy Carlile. 464p. 2000. pap. 14.00 (*0-7867-0753-4*, Pub. by Carroll & Graf) Publishers Group.

Paris Pilgrims. Clancy Carlisle. 496p. 1999. 25.00 (*0-7867-0615-5*) Carroll & Graf.

***Paris Plan Poche, 1.** Michelin Staff. 1999. 2.95 (*2-06-000003-3*) Michelin.

Paris Plenary. Ed. by Andrew V. Frankel & Charles B. Heck. (Trialogue Ser.: No. T41). (Illus.). 96p. (Orig.). 1989. pap. 6.00 (*0-930503-08-2*) Trilateral Comm.

***Paris Pocket Guide.** Berlitz Editors. (Pocket Guides Ser.). (Illus.). 144p. 2000. pap. 8.95 (*2-8315-7703-9*) Berlitz.

Paris Porcelains in the New Orleans Museum. John W. Keefe et al. LC 98-68122. (Illus.). 60p. 1998. pap. 22.95 (*0-89494-071-6*) New Orleans Mus Art.

Paris, Pretoria & the African Continent: The International Relations of States & Societies in Transition. Ed. by Chris Alden & Jean-Pascal Daloz. 256p. 1996. text 69.95 (*0-312-15824-6*) St Martin.

Paris Psalter & Meters of Boethius. Ed. by George P. Krapp. LC 33-2302. 239p. 1932. text 57.50 (*0-231-08769-1*) Col U Pr.

Paris Rainstorms Poetry. Vince S. Knight. 80p. 1998. pap. 8.00 (*0-8059-4280-7*) Dorrance.

Paris Register, 1906 (Town History & Directory) Compiled by Mitchell & Davis. 154p. 1997. reprint ed. pap. 23.50 (*0-8328-5887-0*) Higginson Bk Co.

Paris Review, 140. George Plimpton. 1996. pap. 10.00 (*0-679-77369-X*) Random.

Paris Review, 143. Paris Review Staff. 1997. pap. 10.00 (*0-679-77847-0*) Random.

Paris Review, 151. Ed. by George Plimpton. 304p. 1999. pap. 12.00 (*0-375-75517-9*) Random.

Paris Review, No. 13. George Plimpton. 1995. pap. 10.00 (*0-679-76053-9*) Random.

Paris Review, No. 13. George Plimpton. (Illus.). 304p. 1996. pap. 10.00 (*0-679-76418-6*) Random.

Paris Review, No. 14. Paris Review Staff. Vol. 144. 304p. 1998. pap. 10.00 (*0-375-75049-5*) Random.

Paris Review, No. 138. Ed. by George Plimpton. 1996. pap. 10.00 (*0-679-77143-3*) Fodors Travel.

Paris Review, No. 139. Ed. by George Plimpton. 1996. pap. 10.00 (*0-679-77144-1*) Fodors Travel.

Paris Review, No. 142. George Plimpton. 1997. pap. 10.00 (*0-679-77846-2*) Random.

Paris Review, No. 146. Paris Review Staff. 1998. pap. 10.00 (*0-375-75178-5*) Random Ref & Info.

Paris Review, No. 147. Paris Review Staff. 1998. pap. 10.00 (*0-375-75177-7*) Random.

Paris Review, Vol. 137. George Plimpton. (Illus.). 304p. 1996. pap. 10.00 (*0-679-76875-0*) Random.

Paris Review, Vol. 145. Paris Review Staff. 1998. pap. 10.00 (*0-375-75110-6*) Random.

Paris Review, Vol. 148. George Plimpton. 1999. pap. 10.00 (*0-375-75361-3*) Random.

Paris Review, Vol. 149. George Plimpton. 1999. pap. 10.00 (*0-375-75362-1*) Random.

Paris Review, Vol. 150. George Plimpton. 1999. pap. 12.00 (*0-375-75435-0*) Random House.

***Paris Review, Vol. 152.** Ed. by George Plimpton. 304p. 1999. pap. 12.00 (*0-375-75518-7*) Random.

Paris Review: Strippable, No. 134. George Plimpton. 1995. pap. 10.00 (*0-679-76299-X*) Random.

Paris Review No. 135: Strippable. George Plimpton. 1995. pap. 10.00 (*0-679-76300-7*) Random.

Paris Rooms: Portfolios from 34 Interior Designers. Stephen Mudge. 1999. 40.00 (*1-56496-499-X*) Rockport Pubs.

Paris Salons: 1895-1914, Objets D'Art & Metalware. Alastair Duncan. (Illus.). 576p. 1999. 99.50 (*1-85149-304-2*) Antique Collect.

Paris Salons Ceramics & Glass. Alastair Duncan. (Paris Salons Ser.). (Illus.). 350p. 1998. 99.50 (*1-85149-229-1*) Antique Collect.

Paris Salons, 1895-1914: Furniture, Vol. 3. Alastair Duncan. (Illus.). 392p. 1995. 99.50 (*1-85149-190-2*) Antique Collect.

Paris Salons, 1895-1914: Jewellery. Alastair Duncan. (Illus.). 306p. 1994. 89.50 (*1-85149-168-6*) Antique Collect.

Paris Salons, 1895-1914: Jewellery. Alastair Duncan. (Jewellery: Vol. 1). (Illus.). 350p. 1994. 89.50 (*1-85149-159-7*) Antique Collect.

***Paris Scene: 1998 to 1999 Edition.** Laurence Phillips. (Illus.). 1999. pap. 12.95 (*1-902644-02-6*) Prowler Pr.

Paris Scene, 1995-1996. Laurence Phillips. (Illus.). 208p. (Orig.). 1995. pap. 10.95 (*0-85449-220-8*, Pub. by Gay Mens Pr) LPC InBook.

Paris School Semiotics I: Theory. Ed. by Paul Perron & Frank Collins. LC 88-24058. (Semiotic Crossroads Ser.: Vol. 2). xxviii, 258p. 1989. 76.00 (*1-55619-040-9*) J Benjamins Pubng Co.

Paris School Semiotics II: Practice. Ed. by Paul Perron & Frank Collins. LC 88-24058. (Semiotic Crossroads Ser.: No. 3). xvi, 225p. 1989. 71.00 (*1-55619-041-7*) J Benjamins Pubng Co.

Paris Ses Chansons. 144p. (Orig.). (YA). 1997. pap. 34.95 (*0-7692-1063-5*, 01020647) Wrner Bros.

Paris, 1789: A Guide to Paris on the Eve of the Revolution. Rachel Wright. LC 98-39804. (Sightseers Ser.). 32p. (J). (gr. 2-6). 1999. 8.95 (*0-7534-5183-2*) LKC.

Paris Sewers & Sewermen: Realities & Representations. Donald Reid. LC 90-40617. (Illus.). 248p. 1991. 45.00 (*0-674-65462-5*, REIPAR) HUP.

Paris Sewers & Sewermen: Realities & Representations. Donald Reid. (Illus.). 248p. (C). 1993. pap. 18.00 (*0-674-65463-3*) HUP.

Paris Shopkeepers & the Politics of Resentment. Philip G. Nord. LC 85-42695. 559p. 1986. reprint ed. pap. 173.30 (*0-7837-9403-7*, 206014800004) Bks Demand.

Paris Shopping Companion: A Personal Guide to the Finest Shops in Paris for Every Pocketbook. 2nd ed. Susan S. Winkler. LC 98-13934. (Illus.). 208p. 1998. pap. 12.95 (*1-888952-70-9*) Cumberland Hse.

***Paris Short Stories.** Penguin Books Staff. (Time-Out Book of... Ser.). 2000. pap. 12.95 (*0-14-028121-5*) Viking Penguin.

Paris Sketch Book & Art Criticisms see Complete Works of William Makepeace Thackeray

Paris Sketchbook: An American Retrospective of a Beautiful City. Bill Olendorf. (Sketchbook Ser.). (Illus.). 144p. 1990. 40.00 (*0-923078-02-9*) Olendorf Graph.

Paris sous le Consulat, 4 vols., Set. Francois V. Aulard. LC 74-161714. (Collection de documents relatifs a l'histoire de Paris pendant la Revolution francaise). reprint ed. 540.00 (*0-404-52580-6*) AMS Pr.

Paris sous le Premier Empire, 3 vols., Set. Francois V. Aulard. LC 74-161706. (Collection de documents relatifs a l'histoire de Paris pendant la Revolution francaise). reprint ed. 405.00 (*0-404-52576-8*) AMS Pr.

Paris Sous L'objectif 1885-1994. Anne Cartier-Bresson. 1999. pap. text 27.95 (*2-85025-649-8*) Hazan.

Paris Southeast Map with Index. 9th ed. Michelin Staff. (Orig.). 1996. pap. 12.95 (*2-06-700024-1*, 24) Michelin.

Paris Southwest Map with Index. 10th ed. Michelin Staff. (Orig.). 1996. pap. text 12.95 (*2-06-700022-5*, 22) Michelin.

Paris Spleen. Charles Baudelaire. Tr. by Louise Varese from FRE. LC 48-5012. 1970. pap. 8.95 (*0-8112-0007-8*, NDP294, Pub. by New Directions) Norton.

***Paris Step by Step.** rev. ed. Christopher Turner. (Illus.). 308p. 2002. reprint ed. pap. text 14.00 (*0-7881-6852-5*) DIANE Pub.

Paris Step by Step: The Definitive Guide to the Streets & Sights of Paris. Christopher Turner. (Illus.). 234p. (Orig.). 1992. pap. 9.95 (*0-312-07486-7*) St Martin.

Paris Street Atlas with Index & Practical Information. 20th ed. Michelin Staff. 1997. per. 12.00 (*2-06-700011-X*, 011) Michelin.

Paris Street Map. 1997. 9.95 (*2-06-700010-1*, 10) Michelin.

Paris Street Map with Index. 16th ed. 1998. 12.95 (*2-06-700012-8*, 12) Michelin.

Paris Talks: Addresses Given by Abdu'l-Baha in 1911. Abdu'l-Baha. 224p. 1969. pap. 6.95 (*1-870989-61-9*) Bahai.

Paris Talks: Addresses Given by Abdu'l-Baha in 1911. Abdu'l-Baha. 224p. 1995. 13.95 (*1-870989-57-0*) Bahai.

Paris 360 Degrees. Attilio Boccazzi-Varotto. LC 99-17755. 144p. 1999. 75.00 (*0-679-44285-5*) Random Hse Value.

***Paris 3D.** Paris Musees Staff. (Illus.). 288p. 2000. 75.00 (*1-86154-162-7*, Pub. by Booth-Clibborn) Dist Art Pubs.

Paris, Tightwad, & Peculiar: Missouri Place Names. Margot F. McMillen. (Missouri Heritage Readers Ser.). (Illus.). 96p. (C). 1994. pap. 8.95 (*0-8262-0972-6*) U of Mo Pr.

Paris to Boulogne: A Guide to Eight Hundred Eighty Kilometres of Footpaths Through the Historic Countryside of Northern France, Picardy & the Tour du Boulonnais. French Ramblers Association Staff. Ed. by Folly Marland. Tr. by Danny Price. (Footpaths of Europe Ser.). (Illus.). 190p. (Orig.). 1990. pap. 19.95 (*1-85365-114-1*, Pub. by McCarta) Seven Hills Bk.

Paris Tourism Map. (FRE.). 1995. 8.95 (*2-06-700008-X*, 8) Michelin.

Paris Tourism Map. 1998. 5.95 (*2-06-701007-7*, 7) Michelin.

***Paris Trance: A Romance.** Geoff Dyer. LC 98-47522. 272p. 1999. 22.00 (*0-374-22981-3*) FS&G.

***Paris Trance: A Romance.** Geoff Dyer. 272p. 2000. pap. 13.00 (*0-86547-600-4*) N Point Pr.

Paris Transportation Map. 1998. 5.95 (*2-06-700009-8*, 9) Michelin.

Paris Trout. Pete Dexter. 320p. 1989. pap. 12.95 (*0-14-012206-0*, Penguin Bks) Viking Penguin.

Paris 2000. Fodors Travel Publications, Inc. Staff. 1999. pap. 15.00 (*0-679-00322-3*) Fodors Travel.

***Paris 2000: The Best of the City.** Fodors Travel Publications, Inc. Staff. (Guides Ser.). (Illus.). 1999. pap. 9.00 (*0-679-00351-7*) Fodors Travel.

***Paris 2001.** Ed. by Eugene Fodor. (Fodor Travel Guides). (Illus.). 2000. pap. 15.00 (*0-679-00550-1*) McKay.

Paris under the Social Revolution. A. F. Sanborn. 1973. 59.95 (*0-8490-0802-6*) Gordon Pr.

Paris Underground. unabridged ed. Etta Shiber. 296p. 1997. reprint ed. pap. 14.95 (*1-57002-042-6*) Univ Publng Hse.

Paris. Universite. Bibliotheque d'Art et d'Archeologie. Catalogue General. Periodiques. 1990. reprint ed. 110.00 (*0-8115-0249-X*) Periodicals Srv.

Paris up Close: District to District, Street by Street. Vivienne Menkes-Ivry. (Illus.). 160p. 1994. pap. 12.95 (*0-8442-9452-7*, 94527, Passprt Bks) NTC Contemp Pub Co.

Paris Vivant see Paris Alive, the Point of View of an American

Paris Walking Guide: Where to Go, Where to Eat, What to Do. 3rd ed. Jeanne Oelerich. 1999. pap. text 6.95 (*1-882546-15-6*) Just Marvelous.

***Paris Walks.** Time Out Magazine Staff. (Time-Out Book of... Ser.). 256p. 2000. pap. 14.95 (*0-14-028721-3*, Penguin Bks) Viking Penguin.

Paris Was a Woman: Portraits from the Left Bank. Andrea Weiss. (Illus.). 256p. 1995. 19.95 (*0-04-440929-X*, Pub. by Rivers Oram) NYU Pr.

An Asterisk (*) at the beginning of an entry indicates that the title is appearing for the first time.

Paris, When It's Naked. Etel Adnan. LC 92-50341. 115p. (Orig.). 1993. pap. 13.50 (*0-942996-20-8*) Post Apollo Pr.

Paris Year: Dorothy & James T. Farell, 1931-1932. Edgar M. Branch et al. LC 98-21295. 225p. 1998. 24.95 (*0-8214-1236-1*) Ohio U Pr.

Paris Years of Rosie Kamin: A Novel. Richard Teleky. LC 97-47402. 218p. 1998. 24.00 (*1-883642-96-5*) Steerforth Pr.

Paris Years of Rosie Kamin: A Novel. Richard Teleky. LC 97-47402. 218p. 1999. pap. 12.00 (*1-883642-59-0*) Steerforth Pr.

Paris Years of Thomas Jefferson. William Howard Adams. LC 97-12330. (Illus.). 368p. 1997. 35.00 (*0-300-06903-0*) Yale U Pr.

***Paris Years of Thomas Jefferson.** William Howard Adams. (Illus.). 368p. 2000. pap. 17.95 (*0-300-08261-4*) Yale U Pr.

***Paris 2001.** Fodors Travel Publications, Inc. Staff. (Pocket Guides Ser.). 2000. pap. 10.00 (*0-679-00573-0*, Pub. by Fodors Travel) Random House.

***Parish.** 2000. pap. 12.95 (*0-8192-3132-0*) Morehouse Pub.

Parish! The Pulitzer Prize-Winning Story of One Vibrant Catholic Community. Robert F. Keeler. LC 97-14701. 192p. 1997. 24.95 (*0-8245-1697-4*) Crossroad NY.

Parish: Where God's People Live. Daniel E. Pilarczyk. LC 91-42032. 88p. 1992. pap. 4.95 (*0-8091-3299-0*) Paulist Pr.

Parish & Democracy in French Canada. Maurice Roy. LC 52-1123. (University of Toronto, Duncan & John Gray Memorial Lecture Ser.). 37p. reprint ed. pap. 30.00 (*0-608-16348-1*, 202654600050) Bks Demand.

Parish & the Hill. Mary D. Curran. LC 86-14247. 272p. 1986. reprint ed. pap. 12.95 (*0-935312-58-7*) Feminist Pr.

Parish at War: Letters from Nicaragua. John Medcalf. 110p. 1989. pap. 7.95 (*0-87243-182-7*) Templegate.

Parish Behind God's Back: The Changing Culture of Rural Barbados. George Gmelch & Sharon B. Gmelch. LC 96-51248. 256p. (C). 1997. pap. text 19.95 (*0-472-06626-9*, 06626) U of Mich Pr.

Parish Boundaries: The Catholic Encounter with Race in the Twentieth-Century Urban North. John T. McGreevy. LC 95-36746. (Historical Studies of Urban America). (Illus.). 362p. 1996. 27.50 (*0-226-55873-8*) U Ch Pr.

Parish Boundaries: The Catholic Encounter with Race in the Twentieth-Century Urban North. John T. McGreevy. (Historical Studies of Urban America). (Illus.). 362p. 1998. pap. text 17.00 (*0-226-55874-6*) U Ch Pr.

Parish by the Sea: A History of Saint James-by-the-Sea Episcopal Church La Jolla, California. Lawrence H. Waddy. LC 88-62583. (Illus.). 250p. (Orig.). (C). 1988. 22.00 (*0-9621167-0-X*); 100.00 (*0-9621167-2-6*); pap. 12.00 (*0-9621167-1-8*) St James Bkshelf.

Parish Cantor: Helping Catholics Pray in Song. Michael Connolly. 67p. 1991. pap. text 8.95 (*0-941050-24-6*, G-3626) GIA Pubns.

Parish Churches: Their Architectural Development in England. Hugh Braun. 1970. 18.00 (*0-571-09045-1*) Transatl Arts.

Parish Churches & Nonconformist Chapels of Wales: Their Records & Where to Find Them Vol. 1: Includes: Cardigan, Carmarthen & Pembroke Counties. Bert J. Rawlins. (Illus.). 648p. 1987. pap. text 28.95 (*0-685-24267-6*) Celtic Heritage Pub.

Parish Clergy in Nineteenth-Century Russia: Crisis, Reform, Counter-Reform. Gregory L. Freeze. LC 82-61361. (Illus.). 540p. reprint ed. pap. 167.40 (*0-608-06336-3*, 206669700008) Bks Demand.

Parish Clergy under the Later Stuarts: The Leicestershire Experience. John H. Pruett. LC 78-8174. (Illus.). 213p. 1978. reprint ed. pap. 66.10 (*0-7837-8085-0*, 204783800008) Bks Demand.

Parish Communities & Religious Conflict in the Vale of Gloucester, 1590-1690, Vol. 129. Daniel C. Beaver. LC 98-16295. (Harvard Historical Studies). 480p. 1998. 49.50 (*0-674-75845-5*) HUP.

Parish Community Profile. Philip J. Murnion et al. (Follow Me! Ser.). 32p. 1997. pap. 9.95 (*1-881307-05-0*, B7050) Natl Pastoral LC.

Parish Counseling. Edgar Jackson. LC 84-45066. 221p. 1983. 40.00 (*0-87668-672-2*) Aronson.

Parish Education in Colonial Virginia. Guy F. Wells. LC 71-89252. (American Education: Its Men, Institutions, & Ideas. Series 1). 1978. reprint ed. 13.95 (*0-405-01490-2*) Ayer.

Parish Faith Formation Assessment & Planning Tool. Janet M. Peterson-Hoormon et al. Ed. by Jeffrey Kaser. LC 98-33291. 24p. 1998. pap., wbk. ed. 14.95 (*1-58051-057-4*) Sheed & Ward WI.

Parish Fed Bastards: A History of the Politics of the Unemployed in Britain, 1884-1939, 37. Richard Flanagan. LC 91-47. (Contributions in Labor Studies: No. 37). 304p. 1991. 55.00 (*0-313-27439-8*, FPU, Greenwood Pr) Greenwood.

Parish for the Federal City: St. Patrick's in Washington, 1794-1994. Morris J. MacGregor. LC 93-49694. (Illus.). 475p. (C). 1994. 29.95 (*0-8132-0801-7*); pap. 19.95 (*0-8132-0802-5*) Cath U Pr.

Parish in the Catholic Tradition: History, Theology & Canon Law. James A. Coriden. LC 96-33120. 192p. 1996. pap. 12.95 (*0-8091-3685-6*) Paulist Pr.

Parish Law: Or, a Guide to Justices of the Peace, Ministers, Churchwardens, Overseers of the Poor, Constables, Surveyors of the Highways, Vestry Clerks, & All Others Concerned in Parish Business. 6th ed. Joseph Shaw. 378p. 1991. reprint ed. 65.00 (*0-8377-2624-7*, Rothman) W S Hein.

Parish Life Coordinator: An Institute for Pastoral Life Study. Gary P. Burkart. LC 92-26970. 140p. (Orig.). 1992. pap. 8.95 (*1-55612-569-0*, LL1569) Sheed & Ward WI.

Parish Life in 18th Century Scotland: A Review of the Old Statistical Account. Ed. by Maisie Steven. 256p. 1990. pap. 45.00 (*1-898218-28-5*) St Mut.

Parish Lines: Diocese of Southern Virginia. 3rd ed. Charles F. Cocke. (Publication Ser.: No. 22). 287p. 1996. reprint ed. pap. 15.00 (*0-88490-049-5*) Library of VA.

Parish Lines, Diocese of Southwestern Virginia. Charles F. Cocke. (Publication Ser.: No. 14). 196p. 1980. reprint ed. 10.00 (*0-88490-081-9*) Library of VA.

Parish Lines, Diocese of Virginia. Charles F. Cocke. LC 78-19035. (Publication Ser.: No. 28). xv, 321p. 1978. reprint ed. 10.00 (*0-88490-062-2*) Library of VA.

Parish Liturgy: A Handbook for Renewal. Robert Duggan. LC 96-1794. 192p. (Orig.). 1996. pap. 12.95 (*1-55612-909-2*, LL1909) Sheed & Ward WI.

Parish Liturgy Basics. William Belford. (Orig.). 1992. pap. text 9.95 (*0-912405-96-1*, Pastoral Press) OR Catholic.

Parish Maps of Ireland: (Depicting All Townlands in the Four Ulster Counties of Armagh, Donegal, Londonderry & Tyrone) Brian Mitchell. 288p. 1988. pap. text 29.95 (*0-933227-33-7*, 514) Closson Pr.

Parish Ministry for Returning Catholics. Patricia Barbernitz. LC 93-5901. 128p. (Orig.). 1994. pap. 6.95 (*0-8091-3441-1*) Paulist Pr.

Parish Nurse: Providing a Minister of Health for Your Congregation. Granger E. Westburg & Jill W. McNamara. LC 90-43206. 80p. (Orig.). 1990. pap. text 8.99 (*0-8066-2458-2*, 9-2458) Augsburg Fortress.

Parish Nursing: Promoting Whole Person Health Within Faith Communities. Phyllis A. Solari-Twadell & Mary A. McDermott. LC 98-25454. 1998. pap. 28.95 (*0-7619-1183-9*) Sage.

Parish Nursing: Promoting Whole Person Health Within Faith Communities. Phyllis A. Solari-Twadell & Mary A. McDermott. LC 98-25454. 316p. 1999. 65.00 (*0-7619-1182-0*) Sage.

Parish of All Hallows Barking Pt. 1: The Parish Church. Ed. by Lilian J. Redstone. LC 74-138273. (London County Council. Survey of London Ser.: No. 12). reprint ed. 84.50 (*0-404-51662-9*, DA685) AMS Pr.

Parish of All Saints Vols. 43 & 44: Survey of London: Poplar, Blackwall, & the Isle of Dogs, 2 vols. LC 95-229541. (Illus.). 928p. (C). 1994. text 260.00 (*0-485-48244-4*, Pub. by Athlone Pr) Humanities.

Parish of Bromley-by-Bow. Ed. by Charles R. Ashbee. LC 73-138270. (London County Council. Survey of London Ser.: No. 1). 1990. reprint ed. 84.50 (*0-404-51651-3*) AMS Pr.

Parish of Chelsea, Pt. 1. Ed. by Walter H. Godfrey. LC 71-138271. (London County Council. Survey of London Ser.: No. 2). reprint ed. 84.50 (*0-404-51652-1*, DA585) AMS Pr.

Parish of Chelsea, Pt. 4. Ed. by Walter H. Godfrey. LC 71-138271. (London County Council. Survey of London Ser.: No. 11). reprint ed. 84.50 (*0-404-51661-0*, DA685) AMS Pr.

Parish of Rich Women. James Buchan. LC 98-27440. 192p. 1998. pap. 13.95 (*1-56924-692-0*) Marlowe & Co.

Parish of Saint Martin-in-the Fields Pt. 2: The Strand. Ed. by George H. Gater & E. P. Wheeler. LC 70-37852. (London County Council. Survey of London Ser.: No. 18). reprint ed. 84.50 (*0-404-51668-8*, DA685) AMS Pr.

Parish of St. Margaret, Westminster, Pt. 1. Ed. by Montagu H. Cox. LC 70-138272. (London County Council. Survey of London Ser.: No. 10). (Illus.). reprint ed. 84.50 (*0-404-51660-2*, DA685) AMS Pr.

Parish of St. Margaret, Westminster Vol. 1: Neighbourhood of Whitehall, Pt. 2. Montagu H. Cox & G. Topham Forrest. LC 70-138272. (London County Council. Survey of London Ser.: No. 13). reprint ed. 84.50 (*0-404-51663-7*, NA995) AMS Pr.

Parish of St. Martin-in-the Fields Pt. 3: Trafalgar Square & Neighborhood. George H. Gater & F. R. Hiorns. LC 70-37852. (London County Council. Survey of London Ser.: No. 20). reprint ed. 84.50 (*0-404-51670-X*, NA995) AMS Pr.

Parish of St. Mary Lambeth Pt. 2: Southern Area. London County Council Staff & Parish of St. Mary Labeth Staff. LC 74-6546. (London County Council Survey of London Ser.: No. 26). 1995. reprint ed. 84.50 (*0-404-51676-9*, NA995) AMS Pr.

Parish of St. Pancras Pt. 1: The Village of Highgate. Ed. by Percy Lovell & William Marcham. LC 70-37855. (London County Council. Survey of London Ser.: No. 17). reprint ed. 84.50 (*0-404-51667-X*) AMS Pr.

Parish of St. Pancras Pt. 2: Old St. Pancras & Kentish Town. Ed. by Percy Lovell & William Marcham. LC 70-37855. (London County Council. Survey of London Ser.: No. 19). reprint ed. 84.50 (*0-404-51669-6*) AMS Pr.

Parish of St. Pancras Pt. 4: King's Cross Neighbourhood. Ed. by Walter H. Godfrey. LC 76-37851. (London County Council. Survey of London Ser.: No. 24). reprint ed. 84.50 (*0-404-51674-2*, NA995) AMS Pr.

Parish of St. Sampson. John Fenwick. (C). 1989. text 75.00 (*1-85022-018-2*, Pub. by Dyllansow Truran) St Mut.

Parish of the Next Millennium. Bill Bausch. LC 97-60028. 304p. 1997. pap. 14.95 (*0-89622-719-7*) Twenty-Third.

Parish of the Psychic Moon. Don Domanski. LC 98-151609. 120p. 1998. pap. 9.95 (*0-7710-2874-1*) McCland & Stewart.

Parish Pantry Vol. 1: Spizarnia Kosciol. Ed. by Judy H. Seikel. LC 96-70267. 416p. 1996. spiral bd. 19.95 (*0-9619314-1-8*) CDACCK.

Parish Pastoral Councils. John Heaps. 1994. pap. 4.95 (*0-85574-221-6*, Pub. by E J Dwyer) Morehouse Pub.

Parish Planning: A Practical Guide to Shared Responsibility. Robert Howes. 160p. (Orig.). 1994. pap. 9.95 (*0-8146-2165-1*) Liturgical Pr.

Parish Priest of Ars: The Story of Saint John Narie Vianney see Cure of Ars: The Story of Saint John Vianney, Patron Saint of Parish Priests

Parish Priests among the Saints. Walter Gumbley. LC 76-148214. (Biography Index Reprint Ser.). 1977. 18.95 (*0-8369-8061-1*) Ayer.

Parish Priests & Their People in the Middle Ages in England. Edward L. Cutts. LC 74-107457. reprint ed. 42.50 (*0-404-01898-X*) AMS Pr.

Parish Reconciliation Services: Seasonal Celebrations for Adults & Children. Margrit A. Banta. LC 93-61483. 80p. (Orig.). 1994. pap. 12.95 (*0-89622-586-0*) Twenty-Third.

Parish Records of Christ Episcopal Church, 1831-1863. Sharon Kraynek. 146p. 1988. per. 16.00 (*0-933227-43-4*, 413) Closson Pr.

Parish Register of Christ Church, Middlesex Co., Virginia, from 1625 to 1812. National Society of the Colonial Dames of America. 360p. 1988. reprint ed. 37.50 (*0-89308-631-2*, VA 91) Southern Hist Pr.

Parish Register of Christ Church, Middlesex County, Virginia, from 1653 to 1812. LC 64-20864. 341p. 1997. reprint ed. pap. 31.50 (*0-8063-0073-6*) Clearfield Co.

Parish Register of St. Peter's, New Kent County, Virginia, 1680-1787. National Society of the Colonial Dames of America. 206p. 1996. reprint ed. pap. 12.50 (*0-8063-0306-9*, 5100, Pub. by Clearfield Co) ACCESS Pubs Network.

Parish Registers of Gulval in the County of Cornwall, 1598-1812. Ed. by George Millet & William Bolitho. LC 95-221019. 182p. (Orig.). 1893. reprint ed. pap. 23.00 (*0-7884-0273-0*) Heritage Bk.

Parish Registers of Halifax, County York, England Vol. II: Marriages & Burials, 1538-1593. Ed. by E. W. Crossley. 423p. (Orig.). 1995. reprint ed. pap. text 27.00 (*0-7884-0164-5*) Heritage Bk.

Parish Registers of Prince George Winyah Church, Georgetown, SC 1815-1936. Brent H. Holcomb. (Illus.). 200p. 1996. 30.00 (*0-913363-24-3*) SCMAR.

Parish Registers of Prince George Winyah Church, Georgetown, South Carolina, 1815-1936. Brent H. Holcomb. 191p. pap. 22.50 (*0-8063-4827-5*) Clearfield Co.

Parish Renewal at the Grassroots. David Prior. 1987. 14.95 (*0-310-38370-6*, 18409) Zondervan.

Parish School: A History of American Catholic Parochial Education from Colonial Times to the Present. Timothy Walch. 320p. 1995. 39.95 (*0-8245-1532-3*) Crossroad NY.

Parish-Side. Samuel H. Elliot. LC 70-76924. (American Fiction Reprint Ser.). 1977. 17.95 (*0-8369-7003-9*) Ayer.

Parish Small Group System. Angeline Bukowiecki. (Evangelizer's Handbook, Evangelistic Series Sisters of the New Convenant). (Illus.). 14p. (Orig.). (C). 1989. pap. text 5.00 (*0-924333-19-7*) Sisters New Covenant.

Parish Small Group System: A Long Term Goal for Evangelization. Angeline Bukowiecki. (Evangelizer's Handbook, Coordinators & Pastoral Leaders Evangelistic Series, Catholic Evangelization Training Center). (Illus.). 38p. (Orig.). (C). 1988. pap. text 19.00 (*0-317-92540-7*) Sisters New Covenant.

Parish Small Group System, Policy Manual: A Long Term Goal for Evangelization. rev. ed. Angeline Bukowiecki. (Evangelizer's Handbook, Coordinators & Pastoral Leaders Evangelistic Series, Catholic Evangelization Training Center). (Illus.). 40p. (Orig.). (C). pap. text 19.00 (*0-924333-11-1*) Sisters New Covenant.

Parish Social Ministry: A Vision & Resource. Alexandra Peeler. 194p. 1986. 14.95 (*0-318-20492-4*) Catholic Charities.

Parish, Town & Community Council Finance: A Practical Guide. Ron Harrop. 128p. 1992. 40.00 (*0-85314-422-2*, Pub. by Tolley Pubng) St Mut.

Parish, Town & Community Councils: A Guide to Law & Administration. Harold Clarke. 160p. 1991. 42.00 (*0-85314-368-4*, Pub. by Tolley Pubng) St Mut.

Parish Weddings. Austin Fleming. 55p. 1987. pap. 6.00 (*0-930467-66-3*, PARWED) Liturgy Tr Pubns.

***Parishes & Parish Ministers: A Study of Parish Lay Ministry.** Philip J. Murnion & David DeLambo. Ed. by Karen S. Smith. 80p. 1999. pap. 15.95 (*1-881307-21-2*) Natl Pastoral LC.

Parishes That Excel: Models of Excellence in Ministry, Education, & Evangelization. Patrick J. Brennan. 144p. 1992. 13.95 (*0-8245-1156-5*) Crossroad NY.

Parishes, Tithes, & Society in Earlier Medieval Poland, c. 1100-c. 1250. Piotr Gorecki. LC 92-75294. (Transactions Ser.: Vol. 83, Pt. 2). 125p. 1993. pap. 15.00 (*0-87169-832-3*, T832-GOP) Am Philos.

Parisian Bourgeois' Sundays & Other Stories. Guy de Maupassant. Tr. by Marlo Johnston from FRE. LC 98-111578. 176p. 1998. 29.95 (*0-7206-1033-8*, Pub. by P Owen Ltd) Dufour.

Parisian Education of an American Surgeon: Letters of Jonathan Mason Warren, 1832-1835. Jonathan M. Warren. LC 78-56709. (American Philosophical Society, Memoirs Ser.: No. 128). (Illus.). 280p. reprint ed. pap. 86.80 (*0-8357-7915-7*, 203634400002) Bks Demand.

Parisian Encounters. Charles Hobson. LC 93-43032. (Illus.). 70p. 1994. 18.95 (*0-8118-0703-7*) Chronicle Bks.

Parisian Fields. Ed. by Michael Sheringham. LC 97-152638. (Critical Views Ser.). (Illus.). 288p. 1997. pap. 24.95 (*0-948462-85-X*, Pub. by Reaktion Bks) Consort Bk Sales.

***Parisian Frolics.** 2000. mass mkt. 7.95 (*1-56201-210-X*) Blue Moon Bks.

Parisian from Kansas. Philippe Tapon. 1998. pap. 13.95 (*0-452-27735-3*, Plume) Dutton Plume.

***Parisian Home Cooking: Conversations, Recipes, And Tips From The Cooks And Food Merchants Of Paris.** Michael Roberts. LC 98-41750. (Illus.). 352p. 1999. 25.00 (*0-688-13868-3*, Wm Morrow) Morrow Avon.

Parisian Order of Barristers & the French Revolution. Michael P. Fitzsimmons. LC 86-19519. (Historical Monographs: No. 74). (Illus.). 320p. 1987. 29.95 (*0-674-65464-1*) HUP.

Parisian Points of View. Ludovic Halevy. Tr. by Edith V. Matthews. LC 71-98572. (Short Story Index Reprint Ser.). 1977. 19.95 (*0-8369-3146-7*) Ayer.

Parisian Prowler: Le Spleen de Paris, Petits Poemes en Prose. 2nd ed. Charles Baudelaire. Tr. by Edward K. Kaplan. LC 96-32135. 1997. pap. text 14.95 (*0-8203-1879-5*) U of Ga Pr.

Parisian Questions & Prologues. Eckhart. Tr. by Armand A. Maurer from LAT. 123p. pap. 9.14 (*0-88844-264-5*) Brill Academic Pubs.

Parisian Sans-Culottes & the French Revolution, 1793-94. Albert Soboul. Tr. by Gwynne Lewis from FRE. LC 78-26780. 280p. 1979. reprint ed. lib. bdg. 38.50 (*0-313-20913-8*, SOTP, Greenwood Pr) Greenwood.

Parisian Scholars in the Early Fourteenth Century: A Social Portrait. William J. Courtenay. LC 98-34292. (Cambridge Studies in Medieval Life & Thought: No. 41). (Illus.). 285p. (C). 1999. text 64.95 (*0-521-64212-4*) Cambridge U Pr.

Parisian Sketches: Letters to the New York Tribune, 1875-1876. Henry James. Ed. by Edel Leon & Lind I. Dusoir. LC 78-5995. 262p. 1978. reprint ed. lib. bdg. 65.00 (*0-313-20448-9*, JAPS, Greenwood Pr) Greenwood.

Parisian Stage Pt. 3: Alphabetical Indexes of Plays & Authors. Charles B. Wicks & Jerome W. Schweitzer. LC 50-2939. (University of Alabama Studies: No. 6, 8, 14, 17). 287p. 1961. pap. 81.80 (*0-7837-8416-3*, 2059227) Bks Demand.

Parisian Two-Part Organa: Complete Comparative Edition, 2 vols. Hans Tischler. LC 87-752521. 1400p. 1989. lib. bdg. 400.00 (*0-918728-89-4*) Pendragon NY.

Parisian Views. Shelley Rice. LC 97-7986. 1997. 35.00 (*0-262-18184-3*) MIT Pr.

Parisian Views. Shelley Rice. (Illus.). 288p. 1999. pap. 18.00 (*0-262-68107-2*) MIT Pr.

Parisian Woman's Guide to Style. Virginie Morana & Veronique Morana. 128p. 1999. pap. 19.95 (*0-7893-0372-8*, Pub. by Universe) St Martin.

***Parisian Worlds of Frederic Chopin.** William G. Atwood. LC 99-27886. (Illus.). 447p. 1999. 35.00 (*0-300-07773-4*) Yale U Pr.

***Parisians.** Photos & Text by Peter Turnley. LC 00-26381. (Illus.). 168p. 2000. 50.00 (*0-7892-0650-1*) Abbeville Pr.

Parisians (1872) Edward Bulwer Lytton. 332p. 1999. reprint ed. pap. 24.95 (*0-7661-0787-6*) Kessinger Pub.

***Parisian's Paris.** Phillippe Meyer. 268p. 2000. pap. 16.95 (*2-08-013664-X*, Pub. by Flammarion) Abbeville Pr.

Parisienne see Woman of the Pharisees

Parisienne. Hari Becque. (Livret Ser.). pap. 6.95 (*0-685-34881-4*) Fr & Eur.

Paris/Reims/Chalons-sur-Marne Map. 1997. 6.95 (*2-06-700056-X*, 56) Michelin.

Paris/Troyes/Chaumont Map. 1997. 6.95 (*2-06-700061-6*, 61) Michelin.

Parisville Poles. Ed. by Harry Milostan. LC 77-77917. 1977. lib. bdg. 12.00 (*0-918020-03-4*) Masspac Pub.

Pariswalks. rev. ed. Alison Landes & Sonia Landes. LC 98-42822. (Henry Holt Walks Ser.). (Illus.). 320p. 1999. pap. 15.95 (*0-8050-6127-4*, Pub. by H Holt & Co) VHPS.

Pariswalks. 4th ed. Alison Landes. 1995. pap. 12.95 (*0-8050-1186-2*, Owl) H Holt & Co.

Parity & Time Reversal Violation in Compound Nuclear States & Related Topics. 400p. 1996. lib. bdg. 60.00 (*981-02-2798-1*) World Scientific Pub.

Parity & War: Evaluations & Extensions of the War Ledger. Ed. by Jacek Kugler & Douglas Lemke. LC 95-23699. 402p. 1996. text 57.50 (*0-472-09602-8*, 09602); pap. text 25.95 (*0-472-06602-1*, 06602) U of Mich Pr.

***Parity in Financing Mental Health Services: Managed Care Effects on Cost, Access & Quality.** Harold E. Varmus. 112p. 1999. pap. text 25.00 (*0-7881-7630-7*) DIANE Pub.

Parity Nonconservation in Atomic Phenomena. I. B. Khriplovich. xii, 314p. 1991. text 337.00 (*2-88124-772-5*) Gordon & Breach.

Parity, Parity, Parity. John D. Black. LC 72-2364. (FDR & the Era of the New Deal Ser.). 367p. 1972. reprint ed. 45.00 (*0-306-70482-X*) Da Capo.

Parity Violation in Atoms & in Electron Scattering: Ens, Paris, France 21-31 October 1997. Bernard Frois. 1999. 112.00 (*981-02-3731-6*) World Scientific Pub.

Parity Violation in Electron Scattering. Ed. by R. D. McKeown & E. J. Beise. 244p. (C). 1990. text 66.00 (*981-02-0265-2*) World Scientific Pub.

Park. J. Matthews. (Longman African Writers Ser.). (C). 1995. pap. text 8.95 (*0-582-26435-9*) Addison-Wesley.

Park. Phillipe Sollers. Tr. by A. Sheridan Smith. LC 76-90910. Orig. Title: Le Parc. 96p. 1969. pap. 4.95 (*0-87376-012-3*) Red Dust.

Park. Cole Swensen. 64p. (Orig.). 1991. pap. 8.00 (*0-912449-40-3*) Floating Island.

Park: A Guide to the Crags & High Peaks of Rocky Mountain National Park. Fred Knapp & Mike Stevens. 1998. pap. 9.95 (*0-9657079-9-7*) Sharp End.

Park & Recreation Maintenance Management. 3rd ed. Sternloff. 1993. pap. text 35.15 (*0-13-776477-4*) P-H.

Park & Recreation Maintenance Management. 3rd ed. Robert E. Sternloff & Roger Warren. LC 93-598. 1993. pap. text 34.00 (*0-942280-62-8*) Pub Horizons.

P

Park & Recreation Structures. Albert H. Good. (Illus.). 624p. 1999. reprint ed. 85.00 (*1-56898-171-6*) Princeton Arch.

Park & Recreation Structures. 2nd ed. Albert H. Good. (Illus.). 640p. 1989. reprint ed. 69.95 (*0-317-94106-2*) Ideaworks Pubns.

Park & the People. Roy Rosensweig. 1995. pap. 19.95 (*0-8050-3242-8*) H Holt & Co.

Park & the People: A History of Central Park. Roy Rosenzweig & Elizabeth Blackmar. LC 92-7062. (Illus.). 600p. 1992. text 45.00 (*0-8014-2516-6*) Cornell U Pr.

Park & the People: A History of Central Park. Roy Rosenzweig & Elizabeth Blackmar. (Illus.). 640p. 1998. pap. text 22.50 (*0-8014-9751-5*) Cornell U Pr.

Park Art: With Pad & Pencil in the Parks for 31 Years From the Sunday Star-ledger. Kay Kato. LC 99-10113. 1999. write for info. (*1-57864-063-6*) Donning Co.

Park Attendant. Jack Rudman. (Career Examination Ser.: C-1541). 1994. pap. 23.95 (*0-8373-1541-7*) Nat Learn.

***Park Avenue Chorus Boy.** Michael Mason. 272p. 2000. 29.95 (*1-58374-007-4*) Chicago Spectrum.

Park Bench. Fumiko Takeshita. Tr. by Ruth A. Kanagy from JPN.Tr. of Bench Ga Hitotsu. (Illus.). 40p. (J). (ps-3). 1988. 13.95 (*0-916291-15-4*) Kane-Miller Bk.

Park Bench. Fumiko Takeshita. Tr. by Ruth A. Kanagy from JPN.Tr. of Bench Ga Hitotsu. (Illus.). 40p. (J). (gr. 3-8). 1989. reprint ed. pap. 7.95 (*0-916291-21-9*) Kane-Miller Bk.

Park Builders: A History of State Parks in the Pacific Northwest. Thomas R. Cox. LC 88-5462. (Illus.). 280p. 1988. pap. 14.95 (*0-295-96620-3*) U of Wash Pr.

Park Cities: A Photohistory. Diane Galloway. LC 89-91112. (Illus.). 176p. (Orig.). (C). 1989. pap. write for info. (*0-9621907-0-5*) D Galloway.

Park City. Katherine Reynolds & John Wiebvsch. (Illus.). 72p. 1984. 23.00 (*0-916873-50-1*) Weller Inst.

Park City: New & Selected Stories. Ann Beattie. 496p. 1999. pap. 14.00 (*0-679-78133-1*) Vin Bks.

Park City - A Taste of Past & Present. Park City Education Foundation Staff. 224p. 1996. 19.95 (*1-883004-02-0*) Game of Work.

***Park City Trails.** Raye C. Ringholz. 1999. pap. 7.95 (*0-87480-634-8*) U of Utah Pr.

Park City Trails. Raye C. Ringholz. LC 84-60807. (Illus.). 104p. 1984. pap. 7.95 (*0-915272-26-1*) Wasatch Pubs.

Park City Underfoot: Self-Guided Tours of Historic Neighborhoods. Brent Corcoran. LC 94-36029. (Illus.). 180p. (Orig.). 1995. pap. 10.95 (*1-56085-065-5*) Signature Bks.

Park Construction Coordinator. Jack Rudman. (Career Examination Ser.: C-3278). 1994. pap. 34.95 (*0-8373-3278-8*) Nat Learn.

Park County, Wyoming Facts & Maps Through Time. unabridged ed. Bruce H. Blevins. (Illus.). 81p. 1999. pap. 14.95 (*1-893771-03-2*) W I M.

Park Engineer. Jack Rudman. (Career Examination Ser.: C-3191). 1994. pap. 34.95 (*0-8373-3191-9*) Nat Learn.

Park Foreman. Jack Rudman. (Career Examination Ser.: C-571). 1994. pap. 29.95 (*0-8373-0571-3*) Nat Learn.

Park Genealogy: Relating to Descendants of John B. Park, 1794-1891, of Wells VT, Moriah NY & Trumbull Co. OH. C. A. Harrington & D. H. Richeson. (Illus.). 36p. 1995. reprint ed. pap. 7.50 (*0-8328-4812-3*); reprint ed. lib. bdg. 17.50 (*0-8328-4811-5*) Higginson Bk Co.

Park Guell. Conrad Kent & Dennis Prindle. LC 93-32481. (Illus.). 224p. (Orig.). 1993. pap. 17.95 (*1-56898-000-0*) Princeton Arch.

Park Hill Cemetery: Vol. 1: A-G; Vol. 2: H-Q; Vol. 3: R-Z, 3 vols. Compiled by CCGS Staff. (Clark County Washington Cemetery Records Ser.: No. 9, 10 & 11). 1267p. 1995. 58.00 (*1-892685-08-6*) Clark Cnty Gene.

Park Interpretive Specialist. (Career Examination Ser.). pap. 34.95 (*0-8373-3779-8*, C3779) Nat Learn.

Park It! How to Get Jobs with Concessioners in National Parks. Chloe R. Young. (Illus.). 32p. 1998. pap. write for info. (*0-9660214-0-1*) Sun Chaser Pub.

***Park It Here! 2000: Parking Guide for New York City Streets.** Doris E. Blendinger. (Illus.). 320p. 2000. pap. 13.95 (*1-891160-44-3*) Alixa.

Park Maintenance Supervisor. Jack Rudman. (Career Examination Ser.: C-2942). 1994. pap. 29.95 (*0-8373-2942-6*) Nat Learn.

Park Maker: A Life of Frederick Law Olmsted. Elizabeth Stevenson. LC 99-28638. 484p. 1999. pap. 29.95 (*0-7658-0614-2*) Transaction Pubs.

Park Management. Dwight R. McCurdy. LC 84-27653. 272p. 1985. 41.95 (*0-8093-1226-3*); pap. 31.95 (*0-8093-1202-6*) S Ill U Pr.

Park Manager. Jack Rudman. (Career Examination Ser.: C-2247). 1994. pap. 29.95 (*0-8373-2247-2*) Nat Learn.

Park Manager I. Jack Rudman. (Career Examination Ser.: C-383). 1994. pap. 29.95 (*0-8373-0383-4*) Nat Learn.

Park Manager III. Jack Rudman. (Career Examination Ser.: C-385). 1994. pap. 29.95 (*0-8373-0385-0*) Nat Learn.

Park Manager II. Jack Rudman. (Career Examination Ser.: C-384). 1994. pap. 29.95 (*0-8373-0384-2*) Nat Learn.

***Park Naturalist.** Jim Dawson. LC 99-30637. (Career Exploration Ser.). 48p. (YA). 1999. 19.93 (*0-7368-0332-7*) Capstone Pr.

***Park Naturalist.** Jennifer Wendt. 1999. 19.93 (*0-516-21891-3*) Capstone Pr.

Park Patrol Supervisor. (Career Examination Ser.: C-3643). pap. 29.95 (*0-8373-3643-0*) Nat Learn.

Park Patrolman. Jack Rudman. (Career Examination Ser.: C-1688). 1994. pap. 23.95 (*0-8373-1688-X*) Nat Learn.

Park Profile: America's Hid. National Geographic Staff. 1997. pap. 12.95 (*0-7922-7033-9*) Natl Geog.

Park Profile: Grand Canyon. National Geographic Staff. 200p. 1997. per. 15.00 (*0-7922-7032-0*, Pub. by Natl Geog) S&S Trade.

Park Ranger. Jack Rudman. (Career Examination Ser.: C-650). 1994. pap. 23.95 (*0-8373-0650-7*) Nat Learn.

Park Ranger Guide to Rivers & Lakes: What to See & Learn on America's Freshwaters. Arthur P. Miller, Jr. & Marjorie L. Miller. LC 90-10291. (Park Ranger Guides Ser.). (Illus.). 224p. (Orig.). 1991. pap. 10.95 (*0-8117-3038-7*) Stackpole.

Park Ranger Guide to Wildlife. Arthur P. Miller, Jr. LC 89-39934. (Park Ranger Guides Ser.: Bk. 1). (Illus.). 224p. (Orig.). 1990. pap. 12.95 (*0-8117-2289-9*) Stackpole.

***Park Ranger's Guide to the Federal Criminal Code, 2000-2001.** Steven T. Kernes. (Peace Officer's Guide Ser.). 206p. 2000. pap. 10.95 (*0-937935-46-8*) Justice Syst Pr.

Park Rangers of California. William B. Hedges & Janice M. Hedges. LC 93-91513. (Illus.). (Orig.). 1993. pap. text 12.95 (*0-9620487-3-9*) Baird-Hedges Pub.

Park Recreation Activities Specialist. (Career Examination Ser.). pap. 27.95 (*0-8373-3780-1*, C3780) Nat Learn.

Park, Recreation, Leisure Film Bibliography: Annotated & Cross Indexed Bibliography of Audiovisual Materials Relating to Parks, Recreation & Leisure. Joseph P. Price. LC GV0014.6.S59. 119p. reprint ed. pap. 36.90 (*0-7837-1545-5*, 204183000024) Bks Demand.

Park Row. Allen Churchill. LC 73-14193. 344p. 1973. reprint ed. lib. bdg. 55.00 (*0-8371-7146-6*, CHPR, Greenwood Pr) Greenwood.

Park Service Worker. Jack Rudman. (Career Examination Ser.: C-2468). 1994. pap. 23.95 (*0-8373-2468-8*) Nat Learn.

Park Slope NY. Mark Sonnenfeld. 20p. 1998. pap. 3.00 (*1-887379-17-7*) M Sonnenfeld.

Park-Street Papers. Bliss Perry. LC 73-117826. (Essay Index Reprint Ser.). 1977. 21.95 (*0-8369-2012-0*) Ayer.

Park Superintendent. Jack Rudman. (Career Examination Ser.: C-2268). 1994. reprint ed. pap. 29.95 (*0-8373-2268-5*) Nat Learn.

Park Supervisor. Jack Rudman. (Career Examination Ser.: C-1563). 1994. pap. 29.95 (*0-8373-1563-8*) Nat Learn.

Park the Car. Francis H. Wise & Joyce M. Wise. (Phonetic Readers Ser.: No. 12). (Illus.). (J). (ps-1). 1975. pap. text 2.00 (*0-915766-32-9*) Wise Pub.

Park Trailers, Standards For. 31p. 1993. 18.75 (*0-318-16432-9*) RV Indus Assn.

Park Walking in San Diego County. William Carroll. LC 91-73240. (Explore San Diego County Ser.). (Illus.). 144p. (Orig.). 1991. pap. 10.00 (*0-910390-32-0*) Coda Publications.

Park Waters in Peril. Terri Martin & William J. Lockhart. (Illus.). 126p. (C). 1993. pap. text. write for info. (*0-940091-33-X*) Natl Parks & Cons.

Park Weaves: Based on Dr. William G. Bateman's Manuscript. Ed. by Virigina I. Harvey. LC 84-48359. (Guild Monographs: No. 37). (Illus.). 96p. 1984. pap. 14.95 (*0-916658-39-2*) Shuttle Craft.

Parkander Papers. Ed. by Jane Teleen et al. LC 88-80873. (Augustana College Library Occasional Papers, Wallin Lecture: No. 18). 60p. 1988. pap. 5.95 (*0-910182-45-0*) Augustana Coll.

Parker: Collected Stories. Dorothy D. Parker. 1999. pap. 22.95 (*0-670-86442-0*) Viking Penguin.

Parker: Gleanings from Colonial & American Records of Parker & Morse Families, 1585-1915. William T. Parker. (Illus.). 62p. 1993. reprint ed. pap. 13.00 (*0-8328-3377-0*) Higginson Bk Co.

Parker: Lineage of Malcolm Metzger Parker from Johannes DeLang. I. H. DeLong. (Illus.). 62p. 1994. reprint ed. pap. 13.00 (*0-8328-4230-3*) Higginson Bk Co.

Parker: The History of Peter Parker & Sarah Ruggles. J. W. Linzee. (Illus.). 609p. 1991. reprint ed. pap. 89.50 (*0-8328-2893-9*); reprint ed. lib. bdg. 99.50 (*0-8328-2894-7*) Higginson Bk Co.

Parker & Hulme: A Lesbian View. Julie Glamuzina & Alison J. Laurie. LC 95-25420. 224p. 1995. pap. 12.95 (*1-56341-065-6*); lib. bdg. 26.95 (*1-56341-066-4*) Firebrand Bks.

Parker & Mellows: The Modern Law of Trusts. 6th ed. A. J. Oakley. 1994. pap. 44.00 (*0-421-48750-X*, Pub. by Sweet & Maxwll) Gaunt.

Parker & the Gypsy. Susan Carroll. 1997. per. 3.50 (*0-373-76068-X*, 1-76068-5) Silhouette.

Parker Chronicle. Ed. by A. H. Smith. (Old English Ser.). 1966. pap. text 9.95 (*0-89197-569-1*) Irvington.

Parker Chronicle. Ed. by A. H. Smith. 80p. 1981. pap. text 9.95 (*0-85989-099-6*, Pub. by Univ Exeter Pr) Northwestern U Pr.

Parker Chronicle & Laws: Corpus Christi College, Cambridge, MS 173. Ed. by R. Flower & H. Smith. (EETS Original Ser.: No. 208). 1972. reprint ed. 50.00 (*0-19-722208-0*, Pub. by EETS) Boydell & Brewer.

Parker Chronicle & Laws: Facsimile. rev. ed. Ed. by R. Flower & A. H. Smith. (EETS, OS Ser.: Vol. 208). 1973. reprint ed. 50.00 (*0-8115-3384-0*) Periodicals Srv.

Parker Directory of California Attorneys: The Comprehensive Guide to the California Legal Community. Ed. by Parker Directory Staff. 1700p. 1999. 54.95 (*1-56160-430-5*) Martindale-Hubbell.

Parker Gun. Larry L. Baer. 35.00 (*0-88227-047-8*) Gun Room.

Parker Guns - The Old Reliable: A Concise History of the Famous American Shotgun Manufacturing. Ed Muderlak. (Illus.). 325p. 1997. 40.00 (*1-57157-054-3*) Safari Pr.

Parker Hides. large type ed. Norma A. Callender. (Beginning Reader Comprehension Ser.; Vol. 3). (Illus.). 12p. (Orig.). (J). (ps-2). 1997. pap. 4.95 (*1-890274-03-8*) BATA Bks.

Parker in America, Sixteen Thirty to Nineteen Ten, Genealogy, Biography, & History. A. Parker. (Illus.). 608p. 1989. reprint ed. pap. 91.00 (*0-8328-0937-3*); reprint ed. lib. bdg. 99.00 (*0-8328-0936-5*) Higginson Bk Co.

Parker Master Guide to Personal & Business Success. Lawrence Talbott. LC 81-3929. 240p. 1981. 17.95 (*0-13-650291-1*, Parker Publishing Co) P-H.

Parker on the Iroquois: Iroquois Uses of Maize & Other Food Plants. Arthur C. Parker. Ed. by William N. Fenton. LC 68-31036. (Illus.). 478p. 1981. pap. 16.95 (*0-8156-0115-8*) Syracuse U Pr.

Parker on Writing. Robert B. Parker. 50p. 1985. 50.00 (*0-935716-34-3*) Lord John.

Parker Penguin & the Winter Games. Jon Chardiet. LC 98-27869. (Read with Me Paperback Ser.). (Illus.). 32p. (J). (gr. k-2). 1999. 3.25 (*0-590-14925-3*) Scholastic Inc.

Parker Penguin, Big Brother Blues. Jon Chardiet. LC 98-34154. (Read with Me Paperback Ser.). (Illus.). (J). 1998. write for info. (*0-590-14924-5*) Scholastic Inc.

***Parker Pillsbury: Radical Abolitionist, Male Feminist.** Stacey M Robertson. LC 99-46230. 2000. 35.00 (*0-8014-3634-6*) Cornell U Pr.

Parker Pinecone Catalog. (Illus.). 34p. 1995. pap. 20.00 (*1-884849-15-6*) R&R Bks.

Parker Pyne Investigates. Agatha Christie. 1992. 10.60 (*0-606-12473-X*, Pub. by Turtleback) Demco.

Parker Ranch. Joseph Brennan. pap. 4.95 (*0-686-79501-6*, PBN 5102) HarpC.

Parker Story, Vol. 1 & 2. Charles Price et al. (Illus.). 450p. 1997. write for info. (*0-9657748-1-3*); pap. write for info. (*0-9657748-2-1*) Double Gun.

Parkers' Astrology. Derek Parker & Julia Parker. LC 91-60388. (Illus.). 416p. 1994. pap. 24.95 (*1-56458-710-X*) DK Pub Inc.

Parker's Astrology Pack. Julia Parker & Derek Parker. (Illus.). 96p. 1997. 29.95 incl. audio compact disk (*0-7894-1441-4*) DK Pub Inc.

***Parker's CA 2000 Family Code.** 777p. 1999. pap. 39.00 (*0-327-09954-2*, 2122315) LEXIS Pub.

Parker's California Business & Professions Code Advance Legislative Service. Lexis Law Publishing Staff. 611p. 1998. pap. write for info. (*0-327-06538-9*, Lexis Law PR) LEXIS Pub.

Parker's California Code of Civil Procedure: 1999 Softbound Edition. 762p. pap. 32.00 (*0-327-06562-1*) LEXIS Pub.

Parker's California Corporations Code, 1994. Ed. by Butterworth Staff. 220p. 1993. pap. 39.50 incl. disk (*0-250-47212-0*, MICHIE) LEXIS Pub.

Parker's California Education Code, 1999 Edition. 1265p. Date not set. pap. write for info. (*0-327-07455-8*, 2123010) LEXIS Pub.

Parker's California Family Code, 1994. Ed. by Butterworth Staff. 190p. 1993. pap. 39.50 incl. disk (*0-250-47213-9*, MICHIE) LEXIS Pub.

Parker's California Fire Laws, 1999 Edition. 384p. Date not set. pap. 25.00 (*0-327-07456-6*, 2125210) LEXIS Pub.

***Parker's California Government Code: 1999 Edition, 2 vols.** 5205p. 1999. pap. 125.00 (*0-327-09117-7*, 2131010) LEXIS Pub.

Parker's California Probate Code, 1999 Softbound Edition. 464p. pap. 30.00 (*0-327-06553-2*) LEXIS Pub.

***Parker's California 2000 Civil Code Advance Legislative Service.** 216p. 1999. pap. write for info. (*0-327-09903-8*, 2122011) LEXIS Pub.

***Parker's California 2000 Corporations Advance Legislative Service.** 320p. 1999. pap. write for info. (*0-327-09926-7*, 2129510) LEXIS Pub.

***Parker's California 2000 Evidence Code.** 202p. 1999. pap. 24.00 (*0-327-09904-6*, 2121915) LEXIS Pub.

***Parker's California 2000 Insurance Code.** 1088p. 1999. pap. 40.00 (*0-327-09955-0*, 2122715) LEXIS Pub.

Parker's California 1999 Civil Code. Lexis Law Publishing Staff. 777p. 1998. pap. 32.00 (*0-327-06558-3*) LEXIS Pub.

Parker's California 1999 Evidence Code. Lexis Law Publishing Staff. 233p. 1998. pap. write for info. (*0-327-06555-9*, Lexis Law PR) LEXIS Pub.

Parker's California 1999 Family Code. Lexis Law Publishing Staff. 739p. 1998. pap. 34.00 (*0-327-06559-1*) LEXIS Pub.

Parker's California 1999 Insurance Code. Lexis Law Publishing Staff. 1,035p. 1998. pap. 35.00 (*0-327-06560-5*) LEXIS Pub.

***Parker's California 2000 Civil Code.** 818p. 1999. pap. 37.00 incl. cd-rom (*0-327-09951-8*, 2120715) LEXIS Pub.

***Parker's California 2000 Code of Civil Procedure.** 800p. 1999. Price not set. (*0-327-09953-4*, 2121115) LEXIS Pub.

Parker's Complete Book of Dreams. Dorling Kindersley Staff. LC 98-164415. 1998. pap. 13.95 (*0-7894-3295-1*, D K Ink) DK Pub Inc.

Parkers' Complete Book of Dreams. Julia Parker & Derek Parker. LC 94-27918. (Illus.). 208p. 1995. 24.95 (*1-56458-855-6*) DK Pub Inc.

Parker's Ferry. E. Frank Stephenson, Jr. LC 95-78084. (Illus.). 140p. 1995. mass mkt. 20.00 (*0-9637671-2-7*) Meherrin Riv.

Parker's History of Bedford County, Virginia. rev. ed. Lula J. Parker. Ed. & Pref. by Peter Viemeister. LC 88-82103. (Indexed Edition Ser.). 160p. 1988. reprint ed. pap. 17.95 (*0-9608598-4-5*) Hamiltons.

Parker's Modern Conveyancing Precedents. 2nd ed. Ed. by E. Taylor et al. 228p. 1989. boxed set 89.00 (*0-406-33451-X*, U.K., MICHIE) LEXIS Pub.

Parker's Modern Wills Precedents. 2nd ed. Ed. by E. Taylor et al. 152p. 1987. boxed set 70.00 (*0-406-33461-7*, U.K., MICHIE) LEXIS Pub.

Parker's Modern Wills Precedents. 3rd ed. Ed. by E. Taylor. 1996. write for info. (*0-406-08140-9*, PMWP3, MICHIE) LEXIS Pub.

Parker's 1995 California Civil Code. Ed. by Butterworth Staff. 1020p. 1994. pap. 25.00 incl. disk (*0-250-44768-1*, MICHIE) LEXIS Pub.

Parker's 1995 California Code of Civil Procedure. Ed. by Butterworth Staff. 840p. 1994. pap. 25.00 incl. disk (*0-250-44767-3*, MICHIE) LEXIS Pub.

Parker's 1995 California Evidence Code. Ed. by Butterworth Staff. 270p. 1994. pap. 17.50 incl. disk (*0-250-44770-3*, MICHIE) LEXIS Pub.

Parker's 1995 California Family Code. Ed. by Butterworth Staff. 1994. pap. 28.00 incl. disk (*0-250-44771-1*, MICHIE) LEXIS Pub.

Parker's 1995 California Insurance Code. Ed. by Butterworth Staff. 1150p. 1994. pap. 32.00 incl. disk (*0-250-44772-X*, MICHIE) LEXIS Pub.

Parker's 1995 California Labor Code. Ed. by Butterworth Staff. 620p. 1994. pap. 28.00 incl. disk (*0-250-44773-8*, MICHIE) LEXIS Pub.

Parker's 1995 California Probate Code. Ed. by Butterworth Staff. 600p. 1994. pap. 24.00 incl. disk (*0-250-44774-6*, MICHIE) LEXIS Pub.

Parker's 1995 California Uniform Commercial Code. Ed. by Butterworth Staff. 270p. 1994. pap. 19.50 incl. disk (*0-250-44800-9*, MICHIE) LEXIS Pub.

Parker's 1995 California Vehicle Code. Ed. by Butterworth Staff. 830p. 1994. pap. 32.00 incl. disk (*0-250-44801-7*, MICHIE) LEXIS Pub.

Parker's 1995 California Business & Professions Code, 2 vols., Set. Ed. by Butterworth Staff. 1720p. 1994. pap. 55.00 incl. disk (*0-614-05941-0*, MICHIE) LEXIS Pub.

Parker's 1999 California Business & Professions Code, 2 vols. Lexis Law Publishing Staff. 2024p. 1998. pap. 65.00 (*0-327-06557-5*, Lexis Law PR) LEXIS Pub.

Parker's One Minute Designer. Roger C. Parker. LC 97-37145. 304p. 1997. pap. 24.95 (*1-55828-593-8*, MIS Pr) IDG Bks.

***Parker's 2000 California Business & Professions Code, 2 vols., Set.** 1896p. 1999. pap. 70.00 (*0-327-09952-6*, 2120215) LEXIS Pub.

***Parker's 2000 California Business & Professions Code: Advance Legislative Service.** 680p. 1999. pap. write for info. (*0-327-09922-4*, 2121611) LEXIS Pub.

***Parker's 2000 California Code of Civil Procedure Advance Legislative Service.** 370p. 1999. pap. write for info. (*0-327-09925-9*, 2119911) LEXIS Pub.

***Parker's 2000 California Labor Advance Legislative Service.** 196p. 1999. pap. write for info. (*0-327-09924-0*, 2124011) LEXIS Pub.

***Parker's 2000 California Labor Code.** 521p. 1999. pap. Price not set. (*0-327-09956-9*, 2123115) LEXIS Pub.

***Parker's 2000 California Probate Code.** 487p. 1999. pap. 35.00 (*0-327-09957-7*, 2124215) LEXIS Pub.

***Parker's 2000 California Probate Advance Legislative Service.** 196p. 1999. pap. write for info. (*0-327-09927-5*, 2125010) LEXIS Pub.

***Parker's 2000 California Uniform Commercial Code.** 218p. 1999. pap. 24.50 (*0-327-09905-4*, 2124515) LEXIS Pub.

***Parker's 2000 California Vehicle Code.** 884p. 1999. pap. 32.00 (*0-327-09958-5*, 2124915) LEXIS Pub.

Parker's Virginia Battery, CSA. Robert K. Krick. 487p. 1989. reprint ed. 35.00 (*0-916107-78-7*) Broadfoot.

Parker's Virginia Battery, CSA. 2nd rev. ed. Robert K. Krick. (Illus.). 487p. 1989. 30.00 (*0-685-34626-9*) VA Bk.

Parkers Wine Buyers Guide: Complete Easy to Use Reference on Recent Vintages Prices & Ratings for More. 5th ed. Robert M. Parker, Jr. LC 99-47380. 1704p. 1999. 60.00 (*0-684-84184-3*); per. 30.00 (*0-684-80014-4*) S&S Trade.

Parker's Wine Buyer's Guide: Third Edition. 3rd ed. Robert M. Parker, Jr. Orig. Title: Wine Buyer's Guide. (Illus.). 1168p. 1995. 45.00 (*0-684-80282-1*, Fireside) S&S Trade Pap.

Parker's Wine Buyer's Guide: Third Edition. 3rd rev. ed. Robert M. Parker, Jr. Orig. Title: Wine Buyer's Guide. (Illus.). 960p. 1993. pap. 21.00 (*0-671-79914-2*, Fireside) S&S Trade Pap.

Parker's Wine Buyer's Guide: Third Edition. 4th ed. Robert M. Parker, Jr. LC 95-23983. Orig. Title: Wine Buyer's Guide. (Illus.). 1216p. 1995. per. 25.00 (*0-684-80283-X*) S&S Trade Pap.

Parker's 1997 Texas Business Statutes & Security Rules. 519p. 39.50 (*1-55834-767-4*) LEXIS Pub.

Parker's 1997 Texas Uniform Commercial Code. 193p. pap. 22.50 (*1-55834-797-6*) LEXIS Pub.

Parker's 1999 California Civil Code Advance Legislative Service. Lexis Law Publishing Staff. 161p. 1998. pap. write for info. (*0-327-06530-3*, Lexis Law PR) LEXIS Pub.

***Parker's 1999 California Code of Civil Procedure Advance Legislative Service.** Lexis Law Publishing Staff. 293p. 1998. pap. write for info. (*0-327-06526-5*, Lexis Law PR) LEXIS Pub.

Parker's 1999 California Labor Code. Lexis Law Publishing Staff. 95p. 1998. pap. write for info. (*0-327-06527-3*) LEXIS Pub.

Parker's 1999 California Labor Code. Lexis Law Publishing Staff. 496p. 1998. pap. 40.00 (*0-327-06561-3*, Lexis Law PR) LEXIS Pub.

Parker's 1999 California Uniform Commerical Code. Lexis Law Publishing Staff. 274p. 1998. pap. write for info. (*0-327-06556-7*) LEXIS Pub.

Parker's 1999 California Vehicle Code. Lexis Law Publishing Staff. 841p. 1998. pap. 27.00 (*0-327-06563-X*) LEXIS Pub.

Parker's 1999 Larmac Index to California Laws. Lexis Law Publishing Staff. 1201p. 1998. pap. 90.00 (*0-327-06326-2*) LEXIS Pub.

P

An Asterisk (*) at the beginning of an entry indicates that the title is appearing for the first time.

Parkerstown Delegate. Grace Livingston Hill. 15.95 (*0-89190-064-0*) Amereon Ltd.

***Park/e/s & Bunch on the Trail West.** rev. fac. ed. Alice Crandall Park. LC 74-16831. 487p. 2000. 84.50 (*0-7404-0025-8*); pap. 74.50 (*0-7404-0026-6*) Higginson Bk Co.

Parkett, No. 42. Lawrence Weiner & Rachel Whiteread. 200p. 1995. pap. 19.50 (*3-907509-92-7*, Pub. by Parkett Verlag AG) Dist Art Pubs.

Parkett, No. 43. Juan Munoz & Susan Rothenberg. 200p. 1995. pap. 19.50 (*3-907509-93-5*, Pub. by Parkett Verlag AG) Dist Art Pubs.

Parkett, No. 45. 200p. 1996. pap. 29.00 (*3-907509-95-1*) Dist Art Pubs.

Parkett, No. 49. Laurie Anderson et al. 240p. 1997. pap. 29.00 (*3-907509-99-4*, 710553, Pub. by Parkett Verlag AG) Dist Art Pubs.

Parkett, No. 54. (Illus.). 1998. pap. 32.00 (*3-907582-03-9*, 821202, Pub. by Parkett Verlag AG) Dist Art Pubs.

***Parkett, No. 55.** Roni Horn et al. (Illus.). 250p. 1999. pap. 32.00 (*3-907582-05-5*, 821202, Pub. by Parkett Verlag AG) Dist Art Pubs.

Parkett, No. 56. Contrib. by Vanessa Beecroft et al. 250p. 1999. pap. 32.00 (*3-907582-06-3*, Pub. by Parkett Verlag AG) Dist Art Pubs.

***Parkett, No. 57.** Doug Aitken. 2000. pap. 32.00 (*3-907582-07-1*) Parkett Verlag AG.

***Parkett, No. 58.** Parkett Publishing Staff. 2000. pap. 32.00 (*3-907582-08-X*) Parkett Verlag AG.

Parkett, Vol. 48. Gary Hume. 1997. pap. text 29.00 (*3-907509-98-6*, Pub. by Parkett Verlag AG) Dist Art Pubs.

Parkett: Distance, Nos. 44-45. Lothar Baumgarten et al. 200p. pap. 29.50 (*3-907509-94-3*) Dist Art Pubs.

Parkett No. 32: Collaboration: Imi Knoebel, Sherrie Levine with Damien Hirst, Vija Celmins, Larry Clark. (Illus.). pap. 19.50 (*3-907509-82-X*, Pub. by Parkett Verlag AG) Dist Art Pubs.

Parkett No. 34: Collaboration: Ilya Kabakov, Richard Prince with Tatsuo Miyajima, Gary Hill, Stephen Ellis. (Illus.). pap. 19.50 (*3-907509-84-6*, Pub. by Parkett Verlag AG) Dist Art Pubs.

Parkett No. 36: Collaboration: Stephen Balkenhol, Sophie Calle with Richmond Burton, Eva Hesse. (Illus.). pap. 19.50 (*3-907509-86-2*, Pub. by Parkett Verlag AG) Dist Art Pubs.

Parkett No. 37: Collaboration: Charles Ray, Franz West with Pipilotti Rist, Luc Tuymans. (Illus.). pap. 19.50 (*3-907509-87-0*, Pub. by Parkett Verlag AG) Dist Art Pubs.

Parkett No. 38: Collaboration: Ross Bleckner, Marlene Dumas with Rudi Molacek, Adrian Schiess, Rachel Whiteread. (Illus.). pap. 19.50 (*3-907509-88-9*, Pub. by Parkett Verlag AG) Dist Art Pubs.

Parkett No. 39: Collaboration: Felix Gonzalez-Torres, Wolfgang Laib with Gabriel Orozco, Matthew Barney, Roni Horn, Burt Barr, Meyer Vaisman. (Illus.). pap. 19.50 (*3-907509-89-7*, Pub. by Parkett Verlag AG) Dist Art Pubs.

Parkett No. 46: Collaboration Richard Artschwager, Cady Noland, Hiroshi Sugimoto. 200p. 1996. pap. 29.00 (*3-907509-96-X*, 620511, Pub. by Parkett Verlag AG) Dist Art Pubs.

Parkett No. 47: Collaboration: Tony Oursler, Raymond Pettibon, Thomas Schtte with Zoe Leonard & Cheryl Dunye, Emma Kunz, Diane Arbus. (Illus.). pap. 30.00 (*3-907509-97-8*, Pub. by Parkett Verlag AG) Dist Art Pubs.

Parkett No. 52: Karen Kilimnick, Malcolm Morley & Ugo Rondinone. Text by Jean-Claude Lebensztejn et al. (Illus.). 250p. 1998. pap. 32.00 (*3-907582-01-2*, 811142, Pub. by Parkett Verlag AG) Dist Art Pubs.

Parkett No. 53: Tracey Moffatt, Elizabeth Peyton, Wolfgang Tillmans. (Illus.). 240p. 1998. pap. 32.00 (*3-907582-02-0*, 821201, Pub. by Parkett Verlag AG) Dist Art Pubs.

Parkett Nos. 40 & 41: Collaboration: Francesco Clemente, Gunther Forg, Peter Fischli/David Weiss, Damien Hirst, Jenny Holzer, Rebecca Horn, Sigmar Polke. (Illus.). pap. 19.50 (*3-907509-90-0*, Pub. by Parkett Verlag AG) Dist Art Pubs.

Parkett Nos. 50/51: Special Double Issue. Laurie Anderson et al. (Illus.). 350p. 1998. pap. 48.00 (*3-907582-00-4*, 720991, Pub. by Parkett Verlag AG) Dist Art Pubs.

Parkhurst Tales 2. Norman S. Parker. (Illus.). 314p. 1999. pap. 7.95 (*1-85782-317-6*, Pub. by Blake Publng) Seven Hills Bk.

Parkin & Bade Microeconomics: Economics in Action. Michael Parkin. 1997. pap. text, student ed. write for info. (*0-201-38838-3*) Addison-Wesley.

Parkin Economics Plus Graphpad. 2nd ed. Michael Parkin. 1994. write for info. (*0-201-87623-X*) Addison-Wesley.

Parkin Microeconomics Plus Graphpad. 2nd ed. Michael Parkin. 1994. write for info. (*0-201-87624-8*) Addison-Wesley.

Parkin Study Guide Chapters 1-3: University of Guelph. 1996. (*0-201-93131-1*) S&S Trade.

Parking Enforcement Agent. Jack Rudman. (Career Examination Ser.: C-572). 1994. pap. 23.95 (*0-8373-0572-1*) Nat Learn.

Parking for Downtown's Spenders. Dolores P. Palma & Doyle G. Hyett. (Publications Ser.). (Illus.). ii, 32p. 1995. pap. 21.00 (*1-893312-06-2*) HyettPalma Pubns.

Parking Lot Landscape Development. 2nd ed. Gary O. Robinette. (Community Landscape Development Ser.). (Illus.). 200p. 1994. pap. text 29.95 (*1-882240-01-4*) Agora Comms.

Parking Meter Attendant. Jack Rudman. (Career Examination Ser.: C-1063). 1994. pap. 23.95 (*0-8373-1063-6*) Nat Learn.

Parking Meter Collector. Jack Rudman. (Career Examination Ser.: C-573). 1994. pap. 23.95 (*0-8373-0573-X*) Nat Learn.

Parking Meter Supervisor. Jack Rudman. (Career Examination Ser.: C-2592). 1994. pap. 29.95 (*0-8373-2592-7*) Nat Learn.

Parking Principles. (Special Reports: No. 125). 217p. 1971. 8.00 (*0-309-01958-3*, SR125); pap. 8.00 (*0-317-36096-5*) Transport Res Bd.

Parking Publications for Planners. Dennis Jenks. 18p. 1993. pap. 10.00 (*0-86602-293-7*, Sage Prdcls Pr) Sage.

Parking Requirements for Shopping Centers: Summary Recommendations & Research Study Report. Uli & Urban Land Institute Staff. 1982. 40.95 (*0-87420-605-7*) Urban Land.

Parking Spaces. Childs. LC 98-48077. 289p. 1999. 59.95 (*0-07-012107-9*) McGraw.

Parking Structures: Planning, Design, Construction, Maintenance, & Repair. Anthony P. Chrest et al. (Illus.). 432p. 1989. mass mkt. 65.00 (*0-442-20655-0*) Chapman & Hall.

Parking Structures: Recommended Practice for Design & Construction. 2nd ed. PCI Committee on Parking Structures Staff & PCI Committee on Parking Marketing & Promotion Staff. LC 98-159940. (Illus.). 141p. 1998. pap. text 50.00 (*0-937040-58-4*, MNL-129-98) P-PCI.

Parkins Symposium on Fundamental Aspects of Stress Corrosion Cracking: Proceedings of a Symposium Sponsored by TMS - ASM-MSD Corrosion & Environmental Effects Committee Held at the 1991 Fall Meeting in Cincinnati, OH, October 21-24, 1991. Parkins Symposium on Fundamental Aspects of Stress. Ed. by S. M. Bruemmer et al. LC 92-64425. 598p. 1992. reprint ed. pap. 185.40 (*0-608-03830-X*, 206279200004) Bks Demand.

Parkinson - Specific Motor & Mental Disorders: Role of the Pallidum: Pathophysiological, Biochemical, & Therapeutic Aspects. Ed. by R. G. Hassler & J. F. Christ. LC 82-42604. (Advances in Neurology Ser.: Vol. 40). (Illus.). 611p. 1984. reprint ed. pap. 189.50 (*0-608-07236-2*, 206746100009) Bks Demand.

Parkinson Predicament & a Spoonful of Sugar: My Life with Parkinson's Disease/A Prescription for Living with Parkinson's Disease. Barbara T. Coleman. Ed. by Barry Green. (Illus.). 112p. 1997. pap. text 24.95 (*0-9642109-2-4*) Parkinsonian.

Parkinsonian Syndromes. Ed. by Matthew B. Stern & William C. Koller. LC 93-6644. (Neurological Disease & Therapy Ser.: Vol. 18). (Illus.). 592p. 1993. text 255.00 (*0-8247-8838-9*) Dekker.

Parkinsonism. Calne. (Pharmacology & Therapeutics Ser.). Date not set. pap. write for info. (*0-08-034187-X*, Pergamon Pr) Elsevier.

Parkinsonism: Diagnosis & Treatment. 256p. 1989. pap. text 39.50 (*0-9621697-0-6*) Laurel Hse NJ.

Parkinsonism: Physiology, Pharmacology & Treatment. Donald B. Calne. LC 74-500723. xii, 136 p. 1970. write for info. (*0-7131-4175-1*) St Martin.

Parkinsonism-Symptoms, Syndrome & Tardive Dyskinesia: Index of New Information with Authors & Subjects. Roscoe J. Sacks. LC 92-54188. 180p. 1993. 47.50 (*1-55914-748-2*); pap. 44.50 (*1-55914-749-0*) ABBE Pubs Assn.

Parkinsonism Treatment to Photoelectricity see Ullmann's Encyclopedia of Industrial Chemistry

Parkinson's: A Patient's View. Sidney Dorros. LC 89-10122. 1989. pap. 12.95 (*0-929765-20-6*) Seven Locks Pr.

Parkinson's - A Personal Story of Acceptance. Sandi Gordon. (Illus.). 162p. 1993. pap. 12.95 (*0-8283-1949-9*) Branden Bks.

Parkinson's Challenge: A Beginner's Guide to a Good Life in the Slow Lane. rev. ed. Jan P. Stern. (Illus.). 60p. 1989. reprint ed. pap. 3.85 (*0-9623549-0-2*, TX2156483) DMS Pubs.

Parkinson's Disease. Elaine Landau. LC 98-22450. (Venture Ser.). 112 p. (J). 1999. 24.00 (*0-531-11423-6*) Watts.

***Parkinson's Disease.** Ed. by M. Maral Mouradian. 350p. 2000. 99.50 (*0-89603-761-4*) Humana.

Parkinson's Disease. Porter. LC 92-49799. (One Hundred Maxims in Neurology Ser.). 169p. 1992. 35.95 (*0-8016-7279-1*) Mosby Inc.

Parkinson's Disease. F. Clifford Rose. (Current Problems in Neurology Ser.: Vol. 6). 224p. 1987. 74.95 (*0-86196-110-2*, Pub. by J Libbey Med) Bks Intl VA.

Parkinson's Disease. Tony Smith. (ACP Home Medical Guides). 96p. 2000. pap. 6.95 (*0-7894-4169-1*, D K Ink) DK Pub Inc.

Parkinson's Disease. Ed. by Gerald M. Stern. LC 89-19818. (Series in Contemporary Medicine & Public Health). (Illus.). 670p. 1990. text 125.00 (*0-8018-3975-0*) Johns Hopkins.

***Parkinson's Disease.** Sue Vander Hook. LC 99-29939. (Understanding Illness Ser.). (Illus.). 32p. (YA). (gr. 4-10). 2000. lib. bdg. 22.60 (*1-58340-055-9*) Smart Apple.

Parkinson's Disease. Ed. by Melvin D. Yahr & Kenneth J. Bergmann. LC 86-10183. (Advances in Neurology Ser.: Vol. 45). 640p. 1987. reprint ed. pap. 198.40 (*0-608-04694-9*, 206541500004) Bks Demand.

***Parkinson's Disease.** 3rd ed. Robert Hauser & Theresa Zesiewicz. (Questions & Answers Ser.). (Illus.). 2000. pap. text 17.95 (*1-873413-92-0*) Merit Pub Intl.

Parkinson's Disease, Pt. 69. Ed. by Leontino Battistin et al. (Advances in Neurology Ser.: Vol. 69). (Illus.). 752p. 1995. text 173.00 (*0-7817-0341-7*) Lppncott W & W.

Parkinson's Disease, Vol. 80. Gerald M. Stern. 704p. text 159.00 (*0-7817-1598-9*) Lppncott W & W.

***Parkinson's Disease: A Complete Guide for Patients & Families.** William J. Weiner et al. LC 00-9630. (Health Bks.). 2001. write for info. (*0-8018-6556-5*) Johns Hopkins.

Parkinson's Disease: A Guide for Patient & Family. 4th ed. Roger C. Duvoisin & Jacob I. Sage. 200p. 1995. pap. text 26.00 (*0-7817-0312-3*) Lppncott W & W.

***Parkinson's Disease: A Self-Help Guide.** Marjan Jahanshahi et al. 400p. 2000. pap. 24.95 (*1-888799-38-2*, Pub. by Demos Medical) SCB Distributors.

Parkinson's Disease: Biochemistry, Clinical Pathology, & Treatment. W. Birkmayer & P. Riederer. Tr. by G. Reynolds from GER. (Illus.). 194p. 1983. 82.95 (*0-387-81722-0*) Spr-Verlag.

Parkinson's Disease: Experimental Models & Therapy. Contrib. by Riederer. 350p. 1996. pap. 190.00 (*3-211-82749-8*) Spr-Verlag.

Parkinson's Disease: From Basic Research to Treatment. Ed. by Hirotaro Narabayashi et al. LC RC0321.A276. (Advances in Neurology Ser.: No. 60). (Illus.). 799p. 1993. reprint ed. pap. 200.00 (*0-608-05812-2*, 205977700007) Bks Demand.

Parkinson's Disease: From Clinical Aspects to Molecular Basis. Ed. by P. Riederer et al. (Key Topics in Brain Research Ser.). (Illus.). 240p. 1992. 91.95 (*0-387-82272-0*) Spr-Verlag.

Parkinson's Disease: Neurobehavioral Aspects. Steven J. Huber & Jeffrey L. Cummings. (Illus.). 384p. 1992. text 69.50 (*0-19-506969-2*) OUP.

Parkinson's Disease: Questions & Answers. Robert Hauser & Theresa Zesiewicz. (Questions & Answers Ser.). (Illus.). 136p. 1997. pap. 15.95 (*1-873413-01-7*) Merit Pub Intl.

Parkinson's Disease: The Complete Guide for Patients & Caregivers. Abraham N. Lieberman et al. 272p. (Orig.). 1993. per. 12.00 (*0-671-76819-0*) S&S Trade Pap.

Parkinson's Disease: The Mystery, the Search & the Promise. Sue Dauphin. LC 92-93912. (Illus.). 229p. 1995. pap. 16.95 (*0-9620354-1-6*) Pixel Pr.

***Parkinson's Disease: The Treatment Options.** Ed. by Peter A. LeWitt & Wolfgang H. Oertel. 260p. 1999. 125.00 (*1-85317-379-7*) Martin Dunitz.

Parkinson's Disease - Questions & Answers, 2nd Edition. 2nd rev. ed. Robert Hauser & Theresa Zesiewicz. (Illus.). 150p. 1998. pap. 15.95 (*1-873413-46-7*) Merit Pub Intl.

Parkinson's Disease & Its Management. J. Malcolm Pearce. (Illus.). 160p. 1992. 39.95 (*0-19-262177-7*) OUP.

Parkinson's Disease & Movement Disorders. 2nd ed. Ed. by Joseph Jankovic & Eduardo Tolosa. LC 92-49846. (Illus.). 640p. 1993. 95.00 (*0-683-04380-3*) Lppncott W & W.

Parkinson's Disease & Movement Disorders. 3rd ed. Joseph Jankovic & Eduardo Tolosa. LC 97-45686. 1178p. 1998. 99.00 (*0-683-30016-4*) Lppncott W & W.

***Parkinson's Disease & Movement Disorders: Diagnosis & Treatment Guidelines for the Practicing Physician.** Ed. by Charles H. Adler & J. Eric Ahlskog. (Current Clinical Practice Ser.). 496p. 2000. 125.00 (*0-89603-607-3*) Humana.

***Parkinson's Disease & Parkinson's Syndrome in the Elderly.** Ed. by R. J. Meara & W. C. Koller. (Illus.). 280p. (C). 2000. text. write for info. (*0-521-62884-9*) Cambridge U Pr.

Parkinson's Disease & Quality of Life. Ed. by Lucian Cote et al. LC 00-28034. 223p. 2000. 49.95 (*0-7890-0763-0*) Haworth Pr.

***Parkinson's Disease & Quality of Life.** Ed. by Lucien A. Cote et al. LC 00-28034. 223p. 2000. pap. text 19.95 (*0-7890-0810-6*) Haworth Pr.

***Parkinson's Disease & the Art of Moving.** John Argue. (Illus.). 176p. 2000. pap. text 15.95 (*1-57224-183-7*) New Harbinger.

Parkinson's Disease Management Package. Kate Swinburn. 1996. pap. 125.00 (*1-56593-498-9*, 1154) Singular Publishing.

Parkinson's Handbook. Dwight C. McGoon. 1994. pap. 12.95 (*0-393-31143-0*) Norton.

Parkinson's Law. 126p. 1994. pap. text 7.00 (*957-9091-59-5*) Global Pub NJ.

Parkinson's Law. C. Northcote Parkinson. 1993. reprint ed. lib. bdg. 25.95 (*1-56849-015-1*) Buccaneer Bks.

Parkland Pocket Guide to HIV Care. Nassar. 1997. pap. text 12.50 (*0-01-605400-8*) Collins.

Parkland Trauma Handbook, 2. 2nd ed. Ed. by Fiemu Nwariaku & Erwin R. Thal. LC 98-54476. (Illus.). 544p. (C). (gr. 13). 1999. pap. text 36.95 (*0-8151-2618-2*, 31645) Mosby Inc.

Parkman Reader see Francis Parkman Reader

Parkramya Likhat: (Negotiable Instruments in Hindi) 2nd ed. Avtar Singh. 110p. 1979. 35.00 (*0-7855-1686-7*) St Mut.

Parks: Design & Management. Leonard E. Phillips. LC 95-37116. (Illus.). 229p. 1996. 64.95 (*0-07-049871-7*) McGraw.

Parks Vol. 1: Law of Tug, Tow & Pilotage. 3rd ed. Edward V. Cattell, Jr. 1994. 192.00 (*0-421-52370-0*, Pub. by Sweet & Maxwll) Gaunt.

Parks & Mountains of Colorado: A Summer Vacation in the Switzerland of America, 1868. Samuel Bowles. LC 92-28589. (Illus.). 256p. 1994. pap. 12.95 (*0-8061-2625-6*) U of Okla Pr.

Parks & Open Spaces: Maryland, Delaware & the District of Columbia. Marion J. Kaminkow. LC 96-6476. 150p. 1996. per. 7.75 (*0-917882-44-X*) MD Hist Pr.

Parks & Recreation: An Economic Justification. Robert L. Wilder. LC GV0182.15.W5. (Management Information Systems Ser.: No. 4000). 67p. reprint ed. pap. 30.00 (*0-7837-1541-2*, 204182500024) Bks Demand.

Parks & Recreation Assistant. (Career Examination Ser.: C-3399). 1994. pap. 27.95 (*0-8373-3399-7*) Nat Learn.

Parks & Recreation Program Specialist. (Career Examination Ser.). pap. 29.95 (*0-8373-3782-8*, C3782) Nat Learn.

Parks Are to Share. LC 96-37457. (Building Block Bks.). (J). 1997. 14.95 (*1-57505-068-4*, Carolrhoda) Lerner Pub.

Parks Directory of the United States: A Guide to 4,700 National & State Parks, Recreational Areas, Historic Sites, Battlefields, Monuments, Forests, Preserves, Memorials, Seashores, & Other Designated Recreation Areas in the United States Administered by National & State Park Agencies. 2nd ed. Ed. by Darren L. Smith. LC 94-16925. (Illus.). 831p. 1994. lib. bdg. 145.00 (*0-7808-0018-4*) Omnigraphics Inc.

Parks for Texas: Enduring Landscapes of the New Deal. James Wright Steely. LC 98-28537. 350p. 1999. 29.95 (*0-292-77734-5*) U of Tex Pr.

Parks for the People: A Story about Frederick Law Olmsted. Julie Dunlap. LC 93-40988. (Carolrhoda Creative Minds Bks.). (Illus.). (J). (gr. 3-6). 1994. lib. bdg. 19.95 (*0-87614-824-0*, Carolrhoda) Lerner Pub.

Parks in Peril: People, Politics & Protected Areas. Ed. by Kent H. Redford et al. LC 98-23680. 400p. 1998. text 50.00 (*1-55963-607-6*); pap. text 30.00 (*1-55963-608-4*) Island Pr.

Parks in Peril Source Book. Nature Conservancy Staff. Ed. by Jane A. Mansour. 131p. 1995. pap. 15.00 (*1-886765-01-4*) Nature VA.

Parks on the Borderline: Experience in Transfrontier Conservation. Ed. by Jim Thorsell. (IUCN Protected Area Programme Ser.: No. 1). (Illus.). 98p. (Orig.). 1990. pap. 17.00 (*2-8317-0011-6*, Pub. by IUCN) Island Pr.

Parks, Preserves & Rivers: A Guide to Outdoor Adventures in Virginia's Capital Region. Louise L. Burke & Keith F. Ready. LC 85-7255. (Illus.). 285p. (Orig.). 1985. pap. 3.00 (*0-9615016-0-X*) Metro Found.

Park's Quest. Katherine Paterson. (Horn Book "Fanfare" Ser.). 160p. (J). (gr. 5 up). 1989. pap. 4.99 (*0-14-034262-1*, PuffinBks) Peng Put Young Read.

Park's Quest. Katherine Paterson. 1988. 9.09 (*0-606-02743-2*, Pub. by Turtleback) Demco.

Park's Quest: A Study Guide. Norma Marsh. Ed. by Joyce Friedland & Rikki Kessler. (Novel-Ties Ser.). (J). (gr. 5-7). 1991. pap. text 15.95 (*0-88122-581-9*) Lrn Links.

Parks Recreation & Leisure. Ibrahim-Cordes. 2000. 36.74 (*0-697-27701-1*, WCB McGr Hill) McGrw-H Hghr Educ.

Parks, Recreation & Leisure Services Career Information. 2nd ed. (Illus.). 50p. (Orig.). 1991. pap. text 13.00 (*0-88314-853-6*, 300-10001) AAHPERD.

Parks. Rufus Parks Pedigree: 17 Centuries of One Family's Ancestry. Brian J. L. Berry. (Illus.). 166p. 1995. reprint ed. pap. 29.00 (*0-8328-4884-0*); reprint ed. lib. bdg. 39.00 (*0-8328-4883-2*) Higginson Bk Co.

Parkside Pranks & Sunset Stunts: Growing up with San Francisco. Mary A. Williams. Ed. by Kali Sichen. (Illus.). 83p. (J). (gr. 4-9). 1986. pap. 7.95 (*0-916299-02-3*) North Scale Co.

Parksville. William Lynch. 120p. 1994. pap. text 10.95 (*0-88982-132-1*, Pub. by Oolichan Bks) Genl Dist Srvs.

Parkway Byways: Explore the Charming Countryside Close to the Blue Ridge Parkway, the Shenandoah National Park, the Great Smoky Mountain National Park. James R. Hinkel. LC 97-42177. 1998. pap. 18.95 (*1-887905-07-3*) Pkway Pubs.

Parkway Palate: Recipes & Menus from the Parties. San Joaquin River Parkway Trust Staff. Ed. & Frwd. by Jane C. Groff. Frwd. by Coke Hollowell. (Illus.). 108p. 1996. spiral bd. 23.20 (*0-9654690-0-X*) San Joaquin Riv.

Parkways: Past, Present, & Future: Proceedings of the Second Biennial Linear Parks Conference, 1987. 1989. pap. 15.95 (*0-913239-66-6*) Appalach Consortium.

Parkways, Greenways, Riverways: A Partnership for Beauty & Progress: Marrying Beauty with Utility. (Illus.). 268p. (Orig.). 1995. pap. write for info. (*0-614-09743-6*) Appalach Consortium.

Parkwood. Stephanie Beattie & Sue G. Hall. (Illus.). 68p. 1999. pap. 7.50 (*1-55046-300-4*, Pub. by Boston Mills) Genl Dist Srvs.

Parlamentsrecht des Deutschen Reiches: Im Auftrage des Deutschen Reichstages Dargestellt, Pt. 1. Julius Hatschek. (GER.). xiii, 628p. (C). 1973. reprint ed. 138.45 (*3-11-002157-9*) De Gruyter.

***Parlando: Selected Poems.** Ray Clark Dickson. xvii, 295p. 2000. 14.95 (*0-615-11586-1*) Kerouac Con.

Parlay. Mychal-Jerome Manley. LC 96-90050. 221p. (Orig.). 1996. reprint ed. pap. text 12.95 (*0-533-11863-8*) Vantage.

PARLE: Parallel Architectures & Languages Europe. Ed. by J. W. De Bakker et al. (Lecture Notes in Computer Science Ser.: Vol. 258). xii, 480p. 1987. pap. 49.00 (*0-387-17943-7*) Spr-Verlag.

PARLE: Parallel Architectures & Languages Europe. Ed. by J. W. De Bakker et al. Vol. 259. xii, 464p. 1987. pap. 49.00 (*0-387-17945-3*) Spr-Verlag.

PARLE '89 Vol. II: Parallel Architectures & Languages Europe: Parallel Languages. Ed. by E. Odijk et al. (Lecture Notes in Computer Science Ser.: Vol. 366). xiii, 442p. 1989. 44.00 (*0-387-51285-3*) Spr-Verlag.

Parle Express Basic French. Helene Lucille. 82p. 1993. 95.00 incl. audio (*1-882874-25-0*) Truespeech.

PARLE '94: Parallel Architectures & Languages Europe: Sixth International PARLE Conference, Athens, Greece, July 1994, Proceedings. Ed. by C. Halatsis et al. LC 94-21759. 1994. 112.95 (*0-387-58184-7*) Spr-Verlag.

PARLE '93: Proceedings of the 5th International PARLE Conference, Munich, Germany, June 14-17, 1993. Ed. by Arndt Bode et al. (Lecture Notes in Computer Science Ser.: Vol. 694). xvii, 770p. 1993. 108.95 (*0-387-56891-3*) Spr-Verlag.

P

PARLE '92: Parallel Architectures & Languages Europe: Proceedings, 4th International PARLE Conference, Paris, France, June 15-18, 1992. Ed. by D. Etiemble et al. LC 92-16902. (Lecture Notes in Computer Science Ser.: Vol. 605). xvii, 984p. 1992. 136.95 (*0-387-55599-4*) Spr-Verlag.

PARLE '92 Vol. I: Parallel Architectures & Languages Europe: Parallel Architectures. Ed. by E. Odijk et al. (Lecture Notes in Computer Science Ser.: Vol. 365). xiii, 478p. 1989. 51.00 (*0-387-51284-5*) Spr-Verlag.

***Parle Pas.** Patrick Williams. 1998. pap. text 13.00 (*0-226-89924-1*); lib. bdg. 29.00 (*0-226-89923-3*) U Ch Pr.

Parlement of Giraffes: Poems for the World's Children. Jose G. Villa. Tr. & Illus. by Hilario S. Francia. (TAG.). 150p. (Orig.). (J). (gr. 4-12). 1994. 30.00 (*1-884861-03-2*); pap. 20.00 (*1-884861-04-0*) Bravo Edit.

Parlement of Paris. J. H. Shennan. LC 99-226832. 416p. 1998. pap. 29.95 (*0-7509-1830-6*, Pub. by Sutton Pub Ltd) Intl Pubs Mktg.

Parlement of Paris, 1774-1789. Bailey S. Stone. LC 79-27732. 237p. reprint ed. pap. 73.50 (*0-7837-3764-5*, 204358100010) Bks Demand.

Parler Acadien du Sud-Est du Nouveau-Brunswick: Elements Gammaticaux et Lexicaux. Louise Peronnet. (American University Studies: Foreign Language Instruction: Ser. VI, Vol. 8). (FRE.). 275p. (C). 1988. text 37.50 (*0-8204-0794-1*) P Lang Pubng.

Parler Arabe des Juifs de Tunis Tome 2: Etude Linguistique. David Cohen. LC 72-94452. (Janua Linguarum, Ser. Practica: No. 161). (FRE.). 318p. 1975. 85.40 (*90-279-3296-4*) Mouton.

Parler Bordelais. Guy Suire. (FRE.). 158p. 1988. pap. 24.95 (*0-8288-1717-0*, M 2051) Fr & Eur.

Parler de la Lozere. A. Polverel. (FRE.). 83p. 1994. 34.95 (*0-320-00915-7*) Fr & Eur.

Parler des Bouches-du-Rhone. C. Armanel. (FRE.). 105p. 1993. 34.95 (*0-320-03042-3*) Fr & Eur.

Parler Gascon. (FRE.). 1988. pap. 24.95 (*0-8288-1711-1*, M 2056) Fr & Eur.

Parler Lyonnais. (FRE.). 1988. pap. 24.95 (*0-8288-1712-X*, M2054) Fr & Eur.

Parler Marseillais Dictionnaire Argotique. Robert Bouvier. (FRE.). 182p. 1987. pap. 30.95 (*0-7859-8127-6*, 2862760900) Fr & Eur.

Parler Provencal: Lexique. (PRO.). 197p. 1988. pap. 29.95 (*0-8288-1718-9*, M 2053) Fr & Eur.

Parlers Alsaciens. (FRE.). 1988. pap. 24.95 (*0-8288-1713-8*, M 2055) Fr & Eur.

Parlers Dialectaux et Populaires dans l'Oeuvre de Guy de Maupassant. Butler. (Publ. Romanes et Franc.). 15.50 (*0-685-34943-8*, F67900) Fr & Eur.

Parlers Dialectaux et Populaires Dans l'Oeuvre de Guy de Maupassant. Butler. 15.50 (*0-8288-7636-3*, F67900) Fr & Eur.

Parleuses, Vol. 44. Marguerite Duras & Xaviere Gauthier. (FRE.). 25p. 1974. 31.95 (*0-8288-9922-3*, F33220) Fr & Eur.

Parley's Hollow: Gateway to the Great Salt Lake Valley. rev. ed. Florence C. Youngberg. LC 98-71298. (Illus.). 150p. 1998. pap. 16.00 (*1-888106-13-1*) Agreka Bks.

Parlez-Vous Franglais. Rene Etiemble. (FRE.). 438p. 1991. pap. 10.95 (*0-7859-2251-2*, 2070326357) Fr & Eur.

Parlez-Vous Macintosh? Dictionnaire des Termes Macintosh. Marie-Pierre Teuler. (FRE.). 186p. 1990. pap. 55.00 (*0-7859-7933-6*, 2709111039) Fr & Eur.

Parliament. 3rd ed. Central Office of Info. (Aspects of Britain Ser.). (Illus.). 171p. 1996. pap. 15.00 (*0-11-702046-X*, HM02046X, Pub. by Statnry Office) Bernan Associates.

Parliament & Administration: The Estimates Committee, 1945-65. Nevil Johnson. LC 67-3034. 187p. 1966. 35.00 (*0-678-06022-3*) Kelley.

Parliament & Congress. Kenneth Bradshaw & David Pring. 9.95 (*0-7043-3353-8*, Pub. by Quartet) Charles River Bks.

Parliament & Democratic Consolidation in Southern Europe: Italy, Spain, Portugal, Greece & Turkey in Comparison. Ed. by Ulrike Liebert & Maurizio Cotta. 300p. 1990. text 55.00 (*0-86187-819-1*) St Martin.

Parliament & Industry. David Judge. 300p. 1990. text 72.95 (*1-85521-085-1*, Pub. by Dartmth Pub) Ashgate Pub Co.

Parliament & Liberty from the Reign of Elizabeth to the English Civil War. Ed. by J. H. Hexter. (Making of Modern Freedom Ser.). 360p. 1991. 47.50 (*0-8047-1949-7*) Stanford U Pr.

Parliament & Locality, 1660-1939. D. M. Dean et al. LC 98-196681. 145 p. 1998. write for info. (*0-7486-1027-8*) Edinburgh U Pr.

Parliament & Politics in Late Medieval England, 3 Vols., Vol. 2. J. S. Roskell. 360p. (C). 1985. 60.00 (*0-9506882-9-0*) Hambledon Press.

Parliament & Politics in Late Medieval England, 3 vols., Vol. 3. J. S. Roskell. 424p. (C). 1985. 65.00 (*0-907628-30-3*) Hambledon Press.

***Parliament & Politics in the Age of Churchill & Attlee: The Headlam Diaries, 1935-1951.** Cuthbert Morley Headlam & Stuart Ball. LC 99-59672. 2000. write for info. (*0-521-66143-9*) Cambridge U Pr.

Parliament & Pressure Politics. Ed. by Michael Rush. (Illus.). 320p. 1990. 65.00 (*0-19-827576-5*) OUP.

Parliament & Public Enterprise in India. Laxmi Narain. 1979. text 20.00 (*0-685-14088-1*) Coronet Bks.

Parliament & Public Spending. Ann Robinson. LC 79-307097. 1978. text 77.95 (*0-435-83750-8*) Ashgate Pub Co.

Parliament & Specialist Advice. P. Laugharne. 1993. 75.00 (*1-873534-03-5*, Pub. by Manutius Pr) St Mut.

Parliament & the Atlantic Empire. Ed. by Philip Lawson. 130p. 1996. pap. 23.00 (*0-7486-0628-9*, Pub. by Edinburgh U Pr) Col U Pr.

Parliament & the Media: A Study of Britain, Germany & France. Ralph M. Negrine. LC 97-52202. (Chatham House Papers Ser.). 140p. 1998. 44.95 (*1-85567-555-2*, Pub. by P P Pubs); pap. 15.95 (*1-85567-556-0*, Pub. by P P Pubs) Cassell & Continuum.

Parliament & the People: The Reality & the Public Perception. Philip Laundy. LC 97-15772. 240p. 1997. text 72.95 (*1-85521-949-2*, JF1051.P316, Pub. by Dartmth Pub) Ashgate Pub Co.

Parliament & Welfare Policy. Hugh M. Bochel. 164p. 1992. 72.95 (*1-85521-279-X*, Pub. by Dartmth Pub) Ashgate Pub Co.

Parliament at Work: A Casebook of Parliamentary Procedure. Albert Hanson & H. V. Wiseman. LC 74-29640. 358p. 1975. reprint ed. lib. bdg. 65.00 (*0-8371-8004-X*, HAPA, Greenwood Pr) Greenwood.

Parliament for Wales. Ed. by John Osmond. LC 95-233324. 288p. 1994. pap. 30.00 (*1-85902-173-5*, Pub. by Gomer Pr) St Mut.

***Parliament House, Canberra: A Building for the Nation.** Haig Beck. (Illus.). 280p. 2000. 49.95 (*0-949284-33-5*, Pub. by Watermark) Antique Collect.

Parliament in Elizabethan England: John Hooker's "Order & Usage" Vernon F. Snow. LC 77-23301. (Illus.). 1977. 32.00 (*0-300-02093-7*) Yale U Pr.

Parliament in Perspective. David Menhennet & John Palmer. LC 67-73291. 1967. 18.95 (*0-8023-1125-3*) Dufour.

***Parliament in the Age of the Internet.** Stephen Coleman et al. (Hansard Society Series in Government & Politics). 217p. 2000. pap. text 24.95 (*0-19-922422-6*) OUP.

Parliament of Animals: Anecdotes & Legends from Books of Natural History, 1775-1900. Boria Sax. 240p. (C). 1992. lib. bdg. 55.00 (*0-944473-07-5*) Pace Univ Pr.

Parliament of Canada. C. E. S. Franks. 314p. 1987. pap. text 18.95 (*0-8020-6651-8*) U of Toronto Pr.

Parliament of Minds: Philosophy for a New Millennium. Ed. by Michael Tobias et al. LC 99-43557. 1999. pap. text 21.95 (*0-7914-4484-8*) State U NY Pr.

Parliament of Minds: Philosophy for a New Millennium. Ed. by Michael Tobias et al. LC 99-43557. 2000. text 65.50 (*0-7914-4483-X*) State U NY Pr.

Parliament of Ravens. Laurence Millman. 32p. 1986. pap. 5.00 (*0-910477-03-5*) LoonBooks.

Parliament of 1624: Politics & Foreign Policy. Robert E. Ruigh. LC 72-135548. (Historical Studies: No. 87). (Illus.). 448p. 1971. 27.50 (*0-674-65225-8*) HUP.

Parliament of Souls: In Search of Global Spirituality. Ed. by Michael Tobias et al. LC 95-10093. (Illus.). 304p. (Orig.). 1995. pap. 18.95 (*0-912333-35-9*) BB&T Inc.

Parliament of Souls: Limits & Renewals, Vol. 2. Stephen R. Clark. 202p. 1990. text 55.00 (*0-19-824236-0*) OUP.

Parliament of Whores: A Lone Humorist Attempts to Explain the Entire U. S. Government. P. J. O'Rourke. 1992. pap. 12.00 (*0-679-73789-8*) Vin Bks.

Parliament, Parties & People. 2nd ed. Jaensch. 1994. pap. text. write for info. (*0-582-80250-4*, Pub. by Addison-Wesley) Longman.

Parliament, Party & Politics in Victorian Britain. T. A. Jenkins. LC 95-30845. (New Frontiers in History Ser.). 174p. 1996. text 24.95 (*0-7190-4747-1*, Pub. by Manchester Univ Pr) St Martin.

Parliament, Party & Politics in Victorian Britain. T. A. Jenkins. LC 95-30845. (New Frontiers in History Ser.). 174p. (C). 1996. text 79.95 (*0-7190-4746-3*) Manchester Univ Pr.

Parliament, Policy & Politics in the Reign of William III. Henry Horwitz. LC 76-27126. 385p. 50.00 (*0-87413-124-3*) U Delaware Pr.

Parliament, Politics & People: Essays in Eighteenth Century Irish History. Gerard O'Brien. 200p. 1988. 14.95 (*0-7165-2421-X*, I2421, Pub. by Irish Acad Pr) Intl Spec Bk.

Parliament under Pressure. Peter Riddell. 256p. 1998. 40.00 (*0-575-06435-8*, Pub. by V Gollancz) Trafalgar.

Parliamentarians: The History of the Commonwealth Parliamentary Association 1911-1985. Ian Grey. 380p. 1986. text 82.95 (*0-566-05199-0*, Pub. by Dartmth Pub) Ashgate Pub Co.

Parliamentarism & Government in a One Party System. G. Kilenyi & V. Lamm. (Studies on Hungarian State & Law: Vol. 1). 237p. (C). 1988. pap. 60.00 (*963-05-4882-8*, Pub. by Akade Kiado) St Mut.

Parliamentary & Media Workshop on Africa's Children: Needs & Opportunities. UNICEF Staff. Ed. by Mariam Hughes et al. Tr. by Language Inc. Staff from ENG. LC 88-83434. 66p. 1988. pap. text. write for info. (*0-922684-00-6*) GFSPL.

Parliamentary & Presidential Systems. Don K. Price. (Reprint Series in Social Sciences). (C). 1993. reprint ed. pap. text 5.00 (*0-8290-3375-0*, PS-232) Irvington.

Parliamentary Army Chaplains, 1642-1651. Anne Laurence. (Royal Historical Society: Studies in History: No. 59). 222p. (C). 1990. 75.00 (*0-86193-216-1*) Boydell & Brewer.

Parliamentary Assembly: Procedure & Practice. 9th ed. Council of Europe Staff. (Parliamentary Assembly Ser.). 1990. 45.00 (*92-871-1801-9*, Pub. by Council of Europe) Manhattan Pub Co.

Parliamentary Change in the Nordic Countries. Ed. by Erik Damgaard et al. (Illus.). 224p. 1993. 39.00 (*82-00-21510-5*) Scandnvan Univ Pr.

Parliamentary Commissioner for Administration Reports, 5th Report Session 1995-96: Selected Cases, 1996, Vol. 2. 124p. 1996. pap. 35.00 (*0-10-280396-X*, HM0396X, Pub. by Statnry Office) Bernan Associates.

***Parliamentary Constituencies & Their Registers since 1832.** Richard Cheffins. 247p. 1998. pap. 62.00 (*0-7123-0844-X*) L Erlbaum Assocs.

Parliamentary Control over Finance. S. Seshadri. LC 75-905958. 1975. 11.00 (*0-88386-054-6*) S Asia.

Parliamentary Control over Foreign Policy. Antonio Cassese. 216p. 1980. lib. bdg. 75.50 (*90-286-0019-1*) Kluwer Academic.

Parliamentary Debates, House of Commons. TSO Staff. (Sixth Series, 14 July-25 July 1997: Vol. 298). 955p. 1998. 150.00 (*0-10-681298-X*, HM81298X, Pub. by Statnry Office) Bernan Associates.

Parliamentary Debates, House of Commons, Vol. 281. TSO Staff. 955p. 1997. 150.00 (*0-10-681281-5*, HM12815, Pub. by Statnry Office) Bernan Associates.

Parliamentary Debates, House of Commons: 1996-97, 10 February-20 February 1997, No. 290. 955p. 1997. 155.00 (*0-10-681290-4*, HM12904, Pub. by Statnry Office) Bernan Associates.

Parliamentary Debates, House of Commons: 1996-97, 10 March-21 March 1997, No. 292. 955p. 1998. 155.00 (*0-10-681292-0*, HM12920, Pub. by Statnry Office) Bernan Associates.

Parliamentary Debates, House of Commons: 1996-97, 24 February-6 March 1997, No. 291. 955p. 1997. 155.00 (*0-10-681291-2*, HM12912, Pub. by Statnry Office) Bernan Associates.

Parliamentary Debates, House of Commons: 1997-98, 16 June-27 June 1997, No. 296. 955p. 1998. 155.00 (*0-10-681296-3*, HM12963, Pub. by Statnry Office) Bernan Associates.

Parliamentary Debates, House of Commons: 1997-98, 2 June-12 June 1997, No. 295. 955p. 1998. 155.00 (*0-10-681295-5*, HM12955, Pub. by Statnry Office) Bernan Associates.

Parliamentary Debates, House of Commons: 1997-98, 7 May-22 May, No. 294. 955p. 1998. 155.00 (*0-10-681294-7*, HM12947, Pub. by Statnry Office) Bernan Associates.

Parliamentary Debates, House of Commons No. 299: 28 July-30 October, 1997, 1997-98. Tso. 1998. 155.00 (*0-10-681299-8*, Pub. by Statnry Office) Bernan Associates.

Parliamentary Debates, House of Commons - Bound Volumes Vol. 297: 1997-98, 6th Series, 30 June-11 July 1997. TSO Staff. 955p. 1998. 155.00 (*0-10-681297-1*, HM12971, Pub. by Statnry Office) Bernan Associates.

Parliamentary Debates, House of Commons - Bound Volumes, 1997-98. TSO Staff. (Sixth Series, 26 January-6 February, 1998: Vol. 305, 1). 955p. 1998. 150.00 (*0-10-681305-6*, HM13056, Pub. by Statnry Office) Bernan Associates.

***Parliamentary Debates, House of Commons - Bound Volumes, 1997-98.** TSO Staff. (Sixth Series, 9 March-20 March, 1998: Vol. 308). 955p. 1999. 155.00 (*0-10-681308-0*, HM13080, Pub. by Statnry Office) Bernan Associates.

Parliamentary Debates, House of Commons - Bound Volumes, 1997-98. TSO Staff. (Sixth Series, 23 March-2 April, 1998: Vol. 309). 955p. 1999. 155.00 (*0-10-681309-9*, HM13099, Pub. by Statnry Office) Bernan Associates.

Parliamentary Debates, House of Commons - Bound Volumes, 1997-98. TSO Staff. (Sixth Series, April 6-April 24, 1998: Vol. 310). 955p. 1999. 155.00 (*0-10-681310-2*, HM13102, Pub. by Statnry Office) Bernan Associates.

Parliamentary Debates, House of Commons - Bound Volumes, 1997-98. TSO Staff. (Sixth Series, 27 April-8 May 1998: Vol. 311). 955p. 1999. 150.00 (*0-10-681311-0*, HM13110, Pub. by Statnry Office) Bernan Associates.

Parliamentary Debates, House of Commons, Bound Volumes Vol. 282, 1995-96, 6th Series: 22 July-17 October 1996. TSO Staff. 955p. 1997. 150.00 (*0-10-681282-3*, HM12823, Pub. by Statnry Office) Bernan Associates.

Parliamentary Debates, House of Commons, Bound Volumes Vol. 284, 1996-97, 6th Series: 23 October-7 November 1996. TSO Staff. 955p. 1997. 150.00 (*0-10-681284-X*, HM1284X, Pub. by Statnry Office) Bernan Associates.

Parliamentary Debates, House of Commons, Bound Volumes Vol. 285, 1996-97, 6th Series: 11 November-21 November 1996. TSO Staff. 955p. 1997. 150.00 (*0-10-681285-8*, HM12858, Pub. by Statnry Office) Bernan Associates.

Parliamentary Debates, House of Commons, Bound Volumes Vol. 286, 1996-97, 6th Series: 25 November-6 December 1996. TSO Staff. 955p. 1997. 150.00 (*0-10-681286-6*, HM12866, Pub. by Statnry Office) Bernan Associates.

Parliamentary Debates, House of Commons Bound Volumes 1994-95 5th Series 16 November - 2 December 1994. H. M. S. O. Staff. (Parliamentary Debates Ser.: Vol. 250). 695p. 1995. 185.00 (*0-10-681250-5*, HM12505, Pub. by Statnry Office) Bernan Associates.

Parliamentary Debates, House of Commons, 1994-95, 2 vols. HMSO Staff. (Sixth Series, 3 July - 19 July 1996: Vol. 263). 955p. 1996. boxed set 180.00 (*0-10-681263-7*, HM12637, Pub. by Statnry Office) Bernan Associates.

Parliamentary Debates, House of Commons, 1994-95. HMSO Staff. (Sixth Series, 30 October - 8 November 1995: Vol. 265). 955p. 1996. 180.00 (*0-10-681265-3*, HM12653, Pub. by Statnry Office) Bernan Associates.

Parliamentary Debates, House of Commons, 1995-96. HMSO Staff. (Sixth Series, 15 November - 30 November 1995: Vol. 267). 955p. 1996. 140.00 (*0-10-681267-X*, HM1267X, Pub. by Statnry Office) Bernan Associates.

Parliamentary Debates, House of Commons, 1995-96. HMSO Staff. (Sixth Series, 4 December - 20 December, 1995: Vol. 268). 955p. 1996. 145.00 (*0-10-681268-8*, HM12688, Pub. by Statnry Office) Bernan Associates.

Parliamentary Debates, House of Commons, 1995-96. HMSO Staff. (Sixth Series, 22 January - 2 February 1996: Vol. 270). 955p. 1996. 145.00 (*0-10-681270-X*, HM1270X, Pub. by Statnry Office) Bernan Associates.

Parliamentary Debates, House of Commons, 1995-96, 6th Series, Sessional Index, Vol. 283. TSO Staff. 955p. 1998. 155.00 (*0-10-681283-1*, HM12831) Statnry Office.

***Parliamentary Debates, House of Commons, 1997-98 Vol. 315: 6th Series, 29 June-10 July 1998.** TSO Staff. 955p. 1999. 140.00 (*0-10-681315-3*, HM13153, Pub. by Statnry Office) Bernan Associates.

Parliamentary Debates, House of Commons, 1997-98, 6th Series, 12 January-23 January 1998, Vol. 304. TSO Staff. 955p. 1998. 155.00 (*0-10-681304-8*, HM13048) Statnry Office.

***Parliamentary Debates, House of Commons, 1998-99 Vol. 332: 6th Series, 24 May-11 June, 1999.** 955p. 2000. 150.00 (*0-10-681332-3*, HM13323, Pub. by Statnry Office) Bernan Associates.

***Parliamentary Debates, House of Commons, 1998-99 Vol. 333: 6th Series, 14 June-25 June 1999.** 955p. 2000. 150.00 (*0-10-681333-1*, HM13331, Pub. by Statnry Office) Bernan Associates.

***Parliamentary Debates, House of Commons, 1998-99 Vol. 334: 6th Series, 28 June-8 July 1999.** 955p. 2000. 150.00 (*0-10-681334-X*, HM1334X, Pub. by Statnry Office) Bernan Associates.

***Parliamentary Debates, House of Commons, 1998-99 Vol. 335: 6th Series, 12 July-23 July 1999.** 955p. 2000. 150.00 (*0-10-681335-8*, HM13358, Pub. by Statnry Office) Bernan Associates.

Parliamentary Debates, House of Lords. (5th Series, 1996-97, 23 October-21 November 1996: Vol. 575). 790p. 1997. 90.00 (*0-10-780575-8*, HM05758, Pub. by Statnry Office) Bernan Associates.

Parliamentary Debates, House of Lords: 1997-98, 30 June-July 1997, No. 581. 790p. 1997. 90.00 (*0-10-780581-2*, HM05812, Pub. by Statnry Office) Bernan Associates.

Parliamentary Debates, House of Lords: 1997-98, 7 May-26 June 1997. (5th Ser.: No. 580). 90.p. 1998. 90.00 (*0-10-780580-4*, HM05804, Pub. by Statnry Office) Bernan Associates.

Parliamentary Debates, House of Lords No. 583: 10 November-4 December 1997, 1997-98 Edition. Office Stationary Staff. (Parliamentary Debates, House of Lords Ser.). 1998. 90.00 (*0-10-780583-9*, Pub. by Statnry Office) Bernan Associates.

***Parliamentary Debates, House of Lords Vol. 591: 5th Series, 1997-98, 13-24 July, 1998.** TSO Staff. 790p. 1999. 85.00 (*0-10-780591-X*, HM80591X, Pub. by Statnry Office) Bernan Associates.

Parliamentary Debates, House of Lords, Bound Volumes Vol. 576, 1996-97, 5th Series: 25 November-19 December 1996. TSO Staff. 790p. 1997. 85.00 (*0-10-780576-6*, HM05766, Pub. by Statnry Office) Bernan Associates.

Parliamentary Debates, House of Lords, Bound Volumes Vol. 577, 1996-97, 5th Series: 13 January-6 February 1997. TSO. 790p. 1997. 85.00 (*0-10-780577-4*, HM05774, Pub. by Statnry Office) Bernan Associates.

Parliamentary Debates, House of Lords, Bound Volumes Vol. 578, 1996-97, 5th Series: 10 February-6 March 1997. TSO Staff. 790p. 1997. 85.00 (*0-10-780578-2*, HM05782, Pub. by Statnry Office) Bernan Associates.

Parliamentary Debates, House of Lords, 1995-96. HMSO Staff. (Fifth Series, 9 January - 1 February: Vol. 568). 790p. 1996. 80.00 (*0-10-780568-5*, HM05685, Pub. by Statnry Office) Bernan Associates.

Parliamentary Debates, House of Lords, 1995-96. HMSO Staff. (Fifth Series, 5 February - 1 March 1996: Vol. 569). 790p. 1996. 80.00 (*0-10-780569-3*, HM05693, Pub. by Statnry Office) Bernan Associates.

Parliamentary Debates, House of Lords, 1995-96. HMSO Staff. (Fifth Series, 4 March - 28 March 1996: Vol. 570). 790p. 1996. 85.00 (*0-10-780570-7*, HM05707, Pub. by Statnry Office) Bernan Associates.

Parliamentary Debates, House of Lords, 1995-96. HMSO Staff. (Fifth Series, 1 April - 2 May 1996: Vol. 571). 790p. 1996. 85.00 (*0-10-780571-5*, HM05715, Pub. by Statnry Office) Bernan Associates.

Parliamentary Debates, House of Lords, 1997-98. TSO Staff. (Fifth Series, 28 July-6 November 1997: Vol. 582). 790p. 1998. 90.00 (*0-10-780582-0*, HM05820, Pub. by Statnry Office) Bernan Associates.

Parliamentary Debates, House of Lords, 1997-98, 5th Series 16 February-5 March 1998, Vol. 586. TSO Staff. 790p. 1998. 90.00 (*0-10-780586-3*, HM05863) Statnry Office.

Parliamentary Debates, House of Lords, 1997-98, 5th Series, 30 March-23 April 1998, Vol. 588. TSO Staff. 790p. 1998. 90.00 (*0-10-780588-X*, HM0588X) Statnry Office.

Parliamentary Debates, House of Lords, 1997-98, 5th Series, 9 March-27 March 1998, Vol. 587. TSO Staff. 790p. (Orig.). 1998. pap. 90.00 (*0-10-780587-1*, HM05871) Statnry Office.

***Parliamentary Debates, House of Lords, 1998-99 Vol. 602: 5th Series, 14 June-25 June, 1999.** TSO Staff. 790p. 2000. 85.00 (*0-10-780602-9*, HM806029, Pub. by Statnry Office) Bernan Associates.

***Parliamentary Debates, House of Lords, 1998-99 Vol. 603: 5th Series, 28 June-9 July, 1999.** TSO Staff. 790p. 2000. 85.00 (*0-10-780603-7*, HM06037, Pub. by Statnry Office) Bernan Associates.

***Parliamentary Democracy: Democratization Destabilization Reconsol.** Klaus Von Beyme. LC 99-52085. 2000. text 59.95 (*0-312-22779-5*) St Martin.

Parliamentary Diaries of Sir John Trelawny, 1858-1865. Geraint H. Jenkins. (Camden Fourth Ser.: No. 40). 355p. 27.00 (*0-86193-125-4*) David Brown.

P

An Asterisk (*) at the beginning of an entry indicates that the title is appearing for the first time.

Parliamentary Diary of Sir Edward Knatchbull 1722-30. A. N. Newman. (Camden Third Ser.). 63.00 (*0-86193-094-0*) David Brown.

Parliamentary Diary of Sir Richard Cocks 1698-1702. Richard Cocks. Ed. by D. W. Hayton. LC 95-49947. (Illus.). 434p. (C). 1996. text 125.00 (*0-19-822370-6*, Clarendon Pr) OUP.

Parliamentary Elections. 2nd ed. Central Office of Info. LC 95-204049. (Aspects of Britain Ser.). (Illus.). 86p. 1995. pap. 11.95 (*0-11-701939-9*, HM19399, Pub. by Statnry Office) Bernan Associates.

Parliamentary Enclosure in England: An Introduction to Its Causes, Incidence, & Impact, 1750-1850. G. E. Mingay. LC 97-25200. 176p. (C). 1997. pap. 33.53 (*0-582-25725-5*) Longman.

Parliamentary Gazetteer of Ireland, 6 Vol. 2318p. 1998. 795.00 (*1-85506-634-3*) Thoemmes Pr.

Parliamentary Guide for Church Leaders. C. Barry McCarty. 1990. pap. 9.99 (*0-8054-3116-0*, 4231-16) Broadman.

Parliamentary History of England from the Norman Conquest in 1066 to the Year 1803, 36 vols. Ed. by William Cobbett et al. LC 54-54297. reprint ed. 4140.00 (*0-404-01650-2*) AMS Pr.

Parliamentary Law see Reglas Parlamentarias

Parliamentary Law. Henry M. Robert. 610p. (C). 1975. lib. bdg. 46.50 (*0-8290-0874-8*) Irvington.

Parliamentary Law & Practice for Nonprofit Organizations. 2nd ed. Howard L. Oleck & Cami Green. LC 91-72549. 180p. 1991. pap. 20.00 (*0-8318-0598-6*, B598) Am Law Inst.

Parliamentary Law at a Glance. rev. ed. Ethel C. Utter. LC 97-19712. 368p. 1975. reprint ed. pap. 12.95 (*0-8092-8891-5*, 889150) NTC Contemp Pub Co.

Parliamentary Libraries & Information Services of Asia & the Pacific: Papers Prepared for the 62cnd Conference, Beijing, China, August 25-31, 1996. Rob Brian. (IFLA Publications: 83). iv, 106p. 1997. write for info. (*3-598-21808-7*) K G Saur Verlag.

Parliamentary Libraries & Research Services in Central & Eastern Europe: Building More Effective Legislatures. William H. Robinson. (IFLA Publications: 87). x, 238p. 1998. write for info. (*3-598-21813-3*) K G Saur Verlag.

Parliamentary Motions: A Pocket Guide to Parliamentary Decision-Making (Sturgis) rev. ed. Hermon W. Farwell. 48p. 1992. reprint ed. pap. 4.50 (*0-9604216-3-7*) High Pubs.

Parliamentary Opinion of Delegated Legislation. Chen & Chin-Mai. LC 70-76628. (Columbia University. Studies in the Social Sciences: No. 394). reprint ed. 20.00 (*0-404-51394-8*) AMS Pr.

Parliamentary Opinions: A Compilation & Revision of Opinions of the Opinions Committee, American Institute of Parliamentarians, 1958 to 1982. Virginia H. Schlotzhauer et al. LC 81-71425. viii, 199p. (Orig.). 1982. pap. 12.50 (*0-942736-00-1*) Am Inst Parliamentarians.

Parliamentary Papers: House of Commons & Command, Index. (Sessional Index for Session 1991-92 Ser.). 1000p. 1997. 35.00 (*0-10-238992-6*, HM89926, Pub. by Statnry Office) Bernan Associates.

Parliamentary Papers (House of Commons & Command) Index: Sessional Index for Session 1992-93. 1000p. 1998. 55.00 (*0-10-025003-3*, HM50033, Pub. by Statnry Office) Bernan Associates.

Parliamentary Parallels. Ed. by W. Craig Henry. LC 98-231009. 66p. 1997. text 25.00 (*1-884048-23-4*) Natl Assn Parliamentarians.

Parliamentary Participation in the Making & Operation of Treaties: A Comparative Study. Ed. by Stefan A. Riesenfeld. LC 93-13382. (Current Legal Issues in International & Comparative Law Ser.). 612p. (C). 1994. lib. bdg. 221.00 (*0-7923-1735-1*) Kluwer Academic.

***Parliamentary Party Groups in European Democracies: Political Parties Behind Closed Doors.** Knut Heidar & R. A. Koole. LC 99-45000. (ECPR Studies in European Political Science). 336p. 2000. 90.00 (*0-415-22336-9*) Routledge.

Parliamentary Politics & the Home Rule Crisis: The British House of Commons in 1886. W. C. Lubenow. 450p. 1988. 85.00 (*0-19-822966-6*) OUP.

Parliamentary Politics in Revolutionary Iran: The Institutionalization of Factional Politics. Bahman Baktiari. (Illus.). 312p. 1996. 49.95 (*0-8130-1461-1*) U Press Fla.

Parliamentary Practice: An Introduction to Parliamentary Law. Henry M. Robert. 209p. (C). 1975. 15.95 (*0-8290-0875-6*) Irvington.

Parliamentary Privilege in Canada. 2nd ed. Joseph P. Maingot. LC 98-223747. 432p. 1997. text 65.00 (*0-7735-1718-9*, Pub. by McG-Queens Univ Pr) CUP Services.

Parliamentary Procedure. (Quick Study Academic Ser.). 4p. pap. 3.95 (*1-57222-293-X*) Barcharts.

Parliamentary Procedure: A Programmed Introduction. 2nd ed. Richard G. Rea & John W. Gray. 124p. 1993. per. 15.95 (*0-8403-8882-9*) Kendall-Hunt.

Parliamentary Procedure: Essential Principles. M. Stanley Ryan. LC 83-45012. 232p. 1985. 14.95 (*0-8453-4771-3*, Cornwall Bks) Assoc Univ Prs.

Parliamentary Procedure at A . . . O. Garfield Jones. 1992. mass mkt. 4.25 (*0-89197-877-1*) Irvington.

Parliamentary Procedure at a Glance. Garfield Jones. 1990. pap. 9.95 (*0-14-015328-4*, Penguin Bks) Viking Penguin.

Parliamentary Procedure Guide to Elections: For Voluntary Organizations. Joyce L. Stephens. Ed. by Marjorie N. Picot. LC 98-93560. (Illus.). 114p. 1998. spiral bd. 14.95 (*1-893106-00-4*) Frederick Pubs.

Parliamentary Procedure in India. 3rd ed. Ajita R. Mukherjea. 396p. 1983. 37.50 (*0-19-561133-0*) OUP.

Parliamentary Procedure Without Stress. 64p. 1985. 11.00 (*0-88210-071-8*, 6208616) Natl Assn Student.

Parliamentary Questions. Ed. by Mark N. Franklin & Philip Norton. LC 92-32478. 232p. (C). 1993. 48.00 (*0-19-827317-7*, Clarendon Pr) OUP.

Parliamentary Questions & Answers III. LC 97-227490. 221p. 1997. 30.00 (*1-884048-14-5*) Natl Assn Parliamentarians.

Parliamentary Reform 1640-1832. Cannon. 352p. 1994. 61.95 (*0-7512-0271-1*) Ashgate Pub Co.

***Parliamentary Reform 1770-1918.** Eric J. Evans. LC 99-20830. (Seminar Studies in History Ser.). 154p. 1999. pap. 12.66 (*0-582-29467-3*) Longman.

Parliamentary Reform, 1785-1928. Sean Lang. LC 98-31486. (Questions & Analysis in History Ser.). (Illus.). 112p. (C). 1999. pap. 11.99 (*0-415-18399-5*) Routledge.

Parliamentary Representation: The Case of the Norwegian Storting. Donald R. Matthews & Henry Valen. LC 98-35317. (Parliaments & Legislatures Ser.). 1999. text 60.00 (*0-8142-0798-7*); pap. text 23.95 (*0-8142-5002-5*) Ohio St U Pr.

***Parliamentary Representatives in Europe 1848-2000: Legislative Recruitment & Careers in Eleven European Countries.** Ed. by Heinrich Best & Maurizio Cotta. LC 99-87409. 420p. 2000. text 95.00 (*0-19-829793-9*) OUP.

Parliamentary Sauce: More Helpings of Political Invective. Greg Knight. (Illus.). 242p. 1995. 21.95 (*0-86051-826-4*, Robson-Parkwest) Parkwest Pubns.

Parliamentary Scrutiny of Government Bills. J. A. Griffith. 285p. 1974. 32.95 (*0-8464-1294-2*) Beekman Pubs.

Parliamentary Selection: Social & Political Choice in Early Modern England. Mark A. Kishlansky. 272p. 1986. pap. text 20.95 (*0-521-31116-0*) Cambridge U Pr.

Parliamentary State. David Judge. (Illus.). 240p. 1993. 65.00 (*0-8039-8871-0*); pap. 19.95 (*0-8039-8872-9*) Sage.

Parliamentary Taxation in Seventeenth Century England: Local Administration & Response. M. J. Braddick. (Royal Historical Society Studies in History: Vol. 70). (Illus.). 365p. (C). 1995. 75.00 (*0-86193-278-1*, Royal Historical Soc) Boydell & Brewer.

Parliamentary Texts of the Later Middle Ages. Nicholas Pronay & John Taylor. 1980. 68.00 (*0-19-822368-4*) OUP.

Parliamentary vs. Presidential Government. Arend Lijphart. (Oxford Readings in Politics & Government Ser.). 270p. 1992. pap. text 24.95 (*0-19-878044-3*) OUP.

***Parliaments & Citizens in Western Europe.** Ed. by Philip Norton. 200p. 1999. 52.50 (*0-7146-4835-3*); pap. 22.50 (*0-7146-4387-4*) F Cass Pubs.

Parliaments & English Politics, 1621-1629. J. F. Willard. (Mediaeval Academy of America Publications: Vol. 19). 1934. 45.00 (*0-527-01691-8*) Periodicals Srv.

Parliaments & Governments in Western Europe. Ed. by Philip Norton. LC 98-16206. (Parliaments in Contemporary Western Europe Ser.). 232p. 1998. 52.50 (*0-7146-4833-7*, Pub. by F Cass Pubs); pap. 22.50 (*0-7146-4385-8*, Pub. by F Cass Pubs) Intl Spec Bk.

Parliaments & Parliamentarians in Democratic Politics. Ed. by Ezra N. Suleiman. LC 85-17562. 300p. (C). 1986. pap. 19.95 (*0-8419-1040-5*) Holmes & Meier.

***Parliaments & Pressure Groups in Western Europe.** Ed. by Philip Norton. 200p. 1999. pap. 22.50 (*0-7146-4386-6*, Pub. by F Cass Pubs) Intl Spec Bk.

***Parliaments & Pressure Groups in Western Europe: Philip Norton, the Lord Norton of Louth.** Ed. by Philip Norton. 181p. 1999. 52.50 (*0-7146-4834-5*, Pub. by F Cass Pubs) Intl Spec Bk.

Parliaments & Technology: The Development of Technology Assessment in Europe. Ed. by Norman J. Vig & Herbert Paschen. LC 99-26085. 288p. (C). 1999. text 75.50 (*0-7914-4303-5*, Suny Pr); pap. text 25.95 (*0-7914-4304-3*, Suny Pr) State U NY Pr.

Parliaments & the United Nations. (United Nations Studies). 10.00 (*92-1-157065-4*, E.79.XV.ST/14) UN.

***Parliaments Estates & Representation, Vol. 18.** Upton. 288p. 1998. 122.50 (*0-86078-694-3*) Ashgate Pub Co.

Parliaments Estates & Representation, Vol.19. Upton. 127.50 (*0-86078-790-7*) Ashgate Pub Co.

Parliaments, Estates & Representation: Parliaments, Etats & Representation. A. F. Upton. (Parliaments, Estates & Representation Ser.: No. 16). 256p. 1996. text 122.50 (*0-86078-577-7*, Pub. by Variorum) Ashgate Pub Co.

Parliaments, Estates & Representation, 1997, Vol. 17. A. F. Upton. 256p. 1997. text 122.50 (*0-86078-635-8*) Ashgate Pub Co.

Parliaments, Estates & Representations, 1995, Vol. 15. Ed. by A. F. Upton. 240p. 1995. text 122.50 (*0-86078-536-X*, Pub. by Variorum) Ashgate Pub Co.

***Parliaments in Asia.** Ed. by Nizam Ahmed & Philip Norton. LC 98-49311. (Library of Legislative Studies). 180p. 1999. 49.50 (*0-7146-4951-1*, Pub. by F Cass Pubs) Intl Spec Bk.

***Parliaments in Asia.** Ed. by Nizam Ahmed & Philip Norton. LC 98-49311. (Library of Legislative Studies). 180p. 1999. pap. 24.50 (*0-7146-8010-9*, Pub. by F Cass Pubs) Intl Spec Bk.

Parliaments in the Modern World. Philip Laundy. 250p. 1989. text 72.95 (*1-85521-042-8*, Pub. by Dartmth Pub); pap. text. write for info. (*1-85521-055-X*, Pub. by Dartmth Pub) Ashgate Pub Co.

Parliaments in the Modern World: Changing Institutions. Ed. by Gary W. Copeland & Samuel C. Patterson. LC 94-1743. 192p. (C). 1994. pap. text 20.95 (*0-472-08255-8*, 08255) U of Mich Pr.

Parliaments in Western Europe. 2nd ed. Ed. by Philip Norton. 176p. (C). 1996. pap. text 19.50 (*0-7146-4331-9*, Pub. by F Cass Pubs) Intl Spec Bk.

Parliamo! An Introduction to Italian. 2nd ed. Kaufman. (C). 1995. text. write for info. (*0-07-034064-1*) McGraw.

Parliamo Glasgow Omnibus. Stanley Baxter. 92p. pap. 9.95 (*1-874744-00-9*, Pub. by Birlinn Ltd) Dufour.

Parliamo Insieme: Communication Activities in Italian. Julie Docker & Deborah Thawley. (Illus.). 112p. (C). 1995. pap. 21.95 (*0-521-35656-3*) Cambridge U Pr.

Parliamo Italian. Brancifort. (C). 1997. pap. text, wbk. ed. 32.36 (*0-395-75768-1*) HM.

Parliamo Italiano! Suzanne Branciforte & Anna G. Reintjes. (ITA.). (C). 1997. text, teacher ed. 11.96 (*0-395-83508-9*) HM.

Parliamo Italiano. Etta Publishing Staff & Elvira Bellegoni. 96p. 1999. pap. text 14.95 (*0-9662542-3-6*) Etta Pub Co.

Parliamo Italiano! annot. ed. Suzanne Branciforte & Anna G. Reintjes. (ITA.). (C). 1997. text, teacher ed. 63.16 (*0-395-83506-2*) HM.

Parlo Italiano. L. Rapaccini. (Monnier Ser.). 27.95 (*88-00-85275-0*) Schoenhof.

Parlons Affaires. Berg. (C). 1998. text 53.00 (*0-03-022528-0*, Pub. by Harcourt Coll Pubs) Harcourt.

Parlons Affaires. Annie Rouxeville. 160p. 1998. pap. 24.50 (*1-85075-388-1*, Pub. by Sheffield Acad) CUP Services.

Parlons de Tout: Livre Pour Cours de Conversation Francaise. Paule M. Miller. 278p. (C). 1990. reprint ed. 34.00 (*0-89464-495-5*) Krieger.

Parlons Wolof & Lexique Wolof/Francais/Wolof. Malherbe & Sall. 181p. 1989. 39.95 (*0-320-00830-4*) Fr & Eur.

Parlor Cards, Vol. 3. Becker & Mayer, Ltd. Staff. 1999. text 14.50 (*0-670-86518-4*) Viking Penguin.

Parlor Cards, Vol. 4. Becker & Mayer, Ltd. Staff. 1999. text 14.95 (*0-670-86519-2*) Viking Penguin.

Parlor Cats: A Victorian Celebration, Cynthia Hart & John Grossman. LC 91-50381. (Illus.). 96p. 1991. 15.95 (*1-56305-118-4*, 3118) Workman Pub.

Parlor Games. James C. Wall. 94p. Date not set. pap. 5.60 (*0-87129-992-5*, P93) Dramatic Pub.

Parlor Ladies & Ebony Drudges: African American Women, Class, & Woek in a South Carolina Community. Kibibi C. Mack. LC 98-25345. (Illus.). 264p. 1999. text 34.00 (*1-57233-030-9*) U of Tenn Pr.

***Parlor Politics: In Which the Ladies of Washington Help Build a City & a Government.** Catherine Allgor. 352p. 2000. 29.95 (*0-8139-1998-3*) U Pr of Va.

Parlor Radical: Rebecca Harding Davis & the Origins of American Social Realism. Jean Pfaelzer. 272p. 1996. pap. 19.95 (*0-8229-5654-3*) U of Pittsburgh Pr.

Parlour & the Streets: Elite & Popular Culture in 19th Century Calcutta. Sumanta Banerjee. 1989. 26.50 (*81-7046-063-8*, Pub. by Seagull Bks) S Asia.

Parlour & the Streets: Elite & Popular Culture in 19th Century Calcutta. Sumanta Banerjee. 1998. 29.50 (*81-7046-099-9*, Pub. by Seagull Bks) S Asia.

Parlour Dulcimer. Rosamond Campbell. 104p. 1995. pap. 12.95 (*0-7866-0315-1*, 95377) Mel Bay.

Parlour Games: Pocket Entertainment. Lorenz Staff. (Illus.). 96p. 1998. 7.95 (*1-85967-765-7*) Anness Pub.

Parlour Games of Sherlock Holmes. William S. Dorn. (Illus.). 65p. 1996. pap. 8.00 (*1-896648-67-3*) Battered Silicon.

Parlour Poetry: A Casquet of Gems see Victorian Parlour Poetry: An Annotated Anthology

Parma Fabula: The Ars Magica 4th Edition Storyguide Screen. 4th ed. Ed. by Jeff Tidball. (Ars Magica Ser.). (Illus.). 32p. (Orig.). 1997. pap. 14.95 (*1-887801-57-X*, Atlas Games) Trident MN.

Parma's Best Kept Secrets. Robert E. Harley. (Illus.). 175p. write for info. (*0-9661721-2-4*); lib. bdg. write for info. (*0-9661721-1-6*) Parma Hist Soc.

Parma's Best Kept Secrets. Ed. by Robert E. Horley. LC 99-178272. (Illus.). 175p. (Orig.). 1998. pap. 15.95 (*0-9661721-0-8*) Parma Hist Soc.

Parmenides. Martin Heidegger. LC 91-19431. (Studies in Continental Thought). 192p. 1998. pap. 14.95 (*0-253-21214-6*) Ind U Pr.

Parmenides. Martin Heidegger. Tr. by Richard Rojcewicz & Andre Schuwer. LC 91-19431. (Studies in Continental Thought). 192p. 1998. text 35.00 (*0-253-32726-1*) Ind U Pr.

Parmenides. Plato. Tr. by Mary L. Gill & Paul Ryan. LC 95-48981. 144p. 1996. pap. text 9.95 (*0-87220-328-X*); lib. bdg. 32.95 (*0-87220-329-8*) Hackett Pub.

Parmenides: Der Beginn der Altheia: Untersuchungen Zu B2 - B3 - B6. Jurgen Wiesner. (GER.). ix, 280p. (C). 1996. lib. bdg. 146.70 (*3-11-014513-8*) De Gruyter.

Parmenides: The Fragments. David Sider & Henry W. Johnstone, Jr. (Greek Commentaries Ser.). 38p. (Orig.). (C). 1986. pap. text 5.00 (*0-929524-21-7*) Bryn Mawr Commentaries.

Parmenides & Empedocles. Pref. by Stanley Lombardo. LC 81-7212. 76p. (Orig.). 1982. pap. 4.95 (*0-912516-66-6*) Grey Fox.

Parmenides & Plato's Late Philosophy: Translation of & Commentary on the Parmenides with Interpretative Chapters on the Timaeus, the Theaetetus, the Sophist, & the Philebus. Robert G. Turnbull. LC 98-171166. (Toronto Studies in Philosophy). 240p. 1997. text 50.00 (*0-8020-4236-8*) U of Toronto Pr.

Parmenides' Lesson: Translation & Explication of Plato's Parmenides. Kenneth M. Sayre & Plato. LC 96-26442. 424p. (C). 1996. text 50.00 (*0-268-03817-1*) U of Notre Dame Pr.

Parmenides of Elea: Fragments: A Text & Translation with an Introduction. Parmenides of Elea. Ed. by David Gallop. (Phoenix Supplementary Volumes Ser.: Vol. XVIII; Pre-Socratics I). 160p. 1991. pap. text 17.95 (*0-8020-6908-8*) U of Toronto Pr.

Parmenides of Elea: Fragments: A Text & Translation with an Introduction. David Gallop. LC B 0235.P22E6. 157p. reprint ed. pap. 48.70 (*0-8357-3648-2*, 203637600003) Bks Demand.

Parmenides, Philebus, Symposium, Phaedrus, Alcibiades 1 & 2, Hipparchus, Amatores see Opera

Parmenides, Plato & the Semantics of Not-Being. Francis Jeffry Pelletier. LC 89-27650. 188p. 1997. 35.95 (*0-226-65390-0*) U Ch Pr.

Parmigianino. Gould. Date not set. 150.00 (*0-302-00616-8*) St Martin.

Parmigianino. Cecil Gould. LC 94-39742. (Illus.). 214p. 1995. 95.00 (*1-55859-892-8*) Abbeville Pr.

Parmigiano! Pamela S. Johns & Jennifer B. Design. LC 97-13569. (Illus.). 111p. 1997. 17.95 (*0-89815-937-7*) Ten Speed Pr.

***Parmotrema & Allied Lichen Genera in Papua New Guinea.** S. H. Louwhoff. (Bibliotheca Lichenologica Ser.: Band 73). (Illus.). 152p. 1999. 56.00 (*3-443-58052-1*, Pub. by Gebruder Borntraeger) Balogh.

Parnall Aircraft since 1914. Kenneth E. Wixey. (Putnam Aviation Ser.). (Illus.). 240p. 1990. 44.95 (*1-55750-930-1*) Naval Inst Pr.

***Parnalls Aircraft.** Ken Wixey. (Transport Ser.). 1999. pap. 18.99 (*0-7524-1508-5*) Arcadia Publng.

Parnas. Meir Bar Am. Tr. by Esther Van Handel. 1986. pap. 6.95 (*0-87306-400-3*) Feldheim.

***Parnas: A Scene from the Holocaust.** Silvano Arieti. LC 99-41323. (Illus.). xii, 147p. 2000. pap. 14.95 (*0-9664913-0-0*, Pub. by Paul Dry Bks) IPG Chicago.

Parnasse et Symbolisme. Pierre Martino. 191p. 1970. 29.95 (*0-8288-7432-8*) Fr & Eur.

Parnasse Francois: Titon du Tillet & the Origins of the Monument to Genius. Judith Colton. LC 78-9878. (Yale Publications in the History of Art: No. 27). 323p. reprint ed. pap. 100.20 (*0-8357-8745-1*, 203369500087) Bks Demand.

Parnassians Personally Encountered. limited ed. Edgar E. Saltus. 1923. boxed set 30.00 (*0-686-17411-9*) R S Barnes.

Parnassians Personally Encountered. Edgar E. Saltus. LC 75-175430. reprint ed. 37.50 (*0-404-05548-6*) AMS Pr.

Parnassus. Ed. by Ralph Waldo Emerson. LC 73-116400. (Granger Index Reprint Ser.). 1977. 28.95 (*0-8369-6141-2*) Ayer.

Parnassus. 2nd ed. Ralph Waldo Emerson. (C). 1972. reprint ed. lib. bdg. 24.00 (*0-8422-8043-X*) Irvington.

Parnassus. 2nd ed. Ralph Waldo Emerson. (C). 1986. reprint ed. pap. text 8.95 (*0-8290-1862-X*) Irvington.

Parnassus: Twenty Years of Poetry in Review. Ed. by Herbert Leibowitz. 432p. 1994. pap. 17.95 (*0-472-06577-7*, 06577) U of Mich Pr.

Parnassus: Twenty Years of Poetry in Review. Ed. by Herbert Leibowitz. 432p. 1995. text 42.50 (*0-472-09577-3*, 09577) U of Mich Pr.

Parnassus Biceps: Or Several Choice Pieces of Poetry, 1656. Abraham Wright. (Verse Miscellanies of the Seventeenth Century Ser.). 232p. 1990. 51.95 (*0-85967-782-6*, Pub. by Scolar Pr) Ashgate Pub Co.

Parnassus en Route: An Anthology of Poems about Places, Not People, on the European Continent. Ed. by Kenneth Horan. LC 70-38600. (Granger Index Reprint Ser.). 1977. reprint ed. 18.95 (*0-8369-6332-6*) Ayer.

Parnassus Flowers. 3rd rev. ed. Robert F. Mainone. Ed. by David Mohrhardt. (Haiku Series: Vol. 2). (Illus.). 32p. 1982. pap. 7.00 (*1-888693-02-9*) Wnderlnd MI.

Parnassus Mad Ward: Michael Dransfield & the New Australian Poetry. Livio Dobrez. 1990. pap. 14.95 (*0-7022-2330-1*, Pub. by Univ Queensland Pr) Intl Spec Bk.

Parnassus on Main Street: A History of the Detroit Public Library. Frank B. Woodford. LC 65-11820. (Illus.). 488p. reprint ed. pap. 151.30 (*0-7837-3600-2*, 204346500009) Bks Demand.

Parnassus on the Mississippi: The Southern Review & the Baton Rouge Literary Community, 1935-1942. Thomas W. Cutrer. LC 83-24913. (Southern Literary Studies). (Illus.). 291p. 1984. text 35.00 (*0-8071-1143-0*) La State U Pr.

Parnassus on Wheels. Christopher Morley. 1976. 18.95 (*0-8488-0594-1*) Amereon Ltd.

Parnassus on Wheels. Christopher Morley. (Illus.). 150p. 1992. reprint ed. pap. 12.95 (*1-879923-01-7*) Booksellers Pub.

Parnassus on Wheels: The Haunted Bookshop. Christopher Morley. LC 98-85931. 200p. 1998. reprint ed. pap. 12.00 (*1-892323-10-9*) Vivisphere.

Parnell: A Documentary History. Noel Kissane. (Illus.). 128p. (C). 1994. text 24.95 (*0-907328-19-9*, Pub. by Natl Lib Ireland) Syracuse U Pr.

Parnell Split, 1890-91. Frank Callanan. LC 92-32592. (Irish Studies). (Illus.). 320p. 1993. 42.50 (*0-8156-2597-9*); pap. 19.95 (*0-8156-2598-7*) Syracuse U Pr.

Paro: Dreams of Passion. Namita Gokhale. (C). 1991. text 6.00 (*0-8364-2887-0*, Pub. by Rupa) S Asia.

***Parochial.** Mark Reid. 2000. pap. 16.95 (*1-86368-277-5*, Pub. by Fremantle Arts) Intl Spec Bk.

Parochial & Plain Sermons. John Henry Newman. 1997. 49.95 (*0-89870-638-6*) Ignatius Pr.

Parodia en la Nueva Novela Hispanoamericana (1960-1985) Elzbieta Sklodowska. LC 90-28664. (Purdue University Monographs in Romance Languages: Vol. 34). (SPA.). xx, 220p. 1991. 71.00 (*1-55619-087-5*); pap. 27.95 (*1-55619-088-3*) J Benjamins Pubng Co.

Parodies of the American Masters: Rediscovering the Society of American Fakirs, 1891-1914. Bruce Weber & Ronald G. Pisano. (Illus.). 48p. 1993. pap. 5.00 (*0-943924-18-9*) Mus Stony Brook.

Parodies of the Gothic Novel. Leland C. May. Ed. by Devendra P. Varma. (Gothic Studies & Dissertations). 1980. lib. bdg. 19.95 (*0-405-12654-9*) Ayer.

P

An Asterisk (*) at the beginning of an entry indicates that the title is appearing for the first time.

Parodies of the Romantic Age: The Poetry of the Anti-Jacobin & Other Parodic Writings, 5 vols. Ed. by Graeme Stones & John Strachen. LC 98-8844. 1700p. 1999. 650.00 (*1-85196-475-4*, Pub. by Pickering & Chatto) Ashgate Pub Co.

Parodies of the Works of English & American Authors, 6 vols., Set. Walter Hamilton. (Anglistica & Americana Ser.: No. 169). 1970. reprint ed. 258.70 (*0-685-66474-0*, 05102264) G Olms Pubs.

Parodies on Walt Whitman. Ed. by Henry S. Saunders. LC 70-119648. reprint ed. 32.00 (*0-404-05564-8*) AMS Pr.

Parodies on Walt Whitman. Henry S. Saunders. (BCL1-PS American Literature Ser.). 171p. 1992. reprint ed. lib. bdg. 69.00 (*0-7812-6900-8*) Rprt Serv.

***Parody.** Simon Dentith. LC 99-88778. 200p. 2000. pap. 14.99 (*0-415-18221-2*) Routledge.

***Parody.** Simon Dentith. LC 99-88778. (New Critical Idiom Ser.). 200p. 2000. 50.00 (*0-415-18220-4*) Routledge.

Parody & Decadence: Laforgue's Moralites Legendaires. Michele Hannoosh. LC 89-2996. 285p. reprint ed. pap. 88.40 (*0-608-09681-4*, 206979600006) Bks Demand.

***Parody & the Praise of Folly.** Jon Haarberg. 280p. 1998. pap. 36.00 (*82-00-12981-0*) Scandnvan Univ Pr.

Parody Anthology. Carolyn Wells. 1972. 59.95 (*0-8490-0803-4*) Gordon Pr.

Parody As Film Genre: Never Give a Saga an Even Break, 69. Wes D. Gehring. LC 99-18592. 248p. 1999. 59.95 (*0-313-26186-5*, Greenwood Pr) Greenwood.

Parody in Jewish Literature. Israel Davidson. LC 77-163670. (Columbia University. Oriental Studies: No. 2). reprint ed. 37.50 (*0-404-50492-2*) AMS Pr.

Parody in the Middle Ages: The Latin Tradition. Martha Bayless. LC 96-19030. 440p. (C). 1996. text 54.50 (*0-472-10649-X*, 10649) U of Mich Pr.

Paroi. Pierre Moustiers. (FRE.). 224p. 1969. pap. 15.95 (*0-7859-3961-X*, 2070246590) Fr & Eur.

Parole: Crime Prevention or Crime Postponement? Howard R. Sacks & Charles H. Logan. LC 80-52358. 132p. 1980. pap. 9.00 (*0-939328-04-6*) U CT Law Sch Found.

Parole & Pensee. 5th ed. Lenard. (College French Ser.). (C). 1991. mass mkt., teacher ed. 7.95 (*0-8384-3692-7*) Heinle & Heinle.

Parole & the Community-Based Treatment of Offenders in Japan & the United States. L. Craig Parker, Jr. LC 86-50431. (Illus.). 200p. (Orig.). 1986. pap. text 8.95 (*0-936285-03-6*) U New Haven Pr.

Parole Chez Paul Claudel et les Negro-Africains. Leopold S. Senghor. (FRE.). 1973. pap. 9.95 (*0-7859-5401-5*) Fr & Eur.

Parole Crociate Per Gli Studenti. Nancy P. Goldhagen. (ITA., Illus.). 38p. (J). (gr. 3 up). 1979. pap. 6.60 (*0-8442-8021-6*, Natl Textbk Co) NTC Contemp Pub Co.

Parole de L'Ange: L'Ecriture at le Corps. Dominique De Courcelles. LC 91-19568. (Reading Plus Ser.: Vol. 9). XII, 291p. (C). 1992. text 61.95 (*0-8204-1639-8*) P Lang Pubng.

Parole en Archipel. Rene Char. (FRE.). 160p. 1986. 11.95 (*0-7859-1158-8*, 2070708098) Fr & Eur.

Parole Game: Know Your Rights! Julian Law. 37p. 1998. 12.00 (*0-9639452-1-1*) Lerner Pub.

Parole Nuovo. O. Lurati. 1991. 49.95 (*0-8288-3918-2*, F112072) Fr & Eur.

Parole Officer. Jack Rudman. (Career Examination Ser.: C-574). 1994. pap. 27.95 (*0-8373-0574-8*) Nat Learn.

Parole-Quebec, Countersign-Ticonderoga: Second New Jersey Regimental Orderly Book, 1776. Ed. by Doyen Salsig. LC 77-74398. (Illus.). 312p. 1980. 39.50 (*0-8386-1793-X*) Fairleigh Dickinson.

Parole Rights, Vol. XI. Jack L. Kunsman, Jr. (Encyclopedia of Prisoner's Rights Ser.). 175p. 1983. pap. text 14.50 (*0-914235-11-7*) J L Kunsman.

Paroles. Magnan. (C). 1999. pap. text, wbk. ed., lab manual ed. 41.50 (*0-03-020797-5*) Harcourt.

***Paroles.** Sally S. Magnan. 1998. 82.00 (*0-03-021243-X*) H Holt & Co.

Paroles. Sally S. Magnan et al. (C). 1998. text 44.50 (*0-03-022782-8*) Harcourt Coll Pubs.

Paroles. Jacques Prevert. (FRE.). 251p. 1976. pap. 10.95 (*0-7859-2400-0*, 2070367622) Fr & Eur.

Paroles. Jacques Prevert. (FRE.). (C). 1972. pap. 9.95 (*0-8442-1837-5*, VF1837-5) NTC Contemp Pub Co.

Paroles. Jacques Prevert. (Folio Ser.: No. 762). (FRE.). 1957. pap. 10.50 (*2-07-036762-2*) Schoenhof.

Paroles: Selected Poems. rev. ed. Jacques Prevert. Tr. by Lawrence Ferlinghetti from FRE. (Pocket Poets Ser.: No. 9). (FRE.). 176p. 1990. pap. 8.95 (*0-87286-249-6*) City Lights.

Paroles et Musique see Comedies et Actes Divers

Paroles et Musique. Samuel Beckett. (Coll. Bilingue). (ENG & FRE.). pap. 4.50 (*0-685-37196-4*, F85990) Fr & Eur.

Paroles et Pensees Lyriques. Bernice B. Feinsot. LC 55-9916. (FRE., Illus.). 127p. 1975. pap. 6.95 (*0-915526-01-8*) B B Feinsot.

Paroling Authorities: Recent History & Current Practice. William Robertson Smith et al. 207p. 1991. 23.00 (*0-929310-51-9*, 313H) Am Correctional.

Parousia: A Critical Inquiry into the New Testament Doctrine of Our Lord's Second Coming. James S. Russell. 561p. (Orig.). 1996. reprint ed. pap. 16.95 (*0-9621311-3-X*) Intl Preterist Assn.

Parousia: . . . And Man Made God. M. Jerista Lampman. 1997. pap. 11.95 (*0-9673430-0-3*) Da Hood Pubg Inc.

Parousia: The New Testament Doctrine of Our Lord?s Second Coming. J. Stuart Russell. 608p. (Orig.). (C). (gr. 8 up). 1999. reprint ed. pap. 24.99 (*0-8010-7725-7*) Baker Bks.

Paroxisms: A Guide to the Isms. Edwin Brock. LC 74-8647. (Illus.). 96p. 1974. 5.95 (*0-8112-0549-5*, Pub. by New Directions) Norton.

Paroxysm. Jean Baudrillard. Tr. by Chris Turner. LC 98-39610. 120p. 1998. 60.00 (*1-85984-844-3*, Pub. by Verso); pap. 18.00 (*1-85984-241-0*, Pub. by Verso) Norton.

Parque Jurasico, 1. Michael Crichton. 1998. pap. text 6.95 (*84-01-49236-X*) Lectorum Pubns.

Parque Nacional del Este, D. R. Tomo 1: Recursos Terrestres. Ed. by Domingo Abreu & Kelvin Guerrero. (SPA., Illus.). 134p. (Orig.). 1997. pap. 25.00 (*0-9643786-4-7*) Media Pubng.

Parque Nacional del Este, D. R. Tomo 2: Recursos Marinos. Monica Vega et al. Tr. by Paula Vega & Georgina Bustamante. (SPA., Illus.). 93p. (Orig.). 1997. pap. 25.00 (*0-9643786-7-1*) Media Pubng.

Parque Nacional el Cusuco y Cordillera del Merendon, Honduras. Fundacion Ecologista Staff et al. Ed. by Douglas S. Baker. (America Verde Publications). (SPA., Illus.). 85p. (Orig.). (C). 1996. pap. 10.00 (*1-886765-04-9*) Nature VA.

Parque Nacional San Pedro Martir (San Pedro Martir National Park) Jerry Schad. 1988. 4.95 (*0-9617288-2-5*) Centra Pubns.

Parque Nacional Yellowstone. Jenny Markert. (Libro Vision Ser.). (SPA., Illus.). 32p. (J). (gr. 2-6). 1993. lib. bdg. 22.79 (*1-56766-031-2*) Childs World.

Parr: Common Sense. Martin Parr. (Illus.). 160p. 1999. 50.00 (*1-899235-07-8*, Pub. by Dewi Lewis) Dist Art Pubs.

Parr Family. Lucille Parr. 176p. 1974. 10.00 (*0-87012-190-1*) McClain.
Over 150 pages of the genealogy of the Parr family with allied branches. Indexed. ***Publisher Paid Annotation.***

Parallel & Distributed Computing & Systems (PDCS-93), 6th International Conference, October 14-16, 1993, Louisville, Kentucky, U.S.A: PDCS-93, Oct. 14-16, 1993, Louisville, KY. Ed. by A. Kumar & K. Kamel. (Conference Proceedings Ser.). 466p. 1993. write for info. (*1-880843-06-4*) Int Soc Comp App.

Parramatta Institution & the Black Town: A History. Jack Brook & James Kohen. 295p. 1991. 42.95 (*0-86840-300-8*, Pub. by New South Wales Univ Pr) Intl Spec Bk.

Parris Island Guidebook. Melinda A. Grismer. LC 95-80709. (Illus.). 88p. (Orig.). 1995. pap. 6.95 (*0-9649192-0-6*) Bulldog Press.

Parris Mitchell of Kings Row. Henry Bellamann & Katherine Bellamann. Ed. & Intro. by Jay M. Karr. (Illus.). 1986. reprint ed. pap. 9.45 (*0-9609926-4-2*) Kingdom Hse.

Parrish & Poetry: A Gift of Words & Art. Laurence S. Cutler & Judy G. Cutler. LC 95-30368. (Illus.). 96p. 1995. 19.95 (*0-87654-486-3*) Pomegranate Calif.

Parrish Art Museum: A History of Its Collections & Building. (Illus.). 10p. (Orig.). 1988. pap. 3.00 (*0-943526-36-1*) Parrish Art.

Parrish. The Parrish Family, Including the Allied Families of Belt, Boyd, Cole-Malone, Clokey, Garrett, Merryman, Parsons, Price & Tipton. Boyd & Gottschalk. 413p. 1991. reprint ed. pap. 63.00 (*0-8328-1980-8*); reprint ed. lib. bdg. 73.00 (*0-8328-1979-4*) Higginson Bk Co.

Parrol. Mark Dunster. 29p. (Orig.). 1989. pap. 4.00 (*0-89642-174-0*) Linden Pubs.

***Parrot.** Pam Adams. 1999. pap. text 1.99 (*0-85953-861-3*) Childs Play.

Parrot: An Italian Folktale. Illus. by Laszlo Gal & Raffaella Gal. LC 98-136903. 32p. (J). (gr. 1-3). 1997. 16.95 (*0-88899-287-4*) Publishers Group.

Parrot: An Owner's Guide to a Happy, Healthy Pet. Arthur Freud. 1996. pap. 12.95 (*0-87605-497-1*) Howell Bks.

Parrot & the Fig Tree. Illus. by Michael Harmon. LC 86-24159. (Jataka Tales Ser.). 32p. (Orig.). (J). (gr. k-4). 1987. lib. bdg. 16.95 (*0-89800-156-0*) Dharma Pub.

Parrot & the Fig Tree. Illus. by Michael Harmon. LC 86-24159. (Jataka Tales Ser.). 32p. (Orig.). (J). (ps-3). 1987. pap. 7.95 (*0-89800-142-0*) Dharma Pub.

Parrot Cage. large type ed. Daphne Wright. (Charnwood Library). 1991. 27.99 (*0-7089-8580-7*, Charnwood) Ulverscroft.

Parrot Family: Their Training, Care, & Breeding see Parrots

***Parrot Fever.** Jan Kerouac. LC 99-23973. 160p. 2000. 18.95 (*1-56025-208-1*, Thunders Mouth) Avalon NY.

Parrot Head Companion: An Insider's Guide to Jimmy Buffett. Thomas Ryan. LC 98-27639. (Illus.). 176p. 1998. pap. 10.95 (*0-8065-2015-9*) Carol Pub Group.

Parrot in Aviculture. Rosemary Low. (Illus.). 1992. 39.95 (*1-56465-179-7*, 16116) Tetra Pr.

Parrot in Health & Illness: An Owner's Guide. Bonnie M. Doane. (Illus.). 320p. 1991. 24.95 (*0-87605-826-8*) Howell Bks.

Parrot in the Oven: Mi Vida: A Novel. Victor Martinez. LC 96-2119. (Joanna Cotler Bks.). 224p. (J). (gr. 7 up). 1996. 15.95 (*0-06-026704-6*) HarpC Child Bks.

Parrot in the Oven: Mi Vida: A Novel. Victor Martinez. LC 96-2119. (Joanna Cotler Bks.). 224p. (YA). (gr. 12 up). 1996. lib. bdg. 15.89 (*0-06-026706-2*) HarpC Child Bks.

Parrot in the Oven: Mi Vida: A Novel. Victor Martinez. LC 96-2119. 224p. (YA). (gr. 12 up). 1998. pap. 5.95 (*0-06-447186-1*) HarpC Child Bks.

***Parrot in the Oven: Mi Vida: A Novel.** Victor Martinez. 1998. 10.05 (*0-606-13695-9*, Pub. by Turtleback) Demco.

Parrot People. Rae Wilder. 200p. write for info. (*0-318-69933-8*) Longitude & Lat.

***Parrot Pie for Breakfast: An Anthology of Women Pioneers.** Ed. by Jane Robinson. LC 99-25636. 177p. 2000. pap. 16.95 (*0-19-288020-9*) OUP.

***Parrot-Toys & Play Areas: How to Put Some Fun into Your Parrot's Life.** Carol S. D'Arezzo & Lauren Shannon-Nunn. (Illus.). viii, 136p. 2000. pap. 16.95 (*0-9678820-0-1*) CrowFire Pubng.

Parrot Training Handbook. Jennifer L. Warshaw. (Illus.). 100p. (Orig.). (C). 1990. pap. 14.95 (*0-9626724-0-8*) Parrot Pr.

***Parrot Tulip: Botanicals Lined.** 160p. 1998. text 11.95 (*1-55156-005-4*, Pub. by Paperblank) Andrews & McMeel.

Parrot Without a Name: The Search for the Last Unknown Birds on Earth. Don Stap. LC 91-24498. (Illus.). 254p. 1991. reprint ed. pap. 15.95 (*0-292-76529-0*) U of Tex Pr.

Parrotfish. Lola M. Schaefer. LC 98-31468. (Ocean Life Ser.). 1999. write for info. (*0-7368-0247-9*, Pebble Bks) Capstone Pr.

Parrotfish. Lola M. Schaefer. 1999. 13.25 (*0-516-21835-2*) Capstone Pr.

***Parrotlet: An Owner's Guide to a Happy Healthy Pet.** Sandee Molenda. (Illus.). 2000. 12.99 (*0-7645-6171-5*) IDG Bks.

Parrotlets. Emmett Cestero. (Illus.). 1999. pap. 12.50 (*1-888417-75-7*) Dimefast.

***Parrotlets: A Complete Pet Owner's Manual.** Matthew Vriends. LC 99-30560. 104p. 1999. pap. text 9.95 (*0-7641-0962-6*) Barron.

Parrots see Zoobooks

Parrots see Endangered! - Group 2

Parrots. David Adlerton. (Illus.). 198p. 1992. 31.95 (*1-56465-100-2*, 16070) Tetra Pr.

Parrots. David Alderton. (Illus.). 128p. text 24.95 (*0-905483-91-X*, Pub. by Whittet Bks) Diamond Farm Bk.

***Parrots.** Linda Jacobs Altman. Ed. by Peter Mavrikis. LC 99-49672. (Perfect Pets Ser.). (Illus.). 32p. (J). (gr. 1-4). 2001. lib. bdg. 22.79 (*0-7614-1102-X*, Benchmark NY) Marshall Cavendish.

Parrots. Andrews & McMeel Staff. LC 97-71539. (Little Bks.). (Illus.). 80p. (J). 1997. 4.95 (*0-8362-3608-4*) Andrews & McMeel.

Parrots. Julien L. Bronson. Orig. Title: Parrot Family: Their Training, Care, & Breeding. (Illus.). 80p. 1985. pap. text 6.95 (*0-86622-874-8*, PB-120) TFH Pubns.

Parrots. Carlienne Frisch. (Responsible Pet Care Ser.: Set II). 32p. (J). (gr. 2-5). 1989. lib. bdg. 21.27 (*0-86625-190-1*) Rourke Pubns.

Parrots. Kurt Kolar. (Mini Fact Finders Ser.). 64p. 1990. pap. 4.95 (*0-8120-4448-7*) Barron.

Parrots. Peter Murray. LC 92-44265. (Nature Books Ser.). (Illus.). 32p. (J). (gr. 2-6). 1994. lib. bdg. 22.79 (*1-56766-015-0*) Childs World.

Parrots. Mark J. Rauzon. LC 96-33773. (First Books-Animals). 64p. (J). (gr. 4-6). 1996. lib. bdg. 22.00 (*0-531-20244-5*) Watts.

Parrots. Mark J. Rauzon. (First Bks.). 64p. 1997. pap. 6.95 (*0-531-15815-2*) Watts.

Parrots. Howard S. Russell. 64p. Date not set. 12.95 (*0-7938-0329-2*) TFH Pubns.

Parrots. Ben Sonder. (Illus.). 72p. 10.98 (*1-57717-067-9*) Todtri Prods.

Parrots. Lynn M. Stone. LC 93-7461. (J). 1993. 9.50 (*0-685-66584-4*) Rourke Corp.

Parrots. Lynn M. Stone. LC 93-7461. (Unusual Animals Discovery Library). 24p. (J). (gr. k-4). 1993. lib. bdg. 10.95 (*0-86593-280-8*) Rourke Corp.

Parrots. Matthew M. Vriends & Herbert R. Axelrod. (Illus.). 96p. 1979. 9.95 (*0-86622-729-6*, KW-032) TFH Pubns.

Parrots. Wildlife Education, Ltd. Staff. (Zoobooks Ser.). (Illus.). 20p. (YA). (gr. 5 up). 1995. pap. text 2.75 (*0-937934-27-5*) Wildlife Educ.

Parrots. Wildlife Education, Ltd. Staff & John B. Wexo. (Zoobooks Ser.). (Illus.). 24p. (J). 1993. 13.95 (*0-937934-84-4*) Wildlife Educ.

Parrots: A Complete Pet Owner's Manual. Annette Wolter. 1992. pap. 6.95 (*0-8120-4823-7*) Barron.

Parrots: A Guide to the Parrots of the World. Tony Juniper & Michael Parr. LC 97-80504. (Illus.). 624p. 1998. 55.00 (*0-300-07453-0*) Yale U Pr.

Parrots: A Natural History. John Sparks & Tony Soper. (Illus.). 224p. 1990. 24.95 (*0-8160-2427-8*) Facts on File.

Parrots: A Selection. (Exotic Miniatures Ser.). (Illus.). 114p. 1994. 12.50 (*981-00-4394-5*) Heian Intl.

Parrots & Macaws. David Alderton. (Birdkeeper's Guide Ser.). (Illus.). 96p. 11.95 (*3-923880-74-X*, 16086) Tetra Pr.

Parrots & Parakeets As Pets. Elaine Landau. LC 97-21768. (True Books--Animals Ser.). 1997. 21.00 (*0-516-20385-1*) Childrens.

Parrots & Parakeets as Pets. Elaine Landau. (True Bks.). (J). 1998. pap. text 6.95 (*0-516-26272-6*) Childrens.

Parrots & Related Birds. Henry J. Bates & Robert I. Busenbark. (Illus.). 494p. 1978. 29.95 (*0-87666-967-4*, H-912) TFH Pubns.

Parrots As a Hobby. Dennis Parker. (Illus.). 96p. 1994. pap. 8.95 (*0-7938-0094-3*, TT037) TFH Pubns.

Parrots As a New Pet. William Wentworth. (Illus.). 64p. 1992. pap. 6.95 (*0-86622-434-3*, TU-027) TFH Pubns.

***Parrot's Beak: U. S. Operations in Cambodia.** Paul B. Morgan. 150p. 2000. pap. 14.95 (*1-55571-543-5*, Pub. by PSI Resch) Midpt Trade.

Parrot's Lament: And Other True Tales of Animal Intrigue, Intelligence, & Ingenuity. Eugene Linden. LC 99-23424. 256p. 1999. 23.95 (*0-525-94476-1*, Dutton Child) Peng Put Young Read.

***Parrot's Lament: And Other True Tales of Animal Intrigue, Intelligence & Ingenuity.** Eugene Linden. 2000. pap. 12.95 (*0-452-28068-0*, Plume) Dutton Plume.

***Parrot's Lament: And Other True Tales of Animal Intrigue, Intelligence, & Ingenuity.** large type ed. Eugene Linden. LC 00-26274. (Core Ser.). 255p. 2000. 27.95 (*0-7838-9031-1*, G K Hall Lrg Type) Mac Lib Ref.

Parrots, Macaws & Cockatoos. Elizabeth Butterworth. (Illus.). 64p. 1994. pap. 19.95 (*0-8109-2585-0*, Pub. by Abrams) Time Warner.

Parrots, Macaws & Cockatoos. Vicki Leon. LC 94-30908. (Close up: A Focus on Nature Ser.). (Illus.). 40p. (YA). (gr. 5 up). 1994. pap. 7.95 (*0-382-24899-6*); lib. bdg. 14.95 (*0-382-24898-8*) Silver Burdett Pr.

Parrots of the World. Joseph M. Forshaw. (Illus.). 584p. 1977. reprint ed. 47.95 (*0-87666-959-3*, PS-753) TFH Pubns.

Parrot's Perch. Michel Rio. Tr. by Leigh Hafrey from FRE. LC 85-744. 96p. 1985. 10.95 (*0-15-170964-5*) Harcourt.

Parry: Legal Aid in Criminal Proceedings. James N. Parry. 1996. pap. write for info. (*0-406-04605-0*, CPPG, MICHIE) LEXIS Pub.

Parry Before Jerusalem: Studies of His Life & Music with Excerpts from His Published Writings. Bernard Benoliel & C. Hubert Parry. LC 96-32134. (Illus.). 275p. 1997. text 87.95 (*0-85967-927-6*, Pub. by Scolar Pr) Ashgate Pub Co.

Parry of the Arctic. Pierre Berton. (Exploring the Frozen North Ser.). (Illus.). 88p. (J). (gr. 6-9). pap. 4.99 (*0-7710-1434-1*) McCland & Stewart.

Pars Quarta Vol. I: Tabulae: Tabulae in Epistulas et Orationes. Dietmar Najock. (Alpha-Omega, Reihe A Ser.: Bd. L, 4.1). (GER.). xlv, 894p. 1996. write for info. (*3-487-10131-9*) G Olms Pubs.

Parscale: IRT Based Test Scoring & Item Analysis for Graded Open-Ended Exercises & Performance Tasks. Eiji Muraki & R. Darrell Bock. 1993. ring bd. 30.00 (*0-89498-032-7*) Sci Ware.

Parsec-Scale Radio Jets. Ed. by J. Anton Zensus & Timothy J. Pearson. 414p. (C). 1990. text 74.95 (*0-521-39226-8*) Cambridge U Pr.

Parsha Parables: Weekly Fax & Online Torah Insights. Mordechai Kamenetsky. 1997. 16.95 (*0-9657697-0-4*, Pub. by Bentsh Pr) Feldheim.

Parshall Family, a.d. 870-1913: A Collection of Historical Records & Notes to Accompany of the Parshall Pedigree. Horace F. Parshall. (Illus.). 186p. 1996. reprint ed. pap. 29.00 (*0-8328-5418-2*); reprint ed. lib. bdg. 39.00 (*0-8328-5417-4*) Higginson Bk Co.

Parshas Beshalach. David Bernstein. (Chumash Study Aid Ser.). (ENG & HEB., Illus.). 192p. (J). (gr. 5-8). 1991. pap. text 8.00 (*0-914131-96-6*, A148) Torah Umesorah.

Parshas Lech. Sinai Malovitzki. (Bible in Yiddish Ser.). (YID., Illus.). 160p. (YA). 1987. teacher ed. 15.00 (*0-944704-03-4*) Sinai Heritage.

Parshas Mishpatim. David Bernstein. (Chumash StudyAid Ser.). (Illus.). 177p. 1997. pap., wbk. ed. 8.00 (*0-914131-89-3*, A150) Torah Umesorah.

Parshas Nitzuvim. Sinai Malovitzki. (Bible in Yiddish Ser.). (YID., Illus.). 150p. (J). 1988. pap. 7.00 (*0-944704-61-1*) Sinai Heritage.

Parshas Yisroy. Sinai Malovitzki. (Bible in Yiddish Ser.). (YID., Illus.). 400p. (J). 1988. lib. bdg. 35.00 (*0-944704-19-0*) Sinai Heritage.

Parshaw Va'Yeilech. Sinai Malovitzki. (Bible in Yiddish Ser.). (YID., Illus.). 95p. (YA). 1988. pap. 5.00 (*0-944704-62-X*) Sinai Heritage.

Parsi Law in India. Mahammod Shabbir & S. C. Manchanda. (C). 1990. 80.00 (*0-89771-145-9*) St Mut.

Parsi Mind: A Zoroastrian Asset to Culture. Jer D. Randeria. 175p. (C). 1993. 33.50 (*81-215-0560-7*, Pub. by M Manoharial) Coronet Bks.

***Parsifal.** Peter Bassett. 2000. pap. 14.95 (*1-86254-512-X*, Pub. by Wakefield Pr) BHB Intl.

***Parsifal.** Marianna Mayer. (J). 2001. 15.99 (*0-8037-2012-2*, Dial Yng Read) Peng Put Young Read.

Parsifal. Peter Vansittart. 256p. 1988. 29.95 (*0-7206-0711-6*, Pub. by P Owen Ltd) Dufour.

Parsifal. Composed by Richard Wagner. pap. 7.95 (*963-8303-06-9*) Konemann.

Parsifal. Richard Wagner. Ed. by Nicholas John. Tr. by Andrew Porter from GER. LC 85-52160. (English National Opera Guide Series: Bilingual Libretto, Articles: No. 34). (Illus.). 128p. (C). 1986. pap. 9.95 (*0-7145-4079-X*) Riverrun NY.

Parsifal: A Study of Wagner's Music Drama. W. L. Wilmshurst. 1990. reprint ed. pap. 6.95 (*1-55818-168-7*, Sure Fire) Holmes Pub.

Parsifal: Libretto. Richard Wagner. (GER.). 52p. 1986. pap. 4.95 (*0-7935-5371-7*, 50340400) H Leonard.

Parsifal: The Finding of Christ Through Art. 2nd ed. Albert R. Parsons. 113p. 1996. reprint ed. spiral bd. 11.00 (*0-7873-0659-2*) Hlth Research.

Parsifal: The Finding of Christ Through Art or Richard Wagner As Theologian. Albert R. Parsons. 113p. 1993. reprint ed. pap. 9.95 (*1-56459-368-1*) Kessinger Pub.

Parsifal & the Finding of Christ Through Art: Richard Wagner As Theologian. Albert R. Parsons. 1991. lib. bdg. 79.95 (*0-8490-4934-2*) Gordon Pr.

Parsifal in Full Score. Richard Wagner. 592p. pap. 24.95 (*0-486-25175-6*) Dover.

Parsifal Mosaic. Robert Ludlum. 704p. 1983. mass mkt. 7.99 (*0-553-25270-4*) Bantam.

Parsifal on Record: A Discography of Complete Recordings, Selections, & Excerpts of Wagner's Music Drama, 48. Compiled by Jonathan Brown. LC 92-12292. (Discographies Ser.: No. 48). 168p. 1992. lib. bdg. 52.95 (*0-313-28541-1*, BPR/, Greenwood Pr) Greenwood.

***Parsifal Piano.** Composed by Richard Wagner. 1998. pap. 7.95 (*963-8303-11-5*) Konemann.

An Asterisk (*) at the beginning of an entry indicates that the title is appearing for the first time.

Parsimonious Universe: Shape & Form in the Natural World. Anthony J. Tromba & Stefan Hildebrandt. LC 95-19692. (Illus.). 477p. 1996. 27.50 (*0-387-97991-3*) Spr-Verlag.

Parsing Below the Segment in a Constraint-Based Framework. Cheryl C. Zoll. LC 98-12873. (Dissertations in Linguistics Ser.: Vol. 13). 256p. (C). 1998. pap. 22.95 (*1-57586-130-5*); text 59.95 (*1-57586-131-3*) CSLI.

Parsing Guide to the Greek New Testament. Nathan E. Han. LC 77-158175. 496p. 1994. pap. 19.99 (*0-8361-3693-4*) Herald Pr.

Parsing Natural Language. Ed. by M. King. 1983. text 76.00 (*0-12-408280-7*) Acad Pr.

Parsing Schemata: A Framework for Specification & Analysis of Parsing Algorithms. Klaas Sikkel. LC 96-45082. (Texts in Theoretical Computer Science Ser.). 398p. 1996. 54.95 (*3-540-61650-0*) Spr-Verlag.

Parsing Theory. S. Sippu & E. Soisalon-Soinnen. (EATCS Monographs on Theoretical Computer Science: Vol. 15). (Illus.). 290p. 1988. 71.95 (*0-387-13720-3*) Spr-Verlag.

Parsing Theory. S. Sippu & E. Soisalon-Soinnen. (EATCS Monographs on Theoretical Computer Science: Vol. 20). 444p. 1990. 105.00 (*0-387-51732-9*) Spr-Verlag.

Parsing Through Customs: Essays by a Freudian Folklorist. Alan Dundes. LC 87-1675. 208p. (C). 1987. text 22.95 (*0-299-11260-8*) U of Wis Pr.

Parsing with Principles & Classes of Information. Paola Merlo & Slap. LC 96-206051. (Studies in Linguistics & Philosophy). 246p. (C). 1996. text 93.50 (*0-7923-4103-1*) Kluwer Academic.

Parsippany Troy Hills. Parsippany Historical Society Staff. (Images of America Ser.). 1997. pap. 16.99 (*0-7524-0479-2*) Arcadia Publng.

Parsis in Western India, 1818 to 1920. Nawaz B. Mody. LC 99-934072. xxxii, 288p. 1998. 0.00 (*81-7023-894-3*) Allied Pubs.

Parsley. Ludwig Bemelmans. LC 55-7682. (Illus.). 48p. (J). (ps-3). 1955. 14.95 (*0-06-020455-9*) HarpC Child Bks.

Parsley & Paisley: Vegetarian Cooking 101. Mamie Rader. Ed. by Lucy Morales. (Illus.). 407p. (Orig.). 1996. pap. write for info. (*0-9652221-0-1*) Veggies Plus.

***Parsley Dumpling & the Peppermint Caribou.** Sean M. Dever. (J). 1999. pap. 4.99 (*0-9658180-6-3*) Fox Bks.

Parsley Garden see Creative Short Stories

Parsley Park. Mieke Tazelaar. (Illus.). 64p. (Orig.). 1983. pap. 7.95 (*0-9613792-0-0*) Tazelaar.

Parsley, Sage, Rosemary & Crime. Tamar Myers. 1996. mass mkt. 5.99 (*0-451-18297-9*, Sig) NAL.

Parsley, Sage, Rosemary & Mine: An Herbal Faire. Susan A. McCreary. LC 91-37719. (Illus.). 160p. (Orig.). 1991. pap. 14.95 (*0-9608428-5-3*) Straw Patchwork.

Parsnip. Sue Porter. LC 98-100920. (Illus.). 24p. (J). (ps-k). 1998. 11.95 (*0-7894-2470-3*) DK Pub Inc.

Parsnip & the Runaway Tractor. Sue Porter. LC 98-13778. 20p. (J). 1999. 11.95 (*0-7894-2494-0*) DK Pub Inc.

Parsnips: Poems from Hollywood. Mark Dunster. 11p. 1998. pap. 5.00 (*0-89642-524-X*) Linden Pubs.

Parsnips in the Snow: Talks with Midwestern Gardeners. Jane A. Staw & Mary Swander. LC 89-20439. (Bur Oak Original Ser.). (Illus.). 223p. 1990. pap. 15.95 (*0-87745-279-2*) U of Iowa Pr.

Parson. Anna Kavan. 111p. 1996. pap. 24.00 (*0-7206-0962-3*, Pub. by P Owen Ltd) Dufour.

***Parson & His Cemetery.** Mary Lee Tiernan. (Early History of Sunland, California Ser.: Vol. 3). (Illus.). 20p. 1999. write for info. (*0-9702393-2-7*) Snoops Desktop.

Parson Harding's Daughter. Caroline Harvey. 320p. 1995. mass mkt. 7.99 (*0-552-14299-9*) Bantam.

Parson Henry Renfro: Free Thinking on the Texas Frontier. William C. Griggs. LC 93-7349. (Illus.). 279p. (C). 1994. 27.95 (*0-292-72762-3*) U of Tex Pr.

Parson of Gunbarrel Basin. large type ed. Nelson Nye. LC 93-43546. (General Ser.). 281p. 1994. lib. bdg. 17.95 (*0-8161-5923-8*, G K Hall Lrg Type) Mac Lib Ref.

Parson on the Hill. Roy Aspin. 136p. (C). 1990. pap. text 45.00 (*0-948706-05-8*, Pub. by Brent Pubns) St Mut.

Parson Packs a Peacemaker. Dean Buckland. (Illus.). 64p. 1997. pap. 7.95 (*0-9658776-0-4*) Cntrl Coast Pr.

Parson, Priest & Master: National Education in Co. Meath, 1824-41. Paul Connell. 64p. 1995. pap. 9.95 (*0-7165-2570-4*, Pub. by Irish Acad Pr) Intl Spec Bk.

Parson Takes a Wife. Maria Sheerin. (American Autobiography Ser.). 204p. 1995. reprint ed. lib. bdg. 79.00 (*0-7812-8638-7*) Rprt Serv.

Parson Weem's Life of Francis Marion. Peter Horry. LC 76-21439. 1976. 15.00 (*0-937684-04-X*) Tradd St Pr.

Parsons: The House of Cornet Joseph Parsons, Together with the Houses of a Line of His Descendants & Their Allied Families, 1655-1941. (Illus.). 49p. 1995. reprint ed. pap. 10.00 (*0-8328-4814-X*); reprint ed. lib. bdg. 20.00 (*0-8328-4813-1*) Higginson Bk Co.

Parson's Daughter. Catherine Cookson. 464p. 1988. mass mkt. 7.99 (*0-552-13088-5*) Bantam.

Parson's Daughter. large type ed. Sheila Bishop. 1991. 27.99 (*0-7089-2383-6*) Ulverscroft.

Parson's Diseases of the Eye. 18th ed. Stephen J. Miller. (Illus.). 442p. 1990. text 59.95 (*0-443-04230-6*) Church.

Parson's House. large type ed. Elizabeth Cadell. LC 98-34389. 280 p. 1999. write for info. (*0-7540-3478-X*) Chivers N Amer.

Parson's House. large type ed. Elizabeth Cadell. LC 98-34389. 1999. pap. text 22.95 (*0-7862-1608-5*) Thorndike Pr.

Parson's Lake. Bruce H. Gadbois. LC 99-61466. 256p. 1999. pap. 11.95 (*1-893162-02-8*) Erica Hse.

Parson's Waiting. Sherryl Woods. (Special Edition Ser.). 1994. per. 3.50 (*0-373-09907-X*, 1-09907-6) Harlequin Bks.

Parson's Waiting. Sherryl Woods. 1997. per. 4.50 (*0-373-87001-9*, 1-87001-3) Harlequin Bks.

Parson's Waiting. large type ed. Sherryl Woods. (Silhouette Romance Ser.). 382p. 1995. 19.95 (*0-373-59630-8*) Mac Lib Ref.

Part: Poems. Wendell Berry. LC 80-18268. 104p. 1985. pap. 6.95 (*0-86547-008-1*) N Point Pr.

Part A: Analytical & Continuum Mechanics see Mathematical Principles in Mechanics & Electromagnetism

Part & Present of Sioux City & Woodbury Co., Iowa. Ed. by Constant R. Marks. (Illus.). 826p. 1996. reprint ed. lib. bdg. 85.00 (*0-8328-5194-9*) Higginson Bk Co.

Part B Billing Guide. James R. Lyle & Hoyt W. Torras. 1995. pap. 99.00 (*1-879249-16-2*) HlthCare Consult.

Part B: Electromagnetism & Gravitation see Mathematical Principles in Mechanics & Electromagnetism

Part Buy-Sell. Pollack. LC 95-78497. 1995. 125.00 (*0-316-71298-1*) Little.

Part Comanche. Troxey Kemper. Ed. by William Whallon. LC 91-70154. (Illus.). v, 67p. 1991. 4.00 (*0-9624631-4-0*) Bennett & Kitchel.

Part de Feu see Work of Fire

Part I: Text & Translation see Divine Comedy: Inferno

Part I: Text & Translation see Divine Comedy, II: Purgatorio

Part I: Text & Translation see Divine Comedy, III: Paradiso

Part II: Commentary see Divine Comedy: Inferno

Part II: Commentary see Divine Comedy, II: Purgatorio

Part II: Commentary see Divine Comedy, III: Paradiso

Part Load Efficiency of Gas & Oil-Fired Boilers. Ed. by M. J. Holmes. 1976. 70.00 (*0-86022-023-0*, Pub. by Build Servs Info Assn) St Mut.

Part Management. Roger Blanpain. 1993. pap. text 66.50 (*90-6544-769-5*) Kluwer Academic.

***Part Of.** Hiram Larew. (Illus.). 32p. 1999. pap. 5.00 (*1-879457-62-8*) Norton Coker Pr.

Part of a Whole. J. Brown. 90p. 1999. pap. 11.95 (*0-7392-0198-0*, P3194) Morris Pubng.

Part of Cape Cod Is Missing!, No. 17. Noel W. Beyle. (Illus.). 48p. (Orig.). 1983. pap. 0.95 (*0-912609-00-1*) First Encounter.

Part of Dispatch from George Simpson, Esquire, Governor of Ruperts Land, to the Governor & Committee of the Hudson's Bay Company, London, March 1, 1829: Continued & Completed March 24 & June 5, 1829. Ed. by E. E. Rich. (Hudson's Bay Record Society Publications: Vol. 10). 1974. reprint ed. pap. 65.00 (*0-8115-3184-8*) Periodicals Srv.

Part of Fortune in Astrology. (Illus.). 32p. 1998. pap. 7.95 (*1-883376-03-3*) Stellium Pr.

Part of His Story. Alfred Dewitt Corn. LC 96-50021. 264p. 1997. 24.00 (*0-922811-29-6*) Mid-List.

***Part of Me.** Mariann Lastoka. (Illus.). 47p. 1998. pap. 15.00 (*1-892860-00-7*, 001) MRL Inc.

Part of My Heart Left Here: Renewal Messages of Donald A. Green. Ed. by Mary Green. LC 85-72072. 1986. pap. 12.50 (*0-913342-53-X*) Barclay Pr.

Part of My Life. Jules A. Ayer. (Illus.). 1978. pap. 7.95 (*0-19-281245-9*) OUP.

Part of My Life: Photographs. Marianne Muller. (Illus.). 128p. 1998. 39.95 (*3-931141-29-2*, 810201, Pub. by Scalo Pubs) Dist Art Pubs.

Part of My Soul Went with Him. Winnie Mandela. Ed. by Anne Benjamin & Mary Benson. LC 85-21632. (Illus.). 164p. 1985. pap. 6.95 (*0-393-30290-3*) Norton.

Part of Myself: I Give to You. 2nd rev. ed. Doris B. Demou. Ed. by Mary Meredith. (More to Give Ser.). (Illus.). (YA). (gr. 6 up). 1990. pap. text 6.00 (*0-9604794-0-6*) Doris Demou.

Part of Myself: Portrait of an Epoch. Carl Zuckmayer. (Illus.). 435p. 1984. pap. 9.95 (*0-88184-083-1*) Carroll & Graf.

Part of Nature: Self-Knowledge in Spinoza's Ethics. Genevieve Lloyd. LC 94-3195. 192p. 1994. text 32.50 (*0-8014-2999-4*) Cornell U Pr.

Part of Nature, Part of Us: Modern American Poets. Helen H. Vendler. LC 79-20308. 387p. 1980. 36.50 (*0-674-65475-7*) HUP.

Part of Nature, Part of Us: Modern American Poets. Helen H. Vendler. LC 79-20308. 387p. 1980. pap. text 17.50 (*0-674-65476-5*) HUP.

Part of Our Time: Some Ruins & Monuments of Thirties. Murray Kempton. LC 98-21215. 1998. 18.95 (*0-679-60310-7*) Modern Lib NY.

Part of Ourselves: Lament for Lives That Ended Too Soon. Ed. by Siobhan Parkinson. LC 98-120095. 188p. 1998. pap. 15.95 (*1-899047-34-4*, Pub. by A A Farmar) Irish Bks Media.

Part of Speech. Joseph Brodsky. Tr. by Anthony Hecht et al from RUS. LC 80-613. 160p. 1980. 15.95 (*0-374-22987-2*) FS&G.

Part of Speech. Joseph Brodsky. Tr. by Anthony Hecht et al from RUS. LC 80-613. 160p. 1981. pap. 11.00 (*0-374-51633-2*) FS&G.

Part of the Bargain. Linda Lael Miller. (Men Made in America Ser.). 1994. per. 3.59 (*0-373-45176-8*, 1-45176-4) Harlequin Bks.

***Part of the Bargain.** Linda Lael Miller. 1999. per. 5.99 (*1-55166-512-3*, 1-66512-4, Mira Bks) Harlequin Bks.

***Part of the Bargain.** Linda Lael Miller. LC 00-30292. 2001. write for info. (*0-7862-2621-8*) Thorndike Pr.

Part of the Climate: American Cubist Poetry. Jacqueline V. Brogan. LC 90-34743. 290p. 1990. 60.00 (*0-520-06848-3*, Pub. by U CA Pr) Cal Prin Full Svc.

***Part of the Community: Strategies for Including Everyone.** Jan Nisbet & David Hagner. LC 00-21848. 2000. write for info. (*1-55766-456-0*) P H Brookes.

Part of the Deeper Sea. Lois M. Harrod. (Illus.). viii, 88p. 1997. 18.00 (*1-889806-18-8*, Palanquin); pap. 12.00 (*1-889806-15-3*, Palanquin) Devils Millhopper.

Part of the Furniture. Mary Wesley. LC 96-46226. 256p. 1998. pap. 12.95 (*0-14-026628-3*) Viking Penguin.

Part of the Furniture. large type ed. Mary Wesley. LC 97-13677. (Core Ser.). 351p. 1997. lib. bdg. 25.95 (*0-7838-8223-8*, G K Hall Lrg Type) Mac Lib Ref.

Part of the Main: Short Stories of the Maine Coast. Edward M. Holmes. LC 73-620088. 1976. pap. 9.95 (*0-89101-031-9*) U Maine Pr.

Part of the Only Of. Sam Cannarozzi. Ed. by Edward Mycue. (Took Modern Poetry in English Ser.: No. 24). (FRE., Illus.). 28p. (Orig.). 1992. pap. 4.00 (*1-879457-25-3*) Norton Coker Pr.

Part of the Ribbon: A Time Travel Adventure Through the History of Korea. Ruth S. Hunter & Debra M. Fritsch. LC 96-61175. (Illus.). 216p. (Orig.). (J). (gr. 4-6). 1997. pap. 5.95 (*1-880336-11-1*) Turtle CT.

Part of the Sky. Robert Newton Peck. (YA). 1997. pap. 4.99 (*0-679-88696-6*, Pub. by Random Bks Yng Read) Random.

Part of the Sky. Robert Newton Peck. (J). 1997. 10.09 (*0-606-12149-8*, Pub. by Turtleback) Demco.

Part of the Sky. unabridged ed. Robert N. Peck. (YA). (gr. 7-12). 1994. 21.95 incl. audio (*1-883332-10-9*) Audio Bkshelf.

Part of the Solution: Innovative Approaches to Nonprofit Funding. Center for Public Policy Staff. 140p. (Orig.). 1988. pap. 15.00 (*1-886949-12-3*) Union Inst.

Part of the Solution: Portrait of a Revolutionary. Margaret Randall. LC 72-93974. 1973. pap. 2.95 (*0-8112-0471-5*, NDP350, Pub. by New Directions) Norton.

Part of the Tree: The Study of the Prodigal Son. Gail Erwin. (Christian Theatre Ser.). 31p. (Orig.). (YA). (gr. 8 up). 1995. pap. 3.00 (*1-57514-120-5*, 0090) Encore Perform Pub.

Part Seen, Part Imagined: Meaning & Symbolism in the Works of Charles Rennie Mackintosh & Margaret Macdonald. Timothy Neat. (Illus.). 208p. 1995. 49.95 (*0-86241-366-4*, Pub. by Canongate Books) Interlink Pub.

Part Taken by Women in American History. Mary S. Logan. LC 72-2613. (American Women Ser.: Images & Realities). (Illus.). 956p. 1978. reprint ed. 59.95 (*0-405-04467-4*) Ayer.

Part-Through Crack Fatigue Life Prediction-STP 687. Ed. by J. B. Chang. 226p. 1979. 26.25 (*0-8031-0532-0*, STP687) ASTM.

Part-Time Academic Employment in the Humanities: A Sourcebook for Just Policy. Ed. by M. Elizabeth Wallace. LC 84-1124. (Options for Teaching Ser.: No. 6). xxii, 166p. 1984. pap. 19.75 (*0-87352-307-5*, J206P); lib. bdg. 37.50 (*0-87352-306-7*, J206C) Modern Lang.

Part-Time Employment: A Bridge or a Trap? May Tam. 288p. 1997. text 73.95 (*1-85972-532-5*, Pub. by Avebry) Ashgate Pub Co.

Part-Time Employment for the Low-Income Elderly: Experiences from the Field. Leslie B. Alexander & Lenard W. Kaye. LC 96-35889. (Issues in Aging Ser.: Vol. 6). 204p. 1997. text 44.00 (*0-8153-1976-2*, SS1016) Garland.

Part-Time Faculty: Higher Education at a Crossroads. Judith M. Gappa. Ed. by Jonathan D. Fife. LC 84-72775. (ASHE-ERIC Higher Education Reports: No. 84-3). (Illus.). 125p. (Orig.). 1984. pap. 24.00 (*0-913317-12-8*) GWU Grad Schl E&HD.

Part-Time Faculty in American Higher Education. David W. Leslie et al. LC 81-13773. 151p. 1982. 45.00 (*0-275-90846-1*, C0846, Praeger Pubs) Greenwood.

Part-Time Faculty Personnel Management Policies. George E. Biles & Howard P. Tuckman. (ACE-Oryx Series on Higher Education). 188p. 1986. 27.95 (*0-02-903500-7*) Free Pr.

Part-Time Faculty Personnel Management Policies. George E. Biles & Howard P. Tuckman. 224p. 1986. text. write for info. (*0-318-62004-9*, 2009) Macmillan.

Part-Time Farming in the Southeast. R. H. Allen et al. LC 74-165677. (Research Monographs: Vol. 9). 1971. reprint ed. lib. bdg. 42.50 (*0-306-70341-6*) Da Capo.

Part-Time Father. Sharon Kendrick. 1996. per. 3.50 (*0-373-11820-1*, 1-11820-7) Harlequin Bks.

Part-Time Glamour Photography: Full-Time Income. Joe Farace. LC 99-18349. 160p. 1999. 29.95 (*1-883403-49-9*, Silver Pixel Pr) Saunders Photo.

Part-Time Higher Education: Policy, Practice & Experience. Tom Schuller. (Higher Education Policy Ser.). 1998. pap. text 34.95 (*1-85302-669-7*) Taylor & Francis.

Part-Time Occupational Faculty: A Contribution to Excellence. Michael H. Parsons. 40p. 1985. 5.50 (*0-317-01306-9*) Ctr Educ Trng Employ.

Part-Time Paradox. Cynthia F. Epstein. LC 98-20948. viii, 179 p. (C). 1998. pap. 18.99 (*0-415-92124-4*) Routledge.

Part-Time Paradox: Time Norms, Professional Lives, Family & Gender. Cynthia F. Epstein. LC 98-20948. 176p. (C). 1998. 70.00 (*0-415-92123-6*) Routledge.

Part-Time Parent: Learning to Live Without Full-Time Kids. Carolyn Pogue. 160p. 1998. pap. 14.95 (*1-896836-23-2*) NStone Publ.

Part-Time Profits from Home: 111 Creative & Pratical Home-Based Money-Making Opportunities. M. Buller & D. Sanders. 1997. pap. 9.00 (*0-517-88721-5*) Random Hse Value.

***Part-Time Prosecutors & Conflicts of Interest.** Richard H. Underwood. 190p. 2000. pap. 28.00 (*1-58757-029-7*, AM036) Univ of KY.

Part Time Prospects: International Comparison of Part Time Work in Europe, North America & the Pacific Rim. Ed. by Jacqueline O'Reilly & Colette Fagan. LC 98-166828. 272p. (C). 1998. pap. 29.99 (*0-415-15670-X*) Routledge.

Part Time Prospects: International Comparison of Part Time Work in Europe, North America & the Pacific Rim. Ed. by Jacqueline O'Reilly & Colette Fagan. LC 98-166828. (Illus.). 304p. (C). 1998. 90.00 (*0-415-15669-6*) Routledge.

Part-Time Public Relations with Full-Time Results: A PR Primer for Libraries. Ed. by Rashelle S. Karp. (Illus.). 54p. (Orig.). 1995. pap. 18.00 (*0-8389-0661-3*, 0661-3-2045) ALA.

Part Time Teacher. Judy Wells. (Orig.). 1991. pap. 5.00 (*1-879082-01-2*) Rainy Day CA.

Part-Time Types of Elementary Schools in New York City: A Comparative Study of Pupil Achievement. Frank M. Quance. LC 72-177173. (Columbia University. Teachers College. Contributions to Education Ser.: No. 249). reprint ed. 37.50 (*0-404-55249-8*) AMS Pr.

Part-Time Wife. Susan Mallery. 1998. 21.95 (*0-373-59933-1*) Harlequin Bks.

Part-Time Wife. Susan Mallery. (That Special Woman, Hometown Heartbreakers Ser.). 1996. per. 3.99 (*0-373-24027-9*, 1-24027-4) Silhouette.

Part-Time Workers Need Full Time Rights. Ann Sedley. 1983. 35.00 (*0-7855-3003-7*, Pub. by NCCL) St Mut.

***Part-Time Workers 1999.** Allan & Daniels. 96p. 2000. pap. 29.99 (*0-8464-5124-7*) Beekman Pubs.

Part to Torts. 5th ed. William L. Prosser & Keeton. (C). 1987. 13.50 (*0-314-24253-8*) West Pub.

Part Tulip, Vol. 1. Mapple. 1998. 30.00 (*0-8212-2526-X*) Little.

Part Two: Reflections on the Sequel. Ed. by Paul Budra & Betty A. Schellenberg. LC 99-217365. (Theory - Culture Ser.). (Illus.). 272p. 1998. text 55.00 (*0-8020-0915-8*); pap. text 19.95 (*0-8020-7895-8*) U of Toronto Pr.

***Part-Whole Reasoning in an Object-Centered Framework.** P. Lambrix. (Lecture Notes in Computer Science Ser.: Vol. 1771). xii, 195p. 2000. pap. 45.00 (*3-540-67225-7*) Spr-Verlag.

Part, Yet Apart: South Asians in Asian America. Ed. by Lavina D. Shankar & Rajini Srikanth. LC 97-38354. (Asian American History & Culture Ser.). 320p. 1998. text 59.95 (*1-56639-577-1*) Temple U Pr.

Part 6 see Diatomeenschalen im Elektronenmikroskopischen Bild

Parta: The Crown Jewels of the Village, Hungarian Folk Art Coronets. Evelyn Domjan. Ed. by Judith Magyar & Lory Skwerer. (Illus.). Date not set. pap. 20.00 (*0-913509-02-7*) Domjan Studio.

Partage de Midi. Paul Claudel. (FRE.). 1972. pap. 10.95 (*0-8288-3631-0*, F94341) Fr & Eur.

Partage de Midi. Paul Claudel. (Folio Ser.: No. 245). (FRE.). 160p. 1972. pap. 6.95 (*2-07-036245-0*) Schoenhof.

Partage des Eaux. Alejo Carpentier. (FRE.). 1976. pap. 11.95 (*0-7859-1827-2*, 2070367959) Fr & Eur.

Partakers of Divine Nature. C. Stavropoulos. 1976. pap. 8.95 (*0-937032-09-3*) Light&Life Pub Co MN.

Partakers of Divine Nature: Study Guide. 22p. (Orig.). 1984. pap. text, student ed. 2.50 (*1-56125-005-8*) Educ Services.

Partakers of Divine Nature: Theosis Group Leader's Guide. 21p. 1984. teacher ed. 5.00 (*1-56125-006-6*) Educ Services.

Partakers of God. Panagiotes Chrestou. (Patriarch Athenagoras Memorial Lectures). 66p. 1984. pap. 4.95 (*0-916586-67-7*, Pub. by Holy Cross Orthodox) BookWorld.

Partakers of the Divine Nature: A Study of 13 Qualities of Spiritual Growth. O. William Cooper. LC 98-93153. 214p. 1998. pap. write for info. (*1-57502-860-3*, PO2349) Morris Pubng.

Partakers (with Christ) Estella M. Pitt. (Illus.). 53p. (Orig.). 1995. pap. text 4.95 (*0-9642764-1-0*) E Pitt.

Parte A Examen de Habilidad. Ellis Richardson. (Linguistic Pattern Ser.). (SPA., Illus.). 4p. (J). (gr. 1-2). 1997. pap. text. write for info. (*1-56775-075-3*) ISM Teach Systs.

Parte B Examen de Habilidad. Ellis Richardson. (Linguistic Pattern Ser.). (SPA., Illus.). 4p. (J). (gr. 1-2). 1997. pap. text. write for info. (*1-56775-076-1*) ISM Teach Systs.

Parte C Examen de Habilidad. Ellis Richardson. (Linguistic Pattern Ser.). (SPA., Illus.). 4p. (J). (gr. 2-3). 1997. pap. text. write for info. (*1-56775-077-X*) ISM Teach Systs.

Parte de Una Historia (Part of a Story) Ignacio De Aldecoa. (SPA.). 1996. pap. 14.95 (*0-679-76849-1*) Vin Bks.

Parte Goelta, Brunelleschi Donatello. Dianne F. Zervas. (Illus.). 471p. 1987. 65.00 (*0-614-14873-1*) J J Augustin.

Parted on Her Wedding Morn. Leland Price. 1942. pap. 3.25 (*0-8222-0873-3*) Dramatists Play.

Parteien-Handbuch, die Parteien der Bundesrepublik Deutschland 1945-1980, Vol. 1. R. Stoss. 1310p. 1983. 185.00 (*0-8288-2259-X*, VOL. 1) Fr & Eur.

Parteien-Handbuch, die Parteien der Bundesrepublik Deutschland 1945-1980, Vol. 2. R. Stoss. (GER.). 1250p. 1984. 175.00 (*0-8288-2258-1*, M15262) Fr & Eur.

Parteien in der Demokratie. Rudolf Wichard. (Hildesheimer Beitrage Zu Den Erziehungs und Sozial Wissenschaften Ser.: Bd. 4). (GER.). 120p. 1977. 25.00 (*3-487-06352-2*) G Olms Pubs.

Partera: Story of a Midwife. Fran L. Buss. 152p. 1980. pap. text 14.95 (*0-472-06322-7*, 06322) U of Mich Pr.

***Partera: Story of a Midwife.** Fran Leeper Buss. (Ann Arbor Paperbacks Ser.). (SPA., Illus.). 184p. (C). 2000. pap. 16.95 (*0-472-08712-6*) U of Mich Pr.

***Partha Chatterjee Omnibus: Nationalist Thought & the Colonial World, the Nation & Its Fragments, A Possible India.** Partha Chatterjee. 802p. 2000. text 29.95 (*0-19-565156-1*) OUP.

Partheneia Sacra, 1633. Henry Hawkins. Ed. by Karl J. Holtgen. LC 93-4443. 312p. 1993. 69.95 (*0-85967-982-9*, Pub. by Scolar Pr) Ashgate Pub Co.

P

An Asterisk (*) at the beginning of an entry indicates that the title is appearing for the first time.

Parthenia: or the Maydenhead of the First Musicke That Ever Was Printed for the Virginalls. William Byrd et al. Ed. by Kurt Stone. (Illus.). 62p. 1952. pap. 17.50 (*0-8450-6001-5*) Broude.

Parthenius of Nicaea. Ed. by J. L. Lightfoot. LC PA4263.P3A2 1999. 622p. 1999. text 135.00 (*0-19-815253-1*) OUP.

Parthenon. Peter Crisp. LC 96-48751. (Great Buildings Ser.). 48p. (J). 1997. lib. bdg. 25.69 (*0-8172-4917-6*) Raintree Steck-V.

Parthenon. Susan Woodford. (Cambridge Introduction to World History Topic Bks.). (Illus.). 49p. (YA). (gr. 7 up). 1981. pap. 12.95 (*0-521-22629-5*) Cambridge U Pr.

Parthenon. Alcman. Ed. by W. R. Connor. LC 78-81590. (Greek Texts & Commentaries Ser.). 1979. reprint ed. lib. bdg. 22.95 (*0-405-11432-X*) Ayer.

Parthenon. rev. ed. Vincent J. Bruno. (Illus.). 352p. 1996. pap. 18.95 (*0-393-31440-5*, Norton Paperbks) Norton.

Parthenon: And Its Impact in Modern Times. Ed. by Panayotis Tournikiotis. (Illus.). 368p. 1996. 75.00 (*0-8109-6314-0*, Pub. by Abrams) Time Warner.

Parthenon & the Mycenaean City on the Heights. J. A. Bundgaard. (Publications of the National Museum: No. 1, Pt. 17). (Illus.). 244p. (C). 1976. pap. 33.00 (*87-480-6701-6*, Pub. by Aarhus Univ Pr) David Brown.

Parthenon & the Origin of the Corinthian Capital. Poul O. Pedersen. (Illus.). 48p. (Orig.). 1989. pap. 27.50 (*87-7492-708-6*) Coronet Bks.

Parthenon Frieze. Ian Jenkins. (Illus.). 120p. 1994. 29.95 (*0-292-74038-7*) U of Tex Pr.

Parthenon Frieze & Other Essays. Thomas Davidson. (Notable American Authors Ser.). 1992. reprint ed. lib. bdg. 75.00 (*0-7812-2617-1*) Rprt Serv.

Parthenon, Its Science of Forms. Robert W. Gardner. 1982. 41.95 (*0-8434-0134-6*) McGrath NH.

Parthenon of Ancient Greece. Don Nardo. LC 98-4279. (Building History Ser.). (Illus.). 96p. (YA). (gr. 5 up). 1998. lib. bdg. 23.70 (*1-56006-431-5*) Lucent Bks.

***Parthenopi: New & Selected Poems.** Michael Waters. (American Poets Continuum Ser.: Vol. 63). 130p. 2000. 25.00 (*1-880238-95-0*); pap. 13.95 (*1-880238-96-9*) BOA Edns.

Parthia. Mark Dunster. (Antony Ser.: Pt. 7). (Orig.). 1979. pap. 4.00 (*0-89642-055-8*) Linden Pubs.

Parthian Period. M. A. Colledge. (Iconography of Religions Ser.: Vol. XIV-3). (Illus.). xiv, 47p. 1986. pap. 66.50 (*90-04-07115-6*) Brill Academic Pubs.

Parthian Stations. Isidore Of Charax. Ed. by W. H. Schoff. 1980. pap. 12.50 (*0-89005-058-9*) Ares.

Parti-Colored Blocks for a Quilt: Poets on Poetry. Marge Piercy. 336p. 1982. pap. 13.95 (*0-472-06338-3*, 06338) U of Mich Pr.

Parti Pris des Choses see Nature of Things

Parti Pris des Choses. Francis Ponge. (Poesie Ser.). (FRE.). 224p. 1966. pap. 9.95 (*2-07-030223-7*) Schoenhof.

Parti Pris des Choses: Douze Petits Ecrits. Francis Ponge. (FRE.). 1966. pap. 11.95 (*0-7859-2764-6*) Fr & Eur.

Parti Social-Democrate Allemand et la Fin de la Quatrieme Republique Francaise (1954-1958) Jean-Paul Cahn. (Contacts Ser.: Series II, Vol. 18). (FRE.). 522p. 1996. 62.95 (*3-906754-69-3*, Pub. by P Lang) P Lang Pubng.

Partial Connections. Marilyn Strathern. (Illus.). 180p. (C). 1991. pap. text 24.95 (*0-8476-7698-6*) Rowman.

Partial Connections. Marilyn Strathern. Ed. by Deborah B. Gewertz. (Illus.). 180p. (C). 1991. lib. bdg. 62.00 (*0-8476-7697-8*) Rowman.

Partial Connections. Marilyn Strathern. Ed. by Deborah B. Gewertz. (Illus.). 180p. (C). 1991. pap. text 37.50 (*0-8191-8085-8*) U Pr of Amer.

Partial Constitution. Cass R. Sunstein. LC 92-32492. 416p. 1993. text 43.50 (*0-674-65478-1*) HUP.

Partial Constitution. Cass R. Sunstein. 424p. 1994. pap. text 19.50 (*0-674-65479-X*, SUNPAX) HUP.

Partial Dentures. Fritz Singer & Fritz Schon. (Illus.). 207p. 1973. text 54.00 (*0-931386-59-4*) Quint Pub Co.

Partial Differential & Integral Equations. Heinrich G. W. Begehr et al. LC 98-47337. (International Society for Analysis, Applications & Computation Ser.). 1998. write for info. (*0-7923-5482-6*) Kluwer Academic.

P

Partial Differential Equation. Sergei L. Sobolev. 427p. 1989. pap. 12.95 (*0-486-65964-X*) Dover.

Partial Differential Equation Methods in Control & Shape Analysis. Giuseppe Da Prato & J. P. Zolesio. LC 96-29978. (Lecture Notes in Pure & Applied Mathematics Ser.: Vol. 188). (Illus.). 352p. 1997. pap. text 145.00 (*0-8247-9837-6*) Dekker.

Partial Differential Equation VI: Elliptic & Parabolic Operators. Yu V. Egorov. (Encyclopedia of Mathematical Sciences Ser.: Vol. 63). (Illus.). 336p. 1994. 118.95 (*0-387-54678-2*) Spr-Verlag.

Partial Differential Equations. R. A. Aleksandrjan et al. LC 76-8428. (Translations Ser.: Series 2, Vol. 105). 346p. 1976. 84.00 (*0-8218-3055-4*, TRANS2/105) Am Math.

Partial Differential Equations. Begehr. 232p. (C). 1992. ring bd. 60.95 (*0-582-09640-5*) CRC Pr.

Partial Differential Equations. Richard Ernest Bellman & George Adomian. 312p. 1984. text 154.50 (*90-277-1681-1*) Kluwer Academic.

Partial Differential Equations. Ed. by A. Bitsadze. 300p. (C). 1993. text 55.00 (*981-02-0593-7*) World Scientific Pub.

Partial Differential Equations. A. A. Dezin. LC 87-9421. (Soviet Mathematics Ser.). 180p. 1987. 159.95 (*0-387-16699-8*) Spr-Verlag.

Partial Differential Equations. Emmanuele DiBenedetto. LC 94-42625. 416p. 1994. 49.00 (*0-8176-3708-7*); write for info. (*3-7643-3708-7*) Birkhauser.

Partial Differential Equations. Lawrence C. Evans. LC 97-41033. (Graduate Studies in Mathematics). 662p. 1998. text 75.00 (*0-8218-0772-2*) Am Math.

Partial Differential Equations. Ed. by A. Jeffrey. 1994. write for info. (*0-8493-8604-7*) CRC Pr.

Partial Differential Equations. Harold Levine. LC 97-27385. (AMS/IP Studies in Advanced Mathematics: Vol. 6). 706p. 1997. text 69.00 (*0-8218-0775-7*) Am Math.

Partial Differential Equations. J. Rauch. Ed. by J. H. Ewing et al. (Graduate Texts in Mathematics Ser.: Vol. 128). (Illus.). 256p. 1997. 43.95 (*0-387-97472-5*) Spr-Verlag.

Partial Differential Equations. Otto Vejvoda. 380p. 1982. lib. bdg. 187.00 (*90-247-2772-3*) Kluwer Academic.

Partial Differential Equations. J. T. Wloka. (Illus.). 530p. 1987. pap. text 49.95 (*0-521-27759-0*) Cambridge U Pr.

Partial Differential Equations. Lipman Bers et al. LC 63-19664. (Lectures in Applied Mathematics: Vol. 3a). 343p. 1975. reprint ed. pap. 45.00 (*0-8218-0049-3*, LAM/3.1) Am Math.

Partial Differential Equations. Edward T. Copson. LC 74-12965. 288p. reprint ed. pap. 82.10 (*0-608-15708-2*, 2031635) Bks Demand.

Partial Differential Equations. George F. Duff. LC 56-4187. (Mathematical Expositions Ser.: No. 9). 258p. reprint ed. pap. 80.00 (*0-608-10040-4*, 201419300095) Bks Demand.

Partial Differential Equations. Kenneth S. Miller. LC 87-16930. 262p. (C). 1987. reprint ed. lib. bdg. 27.50 (*0-89464-234-0*) Krieger.

Partial Differential Equations. Ed. by C. B. Morrey, Jr. LC 50-1183. (Proceedings of Symposia in Pure Mathematics Ser.: Vol. 4). 169p. 1961. reprint ed. pap. 38.00 (*0-8218-1404-4*, PSPUM/4) Am Math.

Partial Differential Equations. Pure Mathematics Symposium Staff. Ed. by D. C. Spencer. LC 72-4071. (Proceedings of Symposia in Pure Mathematics Ser.: Vol. 23). 505p. 1973. reprint ed. pap. 61.00 (*0-8218-1423-0*, PSPUM/23) Am Math.

Partial Differential Equations. 2nd ed. George F. Carrier. 340p. 1988. text 48.00 (*0-12-160451-9*) Acad Pr.

Partial Differential Equations. 2nd ed. Paul R. Garabedian. LC 85-73601. (Illus.). xii, 672p. (C). 1986. text 29.50 (*0-8284-0325-2*) Chelsea Pub.

Partial Differential Equations. 4th ed. F. John. (Applied Mathematical Sciences Ser.: Vol. 1). (Illus.). 249p. 1995. 49.95 (*0-387-90609-6*) Spr-Verlag.

Partial Differential Equations, Vol. 273. Wiener. (Research Notes in Mathematics Ser.). 288p. 1992. ring bd. 51.95 (*0-582-09114-4*, Pub. by Addison-Wesley) Longman.

Partial Differential Equations: An Introduction. Walter A. Strauss. LC 91-43999. 440p. (C). 1992. text 80.95 (*0-471-54868-5*) Wiley.

Partial Differential Equations: An Introduction. Bernard Epstein. LC 75-11905. 284p. 1975. reprint ed. 30.50 (*0-88275-330-4*) Krieger.

***Partial Differential Equations An Introduction with Mathematica & Maple.** Ioannis P. Stavroulakis. LC 99-44792. 1999. 37.00 (*981-02-3891-6*) World Scientific Pub.

***Partial Differential Equations: Analytical Solution Techniques.** 2nd ed. J. Kevorkian. LC 99-16552. (Texts in Applied Mathematics Ser.: Vol. 35). (Illus.). 643p. 1999. 59.95 (*0-387-98605-7*) Spr-Verlag.

Partial Differential Equations: Basic Theory. M. E. Taylor. (Texts in Applied Mathematics Ser.: Vol. 23). (Illus.). 563p. 1996. pap. 39.00 (*0-387-94654-3*) Spr-Verlag.

Partial Differential Equations: Models in Physics & Biology. Ed. by Gunter Lumer et al. LC 94-40002. (Mathematical Research Ser.: Vol. 82). 418p. 1994. text 102.90 (*3-05-501657-2*, Pub. by Akademie Verlag) Wiley.

Partial Differential Equations: Theory & Applications. Robert C. McOwen. LC 95-21357. 420p. 1995. 85.33 (*0-13-121880-8*) P-H.

***Partial Differential Equations: Theory & Numerical Solutions** Jindrich Neicas et al. LC 99-27317. (Research Notes in Mathematics Ser.). 360p. 1999. per. 79.95 (*1-58488-022-8*, Chap & Hall CRC) CRC Pr.

Partial Differential Equations & Applications: Collected Papers in Honor of Carlo Pucci. Ed. by Paolo Marcellini et al. LC 95-50251. (Lecture Notes in Pure & Applied Mathematics Ser.: Vol. 177). (Illus.). 392p. 1996. pap. text 175.00 (*0-8247-9698-5*) Dekker.

***Partial Differential Equations & Boundary Value Problems.** Nakhle H. Asmar. LC 99-43378. 598p. 1999. 82.67 (*0-13-958620-2*) P-H.

Partial Differential Equations & Boundary Value Problems. Viorel Barbu. LC 98-6571. (Mathematics & Its Applications Ser.). 1998. 129.00 (*0-7923-5056-1*) Kluwer Academic.

Partial Differential Equations & Boundary Value Problems with Applications. 2nd ed. Mark A. Pinsky. 488p. (C). 1991. text 86.50 (*0-07-050128-9*) McGraw.

Partial Differential Equations & Boundary-Value Problems with Applications. 3rd ed. Mark A. Pinsky. LC 97-36120. 544p. 1997. 82.81 (*0-07-050227-7*) McGraw.

Partial Differential Equations & Boundary Value Problems with Maple V. George A. Articola. LC 97-48543. (Illus.). 628p. (C). 1998. pap. text 44.95 (*0-12-064475-4*) Morgan Kaufmann.

Partial Differential Equations & Calculus of Variations. Ed. by Stefan Hildebrandt & R. Leis. (Lecture Notes in Mathematics Ser.: Vol. 1357). 423p. 1988. 54.95 (*0-387-50508-3*) Spr-Verlag.

Partial Differential Equations & Complex Analysis. Steven George Krantz. 320p. 1992. boxed set 83.95 (*0-8493-7155-4*, QA347) CRC Pr.

Partial Differential Equations & Continuum Mechanics. Ed. by Rudolph E. Langer. LC 61-600003. (U. S. Army. Mathematics Research Center Publication Ser.: No. 5). 413p. reprint ed. pap. 128.10 (*0-608-10257-1*, 201536400094) Bks Demand.

Partial Differential Equations & Functional Analysis: In Memory of Pierre Grisvard. Ed. by J. Cea et al. LC 96-1384. (Progress in Nonlinear Differential Equations & Their Applications Ser.: Vol. 22). 263p. 1996. 84.50 (*0-8176-3839-3*) Birkhauser.

Partial Differential Equations & Geometry: Proceedings of the Park City Conference. Ed. by Christopher I. Byrnes. LC 79-12725. (Lecture Notes in Pure & Applied Mathematics Ser.: No. 48). (Illus.). 339p. reprint ed. pap. 105.10 (*0-608-18015-7*, 202799300058) Bks Demand.

Partial Differential Equations & Group Theory: New Perspectives for Applications. J. F. Pommaret. LC 94-19352. (Mathematics & Its Applications Ser.: Vol. 293). 484p. (C). 1994. text 289.00 (*0-7923-2966-X*) Kluwer Academic.

Partial Differential Equations & Group Theory: New Perspectives for Applications. 2nd ed. LC 96-47897. (Mathematics & Its Applications Ser.). 1997. write for info. (*0-7923-4312-3*) Kluwer Academic.

Partial Differential Equations & Mathematica. Prem K. Kythe et al. LC 96-36946. 400p. 1996. boxed set 89.95 (*0-8493-7853-2*) CRC Pr.

Partial Differential Equations & Mathematical Physics: The Danish-Swedish Analysis Seminar, 1995. Ed. by Lars Hormander & Anders Melin. (Progress in Nonlinear Differential Equations & Their Applications Ser.: Vol. 21). 380p. 1996. 89.50 (*0-8176-3906-3*) Birkhauser.

Partial Differential Equations & Mathematical Physics: The Danish-Swedish Analysis Seminar, 1995. Ed. by Lars Hormander & Anders Melin. (Progress in Nonlinear Differential Equations & Their Applications Ser.: Vol. 21). 1996. write for info. (*3-7643-3906-3*) Birkhauser.

Partial Differential Equations & the Calculus of Variations, 2 vols., Set. Colombini et al. (Progress in Nonlinear Differential Equations & Their Applications Ser.: Nos. 1 & 2). 900p. 1989. 120.50 (*0-8176-3426-6*) Birkhauser.

Partial Differential Equations & the Calculus of Variations, 2 vols., Vol. 1. Colombini et al. (Progress in Nonlinear Differential Equations & Their Applications Ser.: Nos. 1 & 2). 519p. 1989. 75.50 (*0-8176-3424-X*) Birkhauser.

Partial Differential Equations & the Calculus of Variations, 2 vols., Vol. 2. Colombini et al. (Progress in Nonlinear Differential Equations & Their Applications Ser.: Nos. 1 & 2). 498p. 1989. 75.50 (*0-8176-3425-8*) Birkhauser.

Partial Differential Equations & Their Applications. Ed. by Peter C. Greiner et al. LC 97-27467. (CRM Proceedings & Lecture Notes Ser.: Vol. 12). 315p. 1997. pap. 85.00 (*0-8218-0687-4*) Am Math.

***Partial Differential Equations & Their Applications.** Ed. by Chen Z. Huang & L. Rodino. 400p. 2000. 84.00 (*981-02-4059-7*) World Scientific Pub.

Partial Differential Equations VIII, Vol. 65. Ed. by M. A. Shubin. Tr. by C. Constanda. (Encyclopedia of Mathematical Sciences Ser.). 272p. (C). 1995. 107.95 (*0-387-57036-5*) Spr-Verlag.

Partial Differential Equations V. Ed. by M. V. Fedoryuk. (Encyclopedia of Mathematical Sciences Ser.: Vol. 34). 235p. 1997. 102.00 (*0-387-53371-0*) Spr-Verlag.

Partial Differential Equations V: Asymptotic Methods for Partial Differential Equations. Ed. by M. V. Fedoryuk & R. V. Gamkrelidze. Tr. by J. S. Joel & S. Wolf from RUS. (Encyclopaedia of Mathematical Sciences Ser.: Vol. 34). (Illus.). 240p. 1998. text 99.95 (*3-540-53371-0*) Spr-Verlag.

Partial Differential Equations for Scientists & Engineers. Stanley J. Farlow. 98p. 1982. pap. text, teacher ed. 30.95 (*0-471-09582-6*) Wiley.

Partial Differential Equations for Scientists & Engineers. G. Stephenson. 172p. 1996. pap. 17.00 (*1-86094-024-2*) World Scientific Pub.

Partial Differential Equations for Scientists & Engineers. Stanley J. Farlow. LC 93-4556. (Illus.). ix, 414p. 1993. reprint ed. pap. 12.95 (*0-486-67620-X*) Dover.

Partial Differential Equations for Scientists & Engineers. 3rd ed. T. Myint-U & L. Debnath. 620p. 1987. 45.75 (*0-444-01173-0*) P-H.

Partial Differential Equations in China. Chao-gao Gu et al. 1993. write for info. (*0-318-70230-4*) Longman.

Partial Differential Equations in China. Ed. by Chaohao Gu. (Mathematics & Its Applications Ser.). 192p. (C). 1994. text 115.00 (*0-7923-2857-4*) Kluwer Academic.

Partial Differential Equations in Classical Mathematical Physics. 692p. 1998. pap. text 36.95 (*0-521-55846-8*) Cambridge U Pr.

Partial Differential Equations in Engineering Problems. Kenneth S. Miller. 1953. 47.00 (*0-13-650408-6*) P-H.

***Partial Differential Equations in Mechanics.** A. P. S. Selvadurai. LC 00-44024. 2000. write for info. (*3-540-67284-2*) Spr-Verlag.

Partial Differential Equations in Science. 3rd ed. Myintu. 1987. 60.80 (*0-13-051665-1*) P-H.

Partial Differential Equations IV: Microlocal Analysis & Hyperbolic Equations. Yu V. Egorov & M. A. Shubin. LC 92-22077. (Encyclopedia of Mathematical Sciences Ser.: Vol. 33). 1993. write for info. (*3-540-53363-X*); 118.95 (*0-387-53363-X*) Spr-Verlag.

Partial Differential Equations IX: Ellitic Boundary Value Problems. Yu V. Egorov. (Encyclopaedia of Mathematical Sciences: 79). 296p. 1996. 109.50 (*3-540-57044-6*) Spr-Verlag.

Partial Differential Equations of Applied Mathematics, Vol. 1. 2nd ed. Ed. by Erich Zauderer. LC 88-37525. (Pure & Applied Mathematics: A Wiley-Interscience Series of Texts, Monographs & Tracts). 891p. 1998. pap. 79.95 (*0-471-31516-8*) Wiley.

Partial Differential Equations of Elliptic Type. Ed. by Angelo Alvino et al. (Symposia Mathematica Ser.: No. 35). 233p. (C). 1994. text 69.95 (*0-521-46048-4*) Cambridge U Pr.

Partial Differential Equations of Elliptic Type. 2nd rev. ed. C. Miranda. LC 71-75930. (Ergebnisse der Mathematik und Ihrer Grenzgebiete Ser.: Vol. 2). 1970. 75.95 (*0-387-04804-9*) Spr-Verlag.

***Partial Differential Equations of First Order & Their Applications to Physics.** G. Lopez. 250p. 1999. 58.00 (*981-02-3746-4*) World Scientific Pub.

Partial Differential Equations of Hyperbolic Type & Applications: Torino, Italy, September Second Thru the Fourteenth, Nineteen Eighty-Five. Ed. by G. Geymonat. 188p. 1987. text 54.00 (*9971-5-0205-4*) World Scientific Pub.

Partial Differential Equations of Mathematical Physics & Integral Equations. unabridged ed. Ronald B. Guenther & John W. Lee. LC 95-35578. (Illus.). xii, 592p. 1996. reprint ed. pap. text 17.95 (*0-486-68889-5*) Dover.

Partial Differential Equations I: Basic Theory, Vol. 1. Michael E. Taylor. LC 97-167171. (Applied Mathematical Sciences Ser.: Vol. 115). (Illus.). 584p. 1997. 43.95 (*0-387-94653-5*) Spr-Verlag.

Partial Differential Equations I: Foundations of the Classical Theory. Ed. by Yu V. Egorov et al. Tr. by R. Cooke from RUS. (Encyclopedia of Mathematical Sciences Ser.: Vol. 30). (Illus.). 248p. 1991. 118.95 (*0-387-52002-3*) Spr-Verlag.

Partial Differential Equations, Proceedings, Tianjin, 1986. Ed. by Shiing-Shen Chern. (Lecture Notes in Mathematics Ser.: Vol. 1306). vi, 294p. 1988. 44.95 (*0-387-19097-X*) Spr-Verlag.

Partial Differential Equations VII: Spectral Theory of Differential Operators. M. A. Shubin. (Encyclopedia of Mathematical Sciences Ser.: Vol. 64). 240p. 1994. 118.95 (*0-387-54677-4*) Spr-Verlag.

Partial Differential Equations III: Nonlinear Equations, Vol. 3. Michael E. Taylor. LC 97-167171. (Applied Mathematical Sciences Ser.: Vol. 117). (Illus.). 610p. 1996. 69.00 (*0-387-94652-7*) Spr-Verlag.

Partial Differential Equations III: The Cauchy Problem Qualitative Theory of Partial Differential Equations. Ed. by Yu V. Egorov et al. Tr. by M. Grinfeld from RUS. (Encyclopedia of Mathematical Sciences Ser.: Vol. 32). vii, 197p. 1991. 103.95 (*0-387-52003-1*) Spr-Verlag.

Partial Differential Equations Through Examples & Exercises. Endre Pap et al. LC 97-18393. (Texts in Mathematical Sciences Ser.). 416p. 1997. text 214.00 (*0-7923-4724-2*) Kluwer Academic.

Partial Differential Equations Two: Elements of the Modern Theory; Equations with Constant Coefficients. Ed. by Yu V. Egorov & A. I. Komech. 273p. 1994. 118.95 (*0-387-52001-5*) Spr-Verlag.

Partial Differential Equations II: Qualitative Studies of Linear Equations, Vol. 2. Michael E. Taylor. LC 97-167171. (Applied Mathematical Sciences Ser.: Vol. 116). (Illus.). 528p. 1996. 69.00 (*0-387-94651-9*) Spr-Verlag.

Partial Differential Equations with Maple & Vector Analysis. D. Betounes. LC 97-26381. (Illus.). 592p. 1998. 64.95 (*0-387-98300-7*) Spr-Verlag.

Partial Differential Equations with Mathematica. Dimitri Vvedensky. 304p. (C). 1992. 37.50 (*0-201-54409-1*) Addison-Wesley.

Partial Differential Equations with Minimal Smoothness & Applications. Ed. by B. Dahlberg et al. (IMA Volumes in Mathematics & Its Applications Ser.: Vol. 42). 224p. 1992. 62.95 (*0-387-97774-0*) Spr-Verlag.

Partial Differential Equations with Multiple Characteristics. Maria Mascarello & Luigi Rodino. LC 98-100498. (Mathematical Topics Ser.). 352 p. 1997. write for info. (*3-05-501764-1*) Akademie Verlag.

Partial Differential Equations with Multiple Characteristics. Maria Mascarello & Luigi Rodino. 352p. 1997. 149.95 (*3-527-40115-6*) Wiley.

Partial Differential Operators. Ed. by F. A. Cardoso et al. (Lecture Notes in Mathematics Ser.: Vol. 1324). viii, 433p. 1988. 57.95 (*0-387-50111-8*) Spr-Verlag.

Partial Differential Operators & Mathematical Physics: International Conference in Holzhau, Germany, July 3-9, 1994. Ed. by Michael Demuth & Bert-Wolfgang Schulze. LC 95-10776. (Operator Theory, Advances & Applications Ser.: Vol. 78). 1995. write for info. (*3-7643-5208-6*) Birkhauser.

Partial Differential Operators & Mathematical Physics: International Conference in Holzhau, Germany, July 3-9, 1994. Ed. by Michael Demuth & Bert-Wolfgang Schulze. LC 95-10776. (Operator Theory, Advances & Applications Ser.: Vol. 78). 429p. 1995. 142.00 (*0-8176-5208-6*) Birkhauser.

Partial Differential Operators of Elliptic Type. N. Shimakura. LC 92-2953. (Translations of Mathematical Monographs). 288p. 1992. text 132.00 (*0-8218-4556-X*, MMONO/99) Am Math.

Partial Differential Relations. M. Gromov. (Ergebnisse der Mathematik und Ihrer Grenzgebiete Ser.: Folge 3, Vol. 9). 370p. 1986. 142.95 (*0-387-12177-3*) Spr-Verlag.

Partial Discharge & Breakdown Testing at High DC Voltage. Udo Fromm. (Illus.). 126p. (Orig.). 1995. pap. 59.50 (*90-407-1155-0*, Pub. by Delft U Pr) Coronet Bks.

Partial-Discharge Test Procedure, Guide For. Date not set. 30.00 (*0-614-18676-5*, T-24-380-1994) Insulated Cable.

Partial Eclipse. Tony Sanders. LC 94-16558. 75p. 1994. 15.95 (*0-929398-79-3*); pap. 10.95 (*0-929398-81-5*) UNTX Pr.

Partial Edition of les Fais des Rommains with a Study of Its Style. Thomas J. McCormick, Jr. LC 94-48863. 264p. 1995. text 89.95 (*0-7734-2918-2*) E Mellen.

Partial Evaluation & Mixed Computation: Proceedings of the IFIP TC2 Workshop, Gammel Avernaes, Denmark, 18-24 Oct., 1987. Ed. by D. Bjorner et al. 1988. 207.50 (*0-444-70491-4*, North Holland) Elsevier.

Partial Evaluation International Seminar, Dagstuhl Castle, Germany, February 1996: Selected Papers. Olivier Danvy et al. LC 96-2749. (Lecture Notes in Computer Science Ser.: Vol. 1110). 514p. 1996. 81.00 (*3-540-61580-6*) Spr-Verlag.

Partial Excuses to Murder. Ed. by Stanley Yeo. 287p. 1991. pap. 53.00 (*1-86287-047-0*, Pub. by Federation Pr) Gaunt.

Partial Genealogy of the Name Yarnall-Yarnell, 1683-1970. 507p. 1999. 85.00 (*0-8328-9867-8*); pap. 75.00 (*0-8328-9868-6*) Higginson Bk Co.

Partial History & Genealogical Record of the Bancker or Banker Families of America & in Particular the Descendants of Laurens Mattyse Bancker. Howard J. Banker. (Illus.). 458p. 1988. reprint ed. pap. 68.00 (*0-8328-0179-8*); reprint ed. lib. bdg. 76.00 (*0-8328-0178-X*) Higginson Bk Co.

Partial Hospitalization: A Current Perspective. Ed. by R. F. Luber. LC 78-31915. (Illus.). 222p. 1979. 39.50 (*0-306-40201-7*, Plenum Trade) Perseus Pubng.

***Partial Integral Operators & Integro-Differential Equations.** Jhurgen Appell et al. LC 00-22902. (Monographs & Textbooks in Pure & Applied Mathematics). 2000. write for info. (*0-8247-0396-0*) Dekker.

Partial Justice: Federal Indian Law in a Liberal-Constitutional System. Petra T. Shattuck & Jill Norgren. LC 90-39337. (State, Law & Society Ser.). 223p. 1991. 50.00 (*0-85496-588-2*) Berg Pubs.

Partial Justice: Federal Indian Law in a Liberal-Constitutional System. Petra T. Shattuck & Jill Norgren. (State, Law & Society Ser.). 223p. (C). 1993. pap. text 15.50 (*0-85496-342-1*) Berg Pubs.

Partial Justice: Women in State Prisons, 1800-1935. Nicole H. Rafter. LC 84-7990. (Illus.). 295p. 1985. text 47.50 (*0-930350-63-4*) NE U Pr.

Partial Justice: Women, Prisons & Social Control. 2nd ed. Nicole H. Rafter. 342p. (C). 1990. pap. 24.95 (*0-88738-826-4*) Transaction Pubs.

Partial Left Ventriculectomy: Its Theory, Results & Perspectives; Proceedings of the Cardiac Volume Reduction Forum '97, Tokyo, Japan, October 4, 1997. Ed. by Akira T. Kawaguchi & Leonard M. Linde. LC 98-40591. (International Congress Ser.). 128p. 1998. 126.50 (*0-444-50028-6*, Excerpta Medica) Elsevier.

***Partial Left Ventriculectomy 2: Recent Evolution for Safe & Effective Application: Proceedings of the 2nd International Symposium on Partial Left Ventriculectomy, Tokyo, Japan, 12 December, 1998.** International Symposium on Partial Left Ventriculectomy Staff et al. LC 99-51724. 1999. write for info. (*0-444-50279-3*) Elsevier.

Partial Lighting of Interchanges. (National Cooperative Highway Research Program Report Ser.: No. 256). 81p. 1982. 8.40 (*0-309-03451-5*, NR256) Transport Res Bd.

Partial List of Latin American Music Obtainable in the U. S. Leila F. Thompson. 56p. 1993. reprint ed. lib. bdg. 69.00 (*0-7812-9688-9*) Rprt Serv.

Partial-Order Methods for the Verification of Concurrent Systems: An Approach to the State-Explosion Problem. Patrice Godefroid. LC 95-51354. (Lecture Notes in Computer Science Ser.: Vol. 1032). 131p. 1996. pap. 30.00 (*3-540-60761-7*) Spr-Verlag.

Partial Order Methods in Verification: Workshop on Partial Order Methods in Verification, July 24-26, 1996, Princeton University. Artial Order Methods in Verification Staff et al. LC 96-48739. (Dimacs Series in Discrete Mathematics & Theoretical Computer Science: Vol. 29). 403p. 1997. text 85.00 (*0-8218-0579-7*, DIMACS/29) Am Math.

Partial Payments: Essays on Writers & Their Lives. Joseph Epstein. 1991. pap. 12.95 (*0-393-30716-6*) Norton.

Partial Portraits see Works of Henry James Jr.: Collected Works

Partial Portraits. Henry James. LC 74-98842. 408p. 1970. reprint ed. lib. bdg. 35.00 (*0-8371-2797-1*, JAPA, Greenwood Pr) Greenwood.

Partial Portraits. Henry James. LC 68-24939. (Studies of Henry James: No. 17). 1969. reprint ed. lib. bdg. 75.00 (*0-8383-0208-4*) M S G Haskell Hse.

***Partial Portraits, Vol. 72.** Henry James. 2000. pap. 13.95 (*1-892295-65-2*) Green Integer.

Partial Prestressing, from Theory to Practice: Proceedings of NATO Advanced Research Workshop on Partial Prestressing, from Theory to Practice, 2 vols., Vol. I: Survey Reports. Ed. by M. Z. Cohn. 1987. text 440.00 (*90-247-3372-3*) Kluwer Academic.

Partial Prestressing of Concrete Structures. Hugo Bachmann. (IBA Ser.: No. 95). 20p. 1980. 14.50 (*0-8176-1150-9*) Birkhauser.

Partial Quantum Mechanics II. S. Fluegge. (Grundlehren der Mathematischen Wissenschaften Ser.: Band 178). (Illus.). xii, 287p. 1987. 77.50 (*0-317-61425-8*) Spr-Verlag.

***Partial Reason: Critical & Constructive Transformations of Ethics & Epistemology, 78.** Sally E. Talbot. LC 99-88622. (Contributions in Philosophy Ser.: Vol. 78). 2000. write for info. (*0-313-31273-7*, Greenwood Pr) Greenwood.

Partial Recall: Photographs of Native North Americans. Lucy R. Lippard. LC 92-53737. (Illus.). 200p. (Orig.). 1993. 35.00 (*1-56584-016-X*, Pub. by New Press NY); pap. 19.95 (*1-56584-041-0*, Pub. by New Press NY) Norton.

Partial Recall: Photographs of Native North Americans, Vol. 1. unabridged ed. Contrib. by Lucy R. Lippard & Don Desmett. (Illus.). 32p. (Orig.). (C). 1993. pap. 10.00 (*0-614-13761-6*) Temple U Tyler Gal.

Partial Removable Prosthodontics. F. James Kratochvil. (Illus.). 304p. 1988. pap. text 55.00 (*0-7216-2382-4*, W B Saunders Co) Harcrt Hlth Sci Grp.

Partial Seizures & Interictal Disorders: The Neuropsychiatric Elements. David P. Moore. LC 97-4329. 234p. 1997. text 70.00 (*0-7506-9931-0*) Buttrwrth-Heinemann.

Partial Sm - Elementary Statistics. 5th ed. Johnson. (Statistics Ser.). 112p. (C). 1988. pap. 12.50 (*0-534-91773-9*, 36G0234) PWS Pubs.

Partial Sm - Precalculus. Kaufmann. (Math). 192p. (C). 1988. mass mkt. 12.50 (*0-534-91498-5*, 33L4714) PWS Pubs.

Partial Sm - Trigonometry. Kaufmann. (Math). 88p. (C). 1988. mass mkt. 15.00 (*0-534-92153-1*, 33L4734) PWS Pubs.

Partial Sm Operations Research. Winston. 188p. (C). 1987. pap., student ed. 15.00 (*0-87150-113-9*) PWS Pubs.

Partial Solutions Manual T-A Precalculus. 5th ed. Cole. 232p. (C). 1987. mass mkt., teacher ed. 15.50 (*0-87150-147-3*) PWS Pubs.

Partial Solutions Manual to Accompany Applied Finite Math. 2nd ed. Soo T. Tan. 136p. (C). 1987. mass mkt. 17.50 (*0-87150-075-2*) PWS Pubs.

Partial Stability & Control. V. I. Vorotnikov. LC 97-181. 1997. write for info. (*3-7643-3917-9*) Birkhauser.

Partial Stability & Control. V. I. Vorotnikov. LC 97-181. 350p. 1997. 69.95 (*0-8176-3917-9*) Spr-Verlag.

Partial Student Solutions Manual to Accompany a First Course in Differential Equations with Applications. 3rd ed. Wright. (C). 1986. mass mkt. 16.00 (*0-87150-929-6*, 33L3084) PWS Pubs.

Partial to Home: A Memoir of the Heart. Bob Timberlake & Jerry Bledsoe. (Illus.). 304p. 1999. 26.95 (*1-878086-81-2*, Pub. by Down Home NC) Blair.

Partial to Home: Photographs by Birney Imes. Ed. by Constance Sullivan. LC 93-47976. (Photographers at Work Ser.). (Illus.). 60p. (Orig.). 1994. pap. 16.95 (*1-56098-412-0*) Smithsonian.

Partial Truths: A Memoir & Essays on Reading, Writing & Researching. Glenda L. Bissex. LC 96-26639. 1996. pap. text 25.00 (*0-435-07224-2*) Heinemann.

Partial Unemployment: The Regulation of Short Time Working in Britain. Erika M. Szyszczak. Ed. by Bob Hepple & Paul O'Higgins. (Studies in Labour & Social Law). 248p. 1990. text 130.00 (*0-7201-2067-5*); pap. text 40.00 (*0-7201-2068-3*) Continuum.

Partial View: An Alzheimer's Journal. Cary S. Henderson & Nancy Andrews. Ed. by Jackie H. Main et al. LC 98-38368. (Illus.). 120p. 1998. pap. 24.95 (*0-87074-438-0*) SMU Press.

Partial Visions: Culture & Politics in Britain, Canada, & the United States. Richard M. Merelman. LC 91-9089. 300p. (Orig.). (C). 1991. pap. 14.95 (*0-299-12994-2*); lib. bdg. 32.95 (*0-299-12990-X*) U of Wis Pr.

Partiality, Modality & Nonmonotonicity. Ed. & Intro. by Patrick A. Doherty. (Studies in Logic, Language & Information). 312p. (C). 1996. 64.95 (*1-57586-031-7*) CSLI.

Partiality, Modality & Nonmonotonicity. Ed. & Intro. by Patrick A. Doherty. (Studies in Logic, Language & Information). 312p. (C). 1996. pap. 23.95 (*1-57586-030-9*) CSLI.

Partiality of Harbours. Ed. by Manfred Jurgensen. 118p. (C). 1990. 50.00 (*0-9587801-3-7*, Pub. by Pascoe Pub) St Mut.

Partiality, Truth & Persistence. Tore Langholm. LC 88-15015. (CSLI Lecture Notes Ser.: No. 15). 155p. 1988. 54.95 (*0-937073-35-0*); pap. 16.95 (*0-937073-34-2*) CSLI.

Partially Halogenated Chlorofluorocarbons (Ethane Derivatives) (Environmental Health Criteria Ser.: No. 139). (ENG, FRE & SPA.). 130p. 1992. pap. text 29.00 (*92-4-157139-X*, 1160139) World Health.

Partially Halogenated Chlorofluorocarbons (Methane Derivatives) (Environmental Health Criteria Ser.: No. 126). (ENG, FRE & SPA.). 97p. 1991. pap. text 21.00 (*92-4-157126-8*, 1160126) World Health.

Partially Integrable Evolution Equations in Physics. Ed. by Robert Conte & Nino Boccara. (C). 1990. text 309.50 (*0-7923-0752-6*) Kluwer Academic.

Partially Ionized Gases. Morton Mitchner & Charles H. Kruger, Jr. (Illus.). 518p. (C). 1973. reprint ed. pap. text 4.95 (*0-9635646-0-9*) C H Kruger.

***Partially Linear Models.** W. Hardle et al. (Contributions to Statistics Ser.). (Illus.). x, 203p. 2000. pap. 63.00 (*3-7908-1300-1*, Pub. by Physica-Verlag) Spr-Verlag.

Partially Ordered Abelian Groups with Interpolation. K. Goodearl. LC 86-8776. (Mathematical Surveys & Monographs: Vol. 20). 336p. 1986. text 85.00 (*0-8218-1520-2*, SURV/20) Am Math.

Partially Ordered Algebraic Systems. L. Fuchs & Ian N. Sneddon. LC 62-10262. (International Series of Monographs on Pure & Applied Mathematics: Vol. 28). 1963. 113.00 (*0-08-010065-1*, Pub. by Pergamon Repr) Franklin.

Partially Ordered Groups. A. M. Glass. LC 99-20174. 224p. 1998. 36.00 (*981-02-3493-7*) World Scientific Pub.

Partially Ordered Linear Topological Spaces. fac. ed. Isaac Namioka. LC 52-42839. (American Mathematical Society, Memoirs Ser.: No. 24). 56p. 1957. reprint ed. pap. 30.00 (*0-608-01005-7*, 206186300012) Bks Demand.

Partially Ordered Linear Topological Spaces. Isaac Namioka. LC 52-42389. (Memoirs Ser.: No. 1/24). 50p. 1990. reprint ed. pap. 22.00 (*0-8218-1224-6*, MEMO/1/24) Am Math.

Partially Ordered Rings & Semi-Algebraic Geometry. Gregory W. Brumfiel. LC 80-469087. (London Mathematical Society Lecture Note Ser.: No. 37). (Illus.). 288p. reprint ed. pap. 82.10 (*0-608-17518-8*, 2030604) Bks Demand.

Partially Sage: A Comic Look at Common Songs. Shari Ajemian & Sarah Newcomb. LC 83-90154. 130p. (Orig.). 1983. pap. 8.95 (*0-9611994-0-7*) Robinson Lynn Pubs.

Partially Saturated Ocean Detection: Second Order Process Statistics, PARSAT Computer Program Manual. Efstratios Nikolaidis & Anastassios N. Perakis. LC VM0605.. (University of Michigan, Dept. of Naval Architecture & Marine Engineering, Report Ser.: No. 291). 73p. reprint ed. pap. 30.00 (*0-608-12936-4*, 202468700038) Bks Demand.

Partially Specified Matrices & Operators: Classification, Completion, Applications. Israel Gohberg et al. 344p. 1995. 139.00 (*3-7643-5259-0*, Pub. by Birkhauser) Princeton Arch.

Partially Specified Matrices & Operators: Classification, Completion, Applications. Israel Gohberg et al. LC 95-34042. 333p. 1995. 139.00 (*0-8176-5259-0*, Pub. by Birkhauser) Princeton Arch.

Participacion de Organizaciones no-Gubernamentales en la Reduccion de la Pobreza: Estudio de Caso del Proyecto Fondo Hondureno de Inversion Social. Anna K. Webb et al. LC 95-40240. (Doocumentos Para Discusion del Banco Mundial Ser.: No. 295S). 63p. 1995. pap. 22.00 (*0-8213-3440-9*, 13440) World Bank.

Participacion Del Cristiano en la Vida Publica. Jorge S. Elias.Tr. of Christian Participation: Public Life. (SPA.). 1991. pap. 3.50 (*1-56063-042-6*, 490229) Editorial Unilit.

Participant Directed Investment Answer Book, 1. 2nd ed. John M. Maier. LC 98-193419. (Panel Answer Book Ser.). 680p. 1998. boxed set. write for info. (*1-56706-898-7*) Panel Pubs.

Participant Guidebook: My Life . . . Right Now. Community Intervention, Inc. Staff. (Illus.). 52p. (YA). (gr. 7-12). 1988. student ed. 3.50 (*0-9613416-9-6*) Comm Intervention.

Participant Observation. James P. Spradley. 208p. (C). 1980. pap. text 39.00 (*0-03-044501-9*, Pub. by Harcourt Coll Pubs) Harcourt.

Participant Observation: A Methodology for Human Studies. Danny L. Jorgensen. (Applied Social Research Methods Ser.: Vol. 15). 160p. (C). 1989. text 42.00 (*0-8039-2876-9*); pap. text 18.95 (*0-8039-2877-7*) Sage.

Participant Observation: The Psychotherapy Schools in Action. Leston L. Havens. LC 84-45109. 184p. 1993. pap. 30.00 (*1-56821-108-2*) Aronson.

Participant Observation in Organizational Settings. Robert Bogdan. LC 72-85383. (Segregated Settings & the Problems of Change Ser.: No. 3). 106p. 1972. text 27.50 (*0-8156-8080-5*) Syracuse U Pr.

Participant Observer: An Autobiography. William F. Whyte. LC 93-47550. 376p. 1994. text 57.50 (*0-87546-324-X*, ILR Press) Cornell U Pr.

Participant Observer: An Autobiography. William F. Whyte. LC 93-47550. (Illus.). 376p. 1994. pap. text 24.95 (*0-87546-325-8*, ILR Press) Cornell U Pr.

Participant Workbook. Richard Beckhard. 1985. pap. text 14.95 (*0-201-10722-8*) Addison-Wesley.

Participantes - Participant. Rogelio Archilla. (SPA.). 150p. 1995. write for info. (*1-56063-696-3*) Editorial Unilit.

Participant's Guide to Capturing Joy. Zondervan Publishing Staff. (Women of Faith - Capture the Joy Ser.). 96p. 1999. pap. 6.99 (*0-310-23099-3*) Zondervan.

***Participants in Old Testament Texts & the Translator: Reference Devices & Their Rhetorical Impact.** L. J. De Regt. viii, 125p. 1999. text 70.00 (*90-232-3444-8*, Pub. by Van Gorcum) Eisenbrauns.

Participants in the Trial (Strasbourg, 29-31 May, 1996) (Programme Themis Ser.). 1997. 21.00 (*92-871-3222-4*, Pub. by Council of Europe) Manhattan Pub Co.

Participant's Problem-Solving Manual for Kick down the Door of Complacency: Sieze the Power of Continuous Improvement. Charles C. Harwood. 74p. 1998. per. 19.95 (*1-57444-209-0*, SL2090) St Lucie Pr.

***Participassion 101.** Lisa Bell. 2000. write for info. (*1-893569-07-1*) Accolade Pub Co.

Participating in Explanatory Dialogues: Interpreting & Responding to Questions in Context. Joanna D. Moore. (ACL-MIT Series in Natural Language Processing). (Illus.). 366p. 1994. 55.00 (*0-262-13301-6*, Bradford Bks) MIT Pr.

Participating in Government see Community Service for Teens

Participating in Nature: Outline for an Ecologization of Our World View. Wim Zweers. 320p. 1998. pap. 29.95 (*90-5727-010-2*, Pub. by Intl Bks) Paul & Co Pubs.

***Participating in Nature: Thomas J. Elpel's Field Guide to Primitive Living Skills.** 4th rev. ed. Thomas J. Elpel. LC 99-60832. (Illus.). 151p. 1999. pap. 16.95 (*1-892784-04-1*) HOPS Pr.

Participating in the Management Process. 113p. 1997. pap. 11.00 (*0-16-042718-5*) USGPO.

Participating in the Mission of the Church: First Principles of Community Purpose. Jeff Reed. Ed. by Nancy Reed. (First Principles Ser.). (Illus.). 64p. 1997. pap. 6.99 (*1-891441-02-7*) LearnCorp Res.

Participating in Worship: History, Theory, & Practice. Craig D. Erickson. 216p. 1989. pap. 18.95 (*0-8042-1900-1*) Westminster John Knox.

Participating Life Insurance Sold by Stock Companies. Joseph M. Belth. (C). 1964. 10.00 (*0-256-00639-3*, Irwn McGrw-H) McGrw-H Hghr Educ.

Participating Reader. S. Wittig et al. 1978. pap. 12.95 (*0-685-03888-2*) P-H.

***Participating Watershed Development Challenges for the Twenty-First Century.** John Farrington et al. 368p. 2000. text 25.00 (*0-19-565135-9*) OUP.

Participation: A Platonic Inquiry. fac. ed. Charles P. Bigger. LC 68-21802. 239p. 1968. reprint ed. pap. 74.10 (*0-7837-7935-6*, 204769100008) Bks Demand.

Participation & Commitment Among Malaysian Professionals. Razali Mat Zin. LC 98-944674. 162p. 1998. write for info. (*967-942-411-1*) Penerbit U KB.

Participation & Democracy East & West: Comparisons & Interpretations. Ed. by Dietrich Rueschemeyer et al. LC 97-50400. 304p. (C). (gr. 13). 1998. text 73.95 (*0-7656-0229-6*) M E Sharpe.

Participation & Democracy East & West: Comparisons & Interpretations. Ed. & Intro. by Dietrich Rueschemeyer et al. LC 97-50400. (Illus.). 304p. 1998. pap. text 32.95 (*0-7656-0230-X*) M E Sharpe.

Participation & Democratic Theory. Carole Pateman. LC 71-120193. 122p. 1976. pap. text 20.95 (*0-521-29004-X*) Cambridge U Pr.

Participation & Partnership in Urban Infrastructure Management. LC 96-1616. (Urban Management Programme Ser.). 112p. 1996. pap. 22.00 (*0-8213-3650-9*) World Bank.

Participation & Policy Making in the European Union. Ed. by Helen Wallace & Alasdair R. Young. LC 97-20428. (Illus.). 304p. 1997. text 65.00 (*0-19-828060-2*) OUP.

Participation & Political Equality: A Seven-Nation Comparison. Sidney Verba et al. LC 87-10781. xxii, 416p. (C). 1987. pap. text 29.00 (*0-226-85298-9*) U Ch Pr.

Participation & Social Assessment: Tools & Techniques. Jennifer Rietbergen-McCracken & Deepa Narayan. LC 98-14646. 360p. 1998. 60.00 incl. VHS (*0-8213-4186-3*, 14186) World Bank.

Participation & Substantiality in Thomas Aquinas. Rudi A. Velde. LC 95-193704. xiv, 290p. 1995. 112.50 (*90-04-10381-3*) Brill Academic Pubs.

Participation & the Community see Progress in Planning

***Participation & the Good: A Study of Boethian Metaphysics.** Siobhan Nash-Marshall. LC 99-50966. 320p. 2000. pap. 49.95 (*0-8245-1852-7*, Pub. by Crossroad NY) Natl Bk Netwk.

***Participation & the Quality of Environmental Decision Making.** Frans H. Coenen et al. LC 98-34745. (Environment & Policy Ser.). 27p. 1998. 149.00 (*0-7923-5264-5*) Kluwer Academic.

Participation, Associations, Development & Change. Albert Meister. Tr. by Jack L. Ross from FRE. (Illus.). 286p. 1984. 39.95 (*0-87855-423-8*) Transaction Pubs.

Participation by Citizens-Consumers in the Management of Local Public Services. (Local & Regional Authorities in Europe Ser.: No. 54). 1994. 12.00 (*92-871-2492-2*, Pub. by Council of Europe) Manhattan Pub Co.

Participation by Families of Mentally Handicapped People in Policy Making & Planning. Alan Tyne. 1979. 60.00 (*0-7855-0571-7*, Pub. by Natl Inst Soc Work) St Mut.

Participation, Development, & Social Structure. M. Bazlul Karim. LC 93-31774. 52.50 (*0-8191-9318-6*) U Pr of Amer.

Participation in America: Political Democracy & Social Equality. Sidney Verba & Norman H. Nie. LC 87-10825. xxvi, 452p. (C). 1999. pap. text 18.95 (*0-226-85296-2*) U Ch Pr.

Participation in American Politics: The Dynamics of Agenda Building. 2nd ed. Roger W. Cobb & Charles D. Elder. LC 83-48051. (Illus.). 210p. reprint ed. pap. 65.10 (*0-8357-8259-X*, 203414900088) Bks Demand.

Participation in Congress. Richard L. Hall. LC 96-15778. 288p. 1996. 42.50 (*0-300-06811-5*); pap. 18.00 (*0-300-07651-7*) Yale U Pr.

Participation in Curriculum Making As a Means of Supervision of Rural Schools. William J. Holloway. LC 77-178805. (Columbia University. Teachers College. Contributions to Education Ser.: No. 301). reprint ed. 37.50 (*0-404-55301-X*) AMS Pr.

P

Participation in Government: Making a Difference. 3rd rev. ed. Ralph Ketcham et al. (Illus.). 354p. 1996. text 35.00 (*0-87411-824-7*) Copley Pub.

Participation in Housing No. 1: Theory & Implementation. Ed. by N. Handi & B. Greenstreet. (C). 1981. 35.00 (*0-7855-3860-7*, Pub. by Oxford Polytechnic) St Mut.

Participation in Housing No. 2: The Legal & Administrative Framework. Ed. by N. Handi & B. Greenstreet. (C). 1981. 40.00 (*0-7855-3859-3*, Pub. by Oxford Polytechnic) St Mut.

Participation in Housing No. 3: Two Case Studies. Ed. by N. Handi & B. Greenstreet. (C). 1981. 29.00 (*0-7855-3858-5*, Pub. by Oxford Polytechnic) St Mut.

Participation in Human Inquiry. Ed. by Peter Reason. 240p. 1995. 69.95 (*0-8039-8831-1*); pap. 26.95 (*0-8039-8832-X*) Sage.

Participation in Local Social Services: An Explanatory Study-Discussion Paper. Rose Deakin & Phyllis Willmot. 1979. 30.00 (*0-7855-0570-9*, Pub. by Natl Inst Soc Work) St Mut.

Participation in Organizational Change: The TVA Experiment. Aaron J. Nurick. LC 84-26652. 255p. 1985. 59.95 (*0-275-90149-1*, C0149, Praeger Pubs) Greenwood.

Participation in Practice: The Experience of the World Bank & Other Stakeholders, Vol. 333. Jennifer Rietbergen-McCracken & World Bank Staff. LC 96-22256. (Discussion Papers: No. 333). 112p. 1997. pap. 22.00 (*0-8213-3684-3*, 13684) World Bank.

Participation in Public Policy-Making: The Role of Trade Unions & Employees' Associations. Ed. by Tiziano Treu. xii, 282p. (C). 1992. lib. bdg. 121.55 (*3-11-012913-2*) De Gruyter.

Participation in Rural Life. Mildred B. Young. (C). 1942. pap. 4.00 (*0-87574-019-7*) Pendle Hill.

Participation in Services for the Handicapped: Two Contrasting Models-Discussion Paper. Colin Low et al. 1979. 30.00 (*0-7855-0569-5*, Pub. by Natl Inst Soc Work) St Mut.

Participation in the Social Security System: Experiments in Local Consulation. Paul Swift et al. (Illus.). 192p. 1994. 64.95 (*1-85628-533-2*, Pub. by Avebry) Ashgate Pub Co.

Participation in World Treaties on the Protection of the Environment: A Collection of Data. Ed. by Maria C. Maffei et al. LC 97-113541. (International Environmental Law & Policy Ser.). 290p. 1997. text 114.00 (*90-411-0879-3*, K3583) Kluwer Law Intl.

Participation in Zambia, 1974. Peter Jambrek. LC 79-63205. 1979. write for info. (*0-89138-981-4*) ICPSR.

Participation of Black, Hispanic, Asian, & Native Americans in American Orchestras: 1991-92 Inclusiveness Survey. 111p. 1992. pap. 20.00 (*0-614-04620-3*) Am Symphony Orch.

Participation of Federally Qualified Health Centers in Medicaid Case Management Programs. L. Carl Volpe & Tim M. Henderson. 58p. (Orig.). 1992. pap. text 15.00 (*1-55877-161-1*) Natl Governor.

Participation of Foreigners in Public Life at a Local Level: Explantory Report on the Convention Opened for Signature on 5 February, 1992. Council of Europe Staff. (Conventions & Agreements Ser.: No. 144). (ENG & FRE.). 1993. 12.00 (*92-871-2084-6*, Pub. by Council of Europe) Manhattan Pub Co.

Participation of Nongovernmental Organizations in Poverty Alleviation: A Case Study of the Honduras Social Investment Fund Project, Vol. 295. Anna K. Webb et al. LC 95-19587. (World Bank Discussion Papers: No. 295). 60p. 1995. pap. 22.00 (*0-8213-3423-9*, 13423) World Bank.

Participation of People with Disabilities: International Perspectives. World Congress of Rehabilitation International Sta. 1981. 4.50 (*0-686-94877-7*) Rehab Intl.

Participation of States in International Contracts & Arbitral Settlement of Disputes. Esa Paasivirta. 346p. (Orig.). 1990. pap. 147.50 (*951-640-519-3*) Coronet Bks.

Participation of the Poor in Rural Development Programmes: Selected Case Studies. B. Sam Bob. LC 98-903262. x, 112p. 1998. 21.00 (*81-7141-409-5*, Pub. by Discovery Pub Hse) Nataraj Bks.

Participation of Women in Decision Making for Peace. 50p. Date not set. pap. 12.50 (*92-1-130156-4*, E.93.IV.3) UN.

Participation of Women in Decision-Making for Peace: Case Study on Sweden. 105p. pap. 9.95 (*92-1-130135-1*, E.89.IV.7) UN.

Participation, Organizational Effectiveness & Quality of Work Life in the Year 2000. Ed. by Litsa Nicolaou-Smokoviti & Gyorgy Szell. LC 94-43952. (Illus.). 456p. 1994. pap. 57.95 (*3-631-47924-7*) P Lang Pubng.

Participation, Power-Sharing, & School Improvement. Bernard Trafford. LC 98-194746. 130p. 1997. pap. 15.95 (*1-900219-10-7*, Pub. by Educ Heretics) Intl Spec Bk.

Participation Rates, Efficiency, & Characteristics of Workers. CFNPP Staff & R. Sudarshan Canagarajah. (Working Papers). (C). 1992. pap. 7.00 (*1-56401-130-5*) Cornell Food.

Participation Works: Business Cases from Around the World. Ed. by James P. Troxel. LC 93-31681. (Business Ser.). (Illus.). 154p. (C). 1993. pap. text 24.95 (*0-917917-03-0*) Miles River.

Participative Leader. Suzanne Zoglio. 112p. 1995. pap. 10.95 (*0-7863-0252-6*, Irwn Prfssnl) McGraw-Hill Prof.

Participative Leader: From Autocracy to Empowerment. Jerome M. Rosow & Jill Casner-Lotto. (New Roles for Managers Ser.: Pt. V). 131p. 1993. 95.00 (*0-89361-044-5*) Work in Amer.

Participative Leader, Tower Hill Press Special Edition. Suzanne W. Zoglio. 1994. per. write for info. (*0-7863-0364-6*, Irwn Prfssnl) McGraw-Hill Prof.

Participative Management. William P. Anthony. LC 77-83035. 1978. pap. text. write for info. (*0-201-00253-1*) Addison-Wesley.

Participative Management. Harvard Business Review Staff. (People Management Ser.). 115p. 1991. pap. 19.95 (*0-87584-266-6*) Harvard Busn.

Participative Management. Harvard Business School Press Staff. 100p. 1991. pap. 1995.00 (*0-07-103326-2*) McGraw.

Participative Management. Fred Massarik. (Studies in Productivity: Highlights of the Literature Ser.: Vol. 28). 40p. 1983. pap. 55.00 (*0-08-029509-6*) Work in Amer.

Participative Management: An Analysis of Its Effect on Productivity. Michael H. Swearingen. LC 96-46725. (Garland Studies on Industrial Productivity). 104p. 1997. text 35.00 (*0-8153-2825-7*) Garland.

Participative Management in Academic Libraries, 16. Maurice P. Marchant. LC 76-8740. (Contributions in Librarianship & Information Science Ser.: No. 16). 260p. 1977. 45.00 (*0-8371-8935-7*, MPM/, Greenwood Pr) Greenwood.

Participative Prince: Techniques for Developing Your Organization & Improving Its Performance. Daniel A. Tagliere. LC 79-83886. (Illus.). 1979. 14.95 (*0-9602516-0-X*) ODS Pubns.

Participative Strategies for Science-Based Innovations. Joske F. Bunders. 1995. pap. 25.00 (*90-5383-342-0*) Paul & Co Pubs.

Participative Systems at Work: Creating Quality & Employment Security. Ed. by Sidney P. Rubinstein. LC 86-20044. 180p. 1987. 30.95 (*0-89885-338-9*, Kluwer Acad Hman Sci) Kluwer Academic.

Participative Training Skills. John Rodwell. Ed. by Billie Taylor. LC 94-1072. 192p. 1994. 96.95 (*0-566-07444-3*, Pub. by Gower) Ashgate Pub Co.

Participatory Action Research. Ed. by William F. Whyte. (Focus Editions Ser.: Vol. 123). 248p. (C). 1990. text 59.95 (*0-8039-3742-3*); pap. text 26.00 (*0-8039-3743-1*) Sage.

Participatory Action Research: International Contexts & Consequences. Ed. by Robin McTaggart. LC 96-52807. (SUNY Series, Teacher Preparation & Development). (Illus.). 283p. (C). 1997. pap. text 19.95 (*0-7914-3534-2*) State U NY Pr.

Participatory Action Research: International Contexts & Consequences. Ed. by Robin McTaggart. LC 96-52807. (SUNY Series, Teacher Preparation & Development). (Illus.). 283p. (C). 1997. text 59.50 (*0-7914-3533-4*) State U NY Pr.

Participatory Analysis, Monitoring & Evaluation for Fishing Communities: A Manual. R. A. Maine et al. (Fisheries Technical Papers: No. 364). 142p. 1997. pap. 19.00 (*92-5-103919-4*, F39194, Pub. by FAO) Bernan Associates.

Participatory & Workplace Democracy: A Theoretical Development in Critique of Liberalism. Ronald M. Mason. LC 81-16687. 268p. 1982. 31.95 (*0-8093-0992-0*) S Ill U Pr.

Participatory Approach to Rural AIDS Education: A Workshop Manual. limited ed. Isaac Bekalo. 94p. 1992. 4.00 (*0-942717-40-6*) Intl Inst Rural.

Participatory Approach to Urban Planning. Edmund M. Burke. LC 78-31107. 304p. 1979. 42.95 (*0-87705-393-6*, Kluwer Acad Hman Sci) Kluwer Academic.

Participatory Approaches to Agricultural Research & Development: A State-of-the-Art Paper. William F. Whyte. (Special Series on Agriculture Research & Extension: No. 1). 111p. (Orig.). (C). 1981. pap. 8.15 (*0-86731-053-7*) Cornell CIS RDC.

Participatory Approaches to Poverty Alleviation in Rural Community Development. 34p. 10.00 (*92-1-130194-7*) UN.

Participatory Communication: Working for Change & Development. Joseph R. Ascroft. Ed. by Shirley A. White et al. LC 93-34804. (Communication & Human Values Ser.). 1994. pap. 24.95 (*0-8039-9143-6*) Sage.

Participatory Communication: Working for Change & Development. Joseph R. Ascroft. Ed. by Shirley A. White et al. LC 93-34804. (Communication & Human Values Ser.). 436p. 1994. 52.00 (*0-8039-9142-8*) Sage.

Participatory Communication for Social Change. Ed. by Jan Servaes et al. LC 95-50801. (Communication & Human Values Ser.). 276p. 1996. 38.00 (*0-8039-9295-5*); pap. 17.95 (*0-8039-9296-3*) Sage.

Participatory Communication in Nonformal Education. John Comings. (Technical Notes Ser.: No. 17). 15p. (Orig.). 1981. pap. 2.00 (*0-932288-62-6*) Ctr Intl Ed U of MA.

***Participatory Curriculum Development in Agriculture Education: A Training Guide.** FAO Staff. 162p. 1999. pap. 21.00 (*92-5-104272-1*, Pub. by FAO) Bernan Associates.

Participatory Democracy: Populism Revived. Joseph F. Zimmerman. LC 86-8129. 241p. 1986. 55.00 (*0-275-92132-8*, C2132, Praeger Pubs) Greenwood.

Participatory Democracy for Canada: Workers' Control & Community Control. Ed. by Gerry Hunnius. LC 72-196465. (Black Rose Bks.: Vol. B5). 93p. 1971. reprint ed. pap. 30.00 (*0-608-00456-1*, 206127500007) Bks Demand.

Participatory Democracy in Zambia. Patrick E. Ollawa. 520p. 1985. 60.00 (*0-7855-0784-1*, Pub. by A H S Ltd); pap. 60.00 (*0-7855-0785-X*, Pub. by A H S Ltd) St Mut.

Participatory Democracy in Zambia. Patrick E. Ollawa. 520p. (C). 1990. 60.00 (*0-7855-6535-3*, Pub. by A H S Ltd); pap. 50.00 (*0-7223-1214-8*, Pub. by A H S Ltd) St Mut.

Participatory Design: Perspectives on Systems Design. Ed. by Douglas Schuler & Aki Namioka. LC 92-27297. 312p. 1993. 69.95 (*0-8058-0951-1*); pap. 32.50 (*0-8058-0952-X*) L Erlbaum Assocs.

Participatory Design: Theory & Techniques. Intro. by Henry Sanoff. (Illus.). 210p. (Orig.). (C). 1990. pap. text 15.00 (*0-9622107-3-0*) H Sanoff.

Participatory Development: People & Common Property Resources. Kanchan Chopra et al. (Illus.). 152p. (C). 1990. text 22.00 (*0-8039-9631-4*) Sage.

Participatory Development & the World Bank: Potential Directions for Change. Ed. by Bhuvana Bhatnagar & Aubrey C. Williams. LC 92-34236. (Discussion Papers: Vol. 183). 202p. 1992. pap. 22.00 (*0-8213-2249-4*, 12249) World Bank.

Participatory Development from Advocacy to Action. OECD Staff. Ed. by Hartmut Schneider & Marie-Helene Libercier. 250p. (Orig.). 1995. pap. 50.00 (*92-64-14539-7*, Pub. by Org for Econ) OECD.

Participatory Development Tool Kit: Materials to Facilitate Community Empowerment. Deepa Narayan & Lyra Srinivasan. 1994. pap. 40.00 (*0-8213-2687-2*, 12687) World Bank.

Participatory Development Training Manual. 300p. 1994. write for info. (*92-806-3127-6*) U N I C E.

Participatory Economics see Looking Forward: Participatory Economics for the Twenty-First Century

Participatory Economy: An Evolutionary Hypothesis & a Strategy for Development. Jaroslav Vanek. LC 77-148024. (Illus.). 208p. 1971. 42.50 (*0-8014-0639-0*) Cornell U Pr.

Participatory Economy: An Evolutionary Hypothesis & a Strategy for Development. Jaroslav Vanek. LC 77-148024. (Illus.). 208p. 1975. pap. 15.95 (*0-8014-9148-7*) Cornell U Pr.

Participatory Employee Ownership: How It Works. John Logue et al. (Illus.). 192p. 1998. pap. text 14.95 (*0-933522-24-X*); lib. bdg. 24.95 (*0-933522-23-1*) Kent Popular.

Participatory Ergonomics. Ed. by A. Imada & Kageyu Noro. 350p. 1991. 110.00 (*0-85066-382-2*) Taylor & Francis.

Participatory Evaluation: Tools for Managing Change in Water & Sanitation. Deepa Narayan. LC 93-4478. (Technical Papers: No. 207). 136p. 1993. pap. 22.00 (*0-8213-2477-2*, 12477) World Bank.

Participatory Evaluation in Education: Studies in Evaluation Use & Organizational Learning. Ed. by J. Bradley Cousins & Lorna M. Earl. LC 95-7253. 224p. 1995. 79.95 (*0-7507-0402-0*, Falmer Pr); pap. 34.95 (*0-7507-0403-9*, Falmer Pr) Taylor & Francis.

Participatory Information Systems: Analysis & Design in Developing Countries. 2nd ed. Simon Bell. LC 95-39837. (Studies in Information & Library Management Systems Ser.: Vol. 1). 248p. (C). 1996. 85.00 (*0-415-10603-6*) Routledge.

Participatory Literacy Education. Ed. by Arlene Fingeret & Paul Jurmo. LC 85-644750. (New Directions for Adult & Continuing Education Ser.: No. ACE 42). 1989. pap. 22.00 (*1-55542-861-4*) Jossey-Bass.

Participatory Local Governance: Life's Method & Experience, 1992-1997. (Technical Publications: No. 1). 123p. 1997. pap. 20.00 (*92-1-126073-6*) UN.

Participatory Management in Libraries. Donald J. Sager. LC 82-783. (Library Administration Ser.: No. 3). 216p. 1982. 26.50 (*0-8108-1530-3*) Scarecrow.

Participatory Planning in Community Health Education. Preston L. Schiller et al. LC 86-51164. 210p. 1987. pap. 15.95 (*0-89914-024-6*) Third Party Pub.

Participatory Plant Breeding: Proceedings of a Workshop. Ed. by P. Eyzaguirre & M. Iwanaga. (Illus.). 164p. (Orig.). (C). 1997. pap. text 35.00 (*0-7881-4550-9*) DIANE Pub.

***Participatory Practices in Adult Education.** Ed. by Pat Campbell & Barbara Burnaby. 320p. 2001. write for info. (*0-8058-3704-3*) L Erlbaum Assocs.

***Participatory Practices in Adult Education.** Ed. by Pat Campbell & Barbara J. Burnaby. 320p. 2001. pap. write for info. (*0-8058-3705-1*) L Erlbaum Assocs.

Participatory Process: Producing Photo-Literature. Bonnie Cain & John Comings. (Illus.). 40p. (Orig.). (C). 1977. pap. 4.00 (*0-932288-45-6*) Ctr Intl Ed U of MA.

Participatory Research: An Annotated Bibliography. Ed. by Center for International Education & Center for Co. 56p. 1991. spiral bd. 8.00 (*0-932288-88-X*) Ctr Intl Ed U of MA.

Participatory Research & Health. Ed. by Korrie De Koning. LC 95-41659. 256p. (C). 1996. text 65.00 (*1-85649-351-2*, Pub. by Zed Books) St Martin.

Participatory Rural Appraisal: Methods & Applications in Rural Planning. Ed. by A. Mukherjee. 1995. 38.00 (*0-7069-8466-8*, Pub. by Vikas) S Asia.

Participatory Rural Appraisal Practical Experiences. J. Nabasa et al. 1995. pap. 25.00 (*0-85954-392-7*, Pub. by Nat Res Inst) St Mut.

Participatory Video: A Practical Approach to Using Video Creatively in Group Development Work. Jackie Shaw & Clive Robertson. LC 96-36349. (Illus.). 304p. (C). 1997. 90.00 (*0-415-14104-4*) Routledge.

Participatory Video: A Practical Approach to Using Video Creatively in Group Development Work. Jackie Shaw & Clive Robertson. LC 96-36349. (Illus.). 304p. (C). 1997. pap. 27.99 (*0-415-14105-2*) Routledge.

***Participe Passe en Francais.** Lise Lapierre. (Leipzinger Fachsprachen-Studien: Bd. 13). (Illus.). 175p. 1998. 38.00 (*3-631-33223-8*) P Lang Pubng.

Particle Acceleration & Trapping in Solar Flares. Ed. by G. Trottet & M. Pick. (C). 1987. text 146.00 (*90-277-2609-4*) Kluwer Academic.

Particle Acceleration in Cosmic Plasmas. Ed. by G. P. Zank & Thomas K. Gaisser. LC 92-73316. (AIP Conference Proceedings Ser.: No. 264). 498p. 1992. 120.00 (*0-88318-948-8*) Am Inst Physics.

Particle Acceleration in Space Plasmas. Ed. by J. B. Blake & J. A. Slavin. 128p. 1998. pap. 123.50 (*0-08-043312-X*, Pergamon Pr) Elsevier.

Particle Acceleration Mechanics in Astrophysics. Ed. by J. Arrons et al. LC 79-55844. (AIP Conference Proceedings Ser.: No. 56). (Illus.). 425p. 1979. lib. bdg. 22.00 (*0-88318-155-X*) Am Inst Physics.

Particle Acceleration near Accreting Compact Objects. J. van Paradijs et al. (Verhandelingen der Koninklijke Nederlandse Akademie van Wetenschappen, Afd. Natuurkunde Ser.: No. 35). 132p. 1991. pap. text 27.50 (*0-444-85735-4*) Elsevier.

Particle Acceleration Processes, Shockwaves, Nucleosynthesis & Cosmic Rays: Proceedings of Symposia 6 & 8 & the Joint Sessions 6-8 of the COSPAR Twenty-fifth Plenary Meeting Held in Graz, Austria, 25 June to 7 July 1984. Ed. by L. Koch-Miramond & M. A. Lee. (Illus.). 542p. 1985. pap. 110.00 (*0-08-032711-7*, Pergamon Pr) Elsevier.

Particle Accelerator Physics: Basic Principles & Linear Beam Dynamics. Helmut Wiedemann. LC 93-10040. (Illus.). 461p. 1993. 59.95 (*0-387-56550-7*); write for info. (*3-540-56550-7*) Spr-Verlag.

Particle Accelerator Physics No. II: Nonlinear & Higher-Order Beam Dynamics. 2nd ed. H. Wiedemann. LC 98-34218. (Illus.). xvi, 464p. 1998. 79.95 (*3-540-64504-7*) Spr-Verlag.

Particle Accelerator Physics I: Basic Principles & Linear Beam Dynamics. 2nd ed. Helmut Wiedemann. LC 98-46048. (Illus.). xviii, 469p. 1999. 94.00 (*3-540-64671-X*) Spr-Verlag.

Particle Accelerator Physics II: Nonlinear & Higher-Order Beam Dynamics. Helmut Wiedemann. LC 94-35447. 1995. 59.95 (*0-387-57564-2*) Spr-Verlag.

Particle Accelerators: A Brief History. Milton S. Livingston. LC 69-18038. (Illus.). 128p. reprint ed. pap. 39.70 (*0-7837-4167-7*, 205901600012) Bks Demand.

***Particle Accelerators Beam Measurements.** S. I. Kurokawa. 1999. 156.00 (*981-02-3881-9*) World Scientific Pub.

Particle Accelerators & Their Uses, 2 vols., 1. Waldemar H. Scharf. (Accelerators & Storage Rings Ser.). 1000p. 1986. 138.00 (*3-7186-0034-X*) Gordon & Breach.

Particle Accelerators & Their Uses, 2 vols., 1. Waldemar H. Scharf. xviii, 676p. 1986. text 223.00 (*3-7186-0533-3*) Gordon & Breach.

Particle Accelerators & Their Uses, 2 vols., Set. Waldemar H. Scharf. (Accelerators & Storage Rings Ser.). 1000p. 1986. 235.00 (*3-7186-0318-7*) Gordon & Breach.

Particle Accelerators & Their Uses, 2 vols., Vol. 2. Waldemar H. Scharf. (Accelerators & Storage Rings Ser.). xviii, 374p. 1986. 138.00 (*3-7186-0317-9*) Gordon & Breach.

Particle Accelerators & Their Uses, 2 vols., Vol. 2. Waldemar H. Scharf. xxxvi, 1050p. 1986. text 316.00 (*3-7186-0535-X*); text 223.00 (*3-7186-0534-1*) Gordon & Breach.

Particle Accelerators, 46 - 1-3. Ed. by Eberhard Keil. 196p. 1994. pap. text 813.00 (*2-88449-021-3*) Gordon & Breach.

Particle Analysis in Oceanography. Ed. by S. Demers. (NATO ASI Series G: Ecological Sciences: Vol. 27). (Illus.). 416p. 1991. 288.95 (*0-387-51763-4*) Spr-Verlag.

***Particle & Fields.** Ed. by Joao C. A. Barata et al. 500p. 2000. 96.00 (*981-02-4254-9*) World Scientific Pub.

Particle & Nuclear Astrophysics & Cosmology in the Next Millennium. LC 96-139609. 628p. 1995. 41.00 (*981-02-2488-5*) World Scientific Pub.

Particle & Nuclear Physics: Proceedings of the International Symposium, Beijing, China, September 2-7, 1985. Ed. by N. Hu & C. S. Wu. xii, 452 p. 1986. text 117.00 (*9971-5-0175-9*) World Scientific Pub.

Particle Astrophysics. H. V. Klapdor-Kleingrothaus & K. Zuber. Tr. by S. M. Foster & B. Foster from GER. LC 97-22009. 1997. write for info. (*0-7503-0403-0*) IOP Pub.

***Particle Astrophysics.** rev. ed. H. V. Klapdor-Kleingrothaus & K. Zuber. LC 99-50115. (Studies in High Energy Physics, Cosmology & Gravitation Ser.). 507p. 2000. pap. write for info. (*0-7503-0549-5*) IOP Pub.

Particle Astrophysics: Forefront Experimental Issues. Ed. by E. B. Norman. 388p. (C). 1989. pap. 40.00 (*9971-5-0869-9*); text 108.00 (*9971-5-0835-4*) World Scientific Pub.

Particle Astrophysics: The NASA Cosmic Ray Program for the 1990's & Beyond. Ed. by W. Vernon Jones et al. LC 90-55077. (AIP Conference Proceedings Ser.: No. 203). (Illus.). 344p. 1992. lib. bdg. 70.00 (*0-88318-763-9*) Am Inst Physics.

Particle Astrophysics & Cosmology: Proceedings of the NATO Advanced Study Institute, Erice, Italy, June 20-30, 1992. Ed. by Maurice M. Shapiro. (NATO ASI Series C, Mathematical & Physical Sciences). 160p. (C). 1993. text 120.50 (*0-7923-2235-5*) Kluwer Academic.

Particle Attrition. 55.00 (*0-87849-076-0*, Pub. by Trans T Pub) Enfield Pubs NH.

Particle Beam Microanalysis: Fundamentals, Mods, & Applications. Ekkehad Fuchs et al. (Illus.). 508p. 1990. 120.00 (*3-527-26884-7*, Wiley-VCH) Wiley.

Particle Bombardment for Genetic Engineering of Plants. Paul Christou. (Biotechnology Intelligence Unit Ser.). 1996. text 69.95 (*0-12-174410-8*) Acad Pr.

Particle Bombardment for Genetic Engineering of Plants. Paul Christou. LC 96-21774. (Biotechnology Intelligence Unit Ser.). 173p. 1996. 79.00 (*1-57059-357-4*) Landes Bioscience.

Particle Century. Gordon Fraser. LC 98-41655. xxii, 232p. 1998. 59.50 (*0-7503-0543-6*) IOP Pub.

***Particle Characterization: Light Scattering Methods.** J. Perry Gustafson. 432p. 2000. 172.00 (*0-7923-6300-0*, Kluwer Plenum) Kluwer Academic.

Particle Characterization in Technology. John K. Beddow. Incl. Vol. I. Applications & Microanalysis. 264p. 1984. 147.00 (*0-8493-5784-5*, TA418, CRC Reprint); Vol. II. Morphological Analysis. 288p. 1984. 157.00 (*0-8493-5785-3*, TA418, CRC Reprint); 1984. 170.00 (*0-318-60684-4*) CRC Pr.

Particle Control for Semiconductor Manufacturing. Ed. by R. P. Donovan. (Illus.). 504p. 1990. text 185.00 (*0-8247-8242-9*) Dekker.

Particle Counting in Radioactivity Measurements. Ed. by W. Roger Ney. (ICRU Reports: No. 52). 84p. 1994. pap. text 50.00 (*0-913394-51-3*) Intl Comm Rad Meas.

Particle Deposition & Aggregation: Measurement, Modeling & Simulation. M. Elimelech et al. LC 94-41069. (Colloid & Surface Engineering Ser.). (Illus.). 458p. 1995. pap. 160.00 (*0-7506-0743-2*, Focal) Buttrwrth-Heinemann.

Particle Deposition & Aggregation, Measurement, Modeling & Simulation. John Gregory et al. 440p. 1998. pap. 65.00 (*0-7506-7024-X*) Buttrwrth-Heinemann.

Particle Design Via Crystallization. Ed. by R. Ramanarayanan. LC 91-29216. (AIChE Symposium Ser.: Vol. 87, No. 284). 203p. 1991. pap. text 35.00 (*0-8169-0553-3*) Am Inst Chem Eng.

Particle Detection with Drift Chambers. Werner Blum & L. Roland. LC 94-32036. 1994. 76.95 (*0-387-58322-X*) Spr-Verlag.

P

An Asterisk (*) at the beginning of an entry indicates that the title is appearing for the first time.

Particle Detection with Drift Chambers. Werner Blum & L. Rolandi. LC 93-13632. (Illus.). xv, 346p. 1993. 119.00 (*0-387-56425-X*) Spr-Verlag.

Particle Detection with Drift Chambers. Werner Blum & L. Rolandi. LC 94-32036. 1994. write for info. (*3-540-58322-X*) Spr-Verlag.

Particle Detector BriefBook. R. K. Bock & A. Vasilescu. (Accelerator Physics Ser.). (Illus.). v, 126p. 1998. 29.95 (*3-540-64120-3*) Spr-Verlag.

Particle Detectors. Claus Grupen. (Monographs on Particle Physics, Nuclear Physics & Cosmology: No. 5). (Illus.). 469p. (C). 1996. text 105.00 (*0-521-55216-8*) Cambridge U Pr.

Particle Distributions in Hadronic & Nuclear Collisions. Mark Adams. 300p. 1999. 78.00 (*981-02-3786-3*) World Scientific Pub.

Particle Emission from Nuclei, 3 vols., Vol. I: Nuclear Deformation Energy. Ed. by Dorin N. Poenaru & Marin S. Ivascu. 256p. 1988. 152.00 (*0-8493-4634-7*, QC793, CRC Reprint) Franklin.

Particle Emission from Nuclei, 3 vols., Vol. II: Alpha, Proton, & Heavy Ion Radioactives. Ed. by Dorin N. Poenaru & Marin S. Ivascu. 272p. 1988. 155.00 (*0-8493-4635-5*, QC793, CRC Reprint) Franklin.

Particle Emission from Nuclei, 3 vols., Vol. III: Fission & Beta-Delayed Decay Modes. Ed. by Dorin N. Poenaru & Marin S. Ivascu. 224p. 1988. 147.00 (*0-8493-4636-3*, QC793, CRC Reprint) Franklin.

Particle Entrainment: Measurement of the Fluctuating Lift Force. A. M. Mollinger. 205p. 1994. pap. 57.50 (*90-407-1033-3*, Pub. by Delft U Pr) Coronet Bks.

Particle Field Holography. Chandra S. Vikram. (Studies in Modern Optics: No. 11). (Illus.). 285p. (C). 1992. text 99.95 (*0-521-41127-0*) Cambridge U Pr.

Particle, Fields & Gravitation. Ed. by Jakub Rembielinski. LC 98-88573. 586p. 1998. 145.00 (*1-56396-837-1*) Am Inst Physics.

Particle Flux in the Ocean. V. Ittekkot et al. (Scientific Committee on Problems of the Environment Ser.). 396p. 1996. 160.00 (*0-471-96073-X*) Wiley.

Particle Flux in the Ocean EDS: Egon T. Degens, Erol Izdar & Susumu Honjo. (Illus.). 308p. 1987. pap. 40.00 (*0-614-04963-6*) Woods Hole Ocean.

Particle Garden: Our Universe as Understood by Particle Physicists. Gordon Kane. LC 94-25804. (Illus.). 224p. (C). 1995. 22.00 (*0-201-40780-9*) Addison-Wesley.

Particle Garden: Our Universe as Understood by Particle Physicists. Gordon Kane. Ed. by Heather Mimnaugh. 240p. 1996. pap. 12.00 (*0-201-40826-0*) Addison-Wesley.

Particle Hunters. 2nd ed. Yuval Ne'eman & Yoram Kirsh. (Illus.). 316p. (C). 1996. pap. 27.95 (*0-521-47686-0*); text 69.95 (*0-521-47107-9*) Cambridge U Pr.

Particle Image Velocimetry: A Practical Guide. M. Raffel. 2000. text. write for info. (*0-471-72027-5*) Wiley.

Particle Image Velocimetry: A Practical Guide. M. Raffel et al. LC 97-51315. (Experimental Fluid Mechanics Ser.). (Illus.). xvi, 253p. 1998. 79.95 (*3-540-63683-8*) Spr-Verlag.

***Particle Image Velocimetry - Progress Towards Industrial Application.** M. Stanislas et al. LC 99-89036. 552p. 2000. 234.00 (*0-7923-6160-1*) Kluwer Academic.

Particle Induced Electron Emission, No. I. Ed. by Joachim Treusch et al. (Tracts in Modern Physics Ser.: Vol. 122). ix, 130p. 1991. 97.95 (*0-387-53431-8*) Spr-Verlag.

Particle-Induced X-Ray Emission Analysis: Application to Analytical Problems, Vol. 1, No. 2. I. V. Mitchell & K. M. Barfoot. (Nuclear Science Applications Ser.). 63p. 1981. text 74.00 (*3-7186-0085-4*) Gordon & Breach.

Particle-Induced X-Ray Emission Spectrometry (PIXE) Ed. by Sven A. Johansson et al. LC 94-44471. (Chemical Analysis: A Series of Monographs on Analy). 451p. 1995. 120.00 (*0-471-58944-6*) Wiley.

Particle-Interaction Physics at High Energies. S. J. Lindenbaum. (International Series of Monographs on Physics). (Illus.). 1973. 65.00 (*0-19-851267-8*) OUP.

Particle Kinematics. Eero Byckling & K. Kajantie. LC 72-8595. (Illus.). 329p. reprint ed. pap. 102.00 (*0-608-18775-5*, 202979600065) Bks Demand.

Particle-Lung Interactions. Ed. by Peter Gehrung & Joachim Heyder. (Lung Biology in Health & Disease Ser.). 143p. Date not set. 225.00 (*0-8247-9891-0*) Dekker.

Particle Mechanics. Collinson. (Plastics Ser.). 1997. pap. 15.95 (*0-340-61046-8*, VNR) Wiley.

Particle Modeling. D. Greenspan. LC 97-20692. (Modeling & Simulation in Science, Engineering & Technology Ser.). 350p. 1997. text 69.95 (*0-8176-3985-3*) Birkhauser.

Particle Modeling. Donald Greenspan. LC 97-20692. (Modeling & Simulation in Science, Engineering & Technology Ser.). 1997. write for info. (*3-7643-3985-3*) Birkhauser.

Particle Nuclear Physics. Armand Faessler. (Progress in Particle & Nuclear Physics Ser.: Vol. 35). 1995. 482.50 (*0-08-042647-6*, Pergamon Pr) Elsevier.

Particle Overload in the Rat Lung & Lung Cancer - Implications for Human Risk Assessment: Proceedings of MIT Conference Held March 29-30, 1995. Ed. by Robert J. McCunney & Joe L. Mauderly. LC 95-47904. 320p. 1996. 89.95 (*1-56032-543-7*) Hemisp Pub.

Particle Packing Characteristics. Randall M. German. LC 89-50340. (Illus.). 443p. 1989. 50.00 (*0-918404-83-5*) Metal Powder.

Particle-Particle Adhesion in Pharmaceutical Powder Handling. Fridrun Podczeck. 260p. 1998. 48.00 (*1-86094-112-5*, Pub. by Imperial College) World Scientific Pub.

Particle Phenomenology in the Nineties: Workshop on High Energy Phenomenology II, 2-15 January 1991, Calcutta, India. Ed. by A. Datta et al. LC 92-11874. 700p. (C). 1998. text 130.00 (*981-02-0699-2*) World Scientific Pub.

Particle Physics. Murray Gell-Mann. (Science Masters Ser.). 176p. Date not set. pap. write for info. (*0-465-07268-2*) Basic.

Particle Physics, Vol. 2. Murray Gell-Mann. (Science Masters Ser.). 176p. 1998. 20.00 (*0-465-07267-4*, Pub. by Basic) HarpC.

Particle Physics: Cargese, 1985. Ed. by Maurice Levy et al. Tr. by Jacques Weyers & Raymond Castamans. (NATO ASI Series B, Physical Sciences: Vol. 150). 447p. 1987. 110.00 (*0-306-42562-9*, Plenum Trade) Perseus Pubng.

Particle Physics: Cargese, 1987. Ed. by Maurice Levy et al. LC 88-4180. (NATO ASI Series B, Physics: Vol. 173). (Illus.). 684p. 1988. 155.00 (*0-306-42835-0*, Plenum Trade) Perseus Pubng.

Particle Physics: Cargese, 1989. Ed. by Maurice Levy et al. (NATO ASI Series B, Physics: Vol. 223). (Illus.). 368p. 1990. 110.00 (*0-306-43601-9*, Plenum Trade) Perseus Pubng.

Particle Physics: One Hundred Years of Discoveries, an Annotated Chronological Bibliography. annot. ed. Ed. by V. V. Ezhela et al. 340p. 1997. pap. 52.00 (*1-56396-642-5*, AIP Pr) Spr-Verlag.

Particle Physics: Superstring Theory. Ed. by R. Ramachandran & H. S. Mani. 592p. (C). 1988. text 135.00 (*9971-5-0592-4*) World Scientific Pub.

Particle Physics: The Quest for Substance of Substance. L. B. Okun. (Contemporary Concepts in Physics Ser.: Vol. 2). xiv, 224p. 1985. text 132.00 (*3-7186-0228-8*); pap. text 36.00 (*3-7186-0229-6*) Gordon & Breach.

Particle Physics - Perspectives & Opportunities: Report of the DPF Committee on Long-Term Planning. Jonathan Bagger et al. Ed. by Roberto Peccei. LC 95-24956. 400p. 1995. text 82.00 (*981-02-2271-8*) World Scientific Pub.

Particle Physics & Cosmology. P. D. Collins et al. LC 88-33938. 512p. 1989. 186.95 (*0-471-60088-1*) Wiley.

Particle Physics & Cosmology. F. C. Khanna. 568p. 1995. text 141.00 (*981-02-2100-2*) World Scientific Pub.

Particle Physics & Cosmology at the Interface: Puri India 1-17 January, 1993. P. Ghose et al. 570p. 1995. text 118.00 (*981-02-2452-4*, Pha-P294) World Scientific Pub.

Particle Physics & Cosmology/High Energy Physics: First Tropical Workshop/Second Latin American Symposium. Ed. by J. F. Nieves. LC 98-87300. (Conference Proceedings Ser.: Vol. 444). (Illus.). 590p. 1998. 155.00 (*1-56396-775-8*) Am Inst Physics.

Particle Physics & Inflationary Cosmology. A. Linde. Ed. by Herman Feshbach. (Contemporary Concepts in Physics Ser.: Vol. 1). xviii, 362p. 1990. text 101.00 (*3-7186-0489-2*); pap. text 48.00 (*3-7186-0490-6*) Gordon & Breach.

Particle Physics & Introduction to Field Theory. Ed. by T. D. Lee. (Contemporary Concepts in Physics Ser.: Vol. 1). xvii, 866p. 1981. text 229.00 (*3-7186-0032-3*); pap. text 68.00 (*3-7186-0033-1*) Gordon & Breach.

Particle Physics & the Schrodinger Equation. Harald Grosse & Andre Martin. (Monographs on Particle Physics, Nuclear Physics & Cosmology: Vol. 6). (Illus.). 180p. (C). 1998. text 57.95 (*0-521-39225-X*) Cambridge U Pr.

Particle Physics at the Fermi Scale: Proceedings of the CCAST (World Laboratory) Symposium - Workshop Held at China Center of Advanced Science & Technology, World Laboratory, Beijing, People's Republic of China, May 26-June 4, 1993. Ed. by Yang Pang et al. LC 93-49478. (China Center of Advanced Science & Technology (World Laboratory) Symposium - Workshop Proceedings Ser.: Vol. 10). xiv, 492p. 1994. text 131.00 (*2-88449-108-2*) Gordon & Breach.

Particle Physics at the New Millennium. Byron P. Roe. LC 95-44879. 406p. 1996. 59.00 (*0-387-94615-2*) Spr-Verlag.

Particle Physics from Underground to Heaven. G. Domokos & S. Kovesi-Domokos. 350p. 1992. text 98.00 (*981-02-0887-1*) World Scientific Pub.

Particle Physics in the Cosmos. Ed. by Richard A. Carrigan, Jr. & W. Peter Trower. LC 88-32220. (Illus.). 228p. (C). 1989. pap. text 16.95 (*0-7167-1919-3*) W H Freeman.

Particle Physics, 1971: Univ. of California, Irvine, Dec., 1971, No. 6. American Institute of Physics. Ed. by M. Bander et al. LC 72-81239. (AIP Conference Proceedings Ser.). 185p. 1972. 11.00 (*0-88318-105-3*) Am Inst Physics.

Particle Physics Phenomenology. 300p. 1997. text 39.00 (*981-02-3147-4*) World Scientific Pub.

***Particle Physics Phenomenology: Proceedings of IV International Workshop Taiepi, Roc 18 - 21 Jun.** Hai-Yang Cheng. 350p. 1999. 78.00 (*981-02-3817-7*) World Scientific Pub.

Particle Physics, the Factory Era: Proceedings of the Sixth Lake Louise Winter Institute Chateau Lake Louise, Canada, 17-23 February 1991. Ed. by B. A. Campbell et al. 600p. (C). 1991. text 118.00 (*981-02-0733-6*) World Scientific Pub.

Particle Production in Highly Excited Matter. H. H. Gutbrod & J. Rafelski. (NATO ASI Ser.: Vol. 303). (Illus.). 700p. (C). 1993. text 165.00 (*0-306-44413-5*, Kluwer Plenum) Kluwer Academic.

Particle Production near Threshold. Ed. by Hermann Nann & Edward J. Stephenson. (AIP Conference Proceedings Ser.: No. 221). (Illus.). 488p. 1991. 95.00 (*0-88318-829-5*) Am Inst Physics.

***Particle Production Spanning MEV & TEV Energies.** W. Kittel et al. LC 00-42085. (NATO Science Ser.). 2000. write for info. (*0-7923-6431-7*) Kluwer Academic.

Particle Searches & Discoveries: Proceedings, International Conference, Vanderbilt University, 1-3 March 1976. Ed. by R. S. Panvini. LC 76-19949. (AIP Conference Proceedings Ser.: No. 30). 1976. 18.50 (*0-88318-129-0*) Am Inst Physics.

Particle Size - Selective Sampling for Health-Related Aerosols. Ed. by James H. Vincent. (Illus.). 240p. 1998. 39.00 (*1-882417-30-5*, 0830) Am Conf Govt Indus Hygienist.

Particle Size Analysis. Royal Society of Chemistry Staff. 1989. 28.00 (*0-85990-104-1*) CRC Pr.

Particle Size Analysis, 1981: Proceedings of the Fourth Particle Size Analysis Conference, Loughborough University of Technology, 21-24 September 1981. Particle Size Analysis Conference Staff. Ed. by N. G. Stanley-Wood & T. Allen. LC TR0418.. 471p. reprint ed. pap. 146.10 (*0-608-14539-4*, 202480500038) Bks Demand.

Particle Size Analysis, 1988: Proceedings of the Sixth Particle Size Analysis Conference, University of Surrey, Guildford, U. K., 19-20th April, 1988 Organized by the Analytical Division of the Royal Society of Chemistry. fac. ed. Particle Size Analysis Conference Staff. Ed. by Peter John Lloyd. LC 88-5633. (Illus.). 371p. 1987. pap. 115.10 (*0-7837-7654-3*, 204740700007) Bks Demand.

Particle Size Classifiers. 64p. 1992. pap. 65.00 (*0-8169-0594-0*, E-29) Am Inst Chem Eng.

Particle Size Distribution: Assessment & Characterization. Ed. by Theodore Provder. LC 86-32185. (ACS Symposium Ser.: Vol. 332). 320p. 1987. reprint ed. pap. 99.20 (*0-608-03544-0*, 206426300008) Bks Demand.

Particle Size Distribution: Assessment & Characterization: Symposium of the 190th Meeting, Chicago, IL, September 8-13, 1985. Polymetric Materials Division Staff. Ed. by Theodore J. Provder. LC 86-32185. (ACS Symposium Ser.: No. 332). (Illus.). x, 308p. 1987. 59.95 (*0-8412-1016-0*) Am Chemical.

Particle Size Distribution II. 408p. 1991. text 98.00 (*0-8412-2117-0*, Pub. by Am Chemical) OUP.

***Particle Size Distribution in the Exhaust of Diesel & Gasoline Engines.** (Special Publications). 100p. 2000. 49.00 (*0-7680-0621-X*, SP-1552) Soc Auto Engineers.

Particle Size Distribution III: Assessment & Characterization. Ed. by Theodore Provder. LC 98-16110. (Symposium Ser.: No. 693). (Illus.). 368p. 1998. text 120.95 (*0-8412-3561-9*, Pub. by Am Chemical) OUP.

Particle Size Distribution II: Assessment & Characterization. Ed. by Theodore Provder. LC 91-25166. (ACS Symposium Ser.: No. 472). (Illus.). 408p. 1991. 89.95 (*0-685-50550-2*) Am Chemical.

Particle Size Measurement. 4th ed. Terence Allen. (Illus.). 736p. 1990. mass mkt. 182.95 (*0-412-35070-X*, A4396) Chapman & Hall.

Particle Size Measurement Surface Area & Pore Size Determination. 5th ed. Chapman & Hall Staff. text 117.00 (*0-412-75330-8*) Chapman & Hall.

Particle Strengthening of Metals & Alloys. Eckhard Nembach. LC 96-14932. 285p. 1996. 98.50 (*0-471-12072-3*) Wiley.

Particle Symmetries see Brandeis University Summer Institute in Theoretical Physics: 1965 Lectures

Particle Systems, Random Media & Large Deviations. Ed. by Richard Durrett. LC 85-6181. (Contemporary Mathematics Ser.: Vol. 41). 380p. 1985. reprint ed. pap. 44.00 (*0-8218-5042-3*, CONM/41C) Am Math.

Particle Technology & Surface Phenomena in Minerals. Ed. by M. K. Sharma & G. D. Sharma. (Illus.). 317p. (C). 1992. text 132.00 (*0-306-44181-0*, Kluwer Plenum) Kluwer Academic.

Particle Theory. Francois Deschamps & Judith Mohns. 1991. pap. 15.00 (*0-932526-35-7*) Nexus Pr.

Particle Theory & Phenomenology. LC 97-140729. 500p. 1996. lib. bdg. 67.00 (*981-02-2903-8*) World Scientific Pub.

Particle-Transport Simulation with the Monte Carlo Method. L. L. Carter & E. D. Cashwell. LC 75-25993. (ERDA Critical Review Ser.). 124p. 1975. pap. 11.00 (*0-87079-021-8*, TID-26607); fiche 9.00 (*0-87079-382-9*, TID-26607) DOE.

Particles. Randy Blasing. LC 83-10052. 57p. (Orig.). 1983. pap. 8.00 (*0-914278-40-1*) Copper Beech.

Particles: On the Syntax of Verb-Particle, Triadic & Causative Constructions. Marcel den Dikken. (Oxford Studies in Comparative Syntax). (Illus.). 304p. 1995. text 65.00 (*0-19-509134-5*); pap. text 35.00 (*0-19-509135-3*) OUP.

Particles & Cosmology. 340p. 1996. 65.00 (*981-02-2529-6*) World Scientific Pub.

Particles & Cosmology: International School, Bakson Valley, Moscow, 6-12 May 1991. V. A. Matveev et al. Ed. by E. N. Alexeev et al. 400p. 1992. text 109.00 (*981-02-1002-7*) World Scientific Pub.

Particles & Cosmology: Proceedings of the International School. E. N. Alexeev et al. 332p. 1994. text 106.00 (*981-02-1834-6*) World Scientific Pub.

Particles & Fields. 544p. 1996. 89.00 (*981-02-2917-8*) World Scientific Pub.

Particles & Fields. Ed. by G. W. Semenoff & L. Vinet. LC 97-46958. (CRM Series in Mathematical Physics). (Illus.). 499p. 1998. text 79.00 (*0-387-98402-X*) Spr-Verlag.

Particles & Fields: Proceedings. H. D. Doebner et al. 308p. 1994. text 95.00 (*981-02-1698-X*) World Scientific Pub.

Particles & Fields: Proceedings of the Banff Summer Instruction (CAP), 1988, 3. Ed. by Abdul N. Kamal & F. C. Khanna. 800p. (C). 1989. text 190.00 (*9971-5-0812-5*) World Scientific Pub.

Particles & Fields: Proceedings of the Sixth Mexican School. J. C. D'Olivo et al. 500p. 1995. text 122.00 (*981-02-2121-5*) World Scientific Pub.

Particles & Fields: Proceedings of the VII Ja Swieca Summer School. O. J. Peboli & V. O. Rivelles. 812p. 1994. text 135.00 (*981-02-1597-5*) World Scientific Pub.

Particles & Fields: Proceedings of the 1993 Workshop. R. Huerta et al. 388p. 1994. text 109.00 (*981-02-1709-9*) World Scientific Pub.

Particles & Fields: Proceedings of the 9th Jorge Andre Swieca Summer School Brazil 16 - 28 February 1997. Ed. by Joao C. Barata et al. LC 98-213675. 500p. 1998. 84.00 (*981-02-3453-8*) World Scientific Pub.

Particles & Fields: Sixth Mexican Workshop. Ed. by J. C. D'Olivo et al. (Conference Proceedings Ser.: Vol. 445). (Illus.). 388p. 1998. 105.00 (*1-56396-791-X*) Am Inst Physics.

Particles & Fields: Third Mexican School. 3rd ed. Ed. by J. L. Lucio & A. Zepeda. 310p. (C). 1989. text 113.00 (*9971-5-0967-9*) World Scientific Pub.

***Particles & Fields: 8th Mexican School.** Ed. by Juan Carlos D'Olivo et al. LC 99-67150. (Conference Proceedings Ser.: Vol. 490). (Illus.). 455p. 1999. 135.00 (*1-56396-895-9*) Am Inst Physics.

Particles & Fields - Fourth Mexican School. Ed. by J. L. Lucio & A. Zepeda. 500p. (C). 1992. text 130.00 (*981-02-0666-6*) World Scientific Pub.

Particles & Fields, APS-DPF, University of Maryland, 1982: AIP Conference Proceedings No. 98, Particles & Fields Subseries, 29th. W. E. Caswell & G. A. Snow. LC 83-70807. 413p. 1983. lib. bdg. 37.75 (*0-88318-197-5*) Am Inst Physics.

Particles & Fields in the Magnetosphere: Proceedings of the Summer Advanced Study Institute, University of California, Santa Barbara, California, August 4-15, 1969. Summer Advanced Study Institute Staff. Ed. by Billy M. McCormac. LC 78-115884. (Astrophysics & Space Science Library: No. 17). 453p. 1970. text 201.00 (*90-277-0131-8*) Kluwer Academic.

Particles & Gravity: Proceedings of the Eighth Johns Hopkins Workshop on Current Problems in Particle Theory, Johns Hopkins University, June 20-22, 1984. Ed. by G. Domokos & S. Kovesi-Domokos. 400p. 1984. 70.00 (*9971-966-90-5*); pap. 48.00 (*9971-966-91-3*) World Scientific Pub.

Particles & Ideas: Bishop Berkeley's Corpuscularian Philosophy. Gabriel Moked. 256p. 1988. text 59.00 (*0-19-824990-X*) OUP.

Particles & Luck. Louis B. Jones. LC 93-43715. 305p. 1994. pap. 14.00 (*0-679-74599-8*) Vin Bks.

Particles & Nuclei. 800p. 1997. 89.00 (*981-02-3003-6*) World Scientific Pub.

***Particles & Nuclei: An Introduction to the Physical Concepts.** 2nd rev. enl. ed. B. Povh et al. Tr. by M. Lavelle from GER. LC 99-16711. (Illus.). xviii, 376p. 1999. 36.00 (*3-540-66115-8*) Spr-Verlag.

Particles & Nuclei: An Introduction to the Physical Concepts, Vol. IX. Bogdan Povh et al. Tr. by Martin Lavelle from GER. (Illus.). 340p. 1995. 32.95 (*3-540-59439-6*) Spr-Verlag.

Particles & Nuclei: Essays in Honor of the 60th Birthday of Professor Yoshio Yamaguchi. Ed. by H. Terazawa. 356p. 1987. text 89.00 (*9971-5-0202-X*) World Scientific Pub.

Particles & Policy. Wolfgang K. Panofsky. LC 93-14011. (Masters of Modern Physics Ser.: Vol. 8). 232p. 1994. 34.95 (*1-56396-060-5*) Spr-Verlag.

Particles & Projections in Irish Syntax. Nigel Duffield. LC 95-11030. (Studies in Natural Language & Linguistic Theory: Vol. 32). 374p. (C). 1995. text 161.50 (*0-7923-3550-3*) Kluwer Academic.

Particles & Sources. Julian Seymour Schwinger. x, 92p. 1969. pap. text 85.00 (*0-677-02065-1*) Gordon & Breach.

Particles & the Universe: Proceedings of the Twelfth Lake Louise Winter Institute. Anthony Astbury. 1998. 86.00 (*981-02-3467-8*) World Scientific Pub.

Particles & the Universe: Proceedings of the 17th Johns Hopkins Workshop. Z. Horvath et al. 512p. 1994. text 99.00 (*981-02-1800-1*) World Scientific Pub.

Particles & Waves: Historical Essays in the Philosophy of Science. Peter Achinstein. (Illus.). 352p. 1991. pap. text 39.95 (*0-19-506755-X*, 6122) OUP.

Particles in Gases & Liquids No. 1: Detection, Characterization & Control. Ed. by K. L. Mittal. (Illus.). 312p. (C). 1989. text 114.00 (*0-306-43151-3*, Kluwer Plenum) Kluwer Academic.

Particles in Gases & Liquids No. 2: Detection, Characterization & Control. Ed. by K. L. Mittal. (Illus.). 416p. (C). 1991. text 132.00 (*0-306-43809-7*, Kluwer Plenum) Kluwer Academic.

Particles in Gases & Liquids 3: Detection, Characterization & Control. K. L. Mittal. LC 93-17795. (Illus.). 300p. (C). 1993. text 95.00 (*0-306-44485-2*, Kluwer Plenum) Kluwer Academic.

Particles in Nature: The Chronological Discovery of the New Physics. John H. Mauldin. (Illus.). 288p. 1986. 23.95 (*0-8306-0416-2*, 2616); pap. 16.95 (*0-8306-0516-9*, 2616P) McGraw-Hill Prof.

Particles in Our Air: Exposures & Health Effects. Ed. by John D. Spengler & Richard Wilson. LC 96-79259. (Illus.). 300p. Date not set. 20.00 (*0-674-24077-4*) HUP.

Particles in the Nineties. Ed. by J. Iliopoulos & J. Zinn-Justin. 1996. write for info. (*0-614-17906-8*, North Holland) Elsevier.

Particles, Nuclei, & the Universe. Yakov B. Zeldovich. Ed. by J. P. Ostriker et al. Tr. by E. Jackson & A. Granik. LC 91-14814. (Selected Works of Yakov Borisovich Zeldovich: No. 2). (Illus.). 660p. 1993. reprint ed. pap. 200.00 (*0-608-07145-5*, 206737100009) Bks Demand.

P

Particles of Light: Jackson County & Its Authors. David L. Rosheim. 214p. (Orig.). 1995. pap. 20.00 (*0-9602996-3-7*) Andromeda.

Particles of the Past: Sandmining on Long Island, 1870s-1980s. 2nd ed. Ed. by Elly Shodell. (Illus.). 43p. (YA). (gr. 9-12). reprint ed. pap. 8.95 (*0-9615059-0-7*) Pt WA Pub Lib.

Particles on Surfaces: Detection, Adhesion & Removal. K. L. Mittal. (Illus.). 440p. 1994. text 199.00 (*0-8247-9535-0*) Dekker.

Particles on Surfaces: Detection, Adhesion & Removal, Vol. 1. K. L. Mittal. LC 88-28841. (Illus.). 394p. (C). 1988. text 120.00 (*0-306-43030-4*, Kluwer Plenum) Kluwer Academic.

Particles on Surfaces: Detection, Adhesion & Removal, Vol. 2. K. L. Mittal. (Illus.). 336p. (C). 1989. text 110.00 (*0-306-43367-2*, Kluwer Plenum) Kluwer Academic.

Particles on Surfaces: Detection, Adhesion & Removal, Vol. 3. K. L. Mittal. (Illus.). 336p. (C). 1992. text 110.00 (*0-306-44180-2*, Kluwer Plenum) Kluwer Academic.

***Particles on Surfaces Vols. 5 & 6: Detection, Adhesion & Removal.** Ed. by K. L. Mittal. 362p. 1999. 130.00 (*90-6764-312-2*, Pub. by VSP) Coronet Bks.

Particles, Quantum Groups, HTC Phase Transitions & All That. Ed. by K. Kang & C. W. Kim. 412p. (C). 1991. text 101.00 (*981-02-0575-9*) World Scientific Pub.

Particles, Sources & Fields. Julian Seymour Schwinger. (Classics Ser.). (Illus.). 425p. (C). 1989. text 29.95 (*0-685-74065-X*) Addison-Wesley.

Particles, Sources & Fields, Vol. 1. Julian Seymour Schwinger. LC 98-87896. (Advanced Book Classics Ser.). 448p. 1998. pap. text 39.00 (*0-7382-0053-0*) Perseus Pubng.

Particles, Sources & Fields, Vol. 2. Julian Seymour Schwinger. LC 98-87896. (Advanced Book Classics Ser.). 320p. 1998. pap. text 35.00 (*0-7382-0054-9*) Perseus Pubng.

Particles, Sources & Fields, Vol. 3. Julian Seymour Schwinger. LC 98-87896. (Advanced Book Classics Ser.). 336p. 1998. pap. text 35.00 (*0-7382-0055-7*) Perseus Pubng.

Particles, Strings & Cosmology: Proceedings of the Johns Hopkins Workshop on Current Problems in Particle Theory 19 & the Pascos Interdisciplinary Symposium 5, Baltimore, 1995, March 22-25. Jonathan Bagger. LC 96-16481. 496p. 1996. write for info. (*981-02-2512-1*) World Scientific Pub.

Particles, Strings & Cosmology: Proceedings of the Second International Symposium, Northeastern Univ., Boston, 25-30 March 1991. Ed. by Pran Nath & Stephen Reucroff. 800p. 1992. text 121.00 (*981-02-0971-1*) World Scientific Pub.

Particles, Strings & Cosmology - 90: Proceedings of the First International Symposium on Particles, Strings & Cosmology, Boston, U. S. A., March 27-31, 1990. Ed. by Pran Nath & Stephen Reucroft. 716p. 1991. pap. 55.00 (*981-02-0393-4*); text 167.00 (*981-02-0392-6*) World Scientific Pub.

Particles, Strings & Cosmology (PASCOS '98) Proceedings of the 6th International Symposium Boston, U. S. A., 22-29 March 1998. Ed. by P. Nath. LC 98-51619. 950p. 1999. 128.00 (*981-02-3612-3*) World Scientific Pub.

Particles, Strings & Supernovae. Ed. by A. Jevicki & C. I. Tan. 1092p. (C). 1989. text 109.00 (*9971-5-0792-7*); pap. text 61.00 (*9971-5-0793-5*) World Scientific Pub.

Particular Condition in Life: Self-Employment & Social Mobility in Mid-Victorian Brantford, Ontario. David G. Burley. 328p. 1994. 60.00 (*0-7735-1199-7*, Pub. by McG-Queens Univ Pr) CUP Services.

Particular Friends: The Correspondence of Samuel Pepys & John Evelyn. Ed. by Guy de la Bedoyere. (Illus.). 354p. 1998. pap. 29.95 (*0-85115-697-5*, Boydell Pr) Boydell & Brewer.

Particular History of the Five Years French & Indian War. Samuel Drake. (Illus.). 312p. 1995. reprint ed. pap. 22.00 (*0-7884-0294-3*) Heritage Bk.

Particular History of the Five Years French & Indian War in New England & Parts Adjacent. Samuel G. Drake. (Select Bibliographies Reprint Ser.). 1977. 21.95 (*0-8369-5575-7*) Ayer.

Particular Place: Urban Restructuring & Religious Ecology in a Southern Exurb Nancy L. Eiesland. LC 99-15069. 256p. 2000. pap. 21.00 (*0-8135-2738-4*) Rutgers U Pr.

Particular Place: Urban Restructuring & Religious Ecology in a Southern Exurb. Nancy L. Eiesland. LC 99-15069. 256p. 2000. text 52.00 (*0-8135-2737-6*) Rutgers U Pr.

Particular Places: A Traveler's Guide to Inner Ohio, Vol. 2. Orange Frazer Press Editors. LC 90-61654. (Illus.). 301p. 1993. pap. 14.95 (*0-9619637-9-4*) Orange Frazer.

Particular Requirements for Batter-Operated Drain Cleaners: 745-4-35. 1995. write for info. (*1-55989-795-3*, UL 745-4-35) Underwrtrs Labs.

Particular Requirements for Battery-Operated Circular Saws & Circular Knives: 745-4-5. 1995. write for info. (*1-55989-789-9*, UL 745-4-5) Underwrtrs Labs.

Particular Requirements for Battery-Operated Drills: 745-4-1. 1995. write for info. (*1-55989-785-6*, UL 745-4-1) Underwrtrs Labs.

Particular Requirements for Battery-Operated Grinders, Polishers, & Disk-Type Sanders: 745-4-3. 1995. write for info. (*1-55989-787-2*, UL 745-4-3) Underwrtrs Labs.

Particular Requirements for Battery-Operated Hammers: 745-4-6. 1995. write for info. (*1-55989-790-2*, UL 745-4-6) Underwrtrs Labs.

Particular Requirements for Battery-Operated Hand Motor Tools: 745 4-36. 1995. write for info. (*1-55989-796-1*, UL 745-4-36) Underwrtrs Labs.

Particular Requirements for Battery-Operated Reciprocating Saws: 745-4-11. 1995. write for info. (*1-55989-792-9*, UL 745-4-11) Underwrtrs Labs.

Particular Requirements for Battery-Operated Routers & Trimmers: 745-4-17. 1995. write for info. (*1-55989-794-5*, UL 745-4-17) Underwrtrs Labs.

Particular Requirements for Battery-Operated Sanders: 745-4-4. 1995. write for info. (*1-55989-788-0*, UL 745-4-4) Underwrtrs Labs.

Particular Requirements for Battery-Operated Screwdrivers & Impact Wrenches: 745-4-2. 1995. write for info. (*1-55989-786-4*, UL 745-4-2) Underwrtrs Labs.

Particular Requirements for Battery-Operated Shears & Nibblers: 745-4-8. 1995. write for info. (*1-55989-791-0*, UL 745-4-8) Underwrtrs Labs.

Particular Requirements for Circular Saws & Circular Knives: 745-2-5. 1995. write for info. (*1-55989-768-6*, UL 745-2-5) Underwrtrs Labs.

Particular Requirements for Concrete Vibrators: 745-2-12. 1995. write for info. (*1-55989-773-2*, UL 745-2-12) Underwrtrs Labs.

Particular Requirements for Diamond Core Drills: 745-2-31. 1995. write for info. (*1-55989-777-5*, UL 745-2-31) Underwrtrs Labs.

Particular Requirements for Drain Cleaners: 745-2-35. 1995. write for info. (*1-55989-781-3*, UL 745-2-35) Underwrtrs Labs.

Particular Requirements for Drills: 745-2-1. 1995. write for info. (*1-55989-764-3*, UL 745-2-1) Underwrtrs Labs.

Particular Requirements for Grinders, Polishers & Disk-Type Sanders: 745-2-3. 1995. write for info. (*1-55989-766-X*, UL 745-2-3) Underwrtrs Labs.

Particular Requirements for Hammers: 745-2-6. 1995. write for info. (*1-55989-769-4*, UL 745-2-6) Underwrtrs Labs.

Particular Requirements for Hand Motor Tools: 745-2-36. 1995. write for info. (*1-55989-782-1*, UL 745-2-36) Underwrtrs Labs.

Particular Requirements for Magnetic Drill Presses: 745-2-32. 1995. write for info. (*1-55989-778-3*, UL 745-2-32) Underwrtrs Labs.

Particular Requirements for Planers: 745-2-14. 1995. write for info. (*1-55989-774-0*, UL 745-2-14) Underwrtrs Labs.

Particular Requirements for Plate Jointers: 745-2-37. 1995. write for info. (*1-55989-783-X*, UL 745-2-37) Underwrtrs Labs.

Particular Requirements for Portable Bandsaws: 745-2-33. 1995. write for info. (*1-55989-779-1*, UL 745-2-33) Underwrtrs Labs.

Particular Requirements for Reciprocating Saws: 745-2-11. 1995. write for info. (*1-55989-772-4*, UL 745-2-11) Underwrtrs Labs.

Particular Requirements for Routers & Trimmers: 745-2-17. 1995. write for info. (*1-55989-775-9*, UL 745-2-17) Underwrtrs Labs.

Particular Requirements for Sanders: 745-2-4. 1995. write for info. (*1-55989-767-8*, UL 745-2-4) Underwrtrs Labs.

Particular Requirements for Screwdrivers & Impact Wrenches: 745-2-2. 1995. write for info. (*1-55989-765-1*, UL 745-2-2) Underwrtrs Labs.

Particular Requirements for Shears & Nibblers: 745-2-8. 1995. write for info. (*1-55989-770-8*, UL 745-2-8) Underwrtrs Labs.

Particular Requirements for Staplers: 745-2-30. 1995. write for info. (*1-55989-776-7*, UL 745-2-30) Underwrtrs Labs.

Particular Requirements for Strapping Tools: 745-2-34. 1995. write for info. (*1-55989-780-5*, UL 745-2-34) Underwrtrs Labs.

Particular Requirements for Tappers: 745-2-9. 1995. write for info. (*1-55989-771-6*, UL 745-2-9) Underwrtrs Labs.

Particular Saints: Shakespeare's Four Antonios, Their Contexts, & Their Plays. Cynthia Lewis. LC 96-38090. (Illus.). 256p. 1997. 39.50 (*0-87413-630-X*) U Delaware Pr.

Particular Voices: Portraits of Gay & Lesbian Writers. Robert Giard. LC 96-47002. 332p. 1997. 45.00 (*0-262-07180-0*) MIT Pr.

Particular Voices: Portraits of Gay & Lesbian Writers. Robert Giard. (Illus.). 352p. 1998. pap. text 25.00 (*0-262-57125-0*) MIT Pr.

Particularis de Computis: Accounting Books & Records. Luca Pacioli. Ed. by Marianne Thompson. Tr. by Jeremy Cripps. (Illus.). 109p. 1995. 45.00 (*0-9647778-0-0*) Pacioli Soc.

***Particularities: Collected Essays on Ethnography & Education.** George W. Noblit. LC 97-17054. (Counterpoints Ser.: Vol. 44). VII, 224p. (C). 1999. pap. text 29.95 (*0-8204-3674-7*, 36747) P Lang Pubng.

***Particularly Cats.** Doris Lessing. LC 99-89340. (Illus.). 160p. 2000. reprint ed. pap. 14.95 (*1-58080-036-X*) Burford Bks.

Particulars: Selections from the Miller-Plummer Collection. (Illus.). 52p. (Orig.). 1983. pap. 12.50 (*0-935398-08-2*) G Eastman Hse.

Particulars, Actuality, & Identity over Time see Analytical Metaphysics

Particulate Air Pollution: Problems & Solutions. Louis Theodore et al. 112p. 1980. 70.00 (*0-8493-5541-9*, TD884, CRC Reprint) Franklin.

Particulate & Multiphase Processes, 3 vols., Set. Ed. by Teoman Ariman & T. Nejat Veziroglu. (Illus.). 2236p. 1987. 730.00 (*0-89116-636-X*) Hemisp Pub.

Particulate Debris from Medical Implants: Mechanisms of Formation & Biological Consequences. Ed. by Kenneth R. St. John. LC 91-47039. (Special Technical Publication Ser.: No. 1144). (Illus.). 215p. 1992. text 59.00 (*0-8031-1441-9*, STP1144) ASTM.

Particulate Filled Polymer Composites. Ed. by R. N. Rothon. 1996. (*0-582-08782-1*) Addison-Wesley.

Particulate Flows: Processing & Rheology. Ed. by Donald A. Drew et al. LC 97-41795. (IMA Volumes in Mathematics & Its Applications Ser.: Vol. 98). (Illus.). 156p. 1997. 49.95 (*0-387-98378-3*) Spr-Verlag.

Particulate Laden Flows in Turbomachinery: Presented at 1982 AIAA-ASME Joint Fluids, Plasma, Thermophysics, & Heat Transfer Conference, St. Louis, Missouri, June 7-11, 1982. American Society of Mechanical Engineers Staff. Ed. by W. Tabakoff et al. LC 82-71170. (Illus.). 156p. reprint ed. pap. 48.40 (*0-8357-2846-3*, 203908100010) Bks Demand.

Particulate Materials & Processes, Vol. 9. 544p. 1992. 140.00 (*1-878954-28-8*) Metal Powder.

Particulate Materials & Waves. Santamarina. text. write for info. (*0-471-49058-X*) Wiley.

***Particulate Matter: Properties & Effects upon Health.** Robert L. Maynard & Vyvyan Howard. LC 99-39157. (Illus.). 208p. 1999. 115.00 (*0-387-91588-5*) Spr-Verlag.

Particulate Matter: Sources & Resources for Healthcare Manufacturers. Michael J. Groves. 299p. 1993. 86.95 (*0-935184-40-6*) Interpharm.

Particulate Matter & Aquatic Contaminants. 224p. 1993. lib. bdg. 110.00 (*0-87371-678-7*, 678) Lewis Pubs.

Particulate Polycyclic Organic Matter: Proceedings. 173p. 1976. 21.00 (*0-911890-16-5*) Indus Health Inc.

Particulate Two-Phase Flow. Ed. by M. C. Roco. 1002p. 1993. text 115.00 (*0-7506-9275-8*) Buttrwrth-Heinemann.

Particulates & Continuum: Multiphase Fluid Dynamics. Shao L. Soo. (C). 1989. 95.00 (*0-89116-918-0*) Hemisp Pub.

Particulates & Continuum: Multiphase Fluid Dynamics. Shao L. Soo. (C). 1989. student ed. 20.95 (*0-89116-539-8*) Hemisp Pub.

Particulates in Water: Characterization, Fate, Effects, & Removal. Ed. by Michael C. Kavanaugh & James O. Leckie. LC 80-19663. (Advances in Chemistry Ser.: No. 189). 1980. 71.95 (*0-8412-0499-3*) Am Chemical.

Particulates in Water: Characterization, Fate, Effects, & Removal. Ed. by Michael C. Kavanaugh & James O. Leckie. LC 80-19663. (Advances in Chemistry Ser.: Vol. 189). 414p. 1980. reprint ed. pap. 128.40 (*0-608-03860-1*, 206430700008) Bks Demand.

Partido de Futbol. Grace MacCarone. (Mariposa Ser.). (SPA., Illus.). 32p. (J). (ps-1). 1998. pap. text 3.50 (*0-590-27499-6*, Cartwheel) Scholastic Inc.

Partido de Futbol. Grace MacCarone. (Mariposa Scholastica en Espanol Ser.). (J). 1998. 8.70 (*0-606-13882-X*, Pub. by Turtleback) Demco.

***Partie de Campagne.** Caroline Anderson. (FRE.). 2000. mass mkt. 3.99 (*0-373-34811-8*) Harlequin Bks.

Partiendo el Jon . . . Estampas Cubanas de Aqui . . . y de Alla. Jose Sanchez-Boudy. LC 90-83486. (Coleccion Caniqui). (SPA.). 144p. (Orig.). 1991. pap. 9.95 (*0-89729-575-7*) Ediciones.

Partier's Guide to 51 Drinking Games. Brian L. Pellham. Ed. by Amy Neises. (Illus.). 104p. (Orig.). 1995. pap. 9.95 (*0-9649678-0-4*, B106) Kheper Pubg.

Parties. Carl Van Vechten. LC 70-153004. (Select Bibliographies Reprint Ser.). 1977. 23.95 (*0-8369-5758-X*) Ayer.

Parties. Carl Van Vechten. (Sun & Moon Classics Ser.: No. 31). 266p. 1993. reprint ed. pap. 13.95 (*1-55713-029-9*) Sun & Moon CA.

Parties: A Literary Companion. Ed. by Susanna Johnston. LC 96-29268. 286p. 1997. 24.95 (*0-87951-752-2*, Pub. by Overlook Pr) Penguin Putnam.

Parties: A Literary Companion. Ed. by Susanna Johnston. 286p. 1998. pap. 14.95 (*0-87951-842-1*, Pub. by Overlook Pr) Penguin Putnam.

Parties & Democracy. Rick Hofferbert. LC 98-49541. (Political Studies Special Issues). 240p. 1998. pap. 26.95 (*0-631-20930-1*) Blackwell Pubs.

Parties & Democracy: Coalition Formation & Government Functioning in Twenty States. Ian Budge & Hans Keman. (Comparative Politics Ser.). (Illus.). 256p. (C). 1993. reprint ed. pap. text 22.00 (*0-19-827925-6*) OUP.

Parties & Democracy in Britain & America. Ed. by Vernon Bogdanor. LC 83-24794. (American Political Parties & Elections Ser.). 282p. 1984. 65.00 (*0-275-91131-4*, C1131, Praeger Pubs) Greenwood.

***Parties & Democracy in France: Parties under Presidentialism.** David S. Bell. (Parties & Democracy Ser.). 256p. 2000. pap. 30.95 (*1-85521-864-X*, Pub. by Ashgate Pub); text 73.95 (*1-85521-861-5*, Pub. by Ashgate Pub) Ashgate Pub Co.

***Parties & Democracy in Italy.** James L. Newell. (Parties & Democracy Ser.). 224p. 2000. pap. 34.95 (*1-85521-863-1*, Pub. by Ashgate Pub); text 70.95 (*1-85521-859-3*, Pub. by Ashgate Pub) Ashgate Pub Co.

Parties & Democracy in the Post-Soviet Republics: The Case of Estonia. David Arter. 304p. 1996. 81.95 (*1-85521-466-0*, Pub. by Dartmth Pub) Ashgate Pub Co.

Parties & Elections in America: The Electoral Process. 2nd ed. Louis S. Maisel. LC 92-37941. 384p. (C). 1992. pap. 49.06 (*0-07-039738-4*) McGraw.

Parties & Elections in America: The Electoral Process. 3rd ed. L. Sandy Maisel. LC 99-28825. 616p. 1999. pap. text 35.00 (*0-8476-8549-7*) Rowman.

Parties & Elections in an Anti-Party Age: American Politics & the Crisis of Confidence. Jeff Fishel. LC 76-26426. 384p. reprint ed. pap. 119.10 (*0-608-17090-9*, 205622700056) Bks Demand.

Parties & Elections in Greece: The Search for Legitimacy. Richard Clogg. LC 87-30376. xvii, 268p. (C). 1988. text 53.00 (*0-8223-0794-4*); pap. text 23.95 (*0-8223-0823-1*) Duke.

Parties & Leaders in the PostReform House. David W. Rohde. LC 90-22984. (American Politics & Political Economy Ser.). (Illus.). 244p. 1991. pap. text 14.95 (*0-226-72407-7*) U Ch Pr.

Parties & Leaders in the PostReform House. David W. Rohde. LC 90-22984. (American Politics & Political Economy Ser.). (Illus.). 244p. 1991. lib. bdg. 45.00 (*0-226-72406-9*) U Ch Pr.

Parties & Party Systems in Liberal Democracies: Continuity Amid Change. Ed. by Steven B. Wolinetz. 320p. (C). 1988. lib. bdg. 59.50 (*0-415-01276-7*) Routledge.

Parties & Politics in America. Clinton Rossiter. 212p. 1960. pap. text 13.95 (*0-8014-9021-9*) Cornell U Pr.

Parties & Politics in American History: A Reader. Ed. by Sandy L. Maisel & William G. Shade. LC 94-8022. 296p. 1994. text 15.00 (*0-8153-1690-9*, H1724) Garland.

Parties & Politics in Contemporary Japan. Robert A. Scalapino & Junnosuke Masumi. LC 61-14279. (C). 1962. pap. 12.00 (*0-520-01132-5*, Pub. by U CA Pr) Cal Prin Full Svc.

Parties & Politics in Modern Germany. Gerard Braunthal. 224p. (C). 1996. pap. 75.00 (*0-8133-2382-7*, Pub. by Westview); pap. 25.00 (*0-8133-2383-5*, Pub. by Westview) HarpC.

Parties & Politics in North Carolina, 1836-1865. Marc W. Kruman. LC 82-20364. xix, 384p. 1983. pap. text 19.95 (*0-8071-1061-2*) La State U Pr.

Parties & Politics in the Early Republic, 1789-1815. Morton Borden. Ed. by A. S. Eisenstadt & John H. Franklin. LC 67-14298. (American History Ser.). 128p. (C). 1967. pap. text 11.95 (*0-88295-704-X*) Harlan Davidson.

Parties & Power in Modern Argentina, 1930-1946. Alberto Ciria. Tr. by Carlos A. Astiz & Mary F. McCarthy. LC 70-129642. 357p. (C). 1974. text 24.50 (*0-87395-079-8*) State U NY Pr.

Parties & Primaries: Nominating State Governors. Malcolm E. Jewell. LC 83-24688. (American Political Parties & Elections Ser.). 308p. 1984. 57.95 (*0-275-91196-9*, C1196, Praeger Pubs) Greenwood.

***Parties & Projects for the Holidays.** Ed. by Martha Stewart Living Editors. (Illus.). 144p. 2000. pap. 22.00 (*0-609-80593-2*) C Potter.

Parties & Slavery, 1850-1859. Theodore Smith. LC 68-24997. (Studies in Black History & Culture: No. 54). 1969. reprint ed. lib. bdg. 75.00 (*0-8383-0242-4*) M S G Haskell Hse.

Parties & Their Members: Organizing for Victory in Britain & Germany. Susan E. Scarrow. (Comparative Politics Ser.). (Illus.). 290p. 1996. text 72.00 (*0-19-827918-3*) OUP.

Parties, Candidates, & Voters in Japan: Six Quantitative Studies. Ed. by John C. Campbell. LC 81-6190. (Michigan Papers in Japanese Studies: No. 2). viii, 169p. 1981. pap. 8.25 (*0-939512-07-6*) U MI Japan.

Parties, Conflicts & Coalitions in Western Europe: Organizational Determinants of Coalition Bargaining. Moshe Maor. LC 97-14940. 216p. (C). 1997. 90.00 (*0-415-11602-3*) Routledge.

***Parties, Elections & Cleavages: Israel in Comparative & Theoretical Perspective.** Ed. by Moshe Maor & Reuven Y. Hazan. (Israeli History, Politics & Society Ser.). 224p. 2000. 59.50 (*0-7146-5076-5*, Pub. by F Cass Pubs); pap. 26.50 (*0-7146-8123-7*, Pub. by F Cass Pubs) Intl Spec Bk.

Parties, Elections, & Political Participation in Latin America. Intro. by Jorge I. Dominguez. LC 93-42685. (Essays on Mexico, Central & South America Ser.: Vol. 5). 424p. 1994. text 79.00 (*0-8153-1489-2*) Garland.

Parties for Children: Ideas & Instructions for Invitations, Decorations, Refreshments, Favors, Crafts & Games for 19 Theme Parties. Debra K. Moore & Jackie A. Kutter. LC 95-2594. (Illus.). 182p. 1995. pap. 26.50 (*0-7864-0104-4*) McFarland & Co.

Parties for Home & School: A Piece of Cake. Dena K. Bellows & Sandra C. Lamb. (Illus.). 144p. (J). (ps-4). teacher ed. 8.99 (*0-86653-328-1*, GA647) Good Apple.

Parties for Kids. (Illus.). 64p. 1993. 5.98 (*0-7853-0278-6*, 3616100) Pubns Intl Ltd.

Parties for Kids. Judy Bastyra. LC 97-31788. (Illus.). 80p. (YA). (gr. 5 up). 1998. 10.95 (*0-7534-5092-5*) LKC.

Parties for Kids. Michaeline Bresnahan. (Art-Crafts-Cooking-Drawing Books for Children Ser.). (Illus.). 64p. (J). (ps up). 1995. lib. bdg. 17.95 (*1-56674-100-9*, HTS Bks) Forest Hse.

Parties for Kids - Stories & Activities Plus Ideas. Story Time Stories That Rhyme Staff. (Illus.). 52p. (Orig.). 1995. pap. text 15.95 (*1-56820-127-3*) Story Time.

Parties Kids Love: Great New Party Ideas for Birthdays, Holidays, or Just Fun. Mike Artell & Pam Shiller. 1996. pap. 12.95 (*0-673-36229-9*, GoodYrBooks) Addison-Wesley Educ.

Parties Out of Power in Japan, 1931-1941. Gordon Mark Berger. LC 76-3243. 432p. reprint ed. pap. 123.20 (*0-8357-3429-3*, 2039687) Bks Demand.

Parties, Patriots & Undertakers: Parliamentary Politics in Early Hanoverian Ireland. Patrick McNally. LC 98-103973. 240p. 1997. boxed set 45.00 (*1-85182-255-0*, Pub. by Four Cts Pr) Intl Spec Bk.

***Parties, Politics & Democracy in the New Southern Europe.** Nikiforos P. Diamandouros & Richard Gunther. Ed. by Social Science Research Council Staff & American Council of Learned Societies. LC 00-8848. 2001. pap. write for info. (*0-8018-6518-2*) Johns Hopkins.

Parties, Politics & Public Policy in America. 8th ed. William J. Keefe. LC 97-37702. 332p. (YA). 1997. text 29.95 (*1-56802-352-9*) Congr Quarterly.

Parties, Politics, & the Sectional Conflict in Tennessee, 1832-1861. Jonathan M. Atkins. LC 96-1002. 1997. 38.00 (*0-87049-950-5*) U of Tenn Pr.

P

An Asterisk (*) at the beginning of an entry indicates that the title is appearing for the first time.

Parties Respond: Changes in American Parties & Campaigns. 3rd ed. Ed. by L. Sandy Maisel. LC 97-32510. (Transforming American Politics Ser.). 432p. (C). 1997. pap. text 31.00 (*0-8133-9960-2*, Pub. by Westview) HarpC.

Parties, Slavery, & the Union in Antebellum Georgia. Anthony G. Carey. LC 96-30786. 1997. 60.00 (*0-8203-1898-1*) U of Ga Pr.

Parties to a Contract of Carriage. Chris Cahsmore. 252p. 1990. 130.00 (*1-85044-329-7*) LLP.

Parties to the Agreement Dated 1950 & Revised 1977. Witherby & Co. Ltd. Staff. (C). 1989. pap. 30.00 (*0-7855-3921-2*, Pub. by Witherby & Co) St Mut.

Parties, Trade Unions, & Society in East-Central Europe. Ed. by Michael Waller & Martin R. Myant. LC 94-6312. 1994. 37.50 (*0-7146-4583-4*, Pub. by F Cass Pubs) Intl Spec Bk.

Parties with a Purpose: A Handbook for Activity Directors. Shirley L. Barrett. 128p. 1980. pap., spiral bd. 33.95 (*0-398-03986-0*) C C Thomas.

Parties Without Pain: Your Guide to Healthy Humor. Richard D. Taber & Pat Taber. (Illus.). 144p. (Orig.). 1999. pap. 9.95 (*0-941042-24-3*) Dog Eared Pubns.

***Parties Without Partisans: Political Change in Advanced Industrial Democracies.** Ed. by Russell J. Dalton & Martin P. Wattenberg. (Comparative Politics Ser.). 280p. 2000. text 45.00 (*0-19-924082-5*) OUP.

Partikeln der Deutschen Sprache. Ed. by Harald Weydt. (C). 1979. 161.55 (*3-11-007833-3*) De Gruyter.

Partikeln des Ugaritischen, Vol. 2. Kjell Aartun. (Alter Orient und Altes Testament Ser.: Vol. 21). (GER.). x, 177p. 1978. text 29.50 (*3-7887-0567-1*, Pub. by NeukirchenerV) Eisenbrauns.

Partilkeln des Ugaritischen Vol. 1: Adverbien, Verneinungspartikeln, Bekraftigungspartikeln, Hervorhebungspartikeln. Kjell Aartun. (Alter Orient und Altes Testament Ser.: Vol. 21/1). (GER.). 124p. 1974. text 22.50 (*3-7887-0426-8*) NeukirchenerV.

Parting: Celebrate a Life by Planning a Meaningful, Creative Funeral. Karen Moderow. LC 95-60950. 104p. (Orig.). 1996. pap. 8.99 (*0-9643189-0-3*) K Moderow.

Parting: The Aftermath of Separation & Divorce. Graham B. Spanier & Linda Thompson. LC 87-9796. 248p. reprint ed. pap. 76.90 (*0-7837-4569-9*, 204409800003) Bks Demand.

Parting at the Crossroads: The Emergence of Health Insurance in the United States & Canada. Antonia Maioni. LC 97-43548. 216p. 1998. text 37.50 (*0-691-05796-6*, Pub. by Princeton U Pr) Cal Prin Full Svc.

Parting, Clinging, Individulization. J. W. Redfearn. 1985. 20.00 (*0-7855-1943-2*) St Mut.

Parting Company: How to Survive the Loss of a Job & Find Another Successfully. William J. Morin & James C. Cabrera. LC 82-48045. 264p. 1984. pap. 6.95 (*0-15-671046-3*, Harvest Bks) Harcourt.

Parting Company: How to Survive the Loss of a Job & Find Another Successfully. 2nd ed. William J. Morin & James C. Cabrera. 416p. 1991. pap. 13.00 (*0-15-671047-1*, Harvest Bks) Harcourt.

Parting Company: Innovative Strategies to Plan for Succesion, Manage the Transition, Sell or Transfer Your Bussiness. Andrew J. Sherman. LC 99-37347. (Kiplinger's Business Management Library). 254p. 1999. 34.95 (*0-938721-66-6*, Pub. by Kiplinger Bks) Natl Bk Netwk.

Parting Company: Understanding the Loss of a Loved One - The Caregiver's Journey. Margaret Stubbs & Cynthia Pearson. LC 99-23702. 350p. 1999. pap. 18.95 (*1-58005-019-0*) Seal Pr WA.

Parting Curtain. Walter Hixson. LC 95-52253. 295p. 1997. text 45.00 (*0-312-16080-1*) St Martin.

Parting from Phantoms: Selected Writings, 1990-1994. Christa Wolf. Tr. by Jan Van Heurck. LC 97-8799. 248p. 1997. 24.95 (*0-226-90496-2*) U Ch Pr.

Parting from Phantoms: Selected Writings, 1990-1994. Christa Wolf. 1998. pap. 17.00 (*0-226-90503-9*) U Ch Pr.

Parting Gestures: Three by Pedrero (El Color De Agosto, La Noche Dividida, Resguardo Personal) Paloma Pedrero. Ed. by Martha T. Halsey. Tr. by Phyllis Zatlin from SPA. LC 93-73773. xvi, 67p. 1994. pap. 6.00 (*0-9631212-5-1*) Estreno.

Parting Gestures with a Night in the Subway. rev. exp. ed. Paloma Pedrero. Tr. by Phyllis Zatlin from SPA. LC 98-73219. (Contemporary Spanish Plays Ser.: Vol. 6). (Illus.). xiv, 60p. 1999. pap. 8.00 (*1-888463-06-6*) Estreno.

***Parting Gift.** Ben Erickson. LC 99-43018. 288p. 2000. 19.95 (*0-446-52530-8*, Pub. by Warner Bks) Little.

Parting Glass: An American Book of Drink. Ed. by B. Lanzerotti. xi, 76p. 1993. pap. 9.95 (*1-891413-00-7*) Twin Willows.

Parting Is Not Goodbye. Kelly Osmont & Marilyn McFarlane. LC 86-63796. 144p. (Orig.). 1987. 10.95 (*0-941211-00-2*); pap. 9.95 (*0-941211-01-0*) Nobility Pr.

Parting of the Way see Taoism: The Parting of the Way

***Parting of the Ways: Carnap, Cassirer & Heidegger.** Michael Friedman. 2000. 49.95 (*0-8126-9424-4*); pap. 24.95 (*0-8126-9425-2*) Open Court.

Parting Sense: A Couple's Guide to Divorce Mediation. rev. ed. Jack J. Shapiro & Maria S. Caplan. 130p. 1986. pap. 6.95 (*0-89709-146-9*) Liberty Pub.

***Parting Shot.** large type ed. Roger Ormerod. 336p. 1999. 31.99 (*0-7089-4126-5*, Linford) Ulverscroft.

Parting Shots. large type ed. Freda Bright. LC 93-15831. 599p. 1993. 18.95 (*1-56054-763-4*) Thorndike Pr.

Parting the Curtain: Propaganda, Culture, & the Cold War. Walter L. Hixson. 299p. 1997. pap. 17.95 (*0-312-17680-5*) St Martin.

Parting the Curtains: Interviews with Southern Writers. Dannye R. Powell. LC 94-24853. (Illus.). 353p. 1994. 12.95 (*0-89587-116-5*) Blair.

***Parting the Veil: Stories from a Mormon Imagination.** Phyllis Barber. LC 98-47294. 142p. 1999. pap. 16.95 (*1-56085-120-1*) Signature Bks.

Parting the Waters: America in the King Years, 1954-1963. Taylor Branch. 1038p. 1989. pap. 16.00 (*0-671-68742-5*, Touchstone) S&S Trade Pap.

Parting the Waters: How Vision & Faith Make Good Business. James M. Vincent. 1997. pap. 11.99 (*0-8024-5934-X*, 9) Moody.

Parting Visions. Melvin Morse. 1995. mass mkt. 5.99 (*0-8041-1366-1*) Ivy Books.

Partings. Leonid Borodin. 1987. 15.95 (*0-15-170978-5*) Harcourt.

Partings at Dawn: An Anthology of Japanese Gay Literature. Ed. & Pref. by Stephen Miller. (Illus.). 352p. 1996. 50.00 (*0-940567-17-2*); pap. 19.95 (*0-940567-18-0*) Gay Sunshine.

Partings Welded Together: Politics & Desire in the Nineteenth Century English Novel. David Musselwhite. 304p. 1987. text 57.50 (*0-416-06162-1*); pap. text 14.95 (*0-416-06172-9*) Routledge.

Partisan. Yitzhak Arad. LC 78-71299. (Illus.). 288p. 1979. 9.95 (*0-89604-010-0*, Holocaust Library) US Holocaust.

Partisan. large type ed. Benjamin Cheever. LC 94-14546. (Americana: the Making of the Cities Ser.). 445p. 1994. lib. bdg. 21.95 (*0-7862-0253-X*) Thorndike Pr.

Partisan: A Romance of the Revolution. William Gilmore Simms. (BCL1-PS American Literature Ser.). 531p. 1992. reprint ed. lib. bdg. 99.00 (*0-7812-6860-5*) Rprt Serv.

Partisan: A Romance of the Revolution. rev. ed. William Gilmore Simms. LC 68-55650. reprint ed. 39.50 (*0-404-06054-4*) AMS Pr.

Partisan: A Tale of the Revolution, 2 vols. in 1. William Gilmore Simms. LC 68-23728. (Americans in Fiction Ser.). 530p. reprint ed. pap. text 7.95 (*0-89197-878-X*); reprint ed. lib. bdg. 28.00 (*0-8398-1859-9*) Irvington.

Partisan: Hostile Takeover, No. 2. S. Andrew Swann. 352p. 1995. mass mkt. 4.99 (*0-88677-670-8*, Pub. by DAW Bks) Penguin Putnam.

Partisan Approaches to Postwar American Politics. Ed. by Byron Shafer. LC 98-8999. (Illus.). 288p. (C). 1998. pap. text 24.95 (*1-56643-064-X*, Chatham House Pub) Seven Bridges.

Partisan Century: Political Writings from Partisan Review. Ed. by Edith Kurzweil. LC 96-982. 416p. 1996. 51.50 (*0-231-10330-1*) Col U Pr.

Partisan Century: Political Writings from Partisan Review. Ed. by Edith Kurzweil. LC 96-982. 416p. (C). 1996. pap. 20.50 (*0-231-10331-X*) Col U Pr.

Partisan Leader: A Tale of the Future. Nathaniel B. Tucker. LC 68-57557. (Muckrakers Ser.). 392p. reprint ed. lib. bdg. 39.00 (*0-8398-1975-7*) Irvington.

Partisan Leader: A Tale of the Future. Nathaniel B. Tucker. (Americans in Fiction Ser.). 392p. (C). 1986. reprint ed. pap. text 8.95 (*0-8290-1863-8*) Irvington.

Partisan Life with Col. John S. Mosby. Major J. Scott. 36.00 (*0-8488-1159-3*) Amereon Ltd.

Partisan Life with Col. John S. Mosby. John Scott. 492p. 1985. reprint ed. 30.00 (*0-942211-89-8*) Olde Soldier Bks.

***Partisan Linkages in Southern Politics: Elites, Voters & Identifiers.** Michael A. Maggiotto & Gary D. Wekkin. LC 00-8218. 208p. 2000. 38.00 (*1-57233-088-0*) U of Tenn Pr.

Partisan or Neutral? The Futility of Public Political Theory. Michael J. White. LC 96-48980. (Studies in Social, Political, & Legal Philosophy: No. 70). 160p. 1997. 55.50 (*0-8476-8453-9*); pap. 23.95 (*0-8476-8454-7*) Rowman.

Partisan Politics, Divided Government, & the Economy. Alberto Alesina & Howard Rosenthal. LC 93-48512. (Political Economy of Institutions & Decisions Ser.). 298p. (C). 1995. text 69.95 (*0-521-43029-1*) Cambridge U Pr.

Partisan Politics, Divided Government, & the Economy. Alberto Alesina & Howard Rosenthal. LC 93-48512. (Political Economy of Institutions & Decisions Ser.). 298p. (C). 1995. pap. text 19.95 (*0-521-43620-6*) Cambridge U Pr.

Partisan Politics in the Global Economy. Geoffrey Garrett. LC 97-16731. (Cambridge Studies in Comparative Politics). (Illus.). 200p. (C). 1998. text 54.95 (*0-521-44154-4*); pap. text 17.95 (*0-521-44690-2*) Cambridge U Pr.

Partisan, Racial, & Gender Makeup of Georgia County Offices. Charles S. Bullock, III. LC 93-19837. (Public Policy Research Ser.). 1993. 5.00 (*0-89854-168-9*) U of GA Inst Govt.

Partisan Rangers of the Confederate States Army: Memoirs of Adam R. Johnson. A. R. Johnson. Ed. by William J. Davis. LC 95-16738. 640p. 1995. reprint ed. 32.95 (*1-880510-29-4*) State House Pr.

Partisan Spirit: Kentucky Politics, 1779-1792. Patricia Watlington. LC 76-181463. 288p. reprint ed. pap. 89.30 (*0-8357-3922-8*, 203665700004) Bks Demand.

Partisan Warfare in Nineteenth Century Poland. Emanuel Halicz. (Odense Studies in History & Social Sciences: No. 25). 217p. (Orig.). 1975. pap. 22.50 (*87-7492-135-5*, Pub. by Odense Universitets Forlag) Coronet Bks.

Partisan Warfare, 1941-1945. N. Thomas & P. Abbott. (Men-at-Arms Ser.: No. 142). (Illus.). 48p. pap. 11.95 (*0-85045-513-8*, 9074, Pub. by Ospry) Stackpole.

Partisan Wedding. Renata Vigano. Tr. & Intro. by Suzanne Branciforte. LC 99-37940. 248p. 1999. pap. 19.95 (*0-8262-1228-X*) U of Mo Pr.

***Partisanas, 1936-1945: Women & Armed Resistance to Fascism.** Ingrid Strobl. 2000. pap. text 18.95 (*1-902593-28-6*) AK Pr.

Partisans. Piet Prins. Tr. by James C. Van Oosterom from DUT. (Illus.). 102p. (J). 1989. pap. 7.20 (*0-921100-07-8*) Inhtce Pubns.

Partisans. Rodrigo Toscano. 55p. 1999. pap. 10.00 (*1-882022-37-8*) O Bks.

Partisans: Marriage, Politics & Betrayal among the New York Intellectuals. David Laskin. LC 99-41977. 320p. 2000. 26.00 (*0-684-81565-6*) S&S Trade.

***Partisans & Guerrillas.** (Illus.). 208p. 2000. 29.95 (*0-7835-5719-1*) T-L Custom Pub.

Partisans & Poets: The Political Work of American Poetry in the Great War. Mark W. Van Wienen. (Cambridge Studies in American Literature & Culture Ser.: No. 107). (Illus.). 325p. (C). 1997. text 64.95 (*0-521-56396-8*) Cambridge U Pr.

Partisans & Progressives: Private Interest & Public Policy in Illinois, 1870-1922. Thomas R. Pegram. 312p. 1992. text 42.50 (*0-252-01847-8*) U of Ill Pr.

Partisans & the War in Italy. Dante A. Puzzo. LC 92-10256. (Studies in Modern European History: Vol. 7). 101p. (C). 1993. text 38.95 (*0-8204-1951-6*) P Lang Pubng.

Partisan's Memoirs: Woman of the Holocaust. Fay Schulman. LC 96-111281. (Illus.). 200p. 1995. pap. 15.95 (*0-929005-76-7*, Pub. by Sec Story Pr) LPC InBook.

Partisans of the Southern Press: Editorial Spokesman of the Nineteenth Century. Carl R. Osthaus. LC 94-16880. 288p. 1994. 39.95 (*0-8131-1875-1*) U Pr of Ky.

Partisanship, Politics & Partners: America's 'French Party,' 1796-1800, 387. Mathew Q. Dawson. LC 99-22145. 387. 264p. 2000. 62.95 (*0-313-31046-7*, Greenwood Pr) Greenwood.

Partision of India: Literary Responses. Ed. by S. R. Chakravarty & Mazhar Hussain. 1998. 26.00 (*81-241-0583-9*) Har-Anand Pubns.

Partita for Solo Violin. E. Laderman. 24p. 1993. per. 12.95 (*0-7935-2294-3*) H Leonard.

Partita in Nothing Flat. Judson Jerome. 16p. (Orig.). 1983. pap. 2.25 (*0-935306-17-X*) Barnwood Pr.

***Partita in Venice: A Novel.** unabridged ed. Curt Leviant. LC 99-64440. 208p. 1999. 24.00 (*0-942979-64-8*) Livingston AL.

***Partita in Venice: A Novel.** unabridged ed. Curt Leviant. 192p. 2000. pap. 12.00 (*0-942979-63-X*) Livingston U Pr.

Partita on "Hymn to Joy" Ed. by Dale Tucker. (St Cecilia Ser.). 20p. (Orig.). (C). 1997. pap. text 4.95 (*0-7692-0077-X*) Wrner Bros.

Partitas: Poems from Hollywood. Mark Dunster. 11p. 1999. pap. 5.00 (*0-89642-621-1*) Linden Pubs.

Partiti & Sindacati Nella Crisi Del Regime Parlamentare: Parties & Labor Unions in the Crisis of the Parliamentary Regime. Gaetano Mosca. LC 74-25771. (European Sociology Ser.). 348p. 1975. reprint ed. 28.95 (*0-405-06525-6*) Ayer.

Partition & Aftermath: Memoirs of an Ambassador. Kewal Singh. (Illus.). 1991. 40.00 (*0-7069-5811-X*) Advent Bks Div.

Partition by Tomas Segovia. Ed. & Tr. by Myra S. Gann from SPA. LC 96-69216. (Illus.). 160p. 1996. 20.00 (*0-938972-27-8*) Spanish Lit Pubns.

Partition of India: Indo-Pak Wars & the UNO. Ed. by Verinder Grover & Ranjana Arora. 1999. 88.00 (*81-7629-057-2*, Pub. by Deep & Deep Pubns) S Asia.

Partition of Palestine: Decision Crossroads in the Zionist Movement. Itzhak Galnoor. LC 93-51016. (SUNY Series in Israeli Studies). 379p. (C). 1994. text 74.50 (*0-7914-2193-7*); pap. text 24.95 (*0-7914-2194-5*) State U NY Pr.

Partition of the Steppe: The Struggle of the Russians, Manchus, & the Zunghar Mongols for Empire in Central Asia, 1619-1758: a Study in Power Politics. Fred W. Bergholz. LC 92-35176. (American University Studies: History: Ser. IX, Vol. 109). VII, 522p. (C). 1993. text 79.95 (*0-8204-1575-8*) P Lang Pubng.

Partition Principle: Remapping Quebec after Separation. Trevor McAlpine. (Illus.). 80p. 1996. pap. 9.95 (*1-55022-291-0*, Pub. by ECW) Genl Dist Srvs.

Partition Problems in Topology. S. Todorcevic. LC 88-39032. (Contemporary Mathematics Ser.: Vol. 84). 116p. 1989. pap. 29.00 (*0-8218-5091-1*, CONM/84) Am Math.

Partitioned Representations: A Study in Mental Representation, Language Understanding & Linguistic Structure. John Dinsmore. 352p. (C). 1991. lib. bdg. 122.00 (*0-7923-1348-8*) Kluwer Academic.

Partitioning Data Sets: DIMACS Workshop, April 19-21, 1993. Ed. by Ingemar J. Cox et al. LC 94-25120. (DIMACS Series in Discrete Mathematics & Theoretical Computer Science: Vol. 19). 408p. 1995. text 85.00 (*0-8218-6606-0*, DIMACS/19) Am Math.

Partitions. Michael Blitz. (Illus.). 50p. (Orig.). 1982. 11.00 (*0-916258-13-0*); pap. 7.50 (*0-916258-12-2*) Woodbine Pr.

Partitions & Atoms of Clause Structure: Subjects, Agreement, Case, & Clitics. Dominique Sportiche. LC 97-30512. 448p. (C). 1998. 110.00 (*0-415-16926-7*) Routledge.

Partitions of Poland 1772 93 95. Jerzy Lukowski. LC 98-8061. 248p. (C). 1998. pap. 30.13 (*0-582-29274-3*) Longman.

Partitions Poland 1772. Jerzy Lukowski. LC 98-8061. (C). 1998. 63.95 (*0-582-29275-1*) Longman.

Partitives: Studies on the Syntax & Semantics of Partitive & Related Constructions. Ed. by Jacob Hoeksema. LC 96-663. (Groningen-Amsterdam Studies in Semantics: Vol. 14). vi, 238p. (C). 1996. lib. bdg. 117.05 (*3-11-014794-7*) Mouton.

***Partitivitat und Indefinitheit: Die Entstehung und Entwicklung des indefiniten Artikels in den germanischen und romanischen Sprachen am Beispiel des Deutschen, Niederlandischen, Franzosischen und Italienischen.** Marion Presslich. 2000. 47.95 (*3-631-35775-3*, Pub. by P Lang) P Lang Pubng.

***Partizipien und Partizipialsatze Aus Kontrastiver Deutsch-Russischer Sicht: Ubersetzungstraining Mit Grammatischen Schwerpunkten.** Hilde Paul & Nina Maslova. (Beitrage Zur Slavistik Ser.). 246p. 1999. 45.95 (*3-631-35149-6*) P Lang Pubng.

Partly Chosen. Kirk Wulf. 40p. (Orig.). 1995. pap. 5.00 (*1-887289-10-0*) Rodent Pr.

Partly Right. Tony Campolo. 1995. pap. 10.99 (*0-8499-3633-0*) Word Pub.

Partner. John Grisham. 1997. mass mkt. 7.99 (*0-440-29555-6*) Dell.

Partner. John Grisham. 480p. 1998. mass mkt. 7.99 (*0-440-22476-4*, Island Bks); mass mkt. 7.99 (*0-440-22604-X*, Island Bks) Dell.

Partner. John Grisham. LC 96-54702. 368p. 1997. 26.95 (*0-385-47295-1*) Doubleday.

Partner & I. Susan Ware. LC 86-33972. 342p. 1987. 45.00 (*0-300-03820-8*) Yale U Pr.

Partner & I: Molly Dewson, Feminism, & New Deal Politics. Susan Ware. 342p. (C). 1989. reprint ed. pap. 20.00 (*0-300-04621-9*) Yale U Pr.

Partner Earth: A Spiritual Ecology. Pam Montgomery. LC 97-27281. (Illus.). 176p. 1997. pap. 12.95 (*0-89281-741-0*) Inner Tradit.

Partner for Love. large type ed. Jessica Hart. 1995. 23.99 (*0-263-14235-3*, Pub. by Mills & Boon) Ulverscroft.

Partner for Penny. large type ed. Paula Forest. (Linford Romance Library). 368p. 1997. pap. 16.99 (*0-7089-5031-0*, Linford) Ulverscroft.

Partner in Revolution: Abigail Adams see Benchmark Biographies - Group 2

Partner in the Dynamic of Creation: Womanhood in the Teachings of the Lubavitcher Rebbe, Rabbi Menachem M. Schneerson. Ed. by Uri Kaploun. LC 95-237464. 128p. 1994. 16.00 (*1-881400-11-5*) S I E.

Partner or Pariah? Attitudes Toward Israel in Syria, Lebanon, & Jordan. Hilal Khashan. LC 95-35618. (Policy Papers: No. 41). 52p. 1996. pap. 8.00 (*0-944029-63-9*) Wash Inst NEP.

Partner Power: Positive Spouse Support - a Key to Success. Chuck Dean. (Network Marketing Today Ser.: Vol. II). 112p. (Orig.). 1993. pap. 10.00 (*1-883893-00-3*) WinePress Pub.

***Partner Risk.** Warnock Davies. 2000. 34.95 (*1-55753-210-9*) Purdue U Pr.

Partner Schools: Centers for Educational Renewal. Ed. by Russell T. Osguthorpe et al. 348p. 1995. text 36.45 (*0-7879-0065-6*) Jossey-Bass.

***Partner Selling.** Bob Frare. LC 99-55559. 240p. 2000. pap. 10.95 (*1-58062-290-9*) Adams Media.

Partner to Partition: The Shaping of the Jewish Agency's Partition Plan in the Mandate Era. Yossi Katz. LC 97-28250. 224p. 1998. 52.50 (*0-7146-4846-9*, Pub. by F Cass Pubs); pap. 24.50 (*0-7146-4401-3*, Pub. by F Cass Pubs) Intl Spec Bk.

Partner Violence: A Comprehensive Review of 20 Years of Research. Jana L. Jasinski & Linda M. Williams. LC 97-33919. 1998. write for info. (*0-7619-1317-3*); pap. write for info. (*0-7619-1318-1*) Sage.

Partner with the Media to Build Safer Communities. Ed. by Jean O'Neil. 72p. 1995. pap. 19.95 (*0-934513-59-7*, K20) Natl Crime DC.

***Partner Yoga: Making Contact for Physical, Emotional & Spiritual Growth.** Cain Carroll & Lori Kimata. (Illus.). 2000. pap. 19.95 (*1-57954-271-9*, Rodale Reach) Rodale Pr Inc.

Partner Your Project. Sue Dyer. LC 96-70849. (Illus.). xvi, 234p. 1997. 34.95 (*0-9652243-0-9*) Pendulum Pubng.

***Partnering.** Frank Carr. LC 99-39379. 1999. write for info. (*1-57073-737-1*) Amer Bar Assn.

Partnering. Mosley & Moore. (GC - Principles of Management Ser.). 1997. text 29.95 (*0-538-84442-6*) S-W Pub.

***Partnering: Foundation Team Building & Networking.** (C). 2001. pap. text 0.00 (*0-201-61559-2*) HEPC Inc.

Partnering: How to Love Each Other Without Losing Yourselves. Hal Stone & Sidra Stone. LC 99-49353. 256p. 2000. pap. 13.95 (*1-57731-107-8*, Pub. by New Wrld Lib) Publishers Group.

Partnering: Starting Life in Another Relationship. Ian Marshall & Cecilia Morris. 1998. pap. 14.95 (*1-86448-342-3*, Pub. by Allen & Unwin Pty) IPG Chicago.

Partnering Dance & Education: Intelligent Moves for Changing Times. Judith L. Hanna. LC 98-34340. (Illus.). 272p. 1998. 30.00 (*0-88011-511-4*, BHAN0511) Human Kinetics.

Partnering for Growth: Entrepreneurial Strategies for Value-Chain Management. rev. ed. Amy Beekman. LC 99-33043. (Studies in Entrepreneurship). (Illus.). 132p. 1999. 43.00 (*0-8153-3402-8*) Garland.

***Partnering for Performance: Harnessing the Power of Finance in the New Organization.** Martin G. Mand. LC 00-29964. 224p. 2000. 27.95 (*0-8144-0556-8*) AMACOM.

Partnering for Success. Thomas R. Warne. LC 94-7661. 112p. 1994. 17.00 (*0-87262-976-7*) Am Soc Civil Eng.

Partnering in Design & Construction. Kneeland A. Godfrey. LC 95-245. 400p. 1995. 45.00 (*0-07-024038-8*) McGraw.

Partnering in the Information Industry. Betty Unruh & Art Elias. Ed. by Dick Kaser. (NFAIS Report Ser.: Vol. 2). 115p. 1996. pap. 75.00 (*0-942308-47-6*) NFAIS.

An Asterisk (*) at the beginning of an entry indicates that the title is appearing for the first time.

P

Partnering Intelligence: Creating Value for Your Business by Building Strong Alliances. Stephen M. Dent. LC 99-22739. 256p. 1999. 29.95 (0-89106-132-0, Pub. by Consulting Psychol) Consulting Psychol.

***Partnering with Chinese Firms: Lessons for International Managers.** Yadong Luo. 360p. 2000. text 73.95 (1-84014-763-6, Pub. by Ashgate Pub) Ashgate Pub Co.

Partnering with Families to Reform Services: Managed Care in the Child Welfare System. Madeleine H. Kimmich & Tracey Feild. (Illus.). 1999. pap. text 22.50 (0-930915-20-8, CMCP01) Am Humane Assn.

Partnering with God: Practical Information for the New Millennium. Lee Carroll. Ed. by Jill Kramer. (Book Six Ser.). 1997. pap. 14.00 (1-888053-10-0) Kryon Writings.

Partners. Grace Livingston Hill. 21.95 (0-89190-071-3) Amereon Ltd.

Partners. Nora Roberts. (NR Flowers Ser.: No. 21). 1992. per. 3.59 (0-373-51021-7, 5-51021-9) Harlequin Bks.

***Partners.** Nora Roberts. LC 00-37751. 2000. write for info. (0-7862-2612-9) Thorndike Pr.

***Partners.** Bernard Stonehouse & John Francis. LC 00-36456. (Illus.). (YA). 2000. pap. write for info. (0-439-20658-8) Scholastic Inc.

Partners. Deborah S. Syme. (Illus.). 32p. 1990. 8.95 (0-8074-0435-7, 103104) UAHC.

Partners. Karen Waggoner. LC 94-21524. (Illus.). 96p. (J). (gr. 4-6). 1995. 14.00 (0-671-86466-1) S&S Bks Yung.

Partners. large type ed. Hill. LC 98-48556. 1999. 30.00 (0-7862-1755-3, G K Hall Lrg Type) Mac Lib Ref.

Partners. large type ed. Stack Sutton. (Linford Western Large Print Ser.). 240p. 1998. pap. 17.99 (0-7089-5200-3, Linford) Ulverscroft.

Partners: A Practical Guide to Corporate Support of the Arts. LC 81-70689. (Illus.). 112p. 1982. 10.95 (0-317-02281-4) Alliance Arts.

Partners: A Three Act Play. Robert F. Morgan. 20p. (J). (gr. 6). 1994. pap. 20.00 (1-885679-05-X) Morgan Fnd Pubs.

Partners: Building Inter-System Cooperation in Aging with Developmental Disabilities. Edward F. Ansello et al. LC 97-80588. (Illus.). 92p. 1997. pap. text 10.00 (0-9664705-0-8) VA Ctr on Aging.

Partners: The Extraordinary Life of an Ordinary Man. Amnon Barness. (Illus.). 508p. 1999. 24.95 (1-58244-010-7) Rutledge Bks.

Partners Pt. 1: Pt. 1: Neighborhood Revitalization Through Partnership; Pt. 2: Whittier Neighborhood, a Minneapolis Case Study, 2 pts., Pts. 1 & 2. Ranae Hanson et al. (Illus.). 218p. 1981. pap. 15.00 (0-9607450-0-9) Dayton Hudson.

***Partners & Parents.** Michael Chinery. (Secrets of the Rainforest Ser.). (Illus.). 32p. (J). (gr. k-8). 2000. pap. 7.95 (0-7787-0226-X); lib. bdg. 19.96 (0-7787-0216-2) Crabtree Pub Co.

***Partners & Rivals: Representation in U. S. Senate Delegations.** Wendy J. Schiller. LC 99-59302. 2000. pap. text 17.95 (0-691-04887-8) Princeton U Pr.

***Partners & Rivals: Representation in U. S. Senate Delegations.** Wendy J. Schiller. LC 99-59302. (Illus.). 192p. 2000. 49.50 (0-691-04886-X, Pub. by Princeton U Pr) Cal Prin Full Svc.

Partners & the Dolphins Who Moved In. J. J. Fun. (Partners Ser.). 24p. (J). (gr. k-8). 1992. pap. write for info. (0-9632622-1-1) J J Fun.

Partners Becoming Parents. Ed. by Christopher Clulow. 1997. pap. 19.95 (0-7657-0024-7) Aronson.

Partner's for Change: A Peer Helping Manual & Guide for Training & Prevention Programs. V. Alex Kehayan. 464p. (J). (gr. k-12). 1992. spiral bd. 49.95 (0-915190-87-7, JP9087-7) Jalmar Pr.

Partners for Change: A Peer Helping Manual & Guide for Training & Prevention Programs. V. Alex Kehayan. 464p. (J). (gr. k-12). 1992. pap. 44.95 (0-915190-69-9, JP9069-9) Jalmar Pr.

Partners for Learning. Kathy Faggella & Janet Horowitz. Ed. by Lisa L. Durkin. (Illus.). 108p. 1986. pap. 10.95 (0-9615005-3-0) First Teacher.

Partners for Life: Making a Marriage That Lasts. Gene A. Getz & Elaine Getz. Ed. by Kathi Mills. LC 88-15798. 262p. 1988. pap. 7.99 (0-8307-1306-9, 5419603, Regal Bks) Gospel Lght.

Partners for Prosperity: The Group of Seven & the European Community. Alan D. Mep & Heidi Ulrich. 53p. (Orig.). (C). 1994. pap. text 25.00 (0-7881-0687-2) DIANE Pub.

Partners for the Dance: Forming Strategic Alliances in Health Care. Ed. by Arnold D. Kaluzny et al. LC 94-47387. 1995. pap. 19.50 (1-56793-025-5, 0955) Health Admin Pr.

Partners in Care? Hospices & Health Authorities. David Clark. (Occasional Papers on Social Administration). 176p. 1993. 64.95 (1-85628-227-9, Pub. by Avebry) Ashgate Pub Co.

Partners in Caring Home Care Aid Video Series. 26p. 1994. teacher ed. 15.00 (0-8273-6542-X) Delmar.

Partners in Catholic Education: Pastor, Professional, Parent. Jane W. Hughes & Mary L. Barnds. 92p. 1989. 8.00 (1-55833-024-0) Natl Cath Educ.

Partners in Change: The 12-Step Referral Handbook for Probation, Parole & Community Corrections. Edward M. Read. LC 96-136647. 270p. 1996. 17.95 (1-56838-101-8) Am Correctional.

Partners in Command: The Relationships Between Leaders in the Civil War. Joseph T. Glaathar. 286p. 1993. 24.95 (0-02-911817-4) Free Pr.

Partners in Community Health: Working Together for a Healthy New York 1998. 392p. 1999. pap. write for info. (1-887748-23-7) Milbank Memorial.

Partners in Community Leadership: Youth & Adults Working Together for Better Communities. Roy E. Hougen et al. Ed. by Julie Stewart. 250p. 1993. student ed., ring bd. 15.00 (0-936913-07-X, RRD 163) NCRCRD.

Partners in Conflict: The United States & Latin America in the 1990s. rev. ed. Abraham F. Lowenthal. 272p. 1990. text 41.00 (0-8018-4061-9) Johns Hopkins.

Partners in Covenant: The Art of Spiritual Companionship. Barbara A. Sheehan. LC 98-50598. 160p. 1999. pap. 15.95 (0-8298-1329-2) Pilgrim OH.

Partners in Creation: Stewardship for Pastor & People. fac. ed. Ronald D. Petry. LC 79-21770. 126p. 1980. pap. 39.10 (0-7837-7340-4, 204729300007) Bks Demand.

Partners in Crime. Agatha Christie. 240p. 1987. pap. text 5.50 (0-425-10352-8) Berkley Pub.

Partners in Crime. Rolando Hinojosa. LC 84-72298. 248p. (Orig.). (C). 1985. pap. 10.00 (0-934770-37-9) Arte Publico.

Partners in Crime. Alicia Scott. (Thirty-Six Hours Ser.). 1998. per. 4.50 (0-373-65014-0, 1-65014-2) Harlequin Bks.

Partners in Crime. large type ed. Agatha Christie. 1986. 15.95 (0-7089-1540-X) Ulverscroft.

Partners in Decision Making. 109p. 1996. pap. 10.00 (0-16-042698-7) USGPO.

Partners in Design Education. 1988. 35.00 (0-318-36148-5) Inst Busn Desn.

Partners in Dialogue: Christianity & Other World Religions. Arnulf Camps. LC 82-18798.Tr. of Christendom en godsdienstein der wereld. 272p. (Orig.). reprint ed. pap. 84.40 (0-8357-8543-2, 203485500091) Bks Demand.

Partners in Educational Improvement: Schools, Parents & the Community. 25p. 1989. 6.00 (0-317-05342-6) NASBE.

Partners in Empowerment: Networks of Innovation in Social Work. Ed. by Giles Darvil & Gerald G. Smale. (Pictures of Practice Ser.: Vol. 2). (C). 1990. 85.00 (0-7855-0089-8, Pub. by Natl Inst Soc Work) St Mut.

Partners in Empowerment Networks of Innovation in Social Work Vol. 2: Pictures of Practice. Ed. by Giles Darvill & Gerald G. Smale. (C). 1990. pap. 27.00 (0-902789-71-6, Pub. by Natl Inst Soc Work) St Mut.

Partners in Enterprise: The Worker Ownership Phenomenon. Ed. by Jack Quarter & George Melnyk. 201p. (Orig.). 1989. 45.99 (0-921689-45-4, Pub. by Black Rose); pap. 16.99 (0-921689-44-6, Pub. by Black Rose) Consort Bk Sales.

Partners in Enterprise: The Worker Ownership Phenomenon. Ed. by Jack Quarter & George Melnyk. LC 89-90248. (Black Rose Bks.: Vol. R135). 214p. (Orig.). 1989. reprint ed. pap. 66.40 (0-608-00460-X, 206127900007) Bks Demand.

***Partners in Eternity.** Amram Ben Yosef. 1998. 18.95 (1-56871-149-2, Pub. by Targum Pr) Feldheim.

Partners in Everyday Communicative Exchanges: A Guide to Promoting Interaction Involving People with Severe Intellectual Disability. Nancy Butterfield et al. 1995. 43.00 (1-55766-241-X) P H Brookes.

Partners in Furs: A History of the Fur Trade in Eastern James Bay, 1600-1870. Daniel Francis & Toby Morantz. (Illus.). 224p. (C). 1983. pap. text 24.95 (0-7735-0386-2, Pub. by McG-Queens Univ Pr) CUP Services.

Partners in Hate: Noam Chomsky & the Holocaust Deniers. Werner Cohn. (Illus.). 164p. (Orig.). 1995. pap. 9.95 (0-9645897-0-2) Avukah Pubns.

Partners in Healing: Healthcare Organizations & Parish Communities. Robert L. Kinast & Lawrence G. Seidl. LC 96-164009. 57p. 1996. pap. 5.00 (0-87125-227-9) Cath Health.

Partners in Healing: Redistributing Power in the Counselor-Client Relationship. Barbara Friedman. LC 92-3111. 200p. (Orig.). (C). 1992. pap. text 14.95 (0-89390-226-8) Resource Pubns.

Partners in Illusion: Albert Binford & William J. McCloskey. Nancy D. Moure. Ed. by Jacqueline Bryant. 120p. (C). 1996. pap. 24.95 (0-9633959-4-7) Bowers Mus.

Partners in Independence: A Success Story of Dogs & the Disabled. Ed Eames. LC 97-5992. 240p. 1997. 25.95 (0-87605-595-1) Howell Bks.

Partners in Independence: A Success Story of Dogs & the Disabled. Ed Eames & Toni Eames. 1997. 25.95 (0-614-27822-8) Macmillan USA.

Partners in Learning: Cooperative Learning with Younger & Older Student Pairs. Sandy Johnson & Ann Porter. (Illus.). 1996. pap. text, teacher ed. 32.50 (1-57091-147-9) Charlesbridge Pub.

Partners in Learning: Manufacturers & Users. Jerome M. Rosow et al. Ed. by Jill Casner-Lotto. (Training for New Technology Ser.: Part V). 87p. 1987. 95.00 (0-89361-054-2) Work in Amer.

Partners in Learning: Students, Teachers, & the School Library. Ray Doiron & Judy Davies. LC 97-30591. (Illus.). 182p. 1998. text 28.00 (1-56308-552-6) Libs Unl.

Partners in Learning: Teachers & Children in Reading Recovery. Carol Lyons et al. (Language & Literacy Ser.). 256p. (C). 1993. text 38.00 (0-8077-3298-2); pap. text 19.95 (0-8077-3297-4) Tchrs Coll.

Partners in Learning & Growing: Linking the Home, School, & Community Through Curriculum-Based Programs. Jan Philpot & Ed Philpot. Ed. by Leslie Britt. (Illus.). 80p. (Orig.). 1994. pap. text 9.95 (0-86530-298-7, 270-8) Incentive Pubns.

Partners in Life: The Handicapped & the Church. Ed. by Geiko Muller-Fahrenholz. LC 80-473412. (Faith & Order Papers: No. 89). 188p. reprint ed. pap. 58.30 (0-7837-6005-1, 204581500008) Bks Demand.

Partners in Life & Love: A Preparation Handbook for the Celebration of Catholic Marriage. Joseph R. Giandurco & John S. Bonnici. LC 96-22274. (Illus.). 96p. (Orig.). 1996. pap. 2.95 (0-8189-0766-5) Alba.

Partners in Life & Love: Rite of Marriage. Joseph R. Giandurco & John S. Bonnici. 1997. 29.95 (0-8189-0767-3) Alba.

Partners in Love. Jean Saunders. 1991. 19.00 (0-7278-4254-4) Severn Hse.

Partners in Love. large type ed. Maggie Kingsley. (Mills & Boon Large Print Ser.). 288p. 1997. 23.99 (0-263-15082-8, Pub. by Mills & Boon) Ulverscroft.

Partners in Love. large type ed. Jean A. Saunders. 272p. 1994. 27.99 (0-7505-0540-0, Pub. by Mgna Lrg Print) Ulverscroft.

Partners in Love: Ingredients for a Deep & Lively Marriage. Alanson B. Houghton. 1988. 16.95 (0-8027-1005-0) Walker & Co.

Partners in Marriage. Allison Hayes. (Special Edition Ser.: No. 1205). 1998. per. 4.25 (0-373-24205-0, 1-24205-6) Harlequin Bks.

Partners in Ministry. James Garlow. (Illus.). 136p. (Orig.). 1986. pap. 9.99 (0-8341-0693-0) Beacon Hill.

***Partners in Ministry: Clergy & Laity.** Roy W Trueblood. LC 99-41109. 1999. pap. text 15.00 (0-687-08123-8) Abingdon.

Partners in Ministry: Priests in Collaboration with Parish Life Coordinators. Ed. by Maurice L. Monette. LC 88-62579. 72p. (Orig.). (C). 1988. pap. 4.95 (1-55612-243-8) Sheed & Ward WI.

Partners in Mission U. S. A. II: A Popular Report. Robert B. Horine. (Illus.). 80p. (Orig.). 1993. pap. 3.95 (0-88028-146-4, 1232) Forward Movement.

***Partners in Movement.** Meade. (C). 1999. pap. text 49.00 (0-12-785026-0) Acad Pr.

Partners in Necessity: A Liaden Adventure, 4 vols. Sharon Lee & Steve Miller. 648p. 2000. reprint ed. pap. 18.00 (1-892065-01-0) Meisha Merlin.

Partners in Parenthood. Raina Lynn. (Intimate Moments Ser.). 1998. per. 4.25 (0-373-07869-2, 1-07869-0) Silhouette.

Partners in Passion. large type ed. Ann Kelly. (Black Satin Romance Ser.). 417p. 1997. 27.99 (1-86110-042-6) Ulverscroft.

Partners in Peace & Education: Roman Catholic-Presbyterian, Reformed Consultation IV: Text & Discussion Guide. Ed. by Ronald C. White, Jr. & Eugene J. Fisher. LC 88-6948. 157p. reprint ed. pap. 48.70 (0-7837-3196-5, 204280100006) Bks Demand.

***Partners in Peace & Prosperity: A Premier & a Governor in Bermuda.** Allison Moir & David Gibbons. LC 99-91943. 2000. 25.00 (0-7388-1406-7); pap. 18.00 (0-7388-1407-5) Xlibris Corp.

Partners in Peacemaking: Family Workshop Models Guidebook for Leaders. Ed. by James McGinnis et al. LC 85-159853. 170p. 1984. pap. text 10.75 (0-912765-08-9) Inst Peace.

Partners in Performance: Successful Performance Management. Tony Moglia. LC 96-72502. (Fifty-Minute Ser.). (Illus.). 120p. (Orig.). 1997. pap. 10.95 (1-56052-446-4) Crisp Pubns.

Partners in Peru. Sylvia DeLoach & Barbara Massey. LC 98-212787. (Child Like Me Ser.). 32p. (J). (gr. 1-6). 1998. per. 6.99 (1-56309-258-1, N987105, New Hope) Womans Mission Union.

Partners in Play: An Adlerian Approach to Play Therapy. Terry A. Kottman. LC 94-31001. 219p. 1995. pap. text 33.95 (1-55620-141-9, 72589) Am Coun Assn.

Partners in Play: Homemade Toys for Toddlers. Rita Anderson & Linda C. Neumann. (Illus.). 184p. 1991. pap. 12.95 (1-880202-01-8) Partners Pr.

Partners in Play: Parent-Made Toys for Toddlers. Linda C. Neumann. LC 94-37777. 1995. pap. 12.95 (0-8050-3673-3, Owl) H Holt & Co.

Partners in Power, Vol. 1. Roger Morris. 1997. pap. 12.95 (0-8050-5219-4) H Holt & Co.

Partners in Power: The Clintons & Their America. Roger Morris. 512p. 1995. 27.50 (0-8050-2804-8) H Holt & Co.

Partners in Power: The Clintons & Their America. Roger Morris. 1999. pap. text 17.95 (0-89526-302-5) Regnery Pub.

Partners in Prayer see Companeros de Oracion

Partners in Prayer: How to Revolutionize Your Church with a Team Strategy. John Maxwell. 180p. 1996. pap. 10.99 (0-7852-7439-1) Nelson.

Partners in Preparation: Training Married Couples for Marriage Preparation Ministry. Mary A. Paulukonis. 112p. (Orig.). 1995. pap. 29.95 (0-8146-2285-2, Liturg Pr Bks) Liturgical Pr.

Partners in Production? Women, Farm & Family in Ireland. Patricia O'Hara. LC 97-38373. 192p. 1998. 55.00 (1-57181-939-8); pap. 16.50 (1-57181-969-X) Berghahn Bks.

Partners in Profit: Partnerships Business Plans. John M. Townsend. LC 94-12045. (Illus.). 224p. (Orig.). 1995. pap. 29.95 (0-9648105-0-6) Gist Pub.

Partners in Profits: The Managing General Agent System under Fire. Ed. by Jerone Shaver. 122p. 1992. pap. 35.00 (0-614-05732-9) CPCU Society.

Partners in Progress. Esse V. Hathaway. LC 68-29213. (Essay Index Reprint Ser.). (Illus.). 1977. reprint ed. 20.95 (0-8369-0518-0) Ayer.

Partners in Progress: National Impaired Driving Goals & Strategies for 2005. Ed. by Ricardo Martinez. 123p. (Orig.). (C). 1997. reprint ed. pap. text 40.00 (0-7881-4030-2) DIANE Pub.

Partners in Prosperity: Report of the Twentieth Century Fund Task Force on the International Coordination of National Economic Policies. Robert Solomon. 132p. 1991. text 18.95 (0-87078-315-7); pap. text 10.95 (0-87078-316-5) Century Foundation.

Partners in Protest: Life with Canon Collins. Diana Collins. (Illus.). 288p. 1993. 55.00 (0-575-04823-9, Pub. by V Gollancz) Trafalgar.

Partners in Protest: Life with Canon Collins. Diana Collins. 384p. 1995. pap. 27.50 (0-575-05753-X, Pub. by V Gollancz) Trafalgar.

Partners in Public Service: Government-Nonprofit Relations in the Modern Welfare State. Lester M. Salamon. LC 94-31040. 304p. 1995. text 55.00 (0-8018-4962-4) Johns Hopkins.

Partners in Rebellion: Alabama Women in the Civil War. H. E. Sterkx. LC 74-99326. (Illus.). 238p. 1975. 34.50 (0-8386-7614-6) Fairleigh Dickinson.

Partners in Recovery: How Mates, Lovers & Other ProSurvivors Can Learn to Support & Cope with Adult Survivors of Childhood Sexual Abuse. Beverly Engel. 176p. 1991. 19.95 (0-929923-61-8) Lowell Hse.

Partners in Revolution: The United Irishmen & France. Marianne Elliott. 352p. (C). 1990. reprint ed. pap. 25.00 (0-300-04302-3) Yale U Pr.

Partners in Rhyme. William J. Middleton & Harvey E. Stanbrough. LC 95-90023. 65p. 1995. pap. 5.50 (1-886467-04-8) WJM Press.

Partners in Science: An NSP Guidebook. (National Science Partnership for Girl Scouts & Science Museums Ser.). (Illus.). 64p. 1997. pap. 10.00 (0-9625622-9-7) Franklin PA.

Partners in Science: Foundation Managers & Natural Scientists, 1900- 1945. Robert E. Kohler. LC 90-43520. (Illus.). 480p. 1991. 37.50 (0-226-45060-0) U Ch Pr.

Partners in Science: Letters of James Watt & Joseph Black. James Watt & Joseph Black. 518p. (C). 1969. 42.50 (0-674-65480-3) HUP.

Partners in Space: International Cooperation in Space - Strategies for the New Century. U. S. Crest Project on Space Cooperation Staff. LC 93-60300. 100p. (Orig.). 1993. pap. text 18.00 (0-9629930-2-6) US CREST.

Partners in the Divine Dance . . . Praying with Our Three Person'd God. Shaun McCarty. (Illumination Bks.). 88p. 1996. pap. 4.95 (0-8091-3655-4, 3655-4) Paulist Pr.

Partners in the Gospel: The Strategic Role of Partnership in World Evangelization. Ed. by James H. Kraakevik & Dotsey Welliver. (BGC Monograph). 204p. 1992. pap. 7.95 (1-879089-11-4) B Graham Ctr.

Partners in the Impossible. Richard W. Patt. 1984. 5.00 (0-89536-678-9, 4854) CSS OH.

Partners in the Kitchen: From Our House to Yours. Habitat for Humanity International Staff. LC 93-72357. (Illus.). 1993. pap. write for info. (0-87197-384-7) Favorite Recipes.

Partners in the Research Enterprise: University-Corporate Relations in Science & Technology. Ed. by Thomas W. Langfitt et al. LC 83-3508. (Illus.). 224p. 1983. pap. text 25.95 (0-8122-1150-2) U of Pa Pr.

Partners in Tyranny: The Nazi-Soviet Non-Agression Pact - August 23, 1939. unabridged ed. John Kolasky. 158p. 1990. reprint ed. pap. 8.00 (0-945001-86-X) GSG & Assocs.

Partners Nevertheless. Norma Hillmer. (C). 1989. pap. text 29.95 (0-7730-4913-4) Addison-Wesley.

Partners, Not Competitors: The Age of Teamwork & Technology. Lawrence Oliva. LC 90-82962. 256p. (C). 1992. pap. text 32.95 (1-878289-09-8) Idea Group Pub.

Partners of the Heart: Vivien Thomas & His Work with Alfred Blalock: An Autobiography. Vivien T. Thomas. LC 97-14222. 264p. (C). (gr. 13). 1998. pap. text 14.95 (0-8122-1634-2) U of Pa Pr.

Partners of the Tide. Joseph C. Lincoln. LC 72-98402. reprint ed. 49.50 (0-404-03987-1) AMS Pr.

Partners on the Frontier: The Future of U. S.-Russian Cooperation in Science & Technology. National Research Council Staff. LC 98-84557. 35p. (C). 1998. pap. text 10.00 (0-309-06042-7) Natl Acad Pr.

Partners or Competitors? The Prospects for U. S. - European Cooperation on Asian Trade. Ed. by Richard H. Steinberg & Bruce Stokes. LC 98-35637. 288p. 1999. 64.00 (0-8476-9321-X) Rowman.

Partners or Competitors? The Prospects for U. S.-European Cooperation on Asian Trade. Richard H. Steinberg. Ed. by Bruce Stokes. LC 98-35637. 288p. 1999. pap. 19.95 (0-8476-9322-8) Rowman.

***Partners or Prisoners: Christians Thinking about Women & Islam.** Ida Glaser & Napoleon John. (Illus.). xv, 331p. 1998. reprint ed. pap. 16.99 (1-900507-35-8, Pub. by Solway) OM Literature.

Partners Program: A Guide for Teachers & Program Leaders. National Helpers Network Staff. (Illus.). 85p. 1991. spiral bd. 30.00 (1-891455-02-8) Natl Helpers.

Partner's Recovery Guide: 100 Empowering Exercises. Douglas Weiss. 130p. (Orig.). 1997. pap., wbk. ed. 39.95 (1-881292-15-0) Discov TX.

Partners with God. Gila Gervirtz. Ed. by Ruby G. Strauss. (Illus.). 128p. (J). (gr. 3-4). 1995. 14.95 (0-87441-594-2); pap. 8.95 (0-87441-580-2) Behrman.

Partners with God. Gila Gevirtz. 1996. pap., teacher ed. 14.95 (0-87441-595-0) Behrman.

Partners with the Poor: An Emerging Approach to Relief & Development. Jerry Aaker. LC 92-35591. 1993. pap. 12.95 (0-377-00252-6) Friendship Pr.

***Partners with the Sun: South Carolina Photographers, 1840-1940.** Harvey S. Teal. (Illus.). 352p. 2000. 24.95 (1-57003-384-6) U of SC Pr.

***Partners Within.** Robert Felix. 150p. 2000. pap. 14.00 (0-9676309-1-6) Partners Grp.

***Partnershift: How to Profit from the Partnering Trend.** 2nd ed. Edwin Richard Rigsbee. LC 00-36652. 288p. 2000. 29.95 (0-471-38653-7) Wiley.

Partnership. Anne McCaffrey & Margaret Ball. 336p. 1992. mass mkt. 5.99 (0-671-72109-7) Baen Bks.

Partnership, 6 vols. Needles. (C). 1996. pap., suppl. ed. write for info. (0-395-81875-3) HM.

P

Partnership, 2 vols., 1. Alan R. Bromberg. 1988. 162.50 (0-316-10927-4, Aspen Law & Bus) Aspen Pub.

Partnership, 2 vols., 2. Alan R. Bromberg. 1988. 162.50 (0-316-10928-2, Aspen Law & Bus) Aspen Pub.

Partnership, Chapter 5. Alan R. Bromberg. 1991. 75.00 (0-316-10937-1, Aspen Law & Bus) Aspen Pub.

Partnership, Vol. 3. Alan R. Bromberg. 1993. 162.50 (0-316-10934-7, Aspen Law & Bus) Aspen Pub.

Partnership, Vol. 4. Alan R. Bromberg. 1993. 162.50 (0-316-10923-1, Aspen Law & Bus) Aspen Pub.

Partnership: An Innovative Curriculum for Disaffected & Disadvantaged Young People. Linda Dyson. 128p. 1992. pap. 24.95 (1-85346-210-1, Pub. by David Fulton) Taylor & Francis.

Partnership: 1994 Supplement. Alan R. Bromberg. 1994. 150.00 (0-316-10942-8) Little.

Partnership Agencies in Brit Ur. Bailey et al. 224p. 1995. 65.00 (1-85728-069-5, Pub. by UCL Pr Ltd); pap. 24.95 (1-85728-070-9, Pub. by UCL Pr Ltd) Taylor & Francis.

Partnership Agreement, Do It Yourself. Timothy J. Smith. 14.95 (0-9625456-7-8) SJT Enterprises.

*Partnership & Cooperation Agreement Between EC & Kazakhstan. (Treaty Series (Great Britain): No. 13 (2000)). 20p. 2000. pap. 16.00 (0-10-146272-7, MH62727, Pub. by Statnry Office) Bernan Associates.

*Partnership & Cooperation Agreement Between EC & Kyrgyz Republic. (Treaty Series (Great Britain): No. 12 (2000)). 20p. 2000. pap. 15.00 (0-10-146252-2, HM62522, Pub. by Statnry Office) Bernan Associates.

Partnership & Joint Venture Agreements. Richard D. Harroch. 1000p. 1992. ring bd. 95.00 (0-317-05391-4, 00616) NY Law Pub.

Partnership & L. L. C. Litigation Manual: Actions for Accounting & Other Remedies. James R. Burkhard. LC 95-76587. 333p. 1995. 215.00 (0-8318-0689-3, B689/B746) Am Law Inst.

*Partnership & Pragmatism: Germany's Response to Aids Prevention & Care. Rolf Rosenbrock & Michael T. Wright. LC 00-31133. 2000. pap. write for info. (0-415-24106-5) Routledge.

Partnership & Profit in Medieval Islam. Abraham L. Udovitch. LC 78-104097. (Princeton Studies on the Near East). 294p. reprint ed. 91.20 (0-8357-9508-X, 201487700093) Bks Demand.

Partnership & Profit-Sharing in Islamic Law. Nejatullah Siddiqi. 107p. 1996. pap. 8.50 (0-614-21530-7, 946) Kazi Pubns.

Partnership & S Corporation Tax Planning Guide: 1991 Edition. Bruce K. Benesh & M. Kevin Bryant. 530p. 1990. pap. text 64.00 (1-878375-16-4) Panel Pubs.

Partnership & Selling. Manning. 125p. 1994. pap. text 25.80 (0-205-15990-7) P-H.

*Partnership & Trust: The Tacis Program Me - The Environment of Russia - House of Lords Paper 157 Session 1997-98. (House of Lords Papers (All) Ser.). 1999. 45.00 (0-10-477098-8, HM70988, Pub. by Statnry Office) Bernan Associates.

Partnership Between Small & Large Firms. Ed. by J. M. Gibb. (C). 1989. lib. bdg. 91.00 (1-85333-160-0, Pub. by Graham & Trotman) Kluwer Academic.

Partnership Bidding: A Workbook, 1. Mary Paul. 1997. 7.95 (0-9698461-0-X) Master Pt Pr.

Partnership Book. 5th ed. Denis Clifford & Ralph E. Warner. (Illus.). 304p. (Orig.). 1997. reprint ed. pap. 34.95 incl. disk (0-87337-371-5) Nolo com.

*Partnership Book: How to Write a Partnership Agreement. 6th ed. Denis Clifford & Ralph E. Warner. LC 99-46091. 2000. write for info. (0-87337-560-2) Nolo com.

Partnership Council Field Book: Strategies & Tools for Co-Creating a Healthy Work Place. Bonnie Wesorick et al. LC 97-69991. (Illus.). 332p. (C). 1998. pap. 25.00 (0-9648264-4-5) Pract Field.

Partnership Debt Workouts. Chris Trower & John B. Spirtos. 1993. ring bd. 125.00 (0-685-69571-9, PWK) Warren Gorham & Lamont.

Partnership Federal & State Income Tax Reporting, 1995. rev. ed. Michael N. Jennings & Daniel R. Bolar. 496p. 1995. pap. 79.00 (0-9635011-1-9) JB Pubns.

Partnership Federal & State Income Tax Reporting, 1996. rev. ed. Michael N. Jennings & Daniel R. Bolar. 496p. pap. 84.00 (0-9635011-2-7) JB Pubns.

Partnership Federal & State Income Tax Reporting, 1997. rev. ed. Michael N. Jennings & Daniel R. Bolar. 508p. Date not set. pap. 84.00 (0-9635011-4-3) JB Pubns.

Partnership for a Drug-Free America: 1999 Partnership Attitude Tracking Study. (Illus.). 75p. pap. text 25.00 (0-7881-8693-0) DIANE Pub.

Partnership for A New Millennium: Addressing the Unmet Health Care Needs in Indian Country : Hearings Before The Committee On Indian Affairs, United States Senate, One Hundred Fifth Congress, Second Session ... May 21, 1998, Washington, Dc. United States. LC 99-162059. (S. Hrg. Ser.). 530 p. 1998. write for info. (0-16-057695-4) USGPO.

Partnership for Building Innovation: A National Strategy to Expedite Implementation of Innovative Building Technologies. 40p. 1995. 21.00 (0-7844-0126-8) Am Soc Civil Eng.

Partnership for Disorder: China, the United States, & Their Policies for the Postwar Disposition of the Japanese Empire, 1941-1945. Liu Xiaoyuan. (Illus.). 356p. (C). 1996. text 69.95 (0-521-55099-8) Cambridge U Pr.

Partnership for Equality - White Paper. (Command Papers: No. 3890). 1998. 25.00 (0-10-138902-7, HM89027, Pub. by Statnry Office) Bernan Associates.

Partnership for Excellence, 1969-1994: The History of EHV-Weidmann Industries, Inc. Jason Mills & Adrian A. Paradis. LC 94-39419. (Illus.). 120p. 1995. 30.00 (0-914659-72-3) Phoenix Pub.

Partnership for Growth: Reshaping Trade & Investment Patterns: New Approaches to Assisting Central & Eastern Europe. Ed. by Peter S. Rashish. LC 94-71785. 136p. (Orig.). 1994. pap. 15.00 (0-9628287-7-7) European Inst.

Partnership for Health: Building Relationships Between Women & Health Caregivers. Christina S. Beck et al. LC 96-54801. (Communication Ser.). 232p. 1997. pap. 21.50 (0-8058-2445-6); text 45.00 (0-8058-2444-8) L Erlbaum Assocs.

Partnership for Humans & Animals. R. E. McDowell. vii, 95p. 1991. pap. text 10.00 (1-880762-03-X) Kinnic Pubs.

Partnership for Peace vs. Relations with Russia. William B. Burks & Thomas G. Weston. (Pew Case Studies in International Affairs). 50p. (C). 1996. pap. text 3.50 (1-56927-468-1, GU Schl Foreign) Geo U Inst Dplmcy.

*Partnership for PFC Emissions Reductions. 1999. 185.00 (1-892568-44-6) Smicndctr Equip.

Partnership for Posterity: The Correspondence of William Maclure & Marie Duclos Fretageot, 1820-1833. William Maclure & Marie D. Fretageot. Ed. by Josephine M. Elliott. LC 94-15045. (Illus.). xxx, 1151p. 1994. 95.00 (0-87195-104-5) Ind Hist Soc.

Partnership for Sustainable Development: The Role of Business & Industry. LC 96-151469. 92p. 1994. 17.00 (1-899159-00-2, E.94.111.D.5) UN.

Partnership Games: The Musings of a Recently Retired Psychiatrist. Sanford L. Billet. LC 97-94034. 298p. 1997. 28.00 (0-9659365-0-3) Auth Village Pubns.

Partnership Guide: Strategies for Supporting Family Day Care in Your Community. National Council of Jewish Women Staff. 49p. 1991. 15.00 (0-685-62944-9) NCJW.

Partnership Handbook. New York State Bar Association Staff. Ed. by Raymond W. Merritt & Martin Helpern. LC 85-62739. 917p. 1985. 70.00 (0-942954-09-2) NYS Bar.

Partnership in Crisis? The United States, Europe & the Fall & Rise of NATO. Paul Cornish. LC 98-130156. (Chatham House Papers). 256p. 44.95 (1-85567-466-1) Continuum.

Partnership in Crisis? The United States, Europe & the Fall & Rise of NATO. Paul Cornish. LC 98-130156. (Chatham House Papers). 256p. 1997. pap. 15.95 (1-85567-467-X) Continuum.

Partnership in Education Management. Ed. by Cyril D. Poster & Christopher Day. LC 89-113195. (Educational Management Ser.). (Illus.). 239p. reprint ed. pap. 74.10 (0-608-20330-0, 207158300002) Bks Demand.

Partnership in Educational Management. Chris Day & Cyril Poster. 224p. (C). 1988. lib. bdg. 55.00 (0-415-00588-4) Routledge.

Partnership in Initial Teacher Training. Martin Booth et al. 192p. 1990. pap. text 45.00 (0-304-31984-8) Continuum.

Partnership in Literacy: Teacher Education in an Urban School. Camille Allen. LC 95-39274. 114p. 1996. pap. text 19.00 (0-435-08859-9, 08859) Heinemann.

Partnership in Practice: The Children Act of 1989. Ann Buchanan. 140p. 1994. 63.95 (1-85628-561-8, Pub. by Avebry) Ashgate Pub Co.

Partnership in Secondary Initial Teacher Education. Ed. by Anne William. 144p. 1995. pap. text 24.95 (1-85346-361-2, Pub. by David Fulton) Taylor & Francis.

Partnership in the German Theatre: Zuckmayer, & Hilpert, 1925-1961. William Grange. LC 90-41220. (Studies in Modern German Literature: Vol. 43). XVIII, 241p. (C). 1991. text 45.95 (0-8204-1405-0) P Lang Pubng.

Partnership in the United States: OECD Reviews of Rural Policy. OECD Staff. (Reviews of Rural Policy Ser.). 152p. 1997. pap. 25.00 (92-64-15467-1, 04-97-02-1, Pub. by Org for Econ) OECD.

*Partnership in Transition: U. S. - Israel Strategic Cooperation Beyond the Cold War. Ilan Berman. Ed. by James Colbert. 81p. 2000. pap. 14.95 (0-9644523-5-9) Jewish Inst Nat Secur.

Partnership Income Taxation. Alan Gunn. (University Textbook Ser.). 159p. 1990. pap. text 11.75 (0-88277-870-6) Foundation Pr.

Partnership Income Taxation. 2nd ed. Alan Gunn. LC 95-123694. 171p. 1994. pap. text 12.95 (1-56662-246-8) Foundation Pr.

Partnership Law Adviser. Claire M. Dickerson. 540p. 1991. 95.00 (0-685-69470-4) PLI.

Partnership Law for Securities Practitioners. John C. Ale. LC 92-12345. (Securities Law Ser.). 1992. ring bd. 145.00 (0-87632-896-6) West Group.

Partnership Management. William Moberly. 250p. (C). 1983. 110.00 (0-906322-28-6, Pub. by Blackstone Pr) St Mut.

Partnership Model: A Family Perspective on College Presidency. 142p. (Orig.). 1986. pap. text 21.00 (0-88044-078-3) AASCU Press.

*Partnership Model in Human Services: Sociological Foundations & Practices. Rosalyn Benjamin Darling. LC 00-38632. (Clinical Sociology Ser.). 2000. write for info. (0-306-46274-5, Kluwer Plenum) Kluwer Academic.

Partnership '95. Alan R. Bromberg. 1995. 175.00 (0-316-11046-9, Aspen Law & Bus) Aspen Pub.

Partnership Paradigm for Competitive Advantage, Pt. 1. Jerome M. Rosow & John V. Hickey. (Strategic Partners for High Performance Ser.). 115p. 1994. 95.00 (0-89361-050-X) Work in Amer.

Partnership Tax Digest. James A. Douglas & Daniel E. Feld. 1992. suppl. ed. 130.00 (0-7913-0880-4); suppl. ed. 130.00 (0-7913-1010-8) Warren Gorham & Lamont.

Partnership Tax Handbook. Prentice-Hall Staff. 176p. 1988. 19.50 (0-13-697104-0) P-H.

Partnership Tax Handbook. Prentice-Hall Staff. 200p. 1989. 21.50 (0-13-705873-X, Busn) P-H.

Partnership Tax Practice Manual: 1991 Edition. Evelyn Brody et al. 467p. 1990. text 99.00 (0-916592-99-5) Panel Pubs.

Partnership Tax Practice Manual: 1992 Edition. Evelyn Biody et al. 550p. 1991. ring bd. 99.00 (1-878375-70-9) Panel Pubs.

Partnership Taxation. Arthur B. Willis. LC 98-191268. 1998. write for info. (0-7913-3478-3) Warren Gorham & Lamont.

*Partnership Taxation. Arthur B. Willis et al. LC 98-191268. 1998. write for info. (0-7913-3477-5) Warren Gorham & Lamont.

Partnership Taxation, 2 vols. 3rd ed. A. Willis. 1989. text 280.00 (0-07-070623-9) McGraw.

Partnership Taxation, Cases & Materials. Curtis J. Berger & Peter J. Wiedenbeck. (American Casebook Ser.). 788p. (C). 1988. 50.50 (0-314-48238-5) West Pub.

Partnership Taxation Handbook. M. Martin & Jill Lockwood. 528p. 1989. text 79.95 (0-13-651407-3) P-H.

Partnership Taxation, Teacher's Manual to Accompany Cases & Materials. Curtis J. Berger & Peter J. Weidenbeck, Jr. (American Casebook Ser.). 167p. (C). 1989. pap. text. write for info. (0-314-67336-9) West Pub.

Partnership Understandings. Lawrence. 4.95 (0-910791-08-2, 0634) Devyn Pr.

Partnership Way: New Tools for Living & Learning. rev. ed. Riane Eisler & David Loye. (Illus.). 214p. 1998. pap. 24.95 (0-9627232-9-0) Psychology Pr.

Partnerships. Michael Griffiths. 124p. 1999. pap. 40.00 (1-85811-150-1, Pub. by CLT Prof) Gaunt.

Partnerships: A Compendium of State & Federal Cooperative Technology Programs. Christopher M. Coburn & Daniel R. Berglund. LC 94-32950. 660p. 1995. pap. text 39.95 (0-935470-78-6) Battelle.

Partnerships: A Natural Evolution in Logistics. Ed. by Joseph E. McKeon. LC 88-81504. (Logistics Resource Forum Ser.: No. 7). 126p. (Orig.). 1988. pap. text 19.95 (0-9610146-5-2) Leaseway Trans Corp.

Partnerships: Complete Tax Practice & Planning Guide. Evelyn Brody & M. Kevin Bryant. 900p. 1996. ring bd. 135.00 (1-886035-02-4) Pro Tax & Business.

Partnerships: Laws of the United States. Daniel Sitarz. LC 99-38111. (Quick Reference Law Ser.). 250p. 1999. pap. 16.95 (0-935755-69-1) Nova Pub IL.

*Partnerships: Small Business Start-Up Kit. Daniel Sitarz. LC 99-27440. 2000. per. 24.95 incl. cd-rom (0-935755-75-6) Nova Pub IL.

Partnerships - Effective Flood Hazard Management: Proceedings of the Thirteenth Annual Conference of the Association of State Floodplain Managers, May 22-27, 1989, Scottsdale, Arizona. (Special Publications: No. 22). 300p. (Orig.). 1990. pap. 20.00 (0-685-49320-2) Natural Hazards.

Partnerships Against Violence Vol. 2: Information Sources, Funding, & Technical Assistance Resource Guide. 166p. (Orig.). (C). 1995. pap. text 35.00 (0-7881-1888-9) DIANE Pub.

Partnerships Can Kill. Connie Shelton. (Charlie Parker Mystery Ser.: No. 3). 240p. 1998. mass mkt. 5.50 (1-890768-02-2) Intrigue Press.

Partnerships for Classroom Learning: From Reading Buddies to Pen Pals to the Community & World Beyond. Kathlene Willing & Suzanne Girard. LC 97-106070. 1996. pap. text 13.50 (0-435-07230-7, 07230) Heinemann.

Partnerships for Community Preparedness. David F. Gillespie et al. LC 92-45774. (Program on Environment & Behavior Monograph Ser.: No. 54). 1993. 20.00 (1-877943-10-X) Natural Hazards.

Partnerships for Global Ecosystem Management: Science, Economics, & Law. Ed. by Ismail Scrageldin & Joan Martin-Brown. LC 99-170366. 280p. 1998. pap. 35.00 (0-8213-4265-7, 14265) World Bank.

Partnerships for Improving Schools, 24. Byrd L. Jones & Robert W. Maloy. LC 87-23774. (Contributions to the Study of Education Ser.: No. 24). 193p. 1988. 52.95 (0-313-25594-6, JPR/, Greenwood Pr) Greenwood.

Partnerships for Lifelong Learning. Lesley S. Farmer. LC 99-32263. (Professional Growth Ser.). 1999. 39.95 (0-938865-79-X) Linworth Pub.

Partnerships for Peace, Democracy & Prosperity. Ed. by Constantine C. Menges. LC 97-17069. 270p. (C). 1997. pap. 29.50 (0-7618-0796-9) U Pr of Amer.

Partnerships for Profit: Structuring & Managing Strategic Alliances. Jordan D. Lewis. 1990. 35.00 (0-02-919050-9) Free Pr.

Partnerships for Prosperity: Museums & Economic Development. Peggy Wireman. LC 97-11411. 175p. 1997. pap. 25.00 (0-931201-39-X) Am Assn Mus.

Partnerships for Sustainable Forest Ecosystem Management: Fifth Mexico/U. S. Biennial Symposium. Ed. by Celedonio Aguirre-Bravo & Avelino B. Villa-Salas. (Illus.). 419p. (Orig.). (C). 1996. pap. text 45.00 (0-7881-2978-3) DIANE Pub.

Partnerships in Birds: The Study of Monogamy. Ed. by Jeffrey M. Black. (Oxford Ornithology Ser.). (Illus.). 432p. (C). 1996. text 125.00 (0-19-854861-3); pap. text 55.00 (0-19-854860-5) OUP.

Partnerships in Chemical Research & Education. Ed. by James E. McEvoy. LC 91-32420. (ACS Symposium Ser.: No. 478). (Illus.). 250p. 1992. text 55.00 (0-8412-2173-1, Pub. by Am Chemical) OUP.

Partnerships in Family-Centered Care: A Guide to Collaborative Early Intervention. Peggy Rosin et al. 1996. 39.95 (1-55766-225-8) P H Brookes.

Partnerships in Healthcare: Transforming Relational Process. Ed. by Anthony L. Suchman et al. LC 97-45065. (Illus.). 368p. 1998. 95.00 (1-878822-80-2) Univ Rochester Pr.

Partnerships in Maths: Parents & Schools: the IMPACT Project. Ed. by Ruth Merttens & Jeff Vass. LC 92-42864. 256p. 1993. pap. 32.95 (0-7507-0155-2, Falmer Pr); boxed set 89.95 (0-7507-0154-4, Falmer Pr) Taylor & Francis.

Partnerships in Preparedness: A Compendium of Exemplary Practices in Emergency Management. Kay C. Goss et al. (Illus.). 90p. 1998. reprint ed. pap. text 25.00 (0-7881-4218-6) DIANE Pub.

Partnerships in Research, Clinical & Educational Settings. Roger Bibace et al. LC 99-26833. (Advances in Applied Developmental Psychology Ser.). 1999. write for info. (1-56750-455-8) Ablx Pub.

Partnerships in Teacher Education: Schools & Colleges Working Together. Ed. by Thomas F. Warren. 196p. 1996. pap. 23.50 (0-7618-0539-7); lib. bdg. 46.50 (0-7618-0538-9) U Pr of Amer.

Partnerships in the Sea: Hong Kong's Marine Symbioses. Brian Morton. (Illus.). 140p. 1988. 49.50 (962-209-211-X, Pub. by HK Univ Pr) Coronet Bks.

Partnerships Made E-Z. E-Z Legal Staff. (Made E-Z Ser.). 272p. 1999. pap. 17.95 (1-56382-437-X) E-Z Legal.

Partnerships Step-by-Step. David Minars. LC 97-2594. (Legal-Ease Ser.). 240p. 1997. pap. text 14.95 (0-7641-0184-6) Barron.

Partnerships That Perform: The Low Income Housing Tax Credit, 4 bks., Pt. 3. Photos by Jeffrey Klimar et al. (Illus.). 10p. 1997. 20.00 (0-942901-12-6) Enterprise Fnd.

*Partnerships Urban Governance. Jon Pierre. LC 97-49943. 206p. 1998. text 59.95 (0-333-68939-9, Pub. by Macmillan) St Martin.

Partnerships with People. Institute of Directors Staff. 1999. pap. text 14.95 (0-7494-2830-9) Kogan Page Ltd.

Partonic Structure of the Photon: Photoproduction at the Lepton-Proton Collider, Hera. Martin Erdmann. LC 97-15160. (Springer Tracts in Modern Physics Ser.: Vol. 138). 1997. write for info. (3-540-62621-2) Spr-Verlag.

Partonopeus de Blois. Ed. by A. T. Boedtker. (EETS, ES Ser.: No. 109). 1974. reprint ed. 65.00 (0-527-00312-3) Periodicals Srv.

Partons in Soft-Hadronic Processes: Proceedings of the Europhysics Study Conference, Erice, Italy, March 8-14, 1981. Ed. by R. T. Van de Walle. 338p. 1981. 48.00 (9971-950-00-6) World Scientific Pub.

*Partos Mentales O los Alemanes Se Extinguen. Gunter Grass. 163p. 1999. pap. 15.98 (84-204-4206-2) Santillana.

Partow Nameh see Book of Radiance

Parts. Tedd Arnold. LC 96-28552. (Illus.). 32p. (J). (ps-3). 1997. 15.99 (0-8037-2040-8, Dial Yng Read) Peng Put Young Read.

*Parts. Tedd Arnold. (Illus.). 32p. (J). (ps-3). 2000. pap. 5.99 (0-14-056533-7, PuffinBks) Peng Put Young Read.

*Parts: A Study In Ontology. Peter Simons. (Illus.). 408p. 2000. pap. 29.95 (0-19-924146-5) OUP.

Parts: Work by Rita McBride. Deborah Leveton & Eleanor Heartney. LC 92-73382. (Illus.). 42p. 1992. pap. 16.00 (1-879003-06-6) Edmundson.

Parts - Environmental Stress Screening Guidelines for Parts. Institute of Environmental Sciences Staff. 1985. pap. 140.00 (0-915414-86-4) IEST.

Parts - 1985 Proceedings of the 4th National Conference on Environmental Stress Screening of Electronic Parts. 1985. pap. 80.00 (0-915414-84-8) IEST.

Parts Added to the Mirrour for Magistrates. John Higgins & Thomas Blenerhasset. Ed. by Lily B. Campbell. LC 76-29439. reprint ed. 55.00 (0-404-15319-4) AMS Pr.

Parts & Assemblies - 1990 Proceedings, 6th National Conference & Workshop - Environmental Stress Screening of Electronic Hardware (ESSGH) 97p. 1990. pap. 90.00 (1-877862-07-X) IEST.

Parts & Assemblies - 1981 Proceedings, 2nd National ESSEH Conference & Workshop on Environmental Stress Screening of Electronic Hardware: Sept. 21-25, 1981, San Jose, CA. 195p. 70.00 (0-915414-67-8) IEST.

Parts & Assemblies - 1984 Proceedings of the 3rd National Conference-Workshop, Environmental Stress Screening of Electronic Hardware. LC 62-38584. 117p. 1984. pap. text 75.00 (0-915414-75-9) IEST.

Parts & Moments: Studies in Logic & Formal Ontology. Ed. by Barry Smith. (Analytica Ser.). 564p. 1982. 132.00 (3-88405-012-5) Philosophia Pr.

Parts & Other Parts. Charles Stein. LC 82-5505. (Illus.). 96p. 1982. pap. 9.95 (0-930794-66-4) Station Hill Pr.

Parts & Places: The Structures of Spatial Representation. Roberto Casati & Achille C. Varzi. LC 98-51512. (Illus.). 429p. 1999. 35.00 (0-262-03266-X, Bradford Bks) MIT Pr.

Parts Cleaning Handbook Without CFCs: How to Manage the Change. John B. Durkee. 110p. 1994. pap. 39.95 (1-56990-143-0) Hanser-Gardner.

Parts Department-Inventory Management. 6th ed. Mike Nicholes. (Illus.). 505p. (Orig.). student ed. 150.00 (0-685-10193-2) Mike Nicholes.

Parts I & II: Text & Commentary see Divine Comedy, II: Purgatorio

Parts I & II: Text & Commentary see Divine Comedy, III: Paradiso

Parts of a Story. 24p. 1994. pap. 9.95 (0-89898-965-5, JPC004) Wrner Bros.

Parts of a Whole. Margie Burton et al. Ed. by Susan Evento. (Early Connections Ser.). 16p. (J). (gr. k-2). 1998. pap. text 4.25 (1-892393-41-7) Benchmark Educ.

Parts of a Whole. Kari Jenson Gold. (Early Math Big Bks.). (Illus.). 16p. (J). (ps-2). Date not set. pap. 16.95 (1-56784-426-X) Newbridge Educ.

Parts of an Andrology: On Representations of Men's Bodies. Lawrence R. Schehr. LC 96-49744. 266p. 1997. 45.00 (0-8047-2919-0); pap. 16.95 (0-8047-2920-4) Stanford U Pr.

P

Parts of Animals. A. L. Peck. (Loeb Classical Library: No. 323). (ENG & GRE.). (C). 15.50 (*0-674-99357-8*) HUP.

Parts of Light: Poems. Vicki Hearne. LC 94-10709. (Poetry & Fiction Ser.). 80p. 1994. 32.50 (*0-8018-4939-X*); pap. 13.95 (*0-8018-4940-3*) Johns Hopkins.

Parts of Man. Witness Lee. 49p. 1969. pap. 2.50 (*0-87083-002-3*, 04-024-001) Living Stream Ministry.

Parts of Speech see Learn Writing & Grammar Quickly

Parts of Speech. 1997. 4.95 (*1-55708-579-X*, MCR249) McDonald Pub Co.

Parts of Speech. Tina Dubuque. 1998. 4.95 (*1-55708-601-X*, MCR314) McDonald Pub Co.

Parts of Speech. Brander Matthews. LC 68-54361. (Essay Index Reprint Ser.). 1977. 22.95 (*0-8369-0697-7*) Ayer.

Parts of Speech. Carol L. Perkins. 1995. 6.95 (*1-55708-456-4*, MCC935) McDonald Pub Co.

Parts of Speech & Linguistic Typology: Open Classes & Conversion in Russian & Tokelau. Arnfinn Muruvik Vonen. 344p. 1997. pap. 43.00 (*82-00-12685-4*) Scandnvan Univ Pr.

***Parts of Speech 1999c: Globe Fearon English.** 45p. 1998. write for info. (*0-13-023258-0*) S&S Trade.

Parts of the Body in Older Germanic & Scandinavian. Torild W. Arnoldson. LC 71-158274. (Chicago. University. Germanic Studies: No. 2). reprint ed. 37.50 (*0-404-50282-2*) AMS Pr.

Parts of the Body in the Later Germanic Dialects. William D. Baskett. LC 75-161725. (Chicago. University. Linguistic Studies in Germanic: No. 5). reprint ed. 29.50 (*0-404-50285-7*) AMS Pr.

Parts of the Sky. large type ed. Eliza Joekay et al. (Illus.). 12p. (J). (gr. k-3). 1999. pap. text 6.00 (*1-58084-097-3*) Lower Kuskokwim.

Parts I & II: Text & Commentary see Divine Comedy: Inferno

Parts Per Million Values for Estimating Quality Levels. Robert E. Odeh & D. B. Owen. (Statistics: Textbooks & Monographs: Vol. 87). (Illus.). 360p. 1987. text 167.50 (*0-8247-7950-9*) Dekker.

Parts Unknown. John Dilmore. 165p. 1999. pap. 13.95 (*0-88739-182-6*) Creat Arts Bk.

Parts Unknown Collected. Beau Smith. (Parts Unknown Ser.). 120p. 1995. pap. 12.95 (*1-888429-02-X*) Knight Pr.

Partsperson. LC 96-967005. xiii, 119p. 1995. write for info. (*0-662-24197-5*, Pub. by Can7 Govern Pub) Intl Spec Bk.

Partus Sequitur Ventrem: The Child Inherits the Mother's Condition. Ricardo A. Scott. (Ras Cardo Speaks to Humanity Ser.). (Illus.). (Orig.). 1995. pap. 9.95 (*1-883427-62-2*) Crnerstone GA.

Party. Mehesh Alkunchwar. Tr. by Ashish R. Marathi. (C). 1989. 9.00 (*81-7046-035-2*, Pub. by Seagull Bks) S Asia.

***Party.** DK Publishing Staff. (Scratch & Sniff Ser.). 12p. (J). 2000. 6.95 (*0-7894-5224-3*, D K Ink) DK Pub Inc.

Party. Lynne Hubbard. (C). 1989. pap. text 39.00 (*1-85821-025-9*, Pub. by Pentland Pr) St Mut.

Party. David McPhail. 1990. 14.95 (*0-316-88860-5*) Little.

Party. David McPhail. (J). (ps-4). 1990. 14.95 (*0-316-56330-7*, Joy St Bks) Little.

Party. Christopher Pike, pseud. (Final Friends Ser.: No. 1). (YA). (gr. 8 up). 1991. mass mkt. 3.99 (*0-671-73678-7*, Archway) PB.

Party. Christopher Pike, pseud. (Final Friends Ser.). (J). 1997. per. 3.99 (*0-671-01926-0*, Archway) PB.

Party. Christopher Pike, pseud. (Final Friends Ser.). (J). 1988. 9.09 (*0-606-04122-2*, Pub. by Turtleback) Demco.

Party. Barbara Reid. LC 98-29778. (Illus.). 32p. (J). (ps-2). 1999. 15.95 (*0-590-97801-2*) Scholastic Inc.

***Party.** Mario Testino. (Illus.). 96p. 2000. pap. 19.95 (*3-570-19252-0*) te Neues.

Party: A Guide to Adventurous Entertaining. Sally Quinn. LC 97-29874. 224p. 1997. 23.50 (*0-684-81144-8*) S&S Trade.

Party: A Guide to Adventurous Entertaining. Sally Quinn. (Illus.). 224p. 1998. pap. 12.00 (*0-684-84960-7*) S&S Trade.

Party: Library Edition. unabridged ed. Anton Chekhov. 1993. lib. bdg. 18.95 incl. audio (*1-883049-23-7*) Sound Room.

***Party Vol. 5026: 18 Acid-Free Papers for Scrapbooks & More!** Ed. by Suzanne McNeill. (Illus.). 18p. 1999. 8.45 (*1-893749-21-5*) Fiskars.

Party Activists in Southern Politics: Mirrors & Makers of Change. Ed. by Charles D. Hadley & Lewis Bowman. LC 97-21074. 240p. (C). 1998. text 48.00 (*0-87049-999-8*) U of Tenn Pr.

Party Ain't Over Yet! Tashia "Thema" McNeil. LC 97-65864. 1997. pap. 10.00 (*0-9647635-3-2*) La Caille-Nous.

Party & Agricultural Crisis Management in the U. S. S. R. Cynthia S. Kaplan. LC 86-32223. (Studies in Soviet History & Society). 223p. reprint ed. pap. 69.20 (*0-608-08537-5*, 206906000002) Bks Demand.

Party & Army: Professionalism & Political Control in the Chinese Officer Corps, 1949-1964. Ellis Joffe. LC 65-29001. (East Asian Monographs: No. 19). 210p. 1965. pap. 20.00 (*0-674-65500-1*) HUP.

Party & Constituency: Pressures on Congress. Julius Turner. Ed. by Edward V. Schneier. LC 75-110374. 332p. reprint ed. pap. 103.00 (*0-608-30974-5*, 202074600018) Bks Demand.

Party & Faction in American Politics: The House of Representatives, 1789-1801, 32. Rudolf Bell. LC 72-782. (Contributions in American History Ser.: No. 32). 311p. 1974. 59.95 (*0-8371-6356-0*, BPF/, Greenwood Pr) Greenwood.

Party & Government. Ed. by Jean Blondel & M. Cotta. 260p. 1996. text 65.00 (*0-312-15917-X*) St Martin.

Party & Holiday Decorations: A Handbook of Wafer Fun. Donna Horn. LC 87-50697. (Illus.). 88p. (Orig.). (J). (gr. 4-12). 1988. pap. 14.95 (*0-935009-97-3*) Wafer Mache.

Party & Other Stories. Anton Chekhov. 1976. 23.95 (*0-8488-0747-2*) Amereon Ltd.

Party & Other Stories. Anton Chekhov. Tr. by Constance Garnett from RUS. LC 84-6122. (Tales of Anton Chekhov Ser.: Vol. 4). 340p. 1984. reprint ed. pap. 9.50 (*0-88001-051-7*) HarpC.

Party & Professionals: The Political Role of Teachers in Contemporary China. Gordon White. LC 81-5256. 371p. 1981. reprint ed. pap. 115.10 (*0-7837-9977-2*, 206070400006) Bks Demand.

Party & Society: The Anglo-American Democracies. Robert R. Alford. LC 72-9541. (Illus.). 396p. 1973. reprint ed. lib. bdg. 69.50 (*0-8371-6584-9*, ALPS, Greenwood Pr) Greenwood.

Party & the Masses: Lenin's Model for the Bolshevik Revolution. Lennart Lundquist. LC 82-8505. 336p. 1982. lib. bdg. 40.00 (*0-941320-03-0*) Transnatl Pubs.

Party at Ground Zero. Elisa Wilson. 1987. 3.00 (*0-685-14074-1*) New Collage.

Party at Jack's: A Novella. Thomas Wolfe. Ed. by Suzanne Stutman & John L. Idol, Jr. LC 94-34179. 290p. 1995. pap. 24.95 (*0-8078-2206-X*) U of NC Pr.

Party at Manny's. Paul Van Loon. (Count Me in Bks.: Bk. 1). (Illus.). 24p. (Orig.). (J). (ps-1). 1994. pap. 4.95 (*1-55037-361-7*, Pub. by Annick) Firefly Bks Ltd.

Party Bag. Parnell. 1997. pap. 8.99 (*1-85792-286-7*, Pub. by Christian Focus) Spring Arbor Dist.

Party Battle. Ed. by Leon Stein. LC 73-19190. (Politics & People Ser.). 282p. 1974. reprint ed. 25.95 (*0-405-05891-8*) Ayer.

Party Boat Murders. Barbara Steiner. (Thumbprint Mysteries Ser.). 128p. (J). 1999. pap. 5.95 (*0-8092-0693-5*, 069350) NTC Contemp Pub Co.

***Party Cakes.** Emma Summer. (Illus.). 2000. 11.95 (*0-7548-0354-6*, Lorenz Bks) Anness Pub.

Party Cakes. James Winterflood. Ed. by Mary Darveau & Jane Johnson. LC 81-66546. (Continental's Creative Cake Ser.). (Illus.). 64p. (Orig.). 1981. pap. 12.95 (*0-916096-26-2*) Books Bakers.

Party Chief. Jack Rudman. (Career Examination Ser.: C-2167). 1994. reprint ed. pap. 34.95 (*0-8373-2167-0*) Nat Learn.

Party Coalitions: Realignment & the Decline of the New Deal Party System. John R. Petrocik. LC 80-22212. (Illus.). 224p. reprint ed. pap. 69.50 (*0-608-09496-X*, 205429700005) Bks Demand.

Party Coalitions: Realignments & the Decline of the New Deal Party System. John R. Petrocik. LC 80-22212. (Illus.). 1993. pap. text 10.00 (*0-226-66378-7*) U Ch Pr.

Party Coalitions in the Nineteen Eighties. Ed. by Seymour M. Lipset. LC 81-83095. 464p. 1981. text 39.95 (*0-917616-45-6*); pap. text 24.95 (*0-917616-43-X*) Transaction Pubs.

Party Conflict & Community Development: Postwar Politics in Ann Arbor. Samuel J. Eldersveld. 280p. 1995. text 52.50 (*0-472-09562-5*, 09562) U of Mich Pr.

Party Conflict & Community Development: Postwar Politics in Ann Arbor. Samuel J. Eldersveld. 280p. 1995. pap. text 20.95 (*0-472-06562-9*, 06562) U of Mich Pr.

***Party Crasher!** Joe Sharpnack. (Finger Flix Ser.). (Illus.). (J). 2000. pap. 3.95 (*0-7407-0465-6*) Andrews & McMeel.

***Party Crasher: A Gay Republican Challenges Politics As Usual.** Richard L. Tafel. LC 99-19345. 256p. 1999. 25.00 (*0-684-83764-1*) Simon & Schuster.

Party Creations: Book of Theme Event Design. Robin Kring. 504p. 1994. 59.95 (*0-9639600-0-8*) Clear Crk Pubg.

Party Day! Cynthia Jabar. (Illus.). (J). (ps-1). 1987. 11.95 (*0-316-43456-6*, Joy St Bks) Little.

Party Decline in America: Policy, Politics, & the Fiscal State. John J. Coleman. LC 96-6801. (Princeton Studies in American Politics). 288p. 1996. text 39.95 (*0-691-02731-5*, Pub. by Princeton U Pr) Cal Prin Full Svc.

Party Discipline & Parliamentary Government. Ed. by Shaun Bowler et al. LC 98-11722. (Parliaments & Legislatures Ser.). (Illus.). 313p. 1999. text 59.95 (*0-8142-0796-0*, BOWPAR); pap. text 22.50 (*0-8142-5000-9*, BOWPAX) Ohio St U Pr.

Party Dress. Kevin Coyne. LC 90-60286. 192p. 1991. pap. 13.95 (*1-85242-197-5*) Serpents Tail.

Party Elites in Divided Societies: Political Parties in Consociational Democracy. Kurt R. Luther & Kris Deschouwer. LC 98-43802. 1999. text. write for info. (*0-415-20127-6*) Routledge.

Party Fabulous: 12 Parties to Change the World. Todd Merrell. LC 96-215956. (Illus.). 224p. 1996. pap. text 14.00 (*0-425-15530-7*) Berkley Pub.

***Party Finance & Political Corruption.** Robert Williams. 2000. text 59.95 (*0-312-23170-9*) St Martin.

***Party Food.** Anness Publishing Staff. 2000. pap. 12.95 (*0-7548-0521-2*) Anness Pub.

Party Food: Small & Savo. Barbara Kafka. (Illus.). 356p. 1992. 27.00 (*0-688-11184-X*, Wm Morrow) Morrow Avon.

Party Food: The Essential Guide to Menus, Drinks, & Planning. Lorna Wing. (Illus.). 160p. 1999. 30.00 (*1-57959-040-3*, SOMA) BB&T Inc.

Party Food for Vegetarians. Linda Majzlik. 1994. pap. 10.95 (*1-897766-04-1*, Pub. by Jon Carpenter) Paul & Co Pubs.

Party Foods Southern Style. Marion B. Sullivan. 36p. (Orig.). 1994. pap. 3.25 (*1-886367-03-5*) Wellspring.

Party for the Girls: Six Stories. H. E. Bates. LC 87-26874. (New Directions Classics Ser.). 224p. 1988. 21.95 (*0-8112-1050-2*, Pub. by New Directions); pap. 10.95 (*0-8112-1051-0*, NDP653, Pub. by New Directions) Norton.

Party Formation & Democratic Transition in Spain: The Creation & Collapse of the Union of the Democratic Centre. Jonathan Hopkin. LC 98-38457. xi, 289p. 1999. text 69.95 (*0-312-21912-1*) St Martin.

Party Formation in East-Central Europe: Post-Communist Politics in Czechoslovakia, Hungary, Poland & Bulgaria. Ed. by Gordon Wightman. (Studies of Communism in Transition). 296p. 1995. 95.00 (*1-85898-132-8*) E Elgar.

Party Fun. (Illus.). 24p. (J). (gr. 2 up). lib. bdg. 12.95 (*0-88110-458-2*) EDC.

Party Games. large type ed. Hans Hellmut Kirst. 432p. 1982. 27.99 (*0-7089-0880-2*) Ulverscroft.

Party Games for Three's to Eight's: And Easy Cakes Too! Maurice Day. 195p. 1995. pap. 8.95 (*0-572-01580-1*, Pub. by Foulsham UK) Assoc Pubs Grp.

***Party Girl.** Lynne Ewing. 120p. (gr. 7-12). 1999. pap. 4.99 (*0-375-80210-X*) Random.

Party Girl. Lynne Ewing. LC 98-7904. 144p. (J). (gr. 9-12). 1998. lib. bdg. 17.99 (*0-679-99285-5*, Pub. by Random Bks Yng Read) Random.

Party Girl. Lynne Ewing. LC 98-7904. 128p. (YA). (gr. 9-12). 1998. 16.00 (*0-679-89285-0*, Pub. by Random Bks Yng Read) Random.

Party Girl Cookbook: Your Complete Guide to Throwing a Smashing Bash, with Ideas for Themes, Invitations, Costumes, & More Than 150 Recipes. Nina Lesowitz & Laura Morris Starr. LC 99-16035. 272p. 1999. pap. 14.95 (*1-57324-167-9*) Conari Press.

Party Going. Henry Green, pseud. LC 76-122053. 255p. 1970. reprint ed. 25.00 (*0-678-03161-4*) Kelley.

Party Government. E. E. Schattschneider. LC 76-56414. 219p. 1977. reprint ed. lib. bdg. 67.50 (*0-8371-9412-1*, SCPG, Greenwood Pr) Greenwood.

Party Handbook. Alison M. Boteler. LC 97-26148. 224p. (J). 1998. lib. bdg. 19.49 (*0-7868-5049-3*, Pub. by Disney Pr) Little.

Party Identification & Beyond: Representations of Voting & Party Competition. Ed. by Ian Budge et al. LC 75-35615. 403p. reprint ed. pap. 125.00 (*0-608-16338-4*, 202668100051) Bks Demand.

Party Identification, Political Behavior & the American Electorate, 125. Sheldon Kamieniecki. LC 84-15692. (Contributions in Political Science Ser.). 228p. 1985. 62.95 (*0-313-24358-1*, KPI/, Greenwood Pr) Greenwood.

Party Ideologies in America, 1828-1996. John Gerring. LC 97-46088. (Illus.). 360p. (C). 1998. text 64.95 (*0-521-59262-3*) Cambridge U Pr.

***Party Ideologies in America, 1828-1996.** John Gerring. (Illus.). 352p. (C). 2000. pap. text 19.95 (*0-521-78590-1*) Cambridge U Pr.

Party Ideology in Britian. Ed. by L. J. Tivey. 240p. 1989. pap. 15.95 (*0-415-02308-4*, A3569) Routledge.

Party in a Box: The Story of the Sundance Film Festival. Lory Smith. LC 98-3895. (Illus.). 256p. 1999. 24.95 (*0-87905-861-7*) Gibbs Smith Pub.

Party in Peking. large type ed. Margaret A. Pemberton. 319p. 1993. 27.99 (*0-7505-0464-1*, Pub. by Mgna Lrg Print) Ulverscroft.

***Party Intellectuals' Demands for Reform in Contemporary China.** Wenfang Tang. LC 99-33972. (Essays in Public Policy Ser.: No. 97). 1999. pap. 5.00 (*0-8179-4322-6*) Hoover Inst Pr.

Party Killer. large type ed. Hugh Pentecost. (Linford Mystery Library). 368p. 1997. pap. 16.99 (*0-7089-5099-X*, Linford) Ulverscroft.

Party Leaders. Joseph G. Baldwin. 1989. reprint ed. lib. bdg. 79.00 (*0-7812-1878-0*) Rprt Serv.

Party Leaders: Sketches of Thomas Jefferson, Alexander Hamilton, Andrew Jackson, Henry Clay, John Randolph of Roanoke; Including Notices of Many Other Distinguished American Statesmen. Joseph G. Baldwin. LC 72-39654. (Essay Index Reprint Ser.). 1977. reprint ed. 25.95 (*0-8369-2741-9*) Ayer.

Party Leadership & Revolutionary Power in China. Ed. by John W. Lewis. LC 72-120056. (Contemporary China Institute Publications). 430p. reprint ed. pap. 122.60 (*0-608-16803-3*, 2027229) Bks Demand.

Party Leadership in the States. Robert J. Huckshorn. LC 75-32487. 320p. 1976. 35.00 (*0-87023-201-0*) U of Mass Pr.

Party Lights: Healthy Party Foods & Environmentally Conscious Decorations. Linda G. Rector-Page & Douglas Van. (Illus.). (Orig.). 1994. pap. 19.95 (*1-884334-53-9*) Hlthy Healing.

Party Line. A. Bates. 176p. (J). (gr. 7 up). 1989. pap. 3.99 (*0-590-44238-4*) Scholastic Inc.

Party Lines, Pumps, & Privies see Memories of Hoosier Homemakers

Party-Military Relations in Eastern Europe: The Case of Romania. Alex Alexiev. (CISA Working Papers: No. 15). 47p. (Orig.). 1979. pap. 15.00 (*0-86682-014-0*) Ctr Intl Relations.

Party Mix: 21 Creative Plans for Fun Fellowship. Karol Ladd. LC 96-26872. 256p. 1996. pap. 10.99 (*0-8054-6095-0*, 4260-95) Broadman.

Party Network: The Robust Organization of Illinois Republicans. Mildred A. Schwartz. LC 89-40536. 336p. reprint ed. pap. 104.20 (*0-608-20474-9*, 207172600002) Bks Demand.

Party Now, Age Later. Jim Davis. (Main Street Editions Ser.). (Illus.). 48p. 1996. 6.95 (*0-8362-0931-1*) Andrews & McMeel.

Party of Five. Wendy C. Staub. LC 98-135346. 1998. pap. 10.00 (*0-425-16495-0*) Berkley Pub.

Party of Five: A Family Album. Wendy C. Staub. 112p. 1998. pap. 10.00 (*1-57297-352-8*) Blvd Books.

Party of Five: The Unofficial Companion. Brenda S. Royce. LC 97-34225. (Illus.). 256p. 1997. pap. 14.95 (*1-58063-000-6*) Renaissance.

Party of Five 3. Megan Stine. (J). 1998. per. 4.50 (*0-671-01772-1*) PB.

***Party of Humanity: Writing Moral Psychology in Eighteenth-Century Britain.** Blakey Vermeule. LC 00-8288. 280p. 2000. 42.00 (*0-8018-6459-3*) Johns Hopkins.

Party of Mad Fellows: The Story of the Irish Regiments in the Army of the Potomac. Frank A. Boyle. 443p. 1996. 29.95 (*0-89029-329-5*) Morningside Bkshop.

Party of the Communist World Statutes. Ed. by William B. Simons & Stephen White. 1984. lib. bdg. 210.50 (*90-247-2975-0*) Kluwer Academic.

Party of the Third Part: The Story of the Kansas Industrial Relations Court. Henry J. Allen & Samuel Gompers. LC 74-156401. (American Labor Ser., No. 2). 1971. reprint ed. 23.95 (*0-405-02911-X*) Ayer.

Party On! Resource Guide for Planning Parties, Wedding & Corporate Events!, Vol. 1. Mark Frendt. Ed. by Meg Galipault. (Illus.). 224p. (Orig.). 1993. pap. text 14.95 (*0-9636661-0-X*) K G Marx.

Party on Ice. Amy Hest. LC 94-43181. (Illus.). 48p. (J). (gr. 2 up). 1995. 15.00 (*0-688-08394-3*, Wm Morrow) Morrow Avon.

Party Organization & Activism in the American South. Ed. by Robert P. Steed et al. LC 96-52004. 272p. 1998. text 34.95 (*0-8173-0894-6*) U of Ala Pr.

Party Organization & Machinery. Jesse Macy. LC 73-19159. (Politics & People Ser.). 336p. 1974. reprint ed. 25.95 (*0-405-05881-0*) Ayer.

Party Organization & Machinery. Jesse Macy. (Notable American Authors Ser.). 1999. reprint ed. lib. bdg. 125.00 (*0-7812-3912-5*) Rprt Serv.

Party Organizations: A Data Handbook. Richard S. Katz & Peter Mair. (Illus.). 960p. (C). 1992. 150.00 (*0-8039-8783-8*) Sage.

Party Organizations in American Politics. Cornelius P. Cotter. LC 89-40205. (Pitt Series in Policy & Institutional Studies). 230p. 1989. pap. 71.30 (*0-608-05084-9*, 206563800005) Bks Demand.

Party, Parliament & Personality: Essays Presented to Hugh Berrington. 224p. (C). (gr. 13). 1995. 85.00 (*0-415-11526-4*, C0561) Routledge.

***Party! Party! Party!** (Rock & Pop Classics: Vol. 4). (Illus.). 30p. 1999. write for info. (*1-892207-33-8*) Intl Masters Pub.

Party Perfect! 40 Original Recipes for 25 Holidays & Celebrations Year-Round. Kai Bravo et al. (Illus.). ii, 60p. (Orig.). 1996. pap. 9.95 (*0-9653072-2-0*) Cookbk CA.

Party Perfect & Pampered: The Complete Party Book. Sally Holbrook. Ed. by Diane MacFarland. LC 94-73987. (Illus.). 224p. 1995. 24.95 (*0-9631225-1-7*) Sabill Pr.

Party Period & Public Policy: American Politics from the Age of Jackson to the Progressive Era. Richard L. McCormick. 384p. (C). 1988. reprint ed. pap. text 23.95 (*0-19-504784-2*) OUP.

Party Plan Sales: A Reference & Workbook. rev. ed. Prosperity & Profits Unlimited Staff. 1992. ring bd. 29.95 (*0-317-04782-5*) Prosperity & Profits.

Party Planner. Ed. by Owen Levy. (Party Planner Ser.). (Illus.). 96p. 1991. 18.95 (*0-9629770-0-4*) Langston Pr.

Party Planner, Vol. 6. B. Harvey. (Little Library Ser.). 1997. pap. 0.99 (*1-57748-108-9*) Barbour Pub.

Party Planning. Jean Pare. (Company's Coming Pint Size Bks.). 80p. 1995. pap. 4.99 (*1-895455-26-X*) Companys Coming.

Party Planning for African American Children: Great Party Ideas for African American Children's Birthdays & Other Special Occasions. Terry Williams. (Illus.). 1997. pap. write for info. (*0-937913-04-9*) W Stery.

Party Pluralism or Monism: Social Movements & the Political System in Yugoslavia, 1944-1949. Vojislav Kostunica & Kosta Cavoski. 256p. 1985. 63.00 (*0-88033-082-1*, Pub. by East Eur Monographs) Col U Pr.

Party Politics. William I. Jennings. LC 61-1035. 503p. reprint ed. pap. 143.40 (*0-608-14803-2*, 2025589) Bks Demand.

Party Politics & Centre-State Relations in India. S. K. Jain. (C). 1994. 20.00 (*81-7017-309-4*, Pub. by Abhinav) S Asia.

Party Politics & Decolonization: The Conservative Party & British Colonial Policy in Tropical Africa 1951-1964. Philip Murphy. (Oxford Historical Monographs). 272p. 1995. text 65.00 (*0-19-820505-8*) OUP.

Party Politics & Electoral Choice in an Indian State. Surya N. Misra. (C). 1989. 34.00 (*81-202-0247-3*, Pub. by Ajanta) S Asia.

Party Politics in Alabama from 1850 Through 1860. Lewy Dorman. LC 94-35291. (Library of Alabama Classics). (Illus.). 256p. 1995. pap. text 19.95 (*0-8173-0780-X*) U of Ala Pr.

Party Politics in America. 8th ed. Paul A. Beck. LC 96-13789. 467p. (C). 1997. pap. 53.00 (*0-673-99578-X*) Addson-Wesley Educ.

***Party Politics in America.** 9th ed. (C). 2000. write for info. (*0-321-05273-0*) Addison-Wesley.

Party Politics in Contemporary Western Europe. Ed. by Stefano Bartolini & Peter Mair. 192p. 1985. 35.00 (*0-7146-3271-6*, Pub. by F Cass Pubs) Intl Spec Bk.

Party Politics in Germany. Geoffrey Roberts. LC 97-16322. (New Germany Ser.). 220p. 1996. pap. 24.95 (*1-85567-311-8*) Bks Intl VA.

P

An Asterisk (*) at the beginning of an entry indicates that the title is appearing for the first time.

Party Politics in Germany. Geoffrey Roberts. LC 97-16322. (New Germany Ser.). 220p. 1997. 75.00 (*1-85567-029-1*) Bks Intl VA.

Party Politics in India. Myron Weiner. 1990. reprint ed. 14.00 (*81-85418-70-5*, Pub. by Low Price) S Asia.

Party Politics in Israel & the Occupied Terrorities, 93. Gershon R. Kieval. LC 82-12000. (Contributions in Political Science Ser.: No. 93). 228p. 1983. 55.00 (*0-313-23325-X*, KIP/, Greenwood Pr) Greenwood.

Party Politics in Japan. Hans H. Baerwald. 160p. (C). 1986. text 49.95 (*0-04-320183-0*); pap. text 16.95 (*0-04-320184-9*) Routledge.

Party Politics in Postcommunist Russia. Ed. by John Lowenhardt. LC 98-16306. (Illus.). 256p. (C). 1998. text 49.50 (*0-7146-4892-2*, Pub. by F Cass Pubs); pap. text 24.50 (*0-7146-4443-9*, Pub. by F Cass Pubs) Intl Spec Bk.

Party Politics in Punjab. Lakhwinder S. Sidhu. LC 94-906414. (C). 1995. 20.00 (*81-85247-08-0*, Pub. by Harman) S Asia.

Party Politics in the Age of Caesar. Lily R. Taylor. (Sather Classical Lectures: No. 22). 272p. (C). 1949. pap. 15.95 (*0-520-01257-7*, Pub. by U CA Pr) Cal Prin Full Svc.

Party Politics in the Continental Congress. H. James Henderson. 494p. 1987. reprint ed. pap. text 35.00 (*0-8191-6525-5*) U Pr of Amer.

Party Politics in the Nehru Era: (A Study of Congress in Delhi) Yogesh Puri. (C). 1993. 28.50 (*81-85135-72-X*) S Asia.

Party Politics in the South. Ed. by Robert P. Steed et al. LC 80-12084. 270p. 1980. 32.95 (*0-03-056586-3*, Praeger Pubs) Greenwood.

Party Possibilities. Virginia Kelley. (Illus.). 109p. (Orig.). 1995. pap. 18.95 (*1-879633-22-1*) Eldersong.

Party Potions: Theme Parties for Any Occasion. Robin Kring. 235p. 1998. pap. 22.95 (*0-9639600-1-6*) Clear Crk Pubg.

Party Potpourri, Scented Decor & More. Scentouri Staff. (Scentouri Instruction Bks.). 1984. ring bd. 24.95 (*0-318-01391-6*) Prosperity & Profits.

Party Punches. Evelyn Page & Tim Page. LC 86-202652. (Illus.). 190p. (Orig.). 1986. pap. 14.95 (*0-942557-00-X*) Page Pr & Assocs.

Party Realignment & State Politics. Ed. by Maureen Maokley. LC 91-40730. (Illus.). 319p. reprint ed. pap. 98.90 (*0-608-09858-2*, 206982300006) Bks Demand.

Party Reborn: The Democrats of Iowa, 1950-1974. James C. Larew. LC 80-51855. (Illus.). 216p. (C). 1980. 3.50 (*0-89033-002-6*); pap. 6.00 (*0-686-69969-6*) State Hist Iowa.

Party Receipts: From the Charleston Junior League: Hors d'Oeuvres, Savories, Sweets. Ed. by Linda G. Conway. 224p. 1993. pap. 13.95 (*0-945575-84-X*) Algonquin Bks.

Party Renewal in America: Theory & Practice. Ed. by Gerald M. Pomper. LC 79-25184. 204p. 1980. 36.95 (*0-275-90539-X*, C0539, Praeger Pubs) Greenwood.

Party! Resource: The Special Event Directory, 1994-1995. Stacy Stern & Gloria Danovitz. 125p. (Orig.). 1994. pap. 14.95 (*0-9642129-0-0*) Direct of Amer.

Party Rivalry & Political Change in Taisho Japan. Peter Duus. LC 68-21972. (Harvard East Asian Ser.: No. 35). 328p. reprint ed. pap. 101.70 (*0-608-30372-0*, 200549000054) Bks Demand.

Party Shakers. Kathy Martin. LC 82-21729. (Illus.). 47p. (J). (gr. k-8). 1982. pap. 3.95 (*0-942752-00-7*) C A M Co.

Party Shakers. Kathy Martin. Ed. by William Martin. (Illus.). 47p. 1982. pap. 3.95 (*0-942752-03-1*) C A M Co.

Party Snacks. (C). 1989. 45.00 (*1-85368-075-3*, Pub. by New5 Holland) St Mut.

Party Snacks Made Easy. (Recipes of the World Ser.). (Illus.). 1998. write for info. (*1-886614-89-X*) Intl Masters Pub.

Party Spirit in a Frontier Republic: Democratic Politics in Ohio, 1793-1821. Donald J. Ratcliffe. LC 98-23575. 357p. 1998. text 60.00 (*0-8142-0775-8*, RATPAR); pap. text 23.95 (*0-8142-0776-6*, RATPAX) Ohio St U Pr.

Party, State & Citizen in the Soviet Union: A Collection of Documents. Ed. by Mervyn Matthews. LC 89-34446. 428p. (gr. 13). 1990. text 97.95 (*0-87332-430-7*) M E Sharpe.

***Party State & Democracy in Germany.** Michaela W. Richter. 1999. text (*0-312-21461-8*) St Martin.

Party, State & Society: Electorial Behaviour in Britain since 1820. Ed. by Miles Taylor & Jon Lawrence. LC 96-33156. (Illus.). 224p. 1996. 78.95 (*1-85928-046-3*, Pub. by Scolar Pr) Ashgate Pub Co.

Party, State, & Society in the Russian Civil War: Explorations in Social History. Ed. by Diane P. Koenker et al. LC 88-46042. (Indiana-Michigan Series in Russian & East European Studies). (Illus.). 464p. 1989. pap. 12.95 (*0-253-20541-7*, MB-541) Ind U Pr.

Party-States & Their Legacies in Post-Communist Transformation. Maria Csanadi. LC 97-25009. (Studies of Communism in Transition). 448p. 1997. 100.00 (*1-85898-645-1*) E Elgar.

Party Strength in the United States, 1872-1970. Paul T. David. LC 77-183897. (Illus.). 324p. reprint ed. pap. 100.50 (*0-7837-4343-2*, 204405300012) Bks Demand.

Party Structure & Organization in East-Central Europe. Ed. by Paul G. Lewis. LC 96-13006. (Studies of Communism in Transition). 256p. 1996. 90.00 (*1-85898-289-8*) E Elgar.

Party Summer. R. L. Stine, pseud. Ed. by Patricia MacDonald. (Fear Street Super Chiller Ser.: No. 2). 176p. (YA). (gr. 7 up). 1991. per. 3.99 (*0-671-72920-9*, Archway) PB.

Party Summer. R. L. Stine, pseud. (Fear Street Super Chiller Ser.: No. 2). (YA). (gr. 7 up). 1991. 9.09 (*0-606-04999-1*, Pub. by Turtleback) Demco.

Party System Change: Approaches & Interpretation. Peter Mair. LC 97-174372. (Illus.). 264p. 1997. text 69.00 (*0-19-829235-X*) OUP.

Party System Change: Approaches & Interpretations. Peter Mair. (Illus.). 260p. 1999. pap. text 29.95 (*0-19-829549-9*) OUP.

Party Systems. Ed. by Steven B. Wolinetz et al. LC 98-74053. (International Library of Politics & Comparative Government). 608p. 1998. text 179.95 (*1-85521-576-4*, Pub. by Ashgate Pub) Ashgate Pub Co.

***Party Systems & Voter Alignments Revisited.** Lauri Karvonen & Stein Kuhnle. LC 00-29115. (Advances in International Relations & Politics Ser.). 2000. write for info. (*0-415-23720-3*) Routledge.

Party Things. A. Wilkes. (First Cookbooks Ser.). (Illus.). 24p. (J). (gr. 1-4). 1993. pap. text 4.50 (*0-7460-0231-9*, Usborne) EDC.

Party Till You Scream! G. G. Garth. (J). 1995. 9.09 (*0-606-07991-2*) Turtleback.

Party Time. (Quick Study Home Ser.). 4p. pap. 3.95 (*1-57222-236-0*) Barcharts.

Party Time. (In Classical Mood Ser.: Vol. 36). (Illus.). 1998. write for info. incl. cd-rom (*1-886614-62-8*) Intl Masters Pub.

Party Time. M. C. Millman. LC 94-73908. (Cheery Bim Band Ser.: Vol. 8). (Illus.). 143p. (J). (gr. 5-6). 13.95 (*1-56062-294-6*) CIS Comm.

***Party Time!** Ellen Weiss. (Bear in the Big Blue House Ser.). (Illus.). 8p. (J). 2001. write for info. (*1-57584-714-0*, Pub. by Rdrs Digest) S&S Trade.

***Party Time: Creative Kids.** Ina Massler Levin & Michael H. Levin. (Illus.). 160p. 1999. pap., teacher ed. 14.95 (*1-57690-510-1*, TCM2510) Tchr Create Mat.

Party Time & the New World Order. Harold Pinter. LC 93-28859. 80p. 1993. pap. 11.00 (*0-8021-3352-5*, Grove) Grove-Atltic.

***Party Time, Critter County Activity Center: Children's CD-ROM.** Educational Publishing Concept Staff. (Celebrate Jesus! 2000 50-Day Spiritual Adventure Ser.). (J). (ps-2). 1999. cd-rom 15.00 (*1-57849-177-0*) Mainstay Church.

Party Train: A North American Collection of Prose Poetry. Ed. by Robert Alexander et al. LC 95-69349. 400p. (Orig.). 1996. pap. 18.95 (*0-89823-165-5*) New Rivers Pr.

Party vs. State in Post - 1949 China: The Institutional Dilemma. Shiping Zheng. (Modern China Ser.). (Illus.). 308p. (C). 1997. text 59.95 (*0-521-58205-9*); pap. text 20.95 (*0-521-58819-7*) Cambridge U Pr.

Party Walls: The New Law. S. Bickford-Smith & Colin Sydenham. LC 98-165409. xxiv, 190p. 1997. write for info. (*0-85308-401-7*) Jordan Pubng.

Party Walls & What to Do with Them. Ed. by A. Anstey. 127p. (C). 1988. text 75.00 (*0-85406-496-6*, Pub. by R-I-C-S Bks) St Mut.

Party Walls & What to Do with Them. John Anstey. 128p. (C). 1988. text 80.00 (*0-85406-413-3*, Pub. by Surveyors Pubns) St Mut.

Party Weekend. Carolyn Keene. (Nancy Drew on Campus Ser.: No. 10). (YA). (gr. 8 up). 1996. mass mkt. 3.99 (*0-671-52758-4*) S&S Trade.

Party Weekend! Created by Francine Pascal. (Sweet Valley High Ser.: No. 143). 208p. (YA). (gr. 7-12). 1998. mass mkt. 3.99 (*0-553-49233-0*, Sweet Valley) BDD Bks Young Read.

Partyboat Fishing with the Experts. Richard Reina & William A. Muller. (With the Experts Ser.). (Illus.). 269p. 1987. text 14.95 (*0-9625187-1-9*) Wavecrest Comns.

Party Campaigning in the 1980s. Paul S. Herrnson. LC 88-1888. (Illus.). 192p. 1988. 36.50 (*0-674-65525-7*) HUP.

Party's Choice. William R. Keech & Donald R. Matthews. LC 75-31757. (Brookings Institution Studies in Presidential Selection). 284p. reprint ed. pap. 88.10 (*0-608-12704-3*, 202538400043) Bks Demand.

Party's Just Begun: Shaping Political Parties for America's Future. Larry J. Sabato. 272p. (C). 1997. pap. text 38.00 (*0-673-39746-7*) Addison-Wesley Educ.

Party's Not Over: A New Vision for the Democrats. Jeff Faux. 256p. 1997. pap. 14.00 (*0-465-00404-0*) Basic.

Party's Over. Caroline B. Cooney. (J). 1991. 8.35 (*0-606-01919-7*, Pub. by Turtleback) Demco.

Party's Over. Caroline B. Cooney. 192p. (YA). (gr. 7-9). 1992. reprint ed. pap. 3.25 (*0-590-42553-6*, Point) Scholastic Inc.

Party's Over: Living Without Leah. Janet Betts et al. 228p. 1999. 25.95 (*1-86105-116-6*, Pub. by Robson Bks) Parkwest Pubns.

Party's Over: The Diary of a Recovering Cocaine Addict. Katy Hendricks. 275p. (C). 1991. pap. 17.50 (*1-879383-06-3*) Am Univ Pr.

Party's Over: The Diary of a Recovering Cocaine Addict. Katy Hendricks & Norman Denzin. 275p. (C). 1992. 29.50 (*1-879383-07-1*) Am Univ Pr.

Parva: A Tale of War, Peace, Love, Death, God & Man. S. L. Bhyrappan. Tr. by K. Raghavendra Rao. (C). 1994. 20.00 (*81-7201-659-X*, Pub. by Indian Pubs) S Asia.

Parvati: Goddess of Love. Harsha Dehejia. 1999. 19.95 (*1-890206-12-1*) Grantha.

Parvatidarpana: An Exposition of Kasmir Saivism Thru the Images of Siva & Parvati. Harsha Dehejia. LC 97-904200. (C). 1997. 18.00 (*81-208-1483-5*, Pub. by Motilal Bnarsidass) S Asia.

Parvenu & Purple: Thumbnail Biographies. 1993. 20.00 (*0-614-13542-7*) R C Rapier.

Parvoviruses. (Virology Monographs: Vol. 15). 1976. 47.00 (*0-387-81355-1*) Spr-Verlag.

Parvoviruses. K. I. Berns. (Viruses Ser.). (Illus.). 424p. (C). 1984. text 115.00 (*0-306-41412-0*, Kluwer Plenum) Kluwer Academic.

***Parvoviruses: From Molecular Biology to Pathology & Therapeutic Uses.** Ed. by S. Faisst & J. Rommelaere. (Contributions to Microbiology Ser.: Vol. 4). (Illus.). xii, 208p. 2000. 155.00 (*3-8055-6946-7*) S Karger.

Parvoviruses & Human Disease. Ed. by John R. Pattison. 208p. 1988. 117.00 (*0-8493-5956-2*, QR201, CRC Reprint) Franklin.

Paryling with Francis de Sales. Thomas F. Dailey. Ed. by Carl Koch. LC 98-130091. (Companions for the Journey Ser.). (Illus.). 120p. 1997. pap. 8.95 (*0-88489-495-9*) St Marys.

***Parzen und Nornen: Die poetische Ausformung der mythologischen Schicksalsfiguren zwischen Aufklarung und Expressionismus.** Hildegard Kirschenknapp. 2000. 34.95 (*3-631-36024-X*) P Lang Pubng.

Parzifal von Claus Wisse und Philipp Colin (1331 bis 1336) Eine Ergaenzung der Dichtung Wolframs von Eschenbach. Ed. by Karl Schorbach. (Elsaessische Litteraturdenkmaeler aus dem 14, bis 17, Jahrhundert Ser.: Vol. 5). 441p. (C). 1974. reprint ed. 165.40 (*3-11-002365-2*) De Gruyter.

Parzival. Wolfram Von Eschenbach. Ed. by Andre Lefevere. LC 87-5084. (German Library). 320p. 1991. 39.50 (*0-8264-0345-X*); pap. 16.95 (*0-8264-0346-8*) Continuum.

Parzival. Wolfram Von Eschenbach. 864p. 1997. text 40.00 (*3-11-015614-8*) De Gruyter.

Parzival. Wolfram Von Eschenbach. Tr. & Intro. by A. T. Hatto. (Classics Ser.). 448p. 1980. pap. 14.00 (*0-14-044361-4*, Penguin Classics) Viking Penguin.

Parzival. Wolfram Von Eschenbach. 1961. pap. 14.00 (*0-394-70188-7*, V-188) Vin Bks.

Parzival: An Introduction. Eileen Hutchins. 96p. (J). 1992. pap. 14.95 (*0-904693-36-8*, Pub. by Temple Lodge) Anthroposophic.

Parzival: Eine Auswahl mit Anmerkungen und Woerterbuch. 4th ed. Wolfram Von Eschenbach. Ed. by Hermann Jantzen & Herbert Kolb. (Sammlung Goeschen Ser.: Vol. 5021). 128p. (C). 1973. pap. 9.85 (*3-11-004615-6*) De Gruyter.

Parzival: The Chalice of Ecstasy. Frater Achad. 82p. 1976. reprint ed. 11.00 (*0-911662-59-6*) Yoga.

***Parzival: The Quest of the Grail Knight.** Retold by Katherine Paterson. LC 97-23891. 144p. (YA). (gr. 5 up). 1998. 15.99 (*0-525-67579-5*, Dutton Child) Peng Put Young Read.

***Parzival: The Quest of the Grail Knight.** Katherine Paterson. 144p. (YA). (gr. 5-9). 2000. pap. 4.99 (*0-14-130573-8*, PuffinBks) Peng Put Young Read.

Parzival of Wolfram Von Eschenbach. Wolfram Von Eschenbach. LC 51-6040. (North Carolina. University. Studies in the Germanic Languages & Literatures: No. 5). reprint ed. 29.50 (*0-404-50905-3*) AMS Pr.

Parzival und der Gral in der Dichtung des Mittelalters und der Neuzeit. Wolfgang Golther. LC 74-178535. reprint ed. 51.00 (*0-404-56611-1*) AMS Pr.

Pas a Pas: Manuel De Lecture C. H. Elizov. 500p. 1992. pap. 40.00 (*0-13-063272-4*) P-H.

Pas a Pas French: Listening, Speaking, Reading, Writing. Thomas H. Brown. 544p. 1991. 84.95 (*0-471-61773-3*); pap., wbk. ed. 34.95 (*0-471-61774-1*) Wiley.

Pas a Pas French: Listening, Speaking, Reading, Writing. Thomas H. Brown. 850p. 1993. text, wbk. ed. 51.00 (*0-471-03750-8*) Wiley.

Pas d'Amour Entre Nous. Patricia Ryan. (Rouge Passion Ser.). (FRE.). 1997. pap. 3.50 (*0-373-37432-1*, 1-37432-1) Harlequin Bks.

Pas D'Armes & Round Tables: Re-enacting Medieval Feats of Arms. Brian R. Price. (Illus.). 296p. 1998. 39.95 (*1-891448-02-1*, CB004) Chivalry Bkshelf.

Pas de Dansa. limited ed. Joan Barcelo. (Ediciones Especiales y de Bibliofilo Ser.). (CAT., Illus.). 1993. 500.00 (*84-343-0321-3*) Elliots Bks.

***Pas de Deux: A Textbook on Partnering.** 2nd rev. expanded ed. Nikolai Serebrennikov. Ed. & Rev. by Marian Horosko. LC 00-27619. (Illus.). 184p. 2000. reprint ed. pap. 19.95 (*0-8130-1768-8*) U Press Fla.

Pas de Quartier pour les Poires. Guy Lavigne. (Novels in the Roman Plus Ser.). (FRE., Illus.). 160p. (YA). (gr. 8 up). 1996. pap. 8.95 (*2-89021-250-5*, Pub. by La Courte Ech) Firefly Bks Ltd.

Pas de Trois, Fun with Ballet Words. Katherine D. Goodale. (Illus.). 25p. (Orig.). (J). (gr. k-7). 1982. pap. 5.95 (*0-9609662-0-X*) Goodale Pub.

Pas de Vacances pour le Commissaire. Apter. text 3.95 (*0-88436-908-0*) EMC-Paradigm.

Pas de Vingt: A Celebration of Ballet Dancers. James Strecker. (Illus.). 80p. 1994. 19.95 (*0-88962-264-7*); pap. 12.95 (*0-88962-263-9*) Mosaic.

Pas d'Orchidees pour Miss Andrea! Chrystine Brouillet. (Novels in the Roman Jeunesse Ser.). (FRE.). 96p. (J). (gr. 4-7). 1994. pap. 8.95 (*2-89021-207-6*, Pub. by La Courte Ech) Firefly Bks Ltd.

Pas Fous, les Jumeaux! Bertrand Gauthier. (Novels in the Premier Roman Ser.). (FRE.). 64p. (J). (gr. 2-5). 1988. pap. 7.95 (*2-89021-104-5*, Pub. by Les Editions) Firefly Bks Ltd.

***Pa's Harvest.** Jan Andrews. (Illus.). (J). 2000. 12.95 (*0-88899-405-2*) Grndwd Bks.

Pas Perdus. Andre Breton. (FRE.). 1990. pap. 15.95 (*0-7859-2943-6*) Fr & Eur.

Pas Perdus: Essai. Andre Breton. (Coll. Soleil). 16.95 (*0-685-37234-0*, S20760); pap. 4.95 (*0-686-66855-3*, F89551) Fr & Eur.

Pasadena. (Shorey Historical Ser.). 22p. reprint ed. pap. 10.00 (*0-8466-0172-9*, S172) Shoreys Bkstore.

Pasadena Armory Show, 1989, Vol. 1. Text by Dave Hickey. LC 89-85569. (Illus.). 67p. (Orig.). 1989. pap. 20.00 (*0-911291-16-4*) Fellows Cont Art.

Pasadena Cowboy: Growing up in Southern California & Montana, 1925-1947. John L. Church. Ed. by Lisa Smith. LC 96-85162. (Illus.). 294p. (Orig.). 1996. pap. 17.95 (*0-9653071-2-3*) Conover-Patterson.

Pasadena Graphic Arts Academy Case Study Report. Anne M. Rogers & Scott Menzel. (Cross Case Report & Case Studies). 50p. 1995. text, teacher ed. 20.00 (*0-614-24542-7*); pap. text, teacher ed. 10.00 (*0-614-24543-5*) Natl Inst Work.

Pasadena Playhouse: A Celebration of One of the Oldest Theatrical Organizations in America. Judy O'Sullivan. (Orig.). 1992. 89.95 (*0-9633603-0-2*); pap. 39.95 (*0-9633603-1-0*) Theatre Corp Am.

Pasado de una Ilusion. Furet. (SPA.). 20.99 (*84-375-0415-5*, Pub. by Fondo) Continental Bk.

Pasado en Claro (The Clear Past) 2nd ed. Octavio Paz. (SPA.). 47p. 1978. pap. 8.99 (*968-16-1800-9*, Pub. by Fondo) Continental Bk.

Pasado Prehispanico en la Cultura Nacional, 2 vols. Sonia Lombardo de Ruiz. Incl. Vol. 1. El Monitor Republicano (1877-1896) (SPA.). 312p. 1994. pap. 12.50 (*968-29-5146-1*, IN067); (Memoria Hemerografica, 1877-1911 Ser.). 1994. pap. write for info. (*968-29-5145-3*) UPLAAP.

Pasado y Presente Del Amazonas: Su Historia Economica y Social. Ed. by Roberto Pineda & Beatriz Alzate. (Memorias del VI Congreso de Antropologia en Colombia Ser.). (SPA.). 180p. 1993. pap. 10.00 (*958-95572-1-X*, UA003) UPLAAP.

Pasaje a la Libertad. Ken Mochizuki. LC 98-47514. (Illus.), 32p. (YA). (gr. 1-4). 1999. 15.95 (*1-880000-81-4*, Pub. by Lee & Low Bks) Publishers Group.

Pasaje a la Libertad: La Historia de Chiune Sugihara. Ken Mochizuki. LC 98-47514. (SPA., Illus.). 32p. (YA). (gr. 2 up). 1997. pap. 6.95 (*1-880000-82-2*, Pub. by Lee & Low Bks) Publishers Group.

Pasajes. 4th ed. Mary L. Bretz et al. LC 96-36735. (ENG & SPA.). 432p. (C). 1996. pap. 45.94 (*0-07-007697-9*) McGraw.

Pasajes. 4th ed. Mary L. Bretz et al. LC 97-12875. (SPA.). 336p. (C). 1997. pap., student ed. 30.00 (*0-07-007699-5*); pap., student ed. 30.00 (*0-07-007698-7*) McGraw.

Pasajes: Actividades. 3rd ed. Mary L. Bretz et al. (C). 1992. text 22.00 (*0-07-007667-7*) McGraw.

Pasajes: Cultura. 3rd ed. Mary L. Bretz et al. (C). 1992. text 21.00 (*0-07-007666-9*) McGraw.

Pasajes: Gramatica. Mary L. Bretz et al. (C). 1982. 10.00 (*0-685-06749-1*) McGraw.

Pasajes: Lengua. 3rd ed. Mary L. Bretz et al. (C). 1992. text 33.50 (*0-07-007668-5*) McGraw.

Pasajes: Lengua. 4th ed. Mary L. Bretz et al. (SPA.). (C). 1997. pap., wbk. ed., lab manual ed. 30.00 (*0-07-007700-2*) McGraw.

Pasajes: Lengua-Cuaderno de Practica. 3rd ed. Mary L. Bretz et al. (C). 1992. pap. text, wbk. ed. 18.74 (*0-07-007669-3*) McGraw.

Pasajes: Lengua List of Comprehension. 3rd ed. Bretz. 1992. 14.06 (*0-07-007670-7*) McGraw.

Pasajes: Literatura. 3rd ed. Mary L. Bretz et al. (C). 1992. text 22.75 (*0-07-007665-0*) McGraw.

Pasajes Biblicos: Padre Nuestro. Tr. of Bible Passages: Our Father. (SPA.). 43p. 1986. pap. 2.50 (*0-8423-6314-9*, 497304) Editorial Unilit.

Pasame Otro Ladrillo. Charles R. Swindoll.Tr. of Hand Me Another Brick. 208p. 1980. 8.99 (*0-88113-315-9*) Caribe Betania.

Pasanella Klein Stolzman & Berg. Ed. by Oscar R. Ojeda. (Contemporary World Architects Ser.). (Illus.). 132p. 1999. pap. 19.99 (*1-56496-505-8*) Rockport Pubs.

Pasaporte: First Year Spanish. 2nd ed. Barbara Mujica et al. 125p. 1984. pap. text 15.00 (*0-471-80161-5*) Wiley.

Pasaporte: First Year Spanish. 2nd ed. Barbara L. Mujica et al. LC 84-125653. (ENG & SPA., Illus.). 475p. reprint ed. pap. 147.30 (*0-7837-3500-6*, 205783300008) Bks Demand.

Pasaporte Al Exito. 2nd ed. Jean Phillips. (Illus.). 232p. reprint ed. pap. text 21.95 (*0-945933-02-9*) Intechnos.

Pasara la Iglesia por la Gran Tribulacion? Yiye Avila.Tr. of Will the Church Go Through the Tribulation?. (SPA.). 82p. 1995. 4.99 (*1-56063-743-9*, 550046) Editorial Unilit.

Pasaso Presente (Past Present) Juan G. Ponce. (SPA.). 352p. 1993. 16.99 (*968-16-4175-2*, Pub. by Fondo) Continental Bk.

Pasatiempos en Espanol, Bk. 1. European Language Institute Staff. (Multilanguage Ser.). (SPA., Illus.). 71p. (Orig.). (J). (gr. 2-6). 1997. pap. 12.95 (*88-85148-50-6*, Pub. by Europ Lang Inst) Distribks Inc.

Pasatiempos en Espanol, Bk. 2. European Language Institute Staff. (Multilanguage Ser.). (SPA., Illus.). 71p. (Orig.). (J). (gr. 2-6). 1997. pap. 12.95 (*88-85148-97-2*, Pub. by Europ Lang Inst) Distribks Inc.

Pascack Valley Line. Wilson E. Jones. (Illus.). 160p. (Orig.). 1996. pap. 39.00 (*0-941652-14-9*) NJ Midland Railroad.

Pascal. Harriet L. Capron. 1995. 56.00 (*0-8053-1146-7*) Addison-Wesley.

Pascal. Corliss. Date not set. pap. text, teacher ed. write for info. (*0-314-65445-3*) West Pub.

Pascal. Samuel L. Marateck. 823p. 1991. 1.00 (*0-471-55016-7*) Wiley.

Pascal. 2nd ed. James Richards. 1986. pap. 37.50 (*0-12-587522-3*) Acad Pr.

Pascal. 4th ed. Nell Dale & Chip Weems. (Computer Science). Date not set. 58.75 (*0-669-34218-1*) Jones & Bartlett.

Pascal. 4th ed. Nell Dale & Chip Weems. (Computer Science Ser.). 1996. pap. 50.00 (*0-7637-0397-4*) Jones & Bartlett.

Pascal. 5th ed. Elliot B. Koffman. LC 94-34314. 731p. (C). 1995. pap. text 57.00 (*0-201-52674-3*) Addison-Wesley.

P

An Asterisk (*) at the beginning of an entry indicates that the title is appearing for the first time.

Pascal: Adversary & Advocate. Robert J. Nelson. LC 81-6330. (Illus.). 296p. 1982. 43.00 (*0-674-65615-6*) HUP.

Pascal: An Introduction to the Art & Science of Programming. 4th ed. Walter J. Savitch. 715p. (C). 1994. pap. text 57.00 (*0-8053-7458-2*) Benjamin-Cummings.

Pascal: Exploring Problem Solving & Program Design. Dennis Corliss & Kathy Seagraves-Higdon. 564p. (C). 1988. mass mkt. 43.75 (*0-314-59360-8*) West Pub.

Pascal: Exploring Problem Solving & Program Design (HC) Dennis Corliss & Kathy Seagraves-Higdon. 564p. (C). 1988. mass mkt. 45.50 (*0-314-59361-6*) West Pub.

*__Pascal: Great Philosophers.__ Bernard Rogers. LC 99-22484. 1999. pap. 6.00 (*0-415-92398-0*) Routledge.

Pascal: Introduction Art & Science Programmng. 4th ed. (C). 1995. 12.00 (*0-8053-7463-9*) Benjamin-Cummings.

Pascal: Introduction Art & Science Programmng. 4th ed. (C). 1995. 15.00 (*0-8053-7464-7*) Benjamin-Cummings.

Pascal: Introduction to Programmig. (C). 1930. text. write for info. (*0-06-041625-4*) Allyn.

Pascal: Introduction to Programming & Problem Solving. Douglas W. Nance. (Illus.). 639p. (YA). (gr. 9-12). 1986. reprint ed. mass mkt. 38.50 (*0-314-93206-2*) West Pub.

Pascal: Problem Solving & Program Design. 3rd ed. Elliot B. Koffman. (Illus.). 704p. (C). 1989. pap. text 26.36 (*0-201-11834-3*) Addison-Wesley.

*__Pascal: Programming with Style.__ 198p. (C). 1999. 14.25 (*0-536-60330-8*) Pearson Custom.

Pascal: Tape & Text Software. Brian W. Kernighan & P. L. Plauger. LC 81-3629. 1981. audio 80.00 (*0-201-10343-5*) Addison-Wesley.

Pascal: Test Item File. 4th ed. Nell Dale & Chip Weems. (Computer Science Ser.). Date not set. pap. 10.00 (*0-669-34221-1*) Jones & Bartlett.

Pascal: The Emergence of Genius. 2nd ed. Emile Cailliet. LC 75-94602. 383p. 1970. reprint ed. lib. bdg. 22.50 (*0-8371-2537-5*, CAP, Greenwood Pr) Greenwood.

Pascal: The Language & Its Implementation. Ed. by David W. Barron. LC 78-1010. (Wiley Series in Computing). 311p. reprint ed. pap. 96.50 (*0-8357-2767-X*, 203989200014) Bks Demand.

Pascal: The Man & His Two Loves. John R. Cole. 304p. (C). 1995. text 45.00 (*0-8147-1510-9*) NYU Pr.

Pascal: The Man & the Message. Roger H. Soltau. LC 73-109850. 216p. 1970. reprint ed. lib. bdg. 35.00 (*0-8371-4341-1*, SOPS, Greenwood Pr) Greenwood.

Pascal: The Software Fundamentals of Computer Science. Richard A. Meyers. 848p. (C). 1992. pap. 65.00 (*0-13-725623-X*) P-H.

Pascal: Understanding Programming & Problem Solving. 2nd alternate ed. Douglas W. Nance. Ed. by Westby. 596p. (C). 1992. reprint ed. pap. text 50.75 (*0-314-93304-2*) West Pub.

Pascal: Understanding Programming & Problem Solving. 3rd ed. Douglas W. Nance. Ed. by Westby. 716p. (C). 1992. pap. text 49.50 (*0-314-90877-3*) West Pub.

Pascal: Understanding Programming & Problem Solving. 3rd alternate ed. Douglas W. Nance. LC 94-37681. 728p. (C). 1995. mass mkt. 71.95 (*0-314-04361-6*) West Pub.

Pascal + Data Structure: Test Item File. 4th ed. Nell Dale & Susan C. Lilly. (Computer Science Ser.). 1995. pap. 10.00 (*0-669-34722-1*) Jones & Bartlett.

Pascal an Interactive Text. J. Abas & J. R. Mondragon. (Illus.). 268p. 1990. pap. 42.00 (*0-7503-0020-5*); disk 175.00 (*0-7503-0023-X*) IOP Pub.

Pascal & Beyond...Data Abstraction & Data Structures Using Turbo Pascal. Stephen Fisher & Atticus Regis. LC 91-31406. 528p. (C). 1991. text 77.95 (*0-471-50261-8*) Wiley.

Pascal & Disbelief: Catechesis & Conversion in the Pensees. David Wetsel. LC 93-51090. 409p. 1995. 69.95 (*0-8132-0808-4*) Cath U Pr.

Pascal & Rhetoric: Figural & Persuasive Language in the Scientific Treatises, the Provinciales, & the Pensees. Erec R. Koch. LC 96-30892. 1997. lib. bdg. 45.00 (*1-886365-05-9*) Rookwood Pr.

Pascal & the Arts of the Mind. Hugh M. Davidson. LC 92-40937. (Cambridge Studies in French: No. 46). 284p. (C). 1993. text 69.95 (*0-521-33193-5*) Cambridge U Pr.

Pascal & Theology. Jan Miel. LC 75-93822. 236p. reprint ed. pap. 73.20 (*0-608-15870-4*, 203074600070) Bks Demand.

Pascal by Example. 1994. teacher ed. 39.99 (*1-56529-480-7*) Que.

Pascal by Example: From Practice to Principle in Computer Science. Barry A. Burd. (Illus.). 1008p. (C). 1995. pap. text 65.00 (*0-15-568162-1*) OUP.

Pascal Compiler Validation. Ed. by Brian A. Wichmann & Z. J. Ciechanowicz. LC 82-23882. 190p. reprint ed. pap. 58.90 (*0-608-17867-5*, 203269800080) Bks Demand.

Pascal et Descartes see Philosophie de Pascal

Pascal et la Casuistique see Philosophie de Pascal

Pascal for BASIC Programmers. Charles Seiter & Robert H. Weiss. (Microbooks Popular Ser.). 224p. 1983. pap. 14.95 (*0-201-06577-0*) Addison-Wesley.

Pascal for Students (Including Turbo Pascal) 3rd ed. 1996. 24.95 (*0-340-64588-1*, Pub. by E A) Routldge.

Pascal for the Humanities. Nancy M. Ide. LC 87-5866. 320p. (Orig.). 1987. pap. text 42.50 (*0-8122-1242-8*) U of Pa Pr.

Pascal for the IBM-PC: Turbo Pascal, PC-DOS Pascal, & UCSD System Pascal. 5th rev. ed. Kevin W. Bowyer & Sherryl J. Tomboulian. (Illus.). 438p. 1995. pap., wbk. ed. 25.67 (*0-89303-766-4*) Brady Pub.

Pascal for the IBM Personal Computer. Theodore G. Lewis. LC 82-22750. 288p. 1983. pap. 15.95 (*0-201-05464-7*) Addison-Wesley.

Pascal for the Macintosh. Andrew Singer & Henry F. Ledgard. LC 84-24503. 456p. (C). 1986. pap. text, teacher ed. 8.00 (*0-201-11773-8*) Addison-Wesley.

Pascal for You. Pramod Koparkar. 1994. pap. 2.75 (*0-07-462205-6*) McGraw-Hill Prof.

Pascal Implementation: The P4 Compiler, 2 vols. Steven Pemberton & Martin Daniels. LC 81-20184. 172p. 1983. pap. text 52.95 (*0-470-27386-0*) P-H.

Pascal in a Nutshell. Ed. by Robert Van de Weyer. (Philosophers of the Spirit Ser.). 96p. 1997. pap. 6.95 (*0-340-69403-3*, Pub. by Hodder & Stought Ltd) Trafalgar.

Pascal in Practice: Using the Language. L. G. Moseley et al. (Computers & Their Applications Ser.). 274p. 1987. pap. text 34.95 (*0-470-20779-5*) P-H.

Pascal Lab Manual. (C). 1995. write for info. (*0-614-32243-X*) West Pub.

Pascal, les Libertins et les Jansenites see Philosophie de Pascal

Pascal Made Simple. McBride. 200p. Date not set. pap. text. write for info. (*0-7506-3242-9*) Buttrwrth-Heinemann.

Pascal Plus Data Structures, Algorithms, & Advanced Programming. 4th ed. Nell B. Dale & Susan C. Lilly. (Computer Science Ser.). 762p. (C). 1996. pap. 57.50 (*0-669-39540-4*) Jones & Bartlett.

Pascal Plus Data Structures, Algorithms & Advanced Programming. 4th ed. Nell B. Dale & Susan C. Lilly. (Computer Science Ser.). (C). 1995. pap., teacher ed. 10.00 (*0-669-34721-3*) Jones & Bartlett.

Pascal Plus Data Structures, Algorithms, & Advanced Programming 4th ed. Nell B. Dale & Susan C. Lilly. LC 94-76241. xxvii, 762p. 1995. write for info. (*0-669-34720-5*) Free Pr.

Pascal Precisely. Judy Bishop. 256p. (C). 1987. pap. text 19.95 (*0-201-17525-8*) Addison-Wesley.

Pascal Problem Solving. 3rd ed. Elliot B. Koffman. 1989. pap. text 27.16 (*0-201-52736-7*) Addison-Wesley.

Pascal Programming. Edward L. Lamie. LC 86-26779. 427p. reprint ed. pap. 132.40 (*0-7837-2819-0*, 205765300006) Bks Demand.

Pascal Programming & Problem Solving. 4th ed. Sanford Lee & Larry Nyhoff. (Illus.). 800p. (C). 1993. pap. 68.00 (*0-02-388731-1*, Macmillan Coll) P-H.

Pascal Programming & Problem Solving: A Systematic Approach. Mario J. Gonzales & Kay A. Robbins. (Illus.). 544p. (C). 1995. pap. text 44.00 (*0-03-060307-2*) OUP.

Pascal Programming for Libraries: Illustrative Examples for Information Specialists, 6. Charles H. Davis et al. LC 87-32293. (Contributions in Librarianship & Information Science Ser.: No. 60). 376p. 1988. lib. bdg. 79.50 (*0-313-22979-1*, DPC) Greenwood.

Pascal Programming for Libraries: Illustrative Examples for Information Specialists, 60. Charles H. Davis et al. LC 87-32292. (Contributions in Librarianship & Information Science Ser.: No. 60). 122p. 1988. 45.00 (*0-313-25259-9*) Greenwood.

Pascal Programming for Music Research. Alexander R. Brinkman. 986p. 1990. lib. bdg. 45.00 (*0-226-07507-9*) U Ch Pr.

Pascal Programming for Music Research. Alexander R. Brinkman. 896p. 1994. pap. text 39.95 (*0-226-07508-7*) U Ch Pr.

Pascal Programming for Problem Solving. Deborah Shands. (C). 1993. student ed. 15.00 (*1-881592-10-3*) Hayden-McNeil.

Pascal Programming Today. Steven L. Mandell. LC 86-24610. (Illus.). 550p. (Orig.). (C). 1987. pap. text 55.50 (*0-314-33935-3*); pap. text, teacher ed. 21.95 (*0-314-97186-6*) West Pub.

Pascal Programming Visual Masters. Donald D. Spencer. 112p. 1988. pap. 15.95 (*0-89218-097-8*, NO. 3042) Camelot Pub.

Pascal Simplified: A Guide for the First-Time User. Susan H. Gray. LC 85-14197. 144p. 1986. text 42.00 (*0-8476-7428-2*) Rowman.

Pascal User's Manual & Report. 3rd ed. K. Jensen & Niklaus Wirth. (Springer Study Edition Ser.). (Illus.). xvi, 266p. 1990. pap. 24.95 (*0-387-96048-1*) Spr-Verlag.

Pascal User's Manual & Report. 4th ed. K. Jensen et al. (Illus.). xvii, 266p. 1991. 45.95 (*0-387-97649-3*) Spr-Verlag.

Pascal-XSC: Language Reference with Examples. R. Klatte et al. x, 344p. 1992. 62.95 (*0-387-55137-9*) Spr-Verlag.

Pascalgorithms. Reilly. (C). 1988. pap. text, teacher ed. 2.76 (*0-395-45300-3*) HM.

Pascalgorithms. Edwin D. Reilly & Francis D. Federighi. 700p. (C). 1987. text. write for info. (*0-318-62601-2*) HM.

Pascalian Fictions: Antagonism & Absent Agency in Pascal's Wager & Other Pensees. Alton Van Kelly. LC 92-64403. 346p. 1993. lib. bdg. 38.95 (*0-917786-88-2*) Summa Pubns.

*__Pascalian Meditations.__ Pierre Bourdieu. 2000. 49.50 (*0-8047-3331-7*); pap. 18.95 (*0-8047-3332-5*) Stanford U Pr.

Pascali's Island. Barry Unsworth. 192p. 1997. pap. 11.00 (*0-393-31721-8*) Norton.

Pascal/Macpascal. Victor J. Law & Kah Lim Teck. (C). 1986. ring bd. 54.37 (*0-697-03145-4*, Irwn McGrw-H) McGrw-H Hghr Educ.

Pascal's Arithmetical Triangle. write for info. (*0-85264-283-0*) Lubrecht & Cramer.

Pascal's Letters: Reasoning & Morals of the Jesuits. Blaise Pascal. 319p. 1997. reprint ed. pap. text 25.00 (*0-87556-836-X*) Saifer.

Pascal's Lettres Provinciales: A Study in Polemic. Richard Parish. (Illus.). 224p. 1989. text 55.00 (*0-19-815155-1*) OUP.

Pascal's Lettres Provinciales: The Motif & Practice of Fragmentation. Louis A. MacKenzie, Jr. LC 88-61122. (ENG & FRE.). 146p. 1988. lib. bdg. 24.95 (*0-917786-63-7*) Summa Pubns.

Pascal's Triangle. Tony Colledge. (Illus.). 28p. (Orig.). 1992. pap., teacher ed. 10.95 (*0-906212-84-7*, Pub. by Tarquin Pubns) Parkwest Pubns.

Pascal's Triangle. V. A. Uspenskii. Tr. by Timothy McLarnan & David J. Sookne from RUS. LC 73-90941. (Popular Lectures in Mathematics). 42p. (C). 1994. pap. text 5.00 (*0-226-84316-5*) U Ch Pr.

Pascha: The Resurrection of Christ. David Drillock et al. (Music Ser.). 274p. 1980. 25.00 (*0-913836-65-6*) St Vladimirs.

Pascha: The Traditions of Easter in Rockland County. Kathleen Mundell. (Illus.). 45p. 1984. pap. 5.00 (*0-911183-19-1*) Rockland County Hist.

Paschal Beverly Randolph: A Nineteenth-Century Black American Spiritualist, Rosicrucian, & Sex Magician. John P. Deveney. LC 95-52244. (SUNY Series in Western Esoteric Traditions). (Illus.). 607p. (C). 1996. text 86.50 (*0-7914-3119-3*); pap. text 29.95 (*0-7914-3120-7*) State U NY Pr.

Paschal Fire in Jerusalem: A Study of the Rite of the Holy Fire in the Church of the Holy Sepulchre. Hieromonk Auxentios. 225p. (Orig.). 1993. pap. 8.95 (*0-9634692-0-7*) St John Chrysostom.

Paschal Life. Marianne Dorman. (C). 1989. text 60.00 (*0-7855-6965-0*, Pub. by Pentland Pr) St Mut.

Paschal Mystery: Core Grace in the Life of the Christian. Augustine Hennessey. (Synthesis Ser.). 37p. 1977. pap. 1.00 (*0-8199-0707-3*, Frncscn Herld) Franciscan Pr.

*__Paschal Mystery of Christ: Foundation for Liturgical Inculturation in Africa.__ Patrick Chukwudezie Chibuko. (Studies in the Intercultural History of Christianity). XVI, 197p. 1999. pap. 35.95 (*3-631-35560-2*) P Lang Pubng.

*__Paschal Mystery of Christ: Foundation for Liturgical Inculturation in Africa.__ Patrick Chukwudezie Chibuko. LC 99-49816. (Studies in the Intercultural History of Christianity: Vol. 120). xvi, 197p. (C). 1999. pap. 35.95 (*0-8204-4703-X*) P Lang Pubng.

Paschal: or Lent Fast. Peter Gunning. LC 70-168214. (Library of Anglo-Catholic Theology: No. 7). reprint ed. 65.00 (*0-404-52088-X*) AMS Pr.

Paschal Service: Hymnal. Lazar Puhalo. 52p. Date not set. pap. 6.00 (*1-879038-78-1*, 9048) Synaxis Pr.

Paschal Service: Priest's Service Book. Ed. by Lazar Puhalo. 55p. Date not set. pap. 6.00 (*1-879038-79-X*, 9049) Synaxis Pr.

Paschal's Principles of Weight Training. John Paschal & John Dorman. (Illus.). 1979. pap. 2.95 (*0-89826-003-5*) Natl Paperback.

Pasco-Kennewick Intercity Bridge & Geometry Control for the Intercity Bridge. Prestressed Concrete Institute Staff. (PCI Journal Reprints Ser.). 36p. 1979. pap. 8.00 (*0-318-19859-2*, JR205) P-PCI.

PASCO '97: International Symposium on Parallel Symbolic Computation. 1997. pap. 32.00 (*0-89791-951-3*, 505971) Assn Compu Machinery.

PASCOS '94 - Proceeding of the Fourth International Symposium on Particles. K. C. Wali. 500p. 1995. text 109.00 (*981-02-2152-5*) World Scientific Pub.

Pascua: A Yaqui Village in Arizona. Edward H. Spicer. LC 83-18312. (Illus.). 325p. (C). 1984. reprint ed. pap. 17.95 (*0-8165-0845-3*) U of Ariz Pr.

Pascual's Magic Pictures. Amy G. Gage. LC 95-22331. (Illus.). 32p. (J). 1996. lib. bdg. 19.95 (*0-87614-877-1*, Carolrhoda) Lerner Pub.

Paseate Con Paco. Tr. by Mary M. Foreman from ENG. (Gus Is Gone Ser.). (SPA., Illus.). 24p. (J). 1929. pap. 3.95 (*1-56288-240-6*) Checkerboard.

Paseo. Donna Reseigh Long & Janice Lynn Maclan. (C). 1994. mass mkt., student ed. 38.95 (*0-8384-2585-2*); mass mkt., wbk. ed., lab manual ed. 31.95 (*0-8384-2582-8*) Heinle & Heinle.

Paseo de Rosie. Pat Hutchins.Tr. of Rosie's Walk. (J). 1997. 12.19 (*0-606-11294-4*, Pub. by Turtleback) Demco.

Paseo de Rosie. Pat Hutchins. Tr. by Alma F. Ada.Tr. of Rosie's Walk. (SPA.). (J). (ps-1). 1997. reprint ed. pap. 6.99 (*0-614-29083-X*) Aladdin.

Paseo en Avion. unabridged ed. Walter N. Kuhn, Jr. Ed. by Jean M. Kuhn. Tr. by Norberto Rivera. (Freddy el Grillo y la Ciudad de Corncob Ser.: Vol. 8S). (SPA., Illus.). 20p. (J). (ps-10). 1997. spiral bd. 6.95 (*1-891547-15-1*) Hoppa Prodns.

*__Paseo Pintoresco por la Isla de Cuba.__ 2nd rev. ed. Fernando De la Costa et al. Ed. by Cuban National Heritage Staff. LC 99-67188. (Coleccion Arte Cubano). (SPA., Illus.). 480p. 1999. pap. 29.95 (*0-89729-900-0*) Ediciones.

Paseo por el Bosque Lluvioso. Kristin Joy Pratt.Tr. of A Walk in the Rainforest. (SPA.). 1993. 13.15 (*0-606-06835-X*) Turtleback.

Paseo por el Bosque Lluvioso (A Walk in the Rainforest) Kristin J. Pratt. (ENG & SPA., Illus.). 36p. (YA). (ps up). 1993. pap. 7.95 (*1-883220-02-5*) Dawn CA.

Paseo Por la Naturaleza, Explorando una Reserva Natural. Lorraine Ward. (Serie Aventuras Al Aire Libre Ser.). 1993. 13.15 (*0-606-10523-9*, Pub. by Turtleback) Demco.

Paseos: Poems from Hollywood. Mark Dunnston. 13p. 1998. pap. 5.00 (*0-89642-439-1*) Linden Pubs.

Paseos en el Horizonte Vol. 15: Fronteras Semioticas En Los Relatos de Julio Cortazar. Jose Sanjines. (American University Studies: No. XXII). (SPA.). XI, 261p. (C). 1995. text 52.95 (*0-8204-1982-6*) P Lang Pubng.

Pasha of Jerusalem. E. Keith-Roach. 1994. text 45.00 (*1-85043-825-0*, Pub. by I B T) St Martin.

Pashto Newspaper Reader. 1994. audio 12.00 (*1-881265-22-6*) Dunwoody Pr.

Pashto Newspaper Reader. MRM Staff. LC 84-72437. iv, 246p. 1984. text 43.00 (*0-931745-04-7*) Dunwoody Pr.

Pasicrisie Internationale, 1794-1900: Histoire Documentaire des Arbitrage Internationaux. Henri LaFontaine. LC 97-17793. 1997. 209.00 (*90-411-0454-2*) Kluwer Law Intl.

Pasiegos: Spaniards in No Man's Land. Susan T. Freeman. LC 78-13928. (Illus.). 319p. 1979. lib. bdg. 31.50 (*0-226-26173-5*) U Ch Pr.

*__Pasillo de la Muerte.__ Stephen King. (SPA.). 2000. pap. 13.95 (*84-01-47473-6*) Plaza.

*__Pasion.__ (Musica Clasica Para Toda Ocasion Ser.: Vol. 8).Tr. of Passion. (SPA., Illus.). 30p. 2000. write for info. (*1-892207-63-X*) Intl Masters Pub.

Pasion Ardiente. Cathy Williams. (Bianca Ser.: No. 436).Tr. of A Burning Passion. (SPA.). 1997. per. 3.50 (*0-373-33436-2*, 1-33436-6) Harlequin Bks.

Pasion de la Escricutura: Hilda Perera. Rosario Hiriart. LC 98-85502. (Coleccion Polymita). (SPA., Illus.). 289p. 1998. pap. 19.00 (*0-89729-873-X*) Ediciones.

Pasion de Multitudes (Passion of the Masses) Dante Gebel. (What You Need to Know about ... in 12 Lessons Ser.). (SPA & ENG.). 192p. 8.99 (*0-88113-537-2*) Caribe Betania.

Pasion de Una Noche (Passion of a Night) Alex Ryder. (SPA.). 1999. mass mkt. 3.50 (*0-373-33494-X*, 1-33494-5) Harlequin Bks.

Pasion en Verano. Daphne Clair. (Harlequin Bianca Ser.).Tr. of Summer Passion. (SPA.). 156p. 1999. per. 3.50 (*0-373-33504-0*, 1-33504-1) Harlequin Bks.

Pasion Ilicita: Forsaking All Others. Susanne McCarthy. (Bianca Ser.: No. 385). (SPA.). 1996. per. 3.50 (*0-373-33385-4*, 1-33385-5) Harlequin Bks.

Pasion Pasajera, Vol. 164. Katherine Garbera. (Silhouette Deseo Ser.). 1999. per. 3.50 (*0-373-35294-8*) Harlequin Bks.

Pasion por las Almas. Oswald J. Smith. Orig. Title: Passion for Souls. (SPA.). 208p. 1985. mass mkt. 5.99 (*0-8254-1672-8*, Edit Portavoz) Kregel.

Pasion Primera. Anita D. De Jones. (SPA.). 80p. 1998. 9.95 (*0-9665989-0-3*) M Iannone.

Pasion Que Consume: Vida y Ministerio de Alberto Mottesi. G. P. Silva.Tr. of Passion That Consumes: Life & Ministry of Alberto Mottesi. (SPA.). 317p. (Orig.). 1993. pap. write for info. (*0-614-27103-7*) Editorial Unilit.

Pasion Que Consume: Vida y Ministerio de Alberto Mottesi. Pablo Silva.Tr. of Passion That Consumes: Life & Ministry of Alberto Mottesi. (SPA.). 1993. 7.99 (*1-56063-590-8*, 497727) Editorial Unilit.

Pasion Santa. P. C. Sproul.Tr. of One Holy Passion. (SPA.). write for info. (*0-7899-0016-5*, 498263) Editorial Unilit.

Pasion Segun Eva. Abel Posse. 1994. pap. 23.95 (*950-04-1452-X*) Emece.

Pasion Turca. Antonio Gala. 1997. pap. text 9.95 (*84-08-01998-8*) Planeta Edit.

Pasion y Pureza. Elisabeth Elliot.Tr. of Passion & Purity. (SPA.). 206p. 1995. 8.99 (*0-88113-062-1*, B067-0621) Caribe Betania.

*__Pasion y Venganza (Passion & Revenge)__ Anne Marie Winston. (Deseo Ser.). (SPA.). 2000. mass mkt. 3.50 (*0-373-35361-8*, 1-35361-4) Harlequin Bks.

Pasionaria: The Spanish Firebrand. Robert Low. (Illus.). 224p. 1993. 39.95 (*0-09-174572-1*, Pub. by Hutchnson) Trafalgar.

Pasionate Intellect: The Poetry of Charles Tomlinson. Michael Kirkam. LC 99-222141. 320p. 1998. 44.95 (*0-85323-543-0*, Pub. by Liverpool Univ Pr); pap. 20.95 (*0-85323-553-8*, Pub. by Liverpool Univ Pr) Intl Spec Bk.

Pasitos English Language Development Books, 11 vols., Set. Darlyne F. Schott. (Pasitos Hacia la Lectura Ser.). (J). (gr. k-1). 1991. pap. text 115.00 (*1-56537-091-0*) D F Schott Educ.

Pasitos Reading Readiness Kit, A E I O U. rev. ed. Darlyne F. Schott. (Pasitos Hacia la Lectura Ser.). (J). (gr. k-1). 1995. 360.00 (*1-56537-001-5*) D F Schott Educ.

Pasitos Spanish Language Development Books, 13 vols. Darlyne F. Schott. (Pasitos Hacia la Lectura Ser.). (J). (gr. k-1). 1990. pap. text 135.00 (*1-56537-090-2*) D F Schott Educ.

Pasitos Student Workbook, Libro 6. Darlyne F. Schott. (Pasitos Hacia la Lectura Ser.). (SPA., Illus.). 8p. (Orig.). (J). (gr. k-1). 1991. pap. text 1.25 (*1-56537-126-7*, 126) D F Schott Educ.

Pasitos Student Workbook, Libro 7. Darlyne F. Schott. (Pasitos Hacia la Lectura Ser.). (SPA., Illus.). 8p. (Orig.). (J). (gr. k-1). 1991. pap. text 1.25 (*1-56537-127-5*, 127) D F Schott Educ.

Pasitos Student Workbook, Libro 8. Darlyne F. Schott. (Pasitos Hacia la Lectura Ser.). (SPA., Illus.). 8p. (Orig.). (J). (gr. k-1). 1991. pap. text 1.25 (*1-56537-128-3*, 128) D F Schott Educ.

Pasitos Student Workbook, Libro 9. Darlyne F. Schott. (Pasitos Hacia la Lectura Ser.). (SPA., Illus.). 8p. (Orig.). (J). (gr. k-1). 1991. pap. text 1.25 (*1-56537-129-1*, 129) D F Schott Educ.

Pasitos Student Workbook, Libro 10. Darlyne F. Schott. (Pasitos Hacia la Lectura Ser.). (SPA., Illus.). 8p. (Orig.). (J). (gr. k-1). 1991. pap. text 1.25 (*1-56537-131-3*, 131) D F Schott Educ.

Pasitos Student Workbook: Pasitos Reading Readiness Kit, A E I O U, Libro 1. Darlyne F. Schott. (Pasitos Hacia la Lectura Ser.). 17p. (J). (gr. k-1). 1984. 1.25 (*1-56537-021-X*) D F Schott Educ.

Pasitos Student Workbook: Pasitos Reading Readiness Kit, A E I O U, Libro 2. Darlyne F. Schott. (Pasitos Hacia la Lectura Ser.). 17p. (J). (gr. k-1). 1984. 1.25 (*1-56537-022-8*) D F Schott Educ.

Pasitos Student Workbook: Pasitos Reading Readiness Kit, A E I O U, Libro 3. Darlyne F. Schott. (Pasitos Hacia la Lectura Ser.). 17p. (J). (gr. k-1). 1985. 1.25 (*1-56537-023-6*) D F Schott Educ.

Pasitos Student Workbook: Pasitos Reading Readiness Kit, A E I O U, Libro 4. Darlyne F. Schott. (Pasitos Hacia la Lectura Ser.). 17p. (J). (gr. k-1). 1985. 1.25 (*1-56537-024-4*) D F Schott Educ.

Pasitos Student Workbook: Pasitos Reading Readiness Kit, A E I O U, Libro 5. Darlyne F. Schott. (Pasitos Hacia la Lectura Ser.). 17p. (J). (gr. k-1). 1985. 1.25 (*1-56537-025-2*) D F Schott Educ.

Pasitos Supplementary Worksheets: Pasitos Reading Readiness Kit, A E I O U. Darlyne F. Schott. (Pasitos Hacia la Lectura Ser.). 56p. 1985. teacher ed. 30.00 (*1-56537-030-9*) D F Schott Educ.

Pasitos Teacher's Manual: Pasitos Reading Readiness Kit, A E I O U, Libro 1. rev. ed. Darlyne F. Schott. (Pasitos Hacia la Lectura Ser.). 54p. (J). (gr. k-1). 1995. 20.00 (*1-56537-011-2*) D F Schott Educ.

Pasitos Teacher's Manual: Pasitos Reading Readiness Kit, A E I O U, Libro 2. rev. ed. Darlyne F. Schott. (Pasitos Hacia la Lectura Ser.). 44p. (J). (gr. k-1). 1995. 20.00 (*1-56537-012-0*) D F Schott Educ.

Pasitos Teacher's Manual: Pasitos Reading Readiness Kit, A E I O U, Libro 3. rev. ed. Darlyne F. Schott. (Pasitos Hacia la Lectura Ser.). 56p. (J). (gr. k-1). 1995. 20.00 (*1-56537-013-9*) D F Schott Educ.

Pasitos Teacher's Manual: Pasitos Reading Readiness Kit, A E I O U, Libro 4. rev. ed. Darlyne F. Schott. (Pasitos Hacia la Lectura Ser.). 33p. (J). (gr. k-1). 1995. 20.00 (*1-56537-014-7*) D F Schott Educ.

Pasitos Teacher's Manual: Pasitos Reading Readiness Kit, A E I O U, Libro 5. rev. ed. Darlyne F. Schott. (Pasitos Hacia la Lectura Ser.). 40p. (J). (gr. k-1). 1995. 20.00 (*1-56537-015-5*) D F Schott Educ.

Paslanije Svatago Ignatija Aniokhiskago I Sviatago Polykarpa Smirnskago. Tr. of Letters of St. Ignatius of Anioch & of St.Polycarp of Smyrna. reprint ed. 2.00 (*0-317-28881-4*) Holy Trinity.

Paso Al Dia. Cathy Wilson. (SPA.). (YA). (gr. 5 up). Date not set. 9.95 (*0-673-36349-X*, GoodYrBooks) Addson-Wesley Educ.

Paso Al Dia: 180 Daily Brainteasers about Hispanic Cultures. Cathy Wilson & William A. Fleig. 192p. (YA). (gr. 5 up). 1996. spiral bd. 9.95 (*0-673-36348-1*, GoodYrBooks) Addson-Wesley Educ.

Paso Al Dia: 180 Daily Brainteasers for Spanish Vocabulary. Cathy Wilson & William A. Fleig. 192p. (YA). (gr. 5 up). 1996. spiral bd. 9.95 (*0-614-17996-3*, GoodYrBooks) Addson-Wesley Educ.

Paso Al Frente. Eduardo De Acha. LC 92-75090. (Coleccion Cuba y sus Jueces). (SPA.). 80p. (Orig.). 1992. pap. 9.95 (*0-89729-664-8*) Ediciones.

Paso Chile Company. W. Park Kerr & Norma Kerr. LC 92-265. 286p. 1992. 17.00 (*0-688-10941-1*, Wm Morrow) Morrow Avon.

Paso Doble. Earl Atkinson. (Ballroom Dance Ser.). 1986. lib. bdg. 250.00 (*0-8490-3629-1*) Gordon Pr.

Paso Doble. Earl Atkinson. (Ballroom Dance Ser.). 1983. lib. bdg. 250.00 (*0-87700-489-7*) Revisionist Pr.

Paso Mas. Joni Eareckson Tada.Tr. of Step Further. (SPA.). 224p. 1979. mass mkt. 1.25 (*0-8297-0663-1*) Vida Pubs.

Paso Mas: An Intermediate Spanish Course. Gene S. Kupferschmid & Thalia Dorwick. 584p. (C). 1990. pap. 62.50 (*0-07-557641-4*) McGraw.

Paso Mas: An Intermediate Spanish Course. Gene S. Kupferschmid & Thalia Dorwick. 576p. (C). 1990. pap., teacher ed. 29.37 (*0-07-557651-1*) McGraw.

Paso Mas: An Intermediate Spanish Course. Gene S. Kupferschmid & Thalia Dorwick. 576p. (C). 1990. teacher ed., student ed. 110.00 (*0-07-557653-8*) McGraw.

Paso Mas: An Intermediate Spanish Course. Gene S. Kupferschmid & Thalia Dorwick. 576p. (C). 1990. pap., wbk. ed. 33.75 (*0-07-557647-3*) McGraw.

Paso Mas: An Intermediate Spanish Course. Gene S. Kupferschmid & Thalia Dorwick. 576p. 1991. audio. write for info. (*0-318-67203-0*) McGraw.

Paso Mas: An Intermediate Spanish Course. 3rd ed. Gene S. Kupferschmid & Thalia Dorwick. 576p. (C). 1990. teacher ed., student ed. 51.25 incl. audio (*0-07-035728-5*) McGraw.

***Paso 2000: Scope & Sequence.** 2000. write for info. (*0-673-65007-3*, Scott Frsmn) Addson-Wesley Educ.

Pasolini: Forms of Subjectivity. Robert S. Gordon. (Illus.). 336p. (C). 1996. text 72.00 (*0-19-815905-6*) OUP.

Pasolini Old & New: Surveys & Studies. Ed. by Zymunt G. Baranski. 440p. 1999. boxed set 45.00 (*1-85182-436-7*, Pub. by Four Cts Pr) Intl Spec Bk.

***Pasos.** Alma Flor Ada. (Puertas al Sol Ser.). (SPA., Illus.). 1999. pap. text 8.95 (*1-58105-411-4*) Santillana.

Pasos Completos. Lope De Rueda. Ed. by Juan M. Martin Martinez. (Nueva Austral Ser.: Vol. 135). (SPA.). 1991. pap. text 24.95 (*84-239-1935-8*) Elliots Bks.

Pasos de un Peregrino, Tras las Huellas de Espana. Manuel Alver. (Nueva Austral Ser.: No. 230). (SPA.). 1991. pap. text 24.95 (*84-239-7230-5*) Elliots Bks.

***Pasos Dentro de las Aguas.** Peg Rankin. (SPA.). 2000. pap. 9.99 (*0-7899-0569-8*) Spanish Hse Distributors.

Pasos Dos: An Intermediate Course in Spanish. Rosa M. Martin & Martyn Ellis. (SPA.). 1995. 29.95 incl. audio (*0-8120-8240-0*) Barron.

Pasos Gigantes Para los Ninos. Kenneth N. Taylor.Tr. of Giants Steps for Little People. (SPA.). 64p. (J). 1985. 9.99 (*0-8423-6334-3*, 490361) Editorial Unilit.

Pasos Hacia el Exito al Inciar y Administrar una Empresa see Steps for Success in Starting & Operating a Business

Pasos Hacia la Libertad en Cristo. Anderson.Tr. of Steps to Freedom in Christ. (SPA.). 1995. write for info. (*0-614-27104-5*) Editorial Unilit.

Pasos Hacia la Libertad en Cristo. N. Anderson.Tr. of Steps to Freedom in Christ. 1.99 (*0-7899-0234-6*, 497646) Editorial Unilit.

Pasos Hacia la Libertad en Cristo - Steps to Freedom in Christ. Anderson. (SPA.). 1995. write for info. (*0-614-24390-4*) Editorial Unilit.

Pasos Hacia la Paz Interior: Sugestiones Para el Uso de Principios. Peace Pilgrim. Tr. by Clandio Zanelli from ENG. (Peace Pilgrim Ser.).Tr. of Steps Towards Inner Peace. (SPA., Illus.). 64p. (Orig.). 1987. pap. 5.00 (*0-943734-09-6*) Ocean Tree Bks.

Pasos I: A First Course in Spanish. Rosa M. Martin & Martyns Ellis. (SPA.). 288p. (YA). (gr. 9-10). 1997. pap. 16.95 (*0-8120-9096-9*) Barron.

Pasos II: An Intermediate Course in Spanish. Rosa M. Martin & Martyn Ellis. (SPA.). 256p. (YA). (gr. 11-12). 1997. pap. 16.95 (*0-8120-9100-0*) Barron.

Pasos para Libertar a Su Iglesia. N. Anderson & Charles Mylander.Tr. of Steps to Setting Your Church Free. (SPA.). 1.99 (*0-7899-0423-3*, 493784) Editorial Unilit.

Pasos para Libertar Su Matrimonio. N. Anderson & Charles Mylander.Tr. of Steps to Setting Your Marriage Free. (SPA.). 1.99 (*0-7899-0422-5*, 493783) Editorial Unilit.

Pasos Perdidos. Alejo Carpentier. (SPA.). 175p. 1953. 11.00 (*0-8288-8563-X*); 11.00 (*0-8288-8589-3*) Fr & Eur.

Pasos Perdidos. Alejo Carpentier. 1998. pap. 13.95 (*0-14-026193-1*) Viking Penguin.

Pasos Perdidos. Alejo Carpentier. (SPA.). pap. 14.95 (*84-376-0502-4*, Pub. by Ediciones Catedra) Continental Bk.

Pasos Uno: A First Course in Spanish. Rosa M. Martin & Martyn Ellis. (SPA.). 1995. 29.95 incl. audio (*0-8120-8238-9*) Barron.

Pasport to Eternal Life. Valery Oisteanu. 68p. 1990. pap. 8.00 (*0-685-46237-4*) Pass.

Pasquala: The Story of a California Indian Girl. Gail Faber & Michele Lasagna. (Whispers Ser.). (Illus.). 33p. 1990. pap., teacher ed. 9.95 (*0-936480-08-4*) Magpie Pubns.

Pasquala: The Story of a California Indian Girl. Gail Faber & Michele Lasagna. (Whispers Ser.). (Illus.). 95p. (J). (gr. 4-8). 1990. 12.95 (*0-936480-07-6*); pap. 9.95 (*0-936480-06-8*) Magpie Pubns.

***Pasquale's Angel.** McAuley. 2000. 22.00 (*0-380-97253-0*) Morrow Avon.

Pasquale's Angel. Paul J. McAuley. 384p. 1997. mass mkt. 5.99 (*0-380-77820-3*, Avon Bks) Morrow Avon.

Pasquale's Gift. Marie Lukic. LC 93-29002. (Voyages Ser.). (Illus.). (J). 1994. 4.25 (*0-383-03768-9*) SRA McGraw.

Pasquils Mad-Cap & Mad-Cappes Message. Nicholas Breton. LC 79-25850. (English Experience Ser.: No. 200). 88p. 1969. reprint ed. 25.00 (*90-221-0200-9*) Walter J Johnson.

Pasquotank County, North Carolina: Record of Deed, 1700-1751. Gwen B. Bjorkman. 502p. (Orig.). 1990. pap. 35.00 (*1-55613-308-1*) Heritage Bk.

Pasquotank Plate. Episcopal Churchwomen Staff. (Illus.). 300p. 1992. 17.95 (*0-9632518-9-9*) Episcopal Church.

Pasro: Pascal & C for Robots. 2nd ed. C. Blume et al. (Illus.). 240p. 1987. pap. 53.00 (*0-387-18093-1*) Spr-Verlag.

Pass! ACLS No. II: Case-Based Scenarios. American Safety Video Publishers. 96p. 1998. 29.95 incl. VHS (*0-8151-0915-6*, A1057) Mosby Inc.

Pass ACLS! No. III: Skills Based. 2nd ed. American Safety Video Publishers. 1998. 29.95 incl. VHS (*0-8151-0940-7*, A8681) Mosby Inc.

Pass ACLS Booklet. American Safety Video Publishers, Inc. Staff. 1993. 9.95 (*0-8016-7985-0*) Mosby Inc.

Pass after Class. rev. unabridged ed. Fred Much. LC 86-90709. 104p. (Orig.). 1987. pap. 5.95 (*0-9618053-0-7*) Fred Much.

Pass & a Prayer. Clair Bee. LC 98-50759. (Chip Hilton Sports Ser.: Vol. 5). 208p. (YA). 1999. reprint ed. pap. 5.99 (*0-8054-1987-X*) Broadman.

P.A.S.S. C.A.L.F. 8 Behaviors of Sales Success in an Agricultural Dealership. Frank Lee. xiii, 95p. 1997. pap. text 10.95 (*0-9701399-0-X*) Sales Acdmy.

Pass CCRN! Robin D. Dennison. (Illus.). 752p. (C). (gr. 13). 1996. pap. text 37.95 (*0-8016-0128-2*, 00128) Mosby Inc.

***Pass CCRN! A Comprehensive Critical Care Review.** 2nd ed. Robin D. Dennison. 750p. 2000. pap. text 44.95 (*0-323-00999-9*) Mosby Inc.

Pass CPR! American Safety Video Publishers Staff. (Illus.). 96p. 1993. pap. text 9.95 (*0-8151-0036-1*) Mosby Inc.

Pass EMT-Basic: New Curriculum. American Safety Video Publishers. 1996. 32.95 (*0-8151-0883-4*, S2046) Mosby Inc.

Pass Engineer! Booklet. Kidd-Czajkowski. 100p. (gr. 13). 1995. pap. text 9.95 (*0-8151-5263-9*) Mosby Inc.

Pass Exams & Write Top Essays. Richard Burns. 127p. 1995. pap. 14.95 (*0-949142-64-6*, Pub. by Stirling Pr) Intl Spec Bk.

Pass It On. Melvin Ford. pap. 6.95 (*1-56794-201-6*) Star Bible.

Pass It On! A Practical Approach to the Fears & Facts of Planning Your Estate. Barbara J. Shotwell & Nancy Randolph Greenway. LC 99-49481. (Illus.). 304p. 2000. 22.95 (*0-7868-6580-6*, Pub. by Hyperion) Time Warner.

Pass It On: A Treasury of Tastes & Traditions. Delta Delta Delta National Fraternity Staff. 288p. 1994. 17.95 (*0-9639957-0-7*) Delta Delta Delta.

Pass It On! A Treasury of Virgin Islands Tales. rev. ed. Jennie N. Wheatley. (Illus.). 92p. (J). 1996. pap. 15.00 (*0-913441-26-0*) Hse of Nehesi.

Pass It On: African-American Poetry for Children. Illus. by Floyd Cooper. LC 92-16034. 32p. (J). (gr. k-4). 1993. 15.95 (*0-590-45770-5*) Scholastic Inc.

Pass It On! All about Notes from Secret Codes & Special Inks to Fancy Folds & Dead Man's Drops. Sharon Bailly. LC 94-46949. (Illus.). 64p. (J). (gr. 4-6). 1995. lib. bdg. 23.40 (*1-56294-588-2*) Millbrook Pr.

Pass It On: Helping Staff to Share Knowledge & Skills with Youth. William V. Griffin & Dorothy Ansell. 96p. 1989. student ed. 15.00 (*1-878848-10-0*); pap. text, wbk. ed. 55.00 (*1-878848-08-9*); teacher ed. 45.00 (*1-878848-09-7*) Natl Res Ctr.

Pass It On! How to Thrive in the Military Lifestyle. Kathleen P. O'Beirne. LC 91-90191. (Illus.). 528p. (Orig.). 1991. pap. 14.95 (*1-879979-00-4*) Lifescape Enter.

***Pass It On! Ready-to-Use Handouts for Asset Builders.** 176p. 1999. pap. 18.95 (*1-57482-317-5*) Search Inst.

Pass It On: The Story of Bill Wilson & How the A. A. Message Reached the World. Alcoholics Anonymous World Services, Inc., Staff. LC 84-72766. 432p. 1984. 6.50 (*0-916856-12-7*) AAWS.

Pass It On! No. II: Living & Leaving the Military Lifestyle. Kathleen P. O'Beirne. LC 91-90191. (Illus.). 400p. (Orig.). 1995. pap. 19.95 (*1-879979-01-2*) Lifescape Enter.

Pass Key to the ACT. 3rd rev. ed. George Ehrenhaft et al. LC 98-6242. 400p. 1998. pap. 7.95 (*0-7641-0452-7*) Barron.

Pass Key to the ASVAB: Armed Services Vocational Aptitude Battery. 2nd ed. Barron's Educational Editors. LC 96-48239. (Barron's Educational Ser.). 288p. 1997. 7.95 (*0-8120-9741-6*) Barron.

***Pass Key to the ASVAB: Armed Services Vocational Aptitude Battery.** 3rd ed. Barron's Educational Series, Inc. Staff. LC 99-87334. 290p. 2000. pap. 8.95 (*0-7641-0783-6*) Barron.

Pass Key to the GED. 3rd rev. ed. Murray Rockowitz et al. LC 98-38864. 400p. 1998. pap. 7.95 (*0-7641-0457-8*) Barron.

***Pass Key to the GED High School Equivalency Exam.** 4th ed. Murray Rockowitz. LC 00-41383. 2001. write for info. (*0-7641-1372-0*) Barron.

Pass Key to the GRE. 2nd ed. Samuel C. Brownstein & Sharon W. Green. LC 97-30086. 420p. 1997. pap. text 7.95 (*0-8120-9742-4*) Barron.

***Pass Key to the GRE Test.** 3rd ed. Sharon Weiner Green & Ira K. Wolf. 496p. 2000. pap. 8.95 (*0-7641-0782-8*) Barron.

Pass Key to the LSAT: Law School Admission Test. 3rd ed. Jerry Bobrow et al. LC 98-37111. 390p. 1999. pap. 7.95 (*0-7641-0468-3*) Barron.

Pass Key to the NTE. Albertina A. Weinlander. (Pass Key Ser.). 464p. 1993. pap. 11.95 incl. audio (*0-8120-8040-8*) Barron.

Pass Key to the PSAT/NMSQT. Samuel C. Brownstein. 1995. pap., student ed. 7.95 (*0-8120-9022-5*) Barron.

Pass Key to the SAT I. 3rd rev. ed. Sharon W. Green & Ira K. Wolf. LC 98-24179. 460p. 1998. pap. 7.95 (*0-7641-0449-7*) Barron.

***Pass Key to the TOEFL: With Compact Disc.** 3rd ed. Pamela Sharpe. LC 99-19549. 450p. 1999. pap. 14.95 incl. audio compact disk (*0-7641-7145-3*) Barron.

Pass Me a Poem. Janet Collins. LC 99-93540. (Illus.). ix, 87p. (J). (gr. 1-7). 13.95 (*0-9674824-0-2*); pap. 7.50 (*0-9674824-1-0*) J Collins.

Pass My Imperfections Lightly By. Vaughn McBride. 1991. 5.60 (*0-87129-144-4*, P69) Dramatic Pub.

Pass NCLEX-LPN Survival Kit. Melodie Chenevert & Martha Bramhall. 1994. write for info. (*0-8151-7881-6*) Mosby Inc.

Pass NCLEX-RN Survival Guide. Melodie Chenevert. 1994. write for info. (*0-8151-1535-0*) Mosby Inc.

Pass on, No Pass Back! Darrell H. Y. Lum. LC 90-85158. (Bamboo Ridge Ser.: Nos. 48-49). 128p. (Orig.). 1990. pap. 8.00 (*0-910043-19-1*) Bamboo Ridge Pr.

Pass PALS. Walt A. Stoy. 1995. pap. text 32.95 (*0-8151-7952-9*) Mosby Inc.

Pass! Performance Assessment Software User's Manual. Susie H. Vanhuss. (Assessment Ser.). 1996. pap., suppl. ed. write for info. (*0-538-65280-2*); pap., suppl. ed. 72.95 (*0-538-65281-0*); pap., suppl. ed. write for info. (*0-538-65282-9*) S-W Pub.

Pass! Performance Assessment Software User's Manual. Vanhuss & Susie H. Vanhuss. (Assessment Ser.). 1996. pap., suppl. ed. 14.95 (*0-538-65279-9*) S-W Pub.

Pass Port to S+T+R+O+N+G Kids: Teacher Handbook. Linda Silbert & Alvin Silbert. (Illus.). 78p. 1995. teacher ed., ring bd. 29.95 (*0-89544-414-3*, 414-3) Silbert Bress.

Pass Program: SSA Work Incentive for Disabled Beneficiaries Poorly Managed. (Illus.). 63p. (Orig.). (C). 1996. pap. text 20.00 (*0-7881-3227-X*) DIANE Pub.

Pass, Set, Crush: Volleyball Illustrated. 3rd rev. ed. Jeff Lucas. (Illus.). 417p. (Orig.). 1993. pap. 24.95 (*0-9615088-6-8*) Euclid NW Pubns.

Pass the Ball. Matthew Ryan. LC 97-61043. (Aesop's Fables Running Start Ser.). (Illus.). 32p. (J). (gr. 1-3). 1997. pap. 4.95 (*1-890570-18-4*) Huckleberry CT.

Pass the Biscuit: Spirited Practices for Youth Hockey Coaches & Players. Gary Wright. 67p. (Orig.). 1991. pap. 10.95 (*0-9629703-0-1*) Ashworth Pr.

Pass the Bottle: Rum Tales of the West Coast. Eric Newsome. LC 96-111429. (Illus.). 144p. (Orig.). 1995. pap. 12.95 (*1-55143-044-4*) Orca Bk Pubs.

Pass the Bread! Karin L. Badt. LC 94-38003. (World of Difference Ser.). (Illus.). 32p. (J). (gr. 2-5). 1995. lib. bdg. 20.30 (*0-516-08191-8*) Childrens.

Pass the Bread! Karin L. Badt. (World of Difference Ser.). (Illus.). 32p. (J). (gr. 3-7). 1995. pap. 6.95 (*0-516-48191-6*) Childrens.

Pass the Butterworms: Remote Journeys Oddly Rendered. Tim Cahill. 283p. 1998. pap. 13.00 (*0-375-70111-7*) Vin Bks.

Pass the Calories, Please! Gail Farmer. LC 94-15821. 1994. spiral bd. 12.95 (*0-88091-134-4*, 0820) Am Dietetic Assn.

Pass the CBEST. 2nd ed. Elna M. Dimock. LC 84-13794. (Illus.). 156p. (Orig.). (C). 1984. pap. 14.50 (*0-914763-01-6*) Educ Development.

Pass the CBEST. 3rd ed. Elna M. Dimock. LC 88-16287. (Illus.). 256p. (Orig.). 1988. pap. 14.50 (*0-914763-02-4*) Educ Development.

***Pass the Celery, Ellery!** Jeffrey Fisher. LC 00-23391. (Illus.). (J). 2000. pap. 14.95 (*1-58479-031-8*) Stewart Tabori & Chang.

Pass the Cheese, Please! Barbara S. Mazen. (Whole-Language Big Bks.). (Illus.). 16p. (Orig.). (J). (ps-2). 1994. pap. 16.95 (*1-56784-057-4*) Newbridge Educ.

***Pass the Energy, Please!** Barbara S. McKinney. LC 99-32181. (Sharing Nature with Children Book Ser.). (Illus.). 36p. (YA). (gr. 1 up). 2000. 16.95 (*1-58469-001-1*); pap. 7.95 (*1-58469-002-X*) Dawn CA.

***Pass the Energy, Please!** Barbara Shaw McKinney. (Illus.). 48p. (J). (gr. 3-6). 2000. pap. text 7.95 (*1-58469-007-0*) Dawn CA.

***Pass the EXCET on Your First Try: Study Manual for the Texas EXCET Exam: Professional Development.** Mark J. Mentze. LC 99-63369. (Illus.). 85p. 1999. pap. 28.95 (*0-9671860-0-5*) Express Design.

Pass the Fritters, Critters. Cheryl Chapman. LC 91-45055. (Illus.). 40p. (J). (ps-k). 1993. lib. bdg. 16.00 (*0-02-717975-3*, Four Winds Pr) S&S Childrens.

Pass the Jam, Jim! Kaye Umansky & Margaret Chamberlain. (Illus.). 32p. (J). (ps-1). 1993. 17.95 (*0-370-31662-2*, Pub. by Bodley Head) Trafalgar.

Pass the Loot: A Fox Trot Collection. Bill Amend. (Illus.). 128p. (Orig.). 1990. pap. 9.95 (*0-8362-1815-9*) Andrews & McMeel.

Pass the Micropsychology. Williams. 1996. pap. text 28.00 (*0-7020-2066-4*, W B Saunders Co) Harcrt Hlth Sci Grp.

Pass the MRC Psycology Essay. Christopher Williams & Peter Trigwell. (Illus.). 215p. 1996. pap. text 31.50 (*0-7020-2154-7*, Pub. by W B Saunders) Saunders.

Pass the MRCP. Mark Elliot et al. (Illus.). 155p. 1996. pap. text 28.95 (*0-7020-2198-9*, Pub. by W B Saunders) Saunders.

Pass the Parcel with Pig. Josephine Lodge. (Illus.). 12p. (J). 1998. 5.95 (*0-7641-5076-6*) Barron.

Pass the Peas, Please: A Book of Manners. Dina Anastasio. LC 99-19163. 32p. (J). 1999. pap. 7.95 (*0-7373-0193-7*, 01937W) NTC Contemp Pub Co.

Pass the Plate. Pass the Plate, Inc. Staff. Ed. by Alice Underhill & Bobbie Stewart. 520p. 1981. pap. 13.95 (*0-939114-13-5*) Pass the Plate.

Pass the Poetry, Please! Lee B. Hopkins. (J). 1987. 17.05 (*0-606-02173-6*, Pub. by Turtleback) Demco.

Pass the Poetry, Please! 2nd ed. Ed. by Lee B. Hopkins. LC 86-45758. 288p. (J). 1987. 19.00 (*0-06-022602-1*) HarpC Child Bks.

Pass the Poetry, Please! 2nd ed. Lee B. Hopkins. LC 86-45758. (Trophy Nonfiction Bk.). 288p. (J). 1987. pap. 11.95 (*0-06-446062-2*, HarpTrophy) HarpC Child Bks.

Pass the Poetry, Please! 3rd rev. ed. Lee Bennett Hopkins. LC 98-19617. 288p. (J). 1998. 25.00 (*0-06-027746-7*) HarpC.

***Pass the Poetry, Please!** 3rd rev. ed. Lee Bennett Hopkins. LC 98-19617. 288p. (J). 1998. pap. 13.95 (*0-06-446199-8*) HarpC.

***Pass the Polenta: And Other Writings from the Kitchen.** Teresa Lust. (Illus.). 288p. 1999. pap. 11.95 (*0-345-43565-6*, Ballantine) Ballantine Pub Grp.

Pass the Polenta: And Other Writings from the Kitchen. Teresa Lust. LC 98-25789. 269p. 1998. 24.00 (*1-883642-95-7*) Steerforth Pr.

Pass the Quill: I'll Write a Draft: A Story of Thomas Jefferson. Robert Quackenbush. (Illus.). 32p. (J). (gr. 2-6). 1989. lib. bdg. 14.95 (*0-945912-07-2*) Pippin Pr.

***Pass the SAT the Humorous Way: Lampooning Fairy Tales.** Evanne Schneider. LC 00-132652. (Illus.). 315p. (YA). 2000. pap. text 18.95 (*0-9700747-2-7*) Westcreek Indust.

Pass the Summative Assessment & MRCGP: All the Techniques You Need. Peter Lindsay et al. 110p. 1996. pap. text 19.95 (*0-7020-2194-6*, Pub. by W B Saunders) Saunders.

Pass the TASP Test. 2nd ed. Wayne Miller et al. Ed. by Robert Hackworth & Joseph W. Howland. LC 96-75619. (Illus.). 257p. 1996. pap. 9.95 (*0-943202-55-8*) H & H Pub.

Pass the Test: An Employee Guide to Drug Testing. Beverly A. Potter et al. (Illus.). 180p. 1999. pap. 16.95 (*1-57951-008-6*) Ronin Pub.

***Pass the U. S. Citizenship Exam, Vol. 1.** Learning Express Staff. LC 99-20290. 1999. pap. 14.95 (*1-57685-222-9*) LrningExprss.

Pass the Word: The Art of Oral Communication. Helen Beall. 68p. 1993. pap. 11.95 (*0-89745-162-7*) Sunflower U Pr.

Pass the Word Science Anytime Guide. HB Staff. 1995. pap. 8.00 (*0-15-306061-1*) Harcourt Schl Pubs.

Pass Those Cabrini Greens, Please!! Richard Blackmon, Jr. 168p. 1994. pap. 10.00 (*0-9642826-1-5*) Seven Hund Fourteen Prods.

Pass Those Cabrini Greens, Please!! (with Hot Sauce) Richard Blackmon, Jr. 170p. (Orig.). 1994. pap. 10.00 (*0-9642826-0-7*) Seven Hund Fourteen Prods.

Pass Thru Fire: The Collected Lyrics. Lou Reed. LC 98-23415. (Illus.). 352p. 1999. 24.95 (*0-7868-6452-4*, Pub. by Hyperion) Time Warner.

Pass Trak Series 65/66, Uniform Investment Adviser Law/Combined State Law Exam: Principles & Practices, Questions & Answers. 4th rev. ed. Dearborn Financial Publishing Staff & Carolyn B. Mitchell. LC 95-44598. 1995. pap. 75.00 (*0-7931-1840-9*, 3665-0104) Dearborn.

Pass Trak Series 3, National Commodity Futures Exam. 9th ed. Dearborn Financial Publishing Staff. LC 96-17902. 1996. pap. 49.00 (*0-7931-2338-0*, 3603-0209) Dearborn.

P

An Asterisk (*) at the beginning of an entry indicates that the title is appearing for the first time.

Pass Trak Series 24, General Securities Principal. 10th ed. LC 96-13977. 1996. pap. 69.00 (0-7931-2293-7, 3624-0210) Dearborn.

Pass Your Driving Test - First Time! 80p. (C). 1989. 120.00 (1-85368-072-9, Pub. by New5 Holland) St Mut.

Passacaglia. Robert Pinget. Tr. by Barbara Wright from FRE. LC 78-53832. (French Ser.). 1979. 6.95 (0-87376-033-6) Red Dust.

***Passacaglia for Orchestra, Op.1, in Full Score.** Anton Webern. 2000. pap. 8.95 (0-486-41167-2) Dover.

Passacaglias: Poems From Hollywood. Mark Dunster. 12p. 1998. pap. 5.00 (0-89642-560-6) Linden Pubs.

Passacaglio & Ciaccona: From Guitar Music to Italian Keyboard Variations in the 17th Century. Richard A. Hudson. LC 81-25. (Studies in Musicology: No. 37). 329p. reprint ed. pap. 102.00 (0-8357-1161-7, 207028600065) Bks Demand.

Passacaille. Robert Pinget. (FRE.). 136p. 1969. pap. 17.95 (0-7859-1508-7, 2707300861) Fr & Eur.

Passage. Fermin Cabal. Ed. by Martha Halsey. Tr. by H. Rick Hite from SPA. LC 97-60261. (Contemporary Spanish Plays Ser.: Vol. 13).Tr. of Travesia. (Illus.). 64p. 1998. pap. 8.00 (1-888463-03-1) Estreno.

***Passage.** Alexander Lawrence. 2000. mass mkt. 5.99 (0-451-40944-2, Onyx) NAL.

Passage. David Poyer. 560p. 1997. mass mkt. 6.99 (0-312-95450-6) St Martin.

Passage: Exhibition, Fall 1997. Jeane Umbreit & Ledbetter Lusk Gallery Staff. LC 98-34565. (Illus.). 26p. 1997. 10.95 (1-881096-62-9) Towery Pub.

Passage: Over the Hill & Around the World. Frank McNeill. 162p. 1998. pap. 10.00 (0-938711-51-2) Tecolote Pubns.

Passage: Return of Indiana Painters from Germany, 1880-1905. Martin F. Krause. (Illus.). 280p. 1990. 42.50 (0-936260-53-X) Ind Mus Art.

Passage & Other Stories. 2nd ed. Aaronna Griffith. 1998. mass mkt. 6.95 (1-56333-599-9, Rosebud) Masquerade.

Passage & Progress in the Works of William Tylee Ranney. Estill C. Pennington. (Illus.). 1993. pap. 14.95 (0-9638753-1-0) Morris Mus Art.

Passage by Night. large type ed. Jack Higgins. 1980. 12.00 (0-7089-0514-5) Ulverscroft.

Passage de Milan. Michel Butor. 1954. pap. 14.95 (0-7859-0657-6, F89990) Fr & Eur.

Passage East. Ian Marshall. Ed. by John Maxtone-Graham. (Illus.). 160p. 1998. 60.00 (1-57427-069-9) Howell Pr VA.

Passage East. John Maxtone-Graham. 160p. 1997. 160.00 (1-86227-039-2, Pub. by Spellmnt Pubs) St Mut.

***Passage Europe.** Philip Levine & Richard Copeland Miller. (Illus.). 156p. 2000. 50.00 (1-888899-05-0) Lodima.

***Passage Europe.** deluxe ed. Richard Copeland Miller & Philip Levine. 2000. 500.00 (1-888899-06-9) Lodima.

Passage V-VI. Ed. by Erika Boehm & Malcolm Berd. LC 74-1564. 1980. 3.95 (0-931672-01-5) Triton Coll.

Passage Four. Ed. by Erika Boehm & Malcolm Berd. LC 74-1564. (Passage Ser.). (Illus.). 1978. pap. 3.95 (0-931672-03-1) Triton Coll.

***Passage from Dark into Light: An Experience in the Grief Process.** Verna Namy. LC 99-63383. (Illus.). 56p. 1999. pap. 9.95 (0-944851-16-9) Earth Star.

Passage from Home. Isaac Rosenfeld. LC 87-40105. (Masterworks of Modern Jewish Writings). 300p. 1988. reprint ed. pap. 9.95 (0-910129-75-4) Wiener Pubs Inc.

Passage from India: Post-Nineteen Sixty-Five Indian Immigrants & Their Children. Priya Agarwal. (Illus.). 102p. 1991. 18.95 (0-9630579-0-1) Yuvati.

Passage from India: The Life & Times of His Divine Grace A. C. Bhaktivedanti Swami Prabhupada. A Summary Study of Satsvarupa Dasa Goswami's Srila Prabhupada Lilamrta. Steven Rosen. (C). 1992. 14.00 (81-215-0558-5, Pub. by M Manoharial) Coronet Bks.

Passage from India to El Dorado: Guyana & the Great Migration. David Hollett. LC 98-43716. (Illus.). 328p. 1999. 54.50 (0-8386-3819-8) Fairleigh Dickinson.

Passage Home. Alison McLeay. 656p. 1991. mass mkt. 5.99 (0-380-71532-5, Avon Bks) Morrow Avon.

Passage in Time. National Library of Poetry Staff. Date not set. 69.95 (1-57553-042-2) Watermrk Pr.

Passage in Time: The Ships That Brought Our Ancestors. Diane S. Ptak. LC 95-92203. 30p. 1992. pap. 17.00 (1-886905-01-0) D S Ptak.

Passage into Light. Judith Pella. (Russians Ser.). 34p. 1998. pap. 10.99 (1-55661-869-7) Bethany Hse.

Passage into Spirit. John-Roger. 1984. pap. 8.00 (0-914829-25-4) Mandeville LA.

***Passage Making.** Tom Cunliffe. (Keelboat Certification Ser.: Vol. 5). (Illus.). 2000. pap. 24.95 (1-882502-86-8, Pub. by US Sail Assn) Partners Pubs Grp.

Passage of Arms. Eric Ambler. 224p. 1992. mass mkt. 3.95 (0-88184-837-9) Carroll & Graf.

Passage of Darkness: The Ethnobiology of the Haitian Zombie. Wade Davis. LC 87-40537. (Illus.). xxi, 344p. (C). 1988. 39.95 (0-8078-1776-7); pap. 19.95 (0-8078-4210-9) U of NC Pr.

***Passage of Discovery: American Rivers Guidebook to the Missouri River of Lewis & Clark.** Daniel B. Botkin. LC 98-56643. 272p. 1999. pap. 15.95 (0-399-52510-6, Perigee Bks) Berkley Pub.

***Passage of Ghosts: Spirit of Modernity & the Aesthetics of Postcolonial Emancipation.** (Routledge Research in Postcolonial Studies: 2). 200p. (C). (gr. 13). 1998. 65.00 (0-415-18238-7) Routledge.

Passage of High-Energy Particles Through Matter. Yu P. Nikitin et al. Tr. by S. J. Amoretty from RUS. (AIP Translation Ser.). (Illus.). 272p. 1989. 79.95 (0-88318-618-7) Spr-Verlag.

Passage of Mrs. Jung. Laura B. Kennelly. Ed. by Edward Mycue. 28p. (Orig.). 1990. pap. 5.00 (0-9625855-0-5) Norton Coker Pr.

Passage of Nature. Dorothy Emmet. 208p. 1992. 49.95 (0-87722-896-5) Temple U Pr.

Passage of Saint Devil. Duncan McNaughton. 1976. pap. 10.00 (0-88922-100-6) Genl Dist Srvs.

Passage of the Barbarians. Miriam Novitch. 176p. 1993. 45.00 (1-870360-10-9) St Mut.

Passage of the Light: The Recursive Science Fiction of Barry N. Malzberg. Barry N. Malzberg. Ed. by Mike Resnick & Anthony R. Lewis. LC 94-65656. x, 281p. 1994. pap. 14.00 (0-915368-59-5) New Eng SF Assoc.

Passage of the Republic: An Interdisciplinary History of Nineteenth-Century America. William L. Barney. LC 86-80489. 429p. (C). 1987. pap. text 31.56 (0-669-04758-9) HM Trade Div.

Passage of the Year: Seventy-Three Poems. Alfred De Grazia. 133p. 1967. 9.00 (0-940268-10-8) Metron Pubns.

Passage of Time: Caspar David Friedrich & Philipp Otto Runge. Werner Busch & Hannah Kohl. (Illus.). 128p. 1996. 60.00 (90-400-9838-7, Pub. by Waanders) U of Wash Pr.

Passage Point: An Amateur's Dig into New Jersey's Colonial Past. Richard B. Marrin. 339p. 1997. pap. 25.50 (0-7884-0777-5, MO66) Heritage Bk.

Passage VII-VIII. Ed. by Erika C. Boehn. LC 74-1564. 1982. 3.95 (0-931672-04-X) Triton Coll.

***Passage, the Gift & the Prophecy.** Jeff Gutterman. 224p. 2000. pap. 13.95 (1-893676-01-3, Pub. by SlvrWind) Partners-West.

Passage Through Crisis: Polio Victims & Their Families. Fred Davis. 256p. (C). 1990. pap. 24.95 (0-88738-853-1) Transaction Pubs.

Passage Through Darkness. T. Davis Bunn. 400p. 1999. 10.99 (0-88486-254-2) Arrowood Pr.

Passage Through Deep Waters. unabridged ed. David Finnern. LC 97-65418. 149p. 1997. mass mkt. 8.95 (0-9651204-1-4) Pearl Pub CA.

Passage Through Divorce. Barbara Baumgardner. LC 99-201110. 1999. 14.99 (0-8054-1117-8) Broadman.

Passage Through El Dorado: Travelling the World's Last Great Wilderness. Jonathan Kandell. 320p. 1991. pap. 9.95 (0-380-71499-X, Avon Bks) Morrow Avon.

Passage Through Grief: An Interactive Journal. Barbara Baumgardner. LC 96-42206. 1999. 12.99 (0-8054-6072-1) Broadman.

Passage Through Hell: Modern Descents, Medieval Underworlds. David L. Pike. LC 96-18284. (Illus.). 280p. 1996. text 37.50 (0-8014-3163-8) Cornell U Pr.

Passage Through India. Robert Hamburger. LC 98-72958. 181p. 1998. pap. 12.00 (1-881471-27-6) S Duyvil.

Passage Through India. Gary Snyder. LC 83-10670. (Illus.). 130p. 1984. 12.95 (0-912516-79-8); pap. 8.95 (0-912516-80-1) Grey Fox.

Passage Through Mourning. Deborah Potter. 29p. (Orig.). 1996. pap. 5.95 (1-888289-24-4) Mythspinner.

Passage Through Pakistan. Orville F. Linck. LC 59-15364. 283p. reprint ed. 87.80 (0-608-17034-8, 202761000055) Bks Demand.

Passage Through Sacred History: Lenten Reflections for Individuals & Groups. Don C. Skinner. LC 97-33603. 104p. (Orig.). 1997. pap. 9.95 (0-8298-1216-4) Pilgrim OH.

Passage Through Silence & Light. Intro. by Raoul Bunschoten. (Illus.). 48p. 1997. 17.95 (0-9521773-5-8, Pub. by Black Dog Pubg) RAM Publications.

Passage Through the Garden see Lewis & Clark & the Image of the American Northwest

Passage Through the Garden: Lewis & Clark & the Image of the American Northwest. John L. Allen. LC 74-14512. 440p. reprint ed. pap. 136.40 (0-608-13450-3, 202277300029) Bks Demand.

Passage through the Wilderness: A Journey of the Soul. Zeb Bradford Long. LC 98-7584. 192p. 1998. pap. 11.99 (0-8007-9262-9) Chosen Bks.

Passage Through Trinidad: Journal of a Surgical Sex Change. Claudine Griggs. LC 95-21031. 224p. 1995. pap. 35.00 (0-7864-0088-9) McFarland & Co.

Passage Times for Markov Chains. R. Syski. LC 91-75446. (Studies in Probability, Optimization & Statistics: Vol. 1). 560p. 1992. 98.00 (90-5199-060-X, Pub. by IOS Pr) IOS Press.

Passage to a Human World: The Dynamics of Creating Global Wealth. Max Singer. LC 87-82068. 360p. 1988. 21.95 (1-55813-000-4) Hudson Instit IN.

Passage to a Human World: The Dynamics of Creating Global Wealth. Max Singer. 390p. 1989. pap. 24.95 (0-88738-259-2) Transaction Pubs.

Passage to a Ringed World: The Cassini-Huygens Mission to Saturn & Titan. Linda J. Spilker. 163p. 1997. per. 20.00 (0-16-061852-5) USGPO.

Passage to America: Ralegh's Colonists Take Ship for Roanoke. Helen H. Miller. (America's 400th Anniversary Ser.). (Illus.). xiv, 84p. 1986. reprint ed. pap. 6.00 (0-86526-202-0) NC Archives.

Passage to Anthropology: Between Experience & Theory. Kirsten Hastrup. LC 95-8619. 232p. (C). 1995. pap. 25.99 (0-415-12923-0) Routledge.

Passage to Anthropology: Between Experience & Theory. Kirsten Hastrup. LC 95-8619. 232p. (C). (gr. 13). 1995. 85.00 (0-415-12922-2) Routledge.

Passage to Ararat. Michael J. Arlen. LC 95-81171. 300p. 1996. reprint ed. pap. 15.00 (1-886913-05-6) Ruminator Bks.

Passage to China: Colin Campbell's Diary of the First Swedish East India Company Expedition to Canton, 1732-1733. Ed. by Paul Hallberg et al. (Acia Regiae Societasis Scientiarum et Litierarum Gothoburgensis Ser.: No. 37). 260p. 1997. 87.50 (91-85252-55-7, Pub. by Almqvist Wiksell) Coronet Bks.

Passage to Dakota. Marcia F. Hill. LC 97-93676. (Illus.). v, 172p. 1997. pap. write for info. (1-57579-068-8) Pine Hill Pr.

Passage to Dawn. TSR Inc. Staff. 1997. pap. 6.99 (0-7869-0750-9, Pub. by TSR Inc) Random.

Passage to England: Barbadian Londoners Speak of Home. John Western. (Illus.). 336p. (C). 1992. pap. 19.95 (0-8166-1985-9); text 49.95 (0-8166-1984-0) U of Minn Pr.

Passage to ESL Literacy. Diane M. Longfield. (Illus.). 422p. (Orig.). 1981. pap., teacher ed. 22.95 (0-937354-03-1); pap. text, student ed. 10.50 (0-937354-01-5) Delta Systems.

Passage to ESL Literacy Visuals. Diane M. Longfield. (Illus.). 182p. (Orig.). 1981. pap., teacher ed. 23.95 (0-937354-11-2) Delta Systems.

Passage to France Vol. 3: The Autobiography of Teahea Husain. Taha Husayn & Kenneth Cragg. LC 77-456820. (Arabic Translation Ser.). xv, 165 p. 1976. write for info. (90-04-04726-3) Brill Academic Pubs.

***Passage to Freedom: The Sugihara Story.** Ken Mochizuki. LC 96-35359. (Illus.). 32p. (YA). (gr. 1 up). 1999. 15.95 (1-880000-49-0) Lee & Low Bks.

Passage to India. Ed. by Tony Davies & Nigel Wood. LC 93-42009. (Theory in Practice Ser.). 1994. pap. 29.95 (0-335-15712-2) OpUniv Pr.

Passage to India. E. M. Forster. LC 79-307919. (Abinger Edition Ser.). xxviii, 371p. 1978. write for info. (0-7131-6107-8, Pub. by E A) Routldge.

Passage to India. E. M. Forster. LC 43-1812. (Modern Classic Ser.). 320p. 1989. 18.00 (0-15-171141-0) Harcourt.

Passage to India. E. M. Forster. LC 92-52900. 1992. 18.00 (0-679-40549-6) Knopf.

Passage to India. E. M. Forster. 1952. 17.10 (0-606-01711-9, Pub. by Turtleback) Demco.

Passage to India. Norma Ostrander. (Cliffs Notes Ser.). 72p. 1964. pap., student ed. 4.95 (0-8220-0985-4, Cliff) IDG Bks.

***Passage to India.** large type ed. E. M. Forster. LC 97-43865. 377p. 1998. pap. 17.95 (1-56000-507-6) Transaction Pubs.

Passage to India. E. M. Forster. LC 43-1812. 372p. 1965. reprint ed. pap. 13.00 (0-15-671142-7, Harvest Bks) Harcourt.

Passage to India. E. M. Forster. 429p. 1981. reprint ed. lib. bdg. 25.95 (0-89966-300-1) Buccaneer Bks.

Passage to India. Walt Whitman. LC 68-24946. (Studies in Whitman: No. 28). (C). 1969. reprint ed. lib. bdg. 75.00 (0-8383-0260-2) M S G Haskell Hse.

Passage to India. Walt Whitman. (BCL1-PS American Literature Ser.). 120p. 1992. reprint ed. lib. bdg. 69.00 (0-7812-6897-4) Rprt Serv.

***Passage to India.** Walt Whitman. (Notable American Authors Ser.). 1999. reprint ed. lib. bdg. 125.00 (0-7812-9947-0) Rprt Serv.

***Passage to India, Set.** unabridged ed. E. M. Forster. 1998. 47.95 incl. audio (1-55685-562-1) Audio Bk Con.

Passage to India: Essays in Interpretation. Ed. by John B. Beer. LC 85-22947. 176p. 1985. 56.00 (0-389-20601-6, N8159) B&N Imports.

Passage to India: Nation & Narration. Judith S. Herz. (Masterwork Studies). 160p. 1992. 23.95 (0-8057-8056-4, Twyne); pap. 13.95 (0-8057-8104-8, Twyne) Mac Lib Ref.

***Passage to Juneau: A Sea & Its Meanings.** Jonathan Raban. 2000. pap. 15.00 (0-679-77614-1) Knopf.

***Passage to Juneau: A Sea & Its Meanings.** Jonathan Raban. LC 99-28777. 448p. 1999. 26.50 (0-679-44262-6) Pantheon.

Passage to Jupiter. E. J. Hall. 1983. text 2.60 (0-07-025747-7) McGraw.

Passage to Light. Ed. by Jewel Beardall. (Personal Enrichment Ser.). 139p. (Orig.). 1991. pap. write for info. (0-929985-58-3) Jackman Pubng.

Passage to Light: Dealing with Death & Dying. Douglas C. Beardall & Jewel N. Beardall. 248p. 1979. pap. 12.95 (1-882371-02-X) LDS Bk Pubns.

Passage to Little Bighorn. Terry Kretzer-Malvehy. LC 98-49481. 210p. (YA). (gr. 7 up). 1999. pap. write for info. (0-87358-713-8, Rising Moon Bks) Northland AZ.

Passage to Love. Barbara Cartland. (Canfield Ser.: No. 147). 176p. 1995. mass mkt. 4.50 (0-515-11751-X, Jove) Berkley Pub.

Passage to Love. large type ed. Barbara Cartland. LC 98-14055. (Paperback Ser.). 194p. 1998. pap. 21.95 (0-7838-0147-5) Thorndike Pr.

Passage to Medicine Practical. A. Mukherji. (C). 1989. 75.00 (0-89771-357-5, Pub. by Current Dist) St Mut.

Passage to Medicine Practical: Long, Short & Spot Cases, Charts, Skiagrams, E. C. G. Instruments & Drugs. Ajoy Mukherjee. 501p. 1997. pap. (81-86793-31-3) Current Bks Intl.

Passage to Medicine Practice. M. Mukherjee. (C). 1990. 75.00 (0-7855-4669-3, Pub. by Current Dist) St Mut.

Passage to Millennium, Vol. 1. Mary Ellen Carter. 1998. 6.99 (0-312-96743-8, Pub. by Tor Bks) St Martin.

Passage to Modernity: An Essay in the Hermeneutics of Nature & Culture. Louis Dupre. 1995. pap. 18.00 (0-300-06501-9) Yale U Pr.

Passage to Mutiny. Alexander Kent. 1993. reprint ed. lib. bdg. 37.95 (1-56849-029-1) Buccaneer Bks.

Passage to Mutiny. Alexander Kent. LC 99-19262. (Richard Bolitho Novels Ser.: Vol. 7). 352p. 1999. reprint ed. pap. 14.95 (0-935526-58-7) McBooks Pr.

Passage to Peru: A Novel of Love & Intrigue. Marie Avant. LC 97-62091. 192p. 1998. pap. 12.99 (1-57921-072-4) WinePress Pub.

Passage to Petrograd. Charles Whiting. 256p. 1995. 20.00 (0-7278-4783-X) Severn Hse.

Passage to Power: K'ang-Hsi & His Heir Apparent, 1661-1722. Silas H. Wu. LC 79-4191. (East Asian Ser.: No. 91). (Illus.). 267p. 1979. 35.00 (0-674-65625-3) HUP.

Passage to Power: Natural Menopause Revolution. 2nd rev. ed. Leslie Kenton. LC 98-14278. 400p. 1998. pap. 14.95 (1-56170-487-3, 550) Hay House.

Passage to Quivira. Norman Zollinger. 1995. mass mkt. 5.99 (0-8125-4844-2, Pub. by Forge NYC) St Martin.

Passage to Quivira. Norman Zollinger. 1996. mass mkt. write for info. (0-614-05529-6) Forge NYC.

Passage to Samoa. large type ed. Day Keene. (Linford Mystery Library). 320p. 1992. pap. 16.99 (0-7089-7303-5, Linford) Ulverscroft.

Passage to Sword Beach: Minesweeping in the Royal Navy. Brendan A. Maher. LC 95-24424. (Illus.). 270p. 1996. 29.95 (1-55750-572-1) Naval Inst Pr.

Passage to the Center: Imagination & the Sacred in the Poetry of Seamus Heaney. Daniel Tobin. LC 98-33280. (Irish Literature, History & Culture Ser.). 288p. 1998. 34.95 (0-8131-2083-7) U Pr of Ky.

Passage to the Heart: Writings from Families with Children from China. Ed. by Amy Klatzkin. xxvi, 341p. 1999. 19.95 (0-9638472-2-8) Yeong & Yeong.

Passage to the North: A Traveler's Companion to the Historic Sites & Frontier Legends along the Alaska Highway. William R. Hunt. LC 91-26856. (Illus.). 192p. 1992. pap. 14.95 (0-8117-2409-3) Stackpole.

Passage to the Paschal Feast, Year B. Ed. by Samuel Torvend. (Orig.). 1993. pap. 5.00 (0-918208-64-5) Liturgical Conf.

Passage to the Paschal Feast: Year A. Ed. by Virginia Sloyan & Blair G. Meeks. 39p. 1992. pap. 5.00 (0-918208-56-4) Liturgical Conf.

Passage to Union: How the Railroads Transformed American Life, 1829-1929. Sarah H. Gordon. LC 96-28259. (Illus.). 416p. 1996. text 30.00 (1-56663-138-6, Pub. by I R Dee) Natl Bk Netwk.

Passage to Union: How the Railroads Transformed American Life, 1829-1929. Sarah H. Gordon. (Illus.). 416p. 1998. pap. 18.95 (1-56663-218-8, Pub. by I R Dee) Natl Bk Netwk.

Passage to Valhalla: The Human Side of Aerial Combat over Nazi Occupied Europe. William J. Fili. LC 91-73148. (Illus.). 336p. 1991. 24.95 (0-9630265-1-8) Filcon PA.

Passage to Vietnam. Rick Smolan. (Illus.). 1995. 70.00 (1-885559-01-1) Against All Odds.

Passage to Vietnam: Seven Days Through the Eyes of Seventy Photographers. Rick Smolan & Jennifer Erwitt. LC 94-71853. (Illus.). 224p. 1994. 49.95 (1-885559-00-3) Against All Odds.

"Passagenkirche" Ueber Einen Bautyp der Romanischen Baukunst in Frankreich. Volker Konerding. (Beitraege zur Kunstgeschichte Ser.: Vol. 12). (GER.). 120p. (C). 1976. 113.85 (3-11-004537-0) De Gruyter.

Passagenwerk. Joseph Kosuth. (Illus.). 96p. (Orig.). 1992. pap. 17.50 (3-89322-499-8, Pub. by Edition Cantz) Dist Art Pubs.

Passager: The Young Merlin Trilogy. Jane Yolen. LC 94-27101. 96p. (J). (gr. 3-8). 1996. 15.00 (0-15-200391-6) Harcourt.

Passager: The Young Merlin Trilogy. Jane Yolen. (Young Merlin Trilogy Ser.). 1998. 8.60 (0-606-13938-9, Pub. by Turtleback) Demco.

Passages. James. (J). 1993. teacher ed. 29.95 incl. audio (0-8384-4269-2); student ed. 18.00 incl. audio (0-8384-4245-5) Heinle & Heinle.

Passages. Gail Sheehy. 576p. 1984. mass mkt. 7.99 (0-553-27106-7) Bantam.

Passages. 3rd ed. Richard F. Nordquist. 1995. pap. text, teacher ed. 5.00 (0-312-10118-X) St Martin.

Passages. 3rd ed. Richard F. Nordquist. 1995. pap. text, teacher ed. 27.50 (0-312-10119-8) St Martin.

Passages. 4th ed. Richard F. Nordquist. 2000. pap. text. write for info. (0-312-15389-9) St Martin.

Passages: A Beginning Writer's Guide. 3rd ed. Richard F. Nordquist. 476p. 1995. pap. text 43.95 (0-312-10117-1) St Martin.

***Passages: A Journal for Growing Home.** Michelle Chalmers. (Illus.). 151p. (YA). (gr. 7 up). 1999. 15.00 (0-9637696-4-2) Human Srv Assocs.

Passages: A Personal Notebook. (Illus.). 96p. (Orig.). 1996. pap. 5.95 (1-56138-699-5) Running Pr.

Passages: A Woman's Personal Journey. Flavia Weedn & Lisa Weedn. (Illus.). 96p. 1998. pap. 14.95 (0-7683-2049-6) CEDCO Pub.

Passages: An Upper-Level Multi-Skills Course - Student's Book 1, No. 1. Jack C. Richards & Chuck Sandy. LC 98-16239. (Illus.). 128p. (C). 1998. pap. text, student ed. 13.50 (0-521-56472-7) Cambridge U Pr.

***Passages: Photographs in Africa.** Carol Beckwith & Angela Fisher. LC 00-31317. (Illus.). 112p. 2000. pap. 24.95 (0-8109-2948-1, Pub. by Abrams) Time Warner.

Passages: Poems. Catharine S. Brosman. LC 95-44605. (C). 1996. pap. 9.95 (0-8071-2050-2); text 16.95 (0-8071-2049-9) La State U Pr.

Passages Beyond the Gate: Jungaian Approach. 2nd ed. Jennings. 288p. 1998. pap. text 43.00 (0-536-01874-X) Pearson Custom.

Passages for Men: Getting Your Life's Worth out of Every Stage. large type ed. Gail Sheehy. 1997. pap. write for info. (0-679-77431-9) Random Hse Lrg Prnt.

Passages from Antiquity to Feudalism. Perry Anderson. (C). 1996. pap. 19.00 (1-85984-107-4, Pub. by Verso) Norton.

Passages from Berlin: Recollections of the Goldschmidt Schule (1935-1939) Ed. by Steve J. Heims. (Illus.). 213p. (Orig.). 1987. pap. 25.00 (0-9622664-1-8) S J Heims.

Passages from Friday: Poems. Charles Martin. 1983. 17.50 (0-317-40788-0) Abattoir.

***Passages from India: Letters, Essays & Poems.** Norman C. Bansen. Ed. by John W. Nielsen. xvi, 201p. 1999. pap. 19.95 (0-930697-05-7) Lur Pubns.

P

Passages from the American Notebooks. Nathaniel Hawthorne. (Notable American Authors Ser.). 1992. reprint ed. lib. bdg. 75.00 (0-7812-3049-7) Rprt Serv.

Passages from the American Notebooks. Nathaniel Hawthorne. (Illus.). 458p. 1976. reprint ed. 59.00 (0-317-20279-0) Scholarly.

Passages from the Diary of a Late Physician, 3 vols., 2 bks. Samuel Warren. LC 79-8214. (Illus.). reprint ed. 84.50 (0-404-62160-0) AMS Pr.

Passages from the English Notebooks. Nathaniel Hawthorne. (Notable American Authors Ser.). 1992. reprint ed. lib. bdg. 75.00 (0-7812-3050-0) Rprt Serv.

Passages from the French & Italian Notebooks. Nathaniel Hawthorne. (Notable American Authors Ser.). 1992. reprint ed. lib. bdg. 75.00 (0-7812-3051-9) Rprt Serv.

Passages from the French & Italian Notebooks. Nathaniel Hawthorne. 574p. 1976. reprint ed. 39.00 (0-403-02463-3) Scholarly.

Passages from the History of Liberty. Samuel Eliot. (Notable American Authors Ser.). 1992. reprint ed. lib. bdg. 75.00 (0-7812-2787-9) Rprt Serv.

Passages from the Letters of Auguste Comte. Auguste Comte. 1972. 59.95 (0-8490-0804-2) Gordon Pr.

Passages from the Letters of John Butler Yeats. John B. Yeats. LC 76-25292. 60p. 1971. write for info. (0-7165-1351-X) Intl Spec Bk.

Passages in Modern Sculpture. Rosalind E. Krauss. (Illus.). 320p. 1981. pap. text 18.50 (0-262-61033-7) MIT Pr.

Passages North Anthology: A Decade of Good Writing. Ed. by Elinor Benedict. LC 90-5457. 336p. (Orig.). 1989. pap. 11.95 (0-915943-48-4) Milkweed Ed.

Passages of a Working Life During a Half Century, 3 vols. Charles Knight. LC 79-148807. reprint ed. 135.00 (0-404-07670-X) AMS Pr.

Passages of African Descent Ancestry: For People Born in February. Vincent C. Sheppard. 88p. 1999. pap. 10.00 (0-8059-4658-6) Dorrance.

***Passages of Light.** C. R. Gibson. (Illus.). 2000. 20.00 (0-7667-5401-4) Gibson.

***Passages of Light.** Thomas Kinkade. (Illus.). 112p. 2000. 12.99 (0-7852-5519-2) Nelson.

Passages of Light. Ed. by Melisa Mitchell. 1998. 69.95 (1-57553-609-9) Watermrk Pr.

Passages of Light, Vol. I. Carlie Collier. 210p. 1991. pap. 16.95 (0-9636489-0-X) Celest Pr.

Passages of Light: Quotations from "A New Way of Living" the Series. Ed. by Katherine Best & Louis Brubaker. (YA). (gr. 6-12). 1995. pap. 6.95 (1-56266-109-4) Anwol.

Passages of Light: Selected Scriptures with Reflections. Thomas Kinkade. (Illus.). 112p. 1998. 19.99 (0-7852-0705-8) Nelson.

Passages of Marriage see Etapas del Matrimonio

Passages of Retirement: Personal Histories of Struggle & Success, 23. Richard S. Prentis. LC 92-1131. (Contributions to the Study of Aging Ser.: No. 23). 240p. 1992. lib. bdg. 49.95 (0-313-28493-8, PPN/, Greenwood Pr) Greenwood.

Passages of the Soul: Rediscovering the Importance of Rituals in Everyday Life. James Roose-Evans. 176p. 1995. pap. 12.95 (1-85230-708-0, Pub. by Element MA) Penguin Putnam.

Passages of the Soul: Rituals for Today. James Roose-Evans. 1994. pap. 19.95 (1-85230-474-X, Pub. by Element MA) Penguin Putnam.

Passages Teacher's Manual: An Upper-Level Multi-Skills Fluency Course, No. 1. Jack C. Richards & Chuck Sandy. 288p. (C). 1998. pap. text, teacher ed. 17.95 (0-521-56468-9) Cambridge U Pr.

Passages Through Recovery: An Action Plan for Preventing Relapse. Terence T. Gorski. 161p. pap. 12.95 (1-56838-139-5, 5687 A) Hazelden.

Passages to Freedom: A Story of Capture & Escape. 2nd ed. Joseph S. Frelinghuysen. (Illus.). 303p. (Orig.). 1990. pap. 18.95 (0-89745-131-7) Sunflower U Pr.

Passages to India. Julian C. Hollick. 250p. 1992. spiral bd. 50.00 (1-56709-000-1, 1036) Indep Broadcast.

Passages to India, 10 curriculum bklts. unabridged ed. Julian C. Hollick. (C). 1989. spiral bd. 125.00 incl. audio (1-56709-002-8, 1001) Indep Broadcast.

Passages to Modernity: Motherhood, Childhood & Social Reform in Early Twentieth Century Japan. Kathleen S. Uno. LC 98-47549. 248p. (C). 1999. pap. 24.95 (0-8248-2137-8) UH Pr.

Passages to Modernity: Motherhood, Childhood & Social Reform in Early Twentieth Century Japan. Kathleen S. Uno. LC 98-47549. (Illus.). 237p. (C). 1999. 47.00 (0-8248-1619-6) UH Pr.

Passages to Power: Legislative Recruitment in Advanced Democracies. Ed. by Pippa Norris. 275p. (C). 1997. text 59.95 (0-521-59099-X); pap. text 22.95 (0-521-59908-3) Cambridge U Pr.

Passages to the Presidency: From Campaigning to Governing. Charles O. Jones. LC 98-9041. 232p. 1998. pap. 16.95 (0-8157-4713-6); text 39.95 (0-8157-4714-4) Brookings.

Passages to the Sea. Ellen C. Gwynn. (Illus.). 209p. 1993. 14.95 (0-9638288-0-0) E C Gwynn.

Passages 2 Student's Book: An Upper-Level Multi-Skills Course. Jack C. Richards & Chuck Sandy. LC 99-58577. (Illus.). 128p. (C). 2000. pap., student ed. 13.95 (0-521-56471-9) Cambridge U Pr.

Passages 2 Teacher's Manual: An Upper-Level Multi-Skills Course. Jack C. Richards & Chuck Sandy. 212p. (C). 2000. pap., teacher ed. 18.50 (0-521-56467-0) Cambridge U Pr.

Passages We Celebrate: Commentaries on the Scriptural Texts for Baptisms, Weddings & Funerals. Patricia D. Sanchez. 240p. (Orig.). 1994. pap. 14.95 (1-55612-663-8) Sheed & Ward WI.

Passages Workbook: An Upper-Level Multi-Skills Fluency Course, No. 1. Jack C. Richards & Chuck Sandy. 76p. (C). 1999. pap. text, wbk. ed. 8.95 (0-521-56470-0) Cambridge U Pr.

***Passages 2 Audio CD: An Upper-Level Multi-Skills Course.** Jack C. Richards & Chuck Sandy. 2000. audio compact disk 40.95 (0-521-56463-8) Cambridge U Pr.

Passages 2 Workbook: An Upper-Level Multi-Skills Course. Jack C. Richards & Chuck Sandy. 80p. (C). 2000. pap., wbk. ed. 9.50 (0-521-56469-7) Cambridge U Pr.

Passageway. Laurel Mouritsen. 1996. pap. 9.95 (1-55503-688-0, 01111663) Covenant Comms.

Passageways. Palmer. (C). 1993. pap. text 20.00 (0-15-501292-4) Harcourt Coll Pubs.

Passageways, Vol. 1. Palmer. LC 97-74864. (C). 1998. pap. text 25.00 (0-15-502482-5, Pub. by Harcourt Coll Pubs) Harcourt.

Passageways, Vol. 2. Palmer. LC 97-74864. (C). 1998. pap. text 25.00 (0-15-502483-3, Pub. by Harcourt Coll Pubs) Harcourt.

Passageways: A History of Black America. Palmer. (C). 1997. pap. text 18.75 (0-03-055139-0) Harcourt Coll Pubs.

Passageways: An Interpretive History of Black America, 2 vols. Colin A. Palmer. 1998. pap. text 50.00 (0-15-510257-5) Harcourt.

Passageways: Vocabulary Activities to Build Writing Skills. Lori Mammen. 96p. 1992. pap. text 12.95 (0-944459-62-5) ECS Lrn Systs.

Passaggi. Josephine C. Del Deo & Giovanna Del Deo. (Illus.). 95p. 1995. pap. 17.50 (0-9673628-1-4) Three Dunes.

Passaic: The Story of a Struggle Against Starvation Wages & for the Right to Organize. Albert Weisbord. LC 74-22764. (Labor Movement in Fiction & Non-Fiction Ser.). reprint ed. 32.50 (0-404-58517-5) AMS Pr.

Passaic County see Hagstrom Atlases

Passaic County Arts Guide. Ed. by Laura Boss & Maria M. Gillan. 1994. pap. text 5.00 (0-9621465-4-4) Poetry Ctr PCCC.

Passaic Valley, New Jersey, in Three Centuries: Historical & Descriptive Records of the Valley & the Vicinity of the Passaic, 2 vols. John Whitehead. (Illus.). 993p. 1992. reprint ed. lib. bdg. 98.00 (0-8328-2353-8) Higginson Bk Co.

Passalong Plants. Steve Bender & Felder Rushing. LC 93-7156. (Illus.). xiv, 2p. (C). 1993. 32.50 (0-8078-2096-2); pap. 18.95 (0-8078-4418-7) U of NC Pr.

Passamaquoddy Dictionary. 184p. (YA). 1986. pap. 24.95 (0-88432-722-1, AFPS94) Audio-Forum.

Passamaquoddy Texts. John D. Prince. LC 73-3545. (American Ethnological Society Publications: No. 10). reprint ed. 20.00 (0-404-58160-9) AMS Pr.

Passante de Sans-Souci. Joseph Kessel. (FRE.). 224p. 1983. pap. 10.95 (0-7859-2478-7, 2070374890) Fr & Eur.

Passante de Sans-Souci. Joseph Kessel. (Folio Ser.: No. 1489). (FRE.). 224p. 1983. pap. 8.95 (2-07-037489-0) Schoenhof.

Passaruna. Veronika Janelsina. Ed. by Astra Moors. (LAV., Illus.). 253p. (Orig.). 1996. pap. 25.00 (1-888640-00-6) Astra Pubng.

Passatempo. Longman Publishing Staff. Date not set. pap. text. write for info. (0-85896-339-6) Addison-Wesley.

Passbook Clubs - Long Island: Coupon Book. 1991. 30.00 (1-56587-000-X) CUC Pub.

Passchendaele & the Royal Navy, 157. Andrew A. Wiest. LC 94-19594. (Contributions in Military Studies Ser.: Vol. 157). 232p. 1995. 62.95 (0-313-29048-2, Greenwood Pr) Greenwood.

Passchendaele. Philip Warner. 1999. pap. text 12.99 (1-84022-207-7) Wrdsworth Edits.

Passchendaele: The Untold Story. Robin Prior & Trevor Wilson. (Illus.). 256p. 1996. 40.00 (0-300-06692-9) Yale U Pr.

Passchendaele: The Untold Story. Robin Prior & Trevor Wilson. 256p. 1998. pap. 16.00 (0-300-07227-9) Yale U Pr.

Passchendaele: Ypres. Nigel Cave. (Illus.). 1998. pap. 16.95 (0-85052-558-6) Leo Cooper.

Passchendaele & the Battles of Ypres. Martin M. Evans. (Illus.). 112p. 1998. 19.95 (1-85532-734-1, Pub. by Ospry) Stackpole.

Passchendaele & the Battles of Ypres, 1914-1918. Martin M. Evans. (Illus.). 112p. 1998. 19.95 (1-85532-769-4, Pub. by Ospry) Stackpole.

Passchendaele in Perspective. Peter Liddle. (Illus.). 1998. pap. 45.00 (0-85052-588-8) Leo Cooper.

Passe Empiete. Marie Cardinal. (FRE.). 1984. pap. 12.95 (0-7859-3123-6) Fr & Eur.

Passe Ennemi. Emma Darcy. (Azur Ser.: Vol. 698). (FRE.). 1998. mass mkt. 3.50 (0-373-34698-0, 1-34698-0) Harlequin Bks.

Passe-Muraille. Ayme. (FRE.). (C). 1958. pap. 9.95 (0-8442-1974-6, VF1974-6) NTC Contemp Pub Co.

Passe-Muraille. Marcel Ayme. 1943. 12.95 (0-7859-0377-1, F84280) Fr & Eur.

Passe-Muraille. Marcel Ayme. (Folio Ser.: No. 961). (FRE.). 1943. pap. 9.25 (2-07-036961-7) Schoenhof.

Passe-Muraille. Marcel Ayme. (FRE.). 1982. pap. 10.95 (0-8288-3620-5, F84282); pap. 10.95 (0-7859-1856-6, F84282) Fr & Eur.

Passe Obscur. Sally T. Hayes. (Amours d'Aujourd'Hui Ser.). 1999. mass mkt. 4.99 (0-373-38328-2, 1-38328-0) Harlequin Bks.

Passe Our Ennemi. Sandy Steen. (Rouge Passion Ser.). 1999. mass mkt. 3.50 (0-373-37514-X, 1-37514-6) Harlequin Bks.

Passe Partout. 2nd ed. Demeo. (C). 1996. pap. text 33.02 (0-201-89211-1) Addison-Wesley.

Passe pour Temoin. Carla Cassidy. (Rouge Passion Ser.: No. 518). (FRE.). 1999. mass mkt. 3.99 (0-373-37518-2, 1-37518-7) Harlequin Bks.

Passe Simple. Driss Chraibi. (FRE.). 273p. 1986. pap. 11.95 (0-7859-2031-5, 2070377288) Fr & Eur.

Passe Simple. Driss Chraibi. (Folio Ser.: No. 1728). (FRE.). 272p. 1987. pap. 10.95 (2-07-037728-8) Schoenhof.

***Passe Trouble.** Elizabeth August. (Rouge Passion Ser.: No. 526). (FRE.). 1999. mass mkt. 3.99 (0-373-37526-3, 1-37526-0) Harlequin Bks.

Passe Vivant de la France: Advanced. (FRE.). (C). 1986. 23.95 (0-8442-1122-2, VF1122-2) NTC Contemp Pub Co.

Passed on: African American Mourning Stories. Karla F. Holloway. text. write for info. (0-374-22991-0) FS&G.

Passed to the Present: Folk Arts along Wisconsin's Ethnic Settlement Trail. Ed. by Robert T. Teske. LC 94-180394. (Illus.). 56p. (Orig.). 1994. pap. 10.00 (0-9625597-1-7) Cedarburg Cultural Ctr.

Passenger. Michelangelo Antonioni et al. (Illus.). 192p. (Orig.). 1986. pap. 6.95 (0-936839-52-X) Applause Theatre Bk Pubs.

***Passenger.** E. F. Benson. Ed. by Jack Adrian. xx, 160p. 1999. 39.00 (1-899562-81-8) Ash-Tree.

Passenger. Patrick A. Davis. LC 99-25579. 384p. 1999. 24.95 (0-399-14491-9, G P Putnam) Peng Put Young Read.

Passenger. Jane Yolen. (Young Merlin Trilogy Ser.). (J). 1998. pap. 3.50 (0-590-37073-1, Apple Paperbacks) Scholastic Inc.

Passenger, Vol. I. W. H. Gunn & D. W. Goodwin. LC 98-90106. 116p. 1998. pap. 10.95 (0-9618817-2-0) Wings Pubns.

Passenger, Vol. 1. Antonio Porta. 80p. pap. 8.00 (0-919349-73-0) Guernica Editions.

***Passenger: Selected Poems, 1958-1979.** rev. ed. Antonio Porta. Tr. by Pasquale Verdicchio. (Picas Ser.: Vol. 13). 84p. 1999. pap. 8.00 (0-920717-64-0) Guernica Editions.

Passenger & Immigration. P. William Filby. 1981. 98.00 (0-8103-1098-8) Gale.

Passenger & Immigration Index Supplement 97. 97th ed. 1996. 225.00 (0-7876-0114-4, 00108824) Gale.

Passenger & Immigration Lists: Annual Supplement, Vol. 2. 1998. suppl. ed. 240.00 (0-7876-1937-X) Gale.

Passenger & Immigration Lists Annual Supplement, 91. 91st ed. P. William Filby. 1991. 225.00 (0-8103-6969-9) Gale.

Passenger & Immigration Lists Annual Supplement, 92. 92nd ed. P. William Filby. 1992. 225.00 (0-8103-7603-2) Gale.

Passenger & Immigration Lists Annual Supplement, 93. 93rd ed. P. William Filby. 1993. 225.00 (0-8103-8041-2) Gale.

Passenger & Immigration Lists Annual Supplement, 94. 94th ed. P. William Filby. 1994. 225.00 (0-8103-8551-1, 009727) Gale.

Passenger & Immigration Lists Annual Supplement, 95. 95th ed. Filby-Byers. 1995. 235.00 (0-8103-5732-1) Gale.

Passenger & Immigration Lists Annual Supplement, 98. 575p. 1997. 225.00 (0-7876-1203-0, 00156329) Gale.

Passenger & Immigration Lists Annual Supplement, 98, Vol. 2. 575p. 1997. 235.00 (0-7876-1879-9, 111304) Gale.

Passenger & Immigration Lists Annual Supplement, 99, Vol. 1. 99th ed. 575p. 1998. 240.00 (0-7876-1936-1, 00157435) Gale.

Passenger & Immigration Lists Bibliography, 1538-1900. 2nd ed. Ed. by P. William Filby. LC 84-13702. 324p. 1988. 235.00 (0-8103-2740-6) Gale.

Passenger & Immigration Lists Bibliography, 1538-1900: Supplement. Ed. by P. William Filby. 125p. 1984. 66.00 (0-8103-1644-7) Gale.

***Passenger & Immigration Lists Index.** 575p. 2000. 245.00 (0-7876-3280-5) Gale.

***Passenger & Immigration Lists Index.** 575p. 2000. 245.00 (0-7876-3281-3, UXL) Gale.

***Passenger & Immigration Lists Index, 3 vols.** Contrib. by Gale Group. 2340p. 1999. 530.00 (0-7876-3721-1) Gale.

Passenger & Immigration Lists Index: A Reference Guide to Published Lists of about 500,000 Passengers Who Arrived in America in the Seventeenth, Eighteenth & Nineteenth Centuries, 3 vols. Ed. by P. William Filby. 2340p. 1981. 440.00 (0-8103-1099-6) Gale.

Passenger & Immigration Lists Index: 2000 Supplement, Pt. 1. 575p. 1999. 240.00 (0-7876-2216-8, GML00299-111731, Gale Res Intl) Gale.

Passenger & Immigration Lists Index: 2000 Supplement, Pt. 2. 575p. 1999. 240.00 (0-7876-2217-6, GML00299-111732, Gale Res Intl) Gale.

Passenger & Immigration Lists Index, 1986-1990, Cumulated Supplements: A Guide to Published Arrival Records of Passengers Who Came to the New World Between the Sixteenth & the Early Twentieth Centuries, 3 Vols. 90th ed. Ed. by P. William Filby & Dorothy M. Lower. LC 84-15404. 2661p. 1990. 530.00 (0-8103-2579-9) Gale.

Passenger & Immigration Lists Index, 1990 Supplement: A Guide to Published Arrival Records of Passengers Who Came to the New World Between the Sixteenth & the Early Twentieth Centuries. 90th ed. Ed. by P. William Filby & Dorothy M. Lower. LC 84-15404. 660p. 1990. 235.00 (0-8103-2578-0, 009651) Gale.

Passenger & Immigration Lists Index, 1982-85: Cumulation, 4 Vols. 85th ed. Ed. by P. William Filby & Mary K. Meyer. 3404p. 1985. 530.00 (0-8103-1795-8, 009639) Gale.

Passenger & Immigration Lists Index, 1991-95: Cumulative, 3 Vols., Vol. 95. 95th ed. P. William Filby. 1995. 530.00 (0-8103-8337-3, 009667) Gale.

Passenger & Immigration Lists Index Supplement, 83. 83rd ed. Ed. by P. William Filby. 1008p. 1984. 235.00 (0-8103-1790-7) Gale.

Passenger & Immigration Lists Index Supplement, 87. 87th ed. Ed. by P. William Filby & Mary K. Meyer. 677p. 1987. 235.00 (0-8103-2575-6) Gale.

Passenger & Immigration Lists Index Supplement, 89. 89th ed. 722p. 1989. 235.00 (0-8103-2577-2, 009650-99584) Gale.

Passenger & Immigration Lists Index, 1991-95, Vol. 1. 1995. write for info. (0-8103-8338-1) Gale.

Passenger & Immigration Lists Index, 1991-95, Vol. 2. 1995. write for info. (0-8103-8339-X) Gale.

Passenger & Immigration Lists Index, 1991-95, Vol. 3. 1995. write for info. (0-8103-8340-3) Gale.

Passenger & Immigration Lists, 1996. 96th ed. P. William Filby & Byers. 559p. 1996. suppl. ed. 235.00 (0-8103-9329-8) Gale.

Passenger Arrivals at the Port of Charleston, 1820-1829. Compiled by Brent H. Holcomb. LC 94-78263. 188p. 1994. 25.00 (0-8063-1450-8, 4420) Genealog Pub.

Passenger Arrivals at the Port of New York, 1820-1829. Elizabeth P. Bentley. LC 98-75654. 1491p. 1999. 95.00 (0-8063-1610-1) Genealog Pub.

***Passenger Arrivals at the Port of New York, 1820-1829.** Elizabeth Petty Bentley. 2000. 85.00 (0-8063-1625-X) Genealog Pub.

Passenger Arrivals at the Port of Philadelphia, 1800-1819. Ed. by Michael H. Tepper. xvii, 913p. 1986. 45.00 (0-8063-1138-X, 4481) Genealog Pub.

Passenger Boats on Inland Waterways. D. D. Gladwin. 64p. (C). 1985. 39.00 (0-85361-261-7) St Mut.

Passenger Car. Joanne Barkan. (Come Aboard Bks.). (Illus.). 12p. (J). (ps). 1992. pap. 3.50 (0-689-71575-7) Aladdin.

Passenger Car & Diesel Engine Lubricants. 170p. 1998. pap. 85.00 (0-7680-0303-2, SP-1389) Soc Auto Engineers.

Passenger Car Distribution No. R302: Trends to 2000. 1993. 985.00 (0-614-12671-1) Economist Intell.

***Passenger Cars & Vans in Taiwan: A Strategic Entry Report, 1997.** Compiled by Icon Group International Staff. (Illus.). 120p. 1999. ring bd. 1200.00 incl. audio compact disk (0-7418-0964-8) Icon Grp.

Passenger Cars of the Burlington 1869 to the 1930's. William L. Glick. LC 86-90543. (Illus.). 166p. 1986. 60.00 (0-940525-00-3); pap. 39.50 (0-940525-01-1) Quincy Hse.

Passenger Conveyors. J. M. Tough & C. A. O'Flaherty. 192p. (C). 1971. text 189.00 (0-677-65360-3) Gordon & Breach.

Passenger Liners from Germany, 1816-1990. Clas B. Hansen. LC 91-65662. (Illus.). 192p. 1991. 35.00 (0-88740-325-5) Schiffer.

Passenger Lists (& Fragments Thereof) from Hamburg & Bremen to Australia & the United States, 1846-1849. Clifford N. Smith. (German-American Genealogical Research Monographs: No. 23). i, 27p. (Orig.). 1988. pap. 20.00 (0-915162-82-2) Westland Pubns.

Passenger Lists from Ireland: (Excerpted from Journal of the American Irish Historical Society, Vols. 28 & 29) J. Dominick Hackett & Charles M. Early. LC 65-29279. 46p. 1998. reprint ed. pap. 10.00 (0-8063-0166-X) Clearfield Co.

Passenger on a Ferry. Jena Woodhouse. LC 94-217436. 1994. pap. 16.95 (0-7022-2642-4, Pub. by Univ Queensland Pr) Intl Spec Bk.

Passenger Pigeon see Extinct Species Collection

Passenger Pigeon: Gone Forever. Susan Dudley Morrison. (Illus.). 48p. (J). (gr. 5-8). 1998. text 12.00 (0-7881-5834-1) DIANE Pub.

Passenger Pigeons. (Wisconsin Stories Ser.). (Illus.). 23p. 1976. pap. 1.25 (0-87020-188-3) State Hist Soc Wis.

Passenger Protection Technology in Aircraft Accident Fires. Neville H. Birch. 200p. 1987. text 86.95 (0-291-39734-4, Pub. by Avebury Technical) Ashgate Pub Co.

Passenger Psychological Dynamics. 189p. 1968. pap. 10.00 (0-87262-020-4) Am Soc Civil Eng.

***Passenger Ship Construction - Classes I, II & II(A) Instructions for the Guidance of Surveyors.** Maritime & Coastguard Agency Staff. 94p. 1999. ring bd. 50.00 (0-11-551998-X, Pub. by Statnry Office) Balogh.

***Passenger Ship Construction Classes III to VI(A) Instructions for the Guidance of Surveyors.** Maritime & Coastguard Agency Staff. 94p. 1999. ring bd. 70.00 (0-11-552114-3, Pub. by Statnry Office) Balogh.

Passenger to Frankfurt. Agatha Christie. 23.95 (0-88411-384-1) Amereon Ltd.

Passenger to Frankfurt. Agatha Christie. 288p. 1992. mass mkt. 5.99 (0-06-100378-6, Harp PBks) HarpC.

***Passenger Trains.** Chelsea House Publishing Staff. LC 99-51667. (Illus.). 64p. 1999. 21.95 (0-7910-5561-2) Chelsea Hse.

***Passenger Trains.** Allison Lassieur. 1999. 14.60 (0-516-21874-3) Capstone Pr.

***Passenger Trains.** Lynn M. Stone. LC 99-13203. (Trains Ser.). 24p. 1999. lib. bdg. write for info. (0-86593-518-1) Rourke Corp.

Passenger Tramways of Pontypridd. R. Large. 52p. (C). 1985. 39.00 (0-85361-208-0) St Mut.

Passenger Transport after 2000 A. D. G. B. R. Feilden et al. (Illus.). 288p. (C). 1994. 70.00 (0-419-19470-3, E & FN Spon) Routledge.

Passenger Transport Planning Management & Policy in Japan. Mervyn Jones. (C). 1984. 29.00 (0-7855-3844-5, Pub. by Oxford Polytechnic) St Mut.

***Passenger Traveller.** Mark W. Fisher. 60p. 2000. pap. 6.00 (0-9674900-5-7) Wordrunner.

Passenger Vehicles in Dominican Republic: A Strategic Entry Report, 1996. Compiled by Icon Group International Staff. (Illus.). 103p. 1999. ring bd. 1030.00 incl. audio compact disk (0-7418-0694-0) Icon Grp.

P

Passenger Vibration in Transportation Vehicles: Presented at the Design Engineering Technical Conference, Chicago, Illinois, September 26-28, 1977. Design Engineering Technical Conference (1977: Chi. Ed. by Alex Berman & Alan J. Hannibal. LC 77-82212. (AMD Ser.: Vol. 24). 136p. reprint ed. pap. 42.20 (*0-608-13159-8*, 201539300093) Bks Demand.

Passengers. Daniel Besnehard. Tr. by Stephen J. Vogel. 89p. (Orig.). 1985. pap. text 8.95 (*0-913745-12-X*) Ubu Repertory.

Passengers. Nancy E. Krulik. (Lost in Space Digest Ser.). (J). (gr. 4-7). 1998. pap. 3.99 (*0-590-18939-5*) Scholastic Inc.

Passengers & Kings. Joe Fuoco. 96p. 1989. 19.95 (*0-89754-055-7*); pap. 8.95 (*0-89754-054-9*) Dan River Pr.

Passengers & Ships Prior to 1684, Penn's Colony, Vol. 1. Marion R. Balderston et al. Ed. by Walter Lee Sheppard, Jr. 245p. 1992. reprint ed. pap. 21.00 (*1-55613-664-1*) Heritage Bk.

Passengers from Ireland, 1811-1817: Lists of Passengers Arriving at American Ports Between 1811 & 1817. Transcribed from the Shamrock or Hibernian Chronicle. Donald M. Schlegel. LC 79-90983. 158p. 1999. pap. 17.50 (*0-8063-0870-2*) Clearfield Co.

Passenger's Guide to Airline Flying. Larry Coy. LC 98-65643. (Illus.). 144p. 1998. pap. 15.95 (*1-57197-123-8*) Pentland Pr.

Passengers to America: A Consolidation of Ship Passenger Lists from the New England Historical & Genealogical Register. Michael H. Tepper. LC 77-72983. 554p. 1988. reprint ed. 25.00 (*0-8063-0767-6*) Genealog Pub.

Passerby: And Other Stories. Ethel M. Dell. LC 72-5867. (Short Story Index Reprint Ser.). 1977. reprint ed. 23.95 (*0-8369-4210-8*) Ayer.

Passerelle: French Grammar in Use. Kate Beeching & Isabelle Le Guilloux. (Illus.). 232p. (C). 1993. pap. 31.95 (*0-521-36857-X*); audio 31.95 (*0-521-36471-X*) Cambridge U Pr.

Passers & Receivers: The NFL's Top Touchdown Duos. Richard Deutsch. Ed. by Scott Gramling & Michael Northrop. 32p. (J). (gr. 2-8). 1999. pap. 3.99 (*1-886749-67-1*) SI For Kids.

Passes of Colorado: An Encyclopedia of Watershed Divides. Ed Helmuth & Gloria Helmuth. LC 93-42044. (Illus.). 317p. 1994. pap. 25.00 (*0-87108-841-X*) Pruett.

Passin' Through. Louis L'Amour. 208p. (Orig.). 1985. mass mkt. 4.50 (*0-553-25320-4*) Bantam.

***Passing.** Patricia Jones Bacchus. LC 99-94869. 384p. 1999. pap. 12.50 (*0-380-80585-5*, Avon Bks) Morrow Avon.

Passing. Ed. by Stacey Herbert & Luca Crispi. (Theory@Buffalo Ser.: No. 4). 121p. (C). 1998. pap. 8.00 (*0-922668-19-1*) SUNYB Poetry Rare Bks.

Passing. Nella Larsen. Ed. & Intro. by Thadious Davis. LC 97-9482. xxxiv, 122p. 1997. pap. 8.95 (*0-14-118025-0*) Penguin Putnam.

***Passing.** Nella Larsen. 2000. 18.95 (*0-375-50446-X*) Random.

Passing. Nella Larsen. LC 76-92233. (American Negro: His History & Literature. Series 3: His History & Literature, Ser. No. 3). 1970. reprint ed. 27.95 (*0-405-01930-0*) Ayer.

Passing. Nella Larsen. LC 69-18567. 226p. 1990. reprint ed. pap. 19.95 (*0-88143-119-2*) Ayer.

Passing. Nella Larsen. LC 73-82056. 215p. 1969. reprint ed. lib. bdg. 38.50 (*0-8371-1541-8*, LAP&, Greenwood Pr) Greenwood.

Passing: Stories. Ferrol Sams. LC 89-63792. 116p. 1990. pap. 6.95 (*0-929264-31-2*) Longstreet.

Passing: The Vision of Death in America, 2. Charles O. Jackson. LC 77-23794. (Contributions in Family Studies: No. 2). 258p. 1977. 59.95 (*0-8371-9757-0*, JPA/, Greenwood Pr) Greenwood.

Passing a Good Time: With Guns, Dogs, Fly Rods, & Other Joys. Gene Hill. LC 96-48148. 208p. 1996. 25.00 (*0-924357-64-9*, 21310-A) Countrysport Pr.

Passing a Note to M'Girls. Andreia Thaxton-Mathis. Ed. by Valencia Robinson et al. LC 97-67419. 64p. 1997. 14.95 (*0-9657952-5-X*) Shonth Bks.

Passing & Pedagogy: The Dynamics of Responsibility. Pamela L. Caughie. LC 98-58007. 304p. 1999. pap. text 18.95 (*0-252-06770-3*) U of Ill Pr.

Passing & Pedagogy: The Dynamics of Responsibility. Pamela L. Caughie. LC 98-58007. (Illus.). 286p. 1999. 42.50 (*0-252-02466-4*) U of Ill Pr.

Passing & Shooting. Clive Gifford. (Soccer School Ser.). (Illus.). 32p. (J). (gr. 3 up). 1997. pap. text 5.95 (*0-7460-2450-9*, Usborne); lib. bdg. 13.95 (*0-88110-911-8*, Usborne) EDC.

Passing & the Fictions of Identity. Ed. by Elaine K. Ginsberg. LC 95-40106. (New Americanists Ser.). (Illus.). 312p. 1996. text 49.95 (*0-8223-1755-9*); pap. text 17.95 (*0-8223-1764-8*) Duke.

Passing By: Gender & Public Harassment. Carol B. Gardner. 274p. 1995. pap. 17.95 (*0-520-20215-5*, Pub. by U CA Pr) Cal Prin Full Svc.

Passing By: Selected Essays, 1962-1991. Jerzy N. Kosinski. LC 95-19519. 272p. 1995. pap. 12.00 (*0-8021-3423-8*, Grove) Grove-Atltic.

***Passing by Samaria.** Sharon Foster. 400p. 2000. pap. 11.99 (*1-57673-615-6*, Pub. by Multnomah Pubs) GL Services.

Passing Ceremony. Helen Weinzweig. 120p. (Orig.). 1973. pap. 5.95 (*0-88784-325-5*, Pub. by Hse of Anansi Pr) Genl Dist Srvs.

Passing down the Farm: The Other Farm Crisis. Donald J. Jonovic & Wayne D. Messick. 230p. 1987. 24.95 (*0-915607-08-5*) Jamieson Pr.

Passing Duration: Prose Poems. Stephen Rodefer. (Burning Deck Poetry Ser.). 80p. 1991. pap. 8.00 (*0-930901-76-2*) Burning Deck.

Passing Duration: Prose Poems. limited ed. Stephen Rodefer. (Burning Deck Poetry Ser.). 80p. 1991. pap. 15.00 (*0-930901-77-0*) Burning Deck.

Passing Exams. Betty L. Randolph. Ed. by Success Education Institute International Staff. 1990. 9.98 incl. audio (*1-55909-275-0*, 53B) Randolph Tapes.

Passing Exams: A Guide for Maximum Success & Minimum Stress. Dawn Hamilton. 128p. 1999. pap. 16.50 (*0-304-70489-X*) Continuum.

Passing Exams Without Anxiety: How to Get Organized, Be Prepared & Feel Confident of Success. 5th ed. David Acres. 144p. 1998. pap. 19.95 (*1-85703-269-1*, Pub. by How To Bks) Trans-Atl Phila.

Passing Faith's Tests with Love & Joy (James, I & II Peter, I-III John, Jude) Ed. by Jack Hayford. LC 97-222146. (Spirit-Filled Life Bible Discovery Guides Ser.: Vol. B24). 160p. pap. 6.99 (*0-7852-1205-1*) Nelson.

Passing Fancy. David Spencer. Ed. by Tyya Turner. (Alien Nation Ser.: No. 6). 320p. (Orig.). 1994. mass mkt. 5.50 (*0-671-79517-1*) PB.

Passing Figure: Racial Confusion in Modern American Literature. 2nd ed. Juda Bennett. (Modern American Literature: Vol. 6). VIII, 142p. (C). 1998. reprint ed. pap. text 24.95 (*0-8204-4265-8*) P Lang Pubng.

Passing for Black: The Life & Careers of Mae Street Kidd. Wade Hall. (Illus.). 208p. 1997. pap. 16.00 (*0-8131-0948-5*) U Pr of Ky.

***Passing for Normal.** Amy S. Wilensky. 256p. 2000. pap. 12.95 (*0-7679-0186-X*) Broadway BDD.

Passing for Normal: A Memoir of Compulsion. Amy S. Wilensky. LC 99-24312. 224p. 1999. 23.00 (*0-7679-0185-1*) Broadway BDD.

Passing Freaks & Other Graces. Reed Bye. 36p. (Orig.). 1996. pap. 5.00 (*1-887289-25-9*) Rodent Pr.

***Passing Game.** Christopher Brookhouse. LC 00-190466. 160p. 2000. 19.95 (*0-9665798-2-8*, Pub. by Safe Harbor Bks) Enfield Pubs NH.

Passing Game: A History of the CFL. Frank Cosentino. 400p. 1995. 21.95 (*0-921368-54-2*, Pub. by Bain & Cox) Genl Dist Srvs.

Passing Gas: The History of Inflight Refueling. Vernon B. Byrd. Ed. by Heidelberg Graphics Staff & Aaron Kenedi. (Illus.). 288p. 1994. 39.95 (*0-9639977-1-8*) Byrd Pubng.

***Passing Gas - the History of Inflight Refueling.** rev. ed. Vernon B. Bryd, Jr. Ed. by Aaron Kenedi. 288p. 1999. 39.95 (*0-9639977-2-6*) Byrd Pubng.

Passing Generations, 1885-1903. Compiled by Carolyn Wimp. 411p. 1998. pap. 34.00 (*1-889221-39-2*) Ancestral Trails.

Passing Glances. Ed. by Bob Hall. (Southern Exposure Ser.). (Illus.). 112p. (Orig.). (C). 1978. pap. 3.00 (*0-943810-74-4*) Inst Southern Studies.

Passing HSC Legal Studies. R. Pickworth & J. Pickworth. 120p. 1991. pap. 30.00 (*0-409-30194-9*, Austral, MICHIE) LEXIS Pub.

Passing in Constantsa (1996 Epilogue Included) And Other Tales of Eastern Europe in Change. Mike Chessier. (Illus.). 116p. (Orig.). 1996. pap., spiral bd. 9.95 (*0-614-30235-8*) M Chessin.

Passing in Contantsa: And Other Tales of Eastern Europe in Change. Mike Chessin. 84p. 1991. pap. 8.95 (*0-9632512-0-1*) M Chessin.

Passing Interviews. Harper Collins Staff. 240p. 1998. pap. text 12.00 (*0-00-472121-7*) Collins.

Passing into History: Nazism & the Holocaust Beyond Memory. Gulie N. Arad. Date not set. 39.95 (*0-253-30021-5*); pap. 25.00 (*0-253-30026-6*) Ind U Pr.

***Passing It On: Music & Irish Culture.** Marie McCarthy. 224p. 1999. 65.00 (*1-85918-178-3*); pap. 20.00 (*1-85918-179-1*) Cork Univ.

***Passing It On: The Inheritance & Use of Summer Houses. Judith Huggins Balfe. 304p. 1999. (*1-57087-486-7*) Prof Pr NC.**

A family summer house can be the repository of generations of family experiences. It simultaneously can be the source of great family discord as new generations increase family size & diversity. Judith Huggins Balfe, a professional sociologist & summer house heir, has interviewed 125 families who share time & ownership at family summer homes in 18 states & Canada. Her book is a professional assessment of the various factors that determine the parameters of summer house inheritance, & their consequences for both families & individuals. These include differences of social class or status, & issues of authority over the summer house & the legacy it preserves. In separate chapters, Balfe describes several family roles & organizing structures. She also explains a variety of formal, legal arrangements, suggests mediation principles, & presents some tested methods of fair division of time at the summer house. Using scores of interview excerpts, she illustrates the difficulties & solutions multi-generational families have had with family summer houses. Each situation is unique, but how relatives perceive legacy, stewardship & family commitment will determine how successful is the passing on of summer houses. *Publisher Paid Annotation.*

Passing Judgment, Vol. 1. Keith Ferrell. 352p. 1998. mass mkt. 6.99 (*0-8125-5537-6*) Forge Pr.

Passing Judgments. George J. Nathan. LC 71-86774. (Essay Index Reprint Ser.). 1977. 18.95 (*0-8369-1150-4*) Ayer.

Passing Judgments: The Theatre World of George Jean Nathan. George J. Nathan. LC 75-120099. 271p. 1975. 25.00 (*0-8386-7722-3*) Fairleigh Dickinson.

Passing of 'Abdu'l-Baha: A Compilation. Shoghi Effendi. (Illus.). 138p. 1991. 14.95 (*0-933770-82-0*) Kalimat.

Passing of American Neutrality, 1937-1941, Vol. 20--20. Donald F. Drummond. LC 68-54416. (Illus.). 409p. 1969. reprint ed. lib. bdg. 35.00 (*0-8371-0394-0*, DRAN, Greenwood Pr) Greenwood.

Passing of an Actor. Willard Simms. 1968. pap. 3.25 (*0-8222-0874-1*) Dramatists Play.

Passing of an Illusion: The Idea of Communism in the Twentieth Century. Francois Furet. Tr. by Deborah Furet from FRE. LC 98-42109. 600p. 1999. 35.00 (*0-226-27340-7*) U Ch Pr.

Passing of Barchester. Clive Dewey. 236p. 1991. 45.00 (*1-85285-039-6*) Hambledon Press.

Passing of Korea. Homer B. Holbert. 1977. 36.95 (*0-8369-7141-8*, 7974) Ayer.

Passing of Marine Griffiths. D. K. Brough. 1981. 35.00 (*0-7223-1413-2*, Pub. by A H S Ltd) St Mut.

***Passing of Octavio Paz: Bilingual Spanish/English Text/Poem.** Seymour Mayne. 2000. pap. 10.00 (*0-88962-696-0*) Mosaic.

Passing of Souls. John T. Ferrier. 32p. 1968. pap. text 6.00 (*0-900235-62-4*) Order Of The Cross.

Passing of Spanish Traditionalism: Deprivation, Transformation, Credence. Lawrence J. Pinnie. LC 95-90395. (Illus.). xvii, 198p. (Orig.). 1996. pap. 13.95 (*0-9655698-0-2*) L J Pinnie.

Passing of Starr Faithfull. Jonathan Goodman. LC 95-38202. (Illus.). 328p. 1996. reprint ed. pap. 17.00 (*0-87338-541-1*) Kent St U Pr.

Passing of the Armies. Joshua L. Chamberlain. 368p. 1992. mass mkt. 6.99 (*0-553-29992-1*) Bantam.

Passing of the Armies. Joshua J. Chamberlain. 1997. reprint ed. 30.00 (*1-56515-022-8*) Collect Reprints.

Passing of the Armies: An Account of the Final Campaign of the Army of the Potomac, Based upon Personal Reminiscences of the Fifth Army Corps. Joshua L. Chamberlain. LC 98-35167. (Illus.). xxxvii, 407p. 1998. pap. 16.95 (*0-8032-6390-2*, Bison Books) U of Nebr Pr.

Passing of the Armies: The Last Campaign of the Armies. Joshua L. Chamberlain. (Illus.). 402p. 1995. reprint ed. 25.00 (*1-879664-18-6*); reprint ed. pap. 17.95 (*1-879664-19-4*) Stan Clark Military.

"THE PASSING OF THE ARMIES is essential reading for those who wish to touch the mind & character of Joshua Lawrence Chamberlain."--John Peterson. "There is real human depth & critical judgement in some of his original opinions of Grant & Lee, formed on the field. His account of the arrival at the front of the news of Lincoln's assassination is a masterly stroke."--Springfield Republican. "...the best study by a contemporary on the last days of the Civil War."--Willard Wallace. "Chamberlain had a most successful military career capped by his being chosen to command the Union troops who were present when the Army of Northern Virginia laid down their arms. His account of the final Virginia campaign is superb. He was as great a writer as he was a fighter...One of the classics of Civil War literature."--The Union Bookshelf. "The fullest account of the surrender of the Army of Northern Virginia, written by the generous Federal general who commanded at the laying down of arms."--Clifford Dowdey. "The climax of Chamberlain's readable reminiscences is his moving description of the surrender ceremonies at Appomattox."--Civil War Books. Stan Clark Military Books, 915 Fairview Avenue, Gettysburg, PA 17325; Phone: 717-337-1728; Fax: 717-337-0581. *Publisher Paid Annotation.*

Passing of the Frontier. Emerson Hough. 1976. lib. bdg. 10.95 (*0-89968-046-1*, Lghtyr Pr) Buccaneer Bks.

Passing of the Frontier: A Chronicle of the Old West. Emerson Hough. (BCL1 - United States Local History Ser.). 181p. 1991. reprint ed. lib. bdg. 69.00 (*0-7812-6322-0*) Rprt Serv.

Passing of the Frontier, 1825-1850 see History of the State of Ohio

Passing of the Great Race: or The Racial Basis of European History. Madison Grant. LC 74-129398. (American Immigration Collection. Series 2). (Illus.). 1970. reprint ed. 18.95 (*0-405-00577-6*) Ayer.

Passing of the Idle Rich. Frederick T. Martin. LC 75-1858. (Leisure Class in America Ser.). 1975. reprint ed. 20.95 (*0-405-06924-3*) Ayer.

Passing of the Manchus. Percy H. Kent. LC 75-32316. (Studies in Chinese History & Civilization). 404p. 1977. lib. bdg. 69.50 (*0-313-26971-8*, U6971, Greenwood Pr) Greenwood.

Passing of the Mill Village: Revolution in a Southern Institution. Harriet L. Herring. LC 76-54298. 137p. 1977. reprint ed. lib. bdg. 59.50 (*0-8371-9406-7*, HEPA, Greenwood Pr) Greenwood.

Passing of the Summer. Miriam M. Batts. 1998. pap. write for info. (*1-57553-710-9*) Watermrk Pr.

***Passing of the Territorial Age.** Maier. 2000. 30.00 (*0-465-04319-4*, Pub. by Basic); pap. 15.00 (*0-465-04320-8*, Pub. by Basic) HarpC.

Passing of the Three-D Ranch. L. Stansberry. (American History & Americana Ser.: No. 47). 1970. lib. bdg. 75.00 (*0-8383-1108-3*) M S G Haskell Hse.

Passing of the Times Vol. 1, Pt. 1, Bk. 1A: Old Virginia. Sam H. Moore. 1994. write for info. (*0-89904-232-5*); pap. write for info. (*0-89904-233-3*) Crumb Elbow Pub.

Passing of the Times Vol. 2, Pt. 2, Bk. 1B: Old Virginia. Sam H. Moore. 1994. write for info. (*0-89904-234-1*); pap. write for info. (*0-89904-235-X*) Crumb Elbow Pub.

Passing of the Times Vol. 3, Pt. 2, Bk. 2A: Old Virginia. Sam H. Moore. 1994. write for info. (*0-89904-236-8*); pap. write for info. (*0-89904-237-6*) Crumb Elbow Pub.

Passing of the Times Vol. 4, Pt. 2, Bk. 2B: Old Virginia. Sam H. Moore. 1994. write for info. (*0-89904-238-4*); pap. write for info. (*0-89904-239-2*) Crumb Elbow Pub.

Passing of the Times Vol. 5, Pt. 1, Bk. 1A: Trips. Sam H. Moore. 1994. write for info. (*0-89904-240-6*); pap. write for info. (*0-89904-241-4*) Crumb Elbow Pub.

Passing of the Times Vol. 6, Pt. 1, Bk. 1B: Trips. Sam H. Moore. 1994. write for info. (*0-89904-242-2*); pap. write for info. (*0-89904-243-0*) Crumb Elbow Pub.

Passing of the Times Vol. 7, Pt. 2, Bk. 2A: Trips. Sam H. Moore. 1994. write for info. (*0-89904-244-9*); pap. write for info. (*0-89904-245-7*) Crumb Elbow Pub.

Passing of the Times Vol. 8, Pt. 2, Bk. 2B: Trips. Sam H. Moore. 1994. write for info. (*0-89904-246-5*); pap. write for info. (*0-89904-247-3*) Crumb Elbow Pub.

Passing of the Times Vol. 9, Pt. 3, Bk. 3A: Trips. Sam H. Moore. 1994. write for info. (*0-89904-248-1*); pap. write for info. (*0-89904-249-X*) Crumb Elbow Pub.

Passing of the Times Vol. 10, Pt. 3, Bk. 3B: Trips. Sam H. Moore. 1994. write for info. (*0-89904-250-3*); pap. write for info. (*0-89904-251-1*) Crumb Elbow Pub.

Passing of the Times Vol. 11, Pt. 3, Bk. 3C: Trips. Sam H. Moore. 1994. write for info. (*0-89904-252-X*); pap. write for info. (*0-89904-253-8*) Crumb Elbow Pub.

Passing of the Times Vol. 12, Pt. 3, Bk. 4: Trips. Sam H. Moore. 1994. write for info. (*0-89904-254-6*); pap. write for info. (*0-89904-255-4*) Crumb Elbow Pub.

Passing of the Times Vol. 13, Pt. 3, Bk. 4A: Trips. Sam H. Moore. 1994. write for info. (*0-89904-256-2*); pap. write for info. (*0-89904-257-0*) Crumb Elbow Pub.

Passing of the Times Vol. 14: Occupations. Sam H. Moore. 1994. write for info. (*0-89904-258-9*); pap. write for info. (*0-89904-259-7*) Crumb Elbow Pub.

Passing of the Times Vol. 15, Pt. 1, Bk. 1: 150 Years of the Moore Family. 1994. write for info. (*0-89904-260-0*); pap. write for info. (*0-89904-261-9*) Crumb Elbow Pub.

Passing of the Times Vol. 16, Pt. 2, Bk. 2A: 150 Years of the Moore Family. Sam H. Moore. 1994. write for info. (*0-89904-262-7*); pap. write for info. (*0-89904-263-5*) Crumb Elbow Pub.

Passing of the Times Vol. 17, Pt. 2, Bk. 2B: 150 Years of the Moore Family. Sam H. Moore. 1994. write for info. (*0-89904-264-3*); pap. write for info. (*0-89904-265-1*) Crumb Elbow Pub.

Passing of the Times Vol. 18, Pt. 2, Bk. 1A: 150 Years of the Moore Family. Sam H. Moore. 1994. write for info. (*0-89904-266-X*); pap. write for info. (*0-89904-267-8*) Crumb Elbow Pub.

Passing of the Times Vol. 19, Pt. 2, Bk. 1B: 150 Years of the Moore Family. Sam H. Moore. 1994. write for info. (*0-89904-268-6*); pap. write for info. (*0-89904-269-4*) Crumb Elbow Pub.

Passing of the Times Vol. 20, Pt. 1, Bk. 1A: These Stories Are True. Sam H. Moore. 1994. write for info. (*0-89904-270-8*); pap. write for info. (*0-89904-271-6*) Crumb Elbow Pub.

Passing of the Times Vol. 21, Pt. 1, Bk. 1B: These Stories Are True. Sam H. Moore. 1994. write for info. (*0-89904-272-4*); pap. write for info. (*0-89904-273-2*) Crumb Elbow Pub.

Passing of the Torch. James Chen. LC 88-63263. 92p. (Orig.). 1988. pap. 9.95 (*0-940232-31-6*) Seedsowers.

Passing of the Whigs 1832-1886. Southgate. 520p. 1993. 79.95 (*0-7512-0217-7*) Ashgate Pub Co.

Passing of Thomas. Thomas A. Janvier. LC 79-94733. (Short Story Index Reprint Ser.). 1977. 19.95 (*0-8369-3113-0*) Ayer.

Passing Off. Tom LeClair. LC 95-22746. 176p. 1996. 22.00 (*1-877946-77-X*) Permanent Pr.

Passing On. large type ed. Penelope Lively. 342p. 1990. 19.95 (*1-85089-329-2*, Pub. by ISIS Lrg Prnt) Transaction Pubs.

Passing On. Penelope Lively. 224p. 1999. reprint ed. pap. 12.00 (*0-8021-3626-5*, Grove) Grove-Atltic.

Passing On. Penelope Lively. LC 90-55666. 224p. 1991. reprint ed. pap. 12.00 (*0-06-097370-6*, Perennial) HarperTrade.

***Passing On: Kinship & Inheritance in England.** Janet Finch & Jennifer Mason. LC 00-42476. 2000. pap. write for info. (*1-85728-277-9*, Pub. by UCL Pr Ltd) Taylor & Francis.

***Passing on Failure: District Promotion Practices & Policies.** Ed. by Barry Leonard. 58p. (C). 1999. reprint ed. pap. text 20.00 (*0-7881-7998-5*) DIANE Pub.

***Passing on the Faith: A Radical New Model for Youth & Family Ministry.** Merton P. Strommen & Richard A. Hardel. (Illus.). 368p. 2000. pap. 22.95 (*0-88489-606-4*) St Marys.

Passing on the Faith: The Story of a Mennonite School. Donald B. Kraybill. LC 91-74054. (Illus.). 315p. 1991. pap. 11.95 (*1-56148-051-7*) Good Bks PA.

Passing on the Gift: The Story of Dan West. Glee Yoder. 168p. 1995. reprint ed. pap. 8.95 (*0-87178-689-3*, 8893) Brethren.

Passing on the Rites of Passage: Girls' Initiation Rites in the Context of an Urban Roman Catholic Community on the Zambian Copperbelt. Thera Rasing. LC 97-136350. (African Studies Center Leiden). 124p. (Orig.). 1996. pap. 43.95 (*1-85972-301-2*, Pub. by Avebry) Ashgate Pub Co.

P

An Asterisk (*) at the beginning of an entry indicates that the title is appearing for the first time.

Passing on the Truth. Bentley. 1997. pap. 15.99 (*0-85234-389-2*, Pub. by Evangelical Pr) P & R Pubng.

Passing on Your Beliefs: First Principles of Family Life. Jeff Reed. Ed. by Nancy Reed. (First Principles Ser.: Series II). (Illus.). 64p. 1998. pap. 6.99 (*1-891441-05-1*) LearnCorp Res.

Passing over Easter: Constructing the Boundaries of Messianic Judaism. Shoshanah Feher. LC 97-45385. 208p. 1998. pap. 23.95 (*0-7619-8953-6*) AltaMira Pr.

Passing over Easter: Constructing the Boundaries of Messianic Judaism. Shoshanah Feher. LC 97-45385. 208p. 1998. 62.00 (*0-7619-8952-8*) AltaMira Pr.

Passing Performances: Queer Readings of Leading Players in American Theater History. Ed. by Robert A. Schanke & Kim Marra. LC 98-19710. (Triangulations Ser.). (Illus.). 352p. 1998. text 49.50 (*0-472-09681-8*, 09681); pap. text 19.95 (*0-472-06681-1*, 06681) U of Mich Pr.

Passing Places. Stephen Greenhorn. 96p. 1999. pap. 13.95 (*1-85459-349-8*) Theatre Comm.

Passing Remarks. Helen Hodgeman. LC 98-19968. 224p. 1998. pap. 11.00 (*0-345-41773-9*) Ballantine Pub Grp.

***Passing Rhythms: Football, Music & Popular Culture in Liverpool.** Ed. by John Williams et al. (Illus.). 224p. 2000. 65.00 (*1-85973-397-2*, Pub. by Berg Pubs); pap. 19.50 (*1-85973-303-4*, Pub. by Berg Pubs) NYU Pr.

Passing Scores. 1988. 7.50 (*0-317-67892-2*) Educ Testing Serv.

Passing Seasons: Paintings by Robert Sudlow. Novelene G. Ross. (Illus.). 24p. (Orig.). 1993. pap. 12.00 (*0-939324-49-0*) Wichita Art Mus.

Passing Strange: True Tales of New England Hauntings & Horrors. Joseph Citro. LC 97-9702. (Illus.). 320p. 1997. pap. 13.00 (*1-57630-059-5*, Chapters Bks) HM.

Passing Strange & Wonderful: Aesthetics, Nature, & Culture. Yi-Fu Tuan. LC 92-37105. 285p. 1993. 30.00 (*1-55963-209-7*) Island Pr.

Passing Strange & Wonderful: Aesthetics, Nature, & Culture. Yi-Fu Tuan. Ed. by John Urda. (Kodansha Globe Trade Paperback Ser.). (Illus.). 304p. 1995. pap. 14.00 (*1-56836-067-3*, Kodansha Globe) Kodansha.

Passing Strangers & Other Stories. large type ed. Marie Joseph. 432p. 1989. 27.99 (*0-7089-2027-6*) Ulverscroft.

Passing the Baton. Vancil. 318p. 1987. 23.96 (*0-07-103273-8*) McGraw.

Passing the Baton: Church Planting That Empowers. Tom A. Steffen. (Illus.). 264p. (Orig.). (C). 1997. pap. text 15.95 (*1-882757-02-5*) Ctr Organ & Minist.

Passing the Buck. Wellons. 1987. 32.50 (*0-07-103276-2*) McGraw.

Passing the Buck: Federalism & Canadian Environmental Policy. Kathryn Harrison. LC 97-112401. 248p. 1996. 70.00 (*0-7748-0557-9*, HC120) U of Wash Pr.

Passing the Buck: Federalism & Canadian Environmental Policy. Kathryn Harrison. LC 97-112401. 248p. 1997. pap. 29.95 (*0-7748-0558-7*) U of Wash Pr.

Passing the Buck: What the Bible Says about Giving. David Hocking. Ed. by M. B. Steele. 88p. (Orig.). 1987. pap. 4.95 (*0-939497-04-2*) Promise Pub.

***Passing the Bucks: Protecting Your Wealth from One Generation to the Next.** Norman A. Pappas. (Illus.). 250p. 1999. 29.95 (*0-9674518-0-9*) Enter Group.

Passing the City University of New York Mathematics Skills Assessment Test. Martin M. Zuckerman. (Illus.). 362p. 1983. pap. text 30.95 (*0-912675-00-4*) Ardsley.

Passing the College Placement Examination. 2nd ed. Frank Pintozzi et al. 262p. (C). 1990. pap. text 29.95 (*0-89892-086-8*) Contemp Pub Co of Raleigh.

Passing the FAA Written Exam: Commercial. Tom McQueen. 1991. pap. 9.95 (*0-8306-3579-3*) McGraw-Hill Prof.

Passing the Florida High School Competency Test. Frank Pintozzi & Colleen Pintozzi. (Illus.). 200p. (Orig.). (YA). (gr. 11-12). 1996. pap. text 15.00 (*0-89892-141-4*) Contemp Pub Co of Raleigh.

Passing the FRCS. Ivor A. Sewell. 331p. 1989. pap. 50.00 (*0-407-00725-3*) Buttrwrth-Heinemann.

Passing the GED. Linda Barnes. LC 97-19485. 1997. 17.28 (*0-02-803076-1*) Macmillan.

Passing the Ged Rev. Scott Foresman. LC 90-55999. (Illus.). 784p. 1991. reprint ed. pap. 17.00 (*0-06-276052-1*, Harper Ref) HarpC.

Passing the Georgia High School Graduation Test. Frank Pintozzi & Colleen Pintozzi. (Illus.). 260p. (Orig.). (YA). (gr. 11-12). 1995. pap. text, student ed. 15.00 (*0-89892-130-9*) Contemp Pub Co of Raleigh.

Passing the Georgia High School Social Studies Test. 2nd ed. Karen Powell & Georgia Hardwick. (Illus.). 200p. (YA). (gr. 11-12). pap. text 12.00 (*0-89892-193-7*) Contemp Pub Co of Raleigh.

Passing the Health Care Buck: Who Pays the Hidden Cost? Jack A. Meyer et al. LC 83-12296. (AEI Ser.: No. 386). 63p. reprint ed. pap. 30.00 (*0-8357-4521-X*, 203738000008) Bks Demand.

Passing the Keys: Cardinals, Conclaves & the Election of the Next Pope. Francis A. Burkle-Young. LC 99-29538. 480p. 1999. 35.00 (*1-56833-130-4*, Pub. by Madison Bks UPA) Natl Bk Netwk.

***Passing the Marker: Lightworker's Guide to the New Millennium Energy.** Lee Carroll. Ed. by Jill Kramer. (C). 2000. 13.50 (*1-888053-11-9*, Pub. by Kryon Writings) New Leaf Dist.

Passing the North Carolina Competency Test in Math (NCCTM) Jane Hereford. (Illus.). 284p. (YA). (gr. 9-12). 1997. reprint ed. pap., wbk. ed. 12.00 (*0-89892-159-7*) Contemp Pub Co of Raleigh.

Passing the North Carolina Competency Test in Reading. Jane Hereford. LC 98-170110. (Illus.). 220p. (YA). (gr. 9-12). 1997. reprint ed. pap., wbk. ed. 12.00 (*0-89892-165-1*) Contemp Pub Co of Raleigh.

Passing the Obesity & Nutrition Exams in Primary Care. Ed. by Jeff Birnbaum et al. 208p. 1997. pap. text 49.95 (*1-888628-22-7*) Southlnd Tutor.

Passing the Ohio Ninth Grade Proficiency. Kevin D. Arnold et al. (Illus.). 304p. (Orig.). (J). (gr. 7-12). 1996. reprint ed. pap. 15.95 (*1-884183-06-9*) Englfld & Arnold.

Passing the Peace: A Counting Book for Kids. Diane Brookes. (ENG & FRE., Illus.). 24p. (J). 1990. pap. 8.95 (*0-921254-20-2*, Pub. by Penumbra Pr) U of Toronto Pr.

***Passing the Prince 2 Examinations: Project Management.** CCTA Staff. 53p. 1999. 20.00 (*0-11-330013-1*, Pub. by Statnry Office) Balogh.

Passing the Reins Vol. I: The Sunhorses of Time. G. Henry Hofer. LC 98-23357. (Sunhorses of Time Ser.). (Illus.). 384p. 1999. pap. 14.95 (*1-56474-282-2*) Fithian Pr.

Passing the Time in Ballymenone: Culture & History of an Ulster Community. Henry H. Glassie. LC 95-7836. (Illus.). 872p. 1995. 59.95 (*0-253-32921-3*); 27.95 (*0-253-20987-0*) Ind U Pr.

Passing the Torch. Donald H. Bowen. (When the Time Comes to Let Go Ser.). 100p. 1998. pap. 8.00 (*0-9663658-0-1*) Sonrise Minist.

Passing the Torch: Preserving Indiana's Heritage. Jim Merritt. 1997. pap. 20.00 (*1-57860-008-1*) Guild Pr IN.

Passing the Torch: The Influence of Economic Incentives on Work & Retirement. Joseph F. Quinn et al. LC 90-12352. 240p. 1990. text 25.00 (*0-88099-091-0*); pap. text 15.00 (*0-88099-092-9*) W E Upjohn.

Passing the USMLE: Step 1, Vol. I. 3rd rev. ed. Southland Staff. 185p. (C). 1996. pap., wbk. ed. 30.00 (*1-888628-00-6*) Southlnd Tutor.

Passing the USMLE: Step 1, Vol. II. 3rd rev. ed. Southland Staff. 171p. (C). 1996. pap., wbk. ed. 30.00 (*1-888628-01-4*) Southlnd Tutor.

Passing the USMLE: Step 1, Vol. III. 3rd rev. ed. Southland Staff. 166p. (C). 1996. pap., wbk. ed. 30.00 (*1-888628-02-2*) Southlnd Tutor.

Passing the USMLE: Step 1, Vol. IV. rev. ed. Southland Staff. 116p. (C). 1996. pap., wbk. ed. 30.00 (*1-888628-03-0*) Southlnd Tutor.

Passing the USMLE: Step 2, Vol. I. 3rd rev. ed. Southland Staff. 189p. (C). 1996. pap., wbk. ed. 30.00 (*1-888628-06-5*) Southlnd Tutor.

Passing the USMLE: Step 2, Vol. II. 3rd rev. ed. Southland Staff. 273p. (C). 1996. pap., wbk. ed. 30.00 (*1-888628-07-3*) Southlnd Tutor.

Passing the USMLE: Step 2, Vol. III. 3rd rev. ed. Southland Staff. 207p. (C). 1996. pap., wbk. ed. 30.00 (*1-888628-08-1*) Southlnd Tutor.

Passing the USMLE: Step 2, Vol. IV. rev. ed. Southland Staff. (C). 1996. pap., wbk. ed. 30.00 (*1-888628-09-X*) Southlnd Tutor.

Passing the USMLE: Step 3, Vol. I. 3rd rev. ed. Southland Staff. 170p. (C). 1996. pap., wbk. ed. 30.00 (*1-888628-13-8*) Southlnd Tutor.

Passing the USMLE: Step 3, Vol. II. 3rd rev. ed. Southland Staff. 209p. (C). 1996. pap., wbk. ed. 30.00 (*1-888628-14-6*) Southlnd Tutor.

Passing the USMLE: Step 3, Vol. III. 3rd rev. ed. Southland Staff. 223p. (C). 1996. pap., wbk. ed. 30.00 (*1-888628-15-4*) Southlnd Tutor.

Passing the USMLE: Step 3, Vol. IV. rev. ed. Southland Staff. (C). 1996. pap., wbk. ed. 30.00 (*1-888628-16-2*) Southlnd Tutor.

Passing the USMLE Case Clusters: Steps 2 & 3. 3rd rev. ed. Southland Staff. 163p. (C). 1996. pap., wbk. ed. 30.00 (*1-888628-21-9*) Southlnd Tutor.

Passing the USMLE Photo Diagnosis: Steps 1, 2 & 3, Vol. I. 3rd ed. Southland Staff. 77p. 1996. pap., wbk. ed. 30.00 (*1-888628-23-5*) Southlnd Tutor.

Passing the USMLE Photo Diagnosis: Steps 1, 2 & 3, Vol. II. Southland Staff. 1996. pap., wbk. ed. 30.00 (*1-888628-24-3*) Southlnd Tutor.

Passing Through. Peter J. Bailey. 1982. pap. 5.25 (*0-8222-0875-X*) Dramatists Play.

Passing Through. Betty Higgins. Ed. by Sun Star Publications Staff. (Jellybean Collection: Vol. II). (Illus.). 26p. (J). (gr. 3-8). 1986. pap. 2.95 (*0-937787-03-5*) Sun Star Pubns.

Passing Through. Edgar A. Guest. 190p. 1980. reprint ed. lib. bdg. 18.95 (*0-89968-191-3*, Lghtyr Pr) Buccaneer Bks.

Passing Through: A Novel. 10th ed. Leon Driskell. (Front Porch Paperbacks Ser.). 252p. 1993. pap. 8.95 (*1-56512-056-6*) Algonquin Bks.

Passing Through: Letters & Documents Written in Philadelphia by Famous Visitors. Compiled by Clive E. Driver. (Illus.). 126p. 1982. pap. 10.00 (*0-939084-23-6*) R Mus & Lib.

Passing Through: Reflections on Life. Joe Black. LC 96-94968. 112p. 1997. 14.95 (*0-9628474-4-5*) Life Vision Bks.

Passing Through: Reflections on the 23rd Psalm. R. Scott Sullender. 68p. 1998. pap. 9.95 (*1-57438-021-4*, 6520) Ed Ministries.

Passing Through: The Later Poems, New & Selected. Stanley Kunitz. LC 95-2651. 176p. 1997. pap. 12.00 (*0-393-31615-7*) Norton.

Passing Through from Exotic Places. Ronald Ribman. 1970. pap. 5.25 (*0-8222-0876-8*) Dramatists Play.

Passing Through Midland: Songs of a Hometown. LC 99-94907. viii, 76p. 1999. pap. 6.95 (*0-9671625-1-3*) Bamosey Pr.

Passing Through the Clouds: Facing the Challenges As We Grow from Glory to Glory. Marilyn Smith. 110p. 1998. pap. 12.99 (*1-57502-951-0*, PO2615) Morris Pubng.

Passing Through the Veil. Peter Paddon. 240p. (Orig.). 1996. pap. 22.95 (*1-898307-42-3*, Pub. by Capall Bann Pubng) Holmes Pub.

Passing Through the Waters - Chinese Edition. Ezra Wu. (CHI.). 129p. 1995. pap. 7.50 (*1-56582-112-2*) Christ Renew Min.

Passing Thru. Ed. & Pref. by Robert Wolf. 82p. (Orig.). 1990. pap. 4.95 (*1-878781-00-6*) Free River Pr.

Passing Time: Memoir of a Vietnam Veteran Against the War. W. D. Ehrhart. LC 89-45009. 291p. 1989. pap. 25.00 (*0-89950-416-7*) McFarland & Co.

Passing Time: Memoir of a Vietnam Veteran Against the War. 2nd ed. W. D. Ehrhart. LC 94-36917. 296p. 1995. pap. 18.95 (*0-87023-958-9*) U of Mass Pr.

Passing Trains. Greg McDonnell. (Illus.). 160p. 1996. 50.00 (*1-55046-183-4*, Pub. by Boston Mills) Genl Dist Srvs.

Passing Wind (A Collection of Essays & Aphorisms) A Superficial Examination of Life & Love by a Politically Incorrect Moralist, a U. S. Marine Veteran, & a Born-Again Roman Catholic. John A. Hopp. 144p. (Orig.). 1997. pap. 10.00 (*0-9656238-0-7*) Freshaire Pubns.

Passing Your Family Business on to Your Family: Creating a Lifetime Succession Plan to Meet Your Changing Tax, Estate & Business Needs. Irving L. Blackman. 440p. 1995. per. 32.50 (*1-55738-898-9*, Irwn Prfssnl) McGraw-Hill Prof.

Passing Your Heritage On: A Guide to Writing Your Family Stories. Sharon Foltz. 85p. 1998. 34.95 (*0-9669059-0-3*) Rain Ridge Pubns.

***Passing Your Heritage On: A Guide to Writing Your Family Stories.** 2nd rev. ed. Sharon Foltz. 96p. 1999. pap. 14.95 (*0-9669059-1-1*) Rain Ridge Pubns.

Passing Your IPM Exams. Elaine Crosthwaite. 208p. (C). 1993. pap. 30.00 (*0-85292-515-8*, Pub. by IPM Hse) St Mut.

Passing Your ISO 9000/QS-9000 Audit: A Step-by-Step Guide. Don Sanders. LC 97-204573. (Illus.). 224p. 1997. boxed set 49.95 (*1-57444-128-0*) St Lucie Pr.

Passio Christi: Reflections on the Passion of Christ As Recorded by Saint John. Charles F. Shepherd. (C). 1990. pap. text 39.00 (*0-7223-2593-2*, Pub. by A H S Ltd) St Mut.

Passio Sanctarum Perpetuae et Felicitatis. James W. Halporn. (Latin Commentaries Ser.). 61p. (Orig.). (C). 1984. pap. text 6.00 (*0-929524-47-0*) Bryn Mawr Commentaries.

Passion see Pasion

Passion. (In Classical Mood Ser.: Vol. 20). (Illus.). 1998. write for info. incl. cd-rom (*1-886614-44-X*) Intl Masters Pub.

Passion. B. Boyd & R. Montanari. LC 97-32291. 416p. 1999. mass mkt. 6.99 (*0-380-79094-7*, Avon Bks) Morrow Avon.

Passion. Donna Boyd. LC 97-32291. 400p. 1998. mass mkt. 15.95 (*0-380-97449-5*, Avon Bks) Morrow Avon.

Passion. Barbara De Angelis. LC 97-51854. 112p. 1998. 14.95 (*0-385-31435-3*) Delacorte.

Passion. Barbara De Angelis. 112p. 1999. pap. 9.95 (*0-440-50815-0*) Dell.

Passion. Nick Earls. (Orig.). 1992. pap. 14.95 (*0-7022-2417-0*, Pub. by Univ Queensland Pr) Intl Spec Bk.

Passion. Ed. by Helen Exley. (Illus.). 60p. 1996. 8.00 (*1-85015-774-X*) Exley Giftbooks.

Passion. Carolyn J. Griffin. (Lyrics on Matters Relating to Ser.). 10p. 1985. 8.00 (*1-929388-09-8*) Griffin Pubg Co Inc.

Passion. Tanya T. Henderson. LC 97-213184. 225p. 1997. pap. 10.95 (*1-885478-21-6*, Pub. by Genesis Press) BookWorld.

Passion. T.T. Henderson. 1999. mass mkt. 5.99 (*0-345-43256-8*) Ballantine Pub Grp.

***Passion.** Nicole Jordan. 2000. mass mkt. 6.99 (*0-449-00485-6*, Ballantine) Ballantine Pub Grp.

Passion. James Lapine & Stephen Sondheim. LC 94-26688. 112p. 1994. 22.50 (*1-55936-087-9*); pap. 10.95 (*1-55936-088-7*) Theatre Comm.

***Passion.** Judith H. Montgomery. 50p. 1999. pap. 6.00 (*0-9673495-0-8*) Defined Prov.

Passion. Naomi Oliver. 24p. 1999. pap. 7.00 (*0-8059-4659-4*) Dorrance.

Passion. Orlean. Date not set. pap. write for info. (*0-449-22423-6*) Fawcett.

Passion. Marilyn Papano. 1996. pap. 5.99 (*0-614-98106-9*) Warner Bks.

Passion. Marilyn Pappano. 416p. (Orig.). 1996. mass mkt. 5.99 (*0-446-60117-9*, Pub. by Warner Bks) Little.

Passion. Duane A. Schmidt. 1983. write for info. (*0-9607858-0-9*) Success Pr.

Passion, 4 vols. Donald Senior. pap. 48.50 (*0-8146-5457-6*, M Glazier) Liturgical Pr.

Passion. L. J. Smith. Ed. by Patricia MacDonald. (Dark Visions Ser.: Vol. III). 224p. (J). (gr. 6 up). 1995. mass mkt. 3.99 (*0-671-87456-X*, Archway) PB.

Passion. Robert Steiner. Ed. by Michael Peich. (Fiction Ser.: No. 2). (Illus.). 1980. 20.00 (*0-915778-33-5*) Penmaen Pr.

Passion. Jeanette Winterson. 176p. 1997. pap. 12.00 (*0-8021-3522-6*, Grove) Grove-Atltic.

Passion. deluxe limited ed. Robert Steiner. Ed. by Michael Peich. (Fiction Ser.: No. 2). (Illus.). 1980. 40.00 (*0-915778-32-7*) Penmaen Pr.

Passion: A Novel. Igino U. Tarchetti. Tr. by Lawrence Venuti from ITA. LC 94-15259. 224p. (Orig.). 1994. pap. 12.95 (*1-56279-064-1*) Mercury Hse Inc.

Passion: A Salon Professional's Handbook for Building a Successful Business. Susie F. Carder. (Illus.). 200p. (Orig.). 1996. pap. 19.95 (*0-9650777-8-0*) Carder Creative.

Passion: An Essay on Personality. Roberto M. Unger. 309p. 1986. pap. 18.95 (*0-02-933180-3*) Free Pr.

Passion! Reclaiming the Fire in Your Heart. Roz Van Meter & Pat Pearson. LC 94-75608. (Life Savor Ser.). 208p. (Orig.). 1994. pap. 12.95 (*0-944486-01-0*) Hollngswrth TX.

***Passion: Ritual Music for Prayer & Contemplation.** T. Shawn Tracy. 12p. 2000. pap. 16.00 (*1-889542-11-3*) Augustinian Pr.

Passion: Salon Professional's Handbook for Building a Successful Business. Susie Fields. 19.95 (*1-56253-419-X*, Pub. by Delmar) Thomson Learn.

Passion: Vocal Score. Ed. by Carol Cuellar. 208p. (Orig.). (C). 1996. pap. text 85.00 (*1-57623-294-8*, PF9608) Wrner Bros.

Passion: Vocal Selections. Ed. by Sy Feldman. (Best of Broadway Ser.). 268p. (Orig.). (C). 1994. pap. text 16.95 (*0-89724-413-3*, VF2164) Wrner Bros.

Passion: 6 New Short Plays by Australian Women. Ed. by Ros Horin. 130p. 1994. 19.95 (*0-86819-423-9*, Pub. by Currency Pr) Accents Pubns.

Passion According to G. H. Clarice Lispector. Tr. by Ronald W. Sousa from POR. LC 88-4763. (Emergent Literatures Ser.).Tr. of A/Paixao Segundo G. H.. ix, 173p. (Orig.). 1988. pap. 13.95 (*0-8166-1712-0*) U of Minn Pr.

Passion According to Luke: The Special Material of Luke 22. Marion L. Soards. (JSNT Supplement Ser.: No. 14). 181p. 1987. pap. 18.95 (*1-85075-037-8*, Pub. by Sheffield Acad) CUP Services.

Passion & Action: The Emotions in Seventeenth-Century Philosophy. Susan James. (Illus.). 328p. 2000. pap. text 19.95 (*0-19-825013-4*) OUP.

Passion & Affect. Laurie Colwin. LC 94-24623. 192p. 1994. pap. 12.00 (*0-06-097633-0*) HarperTrade.

Passion & Compassion: Mga Tula Sa Ingles at Pilipino. Marra P. Lanot. 153p. 1981. pap. 12.50 (*0-686-32581-8*, Pub. by New Day Pub) Cellar.

Passion & Craft: Conversations with Notable Writers. Bonnie Lyons & Bill Oliver. LC 97-33749. 232p. 1998. 19.95 (*0-252-06687-1*); text 39.95 (*0-252-02387-0*) U of Ill Pr.

Passion & Craft: Economists at Work. Michael Szenberg. LC 98-27739. 336p. 1998. pap. 23.95 (*0-472-06685-4*, 06685) U of Mich Pr.

Passion & Defiance: Italian Film from 1942 to the Present. Mira Liehm. LC 83-6667. (Illus.). 450p. (C). 1984. pap. text 18.95 (*0-520-05744-9*, Pub. by U CA Pr) Cal Prin Full Svc.

Passion & Devastation. Christina Georgina Rossetti. (Illus.). 1999. 19.95 (*1-86019-387-0*) Brockhampton Pr Ltd.

Passion & Excess: Blanchot, Bataille, & Literary Theory. Steven Shaviro. 200p. 1990. 49.95 (*0-8130-0977-4*) U Press Fla.

Passion & Folly: A Scriptural Foundation for Peace. Patricia McCarthy. LC 97-41222. ix, 128 p. 1998. pap. 11.95 (*0-8146-2469-3*) Liturgical Pr.

Passion & Illusion. Barbara Delinsky. 256p. 1994. mass mkt. 5.99 (*0-06-104232-3*, Harp PBks) HarpC.

Passion & Illusion. large type ed. Barbara Delinsky. LC 95-47629. (Large Print Bks.). 1996. 23.95 (*1-56895-278-3*) Wheeler Pub.

Passion & Line: The Dance Photography of Howard Schatz. Howard Schatz. (Illus.). 224p. 1997. 50.00 (*1-888001-37-2*) Graphis US.

Passion & Miracles of the Great Martyr & Victorious Wonderworker Saint George. (Illus.). 1988. reprint ed. pap. 5.00 (*0-913026-69-7*) St Nectarios.

Passion & Pain. Stefan Zweig. Tr. by Eden Paul & Cedar Paul from GER. LC 77-152967. (Short Story Index Reprint Ser.). 1977. reprint ed. 18.95 (*0-8369-3882-8*) Ayer.

Passion & Peace: Traditional Torah Thoughts & Contemporary Reflections. Eliyahu Safran. 1988. 20.00 (*0-88125-301-4*) Ktav.

Passion & Policy: A Social Workers Career. Alvin L. Schorr. LC 97-68258. 212p. 1997. 29.95 (*0-940601-12-5*, David Press); pap. 19.95 (*0-940601-13-3*) Octavia Ohio.

Passion & Power: Sexuality in History. Ed. by Kathy Peiss et al. LC 88-21670. (Critical Perspectives on the Past Ser.). (Illus.). 326p. (C). 1989. pap. 22.95 (*0-87722-637-7*) Temple U Pr.

Passion & Prejudice: A Family Memoir. Sallie Bingham. 1993. pap. 12.95 (*1-55783-077-0*) Applause Theatre Bk Pubs.

Passion & Purity see Pasion y Pureza

Passion & Purity: Learning to Bring Your Love Life under Christ's Control. Elisabeth Elliot. LC 83-21122. 192p. (Orig.). (gr. 10). 1989. pap. 8.99 (*0-8007-5137-X*) Revell.

Passion & Reason: Making Sense of Our Emotions. Richard S. Lazarus & Bernice N. Lazarus. LC 94-9320. 336p. 1994. text 30.00 (*0-19-508757-7*) OUP.

Passion & Reason: Making Sense of Our Emotions. Richard S. Lazarus & Bernice N. Lazarus. 336p. 1996. reprint ed. pap. 15.95 (*0-19-510461-7*) OUP.

Passion & Rebellion: The Expressionist Heritage. Ed. by Stephen E. Bronner & Douglas M. Kellner. (Morningside Bk.). 468p. 1988. pap. text 21.00 (*0-231-06763-1*, King's Crown Paperbacks) Col U Pr.

Passion & Rebellion: The Expressionist Heritage. Ed. by Stephen E. Bronner & Douglas M. Kellner. LC 81-40492. 480p. 1983. 32.95 (*0-87663-356-4*, Bergin & Garvey) Greenwood.

Passion & Resurrection: Lazarus Saturday, Entry into Jerusalem, Holy & Great Week, the Pasch of the Lord. Monks of New Skete. Ed. by Laurence Mancuso. 332p. 1995. 65.00 (*0-935129-25-1*) Monks of New Skete.

Passion & Resurrection Narratives of Jesus: A Commentary. Stephen J. Binz. 120p. 1989. pap. 5.95 (*0-8146-1771-9*) Liturgical Pr.

P

An Asterisk (*) at the beginning of an entry indicates that the title is appearing for the first time.

Passion & Scandal. Candace Schuler. LC 96-512. 219p. 1995. per. 3.25 (*0-373-25657-4*, 1-25657-7) Harlequin Bks.

Passion & Scandal: Great Canadian Love Stories. Barbara Smith. LC 97-203918. (Illus.). 266p. (Orig.). 1997. pap. write for info. (*1-55059-148-7*) Detselig Ents.

Passion & the Fashion: Football Fandom in the New Europe. Ed. by Steve Redhead. LC 93-3864. (Popular Cultural Studies). 224p. 1993. 59.95 (*1-85628-462-X*, Pub. by Avebry); pap. 24.95 (*1-85628-464-6*, Pub. by Avebry) Ashgate Pub Co.

Passion & the Intellect: or Andre Malraux. (Yale French Studies: No. 18). 1956. pap. 25.00 (*0-527-01726-4*) Periodicals Srv.

Passion & the Past: Hearts of Fire. Miranda Lee. 1995. per. 3.25 (*0-373-11766-3*) Harlequin Bks.

Passion & Value in Hume's Treatise. 2nd ed. Pall S. Ardal. 222p. 1990. pap. 28.50 (*0-85224-641-2*, Pub. by Edinburgh U Pr) Col U Pr.

Passion at Work: Six Secrets for Personal Success Kevin Thomson. LC 98-186152. 256p. 1998. write for info. (*1-900961-61-X*) Capstone Pub NH.

Passion Bay. Jennifer Fulton. 288p. 1992. pap. 11.95 (*1-56280-028-0*) Naiad Pr.

Passion Becomes You. Michelle Reid. LC 95-13569. (Presents Ser.). 187p. 1995. per. 3.25 (*0-373-11752-3*, 1-11752-2) Harlequin Bks.

Passion below Zero: Essays from Last Chance, Idaho. David Hays. (Illus.). 256p. (Orig.). 1995. pap. 12.95 (*1-885719-01-9*) Lost River Pr.

***Passion! Betrayal! Outrage! Revenge!** Greg Evans. LC 99-33246. (Luann Bk.). 1999. pap. 9.95 (*1-55853-787-2*) Rutledge Hill Pr.

Passion by Design: The Art & Times of Tamara de Lempicka. Baroness K. De Lempicka-Foxhall. (Illus.). 192p. 1987. 35.00 (*0-89659-760-1*) Abbeville Pr.

Passion by Design: The Art & Times of Tamara de Lempicka. Kizette De Lempicka-Foxhall. (Illus.). 192p. 1998. pap. 19.95 (*0-7892-0503-3*) Abbeville Pr.

Passion Conjugale. Charlotte Lamb. (Azur Ser.: No. 722). (FRE.). 1998. mass mkt. 3.50 (*0-373-34722-7*, 1.-34722-8) Harlequin Bks.

Passion Cruelle. Emma Darcy. (Azur Ser.: Vol. 707). 1998. mass mkt. 3.50 (*0-373-34707-3*, 1-34707-9) Harlequin Bks.

Passion d'Amour. Anne-Marie Villefranche. 480p. 1994. 5.95 (*0-7867-0171-4*) Carroll & Graf.

Passion D'Amour. Anne-Marie Villefranche. 520p. 1998. mass mkt. 7.95 (*0-7867-0600-7*) Carroll & Graf.

Passion de Joseph Pasquier see Chronique des Pasquier

Passion de Joseph Pasquier. Georges Duhamel. (Chronique Des Pasquier Ser.: Vol. X). (FRE.). 276p. 1977. pap. 10.95 (*0-7859-1863-9*, 2070369854) Fr & Eur.

Passion de l'Abbe Delance. Michel De Saint Pierre. (FRE.). 1980. pap. 11.95 (*0-7859-4139-8*) Fr & Eur.

Passion des Femmes. Sebastien Japrisot. (FRE.). 469p. 1988. pap. 11.95 (*0-7859-2556-2*, 2070380343) Fr & Eur.

Passion Dream Book: A Novel. Whitney Otto. LC 97-3563. 288p. 1998. pap. 13.00 (*0-06-109623-7*, Harp PBks) HarpC.

Passion Dream Book: A Novel. large type ed. Whitney Otto. LC 97-36730. (Americana Series). 432p. 1997. lib. bdg. 23.95 (*0-7862-1247-0*) Thorndike Pr.

Passion Eternelle. Christine Scott. (Horizon Ser.: No. 520). (FRE.). 1999. mass mkt. 3.99 (*0-373-39520-5*, 1-39520-1) Harlequin Bks.

Passion Fire. Mallory Burgess. 400p. 1988. pap. 3.95 (*0-380-75381-2*, Avon Bks) Morrow Avon.

Passion Flower. Diana Palmer. 256p. 1996. per. 5.50 (*1-55166-168-3*, 1-66168-5, Mira Bks) Harlequin Bks.

Passion Flowers. Celia Parker. (Black Lace Ser.). 300p. 1996. mass mkt. 5.95 (*0-352-33118-6*, Pub. by Virgin Bks) London Brdge.

Passion Flowers. Julia W. Howe. (Notable American Authors Ser.). 1992. reprint ed. lib. bdg. 75.00 (*0-7812-3212-0*) Rprt Serv.

Passion Flowers. 2nd ed. John Vanderplank. (Illus.). 224p. 1996. 44.00 (*0-262-22052-0*) MIT Pr.

***Passion Flowers.** 3rd ed. John Vanderplank. (Illus.). 224p. (C). 2000. pap. 29.95 (*0-262-72035-3*) MIT Pr.

Passion for Acting: Exploring the Creative Process. Allan Miller. Ed. by Fred Weiler. (Illus.). 189p. (Orig.). (C). 1995. pap. 16.95 (*0-9644844-0-4*) Dynmic Prod.

Passion for Apocalypse. Susan Cole. (Illus.). 36p. (Orig.). 1997. pap. 5.00 (*0-9637704-7-0*) Red Dragon VA.

Passion for Art: Selections from the Berman Collection, the Inaugural Exhibition. Lisa T. Barnes. LC 89-24821. (Illus.). 72p. 1989. pap. text 12.95 (*0-9624021-0-9*) Ursinus College.

Passion for Art: The LeFrak Family Collection. Samuel J. LeFrak et al. (Illus.). 120p. text. write for info. (*0-9620593-1-5*) Lefrak Organization.

Passion for Birds: American Ornithology after Audubon. Mark V. Barrow. LC 97-18600. 336p. 1998. text 39.50 (*0-691-04402-3*, Pub. by Princeton U Pr) Cal Prin Full Svc.

***Passion for Birds: Amrican Ornithology after Audubon.** Mark V. Barrow. 2000. pap. text 19.95 (*0-691-04954-8*, Pub. by Princeton U Pr) Cal Prin Full Svc.

Passion for Birds: Eliot Porter's Photography. John Rohrback et al. LC 97-29177. (Illus.). 64p. 1997. pap. 19.95 (*0-88360-089-7*) Amon Carter.

Passion for Books. Terry Glaspey. LC 98-12946. 96p. 1998. 14.99 (*1-56507-781-4*) Harvest Hse.

Passion for Books. Lawrence C. Powell. LC 73-727. 249p. 1973. reprint ed. lib. bdg. 59.50 (*0-8371-6783-3*, POPB, Greenwood Pr) Greenwood.

Passion for Books: A Book Lover's Treasury of Stories, Essays, Humor, Lore & Lists on Collecting, Reading, Borrowing, Lending, Caring for & Appreciating Books. Ed. by Harold Rabinowitz & Rob Kaplan. LC 99-25583. (Illus.). 384p. 1999. 27.50 (*0-8129-3112-2*, Times Bks) Crown Pub Group.

***Passion for Books: A Book Lover's Treasury of Stories, Essays, Humor, Lore & Lists on Collecting, Reading, Borrowing, Lending, Caring for & Appreciating Books.** Ed. by Harold Rabinowitz & Rob Kaplan. 2001. pap. 16.00 (*0-8129-3113-0*, Three Riv Pr) Crown Pub Group.

Passion for Cactus. Jack Kramer. (Illus.). 64p. 1995. 10.95 (*0-8362-0800-5*) Andrews & McMeel.

Passion for Cheese. Paul Gayler. LC 98-4170. 192p. 1998. text 24.95 (*0-312-19204-5*) St Martin.

***Passion for Cheese: More than 130 Innovative Ways to Cook with Cheese.** Paul Gayler. (Illus.). 192p. 2000. pap. 17.95 (*0-312-25405-9*) St Martin.

***Passion for Chocolate: Seductively Sweet Recipes to Melt Your Heart.** Contrib. by Better Homes & Gardens. (Illus.). 96p. 2000. 16.95 (*0-696-21174-2*, Better Homes) Meredith Bks.

***Passion for Christ.** Thomas F. Torrance et al. 160p. 1999. pap. 11.95 (*0-9652602-4-0*) PLC Publns.

Passion for Cigars. Joel Sherman. 1998. pap. text 12.95 (*0-8362-5289-6*) Andrews & McMeel.

Passion for Color. Sarah Burnett & Conran Octopus. Ed. by Elisa Petrini. 160p. 1990. 39.95 (*0-685-32663-2*) Macmillan Info.

Passion for Color: Creating Brilliant Custom Yarns from Simple Natural Dyes, with 20 Exclusive Knit Designs for Adults & Children. Sarah Burnett. (Illus.). 160p. 1990. text 39.95 (*0-02-518625-6*) Macmillan.

***Passion for Compassion: The Formula for Successful Financial Advisors.** Norman G. Levine. 286p. 2000. pap. 24.95 (*1-891042-10-6*, 59934) Million Dollar.

Passion for Creation: The Earth-Honoring Spirituality of Meister Eckhart. Matthew Fox. LC 99-45739. 608p. 2000. pap. 24.95 (*0-89281-801-8*) Inner Tradit.

Passion for Daylilies: The Flowers & the People. Sydney Eddison. LC 92-39985. 352p. 1995. pap. 15.95 (*0-8050-2611-8*, Owl) H Holt & Co.

Passion for Democracy: American Essays. Benjamin R. Barber. LC 97-52582. 282p. 1998. text 26.95 (*0-691-05766-4*, Pub. by Princeton U Pr) Cal Prin Full Svc.

***Passion for Democracy: Amrerican Essays.** Benjamin R. Barber. 2000. pap. text 16.95 (*0-691-05024-4*) Princeton U Pr.

Passion for Detail. Charlotte Moss. 192p. 1991. 42.50 (*0-385-26760-6*) Doubleday.

Passion for Difference: Essays in Anthropology & Gender. Henrietta L. Moore. LC 94-31477. 186p. 1995. 39.95 (*0-253-33858-1*); pap. 14.95 (*0-253-20951-X*) Ind U Pr.

***Passion for DNA: Genes, Genomes & Society.** James D. Watson. LC 99-87131. 2000. 25.00 (*0-87969-581-1*) Cold Spring Harbor.

Passion for Equality. Kenneth Cauthen. 208p. 1987. 55.00 (*0-8476-7544-0*) Rowman.

Passion for Equality: George Wiley & the Movement. Nick Kotz & Mary L. Kotz. (Illus.). (C). 1977. pap. text 5.00 (*0-393-09006-X*) Norton.

***Passion for Equality: The Life of Jimmy Stewart.** Bob Burke & Vicki Miles-LaGrange. Ed. by Kenny Franks & Gini Moore Campbell. LC 99-70170. (Oklahoma Trackmaker Ser.). (Illus.). 224p. 1999. 18.95 (*1-885596-12-X*) OK Heritage.

Passion for Excellence. Tom Peters & Nancy K. Austin. 608p. 1989. mass mkt. 16.99 (*0-446-38639-1*, Pub. by Warner Bks) Little.

Passion for Faithfulness: Wisdom from the Book of Nehemiah. J. I. Packer. LC 94-24366. (Living Insights Ser.). 224p. 1994. 14.99 (*0-89107-733-2*) Crossway Bks.

Passion for Films: Henri Langlois & the Cinematheque Francaise. Richard Roud. LC 99-14614. (Illus.). 218p. 1999. pap. text 16.95 (*0-8018-6206-X*) Johns Hopkins.

Passion for Flavor: Cooking with Infused Vinegar & Oil. Eve Plociennik. (Illus.). 128p. 1997. 24.95 (*0-9660352-0-8*) Verve Edtns.

Passion for Flowers. Penny Black. (Illus.). 144p. 1992. 30.00 (*0-671-75106-9*) S&S Trade.

Passion for Flowers. Carolyne Roehm. LC 98-104832. (Illus.). 288p. 1997. 60.00 (*0-06-757513-7*) HarpC.

Passion for Flying: Exciting Stories of a Boeing Test Pilot. Marvin Michael. LC 96-230331. 192p. (Orig.). 1996. pap. 10.95 (*1-883893-59-3*) WinePress Pub.

Passion for Freedom: The Life of Sharlot Hall. Margaret F. Maxwell. LC 82-4866. (Illus.). 234p. 1995. pap. 18.95 (*0-8165-1506-9*) U of Ariz Pr.

***Passion for Fruit.** Lorenza De' Medici Stucchi. LC 99-51968. (Illus.). 160p. (J). 2000. 35.00 (*0-7892-0630-7*, Abbeville Kids) Abbeville Pr.

Passion for Fullness see Anhelo de Plenitud

Passion for Glass: The Aviva & Jack A. Robinson Studio Glass Collection. Bonita Fike & Detroit Institute of Arts Staff. LC 98-38669. 1998. pap. 14.95 (*0-89558-150-7*) Det Inst Arts.

Passion for God. Greg Laurie. LC 98-5936. 192p. 1998. pap. 8.99 (*1-56507-802-0*) Harvest Hse.

Passion for God: A Book of Prayers & Devotions - Romans Newly Paraphrased. Raymond C. Ortlund, Jr. LC 93-38010. 224p. 1994. 15.99 (*0-89107-765-0*) Crossway Bks.

Passion for God: The Mystical-Political Dimension of Christianity. Johann B. Metz. Ed. & Tr. by J. Matthew Ashley from GER. LC 97-36614. 224p. 1998. pap. 19.95 (*0-8091-3755-0*, 3755-0) Paulist Pr.

Passion for God's Reign: Theology, Christian Learning, & the Christian Self. Jurgen Moltmann et al. Ed. by Miroslav Volf. LC 97-38349. 120p. 1998. pap. 12.00 (*0-8028-4494-4*) Eerdmans.

Passion for Golf. (Passion for...Ser.). (Illus.). 64p. 1996. 10.95 (*0-8362-1328-9*) Andrews & McMeel.

Passion for Golf. Ed. by Schuyler Bishop. LC 98-10263. 384p. 1998. 24.95 (*0-312-19027-1*, Thomas Dunne) St Martin.

***Passion for Golf: A Golfer's Quest for Meaning.** Roland Merullo. (Illus.). 2000. 20.00 (*1-58574-162-0*) Lyons Pr.

Passion for Golf: Celebrity Musings about the Game. Ann Liguori. LC 97-24658. 256p. 1997. 22.95 (*0-87833-972-8*) Taylor Pub.

Passion for Golf: The Best of Golf Writing. Schuyler Bishop. 1999. pap. 15.95 (*0-312-20668-2*) St Martin.

***Passion for Happiness: Samuel Johnson & David Hume.** Adam Potkay. 2000. 42.50 (*0-8014-3727-X*) Cornell U Pr.

Passion for His Presence. LaMar Boschman. 170p. (Orig.). 1992. pap. 9.99 (*1-56043-704-9*) Destiny Image.

Passion for Holiness in a Believer's Life. Charles H. Spurgeon. Ed. by Robert Hall. (Believer's Life Ser.). 190p. (Orig.). 1994. pap. 9.99 (*1-883002-07-9*) Emerald WA.

Passion for Ideas. George Davie. 1994. 16.00 (*0-7486-6147-6*, Pub. by Polygon) Subterranean Co.

Passion for Jazz. Leonard Feather. (Quality Paperbacks Ser.). (Illus.). 208p. 1990. reprint ed. pap. 10.95 (*0-306-80402-6*) Da Capo.

Passion for Jesus. Mike Bickle. 204p. 1993. pap. 12.99 (*0-88419-258-X*) Creation House.

Passion for Justice: Emotions & the Origins of the Social Contract. Robert C. Solomon. 338p. 1995. pap. 22.95 (*0-8476-8087-8*) Rowman.

Passion for Justice: The Legacy of James Chalmers McRuer. Patrick Boyer. (Osgood Society for Canadian Legal History Ser.). (Illus.). 438p. 1994. text 35.00 (*0-8020-0656-6*) U of Toronto Pr.

Passion for Kittens. J. C. Suares. (Illus.). 64p. 1995. 10.95 (*0-86320-797-9*); 10.95 (*0-8362-0797-1*) Andrews & McMeel.

***Passion for Learning.** Arthur G. Powell & Theodore R. Sizer. 128p. 1999. pap. 17.00 (*0-7879-5043-2*) Jossey-Bass.

Passion for Liberty: Alexis de Tocqueville on Democracy & Revolution. Andrew J. Cosentino. LC 89-13051. 61p. 1989. 4.95 (*0-8444-0651-1*) Lib Congress.

Passion for Life. Frank Pina. LC 97-154589. 144p. (Orig.). 1996. pap. 9.95 (*1-883893-38-0*) WinePress Pub.

Passion for Life: Fragments of the Face of God. Joan D. Chittister. LC 95-43388. (Illus.). 132p. 1996. 30.00 (*1-57075-076-9*) Orbis Bks.

***Passion for Life: Fragments of the Face of God.** Joan Chittister. LC 99-56489. (Illus.). 132p. 2000. reprint ed. pap. 24.00 (*1-57075-318-0*) Orbis Bks.

Passion for Life: Lifelong Psychological & Spiritual Growth. Janice Brewi & Anne Brennan. LC 80-5342. 176p. 1998. 17.95 (*0-8264-1181-9*) Continuum.

Passion for Life: The Biography of Elizabeth Taylor. large type ed. Donald Spoto. LC 95-17375. 1995. 27.95 (*0-7838-1379-1*, G K Hall Lrg Type) Mac Lib Ref.

Passion for Life: The Story of Herman & Maurice Spertus. Elliot B. Lefkowitz. 70p. 1994. pap. 8.95 (*0-935982-48-5*) Spertus Coll.

Passion for Living: A Path to Meaning & Joy. Shahan Shammas. LC 97-91378. 340p. 1998. pap. 19.95 (*0-9662028-0-5*) Worthwhile MD.

Passion for Living: The Art of Real Success. Allan Somersalli. 310p. mass mkt. 4.99 (*1-55197-143-7*) Picasso Publ.

Passion for Manufacturing: Real World Advice from Dick Dauch - The Man Who Engineered the Manufacturing Renaissance at Chrysler. Richard E. Dauch & Jack Troyanovich. LC 92-85522. (Illus.). 274p. 1993. 39.00 (*0-87263-436-1*) SME.

Passion for My Provence: Home Cooking from the South of France. Lydie Marshall. LC 98-49394. 320p. 1999. pap. 15.00 (*0-06-093164-7*) HarpC.

Passion for Narrative: A Guide for Writing Fiction. Jack Hodgins. 304p. 1997. pap. text 16.99 (*0-7710-4188-8*) McCland & Stewart.

***Passion for Our Grandchildren: Our Families Need Us... NOW.** Janet Mort. LC 99-32. (Illus.). 297p. 1999. spiral bd. 19.46 (*1-55212-281-6*) Trafford Pub.

Passion for Pasta. Polly Clingerman. Ed. by Marian Levine. 64p. (Orig.). 1990. pap., per. 3.95 (*0-942320-35-2*) Am Cooking.

Passion for Pasta. rev. ed. Ann Carluccio. LC 94-28410. (Illus.). 192p. 1994. 17.95 (*1-56426-065-8*) Cole Group.

Passion for Pasta: Delicious New Recipes for Fresh Pasta. Sue Lloyd & Jacquie Keys. (Illus.). 137p. 1994. 24.95 (*0-85572-222-3*, Pub. by Hill Content Pubng) Seven Hills Bk.

Passion for Peace: The Social Essays. Thomas Merton. Ed. & Intro. by William H. Shannon. 360p. 1995. 29.95 (*0-8245-1494-7*) Crossroad NY.

Passion for Peace: The Social Essays. Thomas Merton. Ed. & Intro. by William H. Shannon. 348p. 1997. pap. 17.95 (*0-8245-1657-5*, Herdr & Herdr) Crossroad NY.

Passion for Pens. Pierre Haury & Jean-Pierre Lacroux. Tr. by Fred Gorstein from FRE. (Illus.). 200p. 1993. 90.00 (*0-9637887-0-1*) Green Tree.

Passion for People: The Story of Mary Mahoney & Her Old French House Restaurant. Ed Lepoma et al. LC 98-28077. 168p. 1998. pap. 9.95 (*0-937552-94-1*) Quail Ridge.

***Passion for Performance: Sarah Siddons & Her Portraitists.** Ed. by Robyn Asleson et al. LC 98-53976. (Illus.). 144p. 1999. 39.95 (*0-89236-556-0*, Pub. by J P Getty Trust) OUP.

***Passion for Performance: Sarah Siddons & Her Portraitists.** Robyn Asleson et al. LC 98-53976. 1999. write for info. (*0-89236-557-9*, J P Getty Museum) J P Getty Trust.

Passion for Physics: The Story of a Woman Physicist. Joan Freeman. LC 99-224371. (Illus.). 240p. 1991. 43.00 (*0-7503-0098-1*) IOP Pub.

Passion for Piedmont. Matt Kramer. LC 97-15456. 368p. 1997. 28.00 (*0-688-11594-2*, Wm Morrow) Morrow Avon.

Passion for Pilgrimage: Notes for the Journey Home. Alan Jones. LC 99-32673. 208p. 2000. pap. 13.95 (*0-8192-1823-5*) Morehouse Pub.

Passion for Place: Between the Vital Spacing & the Creative Horizons of Fulfilment. Anna-Teresa Tymieniecka. LC 96-24921. (Analecta Husserliana Ser.). 1997. text 130.50 (*0-7923-4146-5*) Kluwer Academic.

Passion for Polka: Old-Time Ethnic Music in America. Victor Greene. 1992. 40.00 (*0-520-07584-6*, Pub. by U CA Pr) Cal Prin Full Svc.

Passion for Potatoes. Lydie Marshall. LC 91-50516. 272p. 1992. pap. 16.00 (*0-06-096910-5*, Perennial) HarperTrade.

Passion for Power. Robert DeMaria. Date not set. 22.95 (*0-8488-2425-3*) Amereon Ltd.

Passion for Prayer. Timothy Crosby & Lonnie Melashenko. LC 98-16043. 192p. (Orig.). 1998. pap. 12.99 (*0-8280-1355-1*) Review & Herald.

Passion for Prayer: Experiencing Deeper Intimacy with God. Thomas D. Elliff. LC 97-48676. 208p. 1998. 15.99 (*0-89107-963-7*) Crossway Bks.

Passion for Presence: Finding Key to God's Heart. Louis F. Kayatin. Ed. by JoAnne Cramberg. 96p. 1997. pap. 10.00 (*0-9657706-2-1*) Phos Pub.

Passion for Preserves: Jams, Jellies, Marmalades, Conserves & Butters. Frederica Langeland. LC 97-13132. (Illus.). 128p. 1997. write for info. (*1-56799-533-0*, Friedman-Fairfax) M Friedman Pub Grp Inc.

Passion for Pulses: A Feast of Beans, Peas & Lentils from Around the World. Nancy Longnecker. (Illus.). 1998. pap. 24.95 (*1-876268-20-4*, Pub. by Univ of West Aust Pr) Intl Spec Bk.

Passion for Radio: Radio Waves & Community. Ed. by Bruce Girard. LC 91-72979. 212p. 1993. 48.99 (*1-895431-35-2*, Pub. by Black Rose); pap. 19.99 (*1-895431-34-4*, Pub. by Black Rose) Consort Bk Sales.

Passion for Reason & Reason of Passion in Seventeenth Century Art & Theory in France, 1648-1683. Martin Weyl. LC 89-8090. (Hermeneutics of Art Ser.: Vol. 2). 326p. (C). 1989. text 50.50 (*0-8204-0981-2*) P Lang Pubng.

Passion for Red. Ellen S. Stern & Nancy Weber. (Illus.). 64p. 1995. 10.95 (*0-8362-0801-3*) Andrews & McMeel.

Passion for Renoir: Sterling & Francine Clark Collect, 1916-1951. Steven Kern et al. LC 95-47829. 1996. pap. 22.95 (*0-931102-37-5*) S & F Clark Art.

Passion for Ribbonry. Camela Nitschke. (Illus.). 144p. 1998. pap. 29.95 (*1-56477-211-X*, DB327, PasTimes) Martingale & Co.

Passion for Roses. Mary Engelbreit & J. C. Suares. LC 95-80758. (Passion for...Ser.). (Illus.). 64p. 1996. 10.95 (*0-8362-1330-0*) Andrews & McMeel.

Passion for Shoes. Linda Sunshine & Mary Tiegreen. (Illus.). 64p. 1995. 10.95 (*0-8362-0799-8*) Andrews & McMeel.

Passion for Sicilians: The World Around Danilo Dolici. Jerre Mangione. 320p. (C). 1985. pap. 24.95 (*0-88738-606-7*) Transaction Pubs.

Passion for Souls see Pasion por las Almas

Passion for Souls: The Life of D. L. Moody. Lyle W. Dorsett. LC 98-122137. 464p. 1997. 24.99 (*0-8024-5194-2*, 10) Moody.

Passion for Souls: The Life of D. L. Moody. deluxe ed. Lyle W. Dorsett. 1997. lthr. 89.99 (*0-8024-5243-4*, 11) Moody.

Passion for Success: Practical, Inspirational, & Spiritual Insight from Japan's Leading Entrepreneur. Kazuo Inamori. 192p. 1995. 16.95 (*0-07-031784-4*) McGraw.

Passion for Teaching. Ed. by Sarah L. Levine. LC 99-6340. (Illus.). 209p. 1999. pap. 23.95 (*0-87120-354-5*, 199224) ASCD.

Passion for the Divine. Ruth Lambek. 1979. pap. 5.95 (*0-87516-289-4*) DeVorss.

Passion for the Earth. Sean McDonagh. LC 95-141327. (Ecology & Justice Ser.). 175p. reprint ed. pap. 54.30 (*0-608-20242-8*, 207150100012) Bks Demand.

***Passion for the Game: Keeping Faith in Every Inning of Life.** Ed Anderson. 2000. 19.99 (*1-56292-848-1*) Honor Bks OK.

***Passion for the Gospel: Confessing Jesus Christ for the Twenty-First Century.** P. Mark Achtemeier & Andrew Purves. 160p. 2000. pap. 14.95 (*0-664-50128-1*, Pub. by Geneva Press) Presbyterian Pub.

***Passion for the Impossible: The Life of Lilias Trotter.** Miriam H. Rockness. LC 98-26140. (Illus.). 288p. 1999. pap. 14.99 (*0-87788-512-5*, H Shaw Pubs) Waterbrook Pr.

Passion for the Inner City. J. Smith. 1990. pap. 22.00 (*0-7220-6419-5*) St Mut.

Passion for the Past: Creative Teaching of United States History. James A. Percoco. LC 98-21451. 1998. write for info. (*0-325-00061-1*) Heinemann.

Passion for the Past: Historic Collections of Antiquities from Egypt & the Levant. Norman Hurst. Ed. by Lara Greenwood & Nicole Hawkes. (Illus.). 60p. 1997. pap. 25.00 (*0-9628074-7-8*) Hurst Gal.

Passion for the Possible: A Guide to Realizing Your True Potential. Jean Houston. LC 97-20406. 160p. 1997. 16.00 (*0-06-251531-4*, Pub. by Harper SF) HarpC.

Passion for the Possible: A Guide to Realizing Your True Potential. Jean Houston. LC 97-20406. 208p. 1998. pap. 10.00 (*0-06-251532-2*, Pub. by Harper SF) HarpC.

Passion for the Possible: A Guide to Realizing Your True Potential. large type ed. Jean Houston. LC 98-5615. 210p. 1998. 24.95 (*0-7838-0128-9*, G K Hall & Co) Mac Lib Ref.

P

An Asterisk (*) at the beginning of an entry indicates that the title is appearing for the first time.

Passion for the Possible: A Message to U. S. Churches. William S. Coffin. LC 93-8022. 96p. (Orig.). 1993. pap. 13.95 (*0-664-25428-4*) Westminster John Knox.

Passion for the Possible: A Spirituality of Hope for a New Millennium Daniel J. O'Leary. LC 98-215634. 294p. 1998. write for info. (*1-85607-235-5*) Intl Scholars.

Passion for Trains: A Rail Aficionado's Diary. A. Michael Coleman. Ed. & Illus. by Ron Ziel. 238p. 1989. 59.00 (*0-685-26484-X*) A M Coleman.

Passion for Travel. Jack W. Williams. 300p. 1994. pap. 15.00 (*0-9641884-0-6*) Travel Views.

Passion for Truth. Abraham Joshua Heschel. LC 95-5378. 352p. 1995. pap. 18.95 (*1-879045-41-9*) Jewish Lights.

***Passion For Truth: From Finding JFK's Single Bullet to Questioning Anita Hill to Impeaching Clinton.** Arlen Specter. (Illus.). 320p. 2000. 26.00 (*0-06-019849-4*, Wm Morrow) Morrow Avon.

***Passion for Truth: The Intellectual Coherence of Evangelicalism.** Alister McGrath. 1999. pap. text 15.99 (*0-8308-1591-0*) InterVarsity.

Passion for Truth: The Intellectual Coherence of Evangelicalism. Alister E. McGrath. 195p. 1995. pap. 24.00 (*0-614-97984-6*, Pub. by Hodder & Stought Ltd) Lubrecht & Cramer.

Passion for Truth: The Intellectual Coherence of Evangelicalism. Alister E. McGrath. LC 96-822. 283p. 1996. pap. 21.99 (*0-8308-1866-9*, 1866) InterVarsity.

Passion for Truth: The Selected Writings Of Eric Breindel. Eric Breindel. LC 98-51059. 256p. 1999. 25.00 (*0-06-019327-1*) HarpC.

***Passion for Vegetables: Simple & Inspired Vegetarian Recipes from Around the Globe.** Paul Gayler. 2000. 35.00 (*1-58574-163-9*) Lyon Press.

Passion for Victory: Living Triumphantly Every Day. Bob Moorehead. LC 96-23256. 190p. 1996. 15.99 (*1-878990-64-0*) Howard Pub LA.

***Passion for Watercolor: Painting the Inner Experience.** Stefan Draughon. (Illus.). 144p. 2000. write for info. (*0-8230-0102-4*) Watsn-Guptill.

Passion for Wings: Aviation & the Western Imagination, 1908-1918. Robert Wohl. LC 94-17559. (Illus.). 320p. 1994. 42.50 (*0-300-05778-4*) Yale U Pr.

Passion for Wings: Aviation & the Western Imagination, 1908-1918. Robert Wohl. (Illus.). 320p. 1996. pap. 25.00 (*0-300-06887-5*) Yale U Pr.

Passion for Wisdom: A Very Brief History of Philosophy. Robert C. Solomon & Kathleen M. Higgins. LC 96-42034. 160p. (C). 1997. 25.00 (*0-19-511208-3*) OUP.

Passion for Wisdom: A Very Brief History of Philosophy. Robert C. Solomon & Kathleen M. Higgins. 160p. 1999. reprint ed. pap. 9.95 (*0-19-511209-1*) OUP.

Passion from Within. Adrienne Von Speyr. 158p. 1998. pap. text 11.95 (*0-89870-594-0*) Ignatius Pr.

Passion in Paradise. large type ed. Irene Ord. (Linford Romance Library). 272p. 1989. pap. 16.99 (*0-7089-6705-1*, Linford) Ulverscroft.

Passion in Poe: The Development of a Critical Term. Glen A. Omans. 1986. pap. 2.95 (*0-910556-22-9*) Enoch Pratt.

Passion in Rio. 2nd ed. Paul Little. 1998. reprint ed. mass mkt. 6.95 (*1-56333-663-4*) Masquerade.

***Passion (In the Beginning)** Michael Ansara Hartsfield. 2000. 6.95 (*0-533-13476-5*) Vantage.

Passion in the First Degree. Carla Cassidy. (Harlequin Intrigue Ser.: No. 379). 1996. per. 3.75 (*0-373-22379-X*, 1-22379-1) Harlequin Bks.

Passion in the Soul: A Celebration of Love. Dawn M. Johnson. Ed. by Harry Parson. 190p. (Orig.). pap. write for info. (*0-9640025-0-7*) Twilight Pr.

Passion in Theory: Conceptions of Freud & Lacan. Robyn Ferrell. (Warwick Studies in European Philosophy Ser.). (Illus.). 128p. (C). 1996. 65.00 (*0-415-09019-9*); pap. 18.99 (*0-415-09020-2*) Routledge.

Passion in Tokyo. (Orig.). 1996. mass mkt. 5.95 (*1-56333-454-2*) Masquerade.

Passion Isabeau: Une Edition du Manuscript Fr. 996 de la Bibiotheque Nationale de Paris Avec une Introduction et des Notes. Ed. by Edelgard E. DuBruck. LC 90-5919. (American University Studies: Romance Languages & Literature: Ser. II, Vol. 141). VIII, 236p. (C). 1991. text 44.95 (*0-8204-1272-4*) P Lang Pubng.

Passion Jesu und Christi in der Gnosis. Dietrich Voorgang. (Europaische Hochschulschriften Ser.: Reihe 23, Bd. 432). (GER.). 453p. 1991. 65.80 (*3-631-44244-0*) P Lang Pubng.

Passion Made Public: Elizabethan Lyric, Gender, & Performance. Diana E. Henderson. 296p. 1995. text 44.95 (*0-252-02162-2*); pap. text 17.95 (*0-252-06460-7*) U of Ill Pr.

***Passion Masters: Sex Secrets of a Forbidden Love Cult.** Amal Rafik. 2000. mass mkt. 7.95 (*1-56201-200-2*) Blue Moon Bks.

Passion, Memory, & Identity: 20th Century Latin American Jewish Women Writers. Ed. by Marjorie Agosin. LC 99-6197. 217p. 1999. 39.95 (*0-8263-2045-7*); pap. 18.95 (*0-8263-2049-X*) U of NM Pr.

Passion Moon see Luna de Pasion: Texas Moon

Passion Moon Rising. Rebecca Brandewyne. 480p. 1988. mass mkt. 5.50 (*0-671-61774-5*) PB.

Passion Moon Rising. Rebecca Brandewyne. 448p. 1997. 25.00 (*0-7278-5158-6*) Severn Hse.

Passion Narratives. Herman Hendrickx. (Commentary on the Synoptic Gospels Ser.). 210p. (C). 1984. reprint ed. 14.95 (*0-225-66400-3*, 8524) Harper SF.

Passion Novena: A Scriptural Rosary. Larry London. LC 95-73145. 136p. (Orig.). 1996. pap. 5.95 (*0-87973-733-6*) Our Sunday Visitor.

Passion of an Angel. Kasey Michaels. 400p. 1995. mass mkt. 5.99 (*0-671-79342-X*) S&S Trade.

Passion of Ansel Bourne: Multiple Personality in American Culture. Michael G. Kenny. LC 86-60457. (Series in Ethnographic Inquiry). (Illus.). 258p. 1986. text 38.00 (*0-87474-572-1*, KEPA); pap. text 19.95 (*0-87474-569-1*, KEPAP) Smithsonian.

Passion of Ayn Rand. Barbara Branden. LC 85-20704. 464p. 1987. pap. 16.95 (*0-385-24388-X*, Anchor NY) Doubleday.

Passion of Barbeque: The Kansas City Barbeque Society Cookbook. Kansas City Barbeque Society Staff. LC 92-12. 176p. (J). 1992. pap. 12.45 (*1-56282-965-3*, Pub. by Hyperion) Time Warner.

Passion of Being Woman. 2nd ed. Mary H. Scott. LC 97-32985. 386p. 1998. reprint ed. pap. 16.95 (*0-9659521-1-8*) Divina.

Passion of Chocolate. Patrick Caton. LC 96-76127. 68p. 1996. 6.50 (*1-56245-272-X*) Great Quotations.

Passion of Christ. Veselin Kesich. 84p. 1965. pap. 3.95 (*0-913836-80-X*) St Vladimirs.

Passion of Christ. Shri Kripalvanandji & Yogi A. Desai. LC 83-80214. 51p. 1983. pap. 4.50 (*0-940258-09-9*) Kripalu Pubns.

Passion of Claude McKay. Claude McKay. LC 72-95662. (Negro History Ser.). vii, 363 p. 1973. write for info. (*0-8052-3498-5*) Schocken.

Passion of Creation. Adams. LC 91-76299. 144p. (Orig.). 1992. pap. 9.95 (*1-879384-11-6*) Cypress Hse.

Passion of David Lynch: Wild at Heart in Hollywood. Martha P. Nochimson. LC 97-7732. (Illus.). 296p. 1997. 40.00 (*0-292-75566-X*); pap. 19.95 (*0-292-75565-1*) U of Tex Pr.

Passion of Dellie O'Barr. Cindy Bonner. 362p. 1996. 18.95 (*1-56512-103-1*, 72103) Algonquin Bks.

Passion of Dennis Potter. Gras. LC 99-29924. 1999. text 45.00 (*0-312-21803-6*) St Martin.

Passion of Emily Dickinson. Judith Farr. (Illus.). 400p. (C). 1992. text 29.95 (*0-674-65665-2*) HUP.

Passion of Emily Dickinson. Judith Farr. (Illus.). 408p. 1994. pap. text 16.95 (*0-674-65666-0*, FARPAX) HUP.

Passion of God. Anthony Phillips. 86p. (Orig.). 1995. pap. 9.95 (*1-85311-101-5*, 852, Pub. by Canterbury Press Norwich) Morehouse Pub.

Passion of Ingmar Bergman. Frank Gado. LC 86-19731. (Illus.). xvii, 547p. (C). 1986. text 64.95 (*0-8223-0585-2*) Duke.

Passion of Ingmar Bergman. Frank Gado. LC 86-19731. (Illus.). xvii, 547p. (C). 1986. pap. text 24.95 (*0-8223-0586-0*) Duke.

Passion of Isis & Osiris. Jean Houston. 1998. pap. 14.95 (*0-345-42477-8*) Ballantine Pub Grp.

***Passion of Jerome.** Dermot Bolger. 2000. pap. 10.95 (*0-413-73880-9*, Methuen Drama) Methn.

Passion of Jesus & Its Hidden Meaning. James Groenings. LC 82-50592. 460p. 1992. reprint ed. pap. 15.00 (*0-89555-189-6*) TAN Bks Pubs.

Passion of Jesus in the Gospel of John. Donald Senior. (Passion Ser.). 176p. (Orig.). 1991. pap. 11.95 (*0-8146-5462-2*) Liturgical Pr.

Passion of Jesus in the Gospel of Luke. Donald Senior. (Passion Ser.). 192p. (Orig.). 1988. pap. 11.95 (*0-8146-5461-4*) Liturgical Pr.

Passion of Jesus in the Gospel of Matthew. Donald Senior. LC 84-73566. (Passion Ser.: Vol. 1). 200p. 1985. pap. 14.95 (*0-8146-5460-6*) Liturgical Pr.

Passion of Judas. Carlo Suares. 1974. pap. 2.95 (*0-394-73022-4*) Random.

Passion of Labour. Robert Lynd. LC 73-76909. (Essay Index Reprint Ser.). 1977. 19.95 (*0-8369-0025-1*) Ayer.

Passion of Lizzie Borden: Poems. Ruth Whitman. 1973. 8.50 (*0-8079-0183-0*); pap. 4.95 (*0-8079-0184-9*) October.

Passion of Maggie Higgins. Laurence Howard. LC 96-83352. 315p. 1996. pap. 12.95 (*1-885487-23-1*) Brownell & Carroll.

Passion of Meter: A Study of Wordsworth's Metrical Art. Brennan O'Donnell. LC 94-30735. 340p. 1995. 35.00 (*0-87338-510-1*) Kent St U Pr.

***Passion of Michel Foucault.** James Miller. 2000. pap. 24.95 (*0-674-00157-5*) HUP.

Passion of Molly T. Lawrence Sanders. 400p. 1986. reprint ed. mass mkt. 6.99 (*0-425-10139-8*) Berkley Pub.

Passion of Music & Dance: Body, Gender, & Sexuality. William Washabaugh. LC 98-211637. 224p. 1998. 55.00 (*1-85973-904-0*, Pub. by Berg Pubs); pap. 19.50 (*1-85973-909-1*, Pub. by Berg Pubs) NYU Pr.

Passion of Narcisse Mondoux. Gratien Gelinas. Tr. by Linda Gaboriau. 112p. (Orig.). 1992. pap. 5.95 (*0-88784-527-4*, Pub. by Hse of Anansi Pr) Genl Dist Srvs.

Passion of Our Lord. Tr. by Maria of Agreda. 284p. 1992. pap. 2.50 (*0-911988-38-6*, 44774) AMI Pr.

Passion of Our Lord Jesus Christ. Ed. by Robert J. Batastini. 118p. 1999. 45.00 (*1-57999-043-6*, G-4998) GIA Pubns.

***Passion of Our Lord Jesus Christ.** George R. Szews & Gabe Huck. LC 98-89329. 48p. 1999. pap. 7.00 (*1-56854-310-7*) Liturgy Tr Pubns.

Passion of Our Lord Jesus Christ: Cycles A, B, C. 1998. 4.95 (*0-89942-096-6*, 96/00) Catholic Bk Pub.

Passion of Our Lord Jesus Christ According to John: Arranged for Readers Theatre. Ronald E. Brassard. 1986. 5.95 (*0-912405-29-5*, Pastoral Press) OR Catholic.

Passion of Patrick MacNeill. Virginia Kantra. 1998. per. 4.25 (*0-373-07906-0*, 1-07906-0, Mira Bks) Harlequin Bks.

Passion of Peace. Ciaran McKeown. 320p. 1990. pap. 11.95 (*0-85640-325-3*, Pub. by Blackstaff Pr) Dufour.

Passion of Pier Pablo Pasolini. Sam Rohdie. 224p. 1995. 35.00 (*0-85170-517-0*, Pub. by British Film Inst); pap. 15.95 (*0-85170-518-9*, Pub. by British Film Inst) Ind U Pr.

Passion of Pier Paolo Pasolini. Sam Rohdie. LC 95-38575. (Perspectives Ser.). 230p. 1995. 35.00 (*0-253-32951-5*) Ind U Pr.

Passion of Pier Paolo Pasolini. Sam Rohdie. LC 95-38575. (Perspectives Ser.). 1996. pap. 15.95 (*0-253-21010-0*) Ind U Pr.

Passion of Rodin: Sculpture from the Iris & B. Gerald Cantor Collection. Stephen C. Wicks. (Illus.). 32p. (Orig.). 1995. pap. text 11.95 (*0-9635881-2-5*) Knoxville Mus.

Passion of St. John. Everett Frese. (Orig.). 1995. pap. text 14.95 (*1-56929-056-3*, Pastoral Press) OR Catholic.

Passion of the Holy Martyrs Sts. Perpetua & Felicity. Perpetua. Tr. by R. E. Wallis. 1991. pap. 2.95 (*0-89981-133-7*) Eastern Orthodox.

Passion of the People: Football in Latin Ameica. Tony Mason. (Critical Studies in Latin American Culture). 224p. (C). 1995. 60.00 (*0-86091-403-8*, B3629, Pub. by Verso) Norton.

Passion of the People: Football in Latin America. Tony Mason. (Critical Studies in Latin American Culture). 224p. (C). 1995. pap. 18.00 (*0-86091-667-7*, B3629, Pub. by Verso) Norton.

Passion of the Western Mind: Understanding the Ideas That Have Shaped Our World View. Richard Tarnas. 560p. 1993. pap. 15.00 (*0-345-36809-6*) Ballantine Pub Grp.

Passion of Therese of Lisieux: The Story of the Final Months in the Life of This Modern Saint. rev. ed. Guy Gaucher. 272p. 1998. pap. 14.95 (*0-8245-0987-0*, Crsrd) Crossroad NY.

Passion of Ursula & the 11,000 Virgins. Tr. by Marcelle Thiebaux & Pamela Sheingorn. (Translation Ser.). 58p. 1996. pap. 8.00 (*0-920669-14-X*, Pub. by Peregrina Pubng) Cistercian Pubns.

Passion of Youth: An Autobiography, 1897-1922. Wilhelm Reich. Ed. by Mary B. Higgins & Chester M. Raphael. Tr. by Philip Schmitz & Jerri Tompkins. 240p. 1988. 17.95 (*0-374-22995-3*) FS&G.

Passion of Youth: An Autobiography, 1897-1922. Wilhelm Reich. (Illus.). 178p. 1994. pap. 10.95 (*1-56924-929-6*) Marlowe & Co.

***Passion Partagee.** Carolyn Zane. (Horizon Ser.: No. 529). (FRE.). 1999. mass mkt. 3.99 (*0-373-39529-9*, 1-39529-2, Harlequin French) Harlequin Bks.

Passion Paths. William R. Grimbol. Ed. by Michael L. Sherer. LC 86-25094. (Orig.). 1987. pap. 4.50 (*0-89536-842-0*, 7801) CSS OH.

Passion Play. W. Edward Blain. 320p. 1991. pap. 3.95 (*0-380-71450-7*, Avon Bks) Morrow Avon.

Passion Play. Catherine De Vinck. LC 75-26326. 72p. 1975. 12.75 (*0-911726-16-0*, PPC); pap. 8.75 (*0-911726-18-7*, PPB) Alleluia Pr.

Passion Play. Peter Meredith. 1990. text. write for info. (*0-582-49079-0*, Pub. by Addison-Wesley) Longman.

Passion Play. Peter Nichols. (Methuen Modern Plays Ser.). 106p. (C). 1981. pap. write for info. (*0-413-47800-9*, A0361, Methuen Drama) Methn.

Passion Play. Charles H. Numrich. 1983. 5.25 (*0-89536-601-0*, 1627) CSS OH.

Passion Play. Sid Rowland. (Illus.). 80p. (Orig.). 1996. pap. 10.00 (*0-937158-07-0*) Del Valley.

Passion Play. Sean Stewart. 208p. (Orig.). 1993. mass mkt. 5.50 (*0-441-65241-7*) Ace Bks.

Passion Play. Jerzy N. Kosinski. LC 98-14018. 288p. 1998. reprint ed. pap. 12.00 (*0-8021-3567-6*, Grove) Grove-Atltic.

Passion Play: A Step-by-Step Guide to Discovering, Developing & Living Your Passion. Richard Y. Chang. LC 99-6392. 320p. 1999. 25.00 (*0-7879-4813-6*) Jossey-Bass.

Passion Play: Ancient Secrets for a Lifetime of Health & Happiness Through Sensational Sex. Felice Dunas. 272p. 1998. pap. 14.00 (*1-57322-698-X*, Riverhd Trade) Berkley Pub.

Passion Play: Ancient Secrets for a Lifetime of Health & Happiness Through Sensational Sex. Felice Dunas & Philip Goldberg. LC 97-8420. (Illus.). 304p. 1997. 24.95 (*1-57322-076-0*, Riverhead Books) Putnam Pub Group.

***Passion, Power & Praise: A Model for Men's Spirituality from the Life of David.** James A. Harnish. LC 00-38610. 2000. pap. write for info. (*0-687-03630-5*) Abingdon.

Passion, Power, & Prophecy: Based on Actual Events. A. E. Witte. LC 95-25582. 224p. 1996. 25.00 (*1-888122-00-5*) Status Pubs.

Passion Principles: Pathways to Purpose, Power & Profit! Ed. & Contrib. by Carol Hibler. (Illus.). 254p. 1999. pap., wbk. ed. 24.95 incl. VHS (*1-890896-50-0*) Passion Pub.

Passion Profit & Power. Marshall Sylver. LC 96-38711. 1997. per. 12.00 (*0-684-82521-X*) S&S Trade.

Passion, Profit, & Power: Reprogram Your Subconscious to Create the Relationships, Wealth, & Well-Being that You Deserve. Marshall Sylver. 1995. 23.00 (*0-684-80178-7*) S&S Trade.

Passion Quest. V. Larue. 1997. mass mkt. 11.95 (*0-340-68483-6*, Pub. by Hodder & Stought Ltd) Trafalgar.

Passion, Reason, & Power: Electric Power Planning in the Chicago Area from 1973 Through 1993. James A. Throgmorton. (New Practices of Inquiry Ser.). 368p. 1996. pap. text 19.95 (*0-226-79964-6*); lib. bdg. 61.00 (*0-226-79963-8*) U Ch Pr.

Passion Ruby. Eboni Snoe. 1995. mass mkt. 4.99 (*0-7860-0201-8*, Pinncle Kensgtn) Kensgtn Pub Corp.

***Passion Rules! Inspiring Women in Business.** Alexandra Powe-Allred. 150p. 2000. 21.95 (*1-55571-530-3*, Pub. by PSI Resch) Midpt Trade.

Passion Sans Escale. Lynn Leslie. (Amours d'Aujourd'Hui Ser.). 1999. mass mkt. 4.99 (*0-373-38327-4*, 1-38327-2) Harlequin Bks.

Passion Simple. Annie Ernaux. (Folio Ser.: No. 2545). (FRE.). 77p. 1992. pap. 8.95 (*2-07-038840-9*) Schoenhof.

Passion Song. Catherine FitzGerald. 384p. (Orig.). 1989. pap. 3.95 (*0-380-75691-9*, Avon Bks) Morrow Avon.

***Passion Songs: Poems from Hollywood.** Mark Dunster. 11p. 1999. pap. 5.00 (*0-89642-837-0*) Linden Pubs.

Passion Star. Mallory Burgess. 432p. 1988. pap. 3.95 (*0-380-75383-9*, Avon Bks) Morrow Avon.

Passion That Consumes: Life & Ministry of Alberto Mottesi see Pasion Que Consume: Vida y Ministerio de Alberto Mottesi

Passion to Believe: Autism & the Facilitated Communication Phenomenon. Diane C. Twachtman. LC 97-21567. 1997. 35.00 (*0-8133-9098-2*, Pub. by Westview) HarpC.

Passion to Lead! How to Develop Your Natural Leadership Ability. Michael Plumstead. Ed. by Kelly Scanlon. LC 96-69147. (Self-Study Sourcebook Ser.). (Illus.). 152p. 1997. pap. 15.95 (*1-57294-051-4*, 13-0027) SkillPath Pubns.

***Passion to Liberate: La Guma's South Africa-Images of District Six.** Fritz Pointer. LC 99-59481. 2000. pap. write for info. (*0-86543-818-8*) Africa World.

Passion to Oppose: John Anderson, Philosopher. Brian Kennedy. 272p. 1996. 49.95 (*0-522-84683-1*, Pub. by Melbourne Univ Pr) Paul & Co Pubs.

Passion to Skate. Sandra Bezic. 176p. 1998. pap. 16.95 (*0-8362-6452-5*) Andrews & McMeel.

Passion Within Reasons. Robert H. Frank. (Illus.). (C). 1989. pap. text. write for info. (*0-393-96022-6*) Norton.

Passional Culture: Emotion, Religion, & Society in Southern Spain. Timothy Mitchell. LC 89-40398. (Illus.). 206p. (C). 1990. text 27.50 (*0-8122-8202-7*) U of Pa Pr.

***Passionate: Poems from Hollywood.** Mark Dunster. 11p. 1999. pap. 5.00 (*0-89642-835-4*) Linden Pubs.

Passionate, Accurate Story: Making Your Hearts Truth into Literature. Carol Bly. 216p. 1998. reprint ed. pap. 13.95 (*1-57131-219-6*) Milkweed Ed.

***Passionate Action: Yeats's Mastery of Drama.** David Richman. LC 00-23413. 2000. write for info. (*0-87413-718-7*) U Delaware Pr.

Passionate Adventure. Karen Van Der Zee. (Presents Ser.). 1994. per. 2.99 (*0-373-11686-1*, 1-11686-2) Harlequin Bks.

Passionate Adventure. large type unabridged ed. (Harlequin Ser.). 1993. lib. bdg. 18.95 (*0-263-13459-8*) Mac Lib Ref.

Passionate Apprentice: The Early Journals, 1897-1909. Ed. by Mitchell A. Leaska. 512p. 1992. pap. 14.95 (*0-15-671160-5*, Harvest Bks) Harcourt.

Passionate Apprentice: The Early Journals, 1897-1909. Virginia Woolf. Ed. by Mitchell A. Leaska. 444p. 1991. 24.95 (*0-15-171287-5*) Harcourt.

Passionate Attention: An Introduction to Literary Study. Richard L. McGuire. (C). 1973. pap. text 11.25 (*0-393-09324-7*) Norton.

Passionate Awakening. large type ed. St Clair. LC 98-49002. Date not set. 30.00 (*0-7838-8471-0*, G K Hall Lrg Type) Mac Lib Ref.

***Passionate Awakening.** large type ed. Joy St. Clair. LC 98-49002. (Romance Ser.). 171p. 1999. write for info. (*0-7540-3636-7*) Chivers N Amer.

Passionate Betrayal. Jacqueline Baird. (Presents Ser.: No. 431). 1992. pap. 2.79 (*0-373-11431-1*, 1-11431-3) Harlequin Bks.

Passionate Brood. Margaret C. Barnes. 24.95 (*0-8488-0782-0*) Amereon Ltd.

***Passionate Business.** 1999. per. 4.50 (*0-373-80663-9*) S&S Trade.

Passionate Camera: Photography & the Bodies of Desire. Deborah Bright. LC 98-12079. (Illus.). 456p. 1998. pap. 30.00 (*0-415-14582-1*) Routledge.

Passionate Camera: Photography & the Bodies of Desire. Deborah Bright. LC 98-12079. (Illus.). 456p. (C). 1998. 85.00 (*0-415-14581-3*) Routledge.

Passionate Captivity. Patricia Wilson. (Larger Print Ser.). 1995. pap. 2.99 (*0-373-15592-1*, 1-15592-8) Harlequin Bks.

Passionate Captivity. large type ed. Patricia Wilson. (Harlequin Ser.). 1993. lib. bdg. 19.95 (*0-263-13542-X*) Thorndike Pr.

Passionate Commitment: Recapturing Your Sense of Purpose. Crawford W. Loritts, Jr. pap. 9.99 (*0-8024-5246-9*, 244) Moody.

Passionate Communities: Reading Lesbian Resistance in Jane Rule's Fiction. Marilyn R. Schuster. LC 99-6339. (The Cutting Edge: Lesbian Life & Literature Ser.). 224p. 1999. text 55.00 (*0-8147-8130-6*); pap. text 20.00 (*0-8147-8133-0*) NYU Pr.

Passionate Concerto. Rebecca Benjamin. (Rainbow Romances Ser.). 160p. 1993. 14.95 (*0-7090-4922-6*) Parkwest Pubns.

***Passionate Concerto.** large type ed. Jill Atkins. 264p. 1999. pap. 18.99 (*0-7089-5544-4*, Linford) Ulverscroft.

Passionate Couple. Charles Gallagher. (Celebrate Love Ser.). 74p. (Orig.). 1990. pap. text 3.95 (*0-911905-29-4*) Past & Mat Rene Ctr.

Passionate Deceit. Kate Proctor. (Presents Ser.: Vol. 89). 1998. per. 3.75 (*0-373-18689-4*, 1-18689-9) Harlequin Bks.

Passionate Detachments. Sue Thornham. LC 97-2480. 224p. 1997. text 65.00 (*0-340-65226-8*) OUP.

Passionate Detachments: An Introduction to Feminist Film Theory. Sue Thornham. LC 97-2480. 224p. 1997. pap. text 18.95 (*0-340-65225-X*) OUP.

Passionate Discontent. Mathews. LC 99-22167. 2000. 35.00 (*0-226-51018-2*) U Ch Pr.

Passionate Distance. Joan Gartland. (Illus.). 24p. (Orig.). 1991. pap. text 4.00 (*1-56439-010-1*) Ridgeway.

P

Passionate Doubts: Designs of Interpretation in Contemporary American Fiction. Patrick O'Donnell. LC 85-28865. 213p. 1986. text 27.95 (0-87745-138-9) U of Iowa Pr.

Passionate Enchantment. large type ed. Joan Moules. (Linford Romance Library). 320p. 1989. pap. 16.99 (0-7089-6648-9, Linford) Ulverscroft.

***Passionate Encounters in a Time of Sensibility.** Ed. by Maximillian E. Novak & Anne Kostelanetz Mellor. LC 99-55925. 280p. 2000. 45.00 (0-87413-703-9) U Delaware Pr.

Passionate Enemies. Jean Plaidy, pseud. 24.95 (0-8488-0606-9) Amereon Ltd.

Passionate Enlightenment: Women in Tantric Buddhism. Miranda Shaw. 1998. 36.00 (81-215-0820-7, Pub. by M Manoharial) Coronet Bks.

Passionate Enlightment: Women in Tantric Buddhism. Miranda Shaw. 307p. (C). 1994. text 42.50 (0-691-03380-3, Pub. by Princeton U Pr); pap. text 15.95 (0-691-01090-0, Pub. by Princeton U Pr) Cal Prin Full Svc.

Passionate Enquiry & School Development: A Story about Teacher Action Research. Marion Dadds. LC 94-23561. 202p. 1995. pap. 27.95 (0-7507-0433-0, Falmer Pr) Taylor & Francis.

Passionate Exiles: Madame de Stael & Madame Recamier. Maurice Levaillant. Tr. by Malcolm Barnes from FRE. LC 73-160923. (Biography Index Reprint Ser.). 1977. reprint ed. 23.95 (0-8369-8086-7) Ayer.

Passionate Eye: The Collected Writings of Suzanne Vega. Suzanne Vega. LC 98-47029. 288p. 1999. 23.00 (0-380-97353-7, Avon Bks) Morrow Avon.

***Passionate Eye: The Collected Writings of Suzanne Vega.** Suzanne Vega. 288p. 2000. pap. 14.00 (0-380-78882-9, HarpEntertain) Morrow Avon.

Passionate Fact: Storytelling in Natural History & Cultural Interpretation. Susan Strauss. (Illus.). 140p. (Orig.). 1996. pap. text 16.95 (1-55591-925-1) Fulcrum Pub.

Passionate Fictions: Gender, Narrative, & Violence in Clarice Lispector. Marta Piexoto. LC 93-29690. 1994. pap. 15.95 (0-8166-2159-4); text 39.95 (0-8166-2158-6) U of Minn Pr.

***Passionate Fictions of Eliza Haywood: Essays on Her Life & Work.** Ed. by Kirsten T. Saxton & Rebecca P. Bocchicchio. 288p. (C). 2000. 32.50 (0-8131-2161-2) U Pr of Ky.

Passionate Form: Life Process As Artistic Paradigm in the Writings of D. H. Lawrence. James B. Sipple. LC 92-4899. (American University Studies: English Language & Literature: Ser. IV, Vol. 144). 128p. (C). 1992. text 35.95 (0-8204-1822-6) P Lang Pubng.

Passionate Friends a Novel & Three Essays see Works of H. G. Wells

Passionate G-Man. Dixie Browning. (Silhouette Desire Ser.). 184p. 1998. per. 3.75 (0-373-76141-4, 0-76141-1) Silhouette.

Passionate Gardener. Georgia Raimondi. LC 98-4833. 1999. 26.95 (0-7621-0074-5, Pub. by RD Assn) Penguin Putnam.

Passionate Ghost. large type ed. Sheila R. Allen. 325p. 1991. reprint ed. lib. bdg. 18.95 (1-56054-187-3) Thorndike Pr.

Passionate Ghost Bk. IV: The Lovers of Steadford Abbey, Bk. IV. Sheila R. Allen. 224p. 1991. 19.95 (0-8027-1158-8) Walker & Co.

Passionate Hearts: The Poetry of Sexual Love. Ed. by Wendy Maltz. LC 96-31046. 224p. 1996. 17.00 (1-57731-007-1, Pub. by New Wrld Lib) Publishers Group.

***Passionate Hearts: The Poetry of Sexual Love.** 2nd ed. Ed. by Wendy Maltz. LC 96-31046. 224p. 2000. pap. 14.00 (1-57731-122-1, Pub. by New Wrld Lib) Publishers Group.

Passionate Inheritance, Bk. 1814. Rebecca King. (Presents Ser.). 1996. per. 3.50 (0-373-11814-7, 1-11814-0) Harlequin Bks.

Passionate Intellect: Dorothy L. Sayers' Encounter with Dante. Barbara Reynolds. LC 88-13930. (Illus.). 286p. 1989. reprint ed. pap. 88.70 (0-608-07360-1, 206758800009) Bks Demand.

Passionate Intellect: The Transformation of Classical Traditions. Ed. by Lewis Ayres. LC 95-9847. (Rutgers University Studies in Classical Humanities: Vol. 7). 376p. 1995. 49.95 (1-56000-210-7) Transaction Pubs.

Passionate Journey: A Novel in 165 Woodcuts. Frans Masereel. (Illus.). 160p. 1994. reprint ed. 14.00 (0-87286-174-0) City Lights.

Passionate Journey: Poems & Drawings in the Erotic Mood. Steve Kowit & Arthur Okamura. LC 84-71153. (Illus.). 88p. 1984. 12.00 (0-933944-08-X); pap. 7.95 (0-933944-09-8) City Miner Bks.

***Passionate Journeys: Why Successful Women Joined a Cult.** Marion S. Goldman. LC 99-9632. (Illus.). 312p. 1999. 29.95 (0-472-11101-9, 11101) U of Mich Pr.

Passionate Judaism: An Inspirational Guide for a Happy & Fulfilling Life. Moshe Meir Weiss. LC 98-40489. 320p. 1998. 21.95 (1-880582-33-3) Judaica Pr.

Passionate Judaism: An Inspirational Guide for a Happy & Fulfilling Life. Moshe Meir Weiss. 320p. 1999. pap. 18.95 (1-880582-35-X) Judaica Pr.

Passionate Kiss of Illusion. Scott Shaw. LC 89-71261. 383p. (Orig.). 1990. pap. 12.95 (1-877792-04-7) Buddha Rose.

Passionate Kisses. Cherie Bennett. Ed. by Pat MacDonald. (Wild Hearts Ser.). 192p. (Orig.). (J). (gr. 3-6). 1994. mass mkt. 3.50 (0-671-88782-3, Archway) PB.

Passionate Kisses. Penny Richards. (Crystal Creek Ser.: Vol. 14). 1994. per. 3.99 (0-373-82526-9, 1-82526-4) Harlequin Bks.

Passionate Life. Sam Keen. 1984. pap. 15.00 (0-06-250468-1, Pub. by Harper SF) HarpC.

Passionate Lives: D. H. Lawrence, F. Scott Fitzgerald, Henry Miller, Dylan Thomas, Sylvia Plath.. John Tytell. 1991. 19.95 (1-55972-077-8, Birch Ln Pr) Carol Pub Group.

Passionate Lives: Eight Autobiographical Poem Cycles. Elizabeth Claman et al. LC 98-66538. 216p. 1998. pap. 12.99 (0-9638992-4-4) Queen of Swords.

Passionate Lives: The Love Lives of D. H. Lawrence, F. Scott Fitzgerald, Henry Miller, Dylan Thomas, & Sylvia Plath. John Tytell. LC 94-36983. 1994. pap. 14.95 (0-312-12412-0) St Martin.

Passionate Love of Mankind: Kitt's Law - The Plom Theory, Vol. 1. Henry Kitt. 192p. 1990. pap. 10.95 (0-924694-11-4) Capricornis.

Passionate Man. Joanna Trollope. 288p. 1994. pap. 10.95 (0-552-99442-1) Bantam.

Passionate Marriage: Love, Sex & Intimacy in Emotionally. David Schnarch. LC 97-52796. 432p. 1998. pap. 12.95 (0-8050-5826-5, Owl) H Holt & Co.

Passionate Marriage: Sex, Love, & Intimacy in Emotionally Committed Relationships. David M. Schnarch. LC 96-40893. 352p. 1997. 25.00 (0-393-04021-6) Norton.

Passionate Measure. Ivan V. Lalic. 94p. 1989. pap. 17.95 (0-85646-222-5, Pub. by Anvil Press) Dufour.

Passionate Measure. Ivan V. Lalic. (C). 1989. 23.00 (0-948268-60-3, Pub. by Dedalus) St Mut.

Passionate Mind: A Manual for Living Creatively with One's Self. Joel Kramer. (Illus.). 122p. 1983. reprint ed. pap. 10.95 (0-938190-12-1) North Atlantic.

Passionate Mind: Sources of Destruction & Creativity. Robin Fox. 298p. 1999. 34.95 (1-56000-419-3) Transaction Pubs.

Passionate Mind: Sources of Destruction & Creativity. 2nd ed. Robin Fox. LC 99-40000. 307p. 1999. pap. 24.95 (0-7658-0632-0) Transaction Pubs.

Passionate Mind of Maxine Greene: I Am....Not Yet" William F. Pinar. LC 98-230641. 268p. 1998. 77.00 (0-7507-0812-3) Taylor & Francis.

Passionate Mind Of Maxine Greene: "i Am....not Yet" William F. Pinar. LC 98-230641. 1998. pap. text 29.95 (0-7507-0878-6) Taylor & Francis.

Passionate Minds: The Inner World of Scientists. Ed. by Lewis Wolpert & Alison Richards. (Illus.). 248p. (C). 1998. 25.00 (0-19-854904-0) OUP.

***Passionate Minds: Women Rewriting the World.** Claudia Roth Pierpont. LC 99-33349. (Illus.). 320p. 2000. 26.95 (0-679-43106-3) Knopf.

Passionate Mistakes & Intricate Corruption of One Girl in America. Michelle Tea. (Semiotext(e) Native Agents Ser.). 192p. 1998. pap. 8.00 (1-57027-074-0) Autonomedia.

Passionate Necessity: A View of Human Purpose. Hugh Shearman. 1970. 10.95 (0-8356-0200-1, Quest) Theos Pub Hse.

Passionate Nomad: The Life of Freya Stark. Jane Fletcher Geniesse. LC 99-12094. (Illus.). 400p. 1999. 27.95 (0-394-58396-5) Random.

Passionate Observer: Photographs by Carl Van Vechten. Keith F. Davis. (Illus.). 120p. 1993. 40.00 (0-87529-668-8); pap. 25.00 (0-87529-669-6) Hallmark.

Passionate Observer: Writings from the World of Nature by Jean-Henri Fabre. Jean-Henri Fabre & Linda Davis. LC 97-36636. (Illus.). 144p. 1998. 21.95 (0-8118-0935-8) Chronicle Bks.

Passionate Organization: Igniting the Fire of Employee Commitment. James R. Lucas. LC 98-54184. 240p. 1999. 24.95 (0-8144-0477-4) AMACOM.

***Passionate Palate: Cooking Up a Delicious Life.** Desiree Witkowski. LC 99-35769. (Illus.). 480p. 1999. 21.95 (1-56718-824-9) Llewellyn Pubns.

Passionate Palate: Recipes for Romance & Rapture. Ailene Eberhard. LC 98-45349. 224p. 1999. pap. 10.00 (0-345-42543-X) Ballantine Pub Grp.

Passionate Pen: The Life & Times of Faith Fenton. Jill Downie. (Illus.). 337p. 1998. text 27.00 (0-7881-5354-4) DIANE Pub.

Passionate Penis: Erotic Drawings. Jean Cocteau. 110p. 1993. 50.00 (0-7206-0894-5, Pub. by P Owen Ltd) Dufour.

Passionate Perils of Publishing. Celeste West & Valerie Wheat. LC 77-94898. (Illus.). 1978. pap. 7.00 (0-912932-04-X) Booklegger Pubng.

Passionate Philosopher: A Marquis de Sade Reader. Marquis De Sade, pseud. Tr. & Intro. by Margaret Crosland. 126p. 1991. 40.00 (0-7206-0826-0, Pub. by P Owen Ltd) Dufour.

***Passionate Pilgrim.** Juliet Landon. 320p. 2000. 26.99 (0-263-16473-X, Pub. by Mills & Boon) Ulverscroft.

Passionate Pilgrim & Other Tales see Works of Henry James Jr.: Collected Works

Passionate Pilgrim & Other Tales. Henry James. (BCL1-PS American Literature Ser.). 496p. 1992. reprint ed. lib. bdg. 99.00 (0-7812-6764-1) Rprt Serv.

Passionate Pilgrims. Allison Lockwood. LC 78-66808. (Illus.). 551p. 1981. 37.50 (0-8453-4725-X, Cornwall Bks) Assoc Univ Prs.

Passionate Pilgrims: The American Traveler in Great Britain, 1800-1914. Allison Lockwood. LC 78-66808. 650p. 1981. 37.50 (0-8386-2272-0) Fairleigh Dickinson.

Passionate Possessions of Faith: The Jacob Guenther Family, 1725-1994. Robert G. Guenther. LC 94-96077. 320p. 1994. write for info. (0-9641475-0-5) R G Guenther.

***Passionate Power of Golf: And Other Connections to the Heart of the Game.** Wendi Keene. LC 99-90507. 2000. pap. write for info. (0-9672001-0-5) First Tee.

Passionate Preference: The Story of the North Carolina School of the Arts. Leslie Banner. (Illus.). 438p. 1991. pap. 14.95 (1-878086-01-4, Pub. by Down Home NC) Blair.

Passionate Pretenders. Haviland. LC 97-52120. 1998. 24.95 (0-7862-1390-6) Thorndike Pr.

Passionate Purpose: Awakening the Inner Fire. Reed Daugherity. LC 97-76829. 140p. 1998. pap. 14.95 (1-885221-75-4) BookPartners.

Passionate Pursuit of God: How Knowing God Transforms Your Life. Tim Riter. LC 99-18733. 150p. 1999. pap. 9.99 (0-8308-2205-4, 2205) InterVarsity.

Passionate Reason: Making Sense of Kierkegaard's Philosophical Fragments. C. Stephen Evans. LC 91-30417. (Indiana Series in the Philosophy of Religion). 228p. 1992. 39.95 (0-253-32073-9) Ind U Pr.

Passionate Rebel. large type ed. Danielle De Winters. (Black Satin Romance Ser.). 363p. 1997. 27.99 (1-86110-033-7) Ulverscroft.

Passionate Relationship. Penny Jordan. (Promo Ser.). 1999. per. 4.50 (0-373-83375-X, 1-83375-5) Harlequin Bks.

Passionate Romantic. George Gordon Byron. (Illus.). 1999. 19.95 (1-86019-308-0) Brockhampton Pr Ltd.

Passionate Sage: The Character & Legacy of John Adams. Joseph J. Ellis. 1994. pap. 14.95 (0-393-31133-3) Norton.

Passionate Sage: The Character & Legacy of John Adams. Joseph J. Ellis. (Illus.). 282p. 1998. reprint ed. lib. bdg. 29.95 (0-7351-0022-5) Replica Bks.

Passionate Scandal. Michelle Reid. 1994. per. 2.99 (0-373-11695-0, 1-11695-3) Harlequin Bks.

Passionate Scandal. large type unabridged ed. (Harlequin Ser.). 1994. lib. bdg. 19.95 (0-263-13899-2) Mac Lib Ref.

***Passionate Sex: Discover the Special Power in You.** Daniel S. Stein & Leslie Aldridge Westoff. 256p. 2000. 26.00 (0-7867-0723-2); pap. 14.00 (0-7867-0705-4) Carroll & Graf.

***Passionate Shopper: Finding Beautiful Things for You & Your Home.** Victoria. LC 99-23391. 192p. 1999. 23.00 (0-688-16737-3, Wm Morrow) Morrow Avon.

***Passionate Sisterhood: Women of the Wordsworth Circle.** Kathleen Jones. (Illus.). 313p. 2000. text 29.95 (0-312-22731-0) St Martin.

Passionate Sociology. Ann Game & Andrew Metcalfe. 160p. 1996. 69.95 (0-8039-7460-4); pap. 22.95 (0-8039-7461-2) Sage.

Passionate State of Mind. Eric Hoffer. 1993. reprint ed. 27.95 (1-56849-032-1) Buccaneer Bks.

Passionate Surrender. Sheryl Sage. 384p. (Orig.). 1993. mass mkt. 4.50 (0-380-76684-1, Avon Bks) Morrow Avon.

Passionate Teacher: A Practical Guide. Robert L. Fried. 288p. 1996. pap. 14.00 (0-8070-3115-1) Beacon Pr.

Passionate Technique: Strategic Psychodrama with Individuals, Families & Groups. Antony Williams. 256p. 1989. 49.50 (0-415-00138-2) Routledge.

***Passionate Times.** Emma Blair. 2000. pap. 10.95 (0-553-40615-9, Pub. by Transworld Publishers Ltd) Trafalgar.

Passionate Times. large type ed. Emma Blair. (Charnwood Large Print Ser.). 560p. 1997. 27.99 (0-7089-8952-7, Charnwood) Ulverscroft.

Passionate Torment. large type ed. Lee Stafford. (Dales Large Print Ser.). 304p. 1998. pap. 19.99 (1-85389-795-7, Dales) Ulverscroft.

Passionate Views: Film Cognition & Emotion. Carl R. Plantinga & Greg M. Smith. LC 98-43308. 1999. 49.95 (0-8018-6010-5) Johns Hopkins.

Passionate Views: Film Cognition & Emotion. Carl R. Plantinga & Greg M. Smith. LC 98-43308. (Illus.). 312p. 1999. pap. 17.95 (0-8018-6011-3) Johns Hopkins.

Passionate Virtuosity: The Fiction of John Barth. Charles B. Harris. LC 83-4976. 232p. 1983. text 24.95 (0-252-01037-X) U of Ill Pr.

Passionate Visions of the American South: Self-Taught Artists from the 1940's to the Present. Alice R. Yelen. (Illus.). 351p. 1993. pap. 35.00 (0-614-01219-8) New Orleans Mus Art.

Passionate Visions of the American South: Self-Taught Artists from the 1940's to the Present. Ed. by Alice R. Yelen. LC 93-29397. (Illus.). 353p. 1994. pap. 37.50 (0-87805-677-7); text 65.00 (0-87805-676-9) U Pr of Miss.

Passionate Voice see Unleash the Passion in Your Voice

Passionate Voice: The Secrets to Unlocking Your Powerful Voice. Elizabeth Sabine. Ed. by Anne McGee. (Illus.). 110p. 1995. pap. 16.00 (0-9660123-0-5) E Sabine.

Passionate Volunteerism: The Importance of Volunteerism Today & How Government, Nonprofits & Volunteers Can Make It a More Powerful Force. Jeanne H. Bradner. 82p. (Orig.). 1993. pap. 3.95 (0-9634395-2-9) Conversation Pr.

Passionate Witch. Thorne Smith. 23.95 (0-89190-433-6) Amereon Ltd.

Passionate Women, Passive Men: Suicide in Yiddish Literature. Janet Hadda. LC 87-9911. (SUNY Series in Modern Jewish Literature & Culture). 224p. (C). 1988. pap. text 21.95 (0-88706-597-X) State U NY Pr.

Passionate Women, Passive Men: Suicide in Yiddish Literature. Janet Hadda. LC 87-9911. (SUNY Series in Modern Jewish Literature & Culture). 224p. (C). 1988. text 64.50 (0-88706-595-3) State U NY Pr.

***Passionately Yours... A Collection of Love Letters to My Beloved.** Samuel McCormick. (Illus.). 70p. 1999. pap. 9.95 (0-7414-0021-9) Buy Books.

Passione. Albert F. Innaurato. 1981. pap. 5.25 (0-8222-0877-6) Dramatists Play.

Passionists of the Southwest: A Revelation of the Penitentes. Alex Darley. LC 68-57290. (Beautiful Rio Grande Classics Ser.). 134p. 1968. lib. bdg. 17.50 (0-87380-020-6) Popular E Commerce.

***Passions.** Chris Cooley. Ed. by Sharon Boodry. 100p. 1999. pap. 11.95 (0-9677802-0-9) Coolio.

Passions, 4 vols. Charlotte Dacre. LC 73-22762. (Gothic Novels Ser.). 1979. reprint ed. 96.95 (0-405-06013-0) Ayer.

Passions: Emotions & the Meaning of Life. abr. ed. Robert C. Solomon. LC 92-45228. 352p. (C). 1993. reprint ed. pap. text 12.95 (0-87220-226-7); reprint ed. lib. bdg. 34.95 (0-87220-227-5) Hackett Pub.

Passions: Glimpses of Romance. Patrick Caton. LC 96-76126. 68p. 1996. 6.50 (1-56245-273-8) Great Quotations.

Passions - The Wines & Travel of Thomas Jefferson. James M. Gabler. Ed. by Robert Gabler & Gwinn Owens. LC 95-94318. (Illus.). 318p. 1995. 29.95 (0-9613525-3-1) Bacchus Pr Ltd.

Passions & Constraints. David S. Holmes. 1995. 29.95 (0-226-34968-3) U Ch Pr.

Passions & Constraints: On the Theory of Liberal Democracy. Stephen Holmes. 1997. pap. text 15.95 (0-226-34969-1) U Ch Pr.

Passions & Deceptions: The Early Films of Ernst Lubitsch. Sabine Hake. (Illus.). 224p. 1992. text 49.50 (0-691-03197-5, Pub. by Princeton U Pr) Cal Prin Full Svc.

Passions & Howard Hughes. abr. ed. Terry Moore & Jerry Rivers. 1996. write for info. incl. audio (1-882071-74-3, 636828, Pub. by B&B Audio) Lndmrk Audiobks.

Passions & Impressions. Pablo Neruda. Ed. by Matilde Neruda & Miguel Otero Silva. Tr. by Margaret Sayers Peden from SPA. 400p. 2001. reprint ed. pap. 16.00 (0-374-51811-4) FS&G.

Passions & Interests: Political Party Concepts of American Democracy. Gerald M. Pomper. LC 92-12328. (American Political Thought Ser.). xii, 180p. 1992. 27.50 (0-7006-0551-7); pap. 12.95 (0-7006-0552-5) U Pr of KS.

Passions & Perfection in Christ: Narratives from Evergentinos by the Desert Fathers. Chrysostomos. 200p. 1998. pap. 15.95 (1-886412-24-3) Preserv Press.

Passions & Prejudice: The Secrets of Spindletop. expanded rev. ed. Linda Light. (Illus.). 405p. 1997. 24.95 (0-9645617-2-7) Spindletop Prod.

Passions & the Homilies from Leabhar Breac. Tr. by Robert Atkinson. LC 78-72680. (Royal Irish Academy, Todd Lecture Ser.: Vol. 2). reprint ed. 72.50 (0-404-60562-1) AMS Pr.

Passions & the Interests: Political Arguments for Capitalism Before Its Triumph. Albert O. Hirschman. 1977. pap. 12.95 (0-691-00357-2, Pub. by Princeton U Pr) Cal Prin Full Svc.

Passions & the Interests: Political Arguments for Capitalism Before Its Triumph. Albert O. Hirschman. LC 96-29551. 180p. 1977. pap. text 12.95 (0-691-01598-8, Pub. by Princeton U Pr) Cal Prin Full Svc.

Passion's Bedtime Stories, Vol. 1. 2nd ed. Brianna Nichole. Ed. by L. J. Brott. 139p. 1999. reprint ed. pap. 13.00 (0-9670079-0-9, Pub. by Brianna Nichole) Afrikan Wrld.

Passion's Betrayal. Penelope Neri. 1985. mass mkt. 3.95 (0-8217-1568-2, Zebra Kensgtn) Kensgtn Pub Corp.

Passion's Blood. Lynn Sanders & Cherif Fortin. LC 99-172638. 81p. 1999. 22.95 (1-885478-65-8, Pub. by Genesis Press) BookWorld.

Passion's Bold Caress. 1997. mass mkt. 1.00 (0-8217-5732-6) Kensgtn Pub Corp.

Passion's Child: The Extraordinary Life of Jane Digby. Margaret F. Schmidt. 5.95 (0-7043-3202-7, Pub. by Quartet) Charles River Bks.

Passion's Choice. Gloria D. Skinner. 1990. mass mkt. 4.50 (0-445-21062-1, Mysterious Paperbk) Warner Bks.

Passions de l'Ame. Rene Descartes. (Tel Ser.). (FRE.). 1970. pap. 16.95 (2-07-071318-0) Schoenhof.

Passions et la Sagesse. Alain. (FRE.). 95.00 (0-8288-3413-X, F81190) Fr & Eur.

Passions et la Sagesse. Alain. (FRE.). 1480p. 1960. text 115.00 (0-7859-7572-1, F81190) Fr & Eur.

Passion's Fever. Jane Kidder. 1991. mass mkt. 4.25 (0-8217-3646-9, Zebra Kensgtn) Kensgtn Pub Corp.

Passion's Fire. Cassie Edwards. 496p. 1986. mass mkt. 3.95 (0-8217-1872-X, Zebra Kensgtn) Kensgtn Pub Corp.

Passion's Fortune: The History of Mills & Boon. Joe McAleer. (Illus.). 352p. 2000. text 35.00 (0-19-820455-8) OUP.

Passion's Fury. Patricia Hagan. 400p. 1981. pap. 3.95 (0-380-77727-4, Avon Bks) Morrow Avon.

Passion's Glory. Anne Moore. 1983. mass mkt. 3.50 (0-685-07868-X, Zebra Kensgtn) Kensgtn Pub Corp.

Passions in Roman Thought & Literature. Ed. by Susanna M. Braund & Christopher Gill. 276p. (C). 1997. text 64.95 (0-521-47391-8) Cambridge U Pr.

Passion's Kiss. Jane Kidder. 384p. 1996. mass mkt. 4.99 (0-8217-5317-7) Kensgtn Pub Corp.

Passion's Legacy. Lori A. Paige. 256p. (Orig.). 1991. pap. 8.95 (0-941483-81-9) Naiad Pr.

Passion's Mistress. large type ed. Helen Bianchin. 1994. 19.95 (0-263-13902-6) Thorndike Pr.

Passion's Mistress: (Presents Plus) Helen Bianchin. (Presents Ser.). 1994. per. 2.99 (0-373-11704-3, 1-11704-3) Harlequin Bks.

Passions of Chelsea Kane. Barbara Delinsky. 576p. 1992. mass mkt. 6.99 (0-06-104093-2, Harp PBks) HarpC.

Passions of Emma. Penelope Williamson. 464p. 1998. mass mkt. 6.99 (0-446-60597-2, Pub. by Warner Bks) Little.

Passions of Emma. large type ed. Penelope Williamson. LC 97-48586. (Large Print Bks.). 1998. 25.95 (1-56895-526-X) Wheeler Pub.

Passions of Fatherhood. Osherson. Date not set. pap. write for info. (0-449-91071-7) Fawcett.

Passions of Innocence: Tantric Celibacy & the Mysteries of Eros. Stuart Sovatsky. 224p. (Orig.). 1992. pap. 14.95 (0-89281-405-5, Destiny Bks) Inner Tradit.

Passions of Mr. Desire. Andre Roy. 82p. pap. 8.00 (0-919349-64-1) Guernica Editions.

An Asterisk (*) at the beginning of an entry indicates that the title is appearing for the first time.

Passions of Rhetoric: Lessing's Theory of Argument & the German Enlightenment. Evelyn K. Moore. LC 93-13187. (Library of Rhetorics: Vol. 3). 144p. (C). 1993. text 124.50 (*0-7923-2308-4*) Kluwer Academic.

Passions of the Cut Sleeve: The Male Homosexual Tradition in China. Bret Hinsch. LC 89-49037. 256p. 1990. 40.00 (*0-520-06720-7*, Pub. by U CA Pr) Cal Prin Full Svc.

Passions of the Cut Sleeve: The Male Homosexual Tradition in China. Bret Hinsch. 1992. pap. 16.95 (*0-520-07869-1*, Pub. by U CA Pr) Cal Prin Full Svc.

Passions of the Human Soul, & Their Influence on Society & Civilization, 2 Vols. Francois M. Fourier. Tr. by H. Doherty. LC 67-29504. 1968. reprint ed. 95.00 (*0-678-00383-1*) Kelley.

***Passions of the Mind.** Frances Paige. 1999. 25.00 (*0-7278-5444-5*, Pub. by Severn Hse) Chivers N Amer.

Passions of the Mind. Irving Stone. 1994. reprint ed. lib. bdg. 35.95 (*1-56849-564-1*) Buccaneer Bks.

Passions of the Mind: Selected Writings. A. S. Byatt. LC 92-50586. 332p. 1993. pap. 12.00 (*0-679-73678-6*) Vin Bks.

Passions of the Mind: Unheard Melodies: A 3rd Principle of Mental Functioning. Harold N. Boris. LC 93-15084. 288p. (C). 1993. text 55.00 (*0-8147-1204-5*) NYU Pr.

Passions of the Minde. Thomas Wright. (Anglistica & Americana Ser.: No. 126). 336p. 1973. reprint ed. 57.20 (*3-487-04661-X*) G Olms Pubs.

Passions of the Minde in Generall: A Reprint Based on the 1604 Edition. Thomas Wright. LC 78-139807. 446p. reprint ed. 138.30 (*0-8357-9692-2*, 201113600074) Bks Demand.

Passions of the People. Zakaria. 2000. write for info. (*0-393-04764-4*) Norton.

Passions of the Soul. Rene Descartes. Tr. by Stephen H. Voss from FRE. LC 87-23818. (HPC Classics Ser.). 191p. (C). 1989. lib. bdg. 34.95 (*0-87220-036-1*) Hackett Pub.

Passions of the Soul. Rene Descartes. Tr. by Stephen H. Voss from FRE. LC 87-23818. (HPC Classics Ser.). 191p. (C). 1989. pap. text 11.95 (*0-87220-035-3*) Hackett Pub.

Passions of the Soul. Elain H. Olaoye. 65p. 1998. pap. text. write for info. (*1-880764-14-8*) Northwind NJ.

Passions of the Soul: The 3rd Book of De Anima et Vita. Juan L. Vives. Tr. by Carlos G. Norena from LAT. LC 89-77132. (Studies in Renaissance Literature: Vol. 4). 152p. 1990. lib. bdg. 79.95 (*0-88946-147-3*) E Mellen.

Passions of the Spore. Barbara G. Fisher. 17p. (Orig.). 1991. pap. write for info. (*0-910147-93-0*) World Poetry Pr.

Passions of the Tongue: Language Devotion In Tamil India, 1891-1970. Sumathi Ramaswamy. LC 96-52441. (Studies on the History of Society & Culture). 343p. 1997. 50.00 (*0-520-20804-8*, Pub. by U CA Pr) Cal Prin Full Svc.

Passions of the Tongue: Language Devotion In Tamil India, 1891-1970. Sumathi Ramaswamy. LC 96-52441. (Studies on the History of Society & Culture). 343p. 1997. pap. 20.00 (*0-520-20805-6*, Pub. by U CA Pr) Cal Prin Full Svc.

Passions of the Voice: Hysteria, Narrative, & the Figure of the Speaking Woman, 1850-1915. Claire Kahane. LC 95-18035. 224p. 1995. text 49.95 (*0-8018-5161-0*); pap. text 15.95 (*0-8018-5162-9*) Johns Hopkins.

Passion's Paradise. Sonya T. Pelton. 544p. (Orig.). 1981. mass mkt. 3.25 (*0-89083-765-1*, Zebra Kensgtn) Kensgtn Pub Corp.

Passions, Pedagogies & 21st Century Technologies. Ed. by Gail E. Hawisher & Cynthia L. Selfe. 464p. 1999. pap. 29.95 (*0-87421-258-8*) Utah St U Pr.

Passion's Piano. Emilie E. Khair. Ed. by Carolyn W. Eklin. (Illus.). 124p. 1997. pap. 16.95 (*0-9661136-0-8*) Care Pub.

Passion's Prey. Rebecca King. LC 95-21635. (Romance Ser.). 189p. 1996. per. 2.99 (*0-373-03394-X*, 1-03394-3) Harlequin Bks.

Passion's Promise see Danielle Steel

Passion's Promise. Danielle Steel. 352p. 1976. mass mkt. 6.99 (*0-440-12926-5*) Dell.

Passion's Ransom. Betina M. Krahn. 1989. mass mkt. 3.95 (*0-8217-2703-6*, Zebra Kensgtn) Kensgtn Pub Corp.

Passion's Ransom. Betina M. Krahn. 1995. mass mkt. 5.99 (*0-8217-5130-1*, Zebra Kensgtn) Kensgtn Pub Corp.

Passion's Rapture. Penelope Neri. 1982. mass mkt. 3.50 (*0-89083-912-3*, Zebra Kensgtn) Kensgtn Pub Corp.

Passion's Shadow. Nicole Conn. 320p. 1995. 21.50 (*0-684-80326-7*, Fireside) S&S Trade Pap.

Passion's Shadow. Nicole Conn. 336p. 1997. reprint ed. mass mkt. 5.99 (*0-425-15664-8*) Berkley Pub.

Passion's Slave. Kay McMahon. 1983. mass mkt. 3.50 (*0-685-07884-1*, Zebra Kensgtn) Kensgtn Pub Corp.

Passions Spin the Plot. Vardis Fisher. 428p. 1934. 200.00 (*0-614-22021-1*, Idaho Center for the Bk) Heming W Studies.

***Passions Tell-All.** 1999. pap. write for info. (*0-06-102084-2*) HarpC.

***Passions Tell-All.** 2000. 25.00 (*0-06-107605-8*, HarpEntertain) Morrow Avon.

Passion's Timeless Hour. Vivian Knight-Jenkins. 368p. (Orig.). 1996. mass mkt. 4.99 (*0-505-52079-6*) Dorchester Pub Co.

Passion's Treasure. Betina Krahn. 448p. 1998. mass mkt. 5.99 (*0-8217-6039-4*, Zebra Kensgtn) Kensgtn Pub Corp.

Passion's Triumph. Mary R. Daheim. 432p. 1988. pap. 3.95 (*0-380-89850-0*, Avon Bks) Morrow Avon.

Passion's Verdict. Frances Williams. (Intimate Moments Ser.). 1993. per. 3.50 (*0-373-07508-1*, 5-07508-0) Silhouette.

Passion's Vixen. Carol Finch, pseud. 480p. 1984. mass mkt. 3.75 (*0-8217-1402-3*, Zebra Kensgtn) Kensgtn Pub Corp.

Passion's Web. Cassie Edwards. 1997. mass mkt. 3.50 (*0-8217-1358-2*, Zebra Kensgtn) Kensgtn Pub Corp.

Passion's Web. Cassie Edwards. 464p. 1997. mass mkt. 5.99 (*0-8217-5726-1*, Zebra Kensgtn) Kensgtn Pub Corp.

Passions Wild & Free. Janelle Taylor. 512p. 1992. mass mkt. 4.99 (*0-8217-3828-3*, Zebra Kensgtn) Kensgtn Pub Corp.

Passions Wild & Free. Janelle Taylor. 512p. 1995. pap. 5.99 (*0-8217-5275-8*, Zebra Kensgtn) Kensgtn Pub Corp.

Passions Wild & Free. Janelle Taylor. 1988. pap. 4.99 (*0-8217-3818-6*) NAL.

Passiv. G. Helbig & Fritz Kempter. 128p. 14.95 (*3-324-00706-2*) Langenscheidt.

Passivation of Metals & Semiconductors. Ed. by K. E. Heusler. (Materials Science Forum Ser.: Vols. 185-188). (Illus.). 1112p. (C). 1995. text 400.00 (*0-87849-692-0*, Pub. by Trans T Pub) Enfield Pubs NH.

Passive: A Comparative Linguistic Analysis. Anna Siewierska. LC 84-15606. 224p. 1984. 47.50 (*0-7099-3318-5*, Pub. by C Helm) Routldge.

Passive Activity Loss - Self-Study Guide: Continuing Professional Education Credits-Self-Study Course-Worth 8 CPE Credits. 214p. 1995. pap. 59.40 (*1-57402-308-X*) Athena Info Mgt.

Passive Activity Losses: Audit Technique Guides. (IRS Tax Audit Information Ser.). 186p. 1994. pap. 38.00 (*1-57402-115-X*) Athena Info Mgt.

Passive Activity Losses: Reference Guide. 232p. 1996. pap. 23.00 (*0-16-061975-0*) USGPO.

Passive & Active Filters: Theory & Implementation. Chen Wai-Kai. LC 85-9497. 528p. 1986. text 109.95 (*0-471-82352-X*) Wiley.

Passive & Active Microwave Circuits. Joseph Helszajn. LC 78-5787. 286p. reprint ed. pap. 88.70 (*0-608-15357-5*, 205634000060) Bks Demand.

Passive & Active Network Analysis & Synthesis. Aram Budak. (Illus.). 733p. (C). 1991. reprint ed. text 56.95 (*0-88133-625-4*) Waveland Pr.

Passive & Low Energy Alternatives. Yannas. 1983. 120.00 (*0-08-031109-1*, Pergamon Pr); pap. 60.00 (*0-08-031108-3*, Pergamon Pr) Elsevier.

Passive & Low Energy Alternatives, 3 vols., Vols. 1-3. Plea. 1985. 259.00 (*0-08-032541-6*, Pergamon Pr) Elsevier.

Passive & Low Energy Cooling of Buildings. Baruch Givoni. (Architecture Ser.). 272p. 1994. 69.95 (*0-471-28473-4*, VNR); text 59.95 (*0-442-01076-1*, VNR) Wiley.

Passive Annual Heat Storage: Improving the Design of Earth Shelters. John N. Hait. LC 85-60066. (Illus.). 152p. (Orig.). 1983. pap., spiral bd. 30.00 (*0-915207-00-1*) Rocky Mtn Res.

Passive Building Design: A Handbook of Natural Climatic Control. Narenda K. Bansal et al. LC 93-38991. 340p. 1994. 1874.00 (*0-444-81745-X*) Elsevier.

Passive Circuit Design. Vincent F. Leonard, Jr. (Engineering Design Ser.). (Illus.). 583p. (C). 1983. pap. text 17.95 (*0-87119-020-6*); student ed., ring bd. 10.95 (*0-87119-021-4*); ring bd. 49.95 (*0-87119-019-2*, EE-1001); 9.95 (*0-87119-022-2*) Heathkit-Zenith Ed.

Passive Components: A User's Guide. rev. ed. Ian R. Sinclair. (Illus.). 176p. 1991. pap. text 29.95 (*0-7506-0229-5*) Buttrwrth-Heinemann.

***Passive Components in Circuit Design.** Ian Sinclair. 320p. 2000. pap. 37.95 (*0-7506-4933-X*, Newnes) Buttrwrth-Heinemann.

Passive Components in France: A Strategic Entry Report, 1997. Compiled by Icon Group International Staff. (Illus.). 125p. 1999. ring bd. 1250.00 incl. audio compact disk (*0-7418-0822-6*) Icon Grp.

***Passive Cooling.** Jeffrey Cook. (Illus.). 593p. 2000. pap. 55.00 (*0-262-53171-2*) MIT Pr.

***Passive Damping & Isolation.** Ed. by T. Tupper Hyde. 384p. 1999. pap. text 84.00 (*0-8194-3146-X*) SPIE.

Passive Electronic Component Handbook. 2nd rev. ed. Charles A. Harper. LC 97-10743. (Illus.). 800p. 1997. 89.50 (*0-07-026698-0*) McGraw.

Passive Energy Dissipation Systems for Structural Design & Retrofit. Michael Constantinou et al. (NCEER Monograph Ser.: Vol. 1). 300p. 1998. pap. write for info. (*0-9656682-1-5*, MN-0001) Multidisciplinary Ctr.

Passive Energy Dissipation Systems in Structural Engineering. T. T. Soong & G. F. Dargush. LC 96-49979. 368p. 1997. 125.00 (*0-471-96821-8*) Wiley.

Passive Fit of Implant Supported Superstructures: Fiction or Reality? I. E. Naert. (Illus.). 113p. 1995. pap. 62.50 (*90-6186-716-9*, Pub. by Leuven Univ) Coronet Bks.

Passive Infrared Detection: Theory & Applications Joseph Caniou. LC 99-15354. 1999. write for info. (*0-7923-8532-2*) Kluwer Academic.

Passive Judiciary: Prosecutorial Discretion & the Guilty. fac. ed. Abraham S. Goldstein. LC 81-11749. (Edward Douglass White Lectures). 116p. 1981. reprint ed. pap. 36.00 (*0-7837-7734-5*, 204749000007) Bks Demand.

Passive Man's Guide to Seduction. Eric Weber & Franklin Parlamis. (Illus.). iv, 140p. 1996. pap. 19.95 (*0-914094-75-0*) Symphony Pr.

Passive Microwave Device Applications of High Temperature Superconductors. M. J. Lancaster. LC 96-14062. (Illus.). 356p. (C). 1997. text 85.00 (*0-521-48032-9*) Cambridge U Pr.

Passive Microwave Remote Sensing of Land-Atmosphere Interactions. Ed. by P. Pampaloni. 680p. 1994. 225.00 (*90-6764-186-3*, Pub. by VSP); pap. 85.00 (*90-6764-188-X*, Pub. by VSP) Coronet Bks.

Passive Microwave Remote Sensing of Oceans. Ed. by Victor Y. Raizer & Igor V. Cherny. LC 97-28549. (Illus.). 204p. 1998. 110.00 (*0-471-97170-7*) Wiley.

Passive Millimeter-Wave Imaging Technology. Ed. by Roger M. Smith. LC 98-111021. 29p. 1997. pap. 69.00 (*0-8194-2479-X*) SPIE.

Passive Millimeter-Wave Imaging Technology II. Ed. by Roger M. Smith. LC 98-227284. (Proceedings of SPIE Ser.: Vol. 3378). 184p. 1998. 59.00 (*0-8194-2827-2*) SPIE.

***Passive Millimeter-Wave Imaging Technology III.** Ed. by Roger M. Smith. 200p. 1999. pap. text 62.00 (*0-8194-3177-X*) SPIE.

***Passive Nihilism: Cultural Historiography & the Rhetorics of Scholarship.** Sande Cohen. 1999. pap. 18.95 (*0-312-22747-7*) St Martin.

Passive Optical Components for Optical Fiber Transmission. Norio Kashima. LC 94-39307. 342p. 1995. 37.00 (*0-89006-775-9*) Artech Hse.

Passive Optical Networks (PON) (Fiber Optics Reprint Ser.: Vol. 37). 301p. 1996. 75.00 (*0-614-18432-0*) Info Gatekeepers.

Passive Power: What Is It? Who Has It? How Do You Get It? Tamiko Staff. (Illus.). 160p. (Orig.). 1994. pap. 14.95 (*0-9644677-2-0*) Tamiko Corp.

Passive Pulse Generators. Smith. pap. text. write for info. (*0-471-49065-2*) Wiley.

Passive RF & Microwave Integrated Circuits. Leo G. Maloratsky. 300p. 1999. 69.95 (*0-7803-1191-4*, PC5661-QOE) Inst Electrical.

Passive Sentences in English & Portuguese. Milton M. Azevedo. LC 79-24987. 128p. reprint ed. pap. 39.70 (*0-7837-6305-0*, 204602000010) Bks Demand.

Passive Solar Buildings. J. Douglas Balcomb. (Solar Heat Technologies: Fundamentals & Applications Ser.: Vol. 7). (Illus.). 583p. 1992. 65.00 (*0-262-02341-5*) MIT Pr.

Passive Solar Commercial & Institutional Buildings: A Sourcebook of Examples & Design Insights. Robert Hastings. LC 93-5246. 464p. 1994. 200.00 (*0-471-93943-9*) Wiley.

Passive Solar Design & Construction Handbook. Steven Winter Associates Staff. LC 97-21327. 291p. 1997. 90.00 (*0-471-18308-3*) Wiley.

Passive Solar Energy: The Homeowner's Guide to Natural Heating & Cooling. 2nd ed. Bruce Anderson & Malcolm Wells. (Illus.). 197p. (Orig.). 1993. pap. 24.95 (*0-931790-95-6*) Brick Hse Pub.

Passive Solar Energy: The Homeowner's Guide to Natural Heating & Cooling. 2nd ed. Bruce Anderson & Malcolm Wells. (Illus.). 168p. (Orig.). 1996. pap. 24.95 (*0-931790-22-0*) Brick Hse Pub.

Passive Solar Heating Analysis, Suppl. 1. 60p. 1987. 32.00 (*0-910110-60-3*) Am Heat Ref & Air Eng.

Passive Solar Heating Analysis: A Design Manual. (Illus.). 720p. 1984. 73.00 (*0-910110-38-7*) Am Heat Ref & Air Eng.

Passive Solar Homes: Case Studies. 1996. lib. bdg. 253.95 (*0-8490-5957-7*) Gordon Pr.

Passive Solar Homes: Case Studies. 1997. lib. bdg. 250.95 (*0-8490-8176-9*) Gordon Pr.

Passive Solar House: Using Solar Design to Heat & Cool Your Home. James Kachadorian. LC 97-3264. (Real Goods Independent Living Bks.). 1997. pap. 24.95 (*0-930031-97-0*) Chelsea Green Pub.

Passive Solar House Basics. Peter Van Dresser. LC 95-37695. (Illus.). 136p. 1996. pap. 10.95 (*0-941270-90-4*) Ancient City Pr.

Passive Solar Schools: A Design Guide. (Building Bulletin Ser.: No. 79). 99p. 1994. pap. 45.00 (*0-11-270876-5*, HM08765, Pub. by Statnry Office) Balogh.

Passive Synthesis und Intersubjektivitat bei Edmund Husserl. I. Yamaguchi. 178p. 1982. lib. bdg. 99.50 (*90-247-2505-4*, Pub. by M Nijhoff) Kluwer Academic.

Passive Tranquility: The Sculpture of Filippo della Valle. Vernon H. Minor. LC 97-22739. (Transactions Ser.: Vol. 87, Pt. 5). (Illus.). 304p. 1998. pap. 22.00 (*0-87169-875-7*, T875-miv) Am Philos.

Passive Vibration Control. Mead. LC 98-48784. 554p. 1999. 270.00 (*0-471-94203-0*) Wiley.

Passive Voice. G. C. Scott. LC 96-33132. 256p. 1996. pap. 8.95 (*0-7867-0381-4*) Carroll & Graf.

Passivity: A Study of Its Development & Expression in Boys. Sylvia Brody. LC 64-18623. 184p. 1964. 28.50 (*0-8236-4020-5*) Intl Univs Pr.

Passivity & It's Breakdown. Ed. by P. M. Natishan et al. LC 98-218261. (Proceedings Ser.: Vol. 97-26). 1038p. 1998. 99.00 (*1-56677-179-X*) Electrochem Soc.

Passivity & Protection of Metals Against Corrosion. Nikon D. Tomashov & Galina P. Chernova. Tr. by Boris H. Tytell & Herbert H. Uhlig from RUS. LC 66-19933. (Illus.). 224p. 1967. reprint ed. pap. 69.50 (*0-608-05411-9*, 206588000006) Bks Demand.

Passivity-Based Control of Euler-Lagrange Systems. Romeo Ortega. LC 98-23128. 1998. 89.95 (*1-85233-016-3*) Spr-Verlag.

Passivity, Resistance & Collaboration: Intellectual Choices in Occupied Shanghai, 1937-1945. Poshek Fu. 1996. pap. text 14.95 (*0-8047-2796-1*) Stanford U Pr.

Passivity, Resistance, & Collaboration: Intellectual Choices in Occupied Shanghai, 1937-1945. Poshek Fu. LC 93-10239. (Illus.). 272p. (C). 1993. 35.00 (*0-8047-2172-6*) Stanford U Pr.

Passivsynonyme Als Elemente der Wissenschaftlichen Fachsprache Im Deutschen: Untersucht an Prominenten Fachtexten des 19 und 20 Jahrhunderts aus den Bereichen der Geisteswissenschaften und der Naturwissenschaften. Gook-Jin Gang. (Europaische Hochschulschriften Ser.: Reihe 21, Bd. 188). 189p. 1997. 189.00 (*3-631-32358-1*) P Lang Pubng.

Passkey. Freedom Barry. LC 92-27550. 80p. 1993. 15.00 (*0-9634250-4-8*) J & L Pubns.

***Passkey for Health Insurance Licensing.** 6th ed. 213p. 1999. pap. 26.00 (*0-7931-3537-0*) Dearborn.

Passkey for Health Insurance Licensing. 6th ed. Dearborn Financial Institute Staff. LC 98-46492. 1998. pap. text 26.00 (*0-7931-3233-9*) Dearborn.

***Passkey for Life Insurance Licensing.** 6th ed. Dearborn. 1999. pap. 26.00 (*0-7931-3536-2*) Dearborn.

Passkey for Life Insurance Licensing. 6th ed. Dearborn-R & R Newkirk Staff. LC 98-46603. 1998. pap. text 26.00 (*0-7931-3232-0*) Dearborn.

Passnotes: A Guardian Book. 256p. 1995. pap. 15.95 (*1-85702-267-X*, Pub. by Fourth Estate) Trafalgar.

Passover. 64p. (Orig.). 1986. 11.65 (*0-86683-779-5*) Harper SF.

Passover. Witness Lee. 58p. 1980. per. 3.00 (*0-87083-043-0*, 07-015-001) Living Stream Ministry.

Passover. David Mamet. LC 95-26035. (Illus.). 64p. 1995. text 14.95 (*0-312-13141-0*) St Martin.

***Passover.** David F. Marx. LC 00-29543. (Rookie Read-About Holidays Ser.). (Illus.). 2000. write for info. (*0-516-22214-7*) Childrens.

Passover. Miriam Nerlove. Ed. by Abby Levine. LC 89-35393. (Illus.). 24p. (J). (ps-1). 1989. pap. 4.95 (*0-8075-6361-7*); lib. bdg. 13.95 (*0-8075-6360-9*) A Whitman.

Passover. David Rose. 1999. pap. text 6.95 (*0-8172-3885-9*) Raintree Steck-V.

Passover. David W. Rose & Gill Rose. LC 96-42306. (World of Holidays Ser.). (Illus.). 32p. (J). 1997. lib. bdg. 22.83 (*0-8172-4607-X*) Raintree Steck-V.

Passover. Ed. by San Francisco Harper Staff. 64p. 1986. 21.45 (*0-86683-778-7*) Harper SF.

Passover. David Sokoloff. (Illus.). 12p. (J). (ps-1). 1998. bds. 5.00 (*0-614-30937-9*) Jewish Educ Toys.

Passover A-Z. 1990. 9.95 (*1-55774-049-6*) Lambda Pubs.

Passover & Easter: Origin & History to Modern Times. Ed. by Paul F. Bradshaw & Lawrence A. Hoffman. LC 98-41342. (Two Litugical Traditions Ser.: No. 5). 264p. 1999. 38.00 (*0-268-03857-0*) U of Notre Dame Pr.

Passover & Easter: The Symbolic Structuring of Sacred Seasons. Ed. by Paul F. Bradshaw & Lawrence A. Hoffman. LC 98-41341. (Two Litugical Traditions Ser.: No. 6). 216p. 1999. 38.00 (*0-268-03858-9*) U of Notre Dame Pr.

***Passover & Easter Vol. 5: Origin & History to Modern Times.** Paul F. Bradshaw. LC 98-41342. (Two Litugical Traditions Ser.). 264p. 1999. reprint ed. pap. 25.00 (*0-268-03859-7*) U of Notre Dame Pr.

***Passover & Easter Vol. 6: The Symbolic Structuring of Sacred Seasons.** Paul F. Bradshaw. LC 98-41341. (Two Litugical Traditions Ser.). 216p. 2000. reprint ed. pap. 25.00 (*0-268-03860-0*) U of Notre Dame Pr.

Passover Anthology. Ed. by Philip Goodman. LC 61-11706. (Holiday Anthologies Ser.). (Illus.). 496p. 1993. pap. 19.95 (*0-8276-0410-6*) JPS Phila.

Passover Celebration: A Haggadah for the Seder. Ed. by Leon Klenicki. 58p. 1980. pap. 2.95 (*0-930467-10-8*, PASS) Liturgy Tr Pubns.

Passover Desserts. Penny Eisenberg. 192p. 1996. 24.95 (*0-02-860999-9*) Macmillan.

Passover Fun: For Little Hands. Katherine J. Kahn. (Illus.). 32p. (J). (ps-1). 1991. pap., student ed. 3.95 (*0-929371-56-9*) Kar-Ben.

Passover Gourmet. Nira Rousso. (Illus.). 192p. 1987. 22.95 (*0-915361-66-3*) Lambda Pubs.

Passover Haggadah. (HEB & RUS., Illus.). 123p. 1992. pap. 9.95 (*0-88123-036-7*) Central Conf.

Passover Haggadah. Ben Z. Bokser. 120p. 1974. 8.00 (*0-88482-354-7*) Hebrew Pub.

Passover Haggadah. Nathan Goldberg. (Illus.). Date not set. pap. 2.65 (*0-614-07625-0*); pap. 4.75 (*0-614-07626-9*) Ktav.

Passover Haggadah. Roe Halper. (Illus.). 40p. (Orig.). (J). 1986. pap. 5.00 (*0-916326-03-9*) Bayberry Pr.

Passover Haggadah. Kaplan. 5.00 (*0-88482-350-4*) Hebrew Pub.

Passover Haggadah. Tr. by Aryeh Kaplan. (Torah Anthology - Meam Loez Ser.). 288p. 1989. 16.00 (*0-940118-36-X*) Moznaim.

Passover Haggadah. Walter Orenstein & Hertz Frankel. 197p. 1962. 3.50 (*0-88482-364-4*) Hebrew Pub.

Passover Haggadah. Jacob J. Reinman. Tr. by Armohom Marmorstein. LC 94-70476. (Illus.). 130p. 1994. 12.95 (*1-56062-251-2*); pap. 8.95 (*1-56062-252-0*) CIS Comm.

Passover Haggadah. Menachem M. Schneerson. Ed. by Yosef B. Marcus. Tr. by Yanky Tauber. (ENG & HEB.). 158p. 1999. pap. 10.00 (*0-8266-0283-5*, Merkos LInyonei Chinuch) Kehot Pubn Soc.

Passover Haggadah. Illus. by M. Van Dijk. 60p. (Orig.). 1996. pap. 2.95 (*1-888162-02-3*) Kuperand USA.

Passover Haggadah. Elie Wiesel. (Illus.). 144p. 1993. pap. 15.00 (*0-671-79996-7*) S&S Trade.

Passover Haggadah. Elie Wiesel. Ed. by Marion Wiesel. (Illus.). 144p. 1993. 30.00 (*0-671-73541-1*) S&S Trade.

Passover Haggadah. rev. ed. Ed. by Herbert Bronstein. LC 74-31161. (Illus.). 123p. 1974. pap. 13.95 (*0-916694-05-4*) Central Conf.

Passover Haggadah. rev. ed. Ed. by Morris Silverman. (Illus.). 1986. 10.00 (*0-87677-025-1*); pap. 6.95 (*0-685-04134-4*) Prayer Bk.

Passover Haggadah. 2nd rev. ed. Roe Halper. (Illus.). 40p. (Orig.). 1990. pap. 7.95 (*0-916326-05-5*) Bayberry Pr.

Passover Haggadah: A Family Haggadah for Passover. Illus. by Ismar David. 112p. 1998. pap. 10.95 (*0-9666561-0-5*) Shunammite Pr.

Passover Haggadah: A Messianic Celebration. Eric Lipson. LC 85-82168. (Illus.). 128p. 1986. pap. 8.00 (*0-9616148-5-4*) Purple Pomegranate.

Passover Haggadah: Riskin Haggadah. Shiomo Riskin. 1986. pap. 7.95 (*0-88125-014-7*) Ktav.

Passover Haggadah: The Complete Seder. Arthur M. Silver. 1980. 10.95 (*0-932232-06-X*) Menorah Pub.

Passover Haggadah: The Original Tradition of the Jews of Yemen. 2nd ed. Chaim Ben-Tsur. (Illus.). 120p. 1998. 18.00 (*0-9664128-0-X*) Assoc Jewish Yem.

Passover Haggadah - Mini Haggadah. Philip Birnbaum. 77p. pap. 2.95 (*0-88482-367-9*) Hebrew Pub.

P

An Asterisk (*) at the beginning of an entry indicates that the title is appearing for the first time.

*__Passover Haggadah for All Generations: A Modern Midrash.__ Morris E. Eson. LC 00-131662. (HEB & ENG., Illus.). 128p. 2000. pap. 18.00 (*0-9679517-0-4*) Adraba.

Passover Haggadah for Jewish Believers. rev. ed. Arnold G. Fruchtenbaum. 101p. 1970. reprint ed. pap. 5.00 (*0-914863-04-5*) Ariel Ministries.

Passover Haggaoah: Haggaoah for Passover. 5th ed. C. Schapiro. (ENG & HEB.). 105p. 1989. pap. 2.50 (*1-880880-00-8*) Israeli Trad.

Passover Haggudah Meamloez Russian Ed. Yaahov Kuli. Tr. by Geduliah Spinadel from HEB. (RUS.). 353p. 1998. 16.00 (*1-885220-05-7*) Moznaim.

Passover Journey. Barbara D. Goldin. 1999. pap. write for info. (*0-14-032867-X*, Viking) Viking Penguin.

Passover Journey. Barbara Diamond Goldin. (J). 1997. 11.19 (*0-606-11722-9*, Pub. by Turtleback) Demco.

Passover Journey: A Seder Companion. Barbara D. Goldin. LC 93-5133. (Illus.). 64p. (J). (ps-3). 1994. 15.99 (*0-670-82421-6*, Viking Child) Peng Put Young Read.

Passover Journey: A Seder Companion. Barbara D. Goldin. (Illus.). (J). 1997. pap. 7.99 (*0-14-056131-5*) Viking Penguin.

Passover Lite Kosher Cookbook. Gail Ashkanazi-Hankin. LC 95-50597. (Illus.). 192p. 1996. 19.95 (*1-56554-133-2*) Pelican.

Passover Magic. Roni Schotter. (Illus.). 32p. (J). (gr. k-3). 1998. pap. 5.95 (*0-316-77928-8*) Little.

Passover Magic. Roni Schotter. (J). 1998. 11.15 (*0-606-13696-7*, Pub. by Turtleback) Demco.

Passover Murder. Lee Harris. 1996. mass mkt. 5.99 (*0-449-14963-3*) Fawcett.

Passover Papers: Controversy, Myth, Fairy Tales & Nonsense. Paul Finch. LC 98-231505. 333p. 1998. pap. 13.95 (*1-57502-736-4*, PO2051) Morris Pubng.

Passover Passage. Susan Atlas. (YA). (gr. 4-7). 1991. pap. 5.95 (*0-933873-46-8*) Torah Aura.

Passover Plot: A New Interpretation of the Life & Death of Jesus. Hugh J. Schonfield. 320p. 1996. pap. 7.95 (*1-85230-836-2*, Pub. by Element MA) Penguin Putnam.

Passover Poems. Gertrude Rubin. (Illus.). 64p. (Orig.). 1991. pap. 8.00 (*1-879260-00-X*) Evanston Pub.

Passover Pop-Up Book. Sol Scharfstein. LC 99-179685. (Illus.). (J). 1985. 9.95 (*0-88125-183-6*) Ktav.

Passover Seder. Ron Wolfson. (Art of Jewish Living Ser.). (Illus.). 332p. 1988. teacher ed. 4.95 (*0-935665-04-8*); student ed. 4.00 (*0-935665-20-X*); pap. text 14.95 (*0-935665-18-8*) Fed Jewish Mens Clubs.

Passover Seder. Ron Wolfson. LC 96-46455. (The Art of Jewish Living Ser.). 352p. 1995. pap. 16.95 (*1-879045-93-1*) Jewish Lights.

Passover Seder: An Anthropological Perspective on Jewish Culture. Ruth F. Cernea. LC 95-18665. 190p. (C). 1995. reprint ed. pap. 24.50 (*0-8191-9926-5*) U Pr of Amer.

Passover Seder: Ritual & Menu for an Observance by Christians. Barbara B. Thompson. 24p. 1988. pap. 4.00 (*0-8066-2133-8*, 10-21338) Augsburg Fortress.

Passover Seder No. 2: Art of Jewish Living. Ron Wolfson. Tr. by Igor Kotler from ENG. (Art of Jewish Living Ser.: No. 2). (RUS., Illus.). 280p. (Orig.). 1991. pap. 14.95 (*0-935665-19-6*) Fed Jewish Mens Clubs.

Passover Seder Teacher's Guide. Ron Wolfson. (Art of Jewish Living Ser.). 1996. pap. text, teacher ed. 4.95 (*1-879045-95-8*) Jewish Lights.

Passover Seder Workbook. Ron Wolfson. (The Art of Jewish Living Ser.). 1996. pap. text, wbk. ed. 6.95 (*1-879045-94-X*) Jewish Lights.

Passover Survival Kit. rev. ed. Shimon Apisdorf. 160p. 1997. 16.95 (*1-881927-10-5*) Leviathan OH.

Passover Table: New & Traditional Recipes for Your Seders & the Entire Passover Week. Susan R. Friedland. LC 93-35991. (Illus.). 96p. 1999. pap. 18.00 (*0-06-095026-9*, Perennial) HarperTrade.

*__Passover Table: New & Traditional Recipes for Your Seders & the Entire Passover Week.__ Susan R. Friedland. (Illus.). 95p. (Orig.). 2000. reprint ed. pap. 18.00 (*0-7881-9362-7*) DIANE Pub.

Passover the Two Lambs. George A. McCabe. 136p. 1988. pap. 19.95 (*0-929529-08-1*) Vision Ministry Pr.

*__Passovotchka: Moscow Dynamo in Britain 1945.__ David Downing. 1999. 32.50 (*0-7475-4456-5*, Pub. by Blmsbury Pub) Trafalgar.

Passport. 1995. write for info. (*1-56476-907-0*, Victor Bks) Chariot Victor.

Passport. Mary E. Mark. LC 74-13170. 58p. 1976. pap. 9.95 (*0-912810-14-9*) Lustrum Pr.

Passport. William Mirza & Thom Lemmons. 300p. 1995. pap. 9.99 (*1-56476-390-0*, 6-3390, Victor Bks) Chariot Victor.

Passport. Herta Muller. 96p. 1992. pap. 7.95 (*1-85242-139-8*) Serpents Tail.

Passport: An Introduction to Travel & Tourism Industry. 2nd ed. David W. Howell. 496p. (C). 1992. pap. text 43.00 (*0-538-70617-1*) S-W Pub.

*__Passport: Introduction to Travel & Tourism.__ 3rd ed. Howell. (Hospitality, Travel & Tourism Ser.). (C). 2000. pap. 33.50 (*0-8273-8448-3*) Delmar.

*__Passport: What Really Happened at Calvary.__ Carlisle John Peterson. LC 98-91106. 200p. 1999. pap. 39.00 incl. audio (*1-889448-26-5*) NBN Publishers Group.

Passport & the Door: A Book of 2 Plays. Pierre Bourgeade. Tr. by Sande Zeig from FRE. 120p. (Orig.). 1984. pap. text 8.95 (*0-913745-06-5*) Ubu Repertory.

*__Passport Argentina: Your Pocket Guide to Argentine Business, Customs & Etiquette.__ Andrea Mandell Campbell. Ed. by Barbara Szerlip. LC 99-16124. 1999. pap. text 6.95 (*1-885073-21-6*) Wrld Trade Pr.

Passport Atlas. Rand McNally Staff. (Illus.). 128p. 1996. pap. text 5.95 (*0-528-83883-0*) Rand McNally.

Passport Brazil: Your Pocket Guide to Brazilian Business, Customs & Etiquette. Elizabeth A. Herrington. Ed. by Barbara Szerlip. LC 97-26551. 1997. pap. text 6.95 (*1-885073-18-6*) Wrld Trade Pr.

Passport China: Your Pocket Guide to Chinese Business, Customs & Etiquette. Jenni Li. Ed. by Barbara Szerlip. LC 96-14389. (Passport to the World Ser.). (Illus.). 96p. (Orig.). 1996. pap. 6.95 (*1-885073-16-X*) Wrld Trade Pr.

*__Passport Diver Manual.__ 2nd ed. (Illus.). 12p. 1999. pap. 8.95 (*1-880229-53-6*, 4072 Guide) Concept Sys.

Passport English-Hebrew Learner's Dictionary. (HEB & ENG.). pap. 19.50 (*0-87559-217-1*) Shalom.

Passport Evaluation of Drake SW8 Receiver. Jock Elliott et al. (Radio Database International White Paper). (Illus.). 24p. (Orig.). 1994. pap. 6.95 (*0-914941-34-8*) IBS PA.

Passport Evaluation of Popular Outdoor Antennas. Stephen Bohac et al. (Radio Database International White Paper). (Illus.). 34p. (Orig.). 1993. pap. 6.95 (*0-914941-31-3*) IBS PA.

Passport Evaluation of the ICOM IC-R9000 Receiver. Lawrence Magne et al. (Radio Database International White Paper). (Illus.). 28p. (Orig.). 1990. pap. 6.95 (*0-914941-21-6*, WP14) IBS PA.

Passport Evaluation of YAESU FRG-100 Receiver. Jock Elliott et al. (Radio Database International White Paper). (Illus.). 20p. (Orig.). 1995. pap. 6.95 (*0-914941-53-4*) IBS PA.

Passport for a Pilgrim. large type ed. James Leasor. 381p. 1982. 27.99 (*0-7089-0837-3*) Ulverscroft.

Passport France: Your Pocket Guide to French Business, Customs & Etiquette. Nadine Joseph. Ed. by Barbara Szerlip. LC 96-28184. (Passport to the World Ser.). (Illus.). 96p. (Orig.). 1996. pap. 6.95 (*1-885073-29-1*) Wrld Trade Pr.

Passport French. Cortina Language Institute Staff. (Passport Language Ser.). (ENG & FRE.). 1995. pap. 12.95 incl. audio (*0-8050-2129-9*) H Holt & Co.

Passport German. Cortina Language Institute Staff. (Passport Language Ser.). (ENG & GER.). 1995. pap. 12.95 incl. audio (*0-8050-2130-2*) H Holt & Co.

Passport Germany: Your Pocket Guide to German Business, Customs & Etiquette. Roland Flamini. Ed. by Barbara Szerlip. LC 96-49110. (Passport to the World Ser.). (Illus.). 96p. (Orig.). 1997. pap. 6.95 (*1-885073-20-8*) Wrld Trade Pr.

Passport Handbook see Repertoire des passeports

Passport Handbook. David Henny.Tr. of Repertoire des passeports. 1994. pap. 945.00 (*90-6211-040-1*, Pub. by Keesing Security) Kluwer Law Intl.

Passport Hong Kong: Your Pocket Guide to Hong Kong Business, Customs & Etiquette. Andrew Grzeskowiak. Ed. by Barbara Szerlip. LC 96-14868. (Passport to the World Ser.). (Illus.). 96p. (Orig.). 1996. pap. 6.95 (*1-885073-31-3*) Thomson Learn.

Passport India: Your Pocket Guide to Indian Business, Customs & Etiquette. Manoj Joshi. Ed. by Barbara Szerlip. LC 96-33489. (Passport to the World Ser.). (Illus.). 96p. (Orig.). 1997. pap. 6.95 (*1-885073-23-2*) Wrld Trade Pr.

Passport Indonesia: Your Pocket Guide to Indonesian Business, Culture & Etiquette. Gregory Cole. Ed. by Barbara Szerlip. LC 97-12973. (Passport to the World Ser.). (Illus.). 96p. (Orig.). 1996. pap. 6.95 (*1-885073-37-2*) Thomson Learn.

Passport Israel: Your Pocket Guide to Israeli Business, Customs, & Etiquette. Donna Rosenthal. Ed. by Barbara Szerlip. LC 96-28183. (Passport to the World Ser.). (Illus.). 96p. (Orig.). 1996. pap. 6.95 (*1-885073-22-4*) Wrld Trade Pr.

Passport Italian. Cortina Language Institute Staff. (Passport Language Ser.). (ENG & ITA.). 1995. pap. 12.95 incl. audio (*0-8050-2131-0*) H Holt & Co.

Passport Italy: Your Pocket Guide to Italian Business, Customs & Etiquette. Claudia Gioseffi. Ed. by Barbara Szerlip. (Passport to the World Ser.). (Illus.). 96p. (Orig.). 1997. pap. 6.95 (*1-885073-34-8*) Wrld Trade Pr.

Passport Japan: Your Pocket Guide to Japanese Business, Customs & Etiquette. Dean Engel & Ken Murakami. Ed. by Barbara Szerlip. LC 96-360. (Passport to the World Ser.). (Illus.). 96p. (Orig.). 1996. pap. 6.95 (*1-885073-17-8*) Wrld Trade Pr.

Passport Korea: Your Pocket Guide to Korean Business, Culture & Etiquette. Kevin Keating. Ed. by Barbara Szerlip. LC 96-49290. (Passport to the World Ser.). (Illus.). 96p. (Orig.). 1997. pap. 6.95 (*1-885073-39-9*) Wrld Trade Pr.

Passport, Lotus Approach. Lotus Staff. (NO - Novell/Wordperfect Ser.). 1995. 26.95 (*0-538-65269-1*) S-W Pub.

Passport Lotus Approach Maintenance. Lotus Staff. (NO - Novell/Wordperfect Ser.). 1995. 15.95 (*0-538-65270-5*) S-W Pub.

Passport Lotus Notes Client Maintenance. Lotus Staff. (NO - Novell/Wordperfect Ser.). 1995. 31.95 (*0-538-65268-3*) S-W Pub.

Passport Malaysia: Your Pocket Guide to Malaysian Business, Customs & Etiquette. Ed. by Barbara Szerlip. 96p. 1996. pap. 6.95 (*1-885073-36-4*) Thomson Learn.

Passport Mexico: Your Pocket Guide to Mexican Business, Customs & Etiquette. Randy Malat. Ed. by Barbara Szerlip. LC 96-25689. (Passport to the World Ser.). (Illus.). 96p. (Orig.). 1996. pap. 6.95 (*1-885073-30-5*) Wrld Trade Pr.

Passport Pal: The Pacific Rim: A Business Traveler's Guide to Fifteen Pacific Rim Destinations, 1999 Edition. 4th ed. John W. Brooks. (Illus.). viii, 68p. 1998. pap. 19.95 (*0-9655022-2-8*) Passport Pal Pr.

Passport Pal - The Pacific Rim: A Business Traveler's Guide to Fourteen Pacific Rim Countries, 1998 Edition. 3rd ed. John W. Brooks. (Illus.). viii, 63p. 1997. pap. 19.95 (*0-9655022-1-X*) Passport Pal Pr.

Passport Philippines: Your Pocket Guide to Philippine Business, Customs & Etiquette. Luis Francia. Ed. by Barbara Szerlip. LC 96-39740. (Passport to the World Ser.). (Illus.). 96p. (Orig.). 1997. pap. 6.95 (*1-885073-40-2*) Wrld Trade Pr.

*__Passport Photos.__ Amitava Kumar. LC 99-31257. 368p. 2000. 48.00 (*0-520-21816-7*, Pub. by U CA Pr) Cal Prin Full Svc.

*__Passport Photos.__ Amitava Kumar. LC 99-31257. (Illus.). 340p. 2000. pap. 17.95 (*0-520-21817-5*, Pub. by U CA Pr) Cal Prin Full Svc.

Passport Poland: Your Pocket Guide to Polish Business, Customs & Etiquette. Serge Koperdak. Ed. by Barbara Szerlip. LC 99-32548. 96p. 1996. pap. 6.95 (*1-885073-33-X*) Thomson Learn.

Passport Program: A Journey Through Emotional, Social, Cognitive, & Self-Development (Grades 1-5) Ann Vernon. LC 98-66600. 334p. (gr. 1-5). 1998. pap. text 32.95 (*0-87822-375-4*) Res Press.

Passport Program: A Journey Through Emotional, Social, Cognitive, & Self-Development (Grades 6-8) Ann Vernon. LC 98-66600. 264p. 1998. pap. text 32.95 (*0-87822-376-2*) Res Press.

Passport Program: A Journey Through Emotional, Social, Cognitive, & Self-Development (Grades 9-12) Ann Vernon. LC 98-66597. 288p. (gr. 9-12). 1998. pap. text 32.95 (*0-87822-377-0*) Res Press.

Passport Road Atlas: Europe. 2nd ed. Passport Books Staff. LC 93-86310. 162p. 1995. pap. 16.95 (*0-8442-9474-8*, Passprt Bks) NTC Contemp Pub Co.

Passport Russia: Your Pocket Guide to Russian Business, Customs & Etiquette. Ed. by Barbara Szerlip. LC 97-45163. 96p. 1997. pap. text 6.95 (*1-885073-32-1*) Wrld Trade Pr.

Passport Singapore: Your Pocket Guide to Singaporean Business, Customs & Etiquette. Jane E. Lasky. Ed. by Barbara Szerlip. LC 97-22973. (Computer Science). (Illus.). 96p. (Orig.). 1996. pap. 6.95 (*1-885073-38-0*) Thomson Learn.

Passport South Africa: Your Pocket Guide to South African Business, Customs & Etiquette. Charles Mitchell. Ed. by Barbara Szerlip. LC 97-25259. 96p. 1996. pap. 6.95 (*1-885073-19-4*) Thomson Learn.

Passport Spain: Your Pocket Guide to Spanish Business, Customs & Etiquette. Himilce Novas. Ed. by Barbara Szerlip. LC 96-52741. (Passport to the World Ser.). (Illus.). 96p. (Orig.). 1997. pap. 6.95 (*1-885073-35-6*) Wrld Trade Pr.

Passport Spanish. Cortina Language Institute Staff. (Passport Language Ser.). (ENG & SPA.). 1995. pap. 12.95 incl. audio (*0-8050-2128-0*) H Holt & Co.

Passport Taiwan: Your Pocket Guide to Taiwanese Business, Culture, & Etiquette. Jeffrey Curry. Ed. by Barbara Szerlip. LC 97-8028. (Passport to the World Ser.). (Illus.). 96p. (Orig.). 1997. pap. 6.95 (*1-885073-27-5*) Wrld Trade Pr.

Passport Thailand: Your Pocket Guide to Thai Business, Customs & Etiquette. Naomi Wise. Ed. by Barbara Szerlip. LC 96-14869. (Passport to the World Ser.). (Illus.). 96p. (Orig.). 1997. pap. 6.95 (*1-885073-26-7*) Wrld Trade Pr.

Passport to America Series. 1984. teacher ed. 6.99 (*0-8325-0429-7*) NTC Contemp Pub Co.

Passport to Assassination: The Never Before Told Story of Lee Harvey Oswald by the KGB Colonel. Oleg Nechiporenko. 1993. 22.50 (*1-55972-210-X*, Birch Ln Pr) Carol Pub Group.

Passport to Chinese. Lin Shan. 264p. pap. 14.95 (*0-89346-862-2*) Heian Intl.

Passport to Danger. Carolyn Keene. Ed. by Anne Greenberg. (Nancy Drew & Hardy Boys Super Mystery Ser.: No. 19). 224p. (YA). (gr. 6 up). 1994. mass mkt. 3.99 (*0-671-78177-4*, Archway) PB.

Passport to Danger. Carolyn Keene. (Nancy Drew & Hardy Boys Super Mystery Ser.: No. 19). (YA). (gr. 6 up). 1994. 9.09 (*0-606-06600-4*, Pub. by Turtleback) Demco.

Passport to English: Grammar Exercises in Context, Vol. 1. 2nd ed. Jane Yedlin & Magdala Raupp. LC 95-34043. 1995. pap. text 13.60 (*0-201-82590-2*) Longman.

Passport to Eternal Life: Poetry, 1980-1990. Valery Oisteanu. Ed. by Allen J. Sheinman. (Illus.). 72p. (Orig.). 1990. pap. text 8.00 (*0-685-45645-5*) Pass.

Passport to Europe's Small Hotels & Inns. 9th ed. Beverly Beyer & Ed A. Rabey. 272p. 1993. pap. 9.95 (*0-471-58298-0*) Wiley.

Passport to France Travel Pak. Robert S. Kane. (Illus.). student ed. 29.95 incl. audio (*0-8442-9229-X*, Passprt Bks) NTC Contemp Pub Co.

Passport to Gardening: A Sourcebook for the Twenty-First Century Gardener. Katherine Laliberte & Ben Watson. LC 97-31662. (Illus.). 320p. 1999. pap. 24.95 (*1-890132-00-4*) Chelsea Green Pub.

Passport to Happiness. Jessica Steele. (Romance Ser.: No. 3077). 1990. per. 2.50 (*0-373-03077-0*) Harlequin Bks.

Passport to Heaven: Gender Roles in the Unification Church. Kathleen S. Lowney. LC 92-20892. (Cults & Nonconventional Religious Groups Ser.). 248p. 1992. text 25.00 (*0-8153-0775-6*) Garland.

Passport to Hollywood: Hollywood Films, European Directors. James Morrison. LC 98-13702. (Series in Postmodern Culture). (Illus.). 320p. (C). 1998. text 65.50 (*0-7914-3937-2*); pap. text 21.95 (*0-7914-3938-0*) State U NY Pr.

Passport to Italian. rev. ed. Charles Berlitz. 240p. 1979. mass mkt. 6.99 (*0-451-16764-3*, Sig) NAL.

Passport to Jewish Music: Its History, Traditions & Culture. Irene Heskes. 1998. pap. 14.95 (*0-933676-45-X*) Tara Pubns.

Passport to Jewish Music: Its History, Traditions & Culture, 33. Irene Heskes. LC 93-35835. (Contributions to the Study of Music & Dance Ser.: No. 33). 368p. 1994. 59.95 (*0-313-28035-5*, Greenwood Pr) Greenwood.

Passport to Magonia. Jacques Vallee. LC 93-3427. 384p. 1993. reprint ed. pap. 17.95 (*0-8092-3796-2*, 379620, Contemporary Bks) NTC Contemp Pub Co.

Passport to Manhood. Joseph Desloge, Jr. 150p. 1995. 15.00 (*0-9616369-1-2*) St Louis Human.

Passport to New York Restaurants. 12th rev. ed. Peter D. Meltzer et al. Orig. Title: Passport to New York the 400 Restaurants That Matter Most. (Illus.). 212p. 1998. pap. 10.95 (*0-937413-12-7*) Passport NYC.

Passport to New York the 400 Restaurants That Matter Most see Passport to New York Restaurants

Passport to North American Trade: Rules of Origin & Customs Procedures under NAFTA. Jimmie V. Reyna. LC 95-22565. (NAFTA Ser.). 1995. pap. write for info. (*0-07-172582-2*) Shepards.

Passport to North Carolina Historic Sites. (Illus.). 52p. 1998. pap. 5.00 (*0-86526-281-0*) NC Archives.

Passport to Oblivion. 1964th ed. James Leasor. (Spies & Intrigues Ser.: No. 5). 220p. pap. 5.95 (*0-918172-18-7*) Leetes Isl.

Passport to Palm Springs. Passport Publications Staff & Wayne Cimperman. 120p. 1994. 9.95 (*0-9645114-0-1*) Passprt Publ.

Passport to Palm Springs, Vol. II. 2nd ed. (Illus.). 120p. (Orig.). 1995. pap. 11.95 (*0-614-14270-9*) Passprt Publ.

Passport to Palm Springs, Vol. III. (Illus.). 120p. (Orig.). 1996. 11.95 (*0-9645114-3-6*) Passprt Publ.

Passport to Paradise. large type ed. Kay Winchester. 1990. 27.99 (*0-7089-2267-8*) Ulverscroft.

*__Passport to Paris.__ Mary-Kate Olsen & Ashley Olsen. 2000. mass mkt. 7.95 (*0-694-01043-X*) HarpC.

Passport to Peril. large type ed. James Leasor. 1980. 27.99 (*0-7089-0428-9*) Ulverscroft.

Passport to Peril. James Leasor. (Spies & Intrigues Ser.: No. 6). 240p. reprint ed. pap. 5.95 (*0-918172-19-5*) Leetes Isl.

Passport to Pittsburgh. Beth Marcello & Earl Bohn. Ed. by Mary Hughes & James E. Turner. LC 93-31594. 320p. 1993. text 45.00 (*0-9630029-6-1*) Community Comm.

*__Passport to Practical & Vocational Nursing.__ Linda Blair. (Illus.). 288p. 1998. teacher ed. write for info. (*1-55664-438-8*) Mosby Inc.

*__Passport to Profits: Why the Next Investment Windfalls Will Be Found Abroad - And How to Grab Your Share.__ Mark Mobius & Stephen Fenichell. 2000. pap. 16.95 (*0-446-67605-5*) Warner Bks.

Passport to Profits: Why the Next Investment Windfalls Will Be Found Abroad - And How to Grab Your Share. Mark Mobius & Steve Fenichell. LC 98-38868. 416p. 1999. 25.00 (*0-446-52251-1*, Pub. by Warner Bks) Little.

Passport to Russia. Sukey S. Gross. (Girls of Riukah Gross Academy Ser.). (Illus.). 158p. (J). (gr. 5-8). 1989. 13.95 (*0-935063-59-5*); pap. 10.95 (*0-935063-60-9*) CIS Comm.

Passport to Russia. Ed. by Alla L. Nazarenko & Keith Rawson-Jones. (SAP - Languages Ser.). 200p. 1999. pap. 19.95 (*1-85075-879-4*, Pub. by Sheffield Acad) CUP Services.

Passport to Russian. Charles Berlitz. (ENG & RUS.). 208p. (Orig.). 1992. mass mkt. 6.99 (*0-451-17200-0*, Sig) NAL.

Passport to San Diego. 1996. 19.95 (*0-9645114-2-8*) Passprt Publ.

Passport to Sanity. Ruby Goodwin. (Illus.). 62p. pap. 4.95 (*0-934482-00-4*) Hathor House Bks.

Passport to Spanish. rev. ed. Charles Berlitz. 240p. 1993. mass mkt. 6.99 (*0-451-17831-9*, Sig) NAL.

Passport to the Bible: An Explorer's Guide. Ed. by Fred Wagner. LC 99-21816. 108p. 1999. pap. 6.99 (*0-8308-1171-0*, 1171) InterVarsity.

Passport to the Cosmos: Human Transformation & Alien Encounters. John E. Mack. LC 99-35412. 320p. 1999. 24.00 (*0-517-70568-0*, Crown) Crown Pub Group.

*__Passport to the Cosmos: Human Transformation & Alien Encounters.__ John E. Mack. 224p. 2000. pap. 14.00 (*0-609-80557-6*, Three Riv Pr) Crown Pub Group.

Passport to the Pub: The Tourist's Guide to Pub Etiquette. Kate Fox. 76p. 1996. pap. 8.95 (*1-899344-09-8*) Dufour.

Passport to the World of English, 4 vols., Set. Martha A. Lane. (Illus.). 1486p. 1997. ring bd. 87.00 incl. audio (*1-877596-37-X*) Literacy & Evangelism.

Passport to Treehouse Court. Judy M. Zocchi. (Illus.). 16p. 1998. pap. 4.99 (*1-891997-02-5*) Dingles & Co.

Passport to World Band Radio: 2000 Edition. Ed. by Lawrence Magne et al. (Illus.). 560p. 1999. pap. 19.95 (*0-914941-49-6*, PAW00P, Pub. by IBS PA) Natl Bk Netwk.

Passport to Your National Parks. 2nd rev. ed. Intro. by Eastern National Park & Monument Assoc. Staff. (Illus.). 104p. 1986. pap. 5.95 (*0-915992-53-1*) Eastern National.

Passport to Yugoslavia. Simon Vladovich. (Illus.). 327p. (Orig.). (C). 1990. pap. text 19.95 (*0-9623753-0-6*) Vladovich Intl Pub.

Passport TravelMate & World Atlas. Hammond Staff. LC 97-675020. (Illus.). 128p. 1999. pap. 5.95 (*0-8437-1275-9*) Hammond World.

Passport U. S. A. Your Pocket Guide to North American Business, Customs & Etiquette. Dean Engel. Ed. by Barbara Szerlip. LC 96-34757. (Passport to the World Ser.). (Illus.). 96p. (Orig.). 1996. pap. 6.95 (*1-885073-15-1*) Wrld Trade Pr.

P

An Asterisk (*) at the beginning of an entry indicates that the title is appearing for the first time.

Passport United Kingdom: Your Pocket Guide to British Business, Customs & Etiquette. Timothy Harper. Ed. by Barbara Szerlip. LC 96-28182. (Passport to the World Ser.). (Illus.). 96p. (Orig.). 1996. pap. 6.95 (*1-885073-28-3*) Wrld Trade Pr.

Passport Vietnam: Your Pocket Guide to Vietnamese Business, Customs & Etiquette. Jeffrey Curry & Jim C. Nguyen. Ed. by Barbara Szerlip. LC 96-14867. (Passport to the World Ser.). (Illus.). 96p. (Orig.). 1997. pap. 6.95 (*1-885073-25-9*) Wrld Trade Pr.

PassPorter Walt Disney World: The Unique Travel Guide, Planner, Organizer, Journal & Keepsake. Jennifer Watson & Dave Marx. (PassPorter Ser.). (Illus.). 208p. 1999. pap. 19.95 (*0-9668994-0-7*) MediaMarx Inc.

***PassPorter Walt Disney World 2000: The Unique Travel Guide, Planner, Organizer, Journal.** 2nd ed. Jennifer Watson & Dave Marx. (PassPorter Travel Ser.). (Illus.). 2000. spiral bd. 19.95 (*0-9668994-1-5*, PassPorter) MediaMarx Inc.

***PassPorter Walt Disney World 2000: The Unique Travel Guide, Planner, Organizer, Journal.** 2nd ed. Jennifer Watson & Dave Marx. (PassPorter Travel Ser.). (Illus.). 260p. 2000. ring bd. write for info. (*0-9668994-2-3*, PassPorter) MediaMarx Inc.

***PassPorter's Field Guide to Disneyland.** Jennifer Watson & Dave Marx. (PassPorter Field Guides Ser.). (Illus.). 2000. pap. write for info. (*0-9668994-3-1*, PassPorter) MediaMarx Inc.

Passport's European Atlas for Travelers. 252p. 1992. pap. 24.95 (*0-8442-9488-8*, Passprt Bks) NTC Contemp Pub Co.

Passport's Guide to Ethnic Chicago. Rich Lindberg. (Illus.). 300p. 1995. pap. 14.95 (*0-8442-9541-8*, Passprt Bks) NTC Contemp Pub Co.

Passport's Guide to Ethnic London. (Illus.). 224p. 1991. pap. 11.95 (*0-8442-9549-3*, Passprt Bks) NTC Contemp Pub Co.

Passport's Guide to Ethnic London: A Complete Guide to the Many Faces & Cultures of London. 2nd ed. Ian McAuley. (Illus.). 224p. 1994. pap. 14.95 (*0-8442-9632-5*, 9604X, Passprt Bks) NTC Contemp Pub Co.

Passports Guide to Ethnic New York. Mike Leeds. (Illus.). 408p. 1994. pap. 14.95 (*0-8442-9542-6*, Passprt Bks) NTC Contemp Pub Co.

Passport's Guide to Ethnic New York: A Complete Guide to the Many Faces & Cultures of New York. 2nd ed. Mark Leeds. LC 95-38970. (Illus.). 528p. 1995. pap. 14.95 (*0-8442-9633-3*, 96333, Passprt Bks) NTC Contemp Pub Co.

Passport's Guide to the Best of Scotland. Ed. by Andrew Leslie. (Illus.). 522p. 1996. pap. 17.95 (*0-8442-4874-6*, 48746, Passprt Bks) NTC Contemp Pub Co.

Passport's Guide to the Business Capitals of the World. Ed. by Business Travel Staff. 320p. 1986. 29.95 (*0-8442-9491-8*, Passprt Bks) NTC Contemp Pub Co.

Passport's Guide to the Business Capitals of the World. Ed. by Business Travel Staff. 320p. 1994. pap. 14.95 (*0-8442-9492-6*, Passprt Bks) NTC Contemp Pub Co.

Passport's Health Guide for International Travelers. Thomas P. Sakmar et al. 160p. 1993. pap. 5.95 (*0-8442-9513-2*, Passprt Bks) NTC Contemp Pub Co.

Passport's Health Guide for International Travelers. 2nd ed. Thomas P. Sakmar et al. LC 94-10043. (Illus.). 140p. 1994. pap. 12.95 (*0-8442-9524-8*, Passprt Bks) NTC Contemp Pub Co.

***Passport's Illustrated Guide to Amsterdam.** 3rd ed. Christopher Catling. (Passport's Illustrated Travel Guides from Thomas Cook Ser.). 192p. 2000. pap. 14.95 (*0-658-00151-5*, 001515) NTC Contemp Pub Co.

***Passport's Illustrated Guide to Bali & Java.** 2nd ed. Ben Davies. (Passport's Illustrated Travel Guides from Thomas Cook Ser.). 192p. 2000. pap. 14.95 (*0-658-00152-3*, 001523) NTC Contemp Pub Co.

***Passport's Illustrated Guide to Boston & New England.** 3rd ed. Robert Holmes. (Passport's Illustrated Travel Guides from Thomas Cook Ser.). 192p. 2000. pap. 14.95 (*0-658-00503-0*) NTC Contemp Pub Co.

***Passport's Illustrated Guide to Budapest.** 2nd ed. Louis James. (Passport's Illustrated Travel Guides from Thomas Cook Ser.). 192p. 2000. pap. 14.95 (*0-658-00147-7*, 001477) NTC Contemp Pub Co.

Passport's Illustrated Guide to Caribbean Cruising. 2nd ed. Thomas Cook. (Passport's Illustrated Ser.). (Illus.). 192p. 2000. pap. 14.95 (*0-8442-1176-1*, 11761, Passprt Bks) NTC Contemp Pub Co.

***Passports Illustrated Guide to Egypt.** Michael Haag. (Passport's Illustrated Ser.). (Illus.). 192p. 2000. pap. 14.95 (*0-658-00148-5*, 001485, Passprt Bks) NTC Contemp Pub Co.

***Passport's Illustrated Guide to Florida.** 2nd ed. Eric Bailey. (Passport's Illustrated Travel Guides from Thomas Cook Ser.). 192p. 2000. pap. 14.95 (*0-658-00505-7*, 005057) NTC Contemp Pub Co.

***Passport's Illustrated Guide to Ireland.** 3rd ed. Louis James. (Illus.). 192p. 2000. pap. 14.95 (*0-658-00504-9*) NTC Contemp Pub Co.

Passport's Illustrated Guide to Jamaica. 2nd ed. Christopher Baker. (Passport's Illustrated Ser.). 192p. 2000. pap. 14.95 (*0-8442-1136-2*, 11362, Passprt Bks) NTC Contemp Pub Co.

Passport's Illustrated Guide to Mexico. 2nd ed. Thomas Cook. (Passport's Illustrated Ser.). (Illus.). 192p. 2000. pap. 14.95 (*0-8442-1154-0*, 11540, Passprt Bks) NTC Contemp Pub Co.

Passport's Illustrated Guide to Normandy. 2nd ed. Kathy Arnold. LC 98-67245. (Passport's Illustrated Travel Guides Ser.). (Illus.). 192p. 2000. pap. 14.95 (*0-8442-1151-6*, 11516, Passprt Bks) NTC Contemp Pub Co.

***Passport's Illustrated Guide to Prague.** 3rd ed. Louis James. (illustrated Travel Guides from Thomas Cook Ser.). (Illus.). 192p. 2000. pap. 14.95 (*0-658-00153-1*, 001531, Passprt Bks) NTC Contemp Pub Co.

***Passport's Illustrated Guide to Thailand.** 2nd ed. Ben Davies. (Passport's Illustrated Travel Guides from Thomas Cook Ser.). 192p. 2000. pap. 14.95 (*0-658-00155-8*, 001558) NTC Contemp Pub Co.

***Passport's Illustrated Guides to Turkey.** Kathy Arnold. (Illus.). 192p. 2000. pap. write for info. (*0-658-00150-7*, Passprt Bks) NTC Contemp Pub Co.

Passport's Illustrated Paris. Thomas Cook. (Passport's Illustrated Travel Guides from Thomas Cook Ser.). (Illus.). 192p. 1994. pap. 12.95 (*0-8442-9041-6*, Passprt Bks) NTC Contemp Pub Co.

Passport's Illustrated Travel Guide to Greek Islands. Robin Gauldine. (Illus.). 192p. 1996. pap. 14.95 (*0-8442-4830-4*, 48304, Passprt Bks) NTC Contemp Pub Co.

Passport's Illustrated Travel Guide to Kenya. 2nd rev. ed. Melissa Shales. (Illus.). 192p. 1996. pap. 14.95 (*0-8442-4831-2*, 48312) NTC Contemp Pub Co.

Passport's Illustrated Travel Guide to New Zealand. Nick Hanna. (Illus.). 192p. 1996. pap. 14.95 (*0-8442-4825-8*, Passprt Bks) NTC Contemp Pub Co.

Passports Issued by Governors of Georgia, 1785 to 1809. Mary G. Bryan. 58p. 1959. pap. 8.00 (*0-915156-21-0*, 21) Natl Genealogical.

Passports Issued by Governors of Georgia, 1810 to 1820. William Dumont & Mary G. Bryan. 112p. 1964. 8.00 (*0-915156-28-8*, 28) Natl Genealogical.

Passport's Japan Almanac. Boye L. De Mente. (Illus.). 1987. pap. 17.95 (*0-8442-8508-0*, Passprt Bks) NTC Contemp Pub Co.

Passport's Map of Switzerland, & the Alps. 1991. pap. 9.95 (*0-8442-9598-1*, 95981, Passprt Bks) NTC Contemp Pub Co.

Passport's Regional Guides of Italy: Venice & Northeastern Italy. Paul Blanchard. LC 96-70352. (Illus.). 256p. 1997. pap. text 17.95 (*0-8442-9960-X*, 9960X) NTC Contemp Pub Co.

Passport's Road Atlas: Great Britain. (Illus.). 128p. 1994. pap. 16.95 (*0-8442-9601-5*, Passprt Bks) NTC Contemp Pub Co.

Passports to Adventure: A World Drive in Model A Fords. Diane M. Davis. (Illus.). 160p. (Orig.). 1994. pap. 15.00 (*0-9641026-0-9*) Peardale Pr.

Passport's Trip Planner & Guide: Australia. Paul Strathern. (Illus.). 304p. 1996. pap. 17.95 (*0-8442-4898-3*, 48983, Passprt Bks) NTC Contemp Pub Co.

Passport's Trip Planner & Guide: Central Italy, Florence, Tuscany, Umbria, the Marchs, Northern Lazio. Peter Green. LC 95-71564. (Passport's Trip Planner Ser.). (Illus.). 272p. (Orig.). 1996. pap. 17.95 (*0-8442-9215-X*, Passprt Bks) NTC Contemp Pub Co.

Passport's Trip Planner & Guide: Italy. 2nd rev. ed. Adrian Gardiner et al. (Illus.). 304p. 1997. pap. 17.95 (*0-8442-4897-5*, 48975, Passprt Bks) NTC Contemp Pub Co.

Passport's Trip Planner & Guide: Thailand. Julia Wilkinson. LC 95-71563. (Passport's Trip Planner Ser.). (Illus.). 256p. (Orig.). 1996. pap. 17.95 (*0-8442-9246-X*, 9246X, Passprt Bks) NTC Contemp Pub Co.

Passport's Trip Planner & Travel Diary. Mike Urban. Ed. by Passport Books Editors. (Illus.). 96p. 1995. 7.95 (*0-8442-9484-5*, 94845, Passprt Bks) NTC Contemp Pub Co.

Passtrak Questions & Answers for Life & Health Insurance. 4th ed. Dearborn Financial Institute Staff. (Passtrak Ser.). 1998. pap. 18.00 (*0-7931-2942-7*, 53083904) Dearborn.

Passtrak Series Vol. 6: Questions & Answers. 18th ed. Dearborn Financial Institute Staff. (Passtrak Ser.). 1998. pap. 24.00 (*0-7931-2807-2*, 36060418) Dearborn.

Passtrak Series 4, Registered Options Principal: Principles & Practices. 8th ed. LC 95-1112. (Passtrak Ser.: No. 4). 1996. pap. 145.00 (*0-7931-1451-9*, 3604-0108) Dearborn.

***Passtrak Series 7 License Exam Manual, Vol. 7.** 10th ed. (SPA.). 700p. 1999. pap. text 65.00 (*0-7931-3507-9*) Dearborn.

***Passtrak Series 7 Questions & Answers, Vol. 7.** 10th ed. (SPA.). 500p. 1999. pap. text 65.00 (*0-7931-3508-7*) Dearborn.

Passumpsic River Canoeing & Recreation Guide. Ed. by Alan Boye. (Illus.). 74p. 1997. spiral bd. 2.95 (*0-913473-12-X*) Saltillo Pr.

Password - Anglicky Vykladovy Slovnik So Slovenskymi Ekvivalentmi (Password) 4th ed. I. Kernerman. (ENG & SLO.). 864p. 1997. write for info. (*80-08-02489-5*, Pub. by Slov Pegagog Naklad) IBD Ltd.

Password Management Guideline: Department of Defense. 31p. (Orig.). (C). 1993. pap. text 20.00 (*1-56806-539-6*) DIANE Pub.

Password to Larkspur Lane. Carolyn Keene. (Nancy Drew Mystery Stories Ser.: No. 10). (Illus.). 180p. (J). (gr. 4-7). 1960. 5.95 (*0-448-09510-6*, G & D) Peng Put Young Read.

Password to Larkspur Lane. fac. ed. Carolyn Keene. LC 97-40794. (Nancy Drew Mystery Stories Ser.: No. 10). (Illus.). 210p. (J). (gr. 4-6). 1997. 14.95 (*1-55709-164-1*) Applewood.

Passwords to English Grammar, Bk. 2. Betty C. Moffatt. 1997. pap., student ed. 11.72 (*0-8114-2226-7*) Raintree Steck-V.

Passwords to English Grammar, Bk. 3. Betty C. Moffatt. 1997. pap., student ed. 11.72 (*0-8114-2227-5*) Raintree Steck-V.

Past. limited ed. Galway Kinnell. LC 85-14211. 96p. 1985. 100.00 (*0-685-10562-8*) HM.

Past - Present - Future. Mark A. Savage. LC 90-92260. (Illus.). 180p. (Orig.). 1991. pap., per. 9.95 (*1-878455-01-X*) Markas Pub.

Past - Present - Future. Mark A. Savage. LC 90-92260. 390p. (Orig.). 1995. pap., per. 9.95 (*1-878455-03-6*) Markas Pub.

Past All Reason. Kay Thorpe. (Presents Ser.). 1993. per. 2.99 (*0-373-11603-9*, 1-11603-7) Harlequin Bks.

Past & Future History: A Planner's Guide. Iben Browning & Evelyn M. Garriss. LC 81-69751. 392p. 1981. pap. 21.00 (*0-87034-063-8*) Fraser Pub Co.

Past & Future of Affirmative Action: A Guide for Human Resource Professionals & Corporate Counsel. Ronald Turner. LC 90-8393. 192p. 1990. 65.00 (*0-89930-511-3*, THP, Quorum Bks) Greenwood.

Past & Future of Medieval Studies. Ed. by John H. Van Engen. LC 93-13972. (Conferences in Medieval Studies: Vol. 4). (C). 1994. text 61.00 (*0-268-03800-7*) U of Notre Dame Pr.

Past & Future of Medieval Studies. Ed. by John Van Engen. LC 93-13972. (Notre Dame Conferences in Medieval Studies: Vol. 4). (C). 1994. reprint ed. pap. text 24.95 (*0-268-03801-5*) U of Notre Dame Pr.

Past & Future of Nuclear Deterrence. Stephen J. Cimbala. LC 97-49280. 248p. 1998. 55.00 (*0-275-96239-3*, Praeger Pubs) Greenwood.

Past & Future Rapid Environmental Changes: The Spatial & Evolutionary Responses of Terrestrial Biota, 47. Brian Huntley. LC 96-45079. (NATO ASI Ser.: Vol. 47). 523p. 1997. 239.00 (*3-540-61877-5*) Spr-Verlag.

Past & Present. Thomas Carlyle. Ed. by Richard D. Altick. LC 77-70381. (Gotham Library). 294p. (C). 1977. pap. text 18.50 (*0-8147-0562-6*) NYU Pr.

Past & Present. Reinhold. 1972. 29.95 (*0-88866-508-3*); 39.95 (*0-88866-509-1*) Edgar Kent.

Past & Present see Works of Thomas Carlyle

Past & Present: Sam Houston's Huntsville: The Junior Service League Entertains. Junior Service League Members. (Illus.). 1996. write for info. (*0-9653605-0-4*) Jr Srvc Leag Inc.

Past & Present Condition, & the Destiny of the Colored Race. Henry H. Garnet. LC 77-79010. (Black Heritage Library Collection). 1977. 12.95 (*0-8369-8576-1*) Ayer.

Past & Present in Medieval Spain. Peter Linehan. (Collected Studies: No. CS384). 360p. 1992. 115.95 (*0-86078-341-3*, Pub. by Variorum) Ashgate Pub Co.

Past & Present in the Hunter Gatherers. Ed. by Carmen Schrire. 1984. text 60.00 (*0-12-629180-2*) Acad Pr.

Past & Present (1909) Thomas Carlyle. 348p. 1998. reprint ed. pap. 19.95 (*0-7661-0713-2*) Kessinger Pub.

Past & Present of Alameda County, California, Vol. I. Joseph E. Baker. (Illus.). 456p. 1993. reprint ed. lib. bdg. 48.00 (*0-8328-2935-8*) Higginson Bk Co.

Past & Present of Alameda County, California, Vol. II. Joseph E. Baker. (Illus.). 589p. 1993. reprint ed. lib. bdg. 59.50 (*0-8328-2936-6*) Higginson Bk Co.

Past & Present of Boone County: Containing a History of . . . Its Cities, Towns, Etc.; A Biographical Directory of Its Citizens; Portraits of Early Settlers & Prominent Men; Etc. (Illus.). 416p. 1997. reprint ed. lib. bdg. 45.00 (*0-8328-6638-5*) Higginson Bk Co.

Past & Present of Bureau County, Illinois: Together with Biographical Sketches of Many of Its Prominent & Leading Citizens & Illustrious Dead. George B. Harrington. (Illus.). 968p. 1997. reprint ed. lib. bdg. 95.00 (*0-8328-5716-5*) Higginson Bk Co.

Past & Present of Dekalb County Illinois, 2 Vols. Lewis M. Gross. (Illus.). 1204p. 1998. reprint ed. lib. bdg. 115.00 (*0-8328-7072-2*) Higginson Bk Co.

Past & Present of Greene County. Ed Miner. (Illus.). 645p. 1995. reprint ed. lib. bdg. 67.00 (*0-8328-4680-5*) Higginson Bk Co.

Past & Present of Greene County: Early & Recent History & Genealogical Records of Many of the Representative Citizens, 2 vols., Set. Jonathan Fairbanks & Clyde E. Tuck. (Illus.). 1933p. 1995. reprint ed. lib. bdg. 185.00 (*0-8328-5052-7*) Higginson Bk Co.

Past & Present of Greene County, Illinois. Ed Miner. (Illus.). 645p. 1997. reprint ed. lib. bdg. 67.50 (*0-8328-5743-2*) Higginson Bk Co.

Past & Present of Greene County, Iowa. E. B. Stillman. (Illus.). 664p. 1993. reprint ed. lib. bdg. 67.50 (*0-8328-3518-8*) Higginson Bk Co.

Past & Present of Hardin County. Ed. by William J. Moir. (Illus.). 1051p. 1997. reprint ed. lib. bdg. 105.00 (*0-8328-6682-2*) Higginson Bk Co.

Past & Present of Iroquois County, Illinois, Together with Biographical Sketches of Many of Its Prominent & Leading Citizens & Illustrious Dead. J. W. Kern. (Illus.). 741p. 1997. reprint ed. lib. bdg. 76.50 (*0-8328-5749-1*) Higginson Bk Co.

Past & Present of Japanese Commerce. Yetaro Kinosita. LC 68-56663. (Columbia University. Studies in the Social Sciences: No. 41). reprint ed. 20.00 (*0-404-51041-8*) AMS Pr.

Past & Present of Jasper County, Iowa, 2 vols. James B. Weaver. (Illus.). 1365p. 1994. reprint ed. lib. bdg. 140.00 (*0-8328-3828-4*) Higginson Bk Co.

Past & Present of Kane County Illinois: History of the County - Its Cities, Towns, Etc.; Directory of Its Citizens; Portraits of Early Settlers & Prominent Men. (Illus.). 821p. 1998. reprint ed. lib. bdg. 84.50 (*0-8328-7080-3*) Higginson Bk Co.

Past & Present of Knox County, 2 vols. Ed. by Albert B. Williams. (Illus.). 907p. 1997. reprint ed. lib. bdg. 93.00 (*0-8328-6332-7*) Higginson Bk Co.

Past & Present of Lake County: Containing a History of the County; Its Cities, Towns, Etc.; Biographical Directory of Its Citizens; Portraits of Early Settlers & Prominent Men, Etc. (Illus.). 501p. 1997. reprint ed. lib. bdg. 55.00 (*0-8328-5758-0*) Higginson Bk Co.

Past & Present of LaSalle County, Illinois. (Illus.). 655p. 1994. reprint ed. lib. bdg. 65.00 (*0-8328-3975-2*) Higginson Bk Co.

Past & Present of Marshall & Putnam Counties Illinois, with Biographical Sketches of Many Prominent & Leading Citizens & Illustrious Dead. John S. Burt & W. E. Hawthorne. (Illus.). 511p. 1998. reprint ed. lib. bdg. 54.50 (*0-8328-7083-8*) Higginson Bk Co.

Past & Present of Marshall County, Iowa, Vol. 1 & 2. George W. Battin & F. A. Moscrip. (Illus.). 1168p. 1993. reprint ed. lib. bdg. 115.00 (*0-8328-3517-X*) Higginson Bk Co.

Past & Present of Mercer County, 2 vols. Isaac N. Bassett. (Illus.). 1117p. 1997. reprint ed. lib. bdg. 118.00 (*0-8328-5771-8*) Higginson Bk Co.

Past & Present of O'Brien & Osceola Counties, Iowa, 2 vols., Set. J. L. Peck et al. (Illus.). 1319p. 1994. reprint ed. lib. bdg. 135.00 (*0-8328-3827-6*) Higginson Bk Co.

Past & Present of Rock Island Co, IL. (Illus.). 474p. 1993. reprint ed. lib. bdg. 49.50 (*0-8328-3083-6*) Higginson Bk Co.

Past & Present of Shelby County. Edward S. White. (Illus.). 1511p. 1997. reprint ed. lib. bdg. 145.00 (*0-8328-6705-5*) Higginson Bk Co.

Past & Present of Solomon Sorge. Judith Barnard. 1987. pap. 5.95 (*0-317-56808-6*) PB.

Past & Present of St. Paul, Minnesota. W. B. Hennessy. (Illus.). 814p. 1994. reprint ed. lib. bdg. 82.50 (*0-8328-3835-7*) Higginson Bk Co.

Past & Present of the City of Decatur & Macon County: History & Biographical. (Illus.). 884p. 1995. reprint ed. lib. bdg. 89.50 (*0-8328-4997-9*) Higginson Bk Co.

Past & Present of Will County: With Biographical Sketches, 2 vols. W. W. Stevens. (Illus.). 854p. 1997. reprint ed. lib. bdg. 90.00 (*0-8328-5801-3*) Higginson Bk Co.

Past & Present of Winneshiek County: A Record of Settlement, Organization, Progress & Achievement. Edwin C. Bailey. (Illus.). 934p. 1995. reprint ed. lib. bdg. 101.00 (*0-8328-5027-6*) Higginson Bk Co.

Past & Present of Woodford County: With Biographical Sketches. Ed. by H. H. Hill & William H. Perrin. (Illus.). 660p. 1995. reprint ed. lib. bdg. 69.00 (*0-8328-5011-X*) Higginson Bk Co.

Past & Present Soil Erosion. Ed. by Martin Bell & John Boardman. (Oxbow Monographs in Archaeology: No. 22). (Illus.). 243p. 1992. pap. 48.00 (*0-946897-46-8*, Pub. by Oxbow Bks) David Brown.

Past & Present Variability of the Solar-Terrestrial System: Measurement, Data Analysis & Theoreticcal Models. Ed. by G. Cini Castagnoli & A. Provenzale. (International School of Physics Enrico Fermi Ser.: Vol. 133). 600p. Date not set. 145.00 (*90-5199-358-7*) IOS Press.

Past & Present Vegetation of the Far Northwest Canada. J. C. Ritchie. 272p. (C). 1984. text 37.50 (*0-8020-2523-4*) U of Toronto Pr.

Past & Promise: Lives of New Jersey Women. Women's Project of New Jersey, Inc. Staff. LC 89-34946. (Illus.). 486p. 1990. 50.00 (*0-8108-2201-6*) Scarecrow.

Past & Promise: Lives of New Jersey Women. Women's Project of New Jersey, Inc. Staff. LC 96-30899. 486p. 1996. reprint ed. pap. 26.95 (*0-8156-0418-1*, WOPPP) Syracuse U Pr.

Past & Repast. Betty F. Marsh. (Illus.). 88p. (Orig.). 1981. pap. 5.95 (*0-933992-16-5*) Coffee Break.

Past & the Future. Alan Bullock. 48p. (Orig.). 1982. pap. text 12.50 (*0-8191-5871-2*) U Pr of Amer.

Past & the Present of Political Economy. Richard T. Ely. LC 78-63743. (Johns Hopkins University. Studies in the Social Sciences. Thirtieth Ser. 1912: 3). reprint ed. 27.50 (*0-404-61013-7*) AMS Pr.

Past & the Present of the Pike's Peak Gold Regions. Henry Villard. LC 76-87629. (American Scene Ser.). (Illus.). 186p. 1972. reprint ed. lib. bdg. 25.00 (*0-306-71804-9*) Da Capo.

Past & the Punishments. Yu Hua. Tr. by Andrew F. Jones from CHI. LC 96-5143. (Fiction From Modern China Ser.). (Illus.). 336p. 1996. pap. 11.75 (*0-8248-1817-2*); text 25.50 (*0-8248-1782-6*) UH Pr.

Past as Future. Jurgen Habermas. Tr. by Max Pensky from GER. LC 93-32385. (Modern German Culture & Literature Ser.).Tr. of Vergangenheit als Zukunft. xxvi, 187p. 1994. pap. 12.50 (*0-8032-7266-9*, Bison Books) U of Nebr Pr.

***Past as Legacy.** Marianne Bonz. LC 99-56275. 2000. write for info. (*0-8006-3225-7*) Augsburg Fortress.

***Past as Liberation from History.** Scott P. Culclasure. LC 98-30526. (Counterpoints Studies in the Postmodern Theory of Education: Vol. 63). 184p. (C). 1999. pap. text 29.95 (*0-8204-3840-5*) P Lang Pubng.

Past As Prologue: Essays to Celebrate the 20-50 Anniversary of ASECS. Ed. by Carla H. Hay & Syndy M. Conger. LC 94-8348. (AMS Studies in the Eighteenth Century: Vol. 28). 1995. 62.50 (*0-404-63528-8*) AMS Pr.

Past As Prologue: Sources & Studies in European Civilization, 2 vols. Ed. by Everett U. Crosby & Charles R. Webb, Jr. (Illus.). (C). 1973. write for info. (*0-318-53721-4*) Irvington.

Past As Prologue: Sources & Studies in European Civilization, 2 vols., 1. Ed. by Everett U. Crosby & Charles R. Webb, Jr. LC 70-166559. (Illus.). (C). 1973. pap. text 12.95 (*0-89197-331-1*) Irvington.

P

Past As Prologue: Sources & Studies in European Civilization, 2 vols., 2. Ed. by Everett U. Crosby & Charles R. Webb, Jr. LC 70-166559. (Illus.). (C). 1973. pap. text 12.95 (*0-89197-332-X*) Irvington.

Past As Prologue I: The Underestimation of Price Increases in the Decontrol Debate: A Comparison of Oil & Natural Gas. 27p. 1982. 45.00 (*0-318-13799-2*); 15.00 (*0-318-13800-X*) Consumer Energy Coun.

Past As Prologue II: The Economic Effects of Rising Energy Prices: The Comparison of the Oil Price Shock & Natural Gas Decontrol. 80p. 1982. 60.00 (*0-318-13801-8*) Consumer Energy Coun.

Past As Text: The Theory & Practice of Medieval Historiography. Gabrielle M. Spiegel. LC 96-36987. (Parallax Ser.). 320p. 1997. text 39.95 (*0-8018-5555-1*) Johns Hopkins.

Past as Text: The Theory & Practice of Medieval Historiography. Gabrielle M. Spiegel. (Parallax Ser.). 320p. 1999. pap. 17.95 (*0-8018-6259-0*) Johns Hopkins.

Past at Present in Issaquah, WA. Edwards R. Fish, Jr. (Illus.). 1967. reprint ed. pap. 17.50 (*0-9612344-3-1*) H U Fish.

Past Betrayals. large type ed. Giulia Gray. (Linford Romance Library). 272p. 1997. pap. 16.99 (*0-7089-5014-0*) Ulverscroft.

Past Caring. Robert Goddard. 528p. 1988. mass mkt. 8.99 (*0-552-13144-X*) Bantam.

Past Caring: A History of U. S. Preschool Care & Education for the Poor, 1820-1965. Emily D. Cahan. LC 89-3425. (Illus.). 60p. (Orig.). 1989. pap. 7.95 (*0-926582-00-3*) NCCP.

Past Climate of Arroyo Hondo, New Mexico, Reconstructed from Tree Rings. Martin R. Rose et al. LC 80-21834. (Arroyo Hondo Archaeological Ser.: Vol. 4). (Illus.). 114p. 1981. pap. 14.95 (*0-933452-05-5*) Schol Am Res.

Past Continues. Samuel Bak. (Illus.). 35.00 (*0-8276-0496-3*) JPS Phila.

***Past Crimes.** Intro. by Martin Edwards. (Perfectly Criminal Ser.: Vol. 3). 256p. 1999. 26.00 (*0-7278-2232-2*, Pub. by Severn Hse) Chivers N Amer.

Past Crimson, Past Woe: The Shakespeare Beckett Connection. Ed. by Anne M. Drew. LC 93-17684. (Studies in Modern Drama: Vol. 4). 200p. 1993. text 15.00 (*0-8153-1383-7*, H1756) Garland.

Past Deceit see Enganos del Pasado: One Reckless Night

Past Due! A Debt Collecting Manual for Collections Professionals, Accounts Receivable Personnel & Small Business Owners. Jim Finucan. LC 98-27630. 125p. 1998. pap. 39.95 (*0-936653-80-9*) Tiare Pubns.

Past Due: A Detective Inspector Carol Ashton Mystery. Claire McNab. (Carol Ashton Mystery Ser.: No. 10). 224p. 1998. pap. 11.95 (*1-56280-217-8*) Naiad Pr.

Past Due: A Story of Disability, Pregnancy & Birth. Anne Finger. LC 89-70235. 200p. (Orig.). 1990. pap. 10.95 (*0-931188-87-3*) Seal Pr WA.

Past Due: How to Collect Money. Norman King. LC 82-21151. 177p. reprint ed. pap. 54.90 (*0-608-16045-8*, 203317300084) Bks Demand.

***Past Dying.** Malcolm Shuman. 224p. 2000. mass mkt. 5.99 (*0-380-80486-7*) Morrow Avon.

Past Eras Awaken II: Atlantis-the Realm of the Incas, Abd-Ru-Shin, Cassandra, John the Baptist, Jesus of Nazareth. 507p. pap. 20.00 (*1-898853-07-X*) Grail Fndtn-Amer.

Past Eras Awaken I: Krishna - Nahome - Cassandra - Mary of Magdala. Orig. Title: Verwehte Zest Erwacht I. 295p. (Orig.). 1997. pap. 20.00 (*1-898853-06-1*) Grail Fndtn-Amer.

Past Eras Awaken III: Egypt - Nemare - Pharaohs - Unknown Events from the Life of Jesus, the Son of God - The Apostles. 420p. 1998. pap. 20.00 (*1-898853-08-8*) Grail Fndtn-Amer.

Past Examination Papers: IPS Foundation Stage - May 1986 Onwards. Institute of Purchasing & Supply Staff. (C). 1990. 60.00 (*0-7855-5699-0*, Pub. by Inst Pur & Supply) St Mut.

Past Examination Papers: IPS Professional Stage (New Syllabus) May 1990 Onwards. Institute of Purchasing & Supply Staff. (C). 1990. 50.00 (*0-7855-5697-4*, Pub. by Inst Pur & Supply) St Mut.

Past Examination Papers: IPS Professional Stage (Old Syllabus) May 1986 to November 1990. Institute of Purchasing & Supply Staff. (C). 1990. 50.00 (*0-7855-5698-2*, Pub. by Inst Pur & Supply) St Mut.

Past Examination Papers ASPS First Certificate & ASPS Second Certificate May 1986 Onwards. Institute of Purchasing & Supply Staff. (C). 1990. 30.00 (*0-7855-5696-6*, Pub. by Inst Pur & Supply) St Mut.

Past Examination Papers Case Study. Institute of Purchasing & Supply Staff. (C). 1990. 65.00 (*0-7855-6524-8*, Pub. by Inst Pur & Supply) St Mut.

***Past Fear & Doubt to Amazing Abundance: Secret Knowledge That Brought Me Self-Actualization.** Stephen Hawley Martin. 224p. 2000. pap. 14.95 (*1-892538-24-5*) Oaklea Pr.

Past Forgetting: My Memory Lost & Found. Jill Robinson. LC 99-34975. 288p. 1999. 24.00 (*0-06-019430-8*, Cliff Street) HarperTrade.

Past Forgetting: My Memory Lost & Found. Jill Robinson. 288p. 2000. pap. 13.00 (*0-06-093234-1*, Cliff Street) HarperTrade.

Past Forgiving. Gloria D. Miklowitz. 160p. (YA). (gr. 7 up). 1995. per. 16.00 (*0-671-88442-5*) S&S Bks Yung.

Past Forward: 6 Artists in Search of Their Childhood. Gowri Ramnarayan. LC 97-906438. (Illus.). 82p. (C). 1997. 17.95 (*0-19-563939-1*) OUP.

Past Glacial Environments: Sediments, Forms & Techniques. Ed. by John Menzies. LC 95-34315. (Glacier Environments Ser.: Vol. 2). (Illus.). 605p. 1996. pap. text 85.95 (*0-7506-2352-7*, Prgamon Press) Buttrwrth-Heinemann.

Past Has Another Pattern: Memoirs. George W. Ball. (Illus.). 540p. 1983. pap. 9.95 (*0-393-30142-7*) Norton.

***Past Imperative.** Duncan. 2000. 22.00 (*0-380-97260-3*) Morrow Avon.

Past Imperative: Round 1 of the Great Game. Dave Duncan. 464p. 1996. mass mkt. 6.50 (*0-380-78129-8*, Avon Bks) Morrow Avon.

Past Imperatives: Studies in the History & Theory of Jewish Ethics. Louis E. Newman. LC 97-38798. (Series in Jewish Philosophy). 288p. (C). 1998. text 59.50 (*0-7914-3867-8*); pap. text 19.95 (*0-7914-3868-6*) State U NY Pr.

Past Imperfect: A Museum Looks at Itself. Donna De Salvo. 1994. 25.00 (*1-56584-166-2*, Pub. by New Press NY) Norton.

Past Imperfect: A Museum Looks at Itself. Donna De Salvo. LC 93-87113. (Illus.). 79p. 1994. 25.00 (*0-943526-26-4*) Parrish Art.

Past Imperfect: Essays on History, Libraries, & the Humanities. Lawrence W. Towner. Ed. by Robert W. Karrow, Jr. LC 92-32425. (Illus.). 336p. (C). 1993. 27.50 (*0-226-81042-9*) U Ch Pr.

Past Imperfect: French Intellectuals, 1944-1956. Tony Judt. 348p. (C). 1994. pap. 15.95 (*0-520-08650-3*, Pub. by U CA Pr) Cal Prin Full Svc.

Past Imperfect: History According to the Movies. Mark C. Carnes. (Illus.). 320p. 1995. pap. 17.95 (*0-8050-3760-8*) H Holt & Co.

Past Imperfect: History According to the Movies. Ed. by Mark C. Carnes. LC 95-354. (Reference Bks.). (Illus.). 88p. 1995. 30.00 (*0-8050-3759-4*) H Holt & Co.

Past Imperfect: How Tracing Your Family Medical History Can Save Your Life. Carol Daus. LC 98-32131. 240p. 1999. pap. 12.95 (*1-891661-03-5*, 1035, Offbeat) Snta Monica.

Past in French History. Robert Gildea. LC 93-28536. (Illus.). 416p. 1994. 47.50 (*0-300-05799-7*) Yale U Pr.

Past in French History. Robert Gildea. 1996. pap. text 20.00 (*0-300-06711-9*) Yale U Pr.

Past in Hiding. Mark Roseman. pap. (*0-8050-6325-0*) H Holt & Co.

***Past in Hiding: Memory & Survival in Nazi Germany.** Mark Roseman. (Illus.). 416p. 2001. text 27.50 (*0-8050-6326-9*) H Holt & Co.

***Past in Perspective: An Introduction to Human Prehistory.** 2nd ed. Kenneth L. Feder. LC 99-28265. xxiv, 552p. 2000. pap. text 47.00 (*0-7674-1192-7*, 1192-7) Mayfield Pub.

Past in Pictures: A Further Collection of Photographs of the London Borough of Sutton over the Last Century. J. Broughton. 1986. 20.00 (*0-907335-03-9*, Pub. by Sutton Libs & Arts) St Mut.

Past in Review, 1941-1991. John E. Tashjean. LC 92-16604. 144p. (Orig.). (C). 1992. pap. text 23.50 (*0-8191-8754-2*) U Pr of Amer.

Past in Ruins: Tradition & the Critique of Modernity. David Gross. LC 92-10935. (Critical Perspectives on Modern Culture Ser.). 192p. 1992. 30.00 (*0-87023-821-3*) U of Mass Pr.

Past in the Present: A History of Women's Higher Education in the Twentieth-Century South. Amy T. McCandless. LC 98-40089. 1999. write for info. (*0-8173-0945-4*) U of Ala Pr.

Past in the Present: A Thematic Study of Modern Southern Fiction. Thomas D. Young. LC 80-24074. (Southern Literary Studies). xvi, 176p. 1981. text 30.00 (*0-8071-0768-9*) La State U Pr.

Past in the Present: Essays on Vardis Fisher's Testament of Man. Lester Strong. 1979. lib. bdg. 250.00 (*0-87700-266-5*) Revisionist Pr.

Past in the Present: Proceedings, 5th British & Cultural Studies Conference, Oldenburg, Germany, 1994. Ed. by Jens-Ulrich Davids & Richard Stinshoff. LC 96-10166. (Studien zur Germanistik & Anglistik: Bd. 10). 162p. 1996. pap. 35.95 (*0-8204-2993-7*, DA566) P Lang Pubng.

Past in the Present: What Is Civilisation? Arthur Mitchell. LC 77-86453. reprint ed. 28.00 (*0-404-16674-1*) AMS Pr.

Past in the Present: Women's Higher Education in the Twentieth-Century American South Amy Thompson McCandless. LC 98-40089. 1999. 24.95 (*0-8173-0994-2*) U of Ala Pr.

Past into Present. Gower. Date not set. pap. text. write for info. (*0-582-00992-8*, Pub. by Addison-Wesley) Longman.

Past into Present: Trends & Techniques in First-Person Interpretation. Stacy F. Roth. LC 97-36874. 280p. 1998. pap. 16.95 (*0-8078-4710-0*) U of NC Pr.

Past into Present: Trends & Techniques in First-Person Interpretation. Stacy F. Roth. LC 97-36874. 1998. 45.00 (*0-8078-2407-0*) U of NC Pr.

Past Is a Foreign Country. David Lowenthal. LC 85-10990. (Illus.). 516p. 1988. pap. text 29.95 (*0-521-29480-0*) Cambridge U Pr.

Past Is a Key to the Future: A History of Terra Alta, West Virginia & Its Vicinity. Betty W. White. Ed. by M. E. Lody. (Illus.). 609p. 1990. 40.00 (0-9627086-0-7, 123-26764) McClain.

A thorough look into captivating people & places in the Preston County area. This book, centering on the Terra Alta community, combines factual data with entertaining stories of the history of this rich area & the townspeople who contributed to many of the important establishments existing there today.
Publisher Paid Annotation.

Past is Human John P. White. LC 75-330058. xii, 153 p. 1974. write for info. (*0-207-13067-1*) Angus & Roberts.

Past Is People. Ed. by Simon & Schuster Children's. (J). 2000. 16.00 (*0-689-82333-9*) Atheneum Yung Read.

Past Is Prologue: A 75th Anniversary History of the Speech Communication Association. Ed. by William Work & Robert C. Jeffrey. LC 89-63658. (Illus.). 67p. (C). 1989. pap. text 7.00 (*0-944811-03-5*) Natl Comm Assn.

Past Is the Past & Gettin' It Together: 2 Plays. Richard Wesley. 1979. pap. 5.25 (*0-8222-0879-2*) Dramatists Play.

Past Is the Prelude. large type ed. Gladys Greenaway. 304p. 1988. 27.99 (*0-7089-1878-6*) Ulverscroft.

Past Keeps Changing: Poems. Chana Bloch. LC 92-9628. 85p. (Orig.). 1992. pap. 12.95 (*1-878818-15-5*, Pub. by Sheep Meadow) U Pr of New Eng.

Past Leads a Life of Its Own. Wayne Fields. LC 97-11754. 270p. 1997. pap. 14.95 (*0-226-24858-5*) U Ch Pr.

Past-Life Chronicles: A Journal for Past-Life Regression. Sharon M. Floathe. 126p. (Orig.). 1988. student ed. 11.95 (*0-929984-00-5*) Ion Corp.

Past Life Recovery. Ingrid Vallieres. 1997. pap. text 9.95 (*1-85398-105-2*, Pub. by Ashgrove Pr) Words Distrib.

Past Life Regression Guidebook: How Our Past Lives Influence Us Now. 2nd rev. ed. Bettye B. Binder. 128p. (Orig.). 1993. pap. 13.00 (*1-879005-11-5*) Reincarnation Bks.

Past Life Regression/Future Life Progression: A Technique Manual see New Age Hypnosis Workbook: A Technique Manual

Past Life Therapy: The State of the Art. Rabia L. Clark. 233p. 1995. pap. 14.95 (*0-9646141-0-3*) Rising Star.

Past Life Therapy in Action. Dick Sutphen & Lauren L. Taylor. 144p. 1983. pap. 7.95 (*0-911842-32-2*, B915) Valley Sun.

Past Lifetimes: Keys for Change. Annie O'Grady. (Illus.). 160p. 1997. pap. 12.95 (*1-86351-170-9*, Pub. by Sally Milner) Seven Hills Bk.

Past Links: Studies in the Languages & Cultures of the Ancient Near East. Ed. by Shlomo Izre'el et al. (Israel Oriental Studies: Vol. 18). 459p. 1998. pap. text 59.50 (*1-57506-035-3*) Eisenbrauns.

Past Live, Future Loves. Dick Sutphen. 1990. pap. 5.50 (*0-671-70828-7*) PB.

Past Lives. Alexis Smith & Amy Gerstleramy. (Illus.). 40p. (Orig.). 1989. pap. 15.00 (*0-929335-01-5*) SM Mus Art.

Past Lives: A Key to Your Present Relationships. 2nd ed. Robert Young & Loy Young. Ed. by Kathryn Hall. 328p. pap. write for info. (*1-882888-47-2*) Aquarius Hse.

Past Lives: Case Histories of Previous Existence. large type ed. Dilys Gater. (General Ser.). 1998. pap. 21.95 (*0-7862-1287-X*) Thorndike Pr.

Past Lives: True Stories of Reincarnation. Sue Carpenter. 1995. mass mkt. 5.95 (*0-86369-906-5*, Pub. by Virgin Bks) London Brdge.

***Past Lives Vol. 1: The Edgar Cayce Soul Group.** Elyse Curtis. LC 00-90543. 50p. 2000. pap. 9.95 (*1-891058-23-1*, 134) Astral Projections.

Past Lives, Future Choices: The Astrology of Reincarnation. Maritha Pottenger. 320p. (Orig.). 1997. pap. 16.95 (*0-935127-54-2*) ACS Pubns.

Past Lives, Future Growth. Armand Marcotte & Ann Druffel. 216p. 1993. pap. 8.95 (*1-878901-79-6*) Hampton Roads Pub Co.

Past Lives, Future Lives. Jenny Cockell. LC 98-11094. 1998. per. 10.00 (*0-684-83216-X*, Fireside) S&S Trade Pap.

Past Lives, Future Lives. Bruce Goldberg. 1988. mass mkt. 6.99 (*0-345-35575-X*) Ballantine Pub Grp.

Past Lives of Famous People: Journeys of the Soul. David R. Bengtson. LC 97-9116. 272p. 1997. pap. 15.95 (*1-885394-22-5*) Bluestar Communs.

Past Lives, Present Dreams. Denise Linn. LC 97-92906. 1997. pap. 12.00 (*0-345-40002-X*) Ballantine Pub Grp.

***Past Lives, Present Joy.** Marilyn C. Sunderman. 2000. pap. 13.00 (*1-57566-545-X*, Knsington) Kensgtn Pub Corp.

Past Lives, Present Joy: My Spiritual Journey. Marilyn Sunderman. LC 98-66233. 224p. 1998. 22.00 (*1-57566-377-5*) Kensgtn Pub Corp.

Past Lives, Present Karma Workbook. Bettye B. Binder. 160p. 1986. pap., wbk. ed. 15.00 (*1-879005-01-8*) Reincarnation Bks.

Past Lives, Present Loves. Jeanne Avery. 1999. mass mkt. 6.50 (*0-451-19680-5*) NAL.

Past Lives Present Problems. Manly P. Hall. Date not set. reprint ed. pap. 4.95 (*0-89314-381-2*) Philos Res.

***Past Lives, Present Tense.** Ed. by Elizabeth A. Scarborough. 352p. 1999. pap. 13.00 (*0-441-00649-3*) Ace Bks.

Past Lives, Still Living: Traveling the Pathways to Freedom. Jolivette Anderson. xv, 41p. 1999. pap. 7.95 (*1-893926-00-1*) Sisterlove Prodns.

Past Lives, Universal Energies, & Me. Amelia De Pazos. LC 98-94107. (Illus.). 137p. 2000. pap. 10.95 (*0-533-12970-2*) Vantage.

Past Looking: Historical Imagination & the Rhetoric of the Image. Michael A. Holly. LC 95-40984. (Illus.). 256p. 1996. text 39.95 (*0-8014-3209-X*); pap. text 15.95 (*0-8014-8302-6*) Cornell U Pr.

***Past Love.** large type ed. Rosemary Ellerbeck. 352p. 2000. 31.99 (*0-7505-1461-2*, Pub. by Mgna Lrg Print) Ulverscroft.

Past Loving. Penny Jordan. LC 95-13707. (Presents Ser.). 188p. 1995. per. 3.25 (*0-373-11756-6*, 1-11756-3) Harlequin Bks.

Past Loving. large type ed. Penny Jordan. 1993. reprint ed. lib. bdg. 18.95 (*0-263-13196-3*) Mac Lib Ref.

Past Masters: The History & Hauntings of Destrehan Plantation. Madeline Levatino. (Illus.). 100p. (Orig.). 1991. pap. 9.50 (*0-9630144-6-3*) M Levatino.

Past Masters & Other Papers. Thomas Mann. Tr. by Helen T. Lowe-Porter. LC 68-25605. (Essay Index Reprint Ser.). 1977. 17.95 (*0-8369-0674-8*) Ayer.

Past Meets Future: Saving America's Historic Environment. Ed. by Antoinette J. Lee. (Illus.). 384p. 1995. 25.95 (*0-471-14412-6*) Wiley.

Past Mischief. Clare Curzon. 1997. per. 4.99 (*0-373-26256-6*, 1-26256-7, Wrldwide Lib) Harlequin Bks.

Past Mischief. Clare Curzon. 1997. pap. text 20.95 (*0-7862-0923-2*) Thorndike Pr.

***Past Mischief.** large type ed. Victoria Clayton. 560p. 1999. 31.99 (*0-7089-9121-1*) Ulverscroft.

Past of Jesus in the Gospels. Eugene E. Lemcio. (Society for New Testament Studies Monographs: No. 68). 204p. (C). 1991. text 59.95 (*0-521-40113-5*) Cambridge U Pr.

Past of the Future: The Novelistic Cycle of Manuel Scorza. Arra-Marie Aldaz. LC 90-6178. (American University Studies: Latin American Literature: Ser. XXII, Vol. 8). XI, 193p. (C). 1991. text 35.00 (*0-8204-1287-2*) P Lang Pubng.

Past or Future Crimes: Deservedness & Dangerousness in the Sentencing of Criminals. Andrew VonHirsch. 220p. 1987. pap. 18.00 (*0-8135-1262-X*) Rutgers U Pr.

Past or the Coming Future. L. C. Walker. 287p. 1998. pap. 14.95 (*1-890622-32-X*) Leathers Pub.

Past Pace: Auto Tech - Heating & Air Conditioning. Aspire. (Automotive Technology Ser.). 1989. student ed. 14.00 (*0-8273-5551-3*) Delmar.

***Past Participles from Latin to Romance** Richard Laurent. LC 99-36467. 598p. 1999. pap. 72.00 (*0-520-09832-3*, Pub. by U CA Pr) Cal Prin Full Svc.

Past Passion. Penny Jordan. 1994. per. 2.99 (*0-373-11655-1*, 1-11655-7) Harlequin Bks.

Past Passion. large type ed. Penny Jordan. 1992. reprint ed. 18.95 (*0-263-13036-3*) Mac Lib Ref.

Past Passions: An Anthology of Erotic Fiction by Women for Women. Ed. by Kerri Sharp. 256p. (Orig.). 1997. mass mkt. 9.95 (*0-352-33159-3*, Pub. by BLA4) London Brdge.

***Past Perfect.** Judith P. Stelboum. LC 00-25651. 235p. 2000. 49.95 (*1-56023-200-5*, Harrington Park); pap. text 19.95 (*1-56023-201-3*, Harrington Park) Haworth Pr.

***Past Perfect: True Tales of Town & 'Round - Nevada & Vernon County, Missouri.** Patrick Brophy. LC 99-75655. (Illus.). 375p. 1999. pap. 19.95 (*1-893046-12-5*, Bushwacker Mus) Vernon Cty Hist Soc.

Past Performance in Government Contracting: A Desk Guide for Contractors & Agencies. Laura K. Kennedy et al. Ed. by Elizabeth J. Sherfy. LC 96-127218. 313p. ring bd. 133.00 (*1-56726-038-1*, B598) Mgmt Concepts.

***Past Presence.** Gaye Newton. 288p. 2000. pap. 14.95 (*0-9700849-0-0*) Galibren.

Past-Present. Francois-Marie Banier. LC 96-42082. 1997. write for info. (*0-06-881516-6*, Wm Morrow); 50.00 (*0-688-15156-6*, Wm Morrow) Morrow Avon.

Past-Present: Essays on Historicism in Art from Donatello to Picasso. Irving Lavin. (Una's Lectures: No. 6). (C). 1992. 75.00 (*0-520-06816-5*, Pub. by U CA Pr) Cal Prin Full Svc.

Past, Present & Future. Arthur Adams. (Godzilla Ser.). (Illus.). 1998. pap. text 17.95 (*1-56971-278-6*) Dark Horse Comics.

Past, Present & Future. Isaac Asimov. LC 87-2243. 382p. 1987. 27.95 (*0-87975-393-5*) Prometheus Bks.

***Past, Present & Future.** Paul Beaton. LC 99-65655. 200p. 1999. pap. 5.99 (*1-893181-29-4*, Simon & Northrop) Le Gesse Stevens.

Past, Present & Future. 2nd ed. Gregg. (College ESL Ser.). (J). 1987. pap., teacher ed. write for info. (*0-534-07909-1*) Wadsworth Pub.

Past, Present, & Future: A Philosophical Essay about Time. Irwin C. Lieb. 272p. 1991. text 34.95 (*0-252-01804-4*); pap. text 14.95 (*0-252-06182-9*) U of Ill Pr.

Past, Present, & Future: A Reading-Writing Text. 2nd ed. Joan Y. Gregg & Joan Russell. 384p. (C). 1983. mass mkt. 18.25 (*0-534-01218-3*) Heinle & Heinle.

Past, Present, & Future: A Reading-Writing Text. 2nd ed. Joan Y. Gregg & Joan Russell. 359p. (C). 1987. mass mkt. 20.00 (*0-534-07908-3*) Heinle & Heinle.

Past, Present, & Future: A Reading-Writing Text. 3rd ed. Joan Y. Gregg & Joan Russell. 363p. (C). 1990. mass mkt. 25.95 (*0-534-12762-2*) Heinle & Heinle.

Past, Present, & Future: A Reading-Writing Text. 4th ed. Joan Russell & Joan Y. Gregg. (College ESL Ser.). 375p. (J). 1996. mass mkt. 28.95 (*0-8384-5282-5*) Heinle & Heinle.

Past, Present, & Future: Perspectives in American Education. Gail C. McClay. (Illus.). 663p. 1995. 55.00 (*0-911541-34-9*) Gregory Pub.

Past, Present, & Future: Selected Papers on Latin American Indian Literatures. Ed. by Mary H. Preuss. LC 91-75066. (Illus.). 160p. (C). 1991. pap. text 32.00 (*0-911437-45-2*) Labyrinthos.

***Past, Present & Future Challenges in Renal Anaemia: Technical Forum, Organized by F. Hoffmann-La Roche Ltd. During the 36th ERA/EDTA Congress, Madrid, September 1999.** Ed. by Fernando Valderrabano. (Nephron Ser.: Vol. 85, Suppl. 1). (Illus.). iv, 24p. 2000. pap. 25.25 (*3-8055-7069-4*) S Karger.

Past, Present, & Future in Prose & Poetry. B. Clark. LC 72-947. reprint ed. 39.50 (*0-404-00015-0*) AMS Pr.

***Past, Present & Future Issues in Earthquake Engineering: 50th Anniversary Special Commemorative Volume.** Ed. by Christopher Arnold & Sarah K. Nathe. (Illus.). 207p. 1998. pap. 40.00 (*0-943198-64-X*, AM-98) Earthquake Eng.

Past, Present & Future of Plant Biology. Ed. by Tuan-Hua D. Ho & Himadri Pakrasi. 142p. 1994. pap. text. write for info. (*0-912260-12-2*) Wash U Med Lib.

Past, Present & Future of the Church. Fred Pruitt. 72p. pap. 2.00 (*0-686-29133-6*) Faith Pub Hse.

P

An Asterisk (*) at the beginning of an entry indicates that the title is appearing for the first time.

Past Present & Future 3e-im. 3rd ed. Joan Y. Gregg & Joan Russell. (College ESL). 363p. (J). 1990. pap., teacher ed. 7.50 (*0-534-12763-0*) Heinle & Heinle.

Past Pretense. Sharon G. Short. (Orig.). 1994. mass mkt. 4.99 (*0-449-14915-3*, GM) Fawcett.

Past Promises. Jill M. Landis. 384p. 1993. mass mkt. 6.50 (*0-515-11207-0*, Jove) Berkley Pub.

Past Reason Hated: An Inspector Banks Mystery. Peter Robinson. (Inspector Banks Mystery Ser.). 320p. 1994. mass mkt. 5.99 (*0-425-14489-5*, Prime Crime) Berkley Pub.

***Past Reason Hated: An Inspector Banks Mystery.** Peter Robinson. 384p. 2000. mass mkt. 6.99 (*0-380-73328-5*) Morrow Avon.

Past Reason Hated: An Inspector Banks Mystery. Peter Robinson. mass mkt. write for info. (*0-14-014842-6*) Penguin Putnam.

Past Receipts Present Recipes. Ed. by Ann K. Hoffer et al. LC 98-105147. 299p. 1996. write for info. (*0-9638923-3-9*) Cumberlnd Cnty Hist.

Past Recovered. Glenn A. May. 267p. (Orig.). (C). 1987. pap. 17.50 (*971-10-0260-4*, Pub. by New Day Pub) Cellar.

Past Regret. Marian Babson. 208p. 1993. mass mkt. 4.99 (*0-446-36437-1*, Pub. by Warner Bks) Little.

***Past Remembering.** Catrin Collier. 1999. pap. 11.00 (*0-09-953871-7*, Pub. by Arrow Bks) Trafalgar.

Past Remembering. Catrin Collier. (*0-7126-7513-2*) Random House.

Past Remembering. Vera K. Fish. 64p. 1984. 22.00 (*0-7212-0695-6*, Pub. by Regency Pr GBR) St Mut.

Past Renewed: A Catalog of German-Speaking Refugee Historians in the United States after 1933. Catherine Epstein. LC 92-568. (Publications of the German Historical Institute, Washington, D.C.). 396p. (C). 1993. text 64.95 (*0-521-44063-7*) Cambridge U Pr.

Past Revolutions, Future Transformations: What Can History Tell Us about Transforming the U. S. Military? Richard O. Hundley. LC 99-25786. 120p. 1999. pap. text 15.00 (*0-8330-2709-3*, MR-1029-DARPA) Rand Corp.

***Past Sexual Abuse.** Josh McDowell. (Friendship 911 Ser.). (Illus.). 64p. (gr. 8-12). 2000. pap. write for info. (*0-8499-3797-3*) Word Pub.

Past Souls. Stephen Wagshel. (Illus.). 16p. (Orig.). 1993. pap. 2.95 (*1-879629-66-6*) Galaxy Pub CO.
Death & rebirth, the endless cycles that pass before the eye of man's immortal soul. Reincarnation is the subject of this illustrated booklet that features vignettes in the lives of famous people, both past & present. "...I. Kant perceives those objects before him, the souls from men who've past." Some things don't change, like our attitudes toward death & dying. Being remembered can be everything & there are certainly many ways of going about it. Writing, making a record, or even going before a crowd are some of the ways. Going in a crowd is another. There's strength in numbers. A last minute marriage, as in the case of Barbara Diamond--an ex-Miss at X-mas! Another contender for notoriety, Elton John; meeting for pizza Nov. 10 in 1986. *Publisher Paid Annotation.*

Past, Space & Self. John Campbell. (Representation & Mind Ser.). 282p. 1995. pap. text 16.00 (*0-262-53131-3*) MIT Pr.

Past Tense. Stephen Greenleaf. LC 96-35476. 352p. 1997. 21.50 (*0-684-83249-6*, Scribners Ref) Mac Lib Ref.

Past Tense. Jayne Ann Krentz. 1998. per. 6.50 (*0-671-01947-3*) PB.

Past Tense: The Cocteau Diaries, Vol. 2. Jean Cocteau. Tr. by Richard Howard. (Illus.). 352p. 1988. 24.95 (*0-15-171291-3*) Harcourt.

Past Tense, Future Perfect: Successful Management & the Alice Principle. Malcolm Kerrell. 268p. 1997. 24.95 (*0-285-63345-7*, Pub. by Souvenir Pr Ltd) IPG Chicago.

Past Tense of God's Word see Tiempo Pasado de la Palabra de Dios

Past Tense of God's Word. Kenneth E. Hagin, Jr. 1980. pap. 1.00 (*0-89276-706-5*) Faith Lib Pubns.

***Past Tense of Love.** large type ed. Elizabeth Cadell. 243p. 1999. 27.95 (*0-7838-8593-8*, G K Hall & Co) Mac Lib Ref.

Past That Poets Make. Harold Toliver. LC 80-18825. 262p. (C). 1981. 41.50 (*0-674-65676-8*) HUP.

Past the Age of Miracles. Eleanor Grover. 252p. 1997. pap. 7.95 (*0-9658809-0-7*) Ellie Bks.

Past the Conemaugh Yards: Selected Poems, 1975-1985. Kathleen M. Sewalk. (Illus.). 1987. pap. 9.95 (*0-941461-01-7*) Tunnel Press.

Past the Last Number. Rama L. Shaw. (Illus.). 275p. (Orig.). 1989. 19.95 (*0-9624091-0-3*) AMAR Pub Co.

Past, the Present, & the Future. Henry C. Carey. LC 67-18573. (Reprints of Economic Classics Ser.). 474p. 1967. reprint ed. 49.50 (*0-678-00245-2*) Kelley.

Past, the Present & the Future of the European Union. Roy Jenkins. 50p. (C). 1997. pap. 13.00 (*82-00-12810-5*, Pub. by Scand Univ Pr) IBD Ltd.

***Past the Size of Dreaming.** Nina Kiriki Hoffman. LC 00-32791. 2000. write for info. (*0-441-00802-X*) Ace Bks.

***Past Time: Baseball As History.** Jules Tygiel. 272p. 2000. 25.00 (*0-19-508958-8*) OUP.

***Past Time: Baseball Haiku.** Ed. by Jim Kacian & Cor Van Den Heuvel. 24p. 1999. pap. 6.95 (*1-893959-07-4*) Red Moon Pr.

Past Times: Stories of Early Memphis. Perre M. Magness. (Illus.). 288p. 1994. 25.00 (*0-9642929-0-4*) Parkway Press.

Past Titan Rock: Journeys into an Appalachian Valley. Ellesa C. High. LC 83-23387. 189p. reprint ed. pap. 58.60 (*0-7837-5790-5*, 204545600006) Bks Demand.

Past Trauma in Late Life: European Perspective on Therapeutic Work with Older People. Linda Hunt et al. LC 97-198033. 224p. 1997. pap. 29.95 (*1-85302-446-5*, Pub. by Jessica Kingsley) Taylor & Francis.

Past Watchful Dragons: The Narnian Chronicles of C. S. Lewis. Walter Hooper. LC 79-10672. xi, 140 p. 1979. write for info. (*0-02-051970-2*) Mac Lib Ref.

Past We Share: The Near Eastern Ancestry of Western Folk Literature. E. L. Ranelagh. (Illus.). 288p. 1981. 21.95 (*0-7043-2234-X*, Pub. by Quartet) Charles River Bks.

Past Will Happen Again: A Survey of Biblical Prophecy. John G. Cunningham. LC 94-93860. 250p. (Orig.). 1995. pap. text 11.95 (*0-9643287-6-3*, Shekinah Hse) Cunningham Copywrit.

Past Within Me: Memoirs of a Warsaw Ghetto Fighter. Simha Rotem. Tr. by Barbara Harshav from HEB. LC 94-17452.Tr. of Uve-Tokhi He-Avar. 192p. 1994. 25.00 (*0-300-05797-0*) Yale U Pr.

Past Within Us: An Empirical Approach to Philosophy of History. Raymond Martin. LC 88-32244. 176p. reprint ed. pap. 54.60 (*0-608-20158-8*, 205443900011) Bks Demand.

Past Won't End. large type ed. Lauran Paine. (Sagebrush Large Print Westerns Ser.). 192p. 1995. lib. bdg. 18.95 (*1-57490-010-2*) T T Beeler.

Pasta. LC 94-77976. 1995. 24.95 (*0-916103-23-4*) Am Express Food.

Pasta. (Popular Brands Cookbooks Ser.). (Illus.). 24p. 1995. pap. write for info. (*1-56144-672-6*) Modern Pub NYC.

Pasta. 200p. 1995. spiral bd. 19.95 (*1-870049-76-4*) Oliver Bks.

***Pasta.** LC 99-36485. (Little Guides Ser.). 320p. 1999. pap. 14.95 (*1-875137-61-0*) Weldon Owen.

Pasta. Better Homes & Gardens. (Cooking for Today Ser.). (Illus.). 144p. 1993. 15.95 (*0-696-01990-6*) Meredith Bks.

Pasta. Deni Bown. (101 Essential Tips Ser.). (Illus.). 72p. 1997. 4.95 (*1-56458-988-9*) DK Pub Inc.

***Pasta.** Julia Della Croce. (Living Ser.). 168p. 2000. pap. text 13.95 (*0-7894-5118-2*, D K Ink) DK Pub Inc.

Pasta. Lorenza De'Medici. Ed. by Laurie Lertz. LC 92-10314. (Williams-Sonoma Kitchen Library). (Illus.). 108p. 1992. lib. bdg. write for info. (*0-7835-0213-3*) Time-Life.

Pasta. Lorenza De'Medici. Ed. by Laurie Lertz. LC 92-10314. (Williams-Sonoma Kitchen Library). (Illus.). 108p. (J). (gr. 11). 1999. 18.95 (*0-7835-0212-5*) Time-Life.

Pasta. Tom Griffin. 1987. pap. 5.25 (*0-8222-0878-4*) Dramatists Play.

***Pasta.** Katherine Hawkins. (Portable Chef Ser.). (Illus.). 256p. 1999. 7.98 (*0-7651-0876-3*) Smithmark.

Pasta. Jillian Powell. LC 96-32829. (Everyone Eats Ser.). (Illus.). 32p. (J). (gr. 2-6). 1997. lib. bdg. 22.83 (*0-8172-4760-2*) Raintree Steck-V.

Pasta. Tr. by Michaell Sola. (The Authentic Italian Kitchen Ser.). (Illus.). 224p. 1995. 17.95 (*0-9642027-0-0*) Strawpaper Pr.

Pasta. Sterling Publishing Company, Inc. Staff. (The Magnet Gourmet Ser.). 10p. 1997. pap. text 5.95 (*0-8069-0601-4*) Sterling.

Pasta. Time-Life Books Editors. (Time-Life Favorite Recipes Ser.). 96p. (J). (gr. 5). 1999. pap. 6.95 (*0-7370-1114-9*) T-L Custom Pub.

Pasta. Time-Life Books Editors. LC 95-17783. (Great Taste - Low Fat Ser.). (Illus.). 160p. (gr. 7). 1999. spiral bd. 14.95 (*0-7835-4551-7*) Time-Life.

***Pasta.** Jeni Wright. 96p. 1999. pap. 12.95 (*0-7548-0263-9*) Anness Pub.

***Pasta: A Passion.** Nina Hensley. LC 99-26363. 160p. 1999. pap. text 19.95 (*1-58008-106-1*) Ten Speed Pr.

***Pasta: Every Way for Every Day.** Eric Treuille & Anna Del Conte. 2000. 19.95 (*0-7894-6548-5*) DK Pub Inc.

Pasta: Sauces & Fillings for All Shapes & Sizes. Constance Jones. 1994. pap. 11.95 (*1-56799-020-7*) M Friedman Pub Grp Inc.

Pasta - Make It Tonight. Home Library Editors. (Home Library Mini-Menu Cookbooks). (Illus.). 64p. 1999. pap. 3.95 (*1-56426-205-7*, Pub. by Cole Group) ACCESS Pubs Network.

Pasta - Popcorn - Chocolate Diet. Lenny Neimark. 32p. 1999. pap. 6.75 (*1-893557-03-0*, Pub. by R E P Tech) Soul Proprietor.

Pasta al Dente: Recipes from All the Regions of Italy. Alberta Nocentini. LC 86-22268. (Illus.). 1989. 24.95 (*0-87949-264-3*) Ashley Bks.

***Pasta & Chinese.** 2000. boxed set 30.00 (*0-7548-0413-5*) Anness Pub.

Pasta & Co. by Request: Coveted Recipes from Seattle's Leading Take-Out Foodshop. Marcella Rosene. LC 91-5108. 264p. (Orig.). 1991. 13.95 (*0-912365-49-8*) Sasquatch Bks.

Pasta & Co. Encore: More Famous Foods from Seattle's Leading Take-Out Foodshop. Marcella Rosene. LC 96-29751. 240p. (Orig.). 1997. pap. 16.95 (*1-57061-109-2*) Sasquatch Bks.

Pasta & Co., the Cookbook. Pasta & Co. Staff. Ed. by Marcella Rosene. 223p. (Orig.). 1987. pap. 12.95 (*0-685-19027-7*) Pasta & Co Inc.

Pasta & Garlic: Low-Fat Recipes... That Work! Chris Gluck. LC 97-92294. (Illus.). 96p. (Orig.). 1997. pap. 6.95 (*1-891004-01-8*) Pasta Pr.

***Pasta & More!** Bardi Castellucci. 1999. 24.95 (*0-7370-0071-6*) T-L Custom Pub.

Pasta & Noodle Technology. Ed. by James E. Kruger et al. LC 95-81154. (Illus.). vi, 356p. 1996. 149.00 (*0-913250-89-9*) Am Assn Cereal Chem.

***Pasta & Pizza: Thematic Unit.** Janet A. Hale. (Illus.). 80p. (J). 1999. pap., teacher ed. 9.95 (*1-57690-374-5*, TCM2374) Tchr Create Mat.

Pasta & Pizza Cookbook. Myra Street. 1992. 15.98 (*1-55521-799-0*) Bk Sales Inc.

***Pasta & Pizza Prego.** Gabriella Rossi. 128p. 2000. 14.95 (*0-7548-0081-4*) Anness Pub.

Pasta & Pizza Presto: 100 of the Best, Most Authentic Italian Favourites Made Simple. Maxine Clark. (Illus.). 192p. 1996. pap. text 16.95 (*1-85967-279-5*, Lorenz Bks) Anness Pub.

Pasta & Vegetables: Low-Fat Recipes... That Work! Chris Gluck. LC 98-91496. (Illus.). 96p. 1998. pap. 7.95 (*1-891004-02-6*) Pasta Pr.

Pasta Bible, 1. Lorenz Books Staff. 1999. 24.95 (*1-85967-905-6*) Anness Pub.

Pasta Bible. Silvio Rizzi et al. LC 96-67512. 240p. 1996. 34.95 (*0-670-86996-1*, Viking) Viking Penguin.

Pasta Book: Recipes in the Italian Tradition. Julia Della Croce. 1997. 9.95 (*0-8118-1745-8*) Chronicle Bks.

Pasta, Classic Essential. (Mini Cook Bks.). (Illus.). 64p. 1999. pap. 1.95 (*3-8290-1593-3*) Konemann.

Pasta Classica: The Art of Italian Pasta Cooking. Julia Della Croce. LC 87-13515. (Illus.). 160p. 1996. pap. 21.95 (*0-8118-0248-5*) Chronicle Bks.

***Pasta Cookbook.** Cole's Home Library Edition Staff. 120p. 2000. pap. 11.95 (*1-56426-161-1*, Pub. by Cole Group) ACCESS Pubs Network.

Pasta Cookbook. Carolyn Garner. 64p. 1995. write for info. (*1-57215-019-X*) World Pubns.

Pasta Dishes: La Pastaciutta. Anna Del Conte. LC 93-13291. (Anna del Cotne's Italian Kitchen Ser.). (Illus.). 64p. 1994. 14.00 (*0-671-87031-9*) S&S Trade.

Pasta e Verdura: 140 Vegetable Sauces for Spaghetti, Fusilli, Rigatoni, & All Other Noodles. Jack Bishop. 336p. 1996. 27.00 (*0-06-017402-1*) HarpC.

***Pasta e Verdura: 140 Vegetable Sauces for Spaghetti, Fusilli, Rigatoni, & All Other Noodles.** Jack Bishop. 336p. 2000. pap. 15.00 (*0-06-093245-7*, Quil) HarperTrade.

Pasta East & West. Nava Atlas. LC 98-37970. 1999. pap. text 14.95 (*1-57067-066-8*) Book Pub Co.

Pasta Exotica. Dave DeWitt & Mary J. Wilan. LC 97-24694. (Illus.). 102p. 1997. pap. text 14.95 (*0-89815-905-9*) Ten Speed Pr.

Pasta Favorites. Nancy Berzinec. 36p. (Orig.). 1988. pap. 3.25 (*0-940844-31-1*) Wellspring.

Pasta Favorites. Mayflower Culinary Editors. LC 98-134039. (The Everyday Chef Ser.). 64p. 1997. pap. text 5.99 (*1-58029-015-9*, Everywhere) Hambleton-Hill.

***Pasta for All Seasons: 125 Vegetarian Pasta Recipes for Family & Friends.** Robin Robertson. (Illus.). 192p. 2000. 24.95 (*1-55832-174-8*); pap. 12.95 (*1-55832-175-6*) Harvard Common Pr.

Pasta for Beginners. Fiona Watt. (Illus.). 48p. (J). (gr. 5-9). 1998. pap. 7.95 (*0-7460-2808-3*, Usborne) EDC.

Pasta for Beginners. Fiona Watt. (Cooking for Beginners Ser.). (Illus.). 48p. (YA). (gr. 5 up). 1998. lib. bdg. 15.95 (*0-88110-969-X*, Usborne) EDC.

Pasta Fresca: An Exuberant Collection Of Fresh, Vivid, And Simple Pasta Recipes, 1. Viana La Place & Evan Kleiman. LC 88-9294. (Illus.). 272p. 1999. pap. 12.00 (*0-688-17011-0*, Grenwillow Bks) HarpC Child Bks.

Pasta Fresca: An Exuberant Collection of Fresh, Vivid & Uncomplicated Pasta Recipes from the Authors of Cucina Fresca. Viana La Place & Evan Kleiman. Ed. by Ann Bramson. LC 88-9294. (Illus.). 224p. 1988. 19.95 (*0-688-07763-3*, Wm Morrow) Morrow Avon.

Pasta Gourmet: Creative Pasta Recipes from Appetizers to Desserts. Sunny Baker & Michelle Sbraga. LC 96-148597. (Illus.). 304p. pap. 14.95 (*0-89529-663-2*, Avery) Penguin Putnam.

Pasta Gusto. Norman Kolpas. 176p. 1994. pap. 9.95 (*0-8092-3726-1*, 372610, Contemporary Bks) NTC Contemp Pub Co.

Pasta Harvest: Delicious Recipes for Pasta with Vegetables at Their Seasonal Best. Janet K. Fletcher. (Illus.). 168p. 1995. pap. 15.95 (*0-8118-0567-0*) Chronicle Bks.

***Pasta Improvvisata: How to Improvise in Classic Italian Style.** Erica DeMane. LC 99-21363. (Illus.). 320p. 1999. 24.50 (*0-684-82972-X*) Scribner.

Pasta in Minutes: Exciting Entress, Salads & Side Dishes. Mable Hoffman. LC 93-20767. (Illus.). 128p. (Orig.). 1993. pap. 9.95 (*1-55561-054-4*) Fisher Bks.

Pasta Light. Norman Kolpas. 144p. (Orig.). 1990. pap. 9.95 (*0-8092-4177-3*, 417730, Contemporary Bks) NTC Contemp Pub Co.

Pasta Light: Over 200 Great Taste, Low Fat Pasta Recipes. Time-Life Books Editors. LC 97-51392. 448p. (gr. 11). 1999. 34.95 (*0-7370-0000-7*) Time-Life.

Pasta Machine Cookbook. Donna R. German. 176p. 1993. pap. 8.95 (*1-55867-081-5*, Nitty Gritty Ckbks) Bristol Pub Ent CA.

Pasta Machine Cookbook. Gina Steer. (Illus.). 128p. 1997. 12.98 (*0-7858-0843-4*) Bk Sales Inc.

Pasta Market. Ed. by Peter Allen. 198p. 1988. pap. 1295.00 (*0-941285-40-5*) FIND-SVP.

Pasta Market. Find/SVP (Firm) Staff. LC 99-199520. (Market Intelligence Report Ser.). xv, 223 p. 1997. write for info. (*1-56241-480-1*) FIND-SVP.

Pasta Market. Find/SVP Staff. LC 97-188662. (A Market Intelligence Report Ser.). xii, 285 p. 1996. write for info. (*1-56241-331-7*) FIND-SVP.

Pasta Math Problem Solving for "Alice in Pastaland" 40 Activities to Connect Math & Literature. Mary Chandler. 1997. pap., teacher ed. 12.95 (*1-57091-154-1*) Charlesbridge Pub.

Pasta Menus. Norman Kolpas. LC 92-39914. 224p. 1993. pap. 12.95 (*0-8092-3914-0*, 391400, Contemporary Bks) NTC Contemp Pub Co.

Pasta Perfect. Cole Group Editors Staff. (Cooking Companion Ser.). 96p. (Orig.). 1995. pap. 47.70 (*1-56426-835-7*) Cole Group.

Pasta Perfect. Cole Group Editors Staff. LC 94-40117. (Cole's Cooking Companion Ser.). (Illus.). 96p. (Orig.). 1995. pap. 7.95 (*1-56426-802-0*) Cole Group.

Pasta, Pizza & Rice. (Feast of Good Cooking Ser.). (Illus.). 128p. 1996. 12.99 (*1-57215-070-X*, JG1067) World Pubns.

Pasta, Pizza, & Risotto. Ed. by Anne Hildyard. (Illus.). 464p. 1997. 25.98 (*0-7858-0851-5*) Bk Sales Inc.

Pasta, Please! Melvin Berger. Ed. by Lisa Trumbauer. (Early Science Big Bks.). (Illus.). 16p. (J). (ps-2). 1994. pap. 16.95 (*1-56784-021-3*) Newbridge Educ.

Pasta, Please! Mini Book. Melvin Berger. Ed. by Lisa Trumbauer. (Early Science Big Bks.). 16p. (J). (ps-2). 1996. pap. 3.95 (*1-56784-046-9*) Newbridge Educ.

Pasta, Please! Theme Pack. Melvin Berger. Ed. by Susan Evento. (Macmillan Early Science Big Bks.). (Illus.). (J). (ps-2). 1995. pap. 49.95 (*1-56784-178-3*) Newbridge Educ.

Pasta Possibilities: An Integrated Activity Approach to "Strega Nona" & Other "Magic Pot" Stories. Wendy Boynton & Janet Christie. (Illus.). 48p. 1993. pap., teacher ed. 10.00 (*1-895411-49-1*) Peguis Pubs Ltd.

Pasta Presto. Norman Kolpas. 128p. (Orig.). 1988. pap. 9.95 (*0-8092-4676-7*, 467670, Contemporary Bks) NTC Contemp Pub Co.

Pasta Pronto! Ed. by Jennifer Darling. LC 97-75846. (Fresh & Simple Ser.). 96p. 1998. pap. 15.95 (*0-696-20784-2*, Better Homes) Meredith Bks.

Pasta Sauces. Time-Life Books Editors. Ed. by Catherine Hackett. LC 96-44017. (Great Taste - Low Fat Ser.). (Illus.). 160p. (J). (gr. 7). 1999. spiral bd. 14.95 (*0-7835-4563-0*) Time-Life.

Pasta Sauces. Ed. by Chuck Williams. LC 93-49011. (Williams-Sonoma Kitchen Library). (Illus.). 108p. (gr. 11). 1999. 18.95 (*0-7835-0283-4*) Time-Life.

Pasta Soups & Salads. Joanne Weir. Ed. by Jill Fox. (Williams-Sonoma Pasta Collection). (Illus.). 128p. 1996. 18.95 (*1-875137-09-2*) Weldon Owen.

Pasta Tecnica. Pasquale Bruno, Jr. (Illus.). 128p. 1982. pap. 15.95 (*0-8092-5894-3*, 58943) NTC Contemp Pub Co.

Pasta Verde. Judith Barrett. 288p. 1998. 16.95 (*0-02-862286-3*) Macmillan.

Pasta with Sauces. Michele A. Jordan. Ed. by Jill Fox. (Williams-Sonoma Pasta Collection). (Illus.). 128p. 1996. 18.95 (*1-875137-07-6*) Weldon Owen.

***Pastabilities.** Todd Strasser. (Here Comes Heavenly Ser.: No. 3). 176p. (YA). 2000. mass mkt. 4.99 (*0-671-03628-9*, Archway) PB.

Pastatively Italy. Virginia O. McLean. LC 94-65440. (Illus.). 40p. (J). (gr. k-6). 1997. 21.95 incl. audio compact disk (*0-9606046-6-9*) Redbird.

Paste see Works of Henry James Jr.: Collected Works

Paste Flow & Extrusion. John Benbow & John Bridgwater. LC 92-37398. (Advanced Manufacturing Ser.: No. 10). (Illus.). 168p. (C). 1993. text 77.95 (*0-19-856338-8*, Clarendon Pr) OUP.

Paste Jewels. John K. Bangs. LC 70-96035. (Short Story Index Reprint Ser.). 1977. 19.95 (*0-8369-3081-9*) Ayer.

***Paste Makes Waste.** Laura Dower. (Powerpuff Girls Ser.). (Illus.). (J). 2000. pap. 3.50 (*0-439-19105-X*) Scholastic Inc.

Pasteboard Bandit. Arna Bontemps & Langston Hughes. LC 97-11626. (Iona & Peter Opie Library of Children's Literature). (Illus.). 96p. (J). (gr. 3-7). 1997. 16.95 (*0-19-511476-0*) OUP.

Pastel. Georgette Heyer. 1976. 25.95 (*0-8488-1367-7*) Amereon Ltd.

Pastel. Georgette Heyer. 1976. reprint ed. 35.95 (*0-89966-121-1*) Buccaneer Bks.

Pastel Book. Bill Creevy. (Illus.). 176p. 1999. pap. 19.95 (*0-8230-3905-6*) Watsn-Guptill.

Pastel Book: Materials & Techniques for Today's Artist. Bill Creevy. (Illus.). 176p. 1991. 32.50 (*0-8230-3902-1*) Watsn-Guptill.

Pastel for the Serious Beginner: Basic Lessons in Becoming a Good Painter. Larry Blovits. (Illus.). 144p. 1996. pap. text 19.95 (*0-8230-3907-2*) Watsn-Guptill.

Pastel Light. Wolf Kahn. LC 82-19152. (Contemporary Artists Ser.: No. 1). (Illus.). 50p. 1983. 75.00 (*0-930794-80-X*) Station Hill Pr.

Pastel Painter's Solution Book. David Cuthbert. (Illus.). 144p. 1996. 27.99 (*0-89134-705-4*, North Lght Bks) F & W Pubns Inc.

***Pastel Painting.** Jose M. Parramon. 95p. 1999. pap. 18.95 (*84-89730-96-2*) LEMA.

Pastel Painting Techniques. Guy Roddon. (Illus.). 144p. 1991. pap. 22.99 (*0-89134-396-2*, 30306, North Lght Bks) F & W Pubns Inc.

Pastel Portraits. Gretchen Liu. (Illus.). 156p. 1995. 40.00 (*9971-88-020-2*, Pub. by Select Bks) Weatherhill.

Pastel School: A Practical Guide to Painting & Drawing with Pastels. Hazel Harrison. LC 95-33556. (Reader's Digest Learn-As-You-Go Guide Ser.). (Illus.). 176p. 1996. 21.00 (*0-89577-849-1*, Pub. by RD Assn) Penguin Putnam.

Pastel Techniques. Lionel Aggett. (CW Art Class Techniques Ser.). (Illus.). 80p. 1993. pap. 19.95 (*1-85223-646-9*, Pub. by Cro1wood) Trafalgar.

Pastel Techniques: Explore the Beauty & Versatility of Pastels. James Horton. (Leisure Painter Ser.). 1998. pap. text 19.95 (*0-7134-8480-2*, Pub. by B T B) Branford.

Pastel Workbook: A Complete Course in Ten Lessons. Jackie Simmonds. (Illus.). 128p. 1999. 24.95 (*0-7153-0843-2*, Pub. by D & C Pub) Sterling.

Pastels. John Blockley. (Learn to Paint Ser.). (Illus.). 1999. pap. 15.95 (*0-00-413346-3*, Pub. by HarpC) Trafalgar.

P

An Asterisk (*) at the beginning of an entry indicates that the title is appearing for the first time.

Pastels. Koneman Staff. (Fine Arts for Beginners Ser.). (Illus.). 172p. 1999. pap. 9.95 (*3-8290-1934-3*, 521049) Konemann.

***Pastels.** Parramon's Editorial Team. LC 98-72917. (Art Handbooks). (Illus.). 96p. 1999. 9.95 (*0-7641-5106-1*) Barron.

Pastels: Art School. Lorenz Staff. 1998. 9.95 (*1-85967-825-4*) Anness Pub.

Pastels Book: The Designer's Ultimate Guide to Working with Color. Dale Russell. (Illus.). 144p. 1998. reprint ed. text 25.00 (*0-7881-5885-6*) DIANE Pub.

Pastels in Prose. Stuart Merrill. 1975. 250.00 (*0-87968-310-4*) Gordon Pr.

Pasteprints: A Technical & Art Historical Investigation. Elizabeth Coombs et al. (Illus.). 46p. 1986. pap. 12.00 (*0-916724-62-X*, 362X) Harvard Art Mus.

***Paster Link Resource Handbook 1999-2000: Faith Weaver Bible Curriculum.** 1999. pap. 4.99 (*0-7644-0904-2*, Grps Active Bible Curr) Group Pub.

Pasternak Leonid, 1862-1945. Josephine Pasternak. 1982. pap. 20.00 (*0-905836-34-0*, Pub. by Museum Modern Art) St Mut.

Pasternak's Short Fiction & the Cultural Vanguard. Larissa Rudova. LC 93-22860. (Middlebury Studies in Russian Language & Literature: Vol. 6). 167p. (C). 1994. text 35.95 (*0-8204-2273-8*) P Lang Pubng.

Pasteups & Mechanicals: A Step-by-Step Guide to Preparing Art for Reproduction. Jerry Demoney & Susan E. Meyer. (Illus.). 176p. 1982. 24.95 (*0-8230-3924-2*) Watsn-Guptill.

Pasteur & la Cure d'Ame. Paul Hoff.Tr. of Pastor As a Counselor. (FRE.). 240p. 1986. pap. 12.95 (*0-8297-0692-5*) Vida Pubs.

Pasteur & Modern Science. Rene Jules Dubos. LC 98-12395. (Illus.). 168p. 1998. reprint ed. pap. 29.95 (*1-55581-144-2*) ASM Pr.

Pasteur Exposed. 5th ed. Ethel D. Hume. 260p. pap. 26.95 (*0-8464-4267-1*) Beekman Pubs.

Pasteur, Plagiarist, Impostor! The Germ Theory Exploded! R. B. Pearson. 148p. 1996. reprint ed. spiral bd. 18.00 (*0-7873-0662-2*) Hlth Research.

Pasteur Vaccines Special Sale. 1998. 0.70 (*0-02-862988-4*, Pub. by Macmillan) S&S Trade.

Pasteurellosis in Production Animals. B. E. Patten et al. 256p. (Orig.). 1993. pap. 159.00 (*1-86320-081-9*) St Mut.

Pasteurization of France. Bruno Latour. Tr. by Alan Sheridan & John Law from FRE. LC 88-2670. (Illus.). 288p. 1988. 45.00 (*0-674-65760-8*) HUP.

Pasteurization of France. Bruno Latour. LC 88-2670. (Illus.). 288p. 1988. reprint ed. pap. 21.50 (*0-674-65761-6*) HUP.

Pasteur's Fight Against Microbes. Beverley Birch. LC 96-83307. (Science Stories Ser.). (Illus.). 48p. (J). (gr. 4-7). 1996. pap. text 5.95 (*0-8120-9793-9*) Barron.

Pasteur's Fight Against Microbes. Beverley Birch. (Science Stories Ser.). (Illus.). 48p. (J). (gr. 2-4). 1996. lib. bdg. 14.95 (*1-56674-193-9*) Forest Hse.

Pasteur's Fight Against Microbes. Beverly Birch. (Science Stories). 1996. 11.15 (*0-606-11723-7*, Pub. by Turtleback) Demco.

Pasteur's Quadrant: Basic Science & Technological Innovation. Donald E. Stokes. LC 97-4807. 180p. 1997. 38.95 (*0-8157-8178-4*); pap. 14.95 (*0-8157-8177-6*) Brookings.

Pasticcio & Temperance Plays in America: Il Pesceballo, (1862) & Ten Nights in a Bar-Room (1890) Ed. by Dale Cockrell. LC 94-24997. (Nineteenth-Century American Musical Theater Ser.: No. 8). (Illus.). 216p. 1994. text 88.00 (*0-8153-1380-2*) Garland.

Pasticcios. Ed. by Ernest Warburton. LC 92-33289. (Librettos of Mozart's Operas Ser.: Vol. 5). (Illus.). 752p. 1993. text 40.00 (*0-8153-0112-X*) Garland.

Pastiche & Prejudice. Arthur B. Walkley. LC 79-105046. (Essay Index Reprint Ser.). 1977. 21.95 (*0-8369-1486-4*) Ayer.

Pastiches: Poems from Hollywood. Mark Dunster. 11p. 1999. pap. 5.00 (*0-89642-734-X*) Linden Pubs.

Pastiches de Proust. Marcel Proust. Ed. by Milly. (FRE.). 48.25 (*0-685-37071-2*) Fr & Eur.

Pastiches et Melanges. Marcel Proust. (FRE.). 1970. pap. 8.95 (*0-7859-2836-7*) Fr & Eur.

Pastillage: Executive Chef. Pasquale Rocco. LC 98-92180. (Illus.). 112p. 1998. pap. write for info. (*1-57502-976-6*, PO2669) Morris Pubng.

Pastime. large type ed. Robert B. Parker. (General Ser.). 269p. 1992. pap. 16.95 (*0-8161-5348-5*, G K Hall Lrg Type) Mac Lib Ref.

Pastime. Robert B. Parker. 1992. reprint ed. mass mkt. 6.99 (*0-425-13293-5*) Berkley Pub.

***Pastime: Telling Time from 1879 to 1969.** Philip Collins. (Illus.). 95p. 1999. text 17.00 (*0-7881-6007-9*) DIANE Pub.

Pastime of Pleasure. S. Hâwes. (EETS, OS Ser.: No. 173). 1974. reprint ed. 63.00 (*0-527-00170-8*) Periodicals Srv.

Pastime Stories. Thomas N. Page. LC 76-75784. (Short Story Index Reprint Ser.). (Illus.). 1977. 19.95 (*0-8369-3009-6*) Ayer.

Pastime Stories. Thomas N. Page. (Notable American Authors Ser.). 1999. reprint ed. lib. bdg. 125.00 (*0-7812-4693-8*) Rprt Serv.

***Pastimes.** Ruth Russell. (C). 1999. pap. 50.00 (*0-07-240030-7*) McGrw-H Hghr Educ.

Pastimes: Context Contemporary. Russell. 1995. teacher ed. 9.68 (*0-697-22726-X*) McGraw.

Pastimes: The Context of Contemporary Leisure. Ruth V. Russell. 480p. (C). 1995. text. write for info. (*0-697-22725-1*) Brown & Benchmark.

Pastimes of a Red Summer. Peter Van Sittart. 198p. 1969. 19.95 (*0-8464-0704-3*) Beekman Pubs.

Pastimes of a Red Summer. Peter Vansittart. 198p. 1969. 29.95 (*0-7206-0250-5*) Dufour.

Pastirskoje Bogoslovije. Konstantine Zaitsev.Tr. of Pastoral Theology. 478p. 1960. pap. text 8.00 (*0-317-30273-6*) Holy Trinity.

Pastirskoje Sovjeshchjanije, 1969. Tr. of Pastoral Conference 1969. 95p. 1969. pap. 3.00 (*0-317-30274-4*) Holy Trinity.

Pastissima! Pasta the Italian Way. Photos by Marco Lanza. LC 97-1823. (Pane & Vino Ser.). (Illus.). 128p. (gr. 11). 1997. 17.95 (*0-7835-4942-3*) Time-Life.

Paston Family in the 15th Century: Fastolf's Will, Vol. 2. Colin Richmond. LC 95-44017. (Illus.). 292p. (C). 1996. text 59.95 (*0-521-56238-4*) Cambridge U Pr.

Paston Letters: A Selection in Modern Spelling. Ed. & Intro. by Norman Davis. (Oxford World's Classics Ser.). (Illus.). 320p. 1999. pap. 10.95 (*0-19-283640-4*) OUP.

Paston Letters & Papers of the 15th Century, Pt. 2. Ed. by Norman Davis. (Illus.). 698p. 1977. text 115.00 (*0-19-812555-0*) OUP.

Paston Letters, 1422-1509, 6 vols., Set. Ed. by James Gairdner. LC 77-168090. reprint ed. 315.00 (*0-404-02690-7*) AMS Pr.

Pastons: A Family in the War of the Roses. Ed. by Richard Barber. LC 93-11789. 208p. (C). 1999. reprint ed. pap. 22.95 (*0-85115-338-0*, Boydell Pr) Boydell & Brewer.

Pastons: The Story of a Medieval Family. Frances Gies & Joseph Gies. LC 97-49169. 416p. 1998. 27.50 (*0-06-017264-9*) HarpC.

Pastons & Their England. H. S. Bennett. LC 90-34447. (Canto Book Ser.). 304p. (C). 1990. pap. 11.95 (*0-521-39826-6*) Cambridge U Pr.

Pastor . . . Be Encouraged! Insights for Maintaining Spiritual Victory. C. Neil Strait. 112p. 1996. pap. text 9.99 (*0-8341-1658-8*) Beacon Hill.

Pastor Amos: Tragedy & Triumph. Herbert J. Oyer. 1997. pap. 12.95 (*0-7880-0916-8*, Fairway Pr) CSS OH.

Pastor & His Ministry see Pastor y Su Ministerio: Una Guia Pratica

Pastor & His Work. Homer A. Kent, Sr. pap. 12.99 (*0-88469-079-2*) BMH Bks.

Pastor & Laity in the Theology of Jean Gerson. D. Catherine Brown. 420p. 1987. 85.00 (*0-521-33029-7*) Cambridge U Pr.

Pastor & Parish: The Psychological Care of Ecclesiastical Conflicts. Robert L. Randall. LC 86-27176. 172p. 1987. 38.95 (*0-89885-348-6*, Kluwer Acad Hman Sci) Kluwer Academic.

Pastor & Patient: A Handbook for Clergy Who Visit the Sick. Ed. by Richard Dayringer. LC 80-70247. 292p. 1995. reprint ed. pap. 45.00 (*1-56821-512-6*) Aronson.

Pastor & People. Roy T. Williams. 1990. reprint ed. pap. 3.99 (*0-88019-091-4*) Schmul Pub Co.

Pastor & the Church Musicians: Thoughts on Aspects of a Common Ministry. Carl F. Schalk. 12p. (Orig.). 1984. reprint ed. pap. 2.50 (*0-570-01330-5*, 99-1256) Concordia.

Pastor & the Patient. Kent D. Richmond & David L. Middleton. 144p. (Orig.). 1992. pap. 13.95 (*0-687-30352-4*) Abingdon.

Pastor As a Counselor see Pasteur & la Cure d'Ame

Pastor As a Counselor see Pastor Como Consejero

***Pastor as Moral Guide.** Rebekah L. Miles. LC 98-48893. (Creative Pastoral Care & Counseling Ser.). 128p. 1999. pap. 14.00 (*0-8006-3136-6*, 1-3136, Fortress Pr) Augsburg Fortress.

Pastor As Newcomer. Roy M. Oswald. pap. 7.25 (*1-56699-188-9*, OD123) Alban Inst.

Pastor As Person: Maintaining Personal Integrity in the Choices & Challenges of Ministry. Gary L. Harbaugh. LC 84-24259. 172p. (Orig.). 1984. pap. 15.99 (*0-8066-2115-X*, 10-4889, Augsburg) Augsburg Fortress.

Pastor As Religious Educator. Ed. by Robert L. Browning. 277p. (Orig.). 1989. pap. 25.95 (*0-89135-066-7*) Religious Educ.

Pastor As Spiritual Guide. Howard Rice. Ed. by Rita Collett. LC 97-23359. 208p. 1998. pap. 17.00 (*0-8358-0846-7*, UR846) Upper Room Bks.

Pastor-Bobo in the Spanish Theatre Before the Time of Lope de Vega. John Brotherton. (Monagrafias A Ser.: No. 51). 210p. (C). 1975. pap. 51.00 (*0-7293-0011-0*, Pub. by Tamesis Bks Ltd) Boydell & Brewer.

Pastor Bodvar's Letter. Olafur J. Sigurdsson. Tr. by George Johnston. 63p. 1985. 6.95 (*0-920806-72-4*, Pub. by Penumbra Pr) U of Toronto Pr.

***Pastor, Church & Law.** 3rd ed. Richard R. Hammar. 1120p. 2000. 49.95 (*1-880562-42-1*) Christ Minist.

Pastor, Church & Law Workbook. Richard R. Hammar. 96p. (C). 1992. 5.95 (*1-880562-03-0*) Christ Minist.

Pastor Como Consejero. P. Hoff.Tr. of Pastor As a Counselor. (SPA.). 228p. 1981. pap. 6.99 (*0-8297-0640-2*) Vida Pubs.

Pastor, His Life & Work. rev. ed. Charles U. Wagner. LC 88-32248. 448p. 1988. pap. 17.99 (*0-87227-001-7*, RBP5048) Reg Baptist.

Pastor Hsi. Taylor. 1997. pap. 11.99 (*1-85792-159-3*, Pub. by Christian Focus) Spring Arbor Dist.

Pastor, I Am Gay. Howard H. Bess. LC 94-47332. 224p. (Orig.). 1995. pap. 14.95 (*0-9644123-0-6*) Palmer Pubng.

***Pastor in Every Pew: Equipping Laity for Pastoral Care.** Leroy Howe. 176p. 2000. pap. 15.00 (*0-8170-1366-0*) Judson.

Pastor in Prayer. Charles H. Spurgeon. 1997. pap. text 8.99 (*1-898787-89-1*) Emerald House Group Inc.

Pastor, Our Marriage Is in Trouble: A Guide to Short-Term Counseling. Charles L. Rassieur. 129p. 1992. pap. 10.95 (*1-56024-350-3*) Haworth Pr.

Pastor-People Partnership: The Call & Recall of Pastors from a Believers' Church Perspective. Leland Harder. (Occasional Papers: No. 5). 180p. 1983. pap. 5.00 (*0-936273-04-6*) Inst Mennonite.

Pastor Promotional Magalog: What to Do . . . (Nineteen Ninety-Six 50-Day Spiritual Adventure Ser.). 16p. (Orig.). 1995. pap. 0.50 (*1-879050-94-3*) Chapel of Air.

Pastor Russell's Date System: And Teachings on the Person of Christ, the Atonement, Etc. J. H. Burridge. 32p. 1988. reprint ed. pap. 1.95 (*1-883858-45-3*) Witness CA.

Pastor Russell's Position & Credentials: And His Methods of Interpretation. J. H. Burridge. 32p. 1988. reprint ed. pap. 1.95 (*1-883858-44-5*) Witness CA.

Pastor Russell's Teachings on the Coming of Christ. J. H. Burridge. 32p. 1988. reprint ed. pap. 1.95 (*1-883858-46-1*) Witness CA.

Pastor Search Committee Planbook. Gerald M. Williamson. LC 81-68923. 64p. 1981. pap. 8.99 (*0-8054-3515-8*, 4235-15) Broadman.

***Pastor, Stop Lying on God.** Alvin Williamson. 96p. 1999. pap. 5.95 (*1-56167-525-3*) Am Literary Pr.

Pastor to Pastor: Trackling the Problems of Ministry. expanded rev. ed. Erwin W. Lutzer. LC 97-41096. 128p. 1997. pap. 8.99 (*0-8254-3164-6*) Kregel.

Pastor, Why Can't I Remarry? see Is Marriage Till Death?

***Pastor y Su Ministerio: Una Guia Pratica.** W. A. Criswell. Tr. by Alirio Eustache. Orig. Title: Criswell's Guidbook for Pastors. (SPA.). 368p. 1998. pap. text 14.99 (*0-311-42102-4*) Casa Bautista.

***Pastoral.** Terry Gifford. 1999. pap. 14.99 (*0-415-14733-6*) Routledge.

***Pastoral.** Terry Gifford. (The New Critical Idiom Ser.). 200p. (C). 1999. text 50.00 (*0-415-14732-8*) Routledge.

***Pastoral.** Carl Phillips. 80p. 2000. pap. 14.00 (*1-55597-298-5*, Pub. by Graywolf) SPD-Small Pr Dist.

Pastoral. Nevil Shute. 22.95 (*0-88411-322-1*) Amereon Ltd.

Pastoral. large type ed. Nevil Shute. 384p. 1984. 27.99 (*0-7089-8220-4*, Charnwood) Ulverscroft.

Pastoral Accounting in Colonial Australia: A Case Study of Unregulated Accounting. Garry Carnegie. LC 97-33178. (New Works in Accounting History). (Illus.). 308p. 1997. text 67.00 (*0-8153-3037-5*) Garland.

Pastoral Action of Bishop John Baptist Scalabrini & His Missionaries among Immigrants in the Americas, 1887-1987 see Pastoral Series

Pastoral & Canonical Innovations of Pastoralis Migratiorum Cura see Pastoral Series

Pastoral & Occasional Liturgies. Leonel L. Mitchell. 130p. 1998. pap. 14.95 (*1-56101-158-4*) Cowley Pubns.

Pastoral & Politics in the Old South. John M. Grammer. LC 96-22786. (Southern Literary Studies). 200p. 1997. text 32.50 (*0-8071-2117-7*) La State U Pr.

Pastoral & Practical Theology of Wilhemus a Brakel. Bartel Elshout. 55p. 1997. pap. 3.75 (*1-892777-08-8*) Reform Heritage Bks.

Pastoral & the Academic: Conflict & Contradiction in the Curriculum. Sally Power. LC 97-127205. (Studies in Pastoral Care, Personal & Social Education). (Illus.). 196p. 1996. 80.00 (*0-304-33223-2*); pap. 37.95 (*0-304-33225-9*) Continuum.

Pastoral & the Poetics of Self-Contradiction: Theocritus to Marvell. Judith Haber. LC 93-46826. 232p. (C). 1995. text 59.95 (*0-521-44206-0*) Cambridge U Pr.

Pastoral Associations in Chad: Oxfam Research Discussion Papers. Hedwig Bruggeman. (Oxfam Research Discussions Papers). 40p. (C). 1993. pap. 15.95 (*0-85598-214-4*, Pub. by Oxfam Pub) Stylus Pub VA.

Pastoral Bereavement Counseling: A Structured Program to Help Mourners. Jacob Goldberg. LC 87-30131. 194p. 1989. 34.95 (*0-89885-419-9*, Kluwer Acad Hman Sci) Kluwer Academic.

Pastoral Care: A Parish Planning Workbook. Joseph Champlin. (Follow Me! Ser.). 1998. pap. 9.95 (*1-881307-15-8*, B7158) Natl Pastoral LC.

Pastoral Care Among Friends: Art of the Everyday. Zoe White. LC 88-6221. 1988. pap. 4.00 (*0-87574-281-5*) Pendle Hill.

Pastoral Care & Administration in Mid-14th Century Barcelona: Exercising the "Art of Arts" Kristine T. Utterback. LC 93-2381. ii, 213p. 1993. write for info. (*0-7734-9311-5*) E Mellen.

Pastoral Care & Context. Ed. by Otto Stange. 160p. (Orig.). 1992. pap. text 20.00 (*90-5383-041-3*, Pub. by VU Univ Pr) Paul & Co Pubs.

Pastoral Care & Counseling. James E. Giles. 1984. pap. text 13.99 (*0-311-72535-X*) Casa Bautista.

Pastoral Care & Counselling: A Manual. William K. Kay & Paul C. Weaver. xiv, 200p. 1997. reprint ed. pap. 16.99 (*0-85364-784-4*, Pub. by Paternoster Pub) OM Literature.

Pastoral Care & Counselling in Africa Today. Ed. by Jean M. Ma Mpolo & Daisy Nwachuku. (African Pastoral Studies: Vol. 1). (Illus.). 194p. 1991. pap. 36.80 (*3-631-44131-2*) P Lang Pubng.

Pastoral Care & Liberation Praxis: Studies in Personal & Social Transformation. Ed. by Perry D. LeFevre & W. Widick Schroeder. (Studies in Ministry & Parish Life). 112p. 1986. text 19.95 (*0-913552-31-3*); pap. text 12.95 (*0-913552-32-1*) Exploration Pr.

Pastoral Care & Liberation Theology. Stephen Pattison. (Cambridge Studies in Ideology & Religion: No. 5). 288p. (C). 1994. text 59.95 (*0-521-41822-4*) Cambridge U Pr.

Pastoral Care & PSE: Entitlement & Provision. Ron Best et al. (Cassell Studies in Pastoral Care & PSE). (Illus.). 256p. 1995. pap. 39.95 (*0-304-32780-8*) Continuum.

Pastoral Care & PSE: Entitlement & Provision. Ron Best et al. Ed. by Caroline Lodge. (Cassell Studies in Pastoral Care & PSE). (Illus.). 352p. 1995. 100.00 (*0-304-32781-6*) Continuum.

Pastoral Care & the Means of Grace. Ralph L. Underwood. LC 92-18311. (Resources for Preaching Ser.). 168p. 1993. pap. 18.00 (*0-8006-2589-7*, 1-2589) Augsburg Fortress.

Pastoral Care Before the Parish. Ed. by John Blair & Richard Sharp. 256p. 1992. text 59.00 (*0-7185-1372-X*, Pub. by Leicester U Pr) Cassell & Continuum.

Pastoral Care for Severe Emotional Disorders: Principles of Diagnosis & Treatment. Paul C. Holinger. LC 83-18670. 145p. 1985. text 27.95 (*0-8290-1509-4*) Irvington.

Pastoral Care for Single Parents. Harold I. Smith. 158p. 1982. pap. 9.99 (*0-8341-0782-1*) Beacon Hill.

Pastoral Care for Survivors of Family Abuse. James Leehan. 156p. (Orig.). 1989. pap. 15.95 (*0-664-25025-4*) Westminster John Knox.

Pastoral Care for Young People. Ed. by Paul Hansford. (Oasis Youth Resources Ser.). 224p. 1997. pap. 11.99 (*0-551-03063-1*, Pub. by M Pickering) Harper SF.

Pastoral Care in Context: An Introduction to Pastoral Care. John Patton. LC 93-3262. 288p. 1993. text 24.95 (*0-664-22034-7*) Westminster John Knox.

***Pastoral Care in Emergencies.** David K. Switzer. (Creative Pastoral Care & Counseling Ser.). 2000. pap. 18.00 (*0-8006-3228-1*, Fortress Pr) Augsburg Fortress.

Pastoral Care in Hospitals. Neville Kirkwood. LC 98-35131. 288p. 1999. pap. 14.95 (*0-8192-1790-5*) Morehouse Pub.

Pastoral Care in Hospitals. Neville A. Kirkwood. 288p. 1995. pap. 14.95 (*0-85574-405-7*, Pub. by E J Dwyer) Morehouse Pub.

Pastoral Care in Parishes Without a Pastor: Applications of Canon 517, Section 2. Ed. by Barbara A. Cusack & Therese G. Sullivan. 88p. 1995. pap. 8.00 (*0-943616-68-9*) Canon Law Soc.

Pastoral Care in Pregnancy Loss: A Ministry Long Needed. Thomas Moe. LC 96-9343. 162p. (C). 1996. pap. 19.95 (*0-7890-0196-9*, Haworth Pastrl) Haworth Pr.

Pastoral Care in Pregnancy Loss: A Ministry Long Needed. Thomas Moe. LC 96-9343. 162p. (C). 1997. 39.95 (*0-7890-0124-1*, Haworth Pastrl) Haworth Pr.

***Pastoral Care of Children.** Ed. by Daniel H. Grossoehme. LC 99-34430. 152p. (C). 1999. 29.95 (*0-7890-0604-9*, Haworth Pastrl); pap. 14.95 (*0-7890-0605-7*, Haworth Pastrl) Haworth Pr.

Pastoral Care of Depression: A Guidebook. Binford W. Gilbert. LC 97-19563. 127p. 1997. 29.95 (*0-7890-0264-7*, Haworth Pastrl); pap. 19.95 (*0-7890-0265-5*, Haworth Pastrl) Haworth Pr.

Pastoral Care of Gays, Lesbians & Their Families. David K. Switzer. LC 98-48890. (Creative Pastoral Care & Counseling Ser.). 160p. 1999. pap. 17.00 (*0-8006-2954-X*, 1-2954, Fortress Pr) Augsburg Fortress.

Pastoral Care of Migrants in the Directives of the Church. Velasio De Paolis. 26p. 1989. 5.00 (*0-934733-46-5*) CMS.

Pastoral Care of Older Adults. Harold George Koenig & Andrew J. Weaver. LC 98-28755. 112p. 1998. pap. 15.00 (*0-8006-2964-7*, 1-2964) Augsburg Fortress.

Pastoral Care of the Mentally Disabled: Advancing Care of the Whole Person. Ed. by Sally K. Severino & Richard Liew. LC 94-17287. 116p. (C). 1994. 39.95 (*1-56024-665-0*) Haworth Pr.

Pastoral Care of the Mentally Disabled: Advancing Care of the Whole Person. Ed. by Sally K. Severino & Richard Liew. LC 94-17287. 116p. (C). 1996. pap. 14.95 (*0-7890-0095-4*) Haworth Pr.

Pastoral Care of the Sick. M.A.C.C. Team Staff. (SPA.). 205p. 1986. write for info. (*0-614-04883-4*) Mex Am Cult.

Pastoral Care of the Sick: Rite of Anointing & Viaticum. large type ed. 384p. 1983. vinyl bd. 9.95 (*0-89942-156-3*, 156/04) Catholic Bk Pub.

Pastoral Care of the Sick: Rites of Anointing & Viaticum. 344p. 1983. 14.95 (*0-8146-1321-7*) Liturgical Pr.

Pastoral Care of the Sick: Rites of Anointing & Viaticum. large type ed. 9.95p. 1983. 13.95 (*0-89942-456-2*, 456/22) Catholic Bk Pub.

Pastoral Care of the Sick - Cuidado Pastoral de los Enfermos. abr. ed. Vatican Congregation for Divine Worship Staff. Ed. by Bishops' Committee on the Liturgy, National Confer. Tr. by International Committee on English in the Liturgy from LAT. 205p. 1986. pap. 15.00 (*0-930467-54-X*, BPCARE) Liturgy Tr Pubns.

Pastoral Care Revisited. Frank Wright. 1996. pap. 24.00 (*0-334-01199-X*) TPI PA.

Pastoral Care Through Worship. Howard W. Roberts. 192p. 1995. pap. 15.00 (*1-880837-74-9*) Smyth & Helwys.

Pastoral Care under the Cross: God in the Midst of Suffering. Richard C. Eyer. LC 94-34466. 160p. 1995. pap. 15.00 (*0-570-04643-2*, 12-3224) Concordia.

Pastoral Care with Children in Crisis. Andrew D. Lester. LC 84-21901. 7p. (Orig.). (C). 1985. pap. 15.95 (*0-664-24598-6*) Westminster John Knox.

Pastoral Care with Handicapped Persons. Lowell G. Colston. LC 77-15229. (Creative Pastoral Care & Counseling Ser.). 94p. (Orig.). reprint ed. pap. 30.00 (*0-608-15814-3*, 203124100074) Bks Demand.

***Pastoral Care with Stepfamilies: Mapping the Wilderness.** Loren L. Townsend. LC 00-9141. 2000. 21.99 (*0-8272-2966-6*) Chalice Pr.

Pastoral Catechetics in Action. Kevin Nichols. (C). 1988. 30.00 (*0-85439-144-4*, Pub. by St Paul Pubns) St Mut.

Pastoral Challenges of the New Immigration. Silvano M. Tomasi. (Pastoral Ser.). 15p. 1990. 5.00 (*0-934733-49-X*) CMS.

Pastoral Cities: Urban Ideals & the Symbolic Landscape of America. James L. Machor. LC 87-2171. (History of American Thought & Culture Ser.). 288p. (C). 1987. pap. text 14.95 (*0-299-11284-5*) U of Wis Pr.

An Asterisk (*) at the beginning of an entry indicates that the title is appearing for the first time.

***Pastoral Communications Guide: An Effective Performance Tool for Church Professionals.** Joseph R. Sullivan & Fred Leafgren. Ed. by Arthur Mallison. 115p. 1999. pap. 99.00 (*1-929112-02-5*) Personality Res.

Pastoral Companion: A Canon Law Handbook for Catholic Ministry. expanded rev. ed. John M. Huels. LC 85-29316. 432p. 1997. reprint ed. 25.00 (*0-8199-0968-8*, Frncscn Herld) Franciscan Pr.

Pastoral Conference 1969 see Pastirskoje Sovjeshchjanije, 1969

Pastoral Constitution on the Church in the Modern World: Gaudium et Spes. Second Vatican Council Staff. 112p. 1965. pap. 4.95 (*0-8198-5854-4*) Pauline Bks.

Pastoral Continuum: The Marginalization of Tradition in East Africa. Paul Spencer. LC 97-23105. (Oxford Studies in Social & Cultural Anthropology). (Illus.). 320p. 1998. text 75.00 (*0-19-823375-2*) OUP.

Pastoral Conventions: Poetry, Language, & Thought in Seventeenth-Century Nuremberg. Jane O. Newman. LC 89-49002. 328p. reprint ed. pap. 101.70 (*0-608-06175-1*, 206650800008) Bks Demand.

Pastoral Counseling. 2nd ed. Barry K. Estadt et al. 320p. (C). 1990. pap. text 23.80 (*0-13-653007-9*) P-H.

Pastoral Counseling: The Basics. James E. Dittes. LC 98-33352. 184p. 1999. pap. 16.00 (*0-664-25738-0*) Westminster John Knox.

Pastoral Counseling Across Cultures. David W. Augsburger. 1995. pap. 26.95 (*0-664-25616-3*) Westminster John Knox.

Pastoral Counseling & Personality Disorders. Richard P. Vaughan. LC 93-36373. 180p. (Orig.). 1994. pap. 15.95 (*1-55612-660-3*) Sheed & Ward WI.

Pastoral Counseling in a Global Church: Voices from the Field. Robert J. Wicks & Barry K. Estadt. LC 93-22082. 150p. (Orig.). 1993. pap. 18.00 (*0-88344-865-3*) Orbis Bks.

Pastoral Counseling Treatment Planner. James R. Kok & Arthur E. Jongsma, Jr. LC 98-20502. 166p. 1998. pap. text 175.00 incl. disk (*0-471-25417-7*) Wiley.

***Pastoral Counseling Treatment Planner.** James R. Kok & Arthur E. Jongsma, Jr. LC 98-20502. 176p. 1998. pap. 39.95 (*0-471-25416-9*) Wiley.

Pastoral Deities in Western India. Gunther-Dietz Sontheimer. Tr. by Anne Feldhaus. (Illus.). 296p. 1994. reprint ed. pap. 16.95 (*0-19-563293-1*) OUP.

***Pastoral Democracy.** I. M. Lewis. 392p. 1999. 56.95 (*3-8258-3566-9*, Pub. by CE24); pap. 29.95 (*3-8258-3084-5*, Pub. by CE24) Transaction Pubs.

Pastoral Democracy: A Study of Pastoralism & Politics among the Northern Somali of the Horn of Africa. I. M. Lewis. LC 81-4074. (Illus.). 349p. reprint ed. pap. 108.20 (*0-8357-3015-8*, 205710100010) Bks Demand.

Pastoral Development Planning. Julian Prior. LC 95-204569. 160p. (C). 1994. 39.95 (*0-85598-203-9*, Pub. by Oxfam Pub); pap. 14.95 (*0-85598-204-7*, Pub. by Oxfam Pub) Stylus Pub VA.

Pastoral Diagnosis: A Resource for Ministries of Care & Counseling. Nancy J. Ramsay. 112p. 1998. pap. 18.00 (*0-8006-2629-X*, 1-2629) Augsburg Fortress.

Pastoral Economics in The Kingdom of Naples. John A. Marino. LC 87-9196. (Studies in Historical & Political Science: 106th Series, No. 1). 400p. 1988. text 60.00 (*0-8018-3437-6*) Johns Hopkins.

***Pastoral Education: Teacher's Edition.** Mary Gurney. (Illus.). 176p. (YA). (gr. 6-10). 2000. pap., teacher ed. 99.50 (*0-7487-5166-1*, Pub. by S Thornes Pubs) Trans-Atl Phila.

Pastoral Epistles see Practical Truth Series

Pastoral Epistles. Edward M. Blaiklock. 128p. 1972. pap. 7.99 (*0-310-21233-2*, 9232P) Zondervan.

Pastoral Epistles. Margaret Davies. (New Testament Guides Ser.: Vol. 14). 127p. 1996. pap. 12.50 (*1-85075-743-7*, Pub. by Sheffield Acad) CUP Services.

Pastoral Epistles. Martin Dibelius & Hans Conzelmann. Ed. by Helmut Koester. Tr. by Philip Buttolph & Adela Yarbro from GER. LC 71-157549. (Hermeneia: A Critical & Historical Commentary on the Bible Ser.). 176p. 1972. 38.00 (*0-8006-6002-1*, 1-6002, Fortress Pr) Augsburg Fortress.

Pastoral Epistles. Benjamin Fiore. (Sacra Pagina Ser.: No. 12). Date not set. write for info. (*0-8146-5814-8*, M Glazier) Liturgical Pr.

Pastoral Epistles. Anthony Tyrrell Hanson. (New Century Bible Ser.). 1982. pap. 14.95 (*0-551-00926-8*, Pub. by Sheffield Acad) CUP Services.

Pastoral Epistles. K. Karris. 1989. pap. 21.00 (*0-86217-023-0*, Pub. by Veritas Pubns) St Mut.

Pastoral Epistles. J. N. Kelly. (Black's New Testament Commentary Ser.: No. 14). 272p. 1993. 22.95 (*1-56563-023-8*) Hendrickson MA.

Pastoral Epistles. Homer A. Kent, Jr. 320p. 1982. pap. 14.99 (*0-88469-075-X*) BMH Bks.

***Pastoral Epistles.** I. Howard Marshall. 928p. 1999. 69.95 (*0-567-08661-5*) T&T Clark Pubs.

Pastoral Epistles. William Mounce. (Word Biblical Commentary Ser.: Vol. 46). 592p. 1999. 32.99 (*0-8499-0245-2*) Word Pub.

Pastoral Epistles. Geoffrey B. Wilson. 173p. 1982. pap. 7.99 (*0-85151-335-2*) Banner of Truth.

Pastoral Epistles. rev. ed. Donald Guthrie. Ed. by Leon Morris. (Tyndale New Testament Commentaries Ser.). 240p. 1990. pap. 13.00 (*0-8028-0482-9*) Eerdmans.

Pastoral Epistles. 2nd rev. ed. Gordon H. Clark. Ed. & Intro. by John W. Robbins. (Works of Gordon Haddon Clark). (Illus.). 250p. 1998. pap. 14.95 (*1-891777-05-X*) Trinity Found.

Pastoral Epistles. 2nd rev. ed. Gordon H. Clark. Ed. & Intro. by John W. Robbins. (Works of Gordon Haddon Clark). (Illus.). 250p. 1999. 29.95 (*1-891777-04-1*) Trinity Found.

Pastoral Epistles: A Commentary on I & II Timothy & Titus. J. R. Ensey. LC 90-35717. 235p. (Orig.). 1990. pap. 8.99 (*0-932581-69-2*) Word Aflame.

Pastoral Epistles: A Commentary on the Greek Text. George W. Knight, III. (New International Greek Testament Commentary Ser.). 600p. 1992. text 45.00 (*0-8028-2395-5*) Eerdmans.

***Pastoral Epistles: Blue Prints for 28 Messages Built upon God's Word.** Wayne E. Shaw. Ed. by Jim Eichenberger. (Solid Foundation Sermon Starters Ser.: Vol. 6). 64p. 1999. pap. 5.99 (*0-7847-0936-X*, 23014, Solid Fnd Res) Standard Pub.

Pastoral Epistles: Critical & Exegetical Commentary. Walter Lock. Ed. by Samuel R. Driver et al. (International Critical Commentary Ser.). 212p. 1928. 39.95 (*0-567-05033-5*, Pub. by T & T Clark) Bks Intl VA.

Pastoral Epistles: I & II Timothy & Titus. Margaret Davies. 1997. pap. text 17.00 (*0-7162-0504-1*) Epworth Pr.

Pastoral Epistles: I & II Timothy, Titus. J. L. Houlden. Ed. by Howard C. Kee & Dennis E. Nineham. LC 89-53801. (New Testament Commentaries Ser.). 168p. 1989. 15.00 (*0-334-01327-5*) TPI PA.

Pastoral Epistles: Studies in 1 & 2 Timothy & Titus. Homer A. Kent, Jr. 314p. (C). 1993. pap. text 16.95 (*1-879215-16-0*) Sheffield WI.

Pastoral Foundations of the Sacraments: A Catholic Perspective. Gregory L. Klein & Robert A. Wolfe. LC 97-41747. 224p. 1998. pap. 14.95 (*0-8091-3770-4*) Paulist Pr.

Pastoral Fulbe Family in Gwandu. C. Edward Hopen. LC 58-2505. (Illus.). 183p. reprint ed. pap. 56.80 (*0-8357-3011-5*, 205709700010) Bks Demand.

Pastoral Genetics: Theology & Care at the Beginning of Life. Ronald Cole-Turner & Brent Waters. LC 95-50981. 192p. (Orig.). 1996. pap. 15.95 (*0-8298-1077-3*) Pilgrim OH.

Pastoral Grit: The Strength to Stand & to Stay. Craig B. Larson. Ed. by David L. Goetz. LC 97-45441. (Pastor's Soul Ser.). 176p. 1998. text 16.99 (*1-55661-969-3*) Bethany Hse.

Pastoral Guidelines on Infant Baptism. Archidocese of Dublin Staff. 1993. pap. 24.95 (*1-85390-001-X*, Pub. by Veritas Pubns) St Mut.

Pastoral Instruction on the Means of Social Communication: Communio et Progressio. Pontifical Council for Social Communications Staff. 77p. pap. 0.50 (*0-8198-4749-6*) Pauline Bks.

Pastoral Landscape. Ed. by John D. Hunt. (Illus.). 1996. 45.00 (*0-300-07513-8*) Yale U Pr.

Pastoral Leader's Handbook. Angeline Bukowiecki & Brigid Meierotto. (Evangelizer's Handbook, Evangelistic Series Sisters of the New Convenant). 28p. (Orig.). (C). 1987. pap. text 10.00 (*0-924333-06-5*) Sisters New Covenant.

Pastoral Leadership. Robert E. Dale. 1986. 16.95 (*0-687-30349-4*) Abingdon.

Pastoral Letter to the English Captives in Africa. Cotton Mather. (Notable American Authors Ser.). 1999. reprint ed. lib. bdg. 125.00 (*0-7812-3957-5*) Rprt Serv.

Pastoral Letters. Marcel Lefebvre. Tr. by Society of St. Pius X Staff from FRE. 148p. (Orig.). 1992. pap. text 8.95 (*0-935952-99-3*) Angelus Pr.

Pastoral Letters & Statements of the U. S. Catholic Bishops, 1989 to 1997, Vol. 6. Ed. by Patrick Carey. 916p. (C). 1998. 39.95 (*1-57455-174-4*) US Catholic.

Pastoral Letters As Composite Documents. James D. Miller. (Society for New Testament Studies Monograph Ser.: Vol. 93). 224p. (C). 1997. text 54.95 (*0-521-56048-9*) Cambridge U Pr.

Pastoral Letters of the United States Catholic Bishops, 1792-1940, Vol. I. Ed. by Hugh J. Nolan. 489p. 1984. pap. 24.95 (*1-55586-880-0*) US Catholic.

Pastoral Letters of the United States Catholic Bishops, 1941-1961, Vol. II. Ed. by Hugh J. Nolan. 273p. 1984. pap. 24.95 (*1-55586-885-1*) US Catholic.

Pastoral Letters of the United States Catholic Bishops, 1962-1974, Vol. III. Ed. by Hugh J. Nolan. 511p. 1984. pap. 24.95 (*1-55586-870-3*) US Catholic.

Pastoral Letters of the United States Catholic Bishops, 1975-1983, Vol. IV. Ed. by Hugh J. Nolan. 617p. 1984. pap. 24.95 (*1-55586-875-4*) US Catholic.

Pastoral Letters of the United States Catholic Bishops, 1983-1988, Vol. V. Ed. by Hugh J. Nolan. 797p. 1989. 39.95 (*1-55586-200-4*) US Catholic.

Pastoral Life in the Power of the Spirit. Johannes Hofinger. LC 81-1439. (Illus.). 215p. 1982. pap. 6.95 (*0-8189-0427-5*) Alba.

Pastoral Livelihoods in Danger: Cattle Disease, Drought, & Wildlife Conservation in Mursiland, South-Western Ethiopia. David Turton. (Oxfam Research Papers: 11). (Illus.). 75p. (C). 1996. pap. 15.95 (*0-85598-333-7*, Pub. by Oxfam Pub) Stylus Pub VA.

Pastoral Masquerade: Disguise & Identity in l'Astree. Laurence A. Gregorio. (Stanford French & Italian Studies: Vol. 73). 128p. 1992. pap. 56.50 (*0-915838-89-3*) Anma Libri.

Pastoral Medicine: The Collegial Working of Doctors & Priests. Rudolf Steiner. Tr. by Gladys Hahn from GER.Tr. of Pastoral-Medizinischer Kurs. 172p. 1987. pap. 16.95 (*0-88010-253-5*) Anthroposophic.

Pastoral-Medizinischer Kurs see Pastoral Medicine: The Collegial Working of Doctors & Priests

Pastoral Ministry in the AIDS Era: Focus on Families & Friends of Persons with AIDS. Louis F. Kavar. LC 88-50082. 64p. (Orig.). 1988. pap. 7.95 (*0-934104-07-7*) Woodland.

Pastoral Muse. Thomas Hardy. 1999. 19.95 (*1-86019-392-7*) Brockhampton Pr Ltd.

Pastoral Music in Practice: Introduction. Ed. by Virgil C. Funk. (Pastoral Music in Practice Ser.). 1981. 7.95 (*0-9602378-3-6*, Pastoral Press) OR Catholic.

Pastoral Musician. Ed. by Virgil C. Funk. (Pastoral Music in Practice Ser.). 120p. 1991. pap. 7.95 (*0-912405-76-7*, Pastoral Press) OR Catholic.

***Pastoral Musician's Book of Days.** Gordon E. Truitt. 208p. 2000. pap. 15.00 (*1-888360-02-X*) NPM Pubns.

Pastoral Narcissus: A Study of the 1st Idyll of Theocritus. Clayton Zimmerman. LC 94-8398. (Greek Studies: Interdisciplinary Approaches). 128p. 1994. pap. 19.95 (*0-8476-7962-4*); lib. bdg. 51.50 (*0-8476-7961-6*) Rowman.

Pastoral Nature of Theology: An Upholding Presence. R. John Elford. 1999. 69.95 (*0-264-67489-8*); pap. text 27.95 (*0-264-67490-1*) Continuum.

Pastoral Nomadism in Arid Zones of India: Socio-Demographic & Ecological Aspects. R. R. Prasad. (C). 1994. text 24.00 (*81-7141-237-8*, Pub. by Discovery Pub Hse) S Asia.

Pastoral Novel: Studies in George Eliot, Thomas Hardy, & D. H. Lawrence. Michael Squires. LC 74-75793. 240p. reprint ed. pap. 74.40 (*0-608-13778-2*, 202063900018) Bks Demand.

Pastoral Partners: Affinity & Bond Partnership among the Dassanetch of South-West Ethiopia. Uri Almagor. LC 78-4128. 258p. 1978. 49.50 (*0-8419-0384-0*, Africana) Holmes & Meier.

Pastoral Plan for Church Communication. U. S. Catholic Bishops Staff. 20p. (Orig.). 1997. pap. text 2.95 (*1-57455-141-8*) US Catholic.

Pastoral Poems. Selected by Ron Hawkins. (Jarrold Poets Ser.). 146p. (Orig.). 1994. 5.95 (*0-7117-0680-8*) Seven Hills Bk.

Pastoral Politics: Shepherds, Bureaucrats & Conservation in the Western Himalaya. Basant K. Saberwal. LC 99-932098. (Studies in Social Ecology & Environmental History). (Illus.). 266p. 1999. text 28.95 (*0-19-564308-9*) OUP.

***Pastoral Practice: Books 3 & 4 of the "Regula Pastoralis" by Saint Gregory the Great.** Ed. & Tr. by John Leinenweber from LAT. LC 97-45169. 112p. 1998. pap. 12.00 (*1-56338-237-7*) TPI PA.

Pastoral Practice & the Paranormal. Bonaventure Kloppenburg. Tr. by David Smith. 164p. 1979. 4.95 (*0-8199-0762-6*, Frncscn Herld) Franciscan Pr.

***Pastoral Prayer Book: Occasional Prayers for Times of Change, Concern & Celebration.** Raymond Chapman. LC 99-34672. 128p. 2000. 18.95 (*0-8192-1822-7*) Morehouse Pub.

***Pastoral Prayers for All Seasons.** Rolland Reece. 2000. pap. 17.25 (*0-7880-1567-2*) CSS OH.

Pastoral Process: Spenser, Marvell, Milton. Susan Snyder. LC 97-30363. 241p. 1998. write for info. (*0-8047-3106-3*) Stanford U Pr.

Pastoral Provisions: Married Catholic Priests. Joseph H. Fichter. LC 89-61925. 160p. (Orig.). 1989. pap. 13.95 (*1-55612-306-X*) Sheed & Ward WI.

Pastoral Psychology see Hacia una Sicologia Pastoral Para los Anos 2000

Pastoral Psychology & Inner Conflict. Ioannis K. Kornarakis. Tr. by Esther Williams. LC 90-43815. 150p. (Orig.). 1991. pap. 9.95 (*0-917651-78-2*, Pub. by Holy Cross Orthodox) BookWorld.

Pastoral Psychotherapy: Theory & Practice. Carroll Wise. LC 84-45025. 328p. 1983. 50.00 (*0-87668-661-7*) Aronson.

***Pastoral Reflections: Sunday Homilies - The Full Liturgical Cycle.** Don L. Fischer. Ed. by Debra W. Hampton. 480p. 2000. pap. 30.00 Pastoral Reflections.

Pastoral Responses to Older Adults & Their Families: An Annotated Bibliography, 15. Ed. by Vivienne Pierce. LC 91-43560. (Bibliographies & Indexes in Gerontology Ser.: No. 15). 288p. 1992. lib. bdg. 59.95 (*0-313-28039-8*, SXD/, Greenwood Pr) Greenwood.

Pastoral Responses to Sexual Issues. William V. Arnold. LC 93-10750. 176p. 1993. pap. 15.00 (*0-664-25450-0*) Westminster John Knox.

Pastoral Role in Caring for the Dying & Bereaved: Pragmatic & Ecumenical, 7. Ed. by Austin H. Kutscher et al. LC 86-545. (Foundation of Thanatology Ser.: Vol. 7). 245p. 1986. 75.00 (*0-275-92153-0*, C2153, Praeger Pubs) Greenwood.

Pastoral Romance: The Tribulation & Triumph of Savatterdom. Maurice French. (History of the Darling Downs Frontier Ser.: Vol. 2). (Illus.). xvi, 304p. (Orig.). 1990. pap. 29.95 (*0-949414-50-6*, Pub. by U Sthrn Queenslnd) Accents Pubns.

Pastoral Scenes. (In Classical Mood Ser.: Vol. 29). (Illus.). 1998. write for info. incl. cd-rom (*1-886614-55-5*) Intl Masters Pub.

Pastoral Search Check-Up. Dave Ray. 50p. 1997. pap., wbk. ed. 14.95 (*1-57326-025-8*) Core Ministries.

Pastoral Series. Incl. Bishop Scalabrini's Plan for the Pastoral Care of Migrants of all Nationalities. Mario Francesconi. 38p. 1973. 5.00 (*0-934733-24-4*); Church, The National Parish & Immigration: Same Old Mistakes. A. M. Greely. 8p. 1973. 3.00 (*0-913256-48-X*); Church's Magna Charta for Migrants. Ed. by G. Tessarolo. 300p. 1961. 3.50 (*0-913256-45-5*); Ethnic Heritage & Cultural Pluralism in the U. S. A. C. S. Tomasi & M. Silvano. (ENG, FRE & SPA.). 8p. 1973. 3.00 (*0-913256-51-X*); Ethnicity & Multiculturalism in the Australian Catholic Church. J. J. Smolicz. 40p. 1988. 5.00 (*0-934733-42-2*); Evolution of the Mission of the Scalabrinian Congregation. C. S De Paolis & Velasio. 44p. 1985. 5.00 (*0-913256-84-6*); Itinerant Missions: Alternate Experiences in the History of Scalabrinians in North America. C. S. Battistella. 31p. 1986. 5.00 (*0-934733-02-3*); John B. Scalabrini: An Insight into His Spirituality. Mario Francesconi. 106p. 1973. 5.00 (*0-913256-50-1*); John Baptist Scalabrini: Apostle of the Immigrants. Marco Caliaro & Mario Francesconi. Tr. by Alba Zizzamia. 580p. 1977. 15.00 (*0-913256-24-2*); Lesson from History: The Integration of Immigrants in the Pastoral Practice of the Church in the United States. C. S. Tomasi & M. Silvano. 19p. 1987. 5.00 (*0-934733-22-8*); Pastoral Action of Bishop John Baptist Scalabrini & His Missionaries among Immigrants in the Americas, 1887-1987. C. S. Tomasi & M. Silvano. 31p. 1984. 5.00 (*0-913256-71-4*); Response of the Catholic Church in the United States to Immigrants & Refugees. C. S. Tomasi & M. Silvano. 21p. 1984. 5.00 (*0-913256-74-9*); Theology of the Local Church in Relation to Migration. Bishop Alfred Ancel. 31p. 1974. 5.00 (*0-913256-15-3*); Vol. 31, No. 2. Pastoral & Canonical Innovations of Pastoralis Migratiorum Cura. C. S. Romasi. 10p. 1971. 3.00 (*0-913256-47-1*); write for info. (*0-318-64745-1*) CMS.

Pastoral Sketches. Beverly Carradine. 1987. pap. 9.99 (*0-88019-218-6*) Schmul Pub Co.

Pastoral Societies & Resistance to Change: A Re-evaluation. Nyaga Mwaniki. (Graduate Student Papers Competition: No. 3). 40p. (Orig.). 1980. pap. text 2.00 (*0-941934-32-2*) Indiana Africa.

Pastoral Societies, Stratification & National Integration in Africa. Charles Frantz. (Research Report Ser.: No. 30). 34p. 1975. write for info. (*91-7106-088-X*, Pub. by Nordic Africa) Transaction Pubs.

Pastoral Son & the Spirit of Patriarchy: Religion, Society & Person among East African Stock Keepers. Michael E. Meeker. LC 88-40438. (New Directions in Anthropological Writing Ser.). (Illus.). 215p. reprint ed. pap. 66.70 (*0-608-20452-8*, 207170500002) Bks Demand.

Pastoral Spanish, 2 bks., Set. Romuald Zantua & Karen Eberle-McCarthy. 1993. pap. text, student ed. 199.00 incl. audio (*0-88432-689-6*, SSP320) Audio-Forum.

Pastoral Statement for Catholics on Biblical Fundamentalism English & Spanish. National Conference of Catholic Bishops. Tr. by Marina Herrera. (ENG & SPA.). 20p. (Orig.). 1987. pap. 1.95 (*1-55586-161-X*) US Catholic.

Pastoral Statement on the Catholic Charismatic Renewal. 48p. 1984. pap. 2.95 (*1-55586-931-9*) US Catholic.

Pastoral Stress: Sources of Tension - Resources for Transformation. Anthony G. Pappas. LC 95-75682. 156p. 1995. pap. 15.25 (*1-56699-150-1*, AL160) Alban Inst.

Pastoral Talks for Special Occasion. Harold A. Buetow. LC 94-23339. 238p. (Orig.). 1994. pap. 12.95 (*0-8189-0700-2*) Alba.

Pastoral Teaching of Paul. Edward W. Chadwick. LC 84-7123. 416p. 1984. pap. 15.99 (*0-8254-2325-2*, Kregel Class) Kregel.

Pastoral Themes & Forms in Cervante's Fiction. Dominick Finello. LC 92-56609. (C). 1994. 44.50 (*0-8387-5255-1*) Bucknell U Pr.

Pastoral Theology see Pastirskoje Bogoslovije

Pastoral Theology. LC 53-1007. 272p. 1990. 24.00 (*0-570-04249-6*, 53-1007) Concordia.

Pastoral Theology: A Black-Church Perspective. James H. Harris. LC 91-13457. 160p. 1991. pap. 16.00 (*0-8006-2502-1*, 1-2502, Fortress Pr) Augsburg Fortress.

Pastoral Theology: A Treatise on the Office & Duties of the Christian Pastor. Patrick Fairbairn. 351p. 1992. 19.95 (*0-9632557-0-3*) Old Paths Pubns.

Pastoral Theology: Essentials of Ministry. Thomas C. Oden. LC 82-47753. 384p. (Orig.). 1983. pap. 25.00 (*0-06-066353-7*, RD 415, Pub. by Harper SF) HarpC.

Pastoral Theology: The Pastor in the Various Duties of His Office. unabridged ed. Thomas Murphy. 525p. 1996. 29.95 (*1-889058-01-7*) Old Paths Pubns.

Pastoral Theology from a Global Perspective: A Case Method Approach. Ed. by Judo Poerwowidagdo et al. LC 96-24882. 224p. (Orig.). 1996. pap. 17.00 (*1-57075-079-3*) Orbis Bks.

Pastoral Tradition & the Female Talent: Studies in Augustan Poetry. Ann Messenger. LC 99-40174. (Studies in the Eighteenth Century: No. 25). 1999. write for info. (*0-404-63525-3*) AMS Pr.

Pastoral Transformations: Italian Tragicomedy & Shakespeare's Late Plays. Robert Henke. LC 96-33001. (Illus.). 240p. 1997. 37.50 (*0-87413-620-2*) U Delaware Pr.

Pastoral Transitions: From Endings to New Beginnings. William B. Phillips. LC 88-71755. 77p. 1988. reprint ed. pap. 9.95 (*1-56699-029-7*, AL108) Alban Inst.

Pastoral Tuareg: Ecology, Culture, & Society, 2 vols. Johannes Nicolaison & Ida Nicolaison. LC 96-61101. (Carlsberg Nomad Ser.). (Illus.). 800p. 1997. 70.00 (*0-614-22210-9*) Thames Hudson.

Pastoral Vision of John Paul II. Ed. by Joan Bland. 210p. 1982. pap. 7.50 (*0-8199-0839-8*, Frncscn Herld) Franciscan Pr.

***Pastoral Visitation.** Nancy Gorsuch. LC 99-39380. 128p. 1999. pap. 14.00 (*0-8006-3190-0*, Fortress Pr) Augsburg Fortress.

Pastoral Years of Rev. Anthony Henckel, 1692-1717. Ann H. Gable. LC 91-60989. (Illus.). 125p. 1991. 19.50 (*0-929539-89-3*, 1189, Penobscot Pr) Picton Pr.

Pastorale. Ray Buttigieg. 1978. pap. 4.99 (*0-685-63585-6*) Cykx.

***Pastorale Bezugsrahmen in der Lyrik Wilfred Owens.** Stefan Jeanjour. (Neue Studien zur Anglistik und Amerikanistik). 244p. 1999. 37.95 (*3-631-35028-7*) P Lang Pubng.

Pastoralen Aufgaben der Polnischen Kirche Nach Dem Ende des Kommunismus: Von der Volkskirche zur Kirchlichen Communio. Bernard Gonska. (Europaische Hochschulschriften Ser.: Reihe 23, Bd. 549). (GER.). 330p. 1996. 57.95 (*3-631-49708-3*) P Lang Pubng.

P

*__Pastoralia.__ George Saunders. LC 99-87258. 208p. 2000. 22.95 (*1-57322-161-9*, Riverhead Books) Putnam Pub Group.

Pastoralism in Africa: Origins & Development Ecology. Andrew B. Smith. LC 92-14788. (Illus.). 303p. (C). 1993. text 45.00 (*0-8214-1046-6*); pap. text 19.95 (*0-8214-1047-4*) Ohio U Pr.

Pastoralism in Crisis: The Dasanetch & Their Ethiopian Lands. Claudia J. Carr. LC 77-1252. (University of Chicago, Department of Geography, Research Paper Ser.: No. 180). 373p. 1977. reprint ed. pap. 115.70 (*0-608-02239-X*, 206279900004) Bks Demand.

Pastoralism in Expansion: The Transhuming Shepherds of Western Rajasthan. Purnendu S Kavoori. LC 99-939174. (Studies in Social Ecology & Environmental History). (Illus.). 226p. 2000. text 28.95 (*0-19-564543-X*) OUP.

Pastoralism in Transition see Sustainable Investment & Resource Use

Pastoralism in Tropical Africa: Les Societes Pastorales en Afrique Tropicale: Studies Presented & Discussed at the XIIIth International African Seminar, Niamey, December 1972. International African Seminar Staff. LC 76-353121. (Illus.). 518p. reprint ed. pap. 160.60 (*0-7837-1179-4*, 204170700023) Bks Demand.

Pastoralist Perspectives in Nigeria: The Fulbe of Udubo Grazing Reserve. Jerome O. Gefu. (Research Report Ser.: No. 89). 106p. 1992. 16.95 (*91-7106-324-2*, Pub. by Nordic Africa) Transaction Pubs.

Pastoralists & the Development of Pastoralism. Johan Helland. (Bergen Studies in Social Anthropology, University of Bergen, Norway: No. 20). 214p. (Orig.). 1985. pap. 13.95 (*0-936508-58-2*, Pub. by Bergen Univ Dept Social Anthro) MBIPubg.

Pastoralists at the Periphery: Herders in a Capitalist World. Ed. by Claudia Chang & Harold A. Koster. 262p. 1994. 47.00 (*0-8165-1430-5*) U of Ariz Pr.

Pastoralists under Pressure? Fulbe Societies Confronting Change in West Africa. Ed. by Victor Azarya. LC 99-27461. (Social, Economic & Political Studies of the Middle East & Asia). 454p. 1999. 80.00 (*90-04-11364-9*) Brill Academic Pubs.

Pastorals in Perspective. Charles Ozanne. 40p. (Orig.). 1993. pap. 3.00 (*1-880573-10-5*) Bible Search Pubns.

Pastorals of Dorset. Mary W. Blundell. LC 73-160931. (Short Story Index Reprint Ser.). (Illus.). 1977. reprint ed. 23.95 (*0-8369-3910-7*) Ayer.

*__Pastoreando a los Pastores.__ Arthur R. Baranowski. Tr. by Jerry Frank. (Llamados a ser Iglesia Ser.). 80p. 2000. pap. 6.95 (*0-86716-405-0*) St Anthony Mess Pr.

Pastores. Tr. by M. R. Cole. (AFS Memoirs Ser.: Vol. 9). (SPA., Illus.). 1974. reprint ed. 30.00 (*0-527-01061-8*) Periodicals Srv.

Pastores: History & Performance in the Mexican Shepherd's Play of South Texas. Richard R. Flores. 216p. 1995. pap. text 16.95 (*1-56098-519-4*) Smithsonian.

Pastores da noite see Shepherds of the Night

Pastores de Promesa. J. Hayford.Tr. of Pastors of Promise. (SPA.). 11.99 (*0-7899-0284-2*, 497660) Editorial Unilit.

Pastores Tambien Lloran: They Cry Too! Lucille Lavender. Tr. by Josie H. Smith from ENG. 136p. (Orig.). 1988. reprint ed. pap. 8.99 (*0-311-42075-3*) Casa Bautista.

Pastores y el Rebano. Humberto Casanova Roberts. (SPA.). 222p. 10.95 (*1-55883-105-3*, 6724-0301C) Libros Desafio.

Pastoring by Elders: Reflecting the Heart of the Father. Mike Dowgiewicz & Sue Dowgiewicz. LC 98-209934. 162p. 1998. pap. 10.00 (*1-890592-07-2*) Restrtion Minist.

Pastoring the 'Pastors' Resources for Training & Supporting Pastoral Facilitators for Small Faith Communities. Arthur Baranowski. 68p. 1988. pap. text 6.95 (*0-86716-597-9*) St Anthony Mess Pr.

PastorPower. Martha E. Stortz. LC 92-46305. 144p. (Orig.). 1993. pap. 11.95 (*0-687-08671-X*) Abingdon.

*__Pastors & Educators Guide.__ 1998. 9.95 (*0-664-50067-6*) Geneva Press.

Pastors & Parishioners in Wurttemberg During the Late Reformation, 1581-1621. Bruce Tolley. LC 93-40636. xiv, 199p. 1995. 39.50 (*0-8047-1681-1*) Stanford U Pr.

Pastors & People: German & Lutheran Reformed Churches in the Pennsylvania Field, 1717-1793. Charles H. Glatfelter. LC 80-83400. (Pennsylvania German Folklore Ser.: Vol. 13). (Illus.). 1979. 30.00 (*0-911122-40-0*) Penn German Soc.

Pastors & People: German & Lutheran Reformed Churches in the Pennsylvania Field, 1717-1793, Vol. II, The History. Charles H. Glatfelter. LC 80-83400. (Pennsylvania German Folklore Ser.: Vol. 15). (Illus.). 25.00 (*0-911122-44-3*) Penn German Soc.

Pastors & Pluralism in Wurttemberg, 1918-1933. David J. Diephouse. LC 87-3293. 408p. 1987. reprint ed. pap. 126.50 (*0-608-02594-1*, 206325100004) Bks Demand.

Pastors & the Care of Souls in Medieval England. Ed. by John Shinners & William Dohar. LC 97-21480. (Texts in Medieval Culture Ser.: Vol. 4). 331p. 1998. pap. 25.00 (*0-268-03850-3*) U of Notre Dame Pr.

Pastors & the Care of Souls in Medieval England. Ed. by John Shinners & William Dohar. LC 97-21480. (Texts in Medieval Culture Ser.: Vol. 4). 360p. (C). 1998. 40.00 (*0-268-03821-X*) U of Notre Dame Pr.

Pastors & Visionaries: Religion & Secular Life in Late Medieval Yorkshire. Jonathan Hughes. 428p. 1988. 90.00 (*0-85115-496-4*) Boydell & Brewer.

Pastor's Appreciation Book of Wit & Wisdom. Ed. & Compiled by Douglas J. Brouwer. 96p. 1995. mass mkt. 5.99 (*0-87788-641-5*, H Shaw Pubs) Waterbrook Pr.

Pastor's Best Friend. James O. Davis. LC 97-17775. 240p. 1997. 12.50 (*0-88243-783-6*) Gospel Pub.

*__Pastor's Bible.__ 2000. 49.99 (*0-310-91093-5*) Zondervan.

Pastor's Challenge: Parish Leadership in an Age of Division, Doubt & Spiritual Hunger. George A. Kelly. LC 94-66027. 320p. 1994. 19.95 (*0-87973-738-7*) Our Sunday Visitor.

Pastor's Check-Up. Dave Ray. 36p. 1994. pap. 9.95 (*1-57326-016-9*) Core Ministries.

Pastor's Complete Book of Model Speeches. Rev. by Mary Purcell & Edward Purcell. (C). 1992. text 39.95 (*0-13-653387-6*) P-H.

Pastor's Family: The Challenges of Family Life & Pastoral Responsibilities. Daniel L. Langford. LC 98-18461. 175p. 1998. 29.95 (*0-7890-0584-0*, Haworth Pastrl); pap. 14.95 (*0-7890-0585-9*, Haworth Pastrl) Haworth Pr.

Pastor's Fire-Side, 2 vols. Jane Porter. LC 75-162887. (Bentley's Standard Novels Ser.: Nos. 18 & 19). reprint ed. 25.00 (*0-404-54560-2*); reprint ed. write for info. (*0-318-50685-8*) AMS Pr.

Pastor's Guide to Counseling Ministry. Murray Callahan. 150p. 1995. pap. text 45.00 (*1-888916-01-X*) Counselsource.

Pastor's Guide to Fundraising Success: Step-by-Step Guide Covers It All. Wayne Groner & Dorsey Levell. 150p. 1999. pap. 39.95 (*1-56625-123-0*) Bonus Books.

*__Pastor's Guide to Psychiatric Disorders & Mental Health Resources.__ Ed. by W. Brad Johnson & William L. Johnson. LC 99-462148. 254p. 2000. 49.95 (*0-7890-0712-6*, Haworth Pastrl); pap. text 24.95 (*0-7890-1111-5*, Haworth Pastrl) Haworth Pr.

Pastor's Guidebook: A Manual for Worship. Marion D. Aldridge. LC 83-70213. 160p. 1984. 16.99 (*0-8054-2312-5*, 4223-12) Broadman.

Pastor's Guidebook: Pastor's Guidebook for Special Occasions. Marion D. Aldridge. LC 88-24113. (Orig.). 1988. pap. 19.99 (*0-8054-2318-4*, 4223-18) Broadman.

Pastor's Handbook: (KJV) King James Version. Christian & Missionary Alliance Home Department St. 102p. 1989. 10.99 (*0-87509-118-0*, KJV) Chr Pubns.

Pastor's Handbook: (NIV) New International Version. rev. ed. Christian & Missionary Alliance Home Department St. LC 88-93031. 1989. 10.99 (*0-87509-417-1*, NIV) Chr Pubns.

Pastor's Manual. James R. Hobbs. 1925. 16.99 (*0-8054-2301-X*, 4223-01) Broadman.

Pastor's Manual for a Local Church Planned Giving Program. J. Donald Elam. 96p. 1997. 29.95 (*1-888499-03-6*) Riverview GA.

Pastors of Promise see Pastores de Promesa

Pastors of Promise: A Practical & Passionate Call for Faithful Shepherds. Jack W. Hayford. LC 96-50192. 210p. 1997. pap. 11.99 (*0-8307-1807-9*, 5422684, Regal Bks) Gospel Lght.

Pastor's Opportunities. Ed. by Cyril S. Rodd. 256p. (Orig.). 1989. pap. 29.95 (*0-567-29167-7*, Pub. by T & T Clark) Bks Intl VA.

Pastors, Partners & Paternalists: African Church Leaders & the Development of Missionary Paternalism in Kenya, 1850-1900. Colin Reed. LC 96-48065. 168p. 1997. 78.00 (*90-04-10639-1*) Brill Academic Pubs.

Pastor's Primer for Premarital Guidance. Robert L. Hawkins. 1978. pap. 3.95 (*0-9607764-0-0*) R L Hawkins.

Pastor's Problems. Ed. by Cyril S. Rodd. 240p. 1993. pap. 27.95 (*0-567-29117-0*, Pub. by T & T Clark) Bks Intl VA.

Pastor's Start-Up Manual: Beginning a New Pastorate. Robert H. Ramey, Jr. Ed. by Herb Miller. (Leadership Insight Ser.). 144p. (Orig.). 1995. pap. 12.95 (*0-687-01486-7*) Abingdon.

Pastors Survival Guide. Otto Crumroy, Jr. et al. LC 97-41731. 48p. 1997. pap. 9.95 (*0-8192-1719-0*) Morehouse Pub.

Pastor's Survival Manual: 10 Perils in Parish Ministry & How to Handle Them. Kenneth A. Moe. LC 95-78603. 130p. 1995. pap. 14.95 (*1-56699-157-9*, AL166) Alban Inst.

Pastor's Unauthorized Instruction Book: What Every Church Leader Ought to Know. R. Michael Sanders & Rebecca Sanders. 208p. (Orig.). 1994. pap. 7.95 (*0-687-17700-6*) Abingdon.

Pastor's Underground Guide to the Revised Common Lectionary: Year A. Shelley E. Cochran. 208p. (Orig.). 1995. pap. 18.99 (*0-8272-2946-1*) Chalice Pr.

Pastor's Underground Guide to the Revised Common Lectionary: Year B. Shelley E. Cochran. 180p. (Orig.). 1996. pap. 16.99 (*0-8272-2947-X*) Chalice Pr.

Pastor's Underground Guide to the Revised Common Lectionary: Year C, Year C. Shelley Cochran. 184p. (Orig.). 1997. 16.99 (*0-8272-2948-8*) Chalice Pr.

Pastor's Voice. Walter H. Brooks. (Illus.). 1990. 25.00 (*0-87498-016-X*) Assoc Pubs DC.

Pastor's Wedding & Funeral Record. LC 68-12321. 1967. 14.99 (*0-8054-2306-0*, 4223-06) Broadman.

Pastor's Wedding Manual. Jim Henry. LC 84-17594. 192p. 1984. 16.99 (*0-8054-2313-3*, 4223-13) Broadman.

Pastors! Who Needs Them? Layman's Viewpoint! Shirley Hogg. 100p. (Orig.). 1994. pap. 7.00 (*0-9642597-0-2*) S Hogg.

Pastor's Wife. Elizabeth Von Arnim. 352p. 1993. pap. 7.95 (*0-460-87243-5*, Everyman's Classic Lib) Tuttle Pubng.

Pastor's Wife. Sabina Wurmbrand. 1979. pap. 8.00 (*0-88264-000-3*) Living Sacrifice Bks.

Pastors' Wives Cookbook. Sybil DuBose. Ed. by Janine Buford. (Illus.). 352p. 1978. spiral bd. 13.95 (*0-918544-13-0*) Wimmer Bks.

Pastor's Worship Resource: For Advent, Lent, & Other Occasions. James R. Spruce. 200p. 1987. pap. 9.99 (*0-8341-1215-9*) Beacon Hill.

*__Past/Present: The National Women's Art Anthology.__ Joan Kerr & Jo Holder. (Illus.). 240p. 1999. pap. text 45.00 (*90-5704-141-3*, Harwood Acad Pubs) Gordon & Breach.

Pastries. Fabien Bellahsen & Daniel Rouche. (Eurodelices Ser.). (Illus.). 336p. 1998. 29.95 (*3-8290-1131-8*, 520380) Konemann.

Pastries & Pies: Delicious Desserts. Ed. by G & R Publishing Staff. (Uni-Bks.). 160p. (Orig.). 1994. pap. text 3.00 (*1-56383-015-9*, 1900) G & R Pub.

Pastries & Puddings. Bridgewater Book Co. (Victorian Kitchen Ser.). 41p. 1995. write for info. (*1-57215-050-5*) World Pubns.

Pastry Cold Dishes Croustades. Denis Ruffel. 1999. 239.95 (*0-471-32145-1*) Wiley.

Pastry, Hors d'Oeuvres, Mini-Sandwiches, Canapes, Assorted Snacks, Hot Hors d'Oeuvres. Denis Ruffel. (Professional Caterer Ser.). 244p. 1997. text 69.95 (*0-470-25007-0*) Halsted Pr.

Pastry Magic. Carol Pastor. 96p. 1996. 29.95 (*0-470-23610-8*) Wiley.

Pastuer's Fight Against Microbes. Beverley Birch. LC 96-83307. (Science Stories Ser.). (Illus.). 48p. (J). (gr. 4-7). 1996. 10.95 (*0-8120-6623-5*) Barron.

Pasture & Forage Crop Pathology. Ed. by C. Chakraborty et al. LC 96-84970. 653p. 1996. 42.00 (*0-89118-129-6*) Am Soc Agron.

Pasture Production & Management. Lovett & Scott. 1998. 69.95 (*0-909605-85-8*) Buttrwrth-Heinemann.

Pasture Profits with Stocker Cattle. rev. ed. Allan Nation. LC 97-41057. (Illus.). 224p. (C). 1998. pap. 24.95 (*0-9632460-7-0*) Green Park.

Pastured Poultry Profits. Joel F. Salatin. (Illus.). 330p. 1996. pap. 35.00 (*0-9638109-0-1*) Chelsea Green Pub.

Pastures: Their Ecology & Management. Ed. by R. H. Langer. (Illus.). 506p. 1990. text 65.00 (*0-19-558174-1*) OUP.

Pastures in Vanuatu. D. MacFarlane & M. Shelton. (C). 1986. text 50.00 (*0-949511-15-3*, Pub. by ACIAR) St Mut.

Pastures New. large type ed. Ann Purser. (General Ser.). 518p. 1996. pap. 20.95 (*0-7862-0666-7*) Thorndike Pr.

Pastures of Heaven. John Steinbeck. 256p. 1995. pap. 11.95 (*0-14-018748-0*, Penguin Classics) Viking Penguin.

Pastures of Heaven. John Steinbeck. LC 83-45886. reprint ed. 21.50 (*0-404-20244-6*, PS3537) AMS Pr.

Pastures of Tender Grass. Compiled by James A. Stewart. 1964. 6.99 (*1-56632-052-6*); pap. 4.99 (*1-56632-053-4*) Revival Lit.

Pastwatch. limited ed. Orson Scott Card. 1996. 200.00 (*0-312-86122-2*, Pub. by Tor Bks) St Martin.

Pastwatch: The Flood. Orson Scott Card. 1998. write for info. (*0-312-85845-0*) Tor Bks.

Pastwatch: The Redemption of Christopher Columbus. Orson Scott Card. 352p. 1996. 23.95 (*0-312-85058-1*) Tor Bks.

Pastwatch: The Redemption of Christopher Columbus. Orson Scott Card. 1997. mass mkt. 6.99 (*0-8125-0864-5*, Pub. by Tor Bks) St Martin.

Pastwatch, the Redemption of Christopher Columbus. Orson Scott Card. LC 95-44927. 1997. 12.09 (*0-606-11724-5*, Pub. by Turtleback) Demco.

Pasupathy Communications. Alberto Leon-Garcia. (C). 2000. 95.00 (*0-201-52528-3*) Addison-Wesley.

Pasyon & Revolution: Popular Movements in the Philippines, 1840-1910. Reynaldo C. Ileto. (Illus.). 296p. 1997. pap. text 18.00 (*971-11-3085-8*, Pub. by Ateneo de Manila Univ Pr) UH Pr.

Pat. (Hawkins Scribble Bks.). (Illus.). 16p. (J). 1996. 6.95 (*0-7894-1165-2*) DK Pub Inc.

Pat-a-Cake. Joanna Cole et al. LC 91-32264. (Illus.). 48p. (J). (ps up). 1992. mass mkt. 6.95 (*0-688-11533-0*, Wm Morrow) Morrow Avon.

Pat-a-Cake. Tony Kenyon. LC 95-68787. (Illus.). 16p. (J). (ps). 1998. bds. 3.99 (*0-7636-0431-3*) Candlewick Pr.

Pat a Cake: And Other Play Phymes. Joanna Cole & Stephanie Calmenson. LC 91-32264. (Illus.). 48p. (J). (ps). 1992. 14.00 (*0-688-11038-X*, Wm Morrow) Morrow Avon.

*__Pat-A-Cake Dough Book & Kit.__ Sharon E. McKay. (Illus.). 48p. (J). (ps-k). 1998. pap. 12.95 (*1-895897-62-9*) Somerville Hse.

Pat, a Pinch, a Peck: My Adventures in the Movies. Leona W. Toppel. LC 95-90570. (Illus.). 112p. (Orig.). 1995. pap. 10.00 (*0-9647655-0-0*) L W Toppel.

Pat & Kirby Go to Hell. Robert Kirby. (Illus.). 120p. pap. 9.95 (*1-885628-46-3*, Pub. by Buckaroo Bks) Origin Bk Sales.

Pat & Pat the Cat & Rat. Daryl A. Schietinger-Cachina. (Illus.). 8p. (J). (ps-5). 1999. pap. 5.00 (*1-928641-00-8*) Daryl Ann Pubns.

Pat & Pat the Cat & Rat in "How about a Picnic" Daryl A. Schietinger-Cachina. (Illus.). 10p. (J). (ps-5). 1999. pap. 5.00 (*1-928641-01-6*) Daryl Ann Pubns.

Pat Chapman's Balti Bible. P. Chapman. text 50.00 (*0-340-72858-2*, Pub. by Hodder & Stought Ltd) Trafalgar.

Pat Conroy: A Critical Companion. Landon C. Burns. LC 95-39495. (Critical Companions to Popular Contemporary Writers Ser.). 216p. 1996. 29.95 (*0-313-29419-4*, Greenwood Pr) Greenwood.

*__Pat F. Garrett's the Authentic Life of Billy, the Kid.__ Pat F. Garrett & Frederick W. Nolan. LC 99-48284. 288p. 2000. 24.95 (*0-8061-3227-2*) U of Okla Pr.

Pat Garrett: The Story of a Western Lawman. Leon C. Metz. LC 72-9261. (Illus.). 328p. 1983. pap. 14.95 (*0-8061-1838-5*) U of Okla Pr.

Pat Hall's Hawaiian Animal Families Coloring Book. Illus. by Pat Hall. 24p. (J). (ps-3). 1994. pap. 3.95 (*0-9633493-3-3*) Pacific Greetings.

Pat Hall's Hawaiian Animals Coloring Book. Illus. by Pat Hall. 24p. (J). (ps-3). 1994. pap. 3.95 (*0-9633493-2-5*) Pacific Greetings.

Pat Hobby Stories. F. Scott Fitzgerald. 23.95 (*0-89190-601-0*) Amereon Ltd.

Pat Hobby Stories. F. Scott Fitzgerald. 192p. 1995. per. 10.00 (*0-684-80442-5*) S&S Trade.

Pat Jacobsen's Collector's Guide to Fruit Crate Labels. Thomas P. Jacobsen. LC 94-96071. (Illus.). 560p. 1994. 39.95 (*0-9640703-0-8*) Patco Ent.

Pat Jacobsen's 1st International Price Guide to Fruit Crate Labels, Vol. 1, No. 1. Thomas P. Jacobsen. LC 94-96114. (Illus.). 560p. 1994. 39.95 (*0-9640703-1-6*) Patco Ent.

*__Pat Jacobsen's Millennium Guide to Fruit Crate Labels: A Collector's Guide & Price Catalogue.__ Thomas P. Jacobsen. (Illus.). 300p. 1999. pap. 59.95 (*0-9640703-2-4*, Crate Expectations) Patco Ent.

Pat Martino, Pt. 1. 80p. (Orig.). 1994. pap. 24.95 incl. audio compact disk (*0-7692-0981-5*, REHBK006CD) Wrner Bros.

Pat Martino, Pt. 2. Prod. by Zobeida Perez. 72p. (Orig.). 1994. pap. 21.95 incl. audio compact disk (*0-89898-945-0*, REHBK007CD) Wrner Bros.

Pat Martino, Pt. 2. Ed. by Aaron Stang. 72p. (Orig.). 1994. pap. 21.95 incl. audio (*0-89898-944-2*, REHBK007AT) Wrner Bros.

Pat McCarran: Political Boss of Nevada. Jerome E. Edwards. LC 82-8576. (Wilbur S. Shepperson Series in History & Humanities: No. 17). (Illus.). 248p. (Orig.). 1982. pap. 14.95 (*0-87417-071-0*) U of Nev Pr.

*__Pat Metheny Songbook.__ Pat Metheny. (Illus.). 448p. (J). 2000. pap. 29.95 (*0-634-00796-3*) H Leonard.

Pat Nixon: The Untold Story. Julie N. Eisenhower. 1987. mass mkt. 4.50 (*0-8217-2300-6*, Zebra Kensgtn) Kensgtn Pub Corp.

Pat Nixon of Texas: Autobiography of a Doctor. Pat I. Nixon. Ed. by Herbert H. Lang. LC 78-65575. 248p. 1979. 18.95 (*0-89096-072-0*) Tex A&M Univ Pr.

Pat of Silver Bush. L. M. Montgomery. Date not set. 22.95 (*0-8488-2371-0*) Amereon Ltd.

Pat of Silver Bush. L. M. Montgomery. 288p. (YA). 1988. mass mkt. 4.50 (*0-7704-2247-0*) Bantam.

Pat of Silver Bush. L. M. Montgomery. (Illus.). 380p. (J). pap. 4.98 (*0-7710-6167-6*) McCland & Stewart.

Pat Paragraphs. Elliot Perry. Ed. by George T. Turner & Thomas E. Stanton. LC 81-68198. (Illus.). 648p. 1982. 55.00 (*0-930412-05-2*) Bureau Issues.

Pat-Riots to Patriots: American Irish in Caricature & Comic Art. John Appel & Selma Appel. Ed. by Sue Caltrider & Ruth D. Fitzgerald. (Illus.). 32p. (Orig.). 1990. pap. text 5.95 (*0-944311-03-2*) MSU Museum.

Pat Robertson in Error. Walter E. Adams. 50p. (Orig.). 1983. pap. 2.95 (*0-937408-27-1*) GMI Pubns Inc.

*__Pat Sonnets.__ Max Wickert. (Street Press Editions Ser.). 72p. 2000. pap. 10.00 (*0-935252-55-X*, Pub. by Street Pr) Tlkng Leaves.

Pat Sparkuhl. Ed. by William S. Bartman. (Exploring the Work of Artists in Mid-Career Ser.), (Illus.). 32p. (Orig.). 1991. pap. text 20.00 (*0-923183-05-1*) ART Pr NY.

Pat Stanton: The Quiet Man. Simon Pia. 128p. (C). 1996. 45.00 (*0-85976-288-2*, Pub. by J Donald) St Mut.

Pat Steir. Thomas McEvilley. LC 94-30546. (Illus.). 176p. 1995. 49.50 (*0-8109-4459-6*, Pub. by Abrams) Time Warner.

Pat Steir: Self-Portrait. Marcia Tucker. (Illus.). 29p. 1987. pap. 4.00 (*0-915557-56-8*) New Mus Contemp Art.

Pat Steir: Waterfalls. Lisa Liebmann. (Illus.). 32p. (Orig.). 1990. pap. text 10.00 (*1-879293-01-3*) Contemp Art Mus.

Pat Tap Technology Reviews: TAP-1, Superconductors. Business Communications Co., Inc. Staff. 1990. 450.00 (*0-89336-819-9*) BCC.

Pat Tap Technology Reviews: TAP-10, Supercritical Fluids. Business Communications Co., Inc. Staff. 1991. 350.00 (*0-89336-850-4*) BCC.

Pat Tap Technology Reviews: TAP-2, High Performance Diamond. Business Communications Co., Inc. Staff. 1991. 350.00 (*0-89336-818-0*) BCC.

Pat Tap Technology Reviews: TAP-4, Chromatography. Business Communications Co., Inc. Staff. 1991. 550.00 (*0-89336-844-X*, TAP-04) BCC.

Pat Tap Technology Reviews: TAP-6, Non-Linear Optics. Business Communications Co., Inc. Staff. 1991. 350.00 (*0-89336-846-6*) BCC.

Pat Tap Technology Reviews: TAP-8, Polymers & Alloys. Business Communications Co., Inc. Staff. 1993. 1000.00 (*0-89336-848-2*, TAP-08R) BCC.

Pat Tap Technology Reviews: TAP-9, Electrophoresis. Business Communications Co., Inc. Staff. 1991. 350.00 (*0-89336-849-0*, TAP-09) BCC.

Pat the Beastie: A Pull-&-Poke Book. Henrik Drescher. (Illus.). 18p. (YA). (ps up). 1993. 9.95 (*1-56282-407-4*, Pub. by Hyprn Child) Little.

Pat the Beastie Book & Puppet. Henrik Drescher. (Illus.). (J). (ps-2). 1997. pap. 10.95 (*0-7868-1228-1*, Pub. by Hyprn Ppbks) Little.

Pat the Bunny. Dorothy Kunhardt. (Golden Touch & Feel Bks.). (Illus.). 20p. (J). (ps). 1942. spiral bd. 7.99 (*0-307-12000-7*, Goldn Books) Gldn Bks Pub Co.

Pat the Bunny & Friends Gift Set. Dorothy Kunhardt & Edith Kunhardt. (Golden Touch & Feel Bks.). (Illus.). 20p. (J). (ps-3). 1994. boxed set 17.95 (*0-307-16209-5*, 16209, Goldn Books) Gldn Bks Pub Co.

Pat the Bunny Book & Plush Bunny. Dorothy Kunhardt. 20p. (J). 1998. 14.99 (*0-307-16327-X*, 16327, Goldn Books) Gldn Bks Pub Co.

*__Pat the Bunny Butterfly Roundup.__ Dorothy Kunhardt. (Pat the Bunny Ser.). (Illus.). (J). 2000. 6.99 (*0-307-10651-9*, Goldn Books) Gldn Bks Pub Co.

*__Pat the Bunny Gift Set: On the Playground.__ (Illus.). (J). 2000. write for info. (*0-307-16330-X*) Gldn Bks Pub Co.

*__Pat the Bunny in the Garden.__ (Pat the Bunny Board Bks.). 14p. (J). 1999. bds. 4.99 (*0-307-10630-6*, 10630, Goldn Books) Gldn Bks Pub Co.

P

An Asterisk (*) at the beginning of an entry indicates that the title is appearing for the first time.

***Pat the Bunny on the Playground.** (Pat the Bunny Board Bks.). 14p. (J). 1999. bds. 4.99 (*0-307-10631-4*, 10631, Goldn Books) Gldn Bks Pub Co.

***Pat the Bunny Sweet Dreams.** (Illus.). 6p. (J). 2000. write for info. (*0-307-16329-6*) Gldn Bks Pub Co.

Pat the Cat. (Hawkins Reading Ser.). (J). 1995. write for info. (*0-7894-0154-1*, 5-70600) DK Pub Inc.

Pat the Cat. Edith Kunhardt. LC 83-83106. (Golden Touch & Feel Bks.). (Illus.). 18p. (J). (ps). 1984. 7.99 (*0-307-12001-5*, 12001, Goldn Books) Gldn Bks Pub Co.

***Pat the Christmas Bunny, 1 vol.** Edith Kunhardt. 1999. 14.99 (*0-307-16328-8*, Goldn Books) Gldn Bks Pub Co.

***Pat the Pony.** (Illus.). 20p. (J). 2000. write for info. (*0-307-12164-X*) Gldn Bks Pub Co.

Pat the Puppy. Edith Kunhardt. (Golden Touch & Feel Bks.). (Illus.). 16p. (J). (ps-k). 1993. 7.99 (*0-307-12004-X*, 12004, Goldn Books) Gldn Bks Pub Co.

Pat Trivigno: The Search for Inner Form. Luba B. Glade. LC 94-66789. (Illus.). 48p. 1994. pap. 18.95 (*0-89494-046-5*) New Orleans Mus Art.

Pat Tung's Fried Ice Cream & Other Gourmet Delights. Pat H. Tung. LC 84-91413. (Illus.). 96p. (Orig.). 1985. pap. 6.95 (*0-9614469-0-0*) P Tungs Intl G.

Pat Ward Williams: Probable Cause. Kellie Jones & Moria Roth. Ed. by Elsa Longhauser. LC 91-77827. (Illus.). 32p. 1992. pap. 20.00 (*1-58442-044-8*) Galleries at Moore.

Pat Welsh's Southern California Gardening: A Month-by-Month Guide. Pat Welsh. Ed. by Nion McEvoy. (Illus.). 352p. 1992. pap. 22.95 (*0-87701-629-1*) Chronicle Bks.

Pat Welsh's Southern California Gardening: A Month-by-Month Guide. Pat Welsh. LC 99-10043. 384p. 2000. pap. 24.95 (*0-8118-2214-1*) Chronicle Bks.

Pat, You Have Cancer: A Story of Hope. Robert Burtness & Patricia Burtness. 117p. (Orig.). 1994. pap. 8.95 (*0-9638111-0-X*) Riverhse Lit Creat.

***PATA Arab Gulf Countries Outbound Market Report: November 1999.** PATA Staff. 125p. 1999. pap. 415.00 (*1-882866-18-5*) Pac Asia Trvl.

***PATA Cruise Report: May 1999.** Travel & Tourism Futures Staff. (Illus.). 73p. 1999. pap. 500.00 (*1-882866-16-9*) Pac Asia Trvl.

PATA Destination Database Conference. 106p. 1993. pap. 35.00 (*1-882866-82-7*) Pac Asia Trvl.

***PATA Israel Outbound Market Report, November 1999.** PATA Staff. 27p. 1999. pap. 85.00 (*1-882866-19-3*) Pac Asia Trvl.

***PATA 1999 Conference Delegate Roster.** 127p. 1999. pap. 80.00 (*1-882866-37-1*) Pac Asia Trvl.

PATA Pacific Division Arafura Tourism Zone Workshop: Proceedings from a Workshop Held August 29-30, 1994. 132p. 1994. pap. 30.00 (*1-882866-33-9*) Pac Asia Trvl.

Pata-Paintings of Orissa. B. Mohanty. 52p. 1984. 49.95 (*0-318-36346-1*) Asia Bk Corp.

Pata Pita. Hilda Perera. 1995. pap. 7.95 (*0-8056-0134-1*) Minerva Bks Ltd.

***PATA U. S. A. Report, June 1999: Building Travel to Pacific Asia from the United States Near Term Approaches for Expansion.** Menlo Consulting Group, Inc. Staff. (Illus.). 1999. pap. 500.00 (*1-882866-17-7*) Pac Asia Trvl.

PATA West Coast Task Force: Task Force for the West Coast of New Zealand. 56p. 1988. pap. 35.00 (*1-882866-56-8*) Pac Asia Trvl.

Patagonia see Works of Henry James Jr.: Collected Works

Patagonia: Natural History, Prehistory, & Ethnography at the Uttermost End of the Earth. Colin McEwan et al. LC 97-18348. 200p. 1998. pap. text 24.95 (*0-691-05849-0*, Pub. by Princeton U Pr) Cal Prin Full Svc.

Patagonia: Notes from the Field. Ed. by Nora Gallagher. LC 99-18491. (Illus.). 144p. 1999. 22.95 (*0-8118-2604-X*) Chronicle Bks.

***Patagonia: The Last Wilderness.** Daniel Rivademar. (Illus.). 160p. 1999. 39.95 (*1-894020-65-0*, Pub. by Warwick Publ) Firefly Bks Ltd.

Patagonia Adventure, , Set. Margaret A. Schultz & Kenn Schultz. 64p. 1995. pap. 19.95 incl. audio (*0-9645435-0-8*) M & K Assocs.

Patai's 1992 Guide to the Chemistry of Functional Groups. Saul E. Patai. LC 91-28943. (Chemistry of Functional Groups Ser.: No. 1078). 534p. 1992. 235.00 (*0-471-93022-9*) Wiley.

Pataki: Leyendas Y Misterios de los Orishas Africanos. Julio Garcia-Cortez. LC 79-54684. (Coleccion Ebano y Canela). (SPA., Illus.). 250p. 1980. pap. 15.00 (*0-89729-236-7*) Ediciones.

Pataki: Where I Come From. George Pataki & Daniel Paisner. LC 98-9774. 256p. 1998. 24.95 (*0-670-87339-X*, Viking) Viking Penguin.

Patan Walk About - Inner City Guide. Ratna Pustak Bhandar. 1996. pap. 22.00 (*0-7855-7471-9*, Pub. by Ratna Pustak Bhandar) St Mut.

***Pataniali's Yoga Sutras: With the Commentary of Vyasa & the Gloss of Vachaspati Misra.** 2nd ed. Rama Prasada. 2000. reprint ed. pap. 19.50 (*81-215-0964-5*, Pub. by M Manoharial) S Asia.

***Patanias: A Legacy in Silver & Gold: Contemporary Southwest Images XIV.** Joanne Stuhr & Judith Freeman. LC 99-71416. (Stonewall Foundation Ser.). (Illus.). 32p. 1999. pap. 15.00 (*0-911611-16-9*) Tucson Mus Art.

Patanjala Yoga Philosophy with Reference to Buddhism. Koichi Yamashita. (C). 1994. text 28.00 (*81-7102-013-5*, Pub. by Firma KLM) S Asia.

Patanjali: The Threads of Yoga. Robert Van de Weyer. (Teachers of Healing & Wholeness Ser.). 1997. pap. 5.95 (*0-85305-413-4*, 1930, Pub. by Arthur James) Morehouse Pub.

Patanjali's Meditation Yoga. Vyn Bailey. 1998. pap. text. write for info. (*0-7318-0648-4*) Simon & Schuster.

Patanjali's Model of Human Mind. H. C. Mathur. 345p. 1987. 59.95 (*81-7071-065-0*) Asia Bk Corp.

Patanjali's Remarks on Anga. James W. Benson. (Oxford University South Asian Studies Ser.). 260p. 1990. 16.95 (*0-19-562022-4*) OUP.

Patanjali's Yoga Sutras. Tr. by Rama Prasada. (C). 1995. pap. 22.00 (*0-614-09975-7*, Pub. by M Manoharial) S Asia.

Patanjali's Yoga Sutras. 2nd ed. Tr. by Rama Prasada from SAN. 318p. 1981. reprint ed. 24.00 (*0-89744-220-2*, Pub. by Orient Reprint) S Asia.

Patanjali's Yoga Sutras (The Aphorisms of Yoga, by Patanjali) With the Commentary of Vyasa & the Gloss of Vachaspati Misra. Tr. by Rama Prasada. LC 73-3789. reprint ed. 29.00 (*0-404-57804-7*) AMS Pr.

Patapsco: Baltimore's River of History. Paul J. Travers. LC 89-40785. (Illus.). 234p. 1990. 22.95 (*0-87033-400-X*, Tidewtr Pubs) Cornell Maritime.

Pataqonia see London Life

Patarata Pottery: Classic Period Ceramics of the South-Central Gulf Coast, Veracruz, Mexico. Barbara L. Stark. LC 89-4793. (Anthropological Papers: No. 51). 205p. 1989. 33.50 (*0-8165-1121-7*) U of Ariz Pr.

***PATA's 1998 Issues & Trends Compendium.** 55p. 1998. pap. 25.00 (*1-882866-25-8*) Pac Asia Trvl.

***Patch.** Big Guy Books Staff. (Illus.). (J). 2000. 16.95 (*1-929945-02-7*) Big Guy Books.

Patch. Teacher Created Materials Staff. (Go Bks.). 8p. (J). (gr. k-1). 1997. pap. 2.49 (*1-57690-815-1*) Tchr Create Mat.

Patch: Special Selection of U. S. Military Insignia. Illus. by Hironori Yasuda. (Graphic Design Collection: No. 1). 165p. 1998. pap. text 30.00 (*0-7881-5883-X*) DIANE Pub.

***Patch & the Rabbits.** Mathew Price. LC 99-75919. (Illus.). 12p. (J). (ps-k). 2000. 5.95 (*0-531-30265-2*) Orchard Bks Watts.

Patch Box Corners. G. R. Watkins. 1989. pap. 5.00 (*0-913150-69-X*) Pioneer Pr.

Patch Boys. Jay Parini. LC 86-4823. 1995. pap. 8.95 (*0-8050-0770-9*, Owl) H Holt & Co.

Patch-Clamp Applications & Protocols. Ed. by Alan A. Boulton et al. (Neuromethods Ser.: Vol. 26). (Illus.). 336p. 1995. 115.00 (*0-89603-311-2*) Humana.

Patch Dynamics. Ed. by S. A. Levin et al. (Lecture Notes in Biomathematics Ser.: Vol. 96). xiii, 307p. 1995. 75.95 (*0-387-56525-6*) Spr-Verlag.

***Patch Finds a Friend.** Mathew Price. LC 99-7518. (Illus.). 12p. (J). (ps-k). 2000. 5.95 (*0-531-30264-4*) Orchard Bks Watts.

Patch Goes to the Park. Jo Lodge. LC 96-76302. (J). 1997. pap. 5.95 (*0-15-201379-2*) Harcourt.

Patch Guide: U. S. Navy Ships & Submarines. Turner Publishing Company Staff. (Illus.). 160p. Date not set. 39.95 (*1-56311-083-0*) Turner Pub KY.

Patch in I Want to Be a Pilot. Stephen Bachand. (Booktime Buddies Ser.). (Illus.). (J). (ps-2). 1999. 4.25 (*1-928972-00-4*) Critter Pubns.

Patch Likes Me. Teacher Created Materials Staff. (Go Bks.). 8p. (J). (gr. k-1). 1997. pap. 2.49 (*1-57690-816-X*) Tchr Create Mat.

Patch of Blue. Grace Livingston Hill. 19.95 (*0-89190-060-8*) Amereon Ltd.

Patch of Blue. Elizabeth Kata. 18.95 (*0-89190-119-1*) Amereon Ltd.

Patch of Blue. Elizabeth Kata. 1989. 11.09 (*0-606-13014-4*, Pub. by Turtleback) Demco.

Patch of Blue. Elizabeth Kata. 1988. mass mkt. 5.99 (*0-446-31485-4*, Pub. by Warner Bks) Little.

Patch of Blue: Frst. Dummy. 1989. mass mkt. 3.50 (*0-446-73863-8*, Pub. by Warner Bks) Little.

Patch of Eden: America's Inner-City Gardeners. H. Patricia Hynes. (Illus.). 208p. 1996. pap. 18.95 (*0-930031-80-6*) Chelsea Green Pub.

Patch of Land Owned by the Company. Stephen G. Warfel. (Illus.). 232p. 1993. pap. 7.95 (*0-89271-052-7*, 0111) Pa Hist & Mus.

Patch Pictures: A Creative Guide to Fabric Collage. Norma Slabbert. 72p. (C). 1988. 70.00 (*1-85368-026-5*, Pub. by New5 Holland) St Mut.

Patch. Supplement to Qinoton Patch of Connecticut, & His Descendants. George E. Partch. 48p. 1996. reprint ed. pap. 10.00 (*0-8328-5420-4*); reprint ed. lib. bdg. 20.00 (*0-8328-5419-0*) Higginson Bk Co.

Patch Testing: Test Concentrations & Vehicles for 3700 Chemicals. 2nd ed. De Groot. 334p. 1994. text 188.50 (*0-444-81911-8*) Elsevier.

Patch, the Pirate Dog: A California Pet Story. Carole Marsh. (Carole Marsh California Bks.). (J). (ps-4). 1994. pap. 19.95 (*0-7933-5429-3*); lib. bdg. 29.95 (*0-7933-5428-5*); disk 29.95 (*0-7933-5430-7*) Gallopade Intl.

Patch, the Pirate Dog: A Colorado Pet Story. Carole Marsh. (Carole Marsh Colorado Bks.). (J). (ps-4). 1994. pap. 19.95 (*0-7933-5432-3*); lib. bdg. 29.95 (*0-7933-5431-5*); disk 29.95 (*0-7933-5433-1*) Gallopade Intl.

Patch, the Pirate Dog: A Connecticut Pet Story. Carole Marsh. (Carole Marsh Connecticut Bks.). (J). (ps-4). 1994. pap. 19.95 (*0-7933-5435-8*); lib. bdg. 29.95 (*0-7933-5434-X*); disk 29.95 (*0-7933-5436-6*) Gallopade Intl.

Patch, the Pirate Dog: A Delaware Pet Story. Carole Marsh. (Carole Marsh Delaware Bks.). (J). (ps-4). 1994. pap. 19.95 (*0-7933-5438-2*); lib. bdg. 29.95 (*0-7933-5437-4*); disk 29.95 (*0-7933-5439-0*) Gallopade Intl.

Patch, the Pirate Dog: A Florida Pet Story. Carole Marsh. (Carole Marsh Florida Bks.). (J). (ps-4). 1994. pap. 19.95 (*0-7933-5444-7*); lib. bdg. 29.95 (*0-7933-5443-9*); disk 29.95 (*0-7933-5445-5*) Gallopade Intl.

Patch, the Pirate Dog: A Georgia Pet Story. Carole Marsh. (Carole Marsh Georgia Bks.). (J). (ps-4). 1994. pap. 19.95 (*0-7933-5447-1*); lib. bdg. 29.95 (*0-7933-5446-3*); disk 29.95 (*0-7933-5448-X*) Gallopade Intl.

Patch, the Pirate Dog: A Hawaii Pet Story. Carole Marsh. (Carole Marsh Hawaii Bks.). (J). (ps-4). 1994. pap. 19.95 (*0-7933-5450-1*); lib. bdg. 29.95 (*0-7933-5449-8*); disk 29.95 (*0-7933-5451-X*) Gallopade Intl.

Patch, the Pirate Dog: A Kansas Pet Story. Carole Marsh. (Carole Marsh Kansas Bks.). (J). (ps-4). 1994. pap. 19.95 (*0-7933-5465-X*); lib. bdg. 29.95 (*0-7933-5464-1*); disk 29.95 (*0-7933-5466-8*) Gallopade Intl.

Patch, the Pirate Dog: A Kentucky Pet Story. Carole Marsh. (Carole Marsh Kentucky Bks.). (J). (ps-4). 1994. pap. 19.95 (*0-7933-5468-4*); lib. bdg. 29.95 (*0-7933-5467-6*); disk 29.95 (*0-7933-5469-2*) Gallopade Intl.

Patch, the Pirate Dog: A Louisiana Pet Story. Carole Marsh. (Carole Marsh Louisiana Bks.). (J). (ps-4). 1994. pap. 19.95 (*0-7933-5471-4*); lib. bdg. 29.95 (*0-7933-5470-6*); disk 29.95 (*0-7933-5472-2*) Gallopade Intl.

Patch, the Pirate Dog: A Maine Pet Story. Carole Marsh. (Carole Marsh Maine Bks.). (J). (ps-4). 1994. pap. 19.95 (*0-7933-5474-9*); lib. bdg. 29.95 (*0-7933-5473-0*); disk 29.95 (*0-7933-5475-7*) Gallopade Intl.

Patch, the Pirate Dog: A Maryland Pet Story. Carole Marsh. (Carole Marsh Maryland Bks.). (J). (ps-4). 1994. pap. 19.95 (*0-7933-5477-3*); lib. bdg. 29.95 (*0-7933-5476-5*); disk 29.95 (*0-7933-5478-1*) Gallopade Intl.

Patch, the Pirate Dog: A Massachusetts Pet Story. Carole Marsh. (Massachuseets Bks.). (J). (ps-4). 1994. pap. 19.95 (*0-7933-5480-3*); lib. bdg. 29.95 (*0-7933-5479-X*); disk 29.95 (*0-7933-5481-1*) Gallopade Intl.

Patch, the Pirate Dog: A Michigan Pet Story. Carole Marsh. (Carole Marsh Michigan Bks.). (J). (ps-4). 1994. pap. 19.95 (*0-7933-5483-8*); lib. bdg. 29.95 (*0-7933-5482-X*); disk 29.95 (*0-7933-5484-6*) Gallopade Intl.

Patch, the Pirate Dog: A Minnesota Pet Story. Carole Marsh. (Carole Marsh Minnesota Bks.). (J). (ps-4). 1994. pap. 19.95 (*0-7933-5486-2*); lib. bdg. 29.95 (*0-7933-5485-4*); disk 29.95 (*0-7933-5487-0*) Gallopade Intl.

Patch, the Pirate Dog: A Mississippi Pet Story. Carole Marsh. (Carole Marsh Mississippi Bks.). (J). (ps-4). 1994. pap. 19.95 (*0-7933-5489-7*); lib. bdg. 29.95 (*0-7933-5488-9*); disk 29.95 (*0-7933-5490-0*) Gallopade Intl.

Patch, the Pirate Dog: A Missouri Pet Story. Carole Marsh. (Carole Marsh Missouri Bks.). (J). (ps-4). 1994. pap. 19.95 (*0-7933-5492-7*); lib. bdg. 29.95 (*0-7933-5491-9*); disk 29.95 (*0-7933-5493-5*) Gallopade Intl.

Patch, the Pirate Dog: A Montana Pet Story. Carole Marsh. (Carole Marsh Montana Bks.). (J). (ps-4). 1994. pap. 19.95 (*0-7933-5495-1*); lib. bdg. 29.95 (*0-7933-5494-3*); disk 29.95 (*0-7933-5496-X*) Gallopade Intl.

Patch, the Pirate Dog: A Nebraska Pet Story. Carole Marsh. (Carole Marsh Nebraska Bks.). (J). (ps-4). 1994. pap. 19.95 (*0-7933-5498-6*); lib. bdg. 29.95 (*0-7933-5497-8*); disk 29.95 (*0-7933-5499-4*) Gallopade Intl.

Patch, the Pirate Dog: A Nevada Pet Story. Carole Marsh. (Carole Marsh Nevada Bks.). (J). (ps-4). 1994. pap. 19.95 (*0-7933-5501-X*); lib. bdg. 29.95 (*0-7933-5500-1*); disk 29.95 (*0-7933-5502-8*) Gallopade Intl.

Patch, the Pirate Dog: A New Hampshire Pet Story. Carole Marsh. (Carole Marsh New Hampshire Bks.). (J). (ps-4). 1994. pap. 19.95 (*0-7933-5504-4*); lib. bdg. 29.95 (*0-7933-5503-6*); disk 29.95 (*0-7933-5505-2*) Gallopade Intl.

Patch, the Pirate Dog: A New Jersey Pet Story. Carole Marsh. (Carole Marsh New Jersey Bks.). (J). (ps-4). 1994. pap. 19.95 (*0-7933-5507-9*); lib. bdg. 29.95 (*0-7933-5506-0*); disk 29.95 (*0-7933-5508-7*) Gallopade Intl.

Patch, the Pirate Dog: A New Mexico Pet Story. Carole Marsh. (Carole Marsh New Mexico Bks.). (J). (ps-4). 1994. pap. 19.95 (*0-7933-5510-9*); lib. bdg. 29.95 (*0-7933-5509-5*); disk 29.95 (*0-7933-5511-7*) Gallopade Intl.

Patch, the Pirate Dog: A New York Pet Story. Carole Marsh. (Carole Marsh New York Bks.). (J). (ps-4). 1994. pap. 19.95 (*0-7933-5513-3*); lib. bdg. 29.95 (*0-7933-5512-5*); disk 29.95 (*0-7933-5514-1*) Gallopade Intl.

Patch, the Pirate Dog: A North Carolina Pet Story. Carole Marsh. (Carole Marsh North Carolina Bks.). (J). (ps-4). 1994. pap. 19.95 (*0-7933-5516-8*); lib. bdg. 29.95 (*0-7933-5515-X*); disk 29.95 (*0-7933-5517-6*) Gallopade Intl.

Patch, the Pirate Dog: A North Dakota Pet Story. Carole Marsh. (Carole Marsh North Dakota Bks.). (J). (ps-4). 1994. pap. 19.95 (*0-7933-5519-2*); lib. bdg. 29.95 (*0-7933-5518-4*); disk 29.95 (*0-7933-5520-6*) Gallopade Intl.

Patch, the Pirate Dog: A Ohio Pet Story. Carole Marsh. (Carole Marsh Ohio Bks.). (J). (ps-4). 1994. pap. 19.95 (*0-7933-5522-2*); lib. bdg. 29.95 (*0-7933-5521-4*); disk 29.95 (*0-7933-5523-0*) Gallopade Intl.

Patch, the Pirate Dog: A Oklahoma Pet Story. Carole Marsh. (Oklahoma Bks.). (J). (ps-4). 1994. pap. 19.95 (*0-7933-5525-7*); lib. bdg. 29.95 (*0-7933-5524-9*); disk 29.95 (*0-7933-5526-5*) Gallopade Intl.

Patch, the Pirate Dog: A Oregon Pet Story. Carole Marsh. (Oregon Bks.). (J). (ps-4). 1994. pap. 19.95 (*0-7933-5528-1*); lib. bdg. 29.95 (*0-7933-5527-3*); disk 29.95 (*0-7933-5529-X*) Gallopade Intl.

Patch, the Pirate Dog: A Pennsylvania Pet Story. Carole Marsh. (Pennsylvania Bks.). (J). (ps-4). 1994. pap. 19.95 (*0-7933-5531-1*); lib. bdg. 29.95 (*0-7933-5530-3*); disk 29.95 (*0-7933-5532-X*) Gallopade Intl.

Patch, the Pirate Dog: A Rhode Island Pet Story. Carole Marsh. (Rhode Island Bks.). (J). (ps-4). 1994. pap. 19.95 (*0-7933-5534-6*); lib. bdg. 29.95 (*0-7933-5533-8*); disk 29.95 (*0-7933-5535-4*) Gallopade Intl.

Patch, the Pirate Dog: A South Carolina Pet Story. Carole Marsh. (South Carolina Bks.). (J). (ps-4). 1994. pap. 19.95 (*0-7933-5537-0*); lib. bdg. 29.95 (*0-7933-5536-2*); disk 29.95 (*0-7933-5538-9*) Gallopade Intl.

Patch, the Pirate Dog: A South Dakota Pet Story. Carole Marsh. (South Dakota Bks.). (J). (ps-4). 1994. pap. 19.95 (*0-7933-5540-0*); lib. bdg. 29.95 (*0-7933-5539-7*); disk 29.95 (*0-7933-5541-9*) Gallopade Intl.

Patch, the Pirate Dog: A Tennessee Pet Story. Carole Marsh. (Tennessee Bks.). (J). (ps-4). 1994. pap. 19.95 (*0-7933-5543-5*); lib. bdg. 29.95 (*0-7933-5542-7*); disk 29.95 (*0-7933-5544-3*) Gallopade Intl.

Patch, the Pirate Dog: A Texas Pet Story. Carole Marsh. (Texas Bks.). (J). (ps-4). 1994. pap. 19.95 (*0-7933-5546-X*); lib. bdg. 29.95 (*0-7933-5545-1*); disk 29.95 (*0-7933-5547-8*) Gallopade Intl.

Patch, the Pirate Dog: A Utah Pet Story. Carole Marsh. (Utah Bks.). (J). (ps-4). 1994. pap. 19.95 (*0-7933-5549-4*); lib. bdg. 29.95 (*0-7933-5548-6*); disk 29.95 (*0-7933-5550-8*) Gallopade Intl.

Patch, the Pirate Dog: A Vermont Pet Story. Carole Marsh. (Vermont Bks.). (J). (ps-4). 1994. pap. 19.95 (*0-7933-5552-4*); lib. bdg. 29.95 (*0-7933-5551-6*); disk 29.95 (*0-7933-5553-2*) Gallopade Intl.

Patch, the Pirate Dog: A Virginia Pet Story. Carole Marsh. (Virginia Bks.). (J). (ps-4). 1994. pap. 19.95 (*0-7933-5555-9*); lib. bdg. 29.95 (*0-7933-5554-0*); disk 29.95 (*0-7933-5556-7*) Gallopade Intl.

Patch, the Pirate Dog: A Washington DC Pet Story. Carole Marsh. (Washington, D.C. Bks.). (J). (ps-4). 1994. pap. 19.95 (*0-7933-5441-2*); lib. bdg. 29.95 (*0-7933-5440-4*); disk 29.95 (*0-7933-5442-0*) Gallopade Intl.

Patch, the Pirate Dog: A Washington Pet Story. Carole Marsh. (Washington Bks.). (J). (ps-4). 1994. pap. 19.95 (*0-7933-5558-3*); lib. bdg. 29.95 (*0-7933-5557-5*); disk 29.95 (*0-7933-5559-1*) Gallopade Intl.

Patch, the Pirate Dog: A West Virginia Pet Story. Carole Marsh. (West Virginia Bks.). (J). (ps-4). 1994. pap. 19.95 (*0-7933-5561-3*); lib. bdg. 29.95 (*0-7933-5560-5*); disk 29.95 (*0-7933-5562-1*) Gallopade Intl.

Patch, the Pirate Dog: A Wisconsin Pet Story. Carole Marsh. (Wisconsin Bks.). (J). (ps-4). 1994. pap. 19.95 (*0-7933-5564-8*); lib. bdg. 29.95 (*0-7933-5563-X*); disk 29.95 (*0-7933-5565-6*) Gallopade Intl.

Patch, the Pirate Dog: A Wyoming Pet Story. Carole Marsh. (Wyoming Bks.). (J). (ps-4). 1994. pap. 19.95 (*0-7933-5567-2*); lib. bdg. 29.95 (*0-7933-5566-4*); disk 29.95 (*0-7933-5568-0*) Gallopade Intl.

Patch, the Pirate Dog: An Alabama Pet Story. Carole Marsh. (Carole Marsh Alabama Bks.). (J). (ps-4). 1994. pap. 19.95 (*0-7933-5417-X*); lib. bdg. 29.95 (*0-7933-5416-1*); disk 29.95 (*0-7933-5418-8*) Gallopade Intl.

Patch, the Pirate Dog: An Alaska Pet Story. Carole Marsh. (Carole Marsh Alaska Bks.). (J). (ps-4). 1994. pap. 19.95 (*0-7933-5420-X*); lib. bdg. 29.95 (*0-7933-5419-6*); disk 29.95 (*0-7933-5421-8*) Gallopade Intl.

Patch, the Pirate Dog: An Arizona Pet Story. Carole Marsh. (Carole Marsh Arizona Bks.). (J). (ps-4). 1994. pap. 19.95 (*0-7933-5423-4*); lib. bdg. 29.95 (*0-7933-5422-6*); disk 29.95 (*0-7933-5424-2*) Gallopade Intl.

Patch, the Pirate Dog: An Arkansas Pet Story. Carole Marsh. (Carole Marsh Arkansas Bks.). (J). (ps-4). 1994. pap. 19.95 (*0-7933-5426-9*); lib. bdg. 29.95 (*0-7933-5425-0*); disk 29.95 (*0-7933-5427-7*) Gallopade Intl.

Patch, the Pirate Dog: An Idaho Pet Story. Carole Marsh. (Carole Marsh Idaho Bks.). (J). (ps-4). 1994. pap. 19.95 (*0-7933-5453-6*); lib. bdg. 29.95 (*0-7933-5452-8*); disk 29.95 (*0-7933-5454-4*) Gallopade Intl.

Patch, the Pirate Dog: An Illinois Pet Story. Carole Marsh. (Carole Marsh Illinois Bks.). (J). (ps-4). 1994. pap. 19.95 (*0-7933-5456-0*); lib. bdg. 29.95 (*0-7933-5455-2*); disk 29.95 (*0-7933-5457-9*) Gallopade Intl.

Patch, the Pirate Dog: An Indiana Pet Story. Carole Marsh. (Carole Marsh Indiana Bks.). (J). (ps-4). 1994. pap. 19.95 (*0-7933-5459-5*); lib. bdg. 29.95 (*0-7933-5458-7*); disk 29.95 (*0-7933-5460-9*) Gallopade Intl.

Patch, the Pirate Dog: An Iowa Pet Story. Carole Marsh. (Carole Marsh Iowa Bks.). (J). (ps-4). 1994. pap. 19.95 (*0-7933-5462-5*); lib. bdg. 29.95 (*0-7933-5461-7*); disk 29.95 (*0-7933-5463-3*) Gallopade Intl.

Patch-Word Quilt: A Great Comforter! Paula J. Smith. 113p. (Orig.). 1985. pap. 5.95 (*0-914749-01-3*) RiskTrek.

Patch-Work Voices: The Culture & Lore of a Mining People. Dennis Brestensky et al. LC 91-50104. (Illus.). 96p. 1991. pap. 12.95 (*0-8229-5460-5*) U of Pittsburgh Pr.

Patched Coat Story: A Pattern for Victorious Christian Living, Vol. 1. Emma M. Weston. 104p. (Orig.). 1995. pap. 6.50 (*1-883179-04-1*) Weston Bible.

P

Patched Coat Story: A Pattern for Victorious Christian Living, Vol. 2. Emma M. Weston. 104p. (Orig.). 1995. pap. 24.95 incl. VHS (*1-883179-06-8*) Weston Bible.

Patchen: History & Genealogy of the Patchin-Patchen Family. Grace P. Leggett. Ed. by Myrtle M. Jillson. (Illus.). 1076p. 1995. reprint ed. pap. 145.00 (*0-8328-4816-6*); reprint ed. lib. bdg. 155.00 (*0-8328-4815-8*) Higginson Bk Co.

*__Patches.__ Ann Meredith Todd. LC 99-93621. 71p. (J). (gr. 3-6). 2000. pap. 6.95 (*0-533-13091-3*) Vantage.

Patches. Albert Ward. LC 88-3560. 50p. 1990. pap. 7.00 (*0-940713-02-0*) Broadside Pr.

Patches & Pieces of Christmas. Nona Gobel. (Illus.). 38p. (Orig.). 1996. pap. 9.95 (*0-9650940-1-4*) Patches & Pieces.

Patches & Pieces of Forget-Me-Nots. Nona Gobel. (Illus.). 40p. 1997. pap. 9.95 (*0-9650940-3-0*) Patches & Pieces.

Patches & Pieces of This-n-That. Nona Gobel. (Illus.). 44p. 1997. pap. 9.95 (*0-9650940-2-2*) Patches & Pieces.

Patches Finds a New Home. Edna Miller. (Illus.). (J). (ps-4). 1989. pap. 12.95 (*0-671-66266-X*) S&S Bks Yung.

Patches of Fire: A Story of War & Redemption. Albert French. LC 96-45682. 304p. 1996. 22.95 (*0-385-48363-5*, Anchor NY) Doubleday.

Patches of Fire: A Story of War & Redemption. Albert French. 256p. 1998. pap. 12.95 (*0-385-48366-X*) Doubleday.

Patches of Glory. Deborah Gordon. (Illus.). 48p. (Orig.). 1991. pap. text 12.95 (*0-9633917-1-2*) First Star AZ.

Patches of Iowa. North Iowa Writers Club Staff. Ed. by Catherine Wagner et al. 152p. 1988. 6.75 (*0-317-91216-X*) N Iowa Writers.

Patches of the U. S Coast Guard, an Illustrated Register Vol. 1-A: White Cutters. R. M. Wessling. LC 90-82785. (Illus.). 227p. (Orig.). 1994. pap. 16.00 (*0-9626843-5-X*) R M Wessling.

Patches of the U. S. Coast Guard, an Illustrated Register Vol. 1-B: Black Cutters. R. M. Wessling. LC 90-82785. (Illus.). 132p. (Orig.). 1995. pap. 10.00 (*0-9626843-6-8*) R M Wessling.

Patches of the U. S. Coast Guard, an Illustrated Register Vol. 1-C: Red Cutters. R. M. Wessling. LC 90-82785. (Illus.). 50p. 1992. pap. 6.00 (*0-9626843-1-7*) R M Wessling.

Patches of the U. S. Coast Guard, an Illustrated Register Vol. 2: Aviation. R. M. Wessling. LC 90-82785. (Illus.). 126p. 1990. 12.00 (*0-9626843-2-5*) R M Wessling.

Patches of the U. S. Coast Guard, an Illustrated Register Vol. 3: Stations. R. M. Wessling. LC 90-82785. (Illus.). 215p. 1998. pap. 17.00 (*0-9626843-3-3*) R M Wessling.

Patches of Time. Linda Halpin. 111p. 1991. pap. 19.95 (*0-9627646-1-2*) R C W Publng.

Patches on My Britches. (Illus.). 293p. (J). (gr. k-12). 1998. pap. 14.00 (*0-9662898-0-3*) Selecto Publ.

Patches, the Blessed Beast of Burden. Joyce B. Barnes. (Illus.). 36p. (J). 1990. 15.00 (*0-9628493-0-8*) J B Barnes.

Patching God's Garment: Environment & Mission in the 21st Century. W. Dayton Roberts. 180p. 1994. pap. 5.95 (*0-912552-85-9*) MARC.

Patching the Safety Net: Shifting Health Care Costs & State Policies. Kala Ladenheim. LC 98-116504. 32p. 1997. 35.00 (*1-55516-751-9*, 6735) Natl Conf State Legis.

Patchogue. Hans Henke. (Images of America Ser.). 1997. pap. 16.99 (*0-7524-0904-2*) Arcadia Publng.

Patchogue, Vol. II. Hans Henke. LC 98-85887. (Images of America Ser.). (Illus.). 128p. 1998. pap. 16.99 (*0-7524-1251-5*) Arcadia Publng.

Patchouli Quintet. B. Pierce. 1995. pap. text 20.00 (*0-7935-4823-3*, 00000542) H Leonard.

Patch's House. Jo Lodge. LC 96-80014. (J). 1997. pap. 11.95 (*0-15-201665-1*) Harcourt.

Patchsaddle Drive. Cliff Farrell. 1998. pap. 17.50 (*0-7540-8032-3*) Chivers N Amer.

Patchsaddle Drive. Cliff Farrell. LC 72-79386. (Western Ser.). 184p. (J). 1972. write for info. (*0-385-08472-2*) Doubleday.

Patchsaddle Drive. Cliff Farrell. 1980. mass mkt. 2.50 (*0-451-11603-8*, Sig) NAL.

Patchwork. Pamela Clabburn. 1989. pap. 25.00 (*0-85263-631-8*, Pub. by Shire Pubns) St Mut.

Patchwork. Peggy Gambill. (Illus.). 89p. 1997. pap. 15.00 (*1-880994-25-9*) Mt Olive Coll Pr.

*__Patchwork.__ Sharon Helgens. 236p. 1999. pap. 7.95 (*1-889406-15-5*) Prell Pub.

*__Patchwork.__ Koenemann Inc. Staff. (Illus.). 72p. 2000. pap. text 3.95 (*3-8290-2783-4*) Konemann.

Patchwork. New Holland Publishing Ltd. Staff. (C). 1989. 40.00 (*1-85368-076-1*, Pub. by New5 Holland) St Mut.

Patchwork. Karen Osborn. 324p. 1992. pap. 8.95 (*0-15-671365-9*, Harvest Bks) Harcourt.

Patchwork. large type ed. Maureen Peters. 1991. 11.50 (*0-7089-2378-X*) Ulverscroft.

*__Patchwork: Poetry & Prose & Papers & Pictures.__ (Illus.). 320p. 1999. pap. 10.00 (*0-7392-0426-2*, PO3700) Morris Pubng.

Patchwork Accessor's Manual. David Bowker et al. (Illus.). 1993. 116.00 (*1-873791-75-5*) Taylor & Francis.

Patchwork & Quilting. Jo Finnis. 1995. 7.98 (*0-7858-0127-8*) Bk Sales Inc.

Patchwork & Quilting Book. Ondori Publishing Company Staff. LC 81-80836. (Illus.). 104p. (Orig.). 1981. pap. 16.00 (*0-87040-498-9*) Japan Pubns USA.

Patchwork Angel. Laurel Collins. 320p. 1998. pap. 4.99 (*0-8217-5881-0*, Zebra Kensgtn) Kensgtn Pub Corp.

Patchwork Baby: Original Patchwork & Quilted Designs. Christine Donaldson. (Illus.). 144p. 1995. 24.95 (*1-57076-017-9*, Trafalgar Sq Pub) Trafalgar.

Patchwork Bags. Chuck Nohara. (Illus.). 96p. (Orig.). 1989. pap. 18.95 (*0-87040-820-8*) Japan Pubns USA.

Patchwork Book: Easy Lessons for Creative Quilt Design & Construction. Judy Martin. (Illus.). 184p. 1994. reprint ed. pap. text 9.95 (*0-486-27844-1*) Dover.

Patchwork Bride of Oz. Gilbert M. Sprague. (Illus.). 64p. (J). (gr. 1 up). 1993. 24.95 (*0-929605-28-4*); pap. 7.95 (*0-929605-27-6*) Books of Wonder.

*__Patchwork Christmas.__ Sharon Harmon et al. LC 99-42036. (Illus.). 120p. 1999. pap. 12.00 (*1-884540-47-3*) Haleys.

*__Patchwork Family.__ Judy Christenberry. (American Romance Ser.). 2000. mass mkt. 4.25 (*0-373-16853-5*, 1168533) Harlequin Bks.

*__Patchwork for the Master... From a Poet's Heart.__ Patty Moon Woodruff. LC 99-63567. 144p. 1999. pap. 11.95 (*1-57921-229-8*, Pub. by WinePress Pub) BookWorld.

Patchwork Garden: Unexpected Pleasures from a Country Garden. Sydney Eddison. 240p. 1995. pap. 12.95 (*0-8050-2091-8*, Owl) H Holt & Co.

Patchwork Girl of Oz. L. Frank Baum. (J). 25.95 (*0-8488-0705-7*) Amereon Ltd.

Patchwork Girl of Oz. L. Frank Baum. (Illus.). 336p. (J). 1990. pap. 7.95 (*0-486-26514-5*) Dover.

Patchwork Girl of Oz. L. Frank Baum. LC 94-77238. (Books of Wonder). (Illus.). 352p. (J). (gr. 4-7). 1995. 20.00 (*0-688-13354-1*, Wm Morrow) Morrow Avon.

Patchwork Girl of Oz. L. Frank Baum. LC 94-77238. (J). 1992. 22.50 (*0-8446-6495-2*) Peter Smith.

Patchwork Girl of Oz. L. Frank Baum. (J). 1997. pap. 2.95 (*0-8167-1469-X*) Troll Communs.

Patchwork Girl of Oz No. 7. L. Frank Baum. LC 79-88483. 384p. (J). 1985. mass mkt. 4.99 (*0-345-33290-3*) Ballantine Pub Grp.

Patchwork Girl of Oz - Musical. Adrian Mitchell. 1994. pap. 5.95 (*0-87129-335-8*, P09) Dramatic Pub.

Patchwork Hearts, 1 vol. Cynthia Sterling. 1999. mass mkt. 5.99 (*0-515-12446-X*, Jove) Berkley Pub.

Patchwork House. Sally Fitz-Gibbon. (Illus.). 32p. (J). (gr. k-3). 1996. pap. 6.95 (*1-55143-090-8*) Orca Bk Pubs.

Patchwork Lady. Mary K. Whittington. Ed. by Jane Yolen. LC 89-24606. (Illus.). 32p. (J). (ps-3). 1991. 13.95 (*0-15-259580-5*) Harcourt.

Patchwork Lady. Mary K. Whittington. (Illus.). 1999. pap. 5.00 (*0-15-201489-6*) Harcourt.

Patchwork Made Perfect. Ondori Publishing Company Staff. 1990. pap. 15.95 (*0-87040-855-0*) Japan Pubns USA.

Patchwork Math, No. 1. Ed. by Scholastic, Inc. Staff. (J). 1990. pap. 14.95 (*0-590-49073-7*) Scholastic Inc.

Patchwork Math 2, No. 2. Ed. by Scholastic, Inc. Staff. (J). 1990. pap. 14.95 (*0-590-49076-1*) Scholastic Inc.

Patchwork of Blessings & Grace. Ed. by Mary Daniels. LC 96-11332. 96p. 1996. pap. 5.00 (*1-57312-050-2*) Smyth & Helwys.

Patchwork of Dreams: Voices from the Heart of the New America. Ed. by Morty Sklar & Joseph Barbato. LC 92-42702. (Ethnic Diversity Ser.: No. 5). (Illus.). 224p. 1996. pap. 12.50 (*0-930370-43-0*) Spirit That Moves.

Patchwork of Dreams: Voices from the Heart of the New America, Signed A-Z. limited ed. Ed. by Morty Sklar & Joseph Barbato. LC 92-42702. (Ethnic Diversity Ser.: No. 5). (Illus.). 224p. 1996. pap. 25.00 (*0-930370-44-9*) Spirit That Moves.

Patchwork of Love. Joan W. Anglund. (Little Bks.). (Illus.). 80p. 1998. 4.95 (*0-8362-6788-5*) Andrews & McMeel.

*__Patchwork of Magic: Living in a Pagan World.__ Julia Day. 1998. pap. 19.95 (*1-898307-21-0*, Pub. by Capall Bann Pubng) Holmes Pub.

Patchwork of Programs for Women's Ministries. Nora Burdett & Karen Keller. (Illus.). 160p. 1994. pap. 19.99 (*0-8341-1477-1*, 73546) Beacon Hill.

Patchwork of Programs 2 for Women's Ministries. Nora Burdett. LC 99-18664. 88p. 1999. pap. text 15.99 (*0-8341-1774-6*) Beacon Hill.

Patchwork Pals. Colleen Parry. (Illus.). 44p. 1997. 9.99 (*1-58050-011-0*, 40-6133) Provo Craft.

Patchwork Pantry: Preserving a Tradition. Suzette Halferty & Carol C. Porter. Ed. by Laura M. Reinstatler. LC 96-14944. (Illus.). 96p. (Orig.). 1996. pap. 27.95 (*1-56477-141-5*, B258) Martingale & Co.

Patchwork Patterns. Jinny Beyer. LC 78-32055. (Illus.). 208p. 1979. pap. 21.95 (*0-914440-27-6*, EPM) Howell Pr VA.

Patchwork Patterns. Parrish. 1998. 9.95 (*1-56570-045-7*) Meridian MI.

Patchwork People. Louise Lawrence. LC 93-40830. 240p. (J). 1994. 14.95 (*0-395-67892-7*, Clarion Bks) HM.

Patchwork Persuasion: Fascinating Quilts from Traditional Designs. Joen Wolfrom. Ed. by Joyce E. Lytle & Elizabeth Aneloski. LC 96-29559. (Illus.). 144p. (Orig.). 1997. pap. 25.95 (*1-57120-027-4*, 10151) C & T Pub.

Patchwork Planet. Anne Tyler. 288p. 1999. pap. 12.95 (*0-449-00398-1*) Fawcett.

Patchwork Planet. Anne Tyler. LC 98-84431. 287p. 1998. 24.00 (*0-375-40256-X*) Knopf.

*__Patchwork Planet.__ large type ed. Anne Tyler. 352p. 1999. 31.99 (*0-7089-9085-1*) Ulverscroft.

Patchwork Planner: 350 Original Designs for Traditional Patchwork. Birte Hilberg. (Illus.). 192p. 1997. pap. 17.95 (*0-7153-0612-X*, Pub. by D & C Pub) Sterling.

Patchwork Pocket Palette: A Handy Visual Guide to Mixing & Matching Colored Fabrics. Anne Walker. LC 94-31758. (Illus.). 64p. 1995. pap. 9.95 (*0-8118-0885-8*) Chronicle Bks.

Patchwork Poetry. 3rd rev. ed. Lillian Thorp. LC 97-68328. 130p. 1997. reprint ed. 7.50 (*1-890869-12-0*) Chelsey Publ.

Patchwork Portfolio: A Presentation of 165 Original Quilt Designs with Illustrated Instructions for Easy Drafting, Elegant Fabric Usage, & Dazzling Design Experimentation. Jinny Beyer. LC 88-33446. (Illus.). 248p. 1990. pap. 29.95 (*0-939009-46-3*, EPM) Howell Pr VA.

Patchwork Prince & the Sleeping Beauty. Bill Solly. 44p. (J). (gr. k-5). 1995. mass mkt. 4.00 (*1-58193-170-0*) Brown Bag Prods.

Patchwork Programs: Comprehensive Services for Pregnant & Parenting Adolescents. Richard A. Weatherley et al. (Center for Social Welfare Research Monograph: No. 4). 264p. (Orig.). 1985. pap. text 11.00 (*0-935035-01-X*) U WA Ctr Pol Rsch.

Patchwork Projects: With Full Size Patterns & Easy to Follow Step by Step Instructions. Jan Musgrave. 1984. write for info. (*0-914169-00-9*, Patchwrk Orig) Econ America.

Patchwork Protectionism: Textile Trade Policy in the United States, Japan, & West Germany. H. Richard Friman. LC 89-27499. (Cornell Studies in Political Economy). (Illus.). 248p. 1990. text 39.95 (*0-8014-2423-2*) Cornell U Pr.

Patchwork Puppies: Cuddly Cloth Board Book. Dawn Bentley. (Illus.). 8p. (J). 1999. 9.95 (*1-58117-044-0*, Piggy Toes Pr) Intervisual Bks.

Patchwork Quilt. Valerie Flournoy. LC 84-1711. (Illus.). (J). (gr. 4-8). 1985. 15.99 (*0-8037-0097-0*, Dial Yng Read) Peng Put Young Read.

Patchwork Quilt: Haiku, Senryu, Tanka, Renku, Artwork. Francine Porad et al. (Illus.). 40p. (Orig.). (C). 1993. pap. text 6.75 (*0-9618009-9-2*) Vandina Pr.

Patchwork Quilt Designs. Susan Johnston. (Illus.). 48p. 1979. pap. 3.95 (*0-486-23845-8*) Dover.

Patchwork, Quilting & Applique: The Complete Guide to All the Essential Techniques. Jenni Dobson. LC 97-8241. 1997. 27.95 (*0-89577-971-4*, Pub. by RD Assn) Penguin Putnam.

Patchwork Quilts to Make for Children. Margaret Rolfe. LC 91-21702. (Illus.). 160p. (Orig.). 1991. pap. 14.95 (*0-8069-8498-8*) Sterling.

Patchwork Sampler Legacy Quilt: Intermediate & Advanced Lessons in Patchwork. 2nd rev. ed. Marie Shirer et al. (Illus.). 74p. 1984. reprint ed. pap. 7.95 (*0-9602970-7-3*) Leman Pubns.

Patchwork Santa. LuAnn Stout. 9p. 1990. pap. 6.95 (*0-922705-33-X*) Quilt Day.

Patchwork Shawl: Chronicles of South Asian Women in America. Ed. by Shamita D. DasGupta. LC 97-49650. 256p. (C). 1998. text 49.00 (*0-8135-2517-9*); pap. text 19.00 (*0-8135-2518-7*) Rutgers U Pr.

Patchwork Souvenirs of the 1933 Chicago World's Fair: The Sears National Quilt Contest & Chicago's Century of Progress Exposition. Merikay Waldvogel & Barbara Brackman. LC 93-22421. (Illus.). 176p. 1993. pap. 19.95 (*1-55853-257-9*) Rutledge Hill Pr.

Patchwork Voices: The Culture & Lore of a Mining People. Dennis F. Brestensky et al. LC 78-23824. 95p. reprint ed. pap. 30.00 (*0-608-15897-6*, 203079500074) Bks Demand.

Patchwork Year: A Datebook. Elaine T. Miles. (Illus.). 128p. 1983. pap. 4.95 (*0-936810-03-3*) M & M.

Patchwork Zoo. Sara Nephew. (Illus.). 144p. 1998. pap. 24.95 (*0-9621172-7-7*) Clearview Triangle.

Patchworks of Purpose: The Development of Provincial Social Assistance Regimes in Canada. Gerard W. Boychuk. pap. 22.95 (*0-7735-1739-1*) McG-Queens Univ Pr.

Patchworks of Purpose: The Development of Provincial Social Assistance Regimes in Canada. Gerard W. Boychuk. 184p. 1998. text 60.00 (*0-7735-1699-9*, Pub. by McG-Queens Univ Pr) CUP Services.

Patchworthy Apparel. Jean Wells. (Illus.). 48p. 1981. pap. 8.00 (*0-932946-04-6*) Burdett CA.

Patchy Coastal Fog: From Manhattan to West Marin in 24 Not-So-Easy Stages. Paki Stedwell. LC 83-63554. 51p. 1984. pap. 6.95 (*0-9613145-0-8*) Point Reyes Pr.

Patchy Pumpkin Finds Himself a Home. rev. ed. Sandra Lardinois. Ed. by Jonna C. Gress. (Illus.). 22p. (J). (ps-2). reprint ed. pap. 2.99 (*0-944943-64-0*) Current Inc.

Patckwork Quilt: Stories of My Childhood. Gladys Patnode. (Stories We Tell Ser.). 31p. 1993. pap. 4.00 (*1-884983-03-0*) Homegrown Bks.

Pate: The Facts of Nature Underlying Pate Thinning Hair & Baldness-Its Causes & a Professional Program for Prevention (Also a Self-Help Book) Lawrence Holley. LC 89-92729. (Illus.). 140p. 1989. pap. 11.95 (*0-9625083-0-6*, Pub. by Pate Pub); lib. bdg. 14.95 (*0-9625083-1-4*, Pub. by Pate Pub) BkMstrs TX.

Pate Chronicle: Edited & Translated from MSS 177, 321, 344, & 358 of the Library of the University of Dares Salaam. Marina Tolmacheva. Tr. by Dagmar Weiler. LC 93-12769. (African Historical Sources Ser.: Vol. 4). (ENG & SWA.). 607p. (C). 1993. 45.00 (*0-87013-336-5*) Mich St U Pr.

Pate de Verre: And Kiln Casting of Glass. James Kervin & Daniel Fenton. LC 97-93102. (Illus.). 216p. 1997. per. 40.00 (*0-9651458-1-6*) Glass Wear Studios.

Pate II: A Demonstration for Prevention of Critical Baldness & Risk of Heart Attack; & for Protection of Baldness to Reduce the Risk. Lawrence Holley. 100p. 1999. pap. write for info. (*0-9625083-2-2*, Pub. by Pate Pub) BkMstrs TX.

Patee Byng's Journal. J. L. Cranmer-Byng. (C). 1987. 135.00 (*0-7855-3953-0*) St Mut.

Patek Philippe. Paolo De Vecchi & Giorgio Gregato. (Illus.). 178p. 1999. 29.95 (*3-8290-1449-X*, 810169) Konemann.

Patek Philippe: Identification & Price Guide. Roy Ehrhardt. (Illus.). 448p. 1992. per. 50.00 (*0-913902-60-8*) Heart Am Pr.

Patek Philippe Geneve. Martin Huber & Alan Banbery. (Illus.). 288p. 1982. 140.00 (*0-915706-23-7*) Am Reprints.

*__Patek Philippe Geneve: 1920-1965 Material Catalog.__ Ed. by John Pierson. (Illus.). 40p. 1999. reprint ed. pap. 9.95 (*0-9631669-2-1*) Clockwks Pr.

Patek Philippe Parts & Materials Catalog Book: Patek Parts Book, No. 2. Roy Ehrhardt. 114p. 1997. spiral bd. 25.00 (*0-913902-99-3*) Heart Am Pr.

Patel: A Life. Rajmohan Gandhi. 625p. 1998. reprint ed. 50.00 (*0-934676-82-8*) Greenlf Bks.

Patelin Nomme Estherville. Erskine Caldwell. (FRE.). 213p. 1985. pap. 11.95 (*0-7859-2019-6*, 2070376850) Fr & Eur.

Patella. Giles R. Scuder. LC 94-29936. (Illus.). 448p. 1995. 115.00 (*0-387-94371-4*) Spr-Verlag.

Patella. Giles R. Scuder. LC 94-29936. 1995. write for info. (*3-540-94371-4*) Spr-Verlag.

Patella: A Team Approach. Ronald P. Grelsamer & Jenny McConnell. LC 97-46654. 273p. 1998. 65.00 (*0-8342-0753-2*, 20753) Aspen Pub.

Patellofemoral Joint. Ed. by James M. Fox & Wilson Del Pizzo. LC 92-48244. (Illus.). 416p. 1993. VHS 95.00 (*0-07-021752-1*) McGraw-Hill HPD.

Patellofemoral Joint. Ed. by James M. Fox & Wilson Del Pizzo. LC 92-48244. (Illus.). 416p. 1993. text 110.00 (*0-07-021753-X*) McGraw-Hill HPD.

Patel's Immigration Law Digest, 5 vols. Pravinchandra J. Patel. LC 84-82185. (Immigration Law Ser.). 1985. ring bd., suppl. ed. 575.00 (*0-685-59812-8*) West Group.

Patent Act & Regulations. 212p. 1989. pap., suppl. ed. 31.00 (*0-409-89135-5*, MICHIE) LEXIS Pub.

Patent Alternative Dispute Resolution Handbook. Tom Arnold. (IP Ser.). 1991. pap. 110.00 (*0-87632-775-7*) West Group.

Patent & Antitrust Law: A Legal & Economic Appraisal. Ward S. Bowman, Jr. 1973. lib. bdg. 25.00 (*0-226-06925-7*) U Ch Pr.

Patent & Know-How Licensing in Japan & the United States. Ed. by Teruo Doi & Warren L. Shattuck. LC 76-7785. (Asian Law Ser.: No. 5). 444p. 1977. 40.00 (*0-295-95513-9*) U of Wash Pr.

Patent & Trademark Office Notices. Government Printing Office Staff. pap. 109.00 (*0-16-009737-1*) USGPO.

Patent & Trademark Tactics & Practice. 3rd ed. David A. Burge. LC 98-30870. 304p. 1999. 49.95 (*0-471-32932-0*) Wiley.

Patent Application Practice. 2nd ed. James E. Hawes. LC 93-36378. (IP Ser.). 1993. ring bd. 85.00 (*0-87632-975-X*) West Group.

Patent Applications Simplified for the Independent Petitioner: What Why When Who Where & How. (Illus.). 65p. (Orig.). 1996. pap. text 17.95 (*0-9656034-0-7*, 1001) Jerry L Jay.

Patent Claims, 3 vols. annuals 2nd rev. ed. Anthony W. Deller & Ernest B. Lipscomb, 3rd. LC 76-112643. (IP Ser.). 1971. suppl. ed. 375.00 (*0-685-59813-6*) West Group.

Patent, Copyright & Trademark. 3rd ed. Stephen Elias. LC 98-39731. 1999. 24.95 (*0-87337-508-4*) Nolo com.

*__Patent, Copyright & Trademark.__ 4th ed. Stephen Elias. LC 00-40215. (Illus.). 2000. write for info. (*0-87337-601-3*) Nolo com.

Patent, Copyright & Trademark: A Desk Reference to Intellectual Property Law. 3rd rev. ed. Stephen Elias. LC 97-28876. (Illus.). 448p. (YA). 1999. pap. 24.95 (*0-87337-398-7*) Nolo com.

*__Patent Damages Law & Practice.__ John Skenyon et al. LC 99-46528. 1999. 175.00 (*0-8366-1380-5*) West Group.

Patent Drawings. LC 86-16329. (Milestone Documents in the National Archives Ser.). (Illus.). 20p. 1986. pap. text 1.00 (*0-911333-47-9*, 200106) National Archives & Recs.

Patent Duffer: 101 Incredible Inventions. Jordan Kaiser. (Illus.). 248p. 1992. per. 19.95 (*0-9629318-8-8*) Automatic Pr.

Patent Files: Dispatches from the Frontiers of Invention. David Lindsay. LC 98-38808. 248p. 1999. 19.95 (*1-55821-741-X*) Lyons Pr.

*__Patent Files: Dispatches from the Frontiers of Invention.__ David Lindsay. 2001. pap. 17.95 (*1-58574-072-1*) Lyons Pr.

Patent Fundamentals for Scientists & Engineers. Thomas T. Gordon & Arthur S. Cookfair. 128p. 1995. per. 44.95 (*0-87371-317-6*, L317) Lewis Pubs.

*__Patent Fundamentals for Scientists & Engineers.__ 2nd ed. Thomas T. Gordon & Arthur S. Cookfair. LC 99-56999. 176p. 2000. per. 49.95 (*1-56670-517-7*) Lewis Pubs.

Patent Guide: A Friendly Handbook for Protecting & Profiting from Patents. Carl W. Battle. LC 96-79670. (Illus.). 224p. (Orig.). 1997. pap. 18.95 (*1-880559-72-2*) Allworth Pr.

Patent History of the Phonograph, 1877-1912. Allen Koenigsberg. (Illus.). 162p. (C). 1990. spiral bd. 54.95 (*0-937612-10-3*) A P M Pr.

Patent Infringement in the European Community. Amiran Benyamini. LC 93-2935. (IIC Studies Ser.: Vol. 13). 433p. 1993. pap. 199.00 (*3-527-28530-X*, Wiley-VCH) Wiley.

Patent Infringement Suits: An Executive's Guide to the Litigation Process. William G. Konold. LC 87-8822. (Series of Special Reports: Vol. 19). 99p. reprint ed. pap. 30.70 (*0-608-09006-9*, 206964100005) Bks Demand.

Patent Interference Practice Handbook. Jerome Rosenstock. LC 98-21054. 1998. ring bd. 160.00 (*0-7355-0114-9*) Panel Pubs.

Patent It Yourself. 6th ed. David Pressman. Ed. by Steve Elias. LC 97-18560. (Illus.). 480p. 1997. reprint ed. pap. 44.95 (*0-87337-395-2*) Nolo com.

An Asterisk (*) at the beginning of an entry indicates that the title is appearing for the first time.

Patent It Yourself. 7th ed. David Pressman. Ed. by Stephen Elias. LC 98-6526. (Illus.). 496p. 1998. pap. 46.95 (*0-87337-469-X*) Nolo com.

*__Patent It Yourself.__ 8th ed. David Pressman. LC 99-48778. 2000. write for info. (*0-87337-563-7*) Nolo com.

Patent It Yourself: 1.1.1. EDS Staff & David Pressman. 224p. 1996. student ed. 229.95 incl. disk (*0-87337-249-2*) Nolo com.

Patent Law. Martin J. Adelman et al. LC 98-12716. (Paralegal). 1200p. 1998. text 49.25 (*0-314-06529-6*) West Pub.

Patent Law. David I. Bainbridge. 440p. 1999. boxed set 152.00 (*1-85811-140-4*, Pub. by CLT Prof) Gaunt.

Patent Law. 2nd ed. Aisenberg. 1992. 95.00 (*0-316-02052-4*, Aspen Law & Bus) Aspen Pub.

Patent Law: A Practitioner's Guide. 2nd ed. Ronald B. Hildreth. 587p. 1993. 125.00 (*0-614-17116-4*, G1-1020) PLI.

*__Patent Law: A Primer for Federal District Court Judges.__ James M. Amend. 93p. 1999. pap. 10.00 (*0-9677766-0-7*, BCLT-99-A-1) BCLT Pr.

Patent Law: Adaptable to Courses Utilizing Francis & Collins' Casebook on Patent Law. Casenotes Publishing Co., Inc. Staff. Ed. by Norman S. Goldenberg et al. (Legal Briefs Ser.). 1995. pap. write for info. (*0-87457-111-1*, 1560) Casenotes Pub.

Patent Law: Legal & Economic Principles. John W. Schlicher. LC 92-2970. (IP Ser.). 1992. ring bd. 145.00 (*0-87632-892-3*) West Group.

Patent Law & Policy. 2nd ed. (Michie Contemporary Legal Education Ser.). (Illus.). 70p. 1998. teacher ed. write for info. (*0-327-00741-9*, 1230711) LEXIS Pub.

Patent Law & Policy: Cases & Materials. 2nd ed. Robert P. Merges. LC 96-79718. (Illus.). 1368p. 1997. text 58.00 (*1-55834-445-4*, 12305-11, MICHIE) LEXIS Pub.

Patent Law & Policy Cases & Materials: 1992 Edition. Thomas Merges. 1034p. 1992. text. write for info. (*0-87473-986-1*, 12305-10, MICHIE) LEXIS Pub.

Patent Law & Policy Statutes, Rules & Treaties: 1997 Edition. Robert Merges. 301p. 1997. pap. 12.00 (*1-55834-458-6*, 12306-11, MICHIE) LEXIS Pub.

*__Patent Law & Practice.__ 2nd ed. Herbert F. Schwartz. LC 98-212852. 187p. 1998. 45.00 (*1-57018-055-5*) BNA Books.

Patent Law Annual, Southwestern Legal Foundation: Proceedings, 1st-26th, 1963-1988. 1963. mic. film 1300.00 (*0-318-57621-X*) W S Hein.

Patent Law Annual, Southwestern Legal Foundation: Proceedings, 1st-26th, 1963-1988, Set. 1963. 1300.00 (*0-8377-9148-0*, Rothman) W S Hein.

Patent Law Basics. Peter D. Rosenberg. LC 92-15593. (IP Ser.). 1992. ring bd. 125.00 (*0-87632-897-4*) West Group.

Patent Law Developments in the Federal Circuit, 1996. Alex Chartove. 300p. 1996. pap. 81.25 (*0-614-17117-2*, G1-1027) PLI.

Patent Law Digest. Donald S. Chisum. text 79.00 (*0-8205-4248-2*) Bender.

Patent Law Digest. Donald S. Chisum. 1991. write for info. (*0-8205-3052-2*) Bender.

Patent Law Essentials: A Concise Guide. Alan L. Durham. LC 98-20133. 240p. 1999. 69.50 (*1-56720-242-X*, Quorum Bks) Greenwood.

Patent Law for the Non-Lawyer. 2nd ed. Amernick. (Illus.). 220p. 1994. text 62.95 (*0-412-99171-3*, Chap & Hall NY) Chapman & Hall.

Patent Law Fundamentals, 3 vols. 2nd ed. Peter D. Rosenberg. LC 80-10710. (IP Ser.). (C). 1980. ring bd. 425.00 (*0-87632-098-1*) West Group.

*__Patent Law Handbook.__ Peter S. Canelias. LC 00-38098. 2000. pap. write for info. (*0-7355-1510-7*) Panel Pubs.

Patent Law in Biotechnology, Chemicals & Pharmaceuticals. Harold C. Wegner. 540p. 1992. 170.00 (*1-56159-048-7*) Groves Dictionaries.

Patent Law Index. Christopher M. Pickett. LC 97-154257. (Orig.). 1997. pap. 75.00 (*1-57018-033-4*, 1033) BNA Books.

Patent Law Perspectives, 6 vols. 2nd ed. M. Adelman. 1970. ring bd. 1280.00 (*0-8205-1532-9*) Bender.

Patent Law Practice Forms, 4 vols. Barry Kramer & Allen D. Brufsky. LC 85-10952. (IP Ser.). 1985. ring bd. 495.00 (*0-87632-467-7*) West Group.

Patent Law Precedent. Aisenberg. 1991. 95.00 (*0-316-02043-5*, Aspen Law & Bus) Aspen Pub.

Patent Law Text & Cases. Laurence H. Pretty. (Illus.). 392p. (Orig.). 1995. pap. text 40.00 (*0-9651658-0-9*) Pasadena Legal.

Patent Law Texts & Cases. 2nd rev. ed. Laurence H. Pretty. 439p. 1997. pap. text 47.00 (*0-9651658-1-7*) Pasadena Legal.

Patent License Agreements: Information Technology, Computers, Electronics. Michael J. Lennon. LC 98-40535. 1998. ring bd. 160.00 (*0-7355-0237-4*) Panel Pubs.

Patent Licensing Transactions, 2 vols. Harold Einhorn & Bender's Editors. (Patent Law & Practice Ser.). 1968. ring bd. 500.00 (*0-8205-1531-0*) Bender.

Patent Litigation, 2 vols. (Patents, Copyrights, Trademarks, & Literary Property Ser.). 1600p. 1991. pap. text 80.00 (*0-685-56904-7*, G4-3873) PLI.

Patent Litigation: Procedure & Tactics, 3 vols. Robert A. White & Rodney K. Caldwell. (Patent Law & Practice Ser.). 1971. ring bd. 295.00 (*0-8205-1813-1*) Bender.

Patent Litigation, 1989. (Patents, Copyrights, Trademarks, & Literary Property Ser.). 578p. 1989. 17.50 (*0-317-99793-9*, G4-3842) PLI.

Patent Litigation, 1995, 2 vols., Set. (Patents, Copyrights, Trademarks, & Literary Property Course Handbook, 1994-95 Ser.). Date not set. pap. 149.00 (*0-614-17239-X*, G4-3952) PLI.

Patent Litigation, 1994, 2 vols., Set. (Patents, Copyrights, Trademarks, & Literary Property Ser.). 1848p. 1994. pap. 149.00 (*0-685-65513-X*, G4-3929) PLI.

*__Patent Litigation Strategies Handbook.__ Barry L. Grossman & Gary M. Hoffman. Ed. by American Bar Association Staff. LC 00-31183. 2000. write for info. (*1-57018-197-7*) BNA Books.

Patent Office: Its History, Activities & Organization. Gustavus A. Weber. LC 72-3045. (Brookings Institution. Institute for Government Research. Service Monographs of the U. S. Government: No. 31). reprint ed. 37.50 (*0-404-57131-X*) AMS Pr.

Patent Office Rules & Practice, 12 vols. Lester Horwitz. 1959. ring bd. 1870.00 (*0-8205-1605-8*) Bender.

Patent Pending: Today's Inventors & Their Inventions. Richard L. Gausewitz. LC 82-9341. (Illus.). 240p. 1983. 14.95 (*0-8159-6522-2*) Devin.

Patent Policy: Government, Academic, & Industry Concept. Ed. by Willard Marcy. LC 78-9955. (ACS Symposium Ser.: Vol. 81). 183p. 1978. reprint ed. pap. 56.80 (*0-608-03934-9*, 206438100009) Bks Demand.

Patent Policy: Government, Academic, & Industry Concepts. Ed. by William Marcy. LC 78-9955. (ACS Symposium Ser.: No. 81). 1978. 27.95 (*0-8412-0454-3*) Am Chemical.

Patent Politics Between the U. S. & Japan. Ed. by Mindy L. Kotler. 130p. 1993. pap. text 50.00 (*1-881853-03-9*) Japan Info Access.

Patent Practice & Policy in the Pacific Rim, 2 vols. Thomas T. Moga. 1995. ring bd. 350.00 (*0-379-01263-4*) Oceana.

Patent Prior User Rights Act & the Patent Reexamination Reform Act: Hearing Before the Subcommittee on Patents, Copyrights & Trademarks of the Committee on the Judiciary, United States Senate, 103rd Congress, 2nd Session, on S. 2272. USGPO Staff. LC 96-164630. iv, 77 p. 1996. write for info. (*0-16-052560-8*) USGPO.

Patent Prosecution: Practice & Procedure Before the U. S Patent Office: Includes, 1998 Supplement. Irah Donner. 1997. pap. 255.00 incl. disk (*1-57018-086-5*, 1087) BNA Books.

Patent, Protect, & Sell Your Idea. Delbert L. Earle. LC 95-176628. (Illus.). 240p. 1994. 14.95 (*0-9645922-0-7*) Skyline Indust.

Patent Searching for Librarians & Inventors. Timothy L. Wherry. 90p. (Orig.). 1995. pap. 25.00 (*0-8389-0641-9*, 0641-9-2045) ALA.

*__Patent Searching Made Easy.__ 2nd ed. David Hitchcock. LC 99-45116. 1999. 29.95 (*0-87337-554-8*) Nolo com.

Patent Searching Made Easy: How to Do Patent Searches on the Internet & in the Library. David Hitchcock. LC 98-29046. 256p. 1999. pap. 24.95 (*0-87337-476-2*) Nolo com.

Patent Strategies for Business. 3rd rev. ed. Stephen C. Glazier. LC 97-97126. 468p. 1997. write for info. (*0-9661437-9-5*) L B I.

Patent System & Modern Technology Needs: Meeting the Challenge of the 21st Century: Hearing Before the Committee on Science, U. S. House of Representatives. Ed. by Constance Morella. 54p. (C). 1998. reprint ed. text 25.00 (*0-7881-7068-6*) DIANE Pub.

Patent Technology Review: Flame-Retardant Chemicals & Compositions, No. 3R. Business Communications Co., Inc. Staff. 306p. 1993. 1250.00 (*0-89336-820-2*) BCC.

Patent Technology Reviews: Batteries. Sara Kochummen. LC 99-175691. (Illus.). xvi, 331 p. 1997. 1500.00 (*1-56965-424-7*, TAP16R) BCC.

Patent Term & Patent Disclosure Legislation: Hearing Before the Committee on Small Business, U. S. House of Representatives. 217p. (C). 1998. pap. text 45.00 (*0-7881-4966-0*) DIANE Pub.

Patent, Trademark, & Copyright Laws: 1998. Ed. by Jeffrey M. Samuels. 646p. 1998. pap. 75.00 (*1-57018-113-6*, 1113) BNA Books.

Patent, Trademark, & Copyright Laws, 1999 Edition. Ed. by Jeffrey M. Samuels. 737p. 1999. 85.00 (*1-57018-181-0*, 1181-PR9) BNA Books.

*__Patent, Trademark & Copyright Laws, 2000.__ Ed. by Jeffrey M. Samuels. 787p. 2000. pap. 95.00 (*1-57018-222-1*, 1222-PRYY) BNA Books.

*__Patent, Trademark, & Copyright Regulations: Includes I.P. Regulatory Developments Through October 1, 1999.__ Ed. by James D. Crowne. 582p. 1999. ring bd. 75.00 (*1-57018-209-4*, 1209-PR9) BNA Books.

Patent, Trademark & Copyright Regulations: 1998 Supplement. Ed. by James D. Crowne. 780p. 1999. ring bd., suppl. ed. 75.00 (*1-57018-161-6*, 1161) BNA Books.

Patent, Trademark, & Copyright Regulations, March 1999 Supplement. James D. Crowne. 561p. 1999. ring bd., suppl. ed. 75.00 (*1-57018-199-3*, 1199-PR9) BNA Books.

*__Patent, Trademark & Copyright Searching on the Internet.__ Charles C. Sharpe. LC 99-48014. (Illus.). 240p. 1999. pap. 32.00 (*0-7864-0757-3*) McFarland & Co.

Patent Wars: The Battle to Own the World's Technology. Fred Warshofsky. 298p. 1994. 27.95 (*0-471-59902-6*) Wiley.

Patented American Sawsets Vol. 1: An Illustrated Patent Directory (1812-1925) Todd L. Friberg. LC 96-92207. (Illus.). 280p. (Orig.). 1996. pap. 23.95 (*0-9653719-2-1*) Osage Pr IL.

Patented Transitional & Metallic Planes in America, Vol. II. Roger K. Smith. LC 91-67596. (Illus.). 396p. 1992. 90.00 (*0-940458-05-5*) R K Smith.

Patented Transitional & Metallic Planes in America, 1827-1927. Roger K. Smith. LC 81-90097. (Illus.). 336p. 1990. reprint ed. 65.00 (*0-940458-00-4*) R K Smith.

Patenting in the Biological Sciences: A Practical Guide for Research Scientists in Biotechnology & the Pharmaceutical & Agrochemical Industries. R. S. Crespi. LC 81-19771. (Illus.). 217p. 1982. reprint ed. pap. 67.30 (*0-7837-8870-3*, 204958100001) Bks Demand.

Patenting of Human Genes & Living Organisms. Vogel F. Vogel. LC 94-3561. 1996. 62.00 (*0-387-58148-0*) Spr-Verlag.

Patenting of Life Forms. Ed. by David W. Plant et al. LC 82-4191. (Banbury Report: No. 10). 351p. reprint ed. pap. 108.90 (*0-7837-2001-7*, 204227500002) Bks Demand.

Patenting the Recombinant Products of Biotechnology & Other Molecules. Phillipe G. Ducor. LC 98-194387. 208p. 1997. 87.00 (*90-411-0698-7*) Kluwer Academic.

Patently Murder. large type ed. Ray Harrison. (Magna Large Print Ser.). 492p. 1996. 27.99 (*0-7505-0922-8*, Pub. by Mgna Lrg Print) Ulverscroft.

Patents, 13 vols. Donald S. Chisum. 1978. ring bd. 1735.00 (*0-8205-1525-6*) Bender.

Patents & Deeds & Other Early Records of New Jersey, 1664-1703. William Nelson. LC 76-252. 770p. 2000. reprint ed. 57.50 (*0-8063-0711-0*, Pub. by Clearfield Co) ACCESS Pubs Network.

Patents & Health Sciences: Index of Modern Information. Herbert T. Yarman. LC 88-47599. 141p. 1988. 44.50 (*0-88164-870-1*) ABBE Pubs Assn.

*__Patents & How to Get One: A Practical Handbook.__ U. S. Department of Commerce Staff. 2000. pap. 3.95 (*0-486-41144-3*) Dover.

Patents & How to Get One for an Invention. 2nd ed. C. D. Tuska. LC 70-187721. xiv, 217 p. 1972. write for info. (*0-486-21169-X*) Dover.

Patents & the Federal Circuit. 4th ed. Robert L. Harmon. LC 98-29186. 1064p. 1998. 225.00 (*1-57018-126-8*, 1126) BNA Books.

Patents as Scientific & Technical Literature. Richard D. Walker. LC 94-8506. 1995. 66.00 (*0-8108-2879-0*) Scarecrow.

Patents, Copyrights & Trademarks. 2nd ed. Frank H. Foster & Robert L. Shook. LC 92-33071. 272p. 1993. 125.95 (*0-471-58123-2*); pap. 29.95 (*0-471-58124-0*) Wiley.

Patents, Copyrights, Trademarks & Literary Property Series. 693p. 1991. pap. text 17.50 (*0-685-56900-4*, G4-3869) PLI.

Patents (DOE) Available for Licensing: A Bibliography Covering January, 1974 Through December 1980. DOE Technical Information Center Staff. 284p. 1982. pap. 17.00 (*0-87079-445-0*, DOE/TIC-3398); fiche 9.00 (*0-87079-456-6*, DOE/TIC-3398) DOE.

Patents (DOE) Available for Licensing: A Bibliography for the Period, 1966-1974. DOE Technical Information Center Staff. 64p. 1983. pap. 9.25 (*0-87079-512-0*, DOE/TIC-3398 SU); fiche 6.50 (*0-87079-513-9*, DOE/TIC-3398 SUPPL. 1) DOE.

Patents for Chemical Inventions: Symposia Sponsored by the Division of Chemical Literature & the Division of Industrial & Engineering Chemistry, at the 145th Meeting of the American Chemical Society, New York, NY, September 9 & 13, 1963. American Chemical Society Staff. LC 64-24274. (Advances in Chemistry Ser.: Vol. 46). 125p. 1964. reprint ed. pap. 38.80 (*0-608-06922-1*, 206713000009) Bks Demand.

Patents for Chemicals, Pharmaceuticals & Biotechnology: Fundamentals of Global Law, Practice & Strategy. Philip W. Grubb. LC 98-51392. 472p. 1999. text 80.00 (*0-19-876520-7*) OUP.

Patents for Inventions, 2 vols. Great Britain, Patent Office Staff. Ed. by Peter C. Bunnell & Robert A. Sobieszek. LC 76-23063. (Sources of Modern Photography Ser.). (Illus.). 1979. reprint ed. lib. bdg. 82.95 (*0-405-09626-7*) Ayer.

Patents for Inventions, 2 vols., Vol. 1. Great Britain, Patent Office Staff. Ed. by Peter C. Bunnell & Robert A. Sobieszek. LC 76-23063. (Sources of Modern Photography Ser.). (Illus.). 1979. reprint ed. lib. bdg. 30.95 (*0-405-09627-5*) Ayer.

Patents for Inventions, 2 vols., Vol. 2. Great Britain, Patent Office Staff. Ed. by Peter C. Bunnell & Robert A. Sobieszek. LC 76-23063. (Sources of Modern Photography Ser.). (Illus.). 1979. reprint ed. lib. bdg. 53.95 (*0-405-09628-3*) Ayer.

Patents for Inventions: Class 119 (Small Arms), 1855-1930, 7 vols. Ed. by British Patent Office Staff. (Illus.). 2013p. 1994. reprint ed. boxed set 250.00 (*0-939683-08-3*) Armory Pubns.

Patents, Getting One . . . A Cost Cutting Primer for Inventors. Stuart R. Peterson. LC 89-81531. (Illus.). 472p. 1990. 43.95 (*0-914960-75-X*) Academy Bks.

Patents Handbook: A Guide for Inventors & Researchers to Searching Patent Documents & Preparing & Making an Application. Fred K. Carr. LC 95-7366. 237p. 1995. lib. bdg. 43.00 (*0-7864-0026-9*) McFarland & Co.

Patents, Invention & Economic Change: Data & Selected Essays. Jacob Schmookler. Ed. by Zvi Griliches & Leonid Hurwicz. LC 74-188355. (Illus.). 310p. 1972. reprint ed. pap. 96.10 (*0-7837-6090-6*, 205913600007) Bks Demand.

Patents Law. H. E. Norman. (European Community Law Ser.). (C). 1997. text 90.00 (*0-485-70015-8*) Humanities.

Patents on Transgenic Plants. Andrew Kalinski. 30p. (Orig.). (C). 1995. pap. text 20.00 (*0-7881-1990-7*) DIANE Pub.

Patents Strategy: For Researchers & Research Managers. H. Jackson Knight. LC 95-688. 180p. 1996. 74.00 (*0-471-96095-0*) Wiley.

Patents, Territorial Restrictions, & EEC Law: A Legal & Economic Analysis. Paul Demaret. (IIC Studies Ser.: Vol. 2). 133p. 1978. pap. 44.00 (*3-527-25696-2*, Wiley-VCH) Wiley.

Patents Throughout the World. 4th ed. Ed. by Alan Jacobs & Elizabeth Hanellin. LC 79-978. (IP Ser.). 1979. reprint ed. ring bd. 195.00 (*0-87632-125-2*) West Group.

Patents, Trademarks & Copyrights. Ed. by Richard L. Strohm. LC 96-48013. (Layman's Law Guides Ser.). 128p. 1997. lib. bdg. 16.95 (*0-7910-4440-8*) Chelsea Hse.

Patents, Trademarks & Copyrights: Practical Strategies for Protecting Your Ideas & Inventions. David G. Rosenbaum. 1993. pap. 9.95 (*0-9630356-6-5*) Makai.

Patents, Trademarks, & Related Rights: National & International Protection, 3 vols. Stephen Ladas. LC 73-89709. 1888p. 1975. 197.00 (*0-674-65775-6*) HUP.

Pater: John Lockwood Kipling His Life & Times, 1837-1911. Arthur R. Ankers. 161p. (C). 1988. text 90.00 (*1-871044-00-6*, Pub. by Hawthorns Pubns) St Mut.

*__Pater Bernhardus: Martin Luther & Bernard of Clairvaux.__ Franz Posset. (Cistercian Studies: Vol. CS168). (Illus.). 432p. 2000. write for info. (*0-87907-368-3*); pap. write for info. (*0-87907-668-2*) Cistercian Pubns.

Pater Noster - "Our Father" An Exposition of Christian Prayer. Peter Toon. (Catechetical Ser.). 52p. audio 3.95 (*1-886412-09-X*) Preserv Press.

Paterfamilias: Allen Ginsberg in America. Jane Kramer. LC 71-466963. 202 p. 1970. write for info. (*0-575-00436-3*) V Gollancz.

Paterik of the Kievan Caves Monastery. Tr. by Muriel Heppell. LC 88-82377. (Harvard Library of Early Ukrainian Literature: Vol. 1). 200p. 1990. text 18.00 (*0-916458-27-X*) Harvard Ukrainian.

Paterna: The Autobiography of Cotton Mather. Cotton Mather. Ed. by Ronald A. Bosco. LC 76-10595. (Center for Editions of American Authors). 504p. 1976. lib. bdg. 75.00 (*0-8201-1273-9*) Schol Facsimiles.

*__Paternal Ancestry of Alexandra Leah Aschheim Feld.__ 1999. pap. 21.00 (*0-8328-9884-8*) Higginson Bk Co.

Paternal Ancestry of Alexandra Leah Aschheim Feld: Genealogy of the Norwalk, Eilenberg, Heilperin, Gutman & Kronenberg. Jay Norwalk. LC 97-70572. (Illus.). 170p. 1997. 35.00 (*1-892446-02-2*) Axion Pr.

*__Paternal Ancestry of Alexandra Leah Aschheim Feld: The Genealogy of the Norwalk, Eilenberg, Heilperin, Gutman.__ Jay Norwalk. 128p. 1999. 31.00 (*0-8328-9883-X*) Higginson Bk Co.

Paternal Instincts: Men! Elizabeth August. (Romance Ser.: No. 1265). 1997. per. 3.25 (*0-373-19265-7*, 1-19265-7) Harlequin Bks.

Paternal Romance: Reading God-the-Father in Early Western Culture. Robert C. Davis. 200p. (C). 1993. text 32.50 (*0-252-01949-0*); pap. text 14.95 (*0-252-06265-5*) U of Ill Pr.

*__Paternalism & Politics: The Revival of Paternalism in Early Nineteenth-century Britain.__ Kim Lawes. LC 99-56310. 288p. 2000. 65.00 (*0-312-23116-4*) St Martin.

Paternalism & Protest: Southern Mill Workers & Organized Labor, 1875-1905, 3. Melton A. McLaurin. LC 70-111261. (Contributions in Economics & Economic History Ser.: No. 3). 265p. 1971. 59.95 (*0-8371-4662-3*, MPP&, Greenwood Pr) Greenwood.

Paternalism & the Legal Profession. David Luban. 1981. 2.50 (*0-318-33307-4*) IPPP.

Paternalism, Conflict, & Coproduction: Learning from Citizen Action & Citizen Participation in Western Europe. Lawrence Susskind & Michael Elliott. (Environment, Development, & Public Policy: Public Policy & Social Services Ser.). 374p. 1983. 75.00 (*0-306-40963-1*, Plenum Trade) Perseus Pubng.

Paternalism in the Japanese Economy. John W. Bennett & Iwao Ishino. LC 72-3538. 307p. 1972. reprint ed. lib. bdg. 65.00 (*0-8371-6424-9*, BEJE, Greenwood Pr) Greenwood.

Paternalistic Capitalism. Andreas G. Papandreou. LC 79-187169. 200p. 1972. reprint ed. pap. 62.00 (*0-7837-2929-4*, 205752500006) Bks Demand.

Paternalistic Intervention: The Moral Bounds on Benevolence. Donald VanDeVeer. LC 85-43320. (Studies in Moral, Political, & Legal Philosophy). 465p. 1986. reprint ed. pap. 144.20 (*0-7837-9467-3*, 206020900004) Bks Demand.

Paternidad. D. S. Prince.Tr. of Fatherhood. (SPA.). 3.50 (*0-7899-0242-7*, 550093) Editorial Unilit.

Paternidad Espiritual. M. Fumero.Tr. of Spiritual Fatherhood. (SPA.). 83p. 1996. 4.50 (*0-7899-0175-7*, 497483) Editorial Unilit.

Paternity. Jasmine Cresswell. 1997. per. 4.50 (*0-373-82561-7*, 1-82561-1) Harlequin Bks.

Paternity--Disputed, Typing, PCR & DNA Tests: Index of New Information. Dexter Z. Franklin. 160p. 1998. 47.50 (*0-7883-1720-2*); pap. 44.50 (*0-7883-1721-0*) ABBE Pubs Assn.

*__Paternity Affair.__ large type ed. Robyn Donald. 1999. write for info. (*0-263-16169-2*, Pub. by Mills & Boon) Ulverscroft.

Paternity & Fatherhood: Myths & Realities. Spaas. LC 97-47027. 288p. 1998. text 45.00 (*0-333-64237-6*) St Martin.

Paternity Factor. Caroline Cross. (Desire Ser.: No. 1173). 1998. per. 3.75 (*0-373-76173-2*, 1-76173-3) Harlequin Bks.

Paternity in Primates: Tests & Theories: Implications of Human DNA Fingerprint. Ed. by R. D. Martin et al. (Illus.). xii, 288p. 1991. 215.75 (*3-8055-5494-X*) S Karger.

Paternity Lessons. Maris Soule. (Romance Ser.: No. 1389). 1999. per. 3.50 (*0-373-19389-0*, 1-19389-5) Silhouette.

P

***Paternity Plan: Project: Pregnancy.** Heather MacAllister. (Romance Ser.: Bk. 3625). 2000. mass mkt. 3.50 (*0-373-03625-6*, 1-03625-4) Harlequin Bks.

***Paternity Plan: Project: Pregnancy.** large type ed. 2000. mass mkt. 3.50 (*0-373-15871-8*) Harlequin Bks.

Paternity Question. Andrea Edwards. 1998. per. 4.25 (*0-373-24175-5*, 1-24175-1) Silhouette.

Paternity Test. Pamela Toth. 1997. per. 3.99 (*0-373-24138-0*, 1-24138-9) Silhouette.

Paternoster Bible History Atlas. F. F. Bruce. 96p. 1982. 19.50 (*0-85364-312-1*, Pub. by Paternoster Pub) McClelland & Stewart.

***Paterson.** June Avignone. (Images of America Ser.). 1999. pap. 16.99 (*0-7524-0937-9*) Arcadia Publng.

Paterson. 2nd ed. William Carlos Williams. Ed. by Christopher J. MacGowan. LC 92-22956. 336p. 1995. pap. 12.95 (*0-8112-1298-X*, NDP806, Pub. by New Directions) Norton.

Paterson. 2nd rev. ed. William Carlos Williams. Ed. by Christopher J. MacGowan. LC 92-22956. 352p. 1992. 38.00 (*0-8112-1225-4*, Pub. by New Directions) Norton.

Paterson: Its Advantages for Manufacturing & Residence, Its Industries, Prominent Men, Banks, Schools, Churches, Etc. with Many Photographs. Charles A. Shriner. 326p. 1997. reprint ed. lib. bdg. 39.00 (*0-8328-6073-5*) Higginson Bk Co.

Paterson & Zderad: Humanistic Nursing Theory. Nancy O'Connor. (Notes on Nursing Theories Ser.: Vol. 7). (Illus.). 64p. (C). 1992. text 22.95 (*0-8039-4798-4*) Sage.

Paterson & Zderad: Humanistic Nursing Theory, No. 7. Nancy O'Connor. (Notes on Nursing Theories Ser.: Vol. 7). (Illus.). 64p. (C). 1992. pap. text 9.95 (*0-8039-4489-6*) Sage.

Paterson Pieces: Poems, 1969-1979. William J. Higginson. (Illus.). 80p. (Orig.). 1981. pap. 4.95 (*0-89120-018-5*, Old Plate) From Here.

Paterson's Licensing Acts, 1994. 102nd ed. Matthew Pink. 1900p. 1994. 253.00 (*0-406-02653-X*, MICHIE) LEXIS Pub.

Paterson's Licensing Acts, 1995. 103rd ed. Lawrence Stevens et al. Date not set. write for info. (*0-406-03689-6*, U.K., MICHIE) LEXIS Pub.

Paterson's Licensing Acts 1997. 105th ed. Lawrence Stevens et al. 1996. write for info. (*0-406-99743-8*, PLA1997, MICHIE) LEXIS Pub.

Path. Erik Kongshaug. 384p. (Orig.). 1998. pap. 15.00 (*1-883968-07-0*) Blinking Yellow.

Path. David A. Wilson. 58p. 1977. pap. 3.00 (*0-934852-18-9*) Lorien Hse.

Path. 2nd ed. J. Donald Walters. (Illus.). 420p. 1996. pap. 14.95 (*1-56589-733-1*) Crystal Clarity.

Path: A Career Workbook for Liberal Arts Students. 3rd ed. Howard E. Figler. LC 92-40247. 128p. 1993. 13.50 (*0-910328-45-5*) Sulzburger & Graham Pub.

Path: A New Look at Reality. Richard Matheson. LC 99-12398. 1999. 13.95 (*0-312-87057-4*, Pub. by Tor Bks) St Martin.

Path: A Philosophy of Leadership. William J. Cox. 64p. (Orig.). 1993. pap. 6.95 (*0-9638471-0-4*) WJC Pr.

***Path: A Practical Guide to Improving Your Life on the Job.** Rick Seaman. LC 98-93498. (Illus.). 288p. 1999. pap. 16.95 (*0-9664778-5-5*) Guidance Pr.

Path: A Spiritual Autobiography. J. Donald Walters. LC 77-72787. Orig. Title: The Path: Autobiography of a Western Yogi. (Illus.). 640p. 1977. 16.95 (*0-916124-11-8*, DS11) Crystal Clarity.

Path: (A Way of Life) Luong S. Hang. LC 92-64129. (Illus.). 330p. (Orig.). 1992. pap. 14.95 (*0-9633690-0-8*) VoVi LED.

Path: An Adventure in African History. Michael Markman. Ed. by Wendy Gift. LC 96-22412. (Illus.). 32p. (J). (gr. 1-5). 1997. 7.95 (*1-881316-19-X*) A&B Bks.

Path: An Adventure in African History. Michael Markman. Ed. by Wendy Gift. LC 96-22412. (Illus.). 32p. (J). (gr. 2-9). 1997. pap. 8.95 (*1-881316-35-1*) A&B Bks.

Path: Creating Your Mission Statement for Work & for Life. Laurie Beth Jones. LC 96-846. 224p. (J). 1996. 17.45 (*0-7868-6227-0*, Pub. by Hyperion) Time Warner.

Path: Creating Your Mission Statement for Work & for Life. Laurie Beth Jones. 192p. 1996. pap. 12.00 incl. audio (*0-671-57062-5*, Sound Ideas) S&S Trade.

***Path: Creating Your Mission Statement for Work & for Life.** Laurie Beth Jones. 249p. (J). 1998. reprint ed. pap. 10.45 (*0-7868-8241-7*, Pub. by Hyperion) Time Warner.

Path: Metaphysics for the 90's. 2nd ed. Richard Matheson. 152p. (Orig.). 1998. reprint ed. pap. 10.95 (*0-911650-13-X*) Word Foun.

Path Ahead: Readings in Death & Dying. 3rd ed. Ed. by Lynne A. DeSpelder & Albert L. Strickland. LC 94-30529. 396p. (C). 1995. pap. text 29.95 (*1-55934-256-0*, 1256) Mayfield Pub.

***Path & Practice: The Road Home.** Prophet Andromeda. Ed. by Sherry Knecht. (Illus.). 188p. (Orig.). 1999. pap. 12.95 (*1-929589-01-8*) Branching Leaf.

***Path & Practice: The Road Home.** 2nd rev. ed. Andromeda Knecht. (Illus.). 198p. 1999. pap. 12.95 (*1-929589-16-6*) Branching Leaf.

Path & the Shadow: Short Stories. David D. Anderson. 234p. 1998. pap. 12.95 (*0-941363-44-9*) Lake Shore Pub.

Path: Autobiography of a Western Yogi see Path: A Spiritual Autobiography

***Path Back Home.** large type ed. Nancy J. Cafaro et al. Ed. by Richard Cafaro. LC 99-94317. (Illus.). 725p. 1999. pap. 50.00 (*0-9671894-0-3*) Jo Pubg.

Path Between. Theodore Enslin. 1986. pap. 3.00 (*0-942396-37-5*) Blackberry ME.

Path Between: An Historical Novel of the Dickinson Family of Amherst. Maravene S. Loeschke. LC 88-63314. (Illus.). 300p. (Orig.). (C). 1988. pap. 15.95 (*0-935132-11-2*) C H Fairfax.

***Path Between Houses.** Greg Rappleye. 2000. 11.95 (*0-299-17014-4*); 18.95 (*0-299-17010-1*) U of Wis Pr.

Path Between the Seas: The Creation of the Panama Canal, 1870-1914. David McCullough. 700p. 1977. 14.95 (*0-685-75146-5*, SS09-4) Am Soc Civil Eng.

Path Between the Seas: The Creation of the Panama Canal, 1870-1914. David McCullough. (Illus.). 698p. 1978. pap. 16.00 (*0-671-24409-4*, Touchstone) S&S Trade Pap.

Path Beyond: Exploring the Drunkard's Path. Betty Kiser. LC 95-116863. (Illus.). 64p. (Orig.). 1994. pap. 19.00 (*0-9630557-1-2*) Path Less.

***Path Crossings.** Mark F. Horstmeyer. 73p. 2000. 15.95 (*0-7541-1208-X*) Minerva Pr.

***Path Dependence & Creation.** Ed. by Raghu Garud & Peter Karnoe. (A Volume in LEA's Organization & Management Series). 372p. 2000. write for info. (*0-8058-3272-6*) L Erlbaum Assocs.

Path Finder. Thomas Locke. LC 95-473. (Spectrum Chronicles Ser.: Bk. 3). 16p. (YA). (gr. 7-10). 1995. pap. 5.99 (*1-55661-434-9*) Bethany Hse.

Path for Freedom: The Liberal Project of the Swabian School in Wuerttemberg, 1806-1848. Victor G. Doerksen. LC 93-9961. (GERM Ser.). xvi, 244p. 1993. 65.00 (*1-879751-70-4*) Camden Hse.

Path from Puebla: Significant Documents of the Latin American Bishops since 1979. Ed. by Edward L. Cleary. Tr. by Phillip Berryman. 435p. (Orig.). 1989. pap. 14.95 (*1-55586-225-X*) US Catholic.

***Path from the Cellar.** Betty Owen Trimble. LC 00-131677. (Illus.). 272p. 2000. pap. write for info. (*1-57197-227-7*, Pub. by Pentland Pr) Assoc Pubs Grp.

Path from the Parlor: Louisiana Women, 1879-1920. Carmen Lindig. 195p. 1986. 17.50 (*0-940984-30-X*) Univ LA Lafayette.

Path Functions & Generalized Basic Hypergeometric Functions. Kevin J. Kadell. LC 86-28866. (Memoirs of the American Mathematical Society Ser.: No. 360). 54p. 1987. pap. 15.00 (*0-8218-2420-1*, MEMO/65/360C) Am Math.

Path. Health Related Profession. Damjano. 1996. 365.00 (*0-7216-6850-X*) Harcourt.

***Path in the Garden.** Christopher Herold. (Illus.). 70p. 2000. pap. 14.95 (*0-9638551-3-1*, Pub. by Katsura Pr) Partners-West.

Path in the Law. Robert Satter. (Orig.). 1997. pap. 12.00 (*0-9655561-0-7*) CT Law Bk.

Path Integral Approach to Quantum Physics: An Introduction. Gert Roepstorff. LC 93-43689. (Texts & Monographs in Physics). 1994. 59.00 (*0-387-55213-8*) Spr-Verlag.

Path Integral Approach to Quantum Physics: An Introduction. Gert Roepstorff. 387p. 1996. pap. 59.95 (*3-540-61106-1*) Spr-Verlag.

Path Integral Method, Lattice Gauge Theory & Critical Phenomena. Ed. by A. Shaukat. 304p. (C). 1989. text 108.00 (*9971-5-0724-2*) World Scientific Pub.

Path Integral Methods. 2nd ed. T. Kashiwa et al. (Illus.). 224p. 1997. text 95.00 (*0-19-851771-8*) OUP.

Path Integral Methods & Their Applications. D. C. Khandekar et al. 300p. (C). 1993. text 44.00 (*981-02-0563-5*) World Scientific Pub.

***Path Integral Quantization & Stochastic Quantization.** Michio Masujima. LC 00-29726. 2000. write for info. (*3-540-66542-0*) Spr-Verlag.

Path Integrals & Coherent States of SU(2) & SU(1,1) Akira Inomata et al. 400p. (C). 1992. text 71.00 (*981-02-0656-9*) World Scientific Pub.

Path Integrals & Quantum Processes. Mark Swanson. (Illus.). 444p. 1992. text 59.00 (*0-12-678945-2*) Acad Pr.

Path Integrals from MeV to MeV. Ed. by M. C. Gutzwiller et al. 468p. 1986. pap. 45.00 (*9971-5-0067-1*); text 89.00 (*9971-5-0066-3*) World Scientific Pub.

Path Integrals from meV to MeV: Proceedings of the 3rd International Conference. Ed. by V. Sa-Yakanit. 584p. (C). 1989. text 130.00 (*9971-5-0935-0*) World Scientific Pub.

Path Integrals from MeV to MeV: Tutzing '92. L. S. Schulman et al. 368p. 1993. text 121.00 (*981-02-1497-9*) World Scientific Pub.

***Path Integrals from PeV to TeV: 50 Years after Feynman's Paper Florence, Italy 25-29 August 1998.** Valerio Togent Ti. 600p. 1999. 88.00 (*981-02-3821-5*) World Scientific Pub.

Path Integrals, Hyperbolic Spaces, & Selberg Trace Formulae. Christian Grosche. LC 95-43476. 250p. 1996. 45.00 (*981-02-2431-1*) World Scientific Pub.

Path Integrals in Physics: Proceedings of the International Conference. V. Sa-Yakanit et al. 488p. 1994. text 112.00 (*981-02-2070-7*) World Scientific Pub.

Path Integrals in Quantum Mechanics, Statistics & Polymer Physics. Hagen Kleinart. LC 94-23835. 800p. 1995. pap. text 24.00 (*981-02-1472-3*) World Scientific Pub.

Path Integrals in Quantum Mechanics, Statistics & Polymer Physics. Hagen Kleinert. 688p. (C). 1990. text 99.00 (*981-02-0196-6*); pap. text 28.00 (*981-02-0197-4*) World Scientific Pub.

Path Integrals in Quantum Mechanics, Statistics & Polymer Physics. 2nd ed. Hagen Kleinert. LC 94-23835. 800p. 1995. text 99.00 (*981-02-1471-5*) World Scientific Pub.

Path Integrals on Group Manifolds: Representation-Independent Propagators for General Lie Groups. Wolfgang Tome. LC 99-172639. 200p. 1998. 32.00 (*981-02-3355-8*) World Scientific Pub.

Path Integration: Lectures on Trieste, 1991. Hilda A. Cerdeira et al. 600p. 1993. text 114.00 (*981-02-1070-1*) World Scientific Pub.

Path into His Presence. G. M. Farley. 125p. 1990. pap. 5.95 (*1-882449-17-7*) Messenger Pub.

Path into Metaphysics: Phenomenological, Hermeneutical, & Dialogical Studies. Robert E. Wood. LC 89-38073. (SUNY Series in Philosophy). 387p. (C). 1990. pap. text 21.95 (*0-7914-0306-8*) State U NY Pr.

Path Is the Goal: A Basic Handbook of Buddhist Meditation. Chogyam Trungpa. Ed. by Sherab Chodzin. 1995. pap. 12.00 (*0-87773-970-6*, Pub. by Shambhala Pubns) Random.

Path Less Taken. O'Keefe. 1996. 6.95 (*0-7667-0386-X*) Gibson.

Path Less Taken. JoAnna O'Keefe. (Illus.). 1996. 6.95 (*0-614-20841-6*) Gibson.

Path Less Traveled: Variation on the Drunkard's Path. Betty Kiser. (Illus.). 64p. (Orig.). 1991. pap. 19.00 (*0-9630557-0-4*) Path Less.

Path Master Guide Book: New Resources Mentors, Coaches, Gurus & Angels. Jack Savidge. 86p. 1993. pap. 20.00 (*951-666-399-0*, Pub. by Finnsh Acdmies Tech) J Savidge & Co.

Path Not Taken. Ed. by Caroline Sullivan. 1996. 69.95 (*1-57553-003-1*) Watermrk Pr.

Path Notes of an American Ninja Master. Glenn Morris. LC 93-8031. 264p. (Orig.). 1993. pap. 16.95 (*1-55643-157-0*) North Atlantic.

Path of a Genocide: The Rwanda Crisis from Uganda to Zaire. Ed. by Howard Adelman & Astri Suhrke. 414p. 1999. 44.95 (*1-56000-382-0*) Transaction Pubs.

Path of a Hunter. limited ed. Gilles Tre-Hardy. Ed. by Ellen Enzler-Herring. Tr. by Bernard Laudon. LC 97-60107. (Illus.). 317p. 1997. 85.00 (*1-882458-16-8*) Trophy Rm Bks.

Path of a Pioneer: A Centennial History of the Wisconsin Electric Power Company. John Gurda. 282p. 1996. 30.00 (*0-9652461-0-8*) Wis Elect.

Path of a Pioneer: A Centennial History of the Wisconsin Electric Power Company. unabridged ed. John Gurda. (Illus.). 282p. 1996. 30.00 (*0-614-30318-4*) Wis Elect.

Path of a Pioneer: The Autobiography of Rabbi Leo Jung. Leo Jung. 408p. 1980. 25.00 (*0-900689-51-X*) Soncino Pr.

Path of a Pioneer: The Early Days of Sun Myung Moon & the Unification Church. Ed. by Jonathan G. Gullery. (Illus.). 88p. (Orig.). 1986. pap. 3.95 (*0-910621-50-0*) HSA Pubns.

Path of a Warrior: Teachings of Phil Messina. Elizabeth A. Kennedy. 144p. 1993. pap. text 25.00 (*0-9640670-0-5*) Modern Warrior.

Path of Archaic Thinking: Unfolding the Work of John Sallis. Ed. by Kenneth Maly. LC 94-11959. (SUNY Series in Contemporary Continental Philosophy). 316p. (C). 1995. text 64.50 (*0-7914-2355-7*); pap. text 21.95 (*0-7914-2356-5*) State U NY Pr.

Path of Awakening. Kosho Soga. LC 88-8616. 63p. (Orig.). 1988. pap. 8.95 (*0-938474-07-3*) Buddhist Study.

Path of Beauty. Li Zehou. Tr. by Gong Lizeng from CHI. (Illus.). 271p. 1988. 69.95 (*0-8351-2144-5*) China Bks.

Path of Beauty: A Study of Chinese Aesthetics. Li Zehou. Tr. by Gong Lizeng. (Illus.). 248p. 1995. pap. text 22.00 (*0-19-586526-X*) OUP.

Path of Blessing: Experiencing the Energy & Abundance of the Divine. Marcia Prager. LC 98-2903. 240p. 1998. 21.00 (*0-517-70363-7*) Bell T.

***Path of Blessing: Experiencing the Energy & Abundance of the Divine.** Marcia Prager. 240p. 1999. reprint ed. pap. 13.00 (*0-609-80393-X*) Bell T.

Path of Blood: The True Story of the 33d New York Volunteers. (Illus.). v, 450p. (Orig.). 1997. 32.95 (*0-9659177-0-3*); pap. 22.95 (*0-9659177-1-1*) G W Contant.

Path of Buddhism. Ed. by George D. Chryssides. 160p. (C). 1989. pap. 32.00 (*0-7855-6806-9*, Pub. by St Andrew) St Mut.

Path of Buddhism. George D. Chryssides. 160p. (C). 1988. pap. text 45.00 (*0-7152-0619-2*) St Mut.

***Path of Colored Leaves.** Rachel Carr Klippenstein. LC 00-130995. 87p. 2000. pap. 8.95 (*0-9659164-3-X*) Fountain Publ.

Path of Compassion, Set. unabridged ed. G. De Purucker. LC 86-50300. audio 20.95 (*0-911500-60-X*) Theos U Pr.

Path of Compassion: Time-Honored Principles of Spiritual & Ethical Conduct. G. De Purucker. LC 86-50300. 84p. 1986. pap. 7.95 (*0-911500-69-3*) Theos U Pr.

Path of Compassion: Writings on Socially Engaged Buddhism. rev. ed. Ed. by Fred Eppsteiner. LC 88-9832. 219p. 1988. reprint ed. pap. 16.00 (*0-938077-02-3*) Parallax Pr.

Path of Daggers. Robert Jordan. LC 98-35888. (Wheel of Time Ser.: Bk. 8). 608p. 1998. 27.95 (*0-312-85769-1*, Pub. by Tor Bks) St Martin.

Path of Daggers. Robert Jordan. LC 98-35888. (Wheel of Time Ser.: Bk. 8). 685p. 1999. mass mkt. 7.99 (*0-8125-5029-3*, Pub. by Tor Bks) St Martin.

Path of Destiny. Wade Blevins. LC 96-10308. (Cherokee Indian Legend Ser.: No. 2). (Illus.). 49p. (J). (gr. 2 up). 1993. lib. bdg. 12.95 (*1-56763-071-5*) Ozark Pub.

Path of Devotion. 8th ed. Swami Paramananda. 107p. 1940. 5.95 (*0-911564-00-4*) Vedanta Ctr.

Path of Discrimination. Tr. by Ven Nanamoli from PLI. (C). 1982. 61.00 (*0-86013-074-6*, Pub. by Pali Text) Elsevier.

Path of Dreams. George M. McClellan. LC 70-152925. (Black Heritage Library Collection). 1977. 19.95 (*0-8369-8769-1*) Ayer.

Path of Due Process of Law. Walton H. Hamilton. (Reprint Series in Political Science). (C). 1993. reprint ed. pap. text 5.00 (*0-8290-2750-5*, PS-119) Irvington.

***Path of Emancipation: Talks from a 21-Day Mindfulness Retreat.** Thich Nhat Hanh. 200p. 2000. pap. 13.50 (*1-888375-15-9*, Pub. by Parallax Pr) SCB Distributors.

Path of Empire: A Chronicle of the United States As a World Power. Carl R. Fish. (BCL1 - U. S. History Ser.). 305p. 1991. reprint ed. lib. bdg. 89.00 (*0-7812-6041-8*) Rprt Serv.

Path of Enlightenment According to the Mithraic Mysteries. Julius Evola. Ed. by J. D. Holmes. Tr. & Intro. by Guido Stucco. (Orig.). 1993. pap. 7.95 (*1-55818-228-4*) Holmes Pub.

***Path of Fire.** T. T. Henderson. 2000. pap. 8.95 (*1-58571-012-1*, Pub. by Genesis Press) BookWorld.

Path of Fire. Charles Ingrid. (Patterns of Chaos Ser.: No. 2). 352p. (Orig.). 1992. mass mkt. 4.99 (*0-88677-522-1*, Pub. by DAW Bks) Penguin Putnam.

Path of Fire & Light Vol. 1: Advanced Practices of Yoga. Swami Rama. LC 86-7586. 156p. 1986. pap. 14.95 (*0-89389-097-9*) Himalayan Inst.

Path of Fire & Light Vol. 2: A Practical Companion to Volume One. Swami Rama. LC 86-7586. 226p. (Orig.). 1988. pap. 14.95 (*0-89389-112-6*) Himalayan Inst.

Path of Flowering Thorn: The Life & Poetry of Yosa Buson. Makoto Ueda & Buson Yosa. LC 97-50578. 232p. 1998. 39.50 (*0-8047-3042-3*) Stanford U Pr.

Path of Freedom. Henri J. M. Nouwen. 32p. 1994. pap. 3.95 (*0-8245-2001-7*) Crossroad NY.

Path of Ghosts. large type ed. Robert MacLeod. 248p. 1980. 27.99 (*0-7089-0458-0*) Ulverscroft.

Path of God. Swami P. Saraswati. (Illus.). 56p. 1998. pap. 4.00 (*1-881921-06-9*) Intl Soc Divine Love.

Path of God's Bondsmen: From Origin to Return. Najm A. Razi. Tr. by Hamid Algar from PER. (Persian Heritage Ser.: Vol. 35). 537p. 1982. text 42.00 (*0-88206-052-X*) Bibliotheca Persica.

Path of Grace: Social Organization & Temple Worship in a Vaishnava Sect. Peter Bennett. (C). 1993. 24.00 (*81-7075-024-5*, Pub. by Hindustan) S Asia.

Path of Healing: Finding Your Soul's Potential. H. K. Challoner. LC 76-3660. 175p. 1990. pap. 9.95 (*0-8356-0662-7*, Quest) Theos Pub Hse.

Path of Heroes: Birth of Enlightenment, 2 vols., Set. Zhechen Gyaltsab. LC 95-150. (Tibetan Translation Ser.). 650p. 1995. 75.00 (*0-89800-274-5*) Dharma Pub.

Path of Heroes: Birth of Enlightenment, 2 vols., Set. Zhechen Gyaltsab. Tr. by Deborah Black. LC 95-150. (Tibetan Translation Ser.). 650p. 1995. pap. 44.00 (*0-89800-273-7*) Dharma Pub.

Path of Hope. Tr. by C. A. Thorpe. 70p. 1997. pap. 2.00 (*1-880189-12-7*) Gods Word.

Path of Hope: Fragments from a Theologian's Journey. Leonardo Boff. Tr. by Phillip Berryman from POR. LC 92-35823. (Illus.). 150p. 1993. reprint ed. pap. 15.00 (*0-88344-815-7*) Orbis Bks.

Path of Initiation. rev. ed. Inayat Khan. LC 79-67752. (Sufi Message of Hazrat Inayat Khan Ser.: Vol. 10). 270p. 1979. 19.00 (*90-6325-098-3*, Pub. by Sufi Mvemnt) Omega Pubns NY.

Path of Insight Meditation. Joseph Goldstein & Jack Kornfield. LC 95-9930. (Pocket Classics Ser.). 200p. 1995. pap. 7.00 (*1-57062-069-5*, Pub. by Shambhala Pubns) Random.

Path of Joy. Carla A. Nelson. 96p. (Orig.). 1996. pap. 8.95 (*0-9655078-0-7*) Windsong Pub ME.

Path of Least Resistance: Learning to Become the Creative Force in Your Own Life. Robert Fritz. 1989. pap. 12.00 (*0-449-90337-0*, Columbine) Fawcett.

Path of Least Resistance for Managers: Designing Organizations to Succeed. Robert Fritz. LC 99-12000. 250p. 1999. pap. 18.95 (*1-57675-065-5*) Berrett-Koehler.

Path of Life. Cyprian Smith. 181p. 1996. pap. 12.95 (*0-85244-302-1*, 956, Pub. by Gra1cewing) Morehouse Pub.

Path of Light. Regina E. Lorr & Robert W. Crary. LC 83-71354. 192p. (Orig.). 1983. pap. 10.95 (*0-87516-520-6*) DeVorss.

Path of Light. Santideva. LC 78-70117. reprint ed. 34.50 (*0-404-17374-8*) AMS Pr.

***Path of Light: A Guide to 21st Century Discipleship & Spiritual Practice in the Kriya Yoga Tradition.** Roy Eugene Davis. 155p. 1999. pap. 50.00 (*81-208-1657-9*, Pub. by Motilal Bnarsidass) St Mut.

Path of Loneliness. Elisabeth Elliot. LC 93-11709. 1991. pap. 10.99 (*0-8407-9118-6*) Nelson.

Path of Love. Ed. by Margaret Leuverunk. (Manaham Ser.). (Illus.). 121p. (Orig.). 1996. pap. text 10.00 (*1-880687-10-0*) Chinmaya Pubns.

Path of Love: Commentaries on the Songs of Kabir. 2nd ed. Osho. (Illus.). 306p. 1997. reprint ed. 13.95 (*81-7261-075-0*, Pub. by Rebel Pub) Oshos.

Path of Meditation: A Step by Step Guide to Meditation. Osho. Tr. by Pratap Bharti from HIN. Orig. Title: Dhyan Sutra. (Illus.). 262p. 1997. 12.95 (*81-7261-071-8*, Pub. by Rebel Pub) Oshos.

Path of My Soul: Journey to the Center of Self. William Homestead. 1999. pap. 13.95 (*1-889051-47-0*) Acrpls Bks CO.

Path of Pale Horse. Paul Fleischman. LC 82-48611. (Charlotte Zolotow Bk.). 160p. (J). (gr. 6 up). 1983. lib. bdg. 13.89 (*0-06-021905-X*) HarpC Child Bks.

Path of Parenting: Twelve Principles to Guide You on Your Journey of Parenthood. Vimala McClure. LC 99-22342. 272p. 1999. pap. 14.00 (*1-57731-078-0*, Pub. by New Wrld Lib) Publishers Group.

Path of Peace see Senderos de Paz

Path of Perfect Love. rev. ed. Diogenes Allen. LC 92-3122. Orig. Title: Finding Our Father. 113p. 1992. pap. 9.95 (*1-56101-057-X*) Cowley Pubns.

Path of Perfection. A. C. Bhaktivedanta Swami Prabhupada. (Illus.). 206p. 1997. pap. 2.95 (*91-7149-171-6*, POP) Bhaktivedanta.

Path of Perfection: The Spiritual Teachings of Master Nur Ali. Bahram Elahi. 1993. pap. 15.95 (*1-85230-392-1*, Pub. by Element MA) Penguin Putnam.

P

An Asterisk (*) at the beginning of an entry indicates that the title is appearing for the first time.

Path of Power. Henri J. M. Nouwen. 32p. 1994. pap. 3.95 (*0-8245-2003-3*) Crossroad NY.

***Path of Practice.** Bri Maya Tiwari. 2000. 24.95 (*0-345-43030-1*) Ballantine Pub Grp.

Path of Prayer: Four Sermons on Prayer. Theophan the Recluse. Ed. by Robin Amis. Tr. by Esther Williams from RUS. LC 91-60842. 105p. (Orig.). (C). 1992. text 15.95 (*1-872292-13-5*); pap. text 11.95 (*1-872292-14-3*) Praxis Inst.

Path of Pregnancy: A Handbook of Traditional Chinese Gestational & Birthing Disease, Vol. I. Bob Flaws. LC 92-75136. 235p. 1993. pap. 19.95 (*0-936185-39-2*) Blue Poppy Pr.

Path of Pregnancy Vol. II: A Handbook of Traditional Chinese Postpartum Diseases. Bob Flaws. LC 92-75136. 275p. 1993. pap. 19.95 (*0-936185-42-2*) Blue Poppy Pr.

Path of Promise, Path of Peace: How to Hear Your Higher Self Speak. Barbara Paulin. LC 94-28852. 280p. 1995. pap. 12.95 (*0-87604-328-7*, 397) ARE Pr.

Path of Prosperity. James Allen. 88p. 1998. pap. 8.00 (*0-89540-403-6*, SB-403) Sun Pub.

Path of Prosperity. James Allen. 88p. 1996. reprint ed. spiral bd. 10.00 (*0-7873-0026-8*) Hlth Research.

Path of Prosperity, 1907. James Allen. 88p. 1996. reprint ed. pap. 9.50 (*1-56459-851-9*) Kessinger Pub.

Path of Psychotherapy: Matters of the Heart. David Ira Welch. LC 97-20314. (Counseling Ser.). 200p. 1997. mass mkt. 31.95 (*0-534-34411-9*) Brooks-Cole.

Path of Purification: Visuddhimagga. Acaeiya Buddhaghosa. Tr. by Bhikkhu Nanamoli from PLI. 950p. (C). 1991. 48.00 (*955-24-0023-6*, Pub. by Buddhist Pub Soc) Vipassana Res Pubns.

***Path of Purification: Visuddhimagga.** Bhadantacariya Buddhaghosa. Tr. by Bhikkha Nanamoli. LC 99-90839. 960p. 2000. reprint ed. 50.00 (*1-928706-00-2*, POP, BPS Pariyatti) Vipassana Res Pubns.

***Path of Purification: Visuddhimagga.** Bhadantacariya Buddhaghosa. Tr. by Bhikkha Nanamoli. LC 99-90839. 960p. 2000. reprint ed. per. 38.00 (*1-928706-01-0*, POP, BPS Pariyatti) Vipassana Res Pubns.

Path of Purity, 3 vols. Buddhaghosa. Tr. by Pe Maung Tin. LC 78-72389. reprint ed. write for info. (*0-404-17570-8*) AMS Pr.

Path of Purity, 3 vols. in 1. Tr. by Tin Pe Maung from PLI. (C). 1975. reprint ed. 71.00 (*0-86013-008-8*, Pub. by Pali Text) Elsevier.

Path of Purpose & Pleasure: A Compilation of Sermons. Albert Gani. 332p. (Orig.). 1992. pap. 15.00 (*1-882853-00-8*) A Gani.

***Path of Self-Transformation.** Elizabeth Clare Prophet. 2000. pap. 7.99 (*0-922729-54-9*) Summit Univ.

Path of Serenity & Insight: An Explanation of the Buddhist Jhanas. Henepola Gunaratana. (C). 1996. reprint ed. 26.00 (*81-208-0871-1*, Pub. by Motilal Bnarsidass) S Asia.

Path of Silence. Omraam M. Aivanhov. (Izvor Collection: Vol. 229). 167p. 1990. pap. 7.95 (*2-85566-473-X*) Prosveta USA.

Path of Silence. 2nd ed. Omraam M. Aivanhov. 167p. 1995. pap. 7.95 (*1-895978-19-X*, Pub. by Prosveta) Prosveta USA.

Path of Sorrow (1832), Eonchs of Ruby (1851), Memoralia (1849), Virginalia (1853), Sons of Usna (1858), 5 vols. in 1. Thomas Holley Chivers. LC 79-22103. 580p. 1979. 80.00 (*0-8201-1340-9*) Schol Facsimiles.

Path of Sorrow: or The Lament of Youth: Or the Lament of Youth. Thomas Holley Chivers. (Works of Thomas Holley Chivers Ser.). 1990. reprint ed. lib. bdg. 79.00 (*0-7812-2281-8*) Rprt Serv.

Path of St. Augustine. William A. Banner. LC 96-2934. 122p. 1996. pap. text 19.95 (*0-8476-8292-7*); lib. bdg. 46.50 (*0-8476-8291-9*) Rowman.

Path of Subud. Husein Rofe. 1972. 250.00 (*0-8490-0805-0*) Gordon Pr.

Path of Subud. 2nd ed. Husein Rofe. 162p. 1988. reprint ed. pap. text 8.95 (*0-945126-03-4*) Undiscovd Worlds Pr.

Path of Terror. Gil Dorland. 240p. 1996. pap. 10.95 (*0-9646531-9-2*) New Continents.

Path of the Baal Shem Tov: Early Chasidic Teachings & Customs. David Sears. LC 96-9445. 272p. 1997. pap. 40.00 (*1-56821-972-5*) Aronson.

Path of the Buddha: Buddhism Interpreted by Buddhists. Kenneth W. Morgan. 1986. 24.00 (*81-208-0030-3*, Pub. by Motilal Bnarsidass) S Asia.

Path of the Buddha: Buddhism Interpreted by Buddhists. Kenneth W. Morgan. 432p. 1986. reprint ed. 25.00 (*0-317-60576-3*, Pub. by Motilal Bnarsidass) S Asia.

Path of the Everyday Hero: Drawing on the Power of Myth to Meet Life's Most Important Challenges. Lorna Catford & Michael Ray. (Illus.). 256p. (Orig.). 1991. pap. 14.95 (*0-87477-630-9*, Tarcher Putnam) Putnam Pub Group.

***Path of the Feather.** Michael Samuels & Mary Rockwood Lane. 176p. 2000. pap. 29.95 (*0-399-14572-9*) Putnam Pub Group.

Path of the Fury. David Weber. 512p. 2000. mass mkt. 6.99 (*0-671-72147-X*) Baen Bks.

Path of the Golden Dragon. William B. Kern. 368p. mass mkt. 5.99 (*1-55197-755-9*) Picasso Publ.

Path of the Just-Mesilath Yesharim. Luzzato. 1982. pap. 15.95 (*0-87306-115-2*) Feldheim.

Path of the Just-Mesilath Yesharim. Moshe Chaim Luzzato. Tr. by Shraga Silverstein. 1990. 8.95 (*0-87306-239-6*) Feldheim.

Path of the Kabbalah. David Sheinkin. Ed. by Edward Hoffman. LC 86-18686. (Patterns of World Spirituality Ser.). 195p. 1990. pap. 10.95 (*0-913757-69-1*) Paragon Hse.

***Path of the Law & Its Influence: The Legacy of Oliver Wendell Holmes.** Ed. by Steven J. Burton. (Cambridge Studies in Philosophy & Law). 384p. 2000. 64.95 (*0-521-63006-1*) Cambridge U Pr.

Path of the Lonely Ones. Rosemary Dennis. LC 79-89516. (Illus.). 1979. 4.50 (*0-918482-02-X*) Ageless Bks.

***Path of the Mother.** Savitri L. Bess. 432p. 2000. pap. 14.00 (*0-345-42347-X*, Ballantine) Ballantine Pub Grp.

Path of the Mystic. Ai Gvhdi Waya. 114p. 1997. pap. 11.95 (*0-929385-47-0*) Light Tech Pubng.

Path of the Mystic Lover: Baul Songs of Passion & Ecstasy. Bhaskar Bhattacharyya. Ed. by Nik Douglas. LC 86-19780. (Illus.). 192p. 1993. pap. 19.95 (*0-89281-019-X*) Inner Tradit.

Path of the Paddle: An Illustrated Guide to the Art of Canoeing. 2nd rev. ed. Bill Mason. (Illus.). 200p. 1999. pap. 19.95 (*1-55209-328-X*) Firefly Bks Ltd.

Path of the Pale Horse. Paul Fleischman. LC 82-48611. (Trophy Bk.). 160p. (YA). (gr. 5 up). 1992. pap. 3.95 (*0-06-440442-0*, HarpTrophy) HarpC Child Bks.

Path of the Phoenix. Kendall K. McCabe. Ed. by Michael L. Sherer. (Orig.). 1986. pap. 7.75 (*0-89536-818-8*, 6827) CSS OH.

***Path of the Pole: Cataclysmic Poleshift Geology.** Charles H. Hapgood. 1999. pap. text 16.95 (*0-932813-71-2*) Advent Unltd.

Path of the Righteous: Gentile Rescuers of Jews During the Holocaust. Mordecai Paldiel. 35.00 (*0-88125-376-6*) Ktav.

Path of the Righteous Gentile: An Introduction to the 7 Laws of the Children of Noach. Chaim Clorfene & Yakov Rogalsky. 142p. 1989. reprint ed. 18.95 (*0-87306-433-X*) Targum Pr.

Path of the Soul. White Eagle Staff. 80p. 1959. pap. 12.50 (*0-85487-020-2*) White Eagle.

Path of the Soul: Making Peace with Mortality. Ben Kamin. LC 98-49652. 176p. 1999. pap. 11.95 (*0-452-28093-1*, Plume) Dutton Plume.

Path of the Soul: The Great Initiations White Eagle. LC 98-198307. 94 p. 1997. write for info. (*0-85487-101-2*) White Eagle.

***Path of the Spirited Athlete: A Woman's Guide to a Balanced & Healthy Lifestyle.** Jan C. Takehara. Ed. by Marian Prokop & J. D. Mumma. LC 99-95262. (Illus.). 240p. 1999. pap. write for info. (*0-9673169-0-1*) Life In Balance.

Path of the Star. Naomi Albright. 193p. 1992. spiral bd. 14.75 (*1-882218-04-3*) Blue Star Pubs.

Path of the Storm. large type ed. Douglas Reeman. 1980. 12.00 (*0-7089-0486-6*) Ulverscroft.

Path of the Sun. Al Dempsey. 320p. 1994. mass mkt. 4.99 (*0-8125-8193-8*) Tor Bks.

Path of the Tiger. Jessica E. Campaign. (Illus.). 160p. (J). (gr. 4-8). 1994. pap., per. 10.95 (*0-9644299-1-8*) Tora Prods.

Path of the Tiger. Cleo Cordeli. (Black Lace Ser.). 1995. mass mkt. 5.95 (*0-352-32959-9*, Pub. by Virgin Bks) London Brdge.

Path of the Upright: Mesillat Yesharim. Moshe C. Luzzatto. Tr. by Mordecai Menaheim Kaplan. LC 94-40542. 504p. 1995. 50.00 (*1-56821-427-8*) Aronson.

Path of the Warrior. Chultz. 1998. text 14.95 (*0-312-18444-1*) St Martin.

Path of the Warrior. Lucas E. Schultz. (Illus.). 112p. 1998. 14.95 (*0-312-19313-0*, Thomas Dunne) St Martin.

Path of the Warrior: An Ethical Guide to Personal & Professional Development in the Field of Criminal Justice. unabridged ed. Larry F. Jetmore. Ed. by Linnea Fredrickson. 144p. 1999. pap. 19.95 (*1-889031-05-4*) Looseleaf Law.

Path of the Wise Woman: A Tale of the Spiritual & Mythic Dimensions of Menopause. Roberta C. Bails. 75p. 1994. pap. write for info. (*0-9644354-0-3*) Mid-Life Hse.

Path of the Wrong Way. Arnold Nerenberg. (C). 1987. pap. write for info. (*1-878113-00-3*) Bell Pubns.

***Path of Transformation: How Healing Ourselves Can Change the World.** rev. ed. Shakti Gawain. LC 00-20076. 240p. 2000. pap. 13.95 (*1-57731-154-X*) New Wrld Lib.

Path of Tumors of Oral Tissue. 5th ed. Cawson. (C). 1998. text 195.00 (*0-443-03990-9*) Church.

Path of Virtue. Jonathon Murro. LC 79-54382. (Illus.). 487p. 1980. 14.95 (*0-917189-00-0*) A R Colton Fnd.

***Path of Yoga.** A. C. Bhaktivedanta Swami Prabhupada. 207p. (YA). 1999. pap. 7.95 (*0-89213-327-9*) Bhaktivedanta.

Path on the Rainbow. 4th ed. George W. Cronyn. (Illus.). 360p. 1997. reprint ed. pap. 14.95 (*0-87877-240-5*) Newcastle Pub.

Path I Trod. Terence V. Powderly. LC 77-181971. reprint ed. 31.50 (*0-404-05098-0*) AMS Pr.

Path, Portal Path: Architecture for the Rites. Christopher V. Stroik. Ed. by David Philippart. LC 99-25451. (Meeting House Essays Ser.: Vol. 10). (Illus.). 1999. pap. 6.00 (*1-56854-243-7*, PATH) Liturgy Tr Pubns.

Path Portal Place: Appreciating Public Space in Urban Environments. Edward T. White. LC 99-94751. (Illus.). 116p. 1999. pap. 12.75 (*1-928643-00-0*) Archit Media.

Path Summation: Achievements & Goals. Ed. by S. O. Lundqvist et al. 536p. (C). 1988. pap. 48.00 (*9971-5-0700-5*); text 117.00 (*9971-5-0597-5*) World Scientific Pub.

Path Telecourse. Terry S. Maness. 1996. pap., student ed. 14.50 (*0-314-09707-4*) West Pub.

Path Through Advent for Children. Oden. (J). 1994. 1.00 (*0-687-30263-3*) Abingdon.

Path Through Deep Waters. Betsy Alexander. Ed. by Jane Weinberger. LC 98-75032. 350p. 1998. 10.00 (*1-883650-51-8*) Windswept Hse.

Path Through Grief: A Compassionate Guide. Marguerite Bouvard & Evelyn Gladu. LC 97-44051. 331p. 1998. pap. text 17.95 (*1-57392-189-0*) Prometheus Bks.

Path Through Lent. Joanne Simcik. (Small Group Booklets Ser.: Cyle C). 32p. 1991. pap. text 2.95 (*1-55612-467-8*) Sheed & Ward WI.

Path Through Stone. 2nd ed. Bruce Barton et al. 79p. (C). 1996. pap. 8.95 (*0-9647066-0-1*) Wellstone Pr.

Path Through Suffering. large type ed. Elisabeth Elliot. LC 96-37855. 300p. 1997. pap. 14.95 (*0-8027-2716-6*) Walker & Co.

Path Through Suffering: Discovering the Relationship Between God's Mercy & Our Pain. Elisabeth Elliot. 201p. 1992. pap. 10.99 (*0-89283-801-9*, Vine Bks) Servant.

Path Through the Ashes: Inspiring Stories of the Holocaust. Nisson Wolpin. (ArtScroll Judaiscope Ser.). (Illus.). 352p. 1986. 19.99 (*0-89906-856-1*) Mesorah Pubns.

Path Through the Bible. John H. Piet. LC 81-2258. 318p. reprint ed. pap. 98.60 (*0-7837-2633-3*, 204298300006) Bks Demand.

Path Through the Fire: A Cancer Story. Wendy Allen Wheeler. (Illus.). x, 90p. 1998. pap. 18.00 (*0-9666778-0-3*) W Wheeler.

Path Through the Woods. Barbara K. Wilson. (Illus.). (J). (gr. 7 up). 1958. 26.95 (*0-87599-129-7*) S G Phillips.

Path to a Larger Life: Creating Kentucky's Educational Future. 2nd ed. Prichard Committee for Academic Excellence Staff. LC 89-78107. 176p. 1990. pap. text 15.00 (*0-8131-0199-9*) U Pr of Ky.

Path to a Meaningful & Fruitful Life. Mitrofan Znosko-Borovskii. LC 98-8615. 2000. write for info. (*1-56072-543-5*, Nova Troitsa Bks) Nova Sci Pubs.

Path to a Successful Retirement: A Retirement Authority Shares His Insights in a Unique Style. rev. ed. James F. Smith. LC 95-69056. (Illus.). 300p. (Orig.). 1995. reprint ed. pap. 19.95 (*0-9646809-3-9*) Sligo Pub.

Path to an Understanding of the Foundation Stone Meditation. Ernst Katz et al. Date not set. reprint ed. 12.00 (*0-9674562-9-0*) Anthropos Society.

Path to Arequipa: A Novel. Mark Jacoby. LC 97-47616. 214p. 1998. pap. 12.95 (*1-56825-039-8*, 039-8) Rainbow Books.

Path to Birth. Stanley Drake. 64p. 1990. pap. 7.95 (*0-903540-32-0*, 888, Pub. by Floris Bks) Anthroposophic.

Path to Bliss: A Practical Guide to Stages of Meditation. Dalai Lama XIV. Ed. by Christine Cox. Tr. by G. T. Huboam & Geshe Thupten Jinpa. LC 90-2650. 240p. 1991. pap. 14.95 (*0-937938-92-0*) Snow Lion Pubns.

***Path to Blitzkrieg: Doctrine & Training in the German Army, 1920-1939.** Robert M. Citino. LC 98-5251. 286p. 1999. lib. bdg. 55.00 (*1-55587-714-1*) L Rienner.

***Path to Bodhidharma: The Teachings of Shodo Harada Roshi.** Tr. by Priscilla Daichi Storandt. 192p. 2000. pap. 15.95 (*0-8048-3216-1*, Periplus Eds) Tuttle Pubng.

Path to Christian Democracy: German Catholics & the Party System from Windthorst to Adenauer. Noel D. Cary. LC 95-40145. 320p. 1996. 54.00 (*0-674-65783-7*) HUP.

***Path to Confession: A Book for Family Reading.** Artemy Vladimirov. Tr. by Nectaria McHees & Ivan Gerasimov from RUS. (Illus.). 134p. 2000. 22.95 (*0-9678400-0-7*) Unexpected Joy.

Path to Convertibility & Growth: The Tunisian Experience. Saleh M. Nsouli et al. LC 93-45034. (Occasional Papers: No. 109). 1993. pap. 15.00 (*1-55775-357-1*) Intl Monetary.

Path to Dreams Fulfilled. 115p. write for info. (*0-939509-31-8*); pap. 12.00 (*0-317-58900-8*) L Benton Geneal.

Path to Dropping Out: Evidence for Intervention. Melissa Roderick. LC 92-42905. 240p. 1993. 55.00 (*0-86569-206-8*, T206, Auburn Hse) Greenwood.

Path to Enlightenment. rev. ed. Dalai Lama XIV. Ed. & Tr. by Glenn H. Mullin. LC 94-39647. (Illus.). 237p. 1994. pap. 14.95 (*1-55939-032-8*) Snow Lion Pubns.

Path to Enlightenment, Vol. 4. Dalai Lama XIV. 16.00 (*0-06-061726-8*) HarpC.

Path to Enlightenment, Vol. 5. Dalai Lama XIV. 16.00 (*0-06-061727-6*) HarpC.

Path to Enlightenment, Vol. 6. Dalai Lama XIV. 16.00 (*0-06-061728-4*) HarpC.

Path to Enlightenment, Vol. 7. Dalai Lama XIV. 16.00 (*0-06-061729-2*) HarpC.

Path to Enlightenment, Vol. 8. Dalai Lama XIV. 16.00 (*0-06-061732-2*) HarpC.

Path to Enlightenment: Masterpieces of Buddhist Sculpture from the National Museum of Asian Arts/Musee Guimet, Paris. Jennifer R. Casler et al. LC 96-75653. (Illus.). 72p. (Orig.). 1996. pap. 12.95 (*0-912804-32-7*) Kimbell Art.

Path to Enlightenment Is Not a Highway. Baba Hari Dass. Ed. & Frwd. by Ma Renu. LC 96-67104. (Illus.). 332p. (Orig.). 1996. pap. 12.95 (*0-918100-18-6*) Sri Rama.

Path to Equality: From the Scottsboro Case to the Breaking of Baseball's Color Barrier (1931-1947) Darlene Clark Hine. LC 93-16016. (Milestones in Black American History Ser.). (Illus.). 128p. (YA). (gr. 5 up). 1994. pap. 8.95 (*0-7910-2677-9*); lib. bdg. 19.95 (*0-7910-2251-X*) Chelsea Hse.

Path to European Economic & Monetary Union. Scheherazade S. Rehman. LC 97-17513. 1997. lib. bdg. 154.00 (*0-7923-9951-X*) Kluwer Academic.

Path to European Union: From the Marshall Plan to the Common Market. Hans A. Schmitt & W. Walton Butterworth. LC 81-6470. 272p. 1981. reprint ed. lib. bdg. 65.00 (*0-313-23107-9*, SCPUN, Greenwood Pr) Greenwood.

Path to Excellence: Quality Assurance in Higher Education. Laurence R. Marcus et al. Ed. by Jonathan D. Fife. LC 83-146405. (ASHE-ERIC Higher Education Reports: No. 83-1). 68p. (Orig.). 1983. pap. 24.00 (*0-913317-00-4*) GWU Grad Schl E&HD.

Path to Fairview: New & Selected Poems. Julia Randall. LC 92-19003. 224p. 1992. pap. 14.95 (*0-8071-1783-8*); text 24.95 (*0-8071-1782-X*) La State U Pr.

Path to Follow: Using Parent Stories for Understanding Families & Children. Heather M. Edwards et al. LC 98-53451. 76p. 1999. pap. text 14.00 (*0-325-00152-9*) Heinemann.

Path to Forever - Together: A Practical Guide to Making Love Last - Joyfully. Bill Winn. LC 96-84795. (Illus.). 178p. (Orig.). 1996. pap. 15.95 (*0-9628510-6-X*) Big Sky Pubns.

Path to Freedom: Articles & Speeches. Michael Collins. LC 95-72790. 160p. 1996. pap. 10.95 (*1-57098-064-0*) Roberts Rinehart.

Path to Freedom: Using Rebirthing & Astrology for Emotional & Spiritual Healing. Ken Kizer & Renee Kizer. (Illus.). 232p. 1999. pap. 15.00 (*0-9647010-4-9*) Immortalist.

Path to Funeral Consultancy. Lance Yost. Ed. by Paul M. Howey. 80p. 1998. pap., wbk. ed. 7.95 (*1-877749-31-1*); pap. text 9.95 (*1-877749-30-3*) Five Star AZ.

Path to Genocide: Essays on Launching the Final Solution. Christopher R. Browning. 207p. (C). 1992. text 52.95 (*0-521-41701-5*) Cambridge U Pr.

Path to Genocide: Essays on Launching the Final Solution. Christopher R. Browning. (Canto Book Ser.). 207p. (C). 1995. pap. 12.95 (*0-521-55878-6*) Cambridge U Pr.

Path to Glory: A Pictorial Celebration of the Santa Fe Trail. Jami Parkison. LC 96-77350. (Illus.). 132p. 1996. 29.95 (*1-888903-01-5*) Highwater Edits.

Path to Good Fortune: The Meng. Lily Chung. LC 97-2437. (Illus.). 288p. (Orig.). 1997. pap. 14.95 (*1-56718-133-3*) Llewellyn Pubns.

***Path to Greatness: Studies on Trials.** Max Lucado. (Topical Bible Study Ser.). 2000. pap. 7.99 (*0-8499-5431-2*) Word Pub.

Path to Healing: A Guide to Wellness for Body, Mind & Soul. Andrea D. Sullivan. 304p. 1999. pap. 12.95 (*0-385-48577-8*) Doubleday.

***Path to Healing: Experiencing God as Love.** Craig Bullock. 1999. pap. 14.95 (*1-929342-04-7*) Olde Ridge Bk.

Path to Healing: Report of the National Round Table on Aboriginal Health & Social Issues. 361p. (Orig.). 1993. pap. 32.45 (*0-660-15173-1*, Pub. by Canadian Govt Pub) Accents Pubns.

Path to Hope: For Parents of Aborted Children & Those Who Minister to Them. John J. Dillon. LC 90-70773. 80p. (Orig.). 1990. pap. 6.95 (*1-878718-00-2*, Resurrection Pr) Catholic Bk Pub.

Path to Illumination. Wally G. Richardson et al. LC 82-71211. (Illus.). 248p. (Orig.). 1982. pap. 9.95 (*0-87516-480-3*) DeVorss.

Path to Immortality. Rowland Wickes. LC 93-21702. 54p. (Orig.). 1993. pap. 3.50 (*1-880573-11-3*) Bible Search Pubns.

Path to Language: Toward Bilingual Education for Deaf Children. Danielle Bouvet. 300p. 1990. 99.00 (*1-85359-079-7*, Pub. by Multilingual Matters); pap. 39.95 (*1-85359-078-9*, Pub. by Multilingual Matters) Taylor & Francis.

Path to Liberation: A Spiritual & Philosophical Approach to the Martial Arts. Herman Kauz. (Illus.). 144p. 1992. 17.95 (*0-87951-423-X*, Pub. by Overlook Pr) Penguin Putnam.

Path to Liberation: A Spiritual & Philosophical Approach to the Martial Arts. Herman Kauz. (Illus.). 128p. 1993. pap. 12.95 (*0-87951-457-4*, Pub. by Overlook Pr) Penguin Putnam.

***Path to Light: How to Not Not Make Healthy Choices.** Judy Leighton. LC 00-190853. 327p. 2000. 25.00 (*0-7388-2029-6*); pap. 18.00 (*0-7388-2030-X*) Xlibris Corp.

Path to Love. Chrissie Loveday. 400p. (Orig.). 1997. mass mkt. 3.99 (*1-85487-924-3*, Pub. by Scarlet Bks) London Brdge.

Path to Love: Renewing the Power of Spirit in Your Life. Deepak Chopra. LC 97-133633. 1996. 24.00 (*0-517-70622-9*) Random Hse Value.

Path to Love: Spiritual Strategies for Healing. Deepak Chopra. LC 97-50035. 352p. 1998. pap. 14.00 (*0-609-80135-X*) Crown Pub Group.

Path to Love Is the Practice of Love: An Introduction to Spirituality. Carol Riddell. (Guidebooks for Growth Together). 144p. (Orig.). 1995. pap. 10.95 (*1-899171-20-7*, Pub. by Findhorn Pr) Words Distrib.

Path to Mastership. John-Roger. 77p. 1982. pap. 5.00 (*0-914829-16-5*) Mandeville LA.

Path to Mastery in Chiropractic: Seeking Excellence in Practice. James C. Smith. (Illus.). 450p. (C). 1994. pap. text. write for info. (*0-9637924-5-8*) Chiropract Paradigm.

Path to National Suicide: An Essay on Immigration & Multiculturalism. Lawrence Auster. 96p. (Orig.). 1990. pap. text 3.00 (*0-936247-12-6*) Amer Immigration.

Path to No-Self: Life at the Center. Bernadette Roberts. LC 91-30833. 214p. (C). 1991. pap. text 19.95 (*0-7914-1142-7*) State U NY Pr.

Path to No-Self: Life at the Center. Bernadette Roberts et al. LC 91-30833. 214p. (C). 1991. text 42.50 (*0-7914-1141-9*) State U NY Pr.

***Path to Organizational Skepticism.** James A. Stever. 320p. (C). 2000. pap. 25.95 (*1-57420-072-0*) Chatelaine.

P

An Asterisk (*) at the beginning of an entry indicates that the title is appearing for the first time.

Path to Parent Involvement: An Educator's Guide to Building Better Relationships with Parents. Kathleen O'Donnell Markert & National School Services (Wheeling, Ill.). LC 98-141687. (Illus.). 1997. write for info. (0-932957-04-8) Natl School.

Path to Payment: The Guide for Effectively Using Your Health Insurance Plan to Save You Money. Fred P. Torres. 264p. (Orig.). 1996. mass mkt. 6.95 (0-9651278-0-X) Alverstone Med.

Path to Popularity Through Friends & Self-Confidence. Peggy Bud. 1986. pap. 9.99 (0-89824-147-2) Trillium Pr.

Path to Power. Robert A. Caro. LC 89-40608. 1990. pap. 19.00 (0-679-72945-3) Vin Bks.

Path to Power. Margaret Thatcher. (Illus.). 656p. 1998. pap. text 18.00 (0-7881-5921-6) DIANE Pub.

Path to Power. Margaret Thatcher. 1996. pap. 18.00 (0-614-12552-9, Perennial) HarperTrade.

Path to Power: A Master's Guide to Conquering Crisis. Mack Newton & Michele St. George. LC 99-180128. 181p. 1997. pap. 14.95 (0-9659821-3-0) NTKD Pub.

Path to Power: The Years of Lyndon Johnson, Vol. 1. Robert A. Caro. LC 82-47811. 1982. 29.95 (0-394-49973-5) Knopf.

Path to Responsibility: A Comprehensive Therapist Treatment-Intervention Manual for Working with Sex Offenders. G. Richard Kishur. (Wounding Man Ser.: Unit 1). 396p. 1994. pap. text 39.95 (1-885473-00-1) Wood N Barnes.

Path to Revolution: The Communist Program. Gus Hall. 1968. pap. 0.25 (0-87898-031-8) New Outlook.

Path to Rome. Hilaire Belloc. LC 87-36772. 267p. 1987. pap. 8.95 (0-89526-784-5) Regnery Pub.

Path to Salvation: A Manual of Spiritual Transformation. St. Theophan the Recluse. Tr. by Seraphim Rose & St. Herman of Alaska Brotherhood Staff. LC 96-71062. (RUS., Illus.). 366p. 1996. 24.95 (1-887904-51-4) St Herman Pr.

Path to Salvation: A Manual of Spiritual Transformation. St. Theophan the Recluse. LC 96-71062. (RUS., Illus.). 368p. 19.95 (1-887904-50-6) St Herman Pr.

Path to School Leadership: A Portable Mentor. Lee G. Bolman & Terrence E. Deal. LC 92-38985. (Road Maps to Success Ser.). 80p. 1992. pap. 14.95 (0-8039-6052-2) Corwin Pr.

Path to Serenity see Camino a la Serenidad

Path to Smarter Economic Development: Reassessing the Federal Role. unabridged ed. 1996. pap. 20.00 (1-57744-021-8) Nat Acad Public Admin.

Path to the Brightest Star. Sandy Brainard. (Illus.). 104p. (Orig.). 1984. pap. 6.00 (0-942494-54-7) Coleman Pub.

Path to the City of Gold. C. H. Waller. 1998. pap. 8.95 (1-882701-49-6) Uplook Min.

Path to the Double Helix: The Discovery of DNA. Robert C. Olby. (Illus.). xxvi, 526p. 1994. reprint ed. pap. 13.95 (0-486-68117-3) Dover.

Path to the Hague: Selected Documents on the Origins of the ICTY. 86p. 20.00 (92-1-056702-1) UN.

Path to the Heart: Informal Talks on Personal Soul Winning. Glenn A. Coon. LC BV3790.C66. 191p. reprint ed. pap. 59.30 (0-7837-6434-0, 204643200012) Bks Demand.

Path to the Middle: Oral Madhyamika Philosophy in Tibet: The Spoken Scholarship of Kensur Yeshey Tupden. Ed. by Anne C. Klein. LC 93-39863. (SUNY Series in Buddhist Studies). 303p. (C). 1994. pap. text 23.95 (0-7914-2044-2) State U NY Pr.

Path to the Middle: Oral Madhyamika Philosophy in Tibet: The Spoken Scholarship of Kensur Yeshey Tupden. Ed. by Anne C. Klein. LC 93-39863. (SUNY Series in Buddhist Studies). 303p. (C). 1994. text 59.50 (0-7914-2043-4) State U NY Pr.

Path to the Nest of Spiders see Path to the Spiders' Nests: Revised Edition

Path to the New Music. Anton Webern. Ed. by Willi Reich. Tr. by Leo Black from GER. pap. 14.95 (3-7024-0030-3, UE12947) Eur-Am Music.

Path to the Ph. D. Measuring Graduate Attrition in the Sciences & Humanities. National Research Council Staff. LC 96-67827. 90p. (Orig.). 1997. pap. text 29.00 (0-309-05482-6) Natl Acad Pr.

***Path to the Soul: The Union of Eastern & Western Wisdom to Heal Your Body, Mind & Soul.** Ashok Bedi. LC 00-26122. (Illus.). 272p. 2000. pap. 16.95 (1-57863-187-4) Weiser.

***Path to the Spiders' Nests: Revised Edition.** rev. ed. Italo Calvino. LC 00-28150. Orig. Title: The Path to the Nest of Spiders. 192p. 2000. pap. 12.00 (0-06-095658-5, Ecco Press) HarperTrade.

Path To The Spiders' Nests, The Revised Ed. rev. ed. Italo Calvino. Ed. by Martin McLaughlin. Tr. by Archibald Colquhoun from ITA. LC 98-18174. 192p. 1998. 23.00 (0-88001-621-3) HarpC.

Path to the Spirit. Barbara Pray. Ed. by Sandra Talkington. (Grandmother Ser.). (Illus.). 77p. (Orig.). (C). 1994. pap. 12.95 (0-922863-05-9) Dream Wvrs Pub Co.

***Path to the Throne: The Pattern of Things in Heaven.** Marilyn J. Wright. (Illus.). 450p. (C). 1998. pap. 49.00 (1-886232-15-6) Majesty Pubns.

Path to Tranquillity: Daily Meditations by The Dalai Lama. Ed. & Compiled by Renuka Singh. LC 99-35039. 413p. 1999. 24.95 (0-670-88759-5) Viking Penguin.

Path to Transcendence: From Philosophy to Mysticism in Saint Augustine. Paul Henry. Tr. by Francis F. Burch. (Pittsburgh Theological Monographs: No. 37). 1981. pap. 10.00 (0-915138-49-2) Pickwick.

***Path to True Happiness: John 2.** D. Martyn Lloyd-Jones. 224p. 1999. pap. 16.99 (0-8010-5978-X) Baker Bks.

Path to True Health & Fulfillment. Raymond R. Rickards. Ed. by Beverly Trainer. (Illus.). 85p. (Orig.). 1995. pap. 15.95 (0-9650288-0-1) Sunburst Publns.

Path to Vietnam: Origins of the American Commitment to Southeast Asia. Andrew J. Rotter. LC 87-47603. 304p. (C). 1987. pap. text 17.95 (0-8014-9620-9) Cornell U Pr.

Path to Wing Chun. Samuel Kwok. pap. 13.95 (0-901764-73-6, 93214, Pub. by P H Crompton) Midpt Trade.

Path to Wing Chun. 2nd ed. Samuel Kwok. (Illus.). 112p. 1998. pap. text 18.95 (1-874250-80-4) P H Crompton.

Path to Your Ascension: Rediscovering Life's Ultimate Purpose. Annice Booth. LC 98-88846. 1999. pap. text 12.95 (0-922729-47-6) Summit Univ.

Path Toward Liberation: Understanding the Need for Polygamy in the African-American Community. Moyenda Nosakhere. 110p. (Orig.). 1991. pap. 9.95 (0-9626613-0-9) New Nation Bks.

Path-Way to Knowledge: Containing the Whole Art of Arithmeticke. John Tapp. LC 68-54667. (English Experience Ser.: No. 66). 1968. reprint ed. 25.00 (90-221-0066-9) Walter J Johnson.

Path-Way to Knowledge, Containing the First Principles of Geometrie. Robert Record. LC 74-80206. (English Experience Ser.: No. 687). 1974. reprint ed. 25.00 (90-221-0687-X) Walter J Johnson.

Path-Way to Military Practice. Barnaby Rich. LC 75-25920. (English Experience Ser.: No. 177). 88p. 1969. reprint ed. 20.00 (90-221-0177-0) Walter J Johnson.

Path We Tread: Blacks in Nursing Worldwide, 1854-1994. 3rd ed. Mary E. Carnegie. LC 94-49183. 1995. 30.95 (0-88737-640-1) Natl League Nurse.

Path Wellness Manual. 2nd ed. Eric R. Braverman. (Illus.). 512p. 1995. text 25.00 (0-9638869-5-9) Pubns for Achieving.

Path with a Heart: Ericksonian Utilization with Resistant & Chronic Clients. Yvonne M. Dolan. LC 85-4225. 224p. 1993. pap. text 28.95 (0-87630-718-7) Brunner-Mazel.

Path with Heart: A Guide Through the Perils & Promises of Spiritual Life. Jack Kornfield. LC 92-42894. 368p. 1993. pap. 14.95 (0-553-37211-4) Bantam.

Path Without Destination: An Autobiography. Satish Kumar. LC 98-35572. 320p. 1999. 22.00 (0-688-16402-1, Wm Morrow) Morrow Avon.

***Path without Destination: The Long Walk of a Gentle Hero.** Satish Kumar. 320p. 2000. pap. 13.00 (0-688-16404-8, Wm Morrow) Morrow Avon.

Path Without Form: A Journey Into the Realm Beyond Thought. Robert Powell. LC 98-47967. 246p. (Orig.). 1999. pap. 14.95 (1-884997-21-X) Blue Dove Pr.

Pathan Borderland. Collin M. Enriquez. 1989. reprint ed. 28.50 (81-7141-062-6) S Asia.

***Pathan Unarmed: Opposition & Memory in the Khudai Khidmatgar Movement.** Mukulika Banerjee. (World Anthropology Ser.). 320p. 2000. 65.00 (0-933452-68-3); pap. 29.95 (0-933452-69-1) Schol Am Res.

Pathans: 500 B.C.-A.D., 1957. With a New Epilogue. Olaf Caroe. (Illus.). 544p. 1984. text 39.95 (0-19-577221-0) OUP.

Pathans of the Latter Day. James W. Spain. (Illus.). 174p. 1997. 24.95 (0-19-577576-7) OUP.

Pathar Panchali. B. Banerji. 166p. 1987. 10.95 (0-318-36919-2) Asia Bk Corp.

Pathblazers: 8 People Who Made a Difference. M. K. Fullen. LC 91-46484. (Collection of Short Biographies). (Illus.). 64p. (Orig.). (J). (gr. 3-10). 1992. 12.95 (0-940880-35-0); pap. 6.95 (0-940880-36-9) Open Hand.

Pathbreakers from River to Ocean: Story of the Great West from Coronado to the Present. Grace R. Hebard. LC 71-164604. (Select Bibliographies Reprint Ser.). 1977. reprint ed. 35.95 (0-8369-5888-8) Ayer.

Pathetic Symphony: A Biographical Novel about Tchaikovsky. Klaus Mann. LC 85-50532. (Illus.). 380p. 1985. reprint ed. pap. 9.95 (0-910129-24-X) Wiener Pubs Inc.

Pathetique - Poetical Sketches by Ralph Aquila. Ralph Aquila. 1998. pap. write for info. (1-57553-839-3) Watermrk Pr.

Pathfinder. Burns. 1998. mass mkt. 6.99 (0-8041-1602-4) Ivy Books.

Pathfinder. James Fenimore Cooper. (Airmont Classics Ser.). (YA). (gr. 6 up). 1964. mass mkt. 2.95 (0-8049-0035-3, CL-35) Airmont.

Pathfinder. James Fenimore Cooper. 1976. lib. bdg. 26.95 (0-89968-159-X, Lghtyr Pr) Buccaneer Bks.

Pathfinder. James Fenimore Cooper. (Illus.). 488p. (J). (gr. k-10). 1961. mass mkt. 5.95 (0-451-52257-5, Sig Classics) NAL.

Pathfinder. James Fenimore Cooper. Ed. & Intro. by Kay S. House. LC 88-32956. 496p. 1989. pap. 9.95 (0-14-039071-5, Penguin Classics) Viking Penguin.

Pathfinder. James Fenimore Cooper. 1961. 11.05 (0-606-02759-9, Pub. by Turtleback) Demco.

Pathfinder. Manuel Garcia. 1997. pap. write for info. (1-57553-624-2) Watermrk Pr.

Pathfinder. Roger Wassell-Smith. LC 97-16214. (Fact Packs Ser.). (Illus.). 32p. (J). (gr. 3-7). 1997. pap. text 14.95 (0-7641-7045-7) Barron.

Pathfinder. James Fenimore Cooper. (Works of James Fenimore Cooper). 1990. reprint ed. lib. bdg. 79.00 (0-7812-2386-5) Rprt Serv.

***Pathfinder: A Quick Reference & Intervention Guide for Pastors & Counselors.** Millie McCarty et al. 200p. 1999. 59.95 (1-929643-09-8) Ambris Publ.

***Pathfinder: Exploring Career & Educational Paths.** 2nd rev. ed. Norene Lindsay. 1999. pap. text 6.95 (1-56370-524-9) JIST Works.

Pathfinder: Exploring Career & Educational Paths & Career Plan Portfolio. Norene Lindsay. 1997. pap. text 24.95 (1-56370-122-7) JIST Works.

Pathfinder: How to Choose or Change Your Career for a Lifetime of Satisfaction & Success. Nicholas Lore. LC 97-36944. 400p. 1998. per. 14.00 (0-684-82399-3, Fireside) S&S Trade Pap.

Pathfinder: Inventor, Scientist, Industrialist. Edward G. Acheson. (American Biography Ser.). 63p. 1991. reprint ed. lib. bdg. 59.00 (0-7812-8001-X) Rprt Serv.

***Pathfinder: Or the Inland Sea.** James Fenimore Cooper. Ed. by William P. Kelly. (Oxford World's Classics Ser.). 528p. 2000. pap. 8.95 (0-19-283989-6) OUP.

Pathfinder: 1st Automobile Trip from Newport to Siletz Bay, 1912. Ed. by James E. Stembridge, Jr. (Illus.). 24p. (Orig.). 1976. pap. 2.95 (0-911443-02-9) Lincoln Coun Hist.

Pathfinder - Exploring Career & Educational Paths: Career & Educational Planning for Junior High & High School Students. Norene Lindsay. Ed. by Sara Hall. (Illus.). 112p. (YA). (gr. 8-12). 1994. pap., student ed. 5.99 (1-56370-120-0, J1200) JIST Works.

Pathfinder & Buffalo Hiders, 2 vols. in 1. Judd Cole. (Cheyenne Ser.: Vols. 9 & 10). 352p. 1998. mass mkt. 4.99 (0-8439-4413-7, Leisure Bks) Dorchester Pub Co.

Pathfinder Area Coordinator Master Manual. Bennie Tillman & Emma L. Tillman. 300p. (Orig.). 1987. pap., teacher ed. 35.00 (0-936241-02-0) Cheetah Pub.

Pathfinder Bennett: Airman Extraordinary. A. S. Jackson. 172p. 1990. 65.00 (0-86138-088-6, Pub. by T Dalton) St Mut.

***Pathfinder Dressage.** Hillsdon. 2000. 35.00 (0-85131-745-6, Pub. by J A Allen) Trafalgar.

Pathfinder for Norwegian Emigrants. Johan R. Reiersen. LC 81-132209. (Norwegian-American Historical Association. Travel & Description Ser.: No. 9). 253p. reprint ed. pap. 78.50 (0-608-15446-6, 202929300059) Bks Demand.

Pathfinder History: Napoleon & Europe. Phil Ingram. 64p. 1998. pap. 23.00 (0-7487-3954-8) St Mut.

Pathfinder Mission to Mars. John Hamilton. LC 97-34704. (Mission to Mars Ser.). (J). 1998. lib. bdg. 14.98 (1-56239-831-8) ABDO Pub Co.

Pathfinder: or the Inland Sea. James Fenimore Cooper. 351p. Date not set. 25.95 (0-8488-2541-1) Amereon Ltd.

Pathfinder: or the Inland Sea. James Fenimore Cooper. LC 79-15598. (Writings of James Fenimore Cooper). 569p. (C). 1980. pap. text 19.95 (0-87395-477-7) State U NY Pr.

Pathfinder Press Was Born with the October Revolution. Mary-Alice Waters. LC 98-223333. 76p. 1988. pap. 8.00 (0-87348-875-X) Pathfinder NY.

Pathfinder Psychic Talking Board. Amy Zerner & Monte Farber. 1999. pap. 27.95 (1-885203-89-6) Jrny Editions.

Pathfinder Staff Training Manual. Bennie Tillman & Emma L. Tillman. 200p. (Orig.). 1987. pap., teacher ed. 25.00 (0-936241-03-9) Cheetah Pub.

Pathfinder Teacher's Guide. Norene Lindsau. 56p. (J). (gr. 7-10). 1993. pap., teacher ed. 14.95 (1-56370-121-9) JIST Works.

Pathfinder to U. S. Export Control Laws & Regulations. Wei Luo. LC 94-18558. (Legal Research Guides Ser.: Vol. 18). xiv, 109p. 1994. 42.50 (0-89941-889-9, 308320) W S Hein.

***Pathfinder's Adventure Kit.** Christine Kennedy et al. (Illus.). 56p. (J). 1998. 15.00 (0-921051-79-4) Somerville Hse.

Pathfinders Honors: A Manual for the Requirements of All Pathfinder Honors. Church Ministries Department Staff. (Illus.). 238p. 1989. pap. 8.99 (0-8163-0883-7) Pacific Pr Pub Assn.

Pathfinders of the Texas State Law Library. Texas State Law Library Staff. LC 97-80447. (Pathfinder Ser.: Vol. 28). xi, 126p. 1997. 48.00 (1-57588-397-X, 311460) W S Hein.

Pathfinders of the West. Agnes C. Laut. LC 74-90651. (Essay Index Reprint Ser.). 1977. 30.95 (0-8369-1220-9) Ayer.

Pathfinders of the World Missionary Crusade. George S. Eddy. LC 76-84304. (Essay Index Reprint Ser.). 1977. 22.95 (0-8369-1127-X) Ayer.

Pathki Nana: Kootenai Girl. Kenneth Thomasma. (J). (gr. 3-8). 1991. 9.95 (1-880114-10-0) Grandview.

Pathki Nana: Kootenai Girl Solves a Mystery. Kenneth Thomasma. LC 92-14432. (Amazing Indian Children Ser.). (Illus.). 168p. (YA). (gr. 7-10). 1991. 9.99 (0-8010-8901-8); pap. 5.99 (0-8010-8902-6) Baker Bks.

Pathki Nana: Kootenai Girl Solves a Mystery. Kenneth Thomasma. LC 92-14432. (Amazing Indian Children Ser.). 1991. 12.05 (0-606-10281-7, Pub. by Turtleback) Demco.

PathLab. Patrick C. Ward. 1994. text 400.00 (1-56815-025-3, 10025) Mosby Inc.

Pathless Way: John Muir & American Wilderness. Michael P. Cohen. LC 83-40260. 500p. 1986. pap. 19.95 (0-299-09724-2) U of Wis Pr.

Pathless Woods. Gloria Whelan. LC 80-8725. (Illus.). 192p. (YA). (gr. 7 up). 1981. lib. bdg. 11.89 (0-397-31931-2, Lippncott) Lppncott W & W.

Pathless Woods: Ernest Hemingway's Sixteenth Summer in Northern Michigan. 2nd rev. ed. Gloria Whelan. (Illus.). (J). (gr. 6-10). 1998. 16.95 (1-882376-63-3); pap. 11.95 (1-882376-44-7) Thunder Bay Pr.

Pathlogy Pediatric Tumors. Atayde Perez. 1999. pap. text 195.00 (0-8385-7802-0, Medical Exam) Appleton & Lange.

Pathmarks. Martin Heidegger. Ed. by William McNeil. LC 97-22565. Orig. Title: Wegmarken. 384p. (C). 1998. text 59.95 (0-521-43362-2); pap. text 19.95 (0-521-43968-X) Cambridge U Pr.

Pathobiochemie: Ein Lehrbuch fur Studierende und Aerzte. 2nd ed. Eckhart Buddecke. (Illus.). 477p. 1983. 52.30 (3-11-009658-7) De Gruyter.

Pathobiochemistry, Vol. 5. rev. ed. Andrew H. Kang & Marcel E. Nimmi. LC 87-20946. (Collagen Ser.: Vol. V). 288p. 1992. 146.00 (0-8493-4605-3, QP552) Franklin.

Pathobiologie Oraler Strukturen: Zaehne, Pulpa, Parodont. 2nd rev. ed. H. E. Schroeder. (Illus.). xii, 266p. 1991. pap. 40.00 (3-8055-5268-8) S Karger.

Pathobiologie Oraler Strukturen: Zaehne, Pulpa, Parodont. 3rd ed. H. E. Schroeder. (Illus.). xiv, 256p. 1996. pap. 51.50 (3-8055-6286-1) S Karger.

Pathobiology & Clinics of Basal Ganglia Disorders. Ed. by P. Riederer & W. Wesemann. (Journal of Nonprofit & Public Sector Marketing: Suppl. 38). (Illus.). 155p. 1993. 72.95 (0-387-82425-1) Spr-Verlag.

Pathobiology Annual, Vol. 1. fac. ed. Pathobiology Annual Staff. Ed. by Harry L. Ioachim. LC 78-151816. (Illus.). 368p. pap. 114.10 (0-7837-7231-9, 204706700012) Bks Demand.

Pathobiology of Alzheimer's Disease. Ed. by Alison Goate & Frank Ashall. (Neuroscience Perspectives Ser.). (Illus.). 272p. 1995. text 79.00 (0-12-286965-6) Acad Pr.

Pathobiology of Cardiovascular Injury. Ed. by H. Lowell Stone & William B. Weglicki. (Developments in Cardiovascular Medicine Ser.). 1985. text 186.00 (0-89838-743-4) Kluwer Academic.

Pathobiology of Human Germ Cell Neoplasia. Ed. by J. W. Oosterhuis et al. (Recent Results in Cancer Research Ser.: Vol. 123). (Illus.). 192p. 1991. 106.00 (0-387-53928-X) Spr-Verlag.

Pathobiology of Malignant Melanoma. Ed. by D. E. Elder. (Pigment Cell Ser.: Vol. 8). (Illus.). viii, 224p. 1987. 151.50 (3-8055-4348-4) S Karger.

Pathobiology of Marine & Estuarine Organisms. John A. Couch. 576p. 1992. lib. bdg. 95.00 (0-8493-8662-4, SF997) CRC Pr.

Pathobiology of Marine Mammal Diseases, 2 Vols., Vol. I. Edwin B. Howard. 248p. 1983. 143.00 (0-8493-6311-X, SF997, CRC Reprint) Franklin.

Pathobiology of Marine Mammal Diseases, 2 Vols., Vol. II. Edwin B. Howard. 240p. 1983. 140.00 (0-8493-6312-8, SF997, CRC Reprint) Franklin.

Pathobiology of Neoplasia. A. E. Sirica. LC 88-29012. (Illus.). 606p. (C). 1989. text 130.00 (0-306-42950-0, Kluwer Plenum) Kluwer Academic.

Pathobiology of Ocular Disease, 2 pts., Set. 2nd expanded rev. ed. Ed. by Garner & Klintworth. (Illus.). 1966p. 1994. text 450.00 (0-8247-9136-3) Dekker.

Pathobiology of Ocular Disease: A Dynamic Approach, Pt. A. Ed. by Alec Garner & Gordon K. Klintworth. LC 81-12602. (Illus.). 861p. reprint ed. pap. 200.00 (0-7837-4314-9, 204400100001) Bks Demand.

Pathobiology of Ocular Disease: A Dynamic Approach, Pt. B. Ed. by Alec Garner & Gordon K. Klintworth. LC 81-12602. (Illus.). 907p. reprint ed. pap. 200.00 (0-7837-4315-7, 204400100002) Bks Demand.

Pathobiology of Ocular Disease: A Dynamic Approach, 2 pts., Pt. B. 2nd expanded rev. ed. Ed. by Garner & Klintworth. (Illus.). 1966p. 1994. text 450.00 (0-8247-9137-1) Dekker.

Pathobiology of Soft Tissue Tumours. C. D. Fletcher & P. H. McKee. (Current Problems in Tumor Pathology Ser.). (Illus.). 358p. 1991. text 139.00 (0-443-03790-6) Church.

Pathobiology of the Aging Mouse, 2 vols. Ed. by C. C. Capen et al. Incl. Vol. 1. LC 96-77541. (Illus.). 527p. 1996. 225.00 (0-944398-45-6); Vol. 2. LC 96-77541. (Illus.). 505p. 1996. 225.00 (0-944398-46-4); (Pathobiology of Aging Laboratory Animals Ser.). 325.00 (0-614-23194-9, 398561) ILSI.

Pathobiology of the Aging Rat, 2 vols. Ed. by C. C. Capen et al. Incl. Vol. 1. LC 92-74194. (Illus.). 485p. 1992. 200.00 (0-944398-09-X); Vol. 2. LC 92-74194. (Illus.). 647p. 1994. 200.00 (0-944398-20-0); (Pathobiology of Aging Laboratory Animals Ser.). 325.00 (0-614-23196-5, 398553) ILSI.

Pathobiology of the Human Atherosclerotic Plaque. Ed. by S. Glagov et al. (Illus.). xxxi, 923p. 1989. 160.00 (0-387-97130-0) Spr-Verlag.

Pathogen & Microbial Contamination Management in Micropropagation. A. C. Cassells. LC 97-31344. (Development in Plant Pathology Ser.). 384p. 1997. text 200.50 (0-7923-4784-6) Kluwer Academic.

Pathogen Detection & Remediation for Safe Eating, Vol. 3544. Ed. by Yud-Ren Chen et al. (Proceedings of SPIE Ser.: Vol. 3545). 646p. 1999. 59.00 (0-8194-3006-4) SPIE.

Pathogenesis & Host Response in Helicobacter Pylori Infections. Ed. by A. P. Moran & C. A. O'Morain. 1997. pap. 30.00 (0-926592-19-X) Normed Verlag.

Pathogenesis & Host Specificity in Plant Diseases, 3 vols., Vol. 2. K. Kohmoto & R. P. Singh. 436p. 1996. 196.50 (0-08-042511-9, Pergamon Pr) Elsevier.

Pathogenesis & Host Specificity in Plant Diseases: Prokaryotes, 3 vols., Vol. 1. K. Kohmoto & R. P. Singh. 346p. 1996. 133.50 (0-08-042510-0, Pergamon Pr) Elsevier.

Pathogenesis & Host Specificity in Plant Diseases: Viruses & Viroids, 3 vols., Vol. 3. K. Kohmoto & R. P. Singh. 444p. 1996. 196.50 (0-08-042512-7, Pergamon Pr) Elsevier.

Pathogenesis & Host Specificity in Plant Diseases 3VS: Histopathological, Biochemical, Genetic & Molecular Bases, 3 vols. R. P. Singh et al. 1200p. 1995. 437.25 (0-08-042273-X, Pergamon Pr) Elsevier.

Pathogenesis & Immunity in Pertussis. Ed. by Alastair C. Wardlaw & Roger Parton. LC 88-125. 506p. 1988. 575.00 (0-471-91820-2) Wiley.

Pathogenesis & Immunology of Treponemal Infections. fac. ed. Ed. by Ronald F. Schell & Daniel M. Musher. LC 82-23547. (Immunology Ser.: No. 20). 412p. 1983. reprint ed. pap. 127.80 (0-7837-8321-3, 204910700010) Bks Demand.

An Asterisk (*) at the beginning of an entry indicates that the title is appearing for the first time.

***Pathogenesis & Medical Management of Uterine Fibroids.** I. A. Brosens & Bruno Lunenfeld. LC 99-35362. (Illus.). 158p. 1999. 59.95 (*1-85070-098-2*) Prthnon Pub.

***Pathogenesis & Risk Factors of Glaucoma.** Ed. by E. Gramer & F. Grehn. (Illus.). 255p. 1999. 76.00 (*3-540-65912-9*) Spr-Verlag.

Pathogenesis & Therapy of Amyotrophic Lateral Sclerosis. Ed. by Georges Serratrice & Theodore L. Munsat. (Advances in Neurology Ser.: Vol. 68). (Illus.). 352p. 1995. text 115.00 (*0-7817-0333-6*) Lppncott W & W.

Pathogenesis & Therapy of Duchenne & Becker Muscular Dystrophy. Ed. by Byron A. Kakulas & Frank L. Mastaglia. LC 89-24144. 287p. 1990. reprint ed. pap. 89.00 (*0-608-03419-3*, 206411800008) Bks Demand.

Pathogenesis & Therapy of Lung Cancer. Ed. by Curtis C. Harris. LC 78-17321. (Lung Biology in Health & Disease Ser.: No. 10). 784p. reprint ed. pap. 200.00 (*0-7837-4060-3*, 204401000011) Bks Demand.

Pathogenesis & Treatment of Diabetes Mellitus. J. K. Radder et al. 1986. text 139.00 (*0-89838-828-7*) Kluwer Academic.

Pathogenesis & Treatment of Immunodeficiency. S. H. Horowitz & R. Hong. (Monographs in Allergy: Vol. 10). 1977. 65.25 (*3-8055-2624-5*) S Karger.

Pathogenesis & Treatment of Nephrolithiasis. Ed. by F. Linari et al. (Contributions to Nephrology Ser.: Vol. 58). x, 298p. 1987. 29.75 (*3-8055-4554-1*) S Karger.

Pathogenesis & Treatment of NIDDM & Its Related Problems: Proceedings of the 4th International Symposium on Treatment of Diabetes Melliuts, Nagoya, 23-26 October 1993. Ed. by N. Sakamoto et al. LC 94-10599. (International Congress Ser.: No. 1057). 532p. 1994. 256.25 (*0-444-81712-3*) Elsevier.

Pathogenesis & Treatment of Prostate Obstruction. Ed. by Christopher R. Chapple. LC 93-17266. 1994. 192.00 (*0-387-19681-1*) Spr-Verlag.

Pathogenesis, Complications & Treatment of Glomerulonephritis. Ed. by Shaul G. Massry & G. A. Cinotti. (Journal: American Journal of Nephrology Ser.: Vol. 9, Suppl. 1, 1989). (Illus.). iv, 84p. 1989. pap. 26.25 (*3-8055-4908-3*) S Karger.

Pathogenesis, Diagnosis & Clinical Relevance of Pleural Plaques: International Meeting, Basel, January 1997. Ed. by John A. Hoskins et al. (Indoor & Build Environment Ser.: Vol. 6, No. 2, 1997). 68p. 1997. pap. 29.75 (*3-8055-6467-8*) S Karger.

Pathogenesis of Bacterial Infections. Ed. by George G. Jackson & H. Thomas. (Bayer Symposium Ser.: 8). (Illus.). 430p. 1985. 101.00 (*0-387-15304-7*) Spr-Verlag.

Pathogenesis of Functional Bowel Disease. W. J. Snape, Jr. (Topics in Gastroenterology Ser.). (Illus.). 388p. (C). 1989. text 95.00 (*0-306-43265-X*, Kluwer Plenum) Kluwer Academic.

Pathogenesis of Infectious Disease. 4th ed. Ed. by Cedric A. Mims et al. (Illus.). 414p. 1995. text 48.00 (*0-12-498262-X*); pap. text 33.00 (*0-12-498263-8*) Acad Pr.

Pathogenesis of Intestinal Infections: Microbiological & Pathological Principles. M. V. Voino-Yasenetsky & T. Bakacs. 420p. (C). 1977. 100.00 (*963-05-1131-2*, Pub. by Akade Kiado) St Mut.

Pathogenesis of Invertebrate Microbial Diseases. Ed. by Elizabeth W. Davidson. LC 81-65007. 576p. 1981. text 65.00 (*0-86598-014-4*) Rowman.

Pathogenesis of Leukemias & Lymphomas: Environmental Influences. Ed. by Ian T. Magrath et al. LC 82-42584. (Progress in Cancer Research & Therapy Ser.: Vol. 27). 429p. 1984. reprint ed. pap. 133.00 (*0-608-00402-2*, 206111600007) Bks Demand.

Pathogenesis of Myocarditis & Cardiomyopathy: Recent Experimental & Clinical Studies. Ed. by Chuichi Kawai & Walter H. Abelmann. LC 88-165114. (Cardiomyopathy Update Ser.: No. 1). 322p. 1987. reprint ed. pap. 99.90 (*0-608-01227-0*, 206191500001) Bks Demand.

Pathogenesis of Non-Insulin Dependent Diabetes Mellitus. Ed. by Valdemar Grill & Suad Efendic. LC 88-15816. (Karolinska Institute Nobel Conference Ser.). 331p. 1988. reprint ed. pap. 102.70 (*0-608-00371-9*, 206108400007) Bks Demand.

Pathogenesis of Sodium Retention & of Ascites Formation in Experimental Cirrhosis in Rats. Guy Van Roey. (Acta Biomedica Lovaniensia Ser.: No. 137). (Illus.). 137p. (Orig.). 1996. pap. 42.50 (*90-6186-767-3*, Pub. by Leuven Univ) Coronet Bks.

Pathogenesis of Stress-Induced Heart Disease. Ed. by R. E. Beamish et al. (Developments in Cardiovascular Medicine Ser.). 1985. text 146.50 (*0-89838-710-8*) Kluwer Academic.

Pathogenesis-Related Proteins in Plants. S. K. Datta. LC 99-12438. 304p. 1999. boxed set 129.95 (*0-8493-0697-3*) CRC Pr.

Pathogenic & Therapeutic Aspects of Chronic Renal Failure. Ed. by K. M. Koch & Gunter Stein. (Illus.). 256p. 1997. text 125.00 (*0-8247-9894-5*) Dekker.

Pathogenic Microbiology: Emerging & Reemerging Diseases. Joanne S. Stolen. LC 97-62348. (Illus.). 258p. (C). 1998. pap. text 45.00 (*1-887052-03-8*) SOS Pubns NJ.

Pathogenic Microorganisms. Ellner. write for info. (*0-444-00824-1*) Elsevier.

Pathogenic Microorganisms from a Typical Clinical Sources: Proceedings of a Conference Held at the Yale University School of Medicine, New Haven, Connecticut. Ed. by A. Von Graevenitz. LC 75-3804. (Microorganisms & Infectious Diseases Ser.: No. 1). 245p. reprint ed. pap. 76.00 (*0-7837-0770-3*, 204108400019) Bks Demand.

Pathogenic Mycoplasmas. CIBA Foundation Staff. LC 72-88563. (CIBA Foundation Symposium: New Ser.: No. 6). 414p. reprint ed. pap. 128.40 (*0-608-13512-7*, 202213800024) Bks Demand.

Pathogenic Neisseriae: Proceedings of the 4th International Symposium, Asilomar, California, 21-25 October 1984. American Society for Microbiology Staff. Ed. by Gary K. Schoolnik et al. LC 85-20108. 659p. reprint ed. pap. 200.00 (*0-7837-4044-1*, 204387400011) Bks Demand.

Pathogenic Yeasts & Yeast Infections. Segal & Gerald L. Baum. 256p. 1994. lib. bdg. 189.00 (*0-8493-6426-4*) CRC Pr.

Pathogenicity & Clinical Significance of Coagulase-Negative Staphylococci. Ed. by Gerhard Pulverer et al. (Zentralblatt fur Bakteriologie Ser.: Vol. 16). 290p. 1987. lib. bdg. 140.00 (*0-89574-242-X*, Pub. by Gustav Fischer) Balogh.

Pathogenicity Islands & Other Mobile Virulence Elements. Ed. by James B. Kaper & Jorg Hacker. LC 99-24324. (Illus.). 320p. 1999. 85.95 (*1-55581-161-2*) ASM Pr.

Pathogenicity of Human Herpesviruses Due to Specific Pathogenicity Genes. Ed. by Yechiel Becker & G. Darai. LC 93-38678. 1994. 174.95 (*0-387-57127-2*) Spr-Verlag.

Pathogens in Model Distribution System Biofilms. Anne K. Camper & AWWA Research Foundation Staff. LC 97-31828. 1997. write for info. (*0-89867-932-X*, 90738) Am Water Wks Assn.

Pathogens of Invertebrates: Application in Biological Control & Transmission Mechanisms. Ed. by Thomas C. Cheng. (Comparative Pathobiology Ser.: Vol. 7). 286p. 1984. 79.50 (*0-306-41700-6*, Plenum Trade) Perseus Pubng.

Pathogens of Maize Seeds: Bibliography. Andrew Kalinski. 56p. (C). 1999. reprint ed. pap. text 20.00 (*0-7881-7987-X*) DIANE Pub.

Pathogens of Medically Important Arthropods. (Bulletin Supplement Ser.: No. 55). 419p. 1977. pap. text 25.00 (*92-4-068551-0*) World Health.

Pathogens of Sorghum: Bibliography. Andrew Kalinski. 112p. (C). 1999. reprint ed. pap. text 20.00 (*0-7881-7988-8*) DIANE Pub.

Pathogens of Soybean Seeds: Bibliography. Andrew Kalinski. 90p. (C). 1999. reprint ed. pap. text 20.00 (*0-7881-7989-6*) DIANE Pub.

Pathogens, Parasites & Predators of Medically Important Arthropods. D. W. Jenkins. (WHO Bulletin Supplement Ser.: Vol. 30). 1964. pap. text 9.00 (*92-4-168301-5*, 1033001) World Health.

***Pathoghomonic Signs.** Veerasamy K. Pillay. 2000. pap. 9.00 (*0-8059-4973-9*) Dorrance.

Pathologiae Graeci Sermonis Elementa, 2 vols. C. August Lobeck. xxv, 1099p. 1966. reprint ed. write for info. (*0-318-70968-6*) G Olms Pubs.

Pathologic Basis of Disease: A Self-Assessment & Review. 4th ed. Carolyn C. Compton. 250p. 1995. pap. text 23.00 (*0-7216-4041-9*, W B Saunders Co) Harcrt Hlth Sci Grp.

***Pathological & Regenerative Plant Anatomy.** Siegfried Fink. (Handbuch der Pflanzenanatomie Ser.: Band XIV, Teil 6). (Illus.). xii, 1095p. 1999. 199.00 (*3-443-14027-0*, Pub. by Gebruder Borntraeger) Balogh.

Pathological Basis Disease. 5th ed. Compton. 1999. pap. text. write for info. (*0-7216-7857-2*, W B Saunders Co) Harcrt Hlth Sci Grp.

Pathological Basis of the Connective Tissue Diseases. write for info. (*0-340-57219-1*, Pub. by E A) Routldge.

Pathological Basis of the Connective Tissue Diseases. Dugald L. Gardner. LC 91-37878. 1050p. 1992. 175.00 (*0-8121-1563-5*) Lppncott W & W.

Pathological Christianity: The Dangers & Cures of Extremist Fundamentalisms. Gregory M. Vogt. LC 94-71587. 270p. (Orig.). 1994. pap. 19.95 (*0-940121-31-X*, P216, Cross Roads Bks) Cross Cultural Pubns.

With a passion reminiscent of Martin Luther posting his 95 theses on the church door in 1517, the author here turns the heat on current American evangelieal fundamentalism whose effects, he says, are in every single nook & cranny of current American life whether we recognize it or not. The emphasis here is on the pathological professional Christianity to which our society has become increasingly vulnerable. Christianity is not the issue; freedom to choose as an individual is what is at stake. This book offers a sense of freedom & a breath of fresh air. *Publisher Paid Annotation.*

Pathological Conduction in Nerve Fibers, Electromyography of Sphincter Muscles, Automatic Analysis of Electrogram with Computers see New Developments in Electromyography & Clinical Neurophysiology

Pathological Cry, Stridor & Cough in Infants: A Clinical Acoustic Study. J. Hirschberg & T. Szende. 156p. (C). 1982. 100.00 (*963-05-2820-7*, Pub. by Akade Kiado) St Mut.

Pathological Diagnosis of Acute Ischaemic Heart Disease: Proceedings of the WHO Scientific Group, Geneva, 1969. WHO Staff. (Technical Reports: No. 441). 1970. pap. text 3.00 (*92-4-120441-9*, 1100441) World Health.

***Pathological Diagnosis of Vascular Diseases.** B. Austin et al. 400p. 1999. 165.00 (*2-287-59660-7*) Spr-Verlag.

Pathological Effects of Oral Contraceptives. P. S. Boffa et al. LC 72-13565. (Illus.). 220p. (C). 1973. text 29.00 (*0-8422-7081-7*) Irvington.

Pathological Gambling. National Research Council Staff. LC 99-6598. 300p. 1999. 27.95 (*0-309-06571-2*) Natl Acad Pr.

Pathological Gambling: Conceptual, Diagnostic, & Treatment Issues. Martin C. McGurrin. Ed. by Harold H. Smith, Jr. LC 91-50928. (Practitioner's Resource Ser.). 96p. 1992. pap. 16.45 (*0-943158-69-9*, PGCBP, Prof Resc Pr) Pro Resource.

Pathological Gambling: The Making of a Medical Problem. Brian Castellani. LC 99-40431. (C). 2000. text 57.50 (*0-7914-4521-6*); pap. text 18.95 (*0-7914-4522-4*) State U NY Pr.

Pathological Lying, Accusation & Swindling, a Study in Forensic Psychology. William Healy & Mary T. Healy. LC 69-14932. (Criminology, Law Enforcement, & Social Problems Ser.: No. 63). 1969. reprint ed. 24.00 (*0-87585-063-4*) Patterson Smith.

Pathological Ocular Conditions. Alan Tunnacliffe. (C). 1989. 35.00 (*0-89771-746-5*, Pub. by Assn Brit Dispen Opticians) St Mut.

***Pathological Problems of Economic Crop Plants & Their Management.** S. M. Paul Khurana. LC 98-908794. 1998. pap. 300.00 (*81-7233-178-9*, Pub. by Scientific Pubs) St Mut.

Pathological Self-Criticism: Assessment & Treatment. Raymond M. Bergner. (Series in Social/Clinical Psychology). 220p. 1995. 39.50 (*0-306-44961-7*, Kluwer Plenum) Kluwer Academic.

***Pathologies of Belief.** Ed. by Max Coltheart & Martin Davies. (Readings in Mind & Language Ser.). 112p. 2000. pap. 24.95 (*0-631-22136-0*) Blackwell Pubs.

Pathologies of Rational Choice Theory: A Critique of Applications in Political Science. Donald P. Green. LC 94-11070. 1996. pap. 16.00 (*0-300-06636-8*) Yale U Pr.

***Pathologies of Speech & Language.** Ben Massen. 1999. pap. text 82.50 (*1-86156-122-9*) Whurr Pub.

Pathologist. Jack Rudman. (Career Examination Ser.: C-645). 1994. pap. 49.95 (*0-8373-0645-0*) Nat Learn.

Pathologist in Peril. Harry Chinchinian. 1996. pap. 8.95 (*0-9653535-2-4*) Plum Tree.

Pathologony of Tumours in Laboratory Animals Vol. 1: Tumours of the Rat, Pts. 1 & 2. Ed. by V. S. Turusov. (IARC Scientific Publications: Nos. 5 & 6). 533p. 1987. 120.00 (*92-832-1410-2*) OUP.

Pathology. Bass. 1996. pap. text 27.00 (*0-443-05003-1*, W B Saunders Co) Harcrt Hlth Sci Grp.

Pathology. L. A. Cree. (Illus.). 608p. 1997. pap. text 32.95 (*0-412-47200-7*, Pub. by E A) OUP.

Pathology. Ivan Damjanov & Goldblatt. LC 98-2713. (Rypins' Intensive Reviews Ser.). 432p. 1998. pap. text 21.95 (*0-397-51555-3*) Lppncott W & W.

Pathology. Edward F. Goljan. Ed. by William Schmitt. LC 97-37850. (Saunders Text & Review Series (STARS)). (Illus.). 560p. (C). 1998. pap. text 29.95 (*0-7216-7023-7*, W B Saunders Co) Harcrt Hlth Sci Grp.

Pathology. N. K. Hall & D. L. Feeback. (Oklahoma Notes Ser.). (Illus.). xi, 223p. (C). 1987. pap. 12.95 (*0-387-96338-3*) Spr-Verlag.

Pathology. Emanuel Rubin et al. LC 65-8626. (Illus.). 1824p. 1988. text 62.50 (*0-397-50698-8*, Lippnctt) Lppncott W & W.

Pathology. Schneider. (Board Review Ser.). 1992. 19.95 (*0-685-75192-9*) Lppncott W & W.

Pathology. Arthur S. Schneider & Philip A. Szanto. LC 92-49705. (Board Review Ser.). (Illus.). 412p. 1993. pap. 19.95 (*0-683-07608-6*) Lppncott W & W.

Pathology. Alan Stevens & Jim Lowe. 1994. 49.00 (*0-397-44764-7*) Mosby Inc.

Pathology. 2nd ed. J. B. Holliman et al. xii, 231p. 1991. pap. 16.95 (*0-387-96718-4*) Spr-Verlag.

Pathology. 2nd ed. Ed. by Emanuel Rubin et al. LC 93-15103. (Illus.). 1578p. 1993. text 69.50 (*0-397-51047-0*) Lppncott W & W.

Pathology. 3rd ed. J. H. Holliman. (Oklahoma Notes Ser.). (Illus.). 224p. 1993. 16.95 (*0-387-97780-5*) Spr-Verlag.

Pathology. 3rd ed. Ed. by Virginia A. LiVolsi et al. LC 93-16371. (National Medical Series for Independent Study). (Illus.). 530p. 1994. pap. 26.00 (*0-683-06243-3*) Lppncott W & W.

Pathology. 3rd ed. Emanuel Rubin. LC 98-3831. 18p. 1998. text 71.95 (*0-397-58422-9*) Lppncott W & W.

Pathology. 3rd ed. Schneider. (National Medical Ser.). 1993. 25.00 (*0-685-75180-5*) Lppncott W & W.

Pathology. 4th ed. John H. Holliman. LC 94-47452. (Oklahoma Notes Ser.). 279p. 1995. 17.95 (*0-387-94390-0*) Spr-Verlag.

Pathology. 9th ed. Earl J. Brown. (Basic Sciences: Pretest Self Assessment & Review Ser.). (Illus.). 1998. pap. 18.95 (*0-07-052686-9*) McGraw-Hill HPD.

Pathology: Basic & Science. Woolf. 1998. pap. text 80.00 (*0-7020-2291-8*, W B Saunders Co) Harcrt Hlth Sci Grp.

Pathology: Digging up the Bones, Vol. 3. 2nd ed. Linas M. Linardakis. LC 97-49310. (Digging Up the Bones Medical Review Ser.). (Illus.). 44p. 1997. pap. text 18.95 (*0-07-038216-6*) McGraw-Hill HPD.

Pathology: Examination & Board Review. James R. Newland. 360p. (C). 1995. pap. text 32.95 (*0-8385-7719-9*, A7719-6, Apple Lange Med) McGraw.

Pathology: Examination & Board Review. 2nd ed. James R. Newland. 1999. pap. 31.95 (*0-8385-8264-8*, Medical Exam) Appleton & Lange.

Pathology: Implications for the Physical Therapists. Catherine C. Goodman & William G. Bossonnault. Ed. by Margaret Biblis. LC 97-7701. (Illus.). 864p. 1997. text 65.00 (*0-7216-5636-6*, W B Saunders Co) Harcrt Hlth Sci Grp.

Pathology: International Edition. Goljan. (C). 1998. pap. text 17.50 (*0-8089-2061-8*, Grune & Strat) Harcrt Hlth Sci Grp.

Pathology: Pretest Self-Assessment & Review. 5th ed. Margaret H. Clements. 1988. pap. text 15.95 (*0-07-051965-X*) McGraw.

Pathology No. 2: The Mechanisms of Disease. 2nd ed. Roderick A. Cawson et al. (Illus.). 592p. (C). (gr. 13). 1989. pap. text 49.95 (*0-8016-1246-2*, 01246) Mosby Inc.

***Pathology & Genetics of Tumours of the Nervous System.** 2nd ed. Ed. by P. Kleihues & W. K. Cavanee. 314p. 2000. pap. text 75.00 (*92-832-2409-4*, Pub. by IARC) OUP.

Pathology & Identity: The Work of Mother Earth in Trinidad. Roland Littlewood. LC 92-18251. (Cambridge Studies in Social & Cultural Anthropology: No. 90). (Illus.). 348p. (C). 1993. text 95.00 (*0-521-38427-3*) Cambridge U Pr.

Pathology & Immunology of Transplantation & Rejection. Sathia Thiru & Herman Waldmann. (Illus.). 592p. 2000. 220.00 (*0-632-03676-1*) Blackwell Sci.

Pathology & Laboratory Medicine 2000. (Illus.). 500p. 2000. text 79.95 (*0-8151-2496-1*, 31768) Mosby Inc.

Pathology & Microbiology. Sharon S. Rowland. LC 94-14073. 416p. 1994. pap. text, lab manual ed. 32.00 (*0-316-76049-8*, Little Brwn Med Div) Lppncott W & W.

Pathology & Pathobiology of the Urinary Bladder & Prostate. Ronald S. Weinstein & William A. Gardner, Jr. LC 92-5499. (Monographs in Pathology: No. 34). (Illus.). 221p. 1992. 90.00 (*0-683-08911-0*) Lppncott W & W.

Pathology & Pathogenesis of Human Viral Disease. John E. Craighead. 600p. 1999. 99.95 (*0-12-195160-X*) Acad Pr.

Pathology & Physiology of Allergic Reactions. Ed. by P. S. Norman. (Journal: International Archives of Allergy & Applied Immunology: Vol. 77, No. 1-2). (Illus.). 280p. 1985. pap. 101.00 (*3-8055-4056-6*) S Karger.

Pathology & Therapeutics for Pharmacists. Greene & Harris. (Illus.). 616p. (Orig.). 1994. mass mkt. 58.95 (*0-412-61100-7*, Chap & Hall NY) Chapman & Hall.

Pathology & Therapeutics for Pharmacists: A Basis for Clinical Pharmacy Practice. Russell J. Greene & Norman D. Harris. (Illus.). 736p. 1993. mass mkt. 164.95 (*0-412-36000-4*, A7510) Chapman & Hall.

Pathology & Trauma. 2nd ed. J. K. Mason. 384p. 1993. text 165.00 (*0-340-54820-7*, Pub. by E A) OUP.

Pathology Annual, 1988, Vol. 23, Pt. 1. Ed. by Paul P. Rosen & Robert E. Fechner. (Illus.). 352p. (C). 1988. pap. text 95.00 (*0-8385-7781-4*, A7781-6, Apple Lange Med) McGraw.

Pathology Annual, 1988, Vol. 23, Pt. 2. Ed. by Paul P. Rosen & Robert E. Fechner. (Illus.). 416p. (C). 1992. pap. text 95.00 (*0-8385-7789-X*, A7789-9, Apple Lange Med) McGraw.

Pathology Annual, 1989, Vol. 24, Pt. 1. Ed. by Paul P. Rosen & Robert E. Fechner. 400p. (C). 1989. pap. text 95.00 (*0-8385-7733-4*, A7733-7, Apple Lange Med) McGraw.

Pathology Annual, 1989, Vol. 24, Pt. 1. 2nd ed. Ed. by Paul P. Rosen & Robert E. Fechner. 352p. (C). 1989. pap. text 95.00 (*0-8385-7713-X*, A7713-9, Apple Lange Med) McGraw.

Pathology Annual, 1990, Vol. 25, Pt. 1. Paul P. Rosen & Robert E. Fechner. (Illus.). 416p. (C). 1989. pap. text 95.00 (*0-8385-7714-8*, A7714-7, Apple Lange Med) McGraw.

Pathology Annual, 1990, Vol. 25, Pt. 2. Paul P. Rosen & Robert E. Fechner. (Illus.). 400p. (C). 1990. pap. text 95.00 (*0-8385-7814-4*, A7814-5, Apple Lange Med) McGraw.

Pathology Annual, 1995, Vol. 30, Pt. 1. Robert E. Fechner & Paul P. Rosen. (C). 1995. pap. text 95.00 (*0-8385-7699-0*, A7699-0, Apple Lange Med) McGraw.

Pathology Annual, 1995, Vol. 30, Pt 2. Paul P. Rosen & Robert E. Fechner. (Illus.). 208p. (C). 1995. pap. text 95.00 (*0-8385-8109-9*, A8109-9, Apple Lange Med) McGraw.

Pathology Annual, 1994, Vol. 29, Pt. 1. Paul P. Rosen & Robert E. Fechner. (Illus.). 320p. (C). 1994. pap. text 95.00 (*0-8385-7723-7*, A7723-8, Apple Lange Med) McGraw.

Pathology Annual, 1994, Vol. 29, Pt. 2. Paul P. Rosen & Robert E. Fechner. (C). 1994. pap. text 95.00 (*0-8385-7700-8*, A7700-6, Apple Lange Med) McGraw.

Pathology Annual, 1991, Vol. 26, Pt. 2. Ed. by Paul P. Rosen & Robert E. Fechner. (Illus.). 304p. (C). 1992. pap. text 95.00 (*0-8385-7717-2*, A7717-0, Apple Lange Med) McGraw.

Pathology Annual, 1993, Vol. 28, Pt. 1. Paul P. Rosen & Robert E. Fechner. (Illus.). 304p. (C). 1992. pap. text 95.00 (*0-8385-7721-0*, A7721-2, Apple Lange Med) McGraw.

Pathology Annual, 1993, Vol. 28, Pt. 2. Paul P. Rosen. Ed. by Robert E. Fechner. 272p. (C). 1993. pap. text 95.00 (*0-8385-7722-9*, A7722-0, Apple Lange Med) McGraw.

Pathology Annual, 1992, Vol. 27, Pt. 2. Ed. by Paul P. Rosen & Robert E. Fechner. (Illus.). 320p. (C). 1992. pap. text 95.00 (*0-8385-7720-2*, A7720-4, Apple Lange Med) McGraw.

Pathology for Health Sciences. Vardaxis. 1995. text 66.00 (*0-443-05324-3*, W B Saunders Co) Harcrt Hlth Sci Grp.

Pathology for Massage Technicians: A Companion to the Merck Manual. Usha Honeyman. (Illus.). 116p. 1995. spiral bd. 29.00 (*0-9673767-0-X*, 001-PMT) Oos Pubg.

Pathology for Surgeons. 2nd ed. Roy A. Spence et al. (Illus.). 656p. 1993. 150.00 (*0-7506-1382-3*) Buttrwrth-Heinemann.

Pathology for Surgeons in Training. 2nd ed. David Tweedle. (Arnold Publication). (Illus.). 416p. 1996. pap. text 45.00 (*0-340-60374-7*) OUP.

Pathology for the Health-Related Professions. Ivan Damjanov. (Illus.). 570p. 1996. pap., teacher ed. write for info. (*0-7216-6473-3*, W B Saunders Co) Harcrt Hlth Sci Grp.

An Asterisk (*) at the beginning of an entry indicates that the title is appearing for the first time.

Pathology for the Health-Related Professions. Ivan Damjanov. LC 99-27976. (Illus.). 555p. 2000. pap. text. write for info. (0-7216-8118-2, W B Saunders Co) Harcrt Hlth Sci Grp.

Pathology for the Health Related Professions: Instructor's Manual. 2nd ed. Ivan Damjanov. 95p. Date not set. pap. text, teacher ed. write for info. (0-7216-8119-0, W B Saunders Co) Harcrt Hlth Sci Grp.

Pathology for the Surgeon. Peter M. Banks & William G. Kraybill. Ed. by Larry McGrew. LC 95-11487. 416p. 1996. text 77.00 (0-7216-5288-3, W B Saunders Co) Harcrt Hlth Sci Grp.

Pathology Illustrated. 3rd ed. Alasdair D. Govan et al. LC 90-1981. (Illus.). 882p. (Orig.). 1991. reprint ed. pap. 200.00 (0-7837-9743-5, 206047100005) Bks Demand.

Pathology Illustrated. 4th ed. Alasdair D. T. Govan et al. LC 94-20077. (Illus.). (Orig.). 1995. pap. text 61.00 (0-443-05068-6) Church.

***Pathology Illustrated.** 5th ed. Peter S. Macfarlane et al. LC 99-28979. 2000. write for info. (0-443-05957-8) Church.

Pathology in a Nutshell. Groysman. 1999. pap. text 19.95 (0-8385-8175-7, Medical Exam) Appleton & Lange.

Pathology in Dentistry. Edward Sheffield. (Illus.). 292p. (C). 1996. pap. text 59.50 (0-19-262421-0) OUP.

Pathology in Dentistry: Systems-Based Pathology for Dental Students. Edward Sheffield. (Illus.). 292p. 1996. text 120.00 (0-19-262422-9) OUP.

Pathology in Gynecology & Obstetrics. 4th ed. Claude Gompel. 700p. (C). 1993. text 173.00 (0-397-51226-0) Lppncott W & W.

Pathology in Marine Science. Ed. by Frank O. Perkins & Thomas C. Cheng. 538p. 1990. text 115.00 (0-12-550755-0) Acad Pr.

***Pathology Integrated: An A-Z of Disease & Its Pathologensis.** Peter M. Lydyard et al. (An Arnold Publication). 2000. pap. text 32.50 (0-340-74063-9, Pub. by E A) OUP.

Pathology Medical Transcription: MDT 122. S. Turley. 142p. (C). 1993. student ed., ring bd. write for info. (0-933195-53-2) CA College Health Sci.

Pathology Notes. Parakrama Chandrasoma & Clive R. Taylor. (Illus.). 636p. (C). 1992. pap. text 27.95 (0-8385-5164-5, A5164-7, Apple Lange Med) McGraw.

Pathology Occupational Lung Disease. 2nd ed. Churg. 95.00 (0-683-30386-4) Lppncott W & W.

Pathology of Adrenal & Extra-Adrenal Paragaglia. Ernest E. Lack. LC 93-32870. (Major Problems in Pathology Ser.: Vol. 29). 1994. text 79.00 (0-7216-5263-8, W B Saunders Co) Harcrt Hlth Sci Grp.

Pathology of Aging Syrian Hamsters. R. Schmidt & R. Eason. LC 82-20713. 256p. 1983. 145.00 (0-8493-5099-9, CRC Reprint) Franklin.

Pathology of Asbestos-Associated Diseases. Victor L. Roggli et al. LC 92-13417. 432p. 1992. text 169.00 (0-316-75423-4, Little Brwn Med Div) Lppncott W & W.

Pathology of Bladder Cancer, 2 Vols., Vol. I. Ed. by George T. Bryan & Samuel M. Cohen. 148p. 1983. 118.00 (0-8493-6225-3, RD755, CRC Reprint) Franklin.

Pathology of Bladder Cancer, 2 Vols., Vol. II. Ed. by George T. Bryan & Samuel M. Cohen. 256p. 1983. 141.00 (0-8493-6226-1, CRC Reprint) Franklin.

Pathology of Bone. P. A. Revell. (Illus.). 320p. 1985. 204.00 (0-387-15418-3) Spr-Verlag.

Pathology of Bone & Joint Disorders: With Clinical & Radiographic Correlation. Edward F. McCarthy & Frank J. Frassica. Ed. by Alan Ross. LC 97-27845. (Illus.). 384p. (C). 1998. text 95.00 (0-7216-6336-2, W B Saunders Co) Harcrt Hlth Sci Grp.

Pathology of Bone & Joint Neoplasms. Timothy R. Helliwell & Allan Ross. LC 97-48343. (Major Problems in Pathology Ser.). 415p. (C). 1998. text 75.00 (0-7216-6439-3, W B Saunders Co) Harcrt Hlth Sci Grp.

Pathology of Bone Marrow. Faramarz Naeim. LC 91-35311. (Illus.). 376p. 1992. 175.00 (0-89640-209-6) Igaku-Shoin.

Pathology of Bone Marrow. 2nd ed. Faramarz Naeim. LC 97-42119. 1998. 149.00 (0-683-30336-8) Lppncott W & W.

Pathology of Bone Tumors: Personal Experience. Andre Mazabraud. LC 97-29696. (Illus.). 550p. 1998. 175.00 (3-540-62751-0) Spr-Verlag.

Pathology of Cardiovascular Disease. H. Thomas Aretz. 650p. 1997. text 125.00 (0-397-51455-7) Lppncott W & W.

Pathology of Cerebrospinal Microcirculation. fac. ed. Ed. by Jorge Cervos-Navarro et al. LC 77-84125. (Advances in Neurology Ser.: No. 20). (Illus.). 632p. pap. 196.00 (0-7837-7256-4, 204704900005) Bks Demand.

Pathology of Computer Viruses. David Ferbrache. xiii, 299p. 1994. 64.34 (0-387-19610-2) Spr-Verlag.

Pathology of Congenital Heart Disease: A Personal Experience with More Than 6,300 Congenitally Malformed Hearts, 2 vols. Saroja Bharati & Maurice Lev. (Illus.). 1608p. 1996. 395.00 (0-87993-556-1) Futura Pub.

Pathology of Corruption S. S. Gill. LC 98-904539. xv, 295 p. 1998. write for info. (81-7223-302-7) CE25.

Pathology of Devices. Ed. by C. L. Berry. LC 93-32868. (Current Topics in Pathology Ser.: Vol. 86). 1994. 237.00 (0-387-54393-7) Spr-Verlag.

Pathology of Domestic Animals, 3 vols. 4th ed. Jubb. 1993. 210.00 (0-12-391604-6) Acad Pr.

Pathology of Domestic Animals. 4th ed. Ed. by K. V. Jubb et al. (Illus.). 780p. 1992. text 104.00 (0-12-391605-4) Acad Pr.

Pathology of Domestic Animals, Vol. 2. 4th ed. Ed. by K. V. Jubb et al. (Illus.). 747p. 1992. text 104.00 (0-12-391606-2) Acad Pr.

Pathology of Domestic Animals, Vol. 3. 4th ed. Ed. by K. V. Jubb et al. (Illus.). 653p. 1993. text 104.00 (0-12-391607-0) Acad Pr.

Pathology of Drug Abuse. Steven B. Karch. 416p. 1993. lib. bdg. 80.95 (0-8493-4418-2, R) CRC Pr.

Pathology of Drug Abuse. 2nd ed. Steven B. Karch. (Illus.). 480p. 1996. boxed set 84.95 (0-8493-9464-3) CRC Pr.

Pathology of Drug-Induced & Toxic Diseases. Ed. by Robert H. Riddell. LC 82-4230. (Illus.). 696p. reprint ed. pap. 200.00 (0-7837-2584-1, 204274500006) Bks Demand.

Pathology of Early Cervical Neoplasia. Christopher P. Crum et al. LC 96-29476. (Contemporary Issues in Surgical Pathology Ser.). 1996. text 95.00 (0-443-07590-5) Church.

Pathology of Eating: Psychology & Treatment. Sara D. Gilbert. 256p. 1986. 37.50 (0-7102-0271-7, 02717, Routledge Thoemms) Routledge.

Pathology of Emerging Infections. C. Robert Horsburgh & Ann M. Nelson. LC 97-13857. (Illus.). 325p. 1997. 89.95 (1-55581-120-5) ASM Pr.

Pathology of Emerging Infections 2. Ed. by Ann M. Nelson & C. Robert Horsburgh. LC 98-8770. (Illus.). 460p. 1998. 89.95 (1-55581-140-X) ASM Pr.

Pathology of English Renaissance: Sacred Remains & Holy Ghosts. Elizabeth Mazzola. LC 98-25295. (Studies in the History of Christian Thought: Vol. 86). (Illus.). 168p. 1998. 64.00 (90-04-11195-6) Brill Academic Pubs.

Pathology of Erythroblastic Mitosis in Occupational Benzenic Erythropathy & Erythremia. E. G. Rondanelli et al. (Bibliotheca Haemotologica Ser.: No. 35). (Illus.). 1969. pap. 66.25 (3-8055-0139-0) S Karger.

***Pathology of Eurocentrism.** Charles W. Ephraim. LC 99-23364. 1999. write for info. (0-86543-755-6) Africa World.

Pathology of Fishes. Ed. by William E. Ribelin & George Migaki. LC 73-15261. (Illus.). 1016p. 1975. 75.00 (0-299-06520-0, 652) U of Wis Pr.

Pathology of Food & Pasture Legumes. Ed. by D. J. Allen & J. M. Lenne. LC 97-15283. (A CAB International Publication). (Illus.). 776p. (C). 1998. text 175.00 (0-85199-166-1) OUP.

***Pathology of Genetically Engineered Mice.** Ed. by Jerrold Michael Ward et al. LC 00-38477. (Illus.). 520p. 2000. 174.95 (0-8138-2521-0) Iowa St U Pr.

Pathology of Granulomas. Ed. by Harry L. Ioachim. LC 82-18586. (Illus.). 551p. 1983. reprint ed. pap. 170.90 (0-608-07248-6, 206747400009) Bks Demand.

Pathology of Heart Valve Replacement. A. G. Rose. 1987. text 229.00 (0-85200-984-4) Kluwer Academic.

Pathology of Higher Education. A. P. Srivastava. 294p. 1979. 14.95 (0-318-36830-7) Asia Bk Corp.

Pathology of Homicide: A Vade Mecum for Pathologist, Prosecutor & Defense Counsel. fac. ed. Lester Adelson. (Illus.). 992p. 1974. 141.95 (0-398-03000-6) C C Thomas.

Pathology of Human Placenta. 3rd ed. Kurt Benirschke & Peter Kaufmann. LC 94-25783. (Illus.). 871p. 1995. 179.00 (0-387-94335-8) Spr-Verlag.

Pathology of Implanted Devices. Nir Kossovsky. 1993. write for info. (0-397-51137-X) Lppncott W & W.

Pathology of Incipient Neoplasia. 2nd ed. Ed. by Donald Henson & Jorge Albores-Saavedra. LC 92-11723. (Major Problems in Pathology Ser.: Vol. 28). (Illus.). 590p. 1992. text 99.00 (0-7216-6457-1, W B Saunders Co) Harcrt Hlth Sci Grp.

***Pathology of Incipient Neoplasia.** 3rd ed. Ed. by Donald Earl Henson & Jorge Albores-Saavedra. LC 99-52562. (Illus.). 880p. 2000. text 165.00 (0-19-512338-7) OUP.

Pathology of Infectious Diseases. Franz Von Lichtenberg. LC 88-43371. (Illus.). 383p. 1991. reprint ed. pap. 118.80 (0-608-05804-1, 205976900007) Bks Demand.

Pathology of Infectious Diseases, Vol. I. Connor. (C). 1997. 176.00 (0-8385-7693-1) Appleton & Lange.

Pathology of Infectious Diseases, Vol. II. Connor. (C). 1997. 176.00 (0-8385-7694-X) Appleton & Lange.

Pathology of Influenza. Milton C. Winternitz et al. 1920. pap. 89.50 (0-614-01814-5) Elliots Bks.

Pathology of Lies. Jonathan Keats. LC 98-41168. 288p. 1999. mass mkt. 14.00 (0-446-67445-1, Pub. by Warner Bks) Little.

Pathology of Limb Ischaema. Henry Dible. LC 67-27239. (Illus.). 110p. 1967. 9.00 (0-87527-030-1) Green.

Pathology of Lymph Nodes. Lawrence M. Weiss. LC 96-19840. (Contemporary Issues in Surgical Pathology Ser.). 1996. text 105.00 (0-443-07620-0) Church.

Pathology of Melanocytic Nevi & Malignant Melanoma of the Skin. Raymond L. Barnhill. LC 94-33338. (Illus.). 294p. 1994. pap. text 175.00 (0-7506-9504-8) Buttrwrth-Heinemann.

Pathology of Multiple Pregnancy. Virginia J. Baldwin. LC 92-48343. 1993. 193.00 (0-387-94011-1) Spr-Verlag.

Pathology of Neoplasia in Children & Adolescents. Ed. by Milton Finegold. (Major Problems in Pathology Ser.). (Illus.). 481p. 1986. text 104.00 (0-7216-1337-3, W B Saunders Co) Harcrt Hlth Sci Grp.

Pathology of Neoplastic & Endocrine Induced Diseases of the Breast. R. Bassler & Hubner. 484p. 1987. 220.00 (0-89574-232-2, Pub. by Gustav Fischer) Balogh.

Pathology of Occupational Lung Disease. Andrew M. Churg. LC 87-3296. (Illus.). 416p. 1988. 98.50 (0-89640-121-9) Igaku-Shoin.

Pathology of Occupational Lung Disease. 2nd ed. Andrew Churg & Francis H. Green. LC 97-33344. 1998. write for info. (0-683-30342-2) Lppncott W & W.

Pathology of Organ Transplantation. George E. Sale. (Illus.). 327p. 1990. pap. text 115.00 (0-409-90133-4) Buttrwrth-Heinemann.

Pathology of Perinatal Brain Injury. Lucy B. Rorke. LC 81-40674. (Illus.). 168p. 1982. reprint ed. pap. 52.10 (0-608-00635-1, 206122300007) Bks Demand.

Pathology of Periodontal Disease. David M. Williams et al. (Illus.). 160p. 1992. text 75.00 (0-19-261955-1); pap. text 45.00 (0-19-262120-3) OUP.

Pathology of Politics: Violence, Betrayal, Corruption, Secrecy & Propaganda. Carl J. Friedrich. 1972. text 49.50 (0-8290-0343-6) Irvington.

Pathology of Protoplasm, Pt. 1. Ernst Kuester. (Handbuch der Pflanzenanatomie Encyclopedia of Plant Anatomy - Traite d' Anatomie Vegetale Ser.). (Illus.). 273p. 1996. 45.00 (969-8053-01-8, Pub. by Gebruder Borntraeger) Balogh.

Pathology of Pseudoneoplastic Lesions. Mark R. Wick et al. LC 96-43036. 250p. 1997. text 199.00 (0-7817-0302-6) Lppncott W & W.

Pathology of Public Policy. Brian W. Hogwood & B. Guy Peters. (Illus.). 228p. 1985. pap. text 21.00 (0-19-878010-9) OUP.

Pathology of Pulmonary Disease. Saldana. 984p. (C). 1993. text 271.00 (0-397-51257-0) Lppncott W & W.

Pathology of Pulmonary Hypertension. C. A. Wagenvoort & Noeke Wagenvoort. LC 76-39782. (Wiley Series in Clinical Cardiology). 359p. reprint ed. 111.30 (0-8357-9948-4, 201519800092) Bks Demand.

Pathology of Radiation Injury. Luis Felipe Fajardo. (C). (gr. 13). 1982. 87.00 (0-89352-182-5) Mosby Inc.

Pathology of Simian Primates, 2 pts., Set. Ed. by R. N. Fiennes. Incl. Pt. 1. General Pathology. 1972. 173.25 (3-8055-1307-0); Pt. 2. Infectious & Parasitic Diseases. 1972. 144.50 (3-8055-1308-9); (Illus.). 1972. 285.25 (3-8055-1329-1) S Karger.

Pathology of Skeletal Muscle. Stirling Carpenter & George Karpati. LC 84-1849. (Illus.). 798p. reprint ed. pap. 200.00 (0-8357-4662-3, 203759200008) Bks Demand.

***Pathology of Skeletal Muscle.** 2nd ed. Stirling Carpenter & George Karpati. (Illus.). 584p. 2000. text 195.00 (0-19-506364-3) OUP.

Pathology of Solid Tumours in Children. Ed. by Stoker & Frederic B. Askin. LC 98-118515. 360p. 1997. text 125.00 (0-412-40170-3, Pub. by E A) OUP.

Pathology of Systemic Lupus. Antonovych. (Illus.). 175p. 1995. pap. text 35.00 (1-881041-23-9) Am Registry Path.

Pathology of Systems see Oxford Textbook of Pathology

Pathology of the Adrenal Glands. Ed. by Ernest E. Lack. LC 89-22177. (Contemporary Issues in Surgical Pathology Ser.: No. 14). (Illus.). 399p. 1990. reprint ed. pap. 123.70 (0-7837-6812-5, 204664400003) Bks Demand.

Pathology of the Aging Human Nervous System. Serge Duckett. LC 90-6638. (Illus.). 505p. 1991. text 99.00 (0-8121-1355-1) Lppncott W & W.

Pathology of the Bone Marrow. Ed. by K. Lennert & K. Hubner. (Illus.). 426p. 1984. lib. bdg. 115.00 (0-89574-195-4, Pub. by Gustav Fischer) Balogh.

Pathology of the Breast. Paul P. Rosen. LC 96-6385. 928p. 1996. text 288.00 (0-397-51694-0) Lppncott W & W.

Pathology of the Breast. Silverberg. 1997. text. write for info. (0-7216-5059-7, W B Saunders Co) Harcrt Hlth Sci Grp.

Pathology of the Breast. Fattaneh A. Tavassoli. 669p. (C). 1992. pap. text 215.00 (0-8385-7702-4, A7702-2) Appleton & Lange.

Pathology of the Breast. 2nd ed. Fatteneh A. Tavassoli. LC 98-50680. (Illus.). 669p. 1999. 250.00 (0-8385-7704-0, Apple Lange Med) McGraw.

Pathology of the Colon, Small Intestine & Anus. 2nd ed. Ed. by H. Thomas Norris. (Contemporary Issues in Surgical Pathology Ser.: Vol. 17). (Illus.). 414p. 1991. text 126.00 (0-443-08729-6) Church.

Pathology of the Ear. Harold F. Schuknecht. LC 73-92802. (Illus.). 521p. reprint ed. pap. 161.60 (0-7837-4189-8, 205903900012) Bks Demand.

Pathology of the Ear. 2nd ed. Harold F. Schuknecht. LC 92-49497. (Illus.). 672p. 1993. text 155.00 (0-8121-1562-7) Lppncott W & W.

Pathology of the Ear & Temporal Bone. George T. Nager. LC 93-27739. (Illus.). 1408p. 1993. 295.00 (0-683-63049-0) Lppncott W & W.

Pathology of the Esophagus. H. T. Enterline & J. J. Thompson. (Illus.). 225p. 1984. 150.00 (0-387-90896-X) Spr-Verlag.

Pathology of the Eye. Gottfried O. Naumann & D. J. Apple. (Illus.). xxxv, 998p. 1986. 460.00 (0-387-96044-9) Spr-Verlag.

Pathology of the Fetus & the Infant. Edith L. Potter & John M. Craig. LC 75-16021. 711p. reprint ed. pap. 200.00 (0-608-16240-X, 202650500049) Bks Demand.

Pathology of the Fischer Rat: Reference & Atlas. Ed. by Gary A. Boorman et al. 580p. 1990. text 167.00 (0-12-115640-0) Acad Pr.

Pathology of the Gallbladder, Biliary Tract & Pancreas. David A. Owen & James Kelly. (Illus.). Date not set. text. write for info. (0-7216-1910-X, W B Saunders Co) Harcrt Hlth Sci Grp.

Pathology of the Gastro-Intestinal Tract. Ed. by Si-Chun Ming & Harvey Goldman. (Illus.). 975p. 1991. text 250.00 (0-7216-6398-2, W B Saunders Co) Harcrt Hlth Sci Grp.

Pathology of the Gastrointestinal Tract. 2nd ed. Si-Chun Ming & Harvey Goldman. LC 97-22939. 904p. 1997. write for info. (0-683-18007-X) Lppncott W & W.

Pathology of the Head & Neck. Armed Forces Institute of Pathology Staff. (C). 1992. 700.00 incl. disk (1-56815-011-3) Mosby Inc.

***Pathology of the Head & Neck: With Clinical Correlations.** Yao Shi Fu et al. (Illus.). 1998. text. write for info. (0-443-07558-1) Church.

Pathology of the Human Embryo & Previable Fetus. Dagmar K. Kalousek. (Illus.). 232p. 1990. 142.00 (0-387-97168-8) Spr-Verlag.

Pathology of the Human Placenta. 2nd ed. Kurt Benirschke & P. Kaufmann. (Illus.). xiv, 878p. 1992. 218.00 (0-387-97282-X) Spr-Verlag.

***Pathology of the Human Placenta.** 4th ed. Kurt Benirschke & Peter Kaufmann. LC 99-32440. 944p. 2000. 189.00 (0-387-98894-7) Spr-Verlag.

Pathology of the Kidney, 3 vols. 3rd ed. Robert H. Heptinstall. 1983. 225.00 (0-316-35797-9, Little Brwn Med Div) Lppncott W & W.

Pathology of the Kidney, 3 vols. 4th ed. Heptinstall. 2368p. 1991. text 375.00 (0-316-35803-7) Lppncott W & W.

Pathology of the Liver. 2nd ed. Ed. by Robert MacSween et al. (Illus.). 717p. 1987. 230.00 (0-443-03049-9) Church.

Pathology of the Liver. 3rd ed. Ed. by Roderick N. MacSween et al. LC 94-33377. 1994. text 270.00 (0-443-04454-6) Church.

Pathology of the Lung. Ed. by G. G. Pietra. (Journal: Applied Pathology: Vol. 4, No. 3, 1986). (Illus.). 96p. 1987. pap. 40.00 (3-8055-4573-8) S Karger.

Pathology of the Lung. 2nd ed. Ed. by William M. Thurlbeck & Andrew M. Churg. (Illus.). 1178p. 1995. 219.00 (0-86577-534-6) Thieme Med Pubs.

***Pathology of the Lungs.** B. Corrin. (Illus.). 704p. 1999. text. write for info. (0-443-05713-3, W B Saunders Co) Harcrt Hlth Sci Grp.

Pathology of the Mesothelium. Ed. by J. S. Jones. (Illus.). 1987. 167.00 (0-387-16208-9) Spr-Verlag.

Pathology of the Nucleus. Ed. by J. C. Underwood. (Current Topics in Pathology Ser.: Vol. 82). (Illus.). 352p. 1990. 211.00 (0-387-51018-4) Spr-Verlag.

Pathology of the Pancreas. A. H. Cruickshank. (Illus.). 290p. 1986. 173.00 (0-387-16216-X) Spr-Verlag.

Pathology of the Pancreas. 2nd ed. A. H. Cruickshank & E. W. Benbow. LC 95-33. 358p. 1995. 145.00 (3-540-19923-3) Spr-Verlag.

Pathology of the Parathyroid & Thyroid Glands. Ed. by Virginia A. LiVolsi & Ronald A. DeLellis. LC 92-48313. (Monographs in Pathology: No. 35). (Illus.). 203p. 1993. 90.00 (0-683-04817-1) Lppncott W & W.

Pathology of the Peripheral Nerve. Edward P. Richardson, Jr. & Umberto DeGirolami. LC 94-20440. (Major Problems in Pathology Ser.: No. 32). 176p. 1994. text 64.00 (0-7216-3298-X, W B Saunders Co) Harcrt Hlth Sci Grp.

Pathology of the Placenta. 2nd ed. Steven H. Lewis & Eugene Perrin. LC 98-23008. (Contemporary Issues in Surgical Pathology Ser.: Vol. 23). (Illus.). 432p. (C). 1998. text 99.00 (0-443-07586-7) Church.

Pathology of the Placenta MPP. 2nd ed. Fox. 1997. text 115.00 (0-7020-2196-2) Bailliere Tindall.

Pathology of the Prostate. Christopher S. Foster & David G. Bostwick. Ed. by Lesley Day. LC 96-23370. (Major Problems in Pathology Ser.: Vol. 34). (Illus.). 464p. 1997. text 95.00 (0-7216-6951-4, W B Saunders Co) Harcrt Hlth Sci Grp.

Pathology of the Skin. Evan Farmer & Antoinette F. Hood. (Illus.). 1008p. (C). 1995. pap. text 175.00 (0-8385-7715-6, A7715-4, Apple Lange Med) McGraw.

Pathology of the Skin. 2nd ed. Phillip H. McKee. 1996. 345.00 (1-56375-588-2) Gower-Mosby.

Pathology of the Skin. 2nd rev. ed. Evan R. Farmer. LC 98-18993. (Illus.). 987p. (C). 1999. 210.00 (0-8385-8079-3, Apple Lange Med) McGraw.

Pathology of the Skin Atlas. Hurwitz & Hood. LC 97-37911. 535p. (C). 1997. 195.00 (0-8385-7689-3, A-7689-1, Apple Lange Med) McGraw.

Pathology of the Syrian Hamster. Ed. by F. Homburger. (Progress in Experimental Tumor Research Ser.: Vol. 16). 1972. 163.50 (3-8055-1367-4) S Karger.

Pathology of the Testes. Reuter. 1997. text. write for info. (0-7216-4977-7) Harcourt.

Pathology of the Thymus & Mediastinum. Michael J. Kornstein. LC 94-19417. (Illus.). 256p. 1995. text 68.00 (0-7216-4337-X, W B Saunders Co) Harcrt Hlth Sci Grp.

Pathology of the Thyroid. 2nd ed. Virginia A. Livolsi. 1999. text. write for info. (0-7216-6324-9) Harcourt.

Pathology of the Thyroid MPP. Virginia A. Livolsi. (Illus.). 448p. 1990. text 92.00 (0-7216-5782-6, W B Saunders Co) Harcrt Hlth Sci Grp.

Pathology of the U. S. Economy: The Costs of a Low-Wage System. Michael Perelman. 250p. 1996. pap. 18.95 (0-312-12685-9) St Martin.

Pathology of the Urinary Bladder. Robert H. Young. (Contemporary Issues in Surgical Pathology Ser.: Vol. 13). (Illus.). 413p. 1989. text 112.00 (0-443-08603-6) Church.

Pathology of the Vessel Wall: A Modern Appraisal. Ed. by Neville Woolf. 359p. 1983. 75.00 (0-275-91419-4, C1419, Praeger Pubs) Greenwood.

Pathology of Transcription & Translation. Ed. by Emmanuel Farber. LC 72-83122. (Biochemistry of Disease Ser.: No. 2). (Illus.). 190p. reprint ed. pap. 58.90 (0-8357-6251-3, 205229900090) Bks Demand.

***Pathology of Trauma.** 3rd ed. Ken Mason. Ed. by Basil Purdue. LC 99-16933. (Illus.). 576p. 2000. text 225.00 (0-340-69189-1, Pub. by E A) OUP.

Pathology of Tropical & Extraordinary Diseases, 2 vols. 1994. lib. bdg. 750.95 (0-8490-5629-2) Gordon Pr.

Pathology of Tropical Food Legumes: Disease Resistance in Crop Improvement. D. J. Allen. LC 82-20301. (Illus.). 431p. reprint ed. pap. 133.70 (0-8357-4396-9, 205233900007) Bks Demand.

Pathology of Tuberculosis in Old Age. L. Haranghy & C. Szemenyei. 210p. (C). 1974. 37.50 (963-05-0005-1, Pub. by Akade Kiado) St Mut.

***Pathology of Tumors of the Central Nervous System: A Guide to Histologic Diagnosis.** Roger E. McLendon et al. (An Arnold Publication). 2000. text 179.50 (0-340-70071-8) E A.

Pathology of Tumours. 4th ed. Rupert A. Willis. LC 68-69740. (Illus.). 1077p. reprint ed. pap. 200.00 (0-608-18016-5, 205632200058) Bks Demand.

Pathology of Tumours in Laboratory Animals: Tumours of the Hamster, Vol. 3. 2nd ed. Ed. by V. S.. Turusov & Ulrich Mohr. LC 97-109979. (IARC Scientific Publications: No. 126). (Illus.). 496p. 1996. text 124.00 (92-832-2126-5) OUP.

Pathology of Tumours in Laboratory Animals, 1979 Vol. 2: Tumours of the Mouse. International Agency for Research on Cancer Staff. LC SF0769.I5. (IARC Scientific Publications: No. 23). 678p. reprint ed. pap. 200.00 (0-7837-4000-X, 204383100002) Bks Demand.

Pathology of Tumours of the Nervous System. 5th ed. write for info. (0-340-50905-8, Pub. by E A) Routldge.

Pathology of Tumours of the Nervous System. 5th ed. Russell & Rubinstein. 974p. 1989. 249.00 (0-683-07462-8) Lppncott W & W.

Pathology of Unusual Malignant Cutaneous Tumors. Ed. by Mark R. Wick. LC 85-25361. (Clinical & Biochemical Analysis Ser.: No. 20). 435p. reprint ed. pap. 134.90 (0-7837-3340-2, 204329800008) Bks Demand.

Pathology of Viral Hepatitis. R. D. Goldin et al. LC 98-7631. (Arnold Publications). (Illus.). 192p. 1998. text 125.00 (0-340-59664-3) OUP.

Pathology of Zoo Animals: A Review of Necropsies Conducted over a Fourteen Year Period at the San Diego Zoo. Lynn A. Griner. LC 82-62698. (Illus.). 1983. 25.00 (0-911461-11-6) Zoological Soc.

Pathology Office Assistant. (Career Examination Ser.: C-3400). 1994. pap. 27.95 (0-8373-3400-4) Nat Learn.

Pathology Picture Tests. Alan Stevens & Jim Lowe. (C). (gr. 13). 1995. 21.00 (0-7234-2192-7, Pub. by Wolfe Pub) Mosby Inc.

Pathology Review. Goljan. (C). 1998. pap. text 13.50 (0-8089-2062-6, Grune & Strat) Harcrt Hlth Sci Grp.

Pathology Review. Edward F. Goljan. Ed. by William Schmitt. LC 97-37847. (Saunders Text & Review Series (STARS)). (Illus.). 304p. 1998. pap. text 19.95 (0-7216-7024-5, W B Saunders Co) Harcrt Hlth Sci Grp.

Pathology Review. Ashraf M. Hassanein & Barbara F. Atkins. LC 97-33791. (USMLE Step 1 Review Ser.). 336p. 1997. pap. 24.95 (0-7619-0517-0) Sage.

Pathology Review. Wurzel. 2001. text. write for info. (0-323-00837-2) Harcourt.

Pathology, Review for New National Boards. Frank N. Miller. LC 93-79828. 222p. 1993. pap. text 25.00 (0-9632873-3-8) J & S Pub VA.

Pathology Reviews - 1989. Ed. by Emanuel Rubin & Ivan Damjanov. (Illus.). 307p. 1989. 89.50 (0-89603-162-4) Humana.

Pathology Reviews, 1990. Ed. by Emanuel Rubin & Ivan Damjanov. (Illus.). 268p. 1990. 99.50 (0-89603-195-0) Humana.

Pathomechanism & Prevention of Sudden Cardiac Death Due to Coronary Insufficiency. Ed. by L. Szekeres et al. 319p. (C). 1984. 75.00 (963-05-3658-7, Pub. by Akade Kiado) St Mut.

Pathophys Biological/Behaviora. 2nd ed. Lee-Ellen C. Copstead & Jacquelyn L. Banasik. Ed. by Robin Carter. LC 98-53145. (Illus.). 1230p. 1999. text 66.00 (0-7216-7178-0, W B Saunders Co) Harcrt Hlth Sci Grp.

Pathophysiologic, Diagnostic & Therapeutic Aspects of Headache. Ed. by Mary E. Granger et al. (Pain & Headache Ser.: Vol. 4). 135p. 1976. 54.00 (3-8055-2282-7) S Karger.

Pathophysiologic Foundations of Critical Care. Michael R. Pinsky & Jean-Francois A. Dhainaut. LC 92-15867. (Illus.). 1008p. 1993. 125.00 (0-683-06888-1) Lppncott W & W.

Pathophysiological Aspects of Cancer Epidemiology. Ed. by G. Mathe & P. Reizenstein. (Advances in the Biosciences Ser.: No. 50). (Illus.). 276p. 1985. 99.00 (0-08-030780-9, Pergamon Pr) Elsevier.

Pathophysiological Phenomena in Nursing: Human Responses to Illness. 2nd ed. Carrieri et al. (Illus.). 622p. (C). 1993. text 79.00 (0-7216-3494-X, W B Saunders Co) Harcrt Hlth Sci Grp.

Pathophysiological Principles of Urology. Grannum R. Sant. LC 93-42937. 544p. 1993. pap. 55.00 (0-86542-221-4) Blackwell Sci.

Pathophysiological Problems in Clinical Nephrology: Proceedings of the Heidelberg Seminars in Nephrology, Heidelberg, September, 1978. Heidelberg Seminars in Nephrology Staff. Ed. by Eberhard Ritz et al. (Contributions to Nephrology Ser.: Vol. 14). (Illus.). 1978. 29.75 (3-8055-2910-4) S Karger.

Pathophysiologie. 5th ed. 1991. text 29.95 (3-540-17831-7) Spr-Verlag.

Pathophysiology. Chowdry. 1993. 53.75 (0-697-09850-8) McGraw.

Pathophysiology. Field. 2000. 27.95 (0-07-134499-3) McGraw.

Pathophysiology. Nowak. 1994. teacher ed. 14.06 (0-697-17438-7) McGraw.

Pathophysiology. 2nd ed. Catherine Paradiso. LC 99-11784. (Lippincott's Review Ser.). 1999. write for info. (0-7817-1843-0) Lppncott W & W.

Pathophysiology see Bile Acids: Chemistry, Physiology & Metabolism

Pathophysiology: A Physiological Approach. 2nd ed. Kathryn L. McCance. 1696p. (C). (gr. 13). 1993. text, teacher ed. 34.00 (0-8151-5749-5, 24200) Mosby Inc.

Pathophysiology: A Programmed Approach. Mary Burns. LC 97-41936. (C). 1998. pap. 39.95 (0-8385-8084-X) Appleton & Lange.

Pathophysiology: Adaptations & Alterations in Function. 4th ed. Barbara L. Bullock. LC 95-32143. 1,296p. 1995. text 63.95 (0-397-55164-9) Lppncott W & W.

Pathophysiology: An Introduction to Mechanisms of Disease. 2nd ed. Bernice L. Muir. LC 87-25298. 685p. 1989. text 44.00 (0-8273-4317-5) Delmar.

Pathophysiology: Application to Clinical Practice. Maureen Groer. 688p. pap. text 49.95 (0-7817-2336-1) Lppncott W & W.

Pathophysiology: Biological & Behavioral Perspectives: Instructor's Manual. 2nd ed. Jacquelyn L. Banasik. (Illus.). 335p. Date not set. teacher ed. write for info. (0-7216-7179-9, W B Saunders Co) Harcrt Hlth Sci Grp.

Pathophysiology: Biological & Behavioral: Study Guide for Copstead/Banasik. 2nd ed. Lee-Ellen C. Copstead & Jacquelyn L. Banasik. (Illus.). 350p. 1999. text, student ed. write for info. (0-7216-7183-7, W B Saunders Co) Harcrt Hlth Sci Grp.

Pathophysiology: Clinical Concepts of Disease Processes. 5th ed. Sylvia A. Price & Lorraine M. Wilson. (Illus.). teacher ed. write for info. (0-8151-2543-7) Mosby Inc.

Pathophysiology: Clinical Concepts of Disease Processes. 5th ed. Sylvia Anderson Price. Ed. by Lorraine McCarty Wilson. LC 96-15023. (Illus.). 1232p. (C). (gr. 13). 1996. text 66.00 (0-8151-6621-4, 24418) Mosby Inc.

Pathophysiology: Concepts of Altered Health States. 5th ed. Carol M. Porth. LC 97-49116. 1,328p. 1998. text 64.95 (0-397-55413-3) Lppncott W & W.

Pathophysiology: Foundations of Disease & Clinical Intervention. Margie Hansen. Ed. by Barbara N. Cullen. LC 96-38014. (Illus.). 1152p. 1998. text 61.95 (0-7216-4465-1, W B Saunders Co) Harcrt Hlth Sci Grp.

Pathophysiology: PreTest Self-Assessment & Review. Ed. by Maurice A. Mufson. LC 98-36684. (Basic Sciences: Pretest Self Assessment & Review Ser.). (Illus.). 250p. 1999. pap. text 18.95 (0-07-052692-3) McGraw-Hill HPD.

Pathophysiology: Principles of Disease. Martha J. Miller. (Illus.). 506p. 1983. teacher ed. write for info. (0-7216-2029-9, W B Saunders Co) Harcrt Hlth Sci Grp.

Pathophysiology: Principles of Disease. Martha J. Miller. (Illus.). 528p. 1983. text 62.95 (0-7216-6337-0, W B Saunders Co) Harcrt Hlth Sci Grp.

Pathophysiology: The Biological Basis for Disease in Adults & Children. 3rd ed. Kathryn L. McCance & Sue E. Huether. LC 97-22899. (Illus.). 1728p. (C). (gr. 13). 1997. text 66.00 (0-8151-9481-1, 29322) Mosby Inc.

*__Pathophysiology: The Biological Basis for Disease in Adults & Children.__ 3rd ed. Kathryn L. McCance & Sue E. Huether. (Illus.). 400p. 1998. student ed. write for info. (0-8151-3766-4) Mosby Inc.

*__Pathophysiology: The Biological Basis for Disease in Adults & Children, Includes Testbank.__ 3rd ed. Kathryn L. McCance & Sue E. Huether. (Illus.). 1998. teacher ed. write for info. (1-55664-433-7) Mosby Inc.

Pathophysiology: With Disk. Kathy Lauer & Sally A. Brozenec. LC 98-49667. (Notes Ser.). 320p. 1999. pap. 24.95 (0-87434-964-8) Springhouse Corp.

Pathophysiology Instructor's Manual: Foundations of Disease & Clinical Intervention. Margie Hansen. (Illus.). 1150p. 1998. write for info. (0-7216-4466-X) W B Saunders.

*__Pathophysiology & Clinical Applications of Nitric Oxide.__ Ed. by Gabor Rubanyi. (Endothelial Cell Research Ser.). 396p. 1999. text 220.00 (90-5702-415-2, Harwood Acad Pubs) Gordon & Breach.

Pathophysiology & Pharmacology of Capillary Resistance. M. Gabor. 236p. (C). 1974. 50.00 (963-05-0238-0, Pub. by Akade Kiado) St Mut.

Pathophysiology & Pharmacology of Erythropoietin. Ed. by Horst Pagel et al. LC 92-2312. (Illus.). xv, 328p. 1992. 100.00 (0-387-54777-0) Spr-Verlag.

Pathophysiology & Pharmacology of Heart Disease: Proceedings of the Symposium Held at Chandigarh, India, Feb. 1988. Ed. by Inder S. Anand et al. (Developments in Cardiovascular Medicine Ser.). (C). 1989. text 131.50 (0-7923-0367-9) Kluwer Academic.

Pathophysiology & Rational Pharamacotherapy of Myocardial Ischemia. Ed. by G. Heusch. 300p. 1990. 66.00 (0-387-91360-2) Spr-Verlag.

Pathophysiology & Treatment of Inhalation Injuries. Ed. by Jacob Loke. (Lung Biology in Health & Disease Ser.: Vol. 34). (Illus.). 576p. 1987. text 250.00 (0-8247-7795-6) Dekker.

Pathophysiology & Treatment of Paget's Disease of Bone. John A. Kanis. LC 90-86388. (Illus.). 320p. 1991. lib. bdg. 110.00 (0-89089-447-7) Carolina Acad Pr.

*__Pathophysiology for the Boards & Wards: A Review of the USMLE Step 1.__ 3rd ed. Carlos Ayala & Brad Spellberg. (Boards & Wards Ser.). (Illus.). 305p. 2000. pap. 27.95 (0-632-04485-3) Blackwell Sci.

*__Pathophysiology for the Emt.__ Myers et al. (C). 2002. pap. 25.50 (0-7668-2548-5) Delmar.

Pathophysiology for the Health-Related Professions. Barbara Gould. (Illus.). 1997. pap., teacher ed. write for info. (0-7216-7184-5, W B Saunders Co) Harcrt Hlth Sci Grp.

Pathophysiology for the Health-Related Professions: Health Related Problems. Barbara Gould. Ed. by Selma Kaszczuk. LC 96-42341. (Illus.). 416p. 1997. pap. text 44.95 (0-7216-5954-3, W B Saunders Co) Harcrt Hlth Sci Grp.

Pathophysiology in Small Animal Surgery. Ed. by M. Joseph Bojrab et al. LC 80-25780. 928p. reprint ed. pap. 200.00 (0-7837-1480-7, 205717500023) Bks Demand.

Pathophysiology Made Incredibly Easy. Springhouse Publishing Company Staff. LC 97-46681. (Illus.). 408p. 1998. pap. text 29.95 (0-87434-935-4) Springhouse Corp.

Pathophysiology of Blood. Ed. by Archie A. MacKinney, Jr. LC 83-26040. (Wiley Pathophysiology Ser.). (Illus.). 462p. (Orig.). reprint ed. pap. 143.30 (0-8357-4660-7, 203759000008) Bks Demand.

Pathophysiology of Blood Disorders. Ed. by Ch. Hershko & G. Izak. (Illus.). 1979. pap. 57.50 (3-8055-3021-8) S Karger.

Pathophysiology of Development & Rupture of Cerebral Aneurysms. H. J. Steiger. (Acta Neurochirugica - Supplementum Ser.: Suppl. 48). 100p. 1990. 61.95 (0-387-82192-9) Spr-Verlag.

Pathophysiology of Disease: An Introduction to Clinical Medicine. 2nd ed. Stephen J. McPhee & Ganong. 624p. (C). 1997. pap. text 36.95 (0-8385-7678-8, A-7678-4, Apple Lange Med) McGraw.

Pathophysiology of Disease: An Introduction to Clinical Medicine. 3rd ed. McPhee. (Illus.). 662p. (C). 1999. pap. 39.95 (0-8385-8160-9, Apple Lange Med) McGraw.

Pathophysiology of Head & Neck Musculoskeletal Disorders. Ed. by D. B. Ferguson. (Frontiers of Oral Physiology Ser.: Vol. 7). (Illus.). viii, 180p. 1990. 208.75 (3-8055-5123-1) S Karger.

Pathophysiology of Heart Disease. Ed. by R. E. Beamish et al. (Developments in Cardiovascular Medicine Ser.). 1987. text 161.50 (0-89838-864-3) Kluwer Academic.

Pathophysiology of Heart Disease. Leonard Lilly. (Illus.). 300p. 1992. pap. 26.00 (0-8121-1566-X) Lppncott W & W.

Pathophysiology of Heart Disease: A Collaborative Project of Medical Students & Faculty. 2nd ed. Harvard Medical School Staff. Ed. by Leonard S. Lilly. LC 97-25006. 401p. 1997. pap. 29.00 (0-683-30220-5) Lppncott W & W.

Pathophysiology of Heart Failure. Ed. by Naranjan S. Dhalla et al. (Developments in Cardiovascular Medicine Ser.: No. DICM 168). 624p. (C). 1996. text 272.50 (0-7923-3571-6) Kluwer Academic.

Pathophysiology of Hypertension. A. Zanchetti & G. Mancia. LC 97-132210. (Handbook of Hypertension Ser.: Vol. 17). 1122p. 1997. 465.75 (0-444-82551-7) Elsevier.

Pathophysiology of Hypertension. Alberto Zanchetti & Giuseppe Mancia. LC 97-132210. (Handbood of Hypertension Ser.). xix, 1102p. 1997. write for info. (0-444-90341-0) Elsevier.

Pathophysiology of Hypertension in Blacks. John C. Fray & Janice G. Douglas. (Clinical Physiology Series - An American Physiological Society Book). (Illus.). 320p. 1992. text 89.00 (0-19-506720-7) OUP.

Pathophysiology of Infantile Malnutrition: Protein Energy Malnutrition & Failure to Thrive. E. Kerpel-Pronius. 312p. (C). 1983. 90.00 (963-05-3222-0, Pub. by Akade Kiado) St Mut.

Pathophysiology of Lipid Peroxides & Related Free Radicals: International Symposium on Physiology of Lipid Peroxides & Related Free Radicals, Inuyama, November 1996. Kunio Yagi. LC 98-145628. (Illus.). x, 182p. 1998. 173.25 (3-8055-6590-9) S Karger.

Pathophysiology of Lysosomel Transport. Bodie Thoene. 368p. 1992. lib. bdg. 249.00 (0-8493-6724-7, RC632) CRC Pr.

Pathophysiology of Melanocytes: Proceedings of the International Pigment Cell Conference, 10th, Cambridge, Mass., October, 1977, Pt. 2. International Pigment Cell Conference Staff. Ed. by S. N. Klaus. (Pigment Cell Ser.: Vol. 5). (Illus.). 1979. 121.00 (3-8055-2973-2) S Karger.

Pathophysiology of Parasitic Infections. L. E. Symons. 300p. 1989. text 90.00 (0-12-680125-8) Acad Pr.

Pathophysiology of Plasma Protein Metabolism. Ed. by Giulian Mariant. 416p. 1985. 115.00 (0-306-41771-5, Plenum Trade) Perseus Pubng.

Pathophysiology of Pneumoperitoneum. Ed. by Raul J. Rosenthal et al. LC 97-20208. (Illus.). x, 174p. 1997. write for info. (3-540-63015-5) Spr-Verlag.

Pathophysiology of Puberty. Ed. by E. Cacciari & A. Prader. LC 80-40928. (Serono Symposia Ser.: No. 36). 1981. text 167.00 (0-12-154160-6) Acad Pr.

Pathophysiology of Renal Disease. (Contributions to Nephrology Ser.: Vol. 23). (Illus.). vi, 234p. 1980. pap. 29.75 (3-8055-0943-X) S Karger.

Pathophysiology of Renal Disease. Shaul G. Massry & Eberhard Ritz. (Contributions to Nephrology Ser.: Vol. 33). (Illus.). viii, 276p. 1982. pap. 29.75 (3-8055-3534-1) S Karger.

Pathophysiology of Renal Disease. 2nd ed. Burton D. Rose. (Illus.). 623p. 1987. pap. text 39.00 (0-07-053629-5) McGraw-Hill HPD.

Pathophysiology of Reperfusion Injury. DAS Staff. 528p. 1992. lib. bdg. 219.00 (0-8493-4555-3, RB144) CRC Pr.

Pathophysiology of Severe Ischemic Myocardial Injury. Ed. by Hans M. Piper. 440p. 1990. text 294.00 (0-7923-0459-4) Kluwer Academic.

Pathophysiology of Shock, Sepsis, & Organ Failure. Ed. by Gunther O. Schlag & H. Redl. LC 93-10875. 1993. 317.00 (0-387-54223-X) Spr-Verlag.

Pathophysiology of Splanchnic Circulation, Vol. I. Kvietys & Granger. 184p. 1987. 107.00 (0-8493-4662-2, CRC Reprint) Franklin.

Pathophysiology of Splanchnic Circulation, Vol. II. Kvietys & Granger. 152p. 1987. 93.00 (0-8493-4663-0, CRC Reprint) Franklin.

Pathophysiology of Tachycardia-Induced Heart Failure. Ed. by Francis G. Spinale. LC 96-23241. (American Heart Association Monographs). (Illus.). 248p. 1996. 48.00 (0-87993-649-5) Futura Pub.

Pathophysiology of the Eye No. 1: The Preocular Tear Film. Feher Janos. (Pathophysiology of the Eye Ser.: No. 1). 142p. 1993. pap. 210.00 (963-05-6515-3, Pub. by Akade Kiado) St Mut.

Pathophysiology of the Gastrointestinal System. Sanjiv Chopra & Roger J. May. 400p. 1989. pap. text 46.95 (0-316-13890-8) Lppncott W & W.

Pathophysiology of the Gut & Airways. P. L. Andrews & J. G. Widdicombe. 150p. 1993. 37.40 (1-85578-022-4, Pub. by Portland Pr Ltd) Ashgate Pub Co.

Pathophysiology of the Microcirculation. Nicholas A. Mortillaro. 305p. 1994. lib. bdg. 239.00 (0-8493-4547-2, RC700) CRC Pr.

Pathophysiology of the Motor Systems: Principles & Clinical Presentations. Christopher M. Fredericks & Lisa K. Saladin. LC 95-37900. (Illus.). 594p. (C). 1996. text 44.95 (0-8036-0093-3) Davis Co.

Pathophysiology of the Nervous System. Lewis Sudarsky. 1990. 35.95 (0-316-82117-9, Little Brwn Med Div) Lppncott W & W.

Pathophysiology of the Splanchnic Circulation. Ed. by Granger et al. 1987. 220.00 (0-8493-4661-4, RC802) CRC Pr.

Pathophysiology of the Visual System. Ed. by L. Maffei. (Documenta Ophthalmologica Proceedings Ser.: No. 30). 304p. 1981. text 171.00 (90-6193-726-4) Kluwer Academic.

Pathophysiology with Practical Applications. Phyllis Chowdry. 576p. (C). 1992. text 64.50 (0-697-08538-4) Brown & Benchmark.

Pathos Dramatico en el Teatro Espanol de 1750 a 1808, 2 vols. I. L. McClelland. Tr. by Guillermina Cenoz & Fernando Huerta. (SPA.). 784p. 1998. 99.95 (0-85323-128-1, Pub. by Liverpool Univ Pr); pap. 44.95 (0-85323-138-9, Pub. by Liverpool Univ Pr) Intl Spec Bk.

Paths. Lawrence E. Keith. (Illus.). 1979. 5.00 (0-932222-01-3); pap. 3.00 (0-932222-02-1) Sunrise Tortoise.

*__Paths: Poems from Hollywood.__ Mark Dunster. 11p. 1999. pap. 5.00 (0-89642-957-1) Linden Pubs.

*__Paths along the Hudson: A Guide to Walking & Biking.__ Marilyne Woodsmall & Jeffrey Perls. LC 99-11393. (Illus.). 352p. 1999. pap. 20.00 (0-8135-2657-4) Rutgers U Pr.

Paths & Paving. DK Publishing Staff. LC 99-199902. 80p. 1999. pap. text 8.95 (0-7894-4158-6) DK Pub Inc.

Paths & Places. Alan M. Hofmeister et al. (Reading for All Learners Ser.). (Illus.). (J). pap. write for info. (1-56861-161-7) Swift Lrn Res.

Paths & Stories: Spirituality for Teachers. Kevin Treston. 128p. 1991. pap. 11.95 (1-85390-162-8, Pub. by Veritas Pubns) St Mut.

Paths & Walkways. Daria P. Bowman. LC 97-13134. (For Your Garden Ser.). (Illus.). 72p. 1997. 12.95 (1-56799-482-2, Friedman-Fairfax) M Friedman Pub Grp Inc.

Paths & Walkways: Simple Projects, Contemporary Designs. Hazel White. LC 97-6980. 1998. pap. 16.95 (0-8118-1429-7) Chronicle Bks.

Paths Are Made by Walking: A Step-by-Step Guidebook for Spiritual Self-Discovery. Rosalind Thompson. Ed. by MaryAnn Gutoff. 212p. (Orig.). 1997. pap. 18.95 (0-9657600-0-6) R Thompson.

Paths Are Many, Truth Is One: A Journey into the Essence of Spirituality & Religion. Sujantra G. McKeever. 150p. 1995. pap. text 9.95 (1-885479-01-8) McKeever Pubng.

Paths Are Many Truth Is One: Exploring the Unity of All Religions. 2nd rev. ed. S. G. McKeever. Ed. by Mairi McKeever. 160p. 1998. pap. 12.95 (1-885479-10-7) McKeever Pubng.

Paths Beyond Ego: The Transpersonal Vision. Ed. by Roger Walsh & Frances Vaughan. LC 93-6705. 288p. 1993. pap. 15.95 (0-87477-678-3, Tarcher Putnam) Putnam Pub Group.

Paths, Flows & VLSI-Layout. Ben Korte et al. Ed. by R. L. Graham. (Algorithms & Combinatorics Ser.: Vol. 9). (Illus.). xxii, 383p. 1990. 135.95 (0-387-52685-4) Spr-Verlag.

Paths in Solitude. Eve Baker. 127p. 1994. pap. 39.95 (0-85439-513-X, Pub. by St Paul Pubns) St Mut.

Paths in Spirituality. 2nd ed. John Macquarrie. LC 93-8172. 176p. 1993. pap. 12.95 (0-8192-1602-X) Morehouse Pub.

Paths in the Rainforests: Toward a History of Political Tradition in Equatorial Africa. Jan Vansina. LC 90-50100. 400p. (C). 1990. pap. text 19.95 (0-299-12574-2) U of Wis Pr.

Paths in Utopia. Martin Buber. Tr. by R. F. C. Hull. LC 96-32897. (Martin Buber Library). 152p. 1996. reprint ed. pap. 15.95 (0-8156-0421-1, BUBUP) Syracuse U Pr.

Paths into Poetry. Joanne Collie & Gillian P. Ladousse. (Illus.). 64p. 1993. pap. text 11.95 (0-19-421716-7) OUP.

Paths Less Traveled: The Adirondack Experience for Walkers, Hikers & Climbers of All Ages. Dennis Aprill. LC 98-65509. (Illus.). 150p. (YA). (gr. 9-12). 1998. pap. 14.95 (0-9632476-6-2) Pinto Pr.

*__Paths Less Traveled: The Adirondack Experience for Walkers, Hikers & Climbers of All Ages.__ 2nd rev. ed. Dennis Aprill. (Illus.). 231p. 1999. pap. 16.95 (0-9632476-9-7) Pinto Pr.

Paths Not Taken: British Labour & International Policy in the 1920s. Henry R. Winkler. LC 94-4590. 300p. 1995. text 49.95 (0-8078-2171-3) U of NC Pr.

*__Paths Not Taken: Speculations on American Foreign Policy & Diplomatic History, Interests, Ideals & Power__ Jonathan M. Neilson. LC 99-37524. (Studies in Diplomacy & Strategic Thought). 240p. 2000. 65.00 (0-275-96769-7, Praeger Pubs) Greenwood.

Paths of a Prodigal: Exploring the Deeper Regions of Spiritual Living. Richard G. Young. 272p. (Orig.). 1997. pap. 15.95 (0-943914-81-7) Larson Pubns.

Paths of Abstraction: Painting in New York, 1944-1981 Selections from the Ciba Art Collection. Ed. & Intro. by William C. Agee. (Illus.). 70p. (Orig.). 1994. pap. 15.00 (1-885998-00-7) Hunter College.

*__Paths of Accommodation: Muslim Societies & French Colonial Authorities In Senegal & Mauritania, 1880-1920.__ David Robinson. (Western African Studies). 408p. (C). 2000. text 65.00 (0-8214-1353-8); pap. text 26.95 (0-8214-1354-6) Ohio U Pr.

P

An Asterisk (*) at the beginning of an entry indicates that the title is appearing for the first time.

Paths of African Theology - Percoris di Teologia Africana. Ed. by Rosino Gibellini. LC 94-3706. 208p. 1994. reprint ed. pap. 20.00 (*0-88344-974-9*) Orbis Bks.
Paths of Armor, the 5th Armored Division in World War II. Vic Hillery & Emerson Hurley. (Divisional Ser.: 27th). (Illus.). 358p. 1986. reprint ed. 39.95 (*0-89839-084-2*) Battery Pr.
Paths of Attainment. Arden C. Rizer, Jr. 82p. 1987. pap. 18.00 (*0-939795-13-2*) Amer Spirit.
Paths of Blessings. Carol E. Mitchell. 48p. 1991. pap. write for info. (*0-9631852-0-9*) Sparrow Hse.
Paths of Change: Stragetic Choices for Organizations & Society. Will McWhinney. (Illus.). 280p. 1992. 52.00 (*0-8039-3930-2*); pap. 24.00 (*0-8039-3931-0*) Sage.
Paths of Change: Strategic Choices for Organizations & Society. Will McWhinney. LC 97-4628. 1997. pap. 24.00 (*0-7619-1017-4*) Sage.
Paths of Continuity: Central European Historiography from the 1930s Through the 1950s. Ed. by Hartmut Lehmann & James V. Melton. (Publications of the German Historical Institute, Washington, D.C.). 416p. (C). 1994. text 80.00 (*0-521-45199-X*) Cambridge U Pr.
Paths of Dalit Liberation in Kerala: Interaction with Christianity & Communism, 1854-1966. George Oommen. (Religion & Society in South Asia Ser.). 240p. (C). 1998. text 45.00 (*0-7007-0423-X*, Pub. by Curzon Pr Ltd) UH Pr.
Paths of Death & Glory: The Last Days of the Third Reich. Charles Whiting. (Illus.). 224p. 1996. 24.00 (*0-7278-4835-6*) Severn Hse.
Paths of Desire: Images of Exploration & Mapping in Canadian Women's Writings. Marlene Goldman. LC 97-170131. (Theory/Culture Ser.). 314p. 1997. text 45.00 (*0-8020-0986-7*); pap. text 19.95 (*0-8020-7944-X*) U of Toronto Pr.
Paths of Development in Nordoff-Robbins Music Therapy. Kenneth Aigen. LC 99-163018. 362p. (C). 1998. pap. text 57.50 incl. audio compact disk (*1-891278-03-7*) Barcelona Pubs.
Paths of Discovery, Vol. I. Fredenc Worden. 1991. 99.00 (*0-8176-3506-8*) Birkhauser.
Paths of Emancipation: Jews, States, & Citizenship. Ed. by Pierre Birnbaum & Ira Katznelson. 320p. 1995. text 59.50 (*0-691-03460-5*, Pub. by Princeton U Pr); pap. text 17.95 (*0-691-03461-3*, Pub. by Princeton U Pr) Cal Prin Full Svc.
Paths of Faith. 4th ed. John A. Hutchison. 608p. (C). 1991. 67.50 (*0-07-031543-4*) McGraw.
Paths of Faithfulness: Personal Essays on Jewish Spirituality. Carol Ochs et al. LC 97-5078. 1997. 8.95 (*0-88125-596-3*) Ktav.
Paths of Fire: An Anthropologist's Inquiry into Technology in the Making of the Modern West. Robert M. Adams. 360p. 1996. text 29.95 (*0-691-02634-3*, Pub. by Princeton U Pr) Cal Prin Full Svc.
Paths of Glory. Glenn Utter & John Story. 360p. 1997. pap. 16.95 (*1-887269-32-0*) J Culler & Sons.
Paths of Glory. Glenn Utter & John Story. 360p. 1998. 23.95 (*1-887269-25-8*) J Culler & Sons.
Paths of Glory: Impressions of War Written at & near the Front. Irvin S. Cobb. (Collected Works of Irvin S. Cobb). 414p. 1998. reprint ed. lib. bdg. 108.00 (*1-58201-605-4*) Classic Bks.
Paths of Heaven: The Evolution of Airpower Theory. Phillip S. Meiling. LC 97-24531. (Illus.). 680p. 1997. pap. 39.00 (*1-58566-027-2*) Air Univ.
Paths of Heidegger's Life & Thought. Otto Phoggeler. LC 99-10396. 1999. write for info. (*1-57392-503-9*, Humanity Bks) Prometheus Bks.
Paths of Heidegger's Life & Thought. Otto Poggeler. Tr. by John Bailiff. (Contemporary Studies in Philosophy & the Human Sciences Ser.). 376p. (C). 1996. text 70.00 (*0-391-03964-4*) Humanities.
Paths of History. Igor M. Diakonoff. LC 98-30994. 400p. 1999. pap. 19.95 (*0-521-64398-8*) Cambridge U Pr.
***Paths of History.** Igor M. Diakonoff. LC 98-30994. 400p. 1999. 54.95 (*0-521-64348-1*) Cambridge U Pr.
Paths of Individuation in Literature & Film: A Jungian Approach. Phyllis B. Kenevan. LC 99-11559. 256p. 1999. 60.00 (*0-7391-0016-5*) Lxngtn Bks.
Paths of Innovation: Technological Change in 20th-Century America. David C. Mowery & Nathan Rosenberg. LC 98-28901. (Illus.). 216p. (C). 1998. 27.95 (*0-521-64119-5*) Cambridge U Pr.
***Paths of Innovation: Technological Change in 20th-Century America.** David C. Mowery & Nathan Rosenberg. (Illus.). 224p. (C). 2000. pap. text 16.95 (*0-521-64653-7*) Cambridge U Pr.
***Paths of Kateri's Kin.** Christopher Vecsey. LC 97-21499. (American Indian Catholics Ser.: Vol. 2). 416p. 2000. reprint ed. pap. 18.00 (*0-268-03864-3*, Pub. by U of Notre Dame Pr) Chicago Distribution Ctr.
Paths of Liberation: A Third World Spirituality. Bakole Wa Ilunga. Tr. by Matthew J. O'Connell. LC 84-5177. 224p. 1984. reprint ed. pap. 69.50 (*0-8357-2679-7*, 204021500015) Bks Demand.
Paths of Life see Paths of Life, Cycle B: Reflections on the Readings for Sundays & Holydays
Paths of Life, 3 vols., Set. Ernest Ferlita. LC 92-25495. 660p. (Orig.). 1994. pap. 24.95 (*0-8189-0707-X*) Alba.
***Paths of Life: Advent/Christmas Season: Reflections on the Readings for the Weekdays of Advent & the Christmas Season.** Ernest Ferlita. LC 99-33224. x, 90p. 1999. pap. 7.95 (*0-8189-0828-9*) Alba.
Paths of Life: American Indians of the Southwest & Northern Mexico. T. Sheridan. LC 95-32531. (Illus.). 298p. 1996. pap. 19.95 (*0-8165-1466-6*) U of Ariz Pr.
Paths of Life: Preface to a World Religion. Charles W. Morris. LC 72-94732. 228p. 1993. pap. text 2.25 (*0-226-53879-6*, P541) U Ch Pr.
Paths of Life: Seven Scenarios. Alice Miller. LC 98-17578. 208p. 1998. 23.00 (*0-375-40379-5*) Pantheon.
Paths of Life: Seven Scenarios. Alice Miller. 1999. pap. 12.00 (*0-375-70345-4*) Vin Bks.
Paths of Life, Cycle A: Cycle A, Reflections on the Readings for Sundays & Holidays. Ernest Ferlita. LC 92-25495. 201p. 1992. pap. 9.95 (*0-8189-0649-9*) Alba.
Paths of Life, Cycle B: Reflections on the Readings for Sundays & Holydays. Ernest Ferlita. LC 92-25495. Orig. Title: Paths of Life. 201p. (Orig.). 1993. pap. 9.95 (*0-8189-0677-4*) Alba.
Paths of Life, Cycle C. Ernest Ferlita. LC 94-25495. 224p. (Orig.). 1994. pap. 9.95 (*0-8189-0706-1*) Alba.
***Paths of Love & Faithfulness: Reflections on Lambeth & the Anglican Communion.** Ed. by Phoebe W. Griswold. 88p. 1999. pap. 4.95 (*0-88028-209-6*, 1518) Forward Movement.
Paths of Meditation. Ed. by Vedanta Kesari Staff. 241p. 1980. pap. 3.50 (*81-7120-144-X*, Pub. by Ramakrishna Math) Vedanta Pr.
Paths of Neighborhood Change: Race & Crime in Urban America. Richard P. Taub et al. LC 84-2488. (Illus.). 272p. (C). 1994. 25.00 (*0-226-79001-0*) U Ch Pr.
Paths of Neighborhood Change: Race & Crime in Urban America. Richard P. Taub et al. LC 84-2488. (Illus.). 276p. (C). 1999. pap. text 14.50 (*0-226-79002-9*) U Ch Pr.
Paths of Our Children: Historic Indians of Arkansas. George Sabo, III. LC 92-11216. (Popular Ser.). (Illus.). 144p. 1992. pap. 5.00 (*1-56349-073-0*, PS03) AR Archaeol.
***Paths of Peace: As the Sky Meets the Earth: Selected Papers from the Peace Colloquy (1999), the Temple, Independence, Missouri.** Peace Colloquy Staff et al. LC 00-25506. 2000. write for info. (*0-8309-0939-7*) Herald Pub Hse.
Paths of Prayer: A Textbook of Prayer & Meditation. Gary Giombi. 160p. (YA). (gr. 9-12). 1993. pap. text, student ed. 10.95 (*0-937997-27-7*, 3655) Hi-Time Pflaum.
Paths of Prayer: A Textbook of Prayer & Meditation. Gary Giombi. 231p. 1994. teacher ed., spiral bd. 23.95 (*0-937997-28-5*) Hi-Time Pflaum.
Paths of Renewal for Religious. Ed. by David L. Fleming. (Best of the Review Ser.: Bk. 2). 359p. (C). 1986. pap. text 10.95 (*0-924768-00-2*) Review Relig.
Paths of Resistance: Tradition & Democracy in Industrializing Missouri. David P. Thelen. 344p. (C). 1991. pap. 16.95 (*0-8262-0794-4*) U of Mo Pr.
Paths of Resistance: Tradition & Dignity in Industrializing Missouri. David P. Thelen. 324p. 1986. text 75.00 (*0-19-503667-0*) OUP.
Paths of Soaring Flight. F. G. Irving. LC 97-39187. 200p. 1997. pap. text 28.00 (*1-86094-055-2*) World Scientific Pub.
Paths of Sociological Imagination, Vol. 1. Daniel Kubat. 596p. 1971. pap. 68.00 (*0-685-58451-8*) Gordon & Breach.
Paths of the Ancients . . . Appalachia. Kenneth Murray. (Illus.). 128p. 1993. 22.95 (*0-932807-94-1*) Overmountain Pr.
Paths of the Church: Ecclesiam Suam. Paul, VI, pseud. 60p. 1964. pap. 2.25 (*0-8198-5855-2*) Pauline Bks.
Paths of the Dead. Steven Brust. 1996. write for info. (*0-312-85579-6*) Tor Bks.
Paths of the Heart: Prayers of Medieval Christians. John Blakesley. 1994. pap. text 8.95 (*0-687-85983-2*) Abingdon.
Paths of the Mound Building Indians & Great Game Animals see Historic Highways of America...with Maps & Illustrations
Paths of the Past: Tennessee, 1770-1970. Paul H. Bergeron. LC 79-14896. (Tennessee Three Star Ser.). (Illus.). 136p. 1979. pap. 7.00 (*0-87049-274-8*) U of Tenn Pr.
Paths of the Perambulator. Alan Dean Foster. 1985. 17.00 (*0-932096-39-5*) Phantasia Pr.
Paths of Wisdom: Principles & Practice of the Magical Cabala in the Western Tradition. John M. Greer. LC 96-18581. (High Magick Ser.). (Illus.). 416p. (Orig.). 1996. pap. 16.95 (*1-56718-315-8*) Llewellyn Pubns.
Paths to a Political Settlement in Ireland: Policy Papers Submitted to the Forum for Peace & Reconciliation. LC 95-198886. 152p. 1995. pap. 10.95 (*0-85640-566-3*, Pub. by Blackstaff Pr) Dufour.
***Paths to a Settlement in Northern Ireland, Vol. 9.** Sean Farren. (Ulster Editions & Monographs Ser.). (Illus.). 2000. pap. 14.95 (*0-86140-413-0*) Smyth.
Paths to Asian Medical Knowledge. Ed. by Charles M. Leslie & Allan H. Young. LC 91-796. (Comparative Studies of Health Systems & Medical Care: Vol. 32). 296p. (C). 1992. 50.00 (*0-520-07317-7*, Pub. by U CA Pr); pap. 17.95 (*0-520-07318-5*, Pub. by U CA Pr) Cal Prin Full Svc.
Paths to Asian Medical Knowledge. Ed. by Charles Leslie & Allan Young. 306p. 1993. 39.50 (*81-215-0608-5*, Pub. by M Manoharial) Coronet Bks.
Paths to Authority: The Middle Class & the Industrial Labor Force in France, 1820-48. fac. ed. Peter N. Stearns. LC 78-16222. 234p. 1978. reprint ed. pap. 72.60 (*0-7837-8061-3*, 204781400008) Bks Demand.
Paths to Becoming a Midwife: Getting an Education. 4th ed. Midwifery Today Staff. (Illus.). 332p. 1998. pap. 29.95 (*1-890446-00-9*) Midwifery Today.
***Paths to Civilization: Readings in the Intellectual Heritage of the Western World, Vol. 1.** James Marra et al. 528p. (C). 1999. per. 69.95 (*0-7872-6312-5*) Kendall-Hunt.
***Paths to Civilization: Readings in the Intellectual Heritage of the Western World, Vol. 2.** James Marra et al. 346p. (C). 1999. per. 55.95 (*0-7872-6313-3*, 41631302) Kendall-Hunt.
Paths to Conflagration: Fifty Years of Diplomacy & Warfare in Laos, Thailand, & Vietnam, 1778-1828. unabridged ed. Mayoury Ngaosyvathn & Pheuiphanh Ngaosyvathn. (Studies on Southeast Asia: Vol. 24). 270p. 1998. pap. 17.00 (*0-87727-723-0*) Cornell SE Asia.
Paths to Contemplation. 6th ed. Yves Raguin. Orig. Title: Chemins de la Contemplation. 154p. 1996. reprint ed. pap. 8.95 (*0-940147-04-1*) Source Bks CA.
Paths to Domination, Resistance, & Terror. Ed. by Carolyn Nordstrom & Joanne M. Martin. (C). 1992. pap. 17.95 (*0-520-07316-9*, Pub. by U CA Pr) Cal Prin Full Svc.
Paths to Domination, Resistance, & Terror. Ed. by Carolyn Nordstrom & Joanne M. Martin. (C). 1992. 55.00 (*0-520-07315-0*, Pub. by U CA Pr) Cal Prin Full Svc.
Paths to Economic Opportunity: Case Studies of Local Development Strategies to Reduce Poverty. 176p. 1995. 30.00 (*1-886152-12-8*, No. 3022) Natl League Cities.
Paths to Educational Reform. W. Clark Trow. LC 71-122810. 256p. 1971. 37.95 (*0-87778-002-1*) Educ Tech Pubns.
Paths to Enlightenment: Buddhist Art in the Whitman College Collection. Akira Takemoto & Jonathan S. Walters. Ed. by Ben Mitchell. (Whitman College Asian Art Collections: Vol. II). (Illus.). 1994. 25.00 (*1-880269-12-0*) D H Sheehan.
Paths to Inclusion Vol. 5: The Integration of Migrants in the United States & Germany. Ed. by Peter Schuck & Rainer Munz. LC 97-30105. (Migration & Refugees Ser.). 336p. 1998. 59.95 (*1-57181-091-9*) Berghahn Bks.
***Paths to Justice: What People Do & Think about Going to Law.** Hazel Genn. 288p. 1999. pap. 27.00 (*1-84113-039-7*, Pub. by Hart Pub) Intl Spec Bk.
Paths to Knowledge. Ed. by Barbara Sarter. 246p. 1988. pap. 16.50 (*0-88737-415-8*, 15-2233) Natl League Nurse.
Paths to Knowledge of Higher Worlds. 3rd ed. Rudolf Steiner. (GER.). 36p. 1980. reprint ed. pap. 3.95 (*0-919924-13-1*, Pub. by Steiner Book Centre) Anthroposophic.
Paths to Learning. Chandler. 1999. 30.00 (*0-02-905305-6*) S&S Trade.
Paths to Liberation: The Marga & Its Transformations in Buddhist Thought. Ed. by Robert E. Buswell, Jr. & Robert M. Gimello. LC 91-29277. (Studies in East Asian Buddhism: No. 7). (Illus.). 536p. (C). 1992. text 45.00 (*0-8248-1417-7*) UH Pr.
Paths to Marriage. Bernard I. Murstein. (Family Studies Text Ser.). (Illus.). 160p. (Orig.). (C). 1986. pap. text 18.95 (*0-8039-2383-X*) Sage.
Paths to Marriage. Bernard I. Murstein. LC 86-1884. (Family Studies Text Ser.: Vol. 5). (Illus.). 168p. (Orig.). 1986. reprint ed. pap. 52.10 (*0-608-07685-6*, 206777500010) Bks Demand.
Paths to New Curriculum. Stephen C. Clem & Z. Vance Wilson. 1991. pap. 27.00 (*0-934338-73-6*) NAIS.
Paths to Otherwhere. James Patrick Hogan. 416p. 1996. 22.00 (*0-671-87710-0*) Baen Bks.
Paths to Otherwhere. James Patrick Hogan. 432p. 1997. per. 5.99 (*0-671-87767-4*) Baen Bks.
Paths to Partnership: University & Community As Learners in Interprofessional Education. Michael S. Knapp & Associates Staff. LC 98-21269. 278p. 1998. 60.00 (*0-8476-8875-5*); pap. 24.95 (*0-8476-8876-3*) Rowman.
Paths to Peace. Ed. by Victor H. Wallace. LC 72-134149. (Essay Index Reprint Ser.). 1977. 28.95 (*0-8369-1980-7*) Ayer.
Paths to Peace: Is Democracy the Answer? Ed. by Miriam F. Elman. LC 97-21782. (CSIA Studies in International Security). (Illus.). 542p. 1997. pap. text 27.50 (*0-262-55029-6*) MIT Pr.
Paths to Peace: Major Documents Addressed to the United Nations & Its Organizations by the Popes & the Holy See. 700p. 1987. 13.98 (*0-940169-01-0*) Liturgical Pubns.
Paths to Pedal: Bicycling in the Tri-State. Corky Johnson & Carol Arbaczewski. (Illus.). 96p. (Orig.). 1990. pap. 10.00 (*0-9626054-0-9*) Tailwind Pub.
Paths to Power. A. W. Tozer. 64p. 1986. mass mkt. 4.99 (*0-87509-190-3*) Chr Pubns.
Paths to Power. Floyd B. Wilson. 229p. 1997. pap. 17.00 (*0-89540-306-4*, SB-306) Sun Pub.
Paths to Power. Floyd B. Wilson. 229p. 1996. reprint ed. spiral bd. 17.00 (*0-7873-0974-5*) Hlth Research.
Paths to Power: A Working Woman's Guide from 1st Job to Top Executive. Natasha Josefowitz. 1980. teacher ed. write for info. (*0-201-03479-4*); pap. 9.95 (*0-201-03486-7*) Addison-Wesley.
Paths to Power: A Working Woman's Guide from 1st Job to Top Executive. Natasha Josefowitz. 1990. pap. 6.68 (*0-201-55093-8*) Addison-Wesley.
Paths to Power: Elite Mobility in Contemporary China. David M. Lampton. (Michigan Monographs in Chinese Studies: No. 55). (Illus.). 379p. (Orig.). 1986. pap. text 25.00 (*0-89264-064-2*) Ctr Chinese Studies.
Paths to Power: Elite Mobility in Contemporary China. David M. Lampton. LC 85-16601. (Michigan Monographs in Chinese Studies: No. 55). (Illus.). 379p. (Orig.). 1988. text 50.00 (*0-89264-063-4*) Ctr Chinese Studies.
***Paths to Power: The Historiography of American Foreign Relations to 1941.** Ed. by Michael J. Hogan. 328p. (C). 2000. text 54.95 (*0-521-66287-7*); pap. text 18.95 (*0-521-66413-6*) Cambridge U Pr.
Paths to Power (1901) Floyd B. Wilson. 230p. 1998. reprint ed. pap. 15.95 (*0-7661-0313-7*) Kessinger Pub.
Paths to Prayer: Prayerful Insights from the Catechism. Robert F. Morneau. 160p. 1997. pap. 9.95 (*0-86716-326-7*) St Anthony Mess Pr.
Paths to Privity: The History of Third Party Beneficiary Contracts at English Law. Vernon V. Palmer. LC 92-29490. 250p. 1993. 64.95 (*1-880921-16-2*); pap. 44.95 (*1-880921-15-4*) Austin & Winfield.
Paths to Proficiency. Naylor & Hagger. 1992. pap. text. write for info. (*0-582-06757-X*, Pub. by Addison-Wesley) Longman.
Paths to Prosperity. Amie Angeli. (Illus.). 150p. Date not set. pap. 21.00 (*1-891333-11-9*) AngeLines Pub.
Paths to Recovery: Al-Anon's Steps, Traditions & Concepts. Al-Anon Family Group Headquarters, Inc. Staff. LC 97-70986. 383p. 1997. 15.00 (*0-910034-31-1*) Al-Anon.
Paths to Renewal: The Spiritualities of 6 Religious Founders: Augustine of Hippo, Benedict of Nursia, Dominic Guzman, Francis of Assisi, Ignatius of Loyola, Teresa of Avila. Zachary Grant. LC 97-18268. 1998. pap. 9.95 (*0-8189-0794-0*) Alba.
Paths to School Readiness: An In-Depth Look at 3 Early Childhood Programs. M. Elena Lopez et al. LC 93-79081. 126p. (Orig.). 1993. pap. text 10.95 (*0-9630627-2-7*) Harvard Fam.
Paths to Social Deviance & Conformity: A Model of the Process. Alvin Rudoff. LC 91-39309. 144p. 1992. lib. bdg. 69.95 (*0-7734-9438-3*) E Mellen.
Paths to State Repression: Human Rights Violations & Contentious Politics. Ed. by Christian Davenport. LC 99-59363. 272p. 1999. pap. 24.95 (*0-8476-9391-0*) Rowman.
***Paths to State Repression: Human Rights Violations & Contentious Politics.** Ed. by Christian Davenport. LC 99-59363. 272p. 1999. 69.00 (*0-8476-9390-2*) Rowman.
***Paths to Success: Beating the Odds in American Society.** Charles C. Harrington. (Illus.). 256p. 2000. pap. 19.95 (*0-674-00413-2*) HUP.
Paths to Success: Beating the Odds in American Society. Charles C. Harrington & Susan K. Boardman. LC 97-8380. (Illus.). 288p. 1997. 36.50 (*0-674-65794-2*) HUP.
***Paths to the Absolute: Mondrain, Malevich, Kandinsky, Pollock, Newman, Rothko, & Still.** John Golding. (A. W. Mellon Lectures in the Fine Arts: Vol. 35). (Illus.). 240p. 2000. 60.00 (*0-691-04896-7*) Princeton U Pr.
Paths to the Ancient Past. Tom B. Jones. LC 67-12515. 1967. pap. 18.95 (*0-02-916630-6*) Free Pr.
Paths to the City: Regional Migration in 19th Century France. Leslie P. Moch. LC 83-2955. (New Approaches to Social Science History Ser.: No. 2). (Illus.). 261p. reprint ed. pap. 81.00 (*0-8357-8498-3*, 203477400091) Bks Demand.
Paths to the Middle East: 10 Scholars Look Back. Thomas Naff. LC 93-14597. 360p. (C). 1993. pap. text 21.95 (*0-7914-1884-7*) State U NY Pr.
Paths to the Middle East: 10 Scholars Look Back. Thomas Naff. LC 93-14597. 360p. (C). 1993. text 64.50 (*0-7914-1883-9*) State U NY Pr.
Paths to the Past: African Historical Essays in Honor of Jan Vansina. Ed. by Robert W. Harms et al. LC 94-29771. 1994. 35.00 (*0-918456-72-X*) African Studies Assn.
Paths to the Power of Myth: Joseph Campbell & the Study of Religion. Daniel C. Noel. 228p. 1994. pap. 12.95 (*0-8245-1389-4*) Crossroad NY.
***Paths to the Wind: Poems from Hollywood.** Mark Dunster. 11p. 1999. pap. 5.00 (*0-89642-962-8*) Linden Pubs.
***Paths to Victory: A History & Tour Guide of the Stones River, Chickamauga, Chattanooga, Knoxville.** Jim Miles. (Illus.). 192p. 1999. pap. 12.95 (*1-58182-074-7*, Cumberland Hearthside) Cumberland Hse.
Paths to Victory: A History & Tour Guide of the Stone's River, Chickamauga, Chattanooga, Knoxville, & Nashville Campaigns. Jim Miles. LC 91-29167. (Illus.). 224p. (Orig.). 1991. pap. 12.95 (*1-55853-126-2*) Cumberland Hse.
Paths Toward a Clearing: Radical Empiricism & Ethnographic Inquiry. Michael Jackson. LC 88-46021. (African Systems of Thought Ser.). 256p. 1989. 36.95 (*0-253-33190-0*) Ind U Pr.
Paths Toward Democracy: The Working Class & Elites in Western Europe & South America. Ruth B. Collier. LC 99-12564. (Cambridge Studies in Comparative Politics). (Illus.). 232p. (C). 1999. 49.95 (*0-521-64369-4*); pap. 17.95 (*0-521-64382-1*) Cambridge U Pr.
Paths Towards Universal Grammar: Studies in Honor of Richard S. Kayne. Guglielmo Cinque. Ed. by Jan Koster et al. LC 94-23291. (Georgetown Studies in Romance Linguistics). (Illus.). 507p. reprint ed. pap. 157.20 (*0-608-08036-5*, 206900100002) Bks Demand.
Pathway for Oxygen. Ewald R. Weibel. (Illus.). 448p. 1984. 55.50 (*0-674-65791-8*); pap. 28.50 (*0-674-65790-X*) HUP.
Pathway for Patients & Families Facing Terminal Illness. 46p. 1997. pap. 11.85 (*0-931207-51-7*) Natl Hospice.
Pathway Home: A Journey into Light. Carole S. Langlois. 171p. (Orig.). 1996. pap. 12.95 (*0-9637744-3-3*) Thats The Spirit.
Pathway into Number Theory. 2nd ed. R. P. Burn. (Illus.). 267p. (C). 1996. pap. text 27.95 (*0-521-57540-0*) Cambridge U Pr.
Pathway into the Overcomer's Walk Workbook. Betty Miller. (Overcoming Life Ser.). 92p. 1994. pap. 5.00 (*1-57149-016-7*) Christ Unltd.
Pathway into the Overcomer's Walk Workbook. Betty Miller. (Overcoming Life Ser.). 1995. pap. 10.00 (*1-57149-017-5*) Christ Unltd.
Pathway Mathematics. Glover. 1992. pap. text. write for info. (*0-582-87617-6*, Pub. by Addison-Wesley) Longman.

P

An Asterisk (*) at the beginning of an entry indicates that the title is appearing for the first time.

Pathway of Existence: Quatrains. Aram A. Armand. LC 92-33844. (ARM.). 172p. 1992. pap. 15.00 (*0-9628715-4-0*) Blue Crane Bks.

Pathway of Holiness: A Guide for Sinners. John White. LC 95-50980. 211p. (Orig.). 1996. pap. 9.99 (*0-8308-1980-0*, 1980) InterVarsity.

Pathway of Life: Teaching Love & Wisdom (1919) Leo Tolstoy. 284p. 1998. reprint ed. pap. 24.95 (*0-7661-0661-6*) Kessinger Pub.

Pathway of Mattie Howard: To & from Prison: Autobiography; True Story of the Regeneration of an Ex-Convict & Gangster Woman. Mattie Howard. (American Biography Ser.). 317p. 1991. reprint ed. lib. bdg. 79.00 (*0-7812-8195-4*) Rprt Serv.

Pathway of Non-Duality (Advaitavada) An Approach to Some Key-Points of Gaudapada's Asparsavada & Samkara's Advaita Vedanta by Means of a Series of Questions Answered by an Asparsin. Raphael. xi, 88p. 1992. 10.95 (*1-881338-19-3*) Nataraj Bks.

***Pathway of Peace: Cistercian Wisdom According to Saint Bernard.** Charles Dumont. LC 99-30965. (Cistercian Studies: Vol. CS187). 259p. 1999. write for info. (*0-87907-687-9*) Cistercian Pubns.

Pathway of Peace: Cistercian Wisdom According to Saint Bernard. Charles Dumont. LC 99-30965. (Cistercian Studies). 259p. 1999. pap. write for info. (*0-87907-787-5*) Cistercian Pubns.

Pathway of Prayer. Kathryn Thaller. LC 97-150882. 160p. (Orig.). 1996. pap. 10.00 (*1-883893-57-7*) WinePress Pub.

Pathway of Roses. F. W. Boreham. 1997. pap. 8.99 (*1-898787-10-7*) Emerald House Group Inc.

Pathway of Roses: Paths to the Life Beautiful. Christian D. Larson. 368p. 1994. reprint ed. pap. 12.95 (*0-87877-187-5*) Newcastle Pub.

Pathway of the Sun. large type ed. E. V. Timms. 544p. 1983. 27.99 (*0-7089-1021-1*) Ulverscroft.

Pathway to Empire. Edward Hungerford. 325p. 1993. reprint ed. lib. bdg. 89.00 (*0-7812-5126-5*) Rprt Serv.

Pathway to Energy Sufficiency: The 2050 Study. John Steinhart et al. Ed. by Sidney Hollister. LC 78-74807. (Illus.). 1979. reprint ed. pap. 4.95 (*0-913890-31-6*) Friends of Earth.

Pathway to Glory: Keys to Christian Living. Lila B. Mullins. (Illus.). 128p. (Orig.). 1996. pap. 7.95 (*0-9650991-0-5*) Librom Pubng.

Pathway to Health. Charles A. Stanley. 50p. (Orig.). (C). 1989. pap. 5.95 (*0-9614857-3-6*) Pressure Appli.

Pathway to His Presence: Removing Barriers to Intimacy with God, Vol. 1. John Bevere. LC 99-58695. 1999. 16.99 (*0-88419-654-2*) Creation House.

Pathway to Jerusalem. Rabbi Obadiah of Bartenura. 96p. 1992. 9.95 (*1-56062-130-3*); pap. 6.95 (*1-56062-131-1*) CIS Comm.

Pathway to Light: An Introduction to the Unarius Science of Life. unabridged ed. Charles L. Spiegel. LC 96-60148. (Illus.). 44p. 1996. pap. 10.00 (*0-935097-34-1*) Unarius Acad Sci.

Pathway to Paradise. Winston J. Paradise. LC 93-84542. (Illus.). 113p. 1993. per. 9.95 (*1-883122-02-3*) Pearce Pub.

***Pathway to Passion: From the Pits to Passion.** Joann Contorno. 2000. pap. 14.95 (*0-9678157-0-3*) J Contorno.

***Pathway to Peace.** Compiled by Cathy Burns. 72p. 1999. pap. 2.50 (*1-891117-14-9*) Sharing.

***Pathway to Peace.** Lois Eger. 1999. pap. 7.95 (*0-9628733-1-4*, Pub. by Legacy Pub FL) BookWorld.

Pathway to Peace. John T. Ferrier. 64p. 1986. pap. text 6.00 (*0-900235-63-2*) Order Of The Cross.

Pathway to Perfection. Geoffrey Hodson. 1986. 6.95 (*0-8356-7018-X*) Theos Pub Hse.

Pathway to Prayer. Meyer Birnbaum. 1997. 9.95 (*1-58330-109-7*) Feldheim.

Pathway to Prayer & Pietie. Robert Hill. LC 74-28864. (English Experience Ser.: No. 744). 1975. reprint ed. 55.00 (*90-221-0744-2*) Walter J Johnson.

Pathway to Promise. Michele Lepsky. LC 93-19926. 250p. (Orig.). 1993. pap. 4.99 (*1-56722-008-8*) Word Aflame.

Pathway to Reality. Richard B. Haldane. LC 77-27220. (Gifford Lectures: 1902-03). reprint ed. 32.50 (*0-404-60458-7*) AMS Pr.

Pathway to Reality: Stage the Second. Richard B. Haldane. LC 77-27221. (Gifford Lectures: 1903-04). reprint ed. 32.50 (*0-404-60459-5*) AMS Pr.

Pathway to Spiritual Mastery. Phoebe M. Holmes. (Golden Keys Ser.: No. 2). 38p. 1996. reprint ed. spiral bd. 8.00 (*0-7873-0417-4*) Hlth Research.

***Pathway to Success: Forms Packet.** 96p. (C). 1999. pap. text 4.00 (*0-536-01007-2*) Pearson Custom.

***Pathway to the Light of Inner Peace: A Synopsis of Life's Experiences in Poetry.** Janet Matthews Moore. 93p. 2000. pap. 10.95 (*0-7414-0370-6*) Buy Books.

Pathway to the Presidency: Community College Deans of Instruction. George B. Vaughan. 195p. 1990. 10.00 (*0-87117-200-3*, 1212) Comm Coll Pr Am Assn Comm Coll.

Pathways. Ed. by Robert Drederian. (Illus.). 240p. 1998. 49.95 (*1-885206-60-7*) Cader Pubng.

***Pathways.** Evelyn Collins Safeblade. 1999. pap. 6.00 (*0-9670655-0-X*) E C Safeblade.

Pathways. Jeri Taylor. LC 98-216188. (Star Trek). 448p. 1998. 23.00 (*0-671-00346-1*, Pocket Books) PB.

Pathways. Jeri Taylor. (Star Trek). 528p. 1999. per. 6.50 (*0-671-02626-7*, Star Trek) PB.

Pathways. Jeri Taylor. (Star Trek Voyager Ser.). 1998. 24.00 incl. audio (*0-671-58230-5*, Audioworks) S&S Trade.

Pathways. Mary B. Wodzinski. (Illus.). 36p. (Orig.). 1997. pap. 5.95 (*1-886028-24-9*) Savage Pr.

***PATHways.** 2nd ed. Priscilla Herrington. 48p. 2000. pap. 5.00 (*1-889289-49-3*) Ye Olde Font Shoppe.

Pathways: A Guided Workbook for Youth Beginning Treatment. rev. ed. Timothy J. Kahn. Ed. by Euan Bear. 152p. (Orig.). (YA). (gr. 6-12). 1996. pap., wbk. ed. 15.00 (*1-884444-34-2*) Safer Soc.

Pathways: A Job Search Curriculum. Denise Bissonnette-Lamendella. 275p. (Orig.). (YA). 1987. student ed. 7.95 (*0-942071-05-0*) M Wright & Assocs.

Pathways: A Job Search Curriculum. rev. ed. Denise Bissonnette-Lamendella. 265p. (Orig.). (J). 1987. reprint ed. teacher ed. 87.95 (*0-942071-02-6*) M Wright & Assocs.

Pathways: A Text for Developing Writers. 2nd ed. Jarrett & Lee. LC 98-39807. 385p. (C). 1998. pap. text 44.00 (*0-205-26412-3*) Allyn.

Pathways: Approaches to the Study of Society in India. Triloki N. Madan. (Illus.). 304p. 1996. pap. text 12.95 (*0-19-563650-3*) OUP.

***Pathways: Computer Projects.** Korb. 1999. pap. 19.95 (*0-538-72218-5*) Thomson Learn.

Pathways: Fostering Spiritual Growth among At-Risk Youth. Thomas J. Everson. 210p. 1993. ring bd. 49.95 (*0-938510-64-9*, 32-002) Boys Town Pr.

Pathways: From the Culture of Addiction to the Culture of Recovery: A Travel Guide for Addiction Professionals. 2nd rev. ed. William L. White. LC 96-2446. Orig. Title: The Culture of Addiction. 560p. 1996. 29.95 (*1-56838-123-9*) Hazelden.

***Pathways: Internet Projects.** Berry. 2000. pap. 17.95 (*0-538-72430-7*) Sth-Wstrn College.

***Pathways: Internet Projects, Core.** Berry. (Computer Applications Ser.). 2000. pap., student ed. 21.95 (*0-538-72423-4*) Sth-Wstrn College.

Pathways: Jews Who Return. Richard H. Greenberg. LC 96-28981. 312p. 1997. 40.00 (*1-56821-990-3*) Aronson.

Pathways: Moving Beyond Stroke & Aphasia. Susan A. Ewing & Beth Pfalzgraf. LC 90-12148. (William Beaumont Hospital Speech & Language Pathology Ser.). (Illus.). 198p. (C). 1990. pap. text 21.95 (*0-8143-2075-9*) Wayne St U Pr.

Pathways: Moving Beyond Stroke & Aphasia. Susan A. Ewing & Beth Pfalzgraft. LC 90-12148. (William Beaumont Hospital Speech & Language Pathology Ser.). 198p. reprint ed. pap. 61.40 (*0-608-10594-5*, 2071215) Bks Demand.

Pathways: Simulation for Word Processing. Eisch & Voiers. (Computer Applications Ser.). 1998. mass mkt. 13.95 (*0-538-68767-3*) S-W Pub.

***Pathways & Ceremonies: The Cursus Monuments of Britian & Ireland.** Ed. by Alistar Barclay & Jan Harding. (Neolithic Studies Group Seminar Papers: Vol. 4). 154p. 1999. pap. 45.00 (*1-900188-42-2*, Pub. by Oxbow Bks) David Brown.

Pathways & Participation in Vocational & Technical Education & Training. OECD Staff. LC 98-145090. 396p. 1998. pap. 47.00 (*92-64-15368-3*, 91-98-01-1-P, Pub. by Org for Econ) OECD.

Pathways Child. Bachrach. (JRA Ser.: Vol. 3, No. 4). 1993. 20.00 (*0-8058-9983-9*) L Erlbaum Assocs.

Pathways for Communication: Books & Libraries in the Information Age. D. J. Foskett. LC 83-197716. 148p. reprint ed. pap. 45.90 (*0-7837-5321-7*, 204506000005) Bks Demand.

Pathways for Cytolysis. Ed. by G. Griffiths & J. Tschopp. (Currents Topics in Microbiology & Immunology Ser.: Vol. 198). 256p. 1995. 137.95 (*3-540-58725-X*) Spr-Verlag.

Pathways for Exceptional Children: School, Home, & Culture. Paul S. Kaplan. 600p. (C). 1995. 81.95 (*0-314-04563-5*) West Pub.

***Pathways for Kids & Other People Too...** Prophet Andromeda. Ed. by Sherry Knecht. (Illus.). 52p. (J). (gr. 3-6). 1999. pap. 9.95 (*1-929589-03-4*) Branching Leaf.

***Pathways for Kids & Other People Too...** 2nd rev. ed. Andromeda Knecht. 58p. (J). (gr. 3-6). 1999. pap. 9.95 (*1-929589-17-4*) Branching Leaf.

Pathways for Minorities into the Health Professions. Pedro J. Lecca & Thomas D. Watts. 98p. 1989. 33.00 (*0-8191-7552-8*) U Pr of Amer.

Pathways for the Poet. Viola Jacobson Berg. 130p. 1999. pap. write for info. (*1-889732-18-4*) Word-For-Word.

Pathways for Women in the Sciences: The Wellesley Report, Pt. I. Paula Rayman et al. (Illus.). 154p. (Orig.). 1997. pap. 42.50 (*0-9641921-0-1*) WC Ctr Res Women.

Pathways for Women in the Sciences: The Wellesley Report, Pt. II. Paula Rayman et al. (Illus.). 154p. (Orig.). 1997. pap. 42.50 (*0-9641921-2-8*) WC Ctr Res Women.

Pathways from the Periphery: The Politics of Growth in the Newly Industrializing Countries. Stephan Haggard. LC 90-32300. (Cornell Studies in Political Economy). 294p. 1990. pap. text 15.95 (*0-8014-9750-7*) Cornell U Pr.

Pathways Guide for Parents of Youth Beginning Treatment. Timothy J. Kahn. Ed. by Euan Bear. 48p. (C). 1997. pap., wbk. ed. 8.00 (*1-884444-01-6*) Safer Soc.

Pathways in Applied Immunology: In Memoriam Walter Brendel. Ed. by K. Messmer & M. Stein. (Illus.). 152p. 1991. 38.95 (*0-387-53989-1*) Spr-Verlag.

Pathways in Juggling: Learn How to Juggle with Balls, Rings, Clubs, Devil Sticks, Diabolos & Other Objects. Robert Irving & Mike Edwards. (Illus.). 128p. (Orig.). 1997. pap. 19.95 (*1-55209-121-X*) Firefly Bks Ltd.

Pathways in Medical Ethics. Alan G. Johnson. 176p. pap. text. write for info. (*0-340-50720-9*, Pub. by E A) Routldge.

Pathways in Pediatrics. Brendan G. Loftus. 288p. 1995. 24.95 (*0-340-59036-X*, Pub. by E A) OUP.

Pathways in Surgical Management see Arbeitsdiagnose - Neue Wege der Chirurgischen Diagnose und Therapie

Pathways in the Workplace: The Effect of Race & Gender on Access to Organzational Resources. Jon Miller. (American Sociological Assn. Rose Monographs). (Illus.). 128p. 1986. text 54.95 (*0-521-32365-7*) Cambridge U Pr.

Pathways into Caring. Poole College Staff et al. 240p. 1999. pap. 32.50 (*0-7487-1569-X*, Pub. by S Thornes Pubs) Trans-Atl Phila.

***Pathways Into Jungian World: Phenomenology & Analytical Psychology.** Roger Brooke. LC 98-56540. 1999. pap. 29.99 (*0-415-16999-2*) Routledge.

***Pathways into the Jungian World: Phenomenology & Analytical Psychology.** Ed. by Roger Brooke. LC 98-56540. 274p. (C). 1999. text. write for info. (*0-415-16998-4*) Routledge.

Pathways Literature Circles. 48p. 1997. pap. text 21.95 (*1-58303-021-2*) Pthways Pubng.

Pathways of Addiction: Opportunities in Drug Abuse Research. Institute of Medicine, Committee on Opportunities. 328p. (Orig.). (C). 1996. pap. text 49.95 (*0-309-05533-4*) Natl Acad Pr.

Pathways of Care. Sue Johnson. LC 96-28014. 240p. (Orig.). 1997. pap. text 36.95 (*0-632-04076-9*) Blackwell Sci.

***Pathways of Change: Grammaticalization in English.** Olga Fischer et al. LC 00-42899. (Studies in Language Companion Ser.). 2000. write for info. (*1-55619-939-2*) J Benjamins Pubng Co.

Pathways of Chemistry, Vol. 1. D. P. Goel. 944p. 1996. pap. 150.00 (*81-209-0212-2*, Pub. by Pitambar Pub) St Mut.

Pathways of Chemistry, Vol. 2. D. P. Goel. 944p. 1996. pap. 180.00 (*81-209-0213-0*, Pub. by Pitambar Pub) St Mut.

***Pathways of Faith: A Story of Widening Opportunities in Mission.** Lester A. Dahlen. LC 99-43329. (Illus.). 228p. 1999. pap. 12.00 (*1-886513-04-X*) Kirk Hse Pubs.

Pathways of Growth: Essentials of Child Psychiatry, 1999 Edition, 2 vols., Vol. 1: Introduction to Child Psychiatry. 99th ed. Joseph D. Noshpitz & Robert King. LC 90-12693. 453p. 1991. 150.00 (*0-471-09917-1*) Wiley.

Pathways of Language Development. Department of Education-Arts Staff. (C). 1990. 90.00 (*0-86431-066-8*, Pub. by Aust Council Educ Res) St Mut.

***Pathways of Learning: Teaching Students & Parents about Multiple Intelligences.** David Lazear. (Illus.). 260p. 2000. pap. 37.00 (*1-56976-118-3*, 1115) Zephyr Pr AZ.

Pathways of Learning: Teaching Students & Parents about Multiple Intelligences. David Lazear. LC 93-33054. 256p. 1999. pap. 37.00 (*0-913705-92-6*) Zephyr Pr AZ.

Pathways of Life in Prose & Poetry. large type ed. LaVerne Stevens. (Illus.). 26p. (Orig.). 1995. pap. 5.00 (*0-9630441-4-1*) B&B Pr.

Pathways of Memory & Power: Ethnography & History among an Andean People. Thomas A. Abercrombie. LC 96-38814. (Illus.). 552p. 1997. 60.00 (*0-299-15310-X*); pap. 27.00 (*0-299-15314-2*) U of Wis Pr.

Pathways of My Journey. Patricia A. Bayless Behnken. LC 93-90621. (Illus.). 152p. (Orig.). 1993. pap. 9.95 (*0-9637811-0-3*) Morning Joy.

Pathways of Philosophy. Manly P. Hall. (Illus.). 254p. 1991. reprint ed. pap. 15.95 (*0-89314-836-9*) Philos Res.

***Pathways of Poetry.** Hazel Miller. 2000. write for info. (*1-58235-573-8*) Watermrk Pr.

***Pathways of Power: Building an Anthropology of the Modern World.** Eric R. Wolf. 488p. 2001. pap. 24.95 (*0-520-22334-9*) U CA Pr.

***Pathways of Power: Building an Anthropology of the Modern World.** Eric R. Wolf. Ed. by Sydel Silverman. 488p. 2001. 60.00 (*0-520-22333-0*) U CA Pr.

Pathways of Recovery: New Life for the Diminished Person. James A. Kitchens. 120p. (Orig.). (C). 1991. pap. 7.95 (*0-9624469-1-2*) Ads-Co.

Pathways of Song Vol. 1: Low Voice. 64p. 1994. pap. 8.95 (*0-89724-257-2*, VF0133) Wrner Bros.

Pathways of Song Vol. 4: High. 64p. (Orig.). (YA). 1997. pap. 8.95 (*0-7692-1066-X*, VF2005) Wrner Bros.

Pathways of Song Best of High. 128p. (Orig.). (YA). 1994. pap. 12.95 (*0-7692-1064-3*, VF1359) Wrner Bros.

Pathways of Song Best of Low. 128p. (Orig.). (YA). 1994. pap. 12.95 (*0-7692-1065-1*, VF1360) Wrner Bros.

Pathways of Spiritual Living. 2nd ed. Susan A. Muto. LC 84-15164. 191p. 1988. reprint ed. pap. 12.95 (*0-932506-65-8*) St Bedes Pubns.

Pathways of the Brain: The Neurocogntivie Basis of Language. Sidney M. Lamb. LC 98-31816. (Current Issues in Linguistic Theory Ser.: Vol. 170). xii, 418p. 1999. pap. 34.95 (*1-55619-888-4*) J Benjamins Pubng Co.

Pathways of the Brain: The Neurocogntivie Basis of Language. Sydney M. Lamb. LC 98-31816. (Current Issues in Linguistic Theory Ser.: Vol. 170). xii, 418p. 1999. 95.00 (*1-55619-886-8*) J Benjamins Pubng Co.

Pathways of the Pulp. 7th ed. Stephen Cohen & Richard C. Burns. LC 98-184459. (Illus.). 912p. (C). (gr. 13). 1997. text 89.00 (*0-8151-8613-4*, 30606) Mosby Inc.

***Pathways on a Journey.** Laurel J. Freeman. 160p. 1999. pap. 10.00 (*1-892937-05-0*) Spec Pubns.

Pathways Through Adolescence: Individual Development in Relation to Social Contexts. Ed. by Lisa J. Crockett & Ann C. Crouter. (Penn State Series on Child & Adolescent Development). 280p. 1995. 49.95 (*0-8058-1500-7*) L Erlbaum Assocs.

***Pathways Through Conciousness, 4 vols.** 2nd rev. ed. Andromeda Knecht. 1999. pap. 199.95 (*1-929589-23-9*) Branching Leaf.

***Pathways Through Consciousness, 4 vols.** Prophet Andromeda. Ed. by Sherry Knecht. (Illus.). (Orig.). 1999. pap. text 199.95 (*1-929589-12-3*) Branching Leaf.

Pathways Through Jewish History. rev. ed. Ruth Samuels. LC 98-165318. (Illus.). (J). (gr. 7-10). 1977. pap. 11.95 (*0-87068-520-1*) Ktav.

***Pathways Through Pain: A Spiritual Journey.** Linda Sonnett Carlson. LC 99-44303. 2000. pap. write for info. (*1-880090-96-1*) Galde Pr.

Pathways Through Pain: Women's Journeys. Ann B. Callender. LC 98-54172. 176p. 1999. 16.95 (*0-8298-1306-3*) Pilgrim OH.

Pathways Through Surgical Finals. J. A. Britto & M. J. Dalrymple-Hay. LC 93-12293. 200p. 1993. pap. text 25.00 (*0-443-04806-1*) Church.

Pathways Through Taharss: Ramban's Introduction. Aaron Werner. 121p. 1994. text 11.95 (*1-885006-18-7*); pap. text 8.95 (*1-885006-19-5*) Three Beacons.

Pathways Through the Land of the Hart. Miriam F. Vamosh. (Illus.). 62p. (Orig.). 1993. pap. 12.95 (*965-229-089-0*, Pub. by Gefen Pub Hse) Gefen Bks.

Pathways to a Grand Canyon Adventure. Judith Bisignano & Rayna Gellman. (Illus.). 128p. (Orig.). (J). (gr. 3-9). 1996. pap. 9.95 (*0-9642469-1-0*) Lrning to Lrn.

Pathways to a More Satisfying Life. William Gerber. (Revisioning Philosophy Ser.: Vol. 5). XII, 334p. 1991. 53.95 (*0-8204-1357-7*) P Lang Pubng.

Pathways to Advanced Skills Vol. 1: Learning Less Commonly Taught Languages: An Agreement on the Bases for the Training of Teachers. Galal Walker & Scott McGinnis. LC 96-206237. 28p. (Orig.). 1995. pap. 3.50 (*0-87415-306-9*, PAT-P01) Foreign Lang.

Pathways to Advanced Skills Vol. 2: Chinese Pedagogy: An Emerging Field. Ed. by Scott McGinnis. LC 97-142168. 328p. (Orig.). 1996. pap. 20.95 (*0-87415-313-1*, PA02) Foreign Lang.

Pathways to Agility: Mass Customization in Action. John D. Oleson. LC 97-31608. (Illus.). 263p. 1998. 39.95 (*0-471-19175-2*) Wiley.

Pathways to Anarchism. Philip Edwards. LC 97-71461. (Avebury Series in Philosophy). 152p. 1997. text 59.95 (*1-85972-639-9*, Pub. by Ashgate Pub) Ashgate Pub Co.

Pathways to Asia: The Politics of Engagement. Ed. by Richard Robison. LC 96-185109. 288p. 1997. pap. text 24.95 (*1-86448-102-1*, Pub. by Allen & Unwin Pty) Paul & Co Pubs.

***Pathways to Career Success for Minorities: A Resource Guide to Colleges, Financial Aid, & Work.** J. G. Ferguson Publishing Company Staff. LC 00-21838. 360p. 2000. pap. 29.95 (*0-89434-303-3*) Ferguson.

***Pathways to Career Success for Women.** LC 00-21892. (Pathways to Career Success Ser.). 2000. 29.95 (*0-89434-281-9*) Ferguson.

Pathways to Change: Brief Therapy Solutions with Difficult Adolescents. Matthew D. Selekman. LC 93-848. 186p. 1993. lib. bdg. 28.00 (*0-89862-015-5*) Guilford Pubns.

Pathways to Change: Improving the Quality of Education in Developing Countries. Adriaan M. Verspoor. (Discussion Papers: No. 53). 202p. 1989. pap. 22.00 (*0-8213-1228-6*, 20053) World Bank.

Pathways to Change: Strategic Choices in Labor Negotiations. Joel E. Cutcher-Gershenfeld et al. LC 95-39190. 265p. (C). 1995. 37.00 (*0-88099-156-9*); pap. 19.00 (*0-88099-155-0*) W E Upjohn.

Pathways to Co-Operation: Starting Points for Co-Operative Learning. Dot Walker & Pamela Brown. Ed. by Debra Doyle. (Illus.). 88p. (Orig.). 1994. teacher ed. 15.00 (*1-875327-20-7*, Pub. by E Curtain) Peguis Pubs Ltd.

Pathways to Criminal Violence. Ed. by Neil A. Weiner & Marvin E. Wolfgang. LC 88-30870. (Sage Focus Editions Ser.: No. 102). 240p. 1989. pap. 74.40 (*0-608-05068-7*, 206562300005) Bks Demand.

Pathways to Criminal Violence. Ed. by Neil A. Weiner & Marvin E. Wolfgang. (Focus Editions Ser.: Vol. 102). 320p. (C). 1989. text 59.95 (*0-8039-3343-6*); pap. text 26.00 (*0-8039-3344-4*) Sage.

***Pathways to Critical Thinking: Belle Prater's Boy.** 32p. 1999. pap. text 19.95 (*1-58303-081-6*) Pthways Pubng.

***Pathways to Critical Thinking: Catherine, Called Birdy.** 32p. 2000. pap. text 19.95 (*1-58303-085-9*) Pthways Pubng.

***Pathways to Critical Thinking: My Brother Sam Is Dead.** 32p. 2000. pap. text 19.95 (*1-58303-086-7*) Pthways Pubng.

***Pathways to Critical Thinking: Nothing but the Truth.** 32p. 2000. pap. text 19.95 (*1-58303-087-5*) Pthways Pubng.

***Pathways to Critical Thinking: Out of the Dust.** 32p. 1999. pap. text 19.95 (*1-58303-082-4*) Pthways Pubng.

***Pathways to Critical Thinking: The Outsiders.** 32p. 1999. pap. text 19.95 (*1-58303-083-2*) Pthways Pubng.

***Pathways to Critical Thinking: The Pigman.** 32p. 1999. pap. text 19.95 (*1-58303-084-0*) Pthways Pubng.

***Pathways to Critical Thinking: The Watsons Go to Birmingham - 1963.** 32p. 2000. pap. text 19.95 (*1-58303-088-3*) Pthways Pubng.

Pathways to Culture: Readings on Teaching Culture in the Foreign Language Class. Ed. by Paula R. Heusinkveld. LC 97-18486. 712p. (Orig.). (C). 1997. pap. text 29.95 (*1-877864-48-X*) Intercult Pr.

***Pathways to Democracy: Political Economy of Democratic Transitions.** Ed. by James Frank Hollifield & Calvin C. Jillson. LC 99-35009. 344p. (C). 1999. text. write for info. (*0-415-92433-2*) Routledge.

***Pathways to Democracy: The Political Economy of Democratic Transitions** James F. Hollifield & Calvin C. Jillson. LC 99-35009. 1999. pap. 24.99 (*0-415-92434-0*) Routledge.

Pathways to Discovery, No. 1. Ed. by George Donigian. 1992. 99.95 (*0-687-30342-7*) Abingdon.

Pathways to Discovery, No. 2. Ed. by George Donigian. 1993. 99.95 (*0-687-30362-1*) Abingdon.

P

Pathways to Discovery, No. 3. Ed. by George Donigian. 1994. 99.95 (*0-687-30368-0*) Abingdon.

Pathways to Discovery: Exploring America's National Trails. Ed. by Donald J. Crump. LC 90-20750. (Special Publications Series 25: No. 4). (Illus.). (YA). 1990. 12.95 (*0-87044-792-0*) Natl Geog.

Pathways to Economic Development. Richard Grabowski. LC 99-12124. 208p. 1999. write for info. (*1-84064-112-6*) E Elgar.

Pathways to Elfland: The Writings of Lord Dunsany. Darrell Schweitzer. (Illus.). 180p. 1989. 25.00 (*0-913896-16-0*) Owlswick Pr.

Pathways to English, Bk. 1. National Council of Teachers of English Staff. 1984. pap. text, wbk. ed. 5.37 (*0-07-046605-X*) McGraw.

Pathways to English, Bk. 1. 3rd ed. National Council of Teachers of English Staff. 1984. text, teacher ed. 14.95 (*0-07-046591-6*) McGraw.

Pathways to English, Bk. 2. 3rd ed. National Council of Teachers of English Staff. 1984. text, wbk. ed. 5.37 (*0-07-046616-5*) McGraw.

Pathways to English, Bk. 2. 3rd ed. National Council of Teachers of English Staff. 1984. text 93.92 (*0-07-046619-X*) McGraw.

Pathways to English, Bk. 2. 3rd ed. National Council of Teachers of English Staff. 1984. text, teacher ed. 14.95 (*0-07-046592-4*) McGraw.

Pathways to English, Bk. 3. 3rd ed. National Council of Teachers of English Staff. 1984. text, teacher ed. 14.95 (*0-07-046593-2*); pap. text, wbk. ed. 5.37 (*0-07-046626-2*) McGraw.

Pathways to English, Bk. 4. 3rd ed. National Council of Teachers of English Staff. 1984. text, teacher ed. 14.95 (*0-07-046633-5*); pap. text, wbk. ed. 5.37 (*0-07-046610-6*) McGraw.

Pathways to English, Bk. 4. 3rd ed. National Council of Teachers of English Staff. 1984. text 93.92 (*0-07-046611-4*) McGraw.

Pathways to English, Bk. 5. 3rd ed. National Council of Teachers of English Staff. 1984. text 8.51 (*0-07-046635-1*); pap. text, wbk. ed. 5.37 (*0-07-046620-3*) McGraw.

Pathways to English, Bk. 5. 3rd ed. National Council of Teachers of English Staff. 1984. text 93.92 (*0-07-046621-1*) McGraw.

Pathways to English, Bk. 5. 3rd ed. National Council of Teachers of English Staff. 1984. text, teacher ed. 14.95 (*0-07-046636-X*) McGraw.

Pathways to English, Bk. 6. 3rd ed. National Council of Teachers of English Staff. 1984. text 8.51 (*0-07-046638-6*); text, teacher ed. 14.95 (*0-07-046639-4*) McGraw.

Pathways to English, Bk. 6. 3rd ed. National Council of Teachers of English Staff. 1984. pap. text, wbk. ed. 5.37 (*0-07-046630-0*) McGraw.

Pathways to English, Vol. 1. 3rd ed. National Council of Teachers of English Staff. 192p. 1983. 8.51 (*0-07-046581-9*) McGraw.

Pathways to English, Vol. 2. 3rd ed. National Council of Teachers of English Staff. 1984. text 8.51 (*0-07-046582-7*) McGraw.

Pathways to Excellence: A Report on Improving Library & Information Services for Native American Peoples, 2 vol. set. 1995. lib. bdg. 599.99 (*0-8490-6548-8*) Gordon Pr.

Pathways to Excellence: Improving Library & Information Services for Native American Peoples, 2 vols. 1994. lib. bdg. 654.75 (*0-8490-8515-2*) Gordon Pr.

Pathways to Excellence: Improving Library & Information Services for Native American Peoples. 1995. lib. bdg. 600.99 (*0-8490-6767-7*) Gordon Pr.

Pathways to Fun Animal Mazes: Preschool/Kindergarten. School Zone Publishing Staff. (Illus.). (J). (ps-3). 1995. pap. 2.99 (*0-88743-113-5*) Sch Zone Pub Co.

Pathways to Fundamental Theories. L. Brink & R. Marnelius. 376p. 1993. text 109.00 (*981-02-1411-1*) World Scientific Pub.

Pathways to God: A Study Guide to the Teachings of Sathya Sai Baba. Jonathan Roof. LC 91-61787. 218p. 1991. pap. 12.00 (*0-9629835-0-0*) Leela Pr.

Pathways to Growth: Comparing East Asia & Latin America. Ed. by Nancy Birdsall & Frederick Jaspersen. LC 97-71220. (Inter-American Development Bank Ser.). 330p. 1997. pap. text 21.95 (*1-886938-13-X*) IADB.

***Pathways to Healing: A Guide to Herbs, Ayurveda, Dreambody & Shamanism.** Don Ollsin. (Illus.). 208p. 1999. pap. 14.95 (*1-58394-011-1*) Frog Ltd CA.

Pathways to Holiness. Louis of Granada. Tr. & Adapted by Jordan Aumann. LC 97-36682. 144p. 1998. pap. 7.95 (*0-8189-0805-X*) Alba.

Pathways to Human Ecology: From Observation to Commitment. Ed. by Huib Ernste. LC 95-166296. 277p. 1994. 46.95 (*3-906753-17-4*) P Lang Pubng.

Pathways to Independence: Discovering Independence National Historical Park. Shirley Milgrim. LC 73-89767. (Illus.). 128p. 1975. 16.95 (*0-85699-101-5*) Chatham Pr.

Pathways to Industrialization & Regional Development. Ed. by Michael Storper & Allen J. Scott. LC 92-10397. (Illus.). 412p. (C). (gr. 13). 1992. 110.00 (*0-415-08752-X*, A9632) Routledge.

Pathways to Inner Peace: Lifesaving Processes for Healing Mind-Body-Spirit. James Webb. mass mkt. 14.95 (*0-9663277-1-3*) Prism Pub.

Pathways to Integration: Lebanon & the Euro-Mediterranean Partnership. Wassin Shahin et al. (Illus.). 286p. 1997. pap. write for info. (*1-886604-11-8*) Lebanese Ctr.

Pathways to Intimacy: Communicating with Care & Resolving Differences. Marvel E. Harrison & Terry Kellogg. 113p. 1994. pap. text 7.95 (*1-880257-08-4*, PATH) BRAT Pub.

Pathways to Investigative Skills: Instructional Lessons for Guiding Students from Problem Finding to Final Product, Grades 3-9. Deborah E. Burns. 104p. 1990. ring bd. 49.95 incl. sl. (*0-936386-54-1*) Creative Learning.

Pathways to Leadership: An ABA Roadmap. 24p. 1993. 5.00 (*0-89707-930-2*, 492-0007) Amer Bar Assn.

Pathways to Leadership: How to Achieve & Sustain Success. James L. Powell. LC 94-43956. (Nonprofit Sector Ser.). 279p. 1995. text 28.95 (*0-7879-0094-X*) Jossey-Bass.

Pathways to Learning in Rett Syndrome. Jackie Lewis. LC 98-186005. 1998. pap. 26.95 (*1-85346-533-X*, Pub. by David Fulton) Taylor & Francis.

Pathways to Literacy. Trevor H. Caimey. (Children, Teachers & Learning Ser.). (Illus.). 208p. 1996. 100.00 (*0-304-32721-2*); pap. 33.95 (*0-304-32723-9*) Continuum.

Pathways to Literacy: Process Transactions. 2nd ed. Roach Van Allen et al. 576p. (C). 1994. text 79.50 (*0-15-501316-5*, Pub. by Harcourt Coll Pubs) Harcourt.

Pathways to Manhood: Young Black Males Struggle for Identity. 2nd exp. ed. Janet M. Billson. 382p. 1996. pap. text 24.95 (*1-56000-871-7*) Transaction Pubs.

Pathways to Maturity: Insights from a 30 Year Study. Betty M. Flint et al. LC 96-219800. 192p. 1996. text 50.00 (*0-8020-0785-6*) U of Toronto Pr.

Pathways to Maturity: Insights from a 30 Year Study. Betty M. Flint et al. LC 96-219800. 192p. 1996. pap. text 16.95 (*0-8020-7148-1*) U of Toronto Pr.

Pathways to Multicultural Counseling Competence: A Developmental Journey. Bea Wehrly. LC 95-12691. 247p. 1995. mass mkt. 41.95 (*0-534-33849-6*) Brooks-Cole.

Pathways to Number: Children's Developing Numerical Abilities. rev. ed. Ed. by Jacqueline Bideaud et al. 408p. 1992. text 89.95 (*0-8058-0866-3*) L Erlbaum Assocs.

Pathways to Parliament: Candidate Selection in Britain. Austin Ranney. LC 65-16364. 314p. 1965. reprint ed. pap. 97.40 (*0-608-01898-8*, 206255000003) Bks Demand.

Pathways to Partnerships: Coalitions for EE: Proceedings from NAAEE's 1993 Annual Conference in Big Sky, Montana. Ed. by Rick Mrazek. 516p. (Orig.). 1994. pap. 10.00 (*1-884008-19-4*) NAAEE.

Pathways to Paul Celan Vol. 73: A History of Critical Responses as a Chorus of Discordant Voices. Bianca Rosenthal. LC 94-23691. (Studies in Modern German Literature). VII, 239p. (C). 1996. text 49.95 (*0-8204-2695-4*) P Lang Pubng.

Pathways to Peace. Sri S. Satchidananda. 1998. pap. 3.95 (*0-932040-45-4*) Integral Yoga Pubns.

Pathways to Peace: Forty Steps to a Less Violent America. 2nd rev. ed. Victor La Cerva. (Illus.). 256p. 1997. pap. 15.00 (*0-9661575-0-8*) HEAL Found.

Pathways to Peace: 40 Steps to a Less Violent America. Victor LaCerva. (Illus.). 256p. (Orig.). 1996. pap. 15.00 (*0-9649104-0-3*) Heartsongs Publn.

Pathways to People. Leonard W. Doob. LC 74-29716. 343p. reprint ed. pap. 106.40 (*0-8357-8746-X*, 203371100087) Bks Demand.

Pathways to People. 2nd rev. ed. Eileen Curns & Clyde Lowstuter. (Illus.). 73p. 1978. pap. 12.00 (*0-942968-00-X*) ACCORD IL.

Pathways to Perfect Living. Vernon Howard. 202p. 1969. reprint ed. pap. 9.95 (*0-911203-35-4*) New Life.

Pathways to Perfection. Thomas S. Monson. LC 73-88634. xiv, 302p. 1973. 14.95 (*0-87747-511-3*) Deseret Bk.

Pathways to Performance: A Guide to Transforming Yourself, Your Team, & Your Organization. Jim Clemmer. LC 94-47410. (Illus.). 352p. 1995. 22.95 (*0-7615-0021-9*) Prima Pub.

Pathways to Performance: A Guide to Transforming Yourself, Your Team, & Your Organization. Jim Clemmer. 352p. 1996. per. 15.00 (*0-7615-0735-3*) Prima Pub.

Pathways to Personal Growth: Adjustment in Today's World. George R. Goethals et al. LC 98-5941. 493p. 1998. pap. text 41.00 (*0-205-13955-8*) Allyn.

Pathways to Philosophy: A Multidisciplinary Approach. Douglas W. Shrader & Ashok Malhotra. LC 95-40431. (Illus.). 452p. 1995. pap. text 57.00 (*0-02-410191-5*, Macmillan Coll) P-H.

Pathways to Play: Developing Play Skills in Young Children. Sandra Heidemann & Deborah Hewitt. LC 92-17167. (Illus.). 110p. (Orig.). 1992. pap. 14.95 (*0-934140-65-0*, 4543) Redleaf Pr.

***Pathways to Pleasure: A Woman's Guide to Orgasm.** Robert William Birch & Cynthia Lief Ruberg. 210p. 2000. pap. 14.95 (*1-57074-479-3*, Pub. by PEC) ACCESS Pubs Network.

Pathways to Pluralism Religious Issues in American Culture. Robert A. Spivey. 1990. pap. (*0-201-22177-2*) Addison-Wesley.

Pathways to Pluralism Religious Issues in American Culture Teacher's Guide. 1990. write for info. (*0-201-22178-0*) Addison-Wesley.

Pathways to Poetry: Poetry Fun for Grades 1-3. Phylliss J. Adams & Ellen L. Kronowitz. 288p. (J). (gr. 1-3). 16.99 (*0-86653-914-X*, FE0914) Fearon Teacher Aids.

Pathways to Poetry: Poetry Fun for Grades 4-6. Phylliss J. Adams & Ellen L. Kronowitz. (J). (gr. 4-6). 16.99 (*0-86653-913-1*, FE0913) Fearon Teacher Aids.

Pathways to Poetry: Poetry Fun for Preschool-Kindergarten. Phylliss J. Adams & Ellen L. Kronowitz. 256p. (J). (ps-6). 16.99 (*0-86653-915-8*, FE0915) Fearon Teacher Aids.

Pathways to Poetry: Writing, Reading & Performing. Katherine Kane & Carol Richman. 64p. (J). (gr. 5-8). 1996. pap. text, teacher ed. 11.95 (*1-881641-58-9*) Pencil Point.

Pathways to Poetry Series: Kaleidoscope, Mosaics, Visions. Jeanne Long et al. Ed. by Jo Miller. (J). (gr. 1-12). 1984. pap. text 44.74 (*0-86617-033-2*) Multi Media TX.

Pathways to Power: Keys That Open Doors. Paul N. Tassell. LC 83-9576. 143p. 1983. reprint ed. pap. 5.99 (*0-87227-093-9*, RBP5119) Reg Baptist.

Pathways to Praying with Teens. Maryann Hakowski. LC 94-113924. 96p. 1993. pap. 15.95 (*0-88489-296-4*) St Marys.

Pathways to Pregnancy & Parturition. Phillip L. Senger. LC 98-180612. (Illus.). x, 275p. (C). 1997. text. write for info. (*0-9657648-0-X*) Current Concept.

Pathways to Print: Color. Robin B. McAllister. LC 98-157804. 80p. (C). 1997. mass mkt. 19.95 (*0-8273-7916-1*) Delmar.

Pathways to Print: Conquering Color, Trapping, Designing for Production, 8 modules. McAllister. (Complete Series for Desktop Publishing). (Illus.). 608p. (C). 1997. mass mkt. 55.95 (*0-8273-7926-9*) Delmar.

Pathways to Print: Design for Production. Robin B. McAllister. LC 96-29481. (Illus.). 80p. (C). 1996. mass mkt. 19.95 (*0-8273-7919-6*) Delmar.

Pathways to Print: Introduction to Desktop Publishing. Robin B. McAllister. LC 96-34409. (Illus.). 80p. (C). 1996. mass mkt. 19.95 (*0-8273-7914-5*) Delmar.

Pathways to Print: Quality Assurance. McAllister. (Illus.). 80p. (C). 1997. mass mkt. 19.95 (*0-8273-7924-2*) Delmar.

Pathways to Print: Scanning & Image Manipulation. McAllister. LC 96-34459. (Illus.). 64p. (C). 1996. pap. 19.95 (*0-8273-7917-X*) Delmar.

Pathways to Print: The Business Side. McAllister. LC 98-157800. (Illus.). 80p. (C). 1997. mass mkt. 19.95 (*0-8273-7923-4*) Delmar.

Pathways to Print: Trapping. McAllister. LC 97-15143. (Illus.). 80p. (C). 1997. mass mkt. 19.95 (*0-8273-7915-3*) Delmar.

Pathways to Print: Type Management. Robin B. McAllister. LC 96-36056. (Illus.). 80p. (C). 1996. mass mkt. 19.95 (*0-8273-7921-8*) Delmar.

Pathways to Privatization in Education. Joseph Murphy. LC 97-30771. (Contemporary Studies in Social & Policy Issues in Education). 1998. 73.25 (*1-56750-363-2*); pap. 24.95 (*1-56750-364-0*) Ablx Pub.

Pathways to Proficiency Kit - Spanish. M. Karper & V. Galloway. (Spanish K-12 Ser.). (Illus.). 1989. pap. text, teacher ed. 243.75 (*0-201-17067-1*) Addison-Wesley.

Pathways to Profits. Mike Mason & Brodie Bruner. 100p. (C). 1995. pap. 24.95 (*0-9635096-2-4*) Telsco Indust.

Pathways to Prosperity: Choices for Success in the Information Age. Kenneth D. Wilson & Richard Goldhurst. LC 83-11177. 147p. 1983. 47.95 (*0-275-91104-7*, C1104, Praeger Pubs) Greenwood.

Pathways to Psychology. Sandra Scarry et al. LC 96-78389. 578p. (C). 1996. text 64.00 (*0-15-505331-0*, Pub. by Harcourt Coll Pubs) Harcourt.

Pathways to Psychology. Sandra Scarry et al. LC 96-78389. 578p. (C). 1997. text 58.50 (*0-15-501047-6*, Pub. by Harcourt Coll Pubs) Harcourt.

Pathways to Psychology. Sternbe. (C). 1996. pap. text, student ed. 25.00 (*0-15-504068-5*, Pub. by Harcourt Coll Pubs) Harcourt.

Pathways to Psychology. Sternberg. (C). 1996. pap. text, teacher ed. 28.00 (*0-15-504073-1*) Harcourt.

Pathways to Psychology. 2nd ed. Sternberg. (C). 1999. pap. text, teacher ed. Price not set. (*0-15-508060-1*) Harcourt Coll Pubs.

Pathways to Psychology. 2nd ed. Sternburg. LC 99-64294. (C). 1999. pap. text 65.00 (*0-15-508047-4*, Pub. by Harcourt Coll Pubs) Harcourt.

Pathways to Re-Creating Religious Communities. Patricia Wittberg. 288p. 1996. pap. 14.95 (*0-8091-3640-6*, 3640-6) Paulist Pr.

Pathways to Reality: Erickson-Inspired Treatment Approaches to Chemical Dependency. John D. Lovern. LC 91-13541. 240p. 1991. text 34.95 (*0-87630-633-4*) Brunner-Mazel.

Pathways to Self Determination: Canadian Indians & the Canadian State. Ed. by Leroy Little Bear et al. 192p. (Orig.). 1984. pap. text 15.95 (*0-8020-6539-2*) U of Toronto Pr.

Pathways to Self-Determination: Canadian Indians & the Canadian State. Ed. by Leroy Little Bear et al. LC 84-162255. (Illus.). 223p. reprint ed. pap. 69.20 (*0-8357-4729-8*, 203764500009) Bks Demand.

***Pathways to Sexual Behavior.** Jean Cons. 2000. pap. text. write for info. (*0-7167-3749-3*) W H Freeman.

Pathways to Social Class: A Qualitative Approach to Social Mobility. Daniel Bertaux & Paul Thompson. (Illus.). 344p. 1997. text 78.00 (*0-19-827931-0*) OUP.

Pathways to Spiritual Understanding: An Exciting Introduction to the Basics of the Christian Life. Richard Powers. 245p. 1988. pap. 16.99 (*1-56322-023-7*) Hensley Pub.

Pathways to Success. 140p. (C). 1998. write for info. (*0-536-01006-4*) Pearson Custom.

Pathways to Success. Michael D. Ames. (GB - Basic Business Ser.). 1994. mass mkt., wbk. ed. 19.95 (*0-538-63727-7*) S-W Pub.

Pathways to Success. Ed. by Lloyd R. Sloan & B. James Starr. (Illus.). 18p. 1997. pap. text 21.95 (*0-88258-139-2*, SLPSP) Howard U Pr.

Pathways to Success: Today's Business Leaders Tell How to Excel in Work, Career, & Leadership Roles. Michael D. Ames. LC 94-1870. (Illus.). 320p. (Orig.). 1994. pap. 16.95 (*1-881052-57-5*) Berrett-Koehler.

Pathways to Success: Your Roadmap to Total Happiness & Achievement. Todd L. Mayo. LC 96-67933. 450p. (Orig.). 1996. pap. 14.95 (*0-9647700-1-6*) Capital Com Inc.

Pathways to Success: 1st Steps for Becoming a Christian in Action. Martin Mawyer. LC 94-67320. 176p. (Orig.). 1994. pap. 9.95 (*0-89221-270-5*) New Leaf.

Pathways to Success in School: Culturally Responsive Teaching. Ed. by Etta R. Hollins & Eileenn I. Oliver. 272p. 1998. write for info. (*0-8058-2805-2*) L Erlbaum Assocs.

Pathways to Success in School: Culturally Responsive Teaching. Ed. by Etta R. Hollins & Eileenn I. Oliver. LC 98-34839. 224p. 1999. pap. 24.50 (*0-8058-2806-0*) L Erlbaum Assocs.

Pathways to Suicide: A Survey of Self-Destructive Behaviors. Ronald W. Maris. LC 80-24520. (Illus.). 399p. 1981. reprint ed. pap. 123.70 (*0-7837-1111-5*, 204164100021) Bks Demand.

Pathways to Tax Reform. Stanley S. Surrey. LC 73-87686. 440p. 1974. 43.00 (*0-674-65789-6*) HUP.

***Pathways to Teaching: A Guide for Beginning Early Childhood Teachers.** 3rd ed. Linda Peacock & Willa Johnson. 192p. (C). 1999. spiral bd. 36.95 (*0-7872-5998-5*, 41599803) Kendall-Hunt.

Pathways to Teshuva. Tr. by Shraga Silverstein. 128p. 1991. pap. 9.95 (*1-58330-110-0*) Feldheim.

Pathways to the Afterlife: Early Chinese Art from the Sze Hong Collection. Julia M. White & Ronald Y. Otsuka. LC 92-38637. (Illus.). 112p. 1993. text 30.00 (*0-8248-1537-8*); pap. text 19.95 (*0-8248-1538-6*) UH Pr.

Pathways to the Gods: The Mystery of the Andes Lines. Tony Morrison. (Illus.). 254p. 1983. reprint ed. pap. 9.95 (*0-89733-282-2*) Academy Chi Pubs.

Pathways to the Heart. Lucy P. Stroman. (Orig.). 1997. pap. write for info. (*1-57553-491-6*) Watermrk Pr.

Pathways to the Humanities in Educational Administration. Samuel H. Popper. LC 97-103686. 231p. (C). 1990. reprint ed. pap. text 22.95 (*0-922971-00-5*, NT3) Univ Council Educ Admin.

Pathways to the Soul: 101 Ways to Open Your Heart. Carlos Warter. LC 99-39469. 256p. 2000. pap. 13.95 (*1-56170-665-5*, 5011) Hay House.

Pathways to the Spirit: 100 Ways to Bring the Sacred into Daily Life. Susan Santucci. LC 98-45961. 240p. (Orig.). 1999. pap. 11.95 (*0-7868-8429-0*, Pub. by Hyperion) Time Warner.

Pathways to the Universe. Bernard Lovell & F. Graham Smith. (Illus.). 242p. 1989. text 38.95 (*0-521-32004-6*) Cambridge U Pr.

Pathways to the Way of God. Avraham Y. Katz. LC 94-30795. 1998. write for info. (*0-87306-686-3*) Feldheim.

Pathways to Thinking: Strategies for Developing Independent Learners K-8. Elinor P. Ross. (Illus.). 256p. (C). 1997. pap. text, teacher ed. 36.95 (*0-926842-68-4*) CG Pubs Inc.

Pathways to Thinking: Strategies for Developing Independent Learners K-8. expanded ed. Elinor P. Ross. LC 97-69047. (Illus.). 316p. (C). 1998. text, teacher ed. 52.95 (*0-926842-69-2*) CG Pubs Inc.

Pathways to Translation: Pedagogy & Process. Donald C. Kiraly. LC 94-36521. (Translation Studies: No. 3). 192p. 1995. text 29.00 (*0-87338-516-0*) Kent St U Pr.

Pathways to Ulster's Past: Sources for Local Studies. Peter Collins. LC 99-165840. (Illus.). 150p. 1998. pap. 13.95 (*0-85389-693-3*, Pub. by Inst Irish Studies) Irish Bks Media.

Pathwork of Self Transformation. Eve Pierrakos. 288p. 1990. pap. 12.95 (*0-553-34896-5*) Bantam.

Pathworking. P. Jennings & P. Sawyer. 1994. pap. 17.95 (*1-898307-00-8*, Pub. by Capall Bann Pubng) Holmes Pub.

Pathworkings of Aleister Crowley: The Treasure House of Images. J. F. Fuller et al. LC 94-66060. 160p. (Orig.). 1994. pap. 12.95 (*1-56184-074-2*) New Falcon Pubns.

Patience. (Vocal Score Ser.). 200p. (Orig.). 1986. pap. 13.95 (*0-88188-725-0*, 50337700) H Leonard.

Patience. (Pocket Power Ser.). 16p. (Orig.). 1986. pap. 1.25 (*0-89486-356-8*, 5361B) Hazelden.

Patience. Stephen D. Eyre. (Fruit of the Spirit Bible Studies). 48p. 1991. pap. 5.99 (*0-310-53681-2*) Zondervan.

Patience! Mary Gibbon. LC 94-76135. 443p. (Orig.). 1993. pap. 10.00 (*0-9640664-0-8*) Mainly Novels.

Patience. Elaine Goley. (Learn the Value Ser.). (Illus.). 32p. (J). (gr. 1-4). 1987. 11.95 (*0-685-67574-2*) Rourke Corp.

***Patience.** Lucia Raatma. LC 99-47923. (Character Education Ser.). 24p. (J). (ps-3). 2000. lib. bdg. 15.93 (*0-7368-0508-7*, Bridgestone Bks) Capstone Pr.

***Patience.** Jason Sherman. 96p. 2000. pap. 14.95 (*0-88754-557-2*) Theatre Comm.

Patience. St. Cyprian of Carthage. 1992. pap. 1.95 (*0-89981-129-9*) Eastern Orthodox.

***Patience.** Warner Press Staff. (Lion Cub Upside-Down Books Ser.). (Illus.). (J). 2000. pap. 5.95 (*0-87162-830-9*) Warner Pr.

Patience. Warren W. Wiersbe. (Thirty Day Devotional Ser.). 72p. 1995. pap. 3.50 (*1-56476-400-1*, 6-3400, Victor Bks) Chariot Victor.

Patience: A Book of Quotations. unabridged ed. Ed. by Rosemary C. Anderson. iv, 16p. 1990. write for info. (*1-929706-00-6*) Anderson Pubng.

Patience: How We Wait upon the World. David B. Harned. LC 97-36165. 160p. 1997. 12.95 (*1-56101-147-9*) Cowley Pubns.

Patience: The Little Books of Virtue. Ariel Books Staff. (Illus.). 80p. 1995. 4.95 (*0-8362-3119-8*) Andrews & McMeel.

Patience . . . Teach Me: Encounters along the Way with My Patients, Family & Friends. Roy R. Hall. 100p. (Orig.). 1997. pap. 11.95 (*1-57502-467-5*, P01398) Morris Pubng.

Patience, An Alliterative Version of Jonah. Poet of Pearl. (BCL1-PR English Literature Ser.). 77p. 1992. reprint ed. lib. bdg. 59.00 (*0-7812-7190-8*) Rprt Serv.

An Asterisk (*) at the beginning of an entry indicates that the title is appearing for the first time.

Patience & Humility: A Handbook for Christians. rev. ed. William B. Ullathorne. LC 98-19804. Orig. Title: The Little Book of Humility & Patience. 144p. 1998. pap. 11.95 (*0-918477-74-3*) Sophia Inst Pr.

Patience & Power: The Lives of Morrocan Village Women. Susan S. Davis. 200p. 1985. pap. 15.95 (*0-87073-504-7*) Schenkman Bks Inc.

Patience & Sarah: A Pioneering Love Story. Paula M. Kimper et al. 226p. 1999. pap. 60.00 (*0-9671874-0-0*, 6501) Once in a Blue.

Patience Card Games. Group Diagram Staff. (Collins Gem). 1996. pap. 8.00 (*0-00-472016-4*) Collins.

Patience de Maigret. Georges Simenon. (FRE.). pap. 3.95 (*0-685-36570-0*) Fr & Eur.

Patience de Maigret, le Confessional, la Morte d'Auguste. Georges Simenon. (FRE.). 896p. 1990. 49.95 (*0-7859-0488-3*, 2258033039) Fr & Eur.

Patience in Islam: Sabr. Tallal Alie Turfe. LC 96-60267. (Illus.). 122p. (Orig.). (C). 1996. pap. text 7.95 (*1-879402-32-7*) Tahrike Tarsile Quran.

Patience My Foot: Learning God's Patience Through Life's Difficulties. 2nd ed. Micheal LeFan. 155p. (Orig.). 1994. pap. 8.99 (*0-89900-619-1*) College Pr Pub.

Patience Never Fails. Gary Jones. 45p. 1985. pap. 0.95 (*0-88144-048-5*) Christian Pub.

Patience of a Saint. Andrew M. Greeley. LC 85-40921. 1987. mass mkt. 4.95 (*0-446-34682-9*, Pub. by Warner Bks) Little.

Patience of Hope. Arthur. 1997. pap. 10.99 (*0-85234-385-X*, Pub. by Evangelical Pr) P & R Pubng.

***Patience of Ice.** Renate Wood. 2000. pap. 14.95 (*0-8101-5105-7*) Northwestern U Pr.

Patience of the Cloud Photographer. Elizabeth Holmes. LC 96-83418. 72p. 1997. pap. 11.95 (*0-88748-240-6*) Carnegie-Mellon.

Patience Pays Off. James R. Sherman. LC 87-62215. (Do It! Success Ser.). 72p. 1987. pap. 4.95 (*0-935538-09-7*) Pathway Bks.

Patience Sparhawk & Her Times. Gertrude F. Atherton. LC 75-104407. 488p. reprint ed. lib. bdg. 32.50 (*0-8398-0066-5*) Irvington.

Patience Sparhawk & Her Times. Gertrude F. Atherton. (C). 1986. reprint ed. pap. text 8.95 (*0-8290-1867-0*) Irvington.

Patience the Herd Dog. Joe Kapelos. Ed. by Jeanne Bretschneider. 28p. (J). (ps-3). 1998. pap. 11.95 (*0-9668001-0-9*) L Leeman.

Patience to Wait Vol. I: Sermons by a Patient Black Woman. Nan M. Brown. Ed. by Arnethea H. Brown & Joan T. Kelley. (Illus.). 160p. (Orig.). (C). 1988. 9.95 (*0-317-91214-3*) N M Brown.

Patience to Wait Vol. II: Sermons for Special Days of the Church. Nan M. Brown. Ed. by Joan A. Kelly. 160p. (Orig.). (C). 1992. pap. write for info. (*0-9620736-2-8*) N M Brown.

Patience Worth - A Psychic Mystery. Charles S. Yost. 290p. 1997. pap. 25.00 (*0-89540-308-0*, SB-308) Sun Pub.

Patience Wright, American Artist & Spy in George III's London. Charles C. Sellers. LC 76-7193. (Illus.). 317p. reprint ed. pap. 98.30 (*0-608-09585-0*, 205438700006) Bks Demand.

Patient. Anamaria Shua. Tr. by David William. LC 97-24435. (Discoveries Ser.). 144p. 1997. pap. text 14.95 (*0-935480-90-0*) Lat Am Lit Rev Pr.

***Patient.** large type ed. Michael Palmer. LC 99-87235. 2000. 24.95 (*0-375-40977-7*) Random Hse Lrg Prnt.

***Patient: A Novel.** Michael Palmer. LC 99-57838. 336p. 2000. 24.95 (*0-553-10983-9*) Bantam.

Patient: Biological, Psychological & Social Dimensions of Medical Practice. 3rd ed. Hoyle Leigh & Morton F. Reiser. (Illus.). 528p. (C). 1992. text 45.00 (*0-306-44142-X*, Kluwer Plenum) Kluwer Academic.

Patient: Paramed Eme Care. 4th ed. Porter & Bledsoe. 288p. 1999. 46.60 (*0-13-021597-X*) S&S Trade.

Patient: The True Story of a Rare Illness. Ben Watt. 192p. 1998. reprint ed. pap. 12.00 (*0-8021-3583-8*, Grove) Grove-Atltic.

Patient A. Lee Blessing. 1993. pap. 5.25 (*0-8222-1364-8*) Dramatists Play.

Patient A & Other Plays: Five Plays by Lee Blessing. Lee Blessing. LC 95-2412. 255p. 1995. pap. 15.95 (*0-435-08662-6*, 08662) Heinemann.

Patient Access to Alternative Treatments: Beyond the FDA: Hearings Before the Committee on Government Reform & Oversight, House of Representatives, 105th Congress, Second Session, February 4 & 12, 1998. LC 98-207020. iv, 337p. 1998. write for info. (*0-16-057168-5*) USGPO.

***Patient Account Management Sourcebook, 2000.** annuals HADG Staff. 2000. pap. 89.00 (*0-8342-1770-8*) Aspen Pub.

Patient Account Manager's 1999 Sourcebook. Joann Petaschnick. LC 98-48637. 1999. 89.00 (*0-8342-1155-6*) Aspen Pub.

Patient Accounts Management Handbook. Allan P. DeKaye. LC 97-19454. 480p. 1997. 69.00 (*0-8342-0843-1*, 20843) Aspen Pub.

Patient Advocacy Strategies for Managed Care. Alex D'Alessandro. LC 98-49709. 1998. pap. text 89.00 (*0-935255-62-1*) Of Course Pubns.

Patient Alcohol Abuse: A Guide for Health Care Professionals. Faith S. Schaefer. Ed. by Milton E. Burglass. LC 97-167781. (Illus.). 174p. (Orig.). 1997. pap. text 38.00 (*1-879772-09-4*) Health Studies.

Patient & Decentralised Testing. Ed. by John P. Ashby. (C). 1987. text 102.50 (*0-7462-0036-6*) Kluwer Academic.

Patient & Family Education: A Compliance Guide to the JCAHO Standards. Joan Iacono & Ann Campbell. LC 97-170611. (Illus.). 124p. (Orig.). 1997. pap. text 67.00 (*1-57839-001-X*) Opus Communs.

Patient & Family Education: Teaching Programs for Managing Chronic Disease & Disability. Marcia Hanak. 272p. 1986. pap. 32.95 (*0-8261-5441-7*) Springer Pub.

***Patient & Family Education: The Compliance Guide to the JCAHD Standards.** 2nd ed. Joan Iacono & Ann Campbell. (Illus.). 140p. 2000. pap. text 87.00 (*1-57839-086-9*) Opus Communs.

Patient & Family Education in Managed Care: Seizing the Teachable Moment. Ed. by William B. Bateman et al. LC 99-37810. (Illus.). 264p. 1999. text 36.95 (*0-8261-1295-1*) Springer Pub.

Patient & Person: Developing Interpersonal Skills in Nursing. Jane Stein-Parbury. (Illus.). 280p. (Orig.). 1993. pap. text 26.95 (*0-443-04253-5*) Church.

Patient & the Analyst. 2nd ed. Joseph Sandler et al. LC 92-1727. 250p. 1992. 40.00 (*0-8236-4031-0*) Intl Univs Pr.

Patient & the Plastic Surgeon. Robert M. Goldwyn. 1981. 32.50 (*0-316-31974-0*, Little Brwn Med Div) Lppncott W & W.

Patient & the Plastic Surgeon. 2nd ed. Robert M. Goldwyn. 1991. 75.00 (*0-316-31978-3*, Little Brwn Med Div) Lppncott W & W.

Patient As a Central Construct in Health Communication Research: A Special Issue of "Health Communication", Vol. 9, No. 1, 1997. Sharf & Street. 1996. pap. 20.00 (*0-8058-9880-8*) L Erlbaum Assocs.

Patient as Partner: A Theory of Human-Experimentation. Robert M. Veatch. LC 86-45043. (Medical Ethics Ser.). (Illus.). 255p. Date not set. reprint ed. pap. 79.10 (*0-608-20572-9*, 205448600002) Bks Demand.

Patient As Partner: A Theory of Human Experimentation Ethics. Robert M. Veatch. LC 86-45043. (Medical Ethics Ser.). (Illus.). 256p. 1987. 39.95 (*0-253-35725-X*) Ind U Pr.

Patient As Partner: The Cornerstone of Community Health Improvement. American Organization of Nurse Executives Staff. LC 97-1280. (AONE Leadership Ser.: Vol. 3). 100p. 1997. pap. text 32.00 (*1-55648-200-0*, 054100) AHPI.

Patient As Person: Explorations in Medical Ethics. Paul Ramsey. LC 77-118737. (Lyman Beecher Lectures at Yale University). 305p. reprint ed. pap. 94.60 (*0-8357-8260-3*, 203386300087) Bks Demand.

Patient Assessment. American Dental Hygienists' Association Staff & Block Drug Company. 1980. 30.00 (*0-318-19097-4*) Am Dental Hygienists.

Patient Assessment: A Guide for Health Professionals. 2nd ed. P. Barker. (Illus.). 320p. 1997. pap. 49.95 (*1-56593-329-X*, 0659) Singular Publishing.

Patient at Peacock's Hall. Margery Allingham. 20.95 (*0-89190-165-5*) Amereon Ltd.

***Patient at Peacocks Hall.** large type ed. Margery Allingham. 172p. 2000. pap. 20.95 (*0-7838-8966-6*) Mac Lib Ref.

***Patient-Based Approaches to Cognitive Neuroscience.** Ed. by Martha J. Farah & Todd E. Feinberg. LC 99-34052. (Issues in Clinical & Cognitive Neuropsychology Ser.). 425p. 2000. pap. 45.00 (*0-262-56123-9*) MIT Pr.

Patient Beware--Doctor Take Care! Edward Zebrowski. LC 94-61243. 303p. (Orig.). 1994. pap. 17.95 (*0-9640096-1-7*) Woodstock Books.

Patient Billing: Computerized Simulation using MediSoft. 2nd ed. Greg Harpole. LC 94-19805. 1995. write for info. (*0-02-802557-1*) Glencoe.

Patient Billing: Using Medisoft for Windows. 3rd ed. Greg Harpole. LC 97-51749. 1997. 39.89 (*0-02-801241-0*); 26.10 (*0-02-801242-9*) Glencoe.

Patient Billing Supervisor. (Career Examination Ser.: C-3607). pap. 29.95 (*0-8373-3607-4*) Nat Learn.

Patient Bridegroom. Barbara Cartland. (Camfield Ser.: No. 141). 176p. (Orig.). 1995. mass mkt. 3.99 (*0-515-11615-7*, Jove) Berkley Pub.

Patient Care. Erica K. Williams. Ed. by Stewart C. Bushong. LC 98-20597. (Essentials of Medical Imaging Ser.). (Illus.). 160p. 1999. pap. 26.95 (*0-07-070632-8*) McGraw-Hill HPD.

Patient Care: Basic Skills for the Health Care Provider. Acello. 160p. 1998. pap. text, teacher ed. 20.95 (*0-7668-0182-9*) Delmar.

Patient Care: Basic Skills for the Health Care Provider. Barbara Acello. LC 97-26953. 400p. (C). 1997. mass mkt. 30.95 (*0-8273-8423-8*) Delmar.

Patient Care Advisories. Donald K. Graves. (Illus.). 175p. 1995. spiral bd. 19.00 (*1-884135-23-4*) Mayer-Johnson.

Patient Care Decision-Making: A Legal Guide for Providers. annuals rev. ed. Claire C. Obade. LC 91-22470. (Health Law Ser.). 1991. ring bd. 125.00 (*0-87632-819-2*) West Group.

Patient Care During Operative & Invasive Procedures. Mark L. Phippen & Maryann P. Wells. Ed. by Maura Connor. LC 98-43363. (Illus.). 860p. 1999. text 69.00 (*0-7216-7292-2*) Church.

Patient Care Emergency Handbook. Ed. by James Matheus & Joseph E. Scherger. 650p. (C). 1991. text 60.00 (*1-878487-30-2*, 5421M) Practice Mgmt Info.

Patient Care Flow Chart. 4th ed. Steven R. Alexander. (Illus.). 608p. (C). 1988. text 59.95 (*1-878487-27-2*, 4301M) Practice Mgmt Info.

Patient Care Guidelines for Nurse Practitioners. 4th ed. Axalla J. Hoole. 396p. 1994. spiral bd. 38.95 (*0-397-55060-X*, Lippnctt) Lppncott W & W.

***Patient Care Guidelines for Nurse Practitioners.** 5th ed. Axalla J. Hoole. LC 99-19760. 1999. 38.95 (*0-7817-1732-9*) Lppncott W & W.

Patient Care in Cardiac Surgery. 5th ed. Gus Vlahakes. LC 93-49425. 320p. 1994. pap. text 42.00 (*0-316-08779-3*) Lppncott W & W.

Patient Care in Colorectal Surgery. Beck & Well. 1991. 50.00 (*0-316-08653-3*, Little Brwn Med Div) Lppncott W & W.

Patient Care in Community Practice. Harman. 1989. pap. 22.00 (*0-85369-209-2*, Pub. by Pharmaceutical Pr) Rittenhouse.

Patient Care in Interventional Radiology: A Resource Manual. Sonja Bartolomei & Constance A. Reifsnyder. LC 97-18581. 1998. 135.00 (*0-8342-0816-4*, S306) Aspen Pub.

Patient Care in Neurology. Ed. by A. C. Williams. LC 98-39264. (Illus.). 512p. 1999. text 149.50 (*0-19-262857-7*) OUP.

Patient Care in Neurosurgery, No. 3. 3rd ed. Ryan C. Amacher. 1990. 45.00 (*0-316-03640-4*, Little Brwn Med Div) Lppncott W & W.

Patient Care in Pediatric Surgery. Lucian L. Leape. 448p. 1987. 52.95 (*0-316-51821-2*, Little Brwn Med Div) Lppncott W & W.

Patient Care in Plastic Surgery. 2nd ed. Ed. by Bernard M. Barrett, Jr. LC 95-44090. (Illus.). 528p. (C). (gr. 13). 1995. pap. text 54.00 (*0-8151-0563-0*, 25685) Mosby Inc.

Patient Care in Radiography. 4th ed. Ruth A. Ehrlich & Ellen D. McCloskey. 1993. teacher ed. write for info. (*0-8151-4700-7*) Mosby Inc.

Patient Care in Radiography. 5th ed. Ruth Ann Ehrlich et al. LC 99-180760. (Illus.). 352p. (C). (gr. 13). 1998. pap. text 36.00 (*0-8151-2856-8*, 31846) Mosby Inc.

***Patient Care in Radiography with an Introduction to Medical Imaging.** 5th ed. Ruth A. Ehrlich et al. 1998. teacher ed. write for info. (*0-323-00026-6*) Mosby Inc.

Patient Care in the Operating Room. Kaczmarowski. (Illus.). 258p. 1983. 33.00 (*0-443-03911-9*) Church.

Patient Care Information Systems: Successful Design & Implementation. E. L. Drazen et al. (Computers in Health Care Ser.). (Illus.). 188p. 1995. text 48.00 (*0-387-94255-6*) Spr-Verlag.

Patient Care Procedures for the Multi-Skilled Care Giver. (Illus.). 352p. (Orig.). (C). 1996. pap. text 31.95 (*0-89582-316-0*) Morton Pub.

Patient Care Procedures for Your Practice, 1991. 2nd ed. Charles E. Driscoll & Robert E. Rakel. (Illus.). 320p. (C). 1991. text. write for info. (*1-878487-29-9*, 6584M) Practice Mgmt Info.

Patient Care Redesign: Lessons from the Field. Diana Jane Weaver & American Organization of Nurse Staff. LC 98-53882. (AONE Management Ser.). 1999. 32.00 (*1-55648-248-5*) AHPI.

Patient Care Skills. 3rd ed. Mary A. Minor & Scott D. Minor. (Illus.). 448p. (C). 1994. pap. text 39.95 (*0-8385-7709-1*, A7709-7) Appleton & Lange.

Patient Care Skills. 4th ed. Minor. (C). 1999. 36.95 (*0-8385-8131-5*) Appleton & Lange.

Patient Care Skills. 4th ed. Mary A. Minor & Scott D. Minor. LC 98-25824. (C). 1999. pap. text. write for info. (*0-8385-8157-9*) Appleton & Lange.

Patient Care Standards. Virginia Mason Medical Center Department of Nursing Staff. LC 98-40590. 250p. Date not set. 179.00 (*0-8342-1222-6*, S15) Aspen Pub.

Patient Care Standards - Collaborative Practice Planning Guides. 6th ed. Susan M. Tucker et al. (Illus.). 1056p. (C). (gr. 13). 1996. pap. text 43.95 (*0-8151-8856-0*, 26539) Mosby Inc.

Patient Care Stds No. 7. 7th ed. Tucker. LC 99-43230. 2000. pap. text 46.95 (*0-323-00996-4*) Mosby Inc.

Patient Care Technician Manual. Total Renal Care, Inc., Educ. Dept. Staff. 315p. 1991. pap. 60.00 (*1-56488-004-4*) Dialyrn.

Patient Care Technician, Module 4 - Physical Therapy. University of Alabama Staff. (Illus.). 200p. (C). (gr. 13). 1997. pap. text 50.00 (*0-8151-9164-2*, 31213) Mosby Inc.

Patient Care Technician, Module 3 - Respiratory Care. University of Alabama Staff. (Illus.). 200p. (C). (gr. 13). 1997. pap. text 50.00 (*0-8151-9495-1*, 31212) Mosby Inc.

Patient Care Technician, Module 2 - EKG. University of Alabama Staff. (Illus.). 200p. (C). (gr. 13). 1997. pap. text 50.00 (*0-8151-9494-3*, 31211) Mosby Inc.

Patient Care Techniques. Dorothy J. Hicks. LC 74-18673. (Allied Health Ser.). 1975. pap. 7.75 (*0-672-61394-8*, Bobbs) Macmillan.

Patient Centered Audit. Christine G. Kruse. (Illus.). 69p. 1984. pap. 14.50 (*0-87527-247-9*) Green.

Patient Centered Care. 153p. pap. text. write for info. (*0-7881-8578-0*) DIANE Pub.

Patient Centered Care: A Model for Restructuring. Mickey L. Parsons. 7p. 1994. 89.00 (*0-8342-0573-4*, 20573) Aspen Pub.

Patient Centered Care: A Model for Restructuring. Mickey L. Parsons & Carolyn L. Murdaugh. 646p. 1994. pap. 39.00 (*0-8342-0983-7*, 20983) Aspen Pub.

Patient-Centered Care: Your Prescription for Maximum Patient Satisfaction & Loyalty. K. C. Warner. LC 98-71410. (How-To Book Ser.). 1998. reprint ed. pap. 12.95 (*1-884926-87-8*, PATCA) Amer Media.

Patient-Centered Hospital Care: Reform from Within. Ed. by Kathryn J. McDonagh. LC 93-14569. 222p. 1993. text 44.00 (*1-56793-002-6*, 0936) Health Admin Pr.

Patient-Centered Medicine. Moira Stewart et al. LC 95-25179. (Illus.). 292p. 1995. text 59.00 (*0-8039-5688-6*); pap. text 25.95 (*0-8039-5689-4*) Sage.

Patient Children: Conditions of Poverty & the Use of Hospital-Based Ambulatory Care. Beth C. Weitzman. LC 92-33036. (Children of Poverty Ser.). 150p. 1992. text 15.00 (*0-8153-1121-4*) Garland.

Patient Comes First: A Nurse Speaks Out. Nancy Fox. LC 88-61282. 153p. 1988. pap. 18.95 (*0-87975-479-6*) Prometheus Bks.

Patient Communication for First Responders & EMS Personnel: The First Hour of Trauma. 2nd ed. Donald Jacobs. 144p. (C). 1991. pap. 20.80 (*0-89303-732-X*) P-H.

Patient Compliance in Medical Practice & Clinical Trials. Ed. by Joyce A. Cramer & Bert Spilker. 432p. 1991. text 83.00 (*0-88167-735-3*) Lppncott W & W.

***Patient Confidentiality.** LC 98-209671. iii, 107p. 1998. write for info. (*0-16-057338-6*) USGPO.

Patient-Controlled Analgesia: Confidence in Post-Operative Pain Control. Margaret Heath & Veronica J. Thomas. (Illus.). 224p. 1993. text 45.00 (*0-19-262165-3*) OUP.

***Patient Controlled Epidural Analgesia.** Ramon Pediani. 128p. 2000. pap. text 25.00 (*0-7506-4299-8*) Buttrwrth-Heinemann.

***Patient Counseling Handbook.** 3rd rev. ed. U. S. Pharmacopeial Convention Staff. 933p. 1998. pap. text 45.00 (*0-917330-91-9*) Am Pharm Assn.

Patient Data Management in Intensive Care, No. 6. Ed. by K. Lenz & A. N. Laggner. (Illus.). 157p. 1995. 39.00 (*0-387-82513-4*) Spr-Verlag.

Patient Drug Facts. Bernie R. Olin et al. (C). 59.95 (*0-03-268636-6*) Lppncott W & W.

Patient Drug Facts: Bundled English/Spanish Version. Facts & Comparisons Staff. (ENG & SPA.). 900p. cd-rom 160.00 (*1-57439-022-8*) Facts & Comparisons.

Patient Dumping in Hospital Emergency Rooms. Lauren Dame & Sidney M. Wolfe. 18p. (Orig.). 1996. pap. 10.00 (*0-937188-06-9*) Pub Citizen.

Patient Education. SPC Staff. LC 97-27722. (Health Care Professional Review Ser.: Vol. 4). 288p. 1997. spiral bd. 24.95 (*0-87434-914-1*) Springhouse Corp.

Patient Education. 2nd ed. John H. Murtagh. LC 97-155548. (Illus.). 200p. 1996. pap. text 49.00 (*0-07-470296-3*) McGraw-Hill HPD.

Patient Education: A Practical Approach. Richard D. Muma & Barbara Ann Lyons. 381p. (C). 1996. pap. text 37.95 (*0-8385-2039-1*, A2039-4, Apple Lange Med) McGraw.

Patient Education: Issues, Principles & Practices. 3rd ed. Sally H. Rankin & Karen D. Stallings. LC 95-10728. 400p. 1995. pap. text 29.95 (*0-397-55194-0*) Lppncott W & W.

Patient Education: Nurses in Partnership with Other Health Care Professionals. Ed. by Carol E. Smith. 384p. 1986. text 55.00 (*0-8089-1833-8*, 794144, Grune & Strat) Harcrt Hlth Sci Grp.

Patient Education: Principles & Practice. 4th ed. Sally H. Rankin & Karen Duffy Stallings. 428p. pap. text 32.95 (*0-7817-2022-2*) Lppncott W & W.

Patient Education: Strategies & Skills for Living Well. Gretchen C. Peske et al. LC 95-76320. (Illus.). 300p. (Orig.). 1996. pap. 12.00 (*1-887109-00-5*) Blue Path Pr.

Patient Education & Discharge Planning for Rehabilitation. St. Joseph's Rehabilitation Hospital Staff. 816p. 1995. ring bd. 256.00 (*0-8342-0715-X*, 20715) Aspen Pub.

Patient Education & Health Promotion in Medical Care. Squyres, Wendy D., & Associates Staff. LC 84-60883. xxiii, 410p. (C). 1985. text 52.95 (*0-87484-553-X*, 553) Mayfield Pub.

Patient Education for the Ill & the Well: Index of New Information. Judy A. Plaines. 160p. 1997. 47.50 (*0-7883-1774-1*); pap. 44.50 (*0-7883-1775-X*) ABBE Pubs Assn.

Patient Education in Home Care: A Practical Guide to Effective Teaching & Documentation. Janet E. Jackson & Elizabeth A. Johnson. 240p. 1988. 60.00 (*0-87189-769-5*, 89769) Aspen Pub.

Patient Education Materials & Instructor's Guide: A Supplement to the Manual of Clinical Dietetics. Jo E. Shield & Mary C. Mullen. 1992. 15.00 (*0-88091-109-3*) Am Dietetic Assn.

Patient Education Sourcebook. Ed. by Mary Rydesky & Tanya DeVaughn. 547p. 1986. 50.00 (*0-318-20441-X*) Health Sci Comm.

Patient Elephant: More Exotic Cases from the World's Top Wildlife Vet. David Conrad Taylor. (Illus.). 194p. 1995. 27.95 (*0-86051-835-3*, Robson-Parkwest) Parkwest Pubns.

Patient Emergencies. SPC Staff. LC 97-23888. (Health Care Professional Review Ser.: Vol. 5). 288p. 1997. spiral bd. 24.95 (*0-87434-915-X*) Springhouse Corp.

Patient Encounters: The Experience of Disease. James H. Buchanan. LC 88-19803. 366p. 1989. reprint ed. pap. 113.50 (*0-7837-8574-7*, 204938900011) Bks Demand.

Patient Financial Services. Ed. by Allen G. Herkimer. 150p. (C). 1993. text 65.00 (*1-882198-14-X*) Hlthcare Fin Mgmt.

Patient Financial Services: Organizing & Managing a Cost-Effective Financial Services Operation. Timothy Carse & Jeffrey Slater. (C). 1993. text 65.00 (*0-07-413122-2*, Irwn McGrw-H) McGrw-H Hghr Educ.

Patient Financial Services: Workbook. Allen G. Herkimer, Jr. 126p. (C). 1993. per. 45.00 (*1-55738-600-5*, Irwn Prfssnl) McGraw-Hill Prof.

Patient-Focused Healing: Integrating Caring & Curing in Health Care. Nancy Moore & Henrietta Komras. LC 93-4218. (Health-Management Ser.). 226p. 1993. text 39.95 (*1-55542-584-4*) Jossey-Bass.

***Patient Genrx.** Mosby Year Book Staff. 1999. pap. text 99.00 (*0-8151-3752-4*) Mosby Inc.

Patient Genrx in Spanish. Mosby Year Books Staff. (SPA.). 1999. pap. text 99.00 (*0-8151-3754-0*) Mosby Inc.

Patient Grissil. Henry Chettle et al. LC 78-133653. (Tudor Facsimile Texts. Old English Plays Ser.: No. 101). reprint ed. 59.50 (*0-404-53401-5*) AMS Pr.

Patient Guide to the Human Heart. LC 99-170263. 1 Vp. 1991. 7.95 (*1-879874-00-8*) T Peters & Co.

Patient Impatience. Tomas Borge. Tr. by Russell Bartley et al. LC 91-55410. 452p. (Orig.). 1992. 24.95 (*0-915306-97-2*) Curbstone.

Patient in Love. large type ed. Theresa Charles. 368p. 1988. 27.99 (*0-7089-1817-4*) Ulverscroft.

P

An Asterisk (*) at the beginning of an entry indicates that the title is appearing for the first time.

Patient in Room 18. Mignon G. Eberhart. LC 94-43645. xvi, 304p. 1995. pap. 9.95 (*0-8032-6727-4*, Bison Books) U of Nebr Pr.

Patient in Room 18. large type ed. Mignon G. Eberhart. LC 93-44784. 385p. 1994. lib. bdg. 20.95 (*0-7862-0086-3*) Thorndike Pr.

Patient in Room 18. Mignon G. Eberhart. 1976. reprint ed. lib. bdg. 23.95 (*0-88411-765-0*) Amereon Ltd.

Patient in the Family: An Ethics of Medicine & Families. Hilde L. Nelson & James L. Nelson. LC 94-33652. 224p. (C). (gr. 13). 1995. pap. 18.99 (*0-415-91129-X*, B4914) Routledge.

Patient in the Womb. E. Peter Volpe. LC 84-10746. (Sesquicentennial Ser.: No. 3). 151p. 1984. 14.50 (*0-86554-122-1*, MUP/H110) Mercer Univ Pr.

Patient Information Catalogue Vol. 1: Dental Medicine Topics. Stephen D. Smith. (Illus.). 88p. 1998. pap. text 39.95 (*0-9663370-1-8*) S D Smith.

Patient Information in Medicine. Ed. by Ronald D. Mann. (Illus.). 199p. 1991. text 35.00 (*1-85070-367-1*) Prthnon Pub.

Patient Instructions for the Emergency Physician. Stewart. 1993. text. write for info. (*0-397-51166-3*) Lppncott W & W.

Patient Majority: Mental Health Policy & Services for Women, Vol. 4. Valerie Gerrand. 96p. 1995. pap. 36.00 (*0-7300-2037-1*, PTSSSO, Pub. by Deakin Univ) St Mut.

Patient Management Cluster. rev. ed. Ed. by L. Skrbic. (Illus.). 140p. (C). 1991. reprint ed. write for info. (*0-9626486-0-4*) Postgraduate Med Rev Ed.

Patient Management of Secondary Disability. Walker. 2000. pap. text Price not set. (*0-443-06117-3*) Church.

Patient Management Problems in Psychiatry: For the Mrcpsych Oral Examination. Parimala Moodley et al. (Illus.). 144p. (Orig.). 1991. pap. text 27.95 (*0-443-04374-4*) Church.

Patient Management Skills for Dental Assistants. Barbara D. Ingersoll. (Illus.). 192p. 1986. pap. text 14.95 (*0-13-653718-9*) P-H.

Patient Monitor Markets. (Market Research Reports: No. 421). (Illus.). 122p. 1997. 995.00 (*0-614-09922-6*) Theta Corp.

Patient Monitoring Markets: Integrated Non-Invasive Products Enhance Manufacturer Opportunities. Market Intelligence Staff. 317p. (Orig.). 1992. 1995.00 (*1-56753-396-5*) Frost & Sullivan.

Patient No More: The Politics of Breast Cancer. Sharon Batt. 432p. 1994. pap. 16.95 (*0-921881-30-4*, Pub. by Gynergy-Ragweed) U of Toronto Pr.

Patient Number One: A True Story of How One CEO Took on Cancer & Big Business in the Fight of His Life. Rick Murdock & David Fisher. LC 99-86763. 320p. 2000. 24.00 (*0-609-60391-4*, Crown) Crown Pub Group.

Patient Nurse. Diana Palmer. 1997. per. 3.50 (*0-373-76099-X*, 1-76099-0) Silhouette.

Patient Obituarist. James Kirkup. LC 97-159517. 1996. pap. 12.95 (*3-7052-0981-7*, Pub. by Poetry Salzburg) Intl Spec Bk.

Patient or Person: Living with Chronic Pain. Penney Cowan. 196p. 1992. pap. 21.95 (*0-89876-186-7*) Gardner Pr.

Patient or Pretender: Inside the Strange World of Factitious Disorders. Marc D. Feldman et al. LC 93-13547. 228p. 1995. pap. 14.95 (*0-471-12013-8*) Wiley.

Patient or Profit. David L. Miller. LC 97-91262. 1998. 8.95 (*0-533-12614-2*) Vantage.

Patient-Oriented Research. Edward H. Ahrens. (Illus.). 248p. 1992. text 39.95 (*0-19-505156-4*) OUP.

Patient Outcomes Research Teams (PORTS) Managing Conflict of Interest. Institute of Medicine Staff. Ed. by Molla S. Donaldson & Alexander M. Capron. 184p. 1991. pap. text 19.00 (*0-309-04482-0*) Natl Acad Pr.

Patient Participation in Program Planning. 2nd ed. Mark Ozer et al. (Illus.). 210p. 1999. pap. 29.95 (*0-07-077882-5*) McGraw-Hill HPD.

Patient Participation in Program Planning: A Manual for Therapists. Otto D. Payton et al. LC 89-16154. 97p. (Orig.). (C). 1990. pap. text 13.95 (*0-8036-6803-1*) Davis Co.

Patient Particulars: American Modernism & the Technique of Originality. Christopher J. Knight. LC 94-23967. 256p. (C). 1995. 38.50 (*0-8387-5296-9*) Bucknell U Pr.

Patient-Physician Relation Pt. 2: The Patient As Partner. Robert M. Veatch. LC 90-4261. (Medical Ethics Ser.). (Illus.). 320p. 1991. 28.95 (*0-253-36207-5*) Ind U Pr.

Patient Placement Criteria for the Treatment of Psychoactive Substance Use Disorders. Norman G. Hoffman et al. LC 91-74015. 170p. (Orig.). 1991. pap. 65.00 (*1-880425-01-7*) Am Soc Addict Med.

Patient Placement Criteria for the Treatment of Substance-Related Disorders: ASAM PPC-2. 2nd ed. David Mee-Lee et al. Ed. by Bonnie B. Wilford. LC 97-108914. 170p. 1996. 100.00 (*1-880425-03-3*) Am Soc Addict Med.

Patient Positioning. Mark J. Schubert. Ed. by Stewart C. Bushong. LC 98-35431. (Essentials of Medical Imaging Ser.). (Illus.). 160p. 1999. pap. 26.95 (*0-07-058067-7*) McGraw-Hill HPD.

Patient Positioning & Immobilization in Radiation Therapy. Gunilla Carleson Bentel. LC 98-26930. 211p. 1998. pap. 45.00 (*0-07-134158-7*) McGraw.

Patient Power: Guide to Action. Spiers. 1998. pap. text. write for info. (*0-443-05687-0*) Harcourt.

Patient Power: Overcoming Chronic Illness. James M. Galbraith. (Orig.). 1995. pap. 12.95 (*0-942246-02-0*) Benchmark Bks.

Patient Power: The Free-Enterprise Alternative to Clinton's Health Plan. John C. Goodman & Gerald L. Musgrave. LC 93-41604. 134p. 1993. mass mkt. 4.95 (*1-882577-10-8*) Cato Inst.

***Patient Power? The Politics of Patients' Associations in Britain & America.** Bruce Wood. LC 99-41546. (State of Health Ser.). 208p. 2000. pap. 29.95 (*0-335-20367-1*) OpUniv Pr.

Patient Power! The Smart Patient's Guide to Health Care. Patricia Parsons. LC 97-139173. (Illus.). 240p. 1997. pap. 14.95 (*0-8020-7186-4*) U of Toronto Pr.

Patient Practitioner Interaction: An Experiential Manual for Developing the Art of Health Care. 3rd ed. Carol M. Davis. LC 98-3498. (Illus.). 352p. 1998. pap. text 32.00 (*1-55642-400-0*, 44000) SLACK Inc.

Patient Practitioner Interaction: Instructor's Manual. 3rd ed. Carol M. Davis. 26p. 1998. pap. text, teacher ed. Price not set. (*1-55642-401-9*, 44019) SLACK Inc.

***Patient Presentations in General Practice: A Comprehensive Guide to Diagnosis & Management.** Ian D. Steven. (Illus.). 581p. 2000. pap. text 79.95 (*0-07-470823-6*) McGraw-Hill Prof.

***Patient Presents.** Kelley J. White. Ed. by Shirley Richburg. 60p. 2001. pap. 9.95 (*0-9658432-6-2*) Peoples MD.

Patient Recruitment in Clinical Trials. Bert Spilker & Joyce A. Cramer. LC 92-12023. 368p. 1992. text 97.00 (*0-88167-931-3*) Lppncott W & W.

Patient Resources on the Internet: 1997 Guide to Health Care Professionals. Ed. by Lois Wingerson. (Illus.). 480p. 1997. pap. text 195.00 (*1-57987-000-7*) Faulkner & Gray.

***Patient Safety Improvement Guidebook.** Patrice L. Spath. 100p. 2000. 30.00 (*1-929955-07-3*) Brown Spath.

Patient Safety in Anesthetic Practice. Robert C. Morell & John H. Eichhorn. LC 96-30949. 1996. text 69.00 (*0-443-07682-0*) Church.

Patient Satisfaction: A Guide to Practice Enhancement. Wendy Leebov et al. LC 89-8255. (Illus.). 380p. 1990. 49.95 (*0-87489-546-4*, ME003) Practice Mgmt Info.

Patient Satisfaction Instruments: A Compendium. Contrib. by APTA Staff. 96p. 1995. pap. 29.95 (*1-887759-40-9*, P-127) Am Phys Therapy Assn.

Patient Satisfaction Pays: Quality Service for Practice Success. Stephen W. Brown et al. LC 93-20094. 432p. 1993. 67.00 (*0-8342-0394-4*) Aspen Pub.

Patient Satisfaction Pays: Quality Service for Practice Success. 2nd ed. Anne-Marie Nelson et al. LC 97-7706. 336p. 1997. 55.00 (*0-8342-0922-5*, 20922) Aspen Pub.

Patient Self-Determination Act: Meeting the Challenges in Patient Care. Lawrence P. Ulrich. LC 99-19307. (Clinical Medical Ethics Ser.). 1999. write for info. (*0-87840-748-0*); 65.00 (*0-87840-747-2*) Georgetown U Pr.

Patient Self-Determination Act: Providers Offer Information on Advance Directives but Effectiveness Uncertain. (Illus.). 48p. (Orig.). (C). 1996. pap. text 20.00 (*0-7881-3038-2*) DIANE Pub.

Patient Self-Determination in Long-Term Care: Implementing the PSDA in Medical Decisions. Ed. by Marshall B. Kapp. (Illus.). 240p. 1994. 34.95 (*0-8261-8520-7*) Springer Pub.

Patient Stone. Sadeq Chubak. Tr. & Intro. by Mohammad R. Ghanoonparvar. (Persian Literature in Translation: No. 1). 290p. 1989. 12.95 (*0-939214-62-8*) Mazda Pubs.

Patient Stones. Tim Ray. 54p. (Orig.). 1996. pap. text. write for info. (*1-57579-018-1*) Pine Hill Pr.

Patient Teaching. Springhouse Publishing Company Staff. LC 98-36727. (Incredibly Easy Ser.). 320p. 1998. 29.95 (*0-87434-959-1*) Springhouse Corp.

Patient Teaching Guides. Mosby Staff. 30p. 1996. text, suppl. ed. 19.95 (*0-8151-6907-8*) Mosby Inc.

Patient Teaching Guides in Pharmacology. Leda McKenry. LC 98-45346. (Illus.). 400p. (C). 1999. text 59.95 (*0-8151-2933-5*, 31829) Mosby Inc.

Patient Teaching Guides on Disk. Mosby Staff. 200p. 1996. text 99.95 (*0-8151-8551-0*) Mosby Inc.

Patient Violence & the Clinician. Ed. by Burr S. Eichelman & Anne C. Hartwig. (Clinical Practice Ser.: No. 30). (Illus.). 200p. 1995. text 15.50 (*0-88048-454-3*, 8454) Am Psychiatric.

Patient Who Cured His Therapist: And Other Stories of Unconventional Therapy. 2nd ed. Stanley Siegel & Ed Lowe. LC 93-3435. 196p. 1999. pap. 12.95 (*1-56924-685-8*) Marlowe & Co.

***Patients & Doctors: Life-Changing Stories from Primary Care.** Ed. by Jeffrey M. Borkan et al. LC 99-19758. 240p. 1999. text 24.95 (*0-299-16340-7*) U of Wis Pr.

Patients & Healers in the Context of Culture: An Exploration of the Borderland Between Anthropology, Medicine, & Psychiatry. Arthur Kleinman. LC 78-57311. (Comparative Studies of Health Systems & Medical Care: Vol. 5). 1979. pap. 17.95 (*0-520-04511-4*, Pub. by U CA Pr) Cal Prin Full Svc.

Patients & Methods. Douglas A. Gammon. (Illus.). 144p. 1991. pap. text 35.00 (*0-07-452733-9*) McGraw-Hill HPD.

Patients & Their Hospitals. Winifred Raphael. Ed. by King Edward's Hospital Fund Staff. 46p. 1977. pap. 19.95 (*0-8464-1297-7*) Beekman Pubs.

***Patients As Effective Collaborators in Managing Chronic Conditions.** Frwd. by Daniel M. Fox & Jessie Gruman. 32p. 1999. pap. write for info. (*1-887748-26-1*) Milbank Memorial.

Patients As People see Newer Dimensions of Patient Care

Patients As Victims: Sexual Abuse in Psychotherapy & Counselling. Derek Jehu. LC 93-42345. (Series in Psychotherapy & Counselling). 260p. 1995. pap. 89.95 (*0-471-94398-3*) Wiley.

Patients at Risk: AIDS in the Dentist's Office: Everything You Need to Know to Protect Yourself & Your Family! John P. Sullivan. LC 93-86275. (Illus.). 64p. (Orig.). 1993. pap. 9.95 (*0-9638856-1-8*) Pronet Pr.

***Patients' Book: How to Survive in Today's Medical System.** Sandra McCray & Diane Hartman. 150p. 2000. pap. 12.00 (*0-9676647-3-9*) Colorado Hlth.

Patients Build Your Practice: Word of Mouth Marketing for Healthcare Practitioners. Michael E. Cafferky. 170p. (Orig.). 1994. pap. text 29.95 (*0-07-600676-X*, ME114) Practice Mgmt Info.

Patient's Daily Pain Journal: An Illustrative Reference & Identification Guide to Targeting Chronic Pain for Improved Communication Between Doctor & Patient. Marguerite J. Cantine. Ed. by Elizabeth A. Kilpatrick. (Illus.). 113p. 1996. write for info. (*0-614-13541-9*) Cantine & Kilpatrick.

***Patients Don't Lie.** Marykutty T. Kuriakose. 1999. pap. 16.95 (*0-9672490-0-7*) M Kuriakose.

Patients First: Experiences of a Patient-Focused Pioneer. William J. Leander et al. LC 95-46555. 1996. pap. 44.00 (*1-56793-039-5*, 0974) Health Admin Pr.

Patient's Guide to Anesthesia. A. J. Hill. 288p. 1999. pap. 13.00 (*1-57566-405-4*) Kensgtn Pub Corp.

Patient's Guide to Backache Relief Acupressure & Medication. Avi Brenholz. (Illus.). 50p. Date not set. pap. 2.48 (*1-889958-03-4*) A Ben Aur.

Patient's Guide to COPD & Lung Cancer. Tim Peters. (Humanatomy Board Bks.). (Illus.). 12p. 1991. bds. 9.95 (*1-879874-03-2*) T Peters & Co.

Patient's Guide to Coronary Bypass Surgery & Its Aftermath: Advice from a Survivor. Douglas C. Ewing. (Illus.). 160p. 16.95 (*0-8065-1748-4*, Citadel Pr) Carol Pub Group.

Patient's Guide to Coronary Bypass Surgery & It's Aftermath: Advice from a Survivor. Douglas C. Ewing. (Illus.). 162p. 1996. 16.95 (*1-55972-351-3*, Birch Ln Pr) Carol Pub Group.

Patients Guide to Dialysis & Transplantation. 3rd ed. R. Gabriel. 1987. pap. text 29.00 (*0-85200-981-X*) Kluwer Academic.

***Patient's Guide to Eye Care.** Lawrence Winograd & Melvin L. Rubin. 272p. 2000. pap. 24.95 (*0-937404-63-2*) Triad Pub FL.

***Patient's Guide to Hair Restoration.** William R. Rassman & Robert M. Bernstein. (Illus.). 239p. 1999. pap. 5.95 (*0-9701405-0-9*) New Hair.

Patient's Guide to Headache Relief Using Acupressure & Medication. Avi Brenholz. (Illus.). 50p. 1995. 2.48 (*1-889958-05-0*) A Ben Aur.

Patient's Guide to Homeopathic Medicine. Robert W. Ullman & Judyth Reichenberg-Ullman. 96p. (Orig.). 1995. pap. 10.95 (*0-9640654-2-8*) Picnic Pt Pr.

Patient's Guide to Knee & Hip Replacement: Everything You Need to Know. Irwin Silber. LC 98-44423. (Illus.). 256p. 1999. per. 12.00 (*0-684-83920-2*, Fireside) S&S Trade Pap.

***Patient's Guide to Male Sexual Dysfunction.** Tom F. Lue. (Illus.). 120p. 2000. pap. write for info. (*1-884065-82-1*, Hndbks Hlth Care) Assocs in Med.

Patient's Guide to Medical Terminology. 3rd rev. ed. Charlotte Isler. LC 94-39738. 258p. (Orig.). 1997. reprint ed. pap. 12.95 (*1-885987-08-0*, ME080, Health Info Pr) Practice Mgmt Info.

Patient's Guide to Medical Tests. Yale University School of Medicine Staff. LC 96-53904. 448p. 1997. 40.00 (*0-395-76536-6*) HM.

Patient's Guide to Medical Tests: Everything You Need to Know about the Tests Your Doctor Prescribes. 4th ed. Joseph Stauffer & Joseph C. Segen. LC 97-37944. 432p. 1997. 29.95 (*0-8160-3471-0*); pap. 17.95 (*0-8160-3530-X*) Facts on File.

Patient's Guide to Prostate Cancer: An Expert's Successful Treatment Strategies & Options. Marc Garnick. 274p. 1996. pap. 12.95 (*0-452-27455-9*, Plume) Dutton Plume.

Patient's Guide to Radial Keratotomy. William Ellis. (Illus.). 80p. (Orig.). 1992. pap. text. write for info. (*0-9633665-0-5*) Eye Ctr N CA.

Patient's Guide to Surgery. Edward L. Bradley, III. Ed. by Consumer Reports Books Editors. (Illus.). 256p. (C). 1994. text 26.50 (*0-8122-3280-1*) U of Pa Pr.

Patients Guide to Surgery. Weedwe. 1995. 22.95 (*0-02-624770-4*) Macmillan.

Patient's Guide to Understandng Hemodialysis. rev. ed. Regional Kidney Disease Program, Education Departm. 150p. 1986. reprint ed. ring bd. 30.00 (*1-56488-005-2*) Dialyrn.

Patient's Guide to Urology: Plumbing Problems in Layman's Terms. G. Mark Seal. (Illus.). 273p. 1995. text 21.95 (*0-9645773-0-5*); pap. text 12.95 (*0-9645773-1-3*) High Oaks Pub.

Patient's Impact on the Analyst. Judy L. Kantrowitz. LC 96-38505. 320p. 1996. 47.50 (*0-88163-211-2*) Analytic Pr.

Patients in My Care. large type ed. Bridget Ristori. (Non-Fiction Ser.). 1971. 27.99 (*0-85456-089-0*) Ulverscroft.

Patient's Interest First: The Nature of Medical Ethics & the Dilemma of a Good Doctor. Arthur M. Lim. 120p. pap. 20.00 (*981-02-3548-8*) World Scientific Pub.

Patient's Interest Foremost: The Good Doctor's Ethics. 88p. 1996. pap. 10.00 (*981-02-2841-4*) World Scientific Pub.

Patient's Journey. David Lefkowitz & Robert Siegel. 99p. (Orig.). 1995. pap. 7.95 (*0-9637668-0-5*) Irving Pr.

Patient's Little Instruction Book: Your Health Care Survival Guide. Carolyn Jenks & Gerard Spiniello. LC 97-580. 144p. 1997. text 10.00 (*1-57626-022-4*) Quality Med Pub.

Patient's Midnight Guide to Exercise. Avi Brenholz. (Illus.). 50p. Date not set. pap. 2.48 (*1-889958-09-3*) A Ben Aur.

Patient's Midnight Guide to Headache Relief Using Acupressure/Shiatsu. Avi Brenholz. (Illus.). 20p. 1995. pap. 1.95 (*1-889958-07-7*) A Ben Aur.

Patient's Midnight Guide to Headache Relief Using Nutrition & Acupressure. Avi Brenholz. (Illus.). 20p. 1996. pap. 1.95 (*1-889958-06-9*) A Ben Aur.

Patient's Midnight Guide to Nutrition. Avi Brenholz. (Illus.). 50p. Date not set. pap. 2.48 (*1-889958-08-5*) A Ben Aur.

Patient's Midnight Guide to Toothache Relief Using Acupressure & Medication. Avi Brenholz. (Illus.). 50p. 1995. pap. 2.48 (*1-889958-04-2*) A Ben Aur.

***Patient's Notes: A 30-Day Calendar on the Path to Wellness.** Christine Parker. 64p. 1999. pap. 15.00 (*0-9669179-3-6*) Fifth Wrld.

Patients or Customers: Are the NHS Reforms Working? Ed. by Reginald Murley et al. (Choice in Welfare Ser.: No. 23). 87p. 1995. pap. 16.95 (*0-255-36360-5*, Pub. by Inst Economic Affairs) Coronet Bks.

Patient's Ordeal. William F. May. LC 90-45841. (Medical Ethics Ser.). 240p. 1991. 26.95 (*0-253-33717-8*) Ind U Pr.

Patient's Ordeal. William F. May. LC 90-45841. (Medical Ethics Ser.). 240p. 1994. pap. 11.95 (*0-253-20870-X*) Ind U Pr.

Patients, Pain & Politics: Nursing Home Inspector's Shocking True Story & Expert Advice for You & Your Family. Mary R. Rollins. Ed. by Barbara Davis. 248p. (Orig.). 1994. pap. 11.95 (*1-884348-20-3*) N Century Pubng.

Patients, Physicians, & Illness: A Sourcebook in Behavioral Science & Health. 3rd ed. Ed. by E. Gartly Jaco. LC 78-63407. 1979. text 29.95 (*0-02-915850-8*) Free Pr.

Patient's Point of View: Observations of a Chiropractic Advocate. William D. Esteb. 240p. 1992. pap. text 19.95 (*0-9631711-0-0*) Back Talk Systs.

Patients, Policies, & Politics: Before & after "Working for Patients" John Butler. LC 92-18762. (State of Health Ser.). 160p. 1992. 118.95 (*0-335-15648-7*); pap. 35.95 (*0-335-15647-9*) OpUniv Pr.

Patients, Power & the Poor in 18th Century Bristol. Mary E. Fissell. (Cambridge History of Medicine Ser.). (Illus.). 272p. (C). 1991. text 64.95 (*0-521-40047-3*) Cambridge U Pr.

Patients' Privacy: An Explanatory Study of Patients' Perception of Their Privacy in a German Acute Care Hospital. Irmgard L. Bauer. LC 94-16735. (Developments in Nursing & Health Care Ser.). 184p. 1994. 66.95 (*1-85628-918-4*, Pub. by Avebry) Ashgate Pub Co.

Patients Profits & Power. Harold Stearley. 1998. pap. 9.95 (*1-888315-01-6*) Power NY.

Patient's Progress: Doctors & Doctoring in 18th-Century England. Dorothy Porter & Roy Porter. LC 89-60692. (Illus.). 313p. 1989. 42.50 (*0-8047-1744-3*) Stanford U Pr.

Patient's Progress: Sickness, Health & Medical Care in England, 1650-1850. Dorothy Porter & Roy Porter. (Medicine & Society Ser.: Vol. 4). 25.00 (*0-520-06661-8*) U CA Pr.

Patients, Psychiatrists & Lawyers: Law & the Mental Health System. 2nd ed. Raymond L. Spring et al. LC 99-188645. 938p. (C). 1996. 59.95 (*0-87084-797-X*) Anderson Pub Co.

***Patients, Psychiatrists & Lawyers: Law & the Mental Health System.** 3rd ed. Raymond L. Spring et al. 2000. text. write for info. (*0-87084-311-7*) Anderson Pub Co.

Patient's Right to Know: Information Disclosure, the Doctor & the Law. Sheila A. McLean. 270p. 1989. pap. 33.95 (*1-85521-021-5*, Pub. by Dartmth Pub); text 87.95 (*1-85521-010-X*, Pub. by Dartmth Pub) Ashgate Pub Co.

Patients' Rights - Community Concerns. Ed. by Steven J. Friedman & Thomas M. Hughes. (Issues in Community Mental Health Ser.). 89p. (C). 1991. pap. text 6.95 (*0-88135-057-5*, Prodist) Watson Pub Intl.

Patients' Rights & Responsibilities: An Easy-to-Read Guide for People Taking Medicine. Michael G. Aman et al. (Project Med). (Illus.). 1999. pap. text. write for info. (*0-9658966-1-7*, 1) OSU Nisonger.

Patient's Story: Integrated Patient-Doctor Interviewing. Robert C. Smith. 232p. 1995. 25.95 (*0-316-80266-2*, Little Brwn Med Div) Lppncott W & W.

Patient's Voice: Experiences of Illness. Jeanine Young-Mason. LC 96-28901. (Illus.). 197p. (C). 1996. pap. text 25.95 (*0-8036-0162-X*) Davis Co.

Patients Who Deceive: Assessment & Management of Risk in Providing Health Care & Financial Benefits. Loren Pankratz. LC 98-12041. (American Series in Behavioral Science & Law). 274p. 1998. text 55.95 (*0-398-06866-6*); pap. text 41.95 (*0-398-06867-4*) C C Thomas.

Patients with Communicable Diseases in the Borough of Kittanning, PA 1907-1955. Allen R. Mechling & Marla K. Mechling. 136p. 1995. per. 6.00 (*1-55856-210-9*, 106) Closson Pr.

***Patients with Special Needs Vol. 39-1: Behavioral Aspects of Vision Care.** (Illus.). 103p. 1998. pap. 20.00 (*0-943599-98-9*) OEPF.

Patients Without Frontiers: Negotiations on the Health Care Market. Ivan Wolffers. 70p. 1991. pap. 24.95 (*90-6256-937-4*, Pub. by VU Univ Pr) Paul & Co Pubs.

PatientWise, Version2. Ed. by Peter Wise et al. 500p. 1997. 215.00 (*0-471-96548-0*, MD00) Wiley.

***Patinaje en Linea.** Joel Rappelfeld. 1998. pap. text 9.95 (*84-8327-005-6*) E Martinez Roca.

P

An Asterisk (*) at the beginning of an entry indicates that the title is appearing for the first time.

Patinas for Silicon Bronze. Patrick V. Kipper. Ed. by Nancy Schmachtenberger & Mary Libbey. LC 95-92327. (Illus.). 238p. Date not set. 69.95 (*0-9647269-0-4*, Pub. by Path Pubns) Rodgers & Nelsen.

Patine Al Invierno Con Matematicas y Ciencias - Glide into Winter with Math & Science. R. Adair et al. (ENG & SPA.). 105p. (J). (gr. k-1). 1987. 16.95 (*1-881431-20-7*, 1402) AIMS Educ Fnd.

Patinnova, '90 - Strategies for the Protections of Innovation: Proceedings of the First European Congress on Industrial Property Rights & Innovation. Ed. by U. Tager & A. Von Witzleben. (C). 1991. lib. bdg. 122.00 (*0-7923-1062-4*) Kluwer Academic.

Patio - Porch. Jack Heifner. 1978. pap. 5.25 (*0-8222-0880-6*) Dramatists Play.

Patio Daddy-O: The Golden Age of Barbecue: 50s Recipes with a 90s Twist. Gideon Bosker et al. LC 95-21388. 96p. 1995. 12.95 (*0-8118-0871-8*) Chronicle Bks.

Patio de Mi Casa: Big Book. (SPA.). (J). (gr. k-1). 1997. 25.95 incl. audio (*1-56014-041-0*) Santillana.

Patio de Mi Casa: Big Book. Alma F. Ada. (Early Learning Packs Ser.). (SPA., Illus.). 16p. (Orig.). (J). (gr. 1-3). 1991. pap. text 29.95 (*1-56334-018-6*) Hampton-Brown.

Patio de Mi Casa: Small Book. Alma F. Ada. (Early Learning Packs Ser.). (SPA., Illus.). 16p. (Orig.). (J). (gr. 1-3). 1991. pap. text 36.00 (*1-56334-088-7*) Hampton-Brown.

Patio Games. David Toyne. (Planning & Planting Ser.). (Illus.). 96p. 1997. pap. 12.95 (*0-7063-7636-6*, Pub. by WrLock) Sterling.

***Patio Garden: Month-By-Month.** Michael Jefferson-Brown. (Month-by-Month Gardening Ser.). (Illus.). 1999. pap. 14.95 (*0-7153-0818-1*) D & C Pub.

Patio Garden Month-by-Month. Michael Jefferson-Brown. LC 97-191975. (Illus.). 144p. 1997. 24.95 (*0-7153-0534-4*) Sterling.

Patio Gardening: Step by Step to Growing Success. Yvonne Rees & David Palliser. (Crowood Gardening Guides Ser.). (Illus.). 128p. 1992. pap. 16.95 (*1-85223-507-1*, Pub. by Crolwood) Trafalgar.

Patio Gardens. Lori K. Pupeza. LC 98-11987. (How-To Gardening for Kids Ser.). (J). 2002. lib. bdg. 13.95 (*1-57765-034-4*) ABDO Pub Co.

Patio House: A Suburban House for Urban Living, Its Design Concept & Application to Urban Renewal. William K. Wittausch. Ed. by J. Ross McKeever. LC 63-16409. (Urban Land Institute, Technical Bulletin Ser.: No. 45). (Illus.). 40p. reprint ed. pap. 30.00 (*0-608-11420-0*, 201136800079) Bks Demand.

Patio Roofs & Gazebos. Sunset Books Editors. LC 88-80795. 96p. 1988. pap. 12.95 (*0-376-01439-3*, 201439, Pub. by Sunset Books) Leisure AR.

Patiofarming: A Compendium of Useful Tables. Franklin W. Martin & Ruth M. Ruberte. (Studies in Tropical Agriculture). 1980. lib. bdg. 69.95 (*0-8490-3075-7*) Gordon Pr.

Patios & Gardens of Mexico. Patricia O'Gorman. 17p. 1994. reprint ed. 40.00 (*0-8038-0210-2*) Archit CT.

Patisambhidamagga, 2 vols. in 1. Ed. by Arnold C. Taylor. LC 78-70108. reprint ed. 43.50 (*0-404-17358-6*) AMS Pr.

Patisserie. 2nd ed. John Hanneman. (Illus.). 334p. 1993. 52.95 (*0-7506-0430-1*) Buttrwrth-Heinemann.

Patissier's Art: Professional Breads, Cakes, Pies, Pastries, & Puddings. George Karousos et al. 320p. 1994. 55.00 (*0-471-59716-3*) Wiley.

Patissier's Art: Professional Breads, Cakes, Pies, Pastries & Puddings. George Karousos et al. 320p. 1998. pap. 19.95 (*0-471-31878-7*) Wiley.

Patito Feo. Hans Christian Andersen. (Spanish Well Loved Tales Ser.: No. 700-1). (SPA.). (J). (gr. 1). 1990. boxed set 3.50 (*0-7214-1407-9*, Ladybrd) Penguin Putnam.

Patito Feo. Hans Christian Andersen. (SPA.). (J). 1997. pap. 3.95 (*0-8167-3066-0*) Troll Communs.

***Patito Feo.** Hans Christian Andersen.Tr. of Grimme Aelling. (SPA.). 1999. pap. 7.95 (*88-8148-251-7*) Europ Lang Inst.

Patito Feo (The Ugly Duckling) Hans Christian Andersen. (SPA., Illus.). 32p. (J). (ps-3). 1999. 8.95 (*0-7641-5150-9*) Barron.

Patitucci/Electric Bass. 36p. (YA). 1994. pap. 26.95 (*0-7692-1240-9*, MMBK0006CD) Wrner Bros.

***Patkau Architects: Selected Projects 1983-1993.** 2nd ed. Patkau Architects Staff. Ed. by Brian Carter & ARUP Associates Staff. LC 94-950012. (Documents in Canadian Architecture Ser.). (Illus.). 120p. 1998. reprint ed. pap. 24.50 (*0-929112-28-8*, Pub. by Tuns Pr) Baker & Taylor.

Patkoi Nagas. S. C. Sardeshpande. 1987. 49.95 (*81-7035-032-8*) Asia Bk Corp.

Patmans of Sweet Valley. Created by Francine Pascal. (Sweet Valley Saga). 352p. (YA). (gr. 8 up). 1996. mass mkt. 4.50 (*0-553-57023-4*) Bantam.

Patmos Conspiracy. Bruce Merritt. LC 90-80821. 287p. 1990. pap. 9.95 (*0-916035-38-7*) Evangel Indiana.

Patmos Prediction. Nathan M. Meyer. LC 89-63537. 261p. (Orig.). 1989. pap. 9.95 (*0-941241-04-1*) Prophecy Pubns.

Patmowt'iwn Hayots: History of the Armenians. Agathangelos. Ed. by Robert W. Thomson. LC 79-27282. (Classical Armenian Texts Ser.). 608p. 1980. reprint ed. 60.00 (*0-88206-027-9*) Caravan Bks.

Patmowt'iwn Hayots: History of the Armenians. Hovhannes Draskhanakertetsi. Ed. by Krikor Maksoudian. LC 79-24542. (Classical Armenian Texts Ser.). 488p. 1980. reprint ed. 50.00 (*0-88206-028-7*) Caravan Bks.

Patmowt'iwn Hayots: History of the Armenians. Moses of Khoren. Ed. by Robert W. Thomson. LC 81-3869. (Classical Armenian Texts Ser.). 488p. 1981. reprint ed. 50.00 (*0-88206-032-5*) Caravan Bks.

Patmuwt'iwn Hayots: History of the Armenians. Ghazar Parbetsi. Ed. by Dickran Kouymjian. LC 85-11340. 276p. 1987. reprint ed. 50.00 (*0-88206-031-7*) Caravan Bks.

Patna & Patusan Perspectives: A Study of the Function of the Minor Characters in Joseph Conrad's Lord Jim. Jan A. Verleun. xx, 236p. (Orig.). 1979. pap. 27.00 (*90-6088-062-5*, Pub. by Boumas Boekhuis) Gen Publ ON.

***Pato Paco, 2 vols.** Anna Turner. (SPA.). 2000. pap. 9.98 (*0-89084-900-5*) Bob Jones Univ.

Pato Paco. Anna Turner & Beth Kitching. LC 93-21134. (Illus.). (J). 1994. pap. 5.49 (*0-89084-722-3*, 076398) Bob Jones Univ.

Pato Salvaje. Alfredo Villanueva-Collado & Carlos A. Rodriguez Matos. (SPA.). 88p. (Orig.). 1991. pap. 8.00 (*0-9623552-5-9*) Ed Arcas.

Patografia. Patrick RILEM Technical Committee. 1999. pap. text 24.95 (*968-406-807-7*) F Planeta.

Patologia Estructural y Funcional. 4th ed. Stanley L. Robbins. 1990. text 99.00 (*0-07-104001-3*) McGraw.

Patologie Vascolari Cerebrali Dell'Anziano. Ed. by W. Meier-Ruge. (Insegnamento E Formazione in Medicina Geriatrica Ser.: Vol. 2). viii, 188p. 1991. pap. 24.50 (*3-8055-5365-X*) S Karger.

Paton & Goldberg's Management of Ocular Injuries. 2nd ed. Thomas A. Deutsch & Daniel B. Feller. (Illus.). 248p. 1985. text 82.00 (*0-7216-1173-7*, W B Saunders Co) Harcrt Hlth Sci Grp.

Paton on Accounting: Selected Writings of W. A. Paton. William A. Paton. Ed. by Herbert F. Taggart. LC 64-64728. 729p. reprint ed. pap. 180.00 (*0-608-13524-0*, 2022093) Bks Demand.

Patos. Lynn M. Stone. (Animales de Granja Ser.).Tr. of Ducks. 24p. (J). (gr. k-4). 1991. lib. bdg. 14.60 (*0-86592-953-X*) Rourke Enter.

Patout's Cajun Home Cooking. Alex Patout. 1986. 27.50 (*0-394-54725-X*) Random.

Patpong Sisters: An American Woman's View of the Bangkok Sex World. Cleo Odzer. LC 94-15551. (Illus.). 320p. 1997. pap. 13.45 (*1-55970-372-5*, Pub. by Arcade Pub Inc) Time Warner.

Patpong Sisters: Prostitution in Bangkok. Cleo Odzer. LC 94-15551. (Illus.). 320p. 1994. 24.45 (*1-55970-281-8*, Pub. by Arcade Pub Inc) Time Warner.

Patranuelo. Joan Timoneda. Ed. by Maria P. Cuartero Sancho. (Nueva Austral Ser.: Vol. 175). (SPA.). 1991. pap. text 24.95 (*84-239-1975-7*) Elliots Bks.

Patres Apostolici Pt. IV: Concordantia in Patres Apostolicos. (Alpha-Omega Ser.: Reihe A, Bd. CLXV). (GER.). 227p. 1996. 35.00 (*3-487-10256-0*) G Olms Pubs.

Patria: El Periodico de Jose Marti, Registro General, 1892-1895. Carlos Ripoll. 1971. 9.95 (*0-88303-011-X*); pap. 6.95 (*0-685-73215-0*) E Torres & Sons.

Patria o Muerte: The Great Zoo & Other Poems. Nicolas Guillen. Ed. & Tr. by Robert Marquez. LC 72-81758. (SPA.). 223p. reprint ed. pap. 69.20 (*0-7837-6997-0*, 204681000004) Bks Demand.

Patriachs & Prophets: How It All Began. Ellen Gould Harmon White. (Bible Study Companion Set Ser.: Vol. 1). 607p. (C). 1997. pap. 11.99 (*1-883012-50-3*) Remnant Pubns.

Patriach's Wife: Literary Evidence & the History of the Family. Margaret J. M. Ezell. LC 86-20720. xii, 272p. (C). 1987. 39.95 (*0-8078-1741-4*) U of NC Pr.

Patrian Transgression, No. 69. Simon Hawke. (Star Trek Ser.). 1994. mass mkt. 5.50 (*0-671-88044-6*) PB.

Patriarcas y Profetas. Ellen G. White. (SPA.). 528p. Date not set. pap. 11.99 (*1-883012-84-8*) Remnant Pubns.

Patriarch. Richard N. Smith. 448p. 1997. pap. 15.00 (*0-395-85512-8*) HM.

Patriarch. Susan E. Tifft & Alex S. Jones. Ed. by Julie Rubenstein. 576p. 1992. reprint ed. per. 12.00 (*0-671-75595-1*) PB.

Patriarch & Folk: The Emergence of Nicaragua, 1798-1858. E. Bradford Burns. 320p. (C). 1991. 51.95 (*0-674-65796-9*) HUP.

Patriarch & the Prince: The Letter of Patriarch Photios of Constantinople to Khan Boris of Bulgaria. D. S. White & Joseph R. Berrigan, Jr. 102p. 1982. 14.95 (*0-916586-52-9*, Pub. by Holy Cross Orthodox); pap. 5.95 (*0-916586-53-7*, Pub. by Holy Cross Orthodox) BookWorld.

Patriarch Athenagoras - Man of Love. Gloria Caleina Del Vecchio. 1998. pap. 9.95 (*1-887213-13-9*) Blck Oak Pr.

Patriarch Nicephorus of Constantinople: Ecclesiastical Policy & Image Worship in the Byzantine Empire. Paul J. Alexander. LC 78-63177. (Heresies Ser.: No. II). reprint ed. 55.00 (*0-404-16195-2*) AMS Pr.

Patriarch Photios of Constantinople, His Life, Scholarly Contributions & Correspondence Together with a Translation of Fifty-Two of His Letters. Despina S. White. Ed. by Nomikos M. Vaporis. (Archbishop Iakovos Library of Ecclesiastical & Historical Sources: No. 5). 234p. 1982. 9.95 (*0-916586-26-X*); pap. 9.95 (*0-916586-21-9*, Pub. by Holy Cross Orthodox) BookWorld.

Patriarcha & Other Writings. Robert Filmer. Ed. by Johann P. Sommerville. (Cambridge Texts in the History of Political Thought Ser.). 373p. (C). 1991. text 59.95 (*0-521-37491-X*); pap. text 19.95 (*0-521-39903-3*) Cambridge U Pr.

Patriarchal Attitudes: Women in Society. Eva Figes. 192p. 1987. reprint ed. pap. 9.95 (*0-89255-122-4*) Persea Bks.

Patriarchal Desire & Victorian Discourse: A Lacanian Reading of Anthony Trollope's Palliser Novels. Priscilla L. Walton. 208p. 1995. text 45.00 (*0-8020-0655-8*) U of Toronto Pr.

Patriarchal Paradox: Women Politicians in Turkey. Yesim Arat. LC 88-45715. 160p. 1989. 29.50 (*0-8386-3347-1*) Fairleigh Dickinson.

Patriarchal Politics & Christoph Kress, (1484-1535) of Nuremberg. Jonathan W. Zophy. LC 92-27478. (Studies in German Thought & History: Vol. 14). (Illus.). 300p. 1992. text 89.95 (*0-7734-9605-X*) E Mellen.

Patriarchal Precedents: Sexuality & Social Relations. Rosalind Coward. 280p. (Orig.). 1983. pap. 14.95 (*0-7100-9324-1*, Routledge Thoemms) Routledge.

Patriarchal Representations: Gender & Discourse in Pirandello's Theatre. Margaret Gunsberg. LC 92-21180. 224p. 1993. 39.50 (*0-85496-340-5*) Berg Pubs.

Patriarchs. Behn Boruch. 28p. 1959. 3.95 (*0-88482-729-1*) Hebrew Pub.

Patriarchs: From Abraham Until Jacob see Torah Anthology: Meam Lo'ez

Patriarchs & Parasites: The Gentry of South-West Wales in the Eighteenth Century. David W. Howell. xii, 322p. 1986. 70.00 (*0-7083-0929-1*, Pub. by Univ Wales Pr) Paul & Co Pubs.

Patriarchs & Prophets. Ellen Gould Harmon White. 805p. 1958. 14.99 (*0-8163-0038-0*, 16082-0) Pacific Pr Pub Assn.

Patriarchs & Prophets. Ellen Gould Harmon White. 805p. 1958. pap. 5.99 (*0-8163-0842-X*, 16083-0) Pacific Pr Pub Assn.

Patriarchs & Prophets. Stanley B. Frost. LC 64-7191. 244p. reprint ed. pap. 75.70 (*0-7837-1039-9*, 204135000020) Bks Demand.

Patriarch's Hope. David Feintuch. LC 98-37556. 528p. 1999. 24.00 (*0-446-52458-1*, Pub. by Warner Bks) Little.

***Patriarch's Hope.** David Feintuch. 528p. 2000. mass mkt. 6.50 (*0-446-60846-7*, Aspect) Warner Bks.

Patriarchs in Hebron & Sodom (Genesis 18-19) A Study of the Structure & Composition of a Biblical Story. Talia Rudin-O'Brasky. (Jerusalem Biblical Studies: Vol. 2). (HEB.). 156p. 1982. pap. text 12.00 (*0-685-49415-2*, Pub. by Simor Ltd) Eisenbrauns.

Patriarchs, Judges & Kings. Bernard R. Youngman. (Background to the Bible Ser.: Vol. 1). 94p. (YA). (gr. 8-12). 1984. pap. 9.95 (*0-7175-0414-X*) Dufour.

Patriarchs of Israel. John M. Holt. LC 64-13543. 247p. reprint ed. pap. 76.60 (*0-8357-3258-4*, 203947900013) Bks Demand.

Patriarchy: Notes of an Expert Witness. Phyllis Chesler. LC 94-21995. 150p. (Orig.). 1994. pap. 12.95 (*1-56751-038-8*); lib. bdg. 29.95 (*1-56751-039-6*) Common Courage.

Patriarchy & Accumulation on a World Scale: Women in the International Division of Labour. Maria Mies. 260p. (C). 1986. pap. 22.50 (*0-86232-342-8*, Pub. by St Martin) St Martin.

Patriarchy & Accumulation on a World Scale: Women in the International Division of Labour. Maria Mies. 260p. (C). 1986. text 49.95 (*0-86232-341-X*, Pub. by Zed Books) St Martin.

***Patriarchy & Accumulation on a World Scale; Women in the International Division of Labour.** Maria Mies. 1999. text 65.00 (*1-85649-734-8*) Zed Books.

***Patriarchy & Accumulation on a World Scale; Women in the International Division of Labour.** 2nd ed. Maria Mies. 1999. pap. 22.50 (*1-85649-735-6*) St Martin.

Patriarchy & Economic Development: Women's Position at the End of the Twentieth Century. Ed. by Valentine M. Moghadam. (Illus.). 382p. (C). 1996. text 89.00 (*0-19-829023-3*) OUP.

Patriarchy & Families of Privilege in 15th-Century England. Joel Thomas Rosenthal. LC 91-17228. (Middle Ages Ser.). (Illus.). 304p. (C). 1991. text 39.95 (*0-8122-3072-8*) U of Pa Pr.

Patriarchy & Incest from Shakespeare to Joyce. Jane M. Ford. LC 98-13226. (Illus.). 272p. 1998. 49.95 (*0-8130-1595-2*) U Press Fla.

Patriarchy As a Conceptual Trap. Elizabeth Dodson Gray. 136p. 1982. pap. 14.95 (*0-934512-04-3*) Roundtable Pr.

Patriarchy of Shakespeare's Comedies. Marilyn L. Williamson. LC 86-11151. 208p. 1986. 34.95 (*0-8143-1807-X*) Wayne St U Pr.

Patriarchy on the Line: Labor, Gender, & Ideology in the Mexican Maquila Industry. Susan Tiano. LC 93-43361. 272p. (C). 1994. text 69.95 (*1-56639-195-4*); pap. text 22.95 (*1-56639-196-2*) Temple U Pr.

Patriarchy, Property & Death in the Roman Family. Richard P. Saller. LC 93-45700. (Studies in Population, Economy & Society in Past Time: No. 25). 263p. (C). 1995. text 59.95 (*0-521-32603-6*) Cambridge U Pr.

Patriarchy, Property & Death in the Roman Family. Richard P. Saller. (Cambridge Studies in Population, Economy & Society in Past Time: No. 25). 263p. 1996. pap. text 22.95 (*0-521-59978-4*) Cambridge U Pr.

Patriarchy's Demolition: A Year of Action. Susanna Cuyler. (Illus.). 178p. (Orig.). (C). 1993. pap. 20.00 (*0-9612018-8-6*) B RUGGED.

Patric Walker's Sun Signs. Patric Walker. 2000. mass mkt. write for info. (*0-06-109243-6*, Harp PBks) HarpC.

Patricia. Grace Livingston Hill. Date not set. 23.95 (*0-8488-2325-7*) Amereon Ltd.

Patricia, No. 36. Grace Livingston Hill. (Grace Livingston Hill Ser.: Vol. 36). 272p. 1992. mass mkt. 4.99 (*0-8423-4814-X*) Tyndale Hse.

Patricia & Phillip Frost Collection: American Abstraction, 1930-45. Virginia M. Mecklenburg. LC 89-43055. (Illus.). 200p. (C). 1989. pap. 29.95 (*0-87474-717-1*) Smithsonian.

***Patricia Cornwell: A Reader's Checklist & Reference Guide.** CheckerBee Publishing Staff. 1999. pap. text 4.95 (*1-58598-014-5*) CheckerBee.

Patricia Cornwell: 3 Complete Novels: Postmortem; Body of Evidence; All That Remains. Patricia Cornwell. 832p. 1997. 14.98 (*0-7651-0912-5*) Smithmark.

***Patricia Farr's Costumes for Every Occasion: Over 30 Easy-to-make Costumes for Children & Adults.** Patricia Farr. LC 00-30358. (Illus.). 2000. write for info. (*1-57912-079-2*) Blck Dog & Leventhal.

Patricia Highsmith. Harrison. LC 97-18792. 1997. 32.00 (*0-8057-4566-1*, Twyne) Mac Lib Ref.

Patricia Letters. Kevin Sampsell. 35p. 1996. 3.00 (*0-9653194-0-7*) Future Tense.

Patricia MaClachlan. Russell. LC 97-7224. 1997. 32.00 (*0-8057-4575-0*, Twyne) Mac Lib Ref.

***Patricia Marne's Manual of Graphology.** Patricia Marne. (Illus.). 2000. pap. 15.95 (*0-572-02463-0*) W Foulsham.

Patricia Nix. James Beck et al. 192p. 1995. 100.00 (*0-9648340-0-6*) Dillon Gallery.

Patricia Renick: Triceracopter. Laura H. Chapman. Ed. by Ruth K. Meyer. (Illus.). pap. 6.50 (*0-917562-06-2*) Contemp Arts.

Patricia Ryan Nixon. Barbara S. Feinberg. LC 97-21382. (Encyclopedia of First Ladies Ser.). 112p. 1997. lib. bdg. 33.00 (*0-516-20482-3*) Childrens.

Patricia Seybold Group's Customers.com Collection. Patricia Seybold Group Staff. (Illus.). 213p. 1998. pap. 4695.00 (*1-892815-00-1*) Patricia Seybold.

Patricia Seybold Group's 1997 User Survey of Electronic Commerce Initiatives. David S. Marshad & Judith Lazaro. 89p. 1997. pap. 295.00 (*1-892815-25-7*) Patricia Seybold.

Patricia, the Baby Manatee & Other Stories Janet Jagan. LC 98-833213. 76p. (J). 1995. write for info. (*0-948833-92-0*, Pub. by Peepal Tree Pr) Paul & Co Pubs.

Patricia Va a California, Vol. 2. Blaine Ray. (TPRS First-Year Spanish Novels Ser.). (SPA.). ii, 42p. (YA). (gr. 7-12). 1999. pap. 3.95 (*0-929724-50-X*) Command Performance.

Patricia Wells at Home in Provence: Recipes Inspired by Her Farmhouse in France. Patricia Wells. (Illus.). 40.00 (*0-614-25661-5*, Scribners Ref) Mac Lib Ref.

***Patricia Wells at Home in Provence: Recipes Inspired by Her Farmhouse in France.** Patricia Wells. 352p. 1999. pap. 23.00 (*0-684-86328-6*, Fireside) S&S Trade Pap.

Patricia Wells at Home in Provence: Recipes Inspired by Her Farmhouse in Provence. Patricia Wells. (Illus.). 384p. 1996. 40.00 (*0-684-81569-9*) S&S Trade.

Patricia Wells' Trat Co. Patricia Wells. 352p. 1995. pap. 14.00 (*0-380-71498-1*, Avon Bks) Morrow Avon.

Patricia Wells' Trattori. Patricia Wells. LC 93-16679. 338p. 1993. 25.00 (*0-688-10532-7*, Wm Morrow) Morrow Avon.

Patricia Wright. Pulley. (J). 1995. lib. bdg. 13.95 (*0-8050-2212-0*) H Holt & Co.

Patrician in the Progressive Era: A Biography of George Von Lengerke Meyer. Wayne A. Wiegand. LC 88-10984. (Modern American History Ser.). 296p. 1988. 15.00 (*0-8240-4339-1*) Garland.

Patrician Rhymes. Ed. by Clinton Scollard & Jessie B. Rittenhouse. LC 72-149115. (Granger Index Reprint Ser.). 1977. 26.95 (*0-8369-6240-0*) Ayer.

Patrician Tribune: Publius Clodius Pulcher. W. J. Tatum. LC 98-37096. (Studies in the History of Greece & Rome Series). 400p. (C). 1999. 49.95 (*0-8078-2480-1*) U of NC Pr.

Patricians & Parvenues: Wealth & High Society in Wilhelmine Germany. Dolores L. Augustine. LC 93-29862. 350p. 1994. 47.50 (*0-85496-397-9*) Berg Pubs.

Patricians & Plebeians: The Origin of the Roman State. Richard E. Mitchell. LC 90-1680. 288p. 1990. 37.50 (*0-8014-2496-8*) Cornell U Pr.

Patricians & Popolani: The Social Foundations of the Venetian Renaissance State. Dennis Romano. LC 87-2826. 220p. 1988. text 38.50 (*0-8018-3513-5*) Johns Hopkins.

Patrician's Daughter. Kirsti Vilkama. Ed. by Erkki Piri. Tr. by Miriam Byman et al. (Illus.). 122p. 1995. write for info. (*1-887034-00-5*) Laestadian Lutheran.

Patricians of Nishapur: A Study in Medieval Islamic Social History. Richard W. Bulliet. LC 70-173413. (Harvard Middle Eastern Studies: No. 16). (Illus.). 305p. 1972. reprint ed. pap. 94.60 (*0-7837-4454-4*, 205798400012) Bks Demand.

Patricians, Professors, & Public Schools: The Origins of Modern Educational Thought in America. Allan S. Horlick. LC 94-14314. (Brill's Studies in Intellectual History: Vol. 53). 1994. 94.00 (*90-04-10054-7*) Brill Academic Pubs.

Patricidal Bedside Companion. K. S. Haddock. 208p. (Orig.). 1994. pap. 12.95 (*0-312-10522-3*) St Martin.

***Patricide.** Elizabeth Fackler. LC 99-59538. 316p. 2000. 22.95 (*0-7862-2363-4*) Mac Lib Ref.

Patricios & Plebeyos: Burgueses, Hacendados, Artesanos & Obreros: Las Relaciones de Clase en el Puerto Rico de Cambio de Siglo. Angel G. Quintero-Rivera. LC 87-82379. (Nave y el Puerto Ser.). (SPA.). 332p. 1988. pap. 10.50 (*0-940238-93-4*) Ediciones Huracan.

Patrick: In His Own Words. Joseph Duffy. 108p. 1988. reprint ed. pap. 6.95 (*0-86217-174-1*, Pub. by Veritas Pubns) St Mut.

Patrick: Patron Saint of Ireland. Tomie De Paola. LC 91-19417. (Illus.). 32p. (J). (ps-3). 1992. lib. bdg. 16.95 (*0-8234-0924-4*) Holiday.

Patrick: Patron Saint of Ireland. Tomie De Paola. LC 91-19417. (Illus.). 30p. (J). (ps-3). 1992. pap. 6.95 (*0-8234-1077-3*) Holiday.

Patrick & Emma Lou. large type ed. Nan Holcomb. (Turtle Bks.). (Illus.). 32p. (J). (ps-2). 1989. pap. 7.95 (*0-944727-03-4*) Jason & Nordic Pubs.

Patrick & Emma Lou. large type ed. Nan Holcomb. (Turtle Bks.). (Illus.). 32p. (J). (ps-3). 1992. reprint ed. lib. bdg. 13.95 (*0-944727-14-X*) Jason & Nordic Pubs.

P

Patrick & the Actors. Margaret Keith. 206p. (YA). (gr. 9-12). 1981. 15.95 (0-920806-31-7, Pub. by Penumbra Pr); pap. 10.95 (0-920806-34-1, Pub. by Penumbra Pr) U of Toronto Pr.

Patrick at Bat. Jennifer Armstrong. (Illus.). (J). 1997. pap. 3.99 (0-679-87787-8) Random.

Patrick Cleburne. Howell Purdue & Elizabeth Purdue. 499p. 1973. reprint ed. 35.00 (0-942211-03-0) Olde Soldier Bks.

Patrick County, Virginia, Deed Book, 1791-1801, No. 1. LC 98-121929. 177p. (Orig.). 1997. pap. 20.00 (1-57445-029-8) TLC Genealogy.

Patrick County, Virginia Deed Index Abstracts, 1791-1850. Barbara C. Baughan & Betty A. Pilson. 411p. 1997. pap. 30.00 (1-888265-14-0) Willow Bend.

Patrick Cox: Wit, Irony & Footwear. Patrick Cox. (Cutting Edge Ser.). 1998. pap. text 16.95 (0-8230-1148-8) Watsn-Guptill.

Patrick Demarchalier. Photos by Patrick Demarchalier. (Illus.). 160p. 1998. 39.95 (1-891475-11-8, 810141) T Shafrazi.

***Patrick Demarchelier.** Patrick Demarchalier. 2000. pap. text 19.95 (3-570-19240-7) V C Bertelsman.

Patrick Demarchelier: Photographs. Patrick Demarchelier. (Illus.). 144p. 1995. 65.00 (0-8212-2169-8, Pub. by Bulfinch Pr) Little.

Patrick Demarchelier: Forms. Patrick Demarchalier. 1998. 75.00 (0-8478-2160-9, Pub. by Rizzoli Intl) St Martin.

Patrick Dennis' U. S. Revenue Cutter Vigilant, 1791-1798. Florence Kern. 1976. 3.95 (0-913377-03-1) Alised.

Patrick des Jarlait: Conversations with a Native American Artist. Neva Williams. LC 94-6535. 64p. (YA). (gr. 5 up). 1994. lib. bdg. 22.60 (0-8225-3151-8, Lerner Publctns) Lerner Pub.

Patrick Doyle Is Full of Blarney. Jennifer Armstrong. LC 95-24754. (First Stepping Stone Bks.). (Illus.). (J). (gr. 1-4). 1996. lib. bdg. 17.99 (0-679-97285-4, Pub. by Random Bks Yng Read) Random.

Patrick Doyle Is Full of Blarney. Jennifer Armstrong. (Stepping Stone Books/Fourth of July Ser.). (Illus.). (J). (gr. 1-4). 1997. pap. 3.99 (0-614-28934-3) Random Bks Yng Read.

Patrick Doyle Is Full of Blarney. Jennifer Armstrong. (Stepping Stone Bks.). (J). 1997. 9.19 (0-606-11725-3, Pub. by Turtleback) Demco.

Patrick Ewing. Richard Rambeck. LC 92-11508. (Sports Superstars Ser.). (Illus.). 32p. (J). (gr. 2-6). 1994. lib. bdg. 21.36 (0-89565-967-0); lib. bdg. 21.36 (1-56766-112-2) Childs World.

Patrick Ewing. Paul Wiener. LC 95-18496. (Basketball Legends Ser.). (Illus.). 64p. (J). (gr. 3 up). 1996. lib. bdg. 15.95 (0-7910-2434-2) Chelsea Hse.

Patrick Ewing: Center of Attention. Howard Reiser. LC 94-14399. (Sports Stars Ser.). (Illus.). 48p. (J). (gr. 2-8). 1994. lib. bdg. 19.00 (0-516-04388-9) Childrens.

Patrick Ford & His Search for America: A Case Study of Irish-American Journalism, 1870-1913. James P. Rodechko. LC 76-6362. (Irish Americans Ser.). 1976. 29.95 (0-405-09354-3) Ayer.

Patrick Geddes: Social Evolutionist & City Planner. Helen Meller. LC 93-4323. (Geography, Environment & Planning Ser.). (Illus.). 384p. (C). 1994. pap. 27.99 (0-415-10393-2) Routledge.

Patrick Gets Hearing Aids. Maureen C. Riski & Nikolas Klakow. (Illus.). 48p. (Orig.). (J). 1994. pap. 8.95 (0-9647691-0-7) Phonak.

Patrick Graham. Intro. by Jack V. Rutberg. (Illus.). 28p. 1989. pap. 25.00 (1-880566-05-2) J Rutberg Fine Arts.

Patrick Graham: Plain Nude Drawings, Studies for the Blackbird Suite. Peter Frank. (Illus.). 16p. 1994. pap. 15.00 (1-880566-11-7) J Rutberg Fine Arts.

Patrick Henry. JoAnn A. Grote. LC 99-33135. 1999. 16.95 (0-7910-5357-1) Chelsea Hse.

Patrick Henry. Joanne Grote. (Revolutionary War Leaders Ser.). (Illus.). 80p. (gr. 3 up). 1999. pap. 8.95 (0-7910-5700-3) Chelsea Hse.

Patrick Henry. Stuart A. Kallen. LC 98-4688. (Founding Fathers Ser.). (J). 2002. lib. bdg. 14.95 (1-57765-012-3) ABDO Pub Co.

Patrick Henry. Moses C. Tyler. (American Statesmen Ser.). 1998. 39.95 (0-7910-4543-9) Chelsea Hse.

Patrick Henry. Moses C. Tyler. 1972. 69.95 (0-8490-0806-9) Gordon Pr.

Patrick Henry. Moses C. Tyler. Ed. by John T. Morse, Jr. LC 71-128936. (American Statesmen Ser.: No. 3). reprint ed. 49.50 (0-404-50853-7) AMS Pr.

Patrick Henry. Moses C. Tyler. (Notable American Authors Ser.). 1999. reprint ed. lib. bdg. 125.00 (0-7812-9854-7) Rprt Serv.

Patrick Henry: Patriot & Statesman. Norine D. Campbell. (Illus.). 1969. 24.95 (0-8159-6501-X) Devin.

Patrick Henry: Voice of American Revolution. Louis Sabin. LC 81-23068. (Illus.). 48p. (J). (gr. 4-6). 1996. pap. 3.95 (0-89375-765-9) Troll Communs.

Patrick Henry: Voice of American Revolution. Louis Sabin. LC 81-23068. (Illus.). 48p. (J). (gr. 4-6). 1997. lib. bdg. 17.25 (0-89375-764-0) Troll Communs.

Patrick Henry: Voice of the American Revolution. Louis Sabin. (J). 1982. 8.70 (0-606-01706-2, Pub. by Turtleback) Demco.

Patrick Henry Callahan, 1866-1940: Progressive Catholic Layman in the American South. William E. Ellis. LC 89-33493. (Studies in American Religion: Vol. 46). (Illus.). 144p. 1990. lib. bdg. 69.95 (0-88946-243-7) E Mellen.

Patrick Henry Lake Liquors. Larry Ketron. 1977. pap. 5.25 (0-8222-0881-4) Dramatists Play.

Patrick Henry, Life, Speeches, & Correspondence, 3 vols. W. W. Henry. 1995. 129.99 (0-87377-165-6) GAM Pubns.

Patrick Henry, the Orator, 8. David A. McCants. LC 90-33274. (Great American Orators: Critical Studies, Speeches & Sources: No. 8). 176p. 1990. lib. bdg. 52.95 (0-313-26210-1, MPX, Greenwood Pr) Greenwood.

Patrick Heron. Mel Gooding. (Illus.). 272p. 1995. pap. 35.00 (0-7148-3444-0, Pub. by Phaidon Press) Phaidon Pr.

Patrick Heron. Text by Mel Gooding. (Illus.). 20p. 1996. pap. write for info. (1-58821-036-7) Salander OReilly.

Patrick Heron. Ed. by Vivien Knight. (Illus.). 128p. (C). 1988. 80.00 (0-85331-525-6, Pub. by Lund Humphries) Antique Collect.

***Patrick in His Own Words.** Joseph Duffy. 147p. 2000. pap. 14.95 (1-85390-525-9, Pub. by Veritas Pubns) Irish Bks Media.

Patrick Ireland: Labyrinths, Language, Pyramids, & Related Acts. Ed. by Russell Panczenko. (Illus.). 112p. 1994. pap. 24.95 (0-932900-33-X) Elvehjem Mus.

Patrick Kavanagh: A Critical Study. Antoinette Quinn. LC 91-4284. (Irish Studies). 493p. 1991. reprint ed. pap. 152.90 (0-608-07622-8, 205993700010) Bks Demand.

***Patrick Kavanagh: A Life Chronicle.** Peter Kavanagh. (Illus.). 550p. 2000. write for info. (0-914612-15-8) Kavanagh.

Patrick Kavanagh: A Reference Guide. Jonathan Allison. LC 96-29255. 1996. 45.00 (0-8161-7286-2, G K Hall & Co) Mac Lib Ref.

Patrick Kavanaugh. Darcy O'Brien. (Irish Writers Ser.). 72p. 1975. 8.50 (0-8387-7884-4); pap. 1.95 (0-8387-7985-9) Bucknell U Pr.

Patrick Kavanaugh: Man & Poet. Ed. by Peter Kavanaugh. LC 85-61480. (Irish Art & Man & Poet Ser.). 500p. (Orig.). 1986. pap. 22.95 (0-915032-64-3) Natl Poet Foun.

***Patrick Kennedy: The Rise to Power.** Darrell M. West. 192p. 2000. pap. 18.67 (0-13-017694-X) P-H.

Patrick Lane & His Works. George Woodcock. (Canadian Author Studies). 53p. (C). 1985. pap. 9.95 (0-920802-94-X, Pub. by ECW) Genl Dist Srvs.

Patrick Lose's Whimsical Cross-Stitch. Patrick Lose. LC 94-42099. (Illus.). 144p. 1995. 24.95 (0-8069-1292-8, Chapelle) Sterling.

Patrick Lose's Whimsical Sweatshirts. Patrick Lose. LC 95-16328. (Illus.). 144p. (Orig.). 1995. 27.95 (0-8069-3179-5, Chapelle) Sterling.

Patrick Lose's Whimsical Sweatshirts. Patrick Lose. (Illus.). 144p. (Orig.). 1996. pap. 14.95 (0-8069-3180-9, Chapelle) Sterling.

***Patrick Loves Peaches: A Story to Help Children Understand Peer Pressure & Loyalty.** Julie G. Dickerson. (Helping Children Understand Ser.). (Illus.). 32p. (Orig.). (J). (gr. k-6). 1998. pap. 11.95 (0-9646576-7-8) Cherubic Pr.

Patrick Modiano. Alan Morris. Ed. by John E. Flower. (New Directions in European Writing Ser.). 256p. 1996. 55.00 (1-85973-098-1); pap. 19.50 (1-85973-004-3) Berg Pubs.

Patrick Moore on Mars. Patrick Moore. LC 99-218330. (Illus.). 224p. 1999. 29.95 (0-304-35069-9) Continuum.

***Patrick Moore on Mars.** Patrick Moore. (Illus.). 2000. pap. 19.95 (1-84188-004-3) Seven Dials.

***Patrick Moore's Millennium Yearbook: The View from 1001 AD.** Patrick Moore & A. Chapman. LC 99-37448. (Illus.). xii, 100p. 1999. pap. 19.95 (1-85233-619-6, Pub. by Spr-Verlag) Spr-Verlag.

Patrick N. L. Bellinger & U. S. Naval Aviation. Paolo E. Coletta. (Illus.). 478p. (Orig.). (C). 1987. lib. bdg. 62.00 (0-8191-6534-4) U Pr of Amer.

Patrick O'Brian: A Life Revealed. Dean King. LC 99-48495. (Illus.). 448p. 2000. 26.00 (0-8050-5976-8) H Holt & Co.

Patrick O'Brian: Critical Essays & a Bibliography. Patrick O'Brian. 1994. 23.95 (0-393-03626-X) Norton.

Patrick Pearse: The Triumph of Failure. Ruth Edwards. 416p. 1990. pap. 21.00 (1-85371-068-7, Pub. by Poolbeg Pr) Dufour.

Patrick Pearse & the Politics of Redemption: The Mind of the Easter Rising, 1916. Sean F. Moran. LC 93-26449. 233p. 1994. 42.95 (0-8132-0775-4) Cath U Pr.

Patrick Pearse & the Politics of Redemption: The Mind of the Easter Rising, 1916. Sean F. Moran. 233p. 1998. pap. text 14.95 (0-8132-0912-9) Cath U Pr.

Patrick Procktor. John McEwen. LC 97-39673. (Illus.). 96p. 1997. text 43.95 (1-85928-322-5, Pub. by Ashgate Pub) Ashgate Pub Co.

Patrick Procktor. limited ed. John McEwen. LC 97-39673. (Illus.). 96p. 1997. text 425.95 (1-85928-323-3, Pub. by Ashgate Pub) Ashgate Pub Co.

Patrick Roy. Andrew Podnieks. (Hockey Heroes Ser.). 1998. pap. text 6.95 (1-55054-641-4, Pub. by DGL) Sterling.

Patrick Roy: Champion Goalie. Morgan Hughes. LC 97-30587. (J). 1998. 21.27 (0-8225-3660-9) Lerner Pub.

Patrick Roy: Champion Goalie. Morgan Hughes. LC 97-30587. (Illus.). 64p. (J). (gr. 4-9). 1998. pap. 5.95 (0-8225-9813-2) Lerner Pub.

***Patrick Sarfati.** Patrick Sarfati. Ed. by Klaus Gerhart. (Photorotic Ser.: Vol. 1). (Illus.). 72p. 2000. 24.95 (1-890377-18-X) Pohlmann Pr.

Patrick Sarsfield & the Williamite War. Piers Wauchope. 1992. pap. 22.95 (0-7165-2496-1, Pub. by Irish Acad Pr) Intl Spec Bk.

Patrick Sarsfield & the Williamite War. Piers Wauchope. (Illus.). 356p. 1992. text 45.00 (0-7165-2476-7, Pub. by Irish Acad Pr) Intl Spec Bk.

***Patrick Sellar & the Highland Clearances: Homicide, Eviction & the Price of Progress.** Eric Richards. 352p. 2000. pap. text 25.00 (1-902930-13-4) Col U Pr.

***Patrick Soft Cloth Photo Album.** Mandy Stanley. (Illus.). 8p. (J). 1999. 6.99 (1-58048-061-6) Sandvik Pub.

Patrick Stewart. James Hatfield & George D. Burt. 320p. 1996. mass mkt. 5.99 (0-7860-0315-4, Pinncle Kensgtn) Kensgtn Pub Corp.

Patrick Straram Ou le Bison Ravi. Jean-Gaetan Seguin. (FRE.). 48p. 1991. pap. write for info. (2-89135-030-8) Guernica Editions.

Patrick Suppes. Ed. by Radu J. Bogdan. LC 78-21095. (Profiles 1 Ser.). 274p. 1979. pap. text 73.50 (90-277-0951-3, D Reidel) Kluwer Academic.

Patrick Suppes: Scientific Philosopher, 3 vols. Ed. by Paul Humphreys. Incl. Vol. 2: Philosophy of Physics, Theory Structure & Measurement Theory. 308p. 1994. lib. bdg. 183.00 (0-7923-2553-2, Pub. by Kluwer Academic); Vol. 1: Probability & Probabilistic Causality. 424p. 1994. lib. bdg. 247.00 (0-7923-2552-4, Pub. by Kluwer Academic); Vol. 3: Philosophy of Language & Logic, Learning & Action Theory. 340p. 1994. lib. bdg. 204.50 (0-7923-2862-0, Pub. by Kluwer Academic); (Synthese Library). 395.00 (0-7923-2554-0, Pub. by Kluwer Academic) Kluwer Academic.

Patrick the Pelaganty. Tracy D. Watkins. Ed. by Keith Herbrechtsmeier. LC 93-83730. (Illus.). 40p. (J). (gr. k-6). 1999. 18.95 (1-883261-00-7) Pelaganty.

Patrick, the Pilgrim Apostle of Ireland: St. Patrick's Confession & Epistola. Maire B. De Paor. LC 98-167668. 313p. 1998. 39.95 (1-85390-304-3) Ignatius Pr.

Patrick Tosani. Patrick Tosani. 109p. 1998. pap. text 25.00 (2-85025-579-3) Hazan.

Patrick Wants to Ride. Cristine L. Sommer. LC 94-92029. (Illus.). 28p. (J). (gr. k-4). 1994. boxed set 12.95 (0-9640415-4-5) C Sommer-Simmons.

Patrick White. Simon During. (Australian Writers Ser.). 120p. 1996. pap. text 26.00 (0-19-553497-2) OUP.

Patrick White: Fiction & the Unconscious. David J. Tacey. (Illus.). 288p. 1988. text 42.00 (0-19-554867-1) OUP.

Patrick White: Letters. Patrick White. Ed. by David Marr. (Illus.). 678p. (C). 1996. 35.00 (0-226-89503-3) U Ch Pr.

Patrick White: Selected Writings. Patrick White. LC 94-188208. 304p. 1995. pap. 14.95 (0-7022-2625-4, Pub. by Univ Queensland Pr) Intl Spec Bk.

Patrick White & the Religious Imagination: Arthur's Dream. Michael Giffin. LC 99-11308. (Studies in Art & Religious Interpretation: Vol. 25). 279p. 1999. text 89.95 (0-7734-8171-0) E Mellen.

Patrick White's Fiction: The Paradox of Fortunate Failure. William Walsh. LC 78-310572. 136 p. 1977. write for info. (0-86861-040-2) Allen & Unwin Pty.

Patricks: Hockey's Royal Family. Eric Whitehead. (Illus.). 280p. 1980. mass mkt. 4.95 (0-88780-103-X, Pub. by Formac Publ Co) Formac Dist Ltd.

***Patrick's Christmas Tree.** Geoffrey Hayes. (Jellybean Bks.). (Illus.). 24p. (J). (ps-k). 1999. lib. bdg. 7.99 (0-375-90100-0, Pub. by Random Bks Yng Read) Random.

***Patrick's Christmas Tree.** Geoggrey Hayes. (Jellybean Bks.). (Illus.). 24p. (J). (ps-k). 1999. 1.99 (0-375-80100-6, Pub. by Random Bks Yng Read) Random.

Patrick's Corner. Sean Patrick. LC 91-33634. 224p. 1992. 18.95 (0-88289-878-7) Pelican.

Patrick's Day. Elizabeth L. O'Donnell. LC 92-27421. (Illus.). 32p. (YA). (gr. k up). 1994. 15.00 (0-688-07853-2, Wm Morrow) Morrow Avon.

Patrick's Dinosaurs. Carol Carrick. LC 83-2049. (Illus.). 32p. (J). (gr. k-3). 1983. 15.00 (0-89919-189-4, Clarion Bks) HM.

Patrick's Dinosaurs. Carol Carrick. LC 83-2049. (Illus.). 32p. (J). (gr. k-3). 1985. pap. 5.95 (0-89919-402-8, Clarion Bks) HM.

Patrick's Dinosaurs. Carol Carrick. LC 83-2049. (Carry-Along Book & Cassette Favorites Ser.). 1p. (J). (ps-3). 1993. pap. 9.95 incl. audio (0-395-66496-9, 112725, Clarion Bks) HM.

Patrick's Dinosaurs. Carol Carrick. (J). 1983. 11.15 (0-606-00737-7, Pub. by Turtleback) Demco.

Patrick's Dinosaurs on the Internet. Carol Carrick. LC 97-47300. (Illus.). 32p. (J). (ps-3). 1999. 16.00 (0-395-50949-1, Clarion Bks) HM.

Patrick's Notebook: Words of Love from One Life to Live. Patrick Thornhart. (Illus.). 176p. (J). 1996. pap. 9.70 incl. audio (0-7868-8226-3, Pub. by Hyperion) Time Warner.

Patrick's Tree House. Steven Kroll. LC 93-4571. (Illus.). 64p. (J). (gr. 2-5). 1994. mass mkt. 13.95 (0-02-751005-0, Mac Bks Young Read) S&S Childrens.

Patrick's "Unfinished" An Intellectual History Counterpoint to Franz-Schubert's Symphony No. 8 "Unfinished" unabridged ed. Patrick A. O'Dougherty. LC 96-94077. 60p. (C). 1996. lib. bdg. 15.99 (0-9626665-6-4) Irish Catholic.

Patrie! An Historical Drama in 5 Acts. Victorien Sardou. LC 86-29518. 232p. 1987. reprint ed. lib. bdg. 35.00 (0-86527-355-3) Fertig.

Patrimonial Interpretation of Indian Society. Norman Jacobs. (C). 1989. 33.50 (81-7001-051-9, Pub. by Chanakya) S Asia.

Patrimony: A True Story. Philip Roth. 1996. pap. 12.00 (0-679-75293-5) Vin Bks.

Patrimony: 6 Case Studies on Local Politics & the Environment in the Philippines. Howie G. Severino et al. LC 96-946576. 162p. 1996. write for info. (971-8686-12-6) PCFIJ.

Patrimony of Fishes. Doug Lawson. LC 97-67764. 128p. 1997. pap. 10.95 (1-888996-04-8, Red Hen Press) Valentine CA.

Patrins: To Which Is Added an Inquirendo into the Wit & Other Good Parts of His Late Majesty King Charles the Second. Louise I. Guiney. LC 72-4750. (Essay Index Reprint Ser.). 1977. reprint ed. 23.95 (0-8369-2946-2) Ayer.

Patriot. Gary Hart. 187p. 1996. 22.00 (0-02-874097-1) Free Pr.

***Patriot.** Stephen Molstad. 304p. 2000. mass mkt. 6.99 (0-06-102076-1) HarpC.

Patriot. Nigel Tranter. mass mkt. 11.95 (0-340-34915-8, Pub. by Hodder & Stought Ltd) Trafalgar.

Patriot. large type ed. Piers P. Read. LC 96-23995. 1997. pap. 22.95 (0-7862-0832-5) Thorndike Pr.

Patriot. Mason L. Weems. (Notable American Authors Ser.). 1999. reprint ed. lib. bdg. 125.00 (0-7812-9921-7) Rprt Serv.

Patriot, Vol. 1, No. 1. James L. Berkman. LC 01-464941. (Illus.). (Orig.). 1984. pap. 10.00 (0-943662-05-2) Runaway Pubns.

Patriot, Vol. 3, No. 1. James L. Berkman. (Illus.). (Orig.). 1986. pap. 10.00 (0-943662-07-9, 256-649) Runaway Pubns.

Patriot, Vol. 4-No. 1. James L. Berkman. (Illus.). (Orig.). 1987. pap. 10.00 (0-943662-08-7, 2-098-376) Runaway Pubns.

Patriot, Vol. 5, No. 1. James L. Berkman. LC 02-348479. (Orig.). 1988. pap. 10.00 (0-943662-09-5) Runaway Pubns.

Patriot, Vol. 6, No. 1. James L. Berkman. LC 02-600. (Orig.). 1989. pap. 10.00 (0-943662-10-9, 02-600919) Runaway Pubns.

Patriot: Nach der Originalausgabe Hamburg, 1724-26, 4 vols. Incl. Vol. 1. Jahrgang 1724, Stueck 1-52. Ed. by Wolfgang Martens. vi, 445p. 1969. 116.75 (3-11-000360-0); Vol. 2. Jahrgang 1725, Stueck 53-104. Ed. by Wolfgang Martens. iv, 428p. 1970. 116.75 (3-11-000361-9); Vol. 3. Jahrgang 1726, Stueck 105-156. Wolfgang Martens. iv, 460p. 1970. 126.75 (3-11-002694-5); Vol. 4. Kommentarband. Ed. by Wolfgang Martens. 1984. 220.00 (3-11-009931-4); (Ausgaben Deutscher Literatur des XV bis XVIII Jahrhunderts Ser.). (GER.). (C). write for info. (0-318-51635-7) De Gruyter.

Patriot: Poems by Christopher Davis. Christopher Davis. LC 97-49513. 104p. 1998. pap. 14.95 (0-8203-1991-0) U of Ga Pr.

***Patriot: The Official Companion.** Suzanne Fritz & Rachel Aberly. (Illus.). 96p. 2000. pap. 19.95 (1-84222-076-4) Carlton Bks Ltd.

Patriot: The Scripturion, Vol. 2, No. 1. James L. Berkman. (Orig.). 1985. pap. text 10.00 (0-943662-06-0, 1-751-040) Runaway Pubns.

Patriot above Profit. Neil M. Lee. LC 88-12032. (Illus.). 704p. 1988. 29.95 (0-934395-68-3) Rutledge Hill Pr.

Patriot after All: The Story of a Chicano Vietnam Vet. Juan Ramirez. LC 98-46679. 180p. 1999. pap. 15.95 (0-8263-1959-9) U of NM Pr.

Patriot after All: The Story of a Chicano Vietnam Vet. Juan Ramirez. LC 98-46679. (Illus.). 180p. 1999. 29.95 (0-8263-1958-0) U of NM Pr.

Patriot & Patrician. Hendrik Hooft. LC 98-46828. Orig. Title: Burgher en de Burgemester. (Illus.). 255p. 1999. 40.00 (0-88135-261-6, Sci Hist) Watson Pub Intl.

Patriot Chiefs: A Chronicle of American Indian Resistance. Alvin M. Josephy, Jr. 384p. 1993. pap. 12.95 (0-14-023463-2, Penguin Bks) Viking Penguin.

Patriot Dreams: The Murder of Colonel Rich Higgins. Robin Higgins. 1999. pap. text 14.95 (0-940328-24-0) Marine Corps.

***Patriot Dreams: The Murder of Colonel Rich Higgins.** Robin Higgins. 210p. 2000. 21.95 (1-55571-527-3, Pub. by PSI Resch) Midpt Trade.

Patriot Gambit. Don Pendleton. (Executioner Ser.: No. 222). 1997. per. 3.75 (0-373-64222-9, 1-64222-2, Wrldwide Lib) Harlequin Bks.

Patriot Game. Barnes. 1999. text. write for info. (0-312-00668-3) St Martin.

Patriot Game: A Play. Elizabeth Schlomer & Alex Atkins. Ed. by Jurgen Klein. (Britannia. Texts in English Ser.: Vol. 3). 174p. 1990. 38.00 (3-631-42265-2) P Lang Pubng.

Patriot Game: Canada & the Canadian Question Revisited. Peter Brimelow. (Publication Ser.: No. 368). 310p. 1987. 10.78 (0-8179-8681-2); pap. text 6.78 (0-8179-8682-0) Hoover Inst Pr.

Patriot Games. Tom Clancy. 512p. 1988. mass mkt. 7.50 (0-425-10972-0) Berkley Pub.

Patriot Games. Tom Clancy. 416p. 1987. 25.95 (0-399-13241-4, G P Putnam) Peng Put Young Read.

Patriot Games. Tom Clancy. 1992. 14.00 (0-606-00982-5, Pub. by Turtleback) Demco.

Patriot-Heroes in England & America: Political Symbolism & Changing Values over Three Centuries. Peter Karsten. LC 78-53286. 301p. 1978. reprint ed. pap. 93.40 (0-608-01884-8, 206253600003) Bks Demand.

Patriot-Improvers: Biographical Sketches of Members of the American Philosophical Society. Whitfield J. Bell, Jr. LC 97-44313. (Memoirs Ser.: Vol. 226). (Illus.). 530p. 1997. 40.00 (0-87169-226-0, M226-bew) Am Philos.

Patriot Press: National Politics & the London Press in the 1740s. Robert Harris. LC 92-24882. (Oxford Historical Monographs). (Illus.). 308p. 1993. text 69.00 (0-19-820378-0, Clarendon Pr) OUP.

Patriot Priest: A Life of Reverend James Coigly. Ed. by Daire Keogh. LC 99-175810. 96p. 1998. pap. 12.95 (1-85918-142-2, Pub. by Cork Univ) Intl Spec Bk.

Patriot Royal. Russ Pottle. LC 95-68667. 360p. 1996. 22.95 (0-9646664-0-5) Chestnut VA.

***Patriot Sage: George Washington & the American Political Tradition.** Ed. by Gary L. Gregg, II & Matthew Spalding. LC 99-64472. 320p. 1999. 29.95 (1-882926-38-2) ISI Books.

Patriotic Activities. Teacher Created Materials Staff. (Illus.). 1996. teacher ed. 2.95 (1-55734-795-6, TCM795) Tchr Create Mat.

An Asterisk (*) at the beginning of an entry indicates that the title is appearing for the first time.

Patriotic Addresses In. Henry W. Beecher. (Works of Henry Ward Beecher). 857p. 1985. reprint ed. lib. bdg. 99.00 (*0-932051-04-9*) Rprt Serv.

Patriotic Anthology: Being Poems of American History, Written by Great American Poets. LC 79-168786. (Granger Index Reprint Ser.). 1977. reprint ed. 16.95 (*0-8369-6306-7*) Ayer.

Patriotic Culture in Russia During World War I. Hubertus F. Jahn. LC 95-8512. (Illus.). 256p. (C). 1995. text 39.95 (*0-8014-3131-X*) Cornell U Pr.

Patriotic Culture in Russia During World War I. Hubertus F. Jahn. 256p. 1998. pap. text 16.95 (*0-8014-8571-1*) Cornell U Pr.

Patriotic Games: Sporting Traditions in the American Imagination, 1876-1926. Steven W. Pope. (Sports History & Society). (Illus.). 240p. 1997. text 39.95 (*0-19-509133-7*) OUP.

Patriotic Gems. 64p. 1993. pap. 6.95 (*0-7935-2178-5*, 00110012); pap. 6.95 (*0-7935-2172-6*, 00221801) H Leonard.

Patriotic Gore: Studies in the Literature of the American Civil War. Edmund Wilson. 848p. 1994. pap. 17.95 (*0-393-31256-9*) Norton.

Patriotic Gore: Studies in the Literature of the American Civil War. Edmund Wilson. 1995. 27.00 (*0-8446-6851-6*) Peter Smith.

Patriotic Murders. large type ed. Agatha Christie. 312p. 1989. lib. bdg. 20.95 (*0-8161-4585-7*, G K Hall Lrg Type) Mac Lib Ref.

Patriotic Pacifism: Waging War on War in Europe, 1815-1914. Sandi E. Cooper. 352p. 1991. text 60.00 (*0-19-505715-5*, 8865) OUP.

Patriotic Poems. Selected by Michael Wylie. (Jarrold Poets Ser.). 146p. (Orig.). 1994. 5.95 (*0-7117-0681-6*) Seven Hills Bk.

Patriotic Quilt-Postcards. Ed. by Museum of American Folk Art Staff. (Illus.). 1991. pap. text 1.00 (*0-486-26764-4*) Dover.

Patriotic Recitations & Readings. Ed. by Josephine Stafford. LC 79-108588. (Granger Index Reprint Ser.). 1977. 17.95 (*0-8369-6116-1*) Ayer.

Patriotic Songs: Irving Berlin D. 64p. 1991. per. 10.95 (*0-7935-0382-5*) H Leonard.

Patriotic Symbols Activity Book. Linda Milliken. Ed. by Kathy Rogers. (Hands-On Heritage Activity Bks.). (Illus.). 48p. (J). (gr. 2-6). 1996. pap. 6.95 (*1-56472-075-6*) Edupress Inc.

Patriotic Symbols Photo Fun Activities. Linda Milliken. Ed. by Barb Lorseyedi & Kathy Rogers. (Social Studies Photo Fun Activities Ser.). (Illus.). 8p. 1996. 6.95 (*1-56472-076-4*) Edupress Inc.

Patriotic Tide, 1940-1950 see This Fabulous Century Series

Patriotic Toil: Northern Women & the American Civil War. Jeanie Attie. LC 98-25717. (Illus.). 256p. 1998. 35.00 (*0-8014-2224-8*) Cornell U Pr.

Patrioticas: La Patria No Ha Muerto, No, Esta en el Viento. Jose Sanchez-Boudy. LC 86-81927. (Coleccion Espejo de Paciencia). (SPA.). 62p. (Orig.). 1986. pap. 6.00 (*0-89729-415-7*) Ediciones.

Patriotism. Nancy M. Davis et al. (Davis Teaching Units Ser.: Vol. 2, No. 12). (Illus.). 34p. (Orig.). (J). (ps-5). 1986. pap. 4.95 (*0-937103-19-5*) DaNa Pubns.

***Patriotism.** Lucia Raatma. LC 99-48335. (Character Education Ser.). 24p. (J). (ps-3). 2000. lib. bdg. 15.93 (*0-7368-0509-5*, Bridgestone Bks) Capstone Pr.

Patriotism. Yukio Mishima, pseud. Tr. by Geoffrey W. Sargent from JPN. LC 95-36529. (New Directions Bibelot Ser.). 64p. 1995. reprint ed. pap. 6.00 (*0-8112-1312-9*, NDP814, Pub. by New Directions) Norton.

Patriotism. rev. ed. Linda C. Johnson. (Values Library). (Illus.). 64p. (YA). (gr. 7-12). 1993. lib. bdg. 15.95 (*0-8239-1507-7*) Rosen Group.

Patriotism: Recognizing Stereotypes. Bonnie Szumski. LC 89-37555. (Opposing Viewpoints Juniors Ser.). (Illus.). 36p. (J). (gr. 3-6). 1990. lib. bdg. 16.20 (*0-89908-640-3*) Greenhaven.

Patriotism & Nationalism: Their Psychological Foundations. Leonard W. Doob. LC 76-42309. (Illus.). 297p. 1977. reprint ed. lib. bdg. 65.00 (*0-8371-8978-0*, DOPN, Greenwood Pr) Greenwood.

Patriotism & the Female Sex: Abigail Adams & the American Revolution. Rosemary S. Keller. LC 94-20197. (Scholarship in Women's History Ser.: Vol. 8). 200p. 1994. 50.00 (*0-926019-69-4*) Carlson Pub.

Patriotism for Profit: Georgia's Urban Entrepreneurs & the Confederate War Effort. Mary A. DeCredico. LC 89-39132. (Fred W. Morrison Series in Southern Studies). (Illus.). 233p. 1990. pap. 72.30 (*0-608-05206-X*, 206574300005) Bks Demand.

Patriotism in America. LC 96-34942. (Democracy in Action Ser.). (J). 1997. lib. bdg. 24.00 (*0-531-11310-8*) Watts.

Patriotism in the Work of Joachim du Bellay: A Study of the Relationship Between the Poet & France. David Hartley. LC 93-15106. 200p. 1993. text 79.95 (*0-7734-9265-8*) E Mellen.

Patriotism, Inc & Other Tales by Paul van Ostaijen. Ed. by E. M. Beekman. LC 79-150314. 192p. 1971. 27.50 (*0-87023-084-0*); pap. 13.95 (*0-87023-097-2*) U of Mass Pr.

Patriotism Limited, 1862-1865: The Civil War Draft & the Bounty System. Eugene C. Murdock. LC 67-64665. 296p. reprint ed. 91.80 (*0-8357-9372-9*, 201041300069) Bks Demand.

Patriotism, Morality, & Peace. Stephen Nathanson. LC 92-32412. (Studies in Social & Political Philosophy). 1993. 59.00 (*0-8476-7799-0*); pap. 23.95 (*0-8476-7800-8*) Rowman.

Patriotism on Parade: The Story of Veterans' & Hereditary Organizations in America, 1783-1900. Wallace E. Davies. LC 55-11951. (Historical Studies: No. 66). 402p. 1955. 27.50 (*0-674-65800-0*) HUP.

Patriotism, Politics, & Popular Liberalism in Nineteenth-Century Mexico: Juan Francisco Lucas & the Puebla Sierra. Guy P. Thomson & David G. LaFrance. LC 97-37865. (Latin American Silhouettes Ser.). (Illus.). 416p. (C). 1998. text 65.00 (*0-8420-2683-5*, SR Bks) Scholarly Res Inc.

Patriotism, Profit & Promotion in the German Enlightenment: The Economic & Scientific Societies, 1760-1815. rev. ed. Henry Lowood. LC 91-27131. (Modern European History Ser.: No. 2). 464p. 1991. text 25.00 (*0-8153-0677-6*) Garland.

Patriotismus Deutscher Juden von der Napoleonischen Ara Bis Zum Kaiserreich: Zwischen Korporativem Loyalismus und Individueller Deutsch-Judischer Identitat. Erik Lindner. (Europaische Hochschulschriften Ser.: Reihe 3, Bd. 726). (GER., Illus.). 448p. 1996. 63.95 (*3-631-31356-X*) P Lang Pubng.

Patriotismus und Sozialdemokratie see European Socialism & Internationalism Before World War I

Patriots see Best Plays of the Modern American Theatre: Second Series, 1939-1946

Patriots. 1995. write for info. (*1-56476-919-4*, Victor Bks) Chariot Victor.

Patriots. Jack Cavanaugh. (American Family Portrait Ser.). 475p. 1995. pap. 11.99 (*1-56476-428-1*, 6-3428, Victor Bks) Chariot Victor.

Patriots. David Drake. 1997. mass mkt. 5.99 (*0-8125-9084-8*, Pub. by Tor Bks) St Martin.

Patriots. large type ed. Kenneth Royce. 518p. 1989. 27.99 (*0-7089-1967-7*) Ulverscroft.

***Patriots: Surviving the Coming Collapse.** James Wesley, Rawles. LC 98-75122. 352p. 1998. pap. 15.99 (*1-56384-155-X*) Huntington Hse.

Patriots: The Men Who Started the American Revolution. A. J. Langguth. 640p. 1989. pap. 16.00 (*0-671-67562-1*) S&S Trade Pap.

***Patriots & Heroes: True Stories of the U. S. Merchant Marine in World War II.** unabridged ed. Gerald Reminick. LC 00-26432. (Illus.). xii, 298p. 2000. pap. 21.95 (*1-889901-14-8*) Glencannon Pr.

Patriots & Liberators: Revolution in the Netherlands, 1780-1813. Simon Schama. 768p. 1992. pap. 18.00 (*0-679-72949-6*) Vin Bks.

Patriots & Proletarians: Politicizing Hungarian Immigrants in Interwar Canada. Carmela Patrias. (McGraw & Arnold's Atlas of Muscle & Musculocutaneous Flaps Ser.). (Illus.). 336p. 1994. 60.00 (*0-7735-1174-1*, Pub. by McG-Queens Univ Pr) CUP Services.

Patriots & Redeemers in Japan: Motives in the Meiji Restoration. George M. Wilson. LC 91-20448. 218p. 1991. pap. text 21.00 (*0-226-90092-4*) U Ch Pr.

Patriots & Redeemers in Japan: Motives in the Meiji Restoration. George M. Wilson. LC 91-20448. 189p. 1994. lib. bdg. 37.50 (*0-226-90091-6*) U Ch Pr.

Patriots & the People: The Rebellion of 1837 in Rural Lower Canada. Allan Greer. LC 93-94402. (Social History of Canada Ser.). (Illus.). 385p. 1993. text 50.00 (*0-8020-2792-X*); pap. text 18.95 (*0-8020-6930-4*) U of Toronto Pr.

Patriots & Tyrants: Ten Asian Leaders. Ross Marlay & Clark D. Neher. LC 98-52020. 368p. 1999. pap. 21.95 (*0-8476-8442-3*) Rowman.

Patriots & Tyrants: Ten Asian Leaders. Ross Marlay et al. LC 98-52020. 368p. 1999. text 69.00 (*0-8476-8441-5*) Rowman.

***Patriot's Dream.** Carl Japikse. 2000. pap. 10.99 (*0-89804-682-3*, Pub. by Ariel GA) Alliance Bk Co.

Patriot's Dream. Barbara Michaels, pseud. 352p. 1994. mass mkt. 6.99 (*0-425-13355-9*) Berkley Pub.

Patriot's Handbook. George Grant. LC 96-42167. (Illus.). 256p. 1996. pap. 14.95 (*1-888952-03-2*) Cumberland Hse.

Patriot's Handbook. Nita Scoggan. LC 93-86522. (Illus.). 60p. (Orig.). 1994. pap. 5.00 (*0-910487-29-4*) Royalty Pub.

Patriots Handbook: A Citizenship Primer for a New Generation of Americans. George Grant. 464p. 1996. pap. text 14.99 (*1-888306-21-1*) Holly Hall.

Patriot's Heart. Stobie Piel. 384p. 1998. mass mkt. 5.50 (*0-7860-0472-X*, Pinncle Kensgtn) Kensgtn Pub Corp.

Patriots in Disguise: Women Warriors of the Civil War. Richard Hall. (Illus.). 225p. 1994. pap. 10.00 (*1-56924-864-8*) Marlowe & Co.

Patriots of the American Revolution. W. Edmunds Claussen. (Illus.). 202p. (Orig.). 1975. 7.00 (*0-9616068-1-9*) Boyertown Hist.

Patriots of the American Revolution: True Accounts by Great Americans, from Ethan Allen to George Rogers Clark. Ed. by Richard M. Dorson. LC 98-12871. 352p. 1998. 7.99 (*0-517-20274-3*) Random Hse Value.

Patriots off Their Pedestals. Paul Wilstach. LC 78-117862. (Essay Index Reprint Ser.). 1977. 21.95 (*0-8369-1738-3*) Ayer.

Patriots, Pirates, & Pineys: Sixty Who Shaped New Jersey. Robert A. Peterson. LC 98-15153. (Illus.). 154p. 1998. 29.95 (*0-937548-37-5*); pap. 19.95 (*0-937548-39-1*) Plexus Pub.

Patriots, Pistols, & Petticoats: Poor Sinful Charles Town During the American Revolution. 2nd ed. Walter J. Fraser, Jr. LC 92-37071. (Illus.). 174p. (C). 1993. pap. 9.95 (*0-87249-896-4*) U of SC Pr.

Patriots Point: Naval & Maritime Museum. Photos by Bryan Riggs & Joe McLemore. (Illus.). 28p. 1996. pap. 4.95 (*0-9649686-2-2*) Chrlstn Post Card.

***Patriot's Pride.** Judy East Wells. 8p. 1998. pap. 2.95 (*0-7390-0879-X*, 18158) Alfred Pub.

Patriot's Progress. Henry Williamson. 1999. pap. text 12.95 (*0-7509-2234-6*) Sutton Pubg.

Patriot's Progress: Henry Williamson & the First World War. Anne Williamson. LC 98-230232. (Illus.). 224p. 1998. 35.95 (*0-7509-1339-8*, Pub. by Sutton Pub Ltd) Intl Pubs Mktg.

Patriots' Revolution: How Eastern Europe Toppled Communism & Won Its Freedom. Mark Frankland. 384p. 1992. text 26.50 (*0-929587-80-4*) I R Dee.

Patriots' Revolution: How Eastern Europe Toppled Communism & Won Its Freedom. Mark Frankland. LC 93-11243. 384p. 1993. reprint ed. pap. 13.95 (*1-56663-035-5*, Elephant Paperbacks) I R Dee.

***Patriot's Way: Everything You Need to Know about the POW/MIA Issue!** Joseph M. Corrigan. LC 00-190649. 284p. 2000. 25.00 (*0-7388-1902-6*); pap. 18.00 (*0-7388-1903-4*) Xlibris Corp.

Patristic Christology: Proceedings of the Third Maynooth Patristic Conference, 1996. Ed. by Thomas Finan & Vincent Twomey. LC 98-231843. 245p. 1998. boxed set 55.00 (*1-85182-354-9*, Pub. by Four Cts Pr) Intl Spec Bk.

***Patristic Ethics, Vol. 1.** Stanley S. Harakas. LC 98-56047. (Wholeness of Faith & Life Ser.). 160p. 1999. pap. 12.95 (*1-885652-26-7*, Pub. by Holy Cross Orthodox) BookWorld.

Patristic Greek Lexicon. Ed. by G. W. Lampe. (GRE.). 1,616p. 1969. text 295.00 (*0-19-864213-X*) OUP.

Patristic Scholarship: The Edition of St. Jerome. annot. ed. Desiderius Erasmus. Ed. & Tr. by John C. Olin. Tr. by James F. Brady. (Collected Works of Erasmus: No. 61). 336p. 1992. text 85.00 (*0-8020-2760-1*) U of Toronto Pr.

Patristica: Ausgewahlte Aufsatze zur Alten Kirche. Ed. by Hanns C. Brennecke & Jorg Ulrich. 480p. 1998. 155.00 (*3-11-015763-2*) De Gruyter.

Patro Mia Laca - L'Avantago de l'Vertebroj. Gellu Naum. Tr. by Sasha Vlad & Ionel Onet from RUM. (ESP., Illus.). 44p. (Orig.). 1996. pap. 7.05 (*1-882251-15-6*) Eldonejo Bero.

Patrol. Walter Dean Myers. (Illus.). 40p. (J). (gr. 3-7). 15.95 (*0-06-028363-7*); lib. bdg. 15.89 (*0-06-028364-5*) HarpC.

Patrol Administration. 2nd ed. G. Douglas Gourley. (Illus.). 400p. 1974. 61.95 (*0-398-03126-6*); pap. 45.95 (*0-398-06359-1*) C C Thomas.

Patrol Administration: Management by Objectives Study Guide. 3rd ed. Davis Pub Staff. 204p. 1979. 28.95 (*1-56325-011-X*, DS006) Davis Pub Law.

Patrol Craft Sailors Association: Too Good to Be Forgotten, Vol. I. Turner Publishing Company Staff. LC 90-70481. (Illus.). 112p. 1990. 39.95 (*0-938021-89-3*) Turner Pub KY.

Patrol Craft Sailors Association: Too Good to Be Forgotten, Vol. II. Turner Publishing Company Staff. LC 90-70481. (Illus.). 112p. 1995. 49.95 (*1-56311-204-3*) Turner Pub KY.

Patrol Field Problems & Solutions: 476 Field Situations. John P. Kenney & Harry W. More. 194p. 1986. pap. 28.95 (*0-398-06200-5*) C C Thomas.

Patrol Field Problems & Solutions: 476 Field Situations. John P. Kenney & Harry W. More. 194p. (C). 1986. 39.95 (*0-398-05202-6*) C C Thomas.

Patrol Guide Quizzer - N. Y. P. D. 220p. 2000. ring bd. 16.95 (*0-930137-33-7*) Looseleaf Law.

***Patrol Officer Problem Solving & Solutions.** John M. Memory & Randall Aragon. 450p. 2000. pap. write for info. (*0-89089-857-X*) Carolina Acad Pr.

Patrol Operations & Enforcement Tactics. 10th ed. George T. Payton & Mike Amaral. (Illus.). 450p. (C). 1996. pap. text 25.00 (*0-9649086-1-1*) Crim Just Serv.

Patrol Order. Tom Davis. (Illus.). 104p. 1994. pap. text 7.95 (*1-884778-02-X*) Old Mountain.

Patrol to the Golden Horn. large type ed. Alexander Fullerton. 528p. 1988. 27.99 (*0-7089-1784-4*) Ulverscroft.

Patrolling: A Reprinting of U. S. Army Special Text 21-75-3 Dismounted Patrolling, January 1981. Ed. by Bruce A. Hanesalo. (Illus.). 210p. 1998. reprint ed. vinyl bd. 20.00 (*1-886848-38-6*) Mil-Info.

Patrolman Examinations - All States. Jack Rudman. (Career Examination Ser.: C-575). 1994. pap. 23.95 (*0-8373-0575-6*) Nat Learn.

Patrolman, Police Department. Jack Rudman. (Career Examination Ser.: C-576). 1994. pap. 23.95 (*0-8373-0576-4*) Nat Learn.

Patrolman-Policewoman. Jack Rudman. (Career Examination Ser.: C-1922). 1994. pap. 23.95 (*0-8373-1922-6*) Nat Learn.

Patrolman's Manual (Philadelphia), 1913 see Metropolitan Police Manuals, 1871-1913: Rules & Regulations for the Government of the Richmond County Police Force, of the State of New York. New York, 1871

Patrology, Vol. 1. Johannes Quasten. LC 83-72018. 608p. 1994. pap. 32.95 (*0-87061-084-8*) Chr Classics.

Patrology, Vol. 2. Ed. by Johannes Quasten. LC 83-72018. Vol. 2. 452p. 1994. pap. 36.95 (*0-87061-085-6*, 6912) Chr Classics.

Patrology, Vol. 3. Johannes Quasten. LC 83-72018. Vol. 3. 350p. 1994. pap. 41.95 (*0-87061-086-4*) Chr Classics.

Patrology, Vol. 4. Johannes Quasten. LC 83-72018. 667p. 1994. pap. 52.95 (*0-87061-127-5*) Chr Classics.

Patrology, 4 vols., Vol. 4. Johannes Quasten. LC 83-72018. 668p. 1994. pap. 149.95 (*0-87061-141-0*) Chr Classics.

Patrology: The Lives & Works of the Fathers of the Church, 3 vols. Otto Bardenhewer. 1994. pap. text 37.50 (*0-89981-069-1*) Eastern Orthodox.

***Patron.** Thomas Wakefield Blackburn. LC 00-31960. 2000. write for info. (*0-7838-9112-1*, G K Hall & Co) Mac Lib Ref.

Patron. Tom W. Blackburn. 1998. 17.50 (*0-7540-8018-8*, Gunsmoke) Chivers N Amer.

Patron Access: Issues for Online Catalogs. Walt Crawford. (Professional Librarian Ser.). 258p. 1987. 40.00 (*0-8161-1850-7*, Hall Reference); 30.00 (*0-8161-1852-3*, Hall Reference) Macmillan.

Patron & Pavements in Late Antiquity. Ed. by Signe Isager & Birte Poulsen. LC 98-217384. (Halicarnassian Studies: Vol. 2). (Illus.). 150p. 1997. 32.00 (*87-7838-297-1*, Pub. by Odense Univ) Intl Spec Bk.

Patron Behavior in Libraries: A Handbook of Positive Approaches to Negative Situations. Ed. by Beth McNeil & Denise Johnson. 200p. (Orig.). 1995. pap. 28.00 (*0-8389-0662-1*, 0662-1-2045) ALA.

Patron-Client Politics & Business in Bangladesh. Stanley A. Kochanek. LC 93-34307. 388p. (C). 1994. text 39.95 (*0-8039-9144-4*) Sage.

Patron-Client State Relationships: Multilateral Crises in the Nuclear Age. Christopher C. Shoemaker. LC 83-17822. 211p. 1984. 49.95 (*0-275-91267-1*, C1267, Praeger Pubs) Greenwood.

Patron de Asentamiento Rural en la Region de San Gregorio, Chiapas, para el Clasico Tardio. Sonia Rivero. 380p. 1990. pap. 15.00 (*968-6068-48-1*, IN031) UPLAAP.

Patron de Asentamientos Prehispanicos en la Parte Central del Bajo Balsas: Un Ensayo Metodologico. Noberto Gonzalez Crespo. (SPA., Illus.). 112p. 1979. pap. 5.00 (*1-877812-66-8*, IN049) UPLAAP.

Patron de Asentamientos Prehispanicos en la Parte Central del Bajo Balsas: Un Ensayo Metodologico. Norberto Gonzalez. (Illus.). 112p. 1979. pap. 5.00 (*1-877812-42-0*, IN049) UPLAAP.

Patron de New-York. Bernard B. Dadie. pap. 6.50 (*0-685-35940-9*) Fr & Eur.

Patron Happiness. Sandra McPherson. LC 82-11490. (American Poetry Ser.). 70p. 1984. pap. 6.50 (*0-88001-022-3*) HarpC.

***Patron Saint of Eye-Liner.** Jeremy Reed. 160p. 2000. 19.95 (*1-84068-042-3*, Pub. by Creation Books) Subterranean Co.

Patron Saint of First Communicants: The Story of Blessed Imelda Lambertini. Mary F. Windeatt. LC 90-71824. (Stories of the Saints for Young People Ages 10 to 100 Ser.). Orig. Title: Little Sister: The Story of Blessed Imelda Lambertini, Patroness of First Communicants. (Illus.). 85p. (J). (gr. 5-9). 1995. reprint ed. pap. 6.00 (*0-89555-416-X*) TAN Bks Pubs.

Patron Saint of Liars. Ann Patchett. 1996. pap. 12.00 (*0-449-91205-1*) Fawcett.

Patron Saint of the New World: Spanish American Colonial Images of St. Joseph. Ed. by Joseph F. Chorpenning. LC 95-6648. 61p. 1992. 14.95 (*0-916101-11-8*) St Joseph.

Patron Saint of Unmarried Women. large type ed. Karl Ackerman. LC 94-28583. 399p. 1994. lib. bdg. 21.95 (*0-7862-0273-4*) Thorndike Pr.

Patron Saints. Daughters of St. Paul Staff. 70p. pap. 1.95 (*0-8198-5859-5*) Pauline Bks.

Patron Saints. Michael Freze. LC 92-80498. 252p. 1992. pap. 9.95 (*0-87973-464-7*) Our Sunday Visitor.

Patron Saints: Five Rebels Who Opened America to a New Art, 1928-1943. Nicholas F. Weber. 1995. pap. 22.50 (*0-300-06448-9*) Yale U Pr.

Patron State: Art & Politics in Fascist Italy. Marla Stone. LC 98-9449. 360p. 1998. text 55.00 (*0-691-02969-5*, Pub. by Princeton U Pr); pap. text 24.95 (*0-691-05999-3*, Pub. by Princeton U Pr) Cal Prin Full Svc.

***Patron Trop Serieux.** Donna Clayton. (FRE.). 2000. mass mkt. 3.99 (*0-373-39541-8*) Harlequin Bks.

Patronage & Institutions: Science, Technology & Medicine at the European Court, 1500-1750. Ed. by Bruce T. Moran. (Illus.). 267p. (C). 1991. 75.00 (*0-85115-285-6*) Boydell & Brewer.

Patronage & Performers in Rajasthan: The Subtle Tradition. Joan L. Erdman. 1985. 42.00 (*81-7001-008-X*, Pub. by Chanakya) S Asia.

Patronage & Piety: The Politics of English Roman Catholicism, 1850-1900. Dermot Quinn. LC 91-75051. 320p. (C). 1993. 45.00 (*0-8047-1996-9*) Stanford U Pr.

Patronage & Politics in 19th-Century Brazil. Richard Graham. LC 89-21598. 400p. 1990. 55.00 (*0-8047-1593-9*) Stanford U Pr.

Patronage & Politics in 19th-Century Brazil. Richard Graham. (Illus.). 400p. (C). 1994. pap. 18.95 (*0-8047-2336-2*) Stanford U Pr.

Patronage & Politics in the U. S. S. R. John P. Willerton. (Cambridge Russian, Soviet & Post-Soviet Studies: No. 82). (Illus.). 321p. (C). 1992. text 69.95 (*0-521-39288-8*) Cambridge U Pr.

Patronage & Poverty in the Tobacco South: Louisa County, Virginia, 1860-1900. Crandall A. Shifflett. LC 82-6996. (Illus.). 177p. 1982. reprint ed. pap. 54.90 (*0-608-02952-1*, 206341700006) Bks Demand.

Patronage & Power: Studies on Social Networks in Corinth. John K. Chow. (Journal for the Study of the New Testament, Supplement Ser.: No. 75). 230p. (C). 1992. 65.00 (*1-85075-370-9*, Pub. by Sheffield Acad) CUP Services.

Patronage & Principle: A Political History of Modern Scotland. Michael Fry. 256p. 1987. text 39.90 (*0-08-035063-1*, Pub. by Aberdeen U Pr) Macmillan.

Patronage & Principle: A Political History of Modern Scotland. Michael Fry. 256p. 1991. pap. text 16.95 (*0-08-041407-9*, Pub. by Aberdeen U Pr) Macmillan.

P

An Asterisk (*) at the beginning of an entry indicates that the title is appearing for the first time.

Patronage & Royal Science in 17th-Century France: The Academie de Physique in Caen. David S. Lux. LC 89-1002. 256p. 1989. 37.50 (*0-8014-2334-1*) Cornell U Pr.

Patronage & Society in Nineteenth-Century England. J. M. Bourne. LC 86-213668. ix, 198 p. 1986. 30.00 (*0-7131-6484-0*) E Arnld Pubs.

Patronage, Art & Society in Renaissance Italy. Ed. by F. W. Kent & Patricia Simons. (OUP-Humanities Research Centre Ser.). (Illus.). 350p. 1987. text 79.00 (*0-19-821978-4*) OUP.

Patronage, Brokerage, Entrepreneurship & the Chinese Community of New York. Bernard Wong. LC 83-45363. (Immigrant Communities & Ethnic Minorities in the U. S. & Canada Ser.: No. 30). 1988. 56.00 (*0-404-19416-8*) AMS Pr.

Patronage Bureaucracy in North India: The Robert M. Bird & James Thomason School, 1820-1870. Peter Penner. 380p. 1986. 35.00 (*81-7001-017-9*, Pub. by Chanakya) S Asia.

Patronage in Ancient Society. Ed. by Andrew Wallace-Hadrill. 256p. (C). 1989. lib. bdg. 49.95 (*0-415-00341-5*) Routledge.

Patronage in Renaissance Italy: From 1400 to the Early 16th Century. Mary Hollingsworth. (Illus.). 384p. (Orig.). (C). 1996. pap. 19.95 (*0-8018-5287-0*) Johns Hopkins.

Patronage in 16th Century Italy. Mary Hollingsworth. LC 97-151954. (Illus.). 384p. 1997. 50.00 (*0-7195-5315-6*, Pub. by John Murray); pap. 24.95 (*0-7195-5388-1*, Pub. by John Murray) Trafalgar.

Patronage in the Renaissance. Ed. by Guy F. Lytle & Stephen Orgel. LC 81-47143. (Folger Institute Essays Ser.). (Illus.). 405p. reprint ed. pap. 125.60 (*0-8357-4199-0*, 203697700006) Bks Demand.

Patronage Politics & Literary Traditions in England, 1558-1658. Ed. by Cedric C. Brown. 310p. (C). 1993. pap. 19.95 (*0-8143-2417-7*) Wayne St U Pr.

Patronage, Power & Poverty in Southern Italy: A Tale of Two Cities. Judith Chubb. LC 82-1325. (Cambridge Studies in Modern Political Economies). (Illus.). 304p. 1983. text 85.00 (*0-521-23637-1*) Cambridge U Pr.

Patronage, Practice, & the Culture of American Science: Alexander Dallas Bache & the U. S. Coast Survey. Hugh R. Slotten. (Illus.). 242p. (C). 1994. text 54.95 (*0-521-43395-9*) Cambridge U Pr.

Patrones de Asentamiento de los Agricultores Prehispanicos en "El Limon," Municipio de Chaparral (Tolima) Camilo Rodriguez. (SPA., Illus.). 108p. 1991. pap. 8.50 (*1-877812-29-3*, BR027) UPLAAP.

Patrones de Participacion Politica de los Puertorriquenos en la Ciudad de Nueva York. Rosa Estades. Tr. by Manuel Gardenas-Ruiz. LC 77-12112. 99p. 1978. pap. 3.00 (*0-8477-2446-8*) U of PR Pr.

Patroness of Paris: Rituals of Devotion in Early Modern France. Moshe Sluhovsky. LC 97-40124. (Cultures, Beliefs & Traditions Ser.: No. 3). (Illus.). 280p. 1998. 103.00 (*90-04-10851-3*) Brill Academic Pubs.

Patronio y Lucanor: La Lectura Inteligente "en el Tiempo Que Es Turbio" Ed. by Marta A. Diz. LC 83-51708. (Scripta Humanistica Ser.). (SPA.). 183p. (C). 1984. 26.00 (*0-916379-01-9*) Scripta.

Patrons & Defenders: The Saints in the Italian City-State. Diana Webb. 304p. 1996. text 65.00 (*1-86064-029-X*, Pub. by I B T) St Martin.

Patrons & Painters: A Study in the Relations Between Italian Art & Society in the Age of the Baroque. rev. ed. Francis Haskell. LC 79-56891. (Illus.). 474p. 1980. pap. 27.50 (*0-300-02540-8*) Yale U Pr.

***Patrons & Perceivers: A History of Uses of Art.** Walter A. Woods. 440p. 2000. pap. 24.00 (*0-8059-4765-5*) Dorrance.

Patrons & Performance: Early Tudor Household Revels. Suzanne R. Westfall. (Illus.). 280p. 1990. text 69.00 (*0-19-812880-0*) OUP.

Patrons & Philistines: Arts & the State in British India, 1773-1947. Ed. by Pushpa Sundar. LC 96-900733. (Illus.). 304p. (C). 1996. text 29.95 (*0-19-563693-7*) OUP.

Patrons & Protegees: Gender, Friendship, & Writing in 19th-Century America. Ed. by Shirley Marchalonis. LC 87-42735. 250p. 1988. 40.00 (*0-8135-1270-0*) Rutgers U Pr.

Patrons & Protegees: Gender, Friendship, & Writing in 19th-Century America. Ed. by Shirley Marchalonis. 243p. (C). 1991. pap. text 18.00 (*0-8135-1690-0*) Rutgers U Pr.

Patrons, Artisans & Instruments of Science, 1600-1750. Silvio A. Bedini. LC 98-53851. (Variorum Collected Studies Ser.). (Illus.). 12p. 1999. text 120.95 (*0-86078-781-8*) Ashgate Pub Co.

Patrons, Clients, Brokers: Ontario Society & Politics, 1791-1896. S. J. Noel. 328p. 1990. pap. 19.95 (*0-8020-6774-3*); text 45.00 (*0-8020-5858-2*) U of Toronto Pr.

Patrons, Collectors, & Connoisseurs: Women & Art, 1350-1750. Ed. by Cynthia Lawrence. LC 95-25743. 1996. 42.50 (*0-271-01568-3*) Pa St U Pr.

Patrons, Devotees, & Goddesses. Masakazu Tanaka. LC 98-902296. 1997. reprint ed. 33.00 (*81-7304-183-0*, Pub. by Manohar) S Asia.

Patrons of Maori Culture: Power, Theory & Ideology in the Maori Renaissance. Steven Webster. 275p. 1998. pap. 39.95 (*1-877133-48-5*, DU423, Pub. by Univ Otago Pr) Intl Spec Bk.

Patrons of the Craftsman, (1731) Sedition & Defamation Display'd (1731) John Hervey et al. LC 97-10016. (British Ideas & Issues, 1660-1820 Ser.). 52p. 1997. pap. 24.50 (*0-404-59651-7*) AMS Pr.

Patrons, Painters, & Saints: Studies in Medieval Italian Painting. Julian Gardner. (Collected Studies: No. CS 414). (Illus.). 352p. 1993. 157.95 (*0-86078-379-0*, Pub. by Variorum) Ashgate Pub Co.

Patronymica Britannica: A Dictionary of the Family Names of the United Kingdom. Mark A. Lower. 443p. 1996. pap. 33.00 (*0-7884-0456-3*, L581) Heritage Bk.

Patroon's Domain. S. G. Nissenson. 416p. 1993. reprint ed. lib. bdg. 99.00 (*0-7812-5192-3*) Rprt Serv.

Patrullas Civiles y Su Legado: Superar la Militarizacion y Polarizacion del Campo Guatemalteco. Margaret L. Popkin. Ed. by James J. Silk. Tr. by Gretta T. Siebentritt. 80p. 1996. pap. text. write for info. (*1-881055-07-8*) RFK Mem Ctr HR.

Patrum Nicaenorum Nomina. Ed. by Gelzer et al. (GRE & LAT.). 1995. reprint ed. 59.50 (*3-519-01995-7*, Pub. by B G Teubner) U of Mich Pr.

Pats. Mark Dunster. 24p. (Orig.). (YA). (gr. 9-12). 1996. pap. 5.00 (*0-89642-303-4*) Linden Pubs.

Pats & Praises. Ed. by Scholastic, Inc. Staff. 1990. pap. 16.95 (*0-590-49071-0*) Scholastic Inc.

Pat's First Book of Thoughts in Poetry & Prose. Eunice Paddio-Johnson. 1991. write for info. (*1-880143-00-3*) Paddio-Johnson.

Pat's Sourdough & Favorite Recipes. 2nd ed. Patricia A. Duncan. 200p. 1991. reprint ed. spiral bd. 14.95 (*0-9625098-1-7*) TAP Pub.

Patshalas into Schools: The Development of Indigenous Elementary Education in Bengal, 1854-1905. Kazi Shahidullah. 1987. 27.50 (*0-8364-2027-6*, Pub. by Mukhopadhyaya) S Asia.

Patssi Valdez: A Precarious Comfort. Terezita Romo & Amalia Mesa-Bains. Ed. by Elizabeth Ptak. (Illus.). 104p. 1999. pap. 24.95 (*1-880508-07-9*) Mexican Museum.

***Patsy.** James J. Thornton, Jr. LC 98-90865. 1999. pap. 13.95 (*0-533-12951-6*) Vantage.

Patsy: The Adventures of an Old Gaffer. John Jefferson. 128p. (C). 1990. text 59.00 (*0-906754-57-7*, Pub. by Fernhurst Bks) St Mut.

Patsy: The Life & Times of Patsy Cline. Margaret Jones. LC 98-43424. (Illus.). 368p. 1999. reprint ed. mass mkt. 15.95 (*0-306-80886-2*, Pub. by Da Capo) HarpC.

Patsy & the Declaration. Elizabeth Massie. (Daughters of Liberty Ser.: No. 2). (J). (gr. 3-6). 1997. per. 3.99 (*0-671-00133-7*, Minstrel Bks) PB.

Patsy & the Declaration. Elizabeth Massie. (Daughters of Liberty Ser.). 1997. 9.09 (*0-606-12671-6*, Pub. by Turtleback) Demco.

Patsy & the Subcontractor: A Study of the Expert-Layman Relationship. Barney G. Glaser. 172p. 1972. 22.00 (*1-884156-04-5*) Sociology Pr.

Patsy Cline - Original Keys for Singers. 120p. 1997. otabind 14.95 (*0-7935-7573-7*) H Leonard.

Patsy Cline, Singing Girl from the Shenandoah Valley. Stuart E. Brown, Jr. & Lorraine F. Myers. (Illus.). 110p. 1996. 19.50 (*0-911578-00-5*) VA Bk.

Patsy Doll Family Encyclopedia. Patricia N. Schoonmaker. LC 93-114852. Vol. I. (Illus.). 224p. 1992. 29.95 (*0-87588-375-3*) Hobby Hse.

Patsy Doll Family Encyclopedia, Vol. II. Patricia N. Schoonmaker. LC 93-114852. Vol. II. 176p. 1998. 29.95 (*0-87588-506-3*) Hobby Hse.

***Patsy Kelly Investigates: A Family Affair.** large type ed. Anne Cassidy. (J). 1998. pap. 16.95 (*0-7540-6028-4*, Galaxy Child Lrg Print) Chivers N Amer.

***Patsy 'n Pals.** Cynthia Gaskill. (Illus.). 48p. 2000. 33.00 (*0-912823-94-1*, TS-139, Pub. by Gold Horse) Dollmasters.

Patsy-O. Bryan MacMahon. LC 89-51016. 128p. (Orig.). (J). (gr. 4-7). 1989. pap. 6.95 (*1-85371-036-9*, Pub. by Poolbeg Pr) Dufour.

***Patsy Says.** Leslie Tryon. LC 99-89612. (Illus.). (J). 2001. write for info. (*0-689-82297-9*) Atheneum Yung Read.

Patsy's Discovery. Elizabeth Massie. (Daughters of Liberty Ser.: No. 1). (J). 1997. per. 3.99 (*0-671-00132-9*) PB.

Patsy's Discovery. Elizabeth Massie. (Daughters of Liberty Ser.). 1997. 9.09 (*0-606-11239-1*, Pub. by Turtleback) Demco.

Patt College Writing. 7th rev. ed. Kirszner. 1997. pap. 35.95 (*0-312-19044-1*) St Martin.

Patt College Writing. 7th rev. ed. Kirszner. 1999. pap. text, teacher ed. 5.00 (*0-312-19050-6*) St Martin.

Patte Dans le Sac. Sylvie Desrosiers. (Novels in the Roman Jeunesse Ser.). (FRE.). 96p. (J). (gr. 4-7). 1987. pap. 8.95 (*2-89021-063-4*, Pub. by La Courte Ech) Firefly Bks Ltd.

Patte du Chat. Marcel Ayme. (Folio - Cadet Bleu Ser.: No. 200). (FRE., Illus.). 72p. (J). (gr. 1-5). 1990. pap. 9.95 (*2-07-031200-3*) Schoenhof.

Patten Genealogy: William Patten of Cambridge, 1635 & His Descendants. T. W. Baldwin. (Illus.). 300p. 1989. reprint ed. pap. 45.00 (*0-8328-0941-1*); reprint ed. lib. bdg. 53.00 (*0-8328-0940-3*) Higginson Bk Co.

Patten Genealogy: 1 Line Descending from William Patten. Malcolm C. Patten. LC 90-62211. (Illus.). 402p. 1990. 25.00 (*0-9627321-0-9*) Powell & Taylor.

Patten's Foundations of Embryology. 6th ed. Bruce M. Carlson. LC 96-75396. 752p. (C). 1996. 85.63 (*0-07-009940-5*) McGraw.

Pattens of Bath: A Seagoing Dynasty. Kenneth R. Martin & Ralph L. Snow. LC 96-19324. 1996. pap. 22.95 (*0-937410-15-2*) ME Maritime Mus.

Patter-Paws the Fox: And Other Stories. Brien Masters. (Illus.). 64p. (J). 1992. 10.95 (*0-904693-35-X*, Pub. by Temple Lodge) Anthroposophic.

Patterened Elicitation Syntax Test: (PEST) with Morphophonemic Analysis. rev. ed. Edna C. Young & Joseph J. Perachio. 48p. 1993. pap. text 65.50 (*0-7616-7873-5*) Commun Skill.

Pattern. Vincent Buckley. 64p. 1979. pap. 8.50 (*0-85105-357-2*, Pub. by Smyth) Dufour.

Pattern. Donna Burk et al. (Box It or Bag It Mathematics Ser.). (Illus.). 67p. (C). 1988. teacher ed., ring bd. 12.00 (*1-886131-06-6*, BB5) Math Lrning.

Pattern. James C. Morris. LC 96-61875. 144p. (Orig.). 1997. pap. 10.99 (*1-883893-93-3*) WinePress Pub.

Pattern. Henry Pluckrose. (Math Counts Ser.). (Illus.). 32p. (J). 1995. pap. 4.95 (*0-516-45455-2*) Childrens.

Pattern. C. H. Sisson. 24p. 1993. pap. 7.95 (*1-870612-68-X*, Pub. by Enitha Pr) Dufour.

Pattern. Mignon G. Eberhart. 1976. reprint ed. lib. bdg. 23.95 (*0-88411-758-8*) Amereon Ltd.

Pattern, 1. Joan Evans. 1976. pap. 9.95 (*0-306-80040-3*) Da Capo.

Pattern, 2. Joan Evans. 1976. pap. 9.95 (*0-306-80041-1*) Da Capo.

***Pattern Almanac 2000.** Linda Rising. (Software Patterns Ser.). 448p. 2000. pap. 29.95 (*0-201-61567-3*) Addison-Wesley.

Pattern Alphabets: 100 Complete Fonts. Selected by Dan X. Solo. LC 94-10949. (Pictorial Archive Ser.). 112p. 1994. 7.95 (*0-486-28371-2*) Dover.

Pattern Analysis. H. Nieman. (Information Sciences Ser.: Vol. 4). (Illus.). 305p. 1981. 47.00 (*0-387-10792-4*) Spr-Verlag.

Pattern Analysis: Lectures in Pattern Theory II. Ulf Grenander. (Applied Mathematical Sciences Ser.: Vol. 24). (Illus.). 1978. 89.95 (*0-387-90310-0*) Spr-Verlag.

Pattern Analysis & Dimensionality Reduction. Kirby. 400p. 89.95 (*0-471-23929-1*) Wiley.

Pattern Analysis & Understanding. 2nd ed. H. Niemann. (Information Sciences Ser.: Vol. 4). (Illus.). 360p. 1990. 59.95 (*0-387-51378-7*) Spr-Verlag.

Pattern Analysis in Savanna-Woodlands at Nylsvley, South Africa. R. H. Whittaker et al. (Memoirs of the Botanical Survey of South Africa Ser.: No. 49). (Illus.). 51p. 1984. 15.00 (*0-621-08265-1*, Pub. by Natl Botanical Inst) Balogh.

Pattern-Analytical Clustering: Theory, Method, Research & Configural Findings. Louis L. McQuitty. LC 87-13346. (Illus.). 816p. 1987. lib. bdg. 102.00 (*0-8191-6449-6*) U Pr of Amer.

Pattern & Chaos: Multilinear Novels by Dos Passos, Doblin, Faulkner, & Koeppen. Kathleen L. Komar. LC 82-73875. (GERM Ser.: Vol. 14). (Illus.). x, 150p. 1983. 35.00 (*0-938100-19-X*) Camden Hse.

Pattern & Design with Dynamic Symmetry. Edward B. Edwards. Orig. Title: Dynamarhythmic Design, Ii. 122p. (C). 1967. pap. 7.95 (*0-486-21756-6*) Dover.

Pattern & Problems of Economic Development in a Backward Region. R. S. Tewari. 102p. (C). 1991. 100.00 (*81-85009-38-4*, Pub. by Print Hse) St Mut.

Pattern & Process. Richard D. Laven. (Illus.). pap. 0.00 (*0-691-02514-2*) Princeton U Pr.

Pattern & Process in a Forested Ecosystem: Disturbance, Development & the State Based on the Hubbard Brook Ecosystem Study. F. H. Bormann & Gene E. Likens. LC 94-211107. 264p. 1996. 43.95 (*0-387-94344-7*) Spr-Verlag.

Pattern & Process in a Forested Ecosystem: Disturbance, Development & the Steady State Based on the Hubbard Brook Ecosystem Study. F. H. Bormann & Gene E. Likens. LC 78-6015. (Illus.). 1991. 44.00 (*0-387-90321-6*) Spr-Verlag.

Pattern & Process in Host-Parasitoid Interactions. Bradford A. Hawkins. (Illus.). 200p. (C). 1994. text 44.95 (*0-521-46029-8*) Cambridge U Pr.

***Pattern & Process in Macroecology.** Kevin J. Gaston & Tim M. Blackburn. LC 00-29739. 2000. write for info. (*0-632-05653-3*) Blackwell Sci.

Pattern & The Prophecy: God's Great Code. James Harrison. LC 96-127127. 1996. 14.95 (*0-9698512-0-0*, Pub. by ISPB) Spring Arbor Dist.

Pattern Animal Book. Mogensen. 1995. pap. 8.95 (*0-201-48037-9*) Addison-Wesley.

Pattern Animals Book. Sandra Mogensen & Judy Magarian-Gold. (Illus.). 48p. 1986. pap. text 8.95 (*0-914040-46-4*) Cuisenaire.

Pattern Biology & the Complex Architectures of Life. Michael J. Katz. LC 87-22651. 1987. 25.00 (*0-89341-521-9*, Longwood Academic) Hollowbrook.

Pattern Block Circus. Janine Blinko & Noel Graham. 1997. pap. 12.50 (*1-871098-32-7*, Pub. by Claire Pubns) Parkwest Pubns.

Pattern Blocks Parts & Wholes. Debby Head & Libby Pollett. (Count on Kids Ser.). 154p. 1994. teacher ed. 31.95 (*1-885775-04-0*) BBY Pubns.

Pattern Book: Recipes for Beauty. Clifford A. Pickover. 250p. 1995. text 59.00 (*981-02-1426-X*) World Scientific Pub.

***Pattern Book: 64,000 Pattern Combinations for Your Home.** Chronicle Books Staff. LC 99-89459. (Illus.). 96p. 2000. 24.95 (*0-8118-2557-4*) Chronicle Bks.

Pattern Book for Carving Fish: 18 Patterns & Instructions for Carving, Texturing & Painting Fresh & Saltwater Game Fish. Brian E. McGray. Ed. by Meredith A. McGray. (Illus.). 96p. 1995. pap. 14.95 (*1-886975-01-9*) Goose Hse Pubns.

Pattern Book for Carving Fish: 18 Patterns & Instructions for Carving, Texturing & Painting Fresh & Saltwater Game Fish. 2nd rev. ed. Brian E. McGray. Ed. by Meredith A. McGray. LC 97-94065. (Illus.). 96p. 1998. per. 14.95 (*1-886975-03-5*) Goose Hse Pubns.

Pattern Books of American Classical Architecture: Practice of Architecture & the Builder's Guide. Asher Benjamin. (Illus.). 475p. 1994. reprint ed. pap. 19.95 (*0-306-80572-3*) Da Capo.

Pattern Change Programing: Creating Your Own Destiny, Bk. 1. Rose A. Parvin. Ed. by Marlo Brooks. LC 94-23106. 768p. 1995. lib. bdg. 40.00 (*1-885917-00-7*) Univrsl Pubng.

Pattern Changes: Universal Laws of Success & Spiritual Excellence, Bk. 9. Rose A. Parvin. LC 95-130. 288p. 1995. lib. bdg. 15.00 (*1-885917-08-2*) Univrsl Pubng.

Pattern Changing for Abused Women: An Educational Program. Marilyn S. Goodman & Beth C. Fallon. (Interpersonal Violence: the Practice Ser.: Vol. 9). 204p. 1994. 52.00 (*0-8039-5493-X*); pap. 24.95 (*0-8039-5494-8*) Sage.

Pattern Classification: A Unified View of Statistical & Neural Approaches. Jurgen Schurmann. LC 95-4733. 392p. 1996. 89.95 (*0-471-13534-8*) Wiley.

Pattern Classification & Scene Analyses. Richard O. Duda & Peter E. Hart. 512p. 1973. 98.00 (*0-471-22361-1*) Wiley.

Pattern Classification & Scene Analysis Part 1: Pattern Classification. 2nd ed. Richard O. Duda et al. LC 99-29981. 624p. 2000. text 110.00 (*0-471-05669-3*, Wiley-Interscience) Wiley.

Pattern Cutting for Outwear Fashion. Ward & Martin M. Shoben. 1994. pap. text 49.95 (*0-7506-2138-9*) Buttrwrth-Heinemann.

Pattern Cutting for Women's Outerwear. Gerry Cooklin. LC 94-16577. (Illus.). 192p. 1994. 36.95 (*0-632-03797-0*, Pub. by Blckwll Scitfc UK) Blackwell Sci.

Pattern Dates for British Ordnance Small Arms, 1718-1783. DeWitt Bailey. (Illus.). 128p. 1997. pap. 20.00 (*1-57747-016-8*) Thomas Publications.

Pattern Deposition Checklists. 3rd ed. Douglas Danner & Larry L. Varn. LC 93-77906. 1993. 160.00 (*0-318-02978-2*) West Group.

Pattern Design. Lewis F. Day. LC 99-45781. 318p. 1999. pap. text 9.95 (*0-486-40709-8*) Dover.

Pattern Design: An Introduction to the Study of Formal Ornament. 2nd ed. Archibald H. Christie. 313p. 1969. reprint ed. pap. 9.95 (*0-486-22221-7*) Dover.

Pattern Designing for Dressmakers. Lynn Alexander. (Illus.). 104p. 1998. pap. 14.95 (*0-87588-536-5*, 5553) Hobby Hse.

Pattern Directed Approach Towards an Object Adaptive Decision Support Environment for Water Resources Management. Ying Liu. (Illus.). 201p. (Orig.). 1995. pap. 59.50 (*90-407-1311-1*, Pub. by Delft U Pr) Coronet Bks.

Pattern Disc Product Liability. 3rd ed. Douglas Danner. LC 94-80029. 1995. ring bd. 270.00 (*0-685-59895-0*) West Group.

Pattern Discovery in Biomolecular Data: Tools, Techniques & Applications. Jason T Wang. LC 98-18934. (Illus.). 272p. 1999. text 55.00 (*0-19-511940-1*) OUP.

Pattern Discovery Motor Vehicles, 2 vols. 3rd ed. Douglas Danner. LC 84-82253. 1994. ring bd. 245.00 (*0-685-59892-6*) West Group.

Pattern Discovery Premises Liability. 2nd ed. Douglas Danner. LC 86-80670. 1986. 98.00 (*0-685-59894-2*) West Group.

Pattern Discovery Tort Actions. 3rd ed. Douglas Danner. LC 86-82354. 1994. ring bd. 245.00 (*0-685-59896-9*) West Group.

Pattern Dissemination in the Prehistoric Southwest & Mesoamerica. Bert Zaslow. (Anthropological Research Papers: No. 25). (Illus.). vii, 57p. 1981. pap. 10.00 (*0-318-62451-6*) AZ Univ ARP.

Pattern Drafting for Apparel with PAD System Version 2.5. Sharon B. Underwood & Cynthia L. Istook. 360p. (C). 1996. pap. 42.00 (*1-888452-02-1*) Ascot Publns.

Pattern Electroretinogram, Circulatory Disturbances of the Visual System & Pattern Evoked Responses. Ed. by John R. Heckenlively & Theodore Lawwill. (Documenta Ophthalmologica Proceedings Ser.). 1984. text 219.50 (*90-6193-503-2*) Kluwer Academic.

***Pattern Fish** Trudy Harris. LC 99-34120. (Illus.). 2000. lib. bdg. write for info. (*0-7613-1712-0*) Millbrook Pr.

Pattern for a Tapestry. Autran Dourado. Tr. by John M. Parker from POR. 170p. 1984. 30.00 (*0-7206-0608-X*, Pub. by P Owen Ltd) Dufour.

Pattern for Joint Operations: World War 2 Close Air Support, North Africa. Daniel B. Mortensen. LC 87-19335. (Illus.). 104p. 1987. pap. 7.50 (*0-16-001963-X*, 008-029-00161-6) USGPO.

Pattern for Life: Selected Writings of Thomas a Kempis. Thomas, a Kempis. Ed. by Timothy Jones. LC 97-33488. (Upper Room Spiritual Classics). 96p. 1998. pap. 5.00 (*0-8358-0835-1*, UR835) Upper Room Bks.

Pattern for Terror. large type ed. Hugh Pentecost. LC 92-30149. (Nightingale Ser.). 228p. 1993. pap. 14.95 (*0-8161-5637-9*, G K Hall Lrg Type) Mac Lib Ref.

Pattern Formation. D. C. Stein. LC 97-11981. (C). 1997. 61.00 (*0-201-40844-9*) Addison-Wesley.

Pattern Formation: Symmetry Methods & Applications. Ed. by John Chadam et al. LC 95-33706. (Fields Institute Communications Ser.: Vol. 5). 358p. 1995. text 99.00 (*0-8218-0256-9*, FIC/5) Am Math.

Pattern Formation & Lattice Gas Automata. Ed. by Raymond Kapral & Anna T. Lawniczak. LC 95-43530. (Fields Institute Communications Ser.: Vol. 6). 346p. 1995. text 99.00 (*0-8218-0258-5*, FIC/6) Am Math.

Pattern Formation During Development. (Symposia on Quantitative Biology Ser.: Vol. LXII). (Illus.). 570p. (C). 1998. pap. text 105.00 (*0-87969-536-6*) Cold Spring Harbor.

Pattern Formation During Development Vol. LXII: Cold Spring Harbor Symposia on Quantitative Biology. (Symposia on Quantitative Biology Ser.: Vol. LXII). (Illus.). 770p. (C). 1998. text 250.00 (*0-87969-535-8*) Cold Spring Harbor.

Pattern Formation in Biology, Vision & Dynamics. Marilyne Woodsmall. LC 99-89209. 600p. 1999. 85.00 (*981-02-3792-8*) World Scientific Pub.

Pattern Formation in Complex Dissipative Systems: Fluid Patterns, Liquid Crystals, Chemical Reactions, Kitakyushu, Japan, 18-20 September, 1991. Ed. by S. Kai. LC 92-14203. 500p. 1992. text 130.00 (*981-02-0879-0*) World Scientific Pub.

Pattern Formation in Continuous & Coupled Systems: A Survey Volume. Ed. by M. Golubitsky & S. H. Strogatz. LC 99-15369. (IMA Volumes in Mathematics & Its Applications Ser.: Vol. 115). (Illus.). 344p. 1999. 74.95 (*0-387-98874-2*) Spr-Verlag.

Pattern Formation in Diffusion - Limited Crystal Growth - Beyond the Single Dendrite. Kassner Klaus. 250p. 1996. text 48.00 (*981-02-1532-0*) World Scientific Pub.

***Pattern Formation in Granular Materials.** Gerald H. Ristow. LC 99-56369. (Tracts in Modern Physics Ser.: Vol. 164). (Illus.). xiii, 161p. (C). 2000. 96.00 (*3-540-66701-6*) Spr-Verlag.

Pattern Formation in Liquid Crystals. Ed. by Agnes Buka & Lorenz Kramer. LC 95-39607. (Partially Ordered Systems Ser.). 344p. 1996. 69.95 (*0-387-94604-7*) Spr-Verlag.

Pattern Formation in Plant Tissues. Tsvi Sachs. (Developmental & Cell Biology Monographs). (Illus.). 246p. (C). 1991. text 90.00 (*0-521-24865-5*) Cambridge U Pr.

***Pattern Formation in the Developing Nervous System.** Ed. by E. M. Carpenter. (Developing Neuroscience Ser.: Vol. 22). (Illus.). 74p. 2000. pap. 25.25 (*3-8055-7086-4*) S Karger.

Pattern Formation in the Physical & Biological Sciences. Daniel L. Stein. LC 97-11981. (C). 1997. pap. 35.00 (*0-201-15691-1*) Addison-Wesley.

Pattern Formation in the Physical & Biological World. Daniel Stein. 1999. write for info. (*0-201-15693-8*) Addison-Wesley.

Pattern Formation in Viscous Flows: The Taylor-Couette Problem & Rayleigh-Benard Convection. 2nd ed. R. Meyer-Spasche. LC 99-211198. (International Series in Numerical Mathematics: Vol. 28). 196p. 1999. 69.50 (*3-7643-6047-X*) Birkhauser.

Pattern-Free Fashions. Mary L. Cole. LC 94-23897. (Illus.). 96p. 1995. pap. 15.95 (*0-8019-8497-1*) Krause Pubns.

Pattern Glass Mugs. John Mordock & Walter Adams. (Illus.). 160p. 1995. 44.95 (*1-57080-011-1*); pap. 34.95 (*1-57080-010-3*) Antique Pubns.

Pattern Grading for Men's Clothes: The Technology of Sizing. Gerry Cooklin. (Illus.). 304p. 1992. pap. 39.95 (*0-632-03305-3*) Blackwell Sci.

***Pattern Grammar: A Corpus-Driven Approach to the Lexical Grammar of English.** Susan Hunston & Gill Francis. LC 99-43483. (Studies in Corpus Linguistics: Vol. 4). xiv, 288p. 2000. write for info. (*1-55619-398-X*); pap. 34.95 (*1-55619-399-8*) J Benjamins Pubng.

Pattern Hatching: Design Patterns Applied. John Vlissides. LC 98-20524. (Software Patterns Ser.). 192p. (C). 1998. pap. text 29.95 (*0-201-43293-5*) Addison-Wesley.

Pattern in Corporate Evolution. Neil M. Kay. (Illus.). 336p. 1997. text 65.00 (*0-19-829047-0*) OUP.

***Pattern in Corporate Evolution.** Neil M. Kay. (Illus.). 344p. 2000. pap. 29.95 (*0-19-924211-9*) OUP.

Pattern in Early Christian Worship. Allen Cabaniss. LC 89-2254. 144p. (C). 1989. 17.50 (*0-86554-345-3*, MUPH283) Mercer Univ Pr.

Pattern in the Heavens. R. Pearson. pap. 3.95 (*0-88172-170-0*) Believers Bkshelf.

Pattern in the Material Folk Culture of the Eastern United States. rev. ed. Henry H. Glassie. LC 75-160630. (Illus.). 316p. 1971. reprint ed. pap. text 19.95 (*0-8122-1013-1*) U of Pa Pr.

Pattern in the Teaching & Learning of Mathematics. Anthony Orton. LC 80-5342. 224p. 1999. 75.00 (*0-304-70051-7*); pap. 27.95 (*0-304-70052-5*) Continuum.

Pattern in the Web: The Mythical Poetry of Charles Williams. Roma A. King, Jr. LC 90-33588. 200p. 1990. 28.00 (*0-87338-412-1*) Kent St U Pr.

Pattern Instructions for Kansas. 2nd ed. Kansas Judicial Council, Committee on Pattern Jury. LC 77-88793. 900p. 121.00 (*0-317-00532-4*) West Group.

Pattern Instructions for Kansas. 2nd ed. Kansas Judicial Council, Committee on Pattern Jury. LC 77-88793. 900p. 1992. suppl. ed. 45.00 (*0-317-04329-3*) West Group.

Pattern Jury Instructions Civil Cases, U. S. Fifth Circuit District Judge's Association: 1995 Edition. Martin Feldman. 187p. (C). 1995. pap. text. write for info. (*0-314-06825-2*) West Pub.

Pattern Jury Instructions, Civil Cases U. S. Fifth Circuit District Judge's Association 1997. Fifth Circuit Comm. on Pattern Jury Instructions. 190p. 1997. pap. text. write for info. (*0-314-22610-9*) West Pub.

Pattern Language: Towns, Buildings, Construction. Christopher Alexander et al. LC 74-22874. (Illus.). 1216p. 1977. 60.00 (*0-19-501919-9*) OUP.

Pattern Language of Programming, Vol 1. (C). 1996. write for info. (*0-201-88084-9*) Addison-Wesley.

Pattern Languages of Program Design, Vol. 1. James O. Coplien & Douglas C. Schmidt. 576p. (C). 1995. pap. text 41.95 (*0-201-60734-4*) Addison-Wesley.

Pattern Languages of Program Design, Vol. 2. John Vlissides et al. 624p. (C). 1996. pap. text 42.95 (*0-201-89527-7*) Addison-Wesley.

Pattern Languages of Program Design, Vol. 3. John Vlissides. LC 97-24997. 656p. (C). 1997. pap. text 41.95 (*0-201-31011-2*) Addison-Wesley.

***Pattern Languages of Program Design 4.** Brian Foote et al. LC 99-37085. (Software Patterns Ser.). 640p. 1999. pap. text 42.95 (*0-201-43304-4*) Addison-Wesley.

Pattern Library: Crochet. Dorling Kindersley Staff. 96p. 1985. pap. 9.00 (*0-345-32711-X*) Ballantine Pub Grp.

Pattern Maker's Assistant: Embracing Lathe Work, Branch Work, Core Work, Sweep Work & Practical Gear Construction, & Preparation & Use of Tools. 6th ed. Joshua Rose. (Illus.). 248p. 1995. reprint ed. pap. 19.95 (*1-879335-59-X*) Astragal Pr.

Pattern Making. Jeanne Powell & Carol Foley. (Illus.). 430p. (C). 1987. pap. text 38.00 (*0-13-654211-5*) P-H.

Pattern Making by the Flat Pattern. 8th ed. Norma R. Hollen. LC 98-24667. 356p. 1998. spiral bd. 75.00 (*0-13-938093-0*) P-H.

Pattern Making for Metal Castings. Modern Engineering Practice Staff. 138p. 1991. reprint ed. pap. text 12.00 (*1-877767-46-8*) Univ Publng Hse.

Pattern Matching Algorithms. Ed. by Alberto Apostolico & Zvi Galil. LC 96-49602. (Illus.). 400p. 1997. text 75.00 (*0-19-511367-5*) OUP.

Pattern, Mechanism, & Adaptive Significance of Territoriality in Herring Gulls (Larus argentatus) Joanna Burger. 92p. 1984. 12.50 (*0-943610-41-9*) Am Ornithologists.

Pattern of a Dependent Economy. Carey Jones. LC 77-157955. (Illus.). 162p. 1972. reprint ed. lib. bdg. 65.00 (*0-8371-6178-9*, CADE, Greenwood Pr) Greenwood.

Pattern of a Man & Other Stories. James Still. LC 76-45313. 1976. pap. 13.50 (*0-917788-01-X*) Gnomon Pr.

Pattern of African Decolonization: A New Interpretation. Warren Weinstein & John J. Grotpeter. LC 73-83839. (Foreign & Comparative Studies Program, Eastern Africa Ser.: No. 10). 123p. 1973. pap. 3.00 (*0-915984-07-5*) Syracuse U Foreign Comp.

Pattern of Baha'i Life. 3rd ed. Baha'u'llah et al. 64p. 1984. pap. 4.50 (*0-900125-15-2*, 315-030-10) Bahai.

***Pattern of Behavior: A Short Story Collection.** Paul Bishop. LC 00-30841. (Standard Print Mystery Ser.). 2000. write for info. (*0-7862-2670-6*) Five Star.

Pattern of Chinese History: Cycles, Development or Stagnation. Intro. by John T. Meskill. LC 82-18378. (Problems in Asian Civilizations Ser.). 108p. 1983. reprint ed. lib. bdg. 57.50 (*0-313-23739-5*, MEPC, Greenwood Pr) Greenwood.

Pattern of Christian Truth: A Study in the Relations Between Orthodoxy & Heresy in the Early Church. Henry E. Turner. LC 77-84707. (Bampton Lectures: 1954). 1977. reprint ed. 79.50 (*0-404-16114-6*) AMS Pr.

Pattern of Circles: An Ambassador's Story. John E. Dolibois. LC 89-8008. (Illus.). 333p. 1989. 26.00 (*0-87338-389-3*) Kent St U Pr.

Pattern of Consumer Debt, 1935-36: A Statistical Analysis. Blanche Bernstein. (Financial Research Program II: Studies in Consumer Installment Financing: No. 6). 256p. 1940. reprint ed. 66.60 (*0-87014-465-0*) Natl Bur Econ Res.

Pattern of Corporate Financial Structure: A Cross-Section View of Manufacturing, Mining, Trade, & Construction, 1937. Walter A. Chudson. (Financial Research Program III: Studies in Business Financing: No. 7). 165p. 1945. reprint ed. 42.90 (*0-87014-135-X*) Natl Bur Econ Res.

Pattern of Deceit. Emma Darcy. (Romance Ser.: No. 3085). 1990. per. 2.50 (*0-373-03085-1*) Harlequin Bks.

Pattern of Deceit. large type ed. Emma Darcy. 1990. reprint ed. lib. bdg. 18.95 (*0-263-12075-9*) Mac Lib Ref.

Pattern of Deceit: The Iran-Contra Affair. Malcolm Byrne. Date not set. pap. 55.00 (*0-8133-8175-4*); pap. 17.00 (*0-8133-8176-2*) Westview.

Pattern of Deception: The Media's Role in the Clinton Presidency. Tim Graham. 288p. (Orig.). 1996. pap. text 18.95 (*0-614-14027-7*) Media Res Ctr.

***Pattern of Evolution.** Niles Eldredge. (Illus.). 219p. 2000. pap. text 14.95 (*0-7167-3963-1*, Sci Am Lib) W H Freeman.

Pattern of Evolution. Eldredge Niles. LC 98-34754. 250p. 1998. text 24.95 (*0-7167-3046-4*) W H Freeman.

Pattern of Financial Asset Ownership, Wisconsin Individuals, 1949: A Study by the National Bureau of Economic Research, New York. Thomas R. Atkinson. LC 56-8387. 196p. 1956. reprint ed. pap. 60.80 (*0-608-02881-9*, 206394500007) Bks Demand.

Pattern of God's Truth. Frank E. Gaebelein. 1985. pap. 8.99 (*0-88469-170-5*) BMH Bks.

Pattern of Government Growth, 1800-1860. Oliver MacDonagh. (Modern Revivals in History Ser.). 368p. 1993. 69.95 (*0-7512-0165-0*, Pub. by Gregg Revivals) Ashgate Pub Co.

Pattern of Health. Aubrey T. Westlake. 1963. 16.95 (*0-8159-6514-1*) Devin.

Pattern of Human Concerns Data, 1957-1963. Hadley Cantril. 1977. write for info. (*0-89138-115-5*) ICPSR.

Pattern of Islands. large type ed. Arthur F. Grimble. 1965. 27.99 (*0-85456-840-9*) Ulverscroft.

Pattern of Land Ownership & Backwardness: A Study of 4 Villages in Jaunpur District of Eastern UP. Kripa Shankar. 1986. 12.50 (*81-7024-021-2*, Pub. by Ashish Pub Hse) S Asia.

Pattern of Landscape. Sylvia Crowe & Mary Mitchell. (Illus.). 176p. 1993. pap. 29.50 (*1-85341-020-9*, Pub. by Packard Pubng Ltd) Antique Collect.

Pattern of Life. 2nd ed. Alfred Adler. LC 81-71160. pap. 10.95 (*0-918560-28-4*) Adler Sch Prof Psy.

Pattern of Our Days: Liturgies & Resources For Worship. 2nd ed. Thomas F. O'Meara. Ed. by Kathy Galloway. LC 98-56177. 224p. 1999. pap. 13.95 (*0-8091-3860-3*) Paulist Pr.

Pattern of Prayer. William E. Sangster & Leslie Davison. 160p. (Orig.). 1988. pap. 6.95 (*0-310-51401-0*, 17189P) Zondervan.

Pattern of Redemption: The Theology of Hans Urs von Balthasar. Edward T. Oakes. LC 78-134827. 336p. 1997. pap. 24.95 (*0-8264-1011-1*) Continuum.

Pattern of Responsibility. Dean Acheson. Ed. by McGeorge Bundy. LC 75-128070. xxi, 309p. 1972. reprint ed. 45.00 (*0-678-03560-1*) Kelley.

Pattern of the Chinese Past. Mark Elvin. LC 72-78869. 346p. 1973. pap. 16.95 (*0-8047-0876-2*) Stanford U Pr.

Pattern of the Iliad. John T. Sheppard. LC 68-816. (Studies in Poetry: No. 38). 1969. reprint ed. lib. bdg. 75.00 (*0-8383-0622-5*) M S G Haskell Hse.

Pattern on Pattern: Spectacular Quilts from Simple Traditional Blocks. Ruth B. McDowell. LC 90-29178. (Illus.). 160p. 1991. pap. 24.95 (*0-8442-2631-9*, Quilt Dgst Pr) NTC Contemp Pub Co.

Pattern on the Stone: The Simple Ideas That Make Computers Work. Daniel Hillis. 176p. 1998. pap. 12.00 (*0-465-02596-X*, Pub. by Basic) HarpC.

Pattern-Oriented Software Arch. Frank Buschmann et al. LC 96-196873. 476p. 1996. 64.99 (*0-471-95869-7*) Wiley.

Pattern-Oriented Software Architecture. Buschmann. text. write for info. (*0-471-48907-7*) Wiley.

***Pattern-Oriented Software Architecture: Patterns for Concurrent & Distributed Objects.** Douglas C. Schmidt et al. 450p. 2000. 54.99 (*0-471-60695-2*) Wiley.

Pattern Play: Creating Your Own Quilts. Doreen Speckmann. Ed. by Joyce E. Lytle et al. LC 93-5633. (Illus.). 160p. (Orig.). 1995. pap. 24.95 (*0-914881-70-1*, 10082) C & T Pub.

Pattern Poetry: Guide to an Unknown Literature. Dick Higgins. LC 87-10199. 275p. (C). 1987. text 29.50 (*0-88706-413-2*) State U NY Pr.

Pattern, Price & Time: Using Gann Theory in Trading Systems. James A. Hyerczyk. LC 97-37322. (Trading Advantage Ser.). 320p. 1998. 59.95 (*0-471-25333-2*) Wiley.

Pattern Recognition. Ed. by J. Kittler. (Lecture Notes in Computer Science Ser.: Vol. 301). vii, 668p. 1988. pap. 83.00 (*0-387-19036-8*) Spr-Verlag.

Pattern Recognition. Sergios Theodoridis & Konstantinos Koutroumbas. LC 98-36062. (Illus.). 625p. 1998. boxed set 59.95 (*0-12-686140-4*) Acad Pr.

Pattern Recognition: Applications to Large Data-Set Problems. Sing-Tzo Bow. (Electrical Engineering & Electronics Ser.: Vol. 23). (Illus.). 336p. 1984. text 125.00 (*0-8247-7176-1*) Dekker.

Pattern Recognition: Architectures, Algorithms & Applications. Ed. by R. Plamondon et al. 396p. (C). 1991. text 104.00 (*981-02-0604-6*) World Scientific Pub.

Pattern Recognition: Human & Mechanical. Satosi Watanabe. LC 84-7354. 520p. 1985. 79.95 (*0-471-80815-6*) Wiley.

Pattern Recognition: Statistical, Structural, & Neural Approaches. Robert J. Schalkoff. LC 91-4751. 384p. (C). 1991. text 96.95 (*0-471-52974-5*) Wiley.

Pattern Recognition Analysis via Genetic Algorithms & Multivariate Statistical Methods. Barry K. Levine. (Fundamental & Applied Aspects of Chemometrics Ser.). 1999. 69.95 (*0-8493-7324-7*, 7324) CRC Pr.

Pattern Recognition & Image Analysis: Selected Papers from the 4th Spanish Symposium. N. P. De La Blanca & E. Vidal. (World Scientific Series on Machine Perception & Artificial I: No. 1). 400p. 1992. text 114.00 (*981-02-0881-2*) World Scientific Pub.

Pattern Recognition & Image Processing. F. Aminzadeh. (Handbook of Geophysical Exploration Ser.). 379p. 1986. 258.00 (*0-08-036955-3*, CRC Reprint) Franklin.

Pattern Recognition & Image Processing. Ed. by Sing-Tzo Bow. (Electrical Engineering & Electronics Ser.: Vol. 77). (Illus.). 580p. 1991. text 215.00 (*0-8247-8583-5*) Dekker.

***Pattern Recognition & Image Processing.** Daisheng Luo. 250p. 1999. pap. 45.00 (*1-898563-52-7*, Pub. by Horwood Pub) Paul & Co Pubs.

Pattern Recognition & Machine Learning. Yuichiro Anzai. (Illus.). 407p. 1992. text 94.00 (*0-12-058830-7*) Acad Pr.

Pattern Recognition & Neural Networks. Brian D. Ripley & N. L. Hjort. (Illus.). 415p. (C). 1996. text 57.95 (*0-521-46086-7*) Cambridge U Pr.

Pattern Recognition & Prediction: Application to Signal Characterization. David H. Kil & France B. Shin. (Modern Acoustic & Signal Processing Ser.). (Illus.). 400p. 1996. 60.00 (*1-56396-477-5*) Spr-Verlag.

Pattern Recognition & Signal Processing, No. 29. Ed. by C. H. Chen. (NATO Advanced Study Institute Ser.). 666p. 1978. text 162.50 (*90-286-0978-4*) Kluwer Academic.

Pattern Recognition Approach to Data Interpretation. Diane D. Wolff & Michael L. Parsons. 220p. 1983. 55.00 (*0-306-41302-7*, Plenum Trade) Perseus Pubng.

Pattern Recognition Basis of Artifical Intelligence. Donald Tveter. LC 97-32259. 1997. 46.00 (*0-8186-7796-1*) Inst Electrical.

Pattern Recognition by Man & Machine. Cronly-Dillon. 1991. 137.00 (*0-8493-7514-2*, QP474) CRC Pr.

Pattern Recognition by Self-Organizing Neural Networks. Ed. by Gail A. Carpenter & Stephen Grossberg. 650p. 1991. 65.00 (*0-262-03176-0*, Bradford Bks) MIT Pr.

***Pattern Recognition, Chemometrics & Imaging for Optical Environmental Monitoring.** Ed. by Khalid J. Siddiqui & Delyle Eastwood. 1999. pap. text 62.00 (*0-8194-3447-7*) SPIE.

Pattern Recognition Engineering. Morton Nadler & Eric P. Smith. LC 92-10636. 608p. 1993. 120.00 (*0-471-62293-1*) Wiley.

Pattern Recognition in Practice IV: Multiple Paradigms, Comparative Studies & Hybrid Systems: Proceedings of an International Workshop held in Vlieland, the Netherlands, 1-3 June 1994. Ed. by E. S. Gelsema & L. N. Kanal. LC 94-35056. (Machine Intelligence & Pattern Recognition Ser.: Vol. 16). 592p. 1994. 250.50 (*0-444-81892-8*) Elsevier.

Pattern Recognition, 1996 International Conference On, 4 vols., Set. LC 10-514651. 4000p. 1996. pap. 250.00 (*0-8186-7282-X*, PRO7282) IEEE Comp Soc.

Pattern Recognition, 1996 International Conference On, Vol. 1. LC 10-514651. 1,010p. 1996. pap. 180.00 (*0-8186-7270-6*, PRO7270) IEEE Comp Soc.

Pattern Recognition, 1996 International Conference On, Vol. 2. LC 10-514651. 1996. pap. 180.00 (*0-8186-7273-0*, PRO7273) IEEE Comp Soc.

Pattern Recognition, 1996 International Conference On, Vol. 3. LC 10-514651. 1996. pap. 180.00 (*0-8186-7276-5*, PRO7276) IEEE Comp Soc.

Pattern Recognition, 1996 International Conference On, Vol. 4. 13th ed. LC 10-514651. 820p. 1996. pap. 160.00 (*0-8186-7472-5*) IEEE Comp Soc.

Pattern Recognition Theory & Applications. Ed. by Pierre A. Devijver & J. Kittler. (NATO Asi Series F: Vol. 30). xi, 543p. 1987. 136.95 (*0-387-17700-0*) Spr-Verlag.

Pattern Recognition Using Neural Networks: Theory & Algorithms for Engineers & Scientists. Carl G. Looney. LC 96-29042. (Illus.). 480p. (C). 1997. text 84.00 (*0-19-507920-5*) OUP.

Pattern Recognition with Fuzzy Objective Function Algorithms. J. C. Bezdek. LC 81-4354. (Advanced Applications in Pattern Recognition Ser.). (Illus.). 272p. (C). 1981. text 79.50 (*0-306-40671-3*, Kluwer Plenum) Kluwer Academic.

Pattern Recognition with Neural Networks in C Plus Plus. Abhijit S. Pandya & Robert B. Macy. 432p. 1995. pap. 94.95 (*0-8493-9462-7*, 9462) CRC Pr.

Pattern Sentence: For Elementary Chinese. Vivian H. Lu et al. (CHI.). 1994. pap. 14.95 (*0-88710-182-8*) Yale Far Eastern Pubns.

Pattern Synthesis: Lectures in Pattern Recognition, Vol. 1. Ulf Grenander. LC 76-209. (Applied Mathematical Sciences Ser.: Vol. 18). 1976. 79.95 (*0-387-90174-4*) Spr-Verlag.

Pattern Thinking. L. Andrew Coward. LC 89-16377. 192p. 1990. 57.95 (*0-275-93427-6*, C3427, Greenwood Pr) Greenwood.

Pattern Trains & Hopscotch Paths: Exploring Pattern. Rebeka Eston & Karen Economopoulos. Ed. by Catherine Anderson & Beverly Cory. (Investigations in Number, Data, & Space Ser.). (Illus.). 126p. (J). (gr. k). 1997. pap. text 22.95 (*1-57232-927-0*, 47104) Seymour Pubns.

Pattern-Welded Blade. Jim Hrisoulas. (Illus.). 120p. 1994. text 39.95 (*0-87364-773-4*) Paladin Pr.

Pattern Words: 10 & 11 Letters in Length. Robert W. Wallace. 128p. (Orig.). 1993. pap. 20.80 (*0-89412-204-5*) Aegean Park Pr.

Pattern Words: 12 Letters & Greater in Length. Robert W. Wallace. 167p. (Orig.). 1993. pap. 20.80 (*0-89412-206-1*) Aegean Park Pr.

Pattern Words: 3 Letters to Eight Letters in Length. Sheila Carlisle. 140p. (Orig.). 1986. pap. 20.80 (*0-89412-135-9*) Aegean Park Pr.

Pattern Words: 9-Letters in Length. Sheila Carlisle. 167p. (Orig.). 1986. pap. 20.80 (*0-89412-146-4*) Aegean Park Pr.

Patterned Aimlessness: Iris Murdoch's Novels of the 1970s & 1980s. Barbara S. Heusel. LC 94-28260. 296p. 1995. 55.00 (*0-8203-1707-1*) U of Ga Pr.

Patterned Peatlands of Minnesota. Ed. by H. E. Wright, Jr. et al. (Illus.). 544p. (C). 1992. 44.95 (*0-8166-1917-4*) U of Minn Pr.

Patterning in Shakespearean Drama: Essays in Criticism. William L. Godshalk. LC 72-94504. (De Proprietatibus Litterarum, Ser. Practica: No. 69). 199p. 1973. pap. text 52.35 (*90-279-2472-4*) Mouton.

Patterning of Material Layers in Submicron Region. U. S. Tandon & W. S. Khokle. 183p. 1994. text 59.95 (*0-470-22063-5*) Halsted Pr.

Patterning of Material Layers in Submicron Region. U. S. Tandon & W. S. Khokle. 1993. write for info. (*81-224-0561-4*, Pub. by Wiley Estrn) Franklin.

Patterning of Time. Leonard W. Doob. LC 72-97346. 486p. reprint ed. pap. 150.70 (*0-608-11186-4*, 200754700063) Bks Demand.

Patterning Science & Technology II & Interconnection & Contact Metallization for ULSI. Ed. by W. Greene et al. LC 92-71002. (Proceedings Ser.: Vol. 92-6). 392p. 1992. 43.00 (*1-56677-007-6*) Electrochem Soc.

Patternmaker's Manual. 320p. 1986. 120.00 (*0-87433-069-6*, PM8600) Am Foundrymen.

Patternmaking. 108p. 1982. pap. 52.00 (*0-317-59857-0*, TE8200) Am Foundrymen.

Patternmaking. 2nd ed. Helen J. Armstrong. (C). 1997. 63.67 (*0-06-501789-7*) Addson-Wesley Educ.

Patternmaking for Fashion Design. 2nd ed. Ed. by Armstrong. 814p. (C). 1997. reprint ed. 80.00 (*0-673-98026-X*) Addison-Wesley.

Patternmaking for Fashion Design. 3rd ed. Helen J. Armstrong. LC 99-43802. 821p. (C). 1999. 67.00 (*0-321-03423-6*, Prentice Hall) P-H.

Patternmaking For Fashion Design. 3rd ed. Helen J. Armstrong. (C). 2000. text. write for info. (*0-321-03424-4*) Addson-Wesley Educ.

Patternmaking Guide. 2nd ed. 416p. 1990. 120.00 (*0-87433-120-X*, PM9000) Am Foundrymen.

Patternmaster. Octavia E. Butler. 208p. 1995. reprint ed. mass mkt. 6.50 (*0-446-36281-6*, Pub. by Warner Bks) Little.

Patterns see Mortimer's Math

Patterns see Discovering Shapes

Patterns. (Let's Look Ser.). (Illus.). 20p. (J). (ps). 1997. 3.95 (*1-85967-521-2*, Lorenz Bks) Anness Pub.

Patterns. Samantha Berger & Daniel Moreton. LC 98-54212. (Learning Center Emergent Readers Ser.). 1998. 2.50 (*0-439-04599-1*) Scholastic Inc.

P

Patterns. Ivan Bulloch et al. LC 96-49559. (Action Math Ser.). (Illus.). 32p. (J). (gr. k-3). 1997. write for info. (*0-7166-4902-0*) World Bk.

***Patterns.** Pat Cadigan. LC 98-32220. 1999. pap. 13.95 (*0-312-86837-5*) St Martin.

Patterns. Terrence G. Coburn et al. LC 92-44142. (Curriculum & Evaluation Standards for School Mathematics Addenda Ser.: Grades K-6). (Illus.). 53p. 1993. pap. 13.95 (*0-87353-320-8*) NCTM.

Patterns, 4 vols. Conlin. (C). 1993. pap., teacher ed. 3.56 (*0-395-59344-1*) HM.

Patterns. Conlin. (C). 1993. pap., teacher ed. 60.76 (*0-395-68150-2*) HM.

Patterns. Joan Hamilton. 48p. pap., teacher ed. 5.95 (*0-8192-5115-1*, 1370) Morehouse Pub.

Patterns. Susan Brecht Hibbard. 1995. 3.95 (*1-55708-474-2*, MCT1005) McDonald Pub Co.

Patterns. David Kirkby. LC 95-20596. (Math Live Ser.). (Illus.). (J). 1998. 19.92 (*1-57572-043-4*); (*1-57572-003-5*) Heinemann Lib.

Patterns. Federico Mayor et al. Tr. by Rosemary Wiltshire et al from SPA. LC 93-74145. 95p. 1994. pap. 14.95 (*1-85610-034-0*, Pub. by Forest Bks) Dufour.

Patterns. Brenda Parkes. Ed. by Jennifer Mooney. (Newbridge Links Ser.). 8p. (J). (gr. k up). 1997. pap. 2.75 (*1-56784-908-3*) Newbridge Educ.

Patterns. Peter Patilla. LC 99-24955. (Math Links Ser.). 32p. (J). (gr. k-2). 1999. lib. bdg. 13.95 (*1-57572-967-9*) Heinemann Lib.

***Patterns.** rev. ed. Ivan Bulloch. (Action Math Ser.). (Illus.). (J). 2000. pap. 4.95 (*1-58728-053-1*) Two Can Pub.

Patterns, 4 vols. 4th ed. Conlin. LC 93-78632. (C). 1993. pap. text 30.36 (*0-395-59343-3*) HM.

Patterns, 5 vols. 5th ed. Conlin. (C). 1997. pap. text 30.36 (*0-395-86843-2*) HM.

Patterns, Level 3, Bk. B. Jo M. Stanchfield. LC 77-83336. (Vistas Ser.). (Illus.). (YA). (gr. 9). 1979. 5.08 (*0-685-02303-6*) HM.

Patterns, Vol. 2658. Ed. by Janet Bruno. (Child-Centered Math Ser.: Vol. 8). (Illus.). 80p. 1997. pap. 4.98 (*1-57471-241-1*, 2658) Creat Teach Pr.

***Patterns: A Manual of Club Passing.** 2nd ed. Richard Dingman. LC 99-31734. 1999. pap. 34.95 (*0-917643-11-9*) B Dube.

Patterns: A Short Prose Reader, 4 vols. 4th ed. Mary L. Conlin. (C). 1993. pap. text, teacher ed. 31.56 (*0-395-68425-0*) HM.

***Patterns: Cutwork Embroidery.** Ed. by Jules Kliot & Kaethe Kliot. (Illus.). 96p. (Orig.). 1999. pap. 16.00 (*1-891656-15-5*, LE71) Lacis Pubns.

***Patterns: Embroidery Early 16th Century.** Claude Hourry. (FRE., Illus.). 144p. (Orig.). 1999. pap. 20.00 (*1-891656-16-3*, LE72) Lacis Pubns.

Patterns: Fit-a-Shape. (Fit-A-Shape Ser.). (Illus.). 10p. (J). 1998. bds. 5.95 (*1-56138-798-3*) Running Pr.

Patterns: Personality Expressions of an Evolving Consciousness. A. La Lansun, pseud. (Solar Ser.: Bk. II). Date not set. pap. write for info. (*0-935861-01-7*) Solarium Analy.

Patterns: Poems of Form & Substance - An Exercise in Experimentation or Obfuscation, a Work in Progress. Roberta Mendel. (Chameleon Ser.). 1997. pap. 10.00 (*0-936424-22-2*, 014) Pin Prick.

Patterns: Sewing for a New Class. Carol Parks. Date not set. 3.75 (*0-8069-5966-5*) Sterling.

***Patterns: Sewing for the Apparel Industry.** Shaeffer. 10p. 2000. write for info. (*0-13-027074-1*) P-H.

Patterns Across Spoken & Written French: Empirical Research on the Interaction among Forms, Function, & Genres. Nadine O'Connor Di Vito. LC 96-76941. (FRE.). 256p. (C). 1997. pap. text 35.96 (*0-669-35173-3*) HM Trade Div.

Patterns All Around. Margie Burton et al. Ed. by Susan Evento. (Early Connections Ser.). 16p. (J). (gr. k-2). 1998. pap. text 4.25 (*1-892393-33-6*) Benchmark Educ.

Patterns All Around Me, Vol. 4471. Trisha Callella-Jones. Ed. by Joel Kupperstein. (Learn to Read Math Ser.). (Illus.). 16p. (J). 1998. pap. 2.75 (*1-57471-378-7*, 4471) Creat Teach Pr.

Patterns & Carving Tips for Santas, Snowmen, & More. Ron Ransom. LC 97-80065. (Schiffer Book for Woodcarvers Ser.). (Illus.). 64p. 1997. pap. 14.95 (*0-7643-0361-9*) Schiffer.

Patterns & Ceremonials of the Indians of the Southwest. unabridged ed. Ira Moskowitz & John Collier. LC 95-6513. (Illus.). 192p. 1995. reprint ed. pap. text 14.95 (*0-486-28692-4*) Dover.

Patterns & Coincidences: A Sequel to "All Is But a Beginning" John G. Neihardt. LC 77-24199. x, 123p. 1978. text 20.00 (*0-8032-3312-4*) U of Nebr Pr.

Patterns & Configurations in Finite Spaces. S. Vajda. (Griffin's Statistical Monographs: No. 22). 120p. 1967. pap. 25.00 (*0-85264-025-0*) Lubrecht & Cramer.

Patterns & Designs from the '20's in Color. Ad Verneuil. (Illus.). 32p. 1993. pap. 6.95 (*0-486-27690-2*) Dover.

Patterns & Dynamics in Reactive Media. Harry L. Swinney. Ed. by A. Friedman et al. (IMA Volumes in Mathematics & Its Applications Ser.: Vol. 37). (Illus.). xiii, 206p. 1991. 57.95 (*0-387-97671-X*) Spr-Verlag.

Patterns & Evolutionary Significance of Geographic Variation in the "shistacea" Group of the Fox Sparrow (Passerella iliaca) Robert M. Zink. (Ornithological Monographs: Vol. 40). (Illus.). 119p. 1986. pap. 5.00 (*0-943610-50-8*) Am Ornithologists.

***Patterns & Experiments in Developmental Biology.** 2nd ed. (C). 2000. pap., student ed. 43.75 (*0-07-241691-2*) McGrw-H Hghr Educ.

Patterns & Experiments in Developmental Biology. 2nd ed. Leland G. Johnson & E. Peter Volpe. 180p. (C). 1995. text. write for info. (*0-697-12303-0*, WCB McGr Hill) McGrw-H Hghr Educ.

***Patterns & Forms in God's Word That Illustrate Divine Truth.** B. R. Hicks. (Illus.). 1999. mass mkt. 5.95 (*1-58363-090-2*, RF2608) Christ Gospel.

Patterns & Functions. Elizabeth Phillips et al. Ed. by Frances R. Curcio. LC 91-18820. (Curriculum & Evaluation Standards for School Mathematics Addenda Ser.: Grades 5-8). (Illus.). 72p. 1991. pap. 15.95 (*0-87353-324-0*) NCTM.

Patterns & Functions: A "Hands On" Approach to Teaching... Natalie Hernandez et al. (Hands on Approach Ser.). (Illus.). 200p. 1991. teacher ed. 17.95 (*0-927726-05-X*) Hands On CA.

Patterns & Instructions for a Child's Quiet Book. Joanne Harlow. (J). 6.95 (*1-55517-113-3*) CFI Dist.

Patterns & Instructions for a Child's Quiet Book. Joanne Harlow. 27p. 1977. pap. 3.49 (*0-317-03553-3*) CFI Dist.

Patterns & Instructions for Carving Authentic Birds. H. D. Green. (Illus.). 64p. (Orig.). 1982. pap. 4.95 (*0-486-24222-6*) Dover.

Patterns & Meanings: Using Corpora for English Language Research & Teaching. Alan Partington. LC 98-36312. (Studies in Corpus Linguistics: Vol. 2). x, 158p. 1998. pap. 24.95 (*1-55619-396-3*) J Benjamins Pubng Co.

Patterns & Meanings: Using Corpora for English Language Research & Teaching. Alan Partington. LC 98-36312. (Studies in Corpus Linguistics: Vol. 2). x, 158p. 1998. 50.00 (*1-55619-343-2*) J Benjamins Pubng Co.

Patterns & Options for Managing Information Technology on Campus. Anne Woodsworth. LC 90-878. 89p. (C). 1991. pap. text 25.00 (*0-8389-0546-3*, 0546-3) ALA.

Patterns & Patchwork: Mountain Dulcimer Fingerpicking Made Easy. Sue Carpenter. LC 91-91870. (Illus.). 152p. (Orig.). 1991. pap. 20.00 (*0-9629028-0-2*) S Carpenter.

Patterns & Pathways. Marilynn M. Moe. 88p. 1994. 11.95 (*1-884816-02-9*) M M Moe.

***Patterns & Perspectives: Vol. 1 Through Reconstruction.** 7th ed. Francis G. Couvares. (Interpretations of American History Ser.). 448p. 2000. 17.95 (*0-684-86773-7*) Free Pr.

***Patterns & Perspectives: Vol. 2 from Reconstruction, Vol. 2.** 7th ed. Francis G. Couvares. (Interpretations of American History Ser.). 464p. 2000. 17.95 (*0-684-87118-1*) Free Pr.

Patterns & Perspectives in English Renaissance Drama. Eugene M. Waith. LC 86-40608. (Illus.). 312p. 1988. 40.00 (*0-87413-325-4*) U Delaware Pr.

Patterns & Perspectives in Iowa History. Ed. by Dorothy Schwieder. LC 73-928. 488p. reprint ed. pap. 151.30 (*0-608-15340-0*, 202962600061) Bks Demand.

Patterns & Pictures: Poetry for Junior Students. Hamilton & Colvin. 1991. pap. text. write for info. (*0-582-86967-6*, Pub. by Addison-Wesley) Longman.

Patterns & Pieces. rev. ed. Ed. by Luane Cole. (Illus.). 392p. 1999. write for info. (*0-9672297-1-5*); pap. write for info. (*0-9672297-0-7*) Lyme Historians.

Patterns & Poetry: No Robes from the Lucy Truman Aldrich Collection. Ed. by Susan A. Hay. LC 92-53595. (Illus.). 190p. 1992. 45.00 (*0-911517-60-X*) Mus of Art RI.

Patterns & Poetry: No-Robes from the Lucy Truman Aldrich Collection at the Museum of Art, Rhode Island School of Design. Museum of Art, Rhode Island School Staff. (Illus.). 192p. 1993. pap. 45.00 (*1-55859-641-0*) Abbeville Pr.

Patterns & Policies, 1996: The Changing. (C). 1996. mass mkt. 25.95 (*0-8384-5732-0*) Heinle & Heinle.

***Patterns & Portraits: Women in the History of the Reformed Church in America.** Renee S. House. (Historical Series of the Reformed Church in America). 1999. pap. 14.00 (*0-8028-4705-6*) Eerdmans.

Patterns & Possibilities: Exploring Religious Education in the Catholic Secondary School. James L. Heft. Ed. by Mary F. Taymans. 63p. 1997. pap. 16.00 (*1-55833-188-3*) Natl Cath Educ.

Patterns & Practice in Chinese Medicine. Li Xuemei & Zhao Jingyi. LC 97-61504. (Illus.). 225p. (C). 1998. 45.00 (*0-939616-27-0*) Eastland.

Patterns & Processes: An Introduction to Anthropological Strategies for the Study of Sociocultural Change. Robert L. Bee. LC 73-10791. (C). 1974. pap. 17.95 (*0-02-902090-5*) Free Pr.

Patterns & Processes in Stream Ecology: A Synoptic Review of Hong Kong Running Waters. David Dudgeon. (Binnengewaesser Ser.: Band XXIX). (Illus.). viii, 150p. 1992. 56.00 (*3-510-40040-2*, Pub. by E Schweizerbartsche) Balogh.

Patterns & Processes in Stream Ecology: A Synoptic Review of Hong Kong Running Waters. David Dudgeon. (Binnengewaesser Ser.: Vol. 29). (Illus.). 147p. 1992. lib. bdg. 62.50 (*0-685-67203-4*) Lubrecht & Cramer.

Patterns & Processes of Vertebrate Evolution. Robert L. Carroll. LC 96-44161. (Cambridge Paleobiology Ser.: No. 2). (Illus.). 528p. (C). 1997. text 85.00 (*0-521-47232-6*); pap. text 39.95 (*0-521-47809-X*) Cambridge U Pr.

Patterns & Projects for the Scroll Saw. John A. Nelson & Joyce C. Nelson. LC 90-44284. 224p. (Orig.). 1991. pap. 14.95 (*0-8117-3040-9*) Stackpole.

Patterns & Prospects of Development in Downtown Kearney. Center for Applied Urban Research Staff. 100p. (Orig.). 1982. pap. 6.00 (*1-55719-059-3*) U NE CPAR.

***Patterns & Reasoning.** Carol Greenes. (Illus.). (J). (gr. 3). 1999. pap. 12.95 (*0-7690-0017-7*) Seymour Pubns.

Patterns & Relationships: Answer Key. Jocelyn Walton & Cheryl Klein. 98p. 1995. text, teacher ed. 19.95 (*1-886292-17-5*) CEO Sftware.

Patterns & Relationships Bk. 3: Series E. Jocelyn C. Walton & Sheryl Klein. 98p. (J). (gr. 7-10). 1995. text, wbk. ed. 19.95 (*1-886292-10-8*) CEO Sftware.

Patterns & Results of the 3rd Democratization Wave. Yong-chuan Liu. 142p. (C). 1993. lib. bdg. 39.50 (*0-8191-9124-8*) U Pr of Amer.

Patterns & Site of Adenosine Triphosphate Catabolism in Lung Tissue. P. De Leyn. No. 67. 114p. (Orig.). 1993. pap. 47.50 (*90-6186-550-6*, Pub. by Leuven Univ) Coronet Bks.

Patterns & Sources of Navajo Weaving. 14.95 (*0-9601322-2-8*) Harmsen.

Patterns & Sources of Navajo Weaving. Bill Harmsen. 1981. 18.95 (*0-9601322-9-5*) Harmsen.

Patterns & Sources of Zuni Kachinas. Mary Morgan. 1989. 49.95 (*0-9601322-4-4*) Harmsen.

Patterns & Themes. 4th ed. Glenn C. Rogers. LC 99-16860. 1999. pap. 21.95 (*0-534-26190-6*) Wadsworth Pub.

Patterns & Themes: A Basic English Reader. Judy R. Rogers & Glenn C. Rogers. xi, 228p. (C). 1985. mass mkt. write for info. (*0-534-03348-2*) Wadsworth Pub.

Patterns & Themes: A Basic English Reader. 2nd ed. Judy R. Rogers & Glenn C. Rogers. 267p. (C). 1988. mass mkt. write for info. (*0-534-08832-5*) Wadsworth Pub.

Patterns & Themes: A Basic English Reader. 3rd ed. Judy R. Rogers & Glenn C. Rogers. 240p. (C). 1992. pap. 24.50 (*0-534-17988-6*) Wadsworth Pub.

Patterns & Themes in Indian Politics. Biplab Dasgupta & W. H. Morris-Jones. 364p. 1975. 16.95 (*0-318-36596-0*) Asia Bk Corp.

Patterns & Waves: The Theory & Applications of Reaction-Diffusion Equations. Peter Grindrod. (Oxford Applied Mathematics & Computing Science Ser.). (Illus.). 256p. 1991. 79.00 (*0-19-859676-6*) OUP.

Patterns, Defects & Materials Instabilities. Ed. by D. Walgraef & N. M. Ghoniem. (C). 1990. text 201.00 (*0-7923-0753-4*) Kluwer Academic.

Patterns, Defects & Microstructures in Nonequilibrium Systems: Applications in Materials Science. Ed. by D. Walgraef. 1987. text 218.00 (*90-247-3479-7*) Kluwer Academic.

Patterns Everywhere: Big Book. Kari J. Gold. Ed. by Janet Reed. (Early Learning Program Ser.). (Illus.). 16p. (J). (ps-1). 1996. pap. 16.95 (*1-56784-306-9*) Newbridge Educ.

Patterns Everywhere: Mini-Book. Kari J. Gold. Ed. by Janet Reed. (Early Learning Program Ser.). (Illus.). 16p. (J). (ps-1). 1996. pap. 3.16 (*1-56784-331-X*) Newbridge Educ.

Patterns for a Purpose. Clouse. 1994. 20.93 (*0-07-011426-9*) McGraw.

Patterns for a Purpose. Barbara F. Clouse. LC 94-13172. 512p. (C). 1994. pap. 31.75 (*0-07-011419-6*) McGraw.

Patterns for a Purpose: A Rhetorical Reader. 2nd ed. Barbara F. Clouse. LC 98-2964. 752p. 1998. pap. 30.75 (*0-07-011980-5*) McGraw.

Patterns for America: Modernism & the Concept of Culture. Susan Hegeman. LC 98-37761. 11p. 1999. 55.00 (*0-691-00133-2*, Pub. by Princeton U Pr) Cal Prin Full Svc.

***Patterns for College Writing.** 7th ed. Kirszner & Mandell. 1999. pap. text 36.95 (*0-312-25581-0*) St Martin.

***Patterns for College Writing.** 8th ed. Kirszner & Mandell. 2000. pap. text. write for info. (*0-312-24736-2*) St Martin.

Patterns for College Writing: Instructor's Edition. 7th ed. Laurie G. Kirszner & Stephen R. Mandell. 1997. pap. text, teacher ed. 30.65 (*0-312-15086-5*) St Martin.

Patterns for Every Purpose: How to Adapt a Pattern for Use in a Variety of Crafts. Josephine Kershner-Veal. 1999. pap. 7.95 (*1-881982-11-4*) Stackpole.

Patterns for Fun, Bk. 1. Paul Sheftel & Vera Wills. 32p. 1990. pap. 6.95 (*0-7390-0500-6*, 10147) Alfred Pub.

Patterns for Guernseys, Jerseys & Arans: Fisherman's Sweaters from the British. Gladys Thompson. (Illus.). 171p. 1971. reprint ed. pap. 9.95 (*0-486-22703-0*) Dover.

Patterns for Holiday Games. 1987. 4.00 (*0-939418-48-7*) Ferguson-Florissant.

Patterns for Jazz - Treble Cleff. 176p. (YA). 1982. pap. 24.95 (*0-89898-703-2*, SB1) Wrner Bros.

Patterns for Lifelong Learning. Theodore M. Hesburgh et al. LC 73-10936. (Jossey-Bass Series in Higher Education). 155p. reprint ed. pap. 48.10 (*0-8357-4947-9*, 203787800009) Bks Demand.

Patterns for Living: From the Old Testament. A. L. Gill & Joyce Gill. (RUS.). 110p. (Orig.). 1994. spiral bd. 12.95 (*0-941975-28-2*) Powerhouse.

Patterns for Living: From the Old Testament. A. L. Gill & Joyce Gill. LC 97-148143. 112p. (Orig.). 1996. reprint ed. pap. 9.95 (*0-941975-39-8*) Powerhouse.

***Patterns for Living: Through the Old Testament.** Tr. of Padroes de Vida. (POR.). 117p. 1999. spiral bd. 12.95 (*0-941975-53-3*) Powerhouse.

Patterns for Manipulatives: Basic Skills - Grades K-3. Joanie Campbell et al. Ed. by Kathy Rogers. (Illus.). 192p. 1995. pap., wbk. ed. 15.95 (*1-56472-065-9*) Edupress Inc.

***Patterns for Memory Challenged Systems.** James Noble. (C). 2000. pap. text. write for info. (*0-201-59607-5*) Addison-Wesley.

Patterns for Practical Communications: Composition Package. Doris C. Weddington. 1977. teacher ed. 17.00 (*0-13-653865-7*) P-H.

Patterns for Practical Communications: Script Composition. Doris C. Weddington. 1977. pap. text 18.75 (*0-13-653840-1*) P-H.

Patterns for Practical Communications: Sentence Package. Doris C. Weddington. 1977. text 375.00 (*0-13-653790-1*) P-H.

Patterns for Prayer: 52 Weeks of Prayer Ideas. 380p. 1995. spiral bd. 11.45 (*1-56212-104-9*, 1940-0450) CRC Pubns.

Patterns for Profit. 2nd ed. Sherman McClellan & Marian McClellan. 54p. 1989. reprint ed. pap. 50.00 (*1-879192-07-1*) Fndtn Study Cycles.

Patterns for Quilting. Linda Macho. 80p. 1984. pap. 6.95 (*0-486-24632-9*) Dover.

Patterns for Self-Unfoldment. Randolph Schmelig & Leddy Schmelig. LC 74-29429. 302p. 1975. 3.48 (*0-87159-127-8*) Unity Bks.

Patterns for Success: Taking the Mystery Out of Basic Composition. Rosaline L. Fung & Raymond F. Pike. 387p. 1997. spiral bd. 29.95 (*1-890756-07-5*, 36122-1) VisionKeeper.

Patterns for Success: Taking the Mystery Out of Writing Sentences, Bk. 1. Rosaline L. Fung. 178p. (C). 1997. wbk. ed. 19.95 (*1-890756-02-4*, 36120-1) VisionKeeper.

Patterns for Success: Taking the Mystery Out of Writing Sentences, Bk. 2. Rosaline L. Fung. 203p. (C). 1997. wbk. ed. 19.95 (*1-890756-03-2*, 36120-2) VisionKeeper.

Patterns for Success: Taking the Mystery Out of Writing Sentences, Bk. 3. Rosaline L. Fung. 201p. (C). 1997. wbk. ed. 19.95 (*1-890756-04-0*, 36120-3) VisionKeeper.

Patterns for Success: Taking the Mystery Out of Writing Sentences, Bk. 4. Rosaline L. Fung. 167p. (C). 1997. wbk. ed. 19.95 (*1-890756-05-9*, 36120-4) VisionKeeper.

Patterns for Success Taking the Mystern Out of the Paragraph. Rosaline L. Fung & Raymond F. Pike. (Illus.). xiv, 225p. 1998. pap. 24.99 (*1-890756-09-1*) VisionKeeper.

Patterns for Success Taking the Mystery Out of the Basic Essay. Rosaline L. Fung & Raymond F. Pike. (Illus.). xii, 181p. 1998. pap. 24.95 (*1-890756-12-1*) VisionKeeper.

Patterns for Teacher-Made Games. 1980. 6.00 (*0-939418-01-0*) Ferguson-Florissant.

Patterns for Theatrical Costumes: Trims, Garment & Accessories from Ancient Egypt to 1915. Katherine S. Holkeboer. (Illus.). 352p. 1993. pap. 29.95 (*0-89676-125-8*, Costume & Fashion Pr) QSMG Ltd.

Patterns for Uncertainty? Planning for the Greater Medical Profession. Ed. by Gordon McLachlan et al. 1979. pap. 14.95 (*0-19-721223-9*) OUP.

Patterns for Wood Carving. Harold L. Enlow. 53p. 1981. pap. 5.50 (*1-882475-04-6*) Enlow Wood Carv.

Patterns for World Cultures. Marilynn Barr. (Illus.). 128p. (Orig.). 1995. pap., teacher ed. 12.95 (*1-878279-76-9*, MM1997) Monday Morning Bks.

Pattern's Foundations of Embryology. 5th ed. Bruce M. Carlson. (C). 1988. text 77.25 (*0-07-009902-2*) McGraw.

Patterns from Finished Clothes: Re-Creating the Clothes You Love. Tracy Doyle. LC 95-46185. (Illus.). 128p. 1996. 27.95 (*0-8069-4874-4*) Sterling.

Patterns from Finished Clothes: Re-Creating the Clothes You Love. Tracy Doyle. (Illus.). 128p. 1997. pap. 14.95 (*0-8069-4875-2*) Sterling.

Patterns from the Sod. Margaret B. Bogue. Ed. by Stuart Bruchey. LC 78-56691. (Management of Public Lands in the U. S. Ser.). (Illus.). 1979. reprint ed. lib. bdg. 26.95 (*0-405-11318-8*) Ayer.

Patterns Handbook: Techniques, Strategies & Applications. Ed. by Linda Rising. (SIGS Reference Library: No. 13). 570p. 1998. pap. 44.95 (*0-521-64818-1*) Cambridge U Pr.

Patterns, Hatches, Tactics, & Trout. Charles R. Meck. LC 95-12008. (Illus.). 350p. 1995. 24.95 (*1-55629-050-0*) Vivid Pub.

Patterns in a Revolution: French Printed Textiles, 1759-1821. Anita Jones. LC 90-70960. (Illus.). 36p. (Orig.). 1990. pap. text 8.00 (*0-915577-20-8*) Taft Museum.

Patterns in Biology: Continuity & Change. Fung & Hambur. 1992. pap. text. write for info. (*0-582-66393-8*, Pub. by Addison-Wesley) Longman.

Patterns in Biology: Continuity & Change. Fung & Hamur. 1992. pap. text. write for info. (*0-582-87648-6*, Pub. by Addison-Wesley) Longman.

Patterns in California Government Revenues since Proposition 13. Michael A. Shires. LC 98-56056. (Illus.). xxvii,111p. 1999. pap. 12.00 (*1-58213-006-X*) Pub Policy Inst.

***Patterns in China's Use of Force: Evidence from History & Doctrinal Writings.** Mark Burles & Abram N. Shulsky. LC 99-88091. xv, 106p. (C). 2000. pap. 12.00 (*0-8330-2804-9*, MR-1060-AF) Rand Corp.

Patterns in Comparative Religion. Mircea Eliade. Tr. by Rosemary Sheed. LC 96-30394. xxi, 486p. 1996. pap. 17.95 (*0-8032-6733-9*, Bison Books) U of Nebr Pr.

Patterns in Criminal Homicide. Marvin E. Wolfgang. LC 74-34157. (Criminology, Law Enforcement, & Social Problems Ser.: No. 211). 413p. 1975. 35.00 (*0-87585-211-4*) Patterson Smith.

Patterns in Crystals. Noel F. Kennon. LC 78-4531. 207p. reprint ed. pap. 64.20 (*0-608-17545-5*, 203052400069) Bks Demand.

Patterns in Family Violence. Ed. by Margaret Elbow. LC 80-52785. (Social Casework Reprint Ser.). 148p. reprint ed. pap. 45.90 (*0-608-13788-X*, 202038300017) Bks Demand.

Patterns in Forcible Rape. Menachem Amir. LC 79-14022. (C). 1971. lib. bdg. 35.00 (*0-226-01734-6*) U Ch Pr.

Patterns in Forcible Rape. Menachem Amir. LC 79-140222. 404p. reprint ed. pap. 125.30 (*0-608-08041-1*, 206900600002) Bks Demand.

Patterns in Freshwater Fish Ecology. William J. Matthews. LC 97-21339. 784p. 1998. write for info. (*0-412-02831-X*) Kluwer Academic.

Patterns in Fungal Development. Ed. by Siu W. Chiu & David Moore. 238p. 1996. text 59.95 (*0-521-56047-0*) Cambridge U Pr.

P

An Asterisk (*) at the beginning of an entry indicates that the title is appearing for the first time.

Patterns in Human Needs. Vincent W. Kafka. 12p. 1986. pap. 3.95 (*0-913261-16-5*) Effect Learn Sys.
Patterns in Ibsen's Middle Plays. Richard Hornby. LC 80-67969. 192p. 1981. 29.50 (*0-8387-5014-1*) Bucknell U Pr.
Patterns in Industrial Buying Behavior. Wesley J. Johnson. LC 81-10745. 197p. 1981. 49.95 (*0-275-90656-6*, C0656, Praeger Pubs) Greenwood.
Patterns in Interior Environments: Perception, Psychology, & Practice. Patricia Rodemann. LC 98-33560. 272p. 1999. 49.95 (*0-471-24162-8*) Wiley.
Patterns in Java, Vol. 2. Mark Grand. (Patterns in Java Ser.). (Illus.). 368p. 1999. pap. 49.99 incl. cd-rom, audio compact disk (*0-471-25841-5*) Wiley.
***Patterns in Java, Vol. 3.** Grand. 416p. 2000. pap. text 49.99 incl. cd-rom (*0-471-33315-8*) Wiley.
***Patterns in Java Vol. 1: A Catalog of Reusable Design Patterns Illustrated with UML.** Mark Grand. LC 98-29976. (Patterns in Java Ser.). 480p. 1998. pap. 49.99 incl. cd-rom (*0-471-25839-3*) Wiley.
Patterns in Language: An Introduction to Language & Literary Style. Joanna Thornborrow & Shan Wareing. LC 97-23795. (Interface Ser.). (Illus.). 280p. (C). 1998. 65.00 (*0-415-14063-3*); pap. 20.99 (*0-415-14064-1*) Routledge.
Patterns in Late Medici Art Patronage. Edward L. Goldberg. LC 83-42561. (Illus.). 472p. 1983. reprint ed. pap. 146.40 (*0-7837-8588-7*, 204940300011) Bks Demand.
***Patterns in Life.** Mary Ann Costantini. LC 00-102665. 112p. 2000. 16.95 (*1-56167-612-8*) Noble Hse MD.
Patterns in Magical Christianity. Nicholas Whitehead. (Illus.). 192p. (Orig.). 1996. pap. 12.95 (*0-9650839-7-7*) Sun Chalice.
***Patterns in Mathematics.** 584p. (C). 2000. text 60.00 (*0-536-60238-7*) Pearson Custom.
Patterns in My Head see Como Pienso Patrones!
Patterns in My Head. Karen M. Rogers. LC 98-71334. (Think-Kids Book Collection). (Illus.). 16p. (J). (gr. 1-4). 1998. pap. 2.95 (*1-58237-019-2*) Creat Think.
Patterns in Oral Literature. Ed. by Heda Jason & Dimitri Segal. (World Anthropology Ser.). xii, 334p. 1977. text 43.10 (*90-279-7969-3*) Mouton.
Patterns in Plant Development. 2nd ed. Taylor A. Steeves & Ian M. Sussex. (Illus.). 408p. 1989. text 74.95 (*0-521-24688-1*); pap. text 30.95 (*0-521-28895-9*) Cambridge U Pr.
Patterns in Plato's Thought. Ed. by Julius M. Moravcsik. LC 73-83566. (Synthese Historical Library: No. 6). 220p. 1973. text 126.50 (*90-277-0286-1*, D Reidel) Kluwer Academic.
Patterns in Play: A Model for Text Setting in the Early French Songs of Guillaume Dufay. Graeme M. Boone. LC 98-14767. (American Musicological Society Monographs). (Illus.). 466p. 1998. text 75.00 (*0-8032-1235-6*) U of Nebr Pr.
Patterns in Pluralism: A Portrait of American Religion, 1952-1971. William M. Newman & Peter L. Halvorson. LC 79-55177. 1980. pap. 5.00 (*0-914422-10-3*) Glenmary Res Ctr.
Patterns in Practice: Selections from the Journal of Museum Education. Pref. by Susan K. Nichols. LC 91-66484. 391p. (Orig.). 1992. pap. 35.00 (*1-880437-00-7*) Mus Ed Round.
Patterns in Prehistory: Humankind's First Three Million Years. 4th ed. Robert J. Wenke. LC 95-43456. (Illus.). 720p. (C). 1999. pap. text 45.00 (*0-19-508572-8*) OUP.
Patterns in Protein Sequence & Structure. Ed. by W. R. Taylor & Peter M. Bayley. (Biophysics Ser.: Vol. 7). (Illus.). xii, 262p. 1992. 123.95 (*0-387-54043-1*) Spr-Verlag.
Patterns in Spelling Bk. 1: Patterns with Other Vowel Sounds. 1993. 9.00 (*0-88336-106-X*); teacher ed. 9.95 (*0-88336-107-8*); 0.40 (*0-88336-133-7*) New Readers.
Patterns in Spelling Bk. 1: Patterns with Short Vowels. 1993. 9.00 (*0-88336-100-0*); teacher ed. 9.95 (*0-88336-127-2*); teacher ed. 1.20 (*0-88336-128-0*); student ed. 1.20 (*0-88336-108-6*); 0.40 (*0-88336-130-2*) New Readers.
Patterns in Spelling Bk. 2: Patterns with Long Vowels. 1993. 9.00 (*0-88336-102-7*); teacher ed. 9.95 (*0-88336-103-5*); 0.40 (*0-88336-131-0*) New Readers.
Patterns in Spelling Bk. 3: Patterns with Consonant Blends & Diagraphs. 1993. 9.00 (*0-88336-104-3*); teacher ed. 9.95 (*0-88336-105-1*); 0.40 (*0-88336-132-9*) New Readers.
***Patterns in the Dark: Understanding Risk & Financial Crisis with Complexity Theory.** Edgar E. Peters. LC HB95.P42 1999. (Wiley Investment Classics Ser.). (Illus.). 222p. 1999. 39.95 (*0-471-23947-X*) Wiley.
Patterns in the Dust. large type ed. Lesley Grant-Adamson. 384p. 1989. 27.99 (*0-7089-2010-1*) Ulverscroft.
Patterns in the Dust: Chinese-American Relations & the Recognition Controversy, 1949-1950. Nancy B. Tucker. Ed. by William E. Leuchtenburg. LC 82-14724. (Contemporary American History Ser.). 400p. 1983. text 72.50 (*0-231-05362-2*) Col U Pr.
Patterns in the Landscape. Simon Bell. 1998. 60.00 (*0-419-20340-0*, E & FN Spon) Routledge.
Patterns in the Mind: Language & Human Nature. Ray R. Jackendoff. (Illus.). 256p. 1994. pap. 14.00 (*0-465-05462-5*, Pub. by Basic) HarpC.
***Patterns in the Sand: Computers, Complexity & Everyday Life.** Terry Bossomaier & David Green. 224p. 1999. pap. text 13.00 (*0-7382-0172-3*, Pub. by Perseus Pubng) HarpC.
Patterns in the Structure of Mammalian Communities. Ed. by D. W. Morris et al. LC 89-32598. (Special Publications: No. 28). iv, 266p. (C). 1989. 30.00 (*0-89672-173-6*); pap. 20.00 (*0-89672-174-4*) Tex Tech Univ Pr.
Patterns in Time: Chanuka. Matis Weinberg. 1988. pap. 19.95 (*1-58330-108-9*) Feldheim.
Patterns in Western Civilization. James Woelfel. (C). 1991. 73.00 (*0-536-57963-6*) Pearson Custom.
Patterns in Western Civilization. Woelfel & Trulove. 568p. (C). 1992. pap. text 72.00 (*0-536-58241-6*) Pearson Custom.
Patterns in Western Civilization. 2nd ed. Woelfel & Truelove. 653p. 1998. pap. 49.00 (*0-536-00080-8*) Pearson Custom.
Patterns, Information & Chaos in Neuronal Systems. B. J. West. (Studies of Nonlinear Phenomena in Life). 248p. 1993. text 64.00 (*981-02-1377-8*) World Scientific Pub.
Patterns of a Network Economy. Ed. by Bjore Johansson et al. LC 94-13328. (Advances in Spatial & Network Economics Ser.). 1994. 119.95 (*0-387-57824-2*) Spr-Verlag.
Patterns of Adoption. David Howe. LC 97-21647. 226p. 1997. pap. text 29.95 (*0-632-04149-8*) Blackwell Sci.
Patterns of Ambivalence: The Poetry & Fiction of Stevie Smith. Catherine A. Civello. LC 97-24267. (Studies in English & American Literature, Linguistics, & Culture). 145p. 1997. 45.00 (*1-57113-119-1*) Camden Hse.
Patterns of American Culture: Ethnography & Estrangement. Dan Rose. LC 89-33964. (Contemporary Ethnography Ser.). (Illus.). 138p. (C). 1989. pap. text 14.95 (*0-8122-1285-1*) U of Pa Pr.
Patterns of American Jurisprudence. Neil Duxbury. 530p. 1995. text 59.00 (*0-19-825850-X*) OUP.
Patterns of American Jurisprudence. Neil Duxbury. 530p. 1997. reprint ed. pap. text 27.00 (*0-19-826491-7*) OUP.
Patterns of Anti-Democratic Thought: An Analysis & a Criticism, with Special Reference to the American Political Mind in Recent Times. David Spitz. LC 80-22640. 347p. 1981. reprint ed. lib. bdg. 75.00 (*0-313-22392-0*, SPPD, Greenwood Pr) Greenwood.
Patterns of Antislavery among American Unitarians, 1831-1860. Douglas C. Stange. LC 75-18245. 308p. (C). 1976. 37.50 (*0-8386-1797-2*) Fairleigh Dickinson.
Patterns of Artistic Development: Comparative Studies of Talent. Constance Milbrath. LC 97-32148. (Illus.). 438p. (C). 1998. text 59.95 (*0-521-44313-X*) Cambridge U Pr.
Patterns of Attachment: A Psychological Study of the Strange Situation. M. D. Ainsworth et al. 416p. 1978. 99.95 (*0-89859-461-8*) L Erlbaum Assocs.
Patterns of Authority: A Structural Basis for Political Inquiry. Harry H. Eckstein. LC 75-19003. 506p. reprint ed. pap. 156.90 (*0-608-30075-6*, 201646600004) Bks Demand.
Patterns of Belief Vol. 1: Peoples & Religion. Eric Carlton. 130p. 1973. pap. 6.95 (*0-04-377004-5*) Attic Pr.
Patterns of Belief Vol. 2: Religions in Society. Eric Carlton. 140p. 1973. pap. 6.95 (*0-04-377005-3*) Attic Pr.
Patterns of Belief & Action: Measurement of Student Political Activism. Sharon L. Sutherland. LC 82-108946. (Illus.). 374p. reprint ed. pap. 116.00 (*0-8357-6391-9*, 203574700096) Bks Demand.
Patterns of Bias in Motion Picture Content. John W. Cones. (Hollywood Ser.). (Illus.). 230p. 1996. pap. 24.95 (*1-890341-02-9*) Rivas Canyon.
Patterns of Birthweights. (PAHO Scientific Publication Ser.: No. 504). 124p. 1987. pap. text 20.00 (*92-75-11504-4*) World Health.
Patterns of Breathing. Robert Wynne. 40p. 1997. pap. 6.00 (*1-890887-02-1*) Mille Grazie.
Patterns of Brief Family Therapy: An Ecosystemic Approach. Steve De Shazer. LC 81-7239. (Family Therapy Ser.). 157p. 1982. lib. bdg. 30.00 (*0-89862-038-4*) Guilford Pubns.
Patterns of Cancer in 5 Continents. Ed. by S. L. Whelan et al. (IARC Scientific Publications: No. 102). (Illus.). 188p. 1990. pap. text 67.50 (*92-832-2102-8*) OUP.
Patterns of Caribbean Development: An Interpretive Essay on Economic Change. Jay R. Mandle. (Caribbean Studies: Vol. 2). 168p. 1982. text 39.00 (*0-677-06000-9*) Gordon & Breach.
Patterns of Change: German Drama & the European Tradition. Dorothy James & Silvia Ranawake. (Studies in European Thought). (Illus.). XI, 334p. (C). 1990. text 48.95 (*0-8204-0716-X*) P Lang Pubng.
Patterns of Change: Tables & Graphs. Cornelia Tierney et al. Ed. by Catherine Anderson et al. (Investigations in Number, Data, & Space Ser.). (Illus.). 152p. (J). (gr. 5-6). 1995. teacher ed. 32.95 incl. mac hd (*0-86651-997-1*, DS21433) Seymour Pubns.
Patterns of Change: Tables & Graphs. rev. ed. Cornelia Tierney et al. Ed. by Catherine Anderson et al. (Investigations in Number, Data, & Space Ser.). (Illus.). 159p. (YA). (gr. 5 up). 1997. pap. text 32.95 (*1-57232-802-9*, 47049) Seymour Pubns.
Patterns of Change, Change of Patterns: Linguistic Change & Reconstruction Methodology. Ed. by Phillip Baldi. LC 91-34032. xii, 343p. (Orig.). (C). 1991. pap. text 43.60 (*3-11-013405-5*) Mouton.
Patterns of Child Rearing. Robert R. Sears et al. LC 75-44903. (Illus.). 550p. 1957. pap. 22.50 (*0-8047-0915-7*) Stanford U Pr.
Patterns of Chloroplast Reproduction. T. Butterfass. (Cell Biology Monographs: Vol. 6). (Illus.). 1980. 106.95 (*0-387-81541-4*) Spr-Verlag.
Patterns of Community Structure in Colombo, Sri Lanka: An Investigation of Contemporary Urban Life in South Asia. Neville S. Arachchige-Don. 310p. (C). 1994. lib. bdg. 42.50 (*0-8191-9606-1*) U Pr of Amer.
Patterns of Conflict: The Individual & Society in Spanish Literature to 1700. Sheila R. Ackerlind. (American University Studies: Romance Languages & Literature: Ser. II, Vol. 105). 328p. (C). 1989. text 45.70 (*0-8204-0879-4*) P Lang Pubng.
***Patterns of Conflict, Paths to Peace.** Ed. by Larry Fisk & John Schellenberg. 220p. 2000. pap. 18.95 (*1-55111-154-3*) Broadview Pr.
Patterns of Connection: Photography by Leah King-Smith. Alison D. Nordstrom & Deborah Ely. 24p. 1992. pap. text 12.00 (*1-887040-02-1*) SE Mus Photo.
Patterns of Consciousness: An Essay on Coleridge. Richard Haven. LC 78-76046. 232p. 1969. 30.00 (*0-87023-048-4*) U of Mass Pr.
Patterns of Contention in Mexican History. Ed. by Jaime E. Rodriguez. LC 91-38845. (Latin American Silhouettes Ser.). (ENG & SPA.). 368p. 1992. lib. bdg. 50.00 (*0-8420-2399-2*) Scholarly Res Inc.
***Patterns of Corporate Philanthropy: Passing the Shareholder's Buck** Christopher Yablonski & Capital Research Center Staff. LC 99-206520. (Studies in Philanthropy). v, 262 p. 1998. write for info. (*1-892934-02-7*) Capital Rsrch Ctr.
Patterns of Cultural Identity: Advanced Culture-Tapestry. Rebecca L. Oxford. (College ESL Ser.). (J). 1995. mass mkt. 22.95 (*0-8384-4123-8*) Heinle & Heinle.
Patterns of Culture. Ruth Benedict. 352p. 1989. reprint ed. pap. 14.00 (*0-395-50088-5*) HM.
Patterns of Culture in South Asia. L. P. Vidyarthi. (Illus.). 128p. 1979. 14.00 (*0-88065-206-3*) Scholarly Pubns.
Patterns of Decision Making? D. J. Murray. LC 74-159623. (Decision Making in Britain Ser.). 108p. 1972. write for info. (*0-335-01948-X*) Taylor & Francis.
Patterns of Decision Making in State Legislatures. Eric M. Uslaner & Ronald E. Weber. LC 76-12884. (Special Studies). 210p. 1977. 57.95 (*0-275-90276-5*, C0276, Praeger Pubs) Greenwood.
***Patterns of Democracy: Government Forms & Performance in Thirty-Six Countries.** Arend Lijphart. LC 99-12365. (Illus.). 336p. 1999. pap. text 17.00 (*0-300-07893-5*) Yale U Pr.
Patterns of Democracy: Government Forms & Performance in Thirty-Six Countries. Arend Lijphart. LC 99-12365. 336p. 1999. 40.00 (*0-300-07894-3*) Yale U Pr.
Patterns of Demographic, Economic & Value Change in the Western United States. Pamela Case & Gregory Alward. (Illus.). 52p. (C). 1998. pap. text 30.00 (*0-7881-7549-1*) DIANE Pub.
Patterns of Deposition & Settlement: Studies on the Megalithic Tombs of West Scania. Birgitta Hardh. (Illus.). 107p. (Orig.). 1990. pap. 43.00 (*91-22-01139-0*) Coronet Bks.
Patterns of Deprivation in the Soviet Union under Brezhnev & Gorbachev. Mervyn Matthews. (Publication Ser.: No. 383). 158p. (C). 1989. pap. text 18.95 (*0-8179-8832-7*) Hoover Inst Pr.
Patterns of Derivational Affixation in the Cabraniego Dialect of East-Central Asturian. Yakov Malkiel. LC 70-627777. (U. C. Publ. in Linguistics Ser.: Vol. 64). 203p. reprint ed. 63.00 (*0-8357-9637-X*, 201510300092) Bks Demand.
Patterns of Descent. Richard Foerster. LC 93-12421. 96p. (Orig.). 1993. 21.95 (*0-914061-36-4*); pap. 12.95 (*0-914061-37-2*) Orchises Pr.
Patterns of Desire. Joyce Kozloff. LC 89-26891. (Illus.). 88p. 1990. 35.00 (*1-55595-053-1*); 25.00 (*1-55595-054-X*) Hudson Hills.
Patterns of Destiny. Eleonora Kimmel. LC 84-70906. 204p. 1985. 17.95 (*0-86690-276-7*, K2529-014) Am Fed Astrologers.
***Patterns of Destiny: A Novel.** Thakur Vijai Singh. 192p. 2000. 19.00 (*81-241-0640-1*, Pub. by Har-Anand Pubns) Nataraj Bks.
Patterns of Development. LC 95-176209. write for info. (*0-340-62511-2*, Pub. by E A) Routldge.
Patterns of Development: Resources, Policy & Economic Growth. Richard Auty. LC 95-176209. (Arnold Publications). (Illus.). 320p. 1994. pap. text 35.00 (*0-340-59502-7*) OUP.
Patterns of Development in Latin America. John Sheahan. LC 87-2853. 445p. 1987. pap. text 20.95 (*0-691-02264-X*, Pub. by Princeton U Pr) Cal Prin Full Svc.
Patterns of Discipleship in the New Testament. Ed. by Richard N. Longenecker. (McMaster New Testament Studies). 319p. (Orig.). 1996. pap. 25.00 (*0-8028-4169-4*) Eerdmans.
***Patterns of Disengagement: The Practice & Portrayal of Reclusion in Early Medieval China.** Alan J Berkowitz. LC 99-57586. 1999. 55.00 (*0-8047-3603-0*) Stanford U Pr.
Patterns of Dissonance: A Study of Women in Contemporary Philosophy. Rosi Braidotti. Tr. by Elizabeth Guild. 324p. (C). 1991. pap. 20.99 (*0-415-90491-9*, A6368) Routledge.
Patterns of Distress: Emotional Insults & Human Form. Stanley Keleman. 75p. 1988. pap. 9.00 (*0-934320-13-6*) Center Pr.
Patterns of Distribution of Amphibians: A Global Perspective. William E. Duellman. LC 98-49449. 648p. 1999. 69.95 (*0-8018-6115-2*) Johns Hopkins.
Patterns of Divine Comedy: A Study of Medieval English Drama. R. D. Jack. 188p. 1989. 75.00 (*0-85991-281-7*) Boydell & Brewer.
Patterns of Economic Restructuring for Eastern Europe. Ed. by S. I. Cohen. LC 93-19256. 219p. 1993. 72.95 (*1-85628-516-2*, Pub. by Avebry) Ashgate Pub Co.
Patterns of Education for the Developing Nations: Tao's Work in China, 1917-1946. Don-chean Chu. LC 66-5481. xi, 179p. 1966. 2.00 (*0-913973-11-4*); pap. 1.00 (*0-913973-07-6*) Inst Sino-Amer.
Patterns of Educational Practice: Theories of Curriculum. Richard W. Morshead. 352p. 1995. pap. 28.00 (*0-87650-318-0*) Pierian.
Patterns of Ellipsis in Russian Compound Noun Formations. Steven J. Molinsky. LC 72-94527. (Slavistic Printings & Reprintings Ser.: No. 278). 1973. text 90.80 (*90-279-2474-0*) Mouton.
Patterns of Emergent Literacy: Processes of Development & Transition. Stuart McNaughton. (Illus.). 229p. (C). 1996. pap. text 45.00 (*0-19-558324-8*) OUP.
Patterns of Energy Use in Developing Countries. Ed. by Ashok V. Desai. (Energy Research Group Review Ser.). (C). 1990. 17.50 (*81-224-0201-1*) S Asia.
Patterns of English Spelling: The Teacher's Book of Word Lists Organized by Phonograms. 4th rev. unabridged ed. Don McCabe. Orig. Title: The Basic Patterns of English Spelling. 894p. 1997. teacher ed., ring bd. 149.95 (*1-56400-201-2*, 200) AVKO Educ Res.
Patterns of English Spelling Vol. 1: The Short Vowel - CVC Families. Don McCabe. 86p. 1995. ring bd. 19.95 (*1-56400-221-7*) AVKO Educ Res.
Patterns of English Spelling Vol. 2: The Short Vowel - CVCC Families. Don McCabe. 100p. 1995. ring bd. 19.95 (*1-56400-222-5*) AVKO Educ Res.
Patterns of English Spelling Vol. 3: The Long Vowels - CV, CVV, & CVCe. Don McCabe. 1995. ring bd. 19.95 (*1-56400-223-3*) AVKO Educ Res.
Patterns of English Spelling Vol. 4: The Long Vowel - CVVC & Miscellaneous Relatives. Don McCabe. 98p. 1995. ring bd. write for info. (*1-56400-224-1*) AVKO Educ Res.
Patterns of English Spelling Vol. 5: The -R & W- Controls & Miscellaneous Relatives. Don McCabe. 106p. 1995. ring bd. 19.95 (*1-56400-225-X*) AVKO Educ Res.
Patterns of English Spelling Vol. 6: The Ending "UL" & "UR" Suffixes & Miscellaneous Relatives. Don McCabe. 98p. 1995. ring bd. 19.95 (*1-56400-226-8*) AVKO Educ Res.
Patterns of English Spelling Vol. 7: The Ending -Y Families. 68p. 1995. ring bd. 19.95 (*1-56400-227-6*) AVKO Educ Res.
Patterns of English Spelling Vol. 8: The Advanced Suffixes. Don McCabe. 102p. 1995. ring bd. 19.95 (*1-56400-228-4*) AVKO Educ Res.
Patterns of English Spelling Vol. 9: Advanced Phonic Patterns. Don McCabe. 70p. 1995. ring bd. 19.95 (*1-56400-229-2*) AVKO Educ Res.
Patterns of English Spelling Vol. 10: Prefixes, Roots, Suffixes. Don McCabe. 78p. 1995. ring bd. 19.95 (*1-56400-230-6*) AVKO Educ Res.
Patterns of English Spelling Vols. 1-5: The Teacher's Book of Basic Word Lists by Phonograms, 5 vols. Don McCabe. 480p. 1995. ring bd. 79.95 (*1-56400-235-7*) AVKO Educ Res.
Patterns of English Spelling Vols. 6-10: The Teacher's Book of Advanced Word Lists Organized by Phonograms, 5 vols. 508p. 1995. teacher ed., ring bd. 79.95 (*1-56400-237-3*) AVKO Educ Res.
Patterns of Enlisted Compensation. Rebecca M. Kilburn & Rachel Louie. LC 96-54487. Date not set. pap. 15.00 (*0-8330-2479-5*) Rand Corp.
Patterns of Epiphany: From Wordsworth to Tolstoy, Pater & Barrett Browning. Martin Bidney. LC 96-38623. 1997. 34.95 (*0-8093-2116-5*) S Ill U Pr.
Patterns of European Industrialization: The 19th Century. Ed. by Richard E. Sylla & Gianni Toniolo. (New Library of Economics). 288p. (C). 1993. pap. 29.99 (*0-415-08156-4*, A9785) Routledge.
Patterns of Evolution: The New Molecular View. Roger Lewin. 1999. pap. text 19.95 (*0-7167-6036-3*, Sci Amer Lib Paperbacks) W H Freeman.
Patterns of Evolution in Galapagos Organisms. Ed. by Robert I. Bowman et al. LC 83-62392. 568p. (Orig.). 1983. 32.50 (*0-934394-05-9*) AAASPD.
Patterns of Excellence: Discover the New Principles of Corporate Success. Danny Samson & David Challis. 256p. 1999. 24.99 (*0-273-63876-9*) F T P-H.
Patterns of Exchange. Gary Williams. 1988. pap. 40.00 (*0-86469-084-3*) Intl Spec Bk.
***Patterns of Experience.** Betty Tomson. 124p. 2000. 19.95 (*0-7541-1104-0*, Pub. by Minerva Pr) Unity Dist.
Patterns of Experience in Autobiography. Susanna Egan. LC 83-12508. xiii, 227p. 1984. 39.95 (*0-8078-1581-0*) U of NC Pr.
***Patterns of Exposition.** 16th ed. 2000. teacher ed. write for info. (*0-321-07848-9*) Addison-Wesley.
***Patterns of Exposition.** 16th ed. Robert A. Schwegler. 704p. 2000. pap. 37.80 (*0-321-07242-1*) Longman.
***Patterns of Exposition 16.** Robert A. Schwegler. LC 00-26107. 2000. write for info. (*0-321-07243-X*) Longman.
Patterns of Faith Around the World. Wilfred C. Smith. 1998. pap. 14.95 (*1-85168-164-7*, Pub. by Element MA) Penguin Putnam.
Patterns of Farm Financial Structure: A Cross-Section View of Economic & Physical Determinants. Donald C. Horton. (Financial Research Program VI: Studies in Agricultural Financing: No. 2). 208p. 1957. reprint ed. 54.10 (*0-87014-150-3*) Natl Bur Econ Res.
Patterns of Fashion, 1860 to 1940 Vol. 2: Englishwomen's Dresses & Their Construction. 3rd rev. ed. Janet Arnold. LC 76-189820. (Illus.). 88p. 1977. pap. 34.95 (*0-89676-027-8*, Costume & Fashion Pr) QSMG Ltd.
Patterns of Fashion, 1560-1620: The Art & Construction of Clothes for Men & Women. Janet Arnold. (Illus.). 128p. 1985. pap. 39.95 (*0-89676-083-9*, Costume & Fashion Pr) QSMG Ltd.
Patterns of Fashion, 1660-1860 Vol. 1: Englishwomen's Dresses & Their Construction. 3rd rev. ed. Janet Arnold. LC 76-189820. (Illus.). 76p. 1977. pap. 34.95 (*0-89676-026-X*, Costume & Fashion Pr) QSMG Ltd.
Patterns of Fear in the Gothic Novel, 1790 to 1830. Ann B. Tracy. Ed. by Devendra P. Varma. LC 79-8487. (Gothic Studies & Dissertations). 1980. lib. bdg. 44.95 (*0-405-12682-4*) Ayer.
***Patterns of Feminist Consciousness in Indian Women Writers: A Study of Anita Desai's Cry, the Peacock, Nayantara Sahgal's Storm in Chandigarh, Attia Hosain's Sunlight on a Broken Column, Rama**

P

Mehta's Inside the Haveli, Shashi Despande's That Long Silence. Anuradha Roy. LC 99-932114. 152p. 1999. write for info. (*81-7551-064-1*, Pub. by Prestige) Advent Bks Div.

Patterns of Fertility in Low-Fertility Settings. (Population Studies: No. 131). 134p. pap. 17.00 (*92-1-151248-4*, E.92.XIII.11) UN.

Patterns of First Marriage Timing & Prev. 327p. 1991. 29.00 (*92-1-151225-5*, E 91.XIII.6) UN.

Patterns of Generosity in America: Who's Holding the Safety Net. Julian Wolpert. LC 93-27777. 1993. pap. 9.95 (*0-87078-183-9*) Century Foundation.

Patterns of Global Terrorism, (1993) (Illus.). 73p. (Orig.). (C). 1995. pap. text 30.00 (*0-7881-2359-9*) DIANE Pub.

Patterns of Global Terrorism, (1995) (Illus.). 70p. (Orig.). (C). 1995. pap. text 35.00 (*0-7881-2609-1*) DIANE Pub.

Patterns of Global Terrorism, 1994. (Illus.). 69p. 1998. pap. text 25.00 (*0-7881-4981-4*) DIANE Pub.

Patterns of Global Terrorism, 1997. Ed. by Christopher W. Ross. (Illus.). 85p. (C). 1998. pap. text 25.00 (*0-7881-7558-0*) DIANE Pub.

Patterns of Global Terrorism, 1996. 16th ed. Ed. by Phil Wilcox. (Illus.). 75p. 1998. pap. text 25.00 (*0-7881-7265-4*) DIANE Pub.

***Patterns of Grace Gift Book: The Wonderful Ways God Touches Our Lives.** Roy Lessin & Heather Solum. 1999. 12.99 (*1-58375-464-4*) Garborgs.

Patterns of Health Care Use among HIV-Infected Adults. 1996. lib. bdg. 263.99 (*0-8490-8353-2*) Gordon Pr.

Patterns of High Performance: Discovering the Ways People Work Best. Jerry L. Fletcher. LC 93-17921. (Illus.). 262p. 1993. 27.95 (*1-881052-33-8*) Berrett-Koehler.

Patterns of High Performance: Discovering the Ways People Work Best. Jerry L. Fletcher. LC 93-17921. (Illus.). 266p. 1995. pap. 17.95 (*1-881052-70-2*) Berrett-Koehler.

Patterns of History. Robert Garfield. 96p. (C). 1995. per. 32.95 (*0-7872-1546-5*, 41154601) Kendall-Hunt.

Patterns of History Through Cycles of Time, 2 vols. Nancy Cassidy. Incl. Vol. I. World Events. 299p. 1997. pap. 22.00 (*0-89540-355-2*, Sun Bks); Vol. II. American Presidents. 288p. 1998. pap. 22.00 (*0-89540-356-0*, Sun Bks); 1997. pap. write for info. (*0-89540-357-9*, Sun Bks) Sun Pub.

Patterns of Human Growth. Barry Bogin. (Cambridge Studies in Biological Anthropology: No. 3). (Illus.). 280p. 1988. pap. text 32.95 (*0-521-34690-8*) Cambridge U Pr.

***Patterns of Human Growth.** 2nd ed. Barry Bogin. (Studies in Biological Anthropology: No. 23). (Illus.). 350p. (C). 1999. pap. text 39.95 (*0-521-56438-7*) Cambridge U Pr.

Patterns of Human Variation: The Demography, Genetics, & Phenetics of the Bougainville Islanders. Jonathan S. Friedlaender. LC 74-17858. (Illus.). 315p. 1975. 32.00 (*0-674-65855-8*) HUP.

Patterns of Hypnotic Techniques of Milton H. Erickson, M. D., Vol. 1. Richard Bandler & John Grinder. LC 75-24584. 1975. pap. 19.95 (*0-916990-01-X*) META Pubns.

Patterns of Hypnotic Techniques of Milton H. Erickson, M. D., Vol. 2. Richard Brandler et al. LC 75-24584. 1977. 21.95 (*0-916990-02-8*) META Pubns.

Patterns of Illusion & Change. John R. Stahl. (Illus.). 24p. (Orig.). 1984. pap. 6.00 (*0-945303-09-2*) Evanescent Pr.

Patterns of Image & Structure in the Essays of Alfonso Reyes. James W. Robb. LC 70-94192. (Catholic University of America. Studies in Romance Languages & Literatures: No. 56). 1969. reprint ed. 37.50 (*0-404-50356-X*) AMS Pr.

Patterns of Improvement in Depressed In-Patients. Malcolm H. Lader et al. (Maudsley Monographs: No. 30). 128p. 1987. 45.00 (*0-19-712154-3*) OUP.

Patterns of Indigeneous Capitalist Formations in Pre-Colonial Africa & North America. Joan Nicklin. LC 95-67260. (African Women Ser.: No. 1). 50p. (Orig.). (C). 1995. pap. text 5.00 (*0-943324-56-4*) Omenana.

P

Patterns of Inductive Reasoning: Developing Critical Thinking Skills. 4th ed. Moore. 302p. 1997. per. 22.95 (*0-7872-4408-2*) Kendall-Hunt.

Patterns of Industrial Bureaucracy: A Case Study of Modern Factory Administration. Alvin W. Gouldner. 1964. pap. 15.95 (*0-02-912740-8*) Free Pr.

Patterns of Infidelity & Their Treatment. Emily M. Brown. LC 90-25925. (Frontiers in Couples & Family Therapy Ser.: No. 3). (Illus.). 304p. 1991. text 40.95 (*0-87630-631-8*) Brunner-Mazel.

Patterns of Influence on Gifted Learners: The Home, the Self, & the School. Ed. by Paula Olszewski-Kubilius & Joyce Vantassel-Baska. LC 88-29486. (Education & Psychology of the Gifted Ser.). 261p. 1989. reprint ed. pap. 81.00 (*0-608-03016-3*, 206346600006) Bks Demand.

Patterns of Injury & Illness in Great Apes: A Skeletal Analysis. Nancy C. Lovell. LC 89-600389. (Illus.). 288p. 1990. 45.00 (*0-87474-678-7*) Smithsonian.

Patterns of Intention. Michael Baxandall. LC 85-6049. 180p. 1987. pap. 16.00 (*0-300-03763-5*, Y-699) Yale U Pr.

Patterns of Italian Conversation: Modelli Di Conversazione Italiana. Edward Williamson. (C). 1981. pap. 4.50 (*0-913298-14-X*) S F Vanni.

Patterns of Japanese Economic Development: A Quantitative Appraisal. Ed. by Kazushi Ohkawa et al. LC 78-23317. (Economic Growth Center, Yale University, & the Council on East Asian Studies, Yale University Publication Ser.). (Illus.). 428p. reprint ed. pap. 132.70 (*0-8357-8261-1*, 203384700087) Bks Demand.

Patterns of Juvenile Delinquency. Howard B. Kaplan. LC 84-18015. (Law & Criminal Justice Ser.: No. 2). 160p. 1984. reprint ed. pap. 49.60 (*0-608-01191-6*, 205948900001) Bks Demand.

Patterns of Language: Structure, Variation, Change. Robbins Burling. (Illus.). 461p. 1992. pap. text 39.95 (*0-12-144920-3*) Acad Pr.

Patterns of Lexis in Text. M. P. Hoey. Ed. by John Sinclair & Ronald Carter. (Illus.). 294p. 1991. pap. text 19.95 (*0-19-437142-5*) OUP.

Patterns of Life. Peter Connor. LC 98-85203. 185p. 1999. pap. 14.95 (*1-56315-110-3*, Pub. by SterlingHse) Natl Bk Netwk.

Patterns of Life. Ed. by Steck-Vaughn Staff. 1998. 59.92 (*0-8172-4204-X*) Raintree Steck-V.

Patterns of Life: Biogeography of a Changing World. Howard Mielke. (Illus.). 370p. 1989. 75.00 (*0-04-574032-1*); pap. 29.95 (*0-04-574033-X*) Routledge.

Patterns of Life History: The Ecology of Human Individuality. Ed. by M. D. Mumford et al. 512p. (C). 1990. text 125.00 (*0-8058-0225-8*) L Erlbaum Assocs.

Patterns of Literary Style. Ed. by Joseph P. Strelka. LC 76-123870. (Yearbook of Comparative Criticism Ser.: Vol. 3). (Illus.). 1971. 30.00 (*0-271-00124-0*) Pa St U Pr.

Patterns of Living in Puerto Rican Families. Lydia J. Roberts & Rosa L. Stefani. LC 74-14247. (Puerto Rican Experience Ser.). (Illus.). 440p. 1975. reprint ed. 35.95 (*0-405-06233-8*) Ayer.

Patterns of Love. Christine Holden. (A Quilting Romance Ser.). 320p. 1999. 5.99 (*0-515-12481-8*, Jove) Berkley Pub.

Patterns of Love. large type ed. Robin L. Hatcher. LC 98-4356. 1998. 25.95 (*1-57490-143-5*, Beeler LP Bks) T T Beeler.

Patterns of Madness in 18th Century: A Reader. Ed. by Allan Ingram. LC 99-207405. 352p. 1998. 45.95 (*0-85323-982-7*, Pub. by Liverpool Univ Pr); pap. 19.95 (*0-85323-992-4*, Pub. by Liverpool Univ Pr) Intl Spec Bk.

Patterns of Market Behavior: Essays in Honor of Philip Taft. Ed. by Michael J. Brennan. LC 65-12932. (Studies in the Fields of General Scholarship). 264p. reprint ed. pap. 81.90 (*0-608-14777-X*, 202564300045) Bks Demand.

Patterns of Mass Movements in Arab Revolutionary Progressive States. Enver M. Koury. LC 76-110953. (Studies in the Social Sciences: No. 9). (Orig.). 1970. pap. text 42.35 (*90-279-1259-9*) Mouton.

Patterns of Migration. Ed. by Patrick O'Sullivan. (Irish World Wide Ser.). (Illus.). 256p. 1997. 24.95 (*0-7185-0118-7*) Bks Intl VA.

Patterns of Migration. Ed. by Patrick O'Sullivan. 240p. (C). 1992. text 59.00 (*0-7185-1422-X*, Pub. by Leicester U Pr) Cassell & Continuum.

Patterns of Migration in Southeast Asia. unabridged ed. Ed. by Robert R. Reed. LC 90-86324. (Occasional Papers: Vol. 16). 302p. (Orig.). 1990. pap. text 19.50 (*0-944613-11-X*) UC Berkeley Ctrs SE Asia.

Patterns of Moral Complexity. Charles E. Larmore. 212p. 1987. pap. text 20.95 (*0-521-33891-3*) Cambridge U Pr.

Patterns of Mothering: A Study of Maternal Influence During Infancy. Sylvia Brody. LC 56-8839. 446p. (Orig.). 1970. reprint ed. 65.00 (*0-8236-4040-X*) Intl Univs Pr.

***Patterns of Negro Segregation.** Charles S. Johnson. (African American Intellectual Heritage Ser.). 376p. 2001. reprint ed. pap. 21.95 (*0-268-03865-1*, Pub. by U of Notre Dame Pr); reprint ed. lib. bdg. 34.95 (*0-268-03866-X*, Pub. by U of Notre Dame Pr) Chicago Distribution Ctr.

Patterns of Nursing Theories in Practice. Ed. by Marilyn E. Parker. LC 93-3402. 1993. 25.95 (*0-88737-600-2*, 15-2548) Natl League Nurse.

Patterns of Order & Utopia. Dorothy F. Donnelly. LC 98-3794. 156p. 1998. text 45.00 (*0-312-16496-3*) St Martin.

Patterns of Panchayati Raj in India. G. Ram Reddy. 1977. 9.50 (*0-8364-0046-1*) S Asia.

Patterns of Panic. Joost A. Meerloo. LC 50-5823. 120p. reprint ed. pap. 37.20 (*0-608-11209-7*, 201044500070) Bks Demand.

Patterns of Paradise: The Styles & Significance of Bark Cloth Around the World. Anne Leonard & John Terrell. Ed. by Tanisse Bushman. LC 80-65125. 1980. pap. 10.95 (*0-914868-05-5*) Field Mus.

Patterns of Parish Leadership: Cost & Effectiveness in Four Denominations. Dean R. Hoge et al. LC 88-61722. 214p. (Orig.). 1989. pap. 14.95 (*1-55612-208-X*) Sheed & Ward WI.

Patterns of Person: Studies in Style & Form from Corneille to Laclos. Edward C. Knox. LC 82-82430. (French Forum Monographs: No. 41). 177p. (Orig.). 1983. pap. 12.95 (*0-917058-40-2*) French Forum.

Patterns of Philanthropy: Charity & Society in Nineteenth-Century Bristol. Martin Gorsky. LC 99-36469. (Royal Historical Society Studies in History). (Illus.). 288p. 1999. 75.00 (*0-86193-245-5*, Royal Historical Soc) Boydell & Brewer.

Patterns of Pilage: A Geography of Caribbean-Based Piracy in Spanish America, 1536-1718. Peter Galvin. LC 97-42002. (American University Studies: Vol. 5, No. 25). xiv, 271p. (C). 1998. text 48.95 (*0-8204-3771-9*) P Lang Pubng.

Patterns of Poetry: An Encyclopedia of Forms. Miller Williams. LC 85-23719. (Illus.). xiii, 203p. 1986. pap. text 17.95 (*0-8071-1330-1*) La State U Pr.

Patterns of Policy: Comparative & Longitudinal Studies of Population Events. Ed. by John D. Montgomery et al. LC 77-94305. 300p. 1979. 44.95 (*0-87855-269-3*) Transaction Pubs.

Patterns of Political Leadership: Egypt, Israel, Lebanon. R. Hrair Dekmejian. LC 74-20940. (Illus.). 368p. (C). 1975. text 24.50 (*0-87395-291-X*) State U NY Pr.

Patterns of Political Oppositions in Southeast Asia. Ed. by Justus M. Van Der Kroef. (Council on International Studies & Programs Special Studies: No. 154). 279p. 1984. pap. text 15.00 (*0-924197-05-6*, 154) SUNYB Coun Intl Studies.

Patterns of Political Participation of Puerto Ricans in New York. Rosa Estades. LC 77-11625. 94p. 1978. pap. 3.00 (*0-8477-2445-X*) U of PR Pr.

Patterns of Population Distribution: A Residential Preference Model & Its Dynamic. David J. Morgan. LC 78-18794. (University of Chicago, Department of Geography, Research Paper Ser.: No. 176). 217p. 1978. reprint ed. pap. 67.30 (*0-608-02271-3*, 206291200004) Bks Demand.

Patterns of Power & Politics in the Philippines: Implications for Development. Ed. by James F. Eder & Robert L. Youngblood. LC 98-127598. i, 196p. (C). 1994. pap. text 12.95 (*1-881044-09-2*) ASU Prog SE Asian.

Patterns of Power in Early Wales: O'Donnell Lectures Delivered in the University of Oxford, 1983. Wendy Davies. (Illus.). 128p. 1990. 39.95 (*0-19-820153-2*) OUP.

Patterns of Prayer see Modelos para Orar

Patterns of Prayer in the Psalms. Laurence Dunlop. 160p. (Orig.). 1984. 9.95 (*0-8164-2377-6*) Harper SF.

Patterns of Preaching: A Sermon Sampler. Ed. by Ronald J. Allen. 272p. 1998. pap. 22.99 (*0-8272-2953-4*) Chalice Pr.

Patterns of Preference. Terence Duniho. Date not set. pap. write for info. (*1-878287-33-8*) Type & Temperament.

Patterns of Presumption: Reflections on How We View Reality. David L. Abel. xi, 300p. 1998. 17.99 (*0-9657988-1-X*) LongView Press.

Patterns of Primate Behavior. 2nd rev. ed. Claud A. Bramblett. (Illus.). 292p. (C). 1994. pap. text 23.95 (*0-88133-743-9*) Waveland Pr.

Patterns of Problem Solving. 2nd ed. Moshe F. Rubinstein & Iris R. Firstenberg. LC 94-7371. (C). 1994. text 51.80 (*0-13-122706-8*) Prntice Hall Bks.

Patterns of Professions. Emma B. Donath. LC 84-70084. 112p. 1984. 13.00 (*0-86690-265-1*, P2299-014) Am Fed Astrologers.

Patterns of Progress. Horace M. Kallen. LC 68-55847. (Essay Index Reprint Ser.). 1977. 17.95 (*0-8369-0582-2*) Ayer.

Patterns of Progress: Quilts in the Machine Age. Barbara Brackman. (Illus.). 128p. 1997. 35.00 (*0-614-28310-8*) Autry Mus Wstrn.

Patterns of Progress: Quilts in the Machine Age. Barbara Brackman & Gene Autry Museum of Western Heritage Staff. LC 97-13375. 1997. pap. write for info. (*1-882880-04-8*) Autry Mus Wstrn.

Patterns of Progress: Quilts in the Machine Age. Barbara Brackman & Gene Autry Museum of Western Heritage Staff. LC 97-13375. (Illus.). 128p. 1998. pap. 25.00 (*1-882880-03-X*) Autry Mus Wstrn.

Patterns of Prophecy. Alan Vaughan. 256p. 1985. pap. 22.00 (*0-89540-155-X*, SB-155) Sun Pub.

Patterns of Protestant Church Music. Robert Murrell Stevenson. LC 53-8271. 227p. reprint ed. pap. 70.40 (*0-608-12814-7*, 202345500033) Bks Demand.

***Patterns of Provocation: Police & Public Disorder.** Richard Bessel & Clive Emsley. LC 99-86560. 208p. 2000. 49.95 (*1-57181-227-X*); pap. 18.50 (*1-57181-228-8*) Berghahn Bks.

Patterns of Psychopathology. Melvin Zax & George Stricker. LC 63-9238. (Case Studies of Behavioral Dysfuntion). 320p. reprint ed. pap. 99.20 (*0-608-13752-9*, 205167800001) Bks Demand.

Patterns of Psychosexual Infantilism. Wilhelm Stekel. (C). 1952. 7.50 (*0-87140-840-6*) Liveright.

Patterns of Race in the Americas. Marvin Harris. LC 80-11594. (Illus.). 154p. 1980. reprint ed. lib. bdg. 55.00 (*0-313-22359-9*, HAPS, Greenwood Pr) Greenwood.

Patterns of Redemption in the Fourth Gospel: An Experiment in Structural Analysis. Gunnar H. Ostenstad. LC 98-18598. (Studies in the Bible & Early Christianity: Vol. 38). 404p. 1998. 109.95 (*0-7734-8396-9*) E Mellen.

Patterns of Redemption in Virgil's Georgics. Llewelyn Morgan. LC 98-44171. (Cambridge Classical Studies). 296p. (C). 1999. 59.95 (*0-521-65166-2*) Cambridge U Pr.

Patterns of Redundancy: Psychological Study. Alan C. Staniland. LC 66-10067. 224p. reprint ed. pap. 63.90 (*0-608-11137-6*, 2050797) Bks Demand.

***Patterns of Reflection.** 3rd ed. 2000. teacher ed. write for info. (*0-205-32704-4*) Allyn.

Patterns of Reflection. 3rd ed. Ed. by Dorothy Seyler. LC 97-251. 495p. 1997. pap. text 34.00 (*0-205-26715-7*) P-H.

***Patterns of Reflection.** 4th ed. Dorothy U. Seyler. LC 99-59738. 495p. (Orig.). 2000. pap. 30.00 (*0-205-31481-3*) Allyn.

Patterns of Reflection: A Reader: Examination Copy. 3rd ed. Dorothy U. Seyler. 512p. (C). 1997. pap. text. write for info. (*0-205-27677-6*, T7677-2) Allyn.

Patterns of Reform: Continuity & Change in the Reformation Kirk. James Kirk. 512p. 1990. 69.95 (*0-567-09505-3*, Pub. by T & T Clark) Bks Intl VA.

Patterns of Relating: An Adult Attachment Perspective. Malcolm L. West & Adrienne E. Sheldon-Keller. LC 93-48128. 210p. 1994. lib. bdg. 30.00 (*0-89862-671-4*) Guilford Pubns.

Patterns of Religion. Schmidt. 1999. pap. 61.95 (*0-534-50649-6*) Brooks-Cole.

Patterns of Renewal. Laurens Van Der Post. LC 62-15859. (Orig.). 1962. pap. 4.00 (*0-87574-121-5*) Pendle Hill.

Patterns of Repetition in Trollope. Elizabeth R. Epperly. LC 88-38588. 250p. 1989. reprint ed. pap. 77.50 (*0-7837-9111-9*, 204991300004) Bks Demand.

Patterns of Reproduction of 4 Species of Vespertilionid Bats in Paraguay. Philip Myers. LC 76-3878. (University of California Publications in Social Welfare: No. 107). (Illus.). 71p. reprint ed. pap. 30.00 (*0-608-18308-3*, 203157800075) Bks Demand.

Patterns of Rogerian Knowing. Mary Madrid. LC 96-29676. 1996. 25.95 (*0-88737-688-6*) Natl League Nurse.

Patterns of Russian Ice Dance. Yelena Tchaikovskaya. Ed. by Harrinton Crissey & Lynn Copley-Graves. Tr. by Beatrice Yusem from RUS. (Illus.). 70p. 1994. pap. 18.00 (*1-882849-01-9*) Platoro Pr.

Patterns of Sedimentation. Zal. text. write for info. (*0-471-49099-7*); pap. text. write for info. (*0-471-49100-4*) Wiley.

Patterns of Sedimentation, Diagenesis, & Hydrocarbon Accumulation in Cretaceous Rocks of the Rock Mountains. Dudley D. Rice & Donald L. Gautier. LC QE0571.R53. (SEPM Short Course Ser.: No. 11). (Illus.). 343p. 1983. pap. 106.40 (*0-608-05574-3*, 206603400006) Bks Demand.

Patterns of Sexual Arousal: Psychophysiological Processes & Clinical Applications. Raymond C. Rosen & J. Gayle Beck. LC 87-19726. 404p. 1988. lib. bdg. 49.95 (*0-89862-712-5*) Guilford Pubns.

Patterns of Sexuality & Reproduction. Alan Parkes. (Illus.). 1976. pap. 4.95 (*0-19-289081-6*) OUP.

Patterns of Social & Technological Change in Europe. Mike Campbell et al. 336p. 1994. 72.95 (*1-85628-608-8*, Pub. by Avebry) Ashgate Pub Co.

***Patterns of Social Capital: Stability & Change in Historical Perspective.** Ed. by Robert I. Rotberg. (Studies in Interdisciplinary History: Vol. 6). (Illus.). 340p. (C). 2000. text 49.95 (*0-521-78086-1*); pap. text 18.95 (*0-521-78575-8*) Cambridge U Pr.

Patterns of Social Policy: An Introduction to Comparative Analysis. Catherine Jones. 300p. (Orig.). 1985. pap. text 14.95 (*0-422-77260-7*, 9561, Pub. by Tavistock) Routldge.

Patterns of Societal Development in Iceland, 1930-1980. Ingmar Einarsson. (Studia Sociologica Upsaliensia: No. 26). 152p. (Orig.). 1987. pap. text 37.50 (*91-554-2015-X*) Coronet Bks.

Patterns of Software: Habitability & Piecemeal Growth. Richard P. Gabriel. (Illus.). 256p. (C). 1996. 27.50 (*0-19-510269-X*) OUP.

Patterns of Software: Tales from the Software Community. Richard P. Gabriel. (Illus.). 256p. 1998. reprint ed. pap. 14.95 (*0-19-512123-6*) OUP.

Patterns of Soviet Economic Decisions-Making: An Inside View of the 1965 Reform. Sergei Freidzon. Ed. by Andrew A. Micta. 104p. (Orig.). 1987. pap. text 100.00 (*1-55831-072-X*) Delphic Associates.

Patterns of Soviet Thought: The Origins & Development of Dialectical & Historical Materialism. Richard T. De George. LC 66-17026. (Ann Arbor Paperbacks Ser.: No. AA-160). 308p. reprint ed. pap. 95.50 (*0-608-10899-5*, 205105600074) Bks Demand.

Patterns of Spanish Pronunciation: A Drillbook. J. Donald Bowen & Robert P. Stockwell. LC 60-16841. (Orig.). 1960. pap. text 4.50 (*0-226-06831-5*) U Ch Pr.

Patterns of Spanish Pronunciation: A Drillbook. Jean D. Bowen & Robert P. Stockwell. LC 60-16841. 137p. reprint ed. pap. 42.50 (*0-608-09392-0*, 205413700004) Bks Demand.

Patterns of Spanish Pronunciation, a Drillbook. Jean D. Bowen & Robert P. Stockwell. LC 60-16841. 147p. Date not set. reprint ed. pap. 45.60 (*0-608-20602-4*, 205456700003) Bks Demand.

Patterns of Stylistic Changes in Islamic Architecture: Local Traditions Versus Migrating Artists. Michael Meinecke. LC 95-5508. (Hagop Kevorkian Series on Near Eastern Art & Civilization). 180p. (C). 1996. text 75.00 (*0-8147-5492-9*) NYU Pr.

Patterns of Suicide & Homicide in the World. David Lester. LC 97-130538. (Illus.). (C). 1996. lib. bdg. 95.00 (*1-56072-392-0*) Nova Sci Pubs.

Patterns of Suicide & Homocide in America. David Lester. 143p. (C). 1994. lib. bdg. 115.00 (*1-56072-148-0*) Nova Sci Pubs.

Patterns of the Fantastic I: Academic Programming at Chicon IV. Ed. by Donald M. Hassler. LC 83-587. (Starmont Studies in Literary Criticism: No. 2). vi, 105p. 1983. pap. 17.00 (*0-916732-62-2*) Millefleurs.

Patterns of the Hypnotic Techniques of Milton H. Erickson, M.D., Vol. I. Richard Bandler & John Grinder. LC 96-25682. 280p. 1997. pap. 18.95 (*1-55552-052-9*) Metamorphous Pr.

Patterns of the Quilted Plains. Dorothy Jenks. Ed. by Ruth M. Kempher. LC 96-134191. (Illus.). 50p. (Orig.). 1995. pap. write for info. (*0-9637483-8-6*) Kings Estate.

***Patterns of the Western Mind: A Reformed Christian Perspective.** John H. Kok. 263p. 1998. pap. text 12.50 (*0-932914-41-1*) Dordt Coll Pr.

Patterns of the Whole Vol. 1: Healing & Quartz Crystals (A Journey with our Souls) John D. Rea. (Illus.). 376p. (Orig.). 1986. pap. 12.95 (*0-938183-01-X*) Two Trees Pub.

Patterns of Thinking: Integrating Learning Skills in Content Teaching. John Henrik Clarke. 320p. (C). 1990. 68.00 (*0-205-12361-9*, H23617) Allyn.

Patterns of Thought in Africa & the West: Essays on Magic, Religion & Science. Robin Horton. (Illus.). 483p. 1997. pap. text 29.95 (*0-521-36926-6*) Cambridge U Pr.

Patterns of Thought in Africa & the West: Selected Theoretical Papers in Magic, Religion, & Science. Robin Horton. LC 92-23089. (Illus.). 483p. (C). 1993. text 74.95 (*0-521-36087-0*) Cambridge U Pr.

An Asterisk (*) at the beginning of an entry indicates that the title is appearing for the first time.

Patterns of Thought in Rimbaud & Mallarme. John P. Houston. LC 85-80741. (French Forum Monographs: No. 63). 134p. (Orig.). 1986. pap. 12.95 (*0-917058-64-X*) French Forum.

Patterns of Time: Mizoguchi & the 1930s. Donald Kirihara. LC 91-40951. (Wisconsin Studies in Film). (Illus.). 240p. (Orig.). (C). 1992. pap. 24.95 (*0-299-13244-7*); lib. bdg. 50.00 (*0-299-13240-4*) U of Wis Pr.

Patterns of Time in Hospital Life: A Sociological Perspective. Eviatar Zerubavel. LC 78-11385. (Illus.). 182p. 1979. lib. bdg. 16.50 (*0-226-98160-6*) U Ch Pr.

Patterns of Tool Use: Scanning Electron Miscroscopy of Experimental Quartz Tools. Kjel Knutsson. (Societas Archaeologica Upsaliensis Ser.: No. 10). (Illus.). 112p. (Orig.). 1988. pap. 90.00 (*91-506-0661-1*, Pub. by Uppsala Universitet) Coronet Bks.

Patterns of Trade, Competition & Trade Policies. Beniamino Quintieri. 192p. 1995. reprint ed. text 66.95 (*1-85972-066-8*, Pub. by Avebry) Ashgate Pub Co.

Patterns of Transcendence. Chidester. (Adaptable Courseware-Softside Ser.). Date not set. mass mkt. 28.00 (*0-534-56587-5*) Wadsworth Pub.

Patterns of Transcendence: Religion, Death & Dying. 2nd ed. Chidester. (Religion Ser.). 2000. mass mkt. 27.50 (*0-534-50607-0*) Wadsworth Pub.

Patterns of Undocumented Migration: Mexico & the U. S. Ed. by Richard C. Jones. LC 83-27233. (Illus.). 256p. (C). 1984. 60.50 (*0-86598-130-2*, R3937) Rowman.

Patterns of Urban Growth in the Russian Empire During the 19th Century. Thomas S. Fedor. LC 74-84783. (University of Chicago, Department of Geography, Research Paper Ser.: No. 163). 274p. 1975. reprint ed. pap. 85.00 (*0-608-02245-4*, 206288600004) Bks Demand.

***Patterns of Vengeance.** John P. Reid. LC 99-52258. 1999. write for info. (*0-9635086-1-X*) Ninth Judicial CHS.

Patterns of Verbal Communication in Mathematics Classes. James T. Fey. LC 74-103135. (Theory & Research in Teaching Ser.). 104p. reprint ed. pap. 32.30 (*0-608-14926-8*, 202601100048) Bks Demand.

Patterns of Vertebrate Biology. E. W. Jameson, Jr. (Illus.). 480p. 1981. 59.00 (*0-387-90520-0*) Spr-Verlag.

Patterns of War since the 18th Century. 2nd ed. Larry H. Addington. LC 93-21544. (Illus.). 384p. (Orig.). (C). 1994. 36.95 (*0-253-30132-7*); pap. 15.95 (*0-253-20860-2*) Ind U Pr.

Patterns of War since the Eighteenth Century. Larry H. Addington. (Illus.). 318p. (C). 1999. reprint ed. pap. text 20.00 (*0-7881-6088-5*) DIANE Pub.

Patterns of War Through the 18th Century. Larry H. Addington. LC 89-45190. (Illus.). 176p. 1990. 25.95 (*0-253-30131-9*, MB 551) Ind U Pr.

Patterns of War Through the 18th Century. Larry H. Addington. LC 89-45190. (Illus.). 176p. 1990. pap. 12.95 (*0-253-20551-4*) Ind U Pr.

Patterns of Wealthholding in Wisconsin since 1850. Lee Soltow. LC 77-101506. 182p. 1971. reprint ed. pap. 56.50 (*0-608-01899-6*, 206255100003) Bks Demand.

Patterns of Wholeness: A Case Study. Rita Wienken. 64p. (Orig.). 1996. pap. 5.99 (*0-9652477-0-8*) RDLE INST Bkstre.

***Patterns of Work Culture: Cases & Strategies for Culture-Building.** Jai B. Sinha. LC 99-54592. 2000. pap. write for info. (*0-7619-9410-6*) Sage.

Patterns of World Economy. Wilson. 1983. pap. text. write for info. (*0-582-72252-7*, Pub. by Addison-Wesley) Longman.

Patterns of World Politics. K. Nossal. 1999. pap. text 39.95 (*0-13-907478-3*) P-H.

Patterns on Our Planet see Geography for Educators: Standards, Themes & Concepts

Patterns or Principles & Other Essays. Stanley L. Jaki. LC 95-81661. 235p. 1994. pap. text 12.95 (*1-882926-09-9*) ISI Books.

Patterns Plus. Conlin. (C). Date not set. pap. text, teacher ed., suppl. ed. write for info. (*0-395-60774-4*) HM.

Patterns Plus, 5 vols. 5th ed. Mary Lou Conlin. LC 94-76496. (C). 1994. pap. text 27.56 (*0-395-69918-5*) HM.

Patterns Plus: A Short Prose Reader with Argumentation, 3 vols. 3rd ed. Mary L. Conlin. (C). 1989. pap. text 2.76 (*0-395-51690-0*) HM.

Patterns Plus: A Short Prose Reader with Argumentation, 5 vols. 5th ed. Mary L. Conlin. (C). 1996. text, teacher ed. 11.96 (*0-395-71860-0*) HM.

Patterns Plus: A Short Prose Reader with Argumentation 5th ed. Mary Lou Conlin. LC 94-76496. xxix, 417p. 1995. write for info. (*0-395-71586-5*) HM.

Patterns Plus: A Short Prose Reader with Argumentation. 6th ed. Mary Lou Conlin. LC 98-72012. xxxii, 349p. 1999. pap. text 23.07 (*0-395-89959-1*) HM.

Patterns, Scales & Modes for Jazz Guitar. Arnie Berle. 1994. 21.95 (*0-8256-2552-1*, AM71382) Omnibus NY.

Patterns That Connect: Social Symbolism in Ancient & Tribal Art. Carl Schuster & Edmund Carpenter. LC 96-12825. (Illus.). 320p. 1996. 65.00 (*0-8109-6326-4*, Pub. by Abrams) Time Warner.

Patterns, Thinking, & Cognition: A Theory of Judgement. Howard Margolis. (Illus.). xii, 344p. 1988. pap. text 19.95 (*0-226-50528-6*); lib. bdg. 45.00 (*0-226-50527-8*) U Ch Pr.

Patterson: James Patterson of Conestoga Manor, & His Descendants. Edmund H. Bell & Mary H. Colwell. (Illus.). 313p. 1993. reprint ed. pap. 48.50 (*0-8328-3379-7*); reprint ed. lib. bdg. 58.50 (*0-8328-3378-9*) Higginson Bk Co.

***Patterson & the Great Green Greedy Galumpus.** Sean P. Harrington. LC 00-90290. (Illus.). 20p. (J). (gr. k-4). 2000. pap. 10.95 (*0-9672290-2-2*) D J Harrington.

Patterson Career Center Case Study Report. Bryna S. Fraser & Scott Menzel. (Cross Case Report & Case Studies). 50p. 1995. text, teacher ed. 20.00 (*0-614-24540-0*); pap. text, teacher ed. 10.00 (*0-614-24541-9*) Natl Inst Work.

Patterson Family. Sheridan Patterson. LC 93-71855. (Illus.). 367p. 1993. pap. 30.00 (*0-938041-17-7*) Arc Pr AR.

Patterson Mound: A Comparative Analysis of the Archaeology of Site ALA-328. fac. ed. Adam E. Treganza & James T. Davis. (Reports of the University of California Archaeological Survey: No. 47). (Illus.). 120p. 1959. reprint ed. pap. 13.13 (*1-55567-364-3*) Coyote Press.

Patterson of Tibet: Death Throes of a Nation. George Patterson. 600p. 1998. pap. 19.95 (*1-57901-026-1*, PPA) ProMotion Pub.

Pattersons American Education. Educational Directories Staff. (Patterson's American Education Ser.). 1998. 80.00 (*0-910536-74-0*) Ed Direct.

Patterson's American Education. rev. ed. Ed. by Douglas C. Moody. 900p. 1996. 81.00 (*0-910536-67-8*) Ed Direct.

***Patterson's American Education 2000, Vol. 96.** Educational Directories Staff. 1999. 97.00 (*0-910536-78-3*) Ed Direct.

Pattersons American Education, Vol. 94. 1997. 96.81 (*0-910536-70-8*) Ed Direct.

Patterson's Elementary Education. rev. ed. Ed. by Douglas C. Moody. LC 89-646629. 900p. 1996. 81.00 (*0-910536-68-6*) Ed Direct.

***Patterson's Elementary Education 2000, Vol. 12.** Educational Directories Staff. 1999. 97.00 (*0-910536-79-1*) Ed Direct.

Patterson's German-English Dictionary for Chemists, 4E. 4th ed. James C. Cox et al. LC 90-45365. 944p. 1991. 129.00 (*0-471-66991-1*) Wiley.

Patterson's Volunteers. large type ed. John Smith. 528p. 1987. 11.50 (*0-7089-1672-4*) Ulverscroft.

Patti, No. 2. John Benton. 192p. (Orig.). (YA). (gr. 7-12). 1990. reprint ed. mass mkt. 3.50 (*0-8007-8346-8*) J Benton Bks.

***Patti Playpal Family: Identification & Price Guide.** Carla Marie Cross. (Illus.). 160p. 2000. pap. 29.95 (*0-7643-1146-8*) Schiffer.

Patti Smith: An Unauthorized Biography. Victor Bockris & Roberta Bayley. LC 99-29435. (Illus.). 336p. 1999. 24.50 (*0-684-82363-2*) S&S Trade.

Patti Smith Complete: Lyrics, Reflections & Notes for the Future. Patti Smith. LC 98-23417. (Illus.). 257p. 1998. 35.00 (*0-385-49079-8*) Doubleday.

***Patti Smith Complete: Lyrics, Reflections & Notes for the Future.** Patti Smith. 288p. 1999. pap. 25.00 (*0-385-49080-1*, Anchor NY) Doubleday.

Patti Smith Memoir. Patti Smith. 1999. write for info. (*0-385-49077-1*) Doubleday.

Pattie Round & Wally Square. Priscilla Jean. (Illus.). (J). (gr. k-3). 1965. 8.95 (*0-8392-3048-6*) Astor-Honor.

Pattie's Personal Narrative, 1824-30, Willard's Inland Trade with New Mexico, 1825, & Downfall of the Fredonia Republic. Malte-Brun's Account of Mexico see Early Western Travels, 1748-1846

Patting the Air. Dennis Ciscel. (Illus.). 100p. Date not set. 12.95 (*0-911051-68-6*) Plain View.

Patti's Pet Gorilla. Mauser. (J). 1987. pap. 7.00 (*0-385-22416-8*) Doubleday.

Patti's Pet Gorilla. Patricia R. Mauser. 64p. (J). 1991. pap. 2.95 (*0-380-71039-0*, Avon Bks) Morrow Avon.

Patti's Pumpkin Patch. Illus. by Teri Sloat. LC 98-17475. 32p. (J). (ps-2). 1999. 15.99 (*0-399-23010-6*, G P Putnam) Peng Put Young Read.

Pattison: Portrait of a Capitalist Superstar. Russell Kelly. 350p. 1986. mass mkt. write for info. (*0-919573-55-X*, Pub. by New Star Bks) Genl Dist Srvs.

Patton. Herbert Essame. (Military Commanders Ser.). 1998. pap. 18.95 (*0-938289-99-3*, 289993) Combined Pub.

Patton. Golden Books Staff. pap. 1.59 (*5-550-63079-6*) Nairi.

Patton: A Genius for War. Carlo D'Este. 1996. 35.00 (*0-614-12874-9*) HarpC.

Patton: A Genius for War. Carlo Deste. LC 95-38433. 1024p. 1996. pap. 20.00 (*0-06-092762-5*) HarpC.

Patton: Operation Cobra & Beyond. Michael R. Green et al. LC 98-23722. (Illus.). 160p. 1998. pap. 19.95 (*0-7603-0498-X*) Motorbooks Intl.

Patton: Ordeal & Triumph. Ladislas Farago. (Illus.). 1964. 39.95 (*0-8392-1084-1*) Astor-Honor.

Patton: The Man Behind the Legend, 1885-1945. Martin Blumenson. (Illus.). 320p. 1994. pap. 16.00 (*0-688-13795-4*, Quil) HarperTrade.

***Patton & His Third Army.** Brenton Greene Wallace. LC 00-35752. 2000. write for info. (*0-8117-2896-X*) Stackpole.

Patton & His 3rd Army. Brenton G. Wallace. (Combat Arms Ser.: No. 6). (Illus.). 232p. 1981. reprint ed. 29.95 (*0-89839-048-6*) Battery Pr.

Patton & His 3rd Army. Brenton G. Wallace. LC 78-31806. (Illus.). 232p. 1979. reprint ed. lib. bdg. 65.00 (*0-8371-7755-3*, WAPTA, Greenwood Pr) Greenwood.

Patton & the Battle of the Bulge. Michael R. Green & Gladys Greenaway. LC 99-22933. (Illus.). 160p. 1999. pap. text 19.95 (*0-7603-0652-4*) Motorbooks Intl.

Patton at Bay. John Nelson Rickard. LC 98-36753. (Praeger Series in War Studies). 320p. 1999. 45.00 (*0-275-96354-3*, Praeger Pubs) Greenwood.

Patton Mind: The Professional Development of an Extraordinary Leader. Roger H. Nye. LC 92-10490. (Illus.). 224p. pap. 12.95 (*0-89529-428-1*, Avery) Penguin Putnam.

***Patton on Leadership.** 1999. 23.00 (*0-13-089292-0*) P-H.

Patton on Leadership: Strategic Lessons for Corporate Warfare. Alan Axelrod. LC 99-28533. (Illus.). 271p. 1999. text 23.00 (*0-7352-0091-2*) PH Pr.

Patton Papers, 1885-1940. Martin Blumenson. (Illus.). 1048p. 1998. reprint ed. pap. 24.50 (*0-306-80862-5*) Da Capo.

Patton Papers, 1885-1940, Vol. I. Martin Blumenson. (Illus.). 1010p. 1999. reprint ed. lib. bdg. 53.95 (*0-7351-0076-4*) Replica Bks.

Patton Papers, 1940-1945. George S. Patton. Ed. by Martin Blumenson. LC 96-15251. (Illus.). 936p. 1996. reprint ed. pap. 19.95 (*0-306-80717-3*) Da Capo.

Patton Papers, 1940-1945, Vol. II. Martin Blumenson. 914p. 1999. reprint ed. lib. bdg. 53.95 (*0-7351-0048-9*) Replica Bks.

Pattons: A Personal History of an American Family. Robert H. Patton. (Illus.). 352p. 1996. reprint ed. pap. 21.95 (*1-57488-127-2*) Brasseys.

Patton's Gap: An Account of the Battle of Normandy, 1944. 2nd rev. ed. Richard Rohmer. (Illus.). 264p. 1998. 23.95 (*0-7737-3118-0*) Stoddart Publ.

***Patton's Ghost Corps: Cracking the Siegfried Line.** Nathan N. Prefer. 288p. 2000. pap. 19.95 (*0-89141-708-7*) Presidio Pr.

Patton's GI Photographers. Ed. by Ralph Butterfield. LC 92-5229. (Illus.). 192p. 1992. 39.95 (*0-8138-0216-4*) Iowa St U Pr.

Pattons Lehigh County, Pennsylvania. A. B. Patton. 1997. pap. 10.95 (*1-57381-048-7*, 836801Q) A B Patton.

Patton's One-Minute Messages: Tactical Leadership Skills for Business Managers. Charles M. Province. (Illus.). 104p. 1995. pap. 9.95 (*0-89141-546-7*, Pub. by Presidio Pr) Natl Bk Netwk.

Patton's Tank Drive: D-Day to Victory. Michael Green. LC 95-36435. (Illus.). 160p. 1995. pap. 19.95 (*0-7603-0163-8*) MBI Pubg.

Patton's Third Army. Christopher J. Anderson. LC 99-20139. (G.I. Ser.). 1999. 19.95 (*0-7910-5374-1*) Chelsea Hse.

Patton's Third Army. Christopher J. Anderson. LC 98-130315. (G. I.: Vol. 10). (Illus.). 80p. 1997. pap. 12.95 (*1-85367-290-4*, Pub. by Greenhill Bks) Stackpole.

Patton's Wall. Leo Kessler. 224p. 1999. 24.00 (*0-7278-2261-6*, Pub. by Severn Hse) Chivers N Amer.

Patty & Pop's Picnic: Big Book. large type ed. Susan McCloskey. (Little Books & Big Bks.). (Illus.). 8p. (J). (ps-1). 1998. pap. text 19.89 (*0-8215-0863-6*) Sadlier.

Patty Cat. Barbara DeRubertis. LC 96-75011. (Let's Read Together Ser.). (Illus.). 32p. (J). (ps-2). 1996. pap. 4.95 (*1-57565-000-2*) Kane Pr.

***Patty Dillman of Hot Dog Fame.** Susan Wojciechowski. 180p. (J). (gr. 5-8). 1999. pap. 5.99 (*0-9673794-0-7*) Small Miracles.

Patty Duke: A Bio-Bibliography, 3. Stephen L. Eberly. LC 87-37575. (Bio-Bibliographies in the Performing Arts Ser.: No. 3). 144p. 1988. lib. bdg. 45.00 (*0-313-25675-6*, EPD/, Greenwood Pr) Greenwood.

Patty Hearst: Her Own Story. Patricia C. Hearst & Alvin Moscow. 1988. mass mkt. 6.99 (*0-380-70651-2*, Avon Bks) Morrow Avon.

Patty Helps Out. large type ed. Judy Mullican. (HRL Cuddle Bks.). (Illus.). 8p. (J). (ps-k). 1999. pap. text 10.95 (*1-57332-140-0*); pap. text 10.95 (*1-57332-141-9*) HighReach Lrning.

Patty Horn's Desert Dwellers Fiesta! Patty Horn. (Illus.). 46p. (J). (gr. k-8). 1998. spiral bd. 15.95 incl. audio (*0-9644105-9-1*) Two Geckos Mus.

Patty Jane's House of Curl. Lorna Landvik. 1999. mass mkt. 6.99 (*0-8041-1460-9*) Ivy Books.

Patty Jane's House of Curl. large type ed. Lorna Landvik. (Niagara Large Print Ser.). 488p. 1997. 29.50 (*0-7089-5877-X*) Ulverscroft.

Patty Jane's House of Curl: A Novel. Lorna Landvik. LC 95-15731. 292p. 1995. 19.95 (*1-882593-12-X*) Bridge Wrks.

Patty Jane's House of Curl: A Novel. Lorna Landvik. 292p. 1996. pap. 11.00 (*0-449-91100-4*) Fawcett.

Patty Loveless: Only What I Feel. Ed. by Milton Okun. 57p. (Orig.). (YA). pap. 14.95 (*0-89524-898-0*, Pub. by Cherry Lane) H Leonard.

Patty Loveless: When Fallen Angels Fly. Ed. by Milton Okun. 70p. (Orig.). (YA). pap. 14.95 (*0-89524-897-2*, 02502161) Cherry Lane.

Patty Paper Geometry. Michael Serra. (YA). (gr. 9-12). 1994. 18.95 (*1-55953-072-3*) Key Curr Pr.

Patty Paper Geometry Student Workbook. Michael Serra. (YA). (gr. 9-12). 1994. 3.25 (*1-55953-074-X*) Key Curr Pr.

Patty Reed's Doll: The Story of the Donner Party. Rachel K. Laurgaard. 1989. 13.05 (*0-606-00841-1*, Pub. by Turtleback) Demco.

Patty Reed's Doll: The Story of the Donner Party. Rachel K. Laurgaard. LC 89-51264. (Illus.). 144p. (J). (gr. 3-6). 1989. reprint ed. pap. 7.95 (*0-9617357-2-4*) Tomato Enter.

***Patty Saves the Day! A Tale in Which Patty Discovers Her True Gift.** Kathryn Wheeler. LC 00-24705. (Stories to Grow By Ser.). (Illus.). (J). 2000. write for info. (*0-7424-0012-3*) Instruct Fair.

Patty Sheehan on Golf. Patty Sheehan & Betty Hicks. LC 95-53051. 240p. 1996. 19.95 (*0-87833-910-8*) Taylor Pub.

Patty's Curiosity. unabridged ed. Charlotte Elizabeth, pseud. (Children's Heritage Ser.). (Illus.). 30p. (J). (gr. 4-6). 1996. pap. 4.25 (*1-58339-117-7*) Triangle Press.

Patty's Hygiene & Toxicology no. 5. Harris. text. write for info. (*0-471-31945-7*) Wiley.

***Patty's Industrial Hygiene, 4 Vol.** 5th ed. Robert L. Harris. 3552p. 2000. 895.00 (*0-471-29784-4*) Wiley.

***Patty's Industrial Hygiene, Vol. 1.** 5th ed. Robert L. Harris. LC 99-32462. 784p. 2000. 250.00 (*0-471-29756-9*) Wiley.

***Patty's Industrial Hygiene, Vol. 2.** 5th ed. Robert L. Harris. 864p. 2000. 250.00 (*0-471-29754-2*) Wiley.

***Patty's Industrial Hygiene, Vol. 3.** 5th ed. Robert L. Harris. 816p. 2000. 250.00 (*0-471-29753-4*) Wiley.

***Patty's Industrial Hygiene, Vol. 4.** 5th ed. Robert L. Harris. 1088p. 2000. 250.00 (*0-471-29749-6*) Wiley.

Patty's Industrial Hygiene & Toxicology, 3 vols. 4th ed. Ed. by George D. Clayton & Florence E. Clayton. 9004p. 1995. 2199.00 (*0-471-13654-9*) Wiley.

Patty's Industrial Hygiene & Toxicology, 3 vols., Vol. 3. Ed. by George D. Clayton & Florence E. Clayton. 42p. 1996. cd-rom 2495.00 (*0-471-13530-5*) Wiley.

Patty's Industrial Hygiene & Toxicology, Vol. 3, 2 Pt. Set. 3rd ed. Ed. by Lewis J. Cralley et al. 1649p. 1995. 435.00 (*0-471-58677-3*) Wiley.

Patty's Industrial Hygiene & Toxicology: Theory & Rationale of Industrial Hygiene Practice, Vol. 3, Pt. B, Theory and Rationale of Industrial. 3rd ed. Ed. by Lewis J. Cralley et al. LC 93-23747. 784p. 1995. 249.00 (*0-471-53065-4*) Wiley.

Patty's Industrial Hygiene & Toxicology: Theory & Rationale of Industrial Hygiene Practice-Biological Responses, Vol. 3. 3rd ed. Ed. by Lewis J. Cralley et al. 864p. 1994. 225.00 (*0-471-53066-2*, Pub. by Interscience) Wiley.

Patty's Industrial Hygiene & Toxicology Vol. 1: General Principles, Pts. A & B. 4th ed. Ed. by George D. Clayton & Florence E. Clayton. 2199p. 1991. 435.00 (*0-471-55205-4*) Wiley.

Patty's Industrial Hygiene & Toxicology Vol. 1, Pt. A: General Principles, Vol. 1, Pt. A, General Principles. 4th ed. Ed. by George D. Clayton & Florence E. Clayton. LC 90-13080. 1104p. 1991. 249.00 (*0-471-50197-2*) Wiley.

Patty's Industrial Hygiene & Toxicology Vol. 1, Pt. B: General Principles, Vol. 1, Pt. B, General Principles. 4th ed. Ed. by George D. Clayton & Florence E. Clayton. 1120p. 1991. 249.00 (*0-471-50196-4*) Wiley.

Patty's Industrial Hygiene & Toxicology Vol. 2 & 6: Toxicology, Vol. 2. 4th ed. Ed. by George D. Clayton & Florence E. Clayton. 5130p. 1994. 1295.00 (*0-471-54727-1*) Wiley.

Patty's Industrial Hygiene & Toxicology Vol. 2, Pt. C: Toxicology, Vol. 2. 4th ed. Ed. by George D. Clayton & Florence E. Clayton. 736p. 1994. 249.00 (*0-471-54726-3*) Wiley.

Patty's Industrial Hygiene & Toxicology Vol. 2, Pt. D: Toxicology, Vol. 2, Pt. D, Toxicology. 4th ed. Ed. by George D. Clayton & Florence E. Clayton. 896p. 1994. 249.00 (*0-471-57947-5*) Wiley.

Patty's Industrial Hygiene & Toxicology Vol. 2, Pt. A: Toxicology, Vol. 2. 4th ed. Ed. by George D. Clayton & Florence E. Clayton. 968p. 1993. 249.00 (*0-471-54724-7*) Wiley.

Patty's Industrial Hygiene & Toxicology Vol. 2, Pt. B: Toxicology, Vol. 2. 4th ed. Ed. by George D. Clayton & Florence E. Clayton. 752p. 1993. 249.00 (*0-471-54725-5*) Wiley.

Patty's Industrial Hygiene & Toxicology Vol. 2, Pt. E: Toxicology, Vol. 2. 4th ed. Ed. by George D. Clayton & Florence E. Clayton. 1020p. 1994. 249.00 (*0-471-01282-3*) Wiley.

Patty's Industrial Hygiene & Toxicology Vol. 2, Pt. F: Toxicology, Vol. 2. 4th ed. Ed. by George D. Clayton & Florence E. Clayton. 760p. 1994. 249.00 (*0-471-01280-7*) Wiley.

Patty's Journey: From Orphanage to Adoption & Reunion. Donna S. Norling. 208p. 1996. 17.95 (*0-8166-2866-1*) U of Minn Pr.

Patty's Journey: From Orphanage to Adoption & Reunion. Donna S. Norling. 1998. pap. text 14.95 (*0-8166-2867-X*) U of Minn Pr.

Patty's Last Dance. Jamie Suzanne. (Sweet Valley Twins Ser.: No. 65). (J). (gr. 3-7). 1993. 8.35 (*0-606-02939-7*, Pub. by Turtleback) Demco.

Patty's Poems. Patricia Grindel. LC 98-66621. 240p. 1998. pap. 12.95 (*1-882792-68-8*) Proctor Pubns.

Patty's Story: Straight Talk about Drugs. Gilda Berger. (YA). 1992. pap. 4.80 (*0-395-63558-6*) HM.

***Patty's Toxicology, Vol. 1.** 5th ed. Eula Bingham et al. 1056p. 2000. 295.00 (*0-471-31932-5*) Wiley.

***Patuas & Patua Art in Bengal.** McCutchion & Bhowmik. 1999. 88.00 (*81-7102-061-5*, Pub. by Firma KLM) S Asia.

Patulous: The Prairie Rattlesnake. Jonathan Kahn. Ed. by Nancy R. Thatch. LC 91-13652. (Books for Students by Students). (Illus.). 26p. (J). (gr. k-4). 1991. lib. bdg. 15.95 (*0-933849-36-2*) Landmark Edns.

Patwin & Their Neighbors. fac. ed. A. L. Kroeber. (University of California Publications in American Archaeology & Ethnology: Vol. 29: 4). 181p. (C). 1932. reprint ed. pap. text 19.38 (*1-55567-281-7*) Coyote Press.

Patwin Houses. fac. ed. W. C. McKern. (University of California Publications in American Archaeology & Ethnology: Vol. 20: 10). (Illus.). 15p. (C). 1923. reprint ed. pap. text 1.88 (*1-55567-246-9*) Coyote Press.

***Patzcuaro.** Joanne Kyger. 32p. 1999. 6.00 (*0-9631462-3-8*, Pub. by Blue Millennium) SPD-Small Pr Dist.

Pau d'Arco: Immune Power from the Rainforest. Kenneth Jones. LC 94-1489. (Illus.). 160p. 1994. pap. 8.95 (*0-89281-497-7*, Heal Arts VT) Inner Tradit.

Pau Hana: Plantation Life & Labor in Hawaii, 1835-1920. Ronald Takaki. LC 83-10225. (Illus.). 228p. 1983. pap. text 14.00 (*0-8248-0956-4*) UH Pr.

Pauahi: The Kamehameha Legacy. George H. Kanahele. (Illus.). 223p. 1986. 15.95 (*0-87336-005-2*) Kamehameha Schools.

Pauillac: The Wines & Estates of a Renowned Bordeaux Commune. Stephen Brook. (Illus.). 192p. 1998. 45.00 (*1-85732-352-1*, Pub. by Mitchell Beazley) Antique Collect.

P

Pauk How to Study 6E & Dict CMPC 6, 6 vols. 6th ed. Walter Paukovits. (C). Date not set. pap. 40.76 (*0-395-90540-0*) HM.

Pauk How To Study 6E & ESL Dict, 6 vols. 6th ed. Walter Paukovits. (C). Date not set. 48.76 (*0-395-90541-9*) HM.

Pauk How To Study 6E & PEJSA, 6 vols. 6th ed. Walter Paukovits. (C). Date not set. pap. 39.96 (*0-395-90539-7*) HM.

Pauk How To Study 6E & Roget, 6 vols. 6th ed. Walter Paukovits. (C). Date not set. 44.36 (*0-395-90542-7*) HM.

Paul see Young Readers Christian Library

Paul. Gunther Bornkamm. LC 95-2159. 288p. 1995. pap. 22.00 (*0-8006-2898-5*, 1-2898, Fortress Pr) Augsburg Fortress.

Paul. E. P. Sanders. (Past Masters Ser.). 144p. 1991. pap. text 9.95 (*0-19-287679-1*) OUP.

Paul: A Critical Life. Jerome Murphy-O'Connor. LC 97-10250. (Illus.). 432p. 1998. reprint ed. pap. 19.95 (*0-19-285342-2*) OUP.

Paul: A Man of Two Worlds. C. J. Den Heyer. 320p. Date not set. pap. 29.00 (*1-56338-301-2*) TPI PA.

Paul: A Man Who Changed the World. H. Buckmaster. 1989. pap. 8.95 (*0-933062-27-3*) R H Sommer.

***Paul: A Novel.** Walter Wangerin, Jr. LC 99-58137. 512p. 2000. 22.99 (*0-310-21892-6*) Zondervan.

Paul: A Study in Social & Religious History. Adolph Deissman. Tr. by William W. Wilson. 1958. 16.50 (*0-8446-1965-5*) Peter Smith.

Paul: An Introduction to His Thought. C. K. Barrett. LC 94-1153. 160p. (Orig.). 1994. pap. 14.95 (*0-664-25541-8*) Westminster John Knox.

Paul: An Outline of His Theology. Herman N. Ridderbos. 1997. pap. text 30.00 (*0-8028-4469-3*) Eerdmans.

Paul: Ancestry of Katharine Choate Paul. E. J. Paul. (Illus.). 386p. 1991. reprint ed. pap. 60.00 (*0-8328-1763-5*); reprint ed. lib. bdg. 70.00 (*0-8328-1762-7*) Higginson Bk Co.

Paul: Apostle of the Heart Set Free. F. F. Bruce. LC 77-26127. 1978. 30.00 (*0-8028-3501-5*) Eerdmans.

Paul: Apostle to the Gentiles. Jurgen Becker. Tr. by O. C. Dean, Jr. LC 92-28776. 448p. 1993. pap. 34.95 (*0-664-25707-0*) Westminster John Knox.

Paul: Arbeitsbuch Elektrotechniques. 1996. 33.00 (*3-540-59484-1*) Spr-Verlag.

***Paul: By the Grace of God: Early Life Through Second Missionary Journey.** Casandra Martin. (Women Opening the Word Ser.). 1999. pap. 12.99 (*0-89098-254-6*) Twent Cent Christ.

Paul: Crisis in Galatia: A Study in Early Christian Theology. George Howard. LC 77-84002. (Society for New Testament Studies,: No. 35). 126p. reprint ed. pap. 36.00 (*0-608-14082-1*, 2024478) Bks Demand.

Paul: Follower of Jesus: or Founder of Christ. David Wenham. LC 95-1071. 468p. (Orig.). 1995. pap. 26.00 (*0-8028-0124-2*) Eerdmans.

Paul: His Letters, Message & Heritage: A Reflective Commentary. Michael J. Taylor. LC 97-2014. 285p. (Orig.). 1997. pap. 14.95 (*0-8189-0772-X*) Alba.

Paul: Ideal Man - Model Missionary. A. B. Simpson. (Heritage Ser.). 1996. pap. 1.99 (*0-87509-651-4*) Chr Pubns.

Paul: Joseph Paull of Ilminster, Somerset, Eng., & Some Descendants Who Have Resided in Philadelphia. H. N. Paul. (Illus.). 157p. 1992. reprint ed. pap. 24.00 (*0-8328-2703-7*); reprint ed. lib. bdg. 34.00 (*0-8328-2702-9*) Higginson Bk Co.

***Paul: Living for the Call of Christ.** Gene A. Getz. LC 99-44909. (Men of Character Ser.: Vol. 12). 192p. 2000. pap. 10.99 (*0-8054-1818-0*) Broadman.

Paul: Man of the Millennia. Lester Sumrall. 63p. (Orig.). 1990. pap. text 1.95 (*0-937580-32-5*) Sumrall Pubng.

Paul: One of the Prophets?: A Contribution to the Apostle's Self-Understanding. Karl O. Sanders. (WissUNT Neuen Testament Ser.). 224p. (Orig.). 1990. pap. 52.50 (*3-16-145557-6*, Pub. by JCB Mohr) Coronet Bks.

Paul: Pastor of Communities for Today. Kevin Hanlon. 128p. (C). 1996. pap. 39.95 (*0-85439-365-X*, Pub. by St Paul Pubns) St Mut.

Paul: Pride & Penitence. Cecil J. Bailey. 224p. (Orig.). 1989. pap. 9.95 (*0-940999-50-1*, C-2160) Star Bible.

Paul: Saint of the Inner City. Joseph Fitzpatrick. 144p. 1990. pap. 5.95 (*0-8091-3129-3*) Paulist Pr.

Paul: The Man & the Myth. Calvin Roetzel. 1999. pap. 22.00 (*0-8006-3173-0*, Fortress Pr) Augsburg Fortress.

Paul: The Man & the Myth. Calvin J. Roetzel. LC 98-25446. (Studies on Personalities of the New Testament). 245p. 1998. text 34.95 (*1-57003-264-5*) U of SC Pr.

Paul: The Mind of the Apostle. A. N. Wilson. 1997. 25.00 (*0-614-28042-7*) Norton.

Paul: The Mind of the Apostle. A. N. Wilson. 288p. 1998. pap. 13.95 (*0-393-31760-9*) Norton.

Paul: The Missionary Apostle. John G. Butler. 806p. 1995. 29.50 (*1-889773-11-5*) LBC Publns.

Paul: Thirteenth Apostle (Acts 13-28) Chuck Christensen & Winnie Christensen. (Fisherman Bible Studyguide Ser.). 64p. (Orig.). 1987. pap. 4.99 (*0-87788-652-0*, H Shaw Pubs) Waterbrook Pr.

Paul A. Samuelson: Critical Assessments, 4 vols., Set. Ed. by John C. Wood & Ronald N. Woods. 1360p. 1989. text, boxed set 660.00 (*0-415-02002-6*, A3209) Routledge.

Paul Adrien Maurice Dirac: Reminiscences about a Great Physicist. Ed. by Behram N. Kursunoglu & E. P. Wigner. (Illus.). 320p. 1987. text 120.00 (*0-521-34013-6*) Cambridge U Pr.

Paul Adrien Maurice Dirac: Reminiscences about a Great Physicist. Ed. by Behram N. Kursunoglu & E. P. Wigner. (Illus.). 315p. (C). 1990. pap. text 42.95 (*0-521-38688-8*) Cambridge U Pr.

Paul among Jews & Gentiles & Other Essays. Krister Stendahl. LC 75-36450. 128p. 1976. pap. 14.00 (*0-8006-1224-8*, 1-1224, Fortress Pr) Augsburg Fortress.

Paul: An Outline of His Theology see Pensamiento de Pablo

***Paul & Apostasy: Eschatology, Perseverance & Falling Away in the Corinthian Congregation.** B. J. Oropeza. (Wissenshaftliche Untersuchungen zum Neuen Testament Ser.: Vol. 2). 320p. 2000. pap. 110.00 (*3-16-147307-8*, Pub. by JCB Mohr) Coronet Bks.

Paul & Barnabas Syndrome. Daniel C. Hardin. 201p. (Orig.). 1991. pap. 10.00 (*0-940999-73-0*, C2173) Star Bible.

Paul & Early Christianity Vol. I: Acts 1-9. Kristy L. Christian & Kathryn L. Merrill. (Illus.). 208p. (YA). (gr. 6-12). 1996. spiral bd., wbk. ed. 19.95 (*0-9626535-1-9*) Infinite Discovery.

Paul & Early Christianity Vol. II: Acts 10-28. Kristy L. Christian & Kathryn L. Merrill. (Illus.). 234p. (YA). (gr. 6-12). 1996. spiral bd., wbk. ed. 19.95 (*0-9626535-2-7*) Infinite Discovery.

Paul & Empire: Community & Authority. Ed. by Richard A. Horsley. LC 97-38319. 272p. 1997. pap. 19.00 (*1-56338-217-2*) TPI PA.

Paul & Friends see Pablo y Sus Amigos

Paul & His Converts. Ernest E. Best. 192p. (C). 1988. 39.95 (*0-567-09147-3*) Bks Intl VA.

Paul & his Elephant see Pablo y su Elefante

Paul & His Friends. Vicki Hines. (Great Big Bks.). 16p. (J). (gr. k-1). 1997. pap. text 14.95 (*0-687-06667-0*) Abingdon.

Paul & His Letters. John B. Pohill. LC 99-26826. 1999. 29.99 (*0-8054-1097-X*) Broadman.

Paul & His Letters. 2nd enl. rev. ed. Leander E. Keck. LC 88-7006. (Proclamation Commentaries: The New Testament Witnesses for Preaching). 176p. 1988. pap. 17.00 (*0-8006-2340-1*, 1-2340, Fortress Pr) Augsburg Fortress.

***Paul & His Story: (Re)Interpreting the Exodus Tradition.** Sylvia C. Keesmaat. (Journal for the Study of the New Testament, Supplement Ser.: No. 181). 289p. 1999. 85.00 (*1-85075-964-2*, Pub. by Sheffield Acad) CUP Services.

Paul & His Theology. 2nd ed. Joseph A. Fitzmyer. 144p. (C). 1988. pap. text 23.00 (*0-13-654419-3*) P-H.

Paul & Jesus: Collected Essays. Ed. by A. J. M. Wedderburn. (JSNT Supplement Ser.: Vol. 37). 206p. 1989. 57.50 (*1-85075-218-4*, Pub. by Sheffield Acad) CUP Services.

Paul & Juhl's Essentials of Radiologic Imaging. 6th ed. John H. Juhl. 1,264p. 1993. text 149.00 (*0-397-51099-3*) Lppncott W & W.

Paul & Mary & their Magic Crystals. Uma Silbey. (Illus.). 48p. (Orig.). (J). (ps-3). 1988. pap. 9.95 (*0-938925-07-5*) U-Music.

Paul & Palestinian Judaism: A Comparison of Patterns of Religion. E. P. Sanders. LC 76-62612. 500p. (Orig.). 1977. pap. 30.00 (*0-8006-1899-8*, 1-1899) Augsburg Fortress.

Paul & Philodemus: Adaptability in Epicurean & Early Christian Psychagogy. Clarence E. Glad. LC 95-15083. (Supplements to Novum Testamentum Ser.: Vol. 81). 1995. 145.50 (*90-04-10067-9*) Brill Academic Pubs.

***Paul & Politics: Ekklesia, Israel, Imperium, Interpretation.** Richard A. Horsley. 224p. 2000. pap. 26.00 (*1-56338-323-3*) TPI PA.

Paul & Preseverance: Staying in & Falling Away. Judith M. Volf. (WissUNT Neuen Testament Ser.: No. 37). 300p. (Orig.). 1989. pap. 48.50 (*3-16-145527-4*, Pub. by JCB Mohr) Coronet Bks.

Paul & Rabbinic Judaism: Some Rabbinic Elements in Pauline Theology. W. D. Davies. 456p. 1980. reprint ed. pap. 28.00 (*1-888961-06-6*) Sigler Pr.

Paul & Rabbinic Judaism: Some Rabbinic Elements in Pauline Theology. W. D. Davies. 456p. 1998. reprint ed. 44.00 (*1-888961-07-4*) Sigler Pr.

Paul & Revelation & the Importance It Had to His Weakness. unabridged ed. Richard J. Willoughby. LC 96-96215. 103p. (Orig.). 1996. pap. write for info. (*0-9651120-0-4*) R J Willoughby.

Paul & Sebastian. Rene Escudie. (I Love to Read Collection). (Illus.). 48p. (J). (ps-3). 1992. lib. bdg. 12.79 (*0-89565-806-2*) Childs World.

Paul & Sebastian. Rene Escudie. Tr. by Roderick Townley from FRE. LC 88-12768. (Illus.). 32p. (J). (ps-3). 1988. 11.95 (*0-916291-19-7*) Kane-Miller Bk.

Paul & Sebastian. Rene Escudie. Tr. by Roderick Townley. (FRE., Illus.). 32p. (J). (ps-3). 1994. reprint ed. pap. 6.95 (*0-916291-49-9*) Kane-Miller Bk.

Paul & Silas Go to Jail. (Bible Big Bks.). 2000. 14.99 (*1-55945-577-2*) Group Pub.

Paul & the Anatomy of Apostolic Authority. John H. Schutz. LC 74-76573. (Society for New Testament Studies,: No. 26). 319p. reprint ed. pap. 91.00 (*0-608-18400-4*, 2030619) Bks Demand.

Paul & the Christian Woman. Brendan Byrne. 128p. (C). 1988. 60.00 (*0-7855-2323-5*, Pub. by St Paul Pubns) St Mut.

Paul & the Corinthians. Robert Winegard. Ed. by Sally Sharpe. 144p. 1998. pap. 9.95 (*0-687-07690-0*) Abingdon.

***Paul & the Corinthians.** Robert Winegard. (Life & Letters of Paul Ser.). 128p. 2000. pap. 8.00 (*0-687-07840-7*) Abingdon.

***Paul & the Discourse of Power.** Sandra Hack Polaski. (Biblical Seminar Ser.: No. 62). 151p. 1999. pap. 19.95 (*1-85075-934-0*, Pub. by Sheffield Acad) CUP Services.

***Paul & the Galatians.** Paul E. Stroble. (Life & Letters of Paul Ser.). 72p. 2000. pap. 8.00 (*0-687-09023-7*) Abingdon.

Paul & the Gentiles: Remapping the Apostle's Convictional World. Terence L. Donaldson. LC 97-202. 432p. 1997. pap. 34.00 (*0-8006-2993-0*, 1-2993, Fortress Pr) Augsburg Fortress.

Paul & the Law. 2nd ed. Heikki Raisanen. (Wissenschaftliche Untersuchungen Zum Neuen Testament Ser.: No. 29). 351p. 1987. 67.50 (*3-16-145198-8*, Pub. by JCB Mohr) Coronet Bks.

Paul & the Law: A Contextual Approach. Frank Thielman. LC 94-31571. 280p. (Orig.). 1994. pap. 21.99 (*0-8308-1854-5*, 1854) InterVarsity.

Paul & the Legacies of Paul. Ed. by William S. Babcock. LC 89-78490. (Illus.). 460p. 1990. text 32.50 (*0-87074-305-8*); pap. text 16.95 (*0-87074-306-6*) SMU Press.

Paul & the Nations: The Old Testament & Jewish Background of Paul's Mission to the Nations with Special Reference to the Destination of the Galatians. James M. Scott. LC 96-106633. (WissUNT Zum Neuen Testament Ser.: No. 84). 280p. 1995. 147.50 (*3-16-146377-3*, Pub. by JCB Mohr) Coronet Bks.

Paul & the Parousia: An Exegetical & Theological Investigation. Joseph Plevnik. LC 96-10729. 352p. (C). 1997. 29.95 (*1-56563-180-3*) Hendrickson MA.

Paul & the Rhetoric of Reconciliation: An Exegetical Investigation of the Language & Composition of One Corinthians. Margaret M. Mitchell. (Hermeneutische Untersuchungen zur Theologie Ser.: No. 28). 392p. 1991. 115.00 (*3-16-145794-3*, Pub. by JCB Mohr) Coronet Bks.

Paul & the Roman House Churches: A Simulation. Reta Halteman Finger. LC 93-2312. 208p. (Orig.). 1993. pap. 12.99 (*0-8361-3605-5*) Herald Pr.

Paul & the Scriptures of Israel. Ed. by Craig A. Evans & James A. Sanders. (Journal for the Study of the New Testament, Supplement Ser.: Vol. 83). 296p. 1993. 85.00 (*1-85075-412-8*, Pub. by Sheffield Acad) CUP Services.

***Paul & the Stoics.** Troels Engberg-Pedersen. 448p. 2000. 39.95 (*0-664-22234-X*) Westminster John Knox.

***Paul & the Thessalonians.** Abraham J. Malherbe. 130p. 2000. reprint ed. pap. 14.00 (*1-888961-13-9*) Sigler Pr.

Paul & the Wolf. Margo Lemieux. LC 95-9686. (Illus.). 32p. (J). (gr. k-2). 1995. 13.95 (*0-382-39100-4*) Silver Burdett Pr.

Paul & the Wolf. Margo Lemieux. (Illus.). 32p. (J). (gr. 1-3). 1995. pap. 5.95 (*0-382-39101-2*); lib. bdg. 15.95 (*0-382-39099-7*, Silver Pr NJ) Silver Burdett Pr.

Paul & Third World Women Theologians. Loretta Dornisch. LC 98-51061. 1999. 9.95 (*0-8146-2553-3*) Liturgical Pr.

Paul & Virginia. Bernardin J. De Saint-Pierre. Tr. & Intro. by John Donovan. 1983. 29.95 (*0-7206-0598-9*, Pub. by P Owen Ltd) Dufour.

Paul & Virginia. Bernardin J. De Saint-Pierre. Tr. by Andrew Lang from FRE. LC 87-52. 152p. 1987. reprint ed. lib. bdg. 29.50 (*0-86527-363-4*) Fertig.

Paul Anderson: The Mightiest Minister. Randall J. Strossen. LC 98-75825. (Illus.). 144p. 1999. pap. 24.95 (*0-926888-08-0*) IronMind Enterprises.

Paul Andreau: The Discovery of Universal Space. Pref. by Paul Andreau. (I Talenti Ser.). (FRE, ITA & KOR., Illus.). 144p. 1997. pap. write for info. (*88-7838-036-9*) Rockport Pubs.

Paul, Antioch & Jerusalem: A Study in Relationships & Authority in Earliest Christianity. Nicholas Taylor. (Journal for the Study of the New Testament, Supplement Ser.: No. 66). 271p. (C). 1992. 75.00 (*1-85075-331-8*, Pub. by Sheffield Acad) CUP Services.

Paul, Apostle of Liberty: The Origin & Nature of Paul's Christianity. Richard Longenecker. 310p. 1992. reprint ed. pap. 23.95 (*1-57383-005-4*) Regent College.

Paul as Apostle to the Gentiles: His Apostolic Self-Awareness & Its Influence on the Soteriological Argument in Romans. Daniel J.-S. Chae. (Biblical & Theological Monographs). xiv, 378p. 1997. reprint ed. pap. 40.00 (*0-85364-829-8*, Pub. by Paternoster Pub) OM Literature.

Paul As Missionary: A Comparative Study of Missionary Discourse in Paul's Epistles & Selected Contemporary Jewish Texts. James Y. Pak. (European University Studies: Theology: Ser. 23, Vol. 410). V, 208p. 1990. pap. 52.00 (*3-631-43459-6*) P Lang Pubng.

Paul Ashbrook. Donald P. Hallmark. Ed. by Rod Buffington. (Illus.). (Orig.). 1990. pap. text, boxed set 100.00 (*0-9624999-2-7*) R A Barker Found.

Paul Auster: A Comprehensive Bibliographic Checklist of Published Work 1968-1994. William Drenttel. (Illus.). 96p. 1995. pap. 40.00 (*1-884381-00-6*) W Drenttel Ed.

Paul Auster Signed: A Comprehensive Bibliographic Checklist of Published Work 1968-1994. William Drenttel. (Illus.). 96p. 1995. 125.00 (*1-884381-01-4*) W Drenttel Ed.

Paul Auster's New York. Paul Auster & Frieder Blickle. LC 97-11756. 1997. 0.01 (*0-8050-5667-X*) H Holt & Co.

Paul Azinger. Bill Gutman. LC 97-28813. (Overcoming the Odds Ser.). (J). 1998. 24.26 (*0-8172-4127-2*) Raintree Steck-V.

Paul Bailey & the Westernlore Press: The 1st 40 Years, with Annotated Bibliography. Ronald D. Miller. LC 83-51162. (Illus.). 1984. 25.00 (*0-930704-16-9*) Sagebrush Pr.

Paul Bear Bryant: What Made Him a Winner. W. Delbert Reed. (Illus.). 209p. 1997. 29.95 (*1-885219-01-6*) Vision AL.

Paul Berger: The Machine in the Window. Rod Slemmons. LC 90-52861. (Illus.). 64p. (Orig.). 1991. pap. 14.95 (*0-932216-37-4*) Seattle Art.

Paul Between Damascus & Antioch: The Unknown Years. Martin Hengel & Anna M. Schwemer. Tr. by John Bowden. LC 97-1386. 528p. (Orig.). 1997. pap. 34.95 (*0-664-25736-4*) Westminster John Knox.

Paul Blaisdell, Monster Maker: A Biography of the B Movie Makeup & Special Effects Artist. Randy Palmer. LC 96-45718. (Illus.). 304p. 1997. lib. bdg. 45.00 (*0-7864-0270-9*) McFarland & Co.

Paul Boeder, PhD: Teacher of Physiological Optics. Paul Boeder. (Ophthalmology Oral History Ser.). (Illus.). xxix, 194p. 1992. pap. 35.00 (*0-926866-04-4*) FAAO.

Paul Bound, the Gospel Unbound - Letters from Paul. Bob Utley. 1998. pap. 14.95 (*1-892691-03-5*); ring bd. 19.95 (*0-9661098-4-8*) Bible Lessons.

Paul Bourget. Armand E. Singer. LC 76-2548. (Twayne's World Authors Ser.). 184p. (C). 1976. lib. bdg. 20.95 (*0-317-38182-2*) Irvington.

Paul Bowles. Caponi. LC 98-34789. 1998. 32.00 (*0-8057-4560-2*, Twyne) Mac Lib Ref.

***Paul Bowles.** Cart. 1998. text. write for info. (*0-8057-1658-0*) Mac Lib Ref.

Paul Bowles. Allen Hibbard. (Twayne's Studies in Short Fiction). 288p. 1993. 29.00 (*0-8057-8318-0*, Twyne) Mac Lib Ref.

Paul Bowles: A Descriptive Bibliography. Jeffrey Miller. LC 84-10967. (Illus.). 327p. 1986. 50.00 (*0-87685-609-1*) Black Sparrow.

Paul Bowles: Music. limited ed. Phillip Ramey & Virgil Thomas. Ed. by Claudia Swan. (EOS Ser.: Vol. 1). (Illus.). 152p. 1995. 35.00 (*0-9648083-0-7*) Eos Music.

Paul Bowles: Romantic Savage. Gena D. Caponi. LC 93-35581. (Illus.). xx, 304p. (C). 1994. 36.95 (*0-8093-1923-3*) S Ill U Pr.

Paul Bowles by His Friends. Ed. by Gary Pulsifer. (Illus.). 160p. 1992. pap. 24.00 (*0-7206-0866-X*, Pub. by P Owen Ltd) Dufour.

Paul Bowles Photographs: How Could I Send a Picture into the Desert. Paul Bowles. 1993. 39.95 (*1-881616-07-X*, Pub. by Scalo Pubs) Dist Art Pubs.

Paul Brach & Miriam Shapiro Paintings & Graphic Works. Thomas H. Graver. (Illus.). 31p. 1969. 5.00 (*0-686-99833-2*) Mus Contemp Art.

Paul Brave Site, Oake Reservoir Area, N. Dakota, No. 33. W. Raymond Wood & Alan R. Woolworth. (Smithsonian Institution, Bureau of American Ethnology Ser.: Bulletin 189). (Illus.). 77p. 1964. pap. text 9.35 (*1-55567-702-9*) Coyote Press.

Paul Brewster & Son. Helen E. Chapman. LC 79-85681. (American Fiction Reprint Ser.). 1977. 19.95 (*0-8369-7010-1*) Ayer.

Paul Broca: Founder of French Anthropology, Explorer of the Brain. Francis Schiller. (Illus.). 360p. 1992. pap. text 21.50 (*0-19-507496-3*) OUP.

Paul Brown's Wild Visions. Paul Brown. 128p. 1998. 39.95 (*0-9642595-1-6*) True Exposures.

Paul Brunton: A Personal View. Kenneth T. Hurst. (Illus.). 300p. (Orig.). (gr. 9-12). 1989. pap. 14.95 (*0-943914-49-3*) Larson Pubns.

Paul Brunton: Essential Readings. Ed. by Paul Cash & Timothy Smith. 1991. pap. 12.95 (*1-85274-080-9*, Pub. by Aqrn Pr) Harper SF.

***Paul Bunyan.** Daniel Hoffman. LC 99-27131. (Illus.). 220p. 1999. pap. 16.95 (*0-87013-521-X*) Mich St U Pr.

Paul Bunyan. Steven Kellogg. LC 83-26684. (Illus.). 48p. (J). (gr. 2 up). 1984. 16.89 (*0-688-03850-6*, Wm Morrow) Morrow Avon.

Paul Bunyan. Steven Kellogg. LC 83-26684. (Illus.). 48p. (J). (ps-3). 1985. mass mkt. 5.95 (*0-688-05800-0*, Wm Morrow) Morrow Avon.

Paul Bunyan. Nanci A. Lyman. LC 79-66320. (Illus.). 48p. (J). (gr. 3-6). 1980. pap. 3.95 (*0-89375-309-2*); lib. bdg. 15.85 (*0-89375-310-6*) Troll Communs.

Paul Bunyan. Esther Shephard. LC 85-5448. (Illus.). 233p. (J). (gr. 7 up). 1985. 12.95 (*0-15-259749-2*, Harcourt Child Bks) Harcourt.

Paul Bunyan. Esther Shephard. LC 85-5448. (Illus.). 233p. (YA). (gr. 7 up). 1985. pap. 6.95 (*0-15-259755-7*, Voyager Bks) Harcourt.

Paul Bunyan. abr. ed. Brian Gleeson. LC 90-8558. (Storybook Classics Ser.). (Illus.). 40p. (J). (ps-3). 1991. 19.95 incl. audio (*0-88708-143-6*, Rabbit Ears) Litle Simon.

Paul Bunyan. Brian Gleeson. (Illus.). 64p. (J). 1993. reprint ed. 5.95 (*0-88708-302-1*, Rabbit Ears) Litle Simon.

Paul Bunyan. Brian Gleeson. LC 92-36654. (Illus.). 40p. (J). (ps-3). 1993. reprint ed. 9.95 incl. audio (*0-88708-303-X*, Rabbit Ears) Litle Simon.

Paul Bunyan. James Stevens. 256p. 1987. reprint ed. 3.95 (*0-89174-048-1*) Comstock Edns.

Paul Bunyan: American Folk Tale Story Pak. Retold by K. Hollenbeck. (Graphic Learning Literature Program Series: Folk Tales). (ENG & SPA., Illus.). (J). 1992. 45.00 (*0-87746-267-4*) Graphic Learning.

Paul Bunyan: Lumberjack. Nellie McCaslin. LC 96-30034. 55p. (Orig.). (J). (gr. 1-6). 1996. pap. 5.00 (*0-88734-477-1*) Players Pr.

Paul Bunyan: Spanish Edition. Steven Kellogg. Tr. by Aida E. Marcuse from SPA. LC 83-26684. (SPA., Illus.). 48p. (J). 1994. lib. bdg. 15.93 (*0-688-13614-1*, Wm Morrow) Morrow Avon.

Paul Bunyan: Superhero of the Lumberjacks. Ed. by Edith Fowke. (Illus.). 112p. (Orig.). (J). 1980. pap. 6.95 (*0-919601-63-4*, Pub. by NC Ltd) U of Toronto Pr.

Paul Bunyan: The Tall Tales, Vol. 1. Carl A. Zapffe. (Illus.). 118p. (Orig.). 1984. pap. 13.95 (*0-910623-02-3*) Hist Heart Assn Inc.

Paul Bunyan: Un Cuento Fantastico. Steven Kellogg. (Mulberry Paperback Bks.= Un Libro Mulbe). 1994. 11.15 (*0-606-06657-8*, Pub. by Turtleback) Demco.

Paul Bunyan, a Tall Tale. Steven Kellogg. (J). 1984. 11.15 (*0-606-02489-1*, Pub. by Turtleback) Demco.

Paul Bunyan & His Blue Ox. Patricia Jensen. (Troll First-Start Tall Tale Ser.). (J). 1994. 8.70 (*0-606-07992-0*, Pub. by Turtleback) Demco.

An Asterisk (*) at the beginning of an entry indicates that the title is appearing for the first time.

Paul Bunyan & His Blue Ox. Patricia A. Jensen. LC 93-24802. (First-Start Tall Tale Ser.). (Illus.). 32p. (J). (gr. k-2). 1993. lib. bdg. 17.25 (*0-8167-3162-4*) Troll Communs.

Paul Bunyan (Spanish edition) Steven Kellogg. Tr. by Aida E. Marcuse from ENG. LC 83-26684. (SPA., Illus.). 44p. (J). (gr. k up). 1994. mass mkt. 5.95 (*0-688-13202-2*, Wm Morrow) Morrow Avon.

Paul Bunyan Swings His Axe. Dell J. McCormick. LC 36-33409. (Illus.). (J). (gr. 4-6). 1936. 15.95 (*0-87004-093-6*) Caxton.

Paul Bunyan's Bearskin: Poems. Patricia Goedicke. LC 91-14944. (Illus.). 142p. (Orig.). 1992. pap. 11.00 (*0-915943-54-9*) Milkweed Ed.

Paul Cadmus. Lincoln Kirstein. LC 84-6533. (Imago Monographs). 144p. 1984. 40.00 (*0-915829-50-9*) Chameleon Bks.

Paul Cadmus. Lincoln Kirstein. 1990. 45.00 (*0-915829-65-7*) Chameleon Bks.

Paul Cadmus. 2nd ed. Larry S. Kirstein. 1996. pap. text 30.00 (*0-915829-68-1*, Pub. by Chameleon Bks) D C Moore.

Paul Calle: An Artist's Journey. James Dean & Pam Hait. Ed. by Dana Cooper. LC 92-62400. (Illus.). 152p. 1992. 65.00 (*0-941728-04-8*, 30596) Mill Pond Pr.

Paul Cambon: Master Diplomat. Keith Eubank. LC 78-6089. (Illus.). 221p. 1978. reprint ed. lib. bdg. 59.50 (*0-313-20502-7*, EUPC, Greenwood Pr) Greenwood.

Paul Caponigro & Huntington Witherill. (Lux Ser.: Vol. I). (Illus.). 46p. 1998. pap. 19.95 (*0-9630393-0-X*) Ctr for Photo.

Paul Caponigro "Masterworks from 40 Years" Ed. by Carol W. Christopher. LC 93-84343. (Illus.). 140p. 1993. 100.00 (*0-9616515-5-5*) Photog West Graphics.

Paul Carus Memorial Symposium, Peru, Ill., 1957: Modern Trends in World Religions. Ed. by Joseph M. Kitagawa. 286p. 1977. 18.95 (*0-8369-7294-5*) Ayer.

Paul Celan: A Biography of His Youth. Israel Chalfen. Tr. by Maximilian Bleyleben from GER. LC 91-25855. 176p. 1991. 24.95 (*0-89255-162-3*) Persea Bks.

Paul Celan: Poet, Survivor, Jew. John Felstiner. LC 94-33942. 364p. 1995. 40.00 (*0-300-06068-8*) Yale U Pr.

Paul Celan: Poet, Survivor, Jew. John Felstiner. 364p. 1997. pap. 18.00 (*0-300-06387-3*) Yale U Pr.

Paul Celan, Nelly Sachs: Correspondence. Paul Celan & Nelly Sachs. Ed. by Barbara Wiedemann. Tr. by Christopher Clark from GER. LC 95-26058. (Illus.). 126p. 1995. text 24.95 (*1-878818-37-6*, Pub. by Sheep Meadow) U Pr of New Eng.

Paul Celan, Nelly Sachs: Correspondence. Paul Celan & Nelly Sachs. Ed. by Barbara Wiedemann. Tr. by Christopher Clark from GER. LC 94-24548. (Illus.). 126p. 1998. pap. 13.95 (*1-878818-71-6*, Pub. by Sheep Meadow) U Pr of New Eng.

Paul Cezanne. (Prestel Postcard Bks.). 18p. 1995. pap. 8.95 (*3-7913-1616-8*, Pub. by Prestel) te Neues.

Paul Cezanne. Anna Barskaya & E. Georgievskaya. 200p. 1982. 50.00 (*0-7855-0704-3*, Pub. by Collets) St Mut.

***Paul Cezanne.** Sean Connolly. LC 99-14545. (Life & Work of...Ser.). (Illus.). 32p. (J). (gr. k-3). 1999. lib. bdg. 13.95 (*1-57572-957-1*) Heinemann Lib.

Paul Cezanne. Richard Shiff. LC 94-14283. (Rizzoli Art Ser.). (Illus.). 24p. 1994. pap. 7.95 (*0-8478-1755-5*, Pub. by Rizzoli Intl) St Martin.

Paul Cezanne. Mike Venezia. LC 97-35788. (Getting to Know the World's Greatest Artists Ser.). 32p. (J). 1998. lib. bdg. 21.00 (*0-516-20762-8*) Childrens.

Paul Cezanne. Karen Wilkin. (Tiny Folios Ser.). (Illus.). 288p. 1996. pap. 11.95 (*0-7892-0124-0*) Abbeville Pr.

Paul Cezanne: A Biography. Gerstle Mack. (Illus.). 462p. 1994. pap. 14.95 (*1-56924-904-0*) Marlowe & Co.

Paul Cezanne: A Life in Art. Isabelle Cahn. 144p. 1996. 39.95 (*0-304-34777-9*, Pub. by Cassell) Sterling.

Paul Cezanne: The Basel Sketchbooks. Lawrence Gowing. (Illus.). 152p. 1988. 45.00 (*0-685-58679-0*, 0-8109-6018-4) Abrams.

Paul Cezanne: The Basel Sketchbooks. Lawrence Gowing. (Illus.). 152p. 1993. pap. 19.95 (*0-685-58680-4*, 0-8109-6119-9) Abrams.

Paul Cezanne: Unknown Horizons. Nikolai Novouspensky. (Great Painters Ser.). (Illus.). 176p. 1996. 40.00 (*1-85995-191-0*) Parkstone Pr.

Paul Cezanne: 2 Sketchbooks. Theodore Reff & Innis H. Shoemaker. (Illus.). 244p. (Orig.). 1989. pap. 25.00 (*0-87633-080-4*) Phila Mus Art.

Paul Cezanne, Letters. Paul Cezanne. Ed. by John Rewald. LC 83-45728. (Illus.). reprint ed. 49.50 (*0-404-20053-2*) AMS Pr.

Paul Cezanne, Letters. 4th ed. Paul Cezanne. Ed. by John Rewald. Tr. by Marguerite Kay from FRE. (Illus.). 470p. 1995. reprint ed. pap. 15.95 (*0-306-80630-4*) Da Capo.

Paul Chidlaw: Paintings & Graphics. Owen Findsen. LC 85-71755. 28p. 1985. pap. 5.00 (*0-940784-07-6*) Miami Univ Art.

Paul Claudel: The Man & the Mystic. Louis Chaigne. LC 78-5951. 280p. 1978. reprint ed. lib. bdg. 65.00 (*0-313-20465-9*, CHCL, Greenwood Pr) Greenwood.

Paul Claudel Interroge le Cantique des Cantiques. Paul Claudel. (FRE.). 540p. 1954. 16.95 (*0-8288-9111-7*, F94360) Fr & Eur.

Paul Clifford. Edward Bulwer Lytton. 228p. 1999. reprint ed. pap. 17.95 (*0-7661-0800-7*) Kessinger Pub.

***Paul Confronts the World Again: The Apostle's Voice in Augustine, Luther, Wesley & Barth.** Noel C. Leroque. LC 99-65172. 192p. 1999. pap. 18.95 (*1-57736-153-9*) Providence Hse.

Paul Creston: A Bio-Bibliography, 55. Monica J. Slomski. LC 94-31649. (Bio-Bibliographies in Music Ser.: Vol. 55). 232p. 1994. lib. bdg. 65.00 (*0-313-25336-6*, Greenwood Pr) Greenwood.

Paul Darrow: A Retrospective. Suzanne Muchnic. (Illus.). 62p. 1992. 15.00 (*0-685-62731-4*) Williamson Gallery.

Paul Davis Songbook. Ed. by Carol Cuellar. 100p. (Orig.). (C). 1996. pap. text 18.95 (*1-57623-432-0*, PF9613) Wrner Bros.

Paul de Cassagnac & the Authoritarian Tradition in 19th-Century France. rev. ed. Karen Offen. LC 91-23151. 416p. 1991. text 45.00 (*0-8153-0479-X*) Garland.

Paul de Man. William Cain & Lewis L. B. Fried. (Wellesley Studies in Critical Theory). 700p. Date not set. text 105.00 (*0-8153-1783-2*) Garland.

Paul de Man: Deconstruction & the Critique of Aesthetic Ideology. Christopher Norris. LC 87-31375. 200p. 1988. pap. text 13.95 (*0-416-01971-4*) Routledge.

Paul de Man: Deconstruction & the Critique of Aesthetic Ideology. Christopher Norris. 1988. pap. 14.95 (*0-415-90080-8*) Routledge.

Paul Delaroche: History Painted. Stephen Bann. LC 97-65607. 336p. 1997. text 49.50 (*0-691-01745-X*, Pub. by Princeton U Pr) Cal Prin Full Svc.

Paul Delaroche, 1797-1856. Stephen Duffy. 1997. pap. text 40.00 (*0-900785-62-4*) Wallace Collect.

Paul Delvaux: Surrealizing the Nude. David Scott. LC 93-191729. (Illus.). 152p. 1993. pap. 22.50 (*0-948462-39-6*, Pub. by Reaktion Bks) Consort Bk Sales.

Paul Desmond Collection. 72p. 1996. per. 19.95 (*0-7935-5163-3*, 00672328) H Leonard.

Paul Dickerson. Charles Bowden. LC 99-70530. (Illus.). 1999. pap. 25.00 (*0-9671443-0-2*) P Dickerson Estate.

Paul Dirac: The Man & His Work. Abraham Pais et al. LC 97-22443. (Illus.). 140p. (C). 1998. 19.95 (*0-521-58382-9*) Cambridge U Pr.

Paul Elmer Moore. Francis X. Duggan. LC 66-24144. (Twayne's United States Authors Ser.). 1966. pap. text 4.95 (*0-8290-1868-9*); lib. bdg. 20.95 (*0-8057-0524-4*) Irvington.

Paul Elmer Moore & American Criticism. Robert Shafer. LC 75-41246. reprint ed. 29.50 (*0-404-14813-1*) AMS Pr.

Paul Elmer More. Arthur H. Dakin. LC 59-11076. 434p. 1960. reprint ed. pap. 134.60 (*0-7837-9326-X*, 206006600004) Bks Demand.

Paul Eluard: Shadows & Sun - Ombres et Soleil: Writings from 1913-1952. Paul Eluard. Ed. & Tr. by Cicely Buckley. Tr. by Lloyd Alexander. LC 95-173041. (ENG & FRE., Illus.). 368p. 1995. pap. 29.95 (*0-9617481-7-6*) Oyster River Pr.

Paul Elvard. Robert Nugent. LC 74-4132. (Twayne's World Authors Ser.). (C). 1974. lib. bdg. 20.95 (*0-8057-2299-8*) Irvington.

Paul Elvstrom Explains the Racing Rules of Sailing, 1997-2000 Rules. Soren Krause. (Illus.). 208p. 1997. pap. 22.95 (*0-07-007044-X*) McGraw.

Paul et Virginie. Jean Cocteau & Raymond Radiquet. (FRE.). 128p. 1973. 7.95 (*0-8288-9134-6*, M3312) Fr & Eur.

Paul et Virginie. Rene De Chateaubriand. (FRE.). 1984. pap. 10.95 (*0-7859-1181-2*, 2253012556) Fr & Eur.

Paul et Virginie. Bernardin De Saint-Pierre. (Coll. GF). pap. 8.95 (*0-685-34034-1*) Fr & Eur.

Paul et Virginie. Bernardin De Saint-Pierre. Ed. by Pierre Trahard. (Class. Garnier Ser.). pap. 29.95 (*0-685-34033-3*) Fr & Eur.

Paul et Virginie. Bernardin De Saint-Pierre. (Folio Ser.: No. 1552). (FRE.). 1964. pap. 12.95 (*2-07-037552-8*) Schoenhof.

Paul et Virginie. unabridged ed. Bernardin De Saint-Pierre. (FRE.). pap. 5.95 (*2-87714-138-1*, Pub. by Bookking Intl) Distribks Inc.

Paul Faber, Surgeon. George MacDonald. (George MacDonald Original Works Ser.: Series II). 396p. 1998. reprint ed. 22.00 (*1-881084-08-6*) Johannesen.

Paul Ferroll. Caroline Clive. (Oxford Popular Fiction Ser.). 236p. 1997. pap. 9.95 (*0-19-283247-6*) OUP.

Paul Ferroll: A Tale. Caroline A. Clive. LC 79-8256. reprint ed. 44.50 (*0-404-61821-9*) AMS Pr.

Paul for a New Day. Robin Scroggs. LC 76-9719. 96p. 1977. pap. 12.00 (*0-8006-1242-6*, 1-1242, Fortress Pr) Augsburg Fortress.

Paul G. Hoffman: Architect of Foreign Aid. Alan R. Raucher. LC 85-13406. 224p. 1985. 29.95 (*0-8131-1555-8*) U Pr of Ky.

Paul Gauguin. Howard Greenfeld. LC 93-9454. (First Impressions Ser.). (Illus.). 92p. (J). 1993. 19.95 (*0-8109-3376-4*, Pub. by Abrams) Time Warner.

Paul Gauguin. Mike Venezia. LC 91-35054. (Getting to Know the World's Greatest Artists Ser.). (Illus.). 32p. (J). (ps-4). 1992. lib. bdg. 21.00 (*0-516-02295-4*) Childrens.

Paul Gauguin. Mike Venezia. LC 91-35054. (Getting to Know the World's Greatest Artists Ser.). (Illus.). 32p. (J). (ps-4). 1992. pap. 6.95 (*0-516-42295-2*) Childrens.

Paul Gauguin: A Bio-Bibliography, 1. Russell T. Clement. LC 91-13903. (Bio-Bibliographies in Art Ser.: No. 1). 352p. 1991. lib. bdg. 65.00 (*0-313-27394-4*, CPQ, Greenwood Pr) Greenwood.

Paul Gauguin: A Complete Life. David Sweetman. (Illus.). 608p. 1996. 35.00 (*0-684-80941-9*) S&S Trade.

Paul Gauguin: Images from the South Seas. Eckhard Hollmann. (Pegasus Library). (Illus.). 116p. 1996. 25.00 (*3-7913-1673-7*, Pub. by Prestel) te Neues.

Paul Gauguin: Letters to His Wife & Friends. Paul Gauguin. Ed. by Maurice Malingue. Tr. by Henry J. Stenning. LC 83-45768. reprint ed. 30.00 (*0-404-20106-7*) AMS Pr.

Paul Gauguin: Mysterious Affinities. Anna Barskya. (Great Painters Ser.). (Illus.). 176p. 1996. 40.00 (*1-85995-141-4*) Parkstone Pr.

Paul Gemmill: Recollections of Mining Ventures, Life in Eastern Nevada & the Nevada Mining Association. Intro. by Mary E. Glass. 426p. 1978. lib. bdg. 60.50 (*1-56475-175-9*); fiche. write for info. (*1-56475-176-7*) U NV Oral Hist.

***Paul Georges.** Text by Carter Ratcliff. (Illus.). 31p. 2000. pap. 20.00 (*1-58821-075-8*) Salander OReilly.

Paul Goble Gallery: Three Native American Stories. Paul Goble. (Illus.). 112p. (J). (gr. k-4). 1999. 19.95 (*0-689-82219-7*) S&S Bks Yung.

***Paul, God's Message Sent Apostle Post & Other Bible Stories to Tickle Your Soul.** Mike Thaler & Dennis Adler. LC 00-23760. (Heaven & Mirth Ser.). (Illus.). (YA). 2000. 10.99 (*0-7814-3433-5*, LifeJourney) Chariot Victor.

Paul, God's Special Missionary. Bessie Dean. (Story Books to Color). 72p. (Orig.). (J). (gr. k-5). 1980. pap. 6.98 (*0-88290-152-4*) Horizon Utah.

Paul Graham. Andrew Wilson. (Contemporary Artists Ser.). (Illus.). 160p. (Orig.). 1996. pap. 29.95 (*0-7148-3550-1*, Pub. by Phaidon Press) Phaidon Pr.

Paul Green. Barrett H. Clark. LC 74-1164. (Studies in Drama: No. 39). 1974. lib. bdg. 49.00 (*0-8383-2016-3*) M S G Haskell Hse.

Paul Green. Vincent Kenny. LC 79-125254. (Twayne's United States Authors Ser.). 1971. reprint ed. pap. text 12.95 (*0-8290-0007-0*); reprint ed. lib. bdg. 20.95 (*0-89197-880-1*) Irvington.

Paul Green Reader. Paul Green. Ed. by Laurence G. Avery. LC 97-40365. (Chapel Hill Bks.). 368p. 1998. 45.00 (*0-8078-2386-4*); pap. 18.95 (*0-8078-4708-9*) U of NC Pr.

Paul Green's Celebration of Man: Proceedings of the 6th Annual Southern Writers' Symposium. Ed. by Lynn V. Sadler. (Orig.). pap. text. write for info. (*0-318-65911-5*) Methodist Coll Pr.

Paul Green's Chicago. Paul M. Green. LC 88-82021. 104p. (Orig.). (C). 1988. pap. 6.95 (*0-9620873-1-9*) Illinois Issues.

Paul Green's War Songs. Paul Green. Ed. by John H. Roper. LC 92-63058. 150p. 1994. 20.00 (*0-933598-48-3*) NC Wesleyan Pr.

Paul Green's Wordbook: An Alphabet of Reminiscence, Set, Vols. I & II. Paul Green. Ed. by Rhoda H. Wynn. LC 89-78156. 1245p. 1990. 85.00 (*0-913239-67-4*) Appalach Consortium.

Paul H. Nitze on Foreign Policy, Vol. XIII. Ed. by Kenneth W. Thompson & Steven L. Rearden. LC 89-22607. (W. Alton Jones Foundation Series on Arms Control). 220p. (Orig.). (C). 1990. pap. text 21.00 (*0-8191-7616-8*, Pub. by White Miller Center); lib. bdg. 44.50 (*0-8191-7615-X*, Pub. by White Miller Center) U Pr of Amer.

Paul H. Nitze on National Security & Arms Control. Ed. by Kenneth W. Thompson & Steven L. Rearden. (W. Alton Jones Foundation Series on Arms Control: Vol. XIV). 250p. (C). 1990. pap. text 26.00 (*0-8191-7894-2*); lib. bdg. 46.00 (*0-8191-7893-4*) U Pr of Amer.

Paul H. Nitze on the Future. Kenneth W. Thompson & Steven L. Rearden. (W. Alton Jones Foundation Series on Arms Control: No. XVIII). 286p. (C). 1991. pap. text 28.50 (*0-8191-8455-1*); lib. bdg. 60.00 (*0-8191-8454-3*) U Pr of Amer.

Paul Halmos: Celebrating 50 Years of Mathematics. Ed. by J. H. Ewing & F. W. Gehring. (Illus.). viii, 320p. 1995. 59.95 (*0-387-97509-8*) Spr-Verlag.

Paul Hamilton Hayne. Rayburn S. Moore. Ed. by Sylvia E. Bowman. LC 73-125818. (Twayne's United States Authors Ser.). 184p. (C). 1972. lib. bdg. 20.95 (*0-8290-1711-9*) Irvington.

Paul Harris: Drawings. Illus. by Morris Yarowsky. LC 96-61349. 164p. 1998. pap. 39.95 (*0-295-97703-5*) U of Wash Pr.

Paul Harris & His Successors: Profiles in Leadership. LC 97-65420. (Illus.). 1997. write for info. (*0-915062-41-0*) Rotary Intl.

***Paul Harris Sculpture: Fifty Years.** Theophilus Brown. LC 99-67355. (Illus.). 136p. 2000. pap. 35.00 (*0-295-97928-3*) U of Wash Pr.

Paul Harvey's for What It's Worth. Paul Harvey, Jr. LC 91-8083. 160p. 1992. mass mkt. 6.50 (*0-553-29676-0*) Bantam.

Paul Harvey's the Rest of the Story. Paul Aurandt. 192p. 1984. mass mkt. 6.50 (*0-553-25962-8*) Bantam.

Paul Hasluck: A Political Biography. Robert Porter. 1993. 39.95 (*1-875560-20-3*, Pub. by Univ of West Aust Pr) Intl Spec Bk.

Paul Heald: Selected Works, 1960-1981. Matthew Kangas. LC 81-71891. (Illus.). 32p. (Orig.). 1982. pap. 5.95 (*0-942342-00-3*) Bellevue Art.

***Paul Heathcote's Rhubarb & Black Pudding.** Fort Matthew & Paul Heathcote. (Illus.). 252p. 1998. 45.00 (*1-85702-500-8*, Pub. by Fourth Estate) Trafalgar.

***Paul Henry.** S. B. Kennedy & Paul Henry. LC 00-38167. (Illus.). 184p. 2000. 50.00 (*0-300-08130-8*) Yale U Pr.

Paul Hervieu & French Classicism. Hulet H. Cook. LC 45-37189. (Indiana University Humanities Ser.: No. 14). 56p. reprint ed. pap. 30.00 (*0-608-10180-X*, 205522300011) Bks Demand.

Paul Hindemith in the United States. Luther Noss. LC 88-10694. (Music in American Life Ser.). (Illus.). 248p. 1989. text 27.95 (*0-252-01563-0*) U of Ill Pr.

Paul, His Apostleship & Message. Cornelius R. Stam. 191p. 1985. 12.50 (*1-893874-12-5*) Berean Bibl Soc.

Paul, His Letters & Theology: An Introduction to Paul's Epistles. Stanley B. Marrow. 288p. (Orig.). 1986. pap. 19.95 (*0-8091-2744-X*) Paulist Pr.

Paul Hofhaimer: Ein Lied- und Orgelmeister des Deutschen Humanismus. Hans J. Moser. ix, 231p. 1966. write for info. (*0-318-71931-2*) G Olms Pubs.

Paul Hoy Helms Library in Liberal Adult Education. Compiled by Alexander N. Charters. 1973. 4.55 (*0-686-50191-8*, MSS 20) Syracuse U Cont Ed.

Paul Hunt's Night Diary. Michael Twinn. LC 92-10850. (Illus.). 32p. (YA). 1992. 13.99 (*0-85953-925-3*, Pub. by Childs Play) Random House.

Paul in His Hellenistic Context. Ed. by Troels Engberg-Pedersen. LC 93-13174. 384p. 1995. 47.00 (*0-8006-2648-6*, 1-2648, Fortress Pr) Augsburg Fortress.

***Paul in the Greco-Roman World.** J. Paul. 464p. 2001. 40.00 (*1-56338-266-0*, Pub. by TPI PA) Morehouse Pub.

Paul J. Stankard: Homage to Nature. Ulysses G. Dietz. LC 96-10850. (Illus.). 160p. 1996. 39.95 (*0-8109-4473-1*, Pub. by Abrams) Time Warner.

Paul Jefferson. Ed. by Jeannette DeLisa. 44p. (Orig.). (YA). 1996. pap. text 17.95 (*1-57623-574-2*, PF9636) Wrner Bros.

Paul Jones: Founder of the American Navy, 2 Vols. Augustus C. Buell. LC 70-157326. (Select Bibliographies Reprint Ser.). 1977. reprint ed. 49.95 (*0-8369-5786-5*) Ayer.

Paul, Judaism & Judgment According to Deeds. Kent L. Yinger. LC 98-30667. (Society for New Testament Studies Monograph Ser.: No. 105). (Illus.). 336p. (C). 1999. text 64.95 (*0-521-63243-9*) Cambridge U Pr.

Paul Kane's Great Nor-West. Diane Eaton & Sheila Urbanek. (Illus.). 176p. 1995. text 44.95 (*0-7748-0538-2*) U of Wash Pr.

Paul Kane's Great Nor-West. Diane Eaton & Sheila Urbanek. (Illus.). 176p. 1997. pap. 29.95 (*0-7748-0549-8*) U of Wash Pr.

Paul Kariya. Mike Bonner. (Ice Hockey Legends Ser.). (Illus.). 64p. (YA). (gr. 3 up). 1999. lib. bdg. 16.95 (*0-7910-5015-7*) Chelsea Hse.

***Paul Kariya: Hockey Magician.** Jeff Savage. LC 97-41050. (J). 1998. lib. bdg. 19.93 (*0-8225-3661-7*) Lerner Pub.

Paul Kariya: Hockey Magician. Jeff Savage. LC 97-41050. (Illus.). 64p. (J). (gr. 4-9). 1998. pap. 5.95 (*0-8225-9824-8*) Lerner Pub.

***Paul Kariya: Maine Man.** Cammy Clark. (SuperStar Series: Vol. 3). 96p. 1999. pap. 4.95 (*1-58261-150-5*, Pub. by Sprts Pubng) Partners-West.

Paul Keres: The Quest for Perfection. Paul Keres & John Nunn. (New American Batsford Chess Library). 256p. (Orig.). 1997. pap. 23.95 (*1-879479-49-4*) ICE WA.

Paul Keres: The Road to the Top. 2nd abr. rev. ed. Paul Keres. LC 96-77760. (New American Batsford Chess Library). 256p. 1996. pap. 23.95 (*1-879479-35-4*) ICE WA.

Paul Keres' Best Games. Egon Varnusz. (Chess Ser.). 500p. 1990. pap. 39.95 (*0-08-037149-3*, Pergamon Pr) Elsevier.

Paul Keres' Best Games. Egon Varnusz. 1994. pap. 19.95 (*1-85744-064-1*) S&S Trade.

Paul Keres' Best Games, Vol. 1. Egon Varnusz. (Illus.). 210p. 1987. 35.90 (*0-08-026915-X*, Pergamon Pr); pap. 23.95 (*0-08-032044-9*, Pergamon Pr) Elsevier.

Paul Keres' Best Games, Vol. 1 & 2. Egon Varnusz. (Chess Ser.). 500p. 1990. 69.90 (*0-08-037148-5*, Pergamon Pr) Elsevier.

Paul Keres' Best Games, Vol. 2. Egon Varnusz. (Chess Ser.). 192p. 1990. 37.95 (*0-08-037140-X*, Pergamon Pr) Elsevier.

Paul Keres Chess Master Class. Iakov Neishtadt. 182p. 1983. 29.90 (*0-08-023122-5*, Pergamon Pr); 17.90 (*0-08-029719-6*, Pergamon Pr) Elsevier.

Paul Kirk's Championship Barbecue Sauces: 175 Make-Your-Own Sauces, Marinades, Dry Rubs, Wet Rubs, Mops, & Salsas. Paul Kirk. LC 97-6626. (Illus.). 272p. 1998. 19.95 (*1-55832-124-1*); pap. 11.95 (*1-55832-125-X*) Harvard Common Pr.

Paul Klee. Jean-Louis Ferrier. Tr. by Malcolm Imrie. (Illus.). 207p. 1999. pap. 27.50 (*2-87939-201-2*, Pub. by Pierre Terrail) Rizzoli Intl.

Paul Klee. Mike Venezia. LC 91-12554. (Getting to Know the World's Greatest Artists Ser.). (Illus.). 32p. (J). (gr. 4). 1991. pap. 6.95 (*0-516-42294-4*); lib. bdg. 21.00 (*0-516-02294-6*) Childrens.

Paul Klee: Dialogue with Nature. Ed. by Ernst-Gerhard Guse. (Illus.). 184p. 1997. pap. text 29.95 (*3-7913-1832-2*, Pub. by Prestel) te Neues.

Paul Klee: Dialogue with Nature. Ed. by Ernst Gerhard Guse et al. (Illus.). 184p. 1991. 39.95 (*3-7913-1141-7*, Pub. by Prestel) te Neues.

Paul Klee: His Work & Thought. Marcel Franciscono. LC 90-39006. (Illus.). 396p. 1991. 70.00 (*0-226-25990-0*) U Ch Pr.

Paul Klee: Painting Music. Hajo Duchting. LC 97-36137. 128p. 1997. 25.00 (*3-7913-1872-1*, Pub. by Prestel) te Neues.

Paul Klee: The Bauhaus Years, 1921-1931. James T. Demetrion & Marianne L. Teuber. LC 73-86308. (Illus.). 144p. 1973. pap. 15.00 (*0-614-06998-X*) Edmundson.

Paul Klee: The Berggruen Klee Collection in the Metropolitan Museum of Art. Sabine Rewald. (Illus.). 320p. 1988. pap. 45.00 (*0-87099-513-8*, 0-8109-2447-1) Abrams.

Paul Klee: The Dusseldorf Collection. Werner Schmalenbach et al. (Illus.). 128p. 1986. 40.00 (*3-7913-0794-0*, Pub. by Prestel) te Neues.

Paul Klee: Three Exhibitions: 1930, 1941, 1949. Pref. by M. Wheeler. LC 68-57298. (Museum of Modern Art Publications in Reprint). (Illus.). 1969. reprint ed. 23.95 (*0-405-01518-6*) Ayer.

Paul Klee at the Guggenheim Museum. Andrew Kagan. (Illus.). 208p. 1994. 45.00 (*0-8109-6874-6*) Abrams.

Paul Klee at the Guggenheim Museum. Andrew Kagan. 1993. 42.00 (*0-89207-106-0*) S R Guggenheim.

P

Paul Klee Catalogue Raisonne: The Bauhaus in Weimar (1919-1922), 9 vols. Ed. by Paul Klee Foundation Staff. LC 98-61525. (ENG & GER., Illus.). 500p. 1999. 225.00 (*0-500-09281-8*, Pub. by Thames Hudson) Norton.

Paul Klee Catalogue Raisonne: The Years of Munich & "Der Blaue Reiter" LC 98-61002. (ENG & GER., Illus.). 500p. 1998. 225.00 (*0-500-09278-8*, Pub. by Thames Hudson) Norton.

***Paul Klee Catalogue Raisonne Vol. 2: 1913-1918.** Ed. by Paul Klee Foundation Staff. LC 98-61082. Vol. 2. (Illus.). 500p. 2000. text 225.00 (*0-500-09280-X*, Pub. by Thames Hudson) Norton.

***Paul Klee Catalogue Raisonne Vol. 4: 1923-1928.** Ed. by Paul Klee Foundation Staff. LC 98-61082. (Illus.). 500p. 2001. 225.00 (*0-500-09282-6*, Pub. by Thames Hudson) Norton.

Paul Klee Drawings I, 1883-1920: Catalogue Raisonne. Jurgen Glaesemer. (GER., Illus.). 312p. 1973. 125.00 (*0-8150-0021-9*) Wittenborn Art.

Paul Klee Drawings II, 1921-1936: Catalogue Raisonne. Jurgen Glaesemer. (GER., Illus.). 546p. 1984. 150.00 (*0-8150-0022-7*) Wittenborn Art.

Paul Klee Notebooks: The Nature of Nature, 2 vols., 2. Paul Klee. Ed. by Jurg Spiller. (Illus.). 456p. 1992. 125.00 (*0-87951-468-X*, Pub. by Overlook Pr) Penguin Putnam.

Paul Klee Notebooks: The Thinking Eye, 2 vols., 1. Paul Klee. Ed. by Jurg Spiller. (Illus.). 1992. 125.00 (*0-87951-467-1*, Pub. by Overlook Pr) Penguin Putnam.

Paul Klee Notebooks Vols. 1 & 2: The Thinking Eye & The Nature of Nature, 2 vols. Paul Klee. Ed. by Jurg Spiller. (Illus.). 1047p. 1992. boxed set 300.00 (*0-87951-466-3*, Pub. by Overlook Pr) Penguin Putnam.

Paul Klee on Modern Art. Paul Klee. (Illus.). 164p. 1966. pap. 10.95 (*0-571-06682-8*) Faber & Faber.

***Paul Klee Rediscovered.** Stefan Frey & Josef Helfenstein. (Illus.). 280p. 2000. 65.00 (*1-85894-115-6*, Pub. by Merrell Holberton) Rizzoli Intl.

Paul Lafargue & the Flowering of French Socialism, 1882-1911. Leslie Derfler. LC 97-42404. 384p. 1999. 45.00 (*0-674-65912-0*) HUP.

Paul Lafargue & the Founding of French Marxism, 1842-1882. Leslie Derfler. LC 90-36659. (Illus.). 304p. 1991. 51.95 (*0-674-65903-1*, DERPAU) HUP.

Paul Laffoley: The Phenomenology of Revelation. Paul Laffoley. Ed. by Jeanne M. Wasilik. (Illus.). 112p. 1989. 30.00 (*1-878607-06-5*) Kent Gallery.

Paul Landowski: Le Main et l'Esprit. Jules Romains, pseud. 308p. 39.50 (*0-686-55328-4*) Fr & Eur.

***Paul Landres: A Director's Stories.** Francis M. Nevins. LC 00-30783. (Filmmakers Ser.). 2000. write for info. (*0-8108-3816-8*) Scarecrow.

Paul Laurence Dunbar: An Anthology in Memoriam (1872-1906) Ed. by M. Myers. LC 97-71073. 168p. (Orig.). 1997. pap. text 16.95 (*1-879183-34-X*) Bristol Banner.

Paul Laurence Dunbar: Poet. Tony Gentry. Ed. by Nathan I. Huggins. (Black Americans of Achievement Ser.). (Illus.). 124p. (YA). (gr. 5 up). 1989. pap. 8.95 (*0-7910-0223-3*); lib. bdg. 19.95 (*1-55546-583-8*) Chelsea Hse.

Paul Laurence Dunbar: Poet. Tony Gentry. (Black American Ser.). (Illus.). 192p. (YA). 1993. mass mkt. 3.95 (*0-87067-784-5*, Melrose Sq) Holloway.

***Paul Laurence Dunbar: Portrait of a Poet.** Catherine Reef. LC 99-16456. (African-American Biographies Ser.). (Illus.). 128p. (gr. 6 up). 2000. lib. bdg. 20.95 (*0-7660-1350-2*) Enslow Pubs.

Paul Laurence Dunbar, Critically Examined. V. Lawson. 1972. 59.95 (*0-8490-0808-5*) Gordon Pr.

Paul Laurence Dunbar, Poet of His People. Benjamin Brawley. (BCL1-PS American Literature Ser.). 159p. 1993. reprint ed. lib. bdg. 69.00 (*0-7812-6960-1*) Rprt Serv.

Paul Laurence Dunbar's Roots & Much More: A Scrapbook of His Life & Legacy. Charles M. Austin. (Illus.). 90p. (Orig.). 1989. pap. 20.00 (*0-9625461-0-0*) Sense Roots Pubns.

Paul Leonard: Tales of Northern Nevada - And Other Lies; As Recalled by Native Son, Journalist & Civic Leader. Ed. by Mary E. Glass. 398p. 1980. lib. bdg. 58.50 (*1-56475-199-6*); fiche. write for info. (*1-56475-200-3*) U NV Oral Hist.

Paul Leroy-Beaulieu & Established Liberalism in France. Dan Warshaw. LC 90-28524. 251p. 1991. lib. bdg. 34.00 (*0-87580-159-5*) N Ill U Pr.

Paul M. Butler: Hoosier Politician & National Political Leader. George C. Roberts. LC 87-6275. (Illus.). 210p. (Orig.). (C). 1987. pap. text 22.50 (*0-8191-6296-5*) U Pr of Amer.

Paul M. Fekula Collection, a Catalogue. 904p. 1988. 350.00 (*0-614-24480-3*, 43755) Oak Knoll.

Paul Mace Guide to Data Recovery. 2nd ed. Paul Mace. 1991. pap. 24.95 (*0-13-654500-9*) P-H.

Paul Marchand: Free Man of Color. Charles Waddell Chesnutt. LC 98-24049. 144p. 1998. 20.00 (*1-57806-055-9*) U Pr of Miss.

Paul Marchand, F. M. C. Charles Waddell Chesnutt & Dean McWilliams. LC 98-26423. 1998. 35.00 (*0-691-05993-4*, Pub. by Princeton U Pr) Cal Prin Full Svc.

Paul Marchand, F. M. C. Charles Waddell Chesnutt & Dean McWilliams. LC 98-26423. 1999. pap. 14.95 (*0-691-05994-2*, Pub. by Princeton U Pr) Cal Prin Full Svc.

Paul Martin: Victorian Photographer. Roy Flukinger et al. LC 77-4764. (Illus.). 235p. 1977. 24.95 (*0-292-76436-7*) U of Tex Pr.

Paul Matt Scale Airplane Drawings, Vol. 1. Paul Matt. (Illus.). 160p. 1993. pap. text 24.95 (*0-943691-04-4*) Aviation Heritage.

Paul Matt Scale Airplane Drawings, Vol. 2. Paul Matt. (Illus.). 158p. 1993. pap. text 24.95 (*0-943691-05-2*) Aviation Heritage.

Paul! May I Speak with You? 6 Dialogues for Bible Study. Marion Fairman. LC 92-40072. 1992. pap. 10.95 (*1-55673-601-0*, 9321) CSS OH.

Paul Mazursky's Tempest. Geoffrey Taylor. (Illus.). 96p. (Orig.). 1982. pap. 10.95 (*0-918432-45-6*) Baseline Bks.

Paul McCarthy. Bob Chartain. (Illus.). 128p. 1999. pap. text 29.95 (*88-8158-210-4*, Pub. by Charta) Dist Art Pubs.

Paul McCarthy. Ralph Rugoff. (Contemporary Artists Ser.). (Illus.). 160p. (Orig.). 1996. pap. 29.95 (*0-7148-3552-8*, Pub. by Phaidon Press) Phaidon Pr.

Paul McCartney. Barbara Paul. 1981. 24.95 (*0-671-43123-4*) S&S Trade.

Paul McCartney: All the Best! 128p. 1988. per. 16.95 (*0-7935-0805-3*, 00384245) H Leonard.

Paul McCartney: From Liverpool to Let It Be. Howard A. DeWitt. (Illus.). 276p. (Orig.). 1992. pap. text 14.95 (*0-938840-04-5*) Horizon Bks CA.

***Paul McCartney: I Saw Him Standing There.** Jorie B. Gracen. (Illus.). 176p. 2000. 35.00 (*0-8230-8372-1*) Watsn-Guptill.

Paul McCartney: Many Years from Now. Barry Miles. LC 98-105657. (Illus.). 512p. 1997. 27.50 (*0-8050-5248-8*) H Holt & Co.

Paul McCartney: Many Years from Now. Barry Miles. (Illus.). 696p. 1998. pap. 16.95 (*0-8050-5249-6*, Owl) H Holt & Co.

Paul McCartney: Off the Ground. 1993. 16.95 (*0-7935-2602-7*, 00308192) H Leonard.

Paul McCartney: Tripping the Live Fantastic. (Piano-Vocal-Guitar Ser.). (Illus.). 168p. 1991. reprint ed. otabind 19.95 (*0-7935-0429-5*, 00385216) H Leonard.

Paul McCartney, Composer-Artist. Paul McCartney. 1981. 12.95 (*0-671-43124-2*) S&S Trade.

Paul McCartney Flaming Pie. 112p. 1997. per. 19.95 (*0-7935-8538-4*) H Leonard.

***Paul McCartney's Paintings.** Paul McCartney. (Illus.). 148p. 2000. 50.00 (*0-8212-2673-8*) Bulfinch Pr.

Paul McFedries' Windows 95 Unleashed. 1997. 59.99 (*0-672-31234-4*) Sams.

Paul McFedries' Windows 95 Unleashed: Professional Reference Edition. Paul McFedries. LC 96-72006. 1648p. 1997. 59.99 (*0-672-31039-2*) Sams.

Paul McFedries' Windows 98 Unleashed, Professional Reference Edition. Paul McFedries. LC 97-69136. 1440p. 1998. 54.99 (*0-672-31224-7*) Macmillan.

Paul Metcalf Vol. 1: Collected Works, 1956-1976. Paul Metcalf. LC 96-2777. Vol. 1. 550p. 1996. 35.00 (*1-56689-050-0*) Coffee Hse.

Paul Metcalf Vol. II: Collected Works, 1976-1986. Paul Metcalf. Vol. 2. 600p. 1997. 35.00 (*1-56689-056-X*) Coffee Hse.

Paul Metcalf Vol. III: Collected Works, 1987-1997. Paul Metcalf. 600p. 1997. 35.00 (*1-56689-062-4*) Coffee Hse.

Paul Miliukov & the Quest for a Liberal Russia, 1880-1918. Melissa K. Stockdale. LC 96-27319. (Illus.). 376p. 1996. text 47.50 (*0-8014-3248-0*) Cornell U Pr.

Paul, Missionary to the Gentiles. 1998. pap. 3.95 (*0-8091-9405-8*) Paulist Pr.

Paul Mitchell: Who Was He? Jocelyn Fujii. LC 93-60316. (Illus.). 112p. 1994. 30.00 (*0-9636648-0-8*) P Mitchell Trust.

Paul Mitchell: Who Was He? limited ed. Jocelyn Fujii. LC 93-60316. (Illus.). 112p. 1994. 150.00 (*0-9636648-1-6*) P Mitchell Trust.

Paul Morphy & the Evolution of Chess Theory. Macon Shibut. (Great Masters Ser.). (Illus.). 341p. 1993. 35.00 (*0-939433-16-8*) Caissa Edit.

Paul, Moses, & the History of Israel: The Letter/Spirit Contrast & the Argument from Scripture in 2 Corinthians 3. Scott J. Hafemann. 500p. 1996. pap. 24.95 (*1-56563-241-9*) Hendrickson MA.

Paul Muldoon. Tom Kendall. LC 96-12982. 256p. 1996. 34.95 (*0-8023-1312-4*); pap. 14.95 (*0-8023-1313-2*) Dufour.

Paul Muldoon. Clair Wills. 1996. 49.95 (*1-85224-347-3*, Pub. by Bloodaxe Bks); pap. 23.95 (*1-85224-348-1*, Pub. by Bloodaxe Bks) Dufour.

Paul Myoda Gargoyles. Vasif Kortun et al. (Illus.). 24p. (Orig.). 1995. write for info. (*0-941276-09-0*, Ctr Curatorial Studies) Bard Coll Pubns.

***Paul Naschy: Memoirs of a Wolfman.** Paul Naschy. 256p. 2000. pap. 20.00 (*1-887664-38-6*, Pub. by Midnght Marquee Pr) Koen Bk Distributors.

***Paul Naschy: Memoirs of a Wolfman.** Paul Naschy. (Illus.). 256p. 2000. 55.00 (*1-887664-37-8*, Pub. by Midnght Marquee Pr) Koen Bk Distributors.

Paul Nash - Aerial Creatures. Charles Hall. (Illus.). 88p. 1998. 29.95 (*0-85331-730-5*) Antique Collect.

Paul Nash as Book Illustrator & Designer: V&A National Art Library, Restaurant Foyer, 16 September-29 November 1998. Lucy Dean. LC 98-222075. 25 p. 1998. pap. write for info. (*1-85177-281-2*) V&A Ent.

Paul Natorps Aesthetik. Inge Krebs. (Kantstudien Ergaenzungsheft Ser.). 1976. text 90.00 (*3-11-006587-8*) De Gruyter.

Paul Natorp's Philosophy of Religion Within the Marburg Neo-Kantian Tradition. Judy D. Saltzmann. (Studien und Materialien Zur Geschichte der Philosophie Ser.: Bd. 7). (GER.). xii, 260p. 1980. write for info. (*3-487-07087-1*) G Olms Pubs.

Paul Nesbit's Longs Peak: Its Story & a Climbing Guide. rev. ed. Ed. by Stan Adamson. LC 89-64298. (Illus.). 73p. 1990. pap. 6.95 (*0-9625445-0-7*) Mills Pub KS.

Paul Newman: The Man Behind the Steel Blue Eyes. Lawrence J. Quirk. LC 97-5906. (Illus.). 400p. 1997. 24.95 (*0-87833-962-0*) Taylor Pub.

Paul of Pergula: Logica & Tractatus de Sensu Composito et Diviso. Ed. by Mary A. Brown. xiv, 162p. 1961. pap. 11.00 (*1-57659-053-4*) Franciscan Inst.

Paul of Tarsus: His Gospel & Life. Herold Weiss. LC 86-72148. 202p. 1986. pap. 15.99 (*0-943872-27-8*) Andrews Univ Pr.

Paul of Venice: A Bibliographical Guide. Ed. by Alan R. Perreiah. (Bibliographies of Famous Philosophers Ser.). 175p. (C). 1986. 14.25 (*0-912632-83-6*) Philos Document.

Paul of Venice: Logica Magna, Fascicule 7, Pt. I. Patricia Clarke. (Classical & Medieval Logic Texts Ser.: Vol. IV). (Illus.). 240p. 1982. 135.00 (*0-19-726003-9*) OUP.

Paul of Venice: Logica Magna, Fascicule 8, Pt. II. E. J. Ashworth. (Classical & Medieval Logic Texts Ser.: Vol. V). (Illus.). 426p. 1989. 140.00 (*0-19-726065-9*) OUP.

Paul of Venice. Logica Magna (Tractatus de Suppositionibus) Ed. by Alan R. Perreiah. xiv, 121p. 1971. pap. 16.00 (*1-57659-052-6*) Franciscan Inst.

Paul on Marriage & Celibacy: The Hellenistic Background of First Corinthians 7. Will Deming. (Society for New Testament Studies Monographs: No. 83). 279p. (C). 1995. text 69.95 (*0-521-47284-9*) Cambridge U Pr.

Paul I of Russia, 1754-1801. Roderick E. McGrew. (Illus.). 424p. 1992. 85.00 (*0-19-822567-9*) OUP.

Paul Overstreet - Heroes. Paul Overstreet. Ed. by Milton Okun. pap. 14.95 (*0-89524-626-0*) Cherry Lane.

Paul Overstreet - Love Is Strong. pap. 14.95 (*0-89524-725-9*) Cherry Lane.

Paul Overstreet - Sowin' Love. Paul Overstreet. Ed. by Milton Okun. pap. 12.95 (*0-89524-485-3*) Cherry Lane.

Paul Pakhider Desha. Ahmad Nawaz. LC 98-70825. (BEN.). xiv, 63p. 1998. pap. 10.00 (*1-58225-143-6*) Ananta Prakashani.

Paul Patoff. Francis M. Crawford. (Works of Francis Marion Crawford). 1990. reprint ed. lib. bdg. 79.00 (*0-7812-2533-7*) Rprt Serv.

Paul Poiret. Alice Mackrell. LC 90-4086. (Illus.). 100p. (Orig.). (C). 1990. 39.95 (*0-8419-1279-3*); pap. 25.95 (*0-8419-1280-7*) Holmes & Meier.

Paul, Poverty & Survival. Justin Meggitt. (Studies of the New Testament & Its World Ser.). 288p. 1998. 49.95 (*0-567-08604-6*, Pub. by T & T Clark) Bks Intl VA.

Paul Powell of Illinois: A Lifelong Democrat. Robert E. Hartley. LC 98-51443. 1999. write for info. (*0-8093-2271-4*) S Ill U Pr.

Paul Powell of Illinois: A Lifelong Democrat. Robert E. Hartley. LC 98-51443. 256p. 1999. 17.95 (*0-8093-2272-2*) S Ill U Pr.

Paul Prescott's Charge. Horatio Alger, Jr. (Works of Horatio Alger Jr.). 1989. reprint ed. lib. bdg. 79.00 (*0-7812-1705-9*) Rprt Serv.

Paul Quest: The Renewed Search for the Jew of Tarsus. Ben Witherington, III. LC 98-8647. 356p. 1998. 22.99 (*0-8308-1503-1*, 1503) InterVarsity.

Paul R. Williams, Architect. Karen E. Hudson. 240p. 1993. 50.00 (*0-8478-1763-6*, Pub. by Rizzoli Intl) St Martin.

***Paul R. Williams, Architect: A Legacy of Style.** Karen E. Hudson. (Illus.). 240p. 2000. pap. 35.00 (*0-8478-2242-7*, Pub. by Rizzoli Intl) St Martin.

***Paul Ramsey's Ethics: The Power of 'Agape' in a Postmodern World.** Michael C. McKenzie. 2000. write for info. (*0-275-96988-6*) Greenwood.

Paul Ramsey's Political Ethics. David Attwood. 244p. (C). 1991. pap. 24.50 (*0-8476-7686-2*); text 62.50 (*0-8476-7685-4*) B&N Imports.

Paul Rand. Steven Heller et al. LC 99-494983. (Illus.). 240p. 1998. 69.95 (*0-7148-3798-9*) Phaidon Pr.

***Paul Rand: A Designer's Art.** Paul Rand. (Illus.). 242p. 2000. pap. 30.00 (*0-300-08282-7*) Yale U Pr.

Paul Rand: American Modernist. Jessica Helfand. 86p. 1998. pap. 12.00 (*1-884381-16-2*) W Drenttel Ed.

Paul Renner: The Art of Typography. Christopher Burke. LC 98-41025. (Illus.). 220p. 1999. pap. 35.00 (*1-56898-158-9*) Princeton Arch.

Paul Resika. Text by W. S. Di Piero & Karen Wilken. (Illus.). 18p. 1993. pap. 20.00 (*1-58821-061-8*) Salander OReilly.

Paul Revere. Jan Gleiter & Kathleen Thompson. LC 94-40992. (First Biographies Ser.). (Illus.). 32p. (J). 1995. lib. bdg. 21.40 (*0-8114-8452-1*) Raintree Steck-V.

Paul Revere. JoAnn A. Grote. LC 99-27369. 1999. 16.95 (*0-7910-5355-5*) Chelsea Hse.

Paul Revere. Joanne Grote. (Illus.). 80p. (gr. 3 up). 1999. pap. 8.95 (*0-7910-5698-8*) Chelsea Hse.

Paul Revere. Gail Sakurai. LC 97-717. (Cornerstones to Freedom Ser.). (Illus.). 32p. (J). (gr. 4-6). 1997. lib. bdg. 19.50 (*0-516-20463-7*) Childrens.

Paul Revere. Gail Sakurai. (Cornerstones to Freedom Ser.). (J). 1998. pap. text 5.95 (*0-516-26230-0*) Childrens.

***Paul Revere.** George Sullivan. LC 99-17381. (In Their Own Words Ser.). (Illus.). 128p. (J). (gr. 4-7). 1999. 4.50 (*0-439-09552-2*) Scholastic Inc.

***Paul Revere.** George Sullivan. (In Their Own Words Ser.). (Illus.). 128p. (J). (gr. 4-7). 2000. 12.95 (*0-439-14748-4*) Scholastic Inc.

Paul Revere: Boston Patriot. Augusta Stevenson. LC 86-10743. (Childhood of Famous Americans Ser.). (Illus.). 192p. (J). (gr. 3-7). 1986. reprint ed. mass mkt. 4.95 (*0-02-042090-0*) Macmillan.

Paul Revere: Rider for the Revolution. Barbara Ford. LC 96-8828. (Historical American Biographies Ser.). (Illus.). 128p. (YA). (gr. 6 up). 1997. lib. bdg. 20.95 (*0-89490-779-4*) Enslow Pubs.

Paul Revere: Son of Liberty. Keith Brandt. LC 81-23147. (Illus.). 48p. (J). (gr. 4-6). 1982. pap. 3.95 (*0-89375-767-5*) Troll Communs.

Paul Revere: Son of Liberty. Keith Brandt. LC 81-23147. (Illus.). 48p. (J). (gr. 4-6). 1997. lib. bdg. 17.25 (*0-89375-766-7*) Troll Communs.

Paul Revere & Freemasonry. Edith J. Steblecki. (Illus.). 122p. 1985. pap. 6.00 (*0-9619999-3-4*) Paul Revere Mem Assn.

Paul Revere & Other Story Hours. Franco Pagnucci & Susan Pagnucci. (Illus.). 72p. (Orig.). (J). (gr. k-6). 1988. pap. 8.99 (*0-929326-00-8*) Bur Oak Pr Inc.

Paul Revere & the Raiders: History Rebeats Itself! Claudia M. Doege. (Illus.). 160p. (Orig.). 1985. pap. text 9.95 (*0-9615517-0-4*) Dia Press.

Paul Revere & the World He Lived In. Esther Forbes. (Illus.). 528p. 1999. pap. 16.00 (*0-618-00194-8*, Mariner Bks) HM.

Paul Revere & the World He Lived In. Esther Forbes. 1992. 27.00 (*0-8446-6526-6*) Peter Smith.

Paul Revere, Artisan, Businessman, & Patriot: The Man Behind the Myth. Revere, Paul Memorial Association Staff. (Artisans & the Arts Ser.). (Illus.). 192p. 1988. pap. text 6.00 (*0-9619999-1-8*); lib. bdg. 25.00 (*0-9619999-0-X*) Paul Revere Mem Assn.

Paul Revere, Boston Patriot. Augusta Stevenson. (J). 1986. 10.05 (*0-606-03255-X*, Pub. by Turtleback) Demco.

***Paul Revere Play Set & Booklet: 15 Pieces Include 5" Figures, Horse, Steeple, Lanterns.** (American Adventure Play Sets Ser.). (Illus.). 32p. (J). (gr. k-7). 1999. 28.00 (*0-9677511-1-X*) Child Light.

Paul Revere's Ride. David H. Fischer. (Illus.). 464p. 1994. 35.00 (*0-19-508847-6*) OUP.

Paul Revere's Ride. David H. Fischer. (Illus.). 464p. 1995. pap. 17.95 (*0-19-509831-5*) OUP.

Paul Revere's Ride. Stephen Krensky. (J). 1924. write for info. (*0-688-16409-9*, Wm Morrow); lib. bdg. write for info. (*0-688-16410-2*, Wm Morrow) Morrow Avon.

Paul Revere's Ride. Henry Wadsworth Longfellow. LC 89-25630. (Illus.). 40p. (J). (gr. k-4). 1990. 16.99 (*0-525-44610-9*, Dutton Child) Peng Put Young Read.

Paul Revere's Ride. Henry Wadsworth Longfellow. (Illus.). 40p. (J). (gr. k up). 1996. pap. 6.99 (*0-14-055612-5*, PuffinBks) Peng Put Young Read.

Paul Revere's Ride. Henry Wadsworth Longfellow. 1996. 10.19 (*0-606-08842-3*, Pub. by Turtleback) Demco.

Paul Revere's Ride. Charles Santore. 1924. write for info. (*0-688-16552-4*) Lothrop.

Paul Revere's Ride. Henry Wadsworth Longfellow. LC 92-23319. (Illus.). 48p. (J). (gr. 1 up). 1993. reprint ed. mass mkt. 4.95 (*0-688-12387-2*, Wm Morrow) Morrow Avon.

Paul Revere's Three Accounts of His Famous Ride. 1976. pap. 5.00 (*0-934909-60-1*) Mass Hist Soc.

Paul Ricoeur. E. Peters. 1998. 93.95 (*90-6831-793-8*, Pub. by Peeters Pub) Bks Intl VA.

***Paul Ricoeur: A Bibliography.** Ed. by Joan Nordquist. (Social Theory: Vol. 53). 72p. 1999. pap. 20.00 (*1-892068-05-2*) Ref Rsch Serv.

Paul Ricoeur: His Life & His Work. Charles E. Reagan. (Illus.). 160p. 1996. 24.95 (*0-226-70602-8*) U Ch Pr.

Paul Ricoeur: His Life & His Work. Charles E. Reagan. (Illus.). 152p. 1998. pap. 13.00 (*0-226-70603-6*) U Ch Pr.

Paul Ricoeur: The Hermeneutics of Action. Ed. by Richard Kearney. (Philosophy & Social Criticism Ser.: Vol. 2). 224p. 1996. 65.00 (*0-7619-5138-5*); pap. 22.95 (*0-7619-5139-3*) Sage.

Paul Ricoeur: The Promise & Risk of Politics. Bernard P. Dauenhauer. LC 98-37915. (Twentieth Century Political Thinkers Ser.: No. 100). 320p. 1998. pap. 24.95 (*0-8476-9237-X*); text 68.00 (*0-8476-9236-1*) Rowman.

Paul Ricoeur's Hermeneutics of the Imagination: The Imagination As the Creative Element of Religious Literacy, Vol. 143. Jeanne Evans. LC 93-42528. (American University Studies: Series VII). 213p. (C). 1995. text 42.95 (*0-8204-2060-3*) P Lang Pubng.

Paul Robbrecht & Hilda Daem: Works in Architecture. Text by Steven Jacobs et al. (Illus.). 160p. 1998. 45.00 (*90-5544-098-1*, 820882) Ludion.

Paul Robeson. Phillip H. Dean. LC 97-162150. 1997. pap. 5.25 (*0-8222-1515-2*) Dramatists Play.

Paul Robeson. Martin Duberman. LC 94-43400. 816p. 1995. pap. 19.95 (*1-56584-288-X*, Pub. by New Press NY) Norton.

Paul Robeson. Shirley Graham. 1995. pap. 9.95 (*0-86543-469-7*) Africa World.

Paul Robeson: A Voice of Struggle. Burnham Holmes. LC 94-12665. (American Troublemakers Ser.). 128p. (J). (gr. 7-8). 1994. lib. bdg. 27.11 (*0-8114-2381-6*) Raintree Steck-V.

Paul Robeson: A Voice to Remember. Patricia McKissack & Fredrick McKissack. LC 92-2582. (Great African Americans Ser.). (Illus.). 32p. (J). (gr. 1-4). 1992. lib. bdg. 14.95 (*0-89490-310-1*) Enslow Pubs.

***Paul Robeson: A Voice to Remember.** rev. ed. Pat McKissack & Fredrick McKissack. LC 00-8294. (Great African Americans Ser.). 2000. write for info. (*0-7660-1674-9*) Enslow Pubs.

Paul Robeson: Actor, Singer, Political Activist. David K. Wright. LC 97-34194. (African-American Biographies Ser.). (Illus.). 128p. (YA). (gr. 6 up). 1998. lib. bdg. 20.95 (*0-89490-944-4*) Enslow Pubs.

Paul Robeson: Artist & Citizen. Ed. by Jeffrey C. Stewart. LC 97-31660. (Illus.). 304p. (C). 1998. pap. 22.00 (*0-8135-2511-X*) Rutgers U Pr.

Paul Robeson: Artist & Citizen. Ed. & Intro. by Jeffrey C. Stewart. LC 97-31660. (Illus.). 304p. (YA). (gr. 6 up). 1998. 40.00 (*0-8135-2510-1*) Rutgers U Pr.

Paul Robeson: Athlete, Actor, Singer, Activist. Scott Erlich. (Black American Ser.). (Illus.). 192p. (YA). 1989. reprint ed. mass mkt. 3.95 (*0-87067-552-4*, Melrose Sq) Holloway.

Paul Robeson: Bearer of a Culture. (Illus.). 98p. 1998. pap. 14.95 (*0-9666711-0-4*) P Robeson Fndtn.

Paul Robeson: Citizen of the World. Shirley Graham. (Young Readers Ser.). (J). 1996. 29.95 (*0-86543-468-9*) Africa World.

An Asterisk (*) at the beginning of an entry indicates that the title is appearing for the first time.

Paul Robeson: Hero Before His Time. Rebecca Larsen. LC 89-8880. (Illus.). 160p. (J). (gr. 6-9). 1989. lib. bdg. 24.00 (*0-531-10779-5*) Watts.

Paul Robeson: Mini Play. (People of Conscience Ser.). (J). (gr. 5 up). 1977. 6.50 (*0-89550-371-9*) Stevens & Shea.

Paul Robeson: Singer & Actor. Steven Samuels. Ed. by Nathan I. Huggins. (Black Americans of Achievement Ser.). (Illus.). 124p. (Orig.). (YA). (gr. 5 up). 1987. lib. bdg. 19.95 (*1-55546-608-7*) Chelsea Hse.

Paul Robeson: Singer & Actor. Steven Samuels. Ed. by Nathan I. Huggins. (Black Americans of Achievement Ser.). (Illus.). 124p. (Orig.). (YA). (gr. 5 up). 1989. pap. 8.95 (*0-7910-0206-3*) Chelsea Hse.

Paul Robeson: The Great Forerunner. rev. ed. Ed. by Freedomways Editors. LC 98-12603. (Illus.). 396p. 1998. reprint ed. pap. 14.95 (*0-7178-0724-X*) Intl Pubs Co.

Paul Robeson: The Years of Promise & Achievement. Sheila T. Boyle & Andrew Bunie. (Illus.). 544p. 2001. 39.95 (*1-55849-149-X*) U of Mass Pr.

Paul Robeson, Citizen of the World. Shirley Graham. LC 75-152393. 264p. 1972. reprint ed. lib. bdg. 35.00 (*0-8371-6055-3*, GRR&, Greenwood Pr) Greenwood.

Paul Robeson Collection: Manuscript Collections from the Schomburg Paul Robeson & David H. Werning. LC 92-7993. (Black Studies Research Sources). 9 p. 1991. write for info. (*1-55655-375-7*) U Pubns Amer.

Paul Robeson Handbook: Every. Lenwood Davis. LC 98-152996. 358p. 1998. pap. 14.00 (*1-57502-780-1*, P02156) Morris Pubng.

Paul Robeson, Jr. Speaks to America. Paul Robeson. LC 92-36164. 225p. (C). 1993. 25.00 (*0-8135-1985-3*) Rutgers U Pr.

Paul Robeson, Jr. Speaks to America: The Politics of Multiculturalism. Paul Robeson, Jr. (C). 1996. 15.95 (*0-8135-2322-2*) Rutgers U Pr.

Paul Robeson Research Guide: A Selected Annotated Bibliography. Compiled by Lenwood G. Davis. LC 82-11680. 879p. 1982. lib. bdg. 59.95 (*0-313-22864-7*, DPR/, Greenwood Pr) Greenwood.

Paul Robin: A Chronology. V. Munoz. Tr. by W. Scott Johnson. (Libertarian & Anarchist Chronology Ser.). 1979. lib. bdg. 59.95 (*0-8490-3055-2*) Gordon Pr.

Paul Rudolph: Architectural Drawings. Paul Rudolph & Yukio Futagawa. (Illus.). 218p. 1981. 55.00 (*0-8038-0208-0*) Archit CT.

Paul Rudolph & Louis Kahn: A Bibliography. Charles R. Smith. LC 87-12781. (Illus.). 238p. 1987. 29.00 (*0-8108-2003-X*) Scarecrow.

***Paul Says.** 1999. pap. text 8.00 (*0-687-03376-4*) Abingdon.

Paul Schilder - Mind Explorer. Donald A. Shashkan & William L. Roller. (Illus.). 316p. 1985. 43.95 (*0-89885-144-0*, Kluwer Acad Hman Sci) Kluwer Academic.

Paul Schneider: The Buchenwald Apostle. Claude R. Foster, Jr. (Illus.). 901p. 1995. pap. 42.00 (*1-887732-09-8*) West Chester Univ.

Paul Schneider: The Witness of Buchenwald. Rudolf Wentorf. Tr. & Intro. by C. Franklin Sanders. (Illus.). 121p. (Orig.). 1993. pap. 8.95 (*0-929408-08-X*) Amer Eagle Pubns Inc.

***Paul Scott.** Jacqueline Bannerjee. (Writers & Their Work Ser.). 128p. 1998. pap. text 17.00 (*0-7463-0875-2*, Pub. by Northcote House) U Pr of Miss.

Paul, Scripture & Ethics: A Study of 1 Corinthians 5-7. Brian S. Rosner. (Biblical Studies Library Ser.). 264p. 1999. pap. 23.99 (*0-8010-2212-6*) Baker Bks.

***Paul Sheriff Teaches Visual Basic 6.** Paul Sheriff. (Illus.). 806p. 1999. pap. 24.99 (*0-7897-1898-7*) Que.

***Paul Signac: A Collection of Watercolors & Drawings.** Charles Cachin et al. LC 99-44943. (Illus.). 128p. 2000. 39.95 (*0-8109-4366-2*, Pub. by Abrams) Time Warner.

Paul Signac: Watercolors by Paul Signac. Ed. by Lauri Thompson. Tr. by Isabel Balzer from FRE. (Illus.). 42p. (Orig.). 1990. pap. 15.00 (*0-935037-86-1*) G Peters Gallery.

Paul Signac & Color in Neo-Impressionism. Floyd Ratliff. (Illus.). 317p. 1992. 49.95 (*0-87470-050-7*) Rockefeller.

Paul Sills's Story Theater: Four Shows. Paul Sills & Viola Spolin. (Illus.). 288p. 1999. 26.95 (*1-55783-398-2*) Applause Theatre Bk Pubs.

Paul Simon. Music Sales Corporation Staff. (Playtime for Recorder Ser.). 1997. pap. text 7.95 (*0-7119-2848-7*) Music Sales.

Paul Simon. John Robertson. (Illus.). 136p. (Orig.). pap. 8.95 (*0-7119-5597-2*, OP47829) Omnibus NY.

***Paul Simon: A Bio-bibliography, 78.** James E. Perone. (Bio-Bibliographies in Music Ser.: Vol. 78). 200p. 2000. lib. bdg. 69.50 (*0-313-31016-5*, Greenwood Pr) Greenwood.

Paul Simon: Anthology. Paul Simon. LC 91-751984. (Illus.). 248p. 1996. pap. 22.95 (*0-8256-1278-0*, PS 11196) Music Sales.

Paul Simon: Complete, 2 vols. Paul Simon. Incl. Vol. 1. Paul Simon: Complete. 1996. 23.95 (*0-8256-3313-3*, PS 11329); Vol. 2. Paul Simon: Complete. 1996. 23.95 (*0-8256-3314-1*, PS 11337); LC 91-762121. 544p. 1995. Set pap. 39.95 (*0-8256-3310-9*, PS 11113) Omnibus NY.

Paul Simon: Complete see Paul Simon: Complete

Paul Simon: Concert in the Park. (Illus.). 168p. 1991. pap. 24.95 (*0-8256-1337-X*, PS11261) Music Sales.

Paul Simon: Graceland. (Illus.). 64p. 1986. pap. 15.95 (*0-7119-1109-6*, PS10867) Music Sales.

Paul Simon: Hearts & Bones. (Illus.). 72p. 1983. pap. 14.95 (*0-685-65818-X*, PS10826) Music Sales.

Paul Simon: Negotiations & Love Songs, 1971-1986. (Illus.). 104p. 1988. pap. 14.95 (*0-8256-3307-9*, PS11121) Music Sales.

Paul Simon: One-Trick Pony. (Illus.). 64p. 1978. pap. 14.95 (*0-685-65819-8*, PS11178) Music Sales.

Paul Simon: Piano Solos. (Illus.). 64p. 1992. pap. 17.95 (*0-7119-2987-4*, AM89114) Music Sales.

Paul Simon: Still Crazy after All These Years. (Illus.). 44p. 1975. pap. 14.95 (*0-86001-315-4*, PS10180) Music Sales.

Paul Simon: The Rhythm of the Saints. (Illus.). 88p. 1990. pap. 17.95 (*0-8256-1298-5*, PS11204) Music Sales.

Paul Simon: Themes & Variations, Clarinet. Selected by Marcel Robinson. (Illus.). 48p. 1988. pap. 12.95 (*0-8256-2553-X*, PS10917) Music Sales.

Paul Simon: Themes & Variations, Flute. Selected by Marcel Robinson. (Illus.). 48p. 1988. pap. 12.95 (*0-8256-2554-8*, PS10925) Music Sales.

Paul Simon: Themes & Variations, Trumpet. Selected by Marcel Robinson. (Illus.). 48p. 1988. pap. 12.95 (*0-8256-2555-6*, PS10933) Music Sales.

Paul Simon: There Goes Rhymin' Simon. (Illus.). 80p. 1973. pap. 14.95 (*0-8256-3302-8*, PS10924) Music Sales.

Paul Simon Compact Collection. (Illus.). 64p. 1987. pap. 14.95 (*0-949789-16-X*, PS10891) Music Sales.

Paul Simon Complete. (Illus.). 144p. 1991. pap. 21.95 (*0-7119-2783-9*, AM86342) Music Sales.

Paul Simon for Fingerstyle Jazz Guitar. Arranged by Howard Morgen. (Illus.). 88p. 1998. pap. text 24.95 (*0-8256-3317-6*, PS11436) Music Sales.

Paul Simon Greatest Hits: Songtab Edition. Paul Simon. (Illus.). 120p. 1993. pap. 17.95 (*0-8256-1357-4*, PS11295) Music Sales.

Paul Simon in Concert: Live Rhymin' (Illus.). 72p. 1974. pap. 14.95 (*0-8256-3301-X*, PS10916) Music Sales.

Paul Simon Six Chord Songbook. 40p. pap. 10.95 (*0-7119-0342-5*, PS10818) Omnibus NY.

Paul Simon Songs from the Capeman. Paul Simon. 119p. 1998. pap. text 22.95 (*0-8256-3318-4*, PS1444) Music Sales.

Paul Simon Transcribed. Mark Hanson. 96p. (Orig.). 1993. pap. 19.95 (*0-936799-09-9*, AM 4044) Accent Music.

Paul VI: The First Modern Pope. Peter Hebblethwaite. LC 93-6475. (Illus.). 768p. 1993. 29.95 (*0-8091-0461-X*) Paulist Pr.

Paul Soldner: A Retrospective. Elaine Levin et al. LC 91-53090. (Illus.). 128p. 1992. pap. 24.95 (*0-295-97159-2*) U of Wash Pr.

Paul Speck: Und Die Karlsruher Masolika. H. Siebenmorgen. (GER., Illus.). 152p. 75.00 (*3-925369-68-6*, Pub. by Arnoldsche Art Pubs) Antique Collect.

Paul, Srtemis, & the Jews in Ephesus. Rick Strelan. (Beiheft zur Zeitschrift fuer die Neuetestamentliche Wissenschaft Ser.: No. 80). xxi, 380p. (C). 1996. lib. bdg. 124.95 (*3-11-015020-4*) De Gruyter.

Paul Strand. Photos by Paul Strand. (Masters of Photography Ser.: Vol. 1). (Illus.). 96p. 1987. 34.95 (*0-89381-077-0*) Aperture.

Paul Strand. 2nd ed. Mark Haworth-Booth. (Masters of Photography Ser.). (Illus.). 96p. 1997. reprint ed. 18.95 (*0-89381-746-5*) Aperture.

Paul Strand: An Extraordinary Vision. Gerald P. Peters, 3rd & Megan Fox. LC 94-75850. (Illus.). 40p. (Orig.). 1994. pap. 28.00 (*0-935037-56-X*) G Peters Gallery.

Paul Strand: Essays on His Life & Work. (Illus.). 352p. 1991. 60.00 (*0-89381-420-2*) Aperture.

Paul Strand: Rebecca. Ed. by John Cheim & Alexandra Rowley. (Illus.). 48p. (Orig.). 1996. pap. 35.00 (*0-944680-48-8*) R Miller Gal.

Paul Strand: Sixty Years of Photographs. Paul Strand. (Illus.). 184p. 1999. 50.00 (*0-912334-81-9*); pap. 35.00 (*0-900406-82-8*) Aperture.

Paul Strand: The World on My Doorstep. Catherine Duncan. (Aperture Ser.). (Illus.). 142p. 1997. pap. 37.95 (*0-89381-579-9*) Aperture.

Paul Strand: The World on My Doorstep. 35th ed. Ute Eskildsen & Catherine Duncan. (Aperture Ser.: No. 135). (Illus.). 142p. 1997. pap. 27.95 (*0-89381-578-0*) Aperture.

Paul Strand: The World on My Doorstep, the Years 1950 to 1976. Catherine Duncan. 1994. 68.00 (*0-89381-545-4*) Aperture.

Paul Strand, Ca. 1916. Maria Morris Hambourg et al. LC 97-39005. 1998. 55.00 (*0-87099-846-3*) Metro Mus Art.

***Paul Strand, Circa 1916.** Maria Morris Hambourg. (Illus.). 192p. 1998. 65.00 (*0-8109-6519-4*, Pub. by Abrams) Time Warner.

Paul Strand, Circa 1916. Maria Morris Hambourg et al. LC 97-39005. 1998. pap. 45.00 (*0-87099-847-1*) Metro Mus Art.

***Paul Street Boys.** Ferenc Molnar. 208p. 1999. pap. 21.00 (*963-13-4803-2*, Pub. by Corvina Bks) St Mut.

Paul Street Boys. Ferenc A. Molnar. 208p. (J). 1989. pap. 45.00 (*963-13-3801-0*, Pub. by Corvina Bks) St Mut.

Paul Struggles with His Congregation: The Pastoral Message of the Letters to the Corinthians. Hans Urs von Balthasar. Tr. by Brigitte Bojarska from GER. LC 91-76068. 90p. 1992. pap. 6.95 (*0-89870-386-7*) Ignatius Pr.

Paul Sutinen Portland, Oregon: Five Works, 1982-1987. Terri M. Hopkins. (Illus.). 1987. pap. 1.00 (*0-914435-16-7*) Marylhurst Art.

Paul the Accused: His Portrait in Acts of the Apostles. Marie-Eloise Rosenblatt. LC 94-16103. (Zacchaeus Studies, New Testament). 136p. (Orig.). 1995. pap. 8.95 (*0-8146-5750-8*, M Glazier) Liturgical Pr.

Paul the Apostle. Robert E. Picirilli. pap. 12.99 (*0-8024-6325-8*, 245) Moody.

Paul, the Apostle: His Life & Times. Robert Boyd. LC 95-197275. (Illus.). 479p. (Orig.). 1995. kivar 12.99 (*0-529-10252-8*, PAUL) World Publng.

Paul the Apostle: Jew & Greek Alike, Vol. 1. Romano Penna. Tr. by Thomas P. Wahl. 344p. (Orig.). 1996. pap. 34.95 (*0-8146-5835-0*, M Glazier) Liturgical Pr.

Paul the Apostle: The Triumph of God in Life & Thought. J. Christiaan Beker. LC 79-8904. 480p. 1980. pap. 25.00 (*0-8006-1811-4*, 1-1811) Augsburg Fortress.

Paul the Apostle: Wisdom & Folly of the Cross, Vol. 2. Romano Penna. Tr. by Thomas P. Wahl from ITA. LC 95-37825. 304p. (Orig.). 1996. pap. text 34.95 (*0-8146-5912-8*, M Glazier) Liturgical Pr.

Paul the Apostle 2 vols. A Theological & Exegetical Study. Romano Penna. Tr. by Thomas P. Wahl. 1996. pap. 64.95 (*0-8146-5913-6*, M Glazier) Liturgical Pr.

Paul the Apostle to America: Cultural Trends & Pauline Scholarship. Robert Jewett. 192p. (Orig.). 1994. pap. 19.95 (*0-664-25483-7*) Westminster John Knox.

Paul the Convert: The Apostolate & Apostasy of Saul the Pharisee. Alan F. Segal. 384p. (C). 1992. reprint ed. pap. 19.00 (*0-300-05227-8*) Yale U Pr.

Paul the Jewish Theologian: A Pharisee Among Christians, Jews, & Gentiles. Brad H. Young. LC 97-2478. 164p. 1997. pap. 12.95 (*1-56563-248-6*) Hendrickson MA.

Paul, the Law, & Justification. Colin G. Kruse. LC 97-2792. 320p. 1997. pap. 16.95 (*1-56563-277-X*) Hendrickson MA.

Paul, the Law & the Jewish People. E. P. Sanders. LC 82-17487. 240p. (Orig.). 1983. pap. 23.00 (*0-8006-1878-5*, 1-1878, Fortress Pr) Augsburg Fortress.

Paul the Leader see Paulo, O Lider

Paul the Letter-Writer: His World, His Options, His Skills. Jerome M. O'Connor. LC 94-11566. (Good News Studies: No. 41). 160p. (Orig.). 1995. pap. text 13.95 (*0-8146-5845-8*, M Glazier) Liturgical Pr.

Paul the Letter-Writer & the Second Letter to Timothy. Michael Prior. (JSNT Supplement Ser.: No. 23). 300p. 1989. 85.00 (*1-85075-147-1*, Pub. by Sheffield Acad) CUP Services.

Paul the Man: His Life & His Ministry. Clarence E. Macartney. LC 92-16135. 176p. 1992. reprint ed. pap. 10.99 (*0-8254-3269-3*) Kregel.

Paul the Minstrel & Other Stories. Arthur C. Benson. LC 70-106247. (Short Story Index Reprint Ser.). 1977. 26.95 (*0-8369-3283-8*) Ayer.

Paul the Missionary. 64p. pap. 2.95 (*0-9609302-0-5*) L Imperio.

Paul the Peddler. Horatio Alger, Jr. (Works of Horatio Alger Jr.). 1989. reprint ed. lib. bdg. 79.00 (*0-685-27568-X*) Rprt Serv.

Paul the Peddler, or the Fortunes of a Young Street Merchant. large type ed. Horatio Alger, Jr. LC 98-89121. 280p. 1998. pap. 16.95 (*1-888725-02-8*) Sci & Human Pr.

Paul the Pitcher. Paul Sharp. LC 84-7011. (Rookie Readers Ser.). (Illus.). 32p. (J). (ps-2). 1984. pap. 4.95 (*0-516-42064-X*); lib. bdg. 17.00 (*0-516-02064-1*) Childrens.

Paul, the Spirit, & the People of God. abr. rev. ed. Gordon D. Fee. LC 95-30872. 208p. (C). 1996. pap. 12.95 (*1-56563-170-6*) Hendrickson MA.

Paul Thek: The Wonderful World that Almost Was. Ann Wilson et al. (Illus.). 200p. 1995. pap. 45.00 (*90-73362-32-6*) Dist Art Pubs.

Paul Thek - Processions. Suzanne Delehanty. LC 77-92423. 1977. pap. 12.00 (*0-88454-023-5*) U of Pa Contemp Art.

Paul Tillich: A Comprehensive Bibliography & Keyword Index of Primary & Secondary Writings in English. Richard C. Crossman. LC 83-15026. (American Theological Library Association Monograph: No. 9). 193p. 1983. 24.00 (*0-8108-1650-4*) Scarecrow.

Paul Tillich: A New Catholic Assessment. Ed. by Raymond F. Bulman & Frederick J. Parella. 360p. (Orig.). 1994. pap. text 19.95 (*0-8146-5828-8*, M Glazier) Liturgical Pr.

Paul Tillich: Sein Leben. Renate Albrecht & Werner Schubler. (GER., Illus.). 187p. 1994. 37.95 (*3-631-46487-8*) P Lang Pubng.

Paul Tillich: Theologian of the Boundaries. Ed. by Mark K. Taylor. LC 91-14241. (Making of Modern Theology Ser.). 352p. (Orig.). 1991. pap. 22.00 (*0-8006-3403-9*, 1-3403, Fortress Pr) Augsburg Fortress.

Paul Tillich & Emanuel Hirsch Debate: A Study in the Political Ramifications of Theology. A. James Reimer. LC 89-13568. (Toronto Studies in Theology: Vol. 42). 384p. 1989. lib. bdg. 109.95 (*0-88946-991-1*) E Mellen.

Paul Tillich First-Hand: A Memoir of the Harvard Years. Grace Cali. LC 95-61557. xv, 123p. 1996. 19.95 (*0-913552-58-5*) Exploration Pr.

Paul Tillich in Conversation: Psychotherapy... Religion... Culture... History... Psychology. James B. Ashbrook. LC 88-40118. 156p. (C). 1988. text 40.00 (*1-55605-039-9*); pap. text 20.00 (*1-55605-038-0*) Wyndham Hall.

Paul Tillich Main Works, Vol. 5. Ed. by Carl H. Ratschow. (Writings on Religion). xvii, 325p. 1987. lib. bdg. 75.40 (*3-11-011541-7*) De Gruyter.

Paul Tillich Main Works - Hauptwerke. Ed. by John Clayton. (Writings in the Philosophy of Religion - Religionsphilosophische Schriften: Vol. 4). iv, 421p. 1987. lib. bdg. 95.40 (*3-11-011543-3*) De Gruyter.

Paul Tillich Main Works - Hauptwerke Vol. 4: Writings in the Philosophy of Religion. Ed. by John Clayton. iv, 422p. 1987. 78.00 (*3-11-011342-2*) De Gruyter.

Paul Tillich on Creativity. Ed. by Jacquelyn A. Kegley. LC 88-38073. (Foundation for Philosophy of Creativity Monograph: No. 3). 174p. (Orig.). (C). 1989. pap. text 19.00 (*0-8191-7311-8*); lib. bdg. 34.50 (*0-8191-7310-X*) Foun Phil Creat.

Paul Tillich's Categories for the Interpretation of History: An Application to the Encounter of Eastern & Western Cultures. Jong C. Park. LC 93-11395. (American University Studies: Vol. 165). 1994. write for info. (*0-8204-2281-9*) P Lang Pubng.

Paul Tillich's Dialectical Humanism: Unmasking the God above God. Leonard F. Wheat. LC 74-105365. 303p. reprint ed. pap. 94.00 (*0-8357-8262-X*, 203410900088) Bks Demand.

Paul Tillich's Main Works in Six Volumes - Hauptwerke in 6 Banden Vol. 1: Philosophical Writings. Ed. by Carl H. Ratschow et al. (GER.). xiv, 424p. (C). 1989. lib. bdg. 103.10 (*3-11-011533-6*) De Gruyter.

Paul Tillich's Philosophy of Art. Michael F. Palmer. LC 83-15056. (Theologische Bibliothek Toepelmann Ser.: Vol. 41). xxii, 217p. 1983. 76.15 (*3-11-009681-1*) De Gruyter.

Paul Tillich's Theological Legacy: Spirit & Community: International Paul Tillich Conference, New Harmony, June 17-20, 1993. Ed. by Frederick J. Parrella. LC 95-40723. (Theologishce Bibliothek Toepelmann Ser.: Vol. 73). xxiii, 185p. (C). 1995. lib. bdg. 106.15 (*3-11-014667-3*) De Gruyter.

Paul Tillich's Theology of the Church: A Catholic Appraisal. Ronald Modras. LC 76-6082. 314p. reprint ed. pap. 97.40 (*0-7837-3605-3*, 204347000009) Bks Demand.

Paul Tuttle: Three Evolutions Plus. Aaron Betsky. (Illus.). 33p. 1995. pap. text 18.00 (*1-880658-09-7*) San Barb CAF.

Paul Tuttle Design & the 80s. Phyllis Plous & David Gebhard. (Illus.). 24p. 1987. pap. 7.00 (*0-942006-13-5*) U of CA Art.

Paul U. Kellogg & the Survey: Voices for Social Welfare & Social Justice. Clarke A. Chambers. LC 77-172931. (Illus.). 297p. reprint ed. pap. 92.10 (*0-608-16070-9*, 203321000084) Bks Demand.

Paul Valery. T. Bosanquet. LC 74-6412. (Studies in French Literature: No. 45). 1974. lib. bdg. 75.00 (*0-8383-1969-6*) M S G Haskell Hse.

Paul Valery. Henry A. Grubbs. LC 67-25204. (Twayne's World Authors Ser.). 1968. pap. text 4.95 (*0-8290-1869-7*); lib. bdg. 20.95 (*0-8057-2920-8*) Irvington.

***Paul Valery: A Philosopher for Philosophers, the Sage.** William Kluback. LC 99-23763. 238p. 2000. pap. text 37.95 (*0-8204-4482-0*) P Lang Pubng.

Paul Valery: De l'Enfant et du Reve. Pierre Girardet. xx, 103p. 1998. pap. 26.95 (*3-906760-24-3*, Pub. by P Lang) P Lang Pubng.

Paul Valery: Illusions of Civilization. William Kluback. LC 95-19460. (American University Studies: Series V, Vol. 177). XII, 148p. (C). 1996. 35.00 (*0-8204-2788-8*) P Lang Pubng.

Paul Valery: Philosophical Reflections. William Kluback. (American University Studies: Philosophy: Ser. V, Vol. 22). XI, 166p. (C). 1987. text 30.50 (*0-8204-0386-5*) P Lang Pubng.

Paul Valery: The Continuous Search for Reality. William Kluback. LC 96-17014. (American University Studies II: Vol. 219). XII, 173p. (C). 1997. 38.95 (*0-8204-3067-6*) P Lang Pubng.

Paul Valery: The Realms of the Analecta. William Kluback. LC 97-26604. (American University Studies V: Vol. 180). 163p. (C). 1998. pap. text 34.95 (*0-8204-3489-2*) P Lang Pubng.

Paul Valery: The Search for Intelligence. William Kluback. LC 93-13191. (American University Studies: Romance Languages & Literature: Ser. II, Vol. 204). 148p. (C). 1993. text 39.95 (*0-8204-2088-3*) P Lang Pubng.

***Paul Valery: The Statesman of the Intellect.** William Kluback. X, 161p. (C). 1999. pap. text 36.95 (*0-8204-4113-9*, 41139) P Lang Pubng.

Paul Valery, an Anthology: Selected from the Collected Works of Paul Valery. Paul Valery. LC 76-3026. (Bollingen Ser.: Vol. 45A). 379p. 1977. reprint ed. pap. 117.50 (*0-608-03761-3*, 206458400009) Bks Demand.

Paul Valery & His Critics. A. J. Arnold. LC 72-12808. (Studies in French Literature: No. 45). 1972. reprint ed. lib. bdg. 75.00 (*0-8383-1590-9*) M S G Haskell Hse.

Paul Valery & the Civilized Mind. Norman Suckling. LC 77-25965. (University of Durham Publications). 294p. 1978. reprint ed. lib. bdg. 65.00 (*0-313-20095-5*, SUPV, Greenwood Pr) Greenwood.

***Paul Valery & the Voice of Desire.** Kirsteen Anderson. (Legenda Ser.). 200p. (C). 2000. pap. 49.50 (*1-900755-40-8*, Pub. by E H R C) David Brown.

Paul Valery Revisited. Walter Putnam, III. LC 94-12619. (Twayne's World Authors Ser.: No. 850). 200p. 1994. 32.00 (*0-8057-8291-5*, Twyne) Mac Lib Ref.

Paul Valery's Album de Vers Anciens: A Past Transfigured. Suzanne Nash. LC 82-47606. 339p. reprint ed. pap. 105.10 (*0-7837-1934-5*, 204214900001) Bks Demand.

Paul Verhoeven. Rob Van Scheers. Tr. by Aletta Stevens. (Illus.). 256p. 1997. 21.95 (*0-571-17479-5*) Faber & Faber.

Paul Verlaine. Harold G. Nicolson. LC 77-10281. reprint ed. 49.50 (*0-404-16332-7*) AMS Pr.

Paul Verlaine. Stefan Zweig. Tr. by O. F. Theis from FRE. LC 77-11500. (Symbolists Ser.). (Illus.). reprint ed. 37.50 (*0-404-16359-9*) AMS Pr.

Paul Verlaine: His Absinthe-Tinted Song. Paul M. Verlaine. Tr. by Bergen Applegate from FRE. LC 77-11494. (Illus.). 232p. reprint ed. 42.50 (*0-404-16353-X*) AMS Pr.

Paul Verlaine: His Life, His Work. Edmond A. Lepelletier. Tr. by E. M. Lang. LC 71-128944. (Illus.). reprint ed. 55.00 (*0-404-03968-5*) AMS Pr.

Paul Verlaine Revisited. Schultz. 1999. 22.95 (*0-8057-4603-X*, Twyne) Mac Lib Ref.

Paul Vincent Carroll. Paul A. Doyle. LC 70-126005. (Irish Writers Ser.). 115p. 1975. 8.50 (*0-8387-7764-3*); pap. 1.95 (*0-8387-7659-0*) Bucknell U Pr.

Paul von Hindenburg. Russell Berman. (World Leaders Past & Present Ser.). (Illus.). 120p. (YA). (gr. 5 up). 1987. lib. bdg. 19.95 (*0-87754-532-4*) Chelsea Hse.

Paul Wallach's Guide to the Restaurants of Los Angeles & Southern California. Paul Wallach. 1995. pap. 13.95 (*0-9619156-8-4*) P Wallach.

P

Paul Wallach's Guide to the Restaurants of Los Angeles & Southern California, 1993. Paul Wallach. 1992. pap. 14.95 (*0-9619156-7-6*) P Wallach.

*Paul Wegener - Frühe Moderne im Film / Early Modernism in Film.** Heide Schonemann. (GER & ENG., Illus.). 128p. 2001. 58.00 (*3-932565-14-2*) Edition A Menges.

Paul Weller: In His Own Words. Mick St. Michael. Ed. by Michael Heatley. (Illus.). 96p. (Orig.). 1996. pap. 15.95 (*0-7119-6097-6*, OP 47855) Omnibus NY.

Paul Weller: My Ever Changing Moods. John Reed. (Illus.). 392p. 1996. 24.95 (*0-7119-5495-X*, OP 47810) Omnibus NY.

Paul Weller: The Unauthorized Biography. Steve Malins. (Illus.). 256p. (Orig.). 1997. pap. text 14.95 (*0-7535-0087-6*, Pub. by Virgin Bks) London Brdge.

Paul Weller: Wild Wood. Date not set. 17.95 (*0-7119-3825-3*, AM 91706) Music Sales.

Paul Weller Songbook. Paul Weller. (Illus.). 72p. 1993. pap. 17.95 (*0-7119-3291-3*, AM90230) Music Sales.

Paul Willems' The Drowned Land & La Vita Breve Vol. 1. Tr. by Donald F. Friedman & Suzanne Burgoyne from FRE. LC 93-39515. (Belgian Francophone Library Ser.: Vol. 1). X, 178p. (C). 1994. text 44.95 (*0-8204-2419-6*) P Lang Pubng.

Paul, Women, & Wives: Marriage & Women's Ministry in the Letters of Paul. Craig S. Keener. LC 92-26515. 350p. (Orig.). 1992. pap. 14.95 (*0-943575-96-6*) Hendrickson MA.

Paul, Women Teachers, & the Mother Goddess at Ephesus: A Study of First Timothy 2: 9-15 in Light of the Religious & Cultural Milieu of the First Century. Sharon H. Gritz. 198p. (Orig.). (C). 1991. pap. text 22.50 (*0-8191-8111-0*); lib. bdg. 43.00 (*0-8191-8110-2*) U Pr of Amer.

Paul Wonner: Abstract Realist. Text by George W. Neubert. LC 81-67616. (Illus.). 72p. 1981. pap. 15.00 (*0-911291-07-5*, Pub. by Fellows Cont Art) RAM Publications.

Paul Wrote from the Heart. Tr. & Intro. by Raymond V. Schoder. LC 86-72725. 64p. 1987. 24.50 (*0-86516-181-X*); pap. 12.00 (*0-86516-194-1*) Bolchazy-Carducci.

Paul Wunderlich: Eine Werkmonographie. Jens Christian Jensen. (GER., Illus.). 255p. 1980. pap. 50.00 (*3-921785-15-4*) Huber Volker.

Paul Wunderlich und Karin Szekessy: Correspondenzen. Fritz J. Raddatz et al. (GER., Illus.). 128p. 1977. 75.00 (*3-7630-1661-9*) Christian Belser.

Paul Wunderlich's Graphic Work, 1948-1982. Carsten Riediger. (GER.). 456p. 1983. 150.00 (*1-55660-115-8*) A Wofsy Fine Arts.

Paul Wylie from Cowboy to Cowboy Artist. Bettye Rogers. 96p. 1998. pap. 25.00 (*0-9664491-0-X*) B Rogers.

*Paul Yandell - Fingerstyle Legacy.** Paul Yandell. 72p. 1998. 17.95 (*0-7866-3485-5*, 95495BCD) Mel Bay.

*Paul Ziegelmaier Poems.** Paul Ziegelmaier. 2000. pap. write for info. (*1-58235-428-6*) Watermrk Pr.

Paul Zweitnig-Rotterdam: A Drawing Retrospective, 1995. Townsend Wolfe & Dore Ashton. 87p. 1995. pap. 20.00 (*1-884240-08-9*) Arkansas Art Ctr.

Paula. (Orig.). 1992. mass mkt. 4.95 (*1-56333-036-9*) Masquerade.

Paula. Isabel Allende. LC 95-2452. 336p. 1996. pap. 14.00 (*0-06-092721-6*) HarpC.

Paula. Eva Lecomte.Tr. of Paula la Pequena Valdense. (SPA.). 200p. 1987. pap. 5.20 (*0-7399-0295-4*, 2339.1) Rod & Staff.

Paula. large type ed. Isabel Allende. Tr. by Margaret Sayers Peden from SPA. LC 95-16376. 539p. 1995. 26.95 (*0-7838-1373-2*, G K Hall Lrg Type) Mac Lib Ref.

Paula: A Narrative Poem. limited ed. P. B. Newman. LC 74-25862. (Living Poets' Library). 1975. pap. 2.50 (*0-686-10402-1*) Dragons Teeth.

Paula Abdul. Susan Zannos. LC 98-30669. (Real-Life Reader Biographies Ser.). (Illus.). 32p. (J). (gr. 3-8). 1998. lib. bdg. 15.95 (*1-883845-74-2*) M Lane Pubs.

Paula Abdul: Straight Up. M. Thomas Ford. LC 91-40231. (Taking Part Ser.). (Illus.). 72p. (J). (gr. 3 up). 1992. lib. bdg. 13.95 (*0-87518-508-8*, Dillon Silver Burdett) Silver Burdett Pr.

Paula Cole: This Fire. 72p. 1997. per. 16.95 (*0-7935-8425-6*) H Leonard.

*Paula Cole Band: Amen.** 72p. 1999. otabind 14.95 (*0-634-01048-4*) H Leonard.

Paula Easley's Warehouse Food Cookbook. Paula Easley. LC 99-24389. 222p. 1999. 22.95 (*0-936783-24-9*) Merril Pr.

Paula Gunn Allen. Elizabeth I. Hanson. LC 90-80261. (Western Writers Ser.: No. 96). (Illus.). 50p. (Orig.). 1990. pap. 4.95 (*0-88430-095-1*) Boise St U W Writ Ser.

Paula Jones, Hero! Max. (Illus.). 45p. 1997. pap. 35.00 (*0-922070-91-1*) M Tecton Pub.

Paula la Pequena Valdense see Paula

Paula Modersohn-Becker: Germany's Pioneer Modernist. Jane Kallir. (Illus.). 48p. (Orig.). 1983. pap. 10.00 (*0-910810-23-0*) Johannes.

Paula Newby-Fraser's Peak Fitness for Women. Paula Newby-Fraser & John Mora. LC 94-40070. (Illus.). 232p. (Orig.). 1995. pap. 15.95 (*0-87322-672-0*, PNEW0672) Human Kinetics.

*Paula Poundstone.** Paula Poundstone. 2001. 24.00 (*0-609-60316-7*) Crown Pub Group.

Paula Rego. 2nd ed. John McEwen. LC 99-215820. (Illus.). 288p. 1997. pap. 39.95 (*0-7148-3622-2*, Pub. by Phaidon Press) Phaidon Pr.

Paula Rego: Retrospective. Fiona Bradley et al. LC 96-61422. (Illus.). 148p. (Orig.). 1997. pap. 29.95 (*0-500-27943-8*, Pub. by Thames Hudson) Norton.

Paula Sandburg's Chikaming Goat Herd. Kathleen Byrne. 64p. 1993. pap. 4.50 (*0-915992-59-0*) Eastern National.

Paula SPA. Isabel Allende. (SPA.). 368p. 1996. pap. 13.00 (*0-06-092720-8*, Perennial) HarperTrade.

Paula, the Waldensian. Eva Lecomte. 191p. (J). (gr. 3-7). 1997. pap. 6.95 (*1-881545-76-8*) Angelas Bkshelf.

Paula, the Waldensian. Eva Lecomte. Tr. by W. M. Strong. 433p. (J). (gr. 3-7). 1942. pap. 7.99 (*0-87213-511-X*) Loizeaux.

Paula's Plantscape - A Clerical Skills Simulation. 2nd ed. Lovern. (KM - Office Procedures Ser.). 1990. mass mkt. 11.50 (*0-538-60316-X*) S-W Pub.

Paula's Story. Shirley Flack. (Illus.). 256p. 1997. 35.00 (*0-7472-1772-6*, Pub. by Headline Bk Pub) Trafalgar.

Paula's Story. Shirley Flack. (Illus.). 256p. 1998. pap. 13.95 (*0-7472-5455-9*, Pub. by Headline Bk Pub) Trafalgar.

*Paulding Farnham: Tiffany's Lost Genius.** John Loring & Paulding Farnham. LC 00-22807. 160p. 2000. 49.50 (*0-8109-3511-2*, Pub. by Abrams) Time Warner.

Paulding Short Stories. James K. Paulding. Ed. by Alfred Bendixen. (Masterworks of Literature Ser.). 1999. write for info. (*0-8084-0442-3*) NCUP.

Paule Marshall. Hall. 1998. 24.95 (*0-8057-4528-9*, Twyne) Mac Lib Ref.

Paule Marshall: For a Reading on the Occasion of a Reception in Honor of Her MacArthur Fellowship. Paule Marshall. (InterAmericas Ser.: No. 2). 16p. 1992. 5.00 (*0-9633741-2-5*) RI Study of Man.

Paule Puhmanns Paddelboot. Gerd Neuner et al. 71p. 16.50 (*3-468-49845-4*) Langenscheidt.

Paulette, Tome I. G. Wolinski Pichard. 1981. pap. 11.95 (*0-7859-4140-1*) Fr & Eur.

Paulette, Tome II. G. Wolinski Pichard. (FRE.). 1981. pap. 11.95 (*0-7859-4155-X*, 2070373061) Fr & Eur.

Pauley Pavillion: College Basketball's Showplace. David Smale. Ed. by Richard Silverman et al. (Illus.). 160p. (C). 1989. 24.95 (*0-9624679-2-8*) SportMemories.

Pauli & the Spin-Statistics Theorem. LC 97-36353. 512p. 1997. text 56.00 (*981-02-3114-8*) World Scientific Pub.

Pauli Sententiae: A Palingenesia of the Opening Titles as a Specimen of Research in West Roman Vulgar Law. Ernst Levy. xii, 130p. 1970. reprint ed. 35.00 (*0-8377-2400-7*, Rothman) W S Hein.

Paulina Dlamini: Servant of Two Kings. Ed. & Tr. by S. Bourquin. (Killie Campbell Africana Library Publication: No. 1). (Illus.). 146p. 1986. pap. 14.95 (*0-86980-523-1*, Pub. by Univ Natal Pr) Intl Spec Bk.

Paulina 1880. Pierre J. Jouve. LC 95-37376. (FRE.). 256p. 1988. pap. 10.95 (*0-7859-2634-8*, 207036609X) Northwestern U Pr.

Paulina 1880. Pierre J. Jouve et al. LC 95-37376. 186p. (C). 1995. pap. 14.95 (*0-8101-6004-8*, Marlboro) Northwestern U Pr.

Pauline. Georg Hallensleben. LC 98-8054. 32p. (J). (ps-1). 1999. 16.00 (*0-374-35758-7*, Frances Foster) FS&G.

Pauline. Betty Keller. 317p. 1981. mass mkt. 5.95 (*0-88780-151-X*, Pub. by Formac Publ Co) Formac Dist Ltd.

Pauline & Johannine Mysticism. Sylvia Mary. 1964. 49.50 (*0-614-00266-4*) Elliots Bks.

Pauline Christianity. 2nd rev. ed. John A. Ziesler. (Oxford Bible Ser.). 176p. (Orig.). 1991. text 65.00 (*0-19-826460-7*); pap. text 21.00 (*0-19-826459-3*) OUP.

Pauline Circle. F. F. Bruce. (Biblical Classics Library: Vol. 14). 106p. (Orig.). 1995. reprint ed. mass mkt. 5.99 (*0-85364-706-2*, Pub. by Paternoster Pub) OM Literature.

Pauline Comics Series, 10 bks., 11 Bks. Incl. James Alberione Vol. 10: Hero for the Gospel. Ed. by Virginia H. Richards. Tr. by Mary D. Wickenhiser. (Illus.). 80p. (J). (gr. 5-9). 1996. pap. 2.95 (*0-8198-3964-7*); Vol. 1. St. Maximilian Kolbe. Jean-Marie Laferte & Brigitte Jeanson. Tr. by Marianne L. Trouve' from FRE. (Illus.). 32p. (J). (gr. 3-8). 1995. pap. 1.95 (*0-8198-6978-3*); Vol. 2. St. Francis of Assisi. Justin Lang & Juliette Wehrung. Tr. by Marianne L. Trouve' from FRE. (Illus.). 32p. (J). (gr. 3-8). 1995. pap. 1.95 (*0-8198-6983-X*); Vol. 3. St. Elizabeth. Justin Lang & Juliette Wehrung. Tr. by Marianne L. Trouve' from FRE. (Illus.). 32p. (J). (gr. 3-8). 1995. pap. 1.95 (*0-8198-6981-3*); Vol. 4. St. Joan of Arc. Rene Berthier & Marie Segault. Tr. by Marianne L. Trouve' from FRE. (Illus.). 32p. (J). (gr. 3-8). 1995. pap. 1.95 (*0-8198-6975-9*); Vol. 5. St. Clare of Assisi. Pierre Dhombre. Tr. by Marianne L. Trove' from FRE. (Illus.). 32p. (J). (gr. 3-8). 1995. pap. 1.95 (*0-8198-6976-7*); Vol. 6. St. Martin. Tr. by Marianne L. Trouve' & Raymond Maric from FRE. (Illus.). 32p. (J). (gr. 3-8). 1995. pap. 1.95 (*0-8198-6980-5*); Vol. 7. St. Bernadette. Rene Berthier & Marie Sigault. Tr. by Marianne L. Trouve' from FRE. (Illus.). 32p. (J). (gr. 3-8). 1995. pap. 1.95 (*0-8198-6977-5*); Vol. 8. St. Vincent De Paul. Roland Garel. Tr. by Marianne L. Trouve' from FRE. (Illus.). 32p. (J). (gr. 3-8). 1995. pap. 1.95 (*0-8198-6982-1*); Vol. 9. St. Bernard of Clairvaux. Monk of Citeaux Staff. Tr. by Marianne L. Trouve' from FRE. (Illus.). 32p. (J). (gr. 3-8). 1995. pap. 1.95 (*0-8198-6979-1*); Set pap. 18.45 (*0-8198-5903-6*) Pauline Bks.

Pauline Doctrine of Male Headship: The Apostle vs. Biblical Feminists. James E. Bordwine. 334p. 1996. text 29.95 (*1-884416-17-9*) A Press.

Pauline Epistles. William Kelly. (Introductory Lecture Ser.: Vol. 2). 551p. 7.95 (*0-88172-098-4*) Believers Bkshelf.

Pauline Eschatology. Geerhardus Vos. 380p. 1979. reprint ed. pap. 14.99 (*0-87552-505-9*) P & R Pubng.

*Pauline Hanson Story.** John Pasquarelli. 1999. pap. text 16.95 (*1-86436-341-X*) New Holland.

Pauline Images in Fiction & Film: On Reversing the Hermeneutical Flow. Larry J. Kreitzer. (Biblical Seminar Ser.: Vol. 61). 263p. 1999. pap. 23.00 (*1-85075-933-2*, Pub. by Sheffield Acad) CUP Services.

Pauline in Catalepsy & Psycho Therapeutics. Joseph R. Poulin. 78p. 1996. reprint ed. spiral bd. 10.50 (*0-7873-1263-0*) Hlth Research.

Pauline Jaricot: Foundress of the Living Rosary & the Society for the Propagation of the Faith. Mary F. Windeatt. LC 93-60214. (Illus.). 244p. (J). 1993. reprint ed. pap. 13.00 (*0-89555-425-9*) TAN Bks Pubs.

Pauline Jewett: A Passion for Canada. Judith McKenzie. (Illus.). 232p. 32.95 (*0-7735-1822-3*) McG-Queens Univ Pr.

Pauline Letters. Leander E. Keck et al. LC 84-6171. 160p. (Orig.). 1984. pap. 12.95 (*0-687-30494-6*) Abingdon.

Pauline Notion of Deeds of the Law. Hilary B. Mijoga. LC 98-20475. 200p. 1998. 74.95 (*1-57309-321-1*, U Pr W Africa); pap. 54.95 (*1-57309-320-3*, U Pr W Africa) Intl Scholars.

Pauline Parallels. rev. ed. Fred O. Francis & J. Paul Sampley. LC 83-48920. (Foundations & Facets). 416p. 1984. pap. 28.00 (*0-8006-2094-1*, 1-2094, Fortress Pr) Augsburg Fortress.

Pauline Periwinkle & Progressive Reform in Dallas. Jacquelyn M. McElhaney. LC 97-32344. (Centennial Series of the Association of Former Students: Vol. 73). (Illus.). 224p. 1998. 29.95 (*0-89096-800-4*) Tex A&M Univ Pr.

Pauline Studies, No. Betl 115. E. Peters. LC 95-208618. 1998. 78.00 (*90-6831-622-2*, Pub. by Peeters Pub) Bks Intl VA.

Pauline, the Prima Donna: Memoirs of an Opera Singer. 144p. 1985. mass mkt. 3.95 (*0-446-32608-9*, Pub. by Warner Bks) Little.

Pauline Theology, Vol. 1. Ed. by Jouette M. Bassler. 304p. 1994. pap. 22.00 (*0-8006-2860-8*, Fortress Pr) Augsburg Fortress.

Pauline Theology: Ministry & Theology. E. Ellis Earle. LC 96-39147. 200p. 1996. pap. 27.50 (*0-7618-0612-1*) U Pr of Amer.

Pauline Theology: Romans, Vol. 3. Ed. by E. Elizabeth Johnson & David M. Ray. 320p. 1995. 40.00 (*0-8006-2929-9*, 1-2929) Augsburg Fortress.

Pauline Theology Vol. 2: First & Second Corinthians. David M. Hay. 320p. 1993. 40.00 (*0-8006-2489-0*, Fortress Pr) Augsburg Fortress.

Pauline Theology & Mission Practice. Dean S. Gilliland. 309p. 1996. pap. 26.00 (*1-57910-005-8*) Wipf & Stock.

Pauline Writings: A Sheffield Reader. Ed. by Stanley E. Porter & Craig A. Evans. (Biblical Seminar Ser.: Vol. 34). 300p. 1995. pap. 19.95 (*1-85075-730-5*, Pub. by Sheffield Acad) CUP Services.

Pauline Writings Notes. Robert E. Picirilli. 1967. pap. 4.95 (*0-89265-001-X*) Randall Hse.

Pauling Catalogue: Ava Helen & Linus Pauling Papers at Oregon State University. Ed. by Clifford S. Mead & Janet Wallace. (Illus.). 305p. 1991. 35.00 (*0-9629082-0-7*) Kerr Lib.

Pauling Symposium: A Discourse on the Art of Biography. Ed. by Ramesh Krishnamurthy et al. (Illus.). 260p. 1996. 25.00 (*0-9629082-2-3*) Kerr Lib.

Pauling's Legacy. Z. B. Maksic & W. J. Orville-Thomas. LC 99-10936. (Theoretical & Computational Chemistry Ser.: Vol. 6). 782p. 1999. 360.50 (*0-444-82508-8*) Elsevier.

*Paulinus Noster: Self & Symbols in the Letters of Paulinus of Nola.** Catherine Conybeare. (Oxford Early Christian Studies). 300p. 2001. text 74.00 (*0-19-924072-8*) OUP.

Paulinus of Nola: Life, Letters & Poems. Dennis E. Trout. LC 98-31299. (Transformation of the Classical Heritage Ser.: Vol. XXVII). 404p. 1999. 55.00 (*0-520-21709-8*, Pub. by U CA Pr) Cal Prin Full Svc.

Paull-Irwin, a Family Sketch. Elisabeth M. Paull. (Illus.). viii, 198p. 1993. reprint ed. pap. 32.50 (*0-8328-2985-4*); reprint ed. lib. bdg. 42.50 (*0-8328-2984-6*) Higginson Bk Co.

*Paulo Coelho Las Confesiones del Peregrino.** Juan Arias. 1999. pap. 19.95 (*84-08-02956-8*) Planeta Edit.

Paulo Freire: A Critical Encounter. Ed. by Peter McLaren & Peter Leonard. LC 92-9965. 224p. (C). 1992. pap. 24.99 (*0-415-08792-9*, A9846) Routledge.

Paulo Freire: A Revolutionary Dilemma for the Adult Educator. Ed. by Stanley Grabowski. LC 72-7971. (Occasional Papers: No. 32). 75p. (Orig.). 1972. pap. 6.00 (*0-87060-054-0*) Syracuse U Cont Ed.

Paulo Freire: Pedagogue of Liberation. John L. Elias. LC 92-34530. 172p. (C). 1993. lib. bdg. 21.50 (*0-89464-816-0*) Krieger.

*Paulo Freire Collection, Vol. 4.** Ed. by Stanley F. Steiner et al. LC 99-45875. (Pedagogy & Popular Culture Ser.: No. 4). 284p. 1999. 55.00 (*0-8153-3377-3*, SS1417) Garland.

Paulo Freire on Higher Education: A Dialogue at the National University of Mexico. Paulo Freire et al. LC 93-15732. (SUNY Series, Teacher Empowerment & School Reform). 201p. (C). 1994. text 49.50 (*0-7914-1873-1*); pap. text 16.95 (*0-7914-1874-X*) State U NY Pr.

Paulo Freire Reader. Paulo Freire. Ed. by Ana Man et al. LC 98-17039. 240p. 1998. 24.95 (*0-8264-1088-X*) Continuum.

Paulo, O Lider. J. Oswald Sanders. Orig. Title: Paul the Leader. (POR.). 192p. 1986. write for info. (*0-8297-0756-5*) Vida Pubs.

Paulo's Strange Adventure. Junior African Writers Staff & Carolyn B. Mitchell. (Junior African Writers Ser.). (Illus.). 80p. (J). (gr. 3 up). 1995. pap. 4.95 (*0-7910-3163-2*) Chelsea Hse.

Paul's Bunions. Robert Kraus. 1999. 14.99 (*0-670-86224-X*) Viking Penguin.

Paul's Case: The Kingston Letters. Lynn Crosbie. LC 98-108979. 208p. 1997. pap. text 14.99 (*1-895837-09-X*) Login Pubs Consort.

Paul's Case & Other Stories. Willa Cather. LC 95-49595. (Thrift Editions Ser.). 64p. (Orig.). 1996. pap. text 1.00 (*0-486-29057-3*) Dover.

*Paul's Concept of Baptism & Its Present Implications for Believers: Walking in the Newness of Life.** M. Olusina Fape & Michael O. Fape. LC 99-14401. (Toronto Studies in Theology: Vol. 78). 242p. 1999. pap. 89.95 (*0-7734-8040-4*) E Mellen.

*Paul's Concept of Baptism & Its Present Implications for Believers: Walking in the Newness of Life.** M. Olusina Fape. LC 99-14401. 1999. write for info. (*0-88946-975-X*) E Mellen.

Paul's Early Letters: From Hope, Through Faith, to Love. Paul Wrightman. LC 83-7126. 148p. (Orig.). 1983. pap., student ed. 6.95 (*0-8189-0440-2*) Alba.

*Paul's Epistle to the Ephesians.** Paul M. Sadler. 400p. 1999. 19.50 (*1-893874-27-3*) Berean Bibl Soc.

Paul's Epistle to the Galatians. Vladimir M. Gelesnoff. 1977. pap. text 4.50 (*0-910424-73-X*) Concordant.

Paul's Epistles see Epistolas de Pablo, Vol. 1

Paul's First Letter to Corinth. Marilyn Ganskow. 107p. 1994. pap., wbk. ed. 10.00 (*1-928712-14-2*) New Life Series.

Paul's Gift from Philippi: Conventions of Gift-Exchange & Christian Giving. G. W. Peterman. LC 96-7897. (Society for New Testament Studies Monographs: No. 92). 257p. 1997. text 59.95 (*0-521-57220-7*) Cambridge U Pr.

Paul's Glory - Christology: Tradition & Rhetoric. Carey C. Newman. (Novum Testamentum, Supplements Ser.: Vol. 69). xviii, 305p. 1991. 126.50 (*90-04-09463-6*) Brill Academic Pubs.

Paul's Gospel in an Intercultural Context: Jew & Gentile in the Letter to the Romans. 2nd ed. William S. Campbell. LC 92-20330. VII, 213p. 1992. 45.00 (*3-631-42981-9*) P Lang Pubng.

Paul's Idea of Community: The Early House Churches in Their Cultural Setting. rev. ed. Robert Banks. LC 94-30999. 234p. 1994. pap. 12.95 (*1-56563-050-5*) Hendrickson MA.

Paul's Journeys Lesson Guide. Nancy Fisher. Ed. by Carol Witte. (Illus.). 40p. (J). (gr. 4-8). pap., wbk. ed. 9.95 (*1-890947-00-8*, 308X) Rose Publshg.

Paul's Language about God. Neil Richardson. LC 95-110006. (JSNT Supplement Ser.: Vol. 99). 371p. 1994. 85.00 (*1-85075-485-3*, Pub. by Sheffield Acad) CUP Services.

Paul's Later Letters: From Promise to Fulfillment. Paul Wrightman. LC 84-11039. 238p. (Orig.). 1984. pap., student ed. 9.95 (*0-8189-0441-0*) Alba.

Paul's Later Life & Letters. Frank Dunn. 1983. pap. 1.00 (*0-88027-101-9*) Firm Foun Pub.

Paul's Letter to Ephesus. Marilyn Ganskow. 55p. 1994. pap., wbk. ed. 8.00 (*1-928712-12-6*) New Life Series.

Paul's Letter to Galatia. Marilyn Ganskow. 65p. 1993. pap. 8.00 (*1-928712-13-4*) New Life Series.

Paul's Letter to the Colossians. Philip Melanchthon. Tr. & Intro. by D. C. Parker. (Historic Texts & Interpreters Ser.: Vol. 7). 126p. 1989. 30.00 (*1-85075-210-9*, Pub. by Sheffield Acad) CUP Services.

Paul's Letter to the Corinthians 55 A.D. Sanford G. Shetler. (Compact Commentary Ser.). 1971. pap. 7.95 (*0-87813-503-0*) Christian Light.

Paul's Letter to the Philippians. rev. ed. Gordon D. Fee. LC 95-19691. (New International Commentary on the New Testament Ser.). 543p. 1995. 38.00 (*0-8028-2511-7*) Eerdmans.

Paul's Letter to the Philippians: A Simplified Version of the Bible Book of Philippians. Ed. by Laurie Penner. (Illus.). 16p. 1992. reprint ed. pap. text 3.50 (*1-893916-04-9*, 1006) Project Pr.

Paul's Letter to the Philippians in the Light of Disunity in the Church. Davorin Peterlin. (Supplements to Novum Testamentum Ser.: Vol. 79). xi, 272p. 1995. 116.50 (*90-04-10305-8*) Brill Academic Pubs.

Paul's Letter to the Romans. Robert S. Bell. 1970. pap. 2.75 (*0-88027-036-5*) Firm Foun Pub.

Paul's Letter to the Romans. John A. Ziesler. Ed. by Howard C. Kee & Dennis Nineham. LC 89-35586. (New Testament Commentaries Ser.). 400p. 1989. 25.00 (*0-334-02297-5*) TPI PA.

Paul's Letter to the Romans: A Commentary. Peter Stuhlmacher. Tr. by Scott J. Hafemann. LC 93-40128.Tr. of Der/Brief an die Romer. 320p. (Orig.). 1994. pap. 32.95 (*0-664-25287-7*) Westminster John Knox.

Paul's Letter to the Romans: A Simplified Version of the Bible Book of Romans. Ed. by Laurie Penner. (Illus.). 64p. 1992. reprint ed. pap. text 5.95 (*1-893916-06-5*, 1008) Project Pr.

Paul's Letters of Love. Bessie Dean. (Story Books to Color). (Illus.). 72p. (Orig.). (J). (gr. k-5). 1981. pap. 6.98 (*0-88290-170-2*) Horizon Utah.

Paul's Letters to the Thessalonians. Frederick A. Tatford. LC 90-48180. 128p. 1992. 14.99 (*0-87213-841-0*) Loizeaux.

Paul's Literary Style: A Stylistic & Historical Comparison of II Corinthians 11:16-12:13, Romans 8:9-39, & Philippians 3:2-4:13. Aida B. Spencer. 266p. 1998. 41.00 (*0-7618-1264-4*) U Pr of Amer.

Paul's Metaphors: Their Context & Character. David J. Williams. LC 98-54750. 390p. 1999. 24.95 (*1-56563-287-7*) Hendrickson MA.

Paul's Narrative Thought World: The Tapestry Of Tragedy & Triumph. Ben Witherington, III. LC 93-39391. 352p. (Orig.). 1994. pap. 29.95 (*0-664-25433-0*) Westminster John Knox.

Paul's New Ears. Connie Steiner. (Illus.). 24p. (Orig.). (J). (gr. k-3). 1991. pap. 5.00 (*0-920541-44-5*) Peguis Pubs Ltd.

Paul's Paradigmatic 'I' Personal Example as Literary Strategy. Brian J. Dodd. (JSNTS Ser.: Vol. 177). 288p. 1999. 75.00 (*1-85075-914-6*, Pub. by Sheffield Acad) CUP Services.

An Asterisk (*) at the beginning of an entry indicates that the title is appearing for the first time.

Paul's Pastoral Vision: Pastoral Letters for a Pastoral Church Today. William F. Maestri. LC 89-203. 240p. (Orig.). 1989. pap. 12.95 (*0-8189-0556-5*) Alba.

Paul's Prison Letters. La Taunya Bynum & Mary Jessup. LC 96-84214. (Covenant Bible Studies). 70p. (Orig.). 1996. pap. 5.95 (*0-87178-007-0*, 8070) Brethren.

Paul's Prison Letters: On Paul's Letters to Philemon, the Philippians, & the Colossians. Daniel J. Harrington. LC 96-46245. (Spiritual Commentaries on the New Testament Ser.). 136p. 1997. pap. 9.95 (*1-56548-088-0*) New City.

Paul's Revelation: The Gospel of Reconciliation. Kenneth E. Hagin. 1983. pap. 1.00 (*0-89276-261-6*) Faith Lib Pubns.

Paul's Revenge. large type ed. Jacqueline Baird. 1997. 20.95 (*0-263-14794-0*) Thorndike Pr.

Paul's Rhetoric in First Corinthians 15: An Analysis Utilizing the Theories of Classical Rhetoric. Insawn Saw. LC 93-48905. (Biblical Press Ser.: Vol. 27). 336p. 1994. 99.95 (*0-7734-2351-6*, Mellen Biblical Pr) E Mellen.

Paul's Sermon on Mars' Hill. Mack Lyon. 110p. 1997. pap. 6.99 (*0-89225-466-1*, G54661) Gospel Advocate.

***Paul's Servant-Lord Analogy for the Relationship of a Believer to Christ.** William D. Sprague. LC 99-48620. 224p. 1999. 42.50 (*0-7618-1537-6*) U Pr of Amer.

Paul's Style of Church Leadership Illustrated by His Instructions to the Corinthians on the Collection: To Command or Not to Command. Verlyn D. Verbrugge. LC 91-44887. 420p. 1992. lib. bdg. 109.95 (*0-7734-9802-8*) E Mellen.

Paul's Thorn. John F. Avanzini. Tr. by Dennis Balcombe from CHI. (Illus.). 32p. 1980. pap. 3.00 (*0-941117-01-4*) HIS Publish.

Paul's Three Ministries. 2nd rev. ed. Michael Penny. 32p. 1999. pap. 3.00 (*1-880573-48-2*) Bible Search Pubns.

Paul's Two-Age Construction & Apologetics. William D. Dennison. LC 85-20272. 144p. (Orig.). (C). 1985. pap. text 17.00 (*0-8191-5012-6*) U Pr of Amer.

Paul's Two-Age Construction & Apologetics. William D. Dennison. LC 85-20272. 144p. (Orig.). (C). 1986. lib. bdg. 37.00 (*0-8191-5011-8*) U Pr of Amer.

Paul's Use of Ethos, Pathos, & Logos in Second Corinthians 10-13. Mario M. DiCicco. LC 94-31547. (Biblical Press Ser.: Vol. 31). 316p. 1995. 99.95 (*0-7734-2369-9*) E Mellen.

Paul's Volcano. Beatrice Gormley. 160p. (J). 1988. pap. 2.50 (*0-380-70562-1*, Avon Bks) Morrow Avon.

Paulson on Change. Terry Paulson. (Distilled Wisdom Ser.). 160p. (Orig.). 1995. pap. 12.95 (*1-882180-49-6*) Griffin CA.

Paulus Als Wundertaeter: Redaktionsgeschichtliche Untersuchungen zur Apostelgeschichte und den Authentischen Paulusbriefen. Stefan Schreiber. (Beiheft zur Zeitschrift fuer die Neuetestamentliche Wissenschaft Ser.: Band 79). (GER.). xii, 329p. (C). 1996. lib. bdg. 126.15 (*3-11-015021-2*) De Gruyter.

***Paulus, Then & Now: A Study of Paul Tillich's Theological World & the Continuing Relevance of His Work.** John J. Carey. 2000. 29.95 (*0-86554-681-9*, H531) Mercer Univ Pr.

Paulus und Barnabas in der Provinz Galatien: Studien Zu Apostelgeschichte 13f.; 16,6; 18,23 und Den Adressaten Des Galaterbriefes. Cilliers Breytenbach. (GER.). xvi, 215p. 1996. 94.00 (*90-04-10693-6*) Brill Academic Pubs.

Paulus und Jerusalem: Kollekte und Mission im Theologischen Denken des Heidenapostels. Burkhard Beckheuer. (Europaische Hochschulschriften Ser.: Reihe 23, Bd. 611). (GER.). 287p. 1997. 54.95 (*3-631-32093-0*) P Lang Pubng.

Paulusberufung Nach Lukas und das Erbe der Propheten: Berufen Zu Gottes Dienst. Hans M. Storm. (Arbeiten zum Neuen Testament und Judentum Ser.: Bd. 10). (GER.). 357p. 1995. 55.95 (*3-631-47645-0*) P Lang Pubng.

Paulusbriefe Ohne Paulus? Die Paulusbriefe in der Hollandischen Radikalkritik. Hermann Detering. (Kontexte Ser.: Bd. 10). (GER.). XVII, 535p. 1992. 81.80 (*3-631-44787-6*) P Lang Pubng.

Paumanok's Contemporary Anthology of English Literature Vol. I: Poetry. Ed. by Dennis M. Zogbi. LC 88-61903. 126p. 1988. pap. 22.00 (*0-929717-00-7*) Paumanok Pubns.

PAUP 4.0: Phylogenetic Analysis Using Parsimony (And Other Methods): Software & User's Manual for UNIX & VMS. David L. Swofford. 2000. 150.00 incl. disk (*0-87893-804-4*) Sinauer Assocs.

Pauper & Prince: Ritchey, Hale, & Big American Telescopes. Donald E. Osterbrock. LC 92-42704. (Illus.). 350p. 1993. 46.00 (*0-8165-1199-3*) U of Ariz Pr.

Pauper & the Pregnant Princess: (Opposites Attract) Nancy Martin. (Desire Ser.). 1995. per. 3.25 (*0-373-05916-7*, 1-05916-1) Silhouette.

Pauperising Agriculture: Studies in Agrarian Change & Demographic Structure. N. Krishnaji. (Illus.). 266p. 1993. text 15.95 (*0-19-563187-0*) OUP.

Pauperism: Its Causes & Remedies. Henry Fawcett. LC 74-1334. (Reprints of Economic Classics Ser.). viii, 270p. 1975. reprint ed. lib. bdg. 39.50 (*0-678-01067-6*) Kelley.

Pauperism, 1871: Its Causes & Remedies. (Works of Henry & Millicent Garrett Fawcett). 284p. 1996. reprint ed. 74.00 (*1-85506-370-0*) Bks Intl VA.

Paupers & Pig-Killers: The Diary of William Holland, a Somerset Parson 1799-1818. William Holland. Ed. by Jack Ayres. (Illus.). 320p. 1996. pap. 12.95 (*0-86299-052-1*, Pub. by Sutton Pub Ltd) Intl Pubs Mktg.

Pauranic Ritualism of the Fifth Century: Shri Vishnudharmottara. Priyabala Shah. (C). 1993. 48.50 (*81-85094-66-7*, Pub. by Punthi Pus) S Asia.

Pausal Sighs. Gregory K. Cole. 64p. 2000. pap. 9.95 (*1-56315-209-6*, Pub. by SterlingHse) Natl Bk Netwk.

Pausaniae Vol. I: Libri I-IV. Ed. by Rocha-Pereira. (GRE.). 1989. 57.50 (*3-322-00508-9*, T1700, Pub. by B G Teubner) U of Mich Pr.

Pausaniae Vol. II: Libri V-VIII. Ed. by Rocha-Pereira. (GRE.). 1990. 49.50 (*3-322-00213-6*, T1576, Pub. by B G Teubner) U of Mich Pr.

Pausaniae Vol. III: Libri IX-X Indices. Ed. by Rocha-Pereira. (GRE.). 1989. 53.50 (*3-322-00509-7*, T1577, Pub. by B G Teubner) U of Mich Pr.

***Pausanias: Travel & Memory in Roman Greece.** Pausanias. Ed. by Susan E. Alcock & Jas Elsner. (Illus.). 384p. 2000. text 65.00 (*0-19-512816-8*) OUP.

Pausanias' Greece: Ancient Artists & Roman Rulers. Karim W. Arafat. 262p. (C). 1996. text 64.95 (*0-521-55340-7*) Cambridge U Pr.

Pausanias' Guide to Ancient Greece. Christian Habicht. LC 99-187467. (Sather Classical Lectures Ser.). 223p. 1998. pap. 16.95 (*0-520-06170-5*, Pub. by U CA Pr) Cal Prin Full Svc.

***Pausanias Periegetes.** W. Kendrick Pritchett. LC 98-195507. 1998. 55.00 (*90-5063-518-0*, Pub. by Gieben) J Benjamins Pubng Co.

***Pausanias Periegetes II.** W. Kendrick Pritchett. (Monographs on Ancient Greek History & Archaeology Ser.: No. 7). 363p. 1999. pap. 55.00 (*90-5063-138-X*, Pub. by Gieben) J Benjamins Pubng Co.

***Pausanias the Spartan (1859)** Edward Bulwer Lytton. 96p. 1999. reprint ed. pap. 14.95 (*0-7661-0795-7*) Kessinger Pub.

Pause: A Christmas Book. Keith G. Davis. 1994. pap. 16.95 (*0-9647751-0-7*) Clayton Paige Pubng.

Pause: A Christmas Gift. Ed. by Keith G. Davis. (Illus.). 38p. (Orig.). 1994. pap. 16.95 (*0-9647751-9-0*) Clayton Paige Pubng.

Pause: Positive Approaches to Menopause. Lonnie Barbach. 304p. 1994. mass mkt. 6.99 (*0-451-18035-6*, Sig) NAL.

***Pause: Positive Approaches to Perimenopause & Menopause.** Lonnie G. Barbach. LC 99-32063. 2000. pap. 13.95 (*0-452-28110-5*, Plume) Dutton Plume.

***Pause: 59 Minutes of Motion Graphics.** Peter Hall & Andrea Codrington. (Illus.). 192p. 2000. pap. 35.00 (*0-7893-0477-5*) Universe.

Pause & Effect: An Introduction to the History of Punctuation in the West. M. B. Parkes. 400p. 1993. 65.00 (*0-520-07941-8*, Pub. by U CA Pr) Cal Prin Full Svc.

Pause Button. Kevin Davies. 80p. 1992. pap. 8.95 (*0-921331-10-X*, Pub. by Tsunami Edits) Barnholden.

Pause for Breath. Edith Reveley. LC 82-22293. 210p. 1983. 15.95 (*0-87951-165-6*, Pub. by Overlook Pr) Penguin Putnam.

Pause for Peace: What God's Gift of the Sabbath Can Mean to You. Clifford Golstein. LC 92-8487. 126p. 1992. pap. 1.99 (*0-8163-1108-0*) Pacific Pr Pub Assn.

Pause for Power: A Year in the Word. Warren W. Wiersbe. 1998. 16.99 (*1-56476-757-4*, Victor Bks) Chariot Victor.

Pause in the Light: Poems. Dorian B. Kottler. Ed. by James Perlman. LC 80-82690. 46p. 1980. pap. 3.00 (*0-930100-07-7*) Holy Cow.

Pause Patterns in Elizabethan & Jacobean Drama: An Experiment in Prosody. Ants Oras. LC 60-62779. (University of Florida Humanities Monographs: No. 3). 96p. reprint ed. pap. 30.00 (*0-7837-4920-1*, 204458500004) Bks Demand.

Pauses. Hopkins. LC 94-14641. 248p. pap. 13.95 (*0-06-446172-6*) HarpC Child Bks.

Pauses: Autobiographical Reflections of 101 Creators of Children's Books. Compiled by Lee B. Hopkins. LC 94-14641. 248p. (J). (gr. 8-12). 1995. 23.00 (*0-06-024748-7*) HarpC.

Paustine from Jerusalem to Munich, from Munich to Jerusalem: The Sole Survivor of Black September Tells His Story for the First Time. Abu Daoud & Gilles Du Jonchay. 400p. Date not set. 27.45 (*1-55970-429-2*, Pub. by Arcade Pub Inc) Time Warner.

Pauvre Ani Croche! Bertrand Gauthier. (Novels in the Roman Jeunesse Ser.). (FRE.). 96p. (J). (gr. 4-7). 1990. pap. 8.95 (*2-89021-133-9*, Pub. by La Courte Ech) Firefly Bks Ltd.

Pauvre Bitos Ou le Diner de Tetes see Pieces Grincantes

Pauvre Bitos Ou le Diner de Tetes. Jean Anouilh. (Folio Ser.: No. 301). (FRE.). 1973. pap. 6.95 (*2-07-036301-5*) Schoenhof.

Pauvre Bitos Ou le "Diner de Tetes. Jean Anouilh. (FRE.). 160p. 1973. pap. 10.95 (*0-7859-1725-X*, M2960) Fr & Eur.

Pauvre Christ de Bomba. Mongo Beti. (B. E. Ser.: No. 27). (FRE.). 1956. 25.00 (*0-8115-2978-9*) Periodicals Srv.

Pauvre Type. Erskine Caldwell. (FRE.). 192p. 1980. pap. 10.95 (*0-7859-1906-6*, 2070371646) Fr & Eur.

Pauvrete Economique Et Pauvrete Social a Byzance 4e-7e Siecles. E. Patlagean. 1977. 107.70 (*90-279-7933-2*) Mouton.

Pavanes: Poems from Hollywood. Mark Dunsten. 11p. 1998. pap. 5.00 (*0-89642-582-7*) Linden Pubs.

Pavannes & Divagations. Ezra Pound. (Collected Works of Ezra Pound). 262p. 1999. reprint ed. lib. bdg. 88.00 (*1-58201-812-X*) Classic Bks.

Pavannes & Divagations. Ezra Pound. LC 58-9510. 256p. 1975. reprint ed. pap. 9.95 (*0-8112-0575-4*, NDP397, Pub. by New Directions) Norton.

Pavans. Ian Kreiger. (Dialogues on Dance Ser.: No. 3). 92p. 1985. pap. 6.00 (*0-941240-00-2*) Ommation Pr.

Pavarotti: Life with Luciano. Adua Pavarotti & Wendy Dallas. (Illus.). 159p. 1998. reprint ed. text 35.00 (*0-7881-5200-9*) DIANE Pub.

***Pavarotti: My World.** Luciano Pavarotti & William Wright. (Illus.). 345p. 1999. reprint ed. pap. text 15.00 (*0-7881-6793-6*) DIANE Pub.

Pavarotti Collection. rev. ed. Selected by Frank Booth. (Illus.). 80p. 1998. pap. text 21.95 (*0-7119-2465-1*, AM 944603) Music Sales.

Pave the Way. Rabe. 1997. pap. 5.00 (*0-15-201329-6*) Harcourt.

Paved Track Stock Car Technology. Steve Smith. LC 97-207225. (Illus.). 176p. 1997. pap. 24.95 (*0-936834-37-4*) S S Autosports.

Paved with Gold: The Romance & Reality of the London Street. 2nd ed. Augustus Mayhew. (Illus.). 408p. 1971. reprint ed. 25.00 (*0-7146-1412-2*, BHA-01412, Pub. by F Cass Pubs) Intl Spec Bk.

Paved with Good Intentions: The Failure of Race Relations in Contemporary America. Jared Taylor. 416p. 1993. pap. 11.95 (*0-7867-0025-4*) Carroll & Graf.

Pavel Axelrod & the Development of Menshevism. Abraham Ascher. LC 72-78423. (Russian Research Center Studies: No. 70). 435p. reprint ed. pap. 134.90 (*0-7837-3842-0*, 204366400010) Bks Demand.

Pavel Bure: The Riddle of the Russian Rocket. Kerry Banks. 208p. 1999. 19.95 (*1-55054-714-3*, Greystone) DGL.

Pavel Kohout und die Metamorphosen Des Sozialistischen Realismus. Veronika Ambros. LC 92-39109. (Russian & East European Studies in Aesthetics & the Philosophy of Culture: Vol. 3). 190p. 1993. text 48.95 (*0-8204-2015-8*) P Lang Pubng.

Pavel Korin. N. A. Mikhailov. 102p. 1982. pap. 35.00 (*0-7855-1647-6*) St Mut.

Pavel Kuznetsov: His Life & Art. Peter Stupples. (Cambridge Studies in the History of Art). (Illus.). 390p. (C). 1990. text 42.95 (*0-521-36488-4*) Cambridge U Pr.

Pavel Tchelitchev. Lincoln Kirstein. 188p. 1994. 60.00 (*0-942642-40-6*) Twelvetrees Pr.

***Pavel Tchelitchew: The Landscape of the Body : June 14-September 6, 1998.** Pavel Tchelitchew et al. LC 98-65757. (Illus.). 1998. write for info. (*0-915171-49-X*) Katonah Gal.

Pavement Analysis. P. Ullidtz. (Developments in Civil Engineering Ser.: Vol. 19). 318p. 1987. 190.75 (*0-444-42817-8*) Elsevier.

Pavement Analysis & Design. Yang H. Huang. LC 92-26720. 784p. (C). 1992. 105.00 (*0-13-655275-7*) P-H.

Pavement & Traffic Monitoring & Evaluation (TRR 1435) Ed. by Naomi Kassabian & Susan Taylor Brown. (Transportation Research Record Ser.). (Illus.). 187p. 1994. pap. text 35.00 (*0-309-05512-1*, R1435) Transport Res Bd.

Pavement Design & Rehabilitation. LC 92-42007. write for info. (*0-309-05411-7*) Transport Res Bd.

Pavement Design & Rehabilitation. LC 92-44289. (Transportation Research Record Ser.: No. 1374). 1993. write for info. (*0-309-05416-8*) Transport Res Bd.

Pavement Evaluation & Rehabilitation. (Research Record Ser.: No. 1117). 170p. 1987. 25.00 (*0-309-04470-7*) Transport Res Bd.

***Pavement for My Pillow: A Homeless Woman's Climb from Degradation to Dignity.** Chris Kitch. LC 98-22418. 200p. 1998. 21.95 (*1-56838-191-3*) Hazelden.

Pavement Maintenance & Effectiveness. Thomas Freeman et al. 350p. (C). 1993. pap. text 20.00 (*0-309-05622-5*, SHRP-H-358) SHRP.

Pavement Maintenance & Rehabilitation - STP 881. Ed. by Bernard F. Kallas. LC 85-7550. (Illus.). 107p. 1985. pap. text 20.00 (*0-8031-0424-3*, STP881) ASTM.

Pavement Management & Performance. LC 92-25612. 172p. 1992. 26.00 (*0-309-05211-4*, R1344) Transport Res Bd.

Pavement Management & Rehabilitation, 1990. (Transportation Research Record Ser.: No. 1272). 148p. 1990. 23.00 (*0-309-05051-0*) Transport Res Bd.

Pavement Management & Weight-in-Motion. (Research Record Ser.: No. 1123). 144p. 1987. 21.50 (*0-309-04503-7*) Transport Res Bd.

Pavement Management & Weight-in-Motion. (Research Record Ser.: No. 1200). 106p. 1988. 10.50 (*0-309-04762-5*) Transport Res Bd.

Pavement Management for Airports, Roads & Parking Lots. M. Y. Shahin. LC 93-47382. 1994. 34.95 (*0-442-23821-5*) Chapman & Hall.

Pavement Management Implementation. Ed. by Frank B. Holt & Linda R. Wade. LC 92-3469. (Special Technical Publication Ser.: No. 1121). (Illus.). 500p. 1992. text 66.00 (*0-8031-1421-4*, STP1121) ASTM.

Pavement Management Practices. (National Cooperative Highway Research Program Report Ser.: No. 135). 139p. 1987. 12.40 (*0-309-04419-7*) Transport Res Bd.

Pavement Management Systems (TRR 1397) Ed. by Susan Taylor Brown. (Transportation Research Record Ser.). (Illus.). 128p. 1993. pap. text 28.00 (*0-309-05468-0*) Transport Res Bd.

Pavement Markings: Materials & Application for Extended Service Life. (National Cooperative Highway Research Program Report Ser.: No. 138). 45p. 1988. 8.00 (*0-309-04423-5*) Transport Res Bd.

Pavement Monitoring & Evaluation (TRR 1410) large type ed. Ed. by Susan Taylor Brown. (Transportation Research Record Ser.). (Illus.). 128p. 1994. pap. text 28.00 (*0-309-05557-1*) Natl Res Coun.

Pavement Roughness & Rideability. (National Cooperative Highway Research Program Report Ser.: No. 275). 69p. 1985. 8.80 (*0-309-03859-6*, NR275) Transport Res Bd.

Pavement Roughness & Rideability Field Evaluation. (National Cooperative Highway Research Program Report Ser.: No. 308). 48p. 1988. 9.00 (*0-309-04605-X*, NR308) Transport Res Bd.

Pavement Saw. Sheila E. Murphy et al. 40p. 1994. pap. 3.50 (*1-886350-00-0*) Pavement Saw.

Pavement Saw, 1995. 56p. 1995. pap. 3.50 (*1-886350-01-9*) Pavement Saw.

Pavement Saw 3. Timothy Russell et al. (Illus.). 64p. 1996. pap. 4.00 (*1-886350-02-7*) Pavement Saw.

***Pavement Subgrade, Unbound Materials & Nondestructive Testing: Proceedings of Sessions of Geo-Denver 2000: August 5-8, 2000, Denver, Colorado.** Geo-Denver 2000 Staff et al. LC 00-41607. 2000. write for info. (*0-7844-0509-3*) Am Soc Civil Eng.

Pavement Surface Characteristics & Materials - STP 763. Ed. by C. Hayden. 131p. 1982. pap. 21.00 (*0-8031-0785-4*, STP763) ASTM.

Pavement Surface Courses, Stone Mastic Asphalt Pavements, & Asphalt Concrete Recycling (TRR 1427) Ed. by Luanne Crayton. (Transportation Research Record Ser.). (Illus.). 68p. 1994. pap. text 22.00 (*0-309-05500-8*) Natl Res Coun.

Pavement Surface Properties: Roughness, Rutting, Skid Resistance, & Surface Distress. LC 92-25095. (Transportation Research Record Ser.: No. 1348). 1992. 20.00 (*0-309-05210-6*) Transport Res Bd.

Paves du Diable. Hubert Ponteilhet. (FRE.). 1972. pap. 8.95 (*0-7859-3991-1*) Fr & Eur.

Pavia. Angus Konstam. (Illus.). 96p. 1996. pap. 14.95 (*1-85532-504-7*, Pub. by Ospry) Stackpole.

Pavie in the Borderlands: The Journey of Theodore Pavie to Louisiana & Texas, 1829-1830, Including Portions of His Souvenirs Atlantiques. Betje B. Klier. (Illus.). 248p. 1999. text 49.95 (*0-8071-2414-1*); pap. text 24.95 (*0-8071-2530-X*) La State U Pr.

Pavilion. Hilda Lawrence. 1999. lib. bdg. 22.95 (*1-56723-147-0*, 156) Yestermorrow.

Pavilion: People & Times Remembered. Stark Young. (American Autobiography Ser.). 194p. 1995. reprint ed. lib. bdg. 69.00 (*0-7812-8669-7*) Rprt Serv.

Pavilion Key: Isle of Buried Treasure. Greg Lewbart. LC 99-35645. 212p. 2000. 18.50 (*1-57524-079-3*) Krieger.

Pavilion of Women. Pearl Synderstricker Buck. 316p. 1994. pap. 11.95 (*1-55921-024-9*) Moyer Bell.

***Pavilion of Women.** Pearl Synderstricker Buck. 316p. 2000. reprint ed. pap. 11.95 (*1-55921-287-X*) Moyer Bell.

Pavilions: Poems from Hollywood. Mark Dunster. 19p. (Orig.). (YA). (gr. 9-12). 1996. pap. 5.00 (*0-89642-330-1*) Linden Pubs.

Pavilions of Plenty: Exhibiting American Culture Abroad in the 1950s. Robert H. Haddow. LC 96-43926. (Illus.). 240p. 1997. text 37.50 (*1-56098-705-7*) Smithsonian.

Pavillion D'Or. Yukio Mishima, pseud. (FRE.). 1975. pap. 11.95 (*0-7859-4039-1*) Fr & Eur.

Pavillon pour le Club des Toons: Tiny Toon Adventures. Carol A. Hanshaw. Tr. by DigiPro Staff from ENG. (Comes to Life Bks.).Tr. of Tiny Toon Adventures: A Clubhouse Built for Toons. (FRE.). 16p. (J). (ps-2). 1994. write for info. (*1-57234-003-7*) YES Ent.

Paving Alaska's Trails: The Work of the Alaska Road Commission. Claus M. Naske. LC 86-15850. (Illus.). 354p. (Orig.). (C). 1986. lib. bdg. 62.00 (*0-8191-5576-4*) U Pr of Amer.

Paving over the Past: A History & Guide to Civil War Battlefield Preservation. Georgie H. Boge & Margie Boge. LC 93-12138. (Illus.). 220p. 1993. pap. 17.95 (*1-55963-192-9*); text 35.00 (*1-55963-191-0*) Island Pr.

Pavior Screeds. LC TA0439.G74. (Materials & Techniques in Building Practice Ser.: No. 1). 46p. reprint ed. pap. 30.00 (*0-608-30348-8*, 201771300007) Bks Demand.

Pavlia, Portrait of a Greek Village. Anthony Decaneas. (Illus.). 128p. (Orig.). 1987. 39.95 (*0-945149-00-X*); pap. 22.95 (*0-945149-01-8*) Panopticon Pr.

Pavlov: A Biography. Boris P. Babkin. LC 49-11887. xiv, 366p. 1975. pap. text 4.25 (*0-226-03373-2*, P621) U Ch Pr.

Pavlova, 1881 to 1931: A Biography. Ed. by A. H. Franks. LC 79-1053. (Series in Dance). (Illus.). 144p. 1979. reprint ed. 25.00 (*0-306-79538-8*) Da Capo.

Pavlova's Gift. unabridged ed. Maxine Trottier. (Illus.). 32p. (J). (gr. k-3). 1997. 18.95 (*0-7737-2969-0*) STDK.

Pavlovian Temperament Survey: An International Handbook. Jan Strelau et al. LC 98-75408. 120p. 1999. pap. 39.00 (*0-88937-204-7*) Hogrefe & Huber Pubs.

Pavlov's Children: A Study of Performance-Outcome-Based Education. 2nd ed. Ann Wilson. Ed. by Sue Cooley. 290p. (Orig.). 1994. pap. 12.95 (*0-9640180-1-2*) J W Pubng.

Pavlov's Mistress. Caron Andregg. 30p. (Orig.). 1996. pap. 5.00 (*1-886895-02-3*) Poetry Harbor.

Pavlov's Trout: The Incompleat Psychology of Everyday Fishing. Paul G. Quinnett. LC 98-18117. 224p. 1998. pap. 12.95 (*0-8362-6840-7*) Andrews & McMeel.

Pavlovsk, 2 vols. Ed. by Emmanuel Ducamp. (Illus.). 236p. boxed set 225.00 (*2-909838-03-X*, Pub. by A Gourcuff) Antique Collect.

Pavlovsk: A Guide. V. Belanina. (Illus.). 88p. (C). 1987. 30.00 (*0-7855-5190-5*, Pub. by Collets) St Mut.

Pavlovsk: The Life of a Russian Palace. Suzanne Massie. (Illus.). 394p. (C). 1990. pap. text 28.00 (*0-9644184-0-1*) HeartTree Pr.

PAVN: People's Army of Vietnam. Douglas Pike. 408p. 1986. 46.00 (*0-08-033614-0*, Pergamon Pr) Elsevier.

Pavo para la Cena de Gracias? No, Gracias! Alma F. Ada. (Cuentos para Todo el Ano Ser.). (SPA., Illus.). (J). (gr. k-12). pap. 7.95 (*1-56014-331-2*) Santillana.

Pavologia: A Celebration of Peacocks Past. Evelyn A. Domjan. Ed. by Rose Stein & Lory Skwerer. (Illus.). 200p. 1984. 45.00 (*0-933652-17-8*) Domjan Studio.

***Pavone - Lined.** (Handstitched Tuscany Florals Ser.). 128p. 2000. 15.95 (*1-55156-157-3*) Paperblank.

Pavonia Cav. Malvaceae. Paul A. Fryxell. (Flora Neotropica Monograph Ser.: Vol. 76). 1998. pap. 57.00 (*0-89327-424-0*, FLN76) NY Botanical.

Paw Island Christmas. Corey Maxwell. (Illus.). 16p. (J). (gr. k-3). 1996. pap. 9.95 (*1-890145-00-9*) PetCare.

***Paw Island Christmas.** Corey Maxwell. (Illus.). 32p. (J). 1999. 12.95 (*1-890145-02-5*, Paw Island Ent) PetCare.

P

Paw Paw Chuck's Big Ideas in the Bible. Charles R. Swindoll. LC 95-24897. (Illus.). 160p. (J). (ps-4). 1995. 16.99 (*0-8499-1067-6*) Tommy Nelson.

Paw Paw Lake, Michigan: A 100 Year Resort History, 1890's-1990's. Roderick C. Rasmussen. LC 94-65459. 144p. (Orig.). 1994. pap. 16.70 (*0-9640093-1-5*) SW Mich Pubns.

Paw Paw Lake, Michigan: A 100 Year Resort History, 1890's-1990's. Roderick L. Rasmussen. LC 94-65459. 144p. (Orig.). 1994. 28.40 (*0-9640093-0-7*) SW Mich Pubns.

Paw Paw Lake, Michigan: Images of a Lake. Roderick L. Rasmussen. LC 95-72991. 128p. (Orig.). 1996. 28.30 (*0-9640093-2-3*); pap. 17.45 (*0-9640093-3-1*) SW Mich Pubns.

Paw Paw River Days & Nights. Roy M. Davis. (Illus.). 388p. (Orig.). 1993. pap. 16.95 (*1-883228-03-4*) Invictus MI.

Paw Paw River Times & People, Vol. I. Roy M. Davis. (Illus.). 360p. (Orig.). 1990. pap. 11.95 (*0-9625866-0-9*) R M Davis.

Paw Print. Alyssa Satin Capucilli. (ps-1). pap. 6.95 (*0-694-01519-9*) HarpC.

Paw Prints in My Soul: A True Story. Lou Dean. LC 97-92419. 159p. 1997. pap. 9.95 (*1-56684-305-7*) Evans Bk Dist.

Pawa: A Memoir from the Belgian Congo, 1945-1949. Frank L. Lambrecht. Ed. by Richard Lane. LC 98-104087. (Illus.). 112p. 1994. 17.95 (*0-9643780-0-0*) F L Lambrecht.

***Pawb Yn Coginio!** Childs Play Inc. Staff. 1999. pap. text 2.99 (*0-85953-651-3*) Childs Play.

***Pawcatuck Watershed - Water Resources: A Management Issues Profile.** Alan Desbonnet. (Sustainable Coastal Communities Reports: Vol. 4400). (Illus.). 1999. write for info. (*1-885454-31-7*) Coastal Res.

***Pawing Through the Past.** Rita Mae Brown & Sneaky Pie Brown. LC 99-86213. (Illus.). 368p. 2000. 24.95 (*0-553-10738-0*, Spectra) Bantam.

Pawless Papers. Robert Fagen. LC 93-3112. 176p. 1993. 24.95 (*0-914061-33-X*) Orchises Pr.

Pawlet for 100 Years. Hiel Hollister. (Illus.). 272p. 1995. reprint ed. lib. bdg. 36.00 (*0-8328-4725-9*) Higginson Bk Co.

***Pawlet (Vermont) for One Hundred Years.** Hiel Hollister. 298p. 1999. reprint ed. pap. 24.50 (*0-7884-1243-4*, H547) Heritage Bk.

Pawley's Island: Historically Speaking. Katherine H. Richardson & Charles E. Lee. (Illus.). 132p. 1994. 35.00 (*0-9643909-0-6*) Pawleys Islnd.

Pawloined Paper. Olga Litowinski. LC 97-74831. (Adventures of Wishbone Ser.: No. 11). (Illus.). 137p. (J). (gr. 3-7). 1998. pap. 3.99 (*1-57064-276-1*, Big Red) Lyrick Pub.

Pawloined Paper see Adventures of Wishbone

***Pawmistry: How to Read Your Cat's Paws.** Ken Ring & Paul Romhany. LC 99-23384. (Illus.). 88p. 1999. pap. text 9.95 (*1-58008-111-8*) Ten Speed Pr.

Pawn & Prophet. Charles Kormos. 87p. 1987. 15.00 (*0-89304-065-7*); pap. 7.50 (*0-685-49062-9*) Cross-Cultrl NY.

Pawn Artistry. rev. ed. Eugene A. Furst. (Artistry Series of Chess Encyclopedias: Vol. 4). (Illus.). 320p. 1991. pap. 19.95 (*1-879394-03-0*, 1-603-768) Caissas Pr.

Pawn Endings. Alexander Cvetkov. Tr. by Jim Marfia from BUL. 69p. 1985. pap. 6.00 (*0-931462-47-9*) Chess Ent.

Pawn in Frankincense. Dorothy Dunnett. 1976. 33.95 (*0-8488-1300-6*) Amereon Ltd.

Pawn in Frankincense. Dorothy Dunnett. LC 96-45598. 1997. pap. 14.00 (*0-679-77746-6*) Vin Bks.

Pawn in Frankincense. Dorothy Dunnett. 425p. 1983. reprint ed. lib. bdg. 39.95 (*0-89966-321-4*) Buccaneer Bks.

Pawn of Chaos: Tales of the Eternal Champion. Edward E. Kramer & Nancy A. Collins. 1996. pap. 14.99 (*1-56504-933-0*, Borealis) White Wolf.

Pawn of Prophecy. David Eddings. (Belgariad Ser.: Bk. 1). 256p. 1986. mass mkt. 3.99 (*0-345-33551-1*, Del Rey) Ballantine Pub Grp.

Pawn of Prophecy. David Eddings. (Belgariad Ser.). 1982. 12.09 (*0-606-01238-9*, Pub. by Turtleback) Demco.

Pawn Power. Angus Dunnington. 88p. 1995. pap. 11.95 (*0-8050-3578-8*, Pub. by Batsford Chess) H Holt & Co.

Pawn Power in Chess. Hans Kmoch. (Illus.). 304p. 1990. pap. 8.95 (*0-486-26486-6*) Dover.

Pawn Structure Chess. Andrew Soltis. 1995. pap. 16.00 (*0-8129-2529-7*, Times Bks) Crown Pub Group.

Pawn to King's Bishop. Lee E. Schackleford. (Christian Theatre Ser.). 1997. pap. 4.00 (*1-57514-292-9*, 1004) Encore Perform Pub.

Pawnbroker. Edward L. Wallant. LC 78-7101. 288p. (C). 1978. reprint ed. pap. 11.00 (*0-15-671422-1*, Harvest Bks) Harcourt.

Pawnbroker's Handbook: How to Get Rich Buying & Selling Guns, Gold & Other Good Stuff. V. Alexander Cullen. (Illus.). 208p. 1995. pap. 20.00 (*0-87364-857-9*) Paladin Pr.

Pawnbroker's Operations Manual. P. Taylor Fletcher. (Illus.). 248p. 1993. pap. 39.95 (*1-883103-02-9*) United NC.

Pawnee see Indians of North America

Pawnee. Elizabeth Hahn. (Native American People Ser.: Set III). 32p. (J). (gr. 4-8). 1992. lib. bdg. 21.27 (*0-86625-391-2*) Rourke Pubns.

Pawnee. large type ed. Arthur Myers. (First Bks.). (Illus.). 64p. (J). (gr. 5-8). 1994. pap. 6.95 (*0-531-15702-4*) Watts.

Pawnee. rev. ed. Dennis B. Fradin. LC 88-11820. (New True Books Ser.). (Illus.). 48p. (J). (ps-3). 1992. lib. bdg. 21.00 (*0-516-01155-3*) Childrens.

Pawnee - Great Plains see Indians of North America

Pawnee & Lower Loup Pottery. Roger T. Grange, Jr. (Publications in Anthropology: No. 3). 235p. 1968. pap. 6.00 (*0-933307-10-1*) Nebraska Hist.

Pawnee Bill: A Biography of Major Gordon W. Lillie. Glenn Shirley. 304p. 1993. reprint ed. 22.95 (*0-935269-13-4*); reprint ed. pap. 14.95 (*0-935269-14-2*) Western Pubns.

Pawnee Bill's Historic Wild West: A Photo Documentary of the 1901-1905 Show Tours. Allen Farnum. LC 92-60904. (Illus.). 128p. 1992. pap. 19.95 (*0-88740-437-5*) Schiffer.

Pawnee Ghost Dance Hand Game. Alexander Lesser. LC 79-82340. (Columbia Univ. Contributions to Anthropology Ser.: Vol. 16). 1969. reprint ed. 37.00 (*0-404-50566-X*) AMS Pr.

Pawnee Ghost Dance Hand Game: Ghost Dance Revival & Ethnic Identity. Alexander Lesser. LC 96-28279. (Illus.). xx, 342p. 1996. pap. 17.50 (*0-8032-7965-5*, Bison Books) U of Nebr Pr.

Pawnee Ghost Dance Hand Game: Ghost Dance Revival & Ethnic Identity. Alexander Lesser. LC 77-91056. (Illus.). 368p. reprint ed. pap. 114.10 (*0-608-07016-5*, 206722300009) Bks Demand.

Pawnee Hero Stories & Folk-Tales. George B. Grinnell. LC 61-10153. (Illus.). xiv, 417p. 1961. reprint ed. pap. 11.95 (*0-8032-5080-0*, Bison Books) U of Nebr Pr.

Pawnee Indians. George E. Hyde. LC 72-9260. (Civilization of the American Indian Ser.: Vol. 128). (Illus.). 384p. 1988. pap. 17.95 (*0-8061-2094-0*) U of Okla Pr.

Pawnee Music. Frances Densmore. LC 72-1880. (Music Ser.). 160p. 1972. reprint ed. lib. bdg. 21.50 (*0-306-70508-7*) Da Capo.

Pawnee Music: Bureau of American Ethnology Bulletins. Frances Densmore. (Bureau of American Ethnology Bulletins Ser.). 129p. 1995. lib. bdg. 79.00 (*0-7812-4093-X*) Rprt Serv.

Pawnee Mythology. George A. Dorsey. LC 97-12832. (Sources of American Indian Oral Literature Ser.). (Illus.). xxvii, 546p. 1997. pap. 22.00 (*0-8032-6603-0*, Bison Books) U of Nebr Pr.

***Pawnee Nation.** Anna Lee Walters. (Native Peoples Ser.). 24p. (J). (ps-3). 2000. lib. bdg. 15.93 (*0-7368-0501-X*, Bridgestone Bks) Capstone Pr.

Pawnee Passage, 1870-1875. Martha R. Blaine. LC 90-50228. (Civilization of the American Indian Ser.: Vol. 202). (Illus.). 352p. 1990. 31.95 (*0-8061-2300-1*) U of Okla Pr.

Pawnee Pride: A History of Pawnee County. Kenny A. Franks & Paul F. Lambert. Ed. by Gini Moore Campbell. (Oklahoma County History Ser.). 298p. 1994. 35.00 (*1-86546-087-7*) OK Heritage.

Pawns. Willo D. Roberts. LC 97-36505. 154p. (J). (gr. 6-8). 1998. 16.00 (*0-689-81668-5*) S&S Trade.

Pawns. Willo Davis Roberts. (Illus.). 160p. (YA). (gr. 4-6). 2000. per. 4.99 (*0-689-83320-2*) Aladdin.

Pawns: The Opening Move. Nigel Findley. (Primal Order Ser.). (Illus.). 192p. (Orig.). 1992. pap. 15.00 (*1-880992-08-6*) Wizards Coast.

Pawns Count. E. Phillips Oppenheim. 24.95 (*0-8488-0304-3*) Amereon Ltd.

Pawns in the Game. William G. Carr. 1978. pap. 10.00 (*0-911038-29-9*, 0004, Noontide Pr) Legion Survival.

Pawns in the Game. William G. Carr. 193p. 1997. reprint ed. pap. 10.00 (*0-913022-34-9*) CPA Bk Pub.

Pawns in the Game. unabridged ed. William Guy Carr. 230p. 1958. reprint ed. pap. 15.00 (*0-945001-15-0*) GSG & Assocs.

Pawns of War. Boston Publishing Company Editors et al. (Vietnam Experience Ser.). (Illus.). 192p. 1987. 16.30 (*0-201-11678-2*) Addison-Wesley.

Pawns of Yalta: Soviet Refugees & America's Role in Their Repatriation. Mark R. Elliot. LC 81-7599. (Illus.). 300p. 1981. text 29.95 (*0-252-00897-9*) U of Ill Pr.

Pawns or Potentates. Lorsch. 200p. 1989. 29.95 (*0-07-103252-5*) McGraw.

Pawnshop & Palaces: The Fall & Rise of the Campana Art Museum. Helen Borowitz & Albert Borowitz. LC 90-10228. (Illus.). 322p. (C). 1991. text 32.00 (*1-56098-010-9*) Smithsonian.

Pawnshop in China. Yang Chao-yu. Ed. by T.S. Whelan. LC 79-120430. (Michigan Abstracts of Chinese & Japanese Works on Chinese History: No. 6). 1979. pap. 15.00 (*0-89264-906-2*) Ctr Chinese Studies.

Pawpaw Patch: A Novel. Janice Daugharty. 1996. write for info. (*0-614-96290-0*) HarpC.

***Pawprints.** Ina Hillebrandt. Ed. by Hannah Liebmann. (Illus.). 208p. 1999. pap. 12.00 (*1-880882-01-9*) Pawpress.

Pawprints in Time. Philippa Butler. (Illus.). 32p. 1998. 14.99 (*0-670-87177-X*) Viking Penguin.

***Pawprints on My Heart.** Ed. by Jean C. Keating. 1999. pap. write for info. (*0-9674016-1-5*) Astra Pub VA.

Pawprints on Our Souls. Ken Foley & S. Francis. 183p. 1999. pap. 13.95 (*0-9667174-0-6*) Foley Pub Co.

Paws & Claws. Theresa Greenaway. LC 94-30730. (Head to Tail Ser.). (Illus.). 40p. (J). 1995. lib. bdg. 5.00 (*0-8114-8266-9*) Raintree Steck-V.

Paws & Tales, Vol. 1. Ed. & Photos by Beth Marcus. (Illus.). 163p. (Orig.). 1998. pap. 12.95 (*0-9667491-9-7*) GDI Pub.

Paws Before Dying. Susan Conant. 1991. mass mkt. 5.50 (*0-425-14430-5*) Berkley Pub.

***Paws for a Minute: People Training for Dog Owners.** Inger Martens. LC 00-29692. (Illus.). 192p. 2000. pap. 13.00 (*0-380-80478-6*) Morrow Avon.

Paws for Alarm, Vol. 1. Marian Babson. 1998. 5.99 (*0-312-96513-3*, Pub. by Tor Bks) St Martin.

Paws for Thought: A Look at the Conflicts, Questions & Challenges of Animal Euthanasia. B. J. Ellis. 144p. (Orig.). 1993. pap. 12.95 (*0-9636708-0-8*) Paw Print Pr.

Paws in Typing Town - Keyboarding. Jackson. (PB - Keyboarding Ser.). (J). (gr. k-8). 1996. text 25.95 (*0-538-65149-0*) S-W Pub.

Paws Presents: ClarisWorks 2.0 & 3.0 Macintosh. Thomson Learning TOOLS Staff. (PAWS Presents Elementary Tutorial Ser.). 224p. (J). (gr. 4-9). 1997. spiral bd. 19.95 (*0-538-65455-4*) S-W Pub.

Paws Presents: ClarisWorks 2.0 & 3.0 Windows. Thomson Learning TOOLS Staff. (PAWS Presents Elementary Tutorial Ser.). 224p. (J). (gr. 4-9). 1997. spiral bd. 19.95 (*0-538-65836-3*) S-W Pub.

Paws Presents: ClarisWorks 4.0 Mac Tutorial. Bingham. (DA - K-8 Computer Education Ser.). (YA). 1997. text 22.95 (*0-538-66075-9*) S-W Pub.

Paws Presents: ClarisWorks 4.0 Macintosh. Thomson Learning TOOLS Staff. (PAWS Presents Elementary Tutorial Ser.). 224p. (J). (gr. 4-9). 1997. spiral bd. 19.95 (*0-538-66076-7*) S-W Pub.

Paws Presents: Microsoft Works 3.0 for Windows. Thomson Learning TOOLS Staff. (PAWS Presents Elementary Tutorial Ser.). 208p. (J). (gr. 4-9). 1997. spiral bd. 19.95 (*0-538-65841-X*) S-W Pub.

Paws Presents: Using ClarisWorks for MAC. Bingham. (DA - Computer Education Ser.). (J). (gr. k-8). 1997. text 22.95 (*0-538-65118-0*); text 22.95 (*0-538-65126-1*) S-W Pub.

Paws Presents: Using ClarisWorks for MAC. Bingham. (DA - Computer Education Ser.). (J). (gr. k-8). 1997. text 22.95 (*0-538-65122-9*) S-W Pub.

Paws Presents: Using ClarisWorks for MAC. Bingham. (DA - Computer Education Ser.). (J). (gr. k-8). 1997. text 22.95 (*0-538-65114-8*) S-W Pub.

Paws Presents the Internet & the World Wide Web. Karl Barksdale et al. (Illus.). 192p. 1997. pap. 23.95 (*0-538-66765-6*) S-W Pub.

Paws That Refresh. (Illus.). 15p. (Orig.). 1996. pap. 4.50 (*0-9656253-0-3*); mass mkt. 2.00 (*0-9656253-1-1*) R A Okey.

Paws to Consider: Choosing the Right Dog for You & Your Family. Brian Kilcommons & Sarah Wilson. LC 98-32300. (Illus.). 256p. 1999. 22.95 (*0-446-52151-5*, Pub. by Warner Bks) Little.

Paws to Remember. Diane E. Rulien et al. (Illus.). 80p. 1998. 25.00 (*0-9669801-0-7*) Chameleon Ent.

***Paws to Remember: Maggie Sue.** Debra Ann Govan. (Illus.). 31p. 2000. pap. 12.45 (*0-9702242-1-4*) D A Govan.

Paws, Wings, & Hooves: Mammals on the Move. Keiko Yamashita. LC 92-18506. (Illus.). (J). (gr. 1-3). 1993. lib. bdg. 19.95 (*0-8225-2901-7*, Lerner Publctns) Lerner Pub.

Paws with Language Arts, Level I. Carolee Sormunen. (PO - ELementary Language Arts Ser.). 1990. pap. 8.95 (*0-538-40930-4*) S-W Pub.

Paws with Language Arts, Level II. Carolee Sormunen. (PO - Elementary Language Arts Ser.). 1993. text 22.95 (*0-538-61479-X*) S-W Pub.

Paws with Language Arts, Level II. Carolee Sormunen. (PO - Elementary Language Arts Ser.). 1993. pap., wbk. ed. 22.95 (*0-538-61741-1*) S-W Pub.

Pawsitively Clemson: Tastes of the Tigers. LC 98-93499. 256p. 1998. 19.95 (*0-9665499-0-2*) Clem Univ IPTAY Sch.

Pawtucket. Elizabeth J. Johnson et al. (Images of America Ser.). 1996. pap. 16.99 (*0-7524-0243-9*) Arcadia Publng.

Pawtucket, Vol. II. Elizabeth J. Johnson et al. LC 95-237754. (Images of America Ser.). 1996. pap. 16.99 (*0-7524-0206-4*) Arcadia Publng.

Pawtucket, Rhode Island & Vicinity Marriages & Deaths from the Pawtucket Gazette & Chronicle, Vol. Two, 1835-1844: The History of Mineral Spring Cemetery. Elizabeth J. Johnson & James L. Wheaton, IV. (Illus.). 243p. (Orig.). 1994. pap. 25.00 (*0-9613692-3-X*) Spaulding Hse Pubns.

Pawtucket, Rhode Island & Vicinity Marriages & Deaths from the Pawtucket Gazette & Chronicle, Vol. 1, 1825-1834 - Saga of the Old Jenks Burying Ground. Elizabeth J. Johnson & James L. Wheaton, IV. LC 88-92589. (Illus.). 292p. (Orig.). 1989. pap. 25.00 (*0-9613692-2-1*) Spaulding Hse Pubns.

Pawtucket, RI, 50's. Historical Briefs, Inc. Staff. Ed. by Thomas Antoucci & Michael Antonucci. 176p. 1990. pap. 19.95 (*0-614-03686-0*) Hist Briefs.

Pawtucket, RI, 40's. Historical Briefs, Inc. Staff. Ed. by Thomas Antonucci & Michael Antonucci. 176p. 1989. pap. 19.95 (*0-89677-000-1*) Hist Briefs.

Pawtuxet. Donald D'Amato & Henry Brown. (Images of America Ser.). 1997. pap. 16.99 (*0-7524-0588-8*) Arcadia Publng.

Pax: A Preparation for the Sacrament of Penance for Children see My Confession Book: A Child's Preparation for the Sacrament of Penance

Pax Americana: Hegemony or Decline. Hippler. LC 93-47173. (Transnational Institute Ser.). (C). 49.95 (*0-7453-0695-0*, Pub. by Pluto GBR); pap. 18.95 (*0-7453-0696-9*) Pluto GBR.

Pax Britannica. Muriel E. Chamberlain. (Studies in Modern European History). (Illus.). 224p. (C). 1989. text 37.95 (*0-582-03079-X*, 78199) Longman.

Pax Britannica? British Foreign Policy 1789-1914 (Studies in Modern History) Muriel E. Chamberlain. (Illus.). 224p. (C). 1989. pap. text 23.95 (*0-582-49442-7*, 78199) Longman.

Pax Britannica: The Climax of an Empire. James Morris. LC 79-24725. (Illus.). 552p. 1980. pap. 16.00 (*0-15-671466-3*, Harvest Bks) Harcourt.

Pax Christi et Pax Caesaris: Religionsgeschichtliche, Traditionsgeschichtliche und Sozialgeschichtliche Studien Zum Epheserbrief. Eberhard Faust. (Novum Testamentum et Orbis Antiquus Ser.: Vol. 24). (GER.). 536p. 1993. text 74.25 (*3-7278-0864-0*, Pub. by Presses Univ Fribourg) Eisenbrauns.

Pax Democratica: A Strategy for the 21st Century. Huntley. LC 97-49331. 256p. 1998. text 45.00 (*0-312-21326-3*) St Martin.

Pax et Sapientia: Studies in the Text & Music of Liturgical Tropes & Sequences. Ritva Jacobson. 114p. 1986. pap. text 35.00 (*91-22-00825-X*) Coronet Bks.

Pax Optima Rerum: Friedensessais Zu Grotius und Goethe, Vol. 49. Christian Gellinek. LC 84-47845. (Germanic Studies in America). (GER.). 153p. 1984. text 18.00 (*0-8204-0147-1*) P Lang Pubng.

Pax Pacifica. Steve R. Pieczenik. 1995. write for info. (*0-446-51818-2*) Warner Bks.

PAX Permanent Martian Base: Space Architecture for the First Human Habitat on Mars. Janis Huebner-Moths et al. Ed. by Gary T. Moore. (Publications in Architecture & Urban Planning: No. R92-2). (Illus.). xi, 75p. (C). 1992. 10.00 (*0-938744-79-8*) U of Wis Ctr Arch-Urban.

Pax Pretoriana: The Fall of Apartheid & the Politics of Regional Destabilisation. Elling Tjenneland. (Discussion Paper Ser.: No. 2). 31p. 1989. write for info. (*91-7106-292-0*, Pub. by Nordic Africa) Transaction Pubs.

Pax Romana. Peter Amey. Ed. by Malcolm Yapp et al. (World History Program Ser.). (Illus.). 32p. (YA). (gr. 6-11). 1980. reprint ed. pap. text 5.90 (*0-89908-002-2*) Greenhaven.

Paxos Tiger. Ted Simon. 384p. (Orig.). 1989. spiral bd. 3.95 (*0-373-97092-7*) Harlequin Bks.

Paxton: A Study of Community Structure & Mobility. George W. Franz. (Outstanding Studies in Early American History). 354p. 1989. reprint ed. 25.00 (*0-8240-6179-9*) Garland.

Paxton Court. Diane Salvatore. 256p. 1995. 21.95 (*1-56280-109-0*) Naiad Pr.

Paxton Court. Diane Salvatore. 240p. 1996. pap. 10.95 (*1-56280-114-7*) Naiad Pr.

Paxton, Massachusetts Births, Marriages & Deaths, 1748-1850. Ed. by Marcia L. Memrino & Paul A. Russell. xx, 138p. (Orig.). 1996. pap. 22.00 (*0-7884-0564-0*, R877) Heritage Bk.

Paxton's Botanical Dictionary. Ed. by S. Hereman. 623p. (C). 1980. text 450.00 (*0-89771-637-X*, Pub. by Intl Bk Distr) St Mut.

Paxton's Botanical Dictionary. S. Hereman. 623p. 1980. reprint ed. 325.00 (*0-7855-3051-7*, Pub. by Intl Bk Distr) St Mut.

Pay: Strategy, Design & Negotiation. G. Roberts. 1996. pap. 129.00 (*1-85953-086-9*, Pub. by Tech Comm) St Mut.

PAY - Preparation, Application, Your Interview: The Guide to Job Hunting Success. Lori A. Kramer. (Illus.). 134p. (Orig.). 1994. pap. text 24.95 (*0-9632678-5-X*); pap. text, teacher ed. 15.95 (*0-9632678-6-8*) LK Co.

Pay & Benefits. Ed. by IPM Personnel Management Services Ltd. Staff. 150p. (C). 1991. pap. text 110.00 (*0-85292-454-2*, Pub. by IPM Hse) St Mut.

Pay & Benefits. Joan Keogh. 216p. 1993. 60.00 (*0-85292-534-4*, Pub. by IPM Hse) St Mut.

Pay & Benefits: New Ideas for Local Government. Ed. by John Matzer, Jr. (Practical Management Ser.). (Orig.). 1988. pap. text 23.95 (*0-87326-056-2*) Intl City-Cnty Mgt.

Pay & Benefits Information on Four Federal Banking Agencies. (Illus.). 59p. (Orig.). (C). 1994. pap. text 30.00 (*0-7881-0371-7*) DIANE Pub.

Pay & Employment in the New Europe. Ed. by David Marsden. 272p. 1992. 95.00 (*1-85278-564-0*) E Elgar.

Pay & File. Ned Wilsher. 175p. 1992. pap. 52.00 (*0-406-00351-3*, U.K., MICHIE) LEXIS Pub.

Pay & Organization Development. Edward E. Lawlor, III. 253p. (C). 1981. pap. text 42.00 (*0-201-03990-7*) Addison-Wesley.

Pay & Pensions for Federal Workers. Robert W. Hartman. LC 82-45980. 118p. 1983. 31.95 (*0-8157-3496-4*); pap. 12.95 (*0-8157-3495-6*) Brookings.

Pay & Productivity Bargaining: A Study of the Effect of National Wage Agreements in the Nottinghamshire Coalfields. R. G. Searle-Barnes. LC 71-94226. (Illus.). xxv, 190p. 1969. 37.50 (*0-678-06776-7*) Kelley.

Pay & Productivity in the Water Supply Industry. National Board for Prices & Incomes Staff. LC 79-560507. (Great Britain, Parliament, Papers by Command). vi, 87 p. 1970. write for info. (*0-10-144340-4*) U Pr of Amer.

Pay Any Price. James G. Miles. 288p. 1989. 19.95 (*0-9627006-0-6*, TXU 350 632) J G Miles.

Pay Any Price. large type ed. Ted Allbeury. 1984. 13.95 (*0-7089-8204-2*, Charnwood) Ulverscroft.

Pay Any Price: Lyndon Johnson & the Wars for Vietnam. Lloyd C. Gardner. LC 95-13208. (Illus.). 640p. 1995. text 35.00 (*1-56663-087-8*) I R Dee.

Pay Any Price: Lyndon Johnson & the Wars for Vietnam. Lloyd C. Gardner. LC 97-17237. 636p. 1997. pap. 18.95 (*1-56663-175-0*, Elephant Paperbacks) I R Dee.

Pay-As-You-Throw: Lessons Learned about Unit Pricing of Municipal Solid Waste. Janice L. Canterbury. 86p. 1996. reprint ed. pap. text 30.00 (*0-7881-3175-3*) DIANE Pub.

Pay at Risk, Vol. 4. Diane Gherson. (Innovations Ser.). (Illus.). (Orig.). 1997. pap. 39.95 (*0-614-30485-7*, AO104) Am Compensation.

Pay at the Crossroads. Helen Murlis. 128p. 1995. 90.00 (*0-85292-614-6*, Pub. by IPM Hse) St Mut.

Pay Attention, Slosh! Mark Smith. LC 97-6154. (Concept Bks.). (Illus.). 56p. (J). (gr. 3-5). 1997. lib. bdg. 11.95 (*0-8075-6378-1*) A Whitman.

Pay Attention! Stop, Think & Listen: A Self-Monitoring Program for Classroom & Home Behavior Management. Linda Bowman. 16p. (Orig.). 1995. pap. 19.00 (*1-886941-04-1*, 0980) Spec Pr FL.

P

An Asterisk (*) at the beginning of an entry indicates that the title is appearing for the first time.

Pay Attention to the Children: Lessons for Teachers & Parents from Sylvia Ashton-Warner. Sydney G. Clemens. LC 96-70255. 172p. 1996. pap. 14.95 (*1-883965-41-1*) Rattle OK Pubns.

Pay Board's Progress: Wage Controls in Phase II. Arnold Weber & Daniel J. Mitchell. LC 77-91820. (Studies in Wage-Price Policy). 472p. reprint ed. pap. 146.40 (*0-608-16858-0*, 202774200056) Bks Demand.

Pay Day. Nathan Asch. (Proletarian Literature Ser.). xxxiii, 280p. 1990. reprint ed. lib. bdg. 38.00 (*1-55888-268-5*) Omnigraphics Inc.

Pay Day: Treasures for Stay-At-Home Moms. Cindy Dagnan. 105p. 1999. pap. text 6.99 (*0-89900-829-1*) College Pr Pub.

Pay Determination & Industrial Prosperity. Alan A. Carruth & Andrew J. Oswald. (Illus.). 224p. 1990. 65.00 (*0-19-828692-9*) OUP.

Pay Determination in the Public Sector: An International Comparison Between France, Great Britain, & Italy. Ed. by J. J. Silvestre & F. Eyraud. LC 96-116572. (Occasional Papers - Labour Law & Labour Relations Programme: No. 6). 146p. 1995. 18.00 (*92-2-108516-3*) Intl Labour Office.

Pay Dirt. Rita Mae Brown. 288p. 1996. mass mkt. 6.99 (*0-553-57236-9*) Bantam.

Pay Dirt: Divorces of the Rich & Famous. James A. Albert. (Illus.). 250p. 1989. 19.95 (*0-8283-1927-8*) Branden Bks.

Pay Dirt: Divorces of the Rich & Famous. James A. Albert. (Illus.). 268p. 1998. text 17.00 (*0-7881-5289-0*) DIANE Pub.

Pay Dirt: Fortunes & Misfortunes of an Alaskan Goldminer. Otis Hahn & Alice Vollmar. Ed. by Tricia Brown. (Illus.). 160p. 1998. pap. 14.95 (*0-945397-68-2*) Epicenter Pr.

Pay Dirt: How to Raise & Sell Herbs & Produce for Serious Cash. 2nd rev. ed. Mimi Luebbermann. LC 96-49878. 256p. 1997. per. 15.00 (*0-7615-0844-9*) Prima Pub.

Pay Dirt: How to Raise & Sell Specialty Herbs & Vegetables for Serious Cash. Mimi Luebbermann. LC 92-39923. 208p. (Orig.). 1993. pap. 12.95 (*1-55958-287-1*) Prima Pub.

Pay Dirt: The Business of Professional Team Sports. James Quirk. 576p. 1932. pap. text 19.95 (*0-691-01574-0*, Pub. by Princeton U Pr) Cal Prin Full Svc.

Pay Dirt: The Business of Professional Team Sports. James Quirk & Rodney D. Fort. (Illus.). 400p. 1932. text 55.00 (*0-691-04255-1*, Pub. by Princeton U Pr) Cal Prin Full Svc.

Pay Dirt! The Search for Gold in British Columbia. Laura Langston. LC 96-120391. (Illus.). 80p. (YA). (gr. 8-12). 1995. pap. 8.95 (*1-55143-029-0*) Orca Bk Pubs.

Pay Envelopes: Tales of the Mill, the Mine & the City Street, Vol. 1. James Oppenheim. LC 72-3288. (Short Story Index Reprint Ser.). (Illus.). 1977. reprint ed. 18.95 (*0-8369-4158-6*) Ayer.

Pay Equity: Empirical Inquiries. National Research Council Staff. Ed. by Robert T. Michael et al. 272p. 1989. pap. text 27.95 (*0-309-03978-9*) Natl Acad Pr.

Pay Equity: Experiences of Canada & the Province of Ontario. (Illus.). 88p. (Orig.). (C). 1994. pap. text 20.00 (*0-7881-0557-4*) DIANE Pub.

Pay Equity: The Labour-Feminist Challenge. Carl J. Cuneo. 240p. 1990. pap. 17.95 (*0-19-540782-2*) OUP.

Pay, Equity, & Discrimination. Robert Hauser. (C). 1996. text 38.50 (*0-8133-7876-1*) Westview.

Pay Equity in Ontario: A Manager's Guide. Ed. by David Conklin & Paul Bergman. 115p. 1990. pap. text 23.95 (*0-88645-110-8*, Pub. by Inst Res Pub) Ashgate Pub Co.

Pay for Performance: Evaluating Performance Appraisal & Merit Pay. Ed. by George T. Milkovich et al. 224p. 1991. pap. text 24.95 (*0-309-04427-8*) Natl Acad Pr.

Pay for Performance: Exploring the Merit System. Robert L. Heneman. (Studies in Productivity: Highlights of the Literature Ser.: Vol. 38). 64p. 1984. 55.00 (*0-08-029513-4*) Work in Amer.

Pay for Performance: History, Controversy, & Evidence. Ed. by Thomas C. Mawhinney. LC 91-41350. (Journal of Organizational Behavior Management: Vol. 12, No. 1). 1992. text 49.95 (*1-56024-254-X*) Haworth Pr.

Pay for Performance: History, Controversy, & Evidence. Ed. by Thomas C. Mawhinney. LC 91-41350. (Journal of Organizational Behavior Management: Vol. 12, No. 1). 1992. pap. text 19.95 (*1-56024-255-8*) Haworth Pr.

Pay for Performance: State & International Public Sector Pay-for-Performance Systems. (Illus.). 49p. (Orig.). (C). 1994. pap. text 25.00 (*0-7881-0591-4*) DIANE Pub.

Pay for Play. Reed Bunzel. 240p. (Orig.). 1992. mass mkt. 4.50 (*0-380-76589-6*, Avon Bks) Morrow Avon.

Pay for Results: A Practical Guide to Effective Employee Compensation. Karen Jorgensen. LC 96-75085. (Taking Control Ser.). 320p. 1996. pap. 29.95 (*1-56343-136-X*) Silver Lake.

Pay-Grab Murders. large type ed. Peter Chester. 264p. 1989. 23.95 (*0-7451-0985-3*, G K Hall Lrg Type) Mac Lib Ref.

***Pay It Forward.** Catherine Ryan Hyde. 2000. per. 7.99 (*0-7434-1202-8*, PB Trade Paper) PB.

***Pay It Forward: A Novel.** Catherine Ryan Hyde. LC 99-26419. 288p. 2000. 22.50 (*0-684-86271-9*) S&S Trade.

Pay Nothing for Everything. Eric W. Gershman. Date not set. pap. 11.95 (*1-893977-02-1*) Great Pines Publishing Inc.

Pay Nothing for Kids Stuff. Eric W. Gershman. Date not set. pap. 11.95 (*1-893977-03-X*) Great Pines Publishing Inc.

Pay Nothing in Your Home & Garden. Eric W. Gershman. (Illus.). (Orig.). 1999. pap. 11.95 (*1-893977-01-3*) Great Pines Publishing Inc.

Pay Nothing to Travel Anywhere You Like. Eric W. Gershman & PayNada.com Editors. (Pay Nothing Book Ser.). (Illus.). (Orig.). 1999. pap. 8.95 (*1-893977-00-5*) Great Pines Publishing Inc.

Pay Now or Pay Later: Controlling Cost of Ownership from Design Throughout the Service Life of Public Buildings. National Research Council Staff. 72p. (C). 1991. pap. text 19.00 (*0-309-04481-2*) Natl Acad Pr.

Pay-Off. large type ed. Domini Wiles. 416p. 1985. 27.99 (*0-7089-1247-8*) Ulverscroft.

Pay-Off in Switzerland. large type ed. Bill Knox. (Linford Mystery Library). 320p. 1997. pap. 16.99 (*0-7089-5061-2*) Ulverscroft.

***Pay-Off Pitch.** rev. ed. Clair Bee. (Chip Hilton Sports Ser.: No. 16). 208p. 2000. pap. 5.99 (*0-8054-2095-9*) Broadman.

Pay or Play. Jon Boorstin. LC 99-89202. 278p. 2000. pap. 12.95 (*1-890085-04-9*, Pub. by Siles Pr) SCB Distributors.

Pay or Play: The Rise & Rise of Hollywood Agents. Nikki Finke. 1992. 25.00 (*0-679-40072-9*) Random.

Pay Pack & Follow. Mary Lovell. Date not set. write for info. (*0-393-04551-X*) Norton.

***Pay People Right! Breakthrough Reward Strategies to Create Great Companies.** Zin Schuster & Zingheim. LC 99-50437. 416p. 1999. 34.95 (*0-7879-4016-X*) Jossey-Bass.

Pay-per-Society: Computers & Communication in the Information Age. Vincent Mosco. Ed. by Brenda Dervin. LC 89-6665. (Communication & Information Science Ser.). 224p. (Orig.). (C). 1989. pap. 39.50 (*0-89391-604-8*) Ablx Pub.

Pay Reform in the Public Service: Initial Impact on Pay Dispersion in Australia, Sweden, & the United Kingdom. Robert F. Elliott. (Public Management Occasional Papers: No. 10). 60p. (Orig.). 1996. pap. 8.00 (*92-64-15293-8*, 42-96-60-1) OECD.

Pay Severance or Die. Tyler Erickson. LC 96-69870. 192p. 1996. 24.95 (*0-9651213-7-2*) Sligo Pr.

***Pay the Devil.** Jack Higgins. 1999. pap. 7.50 (*0-425-17189-2*) Berkley Pub.

Pay the Doctor. large type ed. Elizabeth Seifert. LC 90-45017. 364p. 1990. reprint ed. lib. bdg. 18.95 (*1-56054-062-1*) Thorndike Pr.

Pay the Doctor. Elizabeth Seifert. 1974. reprint ed. lib. bdg. 20.95 (*0-88411-055-9*) Amereon Ltd.

Pay the Piper. Kate Kingsbury. 224p. (Orig.). 1996. mass mkt. 5.50 (*0-425-15231-6*) Berkley Pub.

***Pay the Rent or Feed the Kids: The Tragedy & Disgrace of Poverty in Canada.** Mel Hurtig. (Illus.). 376p. 2000. 34.99 (*0-7710-4213-2*) McCland & Stewart.

***Pay TV Market in Brazil: A Strategic Entry Report, 1996.** Compiled by Icon Group International Staff. (Illus.). 183p. 1999. ring bd. 1830.00 incl. audio compact disk (*0-7418-1473-0*) Icon Grp.

Pay You in Hay. William J. Henry. 96p. 1999. pap. 10.00 (*1-880222-32-9*) Red Apple Pub.

Pay Your Bills on Time! see Unlock the Power of Your Paycheck Now!: 10 Easy Steps You Can Take for On-Time Bill Paying & Debt-Free Living

Pay Your Respects. Richard Graber. LC 78-22486. 240p. (YA). (gr. 7 up). 1979. 10.95 (*0-06-022063-5*) HarpC Child Bks.

Pay Yourself First: A Commonsense Guide to Life Cycle Retirement Investing. Timothy W. Cunningham & Clay B. Mansfield. LC 96-29256. (Illus.). 272p. 1996. pap. 16.95 (*0-471-16248-5*) Wiley.

Pay Yourself First - A Guide to Financial Success. Jesse B. Brown. LC 97-93987. (Illus.). 152p. 1997. 29.95 (*0-9659384-0-9*) Krystal Pr Pub.

Pay Zero Estate Tax: The Super Trust Way. Irving L. Blackman & Donald J. Russ. (Special Report Ser.: No.21). 52p. (Orig.). 1998. pap. 25.00 (*0-916181-29-4*) Blackman Kallick Bartelstein.

Payamber Vol. I, II, III: The Messenger. Z. Rehman. 1991. 12.50 (*0-933511-96-5*) Kazi Pubns.

Payasos y Otros Cuentos. Cristina M. Higuero. LC 93-74473. (SPA., Illus.). 21p. (Orig.). (J). (gr. 1-3). 1993. pap. 10.00 (*0-9605082-4-4*) Allied Ent.

Payatz: Around the World with Yiddish Theater. Herman Yablokoff. Tr. by Bella Mysell from YID. LC 94-30515. (Illus.). 544p. (C). 1995. 24.95 (*0-910155-28-3*) Bartleby Pr.

Payback. Jack Gatton. 185p. mass mkt. 4.99 (*1-55197-094-5*) Picasso Publ.

Payback. R. J. Kaiser. 448p. 1998. per. 5.99 (*1-55166-460-7*, 1-66460-6, Mira Bks) Harlequin Bks.

***Payback.** Francine Pascal. (Fearless Ser.: No. 6). 240p. (YA). (gr. 7-12). 2000. per. 5.99 (*0-671-03946-6*, Pocket Pulse) PB.

Payback. James A. Ritchie. 172p. 1992. 19.95 (*0-8027-1233-9*) Walker & Co.

Payback. Richard Stark. LC 98-5298. 208p. 1999. mass mkt. 12.00 (*0-446-67464-8*, Pub. by Warner Bks) Little.

Payback: A Novel. Thomas Kelly. 1998. mass mkt. 6.99 (*0-449-00223-3*, Crest) Fawcett.

Payback! Advanced Backstabbing & Mudslinging Techniques. George Hayduke. (Illus.). 196p. 1989. pap. 19.95 (*0-87364-537-5*) Paladin Pr.

Payback: America's Long War in the Middle East. John K. Cooley. 257p. 1997. reprint ed. text 20.00 (*0-7881-5137-1*) DIANE Pub.

Payback: The Logic of Retribution in Melanesian Religions. Garry W. Trompf. LC 93-31388. (Illus.). 565p. (C). 1994. text 69.95 (*0-521-41691-4*) Cambridge U Pr.

***Payback at the Capricornia Casino.** Donald Fuller. 1998. pap. 16.95 (*1-875998-47-0*, Pub. by Central Queensland) Accents Pubns.

Paybed. Nicholas Bentley. 1977. 12.00 (*0-233-96845-8*) Transatl Arts.

PayCalc: How to Create Customized Payroll Spreadsheets. Thomas E. Towle. 96p. (Orig.). 1984. 35.50 incl. disk (*0-8306-5072-5*) McGraw-Hill Prof.

PayCalc: Payroll Spreadsheets. Thomas E. Towle. 1991. 29.95 (*0-8306-6611-7*) McGraw-Hill Prof.

Payday at the Races. Les Conklin. 1982. pap. 7.00 (*0-87980-269-3*) Wilshire.

Payday Someday & Other Sermons. R. G. Lee. (Library of Baptist Classics). 1999. pap. 9.99 (*0-8054-1865-2*) Broadman.

Paydirt. Garry Disher. 176p. (Orig.). 1994. mass mkt. 5.95 (*1-86373-581-X*, Pub. by Allen & Unwin Pty) IPG Chicago.

Paydirt: Canadian Mining. Charles Pelley. LC 97-137490. (Illus.). 144p. 1996. 32.00 (*1-55046-085-4*, Pub. by Boston Mills) Genl Dist Srvs.

Payer, Provider, Consumer: Industry Confronts Health Care Costs. R. H. Egdahl. LC 77-21020. (Springer Series in Industry & Health Care: No. 1). (Illus.). 1977. 63.00 (*0-387-90295-3*) Spr-Verlag.

Paying Attention: Visitors & Museum Exhibitions. Beverly Serrell. Ed. by Roxana Adams. (Professional Practice Ser.). 220p. 1998. pap. 15.00 (*0-931201-46-2*, 857) Am Assn Mus.

Paying Attention to Children in a Changing Health Care System: Summaries of Workshops. Board on Children, Youth, & Families Staff et al. LC 96-230003. 104p. (Orig.). 1996. pap. text 26.00 (*0-309-05588-1*, Joseph Henry Pr) Natl Acad Pr.

Paying Attention to God: Discernment in Prayer. William A. Barry. LC 89-85963. 128p. (Orig.). 1990. pap. 7.95 (*0-87793-413-4*) Ave Maria.

Paying Back the Sea. Philip Dow. LC 78-71891. (Poetry Ser.). 1979. 20.95 (*0-915604-54-X*); pap. 11.95 (*0-915604-55-8*) Carnegie-Mellon.

Paying for Agricultural Productivity. Julian M. Alston. LC 99-17315. (International Food Policy Research Institute Ser.). (Illus.). 304p. 1999. pap. 21.50 (*0-8018-6278-7*) Johns Hopkins.

Paying for Agricultural Productivity. Julian M. Alston et al. LC 99-17315. (International Food Policy Research Institute Ser.). (Illus.). 315p. 1999. 59.95 (*0-8018-6185-3*) Johns Hopkins.

***Paying for Auto Injuries: A Consumer Panel Survey of Auto Accident Victims.** Insurance Research Council Staff. 111p. 1999. pap. text 25.00 (*1-56594-050-4*) Ins Res Coun.

***Paying for College Without Going Broke 2000, Vol. 1.** A. Chany Kalman. 319p. 1999. pap. 18.00 (*0-375-75467-9*, Pub. by PRP NY) Random.

***Paying for College, 2001.** Kalman A. Chany. 2000. pap. 18.00 (*0-375-76156-X*) Random.

***Paying for Contribution: Real Performance Related Pay Strategies.** Duncan Brown & Michael Armstrong. 435p. 1998. 34.95 (*0-7494-2899-6*) Kogan Page Ltd.

Paying for Crime. Pat Carlen & Dee Cook. 176p. 1989. 113.00 (*0-335-09938-6*); pap. 34.95 (*0-335-09937-8*) OpUniv Pr.

Paying for Crime: The Policies & Possibilities of Crime Victim Reimbursement. Susan K. Sarnoff. LC 96-20683. 136p. 1996. 52.95 (*0-275-95709-8*, Praeger Pubs) Greenwood.

Paying for Elections: The Campaign Finance Thicket - A Twentieth Century Fund Paper. Larry J. Sabato. 93p. 1989. 18.95 (*0-87078-247-9*); pap. 8.95 (*0-87078-246-0*) Century Foundation.

Paying for Europe. Iain Begg & Nigel Grimwade. (Contemporary European Studies: Vol. 2). 208p. 1998. pap. 15.00 (*1-85075-858-1*, Pub. by Sheffield Acad) CUP Services.

Paying for Growth: Using Development Fees to Finance Infrastructure. Thomas P. Snyder & Michael A. Stegman. LC 86-51156. 133p. 1986. pap. 49.95 (*0-87420-663-4*, P40) Urban Land.

Paying for Health Care: Public Policy Choices for Illinois. Ed. by Lawrence B. Joseph. (Chicago Assembly Ser.). 304p. (C). 1992. pap. text 14.95 (*0-9626755-1-2*) UC Ctr UR&PS.

***Paying for Health Care Trends.** Kathleen O'Leary Morgan. 100p. 1999. pap. 50.00 (*0-7401-0010-6*, M Quitno Pr) Morgan Quitno Corp.

***Paying for Health, Education & Housing: How Does the Centre Pull the Purse Strings?** Howard Glennerster et al. 280p. 2000. text 65.00 (*0-19-924078-7*) OUP.

Paying for Highways, Airways & Waterways. 1995. lib. bdg. 250.00 (*0-8490-6511-9*) Gordon Pr.

Paying for Highways, Airways & Waterways: How Can Users Be Charged? (Illus.). 75p. (Orig.). (C). 1993. pap. text 30.00 (*1-56806-720-8*) DIANE Pub.

Paying for India's Health Care. Ed. by Peter Berman & M. E. Khan. LC 92-48184. (Illus.). 326p. 1993. 38.00 (*0-8039-9463-X*) Sage.

Paying for Long Term In-Home & Nursing Home Care, 1991: Washington State. Cheryl C. Mitchell & F. H. Mitchell, Jr. 120p. 1991. pap. text 25.00 (*1-879909-00-6*) Mitchell WA.

Paying for Medicare: The Politics of Reform. David G. Smith. (Social Institutions & Social Change Ser.). 284p. 1992. pap. text 24.95 (*0-202-30394-2*); lib. bdg. 47.95 (*0-202-30393-4*) Aldine de Gruyter.

Paying for Military Readiness & Upkeep: Trends in Operation & Maintenance Spending. Amy Belasco. (Illus.). 75p. (C). 1998. pap. text 20.00 (*0-7881-7381-2*) DIANE Pub.

Paying for Performance: A Guide to Compensation Management. KPMG Peat Marwick & Peter T. Chingos. LC 96-49180. 384p. 1997. 100.00 (*0-471-17487-4*) Wiley.

Paying for Pollution: Water Quality & Effluent Charges. Conservation Foundation Staff. LC 78-52289. (Conservation Foundation: Issue Reports). 64p. reprint ed. pap. 30.00 (*0-608-11748-X*, 201578400097) Bks Demand.

Paying for Presidents: Public Financing in National Elections. Anthony Corrado. LC 93-38548. (Orig.). 1993. pap. 9.95 (*0-87078-185-5*) Century Foundation.

Paying for Productivity: A Look at the Evidence. Ed. by Alan S. Blinder. 275p. 1990. pap. 18.95 (*0-8157-0999-4*) Brookings.

Paying for Productivity: A Look at the Evidence. fac. ed. Ed. by Alan S. Blinder. LC 89-25328. (Illus.). 320p. 1990. pap. 99.20 (*0-7837-7678-0*, 204743100007) Bks Demand.

Paying for Progress: Perspectives on Financing Environmental Protection. (Illus.). 86p. (Orig.). (C). 1992. pap. text 25.00 (*1-56806-067-X*) DIANE Pub.

Paying for Rented Housing. S. Witherspoon et al. (DSS Research Report Ser.). 1996. write for info. (*0-11-762370-9*, Pub. by Statnry Office) Bernan Associates.

Paying for the German Inflation. Michael L. Hughes. LC 87-24631. xv, 267p. (C). 1988. 45.00 (*0-8078-1777-5*) U of NC Pr.

Paying for the German Inflation. Michael L. Hughes. LC 87-24631. 283p. 1988. reprint ed. pap. 87.80 (*0-608-02072-9*, 206272500003) Bks Demand.

Paying for the Past: The Struggle over Reparations for Surviving Victims of the Nazi Terror. Christian Pross. Tr. by Belinda Cooper from GER. LC 97-39245. 276p. 1998. 29.95 (*0-8018-5824-0*) Johns Hopkins.

Paying for the Piper: Capital & Labour in Britain's Offshore Oil Industry. Charles Woolfson et al. LC 96-36069. (Employment & Work Relations in Context Ser.). (Illus.). 480p. 1997. 130.00 (*0-7201-2348-8*); pap. 59.95 (*0-7201-2350-X*) Continuum.

Paying for Time Not Worked: An Approach to Developing a Comprehensive Workplace Policy. John A. Dantico. (Building Blocks Ser.: Vol. 9). (Illus.). 19p. (Orig.). 1993. pap. 24.95 (*1-57963-012-X*, A0028) Am Compensation.

***Paying for University Research Facilities & Administration.** Charles A. Goldman & T. Williams. LC 99-88423. (C). 2000. pap. 12.00 (*0-8330-2805-7*, MR-1135-OSTP) Rand Corp.

Paying for Your Child's College Education. Marguerite Smith. 192p. (Orig.). 1996. mass mkt. 9.99 (*0-446-67165-7*, Pub. by Warner Bks) Little.

Paying for Your First Car. Larry Burkett. 2000. pap. 7.99 (*0-8024-0978-4*) Moody.

Paying Guest. George R. Gissing. LC 68-54267. reprint ed. 27.50 (*0-404-02799-7*) AMS Pr.

Paying Guests. large type ed. Claire Rayner. 1996. 27.99 (*0-7089-8882-2*, Charnwood) Ulverscroft.

Paying Office Expenses: Piggy-Backing, Cooperative, Sharing, Entrepreneurial Services, Bartering: A Possibility Workbook. Carrol, Frieda, Research Division Staff. 1984. ring bd. 23.95 (*0-318-04335-1*) Prosperity & Profits.

Paying Our Way: Estimating Marginal Social Costs of Feight Transportation Committee for Study of Public Policy for Surface Freight Transportation. Committee for Study of Public Policy for Surface F. LC 96-21831. (Special Reports: No. 246). 171p. 1996. 16.00 (*0-309-06217-9*) Transport Res Bd.

Paying People Not to Work: The Economic Cost of the Social Security Retirement Earnings Limit. Aldona Robbins & Gary Robbins. 1989. pap. 10.00 (*0-943802-45-8*, 142) Natl Ctr Pol.

Paying Physicians: Choices for Medicare, Controlling Medicare Costs Through Competitive Consumer Choices. 1992. lib. bdg. 99.95 (*0-8490-5507-5*) Gordon Pr.

Paying Teachers for What They Know & Do: New & Smarter Compensation Strategies to Improve Schools. Allan R. Odden & Carolyn Kelley. LC 96-25312. (Illus.). 208p. 1996. pap. 24.95 (*0-8039-6459-5*) Corwin Pr.

Paying the Doctor: Health Policy & Physician Reimbursement. Ed. by Jonathan D. Moreno. LC 90-37837. 208p. 1990. 52.95 (*0-86569-006-5*, T006, Auburn Hse) Greenwood.

Paying the Farm Bill: U. S. Agricultural Policy & the Transition to Sustainable Agriculture. Paul Faeth et al. 70p. 1991. pap. 10.00 (*0-915825-64-3*, FAPFP) World Resources Inst.

Paying the Jobless: A Comparison of Unemployment Benefit Policies in Great Britain & Germany. Jochen Clasen. 256p. 1994. 72.95 (*1-85628-519-7*, Pub. by Avebry) Ashgate Pub Co.

Paying the Piper. Sharyn McCrumb. 1999. mass mkt. 5.99 (*0-345-34518-5*) Ballantine Pub Grp.

***Paying the Piper.** Sharyn McCrumb. 1999. 5.99 (*0-345-91576-3*) Ballantine Pub Grp.

Paying the Piper: Causes & Consequences of Art Patronage. Ed. by Judith H. Balfe. LC 92-38280. 344p. 1993. text 45.95 (*0-252-02005-7*); pap. text 17.95 (*0-252-06310-4*) U of Ill Pr.

Paying the Piper: Productivity, Incentives, & Financing in U. S. Higher Education. Ed. by Michael S. McPherson et al. (Economics of Education Ser.). 344p. (C). 1994. text 70.00 (*0-472-10404-7*, 10404) U of Mich Pr.

Paying the Piper: Subsidies, Politics, & the Environment. David M. Roodman. 70p. (Orig.). 1996. pap. 5.00 (*1-878071-35-1*) Worldwatch Inst.

Paying the Political Price: A Handbook on Political Reform. Robert F. Bauer. (Orig.). 1996. pap. write for info. (*1-879650-02-9*) Perkins Coie.

Paying the Political Price: (Summer 1996 Supplement) Robert F. Bayer. 1996. pap. 14.00 (*1-879650-03-7*) Perkins Coie.

P

An Asterisk (*) at the beginning of an entry indicates that the title is appearing for the first time.

Paying the Premium: A Military Insurance Policy for Peace & Freedom, 140. Ed. by Walter Hahn & H. Joachim Maitre. LC 92-35552. (Contributions in Military Studies Ser.: No. 140). 216p. 1993. 55.00 (0-313-28849-6, GM8849, Greenwood Pr) Greenwood.
Paying the Price. Vaughan-Whitehead. LC 97-24798. 416p. 1997. text 79.95 (0-312-17729-1) St Martin.
Paying the Price, Vol. 6. James Humphrey. Ed. by Woody Kaplan et al. LC 99-183579. (Illus.). 113p. 1998. pap. 17.00 (0-936641-23-1) Poets Alive Pr.
Paying the Price: Ignacio Ellacuria & the Murdered Jesuits of El Salvador. Teresa Whitfield. LC 94-20361. (Illus.). 500p. (C). 1994. pap. 22.95 (1-56639-253-5); text 79.95 (1-56639-252-7) Temple U Pr.
Paying the Price: Pesticide Subsidies in Developing Countries. Robert C. Repetto. 40p. 1985. pap. text 10.00 (0-915825-12-0) World Resources Inst.
Paying the Price: The Status & Role of Insurance Against Natural Disasters in the United States. Ed. by Howard Kunreuther & Richard Roth, Sr. LC 98-12369. 270p. 1998. 47.95 (0-309-06361-2, Joseph Henry Pr) Natl Acad Pr.
Paying the Price: What Entrepreneurs Have to Give & Give up to Win Lasting Success. Robert J. Fierle. 196p. 1992. 24.95 (1-881837-00-9) Mgmt Resources Inc.
Paying the Price: Women & the Politics of International Economic Strategy. Ed. by Mariarosa D. Costa & Giovanna F. Costa. LC 95-13679. 112p. (C). 1995. text 19.95 (1-85649-298-2, Pub. by Zed Books) St Martin.
Paying the Price of Freedom: Family & Labor among Lima's Slaves, 1800-1854. Christine Hunefeldt. Tr. by Alexandra M. Stern. (Illus.). 252p. (C). 1994. 50.00 (0-520-08235-4, Pub. by U CA Pr); pap. 17.95 (0-520-08292-3, Pub. by U CA Pr) Cal Prin Full Svc.
Paying the Social Debt: What White America Owes Black America. Richard F. America. LC 93-2861. 160p. 1993. 57.95 (0-275-94450-6, C4450, Praeger Pubs) Greenwood.
Paying the Words Extra: Religious Discourse in the Supreme Court of the United States. Winnifred F. Sullivan. LC 94-29503. (Religions of the World Ser.). 236p. 1994. 25.95 (0-945454-06-6); pap. 15.50 (0-945454-07-4) Harvard U Wrld Relig.
Paying with Plastic: The Digital Revolution in Buying & Borrowing. David Evans & Richard Schmalensee. LC 99-23902. (Illus.). 348p. 1999. 29.95 (0-262-05062-5) MIT Pr.
***Paying with Plastic: The Digital Revolution in Buying & Borrowing.** David Evans & Richard Schmalensee. (Illus.). 392p. (C). 2000. reprint ed. pap. 16.95 (0-262-55037-7) MIT Pr.
Paying Without Money. Patricia Armentrout. LC 96-4568. (Money Ser.). (Illus.). (J). 1996. lib. bdg. 14.60 (1-57103-121-9) Rourke Pr.
Paying Your Sickness Bills. Michael M. Davis. LC 77-180572. (Medicine & Society in America Ser.). 292p. 1972. reprint ed. 21.95 (0-405-03947-6) Ayer.
Payloader (Action-Trucks) David Hawcock. LC 96-131248. (Illus.). 10p. (J). (ps-2). 1995. 3.95 (0-8050-3379-3) H Holt & Co.
Paymaneh-ye Zarin. Georg Trakl. Tr. by Jamshid Shirani & A. Maziar from GER. LC 93-61223. Orig. Title: Aus Goldenem Kelch. (PER., Illus.). 96p. (Orig.). 1994. pap. 7.50 (0-936347-37-6) IBEX.
Payment Bond Manual. 2nd ed. LC 95-79665. 568p. 1995. pap. 79.95 (1-57073-161-6, 51-0164, ABA Tort) Amer Bar Assn.
Payment by Results. xii, 164p. (Orig.). 1984. 31.50 (92-2-103651-0); pap. 22.50 (92-2-103652-9) Intl Labour Office.
Payment Clearing. Greg Gerdes. 1992. ring bd. 115.00 (1-55738-350-2, Irwn Prfssnl) McGraw-Hill Prof.
Payment Deferred. C. S. Forester. 302p. reprint ed. lib. bdg. 23.95 (0-88411-925-4) Amereon Ltd.
Payment Deferred. C. S. Forester. 1991. reprint ed. lib. bdg. 21.95 (1-56849-049-6) Buccaneer Bks.
Payment Due. Penny Jordan. (Presents Ser.). 1992. per. 2.89 (0-373-11491-5, 1-11491-7) Harlequin Bks.
Payment Due. Penny Jordan. (Promo Ser.). 1999. per. 4.50 (0-373-83377-6, 1-83377-1) Harlequin Bks.
Payment Due: A Nation in Debt, a Generation in Trouble. Timothy J. Penny & Steven E. Schier. (Dilemmas in American Politics Ser.). 2p. (C). 1996. pap. 65.00 (0-8133-2598-6, Pub. by Westview) HarpC.
Payment for Mental Health Inpatient Care in California. Mark Juretic et al. (Working Paper Ser.: No. 42). 31p. 1987. pap. 5.00 (0-89940-523-1) LBJ Sch Pub Aff.
Payment for Physicians Services: Strategies for Medicare. 1991. lib. bdg. 75.85 (0-8490-4979-2) Gordon Pr.
Payment for the Piper. large type ed. Frances Murray. 596p. 1987. 27.99 (0-7089-1590-6) Ulverscroft.
Payment in Blood. Elizabeth George. LC 89-426. 432p. 1990. mass mkt. 7.50 (0-553-28436-3) Bantam.
Payment in Blood. large type ed. Elizabeth George. LC 90-10797. 591p. 1990. lib. bdg. 20.95 (1-56054-000-1) Thorndike Pr.
Payment in Full. Anne Hampson. 1980. pap. 1.50 (0-373-58023-1) Harlequin Bks.
Payment in Full: A Guide to Successful Bill Collecting. Leonard Bendell. 176p. 1987. 24.95 (0-937404-05-5) Triad Pub FL.
Payment in Kind, Bk. 9. J. A. Jance. (J.P. Beaumont Ser.). 336p. 1991. mass mkt. 6.99 (0-380-75836-9, Avon Bks) Morrow Avon.
Payment in Love. Penny Jordan. 1990. per. 2.50 (0-373-11314-5) Harlequin Bks.
Payment Law. 4th ed. Douglas J. Whaley. 400p. 1995. 40.00 (0-316-93252-3, Aspen Law & Bus) Aspen Pub.
Payment Law: Suitable for Use with Whaley. Richard G. Bell. (Cambridge Ser.). 207p. 1995. pap. text 19.00 (0-685-54297-1, Chicago Law Bk) Cambridge Law.
***Payment Methods for Your Export Sales, 2000.** annuals John R. Jagoe. Ed. by Agnes Brown. (Illus.). 65p. 2000. pap. 50.00 (0-943677-45-9) Export USA.
Payment of Bonus Act, 1965. 6th ed. K. D. Srivastava. (C). 1988. 140.00 (0-7855-5638-9) St Mut.
Payment System: Cases, Materials & Issues. 2nd ed. Edward L. Rubin & Robert Cooter. (American Casebook Ser.). 992p. (C). 1994. 57.50 (0-314-03545-1) West Pub.
Payment System: Design, Management, & Supervision. Ed. by Bruce J. Summers. LC 94-14188. 1994. write for info. (1-55775-386-5) Intl Monetary.
Payment System, Cases, Materials & Issues, Teacher's Manual to Accompany. Edward L. Rubin & Robert Cooter. (American Casebook Ser.). 195p. 1995. pap. text, teacher ed. write for info. (0-314-07605-0) West Pub.
Payment System Integrity: A Compendium of Interviews on the Regulation of Stored Value. Ed. by William W. Streeter. LC 97-224826. 1975. pap. 15.00 (0-89982-054-9) Am Bankers.
***Payment Systems: Aspen Roadmap Law Course Outline.** Lary Lawrence. LC 99-36479. 432p. 1999. pap. text 21.95 (0-7355-0638-8) Panel Pubs.
Payment Systems: Cases, Materials, & Problems. Peter A. Alces & Marion W. Benfield, Jr. LC 93-20285. (American Casebook Ser.). 576p. (C). 1993. 52.50 (0-314-01973-1) West Pub.
Payment Systems: Principles, Practice, & Improvements. David B. Humphries. LC 94-40044. (World Bank Technical Papers: No. 260). 114p. 1995. pap. 22.00 (0-8213-3111-6, 13111) World Bank.
Payment Systems: Teaching Materials. 5th ed. Richard E. Speidel et al. (American Casebook Ser.). 582p. (C). 1993. pap. 45.50 (0-314-02345-3) West Pub.
Payment Systems: Teaching Materials. 5th ed. Richard E. Speidel et al. (American Casebook Ser.). 56p. 1993. pap. text, teacher ed. write for info. (0-314-03028-X) West Pub.
Payment Systems & Credit Instruments. Clayton P. Gillette et al. LC 96-32385. (University Casebook Ser.). 636p. 1996. write for info. (1-56662-345-6) Foundation Pr.
***Payment Systems & Other Financial Transactions: With Teacher's Manual.** Ronald J. Mann. (Casebook Ser.). 650p. 1999. teacher ed. write for info. (0-7355-0014-2, 00142) Panel Pubs.
***Payment Systems in Global Perspective.** Maxwell J. Fry. LC 98-33132. (International Studies in Money & Banking). 1999. 85.00 (0-415-20764-9) Routledge.
Payment Systems, Monetary Policy & the Role of the Central Bank. Omotunde Johnson. LC 97-3846. 1997. write for info. (1-55775-626-0) Intl Monetary.
Payment Systems, Teacher's Manual to Accompany Cases & Materials On. Peter A. Alces & Marion W. Beafield, Jr. (American Casebook Ser.). 200p. 1993. pap. text. write for info. (0-314-02808-0) West Pub.
Payment Tables for Canadian Mortgages, No. 42. Ed. by Financial Publishing Company Staff. 256p. 1974. pap. 15.00 (0-87600-042-1) Finan Pub.
Payment Tables for FHA Title 1 Loan: 30 Days to First Payment. Financial Publishing Co. Staff. 176p. 1983. pap. 20.00 (0-87600-962-3) Finan Pub.
Payment Tables for FHA Title 1 Loans: 45 Days to First Payment. Financial Publishing Co. Staff. 176p. 1999. pap. 20.00 (0-87600-963-1) Finan Pub.
Payment Tables for Leases with Residuals, No. 16. 2nd ed. 768p. 1999. pap. 40.00 (0-87600-016-2) Finan Pub.
Payment Tables for FHA Title 1 Loans: 60 Days to First Payment. Financial Publishing Co. Staff. 176p. 1999. pap. 20.00 (0-87600-964-X) Finan Pub.
Payment Tables Handbook. Michael E. Dugan. 1993. pap. 7.95 (1-882912-03-9) Sunrise TN.
Payments Arrangements & the Expansion of Trade in Eastern & Southern Africa. Shailendra J. Anjaria et al. (Occasional Papers: No. 11). 52p. 1982. pap. 5.00 (1-55775-079-3) Intl Monetary.
Payments Due: Onstage Offstage. rev. ed. Carol Connolly. LC 93-77632. (Illus.). 92p. 1995. pap. 12.00 (0-935697-06-3) Midwest Villages.
Payments for Care. A. Evers et al. 360p. 1994. pap. 41.95 (1-85972-008-0, Pub. by Avebry) Ashgate Pub Co.
Payments in the Financial Services Industry of the 1980s Conference Proceedings. Federal Reserve Bank of Atlanta Staff. LC 84-3398. (Illus.). 203p. 1984. 52.95 (0-89930-079-0, FPA/, Greenwood Pr) Greenwood.
***Payments Systems Risk.** Turner. 256p. 2000. 65.00 (0-471-32848-0) Wiley.
Payne & Ivamy: Carriage of Goods by Sea. 13th ed. E. R. Hardy Ivamy. 436p. 1989. pap. 48.00 (0-406-52560-9, U.K., MICHIE) LEXIS Pub.
Payne & Pleasure of a Black Woman. Carol P. Crystian. (Orig.). 1997. pap. write for info. (1-57553-433-9) Watermrk Pr.
Payne Hollow. Harlan Hubbard. LC 73-84998. (Illus.). 168p. 1974. pap. 25.00 (0-87130-040-0) Eakins.
Payne Hollow: Life on the Fringe of Society. 2nd ed. Harlan Hubbard. LC 97-71033. (Illus.). 176p. 1997. reprint ed. pap. 12.50 (0-917788-66-4) Gnomon Pr.
Payne Hollow Journal. Harlan Hubbard. Ed. by Don Wallis. LC 96-11048. (Illus.). 216p. 1996. 25.00 (0-8131-1954-5) U Pr of Ky.
Payne on Divorce. 2nd ed. Payne. 360p. 1988. 115.00 (0-409-88849-4, MICHIE) LEXIS Pub.
Payne Reproduction Catalogs. 88p. 1994. pap. 13.00 (1-882418-12-3) Centenn Pubns.
***Payne Stewart: A Changed Heart.** Ed. by Good News Publishers Staff. (Illus.). 2000. pap. 8.50 (5-550-03017-9) Nairi.
***Payne Stewart: The Authorized Biography.** Tracey Stewart & Ken Abraham. (Illus.). 256p. 2000. 24.99 (0-8054-2396-6) Broadman.
***Payne Stewart Story.** Larry Guest. (Illus.). 2000. 24.95 (0-7407-1097-4) Andrews & McMeel.
Payne Stewart's Guide to Golf, 1998. Ed. by Robert Yehling & Charles Oldham. (Illus.). 112p. 1998. pap. 5.95 (0-9644712-3-X) Faircount Intl.
Paynes, Edgar & Elsie: American Artists. Rena N. Coen. LC 87-63403. (Illus.). 108p. 1987. 50.00 (0-944699-01-4) DeRus Fine Art.
Payoff Artillery - W. W. II: The Wide-Ranging Combat of the Battalion that Fought under Five Armies & Eight Divisions in the European Theatre. Frank H. Armstrong. LC 93-71275. (Illus.). 208p. 1994. 21.00 (0-9632448-1-7) Bull Run VT.
Payoffs in the Cloakroom: The Greening of the Michigan Legislature, 1938-1946. Bruce A. Rubenstein & Lawrence E. Ziewacz. LC 94-48041. 1995. 28.00 (0-87013-387-X) Mich St U Pr.
Payofski's Dyscovery. Hal Marden. LC 85-45701. 110p. 1986. 6.95 (0-253-34301-1) Ind U Pr.
Payola! Gerry Cagle. 300p. 1989. 17.95 (0-8283-1925-1) Branden Bks.
Payola in the Music Industry: A History, 1880-1991. Kerry Segrave. LC 92-56691. 288p. 1994. lib. bdg. 42.50 (0-89950-882-0) McFarland & Co.
Payols of Trinidad: A Vanishing Culture. Sylvia Moodie-Kublalsingh. 272p. 1994. text 65.00 (1-85043-660-6) I B T.
Payout Dice Machines. Richard M. Bueschel. (Coin-Op Collector's Ser.). (Illus.). 103p. (Orig.). 1994. spiral bd. 24.95 (1-885160-01-1) Coin-Op Classics.
Payroll Accounting Bernard J. Bieg. LC 99-158517. 1999. write for info. (0-324-00389-7) Sth-Wstrn College.
Payroll Accounting. Timothy F. Carse & Jeffrey Slater. (Orig.). 1998. pap. text 59.95 (0-89863-207-2, 207-2) Star Pub CA.
Payroll Accounting, 2 vols. Giove. (C). 1995. pap., teacher ed. 11.96 (0-395-70873-7) HM.
Payroll Accounting, 2 vols. Giove. (C). 1995. pap., teacher ed., suppl. ed. 11.96 (0-395-70874-5) HM.
Payroll Accounting, 4 vols. Giove. (C). 1996. pap. 38.76 (0-395-83392-2) HM.
Payroll Accounting. Giove. LC 98-75249. 1999. pap. text 33.27 (0-395-95993-4) HM.
Payroll Accounting. B. Lewis Keeling. (C). 1991. text. write for info. (0-318-68637-6, AH60B8H81C) S-W Pub.
Payroll Accounting. 2nd ed. Carse-Slater. 1996. 53.44 (0-256-25212-2) McGraw.
Payroll Accounting. 2nd ed. Carse-Slater. 1996. teacher ed. 39.37 (0-256-25197-5) McGraw.
Payroll Accounting. 2nd ed. Timothy Carse. LC 96-225197. 528p. (C). 1996. text 34.95 (0-256-21754-8, Irwn McGrw-H) McGrw-H Hghr Educ.

***Payroll Accounting. 4th ed. Timothy F. Carse & Jeffrey Slater. (Orig.). 2000. pap. text 59.95 (0-89863-222-6) Star Pub CA.**
Payroll Accounting: A Practical Approach, reflects the authors' years of teaching payroll accounting! The authors simplify the discussion of employment & tax laws that affect payroll preparation, using clear, understandable language. The organization of the book matches the major steps a professional takes in calculating the payroll of a business. The book follows the payroll cycle for a company, within which various tasks & activities occur. *Publisher Paid Annotation.*

Payroll Accounting. 7th ed. Bernard Bieg. (Payroll Accounting Ser.). 1996. pap. 46.95 (0-538-86702-7) S-W Pub.
Payroll Accounting. 88th rev. ed. B. Lewis Keeling & Bernard J. Bieg. 368p. (C). 1987. 20.25 (0-538-80126-3, AH60HB) S-W Pub.
Payroll Accounting. 94th ed. Paula Y. Mooney. LC 93-35659. 290p. 1993. pap. text 65.00 (0-13-091308-1) P-H.
Payroll Accounting, 1998 Edition. 8th ed. Bernard J. Bieg. (Miscellaneous/Catalogs Ser.). 416p. 1999. pap. 40.95 (0-538-86742-6) Thomson Learn.
Payroll Accounting, 1997. Frank C. Giove. (C). 1997. text, teacher ed. 11.96 (0-395-83511-9) HM.
Payroll Accounting, 1997. 7th ed. Bernard J. Bieg. (Miscellaneous/Catalogs Ser.). 1999. mass mkt. 39.95 (0-538-86694-2) S-W Pub.
Payroll Accounting, 1996: A Practical Approach. E. L. Whitecomb. 120p. (C). 1999. pap. 24.00 (1-890033-11-1) Grey Thistle.
Payroll Accounting, 1993. 93rd ed. B. Lewis Keeling. (C). 1992. mass mkt. 31.25 (0-538-81207-9) S-W Pub.
Payroll Accounting Project with Peachtree 5.0. 9th ed. Warren. (SWC-Accounting). 1998. 18.00 (0-324-00817-1) Sth-Wstrn College.
Payroll Accounting Test Key. 93rd ed. Bieg. (Swc-Accounting). 1992. mass mkt. 7.00 (0-538-81209-5) S-W Pub.
Payroll Accounting Tests. 93rd ed. Bieg. (Swc-Accounting). 1992. mass mkt. 14.75 (0-538-81208-7) S-W Pub.
Payroll Accounting 1996 Edition. 6th ed. Bernard J. Bieg. (SWC-Accounting). 416p. 1995. mass mkt. 35.75 (0-538-85723-4) S-W Pub.
Payroll Accounting, 8th ed. 8th ed. Bernard J. Bieg. 1999. pap. text 53.95 (0-538-86743-4) S-W Pub.
Payroll Administration Guide, 3 vols. LC 89-902. 1990. ring bd. 543.00 (1-55871-038-8) BNA.
***Payroll Answer Book.** Gregory E. Matthews. LC 99-188134. 1999. write for info. (1-56706-305-5) Panel Pubs.
Payroll Auditor. Jack Rudman. (Career Examination Ser.: C-2074). 1994. reprint ed. pap. 29.95 (0-8373-2074-7) Nat Learn.
Payroll Clerk. Jack Rudman. (Career Examination Ser.: C-1596). 1994. pap. 23.95 (0-8373-1596-4) Nat Learn.
Payroll Discipline Could Stretch Colorado's Budget Dollar. Fred Holden. 15p. 1988. pap. text 8.00 (1-57655-108-3) Independ Inst.
Payroll Guide. write for info. (0-318-57374-1) P-H.
Payroll Made Easy: An Employer's Guide to Payroll. Rondi S. Wahl. (Illus.). 55p. 1989. pap. 12.95 (0-927209-00-4) Better Bus CA.
***Payroll Manager's Report, 2000 Yearbook.** annuals Ed. by Donis W. Ford & David Solomon. (Illus.). 200p. 2000. pap. 199.00 (1-58673-047-9) IOMA.
***Payroll Practice Fundamentals: 2000 Edition.** Ed. by Publisher's Resource Group Staff. 250p. 2000. 95.95 (1-930471-06-8, 0100) American Payroll.
Payroll Practitioner's Compliance Handbook. Debera J. Salam & Howard R. Freedman. 944p. 1995. 134.00 (0-7913-2436-2) Warren Gorham & Lamont.
Payroll Practitioner's Compliance Handbook: Principles of Payroll Administration. Debera J. Salam. 1800p. 1993. 188.00 (0-614-06644-1) Warren Gorham & Lamont.
Payroll Procedures: Manual & Computer. 10th ed. Fuller. (KM - Office Procedures Ser.). 1989. mass mkt. 9.50 (0-538-60265-1) S-W Pub.
Payroll Record & Procedure. 2nd ed. Merle W. Wood. 1989. pap. 46.92 (0-07-909190-3) McGraw.
Payroll Records & Procedures. 2nd ed. Meryl W. Wood. 1989. pap. 35.64 (0-07-071686-2) McGraw.
Payroll Records & Procedures. 3rd ed. Merle Wood & Sherry Cohen. 1994. teacher ed. 9.28 (0-02-800548-1) Glencoe.
Payroll Records & Procedures. 3rd rev. ed. Merle W. Wood & Sherry Cohen. LC 93-24025. 1993. reprint ed. text. write for info. (0-02-800545-7); reprint ed. teacher ed. write for info. (0-02-800546-5) Glencoe.
***Payroll Records & Procedures.** 4th ed. Merle W. Wood. LC 99-40024. (Illus.). 320p. 1999. 35.68 (0-02-804827-X) McGraw.
***Payroll Records & Procedures** 4th ed. Merle W. Wood & Sherry Cohen. LC 99-40024. 1999. 30.50 (0-02-804834-2) Glencoe.
Payroll Records & Procedures: Includes Workbook & Practice Set. 3rd ed. Merle Wood & Sherry Cohen. 1994. text, wbk. ed. 35.94 (0-02-800549-X) Glencoe.
***Payroll Source: 2000 Edition, 2 vols.** 7th rev. ed. Michael P. O'Toole. 1200p. 2000. 162.95 (1-930471-04-1, 0700) American Payroll.
Payroll Supervisor. Jack Rudman. (Career Examination Ser.: C-3154). 1994. pap. 29.95 (0-8373-3154-4) Nat Learn.
Payroll Systems. 2nd ed. (Open Learning Super Ser.). 1991. pap. text 26.00 (0-08-041635-7, Pergamon Pr) Elsevier.
Payroll Systems & Procedures. B. F. Wigge & Merle W. Wood. 1970. text 10.48 (0-07-070152-0) McGraw.
Payroll Toolkit: Nuts & Bolts Techniques to Managing Your Payroll. Timothy F. Carse & Jeffrey Slater. LC 96-40919. 360p. 1996. 35.00 (1-55623-848-7, Irwn Prfssnl) McGraw-Hill Prof.
Payroll Year-End Survival Guide. Vicki Lambert. 350p. 1998. pap. 69.00 (0-8080-0275-9) CCH INC.
***Payroll Year-End Survival Guide, 2000.** Vickie A. Lambert. 500p. 1999. pap. 69.00 (0-8080-0415-8) CCH INC.
Pays de Loire Map. 1997. 8.95 (2-06-700232-5, 232) Michelin.
Pays des Fourrures. Jules Verne. 8.95 (0-686-55938-X) Fr & Eur.
Pays des 36000 Volontes. Andre Maurois. (FRE.). 94p. 1990. pap. 11.95 (0-7859-4614-4) Fr & Eur.
Pays Lointains. Julien Green. (FRE.). 1990. pap. 24.95 (0-7859-2714-X, 2020115271) Fr & Eur.
Pays Rhenans (1794-1814) Le Comportement des Rhenans Face a l'Occupation Francaise. Josef Smets. (GER.). 1997. 56.95 (3-906754-94-4, Pub. by P Lang) P Lang Pubng.
Paysages see Landscapes
Paysages Francais sur Fond D'Amerique. Francoise Dupuy-Sullivan. LC 94-41995. (FRE., Illus.). 309p. 1995. pap. 34.95 (0-7734-1945-4) E Mellen.
Paysages Le'Gendaires & Acts of Recognition. Peter Russell. LC 99-462689. 109p. 1997. pap. 14.95 (3-7052-0106-9, Pub. by Poetry Salzburg) Intl Spec Bk.
Paysages Unbains dans "Les Beaux Quartiers" d'Aragon: Pour une Theorie de la Description dans le Roman. Raphael Lafhail-Molino. (Publications Universitaires Europeennes Ser.: Series 13, Vol. 224). (FRE.). 538p. 1997. 58.95 (3-906757-84-6, Pub. by P Lang) P Lang Pubng.
Paysan de Paris. Louis Aragon. (FRE.). 256p. 1978. pap. 10.95 (0-7859-1824-8, 2070367827) Fr & Eur.
Paysan de Paris. Louis Aragon. (Folio Ser.: No. 782). (FRE.). pap. 8.95 (2-07-036782-7) Schoenhof.
Paysan Parvenu. Pierre Carlet de Chamblain de Marivaux. (Coll. GF). 1966. pap. 7.95 (0-8288-9607-0, M1832) Fr & Eur.
Paysanne: New & Selected Poems, 1960-1990. George D. Economou. (Illus.). 200p. (Orig.). (C). 1991. pap. text 10.00 (0-936556-23-4) Contact Two.
Paysanne de la Garonne. Jacques Maritain. 405p. 1966. 29.95 (0-8288-7445-X) Fr & Eur.
Paysans. Honore de Balzac. (Folio Ser.: No. 675). (FRE.). pap. 9.95 (2-07-036675-8) Schoenhof.
Paysans. Honore de Balzac & Samuel S. de Sacy. 512p. 1975. 12.95 (0-8288-9358-6) Fr & Eur.
Payson de Garonne: Un Vieux Laic s'Interroge a Propos du Temps Present. Jacques Maritain. 19.95 (0-685-34274-3) Fr & Eur.

P

Paz. Camarin Grae. 336p. 1986. reprint ed. pap. 8.95 (*0-930044-89-4*) Naiad Pr.

Paz... A Pesar del Panico. Charles R. Swindoll. (Serie Realidades - Realities Ser.).Tr. of Peace in Spite of Panic. (SPA.). 1.99 (*0-7899-0009-2*, 498114) Editorial Unilit.

Paz Con Dios. 2nd ed. Algernon J. Pollock. Ed. by Alberto Mahecha. Tr. by SAra Bautista from ENG. (Serie Diamante).Tr. of Peace With God. (SPA., Illus.). 48p. 1982. pap. 0.85 (*0-942504-09-7*) Overcomer Pr.

Paz Con Dios: Peace with God. enl. rev. ed. Billy Graham. (SPA.). 220p. 1987. pap. 10.99 (*0-311-46109-3*) Casa Bautista.

Paz del Perdon. Charles Stanley.Tr. of Forgiveness. (SPA.). 160p. (Orig.). 1990. pap. 8.99 (*0-88113-252-7*) Caribe Betania.

***Paz Fishing Chart & Guide.** (Illus.). 1999. 14.95 (*1-929394-07-1*, B007) Baja Directions.

***PAZ 5-Step Method of Learning Drum Beats Quickly on the Drum Set: Quarter Note, Eighth Note & Sixteenth Note Rock Beats.** Phil Zampino. 90p. 1999. spiral bd. 16.95 (*0-942253-12-4*) PAZ Pub.

***PAZ 5-Step Method of Learning Jazz, Swing Dixie & Big Bank on the Drum Set Bk. 1B: Practical & Useful Jazz Rhythms & Sobs on the Drum Set.** Phil Zampino. 111p. 1999. spiral bd. 18.95 (*0-942253-13-2*) PAZ Pub.

Paz, Perfecta Paz. large type ed. F. B. Meyer.Tr. of Peace, Perfect Peace. (SPA.). 56p. 1990. pap. 2.99 (*1-56063-339-5*, 494021) Editorial Unilit.

Paziente Anziano Nella Pratica Medica. Ed. by W. Meier-Ruge. viii, 256p. 1990. pap. 31.50 (*3-8055-5286-6*) S Karger.

Pazifische Kuestenkordillere (Cordillera Costena) Costa Ricas und Ihre Stellung Innerhalb des Sued-Zentralamerikanischen Gebirges: Tektonik, Magmatismus und Krustenbau in Mittelamerika und Westindien. Dierk Henningsen. (Geotektonische Forschungen Ser.: Vol. 23). (GER.). ii, 109p. 1966. pap. 27.00 (*3-510-50914-5*, Pub. by E Schweizerbartsche) Balogh.

Pazifische Press: German Exile Publishing in Los Angeles 1942-1948. Roland Jaeger. Ed. by Victoria Dailey. Tr. by Marion Philadelphia. (Illus.). 75p. 2000. write for info. (*0-9657858-2-3*) V Dailey.

Pazos de Ulloa. Bazan E. Pardo. (SPA.). 1989. 9.95 (*0-8288-2571-8*) Fr & Eur.

Pazos de Ulloa. Emilia Pardo Bazan. (SPA.). 317p. 1984. 10.00 (*0-8288-8586-9*) Fr & Eur.

Pazos de Ulloa, Level 6. Adapted by Emilia Pardo Bazan. (Leer en Espanol Ser.). (SPA.). (C). 1998. pap. 6.95 (*84-294-3615-4*) Santillana.

Pazza Per Amor & Exerpts from il Postiglione Di Longjumeaux. Pietro Antonio Coppola. (Italian Opera II Ser.: Vol. 5). 288p. 1986. text 30.00 (*0-8240-6554-9*) Garland.

PB - Organolead Compounds. (Gmelin Handbook of Inorganic & Organometallic Chemistry Ser.: Pt. 3). (Illus.). xiii, 246p. 1992. 1025.00 (*0-387-93658-0*) Spr-Verlag.

***PB & J Noodle Stories: Bubbles Custom Pub Special Sale Disney First Reader.** 32p. (J). 1999. pap. 3.99 (*0-7868-4326-8*, Pub. by Disney Pr) Time Warner.

***PB & J Noodle Stories: Jelly's Loose Tooth Custom Pub Spec'l Sale Disney First Reader.** 32p. (J). 1999. pap. 3.99 (*0-7868-4328-4*, Pub. by Disney Pr) Time Warner.

***PB & J Noodle Stories: Rainy Day Custom Pub Special Sale Disney First Reader.** 32p. (J). 1999. pap. 3.99 (*0-7868-4327-6*, Pub. by Disney Pr) Time Warner.

PB Bear Goes to School. (Illus.). 24p. (J). 1996. 12.95 (*0-7894-1172-5*) DK Pub Inc.

Pb Lead Pt. 5: Organolead Compounds: R2PbR2', R2PBR'R", RPbR'R"R, & R4-nPbHn (N=1 to 3) Compounds. 8th ed. (Gmelin Ser.). (Illus.). 204p. 1996. 809.00 (*3-540-93748-X*) Spr-Verlag.

***PBA Workers' Compensation Law Section: Fall Section Meeting 1998.** 1998. 99.00 incl. audio PA Bar Inst.

PB&J USA: Recipes for Kids & Adults by Kids & Adults. Connie C. Fisher. LC 98-96451. (Illus.). 128p. (J). (gr. 3-12). 1998. pap. 10.95 (*0-9661200-1-9*) Small Potatoes.

PB4Y. Turner Publishing Company Staff. (Illus.). 120p. Date not set. 49.95 (*1-56311-237-X*) Turner Pub KY.

PBL: An Inquiry Approach. John Barell. LC 98-60465. (Illus.). 181p. 1998. pap. 32.95 (*1-57517-048-5*, 1592) SkyLght.

PBL Project One: Time Management - Work of the Principal. Edwin M. Bridges. viii, 112p. 1994. pap., teacher ed., ring bd. 15.00 (*0-86552-122-0*) U of Oreg ERIC.

PBL Project One: Time Management: Work of the Principal. Edwin M. Bridges. vii, 112p. 1994. pap., student ed., ring bd. 14.00 (*0-86552-127-1*) U of Oreg ERIC.

PBL Project Three: Write Right! Edwin M. Bridges. vii, 22p. 1994. pap., teacher ed., ring bd. 6.00 (*0-86552-125-5*); pap., student ed., ring bd. 5.50 (*0-86552-129-8*) U of Oreg ERIC.

PBL Project Two: Leadership & School Culture. Philip Hallinger & Barbara L. Habschmidt. vii, 160p. 1994. pap., teacher ed., ring bd. 15.50 (*0-86552-123-9*); pap., ring bd. 14.50 (*0-86552-128-X*) U of Oreg ERIC.

PBM-5 Mariner Flight Manual. (Illus.). 90p. 1997. reprint ed. spiral bd. 17.95 (*1-891570-01-3*) Boomerang.

PBMs: Reshaping the Pharmaceutical Distribution Network. Ed. by Sheila R. Shulman et al. LC 98-12622. (Journal of Pharmaceutical Marketing & Management Ser.: Vol. 12, Nos. 2-3). 189p. 1998. 49.95 (*0-7890-0512-3*, Pharmctl Prods) Haworth Pr.

PBO Lab: Particle Beam Optics Laboratory User Manual. (Illus.). 254p. 1998. pap. write for info. (*1-892267-00-4*) AccelSoft.

***PBR: The Making of a Warrior.** Bill Quinn. 310p. 1999. 16.95 (*0-7414-0229-7*) Buy Books.

PBS: Behind the Screen. Laurence Jarvik. LC 96-31422. 368p. 1996. 25.00 (*0-7615-0668-3*) Prima Pub.

PBS: Behind the Screen. Laurence Jarvik. 368p. 1998. per. 16.95 (*0-7615-1291-8*) Prima Pub.

PBS C Workbook. Sathis Menon. 288p. (C). 1993. pap. 41.88 (*0-07-041576-5*) McGraw.

PBS Companion: A History of Public Television. David Stewart. (Illus.). 224p. 1999. 25.00 (*1-57500-050-4*, Pub. by TV Bks) HarpC.

PBS Hornblower. Forester. 1993. 14.95 (*0-07-021546-4*) McGraw.

PBX Equipment Installer & Repairer. Jack Rudman. (Career Examination Ser.: C-1385). 1994. pap. 27.95 (*0-8373-1385-6*) Nat Learn.

PBX Hacking. John J. Williams. Ed. by Clifford Williams. 15p. 1997. pap. 29.00 (*0-934274-41-X*) Consumertronics.

***PBX Security.** unabridged ed. John J. Williams. (Illus.). 35p. 1999. pap. 29.00 (*0-934274-57-6*) Consumertronics.

PBY Catalina in Action. William E. Scarborough. (In Action Ser.: No. 1062). (Illus.). 50p. 1983. pap. 9.95 (*0-89747-149-0*) Squad Sig Pubns.

***PBY Catalina in Detail & Scale.** Bert Kinzey. (Detail & Scale Ser.: Vol. 66). (Illus.). 80p. 2000. pap. 14.95 (*1-888974-19-2*, 8266) Squad Sig Pubns.

PBY Catalina Walk Around. William E. Scarborough. (Walk Around Ser.). (Illus.). 80p. (Orig.). 1996. pap. 14.95 (*0-89747-357-4*) Squad Sig Pubns.

PBY-5A Catalina Flight Manual. (Illus.). 1997. reprint ed. spiral bd. 17.95 (*1-891570-00-5*) Boomerang.

PC: Portable Standard FORTRAN 77. M. W. Clark. (Computers & Their Applications Ser.). 228p. 1986. text 36.95 (*0-470-20756-6*) P-H.

PC - Computing Customizing Windows 3.1. Paul Bonner. (Illus.). 560p. 1992. pap. 34.95 incl. disk (*1-56276-018-1*, Ziff-Davis Pr) Que.

PC - Computing Guide to Excel 4.0 for Windows. Dale Lewallen. (Guide to...Ser.). (Illus.). 643p. (Orig.). 1992. pap. 27.95 (*1-56276-048-3*, Ziff-Davis Pr) Que.

PC - Computing Guide to Excel 3.0. Dale Lewallen. (Guide to...Ser.). (Illus.). 434p. (Orig.). 1991. pap. 24.95 (*1-56276-019-X*, Ziff-Davis Pr) Que.

PC - Computing Guide to Quicken 5.0. Michael E. Kolowich. (Guide to...Ser.). (Illus.). 556p. (Orig.). 1991. pap. 24.95 (*1-56276-023-8*, Ziff-Davis Pr) Que.

PC - Computing Guide to Quicken 6.0. Michael E. Kolowich. (Guide to...Ser.). (Illus.). 675p. 1992. pap. 24.95 (*1-56276-091-2*, Ziff-Davis Pr) Que.

PC - Computing Guide to Shareware. Preston Gralla. (Guide to...Ser.). 413p. (Orig.). 1991. pap. 34.95 incl. disk (*1-56276-036-X*, Ziff-Davis Pr) Que.

PC - Computing Guide to Using Quicken for Windows. Michael E. Kolowich. (Guide to...Ser.). (Illus.). 523p. (Orig.). 1992. pap. 24.95 (*1-56276-053-X*, Ziff-Davis Pr) Que.

PC - Computing 2001 Windows Tips. Michael Edelhart. (Illus.). 561p. (Orig.). 1993. pap. 27.95 (*1-56276-084-X*, Ziff-Davis Pr) Que.

PC - Hardwarebuch. Messmer. (GER.). (C). 1991. text. write for info. (*0-201-55985-4*) Addison-Wesley.

PC - Mail User's Guide. Rational Data Systems, Inc. Staff. 99p. 1992. pap. 3.50 incl. disk (*1-881378-06-3*) Rational Data.

PC - Remote User's Guide. Rational Data Systems, Inc. Staff. 192p. 1992. pap. 4.00 incl. disk (*1-881378-01-2*) Rational Data.

PC - Tax, 1993. Smith. 184p. 1992. teacher ed. 75.00 incl. disk (*0-685-67019-8*) CCH INC.

PC - VS System Managers Guide. Rational Data Systems, Inc. Staff. 84p. 1992. pap. 10.00 incl. disk (*1-881378-03-9*) Rational Data.

PC - VS System Managers Guide, No. 5. Rational Data Systems, Inc. Staff. 1992. pap. 10.00 incl. disk (*1-881378-15-2*) Rational Data.

PC - VS User's Guide. Rational Data Systems, Inc. Staff. 194p. 1992. pap. 4.00 incl. disk (*0-685-55375-2*) Rational Data.

PC - XT - AT Technical Pocket Reference for IBM-PC & Compatibles: Important Information, Tables, Technical Data, 1. Uwe Fernengel. (Illus.). 81p. (Orig.). 1990. pap. 5.00 (*0-911827-04-8*, 70) Elcomp.

PC Affair: A Comic Mystery of Murder, Mayhem, & Data Processing. Clyde J. Aragon. LC 96-92977. 160p. (Orig.). 1997. pap. 7.95 (*0-9648641-1-8*) Cliff Zone Bks.

PC-Aided Numerical Heat Transfer & Convective Flow. Akira Nakayama. LC 95-7112. 320p. 1995. boxed set 139.95 (*0-8493-7656-4*, 7656) CRC Pr.

PC & Electronics: The Technicians Toolbox. (Illus.). 320p. (Orig.). 1997. pap. 39.95 (*1-55755-334-3*, B334) Abacus MI.

PC & Mac Handbook: Systems, Upgrades & Troubleshooting. Steve Heath. 600p. 1995. pap. text 69.95 (*0-7506-2229-6*, Digital DEC) Buttrwrth-Heinemann.

PC & MS DOS Quick Reference Guide. David Segal & Albert M. Berg. (DDC Quick Reference Guides Ser.). 84p. 1990. spiral bd. 12.00 (*0-936862-82-3*, X-17) DDC Pub.

***PC Anywhere for Dummies.** Jill Gilbert. (For Dummies Ser.). (Illus.). 336p. 2000. pap. 19.99 (*0-7645-0680-3*) IDG Bks.

PC Applications for Business, Using Lotus 1-2-3 (Version 2.2), WordPerfect 5.0 & dBase IV. D. Michael Werner & Thomas W. Warner. (C). 1991. 48.67 (*0-673-46256-0*) Addson-Wesley Educ.

PC Architecture from Assembly Language to C. David Hergert & Nancy Thibeault. LC 97-20688. 282p. (C). 1997. pap. text 110.00 (*0-13-653775-8*) P-H.

PC Architectures for the 21st Century. Peter Varhol. LC 96-7212. (Illus.). 172p. 1996. pap. 275.00 (*1-56607-970-5*) Comput Tech Res.

PC Assembly Language Programming: One Byte at a Time. David Y. Wen & Grey G. Whipple. Ed. by Mixter. LC 93-41587. 500p. (C). 1994. text 52.00 (*0-314-02715-7*) West Pub.

***PC @ Home.** Heather Newman. (Illus.). 184p. 1999. pap. 14.95 (*0-937247-31-6*) Detroit Pr.

***PC Audio Editing.** Roger Derry. LC 99-89555. 240p. 2000. pap. 39.95 (*0-240-51596-X*, Focal) Buttrwrth-Heinemann.

PC-Based Instrumentation & Control. 2nd ed. Michael H. Tooley. 384p. 1999. pap. text 44.95 (*0-7506-2093-5*) Buttrwrth-Heinemann.

PC Bible. 3rd ed. Robert Lauriston. (Bible Ser.). 960p. (C). 1998. pap. text 34.99 (*0-201-35382-2*, Pub. by Peachpit Pr) Addison-Wesley.

PC Bios Internals: Maximize Your PC's Bios. Abacus Publishing Staff. 1999. pap. text 29.95 (*1-55755-342-4*) Abacus MI.

PC Buyer's Guide. Allen L. Wyatt. (Illus.). 190p. (Orig.). 1996. pap. 12.95 (*0-9655054-0-5*) Bearlodge Pr.

PC Buyer's Handbook: Summer, 1997. 8th rev. ed. Gordon P. Foreman. 108p. 1997. pap. 10.00 (*0-9642011-8-6*) Core Concep.

***PC Buyer's Handbook 1999.** Gordon P. Foreman. (Illus.). 128p. 1999. pap. 22.50 (*0-7864-0447-7*) McFarland & Co.

***PC Buyer's Handbook 2000.** Gordon P. Foreman. (Illus.). 127p. 2000. per. 22.50 (*0-7864-0907-X*) McFarland & Co.

PC Calc & a Spreadsheet Program. Buttonware. 1986. pap. 21.95 (*0-256-05749-4*, Irwn McGrw-H) McGrw-H Hghr Educ.

PC Card - PCMCIA Software Developer's Handbook. 2nd ed. Steven M. Kipisz et al. LC 98-39278. 400p. 1999. pap. 49.95 (*1-57398-015-3*) Annabooks.

PC Care Manual. Chris Morrison. 1991. 24.95 (*0-8306-6650-8*) McGraw-Hill Prof.

PC Care Manual: Diagnosing & Maintaining Your MS-DOS CP-M or Macintosh System. Chris Morrison & Teresa S. Stover. LC 87-26235. (Illus.). 224p. 1987. 24.95 (*0-8306-0991-1*, 2991) McGraw-Hill Prof.

PC Complete. Sybex, Inc. Staff. LC 98-88753. 1040p. 1998. pap. 19.99 (*0-7821-2422-4*) Sybex.

***PC Complete.** rev. ed. Sybex, Inc. Staff. (Illus.). 1072p. 2000. pap. text 19.99 (*0-7821-2778-9*) Sybex.

PC Concepts. Shelton. (C). 1991. pap. text, teacher ed. 2.76 (*0-395-53252-3*) HM.

***PC Concepts.** 2nd ed. Martin. (C). 1999. pap. text. write for info. (*0-03-025969-X*) Harcourt Coll Pubs.

PC Concepts: A Core Text for the Houghton Mifflin Software Solutions Series. Nelda Shelton. (C). 1990. pap. text. write for info. (*0-395-53251-5*) HM Soft Schl Col Div.

***PC Confidential: Secure Your PC & Privacy from Snoops, Spies, Spouses, Supervisors & Credit Card Thieves.** Michael A. Banks. 288p. 2000. pap. 24.99 incl. cd-rom (*0-7821-2747-9*) Sybex.

PC Dads Guide to Raising a Computer Smart Parent: A Down-Home Guide for Digitally Distressed Parents. Mark Ivey & Ralph Bond. LC 98-45672. 320p. 1999. pap. 13.95 (*0-440-50843-6*, Delta Trade) Dell.

PC Dictionary. 1997. write for info. (*1-884486-34-7*) Wave Tech.

PC-DOS Customized: Create Your Own DOS Commands. rev. ed. David D. Busch. 400p. (C). 1988. pap. 18.95 (*0-685-19362-4*) P-H.

PC-DOS Fundamentals for Diskette-Based Operation. Peter Calingaert. (Illus.). 272p. 1986. 25.95 (*0-13-654906-3*) P-H.

PC DOS 6.1: Everything You Need to Know. Jonathan Kamin. 1993. pap. 24.95 (*1-55958-450-5*) Prima Pub.

PC Economics Handbook, 001. Daniel J. Ehrlich & Joel Millonzi. (C). 1987. pap. 29.96 (*0-395-35685-7*) HM.

***PC 832 Concepts: Peace Officer Required Training.** Derald D. Hunt. LC 86-67429. 193p. 2000. pap. 24.95 (*1-928916-01-5*) Copperhouse.

PC 8042 Keyboard Controller Kit. Gary Konzak. 160p. 1994. 199.00 (*0-929392-21-3*) Annabooks.

PC Equipment & Accessories in Egypt: A Strategic Entry Report, 1998. Compiled by Icon Group International Staff. (Country Industry Report). (Illus.). 164p. 1999. ring bd. 1640.00 incl. audio compact disk (*0-7418-0155-8*) Icon Grp.

PC Essentials. 3rd ed. 1998. 22.99 (*1-58076-089-9*) Que Educ & Trng.

PC Exercises for Construction Industry. J. N. Howell. 45p. 1989. pap. 28.00 (*0-932223-08-7*) Churchill PC.

PC Expert Systems Shootout. Expertise Associates Staff. 1989. 695.00 (*0-471-50885-3*) Wiley.

PC Fingame: Participant's Manual. 2nd ed. Leroy Brooks, II. 168p. (C). 1995. per. 30.45 incl. disk (*0-256-13611-4*, Irwn McGrw-H) McGrw-H Hghr Educ.

PC Fingame: The Financial Management Decision Game Participant's Manual. 2nd ed. Leroy D. Brooks, II. 204p. (C). 1995. text, per. 30.45 incl. disk (*0-256-20989-8*, Irwn McGrw-H) McGrw-H Hghr Educ.

PC Focus. Wojkowski. (C). 1994. text. write for info. (*0-318-70368-8*) S-W Pub.

PC for the Teacher. Brownell. LC 98-48105. 1998. pap. 56.95 (*0-534-53862-2*) Brooks-Cole.

PC for the Teacher: Instructor's Resource Manual. write for info. (*0-534-53865-7*) Wadsworth Pub.

Pc 4: Pendragon. Stephen R. Lawhead. (Pendragon Cycle Ser.: Bk. 4). 448p. 1995. reprint ed. mass mkt. 6.99 (*0-380-71757-3*, Avon Bks) Morrow Avon.

PC Fundamentals with DOS 3.3. 1993. 29.95 (*1-56877-043-X*); teacher ed. 49.95 (*1-56877-044-8*) Catapult WA.

PC Give 8.0. Jurgen A. Doornik & David F. Hendry. LC 95-153695. 256p. 1994. pap., mass mkt. 81.95 incl. disk (*0-534-25050-5*) Wadsworth Pub.

PC Graphics Handbook for C++ Programers. Julio Sanchez & Maria P. Canton. 1998. 69.95 (*0-8493-1678-2*) CRC Pr.

PC Grundlagen. 2nd ed. Jurgen Ortmann. (GER.). (C). 1991. text. write for info. (*0-201-55957-9*) Addison-Wesley.

PC Guide for DOS with Video: The Easiest Way to Master DOS. 2nd ed. Inter Trade Corporation Staff. (PC Guide Ser.). (Illus.). 320p. 1993. pap. 19.95 incl. VHS (*1-881979-03-2*) Inter Trde.

PC Guide for Windows 95 - Book-Video Combination: The Easiest Way to Learn to Use Windows 95. 2nd ed. (Illus.). 320p. 1996. pap. 24.95 incl. VHS (*1-881979-29-6*) Inter Trde.

PC Handbook: For Engineers, Programmers & Other Serious PC Users. 6th ed. John Foster & John Choisser. (Illus.). 96p. 1997. mass mkt. 9.95 (*0-929392-36-1*) Annabooks.

PC Hardware Guide for DOS Solaris. Ron Ledesma. 352p. 1994. pap. 49.00 (*0-13-124678-X*) P-H.

PC Hardware in a Nutshell. Robert Bruce Thompson & Barbara Frichtman Thompson. Ed. by Robert Denn. (In a Nutshell Ser.). (Illus.). 450p. 2000. pap. 24.95 (*1-56592-599-8*) OReilly & Assocs.

PC Hardware Projects, Vol. 2. James Barbarello. (Illus.). 191p. 1997. pap. 29.95 (*0-7906-1109-0*) Prompt Publns.

PC Hardware Projects, Vol. 3. James Barbarello. 205p. 1998. pap. 29.95 (*0-7906-1151-1*) Prompt Publns.

PC Hardware Projects Vol. 1: A Complete Guide to Building Practical Addons to Your Computer. James Barbarello. LC 97-173507. (Illus.). 256p. 1997. pap. 29.95 (*0-7906-1104-X*) Prompt Publns.

PC Hardware Strategies for the 21st Century. 1998. write for info. (*0-7897-9800-X*) Que.

PC Hardware Tuning: How to Improve Your PC's Performance-the Smart Way. Anreas Voss. 1998. pap. text 29.95 (*1-55755-341-6*) Abacus MI.

PC Home Business Book. Martin Fox. 1993. pap. 24.95 (*0-9626660-4-1*) Future Commns.

***PC in My Pocket.** Steve Seroshek. 208p. 2001. pap. 9.99 (*0-7356-1159-9*) Microsoft Pr.

PC in Your Pocket: Information When You Need It: The Best of the HP Palmtop Paper. Ed. by Ed Keefe. LC 96-60976. (Illus.). 292p. (Orig.). 1996. pap. 19.95 (*0-9652187-0-8*) Thaddeus Comput.

Pc+ Installation Guide 5.0. SPSS Inc. 1993. pap. 3.00 (*0-13-177734-3*, Prentice Hall) P-H.

PC Interface Administration. UNIX System Laboratories Staff. 160p. 1993. pap. text 20.00 (*0-13-177213-9*, Pub. by P-H) S&S Trade.

***PC Interfacing Pocket Reference.** Michael Predko. LC 99-35422. 592p. 1999. pap. 29.95 (*0-07-135525-1*) McGraw.

PC Intern. 6th ed. Michael Tischer. LC 97-136180. 1996. pap. text 69.95 incl. cd-rom (*1-55755-304-1*) Abacus MI.

PC-Internet Connection: TCP Networking for DOS & Windows. Bernard Aboba & Britt Bassett. 272p. pap. 34.95 (*1-883979-00-5*) MailCom.

PC Is Not a Typewriter: A Style Manual for Creating Professional-Level Type on Your Personal Computer. Robin Williams. (Illus.). 96p. (C). 1995. pap. text 9.95 (*0-938151-49-5*, Pub. by Peachpit Pr) Addison-Wesley.

PC Keyboard Design. Gary Konzak. 85p. 1993. student ed. 249.00 incl. disk (*0-929392-12-4*) Annabooks.

PC-Kimmo: A Two-Level Processor for Morphological Analysis. Evan L. Antworth. (Occasional Publications in Academic Computing: No. 16). 280p. 1990. pap. 24.00 (*0-88312-639-7*) S I L Intl.

PC Lab:exper/basic Cir. Greg MacMillan. (Primarily Tech Material). 316p. 1992. pap. text 34.95 incl. disk (*0-8273-4821-5*) Delmar.

PC LAN Markets: Downsizing, Peer to Peer & FDDI-Copper Stir the Pot. Market Intelligence Staff. 380p. (Orig.). 1992. 1495.00 (*1-56753-380-9*) Frost & Sullivan.

PC LAN Systems for the Small Law Firm. ALA Staff. 96p. 1993. per. 49.95 (*0-8403-8578-1*) Kendall-Hunt.

PC Learning Lab Teacher 123 for Windows 95. PC Learning Labs Staff. 1996. pap. 29.99 incl. disk (*1-56276-403-9*, Ziff-Davis Pr) Que.

PC Learning Lab Teaches Wordperfect for Windows 95. PC Learning Labs Staff. 1996. pap. 29.99 incl. disk (*1-56276-398-9*, Ziff-Davis Pr) Que.

PC Learning Labs Teaches Ami Pro 3.0. PC Learning Labs Staff. (Learning Labs Ser.). (Illus.). 464p. 1993. pap. 22.95 incl. disk (*1-56276-134-X*, Ziff-Davis Pr) Que.

PC Learning Labs Teaches CC: Mail. PC Learning Labs Staff. (Learning Labs Ser.). (Illus.). 288p. 1993. pap. 22.95 incl. disk (*1-56276-135-8*, Ziff-Davis Pr) Que.

PC Learning Labs Teaches DOS 5. PC Learning Labs Staff. (Learning Labs Ser.). (Illus.). 346p. (Orig.). 1992. pap. 22.95 incl. disk (*1-56276-042-4*, Ziff-Davis Pr) Que.

PC Learning Labs Teaches DOS 6. PC Learning Labs Staff. (PC Learning Labs Ser.). (Illus.). 456p. (Orig.). 1993. pap. 22.95 incl. disk (*1-56276-100-5*, Ziff-Davis Pr) Que.

PC Learning Labs Teaches Excel 4.0 for Windows. PC Learning Labs Staff. (Learning Labs Ser.). (Illus.). 384p. (Orig.). 1992. pap. 22.95 incl. disk (*1-56276-074-2*, Ziff-Davis Pr) Que.

PC Learning Labs Teaches Lotus Notes 4.0. Logical Operations Staff & PC Learning Labs Staff. xxv, 332p. 1996. pap. 29.99 (*1-56276-377-6*, Ziff-Davis Pr) Que.

PC Learning Labs Teaches Microsoft Access 2.0. PC Learning Labs Staff. LC 94-172106. 400p. 1995. 22.95 incl. disk (*1-56276-225-7*, Ziff-Davis Pr) Que.

P

PC Learning Labs Teaches Microsoft Office. PC Learning Labs Staff. LC 95-123977. (Learning Labs Ser.). (Illus.). 208p. (Orig.). 1994. pap. 22.95 incl. disk (*1-56276-272-9*, Ziff-Davis Pr) Que.

PC Learning Labs Teaches Microsoft Powerpoint/ Windows 95. Logical Operations Staff. LC 96-177808. 384p. 1995. 29.99 (*1-56276-330-X*, Ziff-Davis Pr) Que.

PC Learning Labs Teaches Microsoft Project 3.0 for Windows. PC Learning Labs Staff. (Illus.). 399p. (Orig.). 1993. pap. 22.95 incl. disk (*1-56276-124-2*, Ziff-Davis Pr) Que.

PC Learning Labs Teaches 1-2-3 5.0 for Windows. PC Learning Labs Staff. LC 95-114770. 352p. 1994. 22.95 incl. disk (*1-56276-295-8*, Ziff-Davis Pr) Que.

PC Learning Labs Teaches 1-2-3 Release 2.3. PC Learning Labs Staff. (Learning Labs Ser.). (Illus.). 307p. (Orig.). 1991. pap. 22.95 incl. disk (*1-56276-033-5*, Ziff-Davis Pr) Que.

PC Learning Labs Teaches OS-2 2.1. PC Learning Labs Staff. 320p. 1993. pap. 22.95 incl. disk (*1-56276-148-X*, Ziff-Davis Pr) Que.

PC Learning Labs Teaches PowerPoint for Windows. PC Learning Labs Staff. (Learning Labs Ser.). 464p. 1993. pap. 22.95 incl. disk (*1-56276-154-4*, Ziff-Davis Pr) Que.

PC Learning Labs Teaches Windows 95. 336p. 1995. pap. text 24.95 (*1-56276-266-4*, Ziff-Davis Pr) Que.

PC Learning Labs Teaches Word for Windows 2.0. PC Learning Labs Staff. (Learning Labs Ser.). (Illus.). 363p. (Orig.). 1992. pap. 22.95 incl. disk (*1-56276-065-3*, Ziff-Davis Pr) Que.

PC Learning Labs Teaches Word for Windows 95. LC 96-117758. 384p. 1995. pap. text 24.95 incl. disk (*1-56276-319-9*, Ziff-Davis Pr) Que.

PC Learning Labs Teaches Word 6.0 for Windows. PC Learning Labs Staff. (Learning Labs Ser.). 432p. 1993. pap. 22.95 incl. disk (*1-56276-139-0*, Ziff-Davis Pr) Que.

PC Learning Labs Teaches WordPro 95. Logical Operations Staff. 350p. 1995. pap. text 24.95 (*1-56276-358-X*, Ziff-Davis Pr) Que.

***PC, M. D. Hoe Political Correctness Is Corrupting Medicine.** Sally Satel. 2000. 27.00 (*0-465-07182-1*, Pub. by Basic) HarpC.

PC Magazine Assembly Language Lab Notes. Robert L. Hummel. (Lab Notes Ser.). (Illus.). 344p. (Orig.). 1992. pap. 29.95 incl. disk (*1-56276-059-9*, Ziff-Davis Pr) Que.

PC Magazine BASIC Lab Notes. Ethan Winer & Phil Cramer. (Lab Notes Ser.). (Illus.). 238p. (Orig.). 1992. pap. 29.95 incl. disk (*1-56276-068-8*, Ziff-Davis Pr) Que.

PC Magazine BASIC Techniques & Utilities. Ethan Winer. (Techniques & Utilities Ser.). (Illus.). 565p. (Orig.). 1991. pap. 29.95 incl. disk (*1-56276-008-4*, Ziff-Davis Pr) Que.

PC Magazine Buyer's Guide to PCs, Printers, & Monitors, 1992. John C. Dvorak. (Guide to...Ser.). 410p. (Orig.). 1991. pap. 19.95 (*1-56276-004-1*, Ziff-Davis Pr) Que.

PC Magazine C Lab Notes. Bob Flanders & Michael Holmes. (Lab Notes Ser.). 312p. (Orig.). 1992. pap. 29.95 incl. disk (*1-56276-063-7*, Ziff-Davis Pr) Que.

PC Magazine C++ Communication Utilities. Michael Holmes & Bob Flanders. 560p. 1993. pap. 29.95 incl. disk (*1-56276-110-2*, Ziff-Davis Pr) Que.

PC Magazine Delphi 32 Techniques & Utilities. ZDP Development Group Staff. 1996. pap. 39.99 incl. disk (*1-56276-400-4*, Ziff-Davis Pr) Que.

PC Magazine DOS Batch File Lab Notes. Neil J. Rubenking. (Lab Notes Ser.). 309p. 1992. pap. 29.95 incl. disk (*1-56276-067-X*, Ziff-Davis Pr) Que.

PC Magazine DOS 5 Memory Management with Utilities. Jeff Prosise. (Techniques & Utilities Ser.). (Illus.). 244p. (Orig.). 1992. pap. 34.95 incl. disk (*1-56276-050-5*, Ziff-Davis Pr) Que.

PC Magazine DOS 5 Techniques & Utilities. Jeff Prosise. (Techniques & Utilities Ser.). (Illus.). 1012p. (Orig.). 1991. pap. 39.95 incl. disk (*1-56276-007-6*, Ziff-Davis Pr) Que.

PC Magazine DOS 6 Techniques & Utilities. Jeff Prosise. 1072p. 1993. pap. 39.95 incl. disk (*1-56276-095-5*, Ziff-Davis Pr) Que.

PC Magazine Guide to Ami Pro 2.0 & 3.0. Gerry M. Litton. (Guide to...Ser.). (Illus.). 753p. (Orig.). 1992. pap. 24.95 (*1-56276-090-4*, Ziff-Davis Pr) Que.

PC Magazine Guide to Client - Server Databases. Joe Salemi. (Guide to...Ser.). (Illus.). 264p. (Orig.). 1992. pap. 39.95 (*1-56276-070-X*, Ziff-Davis Pr) Que.

PC Magazine Guide to Connectivity. 2nd ed. Frank J. Derfler, Jr. (Guide to...Ser.). (Illus.). 463p. 1992. pap. 39.95 incl. disk (*1-56276-047-5*, Ziff-Davis Pr) Que.

PC Magazine Guide to Connectivity: Intermediate Level. Frank J. Derfler, Jr. (Guide to...Ser.). 448p. (Orig.). 1991. pap. 39.95 incl. disk (*1-56276-001-7*, Ziff-Davis Pr) Que.

PC Magzine Guide to DOS 6 Memory Management with Utilities. Jeff Prosise. (Techniques & Utilities Ser.). 432p. 1993. pap. 29.95 incl. disk (*1-56276-097-1*, Ziff-Davis Pr) Que.

PC Magazine Guide to ISDN. Les Freed. 1996. pap. 34.99 (*1-56276-399-7*, Ziff-Davis Pr) Que.

PC Magazine Guide to Macromedia Backstage Studios. Ziff-Davis Press Staff. 1996. pap. text 39.99 incl. cd-rom (*1-56276-474-8*, Ziff-Davis Pr) Que.

PC Magazine Guide to Notebook & Laptop Computers. Bill Howard. (Guide to...Ser.). (Illus.). 416p. (Orig.). 1991. pap. 29.95 incl. disk (*1-56276-005-X*, Ziff-Davis Pr) Que.

PC Magazine Guide to 1-2-3 for Windows. Michael Lunsford. (Guide to...Ser.). 643p. (Orig.). 1991. pap. 27.95 (*1-56276-021-1*, Ziff-Davis Pr) Que.

PC Magazine Guide to 1-2-3 Release 2.3. Stephen Cobb. (Guide to...Ser.). (Illus.). 640p. (Orig.). 1991. pap. 27.95 (*1-56276-012-2*, Ziff-Davis Pr) Que.

PC Magazine Guide to Persuasion. Deborah Craig & Gerard Kunkel. (Guide to...Ser.). (Illus.). 582p. (Orig.). 1992. pap. 27.95 (*1-56276-015-7*, Ziff-Davis Pr) Que.

PC Magazine Guide to Professional Write Plus. Gerry M. Litton. (Guide to...Ser.). (Illus.). 422p. (Orig.). 1991. pap. 24.95 (*1-56276-027-0*, Ziff-Davis Pr) Que.

PC Magazine Guide to Quattro Pro for Windows. Leblond Group Staff. (Guide to...Ser.). (Illus.). 1221p. (Orig.). 1992. pap. 27.95 (*1-56276-044-0*, Ziff-Davis Pr) Que.

PC Magazine Guide to Turbo Pascal Techniques & Utilities. Neil J. Rubenking. (Techniques & Utilities Ser.). 892p. (Orig.). 1991. pap. 39.95 incl. disk (*1-56276-010-6*, Ziff-Davis Pr) Que.

PC Magazine Guide to Using NetWare. Les Freed & Frank J. Derfler, Jr. (Guide to...Ser.). (Illus.). 318p. (Orig.). 1991. pap. 39.95 incl. disk (*1-56276-022-X*, Ziff-Davis Pr) Que.

PC Magazine Guide to Using Quattro Pro 3.0. Leblond Group Staff. (Guide to...Ser.). (Illus.). 1040p. (Orig.). 1991. pap. 27.95 (*1-56276-003-3*, Ziff-Davis Pr) Que.

PC Magazine Guide to Using Quattro Pro 3.0 - 4.0. Leblond Group Staff. (Guide to...Ser.). 1064p. (Orig.). 1992. pap. 27.95 (*1-56276-071-8*, Ziff-Davis Pr) Que.

PC Magazine Guide to Using Word 2.0 for Windows. Edward Jones. (Guide to...Ser.). 432p. 1991. pap. 27.95 (*1-56276-030-0*, Ziff-Davis Pr) Que.

PC Magazine Guide to Windows for Workgroups. Frank Derfler, Jr. & Les Freed. (Guide to...Ser.). (Illus.). 219p. (Orig.). 1992. pap. 22.95 (*1-56276-120-X*, Ziff-Davis Pr) Que.

PC Magazine Guide to Windows 3.1. Gus Venditto. (Guide to...Ser.). (Illus.). 472p. (Orig.). 1992. pap. 27.95 (*1-56276-009-2*, Ziff-Davis Pr) Que.

PC Magazine Guide to WordPerfect for Windows. Karen L. Acerson. (Guide to...Ser.). (Illus.). 1021p. (Orig.). 1991. pap. 27.95 (*1-56276-013-0*, Ziff-Davis Pr) Que.

PC Magazine Netscape Navigator 2.0 Gold. Ziff-Davis Press Staff. 528p. 1996. pap. 39.99 (*1-56276-396-2*, Ziff-Davis Pr) Que.

PC Magazine 1995 Computer Buyer's Guide. rev. ed. Ed. by John C. Dvorak. (Buyer's Guide Ser.). 528p. (Orig.). 1994. pap. 19.95 (*1-56276-251-6*, Ziff-Davis Pr) Que.

PC Magazine 1996 Computer Buyer's Guide. John C. Dvorak. 1995. pap. text 19.95 (*1-56276-343-1*, Ziff-Davis Pr) Que.

PC Magazine Programmer's Technical Reference: The Processor & CoProcessor. Robert A. Hummel. (Technical Reference...Ser.). 761p. (Orig.). 1991. pap. 49.95 (*1-56276-016-5*, Ziff-Davis Pr) Que.

PC Magazine Programming Access 97. Miriam Liskin. 1190p. 1997. 49.99 (*1-56276-437-3*, Ziff-Davis Pr) Que.

PC Magazine Programming FoxPro for Windows. Miriam Liskin. pap. 39.95 (*1-56276-173-0*, Ziff-Davis Pr) Que.

PC Magazine Programming FoxPro 2.0. Miriam Liskin. (Programming Ser.). (Illus.). 1516p. (Orig.). 1992. pap. 39.95 incl. disk (*1-56276-038-6*, Ziff-Davis Pr) Que.

PC Magazine Programming Visual BASIC. Ted Young. 400p. 1999. pap. text 39.99 incl. cd-rom (*1-56276-424-1*, Ziff-Davis Pr) Que.

PC Magazine Programming VRML. Clay Graham. 1996. pap. 59.99 incl. cd-rom (*1-56276-380-6*, Ziff-Davis Pr) Que.

PC Magazine Programming Windows with Borland C++ William Roetzheim. (Illus.). 464p. (Orig.). 1992. pap. 39.95 incl. disk (*1-56276-040-8*, Ziff-Davis Pr) Que.

PC Magazine Take Word for Windows to the Edge. Guy Gallo. (Customizing Ser.). (Illus.). 470p. (Orig.). 1992. pap. 29.95 incl. disk (*1-56276-079-3*, Ziff-Davis Pr) Que.

PC Magazine Turbo Pascal 6.0 for Windows Techniques & Utilities. Neil J. Rubenking. (Techniques & Utilities Ser.). (Illus.). 1100p. (Orig.). 1992. pap. 39.95 incl. disk (*1-56276-035-1*, Ziff-Davis Pr) Que.

PC Magazine Visual Basic Programmers Guide to Windows API. Dan Appleman. (Programming Ser.). 1056p. 1993. pap. 34.95 incl. disk (*1-56276-073-4*, Ziff-Davis Pr) Que.

PC Magazine Visual BASIC Utilities. Paul Bonner. (Techniques & Utilities Ser.). 480p. 1993. pap. 29.95 incl. disk (*1-56276-106-4*, Ziff-Davis Pr) Que.

PC Magazine Webmaster's Ultimate Resource Guide. Robert McDaniel et al. LC 97-159624. 576p. 1996. 34.99 (*1-56276-435-7*, Ziff-Davis Pr) Que.

PC Magazine Windows Rapid Application Development. David Sarna & George F. Febish. 480p. 1992. pap. 39.95 incl. disk (*1-56276-088-2*, Ziff-Davis Pr) Que.

PC Magazine Windows 3.1 Graphics Programming. Ben R. Ezzell. (Programming Ser.). (Illus.). 480p. (Orig.). 1992. pap. 34.95 incl. disk (*1-56276-055-6*, Ziff-Davis Pr) Que.

PC Magazine's 1997 Computer Buyer's Guide. Sally Neuman. 544p. 1996. 24.99 (*1-56276-434-9*, Ziff-Davis Pr) Que.

PC Maintenance: An Introduction to Upgrade & Repair. Colin Grimston. 213p. 1997. pap. text 21.95 (*0-340-64545-8*, Pub. by E A) OUP.

PC Maintenance & Repair. Adamson. 1997. pap., wbk. ed. 7.00 (*0-8064-1318-2*, E40) Bergwall.

PC Management: A How-to-Do-It Manual for Librarians. Michael Schuyler & Jake Hoffman. (How-to-Do-It Ser.). 180p. 1990. pap. text 45.00 (*1-55570-076-4*) Neal-Schuman.

PC-mom: The Mother of All PC Books. Woody Leonhard & Barry Simon. 784p. 1994. pap. 49.95 (*0-201-40681-0*) Addison-Wesley.

PC-MS-DOS Quick Reference Guide with Template. 1989. pap. 24.95 (*0-913365-54-8*) Microref Educ Systs.

PC, MS-DOS Version 2-5 Quick Reference Guide with Template. 24.95 (*1-56351-036-7*, S163) Microref Educ Systs.

PC Music Handbook. 2nd ed. Brian Heywood & Roger Evan. (Illus.). 192p. 1995. pap. 15.95 (*1-870775-42-2*) Cimino Pub Grp.

PC Music-The Easy Guide. Robin Vincent. 1999. pap. text 15.95 (*1-878427-72-5*) Cimino Pub Grp.

***PC Netlink Server Software: Performance, Scalability & Deployment.** Prentice-Hall Staff & Don Devitt. (Official Sun Microsystems Resource Ser.). 478p. 2000. pap. text 45.00 (*0-13-026686-8*) P-H.

PC Network Administration. Andres Fortino & Peter Rybaczyk. LC 95-22073. (Illus.). 416p. 1995. text 44.95 (*0-07-912110-1*) McGraw.

PC Networking for the Systems Programmer. Stanley Schatt. LC 91-47969. 224p. 1992. pap. 34.95 (*0-471-55268-2*) Wiley.

PC Networking Handbook. Ed Tittel. LC 95-20918. (Illus.). 857p. 1995. pap. text 42.00 (*0-12-691398-6*) Morgan Kaufmann.

PC 98 System Design Guide. Microsoft Corporation Staff et al. LC 97-37612. 672p. 29.99 (*1-57231-716-7*) Microsoft.

PC Nomad. Wojkowski. (C). 1994. text. write for info. (*0-318-70369-6*) S-W Pub.

PC Operations with MS-DOS 6.0: Student Guide. (Illus.). ii, 88p. 1994. student ed., spiral bd., wbk. ed. 15.95 (*0-7402-0267-7*, MSOPD601WB) Accelerated Comput Train.

PC Pagemaker: A Comprehensive User's Manual. Bud E. Smith. 1987. pap. 19.95 (*0-8306-2911-4*) McGraw-Hill Prof.

PC para Dummies. Goodwin. (For Dummies Ser.). 1997. pap. text 37.95 (*84-283-2381-X*) IBD Ltd.

PC Patrol Craft of World War II: A History of the Ships & Their Crews. William J. Veigele. LC 97-78091. (Illus.). 400p. 1998. 39.95 (*0-9645867-1-1*) Astral Pub.

***PC Ph.D.** Myke Predko. LC 99-35904. 960p. 1999. pap. text 59.95 incl. audio compact disk (*0-07-134186-2*) McGraw.

PC Photography Book. 2nd ed. Heinz Von Buelow & Dirk Paulissen. LC 97-129846. (Illus.). 420p. (Orig.). 1996. pap. 34.95 incl. cd-rom (*1-55755-293-2*) Abacus MI.

PC Policies & Procedures Handiguide. M. Victor Janulaitis. LC 97-104173. (PC Handiguide Ser.). 296p. (Orig.). 1995. pap. 395.00 (*1-881218-23-6*) Pos Support Rev.

PC pour les Nuls. 3rd ed. Dan Gookin. (FRE.). 304p. 1995. 49.95 (*0-7859-9851-9*) Fr & Eur.

PC Principles. Gunnar Forst. 400p. 1990. 60.00 (*0-262-06134-1*) MIT Pr.

PC Printers Pocket Book. Stephen Morris. LC 92-166290. 336p. 1992. pap. 104.20 (*0-608-04991-3*, 206560900004) Bks Demand.

PC Programming Techniques: Creative BASIC Skills for IBM Personal Computers. Alan C. Elliott. (Illus.). 176p. 1984. pap. 14.95 (*0-89303-755-9*) P-H.

PC Projects for Human Resource Management. 2nd ed. Nicholas J. Beutell. Ed. by Fenton. 300p. (C). 1993. pap. text 28.75 incl. audio (*0-314-01250-8*) West Pub.

PC Projects for Human Resource Management. 3rd ed. Nicholas J. Beutell. LC 96-128897. 270p. 1996. pap. 41.95 (*0-314-07135-0*) West Pub.

PC Record Book. Diane L. Simison. (Orig.). 1991. pap. write for info. (*0-9628602-0-4*, Inquiry Bks) Simison-Parada.

PC Scheme: Users Guide & Language Reference Manual. 3rd ed. Texas Instruments, Inc. Staff et al. 1990. pap. text 47.50 (*0-262-70040-9*) MIT Pr.

PC Secrets. Caroline M. Halliday. (InfoWorld Technical Bks.). 800p. 1992. disk 39.95 (*1-878058-49-5*) IDG Bks.

PC Security & Virus Protection Handbook: The Ongoing War Against Information Sabotage. Pamela Kane. LC 94-14134. 1994. pap. 39.95 incl. disk (*1-55851-390-6*, M&T Bks) IDG Bks.

PC Security Guide, 1993-94. T. Monk. viii, 213p. 1992. 325.00 (*1-85617-127-2*, Pub. by Elsvr Adv Tech) Elsevier.

***PC Spartan Plus Tutorial Version 2.0.** Warren J. Hehre et al. (Illus.). 98p. 1999. pap. text 20.00 (*1-890661-11-2*) Wavefunction.

***PC Spartan Plus User's Guide Version 2.0.** (Illus.). 85p. 1999. pap. text 35.00 (*1-890661-12-0*) Wavefunction.

PC Spartan Pro Tutorial. Warren J. Hehre et al. (Illus.). 128p. 1999. pap. text 20.00 (*1-890661-08-2*) Wavefunction.

PC Spartan Pro User's Guide. (Illus.). 112p. 1999. pap. text 35.00 (*1-890661-09-0*) Wavefunction.

***PC Study Bible: Complete Reference Library.** 1999. pap. 349.95 (*1-56514-043-5*) Biblesoft.

PC-SYNC Release 88. Barr Systems, Inc. Staff. 84p. (Orig.). 1988. pap. text 10.00 (*0-938835-12-2*) Barr Syst Inc.

PC Technical Source-Book, 1988. Chuck Philyaw & David Lippincott. Ed. by Marty Kleine. (Illus.). 95p. 1996. pap. 9.95 (*1-882069-54-4*) Industrial Computer Source.

PC Technician Training Guide see Guia de Entrenamiento del Tecnico de Computadoras

***PC Technician Training Guide, Vol. I.** 2nd rev. ed. Richard Harrison. Ed. by Susan Schmidt. 1998. pap. text. write for info. (*0-9663920-9-4*) Specialized Solns.

***PC Technician Training Guide, Vol. I.** 3rd ed. Richard Harrison. Ed. by Susan Schmidt. (Illus.). 390p. 1999. pap. text. write for info. (*1-893596-04-4*) Specialized Solns.

PC Technician Training Guide, Vol. II. Richard Harrison. Ed. by Susan Schmidt. 243p. 1998. pap. text 69.00 (*0-9663920-1-9*, 88249-N) Specialized Solns.

PC Technician Training Guide, Vol. II. 2nd rev. ed. Richard Harrison. Ed. by Susan Schmidt. (Illus.). 289p. 1998. pap. text 69.00 (*0-9663920-0-0*, 88243-N) Specialized Solns.

***PC Technician Training Guide, Vol. II.** 3rd rev. ed. Richard Harrison. Ed. by Susan Schmidt. (Illus.). 267p. 1999. pap. text. write for info. (*1-893596-05-2*) Specialized Solns.

PC Technologies. 1997. write for info. (*1-884486-25-8*) Wave Tech.

PC Telephony: How to Design, Build & Program Systems Using Industry-Standard Dialogic Hardware. 3rd ed. Bob Edgar. Date not set. 34.95 (*0-936648-71-6*) Telecom Bks.

***PC Telephony: The Complete Guide to Designing, Building, & Programming Systems.** 5th ed. Bob Edgar. 800p. 1999. pap. 39.95 (*1-57820-033-4*) Telecom Bks.

PC Telephony: The Complete Guide to Designing, Building & Programming Systems Using Dialogic Related Hardware. 4th ed. Bob Edgar. 776p. 1997. per. 34.95 (*1-57820-017-2*) Telecom Bks.

PC Tools Deluxe. Jonathan Kamin. 1990. pap. text 19.95 (*0-201-55036-9*) Addison-Wesley.

PC Tools 8 Quick Reference. David Wolfe. (Illus.). 182p. (Orig.). 1992. 9.99 (*1-56529-148-4*) Que.

PC Troubleshooting Pocket Book. Michael H. Tooley. (Pocket Bks.). (Illus.). 266p. 1994. 29.95 (*0-7506-1727-6*) Buttrwrth-Heinemann.

PC Upgrade & Repair: Simplified. Ruth Maran. LC 98-72810. (3-D Visual Ser.). (Illus.). 240p. 1998. pap. 24.99 (*0-7645-6049-2*) IDG Bks.

***PC Upgrade & Repair Bible** 3rd ed. Barry Press & Marcia Press. LC 99-38351. 1450p. 1999. 49.99 (*0-7645-3357-6*) IDG Bks.

PC Upgrade & Repair Bible, Professional Edition. Barry Press. LC 97-76687. 1400p. 1998. pap. 49.99 (*0-7645-3148-4*) IDG Bks.

PC Upgrading & Maintenance. 2nd ed. Computing Smart Staff. LC 98-83176. (No Experience Required Ser.). (Illus.). 704p. 1999. pap. 24.99 (*0-7821-2471-2*) Sybex.

PC User's Essential Accesible Pocket Dictionary. 2nd ed. Peter Dyson. LC 95-69363. 656p. 1995. 14.99 (*0-7821-1684-1*) Sybex.

PC User's Guide: Simple Steps to Powerful Personal Computing. Peter Turner. (IBM Ser.). 288p. 1993. pap. 19.95 (*0-07-707421-1*) McGraw.

PC Video Book: Putting Digital Video into Action. Kerstin Eisenkolb. 1994. pap. 34.95 incl. cd-rom (*1-55755-265-7*) Abacus MI.

PC Viruses: Detection, Analysis & Cure. A. Solomon. 304p. 1991. 62.04 (*0-387-19691-9*) Spr-Verlag.

PC Wars: Politics & Correctness in the Academy. Ed. by Jeffrey Williams. 288p. (C). 1994. pap. 25.99 (*0-415-91073-0*, B4479) Routledge.

PC Week: The Internet Advantage. Lauren Paul. LC 98-160796. 416p. 1996. pap. text 34.99 (*1-56276-427-6*, Ziff-Davis Pr) Que.

PC Week Guide to Lotus Notes & Domino. Eric Mann et al. 1997. pap. 49.99 (*0-614-28489-9*, Ziff-Davis Pr) Que.

PC Week Guide to Lotus Notes Release 4. John Helliwell. LC 96-202856. 1008p. 1996. pap. 39.99 (*1-56276-378-4*, Ziff-Davis Pr) Que.

PC Week How to Implement Netscape Livewire Pro. Amy Johnson. LC 98-159769. 384p. 1997. pap. text 39.99 (*1-56276-458-6*, Ziff-Davis Pr) Que.

PC Week Microsoft Windows NT Security: System Administrator's Guide. Nevin Lambert & Manish Patel. 416p. 1997. 39.99 (*1-56276-457-8*, Ziff-Davis Pr) Que.

PC Week Network Buyer's Guide. Strategic Resource Systems Staff. LC 98-159778. 736p. 1996. 49.99 (*1-56276-438-1*, Ziff-Davis Pr) Que.

PC Week Programming Perl 5.0 Web Pages. Ziff Development Staff. LC 96-215439. 416p. 1996. pap. text 34.99 incl. cd-rom (*1-56276-420-9*, Ziff-Davis Pr) Que.

PC-Woerterbuch English. Langenscheidt Staff. (ENG & GER.). 495p. 1994. write for info. (*0-614-00362-8*, 3468909128); write for info. (*0-614-00363-6*, 3468909128) Fr & Eur.

PC-Woerterbuch Franzoesich. Langenscheidt Staff. (FRE & GER.). 495p. 1994. 150.00 (*0-614-00361-X*, 3468909187) Fr & Eur.

PC World DOS 5 Complete Handbook. John Socha. LC 91-75701. 588p. 1991. 34.95 (*1-878058-13-4*) IDG Bks.

PC World DOS 6 Command Reference & Problem Solver. John Socha & Devra Hall. 500p. 1993. pap. 24.95 (*1-56884-055-1*) IDG Bks.

PC World Excel 5 for Windows Handbook. 2nd ed. John Walkenbach & David Maguiness. 900p. 1994. pap. 34.95 (*1-56884-056-X*) IDG Bks.

PC World Excel 4 for Windows Handbook. John Walkenbach & David Maguiness. 719p. 1992. 29.95 (*1-878058-46-0*) IDG Bks.

PC World Microsoft Access Bible. Michael Irwin & Cary N. Prague. 1324p. 1993. pap. 39.95 (*1-878058-81-9*) IDG Bks.

PC World 1-2-3 for Windows Complete Handbook. Phillip R. Robinson & John Walkenbach. LC 91-75964. 680p. 1991. pap. 29.95 (*1-878058-21-5*) IDG Bks.

PC World Paradox 3.5 Power Programming Techniques. Gregory B. Salcedo. 754p. 1990. pap. 39.95 (*1-878058-02-9*) IDG Bks.

PC World Q & A Bible, Version 4. Tom Marcellus. LC 90-84495. 888p. 1991. pap. 39.95 (*1-878058-03-7*) IDG Bks.

PC World Word for Windows 6 Handbook. Brent Heslop et al. LC 93-61311. 900p. 1994. pap. 34.95 (*1-56884-054-3*) IDG Bks.

PC World Wordperfect for Windows DOS to Windows Users Guide. Greg Harvey. LC 91-77471. 340p. 1991. pap. 19.95 (*1-878058-44-4*) IDG Bks.

PC World You Can Do It with DOS. Gordon McComb & Christopher Van Buren. (You Can Do It Ser.). 214p. 1992. 19.95 (*1-878058-38-X*) IDG Bks.

PC World You Can Do It with Windows. Christopher Van Buren. (You Can Do It Ser.). 274p. 1992. 19.95 (*1-878058-37-1*) IDG Bks.

PC Write for Students. 2nd ed. John N. Rogers. LC 90-42093. 64p. (Orig.). 1991. pap. 5.00 (*0-914061-19-4*) Orchises Pr.

PC Write-Lite. 11th ed. Elizabeth Houser & Bob Wallace. 192p. (C). 1990. 43.50 incl. disk (*0-15-531879-9*); pap. text 43.50 incl. disk (*0-15-531880-2*) Harcourt Coll Pubs.

PC-XT-AT Lexikon. 2nd ed. Wolfgang Wienicke. (GER.). 541p. 1991. 85.00 (*0-7859-8464-X*, 3772355137) Fr & Eur.

PC-XT-AT-386 Hardware Reference: Concise Explanations of Hardware Elements, with Illustrations. S. Roberts. (Info Compact Ser.). (Illus.). 100p. (C). 1991. pap. 5.00 (*0-911827-07-2*) Elcomp.

PC-XT-AT-386 Technical Pocket Reference for IBM-PC & Compatibles Pt. 2: Important Information, Tables, Technical Data, 2. S. Roberts. (Info Compact Ser.). (Illus.). 100p. (C). 1991. pap. 5.00 (*0-911827-08-0*) Elcomp.

PC 99 System Design Guide. Intel Corporation Staff & Microsoft Corporation Staff. LC 98-44330. 520p. 1998. pap. 49.99 (*0-7356-0518-1*) Microsoft.

PCA Polity: Documents Illustrative of Historic Presbyterian Church Government. Robert C. Cannada & W. Jack Williamson. 1997. 29.50 (*1-884416-19-5*) A Press.

PCA Soil Primer. rev. ed. 40p. 1992. reprint ed. pap. 14.00 (*0-89312-105-3*, EB007S) Portland Cement.

***PCAT: Pharmacy College Admission Test.** 1999. pap. text 19.95 (*0-02-863699-6*) S&S Trade.

PCAT: Pharmacy College Admission Test. 3rd ed. D. B. Gourley. (Illus.). 176p. 1997. pap. 19.95 (*0-02-861706-1*, Arc) IDG Bks.

PCAT - Pharmacy College Admission Test: Comprehensive Review for Self Study. David M. Tarlow. 145p. (C). 1999. pap. text 19.95 (*1-57732-111-1*) Datar Pub.

PCAT - Pharmacy College Admission Test No. 1: Practice Exam Annotated Answers. 2nd rev. ed. David M. Tarlow. 20p. (C). 1999. pap. text 6.95 (*1-57732-113-8*) Datar Pub.

PCAT - Pharmacy College Admission Test No. 2: Practice Exam Annotated Answers. 2nd rev. ed. David M. Tarlow. (C). 1999. pap. text 6.95 (*1-57732-115-4*) Datar Pub.

PCAT - Pharmacy College Admission Test No. 2: Practice Examination. 2nd rev. ed. David M. Tarlow. 40p. (C). 1999. pap. text 18.95 (*1-57732-114-6*) Datar Pub.

PCAT - Pharmacy College Admission Test No. 3: Practice Exam Annotated Answers. 2nd rev. ed. David M. Tarlow. 20p. (C). 1999. pap. text 6.95 (*1-57732-117-0*) Datar Pub.

PCAT - Pharmacy College Admission Test No. 3: Practice Examination. 2nd rev. ed. David M. Tarlow. 40p. (C). 1999. pap. text 18.95 (*1-57732-116-2*) Datar Pub.

PCAT - Pharmacy College Admission Test No. 4: Practice Exam Annotated Answers. 2nd rev. ed. David M. Tarlow. 20p. (C). 1999. pap. text 6.95 (*1-57732-119-7*) Datar Pub.

PCAT - Pharmacy College Admission Test No. 4: Practice Examination. 2nd rev. ed. David M. Tarlow. 40p. (C). 1999. pap. text 18.95 (*1-57732-118-9*) Datar Pub.

PCAT - Pharmacy College Admission Test No. 5: Practice Exam Annotated Answers. 2nd rev. ed. David M. Tarlow. 20p. (C). 1999. pap. text 6.95 (*1-57732-121-9*) Datar Pub.

PCAT - Pharmacy College Admission Test No. 5: Practice Examination. 2nd rev. ed. David M. Tarlow. 40p. (C). 1999. pap. text 18.95 (*1-57732-120-0*) Datar Pub.

PCAT - Pharmacy College Admission Test Vol. I: Practice Examination. 2nd rev. ed. David M. Tarlow. 40p. (C). 1999. pap. text 18.95 (*1-57732-112-X*) Datar Pub.

PCAT - Pharmacy College Admission Test - Core Content. 2nd rev. ed. David M. Tarlow. (Illus.). 400p. 1999. pap. 49.95 (*1-57774-008-4*) Educ Tsting Cnslts.

***PCAT- Pharmacy College Admission Test.** 4th ed. D. R. Gourley. 230p. 2000. pap. 19.95 (*0-7645-6100-6*) IDG Bks.

PCAT Exam No. 1: Annotated Answers (Pharmacy College Admission Test) 7th ed. David M. Tarlow. (Orig.). 1996. pap. 5.95 (*1-57732-039-5*) Datar Pub.

PCAT Exam No. 1: Pharmacy College Admissions Test. 7th ed. David M. Tarlow. (Illus.). (Orig.). 1996. pap. 19.95 (*1-57732-034-4*) Datar Pub.

PCAT Exam No. 2: Annotated Answers (Pharmacy College Admissions Test) 7th ed. David M. Tarlow. (Orig.). 1996. pap. 5.95 (*1-57732-040-9*) Datar Pub.

PCAT Exam No. 2: Pharmacy College Admission Test. 7th ed. David M. Tarlow. (Orig.). 1996. pap. 19.95 (*1-57732-035-2*) Datar Pub.

PCAT Exam No. 3: Annotated Answers (Pharmacy College Admissions Test) 7th ed. David M. Tarlow. (Orig.). 1996. pap. 5.95 (*1-57732-041-7*) Datar Pub.

PCAT Exam No. 3: Pharmacy College Admission Test. 7th ed. David M. Tarlow. (Illus.). (Orig.). 1996. pap. 19.95 (*1-57732-036-0*) Datar Pub.

PCAT Exam No. 4: Annotated Answers (Pharmacy College Admission Test) 7th ed. David M. Tarlow. 1996. pap. 5.95 (*1-57732-042-5*) Datar Pub.

PCAT Exam No. 4: Pharmacy College Admission Test. 7th ed. David M. Tarlow. (Illus.). (Orig.). 1996. pap. 19.95 (*1-57732-037-9*) Datar Pub.

PCAT Exam No. 5: Annotated Answers (Pharmacy College Admission Test) 7th ed. David M. Tarlow. (Illus.). 1996. pap. 5.95 (*1-57732-043-3*) Datar Pub.

PCAT Exam No. 5: Pharmacy College Admission Test. 7th ed. David M. Tarlow. (Illus.). (Orig.). 1996. pap. 19.95 (*1-57732-038-7*) Datar Pub.

PCAT (Pharmacy College Admission Test) Practice Examination, No. 1. David M. Tarlow. (Practice Examination Ser.). 40p. 1992. pap. 16.95 (*0-931572-22-3*) Datar Pub.

PCAT (Pharmacy College Admission Test) Practice Examination, No. 2. David M. Tarlow. (Practice Examination Ser.). 40p. 1992. pap. 16.95 (*0-931572-23-1*) Datar Pub.

PCAT (Pharmacy College Admission Test) Practice Examination, No. 3. David M. Tarlow. (Practice Examination Ser.). 40p. 1992. pap. 16.95 (*0-931572-24-X*) Datar Pub.

PCAT (Pharmacy College Admission Test) Practice Examination, No. 4. David M. Tarlow. (Practice Examination Ser.). 40p. 1992. pap. 16.95 (*0-931572-25-8*) Datar Pub.

PCAT (Pharmacy College Admission Test) Practice Examination, No. 5. David M. Tarlow. (Practice Examination Ser.). 40p. 1992. pap. 16.95 (*0-931572-26-6*) Datar Pub.

PCAT (Pharmacy College Admissions Test) For Comprehensive Review. 7th ed. David M. Tarlow. (Illus.). (Orig.). 1996. pap., student ed. 19.95 (*1-57732-033-6*) Datar Pub.

PCAT Practice Examination: Annotated Master Answer Guide, No. 2. David M. Tarlow. 1992. 4.95 (*0-931572-48-7*) Datar Pub.

PCAT Practice Examination: Annotated Master Answer Guide, No. 3. David M. Tarlow. 1992. 4.95 (*0-931572-49-5*) Datar Pub.

PCAT Practice Examination: Annotated Master Answer Guide, No. 4. David M. Tarlow. 1992. 4.95 (*0-931572-50-9*) Datar Pub.

PCAT Practice Examination: Annotated Master Answer Guide, No. 5. David M. Tarlow. 1992. 4.95 (*0-931572-51-7*) Datar Pub.

PCB Assembly Systems, 1989. Ed. by T. Leicht et al. (Illus.). 200p. 1989. 135.95 (*0-387-50938-0*) Spr-Verlag.

PCB Compliance Guide for Electrical Equipment. John W. Coryell & Jack E. Cearley. LC 92-657320. 234p. reprint ed. pap. 72.60 (*0-7837-6796-X*, 204662800003) Bks Demand.

***PCB Design Techniques for EMC Compliance.** 2nd ed. Mark I. Montrose. (Series on Electronics Technology). 336p. 2000. 79.95 (*0-7803-5376-5*) Inst Electrical.

PCB Design Using AutoCAD. Chris Schroeder. LC 97-22001. 336p. 1997. pap. text 44.95 (*0-7506-9834-9*) Buttrwrth-Heinemann.

PCB Management Handbook. John P. Woodyard & James J. King. 1992. pap. 49.95 (*0-7816-0047-2*) Exec Ent Pubns.

PCB Mounted Thermal Management Component Markets. Market Intelligence Staff. 1993. 1750.00 (*1-56753-476-7*) Frost & Sullivan.

PCB Preproduction Tooling: Preproduction Automation & Intelligent Tooling for Printed Circuit Board Manufacturing. Ed. by Laura Scholten. (Illus.). 240p. (Orig.). 1994. pap. 49.00 (*0-87930-339-5*) Miller Freeman.

PCB Reference Manual: Operation & Management of Electrical Equipment Containing PCBs. LC 93-41863. 1993. write for info. (*0-917599-14-4*) Natl Rural.

PCBs. Richard K. Miller & Marcia E. Rupnow. LC 90-83852. (Survey on Technology & Markets Ser.: No. 147). 50p. 1991. pap. text 200.00 (*1-55865-172-1*) Future Tech Surveys.

PCBs, a Case Study: Proceedings of a Workshop on Great Lakes Research Coordination, Held at the Holiday Inn, Windsor, Ontario, November 20-22, 1985 - Report to the Great Lakes Research Managers. fac. ed. Workshop on Great Lakes Research Coordination Staf. LC 89-130762. (Illus.). 129p. 1985. pap. 40.00 (*0-7837-7720-5*, 207523200007) Bks Demand.

PCBs & Environment. John S. Waid. LC 86-17549. 240p. 1987. reprint ed. 137.00 (*0-8493-5923-6*, CRC Reprint) Franklin.

PCBs & the Environment, 3 vols. John S. Waid. 256p. 1986. 489.95 (*0-8493-5929-5*, SB608) CRC Pr.

PCBs & the Environment, 3 vols. set, Vol. 2. John S. Waid. 240p. 1987. 200.00 (*0-8493-5924-4*) CRC Pr.

PCBs & the Environment: Analytical Chemistry of PCBs, 3 vols., Vol. 1. John S. Waid. 240p. 1987. 415.00 (*0-685-18753-5*, CRC Reprint) Franklin.

PCBs & the Environment: Differences Between Yusho & Other Kinds of Poisoning Involving Only PCBs, 3 vols. Ed. by John S. Waid. 304p. 1987. 415.00 (*0-317-61078-3*, CRC Reprint) Franklin.

PCBs & the Environment: Polychlorinated Biphenyls: Accumulation & Effects upon Plants, 3 vols., Vol. II. Ed. by John S. Waid. 200p. 1987. 415.00 (*0-317-61073-2*, CRC Reprint) Franklin.

***PCC's 1041 Deskbook, 2 vols.** Hugh H. Sprunt et al. 1999. ring bd. 150.00 (*0-7646-0785-5*) Prctnrs Pub Co.

PCDex: Magazine Resource Guide for Commodore 64, VIC-20 & PET-CBM Personal Computers. Ed. by Alan M. Smith. 216p. (Orig.). 1984. pap. 14.95 (*0-918391-00-8*) Altacom.

PCF1: Palliative Care Formulary. Robert Twycross et al. 254p. 1998. pap. 36.75 (*1-85775-264-3*, Radcliffe Med Pr) Scovill Paterson.

PCI Architectural Precast Concrete. (Illus.). 352p. write for info. (*0-937040-01-0*, MNL-122-89) P-PCI.

***PCI Bus Demystified.** Doug Abbott. (Demystified Ser.). 312p. 2000. pap. 49.95 (*1-878707-54-X*, Pub. by LLH Tech Pub) IPG Chicago.

PCI Design for Fire Resistance of Precast Prestressed Concrete. 88p. pap. 20.00 (*0-937040-08-8*, MNL-124-89) P-PCI.

***PCI Design Handbook: Precast & Prestressed Concrete.** 5th ed. Precast/Prestressed Concrete Institute. LC 99-233856. (Illus.). 1999. write for info. (*0-937040-60-6*) P-PCI.

PCI Handbook: For Hardware & Software Engineers. Brian Dipert. (Illus.). 96p. 1997. mass mkt. 14.95 (*0-929392-25-6*) Annabooks.

PCI Hardware & Software: Architecture & Design. 4th rev. ed. Edward Solari & George Willse. (Illus.). 884p. 1998. 97.95 (*0-929392-59-0*, PCI929-4) Annabooks.

PCI Hot-Plug: Application & Design. Alan Goodrum. (Illus.). 184p. 1998. pap. 34.95 (*0-929392-60-4*, PHP929) Annabooks.

PCI Journal 25 Year Index, 1956-1981. 224p. 30.00 (*0-937040-21-5*, JR-1-82) P-PCI.

PCI Manual for the Design of Hollow-Core Slabs. PCI Staff. 120p. 1985. 60.00 (*0-937040-25-8*) P-PCI.

PCI Membership Directory, 1988. 148p. pap. 150.00 (*0-937040-13-4*, SP-M) P-PCI.

PCI Power Management. George Willse. Ed. by Edward Solari. (Illus.). 240p. 2000. pap. 39.95 (*0-929392-62-0*, PPM929) Annabooks.

PCI Safety & Loss Prevention Manual. (Illus.). 310p. ring bd. 120.00 (*0-937040-03-7*, SLP-100-73) P-PCI.

PCI System Architecture. Tom Shanley. (Architecture Ser.). 250p. 1993. pap. 29.95 (*1-881609-06-5*) Mindshare Pr.

***PCI System Architecture.** 4th ed. Mindshare Inc. Staff. LC 99-32447. 832p. (C). 1999. pap. text 39.95 (*0-201-30974-2*) Addison-Wesley.

PCjr Assembly Programming: A Gentle Introduction. Richard L. Taylor. (Illus.). 256p. 1985. 14.95 (*0-13-655028-2*) P-H.

PCMCIA Developer's Guide. 2nd ed. Michael T. Mori & W. Dean Welder. LC 94-93969. (Illus.). 618p. (C). 1995. pap. 89.95 (*0-9640342-1-2*) Sycard Tech.

PCMCIA Developer's Guide. 3rd ed. Michael T. Mori & W. Dean Welder. (Illus.). 710p. 1999. pap. 89.95 (*0-9640342-2-0*) Sycard Tech.

PCMCIA Primer. Larry Levine. LC 95-24177. 89p. 1995. pap. 24.95 (*1-55828-437-0*, MIS Pr) IDG Bks.

PCMCIA System Architecture. 2nd ed. Don Anderson. (PC System Architecture Ser.). 464p. (Orig.). (C). 1995. pap. text 34.95 (*0-201-40991-7*) Addison-Wesley.

PCMCIA Technology: Impressive Growth Through 2000. Fayreau. LC 96-120786. 156p. 1995. 2650.00 (*1-56965-066-7*, G-152) BCC.

PCMR 16th Annual Report to the President: Citizen With Mental Retardation--Equality Under the Law. 53p. 1987. write for info. (*1-55672-026-2*) US HHS.

PCNs of the Coast Ranger of California: Religious Expressions on the Result of Quarring? Donna L. Gillette. (Illus.). 155p. (C). 1998. pap. text 16.88 (*1-55567-686-3*) Coyote Press.

***PCOS: A Woman's Guide to Dealing with Polycystic Ovary Syndrome.** Colette Harris. 2000. pap. 16.00 (*0-7225-3975-4*) Thorsons PA.

***PCOS: The Silent Epidemic.** Samuel S. Thatcher. LC 00-37316. 2000. pap. write for info. (*0-944934-27-7*) Perspect Indiana.

***PCOS (Polycystic Ovarian Syndrome) The Hidden Epidemic.** Samuel Thatcher. (Illus.). 250p. 2000. 24.95 (*0-944934-25-0*) Perspect Indiana.

PCP. Gerald Newman & Eleanor N. Layfield. LC 97-484. (Drug Library Ser.). (Illus.). 128p. (YA). (gr. 6 up). 1997. lib. bdg. 20.95 (*0-89490-852-9*) Enslow Pubs.

PCP: High Risk on the Streets. Jennifer Croft. LC 98-13882. (Drug Abuse Prevention Library). (Illus.). 64p. (J). (gr. 7-12). 1998. lib. bdg. 16.95 (*0-8239-2774-1*) Rosen Group.

PCP: The Dangerous Angel. Marilyn Carroll. (Encyclopedia of Psychoactive Drugs Ser.: No. 1). (Illus.). 124p. (YA). (gr. 7 up). 1985. lib. bdg. 19.95 (*0-87754-753-X*) Chelsea Hse.

PCP (Phencyclidine) Historical & Current Perspectives. Ed. by E. F. Domino. LC 80-81498. (Illus.). 537p. 1981. 50.00 (*0-916182-03-7*) NPP Bks.

PCP, Phencyclidine, "Angel Dust" Brent Q. Hafen & Kathryn J. Frandsen. 21p. 1988. 2.00 (*0-89486-074-7*, 1942B) Hazelden.

PCP's Guide to Occupational/Environmental Medicine. Hodgson. (Illus.). 550p. 1999. text. write for info. (*1-55664-467-1*) Mosby Inc.

***PCR.** M. J. McPherson & S. Moller. Ed. by R. J. Beynon & C. D. Howe. (Basics Ser.). 120p. 2000. pap. text (*0-387-91600-8*) Spr-Verlag.

PCR. 2nd ed. C. R. Newton & A. Graham. LC 97-6925. (Introduction to Biotechniques Ser.). 208p. 1997. pap. 34.95 (*0-387-91506-0*) Spr-Verlag.

PCR: A Practical Approach. Ed. by M. J. McPherson et al. (Practical Approach Ser.). (Illus.). 274p. 1991. pap. text 55.00 (*0-19-963196-4*) OUP.

PCR: Clinical Diagnostics & Research. Ed. by A. Rolfs et al. (Laboratory Ser.). (Illus.). 280p. 1992. 59.00 (*0-387-55440-8*) Spr-Verlag.

PCR: Clinical Diagnostics & Research. 2nd ed. A. Rolfs. 300p. 1997. pap. text 68.00 (*3-540-59432-9*) Spr-Verlag.

PCR: Essential Data. Ed. by C. R. Newton. (Essential Data Ser.). 236p. 1995. pap. 39.95 (*0-471-95222-2*) Wiley.

PCR: Essential Techniques. Julian F. Burke. LC 96-28414. 168p. 1996. pap. 47.95 (*0-471-95697-X*) Wiley.

PCR: Protocols for Diagnosis of Human & Animal Virus Diseases. Ed. by Gholamreza Darai & Yechiel Becker. LC 95-9546. (Illus.). 448p. 1995. 139.95 (*3-540-58899-X*) Spr-Verlag.

PCR Applications in Pathology: Principles & Practice. Ed. by David S. Latchman. (Modern Methods in Pathology Ser.). (Illus.). 288p. 1995. text 55.00 (*0-19-854835-4*) OUP.

PCR-Based Diagnostics in Infectious Diseases. Ed. by Garth D. Ehrlich & Steven J. Greenberg. LC 93-28476. (Illus.). 720p. 1993. 135.00 (*0-86542-252-4*) Blackwell Sci.

PCR Cloning Protocols: From Molecular Cloning to Genetic Engineering. Ed. by Bruce A. White. LC 96-30876. (Methods in Molecular Biology Ser.: Vol. 67). 512p. 1996. 79.50 (*0-89603-343-0*) Humana.

PCR in Bioanalysis. Ed. by Stephen Meltzer. LC 97-37496. (Methods in Molecular Biology Ser.: Vol. 92). (Illus.). xi, 281p. 1998. 69.50 (*0-89603-361-9*) Humana.

PCR in Bioanalysis. Ed. by Stephen J. Meltzer. (Methods in Molecular Biology Ser.: Vol. 92). (Illus.). 292p. 1998. 89.50 (*0-89603-497-6*) Humana.

PCR in Situ Hybridization: Protocols & Applications. 3rd ed. Gerard J. Nuovo. LC 96-25449. 512p. 1996. text 97.00 (*0-397-58749-X*) Lppncott W & W.

PCR Methods Manual. Innis. LC 99-211203. 566p. 1999. 89.95 (*0-12-372185-7*) Acad Pr.

PCR Methods Manual. Innis. LC 99-211203. 584p. 1999. 59.95 (*0-12-372186-5*) Acad Pr.

PCR Primer: A Laboratory Manual. Ed. by Carl Dieffenbach & Gabriela Dveksler. (Illus.). 350p. (C). 1995. pap. 102.00 (*0-87969-448-3*) Cold Spring Harbor.

***PCR Protocols.** 2nd ed. Ed. by John M. Bartlett & David Stirling. 450p. 2000. 79.50 (*0-89603-627-8*); 119.50 (*0-89603-642-1*) Humana.

PCR Protocols: A Guide to Methods & Applications. Ed. by David H. Gelfand et al. 482p. 1989. pap. 68.00 (*0-12-372181-4*); text 100.00 (*0-12-372180-6*) Acad Pr.

PCR Protocols: Current Methods & Applications. Ed. by Bruce A. White. LC 92-34874. (Methods in Molecular Biology Ser.: Vol. 15). (Illus.). 392p. 1993. pap. 64.50 (*0-89603-244-2*) Humana.

PCR Protocols for Emerging Infectious Diseases. Ed. by David H. Persing. 180p. 1996. spiral bd., suppl. ed. 39.95 (*1-55581-108-6*) ASM Pr.

PCR Protocols in Molecular Toxicology. Ed. by John P. Vanden Heuvel. LC 97-20678. (CRC Press Methods in Toxicology Ser.). 256p. 1997. per. 84.95 (*0-8493-3344-X*) CRC Pr.

PCR Sequencing Protocols. Ed. by Ralph Rapley. (Methods in Molecular Biology Ser.: Vol. 65). 236p. 1996. 69.50 (*0-89603-344-9*) Humana.

PCR Strategies. Ed. by Michael Innis et al. (Illus.). 373p. 1995. text 84.00 (*0-12-372182-2*) Acad Pr.

PCR Strategies. Ed. by Michael Innis et al. LC 94-42506. (Illus.). 373p. 1995. pap. text 42.00 (*0-12-372183-0*) Acad Pr.

PCR Technique DNA Sequencing. Ulf B. Gyllensten. Ed. by James Ellingboe. (BioTechniques Books Update Ser.). (Illus.). 170p. (Orig.). 1992. pap. 24.00 (*1-881299-00-7*, BioTechniques) Eaton Pub Co.

PCR Technique DNA Sequencing II. Ed. by U. Gyllensten & J. Ellingboe. (Update Ser.). (Illus.). 346p. 1997. pap. 34.95 (*1-881299-05-8*, BioTechniques) Eaton Pub Co.

PCR Technique Quantitative PCR. James W. Larrick. LC 97-17660. (Update Ser.). (Illus.). 325p. 1997. pap. text 36.95 (*1-881299-06-6*, BioTechniques) Eaton Pub Co.

PCR Technique RT-PCR. Ed. by Paul Siebert. LC 97-39313. (Update Ser.). (Illus.). 315p. 1997. pap. text 36.95 (*1-881299-13-9*, BioTechniques) Eaton Pub Co.

PCR Technology: Principles & Applications for DNA Amplification. Ed. by Henry A. Erlich. (Breakthroughs in Molecular Biology Ser.). (Illus.). 256p. 1993. pap. text 40.00 (*0-19-509875-7*) OUP.

PCR 3: 3 In Situ Hybridization: A Practical Approach. Ed. by C. Simon Herrington & John J. O'Leary. LC 97-17904. (The Practical Approach Ser.: No. 186). (Illus.). 224p. 1998. pap. text 55.00 (*0-19-963632-X*) OUP.

PCR 3: PCR In Situ Hybridization: A Practical Approach. Ed. by C. Simon Herrington & John J. O'Leary. LC 97-17904. (The Practical Approach Ser.: No. 186). (Illus.). 224p. 1998. text 105.00 (*0-19-963633-8*) OUP.

PCR 2: A Practical Approach. Ed. by M. J. McPherson et al. LC 96-176054. (The Practical Approach Ser.: No. 150). (Illus.). 3360p. 1995. text 95.00 (*0-19-963425-4*); pap. text 55.00 (*0-19-963424-6*) OUP.

***PCS & Cellular Base Station Equipment Vol. 3: U. S. Markets, Competitors & Opportunities: 1998-2003 Analysis & Forecasts.** Frank Kuzler. 1000p. 1999. pap. text 2900.00 (*1-878218-96-4*) World Info Tech.

PCS & Cellular Base Station Equipment - U. S. Markets, Competitors, & Opportunities: 1997-2001 Analysis & Forecasts. Frank Kuzler. 225p. 1997. pap. text 2900.00 (*1-878218-82-4*) World Info Tech.

PCS & Cellular Base Station Equipment - U. S. Markets, Competitors, & Opportunities: 1998-2003 Analysis & Forecasts, Vol. 2. Frank Kuzler. 250p. 1998. pap. text 2900.00 (*1-878218-95-6*) World Info Tech.

PC's Cheat Sheet. Shelley O'Hara. LC 98-87210. 334p. 1999. 14.99 (*0-7897-1874-X*) Que.

PCs for Dummies. Dan Gookin & Andy Rathbone. (For Dummies Ser.). (Illus.). 350p. 1992. pap. 16.95 (*1-878058-51-7*) IDG Bks.

PCs for Dummies. 2nd ed. Andy Rathbone & Dan Gookin. (For Dummies Ser.). (Illus.). 350p. 1994. pap. 16.95 (*1-56884-078-0*) IDG Bks.

PCs for Dummies. 3rd ed. Andy Rathbone. 432p. 1995. pap. 16.99 (*1-56884-904-4*) IDG Bks.

***PCs for Dummies.** 7th ed. Dan Gookin. (For Dummies Ser.). 456p. 1999. pap. 19.99 (*0-7645-0594-7*) IDG Bks.

Pcs for Dummies: Gookin,&Dan. abr. ed. Dan Gookin. 1997. audio 12.00 (*0-694-51824-7*, CPN 10114) HarperAudio.

***PCs for Dummies Quick Reference.** Ed. by Dummies Technology Press Staff. (For Dummies Ser.). 224p. 2000. spiral bd. 12.99 (*0-7645-0722-2*) IDG Bks.

***PCs for Dummies/Illustrated Computer Dictionary FD, 2 vols.** IDG Books Staff. (For Dummies Ser.). (Illus.). 2000. pap. 29.99 (*0-7645-8125-2*) IDG Bks.

***PCs for Dummies/Internet for Dummies, 2 vols.** IDG Books Staff. (For Dummies Ser.). (Illus.). 2000. pap. 24.99 (*0-7645-8130-9*) IDG Bks.

***PCs for Dummies/Windows 98 for Dummies, 2 vols.** IDG Books Staff. (For Dummies Ser.). (Illus.). 2000. pap. 24.99 (*0-7645-8132-5*) IDG Bks.

P

PCs for Teachers. Pam Toliver. 384p. 1996. pap. 24.99 (*1-56884-602-9*) IDG Bks.

PCS Handsets in Hong Kong: A Strategic Entry Report, 1998. Compiled by Icon Group International Staff. (Country Industry Report). (Illus.). 124p. 1999. ring bd. 1240.00 incl. audio compact disk (*0-7418-0566-9*) Icon Grp.

PCs in Pieces. Rob Young. LC 96-48476. (C). 1997. 29.95 (*0-13-617952-5*) P-H.

PCs in Plain English. Bryan Pfaffenberger. 89p. 1995. pap. 19.95 (*1-55828-384-6*, MIS Pr) IDG Bks.

PCs Made Easy. 2nd ed. James L. Turley. 464p. 1993. pap. 19.95 (*0-07-881929-6*) Osborne-McGraw.

PCs Network Deployment. John Tsakalakis. LC 96-47049. (Illus.). 261p. 1996. 65.00 (*0-07-065342-9*) McGraw.

PCs Networking. Rifaat A. Dayem. LC 97-172305. 256p. (C). 1997. 63.00 (*0-13-616574-5*) P-H.

PCs to Corporate America: From Military Tactics to Corporate Interviewing Strategy. 2nd ed. Roger Cameron. LC 92-21911. 288p. (Orig.). 1992. pap. 19.95 (*0-9623216-5-6*) Odenwald Pr.

***PCS to Corporate America: From Military Tactics to Corporate Interviewing Strategy.** 3rd rev. ed. Roger Cameron. 240p. 2000. pap. 19.95 (*1-884363-18-0*) Odenwald Pr.

***PCT Bird Management Field Guide: A Comprehensive Manual for Preventing & Resolving Pest Bird Problems.** Richard Kramer. Ed. by Steve Smith. (Illus.). 122p. 1999. pap. 12.95 (*1-883751-11-X*) GIE Media.

PCT Field Guide for the Management of Structure-Infesting Ants. 2nd rev. ed. Stoy Hedges. Ed. by Daniel Moreland. LC 97-78149. (Illus.). 300p. 1998. pap. 12.95 (*1-883751-09-8*) GIE Media.

***PCT, Spin & Statistics & All That.** Raymond F. Streater. (Landmarks in Mathematics & Physics Ser.). 2000. pap. 19.95 (*0-691-07062-8*) Princeton U Pr.

PCT, Spin & Statistics & All That. WI Streater. pap. 22.00 (*0-8053-9252-1*) Benjamin-Cummings.

PCT Technician's Handbook: A Guide to Pest Identification & Management. 3rd rev. ed. Richard Kramer. Ed. by Jeff Fenner. LC 97-77870. (Illus.). 320p. 1998. pap. 14.95 (*1-883751-08-X*) GIE Media.

PC/Tax Software, 1997 Edition. 324p. 1996. pap., teacher ed., wbk. ed. 78.00 incl. 3.5 ld (*0-614-26804-4*, 14496BLS02) CCH INC.

PC/Tax Workbook, 1997 Edition. 200p. 1996. pap. 17.00 (*0-8080-0110-8*, 14496BLS02) CCH INC.

PCworld DOS 6 Handbook. 2nd ed. John Socha et al. 1000p. 1993. pap. 34.95 incl. disk (*1-878058-79-7*) IDG Bks.

PCworld WordPerfect 6 Handbook. Greg Harvey. 600p. 1993. pap. 34.95 incl. disk (*1-878058-80-0*) IDG Bks.

***P.D. James: A Reader's Checklist & Reference Guide.** CheckerBee Publishing Staff. 1999. pap. text 4.95 (*1-58598-022-6*) CheckerBee.

PD-1 1982 Industry Product Definitions. (ANSI/BIFMA Standards Ser.). 1982. 15.00 (*0-614-30055-X*) BIFMA Intl.

PDA International Conference on Liquid Borne Particle Inspection & Metrology: Conference Proceedings. Parenteral Drug Association Incorporated Staff. Ed. by Marcy Feldman. (Illus.). 662p. 1987. pap. text 95.00 (*0-939459-12-4*) PDA.

***PDCA Test: A Quality Framework for Software Testing.** 2nd ed. William E. Lewis. LC 99-86186. 656p. 2000. boxed set 69.95 (*0-8493-9833-9*) CRC Pr.

PDEase2D Lite. Macsyma, Inc. Staff. 40p. 1999. pap. 97.00 incl. cd-rom (*3-540-14768-3*) Spr-Verlag.

PDF Bible: The Complete Guide to Adobe Acrobat 3.0. Mark Witkowski. (Illus.). 450p. (Orig.). 1998. pap. 39.95 (*0-941845-23-0*) Micro Pub Pr.

PDF Printing & Publishing: The Next Revolution after Gutenberg. Frank Romano et al. (Illus.). 208p. (Orig.). 1997. pap. 27.95 (*0-941845-22-2*) Micro Pub Pr.

***PDF Reference.** 2nd ed. Adobe Systems, Inc. 784p. 2000. pap. 49.95 incl. cd-rom (*0-201-61588-6*) Addison-Wesley.

***PDF with Acrobat 4: Visual QuickStart Guide.** Ted Alspach. 208p. (C). 1999. pap. text 17.99 (*0-201-35461-6*) Peachpit Pr.

PDM No. 1: Piano for the Developing Musician. Martha Hilley & Lynn F. Olson. Ed. by Baxter. 325p. (C). 1993. disk. write for info. (*0-318-70638-5*) West Pub.

PDM No. 1: Piano for the Developing Musician, Vol. I. 3rd ed. Martha Hilley & Lynn F. Olson. Ed. by Baxter. 325p. (C). 1993. pap. 40.50 (*0-314-01260-5*) West Pub.

PDM No. 2: Piano for the Developing Musician. 2nd ed. Martha Hilley & Lynn F. Olson. Ed. by Baxter. 252p. (C). 1992. 33.50 (*0-314-93368-9*) West Pub.

***PDM Business Appraisal Guide: Business Justification of Product Data Management Systems for Industrial Organizations.** 3rd rev. ed. Stanley Port & John MacKrell. (Illus.). 1999. ring bd. (*1-889760-11-0*) CIMdata Inc.

***PDM Buyer's Guide: PDM Systems for Improving Processes & Methods.** 7th rev. ed. Ed Miller et al. (Illus.). 400p. 1999. ring bd. (*1-889760-10-2*) CIMdata Inc.

PDM Buyer's Guide: Product Data Management for Engineering, Vol. 2. 6th rev. ed. Eddy Miller et al. (Illus.). 1200p. 1996. ring bd. 995.00 (*1-889760-02-1*) CIMdata Inc.

PDM Buyer's Guide: Product Data Management Systems for Engineering & Manufacturing, Vol. 1. 6th rev. ed. Eddy Miller et al. (Illus.). 1200p. 1996. ring bd. 995.00 (*1-889760-01-3*) CIMdata Inc.

PDM Case Studies: User Experiences with PDM Systems. Stanley Port & John MacKrell. (Illus.). 150p. 1996. ring bd. 295.00 (*1-889760-04-8*) CIMdata Inc.

PDM Selection Guide: From Needs to Selection; a Business Solution - Guide for the Selection of Product Data Management Systems. Maarten Cornelissen et al. 204p. (Orig.). 1995. pap. 115.00 (*90-407-1142-9*, Pub. by Delft U Pr) Coronet Bks.

PDMA Handbook of Product Development. Milton D. Rosenau, Jr. LC 96-33743. 656p. 1996. 99.00 (*0-471-14189-5*) Wiley.

PDOF. 147p. (Orig.). 1996. pap. 12.00 (*0-9652845-1-4*) Thirteen Enter.

PDQ Embryology. Moore. 1986. 27.95 (*0-8016-3533-0*) Mosby Inc.

***PDQ Epidemiology.** 2nd ed. David L. Streiner & Geoffrey R. Norman. (Illus.). 160p. 1998. pap. 19.95 (*1-55009-077-1*) DEKR.

***PDQ Evidence-Based Principles & Practice.** Ann K. McKibbon et al. (Evidence-Based Ser.). 212p. 1999. boxed set 27.95 incl. cd-rom (*1-55009-118-2*) DEKR.

PDQ Statistics. Norman & David L. Steiner. 1986. 13.95 (*0-8016-3840-2*) Mosby Inc.

***PDQ Statistics.** 2nd ed. Geoffrey R. Norman & David L. Streiner. (Illus.). 188p. 1999. pap. 19.95 (*1-55009-076-3*) DEKR.

PDR Atlas of Anatomy. Todd Olson. LC 98-171711. (Illus.). 500p. 1997. text 54.95 (*1-56363-279-9*) Med Econ.

***PDR Companion Guide 2000. 54th rev. ed. Ed. by Medical Economics Staff. (Illus.). 2000p. 2000. 59.95 (*1-56363-340-X*, PDR) Med Econ.**

Cross-referenced to the 2000 editions of the PDR, PDR for Opthalmology & PDR for Nonprescription Drugs & Dietary Supplements, this unique, time-saving, all-in-one clinical reference assures safe & appropriate drug selection with nine critical checkpoints: Interactions Index, Food Interactions Cross-Reference, Side Effects Index, Indications Index, Contraindications Index, Off-Label Treatment Guide, Cost of Therapy Guide, International Drug Guide, Generic Availability Table, New for 2000, an Imprint Identification Guide which enables readers to quickly identify thousands of drugs by imprint alone. (i.e. strength, color, form, shape, etc.) *Publisher Paid Annotation.*

PDR Family Guide Encyclopedia of Medical Care. Medical Economics Company Staff. LC 97-170. 400p. pap. text 23.00 (*0-609-80069-8*, PDR) Med Econ.

of common medical problems & procedures, follow-up care, vital warnings about complications & emergencies. Concise summaries of what to expect before, during & after hospitalization or clinic treatment. Invaluable when the doctor's instructions are sketchy, forgotten, or misunderstood. Includes a checklist of the complications that signal the need for immediate medical attention. Available now. *Publisher Paid Annotation.*

PDR Pocket Guide to Prescription Drugs. 2nd ed. Ed. by PDR Staff. 1997. per. 6.99 (*0-671-01454-4*) PB.

***PDR Family Guide to Natural Medicines & Healing Therapies.** Physicians' Desk Reference Staff. 752p. 2000. mass mkt. 7.99 (*0-345-43377-7*, Ballantine) Ballantine Pub Grp.

PDR Family Guide to Natural Medicines & Healing Therapies. Physicians' Desk Reference Staff. LC 99-13367. 576p. 1999. pap. 23.00 (*0-609-80071-X*) Crown Pub Group.

Take advantage of all your health options & reap the rewards of better health with this unique consumer's guide to affordable, effective healthcare alternatives. From age-old secrets of harmony, balance & well-being to the very latest nutritional discoveries, readers will find dozens of alternative treatments discussed in this one home handbook. Here are all the latest findings on acupuncture & acupressure, aromatherapy, chiropractic adjustments, environmental medicine, naturopathic medicine, tai chi, yoga & more. Available now. *Publisher Paid Annotation.*

***PDR Family Guide to Prescription Drugs No. 5, Vol. 1.** 7th ed. Physicians' Desk Reference Staff. 1999. pap. 23.00 (*0-609-80491-X*, Three Riv Pr) Crown Pub Group.

PDR for Herbal Medicines. Medical Economics Staff. (Physicians' Desk Reference for Herbal Medicines Ser.). (Illus.). 800p. 1998. 59.95 (*1-56363-292-6*, PDR) Med Econ.

An invaluable resource for prescribing information on over 600 herbs, PDR for Herbal Medicines is the most comprehensive prescribing reference of its kind. Draws on the work conducted by Joerg Gruenwald, a renowned botanist & expert on herbal medicines, as well as the German Federal Health Authority's Commission E, the governmental body which is widely recognized as having done the most authoritative evaluation of herbs in the world. However, PDR for Herbal Medicines also includes hundreds of herbs not reviewed by Commission E & provides detailed reference in support of its finding. Entries include: thorough description of the plant & derived compounds; summarized pharmacological effects of each plant; documented indications & a concise summary of other uses; any applicable precautions, warnings & contraindications; adverse reactions & overdose data; scientific & common English names; modes of administration & typical dosage; exhaustive literature citations & hundreds of color photographs for easy identification of herbs. 900 pages. Available: December 1998. *Publisher Paid Annotation.*

***PDR for Herbal Medicines. 2nd rev. ed. Medical Economics Staff. (Illus.). 1,000p. 2000. 59.95 (*1-56363-361-2*) Med Econ.**

An invaluable resource for prescribing information on over 700 herbs, PDR for Herbal Medicines is the most comprehensive prescribing reference of its kind. Draws on the work conducted by Joerg Gruenwald, a renowned botanist & expert on herbal medicines, as well as the German Federal Health Authority;s Commission E, the governmental body which is widely recognized as having done the most authoritative evaluation of herbs in the world. However, PDR for Herbal Medicines also includes hundreds of herbs not reviewed by Commission E & provides detailed reference in support of its finding. The 2001 edition includes: Over 100 NEW herb monographs added; critical updates to existing monographs; extensive new research data on safety & efficacy; organized to common name; expanded coverage of drug/herb interactions guide; expanded side effects & indications indices; new Asian & homeopathic indices; Safety Guide; daily dosage information for unprocessed herbs & commercially available products; Manufacturers' Directory; Trade names; Expanded therapeutic category index; exhaustive literature citations & hundreds of color photographs for easy identification of herbs. 1,000 pages. Available April 2000. *Publisher Paid Annotation.*

***PDR for Nonprescription Drugs & Dietary Supplements. 21st rev. ed. Ed. by Medical Economics Staff. (Illus.). 500p. 2000. 49.95 (*1-56363-341-8*, PDR) Med Econ.**

The 2000 PDR for Nonprescription Drugs & Dietary Supplements provides critical information on those ingredients that move from prescription to nonprescription status as well as new over-the-counter drugs that are introduced every year. The 2000 edition contains: a section on dietary supplements including nutritionals, herbals, & functional foods; full detailed descriptions of the most commonly used nonprescription drugs & products; color photos of hundreds of OTC drugs for quick ID - cross referenced to the detailed descriptions; four separate indices for quick ID (by category, product name, manufacturer & active ingredient), comprehensive coverage of ingredients, indications, drug interactions, dosage, administration & more. And a Companion Drug Index to common diseases & frequently encountered side effects. *Publisher Paid Annotation.*

***PDR for Nonprescription Drugs & Dietary Supplements, 2001.** 22nd ed. 400p. 2001. 53.95 (*1-56363-381-7*, PDR) Med Econ.

***PDR for Nutritional Supplements. 2000. 59.95 (*1-56363-364-7*, PDR) Med Econ.**

Science based research on over 300 nutritional supplements including vitamins, minerals, probiotics, amino acids & more. Includes convenient indexes listing the supplements in a variety of ways - Supplement Name Index; Indications Index; Side Effects Index; Supplement Category Index; Interactions Index; Supplement Manufacturer Index & a Visual Identification Section. Each entry provides: Scientific & common name of each supplement; chemical & physical attributes, including chemical structure; indications & usage; complete review of the supplement's pharmacology including pharmacokinetics; research summary; precautions, adverse reactions & contraindications; interactions with other supplements, drugs, food, alcohol & herbs; dosage & administration; the most comprehensive literature citations,. Available December 2000. *Publisher Paid Annotation.*

***PDR for Ophthalmic Medicines, 2001. 29th ed. 250p. 2000. 58.95 (*1-56363-366-3*, PDR) Med Econ.**

Exclusive product information on the care & treatment of the eye. This indispensable guide is the definitive directory of drug & product data relating uniquely to the practice of Ophthalmology & Optometry. Available November 2000. *Publisher Paid Annotation.*

***PDR for Ophthalmology 2000. 28th rev. ed. Ed. by Medical Economics Staff. (Illus.). 250p. 1999. 54.95 (*1-56363-339-6*, PDR) Med Econ.**

Exclusive product information on the care & treatment of the eye. This indispensable guide is the definitive directory of drug & product data relating uniquely to the practice of Ophthalmology & Optometry. 230 pages. Available: November 1999 *Publisher Paid Annotation.*

PDR Guide to Over-the-Counter. Physicians Desk Reference. LC 97-97165. 1998. mass mkt. 6.99 (*0-345-41716-X*, Ballantine Epiphany) Ballantine Pub Grp.

***PDR Medical Dictionary.** 2nd rev. ed. Medical Economics Staff & Williams & Wilkins Staff. 2100p. 2000. 49.95 (*1-56363-338-8*, PDR) Med Econ.

PDR Nurse's Dictionary. LC 97-156486. 1350p. 1996. pap. text 19.95 (*1-56363-213-6*) Med Econ.

***PDR Nurses Drug Handbook, 2000. 6th ed. Ed. by Medical Economics Staff. (C). 1999. pap. 29.95 (*0-7668-1086-0*) Thomson Learn.**

Lightweight & portable, the PDR Nurse's Handbook puts essential drug data at your fingertips & offers crystal-clear explanations of the information the practicing nurse needs to do their job effectively. Published in cooperation with Delmar Publishers, the 2000 edition is easier & quicker to use than ever. Arranged in a handy A-Z format, the Handbook provides complete, alphabetically arranged descriptions of each drug, including contents, dosage, side effects, overdose symptoms & treatments. Free internet updates. Instructions included with the book. Detailed listings for the most widely prescribed retail drugs, commonly administered hospital medications, & numerous drugs used in long-term & home health care. Available: August 1999. Also available in CD-ROM format. Call for details. *Publisher Paid Annotation.*

***PDR Nurse's Drug Handbook 2001.** George R. Spratto. 2000. pap. 31.95 (*0-7668-2136-6*) Delmar.

PDR Nurses Handbook. 4th ed. George R. Spratto & Adrienne L. Woods. 1300p. (C). 1998. pap. text 29.95 (*0-7668-0913-7*) Delmar.

PDR Nurses Handbook Network CD-Rom 1999 Edition. George R. Spratto et al. 831.95 (*0-7668-0697-9*, Pub. by Delmar) Thomson Learn.

PDR Nurse's Handbook, 1999 ed. 1998. pap. text 40.95 (*0-7668-0639-1*) Delmar.

***PDR Pharmacopoeia, Pocket Edition, 2001. Medical Economics Staff. (Illus.). 200p. 2000. pap. text 9.95 (*1-56363-365-5*, PDR) Med Econ.**

FDA-approved dosing information for more than 1,200 chemical/biological entities. Based on the latest edition of the Physicians Desk Reference, this book features: small, convenient, pocket-sized format; easy-to-read tabular format; organized by drug indication & therapeutic class; symbols indicate important warnings for nursing or pregnant women; Dosing adjustments for the hepatically or renally impaired; pediatric dosing; valuable additional reference tables. Available July 2000. *Publisher Paid Annotation.*

PDR Pocket Guide to Prescription Drugs. Medical Economics Data Staff. LC 96-213121. (TTL Ser.). 1996. pap. 6.99 (*0-671-52520-4*) PB.

PDR Pocket Guide to Prescription Drugs. 3rd rev. ed. Ed. by Physicians' Desk Reference Staff. (Illus.). 1480p. 1998. per. 6.99 (*0-671-02585-6*) PB.

***PDR Pocket Guide to Prescription Drugs.** 4th rev. ed. Medical Economics Company Staff. (Illus.). 1608p. 2000. per. 6.99 (*0-671-78643-1*, Pocket Books) PB.

***PDR Supplement A.** 54th rev. ed. Medical Economics Staff. (Illus.). 300p. 2000. pap. 29.95 (*1-56363-342-6*, PDR) Med Econ.

***PDR Supplement B.** rev. ed. Medical Economics Staff. (Illus.). 300p. 2000. pap. 29.95 (*1-56363-343-4*, PDR) Med Econ.

***PDR Supplements, 2000: Combined Supplements A & B. 54th rev. ed. Ed. by Medical Economics Staff. (Illus.). 300p. 2000. 29.95 (*1-56363-344-2*, PDR) Med Econ.**

PDR Supplements provide every important update between annual editions of the PDR. And they fit neatly inside the front cover of the PDR where they are always available for ready reference. ***Publisher Paid Annotation.***

***PDR Supplements, 2001.** 55th ed. 2001. 62.95 (*1-56363-379-5*, PDR) Med Econ.

***PDR 3-Pack Configuration, 2000.** 54th rev. ed. Medical Economics Staff. 1999. write for info. (*1-56363-345-0*, PDR) Med Econ.

***PDR 2000: Bookstore Version. 54th rev. ed. Ed. by Medical Economics Staff. (Illus.). 3000p. 1999. 82.95 (*1-56363-335-3*, PDR) Med Econ.**
Completely revised & updated, the 2000 PDR provides FDA-approved drug information on more than 4,000 prescription drugs, over 2,100 full-color, actual-size photos of medicines for instant identification, & important data on over 250 drug manufacturers. New medicines, new drug interaction data, the most recent side effects findings, & certain drugs now removed from the market make it absolutely critical that medical professionals keep up-to-date with the very latest prescription drug information. The 2000 PDR contains: the newest drugs--which drugs are indicated for the diagnosed condition; how different drugs interact; latest findings on side effects caused by the prescribed drug; recommended dosages; clinical pharmacology; pediatric use; contraindications; FDA use-in-pregnancy ratings; & more. Hundreds of new drugs added including: Avandia, Celebrex, Vioxx, Enbrel, Pletal, Agenerase, & many more. New larger trim allows dramatically improved readability. 3,000 pages. Available: November 1999 ***Publisher Paid Annotation.***

PDS in Depth. Trager. 208p. 1983. pap. text 18.00 (*0-13-730987-2*) P-H.

PD's in Depth. Edith C. Trager. (Orig.). 1982. audio. write for info. (*0-87789-216-4*, 1601) ELS Educ Servs.

PD's in Depth. Edith C. Trager. (Orig.). (gr. 9-12). 1982. pap. 4.95 (*0-87789-215-6*, 1600) ELS Educ Servs.

***PDU - 1: A Novella of the Remote Future.** F. E. Potts. LC PS3566.074P37 2000. (Illus.). xii, 132p. 2000. 19.95 (*0-9635210-4-7*) ACS.

PDXI Activity Model Vol. 2: Includes Entire Activity Model. Process Data Exchange Institute Staff. 344p. 1997. pap. 150.00 (*0-8169-0756-0*, I-2) Am Inst Chem Eng.

PDXI Data Models, Vol. 1. Process Data Exchange Institute Staff. 380p. 1997. pap. 300.00 (*0-8169-0755-2*, I-1) Am Inst Chem Eng.

PE Biology 4/E. 95th ed. Arms. (C). 1995. text 93.00 (*0-03-015434-0*) Harcourt Coll Pubs.

P/E Biology Prnciples & Expl. 98th ed. Johnson. 1997. 63.80 (*0-03-051433-9*) H Holt & Co.

Pe Drumul Credintei: Arhimandrit Roman Braga. Roman Braga et al. Ed. & Intro. by HDM Press, Inc. Staff. (Illus.). 358p. (Orig.). 1995. pap. 17.00 (*0-9643478-0-6*) HDM Pr.

PE for You. Jan Wyse. Ed. by John Honeybourne et al. (Illus.). 256p. 1999. pap. 33.50 (*0-7487-3277-2*, Pub. by S Thornes Pubs) Trans-Atl Phila.

PE Informant: Your Personal Guide to Becoming a Professional Engineer. 2nd ed. Ed Brennan & Larry Weng. Ed. by Susan Perry. (Illus.). 150p. (C). 1998. pap. text 19.95 (*0-9663795-0-0*) Avalon Pr PA.

P/E Modern Chemistry 1999, 99th ed. 99th ed. HRW Staff. 1997. 64.50 (*0-03-051122-4*) H Holt & Co.

Pe-Resh: Hebrew-English Dictionary. (Complete Biblical Library: Vol. 6). (ENG & HEB.). 637p. 2000. 49.95 (*1-884642-46-2*) World Library.

Pe Set: Powem. Josaphat Large. Ed. by Edisyon Mafrou. 1994. text. write for info. (*0-9641162-0-0*) Edit La Jeremienne.

***P.E. Teacher's Complete Fitness & Skills Development Activities Program.** Jeff Carpenter. LC 99-37792. 2000. write for info. (*0-13-022817-6*) P-H.

Pe World History: Continuity & Change 1999. 99th ed. Hanes. 1998. text 73.20 (*0-03-052452-0*) Harcourt.

Pe World of Biology. 95th ed. Solomon. (C). 1995. text 83.50 (*0-03-015433-2*) Harcourt Coll Pubs.

Pea. R. K. Makasheva. Tr. by B. R. Sharma from RUS. 275p. (C). 1984. text 97.00 (*90-6191-431-0*, Pub. by A A Balkema) Ashgate Pub Co.

Pea in the Pod, Bk. 3. Ralph F. Parkison. Ed. by Marion O. Withrow. (Illus.). 10p. (Orig.). (J). (gr. 2-6). 1988. pap. text 3.00 (*0-929949-02-1*) Little Wood Bks.

Pea Island Rescue. Pepper Bird Staff. (Multicultural Historical Fiction Ser.). (Illus.). 48p. (Orig.). (J). (gr. 4-7). 1993. pap. 4.95 (*1-56817-002-5*) Pepper Bird.

***Pea or the Flea?** School Zone Publishing Staff. (Start to Read Board Bks.). (Illus.). (J). 2000. bds. 4.99 (*0-88743-810-5*) Sch Zone Pub Co.

Pea Patch Jig. Thacher Hurd. (J). 1995. 10.15 (*0-606-07996-3*) Turtleback.

Pea Ridge: Civil War Campaign in the West. William L. Shea & Earl J. Hess. LC 92-4465. (Illus.). xiv, 418p. 1992. 37.50 (*0-8078-2042-3*) U of NC Pr.

Pea Ridge: Civil War Campaign in the West. William L. Shea & Earl J. Hess. 432p. 1997. pap. 17.95 (*0-8078-4669-4*) U of NC Pr.

***Pea Ridge & Prairie Grove.** Williams Baxter. LC 99-59554. 136p. 2000. pap. 16.00 (*1-55728-591-8*) U of Ark Pr.

Pea Ridge & Prairie Grove. William Baxter. Ed. by Phillip A. Sperry. 270p. 1993. reprint ed. 32.95 (*1-56869-038-X*); reprint ed. pap. 19.95 (*1-56869-039-8*) Oldbuck Pr.

Pea Soup Andersen's Scandinavian-American Cookbook. Ulrich Riedner & Patricia Rain. LC 88-70661. (Illus.). 180p. 1995. pap. 9.95 (*0-89087-523-5*) Celestial Arts.

Peabody. Earl Atkinson. (Ballroom Dance Ser.). 1986. lib. bdg. 250.00 (*0-8490-3630-5*) Gordon Pr.

Peabody. Stephen J. Schier. (Images of America Ser.). 1997. pap. 16.99 (*0-7524-0548-9*) Arcadia Publng.

Peabody: A Living Tradition. Lawrence Wells. (Illus.). 8p. 1981. reprint ed. pap. 1.99 (*0-916242-51-X*) Yoknapatawpha.

Peabody Holmes Inert Gas System. Ed. by Lorne & MacLean Marine & Offshore Productions Staf. 1985. 95.00 (*0-7855-1042-7*, Pub. by Lorne & MacLean Marine) St Mut.

Peabody Holmes Inert Gas System Manual. Lorne & MacLean Marine & Offshore Publications Sta. (C). 1987. 140.00 (*0-7855-4381-3*, Pub. by Lorne & MacLean Marine) St Mut.

Peabody Language Development Kit, Lesson Manual 1 - Level P. Lloyd Dunn et al. 1981. pap. text 47.95 (*0-88671-026-X*, 8551) Am Guidance.

Peabody Language Development Kit, Level P Lesson Manual 2. rev. ed. Lloyd Dunn et al. 1981. pap. text 47.95 (*0-88671-027-8*, 8552) Am Guidance.

Peabody Language Development Kit, Level P Teachers Guide. Lloyd Dunn et al. 1981. teacher ed. 12.95 (*0-88671-028-6*, 8554) Am Guidance.

Peabody Language Development Kit, Level 1 Lesson Manual 1. Lloyd Dunn et al. 1981. pap. text 47.95 (*0-88671-030-8*, 8701) Am Guidance.

Peabody Language Development Kit, Level 1, Lesson Manual 2. Lloyd Dunn et al. 1981. pap. text 47.95 (*0-88671-031-6*, 8702) Am Guidance.

Peabody Language Development Kit, Level 1 Teachers Guide. Lloyd Dunn et al. 1981. teacher ed. 12.95 (*0-88671-032-4*, 8704) Am Guidance.

Peabody Law Review: Portland, Me, 1936-1941, 5 vols. 1936. 87.50 (*0-8377-9197-9*, Rothman) W S Hein.

Peabody (Massachusetts) Story: Events in Peabody's History, 1626-1972. John A. Wells. (Illus.). 531p. 1992. reprint ed. lib. bdg. 49.00 (*0-8328-2379-1*) Higginson Bk Co.

Peabody Museum Collection of Navigating Instruments: With Notes on Their Makers. Marion V. Brewington. (Illus.). xii, 144p. 1996. reprint ed. 75.00 (*1-888262-00-1*) Martino Pubng.

Peabody (Paybody, Pabody, Pabodie) Genealogy. S. Peabody. (Illus.). 614p. 1989. reprint ed. pap. 92.00 (*0-8328-0943-8*); reprint ed. lib. bdg. 100.00 (*0-8328-0942-X*) Higginson Bk Co.

Peabody Sister of Salem. Louise H. Tharp. (Illus.). 380p. 1988. pap. 8.95 (*0-316-83919-1*) Little.

Peabody Steps. Earl Atkinson. 1983. lib. bdg. 250.00 (*0-87700-484-6*) Revisionist Pr.

Peacable & Prosperous Regiment of Blessed Queene Elisabeth: A Facsimile from Holinshed's Chronciles (1587) Intro. by Cyndia S. Clegg. (Illus.). 500p. 2000. 250.00 (*0-87328-161-6*) Huntington Lib.

Peace. (In Classical Mood Ser.: Vol. 17). (Illus.). 1997. write for info. incl. cd-rom (*1-886614-41-5*) Intl Masters Pub.

***Peace.** (Designer Black Shufa Ser.). 160p. 2000. (*1-55156-187-5*); 8.95 (*1-55156-169-7*) Paperblank.

Peace. Molana S. Angha. LC 87-63381. (ENG & PER.). 79p. 1987. pap. 11.55 (*0-910735-12-3*) MTO Printing & Pubn Ctr.

Peace. Deseret Book Company Editors. LC 98-12794. 1998. write for info. (*1-57345-271-8*) Deseret Bk.

***Peace.** Laura Dower. (J). 2001. pap. write for info. (*0-06-440811-6*, HarpTrophy) HarpC Child Bks.

***Peace.** Honor Books Publishing Staff. (Fruit of the Spirit Ser.). 2000. 9.99 (*1-56292-659-4*) Honor Bks OK.

Peace. Jack Kuhatschek. (Fruit of the Spirit Bible Studies). 48p. 1991. pap. 5.99 (*0-310-53741-X*) Zondervan.

Peace. Carole MacKenthun & Paulinus Dwyer. (Fruit of the Spirit Ser.). (Illus.). 48p. (J). (gr. 2-7). 1986. student ed. 7.95 (*0-86653-365-6*, SS 877, Shining Star Pubns) Good Apple.

Peace. Joyce Meyer. 80p. 1995. mass mkt. 4.99 (*0-89274-924-5*, HH-924) Harrison Hse.

Peace. Mary E. Sterling. (Thematic Unit Ser.). (Illus.). 80p. 1993. pap., teacher ed. 9.95 (*1-55734-233-4*) Tchr Create Mat.

Peace, 9 vols. Robert Strand. (Nine Fruits of the Spirit Ser.). 48p. 1999. 3.99 (*0-89221-463-5*) New Leaf Pr.

Peace. Gene Wolfe. LC 95-15464. 272p. 1995. pap. 12.95 (*0-312-89033-8*, Pub. by Tor Bks) St Martin.

Peace. unabridged ed. Aristophanes. Ed. by William-Alan Landes. Tr. by S. H. Landes. LC 98-10740. 55p. (Orig.). 1998. pap. 7.00 (*0-88734-781-9*) Players Pr.

Peace: A Dream Unfolding. Kome & Crean. 24.95 (*0-921051-14-X*) Somerville Hse.

Peace: A Thematic Unit. Mary P. Martin. (Thematic Units Ser.). (Illus.). 80p. (J). (gr. 1-3). 1994. student ed. 9.95 (*1-55734-248-2*) Tchr Create Mat.

Peace: Abstracts of Psychological & Behavioral Literature, 1967-1990. Ed. by Herbert H. Blumberg & Christopher C. French. (Bibliographies in Psychology Ser.: No. 10). 229p. 1992. pap. text 19.95 (*1-55798-137-X*) Am Psychol.

Peace: An Idea Whose Time Has Come. Anatol Rapoport. 224p. (C). 1992. text 42.50 (*0-472-10315-6*, 10315) U of Mich Pr.

Peace: By the Wonderful People Who Brought You Korea & Viet Nam. Archibald E. Roberts. 377p. 1972. 6.95 (*0-318-13713-5*) Comm Restore Const.

Peace: Christian Living in a Violent World. Mary I. Farr. (Intersections: Small Group Ser.). 1995. pap. 5.49 (*0-8066-0135-3*, 15-170) Augsburg Fortress.

Peace: Meanings, Politics, Strategies. Ed. by Linda R. Forcey. LC 89-3625. 242p. 1989. 55.00 (*0-275-92833-0*, C2833, Praeger Pubs); pap. 20.95 (*0-275-92834-9*, B2834, Praeger Pubs) Greenwood.

Peace: More Than an End to War. Ed. by Richard A. Hill et al. 308p. 1986. pap. 3.00 (*0-87743-204-X*) Bahai.

***Peace: New Method, New Light.** Olivier Manitara.Tr. of Paix - Nouvelle Methode, Nouvelle Lumiere. (Illus.). 232p. (Orig.). 1999. pap. 0.00 (*1-894341-01-5*) Telesma-Evida.

Peace: Perspectives on Peace/Conflict. Bob Haverluck & Linda Bilon. 96p. (J). (gr. 1-12). 1990. pap., teacher ed. 7.00 (*0-920541-42-9*) Peguis Pubs Ltd.

Peace: Quotations from the Writings of Ellen G. White. Ellen Gould Harmon White. LC 97-19422. 143p. 1997. pap. 5.99 (*0-8163-1403-9*) Pacific Pr Pub Assn.

***Peace: The Arabian Caricature: A Study of Anti-Semitic Imagery.** Ariem Stav. Tr. by Martin Kett from HEB. LC 99-20730. Orig. Title: Shalom, Karikaturah Arvit. 288p. 1999. 30.00 (*965-229-215-X*) Gefen Bks.

Peace - The Womb of Power. Arun A. Amin. 20p. 1997. pap. 4.95 (*1-891253-04-2*) Aurovision Bks.

***Peace , Power & Resistence in Cambodia.** Lizee. LC 99-15386. 240p. 1999. text 65.00 (*0-312-22406-0*) St Martin.

Peace above the Storm: Freedom from Worry Guilt & Fear. Ellen Gould Harmon White. 112p. 1994. pap. 11.95 (*1-885204-00-0*) Fmly Heritage.

Peace above the Storm Magabook: Freedom from Worry, Guilt & Fear. Ellen G. White. (Illus.). 111p. 1994. pap. 5.99 (*0-8163-1385-7*) Pacific Pr Pub Assn.

Peace Accords & Ethnic Conflict. Ed. by K. M. De Silva & S. W. Samarasinghe. 280p. 1993. text 59.00 (*1-85567-079-8*, Pub. by P P Pubs) Cassell & Continuum.

Peace Action in the 1980s: Social Science Perspectives. Ed. by Sam Marullo & John Lofland. LC 89-49216. 300p. (C). 1990. text 40.00 (*0-8135-1560-2*); pap. text 16.00 (*0-8135-1561-0*) Rutgers U Pr.

Peace after Abortion. 2nd rev. ed. Ava Torre-Bueno. LC 96-72071. 192p. (Orig.). 1997. pap. 9.95 (*0-9651383-1-3*) Pimpernel Pr.

Peace Agitator: The Story of A. J. Muste. rev. ed. Nat Hentoff. LC 82-71646. (Illus.). 275p. 1982. pap. 6.50 (*0-9608096-0-0*) Muste.

***Peace Agreements & Human Rights.** Christine Bell. 380p. 2000. text 74.00 (*0-19-829889-7*) OUP.

Peace among Ourselves: Facing the Vietnam Veterans Memorial. Jane E. Hughes. LC 94-92161. (Illus.). 144p. (Orig.). 1995. pap. 13.95 (*0-9645812-7-2*) J E Hughes.

Peace & Adventure. Ellen Murray. (C). 1990. 20.00 (*0-9501351-6-X*, Pub. by Wild Goose Pubns) St Mut.

Peace & Bread: The Story of Jane Addams. Stephanie S. McPherson. LC 93-6736. (J). (gr. 4-7). 1993. lib. bdg. 22.60 (*0-87614-792-9*, Carolrhoda) Lerner Pub.

Peace & Bread in Time of War. Jane Addams. LC 83-80835. (NASW Classics Ser.). 264p. reprint ed. pap. 81.90 (*0-7837-6538-X*, 204567500007) Bks Demand.

Peace & Conflict Studies. Jeong. 78.95 (*1-84014-095-X*); pap. 30.95 (*1-84014-098-4*) Ashgate Pub Co.

Peace & Conflict Studies in Tolkien's Middle-Earth, Vol. 1. Philip W. Helms et al. 51p. (Orig.). 1993. pap. 7.50 (*1-881799-05-0*) Am Tolkien Soc.

Peace & Development. Ed. by Narindar Singh. (C). 1988. 23.00 (*81-7062-050-3*, Pub. by Lancer International) S Asia.

Peace & Development in the Pacific Hemisphere. Johan Galtung. 68p. 1989. pap. text 5.00 (*0-8248-1262-X*) S M Matsunaga.

Peace & Disarmament: Naval Rivalry & Arms Control, 1922-1933. Richard W. Fanning. LC 94-18444. (Illus.). 248p. (C). 1995. 36.00 (*0-8131-1878-6*) U Pr of Ky.

Peace & Disputed Sovereignty: Reflections on Conflict over Territory. Friedrich V. Kratochwil et al. LC 85-91271. 172p. (Orig.). 1985. pap. text 19.50 (*0-8191-4954-3*); lib. bdg. 47.50 (*0-8191-4953-5*) U Pr of Amer.

***Peace & Friendship: Denmark's Official Relations with China, 1675-2000.** Christopher Bo Bramsen. (Illus.). 160p. 2000. 39.95 (*87-87062-82-8*, Pub. by NIAS) Paul & Co Pubs.

Peace & Its Discontents: Essays on Palestine in the Middle East Peace Process. Edward W. Said. LC 95-34226. 256p. 1996. pap. 12.00 (*0-679-76725-8*) Vin Bks.

Peace & Justice Ministry: A Practical Guide. R. Taylor. LC 95-145308. 1994. pap. 7.50 (*0-697-17798-X*) Harcourt Religion.

***Peace & Justice Shall Embrace: Power & Theopolitics in the Bible.** unabridged ed. Millard C. Lind. Ed. by Ted Grimsrud & Loren L. Johns. LC 99-41416. 252p. 2000. pap. 22.95 (*0-9665021-1-6*, Pub. by Pandora PA) Herald Pr.

Peace & Nuclear War Dictionary. Sheikh R. Ali. LC 89-14971. (Clio Dictionaries in Political Science Ser.). 350p. (C). 1989. lib. bdg. 49.00 (*0-87436-531-7*) ABC-CLIO.

***Peace & Power: Building Communities for Future.** 4th ed. Peggy L. Chinn. (Illus.). 148p. (C). 1998. pap. text 22.50 (*0-7637-0944-1*) JB Pubns.

Peace & Power: Building Communities for the Future. 4th rev. ed. Peggy L. Chinn. LC 95-22950. 1995. 14.95 (*0-88737-657-6*) Natl League Nurse.

Peace & Revolution: The Moral Crisis of American Pacifism. Guenter Lewy. LC 88-1374. 293p. reprint ed. pap. 90.90 (*0-8357-4364-0*, 203719300007) Bks Demand.

Peace & Security: The Next Generation. Ed. by George A. Lopez & Nancy J. Myers. (Illus.). 294p. 1997. 68.50 (*0-8476-8594-2*); pap. 17.95 (*0-8476-8595-0*) Rowman.

Peace & Security Bk. Three. J. Mohan Malik. (Asian Defense Policies Ser.: Bk. 3). 96p. (C). 1995. pap. 40.00 (*0-7300-1811-3*, Pub. by Deakin Univ) St Mut.

Peace & Security in Northeast Asia: The Nuclear Issue & the Korean Peninsula. Ed. by Young W. Kihi & Peter Hayes. LC 96-6318. 512p. (gr. 13). 1997. pap. text 27.95 (*1-56324-790-9*, East Gate Bk) M E Sharpe.

Peace & Security in Northeast Asia: The Nuclear Issue & the Korean Peninsula. Ed. by Young W. Kihl & Peter Hayes. LC 96-6318. 510p. (YA). (gr. 13). 1996. text 87.95 (*1-56324-789-5*, East Gate Bk) M E Sharpe.

Peace & Stability in Korea: Prospects & Pitfalls. Christopher J. Sigur. 21p. (Orig.). 1996. pap. write for info. (*0-87641-146-4*) Carnegie Ethics & Intl Affairs.

Peace & Survival: West Germany, the Peace Movement, & European Security. David Gress. (Publication Ser.: No. 309). 266p. (Orig.). 1988. pap. 3.58 (*0-8179-8092-X*) Hoover Inst Pr.

Peace & the Peacemakers: The Treaty of 1783. Ed. by Ronald Hoffman & Peter J. Albert. LC 85-10618. (U. S. Capitol Historical Society, Perspectives on the American Revolution Ser.). xvi, 263p. 1986. text 35.00 (*0-8139-1071-4*) U Pr of Va.

Peace & the War Industry. rev. ed. Ed. by Kenneth E. Boulding. LC 72-87664. 159p. 1975. reprint ed. pap. text 18.95 (*0-87855-545-5*) Transaction Pubs.

Peace & the War Industry. 2nd rev. ed. Ed. by Kenneth E. Boulding. LC 72-87664. 159p. 1975. reprint ed. 29.95 (*0-87855-052-6*) Transaction Pubs.

Peace & Union. William Frend. LC 91-16954. 62p. 1991. reprint ed. 35.00 (*1-85477-066-7*) Continuum.

Peace & War. Guglielmo Ferrero. Tr. by B. Pritchard. LC 69-18927. (Essay Index Reprint Ser.). 1977. 20.95 (*0-8369-0041-3*) Ayer.

Peace & War: A Theory of International Relations. Raymond Aron. LC 81-14296. 838p. 1981. reprint ed. 89.50 (*0-89874-391-5*) Krieger.

Peace & War: Armed Conflicts & the International Order, 1648-1989. Kalevi J. Holsti. (Studies in International Relations: No. 14). (Illus.). 397p. (C). 1991. pap. text 22.95 (*0-521-39929-7*) Cambridge U Pr.

Peace & War: Cross-Cultural Perspectives. Ed. by Robert A. Rubenstein & Mary L. Foster. 350p. (C). 1985. pap. 21.95 (*0-88738-619-9*) Transaction Pubs.

Peace & War: Readings for Writers. Dennis Okerstrom & Sarah J. Morgan. 512p. (C). 1992. pap. 37.00 (*0-205-13603-6*, H3603-1) Allyn.

Peace & War: Reminiscences of a Life on the Frontiers of Science. Robert Serber & Robert Crease. LC 97-38065. (Illus.). 240p. 1998. 31.50 (*0-231-10546-0*) Col U Pr.

Peace & War? Understanding the Peace Process in Northern Ireland. Ed. by Chris Gilligan & Jon Tonge. LC 97-73871. (Illus.). 192p. 1997. text 64.95 (*1-85972-519-8*, Pub. by Ashgate Pub) Ashgate Pub Co.

Peace & War in Byzantium: Essays in Honor of George T. Dennis, S.J. Ed. by Timothy S. Miller & John Nesbitt. LC 94-19723. 282p. 1995. 49.95 (*0-8132-0805-X*) Cath U Pr.

***Peace & War on the Anglo-Cherokee Frontier, 1756-63.** John Oliphant. 272p. 2000. 39.95 (*0-8071-2637-3*) La State U Pr.

Peace & Wartime Applications & Techincal Issues for Unattended Ground Sensors. Ed. by Gerold Yonas. LC 98-122036. 31p. 1997. pap. 69.00 (*0-8194-2496-X*) SPIE.

***Peace & Waste.** Shaykh Nazim Al-Naqshbandi. 100p. (C). 2000. pap. 9.95 (*1-898863-13-X*, Pub. by Zero Prods) Kazi Pubns.

Peace & World Security Studies: A Curriculum Guide. Ed. by Michael T. Klare. LC 93-28833. 432p. 1994. pap. text 8.00 (*1-55587-432-0*) L Rienner.

Peace As a Women's Issue: A History of the U. S. Movement for World Peace & Women's Rights. Harriet H. Alonso. (Studies on Peace & Conflict Resolution). (Illus.). 360p. 1993. pap. text 19.95 (*0-8156-0269-3*) Syracuse U Pr.

Peace at Heart: An Oregon Country Life. Barbara Drake. LC 98-23928. 192p. 1998. pap. 15.95 (*0-87071-455-4*) Oreg St U Pr.

Peace at Last. Jill Murphy. 1992. pap. 5.99 (*0-14-054685-5*) NAL.

Peace at Last. Jill Murphy. 1980. 9.15 (*0-606-12475-6*, Pub. by Turtleback) Demco.

Peace at Last: The After-Death Experiences of John Lennon. Jason Leen. Ed. by John M. Thompson et al. LC 89-2223. (Illus.). 152p. 1989. pap. 11.95 (*0-935699-00-7*) Illum Arts.

Peace at the Center. David B. Dick. LC 94-92164. (Illus.). 242p. 1994. 17.95 (*0-9632886-2-8*) Plum Lick Pub.

Peace Be on Your Home: An Illustrated Treasury. Moody Press Editors. 1999. 9.99 (*0-8024-4626-4*) Moody.

Peace Be Still: A Meditation Coloring Book. A. J. Wolff. (Illus.). 64p. 1997. pap. 7.95 (*0-931481-05-8*) Rosebush Pub.

Peace Be Still: Inner Healing for Racial Harmony. Cynthia L. Davis. (Illus.). 75p. 1997. pap. 5.00 (*0-9659539-0-4*) Unications Pub.

Peace Be with You. Illus. by Jenny Faw. (Charming Petites Ser.). 80p. 1996. 4.95 (*0-88088-798-2*) Peter Pauper.

Peace Be with You. Cornelia Lehn. LC 80-70190. (Illus.). 126p. (J). (gr. k-5). 1981. 6.95 (*0-87303-061-3*) Faith & Life.

Peace Be with You. Peggy Sneller. 1999. 7.95 (*1-56245-358-0*) Great Quotations.

Peace Be with You. rev. ed. Redemptorist Pastoral Pubns. Staff. (Illus.). 16p. 1987. pap. 2.95 (*0-89243-417-1*) Liguori Pubns.

P

Peace Be with You: Justified Warfare or the Way of Nonviolence. Eileen Egan. LC 99-17247. 350p. 1999. pap. 22.00 (*1-57075-243-5*) Orbis Bks.

Peace Begins with You. Katherine Scholes. (Illus.). 40p. (J). (gr. k-3). 1994. pap. 7.95 (*0-316-77440-5*) Little.

Peace Behind Bars: A Peacemaking Priest's Journal from Jail. John Dear. 320p. (Orig.). 1995. pap. 14.95 (*1-55612-771-5*) Sheed & Ward WI.

Peace Betrayed: Essays on Pacifism & Politics. Ed. by Michael Cromartie. 275p. (C). 1990. pap. text 22.75 (*0-89633-144-X*); lib. bdg. 39.50 (*0-89633-143-1*) Ethics & Public Policy.

Peace Book. Ireni K. Eleftheria. LC 87-90038. (Black Rose Bks.: Vol. P114). 96p. 1987. reprint ed. pap. 30.00 (*0-608-00461-8*, 206128000007) Bks Demand.

Peace Book. Ed. by Ireni K. Eleftheria. (Illus.). 150p. 1987. reprint ed. write for info. (*0-920057-98-5*); reprint ed. pap. write for info. (*0-920057-99-3*) Black Rose.

Peace Breaks Out. John Knowles. 192p. 1997. mass mkt. 5.99 (*0-553-27574-7*, Bantam Classics) Bantam.

Peace Breaks Out. John Knowles. (J). 1982. 10.60 (*0-606-02819-6*, Pub. by Turtleback) Demco.

Peace Breaks Out. Angela M. Thirkell. LC 96-36738. 328p. 1997. pap. 12.95 (*1-55921-188-1*) Moyer Bell.

Peace Brokers: Mediators in the Arab-Israeli Conflict, 1948-1979. Saadia Touval. LC 81-47955. 392p. reprint ed. pap. 121.60 (*0-8357-2554-5*, 204024500015) Bks Demand.

***Peace Building & Police Reform.** Ed. by Espen Barth Eide & Tor Tanke Holm. LC 99-86860. (Peacekeeping Ser.). 240p. 2000. 52.50 (*0-7146-4987-2*, Pub. by F Cass Pubs) Intl Spec Bk.

***Peace Building in Northern Ireland.** Colin Knox. 2000. text 59.95 (*0-312-23410-4*) St Martin.

Peace Building in the Asia Pacific Region. Peter King & Yoichi Kibata. LC 96-202922. 160p. 1997. pap. text 29.95 (*1-86448-115-3*, Pub. by Allen & Unwin Pty) Paul & Co Pubs.

Peace Building Through Reconciliation in Northern Ireland. Mervyn Love. LC 95-78515. 336p. 1995. 77.95 (*1-85972-136-2*, Pub. by Avebry) Ashgate Pub Co.

Peace by Forceful Means? A Special Issue of "Peace & Conflict" Ed. by Milton Schwebel. 87p. 1998. pap. write for info. (*0-8058-9830-1*) L Erlbaum Assocs.

Peace by Peace: Conflict Resolution Through Peer Mediation. (Illus.). (Orig.). (YA). (gr. 7-12). 1995. pap. 0.39 (*1-56688-292-3*); pap., teacher ed. 24.95 (*1-56688-291-5*); pap., student ed. 9.95 (*1-56688-290-7*) Bur For At-Risk.

Peace by Peace: Conflict Resolution Through Peer Mediation, 9 posters, Set. (Poster Ser.). (Illus.). (Orig.). (YA). (gr. 7-12). 1995. 19.95 (*1-56688-293-1*) Bur For At-Risk.

Peace by Peaceful Means: Peace & Conflict, Development & Civilization. Johan Galtung. LC 96-68424. (Peace Research Institute, Oslo Ser.). 320p. 1996. 75.00 (*0-8039-7510-4*); pap. 26.95 (*0-8039-7511-2*) Sage.

Peace by Pieces - United Nations Agencies & Their Roles: A Reader & Selective Bibliography. Ed. by Robert N. Wells, Jr. 494p. 1991. 55.00 (*0-8108-2510-4*) Scarecrow.

Peace by Revolution: An Interpretation of Mexico. Frank Tannenbaum. LC 72-169776. (Select Bibliographies Reprint Ser.). (Illus.). 1977. reprint ed. 29.95 (*0-8369-5996-5*) Ayer.

Peace Calling from the Chasm. Clara P. Schultz. 70p. (Orig.). 1996. pap. write for info. (*1-57502-244-3*) Morris Pubng.

Peace Catalog: A Guidebook to a Positive Future. Ed. by Duane Sweeney. LC 84-62428. (Illus.). 368p. 1984. pap. 14.95 (*0-9614103-0-2*) Press for Peace.

Peace Chief: A Novel of the Real People. Robert J. Conley. LC 98-21125. 336p. 1998. text 25.95 (*0-312-19314-9*) St Martin.

Peace Chiefs of the Cheyennes. Stan Hoig. LC 79-4739. (Illus.). 224p. 1990. pap. 13.95 (*0-8061-2262-5*) U of Okla Pr.

Peace Child *see* **Hijo de Paz**

Peace Commandos: Nonviolent Heroes in the Struggle Against War & Injustice. Michael Kronenwetter. LC 93-31204. (Timestop Bks.). (Illus.). 160p. (J). (gr. 4-6). 1994. lib. bdg. 22.00 (*0-02-751051-4*, New Dscvry Bks) Silver Burdett Pr.

Peace (Compilation) Baha'u'llah et al. 46p. 1986. pap. 3.95 (*0-909991-32-4*) Bahai.

Peace Conference of 1919: Organization & Procedure. Frank S. Marston. LC 80-28997. 276p. 1981. reprint ed. lib. bdg. 45.00 (*0-313-22910-4*, MAPEC, Greenwood Pr) Greenwood.

Peace Conference of 1919, Organization & Procedure. Frank S. Marston. LC 76-29412. reprint ed. 32.50 (*0-404-15349-6*) AMS Pr.

Peace Consciousness: In North Ireland & Findhorn, Scotland. Patricia Hamilton. (Illus.). 114p. 1995. spiral bd. 25.00 (*1-877809-55-1*) Park Pl Pubns.

Peace Conspiracy: Wang Ching-Wei & the China War, 1937-1941. Gerald E. Bunker. LC 78-180149. (Harvard East Asian Ser.: No. 67). 342p. reprint ed. pap. 106.10 (*0-608-30389-5*, 200548600054) Bks Demand.

Peace Conspiracy: Yishiro Fujimura: Warrior-Businessman. Jim McDowell. 264p. (Orig.). 1993. pap. write for info. (*0-9635944-0-0*) McBo Corp Pubs.

Peace Corps: An Annotated Bibliography. Robert B. Ridinger. 300p. (C). 1989. 40.00 (*0-8161-8912-9*, Hall Reference) Macmillan.

Peace Corps: 10,000 Volunteers by the Year 2000: Hearing Before the Committee on International Relations, House of Representatives, 105th Congress, 2nd Session, March 18, 1998. USGPO Staff. LC 98-190606. iii, 66 p. 1998. pap. write for info. (*0-16-057064-6*) USGPO.

Peace Corps & More: 120 Ways to Work, Study & Travel in the Third World. rev. ed. Medea Benjamin. LC 90-27827. 107p. (Orig.). 1991. pap. 6.95 (*0-929765-04-4*) Seven Locks Pr.

Peace Corps Examination. Jack Rudman. (Career Examination Ser.: C-646). 1994. pap. 23.95 (*0-8373-0646-9*) Nat Learn.

Peace Corps Experience: Challenge & Change, 1969-1976. P. David Searles. LC 96-38656. (Illus.). 288p. 1997. 34.95 (*0-8131-2009-8*) U Pr of Ky.

Peace Corps in Cameroon. Julius A. Amin. LC 91-29956. (Illus.). 248p. 1992. 32.00 (*0-87338-450-4*) Kent St U Pr.

Peace Corps, 1966. Eugen Rosenstock-Huessy. (Eugen Rosenstock-Huessy Lectures: Vol. 30). 40p. 1997. pap. 21.00 incl. audio (*0-912148-49-7*) Argo Bks.

Peace Corps Roller Coaster. Dan Hebl et al. Ed. by Sharon Hebl. LC 93-80267. 200p. 1994. pap. 13.00 (*0-9638995-0-3*) Roller Coaster.

Peace Crane. Sheila Hamanaka. LC 95-1772. (Illus.). 40p. (J). (ps up). 1995. 16.00 (*0-688-13815-2*, Wm Morrow) Morrow Avon.

Peace Curriculum. Noreen Teachout. (Illus.). 55p. 1988. teacher ed. 60.00 (*0-317-93649-2*) Peace Curriculum.

Peace Dale. Betty Cotter. LC 98-87322. (Images of America Ser.). (Illus.). 128p. 1998. pap. 16.99 (*0-7524-1296-5*) Arcadia Publng.

Peace Denied: The United States, Vietnam, & the Paris Agreement. Gareth Porter. LC 75-3890. (Illus.). 381p. reprint ed. pap. 118.20 (*0-608-17410-6*, 205643400067) Bks Demand.

Peace, Detente, Cooperation. Leonid I. Brezhnev. LC 80-25943. 213p. 1981. reprint ed. pap. 66.10 (*0-608-05406-2*, 206587500006) Bks Demand.

Peace, Development & People of the Horn of Africa. John Prendergast & Sharon Pauling. (Hunger Policy Occasional Papers: No. 1). (Orig.). (C). 1992. pap. text 5.00 (*0-685-48887-X*) Bread for the World.

Peace Diet: The 44 Day Feast for Personal Peace. Susan Corso. (Illus.). 64p. (Orig.). 1996. pap. 12.95 (*0-9651541-4-9*) Dona Nobis Pacem.

Peace Dividend. Ed. by Nils P. Gleditsch et al. LC 96-9477. (Contributions to Economic Analysis Ser.: Vol. 235). 638p. 1996. text 135.00 (*0-444-82482-0*, North Holland) Elsevier.

Peace Education. Ian M. Harris. LC 88-42509. 245p. 1988. lib. bdg. 38.50 (*0-89950-354-3*) McFarland & Co.

Peace Education: Global Perspectives. Ed. by Ake Bjerstedt. (Studia Psychologica et Paedagogica.: Vol. CVII). 214p. 1993. 45.00 (*91-22-01564-7*) Coronet Bks.

Peace Education in a Postmodern World: A Special Issue of the Peabody Journal of Education, Vol. 71, No. 3, 1996. Ed. by Ian M. Harris. 176p. 1996. pap. 24.50 (*0-8058-9912-X*) L Erlbaum Assocs.

Peace Education in America, 1828-1990: Sourcebook for Education & Research. Aline M. Stomfay-Stitz. LC 93-993. (Illus.). 492p. 1993. 60.00 (*0-8108-2595-3*) Scarecrow.

Peace Eyes. Richard McSorley. LC 77-9240. 219p. 1978. pap. 3.75 (*0-912239-03-4*) Ctr Peace Studies.

Peace, Faith, Nation: Mennonites & Amish in Nineteenth-Century America. Theron F. Schlabach. LC 88-28443. (Mennonite Experience in America Ser.: Vol. 2). 400p. (Orig.). 1988. pap. 19.99 (*0-8361-3102-9*) Herald Pr.

Peace for Beginners. Ian Kellas. 1984. 14.95 (*0-86316-008-5*); pap. 6.95 (*0-86316-009-3*) Writers & Readers.

Peace for Lebanon? From War to Reconstruction. Ed. by Deirdre Collings. LC 93-39746. 342p. 1994. pap. text 22.00 (*1-55587-501-7*); lib. bdg. 46.00 (*1-55587-367-7*) L Rienner.

Peace for Palestine: First Lost Opportunity. Elmer Berger. LC 92-45726. 304p. (C). 1993. 49.95 (*0-8130-1207-4*) U Press Fla.

Peace for the Arsonist. Bart Baxter. 68p. (Orig.). 1995. pap. 7.00 (*0-9637849-7-8*) Bacchae Pr.

Peace from Nervous Suffering. Claire Weekes. 1990. mass mkt. 6.50 (*0-451-16723-6*, Sig) NAL.

Peace from Pieces: Leader's Manual. Diana Stasey. (Illus.). 83p. 1993. pap. text 25.00 (*1-58302-061-6*, BRE-07) One Way St.

Peace from Pieces: Student Workbook. Diana Stasey. (Illus.). 74p. 1993. wbk. ed. 5.00 (*1-58302-062-4*, BRE-07W) One Way St.

Peace, from War to War. John S. Boeman. 450p. 1991. pap. text 57.95 (*0-89126-170-2*) MA-AH Pub.

Peace Has No Space for Memories, Vol. 1. Sheilana Massey. Ed. by Barbara Gabel. LC 96-92569. 144p. 1996. pap. 11.95 (*0-9651004-1-3*) Spiral Pubs.

Peace Heroes. Christine Neufeld. (Fast Lane Bible Studies Ser.). 48p. (J). (gr. 7-9). 1996. pap. 9.95 (*0-87303-306-X*) Faith & Life.

Peace Heroes in 20th-Century America. Ed. & Intro. by Charles DeBenedetti. LC 85-45031. (Illus.). 288p. reprint ed. pap. 89.30 (*0-608-01057-X*, 205936500001) Bks Demand.

Peace I Leave with You. Gary A. Smith. 1.25 (*0-687-02742-X*) Abingdon.

Peace Impossible - War Unlikely: The Cold War Between the United States & the Soviet Union. Joseph L. Nogee & John W. Spanier. (C). 1988. pap. text 21.00 (*0-673-39783-1*) Addson-Wesley Educ.

***Peace in a Violent World.** Susan Field & Taylor Field. Ed. by Jan Turrentine. (Illus.). 63p. 1999. pap. 5.99 (*1-56309-290-5*) Womans Mission Union.

Peace in Exile: Poems. David Oates. 1992. pap. 12.95 (*0-9617481-9-2*); audio 10.00 (*1-882291-50-6*) Oyster River Pr.

Peace in Friendship Village. Zona Gale. 1977. 20.95 (*0-8369-4244-2*, 6055) Ayer.

Peace in 100 Languages: A One-Word Multilingual Dictionary. Contrib. by Mikhail Kabattchenko et al. LC 91-30757. (Illus.). 48p. pap. 9.95 (*0-915190-74-5*, JP9074-5) Jalmar Pr.

Peace in Our Time. Matthew Melko. 217p. 1990. 24.95 (*1-55778-055-2*) Prof World Peace.

Peace in Palestine. Mohammad T. Mehdi. LC 75-43266. 1976. pap. 10.00 (*0-911026-08-8*) New World Press NY.

Peace in Parts: Integration & Conflict in Regional Organization. Joseph S. Nye. LC 87-10480. (Illus.). 224p. (Orig.). (C). 1987. reprint ed. lib. bdg. 46.00 (*0-8191-6393-7*) U Pr of Amer.

***Peace in Passing: How to Find Peace in the Passing of Someone You Love.** unabridged ed. Lolita Walker Snipes. LC 99-91720. 112p. 2000. pap. 10.95 (*0-9677108-9-8*) Roman Pubng.

Peace in Space. David Baker. LC 87-19885. (Today's World in Space Bks.). (Illus.). 48p. (J). (gr. 3-8). 1987. 13.95 (*0-685-67601-3*) Rourke Corp.

Peace in Space. David Baker. LC 87-19885. (Today's World in Space Ser.). (Illus.). 48p. (J). (gr. 3-8). 1987. lib. bdg. 23.93 (*0-86592-408-2*) Rourke Enter.

Peace in Spite of Panic *see* **Paz... A Pesar del Panico**

Peace in the Classroom: Practical Lessons in Living for Elementary-Age Children. Hetty Adams. (Illus.). 144p. 1994. pap., teacher ed. 16.00 (*1-895411-68-8*) Peguis Pubs Ltd.

Peace in the Corazon. Victoria Garcia-Zapata. (Poesia Tejana Ser.: Vol. 2). x, 46p. 1999. pap. 12.00 (*0-930324-46-3*) Wings Pr.

Peace in the Country. C. R. Gibson Company Staff. 1997. 6.00 (*0-7852-2772-5*) Gibson.

Peace in the Lord. Melva J. Harris. 67p. (Orig.). 1995. pap. text 12.00 (*0-614-29914-4*) M J Harris.

Peace in the Making. Ed. by Rohana Mahmood. 108p. 1992. 56.50 (*0-7103-0419-6*, A7252) Routledge.

Peace in the Meadow: And Other Encounters with Life. Ilene Smith. (Illus.). 104p. (Orig.). 1988. pap. 3.95 (*0-88028-087-5*, 965) Forward Movement.

Peace in the Middle East: Israeli-Palestinian Peace Proposal. George D. Mullen. (C). 1994. 19.95 (*1-881116-46-8*, Pub. by Black Forest Pr) Epic Bk Promo.

Peace in the Middle East: The Challenge for Israel. Ed. by Efraim Karsh. 167p. 1994. 42.50 (*0-7146-4614-8*, Pub. by F Cass Pubs); pap. 22.50 (*0-7146-4141-3*, Pub. by F Cass Pubs) Intl Spec Bk.

***Peace in the Midst of the Storm, 2 vols.** Randy Phillips. 1999. pap. 16.97 (*5-550-10701-5*) Nairi.

Peace in the Parish: How to Use Conflict Redemption Principles & Process. James D. Qualben. LC 91-214809. 302p. (Orig.). 1992. pap. text 15.95 (*1-880292-00-9*) LangMarc.

Peace in the Parsonage: A Handbook for Pastors' Wives. Jean Meppelink. 78p. (Orig.). 1992. pap. 5.95 (*0-9657979-0-2*) Growing Life.

Peace in the Post-Reformation: The Birkbeck Lectures, 1995. John Bossy. LC 98-24990. 120p. (C). 1998. text 49.95 (*0-521-64061-X*); pap. text 14.95 (*0-521-64605-7*) Cambridge U Pr.

Peace in the Streets: Breaking the Cycle of Gang Violence. Arturo Hernandez. LC 97-49125. 216p. 1998. pap. 14.95 (*0-87868-692-4*, 6924, CWLA Pr) Child Welfare.

Peace in Their Time. Weiss. 1999. text 49.50 (*1-86064-403-1*) St Martin.

Peace in War: A Novel. Miguel de Unamuno. Tr. by Anthony Kerrigan et al. LC 82-61390. (Selected Works of Miguel de Unamuno: Vol. 1). 452p. 1983. reprint ed. pap. 140.20 (*0-608-02900-9*, 206396400008) Bks Demand.

Peace Is a Circle of Love. Joan W. Anglund. LC 92-28855. (Illus.). 32p. (J). 1993. 8.95 (*0-15-259922-3*, Gulliver Bks) Harcourt.

Peace Is a Fire: A Collection of Writings & Sayings. 2nd ed. Sangharakshita. (Illus.). 160p. 1996. pap. 13.95 (*0-904766-84-5*) Windhorse Pubns.

Peace Is Every Step. Thich Nhat Hanh. 160p. 1992. pap. 12.95 (*0-553-35139-7*, New Age Bks) Bantam.

***Peace Is Everybody's Business: Half a Century of Peace Education with Elizabeth Evans Baker.** Marta Daniels. (Illus.). 1999. pap. 7.95 (*0-9636610-0-0*) Juniata Coll.

Peace Is Everything: World View of Muslims in the Senegambia. David E. Maranz. LC 92-83905. (International Museum of Cultures Publications: No. 28). xiv, 314p. 1993. pap. 32.00 (*0-88312-816-0*) S I L Intl.

Peace Is in the Eye of the Beholder. Raphael Israeli. xxiv, 389p. 1985. text 100.00 (*0-89925-077-7*) Mouton.

***Peace Is the Way: Writings on Nonviolence from the Fellowship of Reconciliation.** Ed. by Walter Wink. LC 00-22077. 275p. 2000. pap. 20.00 (*1-57075-315-6*) Orbis Bks.

***Peace Journey.** Carl Bildt. LC 99-220726. 1998. 50.00 (*0-297-84131-9*, Pub. by Weidenfeld & Nicolson) Trafalgar.

Peace-Just Live It! A Challenge to Youth for the 21st Century. Christine Neufeld. LC 94-61723. 104p. (YA). (gr. 9-12). 1995. pap., spiral bd. 18.95 (*0-87303-239-X*) Faith & Life.

Peace, Justice, & Unity. Raymond L. Flynn. 48p. 1985. pap. 2.50 (*0-317-61836-9*) Quinlin C Pubs.

Peace, Justice, & Unity: Ireland's Unfinished Agenda. Raymond L. Flynn. 48p. (Orig.). 1985. pap. 2.50 (*0-934665-01-X*) Quinlin C Pubs.

Peace Keeper. large type ed. Ray Hogan. LC 94-32527. 219p. 1995. 18.95 (*0-7862-0345-5*) Thorndike Pr.

Peace Keeping in a Democratic Society: The Lessons of Northern Ireland. Robin Evelegh. 1978. 55.00 (*0-7735-0502-4*, Pub. by McG-Queens Univ Pr) CUP Services.

Peace Labyrinth: Sacred Geometry. Beatrice Bartnett. (Illus.). 52p. (Orig.). 1995. pap. 9.95 (*0-9622182-7-8*) Lifestyle Inst.

Peace, Land, Bread! A History of the Russian Revolution. John J. Vail. LC 94-26634. (World History Library). 160p. (YA). (gr. 7-12). 1995. lib. bdg. 19.95 (*0-8160-2818-4*) Facts on File.

Peace Like a River. Vardis Fisher. (Testament of Man Ser.). 1962. 50.00 (*0-614-22022-X*, Idaho Center for the Bk) Heming W Studies.

Peace Like a River: A Personal Journey Across America. Sue Guist. LC 90-21139. (Peacewatch Editions Ser.). 224p. 1991. per. 8.95 (*0-943734-17-7*) Ocean Tree Bks.

Peace Like a Spider & Other Devotions for Teens. Karl Haffner. LC 94-239155. Date not set. pap. 7.99 (*0-8280-0888-4*) Review & Herald.

Peace, Love & Healing: Bodymind Communication & the Path to Self-Healing: An Exploration. Bernie S. Siegel. 304p. 1998. pap. 14.00 (*0-06-091705-9*, Perennial) HarperTrade.

Peace, Love & Healing: Siegel,&Bernie S. abr. ed. Bernie Siegel. 1994. audio 18.00 (*0-89845-918-4*, CPN 2121) HarperAudio.

Peace, Love & Healing: The Bodymind & the Path to Self-Healing - An Exploration. large type ed. Bernie S. Siegel. 312p. 1990. reprint ed. pap. 14.95 (*0-8027-2641-0*) Walker & Co.

Peace-Maintenance: The Evolution of International Political Authority. Jarat Chopra. LC 98-27103. xviii, 261p. 1999. write for info. (*0-415-19483-0*) Routledge.

Peace Makers. Carol M. Baldwin. LC 99-187137. (Illus.). 75p. 1998. pap. 19.95 (*0-9666358-1-7*) Lamp Lighter.

Peace-Making & the Settlement with Japan. Frederick S. Dunn. LC 81-6223. 210p. 1981. reprint ed. lib. bdg. 59.50 (*0-313-23076-5*, DUPM, Greenwood Pr) Greenwood.

Peace Manual: A Guide to Personal-Political Integration. Frank Rubenfeld. (Illus.). 85p. 1986. pap. 7.95 (*0-9616424-0-8*) Lion Lamb Pr.

Peace Manual or War & Its Remedies. George C. Beckwith. LC 73-137529. (Peace Movement in America Ser.). 252p. 1972. reprint ed. lib. bdg. 31.95 (*0-89198-056-3*) Ozer.

Peace Marshal. large type ed. Frank Gruber. (Western Ser.). 384p. 1995. pap. 16.99 (*0-7089-7694-8*, Linford) Ulverscroft.

***Peace Matters: A Philippine Peace Compendium.** Ed. by Miriam Coronel-Ferrer. LC 97-946611. (Illus.). 308p. 1999. pap. text 30.00 (*971-8797-95-5*, Pub. by U of Philippines Pr) UH Pr.

Peace Ministry: A Handbook for Local Churches. Daniel L. Buttry. LC 94-42198. 240p. 1995. pap. 16.00 (*0-8170-1214-1*) Judson.

Peace-Mir: An Anthology of Historic Alternatives to War. Ed. by Charles Chatfield & Ruzanna Ilukhina. (Studies on Peace & Conflict Resolution). 386p. 1994. text 49.50 (*0-8156-2601-0*) Syracuse U Pr.

Peace Mission Movement. M. J. Divine. LC 82-90163. (Illus.). 192p. (Orig.). 1982. 8.00 (*0-9609078-0-7*); pap. 6.00 (*0-9609078-1-5*) Palace Mission.

Peace Movement Organizations & Activists in the U. S. An Analytic Bibliography. Ed. by John Lofland et al. LC 90-5380. (Behavioral & Social Sciences Librarian Ser.: Vol. 10, No. 1). 141p. 1991. 49.95 (*1-56024-075-X*) Haworth Pr.

Peace Movements & Political Cultures. Ed. by Charles Chatfield & Peter Van Den Dungen. LC 88-1902. 320p. 1988. text 41.00 (*0-87049-576-3*) U of Tenn Pr.

Peace Movements Between the Wars: One Man's Work for Peace. William Solzbacher. Ed. by Josephine Solzbacher Kennon. LC 98-44212. (Studies in World Peace: Vol. 9). 356p. 1998. text 99.95 (*0-7734-8235-0*) E Mellen.

Peace Movements Between the Wars: One Man's Work for Peace. William Solzbacher & Josephine S. Kennon. LC 98-44212. (Studies in World Peace). xviii, 333p. 1999. write for info. (*0-88946-586-X*) E Mellen.

Peace Negotiations: A Personal Narrative. Robert Lansing. LC 74-110852. (Illus.). 328p. 1971. reprint ed. lib. bdg. 65.00 (*0-8371-4519-8*, LAPN, Greenwood Pr) Greenwood.

Peace Notebook: An Illustrated Journal, with Quotes. Running Press Staff. (Illus.). 96p. 1998. pap. 5.95 (*0-7624-0268-7*) Running Pr.

Peace Now! American Society & the Ending of the Vietnam War. Rhodri Jeffreys-Jones. LC 99-19725. (Illus.). 320p. 1999. 25.00 (*0-300-07811-0*) Yale U Pr.

Peace of Aristophanes. Aristophanes. Tr. by Robert Webb from GRE. LC 64-22630. 107p. reprint ed. pap. 33.20 (*0-608-15495-4*, 202968400063) Bks Demand.

Peace of Body, Peace of Mind: Practical, Effective Techniques for Mental Fitness. Rose VanSickle. LC 95-92855. 264p. (Orig.). 1996. pap. 14.95 (*0-9649506-1-8*) P L J Unltd.

Peace of Europe, the Fruits of Solitude: And Other Writings. William Penn. 376p. 1993. pap. 6.95 (*0-460-87302-4*, Everyman's Classic Lib) Tuttle Pubng.

Peace of God: Social Violence & Religious Response Around the Year 1000. Ed. by Thomas Head & Richard Landes. LC 92-52758. (Illus.). 384p. (C). 1992. text 52.50 (*0-8014-2741-X*); pap. text 19.95 (*0-8014-8021-3*) Cornell U Pr.

Peace of Heart: Based on the Life & Teachings of Francis of Assisi. John Kirvan. LC 95-77235. (30 Days with a Great Spiritual Teacher Ser.). 216p. (Orig.). 1995. pap. 7.95 (*0-87793-564-5*) Ave Maria.

Peace of Heart in All Things: Meditations for Each Day of the Year. Brother Roger. LC 96-53041. 1996. 9.95 (*0-941050-96-3*) GIA Pubns.

An Asterisk (*) at the beginning of an entry indicates that the title is appearing for the first time.

Peace of Jesus: Reflections on the Gospel for the A-Cycle. Joseph G. Donders. LC 83-4240. 319p. (Orig.). reprint ed. pap. 98.90 (*0-8357-4069-2*, 2036790005) Bks Demand.

Peace of Mind. Compiled by John Cook. LC 97-31316. (Pocket Positives Ser.). 256p. 1997. pap. 8.95 (*1-57749-057-6*) Fairview Press.

Peace of Mind: Daily Meditations for Easing Stress. Amy E. Dean. LC 94-21563. 384p. 1995. pap. 10.95 (*0-553-35454-X*) Bantam.

Peace of Mind: How You Can Learn to Meditate & Use the Power of Your Mind. Ian Gawler. 224p. pap. 10.95 (*0-89529-447-8*, Avery) Penguin Putnam.

Peace of Mind During Pregnancy: An A-Z Guide to the Substances That Could Affect Your Unborn Baby. Christine Kelley-Buchanan. LC 88-45295. 381p. reprint ed. pap. 118.20 (*0-7837-2667-8*, 204303200006) Bks Demand.

Peace of Mind in Earthquake Country. rev. ed. Peter I. Yanev. (Illus.). 200p. 1991. pap. 14.95 (*0-87701-771-9*) Chronicle Bks.

Peace of Mind Is a Blanket That Purrs: A Rose Is Rose Book. Pat Brady. LC 98-12867. (Illus.). 128p. 1998. 9.95 (*1-55853-615-9*) Rutledge Hill Pr.

Peace of Mind Is a Piece of Cake. Joseph Sinclair & Michael Mallows. (Illus.). 110p. 1998. pap. 14.50 (*1-899836-24-1*, Pub. by Crown Hse) LPC Group.

Peace of Mind Through Possibility Thinking. Robert H. Schuller. 192p. 1986. mass mkt. 4.50 (*0-515-08985-0*, Jove) Berkley Pub.

Peace of Nicias & the Sicilian Expedition. Donald Kagan. LC 81-3150. (Illus.). 400p. 1981. text 49.95 (*0-8014-1367-2*) Cornell U Pr.

Peace of Nicias & the Sicilian Expedition. Donald Kagan. LC 81-3150. (Illus.). 400p. 1991. reprint ed. pap. text 18.95 (*0-8014-9940-2*) Cornell U Pr.

Peace of Soul: Timeless Wisdom on Finding Serenity & Joy by the Century's Most Acclaimed Catholic Bishop. Fulton J. Sheen. LC 95-26419. (Liguori Classic Ser.). 288p. 1996. reprint ed. pap. 13.95 (*0-89243-915-7*, Liguori Triumph) Liguori Pubns.

*__Peace of Traveling Girl: Vagabond Virgin.__ Kyoto Shoin. (Kyoto Shoin Arts Collection Series). (Illus.). 144p. 1998. pap. 12.00 (*4-7636-1719-2*, Pub. by Kyoto Shoin) RAM Publications.

Peace Offering - Gift to the U. N. 1991. write for info. (*0-318-68404-7*, 91.I.8) UN.

Peace Officer. large type ed. Elliot Conway. (Linford Western Library). 272p. 1993. pap. 16.99 (*0-7089-7433-3*, Linford) Ulverscroft.

Peace Officers' Guide to California's Dangerous Weapons Laws. Rick Bryce. LC 96-85775. (Illus.). 128p. (C). 1998. pap. 9.95 (*0-9653621-1-6*) Copperhouse.

Peace Officer's Guide to Criminal Law. 19th rev. ed. George T. Payton & Jim Guffy. (Illus.). 244p. (C). 1998. pap. text 20.00 (*0-9649086-4-6*) Crim Just Serv.

*__Peace Officer's Guide to the Georgia Criminal Code, 1999-2000.__ Barbara J. Birkland & Steven T. Kernes. 164p. 1999. 8.95 (*0-937935-44-1*) Justice Syst Pr.

*__Peace Officer's Guide to the Georiga Traffic Code, 1999-2000.__ Steven T. Kernes & Barbara J. Birkland. 147p. 1999. pap. 8.95 (*0-937935-45-X*) Justice Syst Pr.

Peace Officer's Guide to the Hawaii Criminal Code. Barbara J. Birkland & Steven T. Kernes. 100p. 1994. pap. 8.95 (*0-937935-29-8*) Justice Syst Pr.

Peace Officer's Guide to the Idaho Criminal Code, 1998-1999. Barbara J. Birkland & Steven T. Kernes. 164p. 1998. pap. 9.95 (*0-937935-35-2*) Justice Syst Pr.

*__Peace Officer's Guide to the Washington Criminal Code, 2000-2001.__ Barbara J. Birkland & Steven T. Kernes. 178p. 2000. pap. 9.95 (*0-937935-47-6*) Justice Syst Pr.

*__Peace Officer's Guide to the Washington Traffic Code, 2000-2001.__ Barbara J. Birkland & Steven T. Kernes. 143p. 2000. reprint ed. pap. 9.95 (*0-937935-48-4*) Justice Syst Pr.

*__Peace Officer's Pocket Guide to the Criminal Code of Alabama: Edition 2000.__ Ed. by Bruce Coorpender. 128p. 1999. pap. 4.95 (*1-884493-47-5*) Pocket Pr.

*__Peace Officer's Pocket Guide to the Criminal Code of Alaska: Edition 2000.__ Ed. by Bruce Coorpender. 144p. 2000. pap. 4.95 (*1-884493-49-1*) Pocket Pr.

*__Peace Officer's Pocket Guide to the Criminal Code of Florida: Edition 2000.__ Ed. by Bruce Coorpender. 192p. 1999. pap. 4.95 (*1-884493-46-7*) Pocket Pr.

*__Peace Officer's Pocket Guide to the Criminal Code of Indiana: Edition 2000.__ Ed. by Bruce Coorpender. 128p. 1999. pap. 4.95 (*1-884493-44-0*) Pocket Pr.

*__Peace Officer's Pocket Guide to the Criminal Code of Missouri: Edition 2000.__ Ed. by Bruce Coorpender. 144p. 2000. pap. 4.95 (*1-884493-53-X*) Pocket Pr.

*__Peace Officer's Pocket Guide to the Criminal Code of New Jersey: Edition 2000.__ Ed. by Bruce Coorpender. 160p. 1999. pap. 4.95 (*1-884493-45-9*) Pocket Pr.

*__Peace Officer's Pocket Guide to the Criminal Code of New York: Edition 2000.__ Ed. by Bruce Coorpender. 160p. 2000. pap. 4.95 (*1-884493-57-2*) Pocket Pr.

*__Peace Officer's Pocket Guide to the Criminal Code of Ohio: Edition 2000.__ Ed. by Bruce Coorpender. 160p. 1999. pap. 4.95 (*1-884493-48-3*) Pocket Pr.

Peace Officer's Pocket Guide to the Criminal Code of Oregon: Edition 2000. Bruce Coorpender. 160p. 2000. per. 4.95 (*1-884493-28-9*) Pocket Pr.

*__Peace Officer's Pocket Guide to the Criminal Code of Pennsylvania: Edition 2000.__ Ed. by Bruce Coorpender. 128p. 2000. pap. 4.95 (*1-884493-56-4*) Pocket Pr.

*__Peace Officer's Pocket Guide to the Criminal Code of Tennessee: Edition 2000.__ Ed. by Bruce Coorpender. 144p. 1999. pap. 4.99 (*1-884493-50-5*) Pocket Pr.

Peace Officer's Pocket Guide to the Criminal Code of Texas: Edition 2000. Ed. by Bruce Coorpender. 176p. 1998. per. 4.95 (*1-884493-32-7*) Pocket Pr.

*__Peace Officer's Pocket Guide to the Criminal Code of the United States: Edition 2000.__ Ed. by Bruce Coorpender. 192p. 2000. pap. 4.95 (*1-884493-58-0*) Pocket Pr.

*__Peace Officer's Pocket Guide to the Criminal Code of Washington: Edition 2000.__ Ed. by Bruce Coorpender. 160p. 1999. pap. 4.95 (*1-884493-42-4*) Pocket Pr.

*__Peace Officer's Pocket Guide to the Criminal Code of Wisconsin: Edition 1999.__ Ed. by Bruce Coorpender. 160p. 1999. pap. 4.95 (*1-884493-54-8*) Pocket Pr.

*__Peace Officer's Pocket Guide to the Criminal Code of Wyoming: Edition 2000.__ Ed. by Bruce Coorpender. 92p. 1999. pap. 4.95 (*1-884493-41-6*) Pocket Pr.

Peace Officer's Pocket Guide to the Oregon Vehicle Code: Edition 2000. Bruce Coorpender. 160p. 2000. per. 4.95 (*1-884493-29-7*) Pocket Pr.

*__Peace Officer's Pocket Guide to the Vehicle Code of Alabama: Edition 2000.__ Ed. by Bruce Coorpender. 128p. 1999. pap. 4.95 (*1-884493-52-1*) Pocket Pr.

*__Peace Officer's Pocket Guide to the Vehicle Code of New Jersey: Edition 2000.__ Ed. by Bruce Coorpender. 160p. 1999. pap. 4.95 (*1-884493-55-6*) Pocket Pr.

*__Peace Officer's Pocket Guide to the Vehicle Code of Tennessee: Edition 2000.__ Ed. by Bruce Coorpender. 144p. 1999. pap. 4.95 (*1-884493-51-3*) Pocket Pr.

*__Peace Officer's Pocket Guide to the Vehicle Code of Washington: Edition 2000.__ Ed. by Bruce Coorpender. 92p. 1999. pap. 4.95 (*1-884493-43-2*) Pocket Pr.

Peace Officer's Promotional Manual. George T. Payton. 316p. 1996. pap. 25.00 (*0-9649086-0-3*) Crim Just Serv.

Peace on Earth. Stanislaw Lem. Tr. by Elinor Ford & Michael Kandel from POL. 240p. 1996. pap. 12.00 (*0-15-600242-6*, Harvest Bks) Harcourt.

Peace on Earth: Pacem in Terris. John XXIII, pseud. 53p. 1963. 3.95 (*1-55586-342-6*) US Catholic.

Peace on Earth: (Pacem in Terris) Encyclieal. John XXIII, pseud. 52p. 1963. pap. 3.95 (*0-8198-5856-0*) Pauline Bks.

Peace on Earth: Your Dreams, My Dreams of Peace & Love. Josephine T. Bozoukoff. (Illus.). 72p. 1999. pap. 9.00 (*0-8059-4588-1*) Dorrance.

Peace on Earth Advent Calendar. (J). 1995. 44.99 (*1-888074-02-7*) Pckts Lrning.

*__Peace on Earth & Goodwill among Peoples.__ William Sher. LC 93-97491. 9p. 2000. 11.95 (*0-533-13403-X*) Vantage.

Peace on Earth Begins with You: Simple Steps Each of Us Can Take to Bring Harmony to Our World. Faridi McFree. LC 97-22827. (Illus.). 112p. (Orig.). 1997. pap. 9.95 (*0-688-15651-7*, Wm Morrow) Morrow Avon.

Peace on Earth Christmas Around the World. 144p. 1996. otabind 10.95 (*0-7935-6679-7*) H Leonard.

Peace on the Move: A Sociological Survey of the Members of Swedish Peace Organizations. Katsuya Kodama. 196p. (Orig.). 1990. pap. 43.50 (*91-22-01365-2*) Coronet Bks.

Peace on the Wing: Life's Unfolding, a Personal Journey Possibilities with MCSS. Mary Chloe School Craft Saunders Staff. (Illus.). 1997. spiral bd. 12.95 (*0-9662892-0-X*) Possib MCSS.

Peace on This House. Ed. by Mark Water. (Words of Joy & Comfort Ser.). (Illus.). 92p. 1996. 4.95 (*0-8192-1660-7*) Morehouse Pub.

Peace Operations: Cost of Defense Department Operations in Somalia. (Illus.). 54p. (Orig.). (YA). (gr. 12 up). 1994. pap. text 20.00 (*0-7881-0856-5*) DIANE Pub.

Peace Operations: Cost of DOD Operations in Somalia. (Illus.). 54p. 1994. pap. text 45.00 (*1-57979-125-5*) DIANE Pub.

Peace Operations: Developing an American Strategy. 1997. lib. bdg. 250.95 (*0-8490-7639-0*) Gordon Pr.

Peace Operations: Developing an American Strategy. Antonia Handlert Chayes. 188p. 1995. per. 6.00 (*0-16-051681-1*) USGPO.

Peace Operations: Heavy Use of Key Capabilities May Affect Response to Regional Conflicts. (Illus.). 80p. (Orig.). (C). 1995. pap. text 25.00 (*0-7881-2053-0*) DIANE Pub.

Peace Operations: Information on U. S. & U. N. Activities. 40p. (Orig.). 1995. pap. text 25.00 (*1-57979-126-3*) DIANE Pub.

Peace Operations: Information on U. S. & U. N. Activities. 40p. (Orig.). (C). 1995. pap. text 25.00 (*0-7881-1786-6*) DIANE Pub.

Peace Operations: Tackling the Military Legal & Policy Challenges. Michael J. Kelly. (Illus.). 1997. pap. 42.00 (*0-644-47533-1*, Pub. by Aust Gov Pub) Accents Pubns.

Peace Operations: Update on the Situation in the Former Yugoslavia. (Illus.). 44p. (Orig.). (C). 1996. pap. text 25.00 (*0-7881-3429-9*) DIANE Pub.

Peace Operations & Common Sense Replacing Rhetoric with Realism. 31p. pap. text 30.00 (*0-9999012-9-X*) DIANE Pub.

*__Peace Operations & Intrastate Conflict: The Sword or the Olive Branch?__ Thomas R. Mockaitis. LC 98-50237. (Illus.). 184p. 1999. 55.00 (*0-275-96173-7*, C6173, Praeger Pubs) Greenwood.

*__Peace Operations Between War & Peace.__ Ed. by Erwin A. Schmidl. LC 99-56535. (Illus.). 184p. 2000. 52.50 (*0-7146-4989-9*, Pub. by F Cass Pubs); pap. 24.50 (*0-7146-8052-4*, Pub. by F Cass Pubs) Intl Spec Bk.

Peace or War: The American Struggle, 1636-1936. Merle E. Curti. LC 70-143428. (Peace Movement in America Ser.). 374p. 1972. reprint ed. lib. bdg. 45.95 (*0-89198-064-4*) Ozer.

Peace Paint. Larry Simpson. LC 97-94452. 218p. 1998. pap. 10.00 (*1-891429-02-7*) Armadillo Pubng.

Peace Patrol: Creating a New Generation of Problem Solvers & Peacemakers. Eden Steele. Ed. & Illus. by Dianne Schilling. 154p. (Orig.). (J). (gr. k-8). 1994. pap. text 24.95 (*1-56499-020-6*, IP9020) Innerchoice Pub.

Peace, Perfect Peace see Paz, Perfecta Paz

Peace Pilgrim: Her Life & Work in Her Own Words. Peace Pilgrim. LC 82-18854. (Illus.). 214p. 1991. 14.95 (*0-943734-20-7*) Ocean Tree Bks.

Peace Pilgrim: Her Life & Work in Her Own Words. Peace Pilgrim. Ed. by Ann Rush et al. LC 82-18854. (Illus.). 224p. 1994. pap. 12.00 (*0-943734-29-0*) Ocean Tree Bks.

Peace Pilgrim's Wisdom: A Very Simple Guide. Peace Pilgrim. Ed. by Cheryl Canfield. LC 95-41443. 224p. 1996. pap. 14.00 (*1-884997-11-2*) Blue Dove Pr.

Peace Pilgrim's Wisdom: A Very Simple Guide. Peace Pilgrim. (Illus.). 224p. 1996. per. 14.00 (*0-943734-30-4*) Ocean Tree Bks.

Peace Planning for Central & Eastern Europe. Feliks Gross. 70p. 1944. 3.00 (*0-940962-21-7*) Polish Inst Art & Sci.

Peace Plays. Adrian Mitchell et al. Ed. by Stephen Lowe. (Methuen Theatrescripts Ser.). 135p. (C). 1988. pap. write for info. (*0-413-56000-7*, A0206, Methuen Drama) Methn.

Peace Plays 2. Richard Stayton et al. Ed. by Stephen Lowe. Tr. by Daphne Skillen & Michael Glenny from RUS. (Methuen New Theatrescripts Ser.). (Illus.). 160p. (Orig.). (C). 1990. pap. write for info. (*0-413-16529-9*, A0435, Methuen Drama) Methn.

Peace Poem. 68p. 9.95 (*92-1-002069-3*) UN.

Peace Policy of Nations: Egypt, Palestine & India. Jagdish P. Sharma. x, 376p. 1995. 45.00 (*81-85445-92-3*, Pub. by Manak Pubns Pvt Ltd) Nataraj Bks.

Peace Politics: The United States Between the Old & New World Orders. Paul Joseph. 304p. 1993. 54.95 (*1-56639-022-2*); pap. 22.95 (*1-56639-023-0*) Temple U Pr.

Peace, Politics & Violence in the New South Africa. Ed. by Norman Etherington. LC 92-25670. (African Discourse Ser.: No. 4). 370p. 1993. 75.00 (*1-873836-75-9*, Pub. by H Zell Pubs) Seven Hills Bk.

*__Peace Pond.__ Katina Kefalos. (Illus.). 14p. (YA). (gr. 5-8). 1999. 0.95 (*1-929172-09-5*) Emerald Prodns.

Peace Porridge 3: Where Now? Teddy Milne. (J). 1995. pap. 10.95 (*0-938875-32-9*) Pittenbruach Pr.

Peace, Power, & Plenty. Orison S. Marden. 323p. 1997. pap. 28.00 (*0-89540-343-9*, SB-343) Sun Pub.

Peace, Power & Righteousness: An Indigenous Manifesto. Taiaiake Alfred. LC 99-233319. 200p. 1999. pap. 19.95 (*0-19-541216-8*) OUP.

Peace, Power & the United Nations: A Security System for the Twenty-First Century. Joseph P. Lorenz. LC 98-42242. 185p. (C). 1998. 65.00 (*0-8133-8061-8*, Pub. by Westview) HarpC.

Peace Process: American Diplomacy & the Arab-Israeli Conflict since 1967. William B. Quandt. 612p. (C). 1993. 48.00 (*0-520-08388-1*) Brookings.

*__Peace Process American Diplomacy & the Arab-Israeli Conflict since 1967.__ rev. ed. William B. Quandt. 1999. pap. 19.95 (*0-8157-7275-0*) Brookings.

Peace Process in the Former Yugoslavia: Hearings Before the Committee on Foreign Relations, United States Senate, 104th Congress, 1st Session, October 17 & December 1, 1995. USGPO Staff. LC 96-128568. iii, 137p. 1996. pap. write for info. (*0-16-052270-6*) USGPO.

Peace Process in the Holy Land & the Third Way Between Capitalism & Communism: And the Future Abridged & Refined 1981-1999: Correspondence with Judah (Israel) & Ephraim (Philastina) Arichitecture & the Universe. Thomas J. Kuna-Jacob. 99p. 1999. ring bd. 12.00 (*1-878030-04-3*) Assn World Peace.

Peace Progressives & American Foreign Relations. Robert D. Johnson. LC 94-25609. (Harvard Historical Studies: Vol. 119). 464p. 1995. text 45.00 (*0-674-65917-1*, JOHPEA) HUP.

*__Peace, Prosperity & Politics.__ John E. Mueller. LC 99-46218. (Political Economy of Global Interdependence Ser.). 1999. 75.00 (*0-8133-6761-1*) Westview.

Peace Reader: Essential Readings on War & Justice, Non-Violence, & World Order. rev. ed. Ed. by Joseph J. Fahey & Richard Armstrong. LC 92-15129. 480p. (C). 1992. pap. 21.95 (*0-8091-3317-2*) Paulist Pr.

*__Peace Rebel.__ Robert Elmer. LC 99-51015. (Promise of Zion Ser.: Vol. 2). 144p. (J). (gr. 4-7). 2000. pap. 5.99 (*0-7642-2297-X*) Bethany Hse.

Peace Reform in American History. Charles DeBenedetti. LC 79-2173. 264p. 1980. reprint ed. 12.95 (*0-253-13095-6*) Ind U Pr.

Peace Reform in American History. Charles DeBenedetti. LC 79-2173. 264p. 1984. reprint ed. pap. 4.95 (*0-253-20320-1*, MB-320) Ind U Pr.

Peace Register, 1993: Drawing the Peace Dividend. Ed. by Ken Coates. (Endpapers Ser.: No. 23). 144p. (Orig.). 1993. pap. 24.50 (*0-85124-548-X*, Pub. by Spkesman) Coronet Bks.

Peace Research for the 1990s. Ed. by Judit Balazs & Hakan Wiberg. 271p. (C). 1994. 35.00 (*963-05-6620-6*, Pub. by Akade Kiado) Intl Spec Bk.

Peace Research in Western Europe: A Directory Guide. Ed. by Robert Rudney. 45p. (Orig.). 1989. pap. text 4.00 (*1-878597-05-1*) Access Sec Info Serv.

Peace Revolution: Ethos & Social Process, 7. John Somerville. LC 74-5993. (Contributions in Philosophy Ser.: No. 7). 236p. 1975. 55.00 (*0-8371-7532-1*, SPR/, Greenwood Pr) Greenwood.

Peace River. Michael Walton. (C). 1988. 50.00 (*0-900657-00-6*, Pub. by W Sessions) St Mut.

Peace River. Michael Walton. (C). 1990. 115.00 (*0-7855-5092-5*, Pub. by W Sessions) St Mut.

Peace River: A Collectors Volume. Ed. by Michael Walton. (C). 1988. 95.00 (*0-7855-5033-X*, Pub. by W Sessions) St Mut.

Peace River Pioneers. 3rd ed. Louise K. Frisbie. LC 74-81530. (Illus.). 1986. 9.95 (*0-912458-47-X*) Imperial Pub Co.

Peace Scholars: Learning Through Literature, Grade 3. Diane Carlebach. Ed. by James A. Burke, II et al. (Illus.). 206p. (J). (gr. 3). 1996. pap. text, teacher ed. 29.95 (*1-878227-44-0*) Peace Educ.

Peace Scholars: Learning Through Literature, Grade 4. Diane Carlebach & Catherine H. Dickmann. Ed. by James A. Burke, II. (Peace Scholars: Learning Through Literature Ser.). (Illus.). (J). 1999. pap., teacher ed. 29.95 (*1-878227-55-6*) Peace Educ.

Peace Scholars: Learning Through Literature, Student Activity Book. Diane Carlebach. Ed. by James A. Burke, II et al. (Illus.). 72p. (J). (gr. 3). 1996. pap. text 3.39 (*1-878227-45-9*) Peace Educ.

Peace, Security & Conflict Prevention: SIPRI-UNESCO Handbook. Stockholm International Peace Research Institute. LC 98-151621. (A SIPRI Publication). (Illus.). 248p. 1998. text 75.00 (*0-19-829429-8*); pap. text 35.00 (*0-19-829435-2*) OUP.

Peace, Security & the United Nations. Ed. by Hans J. Morgenthau. LC 72-10841. (Essay Index Reprint Ser.). 1977. reprint ed. 18.95 (*0-8369-7232-5*) Ayer.

Peace Seekers: The Nobel Peace Prize. Nathan Aaseng. (Nobel Prize Winners Ser.). (Illus.). 80p. (J). (gr. 5 up). 1987. lib. bdg. 18.60 (*0-8225-0654-8*, Lerner Publctns) Lerner Pub.

Peace Seekers: The Nobel Peace Prize. Nathan Aaseng. (Illus.). 80p. (J). (gr. 5 up). 1991. pap. 5.95 (*0-8225-9604-0*, Lerner Publctns) Lerner Pub.

Peace Soldiers: The Sociology of a United Nations Military Force. Charles C. Moskos, Jr. 1992. lib. bdg. 12.50 (*0-226-54225-4*) U Ch Pr.

Peace Soup: The Recipe for a Peaceful Life in the New Millennium. Gerald Bartholow. 288p. mass mkt. 19.95 (*0-9679005-0-6*) P S I Pubng AL.

Peace Studies: A Critical Survey. Ed. by Caroline Cox & Roger Scruton. (C). 1990. 35.00 (*0-907967-15-9*, Pub. by Inst Euro Def & Strat) St Mut.

Peace Tales: World Folktales to Talk About. Margaret R. MacDonald. LC 92-8994. 128p. (J). (gr. 1-6). 1992. pap. text 17.50 (*0-208-02329-1*, Linnet Bks); lib. bdg. 25.00 (*0-208-02328-3*, Linnet Bks) Shoe String.

Peace Terrorist: And Other Stories. Carol Masters. LC 93-83979. (Minnesota Voices Project Ser.). 106p. (Orig.). 1994. pap. 9.95 (*0-89823-156-6*) New Rivers Pr.

Peace That Defies Pain. Max Lucado. 32p. 1995. pap. 2.99 (*0-8499-5211-5*) Word Pub.

Peace That Passes All Misunderstanding. Thomas E. Witherspoon. LC 87-50929. 144p. 1988. 3.48 (*0-87159-126-X*) Unity Bks.

Peace That You Seek. Alan Cohen. (Illus.). 193p. (Orig.). 1985. 13.95 (*0-910367-35-3*, 157) A Cohen.

Peace, the Enemy of Freedom: The Myth of Non-Violence. Terrence Webster-Doyle. (Sane & Intelligent Living Ser.). (Illus.). 157p. 1991. pap. 9.95 (*0-942941-12-8*) Atrium Soc Educ.

Peace Theology & Violence Against Women. Ed. by Elizabeth G. Yoder. (Occasional Papers: No. 16). 124p. (Orig.). 1992. pap. text 10.00 (*0-936273-20-8*) Inst Mennonite.

Peace Therapy. Carol A. Morrow. LC 94-96664. 80p. 1995. pap. 4.95 (*0-87029-273-0*) Abbey.

Peace Thinking in a Warring World. Edward L. Long. LC 83-14675. 118p. reprint ed. pap. 36.60 (*0-7837-2634-1*, 204298400006) Bks Demand.

Peace Through Agreement: Replacing War with Non-Violent Dispute-Resolution Methods. Gerald Rabow. LC 89-71110. 200p. 1990. 52.95 (*0-275-93505-1*, C3505, Greenwood Pr) Greenwood.

*__Peace Through Law.__ Hans Kelsen. LC 00-36236. 2000. write for info. (*1-58477-103-8*) Lawbk Exchange.

Peace Through Law: Britain & the International Court in the 1920s. Lorna Lloyd. LC 96-46636. (Royal Historical Society Studies in History: No. 74). 320p. 1997. 75.00 (*0-86193-235-8*) Boydell & Brewer.

Peace Thru People: A Human Philosophy of Survival for the Pan-Atomic Age. W. John Weilgart. 72p. 1977. pap. 4.00 (*0-912038-17-9*) Cosmic Comm.

Peace to End All Peace. David Fromkin. LC 93-205528. 635p. 1990. pap. 14.95 (*0-380-71300-4*, Avon Bks) Morrow Avon.

Peace Train: A School-Wide Violence Prevention Program. Joe Wittmer et al. LC 99-60707. (Illus.). 194p. 1999. spiral bd. 29.95 (*0-932796-92-3*) Ed Media Corp.

Peace Treaty: The Crystal-Clear Decision to Respect the Child. Alexej Sesterheim. (Illus.). 4p. 1999. pap. 4.70 (*0-9669229-9-9*) Chld Inter.

Peace Tree: A Modern Christmas Fable. David O'Hooper. (Illus.). 32p. (J). (gr. k-8). 1994. 12.50 (*0-9640684-3-5*) Pixie Dust.

Peace, Truth, Love: NIV Gospel of John. 58p. 1996. write for info. (*1-880349-05-1*) Pocket Testament.

Peace, Truth, Love: The Gospel of John. (New International Version Ser.). 64p. 1990. pap. write for info. (*1-880349-52-3*) Pocket Testament.

Peace under Heaven: A Modern Korean Novel. Man-Sik Ch'ae. Tr. by Chun Kyung-Ja from KOR. LC 92-31807. 272p. (C). 1993. 51.95 (*1-56324-112-9*, East Gate Bk) M E Sharpe.

Peace under Heaven: A Modern Korean Novel. Chae Man-Sik. Tr. by Chun Kyung-Ja from KOR. LC 92-31807. 272p. (C). 1993. pap. text 24.95 (*1-56324-172-2*, East Gate Bk) M E Sharpe.

Peace Versus Power in the Family: Domestic Discord & Emotional Distress. Abraham A. Low. LC 84-51729. 197p. 1984. reprint ed. 20.00 (*0-915005-03-4*) Willett Pub Co.

P

An Asterisk (*) at the beginning of an entry indicates that the title is appearing for the first time.

Peace, Violence & the New Testament. Michel Desjardins. (Biblical Seminar Ser.: Vol. 46). 130p. 1997. pap. 17.95 (*1-85075-799-2*, Pub. by Sheffield Acad) CUP Services.

Peace War. Vernor Vinge. LC 84-14513. 286p. 1984. 25.00 (*0-89366-252-6*) Ultramarine Pub.

Peace, War & European Powers. Bartlett. LC 96-6785. 224p. 1996. text 49.95 (*0-312-16137-9*) St Martin.

Peace, War, & Mental Health: Couples Therapists Look at the Dynamics. Ed. by Barbara J. Brothers. LC 93-18004. (Journal of Couples Therapy: Vol. 3, No. 4). (Illus.). 181p. 1993. lib. bdg. 39.95 (*1-56024-437-2*) Haworth Pr.

***Peace War & Politics.** Jack Anderson & Daryl Gibson. 432p. 2000. pap. 14.95 (*0-312-87497-9*) St Martin.

Peace, War & Politics: An Eyewitness Account. Jack Anderson. LC 99-26647. 1999. 27.95 (*0-312-85602-4*, Pub. by Forge NYC) St Martin.

Peace Was in Their Hearts: Conscientious Objectors in World War II. Richard C. Anderson. 318p. 1996. pap. 17.99 (*0-8361-9053-X*) Herald Pr.

Peace Was Their Profession: Strategic Air Command: A Tribute. Michael Hill & John M. Campbell. LC 94-66967. (Illus.). 304p. (YA). (gr. 10-13). 1995. 49.95 (*0-88740-688-2*) Schiffer.

Peace We Knew. Ed. by Rick Schaub. 1998. 69.95 (*1-57553-733-8*) Nat Lib Poetry.

Peace-Weavers & Shield-Maidens: Women in Early English Society. Kathleen Herbert. LC 98-114818. 64p. 1997. pap. 9.95 (*1-898281-11-4*, Pub. by Anglo-Saxon Bks) Paul & Co Pubs.

Peace with China? U. S. Decisions for Asia. Ed. by Earl C. Ravenal. LC 71-162433. 1971. pap. 2.95 (*0-87140-257-2*, Pub. by Liveright) Norton.

Peace With God see Paz Con Dios

Peace with God. Billy Graham. 220p. 1997. 16.99 (*0-8499-1479-5*) Word Pub.

***Peace with God.** Billy Graham. 2000. pap. 8.99 (*0-8499-4215-2*) Word Pub.

Peace with God: Minibook. Billy Graham. 1994. 4.99 (*0-8499-5075-9*) Word Pub.

Peace with God the Creator, Peace with All Creation. Tom Bright et al. 53p. 1995. 7.95 (*1-55586-032-X*) US Catholic.

Peace with Justice. Dwight D. Eisenhower. LC 61-7096. 273p. 1960. text 67.00 (*0-231-02472-X*) Col U Pr.

***Peace with Justice: A History of the Israeli-Palestinian Declaration.** Andrew S. Buchanan. 2000. text 65.00 (*0-312-22953-4*) St Martin.

Peace with Security: Israel's Minimal Security Requirements in Negotiations with Syria. Ze'ev Schiff. LC 93-12301. (Policy Papers: No. 34). 107p. 1993. pap. 8.00 (*0-944029-23-X*) Wash Inst NEP.

Peace with the Apaches of New Mexico & Arizona. Vincent Colyer. LC 70-165622. (Select Bibliographies Reprint Ser.). 1977. reprint ed. 15.95 (*0-8369-5929-9*) Ayer.

Peace with Your Partner: A Practical Guide to Happy Marriage. Erik Blumenthal. 160p. 1997. pap. 10.95 (*1-85168-136-1*, Pub. by Onewrld Pubns) Penguin Putnam.

Peace Within My Borders: A Bible Study. Phyllis J. Levy. 63p. 1998. pap. 5.00 (*0-9660929-1-0*) Glory Communs.

Peace Within the Stillness: Relaxation & Meditation for True Happiness. Eddie Shapiro & Debbie Shapiro. LC 98-24640. Orig. Title: Meditation for Inner Peace: Your Guide to Relaxation & True Happiness. (Illus.). 181p. 1998. pap. 14.95 (*0-89594-926-1*) Crossing Pr.

Peace Within Your Borders: Devotionals for Home School Teachers. Beth Sharpton. LC 99-60965. 160p. 1999. pap. 9.99 (*1-57921-219-0*, Pub. by WinePress Pub) BookWorld.

Peace Within Yourself. Joseph Murphy. 300p. 1972. pap. 9.00 (*0-87516-188-X*) DeVorss.

Peace Without Hiroshima: Secret Action at the Vatican in Spring, 1945. Martin S. Quigley. 300p. 1991. 22.95 (*0-8191-8056-4*) Madison Bks UPA.

***Peace Without Justice: Obstacles to Building the Rule of Law in El Salvador.** Margaret L. Popkin. 2000. 45.00 (*0-271-01997-2*); pap. 18.95 (*0-271-01998-0*) Pa St U Pr.

P

Peace Without Profit: How the IMF Blocks Rebuilding in Mozambique. LC 96-49146. (African Issues Ser.). 1996. 65.00 (*0-435-07409-1*); write for info. (*0-85255-800-7*) Heinemann.

Peace Without Profit: How the IMF Blocks Rebuilding in Mozambique. J. Hanlon. LC 96-49146. (African Issues Ser.). 1996. pap. 18.95 (*0-435-07410-5*) Heinemann.

Peace Without Profit: How the IMF Blocks Rebuilding in Mozambique. Joseph Hanlon. LC 96-49146. (African Issues Ser.). 1996. write for info. (*0-85255-801-5*) Heinemann.

Peace Without Promise: Britain & the Peace Conferences, 1919-1923. Michael Dockerill & J. Douglas Goold. 287p. 1981. 79.50 (*0-208-01909-X*) Elliots Bks.

Peace Without Victory for the Allies, 1918-1932. Sara Moore. 352p. 39.50 (*1-85973-026-4*) Berg Pubs.

Peace Work. Spike Milligan. 240p. 1992. pap. 12.95 (*0-14-014970-8*, Pub. by Pnguin Bks Ltd) Trafalgar.

Peace Works. Kathleen Fry-Miller & Judith Myers-Walls. (Illus.). 128p. (Orig.). 1989. pap. 14.95 (*0-87178-977-9*, 8779) Brethren.

***Peaceability.** Linda Eyre & Richard Eyre. (Teaching Your Children Values Ser.). 32p. (J). (ps-7). 2000. pap. 16.95 incl. audio (*1-56015-788-7*) Penton Overseas.

Peaceable Classroom. Mary O'Reilley. LC 93-17781. 160p. 1993. pap. text 21.50 (*0-86709-328-5*, 0328, Pub. by Boynton Cook Pubs) Heinemann.

Peaceable Kingdom. Francine Prose. LC 93-10080. 231p. 1993. 20.00 (*0-374-23042-0*) FS&G.

Peaceable Kingdom. Francine Prose. LC 98-21553. 240p. 1998. pap. 12.00 (*0-8050-5939-3*, Owl) H Holt & Co.

Peaceable Kingdom. Ewa Zadrzynska. (Illus.). 32p. (J). (ps-3). 1994. 14.95 (*0-9638904-0-9*) M M Art Bks.

Peaceable Kingdom. Jan DeHartog. 1995. reprint ed. lib. bdg. 39.95 (*1-56849-645-1*) Buccaneer Bks.

Peaceable Kingdom: A Primer in Christian Ethics. Stanley Hauerwas. LC 83-14711. 224p. (C). 1983. text 26.50 (*0-268-01553-8*); pap. text 13.00 (*0-268-01554-6*) U of Notre Dame Pr.

Peaceable Kingdom: Poems by Jon Silkin. deluxe rev. ed. Jon Silkin. (Illus.). 1975. 145.00 (*0-685-52386-1*) Heron Pr.

Peaceable Kingdom & Other Fantasies of Faith. Joel Kauffmann. LC 98-176546. (Pontius' Puddle Presents Ser.). 104p. 1997. pap. 5.95 (*0-687-45919-2*) Abingdon.

Peaceable Kingdom in Hartsdale: A Celebration of Pets & Their People. LC 82-99850. (Illus.). 192p. 1983. 20.00 (*0-9608712-0-9*) Rosywick Pr.

***Peaceable School.** Vicky Schreiber Dill. 114p. 1998. pap. 12.00 (*0-87367-810-9*) Phi Delta Kappa.

***Peaceable Witness among Muslims.** Gordon D. Nickel. 152p. 2000. pap. 14.99 (*0-8361-9105-6*) Herald Pr.

Peacebound Trains. Haemi Balgassi. LC 94-26797. (Illus.). 32p. (J). (gr. 2-5). 1996. 14.95 (*0-395-72093-1*, Clarion Bks) HM.

***Peacebound Trains.** Haemi Balgassi. (Illus.). 48p. (J). (gr. 2-5). 2000. pap. 5.95 (*0-618-04030-7*, Clarion Bks) HM.

***Peacebuilding: A Field Guide.** Ed. by Luc Reychler & Thania Paffenholz. 600p. 2001. 65.00 (*1-55587-912-8*); pap. 29.95 (*1-55587-937-3*) L Rienner.

***Peacebuilding & Police Reform.** Espen Barth Eide & Tor Tanke Holm. LC 99-86860. (Series on Peacekeeping: No. 7). 240p. 2000. pap. 24.50 (*0-7146-8040-0*, Pub. by F Cass Pubs) Intl Spec Bk.

***Peacebuilding as Politics: Cultivating Peace in Fragile Societies.** Ed. by Elizabeth M. Cousens & Chetan Kumar. (Project of the International Peace Academy Ser.). 220p. 2000. 45.00 (*1-55587-921-7*); pap. 16.95 (*1-55587-946-2*) L Rienner.

***Peacebuilding for Adolescents: Strategies for Educators & Community Leaders.** Ed. by Linda Forcey & Ian Harris. LC 98-46242. (Adolescent Cultures, School & Society Ser.: Vol. 2). (Illus.). 364p. (C). 1999. pap. text 32.95 (*0-8204-3745-X*) P Lang Pubng.

Peaceful Air Warfare: The United States, Britain, & the Politics of International Aviation. Alan P. Dobson. 328p. 1991. text 75.00 (*0-19-827531-5*) OUP.

Peaceful & Working People: Manners, Morals, & Class Formation in Northern Mexico. William E. French. LC 95-32446. (Illus.). 263p. (C). 1996. 24.00 (*0-8263-1683-2*) U of NM Pr.

***Peaceful Arts: Medication, Yoga, Tai Chi, Stretching.** 2000. 19.95 (*1-84038-230-9*) Hermes Hse.

Peaceful Change & the Colonial Problem. Bryce Wood. LC 70-76639. (Columbia University. Teachers College. Contributions to Education Ser.: No. 464). reprint ed. 20.00 (*0-404-51464-2*) AMS Pr.

Peaceful Children, Peaceful World: The Challenge of Maria Montessori. Aline D. Wolf. (Illus.). 72p. (Orig.). 1989. pap. 8.95 (*0-939195-02-X*) Parent-Child Pr.

Peaceful Classroom: 162 Easy Activities to Teach Preschoolers Compassion & Cooperation. Charles A. Smith. (Illus.). 208p. (Orig.). 1993. pap. text 16.95 (*0-87659-165-9*) Gryphon Hse.

***Peaceful Classroom in Action: How to Create One & How to Keep It!** Naomi Drew. 154p. 1999. pap. 24.95 (*1-880396-61-0*) Jalmar Pr.

Peaceful Coexistence: International Law in the Building of Communism. Bernard A. Ramundo. LC 67-12421. 176p. reprint ed. pap. 54.60 (*0-608-06190-5*, 206652200008) Bks Demand.

Peaceful Conquest: The Industrialization of Europe, 1760-1970. Sidney Pollard. (Illus.). 464p. 1981. pap. text 24.95 (*0-19-877095-2*) OUP.

Peaceful Cook: More Than a Cookbook. Harriet Kofalk. LC 92-41331. 160p. 1993. 8.95 (*0-913990-46-9*) Book Pub Co.

Peaceful Divorce or Separation - How to Draw up Your Own Settlement Agreement with Your Spouse: The National Marital Settlement Kit. Benji O. Anosike. LC 97-4168. (Illus.). 125p. (Orig.). 1997. pap. 24.95 (*0-932704-43-3*) Do It Yourself Legal Pubs.

***Peaceful Dwelling: Meditations for Healing & Living.** Madeline K. Bastis. LC 00-32594. 2001. pap. write for info. (*0-8048-3234-X*) Tuttle Pubng.

Peaceful Dying: The Step-by-Step Guide to Preserving Your Dignity, Your Choice & Your Inner Peace. Daniel R. Tobin & Karen Lindsey. 224p. 1968. pap. text 14.00 (*0-7382-0034-4*) Perseus Pubng.

Peaceful Easy Feeling. 192p. (Orig.). (YA). 1992. pap. 16.95 (*0-7692-1067-8*, VF1820) Wrner Bros.

Peaceful Easy Feeling: Easy Piano. 128p. (Orig.). 1977. pap. 8.95 (*0-7692-1145-3*, PF0063) Wrner Bros.

***Peaceful Edge: Staying Stress Free & Productive in a World of Too Much to Do.** David Allen. 192p. 2001. text 24.95 (*0-670-88906-7*, Viking) Viking Penguin.

***Peaceful Empire.** McIntosh. 2000. 40.00 (*0-8133-3532-9*, Pub. by Westview) HarpC.

Peaceful Gunman. large type ed. Bill Foord. (Dales Large Print Ser.). 216p. 1997. pap. 18.99 (*1-85389-709-4*) Ulverscroft.

***Peaceful Guns.** large type ed. Ron Pritchett. 256p. 1999. pap. 18.99 (*0-7089-5542-8*, Linford) Ulverscroft.

***Peaceful Hearts: For the Right Hand Alone.** Dennis Alexander. 1999. mass mkt. 2.50 (*0-7390-0318-6*, 18995) Alfred Pub.

Peaceful Home-Country Living. Country Living Magazine Staff. LC 97-21898. 1998. 30.00 (*0-688-15618-5*, Hearst) Hearst Commns.

Peaceful Invasions: Immigration & Changing America. Leon F. Bouvier. 244p. (C). 1991. pap. text 24.50 (*0-8191-8403-9*); lib. bdg. 51.00 (*0-8191-8402-0*) U Pr of Amer.

Peaceful Kingdom Vol. 1: Random Acts of Kindness by Animals. Stephanie Laland. (Illus.). 224p. (Orig.). 1997. pap. 11.95 (*1-57324-094-X*) Conari Press.

Peaceful Management of Transboundary Resources. Gerald H. Blake. LC 95-3397. (International Environmental Law & Policy Ser.). 1995. lib. bdg. 155.00 (*1-85966-173-4*, Pub. by Graham & Trotman) Kluwer Academic.

Peaceful Measures: Canada's Way Out of the "War on Drugs" Bruce K. Alexander. 415p. 1990. text 50.00 (*0-8020-2722-9*); pap. text 20.95 (*0-8020-6753-0*) U of Toronto Pr.

Peaceful Ocean? Maritime Security in the Pacific in the Post-Cold War Era. Ed. by Andrew Mack. 200p. 1994. pap. 24.95 (*1-86373-593-3*, Pub. by Allen & Unwin Pty) Paul & Co Pubs.

Peaceful P. A. L. George H. Quester. (CISA Working Papers: No. 9). 23p. (Orig.). 1977. pap. 15.00 (*0-86682-008-6*) Ctr Intl Relations.

Peaceful Palate: Vegetarian's Favorite Cookbook. rev. ed. Jennifer Raymond. LC 96-3806. (Illus.). 162p. 1996. pap. 15.00 (*1-57067-031-5*) Book Pub Co.

Peaceful Parenting in a Violent World. Joseph N. Cress & Burt Berlowe. 275p. 1995. pap. 14.95 (*0-9645335-0-2*) Perspect Pubns.

***Peaceful Parents, Peaceful Kids: Practical Ways to Create a Calm & Happy Home.** Naomi Drew. 2000. pap. 14.00 (*1-57566-608-1*) Kensgtn Pub Corp.

***Peaceful Passing: Die When You Choose with Dignity & Ease.** Robert S. Wood. Ed. by Tomi Keitlen. LC 00-130441. (Illus.). 240p. 2000. pap. 14.95 (*1-886966-17-6*, Pub. by In Print) Quality Bks IL.

Peaceful Patriot: The Story of Tom Bennett. Bonni McKeown. 224p. 1987. pap. 8.00 (*0-9621483-0-X*) Peaceful Patriot Pr.

Peaceful Peoples: An Annotated Bibliography. Bruce D. Bonta. 301p. 1993. 40.00 (*0-8108-2785-9*) Scarecrow.

Peaceful Procedures: A Master Teacher's Approach to Peaceful Classroom Management. Kathy Gritzmacher. Ed. by Ron Marson. (Master Teacher Ser.). (Illus.). 84p. 1987. teacher ed. 15.00 (*0-941008-63-0*) Tops Learning.

Peaceful Retirement, Set. Miss Read. (Fairacre Chronicles Ser.). 1998. audio 24.95 (*0-7540-7522-2*) Chivers N Amer.

***Peaceful Revolution: Constitutional Change & American Culture from Progressivism to the New Deal.** Maxwell H. Bloomfield. LC 00-26108. (Illus.). 224p. 2000. 35.00 (*0-674-00304-7*) HUP.

Peaceful Season: Daily Advent Meditations for Everyday Christians. Roger A. Swenson. LC 87-1047. 104p. 1987. pap. 7.95 (*0-8189-0519-0*) Alba.

Peaceful Seed Living, Vols. 1 & 2. 2nd ed. Jerome F. Coniker. LC 78-66369. (Living Meditation & Prayerbook Ser.). (Illus.). 156p. 1981. pap. text 3.00 (*0-932406-00-9*) AFC.

Peaceful Settlement of Disputes Between States: A Selective Bibliography. 209p. 25.00 (*92-1-100464-0*, 91.I.49) UN.

Peaceful Settlement of International Disputes in Europe: Future Prospects. Ed. by Daniel Bardonnet. 704p. (C). 1992. pap. text 155.00 (*0-7923-1573-1*) Kluwer Academic.

Peaceful Settlement of International Disputes in Europe: Future Prospects: Colloque, 1990 - Workshop 1990. Ed. by Daniel Bardonnet. (Hague Academy of International Law Recueil des Cours, Colloque Ser.). 704p. (C). 1992. lib. bdg. 215.00 (*0-7923-1572-3*) Kluwer Academic.

***Peaceful Settlement of International Environmental Disputes: A Pragmatic Approach.** Cesare Romano. LC 00-42083. (International Environmental Law & Policy Ser.). 2000. write for info. (*90-411-9808-3*) Kluwer Law Intl.

***Peaceful Solution: Yahweh's 613 Laws Will Bring Peace to All Nations.** Yisrayl Hawkins. 588p. 1999. 29.95 (*1-890967-24-6*) Hse of Yahweh.

Peaceful Soul Within: Reflective Steps Toward Awareness. Margot Robinson. (Illus.). 97p. (Orig.). 1996. per. 14.95 (*0-7872-2221-6*) Kendall-Hunt.

Peaceful Territorial Change. Arie M. Kacowicz. LC 94-6688. (Studies in International Relations). 390p. 1994. text 49.95 (*0-87249-989-8*) U of SC Pr.

Peaceful Transition: The Art of Conscious Dying & the Liberation of the Soul. Bruce Goldberg. LC 97-20431. (Illus.). 264p. (Orig.). 1999. pap. 12.95 (*1-56718-319-0*) Llewellyn Pubns.

Peaceful Use of Nuclear Explosives: Some Economic Aspects. David B. Brooks & John V. Krutilla. LC 69-15904. 55p. reprint ed. pap. 30.00 (*0-608-12239-4*, 202378800034) Bks Demand.

***Peaceful Uses of Trans-Boundary Watercourses in International Law & Politics: The Case of the Euphrates & Tigris Rivers.** Hilal Elver. (Innovation in International Law Ser.). 300p. 2000. 115.00 (*1-57105-089-2*) Transnatl Pubs.

Peaceful Valley Story: Fulfillment of a Dream. Silvia Pettem. LC 94-200416. (Illus.). 64p. (Orig.). 1994. pap. 5.95 (*0-9617799-5-0*) Book Lode.

Peaceful Warrior: A Biography of Horace Porter, 1837-1921. Richard Owens. LC 90-48478. (Dissertations in Nineteenth-Century American Political & Social History: Vol. 1). 300p. 1990. 20.00 (*0-8240-8195-1*) Garland.

***Peaceful Warrior Collection.** Dan Millman. 464p. 2000. 9.98 (*1-56731-399-X*, MJF Bks) Fine Comms.

Peacefully Working to Conquer the World: Singer Sewing Machine in Foreign Markets, 1854-1920. Robert B. Davies. Ed. by Stuart Bruchey & Eleanor Bruchey. LC 76-5000. (American Business Abroad Ser.). 1976. 39.95 (*0-405-09270-9*) Ayer.

***Peacefulness.** Lucia Raatma. (Character Education Ser.). 24p. (gr. k-3). 1999. 14.60 (*0-516-21858-1*, Bridgestone Bks) Capstone Pr.

Peacefulness: Teacher & Parent Handbook. (Excellence in Character Ser.). (Illus.). 90p. 1998. pap. text 14.95 (*1-58259-008-7*); pap. text 14.95 (*1-58259-038-9*) Global Classrm.

Peacefulness: Teacher & Parent Handbook. Lucia Raatma. LC 99-29181. (Character Education Ser.). 24p. (J). 1999. 14.60 (*0-7368-0370-X*, Bridgestone Bks) Capstone Pr.

Peacekeeper. Marisa Carroll. LC 96-572. 296p. 1995. per. 3.75 (*0-373-70655-3*, 1-70655-5) Harlequin Bks.

Peacekeeper. Jeffrey A. Poston. LC 97-7300. 192p. 1997. 20.95 (*0-8027-4160-6*) Walker & Co.

Peacekeeper Series, Level 2. Marianne Bivins. (Illus.). 9p. (J). (ps-k). 1997. pap. 22.00 (*1-890697-09-5*) Bivins Pubs.

Peacekeeper Series Level III. Marianne Bivins. (Illus.). 9p. (J). (ps-1). 1997. pap. 22.00 (*1-890697-26-5*) Bivins Pubs.

Peacekeepers. Ben Bova. 384p. 1989. mass mkt. 4.95 (*0-8125-0238-8*, Pub. by Tor Bks) St Martin.

Peacekeepers. DeWeese. (Star Trek: The Next Generation Ser.: No. 2). 1990. mass mkt. 5.50 (*0-671-73653-1*) PB.

Peacekeepers: An Assessment of Peacekeeping Operations at the Arab-Israel Interface. John Mackinlay. 208p. 1989. 29.95 (*0-685-29202-9*) Routledge.

Peacekeepers & Their Wives: American Participation in the Multinational Force & Observers, 147. David R. Segal & Mady W. Segal. LC 93-7699. (Contributions in Military Studies Ser.: No. 147). 200p. 1993. 57.95 (*0-313-27484-3*, SKG/, Greenwood Pr) Greenwood.

Peacekeeper's Handbook. 439p. 1984. 50.00 (*0-685-43369-2*) Intl Peace.

Peacekeeper's Handbook. International Peace Academy Staff. 416p. 1984. 55.00 (*0-685-08847-2*, Pergamon Pr) Elsevier.

Peacekeepers of Kashmir: The U. N. Military Observer Group in India & Pakistan. Pauline Dawson. 300p. 1996. text 49.95 (*0-312-07589-8*) St Martin.

***Peacekeepers, Politicians & Warlords: The Liberian Peace Process.** Abiodun Alao et al. LC 99-6832. 192p. 1999. 19.95 (*92-808-1031-6*) UN Univ Pr.

Peacekeeping: A Selected Bibliography. Ed. by Diane Publishing Staff. 47p. 1998. pap. text 20.00 (*0-7881-4326-3*) DIANE Pub.

Peacekeeping: Assessment of U. S. Participation in the Multinational Force & Observers. (Illus.). 66p. (Orig.). (C). 1996. pap. text 20.00 (*0-7881-3023-4*) DIANE Pub.

Peacekeeping: Outspoken Observations by a Field Officer. James H. Allan. LC 95-37754. (Praeger Series in War Studies). 224p. 1996. 59.95 (*0-275-95361-0*, Praeger Pubs) Greenwood.

***Peacekeeping & Conflict Resolution.** Tom Woodhouse & Oliver Ramsbotham. (Cass Series on Peacekeeping Ser.). 180p. 1999. 47.50 (*0-7146-4976-7*) F Cass Pubs.

***Peacekeeping & Conflict Resolution.** Tom Woodhouse & Oliver Ramsbotham. (Cass Series on Peacekeeping). 180p. 2000. pap. 24.50 (*0-7146-8039-7*) F Cass Pubs.

***Peacekeeping & Peace Enforcement in Africa: Methods of Conflict Prevention.** Robert I. Rotberg. 2000. 42.95 (*0-8157-7576-8*) Brookings.

Peacekeeping & Peacemaking. Woodhouse. LC 97-40269. 1998. text 65.00 (*0-312-21180-5*) St Martin.

Peacekeeping & Peacemaking after the Cold War. Lynn E. Davis. LC 93-24111. 1993. pap. 15.00 (*0-8330-1410-2*, MR-281-RC) Rand Corp.

Peacekeeping & Public Information: Caught in the Crossfire. Ingrid A. Lehmann. LC 98-47853. (Series on Peacekeeping: No. 5). (Illus.). 192p. 1999. 52.50 (*0-7146-4930-9*, Pub. by F Cass Pubs); pap. 24.50 (*0-7146-4490-0*, Pub. by F Cass Pubs) Intl Spec Bk.

Peacekeeping & the Rule of Russia in Eurasia. Ed. by Lena Jonson & Clive Archer. 240p. (C). 1996. text 69.00 (*0-8133-8958-5*, Pub. by Westview) HarpC.

Peacekeeping & the Un Specialized Agencies. Ed. by Jim Whitman & Michael Pugh. LC 98-52038. 192p. 1999. pap. 24.50 (*0-7146-4451-X*, Pub. by F Cass Pubs) Intl Spec Bk.

Peacekeeping & the Un Specialized Agencies. Ed. by Jim Whitman & Michael Pugh. LC 98-52038. (Series on Peacekeeping: No. 4). 192p. 1999. 52.50 (*0-7146-4897-3*, Pub. by F Cass Pubs) Intl Spec Bk.

Peacekeeping & the United Nations. Ed. by Stephen M. Hill & Shahin P. Malik. LC 96-19228. (Issues in International Security Ser.). 244p. (Orig.). 1996. 81.95 (*1-85521-620-5*, Pub. by Dartmth Pub); pap. 32.95 (*1-85521-613-2*, Pub. by Dartmth Pub) Ashgate Pub Co.

Peacekeeping & U. N. Operational Control: A Study of Their Effect on Unit Cohesion. Ernest G. Cunningham & Richard H. Rongstad. 222p. 1995. pap. text 19.95 (*1-887897-02-X*) Vikng-Phoenix.

Peacekeeping in Africa. Ed. by Oliver Furley & Roy May. 336p. 1998. text 74.95 (*1-85972-492-2*, Pub. by Ashgate Pub) Ashgate Pub Co.

Peacekeeping in Transition: The United Nations in Cambodia. Janet Heininger. LC 94-31673. 183p. (C). 1994. pap. 11.95 (*0-87078-362-9*) Century Foundation.

Peacekeeping, Peacemaking or War: International Security Enforcement. Ed. by Alex Morrison. 159p. 1994. reprint ed. pap. text 40.00 (*0-7881-1287-2*) DIANE Pub.

***Peacemaker.** Gordon Kent. LC 00-40298. 2001. write for info. (*0-399-14663-6*, G P Putnam) Peng Put Young Read.

Peacemaker: A Biblical Guide to Resolving Personal Conflict. 2nd ed. Ken Sande. LC 96-40967. 286p. (gr. 12). 1997. pap. 14.99 (*0-8010-5741-8*) Baker Bks.

Peacemaker: Comanche! large type ed. William S. Brady. (Linford Western Library). 282p. 1985. pap. 16.99 (*0-7089-6089-8*, Linford) Ulverscroft.

An Asterisk (*) at the beginning of an entry indicates that the title is appearing for the first time.

Peacemaker: The Lost. large type ed. William S. Brady. (Linford Western Library). 256p. 1986. pap. 16.99 (*0-7089-6201-7*, Linford) Ulverscroft.

Peacemaker: War Party. large type ed. William S. Brady. (Linford Western Library). 256p. 1986. pap. 16.99 (*0-7089-6193-2*, Linford) Ulverscroft.

Peacemaker: 1000 Dollar Death. large type ed. William S. Brady. (Linford Western Library). 256p. 1985. pap. 16.99 (*0-7089-6133-9*, Linford) Ulverscroft.

Peacemaker Bounty. Peacemaker Bounty Staff. LC 98-96620. 192p. 1998. 18.95 (*0-8034-9331-2*, Avalon Bks) Bouregy.

Peacemaker Evolution & Variations. 2nd rev. ed. Keith Cochran. LC 97-94604. (Illus.). 94p. 1997. pap. 17.50 (*0-936259-27-2*) Cochran Pub.

Peacemaker for Hire. Clifford Blair. (Peacemaker Western Ser.: Bk. 1). 1995. 18.95 (*0-8034-9110-7*, 095141, Avalon Bks) Bouregy.

Peacemaker Law. Clifford Blair. LC 96-95285. (Peacemaker Western Ser.: Bk. 2). 192p. 1997. 18.95 (*0-8034-9195-6*, Avalon Bks) Bouregy.

***Peacemaker Prey.** Clifford Blair. LC 00-190023. 192p. 2000. 18.95 (*0-8034-9420-3*, Avalon Bks) Bouregy.

Peacemaker Rawhide. Clifford Blair. LC 97-94277. (Peacemaker Western Ser.: Bk. 3). 192p. 1997. 17.95 (*0-8034-9271-5*, Avalon Bks) Bouregy.

Peacemakers. Jack Cavanaugh. LC 99-18695. (American Family Portrait Ser.: Vol. 8). 512p. 1999. pap. 11.99 (*1-56476-681-0*, Victor Bks) Chariot Victor.

Peacemakers. Waldo Williams. Tr. by Tony Conran. 1997. pap. 27.00 (*1-85902-444-0*, Pub. by Gomer Pr) St Mut.

Peacemakers. Waldo Williams & Tony Conran. 1997. pap. 26.95 (*0-8464-4590-5*) Beekman Pubs.

Peacemakers: Arms & Adventure in the American West. R. L. Wilson. 1992. 65.00 (*0-679-40494-5*) Random.

Peacemakers: Winners of the Nobel Peace Prize. Ann T. Keene. LC 98-13522. (Oxford Profiles Ser.). (Illus.). 304p. 1998. 35.00 (*0-19-510316-5*) OUP.

Peacemaker's ABCs for Young Children: A Guide for Teaching Conflict Resolution with a Peace Table. Rebecca A. Janke & Julie P. Peterson. (Illus.). 68p. (Orig.). (J). (ps-3). 1995. teacher ed. 9.95 (*0-9646676-0-6*) GCFP.

Peacemakers' Dilemma. Bertram Pickard. (C). 1936. pap. 4.00 (*0-87574-016-2*) Pendle Hill.

Peacemakers, 1814 to 1815. John G. Lockhart. LC 68-8479. (Essay Index Reprint Ser.). 1977. reprint ed. 21.95 (*0-8369-0622-5*) Ayer.

Peacemakers of 1864. Edward C. Kirkland. LC 74-97888. reprint ed. 43.00 (*0-404-03706-2*) AMS Pr.

Peacemakers of 1864. Edward C. Kirkland. (History - United States Ser.). 279p. 1992. reprint ed. lib. bdg. 79.00 (*0-7812-6181-3*) Rprt Serv.

Peacemaking: A Systems Approach to Conflict Management. Lynn S. Kahn. LC 87-31649. (Illus.). 280p. (Orig.). (C). 1988. pap. text 22.00 (*0-8191-6783-5*) U Pr of Amer.

Peacemaking: Moral & Policy Challenges for a New World. Drew Christiansen. 368p. 1995. pap. 19.95 (*1-55586-682-4*) US Catholic.

Peacemaking: The Quiet Power: Conflict Resolution for Churches Through Mediation. Terje C. Hausken. 181p. 1992. pap. 11.95 (*1-881111-00-8*) CPI Pub MN.

Peacemaking among Primates. Frans B. De Waal. LC 88-11067. (Illus.). 320p. 1989. 44.50 (*0-674-65920-1*) HUP.

Peacemaking among Primates. Frans B. De Waal. (Illus.). 320p. 1989. pap. text 17.50 (*0-674-65921-X*) HUP.

Peacemaking & Democratization in the Western Hemisphere: Multilateral Missions. Ed. by Tommie Sue Montgomery. 360p. 2000. pap. 26.95 (*1-57454-045-9*, Pub. by U Miami N-S Ctr) L Rienner.

Peacemaking & International Conflict: Methods & Techniques. I. William Zartman & J. Lewis Rasmussen. LC 96-31298. (C). 1996. pap. text 19.95 (*1-878379-60-7*) US Inst Peace.

Peacemaking & International Conflict: Methods & Techniques. I. William Zartman et al. LC 96-31298. (C). 1996. 35.00 (*1-878379-61-5*) US Inst Peace.

Peacemaking & Peacekeeping for the New Century. Ed. by Olara A. Otunnu & Michael W. Doyle. LC 97-13387. 368p. (C). 1998. 69.00 (*0-8476-8726-0*); pap. 26.95 (*0-8476-8727-9*) Rowman.

Peacemaking & Peacekeeping in Yugoslavia. Bertrand De Rossanet. LC 95-48134. (Nijhoff Law Specials Ser.: Vol. 17). 1996. pap. 87.50 (*90-411-0192-6*) Kluwer Law Intl.

Peacemaking Christians: The Future of Just Wars, Pacifism & Nonviolent Resistance. Michael K. Duffey. LC 95-14284. (Illus.). 176p. 1995. pap. 14.95 (*1-55612-764-2*) Sheed & Ward WI.

Peacemaking Creatively Through the Arts: A Handbook for Educational Activities & Experiences for Children. Phyllis Vos Wezeman. (Illus.). 238p. (Orig.). 1990. pap. 19.95 (*1-877871-01-X*) Ed Ministries.

Peacemaking for Churches. Yvonne Craig. 1999. pap. text 17.95 (*0-281-05177-1*) Society Prom Christ Know.

Peacemaking in a Troubled World. Ed. by Tom Woodhouse. 384p. 1991. 75.00 (*0-85496-594-7*) Berg Pubs.

Peacemaking in Civil War: International Mediation in Zimbabwe, 1974-1980. Stephen J. Stedman. LC 90-42271. 258p. 1990. lib. bdg. 42.00 (*1-55587-200-X*) L Rienner.

Peacemaking in Early Modern Europe: Cardinal Mazarin & the Congress of Westphalia, 1643-1648. Derek Croxton. LC 98-35304. (Illus.). 400p. 1999. 52.50 (*1-57591-017-9*) Susquehanna U Pr.

***Peacemaking in Israel after Rabin.** Ed. by Sasson Sofer. (Israeli History, Politics & Society Ser.). (Illus.). 256p. 1999. 52.50 (*0-7146-5010-2*); pap. (*0-7146-8064-8*) F Cass Pubs.

Peacemaking in Medieval Europe: A Historical & Bibliographical Guide. Udo Heyn. LC 97-9236. (Guides to Historical Issues Ser.: No. 7). 192p. 1997. text 34.95 (*0-941690-71-7*); pap. text 13.95 (*0-941690-72-5*) Regina Bks.

Peacemaking in the 1990s: A Guide for Canadians. Ed. by Thomas L. Perry. (Illus.). 312p. (Orig.). 1991. pap. 14.95 (*0-919574-93-9*) Gordon Soules Bk.

Peacemaking Made Practical: A Conflict Management Curriculum for the Elementary School. Elizabeth Loescher. 86p. (J). (gr. 1-5). 1991. teacher ed. 25.00 (*1-887249-03-6*) Conflict Ctr.

***Peacemaking Power of Prayer: Equipping Christians to Transform the World.** John D. Robb & Jim Hill. LC 00-23059. 240p. 2000. pap. 14.99 (*0-8054-2291-9*) Broadman.

Peacemaking Skills for Little Kids: Grade 1. Sandy T. Rizzo et al. Ed. by James A. Burke, II et al. (Illus.). 104p. 1997. pap. text, teacher ed. 23.95 (*1-878227-37-8*) Peace Educ.

Peacemaking Skills for Little Kids: Grade 2. Elyse Brunt. Ed. by James A. Burke, II et al. (Illus.). 128p. 1997. pap. text, teacher ed. 23.95 (*1-878227-41-6*) Peace Educ.

Peacemaking Skills for Little Kids: Student Activity Book. Sandy T. Rizzo et al. Ed. by James A. Burke, II et al. (Illus.). 56p. (Orig.). (J). (gr. 1). 1996. pap. text 2.79 (*1-878227-38-6*) Peace Educ.

Peacemaking Skills for Little Kids: Student Activity Book. Fran Schmidt et al. (Illus.). 56p. (Orig.). (J). (gr. 2). 1996. pap. text 2.79 (*1-878227-40-8*) Peace Educ.

Peacemaking Skills for Little Kids, Concept Book. 2nd ed. Fran Schmidt & Alice Friedman. (FRE., Illus.). 76p. (Orig.). (J). (ps-2). 1993. teacher ed., ring bd. 23.95 incl. audio (*1-878227-16-5*) Peace Educ.

Peacemaking Struggle: Militarism & Resistance. Ed. by Ronald H. Stone & Dana W. Wilbanks. (Essays Prepared for the Advisory Council on Church & Society of the Presbyterian Church (U. S. A.) Ser.). 304p. (Orig.). 1985. pap. text 24.00 (*0-8191-4773-7*) U Pr of Amer.

Peacemongers: Conscientious Objectors to Military Service in Australia, 1811-1845. Bobbie Oliver. 1997. pap. 19.95 (*1-86368-184-1*, Pub. by Fremantle Arts) Intl Spec Bk.

PeaceRites. Carla DeSola. Ed. by Thomas A. Kane. (Illus.). 1993. spiral bd. 11.95 (*1-56929-006-7*, Pastoral Press) OR Catholic.

Peacetalk 101: An Eight-Step Program for Ending Verbal Abuse. (Orig.). 1993. pap. 10.00 (*1-878709-06-2*) Ozark Ctr Lang Studies Pr.

Peacetalks Student Activity Book. (Illus.). 24p. (YA). (gr. 7-12). 1997. pap., wbk. ed. 2.49 (*1-56688-438-1*, 3800C) Bur For At-Risk.

Peacetime Army, 1900 to 1941: A Research Guide, 1. Marvin E. Fletcher. LC 88-21433. (Research Guides in Military Studies: No. 1). 198p. 1988. lib. bdg. 59.95 (*0-313-25987-9*, FPI/, Greenwood Pr) Greenwood.

Peacetime Unilateral Remedies: An Analysis of Countermeasures. Elizabeth Zoller. LC 84-2407. 224p. 1984. lib. bdg. 45.00 (*0-941320-21-9*) Transnatl Pubs.

Peacetime Use of Foreign Military Installations under Modern International Law. John Woodliffe. LC 92-20901. 268p. (C). 1992. lib. bdg. 131.00 (*0-7923-1879-X*) Kluwer Academic.

Peacetime Uses of Outer Space. Ed. by Simon Ramo et al. LC 76-52430. (Illus.). 279p. 1977. reprint ed. lib. bdg. 38.50 (*0-8371-9368-0*, RAPU, Greenwood Pr) Greenwood.

Peacetime War Plans, 1919-1935. Ed. by Steven T. Ross. LC 92-20669. (American War Plans, 1919-1941 Ser.: Vol. 1). 248p. 1992. text 40.00 (*0-8153-0689-X*) Garland.

Peacewatch Anthology: Analysis of the Arab-Israeli Peace Process from the Madrid Peace Conference to the Eve of President Clinton's Inauguration. Marvin Feuerwerger et al. LC 93-12534. 173p. 1993. pap. 10.00 (*0-944029-50-7*) Wash Inst NEP.

Peacewatch Anthology: The Arab-Israeli Peace Process & U. S. Policy. Ed. by Judith Wrubel et al. LC 94-13714. 255p. 1994. pap. 10.00 (*0-944029-56-6*) Wash Inst NEP.

***Peacewatch/Policywatch: Anthology 1998: Inching Toward Peace, Inching Toward War.** Monica N. Hertzman. Ed. by Elyse G. Aronson. LC 99-21957. 1999. pap. 10.00 (*0-944029-30-2*) Wash Inst NEP.

Peacework: Life Stories of Women Peace Activists. Judith P. Adams. (Oral History Ser.: No. 5). 320p. 1990. 19.95 (*0-685-29287-8*, Twyne); 25.95 (*0-8057-9106-X*, Twyne) Mac Lib Ref.

Peacework: Oral Histories of Women Peace Activists. Judith Porter Adams. 1992. pap. 14.95 (*0-8057-9119-1*) Mac Lib Ref.

Peacework: 20 Years of Nonviolent Social Change. Ed. by Pat Farren. (Illus.). 288p. (Orig.). (C). 1991. pap. 19.95 (*1-879175-09-6*) Fortkamp.

Peaceworld. Michael McIntyre et al. LC 76-12410. (Illus.). 152p. (Orig.). reprint ed. pap. 47.20 (*0-7837-1955-8*, 204217200001) Bks Demand.

Peach. Elizabeth A. Adler. 544p. 1989. mass mkt. 6.99 (*0-440-20111-X*) Dell.

Peach & Blue. Sarah S. Kilborne. LC 93-26562. (Illus.). 40p. (J). (ps-2). 1994. 18.00 (*0-679-83929-1*, Pub. by Knopf Bks Yng Read) Random.

Peach & Blue. Sarah S. Kilborne. 1998. 12.19 (*0-606-13697-5*, Pub. by Turtleback) Demco.

Peach & Blue. Sarah Kilbourne. 32p. (J). 1998. pap. 6.99 (*0-679-89095-5*) Knopf.

***Peach Basket to Prime Time: Saluting a Century of College Basketball.** Andy Geerken. (Illus.). 208p. 2000. 29.95 (*1-58497-006-5*, Pub. by Addax Pubng) Midpt Trade.

Peach Blossom Cologne Company. 3rd ed. Paul. 1997. pap. text. write for info. (*0-256-21801-3*, Irwn McGrw-H) McGrw-H Hghr Educ.

Peach Blossom Cologne Company: A Short Audit Case. 2nd ed. Jack W. Paul. 166p. (C). 1993. text 38.95 (*0-256-09546-9*, Irwn McGrw-H) McGrw-H Hghr Educ.

Peach Blossom Cologne Company Microcomputer IBM Version for Use with 1-2-3 from Lotus. 2nd ed. John W. Paul. 32p. (C). 1993. text 41.87 incl. 3.5 hd (*0-256-13096-5*, Irwn McGrw-H) McGrw-H Hghr Educ.

Peach Blossom Fan. abr. ed. Tr. & Abr. by T. L. Yang. 335p. 36.00 (*962-209-477-5*) Intl Spec Bk.

Peach Blossum Cologne. 3rd ed. Paul. 1998. pap., student ed. 49.06 (*0-256-21672-X*) McGraw.

Peach Boy see Bank Street Ready-to-Read Books: Levels 1, 2 & 3

Peach Boy. Gail Sakurai. LC 93-43178. (Legends of the World Ser.). (Illus.). 32p. (J). (gr. 2-5). 1997. pap. 4.95 (*0-8167-3410-0*) Troll Communs.

Peach Boy. Gail Sakurai. LC 93-43178. (Legends of the World Ser.). (Illus.). 32p. (J). (gr. 2-5). 1997. lib. bdg. 17.25 (*0-8167-3409-7*) Troll Communs.

Peach Boy: A Japanese Legend. Gail Sakurai. LC 93-43178. (Legends of the World Ser.). 1994. 9.15 (*0-606-06660-8*, Pub. by Turtleback) Demco.

Peach Boy & Other Japanese Children's Favorite Stories. Florence Sakade. (Illus.). 58p. (J). (gr. 1-5). 1958. pap. 9.95 (*0-8048-0469-9*) Tuttle Pubng.

Peach Cobbler Lady. Raymond L. Smith. LC 95-71284. 256p. 1995. 27.95 (*1-56167-227-0*) Noble Hse MD.

Peach County: The World's Peach Paradise. Marilyn Neisler Windham. LC 97-191373. (Images of America Ser.). (Illus.). 128p. 1997. pap. 18.99 (*0-7524-0549-7*) Arcadia Publng.

***Peach Girl.** Miwa Ueda. (Illus.). (J). 2000. pap. 11.95 (*1-892213-62-1*) Talisman Hse.

Peach Groves. Barbara Hanrahan. (Illus.). 228p. 1980. pap. 16.95 (*0-7022-1459-0*) Intl Spec Bk.

Peach, Jacquard. 80p. 1990. 3.00 (*0-9620519-5-0*) Iris Bks.

Peach Orchard: Gettysburg, July 2, 1863. John Bigelow. 57p. 1987. reprint ed. pap. 10.00 (*0-942211-25-1*) Olde Soldier Bks.

Peach Perfect. Sherri Eldridge. (Illus.). 32p. 1998. pap. 2.95 (*1-886862-25-7*, MN PCH, Coastal New England Pubns) Harv Hill ME.

Peach Pit Popularity. Nancy Levene. LC 89-33900. (Illus.). 128p. (J). (gr. 2-5). 1994. pap. 4.99 (*1-55513-529-3*, Chariot Bks) Chariot Victor.

***Peach Pit Popularity.** Nancy Simpson. 2000. pap. 4.99 (*0-7814-3407-6*) Chariot Victor.

Peach Pits at My Door: And Other Adventures. John Jopes. 172p. 1996. 17.95 (*0-944933-06-8*) Dragonflyer Pr.

Peach Point Plantation: The First 150 Years. Marie B. Jones. 213p. 1992. 23.50 (*0-9630042-0-4*) M B Jones.

Peach Roses. Lawson Falle Limited Company Staff. (Illus.). 1996. (*1-895911-29-X*) LAW.

Peach Slices. Donna Barr. (Illus.). 96p. 1993. pap. 9.95 (*1-883847-01-X*) MU Press.

Peach State Glovebox Guide to BBQ: Georgia. BBQ Digest Staff. 192p. (Orig.). 1997. pap. 12.95 (*1-56352-375-2*) Longstreet.

Peach State Paradise: A Guide to Gardens & Natural Areas of Georgia. Cindy Spicer. LC 97-22003. (Illus.). 1997. 29.95 (*0-89587-206-4*) Blair.

Peach Train to Beijing: And Beyond. Beth Glick-Rieman. 288p. 1998. pap. 19.95 (*1-896836-15-1*) NStone Publ.

Peach Tree. Norman Pike. (Illus.). 36p. (J). (ps up). 1984. 12.95 (*0-88045-014-2*) Stemmer Hse.

Peach Tree Family Cookbook. Cynthia C. Pedregon. LC 94-66692. 1994. 19.95 (*0-9627590-0-7*) Peach Tree & Tea.

Peach Tree Tea Room. Cynthia C. Pedregon. 1990. 19.95 (*0-9627590-7-4*) Peach Tree & Tea.

Peach-World Cultivars to Marketing. Ed. by Norman F. Childers & Wayne B. Sherman. 1000p. 1998. 35.00 (*0-938378-03-1*) N F Childers.

Peachboy: A Japanese Folktale. Eric Metaxas. LC 91-15251. (Illus.). 36p. (J). (ps-3). 1995. pap. 19.95 (*0-689-80192-0*, Rabbit Ears) Litle Simon.

Peaches. Lawson Falle Limited Company Staff. (Illus.). 1997. pap. 5.99 (*1-895911-51-6*) LAW.

Peaches. Robert Vandermolen. 48p. 1998. pap. 8.00 (*0-9646557-1-3*) Skybooks MI.

Peaches & Pines Vol. 1: A Collection of Recipes from Junior Auxiliary of Ruston. 454p. write for info. (*0-614-15351-4*) Junior Auxiliary.

Peaches of New York. U. P. Hedrick. 541p. 1993. reprint ed. lib. bdg. 99.00 (*0-7812-5235-0*) Rprt Serv.

Peaches! Peaches! Peaches! M. Mosley. (Illus.). 176p. 1997. spiral bd. 5.95 (*1-57166-088-7*) Hearts N Tummies.

***Peaches, Pears & Plums.** Elaine Elliott. (Flavours Ser.). (Illus.). 64p. 1999. pap. 9.95 (*0-88780-471-3*, Pub. by Formac Publ Co) Seven Hills Bk.

Peaches, Plums & Nectarines: Growing & Handling for Fresh Market. Ed. by James H. LaRue & R. Scott Johnson. LC 89-83832. (Illus.). 252p. (Orig.). 1989. pap. 45.00 (*0-931876-88-5*, 3331) ANR Pubns CA.

Peachtree Accounting for Windows Made Easy: The Basics & Beyond! 2nd ed. John V. Hedtke. (Made Easy Ser.). 512p. 1995. pap. text 29.95 (*0-07-882127-4*) McGraw.

***PeachTree Accounting Introduction.** (Illus.). (YA). 1999. pap. write for info. (*0-7423-0396-9*, PTACCT001LG) ComputerPREP.

***PeachTree Accounting Introduction: Instructor Guide.** (Illus.). 192p. 1999. pap., teacher ed. write for info. (*0-7423-0421-3*) ComputerPREP.

Peachtree Bouquet. Junior League Staff. 1987. 14.95 (*0-9618508-1-7*) Jr Lgue Dekalb Cty.

Peachtree Complete Business Toolkit. John Hedtke. LC 98-149907. (Illus.). 560p. (Orig.). 1998. pap. text 39.99 incl. cd-rom (*0-07-882373-0*) Osborne-McGraw.

***Peachtree for College Accounting.** Errol Esterraa. 240p. 1998. pap. text 23.60 (*0-13-982216-X*) P-H.

***Peachtree for Dummies.** Elaine J. Marmel. (For Dummies Ser.). (Illus.). 384p. 2000. pap. 19.99 (*0-7645-0640-4*) IDG Bks.

Peachtree Garden Book: Gardening in the Southeast. 5th rev. ed. Ed. by Olive Robinson. LC 96-38994. (Illus.). 112p. 1997. 7.95 (*1-56145-144-4*) Peachtree Pubs.

Peachtree Made Easy: The Basics & Beyond. 4th ed. John V. Hedtke. 600p. 1998. pap. 24.99 (*0-07-882527-X*) Osborne-McGraw.

***Peachtree Made Easy: The Basics & Beyond!** 5th ed. John V. Hedtke. (Illus.). 592p. 2000. pap. text 29.99 (*0-07-212507-1*) Osborne-McGraw.

Peachtree Mount & Village Site, Cherokee County, North Carolina. Setzler & Jennings. (Bureau of American Ethnology Bulletins Ser.). 103p. 1995. lib. bdg. 79.00 (*0-7812-4131-6*) Rprt Serv.

Peachtree Road. Anne Rivers Siddons. 608p. 1989. mass mkt. 6.99 (*0-345-36272-1*) Ballantine Pub Grp.

Peachtree Road. large type ed. Anne Rivers Siddons. LC 94-20256. 998p. 1994. lib. bdg. 26.95 (*0-8161-7412-1*, G K Hall Lrg Type) Mac Lib Ref.

Peachtree Road. Anne Rivers Siddons. 576p. 1996. reprint ed. 27.50 (*0-937036-05-6*) Old NY Bk Shop.

***Peachtree Road 10th anniv edition.** Anne Rivers Siddons. 832p. 1998. mass mkt. 6.99 (*0-06-109723-3*) HarpC.

Peachy's Proposal. Carole Buck. (Desire Ser.). 1996. per. 3.25 (*0-373-05976-0*, 1-05976-5) Silhouette.

Peacock: The Satirical Novels : A Casebook Lorna Sage. LC 77-354412. (Casebook Ser.). 253 p. 1976. write for info. (*0-333-18410-6*) Macmillan.

***Peacock & other Poems.** Valerie Worth. 2000. text. write for info. (*0-374-35766-8*) St Martin.

***Peacock & the Dragon: India-China Relations in the 21st Century.** Ed. by Kanti P. Bajpai. 2000. 44.00 (*81-241-0642-8*, Pub. by Har-Anand Pubns) S Asia.

Peacock Angel: Being Some Account of Votaries of a Secret Cult & Their Sanctuaries. Ethel S. Drower. LC 77-87643. reprint ed. 20.00 (*0-404-16425-0*) AMS Pr.

Peacock Bass Addiction: The Newest Spots & Latest Tactical Secrets. Larry Larsen. (Illus.). 192p. 1999. pap. 14.95 (*0-936513-49-7*) Larsens Outdoor.

Peacock Bass & Other Fierce Exotics: Where, When & How to Catch Latin America's Most Exciting Freshwater Fish. Larry Larsen. LC 95-95343. (Illus.). 192p. (Orig.). 1996. pap. 13.95 (*0-936513-33-0*) Larsens Outdoor.

Peacock Bass Explosions: Where, When & How to Catch America's Greatest Gamefish. Larry Larsen. LC 93-79801. (Illus.). 192p. (Orig.). 1993. pap. text 12.95 (*0-936513-35-7*) Larsens Outdoor.

Peacock Emperor Moth: Short Fictions. Marcel Cohen. Tr. by Cid Corman from FRE. (Serie d'Ecriture: No. 9). 112p. (Orig.). 1995. pap. 8.00 (*1-886224-07-2*) Burning Deck.

Peacock Fan. Katherine Gordon. (Peacock Ser.). 320p. 1996. 24.00 (*0-7278-4895-X*) Severn Hse.

Peacock Fan. large type ed. Katharine Gordon. (Ulverscroft Large Print Ser.). 320p. 1997. 27.99 (*0-7089-3862-0*) Ulverscroft.

Peacock Feather. Nancy Adams. LC 95-95219. (Illus.). 56p. 1995. 10.00 (*0-9655909-0-9*) N D Adams.

Peacock Feather Murders. Carter Dickson, pseud. LC 87-82443. 192p. 1987. reprint ed. pap. 5.95 (*0-930330-68-4*) Intl Polygonics.

Peacock Festival: Selected Color Woodcuts. John F. Mills. LC 64-8130. (Illus.). 80p. 1964. pap. 20.00 (*0-933652-00-3*) Domjan Studio.

Peacock Has Landed. Ralph E. Martin. LC 97-60659. (Illus.). 52p. 1997. pap. 5.00 (*1-886467-18-8*) WJM Press.

Peacock House, & Other Mysteries. Eden Phillpotts. LC 73-128749. (Short Story Index Reprint Ser.). 1977. 19.95 (*0-8369-3640-X*) Ayer.

Peacock in the Land of Penguins: A Tale of Diversity & Discovery. 2nd ed. Barbara Hateley & Warren H. Smith. LC 97-11540. (Illus.). 152p. (Orig.). 1997. pap. 12.95 (*1-57675-010-8*) Berrett-Koehler.

Peacock on the Roof. Paul Adshead. LC 90-49099. 32p. 1990. 13.99 (*0-85953-295-X*); pap. 6.99 (*0-85953-307-7*) Childs Play.

Peacock on the Roof. Paul Adshead. (GRE.). (J). 1990. pap. 6.99 (*0-85953-804-4*) Childs Play.

Peacock on the Roof. Paul Adshead. (J). 1996. lib. bdg. 15.95 (*0-85953-889-3*) Childs Play.

Peacock or a Crow? Stories, Interviews & Commentaries of Romanian Adoptees in the United States. Victor Groza et al. (Illus.). 240p. 1998. pap. 22.00 (*1-893435-02-4*) Lakeshore Comm.

Peacock Pagoda. large type ed. Alex Stuart. 384p. 1988. 27.99 (*0-7089-1793-3*) Ulverscroft.

Peacock Poems. Sherley A. Williams. LC 75-12531. (Wesleyan Poetry Program Ser.: Vol. 79). 88p. 1975. pap. 12.95 (*0-8195-1079-3*, Wesleyan Univ Pr) U Pr of New Eng.

Peacock Princess: Three American Women Held Captive in Royal & Revolutionary Iran. Sara Harris & Barbara Bell. LC 95-14884. 317p. 1995. 19.99 (*1-56790-006-2*) BookWorld.

Peacock Rider. large type ed. Katharine Gordon. (Large Print Ser.). 528p. 1996. 27.99 (*0-7089-3604-0*) Ulverscroft.

Peacock Room: A Cultural Biography. Linda Merrill. LC 98-21534. (Illus.). 408p. 1998. 65.00 (*0-300-07611-8*) Yale U Pr.

Peacock Season. Otis Bigelow. 1971. pap. 13.00 (*0-8222-0882-2*) Dramatists Play.

Peacock Throne: The Drama of Moghul India. Waldemar Hansen. (Illus.). 560p. 1986. 28.00 (*0-317-60577-1*, Pub. by Motilal Bnarsidass) S Asia.

P

Peacock Throne: The Drama of Moghul India. Waldemar Hansen. (Illus.). 560p. 1986. reprint ed. 26.50 (*81-208-0225-X*, Pub. by Motilal Bnarsidass) S Asia.

Peacocks. Ruth Berman. LC 95-12204. (Early Bird Nature Bks.). (Illus.). 47p. (J). (gr. 2-5). 1996. lib. bdg. 19.95 (*0-8225-3009-0*, Lerner Publctns) Lerner Pub.

***Peacocks.** Yukio Mishima, pseud. (Short Stories Ser.). 22p. 2000. pap. 3.95 (*1-86092-029-2*, Pub. by Travelman Pub) IPG Chicago.

Peacock's Acre. J. Curry. mass mkt. 13.95 (*0-340-68021-0*, Pub. by Hodder & Stought Ltd) Trafalgar.

Peacocks & Beans. Valerie Tekavec. (Illus.). 48p. (Orig.). 1996. pap. text 6.00 (*1-56439-051-9*) Ridgeway.

Peacocks & Pagodas. Paul Edmonds. LC 77-87012. (Illus.). reprint ed. 42.50 (*0-404-16813-2*) AMS Pr.

Peacocks in Paradise. Elisabeth I. Jones. 254p. (C). 1993. pap. 25.00 (*0-86383-672-0*, Pub. by Gomer Pr) St Mut.

Peacocks in Paradise. 3rd ed. Elisabeth Inglis-Jones. 254p. 1996. reprint ed. pap. 22.95 (*0-8464-4695-2*) Beekman Pubs.

Peacock's Memoir of Shelley, with Shelley's Letters to Peacock. Thomas Love Peacock. (BCL1-PR English Literature Ser.). 219p. 1992. reprint ed. lib. bdg. 79.00 (*0-7812-7655-1*) Rprt Serv.

Peacocks on Parade: A Narrative of a Unique Period in American Social History & Its Most Colorful Figures. Albert S. Crockett. LC 75-1836. (Leisure Class in America Ser.). (Illus.). 1975. reprint ed. 24.95 (*0-405-06905-7*) Ayer.

Peacocks, Pagodas & Professor Hall: A Critique of the Persisting Use of Historiography as an Apology for British Empire-Building in Burma. Emanuel Sarkisyanz. LC 72-619652. (Papers in International Studies: No. 24). 74p. reprint ed. pap. 30.00 (*0-608-30136-1*, 200437500051) Bks Demand.

Peacock's Pride. Melissa Kajpust. LC 96-33664. (Illus.). 32p. (J). (ps-2). 1997. 14.95 (*0-7868-0293-6*, Pub. by Hyprn Child); lib. bdg. 14.89 (*0-7868-2233-3*, Pub. by Hyprn Child) Little.

Peacock's Pride. large type ed. Melissa Kajpust. (Illus.). 32p. (J). (ps-3). 1996. write for info. (*1-895340-12-8*) Hyperion Pr.

Peacock's Progress: Aspects of Artistic Development in the Novels of Thomas Love Peacock. Margaret McKay. (Studia Anglistica Upsaliensia Ser.: No. 78). 170p. (Orig.). 1992. pap. 41.00 (*91-554-2914-9*) Coronet Bks.

Peadar O'Donnell. Grattan Freyer. (Irish Writers Ser.). 128p. 1973. pap. 1.95 (*0-8387-1369-6*) Bucknell U Pr.

***Peadar O'Donnell.** Peter Hegarty. (Illus.). 280p. 1999. pap. 19.95 (*1-85635-204-8*) Irish Bks Media.

Peadar O'Donnell: A Reader's Guide. Alexander G. Gonzalez. LC 96-33090. 128p. 1997. pap. 16.95 (*0-8023-1314-0*) Dufour.

Peagius's Commentary on St. Paul's Epistle to the Romans. Pelagius. Tr. & Intro. by Theodore De Bruyn. (Oxford Early Christian Studies). 248p. 1998. reprint ed. pap. text 24.95 (*0-19-826980-3*) OUP.

Peah. (Mishnah Ser.: No. 2a). pap. 15.99 (*0-89906-329-2*, R2AP) Mesorah Pubns.

Peak: Practical Exercises in Applying Knowledge - PeakMath. 2nd rev. ed. Oklahoma Dept. of Vo-Tech Education Staff. (Illus.). 300p. (YA). (gr. 9-12). 1995. ring bd. 195.00 (*1-892312-06-9*) Coin Eductnl.

Peak: Practical Exercises in Applying Knowledge - PeakScience. 2nd rev. ed. Oklahoma Dept. of Vo-Tech Education Staff. (Illus.). 300p. (YA). (gr. 9-12). 1995. ring bd. 195.00 (*1-892312-16-6*) Coin Eductnl.

Peak & Prairie. Anna Fuller. LC 75-94724. (Short Story Index Reprint Ser.). 1977. 24.95 (*0-8369-3103-3*) Ayer.

Peak District. (Ordnance Survey Landranger Guides Ser.). (Illus.). 144p. 1993. pap. 15.95 (*0-7117-0541-0*) Seven Hills Bk.

Peak District. Insight Guides Staff. (Insight Guides). 1998. pap. text 7.95 (*0-88729-554-1*) Langenscheidt.

Peak District. Rob Talbot & Robin Whiteman. LC 99-223056. (Country Ser.). (Illus.). 160p. 1998. pap. 17.95 (*0-7538-0207-4*, Pub. by Orion Pubng Grp) Trafalgar.

Peak District. Rob Talbot & Robin Whiteman. (Country Ser.). (Illus.). 160p. 1997. 29.95 (*0-297-83605-6*, Pub. by Weidenfeld & Nicolson) Trafalgar.

Peak District . . . Something to Remember Her By. John N. Merrill. (Illus.). 96p. (C). 1989. 50.00 (*0-907496-53-9*, Pub. by JNM Pubns) St Mut.

Peak District Challenge Walk - 25 Miles. John N. Merrill. 32p. 1987. 29.00 (*0-907496-43-1*, Pub. by JNM Pubns) St Mut.

Peak District End to End Walks - 23 & 24 Miles. John N. Merrill. 52p. 1987. 29.00 (*0-907496-39-3*, Pub. by JNM Pubns) St Mut.

Peak District Walks. Jarrold Staff. (Ordnance Survey Pathfinder Guides Ser.). (Illus.). 80p. 1993. pap. 14.95 (*0-7117-0464-3*) Seven Hills Bk.

***Peak Experiences: Hiking the Highest Summits in New York, County by County.** Gary Fallesen. 288p. 2000. pap. 16.95 (*0-9656974-0-1*) Footprint Pr NY.

Peak Experiences: Write 'Em Down. Rudarmel. 1994. pap. text 9.95 (*1-880133-44-X*) AHA Calligraphy.

Peak Flow Measurement: An Illustrated Guide. J. G. Ayres et al. LC 96-83632. (Illus.). 144p. 1996. pap. text 22.95 (*0-412-73620-9*, Pub. by E A) OUP.

Peak Flow Meter Book: A Guide for People with Asthma. rev. ed. Nancy J. Sander & Guillermo R. Mendoza. Ed. by Martha White. (Illus.). 28p. 1995. pap. text 5.95 (*1-885543-01-8*) Allergy & Asthma.

Peak-Hour Traffic Signal Warrant. (National Cooperative Highway Research Program Report Ser.: No. 249). 71p. 1982. 7.60 (*0-309-03419-1*, NR249) Transport Res Bd.

Peak in Darien. Freya Stark. 1977. 16.95 (*0-7195-3291-4*) Transatl Arts.

Peak Learning. abr. ed. Ron Gross. 1994. pap. text 10.95 incl. audio (*1-55927-240-6*) Audio Renaissance.

Peak Learning: How to Create Your Own Lifelong Education Program for Personal Enlightenment & Professional Success. rev. ed. Ronald Gross. LC 98-53158. (Illus.). 320p. 1999. 16.95 (*0-87477-957-X*, Tarcher Putnam) Putnam Pub Group.

Peak Line: The Midland Railway. John M. Stephenson. 88p. (C). 1985. 39.00 (*0-85361-282-X*) St Mut.

Peak Log. Kenneth G. Hukari & Scott Griebel. 62p. 1993. 14.95 (*1-884751-00-8*) Wy East LogBk.

Peak of Danger. Franklin W. Dixon. (Hardy Boys Casefiles Ser.: No. 101). (Illus.). 160p. (J). (gr. 6 up). 1995. per. 3.99 (*0-671-88212-0*) PB.

Peak of Danger. Franklin W. Dixon. (Hardy Boys Casefiles Ser.: No. 101). (YA). (gr. 6 up). 1995. 9.09 (*0-606-07614-X*, Pub. by Turtleback) Demco.

Peak of Eloquence - Nahjul Balagha. rev. ed. Ali B. Abi Talib. Ed. by Sayyid Razi. Tr. by Askari Jafery from ARA. 700p. (C). 1987. reprint ed. 12.00 (*0-941724-18-2*) Islamic Seminary.

Peak Performance. Sharon K. Ferrett. LC 92-17061. 400p. (C). 1993. text 18.30 (*0-256-12160-5*, Irwn McGrw-H) McGrw-H Hghr Educ.

Peak Performance. 2nd ed. Sharon K. Ferrett. 416p. (C). 1996. text 18.30 (*0-256-21995-8*, Irwn McGrw-H) McGrw-H Hghr Educ.

Peak Performance: A Guide to Total Sexual Fitness. Lynn Sonberg. (Natural Pleasure Ser.). 1999. mass mkt. 5.99 (*0-440-23452-2*) Dell.

***Peak Performance: Aligning the Hearts & Minds of Your Employees.** Jon R. Katzenbach. LC 99-48878. 2000. 29.95 (*0-87584-936-9*, HBS Pr) Harvard Busn.

***Peak Performance: Business Lessons from the World's Top Sports Organizations.** Clive Gilson. (Illus.). 2000. 27.95 (*1-58799-006-7*) Texere.

Peak Performance: Coaching the Canine Athlete. 2nd rev. ed. M. Christine Zink. (Illus.). 224p. 1997. pap. 24.95 (*1-888119-02-0*) Canine Spts.

Peak Performance: Success in College & Beyond 3rd ed. Sharon K. Ferrett. LC 99-23302. 2000. write for info. (*0-02-804305-7*) Glencoe.

Peak Performance: Training & Nutritional Strategies for Sport. John Hawley & Louise Burke. (Illus.). 456p. 1998. pap. 16.95 (*1-86448-469-1*) IPG Chicago.

Peak Performance: You Can Be a Winner. Ron Brown & Gordon Thiessen. 1999. pap. 3.95 (*1-887002-59-6*) Cross Trng.

Peak Performance . . . & More. Robert N. Singer. 1986. pap. 24.95 (*0-317-44765-3*) Mouvement Pubns.

Peak Performance Course for Traders & Investors, 5 vols., Set. Van K. Tharp. (Orig.). 1987. pap. 595.00 (*0-935219-05-6*) Intl Trading Mastery.

***Peak Performance Fitness: Maximizing Your Fitness Potential Without Injury or Strain.** Jennifer D. Rhodes. (Illus.). 2000. 24.95 (*0-89793-297-8*); pap. 14.95 (*0-89793-296-X*) Hunter Hse.

***Peak Performance Golf: How Good Golfers Become Great Ones.** Patrick J. Cohn. LC 99-40995. 224p. 2000. pap. 16.95 (*0-8092-2432-1*, 243210, Contemporary Bks) NTC Contemp Pub Co.

Peak Performance Kit: Being More Effective on the Job. Jim L. Evers. (Peak Performance Ser.). 1995. 32.95 (*0-9628230-6-6*) J L Evers Assocs.

Peak Performance Principles for High Achievers. John R. Noe. 192p. 1986. mass mkt. 4.50 (*0-425-10150-9*) Berkley Pub.

Peak Performance Selling: How to Increase Your Sales by 70 Percent in Six Weeks. Kerry L. Johnson. (Illus.). 256p. 1990. 22.50 (*0-13-655358-3*) P-H.

Peak Performance Workbook: Self-Empowerment Activities for a Constantly Changing Workplace. Jim L. Evers. (Peak Performance Ser.). (Illus.). 59p. (Orig.). 1998. pap., wbk. ed. 10.95 (*0-9628230-7-4*) J L Evers Assocs.

Peak Performers: The New Heroes of American Business. Charles Garfield. 336p. 1987. pap. 12.00 (*0-380-70304-1*, Avon Bks) Morrow Avon.

Peak-Period Traffic Congestion - Options for Current Programs. (National Cooperative Highway Research Program Report Ser.: No. 169). 65p. 1976. 4.80 (*0-309-02509-5*) Transport Res Bd.

***Peak Sanctuaries & Sacred Caves in Minoan Crete: A Comparison of Artifacts.** Donald W. Jones. (Studies in Mediterranean Archaeology & Literature Pocket Bk.: Vol. 156). 104p. 1999. pap. 37.50 (*91-7081-153-9*, Pub. by P Astroms) Coronet Bks.

Peak to Peak: Colorado Front Range Ski Trails Guidebook & Map. rev. ed. Harlan N. Barton. (Illus.). 232p. 1995. pap. 18.95 (*0-9624606-1-3*) Frnt Range Pub.

Peak to Peek Principle. Robert H. Schuller. 192p. 1984. mass mkt. 4.99 (*0-515-07860-3*, Jove) Berkley Pub.

Peak When It Counts: Periodization for American Track & Field. 3rd rev. ed. William H. Freeman. (Illus.). 136p. 1996. pap. 15.95 (*0-911521-46-1*) Tafnews.

Peak with Books: An Early Childhood Resource for Balanced Literacy. 3rd ed. Marjorie R. Nelsen & Jan Nelsen-Parish. LC 99-6080. (1-Off Ser.). (Illus.). 288p. 1999. pap. 34.95 (*0-8039-6796-9*) Corwin Pr.

Peak with Books: An Early Childhood Resource Guide. 2nd rev. ed. Marjorie R. Nelsen & Jan L. Nelsen. (Illus.). 228p. 1991. 21.95 (*0-9630495-1-8*) Partners in Learn.

Peake's Commentary on the Bible. Ed. by Matthew Black & H H Rowley. (Illus.). 1142p. (C). 1997. 160.00 (*0-415-05147-9*) Routledge.

Peake's Progress: Selected Writings & Drawings of Mervyn Peake. Mervyn Peake. Ed. by Maeve Gilmore. LC 80-83054. (Illus.). 592p. 1981. 37.50 (*0-87951-121-4*, Pub. by Overlook Pr) Penguin Putnam.

Peaking Power Generation: Presented at the Winter Annual Meeting of the American Society of Mechanical Engineers, Chicago, Illinois, November 16-21, 1980. American Society of Mechanical Engineers Staff. Ed. by E. S. Miliaras. LC 80-69795. (Illus.). 58p. reprint ed. pap. 30.00 (*0-8357-2888-9*, 203912400011) Bks Demand.

Peaks: Northern Arizona's High Country. Text by Rose Houk. LC 94-79757. (Illus.). 64p. 1995. pap. 10.95 (*0-916179-48-6*) Ariz Hwy.

Peaks & Lamas. Marco Pallis. 1975. lib. bdg. 300.00 (*0-87968-327-9*) Gordon Pr.

Peaks & People of the Adirondacks. Russell Carson. 269p. 1993. reprint ed. lib. bdg. 79.00 (*0-7812-5120-6*) Rprt Serv.

Peaks of Faith: Protestant Mission in Revolutionary China. T'ien Ju-K'ang. LC 92-30549. (Studies in Christian Mission: Vol. 8). (Illus.). viii, 166p. 1993. 71.00 (*90-04-09723-6*) Brill Academic Pubs.

Peaks of Medical History. 2nd ed. Charles L. Dana. LC 75-23703. (Illus.). reprint ed. 55.00 (*0-404-13255-3*) AMS Pr.

Peaks of Otter: Life & Times. Peter Viemeister. LC 92-70103. (Illus.). 278p. 1992. lib. bdg. 26.50 (*0-9608598-9-6*) Hamiltons.

***Peaks of Power: How Mountains Are Made.** Rosanna Hansen & Linda Falken. (Three-D Science Ser.). (Illus.). 18p. (J). (gr. 1-5). 2001. 12.99 (*1-57584-743-4*, Pub. by Rdrs Digest) S&S Trade.

***Peaks of San Jacinto.** large type ed. Terry Murphy. 232p. 2000. pap. 18.99 (*0-7089-5633-5*, Linford) Ulverscroft.

Peaks of Yemen I Summon: Poetry As Cultural Practice in a North Yemeni Tribe. Steven C. Caton. LC 89-20524. 330p. 1990. 55.00 (*0-520-06766-5*, Pub. by U CA Pr); pap. 18.95 (*0-520-08261-3*, Pub. by U CA Pr) Cal Prin Full Svc.

Peaks, Palms & Picnics: Day Journeys in the Mountains & Deserts of Palm Springs. Linda M. Pyle. LC 99-61932. 365p. 1999. 25.00 (*0-7388-0362-6*); pap. 15.00 (*0-7388-0363-4*) Xlibris Corp.

Peaks, Plateaus & Canyons: Colorado Plateau. Ed. by Jeff Nicholas. (Wish You Were Here Postcard Book Ser.). (Illus.). 32p. 1998. 4.95 (*0-939365-95-2*) Panorama Intl.

Peal of Bells. Robert Lynd. LC 78-90660. (Essay Index Reprint Ser.). 1977. 20.95 (*0-8369-1226-8*) Ayer.

Peal of Bells. Robert Lynd. LC 75-131772. 1971. reprint ed. 16.00 (*0-403-00659-7*) Scholarly.

Peale Family: Creation of a Legacy, 1770-1870. Ed. by Lillian B. Miller. LC 96-13975. (Illus.). 320p. 1996. pap. 48.00 (*0-7892-0248-4*) Abbeville Pr.

Peano: Life & Works of Giuseppe Peano. Hubert Kennedy. (Studies in the History of Modern Science: No. 4). 242p. 1980. pap. text 62.50 (*90-277-1068-6*, D Reidel); lib. bdg. 88.00 (*90-277-1067-8*, D Reidel) Kluwer Academic.

***Peanut Allergy Answer Book.** Michael Young. 2000. pap. 8.95 (*1-86204-823-1*, Pub. by Element MA) Penguin Putnam.

Peanut Butter. Arlene Erlbach. LC 93-20217. (How It's Made Ser.). (J). (gr. 2-5). 1993. lib. bdg. 19.95 (*0-8225-2387-6*, Lerner Publctns) Lerner Pub.

Peanut Butter. Arlene Erlbach. (Illus.). 48p. (J). 1995. pap. 6.95 (*0-8225-9709-8*) Lerner Pub.

Peanut Butter. 2nd ed. Illus. & Retold by Robin Oz. (Let Me Read Ser.). 16p. (J). (ps-1). 1995. bds. 2.95 (*0-673-36271-X*, GoodYrBooks) Addson-Wesley Educ.

Peanut Butter & Jelly see All Day & Night Set

Peanut Butter & Jelly: A Play Rhyme. Nadine Bernard Westcott. (Illus.). 24p. (J). (ps). 1992. pap. 5.99 (*0-14-054852-1*, PuffinBks) Peng Put Young Read.

Peanut Butter & Jelly: Reproducible Worksheets for Young Students of ESL. Solveig Villicana. Ed. by Charles Chapman. (Illus.). 75p. (Orig.). 1991. pap. write for info. (*1-878598-08-2*) Alta Bk Co Pubs.

Peanut Butter & Jelly Big Book: Black & White Nellie Edge I Can Read & Sing Big Book. Illus. by Tani Draper. (J). (ps-2). 1988. pap. text 21.00 (*0-922053-10-3*) N Edge Res.

Peanut Butter & Jelly for Shabbos. Dina Rosenfeld. LC 95-75435. (Illus.). 32p. (J). (ps-1). 1995. 9.95 (*0-922613-69-9*) Hachai Pubng.

Peanut Butter & Jelly Game. Adam Eisenson. Ed. by Nancy Castleman. (Magic Word Book). (Illus.). 32p. (J). (gr. k-3). 1996. lib. bdg. 14.95 (*0-943973-16-3*) Good Advice Pr.

***Peanut Butter & Jelly Management: Tales from Parenthood - Lessons for Managers.** Chris Komisarjevsky & Reina Komisarjevsky. LC 99-58728. (Illus.). 171p. 2000. 16.95 (*0-8144-7062-9*) AMACOM.

Peanut Butter & Jelly Secrets. Nancy Levene. LC 87-5247. 128p. (J). (gr. 3-6). 1987. pap. 4.99 (*1-55513-303-7*, Chariot Bks) Chariot Victor.

Peanut Butter & Jelly Secrets. Nancy Simpson. 1999. pap. text 4.99 (*0-7814-3256-1*) Chariot Victor.

Peanut Butter & Worms? Craig Strasshofer. (Illus.). 10p. (J). (gr. k-2). 1998. bds. 6.99 (*1-57151-608-5*, Nibble Me Bks) Picture Me Bks.

Peanut Butter, Apple Butter, Cinnamon Toast: Food Riddles for You to Guess. Argentina Palacios. (Ready-Set-Read Ser.). (Illus.). 32p. (J). (ps-3). 1990. lib. bdg. 21.40 (*0-8172-3584-1*) Raintree Steck-V.

Peanut Butter, Apple Butter, Cinnamon Toast: Food Riddles for You to Guess. Argentina Palacios. 28p. (J). (ps-3). 1995. pap. text 4.95 (*0-8114-6745-7*) Raintree Steck-V.

Peanut Butter Bob. Cathy Delittle. LC 98-93049. (Illus.). 9p. (J). (ps-1). 1998. spiral bd. 7.95 (*1-892633-00-0*, OOCD203) Delittle Story.

Peanut Butter Cookbook for Kids. Judy Ralph & Ray Gompf. LC 94-37852. (Illus.). 96p. (J). (gr. 3 up). 1995. lib. bdg. 14.89 (*0-7868-2110-8*, Pub. by Hyprn Child) Little.

Peanut Butter Cookbook for Kids. Judy Ralph & Ray Gompf. LC 94-37852. (Illus.). 96p. (YA). (gr. 3 up). 1995. pap. 10.45 (*0-7868-1028-9*, Pub. by Hyprn Ppbks) Little.

Peanut Butter Delights: Peanut Butter Cookbook - 200 Recipes. Betty Brass & Mary Einsel. LC 86-63090. Orig. Title: Peanut Butter Madness. (Illus.). 174p. 1986. reprint ed. pap. 13.95 (*0-9660552-0-9*) Peanut But Del.

Peanut Butter Friends in a Chop Suey World. Deb Brammer. LC 94-38216. (Illus.). (J). 1994. pap. 6.49 (*0-89084-751-7*, 082685) Bob Jones Univ.

Peanut Butter Gang. Catherine Siracusa. (J). 1997. lib. bdg. 14.49 (*0-7868-2300-3*, Pub. by Hyperion) Little.

Peanut Butter Gang. Catherine Siracusa. LC 95-21937. (Illus.). 48p. (J). (gr. 1-3). 1996. 13.95 (*0-7868-0148-4*, Pub. by Hyprn Child) Time Warner.

Peanut Butter Glasses. Barbara E. Mauzy. LC 96-35800. 128p. (YA). (gr. 10). 1997. pap. 19.95 (*0-7643-0107-1*) Schiffer.

Peanut Butter Kid. Gertrude Stonesifer. LC 95-80766. (Illus.). 32p. (J). (gr. 1-4). 1995. pap. 9.95 (*1-878044-44-3*, Wld Rose) Mayhaven Pub.

***Peanut Butter Kisses & Mudpie Hugs: Stories of Love, Laughter & Being a Mom.** Becky Freeman. 200p. 2000. pap. 8.99 (*0-7369-0240-6*) Harvest Hse.

***Peanut Butter Lover Boy.** Bruce Coville. (I Was a Sixth Grade Alien Ser.: Vol. 4). (Illus.). 192p. (J). 2000. per. 3.99 (*0-671-02653-4*, Minstrel Bks) PB.

***Peanut Butter Lover Boy.** Bruce Coville. (Illus.). (J). 2000. 9.34 (*0-606-18307-8*) Turtleback.

Peanut Butter Madness see Peanut Butter Delights: Peanut Butter Cookbook - 200 Recipes

Peanut Butter Market. 118p. 1996. 895.00 (*0-686-31519-7*) Busn Trend.

Peanut Butter Murders. Corinne H. Sawyer. 1995. mass mkt. 4.99 (*0-449-22172-5*) Ballantine Pub Grp.

Peanut Butter Party: Including the History, Uses & Future of Peanut Butter. Remy Charlip. LC 98-43378. (Illus.). (J). (gr. 1-5). 1999. 14.95 (*1-883672-69-4*) Tricycle Pr.

Peanut Butter Pilgrims. Judy Delton. (Pee Wee Scouts Ser.: No. 6). 80p. (Orig.). (J). (gr. k-6). 1988. pap. 3.99 (*0-440-40066-X*, YB BDD) BDD Bks Young Read.

Peanut-Butter Pilgrims. Judy Delton. (Pee Wee Scouts Ser.). (J). 1988. 9.19 (*0-606-04053-6*, Pub. by Turtleback) Demco.

Peanut Butter Promises: Nap 'n Snack Devotions. Robin Currie. LC 99-19055. 96p. 1999. 10.00 (*0-570-05557-1*) Concordia.

Peanut Butter Sticks to the Roof of Your Mouth: Light-Hearted Reflections & Recipes with a Northwest Flavor. Joan Howard. LC 94-78435. 179p. 1994. pap. 12.95 (*1-885221-10-X*) BookPartners.

Peanut Butter, Tarzan & Roosters Activity Book: Developmental Activities. Jackie Silberg. 1987. 10.95 incl. audio (*0-685-14538-7*); pap. 10.95 (*0-939514-09-5*) Miss Jackie.

Peanut Butter Trap. Elaine Moore. (Illus.). 64p. (Orig.). (J). (gr. 1-4). 1996. pap. 3.95 (*0-8167-3624-3*, Little Rainbow) Troll Communs.

Peanut Butter Trap. Elaine Moore. (Orig.). (J). 1996. 9.15 (*0-606-09732-5*, Pub. by Turtleback) Demco.

Peanut Butter Waltz. Joan B. Stuchner. (Annikins Ser.: Series 10). (Illus.). 24p. (Orig.). (J). (ps-2). 1990. pap. 0.99 (*1-55037-126-6*, Pub. by Annick) Firefly Bks Ltd.

Peanut Health Management. Ed. by H. A. Melouk & F. M. Shokes. LC 95-76524. (Health Management Ser.). (Illus.). 137p. (Orig.). 1995. pap. 55.00 (*0-89054-203-1*) Am Phytopathol Soc.

Peanut Improvement: A Case Study in Indonesia. Ed. by G. C. Wright & K. J. Middleton. 108p. 1992. pap. 72.00 (*1-86320-065-7*, Pub. by ACIAR) St Mut.

Peanut Scale Models. Ed. by Nexus Special Interests Staff. (Planbooks Series 7). (Illus.). 32p. (Orig.). 1995. pap. 13.95 (*1-85486-162-X*, Pub. by Nexus Special Interests) Trans-Atl Phila.

Peanut Soup & Spoonbread: An Informal History of Hotel Roanoke. Donlan Piedmont. Ed. by Virginia Tech Real Estate Foundation Staff. LC 94-44863. 1994. 19.95 (*0-9617635-1-5*) VA Tech Found.

Peanuts. Date not set. 5.95 (*0-89868-353-X*); pap. 4.95 (*0-89868-409-9*); lib. bdg. 10.95 (*0-89868-352-1*) ARO Pub.

Peanuts. Claire Llewellyn. LC 97-34925. (What's for Lunch? Ser.). (J). (gr. k-2). 1998. 20.00 (*0-516-20839-X*) Childrens.

Peanuts. Claire Llewellyn. Ed. by Helaine Cohen. LC 97-34925. (What's for Lunch? Ser.). (Illus.). 32p. (J). 1998. pap. 6.95 (*0-516-26222-X*) Childrens.

Peanuts, Bk. 1. June Edison. (Peanuts Piano Course Ser.). (Illus.). 40p. (Orig.). (J). (gr. 1-6). 1989. pap. 5.50 (*1-56516-038-X*) H Leonard.

Peanuts, Bk. 2. June Edison. (Peanuts Piano Course Ser.). (Illus.). 38p. (Orig.). (J). (gr. 1-6). 1989. pap. 5.50 (*1-56516-039-8*) H Leonard.

Peanuts, Bk. 3. June Edison. (Peanuts Piano Course Ser.). (Illus.). 40p. (Orig.). (J). (gr. 1-6). 1989. pap. 5.50 (*1-56516-040-1*) H Leonard.

Peanuts, Bk. 4. June Edison. (Peanuts Piano Course Ser.). (Illus.). 40p. (Orig.). (J). (gr. 1-6). 1989. pap. 5.50 (*1-56516-041-X*) H Leonard.

Peanuts, Bk. 5. June Edison. (Peanuts Piano Course Ser.). (Illus.). 40p. (Orig.). (J). (gr. 1-6). 1989. pap. 5.50 (*1-56516-042-8*) H Leonard.

Peanuts, Bk. 6. June Edison. (Peanuts Piano Course Ser.). (Illus.). 38p. (Orig.). (J). (gr. 1-6). 1989. pap. 5.50 (*1-56516-043-6*) H Leonard.

***Peanuts: A Golden Celebration: The Art & Story of the World's Best-Loved Comic Strip.** Charles M. Schulz. 256p. 1999. 43.00 (*0-06-099617-X*, HarpRes) HarpInfo.

An Asterisk (*) at the beginning of an entry indicates that the title is appearing for the first time.

***Peanuts: A Golden Celebration: The Art & Story of the World's Best-Loved Comic Strip.** Charles M. Schulz. Ed. by David Larkin et al. LC 99-30314. 256p. 1999. 45.00 (0-06-270244-0, HarpRes) HarpInfo.

***Peanuts: The 50th Year of the World's Most Favorite Comic Strip Featuring Charlie Brown, Snoopy.** Charles M. Schulz. (Illus.). 112p. 2000. pap. 9.95 (0-345-44239-3, Ballantine) Ballantine Pub Grp.

Peanuts . . . A Southern Tradition: Cookbook. 122p. 1992. 5.00 (0-318-17774-9) GA Peanut Comm.

Peanuts & Crackerjacks: A Treasury of Baseball Legends & Lore. David Cataneo. (Illus.). 304p. 1994. pap. 11.95 (0-15-671568-6) Harcourt.

Peanuts Christmas Album. June Edison. (Peanuts Piano Course Ser.). (Illus.). 38p. (Orig.). (J). (gr. 1-6). 1989. pap. 5.50 (1-56516-049-5) H Leonard.

Peanuts Collectibles Identification & Values Guide: I. Andrea Podley & Derrick Bang. 304p. 1999. pap. 24.95 (1-57432-147-1) Collector Bks.

***Peanuts Collection.** Charles M. Schulz. (Illus.). 2000. pap. 10.95 (0-7407-1165-2) Andrews & McMeel.

Peanuts Every Sunday. Charles M. Schulz. (Illus.). (J). 1995. pap. 6.95 (0-8050-3310-6) H Holt & Co.

Peanuts First Program Book. June Edison. (Peanuts Piano Course Ser.). (Illus.). 30p. (Orig.). (J). (gr. 1-6). 1989. pap. 5.50 (1-56516-044-4) H Leonard.

Peanuts First Program Book: Clavinova Software. June Edison. (Peanuts Piano Course for Clavinova Ser.). (Illus.). 30p. (Orig.). (J). (gr. 1-6). 1992. pap. 34.95 (1-56516-018-5) H Leonard.

Peanuts Gang Collectibles: An Unauthorized Handbook & Price Guide. Jan Lindenberger. LC 98-85649. 176p. 1998. pap. 29.95 (0-7643-0671-5) Schiffer.

Peanuts Musical Storybook: Around the World with Charlie Brown. Sideline. 1989. 12.99 (0-88704-131-0) Sight & Sound.

Peanuts Musical Storybook: Snoopy's Musical Adventures. Sideline. 1989. 12.99 (0-88704-130-2) Sight & Sound.

***Peanuts' New Friend.** Ellen A. Wade. (Illus.). 26p. (J). (gr. 2-4). 1999. pap. 8.00 (0-9653635-2-X) LNA Pub.

Peanuts Piano Bk. 1: Clavinova Software. June Edison. (Peanuts Piano Course for Clavinova Ser.). (Illus.). 40p. (Orig.). (J). (gr. 1-6). 1992. pap. 34.95 (1-56516-015-0) H Leonard.

Peanuts Piano Bk. 2: Clavinova Software. June Edison. (Peanuts Piano Course for Clavinova Ser.). (Illus.). 38p. (Orig.). (J). (gr. 1-6). 1992. pap. 34.95 (1-56516-016-9) H Leonard.

Peanuts Piano Course, Bk. 1. Charles M. Schulz. (J). 1995. pap. 5.95 (0-7935-6295-3) H Leonard.

Peanuts Piano Course, Bk. 2. Charles M. Schulz. (J). 1995. pap. 5.95 (0-7935-6297-X) H Leonard.

Peanuts Piano Course, Bk. 3. Charles M. Schulz. 40p. (J). 1995. pap. 5.95 (0-7935-6299-6) H Leonard.

Peanuts Piano Course, Bk. 4. Charles M. Schulz. 40p. (J). 1995. pap. 5.95 (0-7935-6300-3) H Leonard.

Peanuts Piano Course, Bk. 5. Charles M. Schulz. (J). 1995. pap. 5.95 (0-7935-6301-1) H Leonard.

Peanuts Piano Course, Bk. 6. Charles M. Schulz. (J). 1995. pap. 5.95 (0-7935-6302-X) H Leonard.

Peanuts Piano Course: First Program, Bk. 1A. Charles M. Schulz. 32p. (J). 1995. pap. 5.95 (0-7935-6296-1) H Leonard.

Peanuts Piano Course: Second Program, Bk. 2A. Charles M. Schulz. (J). 1995. pap. 5.95 (0-7935-6298-8) H Leonard.

Peanuts Second Program Book. June Edison. (Peanuts Piano Course Ser.). (Illus.). 36p. (Orig.). (J). (gr. 1-6). 1989. pap. 5.50 (1-56516-045-2) H Leonard.

Peanut's Shapes. Mouseworks Staff. 8p. (J). 1999. 3.50 (0-7364-0183-0, Pub. by Mouse Works) Time Warner.

Peanuts the Home Collection: Collector's Guide to Identification & Value. Freddi Margolin. LC 99-61592. (Illus.). 352p. 1999. pap. 26.95 (0-930625-82-X, AT2582) Krause Pubns.

***Peanuts Treasury.** Charles M. Schulz. (Illus.). 256p. 2000. 9.98 (1-58663-068-7) M Friedman Pub Grp Inc.

Peapatch Politics: The Earl K. Long Era in Louisiana Politics. W. J. Dodd. 1991. 25.00 (0-87511-932-8) Claitors.

Peapod Dollhouse Text. Playland Staff. (J). 0.00 (0-698-13003-0) Putnam Pub Group.

Pear: Culture, Varieties, Breeding, Propagation, Nutrition, Pruning & Training, Disease & Insects, Harvesting, Storage & Marketing. Ed. by Tom Van der Zwet & Norman F. Childers. LC SB0373.P44. (Illus.). 524p. 1982. reprint ed. pap. 162.50 (0-608-04330-3, 206511000012) Bks Demand.

Pear Blossoms Drift. Emily Romano. 20p. 1981. pap. 2.00 (0-913719-51-X, High Coo Pr) Brooks Books.

Pear Flat Philosophies. deluxe limited ed. L. Weishuhn. (Illus.). 196p. 1993. boxed set 35.00 (0-940143-86-0) Safari Pr.

Pear Flat Philosophies. 2nd ed. L. Weishuhn. (Illus.). 182p. 1993. 24.95 (0-940143-85-2) Safari Pr.

Pear for the Teacher. Daisy M. Styles. (Illus.). 165p. (Orig.). 1987. pap. 9.95 (0-943487-04-8) Sevgo Pr.

Pear Stories - Cognitive, Cultural & Linguistic Aspects of Narrative Production. Ed. by Wallace L. Chafe. (Advances in Discourse Processes Ser.: Vol. 3). (Illus.). 352p. 1980. text 78.50 (0-89391-032-5) Ablx Pub.

***Pear Tree: An Animal Counting Book.** Meredith Hooper. (Illus.). 32p. (J). 2000. pap. 11.99 (0-333-73253-7) Mcm Child Bks.

Pear Tree That Bloomed in the Fall. Will D. Campbell. LC 96-70723. (Father Thyme Bks.). (Illus.). 32p. (J). (gr. 1-5). 1996. 14.95 (1-57736-017-6) Providence Hse.

Pearl. (Assessment Packs Ser.). 15p. (Orig.). 1998. pap. text 15.95 (1-58303-056-5) Pthways Pubng.

Pearl. John Arden. 80p. 1995. pap. 9.95 (0-413-40100-6, A0207) Heinemann.

***Pearl.** Debby Atwell. LC 00-35110. (Illus.). (J). 2001. write for info. (0-395-88416-0) HM.

Pearl. Carroll & Graf Staff. 656p. 1999. mass mkt. 8.95 (0-7867-0670-8) Carroll & Graf.

Pearl. Lynn Crosbie. 62p. (Orig.). 1996. pap. 11.95 (0-88784-578-9, Pub. by Hse of Anansi Pr) Genl Dist Srvs.

***Pearl.** Mary L. Dennis. 28p. 1999. 9.95 (1-56137-325-7) Novel Units.

Pearl. Helme Heine. LC 88-3220. Orig. Title: Dei Perle. (Illus.). 32p. (J). (gr. k-4). 1988. pap. 3.95 (0-689-71262-6) Aladdin.

Pearl. James Jennings. LC 96-207655. 1996. pap. 12.95 (0-345-41004-1) Ballantine Pub Grp.

Pearl. James Jennings. 608p. 1995. mass mkt. 6.95 (0-7867-0294-X) Carroll & Graf.

Pearl. Ed. by Jill Karson. LC 98-21204. (Literary Companion Ser.). (YA). (gr. 9-12). 1998. pap. 17.45 (1-56510-854-X); lib. bdg. 27.45 (1-56510-855-8) Greenhaven.

Pearl. Vincent Katz. LC 97-51307. (Illus.). 72p. 1998. 30.00 (1-57687-016-2, pwerHse Bks) pwerHse Cultrl.

***Pearl.** Maureen Kirchhoefer & Mary L. Dennis. 32p. (YA). 1999. 11.95 (1-56137-326-5) Novel Units.

Pearl. Ruth R. Langan. (Historical Ser.). 1996. per. 4.99 (0-373-28929-4, 1-28929-7) Harlequin Bks.

Pearl. Anne Ruck. 1986. pap. 4.95 (9971-972-37-9) OMF Bks.

Pearl. John Steinbeck. (Barron's Book Notes Ser.). 1985. mass mkt. 3.95 (0-8120-3534-8) Barron.

Pearl. John Steinbeck. 76p. 1975. pap. 5.50 (0-87129-694-2, P18) Dramatic Pub.

Pearl. John Steinbeck. 10.00 (0-89064-048-3) NAVH.

Pearl. John Steinbeck. 1992. 11.05 (0-606-00106-9, Pub. by Turtleback) Demco.

Pearl. John Steinbeck. 96p. (C). 1993. pap. 5.95 (0-14-017737-X) Viking Penguin.

Pearl. large type ed. Newlyn Nash. 1990. pap. 16.99 (0-7089-6885-6, Linford) Ulverscroft.

Pearl. Tr. by Israel Gollancz. LC 66-27657. (Medieval Library). (Illus.). reprint ed. lib. bdg. 53.00 (0-8154-0084-5) Cooper Sq.

Pearl. Stirling Silliphant. 480p. 1991. reprint ed. mass mkt. 5.95 (0-935180-91-5) Mutual Pub HI.

***Pearl: A Handbook for the Orthodox Convert.** Michael Whelton. 208p. 1999. pap. 19.95 (0-9649141-9-0) Regina Orthodox.

Pearl: A Literature Unit. Philip Denny. Ed. by Ina M. Levin. (Literature Units Ser.). (Illus.). 48p. (Orig.). 1992. pap., student ed. 7.95 (1-55734-407-8) Tchr Create Mat.

Pearl: A New Verse Translation. Marie Borroff. 40p. (C). 1977. pap. text 11.25 (0-393-09144-9) Norton.

Pearl: A Unit Plan. Mary B. Collins. 140p. 1994. teacher ed., ring bd. 26.95 (1-58337-006-4) Teachers Pet Pubns.

Pearl: An Edition with Verse Translation. Tr. by William Vantuono. LC 95-16890. (C). 1995. text 29.95 (0-268-03810-4); pap. text 15.95 (0-268-03811-2) U of Notre Dame Pr.

Pearl: Hymn of the Robe of Glory. Illus. by Nonny Hogrogian. LC 79-66092. 1979. 7.95 (0-89756-002-7) Two Rivers.

Pearl: Including Signed Original Artwork. deluxe ed. Vincent Katz. LC 97-34501. (Illus.). 96p. 1998. boxed set 400.00 (1-57687-017-0) pwerHse Cultrl.

***Pearl: My Heart, the Spirit, One Purpose.** Pearlie Nicole Harris. 57p. 2000. pap. 10.00 (0-615-11352-4) Pearls Bk.

Pearl: Reproducible Teaching Unit. rev. ed. James Scott. 27p. (YA). (gr. 7-12). 1985. teacher ed., ring bd. 29.50 (1-58049-027-1, TU38/U) Prestwick Hse.

Pearl: The Obsessions & Passions of Janis Joplin. Ellis Amburn. 384p. 1993. mass mkt. 13.95 (0-446-39506-4, Pub. by Warner Bks) Little.

Pearl: 1 - Act. John Steinbeck. 1975. 3.95 (0-87129-580-6, P57) Dramatic Pub.

Pearl Vol. 1: Monthly Journal of Facetiae & Voluptious Reading. 350p. 1999. reprint ed. pap. text 4.00 (0-7881-6352-3) DIANE Pub.

Pearl - Study Guide. Joyce Friedland & Rikki Kessler. Ed. by Barbara Reeves. (Novel-Ties Ser.). (J). (gr. 6-8). 1993. pap. text, student ed. 15.95 (0-88122-031-0) Lrn Links.

Pearl a Day: Wise Sayings for Living Well. Lawrence M. Ventline. LC 98-75729. 96p. 1999. wbk. ed. 7.95 (1-883520-16-9) Jeremiah Pr.

Pearl, a Middle English Poem. Ed. by Charles G. Osgood, Jr. LC 78-144438. (Belles Lettres Ser. Section II: No. 4). reprint ed. 30.00 (0-404-53614-X) AMS Pr.

Pearl & Hermes Reef, Hawaii, Hydrographical & Biographical Observations. Paul S. Galtsoff. (BMB Ser.: No. 107). 1974. reprint ed. pap. 25.00 (0-527-02213-6) Periodicals Srv.

Pearl & May at the Bowling Alley. Cassi Harris. 70p. 1997. pap. 5.60 (0-87129-769-8, P83) Dramatic Pub.

Pearl & the Dragon. S. Winifred Jacobson. (Junior Jaffray Collection of Missionary Stories: No. 17). 1997. pap. 3.99 (0-87509-716-2) Chr Pubns.

***Pearl & the Dragon: A Study of Vietnamese Pearls & a History of the Oriental Pearl Trade.** Derek J. Content et al. 125p. 1999. write for info. (0-935681-07-8) D J Content.

Pearl & the Dragon: The Story of Gerhard & Alma Jacobson. S. Winifred Jacobson. LC 97-191758. (Jaffray Collection of Missionary Portraits: No. 17). 1997. pap. 9.99 (0-87509-700-6) Chr Pubns.

Pearl & the Princes. Shirley L. Morrison. LC 84-23349. vi, 170p. 1985. 14.95 (0-9613978-0-2); pap. 7.95 (0-9613978-1-0) Laurel Pr.

Pearl at a Great Price Theresa H. Raffael. LC 96-110902. xii, 238p. 1995. write for info. (1-56043-559-3) Destiny Image.

Pearl Bailey: With a Song in Her Heart. Keith Brandt. LC 92-20190. (Easy Biographies Library). (Illus.). 48p. (J). (gr. 4-6). 1992. lib. bdg. 17.25 (0-8167-2921-2, BP275) Troll Communs.

Pearl Bailey: With a Song in Her Heart. Keith Brandt. LC 92-20190. (Illus.). 48p. (J). (gr. 4-6). 1996. pap. 4.95 (0-8167-2922-0) Troll Communs.

Pearl Bailey: With a Song in Her Heart. Keith Brandt. 1993. 8.15 (0-606-02828-5, Pub. by Turtleback) Demco.

Pearl Bastard. Lillian Halegua. 2.50 (0-7043-3828-9, Pub. by Quartet) Charles River Bks.

Pearl Beach Legacy. Surrey Beatty & Sons Pty. Ltd. Staff. 1993. 95.00 (0-949324-53-1, Pub. by Surrey Beatty & Sons) St Mut.

Pearl Beach Legacy: The Story of Minnard Crommelin Visionary. Ed. by Surrey Beatty Staff. LC 94-166909. 174p. 1999. pap. 48.00 (0-949324-55-8, Pub. by Surrey Beatty & Sons) St Mut.

Pearl Beyond Price. Claire Delacroix. LC 95-8361. (Historical Ser.). 299p. 1995. per. 4.50 (0-373-28864-6, 1-28864-6) Harlequin Bks.

Pearl Beyond Price. Susan Westoby. 1998. mass mkt. 5.99 (0-9525543-9-9) Pharaoh Pr.

Pearl Beyond Price: Integration of Personality into Being: An Object Relations Approach. A. H. Almaas. LC 87-51720. (Diamond Mind Ser.: Bk. 2). 506p. 1988. pap. 19.50 (0-936713-02-X) Diamond Bks CA.

***Pearl Book: The Definite Buying Guide: How to Select, Buy, Care for & Enjoy Pearls.** 2nd ed. Antoinette L. Matlins. LC 99-55463. 2000. pap. text 19.95 (0-943763-28-2) GemStone Pr.

Pearl Buck: Author see Women of Achievement

Pearl Buying Guide. 2nd ed. Renee Newman. LC 93-43758. (Illus.). 188p. (C). 1994. pap. 19.95 (0-929975-22-7) Intl Jewelry Pubns.

Pearl Buying Guide. 3rd ed. Renee Newman. LC 98-29627. (Illus.). 156p. 1999. pap. 19.95 (0-929975-27-8) Intl Jewelry Pubns.

Pearl Cannon: Sadeq Hedayat's Greatest Works: Book One. Sadiq Hidayat. Tr. by Iraj Bashiri from PER. LC 85-43495. (Mazda Special Persian Language Publications). 203p. (Orig.). 1986. pap. 9.95 (0-939214-05-9) Mazda Pubs.

***Pearl City Control Theory.** Karen Allen. 310p. 1999. pap. 13.00 (0-9671784-0-1) Cabbages & Kings.

Pearl City, Florida: A Black Community Remembers. Arthur S. Evans & David Lee. 184p. 1990. 29.95 (0-8130-0999-5) U Press Fla.

Pearl, Cleanness, Patience & Sir Gawain. Cotton Nero. (OS 162 Ser.). 1972. reprint ed. 76.00 (0-19-722162-9) OUP.

***Pearl Cove.** Elizabeth Lowell. LC 99-21639. 376p. 1999. 24.00 (0-380-97404-5, Avon Bks) Morrow Avon.

***Pearl Cove.** Elizabeth Lowell. 432p. 2000. mass mkt. 7.50 (0-380-78988-4, Avon Bks) Morrow Avon.

***Pearl Cove.** Elizabeth Lowell. LC 99-31381. (Large Print Book Ser.). 1999. write for info. (1-56895-746-7, Wheeler) Wheeler Pub.

***Pearl Cove.** large type ed. Elizabeth Lowell. 2000. pap. 11.95 (1-56895-964-8) Wheeler Pub.

***Pearl Cove, Set.** unabridged ed. Elizabeth Lowell. 1999. audio 73.25 Highsmith Pr.

Pearl Dictionary. 4th ed. Matthew Kurlan. LC 99-213905. (Illus.). 380p. 1999. ring bd. 27.00 (0-9668187-1-7) Pocket Brain.

Pearl Dictionary: Pocket Brain. Matthew Kurlan. 1998. vinyl bd. 27.00 (0-9668187-0-9) Pocket Brain.

Pearl Divers see Deep Sea Adventure Series: Low Vocabulary, High Interest Level

Pearl from the Dragon's Mouth: Evocation of Feeling & Scene in Chinese Poetry. Cecile C. C. Sun. LC 93-50078. (Michigan Monographs in Chinese Studies: No. 67). 1994. text 50.00 (0-89264-110-X) Ctr Chinese Studies.

Pearl Harbor. (Illus.). 34p. 1983. pap. 4.95 (0-930492-16-1) Hawaiian Serv.

Pearl Harbor! Wallace B. Black & Jean F. Blashfield. LC 90-45621. (World War II 50th Anniversary Ser.). (Illus.). 48p. (J). (gr. 5-6). 1991. lib. bdg. 4.95 (0-89686-555-X, Crstwood Hse) Silver Burdett Pr.

Pearl Harbor. Sue L. Hamilton. Ed. by John C. Hamilton. LC 91-73041. (Day of the Disaster Ser.). 32p. (J). 1991. lib. bdg. 12.98 (1-56239-059-7) ABDO Pub Co.

***Pearl Harbor.** Judy L. Hasday. (Great Disasters Ser.). (Illus.). 128p. (YA). (gr. 5 up). 2000. write for info. (0-7910-5271-0) Chelsea Hse.

Pearl Harbor. Deborah Hopkinson. LC 91-22472. (Places in American History Ser.). (Illus.). 64p. (J). (gr. 4-6). 1991. lib. bdg. 14.95 (0-87518-475-8, Dillon Silver Burdett) Silver Burdett Pr.

Pearl Harbor. Edwin P. Hoyt. 192p. (Orig.). 1991. mass mkt. 4.99 (0-380-76195-5, Avon Bks) Morrow Avon.

***Pearl Harbor.** Earle Rice. LC 99-50970. (World History Ser.). (Illus.). 2000. write for info. (1-56006-652-0) Lucent Bks.

Pearl Harbor. Charles Wills. (Illus.). 64p. (J). (gr. 5 up). 1991. lib. bdg. 14.95 (0-382-24125-8) Silver Burdett Pr.

Pearl Harbor. Charles Wills. (Illus.). 64p. (YA). (gr. 5 up). 1991. pap. 7.95 (0-382-24119-3) Silver Burdett Pr.

Pearl Harbor, Vol. 62. Carl Smith. (Campaign Ser.). 1999. pap. text 17.95 (1-85532-798-8) Greenhill Bks.

Pearl Harbor: A Narrative Poem. John Guenther. LC 80-83810. (Illus.). 64p. (Orig.). 1980. pap. 10.00 (0-938266-00-4) Purchase Pr.

Pearl Harbor: Roosevelt & the Coming of the War. 3rd ed. Ed. by George M. Waller. (Problems in American Civilization Ser.). 263p. (C). 1976. pap. text 18.36 (0-669-98376-4) HM Trade Div.

Pearl Harbor: Roosevelt's Betrayal of the American People - Fifty Years After. 1992. lib. bdg. 75.00 (0-8490-5438-9) Gordon Pr.

Pearl Harbor: The Continuing Controversy. Hans L. Trefousse. LC 81-14237. (Anvil Ser.). 218p. (Orig.). (C). 1982. pap. text 12.50 (0-89874-261-7) Krieger.

Pearl Harbor: The Story of the Secret War. George Morgenstern. LC 42-1121. xx, 425p. (Orig.). 1991. reprint ed. pap. 8.95 (0-939484-38-2, 0978, Inst Hist Rev) Legion Survival.

***Pearl Harbor: The U. S. Enters World War II.** Richard Tames. LC 00-24356. (YA). 2001. lib. bdg. write for info. (1-57572-416-2) Heinemann Lib.

Pearl Harbor: The Way It Was. 2nd ed. Scott C. Stone. (Illus.). 64p. 1977. pap. 7.95 (0-89610-219-X) Island Heritage.

***Pearl Harbor: "This Is No Drill!"** Ed. by Ray Merriam. (World War II Journal Ser.: Vol. 2). (Illus.). 96p. 1999. pap. 12.50 (1-57638-154-4, J2-S) Merriam Pr.

Pearl Harbor: Warning & Decision. Roberta Wohlstetter. xvi, 426p. 1962. 57.50 (0-8047-0597-6); pap. 17.95 (0-8047-0598-4) Stanford U Pr.

Pearl Harbor: Why, How - a Final Appraisal, What Really Happened December 7, 1941. 1992. lib. bdg. 285.85 (0-8490-8859-3) Gordon Pr.

Pearl Harbor after a Quarter of a Century. Harry E. Barnes. LC 75-172203. (Right Wing Individualist Tradition in America Ser.). 1979. reprint ed. 19.95 (0-405-00413-3) Ayer.

Pearl Harbor & The Coming of the Pacific War: A Brief History with Documents & Essays. Akira Iriye. LC 98-87529. 200p. 1999. text 39.95 (0-312-21818-4) St Martin.

Pearl Harbor Attack. Arnold S. Lott & Robert F. Sumrall. (Illus.). 32p. 1992. reprint ed. pap. 2.95 (0-9631388-1-2) AZ Mem Mus.

***Pearl Harbor Casualties: Military & Civilian Plus Casualties & Survivors of the U. S. S. Arizona.** Ray Merriam. (World War II Monograph Ser.: Vol. 39). (Illus.). 70p. 1999. pap. 10.50 (1-57638-155-2, 39-S) Merriam Pr.

Pearl Harbor Fact & Reference Book: Everything to Know about Dec. 7, 1941. Terence McComas. 132p. 1991. pap. 9.95 (0-935180-02-8) Mutual Pub HI.

Pearl Harbor in Perspective. Michael Slackman et al. (Illus.). 92p. 1991. reprint ed. pap. 2.95 (0-9631388-5-5) AZ Mem Mus.

Pearl Harbor is Burning! A Story of World War II. Kathleen V. Kudlinski. LC 93-15135. (Once Upon America Ser.). (Illus.). 64p. (J). (gr. 2-6). 1993. pap. 4.99 (0-14-034509-4, PuffinBks) Peng Put Young Read.

***Pearl Harbor, 1941.** Nancy Holder. (Illus.). 224p. 2000. 4.99 (0-671-03927-X, Archway) PB.

***Pearl Harbor 1941.** Carl Smith. (Illus.). 96p. 2000. pap. 17.95 (1-84176-075-7) Osprey.

Pearl Harbor, 1941: A Bibliography, 4. Myron J. Smith, Jr. LC 90-49167. (Bibliographies of Battles & Leaders Ser.: No. 4). 224p. 1991. lib. bdg. 69.50 (0-313-28121-1, SQH, Greenwood Pr) Greenwood.

***Pearl Harbor Operations: General Outline of Orders & Plans.** Military History Section, Headquarters, Army Forces Far East Staff. (World War II Monograph Ser.: Vol. 32). (Illus.). 30p. 1999. pap. 4.50 (1-57638-156-0, 32-S) Merriam Pr.

Pearl Harbor Papers: Inside the Japanese Plans. Donald M. Goldstein. Ed. by Katherine V. Dillon. (World War II Commemorative Ser.). 400p. 1993. 30.00 (0-02-881001-5) Brasseys.

***Pearl Harbor Papers: Inside the Japanese Plans.** Donald M. Goldstein. 1999. pap. 21.95 (1-57488-222-8) Brasseys.

Pearl Harbor Reexamined: Prologue to the Pacific War. Ed. by Hilary Conroy & Harry Wray. LC 89-37487. (Illus.). 224p. 1989. text 24.00 (0-8248-1235-2) UH Pr.

Pearl Harbor Remembered: No Apology for the Bomb Is Necessary. Ray F. Zuker. 21p. 1994. pap. 5.95 (1-882194-11-X) TN Valley Pub.

Pearl Harbor Story. William T. Rice. pap. 4.95 (1-884485-01-4) Tongg Pub.

Pearl Harbor Survivors: 50th Anniversary. anniversary ed. Turner Publishing Company Staff. LC 92-61188. (Illus.). 480p. 1998. 52.50 (1-56311-042-3) Turner Pub KY.

Pearl, Image of the Ineffable: A Study in Medieval Poetic Symbolism. Theodore Bogdanos. LC 82-42783. 184p. (C). 1983. 28.50 (0-271-00339-1) Pa St U Pr.

Pearl in the Egg. Dorothy O. Van Woerkom. LC 79-8040. (Illus.). 128p. (J). 1980. lib. bdg. 10.89 (0-690-04030-X) HarpC Child Bks.

Pearl in the Mist. V. C. Andrews. Ed. by Linda Marrow. 384p. 1994. per. 7.99 (0-671-75936-1) PB.

Pearl in the Mist. V. C. Andrews. 1994. 12.09 (0-606-07067-2, Pub. by Turtleback) Demco.

Pearl in the Mist. large type ed. V. C. Andrews. 1995. 24.95 (0-7838-1164-0, G K Hall Lrg Type) Mac Lib Ref.

Pearl Inlay: An Instruction Manual for Inlaying Abalone & Mother-of-Pearl. James E. Patterson. 82p. 1991. pap. 13.90 (0-9644752-2-7) Stewart MacDonald.

Pearl Inside the Body: Poems Selected & New. Allan Cooper. (Poetry Ser.). 1991. pap. 11.25 (0-920187-04-8) Genl Dist Srvs.

Pearl Jam. Mick Wall. (Illus.). 175p. 1994. pap. 24.00 (0-283-06207-X, Pub. by S1 & J) Trans-Atl Phila.

Pearl Jam: Place/Date. Photos by Charles Peterson & Lance Mercer. (Illus.). 128p. 1998. pap. 19.95 (0-7893-0269-1, Pub. by Universe) St Martin.

Pearl Jam: The Illustrated Story. Allan Jones. (Illus.). 80p. 1994. pap. 12.95 (0-7935-4035-6, HL00330009) H Leonard.

Pearl Jam: The Illustrated Story. Allan Jones. 1997. pap. text 12.95 (0-600-58426-7) Hamlyn Publishing Group Ltd.

Pearl Jam - Dark Corners: An Illustrated Biography. Martin Power. (Illus.). 95p. 1997. pap. 21.95 (0-7119-6374-6, OP47895) Omnibus NY.

An Asterisk (*) at the beginning of an entry indicates that the title is appearing for the first time.

P

Pearl Jam 10: With Notes & Tablature. 112p. 1992. otabind 19.95 (0-7935-1902-0, 00694855) H Leonard.

Pearl Jam 10: With Notes & Tablature. 56p. 1993. pap. 14.95 (0-7935-2368-0, 00694882) H Leonard.

Pearl Killifishes: The Cynolebiatinae. Wilson J. Costa. (Illus.). 128p. 1996. 23.95 (0-7938-2089-8, TS239) TFH Pubns.

Pearl Lakes Trout Club, Inc. A History. Raye Carrington. (Orig.). 1990. 25.00 (0-9627071-0-4) Kitty Creek.

Pearl Maiden. H. Rider Haggard. (Golden Age of Rome Ser.). 1978. mass mkt. 2.50 (0-89083-352-4, Zebra Kensgtn) Kensgtn Pub Corp.

Pearl Maiden. H. Rider Haggard. reprint ed. lib. bdg. 30.95 (0-89190-708-4) Amereon Ltd.

Pearl Makers: Six Stories about Children in the Philippines. Vilma M. Fuentes. (Illus.). (Orig.). (J). (gr. 1-6). 1989. pap. 4.95 (0-377-00191-0) Friendship Pr.

Pearl Makers: The Tidemarsh Guide to Clams, Oysters, Mussels & Scallops. Mervin F. Roberts. LC 84-50701. (Tidemarsh Guides Ser.). (Illus.). 168p. 1984. 6.95 (0-917941-00-4) M Roberts.

Pearl Millet: Seed Production & Technology. Ishwar S. Khairwal et al. 1990. 38.50 (81-85425-08-6, Pub. by Manohar) S Asia.

*Pearl Millet Breeding. Ed. by I. S. Khairwal et al. LC 99-55707. 535p. 1999. text 95.00 (1-57808-089-4) Science Pubs.

Pearl Millet Science. R. K. Maiti. (Illus.). 246p. 1997. 58.00 (1-886106-96-7, 6967) Science Pubs.

Pearl Moon. Katherine Stone. 1996. mass mkt. 5.99 (0-449-22415-5, Crest) Fawcett.

Pearl Necklace: Toward an Archaeology of the Brazilian Transition Discourse. Roberto Reis. (Illus.). 192p. (C). 1992. 49.95 (0-8130-1105-1) U Press Fla.

Pearl, 91. 1991. 31.00 (0-387-54909-9) Spr-Verlag.

Pearl, 92. 1992. 36.95 (0-387-56267-2) Spr-Verlag.

Pearl Notes. Eva Fitzwater. (Cliffs Notes Ser.). 48p. 1966. pap. 4.95 (0-8220-0994-3, Cliff) IDG Bks.

Pearl of Christian Comfort (Paarl of Christelijke Vertroosting) Petrus Dathenus. Tr. by Arie W. Blok & Joel R. Beeke from DUT. 87p. 1997. 7.50 (1-892777-10-X) Reform Heritage Bks.

Pearl of Cripple Creek: The Story of Cripple Creek's Most Famous Madam, Pearl DeVere. Celeste Black. (Illus.). 32p. 1997. pap. 4.95 (0-9658535-0-0) Blck Bear Pubns.

Pearl of Great Price. Agnes Adam. LC 96-18029. 55p. (Orig.). 1996. pap. 5.00 (0-88734-377-5) Players Pr.

Pearl of Great Price. Ethel Pruitt. 40p. 1998. pap. 8.00 (0-8059-4289-0) Dorrance.

Pearl of Great Price: A History & Commentary. H. Donl Peterson. LC 87-15672. xiii, 400p. 1987. pap. 14.95 (0-87579-665-6) Deseret Bk.

Pearl of Great Price: Healing for Adults Raised in Dysfunctional Families. Jacqueline M. Sitte. 187p. (Orig.). 1993. pap. 12.00 (0-9636568-0-5) J M Sitte.

Pearl of Great Price: Revelations from God. Ed. by H. Donl Peterson & Charles D. Tate. (Monograph Ser.: Vol. 14). 1989. 10.95 (0-88494-683-5) Bookcraft Inc.

Pearl of Great Price: The Life of Mother Maria Skobtsova 1891-1945. rev. ed. Sergei Hackel. LC 81-21356. 192p. 1982. pap. 9.95 (0-913836-85-0) St Vladimirs.

*Pearl of Hong Kong. Henry Kwun Chen. 384p. 1999. write for info. (0-7541-0799-X, Pub. by Minerva Pr) Unity Dist.

Pearl of Orr's Island. Harriet Beecher Stowe. LC 79-18303. (Illus.). 1979. pap. 9.95 (0-917482-18-2) Stowe-Day.

Pearl of Orr's Island. Harriet Beecher Stowe. (Notable American Authors Ser.). 1999. reprint ed. lib. bdg. 125.00 (0-7812-8960-2) Rprt Serv.

Pearl of Orr's Island. Harriet Beecher Stowe. reprint ed. 14.00 (0-403-00280-X) Scholarly.

*Pearl of Orr's Island: A Story of the Coast of Maine. Harriet Beecher Stowe. 304p. 2001. reprint ed. 13.00 (0-618-08347-2) HM.

Pearl of Orr's Island: A Story of the Coast of Maine. Harriet Beecher Stowe. (BCL1-PS American Literature Ser.). 437p. 1992. reprint ed. lib. bdg. 99.00 (0-7812-6874-5) Rprt Serv.

Pearl of Ruby City. Jana Harris. LC 98-23932. 368p. 1998. text 23.95 (0-312-19315-7) St Martin.

*Pearl of the Antilles. Andrea Herrera. 2000. pap. write for info. (0-927534-95-9) Biling Rev-Pr.

Pearl of the Antilles. Roberto Machado. 1996. 45.00 (0-9638703-9-4) Shade Tree Pr.

Pearl of the Soul of the World Vol. III: The Darkangel Trilogy. Meredith Ann Pierce. LC 98-35707. (Darkangel Trilogy Ser.). 320p. (YA). 1999. pap. 6.00 (0-15-201800-X) Harcourt.

Pearl Pagoda. large type ed. Susannah Broome. 505p. 1982. 27.99 (0-7089-0765-2) Ulverscroft.

Pearl Pass - Crested Butte, Co. rev. ed. Ed. by Trails Illustrated Staff. 1997. 8.99 (0-925873-51-9) Trails Illustrated.

Pearl Penguin. John Steinbeck. LC 94-8790. (Illus.). 128p. 1994. pap. 13.99 (0-14-018738-3) Viking Penguin.

Pearl Plants a Tree. Jane Breskin Zalben. LC 94-38404. (Illus.). 32p. (J). (ps-3). 1995. per. 14.00 (0-689-80034-7) S&S Bks Yung.

Pearl Poem: An Introduction & Interpretation. George D. Bond. LC 90-6163. (Studies in Medieval Literature: Vol. 6). 150p. 1991. lib. bdg. 69.95 (0-88946-309-3) E Mellen.

Pearl-Poet. Charles Moorman. Ed. by Sylvia E. Bowman. LC 68-17243. (Twayne's English Authors Ser.). 148p. (C). 1968. lib. bdg. 20.95 (0-8290-1722-4) Irvington.

Pearl Poet Revisited. Sandra P. Prior. (Twayne's English Authors Ser.: No. 512). 176p. 1994. 32.00 (0-8057-4516-5, Twyne) Mac Lib Ref.

Pearl Polto's Easy Guide to Good Credit. Pearl B. Polto. 128p. 1996. mass mkt. 5.50 (0-425-15297-9) Berkley Pub.

Pearl Polto's Easy Guide to Good Credit. Pearl B. Polto & B. Oskam. 1990. pap. 7.95 (0-425-12059-7) Berkley Pub.

*Pearl River Delta: Project on the City. Ed. by Rem Koolhaas et al. (Illus.). 768p. 2000. pap. 39.95 (1-58093-064-6, Pub. by Monacelli Pr) Penguin Putnam.

Pearl S. Buck. rev. ed. Paul A. Doyle. (United States Authors Ser.: No. 85). 184p. 1980. 22.95 (0-8057-7325-8, Twyne) Mac Lib Ref.

Pearl S. Buck: A Cultural Biography. Peter Conn. (Illus.). 494p. (C). 1996. text 34.95 (0-521-56080-2) Cambridge U Pr.

Pearl S. Buck: A Cultural Biography. Peter Conn. (Illus.). 470p. (C). 1998. reprint ed. pap. 18.95 (0-521-63989-1) Cambridge U Pr.

Pearl S. Buck: A Cultural Bridge Across the Pacific, 77. Kang Liao. LC 96-25016. (Contributions to the Study of World Literature Ser.). 200p. 1997. 52.95 (0-313-30146-8) Greenwood.

Pearl S. Buck: Good Earth Mother. Warren Sherk. Ed. by Craig J. Battrick. 248p. 1992. 18.95 (0-9626441-3-7) Drift Creek Pr.

Pearl S. Buck: The Final Chapter. Beverly Rizzon. LC 88-7002. (Illus.). 444p. 1989. 23.95 (0-88280-120-1) ETC Pubns.

*Pearl S. Buck's Chinese Women Characters. Xiongya Gao. LC 99-86340. (Illus.). 136p. 2000. 31.50 (1-57591-025-X) Susquehanna U Pr.

Pearl-Shellers of Torres Strait: Resource, Development & Decline 1860s-1960s. Regina Ganter. LC 94-237419. 256p. 1994. pap. 29.95 (0-522-84547-9, Pub. by Melbourne Univ Pr) Paul & Co Pubs.

Pearl Sic see Deep Sea Adventure Series: Low Vocabulary, High Interest Level

Pearl Within the Shell: A Collection of Inspirational Poetry that Speaks tp You. Dolores Dahl. LC 83-60744. (Illus.). 119p. (Orig.). 1983. pap. 10.95 (0-9608960-1-5) Single Vision.

Pearl 97. 1997. write for info. (3-540-63562-9) Spr-Verlag.

Pearland, Texas: A Centennial History. Bartee Haile. LC 94-27875. 1994. write for info. (0-89865-909-4) Donning Co.

*Pearlhanger. large type ed. Jonathan Gash. LC 99-87742. (Mystery Ser.). 320p. 2000. 26.95 (0-7862-2456-8) Thorndike Pr.

Pearlie Oyster: A Tale of an Amazing Oyster. Suzanne Tate. LC 89-92226. (Nature Ser.: No. 5). (Illus.). 28p. (J). (gr. k-4). 1989. pap. 4.95 (0-9616344-7-2) Nags Head Art.

Pearlie Oyster: A Tale of an Amazing Oyster. Suzanne Tate. LC 89-92226. 1989. 9.15 (0-606-10323-6) Turtleback.

*Pearl/La Perla. Cecilia Romero Cooper. 1999. mass mkt. 5.99 (0-7860-1036-3) Kensgtn Pub Corp.

Pearlmaker. Jim Cornwall. 168p. (Orig.). 1997. pap. 7.99 (0-88270-734-5, Logos NJ) Bridge-Logos.

Pearls. Shellei Addison & Kristin Joyce. 1992. pap. 45.00 (0-13-655374-5) P-H.

Pearls. Fred Ward. Ed. by Charlotte Ward. (Fred Ward Gem Book Ser.). (Illus.). 64p. (Orig.). 1998. pap. 14.95 (0-9633723-3-5) Gem Bk Pubs.

Pearls. 2nd rev. ed. Fred Ward. 64p. (Orig.). 1998. pap. 14.95 (0-9633723-9-4) Gem Bk Pubs.

Pearls: Bedtime Stories. Roger Speirs. (Illus.). (Orig.). (J). (ps-5). 1998. pap. 5.95 (0-9667544-0-9) UCanDo.

Pearls: Ornament & Obsession. Kristin Joyce & Shellei Addison. LC 92-15087. 1993. 65.00 (0-671-75928-0) S&S Trade.

Pearls Along the Path: Lessons for Living Life Passionately. Ronald P. Hill. LC 99-61698. 104p. 1999. pap. 6.95 (0-9652615-0-6, Pub. by Bialkin Bks) Midpt Trade.

Pearls among the Swine. Helen Forelle. Ed. by Janet Leih. LC 89-50033. 40p. (Orig.). 1989. pap. 3.00 (1-877649-05-8) Tesseract SD.

Pearls & Lace: Poems. Magdalena Klein. Tr. by Susan S. Geroe. LC 96-20488. (Illus.). 64p. (Orig.). 1997. pap. 9.00 (1-56474-190-7) Fithian Pr.

Pearls & Pepper. Robert P. Utter. LC 70-152219. (Essay Index Reprint Ser.). 1977. reprint ed. 20.95 (0-8369-2335-9) Ayer.

Pearls & Peril. Lynn Gardner. LC 96-28361. 1996. pap. 10.95 (1-55503-932-4, 01112422) Covenant Comms.

Pearls & Pitfalls in Electrocardiography: Pithy Practical Pointers. 2nd ed. Henry J. Marriott. LC 97-13639. 1997. write for info. (0-683-03017-5) Lppncott W & W.

Pearls & Pitfalls in Electrocardiography: Pithy Practical Points. Henry J. Marriott. LC 90-5594. (Illus.). 157p. 1990. pap. text 29.00 (0-8121-1334-9) Lppncott W & W.

Pearls & Pitfalls in Electrocardiology. 2nd ed. Henry J. Marriott. (Illus.). 168p. 1997. pap. 32.00 (0-683-30170-5) Lppncott W & W.

Pearls Before Swine. Margery Allingham. 224p. 1996. mass mkt. 4.95 (0-7867-0338-5) Carroll & Graf.

Pearls Before Swine. Margery Allingham. 240p. 1998. lib. bdg. 21.95 (1-56723-016-4) Yestermorrow.

Pearls Before Swine. Margery Allingham. 192p. reprint ed. lib. bdg. 18.95 (0-89190-196-5, Rivercity Pr) Amereon Ltd.

Pearl's Delicious Jamaican Dishes: Recipes from Pearl Bell's Repertoire. Vivien Goldman. 1992. pap. 16.95 (1-881047-00-8) Island Trad.

Pearl's Eight Days of Chanukah. Jane Breskin Zalben. LC 97-37917. (Illus.). 48p. (J). (ps-2). 1998. 16.00 (0-689-81488-7) S&S Trade.

Pearls for Parents. Joyce V. Brown. 40p. 1995. 8.95 (0-8378-9860-9) Gibson.

*Pearls for Personal Trainers. Teri S. O'Brien. (Illus.). 128p. 2000. pap. 16.95 (1-57167-465-9) Coaches Choice.

*Pearls for Physical Therapists. 30p. 1999. write for info. (1-887759-84-0, P-130) Am Phys Therapy Assn.

Pearls from a Pediatric Practice I. William Wadlington & Clifton K. Meador. 160p. 1998. pap. text 15.95 (1-56053-267-X) Hanley & Belfus.

Pearls from My Memory Box: Some Very Personal Poems. limited ed. 1987. pap. 5.00 (0-930061-14-4) Interspace Bks.

Pearls from the Moon: Rays from the Sun. Sharon O'Hara. 176p. 1995. 17.95 (0-9646460-0-5) Growing Place.

Pearls in Arabian Waters: The Heritage of Bahrain. Peter Vine. 160p. 1995. pap. 86.85 (0-7855-2702-8, Pub. by IMMEL Pubng) St Mut.

Pearls in Arabian Waters: The Heritage of Bahrain. Peter Vine. 160p. (C). 1995. 125.00 (0-907151-28-0, Pub. by IMMEL Pubng) St Mut.

Pearls in Diagnostic Radiology. Harold D. Rosenbaum. LC 80-19014. 296p. reprint ed. pap. 91.80 (0-7837-3148-5, 204283700006) Bks Demand.

Pearls in the Muddle: Twelve Christian Stories. Zoe McCarthy. LC 98-72101. (Illus.). 128p. 1998. pap. 9.95 (0-9662499-0-9) Holy Ghost Writ.

Pearls in the Ocean: Security Perspectives in South-West Pacific. Man M. Kaul. (C). 1993. text 26.00 (81-85674-88-4, Pub. by UBS Pubs Dist) S Asia.

Pearls in the Shell: A Collection of Best Loved Short Verses from the Chinese Language. Ed. & Tr. by J. S. Soong. LC 98-41189. (Illus.). 216p. 1999. 30.00 (0-89581-942-2) Asian Humanities.

Pearl's Kitchen. Pearl Bailey. LC 73-6624. 211p. 1973. 9.95 (0-15-171600-5) Harcourt.

Pearl's Marigolds for Grandpa. Jane Breskin Zalben. LC 96-21596. (Illus.). 32p. (J). (ps-3). 1997. per. 15.00 (0-689-80448-2) S&S Childrens.

Pearls of Black Wisdom. Illus. by Angela Williams. (Charming Petites Ser.). 80p. 1998. 4.95 (0-88088-382-0) Peter Pauper.

Pearls of Childhood: The Poignant True Wartime Story of a Young Girl Growing up in an Adopted Land. Vera Gissing. (Illus.). 176p. 1995. pap. 11.95 (0-86051-945-7, Robson-Parkwest) Parkwest Pubns.

Pearls of Consciousness. Christa F. Burka. 73p. (Orig.). 1987. pap. 5.95 (0-914732-20-X) Bro Life Inc.

Pearls of Coromandel. large type ed. Keron Bhattacharya. (Large Print Ser.). 576p. 1997. 27.99 (0-7089-3679-2) Ulverscroft.

*Pearls of Country Wisdom: Hints from a Small Town on Keeping Garden & Home. Ed. & Compiled by Deborah S. Tukua. (Illus.). 320p. 2000. 19.95 (1-58574-105-1) Lyons Pr.

*Pearls of Country Wisdom: Homesteaders Quick Reference Guide to Simple Living. Deborah S. Tukua. (Illus.). 132p. 1999. pap. 9.95 (0-9675493-0-2) Holly Creek.

Pearls of Faith. Mary B. O'Neill. 1997. pap. write for info. (1-57553-546-7) Watermrk Pr.

Pearls of Faith (1883) Edwin Arnold. 320p. 1998. reprint ed. pap. 24.95 (0-7661-0243-2) Kessinger Pub.

*Pearls of Freedom. T. D. Jakes. (Illus.). 208p. 2000. 12.99 (0-7852-5520-6) Nelson.

*Pearls of Love: How to Write Love Letters & Love Poems. Ara John Movsesian. 307p. 1999. reprint ed. pap. text 13.00 (0-7881-6593-3) DIANE Pub.

*Pearls of Love & Logic for Parents & Teachers. Jim Fay et al. 288p. 2000. pap. 14.95 (1-930429-01-0, Pub. by Cline-Fay Inst) Midpt Trade.

Pearls of Lutra. Brian Jacques. (Redwall Ser.: Vol. 9). (Illus.). 351p. (J). (gr. 5-9). 1998. mass mkt. 5.99 (0-441-00508-X) Ace Bks.

Pearls of Lutra. Brian Jacques. LC PZ7.J15317Pe 1997. (Redwall Ser.). (Illus.). 416p. (J). (gr. 4-8). 1997. 19.95 (0-399-22946-9, Philomel) Peng Put Young Read.

Pearls of Lutra. Brian Jacques. (Redwall Ser.). (J). (gr. 4-8). 1998. 11.09 (0-606-13015-2, Pub. by Turtleback) Demco.

Pearls of Passion. Ed. by C. Allyson Lee & Makeda Silvera. 208p. 1994. pap. 12.95 (0-920813-99-2) LPC InBook.

Pearls of Pearl Harbor & the Islands of Hawaii: The History, Mythology & Cultivation of Hawaiian Pearls. Michael Walther. Ed. by C. Richard Fassler. LC 97-68646. Date not set. mass mkt. 7.95 (0-9659148-0-1) Natural Images HI.

Pearls of Power: For Possibility Thinkers. Robert H. Schuller. Ed. & Compiled by Terri Gibbs. LC 98-116073. (Illus.). 128p. 1997. 9.99 (0-8499-1513-9) Word Pub.

Pearls of the Concho: A Cookbook by the Junior League of San Angelo, Inc. rev. ed. Sue Sims et al. (Illus.). 298p. 1996. 22.95 (0-9611624-0-6) Jr Leag San Angelo.

Pearls of the Faith. A. Arnold. 1996. pap. 4.00 (0-933511-97-3) Kazi Pubns.

Pearls of the Faith. Edwin Arnold. 368p. 1984. 250.00 (1-85077-004-2, Pub. by Darf Pubs Ltd) St Mut.

Pearls of the Middle Kingdom. (Collections of the National Palace Museum, Taipei). 170p. 1984. 54.50 (957-562-015-1) Heian Intl.

Pearls of Wisdom. Beth M. Conny. (Charming Petites Ser.). (Illus.). 80p. 1996. 4.95 (0-88088-801-6) Peter Pauper.

*Pearls of Wisdom. Dadi Janki. LC 99-29272. 200p. 1999. pap. 6.95 (1-55874-723-0) Health Comm.

Pearls of Wisdom: A Harvest of Gems from All Ages. Jerome Agel & Walter Glanze. LC 87-45016. 160p. 1987. pap. 14.00 (0-06-096200-3, PL/6200, Perennial) HarperTrade.

Pearls of Wisdom: For the Job & for Life. Roger Kirkham. 1994. pap. 6.95 (1-880184-40-0) Compact Classics.

Pearls of Wisdom from Grandma. Ed J. Hayes. LC 97-620. 224p. 1997. 15.95 (0-06-039202-9, ReganBks) HarperTrade.

Pearls of Yiddish Song: Favorite Folk, Art & Theatre Songs. Eleanor G. Mlotek & Joseph Mlotek. 286p. (Orig.). 1988. 17.95 (1-877909-64-5) Jwsh Bk Ctr Wrkmns Cir.

Pearl's Paints. Abigail Thomas. (J). 1995. write for info. (0-8050-2976-1) H Holt & Co.

Pearl's Paints. Abigail Thomas. (J). (ps-2). 1996. reprint ed. pap. 5.95 (0-614-15659-9) H Holt & Co.

Pearls, Palms & Riots. Mirable Hawkes. 104p. (C). 1988. 35.00 (0-7212-0757-X, Pub. by Regency Pr GBR) St Mut.

Pearly Days - Oyster Days. Serenity Bohon. (Fresh Perspective Ser.: Vol. 2). 23p. 1998. pap. 3.50 (0-9660886-3-8) Scribbles & Scribes.

*Pearly Everlasting. Thomas Reiter. LC 99-55820. 80p. 2000. 22.50 (0-8071-2542-3); pap. 14.95 (0-8071-2543-1) La State U Pr.

Pearly Gates of Cyberspace: A History of Space from Dante to the Internet. Margaret Wertheim. LC 98-38200. (Illus.). 336p. 1999. 24.95 (0-393-04694-X) Norton.

*Pearly Gates of Cyberspace: A History of Space from Dante to the Internet. Margaret Wertheim. (Illus.). 336p. 2000. pap. text 14.95 (0-393-32053-7) Norton.

Pearly Mussels of New York State. David Lowell Strayer & Kurt J. Jirka. LC 97-61531. 113 p. 1997. write for info. (1-55557-155-7) NYS Museum.

*Pearly Queen. Mary Jane Staples. (J). 2000. pap. 6.95 (0-552-13856-8, Pub. by Transworld Publishers Ltd) Trafalgar.

Pears: Dialogues. Heather Stephens. LC 97-21751. 1997. pap. 12.00 (0-88734-924-2) Players Pr.

Pears & Planes. Alan M. Hofmeister et al. (Reading for All Learners Ser.). (Illus.). (J). pap. write for info. (1-56861-181-1) Swift Lrn Res.

*Pears Cyclopedia. 107th ed. Chris Cook. 1056p. 1998. text 29.95 (0-14-027737-4, Pub. by Pnguin Bks Ltd) Trafalgar.

Pears from the Willow Tree. Violet D. Lannoy. LC 86-50770. 151p. (Orig.). 1989. 35.00 (0-89410-564-7, Three Contnts); pap. 14.50 (0-89410-565-5, Three Contnts) L Rienner.

Pears, Lake, Sun. Sandy Solomon. LC 96-25238. (Poetry Ser.). 81p. 1996. text 24.95 (0-8229-3961-4) U of Pittsburgh Pr.

Pears of New York. U. P. Hedrick. 636p. 1993. reprint ed. lib. bdg. 109.00 (0-7812-5236-9) Rprt Serv.

Pears on a Willow Tree. Leslie Pietrzyk. 288p. 1999. pap. 12.50 (0-380-79910-3, Avon Bks) Morrow Avon.

*Pear's Ultimate Quiz Companion. 544p. 1998. pap. 13.95 (0-14-027042-6, Pub. by Pnguin Bks Ltd) Trafalgar.

Pearsall Guide to Successful Dog Training. 3rd ed. Margaret Pearsall. LC 80-16840. (Illus.). 352p. 1973. 25.95 (0-87605-759-8) Howell Bks.

Pearson: Crispin Pearson of Bucks County, PA, 1748-1806. A. P. Darrow. Ed. by William C. Armstrong. (Illus.). 166p. 1991. reprint ed. pap. 25.00 (0-8328-1753-8); reprint ed. lib. bdg. 35.00 (0-8328-1752-X) Higginson Bk Co.

Pearson: The Unlikely Gladiator. Ed. by Norman Hillmer. 240p. 1998. 39.95 (0-7735-1768-5, Pub. by McG-Queens Univ Pr) CUP Services.

Pearson & Canada's Role in Nuclear Disarmament & Arms Control Negotiations, 1945-1957. Joseph Levitt. (Illus.). 344p. 1993. 60.00 (0-7735-0905-4, Pub. by McG-Queens Univ Pr) CUP Services.

Pearson Girls: A Family Memoir of the Dakota Plains. Kathy L. Plotkin. LC 98-66956. (Illus.). 260p. 1999. pap. 16.95 (0-911042-51-2) NDSU Inst Reg.

Pearson on the Orchard-House: Hints on the Construction & Management of Orchard-Houses. J. R. Pearson. (Illus.). 63p. 1994. pap. 10.35 (1-881763-00-5) C Barnett Bks.

Pearson's Canal Companions: Birmingham Canal Navigations. Wilson Ltd. Staff & Imray L. Norie. (C). 1989. 53.00 (0-907864-49-X, Pub. by Laurie Norie & Wilson Ltd) St Mut.

Pearson's Canal Companions: Cheshire Ring & Wigan Pier. Wilson Ltd. Staff & Imray L. Norie. (C). 1989. 60.00 (0-907864-52-X, Pub. by Laurie Norie & Wilson Ltd) St Mut.

Pearson's Canal Companions: Four Counties Ring & Caldon Canal. Wilson Ltd. Staff & Imray L. Norie. (C). 1989. 60.00 (0-907864-46-5, Pub. by Laurie Norie & Wilson Ltd) St Mut.

Pearson's Canal Companions: Midland Rings (Stourport & Black Country) Wilson Ltd. Staff & Imray L. Norie. (C). 1989. 35.00 (0-907864-53-8, Pub. by Laurie Norie & Wilson Ltd) St Mut.

Pearson's Canal Companions: Oxford & Grand Union. Wilson Ltd. Staff & Imray L. Norie. (C). 1989. 60.00 (0-907864-55-4, Pub. by Laurie Norie & Wilson Ltd) St Mut.

Pearson's Canal Companions: Severn & Avon. Wilson Ltd. Staff & Imray L. Norie. (C). 1989. 60.00 (0-907864-54-6, Pub. by Laurie Norie & Wilson Ltd) St Mut.

Pearson's Canal Companions: Shropshire Union & Llangollen Canals. Wilson Ltd. Staff & Imray L. Norie. (C). 1989. 32.00 (0-907864-51-1, Pub. by Laurie Norie & Wilson Ltd) St Mut.

Pearson's Canal Companions: South Midlands & Warwickshire Ring. Wilson Ltd. Staff & Imray L. Norie. (C). 1989. 35.00 (0-907864-50-3, Pub. by Laurie Norie & Wilson Ltd) St Mut.

Pearson's Handbook: Desk Edition, 2. P. Villars. 853.00 (0-87170-603-2, 57763G) ASM.

Pearson's Handbook of Crystallographic Data for Intermetallic Phases, 4 vols. 2nd ed. Ed. by Pierre Villars & L. D. Calvert. 5366p. (C). 1991. 1973.00 (0-87170-416-1, 57732G) ASM.

An Asterisk (*) at the beginning of an entry indicates that the title is appearing for the first time.

Peartheayarna: The Journeying of Partha--An Eighteen-Century Balenese Kalzawin. Helen Creese. LC 98-214792. (Bibliotheca Indonesica Ser.). xi, 504 p. 1998. pap. write for info. (*90-6718-117-X*, Pub. by KITLV Pr) Book Bin.

Peary & Amundsen: Race to the Poles. Antony Mason. LC 94-36722. (Beyond the Horizons Ser.). 48p. (J). 1995. lib. bdg. 24.26 (*0-8114-3977-1*) Raintree Steck-V.

Peary Reaches the North Pole. Gordon Charleston. LC 92-44500. (Great Twentieth Century Expeditions Ser.). (Illus.). 32p. (J). (gr. 5 up). 1993. lib. bdg. 13.95 (*0-87518-535-5*, Dillon Silver Burdett) Silver Burdett Pr.

Peas. Nicholas Heller. LC 92-29740. (Illus.). 24p. (J). (ps-3). 1993. 13.93 (*0-688-12407-0*, Grenwillow Bks) HarpC Child Bks.

Peas. Claire Llewellyn. LC 99-25903. (What's for Lunch? Ser.). 32p. (J). (gr. k-2). 1999. 20.50 (*0-516-21549-3*) Childrens.

Peas: Genetics, Molecular Biology & Biotechnology. Ed. by R. Casey & D. R. Davies. (Biotechnology in Agriculture Ser.: No. 10). (Illus.). 336p. 1993. text 110.00 (*0-85198-863-6*) OUP.

***Peas & Honey: A Young Persons Guide to Gracious Dining.** Lynn Evans. (Illus.). (J). (gr. k-5). 1999. 10.00 (*0-9669658-6-8*) Poole & Smith.

Peas & Honey: Recipes for Kids (with a Pinch of Poetry) Kimberly Colen. LC 91-68052. (Illus.). 64p. (J). (gr. 4-6). 1995. 15.95 (*1-56397-062-7*, Wordsong) Boyds Mills Pr.

Peas & Peanuts see NGA Garden Library

***Peas off the Rocks.** Sidney Sideman. LC 98-227318. xiii, 320 p. 1998. write for info. (*1-57279-139-X*) YPP.

Peas-Utilisation in Animal Feeding. Contrib. by F. Gatel & B. Carrouee. 99p. 1997. pap. 48.00 (*2-9508706-1-9*, Pub. by Univ Nottingham) St Mut.

Peasant & French: Cultural Contact in Rural France During the Nineteenth Century. James R. Lehning. (Illus.). 251p. (C). 1995. text 64.95 (*0-521-46210-X*); pap. text 21.95 (*0-521-46770-5*) Cambridge U Pr.

Peasant & Nation: The Making of Postcolonial Mexico & Peru. Florencia E. Mallon. LC 93-34677. 1994. pap. 24.95 (*0-520-08505-1*, Pub. by U CA Pr) Cal Prin Full Svc.

Peasant & Nation: The Making of Postcolonial Mexico & Peru. Florencia E. Mallon. LC 93-34677. 1995. 55.00 (*0-520-08504-3*, Pub. by U CA Pr) Cal Prin Full Svc.

Peasant & Peasant Protests. K. N. Karna. (C). 1989. 39.50 (*81-7076-022-4*, Pub. by Intellectual) S Asia.

Peasant & the City in Eastern Europe: Interpenetrating Structures. Ed. by Thomas G. Winner & Irene P. Winner. 240p. 1982. 24.95 (*0-87073-275-7*) Schenkman Bks Inc.

Peasant Betrayed: Agriculture & Land Reform in the Third World. John P. Powelson & Richard Stock. LC 86-21770. (Lincoln Institute of Land Policy Bk.). 322p. reprint ed. pap. 99.90 (*0-7837-5769-7*, 204543400006) Bks Demand.

Peasant Betrayed: Agriculture & Land Reform in the Third World. rev. ed. John P. Powelson & Richard Stock. 400p. 1990. reprint ed. pap. 20.00 (*0-932790-74-7*) Cato Inst.

Peasant Classes: The Bureaucratization of Property & Family Relations under Early Habsburg Absolutism, 1511-1636. Hermann Rebel. LC 82-47610. (Illus.). 373p. 1983. reprint ed. pap. 115.70 (*0-7837-9431-2*, 206017300004) Bks Demand.

Peasant Community in Changing Thailand. Steven Piker. (Anthropological Research Papers: No. 30). (Illus.). ix, 157p. 1983. pap. 15.00 (*0-685-73906-6*) AZ Univ ARP.

Peasant Consciousness & Guerilla War in Zimbabwe: A Comparative Study. Terence O. Ranger. LC 85-40286. (Perspectives on Southern Africa Ser.: No. 37). 399p. reprint ed. pap. 123.70 (*0-7837-4693-8*, 204444000003) Bks Demand.

Peasant Cooperatives & Political Change in Peru. Cynthia McClintock. LC 80-8563. 437p. 1981. reprint ed. pap. 135.50 (*0-7837-9386-3*, 206013000004) Bks Demand.

Peasant Culture of Bosnia & Herzegovina. Ivo Sivric. 200p. 4.95 (*0-8199-0850-9*, Frncscn Herld) Franciscan Pr.

Peasant Customs & Savage Myths: Selections from the British Folklorists, 2 vols. Ed. by Richard M. Dorson. LC 68-16690. 766p. 1969. lib. bdg. 72.00 (*0-226-15867-5*) U Ch Pr.

Peasant Designs for Artists & Craftsmen. Ed Sibbett, Jr. LC 76-58079. (Needlepoint Ser.). (Illus.). 112p. 1977. pap. 7.95 (*0-486-23478-9*) Dover.

Peasant Designs for Artists & Craftsmen. Ed Sibbett. 1990. 16.50 (*0-8446-5610-0*) Peter Smith.

Peasant Differentiation & Development: The Case of a Mexican Ejido. Lasse Krantz. (Stockholm Studies in Social Anthropology: No. 28). (Illus.). 233p. (Orig.). 1991. pap. 47.50 (*91-7146-939-7*) Coronet Bks.

Peasant Dreams & Market Politics: Labor Migration & the Russian Village, 1861-1905. Jeffrey Burds. LC 97-33876. (Pitt Series in Russian & East European Studies). (Illus.). 407p. 1998. pap. 22.95 (*0-8229-5655-1*); text 50.00 (*0-8229-4049-3*) U of Pittsburgh Pr.

Peasant Economic Development within the English Manorial System. J. A. Raftis. LC 97-193250. 256p. 1996. 55.00 (*0-7735-1403-1*, Pub. by McG-Queens Univ Pr) CUP Services.

Peasant Economics: Farm Households & Agrarian Development. Frank Ellis. (Wye Studies in Agricultural & Rural Development). (Illus.). 327p. (C). 1994. pap. text 34.95 (*0-521-45711-4*) Cambridge U Pr.

Peasant Economy & Social Change in North China. Philip C. Huang. LC 83-40106. 384p. 1985. 52.50 (*0-8047-1220-4*); pap. 18.95 (*0-8047-1467-3*) Stanford U Pr.

Peasant Economy, Culture, & Politics of European Russia, 1800-1921. Ed. by Esther Kingston-Mann et al. LC 90-8643. 461p. 1991. reprint ed. pap. 143.00 (*0-608-02916-5*, 206398000008) Bks Demand.

Peasant Family & Rural Development in the Yangzi Delta, 1350-1988. Philip C. Huang. LC 89-49546. 440p. 1990. 55.00 (*0-8047-1787-7*); pap. 18.95 (*0-8047-1788-5*) Stanford U Pr.

Peasant Fires: The Drummer of Niklashausen. Richard Wunderli. LC 92-6104. (Illus.). 160p. 1992. 24.95 (*0-253-36725-5*); pap. 10.95 (*0-253-20751-7*, MB-751) Ind U Pr.

Peasant History in South India. David E. Ludden. LC 85-42692. (Illus.). 332p. reprint ed. pap. 103.00 (*0-608-04521-7*, 206526600001) Bks Demand.

Peasant Icons: Representations of Rural People in Late Nineteenth Century Russia. Cathy A. Frierson. LC 92-7783. (Illus.). 272p. (C). 1993. text 49.95 (*0-19-507293-6*); pap. text 23.95 (*0-19-507294-4*) OUP.

Peasant in Economic Thought: A Perfect Republic. Ed. by Evelyn L. Forget & Richard A. Lobdell. LC 95-13482. 168p. 1995. 80.00 (*1-85278-856-9*) E Elgar.

Peasant in 19th-Century Russia. Ed. by Wayne S. Vucinich. LC 67-26532. xxii, 314p. 1968. pap. 15.95 (*0-8047-0638-7*) Stanford U Pr.

Peasant Innovation & Diffusion of Agricultural Technology in China. Mary Sheridan. (Special Series on Agriculture Research & Extension: No. 4). 83p. (Orig.). (C). 1981. pap. 7.35 (*0-86731-051-0*) Cornell CIS RDC.

Peasant Intellectuals: Anthropology & History in Northern Tanzania. Steven Feierman. LC 90-50086. 352p. 1990. reprint ed. pap. 109.20 (*0-608-01861-9*, 206251200003) Bks Demand.

Peasant Iron-On Transfer Patterns. E. Sibbett. 1985. pap. text 3.95 (*0-486-23456-8*) Dover.

Peasant Labour & Colonial Capital: Rural Bengal since 1770. Sugata Bose. LC 92-12666. (New Cambridge History of India Ser.: III: 2). (Illus.). 248p. (C). 1993. 47.95 (*0-521-26694-7*) Cambridge U Pr.

Peasant Land Market in Medieval England. P. D. Harvey. (Illus.). 1984. 67.00 (*0-19-822661-6*) OUP.

Peasant Life in China: A Field Study of Country Life in the Yangtze Valley. Hsiao-Tung Fei. LC 75-41090. reprint ed. 49.50 (*0-404-14539-6*) AMS Pr.

Peasant Life in Sweden. Llewelyn Lloyd. LC 77-87710. 496p. reprint ed. 47.50 (*0-404-16501-X*) AMS Pr.

Peasant Life in Yugoslavia. Olive Lodge. LC 77-87722. (Illus.). 352p. reprint ed. 57.50 (*0-404-16582-6*) AMS Pr.

Peasant Literature: A Bibliography of Afro-American Nationalism & Social Protest from the Caribbean, No. 822. Ed. by Joan V. Feeney. 1975. 7.00 (*0-686-20358-5*, Sage Prdcls Pr) Sage.

Peasant, Lord, & Merchant: Rural Society in Three Quebec Parishes 1740-1840. Allan Greer. (Social History of Canada Ser.: No. 39). 320p. 1985. pap. text 20.95 (*0-8020-6578-3*) U of Toronto Pr.

Peasant, Lord, & Merchant: Rural Society in Three Quebec Parishes, 1740-1840. Allan Greer. LC 86-145305. (Social History of Canada Ser.: No. 39). 320p. reprint ed. pap. 99.20 (*0-7837-2048-3*, 204232300004) Bks Demand.

Peasant Maids, City Women: From the European Countryside to Urban America. Ed. by Christiane Harzig. LC 97-5368. (Illus.). 312p. 1996. text 47.50 (*0-8014-3273-1*); pap. text 19.95 (*0-8014-8395-6*) Cornell U Pr.

Peasant Metropolis: Social Identities in Moscow, 1929-1941. David L. Hoffmann. LC 94-10913. (Studies of the Harriman Institute). (Illus.). 296p. 1994. text 37.50 (*0-8014-2942-0*) Cornell U Pr.

***Peasant Metropolis: Social Identities in Moscow, 1929-1941.** David L. Hoffmann. 2000. pap. text 16.95 (*0-8014-8660-2*) Cornell U Pr.

Peasant Mobilization & Rural Development. Edgar G. Nesman. 148p. 1981. pap. text 13.95 (*0-87073-718-X*) Schenkman Bks Inc.

Peasant Moorings: Village Ties & Mobility Rationales in South India. Ed. by Jean-Luc Racine. LC 96-34882. 1996. 49.95 (*0-8039-9349-8*) Sage.

Peasant Movement in Modern India. Sunil Sahasraludhey. (C). 1989. 31.00 (*81-85076-66-9*, Pub. by Chugh Pubns) S Asia.

Peasant Movement in PEPSU Punjab. Mohinder Singh. 1990. 36.00 (*81-85135-54-1*) S Asia.

Peasant Movement Today. Sunil Sahasraludhey. 1986. 28.50 (*81-7024-040-9*, Pub. by Ashish Pub Hse) S Asia.

Peasant Movements in India, 1920 to 1950. D. N. Dhanagare. 1983. 34.50 (*0-19-561390-2*) OUP.

Peasant Movements in Twentieth Century China. Lucien Bianco. 300p. 2000. 64.95 (*1-56324-839-5*) M E Sharpe.

Peasant of El Salvador. rev. ed. Peter Gould & Stephen Stearns. LC 87-50566. (Illus.). 79p. (C). 1987. pap. 7.95 (*0-915731-01-0*) Whetstone Bks.

Peasant of West Brattleboro. David Chase. 192p. (Orig.). 1987. pap. 9.95 (*0-9618750-0-3*) Elm Corners Pr.

Peasant or Proletarian? Wage Labour & Peasant Economy during Industrialization (The Algerian Experience) Christian Andersson. (Illus.). 236p. 1985. pap. text 51.00 (*91-22-00771-7*) Coronet Bks.

Peasant Politics: Struggle in a Dominican Village. Kenneth E. Sharpe. LC 77-4782. (Johns Hopkins Studies in Atlantic History & Culture Ser.). 284p. reprint ed. pap. 88.10 (*0-7837-2201-X*, 204253900004) Bks Demand.

Peasant Politics & Religious Sectarianism: Peasant & Priest in the Cao Dai in Viet Nam. Jayne S. Werner. LC 81-52078. (Monographs: No. 23). 123p. 1981. 10.50 (*0-938692-07-0*) Yale U SE Asia.

Peasant Protest & Social Change in Colonial Korea. Gi-Wook Shin. LC 96-31636. (Korean Studies of the Henry M. Jackson School of International). (Illus.). 264p. 1996. text 40.00 (*0-295-97548-2*) U of Wash Pr.

Peasant Protests & Uprisings in Tokugawa, Japan. Stephen Vlastos. 184p. 1986. pap. 16.95 (*0-520-07203-0*, Pub. by U CA Pr) Cal Prin Full Svc.

Peasant Protests & Uprisings in Tokugawa, Japan. Stephen Vlastos. LC 85-5832. 196p. reprint ed. pap. 60.80 (*0-7837-4800-0*, 204444700003) Bks Demand.

Peasant Rebellion & Communist Revolution in Asia. Ed. by John W. Lewis. LC 73-89860. xvi, 364p. 1974. pap. 17.95 (*0-8047-0924-6*) Stanford U Pr.

Peasant Rebellions of the Late Ming Dynasty. James B. Parsons. LC 68-9341. (Monographs: No. 26). xv, 292p. 1993. reprint ed. 23.00 (*0-8165-0155-6*) Assn Asian Studies.

Peasant Rebels under Stalin: Collectivization & the Culture of Peasant Resistance. Lynne Viola. 328p. 1999. pap. 19.95 (*0-19-513104-5*) OUP.

Peasant Renaissance in Yugoslavia, 1900-1950. Ruth Trouton. LC 72-11399. 344p. 1973. reprint ed. lib. bdg. 69.50 (*0-8371-6662-4*, TRPR, Greenwood Pr) Greenwood.

Peasant Resistance in India, 1858-1914. Ed. by David Hardiman. (India Readings: Themes in Indian History Ser.). 320p. 1994. reprint ed. pap. 8.95 (*0-19-563390-3*) OUP.

Peasant Response to Price Incentives in Tanzania: A Theoretical & Empirical Investigation. Gun Eriksson. (Research Report Ser.: No. 91). 84p. 1993. 12.95 (*91-7106-334-X*, Pub. by Nordic Africa) Transaction Pubs.

Peasant Revolt in Malabar. Ed. by Robert Hardgrave. 1984. 50.00 (*0-8364-1067-X*, Pub. by Usha) S Asia.

Peasant Revolt in Malabar. Robert Hardgrave. 1981. reprint ed. 48.00 (*0-8364-0010-0*) S Asia.

Peasant Revolution in Ethiopia: The Tigray People's Liberation Front, 1975-1991. John Young. (African Studies: Vol. 91). (Illus.). 288p. (C). 1997. text 59.95 (*0-521-59198-8*) Cambridge U Pr.

Peasant Robbers of Kedah, 1900-1929: Historical & Folk Perceptions. Cheah Boon Kheng. (East Asian Historical Monographs). (Illus.). 168p. 1988. text 26.00 (*0-19-588882-0*) OUP.

Peasant Russia: Family & Community in the Post-Emancipation Period. Christine D. Worobec. (Illus.). 272p. 1991. text 45.00 (*0-691-03151-7*, Pub. by Princeton U Pr) Cal Prin Full Svc.

Peasant Russia: Family & Community in the Post-Emancipation Period. rev. ed. Christine D. Worobec. LC 95-37345. (Illus.). xiv, 257p. 1995. pap. text 16.00 (*0-87580-570-1*) N Ill U Pr.

Peasant Russia, Civil War: The Volga Countryside in Revolution (1917-1921) Orlando Figes. (Illus.). 432p. 1991. reprint ed. pap. 32.00 (*0-19-822169-X*) OUP.

Peasant Sage of Japan: The Life & Work of Sontoku Ninomiya. Kokei Tomita. LC 79-65366. (Studies in Japanese History & Civilization). 254p. 1979. reprint ed. lib. bdg. 72.50 (*0-313-26985-8*, U6985, Greenwood Pr) Greenwood.

Peasant Society & Marxist Intellectuals in China: Fang Zhimin & the Origin of a Revolutionary Movement in the Xinjiang Region. Kamal Sheel. LC 88-37476. 283p. 1989. reprint ed. pap. 87.80 (*0-608-07157-9*, 206738200009) Bks Demand.

Peasant Struggle & Action Research in Colombia. Anders Ruqvist. (Uppsala University Research Report Series, 1986: No. 3). 396p. (Orig.). 1986. pap. text 50.00 (*0-317-57954-1*) Coronet Bks.

Peasant Struggles, Land Reforms & Social Change: Malabar, 1836-1982. P. Radhakrishnan. 290p. (C). 1989. text 24.00 (*0-8039-9593-8*) Sage.

Peasant Uprisings in 17th-Century France, Russia, & China. Roland Mousnier. Tr. by Brian Pearce. LC 76-884549. (Great Revolutions Ser.: 1). 381p. reprint ed. pap. 118.20 (*0-608-11933-4*, 202331400032) Bks Demand.

Peasant Uprisings in Japan: An Anthology of Peasant Histories. Ed. by Anne Walthall. LC 91-9362. 276p. 1991. pap. text 15.95 (*0-226-87234-3*); lib. bdg. 41.50 (*0-226-87233-5*) U Ch Pr.

Peasant Venture: Tradition, Migration & Change among Georgian Peasants in Turkey. Paul J. Magnarella. (Illus.). 175p. 1979. pap. 13.95 (*0-87073-821-6*) Schenkman Bks Inc.

***Peasant War in Germany.** Friedrich Engels. LC 00-26699. (Illus.). 2000. write for info. (*0-7178-0720-7*) Intl Pubs Co.

***Peasant Wars of the Twentieth Century.** Eric R. Wolf. LC 99-26445. 352p. 1999. pap. 15.95 (*0-8061-3196-9*) U of Okla Pr.

***Peasantries of Europe: From the Fourteenth to the Eighteenth Centuries.** Ed. by Tom Scott. LC 97-41897. 432p. (C). 1998. pap. 45.00 (*0-582-10131-X*) Addison-Wesley.

Peasantry & Nationalism. Shirin Mehta. 16.00 (*0-8364-1222-2*, Pub. by Manohar) S Asia.

Peasantry & Society in France since 1789. Annie Moulin. Tr. by M. C. Cleary & M. F. Cleary. (Illus.). 271p. (C). 1991. text 59.95 (*0-521-39534-8*); pap. text 19.95 (*0-521-39577-1*) Cambridge U Pr.

Peasantry in India. G. Krishman-Kutty. 130p. 1986. 18.50 (*81-7017-215-2*, Pub. by Abhinav) S Asia.

Peasantry in the French Revolution. Peter Jones. (Illus.). 324p. 1988. text 59.95 (*0-521-33070-X*); pap. text 22.95 (*0-521-33716-X*) Cambridge U Pr.

Peasantry in the Old Regime: Conditions & Protests. Ed. by Isser Woloch. LC 77-6753. (European Problem Studies). 118p. 1977. reprint ed. pap. text 9.50 (*0-88275-563-3*) Krieger.

Peasantry to Capitalism: Western Ostergotland in the 19th Century. Goran Hoppe & John Langton. (Cambridge Studies in Historical Geography: No. 22). (Illus.). 480p. (C). 1995. text 74.95 (*0-521-25910-X*) Cambridge U Pr.

Peasants. Eric R. Wolf. (Illus.). (Orig.). (C). 1965. pap. text 17.00 (*0-13-655456-3*) P-H.

***Peasants Against Globalization: Rural Social Movements in Costa Rica.** Marc Edelman. LC 99-31301. 1999. pap. text 22.95 (*0-8047-3693-6*) Stanford U Pr.

Peasants Against Politics: Rural Organization in Britanny, 1911-1967. Suzanne Berger. LC 73-174541. (Center for International Affairs Ser.). (Illus.). 312p. 1972. 41.00 (*0-674-65925-2*) HUP.

Peasants Against the State: The Politics of Market Control in Bugisu, Uganda, 1900-1983. Stephen G. Bunker. LC 85-20894. x, 302p. 1991. pap. text 17.95 (*0-226-08031-5*) U Ch Pr.

Peasants Against the State: The Politics of Market Control in Bugisu, Uganda, 1900-1983. Stephen G. Bunker. LC 85-20894. 296p. 1987. text 29.95 (*0-252-01288-7*) U of Ill Pr.

Peasants & Capital: Dominica in the World Economy. Michel-Rolph Trouillot. LC 87-20018. (Atlantic History & Culture Ser.). 400p. 1988. text 55.00 (*0-8018-3481-3*) Johns Hopkins.

Peasants & Classes: A Study in Differentiation in Bangladesh. Atiur Rahman. 272p. (C). 1987. pap. 17.50 (*0-86232-346-0*, Pub. by Zed Books); text 49.95 (*0-86232-345-2*, Pub. by Zed Books) St Martin.

Peasants & Communists: Politics & Ideology in the Yugoslav Countryside, 1941-53. Melissa K. Bokovoy. LC 97-33877. (Pitt Series in Russian & East European Studies). 286p. 1998. text 40.00 (*0-8229-4061-2*) U of Pittsburgh Pr.

Peasants & Governments: An Economic Analysis. David Bevan et al. (Illus.). 362p. 1990. text 95.00 (*0-19-828621-X*) OUP.

Peasants & King in Burgundy: Agrarian Foundations of French Absolutism. Hilton L. Root. (California Series on Social Choice & Political Economy: Vol. 9). (C). 1992. pap. 15.95 (*0-520-08097-1*, Pub. by U CA Pr) Cal Prin Full Svc.

***Peasants & Landlords in Later Medieval England.** E. B. Fryde. (Illus.). 384p. 1999. pap. 26.95 (*0-7509-2255-9*) Sutton Pub Ltd.

Peasants & Landlords Medieval. Fryde. LC 96-23198. 384p. 1996. text 49.95 (*0-312-16370-3*) St Martin.

Peasants & Lords in Modern Germany: Recent Studies in Agricultural History. Ed. by Robert G. Moeller. LC 85-6113. 256p. 1986. text 60.00 (*0-04-943037-8*) Routledge.

Peasants & Masters. Theodor Kallifatides. Tr. by Thomas Teal from SWE. LC 90-2814.Tr. of Bonder och Herrar. 208p. 1990. reprint ed. 17.95 (*0-940242-38-9*); reprint ed. pap. 8.95 (*0-940242-37-0*) Fjord Pr.

Peasants & Monks in British India. William R. Pinch. LC 95-18661. 264p. (C). 1996. 55.00 (*0-520-20060-8*, Pub. by U CA Pr) Cal Prin Full Svc.

Peasants & Monks in British India. William R. Pinch. LC 95-18661. (Illus.). 264p. 1996. pap. 24.95 (*0-520-20061-6*, Pub. by U CA Pr) Cal Prin Full Svc.

Peasants & Nabobs: Agrarian Radicalism in Late 18th Century Tamil Country. Chitra Sivakumar. (C). 1993. 16.00 (*81-7075-031-8*, Pub. by Hindustan) S Asia.

Peasants & Nationalism in Eritrea: A Critique of Ethiopian Studies. Jordan Gebre-Medhin. LC 88-62294. 300p. (C). 24.95 (*0-932415-38-5*) Red Sea Pr.

Peasants & Other Stories. Anton Chekhov. Tr. by Constance Garnett from RUS. LC 99-14551. 480p. 1999. reprint ed. pap. 14.95 (*0-940322-14-5*, Pub. by NY Rev Bks) Midpt Trade.

Peasants & Politics in the Modern Middle East. Ed. by John Waterbury & Farhad Kazemi. 464p. (C). 1991. 49.95 (*0-8130-1088-8*); pap. 24.95 (*0-8130-1102-7*) U Press Fla.

Peasants & Potters see Corridors of Time: New Haven & London, 1927-1956

Peasants & Princes: Agrarian Unrest in Eastern Punjab, 1920-48. S. Gajrani. (C). 1987. 21.50 (*0-8364-2138-8*, Pub. by Usha) S Asia.

Peasants & Proletarians: The Struggles of Third World Workers. fac. ed. Ed. by Robin Cohen et al. LC 79-10020. 505p. pap. 156.60 (*0-7837-7548-2*, 204680800005) Bks Demand.

Peasants & Protest: Agricultural Workers, Politics, & Unions in the Aude, 1850-1914. Laura L. Frader. LC 90-31951. (Illus.). 275p. 1991. 45.00 (*0-520-06809-2*, Pub. by U CA Pr) Cal Prin Full Svc.

Peasants & Religion: A Socioeconomic Study of Dios Olivorio & the Palma Sola Movement in the Dominican Republic Jan Lundius & Mats Lundahl. LC 99-24619. 1999. write for info. (*0-415-17411-2*) Routledge.

Peasants & Resistance in India, 1858-1914. Ed. by David Hardiman. (Themes in Indian History Ser.). 320p. (C). 1992. 19.95 (*0-19-562725-3*) OUP.

Peasants & Strangers: Italians, Rumanians, & Slovaks in an American City, 1890-1950. Josef J. Barton. LC 74-14085. (Harvard Studies in Urban History). 231p. reprint ed. pap. 71.70 (*0-7837-4136-7*, 205795900011) Bks Demand.

Peasants & Their Agricultural Economy in Colonial Malaya, 1874-1941. Lim T. Ghee. (East Asian Historical Monographs). (Illus.). 1978. 27.50 (*0-19-580338-8*) OUP.

Peasants & Tobacco in the Dominican Republic, 1870-1930. Michiel Baud. LC 94-18760. (Illus.). 336p. (C). 1995. text 35.00 (*0-87049-891-6*) U of Tenn Pr.

P

An Asterisk (*) at the beginning of an entry indicates that the title is appearing for the first time.

Peasants by Preference? Socio-Economic & Environmental Aspects of Rural Development in Tanzania. Jan Rudengren. 385p. 1981. write for info. (*91-7258-132-8*, Pub. by Nordic Africa) Transaction Pubs.

Peasants, Class & Capitalism: The Rural Research of L. N. Kritsman & His School. Terry Cox. 280p. 1986. 49.95 (*0-19-878014-1*) OUP.

Peasants, Collectives, & Choice: Economic Theory & Tanzania's Villages. Ed. by Louis Putterman. LC 86-2915. (Contemporary Studies in Economic & Financial Analysis: Vol. 57). 389p. 1986. 78.50 (*0-89232-684-0*) Jai Pr.

Peasants, Dervishes & Traders in the Ottoman Empire. Suraiya Faroqhi. (Collected Studies: No. CS230). 344p. (C). 1986. reprint ed. lib. bdg. 115.95 (*0-86078-179-8*, Pub. by Variorum) Ashgate Pub Co.

Peasants in Africa: Historical & Contemporary Perspectives. Ed. by Martin A. Klein. LC 79-23415. (Sage Series on African Modernization & Development: No. 4). 319p. reprint ed. pap. 98.90 (*0-8357-4812-X*, 203774900009) Bks Demand.

Peasants in Arms: War & Peace in the Mountains of Nicaragua, 1979-1994. Lynn Horton. LC 98-22065. (Monographs in International Studies, Latin America Ser.). 372p. (C). 1998. pap. text 26.00 (*0-89680-204-3*) Ohio U Pr.

Peasants in Asia: Social Consciousness & Social Struggle. Zhanna D. Smirenskaia. Tr. by Michael J. Buckley. LC 86-14733. (Monographs in International Studies; Southeast Asia Ser.: No. 73). 240p. 1986. reprint ed. pap. 74.40 (*0-7837-9597-1*, 206035400005) Bks Demand.

Peasants in Peril: Location & Economy in Italy in the Second Century B.C. P. W. De Neeve. (Illus.). 44p. (C). 1984. pap. 10.00 (*90-70265-26-5*, Pub. by Gieben) J Benjamins Pubng Co.

Peasants in Revolt: A Chilean Case Study, 1965-1971. James F. Petras & Hugo Z. Merino. Tr. by Thomas Flory. LC 72-1578. (Latin American Monographs: No. 28). 168p. reprint ed. pap. 52.10 (*0-8357-7754-5*, 203611200002) Bks Demand.

Peasants in Revolt: Tenants, Landlords, Congress & the Raj in Oudh. Kapil Kumar. 1984. 22.00 (*0-8364-1221-4*, Pub. by Manohar) S Asia.

Peasants in the Middle Ages. Werner Rosener. Tr. & Frwd. by Alexander Stutzer. (Illus.). 352p. (Orig.). (C). 1993. pap. text 21.95 (*0-252-06289-2*) U of Ill Pr.

Peasants into Frenchmen: The Modernization of Rural France, 1870-1914. Eugen Weber. LC 75-7486. xvi, 616p. 1976. 67.50 (*0-8047-0898-3*); pap. 22.50 (*0-8047-1013-9*) Stanford U Pr.

Peasants, Landlords & Governments: Agrarian Reform in the Third World. Ed. by David Lehmann. LC 74-6091. 344p. (C). 1974. 37.00 (*0-8419-0162-7*); pap. 19.50 (*0-8419-0163-5*) Holmes & Meier.

Peasants, Merchants, & Markets: Inland Trade in Medieval England, 1150-1350. James Masschaele. LC 96-52279. 250p. 1997. text 45.00 (*0-312-16035-6*) St Martin.

Peasants of Costa Rica & the Development of Agarian Capitalism. Mitchell A. Seligson. LC 78-65015. (Illus.). 252p. reprint ed. pap. 78.20 (*0-608-09927-9*, 206926500003) Bks Demand.

Peasants of Costa Rica & the Rise of Agrarian Capitalism. Mitchell A. Seligson. LC 78-65015. 258p. 1980. 35.00 (*0-299-07760-8*) U of Wis Pr.

Peasants of Languedoc. Emmanuel L. Ladurie. Tr. by John Day from FRE. LC 74-4286. (Illus.). 382p. 1977. reprint ed. pap. text 16.95 (*0-252-00635-6*) U of Ill Pr.

Peasants of Marlhes: Economic Development & Family Organization in Nineteenth-Century France. James R. Lehning. LC 79-18707. 232p. reprint ed. pap. 72.00 (*0-7837-3760-2*, 204357700010) Bks Demand.

Peasants of the Montes: The Roots of Rural Rebellion in Spain. Michael Weisser. LC 75-43231. (Illus.). 1995. lib. bdg. 17.00 (*0-226-89158-5*) U Ch Pr.

P

Peasants, Officials & Participation in Rural Tanzania: Experience with Villagization & Decentralization. Louise Fortmann. (Special Series on Rural Local Organization: No. 1). 136p. (Orig.). (C). 1980. pap. text 6.95 (*0-86731-028-6*) Cornell CIS RDC.

Peasants on Plantations: Subaltern Strategies of Labor & Resistance in the Pisco Valley, Peru. Vincent C. Peloso. LC 98-27846. (Latin America Otherwise Ser.). 1998. pap. 17.95 (*0-8223-2246-3*) Duke.

Peasants on Plantations: Subaltern Strategies of Labor & Resistance in the Pisco Valley, Peru. Vincent C. Peloso. LC 98-27846. (Latin America Otherwise Ser.). (Illus.). 248p. 1998. lib. bdg. 49.95 (*0-8223-2229-3*) Duke.

Peasants on the World Market: Agricultural Experience of Independent Estonia, 1919-1939. Anu M. Koll. LC 95-166495. (Studia Baltica Stockholmiensia: No. 14). 150p. 1994. pap. 37.50 (*91-22-01654-6*) Coronet Bks.

Peasants, Politicians & Producers: The Organisation of Agriculture in France since 1918. Mark Cleary. (Cambridge Studies in Historical Geography: No. 14). (Illus.). 222p. (C). 1989. text 59.95 (*0-521-33347-4*) Cambridge U Pr.

Peasants, Politics, & Revolution: Pressures Toward Political & Social Change in the Third World. Joel S. Migdal. LC 74-2972. 311p. reprint ed. pap. 96.50 (*0-8357-7889-4*, 203630800002) Bks Demand.

Peasants, Politics, & the Formation of Mexico's National State: Guerrero, 1800-1857. Peter F. Guardino. LC 95-38593. 344p. 1996. 55.00 (*0-8047-2572-1*) Stanford U Pr.

***Peasants, Populism & Postmodernism: The Return of the Agrarian Myth.** Tom Brass. (Library of Peasant Studies: No. 17). 304p. 2000. 52.50 (*0-7146-4940-6*, Pub. by F Cass Pubs); pap. 24.50 (*0-7146-8000-1*, Pub. by F Cass Pubs) Intl Spec Bk.

Peasants, Primitives, & Proletariats: The Struggle for Identity in South America. Ed. by David L. Browman & Ronald A. Schwartz. (World Anthropology Ser.). xiv, 430p. 1980. text 63.10 (*90-279-7880-8*) Mouton.

Peasants, Rebels & Outcasts: The Underside of Modern Japan. Mikiso Hane. LC 81-48222. 336p. 1982. pap. 11.96 (*0-394-71040-1*) Pantheon.

Peasants' Revolt. Compiled by Douglas Hill. 39.00 (*1-56696-058-4*) Jackdaw.

Peasants' Rising & the Lollards. Ed. by Edgar Powell & George M. Trevelyan. LC 78-63202. (Heresies of the Early Christian & Medieval Era Ser.: Second Ser.). reprint ed. 34.50 (*0-404-16238-X*) AMS Pr.

Peasants, Traders, & Wives: Shona Women in the History of Zimbabwe, 1870-1939. Elizabeth Schmidt. LC 91-41251. (Social History of Africa Ser.). 289p. (C). 1992. pap. 22.95 (*0-435-08066-0*, 08066) Heinemann.

Peasants vs. City-Dwellers: Taxation & the Burden of Economic Development. Raaj K. Sah & Joseph E. Stiglitz. (Illus.). 238p. 1993. text 49.95 (*0-19-828581-7*) OUP.

Peasants Wake for Fellini's Casanova & Other Poems. Andrea Zanzotto. Tr. by John P. Welle & Ruth Feldman. LC 96-31442. (ENG & ITA.). 256p. 1997. 18.95 (*0-252-06610-3*); text 39.95 (*0-252-02310-2*) U of Ill Pr.

Peasants' War in Germany, 1525-1526 see Social Side of the Reformation in Germany

Peasants, Warriors, & Wives: Studies in the Popular Imagery of Reformation Nuremburg. Keith Moxey. LC 88-37668. (Illus.). 180p. 1989. 35.95 (*0-226-54391-9*) U Ch Pr.

Pease & Chitty's Law of Markets & Fairs. E. F. Cousins & R. Anthony. 500p. 1993. 60.00 (*0-85314-534-2*, Pub. by Tolley Pubng) St Mut.

***Pease Family from Great Baddow, England.** 1000p. 1999. write for info. (*0-9671415-0-8*) R Bart.

Pease Porridge Hot. Ed. by Katherine Hart. (Illus.). 1967. 17.50 (*0-88426-020-8*) Encino Pr.

***Pease Record: An Essential Genealogical Reference on the Pease Family of New England, Comprising Rev. David Pease's "A Genealogical & Historical Record of the Descendants of John Pease, Sr." & Austin S. Pease's "The Early History of the Pease Family in America"** David Pease & Austin S. Pease. 551p. 1999. reprint ed. pap. 38.00 (*0-7884-1300-7*, P108) Heritage Bk.

Peat. (Metals & Minerals Ser.). 1993. lib. bdg. 250.95 (*0-8490-8985-9*) Gordon Pr.

Peat As an Energy Alternative: 1st Symposium. Institute of Gas Technology Staff. 777p. 1980. pap. 50.00 (*0-910091-36-6*) Inst Gas Tech.

Peat As an Energy Alternative: 2nd Symposium. Institute of Gas Technology Staff. 800p. 1981. pap. 75.00 (*0-910091-37-4*) Inst Gas Tech.

Peat Dictionary. International Peat Society Staff. (ENG, FIN, GER, RUS & SWE.). 595p. 1984. pap. 195.00 (*0-8288-0714-0*, M 8145) Fr & Eur.

Peat Stratigraphy & Climatic Change. K. E. Barber. 242p. (C). 1981. text 123.00 (*90-6191-087-0*, Pub. by A A Balkema) Ashgate Pub Co.

Peatland Forestry: Ecology & Principles. E. Paavilainen & J. Paivanen. LC 95-2115. (Ecological Studies: Vol. 111). (GER.). 1995. write for info. (*3-540-58252-5*) Spr-Verlag.

Peatland Forestry: Ecology & Principles. E. Paavilainen & J. Paivanen. LC 95-2115. (Ecological Studies: Vol. 111). 1995. 117.95 (*0-387-58252-5*) Spr-Verlag.

Peatland Systems & Environmental Change. Daniel J. Charman & Barry G. Warner. 2000. pap. text 49.95 (*0-471-96990-7*) Wiley.

Peatlands, Economy & Conservation. Ed. by M. G. Schouten & M. J. Nooren. (Illus.). xiv, 106p. 1990. pap. 32.00 (*90-5103-042-8*, Pub. by SPB Acad Pub) Balogh.

Peatman. David Deans. 1996. pap. 16.00 (*0-7486-6171-9*, Pub. by Polygon) Subterranean Co.

Peau. Curzio Malaparte. (FRE.). 1982. pap. 13.95 (*0-7859-4021-9*) Fr & Eur.

Peau de Cesar. Rene Barjavel. (FRE.). 243p. 1987. pap. 10.95 (*0-7859-2069-2*, 2070378578) Fr & Eur.

Peau de Chagrin. Honore de Balzac. Ed. by Maurice Allem. (Class. Garnier Ser.). pap. 29.95 (*0-685-34091-0*) Fr & Eur.

Peau de Chagrin. Honore de Balzac. (Coll. GF). 1960. pap. 10.95 (*0-8288-9335-7*, 1701) Fr & Eur.

Peau de Chagrin. Honore de Balzac. (FRE.). 448p. 1966. pap. 10.95 (*0-7859-3469-3*, 2070365557) Fr & Eur.

Peau de Chagrin. Honore de Balzac. 1999. pap. 9.95 (*2-266-08332-5*) Midwest European Pubns.

Peau de Chagrin. Honore de Balzac. (Folio Ser.: No. 555). (FRE.). pap. 8.95 (*2-07-036555-7*) Schoenhof.

Peau des Zebres. Jean-Louis Bory. (FRE.). 1981. pap. 14.95 (*0-7859-1931-7*, 2070372650) Fr & Eur.

Peau Noire, Masques Blancs. Frantz Fanon. (Coll. La Condition Humaine). 8.95 (*0-685-35936-0*); pap. 9.95 (*0-685-35937-9*) Fr & Eur.

***Pebble: Old & New Poems.** Mairi MacInnes. 2000. pap. 19.95 (*0-252-06794-0*) U of Ill Pr.

***Pebble: Old & New Poems.** Mairi MacInnes. 2000. 40.00 (*0-252-02571-7*) U of Ill Pr.

***Pebble & a Pen.** Joan Donaldson. LC 00-21777. 176p. (YA). (gr. 5 up). 2000. 15.95 (*0-8234-1500-7*) Holiday.

Pebble & Pond. S. S. Edward. 70p. 1994. pap. 8.95 (*1-883500-00-1*) RAMSI Bks.

Pebble Beach: A True Story. A. K. Karsky. 350p. 24.50 (*1-883740-19-3*) Pebble Bch Pr Ltd.

***Pebble Beach Golf Links: The Official History.** Neal Hotelling. LC 99-33455. (Illus.). 224p. 1999. 45.00 (*1-886947-04-X*) Sleepng Bear.

***Pebble Books Mixed, 1 vol.** (J). 1998. 848.00 (*0-516-29775-9*) Childrens.

Pebble Creek. Amil Quayle. 80p. 1993. pap. 12.00 (*0-9635559-0-1*) Slow Tempo.

Pebble in My Pocket: A History of Our Earth. Meredith Hooper. LC 95-61828. (Illus.). 40p. (J). (gr. 2-6). 1996. 14.99 (*0-670-86259-2*, Viking Child) Peng Put Young Read.

***Pebble in the Shoe: Detecting the Causes of Distress & Pain in the Human Body.** John P. Streicher & Karen B. Alexander. LC 99-68539. 192p. 2000. pap. 24.95 (*1-57921-266-2*) WinePress Pub.

Pebble in the Sky. Isaac Asimov. LC 81-15516. 224p. 1982. reprint ed. 16.00 (*0-8376-0462-1*) Bentley Pubs.

Pebble Mosaics: Creative Designs & Techniques for Paths, Patios & Walls. Maggy Howarth. (Illus.). 80p. 1994. pap. 24.95 (*0-85532-767-7*, 767-7, Pub. by Srch Pr) A Schwartz & Co.

Pebble Ring. Napoleon St. Cyr. 1966. 3.00 (*0-910380-00-7*) Cider Mill.

Pebble Rings. Judy Ray. 64p. 1980. pap. 3.00 (*0-912678-42-9*, Greenfld Rev Pr) Greenfld Rev Lit.

Pebble Searcher. David H. Steele. 16p. (J). (gr. 7-10). 1986. 25.00 (*0-7855-1213-6*, Pub. by A H S Ltd) St Mut.

Pebbles: A Chapbook Anthology of Short Poems. Ed. by Margaret Holley. 20p. 1993. pap. 5.00 (*1-890044-01-6*) Riverstone PA.

Pebbles & Sand. Louis Newman. LC 77-99935. (Illus.). 96p. 1990. pap. 6.00 (*0-912292-12-1*) Smith.

Pebbles in the Sand. Patricia Hewitt. 120p. 1998. pap. 12.00 (*0-8059-4272-6*) Dorrance.

Pebbles in the Stream: A History of Beale Air Force Base & Neighboring Areas. rev. ed. Peggy Bal. LC 93-20345. (Illus.). x, 118p. 1993. pap. 11.95 (*0-915641-05-4*) Nevada County Hist Society.

Pebbles in the Wind. Jean V. Baldner. (Illus.). 52p. (Orig.). (YA). (gr. 7 up). pap. 5.95 (*0-9615317-0-3*) Baldner J V.

***Pebbles, Monochromes & Other Modern Poems, 1891-1916.** William Dean Howells. Ed. by Edwin Cady. LC 99-89155. 192p. 2000. pap. 16.95 (*0-8214-1319-8*, Ohio U Ctr Intl); text 34.95 (*0-8214-1318-X*, Ohio U Ctr Intl) Ohio U Pr.

Pebbles on the Beach. large type ed. Evelyn Hood. (Magna Large Print Ser.). 576p. 1996. 27.99 (*0-7505-0978-3*, Pub. by Mgna Lrg Print) Ulverscroft.

Pebbles on the Path. Fannie L. Houck. 56p. (Orig.). 1990. pap. 6.50 (*0-9624346-2-0*) Ready Writer.

Pebbles on the Prairie. Gloria Bauske. 108p. 1999. pap. 12.95 (*1-57579-144-7*) Pine Hill Pr.

Pebbles to Slay Goliath. Arthur Burt. Ed. & Intro. by Kathie Walters. (Illus.). 64p. 1996. pap. 4.99 (*0-9629559-7-3*) Good News Min.

Pebbles, Weeds & Lima Beans. Ken Hoffman. 40p. 1999. pap. 6.50 (*0-9655816-4-0*) Wings of Dawn.

***Pebbling the Walk: How to Survive Cancer Treatment When You're Not the Patient.** Steve Reed. 2000. pap. 13.95 (*0-936085-63-0*) Blue Heron OR.

Peboan & Seegwun. Charles Larry. LC 93-10092. 32p. (J). (ps-3). 1993. 16.00 (*0-374-35773-0*) FS&G.

Peboan & Seegwun. Charles Larry. LC 93-10092. 32p. (J). (ps-3). 1995. 4.95 (*0-374-45750-6*) FS&G.

Peboan & Seegwun. Charles Larry. LC 93-10092. (J). 1993. 10.15 (*0-606-09737-6*, Pub. by Turtleback) Demco.

Pecado Despues de la Conversion. 2nd ed. Algernon J. Pollock & Gordon H. Bennett. Tr. by Sara Bautista from ENG. (Serie Diamante).Tr. of Sin After Conversion. (SPA., Illus.). 36p. 1982. pap. 0.85 (*0-942504-04-6*) Overcomer Pr.

Pecadora (Seleccion de Poesias) Olga Rosado. LC 80-68759. (SPA.). 66p. (Orig.). 1984. pap. 5.00 (*0-89729-268-5*) Ediciones.

Pecadores en las Manos de un Dios Airado. J. Edwards.Tr. of Sinners in the Hands of an Angry God. (SPA.). write for info. (*0-7899-0313-X*, 497462) Editorial Unilit.

Pecados de Familia. Anne Mather. (SPA.). 1997. per. 3.50 (*0-373-33404-4*, 1-33404-4) Harlequin Bks.

Pecan Candy & Huck-a-Bucks. Rhodesia Jackson. LC 93-84784. 428p. 1993. 16.00 (*0-9637282-2-9*); pap. text 16.00 (*0-9637282-0-2*) Orgena Ent.

Pecan Cookbook. Kim A. Graham. 1993. 11.95 (*0-9637842-0-X*) Adams Pecan.

Pecan Cultivars - The Orchard's Foundation. Darrell Sparks. LC 91-68464. (Illus.). 443p. 1992. lib. bdg. 49.00 (*0-9631839-0-7*) Pecan Prod Innov.

Pecan Lovers' Cook Book. Mark Blazek. LC 86-25812. 120p. (Orig.). 1986. ring bd. 6.95 (*0-914846-27-2*) Golden West Pub.

Pecan Tree. Jane Manaster. LC 93-49563. (Corrie Herring Hooks Ser.: No. 27). (Illus.). 112p. 1994. 17.95 (*0-292-75153-2*) U of Tex Pr.

Pecan Tree: A True Friend. Barbara A. Langham. LC 94-96074. (Illus.). 32p. (J). (gr. k-3). 1994. lib. bdg. 12.95 (*0-9640804-0-0*) B A Langham.

Pecans - A Grower's Perspective: Popular Varieties, Propagation, Culture, & More. G. Wesley Rice. LC TX-3-864-43. (Illus.). xiii, 198p. 1994. pap. 39.50 (*0-9656644-0-6*) Pecan Creek.

Peccadillos: Poems from Hollywood. Mark Dunster. 13p. 1998. pap. 5.00 (*0-89642-435-9*) Linden Pubs.

Peccary: With Observations on the Introduction of Pigs to the New World. R. A. Donkin. LC 84-45906. (Transactions Ser.: Vol. 75, Pt. 5). 150p. 1985. pap. 25.00 (*0-87169-755-6*, T755-DOR) Am Philos.

Peces. Steve Parker. 1995. 18.95 (*84-372-3729-7*) Santillana.

Peces. Lynn M. Stone. (Depredadores Ser.).Tr. of Fish. 24p. (J). (gr. k-4). 1994. lib. bdg. 10.95 (*0-86593-318-9*) Rourke Corp.

Pecfect Fit, 20. Lynda Simmons. 1999. mass mkt. 3.99 (*0-8217-6376-8*, Zebra Kensgtn) Kensgtn Pub Corp.

Pechat' Russkoi Polshi, 1919-1939: Opyt Bibliographicheskogo Issledowania. Olga Szteins & Emanuel Sztein. (RUS., Illus.). 45p. (C). 1990. pap. write for info. (*1-878445-55-3*) Antiquary CT.

Peche aux Avaros. David Goodis. (FRE.). 187p. 1987. pap. 10.95 (*0-7859-2527-9*, 2070378012) Fr & Eur.

Peche de l'Ange. Jacques Maritain. Ed. by De La Trinite & Journet. (FRE.). 248p. 1961. pap. 39.95 (*0-686-56360-3*) Fr & Eur.

Pechenegs, Cumans & Iasians: Steppe Peoples in Medieval Hungary. Andras Poloczi-Horvath. (Hereditas Ser.). (Illus.). 160p. 1999. pap. 21.00 (*963-13-2740-X*, Pub. by Corvina Bks) St Mut.

Pecheur d'Islande. (Coll. Bleue Ser.). 21.50 (*0-685-34265-4*) Fr & Eur.

Pecheur d'Islande. Pierre P. Loti-Viaud. Ed. by Michel Desbrueres. (FRE., Illus.). 1995. pap. 69.95 (*2-86808-071-5*) Intl Scholars.

Pecheur d'Islande. Pierre P. Loti-Viaud. (Folio Ser.: No. 1982). (FRE.). 338p. 1988. pap. 9.95 (*2-07-038070-X*) Schoenhof.

Pecheur d'Islande. unabridged ed. Loti-Viaud. (FRE.). pap. 5.95 (*2-87714-208-6*, Pub. by Bookking Intl) Distribks Inc.

Pecheurs. Thomastine Le May. (Fropse Ser.: No. 5). write for info. (*0-918728-87-8*) Pendragon NY.

Pechstein (Max) The Graphic Work. Gunter Kruger. (GER., Illus.). 368p. 1988. 250.00 (*1-55660-207-3*) A Wofsy Fine Arts.

Peck of Hecklers! Judy Bradbury. (Illus.). 48p. (J). (ps-2). 1997. text 14.95 (*0-07-007043-1*) McGraw.

Peck, Slither & Slide. Suse MacDonald. LC 96-18439. (Illus.). 48p. (ps-1). 1997. 15.00 (*0-15-200079-8*) Harcourt.

Peck, Stow & Wilcox Company 1900 Catalog: Tinsmiths' Tools & Machines. (Illus.). 150p. 1993. pap. 14.95 (*1-879335-38-7*) Astragal Pr.

Pecked to Death by Ducks. Tim Cahill. LC 93-6328. (Vintage Departures Ser.). 377p. 1994. pap. 13.00 (*0-679-74929-2*) Vin Bks.

Pecked to Death by Ducks. large type ed. Tim Cahill. LC 93-7804. 545p. 1993. lib. bdg. 22.95 (*0-8161-5771-5*, G K Hall Lrg Type) Mac Lib Ref.

Pecker Experimental Astronomy. 1970. text 88.00 (*90-277-0157-1*) Kluwer Academic.

Peckerneck Country. Walt Curtis. 1978. 10.00 (*0-932191-05-3*) Mr Cogito Pr.

***Peckham Cry.** Janice Cooke. 290p. 1999. pap. 8.95 (*1-901442-05-5*) Seven Hills Bk.

Peckham Genealogy: English Ancestors & American Descendants of John Peckham of Newport, RI, 1630. Stephen F. Peckham. (Illus.). 596p. reprint ed. pap. 91.00 (*0-8328-1651-5*); reprint ed. lib. bdg. 101.00 (*0-8328-1650-7*) Higginson Bk Co.

***Pecking Order.** McColley. LC 93-17768. 224p. (YA). (gr. 12 up). 2000. pap. 4.95 (*0-06-440516-8*) HarpC Child Bks.

Pecking Order. Mark Kennedy. LC 73-18561. reprint ed. 32.50 (*0-404-11374-5*) AMS Pr.

Peckinpah: A Portrait in Montage. rev. ed. Garner Simmons. LC 98-38390. (Illus.). 328p. 1997. reprint ed. pap. 18.95 (*0-87910-273-X*) Limelight Edns.

Peckinpah: The Western Films: A Reconsideration. Paul Seydor. LC 79-22208. (Illus.). 324p. 1980. text 29.95 (*0-252-00738-7*) U of Ill Pr.

Peckinpah: The Western Films: A Reconsideration. Paul Seydor. LC 96-4521. (Illus.). 400p. 1996. 29.95 (*0-252-02268-8*) U of Ill Pr.

***Peckinpah: The Western Films: A Reconsideration.** Paul Seydor. LC 96-4521. (Illus.). 410p. 1999. pap. 21.95 (*0-252-06835-1*) U of Ill Pr.

Peckover & the Bog Man. large type ed. Michael Kenyon. LC 95-53280. 1996. pap. 20.95 (*0-7862-0641-1*) Thorndike Pr.

Peckover Holds the Baby. Michael Kenyon. 1988. pap. 3.50 (*0-380-70636-9*, Avon Bks) Morrow Avon.

Peckover Joins the Choir. large type ed. Michael Kenyon. LC 94-18877. 395p. 1994. lib. bdg. 19.95 (*0-7862-0266-1*) Thorndike Pr.

Peck's Bad Boy: Playscript. Aurand Harris. (J). (gr. 1-9). 1974. 6.00 (*0-87602-170-4*) Anchorage.

Peck's Bad Boy & His Pa. George W. Peck. (Illus.). 250p. 1991. reprint ed. lib. bdg. 35.95 (*0-89966-750-3*) Buccaneer Bks.

Peck's Beach: A Pictorial History of Ocean City, New Jersey. Tim Cain. Ed. by Gail Travers. (Illus.). 96p. 1988. reprint ed. 27.00 (*0-945582-04-8*) Down the Shore Pub.

Peck's Title Book: Description of State Laws Regulating Motor Vehicle Titles, Registrations & Transfer of Same. Ed. by Stephens-Peck, Inc. Staff & Marcia Barber. 168p. 1988. ring bd. 39.50 (*0-317-91271-2*) Stephens-Peck.

Peck's Title Book: Description of State Laws Regulating Motor Vehicle Titles, Registrations & Transfer of Same. annuals Ed. by Stephens-Peck, Inc. Staff & Marcia Barber. 168p. 1988. 34.00 (*0-317-91272-0*) Stephens-Peck.

Pecong. Steve Carter. 1993. pap. 6.95 (*0-88145-107-X*) Broadway Play.

Peconic Bay Piano Solo-Duet. 16p. (YA). 1993. pap. 4.00 (*0-7692-1440-1*, F3315P9X) Wrner Bros.

Pecos: Gateway to Pueblo & Plains, the Anthology. Ed. by Joseph P. Sanchez & John V. Bezy. LC 88-60561. (Illus.). 144p. 1988. pap. 10.95 (*0-911408-77-0*) SW Pks Mnmts.

***Pecos Bill.** (J). 1999. 9.95 (*1-56137-333-8*) Novel Units.

Pecos Bill. Brian Gleeson. LC 88-11581. (Illus.). 40p. (J). (gr. k-3). 1997. pap. 22.00 (*0-689-81261-2*, Rabbit Ears) Litle Simon.

 An Asterisk (*) at the beginning of an entry indicates that the title is appearing for the first time.

***Pecos Bill.** Brian Gleeson. LC 88-11581. (J). 1999. pap. 10.95 incl. audio (*0-689-82535-8*, Rabbit Ears) Litle Simon.

Pecos Bill. Brian Gleeson. LC 88-11581. (Illus.). 40p. (J). (gr. k up). 1991. 19.95 incl. audio (*0-88708-086-3*, LC 88-11581, Picture Book Studio) S&S Childrens.

Pecos Bill. Steven Kellogg. LC 86-784. (Illus.). 32p. (J). (gr. 2 up). 1986. 17.00 (*0-688-05871-X*, Wm Morrow) Morrow Avon.

Pecos Bill. Steven Kellogg. Ed. by ALC Staff. LC 86-784. (Illus.). 32p. (J). (ps up). 1992. mass mkt. 5.95 (*0-688-09924-6*, Wm Morrow) Morrow Avon.

Pecos Bill. Steven Kellogg. Tr. by Aida E. Marcuse. LC 86-784. (SPA., Illus.). 48p. (J). (gr. k up). 1995. 15.00 (*0-688-14036-X*, Wm Morrow) Morrow Avon.

Pecos Bill. Steven Kellogg. (J). 1995. 11.15 (*0-606-07997-1*, Pub. by Turtleback) Demco.

Pecos Bill. Nanci A. Lyman. LC 79-66319. (Illus.). 48p. (J). (gr. 3-6). 1980. pap. 3.95 (*0-89375-307-6*) Troll Communs.

Pecos Bill. Illus. by Tim Raglin. LC 88-11581. 36p. (J). (ps up). 1991. 14.95 (*0-88708-081-2*, Rabbit Ears) Litle Simon.

Pecos Bill: A Military Biography of William R. Shafter. Paul H. Carlson. LC 88-36465. (Illus.). 240p. 1989. 39.95 (*0-89096-348-7*) Tex A&M Univ Pr.

Pecos Bill: A Tall Tale. Steven Kellogg. 1986. 11.15 (*0-606-01348-2*, Pub. by Turtleback) Demco.

Pecos Bill (Spanish edition) Steven Kellogg. Ed. by Amy Cohn. Tr. by Aida E. Marcuse from ENG. LC 86-784. (SPA., Illus.). 32p. (J). (ps-3). 1995. mass mkt. 5.95 (*0-688-14020-3*, Wm Morrow) Morrow Avon.

Pecos Bill, the Roughest, Toughest Best. Patricia A. Jensen. LC 93-2217. (First-Start Tall Tale Ser.). (Illus.). 32p. (J). (gr. k-2). 1997. lib. bdg. 17.25 (*0-8167-3165-9*) Troll Communs.

Pecos Bill, the Roughest, Toughest Best. Patricia A. Jensen. LC 93-2217. (First-Start Tall Tale Ser.). (Illus.). 32p. (J). (gr. k-2). 1997. pap. 3.50 (*0-8167-3166-7*) Troll Communs.

Pecos Bill, the Roughest, Toughest Best. Patsy Jensen. (Troll First-Start Tall Tale Ser.). (J). 1994. 8.70 (*0-606-07998-X*, Pub. by Turtleback) Demco.

Pecos Bill's Wild West Show. Lane Riosley. (Illus.). 22p. (Orig.). (J). (gr. k-8). 1992. pap. 3.00 (*1-57514-256-2*, 1060) Encore Perform Pub.

Pecos Blood. Erle Adkins. (Illus.). 224p. 1987. mass mkt. 2.50 (*0-8217-2101-1*, Zebra Kensgtn) Kensgtn Pub Corp.

Pecos Kid. Dan Cushman. LC 99-35656. (Westerns Ser.). (Orig.). 1999. 19.95 (*0-7862-1895-9*, Five Star MI) Mac Lib Ref.

***Pecos Kid: A Western Duo.** Dan Cushman. LC 00-42576. (YA). 2000. write for info. (*0-7862-2779-6*) Thorndike Pr.

***Pecos Kid Returns.** 2000. 30.00 (*0-7862-2114-3*) Mac Lib Ref.

Pecos National Monument. Sarah Gustafson. LC 96-70559. 16p. 1997. pap. 3.95 (*1-877856-70-3*) SW Pks Mnmts.

Pecos, New Mexico: Archaeological Notes, Vol. 5. Alfred V. Kidder. LC 58-4944. 1958. pap. 15.00 (*0-939312-06-9*) Peabody Found.

Pecos Pete. large type ed. Charles H. Redish. Ed. by Greg Redish. (Illus.). 32p. (J). (gr. k-8). 1996. 24.95 (*0-9643885-2-9*) Personal Profiles.

Pecos Ranchers in the Lincoln County War. T. Dudley Cramer. Ed. by Dave Bohn. LC 96-8559. (Illus.). 216p. (Orig.). 1996. 40.00 (*0-9653183-0-3*); pap. 22.95 (*0-9653183-1-1*) Branding Iron.

Pecos River Pilgrim's Poems V. Paul Patterson. 1996. 6.00 (*1-887743-01-4*) Cow Hill Pr.

Pecos River Pilgrim's Poems I. Paul Patterson. 1988. reprint ed. pap. 6.00 (*0-9617714-1-0*) Cow Hill Pr.

Pecos River Pilgrim's Poems VI. Paul Patterson. 1998. pap. 10.00 (*1-887743-03-0*) Cow Hill Pr.

Pecos River Pilgrim's Poems III. Paul Patterson. (Illus.). 1992. pap. 11.00 (*0-9617714-5-3*) Cow Hill Pr.

Pecos River Pilgrim's Poems II. Paul Patterson. (Illus.). 1989. reprint ed. pap. 6.00 (*0-9617714-2-9*) Cow Hill Pr.

Pecos River Rock Art: A Photographic Essay. Jim Zintgraff & Solveig A. Turpin. LC 91-67795. 72p. 1991. 45.00 (*0-9633811-0-5*) McPherson Pub.

Pecos Ruins: Geology, Archaeology, History, & Prehistory. 2nd ed. Ed. by David G. Noble. LC 92-55032. (Illus.). 32p. (C). 1993. reprint ed. pap. 6.95 (*0-941270-76-9*) Ancient City Pr.

Pecos to Rio Grande: Interpretations of Far West Texas by Eighteen Artists. Intro. by Ron Tyler. LC 83-45105. (Joe & Betty Moore Texas Art Ser.: No. 6). (Illus.). 130p. 1983. 29.95 (*0-89096-166-2*) Tex A&M Univ Pr.

Pecs - The Picture Exchange Communication System. Andrew S. Bondy & Lori Frost. (Illus.). 71p. 1996. 45.00 (*1-928598-01-3*) Pyramid Educ.

Pectines & Pectinases: Proceedings of an International Symposium, Wageningen, the Netherlands, December 3-7, 1995. J. Visser & A. G. Voragen. LC 96-36458. (Progress in Biotechnology Ser.). 1010p. 1996. 309.50 (*0-444-82330-1*) Elsevier.

Peculiar: A Tale of the Great Transition. Epes Sargent. LC 72-2121. (Black Heritage Library Collection). 1977. reprint ed. 35.95 (*0-8369-9061-7*) Ayer.

***Peculiar Chemistry.** large type ed. Kitty Ray. 480p. 2000. write for info. (*0-7505-1483-3*, Pub. by Mgna Lrg Print) Ulverscroft.

Peculiar Exploits of Brigadier Fellowes. Sterling E. Lanier. LC 74-188477. (Illus.). 159 p. (J). 1971. write for info. (*0-8027-5548-8*) Walker & Co.

Peculiar Honor: A History of the 28th Texas Cavalry. M. Jane Johansson. LC 98-10997. (Illus.). 192p. 1998. pap. 20.00 (*1-55728-504-7*) U of Ark Pr.

Peculiar Humanism: The Judicial Advocacy of Slavery in High Courts of the Old South, 1820-1850. William E. Wiethoff. LC 95-20993. (Studies in the Legal History of the South). 1996. 40.00 (*0-8203-1797-7*) U of Ga Pr.

Peculiar Institution. Kenneth M. Stampp. 1990. pap. 14.00 (*0-679-72307-2*) Vin Bks.

Peculiar Kind of Politics: Canada's Overseas Ministry in the First World War. Desmond Morton. 280p. 1982. text 30.00 (*0-8020-5586-9*) U of Toronto Pr.

Peculiar Language: Literature as Difference from the Renaissance to James Joyce. Derek Attridge. LC 87-19060. 288p. 1988. pap. text 18.95 (*0-8014-9407-9*) Cornell U Pr.

Peculiar Memories of Thomas Penman. Bruce Robinson. 256p. 1998. 29.95 (*0-7475-3614-7*) Chronicle Bks.

***Peculiar Memories of Thomas Penman,** Bruce Robinson. LC 99-53449. 288p. 2000. pap. 13.00 (*0-06-095540-6*, Perennial) HarperTrade.

Peculiar Memories of Thomas Penman. Bruce Robinson. LC 98-47730. 278p. 1999. 24.95 (*0-87951-914-2*, Pub. by Overlook Pr) Penguin Putnam.

Peculiar Mission of a Friends School. Douglas H. Heath. LC 79-84919. 1979. pap. 4.00 (*0-87574-225-4*) Pendle Hill.

Peculiar Motions. Rosmarie Waldrop & Jennifer MacDonald. Ed. by Rena Rosenwasser. LC 90-39995. (Illus.). 48p. (Orig.). (C). 1990. pap. text 9.00 (*0-932716-26-1*) Kelsey St Pr.

Peculiar Motions. deluxe limited ed. Rosmarie Waldrop & Jennifer MacDonald. Ed. by Rena Rosenwasser. LC 90-39995. (Illus.). 48p. (Orig.). (C). 1990. 35.00 (*0-932716-45-8*) Kelsey St Pr.

Peculiar Pain: A Close Look at Black on Black Sexual Harassment & Its Impact. Patricia W. Carson. Ed. by Michelle Smith. (Illus.). 208p. 1995. 24.95 (*0-7872-1076-5*) Kendall-Hunt.

Peculiar Patents: A Collection of Unusual & Interesting Inventions from the files of the U. S. Patent Office. Rick Feinberg. LC 94-12695. (Illus.). 240p. 1994. 9.95 (*0-8065-1561-9*, Citadel Pr) Carol Pub Group.

Peculiar People. J. J. Gurney. (C). 1988. 100.00 (*0-913408-48-4*, Pub. by W Sessions) St Mut.

Peculiar People. Mark Sorrell. (Illus.). 168p. 1979. text 21.00 (*0-85364-263-X*) Attic Pr.

Peculiar People. Gavin Souter. 1991. pap. 18.95 (*0-7022-2382-4*, Pub. by Univ Queensland Pr) Intl Spec Bk.

Peculiar People. large type ed. Jan De Hartog. LC 92-46333. (General Ser.). 509p. 1993. reprint ed. lib. bdg. 17.95 (*1-56054-670-0*) Thorndike Pr.

Peculiar People: Iowa's Old Order Amish. Elmer Schwieder & Dorothy Schwieder. LC 86-27711. (Iowa Heritage Collection). (Illus.). 188p. 1987. reprint ed. pap. 10.95 (*0-8138-0104-4*) Iowa St U Pr.

Peculiar People: Mormons & Same-Sex Orientation. Ed. by Ron Schow et al. LC 91-31162. 406p. 1993. pap. 19.95 (*1-56085-046-9*) Signature Bks.

Peculiar People: Slave Religion & Community Culture among the Gullah. Margaret W. Creel. (American Social Experience Ser.: No. 7). (Illus.). 416p. (C). 1989. pap. text 18.50 (*0-8147-1422-6*) NYU Pr.

Peculiar People: The Church As Culture in a Post-Christian Society. Rodney Clapp. 276p. (Orig.). 1996. pap. 14.99 (*0-8308-1990-8*, 1990) InterVarsity.

Peculiar People: The Story of My Life. Augustus Hare. Ed. by Anita Miller. (Illus.). 350p. 1995. 26.95 (*0-89733-388-8*) Academy Chi Pubs.

Peculiar People, the Dukhobors. Aylmer Maude. LC 72-131033. reprint ed. 32.50 (*0-404-04275-9*) AMS Pr.

Peculiar Plants! Readings, Writing, & Speaking about Plants. Annalisa McMorrow. (Super-Duper Science Ser.). (Illus.). 80p. (J). (gr. 1-3). 1998. pap. 9.95 (*1-57612-044-9*, MM2058) Monday Morning Bks.

Peculiar Politics: A Romantic Comedy. Katia Spiegelman. LC 92-19663. 240p. 1993. 21.95 (*0-7145-2952-4*) M Boyars Pubs.

Peculiar Power: A Quaker Woman Preacher in 18th-Century America. Cristine Levenduski. LC 95-48862. 208p. 1996. text 36.95 (*1-56098-670-0*) Smithsonian.

Peculiar Problem of Taxing Life Insurance Companies. Henry J. Aaron. LC 83-70788. (Studies of Government Finance). 46p. 1983. pap. 7.95 (*0-8157-0031-8*) Brookings.

Peculiar Prophets: A Biographical Dictionary of New Religions. James Lewis. LC 99-21563. (Illus.). 320p. 1999. pap. 19.95 (*1-55778-768-9*) Paragon Hse.

Peculiar Service. Corey Ford. Date not set. lib. bdg. 21.95 (*0-8488-0753-7*) Amereon Ltd.

Peculiar Speech: Preaching to the Baptized. William H. Willimon. 128p. (Orig.). 1992. pap. 13.00 (*0-8028-0616-3*) Eerdmans.

Peculiar Treasure. Edna Ferber. 1994. lib. bdg. 24.95 (*1-56849-492-0*) Buccaneer Bks.

Peculiar Treasure. Brent A. Top. LC 97-72958. 1997. 15.95 (*1-57008-332-0*) Bookcraft Inc.

Peculiar Treasure: Autobiography. Edna Ferber. (American Biography Ser.). 383p. 1991. reprint ed. lib. bdg. 79.00 (*0-7812-8129-6*) Rprt Serv.

Peculiar Treasures: A Biblical Who's Who. Frederick Buechner. LC 92-54775. 224p. 1993. pap. 12.00 (*0-06-061141-3*, Pub. by Harper SF) HarpC.

***Peculiar, Uncertain & Two Egg: The Unusual Origins of More Than 3,000 American Place Names.** Don Blevins. LC 00-27923. (Illus.). 352p. 2000. pap. 14.95 (*1-58182-094-1*, Cumberland Hearthside) Cumberland Hse.

Peculiar vs. Normal Phenomena in A-Type & Related Stars. Ed. by M. M. Dworetsky et al. (ASP Conference Series Proceedings: Vol. 44). 696p. 1993. 34.00 (*0-937707-63-5*) Astron Soc Pacific.

Peculiar Zoo. Barry Louis Polisar. (Illus.). 32p. (J). (gr. k-5). 1993. 14.95 (*0-938663-14-3*) Rainbow Morn.

Peculiaridades Estilisticas de Fernao Lopes. Julio Lopez-Arias. LC 93-23087. (Iberica Ser.: Vol. 10). 210p. (C). 1994. text 47.95 (*0-8204-2251-7*) P Lang Pubng.

Peculiarities in the Reactivity of Telluriumorganic Compounds in Comparison with Their Sulfur & Selenium Analogs, Vol. 9. I. D. Sadekov. (Sulfur Reports). 40p. 1990. pap. text 75.00 (*3-7186-5032-0*, Harwood Acad Pubs) Gordon & Breach.

Peculiarities of German History: Bourgeois Society & Politics in 19th Century Germany. David Blackbourn & Geoffrey Eley. 308p. 1984. pap. text 23.00 (*0-19-873057-8*) OUP.

Peculiarities of the British Economy. Ben Fine & L. Harris. 220p. (C). 1986. pap. 22.50 (*0-85315-575-5*, Pub. by Lawrence & Wishart) NYU Pr.

Peculiarity of Literature: An Allegorical Approach to Poe's Fiction. Jeffrey DeShell. LC 96-29067. 176p. 1997. 32.50 (*0-8386-3666-7*) Fairleigh Dickinson.

Pecunia. Mary Kelly. 56p. (Orig.). 1990. pap. 4.00 (*0-917061-29-2*) Top Stories.

Pedadogia Desde el Siglo XVII. Guy Avanzini. (SPA.). pap. 13.99 (*968-16-3360-1*, Pub. by Fondo) Continental Bk.

Pedadogical Contract. Yun L. Too. (Body, in Theory Ser.). (Illus.). 240p. (C). text 42.50 (*0-472-11087-X*, 11087) U of Mich Pr.

Pedagodfathers: The Lords of Education. Douglas J. Simpson. 182p. (Orig.). (C). 1994. pap. text 17.95 (*1-55059-088-X*) Temeron Bks.

Pedagogia Ilustrada: Principios Generales, Vol. 1. Leroy Ford.Tr. of Primer for Teachers & Leaders. (SPA., Illus.). 144p. 1970. reprint ed. pap., teacher ed. 10.99 (*0-311-11001-0*, Edit Mundo) Casa Bautista.

Pedagogical Discussions see For the Teaching of Mathematics

***Pedagogical Pleasures.** Erica McWilliam. LC 99-19789. (Eruptions Ser.: Vol. 1). 216p. (C). 1999. pap. text 29.95 (*0-8204-3800-6*) P Lang Pubng.

Pedagogical Sketchbook. Paul Klee. (Illus.). 64p. 1968. pap. 16.95 (*0-571-08618-7*) Faber & Faber.

Pedagogical Symposium on Global Climate Change, Analytical Techniques for Characterizing Coal & Coal Conversion Products, Chemistry of Asphalt & Asphalt-Aggregate Mixes: Preprints of Papers Presented at the 204th ACS National Meeting, Washington, DC, August 23-28, 1992. American Chemical Society, Division of Fuel Chemis. LC TP0315.. (Preprints of Papers: Vol. 37, No. 3). 548p. reprint ed. pap. 169.90 (*0-7837-3203-1*, 204319700007) Bks Demand.

Pedagogical Theatre. Arthur Pittis. Ed. by David Mitchell. 173p. 1997. pap. 15.00 (*1-888365-02-1*) Assn Waldorf Schls.

Pedagogical Thesaurus: Thesaurus Paedagogik. 2nd ed. D. Friedrichs. (GER.). 350p. 1982. 95.00 (*0-8288-1391-4*, M8593) Fr & Eur.

Pedagogicka Psychologia - Terminologicky a Vykladovy Slovnik (Pedagogical Psychology - Dictionary of Terminology) M. Bratska & L. Duric. (SLO.). 500p. 1997. pap. 290.00 (*80-08-02498-4*, Pub. by Slov Pegagog Naklad) IBD Ltd.

Pedagogie de l'experience spirituelle personelle: Bible et Exercices see Biblical Theology & the Spiritual Exercises: A Method Toward a Personal Experience of God as Accomplishing within Us His Plan of Salvation

Pedagogie, Dictionnaire Concepts Cles. F. Reynal. (FRE.). 1998. 110.00 (*0-320-00190-3*) Fr & Eur.

Pedagogie Freinet et l'Enseignement des Langues Vivantes: Approche Historique, Systematique et Theorique. Gerald Schlemminger. (FRE.). 304p. 1996. 47.95 (*3-906756-41-6*, Pub. by P Lang) P Lang Pubng.

Pedagogie Fribourgeoise, du Concile de Trente a Vatican II: Continuite ou Discontinuite? Marie-Therese Weber. (Exploration Ser.). (FRE.). 223p. 1997. 31.95 (*3-906754-64-2*, Pub. by P Lang) P Lang Pubng.

Pedagogie Raisonnee de l'Interpretation - A Systematic Approach to Teaching of Interpretation. Danica Seleskovitch & Marianne Lederer. Tr. by Jacolyn Harmer. 234p. pap. 23.75 (*0-916883-13-2*) RID Pubns.

Pedagogie Scientifique, 3 tomes, Set. Maria Montessori. 99.95 (*0-685-33998-X*) Fr & Eur.

Pedagogies of Resistance: Women Educator Activists, 1880-1960. Margaret Smith Crocco et al. LC 98-54347. 144p. 1999. 44.00 (*0-8077-6298-9*); pap. 19.95 (*0-8077-6297-0*) Tchrs Coll.

Pedagogika M. Montessoriovej. Helmingova. (SLO.). 216p. 1996. write for info. (*80-08-00281-6*, Pub. by Slov Pegagog Naklad) IBD Ltd.

Pedagoginis Lithuanistikos Institutas: 1958-1983 see Lithuanian Institute of Education, 1958-1983

Pedagogue et la Modernite: A l'Occasion du 250e Anniversaire de la Naissance de Johann Heinrich Pestalozzi (1746-1827), Actes du Colloque d'Angers (9-11 Juillet, 1996) Ed. by Michel Soetard. (Pedagogie Ser.). (GER.). ix, 238p. (Orig.). 1998. pap. 35.95 (*3-906760-09-X*) P Lang Pubng.

Pedagogy: Disturbing History, 1820-1930. Ed. by Mariolina R. Salvatori. LC 96-11938. (Series in Composition, Literacy, & Culture). 464p. 1996. text 49.95 (*0-8229-3922-3*) U of Pittsburgh Pr.

Pedagogy: The Question of impersonation. Jane Gallop. LC 94-28325. (Theories of Contemporary Culture Ser.). 192p. (Orig.). 1995. 24.95 (*0-253-32536-6*); pap. text 12.95 (*0-253-20936-6*) Ind U Pr.

Pedagogy & Power: Rhetorics of Classical Learning. Ed. by Yun L. Too & Niall Livingstone. LC 97-29632. (Ideas in Context Ser.: No. 50). (Illus.). 368p. (C). 1998. text 64.95 (*0-521-59435-9*) Cambridge U Pr.

Pedagogy & t Politics of Hope: Theory, Culture & Schooling a Critical Reader. Henry A. Giroux. LC 96-39884. 304p. (C). 1997. pap. text 28.00 (*0-8133-3274-5*, Pub. by Westview) HarpC.

Pedagogy & the Politics of the Body: A Critical Praxis. Sherry Shapiro. (Critical Education Practice Ser.: Vol. 16). 160p. 1998. 50.00 (*0-8153-2781-1*, SS1153) Garland.

Pedagogy & the Shaping of Consciousness: Linguistic & Social Processes. Frances Christie. LC 97-32854. (Open Linguistics Ser.). 320p. 1998. 75.00 (*0-304-70228-5*) Continuum.

***Pedagogy & the Shaping of Consciousness: Linguistic & Social Processes.** Frances Christie. (Open Linguistics Ser.). 2000. pap. text 31.95 (*0-8264-4747-3*) Continuum.

Pedagogy & the Struggle for Voice: Issues of Language, Power, & Schooling for Puerto Ricans. Catherine E. Walsh. LC 90-719. (Critical Studies in Education). 192p. 1990. 55.00 (*0-89789-234-8*, H234, Bergin & Garvey); pap. 17.95 (*0-89789-235-6*, G235, Bergin & Garvey) Greenwood.

Pedagogy, Democracy, & Feminism: Rethinking the Public Sphere. Adriana Hernandez. LC 96-1934. (SUNY Series, Teacher Empowerment & School Reform). 128p. (C). 1997. text 39.50 (*0-7914-3169-X*); pap. text 12.95 (*0-7914-3170-3*) State U NY Pr.

Pedagogy for Liberation: Dialogues on Transforming Education. Ira Shor & Paulo Freire. (Illus.). 207p. 1986. 49.95 (*0-89789-104-X*, Bergin & Garvey); pap. 19.95 (*0-89789-105-8*, Bergin & Garvey) Greenwood.

Pedagogy Is Politics: Literary Theory & Critical Teaching. Ed. by Maria-Regina Kecht. 264p. 1992. text 34.95 (*0-252-01834-6*); pap. text 15.95 (*0-252-06201-9*) U of Ill Pr.

Pedagogy of Domination: Toward a Democratic Education in South Africa. Ed. by Mokubung Nkomo. LC 90-80152. 460p. (C). 1990. 49.95 (*0-86543-153-1*); pap. 16.95 (*0-86543-154-X*) Africa World.

Pedagogy of Freedom. Paulo Freire. LC 98-30184. xxxii, 144p. 1998. pap. 22.95 (*0-8476-9047-4*) Rowman.

Pedagogy of Freedom: Ethics, Democracy & Civic Courage. Paulo Freire. Tr. by Patrick Clarke from POR. LC 98-30184. (Critical Perspectives Ser.). 160p. 1998. 22.95 (*0-8476-9046-6*) Rowman.

Pedagogy of Hope: Reliving "Pedagogy of the Oppressed" Paulo Freire. LC 79-4826. 240p. 1995. pap. 15.95 (*0-8264-0843-5*) Continuum.

Pedagogy of Possibility: Bakhtinian Perspectives on Composition Studies. Kay Halasek. LC 98-8354. 1999. 49.95 (*0-8093-2226-9*); pap. 19.95 (*0-8093-2227-7*) S Ill U Pr.

Pedagogy of Praxis: A Dialectical Philosophy of Education. Moacir Gadotti. Tr. by John Milton. LC 95-32347. (SUNY Series, Teacher Empowerment & School Reform). 216p. (C). 1996. text 57.50 (*0-7914-2935-0*); pap. text 18.95 (*0-7914-2936-9*) State U NY Pr.

***Pedagogy of the Earth: Education for a Sustainable Future.** Ed. by Carlos Hernandez & Rashmi Mayur. 254p. 1999. pap. 16.95 (*81-87404-00-0*, Pub. by International Institute) Kumarian Pr.

***Pedagogy of the Earth: Education for a Sustainable Future.** Ed. by Carols Hernandez & Rashmi Mayur. 254p. 1999. pap. 16.95 (*1-874040-00-1*, Pub. by International Institute) Kumarian Pr.

Pedagogy of the Heart. Paulo Freire. 144p. 1998. reprint ed. pap. 11.95 (*0-8264-1131-2*) Continuum.

***Pedagogy of the Oppressed.** 30th anniversary ed. Paulo Freire. LC 00-30304. 2000. write for info. (*0-8264-1276-9*) Continuum.

Pedagogy of the Oppressed: 20th Anniversary Edition. Paulo Freire. Tr. by Myra B. Ramos from POR. LC 70-81571. 164p. 1993. pap. 12.95 (*0-8264-0611-4*) Continuum.

Pedagogy, Praxis, Ulysses: Using Joyce's Text to Transform the Classroom. Ed. by Robert Newman. LC 95-19276. 280p. (C). 1995. text 44.50 (*0-472-10636-8*, 10636) U of Mich Pr.

Pedagogy, Printing, & Protestantism: The Discourse on Childhood. Carmen Luke. LC 88-13924. (SUNY Series, the Philosophy of Education). 171p. (C). 1989. pap. text 21.95 (*0-7914-0003-4*) State U NY Pr.

***Pedagogy, Symbolic Control & Identity.** Basil Bernstein. LC 99-87951. 256p. 2000. pap. 23.95 (*0-8476-9576-X*); text 65.00 (*0-8476-9575-1*) Rowman.

Pedagogy, Symbolic Control & Identity: Theory, Research, Critique. Basil Berstein. 208p. 1995. 79.95 (*0-7484-0371-X*, Pub. by Tay Francis Ltd); pap. 23.95 (*0-7484-0372-8*, Pub. by Tay Francis Ltd) Taylor & Francis.

Pedagogy, Technology & the Body. Ed. by Erica McWilliam & Peter Taylor. LC 96-848. (Counterpoints Ser.: Vol. 29). VIII, 217p. (C). 1996. pap. text 29.95 (*0-8204-3089-7*) P Lang Pubng.

Pedagon: Interdisciplinary Essays in the Human Sciences, Pedagogy & Culture. David G. Smith. LC 98-25589. (Counterpoint Postmodern Ser.: Vol. 15). XIX, 188p. (C). 1999. pap. text 29.95 (*0-8204-2760-8*) P Lang Pubng.

Pedal Car Restoration & Price Guide. Andrew G. Gurka. LC 95-82423. (Illus.). 240p. 1996. pap. 24.95 (*0-87341-405-5*, PCR01) Krause Pubns.

Pedal Cars. Ed Weirick et al. LC 99-34754. (Illus.). 128p. 1999. pap. 24.95 (*0-7603-0443-2*) Motorbooks Intl.

Pedal Cars: Chasing the Kidillac. Jane Dwyre Garton. (Illus.). 208p. 1999. 49.95 (*0-7643-0836-X*) Schiffer.

Pedal for Your Life: By Bicycle from the Baltic to the Black Sea. Christopher Parkway. LC 96-196828. (Illus.). 202p. 1997. 28.95 (*0-7188-2946-8*, Lutterworth-Parkwest) Parkwest Pubns.

P

An Asterisk (*) at the beginning of an entry indicates that the title is appearing for the first time.

Pedal Power. Judy Delton. (Illus.). 96p. (J). (gr. 4-8). 1998. pap. 3.99 (0-440-41336-2) BDD Bks Young Read.
Pedal Power, 35. Judy Delton. (Pee Wee Scouts Ser.). 1998. 9.09 (0-606-13700-9, Pub. by Turtleback) Demco.
Pedal Steel Guitar. Winnie Winston & Bill Keith. (Illus.). 126p. 1975. pap. 19.95 (0-8256-0169-X, OK63115, Oak) Music Sales.
Pedal Steel Guitar Chord Chart. DeWitt Scott. 4p. 1975. pap. 3.95 (0-87166-370-8, 93394) Mel Bay.
Pedal Steel Guitar Licks for Guitar. Forest Rogers. 1995. pap. text 15.95 incl. audio compact disk (1-57424-019-6) Centerstream Pub.
Pedal to the Metal: The Work Life of Truckers. Lawrence J. Ouellet. LC 93-38954. 336p. (C). 1994. pap. 22.95 (1-56639-176-8); text 59.95 (1-56639-175-X) Temple U Pr.
Pedaling Along: Bikes Then & Now see Here We Go! - Group 1
Pedaling Around Southern Queensland. Julia Thorn. (Illus.). 168p. 1993. pap. 12.95 (0-86417-385-7, Pub. by Kangaroo Pr) Seven Hills Bk.
Pedaling Coast to Coast. Tim Bone. LC 98-8960. 110p. 1999. pap. 9.95 (1-884778-60-7) Old Mountain.
Pedaling Northwards: A Father & Son's Bicycle Adventure from Virginia to Canada. Robin Lind. 108p. 1993. pap. 8.95 (0-9639531-0-9) Hope Springs.
Pedaling Through Burgundy Cookbook. Sarah L. Chase. LC 95-32829. (Illus.). 208p. 1995. pap. 14.95 (1-56305-359-4, 3359) Workman Pub.
Pedaling Through Provence Cookbook. Sarah L. Chase. LC 95-32831. (Illus.). 256p. 1995. pap. 14.95 (0-7611-0233-7, 10233) Workman Pub.
Pedaling to Glory: Victory & Drama in Professional Bicycle Racing. Samuel Abt. LC 97-3485. (Illus.). 160p. 1997. pap. 14.95 (0-933201-83-4) MBI Pubg.
Pedalion see Rudder: Divine Canons of the Seven Decumenical & of Local Synods
Pedalling Backwards. E. M. Goldman. 1999. 14.99 (0-670-87514-7) Viking Penguin.
Pedalling the Modern Pianoforte. York Bowen. 1936. pap. 13.95 (0-19-322105-5) OUP.
Peddlers see Colonial Craftsmen - Group 2
Peddlers & Post Traders: The Army Sutler on the Frontier. rev. ed. David M. Delo. (Illus.). 304p. 1998. pap. 24.00 (0-9662218-1-8) Kingfisher Bks.
Peddlers & Princes: Social Development & Economic Change in Two Indonesian Towns. Clifford Geertz. LC 62-18844. (Comparative Studies of New Nations). (Illus.). 172p. 1968. reprint ed. pap. text 10.95 (0-226-28514-6, P318) U Ch Pr.
***Peddler's Dream.** Janice Shefelman. (Illus.). (YA). 1999. 14.95 (1-57168-294-5, Eakin Pr) Sunbelt Media.
Peddler's Gift. Maxine R. Schur. Ed. by Diane Arico. LC 98-36171. (Illus.). 32p. (J). (gr. k-4). 1999. 15.99 (0-8037-1978-7, Dial Yng Read) Peng Put Young Read.
Peddler's Grandson: Growing up Jewish in Mississippi. Edward Cohen. LC 99-10146. (Illus.). 193p. 1999. 25.00 (1-57806-167-9) U Pr of Miss.
Peddlers of Crisis: The Committee on the Present Danger & the Politics of Containment. Jerry Sanders. LC 83-60176. 371p. 1983. 35.00 (0-89608-182-6); pap. 15.00 (0-89608-181-8) South End Pr.
Peddling My Wares. Ivar Lo-Johansson. Tr. & Intro. by Rochelle Wright. LC 94-42896. (SCAND Ser.). xi, 229p. 1995. 60.00 (1-57113-015-2) Camden Hse.
Peddling Prosperity: Economic Ideas & Ideology in America. Krugman Paul. 180p. 1994. 22.00 (0-393-03602-2) Norton.
Peddling Prosperity: Economic Sense & Nonsense in an Age of Diminished Expectations. Paul R. Krugman. 320p. 1995. pap. 13.95 (0-393-31292-5, Norton Paperbks) Norton.
Pedegrewe of Heretiques. John Barthlet. LC 79-76432. (English Experience Ser.: No. 76). 180p. 1969. reprint ed. 30.00 (90-221-0076-6) Walter J Johnson.
Peder Paars (A Verse Translation of the Original Poem) Ludvig Holberg. LC 63-8122. 230p. reprint ed. pap. 71.30 (0-608-30821-8, 200198700009) Bks Demand.
Peder Victorious: A Tale of the Pioneers 20 Years Later. Ole Edvart Rolvaag. Tr. by Nora O. Solum from NOR. LC 81-16402. xx, 325p. 1982. reprint ed. pap. 13.95 (0-8032-8906-5, Bison Books) U of Nebr Pr.
Pederasty & Pedagogy in Archaic Greece. William A. Percy, III. LC 95-12864. (Illus.). 296p. 1996. 29.95 (0-252-02209-2) U of Ill Pr.
Pederasty & Pedagogy in Archaic Greece. William A. Percy. 1998. pap. text 18.95 (0-252-06740-1) U of Ill Pr.
***Pedernales Country Cookbook.** Lillian Fehrenbach. 162p. 1999. 26.95 (0-7351-0162-0) Replica Bks.
Pedersen Memorial Issue. Ed. by R. M. Izatt & J. S. Bradshaw. LC 92-10361. (Advances in Inclusion Science Ser.: Vol. 7). 410p. (C). 1992. text 269.50 (0-7923-1723-8) Kluwer Academic.
Pedestal. unabridged ed. Daniel F. McCarthy. 114p. 1998. pap. 18.00 (0-9666725-0-X) D F McCarthy.
Pedestalled Offering Tables in the Aegean World. Lefteris Platon & Yannis Pararas. (Studies in Mediterranean Archaeology & Literature: No. 106). (Illus.). 76p. (Orig.). 1991. pap. 29.50 (91-7081-046-X, Pub. by P Astroms) Coronet Bks.
Pedestrian Accident Reconstruction & Litigation. 2nd ed. Jerry J. Eubanks & Paul F. Hill. LC 98-44606. (Illus.). 1008p. 1999. 129.00 incl. VHS (0-913875-56-2, 0977-N) Lawyers & Judges.
Pedestrian Accidents. Ed. by Antony J. Chapman et al. LC HE0336.P43P4. 366p. reprint ed. pap. 113.50 (0-8357-3104-9, 203936000012) Bks Demand.
Pedestrian & Bicycle Planning with Safety Considerations. (Research Record Ser.: No. 1141). 45p. 1987. 6.00 (0-309-04520-7) Transport Res Bd.
Pedestrian Areas: From Malls to Corporate Networks. Klaus Uhlig. (Illus.). 1979. 37.50 (0-8038-0209-9) Archit CT.
Pedestrian, Bicycle, & Older Driver Research (TRR 1405) Ed. by Susan Taylor Brown. (Transportation Research Record Ser.). (Illus.). 100p. 1993. pap. text 24.00 (0-309-05554-7) Transport Res Bd.
***Pedestrian Crash Types: A 1990s Informational Guide.** William W. Hunter et al. (Illus.). 93p. 2000. reprint ed. pap. text 25.00 (0-7881-8824-0) DIANE Pub.
Pedestrian Information Plaques. Traffic Engineering Council Committee. (Illus.). 11p. 1997. pap. text 15.00 (0-935403-13-2, IR-093) Inst Trans Eng.
Pedestrian Malls & Skywalks: Traffic Separation Strategies in American Downtown. Kent A. Robertson. LC 94-8723. 1994. 61.95 (1-85628-687-8, Pub. by Avebry) Ashgate Pub Co.
Pedestrian Malls, Streetscapes, & Urban Spaces. Harvey M. Rubenstein. LC 92-2897. 288p. 1992. 99.00 (0-471-54680-1) Wiley.
Pedestrian Papers. Walter S. Hinchman. LC 68-54350. (Essay Index Reprint Ser.). 1977. 19.95 (0-8369-0542-3) Ayer.
Pedestrian Planning & Design. rev. ed. John J. Fruin. (Illus.). 214p. 1987. pap. text 20.00 (1-886536-01-5) Elevator Wrld.
Pedestrian Slip Resistance: How to Measure It & How to Improve It. William English. LC 95-92829. (Illus.). 208p. 1996. 65.00 (0-9653462-0-X) W English.
Pedestrian Survey of Playa Lake Environments in Beaver & Texas Counties, Oklahoma: Project 40-12040.021. Scott D. Brosowske & Leland C. Bement. (Archeological Resource Survey Report: No. 39). (Illus.). 68p. 1998. pap. 4.00 (1-881346-32-3) Univ OK Archeol.
Pedestrians & Traffic-Control Measures. (National Cooperative Highway Research Program Report Ser.: No. 139). 76p. 1988. 9.00 (0-317-93786-3) Transport Res Bd.
Pedi-Wheel: Pediatric Emergency Pocket Reference. Joseph Rose. (Illus.). 2p. 1995. 9.95 (0-9658618-0-5) EMS Advan.
Pedi-Wheel First Responder: Pediatric Emergency Pocket Reference. Joe Rose. (Illus.). 2p. 1997. 9.95 (0-9658618-1-3) EMS Advan.
Pediatric Acute Care Handbook. Mary Lieh-Lai. LC 95-9591. 258p. 1995. pap. text 32.00 (0-316-09306-8, Little Brwn Med Div) Lppncott W & W.
Pediatric Adapted Motor Development & Exercise: An Innovative Multisystem Approach for Professionals & Families. Jo E. Cowden et al. LC 97-46392. (Illus.). 346p. 1998. text 66.95 (0-398-06848-8); pap. text 53.95 (0-398-06849-6) C C Thomas.
Pediatric Advanced Life Support. rev. ed. Barbara Aehlert. (Illus.). 240p. (C). (gr. 13). 1996. pap. text, student ed. 13.00 (0-8151-1251-3, 29598) Mosby Inc.
Pediatric Advanced Life Support, 1997-99. (Emergency Cardiovascular Care Programs Ser.). (Illus.). 198p. 1997. pap., teacher ed. 25.00 (0-87493-628-4) Am Heart.
Pediatric Advanced Life Support, 1997-99. American Academy of Pediatrics Staff & American Heart Association Staff. Ed. by Leon Chameides & Mary Fran Hazinski. LC 99-179983. (Emergency Cardiovascular Care Programs Ser.). (Illus.). 150p. 1997. pap. 25.00 (0-87493-619-5) Am Heart.
Pediatric AIDS. Shearer. (C). 2001. text. write for info. (0-7216-8284-7, W B Saunders Co) Harcrt Hlth Sci Grp.
Pediatric AIDS: The Challenge of HIV Infection in Infants, Children & Adolescents. 2nd ed. Philip A. Pizzo & Catherine M. Wilfert. (Illus.). 1088p. 1994. 99.00 (0-683-06895-4) Lppncott W & W.
Pediatric AIDS: The Challenge of HIV Infection in Infants, Children & Adolescents. 3rd ed. Ed. by Philip A. Pizzo & Catherine M. Wilfert. LC 98-6398. 849p. 1998. 99.00 (0-683-30399-6) Lppncott W & W.
Pediatric Airway. Borland. 1992. 39.00 (0-316-10276-8, Little Brwn Med Div) Lppncott W & W.
Pediatric Airway. Othersen. (Illus.). 256p. 1991. text 110.00 (0-7216-2778-1, W B Saunders Co) Harcrt Hlth Sci Grp.
Pediatric Airway: An Interdisciplinary Approach. Ed. by Charles M. Myer et al. (Illus.). 400p. 1994. text 79.00 (0-397-51415-8) Lppncott W & W.
Pediatric Anaerobic Performance. Ed. by Emmanuel Van Praagh. LC 97-38460. (Illus.). 392p. 1998. pap. text 49.00 (0-87322-981-9, BVAN0981) Human Kinetics.
Pediatric & Adolescent AIDS. Scott W. Henggler. 160p. (C). 1992. text 38.95 (0-8039-3982-5); pap. text 18.95 (0-8039-3983-3) Sage.
Pediatric & Adolescent Endocrinology, 2 vols., Vol. 10-11. (Illus.). xxvi, 458p. 1983. 235.00 (3-8055-3681-X) S Karger.
Pediatric & Adolescent Gynecology. Ed. by Sue E. Carpenter & John A. Rock. 496p. 1991. text 80.00 (0-88167-839-2) Lppncott W & W.
Pediatric & Adolescent Gynecology. Susan Pokorny. (Current Topics in Obstetrics & Gynecology Ser.). (Illus.). 250p. 1995. text 80.95 (0-412-99471-2, Pub. by E A) OUP.
Pediatric & Adolescent Gynecology. Ed. by Joseph S. Sanfilippo et al. LC 93-162. (Illus.). 744p. 1993. text 115.00 (0-7216-3971-2, W B Saunders Co) Harcrt Hlth Sci Grp.
Pediatric & Adolescent Gynecology. 2nd ed. Sue Ellen Koehler Carpenter & John A. Rock. 576p. text 89.00 (0-7817-1781-7) Lppncott W & W.
Pediatric & Adolescent Gynecology. 2nd ed. S. Jean Emans & Donald P. Goldstein. 1982. 42.50 (0-316-23402-8, Little Brwn Med Div) Lppncott W & W.
Pediatric & Adolescent Gynecology. 4th ed. S. Jean Herriot Emans et al. LC 97-21996. (Illus.). 640p. 1997. pap. text 59.95 (0-316-23395-1, Little Brwn Med Div) Lppncott W & W.
Pediatric & Adolescent Obstetrics & Gynecology. Ed. by Joseph S. Sanfilippo & J. Patrick Lavery. (Clinical Perspectives in Obstetrics & Gynecology Ser.). (Illus.). 350p. 1985. 89.95 (0-387-96073-2) Spr-Verlag.
Pediatric & Adolescent Sports Medicine. Lyle J. Micheli. 218p. 1984. 62.95 (0-316-56949-6, Little Brwn Med Div) Lppncott W & W.
Pediatric & Adolescent Sports Medicine, Vol. 3. Ed. by Carl L. Stanitski et al. (Illus.). 560p. 1993. text 145.00 (0-7216-3216-5, W B Saunders Co) Harcrt Hlth Sci Grp.
Pediatric & Fundamental Eletrocardiography. Ed. by Jerome Liebman et al. (Developments in Cardiovascular Medicine Ser.). 1987. text 242.00 (0-89838-815-5) Kluwer Academic.
Pediatric & Neonatal Critical Care Certification Review. M. K. Gaedeke. (Illus.). 560p. (C). (gr. 13). 1995. pap. text 36.95 (0-8151-3455-X, 27882) Mosby Inc.
Pediatric & Neonatal Tests & Procedures. H. William Taeusch et al. (Illus.). 560p. 1995. text 98.00 (0-7216-5159-3, W B Saunders Co) Harcrt Hlth Sci Grp.
Pediatric & Obstetrical Anesthesia. Ed. by Theodore H. Stanley & Patricia G. Schafer. LC 94-44630. (DCCA Ser.: Vol. 30). 384p. (C). 1995. text 144.00 (0-7923-3346-2) Kluwer Academic.
Pediatric & Post Partum Home Health Nursing: Assessment & Care Planning. Kathryn A. Melson & Maries S. Jaffe. (Illus.). 496p. (C). (gr. 13). 1996. spiral bd. 29.95 (0-8151-4876-3, 25760) Mosby Inc.
Pediatric & Reconstructive Urologic Surgery. 3rd ed. John Libertino. (Illus.). 800p. (C). (gr. 13). 1997. text 165.00 (0-8016-7802-1, 07802) Mosby Inc.
Pediatric Andrology. Ed. by S. J. Kogan & E. S. Hafez. 220p. 1981. text 220.00 (90-247-2407-4) Kluwer Academic.
Pediatric Anesthesia. Gregory. 2001. text Price not set. (0-443-06561-6) Church.
Pediatric Anesthesia. 3rd ed. Ed. by George A. Gregory. LC 94-2785. 1994. text 152.00 (0-443-08904-3) Church.
Pediatric Anesthesia, Vol. 1. Ed. by George A. Gregory. LC 83-7411. (Illus.). 599p. reprint ed. pap. 185.70 (0-8357-6555-5, 203592100001) Bks Demand.
Pediatric Anesthesia, Vol. 1. 2nd ed. Ed. by George A. Gregory. LC 89-775. (Illus.). 739p. reprint ed. pap. 200.00 (0-7837-6242-9, 204595600001) Bks Demand.
Pediatric Anesthesia, Vol. 2. Ed. by George A. Gregory. LC 83-7411. (Illus.). 515p. reprint ed. pap. 159.70 (0-8357-6556-3, 203592100002) Bks Demand.
Pediatric Anesthesia, Vol. 2. 2nd ed. Ed. by George A. Gregory. LC 89-775. (Illus.). 771p. reprint ed. pap. 200.00 (0-7837-6243-7, 204595600002) Bks Demand.
Pediatric Anesthesia: A Pocket Companion. Edmond C. Bloch. LC 94-30840. 352p. 1999. text 32.50 (0-7506-9602-8) Buttrwrth-Heinemann.
Pediatric Anesthesia: A Quick Pocket Reference. 2nd ed. Edmond C. Bloch & Brian Ginsberg. LC 99-19066. 365p. 1999. pap. text 35.00 (0-7506-7142-4) Buttrwrth-Heinemann.
Pediatric Anesthesia Handbook. 2nd ed. Bell & Hughes. (Illus.). 720p. (C). (gr. 13). 1996. pap. text 44.95 (0-8151-0659-9, 25695) Mosby Inc.
Pediatric Applications of Transcranial Doppler Sonography. H. Bode. (Illus.). 150p. 1988. 49.95 (0-387-82073-6) Spr-Verlag.
Pediatric Association: The Medical Secretary Simulation. 3rd ed. Humphrey. (KF -Office Education Ser.). 1996. mass mkt., student ed. 30.95 (0-538-65376-0) S-W Pub.
***Pediatric Asthma.** H. William Kelly. Ed. by Shirley J. Murphy. LC 98-50991. (Lung Biology in Health & Disease Ser.). (Illus.). 608p. 1999. text 195.00 (0-8247-0208-5) Dekker.
***Pediatric Balance Program.** Martin. (C). 1999. pap. text 45.00 (0-12-785025-2) Acad Pr.
Pediatric Balance Program. Martin. 1998. 45.00 (0-7616-6020-8) Commun Skill.
Pediatric Basic Life Support, 1997-99. (Emergency Cardiovascular Care Programs Ser.). (Illus.). 115p. 1997. pap. 5.00 (0-87493-622-5); pap., teacher ed. 25.00 (0-87493-630-6) Am Heart.
Pediatric Basic Life Support Plus, 1997-99: Emergency Cardiovascular Care Programs. 118p. 1998. pap. 7.50 (0-87493-686-1) Am Heart.
Pediatric Basic Trauma Life Support. Ann Marie Dietrich & Steven Shaner. Ed. by American College of Emergency Physicians, Ohio Chapter Staff. (Illus.). (C). 1995. pap. text 24.95 (0-9647418-0-6) Basic Trauma.
***Pediatric Basic Trauma Life Support Update.** Ann Marie Dietrich & Steven Shaner. Ed. by John Campbell. (Illus.). (C). 1998. pap. text 24.95 (0-9647418-1-4) Basic Trauma.
Pediatric Behavioral Medicine. Ed. by Ben J. Williams et al. LC 81-5875. 277p. 1981. 59.95 (0-275-90742-2, C0742, Praeger Pubs) Greenwood.
Pediatric Behavioral Neurology. Ed. by Yitzchak Frank. LC 95-36119. 432p. 1996. boxed set 149.95 (0-8493-2458-0, 2458) CRC Pr.
Pediatric Bibliography. A. G. Mitchell. (SRCD M Ser.: Vol. 6, No. 1). 1941. 25.00 (0-527-01517-2) Periodicals Srv.
***Pediatric Board Certification Review.** 5th ed. D. Kanjilal. 2000. 149.00 (1-58141-045-X) Rivercross Pub.
***Pediatric Board Certification Review: An Excellent Guide.** 5th ed. D. Kanjilal. LC 00-38743. 2000. write for info. (1-58141-049-2) Rivercross Pub.
Pediatric Board Certification Review: An Excellent Guide : An Essential Tool for Board Certification. 4th ed. D. Kanjilal. LC 98-44615. xxxiii, 658p. 1999. 149.00 (1-58141-034-4) Rivercross Pub.
Pediatric Body CT. A. Daneman. (Illus.). 390p. 1986. 377.00 (0-387-16217-8) Spr-Verlag.
Pediatric Body CT. Ed. by Marilyn J. Siegel. (Contemporary Issues in Computed Tomography Ser.: Vol. 10). (Illus.). 426p. 1987. text 85.00 (0-443-08533-1) Church.
Pediatric Body Ct. Marilyn J. Siegel. LC 99-10469. 386p. 1999. write for info. (0-7817-1249-1) Lppncott W & W.
Pediatric Bone Imaging: A Practical Approach. Soroosh Mahboubi. 1989. 120.00 (0-316-54381-0, Little Brwn Med Div) Lppncott W & W.
Pediatric Brain Death & Organ/Tissue Retrieval: Medical, Ethical & Legal Aspects. H. H. Kaufman. (Illus.). 384p. (C). 1989. text 75.00 (0-306-42973-X, Kluwer Plenum) Kluwer Academic.
Pediatric Brain Injury. Sellars. (C). 1998. pap. text 54.50 (0-12-784582-8) Acad Pr.
Pediatric Brain Injury: The Special Case of the Very Young Child. Carole W. Sellars et al. LC 97-3431. 1997. pap. 29.50 (1-882855-55-8) HDI Pubs.
Pediatric Cancer Sourcebook: Basic Consumer Health Information. Ed. by Edward Prucha. LC 99-41613. (Health Reference Ser.). (Illus.). 600p. 1999. lib. bdg. 78.00 (0-7808-0245-4) Omnigraphics Inc.
Pediatric Cardiac Anesthesia. 3rd ed. Lake. LC 97-11876. 698p. (C). 1998. 150.00 (0-8385-7680-X, A-7680-0, Apple Lange Med) McGraw.
Pediatric Cardiac Imaging. William F. Friedman & Charles B. Higgins. (Illus.). 279p. 1984. text 82.00 (0-7216-1287-3, W B Saunders Co) Harcrt Hlth Sci Grp.
Pediatric Cardiac Intensive Care. Anthony C. Chang et al. LC 97-39558. (Illus.). 512p. 1998. 89.00 (0-683-01508-7) Lppncott W & W.
Pediatric Cardiac Pacing. Ed. by Paul C. Gillette & Vicki L. Zeigler. LC 95-12159. (Illus.). 264p. 1995. 45.00 (0-87993-621-5) Futura Pub.
Pediatric Cardiac Surgery. (C). 2002. 215.00 (0-8385-8177-3) Appleton & Lange.
Pediatric Cardiac Surgery. Ross Ungerleider & James Jaggers. (Vademecum Ser.). 2001. spiral bd. 45.00 (1-57059-576-3) Landes Bioscience.
Pediatric Cardiac Surgery: Current Issues. Ed. by Marshall L. Jacobs & William I. Norwood. (Illus.). 264p. 1992. text 125.00 (0-7506-9061-5) Buttrwrth-Heinemann.
Pediatric Cardiology. E. F. Doyle et al. (Illus.). l, 1340p. 1985. 198.00 (0-387-96204-2) Spr-Verlag.
Pediatric Cardiology. Ed. by Milan Samanek. (Illus.). 464p. 1992. 78.01 (0-08-036860-3, Pub. by PPI) McGraw.
Pediatric Cardiology. 2nd ed. Anderson. 2000. text 375.00 (0-443-07990-0, W B Saunders Co) Harcrt Hlth Sci Grp.
Pediatric Cardiology: A Problem Oriented Approach. Ed. by Ira H. Gessner & Benjamin E. Victorica. LC 92-48475. (Illus.). 352p. 1993. text 58.00 (0-7216-4564-X, W B Saunders Co) Harcrt Hlth Sci Grp.
Pediatric Cardiology: An Introduction. N. Archer & M. Burch. (Illus.). 256p. 1999. text 65.00 (0-412-73450-8, Pub. by E A) OUP.
Pediatric Cardiology & Cardiosurgery. Ed. by G. P. Belloli. (Modern Problems in Pediatrics Ser.: Vol. 22). (Illus.). viii, 216p. 1983. pap. 143.50 (3-8055-3593-7) S Karger.
Pediatric Cardiology for Practitioners. 3rd ed. Myung K. Park. (Illus.). 560p. (C). (gr. 13). 1995. text 69.95 (0-8151-6632-X, 24218) Mosby Inc.
Pediatric Cardiology Handbook. Allan H. Rees et al. (Illus.). 194p. 1987. pap. 23.75 (0-87527-348-3) Green.
Pediatric Cardiology Handbook. 2nd ed. Myung K. Park. (Illus.). 368p. (C). (gr. 13). 1996. pap. text 29.95 (0-8151-9005-0, 29094) Mosby Inc.
Pediatric Cardiology Updates. Ed. by H. C. Lue. (Illus.). 200p. 1997. 85.00 (4-431-70179-6) Spr-Verlag.
Pediatric Cardiopulmonary Transplantation. Ed. by Kenneth L. Franco. LC 96-52001. (Illus.). 416p. 1997. 89.00 (0-87993-397-6) Futura Pub.
Pediatric Cardiovascular Imaging. Tonken. (Illus.). 320p. 1991. text 120.00 (0-7216-3665-9, W B Saunders Co) Harcrt Hlth Sci Grp.
Pediatric Cardiovascular Medicine. Moller. 1999. text 115.00 (0-443-07677-4, W B Saunders Co) Harcrt Hlth Sci Grp.
Pediatric Care of the ICN Graduate. Roberta A. Ballard. (Illus.). 368p. 1988. text 75.00 (0-7216-1404-3, W B Saunders Co) Harcrt Hlth Sci Grp.
Pediatric Care Planning. 3rd ed. Speer. LC 98-37811. 320p. 1998. 34.95 (0-87434-943-5) Springhouse Corp.
Pediatric CheckMate. 2nd rev. ed. Angela G. Clarkson & Anne M. Larson. (Critical Care CheckMate Ser.). (Illus.). 108p. 1997. write for info. (0-9700484-2-4) NNCC.
Pediatric Chiropractic. Claudia A. Anrig & Gregory Plaugher. LC 97-26950. 1997. write for info. (1-68301-361-1) Lppncott W & W.
Pediatric Chiropractic. Claudia Anrig & Gregory Plaugher. LC 97-26950. 789p. 1998. 89.00 (0-683-00136-1) Lppncott W & W.
Pediatric Chiropractic Practice Management. 2nd ed. Jennifer B. Peet & Palmer M. Peet. (Illus.). 187p. (C). 1993. 45.00 (0-9638642-0-3) Baby Adjusters.
Pediatric Clinical Advisor. Lynn Garfunkel. 2000. text 54.95 (0-323-01049-0) Mosby Inc.
Pediatric Clinical Electromyography. H. Royden Jones et al. LC 95-43992. 487p. 1995. text 104.00 (0-7817-0288-7) Lppncott W & W.
Pediatric Clinical Gastroenterology. 4th ed. Claude C. Roy. (Illus.). 970p. 1991. 89.95 (0-8016-6216-8) Mosby Inc.
Pediatric Clinical Gastroenterology. 4th ed. Ed. by Claude C. Roy et al. LC 94-12633. (Illus.). 960p. (C). (gr. 13). 1995. text 120.00 (0-8151-7406-3, 24171) Mosby Inc.
Pediatric Clinical Skills. 2nd ed. Richard B. Goldbloom. LC 96-53606. 1997. pap. text 49.95 (0-443-07927-7) Church.
Pediatric Companion. Harjit Singh. 1996. pap. 79.95 (81-85017-79-4, Pub. by Interprint) St Mut.

P

An Asterisk (*) at the beginning of an entry indicates that the title is appearing for the first time.

Pediatric Compliance: A Guide for the Primary Care Physician. Edward R. Christopherson. LC 93-41063. (Critical Issues in Developmental & Behavioral Pediatrics Ser.). (Illus.). 492p. (C). 1994. text 60.00 (*0-306-44454-2*, Kluwer Plenum) Kluwer Academic.

Pediatric Conscious Sedation: Agents & Procedures-Specific Procedures, 2 vols., Pt. II. Thomas J. Abramo. 84p. (C). (gr. 13). 1995. pap. text 155.00 (*0-8151-0804-4*) Mosby Inc.

Pediatric Conscious Sedation Pt. I: Agents & Procedures, Package. Thomas J. Abramo. 36p. 1996. write for info. (*0-8151-0805-2*) Mosby Inc.

Pediatric Conscious Sedation Pt. II: Specific Procedures: Case Studies, Package. Thomas J. Abramo. 48p. 1996. write for info. (*0-8151-0808-7*) Mosby Inc.

Pediatric Consultation Liaison Psychiatry. Ed. by Charles E. Hollingsworth. LC 82-19744. 294p. 1983. text 29.95 (*0-88331-173-9*) R B Luce.

Pediatric Cranial MRI: An Atlas of Normal Development. John H. Bisese & Ay-Ming Wang. LC 93-47186. (Illus.). 208p. 1994. 165.00 (*0-387-94218-1*) Spr-Verlag.

Pediatric Critical Care. SCCM Staff. 154p. 1999. pap. text 175.00 (*0-7872-5752-4*, 41575201) Kendall-Hunt.

Pediatric Critical Care. 2nd ed. Bradley Fuhrman & Jerry J. Zimmerman. LC 98-148809. (Illus.). 1520p. (C). (gr. 13). 1997. text 169.00 (*0-8151-2536-4*, 30772) Mosby Inc.

Pediatric Critical Care: The Essentials. Ed. by Joseph D. Tobias. LC 98-54112. (Illus.). 480p. 1999. 75.00 (*0-87993-428-X*) Futura Pub.

Pediatric Critical Care Nursing. Janis B. Smith. LC 83-10218. (Critical Care Nursing Ser.). (Illus.). 500p. (Orig.). (C). 1989. pap. text 36.95 (*0-8273-4374-4*) Delmar.

Pediatric Cytopathology. Kim Geissinger. (Illus.). 365p. 1995. 90.00 (*0-89189-378-4*) Am Soc Clinical.

Pediatric Day Case Surgery. Ed. by N. S. Morton & P. A. Raine. (Illus.). 130p. 1994. text 69.50 (*0-19-262256-0*) OUP.

Pediatric Decision Making. Pomeranz. (C). 2000. pap. text. write for info. (*0-7216-8246-4*, W B Saunders Co) Harcrt Hlth Sci Grp.

Pediatric Decision Making. 3rd ed. Stephen Berman. (Illus.). 704p. (C). (gr. 13). 1996. text 76.95 (*0-8151-0715-3*, 27677) Mosby Inc.

***Pediatric Dental Care in CHIP & Medicaid: Paying for What Kids Need, Getting Value for State Payments.** Frwd. by John M. Colmers et al. 36p. 1999. pap. write for info. (*1-887748-28-8*) Milbank Memorial.

Pediatric Dental Medicine. Ed. by Donald J. Forrester et al. LC 80-10694. 708p. reprint ed. pap. 200.00 (*0-7837-2701-1*, 204308000006) Bks Demand.

Pediatric Dentistry. Cameron. 1997. text 44.95 (*0-7234-3068-3*) Mosby Inc.

Pediatric Dentistry: Infancy Through Adolescence. 2nd ed. Ed. by James R. Pinkham et al. LC 92-49086. (Illus.). 576p. 1993. text 70.00 (*0-7216-4695-6*, W B Saunders Co) Harcrt Hlth Sci Grp.

Pediatric Dentistry: Infancy Through Adolescence. 3rd ed. J. R. Pinkham et al. Ed. by Judy Fletcher. LC 99-24326. (Illus.). 670p. (C). 1999. text. write for info. (*0-7216-8238-3*, W B Saunders Co) Harcrt Hlth Sci Grp.

Pediatric Dermatology, 2 vols. 2nd ed. Ed. by Lawrence A. Schachner & Ronald C. Hansen. 1511p. 1995. text 375.00 (*0-443-08921-3*) Church.

Pediatric Dermatology, 2 vols., Set. Ed. by Lawrence A. Schachner & Ronald C. Hansen. (Illus.). 1674p. 1988. text 325.00 (*0-443-08432-7*) Church.

Pediatric Dermatology: Proceedings of the IVth International Congress of Pediatric Dermatology, June 7-10, 1986, Tokyo. International Congress of Pediatric Dermatology St. Ed. by Harukuni Urabe et al. LC RJ0511.. 659p. 1987. reprint ed. pap. 200.00 (*0-608-01564-4*, 206198100001) Bks Demand.

Pediatric Dermatology - The World's Reality in the Children's Skin: Proceedings of the 7th International Congress of Pediatric Dermatology, Buenos Aires, September 27-October 1, 1994. International Congress of Pediatric Dermatology St. Ed. by Adrian-Martin Pierini et al. LC 95-37760. (International Congress Ser.: No. 1073). 372p. 1995. 191.50 (*0-444-81917-7*) Elsevier.

Pediatric Dermatology & Dermatopathology, Vol. 3. Ruggero Caputo et al. (Illus.). 516p. 1995. 165.00 (*0-683-01437-4*) Lppncott W & W.

Pediatric Dermatology & Dermatopathology, Vol. IV. Ruggero Caputo et al. (Illus.). 476p. 1995. 165.00 (*0-683-01438-2*) Lppncott W & W.

Pediatric Dermatology & Dermatopathology: A Text & Atlas. Ruggero Caputo et al. LC 88-36885. (Illus.). 391p. write for info. (*0-8121-1166-4*); write for info. (*0-8121-1314-4*); text 150.00 (*0-318-67251-0*) Lppncott W & W.

Pediatric Dermatology & Dermatopathology: A Text & Atlas, IV. Ruggero Caputo et al. LC 88-36885. (Illus.). 391p. write for info. (*0-8121-1316-0*) Lppncott W & W.

Pediatric Dermatology & Internal Medicine: Internal Medicine & External Medicine, Proceedings. Congress of Pediatric Dermatology, 2nd, Mexico Cit. Ed. by Ramon Ruiz-Maldonado. (Modern Problems in Pediatrics Ser.: Vol. 20). (Illus.). 1978. 85.25 (*3-8055-2703-9*) S Karger.

Pediatric Dermatopathology: Clinical & Pathologic Correlations. Bernett L. Johnson et al. (Illus.). 334p. 1994. text 215.00 (*0-7506-9264-2*) Buttrwrth-Heinemann.

Pediatric Diagnosis. 6th ed. Green. (C). 1998. text. write for info. (*0-8089-2086-3*, Grune & Strat) Harcrt Hlth Sci Grp.

Pediatric Diagnosis: Intrepretation of Symptoms & Signs in Children & Adolescent. 6th ed. Morris Green. Ed. by Judy Fletcher. LC 97-33312. (Illus.). 464p. (C). 1998. text 62.00 (*0-7216-7284-1*, W B Saunders Co) Harcrt Hlth Sci Grp.

Pediatric Diagnosis & Treatment. N. M. Jacoby. Date not set. 54.95 (*0-8464-4461-5*) Beekman Pubs.

Pediatric Disease (Fourth Series) Test & Syllabus. Marilyn J. Siegel et al. (Professional Self-Evaluation & Continuing Education Program Ser.: Vol. 35). (Illus.). 800p. 1993. 220.00 (*1-55903-035-6*) Am Coll Radiology.

Pediatric Disease (Third Series) Test & Syllabus. Thomas E. Sumner et al. (Professional Self-Evaluation & Continuing Education Program Ser.: Vol. 26). (Illus.). 800p. (C). 1989. 165.00 (*1-55903-026-7*) Am Coll Radiology.

***Pediatric Disorders of Regulation in Affect & Behavior: A Therapist's Guide to Assessment & Treatment.** Georgia A. Degangi. 316p. 2000. pap. 54.95 (*0-12-208770-4*) Acad Pr.

Pediatric Dosage Handbook, 1998-1999. 5th ed. Carol K. Taketomo et al. (Clinical Reference Library). 1998. pap. 35.95 (*0-916589-64-1*) Lexi-Comp.

Pediatric Drug Formulations. 3rd ed. Milap C. Nahata & Thomas F. Hipple. LC 97-22898. xvi, 118p. (Orig.). 1997. pap. text 31.95 (*0-929375-19-X*) H W Bks.

Pediatric Drug Handbook. 3rd ed. William E. Benitz & Davis S. Tatro. LC 95-6862. (Illus.). 688p. (C). (gr. 13). 1995. pap. text 34.95 (*0-8151-0665-3*, 24727) Mosby Inc.

Pediatric Drug Reference: Current Clinical Strategies. Jane Gennrich. 80p. 1996. pap. 8.75 (*1-881528-22-7*) Current Clin Strat.

***Pediatric Drug Reference: 2000 Edition.** rev. ed. Jane Gennrich. (Current Clinical Strategies Ser.). 88p. 2000. pap. 28.95 incl. cd-rom (*1-881528-76-6*) Current Clin Strat.

Pediatric Drug Reference, Year 2000 Edition: Current Clinical Strategies. rev. ed. Ed. by Jane Gennrich. (Current Clinical Strategies Ser.). 88p. 1998. pap. 8.95 (*1-881528-75-8*) Current Clin Strat.

Pediatric Drugs & Nursing Implications. 2nd rev. ed. Ruth M. Bindler & Linda Berner Howry. LC 96-18530. 640p. (C). 1996. pap. text 39.95 (*0-8385-8085-8*, A8085-1) Appleton & Lange.

Pediatric Drugs & Nursing Intervention. Helen Russell. (Illus.). 1979. text 20.95 (*0-07-054298-8*) McGraw.

Pediatric Dypshagia: Assessment & Intervention Considerations for Children & Young Adults. Joan C. Arvedson et al. 157p. 1998. 72.00 incl. audio (*1-58041-021-9*, 0112156) Am Speech Lang Hearing.

Pediatric Dysphagia: Management Challenges for the School-Based Speech-Language Pathologist. Joan C. Arvedson & Brian T. Rogers. 1998. 110.00 incl. VHS (*1-58041-018-9*, 0112094) Am Speech Lang Hearing.

Pediatric Early Elementary Examination (PEEX 2) 2nd rev. ed. Mel Levine. Ed. by Diane Winkleby. 80p. 1996. pap. 15.40 (*0-8388-2806-X*, 82806) Ed Pub Serv.

***Pediatric ECG Interpreation - A Self Study Text.** 3rd rev. ed. Susan Duszynski. Ed. by Becki Jo Hirshy-Wolkenheim. (Illus.). 189p. 2000. pap. 65.00 (*1-930605-01-3*, 106003) Maxishare.

***Pediatric Echocardiographers Pocket Reference.** Terry Reynolds. Ed. by Yeng Pan & Patricia Dubovec. (Illus.). 250p. 1999. 64.95 (*0-9635767-7-1*) AZ Heart Inst.

Pediatric Echocardiography. David T. Linker. (Illus.). 315p. 1998. text. write for info. (*0-443-07640-5*) Church.

Pediatric Echocardiography. Norman H. Silverman. (Illus.). 640p. 1993. 145.00 (*0-683-07713-9*) Lppncott W & W.

Pediatric EEG. American Journal of END Technology Staff. (Illus.). 1998. per. 28.00 (*1-57797-009-8*) ASET.

Pediatric Emergencies. Ed. by Stephen Ludwig. (Clinics in Emergency Medicine Ser.: Vol. 7). (Illus.). 266p. 1985. text 48.00 (*0-443-08303-7*) Church.

Pediatric Emergencies. 2nd ed. Clark. 1997. pap., teacher ed. 46.00 (*0-8359-5129-4*) P-H.

Pediatric Emergencies. 2nd ed. Pratsch. Ed. by Martin Eichelberger. LC 97-6025. 272p. 1997. pap. text 51.00 (*0-8359-5123-5*) P-H.

Pediatric Emergencies: A Handbook for Nurses. Mary E. Connal & Beverly A. Johnson. 312p. 1990. 69.00 (*0-8342-0102-X*, 20102) Aspen Pub.

Pediatric Emergencies: A Manual for Pre-Hospital Care Providers. Martin R. Eichelberger et al. 240p. 1991. pap. text 28.00 (*0-685-50511-1*) P-H.

***Pediatric Emergencies for Prehospital Personnel.** M. S. Aapro. (Illus.). 256p. (C). 2000. pap. text 36.25 (*0-7637-1219-1*) JB Pubns.

Pediatric Emergency Management: Guidelines for Rapid Diagnosis. Ed. by Stanley Cohen. (Illus.). 416p. (C). 1982. text 32.95 (*0-87619-924-4*) P-H.

Pediatric Emergency Medicine. Earl J. Reisdorff et al. (Illus.). 1190p. 1992. text 164.00 (*0-7216-3281-5*, W B Saunders Co) Harcrt Hlth Sci Grp.

Pediatric Emergency Medicine. 4th ed. Gary R. Fleisher & Stephen Ludwig. LC 99-15002. 1,964p. 1999. text 159.00 (*0-683-30609-X*) Lppncott W & W.

Pediatric Emergency Medicine: A Clinician's Reference. Moses Grossman & Ronald A. Dieckmann. (Illus.). 732p. 1991. spiral bd. 55.00 (*0-397-51017-9*) Lppncott W & W.

Pediatric Emergency Medicine: A Comprehensive Study Guide. Ed. by Gary R. Strange et al. LC 95-7448. (Illus.). 750p. 1995. pap. 68.00 (*0-07-062007-5*) McGraw-Hill HPD.

Pediatric Emergency Medicine: Companion Handbook. Ed. by Gary Strange et al. LC 98-21037. (Illus.). 976p. 1999. pap. text 32.00 (*0-07-062008-3*) McGraw-Hill HPD.

Pediatric Emergency Medicine: Concepts & Clinical Practice. 2nd ed. Roger M. Barkinq. LC 97-10646l. (Illus.). 1328p. (C). (gr. 13). 1996. text 169.00 (*0-8151-1002-2*, 29256) Mosby Inc.

Pediatric Emergency Medicine: Self-Assessment & Review. 2nd ed. David H. Rubin & Roger M. Barkin. LC 98-6926. 1998. 29.95 (*1-55664-453-1*) Mosby Inc.

Pediatric Emergency Medicine Package. Roger M. Barkin & Peter Rosen. 1997. write for info. (*0-8151-2125-3*) Mosby Inc.

Pediatric Emergency Medicine Pearls of Wisdom. Turnstall Smith et al. (Pearls of Wisdom Ser.). 1999. pap. write for info. (*1-890369-14-4*) Boston Medical.

Pediatric Emergency Nursing. David Crosley. Ed. by M. Rosanna Rodriguez. 138p. 1997. pap. write for info. (*1-57801-011-X*) Western Schls.

Pediatric Emergency Nursing. 2nd ed. Susan J. Kelley. (Illus.). 571p. (C). 1995. pap. text 59.95 (*0-8385-7705-9*, A7705-5, Apple Lange Med) McGraw.

Pediatric Emergency Nursing Manual. Ed. by Deborah Henderson & Dena Brownstein. (Illus.). 352p. (C). 1994. pap. text 49.95 (*0-8261-8330-1*) Springer Pub.

Pediatric Emergency Nursing Procedures. Lisa Marie Bernardo. (Nursing-Health Science Ser.). 1992. pap. text 42.50 (*0-86720-330-7*) Jones & Bartlett.

Pediatric Endocrine Disorders. Wales. 1995. text 92.95 (*0-7234-2137-4*) Mosby Inc.

Pediatric Endocrinology. (Journal: Hormone Research Ser.: Vol. 22, No. 1-2, 1985). (Illus.). 128p. 1986. pap. 102.75 (*3-8055-4415-4*) S Karger.

Pediatric Endocrinology. Maria I. New. Ed. by C. Pintor et al. (Illus.). 256p. 1993. 242.00 (*0-387-54321-X*) Spr-Verlag.

Pediatric Endocrinology. Mark A. Sperling. Ed. by Lisette Bralow & Judy Fletcher. LC 95-37080. 608p. 1996. text 95.00 (*0-7216-5522-X*, W B Saunders Co) Harcrt Hlth Sci Grp.

Pediatric Endocrinology. Ed. by Robert Collu et al. LC 85-43385. (Comprehensive Endocrinology Ser.). 704p. 1989. reprint ed. pap. 200.00 (*0-608-03398-7*, 206409500008) Bks Demand.

Pediatric Endocrinology: A Clinical Guide. 3rd expanded rev. ed. Ed. by Fima Lifshitz. (Clinical Pediatrics Ser.: Vol. 8). (Illus.). 992p. 1995. text 215.00 (*0-8247-9369-2*) Dekker.

Pediatric Endocrinology: Physiology, Pathophysiolgy & Clinical Aspects. 2nd ed. Ed. by Jean Bertrand et al. LC 92-49159. (Illus.). 768p. 1993. 129.00 (*0-683-00609-6*) Lppncott W & W.

Pediatric Endoscopic Surgery. James W. Holcolmb, III. (Illus.). 180p. (C). 1993. pap. text 125.00 (*0-8385-8047-5*, A8047-1, Apple Lange Med) McGraw.

Pediatric Enteral Nutrition. Susan S. Baker & Anne Davis. 1993. text 69.95 (*0-442-01341-8*) Chapman & Hall.

Pediatric Epilepsy: Diagnosis & Therapy. Ed. by W. Edward Dodson & John M. Pellock. 464p. 1993. pap. 95.00 (*0-939957-33-7*) Demos Medical.

***Pediatric Epilepsy & Epilepsy Surgery.** Ed. by G. W. Mathern. (Developmental Neuroscience Ser.: Vol. 21, No. 3-5). (Illus.). 250p. 1999. pap. 48.75 (*3-8055-6925-4*) S Karger.

Pediatric Ethics - From Principles to Practice. Ed. by Robert C. Cassidy & Alan R. Fleischman. (Mongraphs in Clinical Pediatrics Ser.). 224p. 1996. text 36.00 (*3-7186-5756-2*, Harwood Acad Pubs) Gordon & Breach.

Pediatric Examination. 3rd ed. Gill. (C). 1998. pap. text 22.00 (*0-443-05961-6*) Church.

Pediatric Eye Care. Ed. by Simon Barnard & David Edgar. (Illus.). 288p. 1995. 125.00 (*0-632-03979-5*) Blackwell Sci.

Pediatric Facial Plastic & Reconstructive Surgery. Ed. by James D. Smith & Robert M. Bumsted. LC 92-49735. 416p. 1992. text 163.00 (*0-88167-973-9*) Lppncott W & W.

Pediatric Foot & Ankle Surgery. Richard M. Jay. Ed. by Stephanie Donley. LC 98-31651. (Illus.). 395p. 1999. text. write for info. (*0-7216-7445-3*, W B Saunders Co) Harcrt Hlth Sci Grp.

Pediatric Fractures: A Practical Approach to Assessment & Treatment. Ed. by G. Dean MacEwen et al. LC 92-48218. (Illus.). 464p. 1993. 120.00 (*0-683-05310-8*) Lppncott W & W.

Pediatric Gastroenterology. Ed. by D. Branski et al. (Frontiers of Gastrointestinal Research Ser.: Vol. 13). (Illus.). viii, 416p. 1986. 292.25 (*3-8055-4331-X*) S Karger.

***Pediatric Gastroenterology & Clinical Nutrition.** Donald Bentley et al. (Illus.). 304p. 2000. text 165.00 (*0-19-262808-9*) OUP.

Pediatric Gastroenterology & Hepatology. 3rd ed. Michael Gracey & V. Burke. (Illus.). 1168p. 1993. 265.00 (*0-86542-238-9*) Blackwell Sci.

Pediatric Gastrointestinal Disease. 2nd ed. Robert Wyllie & Jeffrey S. Hyams. Ed. by Judy Fletcher. LC 98-28621. (Illus.). xviii, 805p. 1999. text 145.00 (*0-7216-7461-5*, W B Saunders Co) Harcrt Hlth Sci Grp.

Pediatric Gastrointestinal Diseases, 2 vols., Set. W. Allan Walker. 1990. 298.00 (*1-55664-209-1*) Mosby Inc.

Pediatric Gastrointestinal Diseases: Pathophysiology, Diagnosis, Management. Ed. by Robert Wyllie & Jeffrey S. Hyams. LC 92-11720. (Illus.). 1248p. 1993. text 210.00 (*0-7216-3128-2*, W B Saunders Co) Harcrt Hlth Sci Grp.

***Pediatric Gastrointestinal Imaging & Intervention.** David A. Stringer & Paul S. Babyn. (Illus.). 700p. 1999. boxed set 199.00 incl. cd-rom (*1-55009-079-8*) DEKR.

Pediatric GI Problems. Paul E. Hyman. LC 96-23054. (Gastroenterology & Hepatology Ser.: Vol. 4). 1996. text 90.00 (*0-443-07852-1*) Church.

Pediatric Head Injuries Handbook. A. Loren Amacher. (Illus.). 138p. 1988. pap. 24.50 (*0-87527-337-8*) Green.

Pediatric Health Certification: Exam Review. Beverly Rothfeld. LC 98-22075. 196p. (C). 1998. pap. text 39.95 (*0-8385-8137-4*, A-8137-0) Appleton & Lange.

Pediatric Heart Surgeon & Facility Directory: Profiles of Individual Surgeons & Congenital Heart Programs. Ed. by James H. Myers. LC 97-68297. (Illus.). 128p. 1997. pap. 40.00 (*0-9658918-0-1*) CHASER.

Pediatric Hematology. 2nd ed. John S. Lilleyman. (C). 1999. text 225.00 (*0-443-05840-7*, W B Saunders Co) Harcrt Hlth Sci Grp.

Pediatric Hepatology. W. F. Balisterri & J. Thomas Stocker. 1990. 250.00 (*0-89116-738-2*) Hemisp Pub.

***Pediatric History & Physical Examination.** 4th ed. Elizabeth K. Albright. (Current Clinical Strategies Ser.). 90p. 2000. pap. 9.95 (*1-881528-92-8*) Current Clin Strat.

***Pediatric History & Physical Examination: 2000 Edition.** rev. ed. Elizabeth K. Albright. (Current Clinical Strategies Ser.). 90p. 2000. pap. 28.95 (*1-881528-93-6*) Current Clin Strat.

***Pediatric HIV.** Ed. by Jay P. Shah et al. 425p. 2000. 99.50 (*0-89603-814-9*) Humana.

Pediatric Home Care. 2nd ed. Wendy Votroubek & Julie Townsend. LC 97-18624. 450p. 1997. 60.00 (*0-8342-0884-9*, 20884) Aspen Pub.

Pediatric Home Care Manual. Mary Ann Chestnut. LC 97-25843. 208p. 1997. pap. text 36.95 (*0-7817-1203-3*) Lppncott W & W.

Pediatric Home Companion: Commonsense Advice about Your Child's Health. Lisa Wiseman. LC 97-22119. 178p. 1997. 15.00 (*1-57626-036-4*) Quality Med Pub.

Pediatric Hospice Care: What Helps. Intro. by Belinda B. Martin. (Illus.). 400p. (C). 1989. write for info. (*0-9623727-0-6*) Child Hosp LA.

Pediatric Hospitalization: Family & Nurse Perspectives. Kathleen A. Knafl et al. 326p. (C). 1988. text 23.00 (*0-673-39732-7*) Lppncott W & W.

Pediatric Hypertension. Ed. by Uri Alon & N. G. DeSanto. (Child Nephrology & Urology Journal: Vol. 12, No. 2-3, 1992). (Illus.). 112p. 1992. pap. 55.75 (*3-8055-5608-X*) S Karger.

Pediatric Images: Casebook of Differential Diagnosis. Eugene Blank. LC 97-4093. (Illus.). 1100p. 1997. text 185.00 (*0-316-09991-0*) Lppncott W & W.

Pediatric Imaging. Cecile Godderidge. LC 94-12234. (Contemporary Imaging Techniques Ser.). 256p. 1995. text 49.95 (*0-7216-4534-8*, W B Saunders Co) Harcrt Hlth Sci Grp.

***Pediatric Imaging: Case Review.** Hans Blickman. (Illus.). 224p. (C). 1999. text. write for info. (*0-323-00505-5*) Mosby Inc.

Pediatric Imaging - Doppler Ultrasound of the Chest: Extracardiac Diagnosis. James C. Huhta. LC 86-2806. 269p. reprint ed. pap. 83.40 (*0-7837-2717-8*, 204309700006) Bks Demand.

Pediatric Imaging for the Technologist. Ed. by D. M. Wilmot & G. A. Sharko. (Illus.). xvii, 285p. 1987. 131.00 (*0-387-96439-8*) Spr-Verlag.

Pediatric Immunology. Ed. by Z. Spirer et al. (Pediatric & Adolescent Medicine Ser.: Vol. 3). (Illus.). x, 228p. 1993. 233.25 (*3-8055-5647-0*) S Karger.

Pediatric Infectious Diseases. Ed. by D. Engelhard et al. (Pediatric & Adolescent Medicine Ser.: Vol. 4). (Illus.). viii, 226p. 1993. 233.25 (*3-8055-5697-7*) S Karger.

Pediatric Infectious Diseases. Jenson. (C). Date not set. text. write for info. (*0-7216-8121-2*) Church.

Pediatric Infectious Diseases: A Comprehensive Guide to the Subspecialty. Gary J. Noel et al. LC 96-31925. (Illus.). 336p. 1997. text 65.00 (*0-8018-5563-2*); pap. text 28.95 (*0-8018-5564-0*) Johns Hopkins.

Pediatric Infectious Diseases: A Problem Oriented Approach. 3rd ed. Hugh L. Moffet. LC 65-10986. (Illus.). 640p. 1989. text 56.00 (*0-397-50933-2*, Lippnctt) Lppncott W & W.

Pediatric Infectious Diseases: Principles & Practices. Hal Jenson & Robert S. Baltimore. 1593p. (C). 1996. pap. text 195.00 (*0-8385-2474-5*, A2474-3, Apple Lange Med) McGraw.

Pediatric Infectious Diseases for the Practitioner. M. I. Marks. (Comprehensive Manuals in Pediatrics Ser.: Vol. 3). (Illus.). 890p. 1984. 185.00 (*0-387-96010-4*) Spr-Verlag.

Pediatric Intensive Care. Ed. by Alan Duncan et al. (Illus.). 288p. 1998. pap. 52.00 (*0-7279-1073-6*, Pub. by BMJ Pub) Login Brothers Bk Co.

Pediatric Intensive Care. Jeffrey P. Morray. (Illus.). 581p. (C). 1992. pap. text 115.00 (*0-8385-7800-4*, A7800-4, Apple Lange Med) McGraw.

Pediatric Intensive Care Unit. Carol Hurst. 208p. 1998. spiral bd. 125.00 (*1-879575-93-0*) Acad Med Sys.

Pediatric Interventional Radiology. Richard Towbin. (Illus.). 528p. 2000. 95.00 (*0-86577-617-2*) Thieme Med Pubs.

Pediatric Kidney Disease, 2 vols., Set. 2nd ed. Ed. by Chester M. Edelmann et al. LC 91-43804. 2225p. 1992. text 409.00 (*0-316-21072-2*, RJ476, Little Brwn Med Div) Lppncott W & W.

Pediatric Laboratory Exercise Testing: Clinical Guidelines. Ed. by Thomas W. Rowland. LC 92-1575. (Illus.). 216p. 1992. text 33.00 (*0-87322-380-2*, BROW0380) Human Kinetics.

Pediatric Laparoscopy & Thoracoscopy. Thom E. Lobe & Kurt P. Schropp. (Illus.). 272p. 1993. text 102.00 (*0-7216-4610-7*, W B Saunders Co) Harcrt Hlth Sci Grp.

Pediatric Laryngology & Bronchoesophagology. Lauren Holinger. LC 96-8295. 350p. 1996. text 188.00 (*0-397-51650-9*) Lppncott W & W.

Pediatric Length of Stay by Diagnosis & Operation. 1995. write for info. (*1-57372-008-9*) HCIA.

Pediatric Length of Stay by Diagnosis & Operation. 1996. write for info. (*1-57372-041-0*) HCIA.

P

Pediatric Length of Stay by Diagnosis & Operation, United States, 1986. Commission on Professional & Hospital Activities S. LC 88-647491. 314p. reprint ed. pap. 97.40 (*0-8357-8614-5*, 203503900091) Bks Demand.

Pediatric Length of Stay by Diagnosis & Operation, United States, 1987. Commission on Professional & Hospital Activities S. LC 88-647491. 330p. reprint ed. pap. 102.30 (*0-8357-6833-3*, 203552000095) Bks Demand.

Pediatric Length of Stay by Diagnosis & Operation, United States, 1988. Commission on Professional & Hospital Activities S. LC 88-647491. 361p. reprint ed. pap. 112.00 (*0-7837-1813-6*, 204201300001) Bks Demand.

Pediatric Lung. Ed. by R. W. Wilmott. (Respiratory Pharmacology & Pharmacotherapy Ser.). 350p. 1997. text 175.00 (*3-7643-5703-7*) Birkhauser.

Pediatric Lung Disease: Diagnosis & Management. Gerald M. Loughlin & Howard Eigen. LC 93-1902. (Illus.). 862p. 1994. reprint ed. 125.00 (*0-683-05190-3*) Lppncott W & W.

Pediatric Magnetic Resonance Imaging. Mervyn D. Cohen. (Illus.). 162p. 1986. text 86.00 (*0-7216-1396-9*, W B Saunders Co) Harcrt Hlth Sci Grp.

Pediatric Manual of Clinical Dietetics. American Dietetic Association Staff. LC 97-33561. 1997. write for info. (*0-88091-160-3*) Am Dietetic Assn.

Pediatric Massage. Drehobl. 1998. pap. 36.00 (*0-12-784569-0*) Acad Pr.

***Pediatric Massage for the Child with Special Needs.** rev. ed. Kathy Fleming Drehobl & Mary Gengler Fuhr. LC 00-8442. 2000. pap. write for info. (*0-7616-4092-4*, Thrpy Skill Bldrs) Commun Skill.

Pediatric Massage Manual: For the Child with Special Needs. Kathy F. Drehobl & Mary G. Fuhr. (Illus.). 128p. 1991. pap. text 38.00 (*0-7616-4703-1*) Commun Skill.

Pediatric Medical Student Pearls of Wisdom. Levin & Emblad. (Pearls of Wisdom Ser.). 1999. pap. 32.00 (*1-890369-24-1*) Boston Medical.

Pediatric Medication Education Text. Marcia L. Buck & Anne Hendrick. Tr. by Babel Communications Staff from SPA.Tr. of Texto Educativo de Medicamentos Pediatricos. 200p. (Orig.). 1997. pap. 35.00 (*1-880401-89-4*) Amer Coll of Clin.

Pediatric Medications: A Handbook for Nurses. Suanne Miller & Joanne Fioravanti. (Illus.). 864p. (C). 1997. text. write for info. (*1-55664-482-5*) Mosby Inc.

Pediatric Medicine. 2nd ed. Mary E. Avery & Lewis R. First. (Illus.). 1632p. 1994. 99.00 (*0-683-00293-7*) Lppncott W & W.

Pediatric Molecular Pathology. Ed. by A. J. Garvin et al. (Perspectives in Pediatric Pathology Ser.: Vol. 15). (Illus.). vi, 248p. 1991. 233.25 (*3-8055-5377-3*) S Karger.

Pediatric Molecular Pathology: Quantitation & Applications. Ed. by H. S. Rosenberg et al. (Perspectives in Pediatric Pathology Ser.: Vol. 16). (Illus.). xii, 170p. 1992. 182.75 (*3-8055-5496-6*) S Karger.

Pediatric MRI. Ed. by Rosalind B. Dietrich. (MRI Teaching File Ser.). 256p. 1991. text 76.00 (*0-88167-708-6*) Lppncott W & W.

Pediatric-Neonatal Review Book. rev. ed. Hill et al. 468p. (C). 1994. pap. 49.95 (*0-933195-50-8*) CA College Health Sci.

Pediatric Neoplasia: Morphology & Biology. Ed. by David M. Parham. LC 95-42517. 576p. 1996. text 187.00 (*0-7817-0273-9*) Lppncott W & W.

Pediatric Nephrology. Ed. by A. Drukker & A. B. Gruskin. (Pediatric & Adolescent Medicine Ser.: Vol. 5). (Illus.). x, 242p. 1994. 238.50 (*3-8055-5835-X*) S Karger.

Pediatric Nephrology. Ed. by Howard Trachtman & Bernard Gauthier. (Monographs in Clinical Pediatrics: Vol. 10). 420p. 1998. text 72.00 (*90-5702-273-7*, Harwood Acad Pubs) Gordon & Breach.

Pediatric Nephrology. 3rd ed. Ed. by Malcolm A. Holliday et al. LC 93-451. (Illus.). 1520p. 1994. 190.00 (*0-683-04104-5*) Lppncott W & W.

Pediatric Nephrology. 4th ed. T. Martin Barratt et al. LC 97-48546. 1998. 189.00 (*0-683-30055-5*) Lppncott W & W.

Pediatric Nephrology: Proceedings of the Pediatric Nephrology International Symposium, 5th, 1980, No. 3. Pediatric Nephrology International Symposium Staff. Ed. by Alan B. Gruskin & Michael E. Norman. 530p. 1981. text 211.50 (*90-247-2514-3*) Kluwer Academic.

Pediatric Neurimaging. William S. Ball. LC 97-7705. 816p. 1997. text 175.00 (*0-316-07987-1*) Lppncott W & W.

Pediatric Neuro-Oncology: New Trends in Clinical Research. Ed. by Roger J. Packer et al. LC 90-4990. (Monographs in Clinical Pediatrics: Vol. 3). 320p. 1991. text 143.00 (*3-7186-0524-4*) Gordon & Breach.

Pediatric Neuro-Ophthalmology. Robert L. Tomsak. LC 94-24894. (Illus.). 204p. 1994. text 95.00 (*0-7506-9315-0*) Buttrwrth-Heinemann.

Pediatric Neuroimaging. 2nd ed. A. James Barkovich. LC 94-9720. 688p. 1994. text 175.00 (*0-7817-0179-1*) Lppncott W & W.

Pediatric Neuroimaging: A Casebook Approach. Charles L. Truwit. (Illus.). 290p. 1992. 89.00 (*0-683-08400-3*) Lppncott W & W.

Pediatric Neurologic Physical Therapy. 2nd ed. Ed. by Suzann K. Campbell. (Clinics in Physical Therapy Ser.). (Illus.). 459p. 1991. text 60.00 (*0-443-08764-4*) Church.

Pediatric Neurological Surgery: Sponsored by the Subcommittee on Continuing Education II (Expanded Program), American Association of Neurological Surgeons & Congress of Neurological Surgeons. fac. ed. Ed. by Mark S. O'Brien. LC 78-3005. (Seminars in Neurological Surgery Ser.). (Illus.). 216p. pap. 67.00 (*0-7837-7277-7*, 204702900005) Bks Demand.

Pediatric Neurology. 3rd ed. Edward M. Brett. LC 97-3033. 1997. text 240.00 (*0-443-05200-X*) Church.

Pediatric Neurology: Behavior & Cognition of the Child with Brain Dysfunction. Ed. by Naomi Amir et al. (Pediatric & Adolescent Medicine Ser.: Vol. 1). (Illus.). x, 186p. 1991. 151.50 (*3-8055-5223-8*) S Karger.

Pediatric Neurology: Principles & Practice, 2 vols. 2nd ed. Ed. by Kenneth F. Swaiman. LC 93-25352. (Illus.). 1696p. (C). (gr. 13). 1993. text 263.00 (*0-8016-6695-3*, 06695) Mosby Inc.

Pediatric Neurology: Principles & Practice. 3rd ed. Ed. by Kenneth F. Swaiman & Stephen Ashwal. LC 99-27972. (Illus.). 1678p. 1999. text 250.00 (*0-8151-3097-X*, 31787) Mosby Inc.

Pediatric Neurology: Theory & Praxis. Ed. by C. P. Panteliadis & B. T. Darras. (Illus.). x, 684p. 1995. 170.50 (*3-8055-6287-X*) S Karger.

Pediatric Neuroophthalmology. Michael C. Brodsky et al. LC 95-16249. (Illus.). 552p. 1995. 160.00 (*0-387-94464-8*) Spr-Verlag.

Pediatric Neuropathology. Ed. by Serge Duckett. LC 93-40970. (Illus.). 1500p. 1994. 169.00 (*0-683-02680-1*) Lppncott W & W.

Pediatric Neuropsychology: Interfacing Assessment & Treatment for Rehabilitation. Ed. by Ervin S. Batchelor, Jr. & Raymond S. Dean. 384p. 1995. pap. text 39.80 (*0-205-16486-2*, Longwood Div) Allyn.

***Pediatric Neuropsychology: Research, Theory & Practice.** Ed. by Keith Owen Yeates et al. (Science & Practice of Neuropsychology Ser.). 425p. 1999. lib. bdg. 62.50 (*1-57230-507-X*, C0507) Guilford Pubns.

Pediatric Neuropsychology in a Medical Setting. Ida S. Baron et al. (Illus.). 464p. 1995. text 59.50 (*0-19-506345-7*) OUP.

Pediatric Neurosonography. Asma Q. Fisher et al. 267p. 1985. text 57.00 (*0-471-89252-1*) Church.

Pediatric Neurosurgery. Ed. by M. Choux et al. LC 98-11502. (Illus.). 700p. 1998. write for info. (*0-443-06149-1*, W B Saunders Co) Harcrt Hlth Sci Grp.

Pediatric Neurosurgery. Anthony J. Raimondi. (Illus.). 550p. 1987. 479.00 (*0-387-96408-8*) Spr-Verlag.

Pediatric Neurosurgery: Proceedings. Congress of the European Society for Pediatric Neu. Ed. by R. Villani & M. Giovanelli. (Modern Problems in Pediatrics Ser.: Vol. 18). (Illus.). 1977. 121.75 (*3-8055-2668-7*) S Karger.

Pediatric Neurosurgery: Surgery of the Developing Nervous System. 3rd ed. Ed. by William R. Checck & Arthur E. Marling. LC 93-38501. (Illus.). 656p. 1994. text 230.00 (*0-7216-3767-1*, W B Saunders Co) Harcrt Hlth Sci Grp.

Pediatric Neurosurgery: Surgery of the Developing Nervous System. 4th ed. David G. McLone. (C). 1999. text. write for info. (*0-7216-8209-X*, W B Saunders Co) Harcrt Hlth Sci Grp.

Pediatric Neurosurgery: Theoretical Principles. Art of Surgical Techniques. 2nd enl. rev. ed. A. L. Schawlow & A. J. Raimondi. LC 98-21390. (Illus.). 656p. 1998. 398.00 (*3-540-62777-4*) Spr-Verlag.

Pediatric Neurosurgical Intensive Care. Ed. by Brian T. Andrews & Gregory B. Hammer. (Neurosurgical Topics Ser.). (Illus.). 250p. 1997. 95.00 (*1-879284-45-6*) Am Assn Neuro.

Pediatric Neurosurgical Patient: A Cooperative Approach. Leslie P. Ivan et al. (Illus.). 340p. 1989. pap. 49.50 (*0-87527-352-1*) Green.

Pediatric Nuclear Imaging. Ed. by John H. Miller & Michael Gelfand. LC 93-38091. 1994. text 115.00 (*0-7216-3685-3*, W B Saunders Co) Harcrt Hlth Sci Grp.

Pediatric Nuclear Medicine. S. T. Treves. (Illus.). 360p. 1984. 132.00 (*0-387-96001-5*) Spr-Verlag.

Pediatric Nuclear Medicine. 2nd ed. S. T. Treves. LC 94-9627. (Illus.). 598p. 1994. 139.00 (*0-387-94229-7*) Spr-Verlag.

Pediatric Nurse & the Life-Threatened Child. Ed. by Penelope Buschman et al. LC 86-82710. (Current Thanatology Ser.). 100p. 1987. pap. 14.95 (*0-930194-39-X*) Ctr Thanatology.

Pediatric Nurse Practioner Certification Study Question Book. Patricia Clinton. 300p. 1999. pap. text, student ed. 35.00 (*1-878028-21-9*) Hlth Lead Assoc.

Pediatric Nurse Practitioner. Jack Rudman. (Certified Nurse Examination Ser.: CN-8). 1994. pap. 23.95 (*0-8373-6108-7*) Nat Learn.

Pediatric Nurse Practitioner Certification Prep Exams. Amelie Hollier et al. 300p. (C). 1999. pap. text. write for info. (*1-892418-03-7*) APEA.

***Pediatric Nurse Practitioner Certification Review.** JoAnn Zerwekh & Jo C. Claborn. Ed. by Robin Carter. LC 99-28365. 220p. 1999. pap. text. write for info. (*0-7216-7745-2*, W B Saunders Co) Harcrt Hlth Sci Grp.

Pediatric Nurse Practitioner Certification Review Guide. 3rd ed. Ed. by Virginia L. Millonig & Mary Baroni. LC 98-29338. 600p. (C). 1998. pap. text 52.00 (*1-878028-17-0*) Hlth Lead Assoc.

Pediatric Nurse Practitioner Pearls of Wisdom. Krieger. (Pearls of Wisdom Ser.). 1999. pap. 32.00 (*1-58409-000-6*) Boston Medical.

Pediatric Nurse's Survival Guide. Lisa Rebeschi & Mary Brown. (Nurse's Survival Guide Ser.). 300p. (Orig.). (C). 1996. per. 29.95 (*1-56930-018-6*) Skidmore Roth Pub.

Pediatric Nursing. Blum-Condon & Gasparis. LC 91-5214. (Nursetest: A Review Ser.). 384p. 1991. pap. 21.95 (*0-87434-305-4*) Springhouse Corp.

Pediatric Nursing. Patricia A. Lesner. (LPN/LVN Nursing Ser.). 1983. pap., teacher ed. 10.00 (*0-8273-1933-9*) Delmar.

Pediatric Nursing. Patricia A. Lesner. LC 81-82910. (Illus.). 544p. 1983. text 35.95 (*0-8273-1932-0*) Delmar.

Pediatric Nursing. Paulette D. Rollant. LC 95-36764. (Mosby's Review Ser.). (Illus.). 432p. (C). (gr. 13). 1995. pap. text 24.95 incl. 3.5 hd (*0-8151-7248-6*, 24861) Mosby Inc.

Pediatric Nursing. Martha Velasco-Whetsell et al. LC 99-32630. (Illus.). 600p. 1999. 39.95 (*0-07-070009-5*) McGraw-Hill HPD.

Pediatric Nursing. rev. ed. Delmar Staff & Monika E. Beuman. LC 95-20855. (Rapid Nursing Interventions Ser.). 224p. (C). 1995. mass mkt. 31.95 (*0-8273-7097-0*) Delmar.

Pediatric Nursing. 2nd ed. Ed. by Mary Muscari. LC 95-39932. (Review Ser.). 416p. 1996. pap. text 21.95 (*0-397-55195-9*) Lppncott W & W.

Pediatric Nursing. 2nd rev. ed. Anne Froese-Fretz et al. (Outline Ser.). (C). 1998. per. 23.95 (*1-56930-067-4*) Skidmore Roth Pub.

Pediatric Nursing. 3rd ed. Janice Selekman. LC 96-29152. (Springhouse Notes Ser.). (Illus.). 240p. 1996. 22.95 incl. disk (*0-87434-863-3*) Springhouse Corp.

Pediatric Nursing: An Introductory Text. 6th ed. Eleanor D. Thompson & Jean W. Ashwill. (Illus.). 1992. pap., teacher ed. write for info. (*0-7216-3126-6*, W B Saunders Co) Harcrt Hlth Sci Grp.

Pediatric Nursing: Caring for Children. 2nd ed. (C). 1998. write for info. (*0-8385-8167-6*, Medical Exam) Appleton & Lange.

Pediatric Nursing: Caring for Children. 2nd ed. Jane Ball & Ruth M. Bindler. LC 98-25825. 1083p. (C). 1998. pap. text 62.95 (*0-8385-8123-4*) Appleton & Lange.

Pediatric Nursing & Drugs Package. Ball. 1996. pap. 75.95 (*0-8385-8105-6*, Prentice Hall) P-H.

Pediatric Nursing Care Plans. 2nd rev. ed. Marie S. Jaffe. (Illus.). 400p. (C). 1997. per. 39.95 (*1-56930-057-7*) Skidmore Roth Pub.

Pediatric Nursing-Resource Manual. 2nd rev. ed. Homrighaus. (C). 1998. pap. text 22.95 (*0-8385-8168-4*, Medical Exam) Appleton & Lange.

Pediatric Nursing Skills Manual. Betty J. Whitson & Judith M. McFarlane. LC 79-27079. 304p. (C). 1990. mass mkt. 27.50 (*0-8273-4384-1*) Delmar.

Pediatric Nursing Transparencies. Jane Ball. (C). 1994. pap. text 225.00 (*0-8385-8076-9*, A8076-0) Appleton & Lange.

Pediatric Nutrition, No. 8. Ed. by R. Reifen et al. LC 98-12387. (Pediatric & Adolescent Medicine Ser.: Vol. 8 (1998)). (Illus.). viii, 262p. 1998. 275.00 (*3-8055-6652-2*) S Karger.

Pediatric Nutrition: Infant Feedings, Deficiencies, Diseases. Ed. by Fima Lifshitz. LC 82-14926. (Clinical Disorders in Pediatric Nutrition Ser.: No. 2). 647p. 1982. reprint ed. pap. 200.00 (*0-608-01287-4*, 206203300001) Bks Demand.

Pediatric Nutrition Handbook. 4th ed. American Academy of Pediatrics Staff. LC 98-70031. 833p. 1998. pap. 69.95 (*1-58110-005-1*) Am Acad Pediat.

Pediatric Nutrition in Clinical Practice. Helene MacLean. (Illus.). 300p. 1984. write for info. (*0-318-58157-4*) Addison-Wesley.

Pediatric Nutrition in Developmental Disorders & Chronic Diseases: Prevention, Assessment & Treatment. Shirley W. Ekvall. (Illus.). 568p. (C). 1992. text 65.00 (*0-19-507224-3*) OUP.

Pediatric Nutrition Self-Study Course. King Helm & Patricia Samour. 60p. 1994. 72.00 (*0-8342-0591-2*, 20591) Aspen Pub.

Pediatric Occupational Therapy: Facilitating Effective Service Provision. Winnie W. Dunn. LC 89-43515. 420p. 1990. pap. 42.00 (*1-55642-014-5*) SLACK Inc.

Pediatric Occupational Therapy & Early Intervention. 2nd ed. Jane Case-Smith. LC 97-18094. 280p. 1997. text 52.50 (*0-7506-9780-6*) Buttrwrth-Heinemann.

***Pediatric Oculoplastic Surgery.** James A. Katowitz. LC 99-32438. (Illus.). 752p. 2000. 250.00 (*0-387-94961-5*) Spr-Verlag.

Pediatric Oncology: Clinical Practice & Controversies. 2nd ed. C. R. Pinkerton & P. N. Plowman. 799p. 1997. text 135.00 (*0-412-63080-X*, Pub. by E A) OUP.

Pediatric Oncology 1. Ed. by G. Bennett Humphrey & Louis P. Dehner. 1981. text 141.50 (*90-247-2408-2*) Kluwer Academic.

Pediatric Ophthalmology. Leonard B. Nelson. (Major Problems in Clinical Pediatrics Ser.: Vol. 25). (Illus.). 288p. 1984. text 84.00 (*0-7216-1191-5*, W B Saunders Co) Harcrt Hlth Sci Grp.

Pediatric Ophthalmology: A Text Atlas. Robert A. Catalano & Leonard B. Nelson. (Illus.). 1099p. (C). 1994. 150.00 (*0-8385-7817-9*, A7817-8, Apple Lange Med) McGraw.

Pediatric Ophthalmology: International Ophthalmology Clinics, No. 1, Winter 1992, Vol. 32, 1992. Frederick A., M.D. Jakobiec & Dimitri M.D. Azar. 1992. 39.00 (*0-316-45652-7*) Little.

Pediatric Ophthalmology: Signs & Symptoms. Kenneth W. Wright. LC 98-21740. 1998. write for info. (*0-683-30485-2*) Lppncott W & W.

Pediatric Ophthalmology & Strabismus. John S. Crawford et al. LC 86-553. (Transactions of the New Orleans Academy of Ophthalmology Ser.). 560p. 1986. reprint ed. pap. 173.60 (*0-608-03400-2*, 206409700008) Bks Demand.

Pediatric Ophthalmology & Strabismus: Section Six. (Basic & Clinical Science Course (1989-90) Ser.). 326p. (C). 1989. pap. text 45.00 (*0-685-26050-X*) Am Acad Ophthal.

Pediatric Optometry. rev. ed. Ray C. Wunderlich. Ed. by Sally M. Corngold. (Introduction to Behavioral Optometry Ser.). (Illus.). (C). 1991. lib. bdg. 18.00 (*0-943599-19-9*) OEPF.

Pediatric Optometry. 2nd ed. Jerome Rosner & Joy Rosner. (Illus.). 538p. 1990. text 65.00 (*0-409-90063-X*) Buttrwrth-Heinemann.

Pediatric Oral Skills Package. Caroline Brindley et al. 80p. 1996. spiral bd. 300.00 (*1-56593-572-1*, 0762) Singular Publishing.

Pediatric Orthopedic Radiology. 2nd ed. M. B. Ozonoff. (Illus.). 815p. 1991. text 179.00 (*0-7216-3618-7*, W B Saunders Co) Harcrt Hlth Sci Grp.

Pediatric Orthopedic Secrets. Lynn T. Staheli. LC 97-25774. (Secrets Ser.). 1997. 35.95 (*1-56053-207-6*) Hanley & Belfus.

Pediatric Orthopedics. Broughton. 1996. text 99.00 (*0-7020-1962-3*, W B Saunders Co) Harcrt Hlth Sci Grp.

Pediatric Orthopedics. Ed. by Harris & Knutson. 164p. 1992. pap. 21.00 (*0-912452-80-3*, P-83) Am Phys Therapy Assn.

Pediatric Orthopedics. Dennis S. Weiner. (Illus.). 170p. 1992. text 55.00 (*0-443-08728-8*) Church.

Pediatric Orthopedics, 3 Vol. Set. 2nd ed. Mihran O. Tachdjian. (Illus.). 3749p. 1990. 510.00 (*0-7216-8726-1*, W B Saunders Co) Harcrt Hlth Sci Grp.

Pediatric Orthopedics. 3rd ed. Tachdjian. 2000. text. write for info. (*0-7216-5682-X*) Harcrt Hlth Sci Grp.

Pediatric Orthopedics: A Guide for the Primary Care Physician. R. J. Mier & T. J. Brower. (Illus.). 340p. (C). 1994. text 49.50 (*0-306-44796-7*, Kluwer Plenum) Kluwer Academic.

Pediatric Orthopedics in Primary Care. Vernon T. Tolo & Beverley Wood. LC 93-13960. (Illus.). 448p. 1993. 59.00 (*0-683-08330-9*) Lppncott W & W.

Pediatric Orthopedics in Primary Practice. Ed. by Peter D. Pizzutillo. LC 96-20621. (Illus.). 369p. 1996. text 65.00 (*0-07-050252-8*) McGraw-Hill HPD.

***Pediatric Otolaryngology.** Ralph F. Wetmore et al. LC 99-39601. 912p. 1999. 169.00 (*0-86577-835-3*) Thieme Med Pubs.

Pediatric Otolaryngology for the General Otolaryngologist. Ed. by Andrew H. Hotaling & James A. Stankiewicz. LC 96-11914. (Illus.). 304p. 1996. text 89.50 (*0-89640-312-2*) Igaku-Shoin.

Pediatric Otoloaryngology, 2 vols., Set. 3rd ed. Charles D. Bluestone et al. LC 95-17701. (Illus.). 1504p. 1995. text 350.00 (*0-7216-5246-8*, W B Saunders Co) Harcrt Hlth Sci Grp.

Pediatric Otology. Ed. by C. Cremers & G. Hogland. (Advances in OtoRhinoLaryngology Ser.: Vol. 40). (Illus.). viii, 168p. 1988. 129.75 (*3-8055-4726-9*) S Karger.

Pediatric Otology & Neurotology. Ed. by Anil K. Lalwani & Kenneth M. Grundfast. LC 97-30730. (Illus.). 400p. 1997. text 149.00 (*0-397-51466-2*) Lppncott W & W.

Pediatric Otorhinolaryngology. Ed. by B. Jazbi. (Advances in OtoRhinoLaryngology Ser.: Vol. 23). (Illus.). 1977. 84.50 (*3-8055-2674-1*) S Karger.

Pediatric Otorhinolaryngology: An Update. D. Passali. (Illus.). x, 432p. 1998. 137.00 (*90-6299-158-0*) Kugler Pubns.

Pediatric Outpatient Procedures. Jacob A. Lohr. (Illus.). 400p. 1991. text 53.00 (*0-397-50897-2*) Lppncott W & W.

Pediatric Outpatient Procedures. Ed. by Jacob A. Lohr et al. LC 90-13405. (Illus.). 399p. reprint ed. pap. 123.70 (*0-608-09743-8*, 206991200007) Bks Demand.

Pediatric Pain. Donald C. Tyler & Elliot J. Krane. (Advances in Pain Research & Therapy Ser.: Vol. 15). 432p. 1989. text 108.50 (*0-88167-584-9*) Lppncott W & W.

Pediatric Pain. Ed. by Donald C. Tyler & Elliot J. Krane. LC 89-24292. (Advances in Pain Research & Therapy Ser.: No. 15). (Illus.). 422p. reprint ed. pap. 130.90 (*0-608-09629-6*, 205440500007) Bks Demand.

Pediatric Pain Pt. 1: A Special Issue of "Children's Health Care", Vol. 25, No. 4, 1996. Brown. 1996. pap. 20.00 (*0-8058-9887-5*) L Erlbaum Assocs.

Pediatric Pain Pt. 2: A Special Issue of "Children's Health Care", Vol. 26, No. 1, 1997. Ronald T. Brown. 64p. 1997. pap. 20.00 (*0-8058-9877-8*) L Erlbaum Assocs.

Pediatric Pain Handbook. Jayant K. Deshpande & Joseph D. Tobias. (Illus.). 384p. (C). (gr. 13). 1995. pap. text 36.95 (*0-8151-2431-7*, 25783) Mosby Inc.

Pediatric Pain Management. L. M. Dahlquist. LC 98-43928. (Clinical Child Psychology Library). (Illus.). 172p. (C). 1999. pap. text 24.95 (*0-306-46085-8*, Kluwer Plenum) Kluwer Academic.

Pediatric Pain Management. L. M. Dahlquist. LC 98-43928. (Clinical Child Psychology Library). (Illus.). 172p. (C). 1999. 75.00 (*0-306-46084-X*, Plenum Trade) Perseus Pubng.

Pediatric Pain Management: A Multi-Disciplinary Approach. Ed. by Alison Twycross et al. 182p. 1998. pap. 29.93 (*1-85775-246-5*, Radcliffe Med Pr) Scovill Paterson.

Pediatric Pain Management & Sedation Handbook. Myron Yaster et al. (Illus.). 608p. (C). (gr. 13). 1997. pap. text 36.95 (*0-8151-9516-8*, 29479) Mosby Inc.

Pediatric Parenteral Nutrition. Robert D. Baker et al. LC 96-34371. (Clinical Nutrition Ser.). 465p. 1997. 79.00 (*0-412-07441-9*) Kluwer Academic.

Pediatric Pathology. 2nd ed. J. Thomas Stocker. 1400p. text 279.00 (*0-7817-1774-4*) Lppncott W & W.

Pediatric Patient: An Approach to History & Physical Examination. Paula S. Algranati. (Illus.). 232p. 1992. 32.00 (*0-683-00073-X*) Lppncott W & W.

Pediatric Patient Education Manual. Aspen Staff. LC 98-21790. 1999. ring bd. 59.00 (*0-8342-1000-2*, 489S1) Aspen Pub.

Pediatric Pearls: The Handbook of Practical Pediatrics. 3rd ed. Fossarelli & Beryl J. Rosenstein. LC 96-34956. (Illus.). 496p. (C). (gr. 13). 1997. pap. text 36.95 (*0-8151-8682-7*, 28973) Mosby Inc.

***Pediatric Perfomance Ranges.** 3rd ed. Ed. by Steven J. Soldin et al. 233p. 1999. pap. 62.00 (*1-890883-22-0*, 202873) Am Assn Clinical Chem.

Pediatric Pharmacology. 2nd ed. Sumner J. Yaffe. 1991. text 152.00 (*0-7216-2971-7*, W B Saunders Co) Harcrt Hlth Sci Grp.

Pediatric Pharmacopoeia. Lott. 1999. pap. text 15.00 (*0-7020-1833-3*) Harcourt.

Pediatric Physical Therapy. Harris. 2000. 52.00 (*0-07-134511-6*) McGraw.

Pediatric Physical Therapy. 2nd ed. Jan S. Tecklin. 468p. 1994. text 42.00 (*0-397-54962-8*, Lippnctt) Lppncott W & W.

Pediatric Physical Therapy. 3rd ed. Jan S. Tecklin. LC 98-18730. 606p. 1998. text. write for info. (*0-7817-1010-3*) Lppncott W & W.

Pediatric Physical Therapy for the Physical Therapist Assistant. Ratliffe. LC 97-29089. (Illus.). 464p. (gr. 13). 1997. text 39.00 (*0-8151-7088-2*, 27167) Mosby Inc.

Pediatric Plastic Surgery. Ed. by Michael L. Bentz. LC 96-53379. 1099p. (C). 1999. 295.00 (*0-8385-7820-9*, A-7820-2, Apple Lange Med) McGraw.

Pediatric Pocket Guide. unabridged ed. Cynthia A. Beard et al. 22p. (Orig.). 1996. pap. 20.00 (*0-935890-07-6*, P31) Emerg Nurses IL.

Pediatric Primary Care: A Handbook for Nurse Practitioners. Catherine E. Burns et al. Ed. by Ilze Rader. (Illus.). 980p. 1996. text 68.00 (*0-7216-5013-9*, W B Saunders Co) Harcrt Hlth Sci Grp.

***Pediatric Primary Care: A Handbook of Nurse Practitioners.** 2nd ed. Catherine E. Burns et al. LC 99-47085. (Illus.). 990p. 2000. text 65.00 (*0-7216-8062-3*, W B Saunders Co) Harcrt Hlth Sci Grp.

Pediatric Primary Care: A Problem Oriented Approach. 3rd ed. M. Wiliam Schwartz & Curry. LC 96-53905. (Illus.). 1040p. (C). (gr. 13). 1997. pap. text 64.95 (*0-8151-8054-3*, 27234) Mosby Inc.

Pediatric Primary Care: Spanish Edition. 2nd ed. M. William Schwartz. (SPA.). 1993. 144.45 (*0-8016-6713-5*) Mosby Inc.

Pediatric Primer: Answers to Questions Most Asked by Parents. Charles Ginsburg. LC 96-35679. (Illus.). 130p. 1996. pap. 8.95 (*1-56530-220-6*) Summit TX.

Pediatric Procedural Sedation & Analgesia. Baruch Krauss & Robert M. Brustowicz. LC 99-10331. 1999. write for info. (*0-683-30558-1*) Lppncott W & W.

Pediatric Procedural Terminology - PPT. 3rd ed. American Academy of Pediatrics Staff. 184p. 1995. pap. 34.95 (*0-910761-67-1*) Am Acad Pediat.

Pediatric Psychiatry. Hale F. Shirley. LC 63-19147. (Illus.). 816p. reprint ed. pap. 200.00 (*0-7837-4469-2*, 204417700001) Bks Demand.

Pediatric Psychooncology: Psychological Perspectives on Children with Cancer. Ed. by David J. Bearison & Raymond K. Mulhern. (Illus.). 272p. 1994. text 60.00 (*0-19-507931-0*) OUP.

Pediatric Pulmonary Disease. J. Thomas Stocker. (Aspen Seminars on Pediatric Disease Ser.). 287p. 1988. 90.00 (*0-89116-830-3*) Hemisp Pub.

Pediatric Pulmonary Heart Disease. Harned. 1990. 125.00 (*0-316-34698-5*, Little Brwn Med Div) Lppncott W & W.

Pediatric Pulmonary Pearls. Ed. by Laura S. Inselman. (Pearls Ser.). (Illus.). 225p. 2000. pap. text 39.00 (*1-56053-350-1*) Hanley & Belfus.

Pediatric Quick Reference. 2nd ed. Donna L. Wong. (Illus.). 64p. 1994. text 8.95 (*0-8151-9396-3*) Mosby Inc.

Pediatric Radiation Oncology. 2nd ed. Edward C. Halperin et al. LC 93-51486. 640p. 1994. text 124.00 (*0-7817-0186-4*) Lppncott W & W.

Pediatric Radiation Oncology. 3rd ed. Edward C. Halperin & Louis S. Constine. LC 98-33919. 672p. 1998. text 135.00 (*0-7817-1500-8*) Lppncott W & W.

Pediatric Radiology. 2nd ed. Johan G. Blickman. LC 97-29332. (Requisites Ser.). (Illus.). 340p. (C). (gr. 13). 1997. text 79.00 (*0-8151-0993-8*, 29191) Mosby Inc.

Pediatric Radiology. 2nd ed. Jack O. Haller & T. L. Slovis. LC 95-32581. (Illus.). 224p. 1995. 82.00 (*3-540-59059-5*) Spr-Verlag.

Pediatric Radiology: A Teaching File. Susan John & Leonard E. Swischuk. 550p. 99.00 (*0-683-30043-1*) Lppncott W & W.

Pediatric Reference Ranges. 2nd rev. ed. Ed. by Stephen J. Soldin. LC 97-20504. 181p. 1997. pap. 55.00 (*0-915274-91-4*, 202738) Am Assn Clinical Chem.

Pediatric Regional Anesthesia. Ed. by Bernard J. Dalens. 528p. 1989. lib. bdg. 159.00 (*0-8493-5629-6*, RD84) CRC Pr.

Pediatric Rehabilitation. 2nd ed. Gabriella E. Molnar. (Illus.). 562p. 1991. 72.00 (*0-683-06118-6*) Lppncott W & W.

Pediatric Rehabilitation. 3rd rev. ed. Gabriella Molnar & Michael A. Alexander. LC 98-31219. (Illus.). 500p. 1998. text 75.00 (*1-56053-306-4*) Hanley & Belfus.

Pediatric Rehabilitation Vol. 17, No. 4: Journal: Pediatrician. Ed. by David W. Kaplan. (Illus.). iv, 108p. 1990. pap. 61.00 (*3-8055-5270-X*) S Karger.

Pediatric Rehabilitation Nursing. Patricia A. Edwards et al. Ed. by Thomas Eoyang. LC 98-5825. (Illus.). 590p. (C). 1999. text. write for info. (*0-7216-5425-8*, W B Saunders Co) Harcrt Hlth Sci Grp.

Pediatric Renal Transplantation. Amir H. Tejani & Richard N. Fine. 572p. 1994. 159.95 (*0-471-59120-3*, Wiley-Liss) Wiley.

***Pediatric Repair Manual.** David Rathkamp & Christopher Siodlarz. Ed. by Quynh Vu. LC 00-91683. (Illus.). 354p. 2000. pap. 19.95 (*0-9700586-0-8*, Pub. by Rocco) BookMasters.

Pediatric Respiratory Care: A Guide for Physiotherapists & Health Professionals. J. Hussey & S. A. Prasad. (Illus.). 204p. 1994. pap. text 47.75 (*1-56593-292-7*, 0616) Singular Publishing.

Pediatric Respiratory Therapy: An Introductory Text. N. Balfour Slonim et al. LC 73-85533. 224p. reprint ed. pap. 69.50 (*0-608-14391-X*, 202183800023) Bks Demand.

Pediatric Rheumatic Diseases. Ed. by Jeanne Melvin & Virginia Wright. (Rheumatologic Rehabilitation Ser.: Vol. 3). (Illus.). Date not set. pap. write for info. (*1-56900-087-5*) Am Occup Therapy.

***Pediatric Rheumatic Diseases.** Ed. by Jeanne Melvin & Virginia Wright. (Rheumatologic Rehabilitation Ser.: Vol. 3). (Illus.). 2000. pap. write for info. (*1-56900-140-5*) Am Occup Therapy.

Pediatric Rheumatology for the Practitioner. J. C. Jacobs. (Comprehensive Manuals in Pediatrics Ser.). (Illus.). 556p. 1982. 106.00 (*0-387-90671-1*) Spr-Verlag.

Pediatric Rheumatology for the Practitioner. 2nd ed. J. C. Jacobs. (Illus.). 520p. 1992. 129.00 (*0-387-97750-3*) Spr-Verlag.

Pediatric Risk Factors for Major Chronic Disease. Christine L. Williams. 176p. 1984. 22.50 (*0-87527-237-1*) Green.

***Pediatric Rotation Value Pak.** Rudolph. 1999. 59.95 (*0-8385-8186-2*, Apple Lange Med) McGraw.

Pediatric Secrets: Questions You Will Be Asked on Rounds, in the Clinic, on Oral Exams. 2nd rev. ed. Ed. by Richard A. Polin & Mark F. Ditmar. LC 96-29336. (Secrets Ser.). (Illus.). 550p. 1997. pap. text 39.00 (*1-56053-171-1*) Hanley & Belfus.

Pediatric Sinus Disease. Rande H. Lazar. (Illus.). 224p. 1998. 59.00 (*0-86577-615-6*) Thieme Med Pubs.

Pediatric Sinusitis. Rodney P. Lusk. 160p. 1992. text 131.50 (*0-88167-894-5*, 2386) Lppncott W & W.

Pediatric Skeletal Scintigraphy. Leonard P. Connolly & S. T. Treves. LC 96-29796. 240p. 1997. text 135.00 (*0-387-94695-0*) Spr-Verlag.

***Pediatric Skills for Occupational Therapy Assistants.** Jean W. Solomon. LC 99-40705. 1999. text. write for info. (*0-323-00092-4*) Mosby Inc.

Pediatric Soft Tissue Tumors: A Clinical, Pathological, & Therapeutic Approach. Cheryl M. Coffin et al. LC 96-27565. (Illus.). 428p. 1997. 99.00 (*0-683-02047-1*) Lppncott W & W.

Pediatric Sonography. 2nd ed. Ed. by Marilyn J. Siegel. LC 94-12237. 612p. 1994. text 164.00 (*0-7817-0214-3*) Lppncott W & W.

Pediatric Specialty Certification Examination Study Guide. Ed. by Jane Case-Smith & Caryl J. Semmler. 90p. (C). 1991. pap. text. write for info. (*0-910317-70-4*) Am Occup Therapy.

Pediatric Spine, Vol. 1. Ed. by Anthony J. Raimondi et al. (Principles of Pediatric Neurosurgery Ser.). (Illus.). 220p. 1989. 195.00 (*0-387-96835-0*) Spr-Verlag.

Pediatric Spine, Vol. 2. Ed. by Anthony J. Raimondi et al. (Principles of Pediatric Neurosurgery Ser.). (Illus.). 255p. 1989. 210.00 (*0-387-96861-X*) Spr-Verlag.

Pediatric Spine, Vol. 3. Ed. by Anthony J. Raimondi et al. (Principles of Pediatric Neurosurgery Ser.). (Illus.). 205p. 1989. 165.00 (*0-387-96804-0*) Spr-Verlag.

Pediatric Spine: Principles & Practice, 2 vols., Set. Ed. by Stuart L. Weinstein. 2096p. 1993. text 314.00 (*0-7817-0028-0*) Lppncott W & W.

Pediatric Splinting. Hogan. (C). 1998. pap. text 45.00 (*0-12-785071-6*) Acad Pr.

Pediatric Surgery. Robert M. Arensman. (Vademecum Ser.). 2000. spiral bd. 45.00 (*1-57059-499-6*) Landes Bioscience.

Pediatric Surgery. 2nd ed. Keith W. Ashcraft & Thomas M. Holder. (Illus.). 1080p. 1992. text 209.00 (*0-7216-3737-X*, W B Saunders Co) Harcrt Hlth Sci Grp.

Pediatric Surgery. 3rd ed. Keith W. Ashcraft. Ed. by Richard Lampert. LC 98-31214. (Illus.). 1055p. 1999. text. write for info. (*0-7216-7312-0*, W B Saunders Co) Harcrt Hlth Sci Grp.

Pediatric Surgery. 5th ed. Coran & Lewis Spitz. (Operative Surgery Ser.). Date not set. write for info. (*0-7506-1704-7*) Chapman & Hall.

Pediatric Surgery. 5th ed. O'Neil & Rowe. LC 97-51987. (Illus.). 2176p. (C). (gr. 13). 1998. text 295.00 (*0-8151-6518-8*, 26544) Mosby Inc.

Pediatric Surgery. 5th ed. Lewis Spitz & Arnold G. Coran. LC 94-68719. (Rob & Smith's Operative Surgery Ser.). (Illus.). 928p. (gr. 13). 1994. text 225.00 (*0-412-59110-3*, Pub. by E A) OUP.

Pediatric Surgery & Urology: Long Term Outcomes. Ed. by Mark D. Stringer et al. (Illus.). 510p. 1998. write for info. (*0-7020-2190-3*) W B Saunders.

Pediatric Surgery of the Liver, Pancreas & Spleen. Schiller. (Illus.). 272p. 1991. text 134.00 (*0-7216-8014-3*, W B Saunders Co) Harcrt Hlth Sci Grp.

Pediatric Surgery Secrets. Ed. by Philip L Glick et al. (Secrets Ser.). (Illus.). 350p. 2000. text 38.00 (*1-56053-317-X*) Hanley & Belfus.

Pediatric Surgical Oncology. Richard J. Andrassy. Ed. by Richard Lampert. LC 96-53983. (Illus.). 400p. 1998. text 165.00 (*0-7216-6378-8*, W B Saunders Co) Harcrt Hlth Sci Grp.

Pediatric Swallowing & Feeding. Arvedson. 1997. 68.00 (*0-7616-1741-8*) Commun Skill.

Pediatric Swallowing & Feeding: Assessment & Management. Ed. by Joan C. Arvedson & Linda Brodsky. LC 92-49930. (Early Childhood Intervention Ser.). (Illus.). 486p. (Orig.). (C). 1992. pap. 59.95 (*1-56593-069-X*, 0376) Thomson Learn.

Pediatric Telephone Advice. 2nd ed. Raymond C. Baker & Barton D. Schmitt. LC 97-3048. 300p. 1998. spiral bd. 35.95 (*0-316-77390-5*) Lppncott W & W.

Pediatric Telephone Medicine: Principles, Triage & Advice. 2nd ed. Jeffrey L. Brown. (Illus.). 275p. 1994. pap. text 35.00 (*0-397-51379-8*) Lppncott W & W.

Pediatric Telephone Medicine: Principles, Triage & Advice. 3rd ed. Jeffrey L. Brown. 320p. 1998. spiral bd. 34.95 (*0-7817-1631-4*) Lppncott W & W.

Pediatric Therapy: A Systems Approach. 5th ed. Susan M. Porr et al. Ed. by Shelly J. Lane. LC 98-55693. (Pediatric Occupational Therapy Ser.). (Illus.). 624p. (C). 1999. pap. text 38.95 (*0-8036-0259-6*) Davis Co.

Pediatric Thoracic Surgery. James C. Fallis et al. Ed. by Georges Lemoine. (Current Topics in General Thoracic Surgery: an International Ser.). 370p. 1991. 137.25 (*0-444-01605-8*) Elsevier.

Pediatric Thromboembolism & Stroke Protocols. Maureen Andrew & Gabrielle DeVebers. 72p. 1997. pap. 15.95 (*1-55009-055-0*) DEKR.

Pediatric Thyroidology. Ed. by F. Delange et al. (Pediatric & Adolescent Endocrinology Ser.: Vol. 14). (Illus.). x, 412p. 1985. 239.25 (*3-8055-3968-1*) S Karger.

Pediatric Toxicology: Handbook of Poisoning in Children. Nicholas Edwards et al. 424p. 1997. 115.00 (*1-56159-162-9*) Groves Dictionaries.

Pediatric TPN: Standard Techniques. Keith Kanarek & Barbara Kellam. LC 85-62891. 128p. 1986. pap. 22.95 (*0-931028-75-2*) Precept Pr.

***Pediatric Transfusion.** (Illus.). 2001. write for info. (*1-56395-129-0*) Am Assn Blood.

Pediatric Transfusion Medicine, Vol. I. Christina A. Kasprisin. 224p. 1987. lib. bdg. 219.00 (*0-8493-5593-1*) CRC Pr.

Pediatric Transfusion Medicine, Vol. II. Christina A. Kasprisin. 216p. 1987. lib. bdg. 219.00 (*0-8493-5594-X*) CRC Pr.

Pediatric Transillumination. Steven M. Donn & Lawrence R. Kuhns. LC 82-11035. (Illus.). 133p. reprint ed. pap. 41.30 (*0-8357-7612-3*, 205693500096) Bks Demand.

Pediatric Trauma: Initial Assessment & Management. Edward G. Ford & Richard J. Andrassy. LC 94-6679. (Principles of the Pediatric Surgical Specialties Ser.). (Illus.). 1994. text 69.00 (*0-7216-2913-X*, W B Saunders Co) Harcrt Hlth Sci Grp.

Pediatric Trauma: Initial Care of the Injured. Ed. by Robert M. Arensman. LC 95-3117. (Illus.). 288p. 1995. text 75.00 (*0-7817-0260-7*) Lppncott W & W.

Pediatric Trauma Anesthesia & Critical Care. Ed. by J. K. Hall & Jeffrey M. Berman. LC 96-23404. (Illus.). 528p. 1996. 98.00 (*0-87993-624-X*) Futura Pub.

Pediatric Trauma Nursing. Connie L. Joy. 284p. 1989. 62.00 (*0-8342-0040-6*, 20040) Aspen Pub.

Pediatric Traumatic Brain Injury. Jeffrey H. Snow & Stephen R. Hooper. (Developmental Clinical Psychology & Psychiatry Ser.: No. 31). 120p. 1994. 42.00 (*0-8039-5181-7*) Sage.

Pediatric Traumatic Brain Injury. Jeffrey H. Snow & Stephen R. Hooper. (Developmental Clinical Psychology & Psychiatry Ser.: Vol. 31). 120p. 1994. pap. 18.95 (*0-8039-5182-5*) Sage.

Pediatric Traumatic Brain Injury 2nd ed. Jean L Blosser. 2000. pap. 36.00 (*0-7693-0055-3*) Singular Publishing.

Pediatric Traumatic Brain Injury: Proactive Intervention. Jean L Blosser & Roberta DePompei. LC 94-11315. (Neurogenic Communication Disorders Ser.). (Illus.). 280p. (Orig.). (C). 1994. pap. text 45.00 (*1-56593-168-8*, 0479) Thomson Learn.

Pediatric Triage Guidelines. Kathleen A. Murphy. (Illus.). 352p. (C). (gr. 13). 1996. text 35.95 (*0-8151-7333-4*, 27931) Mosby Inc.

Pediatric Tumor Boards on CD-ROM, No. 1.1. R. Beverly Raney. 1997. cd-rom 89.95 (*0-412-14411-5*, Pub. by E A) OUP.

Pediatric Tumors: Immunological & Molecular Markers. Ed. by John T. Kemshead. 224p. 1989. lib. bdg. 153.00 (*0-8493-6752-2*, RC281) CRC Pr.

Pediatric Ultrasonography. 2nd ed. Keith C. Hayden, Jr. & Leonard E. Swischuck. (Illus.). 472p. 1992. 98.00 (*0-683-03901-6*) Lppncott W & W.

Pediatric Ultrasound. Jack O. Haller & Morton Schneider. LC 79-24809. (Illus.). 290p. reprint ed. pap. 89.90 (*0-8357-7593-3*, 205691400096) Bks Demand.

Pediatric Upper Extremity: Diagnosis & Management. F. William Bora. (Illus.). 429p. 1986. text 155.00 (*0-7216-1872-3*, W B Saunders Co) Harcrt Hlth Sci Grp.

Pediatric Urology. Keith W. Ashcraft. 544p. 1990. text 156.00 (*0-7216-2746-3*, W B Saunders Co) Harcrt Hlth Sci Grp.

Pediatric Urology. 3rd ed. Ed. by Barry O'Donnell & Stephen A. Koff. LC 96-44087. (Illus.). 848p. 1996. text 300.00 (*0-7506-1365-3*) Buttrwrth-Heinemann.

Pediatric Urology for the General Urologist. Ed. by Jack S. Elder. LC 95-33163. (Topics in Clinical Urology Ser.). (Illus.). 248p. 1996. 75.00 (*0-89640-280-0*) Igaku-Shoin.

Pediatric Urology Practice. Edmond T. Gonzales & Stuart B. Bauer. LC 99-13237. 700p. 1998. text 150.00 (*0-397-51368-2*) Lppncott W & W.

Pediatric Videofluoroscopic Swallow Studies: A Professional Manual with Caregiver Guidelines. Joan C. Arvedson. 1998. pap. text 69.00 (*0-12-785064-3*) Acad Pr.

Pediatric Videofluoroscopic Swallow Studies: A Professional Manual with Caregiver Guidelines. Joan C. Arvedson & Maureen A. Lefton-Greif. LC 98-5487. 1998. 69.00 (*0-7616-3228-X*) Commun Skill.

Pediatric Ward. J. M. Briley, Jr. LC 82-39991. 1986. pap. 13.95 (*0-87949-229-5*) Ashley Bks.

Pediatric Work Physiology. Ed. by E. Jokl et al. (Medicine & Sport Science Ser.: Vol. 11). (Illus.). 1978. 68.00 (*3-8055-2866-3*) S Karger.

***Pediatrician.** Rosemary Wallner. 1999. 19.93 (*0-516-21892-1*) Capstone Pr.

***Pediatrician.** Rosemary Wallner. LC 99-25211. (Career Exploration Ser.). (Illus.). 48p. (YA). (gr. 4-7). 2000. 19.93 (*0-7368-0333-5*) Capstone Pr.

Pediatrician. Samuel Woods. LC 98-3900. (Doctors in Action Ser.). (Illus.). 24p. (J). (gr. 3-5). 1998. lib. bdg. 15.95 (*1-56711-237-4*) Blackbirch.

Pediatricians, Families & Child Care. Audrey Brown & Toby Gross. Ed. by Janet B. McCracken. (Pediatric Round Table Ser.: No. 15). 110p. (Orig.). 1993. pap. text 10.00 (*0-931562-17-1*) J & J Consumer Prods.

Pediatrician's Guide to Managed Care. American Academy of Pediatrics Staff. 270p. 1995. ring bd. 49.95 (*0-910761-62-0*) Am Acad Pediat.

Pediatrician's New Baby Owner's Manual see Manual Pediatrico para los Duenos del Nueva Bebe: Guia para el Cuidado y Mantenimiento de su Nuevo Bebe

Pediatrician's New Baby Owner's Manual: Your Guide to the Care & Fine-Tuning of Your New Baby. Horst D. Weinberg. LC 96-35579. (Illus.). 208p. (Orig.). 1996. pap. 12.95 (*1-884956-07-6*) Quill Driver.

Pediatrics. Daniel Bernstein & Steven P. Shelov. (Illus.). 456p. 1996. pap. 37.95 (*0-683-00640-1*) Lppncott W & W.

Pediatrics. Margaret C. Heagarty. LC 97-3054. (Rypins' Intensive Reviews Ser.). (Illus.). 200p. 1997. pap. text 19.95 (*0-397-51556-1*) Lppncott W & W.

Pediatrics. David Milner. (Self-Assessment Picture Tests in Medicine Ser.). 148p. 1993. text 22.50 (*0-7234-1951-5*, Pub. by Wolfe Pub) Mosby Inc.

Pediatrics. Oborn. Date not set. text. write for info. (*0-323-01199-3*) Mosby Inc.

Pediatrics. H.David Wilson. 1998. pap. text 24.95 (*1-889325-09-0*) Fence Crk Pubng.

Pediatrics. Ed. by Harold M. Maurer. LC 82-9423. 1097p. reprint ed. pap. 200.00 (*0-7837-6247-X*, 204595900010) Bks Demand.

Pediatrics. Robert A. Wood et al. LC 88-626. (Illus.). 591p. 1989. reprint ed. pap. 183.30 (*0-608-07235-4*, 206746000009) Bks Demand.

Pediatrics. 2nd ed. (National Medical Ser.). 1991. 27.00 (*0-685-75181-3*) Lppncott W & W.

Pediatrics. 2nd ed. Richard M. Heller et al. (Exercises in Diagnostic Radiology Ser.). (Illus.). 256p. 1987. text 36.00 (*0-7216-1569-4*, W B Saunders Co) Harcrt Hlth Sci Grp.

Pediatrics. 2nd ed. Ed. by Jane E. Puls & A. E. Osburn. LC 96-13501. (Oklahoma Notes Ser.). 390p. 1996. 17.95 (*0-387-94634-9*) Spr-Verlag.

Pediatrics. 2nd ed. Roslyn Thomas & David R. Harvey. LC 96-39718. (Colour Guide Ser.). 1997. write for info. (*0-443-05776-1*) Harcrt Hlth Sci Grp.

Pediatrics. 3rd ed. Ed. by Paul H. Dworkin. LC 95-37175. (National Medical Series for Independent Study). 679p. 1996. 30.00 (*0-683-06245-X*) Lppncott W & W.

Pediatrics. 3rd ed. Mohsen Ziai. 868p. 1983. 38.50 (*0-316-98753-0*, Little Brwn Med Div) Lppncott W & W.

Pediatrics. 4th ed. Mohsen Ziai. 1990. 49.95 (*0-316-98743-3*, Little Brwn Med Div) Lppncott W & W.

Pediatrics. 2000th ed. Stockman. (Illus.). 550p. 2000. text 67.95 (*0-8151-9038-7*, 29143) Mosby Inc.

Pediatrics: A Primary Care Approach. Berkowitz. (C). text. write for info. (*0-8089-2074-X*, Grune & Strat); text. write for info. (*0-8089-2118-5*, Grune & Strat) Harcrt Hlth Sci Grp.

Pediatrics: A Primary Care Approach. Carol D. Berkowitz. (C). 1996. pap. text 18.00 (*0-8089-1975-X*, Grune & Strat) Harcrt Hlth Sci Grp.

Pediatrics: A Primary Care Approach. Carol D. Berkowitz. Ed. by Bill Schmitt. LC 95-23414. (Saunders Text & Review Ser.). (Illus.). 525p. 1996. pap. text 33.95 (*0-7216-5623-4*, W B Saunders Co) Harcrt Hlth Sci Grp.

Pediatrics: A Primary Care Approach. 2nd ed. Carol Berkkowitz. LC 99-49760. (Text & Review Ser.). (Illus.). 525p. 2000. pap. text. write for info. (*0-7216-8183-2*, W B Saunders Co) Harcrt Hlth Sci Grp.

Pediatrics: An Approach to Independent Learning. Ed. by C. William Daeschner, Jr. LC 82-8438. 658p. reprint ed. pap. 200.00 (*0-8357-3060-3*, 203931600012) Bks Demand.

Pediatrics: An Approach to Independent Learning. 3rd ed. Ed. by C. William Daeschner, Jr. & C. Joan Richardson. LC 96-36967. (Illus.). 400p. 1997. text 65.00 (*0-8018-5603-5*); pap. text 34.95 (*0-8018-5604-3*) Johns Hopkins.

Pediatrics: Pretest Self-Assessment & Review. 8th ed. Ed. by Robert J. Yetman. LC 97-17579. (Pretest Clinical Science Ser.). (Illus.). 200p. 1997. pap. text 18.95 (*0-07-052530-7*) McGraw-Hill HPD.

***Pediatrics: PreTest Self Assessment & Review.** 9th ed. Robert J. Yetman. 250p. 2000. Price not set. (*0-07-135955-9*) McGraw.

***Pediatrics: Review for USMLE, Step 1.** Jerome A. Paulson. Ed. by Kurt E. Johnson. (Illus.). 250p. 2000. pap. text (*1-888308-08-7*) J Majors Co.

Pediatrics: Understanding Child Health. Ed. by Tony Waterston et al. LC 97-218843. (Oxford Core Texts Ser.). (Illus.). 432p. 1997. pap. text 49.95 (*0-19-262563-2*) OUP.

***Pediatrics: 2000 Edition.** rev. ed. Paul D. Chan & Jane Gennrich. (Current Clinical Strategies Ser.). 104p. 2000. pap. 28.95 incl. cd-rom (*1-881528-86-3*) Current Clin Strat.

Pediatrics & Perinatology: The Scientific Basis. 2nd ed. Peter D. Gluckman & Michael A. Heymann. (Illus.). 1008p. 1996. text 125.00 (*0-340-66190-9*) OUP.

Pediatrics at a Glance. Ed. by Steven Altschuler & Stephen Ludwig. LC 97-41516. 450p. (C). 1998. pap. 49.95 (*0-8385-8142-0*, A-8142-0, Apple Lange Med) McGraw.

Pediatrics 5 Minute Review, 98-99 Edition: Current Clinical Strategies. Karen Scruggs. 250p. 1997. pap. 19.95 (*1-881528-61-8*) Current Clin Strat.

P

An Asterisk (*) at the beginning of an entry indicates that the title is appearing for the first time.

***Pediatrics 5-Minute Reviews: 2001-2002 Edition.** Karen Scruggs. (Current Clinical Strategies Ser.). 250p. 2000. pap. 19.95 (*1-881528-98-7*) Current Clin Strat.

***Pediatrics 5-Minute Reviews: 2001-2002 Edition.** rev. ed. Karen Scruggs. (Current Clinical Strategies Ser.). 250p. 2000. pap. 29.95 incl. cd-rom (*1-881528-62-6*) Current Clin Strat.

Pediatrics for Nurses. A. L. Speirs. (Illus.). 244p. 1981. 29.95 (*0-8464-1282-9*) Beekman Pubs.

Pediatrics for the Anesthesiologist. Ed. by Frederick A. Berry & David J. Steward. (Illus.). 400p. 1993. text 72.00 (*0-443-08930-2*) Church.

Pediatrics for the Chiropractor. Sanders. 192p. (C). 1998. pap. 13.00 (*0-536-02087-6*) S&S Trade.

Pediatrics, 1997 Edition: Current Clinical Strategies. Paul D. Chan et al. (Current Clinical Strategies Medical Bks Ser.). 104p. 1997. pap. 12.75 (*1-881528-24-3*) Current Clin Strat.

Pediatrics Pearls of Wisdom. Levin et al. (Pearls of Wisdom Ser.). 1998. pap. 88.00 (*1-890369-07-1*) Boston Medical.

Pediatrics Recall. Eugene D. McGahren & William G. Wilson. LC 96-29736. (Recall Ser.). 456p. 1997. pap. 27.00 (*0-683-05855-X*) Lppncott W & W.

***Pediatrics Through the Eyes of a Child.** (C). 2002. write for info. (*0-8053-8182-1*) Benjamin-Cummings.

Pediatrics, Year 2000 Edition: Current Clinical Strategies. rev. ed. Paul D. Chan. (Current Clinical Strategies Ser.). 100p. 1999. pap. 12.95 (*1-881528-85-5*) Current Clin Strat.

Pediatrics 2001. 2001st ed. Stockman. (Illus.). 550p. 2001. text 67.95 (*0-8151-9039-5*, 29144) Mosby Inc.

Pedicle Flaps of the Upper Limb: Vascular Anatomy, Surgical Technique & Current Indications. Alain Gilbert et al. LC 92-2164. 236p. 1992. text 155.00 (*0-316-20772-1*, RD557, Little Brwn Med Div) Lppncott W & W.

Pedigree Analysis in Human Genetics. Elizabeth A. Thompson. LC 85-9821. (Johns Hopkins Series in Contemporary Medicine & Public Health). 236p. 1986. reprint ed. pap. 73.20 (*0-608-03661-7*, 206448700009) Bks Demand.

Pedigree & History of the Washington Family, Derived from Odin, the Founder of Scandinavia, B. C. 70, down to General George Washington. Albert Welles. (Illus.). 420p. 1989. reprint ed. pap. 63.00 (*0-8328-1229-3*); reprint ed. lib. bdg. 71.00 (*0-8328-1228-5*) Higginson Bk Co.

Pedigree Card Index of the German People see Ahnen Stammkartei des Deutschen Volkes: An Introduction & Register

***Pedigree Charts from the Western Reserve.** LC 98-73862. 5654p. 1999. lib. bdg. 30.00 (*0-9669675-0-X*) Cuyahoga OH.

***Pedigree of Man (1908)** Annie W. Besant. 208p. 1998. reprint ed. pap. 17.95 (*0-7661-0580-6*) Kessinger Pub.

Pedigree of the Devil. Frederic T. Hall. LC 76-173108. (Illus.). 272p. 1980. reprint ed. 30.95 (*0-405-08594-X*, Pub. by Blom Pubns) Ayer.

Pedigree Patterns: 21 Original Counted Cross-Stitch Embroidery Charts of Family Relationships. Jean D. Crowther. 24p. (Orig.). 1981. pap. 6.98 (*0-88290-195-8*, 2880) Horizon Utah.

Pedigree Studies: Index of New Information with Analysis, Research & Results. Lilo G. Cronnet. 160p. 1995. 47.50 (*0-7883-0434-8*); pap. 44.50 (*0-7883-0435-6*) ABBE Pubs Assn.

Pedigree to Die For: A Melanie Travis Mystery. Laurien Berenson. 288p. 1996. mass mkt. 4.99 (*1-57566-003-2*) Kensgtn Pub Corp.

Pedigree to Die For: A Melanie Travis Mystery. Laurien Berenson. 288p. 1997. pap. 9.95 (*1-57566-125-X*, Knsington) Kensgtn Pub Corp.

Pedigree to Die For: A Melanie Travis Mystery, 1. Laurien Berenson. 1999. mass mkt. 5.99 (*1-57566-374-0*) Kensgtn Pub Corp.

Pedigree to Die For: A Melanie Travis Mystery. Laurien Berenson. 1996. pap. 4.99 (*0-8217-5227-8*) NAL.

Pedigreed Cats Photo Postcards: 24 Full-Color Ready-to-Mail Cards. Dorothy Holby. (Illus.). 16p. 1989. pap. 4.50 (*0-486-25888-2*) Dover.

Pedigrees in the Ownership of Law Books. Hampton L. Carson. Ed. by Roy M. Mersky & J. Myron Jacobstein. (Classics in Legal History Reprint Ser.: Vol. 2). 31p. 1968. reprint ed. lib. bdg. 36.00 (*0-89941-001-4*, 300130) W S Hein.

Pedigrees of Leading Winners, 1981-1984. Martin Pickering & Michael Ross. 198p. 1990. 120.00 (*0-85131-413-9*, Pub. by J A Allen) St Mut.

Pedigrees of Leading Winners, 1981-1984. Martin Pickering & Michael Ross. 194p. 1986. 65.00 (*0-8131-1601-5*) U Pr of Ky.

Pedigress of Leading Winners, 1960-1980. Ed. by Michael Ross. 198p. 1990. 120.00 (*0-85131-372-8*, Pub. by J A Allen) St Mut.

Pedigrees of Some of the Emperor Charlemagne's Descendants, Vol. I. Marcellus D. Redlich. LC 71-39170. 320p. 1996. reprint ed. 25.00 (*0-8063-0494-4*) Genealog Pub.

Pedigrees of Some of the Emperor Charlemagne's Descendants, Vol. III. J. Orton Buck, Jr. & Timothy F. Beard. 309p. 1996. reprint ed. 30.00 (*0-8063-1211-4*, 775) Genealog Pub.

Pedimental Sculptures of the Hieron in Samothrace. Phyllis W. Lehmann. LC 62-19124. (Illus.). 25.00 (*0-685-71751-8*) J J Augustin.

Pediments of the Parthenon. Olga Palagia. (Monumenta Graeca et Romana Ser.: Vol. 7). (Illus.). viii, 168p. 1998. reprint ed. 57.00 (*90-04-11198-0*) Brill Academic Pubs.

Pedimos Perdon: Libro de Reconciliacion para Ninos. Ellen Shannon & Corinne Hart. Tr. by P. Fidencio Silva & P. Domenico Di Raimondo from ENG. (SPA., Illus.). 32p. (J). (ps-2). 1991. pap. 1.90 (*1-55944-007-4*) Franciscan Comns.

Pedlar in Divinity: George Whitefield & the Transatlantic Revivals, 1737-1770. Frank Lambert. LC 93-1345. (Illus.). 264p. 1994. text 32.50 (*0-691-03296-3*, Pub. by Princeton U Pr) Cal Prin Full Svc.

Pedlar's Pack. Elizabeth Goudge. LC 78-132116. (Short Story Index Reprint Ser.). 1977. 18.95 (*0-8369-3673-6*) Ayer.

Pedlar's Progress: The Life of Bronson Alcott. Odell Shepard. LC 68-19294. 546p. 1968. reprint ed. lib. bdg. 75.00 (*0-8371-0220-0*, SHPP, Greenwood Pr) Greenwood.

Pedlar's Prophecy. Robert Wilson. LC 79-133719. (Tudor Facsimile Texts. Old English Plays Ser.: No. 74). reprint ed. 59.50 (*0-404-53374-4*) AMS Pr.

Pedlar's Revenge: Short Stories. Liam O'Flaherty. 224p. 1997. pap. 11.95 (*0-86327-536-2*, Pub. by Wolfhound Press) Irish Amer Bk.

Pedogenesis & Soil Taxonomy Pt. 1: Concepts & Interactions. Ed. by L. P. Wilding et al. (Developments in Soil Science Ser.: No. 11A). 304p. 1983. 128.00 (*0-444-42100-9*, I-316-83) Elsevier.

Pedogenesis & Soil Taxonomy Vol. 2: The Soil Orders. Ed. by L. P. Wilding et al. (Developments in Soil Science Ser.: Vol. 11B). 410p. 1983. 128.00 (*0-444-42137-8*, I-422-83) Elsevier.

Pedogogia Fructifera: Edicion Actualizada y Ampliada. Findley B. Edge. Tr. by Arnoldo Canclini.Tr. of Teaching for Results. (SPA.). 272p. 1999. pap. text, teacher ed. 15.50 (*0-311-11041-X*) Casa Bautista.

Pedological Perspectives in Archaeological Research: Proceedings of 2 Symposia Sponsored. Ed. by Mary E. Collins. LC 96-6912. (SSSA Special Publications: No. 44). (Illus.). 157p. 1995. 30.00 (*0-89118-820-7*) Soil Sci Soc Am.

Pedondontics. Das. 1983. 60.00 (*0-7855-0746-9*, Pub. by Current Dist) St Mut.

Pedondontics. Das. 1985. 49.00 (*0-7855-0823-6*, Pub. by Current Dist) St Mut.

Pedophiles & Priests: Anatomy of a Contemporary Crisis. Philip Jenkins. 224p. 1996. 30.00 (*0-19-509565-0*) OUP.

Pedophiles on Parade, 2 vols. David Sonenschein. Incl. Vol. 1. Monster in the Media. (Illus.). 256p. 1998. pap. 19.95 (*0-915289-00-8*); Vol. 2. Popular Imagery of Moral Hysteria. (Illus.). 315p. 1998. pap. 24.95 (*0-915289-01-6*); (Illus.). 571p. 1998. Set pap. 40.00 (*0-915289-02-4*) D Sonenschein.

Pedophilia: Biosocial Dimensions. Ed. by J. R. Feierman. x, 594p. 1990. 79.95 (*0-387-97243-9*) Spr-Verlag.

Pedophilia & Sex Behaviors: Index of New Information Including Analysis & Results. Arlene S. Shank. LC 95-16307. 151p. 1995. 47.50 (*0-7883-0462-3*); pap. 44.50 (*0-7883-0463-1*) ABBE Pubs Assn.

Pedor Salinas. John Crispin. LC 73-17149. (Twayne's World Authors Ser.). 180p. (C). 1974. lib. bdg. 20.95 (*0-8057-2784-1*) Irvington.

***Pedra Canga.** Tereza Albues. 140p. 2000. pap. 12.95 (*1-892295-70-9*) Green Integer.

Pedro. Illus. by Marilyn S. Martin. 152p. (J). (gr. 3-6). 1980. 7.65 (*0-7399-0083-8*, 2340) Rod & Staff.

Pedro. Gordon Stowell. (Serie Pescaditos - Little Fish Ser.).Tr. of Peter. (SPA.). 16p. (J). 1989. pap. write for info. (*0-614-27105-3*) Editorial Unilit.

Pedro - Peter. Gordon Stowell. (Serie Pescaditos - Little Fish Ser.). (SPA.). 16p. (J). 1989. write for info. (*0-614-24391-2*) Editorial Unilit.

Pedro Albizu Campos, 1891-1965. Ed. by Nelida Perez & Amilcar Tirado. (Puerto Rican Bibliographies Ser.). (Illus.). 30p. (C). 1986. reprint ed. pap. 1.00 (*1-878483-43-9*) Hunter Coll CEP.

***Pedro & Donkeeta.** Violet Ramos. Ed. by Catherine Wright & Krissy Elwood. (Illus.). 31p. (J). (ps-4). 2000. 17.95 (*0-9658334-2-9*) VR Pubns.

***Pedro & Me.** Winnick Judd. LC 99-40729. (Illus.). 192p. 2000. pap. 14.95 (*0-8050-6403-6*, Owl) H Holt & Co.

***Pedro & Me.** Winnick Judd. LC 99-40729. 2000. text 19.95 (*0-8050-6379-X*) St Martin.

***Pedro & the Irish Treasure.** John J. Ackert. LC 99-64394. 1999. 25.00 (*0-7388-0500-9*); pap. 18.00 (*0-7388-0501-7*) Xlibris Corp.

Pedro & the Monkey. Robert D. San Souci. LC 95-35385. (Illus.). 32p. (J). 1996. lib. bdg. 15.93 (*0-688-13744-X*, Wm Morrow) Morrow Avon.

Pedro & the Monkey. Robert D. San Souci. LC 95-35385. (Illus.). 32p. (J). (gr. k up). 1996. 16.00 (*0-688-13743-1*, Wm Morrow) Morrow Avon.

Pedro Balderon de la Barca's "The Fake Astrologer" A Critical Spanish Text & English Translation. Max Oppenheimer, Jr. & Pedro Calderon de la Barca. LC 93-12701. (Iberica Ser.: Vol. 9). 258p. (C). 1994. text 48.95 (*0-8204-2166-9*) P Lang Pubng.

Pedro Calderon de la Barca: Konkordanz Zu Calderon, Pt. II: Konkordanz Zu denn Comedias y Dramas. Ed. by Jurgen Rolshoven & Manfred Tietz. write for info. (*0-318-71994-0*) G Olms Pubs.

Pedro Calderon de la Barca: La Desdicha de la Voz. Ed. by T. R. Mason. (SPA.). 288p. 1998. 45.95 (*0-85323-823-5*, Pub. by Liverpool Univ Pr); pap. 23.95 (*0-85323-833-2*, Pub. by Liverpool Univ Pr) Intl Spec Bk.

Pedro Calderon de la Barca, el Segundo Blason Del Austria. (Hamburger Romanistische Studien, Reihe B: Vol. 41). (C). 1978. 53.00 (*3-11-005819-7*) De Gruyter.

Pedro Cano: Jornadas. Ed. by Elizabeth McDougall. LC 88-60324. (Illus.). 77p. (Orig.). (C). 1988. text 20.00 (*0-685-37293-6*) Meadows Mus.

Pedro Cano: Jornadas. Edward J. Sullivan. Ed. by Elizabeth McDougall. LC 88-60324. (Illus.). 77p. (Orig.). (C). 1988. 20.00 (*0-935937-03-X*) Meadows Mus.

Pedro Ciruelo's a Treatise Reproving All Superstitions & Forms of Witchcraft: Very Necessary & Useful for All Good Christians Zealous for Their Salvation. Ed. & Tr. by D'Orsay W. Pearson. Tr. by Eugene Maio. LC 74-4979. 366p. 1976. 38.50 (*0-8386-1580-5*) Fairleigh Dickinson.

Pedro de Guatemala see Pedro of Guatemala

Pedro De Mena, Seventeenth-Century Spanish Sculptor. Janet A. Anderson. LC 98-2589. (Studies in Art & Religious Interpretation: Vol. 22). (Illus.). 316p. 1998. text 99.95 (*0-7734-8481-7*) E Mellen.

Pedro de Rivera & the Military Regulations for Northern New Spain, 1724-1729: A Documentary History of His Frontier Inspection & the Reglamento de 1729. Ed. by Thomas H. Naylor & Charles W. Polzer. LC 88-26098. 367p. 1988. 51.00 (*0-8165-1070-9*) U of Ariz Pr.

Pedro de Valdivia, Conqueror of Chile. R. B. Graham. LC 74-3619. (Illus.). 227p. 1974. reprint ed. lib. bdg. 59.75 (*0-8371-7454-6*, GRPV, Greenwood Pr) Greenwood.

Pedro Fools the Gringo: And Other Tales of a Latin American Trickster. Illus. & Retold by Maria C. Brusca. LC 95-9984. (Redfeather Bks.). 55p. (J). (gr. 3-6). 1995. 14.95 (*0-8050-3827-2*) H Holt & Co.

Pedro, His Perro & the Alphabet Sombrero. large type ed. Lynn R. Reed. LC 94-28215. (Illus.). 32p. (J). (ps-3). 1995. 14.95 (*0-7868-0071-2*, Pub. by Hypm Child) Little.

Pedro Lopez de Ayala. Constance L. Wilkins. (World Authors Ser.: No. 807). 184p. (C). 1989. 30.95 (*0-8057-8247-8*, TWAS 807, Twyne) Mac Lib Ref.

Pedro Lujan: Wood Sculpture. Jeanette Ingberman & Pedro Lujan. (Illus.). 15p. (Orig.). 1985. pap. 10.00 (*0-913263-09-5*) Exit Art.

Pedro Martinez. Jim Gallagher. LC 98-48047. (Latinos in Baseball Ser.). (Illus.). 64p. (YA). (gr. 5 up). 1999. lib. bdg. 18.95 (*1-883845-85-8*) M Lane Pubs.

***Pedro Martinez: Pitcher Perfect.** Mark Stewart. (Sports Stars Ser.). (Illus.). 48p. (J). (gr. 3-4). 2000. pap. 5.95 (*0-516-27073-7*) Childrens.

Pedro Martinez: Throwing Strikes. Michael Shalin. Ed. by Rob Rains. (Super Star Ser.). 96p. (J). 1999. pap. 4.95 (*1-58261-047-9*) Sprts Pubng.

***Pedro Martinez, Pitcher Perfect.** Mark Stewart. LC 00-20808. (Sports Stars Ser.). (Illus.). (J). 2000. 19.50 (*0-516-22048-9*) Childrens.

Pedro Menendez de Aviles. Ed. by Eugene Lyon. LC 94-10710. (Spanish Borderlands Sourcebooks Ser.: Vol. 24). (Illus.). 640p. 1995. text 25.00 (*0-8240-2099-5*) Garland.

Pedro Montengon's Frioleras Eruditas y Curiosas para la Publica Instruccion. Pedro Montengon. Ed. by Luis A. Ramos-Garcia. LC 97-48899. (Hispanic Literature Ser.: Vol. 38). 324p. 1998. text 99.95 (*0-7734-8492-2*) E Mellen.

Pedro Nunes, 1502-1578: His Lost Algebra & Other Discoveries. Nunes Pedro. Ed. & Tr. by John R. Martyn from GRE. (American University Studies: Series 9, Vol. 182). 158p. (C). 1996. text 35.95 (*0-8204-3060-9*) P Lang Pubng.

Pedro of Guatemala. Tr. & Illus. by Marilyn S. Martin.Tr. of Pedro de Guatemala. (SPA.). 160p. (J). (gr. 3-6). 1997. pap. 4.15 (*0-7399-0084-6*, 2340.1) Rod & Staff.

Pedro Paramo. Juan Rulfo. (SPA.). pap. 13.95 (*84-376-0418-4*, Pub. by Ediciones Catedra) Continental Bk.

Pedro Paramo. Juan Rulfo. 1991. pap. 9.99 (*968-16-0502-0*) Fondo.

Pedro Paramo. Juan Rulfo. (SPA.). 1989. 6.50 (*0-8288-2575-0*) Fr & Eur.

Pedro Paramo. Juan Rulfo. Tr. by Margaret S. Paden from SPA. LC 90-2821. 136p. 1990. pap. 11.00 (*0-8021-3390-8*, Grove) Grove-Atltic.

Pedro Paramo, el llano en Llamas. Juan Rulfo. (SPA.). pap. 11.95 (*84-322-0474-9*, Pub. by E Seix Barral) Continental Bk.

Pedro Prado. John R. Kelly. LC 73-16015. (Twayne's World Authors Ser.). 154p. (C). 1974. lib. bdg. 20.95 (*0-8057-2712-4*) Irvington.

Pedro Salinas & His Circumstance. Jean C. Newman. LC 83-10778. (Illus.). 274p. (C). 1984. pap. 11.95 (*0-913480-56-8*) Inter Am U Pr.

Pedro Salinas' Theater of Self-Authentication. Stephanie L. Orringer. LC 94-28221. (AUS II: Vol. 199). 137p. (C). 1995. text 39.95 (*0-8204-1994-X*) P Lang Pubng.

Pedro Sanchez. Jose M. De Pereda. Ed. by Jose M. Gonzalez Herran. (Nueva Austral Ser.: Vol. 149). (SPA.). 1991. pap. text 29.95 (*84-239-1949-8*) Elliots Bks.

Pedro the Cruel of Castile, 1350-1369. Clara Estow. LC 95-7468. (Medieval Mediterranean Ser.: Vol. 6). 1995. 102.50 (*90-04-10094-6*) Brill Academic Pubs.

Pedro II of Brazil: The Son of the Habsburg Express. Gloria Kaiser. Tr. & Afterword by Lowell A. Bangerter. LC 99-35535. (Studies in Austrian Literature, Culture & Thought). 405p. 2000. pap. 23.50 (*1-57241-082-5*) Ariadne CA.

Pedro Vallina: A Chronology. V. Munoz. Tr. by W. Scott Johnson. (Libertarian & Anarchist Chronology Ser.). 1979. lib. bdg. 59.95 (*0-8490-3057-9*) Gordon Pr.

***Pedro y el Capitan.** Mario Benedetti. (SPA.). 2000. pap. 9.95 (*968-19-0495-8*) Aguilar.

Pedro y Juan (Peter & John) (SPA.). (J). 1993. 4.98 (*1-56173-935-9*, P000-9359) Pubns Intl Ltd.

Pedro's Journal see Diario de Pedro

Pedro's Journal. Pam Conrad. (Illus.). 96p. (J). (gr. 3-7). 1992. pap. 2.95 (*0-590-46206-7*, 058, Apple Paperbacks) Scholastic Inc.

Pedro's Journal: A Voyage with Christopher Columbus, Aug. 3, 1492-Feb. 14, 1493. Pam Conrad. LC 90-85723. (Illus.). 96p. (J). (gr. 3-7). 1991. 15.95 (*1-878093-17-7*) Boyds Mills Pr.

Pedro's Journal: A Voyage with Christopher Columbus, August 3, 1492-February 14, 1493. Pam Conrad. (J). 1991. 8.60 (*0-606-01924-3*, Pub. by Turtleback) Demco.

Pedro's Simple Trailside Repair. 2nd ed. Dave Rich & Pete Swenson. 1995. pap. 6.95 (*0-9634607-4-9*) ThreeD Pr.

Pee Wee Christmas. Judy Delton. (Pee Wee Scouts Ser.: No. 7). 96p. (Orig.). (J). (gr. k-6). 1988. pap. 3.99 (*0-440-40067-8*, YB BDD) BDD Bks Young Read.

Pee Wee Christmas. Judy Delton. (Pee Wee Scouts Ser.). (J). 1988. 9.09 (*0-606-04054-4*, Pub. by Turtleback) Demco.

Pee Wee Jubilee. Judy Delton. 96p. (J). (gr. k-6). 1989. pap. 3.99 (*0-440-40226-3*, YB BDD) BDD Bks Young Read.

Pee Wee Jubilee. Judy Delton. (Pee Wee Scouts Ser.). (J). 1989. 9.19 (*0-606-04296-2*, Pub. by Turtleback) Demco.

***Pee Wee Pipes & the Wing Thing.** Illus. by Thomas H. Bone, III. LC 00-91370. (Pee Wee Pipes Adventure Ser.: Vol. 1). 32p. (J). (ps-2). 2000. 15.00 (*0-9674602-1-2*) Blue Marlin Pubns.

Pee Wee Pool Party. Judy Delton. (Pee Wee Scouts Ser.: No. 29). (Illus.). 96p. (J). (gr. 1-4). 1996. pap. 3.99 (*0-440-40980-2*, YB BDD) BDD Bks Young Read.

Pee Wee Pool Party. Judy Delton. (Pee Wee Scouts Ser.). (J). 1996. 9.19 (*0-606-09739-2*, Pub. by Turtleback) Demco.

Pee Wee Scouts, No. 24. Judy Delton. 96p. (J). 1994. pap. 3.99 (*0-440-40976-4*) Dell.

Pee Wee Speaks: A Discography of Pee Wee Russell. Robert Hilbert & David Niven. LC 92-37522. (Studies in Jazz: No. 13). (Illus.). 398p. 1992. 50.00 (*0-8108-2634-8*) Scarecrow.

Pee Wees on First. Judy Delton. LC 95-208324. (Pee Wee Scouts Ser.: No. 25). 96p. (J). 1995. pap. 3.99 (*0-440-40977-2*) Dell.

Pee Wees on First. Judy Delton. (Pee Wee Scouts Ser.). (J). 1995. 9.44 (*0-606-08000-7*) Turtleback.

Pee Wees on Parade. Judy Delton. (Pee Wee Scouts Ser.: No. 17). (Illus.). 96p. (J). (ps-3). 1992. pap. 3.99 (*0-440-40700-1*, YB BDD) BDD Bks Young Read.

Pee Wees on Parade. Judy Delton. (Pee Wee Scouts Ser.). 1992. 9.19 (*0-606-00958-2*, Pub. by Turtleback) Demco.

Pee Wee's on Skis. Judy Delton. 96p. (J). 1993. pap. 3.99 (*0-440-40885-7*) Dell.

Pee Wees on Skis. Judy Delton. (Pee Wee Scouts Ser.). (J). 1993. 9.19 (*0-606-05532-0*, Pub. by Turtleback) Demco.

Pee Yew Bartholomew: A Story about Divorce. Dannell C. Morrison. LC 96-79869. 16p. (Orig.). (J). (gr. 5-8). 1997. pap. 5.95 (*1-57543-028-2*) Mar Co Prods.

***Peebles, Ante 1600-1962.** Anne Bradbury Peebles. 191p. 1999. 37.50 (*0-8328-9891-0*); pap. 27.50 (*0-8328-9892-9*) Higginson Bk Co.

Peedie Peeble's Colour Book. Mairi Hedderwick. (Illus.). 32p. (J). (ps-k). 1995. 17.95 (*0-370-31842-0*, Pub. by Bodley Head) Trafalgar.

Peef the Christmas Bear. Tom Hegg. (Illus.). 48p. (J). (gr. 3 up). 1995. 15.95 (*0-931674-26-3*) Waldman Hse Pr.

***Peek: Photographs from the Kinsey Institute.** Carol Squiers et al. (Illus.). 160p. 2000. 60.00 (*1-892041-35-9*) Arena Editions.

Peek-a-Bible Series. Tracy Harrast. (Peek-a-Bible Ser.). (Illus.). 20p. (J). (ps-1). 1998. 6.99 (*0-310-97585-9*) Zondervan.

Peek-a-Boo. (Illus.). (J). 1998. pap. 5.99 (*1-58048-023-3*) Sandvik Pub.

Peek-a-Boo. Illus. by Ellen Appleby. LC 90-218986. 16p. (J). (ps-k). 1990. 3.95 (*0-671-70722-1*) Litle Simon.

Peek-a-Boo! Michael Evans. (Little Surprises Ser.). (Illus.). 24p. (J). (ps-2). 1992. bds. 2.95 (*0-8249-8528-1*, Ideals Child) Hambleton-Hill.

Peek-a-Boo! Roberta G. Intrater. (Baby Faces Ser.). (Illus.). 12p. (J). (ps). 1997. bds. 4.95 (*0-590-05896-7*, Cartwheel) Scholastic Inc.

Peek-a-Boo. Jane L. Mills & Larry D. Johnson. LC 86-60380. (Search & Find Set Ser.: Level 1). (Illus.). 13p. (Orig.). (J). (ps). 1986. pap. 3.50 (*0-938155-04-0*); pap. 12.00 (*0-685-13530-6*) Read A Bol.

Peek-a-Boo! Nicola Tuxworth. (Very First Picture Bks.). (Illus.). 24p. (J). (ps). 1997. 4.95 (*1-85967-410-0*, Lorenz Bks) Anness Pub.

***Peek-a-Boo!** Ellen Weiss. (Fisher-Price Step-by-Step Ser.). (Illus.). (J). (gr. k-3). 2000. pap. 5.99 (*1-57584-391-9*, Pub. by Rdrs Digest) S&S Trade.

***Peek-A-Boo: A Very First Picture Book.** Nicola Tuxworth. (Illus.). (J). 2000. bds. 4.95 (*0-7548-0064-4*, Lorenz Bks) Anness Pub.

Peek-a-Boo ABC. Demi. LC 82-60108. (Peek-a-Boo Board Bks.). (Illus.). (J). (ps-k). 1982. 5.95 (*0-394-85418-7*, Pub. by Random Bks Yng Read) Random.

***Peek-a-Boo Alaska.** Bernd C. Richter & Susan E. Richter. (J). (ps). 2000. bds. 6.95 (*0-9663495-5-5*) Saddle Pal Creat.

Peek-a-Boo at the Zoo see Encondidas en el Zoologico

Peek-A-Boo At The Zoo. Frank Edwards. (New Reader Ser.). (J). pap. 4.95 (*1-894323-06-8*, Pub. by Pokeweed Pr) Genl Dist Srvs.

Peek-a-Boo at the Zoo. Frank B. Edwards. (New Reader Ser.). (Illus.). 24p. (J). (ps-1). 1997. pap. 5.95 (*0-921285-52-3*, Pub. by Bungalo Books) Firefly Bks Ltd.

Peek-A-Boo at the Zoo. Frank B. Edwards. (New Reader Ser.). (Illus.). 24p. (J). (ps-1). 1997. text 16.95 (*0-921285-53-1*, Pub. by Bungalo Books) Firefly Bks Ltd.

Peek-A-Boo Baby. Amanda Haley. LC 98-181120. 4p. (J). 1998. write for info. (*0-7853-2780-0*) Pubns Intl Ltd.

Peek-a-Boo Baby. Illus. by Lisa Kopper. (Lift & Look Board Bks.). 12p. (J). (ps). 1993. bds. 4.99 (*0-448-40197-5*, G & D) Peng Put Young Read.

An Asterisk (*) at the beginning of an entry indicates that the title is appearing for the first time.

Peek-a-Boo Board Book. Janet Ahlberg & Allan Ahlberg. (Illus.). 32p. 1997. pap. 6.99 (*0-670-87192-3*) Viking Penguin.

Peek-a-Boo Gingerbread House. Illus. by Scott McDougall. LC 96-78084. (Lift & Look Board Book Ser.). 12p. (J). (ps up). 1997. bds. 4.95 (*0-448-41622-0*, G & D) Peng Put Young Read.

***Peek-a-Boo! I See You.** Alan Benjamin. (J). 2001. mass mkt. 4.99 (*0-375-81168-0*, Pub. by Random Bks Yng Read) Random.

Peek-a-Boo! I See You! Joan Phillips. (So Tall Board Bks.). (Illus.). 18p. (J). (ps). 1983. bds. 4.99 (*0-448-03092-6*, G & D) Peng Put Young Read.

***Peek-a-Boo I'm Like You.** Funny Friends, LLC Staff. (Illus.). 18p. (J). 1999. bds. write for info. (*1-929758-00-6*) Funny Friends.

***Peek-a-Boo I'm Like You Value Pack: With Plush Star.** Funny Friends, LLC Staff. (Illus.). 18p. (J). 1999. bds. write for info. (*1-929758-03-0*) Funny Friends.

Peek-a-Boo Kitty. Illus. by Lisa Kopper. (Lift & Look Board Bks.). 12p. (J). (ps). 1993. bds. 4.99 (*0-448-40196-7*, G & D) Peng Put Young Read.

Peek-a-Boo, Little Mouse. Noelle Carter. LC 91-78193. (Illus.). 12p. (J). (ps). 1995. 10.95 (*0-8050-2253-8*, Bks Young Read) H Holt & Co.

Peek-a-Boo, Lizzy Lou! A Daytime Book & Muppet Puppet. Lauren Attinello. (Illus.). 16p. (J). 1997. 16.95 (*0-7611-0948-X*) Workman Pub.

Peek-a-Boo Magic. Pat Bagley. LC 95-15050. (Illus.). 32p. (J). 1995. 12.95 (*1-885628-00-5*, Pub. by Buckaroo Bks) Origin Bk Sales.

Peek-a-Boo, Miffy! A Flip Book. Dick Bruna. LC 97-76168. (Illus.). 16p. (J). (ps-k). 1998. bds. 5.95 (*1-56836-222-6*) Kodansha.

Peek-a-Boo Moon. Illus. by Thierry Courtin. LC 95-77543. (Lift & Look Board Bks.). 12p. (J). (ps-3). 1996. bds. 4.95 (*0-448-41282-9*, G & D) Peng Put Young Read.

Peek-a-Boo Moon: A Picture-It Storybook; A Reader Illustrated Storybook. unabridged ed. Julia Kalin. 8p. (J). (ps-3). 1999. pap. text 10.95 (*0-9672430-3-3*, 9904) Stay Play.

***Peek-A-Boo Park.** Metrobooks Staff. (Illus.). 18p. (J). (ps-k). 2000. 9.99 (*1-58663-107-1*) M Friedman Pub Grp Inc.

Peek-a-Boo, Pooh! Disney Publishing Group Staff. (Pooh's Learn & Grow Ser.: Vol. 7). (Illus.). 12p. (J). 1999. 3.49 (*1-57973-041-8*) Advance Pubs.

Peek-a-Boo Sue. Dick Punnett. LC 84-23003. (Rhyme Time Library). (Illus.). 32p. (J). (ps-2). 1985. lib. bdg. 21.36 (*0-89565-305-2*) Childs World.

Peek-a-Boo Teddy. Illus. by Lisa Kopper. (Lift & Look Board Bks.). 12p. (J). (ps). 1993. bds. 4.99 (*0-448-40195-9*, G & D) Peng Put Young Read.

Peek-A-Boo, Winnie the Pooh! Kathleen W. Zoehfeld. (Illus.). (J). 1999. 5.99 (*0-7364-0051-6*, Pub. by Mouse Works) Time Warner.

Peek-a-Boo Zoo. Susan Hood. (J). 1999. 9.99 (*1-56799-896-8*) M Friedman Pub Grp Inc.

***Peek-a-Boogie: Song-Stretching Activities for Children's Favorite Tunes.** Pamela Ott. (Illus.). 96p. 1999. pap. 14.95 (*0-7619-7543-8*) Corwin Pr.

Peek-A-Moo! Marie Torres Cimarusti. (Illus.). 10p. (J). (ps up). 1998. 9.99 (*0-525-46083-7*, Dutton Child) Peng Put Young Read.

Peek a Moo. Bernard Most. LC 97-33042. (Illus.). 20p. (J). 1998. 5.95 (*0-15-201251-6*, Harcourt Child Bks) Harcourt.

***Peek-a-Who?** Nina Laden. LC 99-44248. (Illus.). 11p. (J). (ps). 2000. bds. 6.95 (*0-8118-2602-3*) Chronicle Bks.

Peek at a Pond. Neecy Twinem. LC 98-73044. (Illus.). 24p. (ps-1). 1999. pap. text 6.99 (*0-448-41953-X*) Putnam Pub Group.

Peek at Japan Vol. 1: A Lighthearted Look at Japan's Language & Culture. 2nd rev. ed. Florence E. Metcalf. (Illus.). 133p. (Orig.). (J). (gr. 1-8). 1992. reprint ed. pap. 14.95 (*0-9631684-3-6*) Metco Pub.

Peek at Life from Another Planet. Gene Laboda. LC 83-62346. 96p. (Orig.). 1983. pap. 4.95 (*0-914279-00-9*) Pyramid Pub Co.

Peek at Occupations. Phyllis Trella. LC 82-73692. (P.A.O. Adventures Ser.). (Illus.). 48p. (J). (gr. 2-6). write for info. (*0-914201-03-4*) Cheeruppet.

Peek into My Church. 2nd rev. ed. Veronica Kelly & Wendy Goody. (Illus.). 44p. (J). (gr. k-5). 1998. 14.95 (*0-9657218-1-7*) WhipperSnapper.

***Peek Through the Curtain: A Trilogy.** Robert H. Phillips. LC 98-91131. 564p. 2000. 24.95 (*0-533-13063-8*) Vantage.

Peeka, Pooka & the Dinosaur. Mary H. Frederick. LC 99-19869. (J). 1999. write for info. (*1-893652-06-8*, Writers Club Pr) iUniversecom.

Peekaboo: Poems from Hollywood. Mark Dunster. 11p. 1999. pap. 5.00 (*0-89642-735-8*) Linden Pubs.

Peekaboo! 101 Ways to Make a Baby Smile. LC 98-22920. 24p. (J). 1998. 9.95 (*0-7894-3449-0*) DK Pub Inc.

Peekaboo & Other Games to Play with Your Baby. Shari Steelsmith. (Illus.). 128p. (Orig.). 1995. pap. 9.95 (*0-943990-81-5*); lib. bdg. 18.95 (*0-943990-99-8*) Parenting Pr.

Peekaboo Babies: A Counting Book. Lionel. LC 96-70373. (Illus.). 12p. (J). (ps-1). 1997. 12.95 (*0-531-30016-1*) Orchard Bks Watts.

***Peekaboo, Baby!** Marcia Leonard. LC 99-66183. (Illus.). 20p. (J). (ps-k). 2000. 7.95 (*0-694-01373-0*, HarpFestival) HarpC Child Bks.

Peekaboo Baby. Publications International, Ltd. Editorial Staff et al. LC 98-208306. 1998. write for info. (*0-7853-2777-0*) Pubns Intl Ltd.

Peekaboo Bunny. Alyssa S. Capucilli. LC 92-62493. (Illus.). 24p. (J). (ps-k). 1994. 6.95 (*0-590-46754-9*, Cartwheel) Scholastic Inc.

Peekaboo Bunny: Friend in the Snow. Alyssa S. Melcher. (Illus.). 24p. (J). (ps-k). 1995. 6.95 (*0-590-50318-9*, Cartwheel) Scholastic Inc.

Peekaboo It's Me! Ed. by Instructional Fair Staff. (J). 1998. 7.95 (*1-56822-774-4*) Instruct Fair.

Peekaboo, Puppy! Anna Ross. LC 93-85494. (My Puppy Loves Me Bk.). (J). (ps). 1994. 3.99 (*0-679-85700-1*, Pub. by Random Bks Yng Read) Random.

Peekaboo, Puppy! A My Puppy Loves Me Book. K. K. Ross. (Chunky Flap Bks. Ser.). (Illus.). 22p. (J). (ps). 1994. 3.50 (*0-685-71037-8*) Random Bks Yng Read.

***Peekaboo You!** Marianne Borgardt. (Illus.). 12p. (J). 1999. reprint ed. 5.95 (*1-892374-15-3*) Weldon Owen.

Peekin Through the Past: Easy Scrapbook Pages. Lisa Berrett. (Illus.). 40p. 1997. 8.99 (*1-58050-073-0*, 40-6117) Provo Craft.

Peekin' Through the Past - Summer Fun. Lisa Berrett. 1998. pap. 8.99 (*1-58050-050-1*, 40-6181) Provo Craft.

Peekin Through the Past "Seasonal Ideas" Lisa Berrett. 44p. 1997. 8.99 (*1-58050-022-6*, 40-6151) Provo Craft.

Peeking Prairie Dogs. Christine Zuchora-Walske. LC 98-28517. (Pull Ahead Bks.). 32p. (J). (gr. k-2). 1999. pap. 6.95 (*0-8225-3622-6*, Lerner Publctns) Lerner Pub.

Peeking Prairie Dogs. Christine Zuchora-Walske. LC 98-28517. (Pull Ahead Bks.). (Illus.). 32p. (J). (gr. k-2). 1999. 15.95 (*0-8225-3616-1*, Lerner Publctns) Lerner Pub.

Peekskill in the American Revolution. Emma L. Patterson. (Illus.). 184p. 1997. reprint ed. lib. bdg. 26.50 (*0-8328-6201-0*) Higginson Bk Co.

Peekskill, NY 1950's. Historical Briefs, Inc. Staff. Ed. by Thomas Antonucci & Michael Antonucci. 176p. 1993. pap. 19.95 (*0-89677-073-7*) Hist Briefs.

Peekskill, NY 1940's. Historical Briefs, Inc. Staff. Ed. by Thomas Antonucci & Michael Antonucci. 176p. 1993. pap. 19.95 (*0-89677-077-X*) Hist Briefs.

Peekskill Pioneers, Patriots & People, Past & Present: History of Peekskill. William T. Horton. (Illus.). 355p. 1997. reprint ed. lib. bdg. 42.00 (*0-8328-6200-2*) Higginson Bk Co.

Peel. James R. Thursfield. LC 77-39213. (Select Bibliographies Reprint Ser.). 1977. reprint ed. 18.95 (*0-8369-6815-8*) Ayer.

***Peel 'n Play Adventure Scenes: Adventure Scene Activity Book.** Ed. by Toon Takes. (Illus.). 20p. (J). (ps-4). 1999. pap. 15.50 (*1-929456-05-0*) Myrtle Seal Pubg.

Peel & Put for Early Childhood. Schrader. 1987. 38.00 (*0-7616-2250-0*) Commun Skill.

Peel My Love Like an Onion. Ana Castillo. LC 99-25057. 240p. 1999. 23.95 (*0-385-49676-1*) Doubleday.

***Peel My Love Like an Onion.** Ana Castillo. 256p. 2000. reprint ed. pap. 12.00 (*0-385-49677-X*, Anchor NY) Doubleday.

Peel 'n Play Bible Adventures: Adventure Scene Activity Book. Ed. by Toon Takes. (Illus.). 20p. (J). (ps-4). 1999. pap. 15.50 (*1-929456-02-6*) Myrtle Seal Pubg.

Peel, Priests & Politics: Sir Robert Peel's Administration & the Roman Catholic Church in Ireland, 1841-1846. Donal A. Kerr. (Oxford Historical Monographs). 400p. 1984. pap. 21.00 (*0-19-822932-1*) OUP.

Peel, the Extraordinary Elephant. Susan Joyce. LC 86-61990. (Illus.). 48p. (J). (gr. 2-12). 1988. pap. 8.95 (*0-939217-01-5*) Peel Prod.

Peeled Fruit. Mark Von Zwehl. 20p. (Orig.). 1995. pap. write for info. (*1-885206-20-8*, Iliad Pr) Cader Pubng.

Peeling. Yuri Kageyama. 80p. (Orig.). 1988. pap. 4.95 (*0-918408-26-1*) Ishmael Reed.

Peeling. Shelley Scott. 64p. 1989. pap. 5.95 (*0-932616-27-5*) Brick Hse Bks.

Peeling Back Eggshells. Melannie Svoboda. LC 94-60499. 120p. (Orig.). 1994. pap. 7.95 (*0-89622-613-1*) Twenty-Third.

Peeling the Onion. Wendy Orr. 166p. (YA). (gr. 7-12). 1999. mass mkt. 4.50 (*0-440-22773-9*, LLL BDD) BDD Bks Young Read.

Peeling the Onion. Wendy Orr. LC 96-42353. 176p. (J). (gr. 7-12). 1997. 16.95 (*0-8234-1289-X*) Holiday.

Peeling the Onion: A Gestact Therapy Manual for Clients. rev. ed. Bud Feder. 50p. 1993. pap. 24.00 (*0-9663109-1-8*) B Feder.

Peeling the Onion: An Anthology of Poems Selected by Ruth Gordon. Selected by Ruth Gordon. LC 92-571. (Charlotte Zolotow Bk.). 112p. (J). (ps up). 1993. 14.89 (*0-06-021728-6*) HarpC Child Bks.

Peeling the Sweet Onion: Unlayering the Veils of Identity & Existence. Martin E. Segal. LC 90-901503. 200p. (Orig.). 1990. pap. 9.95 (*0-934619-03-4*) New Age FL Pub.

Peenemunde Raid. Martin Middlebrook. LC 82-17850. (Illus.). 272p. 1983. write for info. (*0-672-52759-6*) Macmillan.

Peenemunde to Canaveral. Dieter K. Huzel. LC 81-2223. (Illus.). 247p. 1981. reprint ed. lib. bdg. 45.00 (*0-313-22928-7*, HUPC, Greenwood Pr) Greenwood.

Peenemunde Wind Tunnels: A Memoir. Peter P. Wegener. LC 95-50289. (Illus.). 264p. 1996. 32.00 (*0-300-06367-9*) Yale U Pr.

Peep at Number 5: or A Chapter in the Life of a City Pastor. Elizabeth S. Phelps. LC 70-164573. (American Fiction Reprint Ser.). 1977. reprint ed. 25.95 (*0-8369-7050-0*) Ayer.

Peep at Washoe: Sketches of Virginia City, N. T. J. Ross Browne. (Illus.). 48p. 1986. 4.95 (*0-913814-77-6*) Nevada Pubns.

Peep Behind the Scenes. O. F. Walton. LC 82-73063. (Victorian Children's Classics Ser.). 1982. pap. 6.99 (*0-88270-538-5*) Bridge-Logos.

***Peep Behind the Scenes: A Little Girl's Journey of Discovery.** O F WALTON. 1999. pap. text 5.99 (*1-85792-524-6*) Christian Focus.

Peep Land: Paintings, 1983-1993. Jane Dickson. (Illus.). 64p. 1994. pap. 20.00 (*0-945558-21-X*) ISU Univ Galls.

***Peep Show.** Michael Huhn. 1998. pap. text 49.95 (*3-925443-62-2*) Janssen.

Peep-Show Girl. Marion Lomax. 1989. pap. 11.95 (*1-85224-072-5*, Pub. by Bloodaxe Bks) Dufour.

Peeper & the Giant Easter Egg. Rhonda C. Greenberg. (Illus.). (Orig.). (J). (ps-1). 1988. pap. 2.95 (*0-671-64823-3*) Litle Simon.

Peeper Puppets Idea Book. Dick Gruber. (Illus.). 15p. 1995. pap. 3.00 (*1-58302-063-2*, BPR-28) One Way St.

Peepers. Bunting. LC 99-6292. 2000. 15.00 (*0-15-260297-6*) Harcourt.

***Peephole Rhymes.** Emily Bolam. (Illus.). (J). (ps-3). 2000. 7.99 (*0-8431-7594-X*, Price Stern) Peng Put Young Read.

***Peephole Riddles.** Margaret Anastas. (Illus.). (J). (ps-3). 2000. 7.99 (*0-8431-7595-8*, Price Stern) Peng Put Young Read.

Peeping Beauty. Mary J. Auch. (Illus.). 32p. (J). (gr. k-3). 1993. pap. 6.95 (*0-8234-1170-2*) Holiday.

Peeping Beauty. Mary J. Auch. LC 92-16374. (Illus.). 32p. (J). (gr. k-3). 1993. lib. bdg. 16.95 (*0-8234-1001-3*) Holiday.

Peeping Beauty. Mary J. Auch. (Illus.). (J). (gr. k-4). 24.95 incl. audio (*0-87499-327-X*) Live Oak Media.

Peeping Beauty. Mary Jane Auch. (Illus.). (J). (gr. k-4). pap. 15.95 incl. audio (*0-87499-326-1*) Live Oak Media.

Peeping Beauty, 4 bks., Set. Mary J. Auch. (Illus.). (J). (gr. k-4). pap. 37.95 incl. audio (*0-87499-328-8*) Live Oak Media.

Peeping in the Shell: A Whooping Crane Is Hatched. Faith McNulty. LC 85-45837. (Illus.). 64p. (J). (gr. 3-7). 1986. 11.95 (*0-06-024134-9*) HarpC Child Bks.

Peeping Tom. Leo Marks. (Illus.). 160p. 1998. pap. 14.95 (*0-571-19403-6*) Faber & Faber.

Peepo! Janet Ahlberg & Allen Ahlberg. (Illus.). (J). pap. 9.95 (*0-14-050384-6*, Pub. by Pnguin Bks Ltd) Trafalgar.

Peeps & Freaks. Chris Musun. LC 85-73404. 446p. (Orig.). 1986. pap. 3.95 (*0-936729-01-5*) Dare Co.

Peeps at People: Being Certain Papers from the Writings of Anne Warrington Witherup. Anne W. Witherup. Ed. by John K. Bangs. LC 78-166659. (Illus.). 1971. reprint ed. 19.00 (*0-403-01400-X*) Scholarly.

Peeps at the Mighty. Patrick Braybrooke. LC 67-22076. (Essay Index Reprint Ser.). 1977. 19.95 (*0-8369-1321-3*) Ayer.

***Peepshow: A Cartoon Diary.** Joe Matt. (Illus.). 104p. 1999. pap. 14.95 (*1-896597-27-0*, Pub. by Drawn & Quarterly) LPC InBook.

***Peepshow: Media & Politics in an Age of Scandal.** Larry J. Sabato et al. LC 99-88697. 192p. 2000. 22.95 (*0-7425-0010-1*) Rowman.

Peepshows: A Visual History. Richard Balzer. LC 97-33267. (FRE & ENG., Illus.). 160p. 1998. 45.00 (*0-8109-6349-3*, Pub. by Abrams) Time Warner.

Peepshows: An Eye to the World. Richard Balzer. (Illus.). 160p. (Orig.). 1997. write for info. (*0-9656676-0-X*); pap. write for info. (*0-9656676-1-8*) Eye Wndr Pr.

Peer Assistance/Impaired Provider Program: A Model. Contrib. by APTA Staff. 59p. 1994. pap. 15.00 (*1-887759-41-7*, P-111) Am Phys Therapy Assn.

Peer Assisted Learning. Ed. by Keith Topping & Stewart Ehly. LC 98-20777. 320p. 1998. write for info. (*0-8058-2501-0*); pap. write for info. (*0-8058-2502-9*) L Erlbaum Assocs.

Peer Coaching for Educators. Barbara Gottesman & James O. Jennings. LC 94-60469. 140p. 1994. pap. text 24.95 (*1-56676-137-9*) Scarecrow.

***Peer Coaching for Educators.** 2nd ed. Barbara L. Gottesman. 144p. 2000. pap. 27.95 (*0-8108-3745-5*) Scarecrow.

Peer Commentary on Peer Review: A Case Study in Scientific Quality Control. Ed. by Stevan R. Harnad. LC 82-19860. 81p. reprint ed. pap. 25.00 (*0-608-15734-1*, 2031666) Bks Demand.

Peer Counseling. 2nd ed. Salovey D' Andrea. 422p. 1996. pap. 29.95 (*0-8314-0084-6*) Sci & Behavior.

Peer Counselling in Schools: A Time to Listen. Ed. by Helen Cowie & Sonia Sharp. 160p. 1996. pap. 24.95 (*1-85346-367-1*, Pub. by David Fulton) Taylor & Francis.

Peer Counselor's Pocket Book see Peer Helper's Pocketbook

Peer Evangelism. Steve Clapp & Sam Detwiler. (FaithQuest Youth Resources Ser.). 100p. 1993. pap. 16.95 (*0-87178-693-1*, 8931) Brethren.

Peer Focused Therapy. Hogan. (C). 1980. text. write for info. (*0-03-051076-7*) Harcourt Coll Pubs.

Peer Gynt. Henrik Ibsen. Date not set. lib. bdg. 21.95 (*0-8488-1667-6*) Amereon Ltd.

Peer Gynt. Henrik Ibsen. Tr. by Gerry Bamman & Irene B. Berman from NOR. LC 92-2564. (TCG Translations Ser.: Vol. 2). 244p. 1992. 22.95 (*1-55936-046-1*); pap. 12.95 (*1-55936-045-3*) Theatre Comm.

Peer Gynt. Henrik Ibsen. 1999. pap. 7.95 (*1-85459-435-4*, Pub. by Theatre Comm) Consort Bk Sales.

Peer Gynt. Henrik Ibsen. Tr. by Peter Watts. (Classics Ser.). 224p. 1966. pap. 8.95 (*0-14-044167-0*, Penguin Classics) Viking Penguin.

Peer Gynt. rev. ed. Henrik Ibsen. Tr. by Rolf Fjelde from NOR. (Nordic Ser.: Vol. 2). 327p. 1980. pap. 13.95 (*0-8166-0915-2*) U of Minn Pr.

Peer Gynt. unabridged ed. Henrik Ibsen. Ed. by William-Alan Landes. LC 98-10360. 88p. 1997. pap. 7.00 (*0-88734-750-9*) Players Pr.

Peer Gynt: A Dramatic Poem. Henrik Ibsen. Tr. by Christopher Fry & Johann Fillinger. (Oxford World's Classics Ser.). 190p. 1999. pap. 7.95 (*0-19-283746-X*) OUP.

Peer Gynt: A Dramatic Poem. Henrik Ibsen. Tr. by John Northam. 193p. 1995. 12.00 (*82-00-22496-1*) Scandnvan Univ Pr.

Peer Gynt Suite: Piano: Centennial Edition. E. Grieg. 44p. 1995. pap. 4.95 (*0-7935-4517-X*, 50482390) H Leonard.

Peer Gynt Suite No. 1: Piano Four Hands. E. Grieg. 24p. 1986. pap. 7.50 (*0-7935-5222-2*) H Leonard.

Peer Gynt Suite for Piano, No. 1. Edvard Grieg. Ed. by Joseph Gahn. (Carl Fischer Music Library: No. 315). 1910. pap. 5.00 (*0-8258-0105-2*) Fischer Inc NY.

Peer Gynt Suite, Holberg Suite & Other Works for Piano Solo. Edvard Grieg. viii, 261p. pap. 14.95 (*0-486-27590-6*) Dover.

Peer Gynt Suites, Vols. 1 & 2. E. Grieg. 1997. pap. 8.95 (*0-486-29582-6*, 706095Q) Dover.

Peer Helper's Pocketbook. Joan Sturkie & Valerie Gibson. LC 92-11052. Orig. Title: The Peer Counselor's Pocket Book. 120p. 1992. pap. 7.95 (*0-89390-237-3*) Resource Pubns.

Peer Helping: A Practical Guide. 2nd rev. ed. Robert D. Myrick & Don L. Sorenson. LC 97-60266. (Illus.). 160p. 1997. pap. text 9.95 (*0-932796-81-8*) Ed Media Corp.

Peer Helping Skills: A Program for Training Peer Helpers & Peer Tutors for Middle & High School, Peer Helper Handbook. John DeMarco. LC 93-44890. 90p. 1993. pap. 32.95 (*1-56246-090-0*, 3104, HazeldenJohnson Inst); pap. 7.75 (*1-56246-089-7*, 3106, HazeldenJohnson Inst) Hazelden.

Peer Helping Training Course. Joan Sturkie & Maggie Phillips. LC 94-22403. (Illus.). 280p. 1994. teacher ed., ring bd. 69.95 (*0-89390-311-6*) Resource Pubns.

Peer Instruction: A User's Manual. Eric Mazur. LC 96-20088. 253p. (C). 1996. pap. 24.20 (*0-13-565441-6*) P-H.

Peer Interaction of Young Children. Carollee Howes. (Monographs of the Society for Research in Child Development: No. 217 53.1). 100p. 1988. pap. text 15.00 (*0-226-35523-3*) U Ch Pr.

Peer Justice & Youth Empowerment: An Implementation Guide for Teen Court Programs. Tracy M. Godwin et al. (Illus.). 287p. (Orig.). 1997. pap. text 50.00 (*0-7881-4491-X*) DIANE Pub.

***Peer Justice & Youth Empowerment: An Implementation Guide for Teen Court Programs.** Tracy M. Godwin. 325p. (Orig.). (C). 2000. reprint ed. pap. text 40.00 (*0-7567-0023-X*) DIANE Pub.

Peer Leadership: A Human Relations Process to Reduce Substance Abuse & Improve School Climate. Thomas Turney. LC 89-90420. 248p. (Orig.). 1989. pap. text. write for info. (*0-9624365-0-X*) T Turney.

***Peer-Led Team Learning: General Chemistry.** David Gosser et al. 2000. pap. text 15.00 (*0-13-028806-3*, Prentice Hall) P-H.

Peer Listening in the Middle School: Training Activities for Students. Sandra P. Hazouri & Miriam F. Smith. LC 91-75586. (Illus.). 134p. (Orig.). (J). (gr. 6-8). 1991. pap. text 8.95 (*0-932796-34-6*) Ed Media Corp.

Peer Mediation: Conflict Resolution in Schools. 2nd rev. ed. Fred Schrumpf et al. LC 96-69186. (Illus.). 350p. 1996. pap. text, teacher ed. 29.95 (*0-87822-368-1*, 4923); pap. text, student ed. 12.95 (*0-87822-367-3*, 4924) Res Press.

Peer Mediation: Finding a Way to Care. Judith M. Ferrara. LC 96-15507. (Illus.). 184p. (Orig.). (C). 1996. pap. text 17.50 (*1-57110-021-0*) Stenhse Pubs.

Peer Mediation: Training Students in Conflict Resolution. Center for Learning Network Staff. (Communication). 67p. (YA). (gr. 7-12). 1996. spiral bd. 15.95 (*1-56077-368-5*) Ctr Learning.

Peer Mediation Skills: A Handbook for Peer Mediators. John DeMarco. 43p. (YA). (gr. 7-12). 1998. pap. 9.95 (*1-56246-143-5*, 3074, HazeldenJohnson Inst) Hazelden.

Peer Mediation Skills: Leader's Guide for Training Peer Mediators. John DeMarco. 76p. 1998. pap. 35.00 (*1-56246-144-3*, 3075, HazeldenJohnson Inst) Hazelden.

***Peer Ministry: Empowering Teens to Be Salt for the Earth.** Center for Learning Network Staff. (Religion Ser.). 127p. 1998. pap. text, teacher ed. 19.95 (*1-56077-545-9*) Ctr Learning.

Peer Networking on the AS/400: Practical Networking Solutions for Today's Business Applications. Chris Peters. LC 97-186148. (Illus.). 380p. (Orig.). 1997. pap. 79.00 (*1-883884-39-X*, 565) Midrange Comput.

Peer, Peasants & Pheasants. Judy Vowles. (Illus.). 140p. 1996. pap. 12.95 (*0-85236-325-7*, Pub. by Farming Pr) Diamond Farm Bk.

***Peer Potential: Making the Most of How Teens Influence Each Other.** Peter S. Bearman et al. 115p. 1999. pap. 15.00 (*1-58671-010-9*) Natl Cpgn Teen Preg.

Peer Power: Preadolescent Culture & Identity. Patricia Adler & Peter Adler. LC 97-22516. xii, 255p. 1998. 48.00 (*0-8135-2459-8*); pap. 17.00 (*0-8135-2460-1*) Rutgers U Pr.

Peer Prejudice & Discrimination: Evolutionary, Cultural & Developmental Dynamics. Harold D. Fishbein. 304p. (C). 1995. per. write for info. (*0-697-15004-6*) Brown & Benchmark.

Peer Prejudice & Discrimination: Evolutionary, Cultural & Developmental Dynamics. Harold D. Fishbein. (Developmental Psychology Ser.). 291p. (C). 1996. pap. text 25.00 (*0-8133-3053-X*, Pub. by Westview) HarpC.

Peer Pressure. George B. Eager. LC 93-80759. (Illus.). 144p. (YA). (gr. 6-12). 1994. 13.95 (*1-879224-17-8*); pap. 8.95 (*1-879224-13-5*) Mailbox.

Peer Pressure. Bill Rudge. 28p. 1996. pap. 2.00 (*1-889809-15-2*) Liv Truth.

Peer Pressure: A Parent-Child Manual. Maria Sullivan. (Illus.). 1991. pap. 9.99 (*0-8125-9473-8*, Pub. by Tor Bks) St Martin.

***Peer Pressure: How Can I Say No?** Kate Havelin. LC 99-31166. (Perspectives on Relationships Ser.). (Illus.). 64p. (YA). 1999. 22.60 (*0-7368-0291-6*) Capstone Pr.

P

An Asterisk (*) at the beginning of an entry indicates that the title is appearing for the first time.

Peer Pressure: How to Handle It. George B. Eager. (Illus.). 29p. (Orig.). (YA). 1993. pap. 3.00 (*1-879224-10-0*) Mailbox.

*__Peer Pressure, Pain & Death, Heroes: 13 Bible-Based Sessions.__ Domain 456 Staff. (Domain 456 Ser.). 2000. pap. 18.99 (*0-7814-5516-2*) Cook.

Peer Pressure Reversal: An Adult Guide to Developing a Responsible Child. 2nd ed. Sharon Scott. LC 97-185701. 1997. pap. text 14.95 (*0-87425-408-6*) HRD Press.

Peer Programs on College Campuses: Theory, Training, & 'Voice of Peers' Sherry L. Hatcher. LC 95-31772. 466p. 1995. pap. 49.95 (*0-89390-349-3*) Resource Pubns.

Peer Relationships. Emogene Fox. (Comprehensive Health for Middle Grades Ser.). (J). (gr. 6-9). 1996. 24.00 (*1-56071-468-9*, H570) ETR Assocs.

Peer Relationships in Child Development. Ed. by Thomas J. Berndt & Gary W. Ladd. LC 88-5779. (Personality Processes Ser.). 434p. 1989. 175.00 (*0-471-85131-0*) Wiley.

Peer Response Groups in Actions: Writing Together in Secondary Schools. Karen I. Spear. LC 93-13171. 264p. (C). 1993. pap. text 23.50 (*0-86709-318-8*, 0318, Pub. by Boynton Cook Pubs) Heinemann.

Peer Review: Reforms Needed to Ensure Fairness in Federal Agency Grant Selection. (Illus.). 133p. (Orig.). (C). 1995. pap. text 30.00 (*0-7881-1686-X*) DIANE Pub.

Peer Review Improvement Act of 1982: A Legislative History of Pub. Law No. 97-248. Ed. by Bernard D. Reams, Jr. LC 89-83917. (Federal Health Law Ser.: Part 2). 564p. 1990. lib. bdg. 58.00 (*0-89941-692-6*, 305930) W S Hein.

Peer Review in Environmental Technology Programs. National Research Council Staff. LC 99-191406. 126p. (C). 1999. pap. text 29.00 (*0-309-06338-8*) Natl Acad Pr.

*__Peer Review in Health Sciences.__ Ed. by Fiona Godlee & Tom Jefferson. (Illus.). 271p. 1999. pap. 54.00 (*0-7279-1181-3*) BMJ Pub.

Peer Review in the Department of Energy - Office of Science & Technology: Interim Report. National Research Council Staff. 68p. (C). 1997. pap. text 15.00 (*0-309-05943-7*) Natl Acad Pr.

Peer Review Manual, Pt. 1. 4th ed. American Institute of Certified Public Accountants. LC 86-217293. 187p. reprint ed. pap. 58.00 (*0-7837-0086-5*, 204035300001) Bks Demand.

Peer Review Manual, Pt. 2: Instructions & Checklists. American Institute of Certified Public Accountants. LC 86-217293. 475p. reprint ed. pap. 147.30 (*0-7837-0087-3*, 204035300002) Bks Demand.

Peer Review Manual: Instructions & Checklists - American Institute of Certified Public Accountants, Division for CPA Firms, SEC Practice Section. 5th rev. ed. American Institute of Certified Public Accountants. LC 87-108519. 432p. pap. 134.00 (*0-7837-0084-9*, 204034600016) Bks Demand.

Peer Review of Teaching: A Sourcebook. Nancy Van Note Chism. 132p. 1998. 24.95 (*1-882982-25-8*) Anker Pub.

Peer Review Program Materials. American Institute of Certified Public Accountants Staff. LC HF5616.U5A58. 372p. Date not set. reprint ed. pap. 115.40 (*0-608-20779-9*, 207187800003) Bks Demand.

Peer Review Workshop Report on Ecological Risk Assessment: Issue Papers. (Illus.). 198p. (Orig.). (C). 1995. pap. text 50.00 (*0-7881-1918-4*) DIANE Pub.

*__Peer-Reviewed Journal: A Comprehensive Guide Through the Editorial Process.__ Gary Michael Smith. (Illus.). 216p. 2000. pap. 35.00 (*0-9658380-7-2*, Chatgris Pr) G M Smith.

Peer-Reviewed Journal: A Comprehensive Guide Through the Editorial Process: Includes Forms, Letters, & Faxes. Gary M. Smith. (Illus.). 185p. (Orig.). 1996. pap. 35.00 (*0-9658380-0-5*, Chatgris Pr) G M Smith.

Peer Support Handbook for the Police Officer. Rachelle Katz et al. 66p. 1998. pap. text 14.99 (*0-9669496-1-7*, Peer Supp) Manhat Couns.

Peer Talk in the Classroom: Learning from Research. Ed. by Jeanne R. Paratore & Rachael L. McCormick. LC 97-27908. 250p. 1997. pap. text 28.95 (*0-87207-181-2*, 181) Intl Reading.

Peer Teaching: Historical Perspective, 5. Wagner Lilya. LC 82-939. (Contributions to the Study of Education Ser.: No. 5). 266p. 1982. 59.95 (*0-313-23230-X*, WPT/, Greenwood Pr) Greenwood.

Peer Teaching: To Teach Is to Learn Twice. Neal A. Whitman. LC 88-83592. (ASHE-ERIC Higher Education Reports: No. 88-4). 88p. (Orig.). (C). 1989. pap. 24.00 (*0-913317-48-9*) GWU Grad Schl E&HD.

Peer Teaching & Collaborative Learning in the Language Arts. Elizabeth McAllister. Ed. by Warren W. Lewis. (Illus.). 68p. 1990. pap. 15.95 (*0-927516-21-7*) ERIC-REC.

Peer Tutorial Instruction. William R. Endsley. Ed. by Danny G. Langdon. LC 79-23110. (Instructional Design Library). 104p. 1980. 27.95 (*0-87778-148-6*) Educ Tech Pubns.

Peer Tutoring: A Guide for School Psychologists. Stewart W. Ehly. 37p. 1986. pap. 8.00 (*0-932955-01-0*); VHS 75.00 (*0-317-45930-9*) Natl Assn Schl Psych.

Peer Tutoring: A Guide to Program Design. William L. Ashley et al. 124p. 1986. 10.50 (*0-318-22165-9*, RD 260) Ctr Educ Trng Employ.

Peer Tutoring & Mentoring Services for Disadvantaged Secondary School Students, Vol. 2. M. Anne Powell. 10p. 1997. pap. write for info. (*1-58703-065-9*) CA St Libry.

Peer Tutoring for K-12 Success. Elizabeth S. Foster-Harrison. Ed. by Donovan R. Walling. LC 97-65153. (Fastback Ser.: Vol. 415). 35p. 1997. pap. 3.00 (*0-87367-615-7*) Phi Delta Kappa.

Peer Tutoring Handbook: Promoting Co-Operative Learning. Keith J. Topping. (Illus.). 123p. (Orig.). 1987. pap. text 18.95 (*0-914797-43-3*) Brookline Bks.

Peerage & Pedigree: Studies in Peerage Law & Family History, 2 Vols. John H. Round. LC 76-124476. 770p. 1998. reprint ed. pap. 60.00 (*0-8063-0425-1*) Clearfield Co.

*__Peerage Law in England: A Practical Treatise for Lawyers & Laymen with an Appendix of Peerage Charters & Letters Patent.__ Francis B. Palmer. LC 97-77283. xiv, 314p. 1998. reprint ed. 96.00 (*1-56169-358-8*) Gaunt.

Peerage of Ireland, or a Genealogical History of the Present Nobility of That Kingdom, 7 vols. John Lodge. Ed. by Mervyn Archdall. LC 77-172749. reprint ed. 150.00 (*0-404-07970-9*) AMS Pr.

Peerage of Scotland, 2 vols. Robert Douglas & John P. Wood. (Illus.). 1573p. 1994. reprint ed. 149.95 (*1-56869-061-4*) Oldbuck Pr.

Peerage of Scotland. Peerage. (Illus.). 339p. 1995. reprint ed. pap. 25.00 (*0-7884-0289-7*) Heritage Bk.

Peeramid II Pediatric Examination of Educational Readiness at Middle School. rev. ed. Mel Levine. Ed. by Diane Winkleby. (Illus.). 80p. 1996. pap. 15.40 (*0-8388-1994-X*, 81998) Ed Pub Serv.

*__Peerifool.__ Judy Paterson. (Illus.). 32p. (J). (gr. k-4). 1998. pap. write for info. (*1-871512-59-X*) Glowworm Bks.

Peering in on Peers: Coaching Teachers. Carol Cummings. (Illus.). 167p. (C). 1985. pap. 8.95 (*0-9614574-2-2*) Teaching WA.

Peering into the Darkness. Dante A. Puzzo. LC 92-62457. 118p. (Orig.). 1993. pap. 12.00 (*0-9634503-0-1*) Randatamp Pr.

Peering Through the Lattices: Mystical, Magical, & Pietistic Dimensions in the Tosafist Period. Ephraim Kanarfogel. LC 99-14014. 2000. 29.95 (*0-8143-2531-9*) Wayne St U Pr.

Peerless Flats. Esther Freud. 224p. 1993. 19.95 (*0-15-171608-0*) Harcourt.

Peerless Flats. Esther Freud. LC 97-34634. 1998. pap. 14.00 (*0-88001-592-6*) HarpC.

Peerless Leader: William Jennings Bryan. Paxton Hibben. (History - United States Ser.). 446p. 1992. reprint ed. lib. bdg. 99.00 (*0-7812-6193-7*) Rprt Serv.

Peerless Science: Peer Review & U. S. Science Policy. Daryl E. Chubin & Edward J. Hackett. LC 89-21855. (SUNY Series in Science, Technology, & Society). 267p. 1990. text 21.50 (*0-7914-0309-2*) State U NY Pr.

Peerless Theodosia. Rebecca Baldwin. 224p. 2000. 19.95 (*1-929085-12-5*); lib. bdg. 17.95 (*1-929085-13-3*); mass mkt. 4.95 (*1-929085-11-7*) Rgncy Pr.

Peerless Theodosia. large type ed. Rebecca Baldwin. 336p. 2000. lib. bdg. 23.95 (*1-929085-14-1*); per. 19.95 (*1-929085-15-X*) Rgncy Pr.

Peers in the Classroom: Case Studies in Adult Higher Education. Regina L. Logan & Robert M. Fromberg. 172p. (C). 1999. pap. 18.95 (*1-58107-013-6*, Pub. by New Forums) Booksource.

Peers Inquiry of the Massacre at My Lai. William R. Peers et al. LC 97-42604. (Vietnam War Research Collections). 1997. write for info. (*1-55655-660-8*) U Pubns Amer.

Peers, Politics & Power: The House of Lords, 1603-1911. Ed. by Clyve Jones & David L. Jones. 557p. 1986. 65.00 (*0-907628-78-8*) Hambledon Press.

Peers/Rovesniki: Russian Language Through Culture. Maria D. Lekic et al. Ed. by Dan Davidson. (RUS., Illus.). 454p. (Orig.). 1995. pap. text, teacher ed. 20.00 (*0-9643332-2-8*); VHS 35.00 (*0-9643332-3-6*) ACIE.

Peervention: Training Peer Facilitators for Prevention Education. Robert D. Myrick & Betsy E. Folk. LC 90-86235. (Illus.). 210p. 1991. pap. text 14.95 (*0-932796-35-4*) Ed Media Corp.

PEET: Pediatric Examination at Three. Melvin D. Levine. (Pediatric Assessment Systems Ser.). 64p. 1986. pap. 13.75 (*0-8388-1795-5*) Ed Pub Serv.

Peetz: The Reel for All Time. Douglas F. Pollard. 1997. pap. 11.95 (*1-895811-48-1*) Heritage Hse.

*__Peewee's Tale.__ Johanna Hurwitz. (Illus.). (J). 2000. 14.95 (*1-58717-027-2*) SeaStar.

*__Peewee's Tale.__ Johanna Hurwitz & Patience Brewster. LC 00-26177. (Illus.). (J). 2000. write for info. (*1-58717-028-0*) SeaStar.

Pefect Picnic Book. 1998. text 6.98 (*1-84038-079-9*) Hermes Hse.

Peffley: Peffly-Pefley Families in America, & Allied Families, 1729-1938. M. M. Frost & E. C. Frost. 245p. 1993. reprint ed. pap. 42.50 (*0-8328-3383-5*); reprint ed. lib. bdg. 52.50 (*0-8328-3382-7*) Higginson Bk Co.

*__Peg - A Dream Betrayed: Peg.__ Florence Joseph Paul. LC 00-190639. 387p. 2000. 25.00 (*0-7388-1884-4*); pap. 18.00 (*0-7388-1885-2*) Xlibris Corp.

Peg Hoenack's Music Literacy Series: Encompassing "Songs I Can Play" Series (Pre-K-2), "Let's Sing & Play" Series (Gr. 2-6), "Rhythm & Pitch Notation Transparencies" (or Charts), 15 vols. K. Jones et al. Ed. by Kay Jones. (Encompassing "Songs I Can Play" Ser.). (Illus.). 1993. pap., student ed. 381.75 (*0-913500-99-2*) Peg Hoenack MusicWorks.

PEG HOENACK'S MUSIC LITERACY SERIES(TM) (ISBN 0-913500-99-2) enables every child & every current or future music & classroom teacher to participate in music & reach the national literacy standards set under the Goals 2000: Educate America Act. Students sing & play folk songs/classics, using two special Peg Hoenack (R) notations they read independently from stand-up books before adding the music symbols for what they have experienced. Teachers add vocabulary--up, down, beat, pattern--as appropriate, encouraging active listening & creating. Lively synthesized CDs or audio cassettes, charts & transitional writing materials assure success. The pre-K to Gr. 2 program centers on Songs I Can Play (ISBN 0-913500-21-6, & -17-8) & uses major-scale tones 1-8 in stand-up books & on 8-bar instruments. See, Hear, Play! describes a pre-K Music Discovery Program; Songs I Can Play Teacher's Book (ISBN 0-913500-01-1) a K-2 Tune Playing Program. The Music Through Recorder Program (Gr. 2-7) centers on Let's Sing & Play (ISBN 0-913500-43-7, -40-2, -18-6, -19-4 & -49-6) & uses absolute pitch names A-G for melodies & chords. Recorder Teaching: A Classroom Approach (ISBN 0-913500-25-9) describes a complete music program. Let's Write & Read Music (ISBN 0-913500-29-1, -24-0) adds writing staff notation to playing songs on many instruments. Rhythm & Pitch Notation Transparencies (ISBN 0-913500-50-X) (or printed charts) improve literacy with any method of vocal or instrumental teaching. Peg Hoenack's MusicWorks(TM), 800-466-TOOT, 8409 Old Seven Locks Rd., Bethesda, MD 20817-2006; FAX: 301-469-9252; INTERNET: http://www.netcom.com/nphoenack ***Publisher Paid Annotation.***

Peg O'My Heart & Other Favorite Song Hits, 1912 & 1913. Ed. by Stanley Appelbaum. 176p. 1989. pap. 12.95 (*0-486-25998-6*) Dover.

Peg Solitaire: 23 All-on-Your-Own Games. Ed. by Klutz Press Staff. 62p. (J). 1996. 17.95 (*1-57054-033-0*) Klutz.

Peg Woffington: A Tribute to the Actress & the Woman. John A. Daly. LC 70-91489. (Illus.). 182p. 1972. 20.95 (*0-405-08427-7*, Pub. by Blom Pubns) Ayer.

Peg Woffington & Christie Johnstone. Charles Reade. (BCL1-PR English Literature Ser.). 329p. 1992. reprint ed. lib. bdg. 89.00 (*0-7812-7621-7*) Rprt Serv.

Pegabalao. Jerry W. Hardin. Tr. by Camilo De Andrade. 88p. 1992. write for info. (*1-882446-26-7*); pap. 5.95 (*1-882446-25-9*) I p e Alliance.

Pegasus. Mark Dunster. 27p. (Orig.). (YA). (gr. 9-12). 1996. pap. 5.00 (*0-89642-314-X*) Linden Pubs.

Pegasus. Marianna Mayer. LC 96-32442. (Illus.). 40p. (J). (gr. k-3). 1998. 16.00 (*0-688-13382-7*, Wm Morrow) Morrow Avon.

*__Pegasus.__ Marianna Mayer. LC 96-32442. (Illus.). 40p. (J). (gr. k-3). 1998. 15.89 (*0-688-13383-5*, Wm Morrow) Morrow Avon.

Pegasus. unabridged ed. Doris Orgel. (Stories to Remember Ser.). (J). (gr. 1-5). 1993. pap. 8.98 incl. audio (*1-879496-13-5*) Lightyear Entrtnmnt.

Pegasus: Dallas' Own Myth. Gail Thomas. 24p. 1993. pap. 9.95 (*0-911005-21-8*) Dallas Inst Pubns.

Pegasus: Providing Enrichment for the Gifted by Adapting Selected Units of Study. Christine L. Lewis et al. Ed. by Marjorie A. Cantor. 119p. 1980. pap., teacher ed. 15.00 (*0-89824-017-4*) Trillium Pr.

Pegasus & Ooloo-Moo-Loo. Wendy Orr. (Illus.). 32p. (J). 1993. pap. 4.95 (*1-55037-279-3*, Pub. by Annick); lib. bdg. 14.95 (*1-55037-278-5*, Pub. by Annick) Firefly Bks Ltd.

Pegasus Bridge: June 6, 1944. Stephen E. Ambrose. (Illus.). 400p. 1988. pap. 11.00 (*0-671-67156-1*, Touchstone) S&S Trade Pap.

Pegasus in Flight. Anne McCaffrey. 304p. 1991. mass mkt. 5.99 (*0-345-36897-5*, Del Rey) Ballantine Pub Grp.

*__Pegasus in Flight.__ Anne McCaffrey. 2000. mass mkt. 5.99 (*0-345-91643-3*, Del Rey) Ballantine Pub Grp.

Pegasus in Flight. Anne McCaffrey. 1991. 11.09 (*0-606-01229-X*, Pub. by Turtleback) Demco.

Pegasus in Harness: Victorian Publishing & W. M. Thackeray. Peter L. Shillingsburg. LC 92-2805. (Victorian Literature & Culture Ser.). 315p. reprint ed. pap. 97.70 (*0-608-20047-6*, 207131900011) Bks Demand.

*__Pegasus in Space.__ Anne McCaffrey. 464p. 2000. 25.00 (*0-345-43466-8*, Del Rey) Ballantine Pub Grp.

Pegasus Mail for Windows: How to Make Your E-Mail Fly. David J. Kocmoud. 500p. (C). 1996. pap. text 34.95 (*0-13-261900-8*) P-H.

Pegasus Presents: A Culinary & Equine Guide to Germantown, Tennessee. Ed. by Emily Bader et al. (Illus.). 240p. (Orig.). (C). 1989. 14.95 (*0-9622844-0-8*) Pegasus Germantown.

*__Pegasus Project.__ B. Michelaard. 368p. 2000. pap. 5.50 (*0-8439-4707-1*, Leisure Bks) Dorchester Pub Co.

Pegasus, the Flying Horse. Illus. by Ming Li. LC 97-39365. (YA). (gr. 2 up). 1998. 16.99 (*0-525-65244-2*) NAL.

Pegasus, the Winged Horse. Adapted by C. J. Naden. LC 80-50069. (Illus.). 32p. (J). (gr. 4-8). 1980. lib. bdg. 18.60 (*0-89375-361-0*) Troll Communs.

Pegasus, the Winged Horse. Adapted by C. J. Naden. LC 80-50069. (Illus.). 32p. (J). (gr. 4-8). 1997. pap. 3.95 (*0-89375-365-3*) Troll Communs.

Pegasus/Cumbayah Collection. William Morrow & Company Staff. 1998. 16.00 (*0-688-16226-6*, Wm Morrow) Morrow Avon.

Pegatinas de Blancanieves. Sheilah Beckett. 1995. pap. text 1.00 (*0-486-28839-0*) Dover.

Pegatinas de Gatitos. Christopher Santoro. (SPA., Illus.). (J). 1994. pap. 1.00 (*0-486-28377-1*) Dover.

Pegatinas de los Animales de la Granja. Nina Barbaresi. (SPA., Illus.). (J). 1995. pap. 1.00 (*0-486-28838-2*) Dover.

Pegatinas de Mis Animales: Favorite Animals (Spanish Edition) Beylon. (SPA.). 1998. pap. text 1.00 (*0-486-28383-6*) Dover.

Pegeen. Hilda Van Stockum. LC 96-85349. (Hilda Van Stockum Family Collection). (Illus.). 176p. (J). (gr. 4 up). 1996. pap. 11.95 (*1-883937-20-5*, 20-5) Bethlehem ND.

Pegged Joint: Restoring Arts & Crafts Furniture & Finishes. Bruce E. Johnson. 96p. (Orig.). 1995. pap. 14.00 (*1-886840-00-8*) Knock Wood.

Peggles & Primroses. Ed. by Nan Collecott. 136p. 1994. pap. 24.00 (*0-86138-066-5*, Pub. by T Dalton) St Mut.

Peggy. North Callahan. LC 83-45139. 248p. 1983. 14.95 (*0-8453-4717-9*, Cornwall Bks) Assoc Univ Prs.

*__Peggy.__ Pauline Neville. 170p. 1999. pap. write for info. (*1-900850-17-6*) Arcadia Bks.

Peggy: An Affair with the Sea. Peggy Slater & Shelly Usen. 272p. 1992. 24.95 (*0-9634119-1-8*) Edens Pub Grp.

Peggy: The Life of Margaret Ramsay, Play Agent. Colin Chambers. LC 97-42554. 383p. 1998. text 27.95 (*0-312-17713-5*) St Martin.

Peggy Deery: A Derry Family at War. Nell McCafferty. (Orig.). 1992. 25.00 (*0-946211-58-2*) St Mut.

Peggy Glanville-Hicks: A Bio-Bibliography, 27. Deborah Hayes. LC 90-34140. (Bio-Bibliographies in Music Ser.: No. 27). 288p. 1990. lib. bdg. 59.95 (*0-313-26422-8*, HPG/, Greenwood Pr) Greenwood.

Peggy Guggenheim: A Celebration. Karole P. Vail et al. LC 98-219034. 151p. 1998. write for info. (*0-89207-206-7*) S R Guggenheim.

Peggy Guggenheim: A Celebration. Karole Vail. LC 98-219034. (Illus.). 151p. 1998. 49.50 (*0-8109-6914-9*, Pub. by Abrams) Time Warner.

Peggy Guggenheim: A Collector's Album. Laurence Rumney & Jack Altman. (Illus.). 176p. 1996. 45.00 (*2-08-013610-0*, Pub. by Flammarion) Abbeville Pr.

Peggy Lee Songbook. 80p. 1997. per. 14.95 (*0-7935-7281-9*) H Leonard.

Peggy Parish. Jill C. Wheeler. LC 96-29789. (Tribute to the Young at Heart Ser.). (Illus.). 32p. (J). 1997. lib. bdg. 14.95 (*1-56239-785-0*) ABDO Pub Co.

Peggy Pond Church. Shelley Armitage. LC 93-70136. (Western Writers Ser.: No. 108). (Illus.). 52p. 1993. pap. 4.95 (*0-88430-107-9*) Boise St U W Writ Ser.

Peggy Pond Church, New & Selected Poems. 3rd ed. Peggy Pond Church. Ed. by Tom Trusky. LC 75-29917. (Ahsahta Press Modern & Contemporary Poets of the West Ser.). 80p. 1976. pap. 6.95 (*0-916272-02-8*) Ahsahta Pr.

Peggy Porcupine. Dave Sargent & Pat L. Sargent. (Animal Pride Ser.: No. 13). (Illus.). 38p. (J). (gr. 2-8). 1996. pap. 2.95 (*1-56763-045-6*); lib. bdg. 12.95 (*1-56763-044-8*) Ozark Pub.

Peggy Seeger Songbook: Warts & All. Peggy Seeger. 364p. 1998. pap. 29.95 (*0-8256-0320-X*, OK 64985) Music Sales.

Peggy Somerville: An English Impressionist. Stephen Reiss. (Illus.). 200p. 1997. 49.50 (*1-85149-260-7*) Antique Collect.

Peggy Sue: 1957 Chevrolet Restoration: A Step by Step Restoration Guide. Cars & Parts Magazine Staff. (Illus.). 248p. 1992. pap. text 12.95 (*1-880524-05-8*) Cars & Parts.

Peggy Sue Got Murdered. Tess Gerritsen. 288p. 1997. mass mkt. 5.99 (*0-06-108270-8*) HarpC.

Pegleg Paddy's Puppy Factory No. 2. Juanita Phillips. (Newspaper Kids Ser.). 1998. pap. text 5.95 (*0-207-19051-8*) HarpC.

Pegleg Pete, Bk. 4. Michael Salmon. (J). 1998. pap. 3.25 (*0-689-81214-0*) S&S Childrens.

Pegora the Witch: Musical. Carol L. Wright. (J). (gr. 1-7). 1966. 6.00 (*0-87602-171-2*) Anchorage.

Peguin Dictionary of the Third Reich. James Taylor. LC 98-155377. 368p. 1998. pap. 14.95 (*0-14-051389-2*) Viking Penguin.

Peguy, 2 vols. Romain Rolland. (FRE.). 696p. 1973. pap. 16.95 (*0-7859-5456-2*) Fr & Eur.

Peguy et les Cahiers. Charles Peguy. pap. 6.95 (*0-685-37034-8*) Fr & Eur.

Pehea Ke Anita? Illus. by 'Umi Kahalio'umi & Kahanano'eau Morita. (HAW.). (J). (ps-k). 1992. 6.95 (*1-58191-045-2*) Aha Punana Leo.

Pei Ch'i Shu '45: Biography of Yen Chih-T'ui. Albert E. Dien. (Wurzburger Sino-Japonica Ser.: Vol. 6). 184p. 1976. 38.00 (*3-261-01756-2*) P Lang Pubng.

Pei Yu: Boy Actress. George Soulie de Morant. Tr. by Gerald Fabian & Guy Wernham from FRE. LC 91-73943. (Illus.). 160p. 1991. 19.95 (*0-9624751-3-0*); pap. 12.95 (*0-9624751-4-9*) Alamo Sq Pr.

Peig: The Autobiography of Peig Sayers of the Great Blasket Island. Peig Sayers. Tr. by Bryan MacMahon. LC 74-11721. (Illus.). 217p. 1974. reprint ed. pap. 67.30 (*0-608-07624-4*, 205993900010) Bks Demand.

Peines de Coeur d'une Chatte Anglaise. Honore de Balzac. (FRE.). 1985. pap. 10.95 (*0-7859-2988-6*) Fr & Eur.

Peines et les Plaisirs de l'Amour see Chefs-d'Oeuvre Classiques de l'Opera Francais

Peineta Colorada. Fernando Pico & Maria A. Ordonez. (SPA.). 49p. 1991. 10.50 (*980-257-098-2*) Ediciones Huracan.

Peineta Colorado (The Red Shell-Comb) Fernando Pico. (SPA., Illus.). 48p. (YA). (gr. 3 up). 1999. pap. 7.95 (*980-257-174-1*, Pub. by Ediciones Ekare) Kane-Miller Bk.

Peintre du Maitre-Autel de Lautenbach, l'Atelier de Durer et l'Art du Rhin Superieur. Jeanne Peipers. (Publications Universitaires Europeennes, Serie 28: Vol. 245). (FRE., Illus.). 538p. 1996. 88.95 (*3-631-47885-2*) P Lang Pubng.

P

Peintre-Graveur Hollandais et Flamand. Johann P. Van Der Kellen. 245p. 1977. reprint ed. write for info. (*3-487-06389-1*) G Olms Pubs.

Peintre-Graveur Illustre, 32 vols., Vols. 1-16. Incl. Honore Daumier. LC 68-27720. 650.00 (*0-306-78520-X*); 14. Francisco Goya. Ed. by Loys Delteil. LC 68-27720. 1969. 85.00 (*0-306-78514-5*); Vol. 12. Gustave Leheutre. Ed. by Loys Delteil. LC 68-27720. 1969. 35.00 (*0-306-78512-9*); Vol. 19. Henri Leys, Henri de Braekeleer, James Ensor. LC 68-27720. 65.00 (*0-306-78519-6*); Vol. 30. Albert Besnard. LC 68-27720. 55.00 (*0-306-78530-7*); Vol. 31. Jean Frelaut. LC 68-27720. lib. bdg. 55.00 (*0-306-78531-5*); LC 68-27720. (Graphic Art Ser.). 1969. write for info. (*0-318-51595-4*) Da Capo.

Peintre Sumida: Persistence of Vision. Jim Clark et al. Ed. by Janet Lenning. Tr. by Philippe Met & Kayko Watanabe from ENG. (FRE & JPN., Illus.). 1991. 45.00 (*1-879138-47-6*) Beaux-Arts Coterie.

Peintre Sumida: Persistence of Vision. Mark Hoffman et al. Ed. by Janet Lenning. Tr. by Philippe Met & Kayko Watanabe. (ENG, FRE & JPN., Illus.). 1991. pap. 25.00 (*1-879138-48-4*) Beaux-Arts Coterie.

Peintres de Races: Reprint of the 1909 Edition. Marius-Ary Leblond. (FRE., Illus.). 238p. 1981. reprint ed. 50.00 (*0-8150-0006-5*) Wittenborn Art.

Peinture Allemande. Otto Benesch. (FRE., Illus.). 198p. 1966. lib. bdg. 75.00 (*0-8288-3985-9*) Fr & Eur.

Peinture Allemande de Durer a Holbein (Skira) Otto Benesch. lib. bdg. 50.00 (*0-8288-2638-2*) Fr & Eur.

***Peiper: Battle Commander.** Charles Whiting. 1999. 29.95 (*0-85052-695-7*) Pen & Sword Bks Ltd.

Peirce: Arguments of the Philosophers Series. Christopher Hookway. 320p. 1985. 55.00 (*0-7100-9715-8*, Routledge Thoemms) Routledge.

Peirce & Contemporary Thought: Philosophical Inquiries. Ed. by Kenneth L. Ketner. LC 94-38634. (American Philosophy Ser.: No. 1). xvi, 444p. 1994. 35.00 (*0-8232-1553-9*) Fordham.

Peirce & Mark of the Gryphon. Kevelson. LC 99-23098. 1999. text 59.95 (*0-312-17694-5*) St Martin.

Peirce & Pragmatism. W. B. Gallie. LC 75-25534. 247p. 1975. reprint ed. lib. bdg. 35.00 (*0-8371-8342-1*, GAPE, Greenwood Pr) Greenwood.

Peirce & Triadomania: A Walk in the Semiotic Wilderness. C. W. Spinks. LC 91-35718. (Approaches to Semiotics Ser.: No. 103). (Illus.). xii, 256p. (C). 1992. lib. bdg. 113.85 (*3-11-012633-8*, 46-92) Mouton.

Peirce & Value Theory: On Peircian Ethics & Aesthetics. Ed. by Herman Parret. LC 93-39339. (Semiotic Crossroads (SC) Ser.: No. 6). xiii, 381p. 1994. 95.00 (*1-55619-340-8*) J Benjamins Pubng Co.

Peirce Family of the Old Colony: or the Lineal Descent of Abraham Peirce, Who Came to America As Early As 1623. Ebenezer W. Peirce. (Illus.). 510p. 1989. reprint ed. pap. 76.50 (*0-8328-0949-7*); reprint ed. lib. bdg. 84.50 (*0-8328-0948-9*) Higginson Bk Co.

Peirce Means Business: A History of Peirce Junior College, 1865-1989. Carl Fassl. LC 90-60386. (Illus.). 116p. (C). 1990. 10.00 (*0-685-33220-9*) Peirce Jr Coll.

Peirce-Nichols House. Gerald W. Ward. LC 76-16904. (Historic House Booklet Ser.: No. 4). 1976. 3.00 (*0-88389-062-3*, PEMP203, Essx Institute) Peabody Essex Mus.

Peirce on Signs: Writings on Semiotic by Charles Sanders Peirce. Ed. by James Hoopes. LC 91-50253. (Illus.). x, 284p. (C). 1991. pap. 19.95 (*0-8078-4342-3*) U of NC Pr.

Peirce, Paradox, Praxis: The Image, the Conflict, & the Law. Roberta Kevelson. (Approaches to Semiotics Ser.: No. 94). x, 403p. (C). 1990. lib. bdg. 136.95 (*3-11-012313-4*) Mouton.

Peirce, Pragmatism, & the Logic of Scripture. Peter Ochs. 372p. (C). 1998. text 64.95 (*0-521-57041-7*) Cambridge U Pr.

Peirce, Science, Signs. Roberta Kevelson. (Semiotics & the Human Sciences Ser.: Vol. 9). XVI, 206p. (C). 1996. text 53.95 (*0-8204-3016-1*) P Lang Pubng.

Peirce, Semeiotic & Pragamatism: Essays by Max H. Fisch. Ed. by Kenneth L. Ketner & Christian J. Kloesel. LC 85-42525. (Illus.). 480p. 1986. 19.95 (*0-253-34317-8*) Ind U Pr.

Peirce Seminar Papers. Ed. by Michael Shapiro & Michael Haley. (Peirce Seminar Papers Ser.: No. 4). 56p. 1998. 69.95 (*1-57181-732-8*) Berghahn Bks.

Peirce Seminar Papers: An Annual of Semiotic Analysis, Vol. 1. Ed. by Michael Shapiro & Michael Haley. 160p. 1993. text 39.50 (*0-85496-357-X*) Berg Pubs.

Peirce Seminar Papers Vol. II: An Annual of Semiotic Analysis. Ed. by Michael Shapiro. 272p. (C). 1994. text 49.95 (*1-57181-060-9*) Berghahn Bks.

Peirce Seminar Papers Vol. 5: Essays in Semiotic Analysis. Ed. by Michael Shapiro & Michael Haley. 352p. 1998. 39.95 (*1-57181-733-6*) Berghahn Bks.

***Peirce, Semiotics & Psychoanalysis** John P. Muller & Joseph Brent. LC 99-41190. (Psychiatry & the Humanities Ser.). 2000. 38.00 (*0-8018-6288-4*) Johns Hopkins.

Peirce, Signs & Meaning. Floyd Merrell. (Toronto Studies in Semiotics). (Illus.). 408p. 1997. pap. text 24.95 (*0-8020-7982-2*) U of Toronto Pr.

Peirce, Signs & Meaning. Floyd Merrell. LC B945.P44M465 1997. (Illus.). 384p. 1997. text 65.00 (*0-8020-4135-3*, B840) U of Toronto Pr.

Peircean Reduction Thesis: The Foundations of Topological Logic. Robert Burch. (Philosophical Inquiries Ser.: No. 1). 128p. 1991. 30.00 (*0-89672-247-3*) Tex Tech Univ Pr.

Peirce's Concept of Sign. Douglas Greenlee. LC 72-94469. (Approaches to Semiotics Ser.: No. 5). 148p. 1974. pap. text 23.10 (*90-279-2494-5*) Mouton.

Peirce's Esthetics of Freedom: Possibility, Complexity, & Emergent Value. Roberta Kevelson. LC 92-30633. (New Studies in Aesthetics: Vol. 12). 360p. 1993. 69.95 (*0-8204-1898-6*) P Lang Pubng.

Peirce's Logic of Relations & Other Studies. R. M. Martin. 156p. 1980. pap. 34.60 (*90-70176-17-3*) Mouton.

Peirce's Philosophical Perspectives. Vincent G. Potter. Ed. & Intro. by Vincent Colapietro. (American Philosophy Ser.: No. 2). xxviii, 212p. 1996. 30.00 (*0-8232-1615-2*) Fordham.

Peirce's Philosophical Perspectives. Vincent G. Potter. Ed. & Intro. by Vincent Colapietro. LC 96-1328. xxxiii, 212p. 1996. pap. text 16.95 (*0-8232-1616-0*) Fordham.

Peirce's Philosophy of Religion. Michael L. Raposa. LC 88-46016. (Peirce Studies: No. 5). 190p. 1989. reprint ed. pap. 58.90 (*0-7837-9665-X*, 205929900005) Bks Demand.

Peirce's Pragmatism: The Medium As Method. Roberta Kevelson. LC 97-52786. (Critic of Institutions Ser.: Vol. 15). X, 204p. (C). 1998. text 44.95 (*0-8204-3982-7*) P Lang Pubng.

Peirce's Theory of Scientific Discovery: A System of Logic Conceived As Semiotic. Richard A. Tursman. LC 85-45764. (Peirce Studies: No. 3). (Illus.). 175p. reprint ed. pap. 54.30 (*0-7837-1762-8*, 205730000024) Bks Demand.

Peire Vidal. Tr. by Paul Blackburn. LC 72-83856. (Illus.). 6.00 (*0-913142-02-6*) Mulch Pr.

***Peiresc's Europe: Learning & Virtue in the Seventeenth Century.** Peter N. Miller. (Illus.). 288p. 2000. 40.00 (*0-300-08252-5*) Yale U Pr.

Peirol, Troubadour of Auvergne. S. C. Aston. LC 80-2185. reprint ed. 35.00 (*0-404-19012-X*) AMS Pr.

Peizazh S Navodneniem - Landscape with Flood. Joseph Brodsky. (RUS.). 1996. pap. 13.95 (*0-87501-094-6*) Ardis Pubs.

Peizoelectric Transducers. USG/NTIS Staff. 1996. 85.00 (*0-614-18494-0*, 135P33) Info Gatekeepers.

Pekin: A Pictorial History. (Illinois Pictorial History Ser.). (Illus.). 200p. 1998. write for info. (*0-943963-65-6*) G Bradley.

***Pekin & Tremont, Illinois: In Vintage Postcards.** Donald L. Nieukirk. (Postcard History Ser.). (Illus.). 128p. 2000. pap. 18.99 (*0-7385-0705-9*) Arcadia Publng.

Peking. (Panorama Bks.). (FRE., Illus.). 3.95 (*0-685-11484-8*) Fr & Eur.

Peking. Hikotareo Andeo. LC 77-400603. (This Beautiful World Bks.). 150 p. 1968. write for info. (*0-7063-1088-8*, Pub. by WrLock) Sterling.

Peking Felix Greene & Yu Ma. LC 79-313406. 1978. write for info. (*0-224-01413-7*, Pub. by Jonathan Cape) Trafalgar.

Peking. Anthony Grey. 560p. 1988. 19.95 (*0-316-32823-5*) Little.

Peking. Burton Holmes. Ed. by Fred L. Israel & Arthur Meier Schlesinger, Jr. LC 97-39521. (World 100 Years Ago Ser.). (Illus.). 132p. (YA). (gr. 5 up). 1998. pap. 19.95 (*0-7910-4667-2*) Chelsea Hse.

Peking. Burton Holmes. Ed. by Arthur Meier Schlesinger, Jr. & Fred L. Isreal. LC 97-39521. (World 100 Years Ago Ser.). (Illus.). 144p. (YA). (gr. 5 up). 1999. lib. bdg. 29.95 (*0-7910-4666-4*) Chelsea Hse.

***Peking: Temples, Public Space, & Urban Identities, 1400-1900.** Susan Naquin. LC 99-32294. (Illus.). 935p. 2000. 80.00 (*0-520-21991-0*, Pub. by U CA Pr) Cal Prin Full Svc.

Peking & the New Left: At Home & Abroad. Klaus Mehnert. LC 70-627631. (China Research Monographs: No. 4). 156p. reprint ed. pap. 48.40 (*0-608-30357-7*, 200341900025) Bks Demand.

Peking Battles Cape Horn. Irving Johnson. 1996. text 21.75 (*0-07-032912-5*) McGraw.

Peking Battles Cape Horn. Irving Johnson. (Illus.). 1995. 21.95 (*0-930248-07-4*); pap. 11.75 (*0-930248-06-6*) Sea Hist Pr.

Peking Cooking. Kenneth H. Lo. LC 75-882821. 176p. 1971. write for info. (*0-571-09493-7*) Faber & Faber.

Peking Cooking. Kenneth H. Lo. LC 72-11556. 176p. 1973. write for info. (*0-394-48502-5*) Pantheon.

Peking Cuisine. Helen Chen. (Illus.). 40p. pap. 2.95 (*0-297-82278-0*, Pub. by Weidenfeld & Nicolson) Trafalgar.

Peking Duck. Roger L. Simon. 256p. 1987. mass mkt. 3.95 (*0-446-34932-1*, Pub. by Warner Bks) Little.

***Peking Duck.** Roger L. Simon. 2000. 14.00 (*0-7434-0716-4*, Pub. by ibooks) S&S Trade.

Peking Letter: A Novel of Chinese Civil War. Seymour Topping. LC 99-29834. 320p. 1999. 25.00 (*1-891620-35-5*, Pub. by PublicAffairs NY) HarpC.

Peking Opera. Colin Mackerras. LC 97-6887. (Images of Asia Ser.). (Illus.). 80p. 1997. text 18.95 (*0-19-587729-2*) OUP.

Peking Papers. Gary Gentile. 208p. 1992. 20.00 (*0-9621453-6-X*) GGP.

Peking Politics, 1918-1923: Factionalism & the Failure of Constitutionalism. Andrew J. Nathan. LC 98-2892. (Michigan Monographs in Chinese Studies). 320p. 1998. 50.00 (*0-89264-131-2*) Ctr Chinese Studies.

Pekingese. Beverly Pisano. (Illus.). 1997. pap. 9.95 (*0-7938-2399-4*, KW-095S) TFH Pubns.

Pekingese: An Owners Companion. Vandella Williams & Adele Summers. (Illus.). 240p. 1992. 39.95 (*1-85223-262-5*, Pub. by Crolwood) Trafalgar.

Pekingese: Everything about Adoption, Purchase, Care, Nutrition, Behavior, & Training. D. Caroline Coile. LC 96-1967. (Illus.). 112p. 1996. pap. 6.95 (*0-8120-9676-2*) Barron.

Pekingese Champions, 1987-1999. Cameeb, Inc. Staff. (Illus.). 2000. pap. 32.95 (*1-55893-052-3*) Camino E E & Bk.

Pekingese Champions, 1982-1986. Camino E. E. & Bk. Co. Staff. (Illus.). 76p. 1987. pap. 28.95 (*0-940808-57-9*) Camino E E & Bk.

Pekingese Champions, 1952-1981. Jan L. Pata. (Illus.). 236p. 1987. pap. 36.95 (*0-940808-12-9*) Camino E E & Bk.

PEL Annual Update, 1997: Recent Progress in Polymer/Plastics Technology. Morton L. Wallach. xii, 110p. 1999. pap. text 135.00 (*0-9658938-2-0*) PEL Assocs.

PEL Annual Update, 1996: Recent Progress in Polymer/Plastics Technology. Morton L. Wallach. xii, 106p. 1998. pap. text 130.00 (*0-9658938-1-2*) PEL Assocs.

PEL Annual Update 1995: Recent Progress in Polymer - Plastics Technology. Morton L. Wallach. vii, 61p. 1997. pap. text 125.00 (*0-9658938-0-4*) PEL Assocs.

Pelagic Nutrient Cycles: Herbivores As Sources & Sinks. T. Andersen. LC 96-49478. (Ecological Studies: Vol. 129). (Illus.). 192p. 1997. 79.95 (*3-540-61881-3*) Spr-Verlag.

Pelagic Snails: The Biology of Holoplanktonic Gastropod Mollusks. Carol M. Lalli & Ronald W. Gilmer. LC 88-20116. (Illus.). 288p. 1989. 55.00 (*0-8047-1490-8*) Stanford U Pr.

Pelagic Tidal Constants. (Publications Scientifique). 65p. 1979. write for info. (*0-318-14517-0*) Intl Assoc Phys Sci Ocean.

Pelagic Tidal Constants, Pt. 2. S. F. Grace. (Publications Scientifiques: No. 33). write for info. (*0-614-17813-4*) Intl Assoc Phys Sci Ocean.

Pelagie-la-Charrette. Antonine Maillet. 1987. pap. 11.95 (*0-7145-3966-X*) Riverrun NY.

Pelagius: A Historical & Theological Study. John Ferguson. LC 77-84700. reprint ed. 34.50 (*0-404-16107-3*) AMS Pr.

Pelagius: Life & Letters. B. R. Rees. LC 98-28992. 552p. 1998. pap. 55.00 (*0-85115-714-9*, Boydell Pr) Boydell & Brewer.

Pelagius & the Fifth Crusade. Joseph P. Donovan. LC 76-29822. reprint ed. 36.50 (*0-404-15416-6*) AMS Pr.

Pelagius's Commentary on St. Paul's Epistle to the Romans. Theodore De Bruyn. LC 92-33697. (Early Christian Studies). 246p. 1993. text 65.00 (*0-19-814399-0*) OUP.

Pelagonii. Ed. by Fischer. (LAT.). 1980. 47.50 (*3-322-00162-8*, T1579, Pub. by B G Teubner) U of Mich Pr.

Pelagonius - In Pelagonii Artem Veterinariam Concordantiae. Ed. by Klaus-Dietrich Fischer & Dietmar Najock. (Alpha-Omega, Reihe A Ser.: Bd. XLVIII). xiv, 482p. 1983. write for info. (*3-487-07409-5*) G Olms Pubs.

Pelagonius, Veterinary Treatises & the Language of Veterinary Medicine in Latin. J. N. Adams. LC 95-3754. (Studies in Ancient Medicine: Vol. 11). ix, 695p. 1995. 257.00 (*90-04-10281-7*) Brill Academic Pubs.

Pelangi Heaven. large type ed. Karen Van der Zee. 1995. 27.99 (*0-7505-0777-2*, Pub. by Mgna Lrg Print) Ulverscroft.

Pelargoniums. Blaise Cooke. (The New Plant Library). (Illus.). 64p. 1998. 9.95 (*1-85967-594-8*, Lorenz Bks) Anness Pub.

Pelargoniums: A Gardener's Guide to the Species & Their Hybrids & Cultivars. Diana Miller. LC 96-18242. (Illus.). 208p. 1996. 29.95 (*0-88192-363-X*) Timber.

Pelcari Project. Rodrigo R. Rosa. 72p. 1991. 25.00 (*0-7206-0805-8*, Pub. by P Owen Ltd) Dufour.

Pelcari Project - Carcel de Arboles. Rodrigo R. Rosa. Tr. by Paul Bowles from SPA. LC 95-83136. (ENG & SPA.). 117p. pap. 11.95 (*0-932274-48-X*) Cadmus Eds.

Pelcari Project - Carcel de Arboles. deluxe limited ed. Rodrigo R. Rosa. Tr. by Paul Bowles from SPA. LC 95-83136. (ENG & SPA.). 128p. 1997. bds. 35.00 (*0-932274-49-8*) Cadmus Eds.

Peldanos. R. L. Politzer & H. N. Urrutibeheity. LC 72-75117. 382p. (C). 1972. reprint ed. text 118.50 (*0-8357-9949-2*, 201362900086) Bks Demand.

Peldanos: Workbook. R. L. Politzer & H. N. Urrutibeheity. LC 72-75117. 191p. (C). reprint ed. pap., student ed. 59.30 (*0-608-08295-3*, 201647600004) Bks Demand.

Pele: The Fire Goddess. Dietrich Varez & Pua K. Kanahele. 52p. 1991. 16.00 (*0-930897-52-8*) Bishop Mus.

Pele: The King of Soccer. Caroline Arnold. Ed. by V. Mathews. LC 91-33557. (First Bks.). (Illus.). 64p. (J). (gr. 3-6). 1992. lib. bdg. 22.00 (*0-531-20077-9*) Watts.

Pele & Hiiaka: A Myth from Hawaii. Nathaniel B. Emerson. LC 75-35190. reprint ed. 36.50 (*0-404-14218-4*) AMS Pr.

Pele & Hiiaka: A Myth from Hawaii. rev. ed. Nathaniel B. Emerson. LC 97-77108. 250p. 1997. pap. 18.95 (*1-883528-05-4*) Ai Pohaku Pr.

Pele, Goddess of Hawaii's Volcanoes. 2nd rev. ed. Herb K. Kane. LC 87-71076. (Illus.). 72p. 1996. pap. 8.95 (*0-943357-01-2*) Kawainui Pr.

Pele Literature: An Annotated Bibliography of the English-Language Literature on Pele, Volcano Goddess of Hawai'i. H. Arlo Nimmo. (Bulletin in Anthropology Ser.: No. 6). 104p. 1992. 15.00 (*0-930897-72-2*) Bishop Mus.

Pele, the King of Soccer. Susan Canizares & Samantha Berger. LC 98-50493. (Social Studies Emergent Readers Ser.). (J). 1999. 2.50 (*0-439-04577-0*) Scholastic Inc.

Pele, the Volcano Goddess. Sheri Galarza. (Hawaiian Values Ser.: Vol. 6). (Illus.). 24p. (J). (ps-2). 1999. pap. 4.95 (*1-57306-092-5*) Bess Pr.

Peleas de los Animales. Kyle Carter. (Que Hacen los Animales?).Tr. of Animals That Fight. 24p. (J). (gr. k-4). 1995. lib. bdg. 17.27 (*1-55916-150-7*) Rourke Bk Co.

Pelecypod Genus Byssonychia As It Occurs in the Cincinnatian at Cincinnati, Ohio see Palaeontographica Americana: Vol. 4

Pelerin. J. A. Baker. (FRE.). 256p. 1989. pap. 10.95 (*0-7859-2124-9*, 2070381692) Fr & Eur.

Pelerin de Prusse on the Astrolabe: Text & Translation of His Practique de Astrolabe. Ed. by Edgar Laird & Robert Fischer. LC 94-8986. (Medieval & Renaissance Texts & Studies: Vol. 127). 128p. 1995. 24.00 (*0-86698-132-2*, MR127) MRTS.

Pelerinage a la Mekke: Etude d'Histoire Religieuse. Maurice Gaudefroy-Demombynes. LC 77-10690. (Studies in Islamic History: No. 7). viii, 332p. 1977. reprint ed. lib. bdg. 45.00 (*0-87991-456-4*) Porcupine Pr.

Pele's Atlantis. James A. Confer. (Illus.). v, 300p. 1998. pap. 14.95 (*0-9660391-0-6*) RTS Pub.

Pele's Tears: Reclaiming the Lost Gems of Hawaiian Music in Western Music Styles. Kele. 1994. 21.95 (*0-533-10631-1*) Vantage.

Pelham: Or the Adventures of a Gentleman. Edward Bulwer Lytton. LC 77-88085. 512p. reprint ed. pap. 158.80 (*0-8357-7934-3*, 205700700002) Bks Demand.

Pelham a Brief, but Most Complete & True Account of the Settlement of the Ancient Town of Pelham, Westchester County, Known One Time...As the Lordshipp & Monnour of Pelham; Also the Story of the Three Modern Villages Called the Pelhams. Lockwood Barr. (Illus.). 190p. 1997. reprint ed. lib. bdg. 27.00 (*0-8328-6202-9*) Higginson Bk Co.

Pelham, New York: Memories of a Century after Incorporation. Thomas B. Fenlon. 1996. pap. 18.95 (*0-9655001-0-1*) Klein Info Res Inc.

***Pelham or Adventures of a Gentleman (1828)** Edward Bulwer Lytton. 230p. 1999. reprint ed. pap. 19.95 (*0-7661-0799-X*) Kessinger Pub.

Pelican. Siegfried Back. Ed. by John E. Rotelle. Tr. by Matthew J. O'Connell from GER. LC 87-72253. 88p. 1987. pap. 7.95 (*0-941491-07-2*) Augustinian Pr.

Pelican. Ray Ovington. LC 76-3763. (Illus.). 32p. 1977. pap. 2.95 (*0-8200-0905-9*) Great Outdoors.

Pelican & After: A Novel about Emotional Disturbance. Tom W. Lyons. LC 83-3283. 268p. 1983. 22.00 (*0-9609506-0-5*) Prescott Durrell & Co.

Pelican & the Chela: The Teacher-Student Relationship in the Spiritual Life. Ann R. Colton & Jonathan Murro. LC 85-70766. (Illus.). 420p. 1985. 21.95 (*0-917189-04-3*) A R Colton Fnd.

Pelican Bill. Joan Pizzo. (Tales of the Back Bay Ser.). (Illus.). (J). (gr. k-6). 1990. lib. bdg. 11.95 (*0-939126-10-9*) Back Bay Bks.

Pelican Brief see Informe Pelicano

***Pelican Brief.** 1999. 7.00 (*0-582-41796-1*) Pearson Educ.

Pelican Brief. large type ed. John Grisham. 384p. 1992. 24.95 (*0-385-42198-2*) Doubleday.

Pelican Brief. large type ed. John Grisham. (Audio Bks.). 1992. 69.95 incl. audio (*0-7838-8001-4*, G K Hall Lrg Type) Mac Lib Ref.

Pelican Brief. John Grisham. 1995. reprint ed. lib. bdg. 27.95 (*1-56849-573-0*) Buccaneer Bks.

Pelican Brief. John Grisham. 448p. 1993. reprint ed. mass mkt. 7.99 (*0-440-21404-1*, Island Bks) Dell.

Pelican Brief Level 5: Penguin Readers. John Grisham. 1998. pap. 7.00 (*0-14-081485-X*) Viking Penguin.

Pelican Chorus: And Other Nonsense. Edward Lear. LC 94-78570. (Illus.). 40p. (J). (gr. k up). 1995. 14.95 (*0-06-205062-1*) HarpC.

Pelican Guide to Gardens of Louisiana. 2nd ed. Joyce Y. LeBlanc. (Pelican Guide Ser.). (Illus.). 80p. 1989. reprint ed. pap. 7.95 (*0-88289-729-2*) Pelican.

Pelican Guide to New Orleans. 8th rev. ed. Thomas K. Griffin. LC 87-7338. (Illus.). 176p. 1988. pap. 7.95 (*0-88289-846-9*) Pelican.

Pelican Guide to Plantation Homes of Louisiana see Guia Pelican a las Casas de Plantaciones de Louisiana

***Pelican Guide to the Florida Panhandle.** Heidi King. LC 98-45413. (Illus.). 304p. 1999. pap. 15.95 (*1-56554-308-4*) Pelican.

Pelican Paradise. Leonard Bernard. LC 97-48299. (J). 1998. write for info. (*0-9634661-3-5*) Bernard Bks.

Pelican Picture Roo. Pauline Reilly. (Picture Roo Bks.). (Illus.). 32p. (J). 1997. pap. 6.95 (*0-86417-830-1*, Pub. by Kangaroo Pr) Seven Hills Bk.

Pelican Rising. Elizabeth North. 232p. 1978. reprint ed. pap. 7.95 (*0-915864-93-2*) Academy Chi Pubs.

Pelican Rising. Elizabeth North. 232p. 1979. reprint ed. 20.00 (*0-915864-94-0*) Academy Chi Pubs.

Pelican Sketchbook. Julia Frith. LC 93-29013. (Voyages Ser.). (Illus.). (J). 1994. 4.25 (*0-383-03769-7*) SRA McGraw.

Pelican Walking. Gladys Bronwyn Stern. LC 78-134981. (Short Story Index Reprint Ser.). 1977. 19.95 (*0-8369-3711-2*) Ayer.

Pelicanos. Lynn M. Stone. (Aves Ser.).Tr. of Pelicans. 24p. (J). (gr. k-4). 1994. lib. bdg. 10.95 (*0-86593-195-X*) Rourke Corp.

Pelicans see Pelicanos

Pelicans. Lynn M. Stone. LC 88-26428. (Illus.). 24p. (J). (gr. k-4). 1989. lib. bdg. 14.60 (*0-86592-322-1*) Rourke Enter.

Pelicans & Chihuahuas: And Other Urban Legends. Bill Scott. 1996. pap. 18.95 (*0-7022-2774-9*, Pub. by Univ Queensland Pr) Intl Spec Bk.

***Pelicans Belly Can.** Tom Noonen. (Illus.). 38p. (J). (ps-3). 1999. 14.95 (*1-893385-04-3*) Little Leaf.

***Pelican's Complete Guide to American Bed & Breakfasts.** Ed. by Kimberly C. DiGrado. (Illus.). 480p. 2000. pap. 19.95 (*1-56554-735-7*) Pelican.

***Pelicans to Polar Bears: Watching Wildlife to Manitoba.** Catherine M. Senecal. 256p. 1999. pap. text. write for info. (*1-896150-02-0*) HTLD.

P

Pelicar: The Official Game Book. Pharoah Games Staff. LC 96-204994. (Illus.). 237p. (Orig.). 1996. pap. 25.00 (0-9653166-0-2) Ivory & Steel.

Pelicula. Polo Moro. LC 95-60608. (Coleccion Caniqui). (SPA.). 72p. (Orig.). 1995. pap. 9.95 (0-89729-759-8) Ediciones.

Peliculas, la Musica, la Television y Yo (Movies, Music & Television & Me) (Programas Biblicos Activos Ser.). (SPA.). (YA). (gr. 7-12). 1996. pap. 9.99 (1-55945-665-5) Group Pub.

Peligro Imminente. Tom Clancy. Orig. Title: Clear & Present Danger. 1998. pap. 8.50 (84-01-49525-3) Lectorum Pubns.

Peligro Oculto: La Mujr y el Sida en Mexico, Centroamerica, y el Caribe de Habla Hispana. Martin Foreman & Annelise H. De Salazar. Tr. by Patricia Ardila. (SPA., Illus.). 60p. (Orig.). 1997. pap. text 15.00 (1-879358-06-9) Panos Inst.

Peligrosa Tentacion. Kate William. (Sweet Valley High Ser.: No. 6).Tr. of Dangerous Love. (YA). (gr. 7 up). 1993. 13.05 (0-606-10468-2, Pub. by Turtleback) Demco.

***Pelikan.** David Lozell Martin. LC 99-36099. 320p. 1999. 22.50 (0-684-85348-5) S&S Trade.

Pelirrojita (Little Red Hair) Marie-Aude Murail. Tr. by Rafael Segovia. (SPA., Illus.). 46p. (J). (gr. 3-4). 1997. pap. 5.99 (968-16-5417-X, Pub. by Fondo) Continental Bk.

Pelissier's Columbian Melodies: Music for the New York & Philadelphia Theaters. Matthew G. Lewis et al. Ed. by Karl Kroeger. (Recent Researches in American Music Ser.: No. RRAM13-14). (Illus.). 178, xxviiip. 1984. pap. 65.00 (0-89579-199-4) A-R Eds.

Pell de Brau. Salvador Espriu. Tr. by Burton Raffel from CAT. 112p. 1987. 25.95 (0-910395-27-6) Marlboro Pr.

Pell de Brau. Salvador Espriu. 1988. pap. 9.00 (0-910395-28-4) Marlboro Pr.

Pell de la Pell. limited aut. ed. J. V. Foix. (Ediciones Especiales y de Bibliofilo Ser.). (CAT., Illus.). 1993. 22500.00 (84-343-0113-X) Elliots Bks.

Pell Mell. Robin Blaser. 128p. 1988. pap. 11.95 (0-88910-339-9, Pub. by Talonbks) Genl Dist Srvs.

Pella Community, Iowa, Vol. I. Pella Historical Society Staff. (Illus.). 682p. 1988. 45.00 (0-88107-106-4) Curtis Media.

Pella Dutch: The Portrait of a Language & Its Use in One of Iowa's Ethnic Communities. Philip E. Webber. LC 87-35395. (Illus.). 174p. 1988. 19.95 (0-8138-0079-X) Iowa St U Pr.

Pella Museum see Greek Museums

Pella of the Decapolis: The 1967 Season of the College of Wooster Expedition to Pella, Vol. 1. Robert H. Smith. LC 72-619700. (Illus.). 248p. 1973. 75.00 (0-9604658-0-4) Coll Wooster.

Pella of the Decapolis Vol. 1: The 1967 Season of the College of Wooster Expedition to Pella. Robert H. Smith. xxxix, 250p. 1973. text 75.00 (0-614-01895-1) Coll Wooster.

Pella of the Decapolis Vol. 1: The 1967 Season of the College of Wooster Expedition to Pella. Robert H. Smith. (Illus.). xxix, 250p. 1973. text 75.00 (0-614-06071-0) Coll Wooster.

Pella of the Decapolis Vol. 2: Final Report on the College of Wooster Excavations in Area IX, the Civic Complex, 1979-1985. Robert H. Smith & Leslie P. Day. LC 72-619700. (Illus.). xxiii, 168p. 1989. text 75.00 (0-9604658-5-5) Coll Wooster.

Pella of the Decapolis, Vol. 1: The Nineteen Sixty-Seven Season of the College of Wooster Expedition to Pella. Robert H. Smith. LC 72-619700. (Illus.). xxix, 250p. 1973. text 75.00 (0-685-65068-5) Coll Wooster.

Pellas Milisande Chihuly. Speight Jenkins & Dale Chihuly. (Illus.). 90p. 1993. 40.00 (0-295-97298-X) U of Wash Pr.

Pelle Erobreren see Pelle the Conqueror, Vol. 2, Apprenticeship

Pelle the Conqueror Vol. 2: Apprenticeship. Martin Anderson Nexo. Tr. by Steven T. Murray & Tiina Nunnally from DAN. LC 89-7837. (Modern Classics Ser.: No. 4).Tr. of Pelle Erobreren. 224p. (Orig.). 1991. 19.95 (0-940242-49-4) Fjord Pr.

Pelleas & Melisande. Claude Debussy. Ed. by Nicholas John. Tr. by Hugh Mac Donald from FRE. (English National Opera Guide Series: Bilingual Libretto, Articles: No. 9). (Illus.). 128p. (Orig.). 1982. pap. 9.95 (0-7145-3906-6) Riverrun NY.

Pelleas & Melisande Librettos. Claude Debussy. 56p. 1986. pap. 4.95 (0-7935-1547-5, 50339970) H Leonard.

Pelleas et Melisande. Maurice Maeterlinck. (FRE.). 70p. 1968. 14.95 (0-7859-0018-7, F66750) Fr & Eur.

Pelleas et Melisande in Full Score. Claude Debussy. (Music Scores to Play & Study Ser.). 416p. 1985. reprint ed. pap. 18.95 (0-486-24825-9) Dover.

Pelle's New Suit. Elsa Beskow. Tr. by Marion L. Woodburn from SWE. (Illus.). 32p. (J). 1989. reprint ed. 15.95 (0-86315-092-6, Pub. by Floris Bks) Gryphon Hse.

Pelletization in a Rotary Processor Using the Wet Granulation Technique. Jan Vertommen. (Acta Biomedica Lovaniensia Ser.). (Illus.). 200p. 1998. pap. 52.50 (90-6186-871-8, Pub. by Leuven Univ) Coronet Bks.

Pellingell Book of Birding Records. 2nd ed. Noel Pellingell. LC 91-76702. (Illus.). 152p. (Orig.). 1992. pap. 12.95 (1-878788-27-2) Amer Birding Assn.

Pellrigunagg Ghas-Santwarjutal-Qalb. Ray Buttigieg. (MLT.). 3.99 (0-932436-03-X) Cykx.

Pellucid Waters: Selected Poems. Claude Peloquin. Tr. by Lucie Ranger from FRE. LC 97-72261. (Essential Poets Ser.: Vol. 81). 64p. 1998. pap. 8.00 (1-55071-066-4) Guernica Editions.

Pellucidar. Edgar Rice Burroughs. 22.95 (0-8488-0933-5) Amereon Ltd.

Pelly. Dave Glaze. (Illus.). 112p. (gr. 4-7). 1993. pap. 4.95 (1-55050-049-X, Pub. by Coteau) Genl Dist Srvs.

Pelly's Exciting Adventures. Roy R. Manzano. (Illus.). (J). 1993. 9.95 (0-533-10526-9) Vantage.

Pelon Drops Out. Celso A. De Casas. LC 79-84473. (Illus.). 1979. pap. 5.95 (0-89229-006-4) TQS Pubns.

Peloponnesian War. Ed. by Jennifer T. Roberts. Tr. by Walter Blanco. LC 97-30006. (C). 1998. pap. 20.25 (0-393-97167-8) Norton.

Peloponnesian War. Thucydides. Tr. & Intro. by Steven Lattimore. LC 97-46084. 656p. (C). 1998. pap. text 12.95 (0-87220-394-8); lib. bdg. 39.95 (0-87220-395-6) Hackett Pub.

Peloponnesian War. Thucydides. Ed. by Terry Wick. (Modern Library College Editions). 574p. (C). 1982. 8.44 (0-07-554372-9) McGraw.

Peloponnesian War. Intro. by David Grene. LC 89-14647. xiv, 638p. 1989. reprint ed. pap. 19.00 (0-226-80106-3) U Ch Pr.

Peloponnesian War. rev. ed. Thucydides. Tr. by Rex Warner. (Classics Ser.). 656p. 1954. pap. 12.95 (0-14-044039-9, Penguin Classics) Viking Penguin.

Peloponnesian War, Bk. II. Thucydides. Ed. by J. S. Rusten. (Cambridge Greek & Latin Classics Ser.). (Illus.). 272p. (C). 1989. text 65.00 (0-521-32665-6); pap. text 22.95 (0-521-33929-4) Cambridge U Pr.

Pelosi Doing Statistics with Minitab for Windows Release: An Introductory Course Supplement for Explorations in Data Analysis & Minitab Mini-Manual. Marilyn K. Pelosi & Theresa M. Sandifer. 904p. 1996. 53.95 (0-471-17441-6) Wiley.

Peloteros. Edgardo R. Julia. (Aqui y Ahora Ser.). 88p. 1997. pap. 6.95 (0-8477-0292-8) U of PR Pr.

Pelt. Daphne Gotlieb. LC 99-61569. 1999. pap. 9.00 (1-887237-09-7) Odd Girls Pr.

Pelt: A Genealogical History of the Pelt Family Branch of the Van Pelt Family Tree. Chester H. Pelt, Sr. (Illus.). 140p. 1992. pap. 22.00 (0-8328-2383-X); lib. bdg. 32.00 (0-8328-2382-1) Higginson Bk Co.

Pelt of Wasps. David Constantine. 96p. 1998. pap. 15.95 (1-85224-428-3, Pub. by Bloodaxe Bks) Dufour.

Pelted with Petals: The Burmese Poems. Kyi May Kaung. (Illus.). 48p. 1996. pap. 15.00 (0-912767-15-4) Intertxt AK.

Pelton Family in America: 375 Years of Genealogy. Charles L. Pelton & Lois Myers-Pelton. 1167p. 1992. lib. bdg. 84.95 (0-931470-10-2) Fam Health Media.

Peltries or Plantations: The Economic Policies of the Dutch West India Company in New Netherland, 1623-1639. Van Cleaf Bachman. LC 74-91336. (Johns Hopkins University Studies in Historical & Political Science: Ser. 87, No. 2). 193p. reprint ed. pap. 59.90 (0-8357-8263-8, 203414100088) Bks Demand.

Pelts & Promises. Nancy Lohr. LC 96-43861. 103p. (J). 1997. pap. 6.49 (0-89084-899-8, 102731) Bob Jones Univ.

Pelts, Plumes, & Hides: White Traders among the Seminole Indians, 1870-1930. Harry A. Kersey. LC 75-16137. (Illus.). 170p. 1975. reprint ed. pap. 52.70 (0-608-07918-9, 206789200011) Bks Demand.

Peltse: And Pentameron. Volodymyr Dibrova et al. LC 96-27239. (Writings from an Unbound Europe). 236p. 1996. 39.95 (0-8101-1219-1); pap. 14.95 (0-8101-1237-X) Northwestern U Pr.

Pelvic Drop Table Adjusting Technique. unabridged ed. Howard Pettersson. LC 98-96782. (Illus.). x, 148p. (C). 1999. pap. text 35.00 (0-9668191-0-1) H Pettersson.

Pelvic Floor Anatomy & the Surgery of Pulsion Enterocoele. R. F. Zacharin. (Illus.). xvi, 170p. 1985. 93.95 (0-387-81861-8) Spr-Verlag.

Pelvic Floor Re-Education. 1997. 69.00 (3-540-76145-4) Spr-Verlag.

Pelvic Floor Re-Education: Principles & Practice. Ed. by B. Schussler et al. LC 94-34927. 1994. write for info. (3-540-19860-1) Spr-Verlag.

Pelvic Floor Re-Education: Principles & Practice. Ed. by B. Schussler et al. LC 94-34927. 1994. 98.00 (0-387-19860-1) Spr-Verlag.

Pelvic Girdle. Diane Lee. (Illus.). 149p. 1989. text 49.95 (0-443-03795-7) Church.

Pelvic Girdle: An Approach to the Examination & Treatment of the Lumbo-Pelvic-Hip Region. Diane Lee. LC 88-25690. (Illus.). 159p. 1989. reprint ed. pap. 49.30 (0-7837-9748-6, 206047600005) Bks Demand.

Pelvic Girdle: An Approach to the Examination & Treatment of the Lumbo-Pelvic-Hip Region. 2nd ed. Diane Lee. LC 98-40027. 1999. text. write for info. (0-443-05814-8) Church.

Pelvic Inflammatory Disease. Ed. by Daniel V. Landers & Richard L. Sweet. (Illus.). 240p. 1996. 59.00 (0-387-94462-1) Spr-Verlag.

Pelvic Inflammatory Disease. Ed. by Gary S. Berger & Lars V. Westrom. LC 92-9149. (Illus.). 219p. 1992. reprint ed. pap. 67.90 (0-608-05834-3, 205979900007) Bks Demand.

Pelvic Injuries (Beckenverletzungen) Results of a Prospective Multicentre Study (Ergebnisse einer Prospektiven Multizentrischen Studie) Ed. by H. Tscherne et al. LC 97-39899. (Hefte Zur Zetischrift "Der Unfallchirurg" Ser.: Vol. 266). (Illus.). 320p. 1997. pap. text 90.00 (3-540-63312-X) Spr-Verlag.

Pelvic Locomotor Dysfunction. George De Franca. 256p. text. write for info. (0-443-08839-X) Church.

Pelvic Locomotor Dysfunction: A Clinical Approach. Geroge G. De Franca & Geroge G. De Franca. LC 95-47220. (Illus.). 464p. 1996. 69.00 (0-8342-0756-7, 20756) Aspen Pub.

Pelvic Pain: Diagnosis & Management. Fred M. Howard et al. 496p. text 85.00 (0-7817-1724-8) Lppncott W & W.

Pelvic Surgery: Adhesion Formation & Prevention. Gere S. Dizerega. LC 96-35592. (Illus.). 304p. 1996. 135.00 (0-387-94871-6) Spr-Verlag.

Pelvic Ultrasound. Ali Shirkhoda & Beatrice Madrazo. LC 92-5835. (Illus.). 328p. 1992. 85.00 (0-683-07697-3) Lppncott W & W.

Pelvis see Jamieson's Illustrations of Regional Anatomy

Pemaquid Loon from Temple. Donald McIntire. (Illus.). (Orig.). (J). 1988. pap. 5.99 (0-317-92307-2) Herit Pub Inc.

Pemaquid Loon from Temple. Donald McIntire. (Illus.). 24p. (Orig.). (J). (ps-4). 1988. pap. text 5.99 (0-929537-00-9) Herit Pub Inc.

***Pemba: Contos Lusofonos.** unabridged ed. Angie Paraizo. (Coleccao Lusofonia : Vol. 1). (POR.). 96p. 1999. boxed set 12.00 (1-889358-21-5, 17) Peregrinacao.

Pember Museum of Natural History. Alan Pistorius & Delight Gartlein. (Illus.). 96p. (Orig.). 1986. pap. 9.95 (0-9616427-0-X) Pember Lib Mus.

Pemberley: Or Pride & Prejudice Continued. Emma Tennant & Jane Austen. 1993. pap. 18.95 (0-312-10793-5) St Martin.

Pemberton: The General Who Lost Vicksburg. Michael B. Ballard. Orig. Title: Pemberton: A Biography. (Illus.). 250p. 1999. reprint ed. pap. 18.00 (1-57806-226-8) U Pr of Miss.

Pemberton: A Biography see Pemberton: The General Who Lost Vicksburg

Pembroke. Mary E. Wilkins Freeman. 330p. 1978. 20.00 (0-915864-72-X) Academy Chi Pubs.

Pembroke. Mary E. Wilkins Freeman. 330p. 1979. pap. 10.00 (0-915864-71-1) Academy Chi Pubs.

Pembroke. Mary E. Wilkins Freeman. Ed. by Perry D. Westbrook. (Masterworks of Literature Ser.). 1971. 18.95 (0-8084-0022-3); pap. 14.95 (0-8084-0023-1) NCUP.

Pembroke & Pembroke Dock: Postcards of Yesteryear. Brian Cripps. 116p. 1996. pap. 23.95 (0-8464-4612-X) Beekman Pubs.

Pembroke & Tenby Railway. M. R. Price. 112p. (C). 1985. 45.00 (0-85361-327-3) St Mut.

Pembroke College in Brown University: The First 75 Years, 1891-1966. Grace E. Hawk. LC 67-19656. 240p. reprint ed. pap. 74.40 (0-608-14780-X, 202564500045) Bks Demand.

Pembroke in the Twentieth Century, North Carolina. Connee Brayboy. (American Century Ser.). (Illus.). 128p. 1999. pap. 16.99 (0-7524-0950-6) Arcadia Publng.

Pembroke Welsh Corgi. Deborah S. Harper. LC 98-37226. (Owner's Guide to a Happy, Healthy Pet Ser.). (Illus.). 160p. 1998. 9.95 (0-87605-214-6) Howell Bks.

***Pembroke Welsh Corgi: Family Friend & Farmhand.** Susan Ewing. LC 00-38289. (Best of Breed Library). (Illus.). 256p. 2000. 24.95 (1-58245-152-4) Howell Bks.

Pembroke Welsh Corgis. Ria Niccoli. (Illus.). 1996. pap. 9.95 (0-7938-2333-1, KW176S) TFH Pubns.

Pembrokeshire Children in History. Margaret Davies. 126p. (C). 1983. text 40.00 (0-85088-566-3, Pub. by Gomer Pr) St Mut.

Pembrokeshire Coast Path. Brian John. (National Trail Guides Ser.). (Illus.). 168p. 1995. pap. 19.95 (1-85410-023-8, Pub. by Aurum Pr) London Brdge.

Pembrokeshire Coast Path - 168 Miles. 72p. 1987. 29.00 (0-907496-69-5, Pub. by JNM Pubns) St Mut.

Pembrokeshire Coast Path Guide: Of Dragons & Wildflowers. Richard Hayward. (British Footpath Guides Ser.: No. 2). (Illus.). 100p. 1995. pap. 8.95 (1-880848-12-0) Brit Footpaths.

Pembrokeshire Islands. Roscoe Howells. 1995. pap. 21.00 (1-85902-122-0, Pub. by Gomer Pr) St Mut.

Pembrokeshire Walks. (Ordnance Survey Pathfinder Guides Ser.). (Illus.). 80p. 1993. pap. 14.95 (0-7117-0611-5) Seven Hills Bk.

Pemmican. Vardis Fisher. 319p. 1956. 16.95 (0-614-22023-8, Idaho Center for the Bk) Heming W Studies.

Pemmican. Vardis Fisher. 341p. reprint ed. lib. bdg. 24.95 (0-89190-833-1, Rivercity Pr) Amereon Ltd.

Pen. David Attwood & Guy Ryecart. (Illus.). 1999. pap. 9.95 (1-85410-595-7, Pub. by Aurum Press Ltd) London Brdge.

Pen Aficionado (Pen Speak) Glen Bowen. (Illus.). 130p. 1996. 12.95 (0-614-13017-4) Wrld Pubns.

Pen & Ben Adventures, Children's Reader Combined Volume: Pen & Ben. Jill Storm & LoAnne Ramirez. (Illus.). 152p. (J). (gr. k-3). 1999. pap. 34.95 (1-929078-12-9, APB00) Gods Kids.

Pen & Brush Lettering: A Book of Alphabets. Ed. by Stuart Booth et al. (Illus.). 112p. 1994. pap. 12.95 (0-289-80099-4) Sterling.

Pen & Ink. Charles E. Cravey. 1990. pap. 9.95 (0-938645-33-1) In His Steps.

Pen & Ink. Brander Matthews. LC 73-37120. (Essay Index Reprint Ser.). 1977. reprint ed. 18.95 (0-8369-2515-7) Ayer.

Pen & Ink Book. Joseph A. Smith. (Illus.). 176p. 1992. 32.50 (0-8230-3985-4) Watsn-Guptill.

Pen & Ink Book: Materials & Techniques for Today's Artist. Jos A. Smith. (Illus.). 176p. 1999. pap. text 19.95 (0-8230-3986-2) Watsn-Guptill.

Pen & Ink Sailor: Charles Middleton & the King's Navy, 1778-1813. John E. Talbott. LC 98-24026. (Naval Policy & History Ser.). (Illus.). 172p. 1998. 54.50 (0-7146-4898-1, Pub. by F Cass Pubs); pap. 24.50 (0-7146-4452-8, Pub. by F Cass Pubs) Intl Spec Bk.

Pen & Ink Techniques. Paulette Fedarb. (CW Art Class Techniques Ser.). (Illus.). 80p. 1993. pap. 19.95 (1-85223-668-X, Pub. by Crolwood) Trafalgar.

Pen & Ink Techniques. Frank J. Lohan. (Illus.). 96p. 1978. pap. 16.95 (0-8092-7438-8, 74388) NTC Contemp Pub Co.

Pen & Inklings: Haiku, Senryu & Sketches. Francine Porad. (Illus.). 28p. (Orig.). (C). 1986. pap. text 5.00 (0-9618009-1-7) Vandina Pr.

Pen & Inklings: Nostalgic Views of Santa Clara County. Ralph Rambo. Ed. by Kathleen Muller & Roberta Jamison. (Illus.). 192p. 1984. 22.95 (0-914139-01-0) Hist San Jose.

Pen & Papered Hand. Elizabeth A. Hellier. LC 98-159741. ii, 52p. 1998. spiral bd. 7.00 (0-9654727-3-6, 24) Izzybo Prods.

Pen & Pencil Sketches of the Great Riots: An Illustrated History of the Railroad & Other Great American Riots, Including All the Riots in the Early History of the Country. Joel T. Headley. LC 76-89406. (Black Heritage Library Collection). (Illus.). 1977. 23.95 (0-8369-8594-X) Ayer.

Pen & Pencil Sketches of the Great Riots: An Illustrated History of the Railroad & Other Great American Riots, Including All the Riots in the Early History of the Country. Joel T. Headley. LC 77-90179. (Mass Violence in America Ser.). 1969. reprint ed. 23.95 (0-405-01318-3) Ayer.

Pen & Peruke: Spanish Literature of the Eighteenth Century. Ed. by Monroe Z. Hafter. LC 81-50963. (Michigan Romance Studies: Vol. 12). (Illus.). 213p. 1992. pap. 15.00 (0-939730-11-1) Mich Romance.

Pen & Plow. 350p. (Orig.). 1997. pap. 12.95 (0-9659184-1-6) Scribe Pub.

***Pen & the Brush.** Dario Gamboni. 2000. lib. bdg. 35.00 (0-226-28055-1) U Ch Pr.

Pen & the Faith: Eight Modern Muslim Writers & the Qur'an. Kenneth Cragg. 188p. (C). 1985. text 24.95 (0-04-297044-X) Routledge.

Pen & the Sword: Conversations with David Barsamian. Ed. by Edward W. Said. LC 94-15582. 224p. 1994. pap. 9.95 (1-56751-030-2); lib. bdg. 29.95 (1-56751-031-0) Common Courage.

Pen & the Sword: Literature & Revolution in Modern China. Innes Herdan. 192p. (C). 1992. pap. 19.95 (0-86232-330-4, Pub. by St Martin); text 55.00 (0-86232-329-0, Pub. by St Martin) St Martin.

Pen & the Sword: Studies in Bulgarian History. Ed. by Dennis P. Hupchick. (East European Monographs: No. 252). 537p. 1988. text 94.00 (0-88033-149-6, Pub. by East Eur Monographs) Col U Pr.

***Pen Calligraphy Manual.** (Illus.). 126p. 1998. reprint ed. pap. 19.95 (1-880133-04-0) AHA Calligraphy.

Pen Computing Report. Maureen Shipley. Ed. by Christine Hughes. (Illus.). 140p. 1992. pap. text 495.00 (1-879637-02-2) Myriad Tech FL.

Pen Drawings & Pen-Draughtsmen. Joseph Pennell. LC 76-30462. (Quality Paperbacks Ser.). 1977. reprint ed. pap. 10.95 (0-306-80064-0) Da Capo.

Pen Flourishing in the 13th Century Manuscripts. Sonia Scott Fleming. LC 89-766. (Litterae Textuales Ser.). 95p. (Orig.). 1989. pap. text 107.50 (90-04-08351-0) Brill Academic Pubs.

Pen for a Party: Dryden's Tory Propaganda in Its Contexts. Phillip Harth. LC 92-27140. 352p. (C). 1993. text 49.50 (0-691-06972-7, Pub. by Princeton U Pr) Cal Prin Full Svc.

Pen in Hand: Children Become Writers. Ed. by Bernice E. Cullinan. LC 93-25880. (Illus.). 95p. reprint ed. pap. 30.00 (0-608-05989-7, 206631700008) Bks Demand.

***Pen, Ink & Evidence: A Study of Writing & Writing Materials for Penman.** Joe Nickell. LC 99-57973. (Illus.). 240p. 2000. 39.95 (1-58456-017-7) Oak Knoll.

Pen Is Like a Piece . . . You Pick It up. You Use It. Gary Hicks. Ed. by Victoria-Ann Bonanni. LC 97-157627. (Illus.). 48p. (Orig.). (C). 1997. pap. 8.95 (0-9636942-8-6) VB Document.

Pen Is Ours: A Listing of Writings by & about African-American Women Before 1910 with Secondary Bibliography to the Present. Ed. by Cynthia D. Bond. (Schomburg Library of Nineteenth-Century Black Women Writers). (Illus.). 400p. 1991. text 49.95 (0-19-506203-5) OUP.

Pen Lettering. Ann Camp. (Illus.). pap. 6.95 (0-8008-6272-4) Taplinger.

Pen My Own Book? Ed. by John R. Terry. 56p. 1989. pap. 3.95 (0-933704-82-8) Dawn Pr.

Pen Names of Women Writers. Alice K. Marshall. x, 181p. 1986. pap. 9.95 (0-9616387-0-2) A Marshall Collection.

Pen on the Wing. Margaret Deming. (Orig.). 1995. pap. write for info. (1-56167-276-9) Watermrk Pr.

Pen Pal Puzzle. Carolyn Keene. (Nancy Drew Notebooks: No. 11). (J). (gr. 2-4). 1996. 8.60 (0-606-09674-4, Pub. by Turtleback) Demco.

Pen, Palmtop, & Notebook Computer & Peripheral Markets: Applications, Applications, Applications. Market Intelligence Staff. 364p. (Orig.). 1992. 1495.00 (1-56753-069-9) Frost & Sullivan.

***Pen Pals.** Kelly Burkholder. LC 00-28434. (Artistic Adventures Ser.). 2000. write for info. (1-57103-353-X) Rourke Pr.

Pen Pals, 6 vols. Beverly Cleary. (J). (gr. 4-7). 1990. boxed set 17.70 (0-440-36028-5) Dell.

Pen Pals. Joan Holub. LC 97-5680. (All Aboard Reading Ser.: Level 2). (Illus.). 48p. (J). (gr. 1-3). 1997. pap. 3.95 (0-448-41612-3, G & D); lib. bdg. 13.89 (0-448-41613-1, G & D) Peng Put Young Read.

Pen Pals. Joan Holub. (All Aboard Reading Ser.). (J). 1997. 9.15 (0-606-13016-0, Pub. by Turtleback) Demco.

Pen Pals: A Cartoon Collection. Gary Brookins & Bob Gorrell. 132p. (Orig.). 1992. pap. 9.95 (0-9635288-0-7) Richmnd-Times-Dispatch.

Pen Pals: What It Means to Be Jewish in Israel & America. Ruth F. Goodman. 96p. (YA). (gr. 7 up). 1996. 14.95 (1-56474-159-1) Fithian Pr.

***Pen Photographs of Charles Dicken's Readings: Taken from Life.** Carolyn J. Moss. LC 97-61395. (Illus.). xx, 101p. (C). 1998. 28.50 (0-87875-495-4) Whitston Pub.

***Pen Pictures: Interpreting the Secrets of Handwriting.** Peter West. (Illus.). 159p. 1999. pap. 12.95 (1-902809-05-X, London House) Allison & Busby.

An Asterisk (*) at the beginning of an entry indicates that the title is appearing for the first time.

Pen Pictures from Paul. W. G. Heslop. 1991. reprint ed. pap. 6.99 (*0-88019-281-X*) Schmul Pub Co.

Pen Pictures from the Second Minnesota: Personal Recollections by a Private Soldier & Marching Thro' Georgia. T. H. Pendergast & Diane Rosenow. LC 98-11012. 1998. pap. 15.00 (*0-915709-58-9*) Pk Geneal Bk.

Pen Pictures of St. Paul, Minnesota & Biographical Sketches of Old Settlers, Vol. 1. T. M. Newson. 746p. 1994. reprint ed. lib. bdg. 75.00 (*0-8328-3839-X*) Higginson Bk Co.

Pen Portraits & Reviews. George Bernard Shaw. LC 78-145293. 1971. reprint ed. 29.00 (*0-403-01206-6*) Scholarly.

Pen Portraits of Alexandria, Virginia, 1739-1900. T. Michael Miller. 401p. (Orig.). 1987. pap. 20.00 (*1-55613-061-9*) Heritage Bk.

Pen Renderings of Elmer Rising: New England in Black & White. Elmer Rising. LC 85-1463. (Illus.). 112p. 1985. 75.00 (*0-9614380-0-2*) FER Pub Co.

Pen Rose Poems: Personalized Wedding Theme Poems. Casey L. Lathrop. 80p. (Orig.). 1997. pap. 14.95 (*1-57502-489-6*, PO1456) Morris Pubng.

PEN Section to Be Determined, Vol. 131. 1999. write for info. (*0-327-06980-5*) LEXIS Pub.

PEN Section to Be Determined, Vol. 132. 1999. write for info. (*0-327-06981-3*) LEXIS Pub.

PEN Section to Be Determined, Vol. 133. 1999. write for info. (*0-327-06982-1*) LEXIS Pub.

PEN Section to Be Determined, Vol. 134. 1999. write for info. (*0-327-06983-X*) LEXIS Pub.

PEN Sections 1-186.8, Vol. 128. 141p. 1999. write for info. (*0-327-06977-5*, 57754-12) LEXIS Pub.

PEN Sections 1028-1146, Vol. 135. 36p. 1999. write for info. (*0-327-06984-8*, 57760-12) LEXIS Pub.

PEN Sections 1147-1203.1, Vol. 136. 129p. 1999. write for info. (*0-327-06985-6*, 57761-12) LEXIS Pub.

PEN Sections 12000-End, Vol. 141. 391p. 1999. pap. write for info. (*0-327-06990-2*, 57766-12) LEXIS Pub.

PEN Sections 1203.2-1320, Vol. 137. 122p. 1999. write for info. (*0-327-06986-4*, 57762-12) LEXIS Pub.

PEN Sections 1321-1522, Vol. 138. 83p. 1999. write for info. (*0-327-06987-2*, 57763-12) LEXIS Pub.

PEN Sections 1523-3999, Vol. 139. 113p. 1999. write for info. (*0-327-06988-0*, 57764-12) LEXIS Pub.

PEN Sections 187-269.8, Vol. 129. 241p. 1999. write for info. (*0-327-06978-3*, 57755-12) LEXIS Pub.

PEN Sections 270-446, Vol. 130. 240p. 1999. write for info. (*0-327-06979-1*, 57756-12) LEXIS Pub.

PEN Sections 4000-11999, Vol. 140. 167p. 1999. write for info. (*0-327-06989-9*, 57765-12) LEXIS Pub.

Pen Shop: Peppercanister 19. Thomas Kinsella. 24p. 1997. 19.95 (*1-901233-01-4*, Pub. by Dedalus); pap. 12.95 (*1-901233-00-6*, Pub. by Dedalus) Dufour.

Pen, Sword & Camisole: A Fable to Kindle a Hope. Jorge Amado. Tr. by Helen R. Lane from POR. Orig. Title: Farda, fardao, camisola de dormir. 1989. pap. 7.95 (*0-380-75480-0*, Avon Bks) Morrow Avon.

Pena Palace, Sintra. Paulo Pereira. 1998. 35.00 (*1-85759-175-5*) Scala Books.

Penal & Reformatory Institutions. Charles R. Henderson. (Russell Sage Foundation Reprint Ser.). (Illus.). reprint ed. lib. bdg. 32.50 (*0-697-00205-5*) Irvington.

Penal Code: Prepared by the Indian Law Commissioners & Published by Command of the Governor General of India in Council, 1838. LC 99-16486. 2000. reprint ed. write for info. (*1-58477-018-X*) Lawbk Exchange.

Penal Code of Finland: And Related Laws. Tr. by Matti Jousten from FIN. LC 86-31329. (American Series of Foreign Penal Codes: Vol. 27). xvi, 179p. 1987. 28.50 (*0-8377-0047-7*, Rothman) W S Hein.

Penal Code of Puerto Rico, 1998 see Codigo Penal de Puerto Rico, 1998: Con Otras Disposiciones Penales Vigentes Basadas en el Titulo 33 de L. P. R. A.

Penal Code of Sweden. Tr. by Thorsten Sellin from SWE. (American Series of Foreign Penal Codes: Vol. 17). x, 114p. 1972. 20.00 (*0-8377-0037-X*, Rothman) W S Hein.

Penal Code of the Federal Republic of Germany. Tr. by Joseph J. Darby from GER. LC 86-29731. (American Series of Foreign Penal Codes: Vol. 28). xxvi, 257p. 1987. 32.50 (*0-8377-0048-5*, Rothman) W S Hein.

Penal Code of the Polish People's Republic. Tr. by Tadeusz Sadowski from POL. (American Series of Foreign Penal Codes: Vol. 19). xiii, 139p. 1973. 35.00 (*0-8377-0039-6*, Rothman) W S Hein.

Penal Code of the Romanian Socialist Republic. Intro. by Simone-Marie Vrabiescu Kleckner. (American Series of Foreign Penal Codes: Vol. 20). xvi, 143p. 1976. 22.50 (*0-8377-0040-X*, Rothman) W S Hein.

Penal Code of the State of New York, 1865 see New York Field Codes, 1850-1865

Penal Colony, stories, & short pieces. large type ed. Franz Kafka. LC 99-54892. 350p. 2000. 27.95 (*1-56000-476-2*) Transaction Pubs.

***Penal Correctionalism & the Colonial State in Ireland, 1763-1870.** Patrick Carroll-Burke. 256p. 1999. 55.00 (*1-85182-458-8*, Pub. by Four Cts Pr) Intl Spec Bk.

Penal Discipline: Female Prisoners. Mary Gordon. 1992. lib. bdg. 75.00 (*0-8490-5301-3*) Gordon Pr.

Penal Discipline, Reformatory Projects & the English Prison Commission. W. J. Forsythe. 264p. 1991. text 62.00 (*0-85989-344-8*, Pub. by Univ Exeter Pr) Northwestern U Pr.

Penal Law: Condensed Guide. (New York State Ser.). 2000. ring bd. 5.95 (*0-930137-16-7*) Looseleaf Law.

Penal Law & C. P. L. Extracts, N. Y. S. 255p. 2000. ring bd. 10.95 (*0-930137-10-8*) Looseleaf Law.

***Penal Law & Criminal Procedure Law.** 470p. 2000. ring bd. 11.95 (*0-930137-51-5*) Looseleaf Law.

Penal Law Crime Cards, N. Y. S. 2000. 5.95 (*0-930137-20-5*) Looseleaf Law.

Penal Law Explanatory Quizzer N. Y. S. - "Shapiro's" Irving Shapiro. 260p. 2000. ring bd. 11.95 (*0-930137-03-5*) Looseleaf Law.

Penal Law, N. Y. S. 200p. 2000. ring bd. 6.95 (*0-930137-02-7*) Looseleaf Law.

Penal Law of Islam. M. I. Siddiqui. 1980. 18.50 (*0-933511-98-1*) Kazi Pubns.

Penal Law of Islam. Muhammad I. Siddiqui. 190p. 1996. 12.00 (*0-614-21204-9*, 949) Kazi Pubns.

***Penal Philosophy.** Gabriel Tarde. 2000. pap. 39.95 (*0-7658-0705-X*) Transaction Pubs.

Penal Philosophy. Gabriel Tarde. Tr. by Rapalje Howell. LC 68-55783. (Criminology, Law Enforcement, & Social Problems Ser.: No. 16). 1968. reprint ed. 30.00 (*0-87585-016-2*) Patterson Smith.

Penal Policy & Social Justice. Barbara A. Hudson. 232p. 1993. text 50.00 (*0-8020-0567-5*); pap. text 18.95 (*0-8020-6988-6*) U of Toronto Pr.

Penal Servitude in Early Modern Spain. Ruth Pike. LC 82-70551. 223p. 1983. reprint ed. pap. 69.20 (*0-7837-9793-1*, 206052200005) Bks Demand.

Penal System: An Introduction. Michael Cavadino & James Digan. (Illus.). 288p. (C). 1992. 55.00 (*0-8039-8343-3*); pap. 25.95 (*0-8039-8344-1*) Sage.

Penal System: An Introduction. 2nd ed. Michael Cavadino & James Dignan. 352p. (C). 1997. 69.95 (*0-7619-5327-2*, 53272); pap. 27.95 (*0-7619-5328-0*, 53280) Sage.

Penalomah: The Eagle Soars. Royal LaPlante. (Illus.). 278p. 1997. pap. 12.95 (*1-881116-88-3*) Black Forest Pr.

***Penalty.** Redmond. 2000. pap. 6.95 (*0-552-54559-7*, Pub. by Transworld Publishers Ltd) Trafalgar.

Penalty Pt. 20: Internal Revenue Manual. 333p. 1995. ring bd. 82.42 (*1-57402-316-0*) Athena Info Mgt.

Penalty Actions Taken by the Department of Transportation for Violations of the Hazardous Materials Transportation Registrations. 93p. (Orig.). (C). 1994. pap. text 25.00 (*1-56806-161-7*) DIANE Pub.

Penalty God Levied on Your Sins Is Prepaid in Full. Edward A. Friess. LC 94-94611. 153p. 1994. pap., per. 10.00 (*0-9643297-0-0*) E A Friess.

Penalty of Death. Roscoe Pound Foundation Staff. LC 80-54626. (Annual Chief Earl Warren Conference on Advocacy in the U.S. Ser.). 121p. 1980. pap. 25.00 (*0-933067-02-X*) Roscoe Pound Inst.

Penalty of Death. Johan T. Sellin. LC 80-203. (Sage Library of Social Research: No. 102). 197p. reprint ed. pap. 61.10 (*0-8357-4853-7*, 203778400009) Bks Demand.

Penalty Points. Bonnie Bryant. (Pine Hollow Ser.: No. 7). 224p. (YA). (gr. 7-12). 1999. mass mkt. 4.50 (*0-553-49285-3*) Bantam.

Penalty Shot. Matt Christopher. LC 96-9741. (Illus.). 176p. (J). (gr. 3-7). 1997. 15.95 (*0-316-13787-1*); pap. 3.95 (*0-316-14190-9*) Little.

Penalty Shot. Matt Christopher. 1997. 9.05 (*0-606-11728-8*, Pub. by Turtleback) Demco.

Penan: People of the Borneo Jungle. Alexandra Siy. LC 93-10007. (Global Villages Ser.). (Illus.). 72p. (J). (gr. 5 up). 1993. lib. bdg. 14.95 (*0-87518-552-5*, Dillon Silver Burdett) Silver Burdett Pr.

Penance. David Housewright. 304p. 1997. mass mkt. 5.99 (*0-425-15942-6*, Prime Crime) Berkley Pub.

Penance. David Housewright. (Holland Taylor Mystery Ser.). 296p. 1995. 21.00 (*0-88150-341-X*, Foul Play) Norton.

Penance. Kevin McNamara. 1989. pap. 21.00 (*0-86217-216-0*, Pub. by Veritas Pubns) St Mut.

Penance. Karl Rahner. 1998. pap. 4.95 (*0-87193-109-5*) Dimension Bks.

Penance, Contemplation, & Service: Pivotal Experiences of Christian Spirituality. Patrick Madigan. 232p. (Orig.). 1994. pap. text 14.95 (*0-8146-5911-X*, M Glazier) Liturgical Pr.

Penance of John Logan & Two Other Tales. William Black. LC 73-106248. (Short Story Index Reprint Ser.). 1977. 20.95 (*0-8369-3284-6*) Ayer.

***Penang.** Insight Guides Staff. 2000. pap. 12.95 (*0-88729-471-5*) Langenscheidt.

Penang. 3rd ed. Insight Guides Staff. (Insight Guides). 1998. pap. text 9.95 (*0-88729-926-1*) Langenscheidt.

***Pencak's Complete Yet Concise Guide to Successful & Profitable Importing Purchases into These United States of America.** Richard Pencak. 99p. 1999. 15.00 (*0-945663-25-0*) Pencak & Co.

Pencarnan. Jennifer Rigg. LC 76-45573. 1977. 8.95 (*0-672-52288-8*, Bobbs) Macmillan.

Pencarrow. large type ed. Nelle M. Scanlan. 465p. 1982. 27.99 (*0-7089-0820-9*) Ulverscroft.

Pence Funeral Home, Conway, Arkansas, 1881-1904, Vol. I. Ed. by Desmond W. Allen. LC 86-60930. 154p. 1986. pap. 18.00 (*0-941765-06-7*) Arkansas Res.

Pence Funeral Home, Conway, Arkansas, 1904-1926, Vol. II. Ed. by Desmond W. Allen. 212p. 1986. pap. 22.00 (*0-941765-07-5*) Arkansas Res.

Pence Funeral Home, Conway, Arkansas, 1926-1945, Vol. III. Edsel F. Voyles. 202p. 1990. pap. 22.00 (*0-941765-41-5*) Arkansas Res.

Penchant for Prejudice: Unraveling Bias in Judicial Decision-Making. Linda G. Mills. LC 99-6024. 216p. 1999. text 44.50 (*0-472-10950-2*, 10950) U of Mich Pr.

Penchants & Places: Essays & Criticism. Brad Leithauser. LC 94-28629. 289p. 1995. 25.00 (*0-679-42998-0*) Knopf.

Pencil. Ralph F. Parkison. Ed. by Marion O. Withrow. (Illus.). 47p. (Orig.). (J). (gr. 2-8). 1988. pap. write for info. (*0-318-64000-7*) Little Wood Bks.

Pencil: A History of Design & Circumstance. Henry Petroski. LC 89-45362. 448p. 1992. pap. 20.00 (*0-679-73415-5*) Knopf.

Pencil & Paper Puzzle Games. 1996. pap. 1.95 (*0-8167-1680-3*) Troll Communs.

***Pencil Box.** Agnes Frieh. (Illus.). 104p. 1999. pap. 12.95 (*1-884540-36-8*) Haleys.

Pencil Drawing. Gene Franks. (Artist's Library). (Illus.). 64p. (Orig.). 1989. pap. 7.95 (*0-929261-03-8*, AL03) W Foster Pub.

Pencil Drawing. Michael Woods. (Illus.). 118p. 1989. pap. 7.95 (*0-486-25886-6*) Dover.

Pencil Drawing for the Architect. Charles I. Hobbis. (YA). (gr. 10-12). 1954. 9.95 (*0-85458-100-6*); pap. 7.95 (*0-85458-101-4*) Transatl Arts.

Pencil Drawing Kit. Gene Franks. (Illus.). 64p. 1995. pap. 14.95 (*1-56010-189-X*, K02) W Foster Pub.

Pencil Drawing Techniques. Ed. by David Lewis. (Illus.). 144p. 1984. pap. 16.95 (*0-8230-3991-9*) Watsn-Guptill.

Pencil Drawings by David X: 101 Amusing, Artistic & Entertaining Drawings of Pencils. David C. Lowy. LC 79-88698. (Illus.). 1979. pap. 3.25 (*0-9602940-0-7*) Lowy Pub.

Pencil Drawings of Joe Belt. Joe Belt. LC 88-25996. 1988. pap. 15.95 (*0-89672-181-7*) Tex Tech Univ Pr.

Pencil Flowers. Johnny Baranski. LC 82-12057. (Kestrel Ser.). 24p. 1983. 3.00 (*0-914974-36-X*) Holmgangers.

Pencil Fun-Lords Prayer. Debbie Watson. 1988. pap. text 8.90 (*0-7814-1523-3*) Chariot Victor.

Pencil Fun-Samson Gods. Debbie Watson. 1993. pap. text 8.90 (*0-7814-0134-8*) Chariot Victor.

Pencil Fun-Shadrach Mes. Marilyne Woodsmall. 1982. pap. text 8.90 (*1-55513-122-0*) Cook.

Pencil Holder. Lucy Kincaid. (You Can Make It Ser.). (Illus.). 24p. (J). 1997. 3.49 (*1-85854-542-0*) Brimax Bks.

Pencil Letter. Ratushinskay. 1988. pap. write for info. (*0-09-173550-5*, Pub. by Random) Random House.

Pencil Me In: A Memoir of Stanley Olsen. Phyllis Hatfield. (Illus.). 256p. 1996. 29.95 (*0-233-98879-3*, Pub. by Andre Deutsch) Trafalgar.

Pencil of Nature. W. H. Talbot. LC 68-25759. (Photography Ser.). (Illus.). 1969. reprint ed. lib. bdg. 95.00 (*0-306-71135-4*) Da Capo.

Pencil of Nature: Anniversary Facsimile William Henry Fox Talbot, Six Parts Plus Introductory Volume by Larry J. Schaaf, Boxed Limited Edition. limited fac. ed. Photos & Text by William Henry Fox Talbot. (Illus.). 98p. 1989. 1500.00 (*0-9621096-0-6*) H P Kraus Jr.

Pencil Pastimes Book of Fun & Games. Richard B. Manchester. (Illus.). 256p. 1994. pap. 8.95 (*0-88486-098-1*, Bristol Park Bks) Arrowood Pr.

Pencil Pastimes Book of Seek-a-Word. Richard B. Manchester. (Pencil Pastimes Ser.). 256p. 1992. pap. 6.95 (*0-88486-055-8*) Arrowood Pr.

Pencil Pastimes Book of Word Games. Richard B. Manchester. (Pencil Pastimes Ser.). 256p. 1992. pap. 8.95 (*0-88486-056-6*) Arrowood Pr.

Pencil Play, Pt. C. Frances Clark. (Frances Clark Library for Piano Students). 24p. (Orig.). 1962. pap. text 3.95 (*0-87487-672-9*) Summy-Birchard.

Pencil Play, Pt. D. Frances Clark. (Frances Clark Library for Piano Students). 16p. (Orig.). 1962. pap. text 3.50 (*0-87487-673-7*) Summy-Birchard.

Pencil Play, Pt. A. Frances Clark. (Frances Clark Library for Piano Students). 32p. (Orig.). 1962. pap. text 4.95 (*0-87487-670-2*) Summy-Birchard.

Pencil Play, Pt. B. Frances Clark. (Frances Clark Library for Piano Students). 24p. (Orig.). 1962. pap. text 3.95 (*0-87487-671-0*) Summy-Birchard.

Pencil Play Word Games for Girls. Paul Meisel. (gr. 9-12). 1999. pap. text 1.95 (*1-56247-730-7*) Pleasant Co.

Pencil Playground: A Creative Writing Curriculum. E. Jeanne Mulligan. (Illus.). 1991. student ed. 29.95 (*0-9608502-0-1*) Estella Graphics.

Pencil Puzzle Fun. Kathryn R. Marlin. 96p. teacher ed. 11.99 (*0-86653-747-3*, GA1462) Good Apple.

Pencil Puzzlers. Steve Ryan. (Illus.). 96p. (YA). (gr. 7-12). 1992. pap. 5.95 (*0-8069-8542-9*) Sterling.

Pencil Sketching. Thomas C. Wang. (Illus.). 96p. 1977. pap. 24.95 (*0-442-29177-9*, VNR); pap. 27.95 (*0-471-28958-2*, VNR) Wiley.

Pencil Sketching & Drawing & Designing with Confidence: A Step By Step Guide. Lin. 74.95 (*0-471-35777-4*) Wiley.

Pencillings. John M. Murry. LC 70-90666. (Essay Index Reprint Ser.). 1977. 21.95 (*0-8369-1229-2*) Ayer.

***Pencils.** Compiled by Marco Ferreri. (Illus.). 111p. 2000. pap. 35.00 (*88-86250-40-1*, Pub. by Corraini) Dist Art Pubs.

Pencils & Sticks: Scripture Word Searches for LDS Families. Joseph K. Kayne. 48p. (Orig.). 1995. pap. 6.98 (*0-88290-218-0*, 2018) Horizon Utah.

Pencils, Pennies & Popcorn. Robert Young & Vanessa Filkins. 80p. teacher ed. 10.99 (*0-86653-718-X*, GA1435) Good Apple.

Pencils Rhetorique: Renaissance Poets & the Art of Painting. Judith Dundas. LC 91-51090. 1993. 44.50 (*0-87413-459-5*) U Delaware Pr.

Pencils to Pixels-Exploring Freehand: Version 3.1. Susan G. Wheeler & Gary S. Wheeler. 412p. (C). 1992. text 24.28 (*0-697-16564-7*) Bus & Educ Tech.

Pendant la Guerre (Juin 1940-Janv. 1946) see Discours et Messages

PenDelfin Collectors Handbook. Stella Ashbrook. (Illus.). 100p. 1998. pap. 19.95 (*1-870703-62-6*, Pub. by Francis Jos Pubns) Krause Pubns.

Pendennis see Complete Works of William Makepeace Thackeray

Pendennis & St. Mawes: An Historical Sketch of Two Cornish Castles. S. Pasfield Oliver. (C). 1989. 70.00 (*0-907566-90-1*, Pub. by Dyllansow Truran) St Mut.

Pender among the Residents. Forrest Reid. 1988. reprint ed. lib. bdg. 59.00 (*0-7812-0344-9*) Rprt Serv.

Pender among the Residents. Forrest Reid. LC 70-131812. 1971. reprint ed. 39.00 (*0-403-00699-6*) Scholarly.

Pendergast! Lawrence H. Larsen & Nancy J. Hulston. LC 97-33391. (Biography Ser.). (Illus.). 256p. 1997. 29.95 (*0-8262-1145-3*) U of Mo Pr.

Pendergast Machine. Lyle W. Dorsett. LC 80-11581. 179p. reprint ed. pap. 55.50 (*0-7837-0225-6*, 204053300017) Bks Demand.

Pendle Hill Idea. Howard Brinton. LC 50-11234. (Orig.). 1950. pap. 4.00 (*0-87574-055-3*) Pendle Hill.

Pendle Hill Reader. Ed. by Herrymon Maurer. LC 74-142668. (Essay Index Reprint Ser.). 1977. reprint ed. 20.95 (*0-8369-2415-0*) Ayer.

Pendle Witches. Blake Morrison & Paula Rego. 54p. 1996. 49.95 (*1-900564-45-9*, Pub. by Enitha Pr) Dufour.

Pendleton County Builder & His Houses. Ruth K. Heal. LC 84-90690. (Illus.). 77p. (Orig.). 1984. pap. 15.00 (*0-9614132-0-4*) Heal.

***Pendleton County (West) Virginia: Probate Records: Wills, 1788-1866; Inventories, Sale Bills; Settlements, 1788-1846.** Rick Toothman. 326p. 1999. (*0-7884-1226-4*, T556) Heritage Bk.

Pendleton County, West Virginia Deedbook Records, 1788-1813. Rick Toohman. (Orig.). 1995. pap. 19.00 (*0-7884-0315-X*) Heritage Bk.

Pendleton District, S. C., Deeds, 1790 to 1806. Betty Willie. 479p. 1982. 38.50 (*0-89308-246-5*) Southern Hist Pr.

***Pendleton Farm.** Anne Kathryn Killinger. 352p. 2000. pap. 12.95 (*1-887730-09-5*, Plain Vanilla) Angel Books.

Pendleton Pennywise Presents the Money Book - Just for You: A Budget Book for Children. Diana J. Olden & Vicki Smith. 44p. (J). (gr. 3-5). 1991. spiral bd. 11.95 (*0-9630463-0-6*) S & D.

***Pendleton Woolen Mills.** Ed. by University of New Mexico Press Staff. (Illus.). 40p. 2000. pap. 11.95 (*0-936755-24-5*) Avanyu Pub.

***Pendolo Di Foucault.** Umberto Eco. 1999. 17.95 (*88-452-1591-1*) Fabbri.

Pendragon. Catherine Christian. 1984. mass mkt. 3.95 (*0-446-32342-X*, Pub. by Warner Bks) Little.

***Pendragon.** Stephen R. Lawhead. 2000. 23.00 (*0-380-97242-5*) Morrow Avon.

Pendragon. large type ed. Muriel Howe. 304p. 1989. 27.99 (*0-7089-2011-X*) Ulverscroft.

Pendragon: Epic Roleplaying in Legendary Britain. 4th ed. Greg Stafford. (Pendragon Roleplaying Ser.). (Illus.). 1993. pap. 26.95 (*1-56882-006-2*, 2716) Chaosium.

Pendragon: The Wizard's Daughter. large type ed. Katrina Wright. 400p. pap. 18.99 (*0-7089-5441-3*) Ulverscroft.

Pendragon's Brave Rider. Linda Armstrong. 126p. (J). (gr. 6-8). 1998. pap. 9.95 (*1-57532-172-6*) Press-Tige Pub.

Pendules: Poems from Hollywood. Mark Dunster. 11p. 1999. pap. 5.00 (*0-89642-757-9*) Linden Pubs.

Pendulum: New & Selected Poems. Robert Watson. LC 94-31288. 120p. 1995. pap. 10.95 (*0-8071-1973-3*); text 19.95 (*0-8071-1972-5*) La State U Pr.

Pendulum: The Story of America's Three Aviation Pioneers: Wilbur Wright, Orville Wright, & Glenn Curtiss, the Henry Ford of Aviation. LC 92-70481. (Illus.). 409p. 1992. pap. 19.95 (*0-9600736-1-2*) Arsdalen Bosch.

Pendulum Book. Jack F. Chandu. (Illus.). 80p. pap. 20.95 (*0-8464-4268-X*) Beekman Pubs.

Pendulum Book. Jack F. Chandu. 187p. 1990. pap. 13.85 (*0-85207-222-8*, Pub. by C W Daniel) Natl Bk Netwk.

Pendulum Bridge to Infinite Knowing: Beginning Through Advanced Instruction. rev. ed. Dale W. Olson. Ed. by Kalani Goins. Orig. Title: Advanced Pendulum Instruction & Application. (Illus.). 224p. (Orig.). 1997. per. 14.95 (*1-879246-08-2*) Crystalline Pubns.

Pendulum Charts: Knowing Your Intuitive Mind. Dale W. Olson. (Illus.). 25p. 1989. spiral bd. 14.95 (*1-879246-02-3*) Crystalline Pubns.

Pendulum Healing Handbook. Walter Lubeck. LC 97-76439. (Sangri-La Ser.). 208p. 1998. pap. 15.95 (*0-914955-54-3*) Lotus Pr.

Pendulum Impact Machines: Procedures & Specimens for Verification. Ed. by Thomas A. Siewert & A. Karl Schmieder. LC 95-13999. (STP Ser.: Vol. 1248). 1995. write for info. (*0-8031-2018-4*, STP1248) ASTM.

***Pendulum Impact Testing: A Century of Progress.** T. A. Siewert & Michael P. Manahan. LC 00-38123. (STP Ser.). (Illus.). 393p. 2000. pap. 124.00 (*0-8031-2864-9*) ASTM.

Pendulum Kit. Sig Lonegren. 128p. 1990. per. 19.95 (*0-671-69140-6*) S&S Trade.

Pendulum Plus Kit. Janet B. Moore. (Illus.). 32p. 1992. pap. 29.95 (*0-9635665-1-2*) Pendulum Plus.

Pendulum Power. Greg Nielsen & Joseph Polansky. 128p. (Orig.). 1987. pap. 8.95 (*0-89281-157-9*) Inner Tradit.

Pendulum Supplies Re. 1969. 26.96 (*0-07-521216-1*) McGraw.

Pendulum Swings. Bob Buess. 92p. (Orig.). 1974. pap. 2.50 (*0-934244-12-X*, TX 391-560) Sweeter Than Honey.

Pendulum Swings. Mildred Goravica. LC 97-90798. 1998. pap. 12.95 (*0-533-12472-7*) Vantage.

Pendulum, the Bible & Your Survival. Hanna Kroeger. 24p. (Orig.). 1973. pap. 3.00 (*1-883713-08-0*) Hanna Kroeger.

Pendulum Workbook. Marcus Schirner. LC 98-33188. 96p. 1999. pap. 12.95 (*0-8069-5731-X*) Sterling.

Pendulum Workbook. Bote Mikkers. (Illus.). 176p. 1990. reprint ed. pap. text 29.95 (*1-85398-036-6*, Pub. by Ashgrove Pr) Words Distrib.

Pendulums. Ron Marson. (Task Cards Ser.: No. 1). (Illus.). 56p. 1992. teacher ed. 9.50 (*0-941008-71-1*) Tops Learning.

***Pendulums.** Ron Marson. (Science with Simple Things Ser.: No. 34). (Illus.). 64p. 2000. teacher ed. 15.00 (*0-941008-55-X*) Tops Learning.

P

Pendulums. Jared O'Keefe. (Illus.). 128p. 1999. pap. 6.95 (*965-494-090-6*) Astrolog Pub.

Penelope. H. R. Coursen. 304p. mass mkt. 5.99 (*1-55197-031-7*) Picasso Publ.

Penelope. Penelope Farmer. LC 95-18801. 192p. (J). (gr. 5-9). 1996. per. 16.00 (*0-689-80121-1*) McElderry Bks.

Penelope. Franklin Rosemont. (Illus.). 62p. 1998. pap. 9.00 (*0-941194-42-6*) C H Kerr.

Penelope: The Story of the Half-Scalped Woman. Penelope S. Schott. LC 98-45484. 72p. 1999. 19.95 (*0-8130-1638-X*); pap. 12.95 (*0-8130-1639-8*) U Press Fla.

Penelope Goes to Portsmouth. large type ed. Marion Chesney. LC 92-17128. (Travelling Matchmaker Ser.: Vol.). 247p. 1992. pap. 14.95 (*0-8161-5547-X*, G K Hall Lrg Type) Mac Lib Ref.

Penelope Hall's Social Services of England & Wales. 9th ed. Penelope Hall. Ed. by John Barron Mays et al. LC 76-356454. (Illus.). 339p. pap. write for info. (*0-7100-8252-5*, Routledge Thoemms) Routledge.

Penelope Hobhouse on Gardening. Penelope Hobhouse. 216p. 1998. 100.00 (*0-7112-0816-6*, Pub. by F Lincoln) St Mut.

Penelope Hobhouse's Garden Design. Penelope Hobhouse. LC 97-187481. 1997. 45.00 (*0-8050-4862-6*) H Holt & Co.

***Penelope Hobhouse's Natural Planting.** Penelope Hobhouse. (Illus.). 192p. 2000. reprint ed. pap. 29.95 (*1-86205-268-9*, Pub. by Pavilion Bks Ltd) Trafalgar.

Penelope Hobhouses's Garden Design. Storey Publishing Staff. 1997. 45.00 (*0-676-57060-7*) Random.

Penelope Jane: A Fairy's Tale. Rosanne Cash. LC 98-41512. (Illus.). 32p. (J). (ps-3). 2000. 15.95 (*0-06-027543-X*) HarpC Child Bks.

***Penelope Jane Fairy Stickers.** (J). 2000. write for info. (*0-06-029069-2*) HarpC Child Bks.

Penelope Lively. Mary H. Moran. LC 93-7655. (Twayne's English Authors Ser.: Vol. 503). 192p. 1993. 22.95 (*0-8057-7028-3*, Twyne) Mac Lib Ref.

Penelope of the Twentieth Century: Selected Poems. Elisaveta Bagryana. Ed. by Blaga Dimitrova. Tr. by B. Walker et al from BUL. LC 93-70419. 138p. 1994. pap. 19.95 (*1-85610-026-X*, Pub. by Forest Bks) Dufour.

Penelope Pen-Pal. Donald R. Stoltz. (Illus.). 38p. (J). 1994. pap. 12.50 (*0-930329-81-3*) Kabel Pubs.

Penelope Penguin: The Incredibly Good Baby. John Bianchi. (Illus.). 24p. (J). (ps-3). 1992. pap. 4.95 (*0-921285-11-6*, Pub. by Bungalo Books); lib. bdg. 14.95 (*0-921285-13-2*, Pub. by Bungalo Books) Firefly Bks Ltd.

***Penelope Penguin's Pancake Party.** Debbie Pollard. LC 00-131650. 32p. (J). (ps-k). 2000. write for info. (*1-57197-226-9*, Pub. by Pentland Pr) Assoc Pubs Grp.

Penelope Pig. W. K. Hilfiker. (Illus.). 48p. (J). 1995. 9.95 (*0-9648238-4-5*) A Hilfiker.

Penelope P'Nutt & the Spirit of Christmas: Penelope P'Nutt et l'Ambiance de Noel. Nancy Palumbo. (Illus.). 16p. (J). (gr. k-6). 1989. student ed. 0.45 (*0-927024-03-9*) Crayons Pubns.

Penelope P'Nutt & the Spirit of Christmas: Penelope P'Nutt y el Espiritu de la Navidad. Nancy Palumbo. (Illus.). 16p. (J). (gr. k-6). 1989. student ed. 0.45 (*0-927024-02-0*) Crayons Pubns.

Penelope P'Nutt at Play: Los Juegos de Penelope P'Nutt. Nancy Palumbo. (Illus.). 32p. (J). (gr. k-6). 1989. student ed. 0.95 (*0-927024-16-0*) Crayons Pubns.

Penelope P'Nutt at Play: Penelope P'Nutt au Jeu. Nancy Palumbo. (Illus.). 32p. (J). (gr. k-6). 1989. student ed. 0.95 (*0-927024-17-9*) Crayons Pubns.

Penelope to Poppaea: Women in the Classical World. J. Haward. 1996. pap. 18.95 (*1-85399-498-7*, Pub. by Brist Class Pr) Focus Pub-R Pullins.

Penelope Voyages: Women & Travel in the British Literary Tradition. Karen R. Lawrence. (Reading Women Writing Ser.). 288p. 1994. text 42.50 (*0-8014-2610-3*); pap. text 16.95 (*0-8014-9913-5*) Cornell U Pr.

Penelope's Fifth Letter. Lacey Kellett. 25p. 1995. 19.95 (*0-9641221-1-9*) Steamboat ME.

Penelope's Knees. Joanne Burns. 1996. pap. 18.95 (*0-7022-2780-3*, Pub. by Univ Queensland Pr) Intl Spec Bk.

Penelope's Pen Pal. Linda P. Silbert & Alvin J. Silbert. (Little Twirps Understanding People Bks.). (Illus.). (J). (gr. k-4). 1978. pap. 4.98 (*0-89544-053-9*) Silbert Bress.

Penelope's Renown: Meaning & Indeterminacy in the Odyssey. Marylin A. Katz. 229p. 1991. text 42.50 (*0-691-06796-1*, Pub. by Princeton U Pr) Cal Prin Full Svc.

Penelope's Renown: Meaning & Indeterminancy in the Odyssey. Marylin A. Katz. LC 90-24444. 235p. reprint ed. pap. 72.90 (*0-608-20145-6*, 207141700011) Bks Demand.

Penelope's Web: Gender, Modernity, H. D.'s Fiction. Susan S. Friedman. (Cambridge Studies in American Literature & Culture: No. 48). (Illus.). 469p. (C). 1991. text 64.95 (*0-521-25579-1*) Cambridge U Pr.

Penem Antibiotics. Ed. by S. Mitsuhashi & G. Franceschi. (Illus.). 180p. 1991. 79.95 (*0-387-53142-4*) Spr-Verlag.

Penetralia: Being Harmonial Answers to Important Questions. Andrew J. Davis. 516p. 1997. reprint ed. pap. 24.50 (*0-7873-0253-8*) Hlth Research.

Penetrance & Variability in Malformation Syndromes. Ed. by James J. O'Donnell & Bryan D. Hall. LC 79-5115. (Alan R. Liss Ser.: Vol. 15, No. 5b). 1979. 50.00 (*0-685-03295-7*) March of Dimes.

Penetrando la Oscuridad. Frank E. Peretti.Tr. of Piercing the Darkness. (SPA.). 468p. 1990. pap. 14.99 (*0-8297-0753-0*) Vida Pubs.

Penetrating International Markets: From Sales & Licensings to Subsidiaries & Acquisitions. Ed. by Dennis Campbell & Fernando Pombo. 340p. 1991. pap. 76.00 (*90-6544-550-1*) Kluwer Law Intl.

***Penetrating Keratoplasty: Diagnosis & Treatment of Postoperative Complications.** M. Severin & K. U. Bartz-Schmidt. (Illus.). x, 145p. 2000. 84.00 (*3-540-66491-2*) Spr-Verlag.

Penetrating Laughter: Hakuin's Zen Art. Kazuaki Tanahashi. LC 83-43155. (Illus.). 144p. 1984. 16.95 (*0-87951-952-5*, Pub. by Overlook Pr) Penguin Putnam.

Penetrating Laughter: Hakuin's Zen Art. Kazuaki Tanahashi. LC 83-43155. (Illus.). 144p. 1987. pap. 13.95 (*0-87951-280-6*, Pub. by Overlook Pr) Penguin Putnam.

Penetrating Missions' Final Frontier: A New Strategy for Unreached Peoples. rev. ed. Tetsunao Yamamori. LC 93-35651. 192p. 1993. pap. 10.99 (*0-8308-1370-5*, 1370) InterVarsity.

Penetrating Poets. Gerald H. Twombly. 112p. 1982. pap. 6.99 (*0-88469-151-9*) BMH Bks.

***Penetrating Radiation Systems & Applications.** Ed. by F. P. Doty. 1999. pap. text 72.00 (*0-8194-3255-5*) SPIE.

Penetrating the Campus. Barry St. Clair & Keith Naylor. 156p. (Orig.). 1993. pap. 9.99 (*1-56476-085-5*, 6-3085, Victor Bks) Chariot Victor.

Penetrating the U. S. Auto Market: German & Japanese Strategies, 1965-1976. James Rader. Ed. by Gunter Dufey. LC 80-15530. (Research for Business Decisions Ser.: No. 22). 210p. 1980. reprint ed. pap. 65.10 (*0-8357-1106-4*, 207014300064) Bks Demand.

Penetration & Permeability of Concrete: Barriers to Organic & Contaminating Liquids: State-of-the-Art Report Prepared by Members of the RILEM Technical Committee 146-TCF. H. W. Reinhardt. LC 98-107870. (Rilem Report Ser.). x, 331p. 1997. write for info. (*0-419-22560-9*, E & FN Spon) Routledge.

Penetration & Protest in Tanzania: The Impact of the World Economy on the Pare, 1860-1960. Isaria N. Kimambo. LC 90-6791. (Eastern African Studies). 200p. (C). 1990. text 29.95 (*0-8214-0967-0*) Ohio U Pr.

Penetration & Protest in Tanzania: The Impact of the World Economy on the Pare, 1860-1960. Isaria N. Kimambo. LC 90-6791. (Eastern African Studies). (Illus.). 200p. (C). 1991. reprint ed. pap. text 16.95 (*0-8214-0997-2*) Ohio U Pr.

Penetration of Arabia. David G. Hogarth. (Illus.). 359p. reprint ed. write for info. (*0-318-71518-X*) G Olms Pubs.

Penetration of Charges Particles Through Matter, 1912-1954. Ed. by J. Thorsen. (Niels Bohr Collected Works: Vol. 8). xx, 838p. 1987. 425.50 (*0-444-87003-2*, North Holland) Elsevier.

Penetration of Liquids into Fibrous Media: Spontaneous & Forced Processes. B. Miller & H. Heilweil. (Surfactant Science Ser.). Date not set. write for info. (*0-8247-0020-1*) Dekker.

Penetration of Money Economy in Japan & Its Effects Upon Social & Political Institutions. Matsuyo Takizawa. LC 68-54302. (Columbia University. Studies in the Social Sciences: No. 285). reprint ed. 29.50 (*0-404-51285-2*) AMS Pr.

Penetration Testing. Institution of Civil Engineers Staff. 384p. 1989. text 136.00 (*0-7277-1377-9*, 1377, Pub. by T Telford) RCH.

Penetration Testing: Proceedings of the 2nd European Symposium on Penetration Testing, Amsterdam, 24-27 May 1982, 2 vols. Ed. by A. Verruijt et al. 1000p. (C). 1982. text 321.00 (*90-6191-250-4*, Pub. by A A Balkema) Ashgate Pub Co.

Penetration Testing 1st Intl, Vol. 1. 1988. 168.00 (*90-6191-802-2*) Ashgate Pub Co.

Penetration Testing 1st Intl, Vol. 2. 1988. 168.00 (*90-6191-803-0*) Ashgate Pub Co.

Penetration Testing, 1988: Proceedings of the First International Symposium ISOPT-1, Orlando, 20-24 March, 1988, 2 vols. 1096p. 1988. 324.00 (*90-6191-801-4*, Pub. by A A Balkema) Ashgate Pub Co.

Penfield: Genealogy of the Descendants of Samual Penfield, with a Supplement of Dr. Levi Buckingham Line & the Gridley, Dwight, Burlingham, Dewey & Pyncheon Collateral Lines. Florence B. Penfield. 320p. 1994. reprint ed. pap. 49.50 (*0-8328-4369-5*); reprint ed. lib. bdg. 59.50 (*0-8328-4349-0*) Higginson Bk Co.

P'eng P'ai & the Hai-Lu-Feng Soviet. Fernando Galbiati. LC 83-40084. 496p. 1985. 59.50 (*0-8047-1219-0*) Stanford U Pr.

P'eng Te-Huai: The Man & the Image. Jurgen Domes. LC 85-50942. xii, 164p. 1985. 35.00 (*0-8047-1303-0*) Stanford U Pr.

Pengara Summer. large type ed. Anne Goring. 1990. 27.99 (*0-7089-2153-1*) Ulverscroft.

Pengarron Land. large type ed. Gloria Cook. 1995. 27.99 (*0-7505-0692-X*, Pub. by Mgna Lrg Print) Ulverscroft.

Penguin see Living Things - Group 3

***Penguin.** Sally Chambers. (J). 1999. 6.95 (*1-86233-020-4*) Levinson Bks.

Penguin. Sabrina Crewe. LC 96-53248. (Life Cycles Bks.). (Illus.). 32p. (J). (gr. 2-5). 1998. lib. bdg. 21.40 (*0-8172-4379-8*) Raintree Steck-V.

Penguin. Frans Lanting. Ed. by Christine Eckstrom. (Illus.). 168p. 1999. 24.99 (*3-8228-6519-2*) Taschen Amer.

***Penguin.** S. Lazourenko. (Babies Bks.). (Illus.). 8p. (J). 2000. 10.95 (*0-7641-5235-1*); 11.95 (*0-7641-5265-3*) Barron.

Penguin. Mary Ling. LC 93-22105. (See How They Grow Ser.). (Illus.). 16p. (J). (ps-1). 1993. 9.95 (*1-56458-312-0*) DK Pub Inc.

Penguin. Bobby Love, II. (Illus.). (Orig.). 1991. write for info. (*1-879460-50-5*) A Love Memorial.

***Penguin.** Keith Reid. (Natural World Ser.). (Illus.). (J). 2000. 9.95 (*0-7398-3128-3*); 27.12 (*0-7398-2767-7*) Raintree Steck-V.

Penguin. Clarie Robinson. LC 91-44727. (Life Story Ser.). (Illus.). 32p. (J). (gr. 4-6). 1997. pap., teacher ed. 4.95 (*0-8167-2772-4*) Troll Communs.

Penguin, Reading Level 3-4. Ann Marie Dalmais. (World Animal Library). (Illus.). 28p. (J). (gr. 2-5). 1983. 12.50 (*0-685-58823-8*) Rourke Corp.

Penguin, Reading Level 3-4. Ann Marie Dalmais. (World Animal Library). (Illus.). 28p. (J). (gr. 2-5). 1983. lib. bdg. 21.27 (*0-86592-854-1*) Rourke Enter.

Penguin: A Funny Bird. Beatrice Fontanel. LC 92-70578. (Animal Close-Ups Ser.). (Illus.). 28p. (J). (ps-3). 1992. pap. 6.95 (*0-88106-426-2*) Charlesbridge Pub.

***Penguin Anthology of Short Fiction.** (C). 2000. text. write for info. (*0-321-08100-5*) Addson-Wesley Educ.

***Penguin Anthology of Short Fiction.** (C). 1999. (*0-8013-3160-9*) Longman.

Penguin Atlas of African History. 2nd ed. Colin McEvedy. (Illus.). 144p. 1995. pap. 15.95 (*0-14-051321-3*, Penguin Bks) Viking Penguin.

Penguin Atlas of Ancient History. Colin McEvedy. 1986. pap. 12.95 (*0-14-051151-2*, Penguin Bks) Viking Penguin.

Penguin Atlas of Diasporas. Gerard Chaliand & Jean-Pierre Rageau. Tr. by A. M. Berrett et al. 208p. 16.95 (*0-614-26613-0*) Penguin Putnam.

Penguin Atlas of Diasporas. Gerard Chaliand & Jean-Pierre Rageau. 1997. pap. 22.95 (*0-14-017814-7*) Viking Penguin.

***Penguin Atlas of Human Sexual Behavior.** Judith MacKay. 2000. pap. 18.95 (*0-14-051479-1*) Viking Penguin.

Penguin Atlas of Modern History. Colin McEvedy. 1986. pap. 12.95 (*0-14-051153-9*, Penguin Bks) Viking Penguin.

Penguin Atlas of Recent History. Colin McEvedy. 1986. pap. 12.95 (*0-14-051154-7*, Penguin Bks) Viking Penguin.

Penguin Best Australian Short Stories Mary Lord. LC 92-103134. 335p. 1991. write for info. (*0-14-013916-8*) Pnguin Bks Ltd.

Penguin Biology. Ed. by Lloyd S. Davis & John T. Darby. 467p. 1990. text 94.00 (*0-12-206335-X*) Acad Pr.

***Penguin Book of Carols.** Ian Bradley. 480p. 2000. pap. 12.95 (*0-14-027526-6*, Penguin Bks) Viking Penguin.

Penguin Book of Classic Children's Characters. Ed. by Leonard S. Marcus. LC 97-26295. Orig. Title: The Penguin Complete Children's Classics. (J). 1997. 35.00 (*0-525-45826-3*, Dutton Child) Peng Put Young Read.

Penguin Book of Contemporary British Verse. Blake Morrison. pap. 15.95 (*0-14-058552-4*, Pub. by Pnguin Bks Ltd) Trafalgar.

Penguin Book of Contemporary Irish Poetry. Ed. by Peter Fallon & Derek Mahon. 496p. (Orig.). 1991. pap. 15.95 (*0-14-058609-1*) Viking Penguin.

Penguin Book of Curious & Interesting Mathematics. David G. Wells. LC 97-206870. 320p. 1997. pap. 12.95 (*0-14-023603-1*) Viking Penguin.

Penguin Book of Erotic Fiction by Women. Richard G. Jones. 416p. 1996. pap. 13.95 (*0-14-024531-6*) Viking Penguin.

***Penguin Book of Exotic Words.** Janet Whitcut. 176p. 2000. pap. 14.95 (*0-14-051341-8*, Pub. by Pnguin Bks Ltd) Trafalgar.

***Penguin Book of Garden Writing.** Ed. by David Wheeler. 382p. 2000. pap. 15.95 (*0-14-024034-9*, Pub. by Pnguin Bks Ltd) Trafalgar.

Penguin Book of Gay Short Stories. Ed. by David Leavitt & Mark Mitchell. 688p. 1994. reprint ed. pap. 16.95 (*0-14-024249-X*, Penguin Bks) Viking Penguin.

Penguin Book of German Verse. Ed. by Leonard Forster. (GER.). 512p. 1988. pap. 14.95 (*0-14-058546-X*, Penguin Bks) Viking Penguin.

Penguin Book of Ghost Stories. Ed. by J. A. Cuddon. (Fiction Ser.). 512p. 1985. pap. 13.95 (*0-14-006800-7*, Penguin Bks) Viking Penguin.

Penguin Book of Hebrew Verse. Ed. by T. Carmi. (ENG & HEB.). 448p. (Orig.). 1981. pap. 18.95 (*0-14-042197-1*, Penguin Bks) Viking Penguin.

Penguin Book of Horror Stories. Ed. by J. A. Cuddon. (Fiction Ser.). 608p. 1985. pap. 14.95 (*0-14-006799-X*, Penguin Bks) Viking Penguin.

Penguin Book of International Gay Writing. Ed. by Mark Mitchell. 608p. 1996. pap. 14.95 (*0-14-023459-4*, Penguin Bks) Viking Penguin.

***Penguin Book of International Women's Stories.** Kate Figes. 480p. 2000. pap. 15.95 (*0-14-024713-0*, Pub. by Pnguin Bks Ltd) Trafalgar.

Penguin Book of Interviews: An Anthology from 1859 to the Present Day see Norton Book of Interviews

***Penguin Book of Irish Fiction.** Ed. by Colm Toibin. (Penguin Bks.). 1200p. 2000. 40.00 (*0-670-89108-8*, Viking) Viking Penguin.

***Penguin Book of Irish Short Stories.** Ed. by Benedict Kiely. 544p. 2000. pap. 14.95 (*0-14-005340-9*, Pub. by Pnguin Bks Ltd) Trafalgar.

Penguin Book of Irish Verse. Ed. by Brendan Kennelly. 480p. 1987. pap. 13.95 (*0-14-058526-5*, Penguin Bks) Viking Penguin.

Penguin Book of Jewish Short Stories. Ed. by Emanuel Litvinoff. 352p. 1979. pap. 13.95 (*0-14-004728-X*, Penguin Bks) Viking Penguin.

Penguin Book of Lesbian Short Stories. Ed. by Margaret Reynolds. LC 93-34061. 1999. text. write for info. (*0-670-84321-0*, Viking) Viking Penguin.

Penguin Book of Lesbian Short Stories. Ed. by Margaret Reynolds. 464p. 1994. reprint ed. pap. 15.95 (*0-14-024018-7*, Penguin Bks) Viking Penguin.

Penguin Book of Limericks. Compiled by E. O. Parrott. (Illus.). 304p. 1985. pap. 19.99 (*0-14-007669-7*, Penguin Bks) Viking Penguin.

Penguin Book of Modern African Poetry. 4th ed. Beier Moore. 384p. 1999. pap. 15.95 (*0-14-118100-1*) Penguin Putnam.

Penguin Book of Modern British Short Stories. Ed. by Malcolm Bradbury. 448p. 1989. pap. 14.95 (*0-14-006306-4*, Penguin Bks) Viking Penguin.

Penguin Book of Modern Fantasy by Women. Ed. by Susan Williams & Richard Glyn-Jones. 576p. 1997. pap. 13.95 (*0-14-024336-4*) Viking Penguin.

Penguin Book of Renaissance Verse, 1509-1659. David Norbrook. Ed. by H. R. Woudhuysen. 960p. 1993. pap. 23.95 (*0-14-042346-X*, Penguin Classics) Viking Penguin.

Penguin Book of Rock & Roll Writing. Ed. by Clinton Heylin. 704p. 1993. reprint ed. pap. 14.00 (*0-14-023227-3*, Penguin Bks) Viking Penguin.

Penguin Book of Rock & Roll Writing. Ed. by Clinton Heylin. 720p. 1999. reprint ed. pap. 14.95 (*0-14-016836-2*, Penguin Bks) Viking Penguin.

Penguin Book of Spanish Verse. Ed. by John M. Cohen. 640p. 1988. pap. 16.95 (*0-14-058570-2*, Penguin Bks) Viking Penguin.

***Penguin Book of the Guardian, 8 Quick Crosswords.** John Perkin. 160p. 1999. pap. 9.95 (*0-14-027751-X*, Pub. by Pnguin Bks Ltd) Trafalgar.

***Penguin Book of Twentieth Century Speeches.** Brian MacArthur. 525p. 2000. pap. 15.95 (*0-14-028500-8*) Viking Penguin.

Penguin Book of Vampire Stories. Ed. by Alan Ryan. 640p. 1989. pap. 14.95 (*0-14-012445-4*, Penguin Bks) Viking Penguin.

Penguin Book of Victorian Verse. Daniel Karlin. LC 99-461809. 928p. 1999. pap. 17.95 (*0-14-044578-1*, PuffinBks) Peng Put Young Read.

Penguin Book of Welsh Short Stories, Vol. 2. Alun Richards. 416p. 1994. pap. 15.95 (*0-14-016871-0*, Pub. by Pnguin Bks Ltd) Trafalgar.

Penguin Book of Women Poets. Ed. by Carol Cosman et al. (Poetry Ser.). 400p. 1986. pap. 13.95 (*0-14-058533-8*, Penguin Bks) Viking Penguin.

Penguin Book of Women Poets. Carol Cosman. 1978. 19.05 (*0-606-02186-8*, Pub. by Turtleback) Demco.

Penguin Book of Women's Humor. Ed. by Regina Barreca. 658p. 1996. pap. 16.95 (*0-14-017294-7*, Penguin Bks) Viking Penguin.

Penguin Brigade Training Log. John Bingham. (Illus.). 160p. 1998. spiral bd. 12.95 (*1-55821-672-3*, Pub. by Breakaway Bks) Consort Bk Sales.

Penguin Chick see Pinguino Polluelo

***Penguin Chick.** Michelle McKenzie. (Illus.). 12p. (J). (gr. k). 2000. bds. 5.95 (*1-878244-28-0*) Monterey Bay Aquarium.

Penguin Chick. Betty Tatham. (J). pap. write for info. (*0-06-445206-9*, HarpTrophy) HarpC Child Bks.

Penguin Chick. Betty Tatham. (Illus.). 40p. (J). (gr. k-4). 15.95 (*0-06-028594-X*); lib. bdg. 15.89 (*0-06-028595-8*) HarpC Child Bks.

***Penguin Companion to European Union.** Timothy Bainbridge. 528p. 1999. pap. 22.95 (*0-14-026879-0*, Pub. by Pnguin Bks Ltd) Trafalgar.

Penguin Complete Children's Classics see Penguin Book of Classic Children's Characters

Penguin Concise Dictionary of Art History. Nancy Frazier. LC 98-56089. 730p. 1999. 60.00 (*0-670-10015-3*) Viking Penguin.

Penguin Critical Studies. Peter Millson. pap. 7.95 (*0-14-077019-4*, Pub. by Pnguin Bks Ltd) Trafalgar.

***Penguin Desk Encyclopedia of Science & Mathematics.** Bryan Bunch & Jenny Tesar. (Illus.). 704p. 2000. 40.00 (*0-670-88528-2*, Viking) Viking Penguin.

***Penguin Dictionary of American English Usage & Style: A Readable Reference Book, Illuminating Thousands of Traps That Snare Writers & Speakers.** Paul W. Lovinger. LC 99-53704. 2000. 40.00 (*0-670-89166-5*) Penguin Putnam.

Penguin Dictionary of American Folklore. Alan Axelrod et al. LC 99-14073. 527p. 2000. 45.00 (*0-670-88752-8*) Viking Penguin.

***Penguin Dictionary of Architecture & Landscape Architecture.** 5th ed. Nikolas Pevsner et al. 656p. 2000. pap. 16.95 (*0-14-051323-X*) Viking Penguin.

Penguin Dictionary of Art & Artists. 7th ed. Peter Murray & Linda Murray. LC 98-130228. 579p. 1998. pap. 15.95 (*0-14-051300-0*, Penguin Bks) Viking Penguin.

***Penguin Dictionary of Astronomy.** 3rd ed. Ed. by Jacqueline Mitton. 420p. 2000. pap. 14.95 (*0-14-051375-2*, Pub. by Pnguin Bks Ltd) Trafalgar.

Penguin Dictionary of Biology. 9th ed. M. Thain & M. Hickman. (Illus.). 688p. 1995. pap. 14.95 (*0-14-051288-8*, Penguin Bks) Viking Penguin.

Penguin Dictionary of Building. James H. MacLean & John S. Scott. (Illus.). pap. 17.95 (*0-14-051239-X*, Pub. by Pnguin Bks Ltd) Trafalgar.

Penguin Dictionary of Chemistry. 2nd abr. rev. ed. D. W. Sharp. (Illus.). 512p. 1991. pap. 15.95 (*0-14-051232-2*) Viking Penguin.

Penguin Dictionary of Classical Mythology. Pierre Grimal. (Illus.). 480p. 1991. pap. 23.99 (*0-14-051235-7*, Penguin Bks) Viking Penguin.

Penguin Dictionary of Contemporary American History. Ed. by Stanley Hochman & Eleanor Hochman. LC 96-25803. 656p. 1997. pap. 16.95 (*0-14-051372-8*) Viking Penguin.

Penguin Dictionary of Curious & Interesting Geometry. David Wells. (Illus.). 304p. 1992. pap. 21.95 (*0-14-011813-6*, Penguin Bks) Viking Penguin.

Penguin Dictionary of Curious & Interesting Numbers. David Wells. LC 98-155322. 256p. 1998. pap. 13.95 (*0-14-026149-4*) Viking Penguin.

Penguin Dictionary of Economics. 6th ed. Graham Bannock et al. LC 99-214064. (Illus.). 438p. 1999. pap. 16.95 (*0-14-051376-0*) Viking Penguin.

P

An Asterisk (*) at the beginning of an entry indicates that the title is appearing for the first time.

Penguin Dictionary of Electronics. 3rd ed. Valerie Illingsworth. 1999. pap. 16.95 (*0-14-051402-3*) Penguin Putnam.

Penguin Dictionary of English Idioms. Daphne M. Gulland & David G. Hinds-Howell. 304p. 1987. pap. 14.95 (*0-14-051135-0*, Penguin Bks) Viking Penguin.

Penguin Dictionary of English Synonyms & Antonyms. Ed. by Rosalind Fergusson. 448p. (Orig.). 1992. pap. 19.99 (*0-14-051168-7*, Penguin Bks) Viking Penguin.

***Penguin Dictionary of International Relations.** Graham Evans. LC 99-199845. 623p. 1998. pap. 14.95 (*0-14-051397-3*, Penguin Classics) Viking Penguin.

Penguin Dictionary of Jokes. Ed. by Fred Metcalf. LC 96-140729. 240p. 1996. pap. 12.95 (*0-14-016602-5*, Penguin Bks) Viking Penguin.

Penguin Dictionary of Mathematics. 2nd ed. David Nelson. 461p. 1999. pap. 14.95 (*0-14-051342-6*, Pub. by Pnguin Bks Ltd) Trafalgar.

Penguin Dictionary of Modern Humorous Quotations. Ed. by Fred Metcalf. 1988. pap. 13.95 (*0-14-007568-2*, Penguin Bks) Viking Penguin.

Penguin Dictionary of Philosophy. Thomas Mautner. LC 98-155375. 672p. 1998. pap. 15.95 (*0-14-051250-0*) Viking Penguin.

***Penguin Dictionary of Plant Sciences.** Ed. by Jill Bailey. (Illus.). 500p. 2000. pap. 14.95 (*0-14-051403-1*, Pub. by Pnguin Bks Ltd) Trafalgar.

Penguin Dictionary of Proverbs. Laurence Urdang. 256p. 1983. pap. 15.95 (*0-14-051118-0*, Penguin Bks) Viking Penguin.

Penguin Dictionary of Religions. 2nd ed. Ed. by John R. Hinnells. LC 97-228873. 800p. 1997. reprint ed. pap. 16.95 (*0-14-051261-6*) Viking Penguin.

Penguin Dictionary of Saints. 3rd ed. Donald Attwater & Catherine R. John. 400p. 1996. pap. 15.95 (*0-14-051312-4*, Penguin Bks) Viking Penguin.

Penguin Dictionary of Science. M. J. Clugston. LC 99-179482. 880p. 1998. pap. 26.99 (*0-14-051271-3*) Viking Penguin.

Penguin Dictionary of Sociology. 3rd ed. Nicholas Abercrombie et al. 528p. 1995. pap. 14.95 (*0-14-051292-6*, Penguin Bks) Viking Penguin.

Penguin Dictionary of 20th Century History. 5th ed. Alan R. Palmer. (Illus.). 448p. pap. 15.95 (*0-14-051404-X*, Pub. by Pnguin Bks Ltd) Trafalgar.

Penguin Dictionary of Twentieth-Century Quotations. J. M. Cohen & M. J. Cohen. 640p. 1996. pap. 14.95 (*0-14-051165-2*) Viking Penguin.

***Penguin Dreams.** J. Otto Seibold & Vivian Walsh. LC 99-16586. (I Can Sleep Bk.). (Illus.). 40p. (J). (gr. k-3). 1999. 13.95 (*0-8118-2558-2*) Chronicle Bks.

Penguin Encyclopedia of Ancient Civilizations. Ed. by Arthur Cotterell. (Illus.). 384p. 1989. pap. 21.95 (*0-14-011434-3*, Penguin Bks) Viking Penguin.

***Penguin Encyclopedia of Ancient Religions.** John R. Hinnells. 1999. write for info. (*0-7139-9156-9*, A Lane) Viking Penguin.

Penguin Encyclopedia of Classical Civilizations. Ed. by Arthur Cotterell. (Illus.). 320p. 1996. pap. 19.99 (*0-14-051344-2*, Penguin Bks) Viking Penguin.

Penguin Encyclopedia of Horror. Jack Sullivan. 1999. pap. write for info. (*0-14-009491-1*, Penguin Bks) Viking Penguin.

Penguin Encyclopedia of Popular Music. 2nd ed. Ed. by Donald Clarke. LC 99-213528. 1524p. 1999. pap. 22.95 (*0-14-051370-1*) Viking Penguin.

Penguin Family Book. Lauritz Somme. Tr. by Patricia Crampton. LC 95-8256. (Animal Family Ser.). (Illus.). 56p. (J). (gr. 1-5). 1995. pap. 8.95 (*1-55858-379-3*, Pub. by North-South Bks NYC) Chronicle Bks.

Penguin French Phrase Book. Jill Norman & Henri Orteu. 320p. (Orig.). 1988. pap. 7.00 (*0-14-009942-5*, Penguin Bks) Viking Penguin.

Penguin Games. Sea World Staff. 1998. pap. 3.95 (*0-15-260289-5*, Harcourt Child Bks) Harcourt.

Penguin Gandhi Reader. Ed. by Rudrangshu Mukherjee. 320p. 1995. pap. 13.95 (*0-14-023686-4*, Penguin Bks) Viking Penguin.

Penguin German Phrase Book. Jill Norman & Ute Hitchin. 272p. (Orig.). 1988. pap. 7.00 (*0-14-009940-9*, Penguin Bks) Viking Penguin.

***Penguin Guide to American Law Schools.** Harold Doughty. LC 98-28969. 307p. 1999. pap. 17.95 (*0-14-046994-X*) Viking Penguin.

Penguin Guide to Ancient Egypt. 2nd ed. William J. Murnane. LC 97-205405. 1997. pap. 18.95 (*0-14-046952-4*, Penguin Bks) Viking Penguin.

***Penguin Guide to Bargain CDs, 1998-1999.** 2nd ed. Ivan March. 1408p. 1999. pap. 22.95 (*0-14-051409-0*) Viking Penguin.

***Penguin Guide to Compact Discs: The Guide to Excellence in Recorded Classical Music.** Ivan March et al. 1600p. 1999. pap. 24.95 (*0-14-051379-5*, Penguin Bks) Viking Penguin.

Penguin Guide to Punctuation. R. L. Trask. (Illus.). 176p. pap. 13.00 (*0-14-051366-3*, Pub. by Pnguin Bks Ltd) Trafalgar.

Penguin Guide to Vastu: The Classical Indian Science of Architecture & Design. Sashikala Ananth. LC 98-917782. 195 p. 1998. 24.00 (*0-670-88288-7*, Viking) Viking Penguin.

Penguin Historical Atlas of Ancient Egypt. Bill Manley. 1997. pap. 16.95 (*0-14-051331-0*) Viking Penguin.

Penguin Historical Atlas of Ancient Greece. Robert Morkot. 2000. pap. 8.00 (*0-14-051335-3*) Viking Penguin.

Penguin Historical Atlas of Ancient Rome. Christopher Scarre. 144p. 2000. pap. 8.00 (*0-14-051329-9*, Penguin Bks) Viking Penguin.

Penguin Historical Atlas of North America. Eric Homberger. 144p. 1995. pap. 16.95 (*0-14-051327-2*, Penguin Bks) Viking Penguin.

Penguin Historical Atlas of the Dinosaurs. Michael J. Benton. 144p. 1996. pap. 16.95 (*0-614-19893-3*) Viking Penguin.

Penguin Historical Atlas of the Pacific. Colin McEvedy. LC 98-9434. (Illus.). 120p. 1998. pap. 16.95 (*0-14-025428-5*) Viking Penguin.

Penguin Historical Atlas of the Third Reich. Richard Overy. 144p. 1997. pap. 16.95 (*0-14-051330-2*) Viking Penguin.

Penguin Historical Atlas of the Vikings. John Haywood. 144p. 1995. pap. 17.95 (*0-14-051328-0*, Penguin Bks) Viking Penguin.

Penguin History of Canada. rev. ed. Kenneth McNaught. 1991. pap. 16.95 (*0-14-014998-8*, Penguin Bks) Viking Penguin.

Penguin History of Latin America. Edwin Williamson. (Illus.). 640p. 1993. pap. 16.95 (*0-14-012559-0*, Penguin Bks) Viking Penguin.

Penguin History of the Church Vol. 6: A History of Christian Missions. 2nd ed. Stephen Neill. 1991. pap. 15.95 (*0-14-013763-7*) Viking Penguin.

Penguin History of the World. rev. ed. J. M. Roberts. (Illus.). 1152p. 1995. pap. 17.95 (*0-14-015495-7*, Penguin Bks) Viking Penguin.

Penguin Island. Anatole France, pseud. Tr. by A. W. Evans. LC 81-80108. 368p. 1981. pap. 6.95 (*0-918172-09-8*) Leetes Isl.

Penguin Island. Anatole France, pseud. reprint ed. lib. bdg. 25.95 (*0-89190-540-5*, Rivercity Pr) Amereon Ltd.

Penguin Italian Phrase Book. Jill Norman & Pietro Giorgetti. 272p. 1988. pap. 7.00 (*0-14-009938-7*, Penguin Bks) Viking Penguin.

***Penguin London Mapguide.** 4th ed. Michael Middleditch. 64p. 2000. pap. 8.95 (*0-14-027948-2*, Penguin Bks) Viking Penguin.

Penguin London Mapguide: The Essential Guide. rev. ed. Michael Middleditch. (Illus.). 48p. 1993. pap. 7.95 (*0-14-046954-0*, Penguin Bks) Viking Penguin.

Penguin Map of Europe. Michael Middleditch. 1993. pap. 9.95 (*0-14-051286-1*) Viking Penguin.

Penguin Map of the World. Michael Graham. 1993. pap. 8.95 (*0-14-051285-3*) Viking Penguin.

Penguin Opera Guide. Amanda Holden. 1995. pap. 19.95 (*0-14-051385-X*) Penguin Putnam.

Penguin Parade. Robert J. Ollason. LC 94-6433. (Illus.). 40p. (J). (gr. 4-6). 1994. lib. bdg. 19.95 (*0-8225-1491-5*, Lerner Publctns) Lerner Pub.

Penguin Parade. D. Schwenk. 12p. 1990. pap. text 3.50 (*0-913277-28-2*) Summy-Birchard.

Penguin Passnotes Nursing. White & David. pap. 11.95 (*0-14-077055-0*, Pub. by Pnguin Bks Ltd) Trafalgar.

Penguin Persons & Peppermints. Walter P. Eaton. LC 72-93335. (Essay Index Reprint Ser.). 1977. 21.95 (*0-8369-1288-8*) Ayer.

Penguin Pete see Pinguin Pit

Penguin Pete see Pit, le Petit Pingouin

Penguin Pete see Pit il Piccolo Piguino

Penguin Pete see Pinguino Pedro

Penguin Pete. Marcus Pfister. LC 87-1627. (Illus.). 32p. (J). (gr. k-3). 1987. 15.95 (*1-55858-018-2*, Pub. by North-South Bks NYC); lib. bdg. 15.88 (*1-55858-242-8*, Pub. by North-South Bks NYC) Chronicle Bks.

Penguin Pete. Marcus Pfister. LC 87-1627. (Illus.). 32p. (J). (gr. k-3). 1994. pap. 6.95 (*1-55858-356-4*, Pub. by North-South Bks NYC) Chronicle Bks.

Penguin Pete. Marcus Pfister. LC 96-44517. (Illus.). 12p. (J). (ps). 1997. bds. 6.95 (*1-55858-690-3*, Pub. by North-South Bks NYC) Chronicle Bks.

Penguin Pete, Ahoy! see Pit Ahoi!

Penguin Pete, Ahoy! see Cia Ciao, Pit!

Penguin Pete, Ahoy! Marcus Pfister. Tr. by Rosemary Lanning. LC 93-19921. (Illus.). 32p. (J). (gr. k-3). 1993. 15.95 (*1-55858-220-7*, Pub. by North-South Bks NYC); lib. bdg. 15.88 (*1-55858-221-5*, Pub. by North-South Bks NYC) Chronicle Bks.

Penguin Pete, Ahoy! Marcus Pfister. LC 93-19921. (Illus.). 32p. (J). (gr. k-3). 1998. pap. 6.95 (*1-55858-907-4*, Pub. by North-South Bks NYC) Chronicle Bks.

Penguin Pete & Little Tim see Papa Pit und Tim

Penguin Pete & Little Tim see Papa Pit et Tim

Penguin Pete & Little Tim. Marcus Pfister. Tr. by Rosemary Lanning. LC 94-5093. (Illus.). 32p. (J). (gr. k-3). 1994. 15.95 (*1-55858-301-7*, Pub. by North-South Bks NYC) Chronicle Bks.

Penguin Pete & Little Tim. Marcus Pfister. LC 94-5093. (Illus.). 32p. (J). (gr. k-3). 1997. pap. 6.95 (*1-55858-773-X*, Pub. by North-South Bks NYC) Chronicle Bks.

Penguin Pete & Pat see Pit und Pat

Penguin Pete & Pat. Marcus Pfister. LC 88-25296. (Illus.). 32p. (J). (gr. k-3). 1989. lib. bdg. 15.88 (*1-55858-243-6*, Pub. by North-South Bks NYC) Chronicle Bks.

Penguin Pete & Pat. Marcus Pfister. Tr. by Anthea Bell. LC 88-25296. (Illus.). 32p. (J). (gr. k-3). 1989. 15.95 (*1-55858-003-4*, Pub. by North-South Bks NYC) Chronicle Bks.

Penguin Pete & Pat. Marcus Pfister. LC 88-25296. (Illus.). 32p. (J). (gr. k-3). 1996. pap. 6.95 (*1-55858-618-0*, Pub. by North-South Bks NYC) Chronicle Bks.

Penguin Pete's New Friends see Pits Neue Freunde

Penguin Pete's New Friends see Nouveaux Amis de Pit

Penguin Pete's New Friends see Nuovi Amici Per Pit

Penguin Pete's New Friends. Marcus Pfister. LC 87-72037. (Illus.). 32p. (J). (gr. k-3). 1988. 15.95 (*1-55858-025-5*, Pub. by North-South Bks NYC); lib. bdg. 15.88 (*1-55858-244-4*, Pub. by North-South Bks NYC) Chronicle Bks.

Penguin Pete's New Friends. Marcus Pfister. LC 87-72037. (Illus.). 32p. (J). (gr. k-3). 1995. pap. 6.95 (*1-55858-414-5*, Pub. by North-South Bks NYC) Chronicle Bks.

Penguin Pete's New Friends. Marcus Pfister. LC 96-47345. (Illus.). 12p. (J). (ps). 1997. bds. 6.95 (*1-55858-691-1*, Pub. by North-South Bks NYC) Chronicle Bks.

Penguin Pete's New Friends. Marcus Pfister. 1995. 11.15 (*0-606-08843-1*, Pub. by Turtleback) Demco.

Penguin Picture Roo. Pauline Reilly. (Picture Roo Bks.). (Illus.). 32p. (Orig.). (J). (ps-3). 1997. pap. 6.95 (*0-86417-826-3*, Pub. by Kangaroo Pr) Seven Hills Bk.

***Penguin Planet.** Kevin Schafer. (Illus.). 144p. 2000. 24.95 (*1-55971-745-9*, NorthWord Pr) Creat Pub Intl.

Penguin Polish Phrase Book. 3rd ed. Magda Hall & Jill Norman. 304p. 1993. pap. 8.95 (*0-14-011174-3*, Penguin Bks) Viking Penguin.

***Penguin Pond.** Annie J. Lang. 50p. 2000. 10.95 (*1-57377-094-9*, 0-1988-4-02326-5) Easl Pubns.

Penguin Pool Murder. Stuart Palmer. LC 90-84274. 182p. 1990. reprint ed. pap. 7.95 (*1-55882-076-0*) Intl Polygonics.

Penguin Portuguese Phrase Book. 2nd ed. Jill Norman & Antonio De Figuerdo. 288p. 1988. reprint ed. pap. 7.95 (*0-14-009937-9*, Penguin Bks) Viking Penguin.

Penguin Principles. David Belasic & Paul Schmidt. LC 85-15524. 1986. 7.95 (*0-89536-799-8*, 6817) CSS OH.

Penguin Profiles: Pittsburgh's Boys of Winter. Jim O'Brien. (Pittsburgh Proud Ser.). (Illus.). 448p. 1994. 24.95 (*0-916114-16-3*) J P OBrien.

Penguin Psychology: or The Mystery of Bridge Building. Robert Benchley. 19.95 (*0-88411-299-3*) Amereon Ltd.

Penguin Quartet. Peter Arrhenius. LC 97-18239. (Illus.). 28p. (J). (gr. k-3). 1998. 14.95 (*1-57505-252-0*, Carolrhoda) Lerner Pub.

Penguin Readers Easystarts: Hannah & the Hurricane. John Escott. 1998. pap. text 7.00 (*0-582-35290-8*) Addison-Wesley.

Penguin Readers Level 3: King Solomons Mines. H. Rider Haggard. 1998. pap. 7.00 (*0-14-081464-7*) Viking Penguin.

Penguin Readers Level 3: Portrait of a Lady. Henry James. 48p. (C). 1998. pap. 7.00 (*0-14-081626-7*) Viking Penguin.

Penguin Readers Level 3: Sense Sensibility. Jane Austen. 48p. 1998. pap. 7.00 (*0-14-081634-8*) Viking Penguin.

***Penguin Readers New Look For March 2000.** (C). 2000. text. write for info. (*0-13-028189-1*) Pearson Custom.

Penguin Russian Dictionary: English-Russian, Russian-English. W. F. Ryan. LC 96-212668. 1152p. 1996. pap. 22.95 (*0-14-051067-2*, Viking) Viking Penguin.

Penguin Short History of English Literature. Stephen Coote. 784p. 1994. pap. 16.95 (*0-14-012531-0*, Penguin Bks) Viking Penguin.

Penguin Small. Mick Inkpen. LC 92-8514. (Illus.). 32p. (J). (ps-3). 1993. 14.95 (*0-15-200567-6*, Gulliver Bks) Harcourt.

Penguin Soup for the Soul. Tom Tomorrow. LC 98-28821. 128p. 1998. text 9.95 (*0-312-19316-5*) St Martin.

Penguin Spanish Phrase Book. Jill Norman & Maria V. Alvarez. 288p. 1988. pap. 7.00 (*0-14-009936-0*, Penguin Bks) Viking Penguin.

***Penguin Sri Aurobindo Reader.** Aurobindo Ghose & Makarand, R. Paranjape. LC 99-932833. 1999. write for info. (*0-14-027840-0*) Penguin Books.

Penguin Stickers. Cathy Beylon. (Illus.). (J). 1995. pap. 1.00 (*0-486-28779-3*) Dover.

Penguin That Walks at Night. Pauline Reilly. (Picture Roo Bks.). (Illus.). 32p. (Orig.). (J). 1993. pap. 6.95 (*0-86417-034-3*, Pub. by Kangaroo Pr) Seven Hills Bk.

***Penguin Thesaurus of Quotations.** M. J. Cohen. 672p. 2000. pap. 13.95 (*0-14-051440-6*, Penguin Bks) Viking Penguin.

Penguin Triumphant. John Ostrander. Ed. by Dennis O'Neil. (Illus.). 48p. 1992. pap. 4.95 (*1-56389-030-5*) DC Comics.

***Penguin Who Hated the Cold Because He Was All Dressed Up & Had No Place To Go.** Taylor Brandon. LC 96-94846. (The World's Greatest Children's Bks.). (Illus.). 48p. (J). (gr. k-5). 1999. 14.99 (*1-889945-61-7*) Imperius.

Penguin Year. Susan Bonners. 1981. 9.43 (*0-440-00170-6*) Delacorte.

Penguin 25 New Fiction. Gregory Beattie & Stephanie Johnson. LC 98-199941. 249p. 1998. write for info. (*0-14-027502-9*) Viking Penguin.

Penguins see Zoobooks

Penguins see Animals & Critters

Penguins see Animals Series

Penguins see Pinguinos

Penguins. (Eyes on Nature Ser.). 32p. (J). (gr. 1). pap. write for info. (*1-882210-61-1*) Action Pub.

Penguins. Cousteau Society Staff. (J). 1998. 3.95 (*0-87628-987-1*) Ctr Appl Res.

Penguins. Cousteau Society Staff. LC 91-35229. (Illus.). 24p. (J). (ps-1). 1992. 3.95 (*0-671-77058-6*) Litle Simon.

***Penguins!** Gail Gibbons. (Illus.). (J). 1998. pap. 6.95 (*0-8234-1516-3*) Holiday.

Penguins! Gail Gibbons. LC 98-5194. (J). (ps-3). 1998. 16.95 (*0-8234-1388-8*) Holiday.

Penguins. M. C. Helldorfer. (Animal Safari Ser.). (Illus.). 10p. (J). (ps-k). 1999. bds. 5.95 (*0-7922-7105-X*, Pub. by Natl Geog) Publishers Group.

***Penguins.** Judith Hodge. LC 99-25196. (Animals of the Ocean Ser.). 32p. 1999. pap. text 5.95 (*0-7641-1216-3*) Barron.

Penguins. Sylvia A. Johnson. LC 80-28180. (Lerner Natural Science Bks.). (Illus.). 48p. (J). (gr. 4 up). 1981. lib. bdg. 22.60 (*0-8225-1453-2*, Lerner Publctns) Lerner Pub.

Penguins. Wolfgang Kaehler. (Illus.). 80p. 1989. 22.95 (*0-87701-649-6*); pap. 12.95 (*0-87701-637-2*) Chronicle Bks.

Penguins. Bobbie Kalman. LC 95-24624. (Crabapples Ser.). (J). 1995. 11.15 (*0-606-09740-6*, Pub. by Turtleback) Demco.

Penguins. Emilie U. Lepthien. LC 82-17911. (New True Books Ser.). (Illus.). 48p. (J). (gr. k-4). 1983. pap. 5.50 (*0-516-41683-9*) Childrens.

Penguins. John Love. LC 96-48510. (WorldLife Library). (Illus.). 72p. (J). (gr. 5 up). 1997. pap. 16.95 (*0-89658-339-2*) Voyageur Pr.

Penguins. John A. Love. (Illus.). 128p. pap. text 19.95 (*1-873580-16-9*, Pub. by Whittet Bks) Diamond Farm Bk.

Penguins! Wayne Lynch. (Illus.). 64p. (YA). (gr. 4 up). 1999. pap. 9.95 (*1-55209-424-3*); lib. bdg. 19.95 (*1-55209-421-9*) Firefly Bks Ltd.

Penguins. Remy Marion. LC 99-18383. 1999. 21.95 (*0-8069-4232-0*) Sterling.

Penguins. Jenny Markert. LC 97-27836. (Illus.). 32p. (J). 1998. lib. bdg. 22.79 (*1-56766-490-3*) Childs World.

Penguins. Rene Mettler. (First Discovery Book). 60p. (J). (ps-3). 1996. 11.95 (*0-590-73877-1*, Cartwheel) Scholastic Inc.

Penguins. Roger T. Peterson. (Illus.). 256p. 1998. pap. 20.00 (*0-395-89897-8*) HM.

Penguins. Claire Robinson. LC 97-12312. (In the Wild Ser.). (Illus.). 24p. (J). (ps-2). 1998. 18.50 (*1-57572-137-6*) Heinemann Lib.

Penguins. Lynn M. Stone. LC 97-51933. (Early Bird Nature Bks.). 1998. 14.95 (*0-8225-3022-8*) Lerner Pub.

Penguins. Lynn M. Stone. LC 88-31606. (Illus.). 24p. (J). (gr. k-4). 1989. lib. bdg. 14.60 (*0-86592-325-6*) Rourke Enter.

Penguins. John B. Wexo. (Zoobooks). (Illus.). 24p. (J). (gr. 1-7). 1997. 13.95 (*1-888153-30-X*, 263-7) Wildlife Educ.

Penguins. Wildlife Education, Ltd. Staff & John B. Wexo. (Zoobooks Ser.). (Illus.). 20p. (YA). (gr. 5 up). 1998. pap. 2.75 (*0-937934-17-8*) Wildlife Educ.

Penguins. Tony D. Williams. (Bird Families of the World Ser.). (Illus.). 310p. 1995. text 65.00 (*0-19-854667-X*) OUP.

Penguins: A Portrait of the Animal World, 1. Derek Hastings. 1998. pap. text 10.95 (*1-57717-026-1*) Todtri Prods.

Penguins: A Postcard Book. Jonathan Chester. 107.40 (*0-89087-798-X*) Celestial Arts.

Penguins: A Thematic Unit. Lola Willrich. (Thematic Units Ser.). (Illus.). 80p. (J). (gr. 1-3). 1991. student ed. 9.95 (*1-55734-277-6*) Tchr Create Mat.

Penguins: A Theme Unit Developed in Cooperation with P.R.B.O. Biological Research. Robin Bernard. 1994. pap. 10.95 (*0-590-49639-5*) Scholastic Inc.

***Penguins: A Visual Introduction to Penguins.** Bernard Stonehouse. LC 99-23829. (Animal Watch Ser.). (Illus.). 48p. (J). 1999. 16.95 (*0-8160-4011-7*, Checkmark) Facts on File.

Penguins: An Educational Coloring Book. Spizzirri Publishing Co. Staff. Ed. by Linda Spizzirri. (Illus.). 32p. (J). (gr. 1-8). 1989. pap. 1.99 (*0-86545-134-6*) Spizzirri.

Penguins: Biology & Management. Ed. by Surrey Beatty Staff et al. 496p. 1999. pap. 340.00 (*0-949324-58-2*, Pub. by Surrey Beatty & Sons) St Mut.

***Penguins: Lanting.** Angelika Taschen. 1999. pap. (*3-8228-6392-0*) Taschen Amer.

Penguins: Nature's Window. Sheila Buff. LC 97-153218. (Nature's Window Ser.). 48p. 1997. 6.95 (*0-8362-2784-0*) Andrews & McMeel.

***Penguins: The Hands-on Way to Build Reading Skills!, 1 vol.** Professional Books Staff. (Illus.). 4p. 1999. 7.95 (*0-439-04323-9*) Scholastic Inc.

Penguins: 23 Postcards. Jonathan Chester. (Illus.). 48p. 1996. pap. 8.95 (*0-89087-764-5*) Celestial Arts.

Penguins - A Story Samphlet. Story Rhyme Staff. (Illus.). 5p. (Orig.). (J). (gr. 4-10). 1995. pap. 9.95 (*1-56820-123-0*) Story Time.

Penguins & Golden Calves: Icons & Idols. Madeleine L'Engle. (Wheaton Literary Ser.). 192p. 1996. 17.99 (*0-87788-631-8*, H Shaw Pubs) Waterbrook Pr.

Penguins & Polar Bears. National Geographic Society Staff. (Illus.). 32p. (J). 1996. pap. text 4.95 (*0-7922-3604-1*) Natl Geog.

Penguins & Their Homes. Deborah C. Gibson. LC 98-15387. (Animal Habitats Ser.). 24p. (J). (gr. k-4). 1999. 18.60 (*0-8239-5311-4*, PowerKids) Rosen Group.

Penguins & Their Young. Jean C. Echols. Ed. by Lincoln Bergman et al. (Great Explorations in Math & Science (GEMS) Ser.). (Illus.). 80p. (Orig.). (J). (ps-1). 1995. pap., teacher ed. 21.00 (*0-912511-92-3*, GEMS) Lawrence Science.

***Penguins & Their Young: Science & Math Activities for Young Children.** Jean Echols. (Illus.). (J). 2000. pap. 21.00 (*0-924886-50-1*, GEMS) Lawrence Science.

Penguins at Home: Gentoos of Antarctica. Bruce McMillan. LC 92-34769. (Illus.). 40p. (J). 1993. 17.00 (*0-395-66560-4*) HM.

Penguins in the Fridge. Nicola Moon. (Illus.). 32p. (J). (gr. 1-3). 1997. pap. 9.95 (*1-85793-793-7*, Pub. by Pavilion Bks Ltd) Trafalgar.

Penguins, Model Parents. Arthur Morton. (Illus.). (J). (gr. k-3). 1994. 12.50 (*1-57842-067-9*) Delmas Creat.

Penguins of the Galapagos. Carol A. Amato. LC 95-51837. (Young Readers' Ser.). (Illus.). 48p. (J). (gr. 2-4). 1996. pap. 4.95 (*0-8120-9313-5*) Barron.

Penguins of the Galapagos. Carol A. Amato. (Young Reader Ser.). (Illus.). 48p. (J). (gr. 3-6). 1996. lib. bdg. 13.45 (*1-56674-205-6*) Forest Hse.

Penguins of the Galapagos. Carol A. Amato. (Young Readers' Series). (J). 1996. 10.15 (*0-606-11729-6*, Pub. by Turtleback) Demco.

Penguins of the World. Wayne Lynch. (Illus.). 144p. (J). 1997. 35.00 (*1-55209-180-5*) Firefly Bks Ltd.

P

Penguins of the World. Pauline Reilly. (Illus.). 176p. 1994. pap. 17.95 (*0-19-553547-2*) OUP.
Penguins of the World: A Bibliography. A. Williams et al. 268p. 1985. 25.00 (*0-85665-112-5*, Pub. by Brit Antarctic Surv) Balogh.
Penguins, Seals, Dolphins, Salmon & Eels: Sketches for an Imaginative Zoology. Karl Konig. 92p. 1990. pap. 12.95 (*0-86315-014-4*, 930, Pub. by Floris Bks) Anthroposophic.
Penguins Slide. Kees Moerbeek. LC 91-42040. 9p. (J). 1992. 5.99 (*0-85953-544-4*) Childs Play.
***Penguins Through the Year.** Scholastic Professional Books Staff. (Super Science Readers Ser.). (Illus.). 16p. (J). 2000. pap. 10.95 (*0-439-16770-1*) Scholastic Inc.
Penguins with Guns. R. Mathews-Danzer. 2000. pap. 14.95 (*1-888417-42-0*) Dimefast.
Penguins Workbook Based on the Story Rye the Rhyming Detective in the Missing Fairy Penguin. A. Doyle. (Illus.). 20p. 1999. pap., wbk. ed. 15.95 (*1-56820-391-8*) Story Time.
***Penhaligon's Rock.** Betty O'Rourke. 352p. 2000. 31.99 (*0-7089-4208-3*) Ulverscroft.
Penhallow. Georgette Heyer. reprint ed. lib. bdg. 25.95 (*0-89190-646-0*, Rivercity Pr) Amereon Ltd.
Penhallow's Indian Wars. Ed. by Edward Wheelock. LC 71-179534. (Select Bibliographies Reprint Ser.). 1977. reprint ed. 23.95 (*0-8369-6663-5*) Ayer.
Penhally. Caroline Gordon. LC 91-62456. (Southern Classics Ser.). 302p. (C). 1991. reprint ed. pap. 14.95 (*1-879941-03-1*) J S Sanders.
Penia en Ploutos. Jacob Homelrijk. Ed. by Gregory Vlastos. LC 78-19360. (Morals & Law in Ancient Greece Ser.). 1979. reprint ed. lib. bdg. 17.95 (*0-405-11552-0*) Ayer.
Peniarth see Reprints of Welsh Manuscripts
Peniaze - Co S Nimi? Petrjanosova. (SLO.). 224p. 1996. write for info. (*80-08-00992-6*, Pub. by Slov Pegagog Naklad) IBD Ltd.
***Penicillin: A Breakthrough in Medicine.** Richard Tames. LC 00-26088. (Point of Impact Ser.). (Illus.). (J). 2000. pap. write for info. (*1-57572-417-0*) Heinemann Lib.
Penicillin: Meeting the Challenge. Gladys L. Hobby. LC 84-19689. (Illus.). 319p. 1985. 50.00 (*0-300-03225-0*) Yale U Pr.
Penicillin Fermentation: A Model for Secondary Metabolite Production. S. John Pirt. (C). 1993. 75.00 (*1-874685-10-X*, Pub. by Pirtferm Ltd) St Mut.
Penicillin in the Treatment of Syphilis: The Experience of Three Decades. O. Idse et al. (WHO Bulletin Supplement Ser.: Vol. 47). 1972. pap. text 12.00 (*92-4-068471-9*, 1034701) World Health.
Penicillium & Acremonium. J. F. Peberdy. LC 87-12328. (Biotechnology Handbooks Ser.: Vol. 1). (Illus.). 314p. (C). 1987. text 85.00 (*0-306-42345-6*, Kluwer Plenum) Kluwer Academic.
Penick Family: Descendants of Edward Penick-Penix-Pinix of St. Peter's Parish, New Kent County, Virginia. Lyman W. Priest. LC 82-82022. 344p. reprint ed. pap. 106.70 (*0-8357-4711-5*, AU0040700009) Bks Demand.
Penikese - Island of Hope: One of the Elizabeths, a Massachussetts Historical Site. I. Thomas Buckley. Ed. by Meg B. Springer. (Illus.). ix, 140p. 1997. 24.95 (*1-887086-07-2*); pap. 15.95 (*1-887086-06-4*) Stony Brook Pr.
Penile Disorders. Symposium on Penile Disorder Staff. LC 96-53124. 1997. pap. write for info. (*3-540-61674-8*) Spr-Verlag.
Penimin Haggadah. A. L. Scheinbaum. 1997. 14.95 (*0-9635120-7-2*, Pub. by Penimin Pubns) Feldheim.
Peninsula. Louise Dickinson. 1976. 22.95 (*0-8488-0984-X*) Amereon Ltd.
Peninsula. Ed. by Editors of Time-Life Books. LC 97-34623. (Voices of the Civil War Ser.). 180p. (gr. 6). 1999. 29.95 (*0-7835-4715-3*) Time-Life.
Peninsula. Alice H. Rice. 23.95 (*0-89190-728-9*) Amereon Ltd.
***Peninsula: Essays & Memoirs from Michigan.** Illus. by Michael Steinberg. 224p. 2000. pap. 24.95 (*0-87013-544-9*) Mich St U Pr.
Peninsula Campaign of 1862: Yorktown to the Seven Days, 3 vols., Vol. 1. Ed. by William J. Miller et al. (Illus.). 238p. 1995. pap. 16.95 (*1-882810-75-9*) Savas Pub.
Peninsula Campaign of 1862 Vol. 2: Yorktown to the Seven Days, 3 vols. Ed. by William J. Miller et al. (Campaign Chronicles Ser.). (Illus.). 208p. 1995. pap. 16.95 (*1-882810-76-7*, 106) Savas Pub.
Peninsula Campaign of 1862 Vol. 3: Yorktown to the Seven Days. Ed. by William J. Miller. (Illus.). 228p. (Orig.). 1997. pap. 16.95 (*1-882810-14-7*, 14-7) Savas Pub.
***Peninsula Cities, California, 1.** Rand McNally Staff. 1999. 3.95 (*0-528-97759-8*) Rand McNally.
Peninsula of Sinai. 64p. pap. text 9.95 (*88-7009-946-6*, Pub. by Bonechi) Eiron.
Peninsula People Book. John McCleary. LC 96-93128. (Illus.). 124p. 1998. pap. 25.00 (*0-9668687-0-6*) Slow Limbo.
Peninsula Trails: Outdoor Adventures on the San Francisco Peninsula. 3rd rev. ed. Jean Rusmore et al. LC 96-46624. (Illus.). 304p. 1997. pap. 14.95 (*0-89997-197-0*) Wilderness Pr.
Peninsular & Oriental Steam Navigation Company & Steam Line AB: A Report on Monopolies & Mergers Commission Report, Command Paper 3664. (Command Papers (All) Ser.: No. 81011068). 1997. 50.00 (*0-10-136642-6*, HM66426, Pub. by Statnry Office) Bernan Associates.
Peninsular Campaigns of Wellington & Featherstone: A Guide to the Battles in Spain & Portugal. Donald Featherstone. 1994. 35.00 (*0-9626655-9-2*, Pub. by Emperors Pr) Combined Pub.
Peninsular Canaan. Howard Pyle. 1996. 6.00 (*1-886706-08-5*) Hickory Hse.
Peninsular Journal, 1808-17. Benjamin D'Urban. 376p. 1989. 37.50 (*0-947898-87-5*, 5574) Stackpole.
Peninsular Malaysia. Jin-Bee Ooi. LC 75-42166. (Geographies for Advances Study Ser.). 453p. reprint ed. pap. 140.50 (*0-608-17116-6*, 202771000056) Bks Demand.
Peninsular Preparation: The Reform of the British Army, 1795-1809. Richard G. Glover. LC 63-25938. 323p. reprint ed. pap. 92.10 (*0-608-30713-0*, 2051444) Bks Demand.
Peninsular War. Donald Featherstone. Ed. by Stuart Asquith. (Wargaming in History Ser.). (Illus.). 127p. 1998. pap. text 11.00 (*0-7881-5559-8*) DIANE Pub.
***Peninsular War.** Roger Parkinson. (Illus.). 2000. pap. 12.99 (*1-84022-228-X*, Pub. by Wrdsworth Edits) Combined Pub.
Peninsular War: Aspects of the Struggle for the Iberian Peninsula. Ed. by Ian Fletcher. (Illus.). 264p. 1997. 34.95 (*1-873376-82-0*, Pub. by Spellmnt Pubs) St Mut.
Peninsulas. K. C. Thorne. LC 96-27673. 80p. (Orig.). 1997. pap. 9.95 (*1-56474-204-0*) Fithian Pr.
Penis. Azid Hashmat & Sakti Das. (Illus.). 350p. 1993. text 99.50 (*0-8121-1508-2*) Lppncott W & W.
Penis Book, 1. Koneman Music Staff. 1999. pap. text 9.95 (*3-8290-2186-0*) Konemann.
Penis Book: An Owner's Manual for Use, Maintenance & Repair. Margaret Gore. (Illus.). 96p. (Orig.). 1997. pap. 10.95 (*1-86448-329-6*, Pub. by Allen & Unwin Pty) IPG Chicago.
Penis Inserts of Southeast Asia: An Annotated Bibliography with an Overview & Comparative Perspectives. Donald E. Brown et al. LC 88-71425. (Occasional Papers: Vol. 15). (Illus.). 60p. (Orig.). (C). 1988. pap. text 6.00 (*0-944613-05-5*) UC Berkeley Ctrs SE Asia.
Penis Puns, Jokes & One-Liners: A Movie Quote Book. Steve Stewart. 120p. (Orig.). 1997. pap. 5.95 (*1-889138-07-X*) Companion Press.
Penis Size & Enlargement: Facts, Fallacies & Proven Methods. Gary Griffin. LC 96-101429. (Illus.). 200p. 1995. pap. 19.95 (*0-934061-24-6*) Marketscope Bks.
***Penissimo.** Leonard Zett. (Gay Erotic Art Photography Ser.). (Illus.). 2000. 44.95 (*3-925443-90-8*) Janssen.
Penitence: A True Story. Edward J. Armstrong. Ed. by Gifford Stevens. (Illus.). 352p. 1994. pap. 19.95 (*0-9642473-0-5*) L Madden Assocs.
***Penitence in the Age of Reformations.** Katharine Jackson Lualdi & Anne T. Thayer. LC 00-38981. (St. Andrews Studies in Reformation History). 2000. write for info. (*0-7546-0096-3*, Pub. by Ashgate Pub) Ashgate Pub Co.
Penitence of Adam: (A Study of the Andrius MS.) Esther C. Quinn. Tr. by Micheline Dufau. LC 79-19056. (Romance Monographs: No. 36). 192p. 1980. 25.00 (*84-499-3367-6*) Romance.
Penitencia de Amor. De Urrea. (Exeter Hispanic Text Ser.: No. 49). (SPA.). 112p. Date not set. pap. text 17.95 (*0-85989-337-5*, Pub. by Univ Exeter Pr) Northwestern U Pr.
penitente elusivo: Reader 4. Kay Jarvis Sladky. 3.75 (*0-88436-861-0*) EMC-Paradigm.
Penitentes. Ray J. De Aragon. (Illus.). 105p. (Orig.). 1988. pap. 5.95 (*0-932906-16-8*) Pan-Am Publishing Co.
Penitentes of New Mexico. Ed. by Carlos E. Cortes. LC 73-14212. (Mexican American Ser.). (Illus.). 1976. reprint ed. 39.95 (*0-405-05686-9*) Ayer.
Penitentes of the Southwest. Marta Weigle. LC 78-131971. (Illus.). 48p. 1970. pap. 4.95 (*0-941270-00-9*) Ancient City Pr.
Penitential Discipline of the Primitive Church. Nathaniel Marshall. LC 74-172846. (Library of Anglo-Catholic Theology: No. 13). reprint ed. 44.00 (*0-404-52105-3*) AMS Pr.
Penitentiaries in Arizona, New Mexico, Nevada, & Utah from 1900 to 1980. Judith R. Johnson. LC 97-2341. (Criminology Studies: No. 1). 260p. 1997. text 89.95 (*0-7734-8663-1*) E Mellen.
Penitentiaries Reform Chain. Colvin. 2000. pap. 18.95 (*0-312-22128-2*) St Martin.
Penitentiaries, Reformatories & Chain Gangs: Social Theory & the History of Punishment in Nineteenth Century America. Mark Colvin. LC 97-12045. 254p. 1997. text 45.00 (*0-312-17327-X*) St Martin.
Penitentiary in Crisis: From Accommodation to Riot in New Mexico. Mark Colvin. LC 91-3407. (SUNY Series in Deviance & Social Control). 257p. (C). 1992. text 67.50 (*0-7914-0929-5*); pap. text 24.95 (*0-7914-0930-9*) State U NY Pr.
***Penitents: A Story about Love, Death & Freedom.** A. M. Provinzano. 200p. 2000. pap. 11.95 (*1-930185-02-2*, 103) Joan of Arc Pubng.
Penjing - Worlds of Wonderment: A Journey Exploring an Ancient Chinese Art & Its History, Cultural Background, & Aesthetics. Qingquan Zhao. Tr. by Karin Albert from CHI. LC 96-61314. (Illus.). 144p. 1997. 39.95 (*0-9655297-0-3*) Venus Communications.
Penkiln Burn. Burn Penkiln. pap. 15.00 (*1-84166-001-9*, Pub. by Ellipsis) Norton.
Penknife in My Heart. large type ed. Nicholas Blake. (Linford Mystery Library). 400p. 1997. pap. 16.99 (*0-7089-5106-6*, Linford) Ulverscroft.
Penknives & Other Folding Knives. Simon Moore. (Album Ser.: No. 223). (Illus.). 32p. 1989. pap. 25.00 (*0-85263-966-X*, Pub. by Shire Pubns) Parkwest Pubns.
Penlake: Reflections on Peninsula Lake. Ed. by Historical Committee, Peninsula Lake Association Staff. LC 97-138566. (Illus.). 160p. 1996. 32.00 (*1-55046-096-X*, Pub. by Boston Mills) Genl Dist Srvs.
Penland School of Crafts Book of Jewelry Making. Ed. by John Coyne. LC 74-31333. (Illus.). 192p. 1975. 12.95 (*0-672-51967-4*, Bobbs) Macmillan.
Penman: Modern Cartooning. Gary Blehm. LC 94-10479. 112p. 1995. pap. 9.00 (*0-15-600076-8*, Harvest Bks) Harcourt.
Penmanship & Fine Lettering: A Resource for Designers. John Mendenhall. LC 97-73401. (Illus.). 112p. 1997. pap. 11.95 (*0-88108-202-3*) Art Dir.
Penmanship from A to Z. Lafayette Robinson. (Illus.). 72p. (J). (gr. 3-4). 1988. student ed. 7.95 (*0-9621081-1-1*) Educ Graphics.
Penmanship of the XVI, XVII & XVIII Centuries. Lewis F. Day. LC 78-58919. (Illus.). 1979. reprint ed. pap. 7.95 (*0-8008-6277-5*) Taplinger.
Penn. Sara Berkeley. 48p. 1989. pap. 9.95 (*1-85186-013-4*) Dufour.
Penn. Elizabeth J. Vining. LC 86-63992. (Illus.). 298p. (J). (gr. 6-10). 1986. reprint ed. pap. 9.00 (*0-941308-06-5*) Phila Yrly Mtg RSOF.
Penn: Banking Supervision. 2nd ed. Graham Penn. 1997. write for info. (*0-406-05212-3*, PBS2, MICHIE) LEXIS Pub.
Penn & Teller's How to Play in Traffic. Penn Jillette. LC 97-224459. 226p. 1997. pap. 18.95 (*1-57297-293-9*) Blvd Books.
Penn & Teller's How to Play with Your Food. Penn Jillette & Teller. (Illus.). 1992. 160.00 (*0-679-41657-9*) Villard Books.
Penn Central Color Guide to Freight & Passenger Equipment. Jim Kinkaid. LC 97-72729. (Illus.). 128p. 1998. 49.95 (*1-878887-84-X*) Morning NJ.
Penn Central Failure & the Role of Financial Institutions. United States Congress Committee on Banking & Curr. LC 79-39322. 1972. 14.95 (*0-405-00374-9*) Ayer.
Penn Containers:act Based Cstgcase. 3rd ed. Raiborn et al. 1998. pap. text 11.00 (*0-538-88522-X*) Thomson Learn.
***Penn State Blue Band: A Century of Pride & Precision.** Thomas E. Range & Sean P. Smith. LC 99-24468. 1999. 30.00 (*0-271-01960-3*) Pa St U Pr.
Penn State Dairy Housing Plans. 2nd rev. ed. Robert E. Graves. (NRAES Ser.: Vol. 85). 106p. 1997. pap. text 15.00 (*0-935817-17-4*, NRAES-85) NRAES.
Penn State Football Encyclopedia. Louis Prato. (Illus.). 654p. 1998. 39.95 (*1-57167-117-X*) Sports Pub.
Penn State Football Encyclopedia: Second Edition. rev. ed. Lou Prato. (Illus.). 750p. 2000. 39.95 (*1-58261-105-X*, Pub. by Sprts Pubng) Partners-West.
Penn State Sports Stories & More. Mickey Bergstein. Ed. by John Hope. LC 98-65584. (Illus.). xvi, 300p. 1998. pap. 19.95 (*1-879441-45-4*) RB Bks.
***Penn State Students' Unofficial Guide to College: A Book of Bests & Worsts of Penn State Students' Life at College.** Michael Chodroff. (Illus.). 160p. (C). 1999. pap. 9.95 (*0-9662801-1-3*) Arm in Arm.
***Penn State Then & Now.** Pat Little. (Illus.). 192p. 1999. 30.00 (*0-9670580-0-7*) Pa St U Pr.
***Penn Trolleys in Color Vol. 3: Pittsburgh Reg.** B. Volkmer. (Illus.). 128p. 1999. 54.95 (*1-58248-019-2*) Morning NJ.
Penn Valley Phoenix: A True North Mystery. Janet McClellan. LC 97-40427. 240p. (Orig.). 1998. pap. 11.95 (*1-56280-200-3*) Naiad Pr.
Penn Yan & Keuka Lake. Charles Mitchell. (Images of America Ser.). 1999. pap. 16.99 (*0-7524-0558-6*) Arcadia Publng.
Pennant Races: Baseball at Its Best. Dave Anderson. 432p. 1997. 10.99 (*0-88365-981-6*) Galahad Bks.
Pennate Diatoms: A Translation of Hustedt's Die Kieselalgen, Vol. 2. F. Hustedt. Tr. by Norman G. Jensen from GER.Tr. of Die Kieselalgen. (Illus.). 918p. 1985. reprint ed. lib. bdg. 163.00 (*3-7682-1416-8*) Lubrecht & Cramer.
Pennaten Diatomeen Aus Dem Obereozaen Von Oamaru, Neuseeland. H. J. Schrader. (Illus.). 1969. suppl. ed. 24.00 (*3-7682-5428-3*) Lubrecht & Cramer.
Penne Stilografiche see Fountain Pens: Penne Stilografiche
Penned from the Heart, Vol. 4. Ed. by Gloria Clover & Karen Martin. (Illus.). 1997. pap. 9.95 (*0-936369-53-1*) Son-Rise Pubns.
Penned from the Heart Vol. 3: A Book of Devotions for Every Day. Ed. by Gloria Clover & Karen Martin. (Illus.). 196p. 1996. pap. 7.95 (*0-936369-52-3*) Son-Rise Pubns.
Penned in the Spirit. Doris Baker. Ed. by Patricia Demings. LC 99-90524. 52p. 1999. pap. 10.95 (*1-891601-15-6*) Ladies Caliber.
Pennell's Etchings: A Complete Catalogue. Louis A. Wuerth. (Illus.). 334p. 1988. reprint ed. 95.00 (*0-915346-93-1*) A Wofsy Fine Arts.
Pennell's New York City Etchings: 91 Prints. Joseph Pennell & Edward Bryant. (Illus.). 112p. (Orig.). 1981. pap. 7.95 (*0-486-23913-6*) Dover.
Pennies for Charity: Telemarketing by Professional Fundraisers. Dennis C. Vacco. (Illus.). 104p. 1998. reprint ed. pap. text 25.00 (*0-7881-3947-9*) DIANE Pub.
Pennies for the Piper. Susan H. McLean. 160p. (YA). (gr. 5 up). 1993. pap. 4.50 (*0-374-45754-9*, Sunburst Bks) FS&G.
Pennies from Heaven: The American Popular Music Business in the Twentieth Century. rev. ed. Russell Sanjek. Orig. Title: American Popular Music & Its Business, Vol. III, from 1900 to 1984. 800p. 1996. pap. 21.50 (*0-306-80706-8*) Da Capo.
Pennies from Heaven: 101 Meditations for Couples Trying to Get Pregnant. Frances Stone & Philip Stone. LC 97-45615. 176p. 1998. pap. 9.95 (*0-14-025529-X*) Viking Penguin.
Pennies, Nickels & Dimes. Elizabeth Murphy-Melas et al. LC 99-18135. (Illus.). 24p. (J). (gr. k-6). 1999. pap. write for info. (*0-929173-32-5*) Health Press.
Pennies on a Dead Woman's Eyes. Marcia Muller. 304p. 1992. 18.95 (*0-89296-454-5*) Mysterious Pr.
Pennies on a Dead Woman's Eyes. Marcia Muller. 336p. 1993. mass mkt. 5.99 (*0-446-40033-5*, Pub. by Warner Bks) Little.
Pennies to Dollars: The Story of Maggie Lena Walker. Muriel M. Branch & Dorothy M. Rice. LC 97-20280. (Illus.). xi, 100p. (J). (gr. 3-7). 1997. lib. bdg. 17.95 (*0-208-02453-0*, Linnet Bks) Shoe String.
Pennies to Dollars: The Story of Maggie Lena Walker. Muriel M. Branch & Dorothy M. Rice. LC 97-20280. (Illus.). xi, 100p. (J). (gr. 3-7). 1997. pap. 13.95 (*0-208-02455-7*, Linnet Bks) Shoe String.
Penniless Politics: A Satirical Poem. Douglas Oliver et al. 77p. 1995. pap. 16.95 (*1-85224-269-8*, Pub. by Bloodaxe Bks) Dufour.
Pennine & Pieter Vostaert: "Roman Van Walewein" Ed. & Tr. by David F. Johnson. LC 91-42990. (Library of Medieval Literature: Vol. 81A). (DUT., Illus.). 632p. 1992. text 20.00 (*0-8240-7393-2*) Garland.
Pennine Way South. Tony Hopkins. (National Trail Guides Ser.). (Illus.). 144p. 1995. pap. 19.95 (*1-85410-321-0*, Pub. by Aurum Pr) London Brdge.
Pennine Way South: Edale to Bowes. Tony Hopkins. (National Trail Guides Ser.). (Illus.). 168p. 1995. pap. 19.95 (*1-85410-022-X*, Pub. by Aurum Pr) London Brdge.
***Pennington Cookbook.** Kelly Patrick Williams. LC 99-56380. 240p. 2000. 22.50 (*1-56554-679-2*) Pelican.
Pennington Profile. 2nd ed. Margaret J. O'Connell. (Illus.). 452p. 1986. 25.00 (*0-9617592-1-6*); 50.00 (*0-9617592-0-8*) Pennington Lib.
Pennington's Butterflies of Southern Africa. LC 95-117201. 1997. pap. text 180.00 (*0-947430-46-6*, Pub. by New5 Holland) BHB Intl.
Pennington's Company Law. 6th ed. Robert R. Pennington. 750p. 1990. pap. 60.00 (*0-406-51041-5*, U.K., MICHIE) LEXIS Pub.
Pennington's Corporate Insolvency Law. Robert R. Pennington. 484p. 1991. pap. 42.00 (*0-406-00141-3*, U.K., MICHIE) LEXIS Pub.
Pennington's Corporate Insolvency Law. 2nd ed. Robert R. Pennington. 1997. pap. write for info. (*0-406-08177-8*, PCIL2, MICHIE) LEXIS Pub.
Pennock: The Pennocks of Primitive Hall. George V. Massey, II. (Illus.). 139p. 1991. reprint ed. pap. 22.50 (*0-8328-2228-0*); reprint ed. lib. bdg. 32.50 (*0-8328-2227-2*) Higginson Bk Co.
Penn's Colony: Genealogical & Historical Materials Relating to the Settlement of Pennsylvania, Vol. 2. George E. McCracken. xviii, 660p. 1996. pap. 44.00 (*0-7884-0397-4*, M121) Heritage Bk.
Penn's Creek, PA. Dan Shields. (River Journal Ser.: Vol. 3, No. 4). (Illus.). 48p. 1996. pap. 15.95 (*1-57188-008-9*) F Amato Pubns.
Penn's Example to the Nations: 300 Years of the Holy Experiment. Ed. by Robert G. Crist. LC 86-63552. (Illus.). 276p. (Orig.). 1987. 18.95 (*0-9618164-0-6*) PA Coun Churches.
Penns of Pennsylvania & England. Arthur Pound. 1993. reprint ed. lib. bdg. 89.00 (*0-7812-5819-7*) Rprt Serv.
Penn's Promise: Still Life Painting in Pennsylvania, 1795-1930. Paul A. Chew. LC 89-50637. 112p. (Orig.). 1988. 10.00 (*0-931241-20-0*) Westmoreland.
Pennsauken. Kathleen T. Crame. LC 97-191401. (Images of America Ser.). 1997. pap. 16.99 (*0-7524-0550-0*) Arcadia Publng.
Pennsbury Pottery. Lucille Henzke. LC 89-64083. (Illus.). 176p. 1990. pap. 24.95 (*0-88740-229-1*) Schiffer.
Pennsy Diesel Years, Vol. 2. Robert J. Yanosey. (Illus.). 128p. 1989. 45.00 (*0-9619058-3-2*) Morning NJ.
Pennsy Diesel Years, Vol. 3. Robert J. Yanosey. LC 88-92526. (Illus.). 128p. 1990. 45.00 (*0-9619058-7-5*) Morning NJ.
Pennsy Diesel Years, Vol. 4. Robert J. Yanosey. LC 88-92526. (Illus.). 128p. 1991. 45.00 (*0-9619058-9-1*) Morning NJ.
Pennsy Diesel Years, Vol. 5. Robert J. Yanosey. (Illus.). 128p. 1993. 49.95 (*1-878887-15-7*) Morning NJ.
Pennsy Diesel Years, Vol. 6. Robert J. Yanosey. (Illus.). 128p. 1996. 49.95 (*1-878887-54-8*) Morning NJ.
***Pennsy Electric Pictorial.** Martin S. Zak & Paul K. Withers. LC 99-66614. (Illus.). 160p. 1999. 39.95 (*1-881411-23-0*) Withers Pub.
Pennsy Electric Years. William D. Volkmer. LC 90-63156. (Illus.). 128p. 1991. 45.00 (*1-878887-01-7*) Morning NJ.
Pennsy Era on Long Island. Ron Ziel. 29.95 (*0-8488-0405-8*) Amereon Ltd.
Pennsy K-4's Remembered: Class K-4, the Keystone of Steam Passenger Power. F. A. Kramer. 32p. 1992. pap. 6.95 (*1-882727-04-5*) Bells & Whistles.
Pennsy Middle Division in HO Scale. Dave Frary. 64p. (Orig.). 1996. pap. 11.95 (*0-89024-276-3*, 12170) Kalmbach.
Pennsy Power III. Alvin F. Staufer. LC 93-92576. (Illus.). 512p. 1993. 75.00 (*0-944513-10-7*) Staufer Bks.
Pennsy Q Class. E. T. Harley. LC 82-81755. (Classic Power Ser.: No. 5). (Illus.). 1982. reprint ed. pap. 23.95 (*0-934088-09-8*) NJ Intl Inc.
Pennsy Steam Facs & Figures. 52p. 1999. 21.95 (*0-934088-37-3*) NJ Intl Inc.
Pennsy Steam Years, Vol 1. David R. Sweetland. LC 91-62002. (Illus.). 128p. 1992. 45.00 (*1-878887-08-4*) Morning NJ.
Pennsy Steam Years, Vol. 2. Ian S. Fischer. (Illus.). 128p. 1997. 49.95 (*1-878887-87-4*) Morning NJ.
Pennsy Streamliners: The Blue Ribbon Fleet. Joe Welsh. 1999. 49.95 (*0-89024-293-3*) Kalmbach.
***Pennsylvania's Brain Drain: Migration in the Mid-1990s.** Gordon DeJong. (Illus.). 14p. 1999. pap. 20.00 (*1-58036-135-8*) Penn State Data Ctr.
Pennsylvania see Official Precancel Catalog, State Sections
Pennsylvania see From Sea to Shining Sea

An Asterisk (*) at the beginning of an entry indicates that the title is appearing for the first time.

Pennsylvania see One Nation Series

***Pennsylvania.** (Switched on Schoolhouse Ser.). (Illus.). (J). 2000. pap. 24.95 (*0-7403-0290-6*) Alpha AZ.

Pennsylvania. Marjorie A. Ackerman. LC 93-73315. 1994. 39.95 (*1-55868-159-0*) Gr Arts Ctr Pub.

***Pennsylvania.** Alliance for Safe Driving Staff. (Career Education - License to Drive Ser.). 2001. 31.50 (*0-7668-2378-4*) Delmar.

Pennsylvania. Capstone Press Geography Department Staff. (One Nation Ser.). (Illus.). 48p. (J). (gr. 3-7). 1996. 19.00 (*0-516-20265-0*) Childrens.

Pennsylvania. Dennis B. Fradin. LC 93-32757. (From Sea to Shining Sea Ser.). (Illus.). 64p. (J). (gr. 3-5). 1995. pap. 7.95 (*0-516-43838-7*) Childrens.

***Pennsylvania** Ann Heinrichs. LC 99-15200. (America the Beautiful Ser.). 2000. 32.00 (*0-516-20692-3*) Childrens.

Pennsylvania. Rand McNally Staff. 1997. pap. 5.95 (*0-528-96684-7*) Rand McNally.

Pennsylvania. Gwenyth Swain. LC 93-12333. (Hello U. S. A. Ser.). (Illus.). 72p. (J). (gr. 3-6). 1994. lib. bdg. 18.95 (*0-8225-2727-8*, Lerner Publctns) Lerner Pub.

Pennsylvania. Gwenyth Swain. (Illus.). 72p. 1995. pap. text 5.95 (*0-8225-9703-9*) Lerner Pub.

Pennsylvania. Kathleen Thompson. LC 85-9972. (Portrait of America Library). (Illus.). 48p. (J). (gr. 3-6). 1996. lib. bdg. 22.83 (*0-8114-7383-X*) Raintree Steck-V.

Pennsylvania. Anne Welsbacher. LC 97-36202. (United States Ser.). (Illus.). 32p. (J). 1998. lib. bdg. 19.93 (*1-56239-893-8*, Checkerboard Library) ABDO Pub Co.

***Pennsylvania, 5 vols. , Set.** Stephen Peters. LC 99-16414. (Celebrate the States Ser.). 144p. (J). 2000. 35.64 (*0-7614-0644-1*) Marshall Cavendish.

Pennsylvania: A Guide to Backcountry Travel & Adventure. Diana Rupp. 415p. 1999. pap. 16.00 (*1-893695-00-X*) Out There Pr.

Pennsylvania: A Guide to the Keystone State. Federal Writers' Project Staff. (American Guidebook Ser.). 1980. reprint ed. lib. bdg. 95.00 (*0-403-02187-1*) Somerset Pub.

Pennsylvania: A Guide to the Keystone State. Federal Writers' Project Staff & Writers Program-WPA Staff. (American Guide Ser.). 1989. reprint ed. lib. bdg. 89.00 (*0-7812-1037-2*, 1037) Rprt Serv.

Pennsylvania: A Photographic Celebration. Walter Choroszewski. (Illus.). 108p. 1997. 25.00 (*0-933605-07-2*) Aesthetic Pr.

Pennsylvania: Along Interstate 80. Steven C. Price. 64p. 1993. pap. 6.95 (*0-9667091-1-X*) Educ Tours.

Pennsylvania: Off the Beaten Path. 5th ed. Susan Perloff. LC 99-48818. (Off the Beaten Path Ser.). (Illus.). 192p. 1999. pap. text 12.95 (*0-7627-0462-4*) Globe Pequot.

Pennsylvania: Political, Governmental, Military & Civil, 5 vols., Set. Frederick A. Godcharles. 1993. reprint ed. lib. bdg. 375.00 (*0-7812-5461-2*) Rprt Serv.

Pennsylvania: Steam - Locomotives & Trains from 1931-1938. 2nd rev. ed. Robert K. Durham. LC 95-92377. (Steam of the Thirties Ser.). (Illus.). 80p. 1999. pap. 21.00 (*0-9644480-2-5*) Durham Publng.

Pennsylvania: The State & Its Educational System. Harold L. Hodgkinson. 17p. 1988. 7.00 (*0-937846-72-4*) Inst Educ Lead.

Pennsylvania - Collected Works of Federal Writers Project, Vol. 1. Federal Writers' Project Staff. 1991. reprint ed. lib. bdg. 98.00 (*0-7812-5761-1*) Rprt Serv.

Pennsylvania - Collected Works of Federal Writers Project, Vol. 2. Federal Writers' Project Staff. 1991. reprint ed. lib. bdg. 98.00 (*0-7812-5769-7*) Rprt Serv.

Pennsylvania - Collected Works of Federal Writers Project, Vol. 3. Federal Writers' Project Staff. 1991. reprint ed. lib. bdg. 98.00 (*0-7812-5774-3*) Rprt Serv.

***Pennsylvania - Standard RR of World.** Jeremy F. Plant & Robert J. Yanosey. (Illus.). 128p. 1999. 54.95 (*1-58248-017-6*) Morning NJ.

***Pennsylvania Air Permitting Guide.** 110p. 2000. pap. 85.00 (*1-929744-19-6*) Penn Chamber of Bus.

Pennsylvania Allegheny & Butler Counties Federal Census Index, 1860 City of Pittsburgh. (Illus.). 1986. lib. bdg. 300.00 (*0-89593-469-8*, Accel Indexing) Genealogical Srvcs.

Pennsylvania, Allegheny & Butler Counties Federal Census Index, 1870 (Includes City of Pittsburgh) Ronald V. Jackson. 1990. 300.00 (*0-89593-824-3*, Accel Indexing) Genealogical Srvcs.

Pennsylvania Almanac. Jere Martin. LC 97-24386. 416p. 1997. pap. 19.95 (*0-8117-2880-3*) Stackpole.

Pennsylvania & Middle Atlantic States Genealogical Manuscripts: A User's Guide to the Manuscript Collections of the Genealogical Society of Pennsylvania as Indexed in Its Manuscript Materials Index. J. Carlyle Parker. LC 86-45. 1986. pap. 14.95 (*0-934153-01-9*, OCLC 13214741) Marietta Pub.

Pennsylvania & Other State Greats (Biographies) Carole Marsh. (Carole Marsh Pennsylvania Bks.). (Illus.). (J). 1994. pap. 19.95 (*0-7933-1943-9*); lib. bdg. 29.95 (*0-7933-1942-0*); disk 29.95 (*0-7933-1944-7*) Gallopade Intl.

Pennsylvania & the American Constitution. Jacob E. Cooke. (Illus.). 14p. (Orig.). 1989. pap. 3.00 (*1-877701-00-9*) NCH&GS.

Pennsylvania & the Federal Constitution, 1787-1788, 2 vols. John McMaster & Frederick B. Stone. LC 74-87406. (American Constitutional & Legal History Ser). 1970. reprint ed. lib. bdg. 79.50 (*0-306-71550-3*) Da Capo.

Pennsylvania Antiwar Movement, 1861-1865. Arnold M. Shankman. LC 78-75186. 240p. 1970. 33.50 (*0-8386-2228-3*) Fairleigh Dickinson.

Pennsylvania Appellate Practice, 2 vols. G. Ronald Darlington et al. LC 86-82356. 1993. suppl. ed. 72.50 (*0-317-03797-8*) West Group.

Pennsylvania Appellate Practice, 2 vols., Set. G. Ronald Darlington et al. LC 86-82356. 1986. 285.00 (*0-317-04605-5*) West Group.

Pennsylvania Archives, 122 vols. (Series 1-9). reprint ed. 6200.00 (*0-404-19576-8*) AMS Pr.

***Pennsylvania Atlas.** 6th ed. DeLorme Mapping Co. Staff. (Illus.). 2000. pap. 19.95 (*0-89933-280-3*) DeLorme Map.

Pennsylvania Atlas & Gazetteer. 4th ed. DeLorme Mapping Company Staff. (Atlas & Gazetteer Ser.). (Illus.). 96p. (Orig.). 1996. pap. 16.95 (*0-89933-236-6*, AA-000026-000) DeLorme Map.

***Pennsylvania Atlas & Gazetteer: Topographic Maps of the Entire State, Back Roads, Outdoor Recreation.** 5th ed. DeLorme Mapping Co. Staff. (Illus.). 1999. pap. write for info. (*0-89933-269-2*) DeLorme Map.

Pennsylvania Automotive Directory. Ed. by T. L. Spelman. 1985. 24.95 (*1-55527-028-X*) Auto Contact Inc.

Pennsylvania Bandits, Bushwackers, Outlaws, Crooks, Devils, Ghosts, Desperadoes & Other Assorted & Sundry Characters! Carole Marsh. (Carole Marsh Pennsylvania Bks.). (Illus.). (J). 1994. pap. 19.95 (*0-7933-0961-1*); lib. bdg. 29.95 (*0-7933-0962-X*); disk 29.95 (*0-7933-0963-8*) Gallopade Intl.

Pennsylvania Barn: Its Origin, Evolution, & Distribution in North America. Robert F. Ensminger. (Creating the North American Landscape Ser.). (Illus.). 272p. 1995. reprint ed. pap. text 19.95 (*0-8018-5252-8*) Johns Hopkins.

***Pennsylvania Battlefields & Military Landmarks.** Arthur P. Miller, Jr. LC 99-56904. (Illus.). 2000. pap. 18.95 (*0-8117-2876-5*) Stackpole.

Pennsylvania Bed & Breakfast Guide & Cookbook: Central Region. Karen Shughart. LC 98-41976. 1999. pap. text 15.95 (*0-8117-2705-X*) Stackpole.

Pennsylvania Benchbook for Criminal Proceedings. 3rd ed. Carolyn Engel Temin. text 250.00 (*0-8205-4173-7*) Bender.

Pennsylvania (Berks County) Federal Census, 1870 (Includes City of Reading) 1990. 165.00 (*0-89593-623-2*, Accel Indexing) Genealogical Srvcs.

Pennsylvania "BIO" Bingo! 24 Must Know State People for Kids to Learn about While Having Fun! Carole Marsh. (Bingo! Ser.). (Illus.). (J). (gr. 2-8). 1998. pap. 14.95 (*0-7933-8636-5*) Gallopade Intl.

Pennsylvania Birds. James Kavanagh. (Pocket Naturalist Ser.). (Illus.). 1999. 5.95 (*1-58355-009-7*, Pub. by Waterford WA) Falcon Pub Inc.

Pennsylvania Births Berks County, 1781-1800. John Humphrey. LC 98-70018. 1998. 30.00 (*1-887609-16-4*) J T Humphrey.

Pennsylvania Births Berks County, 1710-1780. John T. Humphrey. LC 97-77364. 393p. 1998. 30.00 (*1-887609-15-6*) J T Humphrey.

Pennsylvania Births Bucks County, 1682-1800. John T. Humphrey. 352p. 1993. 31.00 (*1-887609-07-5*) J T Humphrey.

Pennsylvania Births, Delaware County, 1682-1800. John T. Humphrey. 117p. 1995. 18.50 (*1-887609-09-1*) J T Humphrey.

Pennsylvania Births Lancaster County, 1723-1777. John T. Humphrey. 1997. 29.00 (*1-887609-12-1*) J T Humphrey.

Pennsylvania Births Lancaster County 1778-1800. J. T. Humphrey. LC 97-70684. 397p. 1997. 29.00 (*1-887609-14-8*) J T Humphrey.

Pennsylvania Births Lebanon County, 1714-1800. John T. Humphrey. 267p. 1996. 26.50 (*1-887609-11-3*) J T Humphrey.

Pennsylvania Births Lehigh County, 1734-1800. John T. Humphrey. 327p. 1992. 29.50 (*1-887609-05-9*) J T Humphrey.

Pennsylvania Births Montgomery County, 1682-1800. John T. Humphrey. 536p. 1993. 39.50 (*1-887609-06-7*) J T Humphrey.

Pennsylvania Births Philadelphia County, 1644-1765. John T. Humphrey. 567p. 1994. 39.00 (*1-887609-01-6*) J T Humphrey.

Pennsylvania Births Philadelphia County, 1766-1780. John T. Humphrey. 1995. 39.00 (*1-887609-00-8*) J T Humphrey.

Pennsylvania Births, York County, 1730-1800. John T. Humphrey. LC 98-75224. 486p. 1998. 36.00 (*1-887609-17-2*) J T Humphrey.

Pennsylvania Bison Hunt. Henry S. Shoemaker. LC 98-88620. (Pennsylvania History & Legends Ser.: No. 1). (Illus.). 66p. 1998. reprint ed. pap. 8.95 (*1-889037-14-1*) Wennawoods.

***Pennsylvania Blue-Ribbon Fly Fishing Guide.** Barry Beck & Cathy Beck. (Illus.). 96p. 2000. pap. 24.95 (*1-57188-158-1*) F Amato Pubns.

Pennsylvania Bookstore Book: A Surprising Guide to Our State's Bookstores & Their Specialties for Students, Teachers, Writers & Publishers. Carole Marsh. (Pennsylvania Bks.). (Illus.). 1991. pap. 19.95 (*0-7933-2970-1*) Gallopade Intl.

Pennsylvania Bookstore Book: A Surprising Guide to Our State's Bookstores & Their Specialties for Students, Teachers, Writers & Publishers. Carole Marsh. (Pennsylvania Bks.). (Illus.). 1994. lib. bdg. 29.95 (*0-7933-2969-8*); disk 29.95 (*0-7933-2971-X*) Gallopade Intl.

Pennsylvania Breweries. Lew Bryson. LC 98-12060. (Illus.). 256p. 1998. 16.95 (*0-8117-2879-X*) Stackpole.

***Pennsylvania Breweries.** 2nd ed. Lew Bryson. LC 00-35787. (Illus.). 2000. write for info. (*0-8117-2898-6*) Stackpole.

Pennsylvania Bucktails: A Photographic Album of the 42nd, 149th & 150th Pennsylvania Regiments. Patrick A. Schroeder. (Illus.). 150p. 2000. pap. 19.95 (*1-889246-14-X*) P A Schroeder.

***Pennsylvania Business Associations Lawsource: Relevant Sections of Titles 15 & 54 Plus Committee Comments.** William H. Clark, Jr. & W. Edward Sell. 654p. 1999. pap. 64.50 (*1-887024-79-4*) Bisel Co.

Pennsylvania Business Corporations, 1991-1994 Vols. 1-2: Law-Practice Forms & Form Disks. 2nd ed. Edward Sell & William Clark. LC 91-61842. 1998. disk 100.00 (*1-887024-39-5*) Bisel Co.

Pennsylvania Business Corporations 1998: Law-Practice Forms, 3 vols. 2nd ed. Edward Sell & William Clark. LC 91-61842. 1998. ring bd. 275.00 (*1-887024-38-7*) Bisel Co.

***Pennsylvania Business Directory, 2000 Edition.** rev. ed. American Business Directories Staff. 4528p. 1999. boxed set 520.00 incl. cd-rom (*0-7687-0180-5*) Am Busn Direct.

***Pennsylvania Business Handbook.** Parente Randolph Orlando Carey & Associates Staff. Ed. by Pennsylvania Chamber of Business & Industry Educational Foundation Staff. 151p. 1998. pap. 70.00 (*1-929744-01-3*) Penn Chamber of Bus.

Pennsylvania Butter: Tools & Processes, Vol. I. Elizabeth A. Powell. (Illus.). 27p. 1974. pap. 3.00 (*0-910302-09-X*) Bucks Co Hist.

Pennsylvania Case Name Citations. text 210.00 (*0-7698-2348-3*) Shepards.

Pennsylvania Cavalcade. Federal Writers' Project Staff. LC 76-44940. (American Guidebook Ser.). 1980. reprint ed. lib. bdg. 79.00 (*0-403-03821-9*) Somerset Pub.

Pennsylvania Census - Abingden & Birmingham Quaker Index, 1683-1939. Ronald V. Jackson. (Illus.). lib. bdg. 30.00 (*0-89593-547-3*, Accel Indexing) Genealogical Srvcs.

Pennsylvania Census Index, 1860 Central Federal (with Addendum) LC 99-198722. (Illus.). 1999. lib. bdg. 315.00 (*0-89593-465-5*, Accel Indexing) Genealogical Srvcs.

Pennsylvania Census Index, 1850 Mortality Schedule. (Illus.). lib. bdg. 88.00 (*0-89593-464-7*, Accel Indexing) Genealogical Srvcs.

Pennsylvania Census Index, 1860 Mortality Schedule. (Illus.). 1982. lib. bdg. 115.00 (*0-89593-467-1*, Accel Indexing) Genealogical Srvcs.

Pennsylvania Census Index, 1870 Mortality Schedule. (Illus.). lib. bdg. 115.00 (*0-89593-471-X*, Accel Indexing) Genealogical Srvcs.

Pennsylvania Census Index 1860 East Federal (Includes Philadelphia County) Ed. by Ronald Vern Jackson. LC 99-198619. (Illus.). 1997. lib. bdg. 325.00 (*0-89593-466-3*, Accel Indexing) Genealogical Srvcs.

Pennsylvania Census Index 1860 Philadelphia County Federal. LC 99-198735. (Illus.). 1986. lib. bdg. 330.00 (*0-89593-468-X*, Accel Indexing) Genealogical Srvcs.

Pennsylvania Census Index 1860 West Federal (Excludes Allegheny & Butler) Ed. by Ronald Vern Jackson. LC 99-198586. (Illus.). 1990. lib. bdg. 330.00 (*0-89593-470-1*, Accel Indexing) Genealogical Srvcs.

Pennsylvania Central 1870 Index, 2 vols. lib. bdg. 295.00 (*1-877677-78-7*) Herit Quest.

***Pennsylvania Chert: Identifying Some of the Materials Used by the Indians in Pennsylvania & Surrounding Areas.** (Illus.). 72p. 1999. pap. 22.50 (*0-941777-82-0*) Fogelman Pub.

Pennsylvania Child Custody: Law, Practice & Procedure - Including Using Expert Witnesses in Custody Cases. Arthur S. Zanan & Emanuel A. Bertin. LC 82-74396. xxiv, 475p. 1999. 69.50 (*1-887024-80-8*) Bisel Co.

Pennsylvania Civil Practice. 2nd ed. Dale F. Shugart. 812p. 1993. 85.00 (*1-55834-038-6*, MICHIE) LEXIS Pub.

Pennsylvania Civil Practice. 3rd ed. Dale F. Shughart, Jr. et al. LC 99-86894. 718p. 1998. 95.00 (*0-327-00290-5*, 6700011) LEXIS Pub.

Pennsylvania Civil Practice: 1989 Supplement. Dale Shughart. 1990. write for info. (*0-87473-514-9*, 66996-10, MICHIE) LEXIS Pub.

Pennsylvania Civil Practice: 1991 Supplement. Dale Shughart. 107p. 1991. pap. text. write for info. (*0-87473-872-5*, 66998-10, MICHIE) LEXIS Pub.

***Pennsylvania Civil Practice, 1999 Supplement: Pocketpart.** 3rd ed. Kevin A. Hess et al. 75p. 1999. write for info. (*0-327-01534-9*, 669915) LEXIS Pub.

Pennsylvania Civil Trial Guide, 6 vols. Stephen M. Feldman. LC 73-169814. 1999. ring bd. 495.00 (*1-887024-41-7*) Bisel Co.

Pennsylvania Classic Christmas Trivia: Stories, Recipes, Activities, Legends, Lore & More! Carole Marsh. (Carole Marsh Pennsylvania Bks.). (Illus.). (J). 1994. pap. 19.95 (*0-7933-0964-6*); lib. bdg. 29.95 (*0-7933-0965-4*); disk 29.95 (*0-7933-0966-2*) Gallopade Intl.

Pennsylvania Clockmakers & Watchmakers, 1660-1900. James B. Whisker. LC 95-4206. 372p. 1996. 99.95 (*0-7734-8966-5*) E Mellen.

Pennsylvania Clocks & Watches: Antique Timepieces & Their Makers. James W. Gibbs. LC 83-62539. (Illus.). 320p. 1984. 42.50 (*0-271-00367-7*) Pa St U Pr.

Pennsylvania Coal: Resources, Technology & Utilization. Ed. by Shyamal K. Majumdar & E. Willard Miller. LC 82-62857. (Illus.). xxvi, 594p. 1983. 25.00 (*0-9606670-1-6*) Penn Science.

Pennsylvania Coastales. Carole Marsh. (Pennsylvania Bks.). (J). 1994. lib. bdg. 29.95 (*0-7933-7303-4*) Gallopade Intl.

Pennsylvania Coastales. Carole Marsh. (Carole Marsh Pennsylvania Bks.). (Illus.). (J). 1994. pap. 19.95 (*0-7933-1937-4*); lib. bdg. 29.95 (*0-7933-1936-6*); disk 29.95 (*0-7933-1938-2*) Gallopade Intl.

***Pennsylvania Collection Agency.** Michael Burkard. 90p. 2001. pap. 14.00 (*1-930974-00-0*) New Issues MI.

Pennsylvania Colonial Militia. James B. Whisker. LC 97-27189. (American Colonial Militia Ser.: Vol. III). 208p. 1997. text 89.95 (*0-7734-8524-4*) E Mellen.

Pennsylvania Colony. Dennis B. Fradin. LC 88-11975. (Thirteen Colonies Ser.). (Illus.). 160p. (J). (gr. 4 up). 1988. lib. bdg. 30.00 (*0-516-00390-9*) Childrens.

Pennsylvania Condominium Law & Practice: Law, Practice, Checklists, Forms. 3rd ed. Ronald B. Glazer. LC 95-75890. 1000p. 1999. ring bd. 109.50 (*1-887024-42-5*) Bisel Co.

Pennsylvania Consolidated Statutes: Title 75, Vehicles, 1997 Edition. rev. ed. Pennsylvania Legislative Reference Bureau Staff. 378p. (C). 1997. pap. 12.24 (*0-8182-0013-8*) Commonweal PA.

Pennsylvania Consolidated Statutes, Constitution: 1984 Permanent Edition. Legislative Reference Bureau Staff. (Orig.). (C). 1984. pap. 4.00 (*0-8182-0046-4*) Commonweal PA.

Pennsylvania Consolidated Statutes Title: 1992 Special Edition - Names. rev. ed. Intro. by Legislative Reference Bureau Staff. 29p. 1998. pap. text 3.74 (*0-8182-0011-1*) Commonweal PA.

Pennsylvania Consolidated Statutes, Title 13: Commercial Code, 1992 Edition. Legislative Reference Bureau Staff. 310p. (C). 1992. pap. 8.50 (*0-8182-0006-5*) Commonweal PA.

Pennsylvania Consolidated Statutes, Title 18: Crime & Offence, 1995 Edition. rev. ed. Legislative Reference Bureau Staff. 302p. (C). 1995. pap. text 8.74 (*0-8182-0007-3*) Commonweal PA.

Pennsylvania Consolidated Statutes, Title 20 , Decedents, Estates & Fiduciaries: 1992 Edition. Legislative Reference Bureau Staff. 278p. (C). 1992. pap. 7.50 (*0-8182-0008-1*) Commonweal PA.

Pennsylvania Consolidated Statutes, Title 24, Education: 1994 Permanent Edition. Legislative Reference Bureau Staff. (Orig.). (C). 1984. pap. 4.24 (*0-8182-0043-X*) Commonweal PA.

Pennsylvania Consolidated Statutes, Title 30, Fish: 1989 Permanent Edition. Legislative Reference Bureau Staff. (Orig.). (C). 1989. pap. 5.00 (*0-8182-0044-8*) Commonweal PA.

Pennsylvania Consolidated Statutes, Title 42, Judiciary & Judicial Procedure: 1995 Edition. rev. ed. Legislative Reference Bureau Staff. 554p. (C). 1995. pap. text 10.74 (*0-8182-0010-3*) Commonweal PA.

Pennsylvania Consolidated Statutes, Title 71, State Government: 1994 Permanent Edition. Legislative Reference Bureau Staff. (Orig.). (C). 1994. pap. 4.24 (*0-8182-0045-6*) Commonweal PA.

Pennsylvania Constitution of 1776. J. Paul Selsam. LC 77-124925. (American Constitutional & Legal History Ser). 1971. reprint ed. lib. bdg. 35.00 (*0-306-71994-0*) Da Capo.

Pennsylvania Consumer Law. Carolyn L. Carter. 460p. 1999. ring bd. 95.00 (*1-887024-18-2*) Bisel Co.

Pennsylvania Contemporary Criminal Procedure. Larry E. Holtz. Ed. by Gould Editorial Staff. 1360p. 1991. pap. text 49.95 (*0-87526-370-4*) Gould.

Pennsylvania Continuing Education for Real Estate Salespersons & Brokers: Elective Course. 2nd ed. Laurel D. McAdams & James J. Skindzier. LC 95-137515. 88p. (C). 1994. pap. text 9.95 (*0-7931-0938-8*, 152008-01, Real Estate Ed) Dearborn.

Pennsylvania Continuing Education for Real Estate Salespersons & Brokers: Required Course. 2nd ed. Laurel D. McAdams & James J. Skindzier. 112p. (C). 1994. pap. text 9.95 (*0-7931-1144-7*, 152004-02, Real Estate Ed) Dearborn.

Pennsylvania Cooking. B. Carlson. (Illus.). 160p. 1997. spiral bd. 5.95 (*1-57166-078-X*) Hearts N Tummies.

Pennsylvania Corporate Practice & Forms: The Wolf, Block, Schorr & Solis-Cohen Manual, 2 vols. Carl W. Schneider. LC 97-41049. 1990p. 1997. ring bd. 275.00 (*1-57400-024-1*) Data Trace Pubng.

Pennsylvania Corporate Practice for the Paralegal: With Forms. Charles P. Nemeth. LC 94-70887. 494p. 1994. ring bd. 89.50 (*1-887024-43-3*) Bisel Co.

Pennsylvania Corporation: Legal Aspects of Organization & Operation. 2nd ed. James F. Nasuti & Jeffrey B. Rotwitt. (Corporate Practice Ser.: No. 30). 1995. pap. 95.00 (*1-55871-313-1*) BNA.

Pennsylvania Corporation Law & Practice. John W. McLamb, Jr. & Wendy C. Shiba. (National Corporation Law Ser.). 1992. ring bd. 126.00 (*0-13-110462-4*) Aspen Law.

Pennsylvania County Maps. rev. ed. Ed. by C. J. Puetz. (Illus.). 144p. 1995. pap. 16.85 (*0-916514-13-7*) Cnty Maps.

Pennsylvania Crime Code: Annual Edition. Gould Editorial Staff. 8.95 (*0-87526-387-9*) Gould.

Pennsylvania Crime Code: Annual Edition. Gould Editorial Staff. 900p. (C). ring bd. 21.95 (*0-87526-216-3*) Gould.

Pennsylvania Crime Commission: 1984 Report. (Illus.). 54p. (C). 1997. reprint ed. pap. text 25.00 (*0-7881-4562-2*) DIANE Pub.

***Pennsylvania Crime in Perspective 2000.** Ed. by Kathleen O'Leary Morgan & Scott E. Morgan. 22p. 2000. spiral bd. 19.00 (*0-7401-0337-7*) Morgan Quitno Corp.

Pennsylvania Crime Perspective, 1998. Ed. by Kathleen O'Leary Morgan & Scott E. Morgan. 20p. 1998. pap. 19.00 (*1-56692-937-7*) Morgan Quitno Corp.

Pennsylvania Crime Perspectives, 1999. Kathleen O'Leary Morgan. 22p. 1999. spiral bd. 19.00 (*0-7401-0137-4*) Morgan Quitno Corp.

***Pennsylvania Crimes & Defenses.** James T. Ranney. 200p. 1999. spiral bd. 40.00 (*1-57823-056-X*) Juris Pubng.

Pennsylvania Crimes Code, Vol. 1. 2nd annot. ed. Sheldon S. Toll. LC 95-80708. 800p. 1995. pap. text 110.00 (*0-7620-0015-5*) West Group.

Pennsylvania Crimes Code & Criminal Law, Vol. 1. rev. ed. Kingsley A. Jarvis. LC 93-709773. 1999. ring bd. 109.50 (*1-887024-44-1*) Bisel Co.

P

Pennsylvania Crimes Code Annotated. Pennsylvania Department of Corrections Staff & Sheldon S. Toll. LC 98-154128. xxix, 811p. 1998. write for info. (0-314-23112-9) West Pub.

Pennsylvania Crimes Code Annotated, Vol. 1. LC 73-93012. 869p. 1993. suppl. ed. 51.50 (0-317-03205-4) West Group.

Pennsylvania Crimes Code, Vehicles Law & Related Statutes. annuals rev. ed. 1020p. (C). pap. 39.95 (0-87526-559-6) Gould.

Pennsylvania Criminal Justice, 1994. Ed. by Joseph H. Kleinfelter. 812p. 1993. pap. 59.50 (0-8322-0495-1) Banks-Baldwin.

Pennsylvania Criminal Justice, 1996. West Publishing Company Editorial Staff. 950p. (Orig.). 1995. pap. text. write for info. (0-314-06416-8) West Pub.

Pennsylvania Criminal Law & Practice, 3 vols., Set. J. T. Ranney. 2000p. 295.00 (0-8205-1697-X, 697) Juris Pubng.

Pennsylvania Criminal Law Digest: Annual Edition. Gould Editorial Staff. 630p. (C). ring bd. 21.95 (0-87526-237-6) Gould.

***Pennsylvania Criminal Lawsource: The Collected Pennsylvania Statutes & Rules.** Marion E. MacIntyre. LC 99-72786. 856p. 1999. pap. 64.50 (1-887024-78-6) Bisel Co.

Pennsylvania Criminal Trial Guide, 2 vols. Robert L. Evangelista. LC 88-71902. 1999. ring bd. 175.00 (1-887024-45-X) Bisel Co.

Pennsylvania "Crinkum-Crankum" A Funny Word Book about Our State. Carole Marsh. (Pennsylvania Bks.). (Illus.). (J). (gr. 3-12). 1994. 29.95 (0-7933-4922-2); pap. 19.95 (0-7933-4923-0); disk 29.95 (0-7933-4924-9) Gallopade Intl.

Pennsylvania Culture Region: A View from the Barn. Joseph W. Glass. Ed. by Simon J. Bronner. LC 86-1397. (American Material Culture & Folklife Ser.). 279p. reprint ed. 86.50 (0-8357-1679-1, 207045400093) Bks Demand.

Pennsylvania Damages: Personal Injury Verdicts & Settlements. Arthur S. Zanan et al. 595p. 1999. per. 74.50 (1-887024-73-5) Bisel Co.

Pennsylvania Damages, Death Actions & Consortium. Stephen M. Feldman. LC 98-70708. 550p. 1998. ring bd. 125.00 (1-887024-11-5) Bisel Co.

Pennsylvania Dauphin County Federal Census, (City of Harrisburg), 1870. 1990. 160.00 (0-89593-619-4, Accel Indexing) Genealogical Srvcs.

***Pennsylvania Deitsh Dictionary: Deitsh to English - English to Deitsh.** Thomas Beachy. 164p. 1999. 9.95 (1-890050-37-7) Carlisle Press.

Pennsylvania Dingbats! Bk. 1: A Fun Book of Games, Stories, Activities & More about Our State That's All in Code! for You to Decipher, Bk. 1. Carole Marsh. (Pennsylvania Bks.). (Illus.). (J). (gr. 3-12). 1994. pap. 19.95 (0-7933-3888-3); lib. bdg. 29.95 (0-7933-3887-5); disk 29.95 (0-7933-3889-1) Gallopade Intl.

Pennsylvania Divorce Code, with Forms & Form Disks. rev. ed. Norman Perlberger. LC 92-74127. 1998. ring bd. 95.00 (1-887024-47-6); disk 69.50 (1-887024-48-4) Bisel Co.

Pennsylvania Divorces: Dauphin County, 1788-1867 & York County, 1790-1860. Eugene F. Throop. 183p. 1996. pap. 19.50 (0-7884-0376-1, T366) Heritage Bk.

***Pennsylvania Domestic Relations, Issue 9.** Saul D. Levit. 100p. 1999. ring bd. write for info. (0-327-01383-4, 8231515) LEXIS Pub.

Pennsylvania Domestic Relations Forms. Saul D. Levit. 540p. 1989. spiral bd. 169.00 (0-8342-0075-9, MICHIE) LEXIS Pub.

Pennsylvania Domestic Relations Forms. Saul D. Levit. 1994. ring bd., suppl. ed. 80.00 (0-685-74634-8, MICHIE) LEXIS Pub.

Pennsylvania Domestic Relations Forms, Issue 9. Saul D. Levit. LC 89-6074. 200p. 1998. ring bd. write for info. (0-327-00229-8, 82315-14) LEXIS Pub.

Pennsylvania Domestic Relations Forms, Set. Saul D. Levit. 1994. disk 50.00 (0-614-03766-2, MICHIE) LEXIS Pub.

Pennsylvania Domestic Relations Lawsource: Statutes, Rules, Index. Arthur S. Zanan. LC 92-7441. 1999. per. 64.50 (1-887024-20-4) Bisel Co.

Pennsylvania Driving under the Influence Law & Practice, 2 vols. Joseph E. Vogrin. LC 97-78246. 1200p. 1999. ring bd. 225.00 (1-887024-26-3) Bisel Co.

Pennsylvania Dutch. Lucille Wallower. Ed. by Patricia L. Gump. (J). (gr. 3-4). 1971. pap. 4.50 (0-931992-31-1) Penns Valley.

Pennsylvania Dutch. rev. ed. Phebe H. Gibbons. LC 77-134378. reprint ed. 52.50 (0-404-08426-5) AMS Pr.

Pennsylvania Dutch: Folk Spirituality. Richard E. Wentz. LC 92-33184. (Sources of American Spirituality Ser.). 384p. 1993. 29.00 (0-8091-0439-3) Paulist Pr.

Pennsylvania Dutch: The Amish & the Mennonites. Ed. by Kern K. Sawyer. LC 97-77589. (Perspectives on History Ser.: Pt. III). (Illus.). 64p. 1997. pap. 6.95 (1-57960-025-5) Disc Enter Ltd.

Pennsylvania Dutch American Folk Art. Henry J. Kauffman. 146p. 1993. pap. 9.95 (1-883294-00-2) Masthof Pr.

Pennsylvania Dutch & Their Cookery see Pennsylvania Dutch Cookbook

Pennsylvania Dutch & Their Furniture see Making Authentic Pennsylvania Dutch Furniture: With Measured Drawings of Museum Classics

Pennsylvania Dutch Cookbook. (Illus.). 48p. 1997. pap. 2.00 (1-890541-26-5) Americana Souvenirs & Gifts.

Pennsylvania Dutch Cookbook. 10th abr. ed. J. George Frederick. Orig. Title: Pennsylvania Dutch & Their Cookery. 1971. pap. 4.95 (0-486-22676-X) Dover.

Pennsylvania Dutch Cookbook "Fine Old Recipes" (Illus.). 48p. 1996. pap. 2.00 (1-890541-27-3) Americana Souvenirs & Gifts.

Pennsylvania Dutch Cooking Book. (Illus.). 64p. 1996. pap. 2.00 (1-890541-25-7) Americana Souvenirs & Gifts.

Pennsylvania Dutch Country. Margaret Gates et al. (Getaway Guide Ser.). (Illus.). 176p. 1998. pap. 12.95 (0-9656338-1-0) Stone Creek Pr.

Pennsylvania Dutch Country. Lynn M. Stone. LC 93-13976. (Back Roads Ser.). 48p. (J). (gr. 3-6). 1993. lib. bdg. 15.95 (0-86593-301-4) Rourke Corp.

Pennsylvania Dutch Country & Philadelphia. Earl Steinbicker. (Daytrips Ser.). (Illus.). 352p. 1999. pap. 16.95 (0-8038-9394-9, Pub. by Hastings) Midpt Trade.

Pennsylvania Dutch Country Cooking. William W. Weaver. (Illus.). 216p. 1997. 19.98 (0-89660-086-6, Artabras) Abbeville Pr.

Pennsylvania Dutch Country Ghosts, Legends & Lore. Charles J. Adams, III. (Illus.). 163p. 1994. pap. 10.95 (1-880683-03-2) Exeter Hse.

Pennsylvania Dutch Designs. Rebecca McKillip. (International Design Library). (Illus.). 48p. (Orig.). 1983. pap. 5.95 (0-88045-032-0) Stemmer Hse.

Pennsylvania Dutch Designs. Rettich. 1998. pap. 3.95 (0-486-24496-2) Dover.

Pennsylvania Dutch Folklore. (Pennsylvania Dutch Bks.). (Illus.). 1960. 3.00 (0-911410-02-3) Applied Arts.

***Pennsylvania Dutch Night Before Christmas.** Chet Williamson et al. LC 00-27748. (Illus.). 2000. pap. 14.95 (1-56554-721-7) Pelican.

Pennsylvania Early Census, Vol. 1. Ronald V. Jackson. 1978. 50.00 (0-89593-596-1, Accel Indexing) Genealogical Srvcs.

Pennsylvania Early Census, Vol. 2. Ronald V. Jackson. (Illus.). lib. bdg. 60.00 (0-89593-742-5, Accel Indexing) Genealogical Srvcs.

Pennsylvania Early Census, Vol. 3. Ronald V. Jackson. 1979. 50.00 (0-89593-598-8, Accel Indexing) Genealogical Srvcs.

Pennsylvania Early Census, Vol. 4. Ronald V. Jackson. 1980. 60.00 (0-89593-599-6, Accel Indexing) Genealogical Srvcs.

Pennsylvania East 1870 Census Index, 2 vols. lib. bdg. 355.00 (1-877677-77-9) Herit Quest.

Pennsylvania Elementary Energy & Environment Science Activities, vol. 6. 172p. pap. text 25.00 (0-7881-3054-4) DIANE Pub.

Pennsylvania Eminent Domain. Edward L. Snitzer et al. 544p. 1998. text 85.00 (1-887024-49-2) Bisel Co.

***Pennsylvania Employer's Guide: A Handbook of Employment Laws & Regulations.** 9th rev. ed. Mark S. Summers. 632p. 1999. ring bd. 92.50 (1-56759-030-6) Summers Pr.

Pennsylvania Environmental Law Handbook. 5th ed. Mattioni, Mattioni, & Mattioni, Ltd. Staff. 408p. 1997. pap. text 95.00 (0-86587-604-5, 604) Gov Insts.

Pennsylvania Equity Index-Digest, 3 vols. Glenn Troutman & Arthur S. Zanan. 1780p. 1999. text 50.00 (1-887024-50-6) Bisel Co.

Pennsylvania Estate Planning & Drafting, 3 vols. Robert J. Weinberg. LC 95-83231. 1300p. 1999. ring bd. 295.00 (1-887024-02-6) Bisel Co.

Pennsylvania Estate Planning & Drafting Forms Disk. Robert J. Weinberg. 1998. disk 125.00 (1-887024-51-4) Bisel Co.

Pennsylvania Estates Practice, Vol. 1. Nancy Rothkopf & Gilbert M. Cantor. LC 79-91161. (Practice Systems Library Manual). ring bd. 125.00 (0-317-00577-4) West Group.

Pennsylvania Estates Practice, Vol. 1. Nancy Rothkopf & Gilbert M. Cantor. LC 79-91161. (Practice Systems Library Manual). 1991. suppl. ed. 65.00 (0-317-03207-0) West Group.

***Pennsylvania Evidence.** 1998. 99.00 incl. audio PA Bar Inst.

Pennsylvania Evidence: Objections & Responses. Mark S. Greenberg & Anthony J. Bocchino. 146p. 1983. 20.00 (0-87215-629-X, MICHIE) LEXIS Pub.

Pennsylvania Evidence Courtroom Manual. pap. 49.50 (1-58360-204-6) Anderson Pub Co.

***Pennsylvania Experience Pocket Guide.** Carole Marsh. (Pennsylvania Experience! Ser.). (Illus.). (J). 2000. pap. 6.95 (0-7933-9586-0) Gallopade Intl.

Pennsylvania Facts & Factivities. Carole Marsh. (Carole Marsh State Bks.). (Illus.). (J). (gr. 4-7). 1996. pap., teacher ed. 19.95 (0-7933-7923-7, C Marsh) Gallopade Intl.

Pennsylvania Facts & Symbols. Emily McAuliffe. LC 98-7360. (States & Their Symbols Ser.). (J). 1999. write for info. (0-7368-0086-7) Capstone Pr.

***Pennsylvania Facts & Symbols.** Emily McAuliffe. LC 98-7360. (J). 1998. 14.00 (0-531-11610-7) Childrens.

Pennsylvania Fairs & Country Festivals. Craig Kennedy. (Illus.). 256p. 1996. pap. 16.95 (0-8117-2494-8) Stackpole.

Pennsylvania Family Practice Manual. Frederick N. Frank & Christine Gale. 778p. 1990. 65.00 (0-87473-513-0, 61926-10, MICHIE) LEXIS Pub.

Pennsylvania Family Practice Manual: 1992 Supplement. Frederick Frank. 134p. 1992. 25.00 (0-87473-871-7, 61927-10, MICHIE) LEXIS Pub.

Pennsylvania Federal Census Index, 1830. Ronald V. Jackson. LC 77-86096. (Illus.). 1976. lib. bdg. 118.00 (0-89593-118-4, Accel Indexing) Genealogical Srvcs.

Pennsylvania Federal Census Index, 1840. Ronald V. Jackson. LC 77-86097. (Illus.). lib. bdg. 173.00 (0-89593-119-2, Accel Indexing) Genealogical Srvcs.

Pennsylvania Federal Census Index, 1850, 2 vols. Ronald V. Jackson. LC 77-86089. (Illus.). 1976. lib. bdg. 300.00 (0-89593-120-6, Accel Indexing) Genealogical Srvcs.

Pennsylvania Federal Census Index, 1810. Ronald V. Jackson. LC 77-86094. (Illus.). lib. bdg. 85.00 (0-89593-116-8, Accel Indexing) Genealogical Srvcs.

Pennsylvania Federal Census Index, 1800. Ronald V. Jackson & Gary R. Teeples. LC 77-86105. (Illus.). lib. bdg. 80.00 (0-89593-115-X, Accel Indexing) Genealogical Srvcs.

Pennsylvania Federal Census Index, 1820. Ronald V. Jackson & Gary R. Teeples. LC 77-86095. (Illus.). 1978. lib. bdg. 113.00 (0-89593-117-6, Accel Indexing) Genealogical Srvcs.

Pennsylvania Federal Census Index, 1790 (1908) Ronald V. Jackson. (Illus.). 1976. lib. bdg. 70.00 (0-89593-768-9, Accel Indexing) Genealogical Srvcs.

Pennsylvania Festival Fun for Kids! Carole Marsh. (Pennsylvania Bks.). (Illus.). (YA). (gr. 3-12). 1994. pap. 19.95 (0-7933-4041-1); lib. bdg. 29.95 (0-7933-4040-3); disk 29.95 (0-7933-4042-X) Gallopade Intl.

Pennsylvania Fiduciary Guide: A Handbook for Executors & Administrators. 4th rev. ed. Ed. by M. Paul Smith et al. LC 83-72880. 595p. 1999. text 69.50 (1-887024-52-2) Bisel Co.

Pennsylvania Fireside Tales Vol. I: Origins & Foundations of Pennsylvania Mountain Folktales & Legends. unabridged ed. Jeffrey R. Frazier. (Illus.). v, 160p. 1996. pap. 12.00 (0-9652351-0-6) Egg Hill.

***Pennsylvania Fireside Tales Vol. I: Origins & Foundations of Pennsylvania Mountain Folktales & Legends.** 2nd ed. Jeffrey R. Frazier. (Pennsylvania Fireside Tales Ser.). (Illus.). 167p. 1999. 12.00 (0-9652351-3-0) Egg Hill.

Pennsylvania Fireside Tales Vol. III: Origins & Foundations of Pennsylvania Mountain Folktales & Legends. unabridged ed. Jeffrey R. Frazier. (Illus.). 232p. 1999. 12.00 (0-9652351-2-2) Egg Hill.

Pennsylvania Firsts: The Famous, Infamous, & Quirky of the Keystone State. Patrick M. Reynolds. LC 98-49234. (Illus.). 192p. 1999. pap. 9.95 (0-940159-46-5) Camino Bks.

Pennsylvania Folk Art of Samuel L. Plank. James Bonson et al. 68p. 1994. text 29.95 (0-9643721-0-X) Kishacoquillas.

Pennsylvania Gardener: All about Gardening in the Keystone State. Derek Fell. LC 94-33833. (Illus.). 257p. 1995. 24.95 (0-940159-15-5) Camino Bks.

Pennsylvania Gardener: All about Gardening in the Keystone State. Derek Fell. LC 94-33833. (Illus.). 257p. 1998. reprint ed. pap. 14.95 (0-940159-48-1) Camino Bks.

Pennsylvania Genealogical Library Guide. John W. Heisey. LC 97-179060. 73p. (Orig.). 1994. pap. 6.50 (1-883294-15-0) Masthof Pr.

Pennsylvania Genealogical Research. George K. Schweitzer. 201p. 1998. pap. 15.00 (0-913857-09-2) Genealog Sources.

Pennsylvania Genealogies: Chiefly Scotch-Irish & German. 2nd ed. William H. Egle. 798p. 1997. reprint ed. pap. 49.95 (0-8063-0102-3, 1620) Clearfield Co.

Pennsylvania Genealogies & Family Histories: A Bibliography of Books about Pennsylvania Families. Donald O. Virdin. iv, 269p. (Orig.). 1992. pap. text 33.00 (1-55613-590-4) Heritage Bk.

Pennsylvania "GEO" Bingo! 38 Must Know State Geography Facts for Kids to Learn While Having Fun! Carole Marsh. (Bingo! Ser.). (Illus.). (J). (gr. 2-8). 1998. pap. 14.95 (0-7933-8637-3) Gallopade Intl.

Pennsylvania Geography. Randall A. Pellow. (Illus.). 64p. (J). (gr. 4-8). 1999. pap. text 8.35 (0-931992-55-9) Penns Valley.

Pennsylvania Geography: A Collection of Reference Maps. Diane Shoop & Jennifer Shultz. (Illus.). 156p. 1998. 50.00 (1-58036-053-X) Penn State Data Ctr.

Pennsylvania German Anthology. Ed. by Earl C. Haag. LC 86-62816. 1988. 49.50 (0-941664-29-5); pap. 17.95 (0-945636-00-8) Susquehanna U Pr.

Pennsylvania German Art, 1683-1850. Ed. by Philadelphia Museum of Art Staff & Winterthur, Henry du Pont Museum Staff. LC 83-18267. (Chicago Visual Library: No. 43). 376p. (C). 1984. lib. bdg. 108.00 incl. fiche (0-226-69535-2) U Ch Pr.

Pennsylvania German Fraktur & Printed Broadsides: A Guide to the Collections in the Library of Congress. Ed. by Jill Roberts. LC 88-600044. 48p. 1988. 9.95 (0-8444-0600-7) Lib Congress.

Pennsylvania German Fraktur of the Free Library of Philadelphia, 2 vols., Set, Vol. 1: 234p.; Vol. 2: 204p. Frederick S. Weiser & Howell J. Henney. (Illus.). 438p. 1976. pap. write for info. (0-614-00737-2) Viking Penguin.

Pennsylvania German Fraktur of the Free Library of Philadelphia: An Illustrated Catalogue, 2 vols. Compiled by Frederick S. Weiser & Howell J. Heaney. (Illus.). 1976. 60.00 (0-911122-32-X) Phila Free Lib.

Pennsylvania German Immigrants, 1709-1786: Lists Consolidated from Yearbooks of the Pennsylvania German Folklore Society. Don Yoder. LC 80-50502. (Illus.). 394p. 1998. reprint ed. 35.00 (0-8063-0892-3) Genealog Pub.

Pennsylvania-German in the Revolutionary War, 1775-1783. Henry M. Muhlenberg. (Illus.). 542p. 1997. reprint ed. lib. bdg. 55.00 (0-8328-6382-3) Higginson Bk Co.

Pennsylvania-German in the Revolutionary War, 1775-1783. Henry M. Richards. (Illus.). 542p. 1991. reprint ed. 27.50 (0-8063-0793-5, 4890) Clearfield Co.

Pennsylvania German Marriages: Marriages & Marriage Evidence in Pennsylvania German Churches. Donna R. Irish. LC 81-84187. 817p. 1999. reprint ed. pap. 55.00 (0-8063-0965-2, Pub. by Clearfield Co) ACCESS Pubs Network.

Pennsylvania German Pioneers, 3 vols., Set. Ed. by Ralph B. Strassburger & William J. Hinke. LC 91-68445. (Illus.). 2560p. 1992. reprint ed. 175.00 (0-929539-98-2, 1345) Picton Pr.

Pennsylvania German Pioneers, 3 vols., Vol. I. Ed. by Ralph B. Strassburger & William J. Hinke. LC 91-68445. (Illus.). 864p. 1992. reprint ed. 65.00 (0-929539-95-8, 1342) Picton Pr.

Pennsylvania German Pioneers, 3 vols., Vol. II. Ed. by Ralph B. Strassburger & William J. Hinke. LC 91-68445. (Illus.). 928p. 1992. reprint ed. 70.00 (0-929539-96-6, 1343) Picton Pr.

Pennsylvania German Pioneers, 3 vols., Vol. III. Ed. by Ralph B. Strassburger & William J. Hinke. LC 91-68445. (Illus.). 768p. 1992. reprint ed. 60.00 (0-929539-97-4, 1344) Picton Pr.

Pennsylvania German Reader & Grammar. Earl C. Haag. LC 82-80453. 320p. (C). 1982. 22.50 (0-271-00316-2) Pa St U Pr.

Pennsylvania German Secular Folk Songs. Albert F. Buffington. LC 74-78062. (Pennsylvania German Folklore Ser.: Vol. 8). 1974. 15.00 (0-911122-30-3) Penn German Soc.

Pennsylvania-German Settlement of Maryland. Daniel W. Nead. (Illus.). 304p. 1997. reprint ed. lib. bdg. 38.50 (0-8328-5944-3) Higginson Bk Co.

Pennsylvania German Words in Context: A Pennsylvania Dutch-English Word List. (GER.). 220p. 1997. write for info. (0-9658840-0-7); pap. write for info. (0-9658840-1-5) C R Beam.

Pennsylvania Germans. Jesse L. Rosenberger. 1993. reprint ed. lib. bdg. 89.00 (0-7812-5825-1) Rprt Serv.

Pennsylvania Germans: Jesse Leonard Rosenberger's Sketch of Their History & Life. Don H. Tolzmann. (Illus.). 219p. 1998. pap. 22.00 (0-7884-0971-9, T551) Heritage Bk.

Pennsylvania Government! The Cornerstone of Everyday Life in Our State! Carole Marsh. (Carole Marsh Pennsylvania Bks.). (Illus.). (J). (gr. 3-12). 1996. pap. 19.95 (0-7933-6296-2); lib. bdg. 29.95 (0-7933-6295-4); disk 29.95 (0-7933-6297-0) Gallopade Intl.

Pennsylvania Governments Performance Standards, 1990. Ed. by Greg Michels. (Governments Performance Standards Ser.). (Illus.). 150p. 1990. text 125.00 (1-55507-499-5) Municipal Analysis.

Pennsylvania Grand Jury Practice. David N. Savitt & Brian Gottlieb. 356p. 1983. 80.00 (0-8322-0045-X) Banks-Baldwin.

Pennsylvania Grants Guide, 1998-2000. 900p. 1998. pap. 179.00 (0-9658306-4-0) Grantseeker.

Pennsylvania Guide to Real Estate Licensing Examination for Salespersons & Brokers. Ronald M. Friedman. LC 79-48053. 124p. (C). 1982. pap. text 13.95 (0-471-87758-1) P-H.

***Pennsylvania Guidelines for School Library Information Programs.** Ed. by Robert W. Barbash. 66p. (C). 2000. pap. text 20.00 (0-7567-0002-7) DIANE Pub.

Pennsylvania Gun Law Guide: What Every Handgun, Rifle or Shotgun Owner Must Know about Pennsylvania & Federal Gun Laws. Kenneth F. Abel. 160p. (Orig.). 1996. pap. 7.95 (0-944214-07-X) ABELexpress.

***Pennsylvania Health Care in Perspective 2000.** Ed. by Kathleen O'Leary Morgan & Scott E. Morgan. 21p. 2000. spiral bd. 19.00 (0-7401-0237-0) Morgan Quitno Corp.

Pennsylvania Health Care Perspective, 1998. Ed. by Kathleen O'Leary Morgan & Scott E. Morgan. 20p. 1998. pap. 19.00 (1-56692-837-0) Morgan Quitno Corp.

Pennsylvania Health Care Perspective, 1999. Kathleen O'Leary Morgan. 21p. 1999. spiral bd. 19.00 (0-7401-0087-4) Morgan Quitno Corp.

Pennsylvania Herald & York General Advertiser, 1789-1793, Bk. 1. Compiled by Diana L. Bowman. 214p. 1996. per. 19.95 (1-55856-225-7, 033) Closson Pr.

Pennsylvania Herald & York General Advertiser, 1794-1798, Bk. 2. Diana L. Bowman. 132p. 1993. per. 12.95 (1-55856-134-X, 034) Closson Pr.

Pennsylvania Heritage Cookbook: A Cook's Tour of Keystone Cultures, Customs, & Celebrations. Kyle D. Nagurny. LC 97-32175. (PA Traveler's Guide Ser.). (Illus.). 224p. 1998. pap. 16.95 (0-8117-2496-4) Stackpole.

Pennsylvania "HISTO" Bingo! 42 Must Know State History Facts for Kids to Learn While Having Fun! Carole Marsh. (Bingo! Ser.). (Illus.). (J). (gr. 2-8). 1998. pap. 14.95 (0-7933-8638-1) Gallopade Intl.

Pennsylvania Historical & Biographical Index, Vol. 1. Ronald V. Jackson. LC 78-53714. (Illus.). 1984. lib. bdg. 30.00 (0-89593-197-4, Accel Indexing) Genealogical Srvcs.

Pennsylvania Historical Bibliography V: Additions Through 1982. Compiled by John B. Trussell, Jr. 138p. 1986. pap. 6.95 (0-89271-033-0) Pa Hist & Mus.

Pennsylvania Historical Bibliography IV: Additions Through 1979. John B. Trussell, Jr. 121p. (Orig.). 1983. pap. 6.95 (0-89271-026-8) Pa Hist & Mus.

Pennsylvania Historical Bibliography I: Additions Through 1970. Compiled by John B. Trussell, Jr. LC 79-622899. 108p. 1979. 6.95 (0-89271-003-9) Pa Hist & Mus.

Pennsylvania Historical Bibliography VI: Additions Through 1985. John B. Trussell, Jr. 136p. 1989. pap. 7.95 (0-89271-045-4) Pa Hist & Mus.

Pennsylvania Historical Bibliography III: Additions Through 1976. John B. Trussell, Jr. 119p. (Orig.). 1983. pap. 6.95 (0-89271-014-4) Pa Hist & Mus.

Pennsylvania Historical Bibliography II: Additions Through 1973. John B. Trussell, Jr. 100p. (Orig.). 1980. pap. 6.95 (0-89271-004-7) Pa Hist & Mus.

An Asterisk (*) at the beginning of an entry indicates that the title is appearing for the first time.

Pennsylvania Historical Society Memoirs, 14 vols., Set. Pennsylvania Historical Society Staff. Incl. Vol. 1. LC 72-14378. (*0-404-11076-2*); Vol. 2. LC 72-14378. (*0-404-11077-0*); Vol. 3. LC 72-14378. (*0-404-11078-9*); Vol. 4. LC 72-14378. (*0-404-11079-7*); Vol. 5. LC 72-14378. (*0-404-11080-0*); Vol. 6. LC 72-14378. (*0-404-11081-9*); Vol. 7. LC 72-14378. (*0-404-11082-7*); Vol. 8. LC 72-14378. (*0-404-11083-5*); Vol. 9. LC 72-14378. (*0-404-11084-3*); Vol. 10. LC 72-14378. (*0-404-11085-1*); Vol. 11. LC 72-14378. (*0-404-11086-X*); Vol. 12. LC 72-14378. (*0-404-11087-8*); Vol. 13. LC 72-14378. (*0-404-11088-6*); Vol. 14. LC 72-14378. (*0-404-11089-4*); LC 72-14378. reprint ed. write for info. (*0-404-11075-4*) AMS Pr.

Pennsylvania History! Surprising Secrets about Our State's Founding Mothers, Fathers & Kids! Carole Marsh. (Carole Marsh Pennsylvania Bks.). (Illus.). (J). (gr. 3-12). 1996. pap. 19.95 (*0-7933-6143-5*); lib. bdg. 29.95 (*0-7933-6142-7*); disk 29.95 (*0-7933-6144-3*) Gallopade Intl.

Pennsylvania History Told by Contemporaries. Asa E. Martin. 1993. reprint ed. lib. bdg. 89.00 (*0-7812-5489-2*) Rprt Serv.

Pennsylvania Home Education Handbook: Using Your Educational Style in Complying with the Law. 4th rev. ed. Diana Baseman. (Illus.). 1997. pap. 14.95 (*0-9624505-0-2*) Tall Oaks Bks.

Pennsylvania Hot Air Balloon Mystery. Carole Marsh. (Carole Marsh Pennsylvania Bks.). (Illus.). (J). (gr. 2-9). 1994. 29.95 (*0-7933-2660-5*); pap. 19.95 (*0-7933-2661-3*); disk 29.95 (*0-7933-2662-1*) Gallopade Intl.

Pennsylvania Hot Zones! Viruses, Diseases, & Epidemics in Our State's History. Carole Marsh. (Hot Zones! Ser.). (Illus.). (J). (gr. 3-12). 1998. pap. 19.95 (*0-7933-8943-7*); lib. bdg. 29.95 (*0-7933-8942-9*) Gallopade Intl.

Pennsylvania Housing Characteristics: 1990. Diane Shoop. 430p. 1996. pap. 45.00 (*1-885925-01-8*) Penn State Data Ctr.

***Pennsylvania Housing Trends.** Amy Jonas & Diane Shoop. 24p. 2000. pap. 20.00 (*1-58036-139-0*) Penn State Data Ctr.

Pennsylvania Hunter Orphans' Court Commonplace Book, 8 vols. 2nd rev. ed. M. Paul Smith & J. Brooke Aker. 1999. text 395.00 (*1-887024-53-0*) Bisel Co.

Pennsylvania Impressionists. Thomas C. Folk. LC 96-48641. (Illus.). 156p. 1997. 55.00 (*0-8386-3699-3*) Fairleigh Dickinson.

Pennsylvania in Perspective, 1998. Ed. by Kathleen O'Leary Morgan & Scott E. Morgan. 24p. 1998. pap. 19.00 (*1-56692-887-7*) Morgan Quitno Corp.

Pennsylvania in Perspective 1999. Ed. by Kathleen O'Leary Morgan. 26p. 1999. spiral bd. 19.00 (*1-56692-987-3*) Morgan Quitno Corp.

***Pennsylvania in Perspective 2000.** Ed. by Kathleen O'Leary Morgan & Scott E. Morgan. 26p. 2000. spiral bd. 19.00 (*0-7401-0287-7*) Morgan Quitno Corp.

Pennsylvania in the Spanish-American War. Richard Sauers. (Illus.). 200p. 1998. pap. 12.95 (*0-9643048-5-6*) Penn Capitol Presrv.

Pennsylvania Indian Dictionary for Kids! Carole Marsh. (Carole Marsh State Bks.). (J). (gr. 2-9). 1996. 29.95 (*0-7933-7758-7*, C Marsh); pap. 19.95 (*0-7933-7759-5*, C Marsh) Gallopade Intl.

Pennsylvania Inheritance & Estate Tax. 2nd rev. ed. Richard L. Grossman & M. Paul Smith. LC 93-72202. 600p. 1999. ring bd. 109.50 (*1-887024-54-9*) Bisel Co.

Pennsylvania Insurance Law. Franklin L. Best, Jr. LC 90-84169. 1999. ring bd. 109.50 (*1-887024-55-7*) Bisel Co.

***Pennsylvania Investment & Business Guide: Business, Investment, Export-Import Opportunities, 50, 38.** Global Investment Center, USA Staff. (U. S. Regional Investment & Business Library-99: Vol. 38). (Illus.). 350p. (Orig.). 1999. pap. 59.95 (*0-7397-1137-7*) Intl Business Pubns.

Pennsylvania Iron Manufacture in the Eighteenth Century. Arthur C. Bining. LC 72-120547. (Library of Early American Business & Industry: No. 39). 227p. 1970. reprint ed. lib. bdg. 35.00 (*0-678-00678-4*) Kelley.

***Pennsylvania Jeopardy.** Carole Marsh. (Pennsylvania Experience! Ser.). (Illus.). (J). (gr. 2-6). 2000. pap. 7.95 (*0-7933-9588-7*) Gallopade Intl.

Pennsylvania Jeopardy! Answers & Questions about Our State! Carole Marsh. (Pennsylvania Bks.). (Illus.). (J). (gr. 3-12). 1994. pap. 19.95 (*0-7933-4194-9*); lib. bdg. 29.95 (*0-7933-4193-0*); disk 29.95 (*0-7933-4195-7*) Gallopade Intl.

***Pennsylvania Jography.** Carole Marsh. (Pennsylvania Experience! Ser.). (Illus.). (J). (gr. 2-6). 2000. pap. 7.95 (*0-7933-9589-5*) Gallopade Intl.

Pennsylvania "Jography" A Fun Run Thru Our State! Carole Marsh. (Carole Marsh Pennsylvania Bks.). (Illus.). (J). 1994. pap. 19.95 (*0-7933-1923-4*); lib. bdg. 29.95 (*0-7933-1922-6*); disk 29.95 (*0-7933-1924-2*) Gallopade Intl.

Pennsylvania Judicial Directory. Ed. by Debbie Shain. 500p. (Orig.). 1997. per. write for info. (*1-57786-075-6*) Legal Communs.

Pennsylvania Judiciary & Judicial Procedure Title 42: Annual Edition. Gould Editorial Staff. 880p. (C). 1983. ring bd. 21.95 (*0-87526-295-3*) Gould.

Pennsylvania Juvenile Delinquency & Deprivation. John Palmieri et al. 340p. 1997. text 59.50 (*1-887024-56-5*) Bisel Co.

Pennsylvania-Kentucky Rifle. Henry J. Kauffman. (Illus.). 374p. 1997. pap. 14.95 (*1-883294-55-X*) Masthof Pr.

Pennsylvania Keystone Lawyer's Desk Library of Practice, 8 vols. Burton R. Laub & W. Edward Sell. 1999. ring bd. 495.00 (*1-887024-57-3*) Bisel Co.

Pennsylvania Kid's Cookbook: Recipes, How-to, History, Lore & More! Carole Marsh. (Carole Marsh Pennsylvania Bks.). (Illus.). (J). 1994. pap. 19.95 (*0-7933-0973-5*); lib. bdg. 29.95 (*0-7933-0974-3*); disk 29.95 (*0-7933-0975-1*) Gallopade Intl.

***Pennsylvania Labor & Employment Lawsource: Collected Labor & Employment Federal & State Statutes, Regulations, Cases & Commentary.** James O. Castagnera et al. LC 99-73296. 448p. 1999. pap. 64.50 (*1-887024-77-8*) Bisel Co.

Pennsylvania Land Records: A History & Guide for Research. Donna B. Munger. LC 90-21384. 240p. 1991. 75.00 (*0-8420-2377-1*); pap. 29.95 (*0-8420-2497-2*) Scholarly Res Inc.

Pennsylvania Land Recycling & Reclamation. 1997. 99.00 incl. audio PA Bar Inst.

Pennsylvania Land Surveying Law: Questions & Answers. John E. Keen. 42p. (C). 1995. pap. text 25.00 (*1-56569-039-7*) Land Survey.

Pennsylvania Landlord & Tenant Handbook. rev. ed. D. Patrick Zimmerman. Ed. by Jean Harbold & Paul G. Campbell. 320p. 1993. 19.95 (*1-880976-04-8*); pap. 14.95 (*1-880976-05-6*) Brookshire Pubns.

Pennsylvania Landlord-Tenant Law & Practice with Form Disks. Ronald M. Friedman. LC 88-70977. 1994. disk 69.50 (*1-887024-59-X*) Bisel Co.

Pennsylvania Landlord-Tenant Law & Practice with Form Disks. 2nd ed. Ronald M. Friedman. LC 94-79452. 1999. ring bd. 109.50 incl. disk (*1-887024-58-1*) Bisel Co.

Pennsylvania Landmarks. (Pennsylvania History Ser.). (Illus.). 1975. 4.45 (*0-911410-31-7*) Applied Arts.

Pennsylvania Law Encyclopedia, 57 vols. Publisher's Editorial Staff. Date not set. text 2399.00 (*0-318-57516-7*, 63620-10, MICHIE) LEXIS Pub.

Pennsylvania Law Encyclopedia, 53 vols. Publisher's Editorial Staff. 1986. text 2399.00 (*0-327-00963-2*, 63620-10, MICHIE) LEXIS Pub.

***Pennsylvania Law Encyclopedia, 53 vols., Vol. 5.** 2nd ed. Ed. by Heather Hayes. 600p. 1999. write for info. (*0-327-01659-0*, 6362611) LEXIS Pub.

***Pennsylvania Law Encyclopedia, Vol. 7.** 2nd ed. Ed. by Michie Editorial Staff. 600p. 2000. write for info. (*0-327-04944-8*) LEXIS Pub.

***Pennsylvania Law Encyclopedia: Replacement, Vol. 6.** 2nd ed. 500p. 1999. write for info. (*0-327-04981-2*, 6362711) LEXIS Pub.

***Pennsylvania Law Encyclopedia Vol. 1: Transition Supplement, 9/99, 53 vols., Vol. 1.** 2nd ed. Ed. by Heather Hayes. 247p. 1999. pap. write for info. (*0-327-01673-6*, 6369114) LEXIS Pub.

***Pennsylvania Law Encyclopedia Vol. 1: Transition Supplement, 9/99, 53 vols., Vol. 2.** 2nd ed. Ed. by Heather Hayes. 89p. 1999. pap. write for info. (*0-327-01674-4*, 6369214) LEXIS Pub.

***Pennsylvania Law Encyclopedia Vol. 1: Transition Supplement, 9/99, 53 vols., Vol. 3.** 2nd ed. Ed. by Heather Hayes. 171p. 1999. pap. write for info. (*0-327-01675-2*, 6369314) LEXIS Pub.

Pennsylvania Law Encyclopedia Vol. 1: 1998 Replacement Volume. 2nd ed. Ed. by David C. Wagoner. 500p. 1998. 80.00 (*0-327-00645-5*, 6362111) LEXIS Pub.

Pennsylvania Law Encyclopedia Vol. 2: 1998 Replacement Volume. 2nd ed. Ed. by David C. Wagoner. LC 98-89715. 500p. 1998. 80.00 (*0-327-00646-3*, 6362211) LEXIS Pub.

***Pennsylvania Law Encyclopedia Finder's Materials: Table of Cases, 53 vols.** Ed. by Robert J. Warren. 950p. 1999. write for info. (*0-327-01660-4*, 6367411) LEXIS Pub.

Pennsylvania Law Encyclopedia Finder's Materials: Tables of Cases/Statutes, 53 vols. Ed. by David C. Wagoner. 500p. 1998. write for info. (*0-327-00642-0*, 6367410) LEXIS Pub.

Pennsylvania Law Encyclopedia, Interim Index. 2nd ed. Ed. by Catherine Crittenden. 180p. 1999. pap. write for info. (*0-327-00945-4*, 6368010) LEXIS Pub.

Pennsylvania Law Encyclopedia, 1998 Cumulative Supplement, 56 vols. Incl. Vol. 1. 1998. (*0-327-00426-6*, 63691-12); Vol. 2. 1998. (*0-327-00427-4*, 63692-12); Vol. 3. 1998. (*0-327-00428-2*, 63693-12); Vol. 4. 1998. (*0-327-00429-0*, 63694-12); Vol. 4A. 1998. (*0-327-00430-4*, 63695-12); Vol. 5. 1998. (*0-327-00431-2*, 63696-12); Vol. 6. 1998. (*0-327-00432-0*); Vol. 7. 1998. (*0-327-00433-9*, 63698-12); Vol. 7A. 1998. (*0-327-00434-7*, 63699-12); Vol. 8. 1998. (*0-327-00435-5*, 63700-12); Vol. 8A. 1998. (*0-327-00436-3*, 63701-12); Vol. 9. 1998. (*0-327-00437-1*, 63702-12); Vol. 10. 1998. (*0-327-00438-X*, 63703-12); Vol. 10A. 1998. (*0-327-00439-8*, 63704-12); Vol. 11. 1998. (*0-327-00440-1*, 63705-12); Vol. 12. 1998. (*0-327-00441-X*, 63706-12); 1998. (*0-327-00442-8*, 63707-12); Vol. 13. 1998. (*0-327-00443-6*, 63708-12); Vol. 14. 1998. (*0-327-00444-4*, 63709-12); Vol. 15. 1998. (*0-327-00445-2*, 63710-12); Vol. 16. 1998. (*0-327-00446-0*, 63711-12); Vol. 17. 1998. (*0-327-00447-9*, 63712-12); Vol. 18. 1998. (*0-327-00448-7*, 63713-12); Vol. 19. 1998. (*0-327-00449-5*, 63714-12); Vol. 20. 1998. (*0-327-00450-9*, 63715-12); Vol. 20A. 1998. (*0-327-00451-7*, 63716-12); Vol. 21. 1998. (*0-327-00452-5*, 63717-12); Vol. 22. 1998. (*0-327-00453-3*, 63718-12); Vol. 23. 1998. (*0-327-00454-1*, 63719-12); Vol. 24. 1998. (*0-327-00455-X*, 63720-12); Vol. 25. 1998. (*0-327-00456-8*, 63721-12); Vol. 26. 1998. (*0-327-00457-6*, 63722-12); Vol. 27. 1998. (*0-327-00458-4*, 63723-12); Vol. 28. 1998. (*0-327-00459-2*, 63724-12); Vol. 29. 1998. (*0-327-00460-6*, 63725-12); Vol. 30. 1998. (*0-327-00461-4*, 63726-12); Vol. 30A. 1998. (*0-327-00462-2*, 63727-12); Vol. 31. 1998. (*0-327-00463-0*, 63728-12); Vol. 32. 1998. (*0-327-00464-9*, 63729-12); Vol. 33. 1998. (*0-327-00465-7*, 63730-12); Vol. 34. 1998. (*0-327-00466-5*, 63731-12); Vol. 35. 1998. (*0-327-00467-3*, 63732-12); Vol. 36. 1998. (*0-327-00468-1*, 63733-12); Vol. 37. 1998. (*0-327-00469-X*, 63734-12); Vol. 38. 1998. (*0-327-00470-3*, 63735-12); Vol. 39. 1998. (*0-327-00471-1*, 63736-12); Vol. 40. 1998. (*0-327-00472-X*, 63737-12); Vol. 41. 1998. (*0-327-00473-8*, 63738-12); Vol. 42. Vol. 42. 1998. (*0-327-00474-6*, 63739-12); Vol. 42A. 1998. (*0-327-00475-4*, 63740-12); Vol. 43. 1998. (*0-327-00476-2*, 63741-12); Vol. 44. 1998. (*0-327-00477-0*, 63742-12); Vol. 45. 1998. (*0-327-00478-9*, 63743-12); write for info. (*0-327-00191-7*, 6369012) LEXIS Pub.

Pennsylvania Law Encyclopedia, 1999 Interim Supplement. Ed. by Heather Hayes. 96p. 1999. suppl. ed. write for info. (*0-327-00957-8*, 6367510) LEXIS Pub.

Pennsylvania Law Encyclopedia, 1999 Replacement Volume, No. 3. 2nd ed. Ed. by Heather Hayes. 500p. 1999. write for info. (*0-327-00953-5*, 6362311) LEXIS Pub.

***Pennsylvania Law Encyclopedia, 1999 Replacement, Vol. 4.** 2nd ed. Ed. by Heather Hayes. 600p. 1999. write for info. (*0-327-01306-0*, 6362411) LEXIS Pub.

***Pennsylvania Law Encyclopedia, 1999 Cumulative Supplement: Pocketpart, 53 vols.** Incl. Vol. 1. 1999. (*0-327-01596-9*, 6368713); Vol. 2. 1999. (*0-327-01597-7*, 6368813); Vol. 3. 1999. (*0-327-01598-5*, 6368913); Vol. 4. 1999. (*0-327-01599-3*, 6369413); Vol. 4A. 1999. (*0-327-01648-5*, 6369513); Vol. 5. 1999. (*0-327-01600-0*, 6369613); Vol. 6. 1999. (*0-327-01601-9*, 6369713); Vol. 7. 1999. (*0-327-01602-7*, 6369813); Vol. 7A. 1999. (*0-327-01603-5*, 6369913); Vol. 8. 1999. (*0-327-01604-3*, 6370013); Vol. 8A. 1999. (*0-327-01605-1*, 6370113); Vol. 9. 1999. (*0-327-01606-X*, 6370213); Vol. 10. 1999. (*0-327-01607-8*, 6370313); Vol. 10A. 1999. (*0-327-01608-6*, 6370413); Vol. 11. 1999. (*0-327-01609-4*, 6370513); Vol. 12. 1999. (*0-327-01610-8*, 6370613); Vol. 12A. 1999. (*0-327-01611-6*, 6370713); Vol. 13. 1999. (*0-327-01612-4*, 6370813); Vol. 14. 1999. (*0-327-01613-2*, 6370913); Vol. 15. 1999. (*0-327-01614-0*, 6371013); Vol. 16. 1999. (*0-327-01615-9*, 6371113); Vol. 17. 1999. (*0-327-01616-7*, 6371213); Vol. 18. 1999. (*0-327-01617-5*, 6371313); Vol. 19. 1999. (*0-327-01618-3*, 6371413); Vol. 20. 1999. (*0-327-01619-1*, 6371513); Vol. 20A. 1999. (*0-327-01620-5*, 6371613); Vol. 21. 1999. (*0-327-01621-3*, 6371713); Vol. 22. 1999. (*0-327-01622-1*, 6371813); Vol. 23. 1999. (*0-327-01623-X*, 6371913); Vol. 24. 1999. (*0-327-01624-8*, 6372013); Vol. 25. 1999. (*0-327-01625-6*, 6372113); Vol. 26. 1999. (*0-327-01626-4*, 6372213); Vol. 27. 1999. (*0-327-01627-2*, 6372313); Vol. 28. 1999. (*0-327-01628-0*, 6372413); Vol. 29. 1999. (*0-327-01629-9*, 6372513); Vol. 30. 1999. (*0-327-01630-2*, 6372613); Vol. 30A. 1999. (*0-327-01631-0*, 6372713); Vol. 31. 1999. (*0-327-01632-9*, 6372813); Vol. 32. 1999. (*0-327-01633-7*, 6372913); Vol. 33. 1999. (*0-327-01634-5*, 6373013); Vol. 34. 1999. (*0-327-01635-3*, 6373113); Vol. 35. 1999. (*0-327-01636-1*, 6373213); Vol. 36. 1999. (*0-327-01637-X*, 6373313); Vol. 37. 1999. (*0-327-01638-8*, 6373413); Vol. 38. 1999. (*0-327-01639-6*, 6373513); Vol. 39. 1999. (*0-327-01640-X*, 6373613); Vol. 40. 1999. (*0-327-01641-8*, 6373713); Vol. 41. 1999. (*0-327-01642-6*, 6373813); Vol. 42. 1999. (*0-327-01643-4*, 6373913); Vol. 42A. 1999. (*0-327-01644-2*, 6374013); Vol. 43. 1999. (*0-327-01645-0*, 6374113); Vol. 44. 1999. (*0-327-01646-9*, 6374213); Vol. 45. 1999. (*0-327-01647-7*, 6374313); 8450p. 1999. write for info. (*0-327-01595-0*, 6369013) LEXIS Pub.

Pennsylvania Law Encyclopedia, Special Supplement, Vol. 1. 2nd ed. Ed. by M. J. Divine & David C. Wagoner. 500p. 1998. pap. write for info. (*0-327-00864-4*, 6369113) LEXIS Pub.

Pennsylvania Law Encyclopedia, Special Supplement, Vol. 2. 2nd ed. Ed. by M. J. Divine & David C. Wagoner. 500p. 1998. pap. write for info. (*0-327-00865-2*, 6369213) LEXIS Pub.

Pennsylvania Law Encyclopedia, Special Supplement, Vol. 3. 2nd ed. Ed. by Heather Hayes. 200p. 1999. 55.00 (*0-327-01141-6*, 6369313) LEXIS Pub.

Pennsylvania Law Enforcement Handbook: Annual Edition. annuals rev. ed. Larry E. Holtz. 1320p. 1988. ring bd. 49.95 (*0-87526-355-0*) Gould.

Pennsylvania Legislative Reapportionment of 1991. Ken Gormley. LC 95-620994. 92p. 1994. 8.05 (*0-8182-0191-6*) Commonweal PA.

Pennsylvania Library Book: A Surprising Guide to the Unusual Special Collections in Libraries Across Our State for Students, Teachers, Writers & Publishers - Includes Reproducible Mailing Labels Plus Activities for Young People! Carole Marsh. (Pennsylvania Bks.). (Illus.). 1994. pap. 19.95 (*0-7933-3120-X*); lib. bdg. 29.95 (*0-7933-3119-6*); disk 29.95 (*0-7933-3121-8*) Gallopade Intl.

Pennsylvania Limited Liability Company Forms & Practice Manual. Alan H. Molod. LC 96-22275. 644p. 1996. ring bd. 219.90 (*1-57400-003-9*) Data Trace Pubng.

Pennsylvania Line: Regimental Organization & Operations, 1775-1783. John B. Trussell. (Illus.). 368p. 1993. pap. 15.95 (*0-89271-053-5*, 0516) Pa Hist & Mus.

Pennsylvania Longrifles of Note. 3rd ed. George Shumway. LC 93-92790. (Illus.). 64p. 1993. pap. 15.00 (*0-87387-101-4*) Shumway.

Pennsylvania Manual of Penalties & Sentences: Civil & Criminal. Burton R. Laub et al. LC 94-73046. 601p. 1999. per. 97.50 (*1-887024-23-9*) Bisel Co.

Pennsylvania Manufacturers Register. 14th rev. ed. Ed. by Frank Lambing. 1999. 157.00 (*1-58202-065-5*) Manufacturers.

Pennsylvania Manuscripts, 1747-1827, Pt. 1. Lyman Draper. Ed. by Mary L. Henderson. 85p. 1993. pap. 8.95 (*1-55856-154-4*, 075) Closson Pr.

Pennsylvania Math! How It All Adds up in Our State. Carole Marsh. (Carole Marsh Pennsylvania Bks.). (Illus.). (YA). (gr. 3-12). 1996. pap. 19.95 (*0-7933-6602-X*); lib. bdg. 29.95 (*0-7933-6601-1*) Gallopade Intl.

Pennsylvania Matrimonial Practice, 4 vols. Jack A. Rounick. LC 81-85429. (Pennsylvania Practice Systems Library). 1982. ring bd. 400.00 (*0-317-00357-7*) West Group.

Pennsylvania Matrimonial Practice, 4 vols. Jack A. Rounick. LC 81-85429. (Pennsylvania Practice Systems Library). 1993. suppl. ed. 175.00 (*0-317-03160-0*) West Group.

Pennsylvania Mechanics' Liens. Michael G. Walsh. 250p. 1992. ring bd. 75.00 (*0-614-05943-7*, MICHIE) LEXIS Pub.

Pennsylvania Media Book: A Surprising Guide to the Amazing Print, Broadcast & Online Media of Our State for Students, Teachers, Writers & Publishers - Includes Reproducible Mailing Labels Plus Activities for Young People! Carole Marsh. (Pennsylvania Bks.). (Illus.). 1994. pap. 19.95 (*0-7933-3276-1*); lib. bdg. 29.95 (*0-7933-3275-3*); disk 29.95 (*0-7933-3277-X*) Gallopade Intl.

Pennsylvania Mennonites in Mexico. Lester Burkholder. (Illus.). 145p. 1998. pap. 9.95 (*1-883294-73-8*) Masthof Pr.

Pennsylvania Migration Trends. Jennifer Shultz & Amy Jonas. Ed. by Diane Shoop. (Illus.). 36p. 1999. pap. 20.00 (*1-58036-131-5*) Penn State Data Ctr.

Pennsylvania Militia in 1777. Compiled by Hannah B. Roach. (Special Publications: No. 1). 80p. 1994. reprint ed. pap. 5.00 (*1-887099-00-X*) Geneal Soc Pa.

Pennsylvania Mining Families: The Search for Dignity in the Coal Fields. Barry P. Michrina. LC 93-19826. (Illus.). 200p. 1993. 27.50 (*0-8131-1850-6*) U Pr of Ky.

Pennsylvania Modern: Charles Demuth of Lancaster. Betsy Fahlman. LC 83-8116. (Illus.). 74p. 1983. pap. 16.95 (*0-87633-054-5*) Phila Mus Art.

Pennsylvania Motor Vehicle Insurance Lawsource: Statutes, Regulations, Bulletins, Notices, Index. Arthur S. Zanan. LC 93-72897. 545p. 1999. per. 64.50 (*1-887024-22-0*) Bisel Co.

Pennsylvania Municipal Law Lawsource. Darrell M. Zaslow. LC 97-78244. 1998. per. 64.50 (*1-887024-27-1*) Bisel Co.

Pennsylvania Municipal Profiles: Southeast, 1997. 2nd rev. ed. Ed. by Louise L. Hornor. 1200p. 1997. pap. 80.00 (*0-911273-22-0*) Info Pubns.

Pennsylvania Mystery Van Takes Off! Book 1: Handicapped Pennsylvania Kids Sneak Off on a Big Adventure, Bk. 1. Carole Marsh. (Pennsylvania Bks.). (Illus.). (J). (gr. 3-12). 1994. 29.95 (*0-7933-5075-1*); pap. 19.95 (*0-7933-5076-X*); disk 29.95 (*0-7933-5077-8*) Gallopade Intl.

Pennsylvania Negligence Instant Case Finder, 3 vols. Glenn Troutman et al. 1940p. 1999. ring bd. 180.00 (*1-887024-61-1*) Bisel Co.

Pennsylvania 1970 Census Index: Heads of Families. pap. 41.50 (*1-877677-51-5*) Herit Quest.

Pennsylvania Non-Profit Handbook. 3rd rev. ed. Gary M. Grobman. LC 92-80603. 164p. 1994. pap. 24.95 (*0-9643402-0-8*) United Way PA.

Pennsylvania Non-Profit Handbook, 1992. Gary M. Grobman. LC 92-80603. 150p. (Orig.). 1992. pap. 19.95 (*0-9632432-0-9*) Non-Prof Adv Netwk.

***Pennsylvania Nonprofit Corporations & Charities Lawsource: Relevant Sections of Titles 15, 20 & 54 on Nonprofit Corporations & Full Text of Laws on Charities.** William H. Clark, Jr. & W. Edward Sell. LC 99-73295. 260p. 1999. pap. 59.50 (*1-887024-80-8*) Bisel Co.

Pennsylvania Nonprofit Handbook: Everything You Need to Know to Start & Run Your Nonprofit Organization. 5th ed. Gary M. Grobman. 294p. 1999. pap. 27.95 (*0-9653653-1-X*) White Hat.

Pennsylvania Old Assyrian Texts. Gwaltney. 1988. 25.00 (*0-685-21551-2*) Ktav.

Pennsylvania One Hundred Years Ago. Headley et al. (Historical Ser.). (Illus.). 1976. pap. 3.50 (*0-89540-021-9*, SB-021) Sun Pub.

Pennsylvania Orphans' Court Lawsource: Code, Statute, Rules & Index. Richard L. Grossman. LC 94-72556. 410p. 1999. per. 64.50 (*0-614-05666-7*) Bisel Co.

Pennsylvania Parks Guide. Chris Boyce. Ed. by Barbara McCaig. 100p. (Orig.). 1988. pap. text 5.95 (*0-935201-37-8*) Affordable Adven.

Pennsylvania People. Rose B. Green. LC 83-20010. 120p. 1984. 12.95 (*0-8453-4781-0*, Cornwall Bks) Assoc Univ Prs.

Pennsylvania Perspective, 1997. Lesley Nearman. Ed. by Diane Shoop. (Illus.). 20p. 1998. pap. 20.00 (*1-58036-057-2*) Penn State Data Ctr.

Pennsylvania Pete. T. R. Ricekit. LC 98-119936. (Illus.). 171p. (Orig.). (YA). (gr. 7 up). 1995. pap. 9.99 (*0-88092-250-8*, 2508) Royal Fireworks.

Pennsylvania Politics, 1817-1832: A Game Without Rules. Philip S. Klein. LC 73-19839. (Perspectives in American History Ser.: No. 13). (Illus.). vii, 430p. 1974. reprint ed. lib. bdg. 45.00 (*0-87991-327-4*) Porcupine Pr.

Pennsylvania Politics, 1872-1877: A Study in Political Leadership. Frank B. Evans. LC 67-66003. 360p. 1966. 6.95 (*0-911124-22-5*) Pa Hist & Mus.

Pennsylvania Politics, 1746-1770: The Movement for Royal Government & Its Consequences. James H. Hutson. LC 74-173756. 274p. reprint ed. pap. 85.00 (*0-8357-8980-2*, 203264800085) Bks Demand.

Pennsylvania Politics Today & Yesterday: The Tolerable Accommodation. Paul B. Beers. LC 79-65826. (Keystone Bks.). (Illus.). 416p. (C). 1980. 45.00 (*0-271-00238-7*) Pa St U Pr.

Pennsylvania Population Projections Background Report. Don Lichter & Sue Copella. Ed. by Diane Shoop. 82p. 1998. pap. 40.00 (*1-58036-060-2*) Penn State Data Ctr.

Pennsylvania Postal History. John L. Kay & Chester M. Smith, Jr. 538p. 1996. lib. bdg. 75.00 (*0-88000-149-6*) Quarterman.

Pennsylvania Potters, 1660-1900. James B. Whisker. LC 93-62. 336p. 1993. text 99.95 (*0-7734-9262-3*) E Mellen.

Pennsylvania Pottery: Tools & Processes. Elizabeth A. Powell. (Tools of the Nation Maker Ser.: Vol. II). (Illus.). 20p. 1972. pap. 3.00 (*0-910302-10-3*) Bucks Co Hist.

Pennsylvania Power & Light Company: A Guide to the Records. Michael Nash et al. 226p. 1985. 10.00 (*0-914650-22-X*) Hagley Museum.

Pennsylvania Prints. Ed. by Judith W. Hansen. LC 79-49259. (Illus.). 176p. 1980. pap. 12.50 (*0-271-00261-1*) Pa St U Pr.

Pennsylvania Prints from the Collection of John C. O'Connor & Ralph M. Yeager: Exhibition Catalogue. Compiled by Judith W. Hansen. LC 79-49259. (Illus.). 180p. 1979. pap. 10.00 (*0-685-30069-2*) Palmer Mus Art.

Pennsylvania Probate, Estates & Fiduciaries Code Annotated. J. Brooke Aker. 1999. ring bd. 109.50 (*1-887024-62-X*) Bisel Co.

Pennsylvania Products Liability Guide. Larry E. Coben et al. LC 92-74117. 1998. ring bd. 69.50 (*1-887024-21-2*) Bisel Co.

Pennsylvania Profiles, Vol. 11. Patrick M. Reynolds. (Illus.). 56p. 1987. pap. 3.95 (*0-932514-16-2*) Red Rose Studio.

Pennsylvania Profiles Series, Vol. 9. Patrick M. Reynolds. (Pennsylvania Profiles Ser.). (Illus.). 56p. (Orig.). 1985. pap. 3.95 (*0-932514-12-X*) Red Rose Studio.

Pennsylvania Province & State, 1609-1790, 2 vols., Set. Albert S. Bolles. 1993. reprint ed. lib. bdg. 150.00 (*0-7812-5430-2*) Rprt Serv.

Pennsylvania Public Employee Reporter. LRP Publications Staff. text 645.00 (*0-934753-04-0*) LRP Pubns.

Pennsylvania Public Employee Reporter, Vol. 17. Ed. by LRP Publications Staff. 1987. text. write for info. (*0-934753-14-8*) LRP Pubns.

Pennsylvania Public Utility Commission Decisions - August 1994-December 1994, Vol. 83. Pennsylvania Public Utility Commission. Ed. by Shirley Leming. 757p. 1994. 235.61 (*0-8182-0212-2*) Commonweal PA.

Pennsylvania Public Utility Commission Decisions - March 1994-August 1994, Vol. 82. Pennsylvania Public Utility Commission. Ed. by Shirley Leming. 692p. 1994. 235.62 (*0-8182-0211-4*) Commonweal PA.

Pennsylvania Public Utility Commission Decisions, April 1987-August 1987. Pennsylvania P. U. C. Staff. Ed. by Kathryn G. Sophy. (PA P.U.C. Decisions Ser.: Vol. 64). 565p. 1987. text 36.95 (*0-8182-0100-2*) Commonweal PA.

Pennsylvania Quaker in Andersonville: The Diary of Charles Smedley. Charles Smedley. Ed. & Pref. by James Durkin. (Illus.). 150p. 1995. reprint ed. pap. 12.95 (*0-9631314-2-7*) J M S Civil War.

Pennsylvania Quiz Bowl Crash Course! Carole Marsh. (Carole Marsh Pennsylvania Bks.). (Illus.). (J). 1994. pap. 19.95 (*0-7933-1946-3*); lib. bdg. 29.95 (*0-7933-1945-5*); disk 29.95 (*0-7933-1947-1*) Gallopade Intl.

Pennsylvania Railroad: Color History. Schafer et al. LC 97-12593. (Railroad Color History Ser.). (Illus.). 128p. 1997. pap. 21.95 (*0-7603-0379-7*) MBI Pubg.

Pennsylvania Railroad: The 1940s & 1950s. Don Ball, Jr. 1986. 50.00 (*0-393-02357-5*) Norton.

*__Pennsylvania Railroad Diesel Locomotive Pictorial Vol. 4: Baldwin Cab & Transfer Units.__ John D. Hahn, Jr. LC 98-85647. (Illus.). 80p. 1998. 16.95 (*1-881411-17-6*) Withers Pub.

*__Pennsylvania Railroad in Indiana.__ William J. Watt. LC 99-55142. (Railroads Past & Present Ser.). (Illus.). 208p. 2000. 49.95 (*0-253-33708-9*) Ind U Pr.

Pennsylvania-Reading Seashore Lines in Color. John Stroup. (Illus.). 128p. 1996. 49.95 (*1-878887-57-2*) Morning NJ.

Pennsylvania Real Estate. Emil L. Iannelli & Lynne P. Iannelli. LC 84-80494. (Pennsylvania Practice Systems Library). 1984. ring bd. 125.00 (*0-318-01919-1*) West Group.

Pennsylvania Real Estate. Emil L. Iannelli & Lynne P. Iannelli. (Pennsylvania Practice Systems Library). 1993. suppl. ed. 62.50 (*0-317-03247-X*) West Group.

Pennsylvania Real Estate Agreements. Charles P. Nemeth. LC 95-76463. 1996. ring bd. 79.50 (*1-887024-63-8*) Bisel Co.

Pennsylvania Real Estate Brokerage: Statutes, Rules, Regulations, Cases, 2 vols. Greg B. Emmons. 1999. ring bd. 225.00 (*1-887024-25-5*) Bisel Co.

Pennsylvania Real Estate Fundamentals & Practices. Ralph A. Palmer & Kenneth M. Lusht. 478p. (C). 1997. pap. text 19.20 (*0-13-777384-6*) P-H.

Pennsylvania Real Estate Practice. Charles P. Nemeth. LC 95-76462. 1996. ring bd. 79.50 (*1-887024-64-6*) Bisel Co.

Pennsylvania Regulations: Containing Insurance Department Regulations, Statements of Policy, & Notices & Selected Attorney General's Opinions. Pennsylvania. Insurance Dept et al. LC 97-68398. (Illus.). 1997. write for info. (*0-89246-477-1*); write for info. (*0-89246-478-X*) NILS Pub.

Pennsylvania Rifle see Lancaster County During the American Revolution Series

Pennsylvania Road Atlas. 2nd ed. H. M. Gousha. LC 96-675522. 1995. 7.95 (*0-671-53600-1*) S&S Trade.

Pennsylvania Rollercoasters! Carole Marsh. (Pennsylvania Bks.). (Illus.). (YA). (gr. 3-12). 1994. pap. 19.95 (*0-7933-5339-4*); lib. bdg. 29.95 (*0-7933-5338-6*); disk 29.95 (*0-7933-5340-8*) Gallopade Intl.

Pennsylvania Rules of Civil Procedure: Annual Edition. Gould Editorial Staff. 530p. (C). ring bd. 18.95 (*0-87526-300-3*) Gould.

Pennsylvania Rules of Evidence Annotated LLP's. 98th ed. (LLP's Pennsylvania Rules of Evidence Annotated Ser.). 288p. 1998. pap. 30.00 (*0-327-06362-9*, 4731010) LEXIS Pub.

*__Pennsylvania Rules of Evidence with Objections.__ Anthony J. Bocchino. LC 99-209365. 293p. 1998. 25.95 (*1-55681-621-9*) Natl Inst Trial Ad.

Pennsylvania Rules of the Road. Dale G. Larrimore. LC 95-80822. 250p. 1995. pap. text. write for info. (*0-7620-0025-2*) West Group.

Pennsylvania School District Report, 1990. Pennsylvania State Data Center Staff. 1994. pap. 45.00 (*0-939667-22-3*) Penn State Data Ctr.

Pennsylvania School Districts, 1990: Socioeconomic Trends, Vol. II. Colleen Garber. 220p. 1995. pap. 45.00 (*1-885925-05-0*) Penn State Data Ctr.

Pennsylvania School Laws & Rules Annotated: 1997-98 Edition. annuals Michael Levin. (Practice Ser.). 1407p. 1997. pap. text, suppl. ed. write for info. (*0-314-22780-6*) West Pub.

Pennsylvania School Laws & Rules Annotated, 1995-1996. Ed. by Michael Levin. 1050p. 1995. pap. write for info. (*0-314-07660-3*) West Pub.

Pennsylvania School Laws & Rules, 1994-95. Ed. by Michael I. Levin. 905p. 1992. pap. 81.00 (*0-8322-0512-5*) Banks-Baldwin.

Pennsylvania School Personnel Actions. 3rd ed. Michael I. Levin. 428p. 1991. pap. 59.00 (*0-8322-0511-7*) Banks-Baldwin.

Pennsylvania School Trivia: An Amazing & Fascinating Look at Ou State's Teachers, Schools & Students! Carole Marsh. (Carole Marsh Pennsylvania Bks.). (Illus.). (J). 1994. pap. 19.95 (*0-7933-0970-0*); lib. bdg. 29.95 (*0-7933-0971-9*); disk 29.95 (*0-7933-0972-7*) Gallopade Intl.

*__Pennsylvania Search & Seizure.__ James T. Ranney. 142p. 1999. spiral bd. 40.00 (*1-57823-057-8*) Juris Pubng.

Pennsylvania Silly Basketball Sportsmysteries, Vol. 1. Carole Marsh. (Carole Marsh Pennsylvania Bks.). (Illus.). (J). 1994. pap. 19.95 (*0-7933-0967-0*); lib. bdg. 29.95 (*0-7933-0968-9*); disk 29.95 (*0-7933-0969-7*) Gallopade Intl.

Pennsylvania Silly Basketball Sportsmysteries, Vol. 2. Carole Marsh. (Carole Marsh Pennsylvania Bks.). (Illus.). (J). 1994. pap. 19.95 (*0-7933-1949-8*); lib. bdg. 29.95 (*0-7933-1948-X*); disk 29.95 (*0-7933-1950-1*) Gallopade Intl.

Pennsylvania Silly Football Sportsmysteries, Vol. 1. Carole Marsh. (Carole Marsh Pennsylvania Bks.). (Illus.). (J). 1994. pap. 19.95 (*0-7933-1928-5*); lib. bdg. 29.95 (*0-7933-1927-7*); disk 29.95 (*0-7933-1929-3*) Gallopade Intl.

Pennsylvania Silly Football Sportsmysteries, Vol. 2. Carole Marsh. (Carole Marsh Pennsylvania Bks.). (Illus.). (J). 1994. pap. 19.95 (*0-7933-1931-5*); lib. bdg. 29.95 (*0-7933-1930-7*); disk 29.95 (*0-7933-1932-3*) Gallopade Intl.

Pennsylvania Silly Trivia! Carole Marsh. (Carole Marsh Pennsylvania Bks.). (Illus.). (J). 1994. pap. 19.95 (*0-7933-1920-X*); lib. bdg. 29.95 (*0-7933-1919-6*); disk 29.95 (*0-7933-1921-8*) Gallopade Intl.

Pennsylvania Silversmiths, Goldsmiths, & Pewterers, 1684-1900. James B. Whisker. LC 93-2691. 332p. 1993. text 99.95 (*0-7734-9260-7*) E Mellen.

Pennsylvania Society of Sons of the Revolution: Centennial Register, 1888-1988. Ed. by Mark F. Lloyd & Jefferson M. Moak. LC 90-61497. (Illus.). x, 994p. 1990. 35.00 (*0-9626507-0-6*) PA Soc Sons Rev.

Pennsylvania Soldiers of the Revolutionary War. Paul W. Myers. 30p. 1987. per. 5.00 (*0-933227-64-7*, 485) Closson Pr.

Pennsylvania Songs & Legends. George G. Korson. LC 78-19277. 1979. 40.95 (*0-405-10608-4*) Ayer.

Pennsylvania Source Book. PA State Data Staff. 70p. 1998. 20.00 (*1-58036-054-8*) Penn State Data Ctr.

Pennsylvania Spelling Bee! Score Big by Correctly Spelling Our State's Unique Names. Carole Marsh. (Carole Marsh Pennsylvania Bks.). (Illus.). (YA). (gr. 3-12). 1996. pap. 19.95 (*0-7933-6755-7*); lib. bdg. 29.95 (*0-7933-6754-9*) Gallopade Intl.

Pennsylvania Spice Box: Paneled Doors & Secret Drawers. Lee E. Griffith. LC 85-52437. (Illus.). 160p. (Orig.). 1986. pap. 25.00 (*0-929706-03-X*) Chester Co Hist Soc.

Pennsylvania State Census Index, 1842, Chester County. (Illus.). lib. bdg. 99.00 (*0-89593-472-8*, Accel Indexing) Genealogical Srvcs.

Pennsylvania State Census Index, 1857, Chester County. (Illus.). 1989. lib. bdg. 101.00 (*0-89593-473-6*, Accel Indexing) Genealogical Srvcs.

*__Pennsylvania State Credit Directory, 2000 Edition.__ rev. ed. American Business Directories Staff. 1120p. 1999. boxed set 175.00 incl. cd-rom (*0-7687-0319-0*) Am Busn Direct.

Pennsylvania State Grange Cookbook. Pennsylvania State Grange Staff. LC 92-30345. 1992. pap., spiral bd. write for info. (*0-87197-350-2*) Favorite Recipes.

Pennsylvania State Parks: A Guide to Pennsylvania State Parks. Bill Bailey. 375p. 1996. pap. 15.95 (*1-881139-15-8*) Glovebox Guidebks.

Pennsylvania Station: New York, 1905-10, McKim, Mead & White. Steven Parissien. (Architecture in Detail Ser.). 60p. (Orig.). 1996. pap. 29.95 (*0-7148-3466-1*, Pub. by Phaidon Press) Phaidon Pr.

Pennsylvania Stories. Arthur H. Quinn. 1993. reprint ed. lib. bdg. 89.00 (*0-7812-5820-0*) Rprt Serv.

Pennsylvania Student Pocket Part to Accompany Civil Litigation for the Paralegal. Thomas A. Dittoe. 1993. 9.95 (*0-8273-5936-5*) Delmar.

Pennsylvania Student Pocket Part to Accompany the Law of Real Property. Kimberly J. Gallagher. 57p. 1993. 10.50 (*0-8273-6205-6*) Delmar.

Pennsylvania Support Practice. Neil Hurowitz & Arthur S. Zanan. LC 79-8913. 1999. 69.50 (*1-887024-03-4*) Bisel Co.

Pennsylvania Survival. Betty L. Hall & Rose G. Hagopin. 160p. (Orig.). (gr. 10-12). 1979. pap. text 5.84 (*0-03-046961-9*) Westwood Pr.

Pennsylvania Tax Handbook. Charles L. Potter et al. 464p. 1988. 17.50 (*0-13-655994-8*) P-H.

Pennsylvania Tax Handbook, 1985. Charles L. Potter et al. write for info. (*0-318-58212-0*) P-H.

Pennsylvania Tax Handbook, 1989. Charles L. Potter et al. 430p. 1988. 18.95 (*0-13-655648-5*, Busn) P-H.

Pennsylvania Taxation. 1000p. 1987. text 135.00 (*0-07-007809-2*) Shepards.

Pennsylvania Timeline: A Chronology of Pennsylvania History, Mystery, Trivia, Legend, Lore & More. Carole Marsh. (Pennsylvania Bks.). (Illus.). (J). (gr. 3-12). 1994. pap. 19.95 (*0-7933-5990-2*); lib. bdg. 29.95 (*0-7933-5989-9*); disk 29.95 (*0-7933-5991-0*) Gallopade Intl.

Pennsylvania Torts: Law & Advocacy. S. Gerald Litvin & Gerald A. McHugh. LC 96-174233. (West's Pennsylvania Practice Ser.). 1996. write for info. (*0-314-08113-5*) West Pub.

Pennsylvania Transaction Guide: Legal Forms, 16 vols. Joseph N. Bongiovanni & Bender's Editors. 1974. ring bd. 1340.00 (*0-8205-1436-5*) Bender.

Pennsylvania Transportation History. William H. Shank. 1990. 8.00 (*0-933788-81-9*) Am Canal & Transport.

Pennsylvania Trial Advocacy. Milford J. Meyer & Arthur S. Zanan. 288p. 1999. text 59.50 (*1-887024-65-4*) Bisel Co.

Pennsylvania Trial Objections: Responses & Motions. Charles B. Gibbons. 284p. 1994. pap. write for info. (*0-314-03024-7*) West Pub.

Pennsylvania Trivia. rev. ed. Ernie Couch & Jill Couch. LC 95-24376. 192p. 1995. pap. 6.95 (*1-55853-356-7*) Rutledge Hill Pr.

Pennsylvania Trolley Museum: Preserving Pennsylvania's Transit Heritage. Bruce P. Wells. (Illus.). 60p. (Orig.). 1993. 4.95 (*1-881873-01-3*) PA Railway Mus.

Pennsylvania Trolleys in Color, Vol. 1. William D. Volkmer. LC 97-70598. (Illus.). 128p. 1997. 49.95 (*1-878887-77-7*) Morning NJ.

Pennsylvania Trolleys in Color Vol. 2: Philadelphia Region. William D. Volkmer. LC 97-70598. (Illus.). 128p. 1998. 49.95 (*1-878887-99-8*) Morning NJ.

Pennsylvania Turnpike. Dan Cupper. (Pennsylvania History Ser.). (Illus.). 1990. pap. 5.50 (*0-911410-91-0*) Applied Arts.

Pennsylvania 2000! Coming Soon to a Calendar Near You - The 21st Century! - Complete Set of AL 2000 Items. Carole Marsh. (Two Thousand! Ser.). (Illus.). (J). (gr. 3-12). 1998. pap. 75.00 (*0-7933-9385-X*); lib. bdg. 85.00 (*0-7933-9386-8*) Gallopade Intl.

Pennsylvania 2000! Coming Soon to a Calendar near You--The 21st Century! Carole Marsh. (Two Thousand! Ser.). (Illus.). (J). (gr. 3-12). 1998. pap. 19.95 (*0-7933-8790-6*) Gallopade Intl.

Pennsylvania 2000! Coming Soon to a Calendar near You-The 21st Century! Carole Marsh. (Two Thousand! Ser.). (Illus.). (J). (gr. 3-12). 1998. lib. bdg. 29.95 (*0-7933-8789-2*) Gallopade Intl.

Pennsylvania UFO's & Extraterrestrials! A Look at the Sightings & Science in Our State. Carole Marsh. (Carole Marsh Pennsylvania Bks.). (Illus.). (J). (gr. 3-12). 1997. pap. 19.95 (*0-7933-6449-3*); lib. bdg. 29.95 (*0-7933-6448-5*) Gallopade Intl.

*__Pennsylvania Unemployment Compensation Lawsource.__ Kenneth A. Sprang & James O. Castagnera. LC 97-78245. 210p. 1998. per. 59.50 (*1-887024-24-7*) Bisel Co.

Pennsylvania Uninsured & Underinsured Motorists. Stephen N. Huntington. LC 96-75154. 300p. 1996. text. write for info. (*0-7620-0042-2*) West Group.

Pennsylvania Vehicle Code Annotated. 2nd ed. Milford J. Meyer. Ed. by Arthur S. Zanan. LC 94-72323. 1999. ring bd. 109.50 (*1-887024-07-7*) Bisel Co.

Pennsylvania Vehicle Laws: Annual Edition. Gould Editorial Staff. 500p. 1991. ring bd. 21.95 (*0-87526-233-3*) Gould.

Pennsylvania Vehicle Laws: Annual Edition. Gould Editorial Staff. 500p. (C). 1991. 8.95 (*0-87526-388-7*) Gould.

Pennsylvania Vehicle Negligence, 2 vols. Arthur S. Zanan & Milford J. Meyer. 1344p. 1999. ring bd. 165.00 (*1-887024-66-2*) Bisel Co.

Pennsylvania Vital Records from The Pennsylvania Magazine of History & Biography & The Pennsylvania Genealogical Magazine, 3 vols., Set. LC 82-83681. 2491p. 1999. reprint ed. pap. 150.00 (*0-8063-1009-X*, Pub. by Clearfield Co) ACCESS Pubs Network.

Pennsylvania West 1870 Census Index: 2 Volume Set & Addendum, 2 vols. lib. bdg. 295.00 (*1-877677-76-0*) Herit Quest.

Pennsylvania Wildlife: A Viewer's Guide. Kathy Korber. (Illus.). 122p. 1994. pap. text 12.95 (*1-885159-00-5*) Northwoods.

*__Pennsylvania Wineries.__ Richard Carey & Linda Jones McKee. LC 99-43759. 2000. 19.95 (*0-8117-2877-3*) Stackpole.

Pennsylvania Workers' Compensation Lawsource: Statutes, Rules, Regulations, Notices, Forms & Index. Arthur S. Zanan. LC 94-72610. 540p. 1999. per. 84.50 (*1-887024-13-1*) Bisel Co.

Pennsylvania Workers in Brass, Copper, & Tin, 1681-1900. James B. Whisker. LC 93-16080. 236p. 1993. 89.95 (*0-7734-9258-5*) E Mellen.

Pennsylvania Workmen's Compensation & Occupational Disease, 3 vols. with case finder. Alexander F. Babieri et al. LC 96-79930. 1999. per. 275.00 (*1-887024-17-4*) Bisel Co.

Pennsylvania Youth Apprenticeship Program: A Historical Account from Its Origins to September 1991. Richard Kazis. 44p. 1991. pap. 10.00 (*1-887410-69-4*) Jobs for Future.

Pennsylvania Zoning Law & Practice, 2 vols. Robert S. Ryan. 1998. ring bd. 195.00 (*1-887024-67-0*) Bisel Co.

Pennsylvanian Depositional Systems in North-Central Texas, A Guide for Interpreting Terrigenous Clastic Facies in a Cratonic Basin. L. F. Brown, Jr. et al. (Guidebook Ser.: GB 14). (Illus.). 122p. 1973. reprint ed. pap. 5.00 (*0-686-29322-3*) Bur Econ Geology.

Pennsylvanian in Blue: Civil War Diary of Thomas Beck Walton. Ed. by Robert A. Taylor. LC 95-18341. (Civil War Heritage Ser.: Vol. VI). (Illus.). 65p. 1995. pap. 9.95 (*0-942597-82-6*, Burd St Pr) White Mane Pub.

Pennsylvanian Invertebrates of the Mazon Creek Area, Illinois. Eugene S. Richardson. LC 56-969. (Chicago Natural History Museum, Publication 785, Fieldiana, Geology: Vol. 12, No. 14). 80p. reprint ed. pap. 30.00 (*0-608-03775-3*, 206461700009) Bks Demand.

*__Pennsylvania's Big Activity Book.__ Carole Marsh. (Pennsylvania Experience! Ser.). (Illus.). 2000. pap. 9.95 (*0-7933-9590-9*) Gallopade Intl.

Pennsylvania's Capitol. Ruth H. Seitz. LC 95-68756. (Pennsylvania's Cultural & Natural Heritage Ser.: No. 4). (Illus.). 80p. 1995. 19.95 (*1-879441-95-0*) RB Bks.

Pennsylvania's Covered Bridges: A Complete Guide. Benjamin D. Evans & June R. Evans. LC 92-37886. (Illus.). 236p. (C). 1993. pap. 19.95 (*0-8229-5504-0*) U of Pittsburgh Pr.

Pennsylvania's Great Rail-Trails. Tom Sexton & Julie Larison. LC 95-166777. (Illus.). 105p. (Orig.). 1995. 12.95 (*0-925794-07-4*) Rails Trails.

Pennsylvania's Hectic Heritage. Patrick M. Reynolds. (Pennsylvania Profiles Ser.: Vol. VI). (Illus.). 56p. (YA). (gr. 7-12). 1982. pap. 3.95 (*0-932514-06-5*) Red Rose Studio.

Pennsylvania's Historic Places. Photos by Blair Seitz. LC 89-7491. (Illus.). 192p. 1997. pap. 22.95 (*1-56148-242-0*) Good Bks PA.

Pennsylvania's Indian Relations to 1754. Sherman P. Uhler. LC 76-43872. reprint ed. 31.50 (*0-404-15731-9*) AMS Pr.

Pennsylvania's (Most Devastating!) Disasters & (Most Calamitous!) Catastrophies! Carole Marsh. (Carole Marsh Pennsylvania Bks.). (Illus.). (J). 1994. pap. 19.95 (*0-7933-0958-1*); lib. bdg. 29.95 (*0-7933-0959-X*); disk 29.95 (*0-7933-0960-3*) Gallopade Intl.

Pennsylvania's Natural Beauty. Ruth H. Seitz. LC 92-62897. (Pennsylvania's Cultural & Natural Heritage Ser.: Vol. 2). (Illus.). 120p. 1993. 24.95 (*1-879441-79-9*) RB Bks.

*__Pennsylvania's Northeast: Poconos, Endless Mountains & Urban Centers.__ Ruth H. Seitz. (Pennsylvania's Cultural & Natural Heritage Ser.: Vol. 7). (Illus.). 144p. 2000. 29.95 (*1-879441-81-0*, Pub. by RB Bks) Stackpole.

Pennsylvania's Oil Heritage Vol. 1: Columbia Farm. Samuel T. Pees. Ed. by Anne W. Stewart. (Self Guided Tours Ser.: Vol. 1). (Illus.). 32p. (Orig.). Date not set. pap. 5.00 (*0-614-12696-7*) Colonel PA.

Pennsylvania's Rail Trails, 1. 4th ed. Fiel Office of Pennsylvania Staff. 1998. pap. 12.95 (*0-925794-14-7*) Rails Trails.

*__Pennsylvania's Rail-Trails: 1999 Edition.__ 5th ed. Pennsylvania Field Office of Rails-Trails Staff. 1999. pap. text 13.95 (*0-925794-15-5*) Rails Trails.

Pennsylvania's Tapestry: Scenes from the Air. Ruth Hoover Seitz. LC 98-67485. (Pennsylvania's Cultural & Natural Heritage Ser.: Vol. 6). (Illus.). 96p. 1999. 24.95 (*1-879441-80-2*) RB Bks.

Pennsylvania's Unsolved Mysteries (& Their "Solutions") Includes Scientific Information & Other Activities for Students. Carole Marsh. (Pennsylvania Bks.). (Illus.). (J). (gr. 3-12). 1994. pap. 19.95 (*0-7933-5837-X*); lib. bdg. 29.95 (*0-7933-5836-1*); disk 29.95 (*0-7933-5838-8*) Gallopade Intl.

Pennsylvannia. Kathleen Thompson. LC 95-9609. (Portrait of America Ser.). 48p. (gr. 4-8). 1996. pap. text 5.95 (*0-8114-7464-X*) Raintree Steck-V.

Penny: Half Coyote, or Half Wolf - & All Heart. Dolores L. Moore. Ed. by Helen Nielson. (Illus.). 156p. (Orig.). 1996. pap. 10.00 (*1-888844-00-0*) Lghthse Publns.

Penny a Look. Harve Zemach. (Illus.). 48p. (J). (ps-3). 1989. pap. 4.95 (*0-374-45758-1*, Sunburst Bks) FS&G.

P

Penny a Look: An Old Story. Harve Zemach. LC 71-161373. (Illus.). 48p. (J). (gr. 2 up). 1971. 16.00 (*0-374-35793-5*) FS&G.

Penny & the Four Questions. Nancy E. Krulik. LC 93-178541. (Read with Me Paperback Ser.). (Illus.). 32p. (J). (ps-3). 1993. pap. 2.50 (*0-590-46339-X*) Scholastic Inc.

Penny & the Magic Medallion: A Musical Play. Joseph Robinette. (Illus.). 44p. (J). (gr. k up). 1987. pap. 4.50 (*0-88680-283-0*) I E Clark.

Penny & Two Fried Eggs: And Other Stories. Geraldine G. Harder. LC 91-16999. (Illus.). 144p. (Orig.). (J). (gr. 2-5). 1991. pap. 6.99 (*0-8361-3564-4*) Herald Pr.

Penny Ante Earth Science. Fred L. Fifer & Cynthia E. Ledbetter. 183p. (J). 1992. student ed. 15.95 (*1-885568-05-3*) SCE Assocs.

Penny Ante Imperialism: The Mosquito Shore & the Bay of Honduras, 1600-1914. Robert A. Naylor. LC 87-45735. (Illus.). 320p. 1989. 42.50 (*0-8386-3323-4*) Fairleigh Dickinson.

Penny Ante Life Science. Fred L. Fifer & Cynthia E. Ledbetter. 196p. (J). 1992. student ed. 15.95 (*1-885568-04-5*) SCE Assocs.

Penny Ante Physical Science. Fred L. Fifer & Cynthia E. Ledbetter. 198p. (J). 1992. student ed. 15.95 (*1-885568-06-1*) SCE Assocs.

Penny Ante Science. Fred L. Fifer & Cynthia E. Ledbetter. 168p. (J). 1989. student ed. 15.95 (*1-885568-00-2*) SCE Assocs.

Penny Ante Science. 3rd ed. Fred L. Fifer & Cynthia E. Ledbetter. (J). 1991. student ed. 15.95 (*1-885568-02-9*) SCE Assocs.

Penny Ante Science, Revisited. Fred L. Fifer & Cynthia E. Ledbetter. 174p. (J). 1990. student ed. 15.95 (*1-885568-01-0*) SCE Assocs.

Penny Bank Book: Collecting Still Banks. Andy Moore & Susan Moore. (Schiffer Book for Collectors Ser.). (Illus.). 192p. 1997. 49.95 (*0-7643-0377-5*) Schiffer.

Penny Banks Around the World. Don Duer. LC 96-33470. 200p. (gr. 10). 1997. 49.95 (*0-7643-0019-9*) Schiffer.

Penny Black. Susan Moody. (Missing Mysteries Ser.: Vol. 1). 1997. mass mkt. 7.95 (*1-890208-01-9*) Poisoned Pen.

Penny Candy, a Memoir. Hinda R. Minor. 300p. 1989. 9.95 (*0-9623699-0-X*) R Minor Graph Arts.

Penny Candy Days. Ardyce H. Samp. Ed. by Karen M. Samp & Arthur J. Matson. LC 96-723345. (Illus.). 100p. (Orig.). 1997. pap. 9.95 (*0-9624593-4-8*) Rushmore Hse Pub.

Penny Catechism: Three Hundred & Seventy Fundamental Questions & Answers on the Catholic Faith. W. Doyle Gilligan. 74p. (Orig.). (J). (gr. 5-8). 1982. pap. 1.75 (*0-913382-48-5*, 103-12) Marytown Pr.

Penny Crossword Puzzles, No. 38. Ed. by Ned Webster. (Orig.). 1989. lib. bdg. 9.98 (*0-685-03974-9*) PB.

***Penny Dreadful.** Will Christopher Baer. LC 99-39592. 224p. 2000. 22.95 (*0-670-88920-2*) Viking Penguin.

Penny Dreadfuls & Boys' Adventures. Elizabeth James. (Illus.). 128p. 1997. 60.00 (*0-7123-4528-0*, Pub. by B23tish Library) U of Toronto Pr.

Penny Foolish: A Book of Tirades & Panegyrics. Osbert Sitwell. LC 67-28767. (Essay Index Reprint Ser.). 1977. 23.95 (*0-8369-0881-3*) Ayer.

Penny for a Hundred. Ethel Pochocki. LC 96-30287. (Illus.). 32p. (J). (gr. 3-6). 1996. 14.95 (*0-89272-392-0*) Down East.

Penny for a Rembrandt: A Journal of a Pilgrimage to Assisi, the Holy Land, Rome & the Vatican. T. R. Allen. 202p. 1999. 9.00 (*0-9672704-0-5*) T R Allen.

Penny for a Song. large type ed. Louise James. (General Fiction Ser.). 560p. 1992. 27.99 (*0-7089-2663-0*) Ulverscroft.

Penny for Barnaby. large type ed. Wendy W. Rouillard. (Illus.). 32p. (J). (gr. 1-3). 1998. 15.95 (*0-9642836-7-0*) Barnaby.

Penny for Love. large type ed. Jeanne Bowman. (Linford Romance Library). 240p. 1992. pap. 16.99 (*0-7089-7209-8*, Linford) Ulverscroft.

Penny for Them. Betty Powton. 84p. (C). 1989. 50.00 (*0-7223-2365-4*, Pub. by A H S Ltd) St Mut.

Penny for Your Thoughts: Original Poems. Penny Young. (Illus.). vi, 74p. Date not set. 10.00 (*0-9675593-0-8*) Will & Way.

Penny Fortunes: The One & Only Investment Guide You Need to Read. Isaiah Israel. 112p. 1999. 14.00 (*0-8059-3670-X*) Dorrance.

Penny Hen. Barbara DeRubertis. LC 96-75012. (Let's Read Together Ser.). (Illus.). 32p. (J). (ps-2). 1996. pap. 4.95 (*1-57565-001-0*) Kane Pr.

Penny Lancaster. Elizabeth W. Bellamy. (Works of Elizabeth Whitfield Bellamy). 1989. reprint ed. lib. bdg. 79.00 (*0-7812-1949-3*) Rprt Serv.

Penny Lane: A History of Antique Mechanical Toy Banks. Al Davidson. Ed. by Ida Long & Earnest A. Long. (Illus.). 272p. 1987. 70.00 (*0-9604406-0-7*) Deborah Davidson.

Penny Lane: A History of Antique Toy Banks. deluxe ed. Al Davidson. Ed. by Ida Long & Earnest A. Long. (Illus.). 272p. 1987. 70.00 (*0-9604406-1-5*) Deborah Davidson.

Penny Marshall: An Unauthorized Biography. Louis Chunovic. (Illus.). 256p. 1999. 22.95 (*1-58063-074-X*, Pub. by Renaissance) St Martin.

***Penny Marshall: An Unauthorized Biography of the Director & Comedienne.** Lawrence Crown. 256p. 2000. pap. 15.95 (*1-58063-161-4*) Renaissance.

***Penny Maybe.** Kathleen Martin. 160p. 1999. pap. write for info. (*1-896764-21-5*) Sec Story Pr.

Penny on the Stair & Other Poems. Flora B. Adams. LC 98-16332. 96p. (J). (gr. 6-8). 1998. pap. 10.95 (*1-883911-27-3*) Brandylane.

Penny Parker's Pregnant! Twins on the Doorstep. Stella Bagwell. (Special Edition Ser.: Bk. 1258). 1999. per. 4.25 (*0-373-24258-1*, 1-24258-5) Silhouette.

***Penny Penguin.** Illus. by Dave Sargent & Jane Lenoir. LC 99-59548. (J). 2000. pap. write for info. (*1-56763-456-7*) Ozark Pub.

Penny Pincher's Handbook: Hundreds of Ways to Make, Save Money. Alyce W. Kingsley. LC 80-81850. (Illus.). 88p. (Orig.). 1981. pap. 9.95 (*0-937378-00-3*) Poseidon Pubns.

Penny Pincher's Passport to Luxury Travel: The Art of Cultivating Preferred Customer Status. Joel L. Widzer. LC 99-12211. (Travelers' Tales Ser.). 253p. 1999. pap. 12.95 (*1-885211-31-7*) Trvlers Tale.

Penny Pincher's Profit Portfolio: How to Make Dollars in Cents. Mark Laythorpe. (Illus.). 80p. 1981. pap. 19.95 (*0-939230-00-3*) SNOWCO.

Penny Pinching. large type ed. Susan Moody. 1991. 27.99 (*0-7089-2374-7*) Ulverscroft.

Penny-Pinching Hedonist: How to Live Like Royalty with a Peasant's Pocketbook. Shel Horowitz. LC 95-94233. 280p. 1995. pap. 17.00 (*0-9614666-4-2*) Accurate Writing.

Penny Pinching 1999: How to Lower Your Everyday Expenses Without Lowering Your Standard of Living. Lee Simmons & Barbara Simmons. LC 99-197589. 272p. 1999. mass mkt. 5.99 (*0-553-57367-5*) Bantam.

Penny-Pinching Tom: Depression-1930's. Frank Kubic. LC 96-67265. 24p. (YA). (gr. 8-12). 1996. pap. 4.25 (*0-9636320-8-6*) Nuggets Wisdom.

Penny Plain. large type ed. O. Douglas. 1974. 27.99 (*0-85456-302-4*) Ulverscroft.

Penny Plain Two Pence Coloured: A History of the Juvenile Drama. Albert E. Wilson. LC 68-56476. (Illus.). 1972. reprint ed. 26.95 (*0-405-09080-3*) Ayer.

***Penny Polar Bear & Her Loud Snore.** Paul Flemming. (Snappy Fun Bks.). (Illus.). 12p. (J). (ps-k). 2000. bds. 4.99 (*1-57584-695-0*, Pub. by Rdrs Digest) S&S Trade.

Penny Postcards: Growing up in a Small Southern Town During the Great Depression. L. H. Adams. LC 92-82731. 240p. (Orig.). 1992. pap. 15.00 (*0-9634655-0-3*) Abecedarian.

Penny Pot. Stuart J. Murphy. LC 97-19776. (MathStart Ser.). (Illus.). 40p. (J). (gr. 2-4). 1998. 15.95 (*0-06-027606-1*); lib. bdg. 15.89 (*0-06-027607-X*) HarpC.

Penny Pot: Level 3: Counting Coins. Stuart J. Murphy. LC 97-19776. (MathStart Ser.: Level 3). (Illus.). 40p. (J). (gr. 2-4). 1998. pap. 4.95 (*0-06-446717-1*, HarpTrophy) HarpC Child Bks.

Penny Puzzles, No. 44. Ed. by Ned Webster. 1995. pap. 352.00 (*0-671-81068-5*) PB.

Penny Racers: Prima's Official Strategy Guide. Prima Publishing Staff. 80p. 1999. per. 12.95 (*0-7615-1894-0*, Prima Games) Prima Pub.

***Penny Road.** Barbara Cooper. 392p. 2000. 31.99 (*0-7089-4214-8*) Ulverscroft.

Penny Saved. Neale S. Godfrey & Tad Richards. 240p. 1996. per. 12.00 (*0-684-82480-9*, Fireside) S&S Trade Pap.

Penny Saved: Still & Mechanical Banks. Don Duer. LC 93-85081. (Illus.). 176p. 1993. 59.95 (*0-88740-528-2*) Schiffer.

Penny Saved: Teaching Your Children the Values & Life Skills They Will Need to Live in the Real World. Neale S. Godfrey & Tad Richards. 240p. 1998. text 19.00 (*0-7881-5548-2*) DIANE Pub.

Penny Saved: Using Money to Teach Your Child How the World Works. Neale S. Godfrey & Tad Richards. 1995. 18.95 (*0-684-80397-6*) S&S Trade.

Penny Saving. large type ed. Susan Moody. (Mystery Ser.). 464p. 1993. 27.99 (*0-7089-2938-9*) Ulverscroft.

***Penny Stock Winners: True Stories of Successful Investors.** R. Max Bowser. (Illus.). 220p. 2000. pap. 19.95 (*1-928877-00-1*) Marathon Intl Bk.

Penny Stocks. 256p. 1985. mass mkt. 8.95 (*0-446-38379-1*, Pub. by Warner Bks) Little.

Penny Stocks: How to Profit with Low-Priced Stocks. Jerome Wenger. 1993. pap. 8.95 (*0-8306-8150-7*) McGraw-Hill Prof.

Penny Stocks: Regulatory Actions to Reduce Potential for Fraud & Abuse. (Illus.). 74p. (Orig.). (C). 1994. pap. text 30.00 (*0-7881-0397-0*) DIANE Pub.

***Penny Stocks: The Next American Gold Rush.** Dan Holtzclaw. 1999. pap. text 17.95 (*0-9674758-0-5*) Greek Financial.

Penny Tree. 2nd rev. ed. Will Reese & Phil Switzer. LC 94-910814. (Illus.). 30p. (J). 1994. pap. 7.95 (*1-55105-050-1*) Lone Pine.

***Penny Urned.** Tamar Myers. 288p. 2000. mass mkt. 6.50 (*0-380-81189-8*, Avon Bks) Morrow Avon.

Penny Whimsy. William H. Sheldon. LC 90-91500. (Illus.). 1990. lib. bdg. 60.00 (*0-942666-62-3*) S J Durst.

Penny Whistle: A Gift of Hope for the Beloved Teacher Who Had Given Them So Much. B. J. Hoff. LC 96-45767. 16p. 1996. text 11.99 (*1-55661-877-8*) Bethany Hse.

Penny Whistle Any Day Is a Holiday Book. Meredith Brokaw. 1996. 25.50 (*0-684-83192-9*) S&S Trade.

Penny Whistle Birthday Party Book. Meredith Brokaw & Annie Gilbar. (Illus.). 256p. (Orig.). 1992. per. 14.00 (*0-671-73795-3*) S&S Trade.

Penny Whistle Book. Robin Williamson. LC 76-41141. (Illus.). 64p. (Orig.). 1977. pap. 11.95 (*0-8256-0190-8*, OK63271, Oak) Music Sales.

Penny Whistle Christmas Party Book: Including Hanukkah, New Year's, & Twelfth Night Family Parties. Meredith Brokaw & Annie Gilbar. (Illus.). 128p. (Orig.). 1991. per. 13.00 (*0-671-73794-5*, Fireside) S&S Trade Pap.

Penny Whistle Every Day Is a Holiday Party Book. Meredith Brokaw. LC 96-15083. 256p. 1996. pap. 13.00 (*0-684-80917-6*) S&S Trade.

Penny Whistle Halloween Book. Meredith Brokaw & Annie Gilbar. (Illus.). 80p. 1991. per. 11.00 (*0-671-73791-0*, Fireside) S&S Trade Pap.

Penny Whistle Lunch Box Book. Meredith Brokaw & Annie Gilbar. (Illus.). 96p. 1991. pap. 11.00 (*0-671-73793-7*, Fireside) S&S Trade Pap.

Penny Whistle Party Planner. Meredith Brokaw & Annie Gilbar. (Illus.). 256p. 1991. per. 13.00 (*0-671-73792-9*, Fireside) S&S Trade Pap.

Penny Whistle Primer. Peter Pickow. 1982. pap. 5.95 (*0-8256-0268-8*, AM34877, Oak) Music Sales.

Penny Whistle Sick-in-Bed Book: What to Do with Kids When They're Home for a Day, a Week, a Month or More. Meredith Brokaw & Annie Gilbar. LC 92-44300. (Illus.). 160p. 1993. pap. 12.00 (*0-671-78691-1*, Fireside) S&S Trade Pap.

Penny Whistle Traveling with Kids Book: Whether by Boat, Train, Car, or Plane - How to Take the Best Trip Ever with Kids of All Ages. Meredith Brokaw & Annie Gilbar. LC 94-3604. (Illus.). 160p. 1995. 24.50 (*0-671-88135-3*, Fireside) S&S Trade Pap.

Penny Wise. Jean F. Black. 1945. pap. 5.25 (*0-8222-0883-0*) Dramatists Play.

Penny Wishes. Kimberly Burke-Weiner. LC 96-77306. (Illus.). 32p. (J). (gr. 3-6). 1996. 15.95 (*0-9634637-3-X*); pap. 8.95 (*0-9634637-4-8*) Inquir Voices.

Penny Wonder Drug: What the Label on Your Aspirin Bottle Doesn't Tell You. Eugene Cisek & Robert S. Persky. Ed. by Susan P. Levy. 128p. (Orig.). 1993. pap. 9.95 (*0-913069-31-0*) Consultant Pr.

***Pennybank Book.** 3rd ed. Andy Moore & Susan Moore. (Illus.). 192p. 2000. 49.95 (*0-7643-1082-8*) Schiffer.

Pennybox. large type ed. Alice Dwyer-Joyce. 304p. 1995. 27.99 (*0-7089-3237-1*) Ulverscroft.

Pennyland & Hartigans: Two Iron Age & Saxon Sites in Milton Keynes. R. J. Williams. (Milton Keynes Archaeological Reports). (Illus.). 289p. 1993. pap. 40.00 (*0-949003-11-5*) David Brown.

Pennypickle: Drawing from Life. David Jaquith. Ed. by Mary Jaquith. (Illus.). 64p. 1990. write for info. (*0-9622551-1-4*) Sea Hse Pubs.

Pennypincher's Guide to Landscaping. Carol A. Boston. LC 84-17775. 192p. 1984. 17.95 (*0-13-655937-9*, Busn); pap. 7.95 (*0-13-655929-8*, Busn) P-H.

Pennyroyal. Stacy J. Tuthill. LC 91-62475. (SCOP Ser.: No. 17). 72p. 1991. pap. 9.95 (*0-930526-16-3*) SCOP Pubns.

Pennyroyal. large type ed. Stella Whitelaw. (Lythway Ser.). 200p. 1990. 18.95 (*0-7451-1242-0*, G K Hall Lrg Type) Mac Lib Ref.

***Penny's Practical Guide to Advanced Projects.** Penny Muncaster-Jewell. 250p. 1999. pap. 75.00 (*0-9672149-2-0*) Canstar.

Penny's Practical Guide to PE-Design. Penny Muncaster-Jewell. (Illus.). 282p. 1997. pap. 75.00 (*0-9672149-0-4*) Canstar.

***Penny's Practical Guide to PE-Designs, Palette & Deco Wizard.** Penny Muncaster-Jewell. 1999. pap. 75.00 (*0-9672149-1-2*) Canstar.

Penny's Worth of Character. 3rd ed. Jesse H. Stuart. Ed. by Jerry A. Herndon et al. LC 92-31438. (Jesse Stuart Foundation Juvenile Ser.). (Illus.). 62p. (J). (gr. 3-6). 1993. reprint ed. pap. 4.00 (*0-945084-32-3*) J Stuart Found.

Penny's Worth of Minced Ham: Another Look at the Great Depression. Robert J. Hastings. LC 85-31731. (Shawnee Bks.). (Illus.). 114p. (Orig.). 1986. pap. 9.95 (*0-8093-1304-9*) S Ill U Pr.

Pennystock Information: How to Find or Locate Information on Pennystock. rev. ed. Data Notes Research Staff. LC 83-90739. 1997. ring bd. 29.95 (*0-911569-60-X*) Prosperity & Profits.

Pennyweight More. Charlotte D. Hutchens. LC 94-185226. 321p. 1994. pap. 15.95 (*0-934188-38-6*) Evans Pubns.

PennyWise Gifts for Kids. Nancy Goodman & Leslie Rice. (Illus.). 64p. (Orig.). 1990. pap. text 12.95 (*0-941233-75-8*) Source Okla.

***Pennywise Pound Foolish: Self Discovery Exercises Workbook.** Ed. by Carolyn J. Griffin. 60p. 1999. spiral bd., wbk. ed. 20.00 (*1-929388-16-0*) Griffin Pubg Co Inc.

Penobscot. Katherine Doherty. (First Bks., Indians of North America). (Illus.). 64p. (J). (gr. 4-6). 1996. reprint ed. pap. 6.95 (*0-531-15764-4*) Watts.

Penobscot: Nine Poems. Stephen Tapscott. 23p. (Orig.). (C). 1983. pap. 10.00 (*0-913219-37-1*) Pym-Rand Pr.

Penobscot: Nine Poems. deluxe ed. Stephen Tapscott. 23p. (Orig.). (C). 1983. 15.00 (*0-913219-38-X*) Pym-Rand Pr.

Penobscot Island & Other Poems: Saga of a Maine Lobsterman's Family. Phoebe B. Driver. 1992. 15.00 (*0-87233-105-9*); pap. 9.95 (*0-87233-109-1*) Bauhan.

Penobscot Man. Fannie H. Eckstorm. LC 74-128733. (Short Story Index Reprint Ser.). 1977. 21.95 (*0-8369-3624-8*) Ayer.

Penobscot Man. rev. ed. Frank G. Speck. (Native Studies). (Illus.). 404p. 1997. 35.00 (*0-89101-095-5*); pap. 15.00 (*0-89101-092-0*) U Maine Pr.

Penobscot Pioneers, Vol. 5. Philip H. Gray. 224p. 1995. 35.00 (*0-89725-241-1*, 1629, Penobscot Pr) Picton Pr.

Penobscot Pioneers Vol. 2: Bray, Closson, Howard. Philip H. Gray. LC 91-68230. 160p. 1992. 35.00 (*0-929539-58-3*, 1398, Penobscot Pr) Picton Pr.

Penobscot Pioneers Vol. 3: Billings, Gray, Herrick. Philip H. Gray. LC 91-68230. 1993. 35.00 (*0-89725-130-X*, 1443, Penobscot Pr) Picton Pr.

Penobscot Pioneers Vol. 4: Eaton, Haskell, Marchant, Raynes. Philip H. Gray. 192p. 1994. 35.00 (*0-89725-183-0*, 1528) Picton Pr.

Penobscot Pioneers Vol. 6: Lawrence, Michaels, Perry, Wescott. Philip H. Gray. LC 91-68230. (Illus.). 192p. 1996. 35.00 (*0-89725-270-5*, 1764) Picton Pr.

Penobscot River Renaissance: Restoring America's Premier Atlantic Salmon Fishery. deluxe limited ed. James E. Butler & Arthur Taylor. LC 92-90314. (Illus.). 160p. 1992. 50.00 (*0-89272-325-4*, Silver Quill Pr) Down East.

Penobscot, the Forest, River & Bay. Ed. by David D. Platt. (Illus.). 200p. (Orig.). 1997. reprint ed. pap. 16.95 (*0-942719-16-6*) Island Inst.

Penobscot Vital Records. Donna Hoffmann. 125p. 1983. pap. 19.95 (*0-941216-13-6*) Cay-Bel.

Penological Esperanto & Sentencing Parochialism: A Comparative Study of the Search for Non-Prison Punishments. Malcolm Davies et al. (Illus.). 240p. 1996. 87.95 (*1-85521-772-4*, Pub. by Dartmth Pub) Ashgate Pub Co.

Penology for Profit: A History of the Texas Prison System, 1867-1912. Donald R. Walker. LC 87-18048. (Southwestern Studies: No. 7). (Illus.). 232p. 1988. 28.95 (*0-89096-315-0*) Tex A&M Univ Pr.

Penon de las Animas. Orlando R. Lopez. (Romance Real Ser.). 192p. (Orig.). pap. 1.50 (*0-88025-007-0*) Roca Pub.

Penpoint Programming. Andrew Novobilski. LC 92-13076. 400p. (C). 1992. pap. text 26.95 (*0-201-60833-2*) Addison-Wesley.

Penpoints, Gunpoints & Dreams: Towards a Critical Theory of the Arts & the State in Africa. Ngugi wa Thiong'o. (Clarendon Lectures in English). 152p. 1998. text 35.00 (*0-19-818390-9*) OUP.

Penguin Book of 20th-Century Speeches. Ed. by Brian MacArthur. 512p. (C). 1994. pap. 15.95 (*0-14-023234-6*) Viking Penguin.

Penrod. Booth Tarkington. LC 85-42910. (Library of Indiana Classics). (Illus.). 320p. 1985. 25.00 (*0-253-34311-9*); pap. 11.95 (*0-253-20361-9*, MB-361) Ind U Pr.

Penrod. Booth Tarkington. reprint ed. lib. bdg. 25.95 (*0-88411-701-4*) Amereon Ltd.

Penrod. Booth Tarkington. 321p. 1983. reprint ed. lib. bdg. 27.95 (*0-89966-178-5*) Buccaneer Bks.

***Penrod.** Booth Tarkington. (Works of Booth Tarkington). 345p. 1999. reprint ed. lib. bdg. 108.00 (*1-58201-864-2*) Classic Bks.

Penrod & Sam. Booth Tarkington. 1975. lib. bdg. 21.95 (*0-89966-179-3*) Buccaneer Bks.

Penrod de Sam. Booth Tarkington. reprint ed. lib. bdg. 22.95 (*0-88411-702-2*) Amereon Ltd.

***Penrod & Sam.** Booth Tarkington. (Works of Booth Tarkington). 356p. 1999. reprint ed. lib. bdg. 108.00 (*1-58201-865-0*) Classic Bks.

Penrod Jasber. Booth Tarkington. 18.95 (*0-8488-1480-0*) Amereon Ltd.

Penrod Jasber. Booth Tarkington. 321p. 1983. reprint ed. lib. bdg. 17.95 (*0-89966-180-7*) Buccaneer Bks.

Penrod, the Dancing Emperor Penguin. unabridged ed. Henrietta Roginski. LC 96-92654. (Illus.). 24p. (J). (ps-6). 1996. pap. 20.95 incl. VHS (*0-9652248-1-3*, 1) H Roginski.

Penrod, the Dancing Emperor Penguin. unabridged ed. Henrietta Roginski. LC 96-92654. (Illus.). 24p. (J). (ps-6). 1996. pap. 10.95 (*0-9652248-0-5*, 1) H Roginski.

Penrose Mystery. Austin R. Freeman. 274p. 1977. reprint ed. lib. bdg. 13.95 (*0-89966-275-7*) Buccaneer Bks.

Penrose Tiles to Trapdoor Cipers: And the Return of Dr. Matrix. rev. ed. Martin Gardner. LC 97-70505. (Spectrum Ser.). (Illus.). 312p. 1997. pap. text 27.95 (*0-88385-521-6*, TILES/PMDS97) Math Assn.

Penrose Titles (1987-8), Time Travel (1925-8), Knotted Donuts (1799-8), Set. Martin Gardner. 1989. pap. text 28.00 (*0-7167-2066-3*) W H Freeman.

Penrose Transform: Its Interaction with Representation Theory. Robert J. Baston & Michael G. Eastwood. (Oxford Mathematical Monographs). (Illus.). 228p. 1990. text 65.00 (*0-19-853565-1*) OUP.

Penrose Transform & Analytic Cohomology in Representation Theory: AMS-IMS-SIAM Joint Summer Research Conference, June 27-July 3, 1992, Supported by the National Science Foundation. Ed. by Michael Eastwood et al. LC 93-27398. (Contemporary Mathematics Ser.: Vol. 154). 259p. 1993. pap. 47.00 (*0-8218-5176-4*, CONM/154) Am Math.

Penruthin's Wife. large type ed. Pauline Bentley. 350p. 1996. 23.99 (*0-263-14523-9*, Pub. by Mills & Boon) Ulverscroft.

Penry Penalty: Capital Punishment & Offenders with Mental Retardation. Emily F. Reed. LC 92-44124. 1993. 54.50 (*0-8191-9019-5*); pap. 29.50 (*0-8191-9020-9*) U Pr of Amer.

Pens & Pencils. rev. ed. Regina Martini. (Illus.). 148p. 1998. pap. 24.95 (*0-7643-0313-9*) Schiffer.

Pens & Personalities. Joseph Ranald. 25.95 (*0-685-01130-5*) NCUP.

Pens & Writing Equipment: A Collector's Guide. (Illus.). 64p. 1999. 11.95 (*1-84000-146-1*) Antique Collect.

Pens Excellencie or the Secretaries Delight. Martin Billingsley. LC 77-6852. (English Experience Ser.: No. 849). 1977. reprint ed. lib. bdg. 20.00 (*90-221-0849-X*) Walter J Johnson.

Pens from the Wood Lathe. Dick Sing. LC 95-37217. 64p. (YA). (gr. 10). 1996. pap. 12.95 (*0-88740-939-3*) Schiffer.

Pensacola: Spaniards to Space Age. Virginia Parks. (Illus.). 128p. 1986. 9.95 (*0-939566-04-4*) Pensacola Hist.

***Pensacola During the Civil War: A Thorn in the Side of the Confederacy.** George F. Pearce. LC 99-43001. (Florida History & Culture Ser.). (Illus.). 304p. 2000. 29.95 (*0-8130-1770-X*) U Press Fla.

Pensacola Florida, 1. Rand McNally Staff. (Rand McNally Streetfinder Ser.). 1999. pap. text 16.95 (*0-528-97878-0*) Rand McNally.

Pensacola Florida's First Place City. Jesse E. Bowden et al. (Illus.). 207p. 1989. 29.95 (*0-89865-777-6*) Pensacola Hist.

P

Pensacola Fortifications, 1698-1980: Guardians of the Gulf. James C. Coleman & Irene S. Coleman. (Illus.). 120p. 1983. pap. 7.95 (*0-939566-02-8*) Pensacola Hist.

Pensacola, the Old & the New. 1988. pap. 2.95 (*0-939566-05-2*) Pensacola Hist.

Pensacola's Currency Issuing Banks & Their Bank Notes, 1833-1935. Philip A. Pfeiffer. Ed. by Marguerite P. Romond. LC 75-6130. (Illus.). 1975. pap. 19.95 (*0-9601038-1-3*) Pfeiffer.

***Pensacola's Soda Water Legacy, 1837-1998.** Philip A. Pfeiffer. Ed. by Mary M. Dawkins. LC 98-92279. (Illus.). 1998. pap. 19.95 (*0-9601038-3-X*) Pfeiffer.

Pensadores de America Latina see Pensamiento en America

Pensadores de Oriente. Idries Shah. (SPA.). 1989. pap. 15.00 (*84-7245-207-7*) Octagon Pr.

Pensadores Hispano-Americans. Intro. by Jose I. Rasco. LC 95-60332. (SPA.). 218p. (Orig.). 1995. pap. 15.00 (*0-89729-770-9*) Ediciones.

Pensamiento Cristiano Revolucionario en America Latina y el Caribe. Samuel S. Gotay. LC 88-80390. 394p. 1989. pap. 13.50 (*0-940238-97-7*) Ediciones Huracan.

***Pensamiento de Pablo.** Herman Ridderbos. Ed. by Humberto Casanova & Alejandro Pimentel.Tr. of Paul: An Outline of His Theology. (SPA.). 2000. write for info. (*1-55883-119-3*) Libros Desafio.

Pensamiento en America, 2 vols. Incl. No. 1. Panorama de las Ideas en Latinoamerica. 24p. 1971. pap. 1.00 No. 2. Pensadores de America Latina. 16p. 1972. pap. 1.00 (*0-8270-5875-6*); No. 3. pap. 1.00 (*0-8270-5895-0*); No. 4. pap. 1.00 (*0-8270-5890-X*); (SPA.). pap. write for info. (*0-318-54738-4*) OAS.

Pensamiento Geometrico. Livia P. Denis. (SPA.). 134p. 1996. pap. write for info. (*0-929441-59-1*) Pubns Puertorriquenas.

Pensamiento Martiano: Diccionario. 2nd ed. Adalberto Alvarado. Ed. by Lucia Garcia & Maggie Ghazi. 376p. 1994. pap. text 14.95 (*0-9641506-0-3*) Edit Interamerica.

Pensamiento Mexicano en el Siglo XX. Villegas. (SPA.). pap. 10.99 (*968-16-4133-7*, Pub. by Fondo) Continental Bk.

Pensamiento Politico en Europa, 1250-1450. Antony Black.Tr. of Political Thought in Europe, 1250-1450. (SPA.). 337p. (C). 1996. pap. 17.95 (*0-521-47831-6*) Cambridge U Pr.

Pensamiento Positivo para Cada Dia. Norman Vincent Peale.Tr. of Positive Thinking Everyday. (SPA.). 384p. 1995. per. 10.00 (*0-684-81553-2*, Fireside) S&S Trade Pap.

Pensamiento Salvaje. Claude Levi-Strauss. (Breviarios Ser.). (SPA.). pap. 9.99 (*968-16-0933-6*, Pub. by Fondo) Continental Bk.

Pensamiento y Forma en la Prosa de Gabriela Mistral. Luis De Arrigoitia. LC 89-33662. 408p. (Orig.). 1989. pap. 18.50 (*0-8477-3613-X*) U of PR Pr.

Pensamiento y Religion en el Mexico Antiguo. L. Sejourne. (Breviarios Ser.). (SPA.). pap. 8.99 (*968-16-0554-3*, Pub. by Fondo) Continental Bk.

***Pensamientos.** (Musica Clasica Para Toda Ocasion Ser.: Vol. 2).Tr. of Meditations. (SPA., Illus.). 30p. 2000. write for info. (*1-892207-57-5*) Intl Masters Pub.

Pensamientos. Kita Antonia. (SPA.). 108p. (Orig.). 1994. pap. 15.00 (*1-887116-07-9*) Saxon West Pubns.

Pensamientos. Smith & Felix. 172p. 1998. pap. text 26.00 (*0-536-01390-X*) Pearson Custom.

Pensamientos: Esperanza y Paz. Tr. of Hope & Peace. (SPA.). 24p. 1989. pap. write for info. (*0-614-27106-1*) Editorial Unilit.

Pensamientos: Esperanza y Paz (Hope & Peace) (SPA.). 24p. 1989. write for info. (*0-614-24392-0*) Editorial Unilit.

***Pensamientos Cotidianos 2000.** (SPA., Illus.). 366p. 1999. pap. 8.95 (*2-85566-792-5*, Pub. by Prosveta) Prosveta USA.

Pensamientos (Seed Thoughts) El Tiene Cuidado (Someone Who Cares) (SPA.). 1.25 (*0-8423-6400-5*, 497116) Editorial Unilit.

Pensamientos (Seed Thoughts) Para Alguien Especial (For Someone Special) (SPA.). 1.25 (*0-685-74973-8*, 497107) Editorial Unilit.

Pensamientos (Seed Thoughts) Para Mama (For My Mother) (SPA.). 1.25 (*0-685-74974-6*, 497108) Editorial Unilit.

Pensamientos (Seed Thoughts) Para Mi Esposa (For My Wife) (SPA.). 1.25 (*0-8423-6280-0*, 497109) Editorial Unilit.

Pensamientos (Seed Thoughts) Para Mi Esposo (For My Husband) (SPA.). 1.25 (*0-8423-6281-9*, 497110) Editorial Unilit.

Pensamientos (Seed Thoughts) Para Papa (For My Father) (SPA.). 1.25 (*0-8423-6282-7*, 497111) Editorial Unilit.

Pensamientos (Seed Thoughts) Un Saludo Amistoso (A Friendly Hello) (SPA.). 1.25 (*0-8423-6283-5*, 497112) Editorial Unilit.

Pensamientos Sobre la Cultura Intelectural Y Moral (Thoughts on Intellectual & Moral Culture. Enrique Aguilar. 230p. 1967. pap. 7.00 (*1-57659-109-3*) Franciscan Inst.

Pensando en Su Nino. 5th ed. Ed. by Maria E. Alvarez del Real. LC 81-71533. (SPA., Illus.). 448p. 1985. pap. 5.95 (*0-944499-09-0*) Editorial Amer.

Pensando Logicamente Sobre una Sociedad Futura. Harvey Jackins. Tr. by Isabel Flores. Orig. Title: Logical Thinking about a Future Society. (SPA.). 1995. pap. 3.00 (*1-885357-12-5*) Rational Isl.

Pensar a Jose Marti: Notas para un Centenario. Enrico M. Santi. LC 95-72862. (Cuban Literary Studies). (SPA., Illus.). 138p. 1996. pap. 25.00 (*0-89295-085-4*) Society Sp & Sp-Am.

Pensar Bien y Mal. 2nd ed. Kenneth E. Hagin.Tr. of Right & Wrong Thinking. (SPA.). 1983. pap. 2.95 (*0-89276-104-0*) Faith Lib Pubns.

Pensar el Ser, No. 20, Vol. 447. Luis Romera. v, 352p. 1994. 53.95 (*3-906753-28-X*) P Lang Pubng.

Pensar Es un Pecado. Exora Renteros. LC 93-74793. (Coleccion Caniqui). 198p. 1994. pap. 16.00 (*0-89729-720-2*) Ediciones.

Pensar Logico. Jose M. Lazaro. 321p. 1988. 6.50 (*0-8477-2825-0*) U of PR Pr.

Pensari. Robert Katz. (Illus.). 48p. (Orig.). 1986. pap. 14.95 (*0-912938-10-2*) Kepler Pr.

***Pensativo: Poems & Watercolors.** Pat Richards. (Illus.). vi, 76p. 2000. pap. 16.95 (*0-9662263-1-3*) P Richards.

Pensee Chinoise: Chinese Thought. Marcel Granet. LC 74-25753. (European Sociology Ser.). 642p. 1975. reprint ed. 51.95 (*0-405-06507-8*) Ayer.

Pensee et la Mouvant. 4th ed. Henri Bergson. (FRE.). 1993. pap. 28.95 (*0-7859-3447-2*) Fr & Eur.

Pensee et le Mouvement. Henri Bergson. 39.95 (*0-685-37210-3*) Fr & Eur.

Pensee et Structure Text. 2nd ed. Darbelne. 1985. 16.95 (*0-684-14882-X*) S&S Trade.

Pensee Medievale en Occident: Theologie, Magique et Autres Textes du XIIe-XIIe Siecle. Marie T. D'Alverny. Ed. by Charles Burnett. (Collected Studies: No. CS511). 352p. 1995. text 119.95 (*0-86078-538-6*, Pub. by Variorum) Ashgate Pub Co.

Pensee Metaphysique de Descartes. Gouhier. 89.95 (*0-685-34225-5*) Fr & Eur.

***Pensee Pedagogique.** Ed. by Monique Samuel-Scheyder & Philippe Alexandre. (Illus.). xx, 412p. 1999. 55.95 (*3-906762-62-9*) P Lang Pubng.

Pensee Philosophique de Maupertuis, Son Milieu et Ses Sources. Giorgio Tonelli. (Studien und Materialien Zur Geschichte der Philosophie Ser.: No. 25). 160p. 1987. write for info. (*3-487-07823-6*) G Olms Pubs.

Pensee Politique de Platon. Jean Luccioni. Ed. by J. P. Mayer. LC 78-67365. (European Political Thought Ser.). (FRE.). 1980. reprint ed. lib. bdg. 28.95 (*0-405-11715-9*) Ayer.

Pensee Sauvage. rev. ed. Claude Levi-Strauss. (FRE.). 1985. 15.95 (*2-266-03816-8*) Adlers Foreign Bks.

Pensee 68. Luc Ferry & Alain Renaut. (Folio Essais Ser.: No. 101). (FRE.). pap. 12.95 (*2-07-032489-3*) Schoenhof.

Pensee Socio-Politique au Quebec, 1784-1812: Analyse Semantique. John E. Hare. LC 78-373952. (Cahiers du Centre de Recherche en Civilisation Canadienne-Francaise: Vol. 13). (FRE.). 103p. 1977. reprint ed. pap. 32.00 (*0-608-02206-3*, 206287600004) Bks Demand.

Pensees, 2 vols. Blaise Pascal. 4.50 (*0-685-73318-1*); pap. 5.95 (*0-685-34246-8*) Fr & Eur.

Pensees. Blaise Pascal. Ed. by Desgranges. (Coll. Prestige). 29.95 (*0-685-34245-X*) Fr & Eur.

Pensees, 2 vols. Blaise Pascal. 1977. pap. 10.95 (*0-7859-4079-0*); pap. 11.95 (*0-7859-4080-4*) Fr & Eur.

Pensees. Blaise Pascal. Ed. by Desgranges. (FRE.). 657p. 1991. pap. 55.00 (*0-7859-4650-0*) Fr & Eur.

Pensees. Henri Rochard. (Illus.). 1977. reprint ed. pap. 5.00 (*0-686-21180-4*) Maple Mont.

Pensees. rev. ed. Blaise Pascal. Tr. by Alban J. Krailsheimer from FRE. 368p. 1995. pap. 9.95 (*0-14-044645-1*, Penguin Classics) Viking Penguin.

Pensees: Le Spicilege. Charles-Louis De Montesquieu. (FRE.). 1991. pap. 59.95 (*0-7859-3032-9*) Fr & Eur.

Pensees: The Thoughts of Dan Quayle. Michael Martone. 100p. (Orig.). 1994. pap. 8.95 (*0-9639885-0-6*) Broad Ripple.

Pensees - Lettres a un Provincial. unabridged ed. Blaise Pascal. (FRE.). pap. 8.95 (*2-87714-297-3*, Pub. by Bookking Intl) Distribks Inc.

Pensees & Letters of Joseph Joubert. Joseph Joubert. 1977. 17.95 (*0-8369-6945-6*, 7826) Ayer.

Pensees & Other Writings. Blaise Pascal. Tr. by Honor Levi & Anthony Levi. (Oxford World's Classics Ser.). 312p. 1999. pap. 8.95 (*0-19-283655-2*) OUP.

Pensees du Coeur. Louise L. Hay. 256p. 1992. 19.95 (*2-920083-62-7*) Edns Roseau.

Pensees of Pascal: A Study in Baroque Style. M. Julie Maggioni. LC 79-94181. (Catholic University of America. Studies in Romance Languages & Literatures: No. 39). reprint ed. 37.50 (*0-404-50339-X*) AMS Pr.

Pensees Philosophiques. 3rd ed. Denis Diderot. 75p. 1965. 10.95 (*0-8288-9959-2*, F46930) Fr & Eur.

Pensees pour Transformer Votre Vie. Louise L. Hay.Tr. of Meditations to Heal Your Life. 259p. 1995. 22.95 (*2-920083-96-1*) Edns Roseau.

Pensees Sous les Nuages & Beauregard see Under Clouded Skies/Beauregard

Pensees sur l'Interpretation de la Nature: Avec: Varloot, Jean. La Pensee de Diderot dans l'Encyclopedie. 2nd ed. Denis Diderot. 9.95 (*0-686-56023-X*) Fr & Eur.

Penser la Revolution Francaise. Francois Furet. (Folio-Histoire Ser.: No. 3). (FRE.). 315p. 1978. pap. 11.95 (*2-07-032298-X*) Schoenhof.

Penshurst: The Semiotics of Place & the Poetics of History. Don E. Wayne. LC 83-40273. (Illus.). 245p. 1984. reprint ed. pap. 76.00 (*0-608-07450-0*, 206767700009) Bks Demand.

Pensieri. Giacomo Leopardi. Tr. by W. S. Di Piero. LC 81-11745. 180p. reprint ed. pap. 55.80 (*0-7837-8809-6*, 204945500011) Bks Demand.

Pension Administration: Forms System Jeffery Mandell. LC 99-202101. 1998. ring bd. 185.00 (*0-7355-0066-5*) Panel Pubs.

Pension Administrator's Form Book. Paul C. Stein & Lewis Schier. LC 87-2299. 1987. 98.00 (*0-916592-68-5*) Panel Pubs.

Pension & Benefits Law, 1998. 1600p. 1998. pap. text 55.00 (*0-7811-0176-X*) Res Inst Am.

Pension & Benefits Law, 1997. rev. ed. 1900p. 1997. pap. 55.00 (*0-7811-0157-3*) Res Inst Am.

Pension & Benefits Law, 1999. rev. ed. Contrib. by In-House Professionals Staff. 1726p. 1999. pap. text 55.00 (*0-7811-0209-X*) Res Inst Am.

Pension & Benefits Law, 1995. rev. ed. RIA In-House Professional Staff. 1456p. 1995. pap. text 55.00 (*0-7811-0102-6*) Res Inst Am.

Pension & Benefits Law, 1996. rev. ed. RIA In-House Professional Staff. LC 97-117134. 1744p. 1996. pap. text 55.00 (*0-7811-0133-6*) Res Inst Am.

Pension & Benefits Law, 1993. rev. ed. RIA In-House Professional Staff. 2200p. 1993. pap. text 55.00 (*0-7811-0068-2*) Res Inst Am.

Pension & Benefits Law, 1994. rev. ed. RIA In-House Professional Staff. 1712p. 1994. pap. text 55.00 (*0-7811-0087-9*) Res Inst Am.

***Pension & Benefits Law, 2000.** rev. ed. In-House Professionals Staff. 1792p. 2000. pap. 55.00 (*0-7811-0230-8*) Res Inst Am.

Pension & Benefits Regulations, 1994. RIA In-House Professional Staff. 2880p. 1994. pap. text 75.00 (*0-7811-0086-0*) Res Inst Am.

Pension & Benefits Regulations, 1997. rev. ed. 1880p. 1997. pap. text 75.00 (*0-7811-0158-1*) Res Inst Am.

Pension & Benefits Regulations, 1998. rev. ed. 1950p. 1998. pap. text 75.00 (*0-7811-0177-8*) Res Inst Am.

Pension & Benefits Regulations, 1999. rev. ed. Contrib. by In-House Professionals Staff. 2010p. 1999. pap. text 75.00 (*0-7811-0210-3*) Res Inst Am.

Pension & Benefits Regulations, 1995. rev. ed. RIA In-House Professional Staff. 2912p. 1995. pap. text 75.00 (*0-7811-0103-4*) Res Inst Am.

Pension & Benefits Regulations, 1996. rev. ed. RIA In-House Professional Staff. 2192p. 1996. pap. text 75.00 (*0-7811-0134-4*) Res Inst Am.

Pension & Benefits Regulations, 1993. rev. ed. RIA In-House Professional Staff. 2700p. 1993. pap. text 75.00 (*0-7811-0069-0*) Res Inst Am.

***Pension & Benefits Regulations, 2000.** rev. ed. In-House Professionals Staff. 2016p. 2000. pap. 75.00 (*0-7811-0231-6*) Res Inst Am.

Pension & Employee Benefit Changes under 1997 Tax & Budget Acts. CCH Editorial Staff. 272p. Date not set. pap. text 39.00 (*0-8080-0161-2*) CCH INC.

Pension & Employee Benefit Law. John H. Langbein & Bruce A. Wolk. (University Casebook Ser.). 673p. 1990. text 37.95 (*0-88277-780-7*) Foundation Pr.

Pension & Employee Benefit Law. 2nd ed. John H. Langbein & Bruce A. Wolk. (Illus.). xlix, 923p. 1995. text 44.95 (*1-56662-243-3*) Foundation Pr.

Pension & Employee Benefit Law: Teacher's Manual. John H. Langbein & Bruce A. Wolk. (University Casebook Ser.). 202p. 1990. pap. text. write for info. (*0-88277-848-X*) Foundation Pr.

Pension & Employee Benefit Law: 1998 Case Supplement. 2nd ed. Langbein & Wolk. 1998. write for info. (*1-56662-647-1*) Foundation Pr.

Pension & Employee Benefit Law, 1994 Supplement. John H. Langbein & Bruce A. Wolk. (University Textbook Ser.). 175p. 1994. 9.00 (*1-56662-203-4*) Foundation Pr.

Pension & Employee Benefit Law, 1991 Supplement. John H. Langbein & Bruce A. Wolk. 87p. (C). 1991. pap. text. write for info. (*0-318-68679-1*) Foundation Pr.

Pension & Employee Benefit Law, 1997 Supplement. 2nd ed. John H. Langbein & Bruce A. Wolk. (University Casebook Ser.). 83p. 1997. pap. text, write for info. (*1-56662-404-5*) Foundation Pr.

Pension & Employee Benefits Code: ERISA - Regulations - Preambles, As of March 1, 1996, 3 vols., Set. 4680p. 1997. pap. 93.00 (*0-685-67158-5*, 4742) CCH INC.

Pension & Employee Benefits Code: ERISA - Regulations, As of March 1, 1996, 2 vols., Set. 3616p. 1997. pap. 66.00 (*0-685-67157-7*, 4743) CCH INC.

***Pension & Employee Benefits Code - ERISA - Regulations, Vol. 2.** CCH Editors. 2200p. 2000. pap. 57.50 (*0-8080-0460-3*) CCH INC.

Pension & Employee Benefits Code - ERISA - Regulations: ERISA Law & Regulations - Related Laws - Proposed Regulations. rev. ed. CCH Editorial Staff Publication. 4550p. 1998. pap. 39.50 (*0-8080-0235-X*) CCH INC.

***Pension & Employee Benefits Code - ERISA - Regulations Vol. 1: Internal Revenue Code & Regulations.** CCH Editors. 2300p. 2000. pap. 57.50 (*0-8080-0461-1*) CCH INC.

***Pension & Employee Benefits Code - ERISA - Regulations Vol. 3: Preambles.** CCH Editors. 1300p. 2000. pap. 32.00 (*0-8080-0459-X*) CCH INC.

Pension & Employee Benefits Code - ERISA - Regulations Vol. 3: Preambles to Final & Temporary Regulations. rev. ed. CCH Editorial Staff. 1216p. 1998. pap. 30.00 (*0-8080-0236-8*) CCH INC.

Pension & Employee Benefits Code ERISA Regulations Vol. 1: Internal Revenue Code & Regulations. rev. ed. CCH Editorial Staff. 2000p. 1998. pap. 39.50 (*0-8080-0234-1*) CCH INC.

Pension & Employee Benefits, Code, ERISA, Regulations as of January 1, 1999 Vol. 1: Internal Revenue Code & Regulations. CCH Editorial Staff. 2300p. 1999. pap. 54.50 (*0-8080-0341-0*) CCH INC.

Pension & Employee Benefits, Code, ERISA, Regulations as of January 1, 1999 Vol. 2: ERISA Laws & Regulations Related Laws Proposed Regulations. CCH Editorial Staff. 1450p. 1999. pap. 54.50 (*0-8080-0342-9*) CCH INC.

Pension & Employee Benefits, Code, ERISA, Regulations as of January 1, 1999 Vol. 3: Preambles to Final & Temporary Regulations. CCH Editorial Staff. 1250p. 1999. pap. 30.00 (*0-8080-0343-7*) CCH INC.

Pension & Profit Sharing Plans for Small & Medium Size Businesses. Francis X. Roche. LC 79-92397. 1984. 150.00 (*0-916592-48-0*) Panel Pubs.

Pension Answer Book. 6th ed. Stephen J. Krass. Ed. by JoAnne S. Haffeman. 1990. 79.00 (*1-878375-33-4*) Panel Pubs.

Pension Answer Book. 9th ed. J. Carl Shrader & Stuart A. Weisberg. 776p. 106.00 (*1-56706-004-8*, 60048) Panel Pubs.

Pension Answer Book. annuals 11th ed. Stephen J. Krass. 1064p. 1995. 118.00 (*1-56706-115-X*) Panel Pubs.

Pension Answer Book: Forms & Worksheets. J. Carl Shrader & Stuart A. Weisberg. 359p. 59.00 (*1-878375-49-0*); pap. 69.00 (*1-56706-010-2*, 60102) Panel Pubs.

Pension Answer Book: Nonqualified Deferred Compensation. Bruce J. McNeil. Ed. by Mark D. Persons. 277p. 1991. 89.00 (*1-878375-40-7*) Panel Pubs.

Pension Answer Book: Nonqualified Deferred Compensation. Bruce J. McNeil & Mark D. Persons. 169p. 1990. pap. text 49.00 (*1-878375-17-2*) Panel Pubs.

Pension Answer Book: Special Supplement, Forms & Checklists. J. Carl Shrader & Stuart A. Weisberg. Ed. by Mark D. Persons. 560p. 1991. pap. 59.00 (*1-878375-64-4*) Panel Pubs.

Pension Answer Book: 1998 Edition. annuals Stephen J. Krass. 1184p. boxed set 125.00 (*1-56706-429-9*, 64299) Panel Pubs.

Pension Answer Book, 1997. Stephen J. Krass. 1128p. 1997. 125.00 (*1-56706-361-6*, 63616) Aspen Pub.

Pension Answer Book, 1997: Forms & Worksheets. rev. ed. 592p. 1997. 125.00 (*1-56706-430-2*) Aspen Pub.

Pension Answer Book, 1992. Stephen J. Krass. Ed. by JoAnne S. Haffeman. 776p. 1991. text 96.00 (*1-878375-75-X*) Panel Pubs.

Pension Beaurepas see Works of Henry James Jr.: Collected Works

***Pension Benefit Guaranty Corporation 1998 Annual Report.** Government Printing Office Staff. 47p. 1999. per. 4.00 (*0-16-049938-0*) USGPO.

***Pension Benefit Guaranty Corporation 1999 Annual Report.** 47p. 2000. per. 5.00 (*0-16-050314-0*, Pension Benefit) USGPO.

Pension Book: What You Need to Know to Prepare for Retirement. Kate Blackwell & Karen Ferguson. LC 96-84308. (Illus.). 288p. 1996. pap. 12.45 (*1-55970-331-8*, Pub. by Arcade Pub Inc) Time Warner.

Pension Choices. A Survey on Personal Pensions in Comparison with Other Pension Options. T. Williams & J. Field. (DSS Research Report Ser.). 1993. 40.00 (*0-11-762091-2*, Pub. by Statnry Office) Bernan Associates.

Pension Claims: Rights & Obligations. 2nd ed. Stephen R. Bruce. LC 92-42811. 883p. 1993. 145.00 (*0-87179-743-7*, 0743) BNA Books.

***Pension Dispute Resolution: An Easy Guide.** Vuyani Ngalawana. 1999. pap. 17.00 (*0-7021-4914-4*, Pub. by Juta & Co) Gaunt.

Pension Disputes & Settlements, Supplement No. 3. Seymour Goldberg. LC 78-59106. 435p. reprint ed. pap. 134.90 (*0-8357-9482-2*, 201618500001) Bks Demand.

Pension Distribution Answer Book. annuals Melanie N. Aska Knox & Joan Gucciardi. LC 98-171631. 1104p. 1998. boxed set 136.00 (*1-56706-431-0*, 64310) Panel Pubs.

Pension Distribution Answer Book. annuals Melanie Aska & Joan Gucciardi. 1048p. 1995. 118.00 (*1-56706-118-4*) Panel Pubs.

Pension Distribution Answer Book. 2nd ed. Melanie A. Knox & Joan Gucciardi. 1048p. boxed set 136.00 (*1-56706-315-2*, 63152) Panel Pubs.

Pension Distribution Answer Book: Forms & Checklists. Joan Gucciardi. LC 98-210769. 600p. 1996. 89.00 (*1-56706-317-9*) Aspen Pub.

Pension Distribution Answer Book: Forms & Worksheets. annuals 2nd ed. Melanie N. Aska Knox & Joan Gucciardi. LC 97-224404. 672p. 1999. pap. 96.00 (*1-56706-445-0*, 64450) Panel Pubs.

***Pension Fairness for NBA Pioneers: Hearing Before the Subcommittee on Employer-employee Relations of the Committee on Education & the Workforce, House of Representatives, 105th Congress, 2nd Session, Hearing Held in Washington, DC, July 15, 1998.** USGPO Staff. LC 99-184757. iii, 64 p. 1998. write for info. (*0-16-057824-8*) USGPO.

Pension for Death. large type ed. Roy H. Lewis. (Linford Mystery Library). 336p. 1987. pap. 16.99 (*0-7089-6395-1*) Ulverscroft.

***Pension Fund Capitalism.** Gordon L. Clark. LC 99-45918. 320p. 2000. 72.00 (*0-19-924047-7*); 29.95 (*0-19-924048-5*) OUP.

Pension Fund Excellence: Creating Value for Stakeholders. Keith P. Ambachtsheer & D. Don Ezra. LC 97-45105. (Frontiers in Finance Ser.). 464p. 1998. 64.95 (*0-471-24655-7*) Wiley.

Pension Fund Investment Management. 2nd rev. ed. Ed. by Frank J. Fabozzi. (Illus.). 301p. 1997. 95.00 (*1-883249-26-0*) F J Fabozzi.

Pension Fund Investment Management: A Handbook for Sponsors & Their Advisors. Fran K. Fabozzi. 1990. 65.00 (*1-55738-107-0*, Irwn Prfssnl) McGraw-Hill Prof.

Pension Fund Revolution. Peter F. Drucker. 240p. (C). 1995. pap. text 21.95 (*1-56000-626-9*) Transaction Pubs.

Pension Fund Trustee Handbook. Roger Self. 137p. 1993. 45.00 (*0-85459-719-0*, Pub. by Tolley Pubng) St Mut.

Pension Funding & Taxation: Implications for Tomorrow. LC 93-45511. 1994. 15.95 (*0-86643-080-6*) Empl Benefit Res Inst.

Pension Funds: A Commonsense Guide to a Common Goal. Clay B. Mansfield & Timothy W. Cunningham. LC 92-12182. 190p. 1992. text 37.50 (*1-55623-810-X*, Irwn Prfssnl) McGraw-Hill Prof.

P

An Asterisk (*) at the beginning of an entry indicates that the title is appearing for the first time.

Pension Funds: An Annotated Bibliography. Nels L. Gunderson. LC 90-36013. 144p. 1990. 25.00 (*0-8108-2328-4*) Scarecrow.

Pension Funds: Investment & Performance. Sylvio Prodano. (C). 1987. 260.00 (*0-7855-4065-2*, Pub. by Witherby & Co) St Mut.

Pension Funds: Retirement-Income Security & the Development of Financial Systems: An International Perspective. E. Philip Davis. (Illus.). 350p. 1998. reprint ed. pap. text 27.95 (*0-19-829304-6*) OUP.

Pension Funds & Economic Renewal. Lawrence Litvak. Ed. by Michael Barker. (Studies in State Development Policy: Vol. 11). 136p. (C). 1981. pap. 16.95 (*0-934842-10-8*) CSPA.

Pension Funds & Their Advisers: 1998 Edition. 1999. pap. write for info. (*0-906247-84-5*) Kogan Page Ltd.

Pension Funds of Multiemployer Industrial Groups, Unions, & Nonprofit Organizations. H. Robert Bartell & Elizabeth T. Simpson. (Occasional Papers: No. 105). 64p. 1968. reprint ed. 20.00 (*0-87014-491-X*) Natl Bur Econ Res.

Pension Handbook for Union Negotiators. Jeffrey A. MacDonald & Anne Bingham. LC 85-29959. 203p. 1986. reprint ed. pap. 63.00 (*0-608-04275-7*, 206502700012) Bks Demand.

Pension Incentives & Job Mobility. Alan L. Gustman & Thomas L. Steinmeier. 175p. 1995. text 34.00 (*0-88099-152-6*); pap. text 15.00 (*0-88099-151-8*) W E Upjohn.

Pension Investment Guidebook. Joseph T. Chadwick, Sr. Ed. by Mark D. Persons. (Illus.). 800p. 1991. 79.00 (*1-878375-78-4*) Panel Pubs.

Pension Investment Handbook. Scott L. Lummer & Mark W. Riepe. 700p. boxed set 165.00 (*1-56706-432-9*, 64329) Panel Pubs.

Pension Investment Handbook. annuals Scott L. Lummer & Mark W. Riepe. 614p. 1996. 165.00 (*1-56706-145-1*) Panel Pubs.

Pension Lists of 1792-1795: With Other Revolutionary War Pension Records. Murtie J. Clark. 216p. 1996. 25.00 (*0-8063-1318-8*, 1008) Genealog Pub.

***Pension Loss in Personal Injuries.** Denis Carey. 60p. 1999. 30.00 (*1-85811-126-9*, Pub. by CLT Prof) Gaunt.

Pension Mathematics for Actuaries. 2nd ed. Arthur W. Anderson. LC 85-11231. 217p. (C). 1992. text 70.00 (*0-936031-10-7*) Actex Pubns.

Pension Mathematics with Numerical Illustrations. 2nd ed. Howard E. Winklevoss. LC 92-44652. (Pension Research Council Publications). 309p. (C). 1993. text 34.95 (*0-8122-3196-1*) U of Pa Pr.

Pension Plan Investments, 1992. (Tax Law & Estate Planning Course Handbook Ser.). 433p. 1992. pap. 70.00 (*0-685-69471-2*) PLI.

Pension Plan Investments, 1996: Nuts, Bolts & Current Developments. (Tax Law & Estate Planning Course Handbook Ser.). Date not set. pap. 99.00 (*0-614-17279-9*, J4-3682) PLI.

Pension Plan Investments, 1995: Nuts, Bolts & Current Developments. (Tax Law & Estate Planning Course Handbook Ser.). 448p. 1995. pap. 99.00 (*0-685-69746-0*, J4-3676) PLI.

Pension Plan Investor: A Guide for Fund Managers & Sponsors in Today's Complex & Uncertain Times. Daniel M. Kehrer. 325p. 1991. text 32.50 (*1-55738-187-9*, Irwn Prfssnl) McGraw-Hill Prof.

Pension Plan Management Manual: Cumulative Supplementation. James E. Burke. 592p. 1991. suppl. ed. 52.25 (*0-7913-0973-8*) Warren Gorham & Lamont.

Pension Plan Strategies: A Comprehensive Guide to Retirement Planning for Physicians & Other Professionals. 2nd ed. C. Colburn Hardy & Howard J. Weiner. Ed. by Kathryn Swanson. (Illus.). 153p. 1995. 44.95 (*1-878487-60-4*, ME055) Practice Mgmt Info.

Pension Plan Terminations. 2nd ed. Edward T. Veal & Edward R. Mackiewicz. LC 98-46455. 659p. 1999. 145.00 (*1-57018-111-X*, 1111-PR9) BNA Books.

Pension Planning. 7th ed. Jack L. Vanderhei et al. 512p. (C). 1992. text 18.00 (*0-256-11918-X*, Irwn McGrw-H) McGrw-H Hghr Educ.

Pension Planning: Pensions, Profit-Sharing, & Other Deferred Compensation Plans. 7th ed. Everett T. Allen, Jr. et al. 448p. (C). 1992. text 69.75 (*0-256-08296-0*, Irwn McGrw-H) McGrw-H Hghr Educ.

Pension Planning: Pensions, Profit-Sharing & Other Deferred Compensation Plans. 8th ed. Allen et al. LC 97-6226. 1997. 58.44 (*0-256-13601-7*, Irwn Prfssnl) McGraw-Hill Prof.

Pension Planning & Deferred Compensation. 2nd ed. Jeffrey G. Sherman. 1990. teacher ed. write for info. (*0-8205-0305-3*) Bender.

Pension Plans: Stronger Labor ERISA Enforcements Should Better Protect Plan Participants. (Illus.). 51p. (Orig.). (C). 1995. pap. text 25.00 (*0-7881-2095-6*) DIANE Pub.

Pension Plans for Small & Mid-Sized Businesses. John B. Wollenberg. LC 95-48806. 368p. 1996. 145.00 (*0-471-13391-4*) Wiley.

Pension Policies & Public Debt in Dynamic CGE Models. Ed. by D. P. Broer & J. Lassila. LC 98-208537. (Illus.). x, 189p. 1997. pap. 69.95 (*3-7908-0970-5*) Spr-Verlag.

Pension Policy: An International Perspective. 1996. lib. bdg. 255.95 (*0-8490-6028-1*) Gordon Pr.

Pension Policy & Small Employers: At What Price Coverage? Emily S. Andrews. 1989. 39.95 (*0-86643-050-4*) Empl Benefit Res Inst.

Pension Policy for a Mobile Labor Force. John A. Turner. LC 92-47019. 214p. 1993. text 35.00 (*0-88099-134-8*); pap. text 17.00 (*0-88099-133-X*) W E Upjohn.

Pension Portability for State & Local Government. Gary I. Gates. 40p. (Orig.). 1996. pap. write for info. (*1-887748-05-9*) Milbank Memorial.

***Pension Power: How Progressive Social Funds Can Transform Capitalism.** Robin Blackburn. 160p. 2001. 22.00 (*1-85984-795-1*, Pub. by Verso) Norton.

Pension Power: Understanding & Control Your Most Valuable Asset. Debbie Harrison. 1995. pap. text 16.00 (*0-471-95240-0*) Wiley.

Pension Prosave Act & Retirement Security: Hearing of the Committee on Labor & Human Resources, United States Senate, 105th Congress, Second Session, on Examining Retirement Security & the Need for Defined Pension Plans for American Workers, Focusing on S. 957, to Establish a Pension Prosave System ... by Facilitating Pension Portability, March 17, 1998. LC 98-167853. (S. Hrg. Ser.). iii, 72p. 1998. write for info. (*0-16-056527-8*) USGPO.

Pension Reform Handbook. Robert C. Wilkie. 1100p. 1988. 37.50 (*0-13-656018-0*) P-H.

***Pension Reform in Latin America.** Armando Barreintos. LC 98-72852. (Illus.). 266p. 1998. text 67.95 (*1-85972-699-2*) Ashgate Pub Co.

***Pension Reform in Latin America & Its Lessons for International Policymakers.** Tapendra Narayan Sinha. LC 00-55999. (Huebner International Series on Risk, Insurance & Economic Security). 2000. write for info. (*0-7923-7882-2*) Kluwer Academic.

Pension Regimes & Saving, Vol. 153. G. A. Mackenzie et al. LC 97-33432. (Occasional Papers). 1997. write for info. (*1-55775-640-6*) Intl Monetary.

Pension Rights in Welfare Capitalism: The Development of Old-Age Pensions in 18 OECD Countries 1930-1985. Joakim Palme. (Swedish Institute for Social Research Ser.: No. 14). 196p. (Orig.). 1990. pap. 69.50 (*91-7604-039-9*) Coronet Bks.

***Pension Schemes Act 1993 & Its Regulations: Pension Laws in Plain English.** Xenia Frostick. 364p. 1999. pap. 149.60 (*1-902558-03-0*, Pub. by Palladian Law) Gaunt.

Pension Schemes & Pension Funds in the United Kingdom. David Blake. LC 93-33140. (Illus.). 630p. 1995. text 110.00 (*0-19-828623-6*) OUP.

Pension Security: Department of Labor (dol) Enforcement of the Employee Retirement Income Security Act (erisa) & the Limited Scope Audit Exemption : Hearing Before & Subcommittee on Human Resources of the Committee on Government Reform & Oversight, House of Representatives, One Hundred Fifth Congress, Second Session, February 12, 1998. United States. LC 98-208187. iii, 89 p. 1998. write for info. (*0-16-057173-1*) USGPO.

***Pension Systems in the European Union: Competition & Tax Aspects.** Leo Stevens et al. (EFS Brochures Ser.: Vol. 7). 160p. 1999. text 81.00 (*90-411-9752-4*) Kluwer Law Intl.

Pensioned Off: Retirement & Income Examined. LC 96-39951. (Rethinking Aging Ser.). 1997. 94.00 (*0-335-19683-7*) OpUniv Pr.

Pensioned Off: Retirement & Income Examined. Midwinter Staff. LC 96-39951. (Rethinking Aging Ser.). 1997. pap. 29.95 (*0-335-19682-9*) OpUniv Pr.

Pensioners of Revolutionary War-Struck off the Roll. United States Pension Bureau. LC 71-78506. 103p. 1998. reprint ed. pap. 15.00 (*0-8063-0350-6*) Clearfield Co.

Pensioners on the Roll As of January 1, 1883, (Living in Minnesota) with Every Name Index. Ed. by Mary H. Bakeman. LC 94-16879. 84p. 1994. reprint ed. pap. 12.50 (*0-915709-13-9*) Pk Geneal Bk.

Pensioners on the Roll, 1 January 1883, Living in Dakota Territory. Ed. by Mary H. Bakeman. LC 96-27299. (Orig.). 1996. pap. 7.50 (*0-915709-26-0*) Pk Geneal Bk.

Pensioners on the Rolls as of January 1, 1999, Living in Foreign Countries. LC 99-19904. 32p. 1999. pap. 10.00 (*0-915709-68-6*) Pk Geneal Bk.

Pensioners on the Rolls, 1 January 1883, Living in Wisconsin. Ed. by Mary H. Bakeman. LC 98-28939. 140p. 1998. pap. 17.50 (*0-915709-63-5*) Pk Geneal Bk.

Pensions. 2nd ed. Stephen Ward. 490p. 1999. pap. 120.00 (*0-85297-507-4*, Pub. by Chartered Bank) St Mut.

Pensions: A Practical Guide. 2nd ed. J. S. Seres. (C). 1987. 250.00 (*0-7855-4064-4*, Pub. by Witherby & Co) St Mut.

Pensions: Tax Law. Ed. by Xenia Frostrick. (Pensions Law Ser.). 250p. 1997. pap. 32.00 (*1-85811-135-8*, Pub. by CLT Prof) Gaunt.

Pensions: The Problems of Today & Tomorrow. Barnard Benjamin et al. (Studies in Financial Institutions & Markets: No. 4). 272p. text 60.00 (*0-04-332127-5*) Routledge.

Pensions - Involving the Members: A Review & Assessment of Current Practice. Ed. by Stephen Palmer & Theon Wilkinson. (C). 1983. 45.00 (*0-85292-324-4*) St Mut.

Pensions - Profit. Russell K. Osgood. 1984. 125.00 (*0-316-66612-2*, Aspen Law & Bus) Aspen Pub.

Pensions Act 1995 & Its Regulations. Xenia Frostick. 400p. 2000. pap. 99.00 (*1-902558-04-9*, Pub. by Palladian Law) Gaunt.

Pensions & Corporate Restructuring in American Industry: A Crisis of Regulation. Gordon L. Clark. LC 92-34553. 304p. (C). 1993. text 39.95 (*0-8018-4523-8*) Johns Hopkins.

Pensions & Divorce. G. Prior & J. Field. (DSS Research Report Ser.). 1996. write for info. (*0-11-762423-3*, Pub. by Statnry Office) Bernan Associates.

Pensions & Employee Benefits. Ed. by Law & Business Inc. Staff & Legal Times Seminars Staff. (Seminar Course Handbks.). 1983. pap. 30.00 (*0-686-89372-7*, C01473) Harcourt.

Pensions & Employee Benefits under the 1982 Tax Act: Coping with the Greatest Changes Since ERISA. Paul S. Berger & Mayer Siegel. (Illus.). 1982. write for info. (*0-318-57052-1*) Harcourt.

Pensions & Other Employee Benefits: A Financial Reporting & Compliance Guide. 4th ed. Richard M. Steinberg et al. LC 92-17262. 432p. 1993. 195.00 (*0-471-55942-3*) Wiley.

Pensions & Population Ageing: An Economic Analysis. John Creedy. LC 97-39374. 256p. 1998. 85.00 (*1-85898-802-0*) E Elgar.

Pensions & Productivity. Stuart Dorsey et al. LC 98-17997. 139p. (C). 1998. 33.00 (*0-88099-186-0*); pap. 14.00 (*0-88099-185-2*) W E Upjohn.

Pensions & Profit Sharing. 7th ed. Ed. by Dearborn Financial Pub. Staff. LC 99-47910. 300p. 2000. pap. text 50.00 (*0-7931-2690-8*, 5415-1407, R & R Newkirk) Dearborn.

Pensions & the Economy: Sources, Uses, & Limitations of Data. Ed. by Zvi Bodie & Alicia H. Munnell. LC 91-45276. (Pension Research Council Publications). (Illus.). 304p. (C). 1992. text 45.00 (*0-8122-3118-X*) U of Pa Pr.

Pensions Around the World. Kevin Doyle. 82p. 1983. 70.00 (*0-900886-79-X*, Pub. by Witherby & Co) St Mut.

Pensions, Economics & Public Policy. Richard A. Ippolito. (Pension Research Council Publications). 296p. (C). 1991. text 52.95 (*0-87094-760-5*) U of Pa Pr.

Pensions, Employment, & the Law. Richard Nobles. (Monographs on Labour Law). 282p. 1993. text 59.00 (*0-19-825448-2*) OUP.

Pensions for Public Employees. Alicia H. Munnell & Ann M. Connolly. LC 79-89303. 128p. 1979. 7.00 (*0-89068-048-5*) Natl Planning.

***Pensions Handbook 1999-2000: The Pensions System Explained.** Sue Ward. 160p. 1999. pap. 30.00 (*0-86242-299-X*, Pub. by Age Concern Eng) St Mut.

Pensions in a Changing Economy. Ed. by Richard V. Burkhauser. LC 93-2155. 1993. pap. 15.00 (*0-86643-078-4*) Empl Benefit Res Inst.

Pensions in Crisis: Why the System Is Failing America & How You Can Protect Your Future. Karen Ferguson & Kate Blackwell. LC 94-41722. (Illus.). 273p. 1995. 22.45 (*1-55970-296-6*, Pub. by Arcade Pub Inc) Time Warner.

Pensions in Marriage Breakdown. Stephen Gailey. 128p. 1996. pap. 59.50 (*1-85811-074-2*, Pub. by CLT Prof) Gaunt.

Pensions in Perspective: A Guide to Qualified Retirement Plans. 4th rev. ed. Judith B. Gee. LC 93-86898. 304p. 1993. pap. 29.95 (*0-87218-120-0*) Natl Underwriter.

Pensions in the American Economy. Laurence J. Kotlikoff & Daniel E. Smith. LC 83-9193. (National Bureau of Economic Research Monographs). 448p. 1984. lib. bdg. 72.00 (*0-226-45146-1*) U Ch Pr.

***Pensions in the European Union: Adapting to Economic & Social Change.** Gerard Hughes & Jim Stewart. LC 00-35654. 2000. write for info. (*0-7923-7838-5*) Kluwer Academic.

Pensions in the U. S. Economy. Zvi Bodie et al. (National Bureau of Economic Research Project Report Ser.). (Illus.). 208p. 1988. lib. bdg. 34.00 (*0-226-06285-6*) U Ch Pr.

Pensions, Labor & Individual Choice. Ed. by David A. Wise. LC 85-1118. (National Bureau of Economic Research Project Report Ser.). x, 464p. 1985. lib. bdg. 60.00 (*0-226-90293-5*) U Ch Pr.

Pensions Law. Linda Luckhaus. (European Community Law Ser.). (C). 1997. text 90.00 (*0-485-70014-X*) Humanities.

Pensions Law. Robert West. boxed set. write for info. (*0-406-02513-4*, U.K., MICHIE) LEXIS Pub.

Pensions Law & Practice. David A. Chatterton. xxiv, 180p. 1998. pap. 72.00 (*1-85941-340-4*, Pub. by Cavendish Pubng) Gaunt.

Pensions Plans Employee. Richard A. Ippolito. LC 97-16796. 312p. 1997. 34.95 (*0-226-38455-1*) U Ch Pr.

***Pensions, Politics & the Elderly: Historic Social Movements & their Lessons for our Aging Society.** Daniel J. B. Mitchell. LC 99-87497. (Illus.). 224p. 2000. text 64.95 (*0-7656-0518-X*) M E Sharpe.

Pensions Politics & the Elderly: Historic Social Movements & Their Lessons for Our Aging Society. Daniel J. B. Mitchell. Date not set. write for info. (*0-7656-0519-8*) M E Sharpe.

***Pensions, Savings & Capital Flows: From Ageing to Emerging Markets.** Helmut Reisen. LC 99-49040. (Organisation for Economic Co-Operation & Development Ser.). 288p. 2000. 90.00 (*1-84064-308-0*) E Elgar.

Pensions, Savings & Capital Markets. Phyllis A. Fernandez. 169p. 1996. per. 13.00 (*0-16-048524-X*) USGPO.

Pensive Jester: The Literary Career of W. W. Jacobs. John D. Cloy. LC 96-9816. 170p. 1996. lib. bdg. 39.50 (*0-7618-0464-1*) U Pr of Amer.

Pensive Mans Practise. John Norden. LC 77-171776. (English Experience Ser.: No. 401). 192p. 1971. reprint ed. 35.00 (*90-221-0401-X*) Walter J Johnson.

Pensive Musings. Bernice Gatling-Scott. 24p. (Orig.). 1991. pap. 4.95 (*1-877971-05-7*) Mid Atl Reg Pr.

Pensive Penman. rev. ed. Stephanie Stearns. (Illus.). 64p. (Orig.). 1988. pap. text 3.50 (*0-317-90979-7*) Dubless Pubns.

Pensive Thoughts. Ed. by Ginny L. Ballor & Carrie Neumann. 40p. (Orig.). (C). 1996. pap. 3.00 (*1-882294-16-5*) Green Gate.

Penstemons. Robert Nold. LC 98-51574. (Illus.). 307p. 1999. 29.95 (*0-88192-429-6*) Timber.

Penstemons: The Beautiful Beardtongues Of New Mexico. Jean Heflin. LC 98-111240. 50p. 1997. write for info. (*0-9659693-0-4*) Jack Rabbit.

Penta Manual: Personal Energetic Task. Waldo Vieira. Tr. by Kevin De La Tour & Simone De La Tour. (Illus.). 148p. 1996. pap. 11.95 (*85-86019-16-X*) Intl Inst Proj.

Pentachlorophenol Health & Safety Guide. WHO Staff. (Health & Safety Guides: No. 19). 44p. 1989. 5.00 (*92-4-154341-8*) World Health.

Pentacle. Tom Piccirilli. (Illus.). 156p. (Orig.). pap. 5.99 (*0-9640168-2-6*) Pirate Writings.

Pentacle & the Sword: The Story of the American Witchcraft Movement. Rhuddlwm Gawr. LC 85-73753. (Illus.). 427p. (Orig.). 1990. 24.95 (*0-685-25296-5*, CP111725); pap. 15.95 (*0-931760-52-6*) Camelot GA.

Pentacoordinated Phosphorus. Ed. by Robert R. Holmes. Incl. Vol. 1. Pentacoordinated Phosphorus: Structure & Spectroscopy. LC 80-26302. 479p. 1980. text 85.00 (*0-8412-0458-6*, Pub. by Am Chemical); Vol. 2. Pentacoordinated Phosphorus: Reaction Mechanisms. LC 80-26302. 237p. 1980. text 49.95 (*0-8412-0528-0*, Pub. by Am Chemical); Set. LC 80-26302. 1980. 99.95 (*0-8412-0529-9*); LC 80-26302. (ACS Monograph). 1980. write for info. (*0-318-50479-0*) Am Chemical.

Pentacoordinated Phosphorus: Reaction Mechanisms see Pentacoordinated Phosphorus

Pentacoordinated Phosphorus: Structure & Spectroscopy see Pentacoordinated Phosphorus

Pentacost see Pjatidesjatnitsa

Pentacost, Peanuts, Popcorn & Prayer. rev. ed. Center for Learning Network Staff. 128p. 1988. spiral bd. 15.95 (*1-56077-027-9*) Ctr Learning.

***Pentacostal Pastor Spanish Edition.** Goodall Trask. (SPA.). 2000. pap. 19.99 (*0-8297-1584-3*) Vida Pubs.

Pentagon: "A National Institution": Its History, Its Functions, Its People. rev. ed. E. A. Rogner. LC 85-72559. (Illus.). 1986. pap. text 3.50 (*0-935045-05-8*) D-OR Pr.

Pentagon: "A National Showplace"; What to See & Where to See It. E. A. Rogner. (Illus.). 48p. (Orig.). pap. text 4.95 (*0-935045-06-6*) D-OR Pr.

Pentagon: Facts about the Building (Monograph) rev. ed. E. A. Rogner. 1986. pap. text 0.95 (*0-935045-04-X*) D-OR Pr.

Pentagon: Flags Displayed in the Building. E. A. Rogner. LC 85-72558. (Illus.). 36p. (Orig.). 1985. pap. 3.50 (*0-935045-03-1*) D-OR Pr.

Pentagon: Flags Displayed in the Flag Corridor (Monograph) E. A. Rogner. (Orig.). pap. 0.95 (*0-935045-02-3*) D-OR Pr.

Pentagon & the Cities. Ed. by Andrew M. Kirby. (Urban Affairs Annual Review Ser.: Vol. 40). 320p. (C). 1991. text 62.00 (*0-8039-3845-4*); pap. text 26.00 (*0-8039-3846-2*) Sage.

***Pentagon Appointment: A Mid-Career Adventure.** Gary D. Penisten. LC 99-56578. 240p. 2000. pap. 15.00 (*1-58151-066-7*, Pub. by BookPartners) Midpt Trade.

Pentagon of Power: The Myth of the Machine, Vol. 2. Lewis Mumford. LC 70-124836. (Illus.). 496p. 1970. 12.95 (*0-15-163974-4*) Harcourt.

Pentagon Papers. abr. ed. Ed. by George C. Herring. LC 92-32172. 224p. (C). 1993. 11.88 (*0-07-028380-X*) McGraw.

***Pentagon Papers: National Security versus the Public's Right to Know.** Geoffrey A. Campbell. LC 00-8083. (Famous Trials Ser.). 128p. (YA). (gr. 4-12). 2000. 18.96 (*1-56006-692-X*) Lucent Bks.

Pentagon Paradox: The Development of the F-18 Hornet. James P. Stevenson. (Illus.). 445p. 1998. text 30.00 (*0-7881-5641-1*) DIANE Pub.

Pentagon Paradox: The Development of the F-18 Hornet. James P. Stevenson. (Illus.). 445p. 1993. 31.95 (*1-55750-775-9*) Naval Inst Pr.

Pentagon Review. 2nd rev. ed. Nita Scoggan. (Illus.). 32p. 1998. pap. 2.75 (*0-910487-43-X*) Royalty Pub.

Pentagon Spy. Franklin W. Dixon. (Hardy Boys Mystery Stories Ser.: No. 61). (J). (gr. 3-6). 1984. 8.85 (*0-685-42775-7*) PB.

Pentagon Spy. Franklin W. Dixon. Ed. by Anne Greenberg. (Hardy Boys Mystery Stories Ser.: No. 61). 192p. (J). (gr. 3-6). 1988. pap. 3.99 (*0-671-67221-5*, Minstrel Bks) PB.

Pentagon, the First Fifty Years. Alfred Goldberg. 109p. 1997. boxed set 31.00 (*0-16-061117-2*) USGPO.

Pentagon Wars: Reformers Challenge the Old Guard. James G. Burton. LC 93-3424. (Illus.). 306p. 1993. 31.95 (*1-55750-081-9*) Naval Inst Pr.

Pentagram: The Compendium. Perntagram Partners Staff. (Illus.). 304p. 1998. pap. 39.95 (*0-7148-3769-5*, Pub. by Phaidon Press) Phaidon Pr.

Pentagram V. LC 98-31114. (Illus.). 496p. 1999. pap. 45.00 (*1-58093-003-4*, Pub. by Monacelli Pr) Penguin Putnam.

Pentagram V, Vol. 5. Pentagram Staff. 1998. 45.00 (*1-58093-042-5*) Monacelli Pr.

Pentagram Press Commonplace Book: (A Selection of Typographic Interpretations) Ed. by Michael Tarachow. 44p. 1988. 125.00 (*0-937596-11-6*) Pentagram.

Pentalia. Amanda Evans. 100p. (Orig.). (J). (gr. 3-7). 1995. pap. 4.95 (*0-9647783-0-0*) Sunflower TX.

Pentamagic: An Eye-Opening Collection of Optical Illusions & Visual Magic. Des. by Pentagram Partnership Staff. LC 92-15505. 160p. 1993. per. 16.99 (*0-671-79185-0*, Fireside) S&S Trade Pap.

Pentamerone Oder das Marchen Aller Marchen. Giambattista Basile. (Volkskundliche Quellen Ser.: No. III). xxiv, 749p. 1973. reprint ed. 80.00 (*3-487-04921-X*) G Olms Pubs.

Pentateuch see Pentateuco

Pentateuch see Pentateuco

Pentateuch. Joseph Blenkinsopp. 288p. 1992. 34.95 (*0-385-41207-X*) Doubleday.

Pentateuch. William Kelly. (Introductory Lecture Ser.). 524p. 7.95 (*0-88172-099-2*) Believers Bkshelf.

Pentateuch. Ed. by Gene M. Tucker et al. LC 96-33533. (Interpreting Biblical Texts Ser.). 170p. 1996. pap. 19.95 (*0-687-00842-5*) Abingdon.

P

An Asterisk (*) at the beginning of an entry indicates that the title is appearing for the first time.

Pentateuch see Oxford Illustrated Old Testament: With Drawings by Contemporary Artists
Pentateuch: A Liberation-Critical Reading. Alice L. Laffey. LC 98-18082. 1998. pap. text 21.00 (*0-8006-2872-1*, Fortress Pr) Augsburg Fortress.
Pentateuch: A Sheffield Reader. John W. Rogerson. (Biblical Seminar Ser.: No. 39). 371p. 1996. pap. 19.95 (*1-85075-785-2*, Pub. by Sheffield Acad) CUP Services.
***Pentateuch: A Social-Science Commentary.** John Van Seters. (Trajectories Ser.: No. 1). 240p. 1999. 79.00 (*1-84127-027-X*, Pub. by Sheffield Acad); pap. 28.00 (*1-84127-036-9*, Pub. by Sheffield Acad) CUP Services.
***Pentateuch: An Introduction to the First Five Books of the Bible.** Joseph Blenkinsopp. 288p. 2000. pap. 20.00 (*0-385-49788-1*, Anchor Bib) Doubleday.
Pentateuch: Chapter by Chapter. W. H. Griffith Thomas. LC 85-10076. 192p. 1985. reprint ed. pap. 10.99 (*0-8254-3833-0*) Kregel.
***Pentateuch Five Books of Moses.** 1999. pap. 100.00 (*1-57074-449-1*) Greyden Pr.
Pentateuch: Hebrew Text, English Translation & Commentary Digest, 7 vols. Tr. by Isaac Levy from GER. (ENG & HEB.). 4257p. 1962. 149.95 (*0-910818-12-6*) Judaica Pr.
Pentateuch & Haftorahs. Ed. by J. H. Hertz. 1067p. 1960. 30.00 (*0-900689-21-8*) Soncino Pr.
Pentateuch as Narrative: A Biblical-Theological Commentary. John H. Sailhamer. 544p. 1995. 24.99 (*0-310-57421-8*) Zondervan.
Pentateuch-Haftaroth & Sabbath Prayers: Hebrew with English. Isaac Lesser. (ENG & HEB.). 32.50 (*0-87559-197-3*) Shalom.
Pentateuch in the Twentieth Century: The Legacy of Julius Wellhausen. Ernest Nicholson. 304p. 1998. text 75.00 (*0-19-826958-7*) OUP.
Pentateuch, T'rumath Tzvi: Hebrew Text, English Translation & Commentary Digest. deluxe ed. Samson R. Hirsch. Tr. by Gertrude Hirschler from GER. 1058p. 1986. boxed set 100.00 (*0-910818-66-5*) Judaica Pr.
Pentateuch with Rashi, 5 vols. A. M. Silbermann & M. Rosenbaum. LC 30-11064. 1973. 49.95 (*0-87306-019-9*) Feldheim.
Pentateuchal & Deuteronomy Studies. Peeters Publishers Staff. 1998. 46.95 (*90-6831-306-1*, Pub. by Peeters Pub) Bks Intl VA.
Pentateuco. Charles Erdman. Tr. by Humberto Casanova & Viviana Casanova.Tr. of Pentateuch. 396p. 1986. 25.00 (*0-939125-14-5*) CRC Wrld Lit.
Pentateuco. P. Hoff.Tr. of Pentateuch. (SPA.). 276p. 1978. pap. 9.99 (*0-8297-0876-6*) Vida Pubs.
Pentathlon: The Game. Robert E. Grace. (Illus.). 16p. (Orig.). 1989. pap. 18.95 (*0-9622857-0-6*, TPG 101) Top Prize Games.
Pentatomoidea (Hemiptera) of Northeastern North America With Emphasis on the Fauna of Illinois. J. E. McPherson. LC 81-9167. (Illus.). 253p. 1982. 31.95 (*0-8093-1040-6*) S Ill U Pr.
Pentatonic Major Scales for Rock & Blues Guitar. 32p. 1995. pap. 5.95 (*0-7935-4369-X*, 00695013) H Leonard.
Pentatonic Partners. 1990. pap. text 3.95 (*0-634-00228-7*) H Leonard.
Pentatonic Scales for the Jazz/Rock Keyboardist. Jeff Burns. 40p. 1997. pap. 9.95 (*0-7935-7679-2*) H Leonard.
***Pentatonicas Mayores Escalas para Guitarra.** Orig. Title: Major Pentatonic Scales for Guitar. (SPA.). 32p. 1998. pap. 5.95 (*0-7935-9012-4*) H Leonard.
***Pentatonicas Menores Escalas Para Guitarra.** Orig. Title: Minor Pentatonic Sclaes for Guitar. (SPA.). 24p. 1998. pap. 5.95 (*0-7935-9011-6*) H Leonard.
Pentax Classic Cameras. Paul Comon. LC 98-36473. (Magic Lantern Guides Ser.). 1999. pap. write for info. (*1-883403-53-7*, Silver Pixel Pr) Saunders Photo.
Pentax K1000/P30N. (User's Guides Bks.). (Illus.). 220p. pap. 19.95 (*0-906447-83-6*, Pub. by Hove Foto) Watsn-Guptill.
Pentax Modern Classics ES11, Spotmatic F, K2, KC/KM, ME/MX, ME Super. (Modern Classics Ser.). (Illus.). 196p. pap. 19.95 (*0-906447-91-7*, Pub. by Hove Foto) Watsn-Guptill.
***Pentax ZX-M/K 1000.** Joseph Meehan. LC 99-26593. (Magic Lantern Guides Ser.). 176p. 1999. 19.95 (*1-883403-55-3*, Silver Pixel Pr) Saunders Photo.
Pentecost. Joseph Brice. 1983. 9.99 (*0-88019-092-2*) Schmul Pub Co.
Pentecost. David Edgar. 128p. 1996. pap. text 14.95 (*1-85459-292-0*, Pub. by N Hern Bks) Theatre Comm.
***Pentecost: Choral Chants.** Monks of New Skete Staff. Ed. & Tr. by Laurence Mancuso. (Liturgical Music Series I: Vol. 13). 44p. 2000. pap. text 25.00 (*0-935129-43-X*) Monks of New Skete.
Pentecost - Today? The Biblical Basis for Understanding Revival. Iain H. Murray. 1998. 19.99 (*0-85151-752-8*) Banner of Truth.
Pentecost - Today? The Biblical Basis for Understanding Revival. Iain H. Murray. 232p. 1998. 19.99 (*0-9654955-5-8*) Founders Pr.
Pentecost - What's That? T. F. Tenney. LC 91-9524. 192p. 2000. reprint ed. pap. 5.95 (*0-932581-83-8*) Word Aflame.
Pentecost Aftershock. William E. Kruger. 156p. (Orig.). 1991. pap. 9.95 (*0-938736-30-2*) Life Enrich.
Pentecost Alley. Anne Perry. 1997. mass mkt. 6.99 (*0-449-22566-6*, Crest) Fawcett.
Pentecost Alley. large type ed. Anne Perry. LC 96-22225. (Cloak & Dagger Ser.). 683p. 1996. 25.95 (*0-7862-0812-0*) Thorndike Pr.
Pentecost Alphabet. Ed. by Phyllis Wezeman. 75p. 1994. pap. 9.95 (*1-877871-64-8*, 2685) Ed Ministries.
Pentecost & After: Studies in the Book of Acts. M. R. De Haan. LC 96-10337. (M. R. De Haan Classic Library). (Illus.). 192p. 1996. pap. 10.99 (*0-8254-2482-8*) Kregel.
"Pentecost in My Soul" Explorations in the Meaning of Pentecostal Experience in the Early Assemblies of God. Edith L. Blumhofer. LC 89-84296. (Illus.). 266p. (C). 1989. pap. 6.50 (*0-88243-646-5*, 02-0646) Gospel Pub.
Pentecost Is for Living. Charles Whitehead. pap. write for info. (*0-232-51988-9*) S Asia.
Pentecost Journey: A Planning Guide for Hispanic Ministries. Jennie Trevino-Teddlie. LC 98-88813. 80p. 1999. pap. 15.95 (*0-88177-268-2*, DR268) Discipleship Res.
Pentecost, Mission, & Ecumenism's Essays on Intercultural Theology: Festschrift in Honour of Professor Walter J. Hollenweger. Ed. by Jan A. B. Jongeneel. LC 92-23749. (Studies in the Intercultural History of Christianity). (Illus.). 376p. 1992. 73.00 (*3-631-44010-3*) P Lang Pubng.
Pentecost of the Hills in Taiwan: The Christian Faith among the Original Inhabitants. Ralph Covell. LC 97-27762. (Illus.). 320p. 1997. pap. 15.95 (*0-932727-90-5*) Hope Pub Hse.
Pentecost Revolution. Hugh J. Schonfield. 320p. 1985. pap. 14.95 (*0-906540-79-8*, Pub. by Element MA) Penguin Putnam.
Pentecostal Bible Study Course: Study Guide. E. Rohn. 512p. (Orig.). 1978. pap. 24.99 (*0-912315-43-1*) Word Aflame.
Pentecostal-Charismatic Movement Yesterday & Today. David W. Cloud. (Illus.). 49p. 1995. pap. 3.00 (*1-58318-043-5*, WOL470B) Way of Life.
Pentecostal Currents in American Protestantism. Edith W. Blumhofer et al. LC 98-25395. 320p. 1999. 42.50 (*0-252-02450-8*); pap. 19.95 (*0-252-06756-8*) U of Ill Pr.
Pentecostal Daughters ... They Shall Prophesy. Thelma Hostetter. 110p. pap. text 10.00 (*0-9700539-0-8*) T Hostetter.
Pentecostal Experience see Experiencia Pentecostal
Pentecostal Experience: The Writings of Donald Gee. Ed. by David A. Womack. LC 93-13636. 285p. 1993. kivar 11.95 (*0-88243-454-3*, 02-0454) Gospel Pub.
Pentecostal Experience - Donald Gee see Experiencia Pentecostal - Donald Gee
Pentecostal Formation: A Pedagogy among the Oppressed. Cheryl Bridges-Johns. (JPT Supplement Ser.: No. 2). 154p. 1993. pap. 13.95 (*1-85075-438-1*, Pub. by Sheffield Acad) CUP Services.
Pentecostal Grace. Laurence W. Wood. Ed. by Harold Burgess. 1984. pap. 5.95 (*0-310-75041-5*, 17028P) Zondervan.
Pentecostal Minister. Ed. by J. L. Hall & David K. Bernard. LC 91-11843. 320p. (Orig.). 1991. pap. 9.99 (*0-932581-84-6*) Word Aflame.
Pentecostal Minister Sermon Resource Manual, Vol. 5. Compiled by Floyd Carey & Hoyt Stone. Vol. 5. (Illus.). 328p. 1996. 16.99 (*0-87148-968-6*) Pathway Pr.
Pentecostal Minister's Sermon Resource Manual, Vol. I. Carey & Stone. LC 87-72041. Vol. 1. (Illus.). 1987. 15.99 (*0-87148-721-7*) Pathway Pr.
Pentecostal Minister's Sermon Resource Manual, Vol. 2. Carey & Stone. Vol. 2. (Illus.). 1988. 15.99 (*0-87148-950-3*) Pathway Pr.
Pentecostal Movements. Ed. by Karl-Joseph Kuschel & Jurgen Motlmann. LC 96-195366. (Concilium Ser.). 150p. (Orig.). 1996. pap. 15.00 (*1-57075-072-6*) Orbis Bks.
Pentecostal Negro Imi. 1993. 65.99 (*0-8297-1816-8*) Vida Pubs.
Pentecostal Origins & Trends: Early & Modern. 3rd rev. ed. Karl Roebling. LC 85-63631. 112p. 1985. 10.00 (*0-942910-12-5*) Dynapress.
Pentecostal Pastor: A Mandate for the 21st Century. Thomas E. Trask et al. LC 97-13504. 640p. 1997. 34.99 (*0-88243-686-4*, 02-0686) Gospel Pub.
***Pentecostal Perspectives.** Ed. by Keith Warrington. xviii, 222p. 1998. reprint ed. pap. 20.00 (*0-85364-804-2*, Pub. by Paternoster Pub) OM Literature.
Pentecostal Pioneering: An Autobiography. George W. Flattery, Sr. LC 92-93564. (Illus.). 320p. 1992. pap. 7.95 (*0-9634670-0-X*) G Flattery.
Pentecostal Preaching. Ray H. Hughes. LC 81-84606. 159p. (Orig.). 1983. pap. 6.99 (*0-87148-711-X*) Pathway Pr.
Pentecostal Resource Manual, Vol. 3. Carey & Stone. Vol. 3. (Illus.). 1990. 15.99 (*0-87148-951-1*) Pathway Pr.
Pentecostal Spirituality: A Passion for the Kingdom. Steven J. Land. (JPT Supplement Ser.: No. 1). 239p. 1993. pap. 21.95 (*1-85075-442-X*, Pub. by Sheffield Acad) CUP Services.
Pentecostal Theology of Edward Irving. Gordon Strachan. (Illus.). 240p. 1988. pap. 9.95 (*0-943575-04-4*) Hendrickson MA.
Pentecostal Worship: A Biblical & Practical Approach. Gary D. Erickson. LC 89-38786. 224p. (Orig.). 1989. pap. 9.99 (*0-932581-52-8*) Word Aflame.
Pentecostalism: Origins & Developments Worldwide. Walter J. Hollenweger. LC 97-35885. 596p. 1997. 34.95 (*0-943575-36-2*) Hendrickson MA.
Pentecostalism: Purity or Peril? O. Talmadge Spence. (Charismatic Ser.: Vol. 3). 146p. (Orig.). (C). 1989. pap. 8.95 (*0-89084-477-1*) Fndtns NC.
Pentecostalism & the Charismatic Renewal. Frank Sullivan. 1989. pap. 22.00 (*0-86217-275-6*, Pub. by Veritas Pubns) St Mut.
***Pentecostalism & the Future of the Christian Churches: Promises, Limitations, Challenges.** Richard Shaull & Waldo Cesar. LC 00-27983. 256p. 2000. pap. 25.00 (*0-8028-4666-1*) Eerdmans.
Pentecostalism in Brazil. Corten. LC 99-21770. 1999. text 59.95 (*0-312-22506-7*) St Martin.
Pentecostalism in Colombia: Baptism by Fire & Spirit. Cornelia B. Flora. LC 74-4974. 288p. 1976. 38.50 (*0-8386-1578-3*) Fairleigh Dickinson.
Pentecostalism in Context: Essays in Honor of William W. Menzies. Ed. by Wonsuk Ma & Robert P. Menzies. (JPTS Ser.: Vol. 11). 373p. 1997. pap. 21.95 (*1-85075-803-4*, Pub. by Sheffield Acad) CUP Services.
***Pentecostals after a Century: Global Perspectives on a Movement in Transition.** Ed. by Allan H. Anderson & Walter J. Hollenweger. (Journal of Pentecostal Theology Supplement Ser.: No. 15). 232p. 1999. pap. 21.95 (*1-84127-006-7*, Pub. by Sheffield Acad) CUP Services.
Pentekontaetia: The Great Fifty Years. Ann Deagon. (Orig.). 1985. pap. 12.00 (*0-931956-21-8*) Water Mark.
Penthesilea: A Tragic Drama. Heinrich Von Kleist. Tr. by Joel Agee. LC 98-73655. (Illus.). 224p. 1998. 30.00 (*0-06-118015-7*) HarpC.
***Penthesilea: A Tragic Drama.** Heinrich Von Kleist. 224p. 2000. pap. 16.00 (*0-06-095632-1*, Perennial) HarperTrade.
Penthesilee, de Kleist. Julien Gracq. 128p. 25.00 (*0-686-54023-9*) Fr & Eur.
Penthorse. Thomas Hagey. (Orig.). 1991. pap. 9.95 (*0-9628198-0-8*) W Kent.
Penthos. Irenee Hausherr. 1982. pap. 11.95 (*0-87907-953-3*) Cistercian Pubns.
Penthouse Guide to Cybersex. Nancy Tamosaitis. 1995. pap. 12.98 (*1-887298-12-6*) Penthse Images.
Penthouse Letters. Ed. by John Heidenry. 304p. 1989. mass mkt. 7.99 (*0-446-35778-2*, Pub. by Warner Bks) Little.
Celebrate the Rites of Passion, No. VII. Penthouse Magazine Editors. LC 97-186071. (Letters to Penthouse Ser.). 368p. (Orig.). 1997. mass mkt. 7.99 (*0-446-60418-6*, Pub. by Warner Bks) Little.
Penthouse Nurse. large type ed. Jane Converse. (Linford Romance Library). 224p. 1993. pap. 16.99 (*0-7089-7411-2*, Linford) Ulverscroft.
***Penthouse Uncensored.** Penthouse Magazine Editors. 592p. 2000. pap. 14.95 (*0-446-67735-3*) Warner Bks.
***Pentimento.** Lillian Hellman. 320p. 2000. pap. 13.95 (*0-316-35288-8*, Back Bay) Little.
Pentinent Psalm: A Commentary on the Penitential Psalms. Ed. by Alexander Barratt. Tr. by Dame Eleanor Hull. (Early English Text Society-Original Ser.: Vol. 307). (FRE & ENG., Illus.). 368p. (C). 1996. text 75.00 (*0-19-722309-5*) OUP.
Pentium & Pentium Pro Processors & Related Products. (Illus.). 1407p. 1996. pap. 23.95 (*1-55512-251-5*) McGraw.
Pentium Microprocessor. James L. Antonakos. LC 96-43995. 539p. (C). 1996. 106.00 (*0-02-303614-1*, Macmillan Coll) P-H.
Pentium Pro & Pentium II System Architecture. 2nd ed. Mindshare, Inc. Staff. LC 97-39010. 624p. (C). 1997. pap. text 36.95 (*0-201-30973-4*) Addison-Wesley.
Pentium Pro Family Developer's Manual, Vol. 1, Specifications see Pentium Pro Processor Developer's Manual
Pentium Pro Family Developer's Manual, Vol. 2, Programmer's Reference Manual see Pentium Pro Processor Developer's Manual
Pentium Pro Family Developer's Manual, Vol. 3, Operating Systems Writer's Manual see Pentium Pro Processor Developer's Manual
Pentium Pro Processor Developer's Manual. Incl. Pentium Pro Family Developer's Manual Vol. 1: Specifications. 352p. Date not set. pap. 26.95 (*1-55512-259-0*); Pentium Pro Family Developer's Manual Vol. 2: Programmer's Reference Manual. 656p. pap. 27.95 (*1-55512-260-4*); Pentium Pro Family Developer's Manual Vol. 3: Operating Systems Writer's Manual. 352p. pap. 26.95 (*1-55512-261-2*); 79.95 (*0-07-913058-5*) McGraw.
Pentium Pro System Architecture. Tom Shanley. LC 96-49786. 560p. (C). 1996. pap. text 34.95 (*0-201-47953-2*) Addison-Wesley.
Pentium Processing Developers Manual, Vol. 1. Intel Corporation Staff. 1996. pap. text 26.95 (*0-07-032895-1*) McGraw.
Pentium Processing Developers Manual, Vol. 2. Intel Corporation Staff. 1996. pap. text 27.95 (*0-07-032896-X*) McGraw.
Pentium Processing Developers Manual, Vol. 3. Intel Corporation Staff. 1996. pap. text 26.95 (*0-07-032897-8*) McGraw.
Pentium Processor System Architecture. 2nd ed. Don Anderson et al. LC 95-1804. (PC System Architecture Ser.). 464p. (C). 1995. pap. text 34.95 (*0-201-40992-5*) Addison-Wesley.
Pentium Processors & Related Products. Intel Corporation Staff. 1996. pap. text 23.95 (*0-07-032903-6*) McGraw.
Pentomic Era: The U. S. Army Between Korea & Vietnam. A. J. Bacevich. 197p. (Orig.). (C). 1995. pap. text 30.00 (*0-7881-2150-2*) DIANE Pub.
Pentominoes. John Millingrton. (Illus.). 1993. pap. 7.95 (*0-906212-57-X*, Pub. by Tarquin Pubns) Parkwest Pubns.
Pentominoes. Arthur J. Wiebe. (Illus.). 93p. (J). (gr. 1-6). 1973. 8.95 (*1-878669-60-5*) Crea Tea Assocs.
Pentoxifylline & Analogues: Effects on Leukocyte Function. Ed. by G. L. Mandell et al. (Illus.). x, 232p. 1990. 170.50 (*3-8055-5302-1*) S Karger.
Pentoxifylline, Pharmacological & Clinical Research. Ed. by J. L. Ambrus. 35.00 (*0-915340-06-2*) PJD Pubns.
Pentti Sammallahti. Pentti Sammallahti et al. 108p. 1997. pap. 35.00 (*952-9851-10-3*) Dist Art Pubs.
Pentum Mission. Joe Fontana. LC 97-44196. 400p. 1998. 24.95 (*0-914061-72-0*) Orchises Pr.
Penturbia: Where Real Estate Will Boom After the Crash of Suburbia. Jack Lessinger. (Illus.). 1991. 22.95 (*0-9625182-5-5*) Socioeconomics.
Penultimate Truth. Philip K. Dick. 201p. 1989. mass mkt. 3.95 (*0-88184-493-4*) Carroll & Graf.
Penultimate Words, & Other Essays. Lev Shestov. LC 67-22117. (Essay Index Reprint Ser.). 1977. 17.95 (*0-8369-0876-7*) Ayer.
Penumbra. Lalla Romano. Tr. by Sian Williams. 1999. pap. 12.95 (*0-7043-8071-4*) Interlink Pub.
Penumbra: Shadows, Places, & People. Patrick P. Garrett. (Illus.). 80p. 1997. 20.00 (*0-9649194-3-5*) P P Garrett.
Penumbra: The Shadow of Destiny in the Arabic World. Paulo Nozolino. (Illus.). 112p. 39.95 (*3-931141-32-2*, 620352, Pub. by Scalo Pubs) Dist Art Pubs.
***Penumbral Visions: The Making of Polities in Early Modern South India.** Sanjay Subrahmanyam. 320p. 2000. text 29.95 (*0-19-565142-1*) OUP.
Penza Oblast: Economy, Industry, Government, Business. 2nd rev. ed. Russian Information & Business Center, Inc. Staff. (Russian Regional Business Directories Ser.). (Illus.). 200p. 1997. pap. 99.00 (*1-57751-406-8*) Intl Business Pubns.
***Penza Oblast Regional Investment & Business Guide.** Global Investment & Business Center, Inc. Staff. (Russian Regional Investment & Business Guides Ser.: Vol. 58). (Illus.). 350p. 1999. pap. 99.00 (*0-7397-0857-0*) Intl Business Pubns.
***Penza Oblast Regional Investment & Business Guide.** Contrib. by Global Investment & Business Center, Inc. Staff. (Russian Regional Investment & Business Guides Ser.: Vol. 58). (Illus.). 350p. 2000. pap. 99.95 (*0-7397-3006-1*) Intl Business Pubns.
Peonage Files of the U.S. Department of Justice, 1901-1945. Pete Daniel et al. LC 90-12380. (Black Studies Research Sources). 26 p. 1989. write for info. (*0-89093-991-8*) U Pubns Amer.
Peonies see Paeonien: Pfingstrosen
Peonies Jane Fearnley-Whittingstall. LC 99-25414. 384p. 1999. 35.00 (*0-8109-4354-9*, Pub. by Abrams) Time Warner.
Peonies. Allan Rogers et al. LC 94-48535. (Illus.). 384p. 1995. 34.95 (*0-88192-317-6*) Timber.
Peonies & Definitely Inuit Sounds. Penny Skillman. (Chapbook Ser.). 25p. 1994. 2.75 (*0-685-71548-5*) White Owl Bks.
Peonies Kana: Haiku by the Upasaka Shiki. Tr. by Harold J. Isaacson. (Bhaisajaguru Ser.). 1972. pap. 1.85 (*0-87830-547-5*, Thtre Arts Bks) Routledge.
Peony. Pearl Synderstricker Buck. 338p. 1990. pap. 11.95 (*0-8197-0593-4*) Bloch.
Peony. Pearl Synderstricker Buck. LC 95-44446. (Illus.). 338p. 1996. reprint ed. lib. bdg. 24.95 (*0-8197-0617-5*) Bloch.
Peony. Pearl Synderstricker Buck. LC 95-44446. 320p. 1996. reprint ed. pap. 11.95 (*1-55921-168-7*) Moyer Bell.
Peony. rev. ed. Alice Harding. LC 92-32021. (Illus.). 178p. 1993. 29.95 (*0-88192-274-9*) Timber.
Peony Pavilion. Xian Zu Tang. Tr. by Cyril Birch from CHI. LC 79-9631. (Illus.). 350p. 1994. reprint ed. pap. text 19.95 (*0-88727-206-1*) Cheng & Tsui.
Peony Pavilion: A Novel. Xian Zu Tang. LC 99-90422. (Illus.). 256p. 1999. pap. 16.95 (*0-9665421-2-6*) Homa & Sekey.
Peony Pavilion (Mudan Ting) Xian Zu Tang. Tr. by Cyril Birch. LC 79-9631. (Chinese Literature in Translation Ser.). (Illus.). 360p. 1980. 49.95 (*0-253-35723-3*) Ind U Pr.
People see Adams County
People see Working Series
People. 104p. pap. 21.95 (*0-88108-211-2*) Art Dir.
People. (Fit-a-Shapes Ser.). (Illus.). 10p. (J). (ps up). 1999. pap. 5.95 (*0-7624-0445-0*) Running Pr.
People. J. L. Angel. LC 73-139121. (Lerna Ser.: Vol. 2). (Illus.). xi, 160p. 1971. 25.00 (*0-87661-302-4*) Am Sch Athens.
People. Ed. by Roger A. Hammer. LC 91-7567. (Illus.). 64p. 1990. pap. 5.95 (*0-913990-77-9*) Book Pub Co.
People. Pierre Hamp. Tr. by James Whitall. LC 74-121558. (Short Story Index Reprint Ser.). 1977. 18.95 (*0-8369-3515-2*) Ayer.
People. Sally Hewitt. LC 99-35496. 1999. pap. text. write for info. (*0-7613-0829-6*, Copper Beech Bks) Millbrook Pr.
***People.** Sue Lacey. LC 99-35496. (Start with Art Ser.). (Illus.). 32p. (J). (gr. 2-5). 1999. lib. bdg. 21.90 (*0-7613-3262-6*, Copper Beech Bks) Millbrook Pr.
People. June Leaf. (Illus.). 62p. 1994. pap. 19.95 (*1-879886-36-7*) Addison Gallery.
People. Jules Michelet. 1973. 200.00 (*0-8490-0810-7*) Gordon Pr.
People. Molly Perham & Julian Rowe. LC 95-2727. (MapWorlds Ser.). (Illus.). 32p. (J). (gr. 5-8). 1995. lib. bdg. 20.00 (*0-531-14362-7*) Watts.
People. Robert B. Pickering. LC 95-3046. (Prehistoric North America Ser.). (Illus.). 48p. (J). (gr. 2-4). 1996. lib. bdg. 21.90 (*1-56294-550-5*) Millbrook Pr.
People. Gail Saunders-Smith. (J). 1998. 53.00 (*0-516-29778-3*) Childrens.
People. Peter Spier. LC 78-19832. (Illus.). 48p. (J). (gr. 1-3). 1980. 16.95 (*0-385-13181-X*) Doubleday.
People. Peter Spier. LC 78-19832. (Illus.). 48p. (J). (ps up). 1988. pap. 12.95 (*0-385-24469-X*) Doubleday.
People. Peter Spier. 1980. 16.15 (*0-606-03961-9*, Pub. by Turtleback) Demco.
People see Florentine Codex, A General History of the Things of New Spain
People: A Global Agenda. Ed. by Uner Kirdar & Leonard Silk. 420p. (C). 1995. text 45.00 (*0-8147-4670-5*) NYU Pr.
People: And Other Uncollected Fiction. Bernard Malamud. 1989. 18.95 (*0-374-23067-6*) FS&G.
People: Bible Story. Standard Publishing Staff. (Collect-a-Bible Story Bks.). 1998. pap. 1.49 (*0-7847-0778-2*) Standard Pub.
***People: Favorite Pictures.** Editors of People Magazine. (Illus.). 176p. 2000. write for info. (*1-929049-00-5*) Tme Inc.

An Asterisk (*) at the beginning of an entry indicates that the title is appearing for the first time.

People: Indians of the American Southwest. Stephen A. Trimble. (Illus.). 536p. 1993. pap. 34.95 (*0-933452-37-3*) Schol Am Res.

People: Legends in Life & Art. Photos by Roloff Beny. LC 95-60280. (Illus.). 208p. 1995. 50.00 (*0-500-97426-8*, Pub. by Thames Hudson) Norton.

People: No Different Flesh. Zenna Henderson. 224p. 1968. pap. 3.50 (*0-380-01506-4*, Avon Bks) Morrow Avon.

People: No Different Flesh. Zenna Henderson. 1993. reprint ed. lib. bdg. 18.95 (*0-89968-343-6*, Lghtyr Pr) Buccaneer Bks.

People: Private Lives. People Magazine Editors. (Annual Ser.). (Illus.). 144p. 1993. write for info. (*1-883013-00-3*) Tme Inc.

***People: Psychology from a Cultural Perspective.** David Matsumoto. 184p. (C). 2000. pap. 14.95 (*1-57766-113-3*) Waveland Pr.

People: Reflections of Native Peoples on the Catholic Experience in North America. P. Michael Galvin et al. Ed. by Patricia Feistritzer. (Illus.). 97p. (Orig.). 1992. pap. 10.00 (*1-55833-117-4*) Natl Cath Educ.

People: The Diana Years. Time-Life Books Editors. 160p. (gr. 11). 1999. 24.95 (*1-883013-45-3*) Time-Life.

People: The Most Intriguing People of the Century. Time-Life Books Editors. LC 97-68230. 160p. (gr. 7). 1999. 29.95 (*1-883013-14-3*) Time-Life.

People: The Native Americans - Thoughts & Feelings. Ed. by Roger A. Hammer. (Illus.). 32p. 1987. pap. 9.95 (*0-932991-03-3*) Place in the Woods.

People: Who Will Live in Colville Area History. (Illus.). 176p. (Orig.). 1989. pap. 16.95 (*0-940151-15-4*) Statesman-Exam.

People Vol. II: Our Native American Legacy. Max Ferguson. 234p. (C). 1997. pap. write for info. (*1-57502-631-7*, PO1791) Morris Pubng.

People - Neighbor. (Sesame Street Ser.: No. 14). (J). 1989. pap. 1.49 (*0-553-18397-4*) Bantam.

People - Plant Relationships: Setting Research Priorities. Intro. by Joel Flagler. LC 94-3031. (Journal of Home & Consumer Horticulture). (Illus.). 368p. 1994. lib. bdg. 49.95 (*1-56022-050-3*) Haworth Pr.

People - Property - Prospects: Who's Living in America's High Income Neighborhoods. Ed. by Robert Elster. 1542p. 1991. 225.00 (*1-879784-28-9*, 600330) Taft Group.

People--Their Power: The Rural Electric Fact Book. rev. ed. Erma Angevine. (Illus.). 196p. 1981. pap. 3.75 (*0-686-31129-9*) Natl Rural.

***People, a Collection of Poems.** Anastasia Fardella. LC 98-89645. 128p. 1999. 17.95 (*1-56167-481-8*) Noble Hse MD.

***People Advantage: Improving Results Through Better Selection & Performance.** Neville Bain & Bill Mabey. LC 99-41759. 2000. 34.95 (*1-55753-177-3*) Purdue U Pr.

People Affinities. Bernard Jensen. 1988. pap. 7.99 (*0-932615-14-7*) B Jensen.

People along the Sand: Three Stories, Six Poems, a Memoir. Anthony Brandt. 83p. (Orig.). 1992. pap. 9.95 (*0-9630164-1-5*) Canios Edit.

People along the Way: The Autobiography of Dan Smoot. 2nd ed. Dan Smoot. 320p. (Orig.). 1996. pap. 12.95 (*1-884441-50-5*) Tyler Pr.

People among Peoples: Quaker Benevolence in Eighteenth-Century America. Sydney V. James. LC 62-20248. 423p. reprint ed. pap. 131.20 (*0-7837-3864-1*, 204368600010) Bks Demand.

People & a Nation, 3 vols. 3rd ed. Norton et al. (C). 1990. pap. text 4.76 (*0-395-52982-4*) HM.

People & a Nation, 3 vols. 3rd ed. Norton et al. (C). 1990. pap. text 4.76 (*0-395-52981-6*) HM.

People & a Nation: A History of the United States, 4 vols. 4th ed. Mary Norton. (C). 1993. 65.16 (*0-395-69773-5*) HM.

People & a Nation: A History of the United States: Instructor's Resource Manual with Video Guide, 4 vols. 4th ed. Mary B. Norton et al. (C). 1993. text 5.16 (*0-395-67822-6*) HM.

People & a Nation Vol. I: A History of the United States, Brief Edition, 4 vols. 4th ed. Mary B. Norton et al. (C). 1995. pap. text, student ed. 19.56 (*0-395-74571-3*) HM.

People & a Nation Vol. 1: A History of the United States, Brief Edition: To 1877, 4 vols. 4th ed. Mary B. Norton et al. 324p. (C). 1995. pap. text 28.76 (*0-395-74569-1*) HM.

People & a Nation Vol. I: A History of the United States: To 1877, 4 vols. 4th ed. Mary B. Norton et al. 464p. (C). 1993. pap. text 48.76 (*0-395-69774-3*) HM.

People & a Nation Vol. II: A History of the United States. 2nd ed. Mary B. Norton et al. LC 85-60316. 1072p. 1985. trans. 84.76 (*0-685-12000-7*); disk. write for info. (*0-318-60190-7*) HM.

People & a Nation Vol. II: A History of the United States, 4 vols. 4th ed. Mary B. Norton et al. (C). 1994. pap. text, student ed. 21.96 (*0-395-67820-X*); pap. text, student ed. 21.96 (*0-395-67821-8*) HM.

People & a Nation Vol. II: A History of the United States, 1. 2nd ed. Mary B. Norton et al. LC 85-60316. 1072p. 1985. 27.16 (*0-685-11998-X*) HM.

People & a Nation Vol. II: A History of the United States, 2. 2nd ed. Mary B. Norton et al. LC 85-60316. 1072p. 1985. text 27.16 (*0-685-11999-8*) HM.

People & a Nation Vol. II: A History of the United States, Brief Edition, 4 vols. 4th ed. Mary B. Norton et al. (C). 1995. pap. text, student ed. 19.56 (*0-395-74572-1*) HM.

People & a Nation Vol. 2: A History of the United States, Brief Edition: Since 1865, 4 vols. 4th ed. Mary B. Norton et al. 375p. (C). 1995. pap. text 28.76 (*0-395-74570-5*) HM.

People & a Proletariat: Essays in the History of Wales, 1780-1980. Dai Smith & Society for the Study of Welsh Labour History Staff. LC 81-136466. 239 P. ;p. 1980. write for info. (*0-86104-321-9*) Pluto GBR.

People & Change: An Introduction to Counseling & Stress Management. Catherine M. Flanagan. 264p. 1990. 69.95 (*0-8058-0450-1*); pap. 39.95 (*0-8058-0451-X*) L Erlbaum Assocs.

People & Change: Planning for Action. J. Gordon Myers. (Illus.). 60p. 1997. pap. 19.95 (*1-884731-15-5*, 06200) Oriel Inc.

People & Chips: The Human Implications of Information Technology. 3rd ed. Christopher Rowe & Jane Thompson. LC 96-42124. 1996. pap. write for info. (*0-07-709345-3*) McGraw.

People & Computers. Vinsonhaler. Date not set. pap. text, teacher ed. write for info. (*0-314-52511-4*) West Pub.

People & Computers: How to Evaluate Your Company's New Technology. Chris Clegg et al. 268p. 1988. text 51.95 (*0-470-21207-1*) P-H.

People & Computers No. 12: Proceedings of HCI'97. Ed. by H. Thimbleby & B. O'Conaill. xi, 420p. 1997. pap. 84.95 (*3-540-76172-1*) Spr-Verlag.

People & Computers VIII: Proceedings of the HCI '93 Conference. Ed. by J. L. Alty et al. (British Computer Society Conference Ser.: No. 7). (Illus.). 502p. (C). 1994. pap. text 80.00 (*0-521-46633-4*) Cambridge U Pr.

People & Computers XI: Proceedings of the HCI '96 Conference, Vol. 11. M. A. Sasse & J. Cunningham. 398p. 1996. text 78.00 (*3-540-76069-5*) Spr-Verlag.

People & Computers V: Proceedings of the Fifth Conference of the BCS Human-Computer Interaction Specialist Group. Ed. by Alistair G. Sutcliffe & Linda Macaulay. (British Computer Society Conference Ser.). 516p. (C). 1990. text 115.00 (*0-521-38430-3*) Cambridge U Pr.

People & Computers IV. Ed. by Dylan M. Jones & Russell Winder. (British Computer Society Conference Ser.). 608p. (C). 1988. text 105.00 (*0-521-36553-8*) Cambridge U Pr.

People & Computers IX: Proceedings of the HCI '94 Conference. Ed. by Gilbert Cockton et al. (British Computer Society Conference Ser.). (Illus.). 440p. (C). 1995. pap. text 69.95 (*0-521-48557-6*) Cambridge U Pr.

People & Computers VII. Ed. by D. Diaper et al. (British Computer Society Conference Ser.). (Illus.). 544p. (C). 1992. pap. text 95.00 (*0-521-44591-4*) Cambridge U Pr.

People & Computers VI. Ed. by D. Diaper & Nicholas G. Hammond. (British Computer Society Conference Ser.). (Illus.). 464p. (C). 1991. text 95.00 (*0-521-41694-9*) Cambridge U Pr.

People & Computers X: Proceedings of the HCI '95 Conference. Ed. by M. A. Kirby et al. (British Computer Society Conference Ser.). 448p. (C). 1996. pap. text 74.95 (*0-521-56729-7*) Cambridge U Pr.

People & Computers III. Ed. by D. Diaper & Russell Winder. (British Computer Society Conference Ser.). 492p. 1988. text 105.00 (*0-521-35197-9*) Cambridge U Pr.

***People & Computers XIII.** H. Johnson & L. M. Nigay. Ed. by C. R. Roast. 342p. 1998. pap. 99.00 (*3-540-76261-2*) Spr-Verlag.

People & Culture. Chi-Lu Chen. 160p. 1987. 22.00 (*0-89986-370-1*) Oriental Bk Store.

People & Culture of the Middle East. 2nd ed. Bates. 352p. 2000. pap. 36.00 (*0-13-656489-5*) P-H.

People & Cultures of Hawaii: A Psychocultural Profile. Ed. by John F. McDermott, Jr. et al. LC 80-11959. 252p. 1980. pap. 11.95 (*0-8248-0706-5*) UH Pr.

People & Customs of the World. Chelsea House Publishing Staff. 1998. 79.80 (*0-7910-5137-4*) Chelsea Hse.

People & Dog in the Sun. Ronald Wallace. LC 86-25041. (Poetry Ser.). 66p. 1987. pap. 10.95 (*0-8229-5388-9*) U of Pittsburgh Pr.

People & Education in the Third World. W. T. Gould. 1993. pap. 35.95 (*0-582-00560-4*, Pub. by Addison-Wesley) Longman.

People & Empires in African History: Essays in Memory of Michael Crowder. Ed. by J. F. Adeajayi & J. D. Peel. 254p. (C). 1992. text 49.95 (*0-582-08997-2*) Longman.

People & Employment. A. K. Whitehead & L. Baruch. 1981. pap. 21.00 (*0-408-10692-1*, MICHIE) LEXIS Pub.

People & Environment: Behavioral Approaches in Human Geography. 2nd ed. D. J. Walmsley. 1993. pap. 34.95 (*0-582-07866-0*, Pub. by Addison-Wesley) Longman.

People & Environment: Development for the Future. Ed. by Stephen Morse & Michael Stoking. 215p. 1996. pap. 25.95 (*0-7748-0546-3*) U of Wash Pr.

People & Folks: Gangs, Crime & the Underclass in a Rustbelt City. 2nd rev. ed. John M. Hagedorn & Perry Macon. LC 97-25593. (Illus.). 320p. 1998. 35.00 (*0-941702-45-6*, 45-6); pap. 17.95 (*0-941702-46-4*, 46-4) Lake View Pr.

People & Food Tomorrow: The Scientific, Economic, Political, & Social Factors Affecting Food Supplies in the Last Quarter of the 20th Century. Ed. by Dorothy Hollingsworth & Elisabeth Morse. (Illus.). 173p. 1976. 59.50 (*0-85334-701-8*) Elsevier.

***People & Forests: Communities, Institutions & Governance.** Ed. by Clark C. Gibson et al. LC 99-43446. (Politics, Science & the Environment Ser.). (Illus.). 298p. 2000. 52.00 (*0-262-07201-7*); pap. 21.00 (*0-262-57137-4*) MIT Pr.

People & Happenings. Emery Turner. 94p. 1996. pap. 10.00 (*0-941363-42-2*) Lake Shore Pub.

People & Housing in Third World Cities: Perspectives on the Problem of Spontaneous Settlements. 2nd ed. Denis J. Dwyer. LC 74-84346. (Illus.). 310p. reprint ed. pap. 96.10 (*0-8357-6252-1*, 203451000090) Bks Demand.

People & Identity in Ostrogothic Italy, 489-554. Patrick Amory. (Cambridge Studies in Medieval Life & Thought: No. 33). 547p. 1997. text 95.00 (*0-521-57151-0*) Cambridge U Pr.

People & Industries. William H. Chaloner. (Illus.). 151p. 1963. 24.00 (*0-7146-1284-7*, Pub. by F Cass Pubs) Intl Spec Bk.

***People & Issues in Latin American History.** 2nd ed. Lewis Hanke & Jane M. Rausch. LC 99-89843. 2000. pap. write for info. (*1-55876-234-5*) Wiener Pubs Inc.

People & Issues in Latin American History: From Independence to the Present, Vol. 2. Ed. by Lewis Hanke. LC 89-27946. (Illus.). 368p. (Orig.). (C). 1990. pap. 19.95 (*1-55876-018-0*) Wiener Pubs Inc.

People & Issues in Latin American History: The Colonial Experience, Vol. 1. 3rd rev. ed. Ed. by Lewis Hanke. (Illus.). 368p. (C). 1993. pap. text 19.95 (*1-55876-061-X*) Wiener Pubs Inc.

***People & Issues in Latin American History Vol. II: From Independence to the Present.** 2nd rev. ed. Ed. by Jane M. Rausch & Lewis Hanke. (Illus.). 380p. 1999. pap. text 22.95 (*1-55876-195-0*) Wiener Pubs Inc.

People & Kids. Sarellen M. Wuest. 272p. (Orig.). 1986. pap. 9.95 (*0-938545-02-7*) Jennings & Keefe.

People & Land in the Holiness Code: An Exegetical Study of the Ideational Framework of the Law in Leviticus 17-26. Jan Joosten. LC 96-41882. (Vetus Testamentum, Supplements Ser.: Vol. 67). 225p. 1996. 84.00 (*90-04-10557-3*) Brill Academic Pubs.

People & Nations, 3 vols. 3rd ed. Norton. (C). Date not set. pap. text, teacher ed., suppl. ed. write for info. (*0-395-57401-3*) HM.

People & Nations, 3 vols. 3rd ed. Norton. (C). 1991. pap. text, teacher ed. 3.16 (*0-395-56302-X*) HM.

People & Nature Conservation: Perspectives on Private Land Use & Endangered Species Recovery. Ed. by Surrey Beatty Staff et al. 238p. 1999. pap. 180.00 (*0-646-24507-4*, Pub. by Surrey Beatty & Sons) St Mut.

People & Notes: The Southern Oregon Symphonic Band & Its Predecessor the Hillah Temple Shrine Band. Bert Webber. LC 94-424447. (Illus.). 112p. 1994. pap. 10.95 (*1-878815-06-7*) Reflected Images.

People & Notes II: Southern Oregon Concert Band. Bert Webber. Ed. by Margie Webber. LC 98-23420. (Illus.). 1998. pap. 12.95 (*1-878815-08-3*) Reflected Images.

People & Organisations in the Delta Programme, 1992-1995: European Research & Development Projects. (Illus.). 121p. (Orig.). (C). 1993. pap. text 50.00 (*1-56806-397-0*) DIANE Pub.

People & Organizations Interacting. Ed. by Aat Brakel. LC 84-5212. 272p. 1985. 215.00 (*0-471-90476-7*) Wiley.

People & Parks: Linking Protected Area Management with Local Communities. Katrina Brandon et al. 112p. 1992. pap. 22.00 (*0-8213-2053-X*, 12053) World Bank.

People & Parliament in the European Union: Participation, Democracy & Legitimacy. Jean Blondel et al. LC 98-12093. (Illus.). 304p. 1998. text 70.00 (*0-19-829308-9*) OUP.

People & Participation in Sustainable Development. Ganes Sivakoti et al. 1997. pap. 74.00 (*0-7855-7479-4*, Pub. by Ratna Pustak Bhandar) St Mut.

People & Particles. unabridged ed. Cornelius Tobias & Ida Tobias. LC 97-65703. (Illus.). vi, 230p. 1997. 25.00 (*0-911302-75-1*) San Francisco Pr.

People And Pearls: The Magic Endures. Keith Hackney. LC 00-38483. (Illus.). 240p. 2000. 40.00 (*0-06-019331-X*) HarpC.

People & Physical Environment. Eyre. Date not set. pap. text. write for info. (*0-582-02427-7*, Pub. by Addison-Wesley) Longman.

People & Pixels: Linking Remote Sensing & Social Science. National Research Council Staff. LC 98-8945. 1998. pap. 30.00 (*0-309-06408-2*) Natl Acad Pr.

***People & Place: The Extraordinary Geography of Everyday Life.** Lewis J. Holloway & Phil Hubbard. LC 00-33965. 2000. write for info. (*0-582-38212-2*) Pearson Educ.

People & Places see Record Breakers

People & Places. 1999. pap. 169.80 (*0-8172-4683-5*) Raintree Steck-V.

***People & Places.** Michael Chinery. (Secrets of the Rainforest Ser.). (Illus.). 32p. (J). (gr. 3-9). 2000. pap. 7.95 (*0-7787-0230-8*); lib. bdg. 19.96 (*0-7787-0220-0*) Crabtree Pub Co.

People & Places. Margaret Early. 1983. 30.75 (*0-15-331257-2*) Harcourt Schl Pubs.

People & Places. Tom Seims. (In the Picture with Jesus Ser.). (Illus.). 32p. (Orig.). (J). 1993. 4.99 (*1-56476-047-2*, 6-3047, Victor Bks) Chariot Victor.

People & Places. Tom Siems & Arbuckle. (J). 1995. 12.99 incl. audio Chariot Victor.

***People & Places.** Lauren Weidenman & Gail Saunders-Smith. LC 00-36471. (Illus.). (J). 2000. write for info. (*0-7368-0743-8*) Capstone Pr.

People & Places: A Memoir. Jacomena Maybeck. (Illus.). 152p. (Orig.). 1992. pap. 9.95 (*1-879042-01-0*) Stonegarden Pr.

People & Places: Roslyn Logsdon's Imagery in Fiber. Roslyn Logsdon. (Illus.). 56p. 1999. pap. 14.95 (*1-881982-14-9*) Stackpole.

People & Places in Changing World. 2nd ed. (HA - Social Studies). 1995. pap. 149.95 (*0-314-04541-4*) West Pub.

People & Places in Colonial Venezuela. John V. Lombardi. LC 75-25433. 500p. reprint ed. pap. 155.00 (*0-608-13199-7*, 205604300044) Bks Demand.

People & Places in Northern Europe, 500-1600: Essays in Honour of Peter Hayes Sawyer. Ed. by Ian Wood & Niels Lund. (Illus.). 270p. 1996. 90.00 (*0-85115-547-2*, Boydell Pr) Boydell & Brewer.

People & Places in Texas Past. June R. Welch. 1983. 20.95 (*0-912854-05-7*) Yellow Rose Pr.

People & Planet: A Practical Politics for the Environment. Ann Taylor. LC 91-42951. 240p. (C). 1992. pap. 29.99 (*0-415-07946-2*, A6920) Routledge.

People & Politics: Who Should Govern? National Issues Institute Staff. 48p. 1993. 3.25 incl. disk (*0-8403-8091-7*) Kendall-Hunt.

People & Politics in the Middle East. Ed. by Michael Curtis. LC 72-140617. 335p. 1971. 39.95 (*0-87855-000-3*); pap. 24.95 (*0-87855-500-5*) Transaction Pubs.

People & Politics in Urban America. 2nd ed. Robert W. Kweit & Mary G. Kweit. LC 98-6537. (Political Science Ser.). (Illus.). 488p. 1998. 72.00 (*0-8153-2607-6*, SS1147); pap. 34.95 (*0-8153-2606-8*, SS1147) Garland.

People & Politics (1999) 8th ed. Michael Botterweck et al. (Illus.). 501p. 1999. pap. 30.00 (*0-911541-59-4*) Gregory Pub.

People & Politics of the Gulf: A Region in Transition. David E. Long & Lucia Rawls. 225p. 1994. text. write for info. (*0-8133-7668-8*) Westview.

People & Politics Studyguide (1999) 8th ed. Mary K. Hiatt. 288p. 1999. pap., student ed. 12.00 (*0-911541-60-8*) Gregory Pub.

People & Polity: The Organizational Dynamics of World Jewry. Daniel J. Elazar. LC 88-17404. 522p. 1989. pap. 24.95 (*0-8143-1844-4*) Wayne St U Pr.

People & Portrait Photography. Liz Walker. LC 95-49253. (Point & Shoot Ser.). (Illus.). 96p. 1995. 11.95 (*0-8174-5545-0*, Amphoto) Watsn-Guptill.

***People & Portraits.** Lee Hammond. LC 00-29214. (Drawing in Color Ser.). (Illus.). 80p. 2000. 14.99 (*1-58180-037-1*, North Lght Bks) F & W Pubns Inc.

People & Power in Byzantium: An Introduction to Modern Byzantine Studies. Alexander P. Kazhdan & Giles Constable. LC 81-12640. 1982. 15.00 (*0-88402-103-3*) Dumbarton Oaks.

People & Power in Scotland: Essays in Honour of T. C. Smout. John Donald Publ. Ltd. Staff et al. 200p. (C). 1997. text 60.00 (*0-85976-392-7*, Pub. by J Donald) St Mut.

People & Power in the Pacific: The Struggle for the Post-Cold War Order. Bello. LC 92-29810. (Transnational Institute Ser.). 147p. (C). 44.95 (*0-7453-0697-7*, Pub. by Pluto GBR) Stylus Pub VA.

People & Predicaments. Milton Mazer. (Illus.). 332p. 1976. 29.50 (*0-674-66075-7*) HUP.

People & Problems. (Illus.). 1997. write for info. (*0-945100-49-3*) Parlay Intl.

People & Production in Late Precolonial Tanzania: History & Structures. Juhani Koponen. (Finnish Society for Development Studies: Monograph No. 2). (Illus.). 434p. (Orig.). 1988. pap. 58.00 (*951-96156-0-1*) Coronet Bks.

People & Productivity. 3rd ed. Sutermeister. (Management Ser.). (C). 1976. text 24.95 (*0-07-062367-8*) McGraw.

People & Productivity in Japan. Terutomo Ozawa. (Studies in Productivity: Vol. 25). 42p. 1982. pap. 55.00 (*0-08-029506-1*) Work in Amer.

***People & Professions of Charleston, South Carolina, 1782-1802.** James W. Hagy. 112p. 1999. pap. 17.50 (*0-8063-1323-4*) Clearfield Co.

***People & Programs That Make a Difference in a Multicultural Society: Volunteerism in America.** Emma T. Pitts. LC 99-27737. 200p. 1999. text 79.95 (*0-7734-7946-5*) E Mellen.

People & Project Management for IT. Hadi Jassim & Sue Craig. LC 94-23473. (Software Engineering Ser.). 1995. write for info. (*0-07-707884-5*) McGraw.

People & Protected Areas: Toward Participatory Conservation in India. Ed. by Ashish Kothari et al. LC 96-7990. 236p. 1996. 38.00 (*0-8039-9333-1*) Sage.

People & Protest, 1815-1880. Ed. by Trevor Herbert & Gareth E. Jones. (Welsh History & Its Sources Ser.). xxx, 215p. 1990. reprint ed. pap. 14.95 (*0-7083-0988-7*, Pub. by Univ Wales Pr) Paul & Co Pubs.

People & Robbers of Cardemon Town: Musical. Thorbjorn Egner. (J). 1968. 6.00 (*0-87602-172-0*) Anchorage.

People & Self Management. Palmer. 128p. pap. text. write for info. (*0-7506-4865-1*) Buttrwrth-Heinemann.

People & Society in Scotland, 1830-1914, Vol. 2. Ed. by Hamish Fraser & R. J. Morris. (People & Society of Scotland Ser.). (Illus.). 300p. (C). 1996. pap. 48.00 (*0-85976-211-4*, Pub. by J Donald) St Mut.

People & Society in Scotland, Vol. 3. A. D. Dickson & J. H. Treble. (People & Society of Scotland Ser.). (Illus.). 300p. (C). 1998. pap. 48.00 (*0-85976-212-2*, Pub. by J Donald) St Mut.

People & Society in Scotland, 1760-1830: A Social History of Modern Scotland. T. M. Devine & R. Mrrchison. (People & Society of Scotland Ser.). 316p. (Orig.). (C). 1998. pap. 48.00 (*0-85976-210-6*, Pub. by J Donald) St Mut.

People & Technology. Mary Fisher. Ed. by Stephen Hayner & Gordon Aeschliman. (Global Issues Bible Study Ser.). 48p. (Orig.). 1990. wbk. ed. 4.99 (*0-8308-4909-2*, 4909) InterVarsity.

People & Technology in the Workplace. National Academy of Engineering Staff & National Research Council Staff. 336p. 1991. text 29.95 (*0-309-04583-5*) Natl Acad Pr.

People & the British Economy, 1830-1914: Land of Hope & Glory. Roderick Floud. LC 96-52762. (Illus.). 228p. 1997. pap. 16.95 (*0-19-289210-X*) OUP.

People & the Earth: An Environmental Atlas. Andrea Due. LC 98-7395. (J). 1998. lib. bdg. 235.00 (*0-7172-9204-5*) Grolier Educ.

People & the Earth: Basic Issues in the Sustainability of Resources & Environment. John J. Rogers & P. Geoffrey Feiss. LC 97-25901. (Illus.). 360p. (C). 1998. text 80.00 (*0-521-56028-4*); pap. text 32.95 (*0-521-56872-2*) Cambridge U Pr.

***People & the Environment.** 380p. (C). 1999. text 55.00 (*0-536-02045-0*) Pearson Custom.

P

People & the Environment Photography. Jonathan Hilton. (Pro Photo Ser.). 160p. 1999. pap. 35.00 (*2-88046-375-0*, Rotovision) Watsn-Guptill.

People & the Faith of the Bible. Andre N. Chouraqui. Tr. by William V. Gugli. LC 74-21237. 224p. 1975. 30.00 (*0-87023-172-3*) U of Mass Pr.

People & the King: The Comunero Revolution in Columbia. John L. Phelan. LC 76-53654. (Illus.). 331p. reprint ed. pap. 102.70 (*0-608-09920-1*, 206925800003) Bks Demand.

People & the Land: Te Tangata Me Te Whenua an Illustrated History of New Zealand 1820-1920. Judith Bassett et al. 352p. 1996. pap. 39.95 (*0-04-614013-1*) Paul & Co Pubs.

People & the Land Through Time: Linking Ecology & History. Emily W. Russell. LC 96-37098. (Illus.). 320p. 1997. 40.00 (*0-300-06830-1*); pap. 17.00 (*0-300-07730-0*) Yale U Pr.

People & the Mob: The Ideology of Civil Conflict in Modern Europe. Peter Hayes. LC 92-9826. 184p. 1992. 49.95 (*0-275-94336-4*, C4336, Praeger Pubs) Greenwood.

People & the Planet: Lessons for a Sustainable Future. Ed. by Pamela Wasserman. LC 96-36911. (Illus.). 189p. 1996. teacher ed., spiral bd. 22.95 (*0-945219-12-1*) Zero Pop Growth.

People & the Police. Algernon D. Black. LC 75-40991. 246p. 1976. reprint ed. lib. bdg. 59.50 (*0-8371-8699-4*, BLPP, Greenwood Pr) Greenwood.

People & the Promise. Ursula Synge. LC 74-10661. 192p. (J). (gr. 7-10). 1974. 27.95 (*0-87599-208-0*) S G Phillips.

People & the Stones. Heinz W. Sabais & Ruth Mead. 72p. 1983. pap. 14.95 (*0-85646-110-5*, Pub. by Anvil Press) Dufour.

People & Their Opinions. 2nd ed. Eric Shiraev. 118p. (C). 1998. per. 51.95 (*0-7872-5397-9*, 41539701) Kendall-Hunt.

People & Their Planet: A Textbook of Environmental Science. Miller. (Illus.). 640p. 1991. pap. text 39.95 (*0-8016-3301-X*) Mosby Inc.

People & Their Planet: Searching for Balance. Barbara S. Baudot & William Moomaw. LC 98-23533. 336p. 1999. text 75.00 (*0-312-21715-3*) St Martin.

People & Their Quilts. John R. Irwin. LC 83-61649. (Illus.). 214p. 1983. 45.00 (*0-916838-87-0*) Schiffer.

People & Their Quilts. John R. Irwin. LC 83-61649. (Illus.). 214p. 1984. pap. 19.95 (*0-88740-024-8*) Schiffer.

People & Tourism in Fragile Environments. Ed. by Martin F. Price. LC 96-1057. 254p. 1997. 110.00 (*0-471-96584-7*) Wiley.

People & Work: Human & Industrial Relations in Library & Information Work. Ed. by Rosemary Raddon. LC 93-104155. 189p. reprint ed. pap. 58.60 (*0-608-08884-6*, 206952100004) Bks Demand.

People Apart. Kathleen Kenna. (Illus.). 64p. (J). (gr. 3 up). 1995. 18.00 (*0-395-67344-5*) HM.

***People Apart.** Kathleen Kenna. (Illus.). 64p. (J). (gr. 3 up). 1998. 17.95 (*1-895897-59-9*) Somerville Hse.

People Apart: Chosenness & Ritual in Jewish Philosophical Thought. Ed. by Daniel H. Frank. LC 92-35706. (SUNY Series in Jewish Philosophy). 270p. (C). 1993. pap. text 19.95 (*0-7914-1632-1*) State U NY Pr.

People Apart: Chosenness & Ritual in Jewish Philosophical Thought. Ed. by Daniel H. Frank. LC 92-35706. (SUNY Series in Jewish Philosophy). 270p. (C). 1993. text 59.50 (*0-7914-1631-3*) State U NY Pr.

People Apart: Ethnicity & the Mennonite Brethren. John H. Redekop. 198p. 1987. pap. 2.95 (*0-919797-68-7*) Kindred Prods.

People Apart: The Jews in Europe, 1789-1939. David Vital. LC 98-51332. (Illus.). 962p. 1999. 45.00 (*0-19-821980-6*) OUP.

People Are Different, People Are the Same. Marge Passamaneck. 1983. pap. 3.25 (*0-89536-615-0*, 1629) CSS OH.

People Are Funny. Donald R. Byrd & Stanley J. Zelinski, III. (Pictures for Practice Ser.: Bk. 1). 80p. (Orig.). 1987. pap. text 16.91 (*0-582-79829-9*, 75079) Longman.

***People Are Good.** Harold R. Eberle. Ed. by Annette Bradley. LC 98-90360. 58p. 1998. pap. 8.45 (*1-882523-15-6*) Winepress Pubng.

People Are Just Desserts . . . Experience the Sweet Rewards. rev. ed. A. Perry. LC 97-171196. (Illus.). 112p. 1995. pap. 14.95 (*1-887879-00-5*) Perry Prods.

People Are Never the Problem. Robert Watts. 1999. pap. text 19.99 (*1-56292-492-3*) Honor Bks OK.

People Are Not the Same: Leprosy & Identity in Twentieth Century Mali. (Social History of Africa Ser.). 1995. text. write for info. (*0-435-07425-3*) Heinemann.

People Are Not the Same: Leprosy & Identity in Twentieth-Century Mali. Eric Silla. LC 97-39954. (Social History of Africa Ser.). 1998. 60.00 (*0-325-00005-0*); pap. text 26.00 (*0-325-00004-2*) Heinemann.

People Are Our Business. Beryl Williams. LC 79-179745. (Biography Index Reprint Ser.). 1977. reprint ed. 18.95 (*0-8369-8113-8*) Ayer.

People Are Starting to Complain about Too Much Violence on Cave Walls: A Herman Sunday Collection. Jim Unger. (Illus.). 80p. 1999. pap. 6.95 (*0-8362-2058-7*) Andrews & McMeel.

People, Art of Native Americans: Items from the Collection of Sara W. Reeves & I.S.K. Reeves V. I. S. Reeves. (Illus.). 56p. (Orig.). 1992. pap. 15.00 (*0-918548-03-9*) Green APC.

***People As an Agent of Environmental Change.** Ed. by R. A. Nicholson & T. P. O'Connor. (Symposia of the Association for Environmental Archaeology Ser.: Vol. 16). (Illus.). 135p. (C). 2000. pap. 45.00 (*1-84217-002-3*, Pub. by Oxbow Bks) David Brown.

People As Subject, People As Object: Selfhood & Peoplehood in Contemporary Israel. Virginia R. Dominguez. LC 89-40254. (New Directions in Anthropological Writing Ser.). 272p. 1989. pap. text 19.95 (*0-299-12324-3*) U of Wis Pr.

People at Play see In My World Series

People at Play. (Illus.). 1989. text 44.00 (*1-56290-070-6*, 6003) Crystal.

People at Play. Rollin L. Hartt. LC 75-1850. (Leisure Class in America Ser.). (Illus.). 1975. reprint ed. 23.95 (*0-405-06917-0*) Ayer.

People at Work see In My World Series

People at Work see Unblocking Your Organization

People at Work. (Illus.). 1989. text 44.00 (*1-56290-074-9*, 6005) Crystal.

People at Work. LC 97-132999. (Illus.). 536p. (J). 1996. 24.95 (*1-878172-51-4*, Wintergreen-Orchard) Riverside Pub Co.

***People At Work.** 2000. write for info. (*0-13-027904-8*) P-H.

People at Work. Dorine Barbey. LC 97-23938. (Illus.). 80p. (YA). (gr. 4 up). 2000. lib. bdg. 25.30 (*0-88682-954-2*, Creat Educ) Creative Co.

People at Work. Brooman. 1994. pap. text. write for info. (*0-582-24595-8*, Pub. by Addison-Wesley) Longman.

***People at Work.** Steck-Vaughn Company Staff. (Read All about It Ser.). (Illus.). (J). 2000. pap. 4.95 (*0-8114-3801-5*) Raintree Steck-V.

People at Work. Welsh Folk Museum Staff. (Illus.). 73p. 1987. pap. 8.95 (*0-8464-4726-6*) Beekman Pubs.

People at Work: Human Relations in Organizations. 4th ed. Paul R. Timm & Brent D. Peterson. Ed. by Clyde Perlee. LC 92-35569. 475p. (C). 1993. mass mkt. 54.75 (*0-314-00901-9*) West Pub.

People at Work: Human Relations in Organizations. 5th ed. Timm et al. LC 99-23191. 576p. 1999. 72.95 (*0-314-20041-X*) West Pub.

People at Work: Listening & Communicative Skills, Vocabulary Building. Edgar Sather et al. (Illus.). 112p. (YA). (gr. 8 up). 1990. student ed. 14.00 (*0-86647-037-9*) Pro Lingua.

People at Work: Student's Package, 1 bk. & 3 cass. Edgar Sather et al. (Illus.). 112p. (YA). (gr. 8 up). 1990. pap. text, student ed. 25.00 incl. audio (*0-86647-033-6*) Pro Lingua.

People at Work: Teacher's Package, 2 bks. & 3 cass. Edgar Sather et al. (Illus.). 1990. pap. text, teacher ed., student ed. 35.00 incl. audio (*0-86647-040-9*) Pro Lingua.

People at Work: The Independent Study Supplement & Teacher's Book. Edgar Sather et al. (Illus.). 112p. 1990. 14.00 (*0-86647-036-0*) Pro Lingua.

People at Work: The New Millenium. Paul M. Muchinsky. (Psychology). 2001. mass mkt. 54.95 (*0-534-34848-3*) Brooks-Cole.

People at Work at a Vet's. Deborah Fox. LC 98-34214. (People at Work Ser.). 1998. lib. bdg. 22.00 (*0-382-42027-6*, Dillon Silver Burdett) Silver Burdett Pr.

People at Work for an Airline. Deborah Fox. LC 98-28695. (People at Work Ser.). (J). 1998. 22.00 (*0-382-42025-X*, Dillon Silver Burdett); pap. 12.00 (*0-382-42026-8*, Dillon Silver Burdett) Silver Burdett Pr.

People at Work in Mountain Rescue. Deborah Fox. LC 98-8579. (People at Work Ser.). (J). 1998. 22.00 (*0-382-42029-2*, Dillon Silver Burdett); pap. 12.00 (*0-382-42030-6*, Dillon Silver Burdett) Silver Burdett Pr.

People at Work in Tv News. Deborah Fox. LC 98-23445. (People at Work Ser.). (J). 1998. write for info. (*0-382-42019-5*, Dillon Silver Burdett) Silver Burdett Pr.

People at Work In Tv News. Deborah Fox. LC 98-23445. (People at Work Ser.). (J). 1998. pap. write for info. (*0-382-42020-9*, Dillon Silver Burdett) Silver Burdett Pr.

People at Work Making a Film. Deborah Fox. LC 98-29589. (People at Work Ser.). (J). 1998. lib. bdg. write for info. (*0-382-42021-7*, Dillon Silver Burdett) Silver Burdett Pr.

People at Work Making Cars. Deborah Fox. LC 98-23456. (People at Work Ser.). (J). 1998. 22.00 (*0-382-42023-3*, Dillon Silver Burdett); pap. 12.00 (*0-382-42024-1*, Dillon Silver Burdett) Silver Burdett Pr.

People at Work (Pobl Wrth Eu Gwaith) Ed. by Welsh Folk Museum Staff. (Illus.). 85p. (C). 1987. pap. text 30.00 (*0-86383-367-5*, Pub. by Gomer Pr) St Mut.

People Atlas. Philip Steele. (Illus.). 64p. (J). (gr. 3-6). 1991. 18.95 (*0-19-520846-3*, 3395) OUP.

People Behind the Peace: Community & Reconciliation in Northern Ireland. Ronald Wells. LC 99-18022. 136p. 1999. pap. 13.00 (*0-8028-4667-X*) Eerdmans.

People Betrayed: November 1918, A German Revolution. Alfred Doblin. Tr. by John E. Woods from GER. LC 82-25133.Tr. of Verratenes Volk & Heimkehr der Fronttruppen. 642p. 1983. pap. 16.95 (*0-88064-008-1*) Fromm Intl Pub.

***People Betrayed: The Role of the West in Rwanda.** Linda Melvern. 288p. 2000. pap. 19.95 (*1-85649-831-X*, Pub. by Zed Books) St Martin.

***People Betrayed: The Role of the West in Rwanda.** Linda Melvern. 2000. text 69.95 (*1-85649-830-1*, Pub. by Zed Books) St Martin.

People Book. James. pap., teacher ed. 3.88 (*0-201-03280-5*) Addison-Wesley.

People Book, '95: A Marketer's Guide to Consumer Demographics. Ed Papazian. 78p. 1995. pap. 75.00 (*0-9621947-5-1*) Media Dynamics.

People Bug People. David A. Gaunt. (Illus.). 128p. 1996. pap. 11.95 (*1-880470-42-X*) Creative Des.

People Called Cajuns: Introduction to an Ethnohistory. James H. Dormon. LC 83-71493. (Illus.). 110p. (C). 1983. 10.00 (*0-940984-09-1*) Univ LA Lafayette.

People Called Cumberland Presbyterians: A History of the Cumberland Presbyterian Church, 2. Ben M. Barrus et al. 650p. 1998. pap. 45.00 (*1-57910-100-3*) Wipf & Stock.

People Called Quakers. Doris N. Dalglish. LC 78-90628. (Essay Index Reprint Ser.). 1977. 18.95 (*0-8369-1254-3*) Ayer.

People Called Quakers. D. Elton Trueblood. LC 85-7009. 298p. (C). 1971. pap. 13.00 (*0-913408-02-6*) Friends United.

People Called Shakers. enl. ed. Edward D. Andrews. 1990. 23.00 (*0-8446-1535-8*) Peter Smith.

People Called Shakers: A Search for the Perfect Society. Edward D. Andrews. (Illus.). 351p. 1963. pap. 8.95 (*0-486-21081-2*) Dover.

People Came from Everywhere. John D. Horman. 1.50 (*0-687-02660-1*) Abingdon.

***People Capability Maturity Model.** Phillips. 448p. (C). 1999. text. write for info. (*0-201-60445-0*) Addison-Wesley.

People Care in Institutions: A Conceptual Schema & Its Application. Yochanan Wozner. LC 90-4609. (Child & Youth Services Ser.: Vol. 15, No. 1). 238p. 1990. text 7.95 (*1-56024-012-1*); pap. text 4.95 (*1-56024-082-2*) Haworth Pr.

People Celebrate the 70s. 192p. 32.00 incl. cd-rom (*1-883013-99-2*) Tme Inc.

People Celebrates People: The Best of 1974-1996. Time-Life Books Editors. 144p. (gr. 7). 1999. 24.95 (*1-883013-44-5*) Time-Life.

People Celebrates Unforgettable Women. 160p. (gr. 7). 1999. 24.95 (*1-883013-36-4*) Time-Life.

People-Centered Development: Contributions Toward Theory & Planning Frameworks. fac. ed. Ed. by David C. Korten & Rudi Klauss. LC 84-914. (Illus.). 347p. 1984. pap. 107.60 (*0-7837-7580-6*, 204733300007) Bks Demand.

People Centered Profit Strategies: 101 Competitive Advantages. Paul Peyton. LC 99-35939. 260p. 1999. pap. text 18.95 (*1-55571-517-6*) PSI Resch.

People-Centred Health Promotion. John Raeburn & I. Rootman. LC 97-22463. 246p. 1997. pap. 54.95 (*0-471-97137-5*) Wiley.

People Chase Twisters: And Other Amazing Facts about Violent Weather. Kate Petty. LC 97-41607. (I Didn't Know That... Ser.). (Illus.). 32p. (J). (gr. 1-3). 1998. 8.95 (*0-7613-0647-1*, Copper Beech Bks); lib. bdg. 19.90 (*0-7613-0715-X*, Copper Beech Bks) Millbrook Pr.

People Chow: Favorite Recipes of the Famous & Almost Famous. Ed. by Marilyn Marshall. (Illus.). 336p. 1985. spiral bd. 12.00 (*0-9616537-1-X*) Hays Humane Soc.

People, Cities & Wealth: The Transformation of Traditional Society. E. Anthony Wrigley. 352p. 1988. pap. 32.95 (*0-631-16556-8*) Blackwell Pubs.

People Come First: User-Centered Academic Library Service. Dale S. Montanelli & Patricia Stenstrom. LC 98-43719. (ACRL Publications in Librarianship : No. 53). 202p. 1999. 31.00 (*0-8389-7999-8*) Assn Coll & Res Libs.

People, Communications, & Organisations. 2nd ed. Desmond W. Evans. 320p. (Orig.). 1990. pap. text 39.50 (*0-273-03269-0*) Trans-Atl Phila.

People (Community) that Listens: The Listening Ears. Israel Lattiboudeaire & Michael Lattiboudeaire. LC 98-91105. (Illus.). 30p. (YA). (gr. 3 up). 1999. 14.95 (*1-889448-57-5*) NBN Publishers Group.

People Could Fly. Mari L. Robbins. (Literature Unit Ser.). (Illus.). 48p. 1995. pap., teacher ed. 7.95 (*1-55734-524-4*) Tchr Create Mat.

***People Could Fly: American Black Folktales.** Virginia Hamilton. 1999. 19.95 incl. audio compact disk (*0-375-80471-4*) Knopf.

People Could Fly: American Black Folktales. Virginia Hamilton. LC 84-25020. (American Black Folktales Ser.). (Illus.). 192p. (J). (ps-12). 1985. lib. bdg. 18.99 (*0-394-96925-1*, Pub. by Knopf Bks Yng Read) Random.

People Could Fly: American Black Folktales. Virginia Hamilton. LC 85-25020. (Illus.). 192p. (J). 1993. pap. 13.00 (*0-679-84336-1*, Pub. by Knopf Bks Yng Read) Random.

People Could Fly: American Black Folktales. Virginia Hamilton. (J). 1985. 18.10 (*0-606-02830-7*, Pub. by Turtleback) Demco.

People, Countries & the Rainbow Serpent: Systems of Classification among the Lardil of Mornington Island. David McKnight. LC 98-18344. (Oxford Studies in Anthropological Linguistics: No. 12). (Illus.). 280p. 1999. text 75.00 (*0-19-509621-5*) OUP.

People Create Technology. Heiner. (Technology & Industrial Education Ser.). (C). 1980. mass mkt. 25.95 (*0-87192-109-X*) S-W Pub.

People Create Technology. Carol W. Heiner & Wayne R. Hendrix. LC 79-53802. (Technology Ser.). (Illus.). 256p. (J). (gr. 5-9). 1980. teacher ed. 12.74 (*0-87192-111-1*); text 19.95 (*0-87192-119-7*) S-W Pub.

People Create Technology, Activity Manual. Carol W. Heiner & Wayne R. Hendrix. LC 79-53802. (Technology Ser.). (Illus.). 256p. (J). (gr. 5-9). 1980. mass mkt., student ed. 11.95 (*0-87192-110-3*) S-W Pub.

People Detector: A Quick-Guide Handbook Revealing What People in Your Life Are Really Like...Their Hidden Motives & Emotions, Their Qualities & Quirks. Maryanna Korwitts & Jim Gash. 72p. 1994. pap. 15.95 (*1-887270-00-0*) Weve Got Your Number.

People, Development & Environment Complex Interlinkages in Bangladesh: Proceedings of a National Symposium Held in Dhaka, Bangladesh 3-4 November, 1992. 170p. (Orig.). (C). 1993. pap. text 18.75 (*0-614-07073-2*, Pub. by IUCN) Island Pr.

People Dimension: Managing the Transition to World-Class Manufacturing. Ronald J. Recardo & Luigi A. Peluso. LC 92-11950. 224p. 1992. text 29.95 (*0-527-91666-8*, 916668) Productivity Inc.

People Divided: Judaism in Contemporary America. Jack Wertheimer. LC 97-14686. (Brandeis Series in American Jewish History, Culture, & Life). 287p. 1997. reprint ed. pap. text 19.95 (*0-87451-848-2*) U Pr of New Eng.

People Doing Things. Rita G. Gelman. 1924. write for info. (*0-688-16645-8*, Grenwillow Bks); lib. bdg. write for info. (*0-688-16646-6*, Grenwillow Bks) HarpC Child Bks.

People Don't Understand: Children, Young People & Their Families Coping with a Hidden Disability. Judith Cavet. LC 98-200463. 80p. 1998. pap. 18.00 (*1-900990-24-5*, Pub. by Natl Childrens Bur) Paul & Co Pubs.

People down South: Stories. Cary C. Holladay. (Illinois Short Fiction Ser.). 136p. 1989. 14.95 (*0-252-01668-8*) U of Ill Pr.

People Earth. 7th ed. Brian M. Fagan. (C). 1992. pap. text 42.66 (*0-673-52167-2*) Addson-Wesley Educ.

People Earth: Introduction to World Prehistory. (C). 1997. write for info. (*0-321-02385-4*) Addson-Wesley Educ.

People Earth & People Earth Study Guide. 8th ed. Fagan. (C). 1998. pap. text, student ed. 54.00 (*0-673-79090-8*) Addison-Wesley.

People Empowerment: Achieving Success Through Involvement. Michael W. Gozzo & Wayne L. Douchkoff. LC 92-4196. 288p. 1992. 19.95 (*0-945456-07-7*) PT Pubns.

***People Entertainment Almanac.** People Magazine Staff. 610p. 2000. write for info. (*1-929049-07-2*) Tme Inc.

People Entertainment Almanac: 1999 Edition. 5th ed. Prod. & Created by Cader Books Staff. (Illus.). 608p. 1998. pap. 10.95 (*1-883013-48-8*, Pub. by Tme Inc) Natl Bk Netwk.

***People Entertainment Almanac: 2000 Edition.** People Magazine Staff. 608p. 1999. pap. text 11.95 (*1-883013-50-X*, People Bks) Tme Inc.

People Entertainment Almanac, 1995. People Magazine Editors. 1994. pap. 12.95 (*0-316-69885-7*) Little.

People Entertainment Almanac 1998. Camille N. Cline. 1997. pap. text 9.95 (*1-883013-20-8*, People Bks) Tme Inc.

People, Environment, Disease & Death in Britain: A Medical Geography Through the Ages. G. Melvyn Howe. LC 97-177063. 328p. 1998. 98.00 (*0-7083-1373-6*, Pub. by Univ Wales Pr) Paul & Co Pubs.

People Everyday & Other Poems. unabridged ed. Daniel Crocker. ii, 92p. 1998. pap. 12.00 (*1-891408-06-2*, GBP-7) Green Bean.

People Everywhere. Paul Humphrey. LC 94-28426. (Read All about It Ser.). (Illus.). 32p. (J). 1995. lib. bdg. 5.00 (*0-8114-5728-1*) Raintree Steck-V.

People Exceeding the Expectations of Your Internal & External Customers: A Value Focused Customer Care System. Carl Henry. Ed. by Connie Wells. LC 97-93542. 144p. 1997. 29.95 (*0-9657626-0-2*) Henry Assocs.

People Factor: Giving People Top Priority in the Life & Ministry of the Local Church. Oral Withrow. Ed. by Arthur Kelly. 203p. 1997. pap. 10.95 (*0-87162-731-0*, D5201) Warner Pr.

People Factors in Health & Safety. J. Stranks. 1996. pap. 129.00 (*1-85953-042-7*, Pub. by Tech Comm) St Mut.

People-Fear. Vijai P. Stlarma. LC 97-72874. (People Fear: Vol. 2). (Orig.). 1997. pap. 9.95 (*0-9628382-7-6*) Mind Pubns.

People First. (ODS Lecture Ser). 36p. 10.00 (*92-1-126088-4*) UN.

People First: A Guide to Self-Reliant Participatory Rural Development. Stan Burkey. 256p. (C). 1993. text 55.00 (*1-85649-081-5*, Pub. by Zed Books) St Martin.

People First: A Guide to Self-Reliant Participatory Rural Development. Stan Burkey. 256p. (C). 1996. text 25.00 (*1-85649-082-3*, Pub. by Zed Books) St Martin.

People, Food & Resources. Kenneth L. Blaxter. 132p. 1986. text 49.95 (*0-521-32300-2*) Cambridge U Pr.

People Food for Dogs. Katie Merwick. (Illus.). 144p. 1998. pap. 14.95 (*0-9660341-0-4*) Blue-dog.

***People for & Against Gun Control: A Biographical Reference.** Marjolijn Bijlefeld. LC 98-53383. (Making a Difference Ser.). 336p. 1999. 49.95 (*0-313-30690-7*) Greenwood.

People for Business - The Key to Success. Royston Flude. (C). 1991. lib. bdg. 77.00 (*1-85333-468-5*, Pub. by Graham & Trotman) Kluwer Academic.

People for His Name: A Church-Based Missions Strategy. 2nd rev. ed. Paul A. Beals. LC 95-34891. (Illus.). 260p. 1995. pap. text 11.95 (*0-87808-764-8*, WCL764-8) William Carey Lib.

People for Whom Shakespeare Wrote. Charles D. Warner. (Notable American Authors Ser.). 1999. reprint ed. lib. bdg. 125.00 (*0-7812-9895-4*) Rprt Serv.

People Forgotten, a Dream Pursued: The American GI Forum. Henry A. Ramos. LC 98-8679. 224p. 1998. 24.95 (*1-55885-261-1*); pap. 14.95 (*1-55885-262-X*) Arte Publico.

People from Bethlehem. C. Morison. 1995. 2.99 (*0-906731-35-6*, Pub. by Christian Focus) Spring Arbor Dist.

People from Heaven. John B. Sanford. LC 94-45900. (Radical Novel Reconsidered Ser.). 264p. 1995. 15.95 (*0-252-06491-7*) U of Ill Pr.

An Asterisk (*) at the beginning of an entry indicates that the title is appearing for the first time.

People from Jericho. C. Morison. 1995. 2.99 (0-906731-36-4, Pub. by Christian Focus) Spring Arbor Dist.

People from Jerusalem. C. Morison. 1995. 2.99 (0-906731-52-6, Pub. by Christian Focus) Spring Arbor Dist.

People from Mother Goose: A Question Book. Lee B. Hopkins. LC 88-38988. (Illus.). 28p. (J). (ps). 1989. 6.95 (0-15-200558-7, Gulliver Bks) Harcourt.

People from Our Side: A Life Story with Photographs & Oral Biography. Peter Pitseolak & Dorothy H. Eber. Tr. by Ann Hanson. (Illus.). 160p. 1993. 60.00 (0-7735-0996-8, Pub. by McG-Queens Univ Pr); pap. 24.95 (0-7735-1118-0, Pub. by McG-Queens Univ Pr) CUP Services.

People from Outer Space. Cynthia Todd & Debbie Ziemann. (Sing Me a Song Ser.). (Illus.). 9p. (J). 1998. lib. bdg. 15.95 (0-685-51627-X) Alpenhorn Pr.

People from Samaria. C. Morison. 1995. 2.99 (0-906731-53-4, Pub. by Christian Focus) Spring Arbor Dist.

People from the Bible. T. W. Weir. 1997. pap. 5.99 (0-907927-66-1) Emerald House Group Inc.

People from the Bible. Martin Woodrow & E. P. Sanders. (Illus.). 180p. 1987. 25.95 (0-8192-1460-4) Morehouse Pub.

People from the Other World. Henry S. Olcott. 492p. 1996. reprint ed. spiral bd. 31.00 (0-7873-0641-X) Hlth Research.

People from the Other World. Henry S. Olcott. 492p. 1996. reprint ed. pap. 29.95 (1-56459-829-2) Kessinger Pub.

People, Groups, & Organizations. Ed. by Bernard P. Indik & Kenneth Berrien. LC 68-23785. 287p. reprint ed. pap. 89.00 (0-608-14896-2, 202602400048) Bks Demand.

People Have More Fun than Anybody: A Centennial Celebration of Drawings & Writings by James Thurber. James Thurber. Ed. by Michael J. Rosen. (Illus.). 1994. write for info. (0-318-72259-3) Harcourt.

People Have More Fun than Anybody: A Centennial Celebration of Drawings & Writings by James Thurber. James Thurber. Ed. by Michael J. Rosen. (Illus.). 192p. 1995. pap. 15.00 (0-15-600235-3, Harvest Bks) Harcourt.

People Have the Floor: History of the Inter-Parliamentary Union. Yefim Zarjevski. 158p. 1989. text 61.95 (1-85521-045-2, Pub. by Dartmth Pub) Ashgate Pub Co.

People, Health & Environment: Environmental Science Textbook for Non-Science Majors. rev. ed. Sigmund F. Zakrzewski. LC 94-92047. (Illus.). viii, 164p. (C). 1994. pap. text 25.00 (0-9639784-1-1) SFZ Pubng.

People I Could Do Without. Donald G. Smith. Ed. by Laurie Boucke. LC 97-37338. 166p. (Orig.). 1998. pap. 14.50 (1-888580-04-6) White-Boucke.

People I Know. Nancy Zafris. LC 89-34553. (Flannery O'Connor Award for Short Fiction Ser.). 176p. 1990. 19.95 (0-8203-1192-8) U of Ga Pr.

People in a Landscape. Chip Sullivan. Ed. by Garrett Eckbo. LC 97-14575. 276p. 1997. 94.00 (0-13-386640-8) P-H.

People in a Landscape: The New Highlanders. Magnus Lindlater. (Illus.). 96p. 1997. pap. 19.95 (1-85158-958-9, Pub. by Mainstream Pubng) Trafalgar.

People in Antarctica. Lynn M. Stone. LC 95-6894. (Antarctica Discovery Library). 24p. (J). (gr. k-4). 1995. lib. bdg. 15.93 (1-55916-142-6) Rourke Bk Co.

People in Art. National Gallery of London Staff. (Illus.). 144p. 1999. pap. 14.95 (0-8230-0335-3) Watsn-Guptill.

People in Art. Anthea Peppin. (J). (gr. 4-7). 1992. pap. 6.70 (0-395-64556-5) HM.

People in Art. Anthea Peppin. LC 91-34983. (Millbrook Arts Library). (Illus.). 48p. (J). (gr. 2-6). 1992. pap. 8.95 (1-56294-818-0) Millbrook Pr.

People in Bondage. Yirmeyahu Ben Israel. 156p. (YA). (gr. 5 up). 1997. 8.95 (0-936026-69-3) R&M Pub Co.

People in Bondage: African Slavery since the 15th Century. L. H. Ofosu-Appiah. (Illus.). 112p. (YA). (gr. 5 up). 1993. lib. bdg. 17.50 (0-8225-3150-X, Runestone Pr) Lerner Pub.

People in Business: Student Book. Micheal Kleindl & David Pickles. 1991. pap. text, student ed. write for info. (0-582-05143-6, Pub. by Addison-Wesley) Longman.

People in Change. Brooman. 1994. pap. text. write for info. (0-582-22665-1, Pub. by Addison-Wesley) Longman.

***People in Charge: Creating Self Managing Workplaces.** Robert Rehm. (Illus.). 288p. 1999. pap. 29.95 (1-869890-87-6, Pub. by Hawthorn Press) Anthroposophic.

People in Corporations: Ethical Responsibilities & Corporate Effectiveness. Ed. by George Enderle. 272p. (C). 1990. lib. bdg. 151.50 (0-7923-0829-8, Pub. by Kluwer Academic) Kluwer Academic.

People in Crisis: Strategic Therapeutic Interventions. Diana S. Everstine & Louis Everstine. LC 82-23969. 280p. 1987. text 36.95 (0-87630-286-X) Brunner-Mazel.

People in Crisis: Understanding & Helping. 2nd ed. Lee A. Hoff. LC 77-79466. 1984. pap. 23.75 (0-201-11075-X, Health Sci) Addison-Wesley.

People in Crisis: Understanding & Helping. 4th ed. LeeAnn Hoff. LC 94-46309. (Health-Social & Behavioral Sciences Ser.). 503p. 1995. pap. 32.95 (0-7879-0084-2) Jossey-Bass.

People in Culture: A Survey of Cultural Anthropology. Ino Rossi et al. LC 79-11842. (Praeger Special Studies). 626p. 1979. pap. 22.95 (0-275-91481-X, B1481, Praeger Pubs) Greenwood.

People in Culture: A Survey of Cultural Anthropology. Ino Rossi et al. LC 79-11842. (Praeger Special Studies). 626p. 1980. 89.50 (0-275-90542-X, C0542, Praeger Pubs) Greenwood.

People in Distress: A Geographical Perspective on Psychological Well-Being. Sol Daiches. LC 81-4308. (University of Chicago, Department of Geography, Research Paper Ser.: No. 197). 216p. 1981. reprint ed. pap. 67.00 (0-608-02241-1, 206288200004) Bks Demand.

People in Focus: How to Photograph Anyone, Anywhere. Bryan F. Peterson. (Illus.). 144p. 1993. pap. 22.50 (0-8174-5388-1, Amphoto) Watsn-Guptill.

People in French Counter-Revolutionary Thought. Marc A. Goldstein. (American University Studies: History: Ser. IX, Vol. 36). 275p. (C). 1988. text 38.50 (0-8204-0588-4) P Lang Pubng.

People in Humanities. Hoeper. 544p. (C). 2001. write for info. (0-02-355781-8, Macmillan Coll) P-H.

People in Jazz. Bill Lee. 1984. 19.95 (0-89898-358-4, SB258) Wrner Bros.

People in Motion: The Postwar Adjustment of the Evacuated Japanese Americans see U. S. War Relocation Authority

People in My Neighborhood Sticker Book. Anna Nilsen. (Illus.). 16p. (J). (ps-k). 1998. pap. 3.99 (0-7636-0430-5) Candlewick Pr.

People in Organisations. Olf. LC 96-52855. 1997. 47.95 (0-631-20181-5) Blackwell Pubs.

People in Pain. Mark Zborowski. LC 70-92888. (Jossey-Bass Behavioral Science Ser.). 294p. reprint ed. pap. 91.20 (0-8357-9342-7, 201382800087) Bks Demand.

People in Pineapple Place. Anne M. Lindbergh. LC 82-47935. 153p. (J). (gr. 3-7). 1982. 14.95 (0-15-260517-7, Harcourt Child Bks) Harcourt.

People in Pineapple Place. Anne M. Lindbergh. 160p. (J). (gr. 4-5). 1990. pap. 2.95 (0-380-70766-7, Avon Bks) Morrow Avon.

People in Power: Forging a Grassroots Democracy in Nicaragua. Gary Ruchwarger. LC 87-12623. 351p. 1987. 69.50 (0-89789-129-5, Bergin & Garvey); pap. 24.95 (0-89789-130-9, Bergin & Garvey) Greenwood.

People in Public Places. Deborah Frederick. 16p. 1993. 5.00 (0-9637053-0-X) U KY Art Dept.

People in Quandaries. Wendell Johnson. 532p. 1980. pap. 24.95 (0-918970-27-X) Intl Gen Semantics.

People in Rural Development: The Religious Radicals of the 16th & 17th Centuries. 2nd rev. ed. Peter Batchelor. xii, 228p. 1993. pap. 16.99 (0-85364-541-8, Pub. by Paternoster Pub) OM Literature.

People in Schools. Blaine Mercer & Steven Hey. LC 80-13278. 382p. 1981. 39.95 (0-87073-856-9) Schenkman Bks Inc.

People in Space. John Heinerman. (Illus.). 144p. (Orig.). 1990. pap. 9.95 (0-945946-08-2) Cassandra Pr.

People in Space: Policy Perspectives for a "Star Wars" Century. Ed. by James E. Katz. (Illus.). (C). 1985. 39.95 (0-88738-052-2); pap. 24.95 (0-88738-609-1) Transaction Pubs.

People in Texas. Ed. by Robert J. Rosenbaum. (Illus.). 192p. (C). 1982. pap. text 16.95 (0-89641-102-8) American Pr.

People in the Bible: Spot the Difference see Personajes de la Biblia: Localiza la Diferencia

People in the News. 2nd ed. David Brownstone & Irene M. Franck. 403p. 1992. 85.00 (0-02-897074-8) Macmillan.

People in the News. 7th ed. David Brownstone & Franck. 1997. 85.00 (0-02-864711-4) Mac Lib Ref.

People in the News, 1997. David Brownstone & Irene Franck. 1997. 85.00 (0-02-864779-3) S&S Trade.

People in the Past. Ed. by Margaret Mulvihill. LC 92-54483. (Picturepedia Ser.). (Illus.). (J). 1993. write for info. (1-56458-217-5) DK Pub Inc.

People in the Pew Vol. 1: Problems & Temptation. Maralene Wesner & Miles Wesner. LC 88-51865. 121p. 1988. pap. 8.95 (0-936715-09-X) Diversity Okla.

People in the Pew Vol. 2: God & Theology. Maralene Wesner & Miles E. Wesner. 123p. 1991. pap. 8.95 (0-936715-38-3) Diversity Okla.

People in the Pew Vol. 3: Sin & Salvation. Maralene Wesner & Miles E. Wesner. 120p. 1991. pap. 8.95 (0-936715-40-5) Diversity Okla.

People in the Pew Vol. 4: Dedication & Spirituality. Maralene Wesner & Miles Wesner. 122p. 1992. pap. 8.95 (0-936715-41-3) Diversity Okla.

People in the Pew Vol. 5: Determination & Discipleship. Maralene Wesner & Miles E. Wesner. 113p. 1992. pap. 7.95 (0-936715-39-1) Diversity Okla.

People in the Pew Vol. 6: Social Relationships & Service. Maralene Wesner & Miles Wesner. 118p. 1992. pap. 7.95 (0-936715-42-1) Diversity Okla.

People in the Playground. Iona Opie. LC 92-12172. (Illus.). 256p. 1993. 25.00 (0-19-811265-3) OUP.

People in the Rain Forest. Saviour Pirotta. LC 97-48525. (Deep in the Rain Forest Ser.). 1999. write for info. (0-7502-2197-6) Raintree Steck-V.

People in the Rain Forest. Saviour Pirotta. LC 97-48525. (Deep in the Rain Forest Ser.). 32p. (J). 1999. 22.83 (0-8172-5137-5) Raintree Steck-V.

***People in the Rain Forest.** Saviour Pirotta. 1999. pap. text 5.95 (0-8172-8111-8) Raintree Steck-V.

People in the Tobacco Belt: Four Lives. Linda Degh. Ed. by Richard M. Dorson. LC 80-792. (Folklore of the World Ser.). (Illus.). 1981. reprint ed. lib. bdg. 31.95 (0-405-13331-6) Ayer.

People in the Web of Life. 2nd ed. Gwendolyn L. Baines. (J). (gr. 7 up). 1992. pap. 9.95 (0-9614505-1-7) Nevada Pub.

People in Transit: German Migrations in Comparative Perspective, 1820-1930. Ed. by Dirk Hoerder & Jorg Nagler. (Publications of the German Historical Insitute, Washington, D.C.). (Illus.). 451p. (C). 1995. text 95.00 (0-521-47412-4) Cambridge U Pr.

People in Upheaval. Ed. by Scott M. Morgan & Elizabeth Colson. LC 86-33354. 228p. 1987. 19.50 (0-934733-17-1); pap. 14.50 (0-934733-16-3) CMS.

People in Your Life. Town Hall, Inc. Staff. Ed. by Margaret M. Hughes. LC 71-142706. (Essay Index Reprint Ser.). 1977. 20.95 (0-8369-2204-2) Ayer.

People Investment: How to Make Your Hiring Decisions Pay off for Everyone. E. Robert Worthington & Anita E. Worthington. LC 93-19672. (Successful Business Library). (Illus.). 212p. 1993. pap. 19.95 (1-55571-161-8, Oasis Pr) PSI Resch.

People, Issues & Events: Case Studies for Academic Writing. Ed. by Gibson. (C). 1999. text. write for info. (0-321-01258-5) Addison-Wesley Educ.

People I've Known & Places I've Been. Jim DeWitt. (Illus.). (Orig.). 1989. pap. 5.95 (0-938991-49-3) Colonial Pr AL.

People Jesus Helped. Ed. by Chariot Victor Publishing Staff. 1992. pap. 1.99 (0-7814-0888-1) Chariot Victor.

People Jesus Met see Personas Que Jesus Conocio

People Jesus Met. C. Mackenzie. Date not set. pap. 1.75 (0-906731-84-4, Pub. by Christian Focus) Spring Arbor Dist.

People, Jobs & Mobility in the New Europe. Anthony J. Fielding & Hans H. Blotevogal. LC 96-38721. 322p. 1997. 125.00 (0-471-94901-9) Wiley.

People Just Like Us. J. Oswald Sanders. 201p. (Orig.). 1978. pap. 4.99 (1-85030-005-4) Bridge-Logos.

People Just Like Us: Leader's Book. Ed. by Sam Crabtree. (Illus.). 80p. 1994. teacher ed., spiral bd., wbk. ed. 14.95 (0-89827-128-2, BKR11) Wesleyan Pub Hse.

People Just Like Us: Student Book. Norman G. Wilson. LC 95-143905. 94p. 1994. pap. text, student ed. 9.95 (0-89827-127-4, BKR10) Wesleyan Pub Hse.

People, Land, & Community: Collected E. F. Schumacher Society Lectures. Ed. by Hildegarde Hannum. LC 96-46526. (E. F. Schumacher Society Lectures). 352p. 1997. 37.00 (0-300-06966-9); pap. 18.00 (0-300-07173-6) Yale U Pr.

People, Land & Sea: Development Challenges in Eastern Indonesia. Gavin W. Jones & Julfita Rahardjo. LC 96-214992. 174 p. 1995. write for info. (0-7315-2314-8) ANU Res Sch.

People, Land & Time: An Historical Introduction to the Relations Between Landscape, Culture & Environment. Peter Atkins et al. LC 98-175518. (Arnold Publications). (Illus.). 304p. 1998. pap. text 29.95 (0-340-67714-7) OUP.

***People, Land & Water in the Bilad-Ash Sham, the Arabian Peninsula: Indigenous Systems in the Countryside.** William Lancaster & Fidelity Lancaster. 454p. 1999. text 83.00 (90-5702-322-9, Harwood Acad Pubs) Gordon & Breach.

People Left Behind: Early Peoples of the Kenai Coast. M. Walker. (Illus.). 36p. 1995. pap. 4.95 (0-930931-13-0) Alaska Natural.

People Like Us. Clapperton. Date not set. 14.95 (0-06-016762-9) HarperTrade.

People Like Us. Dominick Dunne. 1999. mass mkt. 6.99 (0-345-43054-9) Ballantine Pub Grp.

People Like Us. Dominick Dunne. 464p. 1990. mass mkt. 6.99 (0-553-27891-6) Bantam.

People Like Us. Patricia Souder & Jana Carman. LC 99-178959. 1997. 8.99 (0-8341-9650-6, MP-798) Lillenas.

People Like Us: The Report of the Review of the Safeguards for Children Living Away from Home. LC 98-182438. 1997. 60.00 (0-11-322101-0, HM21010, Pub. by Statnry Office) Bernan Associates.

People Link: Human Resource Linkages Across the Pacific. A. E. Safarian. LC 98-111693. 160p. 1997. pap. text 16.95 (0-8020-8126-6) U of Toronto Pr.

People Link: Human Resource Linkages Across the Pacific. A. E. Safarian. LC 98-111693. (Hongkong Bank of Canada Papers on Asia: Vol. III). 160p. 1997. text 45.00 (0-8020-4299-6) U of Toronto Pr.

People Live, They Have Lives: Poems by Hugh Seidman. Hugh Seidman. LC 92-30495. (Miami University Press Poetry Ser.). 67p. 1992. 16.95 (1-881163-02-4); pap. 10.95 (1-881163-03-2) Miami Univ Pr.

People Living Apart: Indians of the Great Lakes, 1855-1900. Edmund J. Danziger. (Illus.). (C). text. write for info. (0-472-09690-7); pap. text. write for info. (0-472-06690-0) U of Mich Pr.

People Look at Educational Television: A Report of Nine Representative ETV Stations. Wilbur L. Schramm & Ithiel De Sola Pool. LC 77-1923. 209p. 1977. lib. bdg. 35.00 (0-8371-9507-1, SCPL, Greenwood Pr) Greenwood.

People Look at Radio. Columbia University, Bureau of Applied Social Rese. LC 75-22803. (America in Two Centuries Ser.). 1976. reprint ed. 18.95 (0-405-07675-4) Ayer.

People, Love, Sex & Families. Eric W. Johnson. (Illus.). 144p. (J). (gr. 4 up). 1985. lib. bdg. 14.85 (0-8027-6605-6) Walker & Co.

People Make It Happen: The Possibilities of Outreach in Every Phase of Public Library Service. Patricia B. Hanna. LC 78-5923. 165p. 1978. lib. bdg. 21.00 (0-8108-1136-7) Scarecrow.

People Make the Difference. David A. Bice. Ed. by Mary J. Kurten. 134p. 1987. 25.00 (0-940213-15-X) Walsworth Pub.

People Make the Hospital: The History of Washoe Medical Center. Anton P. Sohn et al. LC 98-34645. (Illus.). 300p. 1998. 35.00 (0-9649759-5-5) Greasewood.

People Making People. Ruth Barnett. 168p. (C). 1985. pap. 30.00 (0-09-154931-0, Pub. by S Thornes Pubs) St Mut.

People Movements in the Punjab. Frederick E. Stock & Margaret A. Stock. LC 74-18408. 364p. 1995. pap. 9.95 (0-87808-417-7) William Carey Lib.

People Movers: A History of the Private Bus Companies. John Maddock. (Illus.). 214p. (Orig.). 1994. 39.95 (0-86417-412-8, Pub. by Kangaroo Pr) Seven Hills Bk.

People Named Hanes. Jo W. Linn. LC 80-52426. (Illus.). 281p. 1980. 25.00 (0-918470-12-9) J W Linn.

People Named the Chippewa: Narrative Histories. Gerald R. Vizenor. LC 83-19800. (Illus.). 175p. (C). 1984. pap. 14.95 (0-8166-1306-0) U of Minn Pr.

***People, Nation & State: The Meaning of Ethnicity & Nationalism.** Edward Mortimer. 1999. pap. text 19.95 (1-86064-401-5, Pub. by I B T) St Martin.

People Need Each Other. rev. ed. Cherrie Farnette et al. 80p. (J). (gr. 4-7). 1989. pap. text 9.95 (0-86530-070-4, IP 63-3) Incentive Pubns.

People Need People, Level 8. E. Evertts. 1986. 32.20 (0-03-002348-3) Harcourt Schl Pubs.

People Need People, Level 9. E. Evertts. 1983. 37.95 (0-03-061391-4) Harcourt Schl Pubs.

People Need People: Level 9. E. Evertts. 1986. pap. text, wbk. ed. 14.25 (0-03-002352-1) Holt R&W.

People Need People, 1983, Level 9. E. Evertts. 1983. pap., wbk. ed. 14.75 (0-03-069263-6) Harcourt Schl Pubs.

People Need Stillness. Wanda Nash. pap. write for info. (0-232-51971-4) S Asia.

People Next Door. J. P. Miller. 1969. pap. 5.25 (0-8222-0884-9) Dramatists Play.

People Numerous & Armed: Reflections on the Military Struggle for American Independence. rev. ed. John Shy. 376p. 1990. pap. text 19.95 (0-472-06431-2, 06431) U of Mich Pr.

People of Africa. Jean Hiernaux. LC 74-26003. (Peoples of the World Ser.). xii, 217 p. 1975. 12.50 (0-684-14040-3) S&S Trade.

People of Africa & Their Food see Multicultural Cookbooks

People of Africa & Their Food. Ann L. Burckhardt. (Multicultural Cookbooks Ser.). (Illus.). 48p. (J). (gr. 3-7). 1996. 19.00 (0-516-20261-8) Childrens.

People of Alaska. L. J. Campbell. Ed. by Penny Rennick. LC 72-92087. (Alaska Geographic Ser.: Vol. 21, No. 3). (Illus.). 96p. 1994. pap. 19.95 (1-56661-022-2) Alaska Geog Soc.

People of Alaska. Lynn M. Stone. LC 93-43981. (North to Alaska Discovery Library). 24p. (J). (gr. k-4). 1994. lib. bdg. 15.93 (1-55916-029-2) Rourke Bk Co.

People of Aritama. Gerardo Reichel-Dolmatoff & Alicia D. Reichel. LC 60-14234. (Illus.). 495p. 1962. lib. bdg. 36.00 (0-226-70791-1) U Ch Pr.

People of Bali. Angela Hobart et al. (Peoples of South-East Asia & the Pacific Ser.). (Illus.). 256p. (C). 1996. 60.95 (0-631-17687-X) Blackwell Pubs.

People of Calton Hill. Ann Mitchell. 144p. 1996. pap. 40.00 (1-873644-18-3, Pub. by Mercat Pr Bks) St Mut.

People of Cambodia. Dolly Brittan. LC 97-7982. (Celebrating the Peoples & Civilizations of Southeast Asia Ser.). (J). 1997. lib. bdg. 15.93 (0-8239-5129-4, PowerKids) Rosen Group.

People of Chaco: A Canyon & Its Culture. rev. ed. Kendrick Frazier. (Illus.). 261p. 1999. pap. 17.00 (0-393-31825-7, Norton Paperbks) Norton.

***People of China.** Lynn M. Stone. LC 00-38725. (China Ser.). (Illus.). 2000. write for info. (1-55916-319-4) Rourke Bk Co.

People of China & Their Food see Multicultural Cookbooks

People of China & Their Food. Ann L. Burckhardt. (Multicultural Cookbooks Ser.). (Illus.). 48p. (J). (gr. 3-7). 1996. 19.00 (0-516-20260-X) Childrens.

People of Clarksville & Its Cemetery: El Dorado County, California. Photos by Beth K. Pany. (Illus.). 75p. 1999. pap. 12.00 (0-9672409-0-5) CA Genealogical.

People of Colonial America. Ed. by Alan Quincannon. (Learning & Coloring Bks.). (Illus.). 20p. (YA). (gr. k up). 1992. pap. 3.95 (1-878452-09-6, Tory Corner) Quincannon.

People of Color Vol. 2: Black Genealogical Records & Abstracts from MO Sources. Teresa Blattner. 170p. 1998. pap. 18.00 (0-7884-0927-1, B403) Heritage Bk.

People of Color in the American West. Ed. by Sucheng Chan et al. LC 93-78444. 584p. (C). 1994. pap. text 25.56 (0-669-27913-7) HM Trade Div.

People of Color in the Bible: Preliminaries, Establishing a Foundation. William Emanuel. LC 93-216097. (Illus.). 144p. (Orig.). 1993. pap. text 15.00 (0-9640366-0-6) Faith of Jesus.

People of Color in the Bible Vol. 1: Old Testament Collection: In the Beginning. William Emanuel & Renee Emanuel. (Illus.). 32p. (Orig.). (J). (gr. k-7). 1995. pap. text 3.00 (0-9640366-1-4) Faith of Jesus.

People of Color in the Bible Vol. 2: Old Testament Collection: Adam & Eve. William Emanuel & Renee Emanuel. (Illus.). 32p. (Orig.). (J). (gr. k-7). 1995. pap. text 3.00 (0-9640366-2-2) Faith of Jesus.

People of Color in the Bible Vol. 3: Old Testament Collection: The Garden of Eden. William Emanuel & Renee Emanuel. (Illus.). 32p. (J). (gr. k-7). 1995. pap. text 3.00 (0-9640366-3-0) Faith of Jesus.

People of Colour Illustrations: A Clip Art Booklet, Vol. 1. Illus. by Cheryl Williams & Sheila Williams. 64p. 1996. pap. 19.95 (1-889926-62-0) TwinAtta-Sanaa Village.

People of Colour Illustrations: A Clip Art Booklet, Vol. 2. Illus. by Cheryl Williams & Sheila Williams. 64p. 1996. pap. 19.95 (1-889926-63-9) TwinAtta-Sanaa Village.

People of Colour Illustrations: A Clip Art Booklet, Vol. 3. Illus. by Cheryl Williams & Sheila Williams. 64p. 1996. pap. 19.95 (1-889926-64-7) TwinAtta-Sanaa Village.

People of Colour Illustrations: A Clip Art Booklet, Vol. 4. Illus. by Cheryl Williams & Sheila Williams. 64p. 1996. pap. 19.95 (1-889926-65-5) TwinAtta-Sanaa Village.

People of Colour Illustrations: Klip-Klik Art, 2 disc. Cheryl Williams & Sheila Williams. pap. 39.95 incl. cd-rom (1-889926-98-1) TwinAtta-Sanaa Village.

***People of Consequence.** Cambridge International Reference on Current Affairs Staff. 150p. 1999. pap. (0-11-702657-3, Pub. by Statnry Office) Balogh.

P

An Asterisk (*) at the beginning of an entry indicates that the title is appearing for the first time.

People of Crathie & Braemar (kindrocht) 1696: Taken from List of Pollable Persons in the Shires of Aberdeen 1696. Dorothy H. Morgan & Aberdeen and North-East Scotland Family History Society Staff. LC 98-203450. 1998. write for info. (*1-900173-11-5*) Aberdeen & NE Scot.

People of Dancing Sky. Jensen. text 35.00 (*0-312-26532-8*) St Martin.

People of Darkness. Tony Hillerman. 304p. 1991. mass mkt. 6.50 (*0-06-109915-5*, Perennial) HarperTrade.

People of Darkness. large type ed. Tony Hillerman. LC 84-16164. 344p. 1991. reprint ed. lib. bdg. 21.95 (*0-89621-575-X*) Thorndike Pr.

***People of Denendeh: Ethnohistory of the Indians of Canada's Northwest Territories.** June Helm et al. LC 00-34392. (Illus.). 432p. 2000. text 39.95 (*0-87745-735-2*) U of Iowa Pr.

People of Destiny: Americans at Home & Abroad. LC 73-13132. (Foreign Travelers in America, 1810-1935 Ser.). (Illus.). 216p. 1974. reprint ed. 20.95 (*0-405-05454-8*) Ayer.

***People of Earth: Central Michigan University Custom.** Fagan. (C). 1998. pap. text 33.00 (*0-201-45681-8*) P-H.

People of El Valle: A History of the Spanish Colonials in the San Luis Valley. 3rd ed. Olibama Lopez-Tushar. Ed. by Charlene G. Simms & Edward T. Simms. (Illus.). 276p. 1997. pap. 16.95 (*0-9628974-4-2*) El Escrito.

People of England: A Short Social & Economic History. Maurice Ashley. LC 82-84225. 240p. 1982. pap. 74.40 (*0-7837-8533-X*, 204934300011) Bks Demand.

People of Faith. Kibibi V. Mack-Williams. LC 95-11444. (African American Life Ser.). (J). (gr. 2-6). 1995. lib. bdg. 23.93 (*1-57103-031-X*) Rourke Pr.

People of Faith: Craft Projects That Teach about Peter, John, & the Other Disciples. Carolyn Willmore. 1996. pap. 6.95 (*0-687-01528-6*) Abingdon.

People of Faith: Parishes & Religious Communities of the Diocese of Cleveland. Ed. by Charles R. Kaczynski. (Illus.). 509p. (YA). 1998. pap. 14.00 (*0-9669580-0-4*) Diocese Cleveland.

People of Forrs. Byron Brown. 443p. (Orig.). mass mkt. 4.99 (*1-55197-364-2*) Picasso Publ.

People of Georgia: An Illustrated History. 2nd ed. Mills Lane. (Illus.). 312p. 1992. 50.00 (*0-88322-000-8*) Beehive GA.

People of Glengarry: Highlanders in Transition, 1745-1820. Marianne McLean. (Illus.). 312p. 1991. 65.00 (*0-7735-0814-7*, Pub. by McG-Queens Univ Pr) CUP Services.

People of Glengarry: Highlanders in Transition, 1745-1820. Marianne McLean. (Illus.). 312p. 1993. pap. 22.95 (*0-7735-1156-3*, Pub. by McG-Queens Univ Pr) CUP Services.

People of God. Markus Barth. (JSNT Supplement Ser.: No. 5). 103p. 1983. pap. 12.25 (*0-905774-55-8*, Pub. by Sheffield Acad) CUP Services.

People of God. Markus Barth. (JSNT Supplement Ser.: No. 5). 103p. 1983. 28.50 (*0-905774-54-X*, Pub. by Sheffield Acad) CUP Services.

People of God. Karl Pruter. LC 85-13417. v, 162p. 1985. reprint ed. pap. 21.00 (*0-912134-03-8*) Millefleurs.

People of God: A Plea for the Church. Anton W. Houtepan. LC 85-180515. 224p. reprint ed. pap. 69.50 (*0-8357-2678-9*, 204021400015) Bks Demand.

People of God: A Royal Priesthood. Alwyn Marriage. pap. write for info. (*0-232-51989-7*) S Asia.

***People of God: The History of Catholic Christianity.** Anthony E. Gilles. 264p. 2000. pap. 12.95 (*0-86716-363-1*) St Anthony Mess Pr.

People of God at Prayer: Pastoral Prayers for All Occasions. Ed. by Henry R. Rust. 72p. (Orig.). 1991. pap. 8.95 (*1-877871-25-7*, 3532) Ed Ministries.

***People of God at Prayer: 18 Services in the Spirit of Vatican II.** Bill Huebsch. 72p. 2000. pap. 12.95 (*1-58595-012-2*) Twenty-Third.

People of Gumption & Other Stories. Fran Lehr. 90p. 1987. pap. 7.95 (*0-935153-03-9*) Stormline Pr.

People of Hamilton, Canada West: Family & Class in a Mid-Nineteenth-Century City. Michael B. Katz. LC 75-12642. (Harvard Studies in Urban History). 398p. reprint ed. pap. 123.40 (*0-7837-3844-7*, 204366600010) Bks Demand.

People of Hidden Sussex. Warden Swinfen & David Arscott. 168p. 1987. 45.00 (*0-9509510-1-3*) St Mut.

***People of His Presence.** Cynthia Duggan. 300p. 1998. pap. 10.99 (*1-884369-09-X*) McDougal Pubng.

People of Hope: The Protestant Movement in Central America. Carmelo Alvarez. 1990. pap. 3.95 (*0-377-00212-7*) Friendship Pr.

People of India, Vol. XXXVI. Pondicherry. Ed. by K. S. Singh. (C). 1994. 36.00 (*81-85938-25-3*, Pub. by Manohar) S Asia.

People of India: GOA, Vol. XXI. Ed. by K. S. Singh. (C). 1993. 22.00 (*81-7154-760-5*, Pub. by Popular Prakashan) S Asia.

People of India: National Series; The Scheduled Tribes, 3. K. S. Singh. 1,278p. 1998. pap. text (*0-19-564253-8*) OUP.

People of India: The Biological Variation in Indian Populations, Vol. X. Ed. by K. S. Singh et al. 778p. 1994. text 65.00 (*0-19-563351-2*) OUP.

People of India Vol. I: Dadra & Nagar Haveli. Ed. by K. S. Singh et al. (People of India Ser.: Vol. XVIII). (C). 1995. 16.00 (*81-7154-762-1*, Pub. by Popular Prakashan) S Asia.

People of India Vol. I: Haryana. K. S. Singh. (C). 1995. 36.00 (*81-7304-091-5*, Pub. by Manohar) S Asia.

People of India Vol. III: Nagaland. K. S. Singh. (C). 1995. 22.50 (*81-7046-121-9*, Pub. by Seagull Bks) S Asia.

People of India Vol. III: The Scheduled Tribes. Ed. by K. S. Singh. (Illus.). 1296p. 1995. 59.00 (*0-19-563255-9*) OUP.

People of India Vol. IX: Languages & Scripts. K. S. Singh & S. Manoharan. (People of India Ser.). 446p. 1994. text 35.00 (*0-19-563352-0*) OUP.

People of India Vol. IX: Languages & Scripts, Vol. IX. K. S. Singh & S. Manoharan. (Oxford India Paperbacks Ser.). 448p. 1998. reprint ed. pap. text 16.95 (*0-19-564393-3*) OUP.

People of India Vol. XI: Ecology & Cultural Traits, Languages & Linguistics Traits, Demographic & Biological Traits. Ed. by K. S. Singh. (Illus.). 172p. 1995. text 45.00 (*0-19-563267-2*) OUP.

People of India Vol. XXXIII: Mizoram. Ed. by K. S. Singh. (C). 1995. 24.00 (*81-7046-124-3*, Pub. by Seagull Bks) S Asia.

***People of India Vol. XXXVIII: Rajasthan, 2 vols.** Ed. by K. S. Singh. 1998. 78.00 (*81-7154-769-9*, Pub. by Popular Prakashan) S Asia.

People of India Vol. XLI: Tripura. K. S. Singh. (C). 1996. 35.00 (*81-7046-126-X*, Pub. by Seagull Bks) S Asia.

People of Ireland. Ed. by Patrick Loughrey. (Illus.). 208p. (C). 1989. 25.00 (*0-941533-55-7*, NAB) I R Dee.

People of Kau. Leni Riefenstahl. (Illus.). 224p. 1997. text 40.00 (*0-312-16963-9*) St Martin.

People of Lake Kutubu & Kikori: Changing Meanings of Daily Life. Mark Busse et al. (Illus.). 96p. 1995. pap. text 17.00 (*9980-85-513-4*, Pub. by Papua New Guinea) UH Pr.

People of Laos. Dolly Brittan. LC 97-5879. (Celebrating the Peoples & Civilizations of Southeast Asia Ser.). (J). 1997. lib. bdg. 15.93 (*0-8239-5124-3*, PowerKids) Rosen Group.

People of Mexico see Pueblo de Mexico

People of Mexico. Laura Conlon. (South of the Border Discovery Library). 24p. (J). (gr. k-4). 1994. lib. bdg. 15.93 (*1-55916-052-7*) Rourke Bk Co.

People of Mexico & Their Food see Multicultural Cookbooks

People of Mexico & Their Food. Ann L. Burckhardt. (Multicultural Cookbooks Ser.). (Illus.). 48p. (J). (gr. 3-7). 1996. 19.00 (*0-516-20259-6*) Childrens.

People of Migrants: Ethnicity, State & Religion in Karachi. Oskar Verkaaik. (Comparative Asian Studies: Vol. 15). 85p. 1995. pap. 12.00 (*90-5383-339-0*, Pub. by VU Univ Pr) Paul & Co Pubs.

People of My Pilgrimage. Arthur R. Pitcher. 1989. 8.95 (*0-86544-052-2*) Salv Army Suppl South.

People of Nacogdoches County in the Civil War. 2nd ed. Carolyn R. Ericson. (Illus.). 307p. 1994. reprint ed. pap. 25.00 (*0-911317-59-7*) Ericson Bks.

People of Nepal. Dor B. Bista. 1987. 125.00 (*0-7855-0233-5*, Pub. by Ratna Pustak Bhandar) St Mut.

People of Nepal. Dor B. Bista. 210p. (C). 1987. 285.00 (*0-89771-044-4*, Pub. by Ratna Pustak Bhandar) St Mut.

People of Nepal. 5th ed. Dor Bahadur Bista. (Illus.). 210p. (gr. 9-12). 1987. 44.50 (*0-685-05884-0*) Asia Bk Corp.

People of New France. Allan Greer. LC 98-112694. (Themes in Canadian Social History Ser.). 130p. 1997. text 45.00 (*0-8020-0826-7*); pap. text 12.95 (*0-8020-7816-8*) U of Toronto Pr.

People of Orkney. R. J. Berry & H. N. Firth. (C). 1986. 75.00 (*0-907618-08-1*, Pub. by Orkney Pr) St Mut.

People of Our Neighborhood. Mary E. Wilkins Freeman. LC 76-110192. (Short Story Index Reprint Ser.). 1977. 18.95 (*0-8369-3343-5*) Ayer.

People of Our Parish. Leila H. Bugg. 1978. 23.95 (*0-405-10811-7*) Ayer.

People of Paradox: An Inquiry Concerning the Origins of American Civilization. Michael G. Kammen. LC 90-55186. (Illus.). 368p. 1990. reprint ed. pap. text 17.95 (*0-8014-9755-8*) Cornell U Pr.

People of Paris. Daniel Roche. LC 86-24506. (Studies on the History of Society & Culture: No. 2). 300p. 1987. pap. 17.95 (*0-520-06031-8*, Pub. by U CA Pr) Cal Prin Full Svc.

People of Pascua. Edward H. Spicer. LC 88-20802. 331p. 1988. 45.00 (*0-8165-1069-5*) U of Ariz Pr.

People of Peace. Rose Blue & Corinne J. Naden. LC 93-30547. (Illus.). 80p. (J). (gr. 4-6). 1994. lib. bdg. 25.90 (*1-56294-409-6*) Millbrook Pr.

People of Penn's Woods West. Lee Gutkind. LC 84-2192. 152p. 1984. pap. 12.95 (*0-8229-5360-9*) U of Pittsburgh Pr.

People of Plenty: Economic Abundance & the American Character. David M. Potter. LC 54-12797. 229p. 1958. pap. text 11.95 (*0-226-67633-1*) U Ch Pr.

People of Polonia: The 1910 Census, 5 vols. Ed. by Jeanne S. Davis-White. 1993. pap. 31.95 (*1-887124-04-7*, HP 105A) Historyk Pr.

***People of Polonia: The 1910 Census Ward Two Baltimore City, Maryland, Pt. II.** Jeanne S. Davis-White. 1999. pap. 8.95 (*1-887124-16-0*) Historyk Pr.

People of Polonia Vol. 1: The 1910 Census: Anne Arundel & Baltimore County. Ed. by Jeanne S. Davis-White. 97p. 1993. pap. 4.95 (*1-887124-05-5*, PG 105) Historyk Pr.

People of Polonia Vol. 2: The 1910 Census: Baltimore City - Ward One. Ed. by Jeanne S. Davis-White. 193p. 1993. pap. 7.95 (*1-887124-06-3*, PG 106) Historyk Pr.

People of Polonia Vol. 3: The 1910 Census: Baltimore City - Ward 3. Ed. by Jeanne S. Davis-White. 84p. 1993. pap. 3.95 (*1-887124-07-1*, PG 107) Historyk Pr.

People of Polonia Vol. 4, Pt. 1 (A-M) The 1910 Census: Ward Two. Ed. by Jeanne S. Davis-White. 278p. 1995. pap. 6.95 (*1-887124-08-X*, PG 108) Historyk Pr.

People of Portsmouth & Some Who Came to Town. J. D. Lincoln & Rosemary Lincoln. LC 82-16543. (Illus.). 112p. 1982. pap. 13.95 (*0-914339-00-1*) P E Randall Pub.

People of Promise: Adventure Guidebook. Dan Lupton. Ed. by Laurie Mains. (Nineteen Ninety-Nine 50-Day Spiritual Adventure Ser.). 160p. 1998. pap. 7.00 (*1-57849-111-8*) Mainstay Church.

People of Prowess: Sport, Leisure, & Labor in Early Anglo-America. Nancy L. Struna. 296p. 1995. 18.95 (*0-252-06552-2*); text 34.95 (*0-252-02247-5*) U of Ill Pr.

People of Purpose: 80 People Who Have Made a Difference. Arnold B. Cheyney. LC 98-181588. (Illus.). 192p. 1998. pap. 12.95 (*0-673-36371-6*, GoodYrBooks) Addson-Wesley Educ.

People of Route 601: Life in the Slow Lane. Edward A. Youngman. (Illus.). 124p. 1997. write for info. (*0-9660642-0-8*, Wingate U Pr) Wingate Univ.

People of Russia & Their Food see Multicultural Cookbooks

People of Seldwyla & Seven Legends. Gottfried Keller. Tr. by M. D Hottinger. LC 70-140331. (Short Story Index Reprint Ser.). 1977. 18.95 (*0-8369-3723-6*) Ayer.

People of Short Blue Corn. Courlander. (J). 1996. 9.95 (*0-8050-4585-6*) H Holt & Co.

People of Sikkim, Vol. X. Ed. by K. S. Singh. (C). 1994. 24.00 (*81-7046-120-0*, Pub. by Seagull Bks) S Asia.

People of Skene & Kinellar, 1696: Taken from List of Pollable Persons in the Shires of Aberdeen, 1696 / Aberdeeb & North-East Scotland Family History Society Staff. LC 98-171185. 1998. write for info. (*1-900173-03-4*) Aberdeen & NE Scot.

People of Sonora & Yankee Capitalists. Ramon E. Ruiz. LC 87-30133. (PROFMEX Ser.). 326p. 1988. 43.50 (*0-8165-1012-1*) U of Ariz Pr.

People of South East Asia: Biological Anthropology of India, Pakistan & Nepal. Ed. by John R. Lukacs. 458p. 1984. 110.00 (*0-306-41407-4*, Plenum Trade) Perseus Pubng.

People of Sunlight & Starlight: Barrenland Archaeology in the Northwest Territories. Bryan Gordon. (Mercury Ser.: ASC No. 154). (Illus.). 300p. 1996. pap. 29.95 (*0-660-15963-5*, Pub. by CN Mus Civilization) U of Wash Pr.

People of Taihang: An Anthology of Family Histories. Ed. by Sidney L. Greenblatt. LC 74-15389. (China Book Project Ser.). (Illus.). 358p. reprint ed. pap. 111.00 (*0-608-11675-0*, 202185600024) Bks Demand.

People of Terra Nullius: Betrayal & Rebirth in Aboriginal Canada. Boyce Richardson. LC 94-11955. (Illus.). 408p. 1994. pap. 19.95 (*0-295-97391-9*) U of Wash Pr.

People of Thailand. D. Brittan. LC 96-47347. (Celebrating the Peoples & Civilizations of Southeast Asia Ser.). (J). 1997. lib. bdg. 15.93 (*0-8239-5126-X*, PowerKids) Rosen Group.

People of the Abyss. Jack London. LC 93-2947. (Illus.). 388p. 1995. pap. 14.95 (*1-55652-167-7*, Lawrence Hill) Chicago Review.

People of the Abyss. Jack London. (C). pap. 8.95 (*0-904526-17-8*, Pub. by Pluto GBR) LPC InBook.

People of the Abyss. Jack London. (Pluto Classic Ser.). 1998. pap. 14.95 (*0-7453-1415-5*, Pub. by Pluto GBR) Stylus Pub VA.

***People of the Abyss.** Jack London. (Collected Works of Jack London). 1998. reprint ed. lib. bdg. 98.00 (*1-58201-732-8*) Classic Bks.

People of the Andes. James Richardson, III. LC 94-22754. (Exploring the Ancient World Ser.). (Illus.). 176p. 1995. text 24.95 (*0-89599-041-5*) Smithsonian.

People of the Bays & Headlands: Anthropological History & the Fate of Communities in the Unknown Labrador. John C. Kennedy. (Illus.). 320p. 1995. text 50.00 (*0-8020-0646-9*); pap. text 22.95 (*0-8020-7600-9*) U of Toronto Pr.

People of the Bible. John Philips. LC 98-37055. 432p. 1999. 8.99 (*0-517-20421-5*) Random Hse Value.

People of the Bible: Women. Joy Lawler. (Bible People Ser.). 1996. pap. text 5.95 (*0-687-07395-2*) Abingdon.

People of the Blue Mountains. Helena P. Blavatsky. 227p. 1996. reprint ed. pap. 19.95 (*1-56459-619-2*) Kessinger Pub.

People of the Blue Water. Flora G. Iliff. LC 84-24105. 271p. 1985. reprint ed. pap. 15.95 (*0-8165-0925-5*) U of Ariz Pr.

People of the Body: Jews & Judaism from an Embodied Perspective. Ed. by Howard Eilberg-Schwartz. LC 91-35081. (SUNY Series, The Body in Culture, History, & Religion). 392p. (C). 1992. text 64.50 (*0-7914-1169-9*); pap. text 21.95 (*0-7914-1170-2*) State U NY Pr.

People of the Book: Canon, Meaning, & Authority. Moshe Halbertal. LC 97-18945. 256p. 1997. 35.00 (*0-674-66111-7*); pap. 18.95 (*0-674-66112-5*) HUP.

People of the Book: Christian Identity & Literary Culture. David L. Jeffrey. LC 96-6419. (Studies in a Christian World View). 416p. 1996. pap. 25.00 (*0-8028-4177-5*) Eerdmans.

***People of the Book: Drama, Fellowship, & Religion.** Samuel C. Heilman. 350p. 2000. pap. 29.95 (*0-7658-0747-5*) Transaction Pubs.

People of the Book: Drama, Fellowship, & Religion. Samuel C. Heilman. LC 82-13369. 264p. (C). 1983. 25.00 (*0-226-32492-3*) U Ch Pr.

People of the Book: Drama, Fellowship, & Religion. Samuel C. Heilman. LC 82-13369. 264p. (C). 1995. pap. text 16.00 (*0-226-32493-1*) U Ch Pr.

People of the Book: Thirty Scholars Reflect on Their Jewish Identity. Ed. by Jeffrey Rubin-Dorsky & Shelley F. Fishkin. LC 95-44454. (Wisconsin Studies in American Autobiography). 520p. 1996. 49.95 (*0-299-15010-0*); pap. 24.95 (*0-299-15014-3*) U of Wis Pr.

People of the Breaking Day. Sewall. 1998. pap. 5.99 (*0-87628-988-X*) Ctr Appl Res.

People of the Breaking Day. Marcia Sewall. LC 89-18194. (Illus.). 48p. (J). (gr. 2 up). 1997. per. 5.99 (*0-689-81684-7*) Aladdin.

People of the Breaking Day. Marcia Sewall. (Aladdin Picture Bks.). 1997. 11.19 (*0-606-12789-5*, Pub. by Turtleback) Demco.

People of the Breaking Day. Marcia A. Sewall. LC 89-18194. (Illus.). 48p. (J). (gr. 1 up). 1990. 17.00 (*0-689-31407-8*) Atheneum Yung Read.

People of the Buffalo: How the Plains Indians Lived. Maria Campbell. (How They Lived Ser.). (Illus.). 48p. (J). (gr. 4-7). 1992. pap. 7.95 (*0-88894-329-6*) Firefly Bks Ltd.

***People of the California Gold Rush.** Adam D. Parker. (California Biography Ser.). (Illus.). 64p. (J). (gr. 4-8). 1999. pap. text 14.95 (*1-884925-82-0*) Toucan Valley.

***People of the Century: One Hundred Men & Women Who Shaped the Last One Hundred Years.** Time Magazine Editors. LC 99-48828. 480p. 1999. 34.50 (*0-684-87093-2*) S&S Trade.

People of the Chalice. Colbert S. Cartwright. 112p. (Orig.). (C). 1987. pap. 7.99 (*0-8272-2938-0*) Chalice Pr.

People of the Circle, People of the Four Directions. Scott McCarthy. LC 99-43461. (Illus.). 720p. Date not set. 49.95 (*1-57733-014-5*) B Dolphin Pub.

People of the Coquille Estuary: Native Use of Resources on the Oregon Coast. Roberta L. Hall et al. (Illus.). 234p. (Orig.). 1995. pap. 35.00 (*0-9619886-2-2*) Words & Pictures Unltd.

People of the Covenant: An Introduction to the Hebrew Bible. 4th ed. Henry J. Flanders et al. (Illus.). 576p. 1996. text 52.95 (*0-19-509370-4*) OUP.

People of the Covenant: God's New Covenant for Today. Ed. by Jack W. Hayford. LC 94-166324. 1994. pap. 6.99 (*0-8407-8520-8*) Nelson.

People of the Dalles: The Indians of Wascopam Mission. Robert Boyd. LC 95-38916. (Studies in the Anthropology of North American Indians). (Illus.). xi, 414p. 1996. text 60.00 (*0-8032-1236-4*) U of Nebr Pr.

People of the Dawn - Gryningsfolket. Jan Fridegard. Tr. & Frwd. by Robert E. Bjork. LC 89-4917. (Modern Scandinavian Literature in Translation Ser.: Vol. 2). 213p. 1990. reprint ed. pap. 66.10 (*0-608-02780-4*, 206384700007) Bks Demand.

People of the Dead Sea Scrolls: Their Literature, Social Organization & Religious Beliefs. Florentino G. Martinez & Julio T. Barrera. Tr. by Wilfred G. Watson. LC 95-24822. x, 270p. 1995. pap. 23.50 (*90-04-10085-7*) Brill Academic Pubs.

People of the Deer. Farley Mowat. 25.95 (*0-89190-818-8*) Amereon Ltd.

People Of The Deer. Farley Mowat. 304p. 1984. mass mkt. 5.99 (*0-7704-2254-3*) Bantam.

People of the Desert see American Indians Series

People of the Desert. Time-Life Books Editors. LC 92-22262. (American Indians Ser.). 176p. 1993. lib. bdg. 25.93 (*0-8094-9413-2*) Time-Life.

People of the Desert & Sea: Ethnobotany of the Seri Indians. Richard S. Felger & Mary B. Moser. LC 84-16357. (Illus.). 435p. 1992. reprint ed. pap. text 46.00 (*0-8165-1267-1*) U of Ariz Pr.

People of the Deserts. David Lambert. LC 98-10915. (Wide World Ser.). 48p. (J). 1999. 25.69 (*0-8172-5063-8*) Raintree Steck-V.

***People of the Drum of God - Come?** Paul L. Neeley. (Publications in Ethnography). 1999. pap. 29.00 (*1-55671-013-5*) S I L Intl.

People of the Earth. W. Michael Gear. 608p. 1992. mass mkt. 5.99 (*0-8125-0742-8*, Pub. by Tor Bks) St Martin.

People of the Earth. W. Michael Gear. 1992. 12.09 (*0-606-11730-X*, Pub. by Turtleback) Demco.

People of the Earth. 9th ed. Brian M. Fagan. LC 97-24769. 576p. (C). 1997. pap. text 55.00 (*0-321-01457-X*, Prentice Hall) P-H.

***People of The Earth: Intro World Prehistory.** 9th ed. (C). 1998. pap. text 0.00 (*0-321-02473-7*) HEPC Inc.

People of the Earth: Introduction to World Prehistory. 9th ed. (C). 1997. 67.00 (*0-321-02472-9*) Pearson Custom.

People of the Earth: The New Pagans Speak Out Interviews with Margot Adler, Starhawk, Susun Weed, Z. Budapest, & Many Others. Ellen E. Hopman & Lawrence Bond. LC 95-39794. 416p. 1995. pap. 19.95 (*0-89281-559-0*) Inner Tradit.

People of the Earth/ Instructor's Manual. 9th ed. Fagan. 1997. 24.00 (*0-321-40589-7*) Addison-Wesley.

People of the Finger Lakes Region: The Heart of New York State. Emerson Klees. LC 95-61561. 272p. 1995. pap. 15.00 (*0-9635990-6-2*) Frnds Finger Lks.

People of the Fire. W. Michael Gear. 480p. 1991. mass mkt. 5.99 (*0-8125-2150-1*, Pub. by Tor Bks) St Martin.

People of the Fire. W. Michael Gear. (First North Americans Ser.). 1991. 12.09 (*0-606-11731-8*, Pub. by Turtleback) Demco.

People of the First Crusade. Michael Foss. LC 97-4353. (Illus.). 256p. 1997. 24.45 (*1-55970-414-4*, Pub. by Arcade Pub Inc) Time Warner.

People of the First Crusade. Michael Foss. (Illus.). 240p. 1998. pap. 13.95 (*1-55970-455-1*, Pub. by Arcade Pub Inc) Time Warner.

People of the Fresh Water Lake: A Prehistory. Charles Hoffman. LC 89-13375. (American University Studies: Anthropology & Science: Ser. XI, Vol. 47). (Illus.). XVI, 304p. 1991. text 49.95 (*0-8204-1203-1*) P Lang Pubng.

People of the Grasslands. David Lambert. LC 97-28058. (Wide World Ser.). 48p. (J). 1998. 25.69 (*0-8172-5060-3*) Raintree Steck-V.

People of the Great Ocean: Aspects of Human Biology of the Early Pacific. Philip Houghton. (Illus.). 302p. (C). 1996. text 69.95 (*0-521-47166-4*) Cambridge U Pr.

People of the Holocaust see Holocaust Reference Library

An Asterisk (*) at the beginning of an entry indicates that the title is appearing for the first time.

People of the Holocaust. Linda Schmittroth. LC 98-4988. (J). 1998. 49.00 (*0-7876-1744-X*, UXL); pap. write for info. (*0-7876-1745-8*, UXL) Gale.

People of the Ice: How the Inuit Lived. Heather S. Siska. (How They Lived Ser.). (Illus.). (YA). (gr. 5 up). pap. 6.95 (*0-317-62413-X*, Pub. by DGL) Sterling.

People of the Ice: How the Inuit Lived. Heather S. Siska. (How They Lived Ser.). (Illus.). 48p. (J). (gr. 4-7). 1992. pap. 7.95 (*0-88894-404-7*) Firefly Bks Ltd.

People of the Ice Age. Ruth Goode. LC 72-85191. viii, 151 p. 1973. write for info. (*0-02-736420-8*) Macmillan.

People of the Ice & Snow see American Indians Series

People of the Ice & Snow. Time-Life Books Editors. LC 94-16653. (American Indians Ser.). (Illus.). 192p. 1994. lib. bdg. write for info. (*0-8094-9563-5*) Time-Life.

People of the Islands. Colm Regan. LC 98-10933. (Wide World Ser.). (J). 1998. 25.69 (*0-8172-5064-6*) Raintree Steck-V.

People of the Lakes see American Indians Series

People of the Lakes. Kathleen O'Neal Gear & W. Michael Gear. 816p. 1995. mass mkt. 6.99 (*0-8125-0747-9*, Pub. by Tor Bks) St Martin.

People of the Lakes. W. Michael Gear. (First North Americans Ser.). 1995. 12.09 (*0-606-11732-6*, Pub. by Turtleback) Demco.

People of the Lakes. Richard E. Leakey & Roger Lewin. 272p. 1979. mass mkt. 4.95 (*0-380-45575-7*, Avon Bks) Morrow Avon.

People of the Lakes. Time-Life Books Editors. (American Indians Ser.). (Illus.). 192p. 1994. lib. bdg. write for info. (*0-8094-9567-8*) Time-Life.

People of the Land of Flint. Richard D. Campbell. (Illus.). 130p. (Orig.). 1985. pap. text 19.50 (*0-8191-4551-3*) U Pr of Amer.

People of the Lie. M. Scott Peck. 1998. per. 14.00 (*0-684-84859-7*) S&S Trade Pap.

People of the Lie, Vol. 1. unabridged ed. M. Scott Peck. 1992. audio 12.00 (*0-671-76971-5*) S&S Audio.

People of the Lie: The Hope for Healing Human Evil. M. Scott Peck. 270p. 1985. pap. 12.00 (*0-671-52816-5*, Touchstone) S&S Trade Pap.

People of the Lightning. Kathleen O'Neal Gear. LC 95-34746. 1996. 12.09 (*0-606-11733-4*, Pub. by Turtleback) Demco.

People of the Lightning. Kathleen O'Neal Gear & W. Michael Gear. 1996. mass mkt. 6.99 (*0-8125-1556-0*, Pub. by Tor Bks) St Martin.

People of the Longhouse: How the Iroquoian Tribes Lived. Jillian Ridington & Robin Ridington. (How They Lived Ser.). (Illus.). 48p. (J). (gr. 4-7). 1992. pap. 7.95 (*1-55054-221-4*) Firefly Bks Ltd.

People of the Mandate: The Story of the World Evangelical Fellowship. W. Harold Fuller. xvii, 214p. 1996. reprint ed. pap. 11.99 (*1-900890-00-3*, Pub. by WEF) OM Literature.

People of the Masks. Kathleen O'Neal Gear & W. Michael Gear. LC 98-8695. 416p. 1998. 25.95 (*0-312-85857-4*, Pub. by Forge NYC) St Martin.

People of the Masks. Kathleen O'Neal Gear & W. Michael Gear. (Illus.). 552p. 1999. mass mkt. 6.99 (*0-8125-1561-7*, Pub. by Tor Bks) St Martin.

People of the Middle Place: A Study of the Zuni Indians. Dorothea C. Leighton & John Adair. LC 65-28463. (Monographs). 189p. 1966. pap. 10.00 (*0-87536-320-2*) HRAFP.

***People of the Millennium.** Allen H. Merriam. LC 99-94964. 2000. pap. 12.95 (*0-533-13244-4*) Vantage.

People of the Mist. Kathleen O'Neal Gear & W. Michael Gear. LC 97-14682. 480p. 1997. text 26.95 (*0-312-85854-X*) St Martin.

People of the Mist. Kathleen O'Neal Gear & W. Michael Gear. (The First North Americans Ser.). 1998. mass mkt. 6.99 (*0-8125-1560-9*, Pub. by Tor Bks) St Martin.

People of the Mist. H. Rider Haggard. 357p. 1997. pap. 30.00 (*0-89540-307-2*, SB-307) Sun Pub.

People of the Mist. large type ed. Kathleen O'Neal Gear & W. Michael Gear. LC 98-21082. 677p. 1998. 24.95 (*0-7838-0251-X*, G K Hall Lrg Type) Mac Lib Ref.

People of the Moonshell: A Western River Journal. Nancy M. Peterson. LC 84-15919. (Illus.). 176p. (Orig.). 1984. pap. 18.95 (*0-939650-42-8*) R H Pub.

***People of the Mounds: Ohio's Hopewell Culture.** rev. ed. Bradley T. Lepper. (Illus.). 22p. 1999. reprint ed. pap. 1.95 (*1-888213-48-5*) Eastern National.

People of the Mountains. Jen Green. LC 97-33223. (Wide World Ser.). 48 p. (J). 1998. 25.69 (*0-8172-5062-X*) Raintree Steck-V.

People of the North: Boran. Hussein A. Isack. (Kenya People Ser.). (Illus.). 42p. (YA). (gr. 6-9). 1991. pap. write for info. (*0-237-50724-2*) EVN1 UK.

People of the Old Missury: Years of Conflict. Nancy Peterson. LC 89-10723. (Illus.). 192p. (Orig.). 1989. 29.95 (*1-55838-105-8*) R H Pub.

People of the Old Missury: Years of Conflict. Nancy A. Peterson. LC 89-10723. (Illus.). 192p. (Orig.). 1989. pap. 16.95 (*1-55838-106-6*) R H Pub.

People of the Peyote: Huichol Indian History, Religion & Survival. Ed. by S. Schaefer & Peter Furst. 560p. 1998. pap. 29.95 (*0-8263-1905-X*) U of NM Pr.

People of the Philippines. Dolly Brittan. LC 97-8377. (Celebrating the Peoples & Civilizations of Southeast Asia Ser.). (Illus.). 24p. (J). (gr. k-4). 1997. lib. bdg. 15.93 (*0-8239-5127-8*, PowerKids) Rosen Group.

People of the Pit-Grave Kurgans in Eastern Hungary: (Fontes Archaelogici Hungariae) I. Ecsdey. 148p. (C). 1979. pap. 75.00 (*963-05-1733-7*, Pub. by Akade Kiado) St Mut.

People of the Plain: Class & Community in Lower Andalusia. David D. Gilmore. LC 79-20048. 1980. text 57.50 (*0-231-04754-1*) Col U Pr.

People of the Plains & Mountains: Essays in the History of the West Dedicated to Everett Dick, 25. Ray A. Billington. LC 72-784. (Contributions in American History Ser.: No. 25). (Illus.). 227p. 1973. 55.00 (*0-8371-6358-7*, BID/, Greenwood Pr) Greenwood.

People of the Plateau. Ron McCoy. (Plateau Ser.). 32p. 1993. pap. 6.95 (*0-89734-117-1*) Mus Northern Ariz.

People of the Plow: An Agricultural History of Ethiopia. James C. McCann. LC 94-37124. (Illus.). 304p. 1994. pap. text 24.95 (*0-299-14614-6*) U of Wis Pr.

People of the Plow: An Agricultural History of Ethiopia. James C. McCann. LC 94-37124. (Illus.). 304p. 1995. text 54.00 (*0-299-14610-3*) U of Wis Pr.

People of the Polar North: A Record . . . Knud J. Rasmussen. Ed. by G. Herring. LC 74-5868. (Illus.). reprint ed. 74.50 (*0-404-11675-2*) AMS Pr.

People of the Polar Regions. Jen Green. LC 97-38625. (Wide World Ser.). (Illus.). 48p. (J). (gr. 4-6). 1998. 25.69 (*0-8172-5065-4*) Raintree Steck-V.

People of the Promise Series, 8 vols. James R. Shott. Incl. Bk. 1. Leah. LC 90-35487. 160p. 1996. pap. 9.99 (*0-8361-3526-1*); Bk. 2. Joseph. LC 91-32886. 144p. 1996. pap. 9.99 (*0-8361-3576-8*); Bk. 3. Hagar. LC 91-43498. 168p. (Orig.). 1996. pap. 9.99 (*0-8361-3590-3*); Bk. 4. Esau. LC 92-26950. 216p. (Orig.). 1996. pap. 9.99 (*0-8361-3601-2*); Bk. 5. Deborah. LC 93-13109. 168p. (Orig.). 1996. pap. 9.99 (*0-8361-3643-8*); Bk. 6. Othniel. LC 93-44159. 168p. (Orig.). 1996. pap. 9.99 (*0-8361-3661-6*); Bk. 7. Abigail. LC 95-25415. 144p. (Orig.). 1996. pap. 9.99 (*0-8361-9030-0*); Bk. 8. Bathsheba. LC 95-47733. 152p. (Orig.). 1996. pap. 9.99 (*0-8361-9039-4*); 1996. Set pap. 79.99 (*0-8361-9005-X*) Herald Pr.

People of the Rain Forest. Lynn M. Stone. LC 94-20913. (Rain Forests Discovery Library). 24p. (J). (gr. k-4). 1994. lib. bdg. 10.95 (*0-86593-397-9*) Rourke Corp.

People of the Rain Forest. Mae Woods. LC 98-9982. (Rain Forest Ser.). (Illus.). 24p. (J). (gr. 2-4). 1999. lib. bdg. 18.60 (*1-57765-020-4*, Checkerboard Library) ABDO Pub Co.

People of the Rain Forests. Anna Lewington & Edward Parker. LC 97-38626. (Wide World Ser.). 48p. (J). (gr. 4-7). 1998. 25.69 (*0-8172-5061-1*) Raintree Steck-V.

People of the Rainbow: A Nomadic Utopia. Michael I. Niman. LC 97-4626. 1997. pap. 18.95 (*0-87049-989-0*) U of Tenn Pr.

People of the Rainbow: A Nomadic Utopia. Michael I. Niman. LC 97-4626. (Illus.). 360p. 1997. text 50.00 (*0-87049-988-2*) U of Tenn Pr.

People of the Red Earth: Americans Indians of Colorado. Sally Crum. LC 95-32115. (Illus.). 272p. 1986. 33.95 (*0-941270-88-2*) Ancient City Pr.

People of the Red Earth: Americans Indians of Colorado. Sally Crum. LC 95-32115. (Illus.). 272p. 1996. pap. 17.95 (*0-941270-89-0*) Ancient City Pr.

People of the River. W. Michael Gear. (First North Americans Ser.). 1993. 12.09 (*0-606-11734-2*, Pub. by Turtleback) Demco.

People of the River. W. Michael Gear & Kathleen O'Neal Gear. 544p. 1993. mass mkt. 5.99 (*0-8125-0743-6*, Pub. by Tor Bks) St Martin.

People of the River, People of the Tree: Change & Continuity in Sepik & Asmat Art. Allen Wardwell et al. Ed. by Gloria C. Kittleson. (Illus.). 120p. 1989. pap. 20.00 (*0-934251-03-7*) MN Museum Art.

People of the Road: The Irish Travellers. Photos & Text by Mathias Oppersdorff. LC 97-20568. (Illus.). 96p. 1997. 39.95 (*0-8156-0476-9*) Syracuse U Pr.

People of the Sea. W. Michael Gear. (First North Americans Ser.). (J). 1994. 11.09 (*0-606-11735-0*, Pub. by Turtleback) Demco.

People of the Sea. W. Michael Gear & Kathleen O'Neal Gear. 576p. 1994. mass mkt. 5.99 (*0-8125-0745-2*, Pub. by Tor Bks) St Martin.

People of the Sea. A. G. Jamieson. 500p. 1986. 89.95 (*0-416-40540-1*) Routledge.

People of the Sea. David Thomson. (Classics Ser.). 256p. 1996. pap. 11.95 (*0-86241-550-0*, Pub. by Canongate Books) Interlink Pub.

***People of the Sea.** David Thomson. 2000. 25.00 (*1-58243-086-1*, Pub. by Counterpt DC) HarpC.

People of the Sea: Identity & Descent among the Vezo of Madagascar. Rita Astuti. (Studies in Social & Cultural Anthropology: No. 95). (Illus.). 202p. (C). 1995. text 54.95 (*0-521-43350-9*) Cambridge U Pr.

People of the Sea: The Search for the Philistines. Trude Dothan. 256p. 1992. text 25.00 (*0-02-532261-3*) Macmillan.

People of the Secret. Ernest Scott. 263p. 1983. pap. 16.00 (*0-86304-038-1*, Pub. by Octagon Pr) ISHK.

People of the Seventh Fire: Returning Lifeways of Native America. Ed. by Dagmar Thorpe. LC 96-25058. (Illus.). 237p. (Orig.). 1996. pap. 14.00 (*1-881178-02-1*) Akwe Kon Pr.

People of the Shining Mountains: The Utes of Colorado. Charles S. Marsh. LC 81-21032. (Illus.). 190p. 1982. pap. 12.95 (*0-87108-613-1*) Pruett.

People of the Short Blue Corn: Tales & Legends of the Hopi Indians. Harold Courlander. LC 95-37318. (Illus.). 160p. (J). (gr. 5-9). 1995. pap. 9.95 (*0-8050-3511-7*, Owlet BYR) H Holt & Co.

People of the Short Blue Corn, Tales & Legends fo the Hopi Indians. Harold Courlander. LC 95-37318. 1996. 15.05 (*0-606-10282-5*, Pub. by Turtleback) Demco.

People of the Sierra. 2nd ed. Julian A. Pitt-Rivers. LC 70-153710. 260p. 1996. pap. text 12.00 (*0-226-67010-4*, P55) U Ch Pr.

People of the Silence. Kathleen O'Neal Gear & W. Michael Gear. LC 96-23402. (The First North Americans Ser.). 650p. 1997. mass mkt. 6.99 (*0-8125-1559-5*, Pub. by Tor Bks) St Martin.

People of the Small Arrow. Jack H. Driberg. LC 72-3367. (Short Story Index Reprint Ser.). (Illus.). 1977. reprint ed. 31.95 (*0-8369-4146-2*) Ayer.

People Of The Snow: The Story Of Kitimat. John Kendrick. 160p. 1987. pap. 12.95 (*1-55021-022-X*, Pub. by NC Ltd) U of Toronto Pr.

People of the South-Western Highlands: Gusii. William R. Ochieng. (Kenya People Ser.). (Illus.). 34p. (YA). (gr. 6-9). 1991. pap. write for info. (*0-237-49898-7*) EVN1 UK.

People of the Spirit: Gifts, Fruit, & Fullness of the Holy Spirit. Ed. by Jack W. Hayford. (Spirit-Filled Life Kingdom Dynamics Guide Ser.). 1993. pap. 6.99 (*0-8407-8431-7*) Nelson.

People of the State of California, et al. vs. David Van Horn, et al. fac. ed. (California Court of Appeal, Fourth Appellate District Ser.: No. E005276). 8p. 1990. reprint ed. pap. text 1.25 (*1-55567-550-6*) Coyote Press.

People of the State of California, Plaintiff, vs. David Van Horn & Robert Scott White, Defendants. fac. ed. (Municipal Court of the Desert Judicial District County of Riverside, California Ser.). 257p. 1990. reprint ed. pap. text 26.88 (*1-55567-551-4*) Coyote Press.

People of the Temples: Menaidra. Linda C. Eneix. 370p. (Orig.). 1997. pap. 7.99 (*0-9656252-0-6*) O T S.

People of the Tongass: Alaska Forestry under Attack. K. A. Soderberg & Jackie Durette. Ed. by Ron Arnold. (Free Enterprise Battle Bks.). (Illus.). 360p. 1988. 14.95 (*0-939571-04-8*) Free Enter Pr.

People of the Tonto Rim: Archaeological Discovery in Prehistoric Arizona. Charles L. Redman. LC 92-25213. (Illus.). 224p. 1993. pap. text 17.95 (*1-56098-192-X*) Smithsonian.

People of the Towel & the Water. Catherine D. Doherty. 1991. pap. 12.95 (*0-921440-22-7*) Madonna Hse.

People of the Trail: How the Northern Forest Indians Lived. Robin Ridington & Jillian Ridington. (How They Lived Ser.). (Illus.). 40p. (J). (gr. 4-7). 1992. pap. 7.95 (*0-88894-412-8*) Firefly Bks Ltd.

People of the Tropical Rain Forest: In Association with Smithsonian Institution Traveling Exhibition Service. Ed. by Julie S. Denslow & Christine Padoch. (Illus.). 240p. 1988. pap. 34.95 (*0-520-06351-1*, Pub. by U CA Pr) Cal Prin Full Svc.

People of the Troubled Water: A Missouri River Journal. Nancy M. Peterson. LC 88-26418. (Illus.). 176p. (Orig.). 1988. 24.95 (*1-55838-082-5*); pap. 15.95 (*1-55838-083-3*) R H Pub.

People of the Truth: A Christian Challenge to Contemporary Culture. Robert Webber & Rodney Clapp. LC 93-4461. 144p. 1993. reprint ed. pap. 10.95 (*0-8192-1598-8*) Morehouse Pub.

People of the Twilight. Diamond Jenness. LC 59-16100. 1994. pap. text 9.95 (*0-226-39653-3*, P32) U Ch Pr.

People of the Ucayali: The Shipibo & Conibo of Peru. Lucille Eakin et al. LC 86-82643. (International Museum of Cultures Publications: No. 12). ix, 62p. (Orig.). 1986. pap. 9.00 (*0-88312-163-8*) S I L Intl.

People of the Valley. Frank Waters. LC 78-137435. 201p. 1941. pap. 11.95 (*0-8040-0243-6*) Swallow.

People of the Valley: Awakening & Journey, 2 vols. Frances E. Crary. LC 91-73346. (Orig.). 1992. pap. 14.95 (*0-9629950-3-7*) Ashbrook Pub.

People of the Valley Bk. 1: The Awakening. Frances E. Crary. LC 91-73346. 702p. (Orig.). 1992. pap. 14.95 (*0-9629950-1-0*) Ashbrook Pub.

People of the Valley Bk. 2: The Journey. Frances E. Crary. LC 91-73346. 645p. (Orig.). 1992. pap. 14.95 (*0-9629950-2-9*) Ashbrook Pub.

***People of the Volcanoes, Puyulek Pu'irtug! Aniakchaik National Monument & Preserve Ethnographic Overview & Assessment.** Michele Morseth. Ed. by Frank Norris & Margaret Sucec. (Illus.). 206p. 1998. pap. write for info. (*0-941555-05-4*) Natl Pk AK.

People of the Wachusett: Greater New England in History & Memory, 1630-1860. David Jaffee. LC 99-14578. 1999. 39.95 (*0-8014-3610-9*) Cornell U Pr.

People of the WEB. Gregory L. Little. Ed. by Kenneth D. Robinson. (Illus.). 300p. 1989. pap. 19.95 (*0-940829-03-7*) Eagle Wing Bks.

People of the WEB: What Indian Mounds, Ancient Rituals, & Stone Circles Tell Us about Modern UFO Abductions, Apparitions, & the Near Death. Gregory L. Little. Ed. by Kenneth D. Robinson. LC 89-85686. (Illus.). 229p. 1990. pap. 19.95 (*0-940829-02-9*) Eagle Wing Bks.

People of the West. Dayton Duncan. (West (Television Program) Ser.). (Illus.). 128p. (J). (gr. 3-7). 1996. 19.95 (*0-316-19627-4*) Little.

People of the West Desert: Finding Common Ground. Craig Denton. LC 98-58065. (Illus.). 208p. 1999. 44.95 (*0-87421-263-4*); pap. 24.95 (*0-87421-262-6*) Utah St U Pr.

People of the Whistling Waters. Mardi Oakley Medawar. 442p. 1993. 19.95 (*1-879915-05-7*) Affil Writers America.

***People of the Wind River: The Eastern Shoshones, 1825-1900.** Henry E Stamm. LC 99-33978. 272p. 1999. write for info. (*0-8061-3175-6*) U of Okla Pr.

People of the Wolf. W. Michael Gear. 1990. 11.09 (*0-606-11736-9*, Pub. by Turtleback) Demco.

People of the Wolf. W. Michael Gear & Kathleen O'Neal Gear. 448p. 1992. mass mkt. 5.99 (*0-8125-2133-1*, Pub. by Tor Bks) St Martin.

People of the World. Trundle. (World Geography Ser.). (J). (gr. 3-6). 1978. lib. bdg. 14.95 (*0-88110-116-8*, Usborne) EDC.

People of the World. Trundle. (World Geography Ser.). (Illus.). 32p. (J). (gr. 3-6). 1978. pap. 6.95 (*0-86020-189-9*, Usborne) EDC.

People of the World in Pencil. Gene Franks. (How to Draw & Paint Ser.). (Illus.). 32p. (Orig.). 1991. pap. 6.95 (*1-56010-075-3*, HT-234) W Foster Pub.

People of This Parish. large type ed. Rosemary Ellerbeck. 1995. 27.99 (*0-7505-0731-4*, Pub. by Mgna Lrg Print) Ulverscroft.

People of This Place: Natural & Unnatural Habitats. Ed. by Patra McSharry & Roger Rosen. (Icarus World Issues Ser.). (Illus.). (YA). (gr. 7-12). 1993. pap. 8.95 (*0-8239-1382-1*); lib. bdg. 16.95 (*0-8239-1381-3*) Rosen Group.

People of Tibet. Charles A. Bell. 1980. lib. bdg. 300.00 (*0-87968-481-X*) Krishna Pr.

***People of Tibet.** Charles A. Bell. 338p. 2000. 34.00 (*81-215-0933-5*, Pub. by Munshiram) Coronet Bks.

***People of Truth: Living in an Age of Lies, Hype & Spin.** Os Guinness. 128p. (gr. 13 up). 2000. pap. 10.99 (*0-8010-6323-X*, Hour Glass) Baker Bks.

People of Vietnam. Dolly Brittan. LC 96-39805. (Celebrating the Peoples & Civilizations of Southeast Asia Ser.). (J). 1997. lib. bdg. 15.93 (*0-8239-5125-1*, PowerKids) Rosen Group.

People of Wallingford. Birney C. Batcheller. (Illus.). 317p. 1995. reprint ed. lib. bdg. 39.50 (*0-8328-5130-2*) Higginson Bk Co.

People of Wight. Angela Wigglesworth. (Illus.). 160p. 1996. pap. 15.95 (*0-7509-1091-7*, Pub. by Sutton Pub Ltd) Intl Pubs Mktg.

People of Wilson County, Tennessee, 1800-1899. Thomas E. Partlow. 158p. 1983. 22.00 (*0-89308-308-9*) Southern Hist Pr.

People on a Bridge: Poems. Wislawa Szymborska. Tr. by A. Czerniawski from POL. (Illus.). 96p. (Orig.). 1991. pap. 17.95 (*0-948259-70-1*, Pub. by Forest Bks) Dufour.

People on Earth. Robinson & Jackson. Date not set. pap. text. write for info. (*0-582-33081-5*, Pub. by Addison-Wesley) Longman.

People on Earth: (Book & Map) UNESCO Staff. 1997. 35.00 (*92-3-199770-X*, U9777, Pub. by UNESCO) Bernan Associates.

People on the Edge in the Horn: Displacement, Land Use & the Environment in the Gedaref Region. Gaim Kibreab. LC 97-168751. 1996. pap. 21.95 (*1-56902-039-6*) Red Sea Pr.

People on the Edge in the Horn: Displacement, Land Use & the Environment in the Gedaref Region, Sudan. Gaim Kibreab. LC 97-168751. 352p. 79.95 (*1-56902-038-8*) Red Sea Pr.

People on the Farm: Growing Vegetables. 1991. lib. bdg. 76.95 (*0-8490-4486-3*) Gordon Pr.

People on the Move - New Migration Flows in Europe. Council of Europe Staff. 1992. 21.00 (*92-871-2021-8*, Pub. by Council of Europe) Manhattan Pub Co.

People on the Prowl. Jaime Collyer. Ed. by Yvette E. Miller. Tr. by Lilian L. De Tagle from SPA. LC 95-21099. (Discoveries Ser.). 144p. 1996. pap. 13.95 (*0-935480-73-0*) Lat Am Lit Rev Pr.

People on the Way: Asian North Americans Discovering Christ, Culture, & Community. Ed. by David Ng. 336p. (Orig.). 1996. pap. 18.00 (*0-8170-1242-7*) Judson.

People or Monsters? And Other Stories & Reportage from China after Mao. Liu Binyan. Ed. by Perry Link. LC 82-48594. (Chinese Literature in Translation Ser.). 160p. 1983. pap. 4.95 (*0-253-20313-9*, MB-313) Ind U Pr.

People or Monsters? And Other Stories & Reportage from China after Mao. Liu Binyan. Ed. by Perry Link. LC 82-48594. (Chinese Literature in Translation Ser.). 160p. 1983. 20.00 (*0-253-34329-1*) Ind U Pr.

People or Monsters? Other Stories & Reportage from China after Mao. Pin-Yen Liu. Ed. by Perry Link. LC 82-48594. (Chinese Literature in Translation Ser.). 157p. Date not set. reprint ed. pap. 48.70 (*0-608-20559-1*, 205447300002) Bks Demand.

People-Oriented Enterprise Zone for Denver. Dwight Filley. (Issue Papers: No. 2-91). 10p. 1991. pap. text 8.00 (*1-57655-041-9*) Independ Inst.

People, Participation & Sustainable Development: The Dynamics of Natural Resource Systems. Ed. by Ganesh Shivakoti et al. LC 98-904650. (Illus.). xii, 400p. 1997. pap. 20.00 (*1-889740-02-0*) IN Wrkshp in Political Theory.

People, Partnership, & Profits Pt. 2: The New Labor-Management Agenda. Jerome M. Rosaw & Jill C. Lotto. (Strategic Partners for High Performance Ser.). 138p. 1994. pap. text, per. 95.00 (*0-89361-051-8*) Work in Amer.

People, Passion & Performance. Steven Wiley. LC 99-166666. 120p. 1997. 11.00 (*0-7872-4531-3*) Kendall-Hunt.

People Paths & Purposes: Notations for a Participatory Envirotecture. Thiel. LC 95-26417. (Illus.). 379p. (C). 1996. 60.00 (*0-295-97521-0*) U of Wash Pr.

People, Patients & Politics. Clark R. Cahow. Ed. by Gerald N. Grob. LC 78-22554. (Historical Issues in Mental Health Ser.). (Illus.). 1980. lib. bdg. 23.95 (*0-405-11908-9*) Ayer.

People Pattern Power: The Nine Keys to Business Success. Wyatt Woodsmall & Marilyne Woodsmall. LC 98-230832. 1999. pap. 27.99 (*1-892876-00-0*) Next Step Pr.

People, Penguins, & Plastic Trees: Basic Issues in Environmental Ethics. Donald VanDeVeer & Christine Pierce. 267p. (C). 1986. pap. 23.25 (*0-534-06312-8*) Wadsworth Pub.

People, Penguins, & Plastic Trees: Basic Issues in Environmental Ethics. 2nd ed. Christine Pierce & Donald VanDeVeer. LC 94-13151. 485p. 1994. pap. 56.95 (*0-534-17922-3*) Wadsworth Pub.

***People, People.** large type ed. Judy Mullican. (CB Ser.). (Illus.). 6p. (J). (ps-k). 2000. pap. text 10.95 (*1-57332-159-1*) HighReach Lrning.

P

People, Performance . . . Results! 672p. pap. write for info. (*0-318-59907-4*, NTDSP) Am Soc Train & Devel.

People, Performance & Pay: Dynamic Compensation for Changing Organizations. Thomas P. Flannery et al. (Illus.). 256p. 1995. 26.50 (*0-02-874059-9*) Free Pr.

People, Personal Expression & Social Relations in Late Antiquity: Text from Gaul & Western Europe, Vol. 1. Mathisen. (Illus.). (C). text. write for info. (*0-472-10771-2*) U of Mich Pr.

People, Personal Expression & Social Relations in Late Antiquity: Texts from Gaul & Western Europe, Vol. 2. Mathisen. (Illus.). (C). text. write for info. (*0-472-10772-0*) U of Mich Pr.

People Piece Primer. Peggy McLean & Betty Sternberg. (Illus.). 54p. (Orig.). (J). (gr. k-3). 1975. pap. 7.95 (*0-918932-37-8*, A-1403) Activity Resources.

People Piece Puzzles. Jack McLaughlin. (Illus.). 60p. (J). (gr. 2-8). 1973. pap. 7.95 (*0-918932-38-6*, A-1122) Activity Resources.

People Places: Design Guidelines for Urban Open Space. 2nd ed. Ed. by Clare C. Marcus & Carolyn Francis. 384p. 1997. pap. 49.95 (*0-471-28833-0*, VNR) Wiley.

People Places: Design Guidelines for Urban Open Space. 2nd ed. Francis Marcus. LC 97-1233. (Landscape Architecture Ser.). 384p. 1997. pap. 39.95 (*0-442-02546-7*, VNR) Wiley.

People, Places & Moultonborough, Vol. 1. Naomi G. Topalian. Ed. by Helene Pilibosian. LC 89-61431. (Illus.). 1989. 22.00 (*0-936893-04-4*) Baikar.

People, Places & Quilts: A Modern Folk Artist Re-Creates Her Family's Odyssey with the U. S. Navy. Diane F. Wilson. LC 89-39906. (Illus.). 96p. 1989. pap. 15.00 (*0-939009-30-7*, EPM) Howell Pr VA.

People, Places & Quilts: A Modern Folk Artist Re-Creates Her Family's Odyssey with the U. S. Navy. Diane F. Wilson. (Illus.). 87p. 1999. reprint ed. pap. text 30.00 (*0-7881-6326-4*) DIANE Pub.

***People, Places & Reflections: A Journey with United Nations.** Virgilio Chavez. 200p. 2000. pap. 16.00 (*0-8059-4824-4*) Dorrance.

People, Places, & Things. (Encyclopaedia Britannica Fascinating Facts Ser.). (Illus.). 32p. (J). 1993. 8.98 (*1-56173-320-2*) Pubns Intl Ltd.

***People, Places & Things.** Judy Litman. LC 99-95230. (Illus.). 114p. 2000. reprint ed. pap. 25.00 (*0-9672800-0-1*) J Litman Pubn.

People, Places & Things: An African-American Perspective. Ed. by Jeannetta Holliman. (Illus.). (Orig.). 1993. 9.95 (*0-918881-31-5*) Columbus Mus Art.

People, Places & Things: Thirty Years in Photography. Bernard Fontana et al. (Illus.). 111p. (Orig.). 1997. pap. 35.00 (*0-911611-08-8*) Tucson Mus Art.

People, Places & Things in Henri Joly's Legend in Japanese Art: An Analytical Index. Compiled by John B. Tompkins & Dorothy C. Tompkins. LC 78-61162. 218p. 1978. 12.50 (*0-935034-00-5*) Kirin Bks & Art.

People, Places & Things of Yesterday - Bucks Co., Pa. Janice S. Williams. LC 83-90114. (Illus.). 108p. 1983. 12.50 (*0-9611264-0-X*) Ol' Attic Bks.

People, Places, Processes. G. Wynn. 1990. pap. text. write for info. (*0-7730-4979-7*) Addison-Wesley.

People Planning & Development Studies: Some Reflections on Social Planning. Ed. by Raymond Apthorpe. 168p. 1970. 45.00 (*0-7146-2582-5*, BHA-02582, Pub. by F Cass Pubs) Intl Spec Bk.

People, Plans, & Policies: Essays on Poverty, Racism, & Other National Urban Problems. Herbert J. Gans. (History of Urban Life Ser.). 380p. 1991. text 57.50 (*0-231-07402-6*) Col U Pr.

People, Plans, & Policies: Essays on Poverty, Racism, & Other National Urban Problems. Herbert J. Gans. 1994. pap. 23.00 (*0-231-07403-4*) Col U Pr.

***People, Plants & Justice: The Politics of Nature Conservation.** Charles Zerner. LC 99-53777. 1999. 30.00 (*0-231-10811-7*) Col U Pr.

***People, Plants & Justice: The Politics of Nature Conservation.** Charles Zerner. 2000. 49.50 (*0-231-10810-9*) Col U Pr.

People, Plants, & Landscapes: Studies in Paleoethnobotany. Ed. by Kristen J. Gremillion. LC 96-13617. (Illus.). 296p. (C). 1997. pap. text 29.95 (*0-8173-0827-X*) U of Ala Pr.

People, Plants, & Patents: The Impact of Intellectual Property on Trade, Plant Biodiversity, & Rural Society. (Illus.). 142p. (Orig.). (C). 1994. pap. text 35.00 (*0-7881-1177-9*) DIANE Pub.

***People Pleasers: Helping Others Without Hurting Yourself.** Les Carter. LC 99-59090. 192p. 2000. 17.99 (*0-8054-2146-7*) Broadman.

People Plus Service Equals Success. Marian Wold & Jim White. LC 91-66208. 60p. 1991. pap. text 9.95 (*0-916809-53-6*) Scott Pubns MI.

People Poems. Compiled by Jill Bennett. (Illus.). 32p. (J). 1992. pap. (*0-19-276110-2*) OUP.

People Policy: Australia's Population Choices. Doug Cocks. 272p. 1996. pap. 29.95 (*0-614-17757-X*, Pub. by New South Wales Univ Pr) Intl Spec Bk.

People Policy: Australia's Population Choices. Doug Cocks. 347p. 1997. pap. 29.95 (*0-86840-247-8*, Pub. by New South Wales Univ Pr) Intl Spec Bk.

***People, Politics & Economic Life: Exploring Appalachia with Quantitative Methods.** 2nd ed. Thomas Plaut. 164p. (C). 1999. spiral bd. 34.95 (*0-7872-6419-9*, 41641901) Kendall-Hunt.

***People, Politics & Government: A Canadian Perspective.** 5th ed. 2000. write for info. (*0-13-027345-7*) P-H.

***People, Politics & Government: A Canadian Perspective.** 5th ed. James J. Guy. 569p. 2000. pap. write for info. (*0-13-027246-9*) P-H.

***People, Politics & Ideology: Democracy & Social Change in Nepal.** H. Hoftun. 1999. pap. 109.00 (*0-7855-7618-5*) St Mut.

People, Politics & Public Power. Ken Billington. LC 87-51001. (Illus.). 480p. 1988. 24.95 (*0-9619682-0-6*); pap. 19.95 (*0-9619682-1-4*) WA Public Util Dist Assn.

People Pollution: Sociologic & Ecologic Viewpoints on the Prevalence of People. Milton M. Freeman. LC 73-94315. (Environmental Damage & Control in Canada Ser.: No. 4). 189p. reprint ed. pap. 58.60 (*0-7837-1164-6*, 204169300022) Bks Demand.

People, Pooches & Problems. Job M. Evans. (Illus.). 256p. 1991. 19.95 (*0-87605-783-0*) Howell Bks.

People, Positions, & Power: The Political Appointments of Lyndon Johnson. Richard L. Schott & Dagmar S. Hamilton. LC 83-4814. (Administrative History of the Johnson Presidency Ser.). 256p. 1996. 27.00 (*0-226-74016-1*) U Ch Pr.

People, Potholes & City Politics. Karen Herland. LC 92-74578. 240p. 1993. 45.99 (*1-895431-53-0*, Pub. by Black Rose); pap. 16.99 (*1-895431-52-2*, Pub. by Black Rose) Consort Bk Sales.

People, Poverty, & Politics: Pennsylvanians During the Great Depression. Thomas H. Coode & John F. Bauman. LC 78-75198. (Illus.). 276p. 1981. 32.50 (*0-8387-2320-9*) Bucknell U Pr.

People Power. Jim Castelli. 1995. pap. 14.95 (*0-8050-4299-7*) H Holt & Co.

People Power: A Reference Guide to Resources & Information. Randall L. Voight. LC 76-17934. (Illus.). 1977. 7.95 (*0-930318-02-1*) Intl Res Eval.

People Power: An Oral & Photographic History of the Philippines Revolution of 1986. Ed. by Monina A. Mercado. (Illus.). 320p. (Orig.). 1987. pap. 19.95 (*0-86316-131-6*) Writers & Readers.

***People Power: Grass Roots Politics & Race Relations.** Judith N. DeSena. LC 99-32759. 152p. 1999. 49.00 (*0-7618-1461-2*); pap. 28.50 (*0-7618-1462-0*) U Pr of Amer.

People Power: Service, Advocacy, Empowerment : Selected Writings of Brian O'Connell. limited ed. Brian O'Connell. LC 94-23368. 241p. 1994. pap. 24.95 (*0-87954-563-1*) Foundation Ctr.

People Power: Tapping the Spirit of Quality Performance & Service in Your Organization. Thomas J. Stevenin. pap. 10.99 (*0-8024-7355-5*) Northfield Pub.

People Power: Tapping the Spirit of Quality Performance & Service in Your Organization. Thomas J. Stevenin. LC 96-209701. 1996. pap. 10.99 (*1-881273-55-5*) Northfield Pub.

People Power: The Building of a New European Home. Michael Randle. (Conflict & Peacemaking Ser.). (Illus.). 256p. 1991. 16.95 (*1-869890-29-9*, Pub. by Hawthorn Press) Anthroposophic.

People Power: Together We Can Change Things. Dean Brackley. 1989. pap. 1.50 (*0-8091-5203-7*) Paulist Pr.

People Power: 12 Power Principles to Enrich Your Business, Career, & Personal Network. Donna Fisher. 224p. 1995. pap. 14.95 (*1-885167-11-3*) Bard Press.

People, Power, & Politics. 8th ed. 624p. (C). 1998. pap. 38.00 (*0-536-01102-8*) Pearson Custom.

People, Power & Politics: An Introduction to Political Science. 3rd ed. John C. Donovan et al. 360p. 1993. pap. 27.95 (*0-8226-3025-7*) Rowman.

***People, Power, Places: Perspectives in Vernacular Architecture, VIII.** Ed. by Sally McMurry & Annmarie Adams. (Illus.). 328p. (C). 2000. pap. text 30.00 (*1-57233-075-9*, Pub. by U of Tenn Pr) U Ch Pr.

People Prepared. Terry Virgo. 206p. 1996. pap. 10.95 (*1-878327-70-4*, TV1-001) Morning NC.

People, Princes & Paramount Power: Society & Politics in the Indian Princely States. Ed. by Robin Jeffrey. 1979. 19.95 (*0-19-560886-0*) OUP.

People Principle. Willingham. 272p. 1999. pap. 13.95 (*0-312-24490-8*) St Martin.

People Principle: A Revolutionary Redefinition of Leadership. Ron Willingham. 262p. 1999. text 23.00 (*0-7881-6163-6*) DIANE Pub.

People Principle: A Revolutionary Redefinition of Leadership. Ron Willingham. LC 97-14387. (Illus.). 262p. 1997. 22.95 (*0-312-16871-3*) St Martin.

People Principle: Transforming Laypersons into Leaders. Stan Toler. LC 97-3834. 152p. (Orig.). 1997. pap. 9.99 (*0-8341-1664-2*) Beacon Hill.

People Problems: The Executive's Answer Book. John B. Miner. 1985. text 25.00 (*0-394-55002-1*) Organizat Meas.

People Process. Pam Hollister. LC 92-13286. 63p. 1992. ring bd. 19.95 (*0-88390-328-8*, Pfffr & Co) Jossey-Bass.

People Process: A Manufacturing Story. Bill Beck. Ed. & Illus. by Westmoreland Larson Webster, Inc., Staff. LC 95-75072. 133p. 1994. text. write for info. (*0-9644463-0-8*); pap. text 24.00 (*0-9644463-1-6*) Phillips Plastics.

People, Processes, & Managing Data, No. 11. Gerald W. McLaughlin et al. 87p. (C). 1998. pap. 15.00 (*1-882393-07-4*) Assn Instl Res.

People, Processes & Partnerships: A Report on the Customs Service for the 21st Century. 1997. lib. bdg. 250.95 (*0-8490-8107-6*) Gordon Pr.

People, Programs, & Persuasion: Some Remarks about Promoting University Adult Education. Milton R. Stern. 1961. 2.50 (*0-8156-7016-8*, NES 33) Syracuse U Cont Ed.

People, Progress & Employee Relations: Proceedings. Ed. by Richard A. Beaumont. LC 76-54797. 178p. reprint ed. pap. 55.20 (*0-8357-9811-9*, 201148400078) Bks Demand.

People, Promise & Community: A Practical Guide to Creating & Sustaining Small Communities of Faith. Harriet Burke et al. 160p. (Orig.). 1996. pap. 16.95 (*0-8091-3665-1*) Paulist Pr.

People, Protest & Politics: Case Studies of Popular Movements in 19th Century Wales. David Egan. 117p. 1987. pap. 20.95 (*0-8464-4731-2*) Beekman Pubs.

People, Protest & Politics: Case Studies of Popular Movements in 19th Century Wales. David R. Egan. (Illus.). 117p. (C). 1987. pap. 21.00 (*0-86383-350-0*, Pub. by Gomer Pr) St Mut.

People, Protest & Politics: Case Studies of Popular Movements in 20th Century Wales. Gareth E. Jones. (Illus.). (C). 1986. pap. text 45.00 (*0-86383-345-4*, Pub. by Gomer Pr) St Mut.

People Purple Peacock Poetry. deluxe limited ed. Ed. by Winchinchala. (Illus.). 25p. Date not set. pap. 9.99 (*1-889768-31-6*) People with Wings.

People Raising: A Practical Guide to Raising Support. William R. Dillon. wbk. ed. 15.99 (*0-8024-6447-5*, 246) Moody.

People Rape: How the Haves Deprive the Have-Nots. Chesli Vellian. LC 82-13935. 1988. 13.95 (*0-87949-216-3*) Ashley Bks.

People-Reading: How We Control Others, How They Control Us. Ernst G. Beier & Evans G. Valens. LC 84-43053. 228p. 1980. pap. 12.95 (*0-8128-6263-5*, Scrbrough Hse) Madison Bks UPA.

People Ready for the Return of Jesus. Emilio Knechtle. LC 97-60341. 144p. 1997. per. 6.95 (*1-57258-083-6*) Teach Servs.

People Real & Fictional. James Scott. 86p. (YA). (gr. 7-12). 1992. pap., wbk. ed. 4.50 (*1-58049-368-8*, CU3A) Prestwick Hse.

People Say Hello, Vol. 3904. Will Barber. Ed. by Rozanne L. Williams. (Social Studies Learn to Read Ser.). (Illus.). 8p. (J). (ps-2). 1996. pap. 1.75 (*1-57471-123-7*, 3904) Creat Teach Pr.

People Say Hello, Vol. 3961. Will Barber. Ed. by Rozanne L. Williams. (Social Studies Big Bks.). (Illus.). 8p. (J). (ps-2). 1997. pap. 8.98 (*1-57471-169-5*, 3961) Creat Teach Pr.

People Series, 4 bks. Gail Saunders-Smith. Incl. Children. LC 97-23587. 24p. (J). 1997. lib. bdg. 13.25 (*1-56065-491-0*, Pebble Bks); Communities. LC 97-23589. (J). 1997. lib. bdg. 13.25 (*1-56065-494-5*, Pebble Bks); Families. LC 97-12693. 24p. (J). 1997. lib. bdg. 13.25 (*1-56065-493-7*, Pebble Bks); Parents. LC 97-23588. 24p. (J). 1997. lib. bdg. 13.25 (*1-56065-492-9*, Pebble Bks); 53.00 (*1-56065-676-X*, Pebble Bks) Capstone Pr.

People Set A-P-A-R-T. Thelma Williams. (Illus.). 27p. (Orig.). 1991. pap. 4.00 (*0-945768-04-4*) A-Town Pub Co.

People Set Apart: Scotch-Irish in Eastern Ohio. Lorle Porter. Ed. by Toni M. Leland. LC 98-67105. (Illus.). 986p. 1999. 59.95 (*1-887932-75-5*, New Concord Pr) Equine Graph Pubng.

People Shall Continue. Simon J. Ortiz. LC 88-18929. (Illus.). 32p. (YA). (gr. 1 up). 1988. 14.95 (*0-89239-041-7*) Childrens Book Pr.

People Shall Continue. Simon J. Ortiz. (Illus.). (YA). (gr. 1 up). 1994. pap. 7.95 (*0-89239-125-1*) Childrens Book Pr.

People Shall Continue. Simon J. Ortiz. LC 88-18929. 1994. 12.15 (*0-606-06662-4*, Pub. by Turtleback) Demco.

People Shall Continue. Raintree Staff. 1992. lib. bdg. 5.00 (*0-8172-6741-7*) Raintree Steck-V.

People Shall Judge, 2 vols., Vol. 1, Pt. 1. University of Chicago, College of the Social Scien. LC 49-3028. 358p. 1976. pap. text 19.95 (*0-226-77049-4*) U Ch Pr.

People Shall Judge: Readings in the Formation of American Policy, Vol. 2. Chicago University Staff. LC 49-3028. 945p. reprint ed. pap. 200.00 (*0-608-16365-1*, 202674400002) Bks Demand.

People Sharing Jesus see Pueblo Que Testifica de Cristo

People Sharing Jesus. D. Robinson. 1995. VHS 159.99 (*0-7852-7762-5*) Nelson.

People Sharing Jesus. Darrell W. Robinson. LC 94-45172. 252p. 1995. pap. 9.99 (*0-7852-7929-6*) Nelson.

People Sharing Jesus Leader's Guide. Jerry Pipes & Curt Hamner. LC 95-16643. 1995. pap., teacher ed. 10.99 (*0-7852-7682-3*) Nelson.

People Side of Project Management. Ralph L. Kliem & Irwin S. Ludin. 250p. 1992. 39.95 (*0-566-07363-3*, Pub. by Gower) Ashgate Pub Co.

People Side of Project Management. Ralph L. Kliem & Irwin S. Ludin. 200p. 1995. pap. 26.95 (*0-566-07668-3*, Pub. by Gower) Ashgate Pub Co.

People Skills: How to Assert Yourself, Listen to Others, & Resolve Conflicts. Robert Bolton. 300p. 1986. pap. 12.00 (*0-671-62248-X*, Touchstone) S&S Trade Pap.

People Skills - Learn by Doing. Abe Wagner. (Illus.). 52p. Date not set. pap. 3.95 (*0-926632-01-9*) A Wagner & Assocs.

People Skills for Library Managers: A Common Sense Guide. Lucile Wilson. 125p. 1996. pap. text 19.00 (*1-56308-143-1*) Libs Unl.

People Skills for Young Adults. Mbarianna Csboti. LC 98-45887. 1999. pap. 29.95 (*1-85302-716-2*) Taylor & Francis.

People Skills of Jesus. William Beausay, II. LC 97-3897. 128p. 1997. 14.99 (*0-7852-7164-3*) Nelson.

People Smarts: Powerful Techniques for Turning Every Encounter into a Mutual Win. Tony Alessandra et al. Ed. by Marilyn Ross. 350p. 1989. 19.95 (*0-685-30408-6*) Keynote Pub.

***People Soft Step-by-Step: A Complete Self-Study Book on People Tools.** Holly Ngo. (Illus.). 320p. 1999. pap. 34.95 (*0-9674084-0-7*) M I S Pubns.

People Speak! Anti-Semitism & Emancipation in Nineteenth-Century Bavaria. James F. Harris. (Social History, Popular Culture, & Politics in Germany Ser.). 304p. (C). 1994. text 54.50 (*0-472-10437-3*, 10437) U of Mich Pr.

People, States, & Fear: An Agenda for International Security Studies in the Post-Cold War Era. 2nd ed. Barry Buzan. LC 91-2097. 393p. (C). 1991. pap. text 22.00 (*1-55587-282-4*) L Rienner.

People Studying People: Artifacts & Ethics in Behavior Research. Ralph L. Rosnow. LC 96-48978. 176p. 1997. pap. 16.95 (*0-7167-3071-5*); text 26.95 (*0-7167-3070-7*) W H Freeman.

People Studying People: The Human Element in Fieldwork. Robert A. Georges & Michael O. Jones. LC 79-65767. 1980. pap. 15.95 (*0-520-04067-8*, Pub. by U CA Pr) Cal Prin Full Svc.

People Styles at Work: Making Bad Relationships Good & Good Relationships Better. Robert Bolton & Dorothy G. Bolton. 176p. 1996. pap. text 16.95 (*0-8144-7723-2*) AMACOM.

***People That Anthropologists Do Not Like to Study: (Featuring Negroes with No Known African Origin & Primitive Caucasians)** Robert A. Murray. (Illus.). 160p. 2000. pap. write for info. (*0-9676083-0-9*) R Murray.

People That History Forgot: The Mysterious People Who Originated the World's Religions. 2nd unabridged ed. Ernest L. Martin. (Illus.). 196p. (Orig.). (C). 1993. pap. 11.95 (*0-945657-82-X*) Acad Scriptural Knowledge.

People That Shall Dwell Alone: Judaism as an Evolutionary Group Strategy. Kevin Macdonald. LC 94-16446. (Human Evolution, Behavior & Intelligence Ser.). 320p. 1994. 65.00 (*0-275-94869-2*, Praeger Pubs) Greenwood.

People, the Environment & Responsibility: Case Studies from Rural Pakistan. Ed. by F. Amalric & T. Banuri. LC 95-18100. (Illus.). 116p. 1995. 62.00 (*1-85070-652-2*) Prthnon Pub.

People, the World & I. Illus. & Photos by George Wellington. viii, 94p. (YA). (gr. 7 up). Date not set. mass mkt. 10.95 (*0-9670539-0-0*) S W Thomas.

People Time Forgot. Alice Gibbons. Tr. by James C. Yu. (CHI.). 288p. (Orig.). 1987. pap. text 8.00 (*0-940043-27-0*) Evangel Lit.

People to Know Series. Incl. Al Gore: Leader for the New Millennium. Laura S. Jeffrey. LC 98-52498. (Illus.). 112p. (YA). (gr. 6 up). 1999. lib. bdg. 20.95 (*0-7660-1232-8*); Ernest Hemingway: Writer & Adventurer. Della A. Yannuzzi. LC 97-33351. (Illus.). 112p. (YA). (gr. 6 up). 1998. lib. bdg. 20.95 (*0-89490-979-7*); Jack London: A Writer's Adventurous Life. Elaine S. Lisandrelli. LC 98-50565. (Illus.). 128p. (YA). (gr. 6 up). 1999. lib. bdg. 20.95 (*0-7660-1144-5*); John Glenn: Astronaut & Senator. rev. ed. Michael D. Cole. LC 99-50844. 128p. (YA). (gr. 6 up). 2000. lib. bdg. 20.95 (*0-7660-1532-7*); Robert Ballard: Oceanographer Who Discovered the Titanic. Christine M. Hill. LC 98-54437. (Illus.). 128p. (YA). (gr. 6 up). 1999. lib. bdg. 20.95 (*0-7660-1147-X*); Willa Cather: Writer of the Prairie. Sara M. Wooten. LC 97-30244. (Illus.). 128p. (YA). (gr. 6 up). 1998. lib. bdg. 20.95 (*0-89490-980-0*); (Illus.). (YA). (gr. 6 up). lib. bdg. write for info. (*0-89490-450-7*) Enslow Pubs.

People to Remember. Houghton Mifflin Company Staff. (Literature Experience 1993 Ser.). (J). (gr. 7). 1992. pap. 11.04 (*0-395-61846-0*) HM.

People Trade: Pacific Island Laborers & New Caledonia, 1865-1930. Dorothy Shineberg. LC 98-47371. (Pacific Islands Monographs: No. 16). (Illus.). 352p. (C). 1999. 45.00 (*0-8248-2177-7*) UH Pr.

People Trying to Be Good. 3rd ed. Sanford Phippen. Ed. by Constance Hunting. 150p. 1991. pap. 8.95 (*0-913006-40-8*) Puckerbrush.

People, Twentieth Century. Nieh Hua Ling. 288p. 1990. pap. text 9.00 (*0-9625118-5-4*) World Scientific Pub.

People Types & Tiger Stripes. 3rd ed. Gordon Lawrence. 256p. 1993. 15.00 (*0-935652-16-7*) Ctr Applications Psych.

People under Pressure. Albert M. Barrett. 1960. 16.95 (*0-685-01131-3*) NCUP.

People under the Skin. Clare Dunne. 216p. (C). 1990. 70.00 (*0-7855-6626-0*, Pub. by Pascoe Pub) St Mut.

People Under Three: Young Children in Daycare. Elinor Goldschmied & Sonia Jackson. LC 93-7401. (Illus.). 240p. (C). 1993. pap. 25.99 (*0-415-05976-3*) Routledge.

People Use Tools. Margie Burton et al. Ed. by Susan Evento. (Early Connections Ser.). 16p. (J). (gr. k-2). 1998. pap. text 4.25 (*1-892393-56-5*) Benchmark Educ.

People vs. Big Tobacco: How the States Took on the Cigarette Giants. Jeffrey Rothfeder et al. LC 97-42358. (Illus.). 334p. 1998. 23.95 (*1-57660-057-2*, Pub. by Bloomberg NJ) Norton.

People vs. Global Capital - the G-7, TNCs, SAPs, & Human Rights: Report of the International Peoples Tribunal to Judge the G-7, Tokyo, July 1994. Pacific Asia Resource Center Staff. LC 95-902853. 184p. (Orig.). 1995. pap. 14.95 (*0-945257-23-6*) Apex Pr.

People vs. Judas Iscariot. William C. McCord. LC 98-47230. (Worship & Drama Ser.). 108p. 1999. pap. 10.50 (*0-7880-1311-4*) CSS OH.

People vs. Larry Flynt: The Shooting Script. Scott Alexander & Larry Karaszewski. LC 96-31471. (Shooting Script Ser.). 1996. 24.95 (*1-55704-313-2*, Pub. by Newmarket) Norton.

People vs. Larry Flynt: The Shooting Script. Scott Alexander & Larry Karaszewski. LC 96-31471. (Illus.). 208p. 1996. pap. 15.95 (*1-55704-305-1*, Pub. by Newmarket) Norton.

People vs. Lee Harvey Oswald. Walt Brown. (Illus.). 656p. 1994. pap. 15.95 (*0-7867-0081-5*) Carroll & Graf.

People vs. Maxine Lowe. Luella E. McMahon. 87p. (C). 1955. pap. 5.50 (*0-87129-736-1*, P20) Dramatic Pub.

People vs. McDonald: Opinion of the California Supreme Court Reversing Due to Exclusion of Testimony on Eyewitness Identification by Mask, J. Cal. 3d 351, Crim. No. 21770, Nov. 21, 1984. (Monographs: No. CR-50). 1984. 6.00 (*1-55524-051-8*) Ctr Respon Psych.

People vs. Monopoly: Nineteen Eighty Draft Program of the Communist Party, U. S. A. CPUSA Staff. 62p. (Orig.). 1980. pap. 0.50 (*0-87898-142-X*) New Outlook.

An Asterisk (*) at the beginning of an entry indicates that the title is appearing for the first time.

People vs. the Taipings: Bao Lisheng's "Righteous Army of Dongan" James H. Cole. LC 81-80965. (China Research Monographs: No. 21). 83p. 1981. pap. 7.00 (*0-912966-39-4*) IEAS.

***People vs. There People.** Golden Books Staff. (Illus.). (J). 2000. 9.99 (*0-307-10721-3*, Goldn Books) Gldn Bks Pub Co.

People Walk on Their Heads: Moses Weinberger's Jews & Judaism in New York. Ed. by Jonathan D. Sarna. LC 81-6907. 137p. (C). 1982. 27.95 (*0-8419-0707-2*); pap. 13.95 (*0-8419-0731-5*) Holmes & Meier.

People Walking: Pathological Patterns & Normal Changes over the Life Span. Jan Bruckner. LC 98-125405. 1997. VHS 39.95 (*1-55642-350-0*, 43500) SLACK Inc.

People Wanting Children. Gerald Kaminski. LC 98-15474. 117p. 1998. pap. 9.95 (*0-931896-16-9*) Cove View.

People Watcher's Field Guide: People Watching at Its Funniest. R. S. Bean. Ed. by Cliff Carle. 1992. pap. 5.95 (*0-918259-41-X*) CCC Pubns.

People We Live With. Jill C. Wheeler. Ed. by Stuart A. Kallen. LC 91-73067. (We Can Save the Earth Ser.). (J). 1991. lib. bdg. 12.94 (*1-56239-034-1*) ABDO Pub Co.

People Who Are Going to Pick Berries see Atsiyalriit

People Who Are Homeless: Mental Health Services: A Place in Mind: Commissioning & Providing Mental Health Services for People Who Are Homeless. H. M. S. O. Staff et al. LC 96-209757. 172p. 1995. pap. 25.00 (*0-11-321925-3*, HM19253, Pub. by Statnry Office) Balogh.

People Who Came, Bk. 1. Longman Publishing Staff. Date not set. pap. text. write for info. (*0-582-76648-6*, Pub. by Addison-Wesley) Longman.

People Who Came, Bk. 2. Carnegie. Date not set. pap. text. write for info. (*0-582-76658-3*, Pub. by Addison-Wesley) Longman.

People Who Came, Bk. 3. Brathwaite & Phillips. 1993. pap. text. write for info. (*0-582-76657-5*, Pub. by Addison-Wesley) Longman.

People Who Care. Michael Pollard. Ed. by Rebecca Stefoff. LC 91-36502. (Pioneers in History Ser.). (Illus.). 48p. (J). (gr. 5-8). 1992. lib. bdg. 19.93 (*1-56074-035-3*) Garrett Ed Corp.

People Who Changed the World. Philip Wilkinson & Jacqueline Dineen. LC 93-31357. (Turning Points in History Ser.). (Illus.). 96p. (YA). (gr. 5 up). 1994. lib. bdg. 19.95 (*0-7910-2764-3*) Chelsea Hse.

People Who Didn't Say Goodbye. Merrit Malloy. LC 82-45932. 144p. 1985. pap. 11.95 (*0-385-18784-X*) Doubleday.

People Who Discovered Columbus: The Prehistory of the Bahamas. William F. Keegan. (Ripley P. Bullen, Columbus Quincentenary Series, Ripley P. Bullen). (Illus.). 304p. 1992. 39.95 (*0-8130-1137-X*) U Press Fla.

People Who Do Not Exist, Vol. 1. Abbylynn Bogomolny. LC 96-51185. (Series 2B: Vol. 2B). 60p. (Orig.). 1997. pap. 13.95 (*0-934172-45-5*) WIM Pubns.

People Who Do Things to Each Other. Judith Hubback. LC 87-18236. 217p. 1988. pap. 9.95 (*0-933029-21-7*) Chiron Pubns.

People Who Drank Water from the River. James Kennedy. (Illus.). 109p. (Orig.). 1992. pap. 9.95 (*1-85371-141-1*, Pub. by Poolbeg Pr) Dufour.

People Who Hugged the Trees: An Environmental Folk Tale. Deborah L. Rose. (Illus.). 32p. 1990. lib. bdg. 13.95 (*0-911797-80-7*) Roberts Rinehart.

People Who Hugged the Trees: An Environmental Folk Tale. Deborah L. Rose. LC 90-62832. (Illus.). 32p. (J). (gr. 4-8). 1994. pap. 6.95 (*1-879373-50-5*) Roberts Rinehart.

People Who Knock at the Door. Patricia Highsmith. LC 85-12422. 336p. 1985. 15.45 (*0-89296-137-6*, Pub. by Mysterious Pr) Little.

People Who Led to My Plays. Adrienne Kennedy. (Illus.). 144p. (Orig.). 1996. pap. 14.95 (*1-55936-125-5*) Theatre Comm.

People Who Run Europe. Edward C. Page. LC 96-32409. (Illus.). 188p. (C). 1997. text 60.00 (*0-19-828079-3*) OUP.

People Who Say Goodbye. large type ed. P. Y. Betts. 303p. 1992. 23.95 (*1-85089-570-8*, Pub. by ISIS Lrg Prnt) Transaction Pubs.

***People Who Shaped the Century.** Time-Life Books Editors. LC 99-25626. (Illus.). 192p. (YA). (gr. 7). 1999. 29.95 (*0-7835-5513-X*) Time-Life.

***People Who Shaped the Church.** Todd Temple. (20th Century Reference Ser.). 2000. pap. text 10.99 (*0-8423-1778-3*) Tyndale Hse.

***People Who Sweat: My Middle-Aged Adventures among Tree Climbers, Mall Walkers, Surfing Housewives.** Robin Chotzinoff. 2000. pap. text 13.00 (*0-15-601170-0*) Harcourt.

***People Who Sweat: Ordinary People, Extraordinary Pursuits.** Robin Chotzinoff. LC 98-42847. 224p. (C). 1999. 22.00 (*0-15-100286-X*) Harcourt.

People Who Work There. Remigia Kushner & Madonna Helbing. 89p. 1995. pap. 11.30 (*1-55833-146-8*) Natl Cath Educ.

People Who Would Not Kneel: Panama, the United States, & the San Blas Kuna. James Howe. LC 98-4172. 432p. 1998. text 55.00 (*1-56098-890-8*) Smithsonian.

People Who Would Not Kneel: Panama, the United States, & the San Blas Kuna. James Howe. LC 98-4172. (Smithsonian Series in Ethnographic Inquiry). 432p. 1999. pap. 19.95 (*1-56098-865-7*) Smithsonian.

People Will Talk. Lucianne Goldberg. 1995. pap. 6.50 (*0-671-77671-1*) PB.

People with AIDS. Nicholas Nixon & Bebe Nixon. (Imago Mundi Ser.). (Illus.). 168p. 1991. pap. 25.00 (*0-87923-886-0*) Godine.

People with Dirty Hands. Robin Chotzinhof. 1996. pap. 20.00 (*0-02-525201-1*) Macmillan.

People with Dirty Hands: The Passion for Gardening. Robin Chotzinoff. LC 96-47267. (Harvest Book Ser.). 256p. 1996. pap. 12.00 (*0-15-600515-8*) Harcourt.

People with Dirty Hands: The Passion for Gardening. Robin Chotzinoff. LC 95-30585. 256p. 1996. 22.00 (*0-02-860990-5*) Macmillan Info.

People with Disabilities. Pete Sanders & Steve Myers. LC 97-41645. (What Do You Know about...Ser.). (Illus.). 32p. (J). (gr. 4-6). 1998. lib. bdg. 20.90 (*0-7613-0803-2*, Copper Beech Bks) Millbrook Pr.

People with Disabilities: Federal Programs Could Work Together More Efficiently to Promote Employment. (Illus.). 96p. (Orig.). (C). 1996. pap. text 25.00 (*0-7881-3592-9*) DIANE Pub.

People with Disabilities, Alcohol, Tobacco & Other Drugs: A Resource Guide. 1995. lib. bdg. 251.95 (*0-8490-6799-5*) Gordon Pr.

People with Disabilities Explain It All for You: Your Guide to the Public Accommodations Requirements of the Americans with Disabilities Act. Ed. by Disability Rag Staff & Mary Johnson. 160p. (Orig.). 1992. pap. 15.95 (*0-9627064-2-6*) Advocado Pr.

People with Disabilities Who Challenge the System. Ed. by Donna H. Lehr & Fredda Brown. 1996. 34.00 (*1-55766-229-0*) P H Brookes.

***People with Five Fingers: A Native Californian Creation Tale.** Illus. by Robert Andrew Parker. LC 99-28795. 32p. (J). (gr. k-3). 2000. 15.95 (*0-7614-5058-0*, Cav Child Bks) Marshall Cavendish.

People with Hearing Loss & Healthcare Facilities: A Guide for Hospitals to Comply with the Americans with Disabilities Act. Ed. by Barbara Kelley. 56p. 1993. write for info. (*0-318-72631-9*) SHHH.

People with Hearing Loss & the Workplace: A Guide for Employers to Comply with the Americans with Disabilities Act. Ed. by Barbara Kelley. 33p. 1993. write for info. (*0-318-72632-7*) SHHH.

People with HIV & Those Who Help Them: Challenges, Integration, Intervention. Dennis R. Shelby. LC 94-33087. 1995. 49.95 (*1-56024-922-6*); pap. 14.95 (*1-56023-865-8*) Haworth Pr.

People with Learning Disability & Severe Challenging Behavior: New Developments in Services & Therapy. Ian Fleming & Biza Stenfert Kroese. LC 93-2706. 1993. 79.95 (*0-7190-3690-9*, Pub. by Manchester Univ Pr) St Martin.

People with Mental Health Problems & Learning Disabilities, Report 1, No. RC1. 1993. pap. 20.00 (*0-946088-41-1*, Pub. by NCCL) St Mut.

People with Profound & Multiple Learning Disabilities; A Collaborative Approach to Meeting Penny Lacey. 1998. pap. text 32.95 (*1-85346-488-0*) Taylor & Francis.

People Within a Landscape: A Collection of Images of Nepal. Bert Willison. (Illus.). 128p. 1992. 29.95 (*0-89886-328-7*) Mountaineers.

People Without a Country: The Kurds & Kurdistan. rev. ed. A. R. Ghassemlou et al. Ed. by Gerard Chaliand. Tr. by Michael Pallis. LC 92-14618. (Illus.). 320p. 1993. pap. 14.95 (*0-940793-92-X*, Olive Branch Pr) Interlink Pub.

People Without Government: An Anthology of Anarchy. Harold Barclay. 162p. 1996. reprint ed. pap. 12.95 (*1-871082-16-1*, Pub. by Kahn & Averill) Paul & Co Pubs.

***People Work.** Debbie Ecker. LC 00-36481. (Illus.). (J). 2000. write for info. (*0-7368-0740-3*) Capstone Pr.

People Working. Douglas Florian. (J). 1983. 10.95 (*0-690-04263-9*) HarpC Child Bks.

People Worth Talking About. Cosmo Hamilton. LC 79-107706. (Essay Index Reprint Ser.). 1977. 21.95 (*0-8369-1508-9*) Ayer.

***People Yearbook, 1vol.** People Magazine Staff. 2000. 24.95 (*1-883013-85-2*) Tme Inc.

People Yearbook 1998. Time-Life Books Editors. 147p. (gr. 7). 1999. 24.95 (*1-883013-27-5*) Time-Life.

People Yearbooks: 1997. 144p. (gr. 7). 1999. 19.95 (*1-883013-10-0*) Time-Life.

People Yearbook, 1999. Time Inc., People Books Editors. (Illus.). 144p. (gr. 7). 1999. 24.95 (*1-883013-57-7*) T-L Custom Pub.

People, Yes. Carroll T. Hartwell & Ken Burns. LC 94-70316. (Illus.). 128p. 1995. 60.00 (*0-89381-599-3*) Aperture.

People, Yes. Carl Sandburg. 300p. 1990. pap. 9.95 (*0-15-671665-8*) Harcourt.

People You Know. George Ade. (Works of George Ade Ser.). 224p. 1985. reprint ed. 39.00 (*0-932051-62-6*) Rprt Serv.

People You'd Trust Your Life To. Wallace. 1990. pap. 16.99 (*0-7710-8791-8*) McCland & Stewart.

Peoplepedia: The Ultimate Reference on the American People. Les Krantz. LC 95-8948. (Henry Holt Reference Bks.). (Illus.). 88p. 1995. 35.00 (*0-8050-3727-6*) H Holt & Co.

Peoples. Robert C. Downs. LC 73-10704. 1974. 6.95 (*0-672-51900-3*, Bobbs) Macmillan.

People's Action Party of Singapore: Emergence of a Dominant Party System. Thomas J. Bellows. LC 73-114788. (Monographs: No. 14). xii, 195p. 1970. 8.25 (*0-938692-15-1*) Yale U SE Asia.

Peoples Almanac. 1995. pap. 10.95 (*0-316-69375-8*) Little.

People's Almanac Presents the Book of Lists 4. David Wallechinsky & Amy Wallace. LC 93-17197. 1993. 17.95 (*0-316-92079-7*) Little.

People's Almanac Presents the Twentieth Century. David Wallechinsky. LC 95-11568. (Illus.). 864p. 1995. 24.95 (*0-316-92095-9*) Little.

People's Almanac Presents the Twentieth Century. David Wallechinsky. LC 95-11568. 816p. 1996. pap. 17.95 (*0-316-92056-8*) Little.

People's Almanac Presents the Twentieth Century: History with the Boring Bits Left Out. rev. ed. David Wallechinsky. LC 99-10233. (Illus.). 944p. 1999. text 29.95 (*0-87951-944-4*, Pub. by Overlook Pr) Penguin Putnam.

Peoples' & Civilizations of the Americas Before Contact. John E. Kicza. Ed. by Michael Adas. LC 98-11234. (Essays on Global & Comparative History Ser.). 72p. 1998. pap. 6.00 (*0-87229-103-0*) Am Hist Assn.

Peoples & Cultures. Hunt. 2000. pap. write for info. (*0-312-18370-4*) St Martin.

Peoples & Cultures: From 1787, Vol. C. Hunt & Barbara H. Rosenwein. pap. write for info. (*0-312-18363-1*) St Martin.

Peoples & Cultures from 1560 to the Global Age, Vol. 2. Hunt & Barbara H. Rosenwein. pap. write for info. (*0-312-18368-2*) St Martin.

Peoples & Cultures from 1560 to the Global Age see Challenge of the West: Peoples & Cultures from the Stone Age to the Global Age

Peoples & Cultures from 1787 to the Global Age see Challenge of the West: Peoples & Cultures from the Stone Age to the Global Age

Peoples & Cultures from the Stone Age to 1320: Prologue see Challenge of the West: Peoples & Cultures from the Stone Age to the Global Age

Peoples & Cultures from the Stone Age to 1640: Prologue see Challenge of the West: Peoples & Cultures from the Stone Age to the Global Age

Peoples & Cultures from 1320-1787 see Challenge of the West: Peoples & Cultures from the Stone Age to the Global Age

Peoples & Cultures from 1320 to the Global Age see Challenge of the West: Peoples & Cultures from the Stone Age to the Global Age

Peoples & Cultures Instructors Manual, Vols. 2. Hunt. pap. text. write for info. (*0-312-18388-7*) St Martin.

Peoples & Cultures of the Middle East. Daniel Bates & Amal Rassam. (Illus.). 288p. 1996. pap. text 47.33 (*0-13-656793-2*) P-H.

Peoples & Cultures Study Guide, Vol. 1. Hunt. 2000. pap. text. write for info. (*0-312-18389-5*); pap. text. write for info. (*0-312-18397-6*) St Martin.

Peoples & Cultures to 1320, Vol. A. Hunt & Barbara H. Rosenwein. pap. write for info. (*0-312-18365-8*) St Martin.

Peoples & Cultures to 1740, Vol. 1. Lynn Hunt & Barbara H. Rosenwein. pap. write for info. (*0-312-18369-0*) St Martin.

Peoples & Cutures: 1320-1787, Vol. B. Hunt & Barbara H. Rosenwein. pap. write for info. (*0-312-18364-X*) St Martin.

Peoples & Minorities in International Law. Ed. by Catherine Brolmann et al. LC 93-13379. 384p. (C). 1993. lib. bdg. 123.50 (*0-7923-2315-7*) Kluwer Academic.

Peoples & Problems of the Pacific, 2 vols., Set. John M. Brown. LC 75-35176. reprint ed. 125.00 (*0-404-14250-8*) AMS Pr.

Peoples & Settlement in Anatolia & the Caucasus, 800-1900. Anthony Bryer. (Collected Studies: No. CS274). (Illus.). 336p. (C). 1988. reprint ed. lib. bdg. 115.95 (*0-86078-222-0*, Pub. by Variorum) Ashgate Pub Co.

People's Architects. Ed. by Harry Ransom. LC 64-15812. 156p. reprint ed. pap. 48.40 (*0-8357-9652-3*, 201699100005) Bks Demand.

People's Architecture: Texas Courthouses, Jails & Municipal Buildings. Willard B. Robinson. (Illus.). xxii, 365p. 1983. 35.00 (*0-87611-060-X*) Tex St Hist Assn.

People's Armies. Richard Cobb. Tr. by Marianne Elliott. LC 87-10641. 776p. 1987. 25.00 (*0-300-02728-1*) Yale U Pr.

People's Army: Massachusetts Soldiers & Society in the Seven Years' of War. Fred Anderson. 292p. (C). 1996. pap. text 16.95 (*0-8078-4576-0*) U of NC Pr.

People's Army: Massachusetts Soldiers & Society in the Seven Years' War. Fred Anderson. LC 84-2344. (Illus.). 292p. 1984. reprint ed. pap. 90.60 (*0-7837-9890-3*, 206061600006) Bks Demand.

People's Artist of His Majesty. . . Chaliapin see Narodnyi Artist Ego Velichestva. . . Chaliapin

People's Assessors in the Courts: A Study on the Sociology of Law. Kalman Kulcsar. 140p. (C). 1982. 40.00 (*963-05-2849-5*, Pub. by Akade Kiado) St Mut.

People's Banks. Henry W. Wolff. 1972. 69.95 (*0-8490-0811-5*) Gordon Pr.

People's Biographer Workbook. 2nd ed. Jackson F. Bullock. 182p. 1995. pap., student ed. 19.95 (*0-9639778-0-6*); spiral bd. 19.95 (*0-9639778-1-4*) Peoples Biographer.

People's Biographer Workbook (Afrocentric Version) A Structured Biography Writing Guide for the Nonprofessional Writer. Jackson F. Bullock. (Illus.). 182p. 1996. pap., wbk. ed. 19.95 (*0-9639778-4-9*) Peoples Biographer.

People's Biographer Workbook (Christian Version) A Structured Biography Writing Guide for the Nonprofessional Writer. Jackson F. Bullock. (Illus.). 182p. (Orig.). 1996. pap. 19.95 (*0-9639778-5-7*) Peoples Biographer.

People's Book: A New Translation of the Gospel of John. Wayne Walden. LC 90-91914. 80p. (Orig.). 1991. pap. 2.00 (*1-879200-01-5*) Livingworks.

People's Book of Poetry. E. C. Clemons. (Illus.). 43p. 1998. pap. 15.95 (*1-890301-09-4*) M Bey.

***People's Bread: A History of the Anti-Corn Law League.** Paul A. Pickering & Alex Tyrell. LC 00-24647. 2000. write for info. (*0-7185-0218-3*, Pub. by Leicester U Pr) Cassell & Continuum.

People's Budget: A Common Sense Plan for Shrinking the Government in Washington. Edwin L. Dale et al. LC 95-9253. (Illus.). 240p. (Orig.). 1995. pap. 14.95 (*0-89526-722-5*) Regnery Pub.

People(s) Called Methodist: Forms & Reforms of Their Life. Ed. by William B. Lawrence et al. LC 97-42781. (United Methodism & American Culture Ser.: Vol. 2). 320p. 1997. pap. 19.95 (*0-687-02199-5*) Abingdon.

People's Cancer Guide Book: Practical Information to Help You Understand Cancer: Its Causes, Early Detection, Prevention, Symptoms, Treatments, & Cure. Ronald E. Aigotti. LC 95-76465. 427p. (Orig.). 1995. pap. 29.95 (*0-9648656-0-2*) Belletrist.

Peoples' Capitalism: The Economics of the Robot Revolution. James S. Albus. LC 75-44585. 157p. 1976. 10.50 (*0-917480-01-5*); pap. 6.95 (*0-917480-00-7*) New World Bks.

People's Car: An Investigation into the Design & Performance of Civilian & Military Volkswagens 1938-1946. British Intelligence Sub-Committee. (Illus.). 156p. 1997. pap. 34.95 (*0-11-290555-2*, Pub. by Statnry Office) Seven Hills Bk.

People's Catechism. John R. Klopke. 1984. pap. 3.95 (*0-89942-258-6*, 258/04) Catholic Bk Pub.

People's Catechism: Catholic Faith for Adults. Ed. by Raymond A. Lucker et al. 224p. (Orig.). 1995. pap. 14.95 (*0-8245-1466-1*) Crossroad NY.

People's Cause: A History of Guerrillas in Africa. Basil Risbridger Davidson. LC 81-201497. (Longman Studies in African History). (Illus.). 222p. reprint ed. pap. 68.90 (*0-8357-6590-3*, 203598500097) Bks Demand.

People's Century Student Guide. Findley. 1999. pap. text, student ed. 16.17 (*0-395-92200-3*) HM.

***People's Charter? Forty Years of the National Parks & Access to the Countryside Act 1949 (U. K.)** Ed. by John Blunden & Nigel Curry. (Illus.). 299p. 1999. reprint ed. pap. text 25.00 (*0-7881-6662-X*) DIANE Pub.

People's Charter: Liberty's Bill of Rights: A Consultation Document. NCCL Staff. 80p. (C). 1991. text 45.00 (*0-946088-39-X*, Pub. by NCCL) St Mut.

People's China: A Brief History. 3rd ed. Craig Dietrich. LC 97-18948. (Illus.). 400p. (C). 1997. text 50.00 (*0-19-510628-8*); pap. text 22.95 (*0-19-510629-6*) OUP.

People's China & International Law Vol. 1: A Documentary Study. Jerome A. Cohen & Hungdah Chiu. LC 73-2475. (Studies in East Asian Law). 950p. 1974. reprint ed. pap. 200.00 (*0-608-02921-1*, 206398600001) Bks Demand.

Peoples Choice. 2nd ed. Radke. 1998. 13.75 (*0-07-233197-6*) McGraw.

People's Choice: A History of Albany County in Art & Architecture. Allison P. Bennett. LC 80-66320. (Illus.). 145p. 1980. pap. 11.95 (*0-89062-124-1*) Albany County.

People's Choice: A History of Albany County in Art & Architecture. Allison P. Bennett. LC 95-33616. (Illus.). 135p. 1995. reprint ed. pap. 23.00 (*0-935796-66-5*) Purple Mnt Pr.

People's Choice: A Novel. Jeff Greenfield. LC 96-16389. 320p. 1996. pap. 13.95 (*0-452-27705-1*, Plume) Dutton Plume.

People's Choice: How the Voter Makes up His Mind in a Presidential Campaign. 3rd ed. Paul F. Lazarsfeld et al. LC 68-20443. 224p. reprint ed. pap. 69.50 (*0-608-17713-X*, 203010900067) Bks Demand.

People's Choice, from Washington to Harding: A Study in Democracy. Herbert Agar et al. LC 90-46004. (Illus.). 356p. 1990. reprint ed. 34.95 (*0-87797-178-1*) Cherokee.

People's Chronology. rev. ed. James Trager. 1995. 45.00 (*0-8050-3731-4*) H Holt & Co.

People's Chronology: A Year-by-Year Record of Human Events from Prehistory to the Present. rev. ed. James Trager. 1995. pap. 19.95 (*0-8050-3134-0*) H Holt & Co.

People's City: African Life in Twentieth-Century Durban. Paul Maylam & Iain Edwards. LC 96-50944. 1997. 60.00 (*0-435-07402-4*); pap. 22.95 (*0-435-07401-6*) Heinemann.

People's City: African Life in Twentieth-Century Durban. Ed. by Paul Maylam & Iaina Edwards. (Illus.). 320p. 1996. pap. write for info. (*0-86980-916-4*, Pub. by Univ Natal Pr) Intl Spec Bk.

People's Communes & Rural Development in China. Benedict Stavis. 184p. 1974. 4.50 (*0-86731-088-X*) Cornell CIS RDC.

People's Companion to the Breviary: Revised & Expanded Edition of the New Companion to the Breviary with Seasonal Supplement, 2 vols. Carmelites of Indianapolis Staff. Incl. Vol. 1. LC 96-228014. 576p. 1997. pap. (*1-886873-09-7*); Vol. 2. LC 96-228014. 560p. 1997. pap. (*1-886873-11-9*); LC 96-228014. 1997. Set pap. 29.95 (*1-886873-12-7*) Carmelites IN.

People's Contest: The Union & Civil War, 1861-1865. 2nd ed. Phillip S. Paludan. LC 96-21303. (Modern War Studies). (Illus.). 524p. 1996. pap. 16.95 (*0-7006-0812-5*) U Pr of KS.

***Peoples, Cultures & Nations in Political Philosophy.** Paul Gilbert. 224p. 2000. pap. text 19.95 (*0-87840-817-7*) Georgetown U Pr.

People's Democratic Dictatorship. Mao Tse-Tung. 1951. audio 8.95 (*0-88710-053-8*) Yale Far Eastern Pubns.

People's Democratic Republic of Yemen. Tareq Y. Ismael. (C). 1992. pap. text 17.50 (*0-86187-451-X*, Pub. by P P Pubs) Cassell & Continuum.

People's Democratic Republic of Yemen. Tareq Y. Ismael. (C). 1992. text 49.00 (*0-86187-450-1*) St Martin.

People's Doctor: George Hatem & China's Revolution. Edgar A. Porter. LC 96-3401. 1997. text 60.00 (*0-8248-1840-7*); pap. text 29.95 (*0-8248-1905-5*) UH Pr.

P

***People's Doctors: Samuel Thomson & the American Botanical Movement, 1790-1860.** John S. Haller. LC 99-87340. 2000. write for info. (*0-8093-2339-7*) S Ill U Pr.

Peoples East Hapsburg Lan. Robert A. Kann & David. LC 83-21629. (History of East Central Europe Ser.: No. 6). (Illus.). 560p. 1984. 50.00 (*0-295-96095-7*) U of Wash Pr.

People's Europe: Turning a Concept to Context. Ed. by Stratos V. Konstadinidis. LC 98-42335. (EC International Law Forum Ser.). 276p. 1998. text 74.95 (*1-84014-743-1*, Pub. by Ashgate Pub) Ashgate Pub Co.

People's Farm: English Radical Agrarianism, 1775-1840. Malcolm Chase. 232p. 1988. 59.00 (*0-19-820105-2*) OUP.

People's Farming Workbook. Eda Trust. LC 96-207965. (Illus.). 250p. (Orig.). 1996. pap. 29.50 (*0-86486-112-5*, Pub. by Intermed Tech) Stylus Pub VA.

People's Favorites, Vol. 1. unabridged ed. Dale M. Yocum. 171p. (Orig.). 1994. pap. 10.99 (*0-88019-319-0*) Schmul Pub Co.

People's Favorites, Vol. 2. unabridged ed. Dale M. Yocum. 152p. (Orig.). 1994. pap. 8.99 (*0-88019-328-X*) Schmul Pub Co.

People's Force: A History of the Victoria Police. 2nd ed. Robert Haldane. 380p. 1995. pap. 19.95 (*0-522-84674-2*, Pub. by Melbourne Univ Pr) Paul & Co Pubs.

People's Game: The History of Football Revisited. James Walvin. (Illus.). 224p. 1995. 34.95 (*1-85158-642-3*, Pub. by Mainstream Pubng) Trafalgar.

People's Glorious Revolution. (Paranoia Ser.). 6.00 (*0-87431-150-0*, 12010) West End Games.

People's Guide, 1874: Directory of Henry Co., Indiana. Cline & McHaffie. 398p. 1979. 22.00 (*0-686-27818-6*) Bookmark.

Peoples Guide to Government, the Executive Branch. Ellen M. Kaplan & Joseph Torsella. LC 92-223438. 67p. 1991. 15.75 (*1-56256-008-5*) Peoples Pub Grp.

Peoples Guide to Government, the Legislative Branch. Elliot I. Portnoy. LC 98-178664. 67 p. 1991. 15.75 (*1-56256-011-5*) Peoples Pub Grp.

People's Guide to Mexico: Wherever You Go . . . There You Are!! 11th anniversary ed. Carl Franz. 608p. 1998. pap. 22.95 (*1-56261-419-3*) Avalon Travel.

People's Guide to the United States Constitution: Everything You Need to Know in One Easy Read. Dave Kluge. LC 93-46691. 1994. pap. 16.95 (*1-55972-218-5*, Birch Ln Pr) Carol Pub Group.

People's Guide to the United States Constitution: Everything You Need to Know in One Easy Read. rev. ed. Dave Kluge. 176p. 1996. pap. 9.95 (*0-8065-1784-0*, Citadel Pr) Carol Pub Group.

People's Health: A History of Public Health in Minnesota to 1948. Philip D. Jordan. LC 53-38147. (Publications of the Minnesota Historical Society). 562p. reprint ed. pap. 174.30 (*0-8357-3317-3*, 203954100013) Bks Demand.

People's Health: A Memoir of Public Health & Its Evolution at Harvard. Robin M. Henig. LC 96-41963. 256p. 1996. 29.95 (*0-309-05492-3*, Joseph Henry Pr) Natl Acad Pr.

People's Health, 1830-1910. F. B. Smith. (Modern Revivals in History Ser.). 442p. 1993. 72.95 (*0-7512-0185-5*, Pub. by Gregg Revivals) Ashgate Pub Co.

People's Historian: John Richard Green & the Writing of History in Victorian England, 2. Anthony Brundage. LC 93-10379. (Studies in Historiography: No. 2). 200p. 1993. 62.95 (*0-313-27954-3*, BGK/, Greenwood Pr) Greenwood.

People's History of England. 2nd ed. Arthur L. Morton. 588p. (C). 1989. pap. 19.50 (*0-85315-723-5*, Pub. by Lawrence & Wishart) NYU Pr.

People's History of Kingston, Rondout & Vicinity: The First Capitol of N. Y. State (1820-1943) William C. DeWitt. (Illus.). 445p. 1997. reprint ed. lib. bdg. 46.50 (*0-8328-6891-4*) Higginson Bk Co.

***Peoples History of Religion.** Chidester. 2000. 28.00 (*0-06-061451-X*); pap. 18.00 (*0-06-061452-8*) HarpC.

People's History of the Supreme Court. Peter Irons. LC 98-53706. 542p. 1999. 32.95 (*0-670-87006-4*, Viking) Viking Penguin.

***People's History of the Supreme Court.** Peter H. Irons. 2000. pap. 15.95 (*0-14-029201-2*) Viking Penguin.

People's History of the United States see Otra Historia de los Estados Unidos

People's History of the United States. abr. ed. Howard Zinn. LC 96-52532. 1997. 25.00 (*1-56584-366-5*, Pub. by New Press NY); pap. 13.00 (*1-56584-379-7*, Pub. by New Press NY) Norton.

People's History of the United States: The Wall Charts. Howard Zinn & George Kirschner. (Illus.). 48p. (YA). 1995. pap. 25.00 (*1-56584-171-9*, Pub. by New Press NY) Norton.

People's History of the United States: 1492 to Present, Revised & Updated Edition. rev. ed. Howard Zinn. 688p. 1995. pap. 18.00 (*0-06-092643-0*, Perennial) HarperTrade.

People's History of the United States: 1492 to the Present. 20th anniversary ed. Howard Zinn. LC 99-47393. 720p. 1999. 30.00 (*0-06-019448-0*) HarpC.

People's History of U. S. Howard Zinn. Date not set. pap. text. write for info. (*0-582-48948-2*, Pub. by Addison-Wesley) Longman.

People's Home? Social Rented Housing in Europe & America. Michael Harloe. LC 94-15837. (Studies in Urban & Social Change). 544p. 1995. pap. 34.95 (*0-631-18642-5*) Blackwell Pubs.

People's Idea of God. Mary Baker Eddy. pap. 5.00 (*0-87952-235-6*) Writings of Mary Baker.

People's Idea of God. Mary M. Eddy. (Notable American Authors Ser.). 1992. reprint ed. lib. bdg. 75.00 (*0-7812-2749-6*) Rprt Serv.

People's Law & State Law: The Bellagio Papers. Ed. by A. Allot & Gordon R. Woodman. viii, 354p. 1985. pap. 84.30 (*90-6765-100-1*); pap. 90.75 (*3-11-013108-0*) Mouton.

People's Lawyer: The Life of Eugene A. Rerat. Paul Sevaried. 1969. 6.95 (*0-87018-056-8*) Ross.

People's Liberation Army & China's Nation-Building. Ying-mao Kau. LC 72-77203. 483p. reprint ed. pap. 149.80 (*0-608-30780-7*, 201540800093) Bks Demand.

People's Liberation Army in the Information Age. Ed. by James C. Mulvenon & Richard H. Yang. (Illus.). ix, 288p. 1999. pap. 25.00 (*0-8330-2716-6*) Rand Corp.

***People's Lives: Celebrating the Human Spirit.** Bill Wright. LC 00-8800. 2001. write for info. (*0-292-79138-0*) U of Tex Pr.

People's Lobby: Organizational Innovation & the Rise of Interest Group Politics in the United States, 1890-1925. Elisabeth S. Clemens. LC 97-1339. 1997. pap. text 19.95 (*0-226-10993-3*); lib. bdg. 58.00 (*0-226-10992-5*) U Ch Pr.

People's Medical Answer Book: Plain Answers to One Thousand One Hundred Common Questions from Thirty-Six Leading Specialists. Richard I. Pyatt. 1984. 21.95 (*0-13-656596-4*); pap. 10.95 (*0-13-656588-3*) P-H.

People's Medical Society Health Desk Reference: Information Your Doctor Can't or Won't Tell You - Everything You Need to Know for the Best in Health Care. People's Medical Society Staff & Charles B. Inlander. Orig. Title: The Consumer's Medical Desk Reference. 672p. (J). 1996. pap. 19.45 (*0-7868-8167-4*, Pub. by Hyperion) Time Warner.

People's Medical Society Men's Health & Wellness Encyclopedia. Peoples Medical Society Staff. 518p. 1998. pap. text 29.95 (*0-02-862295-2*) Macmillan.

People's Medical Society Men's Health Desk Reference: Everything a Man Needs. People's Medical Society Staff. LC 97-40601. 480p. 1999. 29.95 (*0-02-862153-0*) Macmillan.

People's Money Pages: Fundraising Edition. Carrol, Frieda, Research Division Staff. 50p. 1984. ring bd. 32.95 (*0-318-04338-6*) Prosperity & Profits.

People's Money Pages at Your Own Pace Workbook. Frieda Carrol. LC 80-70419. 50p. 1981. ring bd. 29.95 (*0-9605246-3-0*) Prosperity & Profits.

People's Names: A Cross-Cultural Reference Guide to the Proper Use of over 40,000 Personal & Familial Names in over 100 Cultures. Holly Ingraham. LC 96-28638. 637p. 1997. lib. bdg. 65.00 (*0-7864-0187-7*) McFarland & Co.

People's Needs for Nursing Care: A European Study. P. Ashworth & A. Bjorn. 1987. pap. text 22.00 (*92-890-1041-X*) World Health.

***Peoples of Africa.** Marshall Cavendish Corporation Staff. LC 99-88550. (Illus.). 700p. 2000. lib. bdg. 329.95 (*0-7614-7158-8*) Marshall Cavendish.

Peoples of Africa. James S. Olson. LC 95-36433. 696p. 1996. lib. bdg. 110.00 (*0-313-27918-7*, Greenwood Pr) Greenwood.

Peoples of Africa: Cultures of Africa South of the Sahara. Ed. by James L. Gibbs, Jr. (Illus.). 594p. (C). 1988. reprint ed. pap. text 26.95 (*0-88133-318-2*) Waveland Pr.

Peoples of Africa Series, 6 vols. Diagram Group Staff. (Illus.). 672p. (YA). (gr. 6-12). 1997. 119.70 (*0-8160-3482-6*) Facts on File.

Peoples of Assam. B. M. Das. 98p. 1987. 16.95 (*0-685-21574-1*) Asia Bk Corp.

Peoples of Borneo. Victor T. King. LC 92-34994. 256p. 1993. 44.95 (*0-631-17221-1*) Blackwell Pubs.

Peoples of Canada: A Post-Confederation History, Vol. 2. J. M. Bumsted. (Illus.). 456p. (C). 1993. pap. text 32.00 (*0-19-540914-0*) OUP.

Peoples of Canada: A Pre-Confederation of Words. J. M. Bumsted. (Illus.). 456p. 1992. pap. text 35.00 (*0-19-540690-7*) OUP.

Peoples of Central Africa. Diagram Group Staff. LC 96-38733. (Peoples of Africa Ser.). (Illus.). 112p. (YA). (gr. 8 up). 1997. 19.95 (*0-8160-3486-9*) Facts on File.

Peoples of East Africa. Diagram Group Staff. LC 96-38735. (Peoples of Africa Ser.). (Illus.). (YA). (gr. 6-12). 1997. 19.95 (*0-8160-3484-2*) Facts on File.

Peoples of Greater Unyamwezi, Tanzania (Nyamwezi, Sukuma, Sumbwa, Kimbu, Konongo) R. G. Abrahams. LC 67-111104. (Ethnographic Survey of Africa: East Central Africa Ser.: Pt. 17). 97p. reprint ed. pap. 30.10 (*0-8357-3207-X*, 205707700010) Bks Demand.

Peoples of Ireland: From Prehistory to Modern Times. Liam De Paor. LC 85-52221. 352p. (C). 1990. pap. text 18.50 (*0-268-01590-2*) U of Notre Dame Pr.

Peoples of Israel: Fifty-Seven Centuries of Presence. enl. rev. ed. Herbert A. Klein. Ed. by Joseph Simon. LC 86-90358. Orig. Title: Israel - Land of the Jews. (Illus.). 240p. (ps-12). 1986. reprint ed. 23.50 (*0-934710-13-9*) Rachelle Simon.

Peoples of Middle Earth. J. R. R. Tolkien. Ed. by Christopher Tolkien. LC 96-44312. 496p. 1996. 27.95 (*0-395-82760-4*) HM.

Peoples of North America Before Columbus. Christine Hatt. LC 98-6037. (Looking Back Ser.). (J). 1999. 25.69 (*0-8172-5426-9*) Raintree Steck-V.

Peoples of North East India: Anthropological Perspectives. Ed. by Sarthak Sengupta. LC 96-900236. xvii, 255p. (C). 1996. 28.00 (*81-212-0519-0*, Pub. by Gyan Publishing Hse) Nataraj Bks.

Peoples of Northern Africa. Diagram Group Staff. LC 96-41273. (Peoples of Africa Ser.). (Illus.). 112p. (YA). (gr. 8 up). 1997. 19.95 (*0-8160-3483-4*) Facts on File.

***Peoples of Philadelphia: A History of Ethnic Groups & Lower-Class Life, 1790-1940.** Ed. by Allen F. Davis. LC 98-20934. (Pennsylvania Paperbacks Ser.). 312p. 1998. pap. 17.50 (*0-8122-1670-9*) U of Pa Pr.

Peoples of Prehistoric South Dakota. fac. ed. Larry J. Zimmerman. LC 84-17324. (Illus.). 153p. 1985. reprint ed. pap. 47.50 (*0-7837-8108-3*, 204791100008) Bks Demand.

Peoples of Russia & China: Facing Dawn New Centenial. 192p. (C). 1999. pap. text 8.40 (*0-536-02453-7*) Pearson Custom.

Peoples of Sierra Leone. Merran McCulloch. LC 67-4643. (Ethnographic Survey of Africa: Western Africa Ser.: Pt. 2). 121p. reprint ed. pap. 37.60 (*0-8357-6961-5*, 203902100009) Bks Demand.

Peoples of Southeast Asia. Bruno Lasker. LC 74-161765. (Institute of Pacific Relations Ser.). reprint ed. 37.50 (*0-404-09029-X*) AMS Pr.

Peoples of Southern Africa. Diagram Group Staff. LC 96-38736. (Peoples of Africa Ser.). (Illus.). (YA). (gr. 6-12). 1997. 19.95 (*0-8160-3487-7*) Facts on File.

Peoples of the American West: Historical Perspectives Through Children's Literature. Mary H. Cordier & Maria A. Perez-Stable. LC 89-10284. 244p. 1989. 29.00 (*0-8108-2240-7*) Scarecrow.

Peoples of the Americas, Vol. 7. LC 98-2801. (J). 1999. 35.00 (*0-7614-7057-3*) Marshall Cavendish.

Peoples of the Arctic, 6 vols., Set. Robert Low et al. LC 96-294. (Peoples & Their Environments Ser.). (Illus.). 24p. (J). (gr. k-4). 1996. lib. bdg. 15.93 (*0-8239-2294-4*, PowerKids) Rosen Group.

Peoples of the Desert, 6 vols., Set. Robert Low. LC 96-7753. (Peoples & Their Environments Ser.). (Illus.). 24p. (J). (gr. k-4). 1996. lib. bdg. 15.93 (*0-8239-2296-0*, PowerKids) Rosen Group.

Peoples of the Golden Triangle. Paul Lewis & Elaine Lewis. LC 84-50047. (Illus.). 200p. (YA). 1980. pap. 24.95 (*0-500-97472-1*, Pub. by Thames Hudson) Norton.

Peoples of the Golden Triangle: Six Tribes in Thailand. Paul Lewis & Elaine Lewis. LC 84-50047. (Illus.). 1984. 40.00 (*0-500-97314-8*, Pub. by Thames Hudson) Norton.

Peoples of the Gran Chaco. Ed. by Elmer S. Miller. LC 98-41385. (Native Peoples of the Americas Ser.). 184p. 1999. 65.00 (*0-89789-532-0*, Bergin & Garvey) Greenwood.

Peoples of the Great North. Valentina Gorbatcheva & Marina Fedorova. (Temporis Ser.). (Illus.). 208p. 2000. 55.00 (*1-85995-479-0*) Parkstone Pr.

Peoples of the Great North. Ed. by Parkstone Press Staff. (Blank Book Ser.). (Illus.). 115p. 2000. 15.95 (*1-85995-154-6*) Parkstone Pr.

Peoples of the Horn of Africa: Somali, Afar & Saho. I. M. Lewis. LC 99-163653. 424p. 1998. 89.95 (*1-56902-104-X*); pap. 24.95 (*1-56902-105-8*) Red Sea Pr.

Peoples of the Horn of Africa: Somali, Afar & Saho. I. M. Lewis. LC 55-4468. (Ethnographic Survey of Africa: North Eastern Africa Ser.: Pt. 1). 212p. reprint ed. pap. 65.80 (*0-8357-3014-X*, 205710000010) Bks Demand.

Peoples of the Middle Niger: The Island of Gold. Roderick J. McIntosh. LC 98-10817. (Peoples of Africa Ser.). (Illus.). 336p. 1998. 59.95 (*0-631-17361-7*) Blackwell Pubs.

Peoples of the Mountains, 6 vols., Set. Robert Low. LC 96-14814. (Peoples & Their Environments Ser.). (Illus.). 24p. (J). (gr. k-4). 1996. lib. bdg. 15.93 (*0-8239-2298-7*, PowerKids) Rosen Group.

Peoples of the Niger-Benue Confluence, the Nupe by Daryll Forde, the Igbira by Paula Brown, the Igala by Robert G. Armstrong, the Idoma-Speaking Peoples, by Robert G. Armstrong. International African Institute Staff. LC 78-23171. (Ethnographic Survey of Africa: Western Africa Ser.: No. 10). 170p. reprint ed. pap. 52.70 (*0-8357-6954-2*, 203901300009) Bks Demand.

Peoples of the Northwest Coast: Their Archaeology & Prehistory. Kenneth M. Ames & Herbert D. Maschner. LC 98-60253. (Illus.). 272p. 1999. 45.00 (*0-500-05091-0*, Pub. by Thames Hudson) Norton.

***Peoples of the Northwest Coast: Their Archaeology & Prehistory.** Kenneth Ames & Herbert D. Maschner. LC 98-60253. (Illus.). 288p. 2000. reprint ed. pap. 24.95 (*0-500-28110-6*, Pub. by Thames Hudson) Norton.

Peoples of the Old Testament World. Ed. by Alfred J. Hoerth et al. (Illus.). 400p. (C). (gr. 13). 1998. pap. 24.99 (*0-8010-2196-0*) Baker Bks.

Peoples of the Plains. Thomas E. Mails. Ed. by Anthony Meisel. LC 97-12698. (Library of Native Peoples). (Illus.). 96p. (Orig.). (YA). 1997. pap. 10.95 (*1-57178-046-7*) Coun Oak Bks.

Peoples of the Rain Forest, 6 vols., Set. Robert Low. LC 96-5551. (Peoples & Their Environments Ser.). (Illus.). 24p. (J). (gr. k-4). 1996. lib. bdg. 15.93 (*0-8239-2297-9*, PowerKids) Rosen Group.

Peoples of the River Valley, 6 vols., Set. Robert Low. LC 96-1532. (Peoples & Their Environments Ser.). (Illus.). 24p. (J). (gr. k-4). 1996. lib. bdg. 15.93 (*0-8239-2295-2*, PowerKids) Rosen Group.

Peoples of the Savanna, 6 vols. Robert Low. LC 96-14279. (Peoples & their Environments Ser.). (Illus.). 24p. (J). (gr. k-4). 1996. lib. bdg. 15.93 (*0-8239-2299-5*, PowerKids) Rosen Group.

Peoples of the Soviet Union. Viktor Kozlov. Tr. by Pauline M. Tiffen from RUS. LC 88-637. (Second World Ser.). (Illus.). 274p. 1988. 41.95 (*0-253-34356-9*) Ind U Pr.

***Peoples of the Steppe.** Wright. LC 99-175433. 178p. (C). 1998. pap. text 23.75 (*0-536-01467-1*) Pearson Custom.

Peoples of the Twilight: European Views of Native Minnesota, 1823-1862. Christian F. Feest et al. LC 98-17026. 1998. 125.00 (*1-890434-06-X*) Afton Hist Soc.

Peoples of the U. S. S. R. An Ethnographic Handbook. Ronald Wixman. LC 83-14833. (Illus.). 264p. (gr. 13). 1988. pap. text 34.95 (*0-87332-506-0*) M E Sharpe.

***Peoples of the World: A Reader for Cultural Anthropology.** Michael Nunley & Karl Rambo. 166p. (C). 1999. per. 36.95 (*0-7872-6400-8*, 41640001) Kendall-Hunt.

Peoples of the World: Africa South Sahara 1, Vol. 3. W. Moss. 443p. 1991. 55.00 (*0-8103-7942-2*) Gale.

Peoples of the World: Asians & Pacific Islanders, Vol. 7. W. Moss & George Wilson. 550p. 1993. 55.00 (*0-8103-8866-9*, 101508) Gale.

Peoples of the World: Customs & Cultures. LC 97-32980. (J). 1998. lib. bdg. 305.00 (*0-7172-9236-3*) Grolier Educ.

Peoples of the World: Eastern Europe & the Post-Soviet Republics, Vol. 5. W. Moss & Wilson. 550p. 1992. 55.00 (*0-8103-8867-7*, 101509) Gale.

Peoples of the World: Latin Americans. Ed. by Joyce Moss & George Wilson. 1989. 55.00 (*0-8103-7445-5*) Gale.

Peoples of the World: North Americans, Vol. 2. Ed. by Joyce Moss & George Wilson. 441p. 1990. 55.00 (*0-8103-7768-3*, 100732-M94800) Gale.

Peoples of the World: The Middle East & North Africa, Vol. 4. W. Moss. 437p. 1991. 55.00 (*0-8103-7941-4*) Gale.

Peoples of the World: Western Europeans, Vol. 6. W. Moss & Wilson. 438p. 1993. 55.00 (*0-8103-8868-5*, 101510) Gale.

Peoples of Washington: Perspectives on Cultural Diversity. Ed. by Sid White & S. E. Solberg. LC 89-22556. (Illus.). 261p. 1990. 18.75 (*0-87422-067-X*); pap. 10.95 (*0-87422-062-9*) Wash St U Pr.

Peoples of West Africa. Diagram Group Staff. LC 96-38737. (Peoples of Africa Ser.). (Illus.). (YA). (gr. 6-12). 1997. 19.95 (*0-8160-3485-0*) Facts on File.

Peoples of Zanzibar: Their Customs & Religious Beliefs. Godfrey Dale. LC 78-90112. 124p. 1969. reprint ed. lib. bdg. 45.00 (*0-8371-2028-4*, DAP&, Greenwood Pr) Greenwood.

***People's Palace: The Story of the Chicago Cultural Center.** Intro. by M. W. Newman. (Illus.). 70p. 1999. pap. 14.95 (*0-938903-25-X*) Cty of Chicago.

People's Palace Book of Glasgow. Liz Carnegie et al. LC 99-219339. 128p. 1998. pap. 19.95 (*1-84018-068-4*, Pub. by Mainstream Pubng) Trafalgar.

People's Panel: The Grand Jury in the United States, 1634-1941. Richard D. Younger. LC 63-12993. 271p. reprint ed. 84.10 (*0-608-16622-7*, 202752700055) Bks Demand.

People's Participation: Challenges Ahead. Ed. & Compiled by Orlando Fals-Borda. LC 99-27651. 272p. 1998. pap. 18.50 (*0-945257-91-0*) Apex Pr.

People's Participation & Irrigation Management: Experiences, Issues, Options. S. Satish. (C). 1990. 15.00 (*81-7169-080-7*, Commonwealth) S Asia.

People's Participation in Community Development. Gracious Thomas. (C). 1992. 20.00 (*81-85565-04-X*, Pub. by Uppal Pub Hse) S Asia.

People's Participation in Family Planning. Vapai A. Panandiker & Ajay K. Mehra. 1987. 29.00 (*81-85024-10-3*, Pub. by Uppal Pub Hse) S Asia.

People's Participation in Himalayan Ecosystem Development. M. L. Dewan. (C). 1990. text 35.00 (*81-7022-298-2*, Pub. by Concept) S Asia.

People's Participation in Rural Development - Philippines: FAO W-NGO in Proj. Food & Agriculture Organization Staff. (People's Participation Ser.: No. 6). 62p. 1994. pap. 11.00 (*92-5-103469-9*, F34699, Pub. by FAO) Bernan Associates.

People's Participation in Sustainable Human Development: A Unified Search. Kamal Taori. LC 98-915503. 276p. 1998. write for info. (*81-7022-734-8*) Concept.

People's Party: Victorian Labor & the Radical Tradition 1875-1914. Frank Bongiorno. LC 96-231084. 240p. 1997. pap. 24.95 (*0-522-84738-2*, Pub. by Melbourne Univ Pr) Paul & Co Pubs.

People's Party Campaign Book. Thomas E. Watson. Ed. by Dan C. McCurry & Richard E. Rubenstein. LC 74-30663. (American Farmers & the Rise of Agribusiness Ser.). 1975. reprint ed. 39.95 (*0-405-06839-5*) Ayer.

People's Party in Texas: A Study in Third-Party Politics. Roscoe Martin. (Texas History Paperbacks Ser.: No. 7). 280p. 1970. reprint ed. pap. 7.95 (*0-292-70032-6*) U of Tex Pr.

People's Past. Ed. by Edward J. Cowan. 1991. 11.95 (*0-7486-6157-3*, Pub. by Polygon) Subterranean Co.

People's Peace: British History since 1945. 2nd ed. Kenneth Morgan. LC 98-30645. (Illus.). 624p. 1999. pap. 14.95 (*0-19-285350-3*) OUP.

People's Pharmacy. Joe Graedon. 1998. mass mkt. 6.99 (*0-312-96416-1*) St Martin.

Peoples Pharmacy. rev. ed. Joe Graedon. 416p. 1996. text 24.95 (*0-312-14125-4*) St Martin.

People's Pharmacy Guide to Home & Herbal Remedies. Joe Graedon & Theresa Graedon. LC 99-26613. 394p. 1999. text 27.95 (*0-312-20779-4*) St Martin.

***People's Pharmacy Guide to Home & Herbal Remedies.** Joe Graedon & Teresa Graedon. 2001. reprint ed. pap. write for info. (*0-312-26764-9*, St Martin Griffin) St Martin.

People's Poetry: Hen Benillion. Tr. & Intro. by Glyn Jones. LC 98-211633. 170p. 1998. pap. 24.95 (*1-85411-178-7*, Pub. by Seren Bks) Dufour.

People's Poland: Patterns of Social Inequality & Conflict, 55. Wladyslaw Majkowski. LC 84-15689. (Contributions in Sociology Ser.). (Illus.). 234p. 1985. 59.95 (*0-313-24614-9*, MJP/, Greenwood Pr) Greenwood.

People's Poll on Schools & School Choice. (Illus.). 192p. 1992. pap. 6.00 (*1-55833-081-X*) Natl Cath Educ.

People's Pottage. Truth Seeker Company Staff. LC 92-82524. 116p. 1992. pap. text 9.95 (*0-8403-7994-3*) Truth Seeker.

An Asterisk (*) at the beginning of an entry indicates that the title is appearing for the first time.

People's Power: Cuba's Experience with Representative Government. Peter Roman. LC 98-55919. (Latin American Perspectives Ser.). 296p. 1999. text 60.00 (*0-8133-3586-8*, Pub. by Westview) HarpC.

People's Reactions to Technology: In Factories, Offices, & Aerospace. Ed. by Stuart Oskamp. (Claremont Symposium on Applied Social Psychology Ser.). 296p. (C). 1990. text 39.95 (*0-8039-3852-7*) Sage.

People's Reactions to Technology: In Factories, Offices, & Aerospace, No. 4. Ed. by Stuart Oskamp. (Claremont Symposium on Applied Social Psychology Ser.). 296p. (C). 1990. pap. text 18.95 (*0-8039-3853-5*) Sage.

People's Remedy: The Struggle for Health Care in El Salvador's War of Liberation. Francisco Metzi. Tr. by Jean Carroll from SPA. 224p. (C). 1988. pap. 10.00 (*0-85345-775-1*, Pub. by Monthly Rev) NYU Pr.

People's Repertory: Your Guide to Jafe, Effective Homeopathic Remedies for First Aid, Cold & Flu, Women's Health, Emotional Upsets. Luc De Schepper. Ed. by Begabati Lennihan. (Illus.). 200p. 1998. pap. 9.95 (*0-942501-09-8*) Full of Life.

People's Representatives: Electoral Systems in the Asia-Pacific Region. Ed. by Graham Hassall & Cheryl Saunders. LC 97-157910. 272p. 1997. 39.95 (*1-86448-258-3*, Pub. by Allen & Unwin Pty) Paul & Co Pubs.

People's Republic. Paul F. Amor. 224p. 1990. 18.95 (*0-8027-1072-7*) Walker & Co.

People's Republic: Vermont & the Sanders Revolution. Greg Guma. LC 89-12170. 208p. (Orig.). 1989. pap. 14.95 (*0-933050-78-X*) New Eng Pr VT.

People's Republic of Albania. Nicholas C. Pano. LC 68-27736. (Integration & Community Building in Eastern Europe Ser.). 203p. 1968. reprint ed. pap. 63.00 (*0-608-04018-5*, 206475400011) Bks Demand.

People's Republic of China. Ed. by Guangming Daily. (Illus.). 608p. 1990. 130.00 (*1-86305-004-3*, Pub. by Lotus Pub) Intl Spec Bk.

People's Republic of China. Kim Dramer. LC 98-17643. (Enchantment of the World Ser.). 144p. (J). (gr. 5-10). 1999. 32.00 (*0-516-21077-7*) Childrens.

People's Republic of China: International Customs Journal, 1993-1994. 5th ed. (Illus.). 277p. (Orig.). (C). 1994. pap. text 95.00 (*0-7881-1221-X*) DIANE Pub.

People's Republic of China: The Human Rights Exception, No. 3. Roberta Cohen. 103p. 1988. 5.00 (*0-942182-89-8*, 86) Occasional Papers.

People's Republic of China: Torture & Ill-Treatment of Prisoners. Amnesty International Staff. 46p. (Orig.). 1987. pap. 5.00 (*0-939994-32-1*, Pub. by Amnesty Intl Pubns) Science Pubs.

***People's Republic of China after 50 Years.** Ed. by Richard Louis Edmonds. LC 99-89423. (Studies on Contemporary China). 192p. 2000. pap. 24.95 (*0-19-924065-5*) OUP.

People's Republic of China after Thirty Years: An Overview. Ed. by Joyce K. Kallgren. LC 79-89491. (China Research Monographs: No. 15). 122p. 1979. pap. 5.00 (*0-912966-21-1*) IEAS.

People's Republic of China after Thirty Years: An Overview. Ed. by Joyce K. Kallgren. LC 79-89491. (University of California, Center for Chinese Studies, China Research Monographs: No. 15). 132p. reprint ed. pap. 41.00 (*0-608-13131-8*, 201946800011) Bks Demand.

People's Republic of China & the Law of Treaties. Hungdah Chiu. LC 72-173411. (Studies in East Asian Law: No. 5). 196p. 1972. 24.00 (*0-674-66175-3*) HUP.

People's Republic of China, International Law & Arms Control. David Salem. 325p. 15.00 (*0-942182-59-6*); pap. 7.00 (*0-942182-58-8*) Occasional Papers.

People's Republic of China, 1978-1990. D. Gale Johnson. 129p. 1990. pap. 9.95 (*1-55815-122-2*) ICS Pr.

People's Republic of China, 1979-1984: A Documentary Survey, 2 vols., Set. Ed. by Harold C. Hinton. LC 85-30391. 1986. 150.00 (*0-8420-2253-8*) Scholarly Res Inc.

People's Republic of China, The Massacre of June 1989 & Its Aftermath. 67p. 1989. 5.00 (*0-939994-56-9*) Amnesty Intl USA.

People's Republic of China Yearbook, 1995-96. 500p. 1996. 150.00 (*0-8002-4343-9*) Intl Pubns Serv.

People's Republic of China Yearbook, 1987. 7th ed. 673p. 1987. 130.00 (*0-8002-4211-4*) Taylor & Francis.

People's Response to Our Global Neighborhood: Dialogues on the Report of the Commission on Global Governance. Ed. by Michael Hays & Amy Morgante. 294p. 1995. 10.00 (*1-887917-01-2*) Boston RCFT-FC.

People's Right to Know. Harold L. Cross. LC 75-170844. reprint ed. 29.50 (*0-404-01859-9*) AMS Pr.

People's Right to Know: Media, Democracy, & the Information Highway. Ed. by Frederick Williams & John V. Pavlik. (Telecommunications Ser.). 272p. 1994. pap. 27.50 (*0-8058-1491-4*); text 59.95 (*0-8058-1490-6*) L Erlbaum Assocs.

People's Rights: Social Movements & the State in the Third World. Manoranjan Mohanty et al. LC 97-31054. 1997. write for info. (*0-7619-9212-X*) Sage.

***People's Rights: The State of the Art.** Ed. by Philip Alston. (Collected Courses of the Academy of European Law: Volume 9). 280p. 2000. text 72.00 (*0-19-829875-7*) OUP.

People's Rising: Wexford, 1798. Daniel Gahan. (Illus.). 320p. 1995. pap. 25.95 (*0-7171-2323-5*, Pub. by Gill & MacMill) Irish Bks Media.

People's Runnymede. R. J. Scrutton. 1972. 69.95 (*0-8490-0812-3*) Gordon Pr.

People's Self Development: Perspectives on Participatory Action Research. Anisur Rahman. LC 93-37607. 256p. (C). 1993. text 65.00 (*1-85649-079-3*, Pub. by Zed Books); text 25.00 (*1-85649-080-7*, Pub. by Zed Books) St Martin.

Peoples Speaking to Peoples: A Report on International Mass Communication from the Commission on Freedom of the Press. Llewellyn White & Robert D. Leigh. LC 72-4685. (International Propaganda & Communications Ser.). 131p. 1972. reprint ed. 18.95 (*0-405-04769-X*) Ayer.

People's Tragedy. Orlando Figes. 1998. pap. 19.95 (*0-14-024364-X*) Viking Penguin.

People's Tragedy: A History of the Russian Revolution. Orlando Figes. (Illus.). 923p. 39.95 (*0-614-28401-5*) Viking Penguin.

People's Travel Book. rev. ed. Compiled by Frieda Carrol. LC 80-70869. 115p. 1992. pap. 29.95 (*0-939476-06-1*) Prosperity & Profits.

People's Travel Book. rev. ed. Compiled by Frieda Carrol. LC 80-70869. 115p. 1996. ring bd. 39.95 (*0-939476-05-3*) Prosperity & Profits.

People's Treasures: Collections in the National Library of Australia. John Thompson & National Library of Australia Staff. LC 95-181905. v, 81 p. 1993. write for info. (*0-642-10597-9*, Pub. by Aust Gov Pub) Accents Pubns.

People's Universities of the U. S. S. R., 29. David C. Lee. LC 88-15486. (Contributions to the Study of Education Ser.: No. 29). (Illus.). 279p. 1988. 55.00 (*0-313-26344-2*, LPU/, Greenwood Pr) Greenwood.

***Peoples Versus States: Minorities at Risk in the New Century.** Ted Robert Gurr. (Illus.). 368p. 2000. 55.00 (*1-929223-03-X*); pap. 29.95 (*1-929223-02-1*) US Inst Peace.

People's Voice: An Annotated Bibliography of American Presidential Campaign Newspapers, 1828-1984, 6. Compiled by William Miles. LC 87-11969. (Bibliographies & Indexes in American History Ser.: No. 6). 259p. 1987. lib. bdg. 75.00 (*0-313-23976-2*, MPN/) Greenwood.

People's Voice: Black South African Writing in the Twentieth Century. Piniel V. Shava. LC 89-30980. 187p. 1989. text 26.95 (*0-8214-0931-X*); pap. text 14.95 (*0-8214-0932-8*) Ohio U Pr.

People's Voice: The Orator in American Society. Barnet Baskerville. LC 79-4001. 269p. reprint ed. pap. 83.40 (*0-608-17704-0*, 203004800067) Bks Demand.

***People's War: Responses to World War II in the Soviet Union.** Robert W. Thurston & Bernd Bonwetsch. LC 00-8493. 296p. 2000. text 39.95 (*0-252-02600-4*) U of Ill Pr.

People's Welfare: Law & Regulation in Nineteenth-Century America. William J. Novak. 416p. (C). 1996. pap. text 19.95 (*0-8078-4611-2*); lib. bdg. 59.95 (*0-8078-2292-2*) U of NC Pr.

People's Will. Robert Norris. 80p. (Orig.). 1989. pap. 16.95 (*0-317-93473-2*) Peoples Birmingham.

People's Writer: Erskine Caldwell & the South. Wayne Mixon. LC 95-8291. (Minds of the New South Ser.). (Illus.). 256p. (C). 1995. 30.00 (*0-8139-1627-5*) U Pr of Va.

People's 25TH Anniversary Celebration Time-Life Books Editors. 160p. (gr. 7). 1999. 24.95 (*1-883013-63-1*) Little.

***PeopleSmart: Developing Your Interpersonal Intelligence.** Mel Silberman & Freda Hansburg. 300p. 2000. pap. 16.95 (*1-57675-091-4*, Pub. by Berrett-Koehler) Publishers Group.

PeopleSoft Administrator's Guide. Darrell Bilbrey. LC 99-60011. 560p. 1999. pap. 59.99 (*0-7821-2396-1*) Sybex.

***PeopleSoft Administrator's Handbook.** Stewart S. Miller. 2000. write for info. (*0-07-212408-3*) McGraw-H Intl.

***PeopleSoft Application Development Tools.** Jami Clott & Stephen Raff. LC 99-53269. (Tools Ser.). 512p. 1999. pap. 49.99 (*0-07-135569-3*) McGraw.

***PeopleSoft Developer's Handbook.** Gillespie Gillespie. 1999. pap. text 59.99 (*0-07-212394-X*) McGraw.

***PeopleSoft Financials: A Beginner's Guide.** Created by Romac International Staff. 512p. 1999. 39.99 (*0-7821-2394-5*) Sybex.

***PeopleSoft HRMS: A Beginner's Guide.** Kisha Gunter. 512p. 1999. pap. 39.99 (*0-7821-2395-3*) Sybex.

PeopleSoft HRMS Reporting. Ed. by Bromwich. LC 99-48943. 464p. 1999. pap. 55.00 (*0-13-021612-7*) P-H.

PeopleSoft Integration. Stewart S. Miller. 1999. write for info. (*0-07-135476-X*) McGraw.

PeopleSoft Integration Tools. Stewart S. Miller. LC 99-42384. 512p. 1999. pap. 49.99 (*0-07-135477-8*) McGraw.

PeopleSoft Pro - A Complete Guide. Greyland Royce. Ed. by Mark Thomas. (Illus.). 800p. 1999. spiral bd. 79.95 (*1-928778-09-7*, M01APEIA-001V1) Royce Pubg.

Peopletalk: The Skills of Positive Communication & Customer Care. Judi James. 96p. 1998. pap. 13.95 (*1-85835-520-6*, Indust Soc) Stylus Pub VA.

Peopleware: Productive Projects & Teams. 2nd ed. Tom DeMarco & Timothy R. Lister. LC 99-11525. 264p. 1999. pap. 33.95 (*0-932633-43-9*) Dorset Hse Pub Co.

Peopling Indiana: The Ethnic Experience. Ed. by Robert M. Taylor, Jr. & Connie A. McBirney. LC 96-2850. (Illus.). xiii, 703p. 1996. 39.95 (*0-87195-112-6*) Ind Hist Soc.

Peopling of Africa: A Geographic Interpretation. James L. Newman. LC 94-28259. 235p. 1995. 37.00 (*0-300-06003-3*) Yale U Pr.

Peopling of Africa: A Geographic Interpretation. James L. Newman. 252p. 1997. pap. text 15.00 (*0-300-07280-5*) Yale U Pr.

Peopling of America: A Synoptic History. Jason H. Silverman. LC 91-91027. (Illus.). 96p. 1996. reprint ed. pap. 12.95 (*1-56192-050-9*) Portfolio DC.

Peopling of America: A Timeline of Events That Helped Shape Our Nation. 4th rev. ed. Portfolio Staff. Ed. by Allan S. Kullen. LC 91-91027. 416p. 1996. 17.95 (*1-56192-096-7*) Portfolio DC.

Peopling of British North America: An Introduction. Bernard Bailyn. LC 87-45916. 192p. 1988. pap. 10.00 (*0-394-75779-3*) Vin Bks.

Peopling of North America: The Visual Atlas of the Great Migrations into North America, from the Ice Age to Ellis Island & Beyond. Helen H. Tanner & Robert C. Ostergren. (Illus.). 208p. 1995. pap. 39.95 (*0-02-616272-5*) Macmillan.

Peopling of Planet Earth: Human Population Growth Through the Ages. Roy A. Gallant. LC 89-34575. (Illus.). 128p. (J). (gr. 3-7). 1990. lib. bdg. 15.95 (*0-02-735772-4*, Mac Bks Young Read) S&S Childrens.

Peopling of the New World. Ed. by Jonathan E. Ericson et al. LC 81-22800. (Anthropological Papers: No. 23). (Illus.). 364p. 1982. pap. 10.00 (*0-87919-095-7*) Ballena Pr.

Peopling of Tompkins County: A Social History. Carol Kammen. LC 85-17563. (Illus.). 250p. 1985. 19.95 (*0-932334-21-0*, NY55028) Hrt of the Lakes.

Peopling the Plains: Who Settled Where in Frontier Kansas. James R. Shortridge. LC 94-45603. (Illus.). 192p. 1995. 27.50 (*0-7006-0697-1*) U Pr of KS.

Peor Senora del Mundo (The Worst Woman in the World) Francisco Hinojosa. (SPA.). 44p. (J). (gr. 3-4). 1992. pap. 5.99 (*968-16-3911-1*, Pub. by Fondo) Continental Bk.

Peoria! Jerry Klein. (Illus.). 276p. 1985. 24.95 (*0-9615759-0-5*) Visual Comm.

Peoria: A Postcard History. Charles Bobbitt & Ladonna Bobbitt. LC 98-86603. (Postcard History Ser.). (Illus.). 128p. 1998. pap. 16.99 (*0-7524-1284-1*) Arcadia Publng.

Peoria - Impressions of 150 Years. limited ed. Ed. by Janet Peterson & Kelli Rude. (Illus.). 180p. 1995. 39.95 (*0-9634793-9-3*) Peoria Jrnl.

Peoria Business: A Pictorial History. Monica V. Wheeler. (Illinois Pictorial History Ser.). 160p. 1998. write for info. (*0-943963-63-X*) G Bradley.

Peoria City & County: Record of Settlement, Organization, Progress & Achievement, 2 vols. James M. Rice. (Illus.). 905p. 1997. reprint ed. lib. bdg. 97.00 (*0-8328-5781-5*) Higginson Bk Co.

***Peoria Collection: A Book of Engravings from 1886.** Ed. by Jane Bodman Converse. 58p. 1999. ring bd. 30.00 (*1-893525-01-5*) Converse Pubg.

Peoria Directory for 1844. Simeon DeWitt Drown. 1978. reprint ed. 10.00 (*0-930358-02-3*) Spoon River.

Peoria Industry: A Pictorial History. Jerry Klein. (Illinois Pictorial History Ser.). (Illus.). 1997. write for info. (*0-943963-59-1*) G Bradley.

Peoria-Pekin MSA. Ed. by Joy Anderson & Steve Burlison. (Illus.). 32p. (C). 1994. pap. text 7.95 (*0-9634793-8-5*) Peoria Jrnl.

Peoria People. Peoria Newspaper Guild Staff. Ed. by Bill Knight. (Illus.). 96p. (Orig.). 1988. pap. 5.95 (*0-9621356-0-7*) Peoria Newspaper Guild.

***Peoria Revisited: In Vintage Postcards.** Charles Bobbitt & Ladonna Bobbitt. (Postcard History Ser.). (Illus.). 128p. 2000. pap. 18.99 (*0-7385-0711-3*) Arcadia Publng.

PEP: Moving As Team - Step 3. 7th ed. Gary B. Spindt. 144p. 1992. per. 9.90 (*0-8403-5915-2*) Kendall-Hunt.

PEP: Moving with Confidence - Step 1. 7th ed. Gary B. Spindt. 112p. 1992. per. 9.90 (*0-8403-5334-0*) Kendall-Hunt.

PEP: Moving with Skill - Step 2. 7th ed. Gary B. Spindt. 144p. 1992. per. 9.90 (*0-8403-5912-8*) Kendall-Hunt.

PEP: The Seven P's to Positively Enhance Performance. Richard Ruffalo & Mike Moretti. LC 96-77150. 128p. (Orig.). 1996. pap. 11.95 (*1-883697-23-9*) Hara Pub.

Pep Puzzles English, PEP 3. Keith Methold et al. (English As a Second Language Bk.). 1978. pap. text 3.50 (*0-582-55259-1*) Longman.

Pep Talk: Inspiration from America's Great Coaches. Ed. by Mike Dowdall & Sheila Meehan. LC 94-33742. (Illus.). 88p. 1995. pap. 5.95 (*0-8118-0542-5*) Chronicle Bks.

Pepacton. John Burroughs. (Works of John Burroughs). 1989. reprint ed. lib. bdg. 79.00 (*0-7812-2182-X*) Rprt Serv.

Pepe Botellas. Gustavo A. Gardeazabal. (SPA.). 344p. 1984. 11.00 (*0-317-46760-3*, 3015) Ediciones Norte.

Pepe Le Moko. Ginette Vincendeau. LC 98-215543. (Film Classics Ser.). (Illus.). 80p. 1998. pap. 10.95 (*0-85170-674-6*) Ind U Pr.

Pepe the Little Turtle & Little Rachel. Florence Howard. Ed. by Tony Rose. LC 99-30827. (Illus.). 25p. (J). (gr. k-5). 1999. pap. 5.95 (*0-9655064-6-0*) Amber Books.

Pepe y la Armadura (Pepe & the Armor) Juan Munoz. (SPA., Illus.). 120p. (YA). 1994. pap. 5.99 (*968-16-4465-4*, Pub. by Fondo) Continental Bk.

Pepi & the Secret Names. Jill Paton Walsh. LC 93-48620. (Illus.). 32p. (J). (gr. 1 up). 1995. 15.00 (*0-688-13428-9*) Lothrop.

***Pepin's Bastard: The Story of Charles Martel.** Diane M. Johnson. LC 98-96684. (Illus.). 296p. 1999. pap. 14.95 (*0-9661504-1-4*) Superior Bk Pub.

***Pepita Jimenez.** J. Valear. (SPA.). 1999. 13.00 (*84-481-0622-9*, McGrw-H College) McGrw-H Hghr Educ.

Pepita Jimenez. Juan Valera. (SPA.). pap. 5.95 (*84-410-0008-5*, Pub. by Bookking Intl) Distribks Inc.

Pepita Jimenez. Juan Valera. (SPA.). pap. 16.95 (*84-376-0800-7*, Pub. by Ediciones Catedra) Continental Bk.

Pepita Jimenez. Juan Valera. (Nueva Austral Ser.: Vol. 44). (SPA.). 1991. pap. text 15.95 (*84-239-1844-0*) Elliots Bks.

Pepita Jimenez. Juan Valera. (SPA.). 1989. 7.95 (*0-8288-2581-5*) Fr & Eur.

Pepita Jimenez see Classics of Spanish Literature

Pepita Jimenez Level 5. Juan Valera. (SPA.). (J). 1998. pap. text 6.95 (*84-294-3494-1*) Santillana.

***Pepita Takes Time/Pepita, Siempre Tarde.** Ofelia D. Lachtman et al. 32p. (J). (ps-2). 2000. 14.95 (*1-55885-304-9*) Arte Publico.

Pepita Talks Twice (Pepita Habla Dos Veces) Ofelia D. Lachtman. LC 95-9869. (ENG & SPA., Illus.). 32p. (J). (gr. k-3). 1995. 14.95 (*1-55885-077-5*, Pinata Bks) Arte Publico.

Pepita Thinks Pink (Pepita y el Color Rosado) Ofelia D. Lachtman. LC 97-29676. (ENG & SPA., Illus.). 32p. (J). (ps-2). 1998. 14.95 (*1-55885-222-0*, Pinata Bks) Arte Publico.

Pepito: The Little Dancing Dog. Mark Evans. LC 78-65354. (Illus.). (J). (gr. k-4). 1979. 11.95 (*0-87592-063-2*) Scroll Pr.

Pepito & the United Nations. 1989. 13.95 (*92-1-100427-6*, E.89.I.17) UN.

Pepito, el Nino Que Nunca de Bio Nacer. Jose M. Dorta. (SPA.). 1998. pap. 10.00 (*0-938693-11-5*) Maya Pubns.

Pepito's Fate. Paul. 2001. pap. write for info. (*0-15-600613-8*) Harcourt.

Pepito's Journey. John T. Moore. 25p. pap. 3.95 (*92-1-100308-3*, E.87.I.4) UN.

Pepito's Speech at the United Nations. pap. 4.95 (*92-1-100265-6*) UN.

Pepito's Speech at the United Nations, 1989. rev. ed. 54p. pap. 5.95 (*92-1-100412-8*) UN.

Pepito's World. John T. Moore. 1988. 4.95 (*92-1-100399-7*, E.88.I.14) UN.

PEPM, 95: ACM Symposium on Partial Evaluation & Semantics-Based Program Manipulation. 269p. 1995. pap. text 38.00 (*0-89791-720-0*, 551951) Assn Compu Machinery.

PEPM, 93: ACM Symposium on Partial Evaluation & Semantics-Based Program Manipulation. 224p. 1993. pap. text 30.00 (*0-89791-594-1*, 551931) Assn Compu Machinery.

Peppe the Lamplighter. Elisa Bartone. LC 92-1397. (Illus.). (J). (ps-3). 1993. 16.00 (*0-688-10268-9*); lib. bdg. 15.93 (*0-688-10269-7*) Lothrop.

Peppe the Lamplighter. Elisa Bartone. LC 92-1397. (Illus.). 32p. (J). (gr. k-3). 1997. mass mkt. 4.95 (*0-688-15469-7*, Wm Morrow) Morrow Avon.

Peppe the Lamplighter. Elisa Bartone. LC 92-1397. 1997. 10.15 (*0-606-11737-7*, Pub. by Turtleback) Demco.

***Pepper.** Stewart Cowley. (Illus.). 10p. (gr. k-3). 2000. bds. 4.99 (*1-57584-350-1*) Rdrs Digest.

***Pepper.** Tristan Hawkins. 1998. mass mkt. 10.95 (*0-00-654626-9*, Pub. by HarpC) Trafalgar.

Pepper: Eyewitness to a Century. Claude D. Pepper & Hays Gorey. 1987. 17.95 (*0-15-171695-1*) Harcourt.

Pepper Ann: Soccer Sensation. Nancy Krulik. (Disney Chapters Ser.). 64p. (J). (gr. 2-4). 1998. pap. 3.95 (*0-7868-4262-8*, Pub. by Disney Pr) Time Warner.

Pepper Collection. 80p. 1996. otabind 19.95 (*0-7935-4007-0*, 00672301) H Leonard.

Pepper Font. 2nd ed. Lawrence Shriberg. (C). 1995. 16.95 (*0-205-17174-5*, Macmillan Coll) P-H.

Pepper Garden. Dave Dewitt. LC 93-30508. (Illus.). 240p. 1993. pap. 15.95 (*0-89815-554-1*) Ten Speed Pr.

Pepper, Guns, & Parleys: The Dutch East India Company & China, 1622-1681. John E. Wills. LC 73-81669. (Harvard East Asian Ser.: No. 75). 254p. 1974. reprint ed. pap. 78.80 (*0-7837-4201-0*, 205905100012) Bks Demand.

Pepper Harvest Cookbook. Barbara Ciletti. LC 97-10086. (Illus.). 172p. 1997. 24.95 (*1-56158-195-X*, 70323) Taunton.

Pepper Harvest Cookbook. Barbara Ciletti. (Illus.). 176p. 1998. pap. 19.95 (*1-56158-276-X*, 070408) Taunton.

***Pepper in Our Eyes: The APEC Affair.** Ed. by W. Wesley Pue. (Illus.). 232p. 2000. 32.95 (*0-7748-0779-2*, Pub. by UBC Pr) U of Wash Pr.

Pepper in the Blood. Brian Dyson. 1996. pap. text 12.95 (*0-9652958-3-4*) Chatham Intl.

Pepper Lady's Pocket Pepper Primer. Jean Andrews. LC 96-51216. (Illus.). 190p. 1998. pap. 17.95 (*0-292-70483-6*, ANDPPP) U of Tex Pr.

Pepper Pantry: Chiptles. Dave DeWitt & Chuck Evans. LC 96-30488. (Pepper Pantry Ser.). (Illus.). 96p. 1997. pap. 5.95 (*0-89087-828-5*) Celestial Arts.

Pepper Pantry: Habaneros. Dave DeWitt & Nancy Gerlach. LC 96-31709. (Pepper Pantry Ser.). (Illus.). 96p. 1997. pap. 5.95 (*0-89087-827-7*) Celestial Arts.

Pepper Sprays: Practical Self-Defense for Anyone, Anywhere. Doug Lamb. (Illus.). 120p. 1994. pap. 16.00 (*0-87364-794-7*) Paladin Pr.

***Pepper Trail: History & Recipes from Around the World.** Jean Andrews. LC 99-22244. (Illus.). 264p. 1999. 50.00 (*1-57441-070-9*, Pub. by UNTX Pr) Tex A&M Univ Pr.

Pepper Tree Rider. Jack Curtis. 144p. 1994. 19.95 (*0-8027-4137-1*) Walker & Co.

Pepper Tree Rider. large type ed. Jack Curtis. LC 94-33228. 224p. 1994. lib. bdg. 19.95 (*0-7838-1130-6*, G K Hall Lrg Type) Mac Lib Ref.

Pepper-Upper. Paul Bates et al. (Illus.). 100p. (Orig.). 1989. pap. 12.00 (*1-56046-127-6*) Interact Pubs.

Peppercanister Poems Nineteen Seventy-Two to Nineteen Seventy-Eight. Thomas Kinsella. LC 79-63669. 159p. 1979. pap. 9.95 (*0-916390-12-8*) Wake Forest.

Pepperdine Management Simulation. unabridged ed. Thomas J. Dudley. 112p. (C). 1998. pap. text 3.00 (*1-893260-03-8*) Harrison Pubg.

P

An Asterisk (*) at the beginning of an entry indicates that the title is appearing for the first time.

Pepperell. Joanne Saunders Foley. (Images of America Ser.). 1996. pap. 16.99 (*0-7524-0448-2*) Arcadia Publng.

Pepperidge Farm, Easy Meals for Busy Days. 96p. 1996. 12.95 (*0-696-20552-1*) Meredith Bks.

Pepperidge Farm Goldfish Counting Board Book. Barbara B. McGrath. (Illus.). 12p. (J). (ps-k). 1998. bds. 4.95 (*1-893017-50-8*) Jennings Pond.

Pepperidge Farm Goldfish Counting Book. (Illus.). 32p. 1999. 6.95 (*1-893017-51-6*, Dancing Star Bks) Jennings Pond.

***Pepperidge Farm Goldfish Counting Fun Book.** Barbara Barbieri McGrath. 16p. (J). (ps-1). 2000. bds. 5.99 (*0-694-01504-0*, HarpFestival) HarpC Child Bks.

***Pepperidge Farm Goldfish Fun Book.** Barbara Barbieri McGrath. (Illus.). 16p. (ps-k). 1999. 5.99 (*0-694-01450-8*) HarpC Child Bks.

Peppermill Public Hearing: A Communication Skill-Building Simulation Exercise. James E. Lukaszewski. 11p. 1995. pap. 30.00 (*1-883291-15-1*) Lukaszewski.

***Peppermint Goose & Baby Giki: Fantasy Land.** Sandi Johnson. Ed. by Britt Johnson. (Little Choo-Choo Bks.). (Illus.). 12p. (J). (ps-6). 1998. 8.99 (*1-929063-14-8*, 114) Moons & Stars.

Peppermint Patty & Marcie. Charles M. Schulz. 32p. 1999. pap. 3.50 (*0-06-107320-2*) HarpC.

Peppermint Patty Dog School Studt. Charles M. Schulz. (Peanuts Ser.). (Illus.). 48p. (J). 2000. 3.75 (*0-694-00975-X*, HarpFestival) HarpC Child Bks.

Peppermint Pig. Nina Bawden. LC 74-26922. 192p. (J). (gr. 3-6). 1975. lib. bdg. 13.89 (*0-397-31618-6*) HarpC Child Bks.

Peppermint Train: Journey to a German-Jewish Childhood. Edgar E. Stern. (Illus.). 232p. 1992. pap. 29.95 (*0-8130-1109-4*) U Press Fla.

Peppermints in the Armoire. Jackie M. Alford. LC 97-94511. (Illus.). 160p. 1997. spiral bd. 19.95 (*0-9660609-0-3*) J M Alford.

Peppermints in the Parlor. 2nd ed. Barbara B. Wallace. (J). 1993. 9.05 (*0-606-05535-5*, Pub. by Turtleback) Demco.

Peppermints in the Parlor. 2nd ed. Barbara Brooks Wallace. LC 92-33031. 216p. (J). (gr. 3-7). 1993. reprint ed. mass mkt. 3.95 (*0-689-71680-X*) Aladdin.

Pepperoni Parade & the Power of Prayer: A Book about Prayer. Barbara Johnson. LC 98-51089. (Geranium Lady Ser.). (Illus.). 32p. (J). (ps-2). 1999. 4.97 (*0-8499-5950-0*) Tommy Nelson.

Peppers. Tony Esolen. 64p. 1992. 6.95 (*0-932616-37-2*) Brick Hse Bks.

Peppers. Ed. by Smallwood & Stewart Staff. LC 96-86648. (Little Books for Cooks). 80p. 1997. 4.95 (*0-8362-2788-3*) Andrews & McMeel.

Peppers: A Cookbook. (Illus.). 128p. 1997. 12.98 (*0-7858-0788-8*) Bk Sales Inc.

Peppers: A Cookbook. Robert Berkley. (Illus.). 120p. (Orig.). 1992. per. 17.00 (*0-671-74598-0*, Fireside) S&S Trade Pap.

Peppers: A Story of Hot Pursuits. Amal Naj. LC 92-50625. 1993. pap. 12.00 (*0-679-74427-4*) Vin Bks.

Peppers: Hotness Testing. Craig C. Dremann. (Illus.). 4p. (Orig.). 1993. pap. 2.50 (*0-933421-28-1*) Redwood Seed.

Peppers: Pickled, Sauces & Salsas. Sue J. Dremann. 54p. (Orig.). 1986. pap. 6.00 (*0-933421-05-2*) Redwood Seed.

Peppers: Seed Cleaning. Craig C. Dremann. (Illus.). 6p. (Orig.). 1993. pap. 2.50 (*0-933421-26-5*) Redwood Seed.

Peppers: The Domesticated Capsicums. 2nd ed. Jean Andrews. (Illus.). 274p. 1995. 65.00 (*0-292-70467-4*) U of Tex Pr.

Peppers: Vegetable & Spice Capsicums. P. Bosland & E. Votava. LC 99-16961. (Crop Production Science in Horticulture Ser.: No. 12). 250p. 2000. pap. text 45.00 (*0-85199-335-4*) OUP.

Peppers, Cracklings & Knots of Wool Cookbook: The Global Migration of African Cuisine. Diane M. Spivey. LC 99-26846. 384p. (C). 1999. text 29.50 (*0-7914-4375-2*, Suny Pr) State U NY Pr.

***Peppers, Cracklings & Knots of Wool Cookbook: The Global Migration of African Cuisine.** Diane M. Spivey. LC 99-26846. (C). 2000. pap. text 24.95 (*0-7914-4376-0*) State U NY Pr.

Peppers Hot & Chili. Georgeanne Brennan. 1988. pap. 9.95 (*0-943186-28-5*) Aris Bks.

Peppers, Hot & Sweet: Over 100 Recipes for All Tastes. Beth Dooley. Ed. by Constance Oxley. LC 90-55044. (Illus.). 144p. (Orig.). 1990. 16.95 (*0-88266-622-3*, Garden Way Pub) Storey Bks.

Pepper's Journal: A Kitten's First Year. Stuart J. Murphy. LC 98-47523. (Illus.). 40p. (YA). (gr. 1-4). 2000. pap. 4.95 (*0-06-446723-6*) HarpC.

Pepper's Journal: A Kitten's First Year. Stuart J. Murphy. LC 98-47523. (MathStart Ser.). (Illus.). 40p. (YA). (gr. 3-7). 2000. lib. bdg. 15.89 (*0-06-027619-3*) HarpC.

Pepper's Journal: A Kitten's First Year. Stuart J. Murphy. LC 98-47523. (MathStart Ser. 2). (Illus.). 40p. (YA). (ps-3). 2000. 15.95 (*0-06-027618-5*) HarpC.

Peppers Love Herbs. Ruth Bass. LC 96-15283. (Illus.). 64p. 1996. 9.95 (*0-88266-932-X*, Storey Pub) Storey Bks.

Peppers of the World: An Identification Guide. Dave DeWitt & Paul W. Bosland. LC 96-15364. (Illus.). 219p. (Orig.). 1997. pap. 19.95 (*0-89815-840-0*) Ten Speed Pr.

***Peppers, Peppers, Peppers: Jalapeno, Chipotle, Serrano, Sweet Bell, Poblano & More - In a Riot of Color & Flavor.** Marlena Spieler. (Illus.). 144p. 1999. pap. 19.95 (*1-55209-319-0*) Firefly Bks Ltd.

***Peppers, Popcorn & Pizza: The Science of Food.** Contrib. by Celeste A. Peters. LC 99-10179. (Science at Work Ser.). (Illus.). (J). 2000. lib. bdg. write for info. (*0-7398-0136-8*) Raintree Steck-V.

Peppy Learns to Play Baseball. Pete Heller. Ed. by Thomas D. Kinsey. (Peppy Learns to Play Ser.). (Illus.). 32p. (J). (gr. k-5). pap. 3.95 (*0-932423-00-0*) Summa Bks.

***Peppy, Phlox & the Postman.** Marisol Sarrazin & David Homel. LC 99-900660. (Little Wolf Bks.). (Illus.). 32p. (gr. 1 up). 1999. pap. 5.95 (*1-894363-08-6*) Doml & Friends.

Peppy's Rescue. Kathryn Dahlstrom. (Good News Club Ser.). (J). (gr. 4-11). Date not set. pap. 4.99 (*1-55976-826-6*) CEF Press.

Pepsi: Cola Bottles: Collectors Guide. James C. Ayers. (Illus.). 148p. 1995. ring bd. 29.50 (*0-9645443-0-X*) RJM Enter.

Pepsi Challenge: From 12 Full Ounces to a New Generation, 100 Years of Pepsi History. Ralph Roberts. LC 96-31414. (Illus.). 320p. 1998. pap. text 14.95 (*1-57090-008-6*) Alexander Dist.

Pepsi-Cola Collectibles, Vol. III. 2nd rev. ed. Bill Behling & Michael Hunt. (Illus.). 156p. 1994. pap. 17.95 (*0-89538-021-8*) L-W Inc.

Pepsi-Cola Collectibles: The Everett Lloyd Book. Mary Lloyd. LC 93-85216. (Illus.). 160p. 1993. pap. 29.95 (*0-88740-533-9*) Schiffer.

Pepsi Generations. Paul Bates et al. (Illus.). 164p. (Orig.). 1992. reprint ed. pap. 14.00 (*1-56046-130-6*) Interact Pubs.

***Pepsi Memorabilia Then & Now: Unauthorized Handbook & Price Guide.** Phillip Dillman & Larry Woestman. (Illus.). 144p. 2000. pap. 29.95 (*0-7643-1105-0*) Schiffer.

Pepsi Now & Then: A History of Pepsi-Cola Print Advertising. Bob Stoddard. (Illus.). 208p. 1999. 29.95 (*0-9654016-1-8*) Double Dot.

Pepsi Safety Progress Review. 254p. (Orig.). Date not set. spiral bd. write for info. (*0-88061-168-5*) Intl Loss Cntrl.

***Peptic Nucleic Acids: Protocols & Applications.** Ed. by Peter E. Nielsen & Michael Egholm. LC 99-494986. 1999. 119.99 (*1-898486-16-6*, Pub. by Horizon Sci) Intl Spec Bk.

Peptic Secretion. F. Di Mario et al. (Advances in Gastroenterology Ser.: No. 1). 116p. text 32.00 (*1-57235-017-2*) Piccin Nuova.

Peptic Secretion. F. Di Mario et al. (Advances in Gastroenterology Ser.: Vol. 1). (Illus.). 116p. 1985. text 36.00 (*88-299-0408-2*, Pub. by Piccin Nuova) Gordon & Breach.

Peptic Ulcer Disease: Investigation & Basis for Therapy. Ed. by Edward A. Swabb & Sandor Szabor. (Clinical Pharmacology Ser.: Vol. 17). (Illus.). 552p. 1991. text 225.75 (*0-8247-8226-7*) Dekker.

Peptic Ulcer Disease & Other Acid-Related Disorders. David Zakim & Andrew J. Dannenberg. (Illus.). 384p. 1991. pap. text. write for info. (*0-9629180-0-8*) Acad Rsch Assocs.

Peptic Ulcer Diseases: Basic & Clinical Aspects. G. F. Nelis et al. (Developments in Gastroenterology Ser.). 1985. text 237.50 (*0-89838-759-0*) Kluwer Academic.

Peptide Analysis Protocols. Ed. by Michael W. Pennington & Ben M. Dunn. LC 94-22663. (Methods in Molecular Biology Ser.: Vol. 36). (Illus.). 352p. 1994. 89.50 (*0-89603-274-4*) Humana.

Peptide & Protein Drug Delivery. H. L. Vincent Lee. (Advances in Parenteral Sciences Ser.: Vol. 4). (Illus.). 912p. 1990. text 250.00 (*0-8247-7896-0*) Dekker.

Peptide & Protein Reviews, 4 vols., Vol. 1. Ed. by Milton T. Hearn. LC 83-647692. (Illus.). 255p. 1983. reprint ed. pap. 79.10 (*0-7837-0612-X*, 204096000001) Bks Demand.

Peptide & Protein Reviews, 4 vols., Vol. 2. Ed. by Milton T. Hearn. LC 83-647692. (Illus.). 311p. 1984. reprint ed. pap. 96.50 (*0-7837-0613-8*, 204096000002) Bks Demand.

Peptide & Protein Reviews, 4 vols., Vol. 3. Ed. by Milton T. Hearn. LC 83-647692. (Illus.). 239p. 1989. reprint ed. pap. 74.10 (*0-7837-0614-6*, 204096000003) Bks Demand.

Peptide & Protein Reviews, 4 vols., Vol. 4. Ed. by Milton T. Hearn. LC 83-647692. (Illus.). 271p. 1984. reprint ed. pap. 84.10 (*0-7837-0615-4*, 204096000004) Bks Demand.

Peptide Antibiotics. Ed. by Horst Kleinkauf & Hans Von Dohren. (Illus.). 479p. 1982. 173.10 (*3-11-008484-8*) De Gruyter.

Peptide Antigens: A Practical Approach. Ed. by G. B. Wisdom. LC 94-11639. (The Practical Approach Ser.: No. 144). (Illus.). 272p. 1995. pap. text 49.95 (*0-19-963451-3*); spiral bd. 95.00 (*0-19-963452-1*) OUP.

Peptide-Based Drug Design: Controlling Transport & Metabolism. Ed. by Michael D. Taylor & Gordon L. Amidon. LC 94-40969. (Professional Reference Book Ser.). (Illus.). 650p. 1995. text 110.00 (*0-8412-3058-7*, Pub. by Am Chemical) OUP.

Peptide Biosynthesis & Processing. Lloyd Fricker. 288p. 1991. lib. bdg. 140.00 (*0-8493-8852-X*, QP552) CRC Pr.

Peptide Chemistry. M. Bodanszky. (Illus.). 240p. 1988. pap. 33.00 (*0-387-18984-X*) Spr-Verlag.

Peptide Chemistry: A Practical Textbook. rev. ed. Miklos Bodanszky. LC 93-26806. (Illus.). 220p. 1993. pap. text. write for info. (*3-540-56675-9*) Spr-Verlag.

Peptide Chemistry: A Practical Textbook. 2nd rev. ed. Miklos Bodanszky. LC 93-26806. (Illus.). 220p. 1993. 38.95 (*0-387-56675-9*) Spr-Verlag.

Peptide Chemistry 1992. N. Yanaihara. 1993. text 312.00 (*90-72199-17-0*) Kluwer Academic.

Peptide Drug Delivery to the Brain. William M. Pardridge. LC 91-7861. (Illus.). 367p. 1991. reprint ed. pap. 113.80 (*0-608-07215-X*, 206744000009) Bks Demand.

Peptide Growth Factors, Pt. C. Ed. by John N. Abelson et al. (Methods in Enzymology Ser.: Vol. 198). (Illus.). 578p. 1991. text 115.00 (*0-12-182099-8*) Acad Pr.

Peptide Growth Factors, Pt. A. Ed. by Sidney P. Colowick et al. (Methods in Enzymology Ser.: Vol. 146). 452p. 1987. text 157.00 (*0-12-182046-7*) Acad Pr.

Peptide Growth Factors, Pt. B. Ed. by Sidney P. Colowick et al. (Methods in Enzymology Ser.: Vol. 147). 487p. 1987. text 157.00 (*0-12-182047-5*) Acad Pr.

Peptide Growth Factors & Their Receptors, 2 vols. Ed. by Michael B. Sporn & A. B. Roberts. (Illus.). 1577p. 1993. 130.00 (*0-387-97729-5*) Spr-Verlag.

Peptide Growth Factors & Their Receptors I. Ed. by Michael B. Sporn & A. B. Roberts. (Handbook of Experimental Pharmacology Ser.: Vol. 95). (Illus.). 785p. 1990. 292.90 (*0-387-51184-9*) Spr-Verlag.

Peptide Hormone Receptors. Ed. by M. Y. Kalimi & J. R. Hubbard. viii, 720p. (Orig.). 1987. lib. bdg. 238.50 (*3-11-010759-7*) De Gruyter.

Peptide Hormone Secreting Tumors. Ed. by X. Bertagna. (Journal: Hormone Research Ser.: Vol. 32, 1-3, 1989). (Illus.). viii, 166p. 1990. pap. 101.00 (*3-8055-5167-3*) S Karger.

Peptide Hormone Secretion - Peptide Hormone Action: A Practical Approach, 2 vols. Ed. by K. Siddle & J. C. Hutton. (The Practical Approach Ser.: Nos. 71 & 72). (Illus.). 648p. 1991. 140.00 (*0-19-963072-0*) OUP.

Peptide Hormones: Effects & Mechanisms of Action, Vol. 1. Ed. by Andrea Negro-Vilar & P. Michael Conn. LC 87-35530. 272p. 1988. 167.00 (*0-8493-6719-0*, QP572, CRC Reprint) Franklin.

Peptide Hormones: Effects & Mechanisms of Action, Vol. II. Ed. by Andrea Negro-Vilar & P. Michael Conn. 224p. 1988. 148.00 (*0-8493-6720-4*, CRC Reprint) Franklin.

Peptide Hormones: Effects & Mechanisms of Action, Vol. 3. Andrea Negro-Vilar & P. Michael Conn. 224p. 1988. 125.00 (*0-8493-6721-2*, CRC Reprint) Franklin.

Peptide Hormones As Prohormones: Processing, Biological Activity, Pharmacology. Ed. by Jean Martinez. 1989. text 115.00 (*0-470-21262-4*) P-H.

***Peptide Receptors.** Ed. by R. Quirion et al. 1999. write for info. (*0-444-82972-5*, Excerpta Medica) Elsevier.

Peptide Science, Present & Future. Yasutsugu Shimonishi. LC 98-36874. 1998. 540.00 (*0-7923-5271-8*) Kluwer Academic.

Peptide Synthesis. 2nd ed. Miklos Bodanszky et al. LC 76-16099. (Illus.). 224p. reprint ed. pap. 69.50 (*0-7837-3430-1*, 205775100008) Bks Demand.

Peptide Synthesis Protocols. Ed. by Michael W. Pennington & Ben M. Dunn. LC 94-26326. (Methods in Molecular Biology Ser.: Vol. 35). (Illus.). 336p. 1994. spiral bd. 79.50 (*0-89603-273-6*) Humana.

Peptide Transport & Hydrolysis. Symposium on Peptide Transport & Hydrolysis (1976:. LC 77-8378. (Ciba Foundation Symposium: New Ser.: No. 50). 395p. reprint ed. pap. 122.50 (*0-608-16201-9*, 201464600093) Bks Demand.

Peptide Transport in Bacteria & Mammalian Cut. CIBA Foundation Staff. LC 72-76006. (Ciba Foundation Symposium: New Ser.: No. 4). 170p. reprint ed. pap. 52.70 (*0-608-13514-3*, 202213600024) Bks Demand.

Peptidergic Neuron. J. Joosse et al. (Progress in Brain Research Ser.: Vol. 92). 408p. 1992. 286.00 (*0-444-81457-4*) Elsevier.

Peptides. Ed. by Alan A. Boulton et al. LC 87-4064. (Neuromethods Ser.: Vol. 6). (Illus.). 509p. 1987. 125.00 (*0-89603-105-5*) Humana.

Peptides: A Target for New Drug Development. S. R. Bloom & G. Burstock. 160p. (C). 1991. 350.00 (*1-85271-056-X*, Pub. by IBC Tech Srvs) St Mut.

***Peptides: Biology & Chemistry.** James P. Tam. 312p. 2000. 140.00 (*0-7923-6279-9*, Kluwer Plenum) Kluwer Academic.

Peptides: Biology & Chemistry. Xiao-Jie Xu et al. LC 97-49018. (Chinese Peptide Symposia Ser.). 260p. 1998. write for info. (*0-7923-4963-6*) Kluwer Academic.

Peptides: Chemistry & Biochemistry; Proceedings of the 1st American Peptide Symposium, Yale University, Aug. 1968. Ed. by Boris Weinstein. LC 70-107760. 556p. reprint ed. pap. 172.40 (*0-608-14173-9*, 202151000022) Bks Demand.

Peptides: Chemistry-Biology-Interactions with Proteins. Ed. by Botond Penke & Angela Torok. 467p. (C). 1988. lib. bdg. 211.55 (*3-11-011546-8*) De Gruyter.

Peptides: Design, Synthesis, & Biological Activity. C. Basava & G. M. Anantharamaiah. 352p. 1994. 76.50 (*0-8176-3703-6*) Birkhauser.

Peptides: Directory of New Medical & Scientific Reviews with Subject Index. Science & Life Consultants Association Staff. 160p. 1995. 47.50 (*0-7883-0572-7*); pap. 44.50 (*0-7883-0573-5*) ABBE Pubs Assn.

Peptides: Frontiers of Peptide Science. James P. Tam & Pravin T. Kaumaya. LC 98-26533. lxii, 871 p. 1999. write for info. (*0-7923-5160-6*) Kluwer Academic.

Peptides: Integrators of Cell & Tissue Function. Ed. by Floyd E. Bloom et al. LC 79-65140. (Society of General Physiologists Ser.: No. 35). 271p. 1980. reprint ed. pap. 84.10 (*0-7837-9524-6*, 206027300005) Bks Demand.

Peptides: Synthesis, Structures, & Applications. Ed. by Bernd Gutte. (Illus.). 511p. 1995. text 79.00 (*0-12-310920-5*) Acad Pr.

Peptides - Chemistry & Biology: Proceedings of the 12th American Peptide Symposium, June 16-21, 1991, Cambridge, Massachusetts, U. S. A. Ed. by John A. Smith & Jean E. Rivier. 1048p. (C). 1992. text 495.00 (*90-72199-12-X*, Pub. by Escom Sci Pubs) Kluwer Academic.

Peptides - Chemistry, Structure & Biology: Proceedings of the 11th American Peptide Symposium, July 9-14, 1989, La Jolla, California, U. S. A. Ed. by Jean E. Rivier & Garland R. Marshall. 1168p. (C). 1990. text 475.00 (*90-72199-06-5*, Pub. by Escom Sci Pubs) Kluwer Academic.

Peptides - Chemistry, Structure & Biology: Proceedings of the 13th American Peptide Symposium, June 20-25, 1993, Edmonton, Alberta, Canada. Ed. by Robert S. Hodges & John A. Smith. 1174p. (C). 1994. text 534.00 (*90-72199-19-7*, Pub. by Escom Sci Pubs) Kluwer Academic.

Peptides & Proteases - Recent Advances: Selected Papers Presented at the 2nd International Meeting on the Molecular & Cellular Regulation of Enzyme Activity, Halle, GDR, August 17-23, 1986. R. L. Schowen & A. Barth. (Advances in the Biosciences Ser.: Vol. 67). 304p. 1987. 139.00 (*0-08-035726-1*, Pergamon Pr) Elsevier.

Peptides & Protein Phosphorylation. Ed. by Kemp. 336p. 1990. lib. bdg. 259.00 (*0-8493-6530-9*, QP552) CRC Pr.

Peptides As Probes in Muscle Research. Ed. by Johann C. Ruegg. (Illus.). 188p. 1991. 119.95 (*0-387-53653-1*) Spr-Verlag.

Peptides Biology & Chemistry. Du. 352p. 1993. text 154.00 (*90-72199-18-9*) Kluwer Academic.

Peptides Biology & Chemistry. Lu. 1995. text 166.00 (*90-72199-20-0*) Kluwer Academic.

***Peptides for the New Millennium: Proceedings of the 16th American Peptide Symposium, June 16-July 1, 1999, Minneapolis, Minnesota, U. S. A.** American Peptide Symposium Staff et al. LC 00-41098. 2000. write for info. (*0-7923-6445-7*) Kluwer Academic.

Peptides, Hormones & Behavior. Ed. by Charles B. Nemeroff & A. J. Dunn. (Illus.). 944p. 1984. text 150.00 (*0-88331-174-7*) R B Luce.

Peptides in Mammalian Protein Metabolism: Tissue Utilisation & Clinical Targetting. Ed. by G. Grimble & C. Backwell. (Portland Press Proceedings Ser.: Vol. 11). 200p. (C). 1997. text 93.50 (*1-85578-104-2*, Pub. by Portland Pr Ltd) Ashgate Pub Co.

Peptides in Oncology Vol. 153: Somatostatin & LH-RH Analogues. Ed. by K. Hoffken & R. Kath. LC 98-36682. (Recent Results in Cancer Research Ser.: Vol. 153). (Illus.). 85p. 1999. 119.00 (*3-540-64429-6*) Spr-Verlag.

Peptides in Oncology 1. Ed. by K. Hoffken et al. (Recent Results in Cancer Research Ser.: Vol. 124). (Illus.). xi, 141p. 1992. 72.00 (*0-387-55287-1*) Spr-Verlag.

Peptides in Oncology 2: Somatostatin Analogues & Bombesin Antagonists. Ed. by K. Hoffken. LC 93-13134. (Recent Results in Cancer Research Ser.: Vol. 129). 1993. 89.00 (*0-387-56669-4*) Spr-Verlag.

Peptides, 1988: Proceedings of the 20th European Peptide Symposium, September 4-9, 1988, University of Tuebingen, Tuebingen, Federal Republic of Germany. lx, 795p. (C). 1989. lib. bdg. 296.95 (*3-11-010949-2*) De Gruyter.

Peptides, 1982: Proceedings of the 17th European Peptide Symposium, Prague, Czechoslovakia, August 29-September 3, 1982. Ed. by K Blaha & P. Malon. (Illus.). 846p. 1982. 253.85 (*3-11-009574-2*) De Gruyter.

Peptides, 1986: Proceedings of the Nineteenth European Peptide Symposium. Ed. by D. Theodoropoulos. xix, 684p. (C). 1987. lib. bdg. 246.15 (*3-11-010687-6*) De Gruyter.

Peptides 1990. Giralt. 955p. 1991. text 331.50 (*90-72199-08-1*) Kluwer Academic.

Peptides 1992. Scheider. 1056p. 1993. text 361.50 (*90-72199-16-2*) Kluwer Academic.

Peptides 1994. Maia. 1000p. 1995. text 349.50 (*90-72199-21-9*) Kluwer Academic.

Peptidomimetics Protocols. Wieslaw M. Kazmierski. LC 98-26947. (Methods in Molecular Medicine Ser.: Vol. 23). (Illus.), 576p. 1998. 99.50 (*0-89603-517-4*) Humana.

Peptidyl-Prolyl Cis/Trans Isomerases: Protein Profile. Andrezj Galat & Sylvie Riviere. (Protein Profile Ser.). (Illus.). 130p. 1999. pap. text 45.00 (*0-19-850288-5*) OUP.

Peptolide & Macromolecular Antibiotics see Handbook of Antibiotic Compounds

Pepys Anthology. Samuel Pepys. Ed. by Robert Latham & Linnet Latham. 350p. 1988. 34.95 (*0-520-06354-6*, Pub. by U CA Pr) Cal Prin Full Svc.

Pepys Anthology. Samuel Pepys. Tr. by Robert Latham & Linnet Latham. 350p. 2000. pap. 18.95 (*0-520-22167-2*, Pub. by U CA Pr) Cal Prin Full Svc.

Pepys Ballads, 5 vols., Vols. I-V. fac. ed. Samuel Pepys. Ed. by W. G. Day. 2327p. 1987. 985.00 (*0-85991-256-6*) Boydell & Brewer.

Pepys' Diary & the New Science. Marjorie H. Nicolson. LC 65-26012. (Illus.). 217p. reprint ed. pap. 67.30 (*0-8357-3139-1*, 203940200012) Bks Demand.

Pepys. Genealogy of the Pepys Family, 1273-1887. Walter C. Pepys. (Illus.). 102p. 1996. reprint ed. pap. 19.50 (*0-8328-5422-0*); reprint ed. lib. bdg. 29.50 (*0-8328-5421-2*) Higginson Bk Co.

Pepys Himself. Cecil S. Emden. LC 80-17177. 146p. 1980. reprint ed. lib. bdg. 52.50 (*0-313-22607-5*, EMPH, Greenwood Pr) Greenwood.

Pepys' Memoires of the Royal Navy. Samuel Pepys. LC 68-25260. (English Biography Ser.: No. 31). 1969. reprint ed. lib. bdg. 75.00 (*0-8383-0228-9*) M S G Haskell Hse.

Pepys of French India with a Foreword. Shafaat A. Khan. (C). 1991. 32.00 (*81-206-0623-X*, Pub. by Asian Educ Servs) S Asia.

Pepys on the Restoration Stage. Samuel Pepys. Ed. by Helen McAfee. LC 63-23195. (Illus.). 1972. 20.95 (*0-405-08848-5*) Ayer.

Pepys, 1683-1689 Vol. III: The Saviour of the Navy. Arthur Bryant. 367p. 1985. pap. 10.00 (*0-586-06472-9*) Academy Chi Pubs.

Pepys, 1669-1683 Vol. II: The Years of Peril. Arthur Bryant. 365p. 1985. pap. 10.00 (*0-586-06471-0*) Academy Chi Pubs.

An Asterisk (*) at the beginning of an entry indicates that the title is appearing for the first time.

Pepys, 1633-1669 Vol. I: The Man in the Making. Arthur Bryant. 334p. 1985. pap. 10.00 (*0-586-06470-2*) Academy Chi Pubs.

Pepysian Garland: Black-Letter Broadside Ballads of the Years 1595-1639, Chiefly from the Collection of Samuel Pepys. Samuel Pepys. Ed. by Hyder E. Rollins. LC 74-176041. (Illus.). 527p. 1971. 32.50 (*0-674-66185-0*) HUP.

Pequena Cronica de Grandes Dias (A Small Chronicle of Great Days) Octavio Paz. (SPA.). 172p. 1990. pap. 9.99 (*968-16-3458-6*, Pub. by Fondo) Continental Bk.

Pequena Enciclopedia de Hierbas (Little Herb Encyclopedia) Jack Ritchason. (SPA.). Date not set. pap. 7.95 (*1-885670-63-X*) Woodland UT.

Pequena Enciclopedia de Hierbas (Little Herb Encyclopedia) Jack Ritchason. 228p. 1992. pap. text 6.95 (*0-913923-00-1*) Woodland UT.

Pequena Enciclopedia Tematica Larousse en Color. Small Thematic Larousse Encyclopedia in Color, 2 vols. Larousse Staff & Ramon Garcia-Pelayo. 1096p. 1978. 175.00 (*0-8288-5260-X*, S30235) Fr & Eur.

Pequena Gran Mujer en la China. Gladys Aylward. Orig. Title: Little Woman in China. (SPA.). 160p. 1974. pap. 4.99 (*0-8254-1048-7*, Edit Portavoz) Kregel.

***Pequena Jija de Jairo.** Enid Blyton. (SPA.). 1999. pap. 4.99 (*0-8254-1068-1*, Edit Portavoz) Kregel.

Pequena Locomotora Que Si Pudo (The Little Engine That Could) Watty Piper. Tr. by Alma F. Ada. (SPA., Illus.). 48p. (J). (ps-6). 1992. 7.99 (*0-448-41096-6*, Plat & Munk) Peng Put Young Read.

***Pequena Mentira (One Small Lie)** Barbara McCauley. (Deseo Ser.). (SPA.). 2000. mass mkt. 3.50 (*0-373-35360-X*, 1-35360-6) Harlequin Bks.

Pequena the Burro. Jami Parkison. LC 93-30377. (Key Concepts in Personal Development Ser.). (Illus.). 32p. (J). (gr. k-4). 1994. teacher ed. 79.95 incl. VHS (*1-55942-058-8*, 9376) Marsh Media.

Pequena the Burro. Jami Parkison. LC 93-30377. (Key Concepts in Personal Development Ser.). (Illus.). 32p. (J). (gr. 1-4). 1994. 16.95 (*1-55942-055-3*, 7657) Marsh Media.

***Pequenas Cosas De Dios.** Jose Maria Gironella. (SPA.). 159p. 1999. pap. 18.95 (*84-270-2443-6*) Planeta.

Pequenas Infamias. Carmen Posadas. LC 99-164545. (Autores Espanoles E Iberoamericanos Ser.). 1999. 24.95 (*84-08-02847-2*) Planeta Edit.

Pequenas Muertes. Anita Arroyo. LC 91-77115. (Coleccion Caniqui). (SPA.). 144p. (Orig.). 1992. pap. 16.00 (*0-89729-629-X*) Ediciones.

Pequenines: Libro de Historias Biblicas. John Walton & Kim Walton. Ed. by Jeannie Harmon.Tr. of Tiny Tots Bible Story Book. (SPA., Illus.). 428p. (J). (gr. 1-3). 1994. pap. write for info. (*0-7814-0161-5*) Chariot Victor.

Pequenines: Los Libro de Historias Biblicas. Walton.Tr. of Tiny Tots Bible Stories Book. (SPA.). (J). write for info. (*0-614-27107-X*) Editorial Unilit.

Pequenines: Los Libro de Historias Biblicas - The Tiny Tots Bible Stories Book. Walton. (SPA.). (J). write for info. (*0-614-24393-9*) Editorial Unilit.

Pequeno - Manzano: Spanish Take-Home Parent Pack, Set. (Take-Home Parent Packs Ser.). (SPA., Illus.). (Orig.). 1993. pap. 16.95 incl. audio (*1-56334-384-3*) Hampton-Brown.

Pequeno Canto a los Mios (Poemario) Efren Rivera Ramos. LC 87-25562. 72p. 1987. pap. 5.00 (*0-8477-3236-3*) U of PR Pr.

Pequeno Coala Busca Casa. Lada J. Kratky. (Cuento Mas Ser.). (SPA., Illus.). 24p. (Orig.). (J). (gr. k-3). 1989. pap. text 6.00 (*0-917837-14-2*) Hampton-Brown.

Pequeno Coala Busca Casa (Big Book) Lada J. Kratky. (Un Cuento Mas Ser.). (SPA., Illus.). 24p. (Orig.). (J). (gr. k-3). 1989. pap. text 29.95 (*0-917837-12-6*) Hampton-Brown.

Pequeno Coco. Serena Romanelli. Tr. by Blanca Rosa Lamas. LC 98-37181. (Illus.). 32p. (J). (gr. k-3). 1999. 15.95 (*0-7358-1121-0*, Pub. by North-South Bks NYC) Chronicle Bks.

Pequeno Coco. Serena Romanelli. Tr. by Blanca Rosas Lamas. LC 98-37181. (Illus.). 32p. (J). (gr. k-3). 1999. pap. 6.95 (*0-7358-1122-9*, Pub. by North-South Bks NYC) Chronicle Bks.

***Pequeno Cowboy.** Sue Heap. 1998. 17.95 (*84-88342-13-6*) SA Kokinos.

Pequeno Diccionario de Teatro Mundial. Genoveva Dieterich. (SPA.). 294p. 1976. pap. 19.95 (*0-8288-5748-2*, S31395) Fr & Eur.

Pequeno Diccionario Espanol-Polaco, Polaco-Espanol. A. Marti et al. (POL & SPA.). 707p. 1991. 24.95 (*0-8288-5749-0*, S32367) Fr & Eur.

Pequeno Diccionario Kapelusz de la Lengua Espanola. Cincel Staff. (SPA.). 612p. 1980. pap. 9.95 (*0-8288-2025-2*, S32728) Fr & Eur.

Pequeno Diccionario Medico Practico: Small Practical Medical Dictionary. 8th ed. Pierre Neuville. (SPA.). 240p. 1987. pap. 10.95 (*0-7859-4945-3*) Fr & Eur.

Pequeno Espasa. 4th ed. (SPA., Illus.). 1472p. 1989. 119.50 (*84-239-6896-0*) Elliots Bks.

Pequeno Espasa. 4th ed. Espasa Staff. (SPA.). 1400p. 1989. lib. bdg. 125.00 (*0-8288-2724-9*) Fr & Eur.

Pequeno Gigante de la Cancion. Ned Nelson. (SPA.). 1998. pap. 6.99 (*0-8297-0372-1*) Zondervan.

***Pequeno Larousse: Ilustrado 2001.** (Illus.). 1794p. 2000. 39.95 (*970-22-0010-5*, Larousse LKC) LKC.

Pequeno Larousse en Color. (SPA.). 1996. 95.00 (*0-7859-9869-1*) Fr & Eur.

Pequeno Larousse Illustrado. Ramon Garcia-Pelayo. (SPA.). 1692p. 1988. 49.95 (*2-03-450173-X*, S12289) Fr & Eur.

Pequeno Larousse Illustrado. Ramon Garcia-Pelayo & Ramon G. Gross. (SPA.). 1692p. 1988. 49.95 (*0-8288-4049-0*, S12289) Fr & Eur.

Pequeno Larousse Illustrado, 1996. Ed. by Larousse Staff. 1776p. 1996. 49.95 (*0-7859-9804-7*) Fr & Eur.

Pequeno Larousse Ilustrado: 1999 Edition. Ed. by Larousse Staff. (Illus.). 1998. 39.95 (*970-607-778-2*) LKC.

Pegueno Larousse Ilustrado, 2000. Larousse. (Illus.). 1794p. 1999. 39.95 (*970-607-910-6*, Larousse LKC) LKC.

Pequeno Larousse Ilustrado 1999. annuals Ed. by Larousse Editorial Staff. (SPA.). 49.95 (*0-320-03691-X*) Fr & Eur.

Pequeno Libro de la Navidad. M. Chamberlain.Tr. of Little Christmas Concertina Book. (SPA.). 30p. (J). 1986. 2.99 (*1-56063-270-4*, 494010) Editorial Unilit.

***Pequeno Libro Devocional de Dios Para Mujeres.** (SPA.). 2000. pap. 10.99 (*0-7899-0717-8*) Spanish Hse Distributors.

***Pequeno Libro Devocional de Dios Para Ninos.** V. Gilbert Beers. (SPA.). (J). (gr. 4-7). 2000. 10.99 (*0-7899-0718-6*) Spanish Hse Distributors.

***Pequeno Michaelis Dicionario Alemao-Portugues/ Portugues-Alemao.** Michaelis. 1999. pap. 18.95 (*85-06-01622-3*) Midwest European Pubns.

***Pequeno Michaelis Dicionario Espanhol-Portugues/ Portugues-Espanhol.** Michaelis. 1999. pap. 18.95 (*85-06-01344-5*) Midwest European Pubns.

***Pequeno Michaelis Dicionario Frances-Portugues/ Portugues-Frances.** Michaelis. 1999. pap. 18.95 (*85-06-01674-6*) Midwest European Pubns.

***Pequeno Michaelis Dicionario Italiano-Portugues/ Portugues-Italiano.** Michaelis. 1999. pap. 18.95 (*85-06-01621-5*) Midwest European Pubns.

Pequeno Rey de las Flores. Kveta Pacovska. LC 95-38557. (SPA., Illus.). 40p. (J). (gr. k-3). 1996. 15.95 (*1-55858-538-9*, Pub. by North-South Bks NYC) Chronicle Bks.

***Pequeno Secreto.** Megan McKinney.Tr. of Small Secret. (SPA.). 2000. per. 3.50 (*0-373-35327-8*) Harlequin Bks.

Pequenos Triunfos: Ayyy! Scandinavia.Tr. of Tiny Triumphs: Double Ugh!. (SPA.). 23p. (J). 1992. write for info. (*0-614-27108-8*) Editorial Unilit.

Pequenos Triunfos: Ayyyy! Scandinavia Staff.Tr. of Tiny Triumphs: Double Ugh!. (SPA.). (J). 1992. 3.99 (*1-56063-587-8*, 490825) Editorial Unilit.

Pequenos Triunfos: Buenos Modales en la Mesa. Scandinavia.Tr. of Tiny Triumphs: Boss of the Table Manners. (SPA.). 23p. (J). 1992. 3.99 (*1-56063-585-1*, 490823) Editorial Unilit.

Pequenos Triunfos: El Lobo Invisible. Scandinavia.Tr. of Tiny Triumphs: The Wolf Who Wasn't. (SPA.). 23p. (J). 1992. write for info. (*0-614-27109-6*) Editorial Unilit.

Pequenos Triunfos: El Lobo Invisible. Scandinavia Staff.Tr. of Tiny Triumphs: The Wolf Who Wasn't. (SPA.). (J). 1992. 3.99 (*1-56063-584-3*, 490822) Editorial Unilit.

Pequenos Triunfos: Los Nuevos Oidos. Scandinavia.Tr. of Tiny Triumphs: The New Ears. (SPA.). 23p. (J). 1992. write for info. (*0-614-27110-X*) Editorial Unilit.

Pequenos Triunfos: Los Nuevos Oidos. Scandinavia Staff.Tr. of Tiny Triumphs: The New Ears. (SPA.). (J). 1992. 3.99 (*1-56063-583-5*, 490821) Editorial Unilit.

Pequenos Triunfos: Por Favor, Querida Mama. Scandinavia.Tr. of Tiny Triumphs: Wonderful Mommy. (SPA.). 23p. (J). 1992. 3.99 (*1-56063-582-7*, 490820) Editorial Unilit.

Pequenos Triunfos: Puede Dios Ver el Viento? Scandinavia.Tr. of Tiny Triumphs: Does God See the Wind?. (SPA.). 23p. (J). 1992. write for info. (*0-614-27111-8*) Editorial Unilit.

Pequenos Triunfos: Puede Dios Ver el Viento? Scandinavia Staff.Tr. of Tiny Triumphs: Does God See the Wind?. (SPA.). (J). 1992. 3.99 (*1-56063-586-X*, 490824) Editorial Unilit.

Pequot War. Alfred A. Cave. LC 95-47282. (Native Americans of the Northeast Ser.). 232p. 1996. pap. 15.95 (*1-55849-030-2*); text 45.00 (*1-55849-029-9*) U of Mass Pr.

***Pequots.** Shirlee Petkin Newman. (Indians of the Americas Library). (Illus.). (YA). 2000. pap. 8.95 (*0-531-16482-9*) Watts.

Pequots in Southern New England: The Fall & Rise of an American Indian Nation. Laurence M. Hauptman. LC 90-50235. (Illus.). 288p. 1993. pap. 15.95 (*0-8061-2515-2*) U of Okla Pr.

Pequots in Southern New England: The Fall & Rise of an American Indian Nation. Shirlee Petkin Newman. LC 99-13702. 2000. 24.00 (*0-531-20327-1*) Watts.

Per. see Fundamentals of Islamic Thought: God, Man & the Universe

Per & the Dala Horse. Rebecca Hickox. LC 93-38596. (Illus.). 32p. (J). (ps-3). 1995. 15.95 (*0-385-32075-2*, DD Bks Yng Read) BDD Bks Young Read.

Per & the Dala Horse. Rebecca Hickox. (Illus.). 32p. (J). (ps-3). 1997. pap. 5.99 (*0-440-41425-3*) BDD Bks Young Read.

Per & the Dala Horse. Rebecca Hickox. (Picture Yearling Book Ser.). 1997. 11.19 (*0-606-12790-9*, Pub. by Turtleback) Demco.

Per Ardua: The Rise of British Air Power 1911-1939. Hillary S. Saunders. LC 79-169436. (Literature & History of Aviation Ser.). 1972. reprint ed. 26.95 (*0-405-03781-3*) Ayer.

Per Axel Rydberg: A Biography, Bibliography & List of His Taxa. Arnold Tiehm & Franz A. Stafleu. LC 89-29406. (Memoirs Ser.: No. 58). (Illus.). 84p. 1990. pap. text 10.00 (*0-89327-351-1*) NY Botanical.

Per Capita Fibre Consumption, 1971-1973: Cotton, Wool, Flax, Silk & Man-Made Fibres see Per Capita Fibre Consumption, 1967-1969: Cotton, Wool, Flax, Silk & Man-Made Fibres

Per Capita Fibre Consumption, 1967-1969: Cotton, Wool, Flax, Silk & Man-Made Fibres. United Nations Food & Agriculture Organization Staff. Incl. Per Capita Fibre Consumption, 1971-1973: Cotton, Wool, Flax, Silk & Man-Made Fibres. 18.75. 1975. pap. 16.00 1970. pap. write for info. (*0-685-12828-8*, F1187) Bernan Associates.

PER Handbook. rev. ed. (Illus.). 400p. 1992. 54.95 (*0-686-32574-5*) CLEA.

Per-Immigrant & Pioneer. E. Palmer Rockswold. 1982. pap. 6.95 (*0-934860-22-X*) Adventure Pubns.

Per Iodistas en los Paises Andinos. John Virtue. (SPA., Illus.). (C). 1995. pap. text 23.45 (*0-9644954-1-4*) Fl Internat Univ.

Per Jonson Rosio, the Agrarian Prophet: A Charismatic Leader's Attempt to Rejuvenate Small Agriculture & Create a Commitment to a Cultural Revolt Against Industrialism in Sweden, 1888-1928. John Toler. (Stockholm Studies in History: No. 47). 354p. (Orig.). 1992. pap. 65.00 (*91-22-01534-5*) Coronet Bks.

Per Kirkeby. (Illus.). 420p. 1986. 175.00 (*3-906127-12-5*, Pub. by Gachnang & Springer) Dist Art Pubs.

Per Kirkeby: Paintings & Drawings, 1982-1989. Helaine Posner. LC 91-50794. (Illus.). 48p. (Orig.). 1991. pap. 15.00 (*0-938437-39-9*) MIT List Visual Arts.

Per Kirkeby: Works from the 60's. Antonsen Lasse. (Illus.). 50p. 1995. 25.00 (*1-885013-08-6*) M Werner.

Per Olof Sundman: Writer of the North, 7. Lars G. Warme. LC 83-26472. (Contributions to the Study of World Literature Ser.: No. 7). (Illus.). 217p. 1984. 49.95 (*0-313-24346-8*, WPS/, Greenwood Pr) Greenwood.

Per Olov Enquist: A Critical Study, 5. Ross Shideler. LC 83-22733. (Contributions to the Study of World Literature Ser.: No. 5). (Illus.). 186p. 1984. 49.95 (*0-313-24236-4*, SHI/, Greenwood Pr) Greenwood.

Per Questions & Answers Handbook. rev. ed. 1994. 19.95 (*0-686-32575-3*) CLEA.

Per Saecula, Pt. 1. H. McArdle & G. Suggitt. 1974. pap. text 10.84 (*0-582-36727-1*, 72516) Longman.

Per Saecula, Pt. 2. H. McArdle & G. Suggitt. 1974. pap. text 10.84 (*0-582-36728-X*, 72517) Longman.

Per Se Notum: Die Logische Beschaffenheit Des Selbstverstandlichen Im Denken Des Thomas Von Aquin. Luca Tuninetti. (Studien und Texte zur Geistesgeschichte des Mittelalters Ser.: No. 47). xii, 216p. 1995. 84.00 (*90-04-10368-6*) Brill Academic Pubs.

Per-sist-ent Ster-e-o-types. Pat Courtney. 1988. pap. 10.00 (*0-932526-19-5*) Nexus Pr.

(Per)Versions of Love & Hate. Renata Salecl. (Illus.). 184p. 1998. 22.00 (*1-85984-839-7*, Pub. by Verso) Norton.

(Per)Versions of Love & Hate. Renata Salecl. 180p. 2000. pap. 18.00 (*1-85984-236-4*, Pub. by Verso) Norton.

Perak Malays: Papers on Malay Subjects. Charles C. Brown. LC 77-87481. 128p. reprint ed. 32.50 (*0-404-16797-7*) AMS Pr.

Perak, the Abode of Grace: A Study of an Eighteen-Century Malay State. Barbara W. Andaya. (East Asian Historical Monographs). 1979. 34.00 (*0-19-580385-X*) OUP.

Peralta Barnuevo & the Discourse of Loyalty: A Critical Edition of Four Selected Texts. Jerry M. Williams. LC 96-24561. 216p. 1996. per. 25.00 (*0-87918-083-8*) ASU Lat Am St.

***Perambulations: The Search for a Self.** C. S. Back. 260p. 1999. 25.00 (*0-7388-0768-0*); pap. 18.00 (*0-7388-0769-9*) Xlibris Corp.

Peranakan Chinese Politics in Jaya, 1917-1942. 2nd ed. Leo Suryadinata. 211p. 1981. 42.00 (*9971-69-037-3*, Pub. by Sngapore Univ Pr) Coronet Bks.

Peranakan's Search for National Identity: Biographical Studies of Seven Indonesian Chinese. Leo Suryadinata. 144p. 1993. pap. 18.50 (*981-210-043-1*, Pub. by Times Academic) Intl Spec Bk.

Perason's Composition & Analysis of Foods. 9th ed. R. Kirk. 1991. 181.35 (*0-582-40910-1*, Pub. by Addison-Wesley) Longman.

Perazzi Shotguns. Karl C. Lippard. LC 93-61609. (Illus.). 121p. 1993. pap. 14.95 (*0-9611880-2-2*) Vietnam Mar.

Perce Judd: Man of Peace. Winifred Sarre. (Illus.). 176p. 1983. pap. 2.00 (*0-8309-0377-1*) Herald Pub Hse.

Perceive - Conceive - Achieve Pt. IV: Sustainable City, European Tetralogy, Aesthetics Functionality & Desirability of the Sustainable City. European Communities Staff. 198p. 1997. pap. 30.00 (*92-827-4923-1*, SY79-95-004-ENC, Pub. by Comm Europ Commun) Bernan Associates.

Perceive - Conceive - Achieve Sustainable City Pt. II: A European Tetralogy, SMES & the Revitalisation of the European Cities. 134p. 1996. pap. 30.00 (*92-827-4919-3*, SY79-95-002-ENC, Pub. by Comm Europ Commun) Bernan Associates.

Perceived Control & Motivation: Stress, Coping & Competence. Ellen A. Skinner. (Individual Differences & Development Ser.: 8). 192p. 1995. text 48.00 (*0-8039-5560-X*); pap. text 21.50 (*0-8039-5561-8*) Sage.

Perceived Effects of the Kentucky Instructional Results Information System (KIRIS) Daniel M. Koretz et al. LC 96-9748. 83p. 1996. pap. 9.00 (*0-8330-2435-3*, MR-792-PCT/FF) Rand Corp.

Perceived Exertion. Bruce Noble & Robert Robertson. LC 96-374. (Illus.). 336p. 1996. text 34.00 (*0-88011-508-4*, BNOB0508) Human Kinetics.

Perceived Images: U. S. & Soviet Assumptions & Perceptions in Disarmament. Daniel Frei. LC 85-14207. 344p. 1986. text 50.00 (*0-8476-7443-6*) Rowman.

Perceived Self: Ecological & Interpersonal Sources of Self Knowledge. Ed. by Ulric Neisser. (Emory Symposia in Cognition Ser.: No. 5). (Illus.). 333p. (C). 1994. text 54.95 (*0-521-41509-8*) Cambridge U Pr.

Perceived Usefulness of Financial Statements for Investors' Decisions. Lucia S. Chang & Kenneth S. Most. LC 84-25788. (Illus.). 141p. 1985. reprint ed. pap. 43.80 (*0-608-04477-6*, 206522200001) Bks Demand.

Perceiving & Behaving. Dale G. Lake. LC 72-77891. 116p. reprint ed. pap. 36.00 (*0-608-14858-X*, 202603800048) Bks Demand.

Perceiving & Remembering Faces. Ed. by G. Davies et al. LC 81-66698. 1981. text 157.00 (*0-12-206220-5*) Acad Pr.

Perceiving Animals: Humans & Beasts in Early Modern English Culture. Erica Fudge. LC 99-15589. 232p. 1999. text 59.95 (*0-312-22572-5*) St Martin.

Perceiving, Behaving, Becoming: Lessons Learned. H. Jerome Freiberg et al. LC 98-58125. 162p. 1999. pap. 20.95 (*0-87120-341-3*, 199031) ASCD.

***Perceiving Energy: Beyond the Physical Form.** Dawn E. Clark. LC 99-90425. (Illus.). 128p. 1999. pap. 12.95 (*1-928532-02-0*) Aarron Pubg.

Perceiving Events & Objects. Ed. by Gunnar Jansson et al. (Resources for Ecological Psychology Ser.). 544p. 1994. text 99.95 (*0-8058-1555-4*) L Erlbaum Assocs.

Perceiving God: The Epistemology of Religious Experience. William P. Alston. LC 91-55068. 336p. 1993. text 47.50 (*0-8014-2597-2*); pap. text 17.95 (*0-8014-8155-4*) Cornell U Pr.

Perceiving in Advaita Vedanta: Epistemological Analysis & Interpretation. Bina Gupta. LC 91-55126. 320p. 1991. 39.50 (*0-8387-5213-6*) Bucknell U Pr.

Perceiving India: Insight & Inquiry. Ed. by Geeti Sen. (Illus.). 286p. (C). 1993. text 49.95 (*0-8039-9138-X*) Sage.

***Perceiving Motherhood & Fatherhood: Swedish Working Parents with Young Children.** Clarissa Kugelberg. (Uppsala Studies in Cultural Anthropology: 26). 300p. 1999. pap. 32.50 (*91-554-4372-9*, Pub. by Uppsala Univ Acta Univ Upsaliensis) Coronet Bks.

Perceiving Other Worlds. Ed. by Edwin Thumboo. 448p. 1991. pap. 28.50 (*981-210-010-5*, Pub. by Times Academic) Intl Spec Bk.

Perceiving Other Worlds. Ed. by Edwin Thumboo. pap. 15.00 (*0-614-25210-5*, Pub. by Univ of West Aust Pr) Intl Spec Bk.

Perceiving Reality. Lily A. Hanes. Ed. by Donna Hagen. 170p. (Orig.). 1989. pap. 7.95 (*0-9623522-0-9*) Great Adventure Pub.

Perceiving Similarity & Comprehending Metaphor. Robin J. Hammeal & Marc H. Bornstein. Ed. by Lawrence E. Marks et al. (CDM 215 Ser.: Vol. 52, No. 1). vi, 108p. 1987. pap. text 15.00 (*0-226-50611-8*) U Ch Pr.

Perceiving Talking Faces: From Speech Perception to a Behavioral Principle. Dominic W. Massaro. LC 97-1575. (Cognitive Psychology Ser.). (Illus.). 507p. 1997. 60.00 (*0-262-13337-7*, Bradford Bks) MIT Pr.

***Perceiving the Arts.** 6th ed. Dennis J. Sporre. LC 99-30566. 245p. 1999. pap. text 36.25 (*0-13-022359-X*) P-H.

Perceiving the Elephant: Essays on Eyesight. Ed. by Frances L. Neer. LC 97-65992. 218p. 1998. pap. 14.95 (*0-88739-122-2*) Creat Arts Bk.

Perceiving the Wheel of God. Mark Hanby. 112p. (Orig.). 1994. pap. 9.99 (*1-56043-109-1*) Destiny Image.

Perceiving Thoughts. Kara J. Kissinger. (Illus.). 56p. 1997. pap. 11.00 (*0-9660836-0-1*) KJK Pub.

Perceiving Time: A Psychological Investigation with Men & Women. Thomas J. Cottle. LC 76-18768. 283p. reprint ed. pap. 87.80 (*0-8357-9950-6*, 201188300080) Bks Demand.

Perceiving, Understanding & Coping with the World Relations of Everyday Life. Chadwick F. Alger. Orig. Title: Internationaliation from Local Areas. 170p. (C). 1993. ring bd. 25.00 (*0-614-02999-6*) Amer Forum.

***Percent.** S. H. Collins. (Straight Forward Math Ser.). 39p. (J). (gr. 4-8). 2000. pap., wbk. ed. 3.95 (*0-931993-25-3*, GP-025) Garlic Pr OR.

Percent see Learn Math Quickly Series: Videotapes & Workbooks

Percent Concepts see Key to Percents Reproducible Tests

Percent Fat Calorie Tables. 2nd ed. Robert Stark. 48p. 1987. pap. text 5.00 (*0-9618415-1-6*) AZ Bariatric Phy.

Percent, Measurement & Formulas, Equations, Ratio & Proportion. James T. Fata. (Basic Essentials of Mathematics Ser.). 1997. pap., student ed. 10.56 (*0-8114-4669-7*) Raintree Steck-V.

Percent Water in a Hydrate. H. Anthony Neidig & James N. Spencer. (Modular Laboratory Program in Chemistry Ser.). 7p. (C). 1990. pap. text 1.50 (*0-87540-387-5*, ANAL 387-5) Chem Educ Res.

Percentage Points of Multivariate Student Distributions. Robert E. Bechhofer & Charles W. Dunnett. LC 74-6283. (Selected Tables in Mathematical Statistics Ser.: Vol. 11). 371p. 1988. text 58.00 (*0-8218-1911-9*, TABLES/11C) Am Math.

Percentages. Wood. (MB - Business/Vocational Math Ser.). 1993. pap. 5.95 (*0-538-70767-4*) S-W Pub.

Percents. Eichorn. 1996. pap. text 9.25 (*0-13-432907-4*) P-H.

Percents. J. L. McCabe. 1993. 4.95 (*1-55708-404-1*, MCR458) McDonald Pub Co.

Percents: Concepts & Operations. David Hudson. Ed. by Kathy Rogers. 32p. 1999. pap., wbk. ed. 3.99 (*1-56472-162-0*) Edupress Inc.

Percents & Applications see Basic Mathematics

Percents & Decimals, Bk. 3. Steven Rasmussen & David Rasmussen. 45p. 1988. pap. text 2.25 (*0-913684-59-7*) Key Curr Pr.

Percents & Fractions see Key to Percents Reproducible Tests

Percents & Proportions. 4th ed. Mary S. Charuhas. (Essential Mathematics for Life Ser.: No. 3). 1995. pap. text 7.95 (*0-02-802610-1*) Glencoe.

***Percents & Ratios.** Lucille Caron & Phil St. Jacques. (Math Success Ser.). (Illus.). 64p. (YA). (gr. 4-10). 2000. lib. bdg. 17.95 (*0-7660-1435-5*) Enslow Pubs.

Percents & Work Rates. Anita Harnadek. 32p. (Orig.). (YA). (gr. 9 up). 1988. pap. 6.95 (*0-89455-338-0*) Crit Think Bks.

P

***Percents 1999c: Globe Fearon Math.** 45p. 1998. write for info. (*0-13-023248-3*) S&S Trade.

***Percepcion Extrasensorial.** Ed. by Usborne Books Staff. (SPA., Illus.). 48p. (gr. 4-7). 2000. pap. 5.95 (*0-7460-3662-0*, Usborne) EDC.

Percepcion Remota. Jorge Lira. (Ciencia para Todos Ser.). (SPA.). pap. 6.99 (*968-16-2568-4*, Pub. by Fondo) Continental Bk.

Perceptanalysis. Z. A. Piotrowski. 523p. 1957. text 49.95 (*0-8058-0102-2*) L Erlbaum Assocs.

Perceptible Processes: Minimalism & the Barque. Ed. by Claudia Swan. (Illus.). 85p. 1997. 30.00 (*0-9648083-1-5*) Eos Music.

Perception. Ed. by Kathleen Akins. (Vancouver Series in Cognitive Science). 352p. 1996. pap. text 40.00 (*0-19-508462-4*) OUP.

Perception. Charles Bernstein et al. Ed. by Don Wellman. Tr. by David M. Guss. (Toward a New Poetics Ser.: Vol. 2). (Illus.). 224p. 1982. pap. 6.95 (*0-942030-02-8*) O ARS.

Perception. Ed. by R. Held et al. (Handbook of Sensory Physiology Ser.: Vol. 8). (Illus.). 1978. 211.00 (*0-387-08300-6*) Spr-Verlag.

Perception. Spencer Kope. 192p. 1994. 17.95 (*0-9638471-2-0*) WJC Pr.

Perception. Spencer Kope. 192p. 1994. pap. 10.95 (*0-9638471-3-9*) WJC Pr.

Perception. Howard Robinson. LC 93-49381. (Problems of Philosophy Series: Their Past & Present). 272p. (C). (gr. 13). 1994. 75.00 (*0-415-03364-0*, B4651) Routledge.

Perception. Irvin Rock. (Illus.). 243p. 1995. pap. text 19.95 (*0-7167-6011-8*) W H Freeman.

Perception. Ed. by Enrique Villanueva. (Philosophical Issues Ser.: No. 7). 384p. (C). 1996. pap. text 25.00 (*0-924922-25-7*); lib. bdg. 42.00 (*0-924922-75-3*) Ridgeview.

Perception. Henry H. Price. LC 81-13236. 332p. 1982. reprint ed. lib. bdg. 65.00 (*0-313-23153-2*, PRPT, Greenwood Pr) Greenwood.

Perception. 3rd ed. Robert Sekuler & Randolph Blake. LC 93-1128. 608p. (C). 1994. 71.56 (*0-07-056085-4*) McGraw.

Perception. 4th ed. G. Robert Carlsen. (Themes & Writers Ser.). (Illus.). 640p. (gr. 8). 1985. text 27.60 (*0-07-009805-0*) McGraw.

Perception. 4th ed. Sekuler. 2000. 73.00 (*0-07-057943-1*) McGraw.

Perception, Vol. 5. Ed. by Kathleen Akins. (Vancouver Series in Cognitive Science). 352p. 1996. text 70.00 (*0-19-508461-6*) OUP.

Perception: A Representative Theory. Jackson. 192p. 1993. 61.95 (*0-7512-0190-1*) Ashgate Pub Co.

Perception: An Essay on Classical Indian Theories of Knowledge. Bimal K. Matilal. 454p. 1992. reprint ed. pap. text 39.95 (*0-19-823976-9*) OUP.

Perception: Its Development & Recapitulation. Estelle Breines. LC 81-81244. (Illus.). 304p. (C). 1981. text 19.00 (*0-941930-01-7*) Geri-Rehab.

***Perception: Theory, Development & Organisation.** Paul Rookes & Jane Willson. LC 99-57668. (Modular Psychology Ser.). 176p. (C). 1999. pap. write for info. (*0-415-19094-0*); text. write for info. (*0-415-19093-2*) Routledge.

Perception - Evaluation - Interpretation. rev. ed. Ed. by B. Boothe et al. LC 95-76265. (Swiss Monographs in Psychology: Vol. 3). (Illus.). 188p. 1995. pap. 37.00 (*0-88937-140-7*) Hogrefe & Huber Pubs.

Perception Analysis Vocal Quality. Kempster. 1998. 35.25 (*1-56593-174-2*) Thomson Learn.

Perception & Action: Recent Advances in Cognitive Neuropsychology. Jean Decety. LC 99-187262. 1998. pap. text 64.95 (*0-86377-600-0*) Taylor & Francis.

Perception & Cognition: Advances in Eye Movement Research. Ed. by Gery D'Ydewalle & Johan van Rensbergen. LC 93-12440. (Studies in Visual Information Processing: Vol. 4). (Illus.). 436p. 1993. 146.50 (*0-444-89938-3*, North Holland) Elsevier.

Perception & Cognition at Century's End. 2nd ed. Ed. by Edward C. Caterette et al. (Handbook of Perception & Cognition Ser.). (Illus.). 487p. (C). 1998. boxed set 99.95 (*0-12-301160-4*) Acad Pr.

Perception & Cognition of Music. Ed. by Irene Deliege & John A. Sloboda. LC 97-202027. (Illus.). xvii, 461p. 1997. write for info. (*0-86377-452-0*, Pub. by Psychol Pr) Taylor & Francis.

Perception & Communication. Donald E. Broadbent. (Illus.). 352p. 1987. pap. text 29.95 (*0-19-852171-5*) OUP.

Perception & Communication. 3rd ed. Donald E. Broadbent. LC 58-11832. 1969. 192.00 (*0-08-009090-7*, Pub. by Pergamon Repr) Franklin.

Perception & Control of Self-Motion. Ed. by Rik Warren & Alexander H. Wertheim. 680p. (C). 1990. pap. 65.00 (*0-8058-0909-0*); text 125.00 (*0-8058-0517-6*) L Erlbaum Assocs.

Perception & Discovery. Norwood Russell Hanson. 1969. pap. 21.25 (*0-87735-509-6*) Jones & Bartlett.

Perception & Identity in Intercultural Communication. Marshall R. Singer. LC 98-14688. 296p. (C). 1998. pap. text 24.95 (*1-877864-61-7*) Intercult Pr.

Perception & Imaging. Richard D. Zakia. LC 96-31366. (Illus.). 304p. 1997. pap. 35.95 (*0-240-80201-2*, Focal) Buttrwrth-Heinemann.

Perception & Its Development: A Tribute to Eleanor J. Gibson. Ed. by A. D. Pick. 272p. 1979. text 49.95 (*0-89859-409-X*) L Erlbaum Assocs.

Perception & Misperception in International Politics. Robert Jervis. (Center for International Affairs at Harvard University Ser.). 464p. 1976. pap. text 24.95 (*0-691-10049-7*, Pub. by Princeton U Pr) Cal Prin Full Svc.

Perception & Motor Control in Birds: An Ecological Approach. Mark N. Davies & Patrick R. Green. LC 93-33022. 1994. 262.95 (*0-387-52855-5*) Spr-Verlag.

Perception & Passion in Dante's "Comedy" Patrick Boyde. LC 92-40938. 362p. (C). 1993. text 69.95 (*0-521-37009-4*) Cambridge U Pr.

Perception & Personal Identity: Proceedings. Oberlin Colloquium in Philosophy Staff. Ed. by Norman S. Care & Robert H. Grimm. LC 68-9427. 205p. reprint ed. pap. 63.60 (*0-608-30646-0*, 200325300021) Bks Demand.

Perception & Photography. Richard D. Zakia. LC 74-3402. (Illus.). 1979. pap. text 7.95 (*0-87992-015-7*) Light Impressions.

Perception & Pictorial Representation. Ed. by Calvin F. Nodine & Dennis Fisher. LC 79-4613. (Praeger Special Studies). 411p. 1979. 38.50 (*0-275-90402-4*, C0402, Praeger Pubs) Greenwood.

Perception & Prejudice: Race & Politics in the United States. Ed. by Jon Hurwitz & Mark Peffley. LC 97-44948. (Illus.). 272p. 1998. 30.00 (*0-300-07143-4*) Yale U Pr.

Perception & Production of Fluent Speech. Ed. by Ronald A. Cole. LC 79-25481. (Illus.). 576p. 1980. text 99.95 (*0-89859-019-1*) L Erlbaum Assocs.

Perception & Reality: A History from Descartes to Kant. John W. Yolton. 248p. 1996. text 42.50 (*0-8014-3227-8*) Cornell U Pr.

Perception & Reality: An Opinion Poll on Defence & Disarmament Commentaries. Clive Rose & Peter Blaker. (C). 1990. 45.00 (*0-907967-72-8*, Pub. by Inst Euro Def & Strat) St Mut.

Perception & Reason. Bill Brewer. LC 98-45925. 299p. 1999. text 55.00 (*0-19-823567-4*) OUP.

Perception & Representation: Current Issues. 2nd ed. Ilona Roth & Vicki Bruce. LC 94-41284. 224p. 1995. 32.95 (*0-335-19474-5*) OpUniv Pr.

Perception & Use of Streams in Suburban Areas: Effects of Water Quality & of Distance from Residence to Stream. Robert E. Coughlin et al. (Discussion Papers: No. 53). 1972. pap. 10.00 (*1-55869-090-5*) Regional Sci Res Inst.

Perception & Valuation of Water Quality: A Review of Research Method & Findings. Robert E. Coughlin. (Discussion Papers: No. 80). 1975. pap. 10.00 (*1-55869-091-3*) Regional Sci Res Inst.

Perception As Byesian Inference. Ed. by David C. Knill & Whitman Richards. (Illus.). 527p. (C). 1996. text 74.95 (*0-521-46109-X*) Cambridge U Pr.

Perception Barriers. Robert Frazier. 46p. 1987. pap. 9.95 (*0-917658-25-6*) BPW & P.

Perception, Cognition & Development: Interactional Analyses. Ed. by Thomas J. Tighe & Bryan E. Shepp. 384p. (C). 1983. text 79.95 (*0-89859-254-2*) L Erlbaum Assocs.

Perception, Cognition & Execution - Mechatronics: Designing Intelligent Machines, Vol. 1. George Rzevski. LC 95-210719. 336p. 1995. pap. text 42.95 (*0-7506-2404-3*) Buttrwrth-Heinemann.

***Perception, Cognition & Language: Essays in Honor of Henry & Lila Gleitman.** Barbara Landau. LC 99-88328. 2000. 39.95 (*0-262-12228-6*) MIT Pr.

Perception, Consciousness, Memory: Reflections of a Biologist. Gerold Adam. Tr. by K. Takacsi-Nagy from HUN. LC 73-20153. (Illus.). 230p. 1980. reprint ed. pap. 71.30 (*0-608-05461-5*, 206593000006) Bks Demand.

Perception, Empathy, & Judgment: An Inquiry into the Preconditions of Moral Performance. Arne J. Vetlesen. LC 92-43991. 400p. (C). 1994. 60.00 (*0-271-01056-8*); pap. text 18.95 (*0-271-01012-6*) Pa St U Pr.

Perception et Langage. E. Peters. 1998. 50.00 (*90-6831-902-7*, Pub. by Peeters Pub) Bks Intl VA.

Perception, Expression, & History: The Social Phenomenology of Maurice Merleau-Ponty. John O'Neill. (Studies in Phenomenology & Existential Philosophy). 101p. 1970. 39.95 (*0-8101-0299-4*) Northwestern U Pr.

Perception, Interaction & Language: Interaction of Daily Living: The Roots of Development. Affolter. 1991. 71.95 (*0-387-51150-4*) Spr-Verlag.

***Perception, Knowledge & Belief: Selected Essays.** Fred Dretske. (Cambridge Studies in Philosophy). (Illus.). 295p. (C). 2000. text 59.95 (*0-521-77181-1*); pap. text 19.95 (*0-521-77742-9*) Cambridge U Pr.

Perception Learning & the Self. Hamlyn. 320p. 1994. 71.95 (*0-7512-0302-5*) Ashgate Pub Co.

Perception, Memory & Emotion: Frontiers in Neuroscience. Taketoshi Ono. LC 96-2868. (Pergamon Studies in Neuroscience: Vol. 13). 632p. 1996. 196.50 (*0-08-042735-9*, Pergamon Pr) Elsevier.

Perception, Mind & Personal Identity: A Critique of Materialism. David H. Lund. LC 94-25527. 286p. (Orig.). (C). 1994. reprint ed. pap. text 29.50 (*0-8191-9616-9*); reprint ed. lib. bdg. 53.00 (*0-8191-9615-0*) U Pr of Amer.

Perception Mongers: Reflections on Soviet Propaganda. George Bailey. (C). 1990. 35.00 (*0-907967-12-4*, Pub. by Inst Euro Def & Strat) St Mut.

Perception of Asian Personality. Asoka Mehta. 264p. 1978. 16.95 (*0-940500-63-9*) Asia Bk Corp.

Perception of Choice & Factors Affecting Industrial Water Supply Decisions in Northeastern Illinois. Shue T. Wong. LC 68-56934. (University of Chicago, Department of Geography, Research Paper Ser.: No. 117). 107p. reprint ed. pap. 33.20 (*0-7837-0395-3*, 204071600018) Bks Demand.

Perception of Complex Tastes & Smells. Ed. by B. W. Ache et al. 450p. 1989. text 104.00 (*0-12-042990-X*) Acad Pr.

Perception of Displayed Information. Ed. by L. M. Biberman. LC 72-97695. (Optical Physics & Engineering Ser.). (Illus.). 346p. 1973. 79.50 (*0-306-30724-3*, Plenum Trade) Perseus Pubng.

Perception of Dotted Forms. William Uttal. 128p. 1987. 24.95 (*0-89859-929-6*) L Erlbaum Assocs.

Perception of Environment. (C). 1987. 75.00 (*0-685-18861-2*, Pub. by Scientific) St Mut.

Perception of Environment. Ed. by AAG Staff. (C). 1987. text 50.00 (*81-85046-55-7*, Pub. by Scientific Pubs) St Mut.

Perception of Form & Forms of Perception. R. M. Granovskaya et al. 224p. (C). 1987. text 59.95 (*0-89859-578-9*) L Erlbaum Assocs.

Perception of Grass Root Democracy & Political Performance. Ed. by Ghandi Palanithural. LC 98-903584. 205p. 1998. pap. 108.00 (*81-7533-068-6*, Pub. by Print Hse) St Mut.

Perception of Illusory Contours. Ed. by S. Petry & G. Meyer. (Illus.). 345p. 1987. 214.00 (*0-387-96518-1*) Spr-Verlag.

Perception of Multiple Objects: A Connectionist Approach. Michael C. Mozer. (Bradford Neural Network Modeling & Connectionism Ser.). 232p. 1991. 27.50 (*0-262-13270-2*, Bradford Bks) MIT Pr.

Perception of Music. Ed. by Robert Frances. Tr. by W. Jay Dowling. 384p. 1987. 79.95 (*0-89859-688-2*) L Erlbaum Assocs.

Perception of Natural Events: By Human Observers. 2nd rev. ed. Yusuf A. Yoler. (Illus.). 375p. (Orig.). (C). 1995. pap. 22.50 (*0-9644397-2-7*) Unipress WA.

Perception of Natural Events: By Human Observers. 4th rev. ed. Y. A. Yoler. (Illus.). 460p. 1998. 49.95 (*0-9644397-4-3*) Unipress WA.

Perception of Natural Events: By Human Observers, Bk. I. 4th rev. ed. Yusuf A. Yoler. (Illus.). 460p. (Orig.). 1998. pap. 25.95 (*0-9644397-3-5*) Unipress WA.

Perception of Nature: British Landscape Art in the Late Eighteenth & Early Nineteenth Centuries. Charlotte Klonk. LC 96-60715. (Illus.). 208p. 1996. 60.00 (*0-300-06950-2*) Yale U Pr.

Perception of Nonverbal Behavior in the Career Interview. Walburga von Raffler-Engel. (Pragmatics & Beyond Ser.: Vol:). viii, 148p. 1983. pap. 41.00 (*90-272-2517-6*) J Benjamins Pubng Co.

Perception of Other People. Franz From. Tr. by Erik Kvan & Brendan Maher. LC 76-138295. 205p. reprint ed. pap. 63.60 (*0-608-18783-6*, 202982800065) Bks Demand.

Perception of Poetry. Eugene R. Kintgen. LC 82-48387. 283p. reprint ed. pap. 87.80 (*0-608-18254-0*, 205670600081) Bks Demand.

Perception of Police Power: A Study in Four Cities. Anastassios D. Mylonas. (N. Y. U. Criminal Law Education & Research Center, Monograph Ser.: Vol. 8). (Illus.). x, 131p. 1974. reprint ed. pap. 19.50 (*0-8377-0418-9*, Rothman) W S Hein.

Perception of Reality in the Volksmarchen of Schleswig-Holstein: A Study in Interpersonal Relationships & World View. Margarethe W. Sparing. LC 84-7321. 208p. (Orig.). 1984. lib. bdg. 48.00 (*0-8191-3987-4*) U Pr of Amer.

Perception of Self in Emotional Disorder & Psychotherapy. L. M. Hartman & K. R. Blankstein. (Advances in the Study of Communication & Affect Ser.: Vol. 11). (Illus.). 354p. (C). 1986. 90.00 (*0-306-42315-4*, Plenum Trade) Perseus Pubng.

Perception of Space & Motion. 2nd ed. Ed. by William Epstein & Sheena J. Rogers. LC 95-2336. (Handbook of Perception & Cognition Ser.). (Illus.). 499p. 1995. text 69.95 (*0-12-240530-7*) Acad Pr.

Perception of Structure. Ed. by Gregory R. Lockhead & James R. Pomerantz. 338p. 1994. pap. 19.95 (*1-55798-263-5*) Am Psychol.

Perception of the Amish Way. Bruce Friesen & John Friesen. 168p. (C). 1996. pap. text, per. 25.95 (*0-7872-2447-2*) Kendall-Hunt.

Perception of the Drought Hazard on the Great Plains. Thomas F. Saarinen. LC 66-22754. (University of Chicago, Department of Geography, Research Paper Ser.: No. 106). 199p. reprint ed. pap. 61.70 (*0-608-13800-2*, 201780500008) Bks Demand.

***Perception of the Elements in the Hindu Tradition.** Ed. by Maya Burger & Peter Schreiner. (Studia Religiosa Helvetica Jahrbuch: Vol. 4-5). 215p. 2000. pap. 29.95 (*3-906764-61-3*) P Lang Pubng.

***Perception of the Environment: Essays on Livelihood, Dwelling & Skill.** Tim Ingold. LC 00-27142. 2000. pap. write for info. (*0-415-22832-8*) Routledge.

Perception of the Past in Twelfth-Century Europe. Ed. by Paul Magdalino. 256p. 1992. 55.00 (*1-85285-066-3*) Hambledon Press.

Perception of the Unborn Across the Cultures of the World. Walburga Von Raffler-Engel. LC 93-61410. 200p. 1994. text 24.50 (*0-88937-120-2*) Hogrefe & Huber Pubs.

Perception of Visual Information. Ed. by William R. Hendee & Peter Wells. LC 92-49928. 1993. 98.00 (*0-387-97904-2*) Spr-Verlag.

Perception of Visual Information. 2nd ed. William R. Hendee. LC 97-10231. 400p. 1997. 79.95 (*0-387-94910-0*) Spr-Verlag.

Perception of Women in Spanish Theater of the Golden Age. Ed. by Anita K. Stoll & Dawn L. Smith. LC 89-46402. (Illus.). 280p. 1991. 42.50 (*0-8387-5189-X*) Bucknell U Pr.

Perception of Work in Tokugawa, Japan: A Study of Ishida Baigan & Ninomiya Sontoku. Eiji Takemura. LC 97-33154. 229p. (C). 1997. 46.00 (*0-7618-0886-8*) U Pr of Amer.

Perception, Opportunity & Profit: Studies in the Theory of Entrepreneurship. Israel M. Kirzner. LC 79-11765. 1994. lib. bdg. 20.00 (*0-226-43773-6*) U Ch Pr.

Perception, Opportunity & Profit: Studies in the Theory of Entrepreneurship. Israel M. Kirzner. LC 79-11765. 1994. pap. text 9.95 (*0-226-43774-4*) U Ch Pr.

Perception, Sensation & Verification. Bede Rundle. 266p. 1972. text 34.00 (*0-19-824390-1*) OUP.

Perception Theory. Mausfield. text. write for info. (*0-471-49149-7*) Wiley.

Perception, Theory & Commitment: The New Philosophy of Science. Harold I. Brown. LC 76-22991. (Illus.). 204p. 1979. pap. text 11.95 (*0-226-07618-0*, P812) U Ch Pr.

Perception, 2001: A Report on Defining the Role of Geo-Engineering in the 21st Century. American Society of Civil Engineers, Hydraulics Di. LC 94-22285. 48p. 1994. 5.00 (*0-7844-0042-3*) Am Soc Civil Eng.

Perceptions. Ed. by Robert L. Derderian & Deborah A. Case. LC 94-72201. (Illus.). 320p. 1995. text 45.00 (*1-885206-07-0*, Iliad Pr) Cader Pubng.

***Perceptions.** Charles L. Peters & Kenneth C. Dillon. LC 98-68492. 168p. 1998. pap. 16.00 (*1-57579-137-4*) Pine Hill Pr.

***Perceptions.** Susie S. Piper. (J). 1999. pap. 6.00 (*0-9618280-3-X*) S S Piper.

Perceptions. Damien Simpson. 172p. (Orig.). 1991. pap. 12.95 (*0-9628393-0-2*) UMS Prodns.

Perceptions: Cultures in Conflict. Ed. by Adrian Kerr et al. (Illus.). 185p. (Orig.). 1996. pap. 11.95 (*0-946451-32-X*, Pub. by Guildhall Pr) Irish Bks Media.

Perceptions: Observations on Everyday Life. 2nd deluxe ed. Maxie Dunnam. 80p. (Orig.). 1990. reprint ed. pap. 9.95 (*0-917851-59-5*) Bristol Hse.

Perceptions: One Man's View of the World. Cral Vincent. 1990. pap. 11.95 (*0-9626396-6-4*) Jct Factor.

Perceptions: The Book of Female Character Types. David Spencer & Donny Elliot. (Illus.). 150p. (Orig.). 1995. pap. 10.95 (*0-9645633-0-4*) Net Worth.

Perceptions & Interactions in a Medical Setting: A Sociological Study of a Woman's Hospital. Aneeta A. Minocha. (C). 1996. 21.00 (*81-7075-043-1*, Pub. by Hindustan) S Asia.

Perceptions & Interests: Developing Countries & the International Economic System. Raymond G. Clemencon. (Illus.). XI, 309p. 1990. pap. 44.00 (*3-261-04185-4*) P Lang Pubng.

Perceptions, Emotions, Sensibilities: Essays on India's Colonial & Post-Colonial Experiences. Tapan Raychaudhuri. 260p. 2000. text 29.95 (*0-19-564863-3*) OUP.

Perceptions in Harmony, Vol. 1. Ed. by Jef Sturm. 300p. 1998. write for info. (*1-888680-28-8*) Poetry Guild.

Perceptions in Public Higher Education. Ed. by Gene A. Budig. LC 71-105647. 177p. reprint ed. pap. 54.90 (*0-7837-1393-2*, 204157400021) Bks Demand.

Perceptions, Motivations, & Performance of Women Legislators. V. Prabhavathi. (C). 1991. 27.50 (*81-7054-145-X*, Pub. by Classical Pubng) S Asia.

Perceptions of Aging in Literature: A Cross-Cultural Study, 11. Ed. by Prisca V. Bagnell & Patricia S. Soper. LC 88-34723. (Contributions to the Study of Aging Ser.: No. 11). 200p. 1989. 52.95 (*0-313-26292-6*, BAJ, Greenwood Pr) Greenwood.

Perceptions of Colour. Cronly-Dillon. 1991. 137.00 (*0-8493-7506-1*, QP464) CRC Pr.

Perceptions of Health & Illness: Current Research & Applications. Ed. by Keith J. Petrie & John Weinman. 320p. 1997. text 68.00 (*90-5702-102-1*, ECU55, Harwood Acad Pubs); pap. text 28.00 (*90-5702-103-X*, ECU20, Harwood Acad Pubs) Gordon & Breach.

Perceptions of History: An Analysis of School Textbooks. Ed. by Volker R. Berghahn & Hanna Schissler. LC 87-15845. 181p. 1988. 19.50 (*0-85496-526-2*) Berg Pubs.

Perceptions of Israeli-Arabs: Territoriality & Identity. Izhak Schnell. (Research in Ethnic Relations Ser.). 133p. 1994. 66.95 (*1-85628-861-7*, Pub. by Avebry) Ashgate Pub Co.

Perceptions of Jewish History. Amos Funkenstein. 1993. 45.00 (*0-520-07702-4*, Pub. by U CA Pr) Cal Prin Full Svc.

Perceptions of Justice: Issues in Indigenous & Community Empowerment. Kayleen M. Hazlehurst. LC 94-73715. (Illus.). 303p. (C). 1995. text 77.95 (*1-85972-079-X*, Pub. by Avebry) Ashgate Pub Co.

Perceptions of Landfill Operations Held by Nearby Residents. Robert E. Coughlin et al. (Discussion Papers: No. 65). 1973. pap. 10.00 (*1-55869-092-1*) Regional Sci Res Inst.

Perceptions of Life Quality in Rural America: An Analysis of Survey Data from Four Studies. Robert W. Marans et al. LC 80-50377. (University of Michigan Institute for Social Research Report Ser.). 118p. reprint ed. pap. 36.60 (*0-608-14964-0*, 202596700047) Bks Demand.

Perceptions of Marginality: Theoretical Issues & Regional Perceptions of Marginality in Geographical Space. Ed. by Heikki Jussila et al. LC 98-70147. 299p. 1998. text 67.95 (*1-85972-683-6*, Pub. by Ashgate Pub) Ashgate Pub Co.

***Perceptions of Palestine: Their Influence on U.S. Middle East Policy.** Kathleen Christison. LC 98-41413. Orig. Title: U.S. Policy on the Palestinians & Israel. 380p. 1999. 40.00 (*0-520-21717-9*, Pub. by U CA Pr) Cal Prin Full Svc.

***Perceptions of Partnership: The Allure & Accessibility of the Brass Ring.** 224p. 1999. pap. 295.00 (*1-55733-019-0*) NALP.

Perceptions of Phobia & Phobics: The Quest for Control. Beulah McNab. (Illus.). 253p. 1993. text 115.00 (*0-12-485960-7*) Acad Pr.

Perceptions of Policy Makers. Ed. by Kenneth W. Thompson. (Papers on Presidential Transitions & Foreign Policy: Vol. VI). 142p. (Orig.). (C). 1987. pap. text 16.50 (*0-8191-6121-7*, Pub. by White Miller Center); lib. bdg. 39.00 (*0-8191-6120-9*, Pub. by White Miller Center) U Pr of Amer.

***Perceptions of Priscilla.** 2nd ed. Priscilla Larkin & Warrior King. 52p. 1998. reprint ed. mass mkt. 7.95 (0-9672329-0-2) CGI Assocs.

Perceptions of Risk, Proceedings of the Fifteenth Annual Meeting, Held on March 14-15, 1979. (Annual Meeting Proceedings Ser.: No. 1). 1980. pap. 25.00 (0-685-16974-X) NCRP Pubns.

***Perceptions of St. Patrick in Eighteenth-Century Ireland.** Bridget McCormack. (Maynooth History Studies Ser.). (Illus.). 136p. 1999. 55.00 (1-85182-457-X, Pub. by Four Cts Pr) Intl Spec Bk.

Perceptions of Security: Public Opinion & Expert Assessments in Europe's New Democracies. Ed. by Richard Smoke. LC 95-16866. 300p. 1996. text 29.95 (0-7190-4813-3, Pub. by Manchester Univ Pr) St Martin.

Perceptions of Social Justice in Southeast Asia. Ambassodor Soedjatmoko. 12p. (Orig.). 1977. pap. text 8.50 (0-8191-5831-3) U Pr of Amer.

Perceptions of South Asia's Visual Past. Ed. by Catherine B. Asher. (C). 1994. 54.00 (0-945921-42-X) South Asia Pubns.

Perceptions of Teaching: Primary School Teachers in England & France. Patricia Broadfoot et al. (Education Ser.). (Illus.). 160p. 1994. 70.00 (0-304-32773-5) Continuum.

Perceptions of Teaching & Learning. Ed. by Martin Hughes. LC 93-50123. (BERA Dialogues Ser.: No. 8). 118p. 1994. 29.95 (1-85359-231-5, Pub. by Multilingual Matters) Taylor & Francis.

Perceptions of Technological Risks & Benefits. Leroy C. Gould. LC 88-15774. 316p. 1988. 39.95 (0-87154-362-1) Russell Sage.

Perceptions of the 1963 Presidential Transition. Survey Research Center Staff. 1973. write for info. (0-89138-062-0) ICPSR.

***Perceptions on Diversity in Pennsylvania.** Diane E. Shoop. Ed. by Mark Gehret. (Illus.). 44p. 2000. pap. 20.00 (1-58036-141-2) Penn State Data Ctr.

Perceptive Listening. 2nd ed. Wolff. (C). 1993. pap. text, teacher ed. 3.75 (0-03-096874-7) Harcourt Coll Pubs.

Perceptive Listening. 2nd ed. Florence I. Wolff & Nadine C. Marsnik. 320p. (C). 1993. teacher ed. write for info. (0-318-70027-1) Harcourt Coll Pubs.

Perceptive I: A Personal Reader & Writer. Edmund J. Farrell & James E. Miller, Jr. 1996. pap. write for info. (0-8442-5957-8) NTC Contemp Pub Co.

Perceptive Salesmanship. T. J. King. 65p. 1986. pap. 8.95 (0-913261-11-4) Effect Learn Sys.

Perceptive Types. Frank Jakubowsky. (Orig.). 1993. pap. 10.00 (0-932588-17-4) Jesus Bks.

Perceptive Winds: From Bergen Beach to the Backwoods Trail. Edith P. Dill. (Illus.). 124p. (Orig.). 1995. pap. 7.95 (1-884707-11-4) Lifestyles.

Perceptives on Perception & Action. Ed. by Herbert Heuer & A. F. Sanders. 480p. 1987. text 89.95 (0-89859-694-7) L Erlbaum Assocs.

Perceptrons: An Introduction to Computational Geometry. expanded ed. Marvin L. Minsky & Seymour A. Papert. 275p. 1987. pap. text 30.00 (0-262-63111-3) MIT Pr.

Percepts, Concepts, & Categories: The Representation & Processing of Information. Ed. by Barbara Burns. LC 92-26533. xviii,696p. 1992. 192.00 (0-444-88734-2, North Holland) Elsevier.

Perceptual Activities: A Multitude of Perceptual Actitivies, Level 2-Advanced, Consumerable (Coloring) Edition. Paul McCreary. 1972. student ed. 12.00 (0-87879-711-4, Ann Arbor Div) Acad Therapy.

Perceptual Activities: A Multitude of Reusable Perceptual Activities, Level 1-Primary. Paul McCreary. 1972. 12.00 (0-87879-708-4, Ann Arbor Div) Acad Therapy.

Perceptual Activities, Level 1 - Primary: A Multitude of Perceptual Activities. rev. ed. Paul McCreary. 62p. (J). (gr. 2-4). 1976. 12.00 (0-87879-710-6, Ann Arbor Div) Acad Therapy.

Perceptual Activities, Level 2 - Elementary. Paul McCreary. 1994. 12.00 (0-87879-709-2) Acad Therapy.

Perceptual Activities Packets. 1994. ring bd. 100.00 (0-87879-696-7) Acad Therapy.

Perceptual & Associative Learning. Geoffrey Hall. (Oxford Psychology Ser.: No. 18). (Illus.). 312p. 1992. text 49.95 (0-19-852182-0) OUP.

Perceptual & Cognitive Development. 2nd ed. Ed. by Rochel Gelman et al. LC 95-50891. (Handbook of Perception & Cognition Ser.). (Illus.). 454p. 1996. text 59.95 (0-12-279660-8) Acad Pr.

Perceptual & Learning Disabilities in Children. Incl. Vol. 1. Psychoeducational Practices. Ed. by William M. Cruickshank & Daniel P. Hallahan. 496p. 1975. 45.00 (0-8156-2165-5); Vol. 2. Research & Theory. 498p. 45.00 (0-8156-2166-3); (Illus.). (C). 1975. write for info. (0-318-55904-8) Syracuse U Pr.

Perceptual Approaches to Communication Disorders. Ed. by Sheila L. Wirz. 161p. 1994. 39.95 (1-56593-256-0, 0550) Singular Publishing.

Perceptual Assurance & the Reality of the World. Errol E. Harris. LC 74-82736. (Heinz Werner Lecturrs: No. 8). 1974. 9.00 (0-914206-23-0) Clark U Pr.

Perceptual Changes in Psychopathology. Ed. by William H. Ittelson & Samuel B. Kutash. LC 61-10263. 276p. reprint ed. pap. 85.60 (0-608-11149-X, 205056000085) Bks Demand.

Perceptual Consequences of Cochlear Damage. Brian C. Moore. (Illus.). 246p. 1995. text 90.00 (0-19-852330-0) OUP.

Perceptual Constancy: Why Things Look As They Do. Ed. by Vincent Walsh & Janusz Kulikowski. LC 97-6655. (Illus.). 560p. (C). 1998. text 69.95 (0-521-46061-1) Cambridge U Pr.

Perceptual Development. Ed. by Seymour Wapner & Heinz Werner. LC 58-17798. (Monographs in Psychology & Related Disciplines: No. 2). 95p. 1957. pap. 6.00 (0-914206-03-6) Clark U Pr.

Perceptual Development: Visual, Auditory & Speech Perception. Ed. by Alan Slater. LC 99-159355. 434p. 1998. 59.95 (0-86377-850-X) L Erlbaum Assocs.

***Perceptual Development: Visual, Auditory & Speech Perception.** Alan Slater. 2000. pap. 34.95 (0-86377-851-8) Psychol Pr.

Perceptual Development in Children. Ed. by Aline H. Kidd & Jeanne L. Rivoire. LC 66-25139. 548p. 1966. 80.00 (0-8236-4060-4) Intl Univs Pr.

Perceptual Development in Early Infancy: Problems & Issues. Ed. by Beryl McKenzie & R. H. Day. (Child Psychology Ser.). 312p. 1987. text 59.95 (0-89859-943-1) L Erlbaum Assocs.

Perceptual Development in Infancy. Ed. by Albert Yonas. (Minnesota Symposia on Child Psychology Ser.: Vol. 20). 326p. 1987. 65.00 (0-8058-0010-7) L Erlbaum Assocs.

Perceptual Dialectology: Nonlinguists' Views of Areal Linguistics. Dennis R. Preston. (Topics in Sociolinguistics Ser.: No. 7). xvi, 141p. 1989. 67.70 (90-6765-392-6); pap. 44.65 (90-6765-393-4) Mouton.

Perceptual Error: The Indian Theories. Srinivasa Rao. LC 98-20652. (Monographs of the Society for Asian & Comparative Philosophy: Vol. 16). 168p. 1998. pap. text 20.00 (0-8248-1958-6) UH Pr.

Perceptual Factors in Braille Word Recognition. Carson Y. Nolan & Cleves J. Kederis. LC 79-9310. (American Foundation for the Blind Research Ser.: No. 20). 192p. reprint ed. pap. 59.60 (0-7837-0224-8, 204053200017) Bks Demand.

Perceptual Issues in Visualization. Ed. by George G. Grinstein & H. Levkowitz. LC 95-7853. (IFIP Series on Computer Graphics). 175p. 1995. 93.00 (0-387-58096-4) Spr-Verlag.

Perceptual Knowledge. Georges Dicker. (Philosophical Studies: No. 22). 235p. 1980. text 96.00 (90-277-1130-5, D Reidel) Kluwer Academic.

Perceptual Learning Style Workbook: Understanding How You Learn. Sanford G. Kulkin. (Illus.). 16p. 1997. pap. text, wbk. ed. 12.00 (1-58034-017-2) IML Pubns.

Perceptual-Motor Activities Book. Jim L. Stillwell. (Illus.). 96p. (Orig.). (J). (gr. k-6). 1990. pap. 10.00 (0-945872-05-4) Great Activities Pub Co.

Perceptual Motor Behavior: Developmental Assessment & Therapy. Judith I. Laszlo & Phillip J. Bairstow. 1985. 37.50 (0-275-91650-2, C1650, Praeger Pubs) Greenwood.

***Perceptual-Motor Behavior in Down Syndrome.** Ed. by Daniel J. Weeks et al. LC 99-42474. (Illus.). 376p. 2000. 45.00 (0-88011-975-6) Human Kinetics.

Perceptual-Motor Development Equipment: Inexpensive Ideas & Activities. Peter H. Werner & Lisa Rini. LC 75-43744. 204p. reprint ed. pap. 63.30 (0-608-13337-X, 205571900032) Bks Demand.

Perceptual Motor Development Series, 5 bks. Jack Capon. Incl. Balance Activities. (J). (gr. k-6). 1975. pap. 6.95 (0-8224-5302-9); Ball, Rope, Hoop Activities. (J). (gr. k-6). 1975. pap. 6.95 (0-8224-5301-0); Basic Movement Activities. (J). (gr. k-6). 1975. pap. 6.95 (0-8224-5300-2); Beanbag, Rhythm-Stick Activities. (J). (gr. k-6). 1975. pap. 6.95 (0-8224-5303-7); Tire, Parachute Activities. (J). (gr. k-6). 1975. pap. 6.95 (0-8224-5304-5); (J). (gr. k-6). 1975. pap. write for info. (0-318-55298-1) Fearon Teacher Aids.

Perceptual-Motor Lesson Plans Level 2: Basic & "Practical" Lesson Plans for Perceptual-Motor Programs in Preschool & Elementary Grades, Level 2. 4th ed. Jack Capon. Ed. by Frank Alexander. (Illus.). 236p. 1999. teacher ed., spiral bd. 23.00 (0-915256-04-5) Front Row.

***Perceptual-Motor Lesson Plans - Level 1: Basic & "Practical" Lesson Plans for Perceptual-Motor Programs in Preschool & Elementary Grades.** 8th ed. Jack Capon. Ed. by Frank Alexander. LC 98-177428. (Illus.). 216p. 1998. pap., teacher ed. 19.00 (0-915256-03-7) Front Row.

Perceptual Neuroscience: The Cerebral Cortex. Vernon B. Mountcastle. LC 98-15241. (Illus.). 448 p. 1998. 59.95 (0-674-66188-5) HUP.

Perceptual Organization & Visual Recognition. David Lowe. 176p. (C). 1985. reprint ed. text 122.00 (0-89838-172-X) Kluwer Academic.

***Perceptual Organization for Artificial Vision Systems.** Kim L. Boyer & Sudeep Sarkar. 368p. 2000. 125.00 (0-7923-7799-0) Kluwer Academic.

Perceptual Psychology. M. S. Lindauer. 1978. text 23.50 (0-685-04011-9, Pergamon Pr); pap. text 17.00 (0-685-04012-7, Pergamon Pr) Elsevier.

Perceptual Quotes for Photographers. Richard D. Zakia. LC 80-15008. (Illus.). (Orig.). 1980. pap. text 5.95 (0-87992-019-X) Light Impressions.

Perceptual Study of Intonation: An Experimental-Phonetic Approach to Speech Melody. J't. Hart et al. (Studies in Speech Science & Communication). (Illus.). 227p. (C). 1990. text 69.95 (0-521-36643-7) Cambridge U Pr.

Perceptual System: A Philosophical & Psychological Perspective. Aaron Ben-Ze'ev. LC 92-6211. (American University Studies: Philosophy: Ser. V, Vol. 138). IX, 220p. (Orig.). (C). 1993. pap. text 29.95 (0-8204-1872-2) P Lang Pubng.

Perceptual Training Activities Handbook: 250 Games & Exercises for Helping Children Develop Sensory Skills. 2nd ed. Betty Van Witsen. LC 79-17371. (Illus.). 112p. 1979. reprint ed. pap. 34.80 (0-7837-8948-3, 204965900002) Bks Demand.

Perceptuo-Motor Difficulties: Theory & Strategies to Help Children, Adolescents, & Adults. Dorothy E. Penso. LC 92-49040. (Therapy in Practice Ser.: Vol. 34). 179p. 1992. 41.50 (1-56593-025-8, 0268) Thomson Learn.

Perceval: The Story of the Grail. Chr Etien & Burton Raffel. LC 98-18938. 1999. write for info. (0-300-07585-5); pap. 16.00 (0-300-07586-3) Yale U Pr.

Perceval: The Story of the Grail. Chretien De Troyes. Tr. by Nigel Bryant. (Arthurian Studies Ser.: No. 5). (Illus.). 334p. 1996. reprint ed. pap. 29.95 (0-85991-224-8) Boydell & Brewer.

Perceval le Gallois ou le Conte du Graal: Avec: Mis en Francais Moderne Par Lucien Foulet. Chretien de Troyes. 226p. 1970. 13.50 (0-7859-0690-8, S31794) Fr & Eur.

Perceval le Gallois: ou Le Conte du Graal, 1866-1871, 3 vols. Chretien de Troyes & Charles Potvin. (FRE.). 1970. pap. 250.00 (0-8288-9102-8) Fr & Eur.

Perceval O el Cuento del Grial. Chretien De Troyes. Ed. & Tr. by Martin De Riquer. (Nueva Austral Ser.: Vol. 227). (SPA.). 1991. pap. text 24.95 (84-239-7227-5) Elliots Bks.

Perceval: or The Story of the Grail. Chretien de Troyes. Tr. by Ruth H. Cline from FRE. LC 85-8600. 280p. 1985. pap. text 15.00 (0-8203-0812-9) U of Ga Pr.

Perceval: or The Story of the Holy Grail. Chretien. 260p. 1983. 74.00 (0-08-026296-1, Pergamon Pr) Elsevier.

Perceval: ou le Roman du Graal: Traducion de l'Ancien Francais. Chretien de Troyes. (Folio Ser.: No. 537). (FRE.). 384p. 1974. pap. 8.95 (2-07-036537-9) Schoenhof.

Perceval: ou le Roman du Graal Suivi de Continuations (Choix) Chretien de Troyes. (FRE.). 384p. 1974. pap. 10.95 (0-7859-1775-6, 2070365379) Fr & Eur.

Perceval's Narrative: A Patient's Account of His Psychosis, 1830-1832. John Perceval. Ed. by Gregory Bateson. LC 61-14652. 353p. 1961. reprint ed. pap. 30.00 (0-7837-1223-5, 204175400023) Bks Demand.

Perch Lake Mounds, with Notes on Other New York Mounds & Some Accounts of Indian Trails. William M. Beauchamp. LC 74-7929. reprint ed. 31.50 (0-404-11815-1) AMS Pr.

***Perchance to Dream.** Ed. by Denise Little. 2000. 6.99 (0-88677-888-3, Pub. by DAW Bks) Penguin Putnam.

Perchance to Dream. Quiche Lloyd-Kemble. 40p. 1997. pap. 3.25 (0-87440-048-1) Bakers Plays.

Perchance to Dream. Robert B. Parker. 288p. 1993. mass mkt. 6.99 (0-425-13131-9) Berkley Pub.

Perchance to Dream. Maura Seger. 320p. (Orig.). 1989. pap. 3.95 (0-380-75338-3, Avon Bks) Morrow Avon.

Perchance to Dream. Howard Weinstein. Ed. by David Stern. (Star Trek: The Next Generation Ser.: No. 19). 288p. (Orig.). 1991. mass mkt. 5.50 (0-671-70837-6) PB.

Perchance to Dream. Kathleen Korbel. 1991. reprint ed. 19.00 (0-7278-4177-7) Severn Hse.

Perchance to Dream: Robert B. Parker's sequel to Raymond Chandler's The big sleep. large type ed. Robert B. Parker. LC 91-3776. 304p. 1991. reprint ed. lib. bdg. 21.95 (1-56054-186-5) Thorndike Pr.

Perchance to Dream: Robert B. Parker's sequel to Raymond Chandler's The big sleep. large type ed. Robert B. Parker. LC 91-3776. 304p. 1992. reprint ed. lib. bdg. 13.95 (1-56054-977-7) Thorndike Pr.

Perchan's Chorea. Robert J. Perchan. 1991. 17.50 (0-922820-15-5) Watermark Pr.

Perche la Violenza? Una Interpretazione Filosofica see Why Violence?: A Philosophical Interpretation

Perched on Nothing's Branch. Attila Jozsef. Tr. by Peter Hargitai. LC 86-73139. (Illus.). 73p. 1987. write for info. (0-940821-00-1) Apalachee Pr.

Perched on Nothing's Branch: Selected Poems of Attila Jozsef. Attila Jozsef. Tr. by Peter Hargitai from HUN. LC 99-43488. (Terra Incognito Ser.: Vol. 6). 88p. 1999. pap. 14.00 (1-893996-00-X, Pub. by White Pine) SPD-Small Pr Dist.

***Perchelli Chronicles.** Tony W. Digiacomo. 200p. 2000. mass mkt. 6.99 (1-58265-019-5, 00024) Orphan Press.

Percheron Horse in America. Joseph Mischka. (Illus.). 179p. 1991. 19.95 (0-9622663-5-3) Heart Prairie Pr.

Perching Birds: Singing in the Trees. Sara S. Miller. LC 97-51591. (Animals in Order Ser.). (J). 1999. 23.00 (0-531-11520-8) Watts.

Perching Birds of North America. Sara Swan Miller. (Animals in Order Ser.). 1999. pap. text 6.95 (0-531-15946-9) Watts.

***Perchlorate in the Environment.** Edward Todd Urbansky & American Chemical Society (ACS) Staff. LC 00-32136. 2000. write for info. (0-306-46389-X) Plenum.

Perchloroethylene (Carbon Dichloride, Tetrachloroethylene, Drycleaner, Fumigant) - Effects on Health & Work: Index of New Information. Michelle S. Leeds. 146p. 1995. 47.50 (0-7883-0352-X); pap. 44.50 (0-7883-0353-8) ABBE Pubs Assn.

Percival & the Presense of God. Jim Hunter. 1997. pap. text 10.95 (1-56882-097-6) Chaosium.

***Percival Keene.** Frederick Marryat. LC 98-54895. (Heart of Oak Sea Classics Ser.). 416p. 1999. pap. 15.00 (0-8050-6139-8, Pub. by H Holt & Co) VHPS.

***Percival Lowell: The Culture & Science of a Boston Brahmin.** David Strauss. (Illus.). 352p. 2000. 45.00 (0-674-00291-1) HUP.

Percival, the Homeless Parrot. Rosemarie Riechel. (Illus.). 16p. (J). (gr. k-3). 1998. pap. 7.00 (0-8059-4481-8) Dorrance.

Percival the Piano. Mary Perkins. (Illus.). (Orig.). (J). (gr. k-4). 1990. pap. 5.75 (0-85398-287-2) G Ronald Pub.

***Percivals Aircraft.** Norman H. Ellison. (Transport Ser.). 1999. pap. 18.99 (0-7524-0774-0) Arcadia Publng.

Percival's Angel. Anne Eliot Crompton. 1999. mass mkt. 5.99 (0-451-45757-9) NAL.

Percival's English-Tamil Dictionary. P. Percival. (C). 1993. reprint ed. 22.00 (81-206-0817-8, Pub. by Asian Educ Servs) S Asia.

Percival's Medical Ethics. Thomas Percival. Ed. by Chauncey D. Leake. LC 75-23750. reprint ed. 39.50 (0-404-13356-8) AMS Pr.

Percolated Faith: Forming New Adult Christians Through Conversion & Baptism. Frank G. Honeycutt. LC 95-36213. (Orig.). 1996. pap. 13.75 (0-7880-0563-4) CSS OH.

Percolation. G. Grimmett. (Illus.). 320p. 1989. 67.95 (0-387-96843-1) Spr-Verlag.

Percolation. 2nd ed. G. Grimmett. Ed. by S. S. Chern et al. LC 99-21041. (Illus.). xiii, 444p. 1999. 99.00 (3-540-64902-6) Spr-Verlag.

Percolation & Fractals in Colloid & Interface Science. A. V. Neimark. 400p. (C). 1997. text 48.00 (981-02-0734-4) World Scientific Pub.

Percolation Models for Transport in Porous Media: With Applications to Reservoir Engineering. V. I. Selyakov & V. V. Kadet. LC 96-48828. (Theory & Applications of Transport in Porous Media Ser.). 256p. (C). 1997. text 120.50 (0-7923-4322-0) Kluwer Academic.

Percolation Processes: Theory & Applications. Ed. by A. Rodriques & D. Tondeur. (NATO Advanced Study Institute Ser.: Applied Science, No. 33). 594p. 1981. text 184.00 (90-286-0579-7) Kluwer Academic.

Percolation Theory & Ergodic Theory of Infinite Particle Systems. Ed. by H. Keston. (IMA Volumes in Mathematics & Its Applications Ser.: Vol. 8). (Illus.). 345p. 1987. 65.95 (0-387-96537-8) Spr-Verlag.

Percussion. Barrie Turner. LC 98-6278. (Musical Instruments of the World Ser.). (Illus.). 32p. (J). 1998. lib. bdg. 21.30 (1-887068-46-5) Smart Apple.

***Percussion & Electronic Instruments.** Robert Dearling. (Encyclopedia of Musical Instruments Ser.). (Illus.). (J). 2000. 17.95 (0-7910-6093-4) Chelsea Hse.

Percussion Anthology. 1987. 44.00 (0-686-15892-X) Instrumental.

Percussion Discography: An International Compilation of Solo & Chamber Percussion Music, 36. Compiled by Fernando A. Meza. LC 89-28647. (Discographies Ser.: No. 36). 117p. 1990. lib. bdg. 49.95 (0-313-26867-3, MPQ/, Greenwood Pr) Greenwood.

Percussion (Drums & Mallets) (Standard of Excellence Ser.: Bk. 1). 1993. 6.95 (0-8497-5945-5, W21PR) Kjos.

Percussion (Drums & Mallets) (Standard of Excellence Ser.: Bk. 2). 1993. 6.95 (0-8497-5970-6, W22PR) Kjos.

Percussion (Drums & Mallets) Bruce Pearson. (Standard of Excellence Ser.: Bk. 3). 1996. 6.95 (0-8497-5991-9, W23PR) Kjos.

Percussion Education: A Source Book of Concepts & Information. Percussive Arts Society Education Committee Staff. Ed. by Garwood Whaley. (Illus.). 89p. 1990. pap. 12.95 (0-9664928-0-3) Percussive OK.

Percussion Ensemble Literature. Ed. by Thomas Siwe. LC 98-67154. 556p. (Orig.). (C). 1998. pap. 45.00 (0-9635891-2-1) Media Press.

Percussion Instruments & Their History. James Blades. (Illus.). 512p. 1992. reprint ed. pap. 50.00 (0-933224-61-3, ST114) Bold Strummer Ltd.

Percussion Manual. F. Michael Combs. 160p. (C). 1977. pap. 20.25 (0-534-00504-7) Wadsworth Pub.

***Percussion Manual.** 2nd ed. F. Michael Combs. (Illus.). 167p. (C). 2000. pap. 21.95 (1-57766-106-0) Waveland Pr.

Percussion Methods. Robert Schietroma. 106p. (C). 1991. student ed. 16.27 (1-56870-013-X) RonJon Pub.

Percussion Methods for the College Music Education Major. Douglas B. Wheeler. (Illus.). 91p. (Orig.). (C). 1987. pap. text 16.00 (0-9622729-0-6) D Wheeler.

Percussion Solo Literature. Ed. by Thomas Siwe. LC 95-79705. 517p. (Orig.). (C). 1995. pap. text 35.00 (0-9635891-1-3) Media Press.

***Percussionists: A Biographical Dictionary.** Stephen L. Barnhart. LC 99-46021. 429p. 2000. lib. bdg. 95.00 (0-313-29627-8) Greenwood.

Percussionist's Guide to Orchestral Excerpts. David W. Vincent. 71p. (Orig.). (C). 1980. pap. text 5.00 (0-932614-01-9) Broad River.

Percussive Slap Bass. Chris Matheos. 72p. 1996. pap. 17.95 (0-7866-1673-3, 95703BCP) Mel Bay.

Percutaneous Absorption: Drugs--Cosmetics--Mechanisms--Methodology. 3rd ed. Robert L. Bronaugh & Howard I. Maibach. LC 99-14994. (Illus.). 992p. 1999. text 225.00 (0-8247-1966-2) Dekker.

Percutaneous Absorption: Mechanisms - Methodology - Drug Delivery. 2nd ed. Howard I. Maibach & Robert L. Bronaugh. (Illus.). 632p. 1989. text 215.00 (0-8247-8036-1) Dekker.

Percutaneous Breast Biopsy. Ed. by Steven H. Parker & William E. Jobe. LC 93-14055. 192p. 1993. text 92.00 (0-7817-0010-8) Lppncott W & W.

Percutaneous Collection of Arterial Blood for Laboratory Analysis: Approved Standard, 1992, Vol. 5. 2nd ed. National Committee for Clinical Laboratory Standar. 1992. 100.00 (1-56238-130-X, H11-A2) NCCLS.

Percutaneous Lumbar Discectomy. Ed. by H. M. Mayer & M. Brock. (Illus.). 225p. 1989. 86.95 (0-387-51032-X) Spr-Verlag.

Percutaneous Penetration Enhancers. Ed. by Howard I. Maibach & Eric W. Smith. LC 95-7119. 512p. 1995. boxed set 159.95 (0-8493-2605-2, 2605) CRC Pr.

Percutaneous Prostate Cryoablation. Ed. by Gary M. Onik et al. LC 94-34029. (Illus.). 172p. 1994. text 75.00 (0-942219-66-X) Quality Med Pub.

Percutaneous Revascularization Techniques. Ed. by Manuel Maynar-Moliner et al. LC 92-49670. 1993. 149.00 (0-86577-441-2) Thieme Med Pubs.

Percutaneous Transluminal Angioscopy. Andreas Beck. LC 92-48747. 1993. write for info. (3-540-51066-4); 164.45 (0-387-51066-4) Spr-Verlag.

P

An Asterisk (*) at the beginning of an entry indicates that the title is appearing for the first time.

Percutaneous Transluminal Coronary Angioplasty: A Clinical Follow-Up Study. F. Stammen. No. 73. 121p. (Orig.). 1994. pap. 32.50 (*90-6186-592-1*, Pub. by Leuven Univ) Coronet Bks.

Percutaneous Venous Blood Sampling in Endocrine Diseases. Ed. by R. Sornesen & Renan Uflacker. (Illus.). 208p. 1992. 149.00 (*0-387-97681-7*) Spr-Verlag.

Percy Alexander McMahon - Collected Papers: Combinatorics, Vol. 1. Percy A. MacMahon. Ed. by George E. Andrews. LC 77-28962. (Mathematicians of Our Time Ser.). 1978. 125.00 (*0-262-13121-8*) MIT Pr.

Percy Alexander McMahon - Collected Papers Vol. II: Number Theory, Invariants & Applications. Percy A. MacMahon. Ed. by George E. Andrews. (Mathematicians of Our Time Ser.: No. 24). (Illus.). 904p. 1986. 105.00 (*0-262-13214-1*) MIT Pr.

Percy & Harold. Reverend Wilbert V. Awdry. (Illus.). (J). 1997. 5.99 (*0-679-88681-8*, Pub. by Random Bks Yng Read) Random.

Percy Blandford's Complete Outdoor Buildings Book. Percy W. Blandford. 472p. 1992. 34.95 (*0-8306-3608-0*, 2803) McGraw-Hill Prof.

Percy Blandford's Favorite Woodworking Projects. Percy W. Blandford. 800p. 1991. 39.95 (*0-8306-2148-2*) McGraw-Hill Prof.

Percy Bysshe Shelley see Modern Critical Views Series

Percy Bysshe Shelley see Romantics: Critical Heritage

Percy Bysshe Shelley. Donald H. Reiman. (Twayne's English Authors Ser.: No. 81). 200p. 1989. 28.95 (*0-8057-6981-1*, Twyne) Mac Lib Ref.

Percy Bysshe Shelley. Percy Bysshe Shelley. (Poets Ser.). 146p. 1993. 5.95 (*0-7117-0439-2*, Pub. by JARR UK) Seven Hills Bk.

Percy Bysshe Shelley: (A Collection of Poems) Percy Bysshe Shelley. Ed. by Edward Thompson. (Augustan Books of English Poetry Ser.). 36p. 1998. reprint ed. 10.00 (*0-89904-730-0*, Silhouette Imprints); reprint ed. pap. 5.00 (*0-89904-731-9*, Silhouette Imprints) Crumb Elbow Pub.

Percy Bysshe Shelley: An Anthology of Recent Criticism. Ed. by N. P. Singh. 1993. 30.00 (*81-85753-03-2*, Pub. by Pencraft International) Advent Bks Div.

Percy Bysshe Shelley: Bicentenary Essays. Ed. by Kelvin Everest. (Essays & Studies 1992: Vol. 45). 144p. (C). 1992. 29.95 (*0-85991-352-X*, DS Brewer) Boydell & Brewer.

Percy Bysshe Shelley: Drafts, Vol. 6. Percy Bysshe Shelley. Ed. & Intro. by Mary A. Quinn. LC 83-49271. (Manuscripts of the Younger Romantics & the Bodleian Shelley Manuscripts). 484p. 1994. 195.00 (*0-8240-5870-4*, SSSHELL) Garland.

Percy Bysshe Shelley: Hellas. Percy Bysshe Shelley. Ed. & Intro. by Donald H. Reiman. (Manuscripts of the Younger Romantics Ser.: Vol. 3). 134p. 1985. text 35.00 (*0-8240-6260-4*) Garland.

Percy Bysshe Shelley: Shelley's 1821-1822 Huntington Notebook, Vol. VII. Percy Bysshe Shelley. Ed. & Intro. by Mary A. Quinn. LC 96-3152. (Manuscripts of the Younger Romantics: Vol. 7). 424p. 1996. text 215.00 (*0-8153-1150-8*, HM 2211) Garland.

Percy Bysshe Shelley: The Frankenstein Notebooks, Vol. 9. Mary Wollstonecraft Shelley. Tr. & Comment by Charles E. Robinson. LC 96-31647. (Manuscripts of the Younger Romantics Ser.: Vol. IX). 952p. 1996. text 374.00 (*0-8153-1608-9*) Garland.

Percy Bysshe Shelley: The Mask of Anarchy Draft Notebook, Vol. 4. Percy Bysshe Shelley. Ed. & Intro. by Mary A. Quinn. (Manuscripts of the Younger Romantics, Shelley: Vol. IV). 580p. 1990. reprint ed. text 80.00 (*0-8240-6975-7*, HM 2177) Garland.

Percy Bysshe Shelley's Major Lyrics. Harold Bloom. LC 87-37509. (Modern Critical Interpretations Ser.). 1988. 19.95 (*1-55546-960-4*) Chelsea Hse.

Percy Bysshe Shelley's "The Triumph of Life" Harold Bloom. LC 87-33846. (Modern Critical Interpretations Ser.). 1988. 24.50 (*1-55546-973-6*) Chelsea Hse.

Percy Grainger. Wilfrid Mellers. (Oxford Studies of Composers). (Illus.). 176p. 1992. pap. text 28.00 (*0-19-816270-7*) OUP.

Percy Grainger. 2nd ed. John Bird. (Illus.). 424p. 1999. text 45.00 (*0-19-816652-4*) OUP.

Percy Grainger: The Man Behind the Music. Eileen Dorum. 260p. 1989. 29.50 (*0-912483-63-6*) Pro-Am Music.

Percy Grainger: The Pictorial Biography. Robert Simon. (Illus.). 1987. pap. 22.00 (*0-912483-64-4*) Pro-Am Music.

Percy Granger. John Bird. (Illus.). (Orig.). pap. 29.95 (*0-86819-570-7*, Pub. by Currency Pr) Accents Pubns.

Percy Greene & the Jackson Advocate: The Life & Times of a Radical Conservative Black Newspaperman, 1897-1977. Julius E. Thompson. LC 94-17974. (Illus.). 208p. 1994. lib. bdg. 32.50 (*0-7864-0015-3*) McFarland & Co.

Percy. History of the House of Percy, from the Earliest Times down to the Present Century, 2 vols., Set. Gerald Brenan. Ed. by W. A. Lindsay. (Illus.). 1996. reprint ed. lib. bdg. 149.00 (*0-8328-5295-3*) Higginson Bk Co.

Percy. History of the House of Percy, from the Earliest Times Down to the Present Century, 2 vols., Set. Gerald Brenan. Ed. by W. A. Lindsay. (Illus.). 1996. reprint ed. pap. 129.00 (*0-8328-5296-1*) Higginson Bk Co.

Percy Ray - A Ray for God. Estus W. Pirkle. (Illus.). 624p. 1998. 26.00 (*0-9663391-0-X*) E Pirkle.

***Percy Shelley.** Harold Bloom. 2000. 19.95 (*0-7910-5930-8*) Chelsea Hse.

Percy to the Rescue. Steven J. Simmons. LC 97-39074. (Illus.). 32p. (J). (ps-3). 1998. 15.95 (*0-88106-390-8*, Talewinds) Charlesbridge Pub.

***Percy's Bumpy Ride.** Nick Butterworth. (Illus.). 28p. (J). 2000. write for info. (*1-58048-091-8*) Sandvik Pub.

Percy's Fancy Face Paint Party. Annie Kubler. (Illus.). 32p. (J). (ps-3). 1995. 9.99 (*0-85953-525-8*) Childs Play.

Percy's Picnic. (J). 2001. 16.00 (*0-689-82561-7*) Atheneum Yung Read.

Percyscapes: The Fugue State in Twentieth-Century Southern Fiction. Robert W. Rudnicki. LC 98-44082. (Southern Literary Studies). 176p. 1999. text 30.00 (*0-8071-2344-7*) La State U Pr.

Perdida del Reino (The Loss of the Kingdom) 2nd ed. Jose Bianco. (SPA.). 382p. 1990. 24.99 (*968-16-3396-2*, Pub. by Fondo) Continental Bk.

Perdida y Hallada. Benda. (Serie Rompecabezas en Libro - Jigsaw Puzzles in Book Ser.).Tr. of Lost & Found. (SPA.). 8p. (J). 1992. bds. 4.99 (*1-56063-309-3*, 490447) Editorial Unilit.

Perdido. Rick Collignon. LC 96-53857. 224p. 1997. 19.50 (*1-878448-76-5*) MacMurray & Beck.

Perdido. Rick Collignon. LC 96-53857. 224p. 1999. pap. 10.00 (*0-380-73220-3*, Avon Bks) Morrow Avon.

Perdido (Lost) Hilda Perera. (SPA., Illus.). (YA). 1993. pap. 5.99 (*968-16-4234-1*, Pub. by Fondo) Continental Bk.

Perdita: The Memoirs of Mary Robinson. Ed. by Martin J. Levy. LC 95-112570. 168p. 1995. 35.00 (*0-7206-0930-5*) Dufour.

Perdita: The Memoirs of Mary Robinson, 1758-1800. Ed. by M. J. Levy. 1995. 35.00 (*0-614-07439-8*, Pub. by P Owen Ltd) Dufour.

Perdita Durango. Barry Gifford. 128p. 1996. reprint ed. pap. 12.00 (*0-8021-3483-1*, Grove) Grove-Atltic.

Perdita's Passion. large type ed. Genevieve Lyons. LC 98-5510. (Romance Ser.). 224 p. 1998. write for info. (*0-7540-3275-2*) Chivers N Amer.

Perdita's Passion. large type ed. Genevieve Lyons. LC 98-5510. 265p. 1998. 18.95 (*0-7838-8459-1*, G K Hall Lrg Type) Mac Lib Ref.

Perdition: A Play in Two Acts. Jim Allen. (C). 1996. 29.95 (*0-86372-099-4*); pap. 10.95 (*0-86372-100-1*) LPC InBook.

Perdition, U. S. A. Gary Phillips. 272p. 1997. mass mkt. 5.99 (*0-425-15900-0*, Prime Crime) Berkley Pub.

Perdition, U. S. A. Gary Phillips. LC 93-61105. 260p. 1994. pap. 13.00 (*0-9639050-6-6*, Pub. by Blue Heron OR) Consort Bk Sales.

Perdition's Keepsake. Charles Behlen. Ed. by Dave Oliphant. (Illus.). 1978. pap. 5.00 (*0-933384-00-9*) Prickly Pear.

Perdon de los Pecados. 2nd ed. Carlos H. Mackintosh. Ed. by Gordon H. Bennett. Tr. by Sara Bautista from ENG. (Serie Diamante).Tr. of Forgiveness of Sins. (SPA.). 36p. 1982. pap. 0.85 (*0-942504-02-X*) Overcomer Pr.

Perdon Es... Irene Fohri. 1997. pap. text 5.98 (*968-38-0707-0*) Panorama Edit.

Perdon y Jesus: El Punto de Encuentro Entre "Un Curso en Milagros" y el Cristianismo. Kenneth Wapnick. LC 95-44293. 464p. 1998. pap. 16.00 (*0-933291-23-X*) Foun Miracles.

Perdona y Ama Otra Vez. John Neider.Tr. of Forgive & Love Again. (SPA.). 210p. 1995. 8.99 (*1-56063-521-5*, 498578) Editorial Unilit.

Perdonar para Ser Libre. David Augsburger. Orig. Title: Freedom of Forgiveness. (SPA.). 160p. 1977. mass mkt. 5.99 (*0-8254-1046-0*, Edit Portavoz) Kregel.

Perdue Chicken Cookbook. Mitzi Perdue. Ed. by Bill Grose. 296p. 1991. 18.95 (*0-671-69143-0*) PB.

***Perdue Chicken Cookbook.** Mitzi Perdue. (Illus.). 2000. 9.99 (*0-7858-1200-8*) Bk Sales Inc.

Perdut. Neil Lehrman. LC 78-20558. 1979. pap. 9.95 (*0-931848-23-7*) Dryad Pr.

Perdut. deluxe limited ed. Neil Lehrman. LC 78-20558. 1979. 15.00 (*0-931848-22-9*) Dryad Pr.

Pere d'Arthur. Ginette Anfousse. (Novels in the Premier Roman Ser.). (FRE.). 64p. (J). (gr. 2-5). 1989. pap. 7.95 (*2-89021-112-6*, Pub. by La Courte Ech) Firefly Bks Ltd.

Pere de Circonstance. Maureen Child. (Rouge Passion Ser.). 1999. mass mkt. 3.50 (*0-373-37512-3*, 1-37512-0) Harlequin Bks.

***Pere en Detresse.** Liz Fielding. (Azur Ser.: No. 793). (FRE.). 1999. mass mkt. 3.99 (*0-373-34793-6*, 1-34793-9, Harlequin French) Harlequin Bks.

***Pere et L'Enfant: Pitit Papa L.** Georges Castera. (FRE., Illus.). 11p. 1999. pap. write for info. (*1-58437-011-4*) Edit Memo.

Pere Goriot. Honore de Balzac. 21.95 (*0-88411-598-4*) Amereon Ltd.

Pere Goriot. Honore de Balzac. Ed. by Pierre-Georges Castex. (Coll. Prestige). 49.95 (*0-685-34093-7*); pap. 29.95 (*0-685-34092-9*) Fr & Eur.

Pere Goriot. Honore de Balzac. 1960. 10.95 (*0-685-58345-7*, 2070367843); pap. 10.95 (*0-8288-9365-9*, 2070367843) Fr & Eur.

Pere Goriot. Honore de Balzac. (Modern Library College Editions). (C). 1950. pap. text 6.25 (*0-07-553572-6*, T2) McGraw.

Pere Goriot. Honore de Balzac. 1962. mass mkt. 6.95 (*0-451-52190-0*, Sig Classics) NAL.

Pere Goriot. Honore de Balzac. (FRE.). (C). 1983. pap. 7.95 (*0-8442-1764-6*, VF1764-6) NTC Contemp Pub Co.

Pere Goriot. Honore de Balzac. (Folio Ser.: No. 784). (FRE.). 1960. pap. 9.95 (*2-07-036784-3*) Schoenhof.

Pere Goriot. Honore de Balzac. Tr. by A. J. Krailsheimer. (Oxford World's Classics Ser.). (Illus.). 300p. 1999. pap. 9.95 (*0-19-283569-6*) OUP.

Pere Goriot. Honore de Balzac. 1992. reprint ed. lib. bdg. 24.95 (*0-89968-260-X*, Lghtyr Pr) Buccaneer Bks.

Pere Goriot. unabridged ed. Honore de Balzac. (FRE.). pap. 7.95 (*2-87714-123-3*, Pub. by Bookking Intl) Distribks Inc.

Pere Goriot: A New Translation: Responses, Contemporaries & Other Novelists, Twentieth-Century Criticism. Honore de Balzac & Peter Brooks. Tr. by Burton Raffel. LC 97-19938. (Norton Critical Editions Ser.). (C). 1997. pap. text 12.50 (*0-393-97166-X*) Norton.

Pere Goriot: Anatomy of a Troubled World. Martin Kanes. LC 92-42511. (Masterwork Studies). 160p. 1993. 23.95 (*0-8057-8363-6*, Twyne); pap. 13.95 (*0-8057-8582-5*, Twyne) Mac Lib Ref.

Pere Goriot: D Level. Honore de Balzac. text 8.95 (*0-88436-043-1*) EMC-Paradigm.

Pere Humile. Paul Claudel. (FRE.). 194p. 1920. 8.95 (*0-686-54414-5*); pap. 10.95 (*0-7859-1106-5*, 2070214826) Fr & Eur.

Pere Jacques: Resplendent in Victory. Francis J. Murphy. LC 98-6863. (Illus.). 214p. 1998. pap. 10.95 (*0-935216-64-2*, RV) ICS Pubns.

Pere Joseph see Father Joseph Wresinski: Voice of the Poorest

Pere Lamy. Paul Biver. Tr. by John O'Connor from FRE. 1992. reprint ed. pap. 12.00 (*0-89555-055-5*) TAN Bks Pubs.

Pere Marquette, MI. Matthew A. Supinski. (River Journal Ser.: Vol. 2, No. 4). 1995. pap. 14.95 (*1-878175-77-7*) F Amato Pubns.

Pere Marquette Power. Arthur B. Million & Thomas W. Dixon, Jr. Ed. by Carl W. Shaver. LC 85-70004. (Illus.). 224p. (Orig.). 1984. pap. 23.95 (*0-939487-06-3*) Ches & OH Hist.

Pere Marquette Railroad Company. Paul W. Ivey. LC 75-120135. (Illus.). 1978. reprint ed. 17.50 (*0-912382-03-1*) Black Letter.

Pere Noel. Ginette Anfousse. (Jiji et Pichou Ser.). (FRE., Illus.). 24p. (J). (ps up). 1993. pap. 6.95 (*2-89021-205-X*, Pub. by La Courte Ech) Firefly Bks Ltd.

Peregination Ver l'Ouest (Xiyou Ji), Vol. 2. deluxe ed. Wu Cheng'en. Ed. by Andre Levy. (FRE.). 1200p. 1991. 145.00 (*0-7859-3894-X*, 2070112039) Fr & Eur.

Peregrina. Judith O. Cofer. (International Poetry Chapbook Ser.). 14p. 1985. write for info. (*0-936600-06-3*) Riverstone Foothills.

Peregrina. United Salvadorean Editors. 80p. 1987. pap. 5.95 (*0-933753-04-7*) Canterbury.

Peregrina Curiositas: Eine Reise Durch den Orbis Antiquus. Dirk Van Damme. Ed. by Andreas Kessler et al. (Novum Testamentum et Orbis Antiquus Ser.: Vol. 27). (GER.). 322p. 1994. text 45.50 (*3-7278-0928-0*, Pub. by Presses Univ Fribourg) Eisenbrauns.

Peregrinacion de Bayoan. annot. rev. ed. Eugenio M. De Hostos. Ed. by Julio C. Lopez. LC 87-25566. 420p. 1988. 20.00 (*0-8477-3603-2*); pap. 13.00 (*0-8477-3604-0*) U of PR Pr.

Peregrinaje see What Happens after Death?: Scientific & Personal Evidence for Survival

Peregrinaje: La Vida Despues de la Muerte. Migene Gonzalez-Wippler. LC 93-44592.Tr. of What Happens After We Die?. (SPA.). 256p. 1999. pap. 9.95 (*1-56718-330-1*) Llewellyn Pubns.

Peregrinaje Desde Roma. Bartholomew F. Brewer & Alfred W. Furrell. Tr. by Jose M. Vargas-Caba from ENG. (SPA., Illus.). 194p. 1986. pap. 11.95 (*0-89084-328-7*, 030353) Bob Jones Univ.

Peregrinajes. Hugo G. Vega. (Aqui y Ahora Ser.). 75p. 1997. pap. 6.95 (*0-8477-0304-5*) U of PR Pr.

Peregrination vers l'Ouest, Vol. 1. Wu Ch'eng-en. Ed. by Andre Levy. (FRE.). 1991. lib. bdg. 145.00 (*0-7859-3895-8*) Fr & Eur.

Peregrinations. Robert Enright. LC 98-138490. 392p. 1998. pap. 19.95 (*0-921368-67-4*) Genl Dist Srvs.

Peregrinations: Adventures with the Green Parrot. Gerda W. Klein. LC 86-80966. (Illus.). 48p. (J). (gr. 3-4). 1986. 12.95 (*0-9616699-0-X*); pap. 5.95 (*0-9616699-1-8*) CHB Goodyear Comm.

Peregrinations of the Word: Essays in Medieval Philosophy. Louis Mackey. LC 96-45815. 248p. (C). 1997. text 44.50 (*0-472-10736-4*, 10736) U of Mich Pr.

Peregrine. John Baker. LC 67-23049. 191p. 1987. reprint ed. pap. 16.95 (*0-89301-115-0*) U of Idaho Pr.

Peregrine: Daring, Exciting, Canoeing Adventures. Stanley Potokar. 128p. 1991. pap. 7.50 (*0-9630056-0-X*) Potokar Pub.

Peregrine Falcon. Houghton Mifflin Company Staff. (Literature Experience 1991 Ser.). (J). (gr. 5). 1990. pap. 10.24 (*0-395-55170-6*) HM.

Peregrine Falcon. Derek A. Ratcliffe. LC 80-65963. (Illus.). 1980. 25.00 (*0-931130-05-0*) Harrell Bks.

Peregrine Falcon. Alvin Silverstein et al. LC 94-17991. (Endangered in America Ser.). (Illus.). 64p. (J). (gr. 4-6). 1995. lib. bdg. 22.40 (*1-56294-417-7*) Millbrook Pr.

Peregrine Falcon. 2nd ed. Derek A. Ratcliffe. (Illus.). 454p. 1993. text (*0-85661-060-7*) Poyser.

Peregrine Falcon: Endangered No More. Mac Priebe. LC 98-74803. (Wildlife Winners). (Illus.). 32p. (J). (gr. 2-6). 1999. 15.95 (*0-9669551-9-6*) Mindfull Pubg.

Peregrine Falcons. Candace C. Savage. LC 92-2681. (Illus.). 160p. 1992. 30.00 (*0-87156-504-8*, Pub. by Sierra) Random.

***Peregrine Falcons.** Doug Wechsler. LC 99-59349. (Really Wild Life of Birds of Prey Ser.). (Illus.). (J). 2000. write for info. (*0-8239-5598-2*) Rosen Group.

Peregrine Falcons. Candace C. Savage. LC 92-2681. (Illus.). 160p. 1993. reprint ed. pap. 20.00 (*0-87156-461-0*, Pub. by Sierra) Random.

Peregrine Sketchbook. C. F. Tunnicliffe. (Illus.). 80p. 1997. 35.00 (*1-900318-02-4*, Pub. by Excellent Pr) Silent River.

Peregrine the Chemistry Place. 2000. 4.17 (*0-395-91920-7*) HM.

Peregrine Watching. Ron Berry. 97p. 1987. pap. 11.95 (*0-8464-4638-3*) Beekman Pubs.

Peregrine Watching. Ron Berry. 97p. (C). 1987. pap. 30.00 (*0-86383-362-4*, Pub. by Gomer Pr) St Mut.

Peregrine's Rest. Jennifer Gostin. 256p. 1996. 24.00 (*1-877946-74-5*) Permanent Pr.

Peregrine's Rest. Jennifer Gostin. 1997. pap. text 16.00 (*1-57962-000-0*) Permanent Pr.

Peregrino: El en un Castellano Actualizado. John Bunyan & John H. Thomas.Tr. of Pilgrim's Progress in Today's English. (SPA.). 138p. 1996. 14.99 (*0-8254-1095-9*, Edit Portavoz) Kregel.

Peregrino en Su Patria. Lope de Vega. (SPA.). 505p. 1973. 17.95 (*0-8288-7164-7*, S29340) Fr & Eur.

Peregrino en Su Patria (The Pilgrim in His Country), 3 vols. Octavio Paz. (Mexico en la Obra de Octavio Paz Ser.: Vols. 1-3). (SPA.). 808p. pap. 27.99 (*968-16-3732-1*, Pub. by Fondo) Continental Bk.

Peregrino en Su Patria (The Pilgrim in His Country) El Cercado Ajeno. Octavio Paz. (Mexico en la Obra de Octavio Paz Ser.: Vol. 3). (SPA.). 238p. pap. 13.99 (*968-16-3166-8*, Pub. by Fondo) Continental Bk.

Peregrino en Su Patria (The Pilgrim in His Country) Historia & Politica de Mexico. 2nd ed. Octavio Paz. (Complete Works of Octavio Paz: Vol. VIII). (SPA.). 600p. 1994. 45.99 (*968-16-3902-2*, Pub. by Fondo) Continental Bk.

Peregrino en Su Patria (The Pilgrim in His Country) Pasados. Octavio Paz. (Mexico en la Obra de Octavio Paz Ser.: Vol. 1). (SPA.). 284p. pap. 13.99 (*968-16-3164-1*, Pub. by Fondo) Continental Bk.

Peregrino en Su Patria (The Pilgrim in His Country) Presente Fluido. Octavio Paz. (Mexico en la Obra de Octavio Paz Ser.: Vol. 2). (SPA.). 291p. pap. 13.99 (*968-16-3165-X*, Pub. by Fondo) Continental Bk.

Peregrinos de Aztlan. Miguel Mendez. LC 90-27640. (Clasicos Chicanos - Chicano Classics Ser.: No. 6). 192p. 1991. pap. 15.00 (*0-927534-14-2*) Biling Rev-Pr.

Peregrinos de la Habana. Paul Hollander. (Biblioteca Cubana Contemporanea Ser.).Tr. of Political Pilgrims. (SPA.). 305p. 1987. pap. 23.00 (*84-359-0502-0*, Pub. by Editorial Playor) Ediciones.

Peregrinos de la Libertad. Felix Ojeda Reyes. (SPA., Illus.). 272p. 1992. pap. 29.95 (*0-8477-5664-5*) U of PR Pr.

Peregrinos de la Libertad. Felix O. Reyes. (Caribbean Collection). 245p. 1992. 29.95 (*0-8477-0898-5*) U of PR Pr.

Peregrinos de N. C. Wyeth (N. C. Wyeth's Pilgrims) Robert D. San Souci. Tr. by Alberto Romo. (Illus.). 34p. (J). (gr. 4-6). 1992. 14.95 (*1-880507-03-X*) Lectorum Pubns.

Peregrinos del Amazonas (Pilgrims of the Amazons) Alfredo G. Cerda. (SPA.). 133p. (YA). 1994. pap. 6.99 (*968-16-4071-3*, Pub. by Fondo) Continental Bk.

Pereira Declares: A Testimony. Antonio Tabucchi. Tr. by Patrick Creagh from ITA. LC 95-43565. 144p. 1996. 19.95 (*0-8112-1319-6*, Pub. by New Directions) Norton.

Pereira Declares: A Testimony. Antonio Tabucchi. Tr. by Patrick Creagh from ITA. LC 95-43565. 136p. 1997. pap. 9.95 (*0-8112-1358-7*, NDP848, Pub. by New Directions) Norton.

Perejaume: Des-Exhibit. Text by Marcia Tucker et al. (Illus.). 210p. 1999. pap. 35.00 (*84-95273-05-5*, 920863, Pub. by Actar) Dist Art Pubs.

Perek Highlights of Astronomy. 1969. text 202.50 (*90-277-0137-7*) Kluwer Academic.

Perekrestki Sudeb: Dve povesti. Mikhail Dyomin. LC 80-54024. (RUS.). 307p. 1983. 29.00 (*0-89830-071-1*); pap. 21.00 (*0-89830-033-9*) Russica Pubs.

Perelandra. C. S. Lewis. (J). 1976. 21.95 (*0-8488-0564-X*) Amereon Ltd.

Perelandra. C. S. Lewis. 1965. 12.05 (*0-606-00445-9*, Pub. by Turtleback) Demco.

Perelandra: A Novel. C. S. Lewis. LC 96-10403. (Space Trilogy Ser.: No. 2). 224p. 1996. per. 6.95 (*0-684-82382-9*) S&S Trade.

Perelandra: A Novel. C. S. Lewis. LC 96-20724. 192p. 1996. 21.50 (*0-684-83365-4*) S&S Trade.

Perelandra: A Novel. C. S. Lewis. (Space Trilogy Ser.: No. 2). 222p. 1990. reprint ed. 40.00 (*0-02-570845-7*, Hudson Rvr Edtn) S&S Trade.

Perelandra Essences Guide see Guide d'Utilisation des Essences de Perelandra

Perelandra Essences Guide. Machaelle Wright. (Illus.). 60p. 1998. pap. 3.00 (*0-927978-26-1*) Perelandra Ltd.

***Perelandra Essences Guide (Japanese)** Machaelle S. Wright. Tr. by Michael Reid from ENG. (JPN., Illus.). 2000. pap. 3.00 (*0-927978-49-0*) Perelandra Ltd.

Perelandra Garden Workbook: A Complete Guide to Gardening with Nature Intelligences. 2nd ed. Machaelle S. Wright. LC 93-83705. (Illus.). 328p. 1993. pap. 19.95 (*0-927978-12-1*) Perelandra Ltd.

Perelandra Garden Workbook II: Co-Creative Energy Processes for Gardening, Agriculture & Life. Machaelle S. Wright. LC 87-90410. (Illus.). 198p. (Orig.). 1990. pap. 16.95 (*0-927978-13-X*) Perelandra Ltd.

Perelandra Guide to Nature Program Essences see Guia de las Esencias de Perelandra del Programa de la Naturaleza

Perelandra Guide to Rose & Garden Essences see Guia de las Esencias de Rosas y del Jardin de Perelandra

Perelandra Guide to Rose & Garden Essences see Leitfaden Zu Perelandra Rosen- und Garten-Essenzen

Perelandra Guide to Soul Ray Essences see Guia de las Esencias de Perelandra de Rayos del Alma

Perelandra Microbial Balancing Program Manual. Machaelle S. Wright. LC 95-92802. (Illus.). 167p. 1996. pap. 16.00 (*0-927978-21-0*) Perelandra Ltd.

Perelandra Study Guide. Michael S. Gilleland. 60p. (YA). (gr. 9-12). 1993. student ed., ring bd. 14.99 (*1-58609-157-3*) Progeny Pr WI.

An Asterisk (*) at the beginning of an entry indicates that the title is appearing for the first time.

Perelman's College Football Companion. Richard B. Perelman. (Illus.). 1998. pap. 14.95 (*0-9649258-7-7*) Perelman Pioneer.

*__Perelman's College Football Companion: 1999 Edition.__ Compiled by Richard B. Perelman. (Illus.). 646p. 1999. pap. 14.95 (*0-9649258-9-3*) Perelman Pioneer.

Perelman's New Rhetoric As Philosophy & Methodology for the Next Century. Mieczyslaw Maneli. LC 93-18161. (Library of Rhetorics: Vol. 1). 151p. (C). 1994. text 115.00 (*0-7923-2166-9*) Kluwer Academic.

Perelman's Pocket Cyclopedia of Cigars. Richard B. Perelman. 296p. 1995. pap. 8.95 (*0-9649258-2-6*) Perelman Pioneer.

*__Perelman's Pocket Cyclopedia of Cigars.__ Richard B. Perelman. 1999. pap. 12.95 (*1-893273-00-8*) Perelman Pioneer.

Perelman's Pocket Cyclopedia of Cigars: 1999 Edition. Richard B. Perelman. (Illus.). 832p. 1998. pap. 12.95 (*0-9649258-8-5*) Perelman Pioneer.

Perelman's Pocket Cyclopedia of Cigars, 1997 Edition. Richard B. Perelman. (Illus.). 442p. 1996. pap. 9.95 (*0-9649258-3-4*) Perelman Pioneer.

Perelman's Pocket Cyclopedia of Cigars, 1998 Edition. 4th ed. Richard B. Perelman. (Illus.). 608p. 1997. pap. 9.95 (*0-9649258-5-0*) Perelman Pioneer.

Perelman's Pocket Cylopedia of Havana Cigars. Richard B. Perelman. (Illus.). 108p. (Orig.). 1996. pap. 9.95 (*0-9649258-4-2*) Perelman Pioneer.

Perelomy Zhizni; (The Turning Points) Anatoliy Golitsyn et al. (RUS., Illus.). 296p. (Orig.). (C). 1991. pap. 16.00 (*0-9616413-8-X*) Multilingual.

Peremeshchennoe Litso. Zinovy Zinik. LC 84-60083. (RUS.). 238p. (Orig.). 1985. pap. 15.00 (*0-89830-023-1*) Russica Pubs.

Peremptory Norms (Jus Cogens) in International Law. Lauri Hannikainen. 783p. 1989. 187.50 (*951-640-394-8*) Coronet Bks.

Perennial: An Image of Moorhead. Ed. by Wayne Gudmundson. (Prairie Documents Photographic Bks.). (Illus.). 170p. (Orig.). 1992. pap. text 10.00 (*0-9629472-1-0*) MSU Mass Commns.

Perennial Adventure: A Tribute to Alice Eastwood, 1859-1943. Susanna Dakin. 48p. 1954. 10.00 (*0-940228-09-2*) Calif Acad Sci.

Perennial Bachelor. Anne Parrish. 1976. lib. bdg. 13.95 (*0-89968-153-0*, Lghtyr Pr) Buccaneer Bks.

Perennial Combinations: Stunning Combinations That Make Your Yard Look Fantastic Right from the Start. C. Colston Burrell. LC 98-40152. (Illus.). 352p. 1999. text 29.95 (*0-87596-806-6*) Rodale Pr Inc.

Perennial Companion. Smith & Hawken Staff. 14.95 (*0-7611-0832-7*, 10832) Workman Pub.

Perennial Cultural Almanac of the Northeast. Cheryl C. Smyers. (Illus.). 14.95 (*0-9656475-0-1*) Cator Ent.

Perennial Decay: On the Aesthetics & Politics of Decadence. Ed. by Liz Constable. LC 98-34373. (New Cultural Studies). (Illus.). 320p. 1998. 45.00 (*0-8122-3470-7*); pap. 19.95 (*0-8122-1678-4*) U of Pa Pr.

Perennial Dictionary of World Religions. Keith Crim. LC 89-45260. 848p. 1990. pap. 36.00 (*0-06-061613-X*, Pub. by Harper SF) HarpC.

Perennial Garden: Color Harmonies Through the Seasons. Jeff Cox & Marilyn Cox. LC 85-14192. (Illus.). 320p. 1992. pap. 16.95 (*0-87596-123-1*, 01-644-1) Rodale Pr Inc.

Perennial Garden Color. William C. Welch. LC 88-24820. 280p. 1989. 29.95 (*0-87833-628-1*) Taylor Pub.

Perennial Garden Plants: or The Modern Florilegium. 3rd ed. Graham S. Thomas. LC 89-48715. 535p. 1990. 39.95 (*0-88192-167-X*) Timber.

Perennial Gardening. Derek Fell. 1996. 22.50 (*0-614-96788-0*, Friedman-Fairfax) M Friedman Pub Grp Inc.

Perennial Gardening with Derek Fell. Derek Fell. LC 95-49634. (Illus.). 120p. 1996. 22.50 (*1-56799-252-8*, Friedman-Fairfax) M Friedman Pub Grp Inc.

Perennial Gardens for Texas. Julie Ryan. LC 97-4692. (Illus.). 400p. 1998. 50.00 (*0-292-78106-7*); pap. 27.95 (*0-292-77089-8*) U of Tex Pr.

Perennial Ground Covers. David S. Mackenzie. LC 96-23737. (Illus.). 452p. 1997. 49.95 (*0-88192-368-0*) Timber.

Perennial Killer: A Gardening Mystery. Ann Ripley. LC 99-33254. 2000. 20.01 (*0-553-10694-5*) Bantam.

*__Perennial Killer: A Gardening Mystery.__ Ann Ripley. 352p. 2000. mass mkt. 5.99 (*0-553-57737-9*) Bantam Dell.

Perennial Philadelphians The Anatomy of an American Aristocracy. Nathaniel Burt. LC 98-56457. 1999. pap. text 29.95 (*0-8122-1693-8*) U of Pa Pr.

Perennial Philadelphians: The Anatomy of an American Aristocracy. Nathaniel Burt. LC 75-1834. (Leisure Class in America Ser.). (Illus.). 1975. reprint ed. 46.95 (*0-405-06903-0*) Ayer.

Perennial Philosophy. Aldous Huxley. LC 76-167362. (Essay Index Reprint Ser.). 1977. reprint ed. 28.95 (*0-8369-2773-7*) Ayer.

Perennial Philosophy. Aldous Huxley. LC 89-46102. 336p. 1990. reprint ed. pap. 14.00 (*0-06-090191-8*, CN191, Perennial) HarperTrade.

*__Perennial Plants for Profit.__ rev. deluxe ed. Francis X. Jozwik. Ed. by John Gist. (Illus.). 300p. 2000. 29.95 (*0-916781-20-8*) Andmar Pr.

Perennial Plants for Profit or Pleasure: How to Grow Perennial Flowers & Herbs for Profit Or Personal Landscape Use. Francis X. Jozwik. (Illus.). 206p. 1995. pap. 19.95 (*0-916781-04-6*) Andmar Pr.

Perennial Political Palate: A Feminist Vegetarian Cookbook. Bloodroot Collective Staff et al. LC 82-83994. (Illus.). 320p. (Orig.). 1993. pap. 16.95 (*0-9605210-3-8*) Sanguinaria.

Perennial Psychology of the Bhagavad Gita. Swami Rama. LC 84-25137. 480p. (C). 1982. pap. 16.95 (*0-89389-090-1*) Himalayan Inst.

Perennial Question. George Grimm. Tr. by Ponisch Schoenwerth from GER. 56p. 1979. text 8.50 (*0-89684-096-4*, Pub. by Motilal Bnarsidass) S Asia.

*__Perennial Struggle: Race, Ethnicity Minority Groups in the United States.__ Michael C. LeMay. LC 99-58622. 350p. 2000. pap. text 42.00 (*0-13-020547-8*) P-H.

Perennial Tradition of Neoplatonism. Ed. by John J. Cleary. (Ancient & Medieval Philosophy Ser.: No. XXIV). 614p. 1997. 117.50 (*90-6186-847-5*, Pub. by Leuven Univ) Coronet Bks.

Perennial Vivekananda: A Selection. Compiled by Swami Lokeswaranada. (C). 1988. 8.00 (*0-8364-2463-8*, Pub. by National Sahitya Akademi) S Asia.

*__Perennial Weeds: Characteristics & Identification of Selected Herbaceous Species.__ Wood Powell Anderson. LC 99-35933. (Illus.). 244p. 1999. 64.95 (*0-8138-2520-2*) Iowa St U Pr.

Perennial Works in Sociology, 34 bks., Set. Ed. by Lewis A. Coser & Walter W. Powell. (Illus.). 1979. lib. bdg. 1064.00 (*0-405-12081-8*) Ayer.

Perennials. Deni Bown. LC 95-43903. (Eyewitness Handbooks Ser.). 352p. 1996. pap. 19.95 (*0-7894-0430-3*) DK Pub Inc.

Perennials. DK Publishing Staff & Ray Edwards. LC 98-41493. (AHS Practical Guides Ser.). (Illus.). 80p. 1999. pap. 8.95 (*0-7894-4151-9*) DK Pub Inc.

Perennials. Derek Fell. (Derek Fell's Handy Garden Guides Ser.). (Illus.). 192p. 1996. pap. 12.95 (*1-56799-374-5*, Friedman-Fairfax) M Friedman Pub Grp Inc.

*__Perennials.__ Marion Ferraudi. 1999. 19.99 (*3-8228-6514-1*) Benedikt Taschen.

*__Perennials.__ Lois Hole. 2000. pap. text 7.95 (*0-9682791-7-1*) Holes G & G.

Perennials. Text by Susan A. McClure. LC 92-45809. (Rodale's Successful Organic Gardening Ser.). (Illus.). 1993. pap. 14.95 (*0-87596-560-1*); text 24.95 (*0-87596-559-8*) Rodale Pr Inc.

Perennials. Maggie Oster. LC 99-216600. (Illus.). 1997. write for info. (*0-914697-89-7*) N Amer Outdoor Grp.

*__Perennials.__ Ed. by Sunset Books Editors. (Illus.). 128p. 2000. pap. 12.95 (*0-376-03574-9*, 203574, Pub. by Sunset Books) Leisure AR.

Perennials. Time-Life Books Editors. Ed. by Janet Cave. (Complete Gardener Ser.). (Illus.). 160p. (gr. 11). 1999. pap. 16.95 (*0-7835-4100-7*) Time-Life.

Perennials: A Beginner's Guide to a Colorful Garden. (Illus.). 64p. 1993. spiral bd. 5.98 (*1-56173-754-2*, 3615600) Pubns Intl Ltd.

*__Perennials: A Complete Guide to Successful Growing.__ Richard Bird. (Illus.). 2000. 16.95 (*0-7548-0562-X*, Lorenz Bks) Anness Pub.

Perennials: A Fiftieth Anniversary Selection from the Berg Collection. Lola L. Szladits. LC 88-15211. (Illus.). ix, 92p. (Orig.). 1988. pap. 15.00 (*0-87104-401-3*) NY Pub Lib.

Perennials: A Gardener's Guide. Ed. by Christopher Woods. (Plants & Gardens Ser.). (Illus.). 1991. pap. 7.95 (*0-945352-68-9*) Bklyn Botanic.

*__Perennials: A Photographic Guide to More Than 1,000 Plants by Type, Size, Season of Interest & Color.__ Linden Hawthorne. Ed. by Helen Parker. LC 99-48242. (Illus.). 352p. 2000. 29.99 (*0-7894-5340-1*, D K Ink) DK Pub Inc.

Perennials: A Southern Celebration of Foods & Flavors. Junior Service League of Gainesville Staff. (Illus.). 417p. 1996. 17.95 (*0-942407-32-6*) Father & Son.

Perennials: A Southern Celebration of Foods & Flavors. Illus. by Gwen Newman. LC 83-81825. vi, 426p. 1984. 14.95 (*0-9612234-0-5*) Perennial Pubns.

Perennials: One Thousand One Gardening Questions Answered. Ed. by Garden Way Publishing Staff & Gwen Steege. LC 88-82824. (Illus.). 160p. 1989. 16.95 (*0-88266-548-0*, Garden Way Pub) Storey Bks.

Perennials: Toward Continuous Bloom. Ed. by Ann Lovejoy. (New Voices from American Gardens Ser.). 304p. 1991. pap. 17.95 (*0-913643-06-8*) Capabilitys.

Perennials for American Gardens. Ruth R. Clausen & Nicolas H. Ekstrom. 631p. 1989. 50.00 (*0-394-55740-9*) Random.

*__Perennials for British Columbia.__ Alison Beck & Marianne Binetti. (Illus.). 352p. 2000. pap. 18.95 (*1-55105-258-X*) Lone Pine.

Perennials for Dummies. Storey Publishing Staff. 1997. pap. 16.99 (*0-676-57107-7*) Random.

Perennials for Dummies. Marcia Tatroe. Ed. by National Gardening Association Editors. LC 96-80236. (For Dummies Ser.). (Illus.). 384p. 1997. pap. 16.99 (*0-7645-5030-6*) IDG Bks.

*__Perennials for Every Purpose: Choose the Plants You Need for Your Conditions, Your Garden, & Your Taste.__ Larry Hodgson. LC 99-6968. (Illus.). 512p. 2000. text 29.95 (*0-87596-823-6*) Rodale Pr Inc.

Perennials for Intermountain & High Desert Gardening. Tova Roseman. LC 99-176299. (Tova's Garden Ser.: No. 1). (Illus.). 104p. 1998. pap. 14.95 (*0-943674-01-8*) Roseman Publng.

*__Perennials for Shade.__ (Essential Gardening Made Easy Ser.: Vol. 7). (Illus.). 128p. 1999. write for info. (*1-892207-20-6*) Intl Masters Pub.

*__Perennials for Sun.__ (Essential Gardening Made Easy Ser.: Vol. 1). (Illus.). 128p. 1999. write for info. (*1-892207-14-1*) Intl Masters Pub.

Perennials for the Landscape. Dianne A. Noland & Kirsten Bolin. LC 99-71696. (Illus.). 216p. 1998. pap. 31.25 (*0-8134-3149-2*, 3149) Interstate.

Perennials for the Lower Midwest. abr. ed. Ezra Haggard. LC 95-46331. (Illus.). 224p. 1996. 35.00 (*0-253-33067-X*); pap. 24.95 (*0-253-21014-3*) Ind U Pr.

Perennials for the Plains & Prairies. Edgar W. Toop & Sara Williams. (Illus.). 190p. 1997. pap. 24.95 (*1-55091-029-9*) Lone Pine.

Perennials for the Prairies. Edgar W. Toop & Sara Williams. (Illus.). 188p. 1991. pap. 24.95 (*1-55091-005-1*) Lone Pine.

*__Perennials for Today's Gardens.__ Better Homes & Gardens. 288p. 2000. 29.95 (*0-696-20952-7*, Bttr Homes & Grdns) Meredith Bks.

*__Perennials for Washington & Oregon.__ Marianne Binetti & Alison Beck. (Illus.). 352p. 2000. pap. 18.95 (*1-55105-162-1*) Lone Pine.

Perennials in the Garden for Lasting Beauty. Charles H. Potter. LC 59-6124. (Illus.). 1959. 34.95 (*0-87599-094-0*) S G Phillips.

Perennidad de la Constitucion de los Estados Unidos y Otros Ensayos. Jose Sanchez-Boudy. LC 92-73252. (SPA.). 215p. (Orig.). 1992. pap. 15.00 (*0-89729-650-8*) Ediciones.

Perepiska A. P. Chekhova, 2 vols. Anton Chekhov. Ed. by Collet's Holdings, Ltd. Staff. 448p. 1984. 110.00 (*0-7855-0900-3*) St Mut.

Perepiska iz Dvnukh Uglov see Correspondence Across a Room

Perepiska, Vospominaniia, Dnevniki, 2 vols. Druz'ta Puskina. 642p. 1984. 75.00 (*0-7855-2931-4*) St Mut.

Peres Saints et Culte Chretien dans l'Englise des Premiers Siecles. Victor Saxer. (Collected Studies). 310p. 1994. 113.95 (*0-86078-441-X*, Pub. by Variorum) Ashgate Pub Co.

*__Perespectives: Connecting Past & Present,World History to 1800.__ Spielvogel. 1998. pap. 12.25 (*0-538-42764-7*) Sth-Wstrn College.

Perestroika: A Comparative Perspective. Ed. by Avraham Shama. LC 91-29219. 152p. 1992. 47.95 (*0-275-94038-1*, C4038, Praeger Pubs) Greenwood.

Perestroika: A Marxist Critique. Sam Marcy. 409p. 1990. pap. 12.95 (*0-89567-102-6*) World View Forum.

Perestroika: A Sustainable Process for Change. John P. Hardt & Sheila N. Heslin. 62p. 1989. pap. 10.00 (*1-56708-072-3*) Grp of Thirty.

Perestroika: An Inquiry into Its Historical, Ideological & Intellectual Roots. Abu F. Dowlah. 274p. (Orig.). 1990. pap. 72.50 (*91-86702-04-1*) Coronet Bks.

Perestroika: From Marxism & Bolshevism to Gorbachev. Svetozar Stojanovic. LC 88-12620. 167p. 1988. 35.95 (*0-87975-488-5*) Prometheus Bks.

Perestroika: Global Challenge & Our Common Future. Ed. by Ken Coates. LC 88-51544. 174p. 1988. 45.00 (*0-85124-501-3*, Pub. by Spkesman); pap. 16.95 (*0-85124-502-1*, Pub. by Spkesman) Dufour.

Perestroika: How New Is Gorbachev's New Thinking? Ed. by Ernest W. Lefever & Robert D. Vander Lugt. LC 88-21855. 259p. 1989. 29.95 (*0-89633-133-4*); pap. 12.95 (*0-89633-134-2*) Ethics & Public Policy.

Perestroika: Its Rise & Fall. Mike Davidow. 1993. pap. 8.95 (*0-7178-0703-7*) Intl Pubs Co.

Perestroika: Soviet Domestic & Foreign Policies. Ed. by Tsuyoshi Hasegawa & Alex Pravda. (Royal Institute of International Affairs Ser.). 288p. (C). 1990. text 39.95 (*0-8039-8289-5*); pap. text 19.95 (*0-8039-8308-5*) Sage.

Perestroika: The Historical Perspective. Ed. by Catherine Merridale & Chris Ward. 256p. 1995. text 19.95 (*0-340-55789-3*, A6288, Pub. by E A) St Martin.

Perestroika & International Law: Current Anglo-Soviet Approaches to International Law. Ed. by Anthony Carty & Gennady Danilenko. 288p. 1992. pap. 27.50 (*0-7486-0187-2*, Pub. by Edinburgh U Pr) Col U Pr.

Perestroika & Soviet-American Relations. Mikhail S. Gorbachev. Tr. by APN Publishers. 270p. (Orig.). 1990. pap. 29.95 (*0-943071-13-5*) Sphinx Pr.

Perestroika & Soviet National Security. Michael McGwire. LC 87-17657. 481p. 1991. 44.95 (*0-8157-5554-6*); pap. 19.95 (*0-8157-5553-8*) Brookings.

Perestroika & the Economy: New Thinking in Soviet Economics. Ed. by Anthony Jones & William Moskoff. LC 91-12127. 304p. (gr. 13). 1989. text 85.95 (*0-87332-569-9*) M E Sharpe.

Perestroika & the Nationality Question in the U. S. S. R. Shams U. Din. 1991. text 25.00 (*0-7069-4962-5*, Pub. by Vikas) Advent Bks Div.

Perestroika & the Rule of Law: Soviet & Anglo-American Perspectives. Ed. by William E. Butler. 300p. 1991. 35.00 (*0-685-52915-0*, Pub. by I B T) St Martin.

Perestroika & the Rule of Law: Soviet & Anglo-American Perspectives. William E. Butler. 1991. text 64.50 (*1-85043-316-X*, Pub. by I B T) St Martin.

Perestroika & the Soviet People. David Mandel. LC 91-72984. 207p. 1991. 45.99 (*1-895431-15-8*, Pub. by Black Rose); pap. 16.99 (*1-895431-14-X*, Pub. by Black Rose) Consort Bk Sales.

Perestroika at the Crossroads. Ed. by Alfred J. Rieber & Alvin Z. Rubinstein. LC 90-8633. 400p. (C). (gr. 13). 1991. text 67.95 (*0-87332-741-1*) M E Sharpe.

Perestroika at the Crossroads. Ed. by Alfred J. Rieber & Alvin Z. Rubinstein. LC 90-8633. 400p. (C). (gr. 13). 1991. pap. text 43.95 (*0-87332-742-X*) M E Sharpe.

Perestroika Deception: The World's Slide Towards the "Second October Revolution" ["Weltoktober]. Anatoliy Golitsyn. LC 95-76304. 248p. (Orig.). 1995. pap. 29.50 (*1-899798-00-5*) E Harle Ltd.

Perestroika Deception: The World's Slide Towards the 'Second October Revolution' ('Weltoktober') 2nd ed. Anatoliy Golitsyn. Ed. & Frwd. by Christopher Story. LC 95-76304. 1998. 35.00 (*1-899798-03-X*) E Harle Ltd.

Perestroika-Era Politics: The New Soviet Legislature & Gorbachev's Political Reforms. Ed. by Robert T. Huber & Donald R. Kelley. LC 91-18983. (Contemporary Soviet - Post Soviet Politics Ser.). 264p. (gr. 13). 1991. text 85.95 (*0-87332-829-9*); pap. text 42.95 (*0-87332-830-2*) M E Sharpe.

Perestroika for America. Lodge. 225p. 1990. 25.00 (*0-07-103250-9*) McGraw.

Perestroika for America: Restructuring Business-Government Relations for World Competitiveness. George C. Lodge. 235p. 1990. 22.95 (*0-87584-234-8*) Harvard Busn.

Perestroika in Partygrad. Alexander Zinoviev. Tr. by Charles Janson from RUS. 192p. 1992. pap. 21.00 (*0-7206-0847-3*) Dufour.

*__Perestroika in Perspectve.__ Brown. 2000. 59.95 (*0-8133-2629-X*, Pub. by Westview) HarpC.

Perestroika in the Countryside: Agricultural Reform in the Gorbachev Era. Ed. by William Moskoff. LC 90-8603. 144p. (gr. 13). 1990. text 85.95 (*0-87332-767-5*) M E Sharpe.

Perestroika, Privatization & Worker Ownership in the U. S. S. R. Jacob Keremetsky & John Logue. LC 91-622559. 56p. (Orig.). 1991. pap. 7.95 (*0-933522-22-3*) Kent Popular.

Perestroika Versus Socialism: Stalinism & the Restoration of Capitalism in the U. S. S. R. David North. 80p. (Orig.). (C). 1989. pap. 7.95 (*0-929087-39-9*) Mehring Bks.

Peretz. Isaac L. Peretz. Ed. & Tr. by Solomon Liptzin. LC 72-5689. (Biography Index Reprints - YIVO Bilingual Ser.). 1977. reprint ed. 23.95 (*0-8369-8137-5*) Ayer.

Perez Galdos & the Spanish Novel of the Nineteenth Century. Leslie B. Walton. LC 77-11400. 261p. 1970. reprint ed. 50.00 (*0-87752-115-8*) Gordian.

Perez on Medicine. Jose Perez & Wayman R. Spence. (Illus.). 64p. 1993. 29.95 (*1-56796-005-7*) WRS Group.

Perez on Sports. Jose Perez & Wayman R. Spence. (Illus.). 64p. 1995. text 29.95 (*1-56796-125-8*) WRS Group.

Perez y Martina. Dorothy S. Bishop et al. (SPA., Illus.). 64p. 6.95 (*0-8442-7167-5*, 71675) NTC Contemp Pub Co.

Perez y Martina (Perez & Martina) Marjorie E. Herrmann. (Bilingual Ser.). (ENG & SPA.). (J). 1978. 10.15 (*0-606-01431-4*, Pub. by Turtleback) Demco.

Perezhyte I Peredumane: My Life & Thoughts in Retrospect. Danylo Shumuk. Ed. by Wasyl Hryshko & Nadia Svitlychna. LC 82-84497. (UKR.). 536p. 1983. 20.00 (*0-912601-00-0*) Ukrainian News.

Perfect. large type ed. Judith McNaught. LC 93-10503. 1008p. 1993. lib. bdg. 24.95 (*1-56054-731-6*) Thorndike Pr.

Perfect. large type ed. Judith McNaught. 1008p. 1994. pap. 16.95 (*1-56054-876-2*) Thorndike Pr.

Perfect. Judith McNaught. Ed. by Linda Marrow. 704p. 1994. reprint ed. per. 7.99 (*0-671-79553-8*) PB.

*__Perfect!, Vol. 1.__ Ed. by Ike Morgan et al. (Illus.). 96p. 2000. pap. 4.63 (*1-890881-03-1*) Talla Dem.

Perfect! The Season. rev. ed. Bill Smith. (Illus.). 145p. 1989. pap. 17.95 (*0-9621896-0-X*) McClain.

Perfect ABC Songbook. Jeffrey McFarland-Johnson. (Illus.). 55p. (J). (ps-1). 1998. spiral bd. 24.95 incl. audio compact disk (*1-892397-03-X*); spiral bd. 19.95 incl. audio (*1-892397-04-8*) JohnSong.

Perfect ABC Songbook. Ed. by Jeffrey McFarland-Johnson. (Illus.). 55p. (J). (ps-1). 1998. spiral bd. 10.00 (*1-892397-00-5*) JohnSong.

*__Perfect Access Word 2000.__ Kaplan. LC 99-29350. (Illus.). 656p. 2000. pap. 34.95 (*0-684-86614-5*) S&S Trade.

Perfect Afternoon Tea Book: Tea Time Favorites for Family & Friends. (Illus.). 64p. 1998. 9.95 (*1-85967-542-5*, Lorenz Bks) Anness Pub.

Perfect Age. Dian Curtis Regan. 192p. 1987. pap. 2.50 (*0-380-75337-5*, Avon Bks) Morrow Avon.

Perfect Agreement. Michael Downing. LC 97-25629. 224p. 1997. 22.00 (*1-887178-45-7*, Pub. by Counterpt DC) HarpC.

Perfect Agreement. Michael Downing. 288p. 1998. reprint ed. pap. 12.95 (*0-425-16628-7*) Berkley Pub.

Perfect Alibi: O. J. Simpson's Strategy for Murder. Amir H. Pourtemour. (Illus.). vi, 328p. (Orig.). 1996. pap. 19.95 (*0-9655126-0-6*) A H Pourtemour.

Perfect, Amicable & Sociable Numbers: A Computational Approach. Song Y. Yan. LC 96-31112. 1996. write for info. (*981-02-2847-3*) World Scientific Pub.

Perfect Analysis Given by a Parrot. Tennessee Williams. 1961. pap. 3.25 (*0-8222-0885-7*) Dramatists Play.

Perfect & Preterite in Contemporary Earlier English. Johan Elsness. LC 96-21755. (Topics in English Linguistics Ser.: Vol. 21). xv, 432p. 1997. lib. bdg. 171.05 (*3-11-014686-X*) Mouton.

Perfect Angel. large type ed. Seth J. Margolis. LC 97-15639. (Cloak & Dagger Ser.). 632p. 1997. 25.95 (*0-7862-1150-4*) Thorndike Pr.

Perfect Angel. Seth J. Margolis. 384p. 1998. reprint ed. mass mkt. 6.99 (*0-380-78748-2*, Avon Bks) Morrow Avon.

Perfect Art: The Ostrander Hut & Ski Touring in Yosemite. Howard Weamer. LC 94-90857. (Illus.). 143p. 1995. pap. 24.95 (*0-9644146-9-4*) Plaine Style.

Perfect Ashlar & Other Masonic Symbols. John T. Lawrence. 376p. 1999. reprint ed. pap. 19.95 (*0-7661-0834-1*) Kessinger Pub.

Perfect Attendance: A Guide to Taking Attendance Using the Mac School Student Information System. Frances M. Kulak. (Illus.). 210p. 1997. spiral bd. 44.00 (*0-9637294-5-4*) Sugar Hill Pr.

Perfect Baby: A Pragmatic Approach to Genetics. Glenn McGee. LC 96-31064. 176p. 1997. 52.50 (*0-8476-8343-5*); pap. 14.95 (*0-8476-8344-3*) Rowman.

*__Perfect Baby: Parenthood in the New World of Cloning & Genetics.__ 2nd ed. Glenn McGee. LC 00-21041. 176p. 2000. 57.00 (*0-8476-9758-4*) Rowman.

*__Perfect Baby: Parenthood in the New World of Cloning & Genetics.__ 2nd ed. Glenn McGee. LC 00-21041. 176p. 2000. pap. 16.95 (*0-8476-9759-2*) Rowman.

Perfect Baby Book. Tracy Fuckinger. (Illus.). 23p. 1998. reprint ed. 29.99 (*1-892953-03-X*) Talus Corp.

Perfect Balance see Balance Perfecto

P

Perfect Balance: Compilation Edition. LC 94-237958. 1994. student ed., ring bd. write for info. incl. disk (*1-56433-461-9*); student ed., ring bd. write for info. (*1-56433-462-7*); student ed., ring bd. write for info. (*1-56433-463-5*) Prctnrs Pub Co.

Perfect Barbecue. Fiona Eaton. 1998. 6.98 (*1-84038-063-2*) Random.

***Perfect Barbecue.** Ed. by Lorenz Books Staff. (Illus.). 2000. pap. 11.95 (*0-7548-0593-X*, Lorenz Bks) Anness Pub.

Perfect Basket: Make Your Own Special Occasion Baskets. Diane Phillips. LC 94-6974. 115p. 1994. 15.00 (*0-688-13031-3*, Hearst) Hearst Commns.

Perfect Bone. Terry Collins & Emilie Kong. (Catdog Chapter Bks.: No. 3). (Illus.). 64p. (J). (gr. 2-5). 1999. pap. 3.99 (*0-689-83010-6*, Simon Spot) Little Simon.

***Perfect Bones: A Six Point Plan to Keep or Regain Healthy Bones.** Pamela Levin. LC 99-96171. 304p. 2000. pap. 39.95 (*0-9672718-0-0*) Nourishing Co.

***Perfect Border: How to Plan, Plant & Maintain Beautiful Borders, with Step-by-Step Photographs.** 2000. 14.95 (*0-7548-0038-5*, Lorenz Bks) Anness Pub.

Perfect Bread: Fun with Creative Shapes. Betsy Oppenneer. 1992. 29.95 incl. VHS (*0-9627665-3-4*) Breadworks.

Perfect Bread: How to Conquer Bread Baking. Betsy Oppenneer. 1991. 29.95 incl. VHS (*0-9627665-1-8*) Breadworks.

Perfect Brew: A Presentation of Coffees & Teas. Debbie Hansen & Patrick Caton. 64p. 1995. 6.50 (*1-56245-213-4*) Great Quotations.

Perfect Bride. Jasmine Cresswell. (Romance Ser.). 1993. per. 2.99 (*0-373-03270-6*, 1-03270-5) Harlequin Bks.

Perfect Business. Michael Le Boeuf. 224p. 1997. per. 11.00 (*0-684-83345-X*) S&S Trade Pap.

Perfect Business Plan Made Simple. William R. Lasher. LC 93-35669. 288p. 1994. pap. 12.95 (*0-385-46934-9*) Doubleday.

Perfect C: Algebras. C. Akemann & F. Shultz. LC 85-4018. (Memoirs of the AMS Ser.: No. 55/326). 117p. 1986. pap. 22.00 (*0-8218-2327-2*, MEMO/55/326) Am Math.

***Perfect Career (And How to Get It!) Master Teachers' Secrets Revealed - How to Get a Teaching Job.** (Illus.). 164p. 1999. pap. 59.50 (*0-9675663-0-4*) Aurous.

***Perfect Catch: Lessons for Life from a Bass Fisherman.** Norman Wright. (Illus.). 240p. 2000. 14.99 (*0-7642-2295-3*) Bethany Hse.

Perfect Cats. Peter Warner. 1993. 10.98 (*1-55521-946-2*) Bk Sales Inc.

Perfect Chance. Amanda Carpenter. (Harlequin Presents Ser.: No. 1826). 1996. per. 3.50 (*0-373-11826-0*, 1-11826-4) Harlequin Bks.

***Perfect Child.** Geoffrey Wilson. 337p. 1999. pap. 12.95 (*0-9674388-0-2*) Dominion TX.

Perfect Children's Dogs: A Complete Authoritative Guide. Jan Mahood. 64p. 1998. 12.95 (*0-7938-0236-9*, WW-070) TFH Pubns.

***Perfect Chocolate Chip Cookies: 101 Melt-in-Your-Mouth.** Gwen Steege. (Illus.). 144p. 2000. pap. 9.95 (*1-58017-312-8*, 67312) Storey Bks.

Perfect Choice: The Ultimate Party & Wedding Location Guide. 2nd rev. ed. Betty M. Dunkins & Joy Gray. Ed. by Nancy Parker. LC 97-94688. viii, 359p. 1998. pap. 19.95 (*0-9641379-1-7*) Gray McPherson.

Perfect Choice: Wedding Location Guide. Betty M. Dunkins & Joy Gray-Miott. LC 93-81089. 294p. 1994. pap. 19.95 (*0-9641379-0-9*) Gray McPherson.

***Perfect Christian: How Sinners Like Us Can Be More Like Jesus.** Tony Evans. 286p. 2000. pap. 12.99 (*0-8499-4251-9*) Word Pub.

Perfect Christian: How to Be More Like Jesus. Tony Evans. 1998. 19.99 (*0-8499-1505-8*) Word Pub.

***Perfect Christian: How to Be More Like Jesus.** Tony Evans. 1998. 16.99 incl. audio (*0-8499-6299-4*) Word Pub.

Perfect Christmas. PUBL Anness Publications Staff. 1999. 7.98 (*1-84038-413-1*) Random.

Perfect Christmas, Vol. 4. unabridged ed. Mary Brewer. (Illus.). 16p. 1998. 20.00 (*1-892082-03-9*) Shoestring Pr.

Perfect Christmas: More Than 40 Recipes & Gifts for a Handmade, Homemade Holiday. (Illus.). 64p. 1997. 9.95 (*1-85967-515-8*, Lorenz Bks) Anness Pub.

Perfect Christmas Gift. Judy Delton. LC 91-6549. (Illus.). 32p. (J). (gr. k-3). 1992. lib. bdg. 13.95 (*0-02-728471-9*, Mac Bks Young Read) S&S Childrens.

Perfect Christmas Picture. Fran Manushkin. LC 79-2678. (I Can Read Bks.). (Illus.). 64p. (J). (gr. k-3). 1980. 11.95 (*0-06-024068-7*) HarpC Child Bks.

***Perfect Christmas Tree.** Judi Brantley & Steven Brantley. Ed. by Pringle Franklin. LC 00-90588. (Illus.). 48p. (J). (ps-6). 2000. 16.95 (*1-892570-05-X*) Spng Hse Bks.

Perfect Circles. Gregory A. Moody. LC 98-11485. 400p. 1998. 12.95 (*1-884737-44-7*) VeloPress.

Perfect Cities: Chicago's Utopias of 1893. James B. Gilbert. LC 90-48235. (Illus.). 296p. 1991. 37.50 (*0-226-29317-3*) U Ch Pr.

Perfect Cities: Chicago's Utopias of 1893. James B. Gilbert. LC 90-48235. (Illus.). xiv, 293p. (C). 1993. pap. 13.95 (*0-226-29318-1*) U Ch Pr.

Perfect City. Photos by Bob Thall. LC 93-34460. (Creating the North American Landscape Ser.). (Illus.). 1994. pap. 29.95 (*0-8018-4726-5*) Johns Hopkins.

Perfect Cocktail: Hints, Tips, & Recipes from a Master Bartender. Greg Dempsey. (Illus.). 208p. 1995. pap. 10.95 (*0-385-47914-X*, Main St Bks) Doubleday.

Perfect Cold Warrior. Gary Geddes. LC 95-179015. 128p. 1995. pap. 14.95 (*1-55082-140-7*, Pub. by Quarry Pr) LPC InBook.

Perfect Competition & the Transformation of Economics. Frank M. Machovec. LC 94-32765. (Foundations of the Market Economy Ser.). 360p. (C). (gr. 13). 1995. 90.00 (*0-415-11580-9*, C0028) Routledge.

Perfect Conduct: Ascertaining the Three Vows. Ngari Panchen. 192p. 1996. pap. 18.00 (*0-86171-083-5*) Wisdom MA.

Perfect Counselling. Max Eggert. (J). pap. 13.95 (*0-09-972881-8*, Pub. by Random) Trafalgar.

Perfect Country Cottage. Bill Laws. (Illus.). 144p. 1994. 35.00 (*1-55859-784-0*) Abbeville Pr.

Perfect Country Garden. Sunniva Harte. LC 97-60166. (Illus.). 144p. 1997. 29.95 (*1-57076-097-7*, Trafalgar Sq Pub) Trafalgar.

Perfect Country Garden. StoreyPublishing Staff. 1997. 29.95 (*0-676-57229-4*) Random.

Perfect Country Rooms. Emma-Louise O'Reilly. (Illus.). 144p. 1996. 35.00 (*0-7892-0121-6*) Abbeville Pr.

Perfect Couple. Donald L. Deffner. 1993. pap. text, teacher ed. 5.50 (*0-570-09349-X*, 20-2414); pap. text, student ed. 5.50 (*0-570-09348-1*, 20-2413) Concordia.

Perfect Couple. Maura Seger. (I'm Extra Ser.). 1997. per. 3.99 (*0-373-07775-0*, 1-07775-9) Silhouette.

Perfect Cover. Linda Chase & Joyce St. George. LC 93-14213. 352p. (J). 1994. 19.45 (*0-7868-6001-4*, Pub. by Hyperion) Time Warner.

Perfect Cover. Linda Chase et al. 320p. 1997. per. 6.99 (*0-671-52296-5*) PB.

Perfect Cover Letter. 2nd ed. Richard H. Beatty. LC 96-20721. 192p. 1996. pap. 12.95 (*0-471-12400-1*) Wiley.

Perfect Crime. Peter Abrahams. 1999. mass mkt. 6.99 (*0-345-42680-0*) Ballantine Pub Grp.

***Perfect Crime.** Peter Abrahams. LC 98-48258. 1999. 28.95 (*0-7838-8476-1*) Macmillan Gen Ref.

Perfect Crime. Jean Baudrillard. Tr. by Chris Turner. LC 96-15755. (FRE.). 224p. 1996. 45.00 (*1-85984-919-9*, Pub. by Verso) Norton.

Perfect Crime: The Annihilation of My Family. Joseph Corrado. LC 98-92396. 1088p. 1998. 27.00 (*0-9662873-0-4*) Joe Corrado.

Perfect Crimes. Marvin J. Wolf & Katherine Mader. 1995. mass mkt. 5.99 (*0-345-37477-0*) Ballantine Pub Grp.

***Perfect Cuddle.** Dee Shulman. (Cuddly Board Bks.). (Illus.). 10p. (J). (ps-k). 2000. bds. 6.95 (*0-439-12914-1*, Cartwheel) Scholastic Inc.

Perfect Cup: A Coffee Lover's Guide to Buying, Brewing, & Tasting. Timothy J. Castle. 1991. pap. 13.00 (*0-201-57048-3*) Addison-Wesley.

***Perfect Dark.** Prima Development Staff et al. LC 99-63698. (Official Strategy Guides Ser.). 174p. 2000. pap. 14.99 (*0-7615-2280-8*) Prima Pub.

***Perfect Dark BradyGAMES Official Strategy Guide.** Brady Games Staff. 128p. 2000. pap. 12.99 (*1-56686-908-0*, BradyGAMES) Brady Pub.

Perfect Date. R. L. Stine, pseud. (Fear Street Ser.: No. 38). (YA). (gr. 7 up). 1996. mass mkt. 3.99 (*0-671-89430-7*, Archway) PB.

Perfect Date. R. L. Stine, pseud. (Fear Street Ser.: No. 38). (YA). (gr. 7 up). 1996. 9.09 (*0-606-09741-4*, Pub. by Turtleback) Demco.

Perfect Daughters: Adult Daughters of Alcoholics. Robert J. Ackerman. 200p. 1989. pap. 8.95 (*1-55874-040-6*) Health Comm.

Perfect Day: Guide for a Better Life. Joseph E. Koob, II. 280p. 1998. pap. 8.50 (*0-9665218-0-3*) NEJS Pubns.

Perfect Day for the Tajar. Richard Brown. (Illus.). 56p. 1987. pap. 5.00 (*0-87603-101-7*) Am Camping.

***Perfect Days.** Liz Lochhead. LC 99-487837. 96p. 1999. pap. 14.95 (*1-85459-437-0*, Pub. by Theatre Comm) Consort Bk Sales.

***Perfect Days.** 2nd ed. Liz Lochhead. 1999. pap. 16.95 (*1-85459-419-2*) Theatre Comm.

***Perfect Deterrence.** Frank C. Zagare & D. Marc Kilgour. LC 99-88000. 2000. write for info. (*0-521-78174-4*); write for info. (*0-521-78713-0*) Cambridge U Pr.

Perfect Digestion. Deepak Chopra. 144p. 1997. pap. 12.00 (*0-609-80076-0*) Harmony Bks.

Perfect Digestion: The Key to Balanced Living. Deepak Chopra. 1997. pap. 12.00 (*0-614-27346-3*, Crown) Crown Pub Group.

Perfect Dinner: Fine Food Cooked with Foil. Jacqueline Mallorca. LC 98-73198. (Illus.). 127p. 1999. 22.95 (*0-9658811-8-0*, 99PD) Fairoaks Pr.

Perfect Directions for All English Gold, Now Currant in This Kingdome. John Reynolds. LC 77-7426. (English Experience Ser.: No. 886). 1977. reprint ed. lib. bdg. 20.00 (*90-221-0886-4*) Walter J Johnson.

***Perfect Disappearance.** Martha Rhodes. 51p. 1999. 22.00 (*0-932826-98-9*); pap. 12.00 (*0-932826-99-7*) WMU Poetry & Prose.

Perfect Divorce! Leigh Michaels. (Romance Ser.). 1997. per. 3.25 (*0-373-03444-X*, 1-03444-6) Harlequin Bks.

Perfect Divorce. large type ed. Michaels. 1997. per. 3.25 (*0-373-15690-1*, Harlequin) Harlequin Bks.

***Perfect Documents.** Virginia Lee Webb et al. LC 99-56119. 2000. pap. write for info. (*0-87099-939-7*) Metro Mus Art.

***Perfect Documents: Walker Evans & African Art, 1935.** Virginia-Lee Webb. (Illus.). 112p. 2000. pap. 24.95 (*0-8109-6549-6*, Pub. by Abrams) Time Warner.

Perfect Double. Merline Lovelace. 1998. 21.95 (*0-373-59932-3*) Harlequin Bks.

Perfect Double. Merline Lovelace. (Intimate Moments Ser.). 1996. per. 3.99 (*0-373-07692-4*, 1-07692-6) Silhouette.

Perfect Dream. George K. Sewell. LC 97-21528. 55p. 1997. pap. 6.00 (*0-88734-238-8*) Players Pr.

Perfect Dress. Mouse Works Staff. LC 96-135924. (Illus.). 24p. (J). 1995. 9.98 (*1-57082-271-9*, Pub. by Mouse Works) Little.

***Perfect Elizabeth.** Libby Schmais. LC 00-24759. 240p. 2000. text 22.95 (*0-312-25225-0*) St Martin.

Perfect Endings: A Conscious Approach to Dying & Death. Robert Sachs. LC 97-52064. 160p. 1998. pap. 12.95 (*0-89281-779-8*, Inner Trad) Inner Tradit.

Perfect Enemies: The Religious Right, the Gay Movement, & the Politics of the 1990s. Christopher Bull & John Gallagher. 1997. pap. 14.00 (*0-614-28099-0*) Crown Pub Group.

Perfect Equality: John Stuart Mill on Well-Constituted Communities. Maria H. Morales. LC 96-19391. (Studies in Social, Political, & Legal Philosophy). 238p. (C). 1996. pap. text 24.95 (*0-8476-8181-5*); lib. bdg. 60.50 (*0-8476-8180-7*) Rowman.

Perfect Everything. Rufus Moseley. 230p. pap. 7.95 (*0-910924-29-5*) Macalester.

***Perfect Evil.** Alex Kava. 384p. 2000. 22.95 (*1-55166-573-5*, 1-66573-6, Mira Bks) Harlequin Bks.

Perfect Example. John Porcellino. 1999. pap. text 9.95 (*0-9665363-5-5*) Highwater Bks.

Perfect Execution. Tim Binding. 320p. 1996. write for info. (*0-385-25587-X*) Doubleday.

Perfect Exposure: A Practical Guide for All Photographers. Roger Hicks & Frances Schultz. 192p. 1999. pap. text 29.95 (*0-8174-5398-9*) Watsn-Guptill.

Perfect Eyes. Paulette Morrissey. (Fast, Fun & Easy Ser.: Bk. 2). (Illus.). 22p. 1996. spiral bd. 9.95 (*1-893502-01-5*) Morrissey Co.

Perfect Eyesight: The Art of Improving Vision Naturally. rev. ed. Robert A. Zuraw & Robert T. Lewanski. Ed. by Jack Goldstein. LC 98-60555. (Illus.). 122p. 1998. pap. 20.00 (*0-9608030-2-5*) Taoist Pubs.

Perfect Family. Nancy Carlson. (Illus.). 32p. (J). (ps-3). 1985. pap. 4.95 (*0-87614-854-2*, Carolrhoda) Lerner Pub.

Perfect Family. Nancy Carlson. LC 85-4123. (Illus.). 32p. (J). (ps-3). 1985. lib. bdg. 17.50 (*0-87614-280-3*, Carolrhoda) Lerner Pub.

Perfect Family. Penny Jordan. (Mira Bks.). 1998. per. 5.99 (*1-55166-414-3*, 1-66414-3, Mira Bks) Harlequin Bks.

***Perfect Father.** Penny Jordan. (Presents Ser.). 2000. per. 3.99 (*0-373-12092-3*) Harlequin Bks.

Perfect Father: (From Here to Maternity) Elizabeth Bevarly. (Desire Ser.). 1995. per. 3.25 (*0-373-05920-5*, 1-05920-3) Silhouette.

Perfect Father's Day. Eve Bunting. (Illus.). 32p. (J). (ps-3). 1993. pap. 5.95 (*0-395-66416-0*, Clarion Bks) HM.

***Perfect Father's Day.** Eve Bunting. (Illus.). 32p. (J). 2000. 9.95 (*0-618-04079-X*, Clarion Bks) HM.

Perfect First Mate: A Woman's Guide to Recreational Boating. Joy Smith. LC 99-49207. (Illus.). 256p. 2000. pap. 16.50 (*1-57409-083-6*) Sheridan.

Perfect Fish: Illusions in Fly Tying. Kenneth J. Abrams. LC 99-229058. 112p. 1999. 39.95 (*1-57188-179-4*) F Amato Pubns.

***Perfect Fish: Illusions in Fly Tying.** Kenneth J. Abrams. LC 99-229058. (Illus.). 112p. 1999. pap. 29.95 (*1-57188-138-7*) F Amato Pubns.

Perfect Fit: Man of the Month/The Tallchiefs. Cait London. (Desire Ser.: No. 1183). 1998. per. 3.75 (*0-373-76183-X*, 1-76183-2) Harlequin Bks.

Perfect Flight. Richard L. Collins. 1988. text 19.95 (*0-02-527161-X*) Macmillan.

Perfect Flight: The Pilot's Greatest Challenge - The Search for Excellence. rev. ed. Richard L. Collins. LC 93-48566. (Aviation Library). 215p. 1994. 29.95 (*1-56566-055-2*, Pub. by Thomasson-Grant) ASA Inc.

***Perfect Food/Perfect Health: More Than 125 Wholesome Recipes.** Weight Watchers Staff. (Weight Watchers Ser.). (Illus.). 2000. pap. 9.95 (*0-8487-2356-2*) Oxmoor Hse.

Perfect Fools. Charlotte Vale Allen. 230p. 1998. pap. 20.00 (*0-9657437-7-2*) Isld Nation.

Perfect Fools. Charlotte Vale Allen. 224p. 1998. reprint ed. 22.95 (*1-892738-12-0*, Pub. by Isld Nation) Brodart.

Perfect Form: Variational Principles, Methods, & Applications in Elementary Physics. Don S. Lemons. LC 96-9639. 144p. 1997. text 39.50 (*0-691-02664-5*, Pub. by Princeton U Pr) Cal Prin Full Svc.

Perfect Formula. Sarah Willson. (Rugrats Chapter Bks.: No. 1). (Illus.). 64p. (J). (gr. 1-4). 1999. pap. 3.99 (*0-689-82677-X*, 076714003996, Simon Spot) Little Simon.

Perfect Freedom. Gordon Merrick. LC 99-11461. 464p. 1999. reprint ed. pap. 14.95 (*1-55583-297-0*, Pub. by Alyson Pubns) Consort Bk Sales.

Perfect Freedom: Religious Liberty in Pennsylvania. J. William Frost. (Studies in Religion & American Public Life). 231p. (C). 1990. text 59.95 (*0-521-38545-8*) Cambridge U Pr.

Perfect Freedom: Religious Liberty in Pennsylvania. J. William Frost. LC 93-18813. 240p. 1993. reprint ed. pap. 18.95 (*0-271-01091-6*) Pa St U Pr.

Perfect Freedom in Buddhism. Tr. by Shinji Takuwa. 200p. 1997. pap. 18.95 (*4-590-00293-0*, Pub. by Hokuseido Pr) Book East.

***Perfect Friend.** Reynolds Price. LC 99-55397. (J). (gr. 7). 2000. 16.00 (*0-689-83029-7*) Atheneum Yung Read.

Perfect Fruit Pies: Award-Winning Recipes from Across America. Storey Publishing Staff. LC 90-50418. (Illus.). 160p. (Orig.). 1991. pap. 9.95 (*0-88266-647-9*) Storey Bks.

Perfect Game. McColley. 1996. pap. 3.99 (*0-689-80896-8*) S&S Bks Yung.

Perfect Ganesh. Terrence McNally. 1994. pap. 5.25 (*0-8222-1379-6*) Dramatists Play.

Perfect Gay Pre-Nuptial Agreement. C. W. Cecil. 100p. 2000. pap. 10.00 (*1-886383-86-3*) Pride & Imprints.

Perfect General 2: The Official Strategy Guide. Marc Dultz. 1995. pap. 19.95 (*1-55958-766-0*) Prima Pub.

Perfect Generosity of Price Vessantara: A Buddhist Epic. Ed. by Margaret Cone & Richard F. Gombrich. (Illus.). 160p. 1977. text 48.00 (*0-19-826530-1*) OUP.

Perfect Gentleman. Danice Allen. 1997. mass mkt. 5.50 (*0-380-78151-4*, Avon Bks) Morrow Avon.

Perfect Gentleman. Ralph W. Bergengren. LC 67-23177. (Essay Index Reprint Ser.). 1977. 12.95 (*0-8369-0202-5*) Ayer.

Perfect Gentleman. Jaye S. Fletcher. 320p. 1996. mass mkt. 5.99 (*0-7860-0263-8*) Kensgtn Pub Corp.

***Perfect Gentleman.** Roy Hall. (Illus.). 256p. 1999. 26.00 (*1-85782-376-1*) Blake Pub.

Perfect Gentleman. Roy Hall. 256p. 1999. pap. text 26.00 (*1-85782-307-9*, Pub. by Blake Publng) Seven Hills Bk.

Perfect Gentleman. large type ed. Liz Pedersen. 256p. pap. 18.99 (*0-7089-5450-2*) Ulverscroft.

***Perfect Gentleman: Masculine Control in Victorian Men's Fiction, 1870-1901.** 2nd ed. Karen V. Waters. (Studies in Nineteenth-Century British Literature: Vol. 3). 171p. (C). 1999. reprint ed. pap. text 29.95 (*0-8204-4888-5*) P Lang Pubng.

Perfect Getaway, No. 12. Franklin W. Dixon. (Hardy Boys Casefiles Ser.: No. 12). (Orig.). (YA). (gr. 6 up). 1991. mass mkt. 3.50 (*0-671-73675-2*) PB.

Perfect Gift. Al Lacy & JoAnna Lacy. LC 99-11742. (Hannah of Fort Bridger Ser.: Vol. 5). 300p. 1999. pap. text 10.99 (*1-57673-407-2*) Multnomah Pubs.

***Perfect Gift.** Yvette Pompa. (Barbie Mini Craft Ser.). (Illus.). 16p. (J). (gr. k-3). 2000. pap. 6.99 (*1-57584-413-3*, Pub. by Rdrs Digest) S&S Trade.

Perfect Gift. Janet Schrader. (Illus.). 36p. 1989. pap. 14.95 (*0-935133-24-0*) CKE Pubns.

***Perfect Gift.** Christina Skye. LC 99-94806. 416p. 1999. mass mkt. 6.50 (*0-380-80023-3*, Avon Bks) Morrow Avon.

Perfect Gift. G. S. Sparrow. 116p. (J). (gr. 3-5). 1998. pap. 7.95 (*0-9665485-0-7*) Blue Mantle Pub.

Perfect Gift. Beverly H. Watson. (Illus.). 16p. (Orig.). (J). (gr. 5). 1995. pap. 1.49 (*0-9623647-6-2*) B H Watson.

***Perfect Gift: A Communion with Angels.** Ellen Vannetter. 108p. 1999. pap. 12.95 (*0-7392-0327-4*, 3483) Morris Pubng.

Perfect Gifts for (Nearly) Perfect Men: How to Choose Gifts for Men According to Personality Temperament. Joan Bannan. LC 90-91994. (Illus.). 272p. (Orig.). 1991. pap. 6.95 (*0-9627624-0-7*) J B Comm CA.

Perfect Girl. Kate William. (Sweet Valley High Ser.: No. 74). (YA). (gr. 7 up). 1991. 8.35 (*0-606-05000-0*, Pub. by Turtleback) Demco.

Perfect Girls. Marilyn Kaye. (Replica Ser.: No. 4). 160p. (J). (gr. 4-7). 1999. pap. 3.99 (*0-553-49241-1*) BDD Bks Young Read.

***Perfect Girls.** Marilyn Kaye. (Replica Ser.: No. 4). (J). (gr. 4-7). 1999. 9.34 (*0-606-16372-7*) Turtleback.

Perfect Glass of Wine: Choosing, Serving, & Enjoying. Brian St. Pierre. LC 96-13341. (Illus.). 120p. 1996. 24.95 (*0-8118-1295-2*) Chronicle Bks.

Perfect Graphs. Alf. text. write for info. (*0-471-48970-0*) Wiley.

Perfect Grilled Meats. Matt Kelly. 1995. 2.95 (*0-88266-054-3*, Storey Pub) Storey Bks.

Perfect Grilled Vegetables. Matt Kelly. LC 96-226. (Bulletin Ser.: No. A-152). 1996. pap. 2.95 (*0-88266-509-X*, Storey Pub) Storey Bks.

Perfect Groom. Ruth Scofield. No. 65. 1999. per. 4.50 (*0-373-87065-5*, 1-87065-8, Harlequin) Harlequin Bks.

Perfect Guide to Making $ in Landscaping & Maintenance: A How to Book. Gene Yezak. (Illus.). 220p. Date not set. pap. 9.95 (*1-884797-05-9*) Moran Pub.

***Perfect Hair Everyday.** Nick Chavez. (Illus.). 2000. 27.50 (*1-928998-36-4*) Q V C Pubg.

***Perfect Hand.** Gwen Renninger. (Illus.). ii, 35p. 2000. spiral bd. 6.99 (*0-9679838-0-0*) G G Renninger.

Perfect Happiness. R. Billington. mass mkt. 15.95 (*0-340-67513-6*, Pub. by Hodder & Stought Ltd) Trafalgar.

Perfect Happiness. large type ed. Rachel Billington. (Charnwood Large Print Ser.). 448p. 1997. 27.99 (*0-7089-8969-1*) Ulverscroft.

Perfect Happiness: The Sequel to Jane Austen's Emma. Rachel Billington & Jane Austen. 240p. 1996. text 29.95 (*0-340-67512-8*, Pub. by Hodder & Stought Ltd) Trafalgar.

Perfect Harmonica Method. J. Perelman. 1992. pap. 15.95 incl. audio (*0-931759-64-1*, 00000147) H Leonard.

Perfect Harmonica Method. Jerry Perelman. (Illus.). 64p. 1992. pap. text 17.95 incl. cd-rom (*1-57424-064-1*) Centerstream Pub.

Perfect Harmony. Roger A. Caras. 256p. 1996. 22.50 (*0-684-81100-6*) S&S Trade.

Perfect Harmony. Barbara Wood. LC 97-37623. 448p. (gr. 8). 1998. 23.95 (*0-316-81653-1*) Little.

Perfect Harmony. Barbara Wood. 480p. 1999. mass mkt. 6.99 (*0-446-60629-4*, Pub. by Warner Bks) Little.

Perfect Harmony: The Faith Hill & Tim McGraw Story. Scott Gray. LC 99-90027. 1999. mass mkt. 5.99 (*0-345-43412-9*) Ballantine Pub Grp.

Perfect Harmony: The Intertwining Lives of Animals & Humans Throughout History. Roger Caras. 272p. 1997. per. 12.00 (*0-684-83531-2*, Fireside) S&S Trade Pap.

Perfect Health. Christian D. Larson. 78p. 1997. pap. 8.00 (*0-89540-397-8*, SB-397) Sun Pub.

***Perfect Health: A Practical System of Mind/Body Medicine.** rev. ed. Deepak Chopra. LC 00-32595. 2000. pap. write for info. (*0-609-80694-7*, Three Riv Pr) Crown Pub Group.

Perfect Health: Accept No Substitutes. Elwood Babbitt. 300p. 1993. pap. 15.95 (*1-881343-01-4*) Channel One.

Perfect Health: Allergies. Deepak Chopra. 1997. pap. 12.00 (*0-614-27347-1*, Crown) Crown Pub Group.

Perfect Health: How to Get It & How to Keep It. Charles C. Haskell. 209p. 1996. reprint ed. spiral bd. 16.00 (*0-7873-0383-6*) Hlth Research.

Perfect Health: The Complete Mind-Body Guide. Deepak Chopra. (Illus.). 336p. 1991. pap. 14.00 (*0-517-58421-2*) Harmony Bks.

P

An Asterisk (*) at the beginning of an entry indicates that the title is appearing for the first time.

Perfect Health Vol. II: How to Be Young at 60 & Live to Be 100. National Health Bureau of America Staff. 55p. 1996. reprint ed. spiral bd. 11.00 (*0-7873-0633-9*) Hlth Research.

Perfect Heart. Contrib. by Tom Fettke. 1984. pap. 1.30 (*0-8341-9118-0*, AN-2569) Lillenas.

Perfect Heart. Jeri Williams. LC 95-174818. 192p. 1995. 14.99 (*0-89274-922-9*, HH-922) Harrison Hse.

Perfect Hell. H. L. Hix. LC 96-17261. (Peregrine Smith Poetry Competition Ser.). 64p. 1996. pap. 9.95 (*0-87905-780-7*) Gibbs Smith Pub.

***Perfect Heresy: The Revolutionary Life & Spectacular Death of the Medieval Cathars.** Stephen O'Shea. (Illus.). 224p. 2000. 24.00 (*0-8027-1350-5*) Walker & Co.

Perfect Hero: Whose Child? Paula D. Riggs. (Intimate Moments Ser.: No. 889). 1998. per. 4.25 (*0-373-07889-7*, 0-07889-9) Silhouette.

Perfect Holiday. Anne Gregg. 223p. 1991. pap. 9.95 (*0-563-20645-4*, Pub. by BBC) Parkwest Pubns.

***Perfect Home Wedding: Inspirations for Planning Your Special Day.** Kerry Eielson. LC 99-35701. (Illus.). 208p. 1999. 40.00 (*1-55670-928-5*) Stewart Tabori & Chang.

Perfect Horse. Patricia Leitch. LC 95-26350. (Horseshoes Ser.). 1996. 9.15 (*0-606-09431-8*, Pub. by Turtleback) Demco.

***Perfect Horsekeeping: Expert Advice on Tack & Barn.** John Lyons. Ed. by Maureen Gallatin. (John Lyons Perfect Horse Library Ser.). (Illus.). viii, 200p. 1999. 26.95 (*1-879620-62-6*) Belvoir Pubns.

Perfect Host. Theodore Sturgeon. Ed. by Paul Williams. LC 98-20023. (Complete Short Stories of Theodore Sturgeon Bks.: Vol. 5). 406p. 1998. 27.50 (*1-55643-284-4*) North Atlantic.

***Perfect Host.** Theodore Sturgeon. Ed. by Paul Williams. (Complete Short Stories of Theodore Sturgeon Bks.: Vol. 5). 350p. (C). 2000. pap. 18.95 (*1-55643-360-3*) North Atlantic.

Perfect Husband. Mark K. Brown. 78p. (Orig.). 1995. pap. 7.95 (*1-56245-197-9*) Great Quotations.

Perfect Husband. large type ed. Lisa Gardner. LC 97-47258. (Mystery Ser.). 394p. 1998. 28.95 (*0-7838-8413-3*, G K Hall & Co) Mac Lib Ref.

Perfect Husband. Gary Provost. Ed. by Claire Zion. 264p. 1992. reprint ed. mass mkt. 5.50 (*0-671-72494-0*) PB.

Perfect Husband: What Would You Do If the Man of Your Dreams Hides the Soul of a Killer? Lisa Gardner. 432p. 1997. mass mkt. 6.99 (*0-553-57680-1*) Bantam.

Perfect Husbands & Other Fairy Tales: Demystifying Marriage, Men & Romance. Regina Barreca. LC 94-32826. 288p. 1994. pap. 15.95 (*0-385-47538-1*, Anchor NY) Doubleday.

Perfect Idiot. Eunice Atkinson & Grant Atkinson. 1949. 5.25 (*0-87129-558-X*, P21) Dramatic Pub.

Perfect Imbalance. Laurie Kirk. Ed. by Shirley Warren. 32p. 1990. pap. 5.00 (*1-877801-12-7*) Still Waters.

***Perfect Impact: Now Anyone Can Play Par Golf, Because Here, Finally, All the Secrets of Perfect Impact, Power & Control Are Revealed.** George Hibbard. (Illus.). 200p. 1999. 89.95 (*0-9673951-0-0*) Pendulum.

Perfect in Christ Jesus. Benjamin Gregory. 78p. 1994. pap. 6.99 (*0-88019-331-X*) Schmul Pub Co.

Perfect in My Sight. Tanya Anne Crosby. 384p. 1998. mass mkt. 5.99 (*0-380-78572-2*, Avon Bks) Morrow Avon.

Perfect Incompressible Fluids. Jean-Yves Chemin. Tr. by Isabelle Gallagher & Dragos Iftimie. LC 98-35385. (Oxford Lecture Series in Mathematics & Its Applications: No. 14). 198p. 1998. text 68.00 (*0-19-850397-0*) OUP.

Perfect Interview: How to Get the Job You Really Want. 2nd ed. John D. Drake. Ed. by Mary Glenn. LC 96-9327. 208p. 1996. pap. 17.95 (*0-8144-7919-7*) AMACOM.

Perfect Joy of St. Francis. Felix Timmermans. 1991. lib. bdg. 21.95 (*1-56849-037-2*) Buccaneer Bks.

Perfect Joy of St. Francis. Felix Timmermans. 1998. pap. 12.95 (*0-89870-666-1*) Ignatius Pr.

Perfect Just the Way I Am. Julie Tamler. Ed. by Donna L. Montgomery. (Illus.). 193p. (Orig.). 1993. pap. 9.95 (*0-938577-08-5*) St Johns Pub.

Perfect Justice. William Bernhardt. 1995. mass mkt. 5.99 (*0-345-39133-0*) Hse Collectbls.

Perfect Kill. large type ed. A. J. Quinnell. (Charnwood Ser.). 448p. 1994. 27.99 (*0-7089-8744-3*, Charnwood) Ulverscroft.

***Perfect Kiss.** 1999. per. 4.50 (*0-373-65116-3*) Harlequin Bks.

Perfect Kitten. Peter Neville et al. Ed. by Reader's Digest Editors. LC 97-17994. (Illus.). 160p. 1998. 19.95 (*0-7621-0038-9*, Pub. by RD Assn) Penguin Putnam.

Perfect Lady. Jel D. Lewis (Jones). LC 95-148997. 200p. 1994. pap. 12.95 (*0-9639917-0-1*) Writers Unltd.

***Perfect Lady: Women Self Help.** deluxe ed. Tera L. Kramer. (Illus.). 100p. 2000. 14.95 (*0-9701962-0-2*) T L Kramer.

Perfect Landing. Lynn Kirby. LC 97-46714. (Winning Edge Ser.). 128p. (J). (gr. 5-9). 1998. 5.99 (*0-8499-5835-0*) Tommy Nelson.

Perfect Lattices in Equilibrium, Vol. 1. William Jones & Norman H. March. 1985. pap. 16.95 (*0-486-65015-4*) Dover.

Perfect Law of Liberty: Elias Smith & the Providential History of America. Michael G. Kenny. LC 93-29969. (Illus.). 392p. (C). 1994. text 55.00 (*1-56098-321-3*) Smithsonian.

Perfect Legacy: How to Establish Your Own Private Foundation. Russ A. Prince et al. LC 99-164255. (Illus.). 80p. 1998. pap. 19.95 (*0-9658391-1-7*) HNW Pr.

Perfect Lesbian Pre-Nuptial Agreement. C. W. Cecil. 100p. 2000. pap. 10.00 (*1-886383-87-1*) Pride & Imprints.

Perfect Letter. Joan Minninger. 224p. 1991. pap. 11.00 (*0-385-41998-8*) Doubleday.

Perfect Lies. Elizabeth Bennett. 400p. 2000. mass mkt. 6.50 (*0-06-101373-0*) HarpC.

Perfect Lies. William Hallberg. 384p. 1990. pap. 13.00 (*0-671-69369-7*) S&S Trade.

Perfect Lies. William Hallberg. 1998. pap. 13.00 (*0-684-85232-2*) Scribner.

Perfect Life. William E. Channing. (Works of William Ellery Channing II). 1990. reprint ed. lib. bdg. 79.00 (*0-685-27694-5*) Rprt Serv.

Perfect Life: The Story of Swami Muktananda Paramahamsa. Margaret Simpson. LC 96-27221. (Illus.). 112p. (Orig.). (J). (gr. 5-9). 1996. pap. 8.95 (*0-911307-49-4*) SYDA Found.

***Perfect Life of Lovers.** Monique Pivot. (Illus.). 120p. 2000. 24.95 (*0-7641-5315-3*) Barron.

Perfect Little Angels. Andrew Neiderman. (Orig.). 1991. 19.00 (*0-7278-4150-5*) Severn Hse.

Perfect Little Girls see Petites Filles Modeles

***Perfect Little Monster.** Judy Hindley. LC 99-58256. 24p. (YA). (ps up). 2001. 10.99 (*0-7636-0902-1*); pap. 3.29 (*0-7636-0903-X*) Candlewick Pr.

Perfect Little Piglet. Disney Enterprises, Inc. Staff. (Disney's "Out & about with Pooh" Library: Vol. 2). (Illus.). 44p. (J). (gr. 1-6). 1996. 3.49 (*1-885222-56-4*) Advance Pubs.

Perfect Little Piglet: Parent's Guide. Disney Enterprises, Inc. Staff. (Disney's "Out & about with Pooh" Library: Vols. 2 & 19). (Illus.). 44p. (J). (gr. 1-6). 1996. 3.49 (*1-885222-74-2*) Advance Pubs.

Perfect Lives: An Opera. John Ashley. (Illus.). 224p. 1992. 35.00 (*0-9627767-7-7*) Archer Fields.

Perfect Lives: An Opera. Robert Ashley. 1991. pap. 35.00 (*0-936050-10-1*) Burning Bks.

Perfect London Walk. Roger Ebert & Daniel Curley. (Illus.). 128p. (Orig.). 1985. pap. 8.95 (*0-8362-7929-8*) Andrews & McMeel.

Perfect Love see Perfecto Amor

***Perfect Love.** Buchan. 1999. mass mkt. write for info. (*0-312-97152-4*) St Martin.

Perfect Love. Elizabeth Buchan. LC 99-25323. 1999. text 24.95 (*0-312-20568-6*) St Martin.

***Perfect Love.** Elizabeth Buchan. 448p. 2000. mass mkt. 6.99 (*0-312-97426-4*) St Martin.

Perfect Love. John Findlater. pap. 8.99 (*0-88019-168-6*) Schmul Pub Co.

***Perfect Love.** Sandra Landry. (Time Passages Romance Ser.). 2000. mass mkt. 5.99 (*0-515-12885-6*) Berkley Pub.

Perfect Love. J. A. Wood. 1989. pap. 14.99 (*0-88019-244-5*) Schmul Pub Co.

Perfect Love: A+ Living in a C- World. James Watkins. 110p. (YA). 1987. pap. 5.95 (*0-89827-036-7*, BKE10) Wesleyan Pub Hse.

Perfect Love: Find Intimacy on the Astral Plane. 2nd ed. D. J. Conway. LC 97-42432. (Illus.). 192p. 1999. pap. 12.95 (*1-56718-181-3*) Llewellyn Pubns.

***Perfect Love: Intensely Personal, Overflowing, & Never Ending...** Ruth Myers. 320p. 1999. pap. 12.95 (*1-57856-255-4*) Waterbrook Pr.

***Perfect Love: Intensely Personal, Overflowing, Never Ending...** Ruth Myers. LC 98-229107. 320p. 1998. 19.95 (*1-57856-002-0*); pap., student ed. 6.95 (*1-57856-083-7*) Waterbrook Pr.

Perfect Love: The Meditations, Prayers & Writings of Teresa of Avila. Teresa of Avila. LC 95-34821. 160p. 1995. pap. 6.00 (*0-385-48049-0*, Image Bks) Doubleday.

Perfect Love with Sequel, 2 vols. in 1. abr. ed. Majel Meyer & J. A. Wood. 217p. 1996. reprint ed. pap. 10.00 (*0-9651740-0-X*) Stndrd of Zion.

***Perfect Lover.** large type ed. Penny Jordan. (Harlequin Ser.). 1999. 21.95 (*0-263-16077-7*) Mills & Boon.

***Perfect Lover: A Perfect Family.** Penny Jordan. (Presents Ser.: No. 2025). 1999. per. 3.75 (*0-373-12025-7*, 1-12025-2) Harlequin Bks.

Perfect Machine: Building the Palomar Telescope. Ronald Florence. (Illus.). 480p. 1995. pap. 14.00 (*0-06-092670-8*, Perennial) HarperTrade.

Perfect Man. Jack Knife. 1974. write for info. (*0-318-64127-5*) Poets Pr.

Perfect Man: And Other Great Works of Fiction. Heather Down. Ed. by Patrick Caton. LC 97-71658. 168p. 1997. pap. 5.95 (*1-56245-301-7*) Great Quotations.

Perfect Man: He's Quiet, He's Sweet, & If He Gives You Any Grief, You Can Bite His Head Off. Day. 1994. pap. 7.99 (*1-57081-768-5*) At-A-Glance Consumer.

Perfect Marriage. Laurey Bright. (Intimate Moments Ser.). 1995. per. 3.75 (*0-373-07621-5*, 1-07621-5) Silhouette.

Perfect Marriage. Hilary Rich & Helaina Kravitz. LC 97-71173. 326p. 1997. pap. 16.95 (*0-02-861729-0*, Alpha Ref) Macmillan Gen Ref.

Perfect Marriage: Yes, One Really Does Exist! It's God's Divine Plan. Joseph Racite. 326p. (YA). 1999. pap. 19.95 (*1-892878-01-1*) You Deserve It.

Perfect Marriage Material. Penny Jordan. (Presents Ser.). 1998. per. 3.75 (*0-373-11948-8*, 1-11948-6) Harlequin Bks.

Perfect Master, 2 vols., Vol. 1. Osho. Ed. by Ma Y. Anurag. LC 83-172954. (Sufi Ser.). (Illus.). 1980. 14.95 (*0-88050-113-8*) Oshos.

Perfect Master, Vol. 2. Osho. Ed. by Ma Y. Anurag. LC 83-172954. (Sufi Ser.). (Illus.). 1980. 14.95 (*0-88050-114-6*) Oshos.

Perfect Match. Ginna Gray. (Men at Work Ser.: Vol. 47). 1998. mass mkt. 4.50 (*0-373-81059-8*, 1-81059-7) Harlequin Bks.

Perfect Match? Penny Jordan. (Presents Ser.). 1998. per. 3.75 (*0-373-11954-2*, 1-11954-4) Harlequin Bks.

Perfect Match. Jill McGown. 192p. 1990. mass mkt. 5.99 (*0-449-21820-1*, Crest) Fawcett.

***Perfect Match.** Hailey North. 384p. 2000. mass mkt. 5.99 (*0-380-81306-8*) Morrow Avon.

Perfect Match. Meg-Lynn Roberts. 320p. 1993. mass mkt. 3.99 (*0-8217-4140-3*, Zebra Kensgtn) Kensgtn Pub Corp.

Perfect Match? large type ed. Penny Jordan. (Harlequin Presents Ser.: No. 1954). 1998. 20.95 (*0-263-15516-1*) Thorndike Pr.

Perfect Match, Vol. 3. Beverly Lewis. LC 99-6718. (Girls Only Go Ser.). 128p. (J). (gr. 3-8). 1999. pap. text 5.99 (*0-7642-2060-8*) Bethany Hse.

Perfect Match: A Dog Buyer's Guide. Chris Walkowicz. LC 96-33471. 288p. 1996. 14.95 (*0-87605-767-9*) Howell Bks.

Perfect Match: A Guide to Precise Machine Piecing. Donna L. Thomas. LC 96-14947. 64p. 1997. pap. 12.95 (*1-56477-153-9*) Martingale & Co.

Perfect Matrimony: The Door to Initiation. Samael A. Weor. Tr. by Shelley Blumberg-Lorenzana from SPA. LC 92-80238. (Illus.). 362p. (Orig.). 1992. pap. write for info. (*1-881219-00-3*) U Christ Gnostic.

Perfect Media Kit. Jack Bernstein. 125p. (Orig.). 1991. pap. 17.50 (*0-9616226-4-4*) JB & Me.

Perfect Memo. Patricia H. Westheimer. (C). 1988. pap. 17.66 (*0-673-38101-3*, Scott Frsmn) Addson-Wesley Educ.

Perfect Memo: Write Your Way to Career Success! Patricia H. Westheimer. LC 94-28472. 180p. (Orig.). 1994. pap. 12.95 (*1-57112-064-5*, PM) Park Ave.

Perfect Misfortune: A Guide to Hope, Healing & Happiness During Personal Crisis. Allan E. Flood. Ed. by Caroline Hall-Otis. LC 92-63352. 70p. (Orig.). 1993. pap. text 13.95 (*0-9630873-2-0*) Pugrose Pub.

Perfect Mistress. Betina Krahn. 464p. 1995. mass mkt. 6.50 (*0-553-56523-0*, Fanfare) Bantam.

Perfect Mistress. Jacqueline Ophir. (Illus.). 144p. 39.95 (*1-899861-14-9*, Pub. by AKS Bks) Xclusiv Distrib.

Perfect Mistress. large type ed. Betina M. Krahn. 1995. pap. 21.95 (*1-56895-274-0*) Wheeler Pub.

Perfect Mistress: And Other Stories. Ronald Frederick Henry Duncan. LC 76-465470. 143 p. (J). 1969. write for info. (*0-246-98564-X*) Grftn HrprClns.

Perfect Mix: Bread, soup, dessert, & other homemade mixes from your kitchen. Diane Phillips. LC 92-41328. 1993. 15.00 (*0-688-12104-7*, Hearst) Hearst Commns.

***Perfect Moderns: A History of the Camden Town Group.** Wendy Baron. LC 99-36706. (Illus.). 180p. 1999. text 78.95 (*1-84014-291-X*, Pub. by Ashgate Pub) Ashgate Pub Co.

Perfect Money Planning. David Dionisi. Ed. by Joan Barrett. (Illus.). 125p. (Orig.). 1995. pap. 12.95 (*0-9635770-7-7*) D Dionisi.

Perfect Monologue. Ginger H. Friedman. LC 98-5709. 400p. 1998. reprint ed. pap. 14.95 (*0-87910-300-0*) Limelight Edns.

Perfect Mortgage: A Book No Home Buyer Can Do Without. Alan Silverstein. 96p. 1989. pap. 9.95 (*0-7737-5276-5*) Genl Dist Srvs.

***Perfect Mother.** Jon Salem. 2000. mass mkt. 5.99 (*0-7860-1130-0*, Pinncle Kensgtn) Kensgtn Pub Corp.

Perfect Mother. Penelope S. Schott. 100p. 1993. pap. 6.00 (*0-9638364-0-4*) Snake Nation.

Perfect Murder. large type ed. Bernard Taylor & Stephen Knight. (Illus.). 592p. 1989. 11.50 (*0-7089-2033-0*) Ulverscroft.

Perfect Murder: A Study in Detection. David Lehman. LC 99-42207. 288p. 2000. pap. 18.95 (*0-472-08585-9*, 08585) U of Mich Pr.

Perfect Murder, Perfect Town: JonBenet & the City of Boulder. Lawrence Schiller. LC 99-207248. (Illus.). 640p. 1999. 26.00 (*0-06-019153-8*) HarpC.

***Perfect Murder, Perfect Town: The Uncensored Story of the JonBenet Murder & the Grand Jury's Search for the Final Truth.** Lawrence Schiller. 832p. 1999. mass mkt. 7.99 (*0-06-109696-2*) HarpC.

Perfect Name for the Perfect Baby. Joan Wilen & Lydia Wilen. LC 96-95198. 1997. mass mkt. 5.99 (*0-345-41235-4*) Ballantine Pub Grp.

Perfect Name for the Perfect Baby. Joan Wilen & Lydia Wilen. 224p. 1993. pap. 8.00 (*0-449-90654-X*, Columbine) Fawcett.

Perfect Neighbor: The MacGregors. Nora Roberts. (Silhouette Special Ser.: No. 1232). 251p. 1999. per. 4.25 (*0-373-24232-8*, 1-24232-0) Harlequin Bks.

Perfect Neighbors. DeAnne Neilson. LC 94-77979. 207p. 1994. pap. 7.95 (*0-9624049-6-9*) Hatrack River.

***Perfect Night.** Penny Jordan. (Presents Ser.). 2000. per. 3.99 (*0-373-12104-0*) Harlequin Bks.

***Perfect Night for Bloodless Love.** Arlene Ang. (Illus.). 36p. 2000. pap. 4.95 (*0-9676660-7-4*, Pick Pocket Pr) Phony Lid Pubns.

Perfect Nonprofit Boards. Block. LC 99-160603. 168p. (C). 1998. pap. text 21.95 (*0-536-01184-2*) Pearson Custom.

Perfect Nose Ralph. Jane Breskin Zalben. (J). Date not set. pap. 3.95 (*0-399-21091-1*) Putnam Pub Group.

Perfect Numbers. Stanley Bezuszka et al. (Motivated Math Project Activity Booklets). 169p. (Orig.). (YA). (gr. 7-12). 1980. pap. text 3.50 (*0-917916-19-0*) Boston Coll Math.

Perfect Office 3 for Dummies. John Heilborn. LC 95-76825. 352p. 1995. pap. 19.99 (*1-56884-374-7*) IDG Bks.

Perfect Office 3.0. Lorilee M. Sadler. (DF - Computer Applications Ser.). 1996. pap. 43.95 (*0-7895-0403-0*) Course Tech.

Perfect Olympic Cyclery Narrative: Keeping Financial Records B. 7th ed. Harold Baron & Steinfeld. (BB - Record Keeping I Ser.: Vol. 1). 1991. 20.95 (*0-538-60997-4*) S-W Pub.

Perfect Orange: A Tale from Ethiopia. Frank P. Araujo. LC 94-67524. (Toucan Tales Ser.: Vol. 2). (Illus.). 32p. (J). (ps-8). 1994. 16.95 (*1-877810-94-0*, ORAN) Rayve Prodns.

Perfect Order: Simple Storage Solutions. Elizabeth Hilliard. LC 98-54587. (Illus.). 160p. 1999. 24.00 (*1-57959-046-2*, SOMA) BB&T Inc.

***Perfect Package: How to Add Value Through Graphic Design.** Catherine Fishel. 2000. 35.00 (*1-56496-623-2*) Rockport Pubs.

Perfect Painting: Conferences de l'Academie Royale de Peinture et de Sculpture, 1669. Andre Felibien Des Avaux. (Printed Sources of Western Art Ser.). (FRE.). 144p. 1981. reprint ed. pap. 40.00 (*0-915346-56-7*) A Wofsy Fine Arts.

Perfect Pair. Karen T. Whittenburg. (Family Continuity Program Ser.: No. 24). 1999. per. 4.50 (*0-373-82172-7*, 1-82172-7) Harlequin Bks.

Perfect Pair see Silver Blades

Perfect Pair: Poor Man's Guide & Walking Map. 8th ed. Ed. by Michael E. Williams. 1998. 17.95 (*0-944101-20-8*) New Pittsburgh.

Perfect Palette: Fifty Inspired Color Plans for Every Room in Your Home. Bonnie R. Krims. LC 97-22343. (Illus.). 144p. 1998. 30.00 (*0-446-52348-8*, Pub. by Warner Bks) Little.

Perfect Palette: Fifty Inspired Color Plans for Painting Every Room in Your Home. Bonnie R. Krims. (Illus.). 144p. 1998. 32.95 (*0-446-91217-4*) Warner Bks.

Perfect Pallette: Fifty Inspired Color Plans for Painting Every Room in Your Home. Bonnie R. Krims. 144p. 1999. mass mkt. 16.99 (*0-446-67519-9*, Pub. by Warner Bks) Little.

Perfect Pals. Susan T. Hall. (Illus.). 12p. (J). (ps). 1989. pap. text 5.95 (*0-927106-00-0*) Prod Concept.

Perfect Paper Beads. Wendy J. Canniff. (Illus.). 16p. (J). (gr. 4-7). 1994. pap. 6.95 (*0-8167-3492-5*) Troll Communs.

Perfect Paradox. Gary M. Lawson. LC 93-30580. (Lewiston Poetry Ser.: Vol. 20). 64p. 1993. pap. 14.95 (*0-7734-2789-9*, Mellen Poetry Pr) E Mellen.

Perfect Parenting. Elizabeth Pantley. LC 98-17024. 368p. 1998. pap. 14.95 (*0-8092-2847-5*, 284750, Contemporary Bks) NTC Contemp Pub Co.

Perfect Parties. Marie-France Jensen. (Crafty Hands Collection). (Illus.). 48p. (Orig.). 1996. pap. text 9.95 (*1-85410-374-1*, Pub. by Aurum Pr) London Brdge.

Perfect Parties: Creative Entertaining Made Easy. LC 96-76037. 128p. 1996. 19.95 (*1-57486-008-9*) Oxmoor Hse.

Perfect Partners? Bob Bullan. 176p. 1988. 45.00 (*1-85283-209-6*, Pub. by Boxtree); pap. 30.00 (*1-85283-214-2*, Pub. by Boxtree) St Mut.

Perfect Partners. Jayne Ann Krentz. 368p. 1992. per. 6.99 (*0-671-72855-5*) PB.

Perfect Partners. Jayne Ann Krentz. 1998. per. 6.99 (*0-671-01967-8*) PB.

Perfect Partners. Joyce Marlow. LC 96-95472. 192p. 1997. 18.95 (*0-8034-9198-0*, Avalon Bks) Bouregy.

Perfect Partners. large type ed. Jayne Ann Krentz. LC 92-16523. 510p. 1992. reprint ed. lib. bdg. 22.95 (*1-56054-474-0*) Thorndike Pr.

Perfect Partners, 1, 4. Karen Dorrin. (Zebra Bouquet Ser.). 1999. mass mkt. 3.99 (*0-8217-6277-X*) Kensgtn Pub Corp.

Perfect Partners: Find Your Perfect Partner Step-by-Step. Carolyn Huff & Wesley Huff. 176p. 1998. pap. 18.95 (*1-891336-01-0*) Empowermnt Solns.

Perfect Partners: Make Your Hopes & Dreams for a Great Marriage Come True. Carolyn Huff & Wesley Huff. 392p. 1998. 24.95 (*1-891336-00-2*) Empowermnt Solns.

Perfect Partners: Should You Stay or Should You Leave? Step-by-Step. Carolyn Huff & Wesley Huff. 238p. 1998. pap. 18.95 (*1-891336-03-7*) Empowermnt Solns.

Perfect Partners: When You Think You've Found Your Perfect Partner Step-by-Step. Carolyn Huff & Wesley Huff. 188p. 1998. pap. 18.95 (*1-891336-02-9*) Empowermnt Solns.

Perfect Parts. Rachel McLish & Joyce L. Vedral. 256p. 1987. mass mkt. 14.99 (*0-446-38534-4*, Pub. by Warner Bks) Little.

Perfect Parts. Vedral. 1993. 12.99 (*0-446-77815-X*) Warner Bks.

Perfect Party. A. R. Gurney. 1986. pap. 5.25 (*0-8222-0886-5*) Dramatists Play.

Perfect Party Food Book: Favorite Recipes for Party Success. (Illus.). 64p. 1997. 9.95 (*1-85967-541-7*, Lorenz Bks) Anness Pub.

***Perfect Party Planner.** Leisure Arts Inc. Staff. (Illus.). 128p. 2000. pap. 19.95 (*1-57486-205-7*) Leisure AR.

Perfect Pasta. (Mini Cook Bks.). 148p. pap. 1.95 (*3-8290-0379-X*, 770117) Konemann.

Perfect Pastries. (Mini Cook Bks.). (Illus.). 64p. 1999. pap. 1.95 (*3-8290-1615-8*) Konemann.

Perfect Patterns - Patrones Perfectos, English ed. Cyrl Silber. (Illus.). 67p. (Orig.). 1992. pap. text 18.95 (*0-9634837-0-6*) C Silber.

Easiest method to make your own pattern. How to take your measurements & draw a pattern for a garment of your choice; including sleeves, collars, blouses, blazers, skirts, culottes, shorts & pants. Method is used in Miami public school adult education classes. Clearly written, understandable diagrams, instruction in inches & metric system & easily taught. It's available in English, PERFECT PATTERNS ISBN 0-9634837-0-6 & in Spanish, PATRONES PERFECTOS ISBN 0-9634837-1-4.

P

Perfect Patterns - Patrones Perfectos, Spanish ed. Cyril Silber. (SPA., Illus.). 67p. (Orig.). 1992. pap. text 18.95 (0-9634837-1-4) C Silber.

Perfect Patterns for Reporting Fact & Fiction. Nancy Polette. (Illus.). 48p. 1998. pap. 8.95 (1-880505-25-8, CLC0213) Pieces of Lrning.

Perfect Peace. Amos Oz. Tr. by Hillel Halkin from HEB. LC 84-25171. (Helen & Kurt Wolff Bk.). 400p. 1985. 16.95 (0-15-171696-X) Harcourt.

Perfect Peace. Amos Oz. 384p. 1993. pap. 13.00 (0-15-671683-6) Harcourt.

***Perfect Peace: Selections from the God of All Comfort.** Hannah Whitall Smith. 96p. 2000. 12.99 (0-8024-6692-3) Moody.

Perfect Personal Statements. Mark A. Stewart. LC 96-110840. 120p. 1995. 9.95 (0-02-861049-0, Arc) IDG Bks.

Perfect Pet. Disney Enterprises, Inc. Staff. (Disney's "Out & about with Pooh" Library: Vol. 11). (Illus.). 44p. (J). (gr. 1-6). 1996. 3.49 (1-885222-65-3) Advance Pubs.

Perfect Pets. Kathryn Hinds. (Illus.). 32p. (YA). (gr. 2 up). lib. bdg. 91.14 (0-7614-0792-8) Marshall Cavendish.

***Perfect Pets, No. 2.** Benchmark Books Staff. (Illus.). (J). 2000. 91.14 (0-7614-1100-3, Benchmark NY) Marshall Cavendish.

Perfect Pic? The Purpose & Practice of Organizational Learning. Mike Pedler & Kath Aspinwall. LC 95-24732. (Developing Organizations Ser.). 1995. write for info. (0-07-709130-2) McGraw.

Perfect Pickle Book. 3rd rev. ed. David Mabey & David Collison. 1995. pap. 9.95 (0-563-37068-8, BBC-Parkwest) Parkwest Pubns.

***Perfect Picnic Book.** Ed. by Lorenz Books Staff. (Illus.). 2000. 11.95 (0-7548-0545-X, Lorenz Bks) Anness Pub.

Perfect Picnic Spot. Mouse Works Staff. LC 97-162788. (J). 1997. 3.98 (1-57082-564-5, Pub. by Mouse Works) Time Warner.

Perfect Picnics for All Seasons. Gail Monaghan. (Illus.). 96p. 1994. 15.95 (1-55859-802-2) Abbeville Pr.

Perfect Pics. Lonnie Daizovi. (Illus.). 53p. 1991. 12.95 (0-935301-62-3) Vibrante Pr.

Perfect Picture Hanging. Judy Sheridan. 1997. 20.00 (0-517-20067-8) Random Hse Value.

Perfect Pie. PUBL Anness Publications Staff. 1999. 7.98 (1-84038-411-5) Random.

***Perfect Pie.** Martha Day. (Illus.). 2000. 11.95 (0-7548-0351-1, Lorenz Bks) Anness Pub.

***Perfect Pie.** Judith Thompson. 96p. 2000. pap. 14.95 (0-88754-590-4) Theatre Comm.

***Perfect Pie: 150 All-Time Favorite Pies & Tarts.** Susan G. Purdy. LC 99-45530. (Illus.). 384p. 2000. pap. 17.95 (0-7679-0262-9) Broadway BDD.

Perfect Piece. Tony Hamill. LC 94-29123. 275p. (C). 1995. pap. 12.95 (0-435-08634-0, 08634) Heinemann.

Perfect Piece. Playwrights Canada Press Staff. LC 91-175301. 276p. 1997. pap. text 16.95 (0-88754-498-3) Theatre Comm.

Perfect Piecing: Rodale's Successful Quilting Library. Ed. by Karen C. Soltys. LC 96-51316. 1997. text 19.95 (0-87596-760-4) Rodale Pr Inc.

Perfect Pies No. 45: From Dinner to Dessert. Polly Clingerman. 64p. 1998. pap. 3.95 (0-942320-62-X) Am Cooking.

Perfect Pigs: An Introduction to Manners. Marc Tolon Brown. (J). 1983. 12.15 (0-606-03991-0, Pub. by Turtleback) Demco.

Perfect Pigs: An Introduction to Manners. Marc Tolon Brown & Stephen Krensky. LC 83-746. (Illus.). 32p. (J). (gr. k-3). 1983. pap. 6.95 (0-316-11080-9, Joy St Bks) Little.

Perfect Pipe. H. Paul Jeffers. LC 98-27065. (Illus.). 192p. 1998. 27.95 (1-58080-065-3) Burford Bks.

Perfect Pirate. large type ed. Mary Edwards. (Linford Romance Library). 256p. 1993. pap. 16.99 (0-7089-7469-4, Linford) Ulverscroft.

Perfect Pitch: How to Sell Yourself for Today's Job Market. David Andrusia. LC 96-48246. 272p. (Orig.). 1997. mass mkt. 13.99 (0-446-67294-7, Pub. by Warner Bks) Little.

Perfect Pitch Ear Training SuperCourse, Set. unabridged ed. David L. Burge. LC 81-85963. 60p. 1999. pap. 145.00 incl. audio (0-942542-94-0) EarTraining.

Perfect Pizza Gift Set. Bramley. 1997. 12.95 (1-85833-565-5, Pub. by CLib Bks) Whitecap Bks.

Perfect Plan see Plan Perfecto

***Perfect Plan, No. 3.** Nancy Butcher. (Illus.). 132p. (J). (gr. 3-7). 2000. pap. 3.99 (0-375-80339-4, Pub. by Random Bks Yng Read) Random.

Perfect Planet & Other Stories. James Kochalka. (Illus.). 208p. 1999. pap. 14.95 (1-891830-08-2) Top Shelf Prodns.

Perfect Plant: For Every Size, Habitat, & Garden Style. David Joyce et al. LC 97-41165. 352p. 1998. 45.00 (1-55670-607-3) Stewart Tabori & Chang.

***Perfect Plants for Every Place.** 2000. pap. 12.95 (0-7548-0070-9, Lorenz Bks) Anness Pub.

Perfect Plants for Your Garden. R. Phillips & Martyn Rix. (Illus.). 320p. 1996. pap. write for info. (0-333-65341-6) Humanities.

***Perfect Pleasures: The Pipe, the Cigar & the Cigarette in British Popular Culture.** Matthew Hilton. LC 99-43345. (Studies in Popular Culture). 1999. pap. 29.95 (0-7190-5257-2, Pub. by Manchester Univ Pr) St Martin.

***Perfect Pleasures: The Pipe, the Cigar & the Cigarette in British Popular Culture.** Matthew Hilton. LC 99-43345. 2000. text 74.95 (0-7190-5256-4, Pub. by Manchester Univ Pr) St Martin.

Perfect Plot. Carolyn Keene. Ed. by Anne Greenberg. LC 93-183919. (Nancy Drew Files: No. 76). 150p. (Orig.). (J). (gr. 6 up). 1992. mass mkt. 3.99 (0-671-73080-0, Archway) PB.

Perfect Plot: A User Manual for Constructing an Indistructable Plot. Pascual Vaquer. 162p. 1998. pap. 30.00 (0-9667785-0-2) P Vaquer.

***Perfect Poems: Teaching Phonics.** Deborah Ellermeyer et al. (Illus.). 64p. 1999. pap. 9.95 (0-590-39019-8) Scholastic Inc.

***Perfect Pony.** Michell Bates. (Sandy Lane Stables Ser.). (Illus.). 112p. (J). (gr. 4-9). 1999. pap. text 3.95 (0-7460-3329-X, Usborne) EDC.

Perfect Pony. Michelle Bates. (Sandy Lane Stables Ser.). (Illus.). 112p. (gr. 4-8). 1999. 11.95 (1-58086-175-X) EDC.

***Perfect Pony.** Corinne Demas. LC 99-46813. (Step into Reading Ser.: A Step 3 Book). (Illus.). 48p. (J). (gr. k-3). 2000. lib. bdg. 11.99 (0-679-99199-9, Pub. by Random Bks Yng Read) Random.

Perfect Pork Stew. Paul B. Johnson. LC 97-21962. (Illus.). 32p. (J). (gr. k-4). 1998. 15.95 (0-531-30070-6); lib. bdg. 16.99 (0-531-33070-2) Orchard Bks Watts.

***Perfect Porridge: A Story about Kindness.** Rochel Sandman. LC 99-65449. (Illus.). 32p. (J). (ps-2). 2000. 9.95 (0-922613-92-3) Hachai Pubng.

Perfect Portfolio. Henrietta Brackman. (Illus.). 144p. 1984. pap. 19.95 (0-8174-5401-2, Amphoto) Watsn-Guptill.

Perfect Posture. Hatherleigh Press Staff. LC 99-87620. 112p. 2000. pap. 14.95 (1-57826-040-X, Pub. by Hatherleigh) Norton.

***Perfect Poultry.** Reader's Digest Editors. LC 99-44148. (Great Healthy Cooking Ser.). (Illus.). 1999. write for info. (0-7621-0275-6) RD Assn.

Perfect Power in Consciousness. Heather A. Harder. LC 93-80636. 164p. 1994. pap. 12.95 (1-884410-01-4) Light Pubng.

Perfect Power Within You. Jack E. Addington & Cornelia Addington. LC 73-87712. 167p. 1973. pap. 8.95 (0-87516-179-0) DeVorss.

Perfect Pr. Iain Maitland. LC 99-187872. (ITBP PROFESSIONAL). 256p. 1998. pap. 24.95 (1-86152-221-5) Thomson Learn.

Perfect Praise see Joy in Praising God

Perfect Pregnancy Week by Week: Practical Handbook. Alison MacKonochie. 1999. pap. 8.95 (0-7548-0011-3, Lorenz Bks) Anness Pub.

Perfect Present. Michael Hague. LC 95-52427. (Illus.). 48p. (J). (ps-3). 1996. 16.00 (0-688-10880-6, Wm Morrow) Morrow Avon.

Perfect Present: The Ultimate Gift Guide for Every Occasion. Robyn F. Spizman. LC 98-17544. 128p. 1998. 16.00 (0-609-60131-8, Crown) Crown Pub Group.

Perfect Presentations. John Collins. LC 98-53806. (Self-Development for Success Ser.: Vol. 8). (Illus.). 96p. 1999. pap. 12.95 (0-8144-7040-8) AMACOM.

Perfect Preserves: Provisions from the Kitchen Garden. Nora Carey. (Illus.). 256p. 1995. pap. 24.95 (1-55670-401-1) Stewart Tabori & Chang.

Perfect Princess. Irene Radford. (Dragon Nimbus Ser.: No. 2). 352p. 1995. mass mkt. 5.99 (0-88677-678-3, Pub. by DAW Bks) Penguin Putnam.

***Perfect Project Manager.** Peter Bartram. 1999. pap. 15.95 (0-09-940506-7, Pub. by Random) Trafalgar.

Perfect Prudence. (Little Monsters Ser.). (J). 1997. write for info. (0-614-21781-4, Pub. by Splash) Assoc Pubs Grp.

Perfect Pumpkin. Gail Damerow. LC 97-12562. (Illus.). 224p. 1997. pap. 12.95 (0-88266-993-1, Storey Pub) Storey Bks.

Perfect Puppy: How to Choose Your Dog by Its Behavior. Lynette A. Hart. (Orig.). 1987. pap. text 12.95 (0-7167-1829-4) W H Freeman.

Perfect Puppy: How to Raise a Well-Behaved Dog. Gwen Bailey. LC 95-49963. (Illus.). 192p. 1996. 19.95 (0-89577-839-4, Pub. by RD Assn) Penguin Putnam.

Perfect Put-Downs & Instant Insults. Joseph Rosenbloom. LC 88-11710. (Illus.). 128p. (J). (gr. 2-8). 1989. pap. 4.95 (0-8069-6940-7) Sterling.

Perfect Questions - Perfect Answers. A. C. Bhaktivedanta Swami Prabhupada. 108p. 1997. pap. 2.95 (91-7149-170-8, PQPA) Bhaktivedanta.

Perfect Ray-Free House: Concise Guide for Radiesthologists. Wilton Kullmann. (Illus.). 62p. 1994. pap. 18.95 (3-85068-440-7, Pub. by Ennsthaler) Am Educ Systs.

Perfect Recipe: Getting It Right Every Time: Making Our Favorite Dishes the Absolute Best They Can Be. Pam Anderson. LC 98-17821. (Illus.). 372p. 1998. 27.00 (0-395-89403-4) HM.

Perfect Relationship: A Domestic Comedy in Two Acts. Doric Wilson. LC 83-61708. 119p. 1983. reprint ed. pap. 7.95 (0-933322-12-7) T n T Class.

***Perfect Relationship: The Guru & the Disciple.** 2nd ed. Swami Muktananda. Tr. by Gurumayi Chidvilasananda. LC 98-35843. 192p. (Orig.). 1999. pap. 12.95 (0-911307-76-1) SYDA Found.

Perfect Remedy. large type ed. Frances Crowne. 306p. 1994. 27.99 (0-7505-0630-X, Pub. by Mgna Lrg Print) Ulverscroft.

Perfect Retriever. Herbert Axelrod. (Cats & Dogs). (Illus.). 84p. (YA). (gr. 3 up). 1999. 19.95 (0-7910-4814-4) Chelsea Hse.

Perfect Retriever. Miriam Fields-Babineau. (Illus.). 64p. 1998. 12.95 (0-7938-0325-X, WW-084) TFH Pubns.

***Perfect Rogue.** Martine Berne. 2000. mass mkt. 5.99 (0-8217-6848-4, Zebra Kensgtn) Kensgtn Pub Corp.

Perfect Rose. Gail Porter & Sue Layman. Ed. by Nita Scoggan. LC 86-61447. 100p. (Orig.). 1986. pap. 3.95 (0-910487-09-X) Royalty Pub.

Perfect Sales Piece: A Complete Do-It-Yourself Guide to Creating Brochures, Catalogs, Fliers. Robert W. Bly. LC 94-11311. 237p. 1994. pap. 14.95 (0-471-00411-1) Wiley.

Perfect Sales Piece: A Complete Do-It-Yourself Guide to Creating Brochures, Catalogs, Fliers, & Pamphlets. Robert W. Bly. (Small Business Editions Ser.). 237p. 1994. 49.95 (0-471-00403-0) Wiley.

Perfect Scoundrel. Virginia Hart. (Romance Ser.). 1994. per. 2.99 (0-373-03305-2, 1-03305-9) Harlequin Bks.

Perfect Season. Phillip Fulmer. LC 99-38547. 1999. pap. 24.95 (1-55853-798-8) Rutledge Hill Pr.

Perfect Season: Why 1998 Was Baseball's Greatest Year. Tim McCarver & Danny Peary. LC 99-13423. 224p. 1999. 19.95 (0-375-50330-7) Villard Books.

Perfect Secretary (Le Parfait Secretaire) G. Vivien. (FRE.). 359p. 1991. pap. 29.95 (0-7859-4783-3, M4756) Fr & Eur.

Perfect Secrets. Brenda Joyce et al. 368p. 1999. mass mkt. 6.50 (0-312-97029-3, St Martins Paperbacks) St Martin.

Perfect Seduction. Penny Jordan. (Presents Ser.). 1998. per. 3.75 (0-373-11941-0, 1-11941-1) Harlequin Bks.

Perfect Seduction. large type ed. Joanna Mansell. 1994. 18.95 (0-263-13931-X) Thorndike Pr.

***Perfect Setting.** Peri Wolfman & Charles Gold. 192p. 2000. pap. 24.95 (0-8109-2749-7, Pub. by Abrams) Time Warner.

***Perfect Setting: Menus & Memories from Cincinnati's Taft Museum.** Catherine L. O'Hara. 144p. 1999. 21.95 (0-915577-30-5) Taft Museum.

Perfect Sex: For Men & for the Women Who Love Them. Chin-Ti Lin. LC 97-68873. 250p. 1998. 22.95 (1-882792-51-3); pap. 18.95 (1-882792-73-4) Proctor Pubns.

Perfect Shepherd: Studies in the Twenty-Third Psalm. John J. Davis. pap. 6.50 (0-88469-110-1) BMH Bks.

Perfect Silence see Porque Hay Silencio

Perfect Silence. Alba N. Ambert. LC 94-29360. 199p. 1995. 9.95 (1-55885-125-9) Arte Publico.

***Perfect Silence.** Jeff Hutton. 304p. 2000. 23.00 (1-891369-20-2, Pub. by Breakaway Bks) Consort Bk Sales.

***Perfect Sin.** Kat Martin. 368p. 2000. mass mkt. 6.99 (0-312-97564-3) St Martin.

Perfect Sinner. Penny Jordan. 376p. 1999. per. 5.99 (1-55166-515-8, 1-66515-7, Mira Bks) Harlequin Bks.

***Perfect Slave Abroad.** Becky Bell. 272p. 1999. pap. 9.95 (1-901388-47-6, Pub. by Chimera Pubns) Firebird Dist.

Perfect Soldier. Ralph Peters. LC 94-45908. 320p. 1995. 23.00 (0-671-86583-8, PB Hardcover) PB.

Perfect Soldier. Ralph Peters. 1996. mass mkt. 6.99 (0-671-86584-6) PB.

Perfect Solution. Jacqueline Brandon. (Rainbow Romances Ser.). 160p. 1993. 14.95 (0-7090-4894-7) Parkwest Pubns.

***Perfect Solution: Heart of the West.** Day Leclaire. 2000. per. 4.50 (0-373-82594-3) Harlequin Bks.

Perfect Solution Independent Reader 5-Pack, Unit 12. (Networks Ser.). 1991. pap. 15.00 (0-88106-798-9, N348) Charlesbridge Pub.

***Perfect Sowing: Reflections of a Bookman.** Henry Regnery. Ed. by Jeffrey Nelson. 406p. 1999. 24.95 (1-882926-32-3) ISI Books.

Perfect Speed: Throw Away That Plan. Toni L. Chinoy. 68p. 1998. pap. 11.95 (0-9668591-5-4, Writers Club Pr) iUniversecom.

Perfect Spot. Robert J. Blake. LC 91-16006. (Illus.). 32p. (J). (ps-3). 1992. 15.95 (0-399-22132-8, Philomel) Peng Put Young Read.

Perfect Spot. Robert J. Blake. (Illus.). 32p. (J). (ps-3). 1997. pap. 5.95 (0-698-11431-0, PapStar) Peng Put Young Read.

Perfect Spot. Robert J. Blake. LC 91-16006. (J). 1997. 11.15 (0-606-11738-5, Pub. by Turtleback) Demco.

***Perfect Spy.** John Le Carre, pseud. 688p. 2000. reprint ed. per. 7.99 (0-671-04275-0, Pocket Books) PB.

Perfect Star. John Bibee. LC 92-5686. (Spirit Flyer Ser.: Bk. 7). (Illus.). 192p. (Orig.). (J). (gr. 5-8). 1992. pap. 6.99 (0-8308-1206-7, 1206) InterVarsity.

***Perfect Starfish.** Rosalind B. Chaikin. LC 98-52876. 115p. 1999. pap. 15.00 (0-912526-80-7) Lib Res.

Perfect State of Health. Peter Way. LC 77-18497. 145p. 1972. 20.00 (0-89388-039-6) Okpaku Communications.

***Perfect Storm.** Sebastian Junger. 2000. 20.00 (0-393-05032-7) Norton.

Perfect Storm: A True Story of Men Against the Sea. Sebastian Junger. 320p. 2000. mass mkt. 6.99 (0-06-101351-X, Torch) HarpC.

Perfect Storm: A True Story of Men Against the Sea. Sebastian Junger. (Illus.). 256p. 1999. pap. 14.00 (0-06-097747-7, Perennial) HarperTrade.

Perfect Storm: A True Story of Men Against the Sea. Sebastian Junger. LC 96-42412. (Illus.). 256p. 1997. 23.95 (0-393-04016-X) Norton.

Perfect Storm: A True Story of Men Against the Sea. abr. ed. Sebastian Junger. 1997. 18.00 incl. audio (0-679-46035-7) Random AudioBks.

Perfect Storm: A True Story of Men Against the Sea. large type ed. Sebastian Junger. LC 97-18106. (Americana Series). 371p. 1997. lib. bdg. 26.95 (0-7862-1217-9) Thorndike Pr.

Perfect Stranger. P. J. Kavanagh. 192p. 1995. pap. 14.95 (1-85754-178-2, Pub. by Carcanet Pr) Paul & Co Pubs.

Perfect Stranger. Danielle Steel. 400p. (Orig.). 1983. mass mkt. 6.99 (0-440-16872-4) Dell.

Perfect Stranger. Gina F. Wilkins. (Temptation Ser.: No. 353). 1991. per. 2.95 (0-373-25453-9) Harlequin Bks.

Perfect Stranger, Vol. 2. Rosalyn Alsobrook. (Seascape Romance Ser.). 1996. mass mkt. 5.99 (0-312-95875-7) St Martin.

Perfect Strangers. Jana Ellis. LC 89-36349. (Merivale Mall Ser.). 160p. (J). (gr. 7 up). 1989. pap. text 2.50 (0-8167-1674-9) Troll Communs.

Perfect Strangers. Laura Martin. (Romance Ser.: Vol. 397). 1998. mass mkt. 3.50 (0-373-17397-0, 1-17397-0) Harlequin Bks.

Perfect Strangers. Rebecca Sinclair. 320p. 1996. mass mkt. 4.99 (0-8217-5266-9, Zebra Kensgtn) Kensgtn Pub Corp.

Perfect Strangers: A Novel of Time Travel. Robert L. Smith, Jr. 408p. 1999. pap. 19.95 (1-892896-80-X) Buy Books.

***Perfect Stranger's Guide to Funerals & Grieving Practices: A Guide to Etiquette in Other People's Religious Ceremonies.** Ed. by Stuart M. Matlins. 2000. pap. 16.95 (1-893361-20-9) SkyLight Paths.

***Perfect Stranger's Guide to Wedding Ceremonies: A Guide to Etiquette in Other People's Religious Ceremonies.** Ed. by Stuart M. Matlins. 2000. pap. 16.95 (1-893361-19-5) SkyLight Paths.

Perfect Style with Grammatik. Jane Davis. 1994. pap. 29.95 incl. disk (0-07-015865-7, Windcrest) TAB Bks.

Perfect Summer. Kate William. (Sweet Valley High Super Edition Ser.). (YA). (gr. 7 up). 1985. 8.60 (0-606-00742-3, Pub. by Turtleback) Demco.

Perfect Surprise. Caroline Peak. (Special Edition Ser.). 1995. per. 3.75 (0-373-09960-6, 1-09960-5) Silhouette.

Perfect Symmetry: The Accidental Discovery of a New Form of Carbon. Jim Baggott. (Illus.). 328p. 1995. 45.00 (0-19-855790-6) OUP.

Perfect Symmetry: The Accidental Discovery of a New Form of Carbon. Jim Baggott. (Illus.). 328p. (C). 1996. pap. 19.95 (0-19-855789-2) OUP.

***Perfect System.** Sydney Kessler. 224p. 2000. 18.95 (0-7737-3235-7) Stoddart Publ.

Perfect 10: Phyto "New-trients" Against Cancers. 3rd rev. ed. Laura Pawlak. (Illus.). 264p. 1999. pap. 25.00 (1-893549-13-5) Biomed Genl.

Perfect 10: The Blessings of Following God's Commandments in a Post Modern World. Michael Moriarty. LC 99-19135. 256p. 2000. pap. 12.99 (0-310-22764-X) Zondervan.

Perfect Term Paper: Step-by-Step. Donald J. Mulkerne, Jr. LC 87-12630. 176p. 1988. pap. 9.95 (0-385-24794-X, Anchor NY) Doubleday.

***Perfect Thanksgiving.** Eileen Spinelli. 2000. pap. text. write for info. (0-8050-6531-8) St Martin.

Perfect Thanksgiving Book: Delicious Recipes for a Fabulous Family Feast. Ed. by Lindley Boegehold. (Illus.). 64p. 1995. 9.95 (1-85967-121-7, Lorenz Bks) Anness Pub.

Perfect the Pig. Susan Jeschke. LC 80-39998. (Illus.). 48p. (J). (ps-2). 1995. 14.95 (0-8050-0704-0, Bks Young Read); pap. 5.95 (0-8050-4704-2) H Holt & Co.

Perfect the Pig. Susan Jeschke. LC 80-39998. (J). 1996. 11.15 (0-606-09742-2, Pub. by Turtleback) Demco.

***Perfect 36: Tennessee Delivers Woman Suffrage.** Carol L. Yellin et al. LC 98-173992. 160 p. 1998. write for info. (1-882595-14-9) New So Archit.

Perfect Time. Richard Jones. LC 94-28582. 96p. 1994. pap. 12.00 (1-55659-068-7) Copper Canyon.

Perfect Times, Perfect Places. Robert Adams. (Illus.). 64p. 1988. 53.00 (0-89381-299-4) Aperture.

Perfect Timing. Olga Bicos. 416p. 1998. pap. 5.99 (0-8217-5947-7, Zebra Kensgtn) Kensgtn Pub Corp.

Perfect Timing. J. Mansell. 1997. text 28.00 (0-7472-2019-0, Pub. by Headline Bk Pub) Trafalgar.

***Perfect Timing.** J. Mansell. 1999. pap. 11.00 (0-7472-5783-3, Pub. by Headline Bk Pub) Trafalgar.

Perfect Timing. Philip L. Williams. 320p. 1991. 17.95 (1-56145-024-3) Peachtree Pubs.

Perfect Timing: A Spiritual Journey. Conrad Wolfman. 168p. 1998. pap. 10.00 (0-9637741-4-X) Clear Stream.

Perfect Timing: The Art of Electional Astrology. Szanto. 1988. pap. 14.95 (0-85030-803-8, Pub. by Aqrn Pr) Harper SF.

Perfect Touch. rev. ed. Eli Glass. (Read-Along Radio Dramas Ser.). (J). (gr. 6-10). 1983. reprint ed. ring bd. 38.00 (1-878298-01-1) Balance Pub.

Perfect Tree: A Story about Unity. (Excellence in Character Series Storybks.). (Illus.). 30p. (J). (gr. k-8). 1998. pap. 6.00 (1-58259-029-X) Global Classrm.

Perfect Tribute. Mary R. Andrews. 56p. 1992. reprint ed. lib. bdg. 15.95 (0-89966-920-4) Buccaneer Bks.

***Perfect Trust, Vol. 1.** Charles R. Swindoll. 1999. 9.99 (0-8499-5510-6) Word Pub.

***Perfect Turk's Head Knots.** Roy-Keith Smith. (Illus.). xi, 79p. 1999. pap. 35.00 (0-9677825-1-1) Apichemical Cons.

Perfect Union, 4 vols. 4th ed. Boller. (C). 1995. pap. text 29.56 (0-395-74524-1) HM.

Perfect Union, 4 vols., Vol. 2. 4th ed. Boller. (C). 1995. pap. text 29.56 (0-395-74525-X) HM.

Perfect Use of Silkworms. Olivier Des Serres. Tr. by N. Geffe. LC 72-232. (English Experience Ser.: No. 345). 100p. 1971. reprint ed. 30.00 (90-221-0345-5) Walter J Johnson.

***Perfect Vacuum.** Stanislaw Lem. Tr. by Michael Kandel from POL. LC 99-42422. 240p. 1999. pap. 14.95 (0-8101-1733-9) Northwestern U Pr.

Perfect Vehicle: What It Is about Motorcycles. Melissa H. Pierson. (Illus.). 240p. 1998. pap. 13.00 (0-393-31809-5) Norton.

Perfect Victim. Christine McGuire & Carla Norton. 384p. 1989. mass mkt. 6.99 (0-440-20442-9) Dell.

Perfect Victim. large type ed. James McKimmey. (Linford Mystery Library). 336p. 1997. pap. 16.99 (0-7089-5102-3, Linford) Ulverscroft.

P

An Asterisk (*) at the beginning of an entry indicates that the title is appearing for the first time.

Perfect-Victim Factor: Taking Control of Destructive Personality Traits. Richard K. Nongard & Paula S. Nongard. LC 97-91576. 120p. (Orig.). 1997. pap. 12.95 (*0-9655979-1-1*, BO2PVF) Peachtree Prof.

***Perfect Vinaigrettes: Appetizer to Desserts.** Linda Dannenberg. LC 99-16263. (Illus.). 112p. 1999. text 19.95 (*1-55670-943-9*) Stewart Tabori & Chang.

Perfect Vision: A Mother's Experience with Childhood Cancer. Sharon H. Brunner. LC 96-69281. 128p. (Orig.). 1996. pap. 10.00 (*1-884570-49-6*) Research Triangle.

Perfect Wagnerite: A Commentary on the Niblung's Ring. George Bernard Shaw. 136p. 1967. pap. 6.95 (*0-486-21707-8*) Dover.

Perfect Wagnerite: A Commentary on the Niblung's Ring. George Bernard Shaw. 151p. 1990. reprint ed. lib. bdg. 59.00 (*0-7812-9159-3*) Rprt Serv.

Perfect War. Al Bucci. LC 97-185708. 320p. 1997. pap. 20.00 (*1-886094-65-9*) Chicago Spectrum.

Perfect War. 2nd ed. Sam Lee. Ed. by Margaret Valentine. 186p. 1990. 15.95 (*0-9621667-1-5*) Chengalera Pr.

***Perfect War: Technowar in Vietnam.** James William Gibson. 544p. 2000. reprint ed. pap. 16.00 (*0-87113-799-2*, Atlntc Mnthly) Grove-Atltic.

Perfect Way in Diet. 5th ed. Anna B. Kingsford. 121p. 1996. reprint ed. spiral bd. 11.50 (*0-7873-0493-X*) Hlth Research.

Perfect Way in Diet: A Treatise Advocating a Return in the Natural & Ancient Food of Our Race (1906) Anna B. Kingsford. 131p. 1996. reprint ed. pap. 10.95 (*1-56459-947-7*) Kessinger Pub.

Perfect Way: or The Finding of Christ. Anna B. Kingsford & Edward Maitland. 385p. 1996. pap. 34.00 (*0-89540-312-9*, SB-312) Sun Pub.

Perfect Way: or The Finding of Christ. enl. rev. ed. Anna B. Kingsford & Edward Maitland. 358p. 1996. reprint ed. spiral bd. 19.50 (*0-7873-0494-8*) Hlth Research.

Perfect Way: or The Finding of Christ. enl. rev. ed. Anna B. Kingsford & Edward Maitland. 430p. 1992. pap. 29.95 (*1-56459-254-5*) Kessinger Pub.

Perfect Way to Lose Weight Pocket Guide see Metodo Perfecto para Bajar de Peso

Perfect Way to Lose Weight: Pocket Guide see Metodo Perfecto para Bajar de Peso: Guia de Bolsillo

Perfect Way to Lose Weight Pocket Guide see Metodo Perfecto para Bajar de Peso

Perfect Wedding. Arlene James. 1997. per. 4.50 (*0-373-87004-3*, 1-87004-7) Harlequin Bks.

Perfect Wedding. Maria McBride-Mellinger. LC 96-19111. (Illus.). 336p. 1997. 40.00 (*0-06-258663-7*) Collins SF.

Perfect Wedding: This Side of Heaven. Arlene James. (Romance Ser.). 1993. per. 2.75 (*0-373-08962-7*, 5-08962-8) Silhouette.

***Perfect Wedding Planner, Set.** abr. ed. Diane Warner. (Learn in Your Car - Discovery Ser.). 2000. pap. 15.95 incl. audio (*1-56015-201-X*) Penton Overseas.

Perfect Wedding Workbook: A Bride's "Best Friend" Reflected Images Staff. 1996. 40.00 (*1-881263-22-3*) Reflect Images.

Perfect Weight: The Complete Mind-Body Program for Acheiving & Maintaining Your Ideal Weight. Deepak Chopra. (Perfect Health Library). 144p. 1996. pap. 12.00 (*0-517-88458-5*) Crown Pub Group.

Perfect Wife. Victoria Alexander. 320p. (Orig.). 1996. mass mkt. 4.99 (*0-8439-4108-1*) Dorchester Pub Co.

***Perfect Wife.** Jane Goodger. 2000. mass mkt. 5.99 (*0-451-20130-2*, Sig) NAL.

Perfect Wife. Shari MacDonald. LC 99-14976. (Salinger Sisters Romantic Comedy Ser.: Vol. 3). 256p. 1999. pap. 6.95 (*1-57856-138-8*) Waterbrook Pr.

Perfect Wife. Christina Odone. 217p. 1998. 27.00 (*0-7528-1219-X*, Pub. by Orion Pubng Grp) Trafalgar.

Perfect Wife & Mother. large type ed. Nicola Thorne. (Dales Large Print Ser.). 401p. 1995. pap. 18.99 (*1-85389-527-X*, Dales) Ulverscroft.

Perfect Wisdom: The Short Prajnaparamita Texts. Tr. by Edward Conze. 224p. 1995. pap. 14.95 (*0-946672-28-8*, Pub. by Buddhist Pub) Assoc Pubs Grp.

Perfect Witness. Barry Siegel. LC 97-31008. 352p. 1998. 24.00 (*0-345-41307-5*) Ballantine Pub Grp.

Perfect Witness. Barry Siegel. 339p. 1999. mass mkt. 6.99 (*0-345-43084-0*) Ballantine Pub Grp.

Perfect Woman. Evan Moore. 304p. 1999. mass mkt. 4.99 (*0-7860-0205-0*) Kensgtn Pub Corp.

Perfect Woman. Carolyn Slaughter. LC 84-8838. 208p. 1985. 14.95 (*0-89919-342-0*, Pub. by Ticknor & Fields) HM.

Perfect Woman: Short Stories. Bulbul Sharma. (C). 1995. 7.00 (*81-86112-53-7*, Pub. by UBS Pubs Dist) S Asia.

Perfect Woman's Flaw: Understanding Perfectionism. Patti Williams. LC 91-78273. 106p. 1992. mass mkt. 4.99 (*0-88270-701-9*) Bridge-Logos.

Perfect Words Vol. 1: For Scrapbookers. George Elliott et al. (Illus.). 30p. 1999. pap. 18.95 (*0-9669509-0-9*) Crazy Star.

Perfect World: A Romance of Strange People & Strange Places. Ella Scrymsour. 316p. 1996. reprint ed. spiral bd. 18.00 (*0-7873-0755-6*) Hlth Research.

Perfect Yankee: The Incredible Story of the Greatest Miracle in Baseball History. Don Larsen & Mark Shaw. LC 96-68629. (Illus.). 272p. 1996. 22.95 (*1-57167-043-2*) Sports Pub.

Perfect You. George Hurst. 96p. 1985. pap. 7.95 (*0-942494-91-1*) Coleman Pub.

Perfect Your Notrump Bidding. C. C. Wei & Ron Anderson. 232p. (Orig.). 1978. pap. 5.95 (*0-87643-036-1*) M Lisa Precision.

Perfecta a los Ojos de Dios - Autoestima en la Mujer: Perfect in His Eyes - Studies on Self-Esteem. Kay M. Strom & Priscila De Patacsil. (SPA.). 96p. (Orig.). 1992. pap. 5.50 (*0-311-12105-5*) Casa Bautista.

Perfecta Casada. Fray L. De Leon. Ed. by Lera J. San Jose. (Nueva Austral Ser.: Vol. 275). (SPA.). pap. text. write for info. (*0-318-69901-X*) Elliots Bks.

Perfecta Casada, No. 51. Fray L. De Leon. (SPA.). 152p. 1980. 20.95 (*0-8288-8555-9*) Fr & Eur.

Perfecta Desconocida. Danielle Steel. 1998. pap. 9.95 (*84-270-2127-5*) Planeta.

Perfecta Salud: La Guia Completa del Mente & Cuerpo. Deepak Chopra. (SPA.). 448p. 1997. pap. 14.00 (*0-609-80104-X*) Harmony Bks.

Perfectability of Man. John Passmore. LC 77-129625. 1978. 25.00 (*0-684-15521-4*) S&S Trade.

Perfected Praise. Richard Malm. 96p. (Orig.). 1988. pap. 8.99 (*0-914903-62-4*) Destiny Image.

***Perfectibility of Man.** 2nd ed. John Passmore. LC 99-87606. 546p. 2000. 25.00 (*0-86597-257-5*); pap. 14.00 (*0-86597-258-3*) Liberty Fund.

Perfectible Body: The Western Ideal of Male Physical Development. Kenneth R. Dutton. LC 94-38092. (Illus.). 400p. 1995. pap. 24.95 (*0-8264-0787-0*) Continuum.

Perfecting Corporate Character: Insightful Lessons for 21st Century Organizations. Frank J. Sherosky. LC 96-93099. 309p. 1997. 26.95 (*1-890170-00-3*) Strategic MI.

Perfecting of the Saints & the Building up of the Body of Christ. Witness Lee. 51p. 1989. pap. 3.75 (*0-87083-468-1*, 08-018-001) Living Stream Ministry.

Perfecting Social Skills: A Guide to Interpersonal Behavior Development. Richard M. Eisler & Lee W. Frederiksen. LC 80-21209. (Applied Clinical Psychology Ser.). 236p. 1981. 45.00 (*0-306-40592-X*, Plenum Trade) Perseus Pubng.

Perfecting the Earth: A Piece of Possible History. Charles W. Wooldridge. LC 78-154467. (Utopian Literature Ser.). (Illus.). 1976. reprint ed. 28.95 (*0-405-03549-7*) Ayer.

Perfecting the Family: Antislavery Marriages in Nineteenth-Century America. Chris Dixon. LC 96-47627. 336p. 1997. text 45.00 (*1-55849-068-X*) U of Mass Pr.

Perfecting the Sounds of American English. Silverstein & Bernard Silverstein. 64p. 1997. spiral bd. 17.95 incl. audio (*0-8442-0479-X*, 0479X) NTC Contemp Pub Co.

Perfecting the World: The Life & Times of Thomas Hodgkin. Photos by Amalie Kass & Edward H. Kass. LC 87-26239. (Illus.). 600p. 1988. 34.95 (*0-15-171700-1*) Harcourt.

Perfecting Woman. Barbara D. Metcalf. 440p. 1996. pap. 17.50 (*0-614-21392-4*, 950) Kazi Pubns.

Perfecting Women: Maulana Ashraf Ali Thanawi's Bihishti. Tr. & Comment by Barbara D. Metcalf. (C). 1992. pap. 18.95 (*0-520-08093-9*, Pub. by U CA Pr) Cal Prin Full Svc.

Perfecting Women: Maulana Ashraf Ali Thanawi's Bihishti Zewar. Ed. & Tr. by Barbara D. Metcalf. 1990. 50.00 (*0-520-06491-7*, Pub. by U CA Pr) Cal Prin Full Svc.

Perfecting Your Golf Swing: New Ways to Lower Your Score. Oliver Heuler. LC 95-20236. (Illus.). 144p. 1995. pap. 14.95 (*0-8069-0875-0*) Sterling.

Perfection in New Testament Theology: Ethics & Eschatology in Relational Dyanamic. John R. Walters. LC 94-13280. (Biblical Press Ser.: Vol. 25). 308p. 1994. 99.95 (*0-7734-2355-9*, Mellen Biblical Pr) E Mellen.

Perfection Mechanical Hand Stamp Machine. Reg Morris & Robert J. Payne. (Illus.). 63p. 1991. pap. 8.00 (*0-9621481-9-9*) Machine Cancel Soc.

Perfection, Never Less: The Vera Way Marghab Story. D. J. Cline. LC 98-61099. (Illus.). 224p. 1998. 44.95 (*0-9666544-0-4*) SD Art Museum.

Perfection of England: Artist Visitors to Devon, 1750-1870. Samuel Smiles. LC 96-166213. (Illus.). 124p. 1995. pap. 29.95 (*0-905227-41-7*, Pub. by Lund Humphries) Antique Collect.

***Perfection of Nothing: Reflections of Spiritual Practice.** Rick Lewis. 180p. 2000. pap. 14.95 (*1-890772-02-X*, Pub. by Hohm Pr) SCB Distributors.

Perfection of Solitude: Hermits & Monks in the Crusader States. Andrew Jotischky. LC 94-12641. (Illus.). 200p. 1995. 38.50 (*0-271-01346-X*) Pa St U Pr.

Perfection of the Morning: A Woman's Awakening in Nature. Sharon Butala. LC 96-78758. 194p. 1997. reprint ed. pap. 14.00 (*1-886913-16-1*) Ruminator Bks.

Perfection of the Universe According to Aquinas: A Teleological Study. Oliva Blanchette. 328p. 1992. text 42.50 (*0-271-00797-4*) Pa St U Pr.

***Perfection of Wisdom.** Craig Jamieson. (Illus.). 109p. 2000. 19.95 (*0-670-88934-2*, Viking Studio) Studio Bks.

Perfection of Wisdom in Eight Thousand Lines & Its Verse Summary. Tr. & Pref. by Edward Conze. LC 72-76540. (Wheel Ser.: No. 1). 348p. 1973. pap. 17.95 (*0-87704-049-4*) Four Seasons Foun.

Perfection of Wisdom in Eight Thousand Lines & Its Verse Summary. Tr. by Edward Conze. (C). 1994. text 28.50 (*81-7030-405-9*, Pub. by Sri Satguru Pubns) S Asia.

Perfection of Yoga. A. C. Bhaktivedanta Swami Prabhupada. LC 72-76302. (Illus.). 56p. 1972. pap. 2.95 (*0-912776-36-6*, POY) Bhaktivedanta.

Perfection Pending & Other Favorite Discourses. Russell M. Nelson. LC 98-24542. 1998. 17.95 (*1-57345-405-2*) Deseret Bk.

Perfection Proclaimed: Language & Literature in English Radical Religion, 1640-1660. Nigel Smith. (Illus.). 416p. 1989. text 105.00 (*0-19-812879-7*) OUP.

Perfectionism. Brian. L. 20p. (Orig.). 1985. pap. 1.55 (*0-89486-259-6*, 1404B) Hazelden.

Perfectionism: What's Bad about Being Too Good? Miriam Adderholdt & Jan Goldberg. LC 99-23088. 136p. (YA). (gr. 8 up). 1999. pap. text 12.95 (*1-57542-062-7*) Free Spirit Pub.

Perfectionist & Other Plays. Joyce Carol Oates. 288p. 1998. reprint ed. pap. 15.00 (*0-88001-580-2*) HarpC.

Perfectionist Persuasion: The Holiness Movement & American Methodism, 1867-1936. Charles E. Jones. LC 74-13766. (American Theological Library Association Monograph: No. 5). (Illus.). 262p. 1974. 31.00 (*0-8108-0747-5*) Scarecrow.

Perfectionist Politics: Abolitionism & the Religious Tensions of American Democracy. Douglas M. Strong. LC 98-37928. (Illus.). 275p. 1999. 39.95 (*0-8156-2793-9*) Syracuse U Pr.

Perfectionist Syndrome: How to Stop Driving Yourself & Everyone Else Crazy. Eve Cappello. 169p. 1990. pap. text 14.95 (*0-8403-5744-3*) Eve Cappello.

Perfectionists: Radical Social Thought in the Northern States, 1815-1860. Laurence R. Veysey. LC 73-4900. (Sourcebooks in American Social Thought). 220p. (C). reprint ed. 68.20 (*0-8357-9951-4*, 201257600081) Bks Demand.

"Perfectionist's" How To: "Custom Draperies" 3rd ed. Dolores P. Lederer. LC 88-91302. ("Perfectionist's" How To Bks.: Bk. 1). (Illus.). 104p. (Orig.). 1982. reprint ed. pap. text 35.00 (*0-9608040-0-5*) Lederer Enterprises.

"Perfectionist's" How To: "Drapery Top Treatments" Dolores P. Lederer. ("Perfectionist's" How To Bks.: Bk. II). (Illus.). 108p. (Orig.). 1983. reprint ed. pap. text 35.00 (*0-9608040-1-3*) Lederer Enterprises.

"Perfectionist's" How To: "Window Specialties" Dolores P. Lederer. ("Perfectionist's" How To Bks.: Bk. III). (Illus.). 112p. (Orig.). 1985. reprint ed. pap. text 35.00 (*0-9608040-2-1*) Lederer Enterprises.

"Perfectionist's" How to Books, 3 vols. Dolores P. Lederer. (Illus.). (Orig.). 1992. reprint ed. pap. text 90.00 (*0-9608040-3-X*) Lederer Enterprises.

Perfectionnement Allemand: Intermediate German for French Speakers. Assimil Staff. (FRE & GER.). 28.95 (*0-8288-4485-2*, F29170) Fr & Eur.

Perfectionnement Anglais. Assimil Staff. (Assimil). 1999. 29.95 (*2-7005-0133-0*, Pub. by Assimil); 75.00 (*2-7005-1028-3*, Pub. by Assimil); 95.00 (*2-7005-1075-5*, Pub. by Assimil) Distribks Inc.

Perfectionnement Anglais: Intermediate English for French Speakers. Assimil Staff. (ENG & FRE.). 28.95 (*0-8288-4483-6*, M1500) Fr & Eur.

Perfectionnement Espagnol. (FRE & SPA.). 1997. 24.95 (*2-7005-0134-9*, Pub. by Assimil) Distribks Inc.

Perfectionnement Espagnol: Intermediate Spanish for French Speakers. Assimil Staff. (FRE & SPA.). 28.95 (*0-8288-4487-9*, M1498) Fr & Eur.

Perfectionnement Italien: Intermediate Italian for French Speakers. Assimil Staff. (FRE & ITA.). 28.95 (*0-8288-4496-8*, F40322) Fr & Eur.

Perfectly Contented Meat-Eater's Guide to Vegetarianism: A Book for Those Who Really Don't Want to Be Hassled about Their Diet. Mark W. Reinhardt. LC 97-41023. (Illus.). 252p. 1998. pap. 17.95 (*0-8264-1082-0*) Continuum.

Perfectly Criminal. Ed. by Martin Edwards. 256p. 1996. 24.00 (*0-7278-5132-2*) Severn Hse.

Perfectly Delightful: The Life & Gardens of Harvey Ladew. Christopher Weeks. LC 98-46387. (Illus.). 132p. 1999. 32.50 (*0-8018-6112-8*) Johns Hopkins.

Perfectly English, Vol. 1. Connie Parkinson. (Illus.). 46p. 1997. write for info. (*1-57377-030-2*) Easl Pubns.

Perfectly Matched. Candice Adams. 1994. per. 3.50 (*0-373-70616-2*, 1-70616-7) Harlequin Bks.

Perfectly Orderly House. Ellen K. McKenzie. (J). 1995. 14.95 (*0-8050-1946-4*) H Holt & Co.

Perfectly Pasta. Ed. by Shawnna Silvius et al. 176p. 1998. 5.95 (*1-57502-629-5*, Cookbks by Morris) Morris Pubng.

***Perfectly Practical Advice on Horsemanship.** John Lyons. Ed. by Maureen Gallatin. (John Lyons' The Making of a Perfect Horse Ser.: Vol. VI). (Illus.). viii, 200p. 1999. 26.95 (*1-879620-60-X*) Belvoir Pubns.

Perfectly Pregnant! Carolyn Coats & Pamela Smith. (Illus.). 174p. 1988. 10.00 (*1-878722-04-2*) C Coats Bestsellers.

Perfectly Proper Murder: A Carl Wilcox Mystery. Harold Adams. LC 93-14721. 1993. 18.95 (*0-8027-3237-2*) Walker & Co.

***Perfectly Pure & Good.** Frances Fyfield. 256p. 2000. pap. 5.99 (*0-14-029195-4*) Viking Penguin.

Perfectly Pure & Good. large type ed. Frances Fyfield. LC 94-19728. 375p. 1994. lib. bdg. 17.95 (*0-7862-0308-0*) Thorndike Pr.

Perfectly Safe Home. Jeanne Miller. 1991. pap. 9.95 (*0-671-70580-6*, Fireside) S&S Trade Pap.

Perfectly Splendid: One Family's Repasts. Ed. by Arlene Troutman. (Illus.). 128p. 1992. text 9.95 (*0-9622837-1-1*) McFaddin-Ward.

Perfectly Square: A Fantasy Fable for All Ages. Dolly A. Berthelot. (Illus.). 60p. 1994. pap. 8.99 (*0-9644406-0-1*) Berthelots Consult.

Perfectly Square: A Fantasy Fable for All Ages. Dolly H. Berthelot. 1996. pap. text 8.99 (*0-9644486-0-2*) Lightsmith Prod.

***Perfectly Still: A Journey Through the Heart of Loss to an Inspiring Discovery of Love Without Barriers.** Patricia B. Moran. 2000. pap. 13.95 (*1-58177-063-4*) Barrytown Ltd.

Perfectly Willing. Hsing Yun. Ed. by Amy Lui-Ma. LC 94-78021. (Hsing Yun's Hundred Sayings Ser.: Vol. 1). 120p. (Orig.). 1994. pap. 6.95 (*0-9642612-0-0*) Hsi Lai Univ Pr.

Perfecto Amor. Yiye Avila.Tr. of Perfect Love. (SPA.). 52p. pap. 3.50 (*0-7899-0070-X*, 550045) Editorial Unilit.

Perfecto Extrano. Steel Publishing Company Staff. (SPA.). pap. 7.50 (*950-04-0274-2*) Emece.

Perfectos Desconocidos. Laura Martin. (SPA.). 1997. per. 3.50 (*0-373-33405-2*, 1-33405-1) Harlequin Bks.

Perfezionamento dell'Inglese. Assimil Staff. 1999. pap. text 95.00 (*2-7005-1096-8*, Pub. by Assimil); pap. text 75.00 (*2-7005-1359-2*, Pub. by Assimil) Distribks Inc.

Perfidia Vol. 24: Complete Plays 24. Manuel P. Garcia. 60p. 1998. 4.95 (*1-885901-74-7*, Liberts) Presbyters Peartree.

Perfidious Brethren. (Novel in England, 1700-1775 Ser.). (C). 1973. reprint ed. lib. bdg. 61.00 (*0-8240-0547-3*) Garland.

Perfidious P. (Novel in England, 1700-1775 Ser.). 1977. lib. bdg. 61.00 (*0-8240-0518-X*) Garland.

Perfidious Parrot. Janwillem Van de Wetering. LC 97-2548. 280p. 1997. 22.00 (*1-56947-102-9*) Soho Press.

Perfidious Parrot. Janwillem Van de Wetering. LC 97-2548. (Amsterdam Cops Ser.: No. 14). 280p. 1998. pap. 12.00 (*1-56947-130-4*) Soho Press.

Perfidy. Ben Hecht. LC 97-70694. 275p. 1997. 24.95 (*0-9646886-3-8*) Milah.

Perfil de Tres Monarcas. G. Edwards.Tr. of Tale of Three Kings. (SPA.). 128p. 1986. pap. 4.99 (*0-8297-1115-5*) Vida Pubs.

Perfil de un Verdadero Discipulo (Real Discipleship) J. Oswald Sanders. (SPA.). 126p. 1997. pap. 5.00 (*0-8254-1668-X*, Edit Portavoz) Kregel.

Perfil de una Mujer de Dios. Gloria Ricardo. 75p. 1994. pap. 3.00 (*1-885630-30-1*) HLM Producciones.

Perfil del Aire: Con Otras Obras Olvidadas e Ineditas Documentos y Espistolario. Luis Cernuda. Ed. by Derek Harris. (Textos B Ser.: No. 11). (SPA.). 204p. (C). 1971. pap. 51.00 (*0-900411-20-1*, Pub. by Tamesis Bks Ltd) Boydell & Brewer.

Perfil Del Discipulado. Karen S. Smith et al. Tr. by Oscar Reyes. (Sigueme! (Follow Me!) Ser.). (ENG & SPA.). 32p. 1997. pap. 2.60 (*1-881307-09-3*, B7093) Natl Pastoral LC.

Perfil del Teatro de la Revolucion Mexicana. Marcela Del-Rio. LC 93-27274. (American University Studies, XXII: Latin American Literature: Vol. 17). XIII, 278p. (C). 1994. text 44.95 (*0-8204-1992-3*) P Lang Pubng.

Perfil Pastoral de Felix Varela. Felipe J. Estevez. LC 88-83026. (Coleccion Cuba y sus Jueces). (SPA.). 40p. (Orig.). 1989. pap. 6.00 (*0-89729-516-1*) Ediciones.

Perfil y Aventura del Hombre en la Historia (1492-1988) Octavio R. Costa. LC 88-82372. (SPA.). 624p. (Orig.). 1988. pap. 30.00 (*0-89729-505-6*) Ediciones.

Perfiles del Ecrito: El Progreso de los Pueblos en Africa, Asia y America Latina. 68p. 1995. write for info. (*92-806-3169-1*) U N I C E.

Perfiles Ensayos Sobre Literatura Mexicana Reciente. Federico Patan. LC 91-68484. (SPA.). 169p. 1992. pap. 36.00 (*0-89295-066-8*) Society Sp & Sp-Am.

Perfluorhalogenorano-Verbindungen der Haupt Gruppenelemente-Perfluorohalogenorgano-Compounds of Main Group Elements. Planck, Max, Society for the Advancement of Scienc. (Gmelin Handbuch der Anorganischen Chemie Ser.: Vol. 24, Pt. 3). 233p. 1975. 315.00 (*0-387-93293-3*) Spr-Verlag.

Perfluorinated Ionomer Membranes. Ed. by Adi Eisenberg & Howard L. Yeager. LC 81-20570. (ACS Symposium Ser.: No. 180). 1982. 60.95 (*0-8412-0698-8*) Am Chemical.

Perfluorinated Ionomer Membranes. Ed. by Adi Eisenberg & Howard L. Yeager. LC 81-20570. (ACS Symposium Ser.: Vol. 180). 509p. 1982. reprint ed. pap. 157.80 (*0-608-03105-4*, 206355800007) Bks Demand.

Perfluorocompound (PFC) Technical Update. 1998. pap. write for info. (*1-892568-09-8*) Smicndctr Equip.

Perforated Sovereignties & International Relations: Trans-Sovereign Contracts of Subnational Governments, 211. Ed. by Ivo D. Duchacek et al. LC 87-36092. (Contributions in Political Science Ser.: No. 211). 256p. 1988. 65.00 (*0-313-26180-6*, DPD/) Greenwood.

Perforated Stones from California. Henry W. Henshaw. (Bureau of American Ethnology Bulletins Ser.). 99p. 1995. lib. bdg. 69.00 (*0-7812-4002-6*) Rprt Serv.

Perforations in the "Latter-Day Pamphlets", by One of the Eighteen Millions of Bores: No. 1; Universal Suffrage; Capital Punishment--Slavery. Ed. by Elizur Wright. LC 72-3157. (Black Heritage Library Collection). 1977. reprint ed. 13.95 (*0-8369-9093-5*) Ayer.

***Perform It! The Complete Guide to Young People's Theater.** Jan Hellig Croteau. (Illus.). 112p. 2000. pap. 13.95 (*0-325-00230-4*) Heinemann.

Performance. Colin MacCabe. LC 98-215547. (Film Classics Ser.). 1998. pap. 10.95 (*0-85170-670-3*) Ind U Pr.

Performance. Ed. by A. Dale Timpe. LC 87-27692. (Art & Science of Business Management Ser.: No. 5). 392p. 1988. reprint ed. pap. 121.60 (*0-7837-8157-1*, 204786200008) Bks Demand.

Performance: A Critical Introduction. Marvin Carlson. LC 95-41701. 256p. (C). 1996. 85.00 (*0-415-13702-0*); pap. 20.99 (*0-415-13703-9*) Routledge.

Performance: Faith at Work, Studies From James. Serendipty House Staff. (201 Deeper Bible Study Ser.). 1998. pap. 5.99 (*1-57494-084-8*) Serendipty Hse.

Performance: Live Art since 1960. Roselee Goldberg. LC 98-22775. (Illus.). 240p. 1998. 60.00 (*0-8109-4360-3*, Pub. by Abrams) Time Warner.

Performance: Practical Examinations in Speech & Drama. P. Ranger. 200p. 1990. pap. 22.95 (*0-419-14460-9*, A3884, E & FN Spon) Routledge.

Performance: Revealing the Orpheus Within. Anthony Rooley. 1993. pap. 13.95 (*1-85230-160-0*, Pub. by Element MA) Penguin Putnam.

Performance: Texts & Contexts. Carol S. Stern & Bruce Henderson. 624p. (C). 1993. boxed set 46.50 (*0-8013-0787-2*, 78841) Longman.

An Asterisk (*) at the beginning of an entry indicates that the title is appearing for the first time.

Performance Acrobatics. unabridged ed. Pietrek Lemanski. Ed. by Bruce Fife. LC 98-38270. (Illus.). 80p. 1998. pap. 10.00 (*0-941599-38-8*, Pub. by Piccadilly Bks) Empire Pub Srvs.

Performance Analysis & Appraisal: A How-to-Do-It Manual for Librarians. Robert D. Stueart & Maureen Sullivan. (How-to-Do-It Ser.). 174p. 1991. 49.95 (*1-55570-061-6*) Neal-Schuman.

*__Performance Analysis of ATM Networks: IFIP TC6 WG6.3/WG6.4 International Workshop on Performance Modelling & Evaluation of ATM Networks, July 21-23, 1997, Ilkley, U. K.__ International Workshop on Performance Modelling & Evaluation of ATM Networks Staff & Demetres D. Kouvatsos. LC 99-42851. 1999. write for info. (*0-412-83640-8*) Chapman & Hall.

*__Performance Analysis of Communication Systems with Non-Markovian Stochastic Petri Nets.__ Reinhard German. LC 00-22168. (Interscience Series in Systems & Optimization). 2000. write for info. (*0-471-49258-2*) Wiley.

*__Performance Analysis of Flow Lines with Non-Linear Flow of Material.__ Stefan Helber. LC 99-23638. (Lecture Notes in Economics & Mathematical Systems Ser.: Vol. 473). (Illus.). x, 280p. 1999. pap. 67.00 (*3-540-65954-4*) Spr-Verlag.

Performance Analysis of Manufacturing Systems. Tayfur Altiok. LC 96-14273. (Series in Operations Research). 355p. 1996. 49.95 (*0-387-94773-6*) Spr-Verlag.

Performance Analysis of Multiple Access Protocols. Shuji Tasaka. (Computer Systems Ser.). 300p. 1986. pap. text 34.00 (*0-262-20058-9*) MIT Pr.

Performance Analysis of Real-Time Embedded Software. Benjamin Ehrenberg & Sharad Malik. LC 98-46053. xvi, 146 p. 1999. write for info. (*0-7923-8382-6*) Kluwer Academic.

*__Performance Analysis of Telecommunications & Local Area Network.__ Wah Chun Chan. LC 99-47410. (International Series in Engineering & Computer Science). 1999. write for info. (*0-7923-7701-X*) Kluwer Academic.

Performance & Authenticity in the Arts. Ed. by Salim Kemal & Ivan Gaskell. LC 98-39969. (Cambridge Studies in Philosophy & the Arts). (Illus.). 284p. (C). 2000. 59.95 (*0-521-45419-0*) Cambridge U Pr.

Performance & Competence in Second Language Acquisition. Ed. by Gillian Brown et al. (Illus.). 221p. (C). 1996. text 54.95 (*0-521-55193-5*); pap. text 21.95 (*0-521-55861-1*) Cambridge U Pr.

*__Performance & Consciousness.__ Ed. by Daniel Meyer Dinkgrfe. (Performing Arts International Ser.: Vol. 1, Part 4). (Illus.). 132p. 1999. pap. text 21.00 (*90-5755-096-2*, Harwood Acad Pubs) Gordon & Breach.

Performance & Control of Network Systems: 3-5 November 1997, Dallas, Texas. Wai Sum Lai et al. LC 98-122055. (Proceedings Ser.). xi, 596p. 1997. 99.00 (*0-8194-2664-4*) SPIE.

Performance & Control of Network Systems II, Vol. 3530. Ed. by Wai S. Lai & Robert B. Cooper. LC 99-159854. 1998. 80.00 (*0-8194-2991-0*) SPIE.

*__Performance & Control of Network Systems III.__ Ed. by Robert D. Van der Mei & Daniel P. Heyman. 280p. 1999. pap. text 62.00 (*0-8194-3434-5*) SPIE.

Performance & Cost Data Phase I: City Services. North Carolina Local Government Performance Measur. 108p. (C). 1997. pap. text 15.00 (*1-56011-337-5*, 97.18A) Institute Government.

Performance & Cost Data Phase III City Services: Medium & Smaller Cities. Prod. by North Carolina Local Government Staff. 1999. pap. 15.00 (*1-56011-355-3*) Institute Government.

Performance & Cost Data Phase III County Services: Medium & Smaller Counties. Prod. by North Carolina Local Government Staff. 1999. pap. 15.00 (*1-56011-356-1*) Institute Government.

Performance & Cost Data Phase II: County Services. North Carolina Local Government Performance Measur. 115p. 1998. pap. text 15.00 (*1-56011-340-5*, 97.18B) Institute Government.

Performance & Cultural Politics. Ed. by Elin Diamond. LC 95-20972. 304p. (C). 1996. 90.00 (*0-415-12767-X*) Routledge.

Performance & Cultural Politics. Erin Diamond. LC 95-20972. 304p. (C). 1996. pap. 27.99 (*0-415-12768-8*) Routledge.

Performance & Durability of Bituminous Materials. Ed. by J. G. Cabrera. (Illus.). 336p. (C). 1995. 150.00 (*0-419-19730-3*, E & FN Spon) Routledge.

Performance & Evaluation of Shipping Containers. George G. Maltenfort. LC 89-63845. (Illus.). 488p. 1990. reprint ed. 97.50 (*0-9616302-3-X*) Jelmar Pub.

*__Performance & Fault Management.__ 800p. 2000. 55.00 incl. cd-rom (*1-57870-180-5*) Macmillan Tech.

Performance & Gender in Ancient Greece: Nondramatic Poetry in Its Setting. Eva Stehle. LC 96-3522. 360p. 1996. text 39.50 (*0-691-03617-9*, Pub. by Princeton U Pr) Cal Prin Full Svc.

Performance & Management of Complex Communication Networks. Routledge Chapman & Hall Inc. Staff. text 159.50 (*0-412-84250-5*) Routledge.

Performance & Motivation Strategies for Today's Workforce: A Guide to Expectancy Theory Applications. Thad B. Green. LC 91-48121. 256p. 1992. 59.95 (*0-89930-678-0*, GPJ, Quorum Bks) Greenwood.

Performance & Perception of Notational Variants: A Study of Rhythmic Patterning in Music. Bengt Edlund. 224p. 1985. pap. text 38.50 (*91-554-1675-6*) Coronet Bks.

Performance & Practice: Oral Narrative Traditions Amongst Teenagers in Britain & Ireland. Michael Wilson. 320p. 1997. text 83.95 (*1-84014-112-3*, Pub. by Ashgate Pub) Ashgate Pub Co.

Performance & Quality Measurement in Government: Issues & Experiences. Ed. by Arie Halachmi. 200p. 1999. pap. text 27.95 (*1-57420-067-4*) Chatelaine.

Performance & Reality: Essays from Grand Street. Ed. by Ben Sonnenberg. 330p. 1989. 45.00 (*0-8135-1395-2*); pap. 18.00 (*0-8135-1409-6*) Rutgers U Pr.

Performance & Reliability Analysis of Computer Systems: An Example-Based Approach Using the SHARPE Software Package. Robin A. Sahner et al. 424p. (C). 1995. text 143.00 (*0-7923-9650-2*) Kluwer Academic.

Performance & Reliability of Corrosion-Resistant Alloy Castings: Phase I, Causes of Unsatisfactory Performance. Donald B. Roach & F. H. Beck. LC TA0462.R54. (MTI Manual Ser.: No. 5). (Illus.). 137p. 1981. reprint ed. pap. 42.50 (*0-608-06694-X*, 206689100009) Bks Demand.

Performance & Reliability of Corrosion-Resistant Alloy Castings: Phase II, Casting Discontinuities. Donald B. Roach & F. H. Beck. LC TA0479.S7R63. (MTI Manual Ser.: No. 6). (Illus.). 209p. 1981. reprint ed. pap. 64.80 (*0-608-06693-1*, 206689000009) Bks Demand.

Performance & Reliability of Corrosion-Resistant Alloy Castings, Phase 1. (MTI Manual Ser.: No. 5). 116p. 1981. pap. 35.00 (*0-685-39493-X*) NACE Intl.

Performance & Reliability of Corrosion-Resistant Alloy Castings, Phase 2, Manual 6. (MTI Manual Ser.: No. 6). 182p. 1981. ring bd. 37.00 (*0-685-39494-8*) NACE Intl.

Performance & Stability of Aircraft. LC 96-207392. write for info. (*0-340-63170-8*, Pub. by E A) Routldge.

Performance & Stability of Aircraft. J. Russell. LC 96-207392. 294p. 1996. pap. 64.95 (*0-470-23598-5*) Wiley.

Performance & Standards in MicroFinance: Accion's Experience with the Camel Instrument. Sonia Saltzman et al. 77p. 1998. pap. 8.00 (*0-9664469-0-9*) ACCION Intl.

Performance & Transformation: A Three Dimensional Approach to Medieval Devotional & Ecstatic Texts. Ed. by Mary A. Suydam & Joanna E. Ziegler. LC 98-40688. 300p. 1999. text 49.95 (*0-312-21281-X*) St Martin.

Performance Anthology: Source Book for a Decade of California Performance Art. Ed. by Carl E. Loeffler & Darlene Tong. LC 79-55054. (Contemporary Documents Ser.: Vol. 1). (Illus.). 500p. 1980. pap. 15.95 (*0-931818-01-X*) Contemporary Arts.

Performance Anthology: Source Book of California Performance Art. Ed. by Carl Loeffler & Darlene Tong. (Illus.). 532p. 1990. pap. 24.95 (*0-86719-366-2*) Last Gasp.

Performance Anxieties. Ann Pellegrini. 198p. (C). 1996. pap. 18.99 (*0-415-91686-0*) Routledge.

Performance Anxieties: Re-Producing Masculinity. David Buchbinder. (Illus.). 224p. 1998. pap. 24.95 (*1-86448-425-X*, Pub. by Allen & Unwin Pty) Paul & Co Pubs.

*__Performance Anxiety.__ Horwitz. 2001. pap. 40.00 (*1-56593-924-7*) Singular Publishing.

Performance Anxiety. Mitchell W. Robin & Rochelle Balter. 240p. 1994. pap. 12.00 (*1-55850-441-9*) Adams Media.

Performance Anxiety: With CD. Amanda Cruz. LC 97-8116. (Illus.). 112p. 1997. pap. text 29.95 (*0-933856-46-6*) Mus Art Chicago.

Performance Appraisal. (Open Learning for Supervisory Management). 1990. pap. text 19.50 (*0-08-070181-7*, Pergamon Pr) Elsevier.

Performance Appraisal. John D. Drake. Ed. by Bill Christopher. LC 97-68251. (Management Library). 90p. 1997. pap. 12.95 (*1-56052-442-1*) Crisp Pubns.

Performance Appraisal. B. Wynne. (Financial Times Management Briefings Ser.). 1997. pap. 89.50 (*0-273-63190-X*) F T P-H.

Performance Appraisal: A Practical Guide. B. Wynne. 1996. pap. 129.00 (*1-85953-035-4*, Pub. by Tech Comm) St Mut.

Performance Appraisal: Alternative Perspectives. Robert L. Cardy & Gregory H. Dobbins. LC 93-19694. (Human Resource Management Ser.). (C). 1993. mass mkt. 37.95 (*0-538-81383-0*, GJ65AA) S-W Pub.

Performance Appraisal: Design Manual. Ferdinand F. Fournies. (Illus.). 340p. 1983. 96.45 (*0-917472-09-8*) F Fournies.

Performance Appraisal: Legal & Effective Management of Performance. (Business Management Ser.). 1994. 106.00 (*1-56706-079-X*) Panel Pubs.

Performance Appraisal: Perspectives on a Quality Management Approach. Ed. by Gary N. McLean et al. LC 94-70393. 218p. 1994. reprint ed. pap. 19.00 (*1-56286-004-6*) Am Soc Train & Devel.

Performance Appraisal: The State of the Art in Practice. James W. Smither. LC 98-9568. 576p. 1998. 44.95 (*0-7879-0945-9*) Jossey-Bass.

Performance Appraisal & Human Development. Howard P. Smith et al. LC 76-52663. 1977. pap. text 16.95 (*0-201-07455-9*) Addison-Wesley.

Performance Appraisal Challenge. American Management Association Staff. (The Challenge Ser.). 1998. 49.95 (*0-8144-1203-3*) AMACOM.

Performance Appraisal Handbook. Associated Equipment Distributors Staff. 20p. 1985. 25.00 (*0-318-19177-6*) Assn Equip Distrs.

Performance Appraisal in the Public Sector: Techniques & Applications. Dennis M. Daley. LC 92-12121. 184p. 1992. 57.95 (*0-89930-701-9*, DPI/, Quorum Bks) Greenwood.

Performance Appraisal Manual for Managers & Supervisors: A Gudie to Effective Performance Appraisals. Hubbartt. 80p. 1992. pap. 12.50 (*0-685-67140-2*, 4816) CCH INC.

Performance Appraisal of School Management: Evaluating the Administrative Team. Donald Langlois & Richard McAdams. LC 91-67571. 175p. 1996. text 29.95 (*0-87762-892-0*) Scarecrow.

Performance Appraisal on the Job. Judy Block. 1982. pap. 5.95 (*0-917386-52-3*) Exec Ent Pubns.

Performance Appraisal on the Line. Ann M. Morrison et al. 160p. pap. 15.00 (*0-912879-93-9*) Ctr Creat Leader.

Performance Appraisal Package. 1999. 7.95 incl. disk (*1-55180-159-0*) Self-Counsel Pr.

Performance Appraisal Revisited. Phil Long. 200p. (C). 1986. 105.00 (*0-85292-367-8*, Pub. by IPM Hse) St Mut.

Performance Appraisal Skills see Productive Supervisor: A Program of Practical Managerial Skills

Performance Appraisals. Martin Fisher. 1997. pap. text 19.95 (*0-7494-2021-9*) Kogan Page Ltd.

Performance Appraisals: A Collection of Samples. 2nd ed. Ed. by SHRM Information Center Staff. Date not set. pap. 35.00 (*0-939900-72-6*) Soc Human Resc Mgmt.

Performance Appraisals in Business Industry: Keys to Effective Supervision. George L. Morrisey. 1983. teacher ed. write for info. (*0-201-13982-0*); pap. write for info. (*0-201-04831-0*) Addison-Wesley.

Performance Appraisals in the Public Sector: Key to Effective Supervision. George L. Morrisey. (Illus.). 160p. 1983. pap. write for info. (*0-201-04847-7*) Addison-Wesley.

Performance Approach in Determining Required Levels of Insulation in Concrete Roof Systems. (PCI Journal Reprints Ser.). 16p. 1981. pap. 14.00 (*0-686-40153-0*, JR250) P-PCI.

Performance Art: From Futurism to the Present. enl. rev. ed. RoseLee Goldberg. (Illus.). 212p. 1988. pap. 12.95 (*0-8109-2371-8*, Pub. by Abrams) Time Warner.

Performance Art: Memoirs, Vol. I. Jeff Nuttall. (Orig.). 1986. pap. 11.95 (*0-7145-3788-8*) Riverrun NY.

Performance Art: Scripts, Vol. II. Jeff Nuttall. (Orig.). 1986. pap. 11.95 (*0-7145-3789-6*) Riverrun NY.

*__Performance Artists: Talking in the Eighties.__ Linda M. Montano. (Illus.). 420p. 2000. 60.00 (*0-520-21021-2*, Pub. by U CA Pr); pap. 24.95 (*0-520-21022-0*, Pub. by U CA Pr) Cal Prin Full Svc.

Performance As Political Act: The Embodied Self. Randy Martin. LC 89-33473. (Critical Perspectives in Social Theory Ser.). (Illus.). 223p. 1990. 57.95 (*0-89789-174-0*, H174, Greenwood Pr) Greenwood.

Performance Assessment: Methods & Applications. Ed. by Ronald A. Berk. LC 86-2947. (Illus.). 560p. 1986. reprint ed. pap. 173.60 (*0-608-05926-9*, 206626200008) Bks Demand.

Performance Assessment & Standards Based Curricula: The Achievement Cycle. Allan A. Glatthorn et al. LC 97-40094. 214p. 1997. pap. 29.95 (*1-883001-48-X*) Eye On Educ.

Performance Assessment & Students with Disabilities: Usage in Outcomes-Based Accountability Systems. Margaret J. McLaughlin & Sandra H. Warren. LC 94-26214. (CEC Mini-Library Performance Assessment). 32p. 1994. pap. text 9.00 (*0-86586-250-8*, P5061) Coun Exc Child.

Performance Assessment for the Workplace, Vol. I. Ed. by B. F. Green & Alexandra K. Wigdor. 272p. 1991. text 34.95 (*0-309-04538-X*, Joseph Henry Pr) Natl Acad Pr.

Performance Assessment Handbook Vol. 1: Portfolios & Socratic Seminars. Bil Johnson. (Illus.). 200p. (Orig.). (C). 1996. pap. 29.95 (*1-883001-16-1*) Eye On Educ.

Performance Assessment Handbook Vol. 2: Performances & Exhibitions. Bil Johnson. (Illus.). 200p. (Orig.). (C). 1996. pap. 29.95 (*1-883001-17-X*) Eye On Educ.

Performance Assessment in Academic Libraries. Steve Morgan. LC 94-45209. 224p. 1995. 89.50 (*0-7201-2188-4*) Continuum.

Performance Assessment in Education & Training: Alternative Techniques. Michael Priestly. LC 81-19598. (Illus.). 280p. 1982. 39.95 (*0-87778-181-8*) Educ Tech Pubns.

Performance Assessment in IEA's Third International Mathematics & Science Study. Maryellen Harmon et al. LC 97-69827. 165p. 1997. pap. write for info. (*1-889938-07-6*) Intl Study Ctr.

Performance Assessment in the Workplace Vol. I: Technical Issues. National Research Council Staff. Ed. by Alexandra K. Wigdor & Bert F. Green, Jr. 344p. 1991. text 45.00 (*0-309-04539-8*) Natl Acad Pr.

*__Performance Assessment of Control Loops: Theory & Applications.__ Biao Huang & S. L. Shah. Ed. by M. J. Grimble & M. A. Johnson. LC 99-31704. (Advances in Industrial Control Ser.). (Illus.). 250p. 1999. 84.00 (*1-85233-639-0*, Pub. by Spr-Verlag) Spr-Verlag.

Performance Assessment Systems: Implications for a National System of Skill Standards. John G. Wirt. Ed. by Gerry Feinstein. 40p. (Orig.). pap. text 15.00 (*1-55877-190-5*) Natl Governor.

Performance Assessments in Science: Hands-On Tasks & Scoring Guides. Ed. by Brian M. Stecher & Stephen P. Klein. 382p. (Orig.). 1996. pap. text 13.00 (*0-8330-2367-5*, MR-660-NSF) Rand Corp.

Performance Audit. Ed. by Roy Chowdhury. (C). 1990. 80.00 (*0-89771-217-X*) St Mut.

Performance Audit of the Regulation of Health Maintenance Organizations & Other Prepaid Health Service Plans (in Florida) Dorothy N. Gray. (Illus.). 43p. (Orig.). (C). 1994. pap. text 20.00 (*0-7881-1475-1*) DIANE Pub.

Performance Auditing & the Modernisation of Government. Ed. by David Shand. 288p. (Orig.). 1996. pap. 49.00 (*92-64-15346-2*, 42-96-03-1, Pub. by Org for Econ) OECD.

Performance-Based Assessments: External, Internal & Self Assessment Tools for Total Quality Management. Paul F. Wilson & Richard D. Pearson. 202p. 1995. text 34.00 (*0-87389-242-9*, H0803) ASQ Qual Pr.

*__Performance-Based Certification: How to Design a Valid, Defensible, Cost-Effective Program.__ Judith A. Hale. LC 99-6896. 256p. 1999. 49.95 incl. disk (*0-7879-4640-0*, Pfffr & Co) Jossey-Bass.

Performance-Based Curriculum for Language Arts: From Knowing to Showing. Helen L. Burz & Kit Marshall. LC 96-35195. (Illus.). 104p. 1997. 55.95 (*0-8039-6508-7*); pap. 24.95 (*0-8039-6509-5*) Corwin Pr.

Performance-Based Curriculum for Mathematics: From Knowing to Showing. Helen L. Burz & Kit Marshall. LC 96-12354. (FKS Ser.). (Illus.). 112p. 1996. 55.95 (*0-8039-6495-1*); pap. 24.95 (*0-8039-6496-X*) Corwin Pr.

*__Performance-Based Curriculum for Music & the Visual Arts: From Knowing to Showing.__ Helen L. Burz & Kit Marshall. LC 99-6280. (FKS Ser.). (Illus.). 136p. 1999. pap. 22.95 (*0-7619-7536-5*); lib. bdg. 55.95 (*0-7619-7535-7*) Sage.

Performance-Based Curriculum for Science: From Knowing to Showing. Helen L. Burz & Kit Marshall. LC 97-4946. (Illus.). 104p. 1997. 55.95 (*0-8039-6506-0*); pap. 24.95 (*0-8039-6507-9*) Corwin Pr.

Performance-Based Curriculum for Social Studies: From Knowing to Showing. Helen L. Burz & Kit Marshall. LC 97-45266. (Illus.). 128p. 1997. 55.95 (*0-8039-6500-1*); pap. 24.95 (*0-8039-6501-X*) Corwin Pr.

Performance-Based Instruction: Linking Training to the Workplace. Dale Brethower & Karolyn Smalley. LC 97-45356. 863p. 1998. 44.95 incl. disk (*0-7879-1119-4*) Jossey-Bass.

Performance-Based Instructional Design. David J. Pucel. (C). 1989. student ed. 31.50 (*0-943919-01-0*) Perf Trning Systs.

*__Performance Based Learning & Assessment in Middle School Science.__ K. Michael Hibbard. 2000. 29.95 (*1-883001-81-1*) Eye On Educ.

Performance Based Organization for Nautical Charting & Geodesy. 126p. 1996. pap. 20.00 (*1-57744-014-5*) Nat Acad Public Admin.

Performance-Based Organization for Nautical Charting & Geodesy. unabridged ed. 1996. pap. 20.00 (*1-57744-017-X*) Nat Acad Public Admin.

Performance Based Placement Manual. rev. ed. Richard Pimentel et al. 52p. 1987. reprint ed. student ed. 19.50 (*0-942071-01-8*) M Wright & Assocs.

*__Performance-Based Ratemaking: Theory & Practice.__ Michael R. Schmidt. (Illus.). 300p. 2000. pap. write for info. (*0-910325-82-0*) Public Util.

Performance Based Statements of Work. Ron Smith. Ed. by Donna Ireton. 260p. 1998. pap. 58.00 (*0-9662828-6-8*) Adv Systs Dev.

Performance-Based Student Assessment: Challenges & Possibilities. Joan B. Baron & Dennie P. Wolf. (Ninety-Fifth Yearbook of the National Society for the Study of Education Ser.: Pt. 1). 350p. 1996. 31.00 (*0-226-03803-3*) U Ch Pr.

Performance Benchmaking for Water Utilities. Bill Kingdom et al. LC 97-106742. (Illus.). 249p. 1996. pap. 262.00 (*0-89867-877-3*, 90710) Am Water Wks Assn.

Performance Breakthroughs for Adolescents with Learning Disabilities or ADD: How to Help Students Succeed in the Regular Education Classroom. Geraldine Markel & Judith Greenbaum. LC 95-73079. 336p. (Orig.). 1995. pap. text 21.95 (*0-87822-349-5*, 4915) Res Press.

Performance Budget Revisited: A Report on State Budget Reform. Karen Carter. LC 97-186872. (Legislative Finance Papers: No. 91). 34p. 1994. 10.00 (*1-55516-553-2*, 5101-91) Natl Conf State Legis.

Performance by Computer Modeling or Prescription by Model Code? David R. Baker. 1986. pap. 7.50 (*0-318-22369-4*, TR 86-5) Society Fire Protect.

Performance by Design: Sociotechnical Systems in North America. James C. Taylor & David F. Felten. LC 92-19141. (Series on Human Resource Development). 224p. 1992. pap. text 48.00 (*0-13-656497-6*) Prntice Hall Bks.

Performance Challenge: Aligning People, Practices & Goals to Maximize Organizational Performance. Jerry W. Gilley et al. 256p. 1998. text 35.00 (*0-7382-0044-1*) Perseus Pubng.

*__Performance Challenge: Developing Management Systems to Make Employees Your Organization's Greatest Asset.__ Jerry W. Gilley et al. 256p. 1999. pap. text 22.00 (*0-7382-0161-8*, Pub. by Perseus Pubng) HarpC.

Performance Characteristics for Devices Measuring PO2 & PCO2 in Blood Samples: Approved Standard, Vol. 9. National Committee for Clinical Laboratory Standar. 1992. 75.00 (*1-56238-135-0*, C21-A) NCCLS.

Performance Characteristics of Hydraulic Turbines & Pumps: Presented at the Winter Annual Meeting of ASME, Boston, MA, November 13-18, 1983. American Society of Mechanical Engineers Staff. Ed. by Walter L. Swift et al. LC 83-72716. (FED Ser.: Vol. 6). 214p. reprint ed. pap. 66.40 (*0-8357-8747-8*, 203365600087) Bks Demand.

*__Performance Characteristics Profile of the North American I M S Fleet 2000.__ 2000. 35.00 (*1-882502-81-7*) US Sail Assn.

Performance Characteristics Profile of the North American IMS Fleet - 1995. U. S. Sailing Staff. 79p. 1994. pap. text 65.00 (*1-882502-22-1*) US Sail Assn.

*__Performance Characterization in Computer Vision.__ Reinhard Klette et al. 336p. 2000. 127.00 (*0-7923-6374-4*) Kluwer Academic.

An Asterisk (*) at the beginning of an entry indicates that the title is appearing for the first time.

Performance Checklists for Clinical Nursing Skills. Ellis. 1995. pap. text 17.95 (0-7216-5848-2) Harcourt.

***Performance Confirmation of Constructed Geotechnical Facilities: Proceedings of Sessions of ASCE Specialty Conference On Performance Confirmation of Constructed Geotechnical Facilities: April 9-12, 2000, Amherst, Massachusetts.** ASCE Specialty Conference on Performance Confirmation of Constructed Geotechnical Facilities Staff et al. LC 00-24611. 2000. write for info. (0-7844-0486-0) Am Soc Civil Eng.

Performance Consultant's Fieldbook: Tools & Techniques for Improving Organization & People. Judith A. Hale. LC 98-9409. 240p. 1998. 39.95 incl. disk (0-7879-4019-4, Pfffr & Co) Jossey-Bass.

Performance Consulting: Moving Beyond Training. Dana G. Robinson & James C. Robinson. LC 94-47066. (Illus.). 320p. 1996. reprint ed. pap. 24.95 (1-881052-84-2) Berrett-Koehler.

Performance Consulting Toolbook: Tools & Activities for Trainers in a Performance Consulting Role. Carolyn Nilson. (ASQ Ser.). (Illus.). 300p. 1998. 128.95 (0-07-913760-1); pap. 57.95 (0-07-047169-X) McGraw-Hill Prof.

Performance Contracting: Expanding Horizons. Hansen. 332p. (C). 1997. text 82.00 (0-13-095819-0, Prentice Hall) P-H.

Performance Contracting: Expanding Horizons. Shirley J. Hansen & Jeannie C. Weisman. LC 97-35101. 1998. write for info. (0-88173-276-1) Fairmont Pr.

Performance Contracting for Energy & Environmental Systems. Shirley J. Hansen. LC 92-24389. 1992. write for info. (0-88173-127-7) Fairmont Pr.

Performance Contracting for Public Enterprises. LC 96-108740. 248p. 35.00 (92-1-123120-5) UN.

Performance Contracting in Education - An Appraisal: Toward a Balanced Perspective. Ed. by Donald N. Levine. LC 72-12681. 192p. 1973. pap. 24.95 (0-87778-046-3) Educ Tech Pubns.

Performance Criteria & Measurements for Doppler Ultrasound Devices: Technical Discussion. (Illus.). 1993. pap. write for info. (1-930047-41-X, DU) Am Inst Ultrasound.

Performance Criteria for Concrete Durability. Ed. by H. K. Hilsdorf & J. Kropp. (Illus.). 352p. (C). 1995. 140.00 (0-419-19880-6, E & FN Spon) Routledge.

Performance-Culture & Athenian Democracy. Ed. by Simon Goldhill & Robin Osborne. LC 98-38083. (Key Themes in Ancient History Ser.). (Illus.). 356p. (C). 1999. text 69.95 (0-521-64247-7) Cambridge U Pr.

Performance, Culture & Identity. Ed. by Elizabeth C. Fine & Jean H. Speer. LC 92-16540. 320p. 1992. 55.00 (0-275-94305-4, C4305, Praeger Pubs) Greenwood.

***Performance Cycling: A Scientific Way to Get the Most Out of Your Bike.** Stuart T. Baird. LC 00-131377. (Cycling Resources Ser.). (Illus.). 256p. 2000. pap. 29.95 (1-892495-28-7, Pub. by Van der Plas) Seven Hills Bk.

Performance-Driven Organizational Change: The Organizational Portfolio. Lex Donaldson. LC 98-25383. 320p. 1998. pap. 14.99 (0-7619-0355-0) Sage.

Performance Driven Sales Management. George S. Odiorne. 262p. 1991. ring bd. 79.95 (0-85013-189-8) Dartnell Corp.

Performance Drivers. Olve. 362p. 1999. 43.95 (0-471-98623-2) Wiley.

Performance Engineering of Computer & Telecommunications Systems: Proceedings of the UKPEW '95, Liverpool John Moores University, 5-6 September 1995. Ed. by Madjid Merabti et al. LC 95-53986. ix, 381p. 1996. pap. 69.95 (3-540-76008-3) Spr-Verlag.

Performance Enhancement - Plans for LTC Employees. Margaret Christian. 309p. 1995. student ed. 39.50 (0-929442-24-5, 2237pp) Prof Prnting & Pub.

Performance Enhancement in Coatings. Edward W. Orr. LC 98-30429. 2p. 1998. 98.00 (1-56990-263-1) Hanser-Gardner.

***Performance Enhancements in a Frequency Hopping GSM Network.** Thomas Nielsen & Jeroen Wigard. 352p. 2000. 126.00 (0-7923-7819-9) Kluwer Academic.

Performance Evaluation. Ed. by Walter C. Borman. (International Library of Management). 500p. 1994. 265.95 (1-85521-402-4, Pub. by Dartmth Pub) Ashgate Pub Co.

***Performance Evaluation.** Hariri. 600p. (C). 2000. write for info. (0-471-33288-7) Wiley.

Performance Evaluation: A Management Basic for Librarians. Ed. by Jonathan A. Lindsey. LC 86-42746. 232p. 1986. 39.50 (0-89774-313-X) Oryx Pr.

Performance Evaluation: An Essential Management Tool. Ed. by Christine S. Becker. (Practical Management Ser.). 209p. 1988. pap. text 23.95 (0-87326-051-1) Intl City-Cnty Mgt.

***Performance Evaluation: Origins & Directions.** Ed. by G. Haring et al. (Lecture Notes in Computer Science Ser.: Vol. 1769). x, 529p. 2000. pap. 54.00 (3-540-67193-5) Spr-Verlag.

***Performance Evaluation & Applications of ATM Networks.** Demetres D. Kouvatsos. 472p. 2000. 147.50 (0-7923-7851-2) Kluwer Academic.

Performance Evaluation, Benchmarks, & Attribution Analysis. Ed. by Jan R. Squires. 170p. (Orig.). 1995. pap. text 30.00 (1-879087-48-0) RFICFA.

Performance Evaluation for Professional Personnel. John E. Newman & John R. Hinrichs. (Studies in Productivity: Highlights of the Literature Ser.: Vol. 14). 48p. 1980. pap. 55.00 (0-89361-021-6) Work in Amer.

Performance Evaluation for Professional Personnel, Vol. 14. John E. Newman & John R. Hinrichs. LC 80-20739. (Studies in Productivity, Highlights of the Literature). 1982. pap. 35.00 (0-685-05451-9, Pergamon Pr) Elsevier.

Performance Evaluation, Goal Setting, & Feedback. Ed. by Gerald R. Ferris & Kendrith M. Rowland. LC 90-5947. (Research in Personnel & Human Resources Management Ser.). 296p. 1990. pap. 25.75 (1-55938-230-9) Jai Pr.

Performance Evaluation in the Human Services. Wayne Matheson et al. LC 93-23223. (Illus.). 145p. 1995. lib. bdg. 39.95 (1-56024-379-1) Haworth Pr.

Performance Evaluation of Communication Networks. Gary Higginbottom. LC 98-9286. (Communications Engineering Ser.). 352p. 1998. 93.00 (0-89006-870-4) Artech Hse.

Performance Evaluation of Computer & Communication Systems: Joint Tutorial Papers of Performance '93 & Sigmetrics '93. Ed. by G. Goos & J. Hartmanis. (Lecture Notes in Computer Science Ser.: Vol. 729). vii, 675p. 1993. 92.00 (0-387-57297-X) Spr-Verlag.

Performance Evaluation of High-Speed Switching Fabrics & Networks: ATM, Broadband ISDN, & MAN Technology. Thomas G. Robertazzi. LC 92-44950. (Illus.). 480p. 1993. text 79.95 (0-7803-0436-5, PC03335) Inst Electrical.

Performance Evaluation, Prediction & Visualization of Parallel Systems. Xingfu Wu. LC 99-12049. (Kluwer International Asian Studies in Computer & Information Science Ser.). 1999. write for info. (0-7923-8462-8) Kluwer Academic.

***Performance Excellence Criteria.** Johnson A. Edosomwan. LC 99-173343. 34p. 1998. write for info. (1-891034-13-8) Contin Improve.

Performance Excellence Planning (PEP) Vital Learning Corporation Staff. 1989. write for info. (0-318-65206-4) Vital Learning.

Performance Fluorine Chemicals & Polymers. Contrib. by Charles Forman. 176p. 1995. 2750.00 (1-56965-047-0, C-193) BCC.

Performance Flying: Hang Gliding Techniques for Intermediate & Advanced Pilots. Dennis Pagen. (Illus.). 342p. (Orig.). 1993. pap. 29.95 (0-936310-11-1, Sport Aviation Pubns) Black Mntn.

Performance Goals for the Internal Quality Control of Multichannel Hematology Analyzers. (Proposed Standard Ser.: Vol. 9). 1989. 75.00 (1-56238-054-0, H26-P) NCCLS.

Performance Goals for the Internal Quality Control of Multichannel Hematology Analyzers: Approved Standard (1996) 1996. 75.00 (1-56238-312-4, H26-A) NCCLS.

***Performance Guarantees in Communication Networks.** Cheng-Shang Chang. LC 99-49543. (Telecommunication Networks & Computer Systems Ser.). 410p. 1999. 99.95 (1-85233-226-3, Pub. by Spr-Verlag) Spr-Verlag.

Performance Guide for Understanding Business & Personal Law. 8th ed. L. Anderson et al. 160p. 1987. pap. text 7.96 (0-07-008434-3) McGraw.

Performance Guidelines for Legal Acceptance Records Pt. 2: Acceptance by Government Agencies: ANSI/AIIM TR31/2-1993 (R1999) Association for Information & Image Management Staff. 27p. 1993. pap. 45.00 (0-89258-276-6) Assn Inform & Image Mgmt.

Performance Guidelines for the Legal Acceptance of Records Pt. 1 Evidence: ANSI/AIIm TR31/1 - 1992 (R1999) Association for Information & Image Management Staff. 28p. 1992. pap. 39.00 (0-89258-245-6, TR31/1) Assn Inform & Image Mgmt.

Performance Guidelines for the Legal Acceptance of Records PT. 3 Implementation: ANSI/AIIM TR31/3 - 1994 (R1999) Association for Information & Image Management Staff. 50p. 1994. 39.00 (0-89258-290-1, TR31/3) Assn Inform & Image Mgmt.

Performance Guidelines for the Legal Acceptance of Records Pt. 4 Model Act & Rule: ANSi/AIIM TR31/4 - 1994 (R1999) Association for Information & Image Management Staff. 28p. 1994. 39.00 (0-89258-289-8, TR31/4) Assn Inform & Image Mgmt.

***Performance Ignition Systems: How to Optimize Your Ignition for High Performance Street & Raci.** Christopher Jacobs. LC 99-11875. 176p. (Orig.). 1999. pap. 17.95 (1-55788-306-8, HP Books) Berkley Pub.

Performance Imperative: Strategies for Enhancing Workforce Effectiveness. Ed. by Charles Fay & Howard W. Risher. (Management Ser.). 488p. 1995. text 37.45 (0-7879-0085-0) Jossey-Bass.

Performance Improvement: Charting Your Career Path with the 360 Degree Feedback Process. Ann J. Ewen & Kathleen Athey. Ed. by Lori L. Schmidt. (Career Navigator Ser.). (Illus.). 101p. (Orig.). 1997. pap., spiral bd., wbk. ed. 19.95 (1-890395-00-5) Teams Inc.

Performance Improvement: Winning Compliance Strategies for Your JCAHO Survey. Jodi Eisenberg & Cynthia Barnard. LC 98-132085. (Illus.). 197p. (Orig.). 1997. pap. text 87.00 (1-57839-002-8) Opus Communs.

***Performance Improvement--Making It Happen.** Darryl D. Enos. LC 99-50959. 2000. 39.95 (1-57444-282-1) St Lucie Pr.

Performance Improvement in Ambulatory Care. Joint Commission on Accreditation of Healthcare Organizations. LC 96-79557. iii, 212p. 1997. write for info. (0-86688-528-5) Joint Comm Hlthcare.

Performance Improvement in Health Information Services. William J. Rudman. Ed. by Lisa Biello. LC 96-46878. 224p. 1997. text 44.00 (0-7216-6009-6, W B Saunders Co) Harcrt Hlth Sci Grp.

***Performance Improvement in Long-Term Care, Subacute Programs & Dementia Special Care Units.** Joint Commission on Accreditation of Healthcare Organizations. (Illus.). 163p. 1998. pap. 45.00 (0-86688-590-0, LTC-500) Joint Comm Hlthcare.

Performance Improvement in Plant, Technology & Safety Management: Enhancing the Environment of Care. Joint Commission on Accreditation of Healthcare Organizations. (Illus.). 150p. 1994. pap. 35.00 (0-86688-394-0, PTM-500) Joint Comm Hlthcare.

Performance Improvement in Psychiatric & Substance Abuse Treatment Services. Patrice L. Spath. (Illus.). 190p. 1997. 40.00 (1-929955-04-9) Brown Spath.

Performance Improvement in Public Service Delivery: A Toolkit for Managers. Lynton Barker & Rom Rubycz. 1996. pap. 77.50 (0-273-61663-3) F T P-H.

Performance Improvement Methods: Fighting the War on Waste. H. James Harrington & Kenneth Lomax. LC 99-30552. (H. James Harrington Performance Improvement Ser.). (Illus.). 240p. 1998. 71.95 incl. cd-rom (0-07-027141-0) McGraw-Hill Prof.

Performance Improvement of Virtual Memory Systems. Edwin J. Lau. Ed. by Harold Stone. LC 82-13393. (Computer Science: Systems Programming Ser.: No. 17). 228p. 1982. reprint ed. pap. 70.70 (0-8357-1366-0, 2070073000063) Bks Demand.

Performance Improvement Programmes in Europe: A Special Issue of the European Journal of Work & Jen A. Algera. 1998. pap. 39.95 (0-86377-777-5, Pub. by Psychol Pr) Taylor & Francis.

Performance Improvement Through Information Management: Health Care's Bridge to Success. Judith V. Douglas. Ed. by K. J. Hannah & Marion J. Ball. LC 98-24445. (Health Informatics Ser.). (Illus.). 264p. 1999. 49.95 (0-387-98452-6) Spr-Verlag.

Performance in Life & Literature. Paul H. Gray & James VanOosting. 320p. 1996. 50.00 (0-205-14045-9) Allyn.

Performance in the Texts of Mallarme: The Passage from Art to Ritual. Mary L. Shaw. 304p. 1993. 45.00 (0-271-00807-5) Pa St U Pr.

Performance Indicators. Carol T. Fitz-Gibbon. 1990. 69.00 (1-85359-093-2, Pub. by Multilingual Matters); pap. 24.95 (1-85359-092-4, Pub. by Multilingual Matters) Taylor & Francis.

***Performance Indicators for Operating Commercial Nuclear Power Reactors: Data Through September 1997.** 488p. 1998. per. 38.00 (0-16-062722-2) USGPO.

***Performance Indicators for Operating Commercial Nuclear Power Reactors: Data Through September 1999.** 452p. 2000. per. 40.00 (0-16-059088-4) USGPO.

Performance Indicators for Permanent Disability: Low-Back Injuries in New Jersey. Sara R. Pease. 1987. 35.00 (0-935149-10-4, WC-87-5) Workers Comp Res Inst.

Performance Indicators for Permanent Disability: Low-Back Injuries in Texas. Sara R. Pease. 1988. 35.00 (0-935149-15-5, WC-88-4) Workers Comp Res Inst.

Performance Indicators for Permanent Disability: Low-Back Injuries in Wisconsin. Sara R. Pease. 1987. 35.00 (0-935149-09-0, WC-87-4) Workers Comp Res Inst.

Performance Indicators for the Road Sector. LC 98-121137. (Road Transport Research Ser.). 168p. 1997. pap. 37.00 (92-64-15586-4, 77-97-04-1, Pub. by Org for Econ) OECD.

Performance Indicators in Education. Michael G. Singh. 102p. (C). 1990. pap. 56.00 (0-7300-0779-0, EED433, Pub. by Deakin Univ) St Mut.

Performance Indicators in Higher Education: U. K. Universities. Jill Johnes & Jim Taylor. 160p. 1990. pap. 41.95 (0-335-09454-6) OpUniv Pr.

Performance Indicators in Logistics. Ed. by P. R. Van der Meulen. (Illus.). 100p. 1989. 43.95 (0-387-50873-2) Spr-Verlag.

Performance Instruction: Planning, Delivering, Evaluating, Analyzing. Daniel E. Vogler. (Illus.). 302p. 1996. 20.00 (0-614-22861-1) Instruct Perf.

***Performance Interventions: Selecting, Implementing & Evaluating the Results.** Ed. by Brenda Sugrue & Jim Fuller. LC 99-72097. 326p. 1999. pap. 38.95 (1-56286-124-7) Am Soc Train & Devel.

Performance Kayaking. Stephen B. U'ren. LC 89-38088. (Illus.). 192p. (Orig.). 1990. pap. 15.95 (0-8117-2299-6) Stackpole.

Performance Limits in Communication Theory & Practice. Ed. by J. K. Skwirzynski. (C). 1988. text 226.50 (90-247-3695-1) Kluwer Academic.

Performance Management. Robert Bacal. LC 98-41555. (Briefcase Books Ser.). (Illus.). xiv, 208 p. 1998. pap. 14.95 (0-07-071866-0) McGraw.

***Performance Management.** Andrew E. Schwartz. LC 99-28520. (Barron's Business Success Ser.). 160p. 1999. pap. text 6.95 (0-7641-0883-2) Barron.

Performance Management. Richard Williams. 208p. 1997. pap. 59.95 (0-415-11813-1) Thomson Learn.

Performance Management: Achieving Credit Union Goals Through Employee Performance. Miriam Cleary. (CUES HR Development Ser.). 54p. (Orig.). 1995. pap. 99.00 (1-889394-26-2) Credit Union Execs.

Performance Management: Creating the Conditions for Results. rev. ed. Michael McMaster. LC 94-2566. 320p. (Orig.). 1995. pap. 18.95 (1-55552-041-3) Metamorphous Pr.

Performance Management: Fact or Fantasy : a Study of Current & Future Practices in Singapore. Christopher Mills et al. LC 97-941514. vii, 76p. 1994. write for info. Miscell Pubs.

Performance Management: How Well Is the Government Dealing with Poor Performers? (Illus.). 88p. (Orig.). (C). 1994. pap. text 25.00 (0-7881-0313-X) DIANE Pub.

Performance Management: Improving Quality & Productivity Through Positive Reinforcement. 3rd rev. ed. Aubrey C. Daniels. LC 82-61868. (Illus.). 1989. 29.95 (0-937100-01-3) Perf Manage.

***Performance Management: Performance Standards & You.** rev. ed. Ralph R. Smith & Gary A. Koca. (Illus.). 66p. 1998. pap. 14.95 (0-936295-88-0) FPMI Comns.

Performance Management: Perspectives on Employee Performance. Richard Williams. LC 98-144541. (SWC-Business Communication). 208p. 1998. pap. 21.95 (1-86152-184-7) Thomson Learn.

Performance Management: Policy & Practice in the U. K. IPM Research Staff. (IPM Research Ser.). 120p. (C). 1992. 93.00 (0-85292-489-5, Pub. by IPM Hse) St Mut.

Performance Management: The New Realities. Ed. by Michael Armstrong & Angela Baron. 320p. 1998. pap. 57.00 (0-85292-727-4, Pub. by IPM Hse) St Mut.

***Performance Management: The New Realities.** Baron & Armstrong. 480p. 2000. pap. 56.95 (0-8464-5125-5) Beekman Pubs.

Performance Management Handbook. Mike Walters. 176p. 1995. pap. 60.00 (0-85292-579-4, Pub. by IPM Hse) St Mut.

Performance Management in Government: Contemporary Illustrations. Ed. by David Shand. (Public Management Occasional Papers: No. 9). 112p. (Orig.). 1996. pap. 16.00 (92-64-15290-3, 42-96-59-1) OECD.

Performance Management in Small Businesses. International Federation of Accountants Staff. LC 96-187966. 132p. (Orig.). 1996. pap. text 20.00 (1-887464-14-X) Intl Fed Accts.

***Performance Management in the 21st Century: Solutions for Business, Education & Family.** Norman Jones. LC 98-32268. 205p. 1999. 18.95 (1-57444-244-9) St Lucie Pr.

Performance Management Manual for Managers & Supervisors. Erich E. Schuttauf. (Supervisor's Tool Kit). 1997. pap. 18.75 (0-8080-0187-6) CCH INC.

***Performance Management Pocketbook.** Pam Jones. 112p. 2000. pap. 8.95 (1-57922-003-7) Stylus Pub VA.

***Performance Management Through Capabilities.** 56p. 2000. pap. 35.95 (0-8464-5126-3) Beekman Pubs.

Performance Management Through Capability. IPD Staff. 1998. pap. 36.00 (0-85292-745-2, Pub. by IPM Hse) St Mut.

Performance Management Workbook. E. James Brennan. 512p. (C). 1989. text 69.95 (0-13-658634-1) P-H.

Performance Management Workbook. Drake Beam Morin, Inc. 50p. (Orig.). 1993. pap. 12.95 (1-880030-15-2) DBM Pub.

Performance Mare: Maximizing What Your Mare Does Best. Sharon B. Smith. (Illus.). 224p. 1993. 30.00 (0-87605-958-2) Howell Bks.

Performance Massage. Robert K. King. LC 92-12303. (Illus.). 160p. 1992. pap. 16.95 (0-87322-395-0, PKIN0395) Human Kinetics.

Performance Materials Strategies. David Savage. 150p. 1999. pap. 995.00 (0-471-36371-5) Wiley.

Performance Matters: New Formations 27. Ed. by Simon Firth. (New Formations Ser.: No. 27). 192p. (C). 1997. pap. 19.50 (0-85315-816-9, Pub. by Lawrence & Wishart) NYU Pr.

***Performance Measurement: Getting Results.** Harry P. Hatry. LC 99-41582. 1999. 28.00 (0-87766-692-X) Urban Inst.

Performance Measurement & Evaluation. Jacky Holloway et al. 320p. 1995. text 75.00 (0-8039-7958-4); pap. text 24.95 (0-8039-7959-2) Sage.

Performance Measurement & Evaluation. Ron Surz. Ed. & Illus. by Investment Management Consultants Association Staff. 43p. 1995. 100.00 (1-928974-02-3) Invest Mgmt Cons.

Performance Measurement & Theory. Ed. by Frank J. Landy et al. 416p. 1983. text 79.95 (0-89859-246-1) L Erlbaum Assocs.

Performance Measurement & Visualization of Parallel Systems: Proceedings of the Workshop, Moravany, Czecho-Slovakia, 23-24 October 1992. Ed. by Gunter Haring & Gabriele Kotsis. LC 93-9512. (Advances in Parallel Computing Ser.: Vol. 7). 370p. 1993. 157.00 (0-444-89902-2, North Holland) Elsevier.

Performance Measurement, Evaluation & Incentives. Ed. by William J. Bruns, Jr. 400p. 1992. 39.95 (0-07-103375-0) McGraw.

***Performance Measurement Examples.** 2nd ed. Jack Zigon. 650p. 1999. reprint ed. per. 150.00 (1-892809-16-8) Zigon Perf Grp.

Performance Measurement Examples, Vol. I. Jack Zigon. (Performance Management Ser.). 650p. 1998. ring bd., wbk. ed. 400.00 (0-9649667-4-3) Zigon Perf Grp.

Performance Measurement for Public Services in Academic & Research Libraries. Mary Cronin. (Occasional Papers: Vol. 9). 36p. 1985. 25.00 (0-918006-31-7, OP09) ARL.

Performance Measurement for World Class Manufacturing: A Model for American Companies. Brian H. Maskell. (Illus.). 429p. 1991. 55.00 (0-915299-99-2) Productivity Inc.

***Performance Measurement in Finance.** Satchell & Knight. 2001. 94.95 (0-7506-5026-5) Buttrwrth-Heinemann.

Performance Measurement in Public Agencies. Ed. by Thomas J. Cook. 196p. (Orig.). 1986. pap. 15.00 (0-918592-87-9) Pol Studies.

Performance Measurement, Management, & Appraisal Sourcebook. Ed. by Craig E. Schneier et al. LC 96-209691. 650p. 1995. pap. 59.95 (0-87425-265-2) HRD Press.

Performance Measurement of Computer Systems. Phillip McKerrow. (Illus.). 256p. (C). 1988. text 35.50 (0-201-17436-7) Addison-Wesley.

Performance Measurement Systems & the JIT Philosophy. Karlene M. Crawford et al. LC 88-72100. (Illus.). 123p. 1988. text 20.00 (1-55822-011-9) Am Prod & Inventory.

An Asterisk (*) at the beginning of an entry indicates that the title is appearing for the first time.

P

Performance Measures & Indicators for Managed Behavioral Health. 151p. spiral bd. 67.00 (*0-929156-64-1*) Atlantic Info Services Inc.

Performance Measures for the Criminal Justice System: Discussion Papers from the BJS-Princeton Project. James Q. Wilson. 167p. (Orig.). (C). 1994. pap. text 40.00 (*0-7881-1410-7*) DIANE Pub.

*__Performance Measures of Effectiveness: Assessing the Performance of the National Drug Control Strategy, 1998-2007.__ 128p. 1998. per. 10.00 (*0-16-061880-0*) USGPO.

*__Performance Measurment Solutions, Vol. 1.__ Practitioners Publishing Co. Staff. 1999. ring bd. write for info. (*0-7646-0890-8*) Prctnrs Pub Co.

Performance Methods for Flutists. James J. Pellerite. 1968. pap. text 4.95 (*0-931200-51-2*) Zalo.

Performance Modeling for Computer Architects. Ed. by C. M. Krishna. LC 95-14981. 408p. 1995. pap. 50.00 (*0-8186-7094-0*, BP07094) IEEE Comp Soc.

*__Performance Modeling of Operating Systems Using Object-Oriented Simulation: A Practical Introduction.__ Jose M. Garrido. LC 00-42335. (Series in Computer Science). 2000. write for info. (*0-306-46459-4*) Plenum.

Performance Modeling of Parallel Systems. Arie J. Van Gemund. (Illus.). 210p. (Orig.). 1996. pap. 57.50 (*90-407-1326-X*, Pub. by Delft U Pr) Coronet Bks.

Performance Modifying Chevy Trucks: For Street, Strip & Off-Road. Rich Johnson. LC 99-222924. (Illus.). 128p. (Orig.). 1996. pap. 18.95 (*1-884089-16-X*, S-A Design) CarTech.

Performance Modifying Ford Trucks: For Street, Strip & Off-Road. Rich Johnson. LC 99-219515. (Illus.). 128p. (Orig.). 1996. pap. 18.95 (*1-884089-19-4*, S-A Design) CarTech.

Performance Monitoring for Geotechnical Construction - STP 584. 204p. 1975. 20.00 (*0-8031-0533-9*, STP584) ASTM.

Performance Monitoring Indicators Handbook. Roberto Mosse & Leigh E. Sontheimer. LC 96-27346. (Technical Papers: No. 334). 54p. 1996. pap. 22.00 (*0-8213-3731-9*, 13731) World Bank.

Performance Movie Guide. Mick Brown. 208p. 1999. pap. 15.95 (*1-58234-043-9*) Bloomsbury Pubg.

Performance Now! Inc Business Resources Staff. 1999. pap. 103.00 (*1-58230-010-0*) Thomson Learn.

Performance Objectives for School Principals. Jack A. Culbertson et al. LC 74-75367. 235p. 1974. 31.00 (*0-8211-0223-0*) McCutchan.

Performance Objectives in Education. LC 72-12722. (Educational Technology Reviews Ser.: Vol. 7). 144p. 1973. pap. 29.95 (*0-87778-055-2*) Educ Tech Pubns.

Performance of a Lifetime: A Practical-Philosophical Guide to the Joyous Life. Fred Newman & Phyllis Goldberg. LC 96-83502. 256p. (Orig.). (C). 1996. pap. 11.95 (*0-9628621-7-7*) Castillo Intl.

Performance of Aggregates in Railroads & Other Track Performance Issues. (Research Record Ser.: No. 1131). 106p. 1987. 15.50 (*0-309-04515-0*) Transport Res Bd.

Performance of Alternative Fuels for SI & CI Engines: 1996 International Congress & Exposition. LC 96-207897. (Special Publications). 179p. 1996. pap. 56.00 (*1-56091-790-3*, SP-1160) Soc Auto Engineers.

Performance of Bolting Materials in High Temperature Plant Applications: 16-17 June 1994: York, U. K. Ed. by A. Strang. 438p. 1995. 130.00 (*0-901716-72-3*, Pub. by Inst Materials) Ashgate Pub Co.

Performance of Buildings & Serviceability of Facilities. Ed. by Gerald Davis & Francis T. Ventre. LC 90-31703. (Special Technical Publication Ser.: No. 1029). (Illus.). 353p. 1990. text 44.00 (*0-8031-1292-0*, STP1029) ASTM.

Performance of Computer Communication Systems: A Model-Based Approach to Performance Evaluation. Boudewijn R. Haverkort. LC 98-27222. 518p. 1998. 100.00 (*0-471-97228-2*) Wiley.

Performance of Concrete. 506p. 1990. 51.50 (*0-685-60169-2*, SP-122BOW6) ACI.

Performance of Concrete: Resistance of Concrete to Sulphate & Other Environmental Conditions: A Symposium in Honour of Thorbergur Thorvaldson. Ed. by Edwin G. Swenson. LC 74-350285. (Canadian Building Ser.: No. 2). (Illus.). 253p. reprint ed. pap. 78.50 (*0-8357-8264-6*, 203406800088) Bks Demand.

Performance of Concrete in Marine Environment. 1980. 53.50 (*0-686-70072-4*, SP-65BOW6) ACI.

Performance of Concurrency Control. Ed. by Vijay Kumar. LC 94-47126. 643p. (C). 1995. 52.60 (*0-13-065442-6*) P-H.

Performance of Conviction: Plainness & Rhetoric in the Early English Renaissance. Kenneth J. Graham. LC 93-33720. (Rhetoric & Society Ser.). 240p. 1994. text 35.00 (*0-8014-2871-8*) Cornell U Pr.

Performance of Deep Foundation under Seismic Loading: Proceedings of Sessions Sponsored by the Deep Foundations & Soil Properties Committees of the Geotechnical Engineering Division of the American Society of Civil Engineers in Conjunction with the ASCE Convention in San Diego, California, October 22-26, 1995. Ed. by John P. Turner. (Geotechnical Special Publications: No. 51). 88p. 1995. 23.00 (*0-7844-0120-9*) Am Soc Civil Eng.

Performance of Earth & Earth-Supported Structures: Proceedings of the Specialty Conference on June 11-14, 1972, Purdue University, Lafayette, Indiana, 3 vols., 2. LC TA0710.A4E27. 160p. 1972. reprint ed. pap. 49.60 (*0-608-08298-8*, 201954600003) Bks Demand.

Performance of Earth & Earth-Supported Structures: Proceedings of the Specialty Conference on June 11-14, 1972, Purdue University, Lafayette, Indiana, 3 vols., 3. LC TA0710.A4E27. 423p. 1972. reprint ed. pap. 131.20 (*0-608-08299-6*, 201954600004) Bks Demand.

Performance of Earth & Earth-Supported Structures: Proceedings of the Specialty Conference on June 11-14, 1972, Purdue University, Lafayette, Indiana, 3 vols., Vol. 1, Pt. 1. LC TA0710.A4E27. 891p. reprint ed. pap. 200.00 (*0-608-08296-1*, 201954600001) Bks Demand.

Performance of Earth & Earth-Supported Structures: Proceedings of the Specialty Conference on June 11-14, 1972, Purdue University, Lafayette, Indiana, 3 vols., Vol. 1, Pt. 2. LC TA0710.A4E27. 678p. 1972. reprint ed. pap. 200.00 (*0-608-08297-X*, 201954600002) Bks Demand.

Performance of Elastomeric Bearings. (National Cooperative Highway Research Program Report Ser.: No. 298). 100p. 1988. 12.00 (*0-309-04567-3*, NR298) Transport Res Bd.

Performance of Electrodes for Industrial Electrochemical Processes: Proceedings of the Symposium. Symposium on Performance of Electrodes for Industr. Ed. by Fumio Hine et al. LC 89-85687. (Electrochemical Society Proceedings Ser.: Vol. 89-10). 327p. 1989. reprint ed. pap. 101.40 (*0-7837-9260-3*, 205927400005) Bks Demand.

Performance of Emotion among Paxtun Women: "The Misfortunes Which Have Befallen Me" Benedicte Grima. LC 91-46493. (Modern Middle East Ser.: No. 17). 255p. 1992. pap. 14.95 (*0-292-72756-9*) U of Tex Pr.

Performance of Engineered Barriers in Deep Geological Depositories. IAEA Staff. (Technical Report: No. 342). 79p. 1992. pap. 35.00 (*92-0-103892-5*, STI/DOC/342, Pub. by IAEA) Bernan Associates.

Performance of European Wind Turbines: Statistical Evaluation from the European Wind Turbine Database Eurowin. J. Schmid & H. P. Klein. (Illus.). 168p. (C). (gr. 13). 1991. text 125.00 (*1-85166-737-7*) Elsevier Applied Sci.

*__Performance of Everyday Life: Gaine of Nepal.__ Ingrid Glad. (Acta Humaniora). 342p. 1998. pap. 46.00 (*82-00-12991-8*) Scandnvan Univ Pr.

*__Performance of Financial Institutions: Efficiency, Innovation, Regulation.__ Ed. by Patrick T. Harker & Stavros A. Zenios. (Illus.). 500p. (C). 2000. text 80.00 (*0-521-77154-4*); pap. text 28.95 (*0-521-77767-4*) Cambridge U Pr.

*__Performance of Gender: An Anthropology of Everyday Life in a South Indian Fishing Village.__ Cecilia Busby. LC 99-86428. (Illus.). 2000. write for info. (*0-485-19571-2*, Pub. by Athlone Pr) Humanities.

Performance of Healing. Ed. by Carol Laderman & Marina Roseman. LC 95-24568. 330p. (C). 1995. pap. 21.99 (*0-415-91200-8*) Routledge.

Performance of Healing. Ed. by Carol Laderman & Marina Roseman. LC 95-24568. 330p. (C). (gr. 13). 1996. 80.00 (*0-415-91199-0*) Routledge.

Performance of Hospitals in Washington State. 1993. write for info. (*1-880678-54-3*) HCIA.

Performance of HUD Assisted Properties During the January 17, 1994 Northridge Earthquake. Ed. by Erik Anderson et al. (Illus.). 47p. 1998. pap. text 30.00 (*0-7881-4161-9*) DIANE Pub.

*__Performance of India's Export Zones: A Comparison with the Chinese Approach.__ Ashok Kundra. LC 00-36613. 2000. write for info. (*0-7619-9453-X*) Sage.

Performance of Information & Communication Systems. Chapman & Hall Staff. text 168.00 (*0-412-83730-7*) Chapman & Hall.

Performance of Jewish & Arab Music in Israel Today Pt. 1, Vol. 1. Ed. by Amnon Shiloah. 98p. 1997. pap. text 15.00 (*90-5702-064-5*, Harwood Acad Pubs) Gordon & Breach.

Performance of Jewish & Arab Music in Israel Today Pt. 2, Vol. 2. Amnon Shiloah. 86p. 1997. pap. text 14.00 (*90-5702-156-0*, Harwood Acad Pubs) Gordon & Breach.

*__Performance of Light Aircraft__ John T. Lowry. LC 99-34583. (Education Ser.). 1999. write for info. (*1-56347-330-5*) AIAA.

Performance of Literature in Historical Perspectives. Ed. by David W. Thompson et al. LC 83-3470. 742p. (Orig.). 1983. pap. text 53.00 (*0-8191-3147-4*) U Pr of Amer.

Performance of Longitudinal Traffic Barriers. (National Cooperative Highway Research Program Report Ser.: No. 289). 169p. 1987. 13.20 (*0-309-04023-X*, NR289) Transport Res Bd.

Performance of Lubricating Oils. 2nd ed. H. H. Zuidema. LC 52-8017. (ACS Monograph: No. 143). 1959. 27.95 (*0-8412-0283-4*) Am Chemical.

Performance of Lubricating Oils. 2nd ed. Hilbert H. Zuidema. LC 59-14570. (ACS Monograph Ser.: Vol. 143). (Illus.). 217p. 1959. reprint ed. pap. 67.30 (*0-608-06929-9*, 206713700009) Bks Demand.

Performance of Middle English Culture: Essays on Chaucer & the Drama in Honor of Martin Stevens. Ed. by James J. Paxson et al. LC 98-24827. (Illus.). 208p. 1998. 75.00 (*0-85991-527-1*) Boydell & Brewer.

*__Performance of Nobility in Early Modern European Literature.__ David M. Posner. LC 98-53637. (Cambridge Studies in Renaissance Literature & Culture: No. 33). 284p. (C). 1999. 59.95 (*0-521-66181-1*) Cambridge U Pr.

Performance of Nominal Five-Eighths Inch Plywood Over Joists Spaced 24 Inches on Center, Vol. 1. NAHB Research Foundation Staff. (Research Report Ser.). 11p. 1981. pap. 5.50 (*0-86718-114-1*) Home Builder.

Performance of Off-Road Vehicles & Machines: Proceedings of the 8th International ISTVS Conference, Cambridge, August 1984. Ed. by M. J. Dwyer. 120p. 1984. pap. 33.00 (*0-08-031655-7*, Pergamon Pr) Elsevier.

*__Performance of Plastics.__ Witold Brostow. LC 00-21005. 2000. write for info. (*1-56990-277-1*) Hanser-Gardner.

Performance of Power: Theatrical Discourse & Politics. Ed. by Sue-Ellen Case & Janelle Reinelt. LC 90-26750. (Studies in Theatre History & Culture). (Illus.). 306p. (C). 1991. pap. text 18.95 (*0-87745-318-7*) U of Iowa Pr.

Performance of Precast Prestressed Hollow Core Slab with Composite Concrete Topping. (PCI Journal Reprints Ser.). 15p. 1973. pap. 12.00 (*0-686-40052-6*, JR126) P-PCI.

Performance of Pressure Vessels with Clad & Overlayed Stainless Steel Linings: Presented at the Joint Conference of the Pressure Vessels & Piping, Materials, Nuclear Engineering, Solar Energy Divisions, Denver, Colorado, June 21-25, 1981. American Society of Mechanical Engineers Staff. Ed. by L. I. Sluzalis & P. E. Dempsey. LC 81-69253. (MPC Ser.: No. 16). (Illus.). 77p. reprint ed. pap. 30.00 (*0-8357-2881-1*, 203911800011) Bks Demand.

Performance of Prestressed Concrete on the Illinois Tollway after 25 Years of Service. (PCI Journal Reprints Ser.). 24p. 1983. pap. 14.00 (*0-318-19798-7*, JR287) P-PCI.

Performance of Protective Clothing, Vol. 4. Ed. by J. P. McBriarty & N. Henry, III. (Special Technical Publication Ser.: No. STP 1133). (Illus.). 1025p. 1992. text 83.00 (*0-8031-1430-3*, STP1133) ASTM.

Performance of Protective Clothing, Vol. 5. Ed. by James S. Johnson & S. Z. Mansdorf. (Special Technical Publication Ser.). (Illus.). 640p. 1996. 78.00 (*0-8031-1987-9*, STP1237) ASTM.

Performance of Protective Clothing, Vol. 6. Ed. by Jeffrey O. Stull & Arthur D. Schwope. (STP Ser.: No. 1273). (Illus.). 368p. 1997. pap. text 69.00 (*0-8031-2402-3*, STP1273) ASTM.

Performance of Protective Clothing, STP 900. Ed. by Roger L. Barker & Gerard C. Coletta. LC 86-10706. (Special Technical Publication Ser.). (Illus.). 625p. 1986. text 60.00 (*0-8031-0461-8*, STP900) ASTM.

Performance of Reinforced Soil Structures. Ed. by A. McGown et al. 485p. 1991. text 200.00 (*0-7277-1637-9*, Pub. by T Telford) RCH.

Performance of Rolled Asphalt Road Surfacings. (Conference Proceedings Ser.). 215p. 1980. 36.00 (*0-7277-0096-0*, Pub. by T Telford) RCH.

Performance of Self in Student Writing. LC 97-38280. 1997. pap. text 20.00 (*0-86709-439-7*, Pub. by Boynton Cook Pubs) Heinemann.

Performance of Small Firms. David J. Storey et al. 365p. 1986. 97.50 (*0-415-04017-5*) Routledge.

*__Performance of Social Systems: Perspectives & Problems.__ Francisco Parra Luna. LC 99-54947. 2000. write for info. (*0-306-46309-1*, Kluwer Plenum) Kluwer Academic.

Performance of Solar Energy Converters: Thermal Collectors & Photovoltaic Cells. Giogio Beghi. 1983. text 226.00 (*90-277-1545-9*) Kluwer Academic.

Performance of Tape-bonded Seams of Epdm Membranes: Factors Affecting the Creep-Rupture Response of Tape-bonded & Liquid-Adhesive-Bonded Seams. Walter J. Rossiter, Jr. 55p. 1998. pap. 7.00 (*0-16-056714-9*) USGPO.

*__Performance of TCP/IP Over ATM Networks.__ Mahbub Hassan & Mohammed Atiquzzaman. LC 00-40622. (Telecommunications Library). 2000. write for info. (*1-58053-037-0*) Artech Hse.

Performance of the Bleeding Time Test: Proposed Guideline (1995) 1995. 25.00 (*1-56238-281-0*, H45-P) NCCLS.

Performance of the British Economy. Ed. by Rudiger Dornbusch & Richard Layard. (Illus.). 288p. 1988. 75.00 (*0-19-877272-6*) OUP.

Performance of Tubular Alloy Heat Exchangers in Sea Water Service in the Chemical Process Industry. (MTI Publication: No. 26). (Illus.). 123p. 1987. 10.00 (*0-685-39489-1*) NACE Intl.

Performance of Weathering Steel in Bridges. (National Cooperative Highway Research Program Report Ser.: No. 272). 164p. 1984. 12.00 (*0-309-03851-0*, NR272) Transport Res Bd.

Performance on Lute, Guitar, & Vihuela: Historical Practice & Modern Interpretation. Ed. by Victor A. Coelho. LC 96-47888. (Studies in Performance Practice: Vol. 6). (Illus.). 252p. (C). 1998. text 64.95 (*0-521-45528-6*) Cambridge U Pr.

*__Performance on the Edge: Transformations of Culture.__ Johannes H. Birringer. LC 99-86429. 2000. write for info. (*0-485-00418-6*) Athlone Pr.

Performance One: Monologues for Women. William-Alan Landes. 128p. (Orig.). 1991. pap. 10.00 (*0-88734-122-5*) Players Pr.

Performance or Compliance? Performance Audit & Public Management in Five Countries. Christopher Pollitt et al. LC 99-25365. (Illus.). 264p. 1999. text 70.00 (*0-19-829600-2*) OUP.

Performance Parameters for Digital Analog Networks. (Satellites in an ISDN World Ser.). 1996. 50.00 (*0-614-18394-4*, 126P6) Info Gatekeepers.

Performance Partnership. Filomena D. Warihay. 100p. 1996. pap. 12.95 (*0-9641834-4-7*) Take Charge Cnslts.

Performance Plus Children Favorites, Bk. 3. Ed. by Carol Cuellar. 24p. 1997. pap. 6.95 (*0-7692-0021-4*) Warner Bros.

Performance Plus Family Favorites, Bk. 4. Ed. by Carol Cuellar. 32p. 1997. pap. 6.95 (*0-7692-0020-6*) Warner Bros.

Performance Poems. John Dancy-Jones. (Illus.). 24p. 1988. pap. 5.00 (*0-929170-08-3*) Paper Plant.

Performance Power: Transforming Stress into Creative Energy. Irmtraud T. Kruger. Tr. by Edward H. Tarr from GER. (Illus.). 252p. 1995. pap. 22.99 (*1-887210-00-8*) Summit Records.

Performance Power: Winning Ways to Face Your Audience. Gloria Shafer. LC 92-2611. (Illus.). 160p. 1992. pap. 49.95 (*0-7734-9924-5*) E Mellen.

Performance Practice, 2 vols., I. Ed. by Howard Mayer Brown & Stanley Sadie. (Grove Handbooks in Music Ser.). (Illus.). (C). 1990. 32.50 (*0-393-02807-0*) Norton.

Performance Practice, 2 vols., II. Ed. by Howard Mayer Brown & Stanley Sadie. (Grove Handbooks in Music Ser.). (Illus.). (C). 1990. 44.50 (*0-393-02808-9*) Norton.

Performance Practice: Ethnomusicological Perspectives, 12. Ed. by Gerard Behague. LC 83-10842. (Contributions in Intercultural & Comparative Studies: No. 12). (Illus.). 262p. 1984. 62.95 (*0-313-24160-0*, BPE/, Greenwood Pr) Greenwood.

Performance Practice & Technique in Marin Marais' "Pieces de Viole" Deborah A. Teplow. Ed. by George J. Buelow. LC 85-20843. (Studies in Musicology: No. 93). 168p. reprint ed. 52.10 (*0-8357-1714-3*, 207047500095) Bks Demand.

Performance Practices in Classic Piano Music: Their Principles & Applications. Sandra P. Rosenblum. LC 87-45437. (Music: Scholarship & Applications Ser.). 544p. 1988. 52.50 (*0-253-34314-3*, MB-680) Ind U Pr.

Performance Practices in Classic Piano Music: Their Principles & Applications. Sandra P. Rosenblum. LC 87-45437. (Music: Scholarship & Applications Ser.). 544p. 1991. pap. 23.95 (*0-253-20680-4*) Ind U Pr.

Performance Practices of the Seventeenth & Eighteenth Centuries. Frederick Neumann. 605p. 1993. 50.00 (*0-02-873300-2*, Schirmer Books) Mac Lib Ref.

Performance Prediction of Public Safety & Law Enforcement Personnel: A Study in Race & Gender Differences & MMPI Subscales. Joseph E. Talley & Lisa D. Hinz. 110p. 1990. pap. 20.95 (*0-398-06453-9*) C C Thomas.

Performance Prediction of Public Safety & Law Enforcement Personnel: A Study in Race & Gender Differences & MMPI Subscales. Joseph E. Talley & Lisa D. Hinz. 110p. (C). 1990. text 33.95 (*0-398-05700-1*) C C Thomas.

Performance Process & Performance Audit Findings: An Explanation of Terms. William Costello. LC 97-61110. (Illus.). 75p. 1997. pap. 22.00 (*1-882194-31-4*) TN Valley Pub.

Performance Profiles of Major Energy Producers. 1995. lib. bdg. 250.00 (*0-8490-6499-6*) Gordon Pr.

Performance Profiles of Major Energy Producers. 1996. lib. bdg. 255.00 (*0-8490-6057-5*) Gordon Pr.

Performance Profiles of Major Energy Producers (1992) (Illus.). 152p. (Orig.). (C). 1994. pap. text 50.00 (*0-7881-1068-3*) DIANE Pub.

Performance Profiles of Major Energy Producers (1993) (Illus.). 189p. (Orig.). (C). 1995. pap. text 50.00 (*0-7881-2470-6*) DIANE Pub.

Performance Profiles of Major Energy Producers, 1995. 189p. 1997. per. 18.00 (*0-16-063480-6*) USGPO.

*__Performance Profiles of Major Energy Producers, 1996.__ 199p. 1998. per. 16.00 (*0-16-063524-1*) USGPO.

*__Performance Profiles of Major Energy Producers, 1997.__ 168p. 1999. per. 15.00 (*0-16-063559-4*) USGPO.

*__Performance Puzzles: And How to Put Them Together.__ limited ed. Richard B. Doss. (Illus.). 235p. 1999. pap. 19.95 (*0-9631680-1-0*) Human Side Pr.

Performance Rankings of Illinois School Districts. Richard Stout et al. 88p. 1993. pap. 20.00 (*1-884203-00-0*) Taxpayers Fed.

*__Performance Readiness: A Situational Approach.__ (Illus.). 24p. 1998. 9.95 (*0-931619-04-1*) Ctr Leadership.

*__Performance Recording of Animals State of the Art, 1998.__ Cathy Linton. (Illus.). 352p. 1998. 96.00 (*90-74134-54-8*) Wageningen Pers.

Performance-Related Testing & Evaluation of Aggregate & New Geomaterials (TRR 1418) Ed. by Norman Solomon. (Transportation Research Record Ser.). (Illus.). 72p. 1994. pap. text 24.00 (*0-309-05566-0*) Natl Res Coun.

Performance Reporting by Government Business Enterprises: The Provision of Financial & Non-Financial Performance Information in General Purpose Financial Results. LC 96-225272. 45p. (Orig.). 1996. pap. text 10.00 (*1-887464-09-3*) Intl Fed Accts.

Performance Requirements, Combustible Gas Detectors: S12.13, Pt. I. ISA Staff. (Hazardous Locations Ser.). 38p. 1995. 40.00 (*1-55617-579-5*, S12.13) ISA.

Performance Requirements for Multinational Corporations: U. S. Management Response. Richard D. Robinson. LC 82-22469. 200p. 1983. 57.95 (*0-275-91066-0*, C1066, Praeger Pubs) Greenwood.

Performance Research: Letters from Europe, Vol. 2. Ed. by Richard Gough & Claire MacDonald. 136p. (C). 1997. pap. 17.99 (*0-415-16178-9*) Routledge.

Performance Research: On Illusion. Ed. by Richard Gough & Claire MacDonald. 162p. (C). 1997. pap. 17.99 (*0-415-16210-6*) Routledge.

Performance Results in Value Added Reporting. Ahmed Riahi-Belkaoui. LC 95-46276. 192p. 1996. 59.95 (*1-56720-024-9*, Quorum Bks) Greenwood.

Performance Results of Multinationality. Ahmed Riahi-Belkaoui. LC 98-44554. 200p. 1999. 65.00 (*1-56720-277-2*, Quorum Bks) Greenwood.

Performance Review & Quality Assurance in Social Work. Ed. by Anne Connor & Stewart Black. (Research Highlights in Social Work Ser.: No. 20). 200p. 1994. 34.95 (*1-85302-017-6*) Taylor & Francis.

An Asterisk (*) at the beginning of an entry indicates that the title is appearing for the first time.

Performance Review in Local Government. Robert Ball. LC 98-71408. 214p. 1998. text 63.95 (*1-84014-123-9*, Pub. by Ashgate Pub) Ashgate Pub Co.

*__Performance Reviews.__ (Ten Minute Guides Ser.). 192p. 2000. 10.95 (*0-02-863967-7*) Macmillan Gen Ref.

Performance Rock Climbing. Dale Goddard & Udo Neumann. LC 93-16842. (Illus.). 208p. 1993. pap. 14.95 (*0-8117-2219-8*) Stackpole.

Performance Sailing. Steve Colgate. (Illus.). 1993. pap. 9.95 (*0-914747-03-7*) Offshore Sail Schl.

*__Performance Scorecards: Measuring the Right Things in the Real World.__ Richard Y. Chang & Mark W. Morgan. LC 99-50888. 2000. 28.00 (*0-7879-5272-9*) Jossey-Bass.

Performance Skiing: Training & Techniques to Make You a Better Alpine Skier. George Thomas. LC 92-3586. (Outdoor Sports Ser.). (Illus.). 168p. 1992. pap. 15.95 (*0-8117-3026-3*) Stackpole.

Performance Specification of Computer Aided Environmental Design, 2 vols. Kaiman Lee. LC 75-309149. (Illus.). 554p. 1975. 150.00 (*0-915250-15-2*) Environ Design.

Performance, Stability, Dynamics, & Control of Airplanes. Bandu N. Pamadi. LC 98-34737. (AIAA Education Ser.). 766p. 1998. write for info. (*1-56347-222-8*) AIAA.

Performance Standards & Authentic Learning. Allan A. Glatthorn. LC 98-50281. 180p. 1999. pap. 29.95 (*1-883001-71-4*) Eye On Educ.

Performance Standards for Antimicrobial Disk & Dilution Susceptibility Tests for Bacteria Isolated from Animals: Proposed Standard (1994) Contrib. by Jeffrey L. Watts. 1994. 75.00 (*1-56238-258-6*, M31-P) NCCLS.

Performance Standards for Antimicrobial Disk & Dilution Susceptibility Tests for Bacteria Isolated from Animals: Tentative Standard (1997) 1997. 75.00 (*1-56238-330-2*, M31-T) NCCLS.

Performance Standards for Antimicrobial Disk Susceptibility Tests: Approved Standard (1997) 5th ed. Contrib. by James H. Jorgensen. (SPA.). 1997. 85.00 (*1-56238-308-6*, M2-A6) NCCLS.

Performance Standards for Antimicrobial Susceptibility Testing: Eighth International Supplement (1998) 1998. 115.00 (*1-56238-337-X*, M100-S8) NCCLS.

Performance Standards for Antimicrobial Susceptibility Testing: Seventh Informational Supplement (1997) Contrib. by James H. Jorgensen. 1997. 85.00 (*1-56238-309-4*, M100-S7) NCCLS.

Performance Standards for Music: Strategies & Benchmarks for Assessing Progress Toward the National Standards, Grades PreK-12. MENC Committee on Performance Standards. 136p. 1996. pap. 20.00 (*1-56545-099-X*, 1633) MENC.

Performance Standards for Navigational Equipment. IMO Staff. (C). 1988. 80.00 (*0-7855-0026-X*, IMO 978E, Pub. by Intl Maritime Org); 80.00 (*0-7855-7110-8*, IMO 979F, Pub. by Intl Maritime Org); 80.00 (*0-7855-7111-6*, IMO 980S, Pub. by Intl Maritime Org) St Mut.

Performance Standards for Safely Conducting Research with Genetically Modified Fish & Shellfish Pt. I: Introduction & Supporting Text & Flowcharts. Ed. by Walter A. Hill. (Illus.). 103p. (C). 1998. reprint ed. pap. text 35.00 (*0-7881-7228-X*) DIANE Pub.

Performance Standards for Safely Conducting Research with Genetically Modified Fish & Shellfish Pt. II: Flowcharts & Accompanying Worksheets. Ed. by Craig Acomb & Carolyn Carr. (Illus.). 62p. (C). 1998. pap. text 20.00 (*0-7881-7229-8*) DIANE Pub.

Performance Standards of Cities & Counties: Annual State & National Review of Performance Potential. 125.00 (*1-55507-170-8*) Municipal Analysis.

*__Performance Studies: The Interpretation of Aesthetic Texts.__ Ronald J. Pelias. 272p. (Orig.). (C). 1999. per. 39.95 (*0-7872-6219-6*, 41621901) Kendall-Hunt.

*__Performance Study of Nitrided Gears in High Speed Epicyclic Gearbox Used in Gas Turbogenerators - A Case Study.__ A. K. Rakhit. (Technical Papers: Vol. 99FTM11). 4p. 1999. pap. 30.00 (*1-55589-749-5*) AGMA.

Performance Task Skill Builder, Geography: People & Places in a Changing World. 2nd ed. English. 1996. pap., wbk. ed. 24.25 (*0-314-21469-0*) Thomson Learn.

*__Performance Tasks & Skill Builder Worksheets, Psychology/You.__ 3rd ed. Romano McMahon & Romano. 1999. pap. text 15.75 (*0-538-42907-0*) Thomson Learn.

Performance Test Procedure Sodium Base Recovery Units. Technical Association of the Pulp & Paper Industry. LC TS1176.6.S91. (Technical Association of the Pulp & Paper Car Ser.: No. 39). 102p. reprint ed. pap. 31.70 (*0-608-14042-2*, 202236200027) Bks Demand.

Performance Testing of Buildings. P. J. Fishwick & F. Alamdari. 1995. pap. 60.00 (*0-86022-391-4*, Pub. by Build Servs Info Assn) St Mut.

Performance Testing of Lubricants for Automotive Engines & Transmissions. Ed. by C. F. McCue et al. (Illus.). 811p. 1974. 99.00 (*0-85334-468-X*) Elsevier.

*__Performance Testing of Passive Autocatalytic Recombiners.__ T. K. Blanchat. 210p. 1998. per. 58.00 (*0-16-062930-6*) USGPO.

Performance Testing of Shipping Containers - Sponsored by ASTM Committee D-10 on Packaging. American Society for Testing & Materials Staff. LC 83-641658. 244p. reprint ed. pap. 75.70 (*0-608-15556-X*, 205638400064) Bks Demand.

Performance Tests. 5th ed. Hoggatt Robinson. 1991. pap. text 2.75 (*0-538-60505-7*) Sth-Wstrn College.

Performance Theory of Order & Constituency. John A. Hawkins. (Cambridge Studies in Linguistics: No. 73). 516p. (C). 1995. pap. text 32.95 (*0-521-37867-2*) Cambridge U Pr.

*__Performance Thru Attitude.__ Keith Harrell. 2000. 25.00 (*0-06-019572-X*) HarpC.

Performance Traditions among African-American Teachers. Rhonda B. Jeffries. 128p. 1997. 69.95 (*1-57292-038-6*); pap. 49.95 (*1-57292-037-8*) Austin & Winfield.

Performance Tuning Microsoft Networks. 2nd rev. ed. Vicki Northcutt. (Illus.). 70p. 1998. pap. 20.00 (*0-9668334-1-4*) Intelligentsia.

Performance Tuning NetWare. 450p. 1997. 34.99 (*0-7821-1563-2*) Sybex.

Performance Tuning the IBM RISC System/6000. Rudy Chukran. LC 97-46800. 240p. (C). 1998. pap. text 49.95 (*0-201-63382-5*) Addison-Wesley.

Performance under Sub-Optimal Conditions. Ed. by P. R. Davis. 104p. 1970. pap. 31.00 (*0-85066-044-0*) Taylor & Francis.

Performance vs. Results: A Critique of Values in Contemporary Sport. John H. Gibson. LC 92-8117. (SUNY Series, the Philosophy of Education). 139p. (C). 1993. text 59.50 (*0-7914-1353-5*); pap. text 19.95 (*0-7914-1354-3*) State U NY Pr.

Performance Welding. Peter Finch. LC 97-841. (Power Pro Ser.). (Illus.). 160p. 1997. pap. 16.95 (*0-7603-0393-2*) MBI Pubg.

Performance Wheels & Tires. Mike Mavrigian. LC 97-45832. 176p. 1998. pap. 16.95 (*1-55788-286-X*, HP Books) Berkley Pub.

Performance Without Pressure. Martin L. Seldman. 1988. 17.95 (*0-8027-1022-0*) Walker & Co.

Performances. Greg Dening. LC 96-5031. (Illus.). 324p. 1996. pap. 21.00 (*0-226-14298-1*); lib. bdg. 45.00 (*0-226-14297-3*) U Ch Pr.

Performances. Linda McCartney. 120p. 1999. write for info. (*0-8212-2486-7*) Little.

Performances & Presentations. Misha Berson. Ed. by Terry Link. 24p. (Orig.). 1994. pap. 5.00 (*0-936434-72-4*, Pub. by Zellerbach Fam Fund) Intl Spec Bk.

Performative Circumstances from the Avant Garde to Ramlila. Richard Schechner. 1983. pap. 16.00 (*0-8364-0963-9*, Pub. by Seagull Bks) S Asia.

Performativity & Performance. Ed. by Eve K. Sedgwick & Andrew Parker. (Essays from the English Institute Ser.). 240p. (C). 1995. pap. 19.99 (*0-415-91055-2*, B4259) Routledge.

Performer-Audience Connection: Emotion to Metaphor in Dance & Society. Judith L. Hanna. LC 83-6720. (Illus.). 283p. (C). 1983. text 25.00 (*0-292-76478-2*) U of Tex Pr.

Performer Prepares. Robert Caldwell. 158p. 1990. 19.95 (*1-877761-26-5*) Pst.

Performer Prepares: A Guide to Song Preparation for Actors, Singers & Dancers. David Craig. (Acting Ser.). 324p. 1993. 21.95 (*1-55783-133-5*) Applause Theatre Bk Pubs.

Performer Prepares: A Guide to Song Preparation for Actors, Singers & Dancers. David Craig. 324p. 1999. pap. 18.95 (*1-55783-395-8*) Applause Theatre Bk Pubs.

Performers, 7 bks. (American Women of Achievement Ser.). (YA). (gr. 5 up). 1990. 139.65 (*0-7910-3501-8*) Chelsea Hse.

Performers. Liz Sonneborn. LC 94-25587. (American Indian Lives Ser.). (Illus.). 128p. (YA). (gr. 5-12). 1995. 19.95 (*0-8160-3045-6*) Facts on File.

*__Performers: Actors, Directors, Dancers & Musicians.__ Karen Covington. LC 00-26831. (Remarkable Women Ser.). (Illus.). (J). 2000. pap. 27.12 (*0-8172-5727-6*) Raintree Steck-V.

Performers at the Purple. Photos by Barney Stein. (Illus.). 144p. 1998. pap. 18.95 (*0-9660471-0-9*) Curfran Prods.

Performers' Car. Joanne Barkan. (Circus Train Come Aboard Bks.). (Illus.). 12p. (J). (ps). 1993. pap. 3.50 (*0-689-71673-7*) Aladdin.

Performer's Goal Book: A Step by Step Plan for Achieving Your Dream. Susan Tucker & Kim Copeland. 1998. pap., wbk. ed. 16.95 (*0-9651705-4-3*) Jrny Publng.

Performer's Guide Through Historical Keyboard Tunings. 2nd rev. ed. Martin B. Tittle. LC 87-27095. (Illus.). 80p. (C). 1988. pap. 9.95 (*0-942479-01-7*); lib. bdg. 14.95 (*0-942479-02-5*) Anderson Pr.

*__Performer's Guide to Medieval Music.__ Ross W. Duffin. 640p. 2000. 39.95 (*0-253-33752-6*) Ind U Pr.

Performer's Guide to Renaissance Music. Ed. by Jeffery T. Kite-Powell. (Early Music America, Studies in Historical Performance Practice: Performer's Guides to Early Music). 400p. 1994. 40.00 (*0-02-871231-5*, Schirmer Books) Mac Lib Ref.

Performer's Guide to Seventeenth-Century Music. Stewart Carter. LC 97-1310. (Early Music America Ser.). 1997. 42.00 (*0-02-870492-4*, Schirmer Books) Mac Lib Ref.

*__Performer's Guide to the Collaborative Creative Process.__ Sheila Kerrigan. 176p. 2001. pap. 18.95 (*0-325-00311-4*) Heinemann.

Performer's Guide to the Keyboard Partitas of J. S. Bach. Fernando Valenti. 144p. (C). 1990. 35.00 (*0-300-04312-0*) Yale U Pr.

Performer's Guide to Theater Songs: The Best Solo Songs for Study, Auditions & Revues. Brian Hall. 1991. write for info. (*0-318-68568-X*) Rovey Res Per Arts.

Performer's Guide to Theater Songs: The Best Solo Songs for Study, Auditions & Revues, Vol. 1. Brian Hall. 201p. (YA). (gr. 5-12). 1991. spiral bd. write for info. (*0-9627847-0-2*) Rovey Res Per Arts.

Performer's Guide to Theater Songs: The Best Solo Songs for Study, Auditions & Revues, Vol. I. Brian Hall. 200p. 1994. spiral bd. 22.50 (*0-9627847-1-0*) Rovey Res Per Arts.

Performer's Guide to Theater Songs: The Best Solo Songs for Study, Auditions & Revues, Vol. II. Brian Hall. 200p. 1994. spiral bd. 22.50 (*0-9627847-2-9*) Rovey Res Per Arts.

Performer's Guide to Theatre Songs Set, Vols. I & II, Vols. I & II. 3rd ed. Brian Hall. 1996. spiral bd. 55.00 (*0-9627847-5-3*) Rovey Res Per Arts.

Performer's Guide to Theatre Songs Vol. I: The Best Solo Songs for Females for Study, Auditions & Revues. 3rd ed. Brian Hall. 202p. 1996. spiral bd. 30.00 (*0-9627847-3-7*) Rovey Res Per Arts.

Performer's Guide to Theatre Songs Vol. II: The Best Solo Songs for Males for Study, Auditions & Revues. 3rd ed. Brian Hall. 182p. 1996. spiral bd. 30.00 (*0-9627847-4-5*) Rovey Res Per Arts.

*__Performing O'Neil: Conversations with Actors.__ Yvonne Shafer. 1999. text 24.95 (*0-312-22626-8*) St Martin.

Performing a Safety Certification for Avionics Components & Systems. (Illus.). 1995. 95.00 (*1-885544-07-3*) Avionics Comm.

*__Performing Acoustic Music.__ Ed. by Jeffrey P. Rodgers. LC 00-23689. (Acoustic Guitar Guides Ser.). (Illus.). 104p. 2000. pap. 19.95 (*1-890490-22-9*) String Letter.

Performing Action: Artistry in Human Behavior & Social Research. Joseph R. Gusfield. 295p. 2000. 39.95 (*0-7658-0016-0*) Transaction Pubs.

Performing America: Cultural Nationalism in American Theater. Ed. by Jeffrey D. Mason & J. Ellen Gainor. LC 99-6219. (Theater: Theory - Text - Performance Ser.). (Illus.). 256p. 1999. text 44.50 (*0-472-10985-5*, 10985) U of Mich Pr.

*__Performing an Operational & Strategic Assessment for a Medical Practice.__ Reed Tinsley & Joey Havens. 256p. 1999. 89.00 (*0-471-29964-2*) Wiley.

Performing & Visual Arts Writing & Reviewing. W. U. McCoy. 182p. (Orig.). (C). 1992. pap. text 24.00 (*0-8191-8774-7*) U Pr of Amer.

Performing Appraisal. 2nd ed. (Open Learning Super Ser.). 1991. pap. text 26.00 (*0-08-041540-7*, Pergamon Pr) Elsevier.

Performing Artists. Richard Rennert. (Profiles of Great Black Americans Ser.). (J). 1994. 12.15 (*0-606-08004-X*) Turtleback.

Performing Artists. Ed. by Richard S. Rennert. (Profiles of Great Black Americans Ser.). (Illus.). 64p. (J). (gr. 3 up). 1993. lib. bdg. 15.95 (*0-7910-2069-X*, Chelsea Juniors) Chelsea Hse.

Performing Artists. Ed. by Richard S. Rennert. (Profiles of Great Black Americans Ser.). (Illus.). 64p. (J). (gr. 3 up). 1994. pap. 5.95 (*0-7910-2070-3*) Chelsea Hse.

Performing Artists: From Alvin Ailey to Julia Roberts, 3 vols. Molly Severson. LC 96-137391. (Illus.). 710p. 1995. text 69.00 (*0-8103-9868-0*, UXL) Gale.

Performing Arts: A Guide to the Reference Literature. Linda K. Simons. LC 93-31465. (Reference Sources in the Humanities Ser.). ix, 244p. 1994. lib. bdg. 42.00 (*0-87287-982-8*) Libs Unl.

Performing Arts: A Step into Our Theatrical Past. 1991. lib. bdg. 89.00 (*0-8490-4360-3*) Gordon Pr.

Performing Arts: Motion Pictures. Ed. by Iris Newsom. (Performing Arts Ser.). (Illus.). 269p. 49.00 (*0-8444-0937-5*) Lib Congress.

Performing Arts: Music & Dance. Ed. by John Blacking & Joann W. Kealiinohomoku. (World Anthropology Ser.). (Illus.). xii, 346p. 1979. text 57.70 (*90-279-7870-0*) Mouton.

Performing Arts: The Economic Dilemma. William J. Baumol & William G. Bowen. (Modern Revivals in Economics Ser.). 600p. 1993. 82.95 (*0-7512-0106-5*, Pub. by Gregg Revivals) Ashgate Pub Co.

Performing Arts & American Society. American Assembly Staff. LC 78-1404. 224p. reprint ed. pap. 69.50 (*0-608-18393-8*, 202986500066) Bks Demand.

Performing Arts at the Library of Congress. Ed. by Iris Newsom. 167p. 1992. 26.00 (*0-16-036054-4*, 030-001-00136-9) Lib Congress.

Performing Arts Business Encyclopedia: For Individuals & Organizations As Well As the Attorneys & Business Advisors Who Assist Them. Leonard Duboff. LC 95-83003. 256p. 1996. pap. 19.95 (*1-880559-42-0*) Allworth Pr.

*__Performing Arts Careers.__ rev. ed. Bonnie Bjorguine Bekken. (Opportunities in . . . Ser.). 2000. 14.95 (*0-658-00470-0*, VGM Career) NTC Contemp Pub Co.

Performing Arts College Guide. 2nd ed. Carole J. Everett. 320p. 1994. per. 20.00 (*0-671-88417-4*) Prntice Hall Bks.

*__Performing Arts Directory, 2000.__ Richard Gottlieb. 2000. 175.00 (*1-891482-67-X*) Grey Hse Pub.

Performing Arts, 1876-1981: Including an International Index of Current Serial Publications. 1656p. 1981. 175.00 (*0-8352-1372-2*) Bowker.

Performing Arts in American Society. Ed. by W. McNeil Lowry. LC 78-1404. (American Assembly Books Ser.). 1978. 10.95 (*0-13-657155-7*); pap. 4.95 (*0-13-657148-4*) Am Assembly.

Performing Arts Information, Nineteen Seventy-Five to Nineteen Eighty: A Bibliography of Reference Works. Paula Elliot. 1982. pap. 4.00 (*0-317-00776-9*) KSU.

Performing Arts Major's College Guide. Carole J. Everett. 288p. 1992. pap. 20.00 (*0-13-086679-2*, Arco) Macmillan Gen Ref.

Performing Arts Major's College Guide. 3rd ed. Carole Everett. 320p. 1998. 19.95 (*0-02-861913-7*, Arc) IDG Bks.

Performing Arts Management & Law, 2 vols. Joseph Taubman. Incl. Vol. 1. Vol. 1, Student Edition. 20.00 Vol. 2. Vol. 2, Student Edition., **2 vols., 16 & 17** 45.00 write for info. (*0-318-60262-8*) Law Arts.

Performing Arts Management & Law. Joseph Taubman. 1974. suppl. ed. 20.00 (*0-317-67907-4*) Law Arts.

Performing Arts Management & Law, 7 vols. Joseph Taubman. LC 74-189328. 1978. 420.00 (*0-685-02951-4*); 495.00 (*0-88238-055-9*) Law Arts.

Performing Arts Management & Law, 2 vols. Joseph Taubman. LC 74-189328. 1981. suppl. ed. 125.00 (*0-685-25465-8*); suppl. ed. 20.00 (*0-317-67909-0*) Law Arts.

Performing Arts Management & Law, Vol. 1. Joseph Taubman. text 60.00 (*0-317-67904-X*) Law Arts.

Performing Arts Management & Law, Vol. 2. Joseph Taubman. text 60.00 (*0-317-67906-6*) Law Arts.

Performing Arts Management & Law: Student Edition, 2 vols., 1. Joseph Taubman. write for info. (*0-318-62743-4*) Law Arts.

Performing Arts Management & Law: Student Edition, 2 vols., 2. Joseph Taubman. write for info. (*0-318-62744-2*) Law Arts.

Performing Arts Management & Law: Student Edition, 2 vols., Set, Vols. 1 & 2. Joseph Taubman. 45.00 (*0-317-67912-0*) Law Arts.

Performing Arts Management & Law Forms Vol. 1: Motion Pictures. Joseph Taubman. 60.00 (*0-317-67913-9*) Law Arts.

Performing Arts Management & Law Forms Vol. 3: Theatre & Dance. Joseph Taubman. 60.00 (*0-317-67917-1*) Law Arts.

Performing Arts Management & Law Forms Vol. 4: Live Performance, Managers, & Agents, Miscellaneous & Book Publishing. 252p. 1989. 60.00 (*0-317-67918-X*) Law Arts.

Performing Arts Management & Law Forms Vol. 5: Sound Recording & Sound. 60.00 (*0-317-67919-8*) Law Arts.

Performing Arts Management & Law Forms Vol. 6: Music Publishing. 60.00 (*0-317-67920-1*) Law Arts.

Performing Arts Management & Law Forms Vol. 7: Litigation. 60.00 (*0-317-67921-X*) Law Arts.

Performing Arts Management & Law Forms Vols. 1 & 2: Motion Pictures & Television. Joseph Taubman. suppl. ed. 20.00 (*0-317-67922-8*) Law Arts.

Performing Arts Management & Law Forms Vols. 2: Television. Joseph Taubman. 60.00 (*0-317-67916-3*) Law Arts.

Performing Arts Management & Law, 1973-1980, 9 vols., Set. Joseph Taubman. 495.00 (*0-317-67903-1*) Law Arts.

Performing Arts Medicine. 2nd ed. Robert T. Sataloff. 1998. 49.95 (*1-56593-965-4*, 1910) Singular Publishing.

Performing Arts Medicine. 2nd ed. Ed. by Robert T. Sataloff et al. (Illus.). 688p. 1998. pap. 289.95 (*1-56593-982-4*, 1944) Thomson Learn.

Performing Arts of Kerala. Ed. by Mallika Sarabhai. (Illus.). 188p. 1994. 85.00 (*81-85822-20-4*, Pub. by Mapin Pubng) Antique Collect.

Performing Arts Resources, Vol. 2. Bowser et al. Ed. by Ted Perry. LC 75-646287. 132p. 1976. 25.00 (*0-910482-73-X*) Theatre Lib.

Performing Arts Resources, Vol. 3. Ed. by Ted Perry. 175p. 1976. 25.00 (*0-910482-84-5*) Theatre Lib.

Performing Arts Resources, Vol. 4. Ed. by Mary C. Henderson. LC 75-646287. 116p. 1978. 25.00 (*0-932610-00-5*) Theatre Lib.

Performing Arts Resources, Vol. 6. Ed. by Mary C. Henderson. LC 75-646287. 115p. 1980. 25.00 (*0-932610-02-1*) Theatre Lib.

Performing Arts Resources, Vol. 10. Intro. by Barbara Cohen-Stratyner & Ginnine Cocuzza. LC 75-646287. (Illus.). 85p. 1985. 25.00 (*0-932610-07-2*) Theatre Lib.

Performing Arts Resources Vol. 5: Recollections of O. Smith, Comedian. O. Smith. Ed. by Mary C. Henderson. LC 75-646287. (Illus.). 72p. 1979. 25.00 (*0-932610-01-3*) Theatre Lib.

Performing Arts Resources Vol. 7: Lazzi: The Comic Routines of Commedia Dell' Arte. Mel Gordon. Ed. by Ginnine Cocuzza & Barbara N. Cohen-Stratyner. Tr. by Claudio Vincentini. LC 75-646287. (Illus.). 82p. 1981. 25.00 (*0-932610-03-X*) Theatre Lib.

Performing Arts Resources Vol. 8: Stage Design: Papers from the 15th International Congress of SIBMAS. Ed. by Ginnine Cocuzza & Barbara N. Cohen-Stratyner. (Illus.). xix, 94p. (C). 1983. 25.00 (*0-932610-04-8*) Theatre Lib.

Performing Arts Resources Vol. 11: Scenes & Machines from the 18th Century: The Stagecraft of Jacopo Fabris & Cityoen Boullet. Jacopo Fabris & Cityoen Boullet. Ed. by Barbara Cohen-Stratyner. Tr. & Intro. by C. Thomas Ault. (Performing Arts Resources Ser.). (Illus.). 146p. 1986. 25.00 (*0-932610-08-0*) Theatre Lib.

Performing Arts Resources Vol. 12: Topical Bibliographies of the American Theatre. Intro. by Barbara Cohen-Stratyner. LC 75-646287. (Performing Arts Resources Ser.). 195p. 1987. 25.00 (*0-932610-09-9*) Theatre Lib.

Performing Arts Resources Vol. 13: The Drews & the Barrymores, a Dynasty of Actors. Intro. by Barbara Cohen-Stratyner. LC 75-646287. (Illus.). 161p. 1988. 25.00 (*0-932610-10-2*) Theatre Lib.

Performing Arts Resources Vol. 14: Performances in Periodicals. Intro. by Barbara Cohen-Stratyner. LC 75-646287. (Illus.). 142p. 1989. 25.00 (*0-932610-11-0*) Theatre Lib.

Performing Arts Resources Vol. 15: Arts & Access: Management Issues for Performing Arts Collections. Intro. by Barbara Cohen-Stratyner. LC 75-646287. 102p. 1990. 25.00 (*0-932610-12-9*, Z6935.P46) Theatre Lib.

Performing Arts Resources Vol. 16: Taking the Pledge & Other Public Amusements. Intro. by Barbara Cohen-Stratyner. LC 75-646287. (Illus.). 129p. 1991. 25.00 (*0-932610-13-7*) Theatre Lib.

Performing Arts Resources Vol. 19: Exhibitions & Collections. Lauren Bufferd et al. LC 75-646287. (Illus.). 96p. 1995. 25.00 (*0-932610-16-1*) Theatre Lib.

Performing Arts Resources Vol. 21: Pleasure Gardens. Katy Matheson & Geraldine Duclow. Ed. by Stephen M. Vallillo & Maryann Chach. LC 75-646287. Date not set. 30.00 (*0-932610-18-8*) Theatre Lib.

Performing Arts Resources Vols. 17 & 18: The New York Hippodrome: A Complete Chronology of Performances from 1905-1939. Milton Epstein. LC 75-646287. (Performing Arts Resources Ser.). 535p. 1994. 50.00 (0-932610-14-5) Theatre Lib.

Performing Arts Resources, Vol. 9: An Essay on Stage Performance, A Translation of Franz Lang's Dissertatio de Actione Scenica (1727) by Alfred Siemon Golding. Franz Lang. Ed. by Gininne Cocuzza & Barbarba N. Cohen-Stratyner. Tr. by Alfred S. Golding from LAT. LC 75-646287.Tr. of Dissertatio de Actione Scenica. (Illus.). 128p. 1984. reprint ed. 25.00 (0-932610-06-4) Theatre Lib.

Performing Arts Yearbook for Europe, 1997. Ed. by Rod Fisher & Martin Huber. 708p. 1997. pap. 78.95 (1-873463-15-4) Am for the Arts.

Performing Asian America: Race & Ethnicity on the Contemporary Stage. Josephine Lee. (Asian American History & Culture Ser.). (Illus.). 256p. (C). 1998. pap. text 19.95 (1-56639-637-9) Temple U Pr.

Performing Asian America: Race & Ethnicity on the Contemporary Stage. Josephine D. Lee. LC 96-31621. (Asian American History & Culture Ser.). (Illus.). 256p. 1997. 34.95 (1-56639-502-X) Temple U Pr.

Performing Bach's Keyboard Music. George A. Kocheuitsky. (Illus.). 168p. 1996. write for info. (1-57784-000-3) Pro-Am Music.

Performing Baroque Music. Mary Cyr. 256p. (C). 1998. pap. 25.95 (1-84014-659-1, Pub. by Ashgate Pub) Ashgate Pub Co.

Performing Baroque Music. Mary Cyr. (Illus.). 254p. 1998. pap. 19.95 (1-57467-043-3, Amadeus Pr) Timber.

Performing Beethoven. Ed. by Robin Stowell. LC 93-31379. (Studies in Performance Practice: Vol. 4). (Illus.). 260p. (C). 1994. text 69.95 (0-521-41644-2) Cambridge U Pr.

*Performing Blackness: Enactments of African-American Modernism. Kimberly W. Benston. LC 99-54173. 336p. 2000. pap. 24.99 (0-415-00949-9) Routledge.

*Performing Blackness: Enactments of African-American Modernism. Kimberly W. Benston. LC 99-54173. 336p. (C). 2000. text 75.00 (0-415-00948-0) Routledge.

Performing Body. Dobrila De Negri. (Illus.). 48p. 1998. pap. 19.95 (88-8158-160-4, Pub. by Charta) Dist Art Pubs.

Performing Brecht. Margaret Eddershaw. LC 95-52603. 200p. (C). 1996. 85.00 (0-415-08010-X); pap. 24.99 (0-415-08011-8) Routledge.

*Performing Chekhov. David Allen. LC 99-31944. 280p. (C). 1999. pap. 24.99 (0-415-18935-7) Routledge.

Performing Collaborative Research with Nontraditional Military Suppliers. Kenneth P. Horn et al. LC 96-53000. (Illus.). xxi, 63p. 1997. pap. text 15.00 (0-8330-2483-3, MR-830-A) Rand Corp.

Performing Complex Calculations. Larry Mikulecky. 1990. mass mkt. 9.00 (0-13-852245-6) P-H.

Performing Definitions: Two Genres of Insult in Old Norse Literature. Karen Swenson. (SCAND Ser.: Vol. 3). 150p. 1992. 55.00 (0-938100-87-4) Camden Hse.

Performing Drama - Dramatizing Performance: Alternative Theater & the Dramatic Text. Michael J. Vanden Heuvel. Ed. by Enoch Brater. (Theater: Theory - Text - Performance Ser.). (Illus.). 272p. (C). 1993. pap. text 18.95 (0-472-08248-5, 08248) U of Mich Pr.

Performing Dreams: Discourses of Immortality among the Xavante of Central Brazil. Laura R. Graham. (Illus.). 304p. 1998. pap. 16.95 (0-292-72803-4) U of Tex Pr.

Performing Feminisms: Feminist Critical Theory & Theatre. Ed. by Sue-Ellen Case. LC 89-24602. 320p. 1990. pap. text 15.95 (0-8018-3969-6) Johns Hopkins.

Performing Gender: Theories, Texts & Contexts. Ed. by Shannon Hengen. LC 98-218189. (Studies in Humor & Gender: Vol. 4). 308p. 1998. text 32.00 (90-5699-539-1); pap. text 15.00 (90-5699-540-5) Gordon & Breach.

Performing Haydn's "The Creation" Reconstructing the Earliest Renditions. A. Peter Brown. LC 84-43053. (Music: Scholarship & Performance Ser.). (Illus.). 142p. 1986. 12.95 (0-253-38820-1) Ind U Pr.

*Performing History: Theatrical Representations of the Past in Contemporary Theatre. Freddie Rokem. (Studies in Theatre History & Culture). (Illus.). 264p. 2000. text 42.95 (0-87745-737-9) U of Iowa Pr.

Performing Hybridity. Ed. by May Joseph & Jennifer N. Fink. LC 98-43817. (Illus.). 256p. 1999. 49.95 (0-8166-3010-0); pap. 19.95 (0-8166-3011-9) U of Minn Pr.

Performing Identities on the States of Quebec. Jill R. MacDougall. LC 95-22893. (Francophone Cultures & Literatures Ser.: Vol. 15). (Illus.). X, 231p. (C). 1998. text 47.95 (0-8204-3004-8) P Lang Pubng.

*Performing in Extreme Environments: Training & Working in Intense Heat, Frigid Cold, under Water, High Altitude, Air Pollution. Lawrence E. Armstrong. LC 99-38795. 344p. 2000. 19.95 (0-88011-837-7) Human Kinetics.

Performing in Japan: Amusing Anecdotes & Helpful Hints. Brad Zupp. 80p. (Orig.). 1994. pap. text 11.95 (0-9641002-5-8) Oasis Pubng.

Performing in Musicals. Elaine A. Novak. 304p. 1988. 28.00 (0-02-871731-7, Schirmer Books) Mac Lib Ref.

*Performing Indianness in New York City: Desi on the Hudson. Suntin Sunder Muhni. LC 99-14194. 200p. 1999. 50.00 (0-8153-3372-2) Garland.

*Performing la Mestiza: Textual Representations of Lesbians of Color & the Negotiation of Identities. Ellen M. Gil-Gomez. LC 99-55077. (Literary Criticism & Cultural Theory Ser.). 160p. 2000. 60.00 (0-8153-3647-0) Garland.

Performing Literature: An Introduction. 2nd ed. Hopkins & Long. 224p. (C). 1997. per. 28.95 (0-7872-3666-7, 41366601) Kendall-Hunt.

*Performing Live: Aesthetic Alternatives for the Ends of Art. Richard Schusterman. 2000. 39.95 (0-8014-3753-9); pap. 17.95 (0-8014-8650-5) Cornell U Pr.

Performing Live with MIDI: A Percussionist's (& Anybody Else's) Guide to the Fundamentals. William L. Cahn. 100p. 1993. spiral bd. 15.00 (0-9634060-1-9) HoneyRock.

Performing Medieval Music Drama. Audrey E. Davidson et al. LC 97-41852. 1997. pap. 5.00 (1-879288-96-6) Medieval Inst.

*Performing Miracles & Healing: A Biblical Guide to Developing a Christ-Like Supernatural. Roger Sapp. 340p. 2000. pap. 14.95 (0-9662085-5-2) All Nations Pubs.

Performing Music: Shared Concerns. Jonathan Dunsby. (Illus.). 112p. 1996. reprint ed. pap. text 13.95 (0-19-816642-7) OUP.

Performing Nostalgia: Shifting Shakespeare & the Contemporary Past. Susan Bennett. LC 95-8574. 208p. (C). 1995. pap. 25.99 (0-415-07326-X) Routledge.

Performing Nostalgia: Shifting Shakespeare & the Contemporary Past. Susan Bennett. LC 95-8574. 208p. (C). (gr. 13). 1995. 90.00 (0-415-07325-1) Routledge.

*Performing Parables: Religious Folk Tales, Legends & Fables for Readers Theatre. Matthew Powell. (Illus.). 80p. 2000. pap. 19.95 (0-89390-502-X) Resource Pubns.

Performing Pedagogy: Toward an Art of Politics. Charles R. Garoian. LC 98-54276. (SUNY Series, Interruptions). (Illus.). 336p. (C). 1999. pap. text 20.95 (0-7914-4324-8) State U NY Pr.

*Performing Pedagogy: Toward an Art of Politics. Charles R. Garoian. LC 98-54276. (SUNY Series, Interruptions). (Illus.). 336p. (C). 1999. text 62.50 (0-7914-4323-X) State U NY Pr.

Performing Postmodernity. Ursula Maynard. X, 92p. (C). 1995. text 36.95 (0-8204-2661-X) P Lang Pubng.

*Performing Processes. Roberta Mock. 128p. 2000. pap. 24.95 (1-84150-010-0, Pub. by Intellect) Intl Spec Bk.

Performing Psychology: A Postmodern Culture of the Mind. Lois Holzman. LC 98-42970. 1999. 80.00 (0-415-92204-6); pap. 22.99 (0-415-92205-4) Routledge.

Performing Rites: On the Value of Popular Music. Simon Frith. 360p. 1996. 27.95 (0-674-66195-8) HUP.

Performing Rites: On the Value of Popular Music. Simon Frith. 368p. 1998. pap. text 16.95 (0-674-66196-6) HUP.

Performing Self: Compositions & Decompositions in the Languages of Contemporary Life. Richard Poirier. LC 91-37410. 224p. (Orig.). (C). 1992. reprint ed. text 40.00 (0-8135-1794-X); reprint ed. pap. text 16.00 (0-8135-1795-8) Rutgers U Pr.

Performing Texts. Ed. by Michael Issacharoff & Robin F. Jones. LC 87-19769. 157p. 1987. text 32.50 (0-8122-8073-3) U of Pa Pr.

Performing Texts. Ed. by Michael Issacharoff & Robin F. Jones. LC 87-19769. 165p. reprint ed. pap. 51.20 (0-608-07409-8, 206763600009) Bks Demand.

Performing the Body/Performing the Text. Amelia Jones. 1999. pap. 24.99 (0-415-19060-6) Routledge.

Performing the Music of Henry Purcell. Ed. by Michael Burden. (Illus.). 320p. 1996. text 85.00 (0-19-816442-4) OUP.

Performing the Past: A Study of Israeli Settlement Museums. Tamar Katriel. LC 96-6601. (Everyday Communication Ser.). 176p. 1997. pap. 19.50 (0-8058-1658-5); text 45.00 (0-8058-1657-7) L Erlbaum Assocs.

Performing the Pilgrims: A Study of Ethnohistorical Role-Playing at Plimoth Plantation. Stephen E. Snow. LC 92-45587. (Performance Studies). (Illus.). 250p. 1993. text 37.50 (0-87805-570-3) U Pr of Miss.

Performing the Power Sector in Africa. M. R. Bhagavan. 1999. pap. text 29.95 (1-85649-668-6) Zed Books.

Performing the Renewal of Community: Indigenous Easter Rituals in North Mexico & Southwest United States. Ed. by Rosamond B. Spicer & N. Ross Crumrine. LC 96-43376. 624p. 1997. 74.50 (0-7618-0578-8); pap. 58.50 (0-7618-0579-6) U Pr of Amer.

Performing the Word: African American Poetry As Vernacular Culture. Fahamisha P. Brown. LC 98-46273. 225p. (C). 1999. pap. text 17.00 (0-8135-2632-9) Rutgers U Pr.

Performing the Word: African American Poetry As Vernacular Culture. Fahamisha P. Brown. LC 98-46273. 225p. (C). 1999. text 48.00 (0-8135-2631-0) Rutgers U Pr.

Performing the Word: Preaching As Theater. Jana Childers. LC 98-28390. 192p. 1998. pap. 16.00 (0-687-07423-1) Abingdon.

Performing Twentieth-Century Music: A Handbook for Conductors & Instrumentalists. Arthur Weisberg. 1996. pap. text 11.00 (0-300-06655-4) Yale U Pr.

Performing under Pressure: Mental Techniques for Handling Pressure in Tennis. Marie Dalloway. LC 97-76203. 155p. 1997. pap. text 18.00 (0-9634933-5-3) Optimal Perf.

*Performing Virginity & Testing Chastity in the Middle Ages. Kathleen C. Kelly. LC 99-40601. (Research in Medieval Studies). 240p. 2000. 85.00 (0-415-22181-1) Routledge.

*Performing with Understanding: The Challenge of the National Standards for Music Education. Bennett Reimer. 216p. (Orig.). 2000. pap. 26.00 (1-56545-118-X, 1672) MENC.

Performing Without a Stage: The Art of Literary Translation. Robert Wechsler. LC 97-35268. 320p. 1998. 21.95 (0-945774-38-9, PN241.W43) Catbird Pr.

*Performing Women. Alison Oddey. LC 99-39867. 299p. 1999. text 39.95 (0-312-22909-7) St Martin.

Performing Women: Female Characters, Male Playwrights, & the Modern Stage. Gay G. Cima. (Illus.). 240p. 1993. text 39.95 (0-8014-2874-2) Cornell U Pr.

Performing Women: Female Characters, Male Playwrights, & the Modern Stage. Gay G. Cima. (Illus.). 248p. 1996. pap. text 15.95 (0-8014-8337-9) Cornell U Pr.

*Perfrmnc Measrmt&control. Simons. 348p. 1999. 59.00 (0-13-021945-2) P-H.

Perfume. Caroline B. Cooney. 176p. (YA). (gr. 7-9). 1992. pap. 3.50 (0-590-45402-1, Point) Scholastic Inc.

Perfume. National Geographic Staff. LC 98-23082. 176p. 1998. per. 34.50 (0-7922-7378-8) Natl Geog.

Perfume. Patrick Suskind. (SPA.). 1998. pap. 10.50 (84-322-1500-7, Pub. by E Seix Barral) Continental Bk.

*Perfume. Patrick Suskind. 2000. reprint ed. pap. 12.00 (0-375-72584-9) Vin Bks.

Perfume: Historia de la Asesino. Patrick Suskind. (SPA.). 1998. pap. 10.50 (84-322-1524-4, Pub. by E Seix Barral) Continental Bk.

Perfume: Perfume. Patrick Suskind. 1997. pap. 7.95 (84-322-0531-1, Pub. by E Seix Barral) Continental Bk.

Perfume: The Story of a Murderer. Patrick Suskind. 320p. 1991. per. 14.00 (0-671-74960-9, WSP) PB.

*Perfume: The Ultimate Guide to the World's Finest Fragrances. Nigel Groom. 1999. 24.95 (0-7624-0606-2) Running Pr.

Perfume Album. 2nd ed. Jill Jessee. LC 74-13588. 194p. 1974. reprint ed. 22.50 (0-88275-216-2) Krieger.

Perfume & Tears. Ben Bohnhorst. 24p. (Orig.). 1995. pap. text 6.00 (1-56439-050-0) Ridgeway.

Perfume Atomizer: An Object with Atmosphere. Tirza T. Latimer. LC 91-67016. (Illus.). 168p. 1992. text 69.95 (0-88740-382-4) Schiffer.

Perfume Bottle Auction Five Vol. V: May 6, 1995. Ed. by Randall B. Monsen. (FRE & GER., Illus.). 96p. 1995. pap. 35.00 (0-9636102-3-6) Monsen & Baer.

Perfume Bottle Auction Four Vol. IV: May 14, 1994. Ed. by Randall B. Monsen. (Illus.). 80p. 1994. pap. 29.00 (0-9636102-1-X) Monsen & Baer.

Perfume Bottle Auction Three: May 1, 1993. Monsen & Baer Staff. (Illus.). 80p. 1993. pap. 28.00 (0-9636102-0-1) Monsen & Baer.

Perfume Bottles: A Collector's Guide. Madeleine Marsh. (Miller's Collector's Guide Ser.). (Illus.). 64p. 1999. 11.95 (1-84000-162-3) Antique Collect.

Perfume Bottles: Profumi Mignon. Carla Bordignon. LC 94-45122. (Bella Cosa Ser.).Tr. of Profumi Mignon. (ENG & ITA., Illus.). 144p. 1995. pap. 12.95 (0-8118-1061-5) Chronicle Bks.

Perfume Bottles Remembered, Vol. I. Emily H. Killian. LC 88-92939. (Illus.). 50p. (Orig.). 1989. 19.95 (0-685-44605-0) E H Killian.

Perfume, Cologne & Scent Bottles. Jacquelyne North. LC 86-61205. (Illus.). 243p. 1986. 69.95 (0-88740-072-8) Schiffer.

Perfume, Cologne & Scent Bottles. 3rd rev. ed. Jacquelyne North. (Illus.). 244p. 1999. 69.95 (0-7643-0714-2) Schiffer.

Perfume Handbook. Nigel Groom. LC 92-15183. 323p. (C). (gr. 13). 1992. text 75.50 (0-412-46320-2, A7478) Chapman & Hall.

Perfume Industry of Mycenaean Pylos. Cynthia W. Shelmerdine. (Studies in Mediterranean Archaeology & Literature: No. 34). (Illus.). 195p. (Orig.). 1985. pap. 42.50 (91-86098-30-6, Pub. by P Astroms) Coronet Bks.

Perfume Legends: French Feminine Fragrances. Michael Edwards. (Illus.). 296p. 1996. 120.00 (0-646-27794-4) Crescent Hse.

Perfume of Egypt & Other Stories. C. W. Leabeater. 270p. 1993. reprint ed. pap. 16.95 (1-56459-381-9) Kessinger Pub.

Perfume of Egypt & Other Weird Stories. C. W. Leadbeater. 306p. 1996. reprint ed. spiral bd. 18.50 (0-7873-1070-0) Hlth Research.

Perfume of Eros: A Fifth Avenue Incident. Edgar E. Saltus. LC 75-182713. reprint ed. 37.50 (0-404-05536-2) AMS Pr.

Perfume of Eros: A Fifth Avenue Incident. Edgar E. Saltus. (BCL1-PS American Literature Ser.). 222p. 1992. reprint ed. lib. bdg. 79.00 (0-7812-6849-4) Rprt Serv.

Perfume of Memory. Michelle Nikly. LC 98-33108. (Illus.). 40p. (J). (ps-3). 1999. 16.95 (0-439-08206-4, Pub. by Scholastic Inc) Penguin Putnam.

Perfume of Paradise. large type ed. Jennifer Blake. LC 98-22080. (Large Print Book Ser.). 511 p. 1998. 24.95 (1-56895-604-5) Wheeler Pub.

Perfume of Roses. large type ed. Julia Ashwell. (Linford Romance Library). 240p. 1992. pap. 16.99 (0-7089-7285-3, Linford) Ulverscroft.

Perfume of the Desert: Inspirations from Sufi Wisdom. Andrew Harvey & Eryk Hanut. LC 98-44314. (Illus.). 192p. 1999. pap. 15.00 (0-8356-0767-4, Quest) Theos Pub Hse.

Perfume of the Lady in Black. Gaston Leroux. 1975. lib. bdg. 16.70 (0-89966-138-6) Buccaneer Bks.

Perfume of the Lady in Black. Gaston Leroux. Ed. by Terry Hale. Tr. by Anon from FRE. (Dedalus European Classics Ser.). 326p. 1998. pap. 13.99 (1-873982-98-4, Pub. by Dedalus) Subterranean Co.

*Perfume of the Lady in Black, Set. unabridged ed. Gaston Leroux. 1998. 47.95 incl. audio (1-55685-589-3) Audio Bk Con.

*Perfume Power: The Values of Scent & Aroma. Joules Taylor. 2000. pap. 10.95 (1-902809-29-7) Allison & Busby.

Perfumed Garden. 25.00 (0-85435-363-1) C W Daniel.

Perfumed Garden. Umar ibn Muhammad Nafzawi. Tr. by Richard F. Burton. (Illus.). 96p. 1992. pap. 19.95 (0-89281-443-8, Park St Pr) Inner Tradit.

Perfumed Garden. Umar ibn Muhammad Nafzawi. Tr. by Richard F. Burton from ARA. LC 98-37553. 224p. 1999. mass mkt. 5.95 (0-451-52659-7, Sig Classics) NAL.

*Perfumed Garden of Sensual Desire. Muhammad Al-Nafzawi. Tr. by Jim Colville. 81p. 1999. 110.00 (0-7103-0644-X, Pub. by Kegan Paul Intl) Col U Pr.

Perfumed Garden of the Shaykh Nefzawi. Tr. by Richard Burton. 1992. reprint ed. lib. bdg. 21.95 (0-89968-296-0, Lghtyr Pr) Buccaneer Bks.

Perfumed Scorpion. Idries Shah. 193p. 1982. 25.00 (0-900860-62-6, Pub. by Octagon Pr) ISHK.

Perfumery: Practice & Principles. Robert R. Calkin & J. Stephen Jellinek. 304p. 1994. 79.95 (0-471-58934-9) Wiley.

Perfumery & Eau de Toilette in Hong Kong: A Strategic Entry Report, 1996. Compiled by Icon Group International Staff. (Illus.). 125p. 1999. ring bd. 1250.00 incl. audio compact disk (0-7418-1114-6) Icon Grp.

Perfumery & Flavoring Materials: Annual Review Articles, 1945-1982. Paul Z. Bedoukian. LC TP0983.. 443p. reprint ed. pap. 137.40 (0-7837-2433-0, 204258100005) Bks Demand.

Perfumery, Cosmetic & Toiletry Chemical Markets in the European Community: Perfumery & Cosmetic Chemicals. Market Intelligence Staff. 189p. 1994. 2750.00 (1-56753-606-9) Frost & Sullivan.

Perfumery, Cosmetic & Toiletry Chemical Markets in the European Community: Toiletry Chemicals. Market Intelligence Staff. 186p. 1994. 2750.00 (1-56753-605-0) Frost & Sullivan.

Perfumery Technology. 2nd ed. F. V. Wells. LC 80-42130. 449p. 1981. text 154.00 (0-470-26958-8) P-H.

Perfumes & Fragrances As a Business - A Report. Frieda Carrol Communication Staff. 60p. 1998. ring bd. 49.95 (1-890928-37-2) Frieda Carrol.

Perfumes & Their Production. Edward S. Maurer. LC 59-17885. 328p. reprint ed. pap. 101.70 (0-608-12620-9, 202542400043) Bks Demand.

Perfumes, Potions & Fanciful Formulas. Kelly Reno. Ed. by Sally Smith. 112p. Date not set. 14.95 (1-891437-00-3, V900) Victorian Essence.

Perfumes, Spashes & Colognes: Discovering & Crafting Your Personal Fragrances. Casey Makela & Nancy M. Booth. Ed. by Deborah Balmuth. LC 97-26374. (Herbal Body Ser.). (Illus.). 171p. 1997. pap. 14.95 (0-88266-985-0, Storey Pub) Storey Bks.

*Pergamon. Wolfgang Radt. 2000. pap. 75.00 (0-226-70244-8) U Ch Pr.

Pergamon: Gesammelte Aufsaetze. (Pergamenische Forschungen Ser.: Vol. 1). (Illus.). 222p. (C). 1972. 120.00 (3-11-001829-2) De Gruyter.

Pergamon: The Telephos Frieze from the Great Altar, Vol. 1. Ed. by Renee Dreyfus & Ellen Schraudolph. LC 95-83343. (Illus.). 120p. 1996. pap. 29.95 (0-88401-089-9) U of Tex Pr.

Pergamon: The Telephos Frieze from the Great Altar, Vol. 2. Ed. by Renee Dreyfus & Ellen Schraudolph. (Illus.). 224p. 1996. pap. 39.95 (0-88401-091-0) U of Tex Pr.

Pergamon - Citadel of the Gods: Archaeological Record, Literary Description & Religious Development. Ed. by Helmut Koester. LC 98-39838. 496p. 1998. 45.00 (1-56338-261-X) TPI PA.

Pergamon Dictionary of Perfect Spelling. 2nd ed. C. Maxwell. LC 78-40291. 335p. 1978. pap. 11.75 (0-08-022865-8, Pergamon Pr) Elsevier.

Pergola: Poems from Hollywood. Mark Dunster. 11p. 1998. pap. 5.00 (0-89642-484-7) Linden Pubs.

Perhaps She'll Die. John B. Spencer. LC 97-129135. (Bloodlines Ser.). 154p. 1997. pap. 12.95 (1-899344-14-4, Pub. by Do-Not Pr) Dufour.

Perhaps This Is a Rescue Fantasy. Heather Fuller. 1997. pap. 10.00 (1-890311-00-6) Edge Bks.

Perhaps to Kill. large type ed. Howard C. Davis. (Mystery Ser.). 1994. pap. 16.99 (0-7089-7626-3, Linford) Ulverscroft.

Perhaps Women (1931) Sherwood Anderson. LC 76-105301. 144p. 1970. reprint ed. 12.50 (0-911858-05-9) Appel.

Peri-Tethyan Platforms: Proceedings of the IFP-Peritethys Research Conference, Aries, France, 1993. Ed. by F. Roure. LC 95-153171. (Illus.). 294p. 1994. 480.00 (2-7108-0679-7, Pub. by Edits Technip) Enfield Pubs NH.

Peri-Tothyan Platforms: Proceedings of the IFP-Peritethys Research Conference, Aries, France, 1993. Editions Technip Staff. 1994. 480.00 (2-7708-0673-4, Pub. by Edits Technip) Enfield Pubs NH.

*PeriAnesthesia CheckMate. Angela G. Clarkson & Anne M. Larson. (Critical Care CheckMate Ser.). (Illus.). 134p. 1998. write for info. (0-9700484-1-6) NNCC.

Periapts, Amulets, Inflections: Three Books of Poems. Mark Dunster. 1978. pap. 4.00 (0-89642-002-7) Linden Pubs.

Peribanez & the Comendador of Ocana. Lope de Vega. Ed. by Lloyd. (Hispanic Classics Ser.). 1990. pap. 25.00 (0-85668-439-2, Pub. by Aris & Phillips) David Brown.

Peribanez & the Comendador of Ocana. Lope de Vega. Ed. by James Lloyd. (Hispanic Classics Ser.). (Illus.). 247p. 1990. 59.95 (0-85668-438-4, Pub. by Aris & Phillips) David Brown.

Peribanez y Comendador de Ocana. 18th ed. Lope de Vega. 200p. 1991. pap. 12.95 (0-7859-5166-0) Fr & Eur.

Peribanez y el Comendador de Ocana. Lope de Vega. Ed. by Jose M. Ruano De La Haza. (Nueva Austral Ser.: No. 225). (SPA.). 1991. pap. text 11.95 (84-239-7225-9) Elliots Bks.

Peribanez y el Comendador de Ocana. Lope de Vega. (SPA.). 221p. 1978. 12.95 (0-8288-7028-4, 8437601703) Fr & Eur.

An Asterisk (*) at the beginning of an entry indicates that the title is appearing for the first time.

Peribanez y el Comendador de Ocana. unabridged ed. Lope de Vega. (SPA.). pap. 5.95 (*84-410-0045-X*, Pub. by Bookking Intl) Distribks Inc.

Peribanez y el Comendador de Ocana. 2nd ed. Lope de Vega. (SPA.). 152p. 1997. pap. text 4.00 (*1-56328-071-X*) Edit Plaza Mayor.

Peribanez y el Comendador de Ocana, No. 43. Lope de Vega. (SPA.). 221p. 1978. 12.95 (*0-8288-8558-3*) Fr & Eur.

Pericardial Disease. Ed. by P. S. Reddy et al. LC 81-23539. (Illus.). 391p. reprint ed. pap. 121.30 (*0-7837-7097-9*, 204692600004) Bks Demand.

Pericardial Disease: New Insights & Old Dilemmas. Ed. by J. Soler-Soler et al. (Developments in Cardiovascular Medicine Ser.). (C). 1990. text 186.00 (*0-7923-0510-8*) Kluwer Academic.

Pericardial Tissue As a Cardiac Valve Substitute: Proceedings of a Symposium. Ed. & Illus. by Silent Partners, Inc. Staff. 221p. (Orig.). 1989. pap. write for info. (*1-878353-10-1*) Silent Partners.

Pericardium: A Comprehensive Textbook. David H. Spodick. LC 96-43173. (Fundamental & Clinical Oncology Ser.: Vol. 27). (Illus.). 496p. 1996. text 180.00 (*0-8247-9316-1*) Dekker.

***Pericias: A Grammar Workbook.** Daniel Whitaker & Antoniet Gallegos-Ruiz. 184p. (C). 1999. per. 25.95 (*0-7872-6480-6*) Kendall-Hunt.

Pericles. William Shakespeare. (BBC Television Plays Ser.). 1984. pap. 5.95 (*0-563-20143-6*, Pub. by BBC) Parkwest Pubns.

Pericles. William Shakespeare. Ed. by Doreen DelVecchio & Antony Hammond. LC 97-1358. (New Cambridge Shakespeare Ser.). (Illus.). 228p. (C). 1998. text 44.95 (*0-521-22907-3*); pap. text 12.95 (*0-521-29710-9*) Cambridge U Pr.

Pericles. William Shakespeare. 1988. pap. 3.99 (*0-671-66914-1*) Folger.

Pericles. William Shakespeare. Ed. by A. L. Rowse. LC 87-14752. (Modern Text with Introduction Ser.). 118p. (C). 1987. pap. text 3.45 (*0-8191-3945-9*) U Pr of Amer.

Pericles. large type ed. William Shakespeare. (Charnwood Large Print Ser.). 1991. pap. 24.95 (*0-7089-4536-8*, Charnwood) Ulverscroft.

Pericles. unabridged ed. William Shakespeare. 1988. audio 30.00 (*0-694-50759-8*, SWC 237, Caedmon) HarperAudio.

Pericles. 2nd ed. William Shakespeare. (English). 1997. pap. 11.95 (*0-17-443585-1*) Thomson Learn.

Pericles. 3rd ed. William Shakespeare. Ed. by F. D. Hoeniger. (Arden Shakespeare Ser.). 1963. pap. 10.95 (*0-416-27850-7*, NO. 2487) Routledge.

Pericles. 3rd ed. William Shakespeare. Ed. by F. D. Hoeniger. (Arden Shakespeare Ser.). 1963. text 45.00 (*0-416-47570-1*, NO. 2486) Thomson Learn.

Pericles. 3rd ed. William Shakespeare. (English Ser.). (C). 1998. mass mkt. 9.95 (*0-17-443531-2*) Wadsworth Pub.

Pericles: Critical Essays. Laurilyn Harris. Ed. by Phillip C. Kolin. (Shakespeare Criticism Ser.). 400p. 1997. text 60.00 (*0-8153-1182-6*) Garland.

***Pericles: Critical Essays.** David Skeele. LC 00-39335. (Reference Library of the Humanities). 2000. write for info. (*0-8153-3891-0*) Garland.

Pericles & His Circle. Anthony J. Podlecki. LC 97-19131. 264p. (C). 1998. 65.00 (*0-415-06794-4*) Routledge.

Pericles' Citizenship Law of 451-450 B. C. Cynthia Patterson. 25.00 (*0-405-14046-0*) Ayer.

Pericles' Citizenship Law of 451-450 B. C. Cynthia Patterson. 1981. 27.95 (*0-88143-022-6*) Ayer.

Pericles, Cymbeline & Two Noble Kinsmen. William Shakespeare. Ed. by Ernest Schanzer et al. 1986. mass mkt. 5.95 (*0-451-52265-6*, Sig Classics) NAL.

Pericles of Athens & the Birth of Democracy. Donald Kagan. 350p. 1990. 29.95 (*0-02-916825-2*) Free Pr.

Pericles on Stage: Political Comedy in Aristophanes' Early Plays. Michael Vickers. LC 96-16242. 1997. 37.50 (*0-292-78727-8*) U of Tex Pr.

Pericles, Prince of Tyre. William Shakespeare. Ed. by Philip Edwards. (New Penguin Shakespeare Ser.). 240p. 1981. pap. 5.95 (*0-14-070729-8*, Penguin Classics) Viking Penguin.

Periclus. Mark Dunster. 22p. 1995. pap. 5.00 (*0-89642-276-3*) Linden Pubs.

Pericopsis Elata, (Afrormosia) P. Howland. 1979. 40.00 (*0-85074-049-5*) St Mut.

***Perictione in Colophon: Reflections on the Aesthetic Way of Life.** Roger Scruton. LC 99-50296. 224p. 2000. 30.00 (*1-890318-59-0*, Pub. by St Augustines Pr) Chicago Distribution Ctr.

Periculum Latinum. William D. Curtis. 87p. (J). 1998. spiral bd. 13.50 (*0-939507-53-6*, L8) Amer Classical.

Pericyclic Reactions. Ian Fleming. (Illus.). 96p. (C). 1998. pap. text 12.95 (*0-19-850307-5*) OUP.

Peridiniens Parasites: Morphologie, Reproduction, Ethologie. Edouard Chatton. (Archives de Zoologic Experimentale et Generale Ser.: Vol. 59, 1920). 475p. 1975. reprint ed. 168.30 (*3-87429-100-6*, 002582, Pub. by Koeltz Sci Bks) Lubrecht & Cramer.

Peridontal Instrumentation. 3rd ed. Pattison. (C). 2002. spiral bd. 39.95 (*0-8385-7690-7*) Appleton & Lange.

Peridontology & Its Origins up to 1980. Arthur J. Held. 240p. 1989. 79.50 (*0-8176-1955-0*) Birkhauser.

Perigee Visual Dictionary of Signing: An A-to-Z Guide to Over 1,250 Signs of American Sign Language. 3rd expanded rev. ed. Rod R. Butterworth. Ed. by Mickey Flodin. LC 95-1380. 512p. (Orig.). 1995. pap. 15.95 (*0-399-51952-1*, Perigee Bks) Berkley Pub.

Periglacial Environment. 2nd ed. Hugh French. 1996. pap. 28.47 (*0-582-30536-5*, Pub. by Addison-Wesley) Longman.

Periglacial Processes & Landforms. Ed. by E. A. Koster & H. M. French. (Annals of Geomorphology Ser.: Suppl. 71). (Illus.). 156p. 1988. pap. text 82.50 (*3-443-21071-6*, Pub. by Gebruder Borntraeger) Balogh.

Periglaciation of Britain. Colin K. Ballantyne & Charles Harris. LC 92-43477. (Illus.). 340p. (C). 1994. text 105.00 (*0-521-32459-9*) Cambridge U Pr.

Periglaciation of Britain. Colin K. Ballantyne & Charles Harris. LC 92-43477. (Illus.). 340p. (C). 1995. pap. text 44.95 (*0-521-31016-4*) Cambridge U Pr.

Periglazial: Geomorphologie und Klima in Gletscherfreien, Kalten Regionen. O. R. Weise. viii, 178p. 1983. 20.00 (*3-443-01019-9*, Pub. by Gebruder Borntraeger) Balogh.

Periglaziale Deckschichten und Boeden im Bayerischen Wald und Seinen Randgebieten als Geogene Grundlagen Landschaftsoekologischer Forschung im Bereich Naturnaher Waldstandorte. J. Voelkel. (Zeitschrift fuer Geomorphologie - Annals of Geomorphology Ser.: Supplementband 96). (GER., Illus.). vi, 301p. 1995. pap. 88.00 (*3-443-21096-1*, Pub. by Gebruder Borntraeger) Balogh.

Perigord-Quercy Green Guide. Michelin Staff. (FRE.). 252p. 1989. pap. 17.95 (*0-7859-7234-X*, 2067003704) Fr & Eur.

Perigord-Quercy Green Guide: France (Guides Regionaux) 4th ed. Michelin Staff. (Green Guides Ser.). (FRE., Illus.). 1997. per. 20.00 (*2-06-037004-3*, 370) Michelin.

***Perihelion.** Cordell Caudron. 85p. 2000. 17.95 (*0-7541-1294-2*, Pub. by Minerva Pr) Unity Dist.

Peril at Delphi. Rob MacGregor. (Indiana Jones Ser.: No. 1). 272p. 1991. mass mkt. 4.99 (*0-553-28931-4*) Bantam.

Peril at End House. Agatha Christie. (Hercule Poirot Mystery Ser.). 1991. 10.60 (*0-606-12477-2*, Pub. by Turtleback) Demco.

Peril at Sea. Jim Gibbs. LC 86-61292. (Illus.). 224p. 1986. pap. 19.95 (*0-88740-066-3*) Schiffer.

Peril at Sea & Salvage: A Guide for Masters. ICS Staff & OCIMF Staff. 1996. pap. 200.00 (*1-85609-095-7*, Pub. by Witherby & Co) St Mut.

Peril at Sea & Salvage: A Guide for Masters. 2nd ed. ICS Staff & OCIMF Staff. 1982. 110.00 (*0-7855-1775-8*, Pub. by Witherby & Co) St Mut.

Peril at Sea & Salvage: A Guide for Masters. 3rd ed. ICS Staff & OCIMF Staff. (C). 1988. 110.00 (*0-948691-46-8*, Pub. by Witherby & Co) St Mut.

Peril at Stone Hall. large type ed. Jane Corby. (Linford Mystery Library). 272p. 1993. pap. 16.99 (*0-7089-7427-9*, Linford) Ulverscroft.

Peril at Thunder Ridge. Anthony Dorame. (Illus.). 128p. (YA). (gr. 7-11). 1993. pap. 9.95 (*1-878610-26-0*) Red Crane Bks.

Peril in Evans Woods: A Story about the Meaning of Easter. Louise Mandrell. 1993. 12.95 (*1-56530-053-X*) Summit TX.

Peril in Panama. Richard A. Delgaudio. (Illus.). 128p. 1998. write for info. (*0-9658348-1-6*) Nat Sec Ctr.

Peril in Paradise. Diana Mars. (Desire Ser.). 1995. per. 2.99 (*0-373-05906-X*, 1-05906-2) Silhouette.

Peril in the Amazon, Vol. 4. W. Howard Stuart. (T-Rex Ser.). 1996. pap. text 6.95 (*0-9696800-3-1*) YOUTH AC.

***Peril in the Bessledorf Parachute Factory.** Phyllis Reynolds Naylor. LC 98-36606. 160p. (J). (gr. 4-6). 2000. 16.00 (*0-689-82539-0*) Atheneum Yung Read.

Peril of Faith. 2nd ed. Martin L. Bard. LC 89-49523. 175p. (Orig.). 1989. pap. 6.50 (*0-910309-64-7*, 5012) Am Atheist.

Peril on the Road. Judith A. Green. (Adult Learner Ser.). (Illus.). 220p. 1985. pap. text 8.98 (*0-89061-427-X*, Jamestwn Pub) NTC Contemp Pub Co.

Peril to the Nerve: Glaucoma & Clinical Neuro-Ophthalmology, Proceedings of the 45th Annual Symposium, New Orleans, La, U. S. A., April 25-28, 1996. New Orleans Academy of Ophthalmology Staff et al. LC 97-13859. (Illus.). xiii, 283p. 1998. 94.50 (*90-6299-153-X*) Kugler Pubns.

***Peril Trek.** (Western Trio Ser.). 2000. 30.00 (*0-7862-2112-7*) Mac Lib Ref.

***Peril Trek: A Western Trio.** large type ed. 2001. 30.00 (*0-7838-8724-8*, G K Hall Lrg Type) Mac Lib Ref.

Peril under the Palms. K. K. Beck. 208p. 1989. 18.95 (*0-8027-5715-4*) Walker & Co.

Perilla: The Genus Perilla. Ed. by He-Ci Yu et al. (Medicinal & Aromatic Plants-Industrial Profiles Ser.: Vol. 2). 177p. 1997. text 58.00 (*90-5702-171-4*, Harwood Acad Pubs) Gordon & Breach.

Perilous Advantage: The Best of Natalie Clifford Barney. Natalie C. Barney. Tr. by Anna Livia. LC 92-13831. (Illus.). 224p. (C). 1992. pap. 10.95 (*0-934678-38-3*); text 19.95 (*0-934678-45-6*) New Victoria Pubs.

Perilous Attraction. Dawn A. Poore. 1996. mass mkt. 4.50 (*0-8217-5339-8*, Zebra Kensgtn) Kensgtn Pub Corp.

Perilous Balance: Poems. Arnold S. Stein. LC 45-4997. 57p. reprint ed. pap. 30.00 (*0-608-14147-X*, 205591800039) Bks Demand.

Perilous Balance: The Tragic Genius of Swift, Johnson & Sterne. Walter B. Watkins. reprint ed. 49.00 (*0-403-03066-8*) Somerset Pub.

Perilous Bargain. Jane Peart. LC 96-29629. (Edgecliffe Manor Mysteries Ser.). 240p. 1997. pap. 9.99 (*0-8007-5626-6*) Revell.

***Perilous Bargain.** large type ed. Jane Peart. LC 99-58075. (Edgecliffe Manor Mysteries Ser.). 2000. 24.95 (*0-7862-2380-4*) Thorndike Pr.

Perilous Calling: The Hazards of Psychotherapy Practice. Michael B. Sussman. LC 94-34135. 332p. 1995. 77.50 (*0-471-05657-X*) Wiley.

Perilous Cemetery (L'Atre Perilleux) Ed. & Tr. by Nancy B. Black. LC 94-18392. (Garland Library of Medieval Literature: Vol. 104A). (Illus.). 480p. 1994. text 20.00 (*0-8153-1897-9*) Garland.

Perilous Chastity: Women & Illness in Pre-Enlightenment Art & Medicine. Laurinda S. Dixon. LC 94-34911. (Illus.). 320p. 1995. text 57.50 (*0-8014-3026-7*); pap. text 25.00 (*0-8014-8215-1*) Cornell U Pr.

***Perilous Eden.** Heather Graham. LC 00-34397. 2001. write for info. (*0-7862-2616-1*) Thorndike Pr.

Perilous Eden. Heather G. Pozzessere. (Mira Bks.). 1997. per. 5.50 (*1-55166-296-5*, 1-66296-4, Mira Bks) Harlequin Bks.

***Perilous Engagement.** Emily Hendrickson. (Regency Romance Ser.). 2000. mass mkt. 4.99 (*0-451-20071-3*, Sig) NAL.

Perilous Forest. Michael Trout et al. Ed. by Sam Shirley. (Pendragon Roleplaying Game System Ser.). (Illus.). 128p. 1992. pap. 18.95 (*0-933635-44-3*, 2712) Chaosium.

Perilous Friends. Carole Epstein. LC 96-23322. (Barbara Simons Mystery Ser.). 224p. 1996. 21.95 (*0-8027-3287-9*) Walker & Co.

Perilous Frontier. Thomas J. Barfield. 1992. pap. 29.95 (*1-55786-324-5*) Blackwell Pubs.

Perilous Hunt: Symbols in Hispanic & European Balladry. Edith R. Rogers. LC 79-4010. (Studies in Romance Languages: No. 22). 187p. reprint ed. pap. 58.00 (*0-7837-5787-5*, 204545300006) Bks Demand.

***Perilous Journey.** large type ed. Caroline Joyce. 208p. 1999. pap. 18.99 (*0-7089-5469-3*, Linford) Ulverscroft.

Perilous Journey. large type ed. Joyce Stranger. 432p. 31.99 (*0-7089-4029-3*) Ulverscroft.

Perilous Journey: The Mennonite Brethren in Russia, 1860-1910. John B. Toews. (Perspectives on Mennonite Life & Thought Ser.: Vol. 5). 94p. (Orig.). 1988. pap. 9.95 (*0-919797-78-4*) Kindred Prods.

Perilous Journey of the Donner Party. Marian Calabro. LC 98-29610. (Illus.). 192p. (YA). (gr. 5 up). 1999. 20.00 (*0-395-86610-3*, Clarion Bks) HM.

Perilous Knowledge: The Human Genome Project & Its Implications. Tom Wilkie. LC 93-26352. 1994. 23.00 (*0-520-08553-1*, Pub. by U CA Pr) Cal Prin Full Svc.

***Perilous Memories: The Asia-Pacific War(s)** Ed. by Takashi Fujitani et al. LC 00-27441. (Illus.). 472p. 2000. lib. bdg. 59.95 (*0-8223-2532-2*) Duke.

***Perilous Memories: The Asia-Pacific War(s)** Takashi Fujitani et al. LC 00-27441. (Illus.). 472p. 2000. pap. 19.95 (*0-8223-2564-0*) Duke.

Perilous Missions: Civil Air Transport & CIA Covert Operations in Asia. William M. Leary. LC 83-3554. (Illus.). 294p. 1984. pap. 91.20 (*0-608-05135-7*, 206569600005) Bks Demand.

Perilous Options: Special Operations As an Instrument of U. S. Foreign Policy. Lucien S. Vandenbroucke. (Illus.). 272p. 1993. text 55.00 (*0-19-504591-2*) OUP.

Perilous Passage: A Narrative of the Montana Gold Rush, 1862-1863. Edwin R. Purple. Ed. by Kenneth N. Owens. LC 95-33196. (Illus.). x, 211p. 1995. 25.95 (*0-917298-35-7*); pap. 15.95 (*0-917298-37-3*) MT Hist Soc.

Perilous Pursuits: Our Obsession with Significance. Joseph M. Stowell. 18.99 (*0-8024-7842-5*, 247) Moody.

Perilous Quest: Image, Myth, & Prophecy in the Narratives of Victor Hugo. Richard B. Grant. LC 68-20494. 268p. reprint ed. pap. 83.10 (*0-608-12734-5*, 202339100033) Bks Demand.

Perilous Refuge. large type ed. Patricia Wilson. 285p. 1991. reprint ed. 18.95 (*0-263-12808-3*) Mac Lib Ref.

Perilous Relations: A Barbara Simons Mystery. Carole Epstein. LC 97-30885. (Barbara Simons Mystery Ser.). 276p. 1997. 22.95 (*0-8027-3309-3*) Walker & Co.

Perilous Road. William O. Steele. LC 58-6820. 192p. (J). (gr. 3-7). 1990. pap. 6.00 (*0-15-260647-5*, Odyssey) Harcourt.

Perilous Road. William O. Steele. 1990. 11.10 (*0-606-04503-1*, Pub. by Turtleback) Demco.

Perilous Road: A Study Guide. Brian Yansky. Ed. by J. Friedland & R. Kessler. (Novel-Ties Ser.). (J). (gr. 4-6). 1998. pap. text, student ed. 15.95 (*0-7675-0313-9*) Lrn Links.

Perilous Seas. Dave Duncan. 352p. (Orig.). 1991. mass mkt. 5.99 (*0-345-36630-1*, Del Rey) Ballantine Pub Grp.

Perilous States: Conversations on Culture, Politics, & Nation. Ed. by George E. Marcus. (Late Editions: Cultural Studies for the End of the Century). (Illus.). 400p. 1993. pap. 20.95 (*0-226-50447-6*) U Ch Pr.

Perilous States: Conversations on Culture, Politics, & Nation. Ed. by George E. Marcus. (Late Editions: Cultural Studies for the End of the Century). (Illus.). 360p. 1995. lib. bdg. 60.50 (*0-226-50446-8*) U Ch Pr.

Perilous Times: A Study in Eschatological Evil. Kenneth L. Gentry, Jr. LC 98-16008. 374p. 1998. 24.95 (*1-57309-249-5*, Christ Univ Pr) Intl Scholars.

Perils & Pitfalls of Practice see Nothing Happens Next: Responses to Questions about Meditation

Perils & Prospects of Southern Black Leadership: Gordon Blaine Hancock, 1884-1970. Raymond Gavins. LC 92-37510. 236p. 1993. pap. text 17.95 (*0-8223-1339-1*) Duke.

Perils & Prospects of Southern Black Leadership: Gordon Blaine Hancock, 1884-1970. Raymond Gavins. LC 76-44090. 231p. reprint ed. pap. 71.70 (*0-608-15273-0*, 205220900060) Bks Demand.

Perils of a Restless Planet: Scientific Perspectives on Natural Disasters. Ernest Zebrowski, Jr. LC 96-37794. (Illus.). 320p. (C). 1997. text 24.95 (*0-521-57374-2*) Cambridge U Pr.

Perils of a Restless Planet: Scientific Perspectives on Natural Disasters. Ernest Zebrowski, Jr. (Illus.). 320p. 1999. pap. 16.95 (*0-521-65488-2*) Cambridge U Pr.

Perils of Anarchy: Contemporary Realism & International Security. Ed. by Michael E. Brown et al. LC 94-24041. (International Security Reader Ser.). 541p. 1995. pap. text 24.50 (*0-262-52202-0*) MIT Pr.

Perils of Democracy. P. C. Alexander. LC 95-901699. ix, 304p. 1995. 25.00 (*81-7039-208-X*, Pub. by Somaiya Publns) Nataraj Bks.

***Perils of Engine #49.** Florence B. Smith. 225p. 2000. pap. 7.00 (*1-893463-34-6*) F B Smith.

Perils of Geography. Helen Humphreys. LC 96-108177. 64p. 1995. pap. 11.95 (*0-919626-83-1*, Pub. by Brick Bks) Genl Dist Srvs.

Perils of Imprudent Writing: How to Watch What You Write & Stay Out of Court. Edward P. Ahrens, Jr. LC 97-90626. (Illus.). 96p. 1997. pap. 15.95 (*0-9658381-3-7*) Van Buren.

***Perils of Imprudent Writing: How to Watch What You Write & Stay Out of Court.** 2nd rev. ed. Edward P. Ahrens, Jr. LC 99-71362. (Illus.). 144p. 1999. pap. 16.95 (*0-9658381-6-1*) Van Buren.

Perils of Lulu. William Gleason. 1981. pap. 5.25 (*0-87129-323-4*, P51) Dramatic Pub.

Perils of Napoleon. C. Brian Kelly. 50p. (Orig.). 1993. pap. 5.95 (*0-9624875-5-4*) Montpelier Pub.

Perils of Partners: How to Protect Yourself Against Crooked, Conniving & Incompetent Partners. Irwin Gray. LC 97-91020. (Illus.). 265p. (Orig.). 1997. pap. 18.95 (*0-9659626-0-1*) Smith-J Pubs.

Perils of Patriotism: John Joseph Henry & the American Attack on Quebec, 1775 see Lancaster County During the American Revolution Series

***Perils of Pauline Peach.** A. North. 1998. mass mkt. 6.95 (*0-7472-5776-0*, Pub. by Headline Bk Pub) Trafalgar.

Perils of Perestroika: Viewpoints from the Soviet Press, 1989-91. Ed. & Tr. by Isaac J. Tarasulo from RUS. LC 91-20267. 348p. 1992. 45.00 (*0-8420-2380-1*); pap. text 17.95 (*0-8420-2398-4*) Scholarly Res Inc.

Perils of Personal Computing. Edward Yourdon. LC 84-52806. (Illus.). 136p. (Orig.). 1985. pap. 14.95 (*0-917072-50-2*, Yourdon) P-H.

***Perils of Poncho.** Mark Randall Schoettmer. 200p. 2002. pap. 12.99 (*1-57532-279-X*, Pub. by Press-Tige Pub) Baker & Taylor.

Perils of Power: Crises in American Foreign Relations since World War II. Timothy P. Maga. 189p. (Orig.). 1995. pap. 10.99 (*0-936285-25-7*) U New Haven Pr.

Perils of Progress. Ashton. 2000. text 19.95 (*1-85649-697-X*, Pub. by Zed Books) St Martin.

Perils of Progress: The Health & Environmental Hazards of Modern Technology & What You Can Do about It. John Ashton & Ron Laura. 360p. 1999. text 55.00 (*1-85649-696-1*) St Martin.

Perils of Progress: The Health & Environmental Hazards of Modern Technology, & What You Can Do about Them. John Ashton & Ron Laura. 350p. 1997. pap. 29.95 (*0-86840-488-8*, Pub. by New South Wales Univ Pr) Intl Spec Bk.

Perils of Prosperity: Nineteen Fourteen to Nineteen Thirty-Two. William E. Leuchtenburg. LC 58-5680. (Chicago History of American Civilization Ser.). 1995. pap. text 9.95 (*0-226-47369-4*, CHAC12) U Ch Pr.

Perils of Prosperity, 1914-1932. 2nd ed. William E. Leuchtenburg. LC 92-44912. (Chicago History of American Civilization Ser.). 325p. (C). 1993. pap. text 13.00 (*0-226-47371-6*) U Ch Pr.

Perils of Prosperity, 1914-1932. 2nd ed. William E. Leuchtenburg. LC 92-44912. (Chicago History of American Civilization Ser.). 320p. (C). 1997. lib. bdg. 33.00 (*0-226-47370-8*) U Ch Pr.

Perils of Quadrant X. J. J. Gardner. (Lost in Space Ser.). (J). (gr. 3-7). 1998. pap. 3.99 (*0-590-18940-9*, Apple Paperbacks) Scholastic Inc.

Perils of Regulation: A Market-Process Approach. Israel M. Kirzner. (LEC Occasional Paper). 1979. pap. 1.00 (*0-916770-09-5*) Law & Econ U Miami.

Perils of the Night. Patricia Hall. LC 98-47259. 224p. 1998. text 22.95 (*0-312-19996-1*) St Martin.

Perils of the Ocean & Wilderness: Narrative of Shipwreck & Indian Captivity. John G. Shea. (Reprints in History Ser.). reprint ed. lib. bdg. 42.00 (*0-697-00057-5*) Irvington.

Perils of the Soul: Ancient Wisdom & the New Age. John R. Haule. LC 98-50576. 288p. 1999. pap. 14.95 (*1-57863-107-6*) Weiser.

Perils of the Young Kingdoms. Fred Behrendt et al. Ed. by Les Brooks. (Stormbringer Roleplaying Game System Ser.). (Illus.). 128p. (Orig.). (YA). (gr. 7 up). 1991. pap. 18.95 (*0-933635-82-6*, 2113) Chaosium.

Perils of Timesetting. Colin D. Standish & Russell R. Standish. 82p. 1992. pap. 7.95 (*0-923309-00-4*) Hartland Pubns.

***Perilymphatic Fistula.** Ed. by J. P. Guyot. (Illus.). 48p. 1999. 25.25 (*3-8055-6909-2*) S Karger.

Perimedes the Blacke-Smith, Ciceronis, Amor; or Tullies Loue, the Royal Exchange, 1589-1590 see Life & Complete Works in Prose & Verse of Robert Greene

Perimenopausal & Geriatric Gynecology. Hugh R. Barber. 640p. 1988. 75.00 (*0-02-305880-3*, Macmillan Coll) P-H.

Perimenopause. Bernard J. Cortese. LC 98-26905. (Vital Information Ser.). 112p. 1998. pap. 11.95 (*0-89594-914-8*) Crossing Pr.

Perimenopause. U. S. A. Serono Symposia Staff. Ed. by Rogerio Lobo. LC 97-16665. (Sereno Symposia U. S. A. Ser.). (Illus.). 376p. 1997. 135.00 (*0-387-94967-4*) Spr-Verlag.

Perimenopause: Changes in Women's Health after 35. James E. Huston & L. Darlene Lanka. LC 97-66079. (Illus.). 416p. (Orig.). 1997. pap. 16.95 (*1-57224-085-7*) New Harbinger.

Perimenopause: Preparing for the Change. Nancy Teaff & Kim W. Wiley. LC 94-21795. 352p. 1994. 22.95 (*1-55958-579-X*) Prima Pub.

P

An Asterisk (*) at the beginning of an entry indicates that the title is appearing for the first time.

Perimenopause - Preparing for the Change: A Guide to the Early Stages of Menopause & Beyond. Kim W. Wiley & Nancy Teaff. 224p. 1996. per. 12.95 (*0-7615-0437-0*) Prima Pub.

Perimenopause - Preparing for the Change: A Guide to the Early Stages of Menopause & Beyond. 2nd rev. ed. Nancy L. Teaff & Kim W. Wiley. LC 99-35567. 204p. 2000. pap. 14.00 (*0-7615-1928-9*) Prima Pub.

Perimenopause Handbook. Carol Turkington. LC 97-51584. 192p. 1998. pap. 14.95 (*0-8092-2935-8*, 293580, Contemporary Bks) NTC Contemp Pub Co.

***Perimenopause the Natural Way.** Deborah Gordon & Kerri Brenner. LC 00-35907. (Women's Natural Health Ser.). 256p. 2000. pap. 14.95 (*0-471-37960-3*) Wiley.

Perimeter. Marianne Hancock. Ed. by Jane Weinberger. LC 92-6212. 224p. 1993. pap. 7.95 (*0-932433-99-5*) Windswept Hse.

Perimeter Action Ships - Markings & Insignia Packet. Todd Guenther. 1994. 9.95 (*0-9656016-3-3*) Mstrcom Data.

Perimeter of Light: Writings about the Vietnam War. Ed. by Vivian V. Balfour. (Illus.). 280p. (Orig.). 1992. pap. 15.95 (*0-89823-140-X*) New Rivers Pr.

Perimetres Irrigues en Droit Compare Africain (Madagascar, Maroc, Niger, Senegal, Tunisie) (FRE.). 152p. 1992. 25.00 (*92-5-203171-5*, Pub. by FAO) Bernan Associates.

Perimetric Standards & Perimetric Glossary. Ed. by International Council of Ophthalmology Staff. 1979. text 85.50 (*90-6193-600-4*) Kluwer Academic.

Perimetrie see Perimetry & Its Clinical Correlations

Perimetry & Its Clinical Correlations. Bernhard J. Lachenmayr & Patrick M. Vivell.Tr. of Perimetrie. 320p. 1993. 99.00 (*0-86577-480-3*) Thieme Med Pubs.

Perimetry, Principles, Technique & Interpretation. Carl Ellenberger. LC 80-18629. (Illus.). 124p. 1980. reprint ed. pap. 38.50 (*0-608-00601-7*, 206118800007) Bks Demand.

Perimetry Update, 1988-1989. Ed. by A. Heijl. LC 89-2267. (Illus.). 477p. 1989. lib. bdg. 143.00 (*90-6299-051-7*, Pub. by Kugler) Kugler Pubns.

Perimetry Update, 1994-1995: Proceedings of the XIth International Perimetric Society Meeting, Washington, D. C., U. S. A., July 3-7, 1994. International Perimetric Society Staff. Ed. by Richard P. Mills & Michael Wall. LC 94-46786. 1994. 126.00 (*90-6299-121-1*) Kugler Pubns.

Perimetry Update, 1996 to 1997. Ed. by Michael Wall. (Illus.). xi, 477p. 1997. 143.00 (*90-6299-139-4*) Kugler Pubns.

Perimetry Update, 1990-1991. Ed. by R. P. Mills & A. Heijl. LC 91-14629. (Illus.). 585p. 1991. lib. bdg. 171.50 (*90-6299-075-4*, Pub. by Kugler) Kugler Pubns.

Perimetry Update, 1992-1993. Ed. by Richard P. Mills. LC 93-1932. 609p. 1993. 171.50 (*90-6299-094-0*) Kugler Pubns.

Perinatal & Multigeneration Carcinogenesis. Ed. by N. P. Napalkov et al. (IARC Scientific Publications: No. 96). (Illus.). 462p. 1989. pap. 110.00 (*92-832-1196-0*) OUP.

Perinatal & Pediatric HIV. Wara. 1998. text. write for info. (*0-7216-6767-8*, W B Saunders Co) Harcrt Hlth Sci Grp.

Perinatal & Pediatric Respiratory Care. Barnhart. 1995. 450.00 (*0-7216-6742-2*) Harcourt.

Perinatal & Pediatric Respiratory Care. Ed. by Sherry L. Barnhart & Michael P. Czervinske. (Illus.). 1995. teacher ed. write for info. (*0-7216-5942-X*, W B Saunders Co) Harcrt Hlth Sci Grp.

Perinatal & Pediatric Respiratory Care. Sherry L. Barnhart & Michael P. Czervinske. LC 94-25347. (Pediatric Respiratory Diseases Ser.). (Illus.). 656p. 1995. text 53.00 (*0-7216-6739-2*, W B Saunders Co) Harcrt Hlth Sci Grp.

Perinatal & Pediatric Respiratory Care. Ed. by Sherry L. Barnhart & Michael P. Czervinske. (Illus.). 1995. pap. text, wbk. ed. 16.95 (*0-7216-6741-4*, W B Saunders Co) Harcrt Hlth Sci Grp.

Perinatal Asphyxia. Ed. by J. Haddad & E. Saliba. LC 92-48789. 1993. 149.00 (*0-387-56135-8*) Spr-Verlag.

Perinatal Asphyxia. A. Lacoius-Petruccelli. (Illus.). 188p. (C). 1987. text 65.00 (*0-306-42358-8*, Kluwer Plenum) Kluwer Academic.

Perinatal Audit: A Report Produced for the European Association of Perinatal Medicine. Ed. by P. M. Dunn & G. McIlwaine. 44p. 1996. pap. 18.00 (*1-85070-933-5*) Prthnon Pub.

Perinatal Autopsy Manual. Marie Valdes-Dapena & Dale Huff. (Illus.). 98p. (C). 1993. pap. text 40.00 (*0-7881-0176-5*) DIANE Pub.

Perinatal Autopsy Manual. 2nd ed. Valdez-Depena & Huff. (Illus.). 98p. 1983. reprint ed. pap. text 15.00 (*1-881041-38-7*) Am Registry Path.

Perinatal Biochemistry. Emilio Herrera. 288p. 1992. lib. bdg. 189.00 (*0-8493-6944-4*, PG615) CRC Pr.

Perinatal Cardiovascular Function. Ed. by Norman L. Gootman & Phyllia M. Gootman. LC 82-23544. (Illus.). 414p. reprint ed. pap. 128.40 (*0-7837-4739-X*, 204454700004) Bks Demand.

Perinatal Death As a Pastoral Problem. Astrid A. Wretmark. (Bibliotheca Theologiae Practicae Kyrkov Studier Ser.: No. 50). 319p. (Orig.). 1993. pap. 52.50 (*91-22-01559-0*) Coronet Bks.

Perinatal Endocrinology & Metabolism. Ed. by J. R. Girard. (Journal: Biology of the Neonate: Vol. 48, No. 4, 1985). (Illus.). 76p. 1985. pap. 38.50 (*3-8055-4235-6*) S Karger.

Perinatal Epidemiology. Michael B. Bracken. (Illus.). 550p. 1984. text 69.50 (*0-19-503389-2*) OUP.

Perinatal Epidemiology & Health Care Organisation: The Case of Belgium. Ed. by P. Buekens et al. (Journal: Biology of the Neonate: Vol. 55, No. 1,1989). (Illus.), iv, 72p. 1989. pap. 51.50 (*3-8055-4978-4*) S Karger.

Perinatal Haematological Problems. Ed. by Tom Turner. (Series on Perinatal Practice). 252p. 1991. 340.00 (*0-471-91557-2*) Wiley.

Perinatal Impact of Alcohol, Tobacco & Other Drugs. Margaret Kearney et al. LC 99-22605. 1999. write for info. (*0-86525-083-9*) March of Dimes.

Perinatal Impact of Substance Abuse. Susan M. Weiner. Ed. by Beverly S. Raff & Ellen Fiore. LC 92-23656. (Nursing Issues for the Twenty-First Century Ser.: Series 4, Module 3). 1992. pap. write for info. (*0-86525-055-3*) March of Dimes.

Perinatal Infections. CIBA Foundation Staff. LC 80-23631. (CIBA Foundation Symposium: New Ser.: No. 77). 304p. reprint ed. pap. 94.30 (*0-608-14280-8*, 202219600024) Bks Demand.

Perinatal Medicine. Ed. by J. Clinch. 1985. text 225.00 (*0-85200-908-9*) Kluwer Academic.

Perinatal Medicine. Ed. by Johan Gentz et al. LC 83-2171. 558p. 1984. 79.50 (*0-275-91431-3*, C1431, Praeger Pubs) Greenwood.

Perinatal Medicine, 2 vols. Manohar L. Rathi & Sudhir Kumar. 1982. text 39.50 (*0-07-051208-6*) McGraw.

Perinatal Medicine, 2 vols., Set. E. Kerpel-Fronius et al. 1448p. (C). 1978. 345.00 (*963-05-1413-3*, Pub. by Akade Kiado) St Mut.

Perinatal Medicine, 2 vols., Vol. 1. Manohar L. Rathi & Sudhir Kumar. 1980. text 35.00 (*0-07-051204-3*) McGraw.

Perinatal Medicine: Proceedings. Congress on Perinatal Medicine, 2nd European, Lond. Ed. by P. J. Huntingford et al. 1971. 69.75 (*3-8055-1224-4*) S Karger.

Perinatal Mental Health. Diana Riley. 1994. 24.75 (*1-870905-78-4*, Radcliffe Med Pr) Scovill Paterson.

Perinatal Mortality & Morbidity Including Low Birth Weight: A South-East Asia Regional Profile. T. Perera & Khing. (SEARO Regional Health Papers: No. 3). 72p. 1984. pap. text 8.00 (*92-9022-172-0*) World Health.

Perinatal Mortality in the United States, 1985-91. LC 95-30868. (Vital & Health Statistics Ser.: Series 20, No. 26). 1995. write for info. (*0-8406-0508-0*) Natl Ctr Health Stats.

Perinatal Nephrology Journal: Biology of the Neonate, Vol. 53, No. 4, 1987. Ed. by J. P. Guignard. (Illus.). 80p. 1988. pap. 37.50 (*3-8055-4798-6*) S Karger.

Perinatal Nursing. Ed. by Kathleen R. Simpson & Patricia A. Creehan. LC 95-44866. 560p. 1996. pap. text 39.95 (*0-397-55134-7*) Lppncott W & W.

Perinatal Nursing. 2nd ed. Kathleen R. Simpson & Patricia A. Creehan. 560p. pap. text 41.95 (*0-7817-2510-0*) Lppncott W & W.

Perinatal Nursing: Care of the High Risk Infant. Janice Ouimette. 461p. (C). 1986. 56.25 (*0-86720-356-0*) Jones & Bartlett.

Perinatal Nursing: Legal Dimensions. Mahlmeiste. pap. text. write for info. (*0-7216-5919-5*, W B Saunders Co) Harcrt Hlth Sci Grp.

Perinatal Pathology. 2nd abr. ed. Jonathan S. Wigglesworth. Ed. by Lesley Day. LC 95-42775. (Major Problems in Pathology Ser.: Vol. 15). 512p. 1996. text 74.00 (*0-7216-4252-7*, W B Saunders Co) Harcrt Hlth Sci Grp.

Perinatal-Pediatric Respiratory Therapeutics: RCP 306 Course. Wojciechowski et al. 213p. (C). 1994. ring bd. 43.95 (*0-933195-74-5*) CA College Health Sci.

Perinatal Practice in the Best Interest of Patients: Four Statements of Policy to Improve the Outcome of Pregnancy. Frwd. by Daniel M. Fox & Jennifer L. Howse. 48p. (Orig.). 1997. pap. write for info. (*1-887748-10-5*) Milbank Memorial.

Perinatal Psychiatric Care. Ed. by Katherine E. Williams & Regina C. Casper. (Illus.). 300p. 2001. text 50.00 (*0-19-510957-0*) OUP.

Perinatal Risk & Newborn Behavior. Ed. by Lewis P. Lipsitt & Tiffany M. Field. LC 82-8909. 208p. (C). 1982. text 73.25 (*0-89391-123-2*) Ablx Pub.

Perinatal Substance Abuse: Research Findings & Clinical Implications. Ed. by Theo B. Sonderegger. (Series in Environmental Toxicology). 336p. 1992. text 95.00 (*0-8018-4275-1*) Johns Hopkins.

Perinatal Thrombosis & Hemastasis. Ed. by S. Suzuki et al. (Illus.). xi, 289p. 1991. 118.00 (*0-387-70055-2*) Spr-Verlag.

Perinatal Transfusion Medicine. Ed. by Melanie S. Kennedy. LC 90-14405. 218p. (C). 1990. text 7.00 (*0-915355-84-1*) Am Assn Blood.

Perinatologie. Ed. by E. Bern Rossi. (Paediatrische Fortbildungskurse fuer die Praxis Ser.: Band 41). 200p. 1975. 68.75 (*3-8055-2115-4*) S Karger.

Perinatology. Ed. by Erich Saling. LC 91-18567. (Nestle Nutrition Workshop Ser.: No. 26). (Illus.). 208p. 1992. reprint ed. pap. 64.50 (*0-608-05880-7*, 205984600007) Bks Demand.

***Period.** Dennis Cooper. LC 99-42765. 128p. 2000. 21.00 (*0-8021-1656-6*, Pub. by Grove-Atltc) Publishers Group.

***Period.** rev. ed. Joann Loulan & Bonnie Worthen. 100p. 2000. pap. 9.99 (*0-916773-96-5*) Book Peddlers.

Period. 10th ed. JoAnn Gardner-Loulan et al. LC 90-46065. (Illus.). 95p. (J). (gr. 4-8). 1991. pap. 9.95 (*0-912078-88-X*) Volcano Pr.

Period: Humorous, Light Hearted Look at Woman's Oldest Dilemma. Danna J. Krause. Ed. by Kathy Douglass & Debra D. Munn. (Illus.). 70p. (Orig.). 1994. pap. write for info. (*0-9638699-0-6*) Red Hot Pr.

Period Batch Control. John L. Burbidge. (Oxford Series on Advanced Manufacturing: Vol. 12). (Illus.). 276p. 1996. text 99.95 (*0-19-856400-7*) OUP.

Period Book: Everything You Don't Want to Ask (But Need to Know) Karen Gravelle. 1996. 14.05 (*0-606-10903-X*, Pub. by Turtleback) Demco.

Period Book: Everything You Don't Want to Ask (But Need to Know) Karen Gravelle & Jennifer Gravelle. LC 95-31101. (Illus.). 128p. (J). (gr. 4-7). 1996. 15.95 (*0-8027-8420-8*); pap. 8.95 (*0-8027-7478-4*) Walker & Co.

Period Costume for Stage & Screen: Medieval-1500. Jean Hunnisett. LC 95-50302. (Illus.). 192p. 1996. 50.00 (*0-88734-653-7*) Players Pr.

Period Costume for Stage & Screen: Patterns for Women's Dress, 1500-1800. Jean Hunnisett. LC 90-50385. (Illus.). 176p. 1991. 50.00 (*0-88734-610-3*) Players Pr.

Period Costume for Stage & Screen: Patterns for Women's Dress, 1800-1909. Jean Hunnisett. LC 90-43905. (Illus.). 192p. 1991. 50.00 (*0-88734-609-X*) Players Pr.

Period Finishes & Effects. Judith Miller & Martin Miller. LC 92-5471. (Illus.). 180p. 1992. 40.00 (*0-8478-1569-2*, Pub. by Rizzoli Intl) St Martin.

Period Fireplaces: A Practical Guide to Period-Style Decorating. Judith Miller. (Illus.). 128p. 1995. 27.95 (*1-85732-397-1*, Pub. by Reed Illust Books) Antique Collect.

Period Furniture Projects: Detailed Plans & Step-by-Step Instructions for 20 Classic Pieces. V. J. Taylor. (Illus.). 160p. 1997. pap. 19.95 (*0-7153-0558-1*, Pub. by D & C Pub) Sterling.

Period House: Style, Detail & Decoration, 1774-1914. Richard R. Lawrence & Teresa Chris. (Illus.). 192p. 1998. pap. 24.95 (*0-7538-0119-1*) Phoenix Hse.

Period Houses & Their Details. Colin Amery. (Illus.). 211p. 1978. pap. text 29.95 (*0-7506-0795-5*) Buttrwrth-Heinemann.

Period Kitchens: A Practical Guide to Period-Style Decorating. Judith Miller. (Illus.). 128p. 1995. 27.95 (*1-85732-398-X*, Pub. by Reed Illust Books) Antique Collect.

Period Make-Up for the Stage Step-by-Step. Rosemarie Swinfield. (Illus.). 128p. 1997. 24.99 (*1-55870-468-X*, Betrwy Bks) F & W Pubns Inc.

Period of Adjustment see Four Plays

Period of Adjustment. Tennessee Williams. 1961. pap. 5.25 (*0-8222-0887-3*) Dramatists Play.

Period of Corneille, 1635-1651 see History of French Dramatic Literature in the Seventeenth Century

Period of Internment: Letters & Drawings from Les Milles 1939-1940. Peter Lipman-Wulf. LC 91-73296. (Illus.). 98p. (Orig.). 1993. pap. 15.00 (*0-9630164-5-8*) Canios Edit.

Period of Moliere, 1652-1672 see History of French Dramatic Literature in the Seventeenth Century

Period of Racine, 1673-1700 see History of French Dramatic Literature in the Seventeenth Century

Period of the Gruesome: Selected Cincinnati Journalism of Lafcadio Hearn. Ed. by Jon C. Hughes. 338p. (Orig.). (C). 1990. lib. bdg. 50.00 (*0-8191-7783-0*) U Pr of Amer.

Period of Warring States see Sengoku: Chanbara Roleplaying in Feudal Japan

Period Patterns. Lucy Barton & Doris Edson. (Illus.). 1942. pap. 11.95 (*0-87440-003-1*) Bakers Plays.

Period Piece. Gwen Raverat. (Ann Arbor Paperbacks Ser.). (Illus.). 290p. (C). 1991. reprint ed. pap. 17.95 (*0-472-06475-4*, 06475) U of Mich Pr.

Period Pieces. Rudy Kikel. (Illus.). 110p. (Orig.). 1997. pap. 9.95 (*1-886383-25-1*) Pride & Imprints.

Period Pieces: An Account of the Grand Rapids Dominicans, 1853-1966. Mona L. Schwind. (Illus.). 386p. (Orig.). 1991. pap. 20.00 (*0-9629233-0-3*) Sisters St Dominic.

Period, Question Mark, Exclamation Mark. rev. ed. Contrib. by Beth Bridgman. (Horizons Grammar Ser.). (Illus.). 24p. (J). (gr. 4-9). 1998. pap. 5.95 (*1-58086-058-3*, Usborne) EDC.

Period Rooms in the Metropolitan Museum of Art. James Parker & Amelia Peck. (Illus.). 256p. 1996. 60.00 (*0-8109-3744-1*, Pub. by Abrams) Time Warner.

Period Rooms of Ruth McChesney. Anne D. Smith. LC 97-136094. (Illus.). 96p. (Orig.). 1997. pap. 24.95 (*0-89024-301-8*, 12182, Kalmbach Books) Kalmbach.

Period Ship Handbook. Keith Julier. (Illus.). 205p. 1992. pap. 37.50 (*1-85486-081-X*) Nexus Special Interests.

Period Ship Handbook, Vol. 2. 2nd ed. Keith Julier. (Illus.). 142p. 1995. pap. 34.50 (*1-85486-132-8*, Pub. by Nexus Special Interests) Trans-Atl Phila.

Period Spaces for P-Divisible Groups. M. Rapoport & T. Zink. 353p. 1996. text 69.50 (*0-691-02782-X*, Pub. by Princeton U Pr); pap. text 35.00 (*0-691-02781-1*, Pub. by Princeton U Pr) Cal Prin Full Svc.

Periode Contemporaine (du XVIIIe Siecle a nos Jours) see Histoire du Catholicisme en France

Periodic Differential Equations: Introduction to Mathieu Lame & Allied Functions. F. Arscott & Ian N. Sneddon. LC 62-8703. (International Series of Monographs on Pure & Applied Mathematics: Vol. 66). 1964. 131.00 (*0-08-009984-X*, Pub. by Pergamon Repr) Franklin.

***Periodic Hamiltonian Flows on Four Dimensional Manifolds** Yael Karshon. LC 99-29338. (Memoirs Ser). 1999. write for info. (*0-8218-1181-9*) Am Math.

Periodic Hemodynamics in Health & Disease. Jan A. Schmidt & Michael W. Parker. LC 96-9385. (Medical Intelligence Unit Ser.). 208p. 1996. 99.00 (*1-57059-366-3*) Landes Bioscience.

Periodic Inspection & Testing, Pt. 3. William Culross & Son Ltd. Staff. (C). 1986. 95.00 (*0-900323-78-7*, Pub. by W Culross & Son Ltd) St Mut.

Periodic Kingdom: A Journey into the Land of the Chemical Elements. P. W. Atkins. (Science Masters Ser.). 1997. pap. 12.00 (*0-465-07266-6*, Pub. by Basic) HarpC.

Periodic Kingdom: A Journey into the Land of the Chemical Elements. P. W. Atkins. (Illus.). 163p. (C). 1998. pap. text 15.00 (*0-7881-5518-0*) DIANE Pub.

Periodic Markets, Urbanization, & Regional Planning: A Case Study from Western Kenya, 22. Robert A. Obudho & P. P. Waller. LC 75-23867. (Contributions in Afro-American & African Studies: No. 22). (Illus.). 289p. 1976. 55.00 (*0-8371-8375-8*, OPM/) Greenwood.

Periodic Motions. Miklos Farkas. LC 93-50623. (Applied Mathematical Sciences Ser.: Vol. 104). (Illus.). 568p. 1994. 69.95 (*0-387-94204-1*) Spr-Verlag.

Periodic Orbits, Stability & Resonances: Proceedings of the Symposium, University of Sao Paulo, 1969. Symposium, University of Sao Paulo Staff. Ed. by G. E. Giacaglia. LC 74-124848. 530p. 1970. text 220.50 (*90-277-0170-9*) Kluwer Academic.

Periodic Screening for Breast Cancer: The Health Insurance Plan Project & Its Sequelae, 1963-1986. Sam Shapiro et al. LC 88-9457. (Johns Hopkins Series in Contemporary Medicine & Public Health). (Illus.). 232p. reprint ed. pap. 72.00 (*0-608-06142-5*, 206647500008) Bks Demand.

Periodic Service Review: A Total Quality Assurance System for Human Services & Education. Gary W. LaVigna et al. LC 93-39241. 256p. 1994. spiral bd. 37.95 (*1-55766-142-1*) P H Brookes.

Periodic Solutions of Perturbed Second-Order Autonomous Equations. Warren S. Loud. LC QA0003.A57. (Memoirs of the American Mathematical Society Ser.: No. 47). 141p. reprint ed. pap. 43.80 (*0-7837-1632-X*, 204192500024) Bks Demand.

Periodic Solutions of Singular Lagrangian Systems. Antonio Ambrosetti & Vittorio C. Zelati. LC 93-24376. (Progress in Nonlinear Differential Equations & Their Applications Ser.: No. 10). xii, 157 p. 1993. 54.50 (*0-8176-3655-2*) Birkhauser.

***Periodic Solutions of the N-Body Problem.** Kenneth R. Meyer. LC 99-49591. (Lecture Notes in Mathematics Ser.: Vol. 1719). ix, 144p. 2000. pap. 36.80 (*3-540-66630-3*) Spr-Verlag.

Periodic Solutions of X Double Prime Plus C Times X Plus G of (X) Equals F of T. Warren S. Loud. LC 52-42839. (Memoirs Ser.: No. 1/31). 58p. 1978. reprint ed. pap. 16.00 (*0-8218-1231-9*, MEMO/1/31) Am Math.

Periodic Solutions of X" Plus CX' Plus G(X) Equals EF(T) fac. ed. Warren S. Loud. LC QA0371.A57. (Memoirs of the American Mathematical Society Ser.: No. 31). 60p. 1959. pap. 30.00 (*0-7837-7552-0*, 204730500007) Bks Demand.

Periodic Stars: An Overview of Science Fiction Literature in the 1980s & 1990s. Tom Easton. LC 95-3914. (I. O. Evans Studies in the Philosophy & Criticism of Literature: No. 24). 264p. 1997. pap. 27.00 (*0-8095-1202-5*) Millefleurs.

Periodic Stars: An Overview of Science Fiction Literature in the 1980s & '90s. Tom Easton. LC 95-3914. (I. O. Evans Studies in the Philosophy & Criticism of Literature: No. 24). 264p. 1997. 37.00 (*0-8095-0202-X*) Millefleurs.

Periodic System, 1920-1923. Niels Bohr. Ed. by J. Rud Nielsen. (Niels Bohr Collected Works: Vol. 4). x, 766p. 1977. 350.75 (*0-7204-1804-6*, North Holland) Elsevier.

Periodic Systems & Their Relation to the Systematic Analysis of Molecular Data. Ray Hefferlin. LC 89-9345. 664p. 1989. lib. bdg. 129.95 (*0-88946-032-9*) E Mellen.

Periodic Table. Primo Levi. Tr. by Raymond Rosenthal. 1996. 17.00 (*0-679-44463-7*) Fodors Travel.

Periodic Table. Primo Levi. 240p. 1995. pap. 11.00 (*0-8052-1041-5*) Schocken.

Periodic Table. Oliver Sacks. write for info. (*0-375-40448-1*) Knopf.

Periodical Abstracts Ondisc User Guide. Dennis Auld. 1989. write for info. incl. cd-rom (*0-914604-33-3*) UMI Louisville.

***Periodical Acquisitions & the Internet.** Nancy Slight-Gibney. LC 98-32065. 214p. 1999. 49.95 (*0-7890-0677-4*) Haworth Pr.

Periodical & Monographic Index to the Literature on the Gospels & Acts Based on the Files of Ecole Biblique in Jerusalem. LC 78-27276. (Bibliographia Tripotamopolitana Ser.: No. 3). 1971. 12.00 (*0-931222-02-8*) Pitts Theolog.

Periodical Cicadas. Gene Kritsky. LC 99-70680. (In Ohio's Backyard Ser.: No. 2). (Illus.). 86p. (gr. 6 up). 1999. ring bd. 10.00 (*0-86727-132-9*) Ohio Bio Survey.

Periodical Classes. Harvard University Library Staff. LC 68-14152. (Widener Library Shelflist: No. 15). 766p. 1968. text 30.00 (*0-674-66300-4*) HUP.

Periodical Essays of the Eighteenth Century. Ed. by George Carver. LC 70-99621. (Essay Index Reprint Ser.). 1977. 28.95 (*0-8369-1555-0*) Ayer.

Periodical Guide for Computerists, 1982: Annual since 1975-76. Intro. by Ellen Levine. 70p. (Orig.). 1982. pap. 15.95 (*0-686-40864-0*) Applegate Comp Ent.

Periodical Indexes in the Social Sciences & Humanities: A Subject Guide. Lois A. Harzfeld. LC 78-5230. 188p. 1978. lib. bdg. 18.50 (*0-8108-1133-2*) Scarecrow.

Periodical Letter on the Principles of the "Equity Movement" Josiah Warren. LC 78-22601. (Free Love in America Ser.). reprint ed. 28.50 (*0-404-60975-9*) AMS Pr.

Periodical Literature in Nineteenth-Century America. Ed. by Kenneth M. Price & Susan B. Smith. (Illus.). 352p. (C). 1995. text 45.00 (*0-8139-1629-1*); pap. text 19.50 (*0-8139-1630-5*) U Pr of Va.

Periodical Literature of Iceland Down to Year 1874, an Historical Sketch. Halldor Hermannsson. LC 19-7907. (Islandica Ser.: Vol. 11). 1918. 25.00 (*0-527-00341-7*) Periodicals Srv.

P

An Asterisk (*) at the beginning of an entry indicates that the title is appearing for the first time.

Periodical Literature on Christ & the Gospels. Watson E. Mills. LC 98-39186. (New Testament Tools & Studies). xxx, 962p. 1998. 243.00 (*90-04-10098-9*) Brill Academic Pubs.

Periodical Literature on United States Cities: A Bibliography & Subject Guide. Barbara S. Shearer & Benjamin F. Shearer. LC 82-24211. 574p. 1983. lib. bdg. 65.00 (*0-313-23511-2*, SPL/, Greenwood Pr) Greenwood.

Periodical Publications: A Bibliography of Bibliographies. Theodore Besterman. LC 70-29733. 1971. write for info. (*0-87471-043-X*) Rowman.

Periodical Publishing in Wisconsin: Proceedings. Conference on Periodical Publishing in Wisconsin, et al. Ed. by Barbara J. Arnold et al. 233p. 1980. pap. 7.00 (*0-936442-08-5*) U Wis Sch Lib.

***Periodical Title Abbreviations, Vol. 3.** 12th ed. 2800p. 2000. 156.00 (*0-7876-2451-9*, UXL) Gale.

***Periodical Title Abbreviations by Abbreviation.** 12th ed. 1800p. 1999. 235.00 (*0-7876-2453-5*) Gale.

***Periodical Title Abbreviations by Title, Vol. 2.** 12th ed. 1800p. 1999. 235.00 (*0-7876-2454-3*) Gale.

Periodicals Circulation Statistics at a Mid-Sized Academic Library: Implications for Collection Management. Ed. by John A. Whisler. (Resource Sharing & Information Networks Ser.: Vol. 5, Nos. 1-2). 363p. (C). 1990. text 11.95 (*0-86656-887-5*) Haworth Pr.

Periodicals Collection. 2nd ed. Donald E. Davinson. LC 78-17873. 243 p. 1978. 18.00 (*0-89158-833-7*) Westview.

Periodicals for School Media Programs. Selma K. Richardson. LC 77-25069. 419p. reprint ed. pap. 129.90 (*0-608-12590-3*, 202395200034) Bks Demand.

Periodicals for South-East Asian Studies: A Union Catalogue of Holdings in British & Selected European Libraries. Compiled by Brenda E. Moon. 630p. 1979. 170.00 (*0-7201-0730-X*) Continuum.

Periodicals, Musical: In His Harvard Dictionary of Music. Willi Apel. 567p. 1993. reprint ed. lib. bdg. 99.00 (*0-7812-9684-6*) Rprt Serv.

Periodicals, Newsletters & Indexes in E. S. Bird Library & Clearinghouse of Resources for Educators of Adults. Alexander N. Charters & D. Holmwood. (MS Ser.: No. 8). 1978. 3.50 (*0-686-63883-2*, MSS 8) Syracuse U Cont Ed.

Periodicals of American Transcendentalism. Clarence L. Gohdes. LC 76-107803. (Select Bibliographies Reprint Ser.). 1977. 21.95 (*0-8369-5206-5*) Ayer.

Periodicals of American Transcendentalism. Clarence Gohdes. LC 77-136380. reprint ed. 37.50 (*0-404-02854-3*) AMS Pr.

Periodicals of Queen Victoria's Empire: An Exploration. Ed. by J. Don Vann & Rosemary T. VanArsdel. (Illus.). 368p. 1996. text 80.00 (*0-8020-0810-0*) U of Toronto Pr.

Periodicals of the Mid-West & West. Ed. by Carolyn Mueller. LC 85-60590. 1986. 35.00 (*0-87650-210-9*) Pierian.

Periodicity. 3rd ed. Joseph R. Buchanan. 138p. 1996. reprint ed. spiral bd. 12.00 (*0-7873-0129-9*) Hlth Research.

Periodicity & Stochastic Trends in Economic Time Series. Philip H. Franses. (Advanced Texts in Econometrics Ser.). (Illus.). 248p. 1996. text 69.00 (*0-19-877453-2*); pap. text 35.00 (*0-19-877454-0*) OUP.

Periodicity & the p-Block Elements. Nicholas C. Norman. LC 93-37708. (Oxford Chemistry Primers Ser.: Vol. 16). (Illus.). 96p. (C). 1994. pap. text 12.95 (*0-19-855763-9*) OUP.

Periodicity & the s- & p-Block Elements. N. C. Norman. LC 97-12676. (Oxford Chemistry Primers: No. 51). (Illus.). 96p. (C). 1997. pap. text 12.95 (*0-19-855961-5*) OUP.

Periodisierung der Deutschen Sprachgeschichte: Analysen & Tabellen. Thorsten Roelcke. (Studia Linguistica Germanica: Vol. 40). (GER.). xi, 494p. 1995. lib. bdg. 169.25 (*3-11-015075-1*) De Gruyter.

Periodismo Literario De Jorge Manach. Jorge L. Marti. LC 76-27678. (Coleccion Mente y Palabra). 333p. 1977. 5.00 (*0-8477-0542-0*); pap. 4.00 (*0-8477-0543-9*) U of PR Pr.

Periodization: Theory & Methodology of Training. 4th rev. ed. Tudor O. Bompa. LC 98-54460. (Illus.). 424p. 1999. pap. 33.00 (*0-88011-851-2*, PBOM0851) Human Kinetics.

Periodization Breakthrough! The Ultimate Training System. Steven J. Fleck & William J. Kraemer. LC 96-85249. (Illus.). 190p. 1996. 19.95 (*1-889462-00-4*) Advanced Research Pr.

Periodization Training for Sports. Tudor Bompa. LC 98-48169. (Illus.). 248p. 1999. pap. 19.95 (*0-88011-840-7*, PBOM0840) Human Kinetics.

Periodo Intertestamentario. D. S. Russell.Tr. of Between the Testaments. (SPA.). 176p. 1997. pap. 7.50 (*0-311-03654-6*) Casa Bautista.

Periodoniken. R. Knab. 83p. 1980. pap. 15.00 (*0-89005-330-8*) Ares.

Periodontal & Prosthetic Management for Advanced Cases. Marvin M. Rosenberg et al. (Illus.). 375p. 1988. text 182.00 (*0-86715-162-5*, 1625) Quint Pub Co.

Periodontal Control. Grace & Smales. 144p. 1989. pap. text 34.00 (*1-85097-009-2*) Quint Pub Co.

Periodontal Disease: Immunological Factors, I. Irving Glickman et al. LC 72-10934. (Illus.). 220p. (C). 1973. text 32.50 (*0-8422-7061-2*) Irvington.

Periodontal Disease: Immunological Factors, II. L. Ivanyi et al. LC 72-10934. (Illus.). 193p. 1973. text 32.50 (*0-8422-7069-8*) Irvington.

Periodontal Disease: Recognition, Interception & Perception. S. Cripps. 292p. 1984. text 104.00 (*0-86715-118-8*) Quint Pub Co.

Periodontal Disease Management. Ed. by M. McGuire & C. Townsend. (Illus.). 100p. (Orig.). 1994. pap. 65.00 (*0-9624699-5-5*) Amer Acad Periodontology.

***Periodontal Diseases: Changing Concepts & Treatment Strategies.** Peter N. Galgut et al. 240p. 2000. 89.95 (*0-948269-84-7*, Pub. by Martin Dunitz) Thieme Med Pubs.

Periodontal Instrumentation. 2nd ed. Anna Pattison & Gordon Pattison. (Illus.). 485p. (C). 1991. pap. text 42.95 (*0-8385-7804-7*, A7804-6) Appleton & Lange.

Periodontal Instrumentation for the Practitioner. Jill S. Nield-Gehrig. LC 98-21882. 459p. 1998. pap. 29.95 (*0-683-30493-3*) Lppncott W & W.

Periodontal Ligament in Health & Disease. Ed. by B. K. Berkovitz et al. (Illus.). 472p. 1982. 203.00 (*0-08-024412-2*, Pub. by Pergamon Repr) Franklin.

***Periodontal Medicine.** Louis F. Rose et al. 352p. 1999. boxed set 89.95 incl. cd-rom (*1-55009-120-4*) DEKR.

Periodontal Regeneration: Current Status & Directions. Ed. by Alan Polson. (Illus.). 224p. 1994. text 72.00 (*0-86715-175-7*) Quint Pub Co.

***Periodontal Regeneration Enhanced: Clinical Applications of Enamel Matrix Proteins.** Thomas G. Wilson. LC 98-47492. 20p. 1999. 72.00 (*0-86715-352-0*) Quint Pub Co.

Periodontal Surgery: A Clinical Atlas. Naoshi Sato. (Illus.). 452p. write for info. (*0-86715-377-6*) Quint Pub Co.

Periodontal Therapy Vol. 1: Clinical Approaches & Evidence of Success, Vol. 1. Ed. by Myron Nevins & James Mellonig. LC 97-42610. (Illus.). 412p. 1998. text 178.00 (*0-86715-309-1*) Quint Pub Co.

Periodontic Syllabus. 3rd ed. Ed. by Peter F. Fedi, Jr. et al. LC 94-33984. (Illus.). 231p. 1995. pap. 39.00 (*0-683-03104-X*) Lppncott W & W.

***Periodontic Syllabus.** 4th ed. Peter F. Fedi, Jr. et al. LC 99-32590. 1999. write for info. (*0-683-30668-5*) Lppncott W & W.

***Periodontics.** W. M. M. Jenkins & C. J. Allan. 184p. 1999. 30.00 (*0-7236-1062-2*, Pub. by John Wright) Buttrwrth-Heinemann.

Periodontics - The Scientific Way. Jan Egelberg. 272p. (C). (gr. 13). 1992. 75.95 (*87-16-11001-3*) Mosby Inc.

Periodontitis in Man & Other Animals. R. C. Page & H. E. Schroeder. (Illus.). x, 330p. 1982. 129.75 (*3-8055-2479-X*) S Karger.

Periodontium. H. E. Schroeder. (Handbook of Microscopic Anatomy Ser.: Vol. 5; Pt. 5). (Illus.). 440p. 1986. 471.00 (*0-387-16604-1*) Spr-Verlag.

Periodontology. Peter A. Heasman et al. LC 97-13822. (Colour Guide Ser.). 1997. pap. text 21.95 (*0-443-05705-2*) Harcrt Hlth Sci Grp.

Periodontology & Periodontics: Modern Theory & Practice. Sigurd P. Ramfjord & M. Ash, Jr. (Illus.). 370p. 1989. 59.50 (*0-912791-40-3*, Ishiyaku EuroAmerica) Med Dent Media.

Periodontology for the Dental Hygienist. Dorothy A. Perry et al. Ed. by Selma Ozmat. LC 95-19487. (Illus.). 336p. 1995. pap. text 36.00 (*0-7216-4063-X*, W B Saunders Co) Harcrt Hlth Sci Grp.

Periodontology Today. Ed. by B. Guggenheim. (Illus.). viii, 350p. 1989. pap. 104.50 (*3-8055-4843-5*) S Karger.

Periodos Biblicos. R. Riggs.Tr. of Dispensations. (SPA.). 160p. 1969. pap. 5.99 (*0-8297-0590-2*) Vida Pubs.

***Periodos Biblicos.** Ralph M. Riggs. 1998. pap. 5.99 (*0-8297-1578-9*) Vida Pubs.

Periods: From Menarche to Menopause. Sharon Golub. (Illus.). 280p. 1992. 42.00 (*0-8039-4205-2*); pap. 19.50 (*0-8039-4206-0*) Sage.

Periods: Selected Writings, 1972-1987, No. 23. Phil Demise & Phil Smith. (Illus.). 472p. (Orig.). 1988. pap. 15.00 (*0-943783-00-3*) Gegenschein.

Periods of Hecke Characters. N. Schappacher. (Lecture Notes in Mathematics Ser.: Vol. 1301). xv, 160p. 1988. 35.95 (*0-387-18915-7*) Spr-Verlag.

Periods of Hilbert Modular Surfaces. Takayuki Oda. (Progress in Mathematics Ser.: Vol. 19). 1982. 40.50 (*0-8176-3084-8*) Birkhauser.

Perioperative Assessment in Vascular Surgery. Ed. by D. Preston Flanigan. LC 86-23987. (Science & Practice of Surgery Ser.: No. 9). 400p. 1987. reprint ed. pap. 124.00 (*0-608-01318-8*, 206206200001) Bks Demand.

Perioperative Autologous Transfusion (Transcripts from a Conference) Linda C. Stehling. LC 90-14536. 177p. (C). 1991. text 20.00 (*0-915355-91-4*) Am Assn Blood.

Perioperative Care. Ed. by Richard M. Peters & Jose Toledo. LC 92-49794. (Current Topics in General Thoracic Surgery: an International Ser.: Vol. 2). 462p. 1992. 163.75 (*0-444-89660-0*) Elsevier.

Perioperative Care: Anesthesia, Medicine & Surgery. David J. Stone & Bogdonoff. LC 97-16896. (Illus.). 864p. (C). (gr. 13). 1997. text 59.95 (*0-8151-4639-6*, 29911) Mosby Inc.

Perioperative Care in Cardiac Anesthesia & Surgery. Tirone E. David & Davy C. Cheng. LC 98-50222. (Vademecum Ser.). 1999. spiral bd. 45.00 (*1-57059-527-5*) Landes Bioscience.

***Perioperative Care of the Eye Patient.** Ed. by Gilli Vajidis et al. (Illus.). 70p. 2002. pap. text 19.95 (*0-7279-1225-9*) BMJ Pub.

Perioperative Management: For House Surgeons. P. R. Hambly & M. C. Sainsbury. (Illus.). 288p. (Orig.). 1996. pap. text 34.95 (*1-85996-185-1*, Pub. by Bios Sci) Bks Intl VA.

Perioperative Management of Pacemaker Patients. Ed. by J. L. Atlee, III et al. LC 92-49912. (Illus.). xi, 155p. 1992. write for info. (*3-540-53874-7*); pap. 59.00 (*0-387-53874-7*) Spr-Verlag.

Perioperative Management of the Patient with Congenital Heart Disease. William J. Greeley. (Society of Cardiovascular Anesthesiologists Monograph). (Illus.). 258p. 1996. 60.00 (*0-683-18302-8*) Lppncott W & W.

***Perioperative Medicine: Managing Surgical Patients with Medical Problems.** Ed. by Anthony Nicholls & Iain Wilson. (Illus.). 400p. 2000. pap. 39.95 (*0-19-262975-1*) OUP.

Perioperative Medicine: The Medical Care of the Surgical Patient. 2nd ed. Ed. by David R. Goldmann et al. LC 93-20975. (Illus.). 768p. 1993. text 89.00 (*0-07-023702-6*) McGraw-Hill HPD.

Perioperative Monitoring in Carotid Surgery: Methods, Limits, & Results, Long-Term Results in Carotid Surgery. Ed. by S. Horsch & K. Ktenidis. (Illus.). 200p. 1998. 54.00 (*3-7985-1074-1*) Spr-Verlag.

Perioperative Nursing. Linda B. Chitwood & Diane C. Swain. LC 91-4737. (Notes Ser.). 128p. 1991. pap. 16.95 (*0-87434-368-2*) Springhouse Corp.

Perioperative Nursing: Perioperative Practice. 3rd rev. ed. Linda K. Groah. LC 95-46563. 512p. (C). 1996. text, pap. text, boxed set 52.95 (*0-8385-7365-7*, A7365-8, Apple Lange Med) McGraw.

Perioperative Nursing: Principles & Practice. Ed. by Mark L. Phippen & Maryann P. Wells. LC 92-24341. (Illus.). 1088p. 1993. text 66.00 (*0-7216-7233-7*, W B Saunders Co) Harcrt Hlth Sci Grp.

Perioperative Nursing: Principles & Practice. 2nd ed. Ed. by Susan S. Fairchild. LC 95-50442. 600p. 1996. text 53.00 (*0-316-25969-1*, Little Brwn Med Div) Lppncott W & W.

Perioperative Nursing Care. Susan S. Fairchild. (Nut Shell Ser.). 900p. (C). 1993. 57.50 (*0-86720-432-X*) Jones & Bartlett.

Perioperative Nursing Care Planning. 2nd ed. Jane C. Rothrock. (Illus.). 656p. (C). (gr. 13). 1996. pap. text 42.95 (*0-8151-7147-1*, 24557) Mosby Inc.

Perioperative Nursing Core Curriculum: Achieving Competency in Clinical Practice. Ed. by Rosemary A. Roth. (Illus.). 392p. 1995. pap. text 41.00 (*0-7216-5197-6*, W B Saunders Co) Harcrt Hlth Sci Grp.

Perioperative Nursing Handbook. Maryann P. Wells. LC 94-25433. (Illus.). 345p. 1994. pap. text 25.00 (*0-7216-3412-5*, W B Saunders Co) Harcrt Hlth Sci Grp.

Perioperative Patient Care. 3rd ed. Julia A. Kneedler & Gwen H. Dodge. (Illus.). 552p. 1994. 61.25 (*0-86720-642-X*) Jones & Bartlett.

Perioperative Transfusion Medicine. Bruce D. Spiess et al. LC 97-4138. 600p. 1997. 89.00 (*0-683-07892-5*) Lppncott W & W.

Peripatetic Club, 1933-1993. Ed. by George Cahill, Jr. (Illus.). 211p. (Orig.). 1994. pap. write for info. (*0-9641132-0-1*) Peripat Club.

Peripatetic Rhetoric after Aristotle. Ed. by William W. Fortenbaugh & David C. Mirhady. LC 93-22586. (Rutgers University Studies in Classical Humanities: Vol. 6). 350p. (C). 1994. text 49.95 (*1-56000-150-X*) Transaction Pubs.

Peripheral Actions of 5-Hydroxytryptamine. Ed. by John R. Fozard. (Illus.). 448p. 1989. text 90.00 (*0-19-261683-8*) OUP.

Peripheral Americans. Frank J. Cavaioli & Salvatore J. Lagumina. LC 82-14019. 268p. (C). 1984. pap. 16.00 (*0-89874-542-X*) Krieger.

***Peripheral & Spinal Mechanisms in the Neural Control of Movement.** Ed. by M. D. Binder. (Progress in Brain Research Ser.). 498p. 1999. 228.50 (*0-444-50288-2*, Excerpta Medica) Elsevier.

Peripheral Arterial Chemoreceptors & Respiratory-Cardiovascular Integration. M. De Burgh Daly. LC 96-9435. (Monographs of the Physiological Society: No. 46). (Illus.). 756p. 1997. text 225.00 (*0-19-857675-7*) OUP.

Peripheral Benzodiazepine Receptors. Ed. by Eva Giesen-Crouse. (Neuroscience Perspectives Ser.). (Illus.). 281p. 1993. text 83.00 (*0-12-282630-2*) Acad Pr.

Peripheral Blood Stem Cell Autografts. Ed. by E. W. Wunder & Philippe R. Henon. (Illus.). 235p. 1993. 130.00 (*0-387-52612-9*) Spr-Verlag.

Peripheral Blood Stem Cell Transplantation: Recommendations for Nursing Education & Practice. Wendy Holmes et al. Ed. by Susan Ezzone. (Illus.). 60p. (Orig.). 1997. pap. text 45.00 (*1-890504-03-3*) Oncology Nursing.

Peripheral Blood Stem Cells. Ed. by Douglas Smith et al. (Illus.). 99p. (C). 1993. text 35.00 (*1-56395-022-7*) Am Assn Blood.

Peripheral Campaigns & the Principles of War: The British Experience, 1914-1918. Charles T. Kamps. 147p. 1982. 29.95 (*0-89126-108-7*) MA-AH Pub.

Peripheral Components. (Illus.). 1546p. 1996. pap. 23.95 (*1-55512-255-8*) McGraw.

Peripheral Dopamine Pathophysiology. Francesco Amenta. LC 89-7255. 408p. 1990. 205.00 (*0-8493-6949-5*, RC409, CRC Reprint) Franklin.

Peripheral Dopaminergic Receptors: Proceedings of Satellite Symposium, 7th International Congress of Pharmacology, Strasbourg, July 1978. Ed. by J. Imbs & J. C. Schwartz. LC 79-40355. (Advances in the Biosciences Ser.). (Illus.). 400p. 1979. 81.00 (*0-08-023189-6*, Pergamon Pr) Elsevier.

Peripheral Endovascular Interventions. Ed. by Rodney A. White & Thomas J. Fogarty. (Illus.). 576p. (C). (gr. 13). 1996. text 134.00 (*0-8151-9260-6*, 25194) Mosby Inc.

Peripheral Endovascular Interventions. 2nd ed. Ed. by Y. P. S. Bajaj. LC 98-44697. (Illus.). 680p. 1999. 150.00 (*0-387-98444-5*) Spr-Verlag.

Peripheral Labour: Studies in the History of Partial Proletarianization. Ed. by Shahid Amin & Marcel Van der Linden. (International Review of Social History Supplements Ser.: Vol. 4). 177p. (C). 1997. pap. text 19.95 (*0-521-58900-2*) Cambridge U Pr.

Peripheral Lymph: Formation & Immune Function. Waldemar L. Olszewski. 176p. 1985. 105.00 (*0-8493-6137-0*, QP115, CRC Reprint) Franklin.

Peripheral Manipulation. 3rd ed. G. D. Maitland. (Illus.). 336p. 1991. pap. text 60.00 (*0-7506-1031-X*) Buttrwrth-Heinemann.

Peripheral Migrants: Haitians & Dominican Republic Sugar Plantations. Samuel Martinez. LC 95-4359. 256p. (C). 1995. text 35.00 (*0-87049-901-7*) U of Tenn Pr.

Peripheral Musculoskeletal Ultrasound Atlas. Ed. by Robert Dondelinger et al. LC 95-39513. (Illus.). 224p. 1996. text 115.00 (*0-86577-592-3*) Thieme Med Pubs.

Peripheral Nerve: Structure, Function, & Reconstruction. Julia K. Terzis & Kevin L. Smith. 192p. 1990. text 61.00 (*0-88167-623-3*) Lppncott W & W.

Peripheral Nerve Block. F. L. Jenkner. LC 77-8317. (Illus.). 1977. 36.95 (*0-387-81426-4*) Spr-Verlag.

Peripheral Nerve Blockade. Pinnock. 1996. text 55.00 (*0-443-05064-3*, W B Saunders Co) Harcrt Hlth Sci Grp.

***Peripheral Nerve Blocks: A Color Atlas.** Ed. by Jacques E. Chelly. LC 99-11892. 1999. 95.00 (*0-7817-1626-8*) Lppncott W & W.

Peripheral Nerve Development & Regeneration. Ed. by E. Scarpini et al. (FIDIA Research Ser.: Vol. 19). 330p. 1990. 104.00 (*0-387-97110-6*) Spr-Verlag.

Peripheral Nerve Disease. Mark J. Brown. 1999. write for info. (*0-7506-9068-2*) Buttrwrth-Heinemann.

Peripheral Nerve Disorders 2, Vol. 2. Ed. by Arthur K. Asbury & P. K. Thomas. LC 95-11157. (Blue Books of Practical Neurology: Vol. 15). 352p. 1995. text 100.00 (*0-7506-1765-9*) Buttrwrth-Heinemann.

Peripheral Nerve in Leprosy & Other Neuropathies. Ed. by Noshir H. Antia & Vanaja P. Shetty. LC 98-124923. (Illus.). 300p. 1997. text 85.00 (*0-19-563429-2*) OUP.

Peripheral Nerve Injuries: Medical Subject Analysis with Reference Bibliography. Paul O. Parker. LC 85-48078. 1987. 44.50 (*0-88164-426-9*); pap. 39.50 (*0-88164-427-7*) ABBE Pubs Assn.

Peripheral Nerve Lesions. Ed. by Madjid Samii. (Illus.). 488p. 1990. 256.00 (*0-387-52432-0*) Spr-Verlag.

Peripheral Nerve Lesions: Diagnosis & Therapy. Ed. by Mark Mumenthaler & H. Schliack. (Illus.). 464p. 1990. text 109.00 (*0-86577-361-0*) Thieme Med Pubs.

Peripheral Nerve Surgery. Julia K. Terzis. 1987. text 155.00 (*0-7216-1268-7*, W B Saunders Co) Harcrt Hlth Sci Grp.

Peripheral Nervous System: Structure, Function, & Clinical Correlations. Lawrence J. Mathers, Jr. (Illus.). 227p. (C). 1984. reprint ed. 37.50 (*0-409-90074-5*) Buttrwrth-Heinemann.

Peripheral Neurology: Case Studies in Electrodiagnosis. 2nd ed. Jay A. Liveson. LC 90-14135. (Illus.). 496p. (C). 1991. text 60.00 (*0-8036-5652-1*) OUP.

***Peripheral Neurology: Case Studies in Electrodiagnosis.** 3rd ed. Jay Liveson. (Illus.). 512p. 2000. pap. text 57.50 (*0-19-513563-6*) OUP.

Peripheral Neuropathies. (Technical Report Ser.: No. 654). 138p. 1980. pap. text 9.00 (*92-4-120654-3*) World Health.

Peripheral Neuropathies, 1988: What Is Significantly New? Ed. by J. P. Assal & C. Liniger. (FIDIA Research Ser.: Vol. 21). 600p. 1990. 139.00 (*0-387-97188-2*) Spr-Verlag.

Peripheral Neuropathy, 2 vols., Set. 3rd ed. Peter J. Dyck et al. LC 92-11721. (Illus.). 1845p. 1992. text 415.00 (*0-7216-3242-4*, W B Saunders Co) Harcrt Hlth Sci Grp.

Peripheral Neuropathy: A Practical Approach to Diagnosis & Management. Didier Cros. 1998. write for info. (*0-397-51781-5*) Lppncott W & W.

Peripheral Neuropathy in Childhood. Robert A. Ouvrier et al. LC 90-8677. (International Review of Child Neurology Ser.). (Illus.). 251p. 1990. reprint ed. pap. 77.90 (*0-608-05873-4*, 205984000007) Bks Demand.

Peripheral Neuropathy in Childhood. 2nd rev. ed. R. A. Ouvrier et al. (International Review of Child Neurology Ser.). 300p. (C). 1998. text 69.95 (*1-898683-17-4*, Pub. by Mc Keith Pr) Cambridge U Pr.

Peripheral Parks, 3. ARCO Editorial Board Staff. (Urban Spaces Ser.). (Illus.). 256p. 1997. 80.00 (*84-8185-007-1*) Watsn-Guptill.

Peripheral Retina in Profile. Norman Byer. (Illus.). 159p. 1982. 295.00 incl. digital audio, sl. (*0-9609428-0-7*) Criterion Pr.

Peripheral Signaling of the Brain: Its Role in Neural-Immune Interactions, Learning & Memory. Ed. by James L. McGaugh & R. C. Frederickson. Tr. by D. L. Felton. (Nueronal Control of Bodily Function Ser.: Vol. 6). (Illus.). 550p. 1991. text 98.00 (*0-88937-035-4*) Hogrefe & Huber Pubs.

***Peripheral Space of Photography.** Murat Nemet-Nejat. (Illus.). 76p. 2000. pap. 9.95 (*1-892295-90-3*) Green Integer.

Peripheral Vascular Diseases. 2nd ed. Ed. by Jess R. Young et al. LC 95-48133. (Illus.). 768p. (C). (gr. 13). 1996. text 160.00 (*0-8151-9785-3*, 25864) Mosby Inc.

***Peripheral Vascular Disorders.** Merlin. 2001. text. write for info. (*0-7216-8971-X*) Harcrt Hlth Sci Grp.

Peripheral Vascular Interventions. Ed. by Jeanne M. LaBerge & Michael D. Darcy. LC 94-69675. (Illus.). 407p. 1997. write for info. (*1-928625-00-2*) Socy Cardio & Inter.

Peripheral Vascular Interventions for Cardiovascular Specialists. Ed. by Christopher J. White et al. (Illus.). 2001. write for info. (*0-87993-416-6*) Futura Pub.

Peripheral Vascular Sonography: A Practical Guide. Joseph F. Polak. (Illus.). 384p. 1992. 82.00 (*0-683-06914-4*) Lppncott W & W.

***Peripheral Vascular Stenting for Cardiologists.** Ed. by Richard R. Heuser. 174p. 1999. 99.95 (*1-85317-621-4*, Pub. by Martin Dunitz) Mosby Inc.

***Peripheral Vascular Ultrasound.** Abigail Thrush & Timothy Hartshorne. LC 99-31336. 1999. text. write for info. (*0-443-06049-5*, W B Saunders Co) Harcrt Hlth Sci Grp.

Peripheral Vision. Eric Gamalinda. 121p. (Orig.). 1992. pap. 8.75 (*971-10-0489-5*, Pub. by New Day Pub) Cellar.

P

An Asterisk (*) at the beginning of an entry indicates that the title is appearing for the first time.

Peripheral Vision: Contemporary Australian Art, 1970-1994. Charles Green. (Illus.). 156p. 1996. text 65.00 (976-641-026-7, Pub. by IPG Chicago) Gordon & Breach.
Peripheral Visions. Elizabeth Claman. 1989. pap. 4.00 (0-9618409-2-7) Five Fingers.
Peripheral Visions. Gloria Pierce. LC 82-80581. (Illus.). 64p. (Orig.). 1982. pap. 4.95 (0-943148-00-6) Nikki Pr.
Peripheral Visions: Deterrence Theory & American Foreign Policy in the Third World, 1965 - 1990. Ted Hopf. LC 94-21495. 320p. 1994. text 54.50 (0-472-10540-X, 10540) U of Mich Pr.
Peripheral Visions: Images of Nationhood in Contemporary British Fiction. Ian A. Bell. 220p. 1996. pap. 24.95 (0-7083-1260-8, Pub. by Univ Wales Pr) Paul & Co Pubs.
Peripheral Visions: Learning along the Way. Mary C. Bateson. 256p. 1995. pap. 15.00 (0-06-092630-9, Perennial) HarperTrade.
Peripheral Weapon? The Production & Employment of British Tanks in the First World War, 173. David J. Childs. LC 98-47130. (Contributions in Military Studies Ser.: No. 173). 232p. 1999. 57.95 (0-313-30832-2, GM0832, Greenwood Pr) Greenwood.
Peripheral Worker. Dean Morse. LC 73-76251. 222p. reprint ed. pap. 68.90 (0-608-15858-5, 203071700070) Bks Demand.
Peripheralisation & Industrial Change Impacts on Nations, Regions, Firms, & People. Ed. by Godfrey J. Linge. 272p. (C). 1988. text 57.50 (0-7099-4865-4, Pub. by C Helm) Routldge.
Peripheries. Helene Littmann. 272p. 1998. pap. 14.95 (1-896951-08-2) Cormor Bks.
Periphery: A Battletech Sourcebook. Chris Hussey. (BattleTech Ser.). (Illus.). 160p. 1995. pap. 18.00 (1-55560-276-2, 1692) FASA Corp.
Periphery of the Southeastern Classic Maya Realm. Ed. by Gary W. Pahl. LC 86-7502. (Latin American Indians Ser.). 304p. (Orig.). 1986. pap. 48.50 (0-87903-061-5) UCLA Lat Am Ctr.
Periplum - Austin. (Orig.). 1987. pap. 10.00 (0-318-37124-3) Open Theatre.
Periplus: Papers on Classical Art & Archaeology. Ed. by G. R. Tsetskhiadze et al. LC 99-70943. 336p. 1999. 60.00 (0-500-05097-X, Pub. by Thames Hudson) Norton.
Periplus: Poetry in Translation. Ed. by Daniel Weissbort & Arvind K. Mehrotra. 204p. (C). 1994. 24.95 (0-19-563234-6) OUP.
Periplus Maris Erythraei: Text with Introduction, Translation, & Commentary. Lionel Casson. LC 88-15178. (Illus.). 338p. reprint ed. pap. 104.80 (0-608-06382-7, 206674300008) Bks Demand.
Periplus of Hanno. 3rd rev. ed. Hanno the Carthaginian. Ed. by Al N. Oikonomides & M. C. Miller. (Ancient Greek & Latin Authors Ser.). (Illus.). 152p. 1995. pap. 15.00 (0-89005-180-1) Ares.
Periplus of the Erythraean Sea: Travel & Trade in the Indian Ocean by a Merchant of the First Century. Wilfred H. Schoff. 1996. 26.50 (81-215-0699-9, Pub. by M Manoharial) Coronet Bks.
Periscopio. Roberto Severino & Maria R. Falconi. (ITA., Illus.). 244p. (Orig.). 1986. 28.00 (0-8191-5234-X) U Pr of Amer.
Perish the Thought: The Stress Connection. Herman Lubens & John C. Kiley. 129p. (Orig.). 1995. pap. 14.95 (0-9633198-4-1) Jason Pr.
***Perish Twice.** Robert B. Parker. 320p. 2000. 23.95 (0-399-14668-7) Putnam Pub Group.
***Perishable Empire: Essays on Indian Writing in English.** Meenakshi Mukherjee. 286p. 2000. text 24.95 (0-19-565147-2) OUP.
Perishable Good: Selected Poems. David Offutt. Ed. by Janet Offutt. LC 98-92400. 53p. 1998. pap. 8.97 (0-9663605-1-6) Inflammable Pr.
Perishing Game. Don Pendleton. (Stony Man Ser.: No. 23). 1996. per. 5.50 (0-373-61907-3, 1-61907-1, Wrldwide Lib) Harlequin Bks.
Perishing Republic. Jerome Bahr. LC 79-129182. 148p. 1971. 10.95 (0-686-63593-0) Trempealeau.
Perissone Cambio. Ed. by Jessie A. Owens. LC 90-751362. (Sixteenth-Century Madrigal Ser.: Vol. 2). 232p. 1990. reprint ed. text 30.00 (0-8240-5502-0) Garland.
Perito en Lunas. M. Hernandez. (SPA.). 173p. 1963. 6.95 (0-8288-7138-8, S8063) Fr & Eur.
Peritoneal Adhesions. Ed. by K. H. Treutner & V. Schumpelick. LC 96-28281. 360p. 1996. pap. 79.50 (3-540-61192-4) Spr-Verlag.
Peritoneal Carcinomatosis: Drugs & Diseases. Ed. by Paul H. Sugarbaker. (Cancer Treatment & Research Ser.). 288p. (C). 1996. text 224.00 (0-7923-3726-3) Kluwer Academic.
Peritoneal Carcinomatosis: Principles of Management. Ed. by Paul H. Sugarbaker. (Cancer Treatment & Research Ser.). 464p. (C). 1996. text 320.50 (0-7923-3727-1) Kluwer Academic.
Peritoneal Dialysis. 2nd ed. Ed. by Karl D. Nolph. 1985. text 326.50 (0-89838-685-3) Kluwer Academic.
Peritoneal Dialysis. 3rd ed. Ed. by Karl D. Nolph. (C). 1988. text 315.00 (0-89838-406-0) Kluwer Academic.
Peritoneal, Ovarian & Recto-Vaginal Endometriosis: The Identification of Three Separate Diseases. M. Nisolle & J. Donnez. (Illus.). 190p. 1996. pap. 48.00 (1-85070-941-6) Prthnon Pub.
Peritoneal Surgery. Gere S. Dizerega. LC 99-12449. 448p. 1999. write for info. (0-387-98610-3) Spr-Verlag.
Peritoneum. Gere S. DiZerega & Kathleen E. Rodgers. LC 92-2221. (Illus.). 340p. 1992. write for info. (3-540-97830-5) Spr-Verlag.
Peritoneum. Gere S. DiZerega & Kathleen E. Rodgers. LC 92-2221. (Illus.). 340p. 1994. 145.00 (0-387-97830-5) Spr-Verlag.
Peritonitis in CAPS. Ed. by R. Augustin. (Contributions to Nephrology Ser.: Vol. 57). (Illus.). viii, 256p. 1987. 29.75 (3-8055-4519-3) S Karger.
Peritrophic Membranes. W. Peters. (Zoophysiology Ser.: Vol. 30). (Illus.). xi, 238p. 1992. 207.95 (0-387-53635-3) Spr-Verlag.
Periwinkle Brooch. large type ed. Kate Frederick. 576p. 1996. 27.99 (0-7089-3500-1) Ulverscroft.
***Periwinkle Isn't Paris.** Marilyn Eisenstein. (Illus.). 24p. (J). (gr. k-3). 1999. 15.95 (0-88776-451-7) Tundra Bks.
***Periwinkle Moves in.** (gr. k-3). 2000. 4.99 (0-689-83584-1, Simon Spot) Litle Simon.
Periwinkle's Ride. Ian Trevaskis. LC 93-18049. (Illus.). (J). 1994. write for info. (0-383-03708-5) SRA McGraw.
Periya Puranam. Sekkizhaar. Ed. by N. Mahalingam. Tr. by G. Vanmikanathan from TAM. 612p. 1985. pap. 6.95 (0-87481-534-7, Pub. by Ramakrishna Math) Vedanta Pr.
Perjury. Stan Latreille. LC 97-40653. 352p. 1998. 24.00 (0-609-60138-5) Crown Pub Group.
Perjury. Stan Latreille. 1999. reprint ed. mass mkt. 6.99 (0-451-19687-2, Onyx) NAL.
Perk! The Story of a Teenager with Bulimia. Liza F. Hall. LC 97-8718. 126p. (Orig.). (J). (gr. 6-9). 1997. pap. 10.95 (0-936077-27-1) Gurze Bks.
Perkey's Nebraska Place Names. Elton A. Perkey. LC 82-80300. (Illus.). 227p. 1990. reprint ed. pap. 12.95 (0-934904-19-7) J & L Lee.
Perkin Warbeck. John Ford. Ed. by Donald K. Anderson, Jr. LC 65-15338. (Regents Renaissance Drama Ser.). 134p. 1965. reprint ed. pap. 41.60 (0-608-02371-X, 206301300004) Bks Demand.
Perkin Warbeck Conspiracy, 1491-1499. Ian Arthurson. (Illus.). 256p. 1998. pap. 19.95 (0-7509-1610-9, Pub. by Sutton Pub Ltd) Intl Pubs Mktg.
Perkins & Hansell's Atlas of Diseases of the Eye. 4th ed. Damian O'Neill. LC 93-9993. 112p. 1993. text 49.95 (0-443-04822-3) Church.
Perkins-Budd: Railway Statesmen of the Burlington, 45. Richard C. Overton. LC 81-6961. (Contributions in Economics & Economic History Ser.: No. 45.). (Illus.). 271p. 1982. 59.95 (0-313-23173-7, OPB/, Greenwood Pr) Greenwood.
Perkins Conference - Meeting in Honor of the Retirement of Professor D H Perkins. R. J. Cashmore & G. Myatt. 216p. 1994. text 74.00 (981-02-1561-4) World Scientific Pub.
Perkins Formerly of Hillmorton. Paul H. Daigle. (Illus.). 385p. 1997. pap. 68.50 (0-8328-9487-7); lib. bdg. 58.50 (0-8328-9486-9) Higginson Bk Co.
Perkins, O. T. - Queen City of the Cimarron. David Sasser & Mahlon Erickson. LC 89-85639. (Illus.). 310p. 1989. 22.50 (0-934188-29-7) Evans Pubns.
Perks & Parachutes: Negotiating Your Best Possible Employment Deal. rev. ed. John Tarrant. LC 97-28117. 1997. 25.00 (0-8129-2677-3) Random.
Perks of Being a Wallflower. Stephen Chbosky. 213p. (YA). (gr. 7-12). 1999. per. 12.00 (0-671-02734-4) PB.
Perk's Path. Stanley C. Perkins. Ed. by Marylin Scheidemantel. (Illus.). 538p. 1999. 30.00 (0-9620249-6-1, 846730F); pap. 25.00 (0-9620249-5-3, 846730F) Broadblade Pr.
Perky - The Penguin Who Didn't Belong. Rose M. Shepherd. LC 96-77671. (Illus.). 12p. (Orig.). (J). 1996. pap. 6.00 (0-9648504-4-3) Ironwd Publns.
Perky Otter. Barbara DeRubertis. LC 97-44314. (Let's Read Together Ser.). (Illus.). 32p. (J). (ps-3). 1998. pap. 4.95 (1-57565-045-2) Kane Pr.
Perky Pelican: A Tale of a Lively Bird. Suzanne Tate. LC 95-72699. (Nature Ser.: No. 18). (Illus.). 28p. (J). (ps-4). 1996. pap. 4.95 (1-878405-13-6) Nags Head Art.
Perky Pelican: A Tale of a Lively Bird. Suzanne Tate. LC 95-72699. 1996. 9.15 (0-606-10319-8) Turtleback.
Perky Puppets with a Purpose: A Complete Guide to Puppetry & Ventriloquism in Christian Ministry. Mary R. Pearson. LC 91-42507. (Illus.). 160p. 1992. pap. 12.95 (0-88243-677-5, 02-0677) Gospel Pub.
***Perl.** Andy Yao. 120p. (C). 2000. 20.00 (1-930360-13-4) Unitd Tech.
Perl: Annotated Archives. Martin C. Brown. LC 99-194897. 800p. 1998. pap. 49.99 incl. cd-rom (0-07-882557-1) McGraw.
Perl: The Complete Reference. Martin C. Brown. (Complete Reference Ser.). 1100p. 1999. pap. text 49.99 (0-07-212000-2) Osborne.
Perl: The Programmer's Companion. Nigel Chapman. 292p. 1997. pap. 44.95 (0-471-97563-X) Wiley.
***Perl & CGI for the World Wide Web: Visual QuickStart Guide.** Elizabeth Castro. LC 99-190538. (Visual QuickStart Guide Ser.). (Illus.). 272p. (C). 1998. pap. 18.99 (0-201-35358-X, Pub. by Peachpit Pr) Addison-Wesley.
Perl Black Book. Steve Holzner. LC 99-34994. 1999. pap. text 49.99 (1-57610-465-6) Coriolis Grp.
Perl By Example. 2nd ed. Ellie Quigley. LC 97-30316. 576p. (C). 1997. pap. text 39.95 (0-13-655689-2) P-H.
Perl CD Bookshelf. O'Reilly & Associates Staff. Ed. by Linda Walsh. (Illus.). 1999. pap. 59.95 incl. cd-rom (1-56592-462-2) OReilly & Assocs.
***Perl, CGI & JavaScript Complete.** Sybex, Inc. Staff. (Complete Ser.). (Illus.). 1008p. 2000. pap. text 19.99 (0-7821-2780-0) Sybex.
Perl Cookbook. Tom Christiansen & Nathan Torkington. LC 99-176053. (Illus.). 794p. 1998. pap. 39.95 (1-56592-243-3) OReilly & Assocs.
***Perl Core Language Little Black Book.** Steve Holzner. LC 98-56151. (Little Black Book Series). 1999. pap. text 24.99 (1-57610-426-5) Coriolis Grp.
***Perl Developer's Guide.** Edward S. Peschko. (Application Development Ser.). 2000. pap. 49.99 (0-07-212630-2) Osborne-McGraw.
Perl Developer's Toolkit. 2nd ed. Jon Orwant & Randy Kobes. 320p. (gr. 9 up). 1998. pap. 39.95 incl. audio compact disk (1-889671-17-7) Advice Pr.
Perl Developer's Toolkit. 3rd ed. Randy Kobes. (Developer's Toolkit Ser.). 400p. 1999. pap. 39.95 (1-889671-27-4) Advice Pr.
Perl 5. Robert Seymour. 250p. 1997. pap. text 39.95 (0-387-94827-9) Spr-Verlag.
Perl 5: A Programmer's Notebook. Jesse Feiler. 288p. 1999. pap. text 34.99 (0-13-021321-7) P-H.
Perl 5 by Example. David Medinets. LC 96-69960. 696p. 1996. 39.99 (0-7897-0866-3) Que.
Perl 5 Complete. Edward S. Peschko & Michele DeWolfe. 1232p. 1998. pap. 54.95 incl. cd-rom (0-07-913698-2) McGraw.
Perl 5 Interactive Course: Certified Edition. Jon Orwant. LC 97-11857. 884p. 1997. 49.99 (1-57169-113-8) Macmillan Gen Ref.
Perl 5 Example. Norman Smith. 1998. pap. text 42.95 (1-55622-596-2) Wordware Pub.
Perl 5 How-To. 2nd ed. Stephen Asbury et al. LC 97-20245. 928p. 1997. 49.99 (1-57169-118-9) Sams.
Perl 5 How-To: The Definitive Perl Programming Problem-Solver. Adian Humphreys et al. (Illus.). 900p. 1996. pap. 44.99 (1-57169-058-1) Sams.
Perl 5 Pocket Reference. 2nd ed. Johan Vromans. Ed. by Gigi Estabrook & Steve Talbott. (Illus.). 71p. 1998. reprint ed. pap. 8.95 (1-56592-495-9) OReilly & Assocs.
***Perl 5 Pocket Reference.** 3rd ed. Johan Vromans. Ed. by Linda Mui. (Illus.). 96p. 2000. 8.95 (0-596-00032-4) OReilly & Assocs.
Perl 5 Unleashed. Sams Development Group Staff. 1996. 45.00 incl. cd-rom (0-614-14453-1) Macmillan.
Perl 5 Windows NT Programming. Carl Sampson & Jim Vogel. 400p. 1997. 44.99 (1-57870-001-9) Macmillan Tech.
Perl for Dummies. 2nd ed. Paul E. Hoffman. LC QA76.73.P22H64 1998. (For Dummies Ser.). 408p. 1998. pap. 29.99 incl. cd-rom (0-7645-0460-6) IDG Bks.
Perl for System Administration. David Blank-Edelman. Ed. by Linda Mui. (Illus.). 250p. 2000. pap. 34.95 (1-56592-609-9) OReilly & Assocs.
Perl from the Ground Up. Michael McMillan. (Illus.). 520p. (Orig.). 1998. pap. 34.99 (0-07-882404-4, Oracle Press) Osborne-McGraw.
Perl in a Nutshell. Stephen Spainhour et al. (In a Nutshell Ser.). 654p. 1999. pap. 29.95 (1-56592-286-7) OReilly & Assocs.
Perl Power! A Jumpstart Guide to Programming in Perl 5. Michael Schilli. LC 98-44427. 440p. 1999. pap. text 38.44 (0-201-36068-3) Addison-Wesley.
***Perl Programmers Interactive.** (C). 1999. wbk. ed. write for info. (0-13-026542-X) P-H.
Perl Programmer's Interactive Workbook. Vincent Lowe. 656p. 1999. pap. text 39.99 (0-13-020868-X) P-H.
Perl Programmer's Reference. Martin C. Brown. 380p. 1999. pap. 16.99 (0-07-212142-4) McGraw.
Perl Programming for NT Blue Book, 1. Michael M McMillan. 1999. pap. text 39.99 (1-57610-404-4) Coriolis Grp.
Perl Resource Kit, Win 32 Edition. Dick Hardt et al. (Illus.). 1900p. 1998. pap. 149.95 (1-56592-409-6) OReilly & Assocs.
***Perl Tools: A Guide to Streamlining & Automating the Software Development Process Using Perl.** Brad J. Murray. (Illus.). 300p. 2000. pap. 39.95 (1-884777-96-1, Pub. by Manning Pubns) IPG Chicago.
Perla. John Steinbeck. 1948. 16.05 (0-606-10444-5, Pub. by Turtleback) Demco.
Perla Meyers' Art of Seasonal Cooking. Perla Meyers. Ed. by Judy Knide. (Illus.). 527p. 1998. text 27.00 (0-7881-5291-2) DIANE Pub.
Perla Negra. 7th ed. Scott O'Dell. (Cuatro Vientos Ser.). (SPA.). (J). 1990. 15.05 (0-606-05404-9, Pub. by Turtleback) Demco.
Perla Negra (The Black Pearl) 7th ed. Scott O'Dell. (Cuatro Vientos). (SPA.). (YA). 1996. pap. 9.75 (84-279-3112-3) Lectorum Pubns.
***Perlas de Sabiduria.** Dadi Janki. (SPA.). 200p. 2000. pap. 12.95 (1-55874-791-5) Health Comm.
Perlas Misticas. A. Nervo. (SPA.). 147p. 1973. 9.95 (0-8288-7122-1) Fr & Eur.
Perle see Pearl
***Perle & Williams on Publishing Law.** 3rd ed. E. Gabriel Perle et al. LC 99-26810. 1999. ring bd. 295.00 (0-7355-0448-2) Panel Pubs.
Perle de la Canebiere. Eugene Labiche. 9.95 (0-686-54245-2) Fr & Eur.
Perle Noire. Paul Claudel. (FRE.). 250p. 1947. 8.95 (0-8288-9110-9, F94390) Fr & Eur.
Perle Si Comori. Nichifor Marcu. Ed. by Genovieva Sfatcu Beattie. (RUM.). 97p. 1995. pap. 5.00 (1-893179-09-5) Eastern Europe Aid.
Perles see Beads
Perles ou les Larmes de la Saincte Magdeleine. Nostredame. Ed. by Corum. (Exeter French Texts Ser.: Vol. 58). (FRE.). 64p. Date not set. pap. text 19.95 (0-85989-207-7, Pub. by Univ Exeter Pr) Northwestern U Pr.
Perley's Reminiscences of Sixty Years in the National Metropolis, 2 vols. Benjamin P. Poore. LC 74-158970. reprint ed. 74.50 (0-404-05076-X) AMS Pr.
Perley's Reminiscences of Sixty Years in the National Metropolis. Benjamin P. Poore. (Notable American Authors Ser.). 1999. reprint ed. lib. bdg. 125.00 (0-7812-8766-9) Rprt Serv.
Perlman's Ordeal. Brooks Hansen. LC 99-14275. (Illus.). 400p. 1999. text 24.00 (0-374-23078-1) FS&G.
***Perlman's Ordeal.** Brooks Hansen. 352p. 2000. pap. 14.00 (0-312-26765-7, Picador USA) St Martin.
***Perlman's Ordeal Reader's Edition.** abr. ed. Brooks Hansen. 1999. write for info. (0-374-96408-4) FS&G.
Perloff's Instructors Manual. PERLOFF. (C). 1998. pap. text 24.00 (0-201-83421-9) Addison-Wesley.
Perloo the Bold. Avi. LC 97-10681. (Illus.). 240p. (J). (gr. 3-7). 1998. 16.95 (0-590-11002-0, Pub. by Scholastic) Scholastic Inc.
***Perloo the Bold.** Avi. (Illus.). 256p. (J). (gr. 3-7). 1999. pap. 4.99 (0-590-11003-9, Pub. by Scholastic Inc) Penguin Putnam.
Perl/Tk Pocket Reference. Stephen Lidie. (Illus.). 104p. 1998. pap. 9.95 (1-56592-517-3) OReilly & Assocs.
Perly's BJ Map Book of Metro Toronto & Vicinity. deluxe ed. (Illus.). 288p. 1991. spiral bd. 14.95 (1-895028-11-6, Pub. by NC Ltd) U of Toronto Pr.
Perm Oblast: Economy, Industry, Government, Business. 2nd rev. ed. Russian Information & Business Center, Inc. Staff. (Russian Regional Business Directories Ser.). (Illus.). 200p. 1997. pap. 99.00 (1-57751-407-6) Intl Business Pubns.
***Perm Oblast Regional Investment & Business Guide.** Global Investment & Business Center, Inc. Staff. (Russian Regional Investment & Business Guides Ser.: Vol. 59). (Illus.). 350p. 1999. pap. 99.00 (0-7397-0858-9) Intl Business Pubns.
***Perm Oblast Regional Investment & Business Guide.** Contrib. by Global Investment & Business Center, Inc. Staff. (Russian Regional Investment & Business Guides Ser.: Vol. 59). (Illus.). 350p. 2000. pap. 99.95 (0-7397-3007-X) Intl Business Pubns.
Perm Waving Styles. Candi Ekstrom & Louise Cotter. LC 95-21219. (HAIR). (Illus.). 64p. 1996. 21.95 (1-56253-312-6) Thomson Learn.
Permaculture: A Designer's Manual. Bill Mollison. (Illus.). 576p. 1997. reprint ed. 45.00 (0-908228-01-5, Pub. by Tagari Pubns) RDLE INST Bkstre.
Permaculture Book of Ferment & Human Nutrition. Bill Mollison. (Illus.). 288p. (Orig.). 1997. pap. 29.95 (0-908228-06-6, Pub. by Tagari Pubns) RDLE INST Bkstre.
Permaculture in a Nutshell. Patrick Whitefield. (Illus.). 96p. 2000. pap. 9.00 (1-85623-003-1, Pub. by Hyden House) Chelsea Green Pub.
Permafrost & Its Effect on Life in the North. Troy L. Pewe. LC 67-2694. 40p. 1966. reprint ed. pap. 30.00 (0-608-01832-5, 206248100003) Bks Demand.
Permafrost in Canada: Its Influence on Northern Development. Roger J. Brown. LC 70-464841. (Canadian Building Ser.: No. 4). (Illus.). 250p. reprint ed. pap. 77.50 (0-8357-8265-4, 203398600088) Bks Demand.
***Permanecerenel Castillo.** Jerry Ross. (SPA., Illus.). 28p. 1999. pap. write for info. (0-7392-0338-X) Morris Pubng.
Permanence & Care of Color Photographs: Traditional & Digital Color Prints, Color Negatives, Slides, & Motion Pictures. Henry Wilhelm & Carol Brower. LC 84-6921. (Illus.). ix, 746p. (C). 1993. 39.95 (0-911515-00-3) Preserv Pub Co.
Permanence & Change: An Anatomy of Purpose. 3rd ed. Kenneth Burke. 1984. pap. 17.95 (0-520-04146-1, Pub. by U CA Pr) Cal Prin Full Svc.
Permanence & Evolution of Behavior in Golden-Age Spain: Essays in Gender, Body, & Religion. Intro. by Alain Saint-Saens. LC 92-2293. 1992. write for info. (0-7734-9527-4) E Mellen.
Permanence & Family Support: Changing Practice in Group Child Care. Ed. by Richard W. Small & Gary D. Carman. 1988. pap. 8.50 (0-87868-241-4, 2414) Child Welfare.
Permanence of Organic Coatings - STP 781. Ed. by G. G. Schurr. 132p. 1982. pap. 15.95 (0-8031-0827-3, STP781) ASTM.
Permanence of Paper for Publications & Documents in Libraries & Archives, Z39.48, 1992 (R1997) National Information Standards Organization Staff. LC 93-148. (National Information Standards Ser.). 10p. 1993. 40.00 (1-880124-00-9) NISO.
Permanence of the Political: A Democratic Critique of the Radical Impulse to Transcend Politics. Joseph M. Schwartz. LC 95-3045. 352p. 1995. text 42.50 (0-691-03357-9, Pub. by Princeton U Pr) Cal Prin Full Svc.
Permanency Planning: The Black Experience. Patricia B. Sipp & Mary H. Whaley. 369p. 1983. teacher ed. 17.00 (0-89695-008-5); 7.00 (0-89695-009-3) U Tenn CSW.
Permanency Planning for Children: Concepts & Methods. Anthony N. Maluccio et al. 350p. 1986. text 32.50 (0-422-78840-6, 4074, Pub. by Tavistock) Routldge.
Permanent Address: New Poems, 1973-1980. Ruth Whitman. LC 80-66182. (Illus.). 72p. 1980. pap. 3.95 (0-914086-30-8) Alice James Bks.
Permanent Ade: The Living Writings of George Ade. George Ade. (BCL1-PS American Literature Ser.). 347p. 1993. reprint ed. lib. bdg. 89.00 (0-7812-6943-1) Rprt Serv.
Permanent & Transient Networks. Ed. by M. Pietralla. (Progress in Colloid & Polymer Science Ser.: Vol. 75). 205p. 1988. 107.00 (0-387-91310-6) Spr-Verlag.
Permanent Book of Explorations. Ed. by John Keay. (Illus.). 443p. 1994. pap. 11.95 (0-7867-0034-3) Carroll & Graf.
Permanent Book of Twentieth Century Eyewitness History: An Enthralling Kaleidoscope of the Great Moments of Our Century. Ed. by Jon Lewis. (Illus.). 512p. 1995. pap. 11.95 (0-7867-0161-7) Carroll & Graf.
***Permanent Campaign & Its Future.** Ed. by Norman J. Ornstein & Thomas E. Mann. 250p. 2000. 39.95 (0-8447-4133-7, Pub. by Am Enterprise); pap. 16.95 (0-8447-4134-5, Pub. by Am Enterprise) Pub Resources Inc.

P

Permanent Change. John Skoyles. LC 90-84775. (Poetry Ser.). 64p. (Orig.). (C). 1991. pap. 11.95 (*0-88748-104-3*) Carnegie-Mellon.

Permanent Collection of Twentieth Century Prints: Ohio University Gallery of Fine Art. Ed. by Paul W. Richelson. LC 84-52582. (Illus.). 360p. (Orig.). 1985. pap. 14.95 (*0-933041-00-4*) Gallery Fine Art Ohio U.

Permanent Connections. Sue E. Bridgers. 272p. 1998. reprint ed. lib. bdg. 29.95 (*0-7351-0043-8*) Replica Bks.

Permanent Cosmetics A to Z. Susan Church. 143p. 1998. pap. 59.95 (*1-887080-05-8*) Action Publ.

***Permanent Cosmetics for the Consumer.** Susan Church. (Illus.). 85p. 1999. pap. 19.95 (*1-887080-08-2*) Action Pub.

***Permanent Court of Arbitration: International Arbitration & Dispute Resolution.** Ed. by P. Hamilton et al. 336p. 1999. text 135.00 (*90-411-1233-2*) Kluwer Law Intl.

Permanent Court of International Justice, 1920-1942: A Treatise. Manley O. Hudson. LC 72-4277. (World Affairs Ser.: National & International Viewpoints). 832p. 1972. reprint ed. 54.95 (*0-405-04571-9*) Ayer.

Permanent Deacons. 3rd ed. Russell B. Shaw. 19p. 1995. pap. text 1.95 (*1-55586-084-2*) US Catholic.

Permanent Deacons in the United States: Guidelines on Their Formation & Ministry. rev. ed. 53p. 1985. pap. 6.95 (*1-55586-974-2*) US Catholic.

Permanent Deformation Response of Asphalt Aggregate Mixes. (SHRP Ser.: A-415). (Illus.). 437p. (C). 1994. pap. text 15.00 (*0-309-05850-3*, PA415) Natl Res Coun.

Permanent Democratic Congress. Norman J. Ornstein. (Essay Ser.: No. 3). 31p. (C). 1991. pap. text 3.00 (*1-878802-02-X*) J M Ashbrook Ctr Pub Affairs.

Permanent Disability Benefits in Workers' Compensation. Monroe Berkowitz & John F. Burton, Jr. LC 87-22874. 440p. 1987. text 36.00 (*0-88099-051-1*); pap. text 18.00 (*0-88099-050-3*) W E Upjohn.

Permanent Education. Schwartz. 1974. pap. text 78.50 (*90-247-1648-9*, Pub. by M Nijhoff) Kluwer Academic.

Permanent Education Between New Illiteracy & High Power Technology. Ed. by Michael Schratz & Ursula Schneider. 1989. write for info. (*0-318-64257-3*); pap. text 10.00 (*0-9621423-0-1*) U New Orleans-ICSPP.

Permanent Establishment As a Basis for Tax - A Case Study. Ed. by J. David Oliver & Ian T. Rogers. 208p. 1991. pap. text 75.00 (*1-56423-003-1*) Ntl Ctr Tax Ed.

Permanent Establishments: A Planning Primer. John Huston & Lee Williams. LC 93-5894. 1993. write for info. (*90-6544-717-2*) Kluwer Law Intl.

Permanent Etcetera: Cross-cultural Perspectives on Post-War America. Lee. LC 93-24953. 199p. (C). 49.95 (*0-7453-0640-3*, Pub. by Pluto GBR); pap. 19.95 (*0-7453-0641-1*, Pub. by Pluto GBR) Stylus Pub VA.

Permanent Exiles: Essays on the Intellectual Migration from Germany to America. Martin Jay. 380p. 1990. pap. text 22.00 (*0-231-06073-4*, King's Crown Paperbacks) Col U Pr.

Permanent Extension of Most-favored-Nation (MNF) Trade Status to Romania: Hearing Before the Subcommittee on International Trade of the Committee on Finance, United States Senate, 104th Congress, Second Session on H. R. 3161 & S. 1644, June 4, 1996. LC 98-160401. (S. Hrg. Ser.). iv, 95p. 1998. write for info. (*0-16-056298-8*) USGPO.

***Permanent Family Placement for Children of Minority Ethnic Origin.** June Thoburn. (Illus.). 2000. pap. 27.95 (*1-85302-875-4*) Jessica Kingsley.

Permanent Fiscal Dictionary: Dictionnaire Permanent Fiscal, 2 vols. Legislative Administrative Staff. (FRE.). 5000p. 1989. 495.00 (*0-7859-4928-3*) Fr & Eur.

Permanent Healing. Daniel R. Condron. 224p. (Orig.). (C). 1992. pap. 13.00 (*0-944386-12-1*) SOM Pub.

***Permanent Heartache: A Portrait of Grief, Survival & Life after Homicide.** Marcella Hammett. 2000. pap. 18.95 (*1-56072-630-X*, Nova Kroshka Bks) Nova Sci Pubs.

Permanent Horizon. Ludwig Lewisohn. LC 73-117818. (Essay Index Reprint Ser.). 1977. 21.95 (*0-8369-1811-8*) Ayer.

Permanent Housing for the Homeless. Diana M. Pearce. 9p. 1989. pap. 4.00 (*0-685-29946-5*) Inst Womens Policy Rsch.

***Permanent Instruction of the Alta Vendita: A Masonic Blueprint for the Subversion of the Catholic Church.** John Vennari. LC 98-61685. 50p. 1999. pap. 2.00 (*0-89555-644-8*, 1591) TAN Bks Pubs.

Permanent Italians: An Illustrated Guide to the Cemeteries of Italy. Judi Culbertson & Tom Randall. LC 95-41353. (Permanent Ser.). (Illus.). 230p. (Orig.). 1996. pap. 16.95 (*0-8027-7431-8*) Walker & Co.

Permanent Job Loss & the U. S. System of Financing Unemployment Insurance. Frank Brechling & Louise Laurence. LC 95-19352. 116p. 1995. text 30.00 (*0-88099-160-7*) W E Upjohn.

Permanent Job Loss & the U. S. System of Financing Unemployment Insurance. Frank P. Brechling & Louise Laurence. LC 95-19352. 116p. 1995. pap. text 11.00 (*0-88099-159-3*) W E Upjohn.

Permanent Londoners: An Illustrated Guide to the Cemeteries of London. Judi Culbertson & Tom Randall. (Permanent Ser.). (Illus.). 230p. (Orig.). 1996. pap. 16.95 (*0-8027-7471-7*) Walker & Co.

Permanent Love: Practical Steps to a Lasting Relationship. 3rd ed. Edward E. Ford & Steven Englund. 148p. 1979. reprint ed. pap. 8.00 (*0-9616716-2-9*) Brandt Pub.

Permanent Magnet & Application Handbook. 2nd ed. Lester R. Moskowitz. LC 85-5629. (Illus.). 970p. (C). 1995. 149.50 (*0-89464-768-7*) Krieger.

Permanent-Magnet DC Linear Motors. Amitava Basak. LC 96-204958. (Monographs in Electrical & Electronic Engineering). (Illus.). 200p. (C). 1996. text 80.00 (*0-19-859392-9*) OUP.

Permanent Magnet Materials - Types, Processing, New Developments. 201p. 1992. 2475.00 (*0-89336-976-4*, GB-149A) BCC.

Permanent Magnet Materials & Devices. S. G. Sankar. 500p. 1998. text 137.00 (*981-02-1133-3*) World Scientific Pub.

Permanent-Magnet Materials & Their Applications. K. H. Buschow. (Materials Science Foundations Ser.: Vol. 5). (Illus.). 88p. (C). 1999. text 48.00 (*0-87849-796-X*, Pub. by Trans T Pub) Enfield Pubs NH.

Permanent Magnet Motor Technology: Design & Applications. Jacek F. Gieras & Mitchell Wing. LC 96-41104. (Electrical Engineering & Electronics Ser.: Vol. 99). (Illus.). 472p. 1996. text 165.00 (*0-8247-9794-9*) Dekker.

Permanent Magnet, Reluctance & Self-Synchronous Motors. Syed A. Nasar. 288p. 1993. boxed set 120.00 (*0-8493-9313-2*, TK2787) CRC Pr.

Permanent Magnet, Reluctance & Self-Synchronous Motors. L. E. Unnewehr et al. LC 66-55773. (Electrical Engineering Handbook Ser.). (Illus.). 300p. 1989. 75.00 (*0-89116-676-9*) CRC Pr.

***Permanent Magnetism.** R. Skomski. LC 99-27211. (Studies in Condensed Matter Physics). 1999. 175.00 (*0-7503-0478-2*) IOP Pub.

Permanent Menu Planning List: Mom's Meal Planners. rev. ed. KayLee Parker. (Illus.). 52p. 1995. pap. 3.95 (*1-883924-06-5*, 250) Your Moms Organizers.

Permanent Midnight. Jerry Stahl. 384p. 1998. mass mkt. 6.99 (*0-446-60726-6*, Pub. by Warner Bks) Little.

Permanent Parisians: An Illustrated Guide to the Cemeteries of Paris. Judi Culbertson & Tom Randall. (Permanent Ser.). (Illus.). 230p. 1996. pap. 16.95 (*0-8027-7470-9*) Walker & Co.

***Permanent Parisians: An Illustrated Guide to the Cemeteries of Paris.** Judi Culbertson & Tom Randall. (Illus.). 230p. 1999. reprint ed. pap. text 16.00 (*0-7881-6841-X*) DIANE Pub.

***Permanent Partial Disability Benefits: Interstate Differences in Approach.** Michael Niss & Peter Barth. LC 99-26093. 1999. 50.00 (*0-935149-79-1*, WC-99-2) Workers Comp Res Inst.

Permanent Partial Disability in Tennessee: Similar Benefits for Similar Injuries? Leslie I. Boden. LC 97-45625. 40p. 1997. pap. 50.00 (*0-935149-70-8*, WC-97-5) Workers Comp Res Inst.

Permanent Partners: Building Gay & Lesbian Relationships That Last. Betty Berzon. 352p. 1990. pap. 14.95 (*0-452-26308-5*, Plume) Dutton Plume.

Permanent Pilgrims: The Role of Pilgrimage in the Lives of West African Muslims in Sudan. C. Bawa Yamba. LC 95-68001. 224p. 1995. text 45.00 (*1-56098-612-3*) Smithsonian.

Permanent Presence - Making It Work, 22nd Goddard Memorial Symposium, Mar. 15-16, 1984, Greenbelt, MD. Ed. by Ivan Bekey. (Science & Technology Ser.: Vol. 60). (Illus.). 190p. 1985. 40.00 (*0-87703-207-6*, Am Astronaut Soc); pap. 30.00 (*0-87703-208-4*, Am Astronaut Soc) Univelt Inc.

***Permanent Prostate Seed Implant Brachytherapy No. 68: Report of the AAPM Radiation Therapy Committee TG No. 64.** Yang Yusheng et al. 22p. 2000. pap. text. write for info. (*1-888340-26-6*) AAPM.

Permanent Record, Military Roster of the Civil War, Town of Masonville, Delaware Co., NY. Compiled & Transcribed by Shirley B. Goerlich. LC 98-68621. 85p. 1999. pap. 25.00 (*1-887530-32-0*) RSG Pub.

Permanent Red: Essays in Seeing. John Berger. 223p. 1981. 12.95 (*0-906495-07-5*) Writers & Readers.

Permanent Red: Essays in Seeing. John Berger. (Illus.). 224p. 1981. pap. 6.95 (*0-904613-92-5*) Writers & Readers.

Permanent Remission: Life Extending Diet Strategies That Can Help Prevent & Reverse Cancer, Heart Disease, Diabetes & Osteoporosis. Robert Haas. 416p. 1998. pap. 14.00 (*0-671-00777-7*) S&S Trade.

Permanent Remissions. Ralph Ranald. LC 97-34766. 320p. 1997. 25.00 (*0-671-00776-9*) PB.

Permanent Representatives Committee. J. W. De Zwaan. LC 95-214946. 336p. 1995. 158.75 (*0-444-82274-7*) Elsevier.

Permanent Resident: or Returning Home: Ambassadors Magazine Collection. Ed. by Edwin Su et al. (Special Topic Ser.: No. 8). (CHI.). 255p. (Orig.). 1995. pap. write for info. (*1-882324-12-9*) Ambssdrs Christ.

Permanent Retirement. John Miles. (Worldwide Library Mysteries). 256p. 1997. per. 4.99 (*0-373-26228-0*, 1-26228-6, Wrldwide Lib) Harlequin Bks.

Permanent Retirement. John Miles. LC 92-12985. 230p. 1992. 19.95 (*0-8027-1243-6*) Walker & Co.

Permanent Revolution see Permanentnaia Revolutsiia: (Russian Original of "The Permanent Revolution")

Permanent Revolution: The French Revolution & Its Legacy, 1789-1989. Ed. by Geoffrey Best. LC 88-26181. 256p. 1994. lib. bdg. 24.95 (*0-226-04427-0*) U Ch Pr.

Permanent Revolution: The French Revolution & Its Legacy, 1789-1989. Ed. by Geoffrey Best. LC 88-26181. 156p. 1996. pap. text 13.50 (*0-226-04428-9*) U Ch Pr.

Permanent Revolution: The French Revolution & Its Legacy, 1789-1989. Geoffrey Best. LC 88-26181. 241p. Date not set. reprint ed. pap. 74.80 (*0-608-21013-7*, 205454100003) Bks Demand.

Permanent Satellite Tracking Networks for Geodesy & Geodynamics. Ed. by Gerald L. Mader. (International Association of Geodesy Symposia Ser.: Vol. 109). (Illus.). 210p. 1993. pap. write for info. (*3-540-55827-6*) Spr-Verlag.

Permanent Satellite Tracking Networks for Geodesy & Geodynamics: Symposium No. 109, Vienna, Austria, August 11-24, 1991. Ed. by Gerald L. Mader. LC 93-2186. (International Association of Geodesy Symposia Ser.: No. 109). 1993. 86.95 (*0-387-55827-6*) Spr-Verlag.

Permanent Settlement to Operation Barga. Samir K. Mukhopadhyay. (C). 1994. text 16.00 (*0-614-04131-7*, Pub. by Minerva) S Asia.

Permanent Temperance Documents of the American Temperance Society. American Temperance Society Staff. LC 77-38433. (Religion in America, Ser. 2). 566p. 1972. reprint ed. 42.95 (*0-405-04054-7*) Ayer.

Permanent Things: Hillsdale College, 1900-1994. Arlan K. Gilbert. LC 97-77191. 350p. 1998. text 15.95 (*0-916308-62-6*) Hillsdale Coll Pr.

Permanent Transcient Networks. 1988. 117.95 (*3-7985-0725-2*) Spr-Verlag.

***Permanent Twilight.** Chuck Freadhoff. LC 99-89805. 352p. 2000. 25.00 (*0-06-019216-X*) HarpC.

Permanent Wave. Siobhan Campbell. LC 96-140207. 86p. 1997. pap. 12.95 (*0-85640-572-8*, Pub. by Blackstaff Pr) Dufour.

Permanent Waves. Willett. text 55.00 (*0-8147-9357-6*); pap. text 18.50 (*0-8147-9358-4*) NYU Pr.

Permanent Weight Loss. abr. ed. Roger W. Breternitz. 1985. pap. 9.95 incl. audio (*1-893417-08-5*) Vector Studios.

Permanent Wood Foundation. Craftsman. 1995. 35.00 (*0-9694527-0-5*) J E Traister.

Permanent Work: Poems, 1981-1992. Gabriel T. Munoz. Tr. by Patricia L. Irby et al from SPA. (Baja California Literature in Translation Ser.). 96p. 1993. pap. 12.50 (*1-879691-13-2*) SDSU Press.

Permanently Bard: Selected Poetry. Tony Harrison. Ed. & Intro. by Carol Rutter. LC 98-126987. 176p. 1996. pap. 17.95 (*1-85224-262-0*, Pub. by Bloodaxe Bks) Dufour.

Permanently Failing Organizations. Marshall W. Meyer & Lynne G. Zucker. 180p. (C). 1989. text 38.95 (*0-8039-3258-8*); pap. text 19.50 (*0-8039-3259-6*) Sage.

Permanentnaia Revolutsiia: (Russian Original of "The Permanent Revolution") Leon Trotsky et al. Tr. & Intro. by Fleix Kreisel. LC 93-77102.Tr. of Permanent Revolution. (RUS., Illus.). 396p. (Orig.). 1994. pap. 16.00 (*1-883468-01-9*) Iskra Res.

Permanents. Henryk Minc. (Encyclopedia of Mathematics & Its Applications Ser.: No. 6). 205p. 1984. text 69.95 (*0-521-30226-9*) Cambridge U Pr.

Permar's Oral Embryology & Microscopic Anatomy: A Textbook for Students in Dental Hygiene. 9th ed. Rudy C. Melfi. LC 93-5248. (Illus.). 278p. 1994. 34.00 (*0-8121-1659-3*) Lppncott W & W.

Permeability & Groundwater Contaminant Transport - STP 746. Ed. by Zimmie & Riggs. 245p. 1981. 38.00 (*0-8031-0797-8*, STP746) ASTM.

Permeability & Other Film Properties of Plastics & Elastomers. Plastics Design Library Staff. (PDL Handbook Ser.). 716p. 1995. text 285.00 (*1-884207-14-6*) William Andrew.

Permeability & Stability of Lipid Bilayers. Ed. by E. A. Disalvo & Sidney A. Simon. LC 94-15447. 288p. 1995. boxed set 254.95 (*0-8493-4531-6*) CRC Pr.

Permeability of Cell Membranes. Abramoff. Date not set. 1.20 (*0-7167-9020-3*) W H Freeman.

Permeability of Concrete. Buenfeld. (Illus.). 224p. 1997. text 55.00 (*0-419-16980-6*, E & FN Spon) Routledge.

Permeability of Concrete. American Concrete Institute Staff. Ed. by David Whiting & Arthur Walitt. LC 88-71000. (ACI Publication: No. SP-108). (Illus.). 231p. reprint ed. pap. 71.70 (*0-7837-5223-7*, 204495500005) Bks Demand.

Permeable Barriers for Groundwater Remediation. Arun R. Gavaskar et al. LC 97-20764. 1998. 44.95 (*1-57477-036-5*) Battelle.

***Permed to Death.** Nancy J. Cohen. 304p. 1999. 20.00 (*1-57566-482-8*, Knsington) Kensgtn Pub Corp.

***Permented Foods of the World.** 2nd ed. Geoffrey Campbell-Platt. 376p. 2000. text 270.00 (*1-85573-502-4*, Pub. by Woodhead Pubng) Am Educ Systs.

Permesta Vol. 57: Half a Rebellion. Barbara S. Harvey. (Modern Indonesia Project Ser.). 174p. 1977. pap. 5.00 (*0-87763-003-8*) Cornell Mod Indo.

Permethrin. (Environmental Health Criteria Ser.: No. 94). 125p. 1990. pap. text 24.00 (*92-4-154294-2*, 1160094) World Health.

Permethrin Health & Safety Guide. WHO Staff. (Health & Safety Guides: No. 33). 29p. 1989. 5.00 (*92-4-154354-X*) World Health.

Permettez, Madame. Eugene Labiche. 9.95 (*0-686-54246-0*) Fr & Eur.

Permian & Triassic Rifting in Northwest Europe. Ed. by S. A. Boldy. (Geological Society Special Publication Ser.: No. 91). (Illus.). 263p. 1995. 100.00 (*1-897799-33-0*, 332, Pub. by Geol Soc Pub Hse) AAPG.

Permian of Northern Pangea. 1996. 183.00 (*0-387-57405-0*) Spr-Verlag.

Permian of Northern Pangea Vol. 2: Paleogeography, Paleoclimates, Stratigraphy. Ed. by Peter A. Scholle & T. M. Peryt. 320p. 1995. 108.95 (*0-387-57352-6*) Spr-Verlag.

Permian Stratigraphy & Fusulinida of Afghanistan. Ed. by E. Ja. Leven et al. Tr. by Tatyana Y. Shalashilina. LC 96-51130. (Special Papers: No. 316). 1997. pap. 45.00 (*0-8137-2316-7*) Geol Soc.

***Permian-Triassic Evolution of Tethys & Western Circum-Pacific.** Yin Hongfu. LC 00-37590. 2000. pap. write for info. (*0-444-50154-1*) Elsevier.

Permian-Triassic Pangean Basins & Foldbelts along the Panthalassan Margin of Gondwanaland. Ed. by J. J. Veevers & C. M. Powell. LC 94-5322. (Memoir Ser.: No. 184). (Illus.). 1994. 75.00 (*0-8137-1184-3*) Geol Soc.

Perming Techniques. Zotos Creative Designers Staff. (HAIR). 55p. 1993. pap. 16.95 (*1-56253-172-7*) Thomson Learn.

Permis de Sejour. Claude Roy. (FRE.). 1985. pap. 14.95 (*0-7859-4238-6*) Fr & Eur.

***Permissible Advantage? The Moral Consequences of Elite Schooling.** Alan Peshkin. 200p. 2000. write for info. (*0-8058-2466-9*) L Erlbaum Assocs.

***Permissible Advantage? The Moral Consequences of Elite Schooling.** Alan Peshkin. 200p. 2000. pap. write for info. (*0-8058-2467-7*) L Erlbaum Assocs.

Permissible Computing in Education: Values, Assumptions, & Needs. Ronald G. Ragsdale. LC 87-35964. 292p. 1988. 59.95 (*0-275-92894-2*, C2894, Praeger Pubs) Greenwood.

***Permissible Dose: A History of Radiation Protection in the Twentieth Century.** J. Samuel Walker. LC 00-23398. (Illus.). 189p. 2000. 35.00 (*0-520-22328-4*, Pub. by U CA Pr) Cal Prin Full Svc.

Permissible Killing: The Self-Defence Justification of Homicide. Suzanne Uniacke. LC 93-31988. (Studies in Philosophy & Law). 254p. (C). 1994. text 54.95 (*0-521-45408-5*) Cambridge U Pr.

Permissible Killing: The Self-Defence Justification of Homicide. Suzanne Uniacke. 253p. 1996. pap. text 17.95 (*0-521-56458-1*) Cambridge U Pr.

Permissible Levels of Occupational Exposure to Airborne Toxic Substances: Report of the ILO-WHO Committee on Occupational Health, 6th, Geneva, 1968. ILO-WHO Committee on Occupational Health Staff. (Technical Reports: No. 415). 1969. pap. text 3.00 (*92-4-120415-X*, 1100415) World Health.

***Permission Granted.** Harry F. Forbes. (Illus.). 521p. 1999. 24.95 (*0-9673657-0-8*); pap. write for info. (*0-9673657-1-6*) H F Forbes.

***Permission Marketing: Turning Strangers into Friends & Friends into Customers.** Seth Godin. LC 98-50352. 256p. 1999. 22.50 (*0-684-85636-0*) S&S Trade.

Permission Not Granted: How People Raised in Crisis-Oriented Families Carry Their Childhood Don'ts into Adulthood. James A. McKenna. LC 90-82212. (Illus.). 180p. (Orig.). 1990. pap. 10.95 (*1-878953-00-1*) Emily Pubns.

Permission to Believe: Four Rational Approaches to God's Existence. Lawrence Keleman. 104p. 1990. pap. 12.95 (*0-944070-55-8*, Pub. by Targum Pr) Feldheim.

Permission to Receive: Four Rational Approaches to the Torah's Divine Origin. Lawrence Keleman. 232p. 1996. pap. 15.95 (*1-56871-099-2*, Pub. by Targum Pr) Feldheim.

***Permission to Succeed.** Noah St. John. LC 99-22215. 150p. 1999. pap. 10.95 (*1-55874-719-2*) Health Comm.

Permission to Win. Ray Pelletier. LC 96-8180. (Illus.). 201p. 1996. 22.95 (*1-886939-10-1*, Pub. by OakHill Pr VA) ACCESS Pubs Network.

Permission/The Perfect Wife. M. J. Rennie. 1998. mass mkt. 6.95 (*1-56333-695-2*) Masquerade.

Permissive Action Links (PAL) A Description & Proposal. Dan Caldwell. (CISA Working Papers: No. 56). 27p. (Orig.). 1986. pap. 15.00 (*0-86682-073-6*) Ctr Intl Relations.

***Permissive Bargaining & Congressional Intent: A Special Report.** 2nd rev. ed. Jim Carroll. 131p. 1999. pap. 34.95 (*1-930542-04-6*) FPMI Comns.

Permissive Garden. Erica L. Pearce. 102p. 1987. 75.00 (*0-9511795-0-0*, Pub. by Sweethaws Pr) St Mut.

Permissiveness in Child Rearing & Education - A Failed Doctrine? New Trends for the 1990s. E. Lakin Philips. LC 92-35833. 134p. (C). 1993. text 42.50 (*0-8191-8978-2*) U Pr of Amer.

Permissiveness in Child Rearing & Education - A Failed Doctrine? New Trends for the 1990s. E. Lakin Phillips. LC 92-35833. 134p. (C). 1993. pap. text 21.50 (*0-8191-8979-0*) U Pr of Amer.

Permit Explosion: Coordination of the Proliferation. Fred P. Bosselman et al. LC 76-55844. (Management & Control of Growth Ser.). 96p. reprint ed. pap. 30.00 (*0-8357-8266-2*, 203394700087) Bks Demand.

Permit for Murder. Valerie Wolzien. 1997. mass mkt. 5.99 (*0-449-14960-9*) Fawcett.

Permit Me Voyage. James Agee. LC 70-144740. (Yale Series of Younger Poets: No. 33). reprint ed. 18.00 (*0-404-53833-9*) AMS Pr.

Permit on a Fly. Jack Samson. (Illus.). 192p. 1996. 29.95 (*0-8117-1244-3*) Stackpole.

Permit Their Flourishing: The First Year at the Palo Alto R C Pre-School. 2nd ed. Tim Jackins & Palo Alto Pre-School Staff. 72p. 1977. pap. 3.00 (*0-913937-99-1*) Rational Isl.

Permits Handbook for Coal Development. Cooper H. Wayman & Gail A. Genasci. Ed. by Jon W. Raese & Jean Goldberg. LC 80-22500. (CSM Press Replica Edition Ser.). (Illus.). 616p. 1981. 19.00 (*0-918062-40-3*) Colo Sch Mines.

Permits, Licenses, & Registrations: New England Edition. Frank Kirkpatrick. Ed. by Roger Griffith. LC 84-51488. 82p. 1985. 6.95 (*0-88266-374-7*, Storey Pub) Storey Bks.

Permitted & Prohibited Desires: Mothers, Comics, & Censorship in Japan. Anne Allison. LC 99-16356. 225p. 2000. pap. 16.95 (*0-520-21990-2*, Pub. by U CA Pr) Cal Prin Full Svc.

Permitted Dissent in the U. S. S. R. "Novy Mir" & the Soviet Regime. Dina Spechler. LC 81-17937. 293p. 1982. 49.95 (*0-275-90907-7*, C0907, Praeger Pubs) Greenwood.

P

Permo-Triassic Events in the Eastern Tethys: Stratigraphy Classification & Relations with the Western Tethys. Ed. by Walter C. Sweet et al. (World & Regional Geology Ser.: No. 2). (Illus.). 195p. (C). 1992. text 95.00 (*0-521-38214-9*) Cambridge U Pr.

Permselective Membranes: Selected Papers. American Chemical Society Symposium on Permselecti. Ed. by C. E. Rogers. LC 77-163051. (Illus.). 222p. reprint ed. pap. 68.90 (*0-7837-0900-5*, 204120500019) Bks Demand.

Permutation: A True UFO Story. Shirle Klein-Carsh & Ann C. Ulrich. (Illus.). 184p. (Orig.). 1993. pap. 11.95 (*0-944851-05-3*) Earth Star.

Permutation City. Greg Egan. 352p. 1995. mass mkt. 4.99 (*0-06-105481-X*) HarpC.

Permutation Groups. Peter Cameron. LC 98-45456. (London Mathematical Society Student Texts Ser.: No. 45). (Illus.). 232p. (C). 1999. text 64.95 (*0-521-65302-9*); pap. text 24.95 (*0-521-65378-9*) Cambridge U Pr.

Permutation Groups. John D. Dixon & Brian Mortimer. Ed. by S. Axler et al. LC 95-44880. (Graduate Texts in Mathematics Ser.: Vol. 163). (Illus.). 346p. (C). 1996. 49.00 (*0-387-94599-7*) Spr-Verlag.

Permutation Tests: A Practical Guide to Resampling Methods for Testing Hypotheses. Philip I. Good. LC 93-9062. (Series in Statistics). (Illus.). 228p. 1995. 58.95 (*0-387-94097-9*) Spr-Verlag.

***Permutation Tests: A Practical Guide to Resampling Methods for Testing Hypotheses.** 2nd ed. Phillip I. Good. LC 99-16557. (Statistics Ser.). (Illus.). 344p. 2000. 69.95 (*0-387-98898-X*) Spr-Verlag.

***Permutations of Permanency: Making Sensible Placement Decisions.** Richard J. Delaney. 32p. 1999. spiral bd. 4.95 (*1-885473-30-3*) Wood N Barnes.

Pernsteiners in America: A Genealogy. Florence P. Strange. LC 82-63174. (Illus.). 288p. 1984. pap. 45.00 (*0-931644-03-8*) Manzanita Pr.

Pero el Diablo Metio el Rabo: Profana y Atortoradora Novelilla Velivola en 22 Trances y 1 Introito. Alberto Andino. LC 85-70433. (Coleccion Caniqui). (SPA.). 97p. (Orig.). 1985. pap. 8.95 (*0-89729-370-3*) Ediciones.

Pero Papi, Porque? Michelle Graham.Tr. of But Daddy, Why?. (SPA., Illus.). 96p. (J). (gr. k-5). 1997. pap. 5.00 (*0-9658766-0-8*) Rays of Hope.

Pero Sigo Siendo el Rey. David S. Juliao. (SPA.). 269p. 1983. 9.00 (*0-317-15038-3*, 3012) Ediciones Norte.

Pero Tafur & Cyprus. Tr. by Colbert I. Nepaulsingh. (Sources for the History of Cyprus Ser.: Vol. IV). 85p. (Orig.). 1997. pap. 25.00 (*0-9651704-4-6*) Greece & Cyprus Res.

Peron & the Enigmas of Argentina. Robert O. Crassweller. (Illus.). 1988. pap. 16.95 (*0-393-30543-0*) Norton.

Peron Novel. Thomas E. Martinez. (SPA.). 1997. pap. 14.00 (*0-679-78146-3*) Vin Bks.

Peron Novel. Tomas E. Martinez. LC 98-46385. 1998. pap. 14.00 (*0-679-76801-7*) Random.

Peron Speaks: Speeches & Addresses of Juan Peron. Juan D. Peron. 1996. lib. bdg. 259.95 (*0-8490-6351-5*) Gordon Pr.

Peronism & Argentina. Ed. by James P. Brennan et al. LC 97-46486. (Latin American Silhouette Ser.). 232p. (C). 1998. 50.00 (*0-8420-2706-8*) Scholarly Res Inc.

Peronism & the Three Perons: A Checklist of Writings on the Peronism & on Juan Domingo, Eva, & Isabel Peron & Their Writings in the Hoover Institution Library & Archives & in the Stanford University Libraries. Compiled by L. Horvath. (Bibliographical Ser.: No. 71). 170p. 1988. pap. text 6.78 (*0-8179-2712-3*) Hoover Inst Pr.

Peronism Without Peron: Unions, Parties, & Democracy in Argentina. James W. Mcguire. LC 96-41942. 1997. 49.50 (*0-8047-2831-3*) Stanford U Pr.

Peronism Without Peron: Unions, Parties, & Democracy in Argentina. James W. Mcguire. 1999. pap. text 22.95 (*0-8047-3655-3*) Stanford U Pr.

Peronnik: A French Fairy Tale of the Grail Quest. Emile Souvestre. (Illus.). 26p. (gr. 1-5). 1984. 9.95 (*0-89281-061-0*) Inner Tradit.

Peron's Argentina. Juan D. Peron et al. 429p. 1973. 250.00 (*0-8490-0814-X*) Gordon Pr.

Peron's Argentina. George I. Blanksten. LC F 2849.B55. (Midway Reprint Ser.). 494p. reprint ed. pap. 153.20 (*0-608-12647-0*, 202408300035) Bks Demand.

Perot: An Unauthorized Biography. Todd Mason. 300p. 1990. text 22.95 (*1-55623-236-5*, Irwn Prfssnl) McGraw-Hill Prof.

Perot & His People: Disrupting the Balance of Political Power. Carolyn Barta. Ed. by Mike Towle. 500p. 1993. 22.95 (*1-56530-065-3*) Summit TX.

Perot Potential: How a Reformed Ross Perot & the American People Can Solve Our Country's Problems. Bob Galbraith. LC 93-87519. 200p. (C). 1993. pap. text 14.95 (*0-9640084-0-8*) Nation Pubs.

Perot Voters & the Future of American Politics. Albert J. Menendez. LC 96-3754. (Illus.). 277p. 1996. 25.95 (*1-57392-044-4*) Prometheus Bks.

Perote Prisoners. Frederick C. Chabot. 1993. reprint ed. lib. bdg. 75.00 (*0-7812-5921-5*) Rprt Serv.

Perouse-Marches see Grande Encyclopedie

Perovskite: A Structure of Great Interest to Geophysics & Materials Sciences. Ed. by Alexandra Navrotsky & D. J. Weidner. (Geophysical Monograph Ser.: Vol. 45). 146p. 1989. 27.00 (*0-87590-071-2*) Am Geophysical.

Perovskites & High Tc Superconductors. Francis S. Galasso. xiii, 294p. 1990. text 203.00 (*2-88124-391-6*) Gordon & Breach.

Peroxidases in Chemistry & Biology, II. Ed. by Johannes Everse et al. 400p. 1990. lib. bdg. 239.00 (*0-8493-6964-9*) CRC Pr.

Peroxidases in Chemistry & Biology, Vol. I. Ed. by Johannes Everse et al. 400p. 1990. lib. bdg. 239.00 (*0-8493-6963-0*, QP603) CRC Pr.

Peroxides & Peroxy Compounds, Inorganic to Piping Systems see Encyclopedia of Chemical Technology

Peroxides, Superoxides, & Ozonides of Alkai & Alkaline Earth Metals. Ilya I. Volnov. Ed. by A. W. Petrocelli. Tr. by J. Woroncow from RUS. LC 66-22125. (Monographs in Inorganic Chemistry). (Illus.). 160p. 1966. reprint ed. pap. 49.60 (*0-608-05407-0*, 206587600006) Bks Demand.

Peroxidizing Herbicides. R. Von Bothmer et al. LC 98-40482. 350p. 1999. 150.00 (*3-540-64550-0*) Spr-Verlag.

Peroximones: A Personal Account. Frank Roels. (Illus.). 151p. 1994. pap. 23.00 (*90-70289-94-6*) Paul & Co Pubs.

Peroxisomal B-Oxidation: Partial Characterization of the Rat Peroxisomal Acyl-CoA Synthetases & Molecular Cloning of the Rat & Human Acyl-Coa Oxidases. Johannes C. Vanhooren. (Acta Biomedica Lovaniensia Ser.: Vol. 141). (Illus.). 130p. 1996. pap. 33.50 (*90-6186-786-X*, Pub. by Leuven Univ) Coronet Bks.

Peroxisome: A Vital Organelle. Colin Masters & Denis Crane. (Illus.). 304p. (C). 1995. text 74.95 (*0-521-48212-7*) Cambridge U Pr.

Peroxisome Biogenesis: Identification & Characterization of the Import Receptor for Peroxisomal Proteins Containing a C-Terminal Targeting Sequence. Marc Fransen. (Acta Biomedica Lovaniensia Ser.: No. 121). (Illus.). 111p. (Orig.). 1996. pap. 39.50 (*90-6186-726-6*, Pub. by Leuven Univ) Coronet Bks.

Peroxisome Proliferation & Its Role in Carcinogenesis: Views & Expert Opinions of an IARC Working Group. (IARC Technical Report Ser.: No. 24). 90p. 1995. text 30.00 (*92-832-1439-0*, 1770024) World Health.

Peroxisome Proliferators: Unique Inducers of Drug-Metabolizing Enzymes. Ed. by David E. Moody. 208p. 1994. lib. bdg. 199.00 (*0-8493-8305-6*, 8305) CRC Pr.

Peroxisomes. Ed. by N. Latruffe & M. Bugaut. 210p. 1994. student ed. 107.95 (*0-387-56860-3*) Spr-Verlag.

Peroxisomes: Biology & Importance in Toxicology & Medicine. Ed. by G. Gordan Gibson & Brian G. Lake. 734p. 1993. 205.00 (*0-7484-0053-2*, Pub. by Tay Francis Ltd) Taylor & Francis.

Peroxisomes: Biology & Role in Toxicology & Disease. Janardan K. Reddy. LC 96-39418. (Annals of the New York Academy of Sciences Ser.). 801p. 1997. 150.00 (*0-89766-967-3*) NY Acad Sci.

Peroxisomes & Related Particles in Animal Tissues. P. Boeck et al. (Cell Biology Monographs: Vol. 7). (Illus.). 250p. 1980. 121.00 (*0-387-81582-1*) Spr-Verlag.

Peroxisomes in Biology & Medicine. Ed. by H. D. Fahimi & Helmut Sies. (Proceedings in Life Sciences Ser.). (Illus.). xii, 446p. 1987. 150.95 (*0-387-16689-0*) Spr-Verlag.

Peroxy Compounds to Polyelectrolytes see Encyclopedia of Polymer Science & Engineering

***Preparation Kit for the TOEFL Test 2001.** Patricia Noble Sullivan. 448p. 2000. pap. 29.95 (*0-7645-6123-5*) IDG Bks.

Perpectives on Communication in the People's Republic of China. James A. Schnell. LC 99-30451. 176p. 1999. 55.00 (*0-7391-0013-0*) Lxngtn Bks.

Perpendicular Magnetic Recording. Ed. by Shun-ichi Iwasaki & Jiro Hokkyo. 225p. (gr. 12). 1991. 80.00 (*90-5199-051-0*, Pub. by IOS Pr) IOS Press.

Perpendiculars see Key to Geometry Series - Book 1-8

Perpendiculars & Parallels, Chords & Tangents, Circles see Key to Geometry Series - Book 1-8

Perpertual Peace: Kant. Lewis W. Beck. 80p. (C). 1957. pap. text 6.00 (*0-02-307750-6*, Macmillan Coll) P-H.

Perpetrators, Victims & the Courts. Ed. by Byrgen P. Finkelman. LC 95-753. (Child Abuse; a Multidisciplinary Survey Ser.: Vol. 9). 440p. 1995. text 79.00 (*0-8153-1821-9*) Garland.

Perpetrators Victims Bystanders: Jewish Catastrophe 1933-1945. Raul Hilberg. LC 92-52551. 352p. 1993. reprint ed. pap. 14.00 (*0-06-099507-6*, A Asher Bks) HarpC.

Perpetua. Olga Broumas. LC 89-61455. 96p. (Orig.). 1989. pap. 11.00 (*1-55659-025-3*) Copper Canyon.

***Perpetua.** Fraser Grace. (Oberon Bks.). 2000. pap. 12.95 (*1-84002-122-5*) Theatre Comm.

Perpetual Angelus: As the Saints Pray the Rosary. Romanus Cessario. LC 94-42253. 1995. pap. 9.95 (*0-8189-0722-3*) Alba.

Perpetual Calendar of Poems: With Twelve Signed Prints. deluxe limited ed. David B. Axelrod. Tr. by Nina Scammacca et al. (Illus.). 31p. 1989. 100.00 (*0-89304-533-0*) Cross-Cultrl NY.

Perpetual Chantries in Britain. Kathleen Wood-Legh. LC 65-28505. 373p. reprint ed. pap. 106.40 (*0-608-12487-7*, 2024564) Bks Demand.

Perpetual Dilemma: Jewish Religion in the Jewish State. S. Zalman Abramov. LC 74-5897. 459p. 1976. 48.50 (*0-8386-1687-9*) Fairleigh Dickinson.

Perpetual Dream: Reform & Experiment in the American College. Gerald Grant & David Riesman. LC 77-11039. 480p. 1997. pap. text 6.95 (*0-226-30606-2*, P839) U Ch Pr.

Perpetual Enterprise Machine: Seven Keys to Corporate Renewal Through Successful Product Development. H. Kent Bowen et al. LC 93-43172. (Illus.). 464p. (C). 1994. 30.00 (*0-19-508052-1*) OUP.

Perpetual Estate Planning. Becker. 1993. 125.00 (*0-316-08663-0*, Aspen Law & Bus) Aspen Pub.

***Perpetual Income: How to Generate Cash Flow from Low-End House Investments.** Bryan Wittenmyer. 183p. 1999. pap. 39.00 (*0-9644380-1-1*) Real Estate Enter.

Perpetual Mirage: Photographic Narratives of the Desert West. May Castleberry. LC 95-25999. (Illus.). 1996. write for info. (*0-87427-100-2*) Whitney Mus.

Perpetual Motif: The Art of Man Ray. Merry Foresta et al. (Illus.). 344p. 1998. pap. 39.95 (*0-7892-0440-1*) Abbeville Pr.

Perpetual Motion. Graeme Gibson. 280p. 1998. pap. text 8.95 (*0-7710-3462-8*) McCland & Stewart.

Perpetual Motion. Ed. by Sue Henger. LC 87-81546. (Illus.). 96p. 1987. pap. 20.00 (*0-911291-14-8*, Pub. by Fellows Cont Art) RAM Publications.

Perpetual Motion. Otis Stuart. (Illus.). 320p. 1995. 24.00 (*0-671-87539-6*) S&S Trade.

***Perpetual Motivation: How to Light Your Fire & Keep It Burning.** Dave Durand. Ed. by Warren Jamison. 2000. pap. 12.00 (*0-9675631-0-0*) ProBalance.

***Perpetual Mourning: Widowhood in Rural India.** Martha A. Chen. 416p. 2000. pap. 24.95 (*0-19-564885-4*) OUP.

Perpetual Orgy. Mario Vargas Llosa. Tr. by Helen Lane from SPA. 275p. 1987. pap. 8.95 (*0-374-52062-3*) FS&G.

Perpetual Orgy. Mario Vargas Llosa & Flaubert & Madame Bovary. Tr. by Helen Lane from SPA. 239p. 1986. 17.95 (*0-374-23077-3*) FS&G.

Perpetual Peace. Immanuel Kant. 1972. 59.95 (*0-8490-0815-8*) Gordon Pr.

Perpetual Peace: A Philosophical Essay (1903 Edition) Immanuel Kant. (Key Texts Ser.). 218p. 1996. reprint ed. pap. 19.95 (*1-85506-159-7*) Bks Intl VA.

Perpetual Peace: Essays on Kant's Cosmopolitan Ideal. Ed. by James Bohman & Matthias Lutz-Bachmann. LC 96-37739. (Studies in Contemporary German Social Thought). (Illus.). 272p. 1997. 38.50 (*0-262-02428-4*) MIT Pr.

Perpetual Peace: Essays on Kant's Cosmopolitan Ideal. Ed. by James Bohman & Matthias Lutz-Bachmann. LC 96-37739. (Studies in Contemporary German Social Thought). (Illus.). 272p. 1997. pap. text 19.50 (*0-262-52235-7*) MIT Pr.

Perpetual Peace & Other Essays on Politics, History, & Moral Practice. Immanuel Kant. Ed. & Tr. by Ted Humphrey from GER. LC 82-11748. (HPC Classics Ser.). 168p. (C). 1982. pap. text 8.95 (*0-915145-47-2*); lib. bdg. 24.95 (*0-915145-48-0*) Hackett Pub.

Perpetual Prisoner Machine: How America Profits from Crime. Joel Dyer. LC 99-45576. 318p. 2000. 26.00 (*0-8133-3507-8*, Pub. by Westview) HarpC.

Perpetual Promotion: How to Contact Producers & Create Media Appearances. Brian Jud. Ed. by Charles Lipka & Roberta Buland. LC 97-72129. (Illus.). 100p. (Orig.). 1997. pap. 14.95 (*1-880218-27-5*) Mktg Dir Inc.

Perpetual Property Law. 2nd ed. Robert C. Ellickson. 576p. 1995. pap. text 28.95 (*0-316-23157-6*, Aspen Law & Bus) Aspen Pub.

***Perpetual War for Perpetual Peace.** Robert A. Divine. LC 00-20198. (Foreign Relations & the Presidency Ser.: Vol. 5). 128p. 2000. 29.95 (*0-89096-953-1*); pap. 14.95 (*1-58544-105-8*) Tex A&M Univ Pr.

Perpetual War for Perpetual Peace. enl. rev. ed. Harry E. Barnes. 1982. lib. bdg. 250.00 (*0-87700-454-4*) Revisionist Pr.

Perpetual Waterfalls. David Ashbee. 68p. 1989. reprint ed. pap. 11.95 (*0-905289-84-6*, Pub. by Enitha Pr) Dufour.

Perpetual Youth: An Occult & Historical Romance. Henry Proctor. 115p. 1993. reprint ed. spiral bd. 13.00 (*0-7873-0678-9*) Hlth Research.

Perpetuality of Marriage: A Matter of Faith. James J. D'Amato. Ed. by Josephine DeStefano. 33p. 1994. 14.95 (*0-9621266-3-2*) IPPD.

***Perpetually Perplexed Parents' Guide to the SAT I: Test Preparation.** Suzee J. Vlk. LC 99-47806. 160p. 2000. pap. text 10.95 (*0-7641-1284-8*) Barron.

Perpetua's Passion: The Death & Memory of a Young Roman Woman. Joyce Salisbury. LC 97-21973. 240p. 1997. pap. 20.99 (*0-415-91837-5*) Routledge.

Perpetua's Passion: The Death & Memory of a Young Roman Woman. Joyce Salisbury. LC 97-21973. (Illus.). 240p. (C). 1997. 75.00 (*0-415-91836-7*) Routledge.

***Perpetuating Our Posterity: Alpha Kappa Alpha Educational Advancement Foundation, a Blueprint for Excellence.** Constance K. Holland et al. (Illus.). xii, 100p. 2000. 20.00 (*0-9677128-0-7*) Alpha Kappa.

Perpetuating Patriotic Perceptions: The Cognitive Function of the Cold War. Matthew S. Hirshberg. LC 92-16209. 248p. 1993. 57.95 (*0-275-94165-5*, C4165, Praeger Pubs) Greenwood.

Perpetuating Poverty: The World Bank, the IMF, & the Developing World. Ed. by Doug Bandow. LC 93-48499. 320p. 1993. 25.95 (*1-882577-06-X*) Cato Inst.

***Perpetuating Power.** Jorge Castaneda. Tr. by Padraic Arthur Smithies from SPA. 2000. 30.00 (*1-56584-616-8*) New Press NY.

Perpetuating the Pork Barrel: Policy Subsystems & American Democracy. Robert M. Stein & Kenneth N. Bickers. (Illus.). 248p. (C). 1995. text 59.95 (*0-521-48298-4*) Cambridge U Pr.

Perpetuating the Pork Barrel: Policy Subsystems & American Democracy. Robert M. Stein & Kenneth N. Bickers. (Illus.). 256p. 1997. pap. text 18.95 (*0-521-59584-3*) Cambridge U Pr.

Perpetuities in a Nutshell & The Nutshell Revisited, 2 vols., Set. W. Barton Leach. 1983. reprint ed. pap. 5.00 (*0-686-89066-3*, MICHIE) LEXIS Pub.

Perpetuity Blues & Other Stories. Neal Barrett. 2000. 21.95 (*0-9655901-4-3*, Pub. by Golden Gryphon) IPG Chicago.

Perpignan City Plan. (Grafocarte Maps Ser.). 1996. 8.95 (*2-7416-0092-9*, 80092) Michelin.

Perplexed Philosopher. Henry George. LC 87-26638. 276p. 1988. 18.00 (*0-911312-80-3*) Schalkenbach.

Perplexed Philosopher. Henry George. (Notable American Authors Ser.). 1992. reprint ed. lib. bdg. 75.00 (*0-7812-2919-7*) Rprt Serv.

Perplexed Prophets: Six Nineteenth Century British Authors. Gaylord C. Le Roy. LC 78-147220. 205p. 1971. reprint ed. lib. bdg. 59.50 (*0-8371-5985-7*, LEPR, Greenwood Pr) Greenwood.

Perplexing Lateral Thinking Puzzles: Scholastic Edition. Paul Sloane. (J). 1997. 3.95 (*0-8069-1769-5*) Sterling.

Perplexing Mazes. Lee D. Quinn. (Illus.). 64p. (Orig.). 1992. pap. 3.95 (*0-486-26945-0*) Dover.

Perplexing Problems see Temas Desconcertantes

Perplexing Problems in Probability: Festschrift in Honor of Harry Kesten. Ed. by R. Durrett & M. Bramson. LC 99-14285. (Progress in Probability Ser.: Vol. 44). (Illus.). 432p. 1999. 79.95 (*0-8176-4093-2*) Birkhauser.

Perplexing Problems in Probability: Festschrift in Honor of Harry Kesten Harry Kesten et al. LC 99-14285. (Progress in Probability Ser.). 1999. write for info. (*3-7643-4093-2*) Birkhauser.

Perplexing Puzzlers. Ann R. Fisher. (Illus.). 80p. (J). (gr. 4-8). 1992. student ed. 10.99 (*0-86653-677-9*, 1411) Good Apple.

Perplexing Puzzles & Tantalizing Teasers. 80th ed. Martin Gardner. (Illus.). 256p. (Orig.). 1988. reprint ed. pap. 5.95 (*0-486-25637-5*) Dover.

Perplexities: Rational Choice, the Prisoner's Dilemma, Metaphor, Poetic Ambiguity, & Other Puzzles. Max Black. LC 89-34777. 224p. 1990. text 37.50 (*0-8014-2230-2*) Cornell U Pr.

***Perplexities of Identification: Anthropological Studies in Cultural Differentiation & the Use of Resources.** Ed. by Henk Driessen & Ton Otto. (Illus.). 265p. (C). 2000. 29.95 (*87-7288-818-0*, Pub. by Aarhus Univ Pr) David Brown.

Perplexity & Knowledge. Clark. 1972. lib. bdg. 94.00 (*90-247-1289-0*, Pub. by M Nijhoff) Kluwer Academic.

Perplexity & Ultimacy: Metaphysical Thoughts from the Middle. William Desmond. LC 94-17003. 263p. (C). 1995. text 59.50 (*0-7914-2387-5*); pap. text 19.95 (*0-7914-2388-3*) State U NY Pr.

Perplexity in the Moral Life: Philosophical & Theological Considerations. Edmund N. Santurri. LC 87-16211. (Studies in Religion & Culture). 251p. 1987. pap. 77.90 (*0-7837-8439-2*, 204924300010) Bks Demand.

Perpsectives in Human Biology. Knapp. (Biology Ser.). 1997. mass mkt., student ed. 15.00 (*0-314-21012-1*) West Pub.

Perquimans County: A Brief History. Alan D. Watson. (Illus.). xi, 122p. (Orig.). 1987. pap. 6.00 (*0-86526-220-9*) NC Archives.

***Perrault's Complete Fairy Tales.** Charles Perrault. (Classics for Young Readers Ser.). (Illus.). (J). 2000. pap. 4.99 (*0-14-130651-3*, PuffinBks) Peng Put Young Read.

Perrault's Fairy Tales. Charles Perrault. LC 72-79522. (Illus.). 117p. (J). (gr. 4-6). 1969. reprint ed. pap. 6.95 (*0-486-22311-6*) Dover.

Perrier Pig. Elizabeth Spurr. 32p. (J). 2000. 15.99 (*0-7868-0302-9*, Pub. by Hyprn Child); lib. bdg. 16.49 (*0-7868-2242-2*, Pub. by Hyprn Child) Little.

Perrin Beacon Hd Bk & Desk Ref. 5th ed. Perrin. Date not set. pap. text 19.17 (*0-395-98207-3*) HM.

Perrine's Literature: Structure, Sound & Sense. 7th ed. Thomas R. Arp. LC 97-72035. 1552p. (C). 1997. text 47.50 (*0-15-503822-2*, Pub. by Harcourt Coll Pubs) Harcourt.

Perrines Sound & Sense. 10th ed. Harcourt Brace Publishers. (C). 2000. write for info. (*0-15-507396-6*) Harcourt Coll Pubs.

Perrine's Sound & Sense: An Introduction to Poetry. 9th ed. William Kornblum. LC 96-77101. 432p. (C). 1996. pap. text 33.50 (*0-15-503028-0*, Pub. by Harcourt Coll Pubs) Harcourt.

Perrine's Story & Structure. 9th ed. Thomas R. Arp & Laurence Perrine. LC 97-72036. 624p. (C). 1997. pap. text 34.00 (*0-15-503721-8*, Pub. by Harcourt Coll Pubs) Harcourt.

Perrine's Story & Structure. 9th ed. Laurence Perrine. (C). 1997. pap. text, teacher ed. 28.00 (*0-15-503722-6*) Harcourt Coll Pubs.

Perrins Ledge Crematory. Jane E. Buikstra & Lynne G. Goldstein. (Reports of Investigations Ser.: No. 28). (Illus.). 40p. 1973. pap. 2.00 (*0-89792-052-X*) Ill St Museum.

Perris Reservoir Archeology No. 14: Late Prehistory Demographic Change in Southeastern California. Ed. by James F. O'Connell et al. (Publications of the Department of Parks & Recreation: No. 14). (Illus.). 187p. (C). 1974. reprint ed. pap. text 20.00 (*1-55567-465-8*) Coyote Press.

Perro de la Sol. Stephen King. 1999. pap. 5.99 (*0-451-18661-3*, Sig) NAL.

Perro del Cerro y la Rana de la Sabana. Ana Maria Machado.Tr. of Hound from the Mound & the Frog from the Bog. (SPA.). (J). 1998. pap. 6.95 (*980-257-021-4*, Pub. by Ediciones Ekare) Kane-Miller Bk.

Perro del Hortelano. Lope de Vega. Ed. by Antonio Carreno. (Nueva Austral Ser.: No. 221). (SPA.). 1991. pap. text 11.95 (*84-239-7221-6*) Elliots Bks.

Perro del Hortelano. 7th ed. Lope de Vega. 184p. 1991. pap. 12.95 (*0-7859-5202-0*) Fr & Eur.

Perro Grande--Pero Pequeno (Big Dog--Little Dog) Un Cuento de las Buenas Noches (A Bedtime Story) P. D. Eastman. (ENG & SPA.). (J). 1982. 8.45 (*0-606-04768-9*, Pub. by Turtleback) Demco.

Perro Grande...Perro Pequeno: (Big Dog...Little Dog) P. D. Eastman. Tr. by Pilar De Cuenca & Ines Alvarez. LC 81-12070. (Bilingual Picturebacks Ser.). (SPA., Illus.). 32p. (J). (ps-3). 1982. reprint ed. pap. 3.25 (*0-394-85142-0*, Pub. by Random Bks Yng Read) Random.

An Asterisk (*) at the beginning of an entry indicates that the title is appearing for the first time.

Perro Huevero Aunque le Quemen el Hocico. Juan F. Valerio. Ed. by Jose A. Escapanter & Jose A. Madrigal. LC 86-60602. (SPA.). 108p. 1986. pap. 18.00 (*0-89295-045-5*) Society Sp & Sp-Am.

Perrone Plan. Tony Perone. Date not set. mass mkt. 7.99 (*0-06-109789-6*) HarpC.

Perros. Anne T. Perkins. Tr. by Maria RRinglstetter. (Big Books - Mini Bks.). (SPA., Illus.). 8p. (J). (ps-k). 1994. 12.00 (*1-884204-10-4*) Teach Nxt Door.

*__Perros en la Escuela.__ Suzanne Hardin. Tr. by Alberto Romo. (Books for Young Learners).Tr. of Dogs at School. (SPA., Illus.). 16p. (J). (gr. k-2). 1999. pap. text 5.00 (*1-57274-338-7*, A2887) R Owen Pubs.

Perros y el Hueso. Natalio Dominguez. (Fabulas Creaticas Ser.). (SPA.). 28p. (J). 1994. pap. write for info. (*0-929441-60-5*) Pubns Puertorriquenas.

Perry. A Branch of the Peery Family Tree: Ancestors & Descendants of James Peery Who Came to Delaware about 1730. Lynn Perry. (Illus.). 125p. 1995. reprint ed. pap. 19.50 (*0-8328-4818-2*); reprint ed. lib. bdg. 29.50 (*0-8328-4817-4*) Higginson Bk Co.

Perry. An Incomplete History of the Descendants of John Perry of London, 1604-1955. Bertram Adams. (Illus.). 738p. 1991. reprint ed. pap. 105.00 (*0-8328-1992-1*); reprint ed. lib. bdg. 115.00 (*0-8328-1991-3*) Higginson Bk Co.

*__Perry & the Professor: A Prairie Dog Story.__ William H. Edwards. LC 99-67184. (Illus.). 52p. 2000. pap. 10.95 (*1-888106-55-7*) Agreka Bks.

Perry Anderson: The Merciless Laboratory of History. Gregory Elliott. LC 98-29687. (Cultural Politics Ser.: Vol. 15). (Illus.). 336p. 1998. 39.95 (*0-8166-2966-8*) U of Minn Pr.

Perry Como Sings. John Gorman. (By-Invitation-Only Ser.). 22p. 1992. pap. 6.00 (*1-882448-00-6*, Machiavellian) Mac-Kinations.

Perry County, a History. Thomas J. De la Hunt. (Illus.). 359p. 1992. reprint ed. lib. bdg. 41.00 (*0-8328-2548-4*) Higginson Bk Co.

Perry County, Arkansas Census, 1850. Courtney York & Gerlene York. (Orig.). 1969. pap. 12.00 (*0-916660-03-6*) Hse of York.

Perry County, Ohio: Clement L. Martzolff 1902 History Index. Fay Maxwell. 18p. 1983. 12.00 (*1-885463-26-X*) Ohio Genealogy.

Perry. Descendants of James Newton Perry. Rachel S. Tefft. 44p. 1997. pap. 9.00 (*0-8328-9489-3*); lib. bdg. 19.00 (*0-8328-9488-5*) Higginson Bk Co.

Perry Farrell: The Saga of a Hypester. Dave Thompson. (Illus.). 256p. 1995. pap. 12.95 (*0-312-13585-8*, St Martin Griffin) St Martin.

Perry in Toyland. Rhoda Blumberg. pap. write for info. (*0-688-16678-4*, Wm Morrow) Morrow Avon.

Perry Mason: The Authorship & Reproduction of a Popular Hero, 56. J. Dennis Bounds. LC 96-5458. (Contributions to the Study of Popular Culture Ser.: Vol. 56). 240p. 1996. 59.95 (*0-313-29809-2*, Greenwood Pr) Greenwood.

Perry Mason in the Case of the Burning Bequest. Thomas Chastain. 224p. 1991. mass mkt. 3.99 (*0-380-71318-7*, Avon Bks) Morrow Avon.

Perry Mason in the Case of Too Many Murders. Thomas Chastain. 256p. 1990. pap. 3.95 (*0-380-70787-X*, Avon Bks) Morrow Avon.

Perry Mason in the Case of Too Many Murders. large type ed. Thomas Chastain. LC 90-10732. 322p. 1990. 19.95 (*0-89621-974-7*) Thorndike Pr.

Perry of London: A Family & a Firm on the Seaborne Frontier, 1615-1753. Jacob M. Price. (Historical Studies: Vol. No. III). (Illus.). 208p. 1992. text 30.00 (*0-674-66306-3*) HUP.

Perry Sources 20th Century Eur. Perry. Date not set. pap. text 24.57 (*0-395-92568-1*) HM.

Perry, the Pet Pig. Eunice A. Pennington. (Illus.). (J). (gr. 4-7). 1966. 3.00 (*0-685-19374-8*, 911120-06-8) Pennington.

Perry, the Pet Pig. Eunice a. Pennington. (Illus.). (J). (gr. 4-7). 1966. pap. 1.00 (*0-685-19375-6*) Pennington.

Perry Western Civ Complete. 6th ed. Perry. 1999. pap. text 54.27 (*0-395-95935-7*) HM.

Perry Western Civ V1. 6th ed. Perry. 1999. pap. text 39.57 (*0-395-95936-5*) HM.

Perry Western Civ V2. 6th ed. Perry. 1999. pap. text 39.57 (*0-395-95937-3*) HM.

Perry's Bay: An Encounter with Japan in Summer of 1853. Bayard Taylor et al. 50p. 1995. pap. 7.95 (*0-910704-94-5*) Hawley.

Perry's Chemical Engineers' Handbook. 7th ed. Robert H. Perry & Don W. Green. LC 96-51648. (Illus.). 2640p. 1991. 150.00 (*0-07-049841-5*) McGraw.

Perry's Dead! (And the "Juice" Is Loose) Legal Humor. Victor A. Fleming. (Illus.). 200p. (Orig.). 1995. pap. write for info. (*0-9649323-0-X*) VAF I Swear.

Perry's Department Store: A Buying Simulation. Guthrie & Pierce. (Fashion Merchandising Ser.). 60p. 1996. text, teacher ed. 12.00 (*0-8273-6728-7*) Delmar.

Perrys of Rhode Island, & Tales of Silver Creek. C. B. Perry. (Illus.). 115p. reprint ed. pap. 23.00 (*0-8328-1655-8*); reprint ed. lib. bdg. 33.00 (*0-8328-1654-X*) Higginson Bk Co.

Perrywinkle's Magic Match. Ross Martin Madsen. LC 95-45185. (Illus.). 40p. (J). (gr. 1-4). 1997. 13.99 (*0-8037-1108-5*, Dial Yng Read) Peng Put Young Read.

*__Perrywinkle's Magic Match, Vol. 1.__ Ross Martin Madsen. (Easy-to-Read Ser.). 1999. pap. 3.99 (*0-14-038215-1*, PuffinBks) Peng Put Young Read.

Persae. (GRE.). 1991. pap. 13.95 (*3-519-01014-3*, T1014, Pub. by B G Teubner) U of Mich Pr.

Persatuan Islam: Islamic Reform in Twentieth Century Indonesia. Howard M. Federspiel. LC 72-632241. (Cornell University, Modern Indonesia Project, Monograph Ser.: No. 47). 255p. (Orig.). reprint ed. pap. 79.10 (*0-8357-6253-X*, 203459700090) Bks Demand.

Perscripcion Para Cerdos Rentables: Una Quia Para la Produccion de Cerdos a Nivel de la Piara. Ed. by Ann Henderson. Tr. by Ludwig M. Johannsen. (SPA., Illus.). 175p. 1995. 42.00 (*1-883274-02-8*) Watt Pub.

Perse: A History of the Perse School 1615-1976. S. J. D. Mitchell. (Cambridge Town, Gown & County Ser.: Vol. 7). (Illus.). 1976. 25.00 (*0-902675-71-0*) Oleander Pr.

Persea. Cary Osborne. 224p. 1996. mass mkt. 5.99 (*0-441-00397-4*) Ace Bks.

Persecucion: Cinco Piezas de Teatro Experimental. Reinaldo Arenas. LC 86-80353. (Coleccion Teatro). (SPA.). 67p. (Orig.). 1986. pap. 7.95 (*0-89729-391-6*) Ediciones.

Persecution & Assassination of Jean-Paul Marat As Performed by the Inmates of the Asylum of Charenton Under the Direction of the Marquis De Sade. Peter Weiss. LC 65-15915. 128p. (Orig.). (C). 1978. pap. 6.95 (*0-689-70568-9*) Atheneum Yung Read.

Persecution & Liberty: Essays in Honor of George Lincoln Burr. George L. Burr. LC 68-26467. (Essay Index Reprint Ser.). 1977. reprint ed. 23.95 (*0-8369-0783-3*) Ayer.

Persecution & the Art of Writing. Leo Strauss. 208p. 1988. pap. text 11.00 (*0-226-77711-1*) U Ch Pr.

Persecution by Proxy: The Civil Patrols in Guatemala. Vince Heplig. Ed. by Helet Merkling et al. (Illus.). 88p. 1993. pap. text. write for info. (*1-881055-02-7*) RFK Mem Ctr HR.

Persecution of Defence Lawyers in South Korea: Report of a Mission to South Korea. Adrian W. DeWind & John Woodhouse. LC KZ0372.. 72p. reprint ed. pap. 30.00 (*0-608-18111-0*, 203271000081) Bks Demand.

Persecution of Gypsies in Romania. Ed. by Human Rights Watch Staff. 136p. (Orig.). 1991. pap. 10.00 (*1-56432-037-5*) Hum Rts Watch.

*__Persecution of Microsoft Hurts Consumers.__ Ron Nehring. 1999. pap. write for info. (*1-57655-180-6*) Independ Inst.

Persecutor Comes Home. Khurram Murad. 40p. (J). 1996. pap. 3.50 (*0-614-21038-0*, 951) Kazi Pubns.

Persecutory Imagination: English Puritanism & the Literature of Religious Despair. John Stachniewski. (Illus.). 416p. 1991. 98.00 (*0-19-811781-7*) OUP.

Persee. Jean-Baptiste Lully. (Tragedies Lyriques in Facsimile Ser.: Vol. 9). 1998. lib. bdg. 200.00 (*0-89371-159-4*) Broude Intl Edns.

Persee see Chefs-d'Oeuvre Classiques de l'Opera Francais

Perseguida Por Toda La Ciudad. Mary Higgins Clark. 1998. pap. 6.50 (*84-01-49310-2*) Lectorum Pubns.

Perseguido por un Sueno. Charlotte Lamb. (Bianca Ser.: No. 383). (SPA.). 1996. per. 3.50 (*0-373-33383-8*, 1-33383-0) Harlequin Bks.

Perseids & Other Stories. Robert Charles Wilson. pap. 12.95 (*0-312-87524-X*) St Martin.

*__Perseids & Other Stories.__ Robert Charles Wilson. 224p. 2000. 22.95 (*0-312-87374-3*) Tor Bks.

Persephone. Jenny Joseph. (Illus.). 304p. 1986. 30.00 (*0-906427-77-0*, Pub. by Bloodaxe Bks); pap. 17.95 (*0-906427-78-9*, Pub. by Bloodaxe Bks) Dufour.

Persephone. Barbara Lekatsas. Ed. by Stanley H. Barkan. Tr. by Katerina Anghelaki-Rooke. (Review Woman Writers Chapbook Ser.: No. 1). (ENG & GRE.). 20p. 1986. 15.00 (*0-89304-400-8*, CCC160); pap. 5.00 (*0-89304-401-6*) Cross-Cultrl NY.

Persephone. Philip Trager. LC 96-68503. (Illus.). 40p. 1996. 19.95 (*0-8195-5303-4*, Wesleyan Univ Pr) U Pr of New Eng.

Persephone: A One-Act Comedy. Ford Ainsworth. (Illus.). 40p. 1977. pap. 3.25 (*0-88680-149-4*) I E Clark.

Persephone: Director's Script. Ford Ainsworth. (Illus.). 40p. 1977. pap. 10.00 (*0-88680-150-8*) I E Clark.

Persephone: Mini Book. Barbara Lekatsas. Ed. by Stanley H. Barkan. Tr. by Katerina Anghelaki-Rooke. (Review Woman Writers Chapbook Ser.: No. 1). (ENG & GRE.). 20p. 1986. 15.00 (*0-89304-402-4*); pap. 5.00 (*0-89304-403-2*) Cross-Cultrl NY.

Persephone Is Transpluto: The Scientific, Mythological & Astrological Discovery of the Planet Beyond Pluto. Valerie Vaughan. (Illus.). 254p. (Orig.). 1995. pap. 12.95 (*0-9628031-2-X*) One Reed Pubns.

Persephone Key. R. Roy Whitney. (Illus.). 89p. (Orig.). 1978. pap. 16.95 (*0-926256-01-7*) Destnne Pub.

Persephone Returns: Victims, Heroes & the Journey from the Underworld. Tanya Wilkinson. LC 96-19832. 264p. (Orig.). 1996. pap. 16.95 (*1-879290-09-X*) PageMill Pr.

*__Persephone's Girdle: Narratives of Rape in Seventeenth Century Spanish Literature.__ Marcia L. Welles. LC 99-6745. (Illus.). 272p. 1999. pap. 20.95 (*0-8265-1351-4*) Vanderbilt U Pr.

*__Persephone's Girdle: Narratives of Rape in Seventeenth-Century Spanish Literature.__ Marcia L. Welles. LC 99-6745. (Illus.). 272p. 1999. 42.00 (*0-8265-1335-2*) Vanderbilt U Pr.

Persephone's Quest: Entheogens & the Origins of Religion. R. Gordon Wasson et al. LC 87-51547. (Illus.). 256p. (C). 1992. reprint ed. 42.50 (*0-300-03877-1*); reprint ed. pap. text 17.00 (*0-300-05266-9*) Yale U Pr.

Persephone's Song. Mary Schmidt. LC 90-72538. 212p. (Orig.). 1992. pap. 9.95 (*1-879603-02-0*) Los Hombres.

Persepolis - The Archaeology of Persa, Seat of the Persian Kings. rev. ed. Donald N. Wilber. LC 87-27438. (Illus.). 129p. 1989. 24.95 (*0-87850-062-6*) Darwin Pr.

Persepolis & Ancient Iran. Oriental Institute Staff. LC 76-7942. 57p. 1976. lib. bdg. 66.00 incl. fiche (*0-226-69493-3*) U Ch Pr.

Persepolis Fortification Tablets. Richard T. Hallock. (Oriental Institute Publications: No. 92). 776p. 1969. lib. bdg. 60.00 (*0-226-62195-2*, OIP92) U Ch Pr.

Persepolis Project. John L. Kirkoff. 145p. 1999. pap. 9.95 (*1-891929-28-3*) Four Seasons.

Persepolis Seal Studies: An Introduction with Provisional Concordances of Seal Numbers & Associated Documents on Fortification Tablets I-2087. Margaret C. Root & Mark B. Garrison. (Achaemenid History Ser.: No. 9). (Illus.). 142p. 1996. text 40.00 (*90-6258-409-8*, Pub. by Netherlands Inst) Eisenbrauns.

Persepolis, Third: The Royal Tombs & Other Monuments. Erich F. Schmidt. LC 53-4329. (Oriental Institute Publications: No. 70). 1970. lib. bdg. 108.00 (*0-226-62170-7*, OIP70) U Ch Pr.

Persepolis Treasury Tablets. George G. Cameron. 1997. lib. bdg. 7.50 (*0-226-09227-5*) U Ch Pr.

Perser. Timotheus Milesius. (Wissenschaftliche Veroffentlichungen der Deutschen Orient-Gesellschaft Ser.: Heft 3). 126p. 1973. reprint ed. write for info. (*3-487-05049-8*) G Olms Pubs.

Perserverence. Shelagh Canning. (Adventures from the Book of Virtues). (J). 1997. pap. 3.25 (*0-689-81282-5*) Litle Simon.

*__Perserving Our Common World.__ Gordon. 2000. 60.00 (*0-8133-6632-1*, Pub. by Westview) HarpC.

Perseus. Warwick Hutton. LC 92-7639. (Illus.). 32p. (J). (ps-3). 1993. 14.95 (*0-689-50565-5*) McElderry Bks.

Perseus, a Study in Greek Art & Legend. Jocelyn M. Woodward. LC 75-41299. reprint ed. 29.50 (*0-404-14633-3*) AMS Pr.

Perseus & Medusa. Illus. by Robert Baxter. LC 80-50083. 32p. (J). (gr. 4-8). 1980. pap. 3.95 (*0-89375-366-1*); lib. bdg. 18.60 (*0-89375-362-9*) Troll Communs.

Perseus Spur. Julian May. 1999. mass mkt. 6.99 (*0-345-39510-7*) Ballantine Pub Grp.

Perseus the Boy with Super Powers. Laura Geringer. LC 97-140289. (Myth & Men Ser.). (Illus.). (J). (ps-3). 1996. pap. 4.99 (*0-590-84532-2*) Scholastic Inc.

Perseus the Deliverer. Sri Aurobindo. 175p. 1991. pap. 4.00 (*81-7058-040-4*, Pub. by SAA) E-W Cultural Ctr.

Perseus 1.0 Manual: Interactive Sources & Studies on Ancient Greece. Ed. by Gregory Crane. (Illus.). (Orig.). 1992. 25.00 (*0-300-05088-7*); vdisk 200.00 (*0-300-05086-0*); cd-rom 125.00 (*0-300-05087-9*) Yale U Pr.

Perseverance see African Americans: Voices of Triumph

Perseverance. (African Americans: Voices of Triumph Ser.). (Illus.). 256p. (YA). (gr. 9 up). 1993. lib. bdg. write for info. (*0-7835-2251-7*) Time-Life.

Perseverance. Robert E. Picirilli. 28p. 1973. pap. 0.95 (*0-89265-108-3*) Randall Hse.

Perseverance: A Long Obedience in the Same Direction. Eugene H. Peterson. (Christian Basics Bible Studies: No. 10). 64p. (Orig.). 1996. pap., wbk. ed. 4.99 (*0-8308-2010-8*, 2010) InterVarsity.

Perseverance: Connecting Children's Favorite Stories to Meaningful Life Experiences. Jeri A. Carroll et al. Ed. by Judy Mitchell. (Illus.). 32p. (J). (ps-2). 1998. pap., teacher ed. 2.95 (*1-57310-124-9*) Teachng & Lrning Co.

Perseverance: Staying on Course, Studies From 1st Peter. Serendipty House Staff. (201 Deeper Bible Study Ser.). 1998. pap. 4.95 (*1-57494-082-1*) Serendipty Hse.

*__Perseverance in Gratitude: A Socio-Rhetorical Commentary on the Epistle "To the Hebrews"__ David A. DeSilva. 560p. 2000. pap. 40.00 (*0-8028-4188-0*) Eerdmans.

Perseverance in Preservation. Ralph Staten. 36p. 1975. pap. 0.95 (*0-89265-109-1*) Randall Hse.

Perseverance in Trials: Reflections on Job. Carlo M. Martini. Tr. by Matthew J. O'Connell. 144p. (Orig.). 1992. pap. 9.95 (*0-8146-2060-4*) Liturgical Pr.

*__Perseverance Pass.__ Richard V. Bennett. LC 99-97512. 2000. 24.95 (*0-533-13421-8*) Vantage.

Pershing: A History of the American Medium Tank T20 Series. R. P. Hunnicutt. (Illus.). 240p. 1999. 70.00 (*0-89141-693-5*) Presidio Pr.

Pershing & His Generals: Command & Staff in the AEF. James J. Cooke. LC 97-12319. 192p. 1997. 59.95 (*0-275-95363-7*, Praeger Pubs) Greenwood.

Pershing, General of the Armies. Donald Smythe. LC 85-42529. (Illus.). 413p. reprint ed. pap. 128.10 (*0-7837-3727-0*, 205790500009) Bks Demand.

Persia. Samuel G. Benjamin. LC 70-39191. (Select Bibliographies Reprint Ser.). 1977. 24.95 (*0-8369-6793-3*) Ayer.

Persia & the Bible. Edwin M. Yamauchi. LC 89-48988. 584p. (gr. 12). 1997. pap. 29.99 (*0-8010-2108-1*) Baker Bks.

Persia & the Greeks: The Defense of the West, 546-478 B. C. rev. ed. Andrew R. Burn. LC 83-40516. 640p. 1984. 65.00 (*0-8047-1235-2*) Stanford U Pr.

Persia & the Gulf: Retrospect & Prospect. John F. Standish. LC 98-17637. (Illus.). 240p. 1998. text 55.00 (*0-312-16142-5*) St Martin.

Persia & the Persian Question, 2 vols., Set. George N. Curzon. 1966. 145.00 (*0-7146-1969-8*, Pub. by F Cass Pubs) Intl Spec Bk.

*__Persia & the West: An Archaeological Investigation of the Genesis of Achaemenid Persian Art.__ John Boardman. LC 99-66194. (Illus.). 272p. 2000. 60.00 (*0-500-05102-X*, Pub. by Thames Hudson) Norton.

Persia Past & Present. Abraham V. Jackson. LC 76-149392. (Illus.). reprint ed. 95.00 (*0-404-09014-1*) AMS Pr.

Persian. Shahrzad Mahootian. (Descriptive Grammars Ser.). 408p. (C). 1997. 185.00 (*0-415-02311-4*) Routledge.

Persian. Barry Sadler. (Casca: No. 6). (Orig.). 1992. mass mkt. 3.99 (*0-515-10796-4*, Jove) Berkley Pub.

Persian, Arabic, & Urdu Printing in Bengal from 1778. Katherine S. Diehl. (Printers & Printing in the East Indies to 1850 Ser.: Vol. V). write for info. (*0-89241-394-8*) Caratzas.

Persian-Arabic Dictionary. Khafafi & Shafaji. (PER.). 158p. 1995. 25.00 (*0-86685-650-1*) Intl Bk Ctr.

Persian Army, 560-300 BC. Nicholas V. Sekunda. (Elite Ser.: No. 42). (Illus.). 64p. pap. 12.95 (*1-85532-250-1*, 9457, Pub. by Ospry) Stackpole.

Persian Boy. Mary Renault. LC 86-46179. 432p. 1988. pap. 13.00 (*0-394-75101-9*) Vin Bks.

*__Persian Bride: A Novel.__ James Buchan. (Illus.). 352p. 2000. 23.00 (*0-618-06740-X*) HM.

Persian Brides. Dorit Rabinyan. Tr. by Yael Lotan from HEB. LC 97-45493. 240p. 1998. 22.50 (*0-8076-1430-0*) Braziller.

*__Persian Brides.__ Dorit Rabinyan. 2000. pap. 15.95 (*0-8076-1461-0*) Braziller.

Persian Calligraphic Designs. Mehry M. Reid. (International Design Library). (Illus.). 48p. (Orig.). 1995. pap. 5.95 (*0-88045-130-0*) Stemmer Hse.

Persian Caravan. Arthur C. Edwards. LC 70-110224. (Short Story Index Reprint Ser.). 1977. 19.95 (*0-8369-3311-7*) Ayer.

Persian Carpet Designs. Mehry M. Reid. (International Design Library). (Illus.). 48p. 1982. pap. 5.95 (*0-88045-005-3*) Stemmer Hse.

Persian Cat. Stuart A. Kallen. LC 95-7580. (Cats Ser.). (Illus.). 24p. (J). (ps-4). 1995. lib. bdg. 13.98 (*1-56239-445-2*) ABDO Pub Co.

*__Persian Cat.__ Joanne Mattern. (Learning about Cats Ser.). 48p. (YA). (gr. 5 up). 2000. lib. bdg. 21.26 (*0-7368-0566-4*, Capstone Bks) Capstone Pr.

Persian Cats. Edward E. Esarde. Ed. by Ed Rugenstein. (Illus.). 128p. 1983. 9.95 (*0-86622-740-7*, KW-061) TFH Pubns.

Persian Cats. Marianne Mays. (Illus.). 160p. 1997. 19.95 (*0-7938-0489-2*, GB-005) TFH Pubns.

Persian Cats. Ulrike Miller. 72p. 1990. pap. 6.95 (*0-8120-4405-3*) Barron.

Persian Cats. Jennifer Quasha. LC 98-53564. (Kid's Cat Library). 24p. (J). 1999. 18.60 (*0-8239-5508-7*, PowerKids) Rosen Group.

*__Persian Cats.__ Lynn M. Stone. LC 99-30628. (Read All About Cats Ser.). 24p. 1999. lib. bdg. write for info. (*0-86593-556-4*) Rourke Corp.

Persian Cats. Sandra L. Toney. 1998. pap. 12.95 (*0-7938-0209-1*) TFH Pubns.

Persian Cats & Other Longhairs. Jeanne Ramsdale. (Illus.). 271p. 1964. 23.95 (*0-86622-718-0*, H-918) TFH Pubns.

Persian Ceramic Designs. Mehry M. Reid. (International Design Library). (Illus.). 48p. (Orig.). 1983. pap. 5.95 (*0-88045-024-X*) Stemmer Hse.

Persian Childhood. Pari Courtauld. (Illus.). 148p. 1990. pap. 17.95 (*0-948695-19-6*, Pub. by Rubicon Pr) David Brown.

Persian Cinderella. Shirley Climo. LC 98-36900. (Illus.). 32p. (J). (gr. k-4). 1999. 15.95 (*0-06-026763-1*) HarpC Child Bks.

Persian Cinderella. Shirley Climo. LC 98-36900. (Illus.). 32p. (J). (gr. 1-4). 1999. lib. bdg. 15.89 (*0-06-026765-8*) HarpC Child Bks.

Persian, Contemporary Spoken, Vol. 2. Mehdi Marashi & Mehdi Merashi. 119p. pap. text 185.00 incl. audio (*0-88432-792-2*, AFPE20) Audio-Forum.

Persian Cooking: A Table of Exotic Delights. Nesta Ramazani. LC 96-45556. (Illus.). 320p. 1997. reprint ed. pap. 17.95 (*0-936347-77-5*) IBEX.

Persian Cooking for a Healthy Kitchen. Najmieh Khalili Batmanglij. LC 94-907. (Illus.). 190p. 1994. 29.95 (*0-934211-40-X*) Mage Pubs Inc.

Persian Cuisine: Regional & Modern Foods, Bk. 2. Mohammad R. Ghanoonparvar. LC 82-61268. (Illus.). (Orig.). 1984. pap. 14.95 (*0-939214-23-7*) Mazda Pubs.

Persian Cuisine: Traditional Foods, Bk. 1. Mohammad R. Ghanoonparvar. LC 82-61281. (Illus.). 250p. (Orig.). 1982. pap. 14.95 (*0-939214-10-5*) Mazda Pubs.

Persian Dawns, Egyptian Nights. Lewis G. Gibbon. LC 99-176715. 256p. 1998. pap. 15.95 (*0-7486-6231-6*, Pub. by Polygon) Subterranean Co.

Persian Designs & Motifs for Artists & Craftsmen. Ali Dowlatshahi. (Illus.). 120p. 1979. pap. 7.95 (*0-486-23815-6*) Dover.

Persian Diary, 1939-1941. Walter N. Koelz. (Anthropological Papers Ser.: No. 71). (Illus.). 227p. (Orig.). 1983. pap. 10.00 (*0-932206-93-X*) U Mich Mus Anthro.

Persian Drawings in the Metropolitan Museum of Art. Sussan Babaie & Marie L. Swietochowski. (Illus.). 96p. 1989. pap. 7.95 (*0-87099-564-2*, 0-8109-6468-6) Metro Mus Art.

Persian Empire see Cultures of the Past - Group 2

Persian Empire. Don Nardo. LC 97-3081. (World History Ser.). (Illus.). (J). (gr. 4-12). 1997. lib. bdg. 22.45 (*1-56006-320-3*) Lucent Bks.

Persian Empire & the West. 2nd ed. John Boardman. (Cambridge Ancient History Ser.: Vol. 4). 960p. 1988. text 150.00 (*0-521-22804-2*) Cambridge U Pr.

Persian-English - English-Persian Glossary for Humanities & Social Sciences. Asadollah Kasraie & Hassan Kasraie. LC 91-6483. 408p. (C). 1991. 65.00 (*0-923687-09-2*) Celo Valley Bks.

Persian-English Dictionary. Soleyman Haim. (ENG & PER.). 1040p. 1984. 75.00 (*0-8288-0543-1*, F 46520) Fr & Eur.

Persian-English Dictionary, Romanized. John A. Boyle. (ENG & PER.). 42.50 (*0-87557-057-7*) Saphrograph.

Persian-English, English-Persian Dictionary. Soleyman Haim. (ENG & PER.). 1444p. 1992. 43.00 (*0-7859-8913-7*) Fr & Eur.

Persian-English Standard Dictionary. Haim Shortet. 700p. 1993. pap. 19.95 (*0-7818-0055-2*) Hippocrene Bks.

Persian Etching Designs. Mehry M. Reid. (International Design Library). (Illus.). 48p. 1985. pap. 5.95 (*0-88045-061-4*) Stemmer Hse.

P

An Asterisk (*) at the beginning of an entry indicates that the title is appearing for the first time.

Persian Expedition. Xenophon. (Great Commanders Ser.). 384p. 1997. reprint ed. 30.00 (*1-56515-010-4*) Collect Reprints.

Persian Expedition. rev. ed. Xenophon. Tr. by Rex Warner. (Classics Ser.). 376p. 1949. pap. 19.99 (*0-14-044007-0*, Penguin Classics) Viking Penguin.

Persian (Farsi) Language/30. rev. ed. Educational Services Corporation Staff. (PER.). 1994. pap. 16.95 incl. audio (*0-910542-75-9*) Educ Svcs DC.

Persian Fiction Reader. Michael Hillman. LC 95-83678. 1996. 49.00 (*1-881265-36-6*) Dunwoody Pr.

Persian Garden: Echoes of Paradise. M. R. Moghtader. LC 96-44429. (Illus.). 176p. 1998. 75.00 (*0-934211-46-9*) Mage Pubs Inc.

Persian Gardens & Garden Pavilions. 2nd ed. Donald N. Wilber. LC 78-13801. (Illus.). 1979. 20.00 (*0-88402-082-7*) Dumbarton Oaks.

Persian Grammar. Ann K. Lambton. 290p. (C). 1953. pap. text 44.95 (*0-521-09124-1*) Cambridge U Pr.

Persian Grammar: History & State of Its Study. Gernot L. Windfuhr. (Trends in Linguistics, State-of-the-Art Reports: No. 12). 303p. 1979. 98.50 (*90-279-7774-7*) Mouton.

Persian Gulf: Iran's Role. Rouhollah K. Ramazani. LC 72-77262. (Illus.). 175p. reprint ed. pap. 54.30 (*0-608-30879-X*, 200229100012) Bks Demand.

Persian Gulf Administration Reports, 1837-1957, 11 vols., Set. Archive Editions Staff. 7500p. (C). 1986. reprint ed. lib. bdg. 2495.00 (*1-85207-010-2*, Pub. by Archive Editions) N Ross.

Persian Gulf after the Cold War. Ed. by Mohammed E. Ahrari & James H. Noyes. LC 93-13535. 264p. 1993. 65.00 (*0-275-94457-3*, Praeger Pubs) Greenwood.

Persian Gulf Air War Encyclopedia. Ed. by Walter Jacob & Pauline Webb. (Illus.). 320p. 1999. 39.00 (*0-913337-32-3*) Southfarm Pr.

Persian Gulf & American Policy. Emile A. Nakhleh. LC 82-13125. 151p. 1982. 45.00 (*0-275-90867-4*, C0867, Praeger Pubs) Greenwood.

Persian Gulf & Indian Ocean in International Politics. Ed. by Abbas Amirie. LC 77-378100. 429p. reprint ed. pap. 133.00 (*0-608-15866-6*, 203073700070) Bks Demand.

Persian Gulf & Red Sea Naval Reports, 1820-1960, 15 vols. Ed. by A. L. Burdett. 11,000p. 1993. reprint ed. lib. bdg. 3995.00 (*1-85207-450-7*, Pub. by Archive Editions) N Ross.

Persian Gulf & South Asia: Prospects & Problems of Inter-Regional Cooperation. Bhabani S. Gupta. 244p. 1987. 21.00 (*81-7003-077-3*, Pub. by S Asia Pubs) S Asia.

Persian Gulf & the Strait of Hormuz. Rouhollah K. Ramazani. (International Straits of the World Ser.: No. 3). 200p. 1979. 35.00 (*0-685-04604-4*) Kluwer Academic.

Persian Gulf & the West: The Dilemmas of Security. Charles A. Kupchan. 272p. 1987. text 49.95 (*0-04-497057-9*); pap. text 16.95 (*0-04-497058-7*) Routledge.

Persian Gulf at Millennium: Essays in Politics, Economy, Security & Religion. Gary G. Sick. Ed. by Lawrence G. Potter. LC 97-13020. 320p. 1997. pap. 18.95 (*0-312-17567-1*) St Martin.

Persian Gulf at Millennium: Essays in Politics, Economy, Security & Religion. Ed. by Gary G. Sick & Lawrence G. Potter. LC 97-13020. 320p. 1997. text 49.95 (*0-312-17449-7*) St Martin.

Persian Gulf at the Dawn of the New Millenium. Gawdat Bahgat. LC 99-25142. 219p. 1999. 49.00 (*1-56072-678-4*) Nova Sci Pubs.

Persian Gulf Crisis. Steve A. Yetiv. LC 96-6554. (The Greenwood Press Reference Guides to Historic Events of the 20th Century Ser.). 240p. 1997. 39.95 (*0-313-29943-9*, Greenwood Pr) Greenwood.

Persian Gulf Crisis: Power in the Post-Cold War World. Ed. by Robert F. Helms & Robert H. Dorff. LC 92-9120. 216p. 1992. 52.95 (*0-275-94120-5*, C4120, Praeger Pubs) Greenwood.

Persian Gulf Crisis & the Final Fall of Babylon. Noah W. Hutchings. 138p. (Orig.). 1990. pap. 6.95 (*0-9624517-6-2*) Hearthstone OK.

Persian Gulf Experience & Health: Current Bibliographies in Medicine: January 1971 Through March 1994. Jacqueline VandeKamp & John H. Ferguson. 24p. 1996. reprint ed. pap. text 20.00 (*0-7881-3345-4*) DIANE Pub.

Persian Gulf Gazette & Supplements, 1953-1972, 6 vols., Set. Archive Editions Staff. 3900p. (C). 1987. reprint ed. lib. bdg. 995.00 (*1-85207-090-0*, Pub. by Archive Editions) N Ross.

Persian Gulf Historical Summaries, 1907-1953, 5 vols., Set. Archives Research Ltd. Staff. (Illus.). 92p. (C). 1987. reprint ed. lib. bdg. 395.00 (*1-85207-105-2*, Pub. by Archive Editions) N Ross.

***Persian Gulf in Transition.** Lawrence G. Potter. LC 97-77153. (Headline Ser.). 72p. 1998. 5.95 (*0-87124-179-X*) Foreign Policy.

Persian Gulf Nations. Paul J. Deegan. LC 91-73072. (War in the Gulf Ser.). (J). (gr. 4 up). 1991. lib. bdg. 13.99 (*1-56239-029-5*) ABDO Pub Co.

Persian Gulf Pilot, 1864-1932, 8 vols., Set. Archives Research Ltd. Staff. 2600p. (C). 1989. reprint ed. lib. bdg. 395.00 (*1-85207-180-X*, Pub. by Archive Editions) N Ross.

Persian Gulf Poems. Jocelyn Hollis. LC 91-22484. 39p. (Orig.). 1992. 19.95 (*0-930933-22-2*); pap. 9.95 (*0-930933-19-2*); text 19.95 (*0-930933-21-4*); pap. text 9.95 (*0-930933-20-6*); lib. bdg. 19.95 (*0-930933-18-4*) Am Poetry & Lit.

Persian Gulf Precis, 8 vols., Set. J. A. Saldanha. 3200p. (C). 1986. reprint ed. lib. bdg. 995.00 (*1-85207-000-5*, Pub. by Archive Editions) N Ross.

Persian Gulf Region in the Twenty-First Century: Stability & Change. Nozar Alaolmolki. 226p. (Orig.). 1996. pap. text 34.00 (*0-7618-0480-3*); lib. bdg. 54.00 (*0-7618-0479-X*) U Pr of Amer.

Persian Gulf States. U. S. Government Staff. (Country Studies). 1995. 25.00 (*0-614-30810-0*, UPERSI) Claitors.

Persian Gulf States. Rupert Hay. LC 80-1926. reprint ed. 23.50 (*0-404-18966-0*) AMS Pr.

Persian Gulf States: A Country Study. Ed. by Helen C. Metz. (Illus.). 472p. (C). 1998. reprint ed. text 50.00 (*0-7881-7502-5*) DIANE Pub.

Persian Gulf States: A General Survey. Ed. by Alvin J. Cottrell et al. LC 79-19452. 736p. 1980. reprint ed. pap. 200.00 (*0-608-03679-X*, 206450500009) Bks Demand.

Persian Gulf States: Country Studies. Helen Chapin Metz. 502p. 1994. boxed set 29.00 (*0-16-061169-5*) USGPO.

Persian Gulf States: Studies, 2 vols. 1997. lib. bdg. 600.25 (*0-8490-6201-2*) Gordon Pr.

Persian Gulf States Country Studies: Area Handbook. 3rd ed. LC 93-46476. (Area Handbook Ser.). 1994. 25.00 (*0-8444-0793-3*) Lib Congress.

Persian Gulf Trade Reports, 1905-1940, 8 vols., Set. Archives Research Ltd. Staff. 3250p. (C). 1987. reprint ed. lib. bdg. 995.00 (*1-85207-050-1*, Pub. by Archive Editions) N Ross.

Persian Gulf War. Leila M. Foster. LC 91-4037. (Cornerstones to Freedom Ser.). (Illus.). 32p. (J). (gr. 3-6). 1991. lib. bdg. 19.50 (*0-516-04762-0*) Childrens.

Persian Gulf War. Kathlyn Gay. LC 96-15579. (Voices from the Past Ser.). 64p. (J). (gr. 5-8). 1996. lib. bdg. 18.90 (*0-8050-4102-8*) TFC Bks NY.

Persian Gulf War. Kathlyn Gay & Martin Gay. 1996. write for info. (*0-8050-5282-8*) H Holt & Co.

Persian Gulf War. Don Nardo. LC 91-23064. (America's Wars Ser.). (Illus.). 112p. (J). (gr. 5-8). 1991. lib. bdg. 26.20 (*1-56006-411-0*) Lucent Bks.

Persian Gulf War: Lessons for Strategy, Law & Diplomacy, 99. Ed. by Christopher C. Joyner. LC 89-25730. 272p. 1990. 57.95 (*0-313-26710-3*, JPW/, Greenwood Pr) Greenwood.

Persian Gulf War: "The Mother of All Battles" Zachary Kent. LC 94-2533. (American War Ser.). (Illus.). 128p. (YA). (gr. 5 up). 1994. lib. bdg. 20.95 (*0-89490-528-7*) Enslow Pubs.

Persian Gulf War: "The Mother of All Battles" Zachary Kent. LC 94-2533. (American War Ser.). (Illus.). 128p. (YA). (gr. 5 up). 1994. pap. 10.95 (*0-7660-1730-3*) Enslow Pubs.

Persian Gulf War: Views from the Social & Behavioral Sciences. Ed. by Herbert H. Blumberg & Christopher C. French. 638p. (Orig.). (C). 1993. pap. text 46.50 (*0-8191-9253-8*); lib. bdg. 78.00 (*0-8191-9252-X*) U Pr of Amer.

Persian Gulf War Almanac. Harry G. Summers, Jr. LC 94-28450. (Illus.). 320p. 1995. 35.00 (*0-8160-2821-4*) Facts on File.

Persian Gulf War Syndromes--Facts, Symptoms & Controversy: Index of New Information. Innis C. Haverhold. 160p. 1997. 47.50 (*0-7883-1768-7*); pap. 44.50 (*0-7883-1769-5*) ABBE Pubs Assn.

Persian Handwriting. rev. ed. Mehdi Marashi. LC 98-84882. (Illus.). 246p. 1998. pap. text. write for info. (*0-9640537-7-2*) Monterey Pubng.

***Persian Handwriting: Book & CD Manual for Persian (Farsi) Handwriting.** Mehdi Marashi. LC 98-84882. (Illus.). xviii, 240p. 2000. pap. 35.00 incl. cd-rom (*1-58814-000-8*) IBEX.

***Persian Historiography.** Julie S. Meisami. 288p. 1999. 72.00 (*0-7486-0743-9*, Pub. by Edinburgh U Pr); pap. 31.00 (*0-7486-1276-9*, Pub. by Edinburgh U Pr) Col U Pr.

Persian Horse: A Novel of War in the Gulf. Marc Iverson. 1992. mass mkt. 4.99 (*0-446-36324-3*, Pub. by Warner Bks) Little.

***Persian Legacy & The Edgar Cayce Material.** Kevin J. Todeschi. LC 00-40128. 2000. write for info. (*0-87604-473-9*) ARE Pr.

Persian Letters. Charles De Montesquieu. Tr. by C. J. Betts. (Classics Ser.). 352p. 1973. pap. 11.95 (*0-14-044281-2*, Penguin Classics) Viking Penguin.

Persian Letters. Charles de Secondat Montesquieu. Tr. by George R. Healy from FRE. LC 62-21265. 1964. 29.50 (*0-672-51053-7*) Irvington.

Persian Letters. Baron de la Brede Montesquieu. Tr. by George R. Healy from FRE. LC 99-36814. 320p. (C). 1999. reprint ed. pap. 9.95 (*0-87220-490-1*); reprint ed. lib. bdg. 34.95 (*0-87220-491-X*) Hackett Pub.

Persian Life & Customs. 3rd ed. Samuel G. Wilson. LC 76-178305. reprint ed. 39.50 (*0-404-06996-7*) AMS Pr.

Persian Limes in North America: An Economic Analysis of the Production & Marketing Channels. Michael Roy et al. LC 96-84267. (Illus.). (Orig.). 1996. pap. 25.00 (*0-944961-02-9*) FL Sci Source.

Persian Medical Manuscripts at the University of California, Los Angeles: A Descriptive Catalogue. Lutz Richter-Bernburg. LC 77-94986. (Humana Civilitas Ser.: Vol. 4). (Illus.). xxiv, 297p. 1978. 57.00 (*0-89003-026-X*) Undena Pubns.

Persian Metaphysics & Mysticism: Selected Works of 'Aziz Nasafi. Tr. & Intro. by Lloyd Ridgeon. 228p. 1997. 75.00 (*0-7007-0666-6*, Pub. by Curzon Pr Ltd) Paul & Co Pubs.

Persian Metres. Laurence P. Elwell-Sutton. LC 75-39392. 299p. reprint ed. pap. 85.30 (*0-608-15718-X*, 2031646) Bks Demand.

Persian Miniature Designs. Mojdeh B. Stephenson. (International Design Library). (Illus.). 48p. (Orig.). 1983. pap. 5.95 (*0-88045-033-9*) Stemmer Hse.

***Persian Mirrors: The Elusive Face of Iran.** Elaine Sciolino. LC 00-41103. (Illus.). 2000. 26.00 (*0-684-86290-5*) Free Pr.

Persian Myths. Vesta S. Curtis. (Legendary Past Ser.). (Illus.). 80p. (Orig.). (C). 1994. pap. 12.95 (*0-292-71158-1*) U of Tex Pr.

Persian Newspaper Reader. Michael C. Hillmann & Ramin Sarraf. LC 97-65705. x, 308 p. 1996. write for info. (*1-881265-50-1*) Dunwoody Pr.

Persian Nightingale in a Cage: Selected Persian Diaspora Poetry, Post Islamic Revolution: A Bilingual Parallel Text in English & Persian. Shmuel Shoshani. LC 97-69854. (ENG & PER.). 1997. write for info. (*1-57087-360-7*) Prof Pr NC.

Persian Nights. Diane Johnson. LC 97-39783. 352p. 1998. pap. 12.95 (*0-452-27958-5*, Plume) Dutton Plume.

Persian Painting: Five Royal Safavid Manuscripts of the Sixteenth Century. Stuart C. Welch. LC 75-38508. (Illus.). 128p. 1976. pap. 20.95 (*0-8076-0813-0*, Pub. by Braziller) Norton.

Persian Painting & the National Epic. B. W. Robinson. (Individual Papers). 1983. 3.98 (*0-85672-455-6*) David Brown.

Persian Pearl: And Other Essays, 1899. Clarence Darrow. LC 97-5174. 175p. 1997. reprint ed. lib. bdg. 50.00 (*1-886363-27-7*) Lawbk Exchange.

Persian Pearl & Other Essays. Clarence Darrow. LC 74-1199. (American Literature Ser.: No. 49). 1974. lib. bdg. 75.00 (*0-8383-1770-7*) M S G Haskell Hse.

Persian Period (Stratum V) W. J. Bennett, Jr. & Jeffrey A. Blakely. LC 80-21724. (Joint Archaeological Expedition to Tell el-Hesi Ser.: No. 3). (Illus.). xxvii, 483p. 1990. text 95.00 (*0-931464-54-4*) Eisenbrauns.

Persian Pickle Club. Sandra Dallas. LC 95-31032. 208p. 1995. text 20.95 (*0-312-13586-6*) St Martin.

Persian Pickle Club. large type ed. Sandra Dallas. (Niagara Large Print Ser.). 270p. 1997. pap. 29.50 (*0-7089-5856-7*, Linford) Ulverscroft.

Persian Pickle Club. 8th ed. Sandra Dallas. 208p. 1996. pap. 11.95 (*0-312-14701-5*) St Martin.

Persian Poetry in England & America: A 200-Year History. John D. Yohannan. LC 75-22418. (Persian Studies Ser.: Vol. 4). xxvi, 373p. 1977. text 25.00 (*0-88206-006-6*) Bibliotheca Persica.

Persian Poetry in Kashmir, 1339-1846: An Introduction. Girdhari L. Tikku. LC 70-627150. (University of California Publications, Occasional Papers: No. 4). 334p. reprint ed. pap. 103.60 (*0-608-10816-2*, 202138400021) Bks Demand.

Persian Poetry, Painting, & Patronage: Illustrations in a 16th Century Masterpiece. Marianna S. Simpson. LC 97-41288. (Illus.). 80p. 1997. pap. 20.00 (*0-300-07483-2*) Yale U Pr.

***Persian Poets.** Ed. by Peter Washington. 256p. 2000. 12.50 (*0-375-41126-7*) Knopf.

Persian Postcards: Iran after Khomeini. Fred A. Reed. 288p. 1994. pap. 16.95 (*0-88922-351-3*, Pub. by Talonbks) Genl Dist Srvs.

Persian Presence in the Islamic World. Ed. by Richard G. Hovannisian & Georges Sabagh. (Levi Della Vida Symposia Ser.: Vol. 13). (Illus.). 280p. (C). 1997. text 64.95 (*0-521-59185-6*) Cambridge U Pr.

Persian Reader: Farsi Biyamuzim: Ravesh-E Tadris. 2nd rev. ed. Lily Ayman. LC 93-61059. (PER.). 96p. (J). (gr. 1). 1994. pap., teacher ed. 18.00 (*0-936347-36-8*) IBEX.

Persian Reader Bk. 1: Farsi Biyamuzim: Ketab-E Aval. 2nd rev. ed. Lily Ayman. LC 93-61060. (PER., Illus.). 104p. (Orig.). 1994. pap. text 9.95 (*0-936347-34-1*) IBEX.

Persian Requiem. Simin Danishvar. Tr. by Roxane Zand from PER. LC 91-40933. 288p. 1992. 22.50 (*0-8076-1273-1*) Braziller.

Persian Revolution of 1905-1909. Edward G. Browne. LC 95-9633. (Illus.). 640p. 1995. reprint ed. 39.95 (*0-934211-45-0*) Mage Pubs Inc.

Persian Ruba'Iya't: A Selection of Quatrains from 100 Persian Poets (10th C. to 20th C.) Tr. by Reza Saberi from PER. LC 97-40058. 264p. (C). 1997. 57.00 (*0-7618-0945-7*); pap. 32.50 (*0-7618-0946-5*) U Pr of Amer.

Persian Rug Motifs for Needlepoint. Lyatif Kerimov. LC 75-3650. (Illus.). 48p. 1975. pap. 3.50 (*0-486-23187-9*) Dover.

Persian-Russian Dictionary, 2 vols. Iu. Rubinchik. 1664p. (C). 1983. 195.00 (*0-7855-6493-4*, Pub. by Collets) St Mut.

Persian-Russian Dictionary, 2 vols. J. Rubincik. (PER & RUS.). 1664p. 1985. 150.00 (*0-8288-1126-1*, F47750) Fr & Eur.

Persian-Russian Dictionary, 2 vols., Set. M. Osmanov. (PER & RUS.). 1600p. 1983. 95.00 (*0-8288-0800-7*, F46360) Fr & Eur.

Persian-Russian, Russian-Persian Exports Economics Dictionary. deluxe ed. 596p. 1957. 18.50 (*0-8288-6859-X*, M-9125) Fr & Eur.

Persian Sphinx: Amir-Abbas Hoveyda & the Riddle of the Iranian Revolution. Abbas Milani. (Illus.). 2000. 29.95 (*0-934211-61-2*) Mage Pubs Inc.

Persian Stronghold of Zoroastrianism: Based on the Ratanbai Katrak Lectures, 1975. Mary Boyce. LC 89-35817. (Persian Studies: No. 12). (Illus.). 308p. (C). 1989. reprint ed. lib. bdg. 43.00 (*0-8191-7529-3*) U Pr of Amer.

Persian Studies in North America, Studies in Honor of Mohammad Ali Jazayery. Ed. & Pref. by Medhi Marashi. LC 93-12142. (ENG & PER., Illus.). 560p. 1994. lib. bdg., boxed set 60.00 (*0-936347-35-X*) IBEX.

Persian Sufi Poetry: An Introduction to the Mystical Use of Classical Persian Poems. J. T. De Bruijn. LC 97-217472. 228p. 1997. 65.00 (*0-7007-0674-7*, Pub. by Curzon Pr Ltd) Paul & Co Pubs.

Persian Sufi Poetry: An Introduction to the Mystical Use of Classical Persian Poems. J. T. De Bruijn. LC 97-217472. (Curzon Sufi Ser.: No. 1). 228p. (C). 1997. pap. 25.00 (*0-7007-0312-8*, Pub. by Curzon Pr Ltd) Paul & Co Pubs.

Persian Tales. D. L. R. Lorimer & E. D. Lorimer. LC 78-63210. (Illus.). reprint ed. 30.00 (*0-614-18074-0*) AMS Pr.

Persian Tales: Fifty-Eight Traditional & Folk Tales from Iran. Tr. by D. L. R. Lorimer & Emily Overend Lorimer. LC 98-42590. (Classics of Persian Literature Ser.: vol. 6). (Illus.). 366p. 2000. reprint ed. pap. 28.00 (*0-936347-91-0*) IBEX.

Persian Textile Designs. Mehry M. Reid. (International Design Library). (Illus.). 48p. (Orig.). 1984. pap. 5.95 (*0-88045-027-4*) Stemmer Hse.

Persian Vocabulary. Ann K. Lambton. (PER.). 406p. (C). 1953. pap. text 44.95 (*0-521-09154-3*) Cambridge U Pr.

Persian War see History of the Wars. Secret History

Persian Wars. Herodotus. Ed. by William Shepherd. LC 81-38532. (Translations from Greek & Roman Authors Ser.). (Illus.). 136p. 1982. pap. text 14.95 (*0-521-28194-6*) Cambridge U Pr.

Persian Wars. Herodotus. Tr. by George Rawlinson. 714p. (C). 1964. 8.44 (*0-07-553640-4*, T54) McGraw.

Persian Women & Their Ways. C. Colliver Rice. 1976. lib. bdg. 59.95 (*0-8490-2424-2*) Gordon Pr.

Persian Words in English. Ed. by Steele Commager. Incl. American Variations. Ed. by A. A. Daryusl. 1979. Dutch Influence on English Vocabulary. Ed. by A. A. Daryusl. 1979. Fine Writing. A. A. Daryusl. 1979. lib. bdg. Formation & Use of Compound Epithets in English Poetry. A. A. Daryusl. 1979. lib. bdg. German Influence on the English Vocabulary. A. A. Daryusl. 1979. lib. bdg. H.W. Fowler. A. A. Daryusl. 1979. lib. bdg. Linguistic Self-Criticism. A. A. Daryusl. 1979. lib. bdg. Names, Designations, & Appelations. A. A. Daryusl. 1979. lib. bdg. Northern Words in Modern English. A. A. Daryusl. 1979. lib. bdg. (Society for Pure English Ser.: Vol. 5). 1979. Set lib. bdg. 46.00 (*0-8240-3669-7*) Garland.

Persianeries: Rapportage dans l'Iran des Mollahs, 1995-1998 see On Persian Roads: Glimpses of Revolutionary Iran, 1985-1998

Persians see Prometheus Bound & Other Plays

Persians. Robert Auletta. (American Theater in Literature - A Mark Taper Forum Play Ser.). (Illus.). 104p. (Orig.). 1993. pap. 9.95 (*1-55713-135-X*) Sun & Moon CA.

Persians. Herbert Axelrod. (Cats & Dogs). (Illus.). 84p. (YA). (gr. 3 up). 1999. 19.95 (*0-7910-4809-8*) Chelsea Hse.

Persians. Tr. by Janet Lembke & C. John Herington. (Greek Tragedy in New Translations Ser.). 144p. 1991. reprint ed. pap. 8.95 (*0-19-507008-9*) OUP.

Persians. unabridged ed. Aeschylus. Ed. by William-Alan Landes. Tr. by Robert Potter from GRE. LC 98-2709. 55p. (Orig.). 1998. pap. 7.00 (*0-88734-779-7*) Players Pr.

Persians: Masters of Empire see Lost Civilizations Series

Persians Amongst the English. Denis Wright. LC 85-178728. (Illus.). 273p. 1985. text 29.50 (*0-936508-15-9*, Pub. by I B T) St Martin.

Persians Amongst the English: Episodes in Anglo-Persian History. Denis Wright. 306p. 1990. text 59.50 (*1-85043-003-9*, Pub. by I B T) St Martin.

Persians/Parsian: Persian Translation. Aeschylus. Tr. by Fu'ad Rouhani. LC 98-3406. (Illus.). 72p. 1999. pap. 10.00 (*0-936347-85-6*) IBEX.

***Persiasion as Intervention: Reclaiming Rhetoric as a Civic Art.** 1999. write for info. (*0-673-97943-1*) S&S Trade.

Persidiskie i Tadzhikskie Rukopisi Instituta Vostokovedeniia Rossiiskoi Akademii Nauk: Kratkii (Alfavitnyi Katalog), Vol. 1. Ed. by N. D. Miklukho-Maklai. LC 95-25791. (PER & RUS.). 1998. lib. bdg. 220.00 (*0-88354-140-8*) N Ross.

Persilscheine und falsche Paesse: Wie die Kirchen den Nazis Halfen. Ernst Klee. (GER.). 192p. 1992. pap. 13.50 (*3-596-10956-6*, Pub. by Fischer Tasch) Intl Bk Import.

Persimmon Wind: A Martial Artist's Journey in Japan. Dave Lowry. LC 97-45548. (Illus.). 272p. 1998. pap. 19.95 (*0-8048-3142-4*) Tuttle Pubng.

Persimmons. Jack W. Hazelton. LC 99-63545. (From Seed to Supper Ser.). (Illus.). 64p. 1999. pap. 9.95 (*1-928907-00-8*) Jacks Bookshelf.

***Persimmons: And Other Lesbian Erotica.** Lilith Rogers. (Illus.). 84p. 1999. pap. 11.95 (*0-9671715-0-4*) Earthy Mama.

Persis Collection of Contemporary Art. Jocelyn Fujii. (Illus.). 112p. 1998. 50.00 (*1-892752-00-X*) Goodale HI.

Persisch-Deutsches Woerterbuch. Farhad Sobhani. (GER & PER.). 254p. 1971. 79.95 (*0-7859-8266-3*, 3110018446) Fr & Eur.

Persisch 1. (Glossare Ser.). (GER.). 64p. 1997. pap. write for info. (*3-468-49951-5*) Langenscheidt.

Persist & Publish: Helpful Hints for Academic Writing & Publishing. Ralph E. Matkin & T. F. Riggar. (Illus.). 176p. (Orig.). 1991. pap. text 17.50 (*0-87081-227-0*) Univ Pr Colo.

Persistance of History: Cinema, Television, & the Modern Event. Ed. by Vivian Sobchack. 288p. (C). 1995. pap. 20.99 (*0-415-91084-6*) Routledge.

Persistant Viral Infections. Ahmed. LC 98-24568. 738p. 1999. 320.00 (*0-471-98083-8*) Wiley.

Persistence & Change: Proceedings of the 1st International Conference on Event Perception. Ed. by William H. Warren, Jr. & Robert E. Shaw. 392p. (C). 1985. 79.95 (*0-89859-391-3*) L Erlbaum Assocs.

Persistence & Change in Nineteenth Century Lebanon: A Sociological Essay. Samir Khalaf. 1979. 24.95 (*0-8156-6053-7*, Pub. by Am U Beirut) Syracuse U Pr.

P

An Asterisk (*) at the beginning of an entry indicates that the title is appearing for the first time.

Persistence & Change in Personality Patterns. Katherine E. Roberts. (SRCD M Ser.: Vol. 8, No. 3). 1943. 25.00 (*0-527-01528-8*) Periodicals Srv.

Persistence & Change in the Protestant Establishment. Ralph E. Pyle. LC 96-10426. (Religion in the Age of Transformation Ser.). 176p. 1996. 57.95 (*0-275-95487-0*, Praeger Pubs) Greenwood.

Persistence & Flexibility: Anthropological Perspectives on the American Jewish Experience. Ed. by Walter P. Zenner. LC 87-24465. (SUNY Series in Anthropology & Judaic Studies). (Illus.). 304p. 1988. text 21.50 (*0-88706-748-4*) State U NY Pr.

***Persistence & Long-Range Transport of Organic Chemicals in the Environment: Guidelines & Criteria for Evaluation & Assessment.** Gary M. Klecka. LC 99-461976. (Illus.). 2000. write for info. (*1-880611-22-8*, SETAC Pr) SETAC.

Persistence in Pattern in Mississippi Choctaw Culture. Ed. by Patti C. Black. (Old Capitol Museum Ser.). (Illus.). 44p. 1987. pap. 9.95 (*0-938896-51-2*) Mississippi Archives.

Persistence of Classicism. Patricia Mainardi et al. LC 95-5958. (Illus.). 68p. (Orig.). 1995. pap. 4.50 (*0-931102-36-7*) S & F Clark Art.

Persistence of East German Independence. Joyce Mushaben. 1999. text. write for info. (*0-312-04787-8*) St Martin.

Persistence of Economic Discrimination: Race, Ethnicity, & Gender: A Comparative Analysis. Elias H. Tuma. LC 95-33202. 203p. 1996. 21.95 (*0-87015-265-3*) Pacific Bks.

***Persistence of Empire: British Political Culture in the Age of the American Revolution.** Eliga H. Gould. LC 99-34607. 336p. 2000. pap. 18.95 (*0-8078-4846-8*) U of NC Pr.

***Persistence of Empire: British Political Culture in the Age of the American Revolution.** Eliga H. Gould. LC 99-34607. (Published for the Omohundro Institute of Early American History & Culture, Williamsburg, Virginia Ser.). (Illus.). 336p. 2000. 49.95 (*0-8078-2529-8*) U of NC Pr.

Persistence of Error: Essays in Developmental Epistemology. Robert Kalechofsky. LC 87-14224. 80p. (Orig.). 1987. pap. text 10.00 (*0-8191-6457-7*); lib. bdg. 16.00 (*0-8191-6456-9*) U Pr of Amer.

Persistence of Ethnicity: Dutch Calvinist Pioneers in Amsterdam, Montana. Rob Kroes. (Illus.). 184p. (C). 1992. text 29.95 (*0-252-01931-8*) U of Ill Pr.

Persistence of External Interest in the Middle East. Mary E. Morris. LC 93-31042. 1994. pap. 15.00 (*0-8330-1486-2*, MR-318-DAG) Rand Corp.

Persistence of Fluctuation in Capitalist Economies. Dibeh. 55.95 (*1-85972-088-9*) Ashgate Pub Co.

Persistence of Forage Legumes. G. C. Marten et al. 596p. 1989. 19.00 (*0-89118-098-2*) Am Soc Agron.

Persistence of High Fertility in Nepal. Jayanti M. Tuladhar. (C). 1989. 54.00 (*81-210-0227-3*, Pub. by Inter-India Pubns) S Asia.

Persistence of History: Cinema, Television, & the Modern Event. Ed. by Vivian Sobchack. 288p. (C). (gr. 13 up). 1995. 70.00 (*0-415-91083-8*) Routledge.

Persistence of Human Passions: Manuel Mujica Lainez's Satirical Neo-Modernism. George O. Schanzer. (Monagrafias A Ser.: Vol. CXIX). 153p. 1986. 51.00 (*0-7293-0233-4*, Pub. by Tamesis Bks Ltd) Boydell & Brewer.

Persistence of Human Rights Violations. 1991. pap. 3.00 (*0-685-53234-8*) Amnesty Intl USA.

Persistence of Memory. Gordon McAlpine. 176p. 1998. 29.95 (*0-7206-1047-8*, Pub. by P Owen Ltd) Dufour.

Persistence of Memory. Carol Stetser. (Illus.). 14p. (Orig.). 1992. reprint ed. spiral bd. 20.00 (*0-917960-07-6*) Padma.

Persistence of Memory: A Biography of Dali. Meredith Etherington-Smith. (Illus.). 518p. 1995. reprint ed. pap. 19.95 (*0-306-80662-2*) Da Capo.

Persistence of Memory: Organism, Myth, Text. Philip Kuberski. LC 92-19844. 1992. 35.00 (*0-520-07909-4*, Pub. by U CA Pr) Cal Prin Full Svc.

Persistence of Modernity: Essays on Aesthetics, Ethics & Post Modernism. Albrecht Wellmer. (McCarthy Studies in Contemporary German Social Thought). 200p. 1991. 31.00 (*0-262-23160-3*) MIT Pr.

Persistence of Modernity: Essays on Aesthetics, Ethics, & Postmodernism. Albrecht Wellmer. (Studies in Contemporary German Social Thought). 200p. 1993. pap. text 15.00 (*0-262-73109-6*) MIT Pr.

Persistence of Patriarchy: Class, Gender & Ideology in Twentieth Century Algeria. Peter R. Knauss. LC 87-7026. 190p. 1987. 57.95 (*0-275-92692-3*, C2692, Praeger Pubs) Greenwood.

Persistence of Poetry: Bicentennial Essays on Keats. Ed. by Robert M. Ryan & Ronald A. Sharp. LC 98-7840. 232p. 1998. 29.95 (*1-55849-175-9*) U of Mass Pr.

Persistence of Prehispanic Chiefdoms on the Rio Daule, Coastal Ecuador. David M. Stemper. Tr. by Juana Camacho. (University of Pittsburgh Memoirs in Latin American Archaeology Ser.: No. 7). (ENG & SPA., Illus.). xvi, 214p. 1993. pap. 19.00 (*1-877812-09-9*, M009) UPLAAP.

Persistence of Purgatory. Richard K. Fenn. 217p. (C). 1996. text 64.95 (*0-521-55039-4*); pap. text 22.95 (*0-521-56855-2*) Cambridge U Pr.

Persistence of Racism in America. Thomas Powell. 344p. (Orig.). (C). 1993. pap. text 23.95 (*0-8191-8588-4*); lib. bdg. 57.50 (*0-8191-8587-6*) U Pr of Amer.

Persistence of Regional Cultures: Rusyns & Ukrainians in Their Carpathian Homeland & Abroad. Ed. by Paul R. Magocsi. 220p. 1993. 46.50 (*0-88033-262-X*, 365, Pub. by East Eur Monographs) Col U Pr.

Persistence of Religions: Essays in Honor of Kees W. Bolle. Ed. by Sara J. Denning-Bolle & Edwin Gerow. LC 96-60545. (Other Realities Ser.: Vol. 9). xxii, 444p. (C). 1996. pap. 45.00 (*0-89003-500-8*) Undena Pubns.

Persistence of Sail in the Age of Steam: Underwater Archaeoloogical Evidence from the Dry Tortugas. D. J. Souza. LC 98-18893. (Plenum Series in Underwater Archaeology). (Illus.). 200p. (C). 1998. 42.50 (*0-306-45843-8*, Plenum Trade) Perseus Pubng.

Persistence of Shakespeare Idolatry: Essays in Honor of Robert W. Babcock. Ed. by Herbert M. Schueller. LC 64-16946. 192p. reprint ed. pap. 59.60 (*0-7837-3681-9*, 204355500009) Bks Demand.

Persistence of Social Inequality in America. 2nd ed. John R. Dalphin. 164p. 1987. pap. 14.95 (*0-87073-615-9*) Schenkman Bks Inc.

Persistence of Social Inequality in America. 3rd ed. John R. Dalphin. 192p. write for info. (*0-87047-119-8*) Schenkman Bks Inc.

***Persistence of Social Inequality in America.** 3rd ed. John R. Dalphin. 1999. pap. 18.95 (*0-87047-118-X*) Schenkman Bks Inc.

Persistence of the Westward Movement & Other Essays. John C. Parish. LC 68-14909. (Essay Index Reprint Ser.). 1977. 19.95 (*0-8369-0767-1*) Ayer.

Persistence of Tragedy: Episodes in the History of Drama. 1985. pap. 5.00 (*0-89073-101-2*, 304) Boston Public Lib.

Persistence of Unemployment: Hysteresis in Canadian Labour Markets. Stephen R. Jones. 184p. 1995. 55.00 (*0-7735-1307-8*, Pub. by McG-Queens Univ Pr) CUP Services.

***Persistence of Victorian Liberalism: The Politics of Social Reform in Britain, 1870-1900, 77.** Robert F. Haggard. LC 00-35320. (Contributions to the Study of World History Ser.: Vol. 77). 244p. 2000. 62.00 (*0-313-31305-9*, Greenwood Pr) Greenwood.

***Persistence of Vision.** David Lubbers. (Illus.). 96p. 2000. 48.00 (*0-8028-3884-7*) Eerdmans.

Persistence of Vision: The Films of Robert Altman. N. Feineman. LC 77-22906. (Dissertations on Film Ser.). 1978. lib. bdg. 20.95 (*0-405-10752-8*) Ayer.

***Persistence of Yellow: A Book of Recipes for Life.** Monique Duval. (Illus.). 2000. 19.95 (*1-888387-38-6*) Compendium Inc.

Persistence of Youth: Oral Testimonies of the Holocaust, 32. Ed. by Josey G. Fisher. LC 89-27926. (Contributions to the Study of World History Ser.: No. 32). 200p. 1991. 55.00 (*0-313-28123-8*, FYO, Greenwood Pr) Greenwood.

Persistent Activist: How Peace Commitment Develops & Survives. Paul Wehr & James Downton. LC 96-53176. 186p. (C). 1997. pap. 69.00 (*0-8133-8139-8*, Pub. by Westview) HarpC.

Persistent & Slow Virus Infections. J. Hotchin. Ed. by Joseph L. Melnick. (Monographs in Virology: Vol. 3). (Illus.). 1971. 53.25 (*3-8055-1176-0*) S Karger.

***Persistent Bacterial Infections.** Ed. by James P. Nataro et al. (Illus.). 500p. 2000. 115.95 (*1-55581-159-0*) ASM Pr.

***Persistent, Bioaccumulative, Toxic Chemicals: Fate & Exposure.** Ed. by Robert L. Lipnick et al. (ACS Symposium Ser.: Vol. 772). 2000. 120.00 (*0-8412-3674-7*, Pub. by Am Chemical) OUP.

***Persistent, Bioaccumulative, Toxic Chemicals Assessment & Emerging Chemicals.** Ed. by Robert L. Lipnick et al. (ACS Symposium Ser.: No. 773). (Illus.). 464p. 2000. text 130.00 (*0-8412-3675-5*, Pub. by Am Chemical) OUP.

Persistent Desire: A Femme-Butch Reader. Ed. by Joan Nestle. LC 92-6166. 502p. (Orig.). 1992. pap. 14.95 (*1-55583-190-7*) Alyson Pubns.

Persistent Disparity: Race & Economic Inequality in the U. S. since 1945. William A. Darity, Jr. & Samuel L. Myers, Jr. LC 97-30626. 208p. 1998. 80.00 (*1-85898-658-3*) E Elgar.

Persistent Disparity: Race & Economic Inequality in the U. S. since 1945. William A. Darity & Samuel L. Myers. LC 97-30626. 208p. 1999. pap. 25.00 (*1-85898-665-6*) E Elgar.

***Persistent Disturbances.** 3rd rev. ed. Cydney Chadwick. (Texture Chapbook Ser.: No. 22). 48p. (Orig.). 1999. reprint ed. pap. 5.00 (*0-9641837-5-7*, Pub. by Texture Pr) SPD-Small Pr Dist.

Persistent Inequalities: Women & World Development. Ed. by Irene Tinker. 320p. (C). 1990. pap. text 28.95 (*0-19-506158-6*) OUP.

Persistent International Issues. Ed. by George B. De Huszar. LC 79-142645. (Essay Index Reprint Ser.). 1977. reprint ed. 23.95 (*0-8369-2772-9*) Ayer.

Persistent Issues in American Librarianship. Ed. by Lester Asheim. LC 61-15650. (University of Chicago Studies in Library Science). 119p. reprint ed. pap. 36.90 (*0-608-09265-7*, 205406700002) Bks Demand.

Persistent Ladies. Michael Yates. Ed. by Wister Miller. (Illus.). 159p. (Orig.). pap. 9.95 (*0-9635793-3-9*) Green Hse Pr.

Persistent Lives. Jeannie Ferber. 200p. 1998. write for info. (*1-885934-04-1*) Andover Green.

Persistent Needs: The State of the Nation's Rural Housing in 1996. Housing Assistance Council Staff. (Illus.). 40p. 1996. 7.00 (*1-58064-012-5*) Housing Assist.

Persistent Object Systems: Proceedings of the 5th International Workshop, San Miniato (Pisa), Italy, 1-4 September 1992. Ed. by Antonio Albano & Ron Morrison. LC 92-27164. (Workshops in Computing Ser.). 1993. 79.00 (*0-387-19800-8*) Spr-Verlag.

Persistent Object Systems: Proceedings of the 6th International Workshop on Persistent Object Systems, Tarascon, Provence, France, 5-9 September 1994. Ed. by Malcolm P. Atkinson et al. LC 94-42659. (Workshops in Computing Ser.). xi, 546p. 1995. 69.00 (*3-540-19912-8*) Spr-Verlag.

Persistent Oligarchs: Elites & Politics in Chihuahua, Mexico, 1910-1940. Mark Wasserman. LC 92-39296. (Illus.). 280p. 1993. text 49.95 (*0-8223-1329-4*); pap. text 18.95 (*0-8223-1345-6*) Duke.

Persistent Pain: Modern Methods of Treatment. Sampson Lipton. Incl. Vol. 1. 282p. 1977. 43.50 (*0-8089-1017-5*, 792571, W B Saunders Co); Vol. 2. 416p. 1980. 69.50 (*0-8089-1018-3*, 792572, W B Saunders Co); write for info. (*0-318-56571-4*, Grune & Strat) Harcrt Hlth Sci Grp.

Persistent Pain: Psychosocial Assessment & Intervention. Ed. by N. Timothy Lynch & Sridhar V. Vasudevan. (Current Management of Pain Ser.). (C). 1988. text 140.50 (*0-89838-363-3*) Kluwer Academic.

Persistent Patterns & Emergent Structures in a Waning Century, 3. Ed. by Margaret P. Karns. LC 85-25590. (New Dimensions in International Studies). 327p. 1986. 69.50 (*0-275-92011-9*, C2011, Praeger Pubs) Greenwood.

Persistent Peasants: Smallholders, State Agencies & Involuntary Migration in Western Venezuela. Miguel M. Diaz. (Stockholm Studies in Social Anthropology: No. 35). (Illus.). 291p. (Orig.). 1996. pap. 67.50 (*91-7153-523-3*) Coronet Bks.

Persistent Pesticides in the Environment. 2nd ed. Edwards. 1974. lib. bdg. 74.00 (*0-8493-5011-5*) CRC Pr.

Persistent Pilgrim: The Life of Mary Baker Eddy. Richard A. Nenneman. LC 97-38216. 1997. 30.00 (*1-891331-02-7*, 1003) Nebbadoon Pr.

Persistent Pollutants. Ed. by J. B. Opschoor. (Economy & Environment Ser.). (C). 1991. lib. bdg. 171.00 (*0-7923-1168-X*) Kluwer Academic.

Persistent Pollutants in Marine Ecosystems. C. H. Walker & D. R. Livingstone. (Society of Environment Toxicology & Chemistry Ser.). 192p. 1992. 97.75 (*0-08-041874-0*, Pergamon Pr) Elsevier.

Persistent Poverty: The American Dream Turned Nightmare. R. H. Ropers. LC 91-14. (Illus.). 268p. (C). 1991. 23.95 (*0-306-43764-3*, Plen Insight) Perseus Pubng.

Persistent Poverty in Developing Countries: Determining the Causes & Closing the Gaps. Ed. by Nancy B. Dyke. 150p. 1998. pap. 12.95 (*0-89843-237-5*) The Aspen Inst.

Persistent Prison? Rethinking Decarceration & Penal Reform. Maeve W. McMahon. 320p. 1992. text 45.00 (*0-8020-2817-9*); pap. text 17.95 (*0-8020-7689-0*) U of Toronto Pr.

Persistent Problems of Philosophy. Mary W. Calkins. LC 75-3096. (Philosophy in America Ser.). reprint ed. 82.50 (*0-404-59092-6*) AMS Pr.

Persistent Problems of Psychology. Robert B. MacLeod. LC 75-15636. 207p. 1975. pap. text 19.50 (*0-8207-0254-4*) Duquesne.

Persistent Renal-Genitourinary Disorders. Jose Strauss. (Developments in Nephrology Ser.). 1986. text 161.50 (*0-89838-845-7*) Kluwer Academic.

Persistent Rumours. Lee Langley. LC 94-6454. 304p. 1994. 21.95 (*1-57131-001-0*) Milkweed Ed.

Persistent Rumours. Lee Langley. 304p. 1998. pap. 14.95 (*1-57131-014-2*) Milkweed Ed.

Persistent Seraching for the True Light: Life & Spiritual Journal of a Taiwanese Immigrant. Robert Lee. 103p. 1993. pap. 4.95 (*0-9631789-4-6*) Evan Formosan.

Persistent Shadows of the Holocaust: The Meaning to Those Not Directly Affected. Ed. by Rafael Moses. 288p. 1993. 42.50 (*0-8236-4062-0*) Intl Univs Pr.

Persistent Spectral Hole-Burning: Science & Applications. LC 92-80642. (1992 Technical Digest Ser.: Vol. 22). 250p. 1992. pap. 75.00 (*1-55752-263-4*) Optical Soc.

Persistent Spectral Hole-Burning: Science & Applications. Ed. by W. E. Moerner. (Topics in Current Physics Ser.: Vol. 44). (Illus.). 325p. 1988. 70.95 (*0-387-18607-7*) Spr-Verlag.

Persistent Spirit: Towards Understanding Aboriginal Health in British Columbia. Ed. by Peter H. Stephenson et al. LC 96-132406. (Illus.). 425p. 1996. pap. 25.00 (*0-919838-21-9*) U of Wash Pr.

Persistent Suitor. Phylis Warady. 288p. 1995. mass mkt. 3.99 (*0-8217-4912-9*, Zebra Kensgtn) Kensgtn Pub Corp.

Persistent Underdevelopment: Change & Economic Modernization in the West Indies, Vol. 10. Jay R. Mandle. (Caribbean Studies). 200p. 1996. pap. text 14.00 (*2-88449-194-5*) Gordon & Breach.

Persistent Underdevelopment: Change & Economic Modernization in the West Indies, Vol. 10. Jay R. Mandle. (Caribbean Studies). 200p. 1996. text 35.00 (*2-88449-193-7*) Gordon & Breach.

Persisting Latinisms in 'El Poema de Mio Cid' & Other Selected Old Spanish Literary Works. C. J. Crowley. (LD Ser.: No. 48). 1952. pap. 25.00 (*0-527-00794-3*) Periodicals Srv.

Persisting Traditions: Artisan Work & Culture in Bangor, Maine, 1820-1860. rev. ed. Carol N. Toner. LC 94-23656. (Garland Studies in the History of American Labor). (Illus.). 192p. 1995. text 20.00 (*0-8153-1936-3*) Garland.

Persius: Satires. Tr. by Richard E. Braun. 1983. 12.50 (*0-87291-139-X*) Coronado Pr.

Persius: The Satires. J. Jenkinson & Persius. 1981. 59.99 (*0-85668-159-8*, Pub. by Aris & Phillips); pap. 22.00 (*0-85668-173-3*, Pub. by Aris & Phillips) David Brown.

Persius Flaccus, Aulus: Auli Persi Flacci Lexicon. Ed. by Domenico Bo. xiii, 199p. 1967. 50.00 (*0-318-71970-3*) G Olms Pubs.

Persius Flaccus, Aulus: Index Verborum Quae in Saturis Auli Persi Flacci Reperiuntur. Ed. by Luci Berkowitz & Theodore F. Brunner. xvi, 160p. 1967. 50.00 (*0-318-71969-X*) G Olms Pubs.

Persius Flaccus, Aulus: Konkordanz zu den Satiren des Persius Flaccus. Persius. Ed. by P. Fleury et al. (Alpha-Omega, Reihe A Ser.: Bd. XXXVI). 280p. 1978. write for info. (*3-487-06557-6*) G Olms Pubs.

Persius Saturae. Carrie Cowherd. (Latin Commentaries Ser.). 129p. (Orig.). (C). 1986. pap. text 7.00 (*0-929524-48-9*) Bryn Mawr Commentaries.

Perske Pencil Portraits, 1971-1990. Illus. by Martha Perske. LC 98-217952. 120p. 1998. 20.00 (*0-687-05080-4*) Abingdon.

Persnickity. Stephen Cosgrove. (Serendipity Bks.). (Illus.). 32p. (J). (gr. 1-4). 1988. pap. 4.99 (*0-8431-2303-6*, Price Stern) Peng Put Young Read.

Persnickity. Stephen Cosgrove. (Serendipity Ser.). (J). 1988. lib. bdg. 18.60 (*0-86592-782-0*) Rourke Enter.

Perso-Arabic Sources of Information on the Life & Conditions in the Sultanate of Delhi. I. Siddiqui. (C). 1992. 22.00 (*81-215-0535-6*, Pub. by M Manoharial) Coronet Bks.

***Person** Ridley Pearson. 2001. mass mkt. write for info. (*0-7868-8960-8*) Disney Pr.

Person. 2nd ed. McAdams. (C). 1994. pap. text, teacher ed. 35.00 (*0-15-501967-8*) Harcourt Coll Pubs.

Person. 3rd ed. McAdams. (C). 1999. text. write for info. (*0-15-508066-0*) Harcourt Coll Pubs.

Person: An Introduction to Personality Psychology. 2nd ed. Dan P. McAdams. (Illus.). 704p. (C). 1994. text 86.00 (*0-15-501274-6*) Harcourt Coll Pubs.

Person: Begriff & Name Derselben im Altertum. Rudolf Hirzel. LC 75-13275. (History of Ideas in Ancient Greece Ser.). (GER.). 1976. reprint ed. 12.95 (*0-405-07315-1*) Ayer.

Person: His & Her Development Throughout the Life Cycle. rev. ed. Theodore Lidz. LC 76-22745. 625p. 1983. pap. 40.00 (*0-465-05541-9*, Pub. by Basic) HarpC.

Person & Being. W. Norris Clarke. LC 92-63402. (Aquinas Lectures). 1993. pap. 15.00 (*0-87462-160-7*) Marquette.

Person & Community: A Philosophical Exploration. Ed. by Robert J. Roth. LC 73-93143. 187p. reprint ed. pap. 58.00 (*0-7837-0470-4*, 204079300018) Bks Demand.

Person & Community: Ghanaian Philosophical Studies I. Ed. by Kwame Gyekye & Kwasi Wiredu. LC 91-58172. (Cultural Heritage & Contemporary Change Series II: Vol. 1). 1992. 45.00 (*1-56518-005-4*); pap. 17.50 (*1-56518-004-6*) Coun Res Values.

Person & Community: Selected Essays. Karol Wojtyla. Tr. by Theresa Sandok from POL. LC 92-28994. (Catholic Thought from Lublin Ser.: Vol. 5). XVI, 370p. (C). 1994. text 39.95 (*0-8204-1446-8*) P Lang Pubng.

Person & God. Ed. by George F. McLean & Hugo Meynell. LC 88-161. (International Society for Metaphysics Studies in Metaphysics: Vol. III). 377p. (Orig.). 1988. 45.00 (*0-8191-6937-4*); pap. 17.50 (*0-8191-6938-2*) Coun Res Values.

Person & God in a Spanish Valley. William A. Christian, Jr. 244p. 1989. pap. text 16.95 (*0-691-02845-1*, Pub. by Princeton U Pr) Cal Prin Full Svc.

Person & Ministry of the Holy Spirit. Charles W. Carter. pap. 15.99 (*0-88019-094-9*) Schmul Pub Co.

Person & Myth: Maurice Leenhardt in the Melanesian World. James Clifford. LC 92-14147. (Illus.). 285p. 1992. pap. text 17.95 (*0-8223-1264-6*) Duke.

Person & Nature. Ed. by George F. McLean & Hugo Meynell. LC 88-14368. (International Society for Metaphysics Studies in Metaphysics: Vol. I). 235p. (Orig.). 1988. 45.00 (*0-8191-7025-9*); pap. 17.50 (*0-8191-7026-7*) Coun Res Values.

***Person & Personality of the Holy Spirit.** Dilley Nadesan. 120p. 1999. pap. write for info. (*0-7392-0480-7*, PO3818) Morris Pubng.

Person & Place of Jesus Christ. Peter T. Forsyth. 377p. 1996. pap. 29.00 (*1-57910-016-3*) Wipf & Stock.

Person & Polis: Max Scheler's Personalism As Political Theory. Stephen F. Schneck. LC 86-23014. (SUNY Series in Political Theory: Contemporary Issues). 188p. (C). 1987. pap. text 21.95 (*0-88706-339-X*) State U NY Pr.

Person & Primary Emotions. Peter A. Bertocci. (Recent Research in Psychology Ser.). 340p. 1988. 58.95 (*0-387-96812-1*) Spr-Verlag.

Person & Religion: An Outline of the Philosophy of Religion. Zofia J. Zdybicka. LC 91-30854. (Catholic Thought from Lublin Ser.: Vol. 3). 418p. (C). 1992. text 65.95 (*0-8204-1447-6*) P Lang Pubng.

Person & Self Value. Max Ferdinand Scheler. 1987. lib. bdg. 151.50 (*90-247-3380-4*, Pub. by M Nijhoff) Kluwer Academic.

Person & Society. Ed. by George F. McLean & Hugo Meynell. LC 88-128. (International Society for Metaphysics Studies in Metaphysics: Vol. II). 145p. (Orig.). 1988. 45.00 (*0-8191-6924-2*); pap. 17.50 (*0-8191-6925-0*) Coun Res Values.

***Person & Society.** Charles Thomas Taylor. LC 99-75261. 144p. 2000. pap. write for info. (*1-57197-204-8*, Pub. by Pentland Pr) Assoc Pubs Grp.

Person & the Common Good. Jacques Maritain. 1966. pap. 7.00 (*0-268-00204-5*) U of Notre Dame Pr.

Person & the Common Life: Studies in a Husserlian Social Ethics. James G. Hart. LC 92-11464. (Phaenomenologica Ser.: No. 126). 480p. (C). 1992. lib. bdg. 203.00 (*0-7923-1724-6*, Pub. by Kluwer Academic) Kluwer Academic.

Person & the Human Mind: Issues in Ancient & Modern Philosophy. Ed. by Christopher Gill. 294p. 1990. text 59.00 (*0-19-824460-6*) OUP.

Person & the Natural Law. Mieczyslaw A. Krapiec. Tr. by Maria Szymenska. LC 91-46414. (Catholic Thought from Lublin Ser.: Vol. 7). (ENG & POL.). XI, 268p. (C). 1993. text 51.95 (*0-8204-1843-9*) P Lang Pubng.

Person & the Situation: Essential Contributions of Social Psychology. Lee Ross & Richard E. Nisbett. 192p. (C). 1991. pap. 39.69 (*0-07-053926-X*) McGraw.

P

An Asterisk (*) at the beginning of an entry indicates that the title is appearing for the first time.

Person & the Situation: Essential Contributions of Social Psychology. Lee Ross & Richard E. Nisbett. 192p. 1991. 49.95 (*0-87722-851-5*) Temple U Pr.

Person & the Work of the Holy Spirit. R. A. Torrey. 298p. 1996. mass mkt. 5.99 (*0-88368-384-9*) Whitaker Hse.

Person & the Work of the Holy Spirit. 2nd ed. R. A. Torrey. 224p. (C). 1985. pap. 10.99 (*0-310-33301-6*, 10902P) Zondervan.

Person & Work of Christ. Benjamin B. Warfield. 1950. 19.99 (*0-87552-529-6*) P & R Pubng.

Person & Work of the Holy Spirit. Benjamin B. Warfield. Ed. by Michael Gaydosh. 192p. (Orig.). 1997. pap. 12.95 (*1-879737-16-7*) Calvary Press.

Person Behind the Mask: A Guide to Performing Arts Psychology. LC 97-22316. 1997. pap. 39.50 (*1-56750-345-4*); text 73.25 (*1-56750-344-6*) Ablx Pub.

Person Behind the Syndrome. Peter H. Beighton & Greta Beighton. LC 96-17384. (Illus.). 248p. 1996. 59.00 (*3-540-76044-X*) Spr-Verlag.

Person Centered Astrology. Dane Rudhyar. 385p. 1983. 14.00 (*0-943358-02-7*) Aurora Press.

Person Centered Counseling: Therapeutic & Spiritual Dimensions. Thorne. 204p. 1991. pap. 49.95 (*1-56593-550-0*, 0303) Singular Publishing.

Person Centered Counselling in Action. Dave Mearns & Brian Thorne. (Counselling in Action Ser.). 160p. (C). 1988. text 49.95 (*0-8039-8049-3*); pap. text 21.50 (*0-8039-8050-7*) Sage.

Person-Centered Counselling Training. Dave Mearns. LC 98-121483. 240p. 1997. 59.95 (*0-7619-5290-X*); pap. 24.50 (*0-7619-5291-8*) Sage.

Person Centered Ergonomics: A Brantonian View of Human Factors. David J. Oborne et al. LC 92-29732. 1993. 89.95 (*0-7484-0051-6*) Taylor & Francis.

Person-Centered Foundation for Counseling & Psychotherapy. 2nd ed. Angelo V. Boy & Gerald J. Pine. LC 99-20307. 274p. 1999. text 54.95 (*0-398-06964-6*); pap. text 39.95 (*0-398-06966-2*) C C Thomas.

Person-Centered Leadership: An American Approach to Participatory Management. Jeanne M. Plas. 240p. (C). 1996. 52.00 (*0-8039-5598-7*) Sage.

Person-Centered Learning: Confluent Learning Processes. Glenn E. Whitlock. 114p. (Orig.). 1984. pap. text 14.00 (*0-8191-3856-8*) U Pr of Amer.

Person Centered Long-Term Care: A Walk in Their Shoes. Jo Horne. (Learning the Continuum: AUPHA Modules for Management Education Ser.). (Illus.). 100p. (Orig.). (C). 1989. pap. text 20.00 (*0-910591-17-2*) AUPHA Pr.

Person-Centered Planning & Outcome Management: Maximizing Organizational Effectiveness in Supporting Quality Lifestyles among People with Disabilities. Jane M. Everson & Dennis H. Reid. (Illus.). 225p. 1999. pap. text 28.00 (*0-9645562-2-7*) Habilit Mgt Consult.

Person-Centred Counselling: An Experimental Approach David L. Rennie. LC 97-62420. vi, 153p. 1998. write for info. (*0-7619-5345-0*) Sage.

Person-centred Therapy: A European Perspective. Ed. by Brian Thorne & Elke Lambers. LC 98-61238. 243 p. 1998. write for info. (*0-7619-5154-7*) Sage.

Person County, North Carolina Compilations: Land Grants, 1794. Katherine K. Kendall & Mary Frances K. Donaldson. 148p. 1997. reprint ed. pap. 17.50 (*0-8063-4713-9*) Clearfield Co.

Person County, North Carolina Deed Books 1792-1825. Katharine K. Kendall. 262p. 1996. reprint ed. pap. 24.00 (*0-8063-4518-7*, 9203) Clearfield Co.

Person County, North Carolina Marriage Records, 1792-1868. Katherine K. Kendall. 96p. 1978. pap. 20.00 (*0-614-04980-6*) N C Genealogical.

Person County, North Carolina Marriage Records, 1792-1868. Katherine K. Kendall. 113p. 1997. reprint ed. pap. 14.00 (*0-8063-4712-0*) Clearfield Co.

Person Des Heiligen Geistes Als Thema der Pneumatologie in der Reformierten Theologie. Hong-Hsin Lin. VIII, 283p. 1998. 48.95 (*3-631-33853-8*) P Lang Pubng.

Person-Environment Practice: The Social Ecology of Interpersonal Helping. Susan P. Kemp et al. LC 97-7417. (Modern Applications of Social Work Ser.). 277p. 1997. pap. text 24.95 (*0-202-36103-9*); lib. bdg. 46.95 (*0-202-36102-0*) Aldine de Gruyter.

Person-Environment Psychiatry. Walsh. 1992. 59.95 (*0-8058-0344-0*) L Erlbaum Assocs.

Person Environment Psychology. 2nd ed. Ed. by W. Bruce Walsh et al. LC 99-30603. 325p. 1999. write for info. (*0-8058-2470-7*) L Erlbaum Assocs.

***Person Environment Psychology.** 2nd ed. Ed. by W. Bruce Walsh et al. LC 99-30603. 325p. 1999. pap. write for info. (*0-8058-2471-5*) L Erlbaum Assocs.

Person-Environment Psychology: Clinical & Counseling Applications for Adolescents & Adults. Ed. by William E. Martin, Jr. & Jody L. Swartz. LC 99-32763. 300p. 2000. write for info. (*0-8058-2953-9*) L Erlbaum Assocs.

Person-Fit Reserach: Theory & Applications. Ed. by Rob R. Meijer. 109p. 1995. pap. write for info. (*0-8058-9929-4*) L Erlbaum Assocs.

Person I Am see Persona Que Soy

Person I Once Was. Cindy L. Johnson. 1985. pap. 5.25 (*0-8222-0888-1*) Dramatists Play.

Person in Analysis: Interpersonhood in Metaphysics & Analytic Theory. Kevin O'Shea. 175p. (C). 1996. text 40.00 (*1-55605-270-7*); pap. text 20.00 (*1-55605-269-3*) Wyndham Hall.

Person in Cosmos: Metaphors of Meaning from Physics, Philosophy, & Theology. Kevin O'Shea. 225p. (C). 1995. text 40.00 (*1-55605-264-2*) Wyndham Hall.

Person in Cosmos: Metaphors of Meaning from Physics, Philosophy & Theology. Kevin O'Shea. 225p. (C). 1995. pap. text 20.00 (*1-55605-263-4*) Wyndham Hall.

Person-in-Distress: On the Biosocial Dynamics of Adaptation. Norris Hansell. LC 74-8096. 248p. 1976. 35.95 (*0-87705-213-1*, Kluwer Acad Hman Sci) Kluwer Academic.

Person-in-Environment System: The PIE Classification System for Social Functioning Problems. Ed. by James M. Karls & Karin E. Wandrei. LC 94-23170. 665p. (C). 1994. pap. 28.95 (*0-87101-240-5*, 2405A) Natl Assn Soc Wkrs.

Person-in-Environment System: The PIE Classification System for Social Functioning Problems. Ed. by James M. Karls & Karin E. Wandrei. LC 94-23170. 65p. (C). 1994. lib. bdg., student ed. 28.95 (*0-87101-254-5*, 2545) Natl Assn Soc Wkrs.

Person in Psychology: A Contemporary Christian Appraisal. fac. ed. Mary S. Van Leeuwen. LC 85-10181. (Studies in a Christian World View: No. 3). 278p. 1985. reprint ed. pap. 86.20 (*0-7837-7975-5*, 204773100008) Bks Demand.

Person in the Social Order. Perry J. Roeta. LC B 0828.5.R64. 390p. reprint ed. pap. 120.90 (*0-608-30610-X*, 202116200021) Bks Demand.

Person in the World: Introduction to the Philosophy of Edith Stein. Mary C. Baseheart. LC 97-2846. 216p. 1997. text 107.00 (*0-7923-4490-1*) Kluwer Academic.

***Person Is Like a Tree: A Sourcebook for Tu BeShvat.** Yitzhak Buxbaum. LC 99-48147. 1999. 25.00 (*0-7657-6128-9*) Aronson.

Person Is Many Wonderful, Strange Things. Marsha Sinetar. 64p. 1990. pap. 5.95 (*0-8091-3159-5*) Paulist Pr.

Person of Christ. Donald MacLeod. LC 98-40356. (Contours of Christian Theology Ser.). 288p. 1998. pap. 16.99 (*0-8308-1537-6*, 1537) InterVarsity.

Person of Christ: Covenant Between God & Man. Jean Galot. Tr. by Angeline Bouchard. LC 84-5982. 94p. 1983. pap. 4.50 (*0-8199-0832-0*, Frncscn Herld) Franciscan Pr.

Person of God: In the Form of Man. Vicky Wilkinson. 32p. (Orig.). 1994. pap. 3.00 (*1-880573-17-2*) Bible Search Pubns.

***Person of Jesus Christ, 3 Vols.** Lester Sumrall. 1999. audio 40.00 (*1-58568-103-2*) Sumrall Pubng.

Person of Jesus Christ: The Savior of Mankind. Lester Sumrall. 141p. (C). 1985. pap. text 12.00 (*0-937580-90-2*) Sumrall Pubng.

Person of the Holy Spirit. Lester Sumrall. 103p. (C). 1986. pap. text 12.00 (*0-937580-83-X*) Sumrall Pubng.

Person of the Holy Spirit & His Works. Jesse W. Norwood. 104p. 1998. pap. 12.95 (*1-888398-20-5*, Lightfall Pub) WJC Designs.

Person or Persons Unknown: A Sir John Fielding Mystery. Bruce Alexander. (Sir John Fielding Mystery Ser.: Bk. 4). 336p. 1998. reprint ed. pap. 5.99 (*0-425-16566-3*, Prime Crime) Berkley Pub.

Person Perception & Attribution. Hans-Werner Bierhoff. (Social Psychology Ser.). (Illus.). 370p. 1989. 86.95 (*0-387-50356-0*) Spr-Verlag.

Person Perception in Childhood & Adolescence. W. J. Livesley & D. B. Bromley. LC 72-8606. 332p. reprint ed. pap. 103.00 (*0-608-12452-4*, 202520400042) Bks Demand.

Person Place & Thing: Interpretative & Empirical Essays in Cultural Geography. 2nd ed. Ed. by Shue T. Wong. (Geoscience & Man Ser.: Vol. 31). (Illus.). 442p. (C). 1996. pap. 25.00 (*0-938909-59-2*) Geosci Pubns LSU.

Person, Place & Thing in Henry James's Novels. Charles R. Anderson. LC 77-75619. 318p. reprint ed. pap. 98.60 (*0-608-17316-9*, 205223400068) Bks Demand.

Person Schemes & Maladaptive Interpersonal Patterns. Ed. by Mardi J. Horowitz. LC 90-49633. (John D. & Catherine T. MacArthur Foundation Series on Mental Health & Development). (Illus.). 444p. 1991. 41.95 (*0-226-35375-3*) U Ch Pr.

***Person-Sein: Freiheit und Geschichtlichkeit Als Grundkonstanten des Menschen Im Denken von Max Muller, 1906-1994.** Kai-Uwe Socha. (Europaische Hochschulschriften Ser.). 345p. 1999. 48.95 (*3-631-34419-8*) P Lang Pubng.

Person to Person. 2nd ed. Sasse. (YA). (gr. 9-12). 1981. teacher ed. 23.77 (*0-02-665330-3*) Glencoe.

Person to Person. 2nd ed. Sasse. (YA). (gr. 9-12). 1982. student ed. 7.77 (*0-02-665340-0*) Glencoe.

Person to Person. 4th ed. Kathleen Galvin. 464p. 1990. 26.60 (*0-8442-5670-6*) NTC Contemp Pub Co.

Person to Person. 5th ed. (C). 1992. write for info. (*0-8087-7910-9*) Pearson Custom.

Person to Person. 5th ed. Kathleen Galvin. LC 92-60376. 512p. 1994. 42.32 (*0-8442-5800-8*) NTC Contemp Pub Co.

Person to Person: A Group Approach to Peer Counseling. unabridged ed. Nate Rockitter. LC 93-77665. 132p. 1993. pap. text 12.95 (*0-932446-04-3*) Jacqueline Enter.

Person to Person: A Guide for Professionals Working with People with Disabilities. 3rd ed. Lindsay Gething. LC 97-20354. 371p. 1997. (*1-55766-320-3*) P H Brookes.

Person to Person: An In-depth Course in Relationships. Sanford G. Kulkin. 1993. ring bd. 445.00 incl. audio (*1-58034-002-4*) IML Pubns.

Person to Person: Communicative Speaking & Listening Skills, Bk. 2. Jack Richards & David Bycina. 1985. teacher ed. write for info. (*0-318-59138-3*) OUP.

Person to Person: Fieldwork, Dialogue, & the Hermeneutic Method. Barry P. Michrina & CherylAnne Richards. LC 95-8930. 176p. (C). 1996. pap. text 16.95 (*0-7914-2834-6*) State U NY Pr.

Person to Person: Friendship & Love in the Life & Theology of Hans Urs von Balthasar. John S. Bonnici. LC 98-51510. 160p. 1999. pap. 9.95 (*0-8189-0858-0*) Alba.

***Person to Person: Positive Relationships Don't Just Happen.** 3rd ed. Hanna. LC 98-40744. 493p. 1999. pap. text 55.00 (*0-13-020740-3*) P-H.

Person to Person: The Gospel of Mark. Paul V. Vickers. LC 98-13695. 160p. 1998. pap. 14.95 (*0-87785-380-0*) Swedenborg.

Person to Person Astrology. Pat Strickland. LC 86-70792. 136p. 1986. 13.00 (*0-86690-320-8*, S2359-014) Am Fed Astrologers.

Person-to-Person Communication Skills see Productive Supervisor: A Program of Practical Managerial Skills

Person to Person Inspiration, Vol. 1. Sunnie D. Kidd & James W. Kidd. (American University Studies: No. V). XXXV, 140p. (C). 1995. text 41.95 (*0-8204-2522-2*) P Lang Pubng.

Person to Person to God: The Power of Prayer. Ed. by Frances Cowder. 2000. pap. 10.00 (*1-884289-19-3*) Grandmother Erth.

Person und Dasein. (Phaenomenologica Ser.: No. 32). 1970. lib. bdg. 61.00 (*90-247-0271-2*) Kluwer Academic.

Person und Gehirn. Gabriele Stotz. (Philosophische Texte und Studien: Vol. 16). (GER.). 364p. 1988. write for info. (*3-487-09024-4*) G Olms Pubs.

Person Unknown. large type ed. Judy Chard. (Linford Mystery Library). 1989. pap. 16.99 (*0-7089-6776-0*, Linford) Ulverscroft.

***Person Who Changed My Life: Prominent Americans Recall Their Mentors.** Ed. by Matilda Raffa Cuomo. LC 98-56541. (Illus.). 240p. 1999. 21.95 (*1-55972-508-7*, Birch Ln Pr) Carol Pub Group.

Person Who Is Me: Contemporary Perspectives on the True & False Self. Val Richards & Gillian Wilce. LC 98-152425. (Illus.). 112p. 1996. pap. 22.00 (*1-85575-130-5*, Pub. by H Karnac Bks Ltd) Other Pr LLC.

Person with HIV/AIDS: Nursing Perspectives. 3rd ed. Ed. by Jerry D. Durham & Felissa R. Lashley. LC 99-16258. (Illus.). 518p. 1999. text 54.95 (*0-8261-1293-5*) Springer Pub.

Persona. Lynn Gumpert & Ned Rifkin. LC 81-81190. (Illus.). 57p. (Orig.). 1981. pap. 4.00 (*0-614-18077-5*) New Mus Contemp Art.

Persona. Steven Reinberg. LC 97-11848. (Illus.). 160p. 1997. pap. 35.00 (*0-8478-2046-7*, Pub. by Rizzoli Intl) St Martin.

Persona: Social Role & Personality. Helen H. Perlman. LC 68-21892. 256p. 1986. pap. text 18.00 (*0-226-66028-1*) U Ch Pr.

Persona: Social Role & Personality. Helen H. Perlman. LC 68-21892. 1992. lib. bdg. 16.00 (*0-226-66030-3*) U Ch Pr.

Persona: The Meaning Behind the Mask. Mehmet Mizanoglu. LC 98-72913. (Illus.). 102p. 1998. pap. 10.95 (*0-9663047-1-3*) BGB Pr.

Persona: Vida y Mascara en el Teatro Puertorriqueno. Matias Montes-Huidobro. LC 84-19721. (SPA., Illus.). 560p. (C). 1984. pap. 15.00 (*0-913480-61-4*) Inter Am U Pr.

Persona & Decorum in Milton's Prose. Reuben Sanchez, Jr. LC 96-41403. 256p. 1997. 38.50 (*0-8386-3680-2*) Fairleigh Dickinson.

Persona & Humor in Mark Twain's Early Writings. Don Florence. 184p. (C). 1995. 34.95 (*0-8262-1025-2*) U of Mo Pr.

Persona & Performance: The Meaning of Role in Drama, Therapy, & Everyday Life. Robert J. Landy. LC 93-2361. 278p. 1996. pap. text 21.00 (*0-89862-598-X*, 2598) Guilford Pubns.

Persona & Performance: The Meaning of Role in Drama, Therapy & Everyday Life. Robert J. Landy. 250p. 1993. write for info. (*1-85302-229-2*, Pub. by Jessica Kingsley) Taylor & Francis.

Persona & Performance: The Meaning of Role in Drama, Therapy & Everyday Life. Robert J. Landy. 250p. 1994. pap. write for info. (*1-85302-230-6*, Pub. by Jessica Kingsley) Taylor & Francis.

Persona & Shame. Ingmar Bergman. Tr. by Keith Bradfield from SWE. 192p. 1989. 12.95 (*0-7145-0756-3*) M Boyars Pubs.

Persona Book: Curriculum-Based Enrichment for School Librarians & Teachers. Katherine G. Lallier & Nancy R. Marino. LC 96-37655. 180p. 1997. pap. text, teacher ed. 24.50 (*1-56308-443-0*) Teacher Ideas Pr.

Persona Granada. D. Forman. 1997. text 40.00 (*0-233-98987-0*, Pub. by Andre Deutsch) Trafalgar.

Persona in Three Satires of Juvenal. Martin M. Winkler. write for info. (*0-318-70688-1*) G Olms Pubs.

Persona in Three Satires of Juvenal. Martin M. Winkler. (Altertumswissenschaftliche Texte und Studien: Vol. 10). (GER.). xii, 248p. 1983. 25.87 (*3-487-07437-0*) G Olms Pubs.

Persona, Larva, Maske: Ikonologische Studien zum 16. bis Fruhen 18. Jahrhundert. Eckhard Leuschner. (Europaische Hochschulschriften, Reihe 28: Bd. 292). (GER., Illus.). 566p. 1997. 95.95 (*3-631-31340-3*) P Lang Pubng.

Persona Non Grata. Jorge Edwards. 1994. 27.95 (*1-56924-974-1*) Marlowe & Co.

Persona Non Grata. Viktor Kortchnoi & Lenny Cavallaro. Tr. by Jim Marfia. Orig. Title: Anti-Chess. (Illus.). 145p. (Orig.). 1981. pap. 8.95 (*0-938650-15-7*) Thinkers Pr.

Persona Principle: How to Succeed in Business with Image-Marketing. Derek L. Armstrong & Kam W. Yu. (Illus.). 256p. 1996. 24.50 (*0-684-80268-6*) S&S Trade.

***Persona Principle: How to Succeed in Business with Image-Marketing.** Derek Lee Armstrong & Kam W. Yu. (Illus.). 240p. 2000. reprint ed. 25.00 (*0-7881-9253-1*) DIANE Pub.

Persona Que Dios Usa. Victor Ricardo. 32p. 1993. pap. 1.15 (*1-885630-05-0*) HLM Producciones.

Persona Que Soy. L. Thompson.Tr. of Person I Am. (SPA.). 10.99 (*0-7899-0254-0*, 491046) Editorial Unilit.

Personae: The Shorter Poems of Ezra Pound. 2nd ed. Ezra Pound. LC 89-14036. 304p. 1990. reprint ed. 23.95 (*0-8112-1120-7*, Pub. by New Directions) Norton.

Personae: The Shorter Poems of Ezra Pound. 2nd ed. Ezra Pound. LC 89-14036. 304p. 1990. reprint ed. pap. 14.95 (*0-8112-1138-X*, NDP697, Pub. by New Directions) Norton.

Personae & Poiesis: The Poet & the Poem in Medieval Love Lyric. Prospero Saiz. (De Proprietatibus Litterarum, Ser. Minor: No. 17). (Illus.). 1976. pap. text 32.30 (*90-279-3494-0*) Mouton.

Personae Comicae. G. M. Lyne. (C). 1982. pap. text 39.00 (*0-900269-11-1*, Pub. by Old Vicarage) St Mut.

Personae Comicae. G. M. Lyne. 48p. 1992. reprint ed. 6.00 (*0-86516-031-7*) Bolchazy-Carducci.

Personae Dramatis in Ludis Sherlociensibus: The Characters in the Canon. Gary L. Heiselberg. LC 99-174983. 1997. pap. 16.00 (*1-55246-001-0*) Battered Silicon.

Personae Non Gratae. Paul Mariah. 32p. 1977. pap. 1.95 (*0-686-19032-7*) Man-Root.

Personaggi del Vangelo see Crowd of Witnesses: Interviews with Famous New Testament Men & Women

Personajes, 2 vols. Klein. (C). Date not set. pap. 39.96 (*0-395-79684-9*); pap., teacher ed. 11.96 (*0-395-79483-8*) HM.

Personajes. Klein. (C). 1992. pap. text, wbk. ed. 22.76 (*0-395-58485-X*) HM.

Personajes. Carol E. Klein & Jorge M. Guitart. (SPA.). (C). 1992. pap. text, teacher ed. 44.36 (*0-395-58484-1*) HM.

Personajes. Carol E. Klein et al. (C). 1992. pap. text 43.16 (*0-395-58483-3*) HM.

Personajes Biblicos a Traves de la Hostoria. Dave Warren & Pat Warren. Ed. by Richard Meyer. (Adult Sunday School Ser.). (SPA.). 110p. 1994. 4.40 (*1-879892-39-1*) Editorial Bautista.

Personajes Biblicos Portavoz. Robert Backhouse. (SPA., Illus.). 32p. 1996. pap. 8.99 (*0-8254-1049-5*, Edit Portavoz) Kregel.

Personajes de la Biblia: Localiza la Diferencia. A. Hudson.Tr. of People in the Bible: Spot the Difference. (SPA.). (J). 1995. 1.89 (*1-56063-964-4*, 497755) Editorial Unilit.

Personal Accident, Life & Other Insurances. 2nd ed. E. R. Ivamy. (C). 1980. 520.00 (*0-7855-4063-6*, Pub. by Witherby & Co) St Mut.

Personal Accountability: Your Path to a Rewarding Work Life. Stephen C. Lundin & James K. Arnold. (Illus.). 52p. 1997. pap. 7.95 (*0-9661944-0-3*) Charthouse Intl.

Personal Accounts of Events, Travels, & Everyday Life in America: An Annotated Bibliography. Compiled by E. Richard McKinstry. LC 97-10832. (Winterthur Book Ser.). (Illus.). 236p. 1997. 40.00 (*0-912724-39-0*) Winterthur.

***Personal Accounts of Northern Ireland's Troubles: Public Conflict, Personal Loss.** Ed. by Marie Smyth & Marie-Therese Fay. 144p. 2000. pap. 17.95 (*0-7453-1618-2*, Pub. by Pluto GBR) Stylus Pub VA.

Personal Action Plan: Building Your Blueprint for Business & Personal Excellence. Gary R. Blair. 40p. 1998. pap. 19.95 (*1-889770-55-8*, PAP) GoalsGuy.

Personal Ad Portraits. Lonny Shavelson. (Illus.). 96p. 1983. pap. text 13.95 (*0-912357-00-2*) De Novo Pr.

Personal Adjustment in Old Age. Ruth S. Cavan et al. Ed. by Robert J. Kastenbaum. LC 78-22188. (Aging & Old Age Ser.). (Illus.). 1979. reprint ed. lib. bdg. 19.95 (*0-405-11806-6*) Ayer.

Personal Adjustment in the 21St Century. Everett L. Worthington. 512p. (C). 2001. 47.00 (*0-02-430041-1*, Macmillan Coll) P-H.

Personal Adjustment, Marriage & Family Living. 6th ed. Judson T. Landis et al. 1975. text 26.48 (*0-13-657338-X*) P-H.

Personal Ads. Robbi Sommers. LC 94-15978. 224p. 1994. pap. 11.95 (*1-56280-059-0*) Naiad Pr.

Personal Ads, Why Not? Lynn Davis. Ed. by Trudy Meehan. LC 83-60285. (Illus.). 128p. 1983. pap. 9.95 incl. audio (*0-9610742-0-5*) Purcell Prods.

Personal Adventures in Upper & Lower California in 1848-9. William R. Ryan. LC 72-9466. (Far Western Frontier Ser.). (Illus.). 822p. 1973. reprint ed. 53.95 (*0-405-04994-3*) Ayer.

Personal Affairs: Family & Estate Records Organizer. Harry H. Montgomery, Jr. LC 94-90049. (Illus.). 139p. 1994. ring bd. 34.95 (*0-9640265-0-3*) Windmark Pubns.

Personal Alchemy: The Neophyte's Path to Spiritual Attainment, Lessons 216-25. C. C. Zain. (Brotherhood of Light Home Study Ser.: Course 21). (Illus.). 193p. 1996. pap. 16.95 (*0-87887-362-7*) Church of Light.

***Personal Ancestral File Users Guide: Version 4.0.** Hope Foundation Staff. LC 99-48381. 305p. 1999. pap. 19.95 (*0-916489-93-0*) Ancestry.

Personal & Business Bartering. James Stout. (Illus.). 392p. (Orig.). 1985. pap. 14.95 (*0-8306-1676-4*, 1676P) McGraw-Hill Prof.

Personal & Business Tax & Financial Planning for Psychiatrists. W. Murray Bradford & Glenn B. Davis. LC 84-6189. (Private Practice Monograph Ser.). 191p. reprint ed. pap. 59.30 (*0-8357-7844-4*, 203621900002) Bks Demand.

Personal & Career Exploration. 5th ed. George P. Schmidt. 416p. (C). 1997. pap. text, per. 26.95 (*0-7872-3413-3*, 41341301) Kendall-Hunt.

Personal & Comprehensive Testimony: The P. A. C. T. Plan. Bob Dutton & Beth Anderson. Ed. by Rachel Thompson. 148p. 1993. student ed. 42.00 (*0-9636798-0-5*) Creat Artforms.

Personal & Family Economic. Kimbrell. (HB - Economics Ser.). (C). 1996. mass mkt., wbk. ed. 17.50 (*0-314-06790-6*) West Pub.

Personal & Family Economics. Grady Kimbrell. LC 94-28844. 1995. write for info. (*0-314-02446-8*) West Pub.

P

An Asterisk (*) at the beginning of an entry indicates that the title is appearing for the first time.

Personal & Family Economics. Grady Kimbrell. LC 94-28844. (HB - Economics Ser.). 1995. mass mkt. 45.50 (*0-314-04518-X*) West Pub.

Personal & Family Economics: Your Rights As a Consumer. Kimbrell. 1996. 99.00 (*0-314-09831-3*, Pub. by West Pub) Thomson Learn.

Personal & Family Finance Workbook. 2nd ed. Craig Israelsen & Robert Weagley. 296p. (C). 1996. spiral bd. 29.95 (*0-8403-9370-9*) Kendall-Hunt.

Personal & Family Finance Workbook. 3rd ed. Weagley Israelsen. 294p. (C). 1997. spiral bd. 29.95 (*0-7872-3717-5*) Kendall-Hunt.

Personal & Family Safety. (Illus.). 104p. 1998. write for info. (*0-945100-42-6*) Parlay Intl.

Personal & Historical Sketches & Facial History of & by Members of the Seventh Regiment Michigan Volunteer Cavalry, 1862-1865. Compiled by William O. Lee. LC 89-83404. (Illus.). 313p. 1990. reprint ed. 25.00 (*0-914905-50-3*) Detroit Bk Pr.

Personal & Impersonal: Six Aesthetic Realists. Sheldon Kranz et al. LC 59-10629. 76p. 1959. pap. 7.50 (*0-910492-21-2*) Definition.

Personal & Mobile Radio Systems. Ed. by Kisha Gunter. (Telecommunications Ser.: No. 25). 329p. 1991. pap. 45.00 (*0-86341-286-6*, TE025Z); boxed set 105.00 (*0-86341-219-X*, TE025) INSPEC Inc.

Personal & Organizational Security Handbook. annuals 424p. 1985. pap. 75.00 (*0-317-01262-2*) Gov Data Pubns.

Personal & Political Ballads of the War. Frank Moore. (Notable American Authors Ser.). 1999. reprint ed. lib. bdg. 125.00 (*0-7812-4580-X*) Rprt Serv.

Personal & Professional Development for Counsellors. Paul Wilkins. (Professional Skills for Counselors Ser.). 160p. (C). 1996. 45.00 (*0-8039-7462-0*, 74620); pap. 18.95 (*0-8039-7463-9*, 74639) Sage.

Personal & Professional Effectiveness. Frank Basile. 150p. (Orig.). 1995. pap. 16.95 (*1-878208-59-4*) Guild Pr IN.

Personal & Professional Keyboarding. 7th ed. James C. Bennett. (TA - Typing/Keyboarding Ser.). 1995. mass mkt. 41.95 (*0-538-62021-8*) S-W Pub.

Personal & Professional Recollections. George G. Scott. LC 77-1202. (Architecture & Decorative Art Ser.). 1977. reprint ed. lib. bdg. 59.50 (*0-306-70873-6*) Da Capo.

Personal & Property Rights of a Citizen of the United States: How to Exercise & How to Preserve Them. Theophilus Parsons. xvi, 744p. 1993. reprint ed. 70.00 (*0-8377-2519-4*, Rothman) W S Hein.

Personal & Social Education. John MacBeath. 90p. 1989. pap. 26.00 (*0-7073-0531-4*, Pub. by Mercat Pr Bks) St Mut.

*__Personal & Social Factors in Pharmacy Practice.__ Paul R. Gard. LC 99-46239. 2000. write for info. (*0-632-05138-8*) Blackwell Sci.

Personal & Social Responsibility: Complete Set, Complete Set. rev. ed. Constance H. Dembrowsky. (YA). (gr. 9-12). 1992. spiral bd. 299.00 (*0-924609-11-7*) Inst Affect Skill.

Personal & Social Responsibility: Drug Prevention Component. rev. ed. Constance H. Dembrowsky. 8p. 1992. spiral bd. write for info. (*0-924609-10-9*) Inst Affect Skill.

Personal & Social Responsibility: Parent Activity Book. rev. ed. Constance H. Dembrowsky. 65p. 1992. spiral bd. 7.95 (*0-924609-07-9*) Inst Affect Skill.

Personal & Social Responsibility: Parent Leader Manual. rev. ed. Constance H. Dembrowsky. 144p. 1992. spiral bd. 59.95 (*0-924609-06-0*) Inst Affect Skill.

Personal & Social Responsibility: Student Activity Book. rev. ed. Constance H. Dembrowsky. 400p. 1992. spiral bd. 16.95 (*0-924609-05-2*) Inst Affect Skill.

Personal & Social Responsibility: Teacher Manual. rev. ed. Constance H. Dembrowsky. 539p. 1992. spiral bd. 199.00 (*0-924609-04-4*) Inst Affect Skill.

Personal & Social Transformation: Freedom, Equality, & Fraternity in Everyday Life. Jorgen Smit. Tr. by Simon Blaxland De Lange. (Biography & Self-Development Ser.). 96p. 1993. pap. 14.95 (*1-869890-39-6*, Pub. by Hawthorn Press) Anthroposophic.

Personal & the Political: Women's Activism in Response to the Breast Cancer & AIDS Epidemics. Ulrike Boehmer. LC 99-41118. 224p. (C). 2000. text 57.50 (*0-7914-4549-6*) State U NY Pr.

*__Personal & the Political: Women's Activism in Response to the Breast Cancer & AIDS Epidemics.__ Ulrike Boehmer. LC 99-41118. 224p. (C). 2000. pap. text 18.95 (*0-7914-4550-X*) State U NY Pr.

Personal & the Political Socialist History. Ed. by Thompson. (Socialist History Ser.: 6). Date not set. pap. 9.99 (*0-7453-0810-4*, Pub. by Pluto GBR) Stylus Pub VA.

Personal & Wireless Communications: Digital Technology & Standards. Kun I. Park. LC 96-16696. (International Series in Engineering & Computer Science, Natural Language Processing & Machine Translation). 240p. (C). 1996. text 115.00 (*0-7923-9727-4*) Kluwer Academic.

Personal Anthology. Jorge Luis Borges. LC 67-29764. 224p. 1968. pap. 12.00 (*0-8021-3077-1*, Grove) Grove-Atltic.

Personal Antique Record Book: A Valuable Insurance Record. 1973. pap. 4.95 (*0-89145-094-7*, 2109) Collector Bks.

Personal Appearance: Personal Appearance/Style, No. 1. Judith A. Rasband. (Wardrobe Strategies Ser.: 1). 1996. 128.95 (*0-8273-6162-9*) Delmar.

Personal Archive of Francisco Morazan see Philological & Documentary Studies

Personal Assistance: The Future of Home Care. Robert Morris et al. LC 98-5933. 205p. 1998. 48.00 (*0-8018-5902-6*); pap. 18.95 (*0-8018-5903-4*) Johns Hopkins.

Personal Astrologer Planetary Wheels. Catherine Santos & John Simonello. (Illus.). 1998. 34.95 (*0-9655640-9-6*) Hoop LaLa.

Personal Atmosphere (1915) Frank C. Haddock. 86p. 1998. reprint ed. pap. 14.95 (*0-7661-0286-6*) Kessinger Pub.

Personal Attacks. James Wolcott. 24.00 (*0-06-019494-4*) HarpC.

Personal Aura. Dora Kunz. 1991. 29.95 (*0-8356-0675-9*, Quest); pap. 21.95 (*0-8356-0671-6*, Quest) Theos Pub Hse.

Personal Auto Policy. 2nd rev. ed. George E. Krauss. 128p. 1998. pap. text 44.00 (*1-56461-257-0*, 26559) Rough Notes.

Personal Auto Policy Analysis. George Krauss. 1996. pap. 38.00 (*1-56461-163-9*, 26559) Rough Notes.

Personal Autonomy & Substituted Judgment: Legal Issues in Medical Decisions for Incompetent Patients. Edward D. Robertson, Jr. (Orig.). 1991. pap. 5.99 (*0-685-50296-1*) Diocesan Pr.

Personal Balance Profile: Charting Your Life's Current Reality. Gary R. Blair. 40p. 1998. pap. 19.95 (*1-889770-23-X*, PBP) GoalsGuy.

*__Personal Banking Fraud: Hearings Before the Committee on Banking & Financial Services, U. S. House of Representatives.__ Ed. by James A. Leach. 144p. 2000. reprint ed. pap. text 25.00 (*0-7881-4538-X*) DIANE Pub.

*__Personal Bankruptcy.__ 3rd ed. Stephen Elias. LC 99-35065. (Law Form Kit Ser.). 1999. write for info. (*0-87337-546-7*) Nolo com.

Personal Bankruptcy: A Guide to Controlling Runaway Debt. rev. ed. Jeffrey Freedman. (Illus.). 132p. 1997. 8.95 (*0-9641995-1-3*) J Freedman Attys.

*__Personal Bankruptcy: Analysis of Four Reports on Chapter 7 Debtors' Ability to Pay.__ Richard M. Stana & William Jenkins, Jr. 92p. (C). 2000. pap. text 25.00 (*0-7881-8819-4*) DIANE Pub.

Personal Bankruptcy: Causes & Consequences. Charlene A. Sullivan & D. Drecnik Worden. 89p. 1992. pap. 100.00 (*1-880572-03-6*) Filene Res.

Personal Bankruptcy: The Credit Research Center Report on Debtors' Ability to Pay. Ed. by Richard M. Stana. (Illus.). 46p. (C). 1998. pap. text 15.00 (*0-7881-7487-8*) DIANE Pub.

Personal Bankruptcy: What Every Debtor & Creditor Needs to Know. William C. Hillman. 1993. pap. 14.95 (*0-87224-060-6*) PLI.

Personal Bankruptcy: What Every Debtor & Creditor Needs to Know. 2nd ed. William C. Hillman. LC 95-69569. 355p. 1995. pap. 15.95 (*0-87224-081-9*, K1-1401) PLI.

Personal Bankruptcy & Debt Adjustment. 2nd ed. K. J. Doran. 172p. 1995. pap. 10.00 (*0-679-76976-5*) Random.

Personal Beauty. D. G. Brinton & George H. Napheys. LC 94-4705. 346p. 1994. pap. 12.95 (*1-55709-226-5*) Applewood.

Personal Becoming: In Honor of Karl Rahner. Andrew Tallon. 188p. 1982. pap. 20.00 (*0-87462-522-X*) Marquette.

Personal Being: A Theory for Individual Psychology. Rom Harre. (Illus.). 304p. 1984. 35.00 (*0-674-66313-6*) HUP.

Personal Being: A Theory for Individual Psychology. Rom Harre. (Illus.). 304p. 1986. pap. 14.95 (*0-674-66314-4*) HUP.

Personal Best. Diane Eble. 160p. (YA). 1991. pap. 7.99 (*0-310-71141-X*) Zondervan.

Personal Best: The Foremost Philosopher of Fitness Shares Techniques & Tactics for Success & Self-Liberation. George Sheehan. 256p. 1989. text 17.95 (*0-87857-858-7*) Rodale Pr Inc.

Personal Best: The Foremost Philosopher of Fitness Shares Techniques & Tactics for Success & Self-Liberation. George Sheehan. 256p. 1992. pap. 14.95 (*0-87857-995-8*, 12-009-1) Rodale Pr Inc.

Personal Best: 1001 Great Ideas for Achieving Success in Your Career. National Business Employment Weekly Staff & Joe Tye. LC 96-20398. 320p. 1996. pap. 12.95 (*0-471-14888-1*) Wiley.

Personal Best: 1001 Great Ideas for Achieving Success in Your Career. Joe Tye. Ed. by National Business Employment Staff. 320p. 2000. 7.98 (*1-56731-349-3*, MJF Bks) Fine Comms.

Personal Board of Directors: Building Your Team of Trusted Advisors. Gary R. Blair. 40p. 1998. pap. 19.95 (*1-889770-61-2*, PBD) GoalsGuy.

Personal Bodyguard see Guardaespaldas Personal (A Personal Bodyguard)

Personal Brand Identity: Creating Brand You! Gary R. Blair. 40p. 1998. pap. 19.95 (*1-889770-53-1*, PBI) GoalsGuy.

Personal Budget Planner: A Guide for Financial Success. Eric Gelb. LC 93-74331. 106p. (Orig.). 1995. pap. 19.95 (*0-9631289-0-6*) Career Advan.

Personal Budget Planner: A Guide for Financial Success. Eric Gelb. 192p. (Orig.). 1995. pap. 19.95 (*0-9631289-6-5*) Career Advan.

Personal Business Management. Herbert M. Jelley et al. 1985. text 21.80 (*0-07-032336-4*) McGraw.

Personal Business Management. 2nd ed. Ryan. (OX - Home Economics Ser.). 1990. mass mkt., wbk. ed. 14.95 (*0-538-60379-8*) S-W Pub.

Personal Care Appliances. Ed. by Peter Allen. 200p. 1988. pap. 1295.00 (*0-941285-32-4*) FIND-SVP.

Personal Care for People Who Care. 8th ed. National Anti-Vivisection Society Staff. Orig. Title: Personal Care with Principle. (Illus.). 200p. (Orig.). 1996. pap. 4.95 (*1-888635-00-2*) Nat Anti-Vivisect.

Personal Care for People Who Care. 9th ed. National Anti-Vivi Section Society Staff. 204p. 1998. pap. 6.95 (*1-888635-01-0*) Nat Anti-Vivisect.

*__Personal Care for People Who Care.__ 10th ed. National Anti-Vivisection Society Staff. Orig. Title: Personal Care with Principle. (Orig.). 2000. pap. 9.50 (*1-888635-02-9*) Nat Anti-Vivisect.

Personal Care Formulas. 256p. 1998. ring bd. 140.00 (*0-931710-63-4*) Allured Publishing Corp.

Personal Care in an Impersonal World: A Multidimensional Look at Bereavement. Ed. by John D. Morgan. LC 92-37430. (Death, Value & Meaning Ser.). 267p. 1993. text 37.95 (*0-89503-109-4*); pap. text 26.56 (*0-89503-110-8*) Baywood Pub.

Personal Care in the Home. (Illus.). 176p. (Orig.). 1995. pap. text 14.95 (*0-89582-315-2*) Morton Pub.

Personal Care with Principle see Personal Care for People Who Care

Personal Career Development Profile Manual. Verne Walter. 70p. (Orig.). (C). 1996. pap. 30.00 (*0-918296-25-0*) Inst Personality & Ability.

*__Personal Catholicism.__ Martin X. Moleski. LC 99-41885. 2000. 64.95 (*0-8132-0964-1*) Cath U Pr.

Personal Causation: The Internal Affective Determinants of Behavior. R. De Charms. 416p. 1983. pap. text 49.95 (*0-89859-336-0*) L Erlbaum Assocs.

Personal Choice in Ethnic Identity Maintenance: Serbs, Croats & Slovenes in Washington, D. C. Linda A. Bennett. LC 77-93261. 230p. 1978. pap. 10.00 (*0-918660-06-8*) Ragusan Pr.

Personal Choices & Goals: Guidelines. Richard L. Crews. 66p. (C). 1988. student ed. write for info. (*0-945864-12-4*); pap. text. write for info. (*0-945864-11-6*) Columbia Pacific U Pr.

Personal Choices & Public Commitments: Perspectives on the Medical Humanities. Ed. by William J. Winslade. (Orig.). 1989. pap. 12.00 (*0-9621294-0-2*) Univ TX Med Humanities.

Personal Civil War Letters. Lawrence S. Ross. Ed. by Shelly O. Morrison. Tr. by Perry W. Shelton. 130p. 1994. 29.50 (*0-926158-22-8*) W M Morrison.

Personal Coaching for Financial Advisors. Edwin P. Morrow. (Illus.). 36p. (C). 1999. 14.00 (*1-893717-01-1*) Finan Plan.

Personal Coaching for Results: How to Mentor & Inspire Others to Amazing Growth. Lou Tice. LC 97-141365. 1997. 22.99 (*0-7852-7355-7*) Nelson.

Personal Collective Services: An International Perspective. 51p. 1992. 28.00 (*92-1-100383-0*, E.GV.92.0.22) UN.

Personal Column. Charles Belgrave. (Illus.). 248p. 1996. 45.00 (*0-86685-004-X*) Intl Bk Ctr.

Personal Combat with & Without Weapons. 1991. lib. bdg. 79.95 (*0-8490-4751-X*) Gordon Pr.

Personal Commitments: Making, Keeping, Breaking. Margaret A. Farley. 175p. 1986. 13.95 (*0-86683-476-1*) Harper SF.

Personal Communication Networks: Practical Implementation. Alan D. Hadden. LC 95-6093. 294p. 1995. 75.00 (*0-89006-762-7*) Artech Hse.

Personal Communication Systems & Technologies. John Gardiner & Barry West. LC 94-23867. 252p. 1995. 79.00 (*0-89006-588-8*) Artech Hse.

Personal Communications: Perspectives, Forecasts, & Impacts. Ralph C. Lenz & Lawrence K. Vanston. 99p. 1993. pap. 45.00 (*1-884154-02-6*) Tech Futures.

Personal Communications Products & Services - A Major Emerging U. S. Market: 1995-2004 Analysis & Forecasts. Richard Whelan. 112p. 1995. pap. text 2400.00 (*1-878218-61-1*) World Info Tech.

Personal Communications Services. IGIC, Inc. Staff. 250p. 1991. 2495.00 (*0-918435-63-3*, IGIC-53) Info Gatekeepers.

Personal Communications Systems Applications. Frederick Ricci. LC 96-42322. (Feher/Prentice Hall Digital & Wireless Communciation Ser.). 304p. 1996. 77.00 (*0-13-255878-5*) P-H.

Personal Communications Systems for (PCS)-Voice & ISDN. (Satellites in an ISDN World Ser.). 1996. 95.00 (*0-614-18390-1*, 126ST3) Info Gatekeepers.

Personal Communities. B. Wellman. 1999. pap. 55.00 (*0-8133-1148-9*) Westview.

Personal Companion: Meditations & Exercises for Keeping the Love You Find. Harville Hendrix & Helen Hunt. Ed. by Claire Zion. 384p. (Orig.). 1995. per. 14.00 (*0-671-86884-5*, PB Trade Paper) PB.

Personal Comptrs. (C). 1995. pap. 12.33 (*0-8053-0826-1*) Benjamin-Cummings.

Personal Computer. Time-Life Books Editors. LC 92-40576. (Understanding Computers Ser.). 1993. 15.50 (*0-8094-7625-8*); lib. bdg. write for info. (*0-8094-7626-6*) Time-Life.

Personal Computer: An Industry Sourcebook. 1987. ring bd. 495.00 (*0-685-17935-4*) Chromatic Comm.

Personal Computer: Operating, Troubleshooting & Upgrading. Mike A. Awwad. LC 97-15811. 88p. (C). 1997. pap. 47.00 (*0-13-674417-6*) P-H.

*__Personal Computer: Operating, Troubleshooting & Upgrading.__ 2nd ed. Mike Mutasen Awwad. 208p. 2000. pap. 48.00 (*0-13-020039-5*, Prentice Hall) P-H.

Personal Computer Applications in the Gas Industry II. vi, 458p. 1988. 75.00 (*0-910091-63-3*) Inst Gas Tech.

Personal Computer Applications in the Gas Industry, 1st Symposium. Institute of Gas Technology Staff. 293p. 1985. 50.00 (*0-910091-55-2*) Inst Gas Tech.

*__Personal Computer Applications in the Social Services.__ David A. Patterson. LC 99-31864. (Illus.). 335p. 1999. pap. 36.00 (*0-205-28537-6*) P-H.

Personal Computer-Based CAD-CAM, CAE Markets & Opportunities. Autodesk, Inc. Staff et al. (Illus.). 225p. 1987. ring bd. 1395.00 (*0-938484-21-4*) Daratech.

Personal Computer BASIC(s) Reference Manual. Donald A. Sordillo. (Illus.). 320p. 1983. pap. text 27.50 (*0-13-658047-5*) P-H.

Personal Computer Buyer's Guide. Patrick Plemmons & David Myers. 184p. (Orig.). pap. 12.95 (*0-685-08848-0*) Random.

*__Personal Computer Communications.__ Robert Perry. (Computer Science Library). (Illus.). (YA). 2000. pap. 8.95 (*0-531-16483-7*) Watts.

*__Personal Computer Communications.__ Robert L. Perry. (Computer Science Library). 2000. 24.00 (*0-531-11758-8*) Watts.

Personal Computer Desk Reference. Steven L. Mandell. 608p. 1993. 32.95 (*0-9637426-0-4*); pap. 23.95 (*0-9637426-1-2*) Rawhide Pr.

Personal Computer Dictionary. Donald D. Spencer. LC 94-23064. (Illus.). 184p. (Orig.). 1995. pap. 19.95 (*0-89218-223-7*) Camelot Pub.

*__Personal Computer Essentials.__ 3rd ed. Suzanne Weixel. LC 99-51341. 176p. 1999. spiral bd. 18.67 (*0-13-016792-4*) P-H.

Personal Computer from the Inside Out: The Programmer's Guide to Low-Level PC Hardware & Software. 3rd ed. Murray Sargent, III & Richard L. Shoemaker. LC 94-41206. 816p. 1994. pap. 44.95 incl. disk (*0-201-62646-2*) Addison-Wesley.

Personal Computer Fundamentals: Hardware, DOS & Windows. Marc E. Herniter. LC 97-18488. 1212p. 1997. pap. text 93.00 (*0-13-230137-7*) P-H.

*__Personal Computer Fundamentals for Technology Students: Hardware, Windows & Applications.__ 2nd ed. Marc E. Herniter. (Illus.). 912p. 2000. pap. 85.00 (*0-13-025519-X*) P-H.

Personal Computer Market in Netherlands: A Strategic Entry Report, 1996. Compiled by Icon Group International Staff. (Illus.). 128p. 1999. ring bd. 1280.00 incl. audio compact disk (*0-7418-1130-8*) Icon Grp.

Personal Computer Market in United Kingdom: A Strategic Entry Report, 1996. Compiled by Icon Group International Staff. (Illus.). 101p. 1999. ring bd. 1010.00 incl. audio compact disk (*0-7418-1132-4*) Icon Grp.

Personal Computer Operation & Troubleshooting. 2nd ed. Roger M. Kersey. LC 95-38789. 632p. 1995. 111.00 (*0-13-656380-5*) P-H.

Personal Computer Secrets. Bob O'Donnell. LC 99-27352. 1008p. 1999. pap. 49.99 (*0-7645-3133-6*) IDG Bks.

Personal Computer Security. Ed Tiley. 360p. 1996. pap. 24.99 (*1-56884-814-5*) IDG Bks.

*__Personal Computer Software in Japan: A Strategic Entry Report, 1996.__ Compiled by Icon Group International Staff. (Illus.). 170p. 1999. ring bd. 1700.00 incl. audio compact disk (*0-7418-1150-2*) Icon Grp.

Personal Computer Solutions for CAD-CAM. Ed. by Thomas J. Drozda. LC 89-60297. (Illus.). 236p. 1989. text 42.00 (*0-87263-357-8*) SME.

Personal Computer Standard: BIOS. (Illus.). 346p. (Orig.). 1995. pap. 29.95 (*0-9653456-1-0*) Sure Path Bios.

Personal Computer Use in Credit & Finance. Credit Research Foundation Staff. 18p. 1986. 40.00 (*0-939050-53-6*) Credit Res NYS.

Personal Computers. Center for Occupational Research & Development Staff. 26p. 1992. teacher ed. 10.00 (*1-55502-465-3*); pap. text 15.00 (*1-55502-464-5*) CORD Commns.

Personal Computers. Charnan Kazunas & Tom Kazunas. (New True Books Ser.). (J). 1997. pap. 6.95 (*0-516-26174-6*) Childrens.

Personal Computers. Tom Kazunas & Charnan Kazunas. LC 96-37344. (True Bk.). (J). 1997. lib. bdg. 21.00 (*0-516-20338-X*) Childrens.

Personal Computers - Introduction to Using Windows 95. Ed. by Ron Pronk. (Illus.). 180p. 1997. pap. 20.00 (*1-58264-065-3*, 107) ActiveEd.

Personal Computers & Peripherals in Indonesia: A Strategic Entry Report, 1997. Compiled by Icon Group International Staff. (Illus.). 165p. 1999. ring bd. 1650.00 incl. audio compact disk (*0-7418-0985-0*) Icon Grp.

Personal Computers & the Family. Ed. by Marvin B. Sussman. LC 85-8459. (Marriage & Family Review Ser.: Vol. 8, Nos. 1-2). 202p. 1985. text 49.95 (*0-86656-361-X*); pap. text 19.95 (*0-86656-362-8*) Haworth Pr.

Personal Computers for Distance Education: The Study of an Educational Innovation. Anne Jones et al. 224p. 1992. pap. 49.50 (*1-85396-187-6*) St Martin.

Personal Computers for Scientists. Glenn I. Ouchi. LC 86-24846. (Illus.). x, 250p. 1986. 34.95 (*0-8412-1000-4*); pap. 22.95 (*0-8412-1001-2*) Am Chemical.

Personal Computers for Scientists: A Byte at a Time. Glenn I. Ouchi. LC 86-25846. 288p. 1987. reprint ed. pap. 89.30 (*0-608-03843-1*, 206429000008) Bks Demand.

Personal Computers for Success. Roger W. Hockney. 1984. 19.18 (*0-02-551870-4*) Macmillan.

Personal Computers in Austria: A Strategic Entry Report, 1996. Compiled by Icon Group International Staff. (Illus.). 101p. 1999. ring bd. 1010.00 incl. audio compact disk (*0-7418-1131-6*) Icon Grp.

Personal Computers in Germany: A Strategic Entry Report, 1998. Compiled by Icon Group International Staff. (Country Industry Report). (Illus.). 110p. 1999. ring bd. 1100.00 incl. audio compact disk (*0-7418-0454-9*) Icon Grp.

Personal Computers in Japan: A Strategic Entry Report, 1997. Compiled by Icon Group International Staff. (Illus.). 163p. 1999. ring bd. 1630.00 incl. audio compact disk (*0-7418-0794-7*) Icon Grp.

Personal Computers in United Arab Emirates: A Strategic Entry Report, 1997. Compiled by Icon Group International Staff. (Illus.). 99p. 1999. ring bd. 990.00 incl. audio compact disk (*0-7418-0986-9*) Icon Grp.

Personal Computing, Level 1. David S. Murphy et al. (Easy Way Ser.). 170p. 1993. pap. 29.95 (*1-57048-000-1*) Trning Express.

P

*Personal Computing Essential Right. unabridged ed. 1999. 16.00 (0-13-026194-7) P-H.

*Personal Computing Essentials. 3rd ed. Suzanne Weixel. LC 99-51341. (Illus.). 189p. 1999. spiral bd. 18.67 (0-13-026195-5) P-H.

*Personal Computing for Business. 2nd ed. Jane Knight. (Illus.). 304p. 1999. pap. 47.50 (0-273-63967-6, Pub. by F T P-H) Trans-Atl Phila.

Personal Computing for Health Professionals. Philip Burnard. 144p. 1993. pap. 49.50 (1-56593-149-1, 0461) Singular Publishing.

Personal Computing for Women: Everything You Always Wanted to Know about Personal Computers but Were Afraid to Ask. Maria A. Hoath. LC 90-70514. (Illus.). 152p. (Orig.). 1990. pap. text 9.95 (0-9626224-7-8) Write Byte Pub.

Personal Computing in Nuclear Medicine. D. P. Pretschner. (Lecture Notes in Medical Informatics Ser.: Vol. 18). 133p. 1982. 29.95 (0-387-11598-6) Spr-Verlag.

Personal Computing Smartstart. Meta Hirschl. LC 93-86974. 301p. 1994. 25.99 (1-56529-455-6) Que.

Personal Conflict of Interest in Government Contracting. 140p. 1988. pap. 30.00 (0-89707-414-9, 539-0076-01) Amer Bar Assn.

Personal Construct Counseling & Psychotherapy. Franz R. Epting. LC 83-6913. (Wiley Series on Methods in Psychotheraphy). 217p. reprint ed. pap. 67.30 (0-8357-8981-0, 205227400085) Bks Demand.

Personal Construct Counselling in Action. Fay Fransella & Peggy Dalton. 160p. (C). 1990. text 49.95 (0-8039-8280-1); pap. text 21.50 (0-8039-8281-X) Sage.

Personal Construct Psychology: Clinical & Personality Assessment. Alvin W. Landfield & Franz R. Epting. LC 86-10477. 327p. 1986. 51.95 (0-89885-315-X, Kluwer Acad Hman Sci); pap. 24.95 (0-89885-318-4, Kluwer Acad Hman Sci) Kluwer Academic.

Personal Construct Psychology in Clinical Practice: Theory, Research & Applications. David Winter. LC 93-47681. 480p. (C). 1994. pap. 37.99 (0-415-00601-5, B3911) Routledge.

Personal Construct Theory: Concepts & Applications. J. R. Adams-Webber. LC 78-8638. 251p. reprint ed. pap. 77.90 (0-608-14906-3, 202598500048) Bks Demand.

Personal Construct Theory & Mental Health: Theory, Research & Practice. Ed. by Eric Button. 404p. 1985. 20.00 (0-914797-15-8) Brookline Bks.

Personal Construct Theory in Educational Psychology: A Practitioner's View. Tom Ravenette. 1999. pap. 34.95 (1-86156-121-0) Whurr Pub.

Personal Construct Therapy: A Handbook. Linda Viney. (Developments in Clinical Psychology Ser.). (Illus.). 250p. 1996. pap. 39.50 (1-56750-230-X); text 73.25 (1-56750-229-6) Ablx Pub.

Personal Construction of Nature & the Natural Destruction of Culture. Michael Thompson. (Working Papers on Risk & Rationality). 1988. 2.50 (0-318-33325-2, RR9) IPPP.

*Personal Control in Action: Cognitive & Motivational Mechanisms. M. Kofta et al. LC 98-21501. (Plenum Series in Social-Clinical Psychology). (Illus.). 460p. (C). 1998. 65.00 (0-306-45720-2, Plenum Trade) Perseus Pubng.

Personal Convictions Philosopoetry. Ronald Cook, Sr. 1998. pap. write for info. (1-57553-859-8) Watermrk Pr.

Personal Coping: Theory, Research, & Application. Ed. by Bruce N. Carpenter. LC 92-8378. 276p. 1992. 65.00 (0-275-93012-2, C3012, Praeger Pubs) Greenwood.

Personal Corporate Liability: A Guide for Planners, Litigators & Creditor's Counsel. Harvey Gelb. 381p. 1991. text 95.00 (0-87224-036-3, B1-1336) PLI.

Personal Correspondence of Sam Houston, 1839-1845, Vol. I. Ed. by Madge T. Roberts. LC 95-36738. 448p. 1996. 32.50 (1-57441-000-8) UNTX Pr.

Personal Correspondence of Sam Houston, 1846-1848, Vol. II. Ed. by Madge T. Roberts. 390p. 1998. 32.50 (1-57441-031-8) UNTX Pr.

Personal Correspondence of Sam Houston, 1848-1852, Vol. III. Ed. by Madge T. Roberts. LC 95-36738. 508p. 1999. 32.50 (1-57441-063-6) UNTX Pr.

Personal Counseling: A Practical Guie That Teaches Basic Counseling Skills. 3rd ed. Elwood N. Chapman & Richard L. Knowdell. LC 92-54366. (Fifty-Minute Ser.). 94p. 1993. pap. 10.95 (1-56052-184-8) Crisp Pubns.

Personal Country. A. C. Greene. LC 79-7410. (Illus.). 348p. 1998. pap. 18.95 (1-57441-053-9) UNTX Pr.

Personal Creation. Nora B. Bynum. 42p. (Orig.). pap. 4.95 (1-56411-033-8) Untd Bros & Sis.

Personal Credentials. Joseph A. Uphoff. LC 94-1672. 136p. 1994. pap. text 7.00 (0-943123-26-7) Arjuna Lib Pr.

Personal Data Directory. Evelyn M. Crawford. 56p. (Orig.). 1982. pap. 5.95 (0-9608966-0-0) WY Specialties.

Personal Debt. G. W. Howells & L. Bently. (Waterlow Practitioner's Library). 192p. 1992. pap. 22.01 (0-08-040851-6) Macmillan.

Personal Decisions. H. Paul LeMaire. LC 81-43668. 220p. (Orig.). 1982. pap. text 21.50 (0-8191-2330-7) U Pr of Amer.

Personal Declension & Revival of Religion in the Soul. Octavius Winslow. 1978. pap. 6.50 (0-85151-261-5) Banner of Truth.

Personal Deductions in the Federal Income Tax. C. Harry Kahn. (Fiscal Studies Ser.: No. 6). 267p. 1960. reprint ed. 69.50 (0-87014-122-8) Natl Bur Econ Res.

Personal Defense Weapons. J. Randall. LC 92-72813. 102p. (Orig.). 1992. pap. 12.00 (1-55950-087-5, 19188) Loompanics.

Personal Demons. Christopher Fowler. 308p. 1998. pap. 13.99 (1-85242-597-0) Serpents Tail.

Personal Development: A One Semester Curriculum Designed to Develop Respect, Reponsibility, & Resiliency in At-Risk Adolescents, Preview Packet. rev. ed. Vicki Phillips. 1991. 15.00 (0-9628482-7-1) Prsnl Dev.

Personal Development: A One Semester Curriculum Designed to Develop Respect, Responsibility, & Resiliency in At-Risk Adolescents, Group & Individualized Version. rev. ed. Vicki Phillips. 1991. 595.00 (0-9628482-6-3) Prsnl Dev.

Personal Development: A One Semester Curriculum Designed to Develop Respect, Responsibility, & Resiliency in At-Risk Adolescents, Group Version. rev. ed. Vicki Phillips. 1991. 375.00 (0-9628482-4-7) Prsnl Dev.

Personal Development: A One Semester Curriculum Designed to Develop Respect, Responsibility, Resiliency in At-Risk Adolescents, Individualized Version. rev. ed. Vicki Phillips. 1991. 350.00 (0-9628482-5-5) Prsnl Dev.

Personal Development: Key to Excellence. Narindra Handa. 74p. 1987. text 15.95 (9971-68-129-3, Pub. by Chopmen Singapore) Advent Bks Div.

Personal Development: Theory & Practice in Management Training. Bert Juch. LC 82-7062. 258p. reprint ed. pap. 80.00 (0-608-16353-8, 202669000051) Bks Demand.

*Personal Development & Discovery Through Leisure. Ernest Olson. 300p. (C). 1999. per. 32.95 (0-7872-6296-X, 41629602) Kendall-Hunt.

*Personal Development for Life & Work. 8th ed. Wallace Masters. 2000. pap. 38.95 (0-538-69795-4) Sth-Wstrn College.

Personal Development in Counselor Training. Hazel Johns. (Counselor Trainer & Supervisor Ser.). (Illus.). 128p. 1996. pap. 25.95 (0-304-32933-9); text 75.00 (0-304-32935-5) Continuum.

Personal Development Plan: A Guide to Accomplishing Your Dreams. William T. Streeter. teacher ed. write for info. (1-886572-05-4); teacher ed. write for info. (1-886572-06-2) Baypointe Pub.

Personal Development Plan: A Guide to Accomplishing Your Dreams, Pt. I. William T. Streeter. 48p. 1994. pap. text. write for info. (1-886572-02-X) Baypointe Pub.

Personal Development Plan: A Guide to Accomplishing Your Dreams, Pt. II. William T. Streeter. 99p. pap. text. write for info. (1-886572-03-8) Baypointe Pub.

Personal Development Plan: A Guide to Accomplishing Your Dreams Manual. William T. Streeter. 148p. pap. text. write for info. (1-886572-01-1) Baypointe Pub.

Personal Development Plan: A Guide to Accomplishing Your Dreams Notebook. William T. Streeter. teacher ed. write for info. (1-886572-04-6) Baypointe Pub.

Personal Development Plan: A Guide to Accomplishing Your Dreams Notebook. William T. Streeter. 148p. 1994. text. write for info. (1-886572-00-3) Baypointe Pub.

Personal Development Through Self-Awareness. Marti Eicholz. 200p. 1997. pap. write for info. (0-9653100-4-3) Inst for Transform.

*Personal Devotion: Taking God's Word to Heart. Kathy Dice. (Bible 101 Ser.). 64p. 2000. pap. 4.99 (0-8308-2068-X) InterVarsity.

Personal Diary of Poetry: A Black Man's View. Ajamu Bandele. 115p. pap. 10.00 (1-891143-50-6) Fantom Pubns.

Personal Digital Assistants: A Comprehensive Guide to the Technology. Raymond P. Wenig. (Illus.). 20p. 1997. pap. text 32.00 (0-07-069343-9) McGraw.

Personal Digital Assistants: U. S. Markets, Technologies & Opportunities 1994 to 2000 Analysis. Stuart Hirschhurn. Ed. by Tim Archdeacon. 100p. 1994. 995.00 (1-883742-09-9) Allied Busn.

Personal Disciplemaking: A Step by Step Guide for Leading a Christian from New Birth to Maturity. Christopher B. Aclsit. 384p. 1988. reprint ed. pap. 13.99 (1-57902-022-4, 1526e) Integrtd Res.

Personal Disciplemaking Toolkit. Christopher B. Adsit. 24p. Date not set. pap. 8.99 (1-57902-021-6) Integrtd Res.

Personal Discipline & Material Culture: An Archaeology of Annapolis, Maryland, 1695-1870. Paul A. Shackel. LC 92-30559. (Illus.). 240p. (C). 1993. 30.00 (0-87049-784-7) U of Tenn Pr.

Personal Disorder & the Family. Peter Lomas. LC 97-31564. 227p. 1997. text 32.95 (1-56000-341-3) Transaction Pubs.

Personal Dispatches: Writers Confront AIDS. Ed. by John Preston. 208p. 1990. pap. 8.95 (0-312-05141-7) St Martin.

Personal Distribution of Income & Wealth. Ed. by James D. Smith. (Studies in Income & Wealth: No. 39). 580p. 1975. 150.80 (0-87014-268-2) Natl Bur Econ Res.

Personal Doll Inventory: Perfect Record for Your Dolls. 1973. pap. 4.95 (0-89145-172-2, 1301) Collector Bks.

Personal Dream Diary: Revolutionary Techniques for Recording, Enhancing, & Creating Your Own Dream Drama. Maryanne E. Hoffman. (Illus.). 112p. (Orig.). 1988. pap. 7.95 (0-943299-02-0) Star Visions.

Personal Dream Journal. Janice F. Baylis. (Illus.). 1977. student ed. 4.00 (0-917738-01-2) Sun Man Moon.

Personal Education: About General Learning, Motivation, Development & Progress. Anton S. Pater. LC 76-56540. 1977. 20.00 (0-918210-01-1, GL-1A); pap. 15.00 (0-918210-00-3, GL-1) Multi Spectral.

*Personal Education Plan for Children & Young People in Public Care. Peter Sandiford. 16p. 2000. 40.95 (1-900990-35-0, Pub. by Natl Childrens Bur) Paul & Co Pubs.

Personal Effectiveness. 2nd ed. Murdock & Scutt. 288p. 1997. pap. text 34.95 (0-7506-3393-X) Buttrwrth-Heinemann.

Personal Effects. Robin Becker et al. LC 75-46406. 88p. 1976. pap. 3.95 (0-914086-15-4) Alice James Bks.

Personal Effects. Charlotte Carter. 92p. (Orig.). 1991. pap. 6.00 (0-935992-16-2) United Art Bks.

Personal Effects. George Peffer. 56p. (Orig.). 1993. pap. 8.00 (0-9637849-1-9) Bacchae Pr.

Personal Effects. Sharon A. Sharp. (Scots Plaid Press Fine Poetry Ser.). 36p. 1998. pap. 12.00 (1-879009-38-2) Old Barn Entrprs.

Personal Efficiency Program: How to Do More Work in Less Time. Kerry Gleeson. 224p. 1994. 69.95 (0-471-02058-3) Wiley.

Personal Efficiency Program: How to Do More Work in Less Time. 2nd ed. Kerry Gleeson. LC 00-23578. (Illus.). 224p. 2000. pap. 16.95 (0-471-36279-4) Wiley.

Personal Efficiency Program: How to Get Organized to Do More Work in Less Time. Kerry Gleeson. 224p. 1997. pap. 5.99 (0-471-19326-7) Wiley.

Personal Employment Portfolio. Jean B. Hill. (RUS & SPA.). 20p. (Orig.). 1995. mass mkt. 2.99 (1-888620-01-3) Common Snse PA.

Personal Empowerment - Taking Control of Your Life: Side-Roads & Main-Roads: A Trip for Discovering Your Personal Empowerment. Robert E. Ripley & Marie J. Ripley. LC 93-70693. (Illus.). 129p. 1993. pap. 19.95 (0-9621133-2-8, B006) Carefree Pr.

Personal Empowerment Program, Set. Bruce Goldberg. 1991. 60.00 incl. audio (1-885577-77-X) B Goldberg.

Personal Empowerment Through Type. Patricia Cranton. (Illus.). viii, 220p. 1997. pap. 19.95 (0-9661480-0-2) Psychol Type Pr.

Personal Encryption Clearly Explained. Pete Loshin. LC 98-19661. (Clearly Explained Ser.). (Illus.). 545p. (C). 1998. boxed set 39.95 (0-12-455837-2) Morgan Kaufmann.

Personal Energy Management. Leonard Orr. 1996. 20.00 (0-945793-20-0) Inspir Univ.

Personal Enmity in Roman Politics, 218-43 B. C. David F. Epstein. 192p. 1987. lib. bdg. 50.00 (0-7099-5304-6, Pub. by C Helm) Routldge.

Personal Equation. Harry T. Peck. LC 79-39121. (Essay Index Reprint Ser.). 1977. reprint ed. 24.95 (0-8369-2709-5) Ayer.

Personal Equation. Harry T. Peck. (Notable American Authors Ser.). 1999. reprint ed. lib. bdg. 125.00 (0-7812-8718-9) Rprt Serv.

Personal Equation: A Biography of Steadman Vincent Sanford. Charles S. Gurr. LC 98-30811. (Illus.). 280p. 1999. text 35.00 (0-8203-2108-7) U of Ga Pr.

Personal Ethics. Burnett H. Streeter et al. Ed. by Kenneth E. Kirk. LC 68-22921. (Essay Index Reprint Ser.). 1977. 18.95 (0-8369-0597-0) Ayer.

Personal Evangelism see Evangelismo Personal

Personal Evangelism. E. W. Kenyon. 88p. (Orig.). 1943. ring bd. 7.00 (1-57770-018-X) Kenyons Gospel.

Personal Evangelism Training, Vol. 1. Beverly C. Burgess. 168p. 1985. pap., student ed. 10.99 (0-8341-1058-X) Beacon Hill.

Personal Evangelism Training, Vol. 2. Beverly Burgess. 152p. 1991. pap., student ed. 11.99 (0-8341-1410-0) Beacon Hill.

Personal Evolution: The Art of Living with Purpose. Veronica Ray. 10.00 incl. audio (0-89486-825-X) Hazelden.

Personal Excellence: A Guide to Getting the Most from Yourself & Others. Jack Messenger. LC 89-85531. 207p. 1989. 19.95 (0-939975-04-1) Exec Pr NC.

Personal Excellence Award: The "Oscar" of Personal Mastery. Gary R. Blair. 40p. 1998. pap. 19.95 (1-889770-59-0, PEA) GoalsGuy.

Personal Excellence for Key People: Classified School Employees. Don M. Essig. (Illus.). 142p. (Orig.). 1989. student ed. 15.95 (0-9621751-1-0) D M Essig.

Personal Excellence for Key People: Support Staff. Don M. Essig. (Illus.). 142p. 1989. student ed. 12.95 (0-9621751-2-9) D M Essig.

Personal Exemptions in the Income Tax. Lawrence H. Seltzer. (Fiscal Studies Ser.: No. 12). 238p. 1968. reprint ed. 61.90 (0-87014-482-0) Natl Bur Econ Res.

Personal Existence after Death: Reductionist Circularities & the Evidence. Robert J. Geis. iii, 130p. (Orig.). 1995. pap. 9.95 (0-89385-044-6) Sugden.

Personal Experiences of S. O. Susag. S. O. Susag. 191p. pap. 4.00 (0-686-29134-4) Faith Pub Hse.

Personal Explorations. 6th ed. Weiten. (Psychology Ser.). 1999. pap., wbk. ed. 2.00 (0-534-36665-1) Brooks-Cole.

Personal Exposures. Elliott Erwitt. 1988. 75.00 (0-393-02616-7) Norton.

Personal Exposures. limited aut. ed. Elliott Erwitt. (Illus.). 1988. 750.00 (0-393-02656-6) Norton.

Personal Expressions: Writing Your Way into English. rev. ed. Sue Dicker. 72p. (C). 1987. pap. text 4.00 (0-317-93602-6) D Blot Pubns.

Personal Faith of Jesus As Revealed in the Lord's Prayer. J. Neville Ward. 128p. 1982. reprint ed. 6.95 (0-86683-678-0) Harper SF.

Personal Favorites: Fine Prints from the Collection of Carl F. Barnes, Jr. & Anna M. Barnes. Carl F. Barnes, Jr. (Illus.). 48p. (Orig.). Date not set. pap. text 5.00 (0-925859-07-9) Mead Brook Art.

Personal Feng Shui Manual. Chuen. LC 97-36663. (Illus.). 140p. 1998. pap. 16.95 (0-8050-5558-4, Owl) H Holt & Co.

Personal Fiction Writing. 2nd rev. ed. Meredith S. Willis. 206p. 2000. pap. 14.95 (0-915924-13-7) Tchrs & Writers Coll.

*Personal Fiction Writing: A Guide to Writing from Real Life for Teachers, Students & Writers. 2nd rev. ed. Meredith Sue Willis. 250p. 2000. pap. 15.95 (0-915924-62-5) Tchrs & Writers Coll.

Personal Filing Systems: Creating Information Retrieval Systems on Microcomputers. Sherri McCarthy. (Orig.). 1988. pap. text 22.40 (0-8108-2428-0) Med Lib Assn.

Personal Finance. 1996. teacher ed. (0-321-40440-8) S&S Trade.

Personal Finance. Alpha Books Staff. (Teach Yourself ...in 24 Hours Ser.). 480p. 2000. pap. 19.99 (0-02-863619-8) Macmillan Gen Ref.

*Personal Finance. Kaarl Biedenweg. (Illus.). 80p. (YA). (gr. 5). 1999. pap. text 9.95 (1-58037-091-8, Pub. by M Twain Media) Carson-Dellos.

Personal Finance. Cameron. write for info. (0-534-92254-6) Wadsworth Pub.

Personal Finance. Eisenberg. 1998. 29.95 (0-446-52467-0, Pub. by Warner Bks) Little.

*Personal Finance. Eisenberg. 1998. 25.95 (0-446-52429-8, Pub. by Warner Bks) Little.

Personal Finance, 4 vols. Garman. LC 93-78676. (C). Date not set. text, teacher ed., suppl. ed. 75.16 (0-395-69296-2) HM.

Personal Finance, 3 vols. Garman. (C). 1990. pap., student ed. 17.96 (0-395-57378-5) HM.

Personal Finance, 4 vols. Garman. (C). 1994. pap., teacher ed. 7.96 (0-395-66854-9) HM.

*Personal Finance. Goldsmith. (Health Sciences Ser.). 2000. pap. 54.00 (0-534-54495-9) Wadsworth Pub.

Personal Finance. Keown. (C). 1998. pap. text, student ed. 21.33 (0-13-095492-6) P-H.

Personal Finance. Ike Mathur. (Thomson Executive Press). (C). 1983. pap. 40.00 (0-538-06010-7, F01) S-W Pub.

Personal Finance. Jack Rudman. (Dantes Subject Standardized Tests (DANTES) Ser.: Vol. 76). 43.95 (0-8373-6576-7) Nat Learn.

Personal Finance. Jack Rudman. (DANTES Ser.: No. 26). 1991. 23.95 (0-8373-6676-3) Nat Learn.

*Personal Finance. Sabrin. 2001. pap., student ed. 15.00 (0-324-04266-3) Thomson Learn.

Personal Finance. 2nd ed. Jack R. Kapoor et al. (Finance Ser.). (C). 1991. text 58.95 (0-256-07905-6, Irwn McGrw-H) McGrw-H Hghr Educ.

Personal Finance. 3rd ed. Jerome B. Cohen. (Plaid Ser.). 1981. pap. 12.00 (0-256-02126-0, Irwn Prfssnl) McGraw-Hill Prof.

Personal Finance. 3rd ed. Jack R. Kapoor et al. LC 93-10019. 688p. (C). 1993. text 64.95 (0-256-11619-9, Irwn McGrw-H) McGrw-H Hghr Educ.

Personal Finance. 3rd ed. Jack R. Kapoor et al. 736p. (C). 1993. text. write for info. (0-256-15741-3, Irwn McGrw-H) McGrw-H Hghr Educ.

Personal Finance, 4 vols. 4th ed. Garman. LC 93-78676. (C). 1993. text 75.16 (0-395-66852-2) HM.

Personal Finance, 4 vols. 4th ed. Garman. (C). 1994. pap. text, student ed. 22.76 (0-395-66853-0) HM.

Personal Finance. 4th ed. Jack R. Kapoor. (C). 1995. text, student ed. 15.00 (0-256-14534-2) McGraw.

Personal Finance. 4th ed. Jack R. Kapoor et al. 688p. (C). 1995. text 67.50 (0-256-14532-6, Irwn McGrw-H) McGrw-H Hghr Educ.

Personal Finance. 4th ed. Jack R. Kapoor et al. 312p. (C). 1995. text, student ed. 22.50 (0-256-14533-4, Irwn McGrw-H) McGrw-H Hghr Educ.

Personal Finance, 5 vols. 5th ed. Garman. (C). 1996. pap. text, student ed. 22.76 (0-395-80879-0) HM.

Personal Finance, 5 vols. 5th ed. E. Thomas Garman. LC 96-76905. (C). 1996. text 71.96 (0-395-80877-4) HM.

Personal Finance. 5th ed. Kapoor. 1998. pap., student ed. 82.50 (0-256-26295-0) McGraw.

Personal Finance. 5th ed. Jack R. Kapoor et al. LC 98-23632. (Irwin/Mcgraw-Hill Series In Finance, Insurance, & Real Estate). 1998. write for info. (0-256-24608-4, Irwn Prfssnl) McGraw-Hill Prof.

Personal Finance. 5th ed. Winger & Frasco Staff. LC 99-22440. 497p. 1999. pap. text 76.00 (0-13-021286-5) P-H.

Personal Finance. 6th ed. Kapoor. 2000. 82.50 (0-07-235084-9) McGraw.

*Personal Finance. 7th ed. Rosefsky. 751p. (C). 1998. text. write for info. (0-471-33064-7) Wiley.

*Personal Finance. 7th ed. Rosefsky. 1999. text 63.00 (0-471-37375-3) Wiley.

Personal Finance. 7th ed. Robert S. Rosefsky. LC 98-5649. 736p. 1998. text 95.95 (0-471-23822-8) Wiley.

Personal Finance. 7th ed. David T. Crary & John K. Pfahl. LC 79-27578. (Illus.). 734p. reprint ed. pap. 200.00 (0-608-10695-X, 202150100021) Bks Demand.

Personal Finance: A Balanced Approach to Financial Security. Reno Hoff. LC 94-209431. 160p. (C). 1994. per. 13.95 (0-8403-9218-4) Kendall-Hunt.

Personal Finance: An American Experience. Ken Long. 256p. 1997. pap. text 26.50 (1-56226-359-5) CAT Pub.

Personal Finance: An American Experience. Ken Long. 406p. 1998. pap. text 25.48 (1-56226-407-9) CAT Pub.

*Personal Finance: An Integrated Planning Approach. 4th ed. Bernard J. Winger. 1998. 98.25 (0-13-628629-1) P-H.

Personal Finance: An Integrated Planning Approach. 4th ed. Bernard J. Winger & Ralph R. Frasca. LC 96-23941. 560p. 1996. text 76.00 (0-13-269630-4) P-H.

*Personal Finance: Building & Protecting Your Wealth. 2nd ed. Arthur J. Keown. 550p. 2000. 85.33 (0-13-026928-X) P-H.

Personal Finance: Casebook. 4th ed. Jack R. Kapoor et al. 64p. (C). 1995. text 16.18 (0-256-17405-9, Irwn McGrw-H) McGrw-H Hghr Educ.

*Personal Finance: English/Spanish Glossary. 5th ed. Jack R. Kapoor et al. (SPA & ENG.). 64p. (C). 1998. pap. 12.81 (0-07-303883-0) McGrw-H Hghr Educ.

Personal Finance: Personal Financial Planner. 4th ed. Jack R. Kapoor et al. (C). 1995. text 9.50 incl. disk (0-256-20601-5, Irwn McGrw-H) McGrw-H Hghr Educ.

P

***Personal Finance: Study Guide.** 7th ed. Rosefsky. 162p. 1998. pap., student ed. 33.95 (*0-471-29954-5*) Wiley.

Personal Finance: Testbank, 5 vols. Garman. (C). 1997. pap., teacher ed. 11.96 (*0-395-80878-2*) HM.

Personal Finance: The Savings & Credit Facilities Market. 1985. 225.00 (*0-7855-7251-1*) St Mut.

Personal Finance: Tools for Decision Making. Judith A. Ramaglia & Diane B. MacDonald. LC 98-20640. 1998. pap. 87.95 (*0-538-89040-1*) Sth-Wstrn College.

Personal Finance: Turning Money into Wealth. Keown. LC 97-40198. 690p. 1998. 80.00 (*0-13-616442-0*) P-H.

***Personal Finance: Turning Money into Wealth.** Keown. 1998. pap. 40.00 (*0-13-028629-X*) P-H.

Personal Finance & Investment. Wilford J. Eiteman. 1952. 5.00 (*0-912164-01-8*) Masterco Pr.

Personal Finance Companies & Their Credit Practices. Ralph A. Young et al. (Financial Research Program II: Studies in Consumer Installment Financing: No. 1). 192p. 1940. reprint ed. 50.00 (*0-87014-460-X*) Natl Bur Econ Res.

Personal Finance English/Spanish Glossary. 4th ed. Les Dlabay et al. 32p. (C). 1995. text 15.00 (*0-256-18544-1*, Irwn McGrw-H) McGrw-H Hghr Educ.

Personal Finance for Busy People. Robert Cooke. LC 98-65407. 272p. 1998. pap. 16.95 (*0-07-012556-2*) McGraw.

Personal Finance for Dummies. Eric Tyson & Roger C. Parker. 350p. 1994. pap. 16.95 (*1-56884-150-7*) IDG Bks.

Personal Finance for Dummies. 2nd ed. Eric Tyson. LC 96-78140. (For Dummies Ser.). 456p. 1996. pap. 19.99 (*0-7645-5013-6*) IDG Bks.

Personal Finance for Dummies. 2nd ed. Martin Tyson. 456p. 1998. pap. 19.99 (*0-7645-5123-X*) IDG Bks.

***Personal Finance for Dummies.** 3rd rev. ed. Eric Tyson & David Silverman. (For Dummies Ser.). 384p. 2000. pap. 19.99 (*0-7645-5231-7*) IDG Bks.

Personal Finance for Dummies: A Reference for the Rest of Us. abr. ed. Eric Tyson. (For Dummies Ser.). 1996. audio 12.00 (*0-694-51666-X*, CPN 10071) HarperAudio.

Personal Finance in Singapore: A Primer. Tan Chwee Huat. LC 98-474022. 324p. 1999. pap. 42.50 (*9971-69-216-3*, Pub. by Sngapore Univ Pr) Coronet Bks.

Personal Finance in Your 20's & 30's. Tracey Longo. (Complete Idiot's Guides (Lifestyle) Ser.). (Illus.). 379p. 1999. pap. 16.95 (*0-02-862415-7*) Macmillan Gen Ref.

Personal Finance on the Web: The Interactive Guide. Jonathan Michaels. LC 97-2919. (Illus.). 316p. 1997. pap. 24.95 (*0-471-16385-6*) Wiley.

Personal Finance on Your Computer: A Starter Kit. Phillip R. Robinson. 352p. 1995. pap., pap. text 29.95 incl. cd-rom (*1-55828-420-6*, MIS Pr) IDG Bks.

Personal Finance on Your Computer: Starter Kit. 293p. pap. text 20.00 (*0-7881-6512-7*) DIANE Pub.

Personal Finance Package: With Personal Finance Planner & Casebook & DOS 3.50 Software. 4th ed. Jack R. Kapoor et al. (C). 1996. text 81.25 incl. 3.5 ld (*0-256-23844-8*, Irwn McGrw-H) McGrw-H Hghr Educ.

Personal Finance Telecourse Study System Set. 6th ed. Rosefsky. 354p. 1995. pap. text 22.00 (*0-471-13143-1*) Wiley.

Personal Finance Telecourse Viewers Guide: Textbook & Study Guide. 6th ed. Robert S. Rosefsky. 1152p. 1996. pap. 113.85 (*0-471-16909-9*) Wiley.

Personal Finance Today. Roger L. Miller et al. (Illus.). 446p. (C). 1983. pap. text, teacher ed. write for info. (*0-314-71112-0*) West Pub.

Personal Finance with 1-2-3. Steve Adams. (Orig.). 1990. pap. 24.95 (*0-13-660457-9*) P-H.

Personal Finances see Finanzas Personales

Personal Finances. Larry Burkett. LC 99-158330. 1998. pap. 6.99 (*0-8024-3738-9*) Moody.

Personal Financial. 7th ed. Lawrence J. Gitman. (C). 1995. pap. text, student ed., wbk. ed. 28.00 (*0-03-015984-9*) Harcourt.

Personal Financial Fact Finding. American College Staff. LC 92-70340. 100p. (Orig.). (C). 1992. pap. text 42.95 (*0-943590-36-1*) Amer College.

***Personal Financial Fitness.** 5th ed. Allen Klosowski. Ed. by Michael G. Crisp. LC 98-74376. (Fifty-Minute Book Ser.). (Illus.). 120p. 2000. pap. 10.95 (*1-56052-552-5*) Crisp Pubns.

Personal Financial Fitness: A Practical Guide to Improve the Health of Your Wealth. 4th rev. ed. Allen Klosowski. Ed. by Michael Crisp. LC 96-86237. 120p. 1997. pap. 9.95 (*1-56052-419-7*) Crisp Pubns.

***Personal Financial Literacy & Awareness.** Stephen Ward. 160p. 2000. pap. 80.00 (*0-85297-527-9*, Pub. by Chartered Bank) St Mut.

***Personal Financial Management.** John English et al. 272p. 2000. pap. 29.95 (*1-86508-064-0*, Pub. by Allen & Unwin Pty) Paul & Co Pubs.

Personal Financial Management: A Forecasting & Control Approach. Dennis J. O'Connor & Alberto T. Bueso. (Illus.). 560p. (C). 1983. text 36.00 (*0-13-657940-X*) P-H.

Personal Financial Management: A Strategic Planning Approach. Richard M. Hodgetts. LC 82-6748. 608p. (C). 1983. text 38.25 (*0-201-12775-X*) Addison-Wesley.

Personal Financial Management: Workbook. Hodgetts. LC 82-6748. 608p. (C). 1983. pap. text, student ed. 8.00 (*0-201-12777-6*) Addison-Wesley.

Personal Financial Plan. 8th ed. Gitman. (C). 1998. pap. text, teacher ed., wbk. ed. 28.00 (*0-03-023696-7*, Pub. by Harcourt Coll Pubs) Harcourt.

Personal Financial Planner. rev. ed. Debbie Harrison. (Investors Chronicle Ser.). 335p. 1999. pap. 41.50 (*0-273-63968-4*, Pub. by Pitman Pbg) Trans-Atl Phila.

Personal Financial Planner. 7th ed. Lawrence J. Gitman. (C). 1995. pap. text, teacher ed., suppl. ed. 42.00 (*0-03-015983-0*) Harcourt Coll Pubs.

***Personal Financial Planning.** (C). 1998. 67.00 (*0-321-00678-X*) Addison-Wesley.

Personal Financial Planning. 125.00 (*0-685-69598-0*, PFP) Warren Gorham & Lamont.

Personal Financial Planning. Ed. by McNamara. (C). 1997. pap. text, student ed. write for info. (*0-673-99925-4*) Addison-Wesley.

Personal Financial Planning. Ed. by Rejda. (C). 1997. text. write for info. (*0-673-99878-9*) Addison-Wesley.

Personal Financial Planning. Rejda. (C). 1998. pap. text. write for info. (*0-321-02102-9*) Addison-Wesley.

***Personal Financial Planning.** Wolf & Greninger. (C). 1999. pap. text 42.00 (*0-536-59998-X*) Pearson Custom.

Personal Financial Planning. Harold A. Wolf. 594p. (C). 1992. 30.80 (*0-536-58197-5*) Pearson Custom.

Personal Financial Planning. rev. ed. Harold A. Wolf. 688p. 1989. teacher ed. write for info. (*0-318-63861-4*, H17544); student ed. 19.00 (*0-685-22010-9*, H1756-9) P-H.

Personal Financial Planning. 2nd ed. George E. Rejda. (C). 2000. text (*0-321-04307-3*) Addson-Wesley Educ.

Personal Financial Planning. 2nd rev. ed. 580p. (C). 1996. text 48.00 (*0-536-58851-1*) Pearson Custom.

***Personal Financial Planning.** 5th ed. 543p. (C). 2000. 55.00 (*0-536-60373-1*) Pearson Custom.

Personal Financial Planning. 5th ed. G. Victor Hallman & Jerry S. Rosenbloom. LC 92-40274. 608p. 1992. 40.00 (*0-07-025680-2*) McGraw.

***Personal Financial Planning.** 6th ed. G. Victor Hallman. LC 00-20215. 592p. 2000. 42.95 (*0-07-026031-1*) McGraw.

Personal Financial Planning. 6th ed. Rejda MacNamara. LC 97-21669. 648p. (C). 1997. 92.00 (*0-321-00927-4*) Addison-Wesley Educ.

Personal Financial Planning. 8th ed. Gitman. LC 98-71884. (C). 1998. text 80.50 (*0-03-023691-6*, Pub. by Harcourt Coll Pubs) Harcourt.

Personal Financial Planning. 8th ed. Lawrence J. Gitman. 1998. 97.50 (*0-03-021027-5*) Dryden Pr.

Personal Financial Planning: How to Fix Your Finances. Stephen Lofthouse. LC 96-3434. 1996. pap. text 33.50 (*0-471-96702-5*) Wiley.

Personal Financial Planning: The Adviser's Guide. 2nd ed. Rolf Auster. 576p. 1993. pap. 49.50 (*0-8080-0003-9*, BLS-3256) CCH INC.

Personal Financial Planning: The Advisor's Guide. 3rd ed. Rolf Austen. Ed. by Lawrence Norris. LC 98-173139. xxvi, 476p. 1998. 65.00 (*0-8080-0264-3*) CCH INC.

Personal Financial Planning: The Team Approach. American Institute of Certified Public Accountants. LC 87-142958. (Management Advisory Services Practice Aids, Small Business Consulting Practice Aid Ser.: Vol. 7). 144p. 1987. reprint ed. pap. 44.70 (*0-608-00517-7*, 206135000008) Bks Demand.

Personal Financial Planning: Understanding Your Financial Calculator. James F. Dalton. LC 98-96599. 247p. (C). 1998. pap. text 35.00 (*1-890260-04-5*) Dalton Pub.

Personal Financial Planning: With Forms & Checklists. Jonathan D. Pond. 352p. 1987. 156.50 (*0-88712-914-5*) Warren Gorham & Lamont.

Personal Financial Planning: With Forms & Checklists. Jonathan D. Pond. 352p. 1992. suppl. ed. 165.00 (*0-7913-2700-0*, PFF) Warren Gorham & Lamont.

***Personal Financial Planning Cases & Applications.** 2nd ed. Michael A. Dalton & James F. Dalton. (Personal Financial Planning Ser.). 433p. (C). 1999. pap. text 70.00 (*1-890260-11-8*) Dalton Pub.

Personal Financial Planning for Gays & Lesbians: Our Guide to Prudent Decision Making. Peter M. Berkery, Jr. 336p. 1996. text 24.95 (*0-7863-0482-0*, Irwn Prfssnl) McGraw-Hill Prof.

Personal Financial Planning for Local Government Employees. Ed. by Bruce K. Blaylock & Kenneth F. Kennedy. LC 87-2948. (Orig.). 1987. pap. text 9.95 (*0-318-39866-4*) Intl City-Cnty Mgt.

Personal Financial Planning Made Easy. Eugene J. Aubert & Matthew Stephens. (Illus.). (Orig.). (C). 1988. pap. 59.95 (*0-929416-00-7*) AFPG Inc.

Personal Financial Planning Made Easy. Eugene J. Aubert & Matthew Stephens. (Illus.). 170p. (Orig.). (C). 1988. pap. text 79.00 (*0-317-90583-X*) Advan Finan Plan.

Personal Financial Planning Manual: Nonauthoritative Explanations & Illustrations as of August 1, 1988, 2 vols., Vol. 1. American Institute of Certified Public Accountants. LC HG0179.. 451p. reprint ed. pap. 139.90 (*0-8357-6901-1*, 203796000001) Bks Demand.

Personal Financial Planning Manual: Nonauthoritative Explanations & Illustrations as of August 1, 1988, 2 vols., Vol. 2. American Institute of Certified Public Accountants. LC HG0179.. 252p. reprint ed. pap. 78.20 (*0-8357-6902-X*, 203796000002) Bks Demand.

Personal Financial Planning Manual, 1996-1997. 12th ed. Robson Rhodes. 368p. 1996. pap. 51.00 (*0-406-99089-1*, MICHIE) LEXIS Pub.

Personal Financial Records. William F. Farren & Norbert J. Janis. 68p. 1991. ring bd. 39.95 (*0-9628383-0-6*) My Account.

Personal Financial Statements. (American Institute of CPAs Audit Guides Ser.). 80p. 1983. pap. 31.00 (*0-87051-035-5*) Am Inst CPA.

Personal Financial Success: Basic Course. John M. Cummuta. 130p. 1991. pap. 49.00 (*1-883113-04-0*) Debt-FREE.

Personal Firearms Inventory: An Important Insurance Record. 1980. pap. 4.95 (*0-89145-156-0*, 5092) Collector Bks.

Personal Fitness. Boy Scouts of America. (Illus.). 92p. (YA). (gr. 6-12). 1990. pap. 2.90 (*0-8395-3286-5*, 33286) BSA.

Personal Fitness. Murray. Date not set. wbk. ed. write for info. (*0-314-09736-8*) West Pub.

Personal Fitness. 2nd ed. Gary Pechar & Nelson Ng. 124p. (C). 1999. spiral bd. 13.95 (*0-7872-5703-6*, 41570304) Kendall-Hunt.

***Personal Fitness & Wellness.** Murray et al. 2001. pap. 35.00 (*0-534-56871-8*) Thomson Learn.

Personal Fitness & You Student Text. 2nd rev. ed. Roberta Stokes et al. 260p. 1996. pap. text 25.90 (*0-88725-217-6*) Hunter Textbks.

Personal Fitness & You Teacher's Edition. 2nd rev. ed. Roberta Stokes et al. 443p. 1996. pap. text 36.95 (*0-88725-218-4*) Hunter Textbks.

***Personal Fitness for You.** Roberta Stokes & Sandra Schultz. (Illus.). 238p. 1998. teacher ed. 69.95 (*0-88725-275-3*); text 45.00 (*0-88725-249-4*); teacher ed., spiral bd. 100.00 (*0-88725-276-1*) Hunter Textbks.

Personal Footprints: A Swagger, a Limp & a Therapist's Journey from Alcoholism to Fundamentalism to Personal Use. Charles Griffin. (Illus.). 191p. (Orig.). 1991. pap. write for info. (*0-9627591-0-4*) Prsnl Footprint.

Personal Forces in Modern Literature. Arthur Compton-Rickett. LC 68-54367. (Essay Index Reprint Ser.). 1977. 19.95 (*0-8369-0824-4*) Ayer.

Personal Forces in Modern Literature. Arthur Compton-Rickett. LC 72-973. reprint ed. 34.50 (*0-404-01649-9*) AMS Pr.

Personal Forms of File: 1999 Edition. 316p. 1999. ring bd. 125.00 (*0-8160-4025-7*, Checkmark) Facts on File.

Personal Forms on File. Facts on File Staff. LC 98-106501. 1997. pap. text 125.00 (*0-8160-3664-0*) Facts on File.

Personal Forms on File: 1998 Edition. Diagram Group Staff. 314p. 1998. ring bd. 125.00 (*0-8160-3818-X*) Facts on File.

Personal Forms on File: 1998 Update. Diagram Group Staff. 1998. ring bd. 45.00 (*0-8160-3819-8*) Facts on File.

Personal Forms on File: 1999 Update. 1999. ring bd. 45.00 (*0-8160-4026-5*, Checkmark) Facts on File.

***Personal Forms on File 2000 Update.** Facts on File Publishing Staff. 2000. ring bd. 45.00 (*0-8160-4066-4*) Facts on File.

***Personal Forms on File 2000: Over 100 Indispensable Forms For Organizing Personal Records.** Facts on File Publishing Staff. 318p. 2000. ring bd. 125.00 (*0-8160-4065-6*) Facts on File.

Personal Fouls. Peter Golenbock. (Illus.). 1989. 18.95 (*0-671-67178-2*) PB.

Personal Freedom & National Resurgence. Ed. by Aleksander Dobrynin & Bronius Kuzmickas. LC 94-6871. (Cultural Heritage & Contemporary Change Series IVA: Vol. 8). 1994. 45.00 (*1-56518-038-0*); pap. 17.50 (*1-56518-039-9*) Coun Res Values.

Personal Gathering: Paintings & Sculpture from the Collection of William I. Koch. unabridged ed. Lisa N. Peters et al. LC 95-62399. (Illus.). 184p. (Orig.). 1996. pap. 35.00 (*0-939324-50-4*) Wichita Art Mus.

Personal Gift Bible. Zondervan Publishing Staff. 1024p. 1999. 9.99 (*0-310-91835-9*); 9.99 (*0-310-91834-0*); 9.99 (*0-310-91833-2*) Zondervan.

Personal Glimpse. Josephine M. Sommo. 1997. pap. 56.95 (*1-57553-635-8*) Watermrk Pr.

Personal Goal Plan: Designing an Extraordinary Life. Gary R. Blair. 40p. 1998. pap. 19.95 (*1-889770-54-X*, PGP) GoalsGuy.

Personal Goal Planner: Your Monthly Companion. Gary R. Blair. 52p. 1998. pap. 2.95 (*1-889770-62-0*, PGP2) GoalsGuy.

***Personal Goal Planner: Your Monthly Goal Setting Companion.** Gary Ryan Blair. (GoalsGuy Library). (Illus.). 72p. 2000. pap. 19.95 (*1-889770-65-5*) GoalsGuy.

Personal Goal Planner No. 12: Your Monthly Companion. Gary R. Blair. 52p. 1997. pap. 19.95 (*1-889770-01-9*, PGP1) GoalsGuy.

Personal Goal Setting for a Purposeful & Fulfilled Life. 2nd rev. ed. Wilberta L. Chinn. (Illus.). 56p. (Orig.). 1996. spiral bd. 6.95 (*0-937673-13-7*) Peacock Ent LA.

Personal Goal-Setting Forms: An Assortment of Planning Sheets & Other Helpful Resources. Gary R. Blair. 40p. 1998. pap. 19.95 (*1-889770-58-2*, PGF) GoalsGuy.

Personal Goal Setting 101: Mastering the Fundamentals of Goal-Setting & Personal Strategic Planning. Gary R. Blair. 40p. 1998. pap. 19.95 (*1-889770-22-1*, PGS) GoalsGuy.

Personal Goals & Work Design. Ed. by Peter B. Warr. LC 75-4568. 278p. reprint ed. pap. 86.20 (*0-608-15634-5*, 203176400076) Bks Demand.

Personal Goals Journal: A Record of Your Life's Accomplishments. Gary R. Blair. 48p. 1998. pap. 6.95 (*1-889770-13-2*, PGJ) GoalsGuy.

Personal God: Is the Classical Understanding of God Tenable? Gerald Bray. 74p. 1998. reprint ed. pap. 12.99 (*0-85364-909-X*, Pub. by Paternoster Pub) OM Literature.

Personal Grief & a Reasonable Faith: A Mother's Journey from Tragedy to Triumph in Understanding the Christian Faith. Norma E. Sawyers. LC 91-73415. 140p. 1992. 11.95 (*0-9630031-0-0*) Dogwood.

Personal Growth. Center for Learning Network Staff. (Junior High Religion Ser.). 72p. (J). (gr. 7-8). 1992. student ed., per. 5.95 (*1-56077-233-6*) Ctr Learning.

Personal Growth: Workshop Models for Gr. 7-8. Center for Learning Network Staff. (Junior High Religion (Grades 7-8) Ser.). 45p. 1992. teacher ed., spiral bd. 7.95 (*1-56077-184-4*) Ctr Learning.

Personal Growth - In a Nutshell: Quick & Easy. Dee Frances. Date not set. pap. 12.00 (*1-885519-11-7*, Pub. by DDDD Pubns) Baker & Taylor.

Personal Growth & Behavior, 1996-1997. annuals 16th ed. Karen Duffy. 256p. (C). 1996. text. write for info. (*0-697-31671-8*) Brown & Benchmark.

Personal Growth & Behavior, 98-99. 18th ed. Karen G. Duffy. (Annual Ser.). (Illus.). 240p. 1998. pap. text 12.25 (*0-697-39175-2*, Dshkn McG-Hill) McGrw-H Hghr Educ.

Personal Growth & Behavior 96. 16th annot. ed. Duffy. 1996. teacher ed. (*0-697-31672-6*, WCB McGr Hill) McGrw-H Hghr Educ.

Personal Growth & Behaviour. 14th ed. Duffy. 1994. 12.74 (*1-56134-284-X*) McGraw.

Personal Growth & Behaviour. 15th ed. Duffy. 1995. 12.74 (*1-56134-366-8*) McGraw.

***Personal Growth Through Adventure.** David Hopkins. 2000. pap. 29.95 (*1-85346-608-5*) David Fulton.

Personal Growth Through Adventure. David Hopkins & Roger Putnam. 160p. 1993. pap. 32.50 (*1-85346-158-X*, Pub. by David Fulton) Taylor & Francis.

Personal Growth Through Martial Arts: Studies in Kendo, Fencing, & Indian Swordsmanship. Ed. by Minoru Kiyota & Jordan Lee. LC 97-35934. (Illus.). 170p. 1997. pap. 25.00 (*0-9659801-0-3*) U Wisconsin-Madison.

Personal Guide for Physical Fitness. George A. Mehale. (Illus.). 63p. 1998. pap. 14.99 (*0-9642960-5-5*) Scientific Sports.

Personal Guide to Achieving Winning Pick 3 Numbers: The Big Three. Hal V. Miles. (Illus.). 115p. (Orig.). Date not set. pap. text 24.95 (*0-9654845-0-5*) Miles Intl Assn.

Personal Guide to Living with Loss. rev. ed. Elaine Vail. LC 95-60822. 227p. 1995. pap. 17.95 (*0-9646427-0-0*, 95LWL01) Yeast & Assocs.

Personal Guide to Respite Care. Mary L. Cody. (Illus.). 28p. (Orig.). 1988. pap. 3.00 (*0-685-31065-5*) Visiting Nurse Assn.

***Personal Guide to the Implementation of the Let Me Learn Process Vol. 1: K-12.** Christine Johnston. (Illus.). 160p. 2000. pap. 25.99 (*1-892385-04-X*) Let Me Learn.

Personal Health. Vivian Bernstein. (Life Skills for Today's World Ser.). 1997. pap., student ed. 9.32 (*0-8114-1915-0*) Raintree Steck-V.

Personal Health: Study Guide & Lecture Notes. 3rd ed. Ruth Engs. 196p. (C). 1997. pap. text, per. 31.95 (*0-7872-3378-1*, 41337801) Kendall-Hunt.

Personal Health Care & Social Security: A Report. ILO-WHO Joint Committee. (Technical Reports: No. 480). 74p. 1971. pap. text 5.00 (*92-4-120480-X*, 1100480) World Health.

Personal Health-Care Organizer: The Original Patient Management Workbook. Craig R. Perkins & Kelly A. Perkins. 110p. 1994. 39.95 (*0-9642711-1-7*); pap. 22.95 (*0-9642711-0-9*) Crakel Pubns.

Personal Health Choices. Christopher Smith & Sandra L. Smith. 1990. pap. 45.00 (*0-86720-130-4*) Jones & Bartlett.

Personal Health Choices. Christopher Smith & Sandra L. Smith. 1990. pap. 25.00 (*0-86720-132-0*) Jones & Bartlett.

Personal Health Notes. Joan Dwyer. 124p. 1999. pap. write for info. (*0-7392-0111-5*, PO3008) Morris Pubng.

Personal Health Profile: Health Information Organizer System. Laura A. Clark & Maxine L. Moon. 130p. 1997. ring bd. 19.95 (*0-9671911-0-6*) Health InFacts.

Personal Health Record: Assuming Responsibility for One's Own Health Management. Arthur Kanowitz & Sandra Kanowitz. 36p. (Orig.). 1987. pap. 1.98 (*0-942933-00-1*) Premier Pub CO.

Personal Health Reporter. Albert E. Rees. 627p. 1992. 105.00 (*0-8103-8392-6*, 101230) Gale.

Personal Hearing Protection in Industry. Ed. by Peter W. Alberti. LC 81-40748. (Illus.). 621p. 1982. reprint ed. pap. 192.60 (*0-7837-9574-2*, 206032300005) Bks Demand.

Personal History. Katharine Graham. LC 96-49638. (Illus.). 642p. 1997. 29.95 (*0-394-58585-2*) Knopf.

Personal History. Katharine Graham. 1998. pap. 15.00 (*0-375-70104-4*) Vin Bks.

Personal History, Adventures, Experience & Observation of David Copperfield. Charles Dickens. (Signet Classics). 1962. 10.05 (*0-606-00529-3*, Pub. by Turtleback) Demco.

Personal History & Health: The Midtown Longitudinal Study, 1954-1974. Leo Srole & Ernest J. Millman. LC 97-26145. 310p. 1997. text 39.95 (*1-56000-325-1*) Transaction Pubs.

Personal History Journal for LDS Youth: From Birth Through High School. Duane S. Crowther. 1993. pap. 9.98 (*0-88290-089-7*, 1504) Horizon Utah.

Personal History of David Copperfield see Oxford Illustrated Dickens

***Personal History of David Copperfield.** Charles Dickens. LC 99-25972. (Focus on the Family Great Stories Ser.). 1999. pap. 14.99 (*1-56179-761-8*) Tyndale Hse.

***Personal History of Thirst.** John Burdett. 301p. 1999. reprint ed. text 23.00 (*0-7881-6629-8*) DIANE Pub.

Personal History Through the Life Course, Vol. 3. Ed. by Zena S. Blau. (Current Perspectives on Aging & the Life Cycle Ser.). 298p. 1990. 73.25 (*0-89232-739-1*) Jai Pr.

Personal History Workbook. Margaret L. Ingram. (Illus.). (Orig.). (C). 1992. pap. text 10.00 (*0-9624721-2-3*) Memories Plus.

Personal Holiness. pap. 6.99 (*0-88019-148-1*) Schmul Pub Co.

Personal Holiness in Times of Temptation. Bruce Wilkinson. LC 98-16521. 260p. 1998. 15.99 (*1-56507-943-4*) Harvest Hse.

***Personal Holiness in Times of Temptation.** Bruce Wilkinson. 264p. 1999. pap. 10.99 (*0-7369-0153-1*) Harvest Hse.

Personal Home Inspection Guide. Larry McKay. LC 91-14522. 96p. 1991. pap. 14.95 (*0-942963-11-3*) Distinctive Pub.

Personal Housekeeping. John Myers. 12p. 1997. pap., wbk. ed. 4.95 (0-929690-38-9) Herit Pubs AZ.

Personal Hygiene & Health Care Appliances, UL 1431. 2nd ed. (C). 1996. pap. text 135.00 (0-7629-0127-6) Underwrtrs Labs.

Personal Hygiene for College Students. Delbert Oberteuffer. LC 77-177126. (Columbia University. Teachers College. Contributions to Education Ser.: No. 407). (C). reprint ed. 37.50 (0-404-55407-5) AMS Pr.

Personal Idealism & Mysticism (1924) William R. Inge. 190p. 1998. reprint ed. pap. 19.95 (0-7661-0328-5) Kessinger Pub.

Personal Identification from Human Remains. Spencer L. Rogers. (Illus.). 94p. 1987. 35.95 (0-398-05307-3) C C Thomas.

Personal Identity. Ed. by Harol W. Noonan. LC 92-29002. (International Research Library of Philosophy). 560p. 1993. 184.95 (1-85521-299-4, Pub. by Dartmth Pub) Ashgate Pub Co.

Personal Identity. Harold W. Noonan. (Problems of Philosophy Series: Their Past & Present). 304p. 1989. 55.00 (0-415-03365-9, A3246) Routledge.

Personal Identity. Harold W. Noonan. (Problems of Philosophy Series: Their Past & Present). 304p. (C). 1991. pap. 17.95 (0-415-07047-3, A6284) Routledge.

Personal Identity. Ed. by John Perry. (Topics in Philosophy Ser.: Vol. 2). 246p. 1975. pap. 16.95 (0-520-02960-7, Pub. by U CA Pr) Cal Prin Full Svc.

Personal Identity & Self-Consciousness. Brian Garrett. LC 97-35430. (International Library of Philosophy). 144p. (C). 1998. 65.00 (0-415-16573-3) Routledge.

Personal Immunization Record. Paula D. Golden. (Illus.). 32p. (Orig.). 1994. pap. 7.95 (1-886730-60-1) Romping Feet.

Personal Impressions. Isaiah Berlin. LC 99-490994. (Illus.). 288p. 1998. pap. 19.95 (0-7126-6601-X, Pub. by Pimlico) Trafalgar.

Personal Impressions of Edward Carpenter. Havelock Ellis. 1972. 59.95 (0-8490-0817-4) Gordon Pr.

Personal Income Distribution: A Multicapability Theory. Joop Hartog. 208p. 1980. lib. bdg. 76.00 (0-89838-047-2) Kluwer Academic.

Personal Income During Business Cycles. Daniel Creamer. LC 84-10763. 166p. 1984. reprint ed. lib. bdg. 69.50 (0-313-24421-9, CRPI, Greenwood Pr) Greenwood.

Personal Income Tax Reduction in a Business Contraction. Melvin I. White. LC 68-58638. (Columbia University. Studies in the Social Sciences: No. 564). reprint ed. 21.50 (0-404-51564-9) AMS Pr.

***Personal Income Tax Saving Handbook: How to Maximize Your Tax Refund & Keep More of Your Hard.** William B. McAllister. 2000. pap. 6.95 (0-9676087-1-6) Interactive Sales & Mktg.

Personal Income Taxation: The Definition of Income As a Problem of Fiscal Policy. Henry C. Simons. LC 38-27193. 250p. reprint ed. pap. 77.50 (0-608-12089-8, 202412500035) Bks Demand.

Personal Index to the New York Times Index, 1975-1993 Supplement see Personal Name Index to the New York Times Index, 1975-1993

Personal Influence. Grace Livingston Hill. 1976. 18.95 (0-8488-0818-5) Amereon Ltd.

Personal Influence: Training Package. Terry R. Bacon et al. (Illus.). 91p. 1996. ring bd. write for info. (1-57740-025-9, ILW025) Intl LrningWrk.

Personal Influence Workbook. Terry R. Bacon et al. (Illus.). 57p. 1996. ring bd., wbk. ed. write for info. (1-57740-026-7, ILW026) Intl LrningWrk.

Personal Information: Privacy & the Law. Raymond I. Wacks. (Illus.). 360p. 1994. reprint ed. pap. text 27.00 (0-19-825867-4) OUP.

Personal Information: Privacy at the Workplace. Jack L. Osborn. LC 78-18223. (AMA Management Briefing Ser.). 52p. reprint ed. pap. 30.00 (0-608-30703-3, 205039100078) Bks Demand.

Personal Information Management: Tools & Techniques for Achieving Professional Effectiveness. Barbara Etzel & Peter J. Thomas. LC 96-18451. 154p. (C). 1996. text 50.00 (0-8147-2199-0) NYU Pr.

Personal Information Management: Tools & Techniques for Achieving Professional Effectiveness. Barbara Etzel & Peter J. Thomas. 176p. 1999. pap. text 17.00 (0-8147-2200-8) NYU Pr.

***Personal Injuries.** Scott Turow. LC 99-30829. 384p. 1999. 27.00 (0-374-28194-7) FS&G.

***Personal Injuries.** Scott Turow. 2000. mass mkt. write for info. (0-446-60860-2) Warner Bks.

***Personal Injuries.** large type ed. Scott Turow. LC 99-30989. 1999. 30.95 (0-7862-2014-7) Thorndike Pr.

***Personal Injuries.** large type ed. Scott Turow. LC 99-30989. 2000. pap. 28.95 (0-7862-2015-5) Thorndike Pr.

Personal Injuries Reader Edition. Scott Turow. write for info. (0-374-96409-2) FS&G.

Personal Injury. Ed. by Derek Morgan. (C). 1991. text 22.00 (1-85431-133-6, Pub. by Blackstone Pr) Gaunt.

Personal Injury. 2nd ed. Gordon Exall. (Practice Notes Ser.). 88p. 1992. pap. write for info. (0-85121-866-0, Pub. by Cavendish Pubng) Gaunt.

Personal Injury: Actions, Defenses, Damages, 25 vols. Louis R. Frumer & R. L. Benoit. 1957. ring bd. 2700.00 (0-8205-1530-2) Bender.

Personal Injury Vols. 8-9: Tort & Insurance Practice, 2 Vols. 2nd ed. Richard B. McNamara. 150.00 (0-327-12470-9) LEXIS Pub.

Personal Injury & Torts. Ed. by Glenn A. Guarino. LC 96-75251. (Indiana Practitioner Ser.). 1800p. 1996. text. write for info. (0-7620-0043-0) West Group.

Personal Injury Awards in EC Countries: An Industry Report. David McIntosh & Majorie Holmes. 199p. 1990. pap. 265.00 (1-85044-349-1) LLP.

Personal Injury Awards in EU & EFTA Countries. 2nd ed. David McIntosh & Marjorie Holmes. 456p. 1994. pap. 265.00 (1-85044-506-0) LLP.

Personal Injury Claims in the County Court. Janet Bettle. 184p. 1992. 60.00 (1-85190-166-3, Pub. by Tolley Pubng) St Mut.

Personal Injury Claims in the County Court: Practice & Procedure. 2nd ed. Janet Bettle & John A. Harney. (Lawyers Practice & Procedure Ser.). 289p. (C). 1994. pap. 195.00 (0-85459-921-5, Pub. by Tolley Pubng) St Mut.

Personal Injury Defense Reporter. text 255.00 (0-8205-2113-2) Bender.

Personal Injury Defense Techniques, 3 vols. Mark A. Dombroff. 1987. ring bd. 610.00 (0-8205-1542-6) Bender.

Personal Injury Deskbook, 1961-1990. 1961. 1650.00 (0-8377-9130-8, Rothman) W S Hein.

Personal Injury Forms: Discovery & Settlement. 2nd ed. John A. Tarantino. 350p. 1992. ring bd. 139.00 incl. disk (0-938065-09-2) James Pub Santa Ana.

Personal Injury Forms: Illinois, 2 vols. Goldstein & Fluxgold. LC 92-20090. 1992. ring bd. 200.00 (0-317-05358-2) West Group.

Personal Injury Forms, 1981-1991. John J. Higgins. (Nebraska Legal Forms Ser.). 200p. 1991. ring bd. 69.95 (0-86678-028-9, 82009-10, MICHIE); ring bd. 85.00 incl. disk (0-685-49531-0, MICHIE) LEXIS Pub.

Personal Injury in Virginia: 1999 Spring Cumulative Supplement. 2nd ed. Charles E. Friend. 75p. 1999. write for info. (0-327-01420-2, 6198416) LEXIS Pub.

Personal Injury Law in Virginia. Charles E. Friend. 935p. 1990. 95.00 (0-87473-637-4, 61982-10, MICHIE) LEXIS Pub.

Personal Injury Liability under the Jones Act: Background Materials. Frwd. by Harry N. Cook. 158p. (Orig.). (C). 1992. pap. text 25.00 (0-934292-11-6) Natl Waterways.

Personal Injury Limitation Law. Rodney Nelson-Jones & Frank Burton. 362p. 1994. pap. text 75.00 (0-406-02447-2, UK, MICHIE) LEXIS Pub.

Personal Injury Litigation: Legal Practice Course Guides. Denis Carey. 251p. 1995. pap. 34.00 (1-85431-463-7, Pub. by Blackstone Pr) Gaunt.

Personal Injury Litigation: Legal Practice Course Guides. rev. ed. Denis Carey. 200p. Date not set. pap. 34.00 (1-85431-514-5, Pub. by Blackstone Pr) Gaunt.

Personal Injury Newsletter. Ed. by Gordon L. Ohlsson & Rima Kittner. text 255.00 (0-8205-2106-X) Bender.

Personal Injury Paralegal: Forms & Procedures, 1. Joyce Walden. (Paralegal Litigation Library). 424p. 1997. boxed set 97.95 (0-471-58799-0) Wiley.

Personal Injury Practice & Procedure in Europe. Martha W. Neocleous. LC 98-158744. xi, 182p. 1997. pap. 68.50 (1-85941-179-7, Pub. by Cavendish Pubng) Gaunt.

Personal Injury Practice Handbook. Lise A. Young. 120p. 1986. pap. 35.00 (0-911110-56-9, MICHIE) LEXIS Pub.

Personal Injury Practice Tech & Technology. Lawrence Charfoos & David Christensen. LC 85-82276. 1986. 98.00 (0-685-59918-3) West Group.

Personal Injury Valuation. Frederick A. Raffa. 1992. write for info. (0-8205-1678-3) Bender.

Personal Injury Valuation Handbooks, 9 vols., Set. Jury Verdict Research Staff. 1987. 545.00 (0-317-55323-2) Jury Verdict.

Personal Injury Verdict Reviews. Jury Verdict Research Staff. LC 84-245660. 1985. 375.00 (0-685-10778-7) Jury Verdict.

Personal Insurance. 3rd ed. George E. Rejda et al. LC 97-73241. 382p. (C). 1997. pap. text 31.00 (0-89462-117-3, 2202) IIA.

Personal Insurance: Issues. Leonard J. Watson et al. LC 97-73243. (Illus.). 1997. write for info. (0-89462-112-2) IIA.

***Personal Insurance: Property & Liability.** 2nd ed. Karen L. Hamilton & Donald S. Malecki. LC 99-73139. 389p. (C). 1999. text 41.00 (0-89463-088-1, 202) Am Inst FCPCU.

Personal Insurance: Underwriting & Marketing Practices. Cheryl L. Ferguson. LC 96-76540. (C). 1996. ring bd. 57.00 (0-89462-101-7, 2802) IIA.

***Personal Insurance & Financial Planning.** Karen L. Hamilton. LC 99-73138. 432p. (C). 1999. text 41.00 (0-89463-087-3, 203) Am Inst FCPCU.

Personal Integrity. William Schuttle. Ed. by Erwin R. Steinberg. 1990. 12.50 (0-8446-2889-1) Peter Smith.

***Personal Intelligences: Promoting Social & Emotional Learning.** Launa Ellison. LC 00-8746. 2000. pap. write for info. (0-7619-7692-2) Corwin Pr.

Personal Inventory/Medical Alert Kit. 2nd rev. ed. George Berrang. i, 10p. 1997. ring bd. 29.95 (0-9663990-0-5) Ancora Pubns.

***Personal Investment Planning.** Carl Burlin. 560p. 1999. pap. 120.00 (0-85297-561-9, Pub. by Chartered Bank) St Mut.

Personal Investment Planning. Adrianne Johnson & Rachel Hirst. Ed. by Lesley Cook & Wendy Telfer. 1997. pap. 90.00 (0-85297-399-3, Pub. by Chartered Bank) St Mut.

***Personal Investment Planning.** 2nd ed. Ed. by Bob Souster. 560p. 1998. pap. 90.00 (0-85297-509-0, Pub. by Chartered Bank) St Mut.

Personal Investment Portfolios. Sarah E. Hutchinson & Stacey Sawyer. 1995. text 29.95 (0-07-413211-3, Irwn McGrw-H) McGrw-H Hghr Educ.

***Personal Isurance: Services & Management.** 2nd ed. Cheryl L. Ferguson & Leonard J. Watson. LC 99-73067. 1999. ring bd. 41.00 (0-89462-131-9) IIA.

Personal Job Power: Discover Your Own Power Style for Work Satisfaction & Success. Clay Carr & Valorie Beer. 224p. 1996. pap. 12.95 (1-56079-599-9) Petersons.

Personal Journal: Fifty Years at Motorola. rev. ed. Andy Affrunti, Sr. 147p. 1994. 10.00 (1-56946-004-3) Motorola Univ.

Personal Journal for Yesterday, Now, & Tomorrow: And Other Selected Poems. S. Gordden Link. 128p. 1992. 12.50 (0-9634744-0-5) B Souders.

Personal Journal on Marriage. 3rd ed. Lauer. 1996. pap. 14.69 (0-697-34016-3) McGraw.

Personal Journey & Prayer Journal. Dawn Vandenberg & Sue Bielinski. 1995. write for info. (0-9649378-1-6) Daysprng Shadowood.

Personal Journey Workbook Vol. 1: A Guide to an Extraordinary Life. Ron Koertge & Mary Rocamona. Ed. by Douglas Ery & Richard MacMirr. (Illus.). 85p. (Orig.). 1996. pap. 19.95 (0-9658989-0-3) Rocamora Sch.

Personal Justice Denied: Report of the Commission on Wartime Relocation & Internment of Civilians. Ed. by Tetsuden Kashima. LC 96-13689. 480p. (C). 1996. reprint ed. pap. 18.95 (0-295-97558-X) U of Wash Pr.

Personal Knowledge: Towards a Post-Critical Philosophy. Michael Polanyi. LC 58-5162. xiv, 442p. 1974. reprint ed. pap. text 17.00 (0-226-67288-3, P583) U Ch Pr.

Personal Lace: A Collection of Bobbin Lace Patterns. Trenna E. Ruffner. 32p. 1993. student ed. 10.00 (0-9636953-0-4) Alembic Arts.

Personal Landscapes. Jonathan Bolton. LC 97-12380. 244p. 1997. text 39.95 (0-312-17350-4) St Martin.

Personal Law Answer Book: Special Supplement, Forms & Checklists. James O. Castagnera & Kristine G. Derewicz. Ed. by Mark D. Persons. 350p. 1991. pap. 49.00 (1-878375-66-0) Panel Pubs.

Personal Law Handbook. Miller. LC 94-156023. Date not set. pap. text 9.00 (0-314-03031-X) West Pub.

Personal Leadership in Marketing. Edwin J. Gross. 189p. 1968. pap. 4.50 (0-912598-04-2) Florham.

Personal Leather Goods in Italy: A Strategic Entry Report, 1997. Compiled by Icon Group International Staff. (Illus.). 123p. 1999. ring bd. 1230.00 incl. audio compact disk (0-7418-1046-8) Icon Grp.

Personal Legacy Statement: Determining How You Will Be Remembered. Gary R. Blair. 40p. 1998. pap. 19.95 (1-889770-51-5, PLS) GoalsGuy.

Personal Letters for Business People. Isabel L. Bosticco. 290p. 1986. text 61.95 (0-566-02593-0) Ashgate Pub Co.

Personal Letters for Living. Booher. (C). 1997. text 34.95 (0-13-264078-3); pap. text 15.95 (0-13-264060-0) P-H.

Personal Letters That Mean Business. Linda B. Sturgeon. (C). 1991. pap. text 15.95 (0-13-656299-X) P-H.

Personal Liability & Disqualification of Company Directors. Stephen Griffin. 270p. 1999. 72.00 (1-84113-075-3, Pub. by Hart Pub) Intl Spec Bk.

Personal Liability for Environmental Violations: Avoiding & Defending Civil Suits & Criminal Prosecutions. Jacob Friedlander. 400p. 1991. pap. text 17.50 (0-685-54381-1, H4-5104) PLI.

***Personal Liability in Public Service Organisations: A Legal Research Study for the Committee on Standards in Public Life.** Elizabeth Hambley & Great Britain. Committee on Standards in Public Life. LC 98-171479. 1998. write for info. (0-11-430150-6) Statnry Office.

Personal Liability of Managers & Supervisors for Employment Discrimination. 2nd ed. Robert E. Williams. LC 86-62798. (Monograph Ser.). 1986. pap. 9.95 (0-916559-05-X) EPF.

Personal Liability of Public Officials under Federal Law. 4th ed. Paul T. Hardy & J. Devereux Weeks. 1988. pap. 5.95 (0-89854-132-8) U of GA Inst Govt.

Personal Liberty & Community Safety: Pretrial Release in the Criminal Court. J. S. Goldkamp et al. LC 95-15677. (Plenum Series in Crime & Justice). (Illus.). 366p. (C). 1995. 49.50 (0-306-44879-3, Kluwer Plenum) Kluwer Academic.

Personal Liberty under Indian Constitution. S. N. Sharma. (C). 1991. 21.00 (81-7100-304-4, Pub. by Deep & Deep Pubns) S Asia.

Personal Life History. Randall K. Mehew. (Personal Enrichment Ser.). 32p. (Orig.). 1991. pap. write for info. (0-929985-73-7) Jackman Pubng.

Personal Life of David Livingstone. William G. Blaikie. LC 69-19353. (Illus.). 508p. 1969. lib. bdg. 35.00 (0-8371-0518-8, BLL&, Greenwood Pr) Greenwood.

Personal Life of the Psychotherapist. James D. Guy. LC 87-8254. (Personality Processes Ser.). 352p. 1987. 69.95 (0-471-84854-9) Wiley.

Personal Lunation Charts. Helen Paul-Wolf. LC 83-71152. 88p. 1984. 11.00 (0-86690-243-0, W2299-014) Am Fed Astrologers.

Personal Magnetism. 80p. 1996. reprint ed. pap. 12.95 (1-56459-682-6) Kessinger Pub.

Personal Magnetism: Discover Your Own Charisma & Learn to Charm, Inspire, & Influence Others. Andrew J. DuBrin. LC 97-11795. 208p. 1997. pap. 17.95 (0-8144-7936-7) AMACOM.

Personal Maintenance Plan: Your 3000-Mile Performance Checkup. Gary R. Blair. 40p. 1998. pap. 19.95 (1-889770-60-4, PMP) GoalsGuy.

Personal Management. Boy Scouts of America. (Illus.). 80p. (YA). (gr. 6-12). 1996. pap. 2.90 (0-8395-5002-2, 35002) BSA.

Personal Management Skills. Stephen W. Mayson. 112p. (C). 1992. 31.00 (1-85431-166-2, Pub. by Blackstone Pr) Gaunt.

Personal Marketing & Quality Resumes. Ed Bagley. LC 97-91974. 184p. (Orig.). 1997. pap. 18.52 (0-9658094-1-2) NW Mktg.

Personal Matter. Kenzaburo Oe. Tr. by John Nathan from JPN. LC 68-22007. 176p. 1970. pap. 10.00 (0-8021-5061-6, Grove) Grove-Atltic.

Personal Meanings: The First Guy's Hospital Symposium on the Individual Frame of Reference. Guy's Hospital Symposium on the Individual Frame o. Ed. by Eric Shepherd & J. P. Watson. LC 82-1986. 210p. pap. 65.10 (0-8357-3092-1, 203934900012) Bks Demand.

Personal Meanings of Death. Ed. by Franz R. Epting & Robert A. Neimeyer. LC 83-8529. (Death Education, Aging & Health Care Ser.). (Illus.). 246p. 1984. text 59.95 (0-89116-363-8) Hemisp Pub.

Personal Medical Information Security, Engineering, & Ethics: Proceedings, Personal Information Workshop, Cambridge, U. K., June 21-22, 1996. Isaac Newton Institute for Mathematical Sciences S et al. Ed. by Ross Anderson. LC 97-27559. x, 251p. pap. write for info. (3-540-63244-1) Spr-Verlag.

Personal Medical Records: A Reference & History Handbook. Beth B. O'Neill. (Illus.). 90p. 1996. wbk. ed. 15.00 (0-9652930-0-9) Sr Assist Essent.

Personal Medical Savings Accounts (Medical IRA's) An Idea Whose Time Has Come. John C. Goodman & Gerald L. Musgrave. 35p. 1993. pap. 5.00 (1-56808-011-5, BG128) Natl Ctr Pol.

Personal Meditations. unabridged ed. Richard F. O'Connor. 1990. pap. 16.95 incl. audio (1-55927-082-9) Audio Renaissance.

Personal Memoirs. Ulysses S. Grant. Ed. by Caleb Carr. LC 98-35757. (Modern Library War Ser.). 1999. pap. 15.95 (0-375-75228-5) Modern Lib NY.

Personal Memoirs, 2 vols. in 1. Ulysses S. Grant. reprint ed. 67.50 (0-404-04599-5) AMS Pr.

Personal Memoirs & Recollections of Editorial Life. Joseph T. Buckingham. LC 76-125682. (American Journalists Ser.). 1971. reprint ed. 26.95 (0-405-01657-3) Ayer.

Personal Memoirs & Recollections of Editorial Life, 2 vols., Vols. 1 - 2. Joseph T. Buckingham. (American Biography Ser.). 1991. reprint ed. lib. bdg. 148.00 (0-7812-8051-6) Rprt Serv.

Personal Memoirs of a Residence of 30 Years with the Indian Tribes on the American Frontiers, 1812-1842. Henry R. Schoolcraft. LC 75-119. (Mid-American Frontier Ser.). 1975. reprint ed. 59.95 (0-405-06885-9) Ayer.

Personal Memoirs of a Residence of Thirty Years with the Indian Tribes on the American Frontiers: With Brief Notices of Passing Events, Facts & Opinions, A.D. 1812 to A.D. 1842. Henry R. Schoolcraft. LC 74-9021. reprint ed. 37.50 (0-404-11899-2) AMS Pr.

Personal Memoirs of John H. Brinton, Major & Surgeon U. S. V., 1861-1865. John H. Brinton. LC 95-49078. (Shawnee Classics Ser.). (Illus.). 384p. (C). 1996. reprint ed. pap. 14.95 (0-8093-2044-4) S Ill U Pr.

Personal Memoirs of Jonathan Thomas Scharf of the First Maryland Artillery. Ed. by Tom Kelley. (Illus.). 81p. (C). 1993. 20.00 (0-935523-30-8) Butternut & Blue.

Personal Memoirs of Julia Dent Grant (Mrs. Ulysses S. Grant) Julia D. Grant. Ed. by John Y. Simon. LC 87-20708. (Illus.). 352p. 1988. reprint ed. lib. bdg. 15.95 (0-8093-1443-6) S Ill U Pr.

Personal Memoirs of Major General David Sloan Stanley. David S. Stanley. 271p. 1988. reprint ed. 25.00 (0-942211-57-X) Olde Soldier Bks.

Personal Memoirs of P. H. Sheridan. Philip H. Sheridan. (Quality Paperbacks Ser.). (Illus.). 416p. 1992. reprint ed. pap. 15.95 (0-306-80487-5) Da Capo.

Personal Memoirs of P. H. Sheridan, 2 vols. Philip H. Sheridan. (Illus.). 1993. reprint ed. 75.00 (1-56837-048-2) Broadfoot.

Personal Memoirs of U. S. Grant. (Illus.). 648p. 1989. 18.95 (0-8306-4011-8) McGraw-Hill Prof.

Personal Memoirs of U. S. Grant. Ulysses S. Grant. (Illus.). 512p. 1995. pap. text 11.95 (0-486-28587-1) Dover.

Personal Memoirs of U. S. Grant, 2 vols. in 1. Ulysses S. Grant. LC 95-47120. (Illus.). xvi, 665p. 1996. pap. 26.00 (0-8032-7060-7, Bison Books) U of Nebr Pr.

Personal Memoirs of U. S. Grant. Ulysses S. Grant & James M. McPherson. LC 98-30532. (Penguin Classics Ser.). 320p. 1999. pap. 14.95 (0-14-043701-0) Viking Penguin.

Personal Memoirs of U. S. Grant, 2 vols. Ulysses S. Grant. 1990. reprint ed. lib. bdg. 150.00 (0-89966-736-8) Buccaneer Bks.

Personal Memoirs of U. S. Grant. Ulysses S. Grant & E. B. Long. (Quality Paperbacks Ser.). 608p. 1982. reprint ed. pap. 15.95 (0-306-80172-8) Da Capo.

Personal Memories: Social, Political, & Literary. Edward D. Mansfield. LC 72-133527. (Select Bibliographies Reprint Ser.). 1977. reprint ed. 23.95 (0-8369-5559-5) Ayer.

***Personal Memories in Poetry.** Sophia Thompkins. 1999. pap. write for info. (1-58235-250-X) Watermrk Pr.

Personal Memories of P. H. Sheridan, General, 2 vols. Philip H. Sheridan. LC 72-78831. 1902. reprint ed. 95.00 (0-403-02023-9) Somerset Pub.

Personal Memories of the Spanish Civil War: Luis Puig Casas. Luis Puig Casas. Ed. by Idoya Puig. LC 99-23079. (Spanish Studies: Vol. 5). (CAT & ENG.). 280p. 1999. text 89.95 (0-7734-7996-1) E Mellen.

Personal Memories, Social, Political & Literary. Edward D. Mansfield. LC 74-125707. (American Journalists Ser.). 1971. reprint ed. 35.95 (0-405-01688-3) Ayer.

Personal Memories, Social, Political & Literary, with Sketches of Many Noted People. Edward D. Mansfield. (American Biography Ser.). 348p. 1991. reprint ed. lib. bdg. 79.00 (0-7812-8264-0) Rprt Serv.

Personal Mission Statement: Defining Your Life's Purpose. Gary R. Blair. 40p. 1998. pap. 19.95 (1-889770-52-3, PMS) GoalsGuy.

Personal Money Management. Da Knowledge Transfer Staff. LC 99-67835. pap. 9.95 (1-885003-34-X, Pub. by R D Reed Pubs) Midpt Trade.

P

An Asterisk (*) at the beginning of an entry indicates that the title is appearing for the first time.

Personal Motivation: A Model for Decision Making. Robert P. Cavalier. LC 99-34426. 176p. 2000. 55.00 (*0-275-96168-0*) Greenwood.

Personal Myth in Psychoanalytic Theory. Ed. by Peter Hartocollis & Ian Graham. 420p. 1992. 75.00 (*0-8236-4065-5*) Intl Univs Pr.

Personal Name Asteroids. Non Gwynn Press Staff. 16p. 1990. pap. 4.00 (*0-917086-93-7*) ACS Pubns.

Personal Name Index to "New Directions", Vols. 1-35. Shelley Cox. LC 37-1751. vi, 167p. 1980. 42.00 (*0-87875-180-7*) Whitston Pub.

Personal Name Index to the Augusta Chronicle (Augusta, Georgia), 4 vols. Compiled by Alice O. Walker. 1993. write for info. (*0-941877-00-0*) Augusta-Richmond Cnty.

Personal Name Index to the Augusta Chronicle (Augusta, Georgia), Vol. I, 1786-1799. Compiled by Alice O. Walker. LC 87-1167. 488p. 1987. lib. bdg. 27.50 (*0-941877-01-9*) Augusta-Richmond Cnty.

Personal Name Index to the Augusta Chronicle (Augusta, Georgia), Vol. II, 1800-1810. Compiled by Alice O. Walker. LC 87-1167. 542p. 1988. lib. bdg. 27.50 (*0-941877-02-7*) Augusta-Richmond Cnty.

Personal Name Index to the Augusta Chronicle (Augusta, Georgia), Vol. III, 1811-1820. Compiled by Alice O. Walker. LC 87-1167. 814p. 1991. lib. bdg. 27.50 (*0-941877-03-5*) Augusta-Richmond Cnty.

Personal Name Index to the Augusta Chronicle (Augusta, Georgia), Vol. IV, 1821-1830. Compiled by Alice O. Walker. LC 87-1167. 872p. 1993. lib. bdg. 27.50 (*0-941877-04-3*) Augusta-Richmond Cnty.

Personal Name Index to the New York Times Index, 1851-1974, 22 vols., Vols. 1-22. Byron A. Falk & Valerie R. Falk. Incl. Vol. 1. LC 76-12217. 351p. 1976. lib. bdg. 28.00 (*0-89902-101-8*); Vol. 2. LC 76-12217. 602p. 1977. lib. bdg. 45.00 (*0-89902-102-6*); Vol. 3. LC 76-12217. 569p. 1977. lib. bdg. 43.50 (*0-89902-103-4*); Vol. 4. LC 76-12217. 494p. 1977. lib. bdg. 39.00 (*0-89902-104-2*); Vol. 5. LC 76-12217. 436p. 1977. lib. bdg. 36.50 (*0-89902-105-0*); Vol. 6. LC 76-12217. 639p. 1978. lib. bdg. 51.00 (*0-89902-106-9*); Vol. 7. LC 76-12217. 769p. 1978. lib. bdg. 60.00 (*0-89902-107-7*); Vol. 8. LC 76-12217. 674p. 1978. lib. bdg. 55.50 (*0-89902-108-5*); Vol. 9. LC 76-12217. 455p. 1978. lib. bdg. 42.00 (*0-89902-109-3*); Vol. 10. LC 76-12217. 492p. 1979. lib. bdg. 45.00 (*0-89902-110-7*); Vol. 11. LC 76-12217. 838p. 1979. lib. bdg. 73.25 (*0-89902-111-5*); Vol. 12. LC 76-12217. 648p. 1979. lib. bdg. 58.00 (*0-89902-112-3*); Vol. 13. LC 76-12217. 600p. 1980. lib. bdg. 54.50 (*0-89902-113-1*); Vol. 14. LC 76-12217. 600p. 1980. lib. bdg. 54.50 (*0-89902-114-X*); Vol. 15. LC 76-12217. 417p. 1980. lib. bdg. 40.25 (*0-89902-115-8*); Vol. 16. LC 76-12217. 624p. 1980. lib. bdg. 60.50 (*0-89902-116-6*); Vol. 17. LC 76-12217. 659p. 1981. lib. bdg. 64.00 (*0-89902-117-4*); Vol. 18. LC 76-12217. 600p. 1981. lib. bdg. 64.00 (*0-89902-118-2*); Vol. 20. LC 76-12217. 669p. 1982. lib. bdg. 65.00 (*0-89902-120-4*); Vol. 21. LC 76-12217. 421p. 1982. lib. bdg. 61.00 (*0-89902-121-2*); Vol. 22. LC 76-12217. 446p. 1983. lib. bdg. 62.00 (*0-89902-122-0*); 19. 636p. 1981. lib. bdg. 64.00 (*0-89902-119-0*); LC 76-12217. Set lib. bdg. 1025.00 (*0-89902-100-X*) Roxbury Data.

Personal Name Index to the New York Times Index, 1975-1993, 6 vols. Incl. Vol. 1, 1975-1993 A-Ch. Personal Index to the New York Times Index, 1975-1993 Supplement. Byron A. Falk & Valerie R. Falk. LC 76-12217. 567p. 1995. lib. bdg. 86.75 (*0-89902-135-2*); Vol. 2, 1975-1993 Ci-Gik. Personal Index to the New York Times Index, 1975-1993 Supplement. Byron A. Falk & Valerie R. Falk. LC 76-12217. 566p. 1995. lib. bdg. 86.75 (*0-89902-136-0*); Vol. 3, 1975-1993 Gil-Kor. Personal Name Index to the New York Times Index, 1975-1993 Supplement. Byron A. Falk & Valerie R. Falk. 566p. 1995. lib. bdg. 86.75 (*0-89902-137-9*); Vol. 4, 1975-1993 Kos-N. Personal Name Index to the New York Times Index, 1975-1993 Supplement. Byron A. Falk, Jr. & Valerie R. Falk. 581p. 1995. lib. bdg. 86.75 (*0-89902-138-7*); Vol. 5. Personal Name Index to the New York Times Index, 1975-1993. 567p. 1996. lib. bdg., suppl. ed. 86.75 (*0-89902-139-5*); Vol. 6. Personal Name Index to the New York Times Index, 1975-1993. Byron A. Falk & Valerie R. Falk. 567p. 1996. lib. bdg., suppl. ed. 86.75 (*0-89902-140-9*); 520.50 (*0-89902-093-3*) Roxbury Data.

Personal Name Index to the New York Times Index, 1975-1993 see Personal Name Index to the New York Times Index, 1975-1993

Personal Name Index to the New York Times Index, 1975-1993 Supplement see Personal Name Index to the New York Times Index, 1975-1993

Personal Name Index to the New York Times Index, 1975-1996, Vol. 3. Byron A. Falk & Valerie R. Falk. LC 76-12217. 600p. 1998. lib. bdg. 87.90 (*0-89902-143-3*) Roxbury Data.

Personal Name Index to the New York Times Index, 1975-1996 Supplement, No. 1. Byron A. Falk & Valerie R. Falk. LC 76-12217. 570p. 1998. lib. bdg. 87.90 (*0-89902-141-7*) Roxbury Data.

Personal Name Index to the New York Times Index, 1975-1996 Supplement, Vol. 2. Byron A. Falk & Valerie R. Falk. LC 76-12217. 600p. 1998. lib. bdg., suppl. ed. 87.90 (*0-89902-142-5*) Roxbury Data.

Personal Name Index to the New York Times Index, 1975-1996 Supplement, Vol. 4. Byron A. Falk & Valerie R. Falk. 600p. 1998. lib. bdg., suppl. ed. 87.90 (*0-89902-144-1*) Roxbury Data.

Personal Name Index to the New York Times Index, 1975-1996 Supplement, Vol. 5. Byron A. Falk & Valerie R. Falk. 602p. 1999. lib. bdg., suppl. ed. 87.90 (*0-89902-145-X*) Roxbury Data.

Personal Name Index to the New York Times Index, 1975-1996 Supplement, Vol. 6. Byron A. Falk & Valerie R. Falk. 596p. 1999. lib. bdg., suppl. ed. 87.90 (*0-89902-146-8*) Roxbury Data.

Personal Name Index to the New York Times Index, 1975-1996 Supplement, Vol. 7. Byron A. Falk & Valerie R. Falk. 598p. 1999. lib. bdg., suppl. ed. 87.90 (*0-89902-147-6*) Roxbury Data.

Personal Name Index to the New York Times Index, 1975-1996 Supplement, Vols. 1-7. Byron A. Falk & Valerie R. Falk. 1999. lib. bdg., suppl. ed. 615.80 (*0-89902-096-8*) Roxbury Data.

Personal Names & Naming: An Annotated Bibliography, 3. Compiled by Edwin D. Lawson. LC 86-31789. (Bibliographies & Indexes in Anthropology Ser.: No. 3). 198p. 1987. lib. bdg. 59.95 (*0-313-23817-0*, LNN/, Greenwood Pr) Greenwood.

Personal Names from Cuneiform Inscriptions of Cappadocia. Ferris J. Stephens. LC 78-63557. (Yale Oriental Series: Researches: No. 13, Pt. 1). 1979. reprint ed. 24.00 (*0-404-60283-5*) AMS Pr.

Personal Names from Cuneiform Inscriptions of the Cassite Period. Albert T. Clay. LC 78-63543. (Yale Oriental Series: Researches: No. I). reprint ed. 37.50 (*0-404-60271-1*) AMS Pr.

Personal Names in Hening's Statutes at Large of Virginia & Shepherd's Continuation. Joseph J. Casey. 159p. 1995. reprint ed. pap. 17.50 (*0-8063-0068-X*, 910) Clearfield Co.

***Personal Names of the Latin Inscriptions in Bulgaria, 118.** Milena Minkova. 346p. 2000. 52.95 (*3-631-35141-0*, Pub. by P Lang) P Lang Pubng.

***Personal Names of the Latin Inscriptions in Bulgaria, 118.** Milena Minkova. (Studien zur Klassischen Philologie: Vol. 118). x, 345p. 2000. pap. 52.95 (*0-8204-4361-1*) P Lang Pubng.

Personal Narrative: A Journey to the Equinoctial Regions of the New Continent. Alexander Von Humboldt & Malcolm Nicolson. Tr. by James Wilson. LC 96-150402. 1996. pap. 12.95 (*0-14-044553-6*) Viking Penguin.

Personal Narrative: Writing Ourselves As Teachers & Scholars. Ed. by Gil Haroian-Guerin. LC 98-49086. 246p. 1999. pap. text 25.00 (*0-9663233-9-4*, 323394) Calendar Islands.

Personal Narrative of a Pilgrimage to Al-Madinah & Meccah, Vol. 1. Richard F. Burton. (Illus.). 1964. pap. 11.95 (*0-486-21217-3*) Dover.

Personal Narrative of a Pilgrimage to Al-Madinah & Meccah, Vol. 2. Richard F. Burton. (Illus.). 1964. pap. 10.95 (*0-486-21218-1*) Dover.

Personal Narrative of James O. Pattie. James O. Pattie. Ed. by Richard Batman. LC 88-5221. 216p. 1988. pap. 14.00 (*0-87842-205-6*) Scurlock Pub.

Personal Narrative of James O. Pattie. James O. Pattie. (American Biography Ser.). 300p. 1991. reprint ed. lib. bdg. 69.00 (*0-7812-8308-6*) Rprt Serv.

Personal Narrative of James O. Pattie of Kentucky. James O. Pattie. Ed. by Timothy Flint. LC 72-9464. (Far Western Frontier Ser.). (Illus.). 314p. 1973. reprint ed. 23.95 (*0-405-04992-7*) Ayer.

Personal Narrative of James O. Pattie, 1831. unabridged ed. James O. Pattie. LC 83-27406. 285p. reprint ed. pap. 88.40 (*0-7837-6011-6*, 204582200008) Bks Demand.

Personal Narrative of Travels to the Equinoctial Regions of America During the Years 1799-1804. Alexander Von Humboldt. 1972. 23.95 (*0-405-18963-X*) Ayer.

Personal Narrative of Travels to the Equinoctial Regions of America During the Years 1799-1804. Alexander Von Humboldt. 1972. 24.95 (*0-405-18109-4*); 24.95 (*0-405-18110-8*) Ayer.

Personal Narrative of Travels to the Equinoctial Regions of America During the Years 1799-1804, 3 vols. Alexander Von Humboldt. Tr. by Thomasina Ross. LC 69-13241. 1468p. 1972. reprint ed. 69.95 (*0-405-08642-3*, Pub. by Blom Pubns) Ayer.

Personal Narrative of Travels to the Equinoctial Regions of America During the Years 1799-1804, 7 vols. in 6 pts. Alexander Von Humboldt & Aime Bonpland. Tr. by Helen M. Williams from FRE. LC 01-20782. (Illus.). reprint ed. 525.00 (*0-404-03440-3*) AMS Pr.

Personal Narratives: Women Photographers of Color. Farah J. Griffin & Fatimah T. Rony. Ed. by Nancy H. Margolis. (Illus.). 16p. 1993. 8.00 (*0-9611560-1-5*) SEC Contemp Art.

Personal Narratives, Multiple Voices: The Worlds of a Swahili Peasant. Patricia Caplan. LC 96-25693. (Illus.). 288p. (C). 1997. 80.00 (*0-415-13723-3*); pap. 24.99 (*0-415-13724-1*) Routledge.

Personal Nature of Notions of Consciousness: A Theoretical & Empirical Examination of the Role of the Personal in the Understanding of Consciousness. Imants Baruss. 228p. (C). 1990. lib. bdg. 42.00 (*0-8191-7707-5*) U Pr of Amer.

Personal Navigation Systems. Contrib. by Thomas Rush. 139p. 1996. 2850.00 (*1-56965-075-6*, G-182) BCC.

Personal Networks: A Rational Choice Theoretic Explanation of Their Size & Composition. M. G. Van Der Poel. x, 210p. 1993. pap. 56.00 (*90-265-1366-6*) Swets.

Personal Note Commitment Workbook. Tom Gossen & Lonnie Schreiber. 52p. 1996. pap., wbk. ed. 9.95 (*0-8192-1680-1*) Morehouse Pub.

Personal Nutrition. 2nd ed. Marie Boyle & Gail Zyla. Ed. by Marshall. 390p. (C). 1992. pap. 45.25 (*0-314-93333-6*) West Pub.

Personal Nutrition. 2nd rev. ed. Boyle. 1994. pap. write for info. (*0-314-04960-6*) West Pub.

Personal Nutrition. 3rd ed. Marie A. Boyle & Gail Zyla. LC 95-45675. 450p. (C). 1996. 60.95 (*0-314-06380-3*) West Pub.

Personal Nutrition. 4th ed. Boyle. (Health Sciences). 2000. pap. 43.75 (*0-534-54603-X*) Wadsworth Pub.

Personal Nutrition Planner. Lisa Hoelscher. (Illus.). 260p. 1995. ring bd. 29.95 (*0-9650352-0-4*) Excell in Hlth.

***Personal Odyssey.** Thomas Sowell. (Illus.). 320p. 2000. 24.50 (*0-684-86464-9*) Free Pr.

Personal Options for Organizational Change: Surviving or Thriving Change Is Inevitable, Growth Is Optional, Stress Is a Choice. Don Boone & Donna Martin. 64p. 1996. pap. 9.95 (*1-56664-096-2*) WorldComm.

Personal Organizers. 39.99 (*1-57040-014-8*) Seiko Instr USA.

Personal Organizers: Antiques & Collectibles. (Illus.). 50p. 1997. spiral bd. write for info. (*1-889588-04-0*); ring bd. write for info. (*1-889588-05-9*) Til the Cows.

Personal Organizers: Doll Organizer. 50p. 1997. spiral bd. write for info. (*1-889588-02-4*); ring bd. write for info. (*1-889588-03-2*) Til the Cows.

Personal Organizers: General Inventory Organizer. (Illus.). 50p. 1997. spiral bd. write for info. (*1-889588-06-7*); ring bd. write for info. (*1-889588-07-5*) Til the Cows.

Personal Organizers: Home & Office Finance Organizer. (Illus.). 50p. 1997. spiral bd. write for info. (*1-889588-08-3*); ring bd. write for info. (*1-889588-09-1*) Til the Cows.

Personal Organizers: Steins & Collectibles. (Illus.). 50p. 1997. spiral bd. write for info. (*1-889588-00-8*); ring bd. write for info. (*1-889588-01-6*) Til the Cows.

Personal Orientation Manual for the NHA. Steven V. Benson. 175p. (Orig.). (C). 1991. pap. text 32.00 (*1-877735-30-2*, 2175PP) Prof Prnting & Pub.

Personal Partnerships: A Marriage Alternative. Dee West. LC 93-78741. 88p. (Orig.). 1993. pap. 9.95 (*0-9637208-6-4*) Lookng Glass.

Personal Pathway to God: Our Song of Freedom. L. David Moore. (Illus.). 288p. (Orig.). 1995. pap. 13.95 (*0-9635665-3-9*) Pendulum Plus.

Personal Patterns by Jinni: A Manual for Flat Pattern Design, Vol. 2. Virginia M. Nastiuk. (Illus.). 347p. 1988. lib. bdg. 39.95 (*0-942003-07-1*) Personal Pattern.

Personal Patterns by Jinni: A Manual for Perfect Patternmaking, 2 vols., Vol. 1. Virginia M. Nastiuk. (Illus.). 281p. 1987. reprint ed. lib. bdg. 36.95 (*0-942003-01-2*) Personal Pattern.

Personal Patterns by Jinni: Fitting Problems & Their Corrections. Virginia M. Nastiuk. (Illus.). 101p. 1987. pap. 14.95 (*0-942003-15-2*); lib. bdg. 14.95 (*0-942003-16-0*) Personal Pattern.

Personal Patterns by Jinni: Introduction to Design. Virginia M. Nastiuk. (Illus.). 110p. 1987. pap. 7.90 (*0-942003-20-9*) Personal Pattern.

Personal Patterns by Jinni: Pants - Fit & Design. Virginia M. Nastiuk. (Illus.). 100p. 1987. pap. 14.95 (*0-942003-25-X*); lib. bdg. 14.95 (*0-942003-27-6*) Personal Pattern.

Personal Patterns by Jinni: Skirts - Fit & Design. Virginia M. Nastiuk. (Illus.). 110p. 1987. pap. 7.90 (*0-942003-30-6*) Personal Pattern.

Personal Peace: Macrobiotic Reflections on Mental & Emotional Recovery. David Briscoe & Charlotte Mahoney-Briscoe. 212p. 1989. 18.95 (*0-87040-698-1*) Japan Pubns USA.

Personal Peace: Transcending Your Interpersonal Limits. Robert L. McKinley. 136p. 1993. pap. 11.95 (*0-934986-57-6*) New Harbinger.

Personal Performance Contracts: Setting Realistic Goals. rev. ed. Roger Fritz. Ed. by Michael Crisp. LC 92-73961. (Fifty-Minute Ser.). 85p. 1993. reprint ed. pap. 10.95 (*1-56052-197-X*) Crisp Pubns.

Personal Perspectives. 2nd ed. Beatrice Paolucci et al. (Illus.). (gr. 9-12). 1978. text 32.80 (*0-07-048438-4*) McGraw.

Personal Perspectives: A Guide to Decision Making. Beatrice Paolucci et al. LC 72-8842. 466 p. 1973. write for info. (*0-07-048437-6*) McGraw.

Personal Perspectives on Emotional Disturbance - Behavioral Disorders. Ed. by Benjamin L. Brooks & David A. Sabatino. LC 94-45064. 495p. (Orig.). (C). 1996. pap. text 38.00 (*0-89079-618-1*, 6929) PRO-ED.

Personal Places: Perspectives on Informal Art Environments. Ed. by Daniel F. Ward. LC 84-70520. 177p. 1984. 22.95 (*0-87972-296-7*) Bowling Green Univ Popular Press.

Personal Planner & Training Guide for the Paraprofessional. Wendy Dover. 75p. 1996. 19.95 (*0-914607-39-1*) Master Tchr.

Personal Planning Manual. Alfred A. Montapert. LC 67-12652. 1967. 14.00 (*0-9603174-1-4*, 85920) Bks of Value.

Personal Planning Manual. Alfred A. Montapert. 1977. pap. 6.95 (*0-87505-364-5*) Borden.

Personal Pleasures. Rose Macaulay. LC 79-152193. (Essay Index Reprint Ser.). 1977. 23.95 (*0-8369-2195-X*) Ayer.

Personal Policies. Michael Bratman. (Working Papers on Risk & Rationality). 1988. 2.50 (*0-318-33324-4*, RR8) IPPP.

Personal Political Power: How Ordinary People Can Get What They Want from Government. Joel Blackwell. 160p. 1998. pap. 19.95 (*0-9669236-0-X*, 1487) Issue Mgmt.

Personal Politics: The Roots of Women's Liberation in the Civil Rights Movement & the New Left. Sara M. Evans. LC 79-22485. 1980. pap. 9.56 (*0-394-74228-1*) Vin Bks.

***Personal Portfolio Management: Fundamentals & Strategies.** George W. Trivoli. LC 99-26648. (Illus.). 151p. 1999. pap. 21.00 (*0-13-020495-1*) P-H.

Personal Possession. large type ed. Jeanne Hart. 248p. 1990. 20.95 (*0-7451-1171-8*, G K Hall Lrg Type) Mac Lib Ref.

Personal Power: An Unorthodox Guide to Success. R. Karp. 1994. pap. 21.95 (*0-89876-226-X*) Gardner Pr.

Personal Power: Sacred Energies of Mind, Body & Spirit. Anna Franklin. (Illus.). 1998. pap. 22.95 (*1-86163-030-1*, Pub. by Capall Bann Pubng) Holmes Pub.

Personal Power: The Guide to Power for Today's Working Woman. 181p. 1983. 15.95 (*0-943066-03-4*) CareerTrack Pubns.

Personal Power - Responding to Challenges. Denise Bissonnette. Ed. by John Lamendella & Anita Lee Wright. (Cultivating True Livelihood Ser.: Course 3). (Illus.). 145p. 1997. teacher ed., student ed., ring bd. 200.00 (*0-942071-43-3*, 273M) M Wright & Assocs.

Personal Power Through Awareness: A Guidebook for Sensitive People. Sanaya Roman. Ed. by Elaine Ratner. (Earth Life Ser.: Bk. II). 216p. 1986. pap. 12.95 (*0-915811-04-9*) H J Kramer Inc.

Personal Prayer. Perpetual. 1998. pap. 9.99 (*0-8423-8815-X*) Tyndale Hse.

Personal Prayer Diary - Burgundy (1999) Daily Planner. Ed. by James P. Shaw. (Illus.). 206p. 1998. 16.99 (*1-57658-021-0*) YWAM Pub.

Personal Prayer Diary - Rose (1999) Daily Planner. Ed. by James P. Shaw. (Illus.). 206p. 1998. 16.99 (*1-57658-023-7*) YWAM Pub.

Personal Prayer Diary Blue (1999) Daily Planner. Ed. by James P. Shaw. (Illus.). 206p. 1998. 16.99 (*1-57658-020-2*) YWAM Pub.

Personal Prayer Diary Green (1999) Daily Planner. Ed. by James P. Shaw. (Illus.). 206p. 1998. 16.99 (*1-57658-022-9*) YWAM Pub.

Personal Prayer Diary, 1999: Daily Planner. Ed. by James P. Shaw. (Illus.). 206p. 1998. 16.99 (*1-57658-024-5*) YWAM Pub.

Personal Prayer Evangelism Guide. Terry Teyk. (Illus.). 47p. (Orig.). 4.00 (*1-57892-001-9*) Prayer Pt Pr.

Personal Prayer Journal. Terry Teykl. 73p. 1996. ring bd. 12.00 (*1-57892-004-3*) Prayer Pt Pr.

Personal Pregnancy Planner: The Expectant Mother's Personal Journal & Record Book. Lori L. Grundy. (Illus.). ix, 132p. 1995. 12.95 (*0-9652556-0-3*) K Hill.

Personal Prescriptions. John M. Drescher. 16p. 1969. pap. 2.99 (*0-8361-1596-1*) Herald Pr.

Personal President: Power Invested, Promise Unfulfilled. Theodore J. Lowi. LC 84-45804. 240p. 1985. pap. text 14.95 (*0-8014-9426-5*) Cornell U Pr.

Personal Principle: Studies in Modern Poetry. Derek S. Savage. 1972. 59.95 (*0-8490-0818-2*) Gordon Pr.

Personal Privacy Protection Guide: A Practical Guide to Protecting Your Privacy. E. Noon. LC 97-75677. (Illus.). 1998. pap. 6.95 (*0-9661641-0-5*) ONOne Inc.

Personal Privacy Through a New Identity, 2 vols. 1991. lib. bdg. 600.00 (*0-8490-4777-3*) Gordon Pr.

***Personal Privacy through Foreign Investing.** Trent Sands. 72p. 2000. pap. 8.00 (*1-893626-38-5*) Breakout Prods Inc.

Personal Problem Solving in the Classroom: The Reality Technique. Donald W. Morrison. LC 76-28419. 200p. reprint ed. pap. 62.00 (*0-608-10826-X*, 201584800097) Bks Demand.

Personal Productivity: How to Increase Your Satisfaction in Living. John W. Kendrick & John B. Kendrick. LC 87-28472. 208p. (gr. 13). 1988. text 68.95 (*0-87332-462-5*); pap. text 34.95 (*0-87332-463-3*) M E Sharpe.

Personal Productivity in Information Technology. Gordon B. Davis & David Naumann. LC 96-78928. (Illus.). 512p. (C). 1997. pap. 45.00 (*0-07-015916-5*) McGraw.

Personal Productivity Tools. Rebecca Courington. 334p. (C). 1994. text 37.40 (*0-536-58704-3*) Pearson Custom.

***Personal Productivity Tools: Introduction to Mac.** 2nd ed. 314p. (C). 2000. 35.80 (*0-536-60732-X*) Pearson Custom.

Personal Productivity with Lotus 1-2-3. Kenneth Gorham. 176p. (C). 1987. spiral bd. write for info. (*0-697-05227-3*) Bus & Educ Tech.

Personal Productivity with Lotus 1-2-3, Version 2.01. Kenneth Gorham. 400p. (C). 1990. spiral bd. write for info. (*0-697-11731-6*) Bus & Educ Tech.

Personal Productivity with Lotus 1-2-3, Version 2.01 Primer. 2nd ed. Kenneth Gorham. 256p. (C). 1990. spiral bd. write for info. (*0-697-07719-5*) Bus & Educ Tech.

Personal Professional Development & the Solo Librarian: Library Training Guide. Sue L. Bryant. 88p. 1995. pap. text 40.00 (*1-85604-141-7*, LAP1417, Pub. by Library Association) Bernan Associates.

***Personal Progress Through Positive Thinking.** Hilary Jones. 2000. pap. text 12.95 (*1-902809-20-3*) Allison & Busby.

Personal Promise Pocketbook see Promesas Personales de la Biblia

Personal Promise Pocketbook. LC 80-52398. (Pocketpac Bks.). 128p. 1980. mass mkt. 2.99 (*0-87788-673-3*, H Shaw Pubs) Waterbrook Pr.

Personal Promises from God's Word. LC 96-90384. 128p. (Orig.). 1996. pap. 4.99 (*0-529-10699-X*, GW21) World Publng.

Personal Promises of the Bible see Promesas Personales de la Biblia

Personal Pronouns in Present-Day English. Katie Wales. LC 95-35080. (Studies in English Language). 251p. (C). 1996. text 59.95 (*0-521-47102-8*) Cambridge U Pr.

Personal Pronouns in the Germanic Languages: A Study of Personal Pronoun Morphology & Change in the Germanic Languages from the First Records to the Present Day. Stephen Howe. LC 96-27271. (Studia Linguistica Germanica: Vol. 43). xxii, 390p. (C). 1996. lib. bdg. 146.70 (*3-11-014636-3*) De Gruyter.

Personal Property. 3rd ed. Fraser & Taintor. 1954. text 22.00 (*0-88277-384-4*) Foundation Pr.

Personal Property: Commentary & Materials. R. G. Hammond. 334p. 1990. 49.95 (*0-19-558217-9*) OUP.

Personal Property: Wives, White Slaves, & the Market in Women. Margit Stange. LC 97-29656. (Illus.). 188p. 1998. text 32.50 (*0-8018-5626-4*) Johns Hopkins.

P

An Asterisk (*) at the beginning of an entry indicates that the title is appearing for the first time.

Personal Property in a Nutshell. 2nd ed. Barlow Burke, Jr. LC 83-6519. (Nutshell Ser.). 399p. (C). 1993. pap. 21.00 (*0-314-01700-3*) West Pub.

Personal Property Insurance Fraud Checklists, 1991. Michael H. Boyer. LC 88-17496. 1991. spiral bd. 68.00 (*0-87632-772-2*) West Group.

Personal Property Inventory: Record All Your Stuff, 1. Della Sheffield. 29p. 1999. pap. 12.95 (*1-882330-53-6*, PPI536) Magni Co.

Personal Property Law. Michael Bridge. 182p. 1993. pap. 36.00 (*1-85431-254-5*, Pub. by Blackstone Pr) Gaunt.

Personal Property Law. 2nd ed. Michael Bridge. 170p. 1996. pap. 26.00 (*1-85431-581-1*, Pub. by Blackstone Pr) Gaunt.

***Personal Property Law: Text & Materials.** Sarah Worthington. 900p. 2000. 80.00 (*1-901362-43-4*, Pub. by Hart Pub); pap. 45.00 (*1-901362-44-2*, Pub. by Hart Pub) Intl Spec Bk.

Personal Property Security Act & Regulations. 112p. 1991. pap. 17.00 (*0-409-89951-8*, MICHIE) LEXIS Pub.

Personal Property Tax Records for 1856 of Northampton Co., VA. Doris R. Adler. 1996. 15.00 (*1-886706-14-X*) Hickory Hse.

Personal Property Taxation of Computer Software. 3rd ed. Ed. by Kutish Publications Staff. LC 95-76471. 250p. 1996. pap. text 135.00 (*1-880815-08-7*) Sftware Taxation.

Personal Protection. Neville Williams. (Safety Instruction Booklet Ser.). (Illus.). 20p. 1994. pap. 45.00 (*1-85573-175-4*, Pub. by Woodhead Pubng) Am Educ Systs.

Personal Protection: The Weapons & Self-Defense Laws of the United States. Doug Briggs. LC 93-71047. (Illus.). 640p. (Orig.). 1993. 19.95 (*1-881287-02-5*) Beverly Bk.

Personal Protection Equipment Program. Mark M. Moran. (OSHA Written Compliance Programs Ser.: No. 21). (Illus.). 60p. 1992. ring bd. 169.00 (*1-890966-15-0*) Moran Assocs.

Personal Protection Safety Product Markets. Market Intelligence Staff. 170p. 1994. 1650.00 (*0-7889-0031-5*); 1650.00 (*0-7889-0032-3*) Frost & Sullivan.

Personal Protective Equipment. Graham Roberts-Phelps. (Gower Health & Safety Workbook Ser.). 80p. 1998. pap., wbk. ed. 29.95 (*0-566-08061-3*, Pub. by Gower) Ashgate Pub Co.

Personal Protective Equipment: Implementing a Protection Program for OSHA Compliance. Theodore J. Hogan. 240p. 1998. pap. 49.00 (*0-8342-1049-5*, 21049) Aspen Pub.

Personal Psalm Journal. Joan Metzner. LC 97-60533. 120p. 1998. pap. 9.95 (*0-89622-733-2*) Twenty-Third.

Personal Psychology for Life & Work. 4th ed. Rita K. Baltus. LC 93-41127. 1994. 19.50 (*0-02-801096-5*) Glencoe.

***Personal Psychology for Life & Work.** 5th ed. Rita Baltus. 1999. teacher ed. 14.95 (*0-02-804295-6*); text 31.28 (*0-02-804294-8*) Glencoe.

Personal Psychopathology: Early Formulations. Harry Stack Sullivan. 416p. 1984. reprint ed. pap. 9.95 (*0-393-30184-2*) Norton.

Personal Publicity Planner: A Guide to Marketing You. Marion E. Gold. LC 97-74587. 88p. (Orig.). 1997. pap. 15.00 (*0-941394-03-4*) Brittany Pubns.

Personal Quests & Quandaries. Ed. by Carol W. Hotchkiss et al. 210p. (Orig.). 1997. pap. 19.95 (*1-890765-01-5*) Avocus Pub.

Personal Quilt Registry: Keep Accurate Records for Your Quilts. 1984. pap. 3.95 (*0-89145-901-4*, 5203, Am Quilters Soc) Collector Bks.

Personal R. E. S. U. M. E. Tracker. Jean B. Hill. (RUS & SPA.). 52p. (Orig.). 1995. mass mkt. 2.99 (*1-888620-02-1*) Common Snse PA.

Personal Reading Journal: Your Record of Quotations, Reflections & Impressions. Gary R. Blair. 48p. 1998. pap. 6.95 (*1-889770-09-4*, PRJ) GoalsGuy.

Personal Reality Assessment: Preparing Your Future by Understanding Your Past. Gary R. Blair. 40p. 1998. pap. 19.95 (*1-889770-24-8*, PRA) GoalsGuy.

***Personal Recalling of the Sioux War: With the 8th Minnesota, Company F.** Thomas C. Hodgson. Tr. by Robert Olson. LC 99-46776. (Illus.). 55p. 1999. pap. 12.00 (*0-915709-69-4*, M328) Pk Geneal Bk.

Personal Recollections & Observations of General Nelson A. Miles, 2 Vols. Nelson A. Miles. Incl. Vol. 1. Personal Recollections & Observations of General Nelson A. Miles. Contrib. by Robert Wooster. LC 91-39603. (Illus.). 319p. Date not set. reprint ed. pap. 11.95 (*0-8032-8180-3*, Bison Books); Vol. 2. Personal Recollections & Observations of General Nelson A. Miles. LC 91-39603. (Illus.). 272p. Date not set. reprint ed. pap. 11.95 (*0-8032-8181-1*, Bison Books); LC 91-39603. Date not set. reprint ed. Set pap. 23.90 (*0-8032-8182-X*, Bison Books) U of Nebr Pr.

Personal Recollections & Observations of General Nelson A. Miles. rev. ed. Nelson A. Miles. LC 68-23812. (American Scene Ser.). (Illus.). 1969. reprint ed. lib. bdg. 69.50 (*0-306-71020-X*) Da Capo.

Personal Recollections & Observations of General Nelson A. Miles see Personal Recollections & Observations of General Nelson A. Miles

Personal Recollections, from Early Life to Old Age, of Mary Somerville. Mary Somerville. LC 73-37723. reprint ed. 47.50 (*0-404-56837-8*) AMS Pr.

Personal Recollections of Arnold Dolmetsch. Mabel Dolmetsch. LC 79-24413. (Music Reprint Ser.). (Illus.). 1980. reprint ed. lib. bdg. 29.50 (*0-306-76022-3*) Da Capo.

Personal Recollections of Captain Enoch Anderson, an Officer of the Delaware Regiments in the Revolutionary War. Enoch Anderson & Henry H. Bellas. LC 76-140851. (Eyewitness Accounts of the American Revolution Ser.). 1971. reprint ed. 14.95 (*0-405-01221-7*) Ayer.

Personal Recollections of Joan of Arc. Mark Twain, pseud. (Works of Samuel Clemens). 1989. reprint ed. lib. bdg. 79.00 (*0-685-28367-4*) Rprt Serv.

Personal Recollections of Joan of Arc, 1896. Mark Twain, pseud. Ed. by Shelley F. Fishkin. (Oxford Mark Twain). (Illus.). 624p. 1997. text 28.00 (*0-19-511416-7*) OUP.

Personal Recollections of Johannes Brahms, Some of His Letters to & Pages from a Journal Kept by George Henschel... George Henschel. LC 74-24110. reprint ed. 32.50 (*0-404-12963-3*) AMS Pr.

Personal Recollections of Many Prominent People Whom I Have Known. John F. Darby. LC 75-94. (Mid-American Frontier Ser.). 1975. reprint ed. 40.95 (*0-405-06860-3*) Ayer.

Personal Recollections of Nathaniel Hawthorne. Horatio Bridge. LC 68-24931. (Studies in Hawthorne: No. 15). 1969. reprint ed. lib. bdg. 75.00 (*0-8383-0916-X*) M S G Haskell Hse.

Personal Recollections of Nathaniel Hawthorne. Horatio Bridge. (Works of Horatio). 1989. reprint ed. lib. bdg. 79.00 (*0-7812-2062-9*) Rprt Serv.

Personal Recollections of the Civil War. unabridged ed. John Gibbon. 426p. 1988. reprint ed. text 30.00 (*0-89029-042-3*) Morningside Bkshop.

Personal Recollections of the Drama. Henry D. Stone. LC 70-81219. 1972. 24.95 (*0-405-09003-X*) Ayer.

Personal Recollections of the Drama. Henry D. Stone. 316p. 1993. reprint ed. lib. bdg. 89.00 (*0-7812-5287-3*) Rprt Serv.

***Personal Recollections of the Use of the Rod.** Margaret Anson. 240p. 2000. mass mkt. 7.95 (*1-56201-188-X*, Pub. by Blue Moon Bks) Publishers Group.

Personal Recollections of the War of 1861. Charles A. Fuller. LC 89-82533. 123p. 1990. reprint ed. pap. 13.95 (*0-9622393-1-3*) Edmonston Publ.

Personal Recollections of Wagner. Angelo Neumann. LC 76-16506. (Music Reprint Ser.). 329p. 1976. reprint ed. 45.00 (*0-306-70843-4*) Da Capo.

Personal Record. Joseph Conrad. Date not set. lib. bdg. 17.95 (*0-8488-1670-6*) Amereon Ltd.

Personal Record. 2nd ed. Joseph Conrad. LC 88-60728. 148p. 1988. reprint ed. pap. 8.95 (*0-910395-46-2*) Marlboro Pr.

Personal Record: A Personal Weight Training Diary. Health for Life Staff. 160p. 1988. pap. 8.95 (*0-944831-19-2*) Health Life.

Personal Record & the Mirror of the Sea. Joseph Conrad. LC 99-185223. 384p. 1998. pap. 13.99 (*0-14-018966-1*) Viking Penguin.

Personal Record, 1920-1972. Gerald Brenan. LC 75-301961. 381p. 1974. write for info. (*0-224-01044-1*) Jonathan Cape.

Personal Record of the Thirteenth Regiment, Tennessee Infantry, C. S. A. Alfred J. Vaughn. 95p. 1977. reprint ed. 15.00 (*0-937130-01-X*) Burkes Bk Store.

Personal Recorder: How to Be Positively Absolutely Organized. 3rd rev. ed. Carole Meneses. (Illus.). 168p. (YA). 1996. ring bd. 30.00 (*0-9653644-4-5*) Potto Publng.

Personal Recordkeeper: Version 5. Albin Renauer. LC 98-16995. 1998. 59.95 (*0-87337-483-5*) Nolo com.

Personal Records. Alice A. Zoerb. (Orig.). 1979. pap. text 5.95 (*0-9602888-1-3*) Heritage Rec.

Personal Recorkeeping Practice Set: The Linden Family. 3rd ed. Merle W. Wood. 1988. pap. text 11.60 (*0-07-071632-3*) McGraw.

Personal Reference Guide: Resources to Assist You on Life's Journey. Gary R. Blair. 40p. 1998. pap. 19.95 (*1-889770-57-4*, PRG) GoalsGuy.

Personal Reflection of the Holocaust. Deli Strummer. Ed. by Nancy Heneson. LC 88-83595. 70p. (Orig.). 1988. pap. 6.95 (*0-317-93134-2*); lib. bdg. 4.67 (*0-9622135-0-0*) Aurich Pr.

Personal Reflections. Gangadhar S. Gouri. LC 97-91299. Date not set. 17.95 (*0-533-12616-9*) Vantage.

Personal Reflections & Meditations: Siegel,&Bernie. abr. ed. Bernie Siegel. 1991. audio 12.00 (*1-55994-430-7*, CPN 1886) HarperAudio.

Personal Relations. large type ed. Pamela Street. 1991. 11.50 (*0-7089-2353-4*) Ulverscroft.

Personal Relations Therapy: The Collected Papers of H. J. S. Guntrip. Ed. by Jeremy Hazell. LC 93-33868. 448p. 1994. 60.00 (*1-56821-164-3*) Aronson.

Personal Relationship Inventory (PRI) Manual for Scoring & Interpretation. Ronald L. Mann. 91p. (Orig.). 1994. pap. 18.00 (*1-879858-03-7*) Behaviordyne.

Personal Relationships. Richard N. Beim. 1992. mass mkt. 4.99 (*0-8125-1884-5*, Pub. by Tor Bks) St Martin.

Personal Relationships, Vol. 5. Steve Duck. 1984. text 120.00 (*0-12-222805-7*) Acad Pr.

Personal Relationships: An Integrated Perspective. Dale E. Wright. LC 98-30174. xviii, 366p. 1998. pap. text 42.95 (*1-55934-952-2*, 1952) Mayfield Pub.

Personal Relationships: Implications for Clinical & Community Psychology. Sarason. pap. text. write for info. (*0-471-49161-6*) Wiley.

Personal Relationships: Instructor's Manual. Dale E. Wright. xviii, 366p. (C). 1998. pap. text, teacher ed. 42.95 (*0-7674-1043-2*, 1043-2) Mayfield Pub.

Personal Relationships: The Art of Living Together. Marti Eicholz. 200p. 1997. pap. write for info. (*0-9653100-3-5*) Inst for Transform.

Personal Relationships: Their Structures & Processes. Harold H. Kelley. 192p. 1979. text 39.95 (*0-89859-470-7*) L Erlbaum Assocs.

Personal Relationships Vol. 1: Studying Personal Relationships. Ed. by Steve Duck & Robin Gilmour. LC 80-41360. 1981. text 120.00 (*0-12-222801-4*) Acad Pr.

Personal Relationships Vol. 3: Personal Relationships in Disorder. Ed. by Steve Duck & Robin Gilmour. LC 80-41360. 1981. text 120.00 (*0-12-222803-0*) Acad Pr.

Personal Relationships Vol. 4: Dissolving Personal Relationships. Ed. by Steve Duck. 1982. text 120.00 (*0-12-222804-9*) Acad Pr.

***Personal Relationships Across Cultures.** Robin Goodwin. LC 98-43680. 1999. 85.00 (*0-415-12860-9*); pap. 25.99 (*0-415-12861-7*) Routledge.

***Personal Relationships Across the Lifespan.** Patricia Noller et al. LC 00-40311. (International Series in Social Psychology). (C). 2000. write for info. (*0-415-18648-X*) Routledge.

Personal Relationships & Communication. Ronald Dingwall. 54p. (C). 1986. 65.00 (*0-86236-000-5*, Pub. by Granary) St Mut.

Personal Relationships & Personal Constructs: A Study of Friendship Formation. Stephen W. Duck. LC 73-8193. 182p. reprint ed. 56.50 (*0-8357-9952-2*, 201489800093) Bks Demand.

Personal Relationships During Adolescence. Ed. by Raymond Montemayer et al. (Advances in Adolescent Development Ser.: Vol. 6). (C). 1994. text 58.00 (*0-8039-5680-0*); pap. text 26.00 (*0-8039-5681-9*) Sage.

Personal Relevance of Truth. Thomas S. Brown. LC 55-7711. (C). 1955. pap. 4.00 (*0-87574-081-2*) Pendle Hill.

Personal Religion among the Greeks. Andre-Jean Festugiere. LC 84-517. (Sather Classical Lecture: No. 26). 186p. 1984. reprint ed. lib. bdg. 49.75 (*0-313-23209-1*, FERG, Greenwood Pr) Greenwood.

Personal Religion & the Life of Devotion. William R. Inge. 96p. 1996. reprint ed. pap. 14.95 (*1-56459-576-5*) Kessinger Pub.

Personal Reminiscences & Experiences. One Hundred & Third Ohio Volunteer Infantry Member. 444p. 1984. reprint ed. 25.00 (*0-9613625-0-2*) OH Volunteer.

Personal Reminiscences, 1840-1890. L. E. Chittenden. LC 72-37302. (Black Heritage Library Collection). 1977. reprint ed. 28.95 (*0-8369-8939-2*) Ayer.

Personal Reminiscences of Abraham Lincoln. LeRoy Fladseth. 100p. (Orig.). 1997. pap. write for info. (*1-57502-388-1*, P01224) Morris Pubng.

Personal Reminiscences of Early Days in California. Stephen J. Field. LC 68-29601. (American Scene Ser.). 1968. reprint ed. lib. bdg. 45.00 (*0-306-71157-5*) Da Capo.

Personal Reminiscences of General Robert E. Lee. J. William Jones. LC 94-18400. (Illus.). 560p. 1994. pap. 27.95 (*0-8071-1959-8*) La State U Pr.

Personal Reminiscences of the Rebellion, 1861-1866. Le Grand Cannon. LC 78-157363. (Black Heritage Library Collection). 1977. 25.95 (*0-8369-8801-9*) Ayer.

Personal Reminiscences of the War of 1861-5. William H. Morgan. LC 74-146868. (Select Bibliographies Reprint Ser.). 1977. reprint ed. 19.95 (*0-8369-5635-4*) Ayer.

Personal Reminiscenses, 1861-1865. George W. Booth. 25.50 (*0-8488-0920-3*) Amereon Ltd.

Personal Renewal: Your Guide to Vitality, Allure & a Joyful Life Using Healing, Herbs, Diet, Movement & Visualizations. Letha Hadady. LC RA776.75.H3199. 1999. pap. 13.00 (*0-609-80229-1*, Three Riv Pr) Crown Pub Group.

Personal Renewal: Your Guide to Vitality, Allure & a Joyful Life Using Healing Herbs, Diet, Movement & Visualizations. Letha Hadady. LC 98-28576. 288p. 1998. 23.00 (*0-609-60163-6*) Harmony Bks.

Personal Resources. (Workmatters Ser.). (YA). (gr. 10-12). teacher ed. 33.26 (*0-8092-0826-1*) NTC Contemp Pub Co.

Personal Response Systems: An International Report of a New Home Care Service. Intro. by Andrew S. Dibner. LC 92-25580. (Home Health Care Services Quarterly Ser.: Vol. 13, Nos. 3 & 4, 1992). (Illus.). 280p. 1993. lib. bdg. 49.95 (*1-56024-272-8*) Haworth Pr.

Personal Responsibility Act: An Analysis. Isaac Shapiro et al. 77p. (Orig.). 1994. pap. 10.00 (*1-57291-002-X*) Ctr on Budget.

Personal Responsibility & Christian Morality. fac. ed. Josef Fuchs. Tr. by William Cleves et al. LC 83-1548. 238p. (Orig.). 1983. reprint ed. pap. 73.80 (*0-7837-7779-5*, 204753400007) Bks Demand.

Personal Responsibility & Therapy: An Integrative Approach. Richard Nelson-Jones. 214p. 1987. 49.95 (*0-89116-777-3*) Hemisp Pub.

Personal Resume Preparation. Michael P. Jaquish. LC 68-20098. (Wiley Series on Human Communication). 158p. reprint ed. pap. 49.00 (*0-608-16166-7*, 205573000034) Bks Demand.

Personal Revelation. JoAnn Hibbert Hamilton. 1998. 15.95 (*1-57734-268-2*, 01113321) Covenant Comms.

Personal Revival: Living the Christian Life in the Light of the Cross. Stanley Voke. (Illus.). 79p. 1997. reprint ed. mass mkt. 4.99 (*1-884543-05-7*) O M Lit.

Personal Revolution & Picasso. Louis Danz. LC 74-3421. (Studies in Philosophy: No. 40). 1974. lib. bdg. 59.00 (*0-8383-2066-X*) M S G Haskell Hse.

Personal Riches for Today's Singles. Cliff Allbritton. Ed. by Stephanie McGuirk. (Orig.). 1992. pap. 6.95 (*1-881834-01-8*) Atlas Crown.

***Personal Risk Management & Insurance (For CPCU 2)** rev. ed. R. Robert Rackley. (CPCU Ser.). 1999. 160.00 (*1-57195-192-X*) Insurance Achiev.

***Personal Road to Hell & Back.** Herb Smith. LC 99-93619. 328p. 2000. 21.95 (*0-533-13089-1*) Vantage.

***Personal Robot Navigator.** Merl K. Miller et al. (Illus.). 198p. 1998. pap. 44.95 (*1-888193-00-X*) AK Peters.

Personal Robotics: Real Robots to Construct, Program & Explore the World. Richard Raucci. LC 98-51745. (Illus.). 250p. 1999. 25.00 (*1-56881-089-X*) AK Peters.

Personal Rule of Charles I. Kevin Sharpe. LC 92-16271. (Illus.). 736p. (C). 1992. 57.00 (*0-300-05688-5*) Yale U Pr.

Personal Rule of Charles I. Kevin Sharpe. 1996. pap. 25.00 (*0-300-06596-5*) Yale U Pr.

***Personal Safety.** Alvin Silverstein et al. LC 99-49662. (My Health Ser.). 2000. 22.50 (*0-531-11639-5*) Watts.

Personal Safety: A Training Resource Manual. Chris Cardy. 218p. 1992. ring bd. 212.95 (*1-85904-045-4*, Pub. by Gower) Ashgate Pub Co.

Personal Safety - Things You Should Know & Understand. 1991. 3.95 (*0-474-02234-X*) My Rain.

***Personal Safety & Security Equipment in Mexico: A Strategic Entry Report, 1995.** Compiled by Icon Group International Staff. (Illus.). 141p. 1999. ring bd. 1410.00 incl. audio compact disk (*0-7418-1661-X*) Icon Grp.

Personal Safety for Health Care Workers. Bibby. 248p. 1995. pap. 33.95 (*1-85742-196-5*) Ashgate Pub Co.

Personal Safety for People Working in Education. Diana Lamplugh & Barbara Pagan. LC 96-86202. 326p. 1996. pap. 33.95 (*1-85742-194-9*, Pub. by Arena) Ashgate Pub Co.

Personal Safety for Social Workers. Ed. by Pauline Bibby. 224p. 1994. pap. 33.95 (*1-85742-195-7*, Pub. by Arena) Ashgate Pub Co.

Personal Saving, Consumption, & Tax Policy. Kosters. (Special Analysis Ser.). 50p. (Orig.). (C). 1992. pap. 9.75 (*0-8447-7013-2*) Am Enterprise.

***Personal Saving, Personal Choice.** Ed. by David A. Wise. LC 99-38033. (Publication Ser.: Vol. 463). 96p. 1999. pap. 16.95 (*0-8179-9712-1*) Hoover Inst Pr.

Personal Secrets: Your True Character Unveiled. Rodney Davies. (Illus.). 176p. 1991. pap. 6.95 (*1-85538-044-7*, Pub. by Aqrn Pr) Harper SF.

Personal Security Equipment in Argentina: A Strategic Entry Report, 1997. Compiled by Icon Group International Staff. (Country Industry Report). (Illus.). 141p. 1999. ring bd. 1410.00 incl. audio compact disk (*0-7418-0337-2*) Icon Grp.

***Personal Security for the American Business Traveler Overseas.** 20p. 1998. pap. 1.00 (*0-16-061931-9*) USGPO.

Personal Security for the American Business Traveler Overseas, November 1994. 60p. 1995. pap. 4.50 (*0-16-061905-X*) USGPO.

Personal Security Guidelines for the American Business Traveler Overseas. 1996. lib. bdg. 250.95 (*0-8490-6939-4*) Gordon Pr.

***Personal Self Improvement Premium.** 1998. write for info. (*0-13-974189-5*) P-H.

Personal Selling. 3rd ed. Ingram. (C). 1999. text 55.50 (*0-03-030452-0*, Pub. by Harcourt Coll Pubs) Harcourt.

Personal Selling: A Relationship Approach. 6th ed. Ron Marks. LC 96-29159. 585p. (C). 1996. 92.00 (*0-13-242884-9*) P-H.

Personal Selling: Function, Theory, & Practice. 3rd ed. R. Wayne Mondy et al. 480p. 1988. teacher ed. write for info. (*0-318-63843-6*, H19185) P-H.

Personal Selling: Function, Theory, & Practice. 4th ed. Mondy et al. LC 97-67107. 1997. 69.95 (*0-87393-638-8*) Dame Pubns.

Personal Sentence Completion Inventory. L. C. Miccio-Fonseca. Ed. by A. Hewat. 88p. (Orig.). 1997. pap. 50.00 (*1-884444-47-4*) Safer Soc.

Personal Shorthand, 3 pts. Carl W. Salser & C. Theo Yerian. (Personal Shorthand Cardinal Ser.). 1980. 936.00 (*0-89420-170-0*) Natl Book.

Personal Shorthand, 3 pts., Set. Carl W. Salser & C. Theo Yerian. Incl. PS, Bk. 1. 1980. pap. text 9.95 (*0-89420-106-9*, 241050); PS, Bk 2. 1980. pap. text 11.50 (*0-89420-107-7*, 241105); PS, Bk. 3. 1980. pap. text 12.95 (*0-89420-108-5*, 241165); (Personal Shorthand Cardinal Ser.). 1980. Set text 31.85 (*0-89420-105-0*) Natl Book.

Personal Shorthand: Individualized Syllabus. Carl W. Salser & C. Theo Yerian. (Personal Shorthand Cardinal Ser.: Bk. 1). 150p. (Orig.). 1983. pap. text 10.95 (*0-89420-232-4*, 241175) Natl Book.

Personal Shorthand: Ps-80, Bks. 1 & 2. Carl W. Salser & C. Theo Yerian. (Personal Shorthand Cardinal Ser.). 369p. 1981. text 13.85 (*0-89420-221-9*, 241180) Natl Book.

Personal Shorthand: Syllabus. 2nd ed. Joanne Piper & C. Theodore Yerian. 1975. pap. text 16.95 (*0-89420-083-6*, 217000) Natl Book.

Personal Shorthand: Teacher's Manual & Key to Syllabus. Joanne Piper & C. Theodore Yerian. 1975. teacher ed. 5.95 (*0-89420-094-1*, 217007) Natl Book.

Personal Shorthand Cardinal Series 2000. Carl W. Salser et al. (Illus.). 450p. 1989. text 19.95 (*0-89420-260-X*, 241280) Natl Book.

Personal Shorthand Cardinal Series 2000: College Edition, Bk. 1. Carl W. Salser et al. 225p. (C). 1991. pap. text 17.85 (*0-89420-257-X*, 244250) Natl Book.

Personal Shorthand Combined Dictionary - Professional Edition. Carl W. Salser et al. 417p. 1984. pap. 18.95 (*0-89420-241-3*, 213000) Natl Book.

Personal Shorthand for College-University Notetaking. C. Theo Yerian & Carl W. Salser. 135p. (Orig.). (C). 1985. pap. 10.95 (*0-89420-247-2*, 421000) Natl Book.

Personal Shorthand for the Administrator, Executive, Manager & Supervisor. M. Herbert Freeman et al. 136p. (C). 1984. pap. text 15.70 (*0-89420-237-5*, 420125) Natl Book.

Personal Shorthand for the Executive Secretary: Syllabus. Piper et al. 211p. 1977. pap. text 14.95 (*0-89420-030-5*, 217150) Natl Book.

An Asterisk (*) at the beginning of an entry indicates that the title is appearing for the first time.

Personal Shorthand for the Journalist. Walter Blum & C. Theo Yerian. 176p. (Orig.). (C). 1980. pap. text 13.95 (*0-89420-214-6*, 242032); audio 237.20 (*0-89420-225-1*, 242000) Natl Book.

Personal Shorthand Handbook for Beginning Legal Assistants & Receptionists. Carl W. Salser et al. 230p. 1989. pap. 19.95 (*0-89420-254-5*, 422150) Natl Book.

Personal Shorthand Handbook for Beginning Medical-Dental Assistants. Carl W. Salser et al. 260p. (Orig.). 1988. pap. 19.95 (*0-89420-253-7*, 422100) Natl Book.

Personal Shorthand Standard Dictionary. Carl W. Salser et al. Ed. by Charlotte A. Butsch. 207p. 1984. pap. 11.95 (*0-89420-239-1*, 213100) Natl Book.

Personal Shorthand Theory Review Workbook. 2nd rev. ed. Carl W. Salser & C. Theo Yerian. (Personal Shorthand Cardinal Ser.). 97p. 1983. pap. text 7.95 (*0-89420-233-2*, 216715) Natl Book.

Personal Side. Jessie A. Bloodworth & Elizabeth J. Greenwood. LC 71-137156. (Poverty U. S. A. Historical Record Ser.). 1971. reprint ed. 29.95 (*0-405-03094-0*) Ayer.

Personal Social Services: Basic Information. 1977. 30.00 (*0-7855-0568-7*, Pub. by Natl Inst Soc Work) St Mut.

Personal Social Services: Clients, Consumers or Citizens? Robert Adams. LC 95-49641. (Social Policy in Britain Ser.). 1996. pap. write for info. (*0-582-25875-8*, Pub. by Addison-Wesley) Longman.

Personal Social Services Council: At Home in a Boarding House. Ed. by National Institue for Social Work Staff. 1981. 30.00 (*0-7855-0839-2*, Pub. by Natl Inst Soc Work) St Mut.

Personal Social Services in an Unsuccessful Economy. Charles Carter. (Younghusband Lectures: 1980). 1981. 25.00 (*0-7855-0835-X*, Pub. by Natl Inst Soc Work) St Mut.

***Personal, Societal, Andecological Values of Wilderness Vol. I: Sixth World Wilderness Congress - Proceedings on Research, Management, & Allocation.** Ed. by Alan E. Watson et al. (Illus.). 158p. (C). 1999. pap. text 35.00 (*0-7881-8163-7*) DIANE Pub.

Personal Sociology. Ed. by Paul C. Higgins & John M. Johnson. LC 87-25894. 174p. 1988. 49.95 (*0-275-92642-7*, C2642, Praeger Pubs) Greenwood.

Personal Speech - Ethics in the Epistle of James. William R. Baker. LC 95-161221. (WissUNT Zum Neuen Testament Ser.). 350p. (Orig.). 1994. pap. text 87.50 (*3-16-145958-X*, Pub. by JCB Mohr) Coronet Bks.

Personal Spiritual Warfare. Betty Miller. (End Times Ser.). 92p. 1991. pap. 5.00 (*1-57149-018-3*) Christ Unltd.

Personal Stereo. Catherine Chambers. LC 97-31458. (Look Inside Ser.). (Illus.). 24p. 1998. write for info. (*1-57572-623-8*) Heinemann Lib.

Personal Stories: A Book for Adults Who Are Beginning to Read, Bk. 1. Kamla D. Koch et al. (Illus.). 78p. (Orig.). 1985. pap., teacher ed. 4.50 (*0-916591-03-4*); 5.99 (*0-916591-02-6*) Linmore Pub.

Personal Stories: A Book for Adults Who Are Beginning to Read, Bk. 2. Kamla D. Koch et al. (Illus.). 113p. (Orig.). 1986. teacher ed. 4.50 (*0-916591-05-0*); pap. text 6.50 (*0-916591-04-2*) Linmore Pub.

Personal Strategic Plan: Putting It All Together. Gary R. Blair. 40p. 1998. pap. 19.95 (*1-889770-56-6*, PSP) GoalsGuy.

Personal Stress Profile. 3rd ed. Greenberg. 1999. 11.25 (*0-697-29435-8*, WCB McGr Hill) McGrw-H Hghr Educ.

Personal Stress Reduction Program. Jeffrey W. Forman & Dave Myers. (Illus.). 160p. 1987. 11.50 (*0-13-659277-5*) P-H.

Personal Style Profile for Intimate Partners. 3rd ed. Susan K. Gilmore & Patrick W. Fraleigh. (Illus.). 40p. 1992. pap. 10.00 (*0-938070-06-1*) Friendly Oregon.

Personal Styles in Greek Sculpture. Evelyn B. Harrison et al. Ed. by Olga Palagia & J. J. Pollitt. (Yale Classical Studies: No. 30). (Illus.). 246p. (C). 1996. text 70.00 (*0-521-55187-0*) Cambridge U Pr.

Personal Styles in Greek Sculpture. Ed. by Olga Palagia & J. J. Pollitt. (Yale Classical Studies: No. 30). (Illus.). 247p. (C). 1999. pap. text 22.95 (*0-521-65738-5*) Cambridge U Pr.

***Personal Success Strategies: Developing Your Potential.** Mel Hensey. LC 99-41071. 124p. 1999. pap. 25.00 (*0-7844-0446-1*) Am Soc Civil Eng.

Personal Tax. Price Waterhouse Staff. 280p. 1995. mass mkt. 12.95 (*0-385-25497-0*) Doubleday.

Personal Tax Planning for Professionals & Owners of Small Businesses. 434p. 1983. 95.00 (*0-88124-115-6*, TX-36630) Cont Ed Bar-CA.

Personal Tax Planning for Professionals & Owners of Small Businesses: May 1994 Update. Philip Starr et al. Ed. by Christopher Dworin. LC 82-73368. 272p. 1994. pap. text 64.00 (*0-88124-755-3*, TX-36638) Cont Ed Bar-CA.

Personal Tax Return Preparation Guide 1994. (C). 1994. pap. 9.95 (*0-13-127234-9*, Macmillan Coll) P-H.

Personal Tax Strategies, 1991. DeJong & Jakabcin. 1990. pap. 4.95 (*0-13-660960-0*) P-H.

***Personal Taxation & the Cost of Living: Comparison Between Montrbeal & Various North American Cities : 1998-1999 Budget.** LC 98-187694. xvii, 72 p. 1998. write for info. (*2-550-32703-9*) Gvt Quebec.

Personal Teaching: Efforts to Combine Personal Love & Professional Skill in the Classroom. J. T. Dillon. 178p. (C). 1990. reprint ed. pap. text 19.00 (*0-8191-7780-6*) U Pr of Amer.

Personal Testament: Essays & Poems. Alex Jackinson. LC 90-63617. 106p. 1991. pap. 12.95 (*0-685-49332-6*) North Lights.

Personal Themes in Literature: The Multicultural Experience. Valerie Whiteson & Sally Jorgensen. LC 92-45100. 176p. (C). 1993. pap. text 26.93 (*0-13-013418-X*) P-H.

Personal Theories. Scroggs. Date not set. pap. text. write for info. (*0-314-87235-3*) West Pub.

Personal Therapy: How to Change Your Life for the Better. Brian Roet. (Illus.). 130p. 1997. pap. 17.95 (*0-09-181305-0*) Trafalgar.

Personal Time Management. rev. ed. Marion E. Haynes. Ed. by Michael Crisp. LC 93-74050. (Fifty-Minute Ser.). (Illus.). 89p. 1994. pap. 10.95 (*1-56052-264-X*) Crisp Pubns.

***Personal Time Management.** 3rd ed. Marion E. Haynes. 108p. 2000. pap. 12.95 (*1-56052-585-1*) Crisp Pubns.

Personal Time Management Manual. 11th ed. John S. Hoyt, Jr. 246p. (C). 1981. 15.00 (*0-943000-08-4*) Telstar Inc.

Personal Time Management Study Guide. 11th ed. John S. Hoyt, Jr. (Illus.). 50p. 1982. pap. text 4.95 (*0-943000-02-5*) Telstar Inc.

Personal Totem Pole: Animal Imagery, the Chakras, & Psychotherapy. 2nd ed. Eligio S. Gallegos. LC 87-90620. 200p. (Orig.). (C). 1990. pap. 12.00 (*0-944164-08-0*) Moon Bear Pr.

Personal Touch. Candace Schuler. (Temptation Ser.). 1994. mass mkt. 2.99 (*0-373-25597-7*, 1-25597-5) Harlequin Bks.

Personal Touch. Elizabeth Wall. 1998. pap. write for info. (*1-57553-939-X*) Watermrk Pr.

Personal Touch. Glenn Wilson. (Illus.). 192p. 1995. pap. 17.95 (*0-7867-0211-7*) Carroll & Graf.

Personal Touch: Encouraging Others Through Hospitality. Rachael Crabb & Raeann Hart. LC 90-63217. 132p. (Orig.). 1991. pap. 8.00 (*0-89109-607-8*) NavPress.

Personal Touch: What You Really Need to Succeed in Today's Fast-Paced Business World. Terrie Williams & Joe Cooney. 256p. 1996. reprint ed. mass mkt. 13.95 (*0-446-67158-4*, Pub. by Warner Bks) Little.

***Personal Tour of a Shaker Village.** Michael Capek. LC 00-9316. (How It Was Ser.). (Illus.). (J). 2001. lib. bdg. write for info. (*0-8225-3584-X*) Lerner Pub.

Personal Tour of Camden Yards. Robert Young. LC 98-19260. (How It Was Ser.). 64p. (J). (gr. 4-6). 1999. lib. bdg. 23.93 (*0-8225-3578-5*, Lerner Publctns) Lerner Pub.

***Personal Tour of Edison's Lab.** Robert Young. (How It Was Ser.). (Illus.). 64p. (J). (gr. 4-7). 2000. 25.26 (*0-8225-3581-5*, Lerner Publctns) Lerner Pub.

***Personal Tour of Ellis Island.** Robert Young. LC 99-42054. (How It Was Ser.). (Illus.). 64p. (J). (gr. 4). 2000. lib. bdg. 25.26 (*0-8225-3579-3*, Lerner Publctns) Lerner Pub.

***Personal Tour of Hull-House.** Laura B. Edge. (How It Was Ser.). (Illus.). 64p. (J). (gr. 4-7). 2000. 25.26 (*0-8225-3582-3*, Lerner Publctns) Lerner Pub.

Personal Tour of La Purisima. Robert Young. LC 97-46908. (How It Looked Ser.). (Illus.). 64p. (J). (gr. 4-7). 1999. lib. bdg. 23.93 (*0-8225-3576-9*, Lerner Publctns) Lerner Pub.

Personal Tour of Mesa Verde. Robert Young. LC 98-9422. (How It Was Ser.). (Illus.). 64p. (J). (gr. 4-7). 1999. 23.93 (*0-8225-3577-7*, Lerner Publctns) Lerner Pub.

Personal Tour of Monticello. Robert Young. LC 97-46662. (How It Looked Ser.). (Illus.). 64p. (J). (gr. 4-7). 1999. lib. bdg. 23.93 (*0-8225-3575-0*, Lerner Publctns) Lerner Pub.

***Personal Tour of Old Ironsides.** Robert Young. LC 99-35500. (How It Was Ser.). (Illus.). 64p. (J). (gr. 4-7). 2000. 25.26 (*0-8225-3580-7*, Lerner Publctns) Lerner Pub.

***Personal Tour of Tuskegee Institute.** Bettye Stroud. LC 00-8905. (How It Was Ser.). (Illus.). (J). 2001. lib. bdg. write for info. (*0-8225-3585-8*) Lerner Pub.

Personal Trainer's Handbook. Teri S. O'Brien. LC 96-41431. (Illus.). 192p. (Orig.). 1997. pap. text 25.00 (*0-88011-593-9*, BOBR0593) Human Kinetics.

Personal Training. Jennifer Wade. LC 98-15953. (Illus.). 160p. 1998. 19.95 (*0-8069-4201-0*) Sterling.

Personal Training Log. John Feeney. (Illus.). 190p. (Orig.). 1996. pap. 12.00 (*1-57502-295-8*, P1008) Morris Pubng.

***Personal Training Profits & A Secure Fitness Future: Explosive Inside Secrets to Skyrocket Your Personal Training Career.** Phil Kaplan. 270p. 2001. pap. 39.99 (*1-887463-12-7*) Grt Atltc.

Personal Training: Why Not You? First Study of the Client-Trainer Partnership. Bill Taylor & Christine C. Yukevich. LC 97-73077. 224p. 1997. pap. text 13.95 (*0-9658822-5-X*) Lion Pr.

Personal Traits & Success in Teaching. Elizabeth H. Morris. LC 76-177087. (Columbia University. Teachers College. Contributions to Education Ser.: No. 342). reprint ed. 37.50 (*0-404-55342-7*) AMS Pr.

Personal Transformations in Small Groups: A Jungian Perspective. Robert D. Boyd. (International Library of Group Psychotherapy & Group Process Ser.). 304p. (C). (gr. 13). 1991. text 49.95 (*0-415-04362-X*, A5080) Routledge.

Personal Transformations in Small Groups: A Jungian Perspective. Robert D. Boyd. LC 94-8489. (International Library of Group Psychotherapy & Group Process Ser.). 256p. (C). 1994. pap. 29.99 (*0-415-04363-8*, B4780) Routledge.

Personal Travel Budgets. Ed. by Howard R. Kirby. 124p. 1981. pap. 32.00 (*0-08-027420-X*, Pergamon Pr) Elsevier.

Personal Typing. 4th ed. Alan C. Lloyd et al. (Illus.). 1978. text 19.96 (*0-07-038208-5*) McGraw.

Personal Typing 30. 5th ed. Philip S. Pepe. 64p. 1974. text 15.96 (*0-07-049299-9*) McGraw.

Personal Value Statements: Writing Your Personal Operating System. Gary R. Blair. 40p. 1998. pap. 19.95 (*1-889770-50-7*, PVS) GoalsGuy.

***Personal Values: The Application of Personal Values to the World of Work.** John M. Stepahin. LC 00-190047. iv, 219p. 2000. 23.95 (*0-9678526-0-9*) Pacific Pr OR.

Personal Values: Writings by Uncommon Women. Elizabeth Croydon et al. LC 94-67994. 56p. (Orig.). 1994. pap. 11.95 (*0-9637704-0-3*) Red Dragon VA.

Personal Values Analysis Handbook. Pref. by James J. Messina. (Professional Handbook Ser.). 26p. (Orig.). 1982. pap. text 7.00 (*0-931975-16-6*) Advanced Dev Sys.

Personal Videoconferencing. Evan Rosen & Manning Publications Staff. (Illus.). 416p. 1996. pap. text 39.50 (*0-13-268327-X*) P-H.

Personal Views. Neal Starkman. LC 89-22302. (Illus.). 43p. (Orig.). (YA). (gr. 6-12). 1989. pap. 8.00 (*0-935529-12-8*) Comprehen Health Educ.

Personal Vision of Ingmar Bergman. Jorn Donner. (Biography Index Reprint Ser.). (Illus.). 276p. 1964. pap. 4.95 (*0-8290-1760-7*) Irvington.

Personal Vision of Ingmar Bergman. Jorn Donner. Tr. by Holger Lundbergh. (Biography Index Reprint Ser.). 1980. reprint ed. 20.95 (*0-8369-8119-7*) Ayer.

Personal Vision of Ingmar Bergman. Jorn Donner. (Biography Index Reprint Ser.). (Illus.). 276p. reprint ed. lib. bdg. 22.25 (*0-8290-0832-2*) Irvington.

***Personal Visions: Conservations with Contemporary Film Directors.** Mario Falsetto. 320p. 1999. pap. 18.95 (*1-879505-51-7*) Silman James Pr.

Personal Voice in Biblical Interpretation. Ingrid R. Kitzberger. LC 98-34313. 1998. write for info. (*0-415-18099-6*); pap. 25.99 (*0-415-18100-3*) Routledge.

Personal Voices: Chinese Women in the 1980's. Emily Honig & Gail Hershatter. LC 87-18013. (Illus.). x, 387p. 1988. 47.50 (*0-8047-1416-9*); pap. 16.95 (*0-8047-1431-2*) Stanford U Pr.

Personal Vote: Constituency Service & Electoral Independence. Bruce Cain et al. LC 86-22839. (Illus.). 288p. 1987. 41.00 (*0-674-66317-9*) HUP.

Personal Vote: Constituency Service & Electoral Independence. Bruce Cain et al. 280p. 1990. pap. 18.50 (*0-674-66318-7*) HUP.

Personal War: Big Trucks...Big...Men...Riding for Justice, 2 vols. Bob Ham. (Overload Ser.). 1999. audio 16.95 (*1-56431-257-7*) Sunset Prod.

Personal War in Vietnam. Robert Flynn. LC 89-4630. (Military History Ser.: No. 13). (Illus.). 160p. 1989. 24.95 (*0-89096-407-6*); pap. 14.95 (*0-89096-418-1*) Tex A&M Univ Pr.

Personal Water Vehicle Service Manual. Intertec Publishing Staff. LC 88-45483. (Illus.). 128p. 1988. pap. 26.95 (*0-87288-307-8*, PWV-1) Intertec Pub.

***Personal WaterCraft Adventures & Guidebook - Texas.** Thomas Bell. LC 98-96980. (Illus.). 210p. 1999. pap. 23.95 (*0-9668333-0-9*) Life Advents.

***Personal Watercraft Safety.** Ed. by Barry Leonard. (Illus.). 98p. 2000. reprint ed. pap. text 25.00 (*0-7881-8870-4*) DIANE Pub.

Personal Way of the Cross. 32p. 1990. pap. 0.99 (*0-89622-319-1*) Twenty-Third.

Personal Wedding Planner. Sharon C. Cook & Elizabeth Gale. (Illus.). 192p. 1992. 20.00 (*1-55850-048-0*) Adams Media.

***Personal Wellness.** Forrest Dolgener. Ed. by Larry Hensley. 368p. (C). 1998. pap. text 34.95 (*0-945483-85-6*) E Bowers Pub.

***Personal Wellness: How to Go the Distance.** Alban Bacchus & Carol Bacchus. Ed. by Margaret Savage. (Illus.). 336p. 1999. pap. 24.95 (*0-9674834-0-9*, Medawellcom) Engin Systms Sol.

Personal Wellness: Your Most Profitable Investment. Rick Griggs. LC 89-81519. (Fifty-Minute Ser.). (Illus.). 104p. 1990. pap. 10.95 (*1-56052-021-3*, C021) Crisp Pubns.

Personal Wireless Comunication with DECT & PWT: Wireless Communications Engineering. John A. Phillips. LC 98-30072. 1998. 93.00 (*0-89006-872-0*) Artech Hse.

***Personal Wisdom: Living from the Inside Out.** M. Jane Miner. 65p. 2000. pap. 8.95 (*1-887476-02-4*) Perf Publns.

Personal Work. Milo Kauffman. 1970. reprint ed. pap. 2.50 (*0-87813-951-6*) Christian Light.

***Personal Worker's New Testament: Psalms & Proverbs.** 1999. pap. text 5.99 (*0-529-11114-4*); pap. text 5.99 (*0-529-11115-2*) World Publng.

Personal World: John MacMurray on Self & Society. Philip Conford. 224p. 1997. pap. text 24.95 (*0-86315-236-8*, Pub. by Floris Bks) Anthroposophic.

Personal Worship, 7 vols., Vol. 2. Don DeWelt. LC 88-62771. (Orig.). 1989. pap. 9.99 (*0-89900-451-2*) College Pr Pub.

Personal Worship, 7 vols., Vol. 3. Don DeWelt. LC 88-62771. (Orig.). 1989. pap. 9.99 (*0-89900-452-0*) College Pr Pub.

Personal Worship, 7 vols., Vol. 5. Don DeWelt. LC 88-62771. (Orig.). 1989. pap. 9.99 (*0-89900-454-7*) College Pr Pub.

Personal Worship, 7 vols., Vol. 6. Don DeWelt. LC 88-62771. (Orig.). 1989. pap. 9.99 (*0-89900-455-5*) College Pr Pub.

Personal Worship, 7 vols., Vol. 7. Don DeWelt. LC 88-62771. (Orig.). 1989. pap. 9.99 (*0-89900-456-3*) College Pr Pub.

Personal Writings. Ignatius of Loyola Staff. LC 97-110462. 1997. pap. 13.95 (*0-14-043385-6*) Viking Penguin.

Personal Writings by Women to 1900: A Bibliography of American & British Writers. Ed. by Beverly A. Joyce. LC 88-37865. 288p. 1989. 67.50 (*0-8061-2206-4*) U of Okla Pr.

***Personal Writings of Eliza Roxcy Snow.** Eliza R. Snow. (Life Writings of Frontier Women Ser.: Vol. 5). (Illus.). 336p. 2000. 34.95 (*0-87421-297-9*); pap. 19.95 (*0-87421-298-7*) Utah St U Pr.

Personal Year of Grace: Spiritual Growth Through the Liturgical Year. Warren Dicharry. LC 95-13676. 104p. (Orig.). 1996. pap. 8.95 (*0-8146-2221-6*, Liturg Pr Bks) Liturgical Pr.

Personalidad Transformada. Orpha Luna. (Serie Actualidades - Actualities Ser.).Tr. of Transformed Personality. (SPA.). 65p. 1993. pap. 2.29 (*1-56063-454-5*, 498158) Editorial Unilit.

Personalidad y Literatura Puertorriquenas. rev. ed. Hilda Quintana et al. (SPA.). 384p. (C). 1996. pap. text 16.95 (*1-56328-102-3*) Edit Plaza Mayor.

Personalidades del Calvario. Fernando L. Rivera.Tr. of Personalities at Calvary. (SPA.). 144p. (Orig.). 1996. pap. 11.99 (*0-8272-2949-6*) Chalice Pr.

Personalidades del Pesebre. Fernando L. Rivera. (SPA., Illus.). (Orig.). 1992. pap. 9.99 (*0-8272-2943-7*) Chalice Pr.

Personalinformationssysteme: Einfuhrung und Einsatz in Schweizer Grossunternehmen. Urs Steiner. (Europaische Hochsculschriften Ser.: Riehe 5, Bd 2372). 1998. 41.95 (*3-906761-57-6*, Pub. by P Lang) P Lang Pubng.

Personalism. Borden P. Bowne. LC 75-949. reprint ed. 34.50 (*0-404-59073-X*) AMS Pr.

Personalism. Emmanuel Mounier. Tr. by Philip Mairet. LC 75-122050. 1970. reprint ed. pap. 8.00 (*0-268-00434-X*) U of Notre Dame Pr.

***Personalism: A Critical Introduction.** Rufus Burrow, Jr. LC 99-43444. 1999. 29.99 (*0-8272-2955-0*) Chalice Pr.

Personalism & Mathematics As Women's Personifestors: Women & the Fior (Which Is Irish for Truth) & the Creation of the Personalist Intuitionist School of Mathematics & Physics. Patrick A. O'Dougherty. LC 95-79957. 106p. (C). 1995. lib. bdg. 20.99 (*0-9626665-5-6*) Irish Catholic.

Personalism & Party Politics: Institutionalization of the Popular Democratic Party of Puerto Rico. Kenneth H. Farr. LC 73-75406. 143p. (Orig.). 1973. 4.95 (*0-913480-12-6*); pap. 2.95 (*0-913480-13-4*) Inter Am U Pr.

Personalism & the Politics of Culture. Patrick Grant. LC 96-11589. 224p. 1996. text 59.95 (*0-312-16176-X*) St Martin.

Personalism & the Problems of Philosophy: An Appreciation of the Works of Borden Parker Bowne. Ralph T. Flewelling. LC 75-3147. reprint ed. 34.50 (*0-404-59154-X*) AMS Pr.

Personalism in Theology. Ed. by Edgar S. Brightman. LC 75-3088. (Philosophy in America Ser.). reprint ed. 37.50 (*0-404-59086-1*) AMS Pr.

Personalismo y Politica de Partidos: La Institucionalizacion del Partido Popular Democratico De Puerto Rico. Kenneth R. Farr. Tr. by Jesus Benitez from ENG. LC 73-75406. 268p. 1975. pap. 2.95 (*0-913480-26-6*) Inter Am U Pr.

Personalismo y Politica de Partidos: La Institucionalizacion del Partido Popular Democratico De Puerto Rico. Kenneth R. Farr. Tr. by Jesus Benitez from ENG. LC 73-75406. 268p. 1975. 4.95 (*0-913480-25-8*) Inter Am U Pr.

Personalist Challenge: Intersubjectivity & Ontology. Maurice Nedoncelle. Tr. by Francois C. Gerard et al. LC 83-26293. (Pittsburgh Theological Monographs: No. 27). 1994. pap. 10.00 (*0-915138-29-8*) Pickwick.

Personalist Economics: Moral Convictions, Economic Realities, & Social Action. Edward J. O'Boyle. LC 98-13615. 1998. 99.95 (*0-7923-8146-7*) Kluwer Academic.

Personalist Ethics & Human Subjectivity: Ethics at the Crossroads, Vol. 2. Ed. by George F. McLean. LC 92-13188. (Cultural Heritage & Contemporary Change Series I: Vol. 8). 300p. 1994. pap. 17.50 (*1-56518-024-0*) Coun Res Values.

Personalitat Durch Humanitat: Das Ethikgeschichtliche Profil Christlicher Handlungslehre Bei Lactanz Denkhorizont - Textubersetzung - Interpretation - Wirkungsgeschichte. Wolfram Winger. (Illus.). 748p. 1998. 113.95 (*3-631-33602-0*) P Lang Pubng.

Personalites of Melvin Hill Cemetary Phelps, Ontario Co., NY. David L. Burnisky. (Illus.). 269p. 1996. pap. 28.50 (*0-7884-0383-4*, B868) Heritage Bk.

Personalities. Arthur A. Baumann. LC 68-54323. (Essay Index Reprint Ser.). 1977. 20.95 (*0-8369-0177-0*) Ayer.

Personalities & Problem: Interpretive Essays in World Civilizations, Vol. I. 2nd ed. Ken Wolf. LC 98-28677. 160p. 1998. pap. 12.50 (*0-07-071348-0*, McGrw-H College) McGrw-H Hghr Educ.

Personalities & Problem: Interpretive Essays in World Civilizations, Vol. I. 2nd ed. Ken Wolf. LC 98-28677. 160p. 1998. pap. 12.50 (*0-07-071349-9*) McGrw-H Hghr Educ.

Personalities & Problems: Interpretive Essays in World Civilizations, 001. Ken Wolf. LC 93-27176. 160p. (C). 1994. 22.19 (*0-07-071343-X*) McGraw.

Personalities & Problems: Interpretive Essays in World Civilizations. Vol. 1, 002. Ken Wolf. 176p. (C). 1994. pap. 22.19 (*0-07-071347-2*) McGraw.

Personalities & Products: A Historical Perspective on Advertising in America, 53. Edd Applegate. LC 97-26893. (Contributions to the Study of Mass Media & Communications: Vol. 53). 192p. 1998. 57.95 (*0-313-30364-9*, Greenwood Pr) Greenwood.

Personalities & Reminiscences of the War. Robert L. Bullard. 1977. 18.95 (*0-8369-6967-7*, 7848) Ayer.

Personalities at Calvary see Personalidades del Calvario

Personalities at Risk: Addiction, Codependency & Psychological Type. 144p. 1992. pap. 14.95 (*1-878287-37-0*) Type & Temperament.

P

Personalities in American Art. William F. Paris. LC 72-107731. (Essay Index Reprint Ser.). 1977. 17.95 (*0-8369-1582-8*) Ayer.

Personalities in Art. Royal Cortissoz. LC 68-55844. (Essay Index Reprint Ser.). 1977. 31.95 (*0-8369-0339-0*) Ayer.

Personalities in the History of Oman. Sultan Qaboos University Staff. (ARA.). 170p. 1991. 19.95 (*0-86685-560-2*, LDL5602, Pub. by Librairie du Liban) Intl Bk Ctr.

Personalities of Antiquity. Arthur E. Weigall. LC 77-90672. (Essay Index Reprint Ser.). 1977. 20.95 (*0-8369-1217-9*) Ayer.

Personalities of Mithra in Archaeology & Literature. A. D. Bivar. LC 98-43663. (Biennial Yarshater Lecture Ser.: Vol. 1). xii, 164p. 1998. text 28.00 (*0-933273-28-2*) Bibliotheca Persica.

Personalities of the Early Church. Ed. by Everett Ferguson. LC 92-36215. (Studies in Early Christianity: Vol. 1). (Illus.). 432p. 1993. text 90.00 (*0-8153-1061-7*) Garland.

Personalities of the Zodiac: A Cartoon Chronicle on How Your Birthday Shapes Your Character. William Schreib. LC 98-90335. (Illus.). iv, 60p. 1998. pap. 8.95 (*0-9614627-0-1*) Starry-Eyed Pubns.

Personalities, War & Diplomacy: Essays on International History. Ed. by Thomas G. Otte & C. Pagedas. LC 97-16760. 291p. 1997. 59.95 (*0-7146-4818-3*, Pub. by F Cass Pubs) Intl Spec Bk.

Personality. Susan C. Cloninger. LC 95-48100. 608p. (C). 1996. pap. text 68.95 (*0-7167-2825-7*) W H Freeman.

Personality. Friedman & Schustack. LC 98-28088. 566p. 1998. 82.00 (*0-205-13953-1*) Allyn.

Personality. Ed. by Lanning. (C). 1999. text. write for info. (*0-321-01191-0*) Addson-Wesley Educ.

Personality. Rabindranath Tagore. 184p. 1985. 5.50 (*0-318-36926-5*) Asia Bk Corp.

Personality. Zirkel. 2000. pap. text 11.97 (*0-395-97207-8*) HM.

Personality. rev. ed. David C. McClelland. 672p. reprint ed. text. write for info. (*0-318-53722-2*) Irvington.

Personality. 2nd ed. Burger. (Psychology Ser.). 1989. text, teacher ed. write for info. (*0-534-11665-5*) Brooks-Cole.

Personality. 2nd ed. Jerry M. Burger. 525p. (C). 1989. mass mkt. 51.50 (*0-534-11664-7*) Brooks-Cole.

Personality. 2nd ed. Christopher Peterson. 700p. (C). 1992. text 86.00 (*0-15-569600-9*) Harcourt Coll Pubs.

Personality. 3rd ed. Jerry M. Burger. (Psychology Ser.). 1993. pap., student ed. 19.95 (*0-534-17222-9*) Brooks-Cole.

Personality. 3rd ed. Jerry M. Burger. (C). 1993. text 45.50 (*0-534-17220-2*) Brooks-Cole.

Personality. 3rd ed. Seymour Feshbach & Bernard Weiner. LC 90-82955. 650p. (C). 1991. text 67.56 (*0-669-20898-1*) HM Trade Div.

Personality. 4th ed. Seymour Feshbach et al. 661p. (C). 1996. text 67.56 (*0-669-35442-2*); text, teacher ed. 2.66 (*0-669-35443-0*) HM Trade Div.

***Personality.** 5th ed. Burger. (Psychology Ser.). (C). 2000. text 18.00 (*0-534-36858-1*) Wadsworth Pub.

Personality: A Cognitive Approach. Jo Brunas-Wagstaff. LC 97-39541. (Psychology Focus Ser.). 184p. (C). 1998. 50.00 (*0-415-16304-8*); pap. 14.99 (*0-415-16305-6*) Routledge.

Personality: A Systems Approach. Emmons. (C). Date not set. text 63.50 (*0-15-501985-6*) Harcourt Coll Pubs.

Personality: An Integrative Approach. F. Stephan Mayer & Karen Sutton. LC 95-38601. 652p. 1996. 87.00 (*0-02-378180-7*, Macmillan Coll) P-H.

Personality: Analysis & Interpretation of Lives. David Winter. 1995. pap. text, teacher ed., suppl. ed. write for info. (*0-07-071130-5*) McGraw.

Personality: Analysis & Interpretation of Lives. David G. Winter. LC 95-15697. 678p. (C). 1995. 69.38 (*0-07-071129-1*) McGraw.

Personality: Classic Theories & Modern Research. (C). 1998. text. write for info. (*0-205-29368-9*, Longwood Div) Allyn.

Personality: Contemporary Theory & Research. 2nd rev. ed. Valerian J. Derlega et al. LC 98-14938. (Psychology). 450p. 1999. pap. text 49.95 (*0-8304-1422-3*) Thomson Learn.

Personality: Critical Concepts, 4 vols. Cary L. Cooper & Lawrence A. Pervin. LC 97-32757. 1664p. (C). 1998. reprint ed. 700.00 (*0-415-13504-4*) Routledge.

Personality: Description, Dynamics, & Development - Instructor's Manual with Test Questions. Fred W. Whitford. 1996. teacher ed. write for info. (*0-7167-2759-5*) W H Freeman.

***Personality: Determinants, Dynamics, & Potentials.** Gian Vittorio Caprara & Daniel Cervone. (Illus.). 480p. 2000. write for info. (*0-521-58310-1*); pap. write for info. (*0-521-58748-4*) Cambridge U Pr.

Personality: Evolutionary Heritage & Human Distinctiveness. Arnold H. Buss. 280p. (C). 1988. text 49.95 (*0-8058-0298-3*) L Erlbaum Assocs.

Personality: In Search of Individuality. Nathan Brody. 270p. 1988. text 69.95 (*0-12-134845-8*) Acad Pr.

Personality: Inquiry & Application. Mark Sherman. LC 78-13540. (General Psychology Ser.: Vol. 74). 560p. 1979. 40.00 (*0-08-019585-7*, Pergamon Pr) Elsevier.

Personality: Its Cultivation & Power & How to Attain. Lily L. Allen. 170p. 1992. pap. 15.00 (*0-89540-218-1*, SB-218) Sun Pub.

Personality: Measurement of Dimensions. LC 68-54939. (Jossey-Bass Behavioral Science Ser.). 262p. reprint ed. pap. 81.30 (*0-608-30838-2*, 201392500087) Bks Demand.

Personality: Selected Readings in Theory. Willard B. Frick. LC 93-86172. 323p. (C). 1994. pap. 35.00 (*0-87581-383-6*, PER) F E Peacock Pubs.

Personality: Strategies & Issues. 5th ed. Robert M. Liebert & Michael D. Spiegler. (C). 1987. pap. 39.00 (*0-534-10675-7*) Brooks-Cole.

Personality: Strategies & Issues. 6th ed. Robert M. Liebert & Michael D. Spiegler. LC 89-22097. 608p. (C). 1989. pap. 54.75 (*0-534-12228-0*) Brooks-Cole.

Personality: Strategies & Issues. 7th ed. Robert M. Liebert & Michael D. Spiegler. LC 93-36565. 1993. pap. 58.00 (*0-534-17580-5*) Brooks-Cole.

Personality: Strategies & Issues. 7th ed. Liebert & Siegler. (Psychology Ser.). 1994. pap., teacher ed. write for info. (*0-534-17582-1*) Wadsworth Pub.

Personality: Strategies & Issues. 7th ed. Liebert & Spiegler. 1994. write for info. (*0-534-22652-3*); pap. write for info. (*0-534-22653-1*) Wadsworth Pub.

Personality: Strategies & Issues. 8th ed. Robert M. Liebert. LC 97-44686. (Psychology Ser.). 643p. 1997. pap. 81.95 (*0-534-26418-2*) Brooks-Cole.

***Personality: Strategies & Issues.** 9th ed. Liebert & Liebert. 2001. pap. 58.50 (*0-534-57987-6*) Wadsworth Pub.

Personality: Test Bank. Ewen. 1998. pap. write for info. (*0-8058-3146-0*) L Erlbaum Assocs.

Personality: The Individuation Process in the Light of C. G. Jung's Typology. C. A. Meier. LC 76-15650. 214p. 1997. pap. 16.95 (*3-85630-549-1*) Continuum.

Personality: The Need for Liberty & Rights. Rubin Gotesky. 1987. 10.00 (*0-87212-012-0*) Libra.

Personality: Theories & Processes. (C). 1992. 12.33 (*0-06-501768-4*) Addison-Wesley.

Personality: Theories, Research & Applications. Lewis R. Aiken. LC 92-30073. 512p. (C). 1992. text 61.00 (*0-13-658733-X*) P-H.

Personality: Theory & Research. Jerry M. Burger. 510p. (C). 1986. mass mkt. 35.00 (*0-534-06126-5*) Brooks-Cole.

Personality: Theory & Research. 4th ed. Jerry M. Burger. LC 96-3311. (Psychology Ser.). 590p. 1996. text 52.25 (*0-534-33924-7*) Brooks-Cole.

Personality: Theory & Research. 4th ed. Jerry M. Burger. 1997. text, teacher ed. write for info. (*0-534-34562-X*) Brooks-Cole.

Personality: Theory & Research. 7th ed. Lawrence A. Pervin. LC 96-7678. 608p. 1996. text 89.95 (*0-471-12804-X*) Wiley.

Personality - A Topical Approach: Theories, Research, Major Controversies, & Emerging Findings. Robert B. Ewen. LC 96-53172. 600p. 1997. 34.50 (*0-8058-2098-1*) L Erlbaum Assocs.

***Personality Accountability: Powerful & Practical Ideas for You & Your Organization.** John G. Miller. 1998. 25.00 (*0-9665832-0-5*) DeVere Pr.

***Personality Accountability: Powerful & Practical Ideas for You & Your Organization.** John G. Miller. 1998. pap. 15.00 (*0-9665832-1-3*) Denver Pr.

Personality & Ability: The Personality Assessment System. Charles J. Krauskopf & David R. Saunders. LC 93-26379. 282p. (Orig.). (C). 1993. text 57.50 (*0-8191-9281-3*); pap. text 29.50 (*0-8191-9282-1*) U Pr of Amer.

Personality & Adversity: Psychospiritual Aspects of Rehabilitation. Carolyn Vash. LC 94-1497. 304p. (C). 1994. text 37.95 (*0-8261-8040-X*) Springer Pub.

Personality & Assessment. Walter Mischel. 376p. 1996. pap. 36.00 (*0-8058-2330-1*) L Erlbaum Assocs.

Personality & Belief: Interdisciplinary Essays on John Henry Newman. Ed. by Gerard Magill. 228p. (C). 1994. lib. bdg. 44.00 (*0-8191-9757-2*) U Pr of Amer.

Personality & Biography: Proceedings of the 6th International Conference on the History of Adult Education, Vols. I & II. Ed. by Martha Friedenthal-Haase. LC 98-17034. (Studies in Pedagogy, Andragogy & Gerontagogy: Vol. 38). (Illus.). LVIII, 886p. (C). 1998. pap. text 85.95 (*0-8204-3267-9*) P Lang Pubng.

Personality & Biography Vols. I & II: Proceedings of the 6th International Conference on the History of Adult Education: General, Comparative, & Synthetic Studies; Biographies of Adult Educators from Five Continents. Ed. by Martha Friedenthal-Haase. (Studies in Pedagogy, Andragogy, & Gerontagogy: Vol. 38). (Illus.). lviii, 886p. 1998. pap. 85.95 (*3-631-31531-7*) P Lang Pubng.

Personality & Democratic Politics. Paul M. Sniderman. LC 72-87201. 379p. reprint ed. pap. 117.50 (*0-7837-4687-3*, 204443400003) Bks Demand.

Personality & Depression: A Current View. Marjorie H. Klein. Ed. by David J. Kupfer et al. LC 92-48737. (MHP Ser.). 195p. 1993. lib. bdg. 31.50 (*0-89862-118-6*) Guilford Pubns.

***Personality & Development.** 350p. (C). 1999. 50.00 (*0-536-60148-8*) Pearson Custom.

***Personality & Development.** 752p. (C). 1999. 68.00 (*0-536-60166-6*) Pearson Custom.

Personality & Deviance: Development & Core Dynamics. S. Giora Shoham. LC 99-21595. 224p. 2000. 65.00 (*0-275-96683-6*) Greenwood.

Personality & Disease. Ed. by Howard S. Friedman. LC 90-11927. (Personality Processes Ser.). 315p. 1990. 145.00 (*0-471-61805-5*) Wiley.

Personality & Family Development: An Intergenerational Longitudinal Comparison. Klaus Schneewind & Stefan Ruppert. Tr. by Jonathan Harrow. LC 97-1096. 312p. 1997. 75.00 (*0-8058-2512-6*) L Erlbaum Assocs.

Personality & Heredity: An Introduction to Psychogenetics. Brian Wells. LC 80-40140. 235p. reprint ed. pap. 72.90 (*0-608-17049-6*, 202771800056) Bks Demand.

Personality & Ideology. Peter Leonard. (Critical Texts in Social Work & the Welfare State). 225p. (C). 1997. text 21.95 (*0-333-34726-9*, Pub. by Macmillan) Humanities.

Personality & Impersonality: Lawrence, Woolf & Mann. Daniel Albright. LC 77-23873. 328p. Date not set. reprint ed. pap. 101.70 (*0-608-20979-1*, 205450700003) Bks Demand.

Personality & Individual Differences: A Natural Science Approach. H. J. Eysenck & M. W. Eysenck. (Perspectives on Individual Differences Ser.). (Illus.). 452p. (C). 1985. 49.50 (*0-306-41844-4*, Plenum Trade) Perseus Pubng.

Personality & Intelligence: Psychometric & Experimental Approaches. Ed. by Robert J. Sternberg & Patricia Ruzgis. LC 93-21757. (Illus.). 351p. (C). 1994. text 59.95 (*0-521-41790-2*); pap. text 21.95 (*0-521-42835-1*) Cambridge U Pr.

Personality & Interpersonal Communication. Ed. by James C. McCroskey & John A. Daly. (Series in Interpersonal Communication: Vol. 6). 288p. 1987. text 52.00 (*0-8039-2645-6*); pap. text 24.50 (*0-8039-2646-4*) Sage.

Personality & Its Disorders: A Biosocial Learning Approach. Theodore Millon & George S. Everly, Jr. LC 84-21995. 304p. (C). 1985. pap. 49.95 (*0-471-87816-2*) Wiley.

Personality & Job Performance: A Special Issue of Human Performance. Ed. by Joyce Hogan. 181p. 1998. pap. 40.00 (*0-8058-9835-2*) L Erlbaum Assocs.

Personality & Love: An Illustrated Primer on Understanding Human Relationships. Frans M. Brandt. (Illus.). 110p. 1998. pap. 14.95 (*1-57502-858-1*, PO2326) Morris Pubng.

Personality & Mood by Questionnnaire. Raymond B. Cattell. LC 73-1853. (Jossey-Bass Behavioral Science Ser.). 552p. reprint ed. pap. 171.20 (*0-608-12258-0*, 202378300034) Bks Demand.

Personality & Morality: A Developmental Approach. Agnes Reardon. (Illus.). 122p. (Orig.). 1983. pap. 8.95 (*0-931474-26-4*) TBW Bks.

Personality & Organizational Influence. Ed. by Barry M. Staw & Larry L. Cummings. LC 90-4524. (Research in Organizational Behavior Ser.). 326p. 1990. pap. 25.75 (*1-55938-217-1*) Jai Pr.

Personality & Peer Influence in Juvenile Corrections, 38. Martin Gold & D. Wayne Osgood. LC 92-9328. (Contributions in Criminology & Penology Ser.: No. 38). 256p. 1992. 59.95 (*0-313-27970-5*, GPK, Greenwood Pr) Greenwood.

Personality & Personal Growth. 4th ed. (C). 1997. 24.00 (*0-321-40120-4*) Addson-Wesley Educ.

Personality & Personal Growth. 4th ed. Frager. (C). 1998. text 67.00 (*0-321-00586-4*) Addson-Wesley Educ.

Personality & Personal Growth. 4th ed. Robert D. Frager & James Fadiman. LC 97-10604. 576p. (C). 1997. 80.00 (*0-321-01192-9*, Prentice Hall) P-H.

Personality & Persuasibility. Janis L. Irving. LC 82-11848. (Yale Studies in Attitude & Communication). 333p. 1982. reprint ed. lib. bdg. 75.00 (*0-313-23320-9*, JAPE, Greenwood Pr) Greenwood.

Personality & Politics: Problems of Evidence, Inference, & Conceptualization. Fred I. Greenstein. LC 87-2427. 245p. 1987. reprint ed. pap. 76.00 (*0-608-02914-9*, 206397800008) Bks Demand.

Personality & Prediction: Principals of Personality Assessment. Jerry S. Wiggins. LC 87-17348. 704p. (C). 1988. reprint ed. lib. bdg. 75.50 (*0-89464-239-1*) Krieger.

Personality & Psychological Assessment. Benjamin Kleinmuntz. LC 85-18142. 462p. (C). 1985. reprint ed. lib. bdg. 52.50 (*0-89874-893-3*) Krieger.

Personality & Psychopathology. Ed. by C. Robert Cloninger. LC 98-30095. (American Psychopathological Association Ser.). xv, 524p. 1999. 59.95 (*0-88048-923-5*, 8923) Am Psychiatric.

Personality & Psychopathology: Building a Clinical Science: Selected Papers of Theodore Millon. Theodore Millon. LC 95-10576. 354p. 1995. 90.00 (*0-471-11685-8*, Wiley-Interscience) Wiley.

Personality & Psychopathology: Feminist Reappraisals. Ed. by Laura S. Brown & Mary Ballou. LC 91-38466. 272p. 1994. pap. text 23.00 (*0-89862-500-9*, 2500) Guilford Pubns.

Personality & Religion. Edgar S. Brightman. LC 75-3084. (Philosophy in America Ser.). reprint ed. 37.50 (*0-404-59083-7*) AMS Pr.

***Personality & Sexuality.** Ferrara. 2001. pap. 25.00 (*0-534-57645-1*) Thomson Learn.

Personality & Sexuality in the Physically Handicapped Woman. Carney Landis & M. Marjorie Bolles. Ed. by William R. Phillips & Janet Rosebberg. LC 79-6912. (Physically Handicapped in Society Ser.). 1980. reprint ed. lib. bdg. 19.95 (*0-405-13121-6*) Ayer.

Personality & Social Adjustment. Charles A. Heidenreich. 1970. 9.95 (*0-9600428-4-9*) Heidenreich.

Personality & Social Behaviour. Adrian Furnham & Patrick C. Heaven. LC 98-37860. 1998. text 75.00 (*0-340-67724-4*, Pub. by E A); pap. text 19.95 (*0-340-67725-2*, Pub. by E A) OUP.

Personality & Social Psychology: Towards a Synthesis. Barbara Krahe. (Illus.). 288p. (C). 1992. 59.95 (*0-8039-8724-2*); pap. 14.99 (*0-8039-8725-0*) Sage.

Personality & the Behavior Disorders: A Handbook Based on Experimental & Clinical Research, 1. Ed. by J. Hunt. LC 44-2163. (Illus.). 632p. reprint ed. pap. 196.00 (*0-608-11423-5*, 201241500081) Bks Demand.

Personality & the Behavior Disorders: A Handbook Based on Experimental & Clinical Research, 2. Ed. by J. Hunt. LC 44-2153. (Illus.). 631p. reprint ed. pap. 195.70 (*0-608-11424-3*, 201241500082) Bks Demand.

Personality & the Cultural Construction of Society: Papers in Honor of Melford E. Spiro. Ed. by David K. Jordan & Marc J. Swartz. LC 89-32993. 414p. 1990. reprint ed. pap. 128.40 (*0-608-01672-1*, 206232800002) Bks Demand.

Personality & the Environment. Ed. by Kenneth H. Craik & George E. McKechnie. LC 77-94068. (Sage Contemporary Social Science Issues Ser.: Vol. 42). 128p. reprint ed. pap. 39.70 (*0-608-30798-X*, 202188300026) Bks Demand.

Personality & the Social Group. Ernest W. Burgess. 230p. 1977. 18.95 (*0-8369-0066-9*) Ayer.

Personality & the Teaching of Composition. George H. Jensen & John K. DiTiberio. Ed. by Marcia Farr. LC 88-10446. (Writing Research Ser.: Vol. 20). 224p. (C). 1989. pap. 39.50 (*1-56750-159-1*) Ablx Pub.

Personality & the Teaching of Composition. George H. Jensen & John K. DiTiberio. Ed. by Marcia Farr. LC 88-10446. (Writing Research Ser.: Vol. 20). 224p. (C). 1989. text 73.25 (*0-89391-504-1*) Ablx Pub.

Personality Assessment. 2nd ed. Richard I. Lanyon & Leonard D. Goodstein. 328p. (C). 1992. pap. text 29.50 (*0-8191-8487-X*) U Pr of Amer.

Personality Assessment. 3rd ed. Richard I. Lanyon & Leonard Goodstein. LC 96-18061. (Series on Personality Processes). 438p. 1996. 74.50 (*0-471-55562-2*) Wiley.

***Personality Assessment: Methods & Practices.** 3rd ed. Lewis R. Aiken. 592p. 1999. 59.00 (*0-88937-209-8*) Hogrefe & Huber Pubs.

Personality Assessment in America: A Retrospective on the Occasion of the Fiftieth Anniversary of the Society for Personality Assessment. Ed. by E. I. Megargee & Charles D. Spielberger. 200p. (C). 1992. text 39.95 (*0-8058-0928-7*) L Erlbaum Assocs.

Personality Assessment in Managed Health Care: Using the MMPI-2 in Treatment Planning. Ed. by James Butcher. LC 96-9456. (Illus.). 264p. (C). 1997. text 40.00 (*0-19-511160-5*) OUP.

Personality at the Crossroads. David Magnusson & Norman S. Endler. LC 77-4190. 464p. (C). 1977. text 79.95 (*0-89859-293-3*) L Erlbaum Assocs.

Personality at Work: The Role of Individual Differences in the Workplace. Adrian F. Furnham. LC 93-30846. 448p. (C). 1994. pap. 25.99 (*0-415-10648-6*) Routledge.

***Personality Characteristics of Patients with Pain.** Ed. by Robert J. Gatchel & James N. Weisberg. LC 99-52773. 272p. 2000. 39.95 (*1-55798-646-0*) Am Psychol.

Personality Characteristics of the Personality Disordered. Ed. by Charles G. Costello. LC 95-7510. 340p. 1995. 75.00 (*0-471-01529-6*) Wiley.

Personality, Cognition, & Social Interaction. Ed. by N. Cantor & John F. Kihlstrom. LC 81-208. 384p. 1981. text 79.95 (*0-89859-057-4*) L Erlbaum Assocs.

Personality Comedians As Genre: Selected Players, 61. Wes D. Gehring. LC 96-47536. (Contributions to the Study of Popular Culture Ser.: Vol. 61). 232p. 1997. 59.95 (*0-313-26185-7*, Greenwood Pr) Greenwood.

Personality Compass: A New Way to Understand People. Diane Turner & Thelma Greco. LC 98-3554. 1998. 16.95 (*1-86204-285-3*); pap. 12.95 (*1-86204-425-2*, Pub. by Element MA) Penguin Putnam.

Personality Conception of the Legal Entity. Alexander Nekam. LC 38-37803. (Harvard Studies in the Conflict of Laws: Vol. 3). 131p. 1978. reprint ed. lib. bdg. 40.00 (*0-89941-128-2*, 301060) W S Hein.

Personality Description in Ordinary Language. Dennis B. Bromley. LC 76-40293. 288p. reprint ed. pap. 89.30 (*0-608-17615-X*, 203046700069) Bks Demand.

***Personality Development: Psychoanalytic Perspective.** Ed. by Debbie Hindle & Marta Vaciago Smith. LC 99-17408. 208p. (C). 1999. text. write for info. (*0-415-17957-2*) Routledge.

Personality Development: Psychoanalytic Perspective. Debbie Hindle & Marta V. Smith. LC 99-17408. 1999. pap. write for info. (*0-415-17958-0*) Routledge.

Personality Development: Theoretical, Empirical, & Clinical Investigations of Loevinger's Conception of Ego Development. P. Michiel Westenberg et al. LC 97-41407. 1998. 89.95 (*0-8058-1649-6*) L Erlbaum Assocs.

Personality Development & Deviation: A Textbook for Social Work. Ed. by George H. Wiedeman & Sumner Matison. LC 73-89439. 539p. 1974. 80.00 (*0-8236-4070-1*) Intl Univs Pr.

Personality Development & Psychopathology: A Dynamic Approach, 2 vols. 2nd ed. Norman Cameron & Joseph F. Rychlak. LC 84-80710. 816p. (C). 1984. text 78.36 (*0-395-34387-9*) HM.

Personality Development & Psychotherapy in Our Diverse Society: A Sourcebook. Rafael A. Javier & William G. Herron. LC 98-5659. (Illus.). 1998. 65.00 (*0-7657-0167-7*) Aronson.

Personality Development by Norma. Norma L. Williams. 100p. (Orig.). 1997. pap., teacher ed. 19.95 (*1-890644-07-2*) Union Cnty.

Personality Development for Work. 5th ed. Russon. (CA - Career Development Ser.). 1981. text 25.95 (*0-538-11420-7*) S-W Pub.

Personality Development for Work. 6th ed. Wallace. (CA - Career Development Ser.). 1988. mass mkt. 23.95 (*0-538-11430-4*); mass mkt. 10.95 (*0-538-11431-2*) S-W Pub.

Personality Development for Work. 7th ed. L. Ann Masters & Harold R. Wallace. LC 95-16940. 1995. mass mkt. 28.95 (*0-538-63665-3*) S-W Pub.

Personality Development for Work. 7th ed. Wallace. (CA - Career Development Ser.). 1995. mass mkt., wbk. ed. 12.95 (*0-538-63666-1*) S-W Pub.

Personality Development for Work: Tests. 6th ed. Wallace. (CA - Career Development Ser.). 1988. 1.95 (*0-538-11432-0*) S-W Pub.

Personality Development for Work: Tests. 7th ed. Wallace. (CA - Career Development Ser.). 1995. 5.95 (*0-538-63677-7*) S-W Pub.

P

An Asterisk (*) at the beginning of an entry indicates that the title is appearing for the first time.

Personality Development in Adolescence: A Cross National & Life Span Perspective. Eva Skoe & Anna L. Von Der Lippe. LC 97-37966. (Adolescence & Society Ser.). (Illus.). 240p. (C). 1998. pap. 24.99 (*0-415-13506-0*) Routledge.

Personality Development in Adolescence: A Cross National & Life Span Perspective. Eva Skoe & Anna L. Von Der Lippe. LC 97-37966. (Adolescence & Society Ser.). (Illus.). 240p. (C). 1998. 75.00 (*0-415-13505-2*) Routledge.

Personality Development in Adolescent Girls. Lawrence K. Frank et al. (SRCD M Ser.: Vol. 16). 1951. 25.00 (*0-527-01552-0*) Periodicals Srv.

Personality Development in Adulthood. Lawrence S. Wrightsman. 320p. 1988. pap. 23.50 (*0-8039-3345-2*); text 48.00 (*0-8039-2776-2*) Sage.

Personality Development in Adulthood. Lawrence S. Wrightsman. LC 87-35762. 312p. reprint ed. pap. 96.80 (*0-608-09790-X*, 206996400007) Bks Demand.

Personality Development in Individuals with Mental Retardation. Ed. by Edward Zigler & Dianne Bennett-Gates. LC 98-46761. (Illus.). 384p. (C). 1999. 64.95 (*0-521-63048-7*) Cambridge U Pr.

Personality Development in Individuals with Mental Retardation. Ed. by Edward Zigler & Dianne Bennett-Gates. LC 98-46761. (Illus.). 284p. (C). 1999. pap. 24.95 (*0-521-63963-8*) Cambridge U Pr.

Personality Development in Preschool Years, Latency, & Adolescence see Teaching Program in Psychiatry

Personality Development of Children. Singh Saraswati. 106p. 1995. pap. 100.00 (*81-7487-028-8*, Pub. by Print Hse) St Mut.

Personality Differences & Biological Variations: A Study of Twins. Gordon S. Claridge et al. LC 72-10132. (C). 1973. 84.00 (*0-08-017124-9*, Pub. by Pergamon Repr) Franklin.

Personality Dimensions & Arousal. J. Strelau & H. J. Eysenck. (Perspectives on Individual Differences Ser.). (Illus.). 344p. (C). 1987. 65.00 (*0-306-42437-1*, Plenum Trade) Perseus Pubng.

Personality Disorder in Children & Adolescents, Vol. 1. Paulina Kernberg. LC 99-46470. 320p. 1999. pap. 48.00 (*0-465-09562-3*, Pub. by Basic) HarpC.

Personality Disorder Interview IV: A Semistructured Interview for the Assessment of Personality Disorders. Thomas A. Widiger et al. LC 94-43676. 309p. 1995. 47.00 (*0-911907-21-1*) Psych Assess.

***Personality Disorders.** Linda N. Bayer. LC 99-28888. (Encyclopedia of Psychological Disorders Ser.). 144p. 2000. 24.95 (*0-7910-5317-2*) Chelsea Hse.

Personality Disorders. J. J. L. Derksen. 1995. pap. text 71.95 (*0-471-95549-3*) Wiley.

***Personality Disorders: Diagnosis, Management & Course.** 2nd ed. Peter J. Tyrer. LC 00-21641. (Illus.). 214p. 2000. pap. 45.00 (*0-7506-3433-2*) Buttrwrth-Heinemann.

Personality Disorders: New Look at the Developmental Self & Object Relations Approach: Theory, Diagnosis & Treatment. James F. Masterson. LC 99-32777. 2000. 35.95 (*1-891944-33-9*) Zeig Tucker.

Personality Disorders: New Perspectives on Diagnostic Validity. John M. Oldham. LC 89-18135. (Progress in Psychiatry Ser.). 217p. 1991. reprint ed. pap. 67.30 (*0-608-06667-2*, 206686400009) Bks Demand.

Personality Disorders: New Symptom-Focused Drug Therapy. Sonny Joseph. LC 96-28626. (Illus.). 274p. (C). 1997. 59.95 (*0-7890-0134-9*, Hawrth Medical); pap. text 29.95 (*0-7890-0195-0*, Hawrth Medical) Haworth Pr.

Personality Disorders: Recognition & Clinical Management. Jonathan H. Dowson & Adrian T. Grounds. (Illus.). 414p. (C). 1996. text 95.00 (*0-521-45049-7*) Cambridge U Pr.

***Personality Disorders & Culture: Clinical & Conceptual Interactions.** Renato D. Alarcon et al. LC 97-46371. 310p. 1998. 75.00 (*0-471-14964-0*) Wiley.

Personality Disorders & the Five-Factor Model of Personality. Ed. by Paul T. Costa, Jr. & Thomas A. Widiger. LC 93-26795. 364p. 1994. text 39.95 (*1-55798-214-7*) Am Psychol.

***Personality Disorders in Modern Life: Character Disorders.** Theodore Millon & Roger D. Davis. LC 99-30334. 581p. 1999. 55.00 (*0-471-32355-1*) Wiley.

Personality Disorders in Older Adults: Emerging Issues in Diagnosis & Treatment. Ed. by Erlene Rosowsky et al. LC 98-49371. (Personality & Clinical Psychology Ser.). 328p. 1999. 39.95 (*0-8058-2683-1*) L Erlbaum Assocs.

Personality Dynamics. B. B. Wilman. (Illus.). 176p. (C). 1991. 39.50 (*0-306-43956-5*, Plenum Trade) Perseus Pubng.

***Personality Effectiveness with Style: Facilitator Guide.** 2nd ed. Joseph R. Sullivan & Fred Leafgren. 59p. 1999. reprint ed. pap. 99.00 (*1-929112-13-0*) Personality Res.

***Personality Effectiveness with Style: Participant Workbook.** 2nd rev. ed. Joseph R. Sullivan. Ed. by Jerry Sheets. 44p. 1999. pap. 8.00 (*1-929112-14-9*) Personality Res.

Personality, Elevated Blood Pressure, & Essential Hypertension. Ed. by Ernest H. Johnson et al. LC 92-1480. (Series in Health Psychology & Behavioral Medicine). 1992. 69.95 (*1-56032-142-3*) Hemisp Pub.

Personality Factor. Jason Leigh. (Illus.). 120p. (Orig.). 1985. 5.95 (*0-934145-01-6*) Airborne Pr.

Personality Factors in Mothers of Excessively Crying Infants. Martin Lakin. (SRCD M Ser.: Vol. 22, No. 1). 1957. pap. 25.00 (*0-527-01569-5*) Periodicals Srv.

Personality, Genetics, & Behavior: Selected Papers. Hans J. Eysenck. Ed. by Charles D. Speilberger. LC 81-15765. (Centennial Psychology Ser.). 340p. 1982. 55.00 (*0-275-90787-2*, C0787, Praeger Pubs) Greenwood.

Personality in Adulthood. Robert R. McCrae & Paul Costa. LC 89-78494. 198p. 1990. pap. text 21.00 (*0-89862-528-9*) Guilford Pubns.

Personality in Culture & Society: An Interdisciplinary & Cross-Cultural Approach. 2nd ed. Won Hurh. 512p. (C). per. 54.95 (*0-7872-6616-7*) Kendall-Hunt.

Personality in German Literature Before Luther. Kuno Francke. LC 72-141480. 221p. 1973. reprint ed. lib. bdg. 22.50 (*0-8371-5865-6*, FRPG, Greenwood Pr) Greenwood.

Personality in Greek Epic, Tragedy, & Philosophy: The Self in Dialogue. Christopher Gill. 520p. (C). 1996. text 85.00 (*0-19-814676-0*) OUP.

Personality in Greek Epic, Tragedy, & Philosophy: The Self in Dialogue. Christopher Gill. 528p. 1998. reprint ed. pap. text 35.00 (*0-19-815232-9*) OUP.

Personality in Handwriting: A Step-by-Step Guide to Unlocking Hidden Talents & Desires In... Alfred O. Mendel. 1990. pap. 14.95 (*0-87877-153-0*) Newcastle Pub.

Personality in Japanese History. Ed. by Albert M. Craig & Donald H. Shively. LC 94-43147. (Michigan Classics in Japanese Studies: No. 13). x, 481p. 1995. reprint ed. pap. 18.95 (*0-939512-67-X*) U MI Japan.

Personality in Literature. Rolfe A. Scott-James. LC 68-22945. (Essay Index Reprint Ser.). 1977. reprint ed. 18.95 (*0-8369-0858-9*) Ayer.

Personality in Middle Life & Late Life: Empirical Studies. Bernice L. Neugarten et al. Ed. by Leon Stein. LC 79-8677. (Growing Old Ser.). (Illus.). 1980. reprint ed. lib. bdg. 25.95 (*0-405-12794-4*) Ayer.

Personality in Roman Private Law. P. W. Duff. xiii, 241p. 1971. reprint ed. 27.50 (*0-8377-2026-5*, Rothman) W S Hein.

Personality in Roman Private Law. Patrick W. Duff. LC 70-138536. xiii, 241p. 1971. reprint ed. lib. bdg. 12.50 (*0-678-04544-5*) Kelley.

Personality in the Depression, Vol. 12. Edward Rundquist & Raymond Sletto. LC 72-142315. (University of Minnesota Institute of Child Welfare Monographs: No. 12). (Illus.). 398p. 1975. reprint ed. lib. bdg. 55.00 (*0-8371-5903-2*, CWRP, Greenwood Pr) Greenwood.

Personality in the Social Process. Joel Aronoff & John P. Wilson. 408p. 1985. text 79.95 (*0-89859-526-6*) L Erlbaum Assocs.

Personality Index: To Hollywood Scandal Magazines, 1952-1966. Alan Betrock & Hillard Schneider. LC 90-92216. (Illus.). 64p. (Orig.). 1990. pap. 6.00 (*0-9626833-1-0*) Shake Bks.

Personality Inventory. Robert G. Bernreuter. 1986. write for info. (*0-8047-1065-1*) Stanford U Pr.

Personality Judgment: A Realistic Approach to Person Perception. David C. Funder. 304p. 1999. 69.95 (*0-12-269930-0*) Acad Pr.

Personality Lite. Date not set. write for info. (*0-926395-09-2*) Anchor Maryland.

Personality, Motivation & Action: Selected Papers. John W. Atkinson. Ed. by Charles D. Spielberger. LC 83-4261. (Centennial Psychology Ser.). 432p. 1983. 38.95 (*0-275-90937-9*, C0937, Praeger Pubs) Greenwood.

Personality Neurosurgery. 1988. 175.00 (*0-387-82088-4*) Spr-Verlag.

Personality of Britain, Its Influence on Inhabitant & Invader in Prehistoric & Early Historic Times. Cyril F. Fox. LC 78-27272. reprint ed. 55.00 (*0-404-14728-3*) AMS Pr.

Personality of Emerson. Franklin B. Sanborn. LC 72-156911. (Studies in Emerson: No. 12). 1971. reprint ed. lib. bdg. 75.00 (*0-8383-1290-X*) M S G Haskell Hse.

Personality of Ireland: Habitat, Heritage & History. rev. ed. E. Estyn Evans. (Illus.). 144p. 1992. pap. 13.95 (*0-946640-81-5*, Pub. by Lilliput Pr) Irish Bks Media.

Personality of the Cat. Ed. by Brant Aymar. (Illus.). 352p. (J). 1993. 9.99 (*0-517-00016-4*) Random Hse Value.

Personality of the Critic. Ed. by Joseph P. Strelka. LC 73-6880. (Yearbook of Comparative Criticism Ser.: Vol. 6). 220p. 1973. 30.00 (*0-271-01120-3*) Pa St U Pr.

Personality of the Dog. Ed. by Brandt Aymar & Edward Sagarin. 368p. 1995. 9.99 (*0-517-14665-7*) Random Hse Value.

Personality of the Holy Ghost. Charles H. Spurgeon. 1977. mass mkt. 0.75 (*1-56186-334-3*) Pilgrim Pubns.

Personality of the Horse. Random House Value Publishing Staff. LC 96-215516. 352p. 1988. 9.99 (*0-517-03785-8*) Random Hse Value.

Personality of the Organization: A Psycho-Dynamic Explanation of Culture & Change. Lionel Stapley. 250p. (C). 1996. pap. 22.50 (*1-85343-342-X*, Pub. by Free Assoc Bks) NYU Pr.

Personality of the Organization: A Psycho-Dynamic Explanation of Culture & Change. Lionel Stapley. 250p. (C). 1997. 55.00 (*1-85343-341-1*, Pub. by Free Assoc Bks) NYU Pr.

Personality of Thoreau. Franklin B. Sanborn. LC 80-2516. reprint ed. 34.50 (*0-404-19064-2*) AMS Pr.

Personality Organization in Cognitive Controls & Intellectual Abilities. Riley W. Gardner et al. (Psychological Issues Monographs: No. 8, Vol. 2, No. 4). 148p. (Orig.). 1961. 27.50 (*0-8236-4080-9*) Intl Univs Pr.

Personality Patterns & Oral Reading: A Study of Overt Behavior in the Reading Situation As It Reveals Reactions of Dependence, Aggression, & Withdrawal in Children. Gladys Natchez. LC 60-6043. 112p. reprint ed. pap. 34.80 (*0-608-11175-9*, 205032200061) Bks Demand.

Personality Plus see Enriquezca Su Personalidad

Personality Plus: How to Understand Others by Understanding Yourself. 2nd expanded rev. ed. Florence Littauer. LC 92-13275. 208p. (gr. 11). 1994. pap. 9.99 (*0-8007-5445-X*) Revell.

Personality Plus: Some Experiences of Emma McChesney & Her Son, Jock. Edna Ferber. LC 77-150473. (Short Story Index Reprint Ser.). (Illus.). 1977. reprint ed. 18.95 (*0-8369-3813-5*) Ayer.

***Personality Plus for Parents: Understanding What Makes Your Child Tick.** Florence Littauer. 2000. pap. 11.99 (*0-8007-5737-8*) Revell.

Personality, Power & Authority: A View from the Behavioral Sciences, 1. Leonard W. Doob. LC 83-1688. (Contributions in Psychology Ser.: No. 1). 218p. 1983. 55.00 (*0-313-23920-7*, DPA/, Greenwood Pr) Greenwood.

Personality, Power, & Politics: The Historical Significance of Napoleon, Bismarck, Lenin, & Hitler. Anthony R. De Luca. 133p. 1983. pap. 13.95 (*0-87073-617-5*) Schenkman Bks Inc.

Personality Power the Specific Action Way: A Complete Course in Management Styles. Owen Allen. LC 87-63535. (Illus.). 110p. (C). 1988. text 25.00 (*0-932569-01-3*) Specific Action.

Personality Probe. Nathan Levy. (J). (gr. k up). 1990. pap. 21.95 (*1-878347-07-1*) NL Assocs.

Personality Projection in the Drawing of the Human Figure: A Method of Personality Investigation. Karen Machover. (Illus.). 192p. 1980. 37.95 (*0-398-01184-2*); pap. 24.95 (*0-398-06260-9*) C C Thomas.

Personality Psychology. Ed. by D. M. Buss & Nancy Cantor. (Illus.). 335p. 1989. 80.95 (*0-387-96993-4*) Spr-Verlag.

Personality Psychology: A Student Centered Approach. Jim McMartin. 216p. 1995. text 42.00 (*0-8039-5343-7*); pap. text 19.50 (*0-8039-5344-5*) Sage.

Personality Psychology: The Science of Individuality. Nathan Brody & Howard Ehrlichman. LC 97-20128. 446p. 1997. 83.00 (*0-13-146903-7*) P-H.

Personality Psychology in Europe, Vol. 3. G. Van Heck et al. xiv, 242p. 1990. pap. 32.00 (*90-265-1037-3*) Swets.

Personality Psychology in Europe Vol. 2: Current Trends & Controversies. Ed. by A. Angleitner et al. xii, 272p. 1986. pap. 57.75 (*90-265-0597-3*) Swets.

Personality Puzzle. David Funder. (C). 1997. pap. text. write for info. (*0-393-98012-X*) Norton.

Personality Puzzle. David C. Funder. LC 96-2140. (C). 1996. pap. text 40.50 (*0-393-96993-2*) Norton.

Personality Puzzle. 2nd ed. David Funder. (C). pap. text. write for info. (*0-393-97541-X*) Norton.

Personality Puzzle: Understanding the People You Work With. Florence Littauer & Marita Littauer. LC 92-5608. 208p. (gr. 11). 1992. pap. 9.99 (*0-8007-1676-0*) Revell.

Personality Research in Marketing: A Bibliography. Ed. by Dik W. Twedt et al. LC 76-45806. (American Marketing Association Bibliography Ser.: No. 23). 58p. reprint ed. pap. 30.00 (*0-608-11940-7*, 202336100032) Bks Demand.

Personality Research, Methods & Theory: A Festschrift Honoring Donald W. Fiske. Ed. by Patrick E. Shrout & Susan T. Fiske. 384p. 1995. pap. 36.00 (*0-8058-1271-7*); text 79.95 (*0-8058-1270-9*) L Erlbaum Assocs.

***Personality Rights & Freedom of Expression: The Modern Actio Injuriarum.** J. Burchell. LC 99-223774. 448p. 1999. pap. 74.50 (*0-7021-4810-5*, Pub. by Juta & Co) Gaunt.

Personality, Roles & Social Behavior. Ed. by W. Ickes & E. S. Knowles. (Social Psychology Ser.). (Illus.). 362p. 1982. 105.00 (*0-387-90637-1*) Spr-Verlag.

Personality Self-Portrait see New Personality Self-Portrait: Why You Think, Work, Love & Act the Way You Do

***Personality Selling: Using NLP & the Enneagram to Understand People & How They Are Influenced.** Albert J. Valentino. 368p. 1999. pap. 17.95 (*0-9667732-3-3*, Pub. by Vantage Point) ACCESS Pubs Network.

Personality, Social, & Biological Perspectives on Personal Adjustment. Bem P. Allen. 550p. (C). 1990. text 48.95 (*0-534-13020-8*) Brooks-Cole.

Personality, Social Skills, & Psychopathology: An Individual Differences Approach. D. G. Gilbert & J. J. Connolly. (Perspectives on Individual Differences Ser.). (Illus.). 312p. (C). 1991. 59.50 (*0-306-43793-7*, Plenum Trade) Perseus Pubng.

Personality, Spirit, & Ethics: The Ethics of Nicholas Berdyaev. Howard A. Slaatte. LC 96-42959. (American University Studies: Vol. 181, No. V). IX, 122p. (C). 1997. pap. text 24.95 (*0-8204-3671-2*) P Lang Pubng.

Personality Structure & Human Interaction: The Developing Synthesis of Psychodynamic Theory. Harry Guntrip. LC 61-12135. 456p. 1964. 67.50 (*0-8236-4120-1*) Intl Univs Pr.

Personality Structure & Measurement. Hans J. Eysenck & Sybil B. G. Eysenck. LC 68-15875. 1968. text 18.00 (*0-912736-08-9*) EDITS Pubs.

Personality Structure in the Life Course. Ed. by Robert A. Zucker et al. LC 91-26162. (Illus.). 400p. 1992. pap. 37.95 (*0-8261-7870-7*) Springer Pub.

Personality Style Workbook: Understanding Yourself. Sanford G. Kulkin. (Illus.). 20p. 1997. pap. text, wbk. ed. 12.00 (*1-58034-016-4*) IML Pubns.

Personality Surgeon. Colin Wilson. LC 85-62423. 322p. (Orig.). 1986. 17.95 (*0-916515-04-4*) Mercury Hse Inc.

Personality Survives Death. Lady Barrett. 1972. 59.95 (*0-8490-0819-0*) Gordon Pr.

Personality System Certification Guide. 80p. 1993. pap. write for info. (*1-58034-023-7*) IML Pubns.

Personality System Workbook. 24p. 1993. pap. 8.00 (*1-58034-015-6*, P001W) IML Pubns.

Personality Test. Ted DeLong. 40p. 1995. pap. text 15.00 (*1-885661-04-5*) Estate Protection.

Personality Test: See Yourself As Others See You. Dan Pape. (Illus.). 32p. (Orig.). (C). 1993. pap. write for info. (*1-882330-16-1*) Magni Co.

Personality Tests & Reviews II. Ed. by Oscar K. Buros. LC 74-13192. (Tests in Print Ser.). xxxi, 841p. 1975. text 65.00 (*0-910674-19-1*) U of Nebr Pr.

Personality Theories. 3rd ed. Hjelle. 1992. teacher ed. 54.68 (*0-07-029080-6*) McGraw.

Personality Theories. 3rd ed. Larry A. Hjelle & Daniel J. Zeigler. 402p. (C). 1992. 78.13 (*0-07-029079-2*) McGraw.

Personality Theories. 3rd ed. Larry A. Hjelle & Daniel J. Zeigler. (C). 1992. text 60.25 (*0-07-911290-0*) McGraw.

Personality Theories, 4 vols. 4th ed. Barbara O. Engler. LC 94-76501. (C). 1994. text 69.56 (*0-395-70835-4*) HM.

Personality Theories. 6th ed. Maddi. 1996. teacher ed. write for info. (*0-534-34078-4*) Thomson Learn.

Personality Theories: A Comparative Analysis. 5th ed. Salvatore R. Maddi. 749p. (C). 1989. text 45.00 (*0-534-10696-X*) Brooks-Cole.

***Personality Theories: An Introduction** 5th ed. Barbara O. Engler. LC 98-72020. xxv, 550 p. 1999. write for info. (*0-395-90765-9*) HM.

***Personality Theories: Development, Growth & Diversity.** 3rd ed. Allen. LC 99-18624. 518p. (C). 1999. 82.00 (*0-205-28709-3*, Macmillan Coll) P-H.

Personality Theories: Journeys into Self - An Experiential Workbook. 2nd ed. Willard B. Frick. 144p. (C). 1991. pap. text, wbk. ed. 14.95 (*0-8077-3088-2*) Tchrs Coll.

Personality Theory, 4 vols. Barbara O. Engler. LC 94-76501. (C). Date not set. text, teacher ed., suppl. ed. 69.56 (*0-395-71710-8*) HM.

Personality Theory, 4 vols. Barbara O. Engler. (C). 1994. pap., teacher ed. 11.96 (*0-395-70836-2*) HM.

***Personality Theory.** Hogan. 2000. 65.00 (*0-8133-6634-8*, Pub. by Westview) HarpC.

Personality Theory & Clinical Practice. Peter Fonagy & Anna Higgitt. 194p. 1985. pap. 8.95 (*0-416-35630-3*, NO. 9182) Routledge.

Personality Theory & Information Processing. Ed. by Harold M. Schroder et al. LC 77-123053. (Illus.). 318p. reprint ed. pap. 98.60 (*0-608-11216-X*, 201237600081) Bks Demand.

Personality ,Theory & Research. Burger. (Psychology). 1986. teacher ed. write for info. (*0-534-06127-3*) Wadsworth Pub.

Personality Theory in Action: Handbook for the Objective-Analytic (O-A) Battery. Raymond B. Cattell & James M. Schuerger. LC 78-50146. 1978. 58.75 (*0-918296-11-0*) Inst Personality & Ability.

Personality Theory Notes. David Dillala. (Adaptable Courseware Ser.). 1997. 6.25 (*0-534-49768-3*) Brooks-Cole.

Personality Traits. Gerald Matthews & Ian J. Deary. LC 97-14349. 320p. (C). 1998. text 59.95 (*0-521-49739-6*); pap. text 19.95 (*0-521-49759-0*) Cambridge U Pr.

Personality Traits in Professional Services Marketing. James B. Wetizul. LC 93-41818. 184p. 1994. 59.95 (*0-89930-877-5*, Quorum Bks) Greenwood.

Personality Type A: Index of New Information with Authors, Subjects, Research Categories & References. Lois A. Hutton. 150p. 1997. 47.50 (*0-7883-1334-7*); pap. 44.50 (*0-7883-1335-5*) ABBE Pubs Assn.

Personality Type & Religious Leadership. Roy M. Oswald & Otto Kroeger. LC 88-70758. 183p. (Orig.). 1988. pap. 17.95 (*1-56699-025-4*, AL103) Alban Inst.

Personality Type & Scripture: Exploring Mark's Gospel. Leslie J. Francis. LC 98-129558. 160p. 1997. pap. 15.95 (*0-304-70087-8*) Continuum.

Personality Type in Congregations: How to Work with Others More Effectively. Lynne M. Baab. LC 97-78129. xvi, 155p. 1998. pap. 15.25 (*1-56699-199-4*, AL190) Alban Inst.

Personality Types. Daryl Sharp. (Illus.). 128p. 1995. pap. 16.00 (*0-919123-30-9*, Pub. by Inner City Bks) BookWorld.

Personality Types. rev. ed. Don R. Riso & Russ Hudson. 456p. 1996. pap. 14.00 (*0-395-79867-1*) HM.

Personality Types & Culture in Later Adulthood. J. Shanan. (Contributions to Human Development Ser.: Vol. 12). (Illus.). xiv, 146p. 1985. 51.25 (*3-8055-3998-3*) S Karger.

Personality Types at Work: Using the Enneagram to Understand the People You Deal With. Don Richard Roso. 1999. 21.95 (*0-07-077997-X*) McGraw.

Personality Typologies: A Comparison of Western & Ancient Indian Approaches. C. Beena. 1990. 59.00 (*81-7169-092-0*, Commonwealth) S Asia.

Personality Unfolded Through Script-Psychology. unabridged ed. Rex Smith. (Illus.). 414p. 1989. pap. text 24.95 (*0-9623117-0-7*) Writeway Servs.

***Personalized & Database Printing: The Complete Guide.** David Broudy. 1999. pap. 49.95 (*0-941845-24-9*) Micro Pub Pr.

Personalized Care Model for the Elderly. Ed. by Clara Nicholson & Judith Nicholson. 540p. 1983. pap. text 21.30 (*0-317-00780-7*) Elder.

***Personalized Instructing: Changing Classroom Practice.** James W. Keefe & John M. Jenkins. 225p. 2000. 29.95 (*1-883001-86-2*) Eye On Educ.

Personalized Parenting Program, Grades K-12. Arden Martenz. (Orig.). 1995. pap. 450.00 (*1-884063-63-2*) Mar Co Prods.

Personalized Perfumes: More than 40 Recipes for Making Fragrances with Essential Oils. Gail Duff. (Illus.). 80p. 1994. 16.00 (*0-671-88029-2*) S&S Trade.

Personalized Prayers for Every Day Living. Coral Kennedy. (Orig.). 1999. pap. 9.95 (*0-9663308-3-8*) North Church.

Personalized Stress Management: A Manual for Everyday Life & Work. Joseph L. Gill. LC 82-90115. (Illus.). 175p. 1983. 14.95 (*0-910819-00-9*); pap. 9.95 (*0-910819-01-7*) Counsel & Consult.

P

An Asterisk (*) at the beginning of an entry indicates that the title is appearing for the first time.

Personalized System of Instruction. J. Gilmour Sherman & Robert S. Ruskin. Ed. by Danny G. Langdon. LC 77-25415. (Instructional Design Library). (Illus.). 128p. 1978. 27.95 (*0-87778-117-6*) Educ Tech Pubns.

Personalized Whole Brain Integration: The Basic II Manual on Educational Kinesiology. Paul E. Dennison & Gail E. Dennison. (Illus.). 98p. (Orig.). 1985. pap. 15.95 (*0-942143-07-8*) Edu-Kinesthetics.

Personalizing Care with Infants, Toddlers & Families. Ed. by Elaine Surbeck & Michael F. Kelley. LC 90-24570. (Illus.). 80p. 1990. 12.00 (*0-87173-122-3*) ACEI.

Personalizing Foreign Language Instruction. Ed. by Robert DiDonato. (Central States Ser.). pap. 14.21 (*0-8442-9305-9*, VF9305-9) NTC Contemp Pub Co.

***Personalizing Language Learning.** Griff Griffiths & Kathy Keohane. LC 99-55435. 1999. write for info. (*0-521-63364-8*) Cambridge U Pr.

Personalizing Music Education. Joan Fyfe. 296p. 1978. pap. 24.95 (*0-88284-063-0*, 1688) Alfred Pub.

Personalizing Professional Growth: Staff Development That Works. Bernadette Marczely. LC 96-10056. (Illus.). 144p. 1996. 49.95 (*0-8039-6433-1*); pap. 21.95 (*0-8039-6434-X*) Corwin Pr.

Personalizing Professional Growth: Staff Development That Works. Bernadette Marczely. 144p. 1996. 43.95 (*2-8106-6433-1*); pap. 18.95 (*2-8106-6434-X*) NEA.

Personalizing Reading Efficiency. 2nd ed. Lyle L. Miller. (C). 1981. pap. text. write for info. (*0-8087-3990-5*) Pearson Custom.

***Personalizing Your PC.** Robert W. Beattie. 72p. 2000. pap. 6.95 (*0-7894-6854-9*) DK Pub Inc.

Personally Conducted. Frank Stockton. (Notable American Authors Ser.). 1999. reprint ed. lib. bdg. 125.00 (*0-7812-8929-7*) Rprt Serv.

***Personally, I Wouldn't Buy It Either.** Joseph T. Neilson. 137p. 1999. pap. 11.95 (*0-7414-0317-X*) Buy Books.

Personally Speaking. James P. Lisante. 144p. 2000. pap. 8.95 (*1-878718-51-7*, Resurrection Pr) Catholic Bk Pub.

Personally Yours. Freda Amsel. 28p. (Orig.). 1989. pap. text. write for info. (*0-9602026-1-7*) Amsel Enterps.

Personas Mexicanas: Chicano High Schoolers in a Changing Los Angeles (Case Studies in Cultural Anthropology) James D. Vigil. LC 96-77233. 176p. (C). 1997. pap. text 23.50 (*0-15-503838-9*) Harcourt Coll Pubs.

Personas Ocupadas. Christian Focus Staff. (Serie Uniendo los Puntos - Dot to Dot Ser.: No. 2).Tr. of Busy People. (SPA.). 17p. (J). 1993. pap. 1.59 (*1-56063-387-5*, 494012) Editorial Unilit.

Personas Que Jesus Conocio. Penny Frank & John Hayson. (Serie Historias de la Biblia - Children's Bible Story Books Ser.).Tr. of People Jesus Met. (SPA.). 24p. (J). 1984. 1.50 (*0-8423-6266-5*, 490345) Editorial Unilit.

Persone - En Familiereg. J. D. Van Der Vyver & D. Joubert. 738p. 1991. pap. write for info. (*0-7021-2549-0*, Pub. by Juta & Co) Gaunt.

Persone- en Familiereg, Die Suid-Afrikaanse. 3rd ed. D. S. Cronje. (AFR.). 388p. 1994. pap. write for info. (*0-409-04625-6*, MICHIE) LEXIS Pub.

***Personen Und Identitaten.** Dieter Teichert. 1999. 124.00 (*3-11-016405-1*) De Gruyter.

Personennamen der Inschriften aus Hatra. Sabri Abbadi. (Texte und Studien Zur Orientalistik Ser.: Vol. 1). xxviii, 217p. 1983. 30.00 (*3-487-07427-3*) G Olms Pubs.

Personennamen in den Altsabaischen Inschschriften. Salem A. Tairan. (Texte und Studien Zur Orientalistik Ser.: Bd. 8). (GER.). viii, 265p. 1992. write for info. (*3-487-09665-X*) G Olms Pubs.

Personereg Bronnebundel. A. Jordaan & T. Davel. 366p. 1992. pap. write for info. (*0-7021-2801-5*, Pub. by Juta & Co) Gaunt.

Personhood. Leo F. Buscaglia. 147p. 1986. pap. 11.00 (*0-449-90199-8*, Columbine) Fawcett.

Personhood. Leo F. Buscaglia. LC 78-66423. 160p. 1978. 9.95 (*0-913590-63-0*) SLACK Inc.

Personhood: Growing in Wholeness & Holiness. Center for Learning Network Staff. (Religion). 60p. (YA). (gr. 9-12). 1996. spiral bd. 12.95 (*1-56077-481-9*) Ctr Learning.

Personhood: Growing in Wholeness & Holiness - Student Text. Center for Learning Network Staff. (Discipleship Ser.). 122p. (YA). (gr. 9-10). 1996. 7.95 (*1-56077-469-X*) Ctr Learning.

Personhood: Growing in Wholeness & Holiness -Teacher Manual. Center for Learning Network Staff. (Discipleship Ser.). 117p. (YA). (gr. 9-10). 1996. spiral bd. 9.95 (*1-56077-470-3*) Ctr Learning.

Personhood: Orthodox Christianity & the Connection Between Body, Mind, & Soul. John T. Chirban. LC 95-34302. 216p. 1996. 57.95 (*0-89789-463-4*, Bergin & Garvey) Greenwood.

Personhood in Advanced Old Age: Implications for Practice. Sheldon S. Tobin. LC 90-10444. 200p. 1991. 30.95 (*0-8261-7580-5*) Springer Pub.

Personification & the Sublime: Milton to Coleridge. Steven Knapp. 192p. 1985. 34.50 (*0-674-66320-9*) HUP.

Personified Street. Thomas R. Crowe. LC 93-92608. (Night Sun Trilogy Ser.: Bk. 1). 88p. 1993. pap. 9.95 (*1-883197-01-5*) New Native Pr.

Personliche Wirken und Werben see Voices of German Pacifism

Personnages. Francoise Mallet-Joris. (FRE.). 462p. 1973. 13.95 (*0-8288-9841-3*, F110790); pap. 3.95 (*0-686-56311-5*) Fr & Eur.

Personnages. Oates. (C). 1995. pap., teacher ed., suppl. ed. 11.96 (*0-395-67104-3*) HM.

Personnages. Oates. (C). 1995. pap., wbk. ed., lab manual ed. 24.76 (*0-395-67103-5*) HM.

Personnages. Michael D. Oates & Jacques F. Dubois. (FRE.). (C). 1994. text, teacher ed. 46.76 incl. audio (*0-395-72678-6*); pap. text 45.56 incl. audio (*0-395-72677-8*) HM.

Personnages Historiques Figurant dans la Poesie Lyrique Francaise des XII et XIIIe Siecles. Holger N. Petersen-Dyggve. LC 80-2166. 1981. 67.50 (*0-404-19031-6*) AMS Pr.

Personnel. 1993. pap. text 41.00 (*0-13-093451-8*) P-H.

Personnel. Edward P. Lazear. LC 97-7933. 560p. 1998. text 89.95 (*0-471-59466-0*) Wiley.

Personnel. Steven Rouse. Date not set. pap. 6.00 (*0-8166-2796-7*) U of Minn Pr.

Personnel. Marie-Elise Wheatwind. 16p. (Orig.). 1983. pap. 3.00 (*0-930012-45-3*) J Mudfoot.

Personnel. 2nd ed. Leon C. Megginson. (C). 1972. 14.50 (*0-256-00360-2*, Irwn McGrw-H) McGrw-H Hghr Educ.

Personnel: Recruiting, Motivating, Rewarding. Ed. by J. R. King, Jr. LC 83-70392. 93p. 1983. pap. 12.00 (*0-87262-365-3*) Am Soc Civil Eng.

Personnel: The Department at Work. Ed. by Penny Hackett. 196p. (C). 1991. pap. text 60.00 (*0-85292-458-5*, Pub. by IPM Hse) St Mut.

Personnel: The Department at Work. Ed. by Penny Hackett. (C). 1992. write for info. incl. audio (*0-85292-477-1*, Pub. by IPM Hse) St Mut.

Personnel - HR Management in Small Organizations & Growing Companies. 500p. 1997. pap. text 99.00 (*0-939900-58-0*) Soc Human Resc Mgmt.

Personnel - Human Resource Management. Floyd A. Patrick. 512p. (C). 1994. per. 52.95 (*0-8403-9435-7*) Kendall-Hunt.

Personnel - Human Resource Management. Jack Rudman. (Dantes Subject Standardized Tests (DANTES) Ser.: Vol. 48). 43.95 (*0-8373-6548-1*) Nat Learn.

Personnel Administration. Jackson Flanigan. (C). 1995. text. write for info. (*0-8013-1105-5*) Addison-Wesley.

Personnel Administration: Its Principles & Practice. Ordway Tead, Jr. & Henry C. Metcalfe. Ed. by Alfred D. Chandler. LC 79-7556. (History of Management Thought & Practice Ser.). 1980. reprint ed. lib. bdg. 50.95 (*0-405-12342-6*) Ayer.

Personnel, Administration & Computer Occupations. Jack Rudman. (Career Examination Ser.: C-3555). 1994. pap. 27.95 (*0-8373-3555-8*) Nat Learn.

Personnel Administration Handbook. John Forsaith & Nick Townsend. 560p. 1997. 380.00 (*0-85292-647-2*, Pub. by IPM Hse) St Mut.

***Personnel Administration Handbook Updates.** John Forsaith & Townsend. 2000. boxed set 75.00 (*0-8464-5128-X*) Beekman Pubs.

***Personnel Administration Handbook 1997.** John Forsaith & Townsend. 560p. 2000. boxed set 295.95 (*0-8464-5127-1*) Beekman Pubs.

Personnel Administration in an Automated Environment. Ed. by Philip E. Leinbach. LC 90-39450. (Journal of Library Administration: Vol. 13, Nos. 1-2). 214p. 1990. text 49.95 (*1-56024-032-6*) Haworth Pr.

Personnel Administration in Education: A Management Approach. 2nd ed. Ronald W. Rebore. (Illus.). 368p. (C). 1987. text 31.95 (*0-13-657719-9*) P-H.

Personnel Administration in Education: A Management Approach. 5th ed. Ronald W. Rebore. LC 97-16286. 360p. 1997. 75.00 (*0-205-26912-5*) Allyn.

Personnel Administration in Higher Education: Handbook of Faculty & Staff Personnel Practices. Ray T. Fortunato & D. Geneva Waddell. LC 81-47769. (Jossey-Bass Higher Education Ser.). 410p. reprint ed. pap. 127.10 (*0-7837-2504-3*, 204266300006) Bks Demand.

Personnel Administration in Libraries. 2nd ed. Shiela Creth & Frederick Duda. 353p. 1989. pap. text 55.00 (*1-55570-036-5*) Neal-Schuman.

Personnel Administration in the Christian School. J. Lester Brubaker. 168p. (Orig.). 1980. pap. 9.99 (*0-88469-130-6*) BMH Bks.

Personnel Administration Made Simple: Forms, Cards & Computers. John Bramham & David Cox. 340p. (C). 1984. 108.00 (*0-85292-306-6*) St Mut.

Personnel Administration Today. Craig E. Schneier & Richard W. Beatty. 1978. pap. text. write for info. (*0-201-00503-4*) Addison-Wesley.

Personnel Administrator. Jack Rudman. (Career Examination Ser.: C-647). 1994. pap. 39.95 (*0-8373-0647-7*) Nat Learn.

Personnel Analyst. Jack Rudman. (Career Examination Ser.: C-2344). 1994. pap. 34.95 (*0-8373-2344-4*) Nat Learn.

Personnel Analyst Trainee. Jack Rudman. (Career Examination Ser.: C-2395). 1994. pap. 27.95 (*0-8373-2395-9*) Nat Learn.

Personnel & Human Resource Management. Andrew F. Sikula & John F. McKenna. 480p. (C). 1990. reprint ed. lib. bdg. 49.50 (*0-89464-414-9*) Krieger.

Personnel & Human Resource Management. 5th ed. Randall S. Schuler & Vandra L. Huber. Ed. by Fenton. LC 92-30205. 650p. (C). 1993. text 60.75 (*0-314-01184-6*) West Pub.

Personnel & Human Resource Management in Canada. Shimon D. Dolan & Randall S. Schuler. 620p. (C). 1987. pap. text, teacher ed. write for info. (*0-314-34766-6*) West Pub.

Personnel & Human Resources Administration. 3rd ed. Leon C. Megginson. (C). 1977. 18.95 (*0-256-01909-6*, Irwn McGrw-H) McGrw-H Hghr Educ.

Personnel & Human Resources Development, Vol. 1. Ed. by Jill Muehrcke. (Leadership Ser.). 95p. 1990. spiral bd. 35.00 (*0-614-07105-4*) Soc Nonprofit Org.

Personnel & Human Resources Development, Vol. 2. Ed. by Jill Muehrcke. (Leadership Ser.). 72p. 1993. spiral bd. 35.00 (*0-614-07106-2*) Soc Nonprofit Org.

Personnel & Operations Manual for Travel Agencies. 3rd ed. Douglas Thompson & Alexander Anolik. 200p. 1992. 65.00 incl. disk (*0-936831-02-2*) Dendrobium Bks.

Personnel & Profit: The Pay-Off from People. Hugo Fair. 160p. (C). 1991. pap. text 75.00 (*0-85292-462-3*, Pub. by IPM Hse) St Mut.

Personnel & the Bottom Line. Michael Armstrong. 256p. (C). 1989. 150.00 (*0-85292-421-6*, Pub. by IPM Hse) St Mut.

Personnel & the Law. Joanne D. Scheuch & Wendy E. Shannon. 106p. 1989. pap. 32.00 (*0-685-50409-3*, 623202) Am Bankers.

***Personnel & the Line.** 96p. 2000. pap. 105.00 (*0-8464-5129-8*) Beekman Pubs.

Personnel & the Line Developing the New Relationship. (IPD Research Ser.). 96p. 1995. pap. 150.00 (*0-85292-606-5*, Pub. by IPM Hse) St Mut.

***Personnel Armor System Ground Troops Helmet: Illust.Study of Us Military Current Issue Helmet.** Mark A. Reynosa. (Illus.). 80p. 2000. pap. 19.95 (*0-7643-1034-8*) Schiffer.

Personnel Assistant. Jack Rudman. (Career Examination Ser.: C-577). 1994. pap. 29.95 (*0-8373-0577-2*) Nat Learn.

Personnel Associate. Jack Rudman. (Career Examination Ser.: C-648). 1994. pap. 29.95 (*0-8373-0648-5*) Nat Learn.

Personnel Classification Board: Its History, Activities & Organization. Paul V. Betters. LC 72-3081. (Brookings Institution. Institute for Government Research. Service Monographs of the U. S. Government: No. 64). reprint ed. 24.00 (*0-404-57164-6*) AMS Pr.

Personnel Clerk. Jack Rudman. (Career Examination Ser.: C-2461). 1994. pap. 23.95 (*0-8373-2461-0*) Nat Learn.

Personnel Decisions in the Family Farm Business. Amy R. Lyman. 64p. 1993. 6.00 (*1-879906-13-9*, 3357) ANR Pubns CA.

Personnel Development in Libraries. Ed. by R. Kay Maloney. (Issues in Library & Information Sciences Ser.: No. 3). 1977. pap. text 15.00 (*0-8135-0843-6*) Rutgers U SICLS.

Personnel Director. Einar J. Westerlund & John R. Talbot. 24p. (C). 1986. pap. 45.00 (*0-86236-003-X*, Pub. by Granary) St Mut.

Personnel Director's Legal Guide. rev. ed. Steven C. Kahn et al. 1994. text 142.00 (*0-685-69667-7*, PDLG) Warren Gorham & Lamont.

Personnel Director's Legal Guide, No. 2745. Steven C. Kahn & Michael Lanzarone. 1200p. 1991. text, suppl. ed. 48.00 (*0-7913-1033-7*) Warren Gorham & Lamont.

Personnel Economics. Edward P. Lazear. (Wicksell Lectures). (Illus.). 184p. 1995. 27.50 (*0-262-12188-3*) MIT Pr.

Personnel Evaluation Standards: How to Assess Systems for Evaluating Educators. Daniel L. Stufflebeam. LC 88-18189. 224p. (C). 1988. 55.95 (*0-8039-3360-6*, D1478); pap. text 24.95 (*0-8039-3361-4*, D1478) Corwin Pr.

Personnel Examiner. Jack Rudman. (Career Examination Ser.: C-578). 1994. pap. 29.95 (*0-8373-0578-0*) Nat Learn.

Personnel Examining Trainee. Jack Rudman. (Career Examination Ser.: C-579). 1994. pap. 27.95 (*0-8373-0579-9*) Nat Learn.

Personnel for Health Care: Case Studies of Educational Programmes, Vol. 1. F. Katz. (Public Health Papers: No. 70). 260p. 1978. text 21.00 (*92-4-130070-1*, 1110070) World Health.

Personnel for Health Care: Case Studies of Educational Programmes, Vol. 2. F. Katz. (Public Health Papers: No. 71). 202p. 1980. pap. text 14.00 (*92-4-130071-X*, 1110071) World Health.

Personnel Forms & Employment Checklist, Issue 7. 2nd ed. Maureen F. Moore. 100p. 1999. ring bd. write for info. (*0-327-01030-4*, 8232417) LEXIS Pub.

Personnel Forms & Employment Checklists. Maureen F. Moore. 440p. 1994. ring bd. 79.50 incl. disk (*0-614-05944-5*, MICHIE) LEXIS Pub.

Personnel Forms & Employment Checklists. 2nd ed. Maureen F. Moore. Date not set. ring bd. 95.00 (*0-327-01026-6*, 82323-11, MICHIE) LEXIS Pub.

Personnel Function in a Changing Environment. T. P. Lyons. (Times Management Library). 1971. pap. 22.95 (*0-8464-0710-8*) Beekman Pubs.

Personnel-Human Resource Management. Jack Rudman. (Dantes Subject Standardized Tests Ser.: DANTES-48). 1994. pap. 23.95 (*0-8373-6648-8*) Nat Learn.

Personnel /Human Resource Management. 2nd ed. (C). 1994. 7.00 (*0-02-368524-7*, Macmillan Coll) P-H.

Personnel-Human Resource Management: An Environmental Approach. Vida G. Scarpello & James Ledvinka. 816p. (C). 1988. text 57.25 (*0-534-08346-3*) S-W Pub.

Personnel Human Resource Management Today. 2nd ed. Craig E. Schneier et al. (C). 1986. pap. text 22.36 (*0-201-05794-8*) Addison-Wesley.

Personnel Human Resources. 5th ed. Randall S. Schuler. Date not set. pap. text. write for info. (*0-314-01840-9*) West Pub.

Personnel-Human Resources Mangement see Human Resource Management: Environments & Functions

Personnel in Context. David Farnham. 336p. (C). 1990. 95.00 (*0-85292-451-8*, Pub. by IPM Hse) St Mut.

Personnel in Context. David Farnham. 336p. (C). 1986. 89.00 (*0-85292-387-2*) St Mut.

Personnel in Practice. Donald Currie. (Illus.). 256p. (Orig.). 1997. pap. 38.95 (*0-631-20089-4*) Blackwell Pubs.

Personnel Issues & Answers. Karen Jorgensen & James Zimmerman. 150p. 1992. pap. 39.50 (*1-55943-159-8*, MICHIE) LEXIS Pub.

Personnel Issues in Reference Services. Ed. by Bill Katz & Ruth Fraley. LC 86-3063. (Reference Librarian Ser.: No. 14). 200p. 1986. text 49.95 (*0-86656-523-X*) Haworth Pr.

Personnel Issues in Reference Services. Ed. by Bill Katz & Ruth Fraley. 200p. 1993. pap. 19.95 (*0-86656-524-8*) Haworth Pr.

Personnel Law. 4th ed. Kenneth L. Sovereign. LC 98-34088. (Illus.). 362p. (C). 1998. pap. text 40.00 (*0-13-020038-7*) P-H.

Personnel Law Answer Book. James O. Castagnera & JoAnne S. Haffeman. 315p. 1988. text 79.00 (*0-916592-89-8*) Panel Pubs.

Personnel Law Answer Book. James O. Castagnera & JoAnne S. Haffeman. 400p. 1991. pap. text, suppl. ed. 49.99 (*1-878375-65-2*) Panel Pubs.

Personnel Law Answer Book, 1991 Supplement. James O. Castagnera. Ed. by Richard K. Walton. 1990. text 49.00 (*1-878375-25-3*) Panel Pubs.

Personnel Law for Community Associations. 3rd ed. William E. Stewart. LC 97-187155. 76p. (C). 1997. pap. 18.95 (*0-941301-39-7*) CAI.

Personnel Law for Community Associations: What Every Homeowners' Association & Manager Should Know. rev. ed. William E. Stewart. LC 93-9388. 1993. 18.95 (*0-941301-22-2*) CAI.

Personnel Law Handbook, 1993. Wake Forest University School of Law Continuing Le. 904p. 1993. pap. 125.00 (*0-942225-70-8*) Wake Forest Law.

Personnel Letters Ready to Go. Cheryl D. Wilson. Ed. by Frank Barnett. LC 94-41439. (. . . Ready to Go! Ser.). (Illus.). 160p. (Orig.). 1995. pap. 12.95 (*0-8442-3542-3*) NTC Contemp Pub Co.

Personnel Management. Jack Rudman. (ACT Proficiency Examination Program (PEP) Ser.: Vol. 20). 43.95 (*0-8373-5570-2*) Nat Learn.

Personnel Management. Jack Rudman. (ACT Proficiency Examination Program Ser.: PEP-20). 1994. pap. 23.95 (*0-8373-5520-6*) Nat Learn.

Personnel Management. A. W. Savage. LC 78-311085. (Library Association Management Pamphlets: Vol. 1). 63p. reprint ed. pap. 30.00 (*0-608-08889-7*, 206952600004) Bks Demand.

Personnel Management. 2nd ed. Keith Sisson. (Industrial Relations in Context Ser.). 500p. (C). 1994. pap. text 43.95 (*0-631-18821-5*) Blackwell Pubs.

Personnel Management. 4th ed. Gary Dessler. (Illus.). 704p. (C). 1988. text. write for info. (*0-318-62356-0*) P-H.

Personnel Management. 8th ed. Michael Jucius. (C). 1975. 14.95 (*0-256-01644-5*, Irwn McGrw-H) McGrw-H Hghr Educ.

***Personnel Management: A Comprehensive Guide to Theory & Practice.** 3rd ed. Keith Sisson & Stephen E. Bach. LC HF5549.2.G7P47 1999. 500p. 1999. 74.95 (*0-631-21291-4*); pap. text 39.95 (*0-631-21292-2*) Blackwell Pubs.

Personnel Management: A Computer Based System. Cary Thorp. Ed. by Sang M. Lee. 1979. pap. 15.00 (*0-89433-053-5*); text 22.50 (*0-89433-052-7*) Petrocelli.

Personnel Management: A New Approach. Derek Torrington & Laura Hall. 602p. (C). 1987. 90.00 (*0-13-658501-9*) St Mut.

Personnel Management: A New Approach. 2nd ed. Ed. by Derek Torrington & Laura Hall. 661p. (C). 1991. pap. 110.00 (*0-13-658667-8*, Pub. by IPM Hse) St Mut.

Personnel Management: Communications. Prentice-Hall Staff. 1984. write for info. (*0-318-58014-4*) P-H.

Personnel Management: Compensation. Prentice-Hall Staff. 1984. write for info. (*0-318-58015-2*) P-H.

Personnel Management: Policies & Practices. Prentice-Hall Staff. 1984. write for info. (*0-318-58013-6*) P-H.

Personnel Management & Banking. T. Cowan. 1985. 50.00 (*0-85297-077-3*, Pub. by Chartered Bank) St Mut.

Personnel Management & Human Relations. Zabka, John R. Associates Inc. Staff. LC 73-142500. 1971. 12.30 (*0-672-96095-8*, Bobbs); teacher ed. 6.67 (*0-672-96097-4*, Bobbs); student ed. 6.75 (*0-672-96096-6*, Bobbs) Macmillan.

Personnel Management & Municipal Administration in India. A. Amruth Rao. 1985. 32.50 (*0-8364-1389-X*, Pub. by Ashish Pub Hse) S Asia.

Personnel Management & the Single European Market, 1992. Incomes Data Services Staff. 60p. (C). 1988. pap. 40.00 (*0-85292-418-6*, Pub. by IPM Hse) St Mut.

Personnel Management for Effective Schools. 2nd ed. John T. Seyfarth. LC 95-9231. 352p. 1995. 78.33 (*0-205-16613-X*) Allyn.

Personnel Management for Effective Schools. 2nd ed. John T. Seyfarth. (C). 1995. pap., teacher ed. write for info. (*0-205-18564-9*, H8564-0) Allyn.

Personnel Management for Printers. Pira Staff. 1998. 70.00 (*1-85802-098-0*, Pub. by Pira Pub) Bks Intl VA.

Personnel Management for Small Business in the Water Service Industries. S. Smith. 50p. 1980. 8.75 (*1-56034-036-3*, T035) Natl Grnd Water.

Personnel Management for Sport Directors. Timothy E. Flannery & Michael L. Swank. LC 98-37669. 176p. 1999. pap. 22.00 (*0-88011-757-5*) Human Kinetics.

Personnel Management for the Small Business. Neville C. Tompkins. LC 95-83115. (Small Business & Entrepreneurship Ser.). 193p. (Orig.). 1996. pap. 15.95 (*1-56052-363-8*) Crisp Pubns.

Personnel Management for the Smaller Company: A Hands-on Manual. Linda A. Roxe. LC 79-10867. 256p. reprint ed. pap. 79.40 (*0-608-12965-8*, 202392000034) Bks Demand.

Personnel Management, Human Capital Theory, & Human Resource Accounting. Eric G. Flamholtz & John M. Lacey. (Monograph & Research Ser.: No. 27). 112p. 1981. 7.00 (*0-89215-111-0*) U Cal LA Indus Rel.

Personnel Management in Government: Politics & Process. 4th ed. Rosenbloom et al. (Public Administration & Public Policy Ser.: Vol. 44). (Illus.). 576p. 1991. text 59.75 (*0-8247-8590-8*) Dekker.

Personnel Management in Local Government. Alan Fowler. 318p. (C). 1980. 75.00 (*0-85292-270-1*) St Mut.

P

An Asterisk (*) at the beginning of an entry indicates that the title is appearing for the first time.

Personnel Management in the Medical Practice: The Physician's Handbook for Successful Management. American Medical Association. (Practice Success Ser.). 1996. pap. 44.95 (*0-89970-756-4*, OP700995WE) AMA.

Personnel Management in the Public Sector. Steven W. Hays & T. Zane Reeves. 524p. (C). 1994. text. write for info. (*0-697-25257-4*) Brown & Benchmark.

Personnel Management Law. Date not set. pap. 43.95 (*0-8464-4410-0*) Beekman Pubs.

Personnel Management, 1913-1963: The Growth of Personnel Management & the Development of the Institute. Mary M. Niven. 174p. (C). 1978. 50.00 (*0-85292-199-3*) St Mut.

Personnel Management of a Medical Practice. (Illus.). 225p. 1999. pap. 65.00 (*1-58383-039-1*, PERMGT9) Robert D Keene.

Personnel: Management Of Human Resources. 3rd ed. Donald P. Crane. LC 81-19295. (SWC-Management). 752p. (C). 1982. mass mkt. 28.25 (*0-534-01070-9*) PWS Pubs.

Personnel Manager. Jack Rudman. (Career Examination Ser.: C-2112). 1994. reprint ed. pap. 39.95 (*0-8373-2112-3*) Nat Learn.

Personnel Manager's Encyclopedia of Prewritten Personnel Policies, 3 vols. rev. ed. Sue Ellen Thompson & Business & Legal Reports Staff. LC 99-186409. 1998. ring bd. write for info. (*1-55645-419-8*) Busn Legal Reports.

Personnel Manager's Encyclopedia of Prewritten Personnel Policies, 3 vols., Set. rev. ed. Ed. by Sue E. Thompson. 1983. ring bd. 159.95 (*1-55645-409-0*, 315000) Busn Legal Reports.

Personnel Manager's Handbook of College Recruiting. rev. ed. Stephen D. Bruce. 90p. 1983. per. 33.95 (*1-55645-507-0*, 507) Busn Legal Reports.

Personnel Manager's Handbook of Performance Evaluation Programs. rev. ed. S. E. Parnes. 85p. 1981. per. 27.95 (*1-55645-117-2*, 404) Busn Legal Reports.

Personnel Manager's Portfolio of Model Letters. Mary F. Cook. LC 84-15065. 198p. 1984. 60.00 (*0-13-659251-1*, Busn) P-H.

Personnel Manual: An Outline for Libraries. rev. ed. Ed. by Charles E. Kratz & Valerie A. Platz. LC 92-41087. (Illus.). 92p. (C). 1993. pap. text 25.00 (*0-8389-3418-8*) ALA.

Personnel Manual: 1994 Edition. rev. ed. Compiled by North State Cooperative Library System Staff. 72p. 1994. ring bd. 9.00 (*1-891367-04-8*) North State Coop.

Personnel Mgt Situational Apprch. Donald P. Crane. (SWC-Management). 1974. pap. 15.75 (*0-534-00356-7*) PWS Pubs.

Personnel Municipal de Paris Pendant la Revolution. Paul Robiquet. LC 73-174332. (Collection de documents relatifs a l'histoire de Paris pendant la Revolution francaise). reprint ed. 135.00 (*0-404-52557-1*) AMS Pr.

Personnel of George Rogers Clark's Fort Jefferson: And the Civilian Community of Clarksville (Kentucky), 1780-1781. Kenneth C. Carstens. LC 99-219504. 189p. 1999. pap. 22.00 (*0-7884-1183-7*, C066) Heritage Bk.

Personnel Officer. Jack Rudman. (Career Examination Ser.: C-2343). 1994. pap. 29.95 (*0-8373-2343-6*) Nat Learn.

Personnel Organization & Procedure: A Manual Suggested for Use in Public Libraries. 2nd ed. American Library Association Staff. LC 68-21023. 59p. reprint ed. pap. 30.00 (*0-608-12794-9*, 202421400035) Bks Demand.

Personnel Policies & Practices. ring bd. write for info. (*0-318-57379-2*) P-H.

Personnel Policies & Practices Made Easy. Minnie Harrington. Ed. by Eugene Harrington. 110p. 1997. pap. 79.95 (*0-9658111-0-7*) Harrington Assocs.

Personnel Policies & Procedures for Health Care Facilities: A Manager's Deskbook & Guide. Eugene P. Buccini & Charles P. Mullaney. LC 88-36491. 311p. 1989. 89.50 (*0-89930-425-7*, BPQ, Quorum Bks) Greenwood.

Personnel Policies for Engineers & Scientists: An Analysis of Major Corporate Practice. Herbert R. Northrup & Margot E. Malin. LC 85-60642. (Manpower & Human Resources Studies: Vol. 11). 331p. 1985. 30.00 (*0-89546-053-X*) U PA Ctr Hum Res.

Personnel Policies in Libraries. Ed. by Nancy P. Van Zant. LC 80-11734. 334p. 1980. 45.00 (*0-918212-26-X*) Neal-Schuman.

Personnel Policies Prewritten. 400p. 1996. pap. text 495.00 (*0-7605-4329-1*) Rector Pr.

Personnel Policy Handbook: How to Develop a Manual That Works. William S. Hubbartt. LC 93-9807. 582p. 1992. 74.95 (*0-07-030833-0*) McGraw.

Personnel Policy in the City: The Politics of Jobs in Oakland (Oakland Project) Frank J. Thompson. 1975. pap. 11.95 (*0-520-03509-7*, Pub. by U CA Pr) Cal Prin Full Svc.

Personnel Practice. Malcolm Martin & Tricia Jackson. 192p. 1997. pap. 60.00 (*0-85292-678-2*, Pub. by IPM Hse) St Mut.

Personnel Practice Ideas. Ed. by Gerard P. Panaro. 125.00 (*0-685-69668-5*, PPI) Warren Gorham & Lamont.

***Personnel Practice 1997.** Martin & Jackson. 192p. 2000. pap. 44.95 (*0-8464-5130-1*) Beekman Pubs.

***Personnel Practice 2000.** Martin & Jackson. 208p. 2000. pap. 44.95 (*0-8464-5181-6*) Beekman Pubs.

Personnel Practices: Presidential Transition Conversions & Appointments: Changes Needed. (Illus.). 73p. (Orig.). (C). 1995. pap. text 20.00 (*0-7881-1694-0*) DIANE Pub.

Personnel Practices: Propriety of Career Appointments Granted Former Political Appointees. (Illus.). 59p. (Orig.). (C). 1993. pap. text 25.00 (*0-7881-0177-3*) DIANE Pub.

Personnel Practices for the Nineties: A Local Government Guide. Ed. by John Matzer, Jr. (Practical Management Ser.). (Orig.). 1988. pap. text 23.95 (*0-87326-055-4*) Intl City-Cnty Mgt.

***Personnel Preparation in Disability & Community Life: Toward Universal Approaches to Support.** Julie Ann Racino. LC 00-37737. 2000. pap. write for info. (*0-398-07078-4*) C C Thomas.

Personnel Psychology. 2nd ed. P. J. D. Drenth. LC 98-186244. (Work & Organizational Psychology Handbks.). 1998. 69.95 (*0-86377-524-1*, Pub. by Psychol Pr) Taylor & Francis.

Personnel Record Keeper. Ed. by Mark D. Persons. (Illus.). 400p. 1991. ring bd. 86.00 (*1-878375-31-8*) Panel Pubs.

Personnel Record Keeper, 1991. Matthew J. DeLuca & Mark D. Persons. 302p. 1990. text 86.00 (*0-916592-95-2*) Panel Pubs.

Personnel Safety in Helicopter Operations: Helirescue Manual. Patrick Lavall & Robert C. Stoffel. (Illus.). 124p. 1988. ring bd. 8.50 (*0-913724-36-X*) Emerg Response Inst.

***Personnel Savings in Competitively Sourced DOD Activities: Are They Real? Will They Last?** Susan Gates & Albert A. Robbert. (Illus.). xxii, 111p. (C). 2000. pap. 15.00 (*0-8330-2826-X*, MR-1117) Rand Corp.

Personnel Security: Pass & Security Clearance Data for the Executive Office of the President. 36p. (Orig.). (C). 1996. pap. text 20.00 (*0-7881-2951-1*) DIANE Pub.

Personnel Selection: A Theoretical Approach. Neal Schmitt & David Chan. LC 98-25336. (Foundations for Organizational Science Ser.). 378p. 1998. 48.50 (*0-7619-0985-0*); pap. 23.50 (*0-7619-0986-9*) Sage.

***Personnel Selection: Adding Value Through People.** 3rd ed. Mark Cook. LC 97-44532. 366p. 1998. pap. 37.00 (*0-471-98158-3*) Wiley.

Personnel Selection: Adding Value Through People. 3rd ed. Mark Cook. LC 97-44532. 366p. 1998. 87.95 (*0-471-98156-7*) Wiley.

Personnel Selection & Placement. Dunnette. (Psychology). 1967. mass mkt. 14.75 (*0-8185-0311-4*) Brooks-Cole.

Personnel Selection & Assessment: Individual & Organizational Perspectives. Ed. by Heinz Schuler et al. (Applied Psychology Ser.). 384p. 1993. text 89.95 (*0-8058-1034-X*) L Erlbaum Assocs.

Personnel Selection & Classification. Ed. by Michael G. Rumsey et al. 504p. 1994. text 49.95 (*0-8058-1644-5*) L Erlbaum Assocs.

Personnel Selection in Organizations. Neal Schmitt et al. LC 92-23346. (Jossey-Bass Management Ser.). 546p. 1992. 43.45 (*1-55542-475-9*) Jossey-Bass.

Personnel Specialist. Jack Rudman. (Career Examination Ser.: C-1386). 1994. pap. 29.95 (*0-8373-1386-4*) Nat Learn.

Personnel Studies of Scientists in the United States. Ching-Ju Ho. LC 76-176867. (Columbia University. Teachers College. Contributions to Education Ser.: No. 298). reprint ed. 37.50 (*0-404-55298-6*) AMS Pr.

Personnel Study of Deans of Girls in High Schools. Sarah M. Sturtevant & Ruth Strang. LC 71-177730. (Columbia University. Teachers College. Contributions to Education Ser.: No. 393). reprint ed. 37.50 (*0-404-55393-1*) AMS Pr.

Personnel Study of Deans of Women in Teachers Colleges & Normal Schools. Sarah M. Sturtevant & Ruth Strang. (Columbia University. Teachers College. Contributions to Education Ser.: No. 319). reprint ed. 17.50 (*0-404-55319-2*) AMS Pr.

Personnel Study of Women Deans in Colleges & Universities. Jane L. Jones. LC 78-176917. (Columbia University. Teachers College. Contributions to Education Ser.: No. 326). reprint ed. 37.50 (*0-404-55326-5*) AMS Pr.

Personnel Systems Analyst. Jack Rudman. (Career Examination Ser.: C-1387). 1994. pap. 34.95 (*0-8373-1387-2*) Nat Learn.

Personnel Technician. Jack Rudman. (Career Examination Ser.: C-1944). 1994. pap. 29.95 (*0-8373-1944-7*) Nat Learn.

Personnel Technician Trainee. Jack Rudman. (Career Examination Ser.: C-2274). 1994. pap. 27.95 (*0-8373-2274-X*) Nat Learn.

Personnel Testing: A Manager's Guide. John W. Jones. Ed. by Sara Schneider. LC 93-72502. (Fifty-Minute Ser.). (Illus.). 98p. (Orig.). 1994. pap. 10.95 (*1-56052-233-X*) Crisp Pubns.

Personnel Transactions Supervisor. Jack Rudman. (Career Examination Ser.: C-3150). 1994. pap. 29.95 (*0-8373-3150-1*) Nat Learn.

Personnel Travel Greenhouse Effect. Peter Hughes. 1992. 30.00 (*1-85383-169-7*, Pub. by Escan Pubns) Island Pr.

Personnel Turbulence: The Policy Determinants of Permanent Change of Station Moves. W. Michael Hix et al. LC 97-42459. (Illus.). 77p. 1998. pap. 15.00 (*0-8330-2582-1*, MR-938-A) Rand Corp.

Personnel Utilization in Libraries: A Systems Approach. Myrl Ricking. LC 74-8688. 168p. reprint ed. pap. 52.10 (*0-608-12591-1*, 202395300034) Bks Demand.

Personnel/Human Resources Program Appraisal Workbook. Gloria A. White. 21p. 1989. 7.50 (*0-910402-90-6*) Coll & U Personnel.

Personology: Method & Content in Personality Assessment & Psychobiography. Irving E. Alexander. LC 89-36230. 294p. (Orig.). (C). 1990. text 54.95 (*0-8223-0996-3*); pap. text 19.95 (*0-8223-1020-1*) Duke.

Persons: A Comparative Account of the Six Possible Theories, 13. F. F. Centore. LC 78-74653. (Contributions in Philosophy Ser.: No. 13). 329p. 1979. 65.00 (*0-313-20817-4*, CPE/, Greenwood Pr) Greenwood.

Persons: What Philosophers Say about You. Warren Bourgeois. LC 96-135942. viii, 340p. (C). 1995. pap. 29.95 (*0-88920-251-6*) W Laurier U Pr.

***Persons & Bodies: A Constitution View.** Lynne Rudder Baker. (Studies in Philosophy). 256p. (C). 2000. text 49.95 (*0-521-59263-1*); pap. text 18.95 (*0-521-59719-6*) Cambridge U Pr.

Persons & Causes: The Metaphysics of Free Will. Timothy O'Connor. LC 99-20501. 160p. 2000. text 35.00 (*0-19-513308-0*) OUP.

Persons & Events. Ludwig Fuerbringer. (American Autobiography Ser.). 274p. 1995. reprint ed. lib. bdg. 79.00 (*0-7812-8524-0*) Rprt Serv.

Persons & Institutions in Early Rabbinic Judaism. Ed. by William S. Green. LC 76-52503. (Brown Judaic Studies: Vol. 3). 316p. reprint ed. pap. 98.00 (*0-608-08688-6*, 206921100003) Bks Demand.

Persons & Minds: The Prospects of Nonreductive Materialism. Joseph Margolis. (Synthese Library: No. 121). 314p. 1977. pap. text 55.50 (*90-277-0863-0*, D Reidel); lib. bdg. 88.00 (*90-277-0854-1*, D Reidel) Kluwer Academic.

Persons & Periods: Studies. George D. Cole. LC 67-26726. (Essay Index Reprint Ser.). 1977. 20.95 (*0-8369-0323-4*) Ayer.

Persons & Periods: Studies by G. D. H. Cole. George D. Cole. LC 73-75412. vii, 332p. 1969. reprint ed. 39.50 (*0-678-00495-1*) Kelley.

Persons & Personal Relationships: Love, Identity & Ethics. Hugh LaFollette. 256p. (C). 1995. 58.95 (*0-631-19684-6*); pap. 25.95 (*0-631-19685-4*) Blackwell Pubs.

Persons & Personality: An Introduction to Psychology. Annette Walters & Kevin O'Hara. LC 52-13695. (Century Psychology Ser.). (C). 1953. 36.00 (*0-89197-550-0*) Irvington.

Persons & Places - Critical Edition: The Autobiography of George Santayana. George Santayana. Ed. by Herman J. Saatkamp & William G. Holzberger. (Illus.). 547p. 1987. 47.50 (*0-262-19238-1*, Bradford Bks) MIT Pr.

Persons & Places - Trade Edition: The Autobiography of George Santayana. George Santayana. Ed. by Herman J. Saatkamp & William G. Holzberger. (Illus.). 661p. 1988. pap. text 16.95 (*0-262-69114-0*, Bradford Bks) MIT Pr.

Persons & Places in One Volume. George Santayana. (Hudson River Editions Ser.). 1981. 35.00 (*0-684-16830-8*) S&S Trade.

Persons & Places of the Bronte Novels. Herbert E. Wroot. (BCL1-PR English Literature Ser.). 237p. 1992. reprint ed. lib. bdg. 79.00 (*0-7812-7453-2*) Rprt Serv.

Persons & Powers of Women in Diverse Cultures. Ed. by Shirley Ardener. (Illus.). 224p. 1992. pap. 19.50 (*0-85496-866-0*, Pub. by Berg Pubs) NYU Pr.

Persons & Powers of Women in Diverse Cultures. Ed. by Shirley Ardener. (Illus.). 224p. 1992. 49.50 (*0-85496-744-3*, Pub. by Berg Pubs) NYU Pr.

Persons & Their Bodies: Rights, Responsibilities, Relationships. Mark J. Cherry. LC 99-25030. (Philosophy & Medicine Ser.). 1999. write for info. (*0-7923-5701-9*) Kluwer Academic.

Persons & Their Minds: A Philosophical Investigation. Elmer Sprague. LC 99-20268. 208p. 1999. 60.00 (*0-8133-9127-X*) Westview.

***Persons & Their Minds: A Philosophical Investigation.** Elmer Sprague. LC 99-20268. 208p. 1999. mass mkt. 23.00 (*0-8133-9128-8*) Westview.

Persons & Their World. Olen. 1983. teacher ed. 16.00 (*0-07-554386-9*) McGraw.

Persons & Their World: An Introduction to Philosophy. Jeffrey Olen. 608p. (C). 1983. text 41.74 (*0-07-554311-7*) McGraw.

Persons, Animals, & Fetuses: An Essay in Practical Ethics. Mary G. Forrester. (Philosophical Studies: Vol. 66). 312p. (C). 1996. text 147.00 (*0-7923-3918-5*) Kluwer Academic.

***Persons, Animals, Ships & Cannons in the Aubrey-Maturin Sea Novels of Patrick O'Brian.** Anthony G. Brown. LC 99-30996. (Illus.). 350p. 1999. pap. 35.00 (*0-7864-0684-4*) McFarland & Co.

Persons, Behavior, & the World: The Descriptive Psychology Approach. Mary M. Shideler. 362p. (Orig.). (C). 1988. pap. text 31.00 (*0-8191-6787-8*) U Pr of Amer.

Persons, Divine & Human. Ed. by Christoph Schwobel & Colin E. Gunton. 216p. 1992. text 44.95 (*0-567-09584-3*, Pub. by T & T Clark) Bks Intl VA.

***Persons, Divine & Human.** Ed. by Christoph Schwobel & Colin E. Gunton. 176p. 1999. pap. 27.95 (*0-567-08660-7*) T&T Clark Pubs.

Persons-Exegese und Christologie bei Augustinus: Zur Herkunft der Formel una Persona. Hubertus R. Drobner. (Philosophia Patrum Ser.: Vol. 8). xiii, 353p. 1986. 74.00 (*90-04-07875-4*) Brill Academic Pubs.

Persons Handicapped by Rubella: Victors & Victims, a Follow-Up Study. Jan J. Van Dijk et al. 180p. 1991. 38.00 (*90-265-1128-0*) Swets.

Persons in Communion: Trinitarian Description & Human Participation. Alan J. Torrance. 400p. 1996. text 54.95 (*0-567-09740-4*, Pub. by T & T Clark) Bks Intl VA.

Persons in Context: Developmental Processes. Ed. by Niall Bolger et al. (Human Development in Cultural & Historical Contexts Ser.). (Illus.). 280p. 1989. text 49.95 (*0-521-35577-X*) Cambridge U Pr.

Persons in Groups: Social Behavior As Identity Formation. Ed. by Richard C. Trexler. LC 84-27211. (Medieval & Renaissance Texts & Studies: Vol. 36). (Illus.). 272p. 1985. 24.00 (*0-86698-069-5*, MR36) MRTS.

Persons in Hiding. J. Edgar Hoover. xix, 325p. 1997. reprint ed. 95.00 (*1-56169-340-5*) Gaunt.

Persons in Love. Luther. 1972. pap. text 65.00 (*90-247-1292-0*) Kluwer Academic.

***Persons in Process: Four Stories of Writing & Personal Development in College.** Anne J. Herrington & Marcia Curtis. LC 99-56816. 445p. 2000. pap. 34.95 (*0-8141-3512-9*, 35129) NCTE.

Persons in Relation. John Macmurray. LC 91-21420. 256p. (C). 1991. pap. 17.50 (*0-391-03716-1*) Humanities.

Persons in Relation. John Macmurray. LC 98-54284. 1998. write for info. (*1-57392-625-6*, Humanity Bks) Prometheus Bks.

Persons Naturalized in the Province of Pennsylvania, 1740-1773: With an Added Index (From the "Pennsylvania Archives," Second Series, Vol. 2, 1890) John B. Linn & William H. Egle. 139p. 1997. reprint ed. pap. 16.00 (*0-8063-0213-5*, 3395) Clearfield Co.

Persons of Hispanic Origin in the United States. (Illus.). 356p. (C). 1994. pap. text 50.00 (*0-7881-0619-8*) DIANE Pub.

Persons of Hispanic Origin in the United States. 1995. lib. bdg. 299.99 (*0-8490-6521-6*) Gordon Pr.

Persons of Hispanic Origin in the United States. 1997. lib. bdg. 255.95 (*0-8490-6085-0*) Gordon Pr.

Persons, Passions & Politics. M. Yunus. 333p. 1980. 16.95 (*0-7069-1017-6*) Asia Bk Corp.

Persons, Places & Things. Sam Adams. 139p. 1998. pap. 15.00 (*0-9665891-0-6*) P S Brown LA.

Persons, Places & Things Around the Finger Lakes Region: The Heart of New York State. Emerson Klees. LC 94-94335. 288p. 1994. pap. 15.00 (*0-9635990-4-6*) Frnds Finger Lks.

Persons, Places & Things in the Finger Lakes Region: The Heart of New York State. 2nd ed. Emerson C. Klees. LC 93-77897. (Illus.). 464p. 2000. reprint ed. pap. 19.95 (*0-9635990-3-8*, Pub. by Frnds Finger Lks) North Country.

***Persons Reported.** Robert Charles. 472p. 2000. 18.99 (*0-7089-5738-2*) Ulverscroft.

Persons, Rights & the Moral Community. Loren E. Lomasky. (Illus.). 296p. 1990. reprint ed. pap. text 21.00 (*0-19-506474-7*) OUP.

***Persons, Situations & Emotions: An Ecological Approach.** Hermann Brandstatter & Andrzej Eliasz. (Series in Affective Science). (Illus.). 272p. 2000. text 49.95 (*0-19-513517-2*) OUP.

Persons with Disabilities: Issues in Health Care Financing & Service Delivery. Ed. by Joshua M. Weiner et al. 324p. (C). 1995. pap. 19.95 (*0-8157-9379-0*) Brookings.

Personwerdung: Eine Theologische Untersuchung Zu Max Schelers Phanomenologie der "Person-Gefuhle" Mit Besonderer Berucksichtigung Seiner Kritik an der Moderne. Xiaofeng Liu. (Basler und Berner Studien zur Historischen und Systematischen Theologie: Bd. 64). (GER.). 245p. 1996. 44.95 (*3-906752-84-4*, Pub. by P Lang) P Lang Pubng.

Persoonia Supplement 2: The Dutch, French & British Species of Psathyrella. E. Kits Van Waveren. (Persoonia Ser.: No. 2). (Illus.). 368p. 1987. reprint ed. pap. 54.00 (*90-71236-01-3*, Pub. by Rijksherbarium) Balogh.

Persoonlikheidsreg. J. Neethling. (AFR.). 332p. 1991. pap. write for info. (*0-409-04560-8*, MICHIE) LEXIS Pub.

Perspecta 30: The Yale Architectural Journal "Settlement Patterns" Ed. by Louise Harpman & Evan M. Supcoff. (Illus.). 120p. 1999. pap. text 20.00 (*0-262-58178-7*) MIT Pr.

***Perspecta 31: The Yale Architectural Journal "Reading Structures"** Ed. by Carolyn Ann Foug & Sharon L. Joyce. (Illus.). 160p. 2000. pap. 20.00 (*0-262-56126-3*) MIT Pr.

Perspecta 28: The Yale Architectural Journal: Architects, Process & Inspiration: A Collection of Essays. Ed. by Robert Joyce et al. (Illus.). 230p. 1997. pap. text 35.00 (*0-262-66102-0*) MIT Pr.

***Perspecta 29: The Yale Architectural Journal "Into the Fire"** Ed. by William Deresiewicz et al. (Illus.). 120p. 1998. pap. text 20.00 (*0-262-54092-4*) MIT Pr.

Perspectiva Humoristica en la Trilogia de Gironella. J. D. Suarez-Torres. 1975. 12.95 (*0-88303-021-7*); pap. 10.95 (*0-685-73222-3*) E Torres & Sons.

Perspectivas. 5th ed. Mary E. Kiddle & Brenda Wegmann. (SPA.). 288p. (C). 1993. pap. text 43.00 (*0-03-072236-5*) Harcourt Coll Pubs.

Perspectivas. 6th ed. Mary Ellen Kiddle & Brenda Wegmann. 848p. (C). 1998. pap. text 23.00 (*0-03-024567-2*, Pub. by Harcourt Coll Pubs) Harcourt.

Perspectivas: Hispanic Ministry. Timothy M. Matovina. Ed. by Yolanda Tarango et al. LC 95-8617. 152p. (Orig.). 1995. pap. 12.95 (*1-55612-770-7*) Sheed & Ward WI.

Perspectivas Criticas de la Psicologia Social. Maria M. Lopez & Ricardo Zuniga Burmester. LC 85-1053. viii, 450p. 1988. pap. 16.00 (*0-8477-2909-5*) U of PR Pr.

Perspectivas Culturales de Espana. J. Kattan-Ibarra. (C). 1989. 65.00 (*0-8442-7653-7*, Pub. by S Thornes Pubs) St Mut.

Perspectivas Culturales de Espana. Juan Kattan-Ibarra. (SPA.). 1995. pap., teacher ed. 5.60 (*0-8442-7162-4*) NTC Contemp Pub Co.

Perspectivas Culturales de Espana: Student Text. 2nd ed. Juan Kattan-Ibarra. (SPA.). 384p. (C). pap., student ed. 28.20 (*0-8442-7159-4*, VS7159-4) NTC Contemp Pub Co.

Perspectivas Culturales de Hispanoamerica. J. Kattan-Ibarra. (C). 1989. 85.00 (*0-8442-7650-2*, Pub. by S Thornes Pubs) St Mut.

Perspectivas Culturales de Hispanoamerica: Student Text. 2nd ed. Juan Kattan-Ibarra. (SPA.). 375p. (C). 1998. pap., student ed. 26.50 (*0-8442-7203-5*, VS7203-5) NTC Contemp Pub Co.

Perspectivas Politicas. rev. ed. Lynn-Darrell Bender. LC 83-82307. 167p. 1983. pap. text 6.95 (*0-913480-59-2*) Inter Am U Pr.

P

Perspectivas Politicas, Vol. II. Lynn-Darrell Bender. LC 79-27350. 115p. 1979. pap. text 4.55 (*0-913480-43-6*) Inter Am U Pr.

Perspectivas Regionales en la Arqueologia del Suroccidente de Colombia y Norte del Ecuador. Ed. by Cristobal Gnecco. 342p. 1995. pap. 17.00 (*958-9451-00-4*, UC001) UPLAAP.

*__Perspective.__ National Gallery London Staff. (Eyewitness Books). 64p. (J). (gr. 4-7). 2000. 15.95 (*0-7894-5585-4*, D K Ink) DK Pub Inc.

Perspective. Ernest Norling. (How to Draw & Paint Ser.). (Illus.). 32p. (Orig.). 1989. pap. 6.95 (*1-56010-013-3*, HT029) W Foster Pub.

Perspective. William F. Powell. (Artist's Library). (Illus.). 64p. (Orig.). 1989. pap. 7.95 (*0-929261-13-5*, AL13) W Foster Pub.

Perspective. Jan Vredeman De Vries. xv, 74p. 1968. pap. 7.95 (*0-486-20186-4*) Dover.

Perspective: A Conceptual, Ecological, Generic Model for Understanding Substance Use & Abuse: the Active Ingredients. 2nd ed. Earl S. Shive. (Illus.). 194p. (Orig.). (C). 1994. pap. text 22.25 (*0-9628229-2-2*) ESS Pubns.

Perspective: A Step-by-Step for Mastering Perspectives by Using the Grid System. Donald A. Gerds. 56p. 1996. pap. 19.95 (*1-56970-511-9*) Bks Nippan.

Perspective: Art, Literature, Participation. Ed. by Mark Neuman & Michael Payne. LC 85-24330. (Review Ser.: Vol. 30, No. 1). (Illus.). 160p. 1986. 22.00 (*0-8387-5104-0*) Bucknell U Pr.

Perspective! For Cartoonists & Illustrators. David Chelsea. LC 97-28757. (Illus.). 176p. 1997. pap. 19.95 (*0-8230-0567-4*) Watsn-Guptill.

Perspective Affranchie. Johann H. Lambert. (FRE., Illus.). 208p. 1998. reprint ed. pap. 240.00 (*1-85297-028-6*, Pub. by Archival Facs) St Mut.

Perspective & Composition. Parramon's Editorial Team. LC 98-74346. (Barron's Handbook Collection). (Illus.). 96p. 1999. 9.95 (*0-7641-5104-5*) Barron.

Perspective As a Problem in the Art, History & Literature of Early Modern England. Ed. by Mark Lussier & S. K. Heninger. LC 92-8707. (Illus.). 152p. 1992. lib. bdg. 69.95 (*0-7734-9620-3*) E Mellen.

Perspective As Symbolic Form. Erwin Panofsky. Tr. by Christopher S. Wood from GER. LC 91-10716. (Illus.). 196p. 1991. 26.00 (*0-942299-52-3*) Zone Bks.

Perspective As Symbolic Form. Erwin Panofsky. Tr. by Christopher S. Wood from GER. LC 91-10716. (Illus.). 196p. 1997. pap. 15.00 (*0-942299-53-1*) Zone Bks.

Perspective Charts. Lawson. Ep. 1940. pap. 44.95 (*0-471-28852-7*, VNR) Wiley.

Perspective Drawing. 2nd rev. ed. Kenneth W. Auvil. LC 96-9382. (Illus.). 87p. (C). 1996. pap. text 14.95 (*1-55934-697-3*, 1697) Mayfield Pub.

Perspective Drawing: A Step-by-Step Handbook. Michael E. Helms. 672p. (C). 1990. pap. text 50.20 (*0-13-659293-7*) P-H.

Perspective Drawing & Applications. 2nd ed. Charles A. O'Connor et al. LC 97-33980. 96p. (C). 1997. pap. text 39.33 (*0-13-633025-8*) P-H.

Perspective Drawing Handbook. Joseph D'Amelio. LC 83-12399. (Illus.). 96p. 1984. pap. 34.95 (*0-442-21828-1*, VNR) Wiley.

Perspective Drawing Handbook. Joseph D'Amelio. (Illus.). 96p. 1984. pap. 34.95 (*0-471-28873-X*, VNR) Wiley.

Perspective Drawing with the Geometer's Sketchpad. Cathi Saunders. (gr. 9-12). 1994. 24.95 (*1-55953-071-5*) Key Curr Pr.

Perspective for Artists. Rex V. Cole. LC 77-15743. (Illus.). 279p. 1976. reprint ed. pap. 7.95 (*0-486-22487-2*) Dover.

Perspective for Artists: Lo Inganno de Gl'occhi Prospettiva Practica, 1625. Pietro Accolti. (Printed Sources of Western Art Ser.). (ITA., Illus.). 168p. 1981. reprint ed. boxed set 50.00 (*0-915346-60-5*) A Wofsy Fine Arts.

Perspective for Interior Designers. John Pile. (Illus.). 160p. 1989. pap. 22.50 (*0-8230-4008-9*, Whitney Lib) Watsn-Guptill.

Perspective for Painters. Howard Etter & Margit Malmstrom. (Illus.). 144p. 1993. reprint ed. pap. 18.95 (*0-8230-3998-6*) Watsn-Guptill.

Perspective Grid Sourcebook: Computer Generated Tracing Guides for Architectural & Interior Design Drawings. Ernest Burden. 208p. 1991. pap. 54.95 (*0-471-28866-7*, VNR) Wiley.

Perspective Grid Sourcebook: Computer-Generated Tracing Guides for Architecture & Interior Design Drawings. Ernest E. Burden. (Illus.). 224p. 1991. pap. 47.95 (*0-442-21132-5*, VNR) Wiley.

Perspective in American Education, & Doctors & Masters. Conrad Bergendoff & Mark Van Doren. (Augustana College Library Occasional Papers, Wallin Lecture: No. 7). 20p. 1961. pap. 1.00 (*0-910182-28-0*) Augustana Coll.

Perspective in Architecture. Andrea Pozzo. (Illus.). 224p. 1989. pap. 12.95 (*0-486-25855-6*) Dover.

Perspective in Botanical Museum. V. S. Agarwal. (C). 1988. 110.00 (*0-7855-3238-2*, Pub. by Scientific) St Mut.

Perspective in Theoretical Computer Science. Ed. by Raghavan Narasimhan. 456p. (C). 1989. pap. 37.00 (*9971-5-0926-1*); text 113.00 (*9971-5-0925-3*) World Scientific Pub.

Perspective in Whitehead's Metaphysics. Stephen D. Ross. LC 82-8332. (SUNY Series in Systematic Philosophy). 295p. (C). 1983. text 59.50 (*0-87395-657-5*); pap. text 19.95 (*0-87395-658-3*) State U NY Pr.

Perspective in Zoosemiotics. Thomas A. Sebeok. LC 72-189708. (Janua Linguarum, Ser. Minor: No. 122). (Illus.). 188p. (Orig.). 1972. pap. text 36.95 (*90-279-2121-0*) Mouton.

Perspective Look at Nonlinear Media: From Physics to Biology & Social Sciences. Ed. by J. Parisi et al. (Lecture Notes in Physics). viii, 372p. 1998. 86.00 (*3-540-63995-0*) Spr-Verlag.

Perspective Made Easie. Bernard Lamy. (Illus.). 256p. 1998. reprint ed. pap. 240.00 (*1-85297-029-4*, Pub. by Archival Facs) St Mut.

Perspective Made Easy. Ernest Norling. LC 99-10310. (Illus.). 224p. 1999. pap. text 7.95 (*0-486-40473-0*) Dover.

Perspective Nutrition. 4th ed. Wardlaw. 256p. 1998. pap., student ed. 24.06 (*0-07-092082-6*) McGraw.

Perspective of Constraint-Based Reasoning: An Introductory Tutorial. Hans Werner Ghusgen & J. Hertzberg. LC 92-16218. viii, 123 p. 1992. write for info. (*3-540-55510-2*) Spr-Verlag.

Perspective of Constraint-Based Reasoning: An Introductory Tutorial. H. W. Guesgen & J. Hertzberg. Ed. by Joerg H. Siekmann. (Lecture Notes in Computer Science, Lecture Notes in Artificial Intelligence Ser.: Vol. 597). viii, 123p. 1992. 34.00 (*0-387-55510-2*) Spr-Verlag.

Perspective of Ethnomethodology. Douglas Benson & John A. Hughes. LC 82-10113. 213p. reprint ed. pap. 66.10 (*0-8357-6584-9*, 203597900097) Bks Demand.

Perspective of God: Jonah 3. Gary Purdy. (Inter Acta Ser.). (Illus.). 6p. (C). 1994. teacher ed., ring bd. 1.25 (*1-885702-49-3*, 741-026t, Inter Acta); student ed., ring bd. 3.25 (*1-885702-48-5*, 741-026s, Inter Acta) WSN Pr.

Perspective of Library Movement in India. M. Esperanza. LC 94-901932. (C). 1994. 22.00 (*81-7018-788-5*, Pub. by BR Pub) S Asia.

*__Perspective on Arabic Linguistics Vol. XI: Papers from the 11th Annual Symposium on Arabic Linguistics, Atlanta, Georgia, 1997.__ Ed. by Elabbas Benmamoun et al. (Current Issues in Linguistic Theory Ser.: Vol. 167). viii, 231p. 1998. 79.00 (*1-55619-883-3*) J Benjamins Pubng Co.

Perspective on Automation: Three Talks to Educators. R. Theobald et al. 1974. 2.50 (*0-8156-7023-0*, NES 43) Syracuse U Cont Ed.

Perspective on Behavior Gained from Lithic Analysis & Archaeological Investigations near Bridgeport, Mono County, California. David G. Bieling. 188p. (C). 1992. pap. text 20.00 (*1-55567-100-4*) Coyote Press.

Perspective on Budgeting. rev. ed. Ed. by Allen Schick. (PAR Classics Ser.: Vol. II). 327p. 1987. 14.95 (*0-936678-09-7*) Am Soc Pub Admin.

Perspective on Citizen Kane. Ronald Gottesman. 1996. 55.00 (*0-8161-1616-4*, G K Hall & Co) Mac Lib Ref.

Perspective on Civil Procedure. Geoffrey C. Hazard, Jr. & Jan Vetter. LC 86-81528. 350p. (Orig.). 1987. pap. 21.00 (*0-316-35259-4*, Aspen Law & Bus) Aspen Pub.

*__Perspective on Control Self-Assessment.__ Institute of Internal Auditors. Ed. by Lee A. Campbell. LC 98-170476. (Professional Practices Pamphlet Ser.: Vol. 98-2). 15p. 1998. pap. 15.00 (*0-89413-406-X*) Inst Inter Aud.

Perspective on Corporate America: Politics, Pitfalls & Downfalls: The Source of Human Suffering & Business Failure. S. Otis Pratt. Ed. by Mark Easland & Kay Woods. 166p. (Orig.). 1997. pap. 14.95 (*0-9651480-0-9*) S O Pratt Stat.

Perspective on Credit Risk. P. Henry Mueller. LC 88-436. (Illus.). 76p. 1988. pap. 43.00 (*0-936742-48-8*, 34131) Robt Morris Assocs.

*__Perspective on Emotional/Behavioral Disorders: Assumptions & Their Implications for Education & Treatment.__ C. Michael Nelson et al. (What Works for Children & Youth with Emotional/Behavior Disorders Ser.). 42p. 1999. pap. 11.40 (*0-86586-350-4*) Coun Exc Child.

Perspective on Infantry. John A. English. LC 81-5230. 345p. 1981. 38.50 (*0-275-90609-4*, C0609, Praeger Pubs) Greenwood.

Perspective on Learning. 3rd rev. ed. D. C. Phillips & Jonas F. Soltis. LC 98-20832. (Thinking about Education Ser.). 128p. 1998. pap. 15.95 (*0-8077-3703-8*) Tchrs Coll.

Perspective on New Church Education: A Collection of Papers & Addresses on Higher Education at the Academy of the New Church. E. Bruce Glenn & Vera P. Glenn. LC 97-15173. 1997. write for info. (*0-910557-51-9*) Acad New Church.

Perspective on New Techniques in Congenital & Acquired Heart Disease: Proceedings of the Cardiovascular Disease Conference, 4th, Snowmass at Aspen, Colorado, Jan. 1973. Cardiovascular Disease Conference Staff. Ed. by J. Vogel. (Advances in Cardiology Ser.: Vol. 11). 1974. 95.00 (*3-8055-1654-1*) S Karger.

Perspective on Orson Welles. Morris Beja. 1995. 55.00 (*0-8161-7344-3*, G K Hall & Co) Mac Lib Ref.

*__Perspective on Outsourcing of the Internal Auditing Function.__ Institute of Internal Auditors. Ed. by Lee A. Campbell. LC 98-170472. (Professional Practices Pamphlet Ser.: Vol. 98-1). 14p. 1998. pap. 15.00 (*0-89413-405-1*) Inst Inter Aud.

Perspective on Reform in Mathematics & Science Education, 2 vols. 1996. lib. bdg. 605.99 (*0-8490-6055-9*) Gordon Pr.

Perspective on Reform in Mathematics & Science Education. 1997. lib. bdg. 251.99 (*0-8490-8115-7*) Gordon Pr.

Perspective on Reform in Mathematics & Science Education: Monograph No. 3. Arnold A. Strassenburg. 63p. 1996. pap. 4.75 (*0-16-063577-2*) USGPO.

Perspective on Safety in Commercial Aviation, 23rd Littlewood Lecture. 20p. 1996. 12.00 (*1-56091-910-8*, SP-1218) Soc Auto Engineers.

Perspective on the American Past Vol. 1: Readings & Commentary, 1620-1877. 2nd ed. Michael Perman. LC 95-76581. 326p. (C). 1996. pap. text 29.16 (*0-669-39720-2*) HM Trade Div.

*__Perspective on the Art of Chinese Healing: Pathways to Wisdom, Vol. II.__ John Walter. 240p. 2000. pap. 15.95 (*1-58151-070-5*, Pub. by BookPartners) Midpt Trade.

Perspective on the Nature of Geography. Richard Hartshorne. LC 59-7032. (Monographs: No. 1). 1959. 15.00 (*0-89291-080-1*) Assn Am Geographers.

Perspective on the Nature of Geography. Richard Hartshorne. 201p. 1987. 75.00 (*0-7855-1981-5*, Pub. by Scientific) St Mut.

Perspective on the Nature of Geography. R. Hartstone. (C). 1992. text 68.00 (*0-7855-6901-4*, Pub. by Scientific Pubs) St Mut.

Perspective on Urban Land & Urban Management Policies in Sub-Saharan Africa. Akin L. Mabogunje. LC 92-43900. (Technical Papers: No. 196). 65p. 1993. pap. 22.00 (*0-8213-2355-5*, 12355) World Bank.

Perspective on War in the Bible. John Wood. LC 98-161258. 192p. 1998. pap. text 17.95 (*0-86554-564-2*, P111) Mercer Univ Pr.

Perspective Rendering for the Theatre. William H. Pinnell. LC 95-45512. (Illus.). 256p. (C). 1996. pap. 24.95 (*0-8093-2053-3*) S Ill U Pr.

Perspective Sketches. 5th ed. Theodore D. Walker. 1989. pap. 34.95 (*0-442-23781-2*, VNR); pap. 34.95 (*0-471-28908-6*, VNR) Wiley.

Perspective Systems Approach to Parameter Identification in Machine Vision. B. Ghosh & E. P. Loucks. (Systems & Control Ser.). 350p. 1997. 74.50 (*0-8176-3955-1*) Birkhauser.

Perspective Without Pain. Phil Metzger. (Illus.). 144p. 1992. pap. 19.99 (*0-89134-446-2*, 30386, North Lght Bks) F & W Pubns Inc.

Perspectives. (Illus.). 440p. 1996. 45.00 (*1-885206-33-X*, Iliad Pr) Cader Pubng.

Perspectives. Hopkins. Date not set. pap. text. write for info. (*0-582-01665-7*, Pub. by Addison-Wesley) Longman.

Perspectives. Edward Riccardo. 238p. 1993. pap. 14.00 (*0-911541-26-8*) Gregory Pub.

*__Perspectives.__ Ed. by UNIVERSITY MARYLAND & DIM STAFF. 290p. 1999. pap. text 26.25 (*0-536-02650-5*) P-H.

Perspectives. David Howard. LC 77-90787. (Illus.). 1978. reprint ed. lib. bdg. 24.95 (*0-930976-00-2*) SF Center Vis Stud.

Perspectives, 10 novels in ea. set, Sets 1&2, Set 1. (Illus.). 48p. (J). (gr. 3-12). 1982. pap. 27.50 (*0-87879-291-0*) High Noon Bks.

Perspectives, 10 novels in ea. set, Sets 1&2, Set 2. (Illus.). 48p. (J). (gr. 3-12). 1982. pap. write for info. (*0-87879-311-9*) High Noon Bks.

Perspectives: A Williams Anthology. Ed. by Frederick Rudolph. LC 83-51219. 340p. 1983. 17.50 (*0-915081-00-8*) Williams Coll.

Perspectives: Angles on African Art. Robert F. Thompson et al. LC 86-26328. (Illus.). 196p. 1987. text 45.00 (*0-9614587-4-7*, CAA) Museum African.

Perspectives: Collected Poems, 1970-1986. George Bruce. 90p. 1987. pap. text 13.90 (*0-08-035062-3*, Pub. by Aberdeen U Pr) Macmillan.

*__Perspectives: Competition in School Sport, Vol. 1.__ 1999. pap. 19.95 (*1-84126-019-3*) Meyer & Meyer.

Perspectives: Connecting Past & Present, Modern World History. Jackson J. Spielvogel. 1998. 10.95 (*0-538-42307-2*) S-W Pub.

Perspectives: From Adult Literacy to Continuing Education. Alice M. Scales & Joanne Burley. 304p. (C). 1991. text. write for info. (*0-697-11793-6*) Brown & Benchmark.

Perspectives: Online Journalism. Kathleen Wickham. LC 97-75311. (C). 1998. pap. 16.36 (*0-395-90226-6*) HM.

Perspectives: Poems. E. F. Pasbach. LC 95-92762. 148p. (Orig.). 1995. pap. 9.95 (*0-9649797-0-5*) E F Pasbach.

Perspectives: Readings for Writers. Robert DiYanni. LC 95-8885. 480p. (C). 1995. pap. 34.69 (*0-07-016967-5*) McGraw.

Perspectives: Readings on Contemporary American Government. 2nd rev. ed. Tim Walker et al. LC 96-72626. (Illus.). 240p. (YA). (gr. 9-12). 1997. pap. text 16.95 (*0-932765-77-7*, 1926-97) Close Up Fnd.

Perspectives: Relevant Scenes for Teens. Mary Krell-Oishi. Ed. by Theodore O. Zapel. LC 97-5405. 256p. (YA). (gr. 8-12). 1997. pap. 12.95 (*1-56608-030-4*, B206) Meriwether Pub.

Perspectives: Saenredam & the Architectural Painters of the 17th Century. Jeroen Giltaij & Guido Jansen. (Illus.). 326p. 1992. 65.00 (*90-6918-080-4*) U of Wash Pr.

Perspectives: Teacher's Guide. 4th ed. Close up Foundation Staff. Ed. by Charles Sass. 1997. pap. text, teacher ed. 15.95 (*0-614-24121-9*, 1927-97) Close Up Fnd.

Perspectives Analysis, Assessment & Fate Toxicity Testing, Risk Assessment, Remediation, Innovative Technologies, Polycyclic Aromatic Hydrocarbons. Ed. by Paul T. Kostecki et al. (Hydrocarbon Contaminated Soils Ser.: Vol. 5). (Illus.). 593p. 1995. text 59.95 (*1-884940-02-1*) Amherst Sci Pubs.

Perspectives Analysis Human Health Risk Assessment Remediation. Ed. by Paul T. Kostecki et al. (Hydrocarbon Contaminated Soils Ser.: Vol. 4). (Illus.). 488p. 1994. text 59.95 (*1-884940-00-5*) Amherst Sci Pubs.

Perspectives & Challenges in the Development of Sudanese Studies. Ed. by Ismail Abdalla & David Sconyers. LC 93-27049. 308p. 1993. text 99.95 (*0-7734-9333-6*) E Mellen.

Perspectives & Identities: The Elizabethan Writer's Search to Know His World. Peter Lloyd. 1989. 35.00 (*0-948695-11-0*) Intl Spec Bk.

Perspectives & Issues in Health Care. Mitchell. (LPN/LVN Nursing Ser.). 1996. teacher ed. 14.95 (*0-8273-6320-6*) Delmar.

Perspectives & Issues in Health Care. Mitchell. (LPN/LVN Nursing Ser.). 1998. pap. 24.95 (*0-8273-6319-2*) Delmar.

Perspectives & Issues in International Political Economy. Ed. by Chronis Polychroniou. LC 92-7496. 288p. 1992. 65.00 (*0-275-94016-0*, C4016, Praeger Pubs) Greenwood.

Perspectives & Points of View: The Early Works of Weiland & Their Background. Lieselotte E. Kurth-Voigt. LC 74-6829. 208p. reprint ed. pap. 64.50 (*0-608-14709-5*, 202585500046) Bks Demand.

Perspectives & Practices in Prison Theatre. James Thompson. LC 96-32681. (Forensic Focus Ser.). 247p. 1997. pap. write for info. (*1-85302-417-1*, Pub. by Jessica Kingsley) Taylor & Francis.

Perspectives & Promises of Clinical Psychology. A. Ehlers et al. (Applied Clinical Psychology Ser.). (Illus.). 262p. (C). 1992. 54.50 (*0-306-44098-9*, Plenum Trade) Perseus Pubng.

Perspectives Arabes et Medievales. E. Peters. 1998. 75.00 (*90-6831-783-0*, Pub. by Peeters Pub) Bks Intl VA.

Perspectives Cavaliere. Andre Breton. Ed. by Bonnet. 14.50 (*0-685-37235-9*) Fr & Eur.

Perspectives Criminal Justice. Calhoun. 1996. 6.75 (*0-07-217377-7*) McGraw.

Perspectives for Agronomy - Adopting Ecological Principles & Managing Resource Use: Proceedings of the 4th Congress of the European Society for Agronomy, Veldoven & Wageningen, The Netherlands, 7-11 July 1996. Ed. by M. K. Van Ittersum & S. C. Van de Geijn. 384p. 1997. reprint ed. 201.00 (*0-444-82852-4*, North Holland) Elsevier.

*__Perspectives for American Society.__ Ivan Parkins. 2000. pap. 12.95 (*0-533-13446-3*) Vantage.

Perspectives for Electroweak Interactions in E+E-Collisions: Proceedings of the Ringberg Workshop: Ringberg Castle, Germany, 5-8 February 1995. Ed. by B. A. Kniehl. LC 95-32928. 350p. 1995. 84.00 (*981-02-2335-8*) World Scientific Pub.

Perspectives for Leisure & Amusement Facilities. Kenchiku-Sha Shoten. (Illus.). 138p. 1998. pap. 39.95 (*4-7858-0116-6*, Pub. by Shotenkenchiku-Sha) Bks Nippan.

Perspectives for Living: Conversations on Bereavement & Love. Bel Mooney. (Illus.). 208p. 1993. pap. 18.95 (*0-7195-5125-0*, Pub. by John Murray) Trafalgar.

Perspectives for Moral Decisions. John Howie. LC 80-6102. 192p. (C). 1981. pap. text 20.00 (*0-8191-1376-X*) U Pr of Amer.

Perspectives for New Detectors in Future Supercolliders: Proceedings of the 9th Workshop of the INFN Eloisatron Project, Erice, Italy, 17-24 October 1990. Ed. by L. Cifarelli et al. 252p. (C). 1991. text 89.00 (*981-02-0652-6*) World Scientific Pub.

Perspectives for Parallel Optical Interconnects: Project 3199 WOIT. Ed. by P. Lalanne & P. Chavel. (ESPRIT Basic Research Ser.). xiii, 417p. 1993. 89.00 (*0-387-56786-0*) Spr-Verlag.

Perspectives for Peas & Lupins As Protein Crops. R. Thompson & R. Casey. 1983. text 176.50 (*90-247-2792-8*) Kluwer Academic.

Perspectives for the Interacting Boson Model: Proceedings on the Occasion of Its 20th Anniversary. R. F. Casten et al. 780p. 1994. text 162.00 (*981-02-2071-5*) World Scientific Pub.

Perspectives from Church History. James P. Eckman. 96p. 1996. pap. text 9.95 (*0-910566-67-4*) Evang Trg Assn.

Perspectives from Church History. James P. Eckman. 96p. 1996. teacher ed., ring bd. 24.95 (*0-910566-68-2*) Evang Trg Assn.

Perspectives from the Past. P. Brophy. 1998. pap. text. write for info. (*0-393-97387-5*) Norton.

Perspectives from the Past: From Early Modern Era through Contemporary Times, Vol. 2. James Brophy. LC 98-13551. 1998. pap. text. write for info. (*0-393-95879-5*) Norton.

Perspectives from the Past: Primary Sources in Western Civilizations, 1. James Brophy et al. LC 98-13551. 1998. pap. text. write for info. (*0-393-95876-0*) Norton.

Perspectives in Aerospace Design. Compiled by Conrad F. Newberry. 1026p. 1991. 79.95 (*1-56347-010-1*) AIAA.

Perspectives in Ageing Research. Rameshwar Singh & G. S. Singhal. (Illus.). 395p. 1990. 59.00 (*1-55528-219-9*, Pub. by Today Tomorrow) Scholarly Pubns.

Perspectives in American Diplomacy. Ed. by Jules David. (Individual Publications). 1979. lib. bdg. 26.95 (*0-405-09162-1*) Ayer.

Perspectives in Animal Behavior. Judith Goodenough et al. LC 92-42640. 816p. 1993. text 77.95 (*0-471-53623-7*) Wiley.

Perspectives in Applied Phonology. Barbara W. Hodson & Mary L. Edwards. LC 96-43784. (Diagnostic & Management Strategies Ser.). 1997. 42.00 (*0-8342-0881-4*) Aspen Pub.

Perspectives in Aridzone Ecology. S. K. Agarwal. (Recent Researches in Ecology, Environment & Pollution Ser.: Vol. 8). (Illus.). 225p. 1991. 59.00 (*1-55528-258-X*) Scholarly Pubns.

Perspectives in Artificial Intelligence: Expert Systems, Applications & Technical Foundations, Vol. 1. Ed. by J. A. Campbell & J. Cuena. 1989. text 64.95 (*0-470-21434-1*) P-H.

Perspectives in Artificial Intelligence: Machine Translation, Nlp, Databases & Computer-Aided Instruction. Ed. by J. A. Campbell & J. Cuena. 1989. text 74.95 (*0-470-21435-X*) P-H.

Perspectives in Asian Cross-Cultural Psychology. Ed. by J. L. Dawson et al. x, 198p. 1981. pap. 29.75 (*90-265-0359-8*) Swets.

P

An Asterisk (*) at the beginning of an entry indicates that the title is appearing for the first time.

Perspectives in Astrophysical Cosmology. Martin J. Rees. (Lezioni Lincee Lectures). (Illus.). 151p. (C). 1995. text 49.95 (*0-521-47530-9*); pap. text 21.95 (*0-521-47561-9*) Cambridge U Pr.

Perspectives in Avian Endocrinology. S. Harvey & R. Etches. 408p. 1996. text 149.95 (*1-898099-09-X*) Blackwell Sci.

Perspectives in Behavior Genetics. Ed. by John L. Fuller & Edward C. Simmel. LC 86-16613. (Illus.). 290p. reprint ed. pap. 89.90 (*0-7837-1136-0*, 204166600022) Bks Demand.

Perspectives in Behavioral Medicine: Eating Regulation & Discontrol. Ed. by Herbert Weiner & Andrew Baum. 248p. 1987. 49.95 (*0-89859-928-8*) L Erlbaum Assocs.

Perspectives in Biochemistry, Vol. 1. Hans Neurath. LC 89-409. (Illus.). 251p. 1989. pap. text 16.95 (*0-8412-1621-5*, Pub. by Am Chemical) OUP.

Perspectives in Bioconjugate Chemistry. Ed. by Claude F. Meares. LC 93-15385. (Illus.). 210p. 1993. pap. text 38.00 (*0-8412-2672-5*, Pub. by Am Chemical) OUP.

Perspectives in Bioethics. R. Lawler & W. May. Ed. by F. Lescoe & D. Liptak. (Pope John Paul II Lecture Series in Bioethics: Vol. I). 66p. (Orig.). 1983. pap. 3.75 (*0-910919-00-3*) Mariel Pubns.

Perspectives in Biogeochemistry. E. T. Degens. (Illus.). 495p. 1989. 85.95 (*0-387-50191-6*) Spr-Verlag.

Perspectives in Biological Chemistry. Ed. by Robert E. Olson. LC 78-103834. (Illus.). 298p. reprint ed. pap. 92.40 (*0-7837-0960-9*, 204126500019) Bks Demand.

Perspectives in Biology. Michael R. Cummings. 225p. 1996. pap. 12.25 (*0-314-07562-3*) West Pub.

Perspectives in Biomechanics: Proceedings of the International Conference on Mechanics in Medicine & Biology, 1st, Aachen, Germany, 1978, Pt. A & B, Vol. 1. International Conference on Mechanics in Medicine. Ed. by I. H. Reul et al. (Perspectives in Biomechanics Ser.). xxiv, 892p. 1980. 857.00 (*3-7186-0006-4*) Gordon & Breach.

Perspectives in Bioregional Education. Ed. by Frank Traina & Susan Darley-Hill. 176p. 1994. 20.00 (*1-884008-17-8*) NAAEE.

Perspectives in Bioremediation Technologies for Environmental Improvement: Proceedings of the NATO Advanced Research Workshop on Biotechnical Remediation of Contaminated Sites, Lviv, Ukraine, March 5-9, 1996. Ed. by J. R. Wild. LC 96-49518. (NATO ASI Series: Partnership Sub-Series 3). 140p. (C). 1996. text 99.50 (*0-7923-4339-5*) Kluwer Academic.

Perspectives in Biotechnology. Ed. by Jose C. Duarte et al. LC 87-11015. (NATO ASI Series A, Life Sciences: Vol. 128). 218p. 1987. 69.50 (*0-306-42569-6*, Plenum Trade) Perseus Pubng.

Perspectives in Botanical Museum: With Preference to India. V. S. Agarwal. viii, 390p. 1983. 49.00 (*0-88065-233-0*) Scholarly Pubns.

Perspectives in British Historical Fiction Today. Neil McEwan. LC 86-7200. 200p. 1987. 25.00 (*0-89341-547-2*, Longwood Academic) Hollowbrook.

Perspectives in Business Ethics. Laura B. Pincus. LC 97-22530. 1997. 71.00 (*0-256-23317-9*, Irwn Prfssnl) McGraw-Hill Prof.

Perspectives in Business Ethics. 2nd ed. Pincus. 2001. 50.00 (*0-07-231405-2*) McGraw.

Perspectives in Business Management. Hurd. 1998. 8.74 (*0-07-228973-2*) McGraw.

Perspectives in Catalysis. J. M. Thomas et al. LC 90-27831. (A "Chemistry for the 21st Century" Monograph). xv, 492 p. 1992. write for info. (*0-632-03165-4*) Blackwell Sci.

Perspectives in Chemoreception & Behavior. Ed. by R. F. Chapman et al. (Proceedings in Life Sciences Ser.). (Illus.). 125p. 1986. 141.00 (*0-387-96374-X*) Spr-Verlag.

Perspectives in Child Care Policy. Lorraine M. Harding. LC 90-5564. 1991. pap. text. write for info. (*0-582-08345-1*) Longman.

Perspectives in Child Care Policy. 2nd ed. Lorraine M. Harding. LC 96-35436. 1997. pap. text. write for info. (*0-582-27684-5*) Longman.

Perspectives in Christian Education: Focus on Parent & Student Relationships. Dan L. Burrell et al. LC 97-61498. 160p. 1997. pap. write for info. (*1-57921-049-X*) WinePress Pub.

Perspectives in Clinical Investigation. Ed. by Thomas P. Stossel. 72p. (Orig.). 1984. pap. 10.00 (*0-87470-040-X*) Rockefeller.

Perspectives in Coastal Dune Management. Ed. by F. Van der Meulen et al. (Illus.). viii, 335p. 1989. pap. 82.50 (*90-5103-025-8*, Pub. by SPB Acad Pub) Balogh.

Perspectives in Cognitive Science: Theories, Experiments & Foundations. Ed. by Peter Slezak et al. (Illus.). 392p. 1995. text 78.50 (*1-56750-105-2*) Ablx Pub.

Perspectives in Cognitive Science Vol. 2: Theories, Experiments, & Foundations. Janet Wiles & Terry Dartnall. LC 98-28984. 1999. 78.50 (*1-56750-382-9*) Ablx Pub.

Perspectives in Cognitive Science Vol 2: Theories, Experiments, & Foundations. Janet Wiles & Terry Dartnall. LC 98-28984. (Perspectives in Cognitive Science Ser.). 1999. pap. 39.50 (*1-56750-383-7*) Ablx Pub.

Perspectives in Communications: Proceedings of the Workshop ICTP, Trieste, Italy, November 14-December 2, 1983, 2 vols. Ed. by U. R. Rao et al. 1504p. 1987. text 291.00 (*9971-978-76-8*) World Scientific Pub.

***Perspectives in Control: New Concepts & Applications.** Tariq Samad & IEEE Control Systems Society Staff. LC 00-38854. 2000. pap. write for info. (*0-7803-5356-0*) IEEE Standards.

Perspectives in Control: Theory & Applications. Ed. by D. Normand-Cyrot. (Illus.). 370p. 1998. 90.00 (*1-85233-042-2*) Spr-Verlag.

Perspectives in Control Theory: Proceedings of the Sielpia Conference, Poland, Sept. 1988. B. Jakubczyk et al. (Progress in Systems & Control Theory Ser.: No. 2). 364p. 1990. 102.00 (*0-8176-3456-8*) Birkhauser.

Perspectives in Criminology. Ed. by S. Venogopal Rao. 250p. 1988. text 40.00 (*0-7069-4000-8*, Pub. by Vikas) S Asia.

***Perspectives in Critical Thinking: Essays by Teachers in Theory & Practice.** Ed. by Danny Wells & Kathl Holly Anderson. (Counterpoints Ser.: Vol. 110). 240p. 1999. pap. text 29.95 (*0-8204-4429-4*) P Lang Pubng.

Perspectives in Cultural Anthropology. Ed. by Herbert Applebaum. LC 86-19168. 614p. (C). 1987. pap. text 23.95 (*0-88706-439-6*) State U NY Pr.

Perspectives in Cultural Anthropology. Betty Smith & Wayne Van Horne. 256p. (C). 1999. per. 39.95 (*0-7872-5662-5*, 41566204) Kendall-Hunt.

Perspectives in Culture. Long. 1998. pap. text 27.00 (*0-205-27478-1*, Longwood Div) Allyn.

Perspectives in Dental Ceramics. Jack D. Preston. (Illus.). 472p. 1988. text 160.00 (*0-86715-136-6*, 1366) Quint Pub Co.

Perspectives in Early Brass Scholarship: Proceedings of the 95 International Historic Brass Symposium 95. Stewart Carter. LC 97-33015. (Historic Brass Ser.: Vol. 2). 1997. text 54.00 (*0-945193-97-1*) Pendragon NY.

Perspectives in Ecological Theory. Ramon Margalef. LC 68-27291. (Illus.). viii, 112p. (C). 1993. pap. text 4.95 (*0-226-50506-5*, P629) U Ch Pr.

Perspectives in Ecological Theory. Ed. by Jonathan Roughgarden et al. 425p. 1989. pap. text 29.50 (*0-691-08508-0*, Pub. by Princeton U Pr) Cal Prin Full Svc.

***Perspectives in Ecology: A Glance from the VII International Congress of Ecology, Florence, 19-25 July 1998.** Ed. by Almo Farina. 497p. 1999. 70.00 (*90-5782-041-2*, Pub. by Backhuys Pubs) Balogh.

Perspectives in Education, Religion, & the Arts. Ed. by Howard Keifer & Milton K. Munitz. LC 69-14641. 435p. reprint ed. 134.90 (*0-8357-9596-9*, 201011100068) Bks Demand.

Perspectives in Endocrine Psychobiology. F. Brambilla & Bridges. LC 76-27305. 590p. reprint ed. 182.90 (*0-8357-9953-0*, 201616000098) Bks Demand.

Perspectives in Entomological Research. O. P. Agrawal. 1994. pap. 180.00 (*81-7233-075-8*, Pub. by Scientific Pubs) St Mut.

Perspectives in Environmental Botany, Vol. 2. Ed. by D. N. Rao et al. (Illus.). xiv, 325p. 1988. 69.00 (*1-55528-098-6*, Pub. by Today Tomorrow) Scholarly Pubns.

Perspectives in Environmental Chemistry. Ed. by Donald L. Macalady. LC 97-4123. (Topics in Environmental Chemistry Ser.). (Illus.). 528p. 1997. text 68.00 (*0-19-510208-8*); pap. text 47.95 (*0-19-510209-6*) OUP.

Perspectives in Environmental Management. R. Buckley. xi, 276p. 1991. 76.95 (*0-387-53815-1*) Spr-Verlag.

Perspectives in Environmental Management. Ed. by T. N. Khoshoo. 484p. (C). 1987. 42.00 (*81-204-0248-0*, Pub. by Oxford IBH) S Asia.

Perspectives in Ethology. Incl. Social Behavior. Ed. by P. P. Bateson & Peter H. Klopfer. 276p. 1978. 49.50 (*0-306-36603-7*, Kluwer Plenum); LC 77-1665. 350p. 1973. 49.50 (*0-306-36601-0*, Kluwer Plenum); LC 77-1665. 352p. 1976. 49.50 (*0-306-36602-9*, Kluwer Plenum); (Illus.). write for info. (*0-318-55333-3*, Plenum Trade) Perseus Pubng.

Perspectives in Ethology Vol. 4: Advantages of Diversity. Ed. by P. P. Bateson & Peter H. Klopfer. LC 73-79427. 276p. 1980. 65.00 (*0-306-40511-3*, Plenum Trade) Perseus Pubng.

Perspectives in Ethology Vol. 5: Ontogeny. Ed. by P. P. Bateson & Peter H. Klopfer. LC 73-79427. 536p. 1982. 79.50 (*0-306-41063-X*, Plenum Trade) Perseus Pubng.

Perspectives in Ethology Vol. 6: Mechanisms. Ed. by P. P. Bateson & Peter H. Klopfer. LC 73-79427. 324p. 1985. 69.50 (*0-306-41846-0*, Plenum Trade) Perseus Pubng.

Perspectives in Ethology Vol. 7: Alternatives. Ed. by P. P. Bateson & Peter H. Klopfer. LC 86-649219. 298p. 1987. 65.00 (*0-306-42429-0*, Plenum Trade) Perseus Pubng.

Perspectives in Ethology Vol. 8: Whither Ethology? P. P. Bateson & P. H. Klopfer. (Illus.). 292p. (C). 1988. text 85.00 (*0-306-42948-9*, Kluwer Plenum) Kluwer Academic.

Perspectives in Ethology Vol. 9: Human Understanding & Animal Awareness. P. P. Bateson & P. H. Klopfer. LC 86-649219. (Illus.). 330p. (C). 1990. text 85.00 (*0-306-43651-5*, Kluwer Plenum) Kluwer Academic.

Perspectives in Ethology Vol. 10: Behavior & Evolution, Vol. 10. P. P. Bateson et al. LC 86-649219. (Illus.). 302p. (C). 1993. text 85.00 (*0-306-44398-8*, Kluwer Plenum) Kluwer Academic.

Perspectives in Ethology Vol. 11: Behavioral Design. Ed. by Nicholas S. Thompson. LC 86-649219. (Illus.). 350p. (C). 1995. text 102.00 (*0-306-44906-4*, Kluwer Plenum) Kluwer Academic.

Perspectives in Ethology Vol. 12: Communication, Vol. 12. Ed. by Donald H. Owings et al. (Illus.). 446p. (C). 1998. text 138.00 (*0-306-45764-4*, Kluwer Plenum) Kluwer Academic.

Perspectives in Exercise Science & Sports Medicine. David R. Lamb et al. LC 88-70343. 1988. write for info. (*0-936157-34-8*) Brown & Benchmark.

Perspectives in Exercise Science & Sports Medicine: Energy Metabolism in Exercise & Sport, Vol. 5. Ed. by David Lamb & Carl V. Gisolfi. LC 91-73932. (Illus.). 495p. 1992. reprint ed. text 49.00 (*1-884125-36-0*) Cooper Pubng.

Perspectives in Exercise Science & Sports Medicine: Exercise, Heat, & Thermoregulation, Vol. 6. Ed. by David Lamb et al. LC 92-73445. (Illus.). 405p. 1993. text 49.00 (*1-884125-37-9*) Cooper Pubng.

Perspectives in Exercise Science & Sports Medicine: Prolonged Exercise, Vol. 1. Ed. by David R. Lamb & Robert Murray. LC 88-70343. (Illus.). 494p. 1988. reprint ed. text 49.00 (*1-884125-34-4*) Cooper Pubng.

Perspectives in Exercise Science & Sports Medicine: Youth, Exercise & Sport, Vol. 2. Ed. by Carl V. Gisolfi & David Lamb. LC 88-70343. (Illus.). 590p. 1989. reprint ed. text 49.00 (*1-884125-35-2*) Cooper Pubng.

Perspectives in Exercise Science & Sports Medicine Vol. 3: Fluid Homeostasis During Exercise. Ed. by Carl V. Gisolfi & David Lamb. LC 88-70343. (Illus.). 456p. 1990. reprint ed. text 49.00 (*1-884125-07-7*) Cooper Pubng.

Perspectives in Exercise Science & Sports Medicine Vol. 4: Ergogenics: Enhancement of Athletic Performance. Ed. by David Lamb & Melvin Williams. LC 88-70343. (Illus.). 444p. 1991. reprint ed. text 49.00 (*1-884125-08-5*) Cooper Pubng.

Perspectives in Exercise Science & Sports Medicine Vol. 7: Physiology & Nutrition of Competitive Sport. Ed. by David Lamb. LC 88-70343. (Illus.). 400p. (C). 1994. text 49.00 (*1-884125-09-3*) Cooper Pubng.

Perspectives in Exercise Science & Sports Medicine Vol. 8: Exercise in Older Adults. Ed. by David Lamb et al. LC 88-70343. (Illus.). 400p. 1995. text 49.00 (*1-884125-20-4*) Cooper Pubng.

Perspectives in Exercise Science & Sports Medicine Vol. 10: Optimizing Sport Performance. Ed. by David R. Lamb & Robert Murray. 450p. 1997. text 49.00 (*1-884125-63-8*) Cooper Pubng.

Perspectives in Exercise Science & Sports Medicine Vol. 11: Exercise, Nutrition, & Weight Control. Ed. by David R. Lamb & Robert Murray. LC 95-67366. 450p. 1998. text 49.00 (*1-884125-70-0*) Cooper Pubng.

Perspectives in Exercise Science & Sports Medicine Vol. 12: The Metabolic Basis of Performance in Sport & Exercise. Ed. by David R. Lamb & Robert Murray. 450p. (C). 1999. text 49.00 (*1-884125-73-5*) Cooper Pubng.

Perspectives in Exercise Science & Sports Medicine Vol. 12: Volume 12: The Metabolic Basis of Performance in Sport & Exercise. Douglas B. McKeag & David Hough. Ed. by David R. Lamb & Robert Murray. (Illus.). 450p. (C). 1999. 49.00 (*1-884125-68-9*) Cooper Pubng.

Perspectives in Experimental Biology: Zoology & Botany, 2 pts. P. Spencer Davies & N. Sunderland. 1090p. 1976. 477.00 (*0-08-019939-9*, Pub. by Pergamon Repr) Franklin.

Perspectives in Experimental Gerontology. Ed. by Nathan W. Shock & Leon Stein. LC 79-8689. (Illus.). 1980. reprint ed. lib. bdg. 40.95 (*0-405-12805-3*) Ayer.

Perspectives in Experimental Linguistics: Papers from the University of Alberta Conference on Experimental Linguistics, Edmonton, 1-14 Oct. 1978. Ed. by Gary D. Prideaux. (Current Issues in Linguistic Theory Ser.: No. 10). xi, 176p. 1979. 46.00 (*90-272-3503-1*) J Benjamins Pubng Co.

Perspectives in Ferrous Metallurgy. Bell. 1985. write for info. (*0-08-033422-9*, Pergamon Pr) Elsevier.

***Perspectives in Fixed Income.** Fabozzi. 200p. 2000. 75.00 (*1-883249-77-5*) F J Fabozzi.

Perspectives in Fluid Mechanics. Ed. by D. Coles. (Lecture Notes in Physics Ser.: Vol. 320). vii, 207p. 1989. 45.95 (*0-387-50644-6*) Spr-Verlag.

Perspectives in Geometry & Relativity: Essays in Honor of Vaclav Hlavaty. Ed. by Banesh Hoffman. LC 65-19704. (Illus.). 508p. reprint ed. pap. 157.50 (*0-608-30274-0*, 200574500058) Bks Demand.

Perspectives in Glaucoma Research, Pt. I. Ed. by E. Luetjen-Drecoll. (Journal: Ophthalmologica: Vol. 210, No. 5, 1996). (Illus.). 70p. 1996. pap. 69.75 (*3-8055-6378-7*) S Karger.

Perspectives in Glaucoma Research, Pt. II. Ed. by Elke Lutjen-Drecoll. (Journal: Vol. 211, No. 3, 1997). (Illus.). 84p. 1997. pap. 60.00 (*3-8055-6515-1*) S Karger.

Perspectives in Grassland Ecology: Results & Applications of the US-IBP Grassland Biome Study. Ed. by N. R. French. LC 78-13971. (Ecological Studies: Vol. 32). (Illus.). 1979. 83.00 (*0-387-90384-4*) Spr-Verlag.

***Perspectives in Gynaecology & Obstetrics: Selected Plenary Papers Presented at the XIV European Congress of Gynaecologists & Obstetricians, Granada, Spain, September, 1999.** Ed. by F. Gonzalez Gomez & S. Palacios. LC 99-51628. (Illus.). 180p. 1999. 65.00 (*1-85070-774-X*) Prthnon Pub.

***Perspectives in Hadronic Physics.** Ed. by S. Boffi et al. LC 99-57214. 630p. 1999. 128.00 (*981-02-4110-0*) World Scientific Pub.

Perspectives in Hadronic Physics: Proceedings of the Conference ICTP, Trieste, Italy 12-16 May, 1997. Ed. by Sigfrido Boffi et al. 562p. 1998. 138.00 (*981-02-3321-3*) World Scientific Pub.

Perspectives in Heavy Ion Physics. C. Signorini. 1998. 78.00 (*981-02-3554-2*) World Scientific Pub.

Perspectives in Heavy-Ion Physics: Proceedings of the 2nd RIKEN/INFN Joint Symposium RIKEN, Saitama, Japan 22 - 26 May 1995. Ed. by M. Ishihara et al. 400p. 1996. text 98.00 (*981-02-2465-6*, Pn-P2936) World Scientific Pub.

Perspectives in Higgs Physics: Reviews & Speculations. Gordon Kane. 488p. 1993. text 137.00 (*981-02-1216-X*) World Scientific Pub.

Perspectives in High Frequency Ventilation. Ed. by P. A. Scheck et al. 1983. text 176.50 (*0-89838-571-7*) Kluwer Academic.

Perspectives in Higher Education Reform, Vol. 1. Ed. & Pref. by David A. Hake. 121p. (Orig.). 1992. pap. text 18.00 (*0-940191-19-9*) Univ TN Ctr Bus Econ.

Perspectives in Higher Education Reform, Vol. 2. Ed. & Pref. by David A. Hake. 211p. (Orig.). 1993. pap. text 18.00 (*0-940191-20-2*) Univ TN Ctr Bus Econ.

Perspectives in Higher Education Reform, Vol. 3. Ed. & Pref. by David A. Hake. 403p. (Orig.). 1994. pap. text 18.00 (*0-940191-21-0*) Univ TN Ctr Bus Econ.

Perspectives in Human Biology. 108p. 1996. write for info. (*981-02-2586-5*); pap. 17.00 (*981-02-2551-2*) World Scientific Pub.

Perspectives in Human Biology. Loren Knapp. LC 97-22459. 1997. pap. 58.95 (*0-314-20110-6*) Wadsworth Pub.

Perspectives in Human Biology: Internet Booklet. Knapp. (Biology Ser.). 1997. pap. 5.00 (*0-534-54071-6*) Wadsworth Pub.

Perspectives in Human Biology - Humans in the Australasian Region. 102p. 1996. pap. 13.00 (*981-02-3007-9*) World Scientific Pub.

Perspectives in Human Biology with Infotrac. Knapp. (Biology Ser.). 1997. 53.25 incl. cd-rom (*0-534-54096-1*) Wadsworth Pub.

Perspectives in Human Sexuality: Contemporary Perspectives. Slaton. 480p. (C). 1997. pap., student ed. 27.00 (*0-06-502182-7*) Addson-Wesley Educ.

Perspectives in Industrial Geography: A Case Study of an Industrial City of Uttar Pradesh. Aruna Saxena. (C). 1989. 27.50 (*81-7022-250-8*, Pub. by Concept) S Asia.

Perspectives in Interest Rate Risk. Fabozzi. 1998. text 60.00 incl. audio (*0-07-067695-X*) McGraw.

Perspectives in International Development. Ed. by Mekki Mtewa. 1987. 18.00 (*0-8364-2063-2*, Pub. by Allied Pubs) S Asia.

Perspectives in Introductory Biology. 7th rev. ed. E. Lane Netherland et al. 168p. 1996. pap. text 21.95 (*0-88725-234-6*) Hunter Textbks.

Perspectives in Islamic Law. Ed. by Mohamed Taher. 1998. 52.00 (*81-7488-940-X*) Anmol.

Perspectives in Jewish Learning, Vol. I. Intro. by Monford Harris. LC 65-27991. 85p. (Orig.). (C). 1965. pap. 3.95 (*0-935982-34-5*, PJL-01) Spertus Coll.

Perspectives in Jewish Learning, Vol. II. Intro. by Moses A. Shulvass. LC 65-27991. 51p. (Orig.). (C). 1966. pap. 3.95 (*0-935982-35-3*, PJL-02) Spertus Coll.

Perspectives in Jewish Learning, Vol. III. Intro. by Judah M. Rosenthal. LC 65-27991. 56p. (Orig.). (C). 1967. pap. 3.95 (*0-935982-36-1*, PJL-03) Spertus Coll.

Perspectives in Jewish Learning, Vol. IV. Intro. by Mordechai M. Friedman. LC 65-27991. 40p. (Orig.). (C). 1972. pap. 3.95 (*0-935982-37-X*) Spertus Coll.

Perspectives in Jewish Learning, Vol. V. Intro. by Byron L. Sherwin. LC 65-27991. 60p. (Orig.). (C). 1973. pap. text 3.95 (*0-935982-38-8*, PJL-05) Spertus Coll.

Perspectives in Judaism: South Africa. S. Rappaport. 378p. 1986. 17.95 (*0-8197-0523-3*) Bloch.

Perspectives in Jurisprudence: An Analysis of H. L. A. Hart's Legal Theory, Vol. 184. Eric J. Boos. LC 97-26603. (American University Studies V). 212p. (C). 1998. pap. text 25.95 (*0-8204-3902-9*) P Lang Pubng.

Perspectives in Kinanthropometry. Olympic Scientific Congress (1984: Eugene, OR) Sta. Ed. by James A. Day. LC 85-18118. (Nineteen Eighty-Four Olympic Scientific Congress Proceedings Ser.: No. 1). (Illus.). 300p. 1986. reprint ed. pap. 93.00 (*0-608-06447-5*, 206728300009) Bks Demand.

Perspectives in Landscape Ecology. Ed. by S. T. Talling. 352p. (C). 1991. text 350.00 (*0-89771-668-X*, Pub. by Intl Bk Distr) St Mut.

Perspectives in Life Cycle Impact Assessment: A Structured Approach to Combine Models of the Technosphere, Ecosphere, & Valuesphere. Patrick Hofstetter. LC 98-46060. 484p. 1998. text 159.00 (*0-7923-8377-X*, GE145) Kluwer Academic.

Perspectives in Linguistics. John T. Waterman. LC 63-9732. (Midway Reprint Ser.). (Illus.). viii, 120p. 1996. pap. text 11.00 (*0-226-87462-1*) U Ch Pr.

Perspectives in Linguistics. 2nd ed. John T. Waterman. LC 74-143212. (Midway Reprint Ser.). 127p. pap. 39.40 (*0-608-09050-6*, 206968500005) Bks Demand.

Perspectives in Literary Symbolism. Ed. by Joseph P. Strelka. LC 67-27116. (Yearbook of Comparative Criticism Ser.: Vol. 1). (Illus.). 1968. 30.00 (*0-271-73137-0*) Pa St U Pr.

P

Perspectives in Lung Cancer: Proceedings of the Frederick E. Jones Memorial Symposium in Thoracic Surgery, Columbus, Ohio, Oct. 1986. Jones, Frederick E., Memorial Symposium in Thoraci. Ed. by T. E. Williams et al. (Illus.). 1977. 38.50 (*3-8055-2649-0*) S Karger.

Perspectives in Many-Particle Physics: Varenna on Lake Como, Villa Monastero, 7-17 July 1992. Ed. by Ricardo A. Broglia et al. LC 94-6889. (Proceedings of the International School of Physics "Enrico Fermi" Ser.: Vol.121). 306p. 1994. 184.00 (*0-444-82004-3*, North Holland) Elsevier.

Perspectives in Marketing Theory. Ed. by Jerome B. Kernan & Montrose S. Sommers. LC 68-19476. (C). 1968. 32.50 (*0-89197-333-8*) Irvington.

Perspectives in Mathematical Physics. Ed. by S. T. Yau & Robert Penner. (Series in Mathematical Physics). 307p. (C). 1994. text 42.00 (*1-57146-009-8*) Intl Pr Boston.

Perspectives in Mathematics: Anniversary of Oberwolfach, 1984. Ed. by W. Jager et al. (ENG & GER.). 520p. 1984. text 114.80 (*3-7643-1624-1*) Birkhauser.

Perspectives in Medical Sociology. 2nd rev. ed. Ed. by Phil Brown. LC 97-205600. (Illus.). 804p. (C). 1996. pap. text 32.95 (*0-88133-903-2*) Waveland Pr.

***Perspectives in Medical Sociology.** 3rd ed. Ed. by Phil Brown. 673p. (C). 2000. pap. 31.95 (*1-57766-134-6*) Waveland Pr.

Perspectives in Medicinal Chemistry. Ed. by B. Testa et al. (Illus.). 645p. (C). 1993. 230.00 (*3-527-28486-9*, Wiley-VCH) Wiley.

Perspectives in Medicine. New York Academy of Medicine Staff. LC 75-152204. (Essay Index Reprint Ser.). 1977. 19.95 (*0-8369-2813-X*) Ayer.

Perspectives in Medieval History. Ed. by Katherine F. Drew & Floyd S. Lear. LC 63-20902. 105p. reprint ed. 32.60 (*0-8357-9653-1*, 201575300097) Bks Demand.

Perspectives in Memory Research. Ed. by Michael S. Gazzaniga. 336p. 1988. 40.00 (*0-262-07112-6*) MIT Pr.

Perspectives in Metallurgical Development. 337p. 1984. text 60.90 (*0-904357-71-6*, Pub. by Inst Materials) Ashgate Pub Co.

Perspectives in Methodology for Study of the Microcirculation. Ed. by F. Hammersen et al. (Progress in Applied Microcirculation Ser.: Vol. 6). (Illus.). vi, 160p. 1984. pap. 64.50 (*3-8055-3988-6*) S Karger.

Perspectives in Mexican American Studies Vol. 2: Mexicans in the Midwest. Dennis N. Valdes et al. LC 88-650023. 185p. (Orig.). (C). 1990. pap. 15.00 (*0-939363-02-X*) U of AZ Mex Am.

Perspectives in Mexican American Studies Vol. 3: Community, Identity & Education. Ed. by Thomas Gelsinon. 210p. (C). 1992. pap. 15.00 (*0-939363-03-8*) U of AZ Mex Am.

Perspectives in Modern Chemical Spectroscopy. Ed. by D. L. Andrews. (Illus.). 352p. 1990. 59.95 (*0-387-52218-2*) Spr-Verlag.

Perspectives in Molecular Sieve Science. Ed. by William H. Flank & Thaddeus E. Whyte. LC 88-6268. (ACS Symposium Ser.: No. 368). ix, 632p. 1988. 99.95 (*0-8412-1476-X*) Am Chemical.

Perspectives in Molecular Sieve Science: Published in Advance of a Symposium Cosponsored by the Divisions of Industrial & Engineering Chemistry Inc., Petroleum Chemistry, Inc., & Fuel Chemistry at the Third Chemical Congress of North America (195th National Meeting of American Chemical Society), Toronto, Ontario, Canada, June 5-11, 1988. Ed. by William H. Flank & Thaddeus E. Whyte, Jr. LC 88-6268. (ACS Symposium Ser.: Vol. 368). 650p. 1988. reprint ed. pap. 200.00 (*0-608-02981-5*, 205255700007) Bks Demand.

Perspectives in Multicultural Education. William E. Sims & Bernice B. Bass De Martinez. LC 81-40171. (Illus.). 230p. (Orig.). 1981. pap. text 24.50 (*0-8191-1688-2*) U Pr of Amer.

Perspectives in Multicultural Education: The Diverse Classroom. Ed. & Intro. by Carlos A. Bonilla. (Illus.). 210p. (Orig.). (C). 1996. pap. text 19.95 (*1-879774-10-0*) ICA Pub Co.

Perspectives in Music Education: Source Book III. Ed. by Bonnie C. Kowall. LC 66-25659. (Illus.). 575p. 1966. reprint ed. pap. 178.30 (*0-608-04219-6*, 206496300011) Bks Demand.

Perspectives in Mycological Research, Vol. 1. G. P. Festschrift. Ed. by S. K. Hasija et al. (International Bioscience Ser.: Vol. XII). (Illus.). 327p. 1987. 65.00 (*1-55528-145-1*) Scholarly Pubns.

Perspectives in Neural Systems & Behavior. Ed. by Thomas J. Carew & Darcy B. Kelley. (MBL Lectures in Biology: Vol. 10). 276p. 1989. pap. 145.00 (*0-471-56218-1*) Wiley.

Perspectives in Nonlinear Dynamics: Proceedings of the Conference Held at NSWC, Virginia May 28-30, 1985. A. W. Saenz et al. 368p. 1986. pap. 52.00 (*9971-5-0114-7*); text 113.00 (*9971-5-0111-2*) World Scientific Pub.

Perspectives in Nuclear Physics. S. Boffi et al. 596p. 1995. text 122.00 (*981-02-1688-2*) World Scientific Pub.

***Perspectives in Nuclear Physics.** Ed. by J. H. Hamilton et al. 368p. 1999. 84.00 (*981-02-4040-6*) World Scientific Pub.

Perspectives in Nuclear Physics at Intermediate Energies: Proceedings of the 1st Workshop ICTP, Trieste, Italy, Oct. 10-14, 1983. Ed. by S. Boffi et al. 560p. (C). 1984. 98.00 (*9971-966-32-8*) World Scientific Pub.

Perspectives in Nuclear Physics at Intermediate Energies: Proceedings of the 2nd Workshop on Perspective in Nuclear Physics Intermediate Energies. Ed. by S. Boffi et al. 640p. 1985. 130.00 (*9971-5-0034-5*) World Scientific Pub.

Perspectives in Nuclear Physics at Intermediate Energies: Proceedings of the 3rd Workshop. Ed. by S. Boffi et al. 712p. 1988. text 138.00 (*9971-5-0487-1*) World Scientific Pub.

Perspectives in Nuclear Physics at Intermediate Energies: Proceedings of the 4th Workshop. Ed. by S. Boffi et al. 748p. (C). 1989. text 161.00 (*981-02-0046-3*) World Scientific Pub.

Perspectives in Nutrition. 3rd ed. Wardlaw. 1996. (*0-8151-9150-2*) Mosby Inc.

Perspectives in Nutrition. 3rd ed. Wardlaw. 1996. (*0-8151-9161-8*) Mosby Inc.

Perspectives in Nutrition. 4th ed. Gordon M. Wardlaw. LC 98-12998. 1999. 64.63 (*0-07-092078-8*) McGraw.

Perspectives in Nutrition. 5th ed. Wandlaw. 2001. 51.50 (*0-07-228784-5*) McGraw.

Perspectives in Nutrition Study Guide. Gordon M. Wardlaw. 352p. (C). 1989. per. write for info. (*0-8016-5344-4*, WCB McGr Hill) McGrw-H Hghr Educ.

Perspectives in Nutrition Study Guide. 3rd ed. Gordon M. Wardlaw. 368p. (C). 1996. text, student ed. 21.87 (*0-8151-9073-5*, WCB McGr Hill) McGrw-H Hghr Educ.

Perspectives in Nutrition Study Guide & Software. Insel & Gordon M. Wardlaw. 1990. 16.95 (*0-8016-5322-3*) Mosby Inc.

Perspectives in Operations Management: Essays in Honor of Elwood S. Buffa. Ed. by Rakesh K. Sarin. 512p. (C). 1993. lib. bdg. 201.50 (*0-7923-9263-9*) Kluwer Academic.

Perspectives in Optoelectronics. S. S. Jha. 900p. 1995. text 235.00 (*981-02-2022-7*) World Scientific Pub.

***Perspectives in Organopalladium Chemistry for the 21st Century.** Ed. by J. Tsuji. 322p. 1999. 147.00 (*0-444-50197-5*) Elsevier.

Perspectives in Particle Physics, '94: Proceedings of the 7th Adriatic Meeting on Particle Physics. D. Klabucar et al. 400p. 1995. text 113.00 (*981-02-2261-0*) World Scientific Pub.

Perspectives in Pediatric Pathology, Vol. 3. Ed. by Harvey S. Rosenberg & Robert P. Bolande. LC 72-88828. 377p. reprint ed. pap. 107.50 (*0-608-11596-7*, 2022730) Bks Demand.

Perspectives in Pediatric Pathology, Vol. 4. Ed. by Harvey S. Rosenberg & Robert P. Bolande. LC 72-88828. 533p. pap. 165.30 (*0-608-15509-8*, 202974000064) Bks Demand.

Perspectives in Peptide Chemistry. Alex N. Eberle. Ed. by T. Wieland et al. (Illus.). xii, 444p. 1980. 126.25 (*3-8055-1297-X*) S Karger.

Perspectives in Personality, 2 pts. Ed. by Robert T. Hogan & Warren H. Jones. 1991. 175.00 (*1-85302-085-0*) Taylor & Francis.

Perspectives in Personality, 2 pts., Pt. A. Ed. by Robert T. Hogan & Warren H. Jones. 1991. 88.00 (*1-85302-086-9*) Taylor & Francis.

Perspectives in Personality, 2 pts., Pt. B. Ed. by Robert T. Hogan & Warren H. Jones. 1991. 88.00 (*1-85302-087-7*) Taylor & Francis.

Perspectives in Philosophy. Michael Boylan. (Illus.). 340p. (C). 1993. text 65.00 (*0-15-500111-6*, Pub. by Harcourt Coll Pubs) Harcourt.

Perspectives in Philosophy, Religion & Art: Essays in Honour of Margaret Chatterjee. Ed. by R. Balasubramanian. (C). 1993. 18.00 (*81-85636-05-2*, Pub. by Manohar Bk Srv) S Asia.

Perspectives in Phonology. Ed. by Jennifer Cole & Charles Kisserberth. LC 94-30497. (CSLI Lecture Notes Ser.: Vol. 51). 328p. 1995. pap. 19.95 (*1-881526-54-2*) CSLI.

Perspectives in Photosynthesis: Proceedings of the 22nd Jerusalem Symposium on Quantum Chemistry & Biochemistry, Held in Jerusalem, Israel, May 15-18, 1989. Ed. by Joshua Jortner & Bernard Pullman. (C). 1990. text 266.50 (*0-7923-0534-5*) Kluwer Academic.

Perspectives in Phycology. Rao V. Raja. (Illus.). 500p. 1991. 69.00 (*1-55528-192-3*, Pub. by Today Tomorrow) Scholarly Pubns.

Perspectives in Physical Acoustics: Dan I Bolef Symposium. Y. T. Fu. 292p. 1992. text 95.00 (*981-02-0908-8*) World Scientific Pub.

Perspectives in Physics. 3rd ed. P. C. Sharma. 240p. (C). 1994. spiral bd. 23.95 (*0-8403-9476-4*) Kendall-Hunt.

Perspectives in Phytopathology: Dr. R. S. Singh Festschrift Volume. Ed. by V. P. Agnihotri et al. (Illus.). xiii, 525p. (Orig.). 1989. 85.00 (*1-55528-167-2*) Scholarly Pubns.

Perspectives in Plant Cell Recognition. Ed. by J. A. Callow & J. R. Green. (Society for Experimental Biology Seminar Ser.: No. 48). (Illus.). 318p. (C). 1992. text 100.00 (*0-521-40445-2*) Cambridge U Pr.

Perspectives in Plant Sciences in India: Proceedings of the Section of Botany of Indian Science Congress Platinum Jubilee Session, June 1988. Ed. by S. S. Bir & M. I. Saggoo. (Aspects of Plant Sciences Ser.: Vol. X). xvi, 279p. 1989. 45.00 (*1-55528-163-X*) Scholarly Pubns.

Perspectives in Political Sociology. Ed. by Andrew Effrat. LC 73-4329. 1973. 37.50 (*0-672-51746-9*) Irvington.

Perspectives in Political Sociology. Ed. by Andrew Effrat. LC 73-4329. 320p. (C). 1973. pap. text 6.50 (*0-672-61322-0*, Bobbs) Macmillan.

Perspectives in Primate Biology, Vol. 1. Ed. by P. K. Seth. (Illus.). 242p. 1983. 69.00 (*1-55528-066-8*, Pub. by Today Tomorrow) Scholarly Pubns.

Perspectives in Primate Biology, Vol. 2. Ed. by P. K. Seth. 208p. 1989. 69.00 (*1-55528-175-3*) Scholarly Pubns.

Perspectives in Primate Biology, Vol. 3. Ed. by P. K. Seth. 260p. 1989. 69.00 (*1-55528-176-1*) Scholarly Pubns.

Perspectives in Primate Biology, Vol. 4. P. K. Seth & Swadesh Seth. (Illus.). 260p. 1991. 59.00 (*1-55528-256-3*, Pub. by Today Tomorrow) Scholarly Pubns.

Perspectives in Professional Child & Youth Care. Ed. by James P. Anglin et al. 359p. 1990. pap. 24.95 (*1-56024-055-5*) Haworth Pr.

Perspectives in Professional Child & Youth Care, Pt. 1. Ed. by James P. Anglin et al. LC 90-4051. (Child & Youth Services Ser.: Vol. 13, No. 1 & 2). 360p. 1990. text 49.95 (*0-86656-891-3*) Haworth Pr.

Perspectives in Psychical Research Series, 34 vols. Ed. by Robert L. Morris. 1975. 1049.00 (*0-405-07020-9*) Ayer.

Perspectives in Psychological Experimentation: Toward the Year 2000. Ed. by Viktor Sarris & Allen Parducci. 384p. (C). 1984. text 79.95 (*0-89859-288-7*) L Erlbaum Assocs.

Perspectives in Psychological Theory: Essays in Honor of Heinz Werner. Ed. by Bernard Kaplan & Seymour Wapner. LC 60-8303. (Illus.). 395p. reprint ed. pap. 122.50 (*0-608-11201-1*, 201044700070) Bks Demand.

Perspectives in Pteridology, Present & Future: Prof. S. S. Bir Commemoration Volume, Pt. 1. T. N. Bhardwaja & C. B. Gena. (Aspects of Plant Sciences Ser.: Vol. 13). (Illus.). 342p. 1991. text 65.00 (*81-7019-385-0*, Pub. by Today Tomorrow) Lubrecht & Cramer.

Perspectives in Pteridology, Present & Future: Prof. S. S. Bir Commemoration Volume, Pt. I. Ed. by T. N. Bhardwaja & C. B. Gena. (Aspects of Plant Sciences Ser.: Vol. 13). (Illus.). xxxviii, 342p. 1992. 65.00 (*1-55528-251-2*, Pub. by Today Tomorrow) Scholarly Pubns.

Perspectives in Pteridology, Present & Future: Prof. S. S. Bir Commemoration Volume, Pt. II. Ed. by T. N. Bhardwaja & C. B. Gena. (Aspects of Plant Sciences Ser.: Vol. 14). (Illus.). xxxviii, 342p. 1992. 65.00 (*0-685-66552-6*, Pub. by Today Tomorrow) Scholarly Pubns.

Perspectives in Quantum Chemistry. Ed. by Joshua Jortner & Bernard Pullman. (C). 1989. text 142.00 (*0-7923-0228-1*) Kluwer Academic.

Perspectives in Quantum Hall Effects: Novel Quantum Liquids in Low-Dimensional Semiconductor Structures. Ed. by Sankar D. Sarma & Aron Pinczuk. LC 96-20452. 448p. 1996. 91.50 (*0-471-11216-X*) Wiley.

Perspectives in Receptor Research. Ed. by D. Giardina et al. (Pharmacochemistry Library: Vol. 24). 422p. 1996. text 227.00 (*0-444-82204-6*) Elsevier.

Perspectives in Recreational Therapy: Issues of a Dynamic Profession. Ed. by Frank Brasile et al. (Illus.). 550p. 1998. pap. 45.00 (*1-882883-26-8*) Idyll Arbor.

Perspectives in Regional Problems & Regional Development in Nepal. D. B. Amatya. 1987. 38.00 (*0-7855-0249-1*, Pub. by Ratna Pustak Bhandar) St Mut.

Perspectives in Regional Problems & Regional Development in Nepal. D. B. Amatya. 160p. (C). 1987. 150.00 (*0-89771-053-3*, Pub. by Ratna Pustak Bhandar) St Mut.

Perspectives in Rehabilitation Ergonomics. Ed. by Shrawan Kumar. LC 97-171564. 408p. 1997. text 120.00 (*0-7484-0644-1*, Pub. by Tay Francis Ltd); pap. text 54.95 (*0-7484-0673-5*, Pub. by Tay Francis Ltd) Taylor & Francis.

Perspectives in Ring Theory. Ed. by Freddy Van Oystaeyen & Lieven Le Bruyn. (C). 1988. text 201.00 (*90-277-2736-8*) Kluwer Academic.

Perspectives in Running Water Ecology. Ed. by Maurice A. Lock & D. D. Williams. LC 81-17838. 440p. 1981. 95.00 (*0-306-40898-8*, Plenum Trade) Perseus Pubng.

Perspectives in Schizophrenia Research. fac. ed. Ed. by Claude F. Baxter & Theodore Melnechuk. LC 80-5052. (Illus.). 463p. pap. 143.60 (*0-7837-7168-1*, 204712900005) Bks Demand.

Perspectives in Scottish Social History: Essays in Honour of Rosalind Mitchison. Leah Leneman. 200p. 1988. pap. text 29.95 (*0-08-036574-4*, Pub. by Aberdeen U Pr) Macmillan.

Perspectives in Social & Economic History of Early India. Ram S. Sharma. LC 95-911601. 340p. (C). 1995. 33.50 (*81-215-0672-7*, Pub. by M Manoharial) Coronet Bks.

Perspectives in Social Gerontology. Compiled by Robert B. Enright, Jr. LC 93-28829. 406p. 1993. pap. text 52.00 (*0-205-15433-6*) Allyn.

Perspectives in Social Science: Three Studies on the Agrarian Structure in Bengal, 1850-1947. Asok Sen et al. 1983. 16.95 (*0-19-561019-9*) OUP.

Perspectives in Social Welfare in India. J. Bulsara. 226p. 1984. 22.95 (*0-318-36854-4*) Asia Bk Corp.

Perspectives in Sociology. 2nd ed. Ed. by E. C. Cuff & G. C. Payne. 1983. pap. text 15.95 (*0-04-301157-8*) Routledge.

Perspectives in Sociology. 3rd ed. E. C. Cuff et al. 257p. (C). 1990. pap. text 16.95 (*0-04-445684-0*) Routledge.

Perspectives in Sociology. 4th ed. E. C. Cuff & W. W. Sharrock. LC 97-30113. 368p. (C). 1998. 85.00 (*0-415-17371-X*) Routledge.

Perspectives in Sociology. 4th ed. E. C. Cuff et al. LC 97-30113. 368p. (C). 1998. pap. 24.99 (*0-415-15979-2*) Routledge.

Perspectives in Spread Spectrum, Vol. 459. Amer A. Hassan et al. LC 98-27924. (International Series in Engineering & Computer Science). 1998. write for info. (*0-7923-8265-X*) Kluwer Academic.

Perspectives in Steroid Receptor Research. fac. ed. Ed. by Francesco Bresciani. LC 79-5398. (Illus.). 334p. pap. 103.60 (*0-7837-7164-9*, 204713300005) Bks Demand.

Perspectives in String Theory: Proceedings of the Niels Bohr Institute-Nordita Meeting, Copenhagen, Denmark. Ed. by P. Di Vecchia & J. L. Petersen. 524p. (C). 1988. pap. 61.00 (*9971-5-0534-7*); text 123.00 (*9971-5-0526-6*) World Scientific Pub.

Perspectives in Surgery. Clare G. Peterson. LC 72-115025. 355p. reprint ed. pap. 110.10 (*0-608-30536-7*, 201457700094) Bks Demand.

***Perspectives in the Philosophy of Language: A Concise Anthology.** Ed. by Robert J. Stainton. 360p. 1999. pap. 19.95 (*1-55111-253-1*) Broadview Pr.

Perspectives in the Science of Sociology. Ed. by Stuart S. Blume. LC 76-30827. 245p. reprint ed. pap. 69.90 (*0-685-20695-5*, 2030484) Bks Demand.

Perspectives in the Standard Model: Proceedings of the 1991 TASI Symposium. 720p. 1992. text 35.00 (*981-02-1990-3*) World Scientific Pub.

Perspectives in the Standard Model (TASI-91) Proceedings in Elementary River Edge, N. J., 1991. Ed. by R. K. Ellis et al. LC 92-10270. 500p. 1992. text 109.00 (*981-02-0921-5*) World Scientific Pub.

Perspectives in the Structure of Hadronic Systems. M. N. Harakeh et al. (NATO ASI Ser.: Vol. 328). (Illus.). 368p. (C). 1994. text 115.00 (*0-306-44739-8*, Kluwer Plenum) Kluwer Academic.

Perspectives in the Study of the Old Testtament & Early Judiasm: A Symposium in Honour of Adams S. Van Der Woude on the Occasion of His 70th Birthday. A. S. Van Der Woude et al. LC 98-47857. (Supplements to Vetus Testamentum Ser.). 1998. write for info. (*90-04-11322-3*) Brill Academic Pubs.

Perspectives in the Vedic & the Classical Sanskrit Heritage. G. V. Davane. (C). 1995. 30.00 (*81-246-0031-7*, Pub. by DK Pubs Ind) S Asia.

Perspectives in Theology & Mission from South Africa: Signs of the Times. Ed. by Daryl M. Balia. LC 93-21574. 1993. pap. 39.95 (*0-7734-1950-0*) E Mellen.

Perspectives in Theoretical Stereochemistry. I. Ugi et al. (Lecture Notes in Chemistry Ser.: Vol. 36). 265p. 1984. pap. 37.00 (*0-387-13391-7*) Spr-Verlag.

Perspectives in Total Quality. Ed. by Michael J. Stahl. LC 98-8587. (Illus.). 320p. 1998. 69.95 (*0-631-20884-4*) Blackwell Pubs.

Perspectives in Transactional Analysis. Muriel James. LC 99-168604. (Illus.). 270p. 1998. pap. 25.00 (*0-89489-005-0*) Intl Transactional.

Perspectives in Tropical Limnology. F. Schiemer & K. T. Boland. (Illus.). 348p. 1996. 160.00 (*90-5103-113-0*, Pub. by SPB Acad Pub) Balogh.

Perspectives in Urban Ecology. Ed. by Elizabeth E. Webb & Susan Q. Foster. (Illus.). 96p. (Orig.). 1990. pap. 14.95 (*0-916278-69-7*) Denver Mus.

Perspectives in Urban Geography Vol. 7: Slums, Urban Decline & Revitalization. C. S. Yadav. 1987. 41.00 (*0-8364-2260-0*, Pub. by Concept) S Asia.

Perspectives in Urban Geography Vol. 8: Contemporary Urban Issues. Ed. by C. S. Yadav. 1987. 54.00 (*0-8364-2241-4*, Pub. by Concept) S Asia.

Perspectives in Urban Geography Vol. 12: Perceptual & Cognitive Image of the City. C. S. Yadav. 1987. 57.00 (*0-8364-2253-8*, Pub. by Concept) S Asia.

Perspectives in Virology Vol. 10: The Gustav Stern Symposium. fac. ed. Ed. by Morris Pollard. LC 59-8415. (Illus.). 276p. pap. 85.60 (*0-7837-7155-X*, 204714200010) Bks Demand.

Perspectives in Western Drama. Avtar Singh. viii, 276p. 1992. 30.00 (*81-85151-54-7*, Pub. by Harman Pub Hse) Advent Bks Div.

Perspectives of Antioxidant Treatment of Emphysema with N-Acetyloysteine: Journal: Respiration, Vol. 50, Suppl. 1, 1986. Ed. by V. Cichetti et al. vi, 74p. 1986. pap. 24.50 (*3-8055-4514-2*) S Karger.

Perspectives of Archeology, Art & Culture in Early Andhra Desa. K. Ramamohan Rao. (C). 1992. text 42.00 (*81-85689-01-6*, Pub. by Aditya Prakashan) S Asia.

Perspectives of Black Popular Culture. Ed. by Harry B. Shaw. LC 90-83464. 185p. (C). 1991. 37.95 (*0-87972-503-6*) Bowling Green Univ Popular Press.

Perspectives of Critical Contract Law. Ed. by Thomas Wilhelmsson. 415p. 1993. 96.95 (*1-85521-319-2*, Pub. by Dartmth Pub) Ashgate Pub Co.

Perspectives of Elementary Mathematics. G. P. Hochschild. 140p. 1983. 71.95 (*0-387-90848-X*) Spr-Verlag.

Perspectives of Event-Related Potentials Research. Ed. by G. Karmos et al. LC 94-48149. (Electroencephalography & Clinical Neurophysiology Ser.; Supplement: No. 44). 478p. 1995. 256.25 (*0-444-82058-2*) Elsevier.

Perspectives of Fundamental Physics, Vol.1. Ed. by Carlo Schaerf. (Studies in High Energy Physics: Vol. 1). viii, 470p. 1979. 252.00 (*3-7186-0007-2*) Gordon & Breach.

Perspectives of Global Responsibility - In Honor of Helmut Schmidt on the Occasion of His 75th Birthday. Ed. by Hans D'Orville. (Illus.). 546p. 1994. 25.00 (*1-885060-01-7*) H dOrville.

Perspectives of Information Processing in Medical Application: Strategic Issues, Requirements & Options for the European Community. Ed. by F. Roger-France & G. Santucci. (Health Systems Research Ser.). 320p. 1991. 71.95 (*0-387-53856-9*) Spr-Verlag.

Perspectives of Information Systems. Ed. by Vesa Savolainen. LC 98-53848. (Illus.). 271p. 1999. 55.95 (*0-387-98712-6*) Spr-Verlag.

Perspectives of Irony in Medieval French Literature. Vladimir Rossman. (De Proprietatibus Litterarum, Ser. Major: No. 35). 198p. (Orig.). 1975. pap. text 60.80 (*90-279-3291-3*) Mouton.

Perspectives of Life in Literature. unabridged ed. Compiled by John D. Martin et al. LC 97-132833. (Illus.). 611p. (YA). (gr. 9). 1996. text 22.95 (*0-87813-927-3*) Christian Light.

Perspectives of Motor Behavior & Its Neural Basis. Ed. by Marie-Claude Hepp-Reymond & Gabriella Marini. LC 97-3035. (Illus.). viii, 138p. 1997. 85.25 (*3-8055-6403-1*) S Karger.

***Perspectives of Mutual Encounters in South Asian History, 1750-1850.** Jamal Malik. LC 00-29732. 492p. 2000. 140.00 (*90-04-11802-0*) Brill Academic Pubs.

Perspectives of Nuclear Physics in the Late Nineties: Proceedings of the International Conference on Nuclear Physics & Relation. Ed. by Nguyen D. Dang et al. 150p. 1995. text 150.00 (*981-02-2086-3*) World Scientific Pub.

Perspectives of Polarons. 250p. 1996. lib. bdg. 38.00 (*981-02-2778-7*) World Scientific Pub.

Perspectives of Psychiatry. Paul R. McHugh & Phillip R. Slavney. LC 83-6157. 176p. 1986. reprint ed. pap. text 13.95 (*0-8018-3302-7*) Johns Hopkins.

Perspectives of Psychiatry. 2nd ed. Paul R. Mchugh. LC 98-26808. 375p. 1998. pap. text 16.95 (*0-8018-6046-6*) Johns Hopkins.

Perspectives of Psychiatry. 2nd ed. Paul R. McHugh & Phillip R. Slavney. LC 98-26808. (Illus.). 375p. 1998. 35.00 (*0-8018-6045-8*) Johns Hopkins.

Perspectives of Strong Coupling Gauge Theories: Proceedings of the 1996 International Workshop, Nagoya, Japan, 13-16 November 1996. Ed. by J. Nishimura & K. Yamawaki. 450p. 1997. 84.00 (*981-02-3187-3*) World Scientific Pub.

***Perspectives of System Informatics: Proceedings of the Third International Andrei Ershov Memorial Conference, PSI '99, Akademgorodok, Novosibirsk, Russia, July 6-9, 1999.** International Andrei Ershov

An Asterisk (*) at the beginning of an entry indicates that the title is appearing for the first time.

Memorial Conference Staff et al. LC 00-21732. (Lecture Notes in Computer Science Ser.: Vol. 1755). xii, 540p. 2000. pap. 85.00 (*3-540-67102-1*) Spr-Verlag.

Perspectives of System Informatics Vol. XVII: Proceedings, 2nd International Andrei Ershov Memorial Conference, Akademgorodok, Novosibirsk, Russia, June 25-28, 1966, Vol. 1181. Ed. by D. Bjorner et al. LC 96-50358. (Lecture Notes in Computer Science Ser.). 447p. 1996. pap. 75.00 (*3-540-62064-8*) Spr-Verlag.

Perspectives of the History of Economic Thought Vol. II: Twentieth-Century Economic Thought. Ed. by Donald A. Walker. (Perspectives on the History of Economic Thought Ser.: Vol. 2). 272p. 1989. text 95.00 (*1-85278-132-7*) E Elgar.

Perspectives of the Scottish City, 1831-1981. Ed. by George Gordon. (Illus.). 224p. 1985. text 39.00 (*0-08-030371-4*, Pergamon Pr) Elsevier.

Perspectives of Truth in Literature. John D. Martin & Lester E. Showalter. (Christian Day School Ser.). (YA). (gr. 12). 1983. 22.95 (*0-87813-921-4*) Christian Light.

Perspectives of Truth in Literature: Teacher's Guiebook. John D. Martin & Lester E. Showalter. (Christian Day School Ser.). (YA). (gr. 12). 1983. teacher ed. 12.00 (*0-87813-922-2*) Christian Light.

Perspectives on a Dynamic Earth. Thomas R. Paton. 176p. 1986. text 55.00 (*0-04-550042-8*) Routledge.

Perspectives on a Dynamic Earth. Thomas R. Paton. 176p. (C). 1986. pap. text 21.95 (*0-04-550043-6*) Routledge.

Perspectives on a Grafted Tree: Thoughts for Those Touched by Adoption. Ed. by Patricia Irwin Johnston. LC 82-2424. (Illus.). 144p. 1983. 14.95 (*0-9609504-0-0*) Perspect Indiana.

Perspectives on a Parent Movement: The Revolt of Parents of Children with Intellectual Limitations. Rosemary F. Dybwad. LC 90-35065. 186p. (Orig.). 1990. pap. text 17.95 (*0-914797-74-3*) Brookline Bks.

Perspectives on a Regional Culture. Ed. by B. Beck. 212p. 1979. 19.95 (*0-318-36977-X*) Asia Bk Corp.

Perspectives on a U. S. - Canadian Free Trade Agreement. Ed. by Robert M. Stern et al. LC 87-17657. 266p. 1987. 32.95 (*0-8157-8132-6*); pap. 12.95 (*0-8157-8131-8*) Brookings.

Perspectives on Abortion. Ed. by Paul Sachdev. LC 84-10573. 293p. 1984. 26.50 (*0-8108-1708-X*) Scarecrow.

Perspectives on Academic Writing. Alice Calderonello et al. 144p. (C). 1996. pap., teacher ed. write for info. (*0-02-318296-2*) Macmillan.

Perspectives on Accounting & Finance in China. Ed. by John Blake & Simon Gao. LC 94-39780. 320p. (C). (gr. 13). 1995. pap. 60.00 (*0-415-11812-3*, C0476) Thomson Learn.

Perspectives on Activity Theory. Ed. by Yrjo Engestrom et al. LC 97-40981. (Learning in Doing Ser.). 568p. (C). 1999. text 80.00 (*0-521-43127-1*) Cambridge U Pr.

Perspectives on Activity Theory. Yrjo Engestrom & Reijo Miettinen. LC 97-40981. (Learning in Doing Ser.). 568p. (C). 1999. pap. text 32.95 (*0-521-43730-X*) Cambridge U Pr.

Perspectives on Adolescent Drug Use. Ed. by Bernard Segal. 170p. 1989. 39.95 (*0-86656-923-5*) Haworth Pr.

Perspectives on Adult Education & Training in Europe. Jarvis. 430p. 1992. 57.50 (*1-872941-19-2*) Krieger.

Perspectives on Adult Learning. Ed. by E. Michael Brady. 92p. (Orig.). 1986. pap. text 5.00 (*0-939561-00-X*) Univ South ME.

***Perspectives on Adults Learning Mathematics: Research & Practice.** Diana Coben et al. LC 00-33084. (Mathematics Education Library). 2000. write for info. (*0-7923-6415-5*) Kluwer Academic.

Perspectives on Affirmative Action . . . & Its Impact on Asian Pacific Americans. Ed. by Gena A. Lew. 39p. (Orig.). (C). 1996. pap. text 25.00 (*0-7881-2330-0*) DIANE Pub.

Perspectives on Africa: A Reader in Culture, History, & Representation. Roy R. Grinker & Christopher B. Steiner. LC 96-21537. 1996. 88.95 (*1-55786-685-6*); pap. 34.95 (*1-55786-686-4*) Blackwell Pubs.

***Perspectives on African Americans.** Walter G. Secada. 194p. 2000. pap. 18.00 (*0-87353-461-1*, 693E1) NCTM.

Perspectives on African Literature. Ed. & Intro. by Christopher Heywood. LC 71-169493. 172p. 1972. 29.50 (*0-8419-0093-0*, Africana) Holmes & Meier.

Perspectives on Aging & Human Development Series, 3 vols. Incl. Vol. 1. Being & Becoming Old. Ed. by Jon Hendricks. 160p. 1980. pap. 15.95 (*0-89503-014-4*); Vol. 2. In the Country of the Old. Jon Hendricks. 160p. 1980. pap. 15.95 (*0-89503-015-2*); Vol. 3. Institutionalization & Alternative Futures. Ed. by Jon Hendricks. 160p. 1980. pap. 14.95 (*0-89503-016-0*); 480p. 1980. Set pap. 37.95 (*0-89503-024-1*) Baywood Pub.

Perspectives on Agriculture, Food & Natural Resources: 10 Year U. S. Agricultural Outlook. Ed. by Stanley R. Johnson et al. (Illus.). 121p. 1997. reprint ed. pap. text 25.00 (*0-7881-4164-3*) DIANE Pub.

Perspectives on Aid & Development. Ed. & Intro. by Catherine Gwin. LC 97-29209. (Overseas Development Council Ser.: No. 22). 108p. (Orig.). 1997. pap. text 13.95 (*1-56517-007-5*) Overseas Dev Council.

Perspectives on Aids: Ethical & Social Issues. Ed. by Christine Overall & William P. Zion. 240p. 1991. pap. text 24.95 (*0-19-540749-0*) OUP.

Perspectives on Akira Kurosawa. James Goodwin. (Illus.). 336p. 1994. 55.00 (*0-8161-1993-7*, Hall Reference) Macmillan.

Perspectives on Alcohol Prevention. Hakan Leifman. (Stockholm Studies in Sociology: NS 3). 195p. 1996. pap. 42.50 (*91-22-01732-1*) Coronet Bks.

Perspectives on Alfred Hitchcock. Ed. by David Boyd. LC 94-35398. (Perspectives on Film Ser.). 200p. 1995. 55.00 (*0-8161-1603-2*, G K Hall & Co) Mac Lib Ref.

Perspectives on American & Texas Politics. 5th ed. Tedin et al. LC 97-202353. 432p. (C). 1997. per. 20.95 (*0-7872-4245-4*, 41424501) Kendall-Hunt.

Perspectives on American Civilization. 3rd ed. Robert A. Goldberg & L. R. Gunn. 384p. (C). 1990. pap. 49.00 (*0-536-57713-7*) Pearson Custom.

Perspectives on American Culture: Essays on Humor, Literature, & the Popular Arts. M. Thomas Inge. LC 94-14908. (Locust Hill Literary Studies: No. 16). (C). 1994. lib. bdg. 32.00 (*0-933951-59-0*) Locust Hill Pr.

Perspectives on American English. Ed. by J. L. Dillard. (Contributions to the Sociology of Language Ser.: No. 29). 468p. 1980. 84.65 (*90-279-3367-7*) Mouton.

Perspectives on American Government. Rick Hardy. 276p. (C). 1995. text 39.60 (*0-536-59127-X*) Pearson Custom.

Perspectives on American Government. 2nd ed. 296p. (C). 1998. text 29.20 (*0-536-01066-8*) Pearson Custom.

Perspectives on American Government: A Comprehensive Reader. William Lasser. 775p. (C). 1992. teacher ed. 2.66 (*0-669-28289-8*) HM Trade Div.

Perspectives on American Government: A Comprehensive Reader. 2nd ed. William Lasser. (C). 1996. text, teacher ed. 28.36 (*0-669-41643-6*) HM Trade Div.

Perspectives on American Government: A Comprehensive Reader, 2 Vols. 2nd ed. William Lasser. 625p. (C). 2000. pap. text 29.16 (*0-669-41642-8*) HM Trade Div.

Perspectives on American Labor History: The Problem of Synthesis. Ed. by Alice Kessler-Harris. 257p. 1990. text 32.00 (*0-87580-150-1*); pap. text 16.00 (*0-87580-551-5*) N Ill U Pr.

Perspectives on American Methodism: Interpretive Essays. Russell E. Richey et al. Ed. by Jean M. Schmidt. 384p. (Orig.). 1993. pap. 26.95 (*0-687-30782-1*) Abingdon.

Perspectives on American Music from 1970 to 1990. James R. Heintze. Ed. by Michael Saffle. (Essays on American Music Ser.). 400p. 1997. text 60.00 (*0-8153-2143-0*) Garland.

Perspectives on American Music from World War I to World War II. Michael Saffle. Ed. by James R. Heintze. (Essays on American Music Ser.). 400p. 1999. text 60.00 (*0-8153-2145-7*) Garland.

Perspectives on American Music Since 1950. Ed. by James R. Heintze & Michael Saffle. LC 99-10967. (Essays in American Music Ser.: Vol. 4). 496p. 1999. text 85.00 (*0-8153-2144-9*, H1953) Garland.

Perspectives on American Political Media. Gary C. Woodward. LC 96-8864. 256p. 1996. pap. text 37.00 (*0-205-26250-3*) Allyn.

Perspectives on American Religion & Culture: A Reader. Ed. by Peter M. Williams. LC 98-47774. 404p. 1998. 64.95 (*1-57718-117-4*) Blackwell Pubs.

Perspectives on American Religion & Culture: A Reader. Ed. by Peter M. Williams. LC 98-47774. 400p. 1999. pap. 29.95 (*1-57718-118-2*) Blackwell Pubs.

Perspectives on an Economic Future: Forms, Reforms, & Evaluations, 116. Ed. by Shripad G. Pendse. LC 90-37841. (Contributions in Economics & Economic History Ser.: No. 116). 216p. 1991. 57.95 (*0-313-26288-8*, PCG/, Greenwood Pr) Greenwood.

Perspectives on Analytic Philosophy. E. M. Barth. (Mededelingen der Koninklijke Nederlandse Akademie van Wetenschappen, Afd. Letterkunde Ser.: No. 42(2)). 48p. 1979. pap. text 18.75 (*0-7204-8484-7*) Elsevier.

***Perspectives on Animal Behavior.** 2nd ed. Judith Goodenough et al. 576p. (C). 2000. text. write for info. (*0-471-29502-7*) Wiley.

Perspectives on Animal Research, Vol. 1. Ed. by Stephen R. Kaufman & Betsy Todd. 160p. 1989. pap. 10.00 (*0-9623858-1-6*) Med Res Modern.

Perspectives on Animal Research, 1989, Vol. 1. Ed. by Stephen R. Kaufman & Betsy Todd. 160p. 1989. 15.00 (*0-9623858-0-8*) Med Res Modern.

Perspectives on Anthropological Collections from the American Southwest. Ed. by Ann L. Hedlund. LC 89-81033. (Anthropological Research Papers: No. 40). (Illus.). iii, 158p. (Orig.). 1989. pap. 15.00 (*0-936249-04-8*) AZ Univ ARP.

Perspectives on Antitrust Policy. Ed. by Almarin Phillips. LC 64-19822. 466p. 1965. reprint ed. pap. 144.50 (*0-7837-9419-3*, 206016000004) Bks Demand.

Perspectives on Applied Physical Geography. 2nd ed. John E. Oliver et al. LC 97-73137. 196p. 1997. per. 52.95 (*0-7872-2516-9*, 41251601) Kendall-Hunt.

Perspectives on Applied Sociolinguistics. Robert St. Clair et al. 257p. 1979. pap. 25.00 (*0-87291-136-5*) Coronado Pr.

Perspectives on Arabic Linguistics Vol. 1: Papers from the First Annual Symposium on Arabic Linguistics, Salt Lake City, Utah 1987. Ed. by Mushira Eid. LC 90-959. (Current Issues in Linguistic Theory Ser.: Vol. 63). xiii, 290p. 1990. 109.00 (*90-272-3560-0*) J Benjamins Pubng Co.

Perspectives on Arabic Linguistics Vol. II: Papers from the 2nd Annual Symposium on Arabic Linguistics, Salt Lake City, Utah 1988. Ed. by Mushira Eid & John McCarthy. LC 90-752. (Current Issues in Linguistic Theory Ser.: Vol. 72). xiv, 332p. 1990. 83.00 (*1-55619-128-6*) J Benjamins Pubng Co.

Perspectives on Arabic Linguistics Vol. III: Papers from the 3rd Annual Symposium on Arabic Linguistics, Salt Lake City, Utah 1989. Ed. by Bernard Comrie & Mushira Eid. LC 91-7898. (Current Issues in Linguistic Theory Ser.: No. 80). xii, 274p. 1991. 71.00 (*1-55619-135-9*) J Benjamins Pubng Co.

Perspectives on Arabic Linguistics Vol. IV: Papers from the 4th Annual Symposium on Arabic Linguistics, Detroit, Michigan 1990. Ed. by Ellen Broselow et al. (Current Issues in Linguistic Theory Ser.: No. 85). viii, 282p. 1992. 71.00 (*1-55619-140-5*) J Benjamins Pubng Co.

Perspectives on Arabic Linguistics Vol. V: Papers from the 5th Annual Symposium on Arabic Linguistics, Ann Harbor, Michigan 1991. Ed. by Mushira Eid & Clive Holes. LC 91-641663. (Current Issues in Linguistic Theory Ser.: No. 101). viii, 347p. 1993. 83.00 (*1-55619-554-0*) J Benjamins Pubng Co.

Perspectives on Arabic Linguistics Vol. VI: Papers from the 6th Annual Symposium on Arabic Linguistics, March 6-8, 1992, The Ohio State University, Columbus, Ohio 1992. Ed. by Mushira Eid et al. LC 91-641663. (Current Issues in Linguistics Theory Ser.: No. 115). viii, 238p. 1994. lib. bdg. 67.00 (*1-55619-569-9*) J Benjamins Pubng Co.

Perspectives on Arabic Linguistics Vol. VII: Papers from the 7th Annual Symposium on Arabic Linguistics, Austin, Texas 1993. Ed. by Mushira Eid. (Current Issues in Linguistic Theory Ser.: No. 130). vii, 192p. 1995. lib. bdg. 57.00 (*1-55619-584-2*) J Benjamins Pubng Co.

Perspectives on Arabic Linguistics Vol. VIII: Papers from the Annual Symposium on Arabic Languages, Amherst, Massachusetts. Ed. by Mushira Eid. (Current Issues in Linguistic Theory Ser.: Vol. 134). vii, 261p. 1996. lib. bdg. 69.00 (*1-55619-589-3*) J Benjamins Pubng Co.

Perspectives on Arabic Linguistics Vol. IX: Papers from the Annual Symposium on Arabic Linguistics, Washington, DC, 1995. Ed. by Mushira Eid & Dilworth B. Parkinson. (Current Issues in Linguistic Theory Ser.: Vol. 141). xiii, 249p. 1996. lib. bdg. 84.00 (*1-55619-596-6*) J Benjamins Pubng Co.

Perspectives on Arabic Linguistics Vol. X: Papers from the Tenth Annual Symposium on Arabic Linguistics, Salt Lake City, 1996. Ed. by Mushira Eid & Robert R. Ratcliffe. (Current Issues in Linguistic Theory Ser.: Vol. 153). vii, 296p. 1997. lib. bdg. 82.00 (*1-55619-869-8*) J Benjamins Pubng Co.

***Perspectives on Arabic Linguistics XIII Vol. XII: Papers from the Twelfth Annual Symposium On Arabic Linguistics, Urbana-Champaign, Illinois, 1998.** Ed. by Elabbas Benmamoun. (Current Issues in Linguistic Theory Ser.: Vol. 190). viii, 204p. 1999. 75.00 (*1-55619-967-8*) J Benjamins Pubng.

Perspectives on Archaeological Resources Management in the Great Plains. Ed. by Robert C. Hassler. (Illus.). ix, 391p. 1987. pap. 16.00 (*0-9619168-0-X*) I & O Pub NE.

Perspectives on Argument: 1998 MLA Update Edition. 2nd ed. Nancy V. Wood. LC 97-12903. (C). 1998. pap. text 36.60 (*0-13-096448-4*) P-H.

Perspectives on Argumentation: Essays in Honor of Wayne Brockreide. Ed. by Robert Trapp & Janice Schuetz. (Illus.). 338p. (C). 1990. pap. text 20.95 (*0-88133-515-0*) Waveland Pr.

Perspectives on Arthur Miller. Atma Ram. (C). 1988. 14.50 (*81-7017-240-3*, Pub. by Abhinav) S Asia.

***Perspectives on Asian Americans & Pacific Islanders.** Ed. by Carole A. Edwards. LC 99-45435. (Changing the Faces of Mathematics Ser.). (Illus.). 96p. 1999. pap. 16.95 (*0-87353-475-1*) NCTM.

***Perspectives on Audiovisuals in the Teaching of History.** Ed. by Susan W. Gillespie. LC 99-29359. 86p. (C). 1999. pap. 8.00 (*0-87229-111-1*) Am Hist Assn.

Perspectives on Australia. Ed. by Dave Oliphant. (Illus.). 204p. 1988. pap. 18.95 (*0-87959-108-0*) U of Tex H Ransom Ctr.

Perspectives on Autoimmunity. Ed. by Irun R. Cohen. 272p. 1987. 136.00 (*0-8493-6431-0*, RC600, CRC Reprint) Franklin.

Perspectives on Availability: A Symposium on Determining Protected Group Representation in Internal & External Labor Markets. Robert J. Flanagan et al. LC 78-63628. 243p. (Orig.). (C). 1977. pap. 12.75 (*0-937856-02-9*) Equal Employ.

Perspectives on Bacterial Pathogenesis & Host Defense. Ed. by Bernhard Urbaschek. 268p. 1988. lib. bdg. 42.00 (*0-226-84275-4*) U Ch Pr.

Perspectives on Behavior & Organizations. 2nd ed. Porter L. Hackman et al. Ed. by Patricia S. Nave. (Illus.). 608p. (C). 1983. 62.81 (*0-07-025414-1*) McGraw.

Perspectives on Behavioral Inhibition. Ed. by J. Steven Reznick. LC 89-32463. (John D. & Catherine T. MacArthur Foundation Series on Mental Health & Development). (Illus.). 326p. 1989. 39.95 (*0-226-71040-8*) U Ch Pr.

Perspectives on Behavioral Self-Regulation, Vol. 12. Ed. by Robert S. Wyer. (Advances in Social Cognition Ser.). 250p. 1999. write for info. (*0-8058-2588-6*) L Erlbaum Assocs.

Perspectives on Behavioral Self-Regulation: Advances in Social Cognition, Vol. 12. Ed. by Robert S. Wyer. (Advances in Social Cognition Ser.). 320p. 1999. pap. 34.50 (*0-8058-2589-4*) L Erlbaum Assocs.

Perspectives on Behaviour: A Practical Guide to Effective Interventions for Teachers (Resource Materials for Teachers) Harry Ayers et al. 64p. 1995. pap. 17.95 (*1-85346-364-7*, Pub. by David Fulton) Taylor & Francis.

Perspectives on Bereavement. Irwin Gerber. 1979. 18.95 (*0-405-12481-3*) Ayer.

Perspectives on Bereavement. Ed. by Irwin Gerber et al. (Thanatology Ser.). 1978. 14.95 (*0-8422-7304-2*) Irvington.

Perspectives on Bias in Mental Testing. Ed. by Cecil R. Reynolds & Robert T. Brown. (Perspectives on Individual Differences Ser.). 594p. 1984. 85.00 (*0-306-41529-1*, Plenum Trade) Perseus Pubng.

Perspectives on Bilingualism & Bilingual Education. Ed. by James E. Alatis & John J. Staczek. LC 85-5457. 462p. (Orig.). reprint ed. pap. 143.30 (*0-7837-7083-9*, 204689500004) Bks Demand.

***Perspectives on Biodiversity: Valuing Its Role in an Everchanging World.** National Research Council Staff. 168p. 1999. pap. 37.00 (*0-309-06581-X*) Natl Acad Pr.

Perspectives on Bioinorganic Chemistry, Vol. 1. Ed. by Robert W. Hay et al. 284p. 1991. 109.50 (*1-55938-184-1*) Jai Pr.

Perspectives on Bioinorganic Chemistry, Vol. 2. Ed. by Robert W. Hay et al. 292p. 1993. 109.50 (*1-55938-272-4*) Jai Pr.

Perspectives on Bioinorganic Chemistry, Vol. 3. Ed. by Robert W. Hay et al. 1996. 109.50 (*1-55938-642-8*) Jai Pr.

Perspectives on Bioinorganic Chemistry, Vol. 4. Ed. by Robert W. Hay et al. Date not set. 109.50 (*0-7623-0352-2*) Jai Pr.

***Perspectives on Biologically Based Cancer Risk Assessment.** Vincent J. Cogliano et al. LC 99-30081. (NATO - Challenges of Modern Society Ser.). 319p. 1999. write for info. (*0-306-46108-0*, Kluwer Plenum) Kluwer Academic.

Perspectives on Black English. Ed. by J. L. Dillard. (Contributions to the Sociology of Language Ser.: No. 4). 391p. 1975. text 46.15 (*90-279-7811-5*) Mouton.

Perspectives on Blacks in Cinema: An Introductory Text on Select Topics. Y. G. Lulat & James G. Pappas. LC 93-11628. 708p. 1993. lib. bdg. 55.50 (*0-944265-11-1*, Cerebrum Bks) Librosmondiale.

Perspectives on Blacks in Cinema: An Introductory Text on Select Topics. Y. G. Lulat & James G. Pappas. LC 93-11628. 512p. 1997. pap. text 45.50 (*0-944265-12-X*, Cerebrum Bks) Librosmondiale.

***Perspectives on British Rural Policy & Planning Policy, 1994-97.** Andrew W. Gilg. (Perspectives on Rural Policy & Planning Ser.). 158p. 1999. text 61.95 (*1-85972-641-0*, Pub. by Ashgate Pub) Ashgate Pub Co.

Perspectives on Buddhist Ethics. Ed. by Mahesh Tiwary. ix, 172p. 1989. 15.00 (*0-685-62633-4*, Pub. by Eastern Bk Linkers) Nataraj Bks.

Perspectives on Budgeting. 2nd ed. Ed. by Allen Schick. LC HJ2052.P47. (PAR Classics Ser.: No. 2). (Illus.). 334p. reprint ed. pap. 103.60 (*0-7837-6152-X*, 204587400009) Bks Demand.

Perspectives on Business Modelling: Understanding & Changing Organizations. Ed. by A. G. Nilsson et al. LC 99-20541. (Illus.). 360p. 1999. 85.00 (*3-540-65249-3*) Spr-Verlag.

Perspectives on Canada's Population: An Introduction to Concepts & Issues. Ed. by Frank Trovato & Carl F. Grindstaff. (Illus.). 440p. (C). 1994. pap. text (*0-19-540960-4*) OUP.

Perspectives on Canadian Marine Fisheries Management. Ed. by L. S. Parsons & W. H. Lear. 486p. 1994. 68.95 (*0-660-15003-4*) NRC Res Pr.

Perspectives on Capitalism: Marx, Keynes, Schumpeter & Weber. Ed. by Krishna Bharadwaj & Sudipta Kaviraj. 260p. (C). 1990. text 26.00 (*0-8039-9619-5*) Sage.

Perspectives on Case Management Practice. Ed. by Carol D. Austin & Robert W. McClelland. LC 96-619. 278p. 1996. reprint ed. pap. 25.95 (*1-896918-12-3*, Manticore Europe) Manticore Pubs.

Perspectives on Cellular Regulation: From Bacteria to Cancer. Ed. by Judith Campisi et al. LC 90-26568. (MBL Lectures in Biology: Vol. 11). 370p. 1991. 195.00 (*0-471-56090-1*, Wiley-Interscience) Wiley.

Perspectives on Childhood: A Resource Book for Teachers. Bob Hill et al. LC 98-191572. (Education Ser.). (Illus.). 128p. 1996. pap. 34.95 (*0-304-33424-3*) Continuum.

Perspectives on Children's Testimony. Ed. by S. J. Ceci et al. (Illus.). 270p. 1989. 90.95 (*0-387-96864-4*) Spr-Verlag.

Perspectives on Chinese Cinema. enl. rev. ed. Ed. by Chris Berry. (Illus.). 244p. 1991. reprint ed. pap. 21.95 (*0-85170-272-4*, Pub. by British Film Inst) Ind U Pr.

Perspectives on Christianity in Korea & Japan: The Gospel & Culture in East Asia. Ed. by Mark R. Mullins & Richard F. Young. LC 95-35989. 1995. write for info. (*0-7734-8868-5*) E Mellen.

Perspectives on Christology: Essays in Honor of Paul K. Jewett. Ed. by Marguerite Shuster & Richard Muller. 208p. 1991. pap. 16.99 (*0-310-39731-6*) Zondervan.

Perspectives on Close Relationships. Ed. by Ann L. Weber & John H. Harvey. LC 93-5205. 1993. pap. text 31.00 (*0-205-13964-7*) Allyn.

Perspectives on Cognitive Change in Adulthood & Aging. Fredda Blanchard-Fields & Thomas Hess. LC 95-81973. 528p. (C). 1996. pap. 45.31 (*0-07-028450-4*) McGraw.

Perspectives on Cognitive Dissonance. R. A. Wicklund & J. W. Brehm. 349p. 1976. 79.95 (*0-89859-419-7*) L Erlbaum Assocs.

***Perspectives on Cognitive, Learning & Thinking Styles.** Ed. by Robert J. Sternberg & L. Zhang. (A Volume in the Educational Psychology Series). 320p. 2000. write for info. (*0-8058-3430-3*) L Erlbaum Assocs.

***Perspectives on Cognitive, Learning & Thinking Styles.** Ed. by Robert J. Sternberg & Li-fang Zhang. (A Volume in the Educational Psychology Series). 320p. 2000. pap. write for info. (*0-8058-3431-1*) L Erlbaum Assocs.

Perspectives on Cognitive Science. Ed. by Donald A. Norman. LC 80-21343. 315p. reprint ed. pap. 97.70 (*0-7837-0201-9*, 204049700017) Bks Demand.

Perspectives on College Student Suicide. Ralph L. Rickgarn. LC 94-41. (Death, Value & Meaning Ser.). 244p. 1994. pap. 23.07 (*0-89503-154-X*); text 32.95 (*0-89503-153-1*) Baywood Pub.

Perspectives on Communities: A Community Economic Development Roundtable. Ed. by Gertrude A. MacIntyre. 160p. 1997. pap. 19.95 (*0-920336-57-4*, Pub. by U Coll Cape Breton) Genl Dist Srvs.

P

An Asterisk (*) at the beginning of an entry indicates that the title is appearing for the first time.

Perspectives on Community Health Education: A Series of Case Studies. Ed. by Raymond W. Carlaw. LC 80-54741. 224p. (C). 1982. pap. text 9.95 (*0-89914-007-6*) Third Party Pub.

Perspectives on Company Law. Fiona M. Patfield & University of London Staff. LC 95-37403. 1995. 108.00 (*90-411-0852-1*) Kluwer Law Intl.

Perspectives on Company Law, Vol. 2. Ed. by Fiona M. Parfield. 352p. 1997. 140.00 (*90-411-0678-2*) Kluwer Academic.

Perspectives on Conceptual Change: Multiple Ways to Understand Knowing & Learning in a Complex World. Ed. by Barbara Guzzetti & Cyndie Hynd. LC 98-9583. 300p. 1998. write for info. (*0-8058-2321-2*); pap. write for info. (*0-8058-2322-0*) L Erlbaum Assocs.

Perspectives on Conflict of Laws: Choice of Law. James A. Martin. 1980. 15.00 (*0-316-54853-7*, Aspen Law & Bus) Aspen Pub.

Perspectives on Conservation: Essays on America's Natural Resources. John Kenneth Galbraith & Luther G. Griffith. Ed. by Henry Jarrett. LC 58-59888. 272p. reprint ed. pap. 84.40 (*0-7837-3122-1*, 202380100034) Bks Demand.

Perspectives on Contemporary Issues: Reading Across the Disciplines. Katherine A. Ackley. LC 96-76367. 128p. (C). 1996. pap. text 33.00 (*0-15-502480-9*, Pub. by Harcourt Coll Pubs); pap. text, teacher ed. 28.00 (*0-15-502487-6*) Harcourt Coll Pubs.

Perspectives on Contemporary New Testament Questions: Essays in Honor of T. C. Smith. Ed. by Edgar V. McKnight. LC 92-41327. 136p. 1992. text 69.95 (*0-7734-2852-6*) E Mellen.

Perspectives on Contemporary Spanish American Theatre. Ed. by Frank Dauster. LC 55-58217. (Bucknell Review Ser.: Vol. XL, No. 2). 160p. 1997. 24.00 (*0-8387-5345-0*) Bucknell U Pr.

Perspectives on Contemporary Statistics. Ed. by David Moore & David Hoaglin. LC 91-62170. (MAA Notes Ser.: Vol. 21). 192p. 1991. pap. text 18.00 (*0-88385-075-3*, NTE-21) Math Assn.

Perspectives on Contemporary Theatre. Oscar G. Brockett. LC 75-154268. 166p. reprint ed. pap. 51.50 (*0-608-09818-3*, 206998600007) Bks Demand.

Perspectives on Contemporary Youth. 268p. 20.00 (*92-808-0643-2*, E.88.III.A.2) UN.

Perspectives on Contract Law. Randy E. Barnett. LC 95-76099. (Reader Ser.). 416p. 1995. pap. 18.95 (*0-316-08129-9*, 81299) Aspen Law.

Perspectives on Contract Law. Randy E. Barnett. 416p. 1995. pap. text 25.95 (*0-7355-1277-9*) Panel Pubs.

Perspectives on Cormac McCarthy. 2nd rev. ed. Ed. by Edwin T. Arnold & Dianne C. Luce. LC 98-36319. 224p. 1998. pap. 18.00 (*1-57806-105-9*); text 40.00 (*1-57806-104-0*) U Pr of Miss.

Perspectives on Corporate Takeovers. Ed. by Thomas J. Kopp. LC 89-34286. (Illus.). 170p. (Orig.). (C). 1989. pap. text 18.00 (*0-8191-7516-1*); lib. bdg. 44.00 (*0-8191-7515-3*) U Pr of Amer.

Perspectives on Counselng Adults. Alan Schlossberg et al. (Counseling). 1978. pap. text 14.50 (*0-8185-0261-4*) Brooks-Cole.

Perspectives on Creativity Research: The Biographical Method. John E. Gedo & Mary M. Gedo. Ed. by Mark A. Runco. (Creativity Research Ser.). 224p. (C). 1992. pap. 39.50 (*0-89391-944-6*); text 73.25 (*0-89391-760-5*) Ablx Pub.

Perspectives on Crime. Hope. 166.95 (*0-7546-2035-2*) Ashgate Pub Co.

Perspectives on Crime & Deviance. 3rd ed. Allen E. Liska & Steven F. Messner. LC 98-6254. 260p. 1998. 38.60 (*0-13-235771-2*) P-H.

***Perspectives on Crime & Justice: 1997-1998 Lecture Series.** George L. Kelling. 125p. (C). 2000. reprint ed. pap. text 25.00 (*0-7881-8202-1*) DIANE Pub.

Perspectives on Crime & Justice, 1996-1997. James Q. Wilson et al. (Lecture Ser.). (Illus.). 132p. (C). 1998. pap. text 25.00 (*0-7881-7257-3*) DIANE Pub.

Perspectives on Cuban Economic Reforms. Jorge Perez-Lopez & Matias F. Travieso-Diaz. LC 97-49289. (Special Studies: Vol. 30). (Illus.). 190p. (Orig.). (C). 1998. pap. 35.00 (*0-87918-087-0*) ASU Lat Am St.

Perspectives on Current Social Problems. Gregg L. Carter. LC 96-29116. 368p. 1996. pap. text 35.00 (*0-205-19836-8*) Allyn.

Perspectives on Death & Dying. Gene B. Fulton & Eileen K. Metress. (Health Science Ser.). 136p. Date not set. pap., teacher ed. 10.00 (*0-86720-911-9*) Jones & Bartlett.

Perspectives on Death & Dying. Gere B. Fulton & Eileen K. Metress. LC 94-33903. 1995. 50.00 (*0-86720-926-7*) Jones & Bartlett.

Perspectives on Death & Dying: Cross-Cultural & Multi-Disciplinary Views. Ed. by Arthur A. Berger et al. LC 88-63424. 270p. 1989. pap. text 22.95 (*0-914783-27-0*) Charles.

Perspectives on Development: The Euro-Mediterranean Partnership. George Joffe. LC 98-42274. 10p. 1999. 49.50 (*0-7146-4939-2*); pap. 22.50 (*0-7146-4499-4*) F Cass Pubs.

Perspectives on Development & Population Growth in the Third World. O. G. Simmons. LC 88-19866. (Illus.). 294p. (C). 1988. 54.00 (*0-306-42941-1*, Plenum Trade) Perseus Pubng.

Perspectives on Development Communication. Ed. by Sadanandan K. Nair & Shirley A. White. LC 93-25691. 256p. 1994. text 36.00 (*0-8039-9132-0*); pap. text 16.50 (*0-8039-9133-9*) Sage.

Perspectives on Dialogue: Making Talk Developmental for Individuals & Organizations. Nancy M. Dixon. LC 95-50957. 46p. 1996. pap. 20.00 (*1-882197-16-X*) Ctr Creat Leader.

Perspectives on Direct Practice Evaluation. Judy Kopp. Ed. by Naomi Gottlieb et al. (Center for Social Welfare Research Monograph: No. 5). 170p. (Orig.). 1987. pap. 16.00 (*0-935035-02-8*) U WA Ctr Pol Rsch.

Perspectives on Disability: Text & Readings on Disability. 2nd ed. Ed. by Mark Nagler. 460p. (C). 1993. text 45.00 (*0-9627640-3-5*) Hlth Mrkts Res.

Perspectives on Drug Use in the United States. Ed. by Bernard Segal. LC 86-7615. (Drugs & Society Ser.: Vol. 1, No. 1). 126p. (C). 1986. text 3.95 (*0-86656-586-8*) Haworth Pr.

Perspectives on Early Childhood Education: Growing with Young Children Toward the 21st Century. Ed. by David Elkind. 262p. 1991. pap. 19.95 (*0-8106-0351-9*) NEA.

Perspectives on Ecological Integrity. Ed. by Laura Westra & John Lemons. LC 95-35895. (Environmental Science & Technology Library: Vol. 5). 287p. (C). 1995. text 144.00 (*0-7923-3734-4*) Kluwer Academic.

Perspectives on Economic & Foreign Policies. Charles Wolf, Jr. LC 95-8388. 75p. 1995. pap. text 9.00 (*0-8330-1638-5*, MR-522-RC) Rand Corp.

Perspectives on Economic Development: Essays in the Honour of W. Arthur Lewis. Ed. by T. E. Barker et al. LC 81-43790. (Illus.). 324p. (Orig.). (C). 1982. pap. text 27.00 (*0-8191-2382-X*) U Pr of Amer.

Perspectives on Economic Development & Thought. Ed. by Kamta Prasad & R. K. Sinha. 1986. 24.00 (*0-8364-1659-7*, Pub. by Somaiya) S Asia.

Perspectives on Economic Development in Africa. Ed. by Fidelis Ezeala-Harrison & Senyo B. Adjibolosoo. LC 93-5415. 264p. 1994. 65.00 (*0-275-94663-0*, Praeger Pubs) Greenwood.

Perspectives on Economic Integration & Business Strategy in the Asia-Pacific Region. Dzever. LC 96-44474. 247p. 1997. text 69.95 (*0-312-17275-3*) St Martin.

Perspectives on Economic Thought. Giovanni Palmerio. (Luiss Ser.). 222p. 1991. 66.95 (*1-85521-189-0*, Pub. by Dartmth Pub) Ashgate Pub Co.

***Perspectives on Economics.** Jeffrey Madrick. 2000. pap. 12.95 (*0-87078-444-7*) Century Foundation.

Perspectives on Ecosystem Management for the Great Lakes: A Reader. Ed. by Lynton K. Caldwell. LC 87-24497. (SUNY Series in Environmental Public Policy). 365p. (C). 1988. pap. text 21.95 (*0-88706-766-2*) State U NY Pr.

Perspectives on Education. 5th ed. Gary L. Peltier. (C). 1991. pap. 52.00 (*0-536-57907-5*) Pearson Custom.

Perspectives on Education Reform: Arts Education As Catalyst. LC 93-32459. 56p. 1993. pap. 5.00 (*0-89236-296-0*, Pub. by J P Getty Trust) OUP.

Perspectives on Educational Certificate Programs. Ed. by Margaret E. Holt & George J. Lopos. LC 85-644750. (New Directions for Adult & Continuing Education Ser.: No. ACE 52). 1991. pap. 22.00 (*1-55542-766-9*) Jossey-Bass.

***Perspectives on Embodiment: Intersection of Nature & Culture.** Ed. by Honi F. Haber & Gail Weiss. LC 98-22730. 1p. (C). (gr. 13). 1999. 55.00 (*0-415-91585-6*) Routledge.

Perspectives on Embodiment: The Intersections of Nature & Culture. Gail Weiss & Honi F. Haber. LC 98-22730. xvii, 270 p. 1999. pap. 22.99 (*0-415-91586-4*) Routledge.

***Perspectives on Employee Performance: Performance Mgmt.** Williams. 1998. pap. write for info. (*1-86152-244-4*) Thomson Learn.

Perspectives on Environmental Conflict & International Politics. Ed. by Jyrki Kakonen. 224p. 1992. text 59.00 (*1-85567-019-4*, Pub. by P P Pubs) Cassell & Continuum.

Perspectives on Environmental Impact Assessment. Brian D. Clark et al. 1984. text 237.50 (*90-277-1753-2*) Kluwer Academic.

Perspectives on Equality: Constructing a Relational Theory. Christine M. Koggel. LC 97-35810. 336p. 1997. 60.50 (*0-8476-8805-4*); pap. 24.95 (*0-8476-8806-2*) Rowman.

Perspectives on Equity & Justice in Social Work. Intro. by Dorothy M. Pearson. LC 93-70219. (Carl A. Scott Memorial Lectures, 1988-1992). (Illus.). 88p. (Orig.). (C). 1993. pap. text 7.00 (*0-87293-034-3*) Coun Soc Wk Ed.

***Perspectives on Equity Indexing.** Frank J. Fabozzi. (Illus.). 266p. 2000. 75.00 (*1-883249-82-1*) F J Fabozzi.

Perspectives on Ethics. Judith A. Boss. LC 97-41495. xxiv, 504p. 1997. pap. text 38.00 (*1-55934-970-0*, 1970) Mayfield Pub.

Perspectives on Ethnicity. Ed. by Regina E. Holloman & Serghei Arutiunov. (World Anthropology Ser.). xii, 460p. 1978. 61.55 (*90-279-7690-2*) Mouton.

Perspectives on Europe. Ed. by Sami Nair et al. (Contemporary European Affairs Ser.: No. JCEA 4). 272p. 1992. pap. 27.25 (*0-08-041923-2*, Pergamon Pr) Elsevier.

***Perspectives on Evil & Violence: A Special Issue of Personality & Social Psychology Review.** Ed. by Arthur G. Miller. 96p. 1999. pap. 20.00 (*0-8058-9784-4*) L Erlbaum Assocs.

Perspectives on Experience. Boston Consulting Group Staff. LC 72-180882. 109p. reprint ed. pap. 33.80 (*0-7837-0000-8*, AU0003900059) Bks Demand.

Perspectives on Faculty Roles in Nursing Education. Ed. by Lynne B. Welch. LC 91-28999. 160p. 1992. 52.95 (*0-275-93789-5*, C3789, Praeger Pubs) Greenwood.

Perspectives on Family Communication. Lynn H. Turner & Richard L. West. LC 97-37782. xiv, 352p. 1997. pap. text 40.00 (*1-55934-690-6*) Mayfield Pub.

Perspectives on Federal Educational Policy: An Informal Colloquium. 64p. 1976. 3.00 (*0-318-03029-2*) Inst Educ Lead.

Perspectives on Federalism: Papers from the First Berkeley Seminar on Federalism. Berkeley Seminar on Federalism (1st, 1987) Staff. Ed. by Harry N. Scheiber. LC 87-2618. 193p. reprint ed. pap. 59.90 (*0-608-20125-1*, 207139700011) Bks Demand.

Perspectives on Feminist Hermeneutics. Ed. by Gayle G. Koontz & Willard M. Swartley. (Occasional Papers: No. 10). 128p. 1987. pap. text 6.50 (*0-936273-10-0*) Inst Mennonite.

Perspectives on Feminist Thought in European History: From the Middle Ages to the Present. Tjitske Akkerman & Siep Stuurman. LC 97-25914. 256p. (C). 1998. 90.00 (*0-415-15220-8*) Routledge.

Perspectives on Film Noir. R. Barton Palmer. 1996. 55.00 (*0-8161-1601-6*, G K Hall & Co) Mac Lib Ref.

Perspectives on Financial Control: Essays in Memory of Kenneth Hilton. Ed. by Mahmoud Ezzamel & David F. Heathfield. LC 92-25127. 1992. mass mkt. 99.95 (*0-412-40980-1*) Chapman & Hall.

Perspectives on Florida's Growth Management Act of 1985. Ed. by John M. DeGrove & Julian C. Jurgensmeyer. 197p. 1986. 15.00 (*0-317-01544-3*) Fla Atlantic.

Perspectives on Florida's Growth Management Act of 1985. Ed. by John M. DeGrove & Julian C. Juergensmeyer. LC KF9909.. (Lincoln Institute of Land Policy Monograph: No. 86-5). 209p. reprint ed. pap. 64.80 (*0-7837-5751-4*, 204541300006) Bks Demand.

***Perspectives on Fluency.** Ed. by Heidi Riggenbach. LC 99-87225. (Illus.). 336p. (C). 2000. text 49.50 (*0-472-11028-4*, 11028); pap. text 29.95 (*0-472-08604-9*, 08604) U of Mich Pr.

***Perspectives on Foreign & Second Language Pedagogy.** Ed. by D. Albrechtsen et al. (Illus.). 304p. 1999. pap. 31.50 (*87-7838-385-4*, Pub. by Odense Univ) Intl Spec Bk.

Perspectives on Foreign Language Policy: Studies in Honor of Theo van Els. Ed. by Theo Bongaerts & Kees De Bot. LC 97-9930. viii, 224p. 1997. lib. bdg. 54.00 (*1-55619-518-4*) J Benjamins Pubng Co.

Perspectives on Forestry Resources Management: Report of an APO Seminar, 17-27 October 1995, Tokyo, Japan. APO Seminar on Forestry Resources Management. LC 98-155144. 275p. 1997. write for info. (*92-833-2198-7*) Asian Prod Organ.

Perspectives on Freedom of Speech: Selected Essays from the Journals of the Speech Communication Association. Ed. by Thomas L. Tedford et al. LC 86-6706. 351p. (Orig.). 1986. pap. text 17.95 (*0-8093-1308-1*) S Ill U Pr.

Perspectives on Freedom of Speech: Selected Essays from the Journals of the Speech Communication Association. Ed. by Thomas L. Tedford et al. LC 86-6706. 351p. (Orig.). 1987. text 36.95 (*0-8093-1307-3*) S Ill U Pr.

Perspectives on Freshman Year: Selected Addresses from the Freshman Year Experience Conferences 1988-89. Alexander W. Astin et al. (Freshman Year Experience Monograph: No. 2). 68p. 1990. pap. 20.00 (*1-889271-01-2*) Nat Res Ctr.

Perspectives on Functional Grammar. 2nd ed. Michael Moortgat. Ed. by Harry Van Der Hulst et al. x, 352p. 1983. reprint ed. pap. 41.45 (*90-70176-27-0*) Mouton.

Perspectives on Fundamental Processes in Intellectual Functioning. Sal Soraci & William J. McIlvane. LC 97-23866. 300p. 1998. 78.50 (*1-56750-358-6*); pap. 39.50 (*1-56750-359-4*) Ablx Pub.

***Perspectives on Garden Histories.** Michel Conan. LC 98-30313. 1999. 35.00 (*0-88402-265-X*); pap. 20.00 (*0-88402-269-2*) Dumbarton Oaks.

Perspectives on Gender: An Anthology. Jane C. Hood. (Sociology Ser.). 2000. pap. 28.95 (*0-534-24714-8*) Wadsworth Pub.

Perspectives on Genes & the Molecular Biology of Cancer. Symposium on Fundamental Cancer Research Staff. Ed. by Donald L. Robberson & Grady F. Saunders. LC 82-18551. (Illus.). 347p. 1983. reprint ed. pap. 107.60 (*0-608-00644-0*, 206123200007) Bks Demand.

***Perspectives on Genetics: Anecdotal, Historical & Critical Commentaries, 1987-1998.** Ed. by James F. Crow & William F. Dove. LC 99-49567. (Illus.). 734p. 2000. pap. 19.95 (*0-299-16604-X*) U of Wis Pr.

Perspectives on German Cinema. Terri Ginsberg & Kirsten Moana Thompson. LC 96-23301. 592p. 1996. 65.00 (*0-8161-1611-3*, G K Hall & Co) Mac Lib Ref.

Perspectives on German Realist Writing: Eight Essays. Ed. by Mark G. Ward. LC 94-12815. 140p. 1994. text 69.95 (*0-7734-9022-1*) E Mellen.

Perspectives on Gerontological Nursing. Elizabeth M. Baines. (Illus.). 400p. 1991. text 65.00 (*0-8039-3722-9*); pap. text 28.95 (*0-8039-4237-0*) Sage.

Perspectives on Gerontological Nursing. Ed. by Elizabeth M. Baines. LC 91-6874. (Illus.). 430p. 1991. reprint ed. pap. 133.30 (*0-608-04297-8*, 206507600012) Bks Demand.

Perspectives on Global Change: The TARGETS Approach. Ed. by Jan Rotmans & Bert De Vries. LC 97-229056. (Illus.). 479p. 1997. text 69.95 (*0-521-62176-3*) Cambridge U Pr.

Perspectives on God: Sociological, Theological & Philosophical. Charles Curtis et al. LC 78-62943. 1978. pap. text 24.00 (*0-8191-0605-4*) U Pr of Amer.

Perspectives on Grammaricalization. Ed. by William Pagliuca. LC 94-14551. (Current Issues in Linguistic Theory Ser.: No. 109). xx, 306p. 1994. lib. bdg. 79.00 (*1-55619-563-X*) J Benjamins Pubng Co.

Perspectives on Gulf Coast Prehistory. Ed. by Dave D. Davis. LC 84-3686. (Ripley P. Bullen Monographs in Anthropology & History: No. 5). (Illus.). 390p. 1984. 49.95 (*0-8130-0756-9*) U Press Fla.

Perspectives on Guru Amardas. Ed. by Fauja Singh. 1985. 8.50 (*0-8364-1518-3*, Pub. by Punjabi U) S Asia.

***Perspectives on Habermas.** Ed. by Lewis E. Hahn. 2000. 64.95 (*0-8126-9426-0*); pap. 29.95 (*0-8126-9427-9*) Open Court.

Perspectives on "Hamlet" Ed. by William G. Holzberger & Peter B. Waldeck. 246p. 1975. 36.50 (*0-8387-1573-7*) Bucknell U Pr.

Perspectives on HCI: Diverse Approaches. Ed. by Petra Ahrweiler & Andrew F. Monk. (Computers & People Ser.). (Illus.). 312p. 1995. text 63.00 (*0-12-504575-1*) Acad Pr.

Perspectives on Health Communication. Barbara C. Thornton & Gary L. Kreps. 237p. (C). 1993. pap. text 18.95 (*0-88133-711-0*) Waveland Pr.

Perspectives on Health Policy: Australia, New Zealand, United States. Ed. by Marshall M. Raffel & Norma K. Raffel. LC 87-2168. (Wiley-Medical Publication). 296p. reprint ed. pap. 91.80 (*0-8357-3477-3*, 203973600013) Bks Demand.

Perspectives on Higgs Physics. Ed. by G. L. Kane. (Advanced Series on Directions in High Energy Physics": Vol. 13). 488p. 1993. pap. 67.00 (*981-02-1241-0*) World Scientific Pub.

Perspectives on Higgs Physics II, 17. LC 98-122584. 500p. 1997. text 60.00 (*981-02-3127-X*); text 37.00 (*981-02-3153-9*) World Scientific Pub.

Perspectives on High Energy Physics Cosmology: Proceedings of the Conference. A. Gonzalez-Arroyo & C. Lopez. 200p. 1994. text 81.00 (*981-02-1574-6*) World Scientific Pub.

Perspectives on Historical Linguistics: Papers From a Conference Held at the Meeting of the Language Theory Division, Modern Language Assn., San Francisco, 27-30 December 1979. Ed. by Winfred P. Lehmann & Yakov Malkiel. (Current Issues in Linguistic Theory Ser.: No. 24). xii, 379p. 1982. 78.00 (*90-272-3516-3*) J Benjamins Pubng Co.

Perspectives on History & Culture: Essays in Honour of Professor D. P. Singhal (1925-1986) Ed. by Arvind Sharma. (Sri Garib Dass Oriental Ser.: No. 141). (C). 1992. text 26.00 (*81-7030-318-4*) S Asia.

Perspectives on History Series, 25 vols., Pt. I. Ed. by JoAnne B. Weisman et al. (Illus.). (YA). (gr. 5 up). 1995. boxed set 150.00 (*1-878668-54-4*) Disc Enter Ltd.

Perspectives on History Series, 25 vols., Pt. II. Incl. Alamo: Flash Point Between Texas & Mexico. Ed. by Mary D. Wade. LC 96-86709. (Illus.). 64p. 1996. pap. 6.95 (*1-878668-95-1*); Echoes of the Civil War: The Blue. Ed. by Stephen M. Forman. LC 96-86661. (Illus.). 64p. (J). (gr. 5-12). 1997. pap. 6.95 (*1-878668-83-8*); Echoes of the Civil War: The Gray. Ed. by Stephen M. Forman. LC 96-86667. (Illus.). 64p. (J). (gr. 5-12). Date not set. 6.95 (*1-878668-84-6*); Frederick Douglass: A Play Incorporating the Words of Douglass. Carolee Brockman. (Illus.). 22p. (Orig.). (J). (gr. 5-8). 1996. pap. 10.00 (*1-878668-78-1*); His Name Was Martin: A Play about Martin Luther King, Jr. Sharon Fennessey. (Illus.). 20p. (J). (gr. 5-8). 1996. pap. 10.00 (*1-878668-69-2*); Orphan Trains: Leaving the Cities Behind. Ed. by Jeanne M. Bracken. LC 96-86719. (Illus.). 64p. (YA). (gr. 8-12). 1997. pap. 6.95 (*1-878668-87-0*); Progressive Movement, 1900-1917. Ed. by A. J. Scopino, Jr. LC 96-86662. (Illus.). 60p. 1996. pap. 6.95 (*1-878668-94-3*); Talkin' Union: The American Labor Movement. Ed. by Juliet H. Mofferd. LC 96-84729. (Illus.). 64p. (YA). (gr. 8-12). 1997. pap. 6.95 (*1-878668-79-X*); Way West: Traveling the Oregon Trail, a Play. Katharine N. Emsden. (Illus.). 13p. (J). (gr. 5-8). 1997. pap. 10.00 (*1-878668-99-4*); World War I: The Great War. Ed. by A. J. Scopino, Jr. LC 96-86739. (Illus.). 64p. (YA). (gr. 8-12). 1998. pap. 6.95 (*1-878668-91-9*); World War II: The European Theatre. Ed. by Phyllis R. Emert. LC 96-86714. (Illus.). 64p. (YA). (gr. 8-12). 1997. pap. 6.95 (*1-878668-76-5*); 1997. Set boxed set 150.00 (*1-878668-97-8*, 1878668978) Disc Enter Ltd.

Perspectives on History Series, Pt. III. 1998. pap. 150.00 (*1-57960-027-1*) Disc Enter Ltd.

Perspectives on Hittite Civilization: Selected Writings of Hans G. Guterbock. Ed. by H. A. Hoffner, Jr. LC 96-67508. (Assyriological Studies: No. 26). (Illus.). xi, 274p. 1997. pap. text 35.00 (*1-885923-04-X*) Orient Inst.

Perspectives on Hong Kong Society. Benjamin K. Leung. LC 96-232403. (Illus.). 210p. 1996. pap. text 28.00 (*0-19-586535-9*) OUP.

***Perspectives on Human Behavior.** 620p. (C). 1999. 55.00 (*0-536-02253-4*) Pearson Custom.

Perspectives on Human Biology. Fox. 1991. pap. 14.06 (*0-697-10998-4*) McGraw.

Perspectives on Human Biology. Stuart I. Fox. 544p. (C). 1991. text. write for info. (*0-697-10785-X*, WCB McGr Hill) McGrw-H Hghr Educ.

Perspectives on Human Communication. Billie J. Wahlstrom. 416p. (C). 1991. text. write for info. (*0-697-10704-3*) Brown & Benchmark.

Perspectives on Human Rights. Ed. by Vijay K. Gupta. LC 96-902426. (C). 1997. 34.00 (*81-259-0139-6*, Pub. by Vikas) S Asia.

Perspectives on Human Sexuality. Anne Bolin & Patricia Whelehan. LC 98-38210. (Illus.). 416p. (C). 1999. text 92.50 (*0-7914-4133-4*) State U NY Pr.

Perspectives on Human Sexuality. Anne Bolin & Patricia Whelehan. LC 98-38210. (Illus.). 503p. (C). 1999. pap. text 34.95 (*0-7914-4134-2*) State U NY Pr.

Perspectives on Human Sexuality: Psychological, Social, & Cultural Research Findings. Ed. by Nathaniel N. Wagner. 517p. 1974. 53.95 (*0-87705-147-X*, Kluwer Acad Hman Sci) Kluwer Academic.

Perspectives on Hydrogen in Metals: Collected Papers on the Effect of Hydrogen on the Properties of Metals & Alloys. Ed. by Michael F. Ashby & J. P. Hirth. 700p. 1986. 339.00 (*0-08-034813-0*) Franklin.

Perspectives on Hysteria. Phillip R. Slavney. 1990. 35.00 (*0-8018-3961-0*) Johns Hopkins.

P

Perspectives on Ideotype of Rice Root System. 200p. 1997. lib. bdg. 34.00 (*981-02-2747-7*) World Scientific Pub.

Perspectives on Imperialism & Decolonization: Essays in Honour of A. F. Madden. Ed. by R. F. Holland et al. LC 84-1886. 222p. 1984. 35.00 (*0-7146-3242-2*, BHA-03242, Pub. by F Cass Pubs) Intl Spec Bk.

Perspectives on Implementation: Arts Education Standards for America's Students. Music Educators National Conference Staff. Ed. by Bruce O. Boston. LC 94-227605. 128p. 1994. pap. 19.50 (*1-56545-042-6*, 1622) MENC.

Perspectives on Improving Education: Project Talent's Young Adults Look Back. Ed. by John C. Flanagan. LC 78-13600. (Praeger Special Studies). 133p. 1978. 47.95 (*0-275-90291-9*, C0291, Praeger Pubs) Greenwood.

***Perspectives on Indian Development: Economy, Polity & Society.** R. V. Rao. 2000. 54.00 (*81-207-2253-1*, Pub. by Sterling Pubs) S Asia.

Perspectives on Indian Drama in English. M. K. Naik & S. Mokashi-Punekar. 1977. text 7.50 (*0-19-560825-9*) OUP.

Perspectives on Indian Fiction in English. Ed. by M. K. Naik. 1985. 20.00 (*0-8364-1412-8*, Pub. by Abhinav) S Asia.

Perspectives on Indian Politics. Roy Rameshray. 489p. 1987. 48.50 (*0-8364-2014-4*, Pub. by Usha) S Asia.

Perspectives on Indian Regionalism. Ed. by G. Palanithurai. (C). 1992. 16.00 (*81-85475-58-X*, Pub. by Kanishka) S Asia.

Perspectives on Indo-European Language, Culture & Religion: Studies in Honor of Edgar C. Polome, Vol. 1. Ed. by Roger Pearson. (Journal of Indo-European Studies: No. 7). (Illus.). 256p. (C). 1991. pap. 36.00 (*0-941694-37-2*) Inst Study Man.

Perspectives on Indo-European Language, Culture & Religion: Studies in Honor of Edgar C. Polome, Vol. 2. K. G. Zysk et al. Ed. by Roger Pearson. (Journal of Indo-European Studies: No. 9). 288p. (C). 1992. lib. bdg. 50.00 (*0-941694-39-9*) Inst Study Man.

Perspectives on Industrial Development in India. Ed. by N. K. Sinha & M. B. Singh. (C). 1993. 30.00 (*81-7033-199-4*, Pub. by Rawat Pubns) S Asia.

Perspectives on Infant Development. (C). 2001. 66.00 (*0-205-28371-3*, Macmillan Coll) P-H.

Perspectives on Infant Mental Health see Handbook of Infant Mental Health

Perspectives on Inflation: Models & Policies. Ed. by David F. Heathfield. LC 78-40186. 248p. reprint ed. pap. 76.90 (*0-608-12173-8*, 202527200043) Bks Demand.

Perspectives on Instructional Time: Research on Teaching Monograph Series. Charles W. Fisher & David C. Berliner. LC 84-15398. (Research on Teaching Monograph). 320p. (C). 1985. text 53.95 (*0-582-28414-7*, 71447) Longman.

Perspectives on Integrated Coastal Zone Management. Ed. by W. Salomons et al. LC 99-23642. (Environmental Science Ser.). (Illus.). 460p. 1999. 189.00 incl. cd-rom (*3-540-65565-4*) Spr-Verlag.

Perspectives on Intellectual Development. Ed. by Marion Perlmutter. (Minnesota Symposia on Child Psychology Ser.: Vol. 19). 280p. (C). 1986. text 59.95 (*0-89859-784-6*) L Erlbaum Assocs.

Perspectives on Interest Rate Risk Management for Money Managers & Traders. Ed. by Frank J. Fabozzi. (Illus.). 280p. 1998. 60.00 (*1-883249-29-5*) F J Fabozzi.

***Perspectives on International Fixed Income Investing.** Fabozzi. 1998. text 60.00 incl. audio (*0-07-067696-8*) McGraw-Hill Prof.

Perspectives on International Fixed Income Investing. Ed. by Frank J. Fabozzi. (Illus.). 296p. 1998. 60.00 (*1-883249-31-7*) F J Fabozzi.

Perspectives on International Law. Ed. by Nandasiri Jasentuliyana. LC 95-43584. 1995. 193.00 (*90-411-0884-X*) Kluwer Law Intl.

Perspectives on Investment Management of Public Pension Funds. Ed. by Frank J. Fabozzi & Robert Paul Molay. (Illus.). 146p. 1999. 65.00 (*1-883249-56-2*) F J Fabozzi.

Perspectives on Irish Drama & Theatre. Ed. by Jacqueline Genet & Richard A. Cave. (Irish Literary Studies: No. 38). 180p. (C). 1990. text 69.00 (*0-389-20914-7*) B&N Imports.

Perspectives on Irish Nationalism. Ed. by Thomas E. Hachey & Lawrence J. McCaffrey. LC 88-20818. 168p. 1989. 29.95 (*0-8131-1665-1*); pap. 15.00 (*0-8131-0188-3*) U Pr of Ky.

Perspectives on Japan: Towards the Twentieth-First Century. Sargent. 208p. 1999. text 49.95 (*0-312-21529-0*) St Martin.

Perspectives on Japan: Towards the Twenty-First Century. John Sargent. 208p. 1998. text 42.00 (*1-873410-75-1*, Pub. by Curzon Pr Ltd) UH Pr.

Perspectives on Jewish Thought & Mysticism. Ed. by Alfred L. Ivery et al. 540p. 1998. text 64.00 (*90-5702-194-3*, Harwood Acad Pubs) Gordon & Breach.

Perspectives on Jews & Judaism: Essays in Honor of Wolfe Kelman. Ed. by Arthur A. Chiel. 25.00 (*0-87068-683-6*) Ktav.

Perspectives on John: Method & Interpretation in the Fourth Gospel. Ed. by Robert B. Sloan & Mikeal C. Parsons. LC 93-13404. 368p. 1993. 99.95 (*0-7734-2856-9*) E Mellen.

Perspectives on John: Method & Interpretation in the Fourth Gospel. Ed. by Robert B. Sloan & Mikeal C. Parsons. LC 93-13404. (NABPR Special Studies Ser.: No. 11). 368p. 1993. text 99.95 (*0-7734-2859-3*) E Mellen.

Perspectives on John Huston. Stephen Cooper. LC 93-46640. (Perspectives on Film Ser.). (Illus.). 224p. 1994. 55.00 (*0-8161-1985-6*, G K Hall & Co) Mac Lib Ref.

Perspectives on John Philip Sousa. 1984. lib. bdg. 79.95 (*0-87700-533-8*) Revisionist Pr.

Perspectives on Judgement & Decision Making. Ed. by Wing H. Loke. 324p. 1996. 37.00 (*0-8108-2642-9*) Scarecrow.

Perspectives on Kate Chopin: Proceedings from the Kate Chopin International Conference, Northwestern State University, Natchitoches, Louisiana. 1990. 14.95 (*0-917898-17-6*) NSU Pr LA.

Perspectives on Korea. Ed. by Sang-Oak Lee & Duk-Soo Park. 640p. (C). 1998. text 60.00 (*0-9586526-6-X*) UH Pr.

Perspectives on Language & Text: Essays & Poems in Honor of Francis I. Andersen's Sixtieth Birthday, July 28, 1985. Ed. by Edgar W. Conrad & Edward G. Newing. LC 86-24349. xxviii, 443p. 1987. text 49.50 (*0-931464-26-9*) Eisenbrauns.

Perspectives on Later Life. Peter R. Day. 200p. 1994. pap. 34.95 (*1-871177-44-8*, Pub. by Whiting & Birch) Paul & Co Pubs.

Perspectives on Latinos. Ed. by Luis Ortiz-Franco et al. LC 99-25206. (Changing the Faces of Mathematics Ser.). (Illus.). 168p. 1999. pap. 18.75 (*0-87353-464-6*) NCTM.

Perspectives on Leadership. Burt Nanus et al. 137p. 1995. pap. 35.00 (*0-614-10808-X*) APPA VA.

Perspectives on Leadership: From the Science of Management to Its Spiritual Heart. Gilbert W. Fairholm. LC 97-48615. 192p. 1998. 55.00 (*1-56720-202-0*, Quorum Bks) Greenwood.

***Perspectives on Leadership: From the Science of Management to Its Spiritual Heart.** Gilbert W. Fairholm. 2000. pap. write for info. (*0-275-97105-8*, Praeger Trade) Greenwood.

Perspectives on Learning. 2nd ed. D. C. Phillips & Jonas F. Soltis. (Thinking about Education Ser.). 128p. (Orig.). (C). 1991. pap. text 11.95 (*0-8077-3116-1*) Tchrs Coll.

Perspectives on Learning & Memory. Ed. by L. G. Nilsson & Trevor Archer. (Comparative Cognition & Neuroscience Ser.). 352p. (C). 1985. 69.95 (*0-89859-628-9*) L Erlbaum Assocs.

Perspectives on Learning Disabilities. Robert J. Sternberg. 1998. pap. 24.95 (*0-8133-3176-5*) Westview.

Perspectives on Learning Disabilities: Biological, Cognitive, Contextual. Ed. by Robert J. Sternberg & Louise Spear-Swerling. LC 98-11327. 396p. (C). 1998. text 75.00 (*0-8133-3175-7*, Pub. by Westview) HarpC.

Perspectives on Legal Aid: An International Survey. Ed. by Fredrick H. Zemans. LC 79-883. 363p. 1979. lib. bdg. 49.95 (*0-313-20986-3*, ZLA/, Greenwood Pr) Greenwood.

Perspectives on Life-Threatening Illness for Allied Health Professionals: History, Approaches, Considerations. Ed. by Leslie M. Thompson et al. LC 92-49281. (Loss, Grief & Care Ser.: Vol. 7, Nos. 1 & 2). (Illus.). 220p. 1993. 49.95 (*1-56024-329-5*) Haworth Pr.

Perspectives on Listening. Ed. by Carolyn G. Coakley. LC 92-42454. 306p. 1993. pap. 39.50 (*0-89391-925-X*) Ablx Pub.

Perspectives on Listening. Ed. by Andrew D. Wolvin & Carolyn G. Coakley. LC 92-42454. 306p. 1993. text 73.25 (*0-89391-879-2*) Ablx Pub.

Perspectives on Literacy. Ed. by Eugene R. Kintgen et al. LC 87-23575. 496p. (C). 1988. text 51.95 (*0-8093-1457-6*); pap. text 24.95 (*0-8093-1458-4*) S Ill U Pr.

Perspectives on Living the Orthodox Faith. Anthony M. Coniaris. 1985. pap. 12.95 (*0-937032-36-0*) Light&Life Pub Co MN.

Perspectives on Local Government. Ed. by Robert S. Ross. 192p. (C). 1987. pap. 14.95 (*0-89863-119-X*) Star Pub CA.

Perspectives on Local Government Reorganization. Steve Leach. LC 97-29368. 1997. pap. write for info. (*0-7146-4416-1*, Pub. by F Cass Pubs) Intl Spec Bk.

Perspectives on Local Public Finance & Public Policy, Vol. 3. Ed. by John M. Quigley. 196p. 1987. 73.25 (*0-89232-648-4*) Jai Pr.

Perspectives on Loss: A Sourcebook. Ed. by John H. Harvey. 370p. 1998. pap. 34.95 (*0-87630-910-4*) Brunner-Mazel.

***Perspectives on Loss: A Sourcebook.** Ed. by John H. Harvey. 370p. 1998. 79.95 (*0-87630-909-0*) Brunner-Mazel.

Perspectives on Loss: A Sourcebook. Ed. by John H. Harvey. LC 98-4026. 356p. 1998. 79.95 (*1-56032-641-7*) Hemisp Pub.

Perspectives on Loss: A Sourcebook. Ed. by John H. Harvey. LC 98-4026. 356p. 1998. pap. 39.95 (*1-56032-642-5*, Pub. by Tay Francis Ltd) Intl Pubns Serv.

Perspectives on Maimonides: Philosophical & Historical Studies. Ed. by Joel L. Kraemer. LC 96-20915. (Library of Jewish Civilization). 332p. 1996. pap. 19.95 (*1-874774-26-9*, Pub. by Littman Lib) Intl Spec Bk.

Perspectives on Management Systems Approaches in Education: A Symposium. Ed. by Albert H. Yee. LC 72-12729. 174p. 1973. pap. 24.95 (*0-87778-044-7*) Educ Tech Pubns.

Perspectives on Marital Interaction. Ed. by Patricia Noller & MaryAnn Fitzpatrick. (Monographs in the Social Psychology of Language). 1988. 99.00 (*0-905028-91-0*, Pub. by Multilingual Matters); pap. 44.95 (*0-905028-90-2*, Pub. by Multilingual Matters) Taylor & Francis.

***Perspectives On Marriage.** 2nd ed. Kieran Scott & Michael Warren. 416p. 2000. pap. text 32.95 (*0-19-513439-7*) OUP.

Perspectives on Marriage: A Reader. Ed. by Michael Warr & Kieran Scott. LC 92-14595. 456p. 1993. pap. text 31.95 (*0-19-507804-7*) OUP.

Perspectives on Marriage: Catholic Wedding Ceremony Edition. Gregory F. Pierce. 88p. 1992. student ed. 4.95 (*0-915388-37-5*, 153) ACTA Pubns.

Perspectives on Marriage: Ecumenical Edition. 72p. 1992. student ed. 4.75 (*0-915388-34-0*, 154) ACTA Pubns.

Perspectives on Marriage: Leader's Guide. William Urbane. 36p. 1992. pap. 7.95 (*0-915388-39-1*, 155) ACTA Pubns.

Perspectives on Mass Communication History. David Sloan. (Communication Textbook Ser.). 392p. 1991. pap. 45.00 (*0-8058-0863-9*); text 89.95 (*0-8058-0835-3*) L Erlbaum Assocs.

Perspectives on Mathematics Education. Ed. by Christiansen et al. 1985. pap. text 73.50 (*90-277-2118-1*) Kluwer Academic.

Perspectives on Max Frisch. Ed. by Gerhard F. Probst & Jay F. Bodine. LC 80-5181. 232p. 1982. 27.50 (*0-8131-1438-1*) U Pr of Ky.

Perspectives on Media Effects. Ed. by Jennings Bryant & Dolf Zillmann. 374p. 1989. pap. text 36.00 (*0-8058-0721-7*) L Erlbaum Assocs.

Perspectives on Medical Research, Vol. 1 & 2. Ed. by Stephen R. Kaufman & Betsy Todd. 1990. pap. 10.00 (*0-9623858-5-9*) Med Res Modern.

Perspectives on Medical Research, Vol. 3. Ed. by Stephen R. Kaufman. (Illus.). 91p. 1992. pap. 10.00 (*0-9623858-7-5*); text 15.00 (*0-9623858-6-7*) Med Res Modern.

Perspectives on Medical Research, Vol. 4, 1993. Ed. by Stephen R. Kaufman & Kathryn Hahner. 80p. 1993. pap. 10.00 (*0-9623858-9-1*); text 15.00 (*0-9623858-8-3*) Med Res Modern.

Perspectives on Medical Research, Vol.2. Ed. by Stephen R. Kaufman & Betsy Todd. 1990. 15.00 (*0-9623858-4-0*) Med Res Modern.

Perspectives on Medieval History. Harbans Mukhia. (C). 1993. 32.00 (*0-7069-6387-3*, Pub. by Vikas) S Asia.

Perspectives on Memory Research. Ed. by L. G. Nilsson. 416p. 1979. text 79.95 (*0-89859-483-9*) L Erlbaum Assocs.

Perspectives on Mental Handicap in South Africa. Susan Lea. Ed. by Don Foster. 1990. pap. text 45.00 (*0-409-10919-3*) Buttrwrth-Heinemann.

Perspectives on Methodology in Consumer Research. Ed. by D. Brinberg & R. Lutz. (Illus.). 325p. 1986. 88.95 (*0-387-96238-7*) Spr-Verlag.

Perspectives on Mexican-American Life. LC 73-14214. (Mexican American Ser.). 1976. reprint ed. 20.95 (*0-405-05688-5*) Ayer.

Perspectives on Mind. Ed. by Herbert A. Otto & James Tuedio. 430p. (C). 1987. text 176.50 (*90-277-2640-X*, D Reidel) Kluwer Academic.

Perspectives on Minority Influence. Ed. by Serge Moscovici et al. (European Studies in Social Psychology). 272p. 1985. text 64.95 (*0-521-24695-4*) Cambridge U Pr.

Perspectives on Minority Women in Higher Education. Ed. by Lynne B. Welch. LC 91-28833. 176p. 1992. 49.95 (*0-275-93742-9*, C3742, Praeger Pubs) Greenwood.

***Perspectives on Modern America: Making Sense of the Twentieth Century.** Ed. by Harvard Sitkoff. 352p. 2000. 30.00 (*0-19-512864-8*) OUP.

***Perspectives on Modern America: Making Sense of The Twentieth Century.** Ed. by Harvard Sitkoff. 352p. (C). 2000. pap. text 22.95 (*0-19-512865-6*) OUP.

Perspectives on Modern Art. Ed. by Linnea H. Wren. 320p. (Orig.). 2000. 35.00 (*0-06-438944-8*) HarperTrade.

Perspectives on Modern Art. Ed. by Linnea H. Wren. (Illus.). 320p. (Orig.). 2000. pap. 20.00 (*0-06-430227-X*) HarperTrade.

Perspectives on Modern China: Four Anniversaries. Ed. by Joyce K. Kallgren et al. LC 91-13410. (Studies on Modern China). 448p. (C). (gr. 13). 1991. text 96.95 (*0-87332-814-0*, East Gate Bk) M E Sharpe.

Perspectives on Modern China: Four Anniversaries. Ed. by Kenneth Lieberthal et al. LC 91-13410. (Studies on Modern China). 448p. (C). (gr. 13). 1991. pap. text 32.95 (*0-87332-890-6*, East Gate Bk) M E Sharpe.

Perspectives on Modern German Economic History & Policy. Knut Borchardt. 295p. (C). 1991. text 69.95 (*0-521-36310-1*); pap. text 24.95 (*0-521-36858-8*) Cambridge U Pr.

Perspectives on Moral Responsibility. Ed. by John M. Fischer & Mark Ravizza. LC 93-25712. 365p. 1993. 45.00 (*0-8014-2943-9*); pap. text 17.95 (*0-8014-8159-7*) Cornell U Pr.

***Perspectives on Multiculturalism & Gender Equity.** Walter G. Secada. LC 00-33865. (Changing the Faces of Mathematics Ser.). 2000. write for info. (*0-87353-478-6*) NCTM.

Perspectives on Multilateral Assistance: A Review by the Nordic U. N. Project. Ed. by Ulf Rundin. 317p. (Orig.). 1990. pap. 79.00 (*91-22-01405-5*) Coronet Bks.

Perspectives on Multiple Personality Disorder. Ross & Lowenstein. (Psychoanalytic Inquiry Book Ser.; Vol. 12, No. 1). 1992. 20.00 (*0-88163-948-6*) Analytic Pr.

Perspectives on Music. Ed. by Dave Oliphant & Thomas Zigal. (Illus.). 235p. 1984. pap. 16.95 (*0-87959-102-1*) U of Tex H Ransom Ctr.

Perspectives on Musical Aesthetics. Ed. by John Rahn. (C). 1995. pap. 18.95 (*0-393-96508-2*) Norton.

Perspectives on Narratology: Papers from the Stockholm Symposium on Narratology. Ed. by Claes Wahlin. 153p. 1996. pap. 35.95 (*3-631-49331-2*) P Lang Pubng.

Perspectives on Narratology: Papers from the Stockholm Symposium on Narratology. Ed. by Claes Wahlin. 153p. 1996. pap. 35.95 (*0-8204-2936-8*) P Lang Pubng.

***Perspectives on National Security in South Asia: In Search of a New Paradigm.** P. R. Chari. 1999. 44.00 (*81-7304-325-6*, Pub. by Manohar) S Asia.

Perspectives on New Economic Policy. Ed. by M. Basheer Ahmed Khan. 1989. 14.00 (*81-202-0235-X*, Pub. by Ajanta) S Asia.

Perspectives on Non-Sexist Early Childhood Education. Ed. by Barbara Sprung. LC 78-6251. 194p. 1978. pap. 60.20 (*0-608-05180-2*, 206565700006) Bks Demand.

Perspectives on Non-Sexist Early Childhood Education. Ed. by Barbara Sprung. LC 78-6251. 224p. 1978. pap. 16.95 (*0-8077-2547-1*) Tchrs Coll.

Perspectives on Non-Violence. Ed. by V. K. Kool. (Illus.). xiv, 283p. 1989. 78.95 (*0-387-97096-7*) Spr-Verlag.

Perspectives on Nonformal Adult Education. Lyra Srinivasan. (Illus.). 122p. 1977. pap. 7.50 (*0-914262-04-1*) World Educ.

Perspectives on Nonpoint Source Pollution. Contrib. by U. S. EPA Staff. (Illus.). 514p. 1985. reprint ed. pap. 29.95 (*1-880686-16-3*) Terrene Inst.

***Perspectives on Nonprofit Board Diversity.** Judith Miller et al. 60p. 1999. pap. text 19.99 (*0-925299-91-X*) Natl Ctr Nonprofit.

Perspectives on Nuclear Accident in Western Europe. Ed. by International Bar Association Staff & Peter Cameron. (C). 1988. lib. bdg. 122.00 (*1-85333-110-4*, Pub. by Graham & Trotman) Kluwer Academic.

Perspectives on Nuclear War & Peace Education, 60. Ed. by Robert Ehrlich. LC 86-27132. (Contributions in Military Studies Ser.: No. 60). 249p. 1987. 59.95 (*0-313-25504-0*, ENW/, Greenwood Pr) Greenwood.

Perspectives on Nursing Leadership: Issues & Research. Ed. by Shake Ketefian. LC 80-27464. 109p. reprint ed. pap. 33.80 (*0-8357-3457-9*, 203971900013) Bks Demand.

Perspectives on Nursing Theory. 3rd ed. Leslie H. Nicoll. LC 96-33075. 736p. 1996. pap. text 36.95 (*0-397-55312-9*) Lppncott W & W.

Perspectives on Nyaya Logic & Epistemology. S. Saha. (C). 1987. 31.00 (*81-7074-006-1*, Pub. by KP Bagchi) S Asia.

Perspectives on Official English: The Campaign for English As the Official Language of the U. S. A. Ed. by Karen L. Adams & Daniel T. Brink. (Contributions to the Sociology of Language Ser.: No. 57). x, 366p. (C). 1990. pap. 25.00 (*3-11-012792-X*); lib. bdg. 113.85 (*3-11-012325-8*) Mouton.

Perspectives on Old Testament Literature. Woodrow Ohlsen. LC 77-91012. (Illus.). 450p. (C). 1978. pap. text 34.00 (*0-15-570484-2*, Pub. by Harcourt Coll Pubs) Harcourt.

Perspectives on Organization Theory. Anna Grandori. LC 87-11359. 240p. 1987. 32.00 (*0-88730-214-9*, HarpBusn) HarpInfo.

Perspectives on Organizational Communication. 3rd ed. Tom D. Daniels & Barry K. Spiker. 360p. (C). 1993. text. write for info. (*0-697-20134-1*) Brown & Benchmark.

Perspectives on Organizational Communication. 4th ed. Tom D. Daniels & Barry K. Spiker. LC 96-83543. 384p. (C). 1996. text. write for info. (*0-697-28896-X*, WCB McGr Hill) McGrw-H Hghr Educ.

Perspectives on Our Age. Jacques Ellul. Ed. by Willem H. Vanderburg. 128p. 1997. pap. 14.95 (*0-88784-595-9*, Pub. by Hse of Anansi Pr) Genl Dist Srvs.

Perspectives on Our Age: Jacques Ellul Speaks on His Life & Work. Jacques Ellul. Ed. by William H. Vanderburg. Tr. by Joachim Neugroschel. 1982. 12.95 (*0-8164-0485-2*) Harper SF.

Perspectives on Pacifism: Christian, Jewish, & Muslim Views on Nonviolence & International Conflict. Ed. by David R. Smock. LC 94-45230. 1995. pap. text 6.95 (*1-878379-42-9*) US Inst Peace.

Perspectives on Packetized Voice & Data Communications. Ed. by William Lidinsky & David Vlack. LC 90-32479. (Illus.). 304p. 1990. text 69.95 (*0-87942-263-7*, PC02527) Inst Electrical.

Perspectives on Pain: Mapping the Territory. Ed. by Bernadette Carter. (An Arnold Publication). (Illus.). 336p. 1998. pap. text 37.50 (*0-340-69254-5*) OUP.

Perspectives on Particle Physics: Festschrift in Honor of Prof. H. Miyazawa. Ed. by S. Matsuda et al. 424p. (C). 1989. text 99.00 (*9971-5-0589-4*) World Scientific Pub.

Perspectives on Partnership: Secondary Initial Teacher Training. Ed. by Anne Williams. LC 94-12289. 192p. 1994. pap. 29.95 (*0-7507-0293-1*, Falmer Pr) Taylor & Francis.

Perspectives on Patch. Ed. by David N. Thomas & Ian Sinclair. 1983. 25.00 (*0-7855-0836-8*, Pub. by Natl Inst Soc Work) St Mut.

Perspectives on Patch. Ed. by Ian S. Thomas & David N. Thomas. (C). 1983. 60.00 (*0-7855-3747-3*, Pub. by Natl Inst Soc Work) St Mut.

Perspectives on Path. Ian Sinclair & David N. Thomas. (C). 1983. 30.00 (*0-7855-5890-X*, Pub. by Natl Inst Soc Work) St Mut.

Perspectives on Pathophysiology. Lee-Ellen C. Copstead. LC 94-21277. (Illus.). 1258p. 1995. text 65.00 (*0-7216-3846-5*, W B Saunders Co) Harcrt Hlth Sci Grp.

Perspectives on Paul. Ernst Kasemann. LC 79-157540. 183p. reprint ed. pap. 56.80 (*0-608-15448-2*, 202929600060) Bks Demand.

Perspectives on Paul. Ernst Kasemann. 184p. 1996. reprint ed. pap. 18.00 (*1-888961-00-7*) Sigler Pr.

Perspectives on Pedagogical Grammar. Ed. by Terence Odlin. (Applied Linguistics Ser.). (Illus.). 350p. (C). 1994. text 69.95 (*0-521-44530-2*); pap. text 26.95 (*0-521-44990-1*) Cambridge U Pr.

Perspectives on Peirce: Critical Essays on Charles Sanders Peirce. Ed. by Richard J. Bernstein. LC 80-13703. 148p. 1980. reprint ed. lib. bdg. 38.50 (*0-313-22414-5*, BEPP, Greenwood Pr) Greenwood.

Perspectives on Pentecost: New Testament Teaching on the Gifts of the Holy Spirit. Richard B. Gaffin, Jr. 1979. pap. 8.99 (*0-87552-269-6*) P & R Pubng.

Perspectives on Perception: Philosophy, Art & Literature. Mary A. Caws. (Reading Plus Ser.: Vol. 3). XII, 265p. (C). 1989. text 49.00 (*0-8204-0469-1*) P Lang Pubng.

Perspectives on Person-Environment Interaction & Drug-Taking Behavior. Ed. & Intro. by Bernard Segal. LC 87-26268. (Drugs & Society Ser.: Vol. 2, No. 1). 170p. 1988. text 39.95 (*0-86656-716-X*) Haworth Pr.

Perspectives on Personality. Michael F. Scheier & Charles S. Carver. 512p. (C). 1988. pap. text 46.00 (*0-205-11120-3*, H11208) Allyn.

Perspectives on Personality. 4th ed. Charles S. Carver & Michael F. Scheier. LC 99-26281. 602p. (C). 1999. 85.00 (*0-205-29394-8*) Allyn.

***Perspectives on Personality: Website.** 4th ed. 1999. write for info. (*0-205-30940-2*) Allyn.

Perspectives on Philippine Historiography: A Symposium. Ed. by John A. Larkin. LC 78-59565. (Monographs: No. 21). iv, 74p. 1979. pap. 9.50 (*0-938692-09-7*) Yale U SE Asia.

Perspectives on Photon Interactions with Hadrons & Nuclei: Proceedings of a Workshop Held at Gottingen, FRG, on 20 & 21 February 1990. Ed. by M. Schumacher et al. (Lecture Notes in Physics Ser.: Vol. 365). ix, 251p. 1990. 40.95 (*0-387-52981-0*) Spr-Verlag.

Perspectives on Plagiarism & Intellectual Property in a Postmodern World. Ed. by Lise Buranen & Alice M. Roy. LC 99-11407. (Illus.). 304p. (C). 1999. text 71.50 (*0-7914-4079-6*); pap. text 23.95 (*0-7914-4080-X*) State U NY Pr.

Perspectives on Planning & Urban Development in Belgium. Ed. by Ashok K. Dutt & Frank J. Costa. LC 92-22979. (GeoJournal Library: Vol. 22). 244p. (C). 1992. text 127.50 (*0-7923-1885-4*) Kluwer Academic.

Perspectives on Political & Economic Transitions after Communism. Ed. by John Micgiel. LC 97-73639. xiv, 267p. (C). 1997. pap. 19.95 (*0-9654520-1-8*) Col U Inst E Cntrl Eur.

Perspectives on Politics: Classic to Contemporary. James Peterson. LC 95-112363. 304p. (C). 1994. pap. text, per. 25.95 (*0-8403-9962-6*) Kendall-Hunt.

Perspectives on Positive Political Economy. Ed. by James E. Alt & Kenneth A. Shepsle. (Political Economy of Institutions & Decisions Ser.). (Illus.). 278p. (C). 1990. text 69.95 (*0-521-39221-7*); pap. text 21.95 (*0-521-39851-7*) Cambridge U Pr.

Perspectives on Power: Reflections on Human Nature & the Social Order. Noam Chomsky. 272p. write for info. (*1-55164-049-X*); pap. write for info. (*1-55164-048-1*) Black Rose.

Perspectives on Prayer. David Hocking. Ed. by M. B. Steele. 144p. (Orig.). 1991. pap. 8.95 (*0-939497-25-5*) Promise Pub.

Perspectives on Presidential Selection. Ed. by Donald R. Matthews. LC 73-1078. (Brookings Insitution Studies in Presidential Selection). 258p. reprint ed. pap. 80.00 (*0-608-12717-5*, 202539000043) Bks Demand.

Perspectives on Prevention & Treatment of Cancer in the Elderly. Rosemary Yancik. Ed. by Paul Carbone et al. LC 83-8632. (Aging Ser.: No. 24). (Illus.). 360p. reprint ed. pap. 111.60 (*0-608-09644-X*, 205442000001) Bks Demand.

Perspectives on Privatization in Municipal Governments. 16p. 1997. 10.00 (*1-886152-38-1*, No. 3537) Natl League Cities.

Perspectives on Psychologism. Ed. by M. A. Notturno. LC 89-9849. (Brill's Studies in Epistemology, Psychology & Psychiatry). 504p. 1989. text 167.50 (*90-04-09182-3*) Brill Academic Pubs.

***Perspectives on Psychology & Social Development: Proceedings of the VII & VIII Congress of the National Academy of Psychology, India** National Academy of Psychology Staff et al. LC 98-915277. (Advances in Psychological Research in India Ser.). xi, 442 p. 1999. write for info. (*81-7022-768-2*, Pub. by Concept) S Asia.

Perspectives on Psychology & the Media. Ed. by Sam Kirschner & Diana A. Kirschner. LC 97-5538. (Psychology & the Media Ser.). 204p. 1997. 24.95 (*1-55798-433-6*) Am Psychol.

Perspectives on Public Choice: A Handbook. Ed. by Dennis C. Mueller. (Illus.). 685p. (C). 1996. pap. text 31.95 (*0-521-55654-6*) Cambridge U Pr.

Perspectives on Public Choice: A Handbook. Ed. by Dennis C. Mueller. (Illus.). 685p. (C). 1996. text 80.00 (*0-521-55377-6*) Cambridge U Pr.

Perspectives on Public Policy-Making. Ed. by William B. Gwyn & George C. Edwards. LC 75-321771. (Tulane Studies in Political Science: No. 15). 257p. Date not set. reprint ed. pap. 79.70 (*0-608-20652-0*, 207208900003) Bks Demand.

Perspectives on Public Policy Making, Vol. 15. Ed. by William B. Gwyn & George C. Edwards, III. LC 75-321771. xi, 241p. 1975. pap. text 11.00 (*0-930598-14-8*); lib. bdg. 15.00 (*0-930598-15-6*) Tulane Stud Pol.

***Perspectives on Public Relations Research.** Danny Moss et al. LC 99-16205. (Advances in Management & Business Studies). 232p. 1999. 90.00 (*0-415-21767-9*) Routledge.

Perspectives on Punishment: An Interdisciplinary Exploration. Ed. by Richard M. Andrews. LC 92-30407. VIII, 200p. (C). 1997. text 44.95 (*0-8204-1791-2*) P Lang Pubng.

Perspectives on Quantization: Proceedings of the 1996 AMS-Siam Joint Summer Research Conference, July 7-11, 1996, Mt. Holyoke College, Vol. 214. Lewis A. Coburn & Marc A. Rieffel. LC 97-34607. (Contemporary Mathematics Ser.). 195p. 1997. pap. 39.00 (*0-8218-0684-X*) Am Math.

Perspectives on Quantum Reality: Non-Relativistic, Relativistic, & Field-Theoretic. Ed. by Rob Clifton. LC 95-40138. (University of Western Ontario Series in Phylosophy of Science). 256p. (C). 1996. text 118.00 (*0-7923-3812-X*) Kluwer Academic.

Perspectives on Quine. Ed. by Robert B. Barrett & Roger F. Gibson. (Philosophers & Their Critics Ser.: No. 6). 358p. 1993. pap. text 31.95 (*0-631-19178-X*) Blackwell Pubs.

Perspectives on Race & Culture in Japanese Society: The Mass Media & Ethnicity. Peter B. Oblas. LC 94-38356. 236p. 1995. text 89.95 (*0-7734-8986-X*) E Mellen.

Perspectives on Racism & the Human Services Sector: A Case for Change. Ed. by Carl E. James. 272p. 1996. text 50.00 (*0-8020-2954-X*) U of Toronto Pr.

Perspectives on Racism & the Human Services Sector: A Case for Change. Ed. by Carl E. James. 272p. 1996. pap. text 25.00 (*0-8020-7779-X*) U of Toronto Pr.

Perspectives on Radio & Television. 4th ed. F. Leslie Smith et al. LC 99-160204. (Communication Ser.). 625p. 1998. text. write for info. (*0-8058-2092-2*) L Erlbaum Assocs.

Perspectives on Raging Bull. Steven G. Kellman. 224p. 1994. 55.00 (*0-8161-7345-1*, Hall Reference) Macmillan.

Perspectives on Rape & Sexual Assault. Ed. by June Hopkins. 160p. 1984. pap. 36.95 (*0-335-09821-5*) OpUniv Pr.

Perspectives on Reactor Safety. F. E. Haskin. 745p. 1997. per. 62.00 (*0-16-062870-9*) USGPO.

Perspectives on Regional Planning & Development. Roberts Chapman. 56.95 (*1-85972-527-9*) Ashgate Pub Co.

Perspectives on Regional Unemployment in Europe. Paolo Mauro et al. LC 99-26825. (Occasional Paper Ser.). 1999. write for info. (*1-55775-800-X*) Intl Monetary.

Perspectives on Research & Scholarship in Composition. Ed. by Ben W. McClelland & Timothy R. Donovan. LC 85-15401. ix, 266p. 1985. pap. 19.75 (*0-87352-145-5*, J304P); lib. bdg. 37.50 (*0-87352-144-7*, J304C) Modern Lang.

Perspectives on Research in Emotional Stress. K. V. Sudakov et al. (Systems Research in Physiology Ser.: Vol. 3). xiv, 400p. 1989. text 367.00 (*2-88124-699-0*) Gordon & Breach.

Perspectives on Research on Effective Mathematics Teaching. Ed. by Douglas A. Grouws et al. LC 88-138073. (Research Agenda for Mathematics Education Ser.: Vol. 1). (Illus.). 272p. reprint ed. pap. 84.40 (*0-608-09127-8*, 206975900001) Bks Demand.

Perspectives on Research on Effective Mathematics Teaching, Vol. 1. Ed. by Douglas A. Grouws et al. (Research Agenda for Mathematics Education Ser.). 272p. 1988. 59.95 (*0-8058-0326-2*) L Erlbaum Assocs.

***Perspectives on Richard Ford.** Ed. by Huey Guagliardo. LC 99-45448. 200p. 2000. text 45.00 (*1-57806-233-0*) U Pr of Miss.

Perspectives on Romanticism: A Transformational Analysis. David Morse. 324p. 1981. 45.00 (*0-389-20164-2*, N6934) B&N Imports.

Perspectives on Safe & Sound Banking: Past, Present, & Future. George J. Benston et al. 352p. 1986. 44.00 (*0-262-02246-X*) MIT Pr.

Perspectives on Scholarly Misconduct in the Sciences. Ed. by John M. Braxton. LC 98-50039. (Illus.). 272p. 1999. text 50.00 (*0-8142-0815-0*) Ohio St U Pr.

***Perspectives on School Algebra.** Rosamund Sutherland. LC 00-42030. (Mathematics Education Library). 2000. write for info. (*0-7923-6462-7*) Kluwer Academic.

Perspectives on School Learning: Selected Writings of John B. Carroll. Ed. by Lorin W. Anderson & John B. Carroll. 440p. (C). 1985. text 99.95 (*0-89859-343-3*) L Erlbaum Assocs.

Perspectives on Self & Community in George Eliot: Dorothea's Window. Ed. by Patricia Gately et al. LC 97-36271. (Studies in British Literature: Vol. 32). 292p. 1997. text 89.95 (*0-7734-8541-4*) E Mellen.

Perspectives on Self Deception. Ed. by Brian P. McLaughlin & Amelia O. Rorty. (Topics on Philosophy Ser.: Vol. VI). (C). 1988. pap. 22.50 (*0-520-06123-3*, Pub. by U CA Pr) Cal Prin Full Svc.

Perspectives on Sentence Processing. Charles Clifton et al. 488p. 1994. pap. 49.95 (*0-8058-1582-1*); text 89.95 (*0-8058-1581-3*) L Erlbaum Assocs.

Perspectives on Sex, Crime & Society. David Selfe & Vincent Burke. 248p. 1998. pap. 49.00 (*1-85941-317-X*, 15672, Pub. by Cavendish Pubng) Gaunt.

Perspectives on Sexuality: A Literary Collection. Ed. by James L. Malfetti & Elizabeth Eidlitz. LC 78-144052. (Illus.). 611p. 1972. pap. text 9.95 (*0-03-082826-0*) Irvington.

***Perspectives on Shakespeare in Performance.** John L. Styan. LC 98-53181. (Studies in Shakespeare: Vol. 11). 183p. 2000. pap. text 24.95 (*0-8204-4426-X*) P Lang Pubng.

Perspectives on Silence. Ed. by Deborah Tannen & Muriel Saville-Troike. LC 84-18465. 272p. 1985. pap. 39.50 (*0-89391-310-3*); text 73.25 (*0-89391-255-7*) Ablx Pub.

Perspectives on Social Change. 4th ed. Robert H. Lauer. 416p. 1991. text 42.00 (*0-205-12575-1*, H25752) Allyn.

Perspectives on Social Issues. Harriet Bicksler. LC 92-72846. 192p. 1992. pap., student ed. 5.95 (*0-916035-54-9*) Evangel Indiana.

Perspectives on Social Issues. Harriet Bicksler. LC 92-73335. 96p. 1992. pap., teacher ed. 4.95 (*0-916035-55-7*) Evangel Indiana.

Perspectives on Social Issues: Leader's Guide for Youth Group Study. Lynda W. Gephart & Harriet Bicksler. 95p. 1996. pap. 4.95 (*0-916035-68-9*) Evangel Indiana.

Perspectives on Social Problems, Vol. 3. Ed. by James A. Holstein & Gale Miller. 309p. 1992. 78.50 (*1-55938-237-6*) Jai Pr.

Perspectives on Social Problems, Vol. 4. Ed. by James A. Holstein & Gale Miller. 299p. 1992. 78.50 (*1-55938-559-6*) Jai Pr.

Perspectives on Social Problems, Vol. 6. Ed. by James A. Holstein & Gale Miller. 1994. 78.50 (*1-55938-880-3*) Jai Pr.

Perspectives on Social Problems, Vol. 9. Gale Miller & J. Holstein. 1998. 78.50 (*0-7623-0296-8*) Jai Pr.

Perspectives on Social Problems Vol. 10. Ed. by Carol B. Gardner. 309p. 78.50 (*0-7623-0456-1*) Jai Pr.

***Perspectives on Social Problems Vol. 11.** 1999. 78.50 (*0-7623-0481-2*) Jai Pr.

Perspectives on Socially Shared Cognition. Ed. by Lauren B. Resnick et al. 429p. 1991. pap. 19.95 (*1-55798-376-3*) Am Psychol.

Perspectives on Software Documentation: Inquiries & Innovations. Ed. by Thomas T. Barker. (Technical Communications Ser.). 279p. 1991. text 38.95 (*0-89503-069-1*); pap. text 29.22 (*0-89503-068-3*) Baywood Pub.

Perspectives on Solvable Models. U. Grimm & M. Baake. 308p. 1995. text 86.00 (*981-02-2107-X*) World Scientific Pub.

Perspectives on Soviet Law of the 1980s. Ed. by Ferdinand J. Feldbrugge & William B. Simons. 180p. 1982. lib. bdg. 75.50 (*90-247-2561-5*) Kluwer Academic.

Perspectives on Spinoza in Works by Schiller, Buchner, & C. F. Meyer: Five Essays. Rodney Taylor. LC 94-15033. (North American Studies in Nineteenth-Century German Literature: Vol. 18). 170p. 1995. text 46.95 (*0-8204-2502-8*) P Lang Pubng.

***Perspectives on Spiritual Well-Being & Aging.** James A. Thorson. 230p. 2000. 45.95 (*0-398-07037-7*); pap. 31.95 (*0-398-07038-5*) C C Thomas.

Perspectives on Stanley Kubrick. Geduld. Ed. by Mario Falsetto. (Perspectives on Film Ser.). 1996. 55.00 (*0-8161-1991-0*, G K Hall & Co) Mac Lib Ref.

Perspectives on Strategic Change. Luca Zan et al. LC 92-44914. 368p. (C). 1993. lib. bdg. 216.50 (*0-7923-9326-0*) Kluwer Academic.

***Perspectives on Strategic Environmental Assessment.** Maria do Rosario Partidario. LC 99-44581. 287p. 1999. 59.95 (*1-56670-360-3*) Lewis Pubs.

Perspectives on Strategic Management. Ed. by James W. Fredrickson. 220p. 1990. text 34.95 (*0-88730-357-9*, HarpBusn) HarpInfo.

Perspectives on Strategy-Contributions of Porter. F. A. Van Den Bosch & Adrianus P. De Man. LC 97-6829. 1997. lib. bdg. 69.95 (*0-7923-9895-5*) Kluwer Academic.

Perspectives on Strategy from the Boston Consulting Group: The Best Strategic Thinking from the Boston Consulting Group. Carl W. Stern & George Stalk. LC 97-43063. 336p. 1998. 29.95 (*0-471-24833-9*) Wiley.

Perspectives on Structure & Mechanism: Solutions Manual. Carroll. (Chemistry Ser.). 1996. mass mkt., student ed. 16.50 (*0-534-34096-2*) Brooks-Cole.

Perspectives on Structure & Mechanism in Organic Chemistry. Felix A. Carroll. teacher ed. write for info. (*0-534-24949-3*) Brooks-Cole.

Perspectives on Structure & Mechanism in Organic Chemistry. Felix A. Carroll. LC 95-37049. 876p. 1997. mass mkt. 110.95 (*0-534-24948-5*) Wadsworth Pub.

Perspectives on Supersymmetry. Gordon L. Kane. (Advanced Series on Directions in High Energy Physics). 1998. 86.00 (*981-02-3553-4*) World Scientific Pub.

Perspectives on Teacher Induction: A Review of the Literature & Promising Program Models. Ellen Newcombe. 98p. 1990. pap. 16.95 (*1-56602-033-6*) Research Better.

***Perspectives on Teaching Innovations: Teaching to Think Historically.** Ed. by Susan W. Gillespie. LC 99-29358. 116p. (C). 1999. pap. 8.00 (*0-87229-113-8*) Am Hist Assn.

***Perspectives on Teaching Innovations: World & Global History.** Ed. by Susan W. Gillespie. LC 99-29362. 102p. (C). 1999. pap. 8.00 (*0-87229-112-X*) Am Hist Assn.

Perspectives on Technological Development in the Arab World. Mujid S. Kazimi & John Makhoul. (Monographs: No. 8). 96p. (Orig.). pap. text 4.95 (*0-937694-03-7*) Assn Arab-Amer U Grads.

Perspectives on Technology. Nathan Rosenberg. LC 84-23495. 360p. 1985. reprint ed. pap. 111.60 (*0-7837-9948-9*, 206067500006) Bks Demand.

Perspectives on Technology & Culture. Egbert Schuurman. Tr. by John H. Kok. 165p. 1995. pap. 10.95 (*0-932914-33-0*) Dordt Coll Pr.

Perspectives on Terrorism. Ed. by Lawrence Z. Freedman & Yonah Alexander. LC 83-3011. 254p. 1983. lib. bdg. 45.00 (*0-8420-2201-5*) Scholarly Res Inc.

Perspectives on Terrorism. Harold J. Vetter & Gary R. Perlstein. LC 90-44316. 268p. (C). 1990. 32.50 (*0-534-14874-3*) Wadsworth Pub.

Perspectives on the American Past Vol. 2: Readings & Commentary: Since 1865. 2nd ed. Michael Perman. LC 95-76581. 363p. (C). 1996. pap. text 29.16 (*0-669-39721-0*) HM Trade Div.

Perspectives on the American South, Vol. 2. Merle Black & John S. Reed. xii, 272p. 1984. text 90.00 (*0-677-16450-5*) Gordon & Breach.

Perspectives on the American South, Vol. 3. Ed. by James C. Cobb & Charles R. Wilson. xiv, 298p. 1985. text 75.00 (*2-88124-108-5*) Gordon & Breach.

Perspectives on the American South: An Annual Review, Vol. 1. Ed. by M. Black & J. Reed. xii, 410p. 1981. text 125.00 (*0-677-16260-X*) Gordon & Breach.

Perspectives on the American South: An Annual Review of Society, Politics & Culture, Vol. 4. Ed. by James C. Cobb & Charles R. Wilson. xvi, 218p. 1987. text 129.00 (*2-88124-157-3*) Gordon & Breach.

Perspectives on the Battle of Kadesh. Ed. by Hans Goedicke. (Illus.). 216p. (Orig.). 1985. pap. 36.00 (*0-9613805-1-9*) Halgo Inc.

Perspectives on the Classification of Specific Developmental Disorders. Ed. by Jan Rispens et al. LC 97-32490. (Neuropsychology & Cognition Ser.). 286p. 1998. 130.50 (*0-7923-4871-0*) Kluwer Academic.

Perspectives on the Constitution. Ed. by Subhash C. Kashyap. xiv, 302p. 1993. 30.00 (*81-85402-25-6*, Pub. by Shipra Pubns) Nataraj Bks.

Perspectives on the Costs & Benefits of Applied Social Research. Ed. by Clark C. Abt et al. LC 78-67240. 1979. text 30.00 (*0-89011-520-6*) Abt Bks.

Perspectives on the Eastern Margin of the Cretaceous Western Interior Basin. Ed. by G. W. Shurr et al. (Special Papers: No. 287). 1994. pap. 45.00 (*0-8137-2287-X*) Geol Soc.

Perspectives on the Education & Training System of the Future. Warren H. Groff. (Eric Information Analysis Ser.). 34p. 1986. 5.25 (*0-318-22358-9*, IN 312) Ctr Educ Trng Employ.

Perspectives on the Educational Use of Animals. William Mayer et al. (Illus.). 77p. 1980. pap. 3.00 (*0-913098-38-8*) Orion Society.

Perspectives on the Emergence of Scientific Disciplines. Gerard Lemaine. 1977. text 38.50 (*90-279-7743-7*) Mouton.

Perspectives on the Environment: Interdisciplinary Research in Action. Interdisciplinary Research Network on the Environm. (Studies in Green Research). 188p. 1993. 61.95 (*1-85628-606-1*, Pub. by Avebry) Ashgate Pub Co.

Perspectives on the Environment Two. 256p. 1995. 77.95 (*1-85628-982-6*) Ashgate Pub Co.

Perspectives on the Executive Personality. Virgil R. Lang & Samuel E. Krug. LC 78-27205. 1983. pap. text 25.00 (*0-918296-12-9*) Inst Personality & Ability.

Perspectives on the Extraterritorial Application of U. S. Antitrust & Other Laws. LC 79-83502. 241p. 1979. pap. 20.00 (*0-685-29709-8*, 521-0022-01) Amer Bar Assn.

Perspectives on the Family. Ed. by Robert C. Moffat et al. LC 90-6472. (Studies in Social & Political Theory: Vol. 8). 400p. 1990. lib. bdg. 109.95 (*0-88946-685-8*) E Mellen.

Perspectives on the Family in Spain: Past & Present. David S. Reher. (Illus.). 372p. 1997. text 85.00 (*0-19-823314-0*) OUP.

Perspectives on the Freshman Year, Vol. II. Ernest Boyer et al. (Freshman Year Experience Monograph Ser.: No. 8). (Orig.). 1992. pap. 20.00 (*1-889271-06-3*) Nat Res Ctr.

Perspectives on the Godfather, Set, Pts. 1 & 2. Cardullo. 1996. 50.00 (*0-8161-1612-1*, Hall Reference) Macmillan.

Perspectives on the Grateful Dead: Critical Writings, 55. Robert G. Weiner. LC 99-10607. 272p. 1999. 59.95 (*0-313-30569-2*) Greenwood.

Perspectives on the History of British Feminism, 6 vols., Set. Ed. by Marie M. Roberts & Tamae Mizuta. (History of British Feminism Ser.). 2301p. (C). (gr. 13). 1994. text, boxed set 700.00 (*0-415-10352-5*, B4783) Routledge.

Perspectives on the History of Economic Thought: Classicals, Marzians & Neo-Classicals. Ed. by Donald E. Moggridge. (Perspectives on the History of Economic Thought Ser.: Vol. 3). 216p. 1990. text 95.00 (*1-85278-293-5*) E Elgar.

Perspectives on the History of Economic Thought: Contributions to the History of Economics. Ed. by S. Todd Lowry. (Perspectives on the Hostory of Economic Thought Ser.: Vol. 8). 288p. 1992. 95.00 (*1-85278-448-2*) E Elgar.

Perspectives on the History of Economic Thought: Perspectives on Administrative Tradition: from Antiquity to the 20th Century. Ed. by S. Todd Lowry. (Perspectives on the History of Economic Thought Ser.: Vol. 7). 240p. 1992. 95.00 (*1-85278-447-4*) E Elgar.

Perspectives on the History of Economic Thought: Themes in Keynesian Criticism & Supplementary Modern Topics, Vol. VI. Ed. by William J. Barber. (Perspectives on the History of Economic Thought Ser.). 176p. 1991. text 90.00 (*1-85278-364-8*) E Elgar.

Perspectives on the History of Economic Thought Vol. 1: Classical & Neoclassical Economic Thought. Ed. by Donald A. Walker. (Perspectives on the History of Economic Thought Ser.: Vol. 1). 232p. 1989. text 95.00 (*1-85278-131-9*) E Elgar.

Perspectives on the History of Economic Thought Vol. IV: Keynes, Macroeconomics & Method. Ed. by Donald E. Moggridge. (Perspectives on the History of Economic Thought Ser.: Vol. 4). (Illus.). 232p. 1990. text 95.00 (*1-85278-294-3*) E Elgar.

Perspectives on the History of Economic Thought Vol. 5: Themes in Pre-Classical & Marxian Economics. Ed. by William J. Barber. (Perspectives on the History of Economic Thought Ser.). 176p. 1991. text 90.00 (*1-85278-363-X*) E Elgar.

Perspectives on the History of Economic Thought Vol. IX: Themes on Economic Discourse, Method, Money & Trade. Ed. by Robert F. Herbert. (Perspectives on the History of Economic Thought Ser.: Vol. 9). 224p. 1993. 90.00 (*1-85278-660-4*) E Elgar.

Perspectives on the History of Economic Thought Vol. X: Method, Competition, Conflict & Measurement in the Twentieth Century. Ed. by Karen I. Vaughn. (Perspectives on the History of Economic Thought Ser.: Vol. 10). 288p. 1994. 95.00 (*1-85278-807-0*) E Elgar.

Perspectives on the History of Mathematical Logic. Ed. by T. Drucker. (Illus.). 232p. 1991. 86.50 (*0-8176-3444-4*) Birkhauser.

P

An Asterisk (*) at the beginning of an entry indicates that the title is appearing for the first time.

Perspectives on the Holocaust. Randolph L. Braham. (Holocaust Studies). 1983. lib. bdg. 73.50 (*0-89838-124-X*) Kluwer Academic.

Perspectives on the Holocaust see Nazi Holocaust

Perspectives on the Hospitality Industry. Carl Borchegrevink. 480p. 1999. per. 39.95 (*0-7872-4864-9*, 41486401) Kendall-Hunt.

Perspectives on the Human Controller. Ed. by Thomas B. Sheridan & Ton Van Lunteren. LC 96-37983. 336p. 1997. 69.95 (*0-8058-2189-9*); pap. 39.95 (*0-8058-2190-2*) L Erlbaum Assocs.

Perspectives on the Informal Economy: Monographs in Economic Anthropology No. 8. Ed. by M. Estellie Smith. (Monographs in Economic Anthropology). 364p. (C). 1990. pap. text 31.00 (*0-8191-7753-9*); lib. bdg. 50.00 (*0-8191-7752-0*) U Pr of Amer.

Perspectives on the Logic & Metaphysics of F. H. Bradley. Ed. & Intro. by W. J. Mander. (Idealism Ser.: No. 2). 310p. 1996. 72.00 (*1-85506-433-2*); pap. 24.00 (*1-85506-432-4*) Bks Intl VA.

Perspectives on the Memorandum: Policy, Practice & Research in Investigative Interviewing. Ed. by Helen Westcott & Jocelyn Jones. LC 97-19596. 280p. 1997. text 59.95 (*1-85742-356-9*, Pub. by Arena) Ashgate Pub Co.

Perspectives on the Molecular Biology & Immunology of the Pancreatic Beta Cell. Ed. by Douglas Hanahan et al. (Current Communications in Molecular Biology Ser.). (Illus.). 212p. (C). 1989. pap. text 24.00 (*0-87969-326-6*) Cold Spring Harbor.

Perspectives on the New Age. Ed. by James R. Lewis & J. Gordon Melton. LC 91-39093. (SUNY Series in Religious Studies). 369p. (C). 1992. text 59.50 (*0-7914-1213-X*); pap. text 19.95 (*0-7914-1214-8*) State U NY Pr.

Perspectives on the New Economics & Regulation of Telecommunications. Ed. by W. T. Stanbury. 200p. 1996. pap. 29.95 (*0-88645-174-4*, Pub. by Inst Res Pub) Ashgate Pub Co.

Perspectives on the Nurturing of Faith. Ed. by Leland Harder. (Occasional Papers: No. 6). 189p. 1983. pap. 5.00 (*0-936273-05-4*) Inst Mennonite.

Perspectives on the Passion. William R. Grimbol. 1984. 7.25 (*0-89536-665-7*, 1645) CSS OH.

Perspectives on the Past: Theoretical Biases in Mediterranean Hunter-Gatherer Research. Ed. by Geoffrey A. Clark. LC 91-16444. (Illus.). 560p. (C). 1991. text 47.95 (*0-8122-8190-X*) U of Pa Pr.

Perspectives on the Politics of Abortion. Ed. by Ted G. Jelen. LC 95-6937. 216p. 1995. 57.95 (*0-275-95225-8*, Praeger Pubs) Greenwood.

***Perspectives on the Precautionary Principle.** Ed. by Ronnie Harding & Elizabeth Fisher. 320p. 1999. pap. 49.95 (*1-86287-318-6*, Pub. by Federation Pr) Gaunt.

Perspectives on the Profession of Technical Communication. Ed. & Intro. by Madelyn Flammia. (Anthology Ser.). (Illus.). 300p. (C). 1995. per. 50.00 (*0-914548-83-2*, 159-95) Soc Tech Comm.

Perspectives on the Role of a Central Bank: Proceedings of a Conference Held in Beijing, China, January 5-7, 1990. xii, 88p. 1991. pap. 12.50 (*1-55775-206-0*) Intl Monetary.

Perspectives on the Role of Science & Technology in Sustainable Development. (Illus.). 101p. (Orig.). (C). 1995. pap. text 30.00 (*0-7881-2058-1*) DIANE Pub.

Perspectives on the Second Republic in Nigeria. Ed. by C. S. Whitaker, Jr. 50p. (Orig.). 1981. pap. 10.00 (*0-918456-43-6*, Crossroads) African Studies Assn.

Perspectives on the Small Community: Humanistic Views for Practitioners. Emilia E. Martinez-Brawley. LC 90-6439. 261p. 1990. 27.95 (*0-87101-183-2*) Natl Assn Soc Wkrs.

Perspectives on the Social Gospel: Papers from the Inaugural Social Gospel Conference at Colgate Rochester Divinity School. Ed. by Christopher H. Evans. LC 99-26293. 2p. 1999. text 89.95 (*0-7734-8042-0*) E Mellen.

Perspectives on the Sociology of Education. Philip Robinson. 250p. (C). 1981. write for info. (*0-318-55559-X*); pap. 15.95 (*0-7100-0787-6*) Routledge.

Perspectives on the Study of Speech. Ed. by Peter D. Eimas & Joanne L. Miller. LC 80-39499. 464p. 1981. text 89.95 (*0-89859-052-3*) L Erlbaum Assocs.

Perspectives on the T'ang. Ed. by Arthur F. Wright et al. LC 72-91310. 468p. reprint ed. pap. 145.10 (*0-608-11729-3*, 201056600069) Bks Demand.

Perspectives on the Teaching of Geometry for the 21st Century. Ed. by Carmelo Mammana. (ICMI Studies). 364p. 1998. pap. 65.00 (*0-7923-4991-1*) Kluwer Academic.

Perspectives on the Teaching of Geometry for the 21st Century. Carmelo Mammana & Vinicio Villani. LC 98-9444. (ICMI Studies). 353p. 1998. 129.00 (*0-7923-4990-3*) Kluwer Academic.

Perspectives on the Telephone Industry: The Challenge for the Future. Ed. by James Alleman & Richard Emmerson. 360p. 1989. text 45.00 (*0-88730-376-5*, HarpBusn) HarpInfo.

Perspectives on the Third World. Denham. 1999. text 49.95 (*0-312-15881-5*) St Martin.

Perspectives on the Unity & Integration of Knowledge. Ed. by Ronald Glasberg et al. LC 96-32418. (Counterpoints: Vol. 39). X, 286p. (C). 1998. pap. text 32.95 (*0-8204-3487-6*) P Lang Pubng.

Perspectives on the Use of Non-Aversive & Aversive Interventions for Persons with Developmental Disabilities. Ed. by Nirbhay N. Singh. (Illus.). 450p. (C). 1990. text 44.95 (*0-9625233-1-3*) Sycamore Pub.

Perspectives on the Use of Nonaversive & Aversive Interventions for Persons with Developmental Disabilities. Ed. by Alan C. Repp & Nirbhay N. Singh. 533p. 1993. 60.25 (*0-534-21672-2*) Brooks-Cole.

***Perspectives on the Word of God: An Introduction to Christian Ethics.** John M. Frame. 76p. (Orig.). 1999. pap. 7.00 (*1-57910-257-3*) Wipf & Stock.

Perspectives on the World: An Interdisciplinary Reflection. Worldviews Group Staff. Tr. by Gregory Ball. LC 96-182428. 246p. 1996. pap. 24.95 (*90-5487-113-X*, Pub. by VUB Univ Pr) Paul & Co Pubs.

Perspectives on the World Christian Movement: A Reader. 2nd ed. Ed. by Ralph D. Winter & Steven C. Hawthorne. LC 81-69924. 880p. 1992. pap. text 16.95 (*0-87808-228-X*, WCL228-X) William Carey Lib.

Perspectives on the World Christian Movement: A Reader. 3rd rev. ed. Ed. by Ralph D. Winter & Steven C. Hawthorne. LC 98-51494. (Illus.). 782p. 1999. pap. 25.99 (*0-87808-289-1*, 0-87808-289-1) William Carey Lib.

Perspectives on the World Christian Movement: A Study Guide, 1997. rev. ed. Steven C. Hawthorne et al. 352p. 1996. pap. 13.95 (*0-87808-762-1*, WCL762-1B) William Carey Lib.

***Perspectives on the World Christian Movement: Study Guide.** 3rd ed. Steven C. Hawthorne. 98p. 1999. pap. 9.99 (*0-87808-290-5*) William Carey Lib.

Perspectives on Theater Air Campaign Planning. David E. Thaler & David A. Shlapak. LC 94-41873. 50p. 1995. pap. text 15.00 (*0-8330-1612-1*, MR-515-AF) Rand Corp.

Perspectives on Theory for the Practice of Occupational Therapy. 2nd ed. Rosalie J. Miller & Kay F. Walker. Orig. Title: Six Perspectives on Theory for the Practice of Occupational Therapy. 320p. 1993. 51.00 (*0-8342-0358-8*, 20358) Aspen Pub.

Perspectives on Third-World Sovereignty. Ed. by Mark E. Denham & Mark O. Lombardi. LC 95-26835. (International Political Economy Ser.). 240p. 1996. text 59.95 (*0-312-16039-9*) St Martin.

***Perspectives on 3rd World Workshop on Oral Medicine, 1998.** Ed. by H. Dean Millard & David Mason. 392p. 2000. pap. text 65.00 (*0-9645852-1-9*) UMI Schl Dentsy.

Perspectives on Thomas Hobbes. Ed. by G. A. Rogers & Alan Ryan. (Mind Association Occasional Ser.). 218p. 1991. pap. text 27.00 (*0-19-823914-9*) OUP.

Perspectives on Time. Ed. by Jan Faye. LC 96-48827. (Boston Studies in the Philosophy of Science: Vol. 189). 472p. (C). 1996. text 151.00 (*0-7923-4330-1*) Kluwer Academic.

Perspectives on Topicalization: The Case of Japanese WA. Ed. by John Hinds et al. LC 87-29982. (Typological Studies in Language: Vol. 14). xi, 307p. (C). 1987. 94.00 (*0-915027-97-6*); pap. 39.95 (*0-915027-98-4*) J Benjamins Pubng Co.

Perspectives on Tort Law. 2nd ed. Robert L. Rabin. 352p. (C). 1983. 12.00 (*0-316-73003-3*, Aspen Law & Bus) Aspen Pub.

Perspectives on Tourism Policy. Ed. by Peter Johnson & Barry Thomas. (Illus.). 224p. 1993. pap. text 37.95 (*0-7201-2164-7*) Continuum.

Perspectives on Trade & Development. Anne O. Krueger. LC 89-35246. 394p. 1990. 59.95 (*0-226-45490-8*) U Ch Pr.

Perspectives on Tsunami Hazard Reduction: Observations, Theory & Planning. Ed. by Gerald Hebenstreit. LC 97-39881. (Advances in Natural & Technological Hazards Research Ser.: No. 9). 224p. 1997. 96.00 (*0-7923-4811-7*) Kluwer Academic.

Perspectives on U. S. Policy Toward the Law of the Sea: Prelude to the Final Session of the Third U. N. Conference of the Sea, Occasional Paper No. 35. David D. Caron & Charles L. Buderi. 98p. 1985. 5.00 (*0-911189-12-2*) Law Sea Inst.

Perspectives on Understanding & Working with Families. Kevin J. Swick. 130p. 1987. pap. text 7.80 (*0-87563-305-6*) Stipes.

Perspectives on Urban America. Ed. by Melvin I. Urofsky. 1980. 12.50 (*0-8446-5091-9*) Peter Smith.

Perspectives on Urban Infrastructure. Ed. by Royce Hanson. LC 80-63272. 221p. 1984. reprint ed. pap. 68.60 (*0-608-02346-9*, 206298700004) Bks Demand.

Perspectives on Urbanization & Migration, India & U. S. S. R. Ed. by Manzoor Alam & Fatima Alikhan. xxiv, 538p. 1987. 26.50 (*0-8364-2155-8*, Pub. by Allied Pubs) S Asia.

***Perspectives on Violence, 8 vols.** Gustav M. Gedatus. LC 99-57553. 2000. write for info. (*0-7368-0439-0*) Capstone Pr.

Perspectives on Vocational Education: Purposes & Performance. Ed. by Morgan V. Lewis & Frank C. Pratzner. 73p. 1984. 7.95 (*0-318-17788-9*, RD247) Ctr Educ Trng Employ.

Perspectives on War & Peace in Central America. Ed. by Sung Ho Kim & Thomas W. Walker. LC 92-8970. (Monographs in International Studies, Latin America Ser.: No. 19). 155p. (Orig.). (C). 1992. pap. text 17.00 (*0-89680-172-1*) Ohio U Pr.

Perspectives on Water: An Integrated Model-Based Exploration of the Future. Arjen Hoekstra. LC 99-182674. 352p. 1998. pap. 35.00 (*90-5727-018-8*, Pub. by Intl Bks) Paul & Co Pubs.

Perspectives on Water: Uses & Abuses. Ed. by David H. Speidel et al. (Illus.). 400p. 1987. pap. text 36.95 (*0-19-504248-4*) OUP.

Perspectives on Welfare: The Experience of Minority Ethnic Groups in Scotland. Alison Bowes & Duncan Sim. LC 97-71720. (Research in Ethnic Relations Ser.). (Illus.). 256p. 1997. text 64.95 (*1-85972-415-9*, Pub. by Ashgate Pub) Ashgate Pub Co.

Perspectives on Western Art, Vol. 1. Ed. by Linnea H. Wren. LC 85-45244. 288p. 1987. pap. 28.00 (*0-06-430154-0*, IN-154, Icon Edns) HarpC.

***Perspectives on Western Culture , Vol. 1.** 304p. (C). 1998. text 18.00 (*0-536-01332-2*) Pearson Custom.

***Perspectives on Western Culture: Rise of Modernity, Vol. 2.** 258p. (C). 1998. text 28.00 (*0-536-02044-2*) Pearson Custom.

Perspectives on Witness & Translation: Essays in Honor of John E. Steely. Clayton N. Jefford. LC 93-29332. 160p. 1993. text 69.95 (*0-7734-2858-5*) E Mellen.

Perspectives on Woody Allen. Renee Curry. 1996. 50.00 (*0-8161-1615-6*) Macmillan.

Perspectives on World Politics. Ed. by Michael Smith et al. 431p. 1981. pap. 16.95 (*0-415-03976-2*, Pub. by C Helm) Routldge.

Perspectives on World Politics. 2nd ed. Ed. by Richard Little & Michael Smith. LC 90-44301. 496p. (C). 1991. pap. 27.99 (*0-415-05624-1*, A5502) Routledge.

Perspectives on World War II. Ed. by Catherine Thoburn & Janet Knapp. 1995. pap. 3.50 (*1-885761-02-3*) Turner Geriatric.

***Perspectives on Writing: Research, Theory & Practice.** Roselmina Indrisano & James R. Squire. 2000. pap., teacher ed. 29.95 (*0-87207-268-1*, 268) Intl Reading.

Perspectives on Written Argument. Ed. by Deborah Berrill & Marcia Tarr. LC 96-24443. (Written Language Ser.). 288p. (Orig.). (C). 1996. text 62.50 (*1-57273-038-2*); pap. text 26.50 (*1-57273-039-0*) Hampton Pr NJ.

***Perspectives, Science & Technologies for Novel Silicon On.** Peter L. F. Hemment et al. 368p. 1999. pap. 75.00 (*0-7923-6117-2*) Kluwer Academic.

Perspectives Towards Sustainable Environmental Development. Ed. by Colin Williams & Graham Haughton. (Studies in Green Research). 212p. 1994. 67.95 (*1-85628-874-9*, Pub. by Avebry) Ashgate Pub Co.

Perspectives 2000: Intermediate English, Level 1. 3rd ed. Lee et al. 180p. (J). 1991. mass mkt. 13.00 (*0-8384-2003-6*); mass mkt., student ed. 9.95 (*0-8384-2005-2*) Heinle & Heinle.

Perspectives 2000: Intermediate English, Level 1. 3rd ed. Lee et al. (J). 1991. mass mkt., teacher ed. 21.95 (*0-8384-2052-4*) Heinle & Heinle.

Perspectives 2000: Intermediate English, Level 1. 3rd ed. Lee et al. (J). 1991. audio 60.95 (*0-8384-2004-4*) Heinle & Heinle.

Perspectives 2000: Intermediate English, Level 1. 3rd ed. Lee et al. (YA). (gr. 8-12). 1991. mass mkt., lab manual ed. 38.95 (*0-8384-2222-5*) Heinle & Heinle.

Perspectives 2000: Intermediate English, Level 1. 3rd ed. Lee et al. (J). 1992. audio 23.95 (*0-8384-4233-1*) Heinle & Heinle.

Perspectives 2000: Intermediate English, Level 1. 3rd ed. Lee et al. (J). 1993. audio 42.95 (*0-8384-4199-8*) Heinle & Heinle.

Perspectives, 2000: Intermediate English, Level 2. 3rd ed. Chamot et al. 182p. (J). 1991. mass mkt. 15.00 (*0-8384-2006-0*) Heinle & Heinle.

Perspectives, 2000: Intermediate English, Level 2. 3rd ed. Chamot et al. (J). 1991. mass mkt., student ed. 9.95 (*0-8384-2008-7*) Heinle & Heinle.

Perspectives, 2000: Intermediate English, Level 2. 3rd ed. Chamot et al. (J). 1991. audio 60.95 (*0-8384-2007-9*) Heinle & Heinle.

Perspectives, 2000: Intermediate English, Level 2. 3rd annot. ed. Chamot et al. (J). 1991. mass mkt., teacher ed. 21.95 (*0-8384-2053-2*) Heinle & Heinle.

Perspectives Whole Language Folio: A Folio of Articles from Perspectives in Education & Deafness. Ed. by Mary Abrams. (Illus.). 62p. (J). 1991. pap. text, teacher ed. 6.95 (*0-88095-205-9*) Gallaudet U Pre Coll.

Perspektive aus Deutschland: Beginning. (GER.). (C). 1991. 8.40 (*0-8442-2290-9*, X2290-9) NTC Contemp Pub Co.

Perspektiven: Texte zur Kultur und Literatur. Manfred Bansleben. 272p. (C). 1987. pap. text 40.50 (*0-03-063238-2*) Harcourt Coll Pubs.

Perspektiven: Ubungen zur Grammatik. Manfred Bansleben. (C). 1987. pap. text 53.00 (*0-03-063239-0*) Harcourt Coll Pubs.

Perspektiven: Ubungen Zur Grammatik & Texte Zur Kultur & Literatur. Manfred Bansleben. (C). 1987. pap. text, student ed. 30.00 (*0-03-063241-2*) Harcourt Coll Pubs.

Perspektiven der Menschheitsentwicklung see Materialism & the Task of Anthroposophy

Perspektiven Transzendental-Phanomelogischer Forschung. U. Claesges & K. Held. (Phaenomenologica Ser.: No. 49). 306p. 1972. lib. bdg. 112.50 (*90-247-1313-7*, Pub. by M Nijhoff) Kluwer Academic.

Persuade Us to Rejoice: The Liberating Power of Fiction. Robert M. Brown. 160p. (Orig.). 1992. pap. 14.95 (*0-664-25381-4*) Westminster John Knox.

Persuaded Passions. Mikhail Armalinskii, pseud. 74p. 1980. pap. 5.00 (*0-935090-03-7*) Almanac Pr.

Persuading Aristotle: The Timeless Art of Persuasion in Business, Negotiation & the Media. Peter Thompson. 1999. pap. 19.95 (*1-86448-739-9*, Pub. by Allen & Unwin Pty) IPG Chicago.

Persuading on Paper: The Complete Guide to Writing Copy That Pulls in Business. Marcia Yudkin. LC 95-34894. 288p. 1996. pap. 12.95 (*0-452-27313-7*, Plume) Dutton Plume.

***Persuading People to Have Safer Sex: Application of Social Science to the AIDS Crisis.** Richard M. Perloff. (A Volume in LEA's Communication Series). 280p. 2000. write for info. (*0-8058-3380-3*); pap. write for info. (*0-8058-3381-1*) L Erlbaum Assocs.

Persuading Science: The Art of Scientific Rhetoric. Ed. by Marcello Pera. 224p. 1991. 39.95 (*0-88135-071-0*, Sci Hist) Watson Pub Intl.

Persuading the People: Government Publicity in the Second World War. Anthony Osley. LC 96-137994. 92p. 1995. pap. 30.00 (*0-11-701885-6*, Pub. by Statnry Office) Balogh.

***Persuals into (Post) Modern Thought.** Claudia Moscovici. LC 99-88671. 120p. 2000. 24.50 (*0-7618-1615-1*) U Pr of Amer.

Persuasion. Jane Austen. Ed. by D. W. Harding. (English Library). 400p. (C). 1998. pap. 5.95 (*0-14-043005-9*) Addson-Wesley Educ.

Persuasion. Jane Austen. 122p. Date not set. 17.95 (*0-8488-2542-X*) Amereon Ltd.

Persuasion. Jane Austen. 240p. 1984. mass mkt. 3.95 (*0-553-21137-4*, Bantam Classics) Bantam.

Persuasion. Jane Austen. Ed. by Linda Bree. LC 98-231555. (Literary Texts Ser.). (Illus.). 306p. 1998. pap. text 7.95 (*1-55111-131-4*) Broadview Pr.

Persuasion. Jane Austen. (Cloth Bound Pocket Ser.). 350p. 1998. 7.95 (*3-8290-0901-1*, 520664) Konemann.

Persuasion. Jane Austen. 1992. 15.00 (*0-679-40986-6*) McKay.

Persuasion. Jane Austen. 1995. 13.50 (*0-679-60191-0*) Modern Lib NY.

Persuasion. Jane Austen. 1996. mass mkt. 4.95 (*0-451-52638-4*) NAL.

Persuasion. Jane Austen. Ed. by Patricia M. Spacks. LC 94-4510. (Critical Editions Ser.). 316p. (C). 1994. pap. text 9.75 (*0-393-96018-8*) Norton.

Persuasion. Jane Austen. Ed. by John Davie. (Oxford World's Classics Ser.). 302p. 1998. pap. 4.95 (*0-19-283361-8*) OUP.

***Persuasion.** Jane Austen. 256p. 1999. mass mkt. 2.99 (*0-8125-6588-6*, Pub. by Tor Bks) St Martin.

Persuasion. Jane Austen. 1984. 9.05 (*0-606-02200-7*, Pub. by Turtleback) Demco.

Persuasion. Jane Austen. Ed. & Intro. by Gillian Beer. LC 99-228376. 236p. (C). 1999. pap. write for info. (*0-14-043467-4*) Viking Penguin.

Persuasion. Jane Austen. (Classics Library). 224p. 1998. pap. 3.95 (*1-85326-056-8*, 0568WW, Pub. by Wrdsworth Edits) NTC Contemp Pub Co.

Persuasion. Adapted by Nick Dear. (Screenplay Ser.). 1996. pap. 10.95 (*0-413-71170-6*) Methn.

Persuasion. Intro. by Pat Rogers. 318p. 1994. 3.95 (*0-460-87529-9*, Everyman's Classic Lib) Tuttle Pubng.

Persuasion. Michael E. Tigar & American Bar Assn. Staff. LC 98-47122. 1998. write for info. (*1-57073-637-5*) Amer Bar Assn.

Persuasion. large type ed. Jane Austen. (Large Print Heritage Ser.). 371p. 1998. lib. bdg. 34.95 (*1-58118-027-6*, 22023) LRS.

Persuasion. large type ed. Jane Austen. 389p. 1990. 27.99 (*0-7089-8534-3*, Charnwood) Ulverscroft.

Persuasion. large type ed. Jane Austen. 405p. 1996. reprint ed. lib. bdg. 24.00 (*0-939495-04-X*) North Bks.

Persuasion. Jane Austen. 240p. 1986. reprint ed. lib. bdg. 18.95 (*0-89966-538-1*) Buccaneer Bks.

Persuasion. Jane Austen. LC 97-10948. 224p. 1997. reprint ed. pap. text 2.00 (*0-486-29555-9*) Dover.

Persuasion. Jane Austen. 243p. 1998. reprint ed. lib. bdg. 24.00 (*1-58287-055-1*) North Bks.

Persuasion, Set. abr. ed. Jane Austen. 1996. pap. 23.95 incl. audio (*0-14-086058-4*, 693419, Png AudioBks) Viking Penguin.

Persuasion: A Language Arts Unit for High-Ability Learners. Center for Gifted Education Staff. 340p. (C). 1998. per. 28.95 (*0-7872-5341-3*, 41534101); boxed set 65.95 (*0-7872-5340-5*, 41534001) Kendall-Hunt.

Persuasion: Advances Through Meta-Analysis. Ed. by Mike Allen & Raymond W. Preiss. LC 98-11061. (Communication Ser.). 304p. (C). 1998. pap. 26.50 (*1-57273-067-6*); text 62.50 (*1-57273-066-8*) Hampton Pr NJ.

Persuasion: Greek Rhetoric in Action. Ed. by Ian Worthington. 320p. (C). 1994. pap. 27.99 (*0-415-08139-4*) Routledge.

Persuasion: New Directions in Theory & Research. Ed. by Michael E. Roloff & Gerald R. Miller. LC 79-21202. (Sage Annual Reviews of Communication Research Ser.: No. 8). 311p. 1980. reprint ed. pap. 96.50 (*0-608-01447-8*, 205949100001) Bks Demand.

Persuasion: Penguin Reader Level 2. Jane Austen. 1998. pap. 7.00 (*0-14-081527-9*) Viking Penguin.

Persuasion: Reception & Respons. 6th ed. Larson. (Speech & Theater Ser.). 1992. mass mkt., teacher ed. write for info. (*0-534-14983-9*) Wadsworth Pub.

Persuasion: Reception & Responsibility. 4th ed. Charles U. Larson. 349p. (C). 1985. pap. write for info. (*0-534-06162-1*) Wadsworth Pub.

Persuasion: Reception & Responsibility. 5th ed. Charles U. Larson. 434p. (C). 1989. pap. write for info. (*0-534-10134-8*) Wadsworth Pub.

Persuasion: Reception & Responsibility. 6th ed. Charles U. Larson. 422p. (C). 1991. pap. 32.95 (*0-534-14982-0*) Wadsworth Pub.

Persuasion: Reception & Responsibility. 7th ed. Larson. (Speech & Theater Ser.). 1994. pap., teacher ed. 49.00 (*0-534-23071-7*) Wadsworth Pub.

Persuasion: Reception & Responsibility. 7th ed. Charles U. Larson. LC 94-12354. 447p. 1994. mass mkt. 41.95 (*0-534-23070-9*) Wadsworth Pub.

Persuasion: Reception & Responsibility. 8th ed. Charles Larson. LC 97-18841. (Speech & Theater Ser.). (C). 1997. 56.95 (*0-534-52281-5*) Wadsworth Pub.

Persuasion: Reception & Responsibility. 9th ed. Larson. (Speech & Theater Ser.). 2000. 34.75 (*0-534-52285-8*) Wadsworth Pub.

Persuasion: Speech & Behavioral Change. Gary Cronkhite. LC 73-75140. (Speech Communication Ser.). (C). 1969. pap. write for info. (*0-672-61075-2*, SC4, Bobbs) Macmillan.

P

Persuasion: Strategies for Public Influence. 3rd ed. John A. Cook & William F. Strong. 208p. 1996. per. 26.95 (*0-8403-8037-2*) Kendall-Hunt.

Persuasion: Theory & Practice. 2nd ed. Kenneth E. Andersen. (Illus.). 431p. 1983. pap. text 24.95 (*0-89641-117-6*) American Pr.

Persuasion: Understanding, Practice & Analysis. 2nd ed. Herbert W. Simons. 400p. (C). 1986. 59.38 (*0-07-553819-9*) McGraw.

Persuasion Analysis: A Companion to Composition. Hugh Rank. LC 88-25696. 160p. (Orig.). 1988. pap. text 10.00 (*0-943468-02-7*) Counter-Prop Pr.

Persuasion & Healing: A Comparative Study of Psychotherapy. 3rd ed. Jerome D. Frank & Julia B. Frank. 384p. 1993. reprint ed. pap. text 17.95 (*0-8018-4636-6*) Johns Hopkins.

***Persuasion & Influence in American Life.** 4th ed. Gary C. Woodward & Robert E. Denton. 445p. (C). 1999. pap. 35.95 (*1-57766-070-6*) Waveland Pr.

Persuasion & Privacy in Cyberspace: The Online Protests Over Lotus Marketplace & the Clipper. Laura J. Gurak. (Illus.). 200p. 1999. pap. text 15.00 (*0-300-07864-1*) Yale U Pr.

Persuasion & Social Movements. 3rd rev. ed. Charles Stewart et al. (Illus.). 326p. (C). 1994. pap. text 19.95 (*0-88133-777-3*) Waveland Pr.

Persuasion As Intervention: Reclaiming Rhetoric As a Civic Art. Ed. by Arwill. (C). 1999. text. write for info. (*0-321-01593-2*) Addson-Wesley Educ.

Persuasion Context People. Lulofs. 410p. 1997. pap. text 53.00 (*0-13-777905-4*) P-H.

Persuasion Engineering. Richard Bandler & John LaValle. LC 95-76816. 1996. 24.95 (*0-916990-36-2*) META Pubns.

***Persuasion Ethics: A Special Issue of the Journal of Mass Media Ethics.** Ralph D. Barney & Jay Black. 64p. 1999. pap. 20.00 (*0-8058-9780-1*) L Erlbaum Assocs.

Persuasion, Getting Your Way with Words. Tarshis. 1995. pap. 22.00 (*0-02-616271-7*) Macmillan.

Persuasion in Cyberspace: Privacy, Community & the Online Protests over Marketplace & Clipper. Laura J. Gurak. LC 96-38472. (Illus.). 200p. 1997. 32.00 (*0-300-06963-4*) Yale U Pr.

Persuasion in Marketing: The Dynamics of Marketing's Great Untapped Resource. Horace S. Schwerin & Henry H. Newell. LC 80-23133. (Illus.). 275p. 1981. reprint ed. pap. 85.30 (*0-7837-3515-4*, 205784900008) Bks Demand.

Persuasion in Practice. 2nd ed. Kathleen K. Reardon. (Illus.). 232p. 1991. 45.00 (*0-8039-3316-9*); pap. 19.95 (*0-8039-3317-7*) Sage.

Persuasion in the Courtroom. rev. ed. Joseph V. Guastaferro. 101p. 1989. pap. 185.00 incl. audio (*0-943380-33-2*) PEG MN.

Persuasion in the French Personal Novel: Studies of Chateaubriand, Constant, Balzac, Nerval, & Fromentin. Richard Bales. LC 96-70889. 154p. 1997. lib. bdg. 34.95 (*1-883479-16-9*) Summa Pubns.

Persuasion Power Skills. Roger Burggraff. 13p. 1991. pap. text 79.50 incl. audio (*0-88432-436-2*, S03040) Audio-Forum.

Persuasion, Social Influence, & Compliance Gaining. Robert Gass & John S. Seiter. LC 98-7618. 354p. 1998. pap. text 47.00 (*0-205-26352-6*) Allyn.

Persuasion, Theory, & Context. Kathleen K. Reardon. LC 81-1892. (Sage Library of Social Research: No. 122). 283p. 1981. reprint ed. pap. 87.80 (*0-608-01446-X*, 205949000001) Bks Demand.

Persuasions: A Dream of Reason Meeting Unbelief. Douglas Wilson. 96p. (Orig.). 1997. pap. 8.00 (*1-885767-29-3*, P-102) Canon Pr ID.

Persuasions: A Dream of Reason Meeting Unbelief. Douglas Wilson. 70p. (Orig.). (C). 1989. pap. 4.50 (*0-317-93503-8*) Oakcross Pubns.

Persuasions & Performances: The Play of Tropes in Culture. James W. Fernandez. LC 85-45311. 320p. (C). 1986. 41.95 (*0-253-34399-2*); pap. 15.95 (*0-253-20374-0*, MB-374) Ind U Pr.

Persuasions & Prejudices: An Information Compendium of Modern Social Science, 1953-1988. Irving L. Horowitz. 645p. 1988. 49.95 (*0-88738-261-4*) Transaction Pubs.

***Persuasion's Domain: An Introduction to Rhetoric & Lucifer State.** Richard Thames & Trevor Melia. (C). 1999. pap. text 52.95 (*0-7872-6494-6*, 41649401) Kendall-Hunt.

Persuasions of the Witch's Craft: Ritual Magic in Contemporary England. Tanya M. Luhrmann. LC 88-33382. (Illus.). 380p. 1989. 32.00 (*0-674-66323-3*) HUP.

Persuasions of the Witch's Craft: Ritual Magic in Contemporary England. Tanya M. Luhrmann. (Illus.). 416p. 1991. pap. text 16.95 (*0-674-66324-1*, LUHPEX) HUP.

Persuasive Advertising for Entrepreneurs & Small Business Owners: How to Create More Effective Sales Messages. Jay P. Granat. LC 92-22807. (Illus.). 200p. 1994. lib. bdg. 39.95 (*1-56024-366-X*) Haworth Pr.

Persuasive Advertising for Entrepreneurs & Small Business Owners: How to Create More Effective Sales Messages. Jay P. Granat. 194p. 1997. pap. 14.95 (*1-56024-994-3*) Haworth Pr.

Persuasive Appeal of the Chronicler. Rodney K. Duke. (JSOT Supplement Ser.: No. 88). 192p. 1990. 57.50 (*1-85075-228-1*, Pub. by Sheffield Acad) CUP Services.

Persuasive Artistry: Studies in New Testament Rhetoric of George A. Kennedy. Ed. by Duane F. Watson. (Journal for the Study of the New Testament, Supplement Ser.: No. 50). 390p. 1991. 85.00 (*1-85075-284-2*, Pub. by Sheffield Acad) CUP Services.

Persuasive Business Proposals: Writing to Win Customers, Clients, & Contracts. Tom Sant. LC 92-18963. 224p. 1992. 26.95 (*0-8144-5100-4*) AMACOM.

Persuasive Business Speaking. Elayne Snyder. LC 90-55213. 256p. (Orig.). 1990. pap. 17.95 (*0-8144-7722-4*) AMACOM.

Persuasive Communication. James B. Stiff. LC 93-23401. (Communication Ser.). 278p. 1993. lib. bdg. 36.95 (*0-89862-308-1*) Guilford Pubns.

Persuasive Communication. 5th ed. Betting. (C). 1994. pap. text 50.00 (*0-03-055352-0*, Pub. by Harcourt Coll Pubs) Harcourt.

Persuasive Communication. 5th ed. Erwin P. Bettingham. (C). 1994. pap. text, teacher ed. 4.75 (*0-03-097621-9*) Harcourt Coll Pubs.

Persuasive Communication & Drug Abuse Prevention. Ed. by L. Donohew et al. (Communication Ser.). 360p. (C). 1991. text 69.95 (*0-8058-0693-8*) L Erlbaum Assocs.

Persuasive Communication Campaigns. Michael Pfau & Roxanne Parrott. 528p. 1995. 73.00 (*0-205-13977-9*) Allyn.

***Persuasive Computing: Using Technology to Change Attitudes.** B. J. Fogg. (Illus.). 2000. pap. 29.95 (*1-55860-643-2*) Morgan Kaufmann.

Persuasive Delivery in the Courtroom. Celia W. Childress. Ed. by David B. Harrison. LC 95-78204. 600p. 1995. text. write for info. (*0-7620-0026-0*) West Group.

Persuasive Encounters. Gary C. Woodward. LC 90-32132. (Case Studies in Constructive Confrontation). 216p. 1990. 55.00 (*0-275-93091-2*, C3091, Praeger Pubs); pap. 19.95 (*0-275-93092-0*, B3092, Praeger Pubs) Greenwood.

Persuasive Fictions: Faith, Faction & Literature in the Reign of Henry VIII. Greg Walker. (Illus.). 229p. 1996. 86.95 (*1-85928-139-7*, Pub. by Scolar Pr) Ashgate Pub Co.

Persuasive Images: Posters of War & Revolution from the Archives of the Hoover Institution. Peter Paret et al. (Illus.). 280p. 1992. 57.50 (*0-691-03204-1*, Pub. by Princeton U Pr) Cal Prin Full Svc.

Persuasive Jury Communication: Case Studies from Successful Trials. Fred Wilkins. LC 93-49763. (Trial Practice Ser.). 1994. write for info. (*0-07-172595-4*) Shepards.

Persuasive Manager: How to Sell Yourself & Your Ideas. Thomas L. Quick. LC 80-70254. 204p. reprint ed. pap. 63.30 (*0-608-15472-5*, 202938900060) Bks Demand.

Persuasive Opening Statements & Closing Arguments. Joseph W. Cotchett & Frank Rothman. 375p. 1988. 80.00 (*0-88124-165-2*, CP-39650) Cont Ed Bar-CA.

Persuasive Opening Statements & Closing Arguments: 12/97. Frank Rothman & Joseph W. Cotchett. LC 88-71394. 454p. 1997. per. 35.00 (*0-7626-0164-7*, CP-39658) Cont Ed Bar-CA.

Persuasive Pen: Reasoning & Writing. Nancy Carrick & Lawrence Finsen. LC 96-43142. (Philosophy Ser.). 320p. 1997. pap. 35.00 (*0-7637-0234-X*) Jones & Bartlett.

Persuasive Person: Communicating More Effectively in Person & in Print. James Watkins. 134p. (Orig.). 1987. pap. 6.95 (*0-89827-040-5*, BKM32) Wesleyan Pub Hse.

Persuasive Public Relations for Libraries. Vicki Northcutt & Esther Perica. LC 83-15473. xii, 199 p. 1983. 15.00 (*0-8389-3284-3*) ALA.

***Persuasive Reports & Proposals.** Andrew Leigh. 96p. 2000. pap. 17.95 (*0-8464-5131-X*) Beekman Pubs.

Persuasive Resume! A Guide to Writing, Formatting & Finishing. Lawrence E. Lensmith. 1991. pap. text 7.95 (*1-880381-00-1*) Desktop Impress.

Persuasive Speaking & Writing. Frank Schaffer Publications, Inc. Staff. (Middle School Bks.). (Illus.). 1996. wbk. ed. 10.95 (*0-7647-0055-3*, FS-10207) Schaffer Pubns.

Persuasive Technical Writing. J. Banks. LC 65-28552. 1966. 36.00 (*0-08-011668-X*, Pub. by Pergamon Repr) Franklin.

Persuasive Writing. Irving Younger. 103p. (Orig.). 1990. pap. 15.95 (*0-943380-02-2*) PEG MN.

***Persuasive Writing, Vol. 4.** Tara McCarthy. (Illus.). (J). (gr. 4-7). 1998. mass mkt. 9.95 (*0-590-20934-5*) Scholastic Inc.

Persuasive Writing: The Writing Teacher's Handbook, No. 2366. June Hetzel & Deborah McIntire. Ed. by Joel Kupperstein. 64p. (J). (gr. 4-6). 1998. pap. 7.98 (*1-57471-356-6*) Creat Teach Pr.

Persuasive Writing for Lawyers & the Legal Profession 1995. annuals Louis J. Sirico, Jr. 1995. text 16.00 (*0-8205-2721-1*) Bender.

Persuasives to Early Piety. J. G. Pike. 362p. (YA). (gr. 5-11). 1996. 29.95 (*1-57358-036-8*) Soli Deo Gloria.

Perth: The Fair City. David Graham-Campbell. 220p. (C). 1996. pap. 30.00 (*0-85976-382-X*, Pub. by J Donald) St Mut.

Perth Amboy. Joan Seguine-Levine. LC 96-231070. (Images of America Ser.). 1996. pap. 16.99 (*0-7524-0411-3*) Arcadia Publng.

Perth Sketchbook. Barry Strickland & Peter Harper. (Illus.). 56p. (C). 1995. 16.95 (*1-875560-40-8*, Pub. by Univ of West Aust Pr) Intl Spec Bk.

Perthshire Book, 1. Donald Omand. LC 99-219555. 1999. 33.95 (*1-874744-84-X*) Dufour.

***Perthshire in History & Legend.** Archie McKerracher. 219p. 2000. pap. 19.95 (*0-85976-517-2*, Pub. by J Donald) Dufour.

Pertinent Commercial Statutes. annuals Gould Editorial Staff. 560p. (C). ring bd. 14.95 (*0-87526-293-7*) Gould.

Pertinent Questions & Answers about Homeopathy. James G. Speight. 109p. 1984. pap. 3.95 (*0-85207-164-7*, Pub. by C W Daniel) Natl Bk Netwk.

Pertinent Questions & Answers about Homoeopathy. Phyllis Speight. 28p. (Orig.). pap. 5.95 (*0-8464-4269-8*) Beekman Pubs.

Pertshire Walks. Compiled by John Watney. (Ordnance Survey Pathfinder Guides Ser.). (Illus.). 80p. (Orig.). 1994. pap. 14.95 (*0-7117-0673-5*) Seven Hills Bk.

Perturbation Analysis of Discrete Event Dynamic Systems. Yu-Chi Ho & Xi-Ren Cao. (C). 1991. text 131.50 (*0-7923-9174-8*) Kluwer Academic.

Perturbation Analysis of Optimization Problems. J. Frederic Bonnans & A. Shapiro. LC 00-20825. (Springer Series in Operations Research). 624p. 2000. 79.95 (*0-387-98705-3*) Spr-Verlag.

Perturbation Methods. E. J. Hinch. (Cambridge Texts in Applied Mathematics Ser.: No. 6). (Illus.). 172p. (C). 1991. text 80.00 (*0-521-37310-7*); pap. text 29.95 (*0-521-37897-4*) Cambridge U Pr.

Perturbation Methods. Ali H. Nayfeh. (Pure & Applied Mathematics: A Wiley-Interscience Series of Texts, Monographs & Tracts). 448p. 1973. 183.95 (*0-471-63059-4*) Wiley.

Perturbation Methods, Bifurcation Theory & Computer Algebra. R. H. Rand & D. Armbruster. (Applied Mathematical Sciences Ser.: Vol. 65). (Illus.). 255p. 1987. 58.95 (*0-387-96589-0*) Spr-Verlag.

Perturbation Methods for Engineers & Scientists. Alan W. Bush. 320p. 1992. per. 72.95 (*0-8493-8614-4*) CRC Pr.

Perturbation Methods for Engineers & Scientists. Alan W. Bush. 320p. 1992. boxed set 104.95 (*0-8493-8608-X*, QA871) CRC Pr.

Perturbation Methods in Applied Mathematics. J. Kevorkian & J. D. Cole. (Applied Mathematical Sciences Ser.: Vol. 34). (Illus.). 558p. 1985. reprint ed. 84.95 (*0-387-90507-3*) Spr-Verlag.

Perturbation Methods in Fluid Mechanics. Milton Van Dyke. LC 75-15072. (C). 1975. 15.00 (*0-915760-01-0*) Parabolic Pr.

Perturbation Methods in Heat Transfer. A. Aziz & Tsung Na. LC 84-6624. (Computational Methods in Mechanics & Thermal Sciences Ser.). (Illus.). 225p. 1984. text 85.00 (*0-89116-376-X*) Hemisp Pub.

Perturbation Methods in the Computer Age. David C. Wilcox. LC 95-92014. (Illus.). xvi, 224 p. (C). 1995. text 50.00 (*0-9636051-2-7*) DCW Industries.

Perturbation Methods, Instability, Catastrophe & Chaos. D. De Kee. LC 99-14412. 1999. 76.00 (*981-02-3726-X*) World Scientific Pub.

***Perturbation Methods, Instability, Catastrophe & Chaos.** Chen Wen-fang et al. 1999. pap. text 38.00 (*981-02-3727-8*) World Scientific Pub.

Perturbation, My Sister: A Study of Max Ernst's "Hundred Headless Woman" Kristin Prevallet. 80p. (Orig.). 1997. pap. 10.00 (*1-889960-02-0*) First Intensity.

Perturbation of Spectra in Hilbert Space. K. O. Friedrichs. LC 60-12712. (Lectures in Applied Mathematics: Vol. 3). 178p. 1965. text 38.00 (*0-8218-1103-7*, LAM/3) Am Math.

Perturbation Techniques for Flexible Manipulators. Anthony R. Fraser & Ron W. Daniel. (C). 1991. text 122.00 (*0-7923-9162-4*) Kluwer Academic.

Perturbation Theory for Linear Operators. 3rd ed. Tosio Kato. LC 94-39131. (Classics in Mathematics Ser.). 619p. 1995. 35.00 (*3-540-58661-X*) Spr-Verlag.

Perturbation Theory for the Schrodinger Operator with a Periodic Potential. Yulia E. Karpeshina. LC 97-22224. (Lecture Notes in Mathematics Ser.: Vol. 166). 1997. pap. write for info. (*3-540-63136-4*) Spr-Verlag.

Perturbation Theory of Eigenvalue Problems. F. Rellich. x, 128p. 1969. text 195.00 (*0-677-00680-2*) Gordon & Breach.

***Perturbations: Theory & Methods.** James A. Murdock et al. LC 99-36132. (Classics in Applied Mathematics: Vol. 27). xx, 509p. 1999. pap. 53.00 (*0-89871-443-5*, CL27) Soc Indus-Appl Math.

Perturbations, Approximations, & Sensitivity Analysis of Optimal Control Systems. A. L. Dontchev. (Lecture Notes in Control & Information Sciences: Vol. 52). 162p. 1983. pap. 19.00 (*0-387-12463-2*) Spr-Verlag.

Perturbations of Banach Algebras. K. Jarosz. (Lecture Notes in Mathematics Ser.: Vol. 1120). v, 118p. 1985. 29.95 (*0-387-15218-0*) Spr-Verlag.

Perturbative & Nonperturbative Aspects of Quantum Field Theory. Ed. by W. Schweiger. LC 96-54731. (Lecture Notes in Physics Ser.: No. 479). 1997. 86.00 (*3-540-62478-3*) Spr-Verlag.

Perturbative QCD. A. Mueller. (Advanced Series on Directions in Hep.: Vol. 5). 624p. 1989. text 110.00 (*9971-5-0564-9*); pap. text 40.00 (*9971-5-0565-7*) World Scientific Pub.

Perturbative Quantum Chromodynamics: Tallahassee, 1981. Ed. by D. W. Duke & J. F. Owens. (AIP Conference Proceedings Ser.: No. 74). 477p. 1981. lib. bdg. 34.75 (*0-88318-173-8*) Am Inst Physics.

***Perturbative Quantum Electrodynamics & Axiomatic Field Theory.** Othmar Steinmann. LC 00-30798. (Texts & Monographs in Physics). 2000. write for info. (*3-540-67024-6*) Spr-Verlag.

Perturbed Spirit: The Life & Personality of Samuel Taylor Coleridge. Oswald Doughty. LC 78-66792. 365p. 1981. 45.00 (*0-8386-2353-0*) Fairleigh Dickinson.

Perturbing the Organism: The Biology of Successful Experience. Herbert Weiner. LC 91-838. (Illus.). 372p. 1992. 40.50 (*0-226-89041-4*) U Ch Pr.

Pertussis. Ed. by C. R. Manclark & W. Hennessen. (Developments in Biological Standardization Ser.: Vol. 61). (Illus.). xii, 600p. 1986. pap. 61.00 (*3-8055-4210-0*) S Karger.

Pertussis: Evaluation & Research on Acellular Pertussis Vaccines. Ed. by Y. Sato et al. (Developments in Biological Standardization Ser.: Vol. 73). (Illus.). xii, 386p. 1991. 61.00 (*3-8055-5457-5*) S Karger.

Pertussis Vaccine Trials: Symposium at the Istituto Superiore di Sanita, Rome, October/November 1995. Ed. by Fred Brown et al. LC 97-202571. (Developments in Biological Standardization Ser.: Vol. 89, 1997). (Illus.). xiv, 418p. 1997. pap. 339.25 (*3-8055-6481-3*) S Karger.

Peru see American Nations Past & Present

Peru see Statements of the Laws of the OAS Member States in Matters Affecting Business

Peru see Festivals of the World

Peru. (Insight Guides Ser.). 1998. 22.95 (*0-88729-129-5*) Langenscheidt.

Peru. Denise Allard. LC 96-1451. (Postcards From Ser.). (Illus.). (J). 1997. lib. bdg. 21.40 (*0-8172-4028-4*) Raintree Steck-V.

***Peru.** Mary Catherine. LC 99-42409. (Illus.). (J). 2000. lib. bdg. write for info. (*1-56766-739-2*) Childs World.

Peru. Colleen Gray. LC 83-8740. (World Education Ser.). (Illus.). 132p. (Orig.). (C). 1983. pap. text 12.00 (*0-910054-77-0*) Am Assn Coll Registrars.

***Peru.** Lisa Halvorsen. LC 00-9008. (Letters Home from... Ser.). (Illus.). 32p. 2000. pap. 16.95 (*1-56711-414-8*) Blackbirch.

***Peru.** Elaine Landau. LC 99-14955. (True Bks.). (Illus.). 48p. (J). (gr. 3-5). 2000. 21.50 (*0-516-21174-9*) Childrens.

***Peru.** Elaine Landau. (Illus.). 48p. (J). (gr. 3-5). 2000. pap. 6.95 (*0-516-27019-2*) Childrens.

Peru Marion Morrison. LC 99-17871. (Enchantment of the World Ser.). (J). 2000. 32.00 (*0-516-21545-0*) Childrens.

Peru. Edward A. Parker. LC 96-18331. (Economically Developing Countries Ser.). (J). 1997. lib. bdg. 24.26 (*0-8172-4525-1*) Raintree Steck-V.

Peru. Reid. pap. text 10.00 (*0-85345-698-4*) Monthly Rev.

***Peru.** Schmidt. 2000. 49.00 (*0-8133-0649-3*, Pub. by Westview) HarpC.

Peru. Kristin Thoennes. LC 98-41778. (Countries of the World Ser.). (J). (gr. 3-4). 1999. write for info. (*0-7368-0155-3*, Bridgestone Bks) Capstone Pr.

Peru. Kristin Thoennes. (Countries of the World Ser.). 24p. (J). (gr. 1-5). 1999. 14.00 (*0-516-21753-4*) Childrens.

Peru. U. S. Government Staff. (Country Studies). 1994. 23.00 (*0-614-30811-9*, UPERU) Claitors.

Peru. annot. ed. Ed. by John R. Fisher. LC 90-158015. (World Bibliographical Ser.: No. 109). 214p. 1990. lib. bdg. 58.00 (*1-85109-100-9*) ABC-CLIO.

Peru. Rosa Q. Mesa. LC 73-180800. (Latin American Serial Documents Ser.: Vol. 10). 307p. 1973. reprint ed. pap. 95.20 (*0-8357-0078-X*, 201354800087) Bks Demand.

Peru see Enchantment of the World Series

Peru. 3rd ed. Gordon Lish. LC 96-37673. 192p. 1997. reprint ed. pap. 12.95 (*1-56858-085-1*) FWEW.

***Peru.** 4th ed. Rough Guides Staff. (Travel Ser.). (Illus.). 2000. pap. 17.95 (*1-85828-536-4*, Pub. by Rough Guides) Penguin Putnam.

Peru see Cultures of the World - Group 11

Peru: A Country Study. Rex A. Hudson. 478p. 1993. boxed set 33.00 (*0-16-061155-5*) USGPO.

***Peru: A Country Study Guide.** Global Investment & Business Center, Inc. Staff. (World Country Study Guides Library: Vol. 135). (Illus.). 350p. 2000. pap. 59.00 (*0-7397-2433-9*) Intl Business Pubns.

Peru: A Short History. David P. Werlich. LC 77-17107. (Illus.). 447p. 1978. 29.95 (*0-8093-0830-4*) S Ill U Pr.

Peru: April 1995 Election Assessment. Rodrigo Villareal. iv, 158p. 1996. pap. text 18.00 (*1-879720-26-4*) Intl Fndt Elect.

Peru: "Disappearances," Torture & Summary Executions by Government Forces after Prison Revolts of June 1986. Amnesty International Staff. 70p. 1987. pap. 5.00 (*0-86210-116-6*, Pub. by Amnesty Intl Pubns) Science Pubs.

Peru: History of Coca, "the Divine Plant" of the Incas. William G. Mortimer. LC 74-15120. reprint ed. 69.50 (*0-404-11980-8*) AMS Pr.

Peru: Incidents of Travel & Exploration in the Land of the Incas. Ephraim G. Squier. LC 72-5003. (Harvard University. Peabody Museum of Archaeology & Ethnology. Antiquities of the New World Ser.: No. 9). (Illus.). reprint ed. 76.50 (*0-404-57309-6*) AMS Pr.

Peru: Lost Cities, Found Hopes see Exploring Cultures of the World - Group 5

Peru: Major World Nations. Garry Lyle. LC 98-6401. (Major World Nations Ser.). (Illus.). 144p. (YA). (gr. 5 up). 1999. lib. bdg. 19.95 (*0-7910-4971-X*) Chelsea Hse.

Peru: Pre-Election Technical Assessment, 1993-1994. J. Ray Kennedy et al. ii, 100p. 1994. pap. text 12.00 (*1-879720-40-X*) Intl Fndt Elect.

Peru: Society & Nationhood in the Andes. Peter Flindell Klaren. LC 99-20062. (Latin American Histories Ser.). (Illus.). 512p. (C). 1999. pap. 26.95 (*0-19-506928-5*); text 55.00 (*0-19-506927-7*) OUP.

Peru: Textiles Unlimited. Harriet Tidball. LC 76-24015. (Guild Monographs: Nos. 25-26). (Illus.). 82p. 1968. pap. 10.95 (*0-916658-25-2*) Shuttle Craft.

Peru: The Authoritarian Tradition. David S. Palmer. LC 80-12176. 134p. 1980. 29.95 (*0-275-90531-4*, C0531, Praeger Pubs) Greenwood.

Peru: The Evolution of a Crisis. James D. Rudolph. LC 91-23655. (Politics in Latin America Ser.). 192p. 1992. 59.95 (*0-275-94146-9*, C4146, Praeger Pubs); pap. 17.95 (*0-275-94181-7*, B4181, Praeger Pubs) Greenwood.

Peru: The Land. Bobbie Kalman. (Lands, Peoples, & Cultures Ser.). (J). 1994. 13.40 (*0-606-08005-8*) Turtleback.

Peru: The New Poetry. Ed. & Tr. by David Tipton. LC 74-10432. 1977. 10.95 (*0-87376-024-7*) Red Dust.

Peru: The Next Step. 2nd ed. E. Lonergan. (Illus.). 200p. 1994. 170.00 (*1-85564-455-X*, Pub. by Euromoney) Am Educ Systs.

P

Peru: Time of Fear. Deborah Poole & Gerardo Renique. (Latin America Bureau Ser.). 200p. (Orig.). (C). 1992. pap. 19.00 (*0-85345-869-3*, Pub. by Lat Am Bur) Monthly Rev.

Peru: Travel Guide. 4th ed. Rob Rachowiecki. (Illus.). 512p. 1996. pap. 17.95 (*0-86442-332-2*) Lonely Planet.

Peru: Ulysses Travel Guide. Alain Legault. Ed. by Ulysses Travel Guide Staff. (Ulysses Travel Guide Ser.). (Illus.). 1999. pap. 19.95 (*2-89464-122-2*) Ulysses Travel.

Peru - A Country Study Guide: Basic Information for Research & Pleasure. Global Investment Center, USA Staff. (World Country Study Guide Library: Vol. 135). (Illus.). 350p. 1999. pap. 59.00 (*0-7397-1532-1*) Intl Business Pubns.

Peru - The Land see Lands, Peoples & Cultures Series

Peru - The People & Culture see Lands, Peoples & Cultures Series

Peru - Violations of Human Rights in the Emergency Zones. 1988. 4.00 (*0-685-23309-X*) Amnesty Intl USA.

Peru & Bolivia: A Bradt Hiking & Trekking Guide. 7th ed. Hilary Bradt. LC 98-27848. (Illus.). 300p. 1998. pap. text 17.95 (*1-898323-75-5*, Pub. by Bradt Pubns) Globe Pequot.

Peru & Ecuador. Griffin Trade Paperbacks Staff. (Let's Go Ser.). (Illus.). 544p. 1999. pap. 19.99 (*0-312-24464-9*) St Martin.

Peru & the Andean Countries. Chantal Deltenre & Martine Noblet. LC 94-25171. (Tintin's Travel Diaries). (Illus.). 76p. (J). (gr. 5 up). 1995. pap. 7.95 (*0-8120-9161-2*) Barron.

Peru & the Andean Countries. Chantal Deltenre & Martine Noblet. Tr. by Maureen Walker from FRE. LC 94-25171. (Tintin's Travel Diaries). (Illus.). 76p. (J). (gr. 5 up). 1995. 11.95 (*0-8120-6490-9*) Barron.

Peru & the History of Coca: Divine Plant of the Incas. W. Golden Mortimer. 1976. lib. bdg. 75.00 (*0-8490-0821-2*) Gordon Pr.

Peru & the United States: The Condor & the Eagle. Lawrence A. Clayton. LC 98-33595. (United States & the Americas Ser.). 1999. 55.00 (*0-8203-2024-2*) U of Ga Pr.

Peru & the United States: The Condor & the Eagle. Lawrene A. Clayton. LC 98-33595. (United States & the Americas Ser.). 1999. pap. 20.00 (*0-8203-2025-0*) U of Ga Pr.

***Peru, Bolivia & Ecuador Including the Galapagos.** rev. ed. Let's Go Staff. (Let's Go 2001 Ser.). (Illus.). 640p. 2000. pap. 22.99 (*0-312-24672-2*, St Martin Griffin) St Martin.

***Peru Business Intelligence Report, 190 vols.** Global Investment & Business Center, Inc. Staff. (World Business Intelligence Library: Vol. 135). (Illus.). 350p. 2000. pap. 99.95 (*0-7397-2633-1*) Intl Business Pubns.

***Peru Business Law Handbook.** Global Investment & Business Center, Inc. Staff. (Global Business Law Handbooks Library: Vol. 135). (Illus.). 2000. pap. 99.95 (*0-7397-2033-3*) Intl Business Pubns.

Peru Business Law Handbook-98. Russian Information & Business Center, Inc. Staff. (World Business Law Library-98). (Illus.). 350p. 1998. pap. 99.00 (*1-57751-843-8*) Intl Business Pubns.

***Peru Business Opportunity Yearbook.** Global Investment & Business Center, Inc. Staff. (Global Business Opportunity Yearbooks Library: Vol. 135). (Illus.). 2000. pap. 99.95 (*0-7397-2233-6*) Intl Business Pubns.

***Peru Business Opportunity Yearbook: Export-Import, Investment & Business Opportunities.** International Business Publications, U. S. A. Staff & Global Investment Center, U. S. A. Staff. (Global Business Opportunity Yearbooks Library: Vol. 135). (Illus.). 350p. 1999. pap. 99.95 (*0-7397-1333-7*) Intl Business Pubns.

***Peru Country Review 2000.** Robert C. Kelly et al. (Illus.). 60p. 1999. pap. 39.95 (*1-58310-559-X*) CountryWatch.

Peru Country Studies: Area Handbook. 4th ed. Ed. by Rex A. Hudson. LC 93-19676. (Area Handbook Ser.). 1993. 23.00 (*0-8444-0774-7*) Lib Congress.

Peru Earthquake of October, 1974. D. F. Moran et al. 85p. 1975. pap. 12.00 (*0-318-16327-6*) Earthquake Eng.

Peru, 1890-1897. Rosemary Thorp & Geoffrey Bertram. Ed. by Stuart Bruchey. (Columbia Economic History of the Modern World Ser.). 1978. text 69.00 (*0-231-03433-4*) Col U Pr.

***Peru Foreign Policy & Government Guide.** Contrib. by Global Investment & Business Center, Inc. Staff. (World Foreign Policy & Government Library: Vol. 129). (Illus.). 350p. 1999. pap. 99.00 (*0-7397-3627-2*) Intl Business Pubns.

***Peru Foreign Policy & Government Guide.** Global Investment & Business Center, Inc. Staff. (World Foreign Policy & Government Library: Vol. 129). (Illus.). 350p. 2000. 99.95 (*0-7397-3833-X*) Intl Business Pubns.

***Peru Handbook.** 2nd ed. Alan Murphy. (Footprint Handbooks Ser.). (Illus.). 512p. 1999. pap. 17.95 (*0-8442-2187-2*, 21872) NTC Contemp Pub Co.

Peru in Crisis: Challenges to a New Government. Washington Office on Latin America Staff. 41p. (Orig.). (C). 1990. pap. text 6.00 (*0-929513-16-9*) WOLA.

Peru in Crisis: Dictatorship or Democracy? Joseph S. Tulchin. LC 94-14646. (Woodrow Wilson Center Current Studies on Latin America). 200p. 1994. pap. text 11.95 (*1-55587-543-2*) L Rienner.

Peru in Focus: A Guide to the People, Politics & Culture. Jane H. De Diaz-Limaco. (In Focus Guides Ser.). (Illus.). 100p. 1998. pap. 12.95 (*1-56656-232-5*) Interlink Pub.

Peru in Peril: The Economy & Human Rights, 1985-1987. Washington Office on Latin America Staff. 38p. (Orig.). 1987. pap. 5.00 (*0-929513-03-7*) WOLA.

Peru in Pictures. Lerner Publications, Department of Geography Staff. (Visual Geography Ser.). (Illus.). 64p. (YA). (gr. 5 up). 1987. lib. bdg. 19.95 (*0-8225-1820-1*, Lerner Publctns) Lerner Pub.

***Peru Investment & Business Guide.** Global Investment & Business Center, Inc. Staff. (Global Investment & Business Guide Library: Vol. 135). (Illus.). 2000. pap. 99.95 (*0-7397-1833-9*) Intl Business Pubns.

Peru Investment & Business Guide: Economy, Export-Import, Business & Investment Climate, Business Contacts. Contrib. by Russian Information & Business Center, Inc. Staff. (Russia, NIS & Emerging Markets Investment & Business Library-98). (Illus.). 350p. 1998. pap. 99.00 (*1-57751-900-0*) Intl Business Pubns.

***Peru Investment & Business Guide: Export-Import, Investment & Business Opportunities.** International Business Publications, USA Staff & Global Investment Center, USA Staff. (World Investment & Business Guide Library-99: Vol. 135). (Illus.). 350p. 1999. pap. 99.95 (*0-7397-0330-7*) Intl Business Pubns.

Peru, 1965: Notes on a Guerrilla Experience. Hector Bejar-Rivera. Tr. by William Rose. LC 75-105309. 142p. 1970. reprint ed. pap. 44.10 (*0-608-08300-3*, 205617400054) Bks Demand.

Peru Reader: History, Culture, Politics. Ed. by Orin Starn et al. LC 94-42125. (Illus.). 552p. 1995. text 59.95 (*0-8223-1601-3*); pap. text 19.95 (*0-8223-1617-X*) Duke.

Peru, the People & Culture. Bobbie Kalman. (Lands, Peoples, & Cultures Ser.). (J). 1994. 13.40 (*0-606-08006-6*) Turtleback.

Perugia Consensus Conference on Antiemetic Therapy. Ed. by R. J. Gralla et al. LC 98-22555. 200p. 1998. 54.00 (*3-540-64076-2*) Spr-Verlag.

Peru's APRA: Parties, Politics, & the Elusive Quest for Democracy. Carol Graham. LC 92-240. 267p. 1992. lib. bdg. 43.00 (*1-55587-306-5*) L Rienner.

Peru's Indian Peoples & the Challenge of Spanish Conquest: Huamanga to 1640. 2nd ed. Steve J. Stern. LC 93-31326. 350p. 1993. pap. 19.95 (*0-299-14184-5*) U of Wis Pr.

Peru's Path to Recovery: A Plan for Economic Stabilization & Growth. Ed. by Carlos Paredes & Jeffrey D. Sachs. 336p. 1991. 44.95 (*0-8157-6914-8*); pap. 19.95 (*0-8157-6913-X*) Brookings.

Peru's "Shining Path" Martin Koppel. 35p. 1993. pap. 3.50 (*0-87348-781-8*) Pathfinder NY.

Perush Rabbenu Perahyah Ben Nissim Al Masskheth Shabbath. Perahyah B. Nissim. Ed. by Boruch Hirschfeld. (HEB.). 339p. (C). 1988. 14.00 (*1-881255-04-2*) OFEQ Inst.

Perush Rashi 'al ha-Torah see Rashi's Torah Commentary: Religious, Philosophical, Ethical & Educational Insights

Perutilis Logica. Saxonia D. Albertus. (Documenta Semiotica Ser.: Vol. 6). (GER.). 103p. 1974. reprint ed. write for info. (*3-487-05253-9*) G Olms Pubs.

Peruvian Anchoveta & Its Upwelling Ecosystem: Three Decades of Change. Ed. by Daniel Pauly & I. Tsukayama. (ICLARM Studies & Reviews: No. 15). 351p. 1987. 36.00 (*971-10-2234-6*, Pub. by ICLARM) Intl Spec Bk.

Peruvian & Other South American Manuscripts in the Rosenbach Foundation: 1536-1914. Ed. by David M. Szewczyk. LC 78-10353. (Illus.). 190p. 1977. 15.00 (*0-939084-06-6*) R Mus & Lib.

Peruvian Antiquities. Francis L. Hawks. (Notable American Authors Ser.). 1992. reprint ed. lib. bdg. 75.00 (*0-7812-3033-0*); reprint ed. lib. bdg. 75.00 (*0-7812-3034-9*) Rprt Serv.

Peruvian Contexts of Change. William W. Stein. 270p. 1984. 39.95 (*0-88738-013-1*) Transaction Pubs.

Peruvian Cumbrous Bowls. fac. ed. Isabel Kelly. (University of California Publications in American Archaeology & Ethnology: Vol. 24(6)). (Illus.). 27p. (C). 1930. reprint ed. pap. text 3.13 (*1-55567-714-2*) Coyote Press.

Peruvian Democracy under Economic Stress: An Account of the Belaunde Administration, 1963-1968. Godard P. Kuczynski. LC 76-24296. 323p. 1977. reprint ed. pap. 100.20 (*0-7837-9364-2*, 206010700004) Bks Demand.

Peruvian Economy & Structural Adjustment: Past, Present, & Future. Ed. by Efrain Gonzales de Olarte. 376p. (C). 1996. pap. 26.95 (*0-935501-97-5*, Pub. by U Miami N-S Ctr) L Rienner.

Peruvian Experiment: Continuity & Change under Military Rule. Ed. by Abraham F. Lowenthal. LC 75-2998. 502p. reprint ed. pap. 155.70 (*0-8357-6254-8*, 203465600090) Bks Demand.

Peruvian Experiment Reconsidered. Ed. by Cynthia McClintock & Abraham F. Lowenthal. LC 82-61377. 464p. 1983. reprint ed. pap. 143.90 (*0-608-03322-7*, 206403400008) Bks Demand.

Peruvian Industrial Labor Force. David Chaplin. LC 66-11965. 342p. 1967. reprint ed. pap. 106.10 (*0-7837-9315-4*, 206005500004) Bks Demand.

Peruvian Labyrinth. Ed. by Maxwell A. Cameron & Philip Mauceri. LC 96-42209. 288p. 1997. 55.00 (*0-271-01660-4*); pap. 19.95 (*0-271-01661-2*) Pa St U Pr.

Peruvian Literature: A Bibliography of Secondary Sources. David W. Foster. LC 81-6957. 324p. 1981. lib. bdg. 59.95 (*0-313-23097-8*, FPL/, Greenwood Pr) Greenwood.

Peruvian Nationalism: A Corporatist Revolution. Ed. by David Chaplin. LC 73-85099. (Third World Ser.). 600p. 1976. 44.95 (*0-87855-077-1*); pap. 24.95 (*0-87855-573-0*) Transaction Pubs.

Peruvian Population Control Program: Hearing Before the Subcommittee on International Operations & Human Rights of the Committee on International Relations, House of Representatives, 105th Congress, Second Session, February 25, 1998. LC 98-176159. iii, 190p. 1998. write for info. (*0-16-056586-3*) USGPO.

Peruvian Pottery. George Bankes. (Ethnography Ser.: No. 15). (Illus.). 72p. pap. 10.50 (*0-7478-0013-8*, Pub. by Shire Pubns) Parkwest Pubns.

Peruvian Prehistory. Ed. by Richard W. Keatinge. (Illus.). 384p. 1988. text 69.95 (*0-521-25560-0*) Cambridge U Pr.

Peruvian Prehistory. Ed. by Richard W. Keatinge. (Illus.). 384p. 1988. pap. text 25.95 (*0-521-27555-5*) Cambridge U Pr.

Peruvian Psychiatric Hospital. William W. Stein. 324p. (C). 1995. lib. bdg. 48.50 (*0-7618-0093-X*) U Pr of Amer.

Peruvian Puzzle: A Twentieth Century Fund Paper. Felipe O. DeZevallos. 85p. 1989. 18.95 (*0-87078-233-9*); pap. 8.95 (*0-87078-232-0*) Century Foundation.

Peruvian Textile Designs. Caren Caraway. (International Design Library). (Illus.). 48p. 1983. pap. 5.95 (*0-88045-026-6*) Stemmer Hse.

Peruvian Textiles. Jane Feltham. (Ethnography Ser.). (Illus.). 72p. 1989. pap. 10.50 (*0-7478-0014-6*, Pub. by Shire Pubns) Parkwest Pubns.

Peruvian Upwelling Ecosystem: Dynamics & Interactions. Ed. by Daniel Pauly et al. 438p. 1989. pap. 27.00 (*971-10-2247-8*, Pub. by ICLARM) Intl Spec Bk.

Perv: Stories. Rabih Alameddine. LC 99-25993. 208p. 1999. text 21.00 (*0-312-20041-2*, Picador USA) St Martin.

***Perv - A Love Story.** Jerry Stahl. 2001. pap. write for info. (*0-688-17787-5*, Perennial) HarperTrade.

Perv--a Love Story. Jerry Stahl. LC 99-21960. 352p. 1999. 24.00 (*0-688-17094-3*, Wm Morrow) Morrow Avon.

Pervaporation & Vapor Permeation, No. C-127R. 170p. 1993. 2675.00 (*0-89336-972-1*) BCC.

Pervaporation Membrane Separation Processes. Ed. by R. Y. Huang. (Membrane Science & Technology Ser.: No. 1). 550p. 1991. 228.50 (*0-444-88227-8*) Elsevier.

Pervasive Developmental Disorders: Finding a Diagnosis & Getting Help. Mitzi Waltz. Ed. by Linda Lamb. LC 99-23708. (Patient-Centered Guides Ser.). (Illus.). 584p. 1999. pap. 24.95 (*1-56592-530-0*) OReilly & Assocs.

Pervasive Image: The Role of Analogy in the Poetry of Ausias March. Robert Archer. LC 85-13360. (Purdue University Monographs in Romance Languages: No. 17). xii, 220p. 1985. pap. 54.00 (*0-915027-56-9*) J Benjamins Pubng Co.

Pervasive Prejudice. Ian Ayres. 1997. 39.95 (*0-226-03351-1*); pap. text 24.95 (*0-226-03353-8*) U Ch Pr.

***Pervasive Role of Science, Technology & Health in Foreign Policy: Imperatives for the Department of State.** National Research Council Staff. 124p. 1999. pap. 29.00 (*0-309-06785-5*) Natl Acad Pr.

Pervasive Subjects. Bill Rees & Saleem Sheikh. 250p. 1993. 34.00 (*1-85431-298-7*, Pub. by Blackstone Pr) Gaunt.

Perverse Christianity: A Ministry of Death. P. J. Logan. 170p. 1995. pap. 10.95 (*0-9649074-0-2*) Uniquely Christian.

Perverse Desire & the Ambiguous Icon. Allen S. Weiss. LC 93-50160. 158p. (C). 1994. pap. text 16.95 (*0-7914-2156-2*) State U NY Pr.

Perverse Desire & the Ambiguous Icon. Allen S. Weiss. LC 93-50160. 158p. (C). 1994. text 49.50 (*0-7914-2155-4*) State U NY Pr.

Perverse Economics of Health Care & How We Can Fix It. David R. Henderson. LC 94-34925. (Essays in Public Policy Ser.: No. 54). 1994. pap. 5.00 (*0-8179-5592-5*) Hoover Inst Pr.

Perverse Gaze of Sympathy: Sadomasochistic Sentiments form Clarissa to Rescue 911. Laura Hinton. LC 99-28288. (SUNY Series in Feminist Criticism & Theory). (Illus.). 320p. (C). 1999. text 57.50 (*0-7914-4339-6*, Suny Pr); pap. text 18.95 (*0-7914-4340-X*, Suny Pr) State U NY Pr.

Perverse History of the Human Heart. Milad Doueihi. LC 97-27437. (Illus.). 256p. 1997. 35.00 (*0-674-66325-X*); pap. 18.95 (*0-674-66327-6*) HUP.

Perverse Incentives: The Neglect of Social Technology in the Public Sector. Theodore Caplow. LC 94-2981. 176p. 1994. 52.95 (*0-275-94911-7*, Praeger Pubs); pap. 16.95 (*0-275-94933-8*, Praeger Pubs) Greenwood.

Perverse Mind: Eugene O'Neill's Struggle with Closure. Barbara Voglino. LC 99-26439. 168p. 1999. 32.50 (*0-8386-3833-3*) Fairleigh Dickinson.

Perverse Person's ABC. Sally Maltby. (Illus.). 64p. 1998. 15.95 (*1-85626-270-7*, Pub. by Cathie Kyle) Trafalgar.

Perverse Serenity. Robyn Rowland. 96p. 1993. pap. 12.95 (*1-875559-13-2*, Pub. by SpiniFex Pr) LPC InBook.

Perverse Spectators. Janet Staiger. text 55.00 (*0-8147-8138-1*); pap. text 18.50 (*0-8147-8139-X*) NYU Pr.

***Perverse Subsidies: How Misused Tax Dollars Harm the Environment & the Economy.** Norman Myers & Jennifer Kent. (Illus.). 240p. 2000. 40.00 (*1-55963-834-6*, Shearwater Bks); pap. 20.00 (*1-55963-835-4*, Shearwater Bks) Island Pr.

Perverse Supply Response in Agriculture: The Importance of Produced Means of Production & Uncertainty. Adam Ozanne. 188p. 1992. 82.95 (*1-85628-375-5*, Pub. by Avebry) Ashgate Pub Co.

Perversion: The Erotic Form of Hatred. Robert J. Stoller. 258p. 1994. pap. text 31.00 (*0-946439-20-6*, Pub. by H Karnac Bks Ltd) Other Pr LLC.

Perversion: The Erotic Form of Hatred. Robert J. Stoller. LC 86-17296. 256p. reprint ed. pap. 79.40 (*0-8357-7856-8*, 203623300002) Bks Demand.

Perversion & Utopia: A Study in Psychoanalysis & Critical Theory. Joel Whitebook. (Studies in Contemporary German Social Thought). (Illus.). 368p. 1995. 35.00 (*0-262-23178-6*) MIT Pr.

Perversion & Utopia: A Study in Psychoanalysis & Critical Theory. Joel Whitebook. (Studies in Contemporary German Social Thought). (Illus.). 360p. 1996. pap. text 17.50 (*0-262-73117-7*) MIT Pr.

Perversion of Autonomy. Willard Gaylin & Bruce Jennings. 272p. 1996. 25.00 (*0-684-82784-0*) Free Pr.

***Perversion of Autonomy: The Proper Uses of Coercion & Constraints in a Liberal Society.** Willard Gaylin & Bruce Jennings. 270p. 1999. reprint ed. text 25.00 (*0-7881-6633-6*) DIANE Pub.

Perversion of Submission: Idols in the Christian Church. Joan Erickson. LC 98-93449. vi, 489p. 1998. pap. 18.50 (*0-9665846-0-0*) Mrcle Lve Min.

Perversions of the Sex Instinct. Albert Moll. LC 72-11289.Tr. of Die/Contraere Sexualempfindung. (ENG.). reprint ed. 38.50 (*0-404-57482-3*) AMS Pr.

Perversity. Ed. by Judith Squires. (New Formations Nineteen Ser.: No. 19). 192p. (C). 1993. pap. 19.95 (*0-85315-760-X*, Pub. by Lawrence & Wishart) NYU Pr.

Pervert. Catherine Lord. (Illus.). 48p. (Orig.). 1995. pap. 16.50 (*1-884355-01-3*) U CA Fine Arts.

Perverted Adult Survey Game. Mark Childs. 160p. 1991. per. 7.95 (*0-8187-0145-5*) Harlo Press.

Perverted Ideal in Dostoevsky's "The Devils" Nancy Anderson. LC 96-5859. (Middlebury Studies in Russian Language & Literature: Vol. 8). VIII, 173p. (C). 1997. text 41.95 (*0-8204-3318-7*) P Lang Pubng.

Perverted Love. Barbara H. Seguin. 62p. 1987. pap. 3.75 (*0-88144-109-0*) Christian Pub.

Perverts by Official Order: The Campaign Against Homosexuals by the United States Navy. Ed. & Intro. by Lawrence R. Murphy. LC 87-33452. (Journal of Homosexuality Ser.: No. 1). (Illus.). 340p. 1988. pap. text 14.95 (*0-918393-44-2*, Harrington Park) Haworth Pr.

Perverts by Official Order: The Campaign Against Homosexuals by the United States Navy. Ed. by Lawrence R. Murphy. LC 90-4451. (Journal of Homosexuality: No. 1). (Illus.). 340p. 1988. text 49.95 (*0-86656-708-9*) Haworth Pr.

Pervin's Science of Personality. Pervin. 256p. 1996. pap. text, teacher ed. 25.00 (*0-471-16082-2*) Wiley.

Pervisions: Deviant Readings by Mandy Merck. Ed. by Mandy Merck. (Illus.). 224p. (C). (gr. 13). 1993. pap. 17.99 (*0-415-90792-6*, B0639) Routledge.

Perv's Guide to the Net. Cyberspace Consortium Staff. 316p. (Orig.). 1996. mass mkt. 6.95 (*1-56333-471-2*, Rhinoceros) Masquerade.

Pervye Shagi K Fizicheskomu Sovershenstvu see First Steps on the Ski Trail: How to Teach Children to Cross-Country Ski

***Pery Government & Business Contacts Handbook: Strategic Government & Business Contacts for Conducting succesful Business, Export-Import & Investment Activity.** International Business Publications, USA Staff & Global Investment Center, USA Staff. (World Export-Import & Business Library: 109). (Illus.). 250p. 2000. pap. 99.95 (*0-7397-6098-X*) Intl Business Pubns.

Pesach. Yaffa Ganz. (ArtScroll Youth Holiday Ser.). (YA). 1991. 8.99 (*0-89906-981-9*) Mesorah Pubns.

Pesach: A Holiday Funtext. Judy Bin-Nun et al. (Illus.). 32p. (Orig.). (J). (gr. 1-3). 1983. pap. text 5.00 (*0-8074-0161-7*, 101310) UAHC.

Pesach - One, Two, Three. A. Backman. 1992. 10.99 (*0-89906-988-6*); pap. 7.99 (*0-89906-989-4*) Mesorah Pubns.

Pesach - Passover - Its History, Observance & Significance. M. Stein & M. Lieber. 1994. 17.99 (*0-89906-447-7*); pap. 14.99 (*0-89906-446-9*) Mesorah Pubns.

Pesach Haggadah with Ideas & Insights of the SEFAS EMES. Yosef Stern. 18.99 (*0-89906-398-5*, HSEH); pap. 14.99 (*0-89906-399-3*, HSEP) Mesorah Pubns.

Pesach, Pesach, Pesach Time Is Here see Kadima Hagim Series

Pesach-Shavos see Festivals in Halachah

***Pesach with the Cohen Family.** Menucha Fuchs. (Illus.). 48p. (J). (gr. k-5). 2000. pap. 4.95 (*1-880582-55-4*) Judaica Pr.

Peschim, No. 1. Schottenstein. 47.99 (*0-89906-714-X*, TPE1) Mesorah Pubns.

Pesadilla En Mi Armario. Mercer Mayer. 1996. 12.70 (*0-606-10528-X*, Pub. by Turtleback) Demco.

Pesadilla en 3 Dimensiones. R. L. Stine, pseud. (Coleccion Fantasmas De Fear Street/Ghosts of Fear Street Ser.: No. 4).Tr. of Nightmare in 3-D. (SPA.). (J). (gr. 4-7). 1997. pap. text 8.50 (*950-04-1658-1*) Emece.

Pesah Is Coming. Hyman Chanover & Alice Chanover. (Holiday Series of Picture Storybooks). (Illus.). (J). (gr. k-2). 1956. 5.95 (*0-8381-0713-3*, 10-713) USCJE.

Pesah Is Here. Hyman Chanover & Alice Chanover. (Holiday Series of Picture Storybooks). (Illus.). (J). (gr. k-2). 1956. 5.95 (*0-8381-0714-1*) USCJE.

Pesahim, 2 vols. (ENG & HEB.). 30.00 (*0-910218-55-2*) Bennet Pub.

Pesante. Raynor Carroll. 4p. 1996. pap. 3.95 (*1-891188-11-9*) Batterie Music.

Pesantren Tradition: The Role of the Kyai in the Maintenance of Traditional Islam in Java. Zamakhsyari Dhofier. (Illus.). xxxii, 254p. 1999. pap. 19.95 (*1-881044-19-X*) ASU Prog SE Asian.

Pesar de Todo Dios Sigue Siendo Amor. Cecilio Arrastia.Tr. of God Is Still Love. (SPA.). 176p. 1994. 7.99 (*0-89922-487-3*, C063-4873) Caribe Betania.

Pesar de Todo, 1997. Josefina Gonzalez. (SPA.). 1997. pap. 9.95 (*0-89729-813-6*) Ediciones.

PESC '95 Record 26th Annual IEEE Power Electronics Specialists Conference. IEEE Staff. LC 80-646675. 1995. pap. text. write for info. (*0-7803-2730-6*); lib. bdg. write for info. (*0-7803-2731-4*, 95CH35818); mic. film. write for info. (*0-7803-2732-2*) Inst Electrical.

P

PESC '96 Record 27th Annual IEEE Power Electronics Specialists Conference. IEEE (Power Electronics Society) Staff. Ed. by IEEE (Institute of Electrical & Electronics Engine. LC 80-646675. 1400p. 1996. pap. text 204.00 (*0-7803-3500-7*, 96CH35962); lib. bdg. 204.00 (*0-7803-3501-5*, 96CB35962); fiche 204.00 (*0-7803-3502-3*, 96CM35962) Inst Electrical.

Pesca de Nessa. Nancy Luenn. (J). 1997. per. 6.99 (*0-689-81467-4*) Aladdin.

Pesca de Nessa. Nancy Luenn. (SPA., Illus.). 32p. (J). (gr. k-3). 1994. mass mkt. 15.95 (*0-689-31977-0*) Atheneum Yung Read.

Pesca de Nessa. Nancy Luenn. 1997. 12.19 (*0-606-12752-6*, Pub. by Turtleback) Demco.

Pesca de Nessa Nessas. Nancy Luenn. (SPA.). (J). 1996. pap. 4.95 (*0-689-31978-9*) S&S Bks Yung.

Pesebre. Gordon Stowell & P. Mara. (Serie Libros de Carton - Board Bks.).Tr. of Manger. (SPA.). 24p. (J). 1991. bds. 4.99 (*1-56063-311-5*, 490449) Editorial Unilit.

Pesharim: Qumran Interpretations of Biblical Books. Maurya P. Horgan. Ed. by Bruce Vawter. LC 78-12910. (Catholic Biblical Quarterly Monographs: No. 8). ix, 308p. 1979. pap. 6.00 (*0-915170-07-8*) Catholic Bibl Assn.

Peshat & Derash: Plain & Applied Meaning in Rabbinic Exegesis. David W. Halivni. 272p. 1998. reprint ed. pap. 19.95 (*0-19-511571-6*) OUP.

Peshat & Derash: Plain & Applied Meaning in Rabbinic Exegesis. David W. Halivni. 264p. 1991. text 65.00 (*0-19-506065-2*) OUP.

Peshawar Nights. rev. ed. Tr. by Charles A. Campbell & Hamid Quinlan from PER. 630p. Date not set. pap. 14.95 (*1-890847-00-3*) Texas Islam.

Peshawar Nights. 2nd rev. ed. Tr. by Charles A. Campbell & Hamid Quinlan from PER. 630p. Date not set. reprint ed. 24.95 (*1-890847-01-1*) Texas Islam.

Peshchera Neozhidannostei (The Fun House) Intro. by Emil Draitser & Vassily Aksyonov. LC 83-63368. (RUS.). 160p. 1984. pap. 7.95 (*0-911971-03-3*) Effect Pub.

Peshine Family in Europe & America: Notes & Suggestions for a Genealogical Tree from the Beginning of the 14th Century to the Present Day, with Some Biographical Sketches & Much Data Relating to the Ball, Mulford & Pye Families. John H. Peshine. 109p. 1996. reprint ed. pap. 19.00 (*0-8328-5328-3*); reprint ed. lib. bdg. 29.00 (*0-8328-5327-5*) Higginson Bk Co.

Peshita Vol. 1, Pt. 5: The Old Testament in Syriac According to the Peshita Version. Ed. by J. A. Emerton. LC 96-46665. (Vetus Testamentum, Supplements Ser.: No. 66). (Illus.). 392p. 1997. 143.50 (*90-04-10687-1*) Brill Academic Pubs.

Peshitta: Its Early Text & History: Papers Read at the Peshitta Symposium Held at Leiden 30-31 August 1988. Ed. by P. B. Dirksen & M. J. Mulder. (Monographs of the Peshitta Institute Leiden: Vol. IV). (Illus.). x, 310p. 1988. 82.00 (*90-04-08769-9*) Brill Academic Pubs.

***Peshitta & the Versions: A Study of the Peshitta Variants in Joshua 1-5 in Relation to Their Equivalents in the Ancient Versions.** Johann E. Erbes. (Studia Semitica Upsaliensia: Vol. 16). (Illus.). 374p. 1999. pap. 62.50 (*91-554-4459-8*, Pub. by Uppsala Univ Acta Univ Uppsaliensis) Coronet Bks.

Peshitta As a Translation: Proceedings; Peshitta Symposium (2nd: 1993: Leiden, Netherlands) Ed. by P. B. Dirksen & A. Van Der Kooij. LC 95-18530. (Monographs of the Peshitta Institute Leiden: Vol. 8). vii, 240p. 1995. 94.00 (*90-04-10351-1*) Brill Academic Pubs.

Peshitta of Exodus: The Development of Its Text in the Course of Fifteen Centuries. M. D. Koster. (Studia Semitica Neerlandica: Vol. 19). xix, 650p. 1977. text 145.00 (*90-232-1503-6*, Pub. by Van Gorcum) Eisenbrauns.

Peshitta of Leviticus. David J. Lane. LC 94-569. (Monographs of the Peshitta Institute Leiden: Vol. 6). xv, 184p. 1994. 92.50 (*90-04-10020-2*) Brill Academic Pubs.

Peshitta of the Twelve Prophets. Anthony Gelston. 232p. 1987. 59.00 (*0-19-826179-9*) OUP.

Peshitta to the Book of Job: Critically Investigated with Introduction, Translation, Commentary & Summary. Gosta Rignell. 382p. (Orig.). 1994. pap. 59.50 (*91-88034-24-0*) Coronet Bks.

Peshitta Version of the Pentateuch & Early Jewish Exegesis. Yeshayahu Maori. (HEB.). 403p. 1995. text 24.00 (*965-223-874-0*, Pub. by Magnes Pr) Eisenbrauns.

Pesikta Rabbati: Homiletical Discourses for Festal Days & Special Sabbaths, 2 vols. Tr. by William G. Braude. LC 68-27748. (Judaica Ser.: No. 18). (Illus.). 1968. 120.00 (*0-300-01071-0*) Yale U Pr.

Pesimismo. Eduardo De Acha. LC 83-82918. (SPA.). 112p. (Orig.). 1984. pap. 5.00 (*0-89729-340-1*) Ediciones.

Pesky Plants. Thor Kommedahl. Ed. by Diane Peltz. (Illus.). 70p. (Orig.). 1989. pap. 6.95 (*0-9623116-7-7*) U MN Ext Serv.

Peso Pluma: Ensayos Periodisticos, 1988-1994. Edgardo S. Santaliz. (Aqui y Ahora Ser.). 138p. 1996. pap. 6.95 (*0-8477-0267-7*) U of PR Pr.

Pessach-Haggadah. fac. limited ed. Comment by Ulf Haxen. (Codices Selecti A Ser.: Vol. LXXXIX). (GER., Illus.). 52p. 1989. lthr. 1321.00 (*3-201-01463-X*, Pub. by Akademische Druck-und) Balogh.

Pessimism. Joe Bailey. 200p. 1988. text 47.50 (*0-415-00247-8*); pap. text 14.95 (*0-415-00248-6*) Routledge.

Pessimism & Contemporary Bengali Literature. Diplab Chakraborti. 1985. 12.00 (*0-8364-1459-4*) S Asia.

Pessimism of Thomas Hardy: A Social Study. G. W. Sherman. LC 74-4982. 518p. 1976. 48.50 (*0-8386-1582-1*) Fairleigh Dickinson.

Pessimist's Guide to History. Stuart B. Flexner & Doris Flexner. 400p. (Orig.). 1992. pap. 12.00 (*0-380-76236-6*, Avon Bks) Morrow Avon.

***Pessimist's Guide To History: An Irresistible Compendium Of Catastrophes, Barbarities, Massacres And Mayhem From The Big Bang To The New Millennium.** Stuart Flexner. (Illus.). 448p. 2000. pap. 14.00 (*0-06-095745-X*, Perennial) HarperTrade.

Pessimist's Handbook: A Collection of Popular Essays. Arthur Schopenhauer. Ed. by Hazel E. Barnes. LC 64-11583. 848p. reprint ed. pap. 200.00 (*0-608-30594-4*, 202247600027) Bks Demand.

Pessimist's Journal of Very, Very Bad Days. Jess M. Brallier & R. P. McDonough. 1989. pap. 9.95 (*0-316-10600-3*) Little.

Pest Animals of Australia. George Wilson et al. (Illus.). 64p. (Orig.). 1993. pap. 14.95 (*0-86417-447-0*, Pub. by Kangaroo Pr) Seven Hills Bk.

Pest Control. (Fix-It-Yourself Ser.). (Illus.). 144p. 1991. 18.60 (*0-8094-7404-2*); lib. bdg. 24.60 (*0-8094-7405-0*) Time-Life.

Pest Control. Bill Fitzhugh. LC 96-28796. 320p. 1998. mass mkt. 5.99 (*0-380-78868-3*, Avon Bks) Morrow Avon.

Pest Control. Jerry Leppart. LC 99-47726. 224p. 2000. pap. 14.95 (*1-880090-95-3*) Galde Pr.

Pest Control: New Studies in Biology. 2nd ed. H. F. Van Emden. (Illus.). 127p. 1991. pap. text 17.95 (*0-521-42788-6*, A3832) Cambridge U Pr.

Pest Control: Operations & Systems Analysis in Fruit Fly Management. Ed. by M. Mangel et al. (NATO ASI Series G Ecological Sciences: No. 11). xii, 465p. 1986. 158.95 (*0-387-16088-4*) Spr-Verlag.

Pest Control Aide. Jack Rudman. (Career Examination Ser.: C-2030). 1994. pap. 23.95 (*0-8373-2030-5*) Nat Learn.

Pest Control in the School Environment: Adopting Integrated Pest Management. (Illus.). 43p. 1996. reprint ed. pap. text 15.00 (*0-7881-3161-3*) DIANE Pub.

Pest Control Strategies for the Future. National Research Council, Agricultural Board Staf. 383p. reprint ed. pap. 118.80 (*0-608-13709-X*, 2055289) Bks Demand.

Pest Control Strategies for the Future. National Research Council, Agricultural Board Staff. LC SB0950.N29. 383p. 1972. reprint ed. pap. 118.80 (*0-608-09962-7*, 205528900013) Bks Demand.

Pest Control Supervisor. Jack Rudman. (Career Examination Ser.: C-3094). 1994. pap. 29.95 (*0-8373-3094-7*) Nat Learn.

Pest Control with Enhanced Environmental Safety. Ed. by Stephen O. Duke et al. LC 93-12098. (ACS Symposium Ser.: No. 524). (Illus.). 358p. 1993. text 95.00 (*0-8412-2638-5*, Pub. by Am Chemical) OUP.

Pest ID Manual. Date not set. write for info. (*1-56918-280-9*) Visual EP.

Pest ID Student Guide. Date not set. student ed. write for info. (*1-56918-282-5*) Visual EP.

Pest ID Supplement Student Guide. Date not set. student ed. write for info. (*1-56918-283-3*) Visual EP.

Pest Lepidopters of Europe. David J. Carter. (Entomologica Ser.). 1984. text 303.50 (*90-6193-504-0*) Kluwer Academic.

Pest Management: A Directory of Information Sources, Vol. 3. C. J. Hamilton. 300p. write for info. (*0-85198-826-1*) C A B Intl.

Pest Management: Biologically Based Technologies: Proceedings of the Beltsville Symposium XVIII, Agricultural Research Service, U. S. Department of Agriculture, Beltsville, Maryland, May 2-6, 1993. Ed. by Robert D. Lumsden & James L. Vaughn. LC 93-26355. 436p. 1993. text 120.00 (*0-8412-2726-8*, Pub. by Am Chemical) OUP.

Pest Management - A Directory of Information Sources: Animal Health, Vol. 2. C. J. Hamilton. 296p. 1995. text 75.00 (*0-85198-743-5*) OUP.

Pest Management - A Directory of Information Sources Vol. 1: Crop Protection, Vol. 1. C. J. Hamilton. 352p. 1991. text 80.00 (*0-85198-675-7*) OUP.

***Pest Management & Food Production: Looking to the Future.** Montague Yudelman et al. LC 99-208200. 1998. write for info. (*0-89629-629-6*) Intl Food Policy.

Pest Management in Cotton. Ed. by M. B. Green & D. J. Lyon. 1989. text 112.50 (*0-470-21451-1*) P-H.

Pest Management in Rice: Published on Behalf of the Society of Chemical Industry. Ed. by B. T. Grayson et al. 536p. 1990. 117.00 (*1-85166-514-5*) Elsevier.

Pest Management, Insect Sex Attractants & Other Behavior-Controlling Chemicals. Ed. by Morton Beroza. LC 76-1873. (ACS Symposium Ser.: Vol. 23). 200p. 1976. reprint ed. pap. 62.00 (*0-608-03553-X*, 206427200008) Bks Demand.

Pest Management with Insect Sex Attractants. Ed. by Morton Beroza. LC 76-1873. (ACS Symposium Ser.: No. 23). 1976. 27.95 (*0-8412-0308-3*) Am Chemical.

Pest-Repellent Plants. Penny Woodward. (Illus.). 128p. pap. 12.95 (*1-86447-028-3*, Pub. by Hyland Hse) Seven Hills Bk.

Pest Resistance to Pesticides. Ed. by G. P. Georghiou & Tetsuo Saito. LC 82-22369. 822p. 1983. 135.00 (*0-306-41246-2*, Plenum Trade) Perseus Pubng.

Pestalozzi. Compiled by Lewis F. Anderson. LC 75-130984. 1975. reprint ed. 14.00 (*0-404-00357-5*) AMS Pr.

Pestalozzi. Johann H. Pestalozzi. Ed. by Lewis F. Anderson. LC 73-10877. 283p. 1975. reprint ed. lib. bdg. 35.00 (*0-8371-7046-X*, PEP, Greenwood Pr) Greenwood.

***Pestalozzi & Education.** Gerald L. Gutek. 178p. 1999. pap. 12.95 (*1-57766-091-9*) Waveland Pr.

Pestalozzi-Bibliographie, 3 vols., Set. August Israel. 1970. reprint ed. write for info. (*0-318-71807-3*) G Olms Pubs.

Pestalozzian Music Teacher. Lowell Mason. 1977. lib. bdg. 59.95 (*0-8490-2425-0*) Gordon Pr.

Pestalozzi's Educational Writings. Ed. by J. A. Green. 1972. 59.95 (*0-8490-0822-0*) Gordon Pr.

Pestalozzi's Educational Writings, 2. Johann H. Pestalozzi. Tr. by John A. Green from GER. LC 77-72191. (Contributions to the History of Psychology Ser.: Vol. II, Pt. B, Psychometrics). 424p. 1977. reprint ed. lib. bdg. 85.00 (*0-313-26937-8*, U6937, Greenwood Pr) Greenwood.

Peste. Albert Camus. (FRE.). 1972. pap. 10.95 (*0-8288-3668-X*, F90691) Fr & Eur.

Peste. Albert Camus. (FRE.). (C). 1947. pap. 9.95 (*0-8442-1765-4*, VF1765-4) NTC Contemp Pub Co.

Peste. Albert Camus. (Folio Ser.: No. 42). (FRE.). pap. 9.25 (*2-07-036042-3*) Schoenhof.

Peste. Albert Camus. 1942. write for info. (*0-318-63575-5*, F90692) Fr & Eur.

Peste, Camus: Critical Monographs in English. Edward J. Hughes. 1993. pap. 32.00 (*0-85261-244-3*, Pub. by Univ of Glasgow) St Mut.

Peste y la Colera. Homer. (Fondo 2000 Ser.). (SPA.). pap. 2.99 (*968-16-5051-4*, Pub. by Fondo) Continental Bk.

Pesticidal Formulations Research: Physical & Colloidal Chemical Aspects: A Symposium Co-Sponsored by the Division of Agricultural & Food Chemistry & the Division of Colloid & Surface Chemistry at the 153rd National Meeting, Miami Beach, FL, April 13-14, 1967. American Chemical Society Staff. LC 74-81252. (Advances in Chemistry Ser.: No. 86). (Illus.). 222p. 1969. reprint ed. pap. 68.90 (*0-608-06817-9*, 206701400009) Bks Demand.

Pesticidal Pollution of Environment & Control: An Annotated Bibliography. Ed. by K. V. Paliwal. 594p. 1994. pap. 375.00 (*81-85880-23-9*, Pub. by Print Hse) St Mut.

Pesticide Alert: A Guide to Pesticides in Fruits & Vegetables. Lawrie Mott & Karen Snyder. 128p. 1987. 6.95 (*0-318-39812-5*) Natl Resources Defense Coun.

Pesticide Alert: A Guide to Pesticides in Fruits & Vegetables. Lawrie Mott & Karen Snyder. LC 87-42965. (Illus.). 128p. 1988. pap. 6.95 (*0-87156-726-1*, Pub. by Sierra) Random.

Pesticide Analytical Methodology. Ed. by John Harvey, Jr. & Gunter Zweig. LC 80-19470. (ACS Symposium Ser.: No. 136). 1980. 49.95 (*0-8412-0581-7*) Am Chemical.

Pesticide Analytical Methodology. Ed. by John Harvey, Jr. & Gunter Zweig. LC 80-19470. (ACS Symposium Ser.: No. 136). (Illus.). 416p. 1980. reprint ed. pap. 129.00 (*0-608-03238-7*, 206375700007) Bks Demand.

Pesticide & Fertilizer Use & Trends in U. S. Agriculture. Biing-Hwan Lin et al. (Illus.). 47p. (Orig.). (C). 1995. pap. text 20.00 (*0-7881-2477-3*) DIANE Pub.

Pesticide & Xenobiotic Metabolism in Aquatic Organisms. Ed. by M. A. Khan et al. LC 79-4598. (ACS Symposium Ser.: No. 99). 1979. 47.95 (*0-8412-0489-6*) Am Chemical.

Pesticide & Xenobiotic Metabolism in Aquatic Organisms. Ed. by M. A. Khan et al. LC 79-4598. (ACS Symposium Ser.: Vol. 99). 447p. 1979. reprint ed. pap. 138.60 (*0-608-03094-5*, 206354700007) Bks Demand.

Pesticide Application Equipment for Use in Agriculture: Manually Carried. G. A. Matthews & E. W. Thronhill. LC 95-214726. (Agricultural Services Bulletin Ser.: No. 112-1). (Illus.). 163p. 1994. pap. 25.00 (*92-5-103582-2*, F35822, Pub. by FAO) Bernan Associates.

Pesticide Application Equipment for Vector Control. (Technical Reports: No. 791). (ENG, FRE & SPA.). 58p. 1990. pap. text 8.00 (*92-4-120791-4*, 1100791) World Health.

Pesticide Application Methods. 2nd ed. Matthews. 1992. pap. text. write for info. (*0-582-40905-5*) Longman.

***Pesticide Application Methods.** 3rd ed. G. A. Matthews. LC 00-33746. 2000. write for info. (*0-632-05473-5*) Blackwell Sci.

Pesticide Applications: States Move to Limit Farmer Liability for Groundwater Contamination. Gordon Meeks, Jr. (State Legislative Reports: Vol. 15, No. 15). 7p. 1990. pap. text 15.00 (*1-55516-271-1*, 7302-1515) Natl Conf State Legis.

Pesticide Bioassays with Arthropods. Jacqueline L. Robertson. 144p. 1991. lib. bdg. 129.00 (*0-8493-6463-9*, QH545) CRC Pr.

Pesticide Book. 5th ed. George W. Ware. 340p. (C). 1999. pap. 35.00 (*0-913702-52-8*) Thomson Pubns.

Pesticide Bound Residues in Soil. Senate Commission on the Assessment of Chemicals Used in Agriculture Staff. LC 98-229736. 196p. 1998. pap. 98.00 (*3-527-27583-5*) Wiley.

Pesticide Chemist & Modern Toxicology. Ed. by Suresh K. Bandal et al. LC 81-10790. (ACS Symposium Ser.: No. 160). 1981. 54.95 (*0-8412-0636-8*) Am Chemical.

Pesticide Chemist & Modern Toxicology. Ed. by Suresh K. Bandal. LC 81-10790. (ACS Symposium Ser.: Vol. 160). 593p. 1981. reprint ed. pap. 183.90 (*0-608-03050-3*, 206350300007) Bks Demand.

Pesticide Chemistry. Ed. by G. Matolcsy et al. (Studies in Environmental Science: No. 32). 800p. 1989. 401.25 (*0-444-98903-X*) Elsevier.

Pesticide Chemistry: Human Welfare & the Environment, Vol. 2. Ed. by J. Miyamoto. (IUPAC Symposium Ser.). (Illus.). 1983. 20.00 (*0-08-029227-5*, Pub. by Pergamon Repr) Franklin.

Pesticide Chemistry: Proceedings of the International IUPAC Congress, 2nd Congress, 6 vols., Vol. 4. International IUPAC Congress Staff. Ed. by A. S. Tahori. 618p. 1971. 271.00 (*0-677-12160-1*) Gordon & Breach.

Pesticide Chemistry - Human Welfare & the Environment: Mode of Action, Metabolism & Toxicology, Vol. 3. Ed. by J. Miyamoto & Philip C. Kearney. (IUPAC Symposium Ser.). (Illus.). 1983. 20.00 (*0-08-029228-3*, Pub. by Pergamon Repr) Franklin.

Pesticide Chemistry - Human Welfare & the Environment: Pesticide Residues & Formulation Chemistry, Vol. 4. Ed. by J. Miyamoto & Philip C. Kearney. (IUPAC Symposium Ser.). 1983. 20.00 (*0-08-029229-1*, Pub. by Pergamon Repr) Franklin.

Pesticide Chemistry - Human Welfare & the Environment: Synthesis & Structure Activity Relationships, Vol. 1. Ed. by J. Miyamoto & Philip C. Kearney. (IUPAC Symposium Ser.). 1983. 20.00 (*0-08-029226-7*, Pub. by Pergamon Repr) Franklin.

Pesticide Chemistry & Biosciences: The Food-Environment Challenge. Ed. by G. T. Brooks & T. Roberts. (Special Publication Ser.: Vol. 233). 400p. 1999. 100.00 (*0-85404-709-3*) Royal Soc Chem.

Pesticide Chemistry in the 20th Century: A Symposium. Ed. by Jack R. Plimmer. LC 76-51748. (ACS Symposium Ser.: No. 37). (Illus.). 320p. 1977. reprint ed. pap. 99.20 (*0-608-04340-0*, 206512000001) Bks Demand.

Pesticide Conspiracy. Robert Van Den Bosch. 1989. pap. 15.95 (*0-520-06823-8*, Pub. by U CA Pr) Cal Prin Full Svc.

Pesticide Control Inspector. Jack Rudman. (Career Examination Ser.: C-2561). 1994. pap. 29.95 (*0-8373-2561-7*) Nat Learn.

Pesticide Dangers: And How to Live Without Them. Deborah A. Murphy. (Sound-Off Ser.). 12p. 1998. pap. 2.50 (*0-9646811-8-8*) Stardust PA.

Pesticide Data Program: Annual Summary Calendar Year 1997. 140p. pap. text. write for info. (*0-7881-8631-0*) DIANE Pub.

***Pesticide Data Program: Annual Summary, Calendar Year 1998.** Ed. by Kathleen A. Merrigan. (Illus.). 160p. 2000. pap. text 25.00 (*0-7567-0033-7*) DIANE Pub.

Pesticide Data Program: Summary of 1992 Data. Lon Hatamiya. (Illus.). 108p. (Orig.). (C). 1994. pap. text 30.00 (*0-7881-1529-4*) DIANE Pub.

***Pesticide Dermatosis.** Howard I. Maibach et al. 500p. 1999. 89.95 (*1-56670-293-3*) Lewis Pubs.

Pesticide Directory, 2000-2001. Lori T. Harvey & W. T. Thomson. 175p. 2000. pap. 49.95 (*0-913702-45-5*) Thomson Pubns.

Pesticide Fact Handbook, Vol. 2. U. S. Environmental Protection Agency Staff. LC 87-31528. (Illus.). 666p. 1990. 145.00 (*0-8155-1239-2*) Noyes.

Pesticide Formulating Industry: Guides to Pollution Prevention. (Illus.). 54p. (Orig.). (C). 1995. pap. text 25.00 (*0-7881-2143-X*) DIANE Pub.

Pesticide Formulation & Adjuvant Formulation. Chester L. Foy & David W. Pritchard. 384p. 1996. boxed set 189.95 (*0-8493-7678-5*, 7678) CRC Pr.

Pesticide Formulations. Ed. by W. Van Valkenburg. LC 72-86610. 491p. reprint ed. pap. 152.30 (*0-8357-9091-6*, 205505300008) Bks Demand.

Pesticide Formulations: Innovations & Developments. Ed. by Barrington Cross & Herbert B. Scher. LC 88-10419. (ACS Symposium Ser.: Vol. 371). 304p. 1988. reprint ed. pap. 94.30 (*0-608-03282-4*, 206380000007) Bks Demand.

Pesticide Formulations & Application System (STP 1146), Vol. 12. Ed. by Bala N. Devsetty. 381p. 1993. 60.00 (*0-8031-1439-7*, STP1146) ASTM.

Pesticide Formulations & Application Systems. Ed. by Paul D. Berger et al. (Special Technical Publication Ser.: Vol. 13, No. STP 1183). (Illus.). 420p. 1993. text 61.00 (*0-8031-1888-0*, STP1183) ASTM.

Pesticide Formulations & Application Systems, Vol. 7. Ed. by G. B. Beestman & D. I. Vander Hooven. LC 87-14461. (Special Technical Publication Ser.: No. 968). (Illus.). 275p. 1987. text 39.00 (*0-8031-0970-9*, STP968) ASTM.

Pesticide Formulations & Application Systems, Vol. 10. Ed. by L. E. Bode et al. (Special Technical Publication Ser.: No. 1078). (Illus.). 260p. 1990. text 39.00 (*0-8031-1388-9*, STP1078) ASTM.

Pesticide Formulations & Application Systems, Vol. 11. Ed. by Loren E. Bode & David G. Chasin. (Special Technical Publication Ser.: No. 1112). (Illus.). 310p. 1992. text 38.00 (*0-8031-1414-1*, STP1112) ASTM.

Pesticide Formulations & Application Systems, Vol. 15. Ed. by Herbert M. Collins et al. (STP Ser.: No. 1268). (Illus.). 215p. 1996. 59.00 (*0-8031-2007-9*, STP1268) ASTM.

Pesticide Formulations & Application Systems, Vol. 16. Ed. by Michael J. Hopkinson et al. 225p. 1997. pap. 57.00 (*0-8031-2035-4*, STP1312) ASTM.

Pesticide Formulations & Application Systems, Vol. 17. Ed. by G. Robert Goss et al. (STP Ser.: No. 1328). (Illus.). 330p. 1997. text 81.00 (*0-8031-2469-4*, STP1328) ASTM.

***Pesticide Formulations & Application Systems, Vol. 18.** Ed. by John D. Nalewaja et al. (STP Ser.: No. 1347). 338p. 1998. pap. text 88.00 (*0-8031-2491-0*, STP1347) ASTM.

Pesticide Formulations & Application Systems: 2nd Conference - STP 795. Ed. by K. G. Seymour. LC 82-72891. 111p. 1983. pap. text 14.00 (*0-8031-0233-X*, STP795) ASTM.

Pesticide Formulations & Application Systems: 3rd Symposium - STP 828. Ed. by Thomas M. Kaneko & N. B. Akesson. LC 83-71898. 152p. 1984. text 19.00 (*0-8031-0221-6*, STP828) ASTM.

Pesticide Formulations & Application Systems: 4th Symposium - STP 875. Ed. by Thomas M. Kaneko & Larry D. Spicer. LC 85-13390. (Illus.). 193p. 1985. text 37.00 (*0-8031-0413-8*, STP875) ASTM.

***Pesticide Formulations & Application Systems Vol. 19: Global Pest Control Formulation for the Next Millennium.** Ed. by R. Scott Tann. (STP Ser.: No. 1373). (Illus.). 149p. 1999. pap. 39.00 (*0-8031-2622-0*, STP 1373) ASTM.

P

An Asterisk (*) at the beginning of an entry indicates that the title is appearing for the first time.

Pesticide Formulations & Applications Systems, Vol. 6. Ed. by D. I. Vander Hooven et al. LC 87-11503. (Special Technical Publication Ser.: No. 943). (Illus.). 186p. 1987. text 36.00 (*0-8031-0943-1*, STP943) ASTM.

Pesticide Formulations & Applications Systems: 5th Symposium. Ed. by Thomas M. Kaneko & Larry D. Spicer. LC 86-22358. (Special Technical Publication Ser.: No. 915). (Illus.). 154p. 1986. text 32.00 (*0-8031-0481-2*, STP915) ASTM.

Pesticide Handbook. Peter Hurst et al. 128p. 1989. text 24.95 (*0-7453-0329-3*) Routledge.

Pesticide Hazard: A Global Health & Environmental Audit. Barbara Dinham. LC 92-36319. (C). 1993. text 59.95 (*1-85649-201-X*, Pub. by Zed Books); text 25.00 (*1-85649-202-8*, Pub. by Zed Books) St Martin.

Pesticide Index. 2nd ed. Hamish Kidd & Hartley. 1992. 63.00 (*0-85186-401-5*) CRC Pr.

Pesticide Interactions in Crop Production. Jack Altman. 592p. 1993. boxed set 229.00 (*0-8493-6339-X*, SB951) CRC Pr.

Pesticide Metabolism. Kaneko & J. Miyamoto. 1991. 32.00 (*0-632-02256-6*) CRC Pr.

Pesticide Movement in Agroecosystems. George P. Cobb & Carol P. Weisskopf. 1999. 69.95 (*0-87371-888-7*) CRC Pr.

Pesticide Policies in Developing Countries: Do They Encourage Excessive Use? Jumanah Farah. LC 94-13584. (Discussion Paper Ser.: No. 238). 54p. 1994. pap. 22.00 (*0-8213-2830-1*, 12830) World Bank.

Pesticide Policy, Production Risk, & Producer Welfare. John M. Antle. LC 88-14120. 134p. 1988. pap. 16.95 (*0-915707-39-X*) Resources Future.

Pesticide Prediction in Soils, Plants, & Aquatic Systems. Mohammed Mansour. 304p. 1993. lib. bdg. 110.00 (*0-87371-616-7*, L616) Lewis Pubs.

Pesticide Problem: An Economic Approach to Public Policy. Joseph C. Headley & J. N. Lewis. LC 66-28503. 159p. reprint ed. pap. 49.30 (*0-608-13828-2*, 202096400020) Bks Demand.

Pesticide Profiles: Toxicity, Environmental Impact & Fat. Michael A. Kamrin. LC 96-34362. 704p. 1997. boxed set 99.95 (*1-56670-190-2*) CRC Pr.

Pesticide Properties in the Environment. A. G. Hornsby et al. LC 95-34367. 232p. 1995. 59.95 (*0-387-94353-6*) Spr-Verlag.

Pesticide Regulation Handbook. McKenna & Cuneo Staff & Technology Staff. 513p. 1994. 110.00 (*0-471-12596-2*) Wiley.

Pesticide Regulation Handbook. rev. ed. McKenna & Cuneo Staff et al. 1991. pap. 75.00 (*1-55840-464-3*) Exec Ent Pubns.

Pesticide Regulation Handbook: A Guide for Users. Jan Greene. 176p. 1994. lib. bdg. 59.95 (*0-87371-967-0*, L967) Lewis Pubs.

Pesticide Remediation in Soils & Water. P. C. Kearney & Terry Roberts. LC 97-48848. (Series in Agrochemicals & Plant Protection). 398p. 1998. 190.00 (*0-471-96805-6*) Wiley.

***Pesticide Removal by Combined Ozonation & Granular Activated Carbon Filtration.** Ervin Orlandini. (IHE Dissertation Ser.: Vol. 16). (Illus.). 182p. (C). 1999. pap. text 40.00 (*90-5410-414-7*, Pub. by A A Balkema) Ashgate Pub Co.

Pesticide Residues: Report of the 1967 Joint Meeting of the FAO Working Party & the WHO Expert Committee, 1968. (Technical Report Ser.: No. 391). 43p. 1968. pap. text 5.00 (*92-4-120391-9*, 1100391) World Health.

Pesticide Residues & Exposure. Ed. by Jack R. Plimmer. LC 81-20568. (ACS Symposium Ser.: No. 182). 1982. 32.95 (*0-8412-0701-1*) Am Chemical.

Pesticide Residues & Exposure. Ed. by Jack R. Plimmer. LC 81-20568. (ACS Symposium Ser.: Vol. 182). 224p. 1982. reprint ed. pap. 69.50 (*0-608-03107-0*, 206356000007) Bks Demand.

Pesticide Residues & Food Safety. B. G. Tweedy. (ACS Symposoium Ser.). 376p. 1990. pap. text 39.95 (*0-8412-1906-0*, Pub. by Am Chemical) OUP.

Pesticide Residues in Food. Hamilton. text. write for info. (*0-471-48991-3*) Wiley.

Pesticide Residues in Food: Joint Report of the FAO Working Party & the WHO Expert Committee on Pesticide, 1967. (Technical Report Ser.: No. 369). 19p. 1967. pap. text 3.00 (*92-4-120370-6*, 1100370) World Health.

Pesticide Residues in Food: Report, Geneva, 1975. FAO-WHO Experts on Pesticide Residues Staff. (Technical Reports: No. 592). 1976. pap. text 6.00 (*92-4-120592-X*, 1100592) World Health.

Pesticide Residues in Food: Report of the FAO-WHO Experts on Pesticide Residues, Geneva, 1968. FAO-WHO Experts on Pesticide Residues Staff. (Technical Reports: No. 417). 1969. pap. text 5.00 (*92-4-120417-6*, 1100417) World Health.

Pesticide Residues in Food: Report of the FAO-WHO Experts on Pesticide Residues, Geneva, 1968. FAO-WHO Experts on Pesticide Residues Staff. (Technical Reports: No. 458). 1970. pap. text 5.00 (*92-4-120458-3*, 1100458) World Health.

Pesticide Residues in Food: Report of the FAO-WHO Experts on Pesticide Residues, Geneva, 1968. FAO-WHO Experts on Pesticide Residues Staff. (Technical Reports: No. 474). 1971. pap. text 5.00 (*92-4-120474-5*, 1100474) World Health.

Pesticide Residues in Food: Report of the FAO-WHO Experts on Pesticide Residues, Geneva, 1968. FAO-WHO Experts on Pesticide Residues Staff. (Technical Reports: No. 502). 1972. pap. text 4.00 (*92-4-120502-4*, 1100502) World Health.

Pesticide Residues in Food: Report of the FAO-WHO Experts on Pesticide Residues, Geneva, 1968. FAO-WHO Experts on Pesticide Residues Staff. (Technical Reports: No. 545). 1974. pap. text 6.00 (*92-4-120545-8*, 1100545) World Health.

Pesticide Residues in Food: Report of the FAO-WHO Experts on Pesticide Residues, Geneva, 1968. FAO-WHO Experts on Pesticide Residues Staff. (Technical Reports: No. 574). 1975. pap. text 6.00 (*92-4-120574-1*, 1100574) World Health.

Pesticide Residues in Food: Report of the 1976 Joint FAO/WHO Meeting, 1977. (Technical Report Ser.: No. 612). 35p. 1977. pap. text 6.00 (*92-4-120612-8*, 1100612) World Health.

Pesticide Residues in Food: Technologies for Detection. (U. S. Congress, Office of Technology Assessment Workshop Ser.). 236p. 1989. pap. 19.95 (*0-87762-667-7*) Technomic.

Pesticide Residues in Food & Human Bodies: Index of New Information. John C. Bartone. 160p. 1997. 47.50 (*0-7883-1670-2*); pap. 44.50 (*0-7883-1671-0*) ABBE Pubs Assn.

***Pesticide Residues in Food Evaluations 1997 Part 2: Toxicological & Environmental.** Food & Agriculture Organization Staff. (Evaluation Ser.). 424p. 1999. pap. 55.00 (*92-4-166513-0*, Pub. by World Health) Bernan Associates.

Pesticide Residues in Food, 1989: Report of the Joint Meeting FAO/WHO, Geneva, 1989. 93p. 1989. 12.00 (*92-5-102887-7*, Pub. by FAO) Bernan Associates.

Pesticide Residues in Food, 1989 Evaluations: Residues, Pt. I. 369p. 1990. 45.00 (*92-5-102935-0*, F9350, Pub. by FAO) Bernan Associates.

Pesticide Residues in Food, 1994. FAO Staff. (Plant Production & Protection Papers: No. 127). 424p. 1995. pap. 35.00 (*92-5-103632-2*, F36322, Pub. by FAO) Bernan Associates.

Pesticide Residues in Food, 1991: Report of the Joint Meeting FAO/WHO, Geneva, 1991. 147p. 1991. 17.00 (*92-5-103112-6*, F0126, Pub. by FAO) Bernan Associates.

Pesticide Residues in Food, 1990: Report of the Joint Meeting FAO/WHO, Rome, 1990. 107p. 1990. 14.00 (*92-5-103007-3*, F0073, Pub. by FAO) Bernan Associates.

Pesticide Residues in Food, 1995 Evaluations: Residues, Pt. 1. FAO Staff. (Plant & Production Paper Ser.: No. 137). (Illus.). 424p. 1996. pap. 79.00 (*92-5-103868-6*, F38686, Pub. by FAO) Bernan Associates.

Pesticide Residues in Food, 1993 Evaluations: Residues, Pt. I. FAO Staff. 852p. 1994. 100.00 (*92-5-103543-1*, F35431, Pub. by FAO) Bernan Associates.

Pesticide Residues in Food, 1994 Evaluations: Residues, Pts. 1 & 2. FAO Staff. (Plant Production Papers). 159p. 1995. pap. 180.00 (*92-5-103717-5*, F37175, Pub. by FAO) Bernan Associates.

Pesticide Residues in Food, 1990 Pt. 2: Toxicology Evaluations. (Joint Meeting of the FAO Panel of Experts on Pesticide Residues in Food & the Environment & the WHO Expert Group on Pesticide Residues Ser.). x, 182p. 1991. pap. text 30.00 (*92-4-166506-8*, 1280006) World Health.

Pesticide Residues in Food, 1992 Pt. 2: Toxicology Evaluations. (Joint Meeting of the FAO Panel of Experts on Pesticide Residues in Food & the Environment & the WHO Expert Group on Pesticide Residues Ser.). x, 422p. 1993. pap. text 50.00 (*92-4-166508-4*, 1280008) World Health.

Pesticide Residues in Food, 1991 Pt. II: Toxicology Evaluations (WHO/PCS/9252) WHO Staff. (WHO Pesticides Residues in Food Ser.: No. 7). 318p. 1992. 35.00 (*92-4-166507-6*, 1280007) World Health.

Pesticide Residues in Food, 1977 Evaluations see Evaluation of Some Pesticide Residues in Food

Pesticide Residues in Food, 1977 Evaluations see Land Use & Environment Law Review, 1984

Pesticide Residues in Food, 1977 Evaluations see Papers of the Dictionary Society of North America

Pesticide Residues in Food, 1977 Evaluations see Statistics on Narcotic Drugs Furnished by Governments in Accordance with the International Treaties & Maximum Levels of Opium Stock

Pesticide Residues in Food, 1977 Evaluations. 879p. 1978. write for info. Modern Lang.

Pesticide Residues in Food, 1977 Evaluations. 144p. write for info. Soc Am Baseball Res.

Pesticide Residues in Food, 1977 Evaluations. pap. 19.00 pap. 6.00 pap. 50.00 pap. 13.00 UN.

Pesticide Residues in Food, 1977 Evaluations. 88p. 1979. 9.00 UN.

Pesticide Residues in Food, 1977 Evaluations, Methodology & Definitions. pap., suppl. ed. 29.00 UN.

Pesticide Residues in Food, 1977 Evaluations, 2 Vols., Set. 1969p. 1983. pap. 70.00 UN.

Pesticide Residues in Food, 1977 Evaluations, Vol. 2. pap. 18.00 UN.

Pesticide Residues in Food, 1977 Evaluations see CCAR Yearbook

***Pesticide Residues in Food, 1998 Evaluations Pt. 1: Residues.** FAO Staff. (Plant Production & Protection Paper Ser.: Vol. 152, Nos. 1 & 2). 424p. 1999. pap. 170.00 (*92-5-104338-8*, F43388, Pub. by FAO) Bernan Associates.

Pesticide Residues in Foods: Methods, Techniques & Regulations. W. George Fong et al. LC 98-27512. (Chemical Analysis). 376p. 1999. 84.95 (*0-471-57400-7*) Wiley.

Pesticide Resistance: Strategies & Tactics for Management. fac. ed. National Research Council U. S. Staff. LC 85-25919. 482p. 1986. pap. 149.50 (*0-7837-7558-X*, 204731100007) Bks Demand.

***Pesticide Science: Pesticide Resistance.** Ed. by J. Marshall Clark & Isamu Yamaguchi. (ACS Symposium Series). (Illus.). 306p. 2001. text 115.00 (*0-8412-3723-9*, Pub. by Am Chemical) OUP.

Pesticide Science & Biotechnology. Greenhlagh. Ed. by T. R. Roberts. 1991. 122.00 (*0-632-01618-3*) CRC Pr.

Pesticide Selectivity. Ed. by Joseph C. Street. LC 75-12365. (Illus.). 211p. reprint ed. pap. 65.50 (*0-7837-0696-0*, 204102900019) Bks Demand.

Pesticide Standards & Enforcement: A Comparison of U. S. & Mexico. 64p. (Orig.). (C). 1992. pap. text 25.00 (*1-56806-035-1*) DIANE Pub.

Pesticide Synthesis Handbook. Thomas A. Unger. LC 96-10904. 1080p. 1996. 195.00 (*0-8155-1401-8*) Noyes.

Pesticide Synthesis Through Rational Approaches: Based on a Symposium Sponsored by the Division of Pesticide Chemistry at the 186th Meeting of the American Chemical Society, Washington, DC, August 28-September 2, 1983. Ed. by Philip S. Magee et al. LC 84-11062. (ACS Symposium Ser.: No. 255). (Illus.). 368p. reprint ed. pap. 114.10 (*0-7837-1965-5*, 205244300001) Bks Demand.

Pesticide Tank Mix Applications: First Conference - STP 764. Ed. by Wright et al. 100p. 1982. pap. 13.95 (*0-8031-0828-1*, STP764) ASTM.

Pesticide Transformation Products. Ed. by L. Somasundaram & Joel R. Coats. LC 91-2034. (Symposium Ser.: No. 459). 308p. 1991. text 78.00 (*0-8412-1994-X*, Pub. by Am Chemical) OUP.

Pesticide Use & Toxicology in Relation to Wildlife: Organophosphorus & Carbamate Compounds. Gregory J. Smith. LC 92-34055. 176p. 1992. lib. bdg. 89.95 (*0-8493-8721-3*, QH545) CRC Pr.

Pesticide Waste Disposal Technology. Ed. by James S. Bridges & Clyde R. Dempsey. LC 87-31548. (Pollution Technology Review Ser.: No. 148). (Illus.). 331p. 1988. 89.00 (*0-8155-1157-4*) Noyes.

Pesticide Waste Management: Technology & Regulation. Ed. by John Bourke et al. LC 92-32304. (ACS Symposium Ser.: No. 510). (Illus.). 273p. 1992. text 70.00 (*0-8412-2480-3*, Pub. by Am Chemical) OUP.

Pesticides: Adulterated Imported Foods Are Reaching U. S. Grocery Shelves. (Illus.). 30p. (Orig.). (C). 1993. pap. text 15.00 (*1-56806-469-1*) DIANE Pub.

Pesticides: Advice & Recommendations to Be Used by National & Other Authorities As Well As Manufacturers Concerned with the Registration of Agricultural & Non-Agricultural Pesticides. 7th ed. Council of Europe Staff. 1992. 21.00 (*92-871-1958-9*, Pub. by Council of Europe) Manhattan Pub Co.

Pesticides: Contemporary Roles in Agriculture, Health & the Environment. Ed. by T. J. Sheets & David Pimentel. LC 78-71497. (Contemporary Issues in Science & Society Ser.). 208p. 1979. 69.50 (*0-89603-005-9*) Humana.

***Pesticides: Managing Risks & Optimizing Benefits.** Nancy N. Ragsdale & James N. Seiber. LC 99-14981. (ACS Symposium Ser.: No. 734). (Illus.). 288p. 1999. text 100.00 (*0-8412-3616-X*, Pub. by Am Chemical) OUP.

Pesticides: Minimizing the Risks. Ed. by Nancy N. Ragsdale & Ronald J. Kuhr. LC 87-1842. (ACS Symposium Ser.: No. 336). (Illus.). vii, 186p. 1987. 34.95 (*0-8412-1022-5*) Am Chemical.

Pesticides: Minimizing the Risks. Ed. by Nancy N. Ragsdale & Ronald J. Kuhr. LC 87-1842. (ACS Symposium Ser.: Vol. 336). 194p. 1987. reprint ed. pap. 60.20 (*0-608-03548-3*, 206426700008) Bks Demand.

Pesticides: Reducing Exposure to Residues of Canceled Pesticides. (Illus.). 42p. (Orig.). (C). 1995. pap. text 20.00 (*0-7881-1711-4*) DIANE Pub.

Pesticides: The Phaseout of Methyl Bromide in the U. S. (Illus.). 41p. (Orig.). (C). 1996. pap. text 20.00 (*0-7881-3020-X*) DIANE Pub.

Pesticides: Thirty Years since Silent Spring. Peter F. Guerrero. 22p. (Orig.). (C). 1992. pap. text 10.00 (*1-56806-036-X*) DIANE Pub.

Pesticides - Developments, Impacts, & Controls: Proceedings: Analytical Division's Symposium of the Royal Society of Chemistry Annual Chemical Congress (1995: Edinburgh, UK) Ed. by Gerry Best et al. 180p. 1995. 78.00 (*0-85404-785-9*, SB) CRC Pr.

Pesticides Analysis. Das. (Illus.). 488p. 1981. text 185.00 (*0-8247-1087-8*) Dekker.

Pesticides & Food Safety. (Illus.). 56p. (Orig.). (C). 1993. pap. text 25.00 (*0-7881-0124-2*) DIANE Pub.

Pesticides & Ground Water. 1993. 12.00 (*92-871-2384-5*, Pub. by Council of Europe) Manhattan Pub Co.

Pesticides & Groundwater Quality: Issues & Problems in Four States. Patrick W. Holden. LC 86-60349. 135p. 1986. reprint ed. pap. 41.90 (*0-608-02344-2*, 206298500004) Bks Demand.

Pesticides & Human Cancer Involvement: Index of New Information. John C. Bartone. 160p. 1997. 47.50 (*0-7883-1650-8*); pap. 44.50 (*0-7883-1651-6*) ABBE Pubs Assn.

Pesticides & Human Health. William H. Hallenbeck & K. M. Burns. vii, 176p. 1984. 55.00 (*0-387-96050-3*) Spr-Verlag.

Pesticides & Nature Conservation: The British Experience, 1950-1975. John Sheail. (Illus.). 300p. 1985. 29.95 (*0-19-854150-3*) OUP.

Pesticides & Neurological Diseases. Ed. by Donald J. Ecobichon & Robert M. Joy. 296p. 1982. 165.00 (*0-8493-5571-0*, RC346, CRC Reprint) Franklin.

Pesticides & Neurological Diseases. 2nd ed. Donald J. Ecobichon & Robert M. Joy. LC 93-1125. 400p. 1993. lib. bdg. 169.00 (*0-8493-4361-5*, RC347) CRC Pr.

Pesticides & Nitrogen Cycle, Vol. 3. LAL R. LC 87-7985. 184p. 1987. 106.00 (*0-8493-4353-4*, CRC Reprint) Franklin.

Pesticides & Nitrogen Cycle: Pesticides, Chemists & Soil Scientists, 3 vol., Set. Ed. by Rup Lal. 1988. 90.00 (*0-8493-4350-X*, QH545, CRC Reprint) Franklin.

Pesticides & Politics: The Life Cycle of a Public Issue. Christopher J. Bosso. LC 86-19245. (Series in Policy & Institutional Studies). (Illus.). 312p. 1987. reprint ed. text 49.95 (*0-8229-3547-3*) U of Pittsburgh Pr.

Pesticides & Politics: The Life Cycle of a Public Issue. Christopher J. Bosso. LC 86-19245. (Series in Policy & Institutional Studies). (Illus.). 312p. 1988. reprint ed. pap. 16.95 (*0-8229-5418-4*) U of Pittsburgh Pr.

Pesticides & the Future: Minimizing Chronic Exposure of Humans & Environment. Ed. by R. J. Kuhr & N. Motoyama. 1999. 150.00 (*90-5199-388-9*) IOS Pr.

Pesticides & the Immune System: The Public Health Risks. Robert C. Repetto & Sanjay S. Baliga. LC 96-12739. 100p. (Orig.). 1996. pap. 20.00 (*1-56973-087-3*) World Resources Inst.

Pesticides & the Living Landscape. Robert L. Rudd. LC 64-14506. 336p. reprint ed. pap. 104.20 (*0-608-14279-4*, 201565300095) Bks Demand.

Pesticides & the Nitrogen Cycle, Vol. I. R. Lal. 152p. 1987. 90.00 (*0-8493-4351-8*, CRC Reprint) Franklin.

Pesticides & the Nitrogen Cycle, Vol. II. R. Lal. 168p. 1987. 46.00 (*0-8493-4352-6*) CRC Pr.

Pesticides, Chemicals & Health. British Medical Association Staff. (Illus.). 224p. 1992. pap. text 29.95 (*0-340-54924-6*, A6602, Pub. by E A) Routldge.

Pesticides for Use in Christmas Tree Production in the North Central Region. Roseann Kachadoorian et al. (Illus.). 52p. (C). 1998. reprint ed. pap. text 25.00 (*0-7881-4221-6*) DIANE Pub.

Pesticides Handbook. Peter Hurst et al. 448p. (C). 47.50 (*1-85172-041-3*, Pub. by Pluto GBR) Stylus Pub VA.

Pesticides, Human Health, Research & Cancer: Index of New Information with Bibliography. Stanley S. Kubiak. (Illus.). 150p. 1999. 47.50 (*0-7883-2206-0*); pap. 44.50 (*0-7883-2207-9*) ABBE Pubs Assn.

Pesticides Identification at the Residue Level: A Symposium Sponsored by the Division of Pesticide Chemistry of the American Chemical Society at the Joint Conference of the Chemical Society of Canada & the American Chemical Society at Toronto, Ontario, Canada, May 26-27, 1970 - Francis J. Biros, Symposium Chairman. American Chemical Society Staff. LC 70-164408. (Advances in Chemistry Ser.: No. 104). (Illus.). 192p. 1971. reprint ed. pap. 59.60 (*0-608-06769-5*, 206696600009) Bks Demand.

Pesticides in Air Pt. II: Development of Predictive Methods for Estimating Pesticide Flux to Air. Dennis P. Hsieh et al. (Illus.). 54p. (C). 1998. pap. text 20.00 (*0-7881-7227-1*) DIANE Pub.

Pesticides in Bed Sediments & Aquatic Biota in Streams: Distribution, Trends, & Governing Factors. Lisa H. Nowell et al. Ed. by Robert J. Gilliom. (Pesticides in the Hydrologic System Ser.). 400p. (C). 1997. text 59.95 (*1-57504-007-7*) CRC Pr.

Pesticides in Drinking Water. David I. Gustafson. LC 92-33462. 256p. 1993. text 70.95 (*0-442-01187-3*, VNR) Wiley.

Pesticides in Drinking Water. David I. Gustafson. (Industrial Health & Safety Ser.). 241p. 1993. 89.95 (*0-471-28497-1*, VNR) Wiley.

Pesticides in Food: A Guide for Professionals. LC 91-40494. 1991. pap. 5.50 (*0-88091-095-X*, 0155) Am Dietetic Assn.

Pesticides in Foods: Residues, Risks & Reality. Winter. 350p. text 64.95 (*0-471-16153-5*) Wiley.

Pesticides in Fruits & Vegetables. Susan E. Kegley & Laura J. Wise. LC 98-10225. (Illus.). 128p. 1998. pap. 19.50 (*0-935702-46-6*) Univ Sci Bks.

Pesticides in Ground & Surface Water: Multimethod Residue Analysis. Ed. by H. J. Stan. LC 94-78363. (Chemistry of Plant Protection Ser.: Vol. 11). 1995. write for info. (*0-387-58794-2*) Spr-Verlag.

Pesticides in Ground & Surface Water: Multimethod Residue Analysis. Ed. by H. J. Stan. LC 94-47363. (Chemistry of Plant Protection Ser.: Vol. 11). 288p. 1995. 180.95 (*3-540-58794-2*) Spr-Verlag.

Pesticides in Ground Water: Distribution, Trends & Governing Factors. Jack E. Barbash & Elizabeth A. Resek. Ed. by Robert J. Gilliom. (Pesticides in the Hydrologic System Ser.). 616p. (C). 1997. boxed set 84.95 (*1-57504-005-0*) CRC Pr.

Pesticides in Groundwater Database: A Compilation of Monitoring Studies. 1994. lib. bdg. 260.75 (*0-8490-6441-4*) Gordon Pr.

Pesticides in Our Communities: Choices for Change. Susan Boyd et al. (Community Action Guides Ser.). (Illus.). 32p. (Orig.). 1992. pap. text 4.00 (*0-937345-08-3*) CONCERN.

Pesticides in Surface Water. 1995. 15.00 (*92-871-2776-X*, Pub. by Council of Europe) Manhattan Pub Co.

Pesticides in Surface Water: Distribution, Trends & Governing Factors. Steven J. Larson et al. Ed. by Robert J. Gilliom. LC 97-22728. (Pesticides in the Hydrologic System: No. 3). 400p. (C). 1997. ring bd. 79.95 (*1-57504-006-9*) CRC Pr.

Pesticides in the Atmosphere: Distribution, Trends & Governing Factors. Michael S. Majewski & Paul D. Capel. Ed. by Robert J. Gilliom. LC 95-34078. (Pesticides in the Hydrologic System Ser.). 215p. (C). 1996. ring bd. 69.95 (*1-57504-004-2*) CRC Pr.

Pesticides in the Diets of Infants & Children. National Research Council Staff. LC 93-14961. 408p. 1993. pap. text 47.95 (*0-309-04875-3*) Natl Acad Pr.

Pesticides in the Environment. Somasundar. 1998. write for info. (*0-12-654625-8*) Acad Pr.

Pesticides in the Environment, 2 pts., Vol. 1, Pt. 1. Ed. by Robert White-Stevens. LC 77-138499. (Illus.). 288p. reprint ed. pap. 89.30 (*0-8357-6256-4*, 202710200001) Bks Demand.

An Asterisk (*) at the beginning of an entry indicates that the title is appearing for the first time.

Pesticides in the Environment, Vol. 1, Pt. 2. Ed. by Robert White-Stevens. LC 77-138499. (Illus.). 366p. reprint ed. pap. 113.50 (*0-8357-6257-2*, 202710200002) Bks Demand.

Pesticides in the Environment, Vol. 2. Ed. by Robert White-Stevens. LC 77-138499. (Illus.). 478p. reprint ed. pap. 148.20 (*0-8357-6255-6*, 205230300002) Bks Demand.

Pesticides in the Environment, Vol. 3. Ed. by Robert White-Stevens. LC 77-138499. 384p. reprint ed. pap. 119.10 (*0-8357-6258-0*, 202710200003) Bks Demand.

Pesticides in the Hydrologic System Series, 4 vols., Set. Ed. by Robert J. Gilliom. 1500p. (C). 1997. text 199.95 (*1-57504-020-4*) CRC Pr.

Pesticides in the Hydrologic System Series, Vol. 4. U. S. Geological Staff. 1040p. 1999. boxed set 89.95 (*1-56670-469-3*) CRC Pr.

Pesticides in the Next Decade: The Challenges Ahead: Third National Research Conference. 111p. (Orig.). (C). 1994. pap. text 30.00 (*0-7881-0424-1*) DIANE Pub.

Pesticides in the Soil Environment: Processes, Impacts, & Modeling. Ed. by H. H. Cheng. (Book Ser.: No. 2). 554p. 1990. 36.00 (*0-89118-791-X*) Soil Sci Soc Am.

Pesticides in Tropical Agriculture. T. Thornton. (C). 1991. text 360.00 (*0-89771-666-3*, Pub. by Intl Bk Distr) St Mut.

Pesticides in Tropical Agriculture: A Collection of Papers Comprising the Symposium on Pesticides in Tropical Agriculture, Presented Before the Division of Agricultural & Food Chemistry at the 126th Meeting of the American Chemical Society, New York, NY, September 1954. American Chemical Society Staff. LC 55-4179. (Advances in Chemistry Ser.: Vol. 13). (Illus.). 106p. 1955. reprint ed. pap. 32.90 (*0-608-06905-1*, 206711300009) Bks Demand.

Pesticides in Tropical Agriculture: Hazards & Alternatives. Arnold Schwab et al. Ed. by Rolf Altenburger. LC 96-173020. 280p. 1997. pap. 24.50 (*3-8236-1243-3*, Pub. by Margraf Verlag) Balogh.

Pesticides in Urban Environments: Fate & Significance. Ed. by Kenneth D. Racke & Anne R. Leslie. LC 92-42060. (Symposium Ser.: Vol. 522). (Illus.). 385p. 1993. 94.95 (*0-8412-2627-X*) Am Chemical.

Pesticides in Urban Environments: Fate & Significance. Ed. by Kenneth D. Racke & Anne R. Leslie. LC 92-42060. (ACS Symposium Ser.: Vol. 522). 392p. 1993. reprint ed. pap. 121.60 (*0-608-02980-7*, 205255600006) Bks Demand.

Pesticides Industry: Pesticides Industry. rev. ed. (UNIDO Guide to Information Sources Ser.: No. 10). pap. 4.00 (*92-1-106142-3*) UN.

Pesticides Industry in India: Issues & Constraints in Its Growth. U. K. Srivastava & N. T. Patel. 1990. 44.50 (*81-204-0503-X*, Pub. by Oxford IBH) S Asia.

Pesticides Laboratory Training Manual. Ed. by C. E. Meloan. (Illus.). xviii, 484p. 1996. pap. 79.00 (*0-935584-60-9*) AOAC Intl.

Pesticides Law Handbook: A Legal & Regulatory Guide for Business. Marshall L. Miller. LC 99-36240. 448p. 1999. text 89.00 (*0-86587-633-9*, 633) Gov Insts.

Pesticides, Man & Biosphere. O. P. Shulka et al. 1998. 74.00 (*81-7024-973-2*) Ashish Pub Hse.

Pesticides, 1998. Orig. Title: Approved Products for Farmers & Growers. 560p. 1998. pap. 40.00 (*0-11-243032-5*, HM30325, Pub. by Statnry Office) Bernan Associates.

Pesticides Nomenclature, Specifications, Analysis, Use & Residues in Food. D. Lowe & A. Stiles. (Progress in Standardization Ser.: No. 1). 40p. 1973. pap. text 6.00 (*92-4-154101-6*, 1260001) World Health.

Pesticides on Millet in Mali. N. D. Jago et al. 1993. pap. 25.00 (*0-85954-303-X*, Pub. by Nat Res Inst) St Mut.

Pesticides Studied in Man. Wayland J. Hayes. LC 81-7410. 685p. reprint ed. pap. 200.00 (*0-608-15555-1*, 205638200063) Bks Demand.

***Pesticides, 2000.** 560p. 2000. pap. 45.00 (*0-11-243051-1*, HM30511, Pub. by Statnry Office) Bernan Associates.

***Pesticides, 2000: Your Guide to Approved Pesticides.** 500p. 2000. pap. 40.00 (*0-11-243048-1*, HM30481, Pub. by Statnry Office) Balogh.

***Pestilence.** William Owen Roberts. Tr. by Elisabeth Roberts. 214p. 2000. pap. 17.95 (*1-85411-198-1*, Pub. by Seren Bks) Dufour.

Pestis 18. Sharon Webb. 1996. pap., mass mkt. 4.99 (*0-8125-4343-2*) Tor Bks.

Pestis Eighteen. Sharon Webb. 416p. 1987. 17.95 (*0-317-52882-3*) St Martin.

Pestline, 2 vols., 1. OCCP Health Ser. Staff. 1991. text. write for info. (*0-442-00697-7*, VNR) Wiley.

Pestline, 2 vols., 2. OCCP Health Ser. Staff. 1991. text. write for info. (*0-442-00698-5*, VNR) Wiley.

Pesto. Illus. by Marvin Scott Jarrett & Steven Salerno. LC 93-24860. 72p. 1994. 9.95 (*0-8118-0426-7*) Chronicle Bks.

Pesto. Lou S. Pappus. 1994. 99.50 (*0-8118-9175-5*) Chronicle Bks.

***Pesto, Loose Ends & Other Love Poems.** Rita Flores Bogaert. 36p. 1999. pap. 5.00 (*0-9674775-0-6*) Coral Bell Pr.

Pesto Pesto! Recipes for the Calculated, the Casual & the Emergency Gourmet. 2nd ed. Victoria Starkey. 128p. 1992. pap. 11.95 (*0-9635334-0-1*) Cucina Pr.

Pestos! Cooking With Herb Pastes. Dorothy Rankin. LC 85-17121. (Illus.). 150p. 1985. pap. 8.95 (*0-89594-180-5*) Crossing Pr.

***Pests & Diseases: A Complete Guide to Preventing, Identifying & Treating Plant Problems.** DK Publishing Staff. (Illus.). 2000. pap. 0.00 (*0-7894-5996-5*) DK Pub Inc.

***Pests & Diseases of Herbaceous Perennials: The Biological Approach.** Stanton Gill et al. LC 99-29388. 320p. 1999. 68.95 (*1-883052-20-3*) Ball Pub.

Pests & Pathogens: Plant Responses to Foliar Attack. Ed. by P. G. Ayres. (Environmental Plant Biology Ser.). 216p. 1992. 152.50 (*1-872748-01-5*, Pub. by Bios Sci) Coronet Bks.

Pests in & Around the Florida Home. Philip G. Koehler. (Illus.). 180p. 1993. pap. text 8.00 (*0-916287-05-X*, SP134) Univ Fla Food.

Pests of Landscape Trees & Shrubs. Steve H. Dreistadt. LC 94-60514. (Illus.). 336p. 1994. pap. 32.00 (*1-879906-18-X*, 3359) ANR Pubns CA.

***Pests of Paradise: First Aid & Medical Treatment of Injuries from Hawai'i's Animals.** Susan Scott & Craig Thomas. LC 99-57565. (Illus.). 168p. 2000. pap. 19.95 (*0-8248-2252-8*) UH Pr.

Pests of Pastures: Weed, Invertebrate & Disease Pests of Australian Sheep Pastures. E. S. Delfosse. (Illus.). 600p. 1992. pap. 75.00 (*0-643-05140-6*, Pub. by CSIRO) Accents Pubns.

Pests of Stored Products & Their Control. Hill. 200p. 1990. text 212.00 (*0-471-94645-1*) Wiley.

Pests of Stored Products & Their Control. D. S. Hill. 200p. (C). 1991. text 465.00 (*0-89771-639-6*, Pub. by Intl Bk Distr) St Mut.

Pests of Stored Products & Their Control. Ed. by Dennis S. Hill. 1990. 71.00 (*0-8493-7704-8*, SB) CRC Pr.

Pests of the Garden & Small Farm: A Grower's Guide to Using Less Pesticide. Mary L. Flint. LC 89-81743. (Illus.). 288p. 1990. pap. text 30.00 (*0-931876-89-3*, 3332) ANR Pubns CA.

***Pests of the Garden & Small Farm: A Grower's Guide to Using Less Pesticide.** 2nd ed. 286p. 1998. pap. 35.00 (*1-879906-40-6*) ANR Pubns CA.

Pests of the Garden & Small Farm: A Grower's Guide to Using Less Pesticide. 2nd ed. Mary L. Flint. LC 98-60419. (Illus.). 286p. 1999. 35.00 (*0-520-21810-8*) U CA Pr.

Pests of the West: Prevention & Control for Today's Garden & Small Farm. Whitney Cranshaw. LC 98-29636. (Illus.). 224p. (Orig.). 1998. pap. 19.95 (*1-55591-401-2*) Fulcrum Pub.

Pests of Vegetables: Their Identification & Control in Ghana. B. B. Critchley. 282p. 1997. pap. 90.00 (*0-85954-463-X*, Pub. by Nat Res Inst) St Mut.

Pests, Pathogens & Plant Communities. J. Burdon & Simon R. Leather. 1990. 155.00 (*0-632-02561-1*) Blackwell Sci.

Pet. Mel Gilden & Ted Pedersen. Ed. by Lisa Clancy. (Star Trek: Deep Space Nine Ser.: No. 4). 128p. (J). (gr. 3-6). 1994. pap. 3.99 (*0-671-88352-6*, Minstrel Bks) PB.

***Pet: The Sound of "P"** Alice K. Flanagan. LC 99-20955. (Wonder Books Ser.). (Illus.). 24p. (J). 1999. lib. bdg. 21.41 (*1-56766-687-6*) Childs World.

Pet-a-Luma. Cyndy Richtik. LC 94-96332. (Luma Ser.). (Illus.). 23p. (J). (gr. k-12). 1994. 14.95 (*0-9643318-0-2*) Vis Bks Intl.

Pet Allergies: Remedies for an Epidemic. Alfred J. Plechner & Martin Zucker. LC 85-51341. 130p. (Orig.). 1986. pap. 6.95 (*0-9615452-0-8*) Very Healthy Ent.

Pet Animals. Lucy Cousins. LC 98-73057. (Illus.). 14p. (J). (ps). 1999. bds. 3.99 (*0-7636-0612-X*, Pub. by Candlewick Pr) Penguin Putnam.

***Pet Boy.** Keith Graves. LC 99-50824. (Illus.). (J). 2000. write for info. (*0-8118-2672-4*) Chronicle Bks.

Pet Budgies. Michael Christian. (Illus.). 48p. (Orig.). 1994. pap. 10.95 (*0-86417-589-2*, Pub. by Kangaroo Pr) Seven Hills Bk.

Pet Bugs: A Kid's Guide to Catching & Keeping Touchable Insects. Sally S. Kneidel. 128p. (J). 1994. pap. 12.95 (*0-471-31188-X*) Wiley.

Pet Care. Betsey Chessen. LC 98-35284. (Learning Center Emergent Readers Ser.). 1998. pap. 2.50 (*0-439-04589-4*) Scholastic Inc.

Pet Clean-Up Made Easy. Don A. Aslett. (Illus.). 145p. (Orig.). 1988. pap. 12.99 (*0-89879-262-2*) Marsh Creek Pr.

Pet Corner, 6 bks. Kath Mellentin & Tim Wood. (Illus.). 8p. (J). (ps-k). 1998. 9.95 (*0-7641-7210-7*) Barron.

***Pet Detectives.** Betty Wright. 1999. 5.95 (*0-8167-5652-X*) Bridgewater Pub.

Pet Detectives. Betty R. Wright. LC 98-31228. (Illus.). 32p. (J). (ps-3). 1999. 15.95 (*0-8167-4952-3*) BrdgeWater.

***Pet ER: Memoirs of an Animal Doctor.** George A. Porter. LC 99-61912. 248p. 1999. 24.95 (*1-57736-149-0*, Hillsboro Pr) Providence Hse.

Pet Ferret Owners' Manual. Ed. by Chris Maggio. (Illus.). 72p. (Orig.). 1995. pap. write for info. (*0-9646477-2-9*); lib. bdg. write for info. (*0-9646477-1-0*) C Maggio.

Pet First Aid: Cats & Dogs. American Red Cross Staff. (gr. 13). 1997. 10.00 (*0-8151-2318-3*) Mosby Inc.

***Pet First Aid: Cats & Dogs - Special Edition.** (Illus.). 1999. write for info. (*1-58480-025-9*) StayWell Co.

Pet Food in Argentina: A Strategic Entry Report, 1998. Compiled by Icon Group International Staff. (Country Industry Report). (Illus.). 145p. 1999. ring bd. 1450.00 incl. audio compact disk (*0-7418-0525-1*) Icon Grp.

Pet Food in Israel: A Strategic Entry Report, 1998. Compiled by Icon Group International Staff. (Country Industry Report). (Illus.). 117p. 1999. ring bd. 1170.00 incl. audio compact disk (*0-7418-0526-X*) Icon Grp.

Pet Food in Taiwan: A Strategic Entry Report, 1997. Compiled by Icon Group International Staff. (Illus.). 112p. 1999. ring bd. 1120.00 incl. audio compact disk (*0-7418-0878-1*) Icon Grp.

Pet Foods & Supplies in Japan: A Strategic Entry Report, 1998. Compiled by Icon Group International Staff. (Country Industry Report). (Illus.). 162p. 1999. ring bd. 1620.00 incl. audio compact disk (*0-7418-0284-8*) Icon Grp.

Pet for Drug Development & Evaluation. Ed. by D. Comar. LC 95-24830. (Developments in Nuclear Medicine Ser.: Vol. 26). 384p. (C). 1995. text 144.00 (*0-7923-3716-6*) Kluwer Academic.

Pet for Dunsworth. Russell K. Hooker. (Dunsworth P. Dragon Coloring Storybooks Ser.). (Illus.). 36p. (J). (ps-6). 1993. pap. 4.95 (*1-884534-01-5*) Duzall Toys.

Pet for Pippa Mouse. Betty Boegehold. (J). 1999. lib. bdg. 7.99 (*0-679-99340-1*) Random.

Pet for Pippa Mouse. Betty Boegehold. (Illus.). (J). 2000. 2.99 (*0-679-89340-7*, Pub. by Random Bks Yng Read) Random.

Pet Gerbils. Jerome Wexler. Ed. by Kathy Tucker. LC 89-5636. (Illus.). 48p. (J). (gr. 3-6). 1990. lib. bdg. 15.95 (*0-8075-6523-7*) A Whitman.

Pet Hamsters. Jerome Wexler. Ed. by Kathleen Tucker. (Illus.). 48p. (J). (gr. 3-6). 1992. lib. bdg. 15.95 (*0-8075-6525-3*) A Whitman.

Pet Health Journal. Laurie Barranti-Teague. 105p. 1997. pap. write for info. (*0-9675257-0-5*) Bananknotcom.

***Pet I'll Get.** Nancy I. Sanders. (Soft Tabs Bk.). (Illus.). 10p. (J). 2000. write for info. (*1-57584-706-X*, Pub. by Rdrs Digest) S&S Trade.

***Pet in Oncology: Basics & Clinical Application.** J. Ruhlmann et al. LC 99-26968. (Illus.). xii, 178p. 1999. 89.00 (*3-540-65077-6*) Spr-Verlag.

Pet Inc. A Report on the Company's Environmental Policies & Practices. (Illus.). 28p. (C). 1994. reprint ed. pap. text 40.00 (*0-7881-0944-8*, Coun on Econ) DIANE Pub.

Pet Industry: Food, Accessories, Health Products & Services. Julia Dvorko. LC 98-143459. (Report Ser.: No. GA-034X). 220p. 1997. 2950.00 (*1-56965-120-5*) BCC.

Pet Industry in France: A Strategic Entry Report, 1997. Compiled by Icon Group International Staff. (Illus.). 123p. 1999. ring bd. 1230.00 incl. audio compact disk (*0-7418-0879-X*) Icon Grp.

Pet Loads, 2 Vol. set. 3rd ed. Ken Waters. Ed. by Dave Wolfe. (Illus.). 432p. 1980. 29.50 (*0-935632-33-6*) Wolfe Pub Co.

Pet Loss: A Spiritual Guide. Eleanor L. Harris. LC 96-47971. (Illus.). 288p. 1999. pap. 9.95 (*1-56718-347-6*) Llewellyn Pubns.

Pet Loss: A Thoughtful Guide for Adults & Children. Herbert A. Nieburg & Arlene Fischer. LC 96-151056. 176p. 1996. pap. 11.00 (*0-06-092678-3*) HarpC.

Pet Loss & Human Bereavement. Ed. by William J. Kay et al. (Illus.). 210p. 1988. reprint ed. pap. 18.95 (*0-8138-1327-1*) Iowa St U Pr.

Pet Loss & Human Emotion: Guiding Clients Through Grief. Cheri B. Ross & Jane B. Sorensen. LC 97-38965. 164p. 1998. pap. 19.95 (*1-56032-652-2*) Hemisp Pub.

Pet Loss Symposiums: Delta Society Conference Lecture Summaries & Writings on Pet Owner's Grief, Bereavement Therapy & Human Nature, 1996-1998. Deborah Antinori et al. 56p. 1999. reprint ed. pap. 15.00 (*1-889785-07-5*) Delta Soc.

***Pet Lover's Collection of Chicken Soup for the Soul.** Jack Canfield. 2000. pap. 4.95 (*0-7407-1141-5*) Andrews & McMeel.

***Pet Medical Records.** Sandrajeanne Bushell. 154p. 1999. 15.00 (*1-58499-001-5*, 120) Full Spectrums.

Pet Memories: Keepsakes & Memories of Our Pet. Naomi M. Zunker. 52p. 1991. pap. 12.95 (*0-9630179-0-X*) Ocotillo Hills.

Pet Names. Jean E. Taggart. LC 62-19730. 387p. 1962. 39.50 (*0-8108-0111-6*) Scarecrow.

***Pet of a Pet.** Marsha Hayles. LC 99-20201. (Illus.). (J). 2001. 13.01 (*0-8037-2512-4*, Dial Yng Read) Peng Put Young Read.

Pet of Frankenstein. Mel Gilden. 96p. (J). (gr. 3-7). 1988. pap. 2.50 (*0-380-75185-2*, Avon Bks) Morrow Avon.

***Pet of My Own: A Caring Guide to Pets.** Moira Butterfield. (Illus.). 2000. pap. 4.95 (*1-902618-22-X*, Pub. by Element Childrns) Penguin Putnam.

Pet of Your Own. George Zappler & Paul Villiard. 1981. pap. 4.95 (*0-385-15429-1*) Doubleday.

Pet or Not? Alvin Silverstein et al. (What a Pet! Ser.). (Illus.). 48p. (YA). (gr. 5-8). 1999. lib. bdg. 21.40 (*0-7613-3230-8*) TFC Bks NY.

Pet-Oriented Child Psychotherapy. 2nd ed. Boris M. Levinson & Gerald P. Mallon. LC 96-8968. 242p. 1996. text 48.95 (*0-398-06673-6*); pap. text 33.95 (*0-398-06674-4*) C C Thomas.

Pet Owner's Guide to Budgerigars. Stan Moizer & Barbara Moizer. (Pet Owner's Guide Ser.). (Illus.). 80p. 1997. 8.00 (*1-86054-038-4*, Pub. by Ringpr Bks) Seven Hills Bk.

Pet Owner's Guide to Coldwater Fishkeeping. Andrew Eade. (Pet Owner's Guide Ser.). (Illus.). 80p. 1997. 8.00 (*1-86054-072-4*, Pub. by Ringpr Bks) Seven Hills Bk.

Pet Owner's Guide to Complete Flea Control: Treating for Fleas Including Pet, Home & Yard. Vance Jackson. (Animal Health Ser.). (Illus.). 110p. (Orig.). 1994. pap. 14.95 (*0-9640526-0-1*) Pet Care Pubng.

Pet Owner's Guide to Greyhounds. Ann Finch. (Pet Owner's Guide Ser.). (Illus.). 80p. 1997. 8.00 (*1-86054-077-5*, Pub. by Ringpr Bks) Seven Hills Bk.

Pet Owner's Guide to Hamsters. Lorraine Hill. (Pet Owner's Guide Ser.). (Illus.). 80p. 1997. 8.00 (*1-86054-043-0*, Pub. by Ringpr Bks) Seven Hills Bk.

Pet Owner's Guide to Rabbits. Marianne Mays. (Pet Owner's Guide Ser.). 80p. 1997. 8.00 (*0-948955-89-9*, Pub. by Ringpr Bks) Seven Hills Bk.

Pet Owner's Guide to the Bearded Collie. Brenda White. (Pet Owner's Guide Ser.). (Illus.). 1998. 8.00 (*1-86054-087-2*, Pub. by Ringpr Bks) Seven Hills Bk.

Pet Owner's Guide to the Border Collie. Adrienne McLeavy. (Pet Owner's Guide Ser.). (Illus.). 1996. 8.00 (*1-86054-070-8*, Pub. by Ringpr Bks) Seven Hills Bk.

Pet Owner's Guide to the Boxer. Andrew Brace. (Pet Owner's Guide Ser.). (Illus.). 1996. 8.00 (*1-86054-065-1*, Pub. by Ringpr Bks) Seven Hills Bk.

Pet Owner's Guide to the Cavalier King Charles Spaniel. Ken Town. (Pet Owner's Guide Ser.). (Illus.). 80p. 1997. 8.00 (*1-86054-011-2*, Pub. by Ringpr Bks) Seven Hills Bk.

Pet Owner's Guide to the Dalmation. M. Gregory. (Pet Owner's Guide Ser.). 80p. 1997. 8.00 (*0-948955-34-1*, Pub. by Ringpr Bks) Seven Hills Bk.

Pet Owner's Guide to the English Springer Spaniel. Don Miller. (Pet Owner's Guide Ser.). (Illus.). 80p. 1997. 8.00 (*1-86054-020-1*, Pub. by Ringpr Bks) Seven Hills Bk.

Pet Owner's Guide to the German Shepherd Dog. Malcolm B. Willis. (Pet Owner's Guide Ser.). (Illus.). 80p. 1997. 8.00 (*0-948955-33-3*, Pub. by Ringpr Bks) Seven Hills Bk.

Pet Owner's Guide to the Golden Retriever. Bernard Bargh. LC 93-9744. (Pet Owner's Guides Ser.). (Illus.). 80p. 1993. pap. 8.00 (*0-87605-979-5*) Howell Bks.

Pet Owner's Guide to the Golden Retriever. Bernard Bargh. (Pet Owner's Guide Ser.). (Illus.). 80p. 1997. 8.00 (*0-948955-43-0*, Pub. by Ringpr Bks) Seven Hills Bk.

Pet Owner's Guide to the Hamster. Lorraine Hill. (Pet Owner's Guide Ser.). (Illus.). 1998. 8.00 (*1-86054-053-8*, Pub. by Ringpr Bks) Seven Hills Bk.

Pet Owner's Guide to the Jack Russell Terrier. John Valentine. (Pet Owner's Guide Ser.). (Illus.). 80p. 1997. 8.00 (*1-86054-007-4*, Pub. by Ringpr Bks) Seven Hills Bk.

Pet Owner's Guide to the Poodle. Barbara Cherry. (Pet Owner's Guide Ser.). (Illus.). 80p. 1997. 8.00 (*0-948955-29-5*, Pub. by Ringpr Bks) Seven Hills Bk.

Pet Owner's Guide to the Rottweiler. Mary MacPhail. (Pet Owner's Guide Ser.). (Illus.). 80p. 1997. 8.00 (*0-948955-38-4*, Pub. by Ringpr Bks) Seven Hills Bk.

Pet Owner's Guide to the Shetland Sheepdog. Mary Davis. (Pet Owner's Guide Ser.). (Illus.). 80p. 1997. 8.00 (*0-948955-24-4*, Pub. by Ringpr Bks) Seven Hills Bk.

Pet Owner's Guide to the Shih Tzu. Dorothy Gurney. (Pet Owner's Guide Ser.). (Illus.). 80p. 1997. 8.00 (*0-948955-44-9*, Pub. by Ringpr Bks) Seven Hills Bk.

Pet Owner's Guide to the Staffordshire Bull Terrier. Clara Lee. (Pet Owner's Guide Ser.). 1998. 8.00 (*1-86054-082-1*, Pub. by Ringpr Bks) Seven Hills Bk.

Pet Owner's Guide to the West Highland White Terrier. Sheila Cleland. (Pet Owner's Guide Ser.). (Illus.). 80p. 1997. 8.00 (*1-86054-015-5*, Pub. by Ringpr Bks) Seven Hills Bk.

Pet Owner's Guide to the Yorkshire Terrier. B. Mackay. (Pet Owner's Guide Ser.). (Illus.). 80p. 1997. 8.00 (*0-948955-39-2*, Pub. by Ringpr Bks) Seven Hills Bk.

Pet Owner's Guide to Tropical Fishkeeping. Mary Bailey. (Pet Owner's Guide Ser.). (Illus.). 80p. 1997. 8.00 (*1-86054-067-8*, Pub. by Ringpr Bks) Seven Hills Bk.

***Pet Pals: Authors & Their Pets.** Fern Michaels et al. (Author Scrapbks.: Vol. 1). (Illus.). 38p. 1999. pap. 5.00 (*1-58365-038-5*, Indigo Publicatns) BT Pub.

Pet Parade. Patricia Reilly Giff. (Polk Street Special Ser.: No. 8). (Illus.). 112p. (J). (gr. 1-7). 1996. pap. 3.99 (*0-440-41232-3*, YB BDD) BDD Bks Young Read.

Pet Parade. Patricia Reilly Giff. (J). 1996. 9.09 (*0-606-09743-0*, Pub. by Turtleback) Demco.

Pet Parrot Book. Peter J. Snyder. LC 98-4264. (Illus.). 136p. 1998. pap. 9.95 (*0-7641-0608-2*) Barron.

Pet Partners Introductory Animal Handlers Skills Course see **Pet Partners Team Training Course: Pets Helping People Manual**

Pet Partners Team Training Course: Pets Helping People Manual. 3rd rev. ed. Ann R. Howie. Orig. Title: Pet Partners Introductory Animal Handlers Skills Course. (Illus.). 234p. pap. 29.00 (*1-889785-08-3*) Delta Soc.

Pet Partners Volunteer Workshop Instructor Guide. Delta Society Staff. (Illus.). Date not set. text. write for info. (*0-9627802-7-8*) Delta Soc.

Pet Parts & Extra Things. Paul Woodbine. (Illus.). 24p. 1984. text 98.00 (*0-916258-14-9*) Woodbine Pr.

Pet Peeves. Virginia Hart. (Romance Ser.). 1993. per. 2.99 (*0-373-03272-2*, 1-03272-1) Harlequin Bks.

Pet Peeves. Taylor McCafferty. Ed. by Jane Chelius. 224p. (Orig.). 1990. mass mkt. 4.99 (*0-671-72802-4*) PB.

Pet Peeves. Daniel R. Vincent. (Illus.). 128p. 1998. pap. 10.95 (*0-9641131-8-X*) DG Publng.

Pet Peeves: And What to Do about Them. rev. ed. M. Edward Burns, Jr. LC 92-6014. (C). 1992. pap. 15.95 (*0-941301-19-2*) CAI.

Pet Peeves: More Than 200 Irritations from Everyday Life. Louie Hulme. LC 94-4397. 128p. (Orig.). 1993. pap. 5.95 (*1-56530-129-3*) Summit TX.

Pet Peeves: Things That Tick Me off about Driving. Jeff Hodge. Ed. by Paulette Hodge. LC 93-60926. (Illus.). 120p. (Orig.). 1993. pap. 5.95 (*0-9633347-5-1*) Talent Wrld Pubns.

Pet Peeves between Partners. 256p. 1998. pap. text 16.95 (*0-87605-626-5*) Howell Bks.

***Pet Peeves: Or Whatever Happened to Doctor Rawff?** George Plimpton. LC PS3566.L5P57 2000. (Illus.). 80p. 2000. 16.95 (*0-87113-820-4*, Atlntc Mnthly) Grove-Atltic.

***Pet Pocketbook: A Record-Keeping Journal for Your Pet.** 2nd ed. Laurie Barranti. 20p. 2000. pap. 8.00 (*0-9675257-1-3*) Bananknotcom.

Pet Power: Amazing True Stories of Animal Bravery & Devotion. Tess Cuming & David Wolstencroft. (Illus.). 128p. 1997. pap. 16.95 (*0-09-185328-1*, Pub. by Ebury Pr) Trafalgar.

***Pet Products in France: A Strategic Entry Report, 1999.** Compiled by Icon Group International. (Illus.). 119p. 1999. ring bd. 1190.00 incl. audio compact disk (*0-7418-1855-8*) Icon Grp.

P

An Asterisk (*) at the beginning of an entry indicates that the title is appearing for the first time.

***Pet Products in Italy: A Strategic Entry Report, 2000.** Compiled by Icon Group International. (Illus.). 133p. 1999. ring bd. 1330.00 incl. audio compact disk (*0-7418-2183-4*) Icon Grp.

Pet Projects for Your Cat: Easy Ways to Pamper Your Kitty. Time-Life Books Editors. LC 99-29322. (Illus.). 80p. 1999. pap. 9.95 (*0-7370-0053-8*) T-L Custom Pub.

Pet Projects for Your Dog: Easy Ways to Pamper Your Puppy. Time-Life Books Editors. LC 99-29321. 80p. 1999. pap. 9.95 (*0-7370-0054-6*) T-L Custom Pub.

Pet Recycling. Richard K. Miller & Marcia E. Rupnow. LC 90-83876. (Survey on Technology & Markets Ser.: No. 171). 50p. 1991. pap. text 200.00 (*1-55865-196-9*) Future Tech Surveys.

Pet Repair. write for info. (*0-9615622-4-2*) McElyea Pubns.

Pet Rescue. Mark Evans. 128p. 1998. 29.95 (*1-85702-733-7*) Trafalgar.

Pet Rescue. large type unabridged ed. Mark Evans. 192p. 1998. 24.95 (*0-7531-5446-3*, 154463) ISIS Pub.

Pet-rified! Dean Marney. 128p. (J). (gr. 4-9). 1997. pap. 3.99 (*0-590-98830-1*) Scholastic Inc.

Pet Sematary. Stephen King. LC 82-45360. 384p. 1983. 30.00 (*0-385-18244-9*) Doubleday.

Pet Sematary. Stephen King. 1984. 12.60 (*0-606-01108-0*, Pub. by Turtleback) Demco.

Pet Sematary. Stephen King. LC 82-45360. 1994. reprint ed. lib. bdg. 29.95 (*1-56849-545-5*) Buccaneer Bks.

Pet Sematary. Stephen King. LC 82-45360. 416p. 1984. reprint ed. mass mkt. 7.99 (*0-451-16207-2*, Sig) NAL.

Pet Shop. Harry Bornstein & Lillian B. Hamilton. (Signed English Ser.). (Illus.). 16p. (J). (ps). 1976. pap. 3.50 (*0-913580-54-6*, Pub. by K Green Pubns) Gallaudet Univ Pr.

Pet Shop Boys. 84p. (YA). 1994. pap. 24.95 (*1-85909-102-4*, UF2152) Wrner Bros.

Pet Shop Boys, Literally. Chris Heath. (Illus.). 368p. 1992. reprint ed. pap. 14.95 (*0-306-80494-8*) Da Capo.

Pet Shop Mouse. Judie Schrecker. LC 93-60231. (Illus.). 35p. (J). (gr. 2-3). 1995. 8.95 (*1-880664-29-1*) E M Pr.

Pet Shop Mystery. Created by Gertrude Chandler Warner. LC 96-30587. (Boxcar Children Special Ser.: No. 7). (Illus.). 128p. (J). (gr. 2-5). 1996. pap. 3.95 (*0-8075-6528-8*); lib. bdg. 13.95 (*0-8075-6527-X*) A Whitman.

Pet Shop Mystery. Created by Gertrude Chandler Warner. (Boxcar Children Ser.: No. 7). (J). (gr. 2-5). 1996. 9.05 (*0-606-10761-4*, Pub. by Turtleback) Demco.

Pet Shop Sticker Activity Book. Cathy Beylon. (J). pap. text 1.00 (*0-486-40312-2*) Dover.

Pet Show! Ezra Jack Keats. (Illus.). 1974. 11.19 (*0-606-01233-8*, Pub. by Turtleback) Demco.

Pet Show! Ezra Jack Keats. LC 86-17225. (Illus.). 32p. (J). (gr. k-3). 1987. reprint ed. mass mkt. 5.99 (*0-689-71159-X*) Aladdin.

Pet-Sitters. Ellen Schecter. LC 95-49339. (West Side Kids Ser.: No. 4). (Illus.). 80p. (J). (gr. 2-5). 1996. pap. 3.95 (*0-7868-1046-7*, Pub. by Hyprn Ppbks) Little.

Pet-Sitters. Ellen Schecter. LC 95-49339. (West Side Kids Ser.). 1996. 9.40 (*0-606-10360-0*) Turtleback.

Pet Sitter's Career Guide. Tammy S. Collins. 80p. (Orig.). pap. 11.95 (*0-9633885-0-9*) Pet Indulgence HPCS.

***Pet Sitters Diary & the Jam Packed Information Manual.** M. J. Price. 400p. 1999. pap. 17.95 (*0-7392-0398-3*, PO3626) Morris Pubng.

Pet Sitting for Profit. Patti J. Moran. (Illus.). 72p. (Orig.). 1987. pap. 9.95 (*0-944165-00-1*) New Beginnings.

Pet Sitting for Profit. rev. ed. Patti J. Moran. (Illus.). 112p. (Orig.). 1988. pap. 9.95 (*0-944165-11-7*) New Beginnings.

Pet Sitting for Profit. 2nd ed. Patti Meran. LC 97-27615. 224p. 1997. 17.95 (*0-87605-596-X*) Howell Bks.

Pet Sitting for Profit: A Complete Manual for Success. Patti J. Moran. (Illus.). 192p. 1992. pap. 15.95 (*0-87605-770-9*) Howell Bks.

Pet-Sitting Peril. Willo D. Roberts. (J). 1983. 10.09 (*0-606-00381-9*, Pub. by Turtleback) Demco.

Pet-Sitting Peril. 2nd ed. Willo D. Roberts. LC 89-77696. 192p. (J). (gr. 4-6). 1990. reprint ed. mass mkt. 4.99 (*0-689-71427-0*) Aladdin.

Pet-Sitting Service. Danae Dobson. (Sunny Street Kids' Club Ser.: Vol. 2). (Illus.). 32p. (J). (ps-3). 1996. pap. 4.99 (*0-8499-5113-5*) Tommy Nelson.

Pet Snoopy. Determined Productions. (Illus.). (J). (ps). 1983. pap. 4.95 (*0-915696-72-X*) Determined Prods.

Pet Store. M. T. Coffin. (Spinetinglers Ser.: No. 13). 144p. (Orig.). (J). (gr. 4-7). 1996. pap. 3.50 (*0-380-78460-2*, Avon Bks) Morrow Avon.

Pet Store. M. T. Coffin. (Spinetinglers Ser.). (Orig.). 1996. 8.60 (*0-606-09744-9*, Pub. by Turtleback) Demco.

***Pet Store: A Complete Theme Unit Including Learning Centers.** Dana McMillan. (Illus.). 32p. (J). (ps). 2000. pap. 5.95 (*1-57310-211-3*) Teachng & Lrning Co.

***Pet-Store Sprite.** Tracey West. (Pixie Tricks Ser.: No. 3). 80p. (J). (gr. 4-7). 2000. pap. 3.99 (*0-439-17978-5*) Scholastic Inc.

Pet Stories for Children of All Ages. Stephen Charak. (Illus.). 48p. (Orig.). 1991. pap. 5.95 (*0-9627201-1-9*) Patcha Pubng.

***Pet Stories You Don't Have to Walk.** Ed. by SeaStar Publishing Staff. (Reading Rainbow Ser.). 2000. 14.88 (*1-58717-032-9*); pap. 3.99 (*1-58717-031-0*) SeaStar.

***Pet Story: Publish Your Own Keepsake Pet Book!** Chimeric Inc. Staff. (Illus.). 2000. 28.95 (*0-9636796-5-1*) Chimeric.

Pet Studies on Amino Acid Metabolism & Protein Synthesis. Ed. by B. M. Mazoyer. (Developments in Nuclear Medicine Ser.). 288p. (C). 1993. text 145.50 (*0-7923-2076-X*) Kluwer Academic.

***Pet Tenant.** Debbie Vallis. 256p. 2000. pap. 14.95 (*1-56167-585-7*) Am Literary Pr.

Pet That I Want. Mary Packard. LC 94-16976. (My First Hello Reader Ser.). (Illus.). 32p. (J). (ps-1). 1995. 3.95 (*0-590-48512-1*, Cartwheel) Scholastic Inc.

Pet That Never Was. Nancy S. Levene. LC 91-33518. Vol. 1. 96p. (J). (gr. 5-7). 1992. pap. 4.99 (*1-55513-394-0*, Chariot Bks) Chariot Victor.

Pet the Baby Farm Animals: Their Fur Feels Real! Lucinda McQueen. LC 93-84532. (Illus.). 16p. (J). (ps-2). 1994. 8.95 (*0-590-47687-4*, Cartwheel) Scholastic Inc.

Pet Tracker: For Dog Owners. Kelly Carroll. (Illus.). 40p. 1997. spiral bd. 23.00 (*0-9657256-0-X*) Falling Sun.

Pet-Trust: A Last Will & Testament for You & Your Pet. Richard E. Faler, Jr. 44p. 1997. pap. 9.95 (*1-881399-17-6*) Beaver Pond P&P.

Pet Vet. Marcia Leonard. LC 98-34285. (Real Kids Readers Ser.). (Illus.). 32p. (J). (ps-1). 1999. pap. 3.99 (*0-7613-2075-X*, Copper Beech Bks); lib. bdg. 16.90 (*0-7613-2050-4*, Copper Beech Bks) Millbrook Pr.

Peta - A Feminist's Problem with Men. Ed. by Moira Walker. LC 94-24085. (In Search of a Therapist Ser.). 168p. 1995. 30.95 (*0-335-19223-8*) OpUniv Pr.

Peta Stories. Tr. by U Ba Kyaw & P. Masefield from PLI. (C). 1980. 71.00 (*0-86013-075-4*, Pub. by Pali Text) Elsevier.

Petagwana to Pele: The Story of Great Lakes Prehistoric & Historic Sites & Their People (Point Edward to Point Pelee) 3rd ed. Al Plant. (Illus.). 116p. (YA). (gr. 7 up). 1995. pap. 12.95 (*0-913611-06-9*) W E C Plant.

Petah Coyne. Petah Coyle et al. LC 96-31061. 1996. pap. write for info. (*0-88675-048-2*) Corcoran.

Petah Coyne. David S. Rubin. (Illus.). 36p. 1992. pap. text 10.00 (*1-880353-02-4*) Cleveland Ctr.

Petain. Nicholas Atkin. LC 97-14220. (Profiles in Power Ser.). 256p. (C). 1997. pap. 23.53 (*0-582-07037-6*) Longman.

Petain Profiles in Power Series. Nicholas Atkin. LC 97-14220. (Profiles in Power Ser.). (C). 1997. text 62.81 (*0-582-07036-8*) Longman.

Petain's Crime: The Complete Story of French Collaboration in the Holocaust. Paul Webster. (Illus.). 240p. 1991. text 24.95 (*0-929587-55-3*) I R Dee.

Petal by Petal. Joan Shay. LC 98-30017. 1998. pap. text 14.95 (*1-57432-707-0*, 5013, Am Quilters Soc) Collector Bks.

Petal Pals Children's Stories, 4 bks. Susan Tate. (Petal Pals Ser.). (J). (gr. k-3). 1993. pap. 15.96 (*1-884395-07-4*) Clear Blue Sky.

Petal Pals Coloring Books, 3 bks., Set. Susan Tate. (Petal Pals Ser.). (Illus.). (J). (gr. k-3). 1993. pap. 1.17 (*1-884395-08-2*) Clear Blue Sky.

Petal Power. Sandra Byrd. (Secret Sisters Ser.: Vol. 8). 112p. (J). (gr. 4-7). 1999. pap. 5.95 (*1-57856-115-9*) Waterbrook Pr.

Petalos. Richard O. Mahoney. (Illus.). (Orig.). Date not set. pap. write for info. (*1-880708-03-5*) U Phoenix Pr.

Petalos Al Viento. V. C. Andrews. 1998. pap. 6.95 (*84-01-49748-5*) Lectorum Pubns.

Petalos de la Rosa. Dalia N. Albert. Ed. by Pepe Carvajal. (SPA.). 28p. 1993. pap. write for info. (*0-942347-01-3*) Ediciones Puerto.

Petals. Georgia Bartlett. 62p. 1995. pap. 10.50 (*1-56770-317-8*) S Scheewe Pubns.

Petals: Change Your Perspective Change Your Life. Annette F. McMahon. (Illus.). 223p. (Orig.). 1987. 24.95 (*0-944005-21-7*); pap. write for info. (*0-944005-22-5*); lib. bdg. write for info. (*0-944005-23-3*) Columbia NY.

***Petals Vol. 5034: 18 Acid-Free Papers for Scrapbooks & More!** Ed. by Suzanne McNeill. (Illus.). 18p. 1999. 8.45 (*1-893749-20-7*) Fiskars.

Petals from a Rose. Tom Pagna. (Illus.). 250p. 1998. 24.95 (*0-89651-556-7*) Hardwood Pr.

Petals from the Rain Gutter. Tamson Weston. 48p. (Orig.). 1995. pap. 6.95 (*1-886963-00-2*) Kettle of Fish.

Petals in the Storm. Mary Jo Putney. 384p. (Orig.). 1993. mass mkt. 6.99 (*0-451-40445-9*, Topaz) NAL.

Petals in the Wind. Helen Burton. LC 95-95062. (Illus.). 82p. 1997. 17.95 (*0-9645769-1-0*) H Burton.

Petals in the Wind. large type ed. Ivy Preston. (Linford Romance Library). 320p. 1992. pap. 16.99 (*0-7089-7207-1*, Linford) Ulverscroft.

***Petals, Mountains, Hearts.** Patricia Sullivan. (Illus.). 24p. 1999. pap. 5.00 (*0-9669897-2-4*) Gravity Presses.

Petals of Blood. Ngugi wa Thiong'o. 344p. 1991. pap. 13.95 (*0-14-015351-9*, Penguin Bks) Viking Penguin.

Petals of Rebirth, Vol. 2, No. 2. Ed. by Lana M. Wegeng et al. 68p. 1998. pap. 9.95 (*0-9659454-5-6*) Columbia Pubns.

Petals of the Rose. Joseph P. Simini. 28p. (Orig.). 1990. pap. 4.50 (*0-943020-04-2*) Bottom Line Pr.

Petals of the Rose: Poems & Epigrams. Louis V. Burrell. LC 70-168513. (Black Heritage Library Collection). 1977. reprint ed. 14.95 (*0-8369-8876-0*) Ayer.

***Petals on a Wet Whitewall.** Kirpal Gordon. 64p. 1999. pap. 9.95 (*0-9674278-0-0*) Hunger Mag.

Petals on the Prairie. Gloria Bauske. 108p. 1999. pap. 12.95 (*1-57579-145-5*) Pine Hill Pr.

Petals on the River. Kathleen E. Woodiwiss. LC 97-29814. 560p. 1998. mass mkt. 6.99 (*0-380-79828-X*, Avon Bks) Morrow Avon.

Petals on the River. large type ed. Kathleen E. Woodiwiss. LC 97-50388. (Americana Series). 708p. 1998. 28.95 (*0-7862-1285-3*) Thorndike Pr.

Petals on the Wind. V. C. Andrews. LC 80-15638. 1980. pap. write for info. (*0-671-82977-7*) Litle Simon.

Petals on the Wind. V. C. Andrews. 1984. write for info. (*0-318-57961-8*) PB.

Petals on the Wind. V. C. Andrews. Ed. by Linda Marrow. LC 00-1495. 1990. per. 7.99 (*0-671-72947-0*) PB.

Petals on the Wind. V. C. Andrews. 1980. 12.09 (*0-606-00253-7*, Pub. by Turtleback) Demco.

Petals Plucked from Sunny Climes. Silvia Sunshine, pseud. LC 76-10700. (Floridiana Facsimile & Reprint Ser.). 507p. 1976. reprint ed. 29.95 (*0-8130-0414-4*) U Press Fla.

Petaluma's Poultry Pioneers: Recall the Heyday of Chicken Ranching. Thea S. Lowry. (Illus.). 128p. (Orig.). 1993. pap. 10.95 (*0-9610116-0-2*) Manifold Pr.

Petanque: The French Game of Boules. Ed. by Garth Freeman. 75p. 1987. pap. 75.00 (*0-9510213-0-3*, Pub. by Carrew Pr) St Mut.

Peta's Pence. Christina Purkus. (Livewire Ser.). (YA). (gr. 6-9). pap. 6.95 (*0-7043-4923-X*, Pub. by Womens Press) Trafalgar.

Pete, 1. Leigh Greenwood. (Coyboys Ser.). 400p. 1999. mass mkt. 5.99 (*0-8439-4562-1*, Pub. by Dorchester Pub Co) CMG.

Pete: The Story of Peter V. Cacchione, New York's First Communist Councilman. Simon W. Gerson. LC 76-29039. 215p. 1976. pap. 3.50 (*0-7178-0473-9*) Intl Pubs Co.

Pete Aguereberry: Death Valley Prospector. George Pipkin. LC 81-84564. (Illus.). 1982. 10.95 (*0-930704-11-8*) Sagebrush Pr.

Pete & His Elves Series, Set. Kate Cavanaugh. (Illus.). 28p. (J). 1992. pap. write for info. (*0-9622353-4-2*) KAC.

Pete & Moe Visit Professor Swizzle's Robots. Vincent Giarrano. (Illus.). 32p. 1994. 14.95 (*1-56971-007-4*) Dark Horse Comics.

***Pete & Polo's Big School Adventure.** Adrian Reynolds. LC 99-51523. (Illus.). 32p. (J). 2000. 15.95 (*0-531-30275-X*) Orchard Bks Watts.

Pete & Roland. Bob Graham. (J). (ps-3). 1988. pap. 3.95 (*0-318-32773-2*, PuffinBks) Peng Put Young Read.

Pete & Shirley: The Great Tar Heel Novel. Clyde Edgerton et al. Ed. by David Perkins. LC 95-83311. 116p. 1995. pap. 13.95 (*1-878086-49-9*, Pub. by Down Home NC) Blair.

Pete Cassidy's Oracle Cookbook for SQL Plus. Pete Cassidy. Ed. by Carole Cassidy. (Illus.). 228p. (Orig.). 1995. pap. 29.95 (*0-9656696-0-2*) Chef Pierre.

Pete Ellis: An Amphibious Warfare Prophet, 1880-1923. Merrill L. Bartlett & Dirk A. Ballendorf. LC 96-43522. (Illus.). 200p. 1996. 27.95 (*1-55750-060-6*) Naval Inst Pr.

Pete Fountain's Transcribed Solos. 52p. 1995. pap. 11.95 (*0-7935-4961-2*, 00030390) H Leonard.

***Pete Frame's Rocking Around Britain.** Pete Frame. (Illus.). 176p. 1999. 24.95 (*0-7119-6973-6*) Omnibus NY.

Pete Goes to Grand Island. Kate Cavanaugh. (Illus.). 24p. (J). 1992. pap. 5.95 (*0-9622353-3-4*) KAC.

Pete Maravich: Basketball Whiz. Musemeche & Ellis. 1969. 4.95 (*0-685-00420-1*) Claitors.

***Pete Newell's Defensive Basketball: Winning Techniques & Strategies.** Pete Newell. (Illus.). 220p. 2000. pap. 16.95 (*1-58382-043-4*) Coaches Choice.

Pete Pig Cleans Up. Jay Hulbert. (Real Readers Ser.: Level Red). (Illus.). 32p. (J). (gr. 1-4). 1989. pap. 4.95 (*0-8114-6703-1*) Raintree Steck-V.

Pete Pig Cleans Up. Jay Hulbert. (Real Readers Ser.: Level Red). (Illus.). 32p. (J). (ps-3). 1989. lib. bdg. 21.40 (*0-8172-3504-3*) Raintree Steck-V.

Pete Rose. Thomas Gilbert. LC 94-30941. (Baseball Legends Ser.). (Illus.). 64p. (J). (gr. 3 up). 1995. lib. bdg. 15.95 (*0-7910-2171-8*) Chelsea Hse.

Pete Rose: My Story. Peter I. Rose & Roger Kahn. 288p. 1989. text 18.95 (*0-02-560611-5*) Macmillan.

Pete Sampras. Calvin C. Miller. LC 97-48344. (Great Athletes Ser.). (Illus.). 64p. (YA). (gr. 3 up). 1998. lib. bdg. 17.95 (*1-883846-26-9*) M Reynolds.

Pete Sampras. Richard Rambeck. LC 95-42610. (Sports Superstars Ser.). (Illus.). 24p. (J). (gr. 2-6). 1996. lib. bdg. 21.36 (*1-56766-262-5*) Childs World.

***Pete Sampras: Strokes of Genius.** Mark Stewart. (Sports Stars Ser.). (Illus.). (J). 2000. 19.50 (*0-516-22049-7*) Childrens.

***Pete Sampras: Strokes of Genius.** Mark Stewart. (Sports Stars Ser.). (Illus.). 48p. (J). (gr. 3-4). 2000. pap. 5.95 (*0-516-27074-5*) Childrens.

Pete the Parakeet. Sharon Gordon. (Illus.). 32p. (J). (gr. k-2). 1980. lib. bdg. 13.05 (*0-89375-384-X*) Troll Communs.

Pete the Parakeet. Sharon Gordon. (Illus.). 32p. (J). (gr. k-2). 1997. pap. 2.50 (*0-89375-284-3*) Troll Communs.

Pete the Python: The Further Adventures of Mark & Deke. Jim Dunlap. 160p. 1996. pap. 8.95 (*1-55622-508-3*, Seaside Pr) Wordware Pub.

Pete Townshend: The Minstrel's Dilemma. Larry David Smith. LC 98-35320. 320p. 1999. 39.95 (*0-275-96472-8*, Praeger Pubs) Greenwood.

Pete Turner. Gruppo Editoriale Fabbri Staff. write for info. (*0-318-58188-4*) P-H.

Peter see Young Readers Christian Library

Peter see Pedro

***Peter.** Robbie Castleman. 1999. pap. 4.99 (*0-8308-3088-X*) InterVarsity.

Peter: A Journey in Faith. R. Scott Sullender. 47p. (Orig.). 1986. pap. 7.95 (*0-940754-37-1*) Ed Ministries.

Peter: An Opera. Composed by Gene Koskey. 90p. 1997. spiral bd. 19.95 (*0-9656757-3-4*) Genteel Pubs.

***Peter: Apostle for the Whole Church.** Pheme Perkins. LC 00-24751. (Personalities of the New Testament Ser.). 224p. 2000. pap. 22.00 (*0-8006-3165-X*, Fortress Pr) Augsburg Fortress.

Peter: Eyewitness of His Majesty. Edward A. Donnelly. 100p. 1998. pap. 9.99 (*0-85151-744-7*) Banner of Truth.

Peter: The Illustrious Disciple. John G. Butler. 394p. 1993. 19.50 (*1-889773-08-5*) LBC Publns.

Peter: Twenty-Six Learning Activities for Children. Phyllis Vos Wezeman et al. LC 97-38010. (Ideas A to Z Ser.). (Illus.). 80p. Date not set. pap. 9.99 (*0-8254-3962-0*) Kregel.

Peter: 8 Lessons on Righteous Living Exclusively for Women. Dee Brestin. 1999. pap. text 6.99 (*1-56476-768-X*) SP Pubns.

Peter - Revelation: Commentary. Paul Gardner. 1988. pap. 4.95 (*0-87508-175-4*) Chr Lit.

Peter - The Apostle. C. Mackenzie. (BibleTime Bks.). (J). 1995. 2.99 (*0-906731-65-8*, Pub. by Christian Focus) Spring Arbor Dist.

Peter - The Fisherman. C. Mackenzie. (BibleTime Bks.). (J). 1995. 2.99 (*0-906731-08-9*, Pub. by Christian Focus) Spring Arbor Dist.

Peter, a Follower of Jesus. Susan Harrison. 1999. pap. text 3.95 (*0-687-05329-3*) Abingdon.

Peter Abelard. Ed. by E. Buytaert. No. 2. 195p. (Orig.). 1974. pap. 34.50 (*90-6186-005-9*, Pub. by Leuven Univ) Coronet Bks.

Peter Abelard. Joseph McCabe. LC 74-148889. (Select Bibliographies Reprint Ser.). 1977. reprint ed. 24.95 (*0-8369-5655-9*) Ayer.

Peter Abelard, Letters IX-XIV. Edme R. Smits. xii, 315p. (Orig.). 1983. pap. 31.00 (*90-6088-085-4*, Pub. by Boumas Boekhuis) Gen Publ ON.

Peter Ackroyd. Ed. by Susana Onega. pap. 22.50 (*0-7463-0839-6*, Pub. by Northcote House) Trans-Atl Phila.

***Peter Ackroyd: The Ludic & Labyrinthine Text.** Jeremy S. Gibson & Julian Wolfreys. LC 99-43171. 300p. 2000. text 55.00 (*0-312-22868-6*) St Martin.

***Peter Alexander: In This Light.** Peter Alexander et al. LC 98-40840. 1999. pap. 29.95 (*0-917493-27-3*) Orange Cnty Mus.

***Peter Alexander: In This Light.** Dave Hickey & Naomi Vine. LC 98-40840. (Illus.). 120p. 1999. 45.00 (*0-917493-28-1*, Pub. by Orange Cnty Mus) Hudson Hills.

Peter & His Friend Jesus. Benton Mayhan. 1999. pap. text 3.95 (*0-687-05338-2*) Abingdon.

Peter & His Pick-Up Truck: A Southwestern Children's Tale. Cynthia V. Nasta. LC 89-80351. (Illus.). 24p. (J). (ps-8). 1989. pap. 6.95 (*0-9622064-0-7*) Little Buckaroo.

Peter & His Pick-up Truck: An Arizona Children's Tale. Cynthia V. Nasta. LC 89-80352. (Illus.). 24p. (J). (ps-8). 1989. pap. 6.95 (*0-9622064-2-3*); lib. bdg. 6.95 (*0-9622064-1-5*) Little Buckaroo.

Peter & Paul. 1996. pap., student ed. 19.99 (*1-56364-185-2*) Vision Vid PA.

Peter & Paul in the Church of Rome: The Ecumenical Potential of a Forgotten Perspective. William R. Farmer & Roch Kereszty. 1989. pap. 11.95 (*0-8091-3102-1*) Paulist Pr.

Peter & Sally Sammartino: Biographical Notes. Margherita Marchione. (Biographical Notes Ser.). (Illus.). 305p. 1994. 24.95 (*0-8453-4855-8*, Cornwall Bks) Assoc Univ Prs.

Peter & the Beloved Disciple: Figures for a Community in Crisis. Kevin B. Quast. (JSNT Supplement Ser.: No. 32). 232p. 1989. 70.00 (*1-85075-217-6*, Pub. by Sheffield Acad) CUP Services.

***Peter & the Blue Witch Baby.** Robert D. San Souci. (Illus.). 32p. (J). (ps-3). 2000. 17.99 (*0-385-90002-3*) Doubleday.

***Peter (& the Boys)** John Seventin. LC 98-61759. 129p. 2000. 16.95 (*0-533-13014-X*) Vantage.

Peter & the Penny Tree. (J). 1997. pap. 2.50 (*0-8167-0033-8*) Troll Communs.

Peter & the Rock. Chrys Caragounis. (Beiheft zur Zeitschrift fuer die Alttestamentliche Wissenschaft Ser.: Vol. 58). ix, 157p. 1990. lib. bdg. 49.25 (*3-11-012396-7*) De Gruyter.

Peter & the Wolf. Illus. & Retold by Ian Beck. LC 95-75918. 32p. (J). (gr. 4-6). 1995. 13.00 (*0-689-80336-2*) Atheneum Yung Read.

***Peter & the Wolf.** Ian Beck. (J). 2000. pap. 8.95 (*0-552-52755-6*, Pub. by Transworld Publishers Ltd) Trafalgar.

Peter & the Wolf. Illus. by Richard Bernal. 32p. (J). (ps-3). 1992. 6.95 (*0-8362-4921-6*) Andrews & McMeel.

Peter & the Wolf. David Brownell. (J). (gr. 1-9). 1992. pap. 4.95 (*0-88388-093-8*) Bellerophon Bks.

Peter & the Wolf. Illus. by Reg Cartwright. LC 86-27004. 32p. (J). (ps-2). 1995. pap. 5.95 (*0-8050-1362-8*, Bks Young Read) H Holt & Co.

Peter & the Wolf. George Doherty. (J). 1994. 7.98 (*1-57042-224-9*) Warner Bks.

Peter & the Wolf. David Eastman. LC 87-11275. (Illus.). 32p. (J). (gr. k-3). 1988. lib. bdg. 15.85 (*0-8167-1057-0*) Troll Communs.

Peter & the Wolf. David Eastman. LC 87-11275. (Illus.). 32p. (J). (gr. k-3). 1997. pap. 3.95 (*0-8167-1058-9*) Troll Communs.

Peter & the Wolf. David Eastman. (J). 1988. 8.15 (*0-606-03636-9*, Pub. by Turtleback) Demco.

Peter & the Wolf. Illus. by Naomi Howland. LC 97-10154. 24p. (J). (ps-3). 1997. 14.98 (*1-56799-540-3*, Friedman-Fairfax) M Friedman Pub Grp Inc.

Peter & the Wolf. Illus. & Retold by Michele Lemieux. 32p. (J). 1991. pap. 4.95 (*1-55074-174-8*) Kids Can Pr.

Peter & the Wolf. Illus. & Retold by Michele Lemieux. LC 90-6486. 32p. 1991. 13.95 (*0-688-09846-0*, Wm Morrow) Morrow Avon.

Peter & the Wolf. Michele Lemieux. (J). (ps-3). 1996. mass mkt. 4.95 (*0-688-14728-3*, Wm Morrow) Morrow Avon.

Peter & the Wolf. Sergei O. Prokofieff. 1994. 22.95 incl. audio (*0-679-86156-4*) Random Hse Chldrns.

***Peter & the Wolf.** Sergei Prokofiev. LC 99-18979. (Illus.). 32p. (J). (gr. k-2). 1999. 15.95 (*0-7358-1188-1*, Pub. by North-South Bks NYC) Chronicle Bks.

P

***Peter & the Wolf.** Sergei Prokofiev. LC 99-18979. (Illus.). 32p. (J). (gr. k-3). 1999. lib. bdg. 15.88 (*0-7358-1189-X*, Pub. by North-South Bks NYC) Chronicle Bks.

Peter & the Wolf. Sergei Prokofiev. Tr. by Maria Carlson. LC 86-3217. (Picture Puffin Ser.). (Illus.). 32p. (J). (ps-3). 1986. pap. 5.99 (*0-14-050633-0*, PuffinBks) Peng Put Young Read.

Peter & the Wolf. Sergei Prokofiev. Tr. by Joe Johnson from FRE. (Illus.). 22p. (J). (gr. 4-8). 1998. 15.95 (*1-56163-200-7*) NBM.

Peter & the Wolf. Sergey Prokofiev. (J). 1986. 10.19 (*0-606-01425-X*, Pub. by Turtleback) Demco.

***Peter & the Wolf.** Vladimir Vasil'evich Vagin & Sergey Prokofiev. LC 99-47590. (Illus.). 32p. (YA). (gr. k up). 2000. 15.95 (*0-590-38608-5*) Scholastic Inc.

Peter & the Wolf. large type ed. Sergei Prokofiev. (Illus.). 1993. 9.50 (*0-614-09851-3*, L-34092-00) Am Printing Hse.

Peter & the Wolf. unabridged ed. Sergei Prokofiev. Tr. by Maria Carlson. (Illus.). (J). (gr. 1-5). 1987. pap. 15.95 incl. audio (*0-87499-073-4*) Live Oak Media.

Peter & the Wolf, 4 bks., Set. Sergei Prokofiev. Tr. by Maria Carlson. (Illus.). (J). (gr. 1-5). 1987. pap., teacher ed. 33.95 incl. audio (*0-87499-075-0*) Live Oak Media.

Peter & The Wolf Level 4. Carin Dewhirst. (J). 1996. 16.98 incl. audio, cd-rom (*1-56799-303-6*) Friedman Pub.

Peter & the Wolf & Tubby the Tuba. unabridged ed. Sergei Prokofiev. (J). (gr. k-5). 1988. audio 14.95 (*0-89845-816-1*, CPN 1623, Caedmon) HarperAudio.

Peter & the Wolf Pop-up-Book. Sergei Prokofiev. (Illus.). (J). (gr. k-12). 1986. 19.99 (*0-670-80849-0*, Viking Child) Peng Put Young Read.

Peter & Veronica. Marilyn Sachs. LC 95-3134. 1995. pap. 4.99 (*0-14-037082-X*, PuffinBks) Peng Put Young Read.

Peter & Veronica. Marilyn Sachs. (J). 1995. 10.09 (*0-606-08009-0*, Pub. by Turtleback) Demco.

Peter Arbiter: The Adventures of a Young Man in Texas. Edwin Shrake. (Illus.). 152p. 1973. 14.95 (*0-88426-030-5*) Encino Pr.

Peter Aureol on Predestination: A Challenge to Late Medieval Thought. James L. Halverson. LC 98-16147. (Studies in the History of Christian Thought). 1998. 85.50 (*90-04-10945-5*) Brill Academic Pubs.

Peter Aureoli: Scriptum Super Primum Sententiarum, 2 vols., Vol. 2. Ed. by Eligius M. Buytaert. (Text Ser.). 1956. 23.00 (*1-57659-119-0*) Franciscan Inst.

Peter B. & the Pelican Man. Betty Z. Watson. (Illus.). 24p. (J). (ps-3). 1994. 9.95 (*1-885181-00-0*) Watson Pubns.

Peter B. Merialdo: Memoirs of a Son of Italian Immigrants, Recorder & Auditor of Eureka County, Nevada State Controller, & Republican Party Worker. Ed. by Mary E. Glass. 155p. 1968. lib. bdg. 37.50 (*1-56475-055-8*); fiche. write for info. (*1-56475-056-6*) U NV Oral Hist.

***Peter Basseler.** Lothar Romain. (ENG & GER., Illus.). 200p. 2001. 89.00 (*3-932565-00-2*) Edition A Menges.

Peter Beagle. Kenneth J. Zahorski. Ed. by Roger C. Schlobin. LC 87-9924. (Starmont Reader's Guide Ser.: Vol. 44). iv, 124p. 1988. pap. 17.00 (*1-55742-008-4*) Millefleurs.

Peter Beard: Beyond the End of the World. Edwards. 2000. pap. 25.00 (*0-7893-0147-4*, Pub. by Universe) St Martin.

***Peter Bedricks Young Peoples Encyclopedia: Plants & Animals.** Editors of Larousse. LC 99-59506. (Peter Bedrick Young People's Encyclopedias Ser.). (Illus.). 96p. (J). (gr. 5-9). 2000. 24.95 (*0-87226-623-0*, 66230B, P Bedrick Books) NTC Contemp Pub Co.

Peter Behrens & a New Architecture for the Twentieth Century. Stanford Anderson. LC 99-49154. (Illus.). 393p. 2000. 59.95 (*0-262-01176-X*) MIT Pr.

Peter Bell. William Wordsworth. Ed. by John E. Jordan. LC 83-21042. (Cornell Wordsworth Ser.). (Illus.). 648p. (C). 1985. text 90.00 (*0-8014-1620-5*) Cornell U Pr.

Peter Bell. William Wordsworth. 110p. 1992. reprint ed. 40.00 (*1-85477-114-0*) Continuum.

***Peter Benchley's Amazon: The Ghost Tribe, No. 1.** Rob MacGregor. 384p. 2000. mass mkt. 6.99 (*0-380-81403-X*, Torch) HarpC.

Peter Benchley's Creature. Peter Benchley. 1998. mass mkt. 6.99 (*0-312-96573-7*) St Martin.

Peter Bently: The Super Sleuth Cat. Albert J. Montesi. 60p. 1987. pap. 5.00 (*0-918476-15-1*) Cornerstone Pr.

Peter Berner: On the Occasion of His 65th Birthday: Journal: Psychopathology, 1990, Vol. 23, No. 2. Ed. by H. G. Zapotoczky & E. Gabriel. (Illus.). 72p. 1990. 35.75 (*3-8055-5311-0*) S Karger.

Peter Bichsel. Ed. by Rolf Jucker. LC 97-147779. 131p. 1997. pap. 14.95 (*0-7083-1380-9*, Pub. by Univ Wales Pr) Paul & Co Pubs.

Peter Blume: The Italian Drawings. Frank A. Trapp. (Illus.). 42p. (Orig.). 1985. pap. 5.00 (*0-914337-06-8*) Mead Art Mus.

***Peter Bogdanovich's Movie of the Week.** Peter Bogdanovich. LC 99-28582. (Illus.). 1999. pap. 11.00 (*0-345-43205-3*) Ballantine Pub Grp.

Peter Brook. Albert Hunt & Geoffrey Reeves. (Directors in Perspective Ser.). (Illus.). 306p. (C). 1995. pap. text 20.95 (*0-521-29605-6*) Cambridge U Pr.

Peter Brook: A Theatrical Casebook. Ed. by David Williams. 398p. (C). 1988. pap. 17.95 (*0-413-15700-8*, A0209) Heinemann.

***Peter Brook: Oxford to Orghast.** Richard Helfer. 324p. 1998. text 57.00 (*90-5702-207-9*, Harwood Acad Pubs) Gordon & Breach.

Peter Brook: Oxford to Orghast. Ed. by Richard Helfer & Glenn Loney. (Contemporary Theatre Studies). 324p. 1998. pap. text 24.00 (*90-5702-208-7*, Harwood Acad Pubs) Gordon & Breach.

Peter Brook - Jean-Claude Carriere Mahabharata: The History of Mankind. David Leeming. 69p. 1986. 49.95 (*0-88946-005-1*) E Mellen.

Peter Brook & The Mahabharata: Critical Perspectives. Ed. by David Williams. (Illus.). 304p. (C). 1991. pap. text 25.00 (*0-415-04778-1*, A6079) Routledge.

***Peter Bruegel.** Jayne Woodhouse. LC 00-25791. 2000. write for info. (*1-57572-344-1*) Heinemann Lib.

Peter Bruegel the Elder: At the Kunsthistoriches Museum in Vienna. Ed. by Wilfried Seipel. (Illus.). 160p. 1999. boxed set 55.00 (*88-8118-320-X*, Pub. by Skira IT) Abbeville Pr.

Peter Brueghel the Elder. Gustave Gluck. Tr. by E. B. Shaw. (Illus.). 34p. 1936. lib. bdg. 35.00 (*0-8288-3936-0*) Fr & Eur.

Peter C. Hiebert: He Gave Them Bread. Ed. by Wesley Prieb. (Illus.). 149p. (Orig.). 1990. pap. 10.00 (*1-877941-02-6*) Ctr Mennonite Brethren Studies.

Peter C. Petersen: Reminiscences of My Work in Nevada Labor, Politics, Post Office & Gaming Control. Jerome E. Edwards. 107p. 1970. lib. bdg. 31.50 (*1-56475-090-6*); fiche. write for info. (*1-56475-091-4*) U NV Oral Hist.

Peter Camenzind. Hermann Hesse. Tr. by Michael Roloff from GER. 208p. 1988. pap. 12.00 (*0-374-50784-8*) FS&G.

Peter Camenzind. Hermann Hesse. (GER., Illus.). (C). 1953. 12.00 (*0-8442-2762-5*, X2762-5) NTC Contemp Pub Co.

Peter Campus: Selected Works, 1973-1987. Judith E. Tannenbaum & David S. Rubin. LC 87-80140. (Illus.). 36p. (Orig.). 1987. pap. text 8.00 (*0-941972-04-6*) Freedman.

Peter Campus - Photographs, David Deutsch - Paintings & Drawings. Kathy Halbreich & Katy Kline. (Illus.). 28p. (Orig.). 1983. pap. 4.00 (*0-938437-07-0*) MIT List Visual Arts.

Peter Can't Wait. Carol T. Plum. LC 90-64471. (I Am Special Story Bks.). (Illus.). 32p. (J). (gr. k-3). 1991. 6.95 (*0-87973-006-4*, 6); pap. 3.95 (*0-87973-007-2*, 7) Our Sunday Visitor.

Peter Capstick's Africa: Return to the Long Grass. Peter H. Capstick. 320p. 1987. text 35.00 (*0-312-00670-5*) St Martin.

Peter Chan's Magical Landscape: Transforming Any Small Space into a Place of Beauty. Peter Chan. Ed. by Gwen Steege. LC 86-45975. (Illus.). 128p. 1988. pap. 10.95 (*0-88266-455-7*, Garden Way Pub) Storey Bks.

Peter Chan's Magical Landscape: Transforming Any Small Space into a Place of Beauty. Peter Chan. Ed. by Gwen Steege. LC 86-45975. (Illus.). 128p. 1988. 21.95 (*0-88266-454-9*, Garden Way Pub) Storey Bks.

Peter Charlie: The Cruise of the PC 477. Arthur S. Bell, Jr. LC 82-71794. (Illus.). 384p. 1982. 14.95 (*0-910355-00-2*) Courtroom Comp.

Peter Christian's Favorites. 1987. write for info. (*0-9619409-0-5*) Enter Edibles.

Peter Christian's Recipes. 1983. write for info. (*0-936988-09-6*) Enter Edibles.

Peter Churchmouse. Margot Austin. (Illus.). 42p. 1992. reprint ed. lib. bdg. 14.95 (*0-89968-307-X*, Lghtyr Pr) Buccaneer Bks.

Peter Claus & the Naughty List. Lawrence David. LC 98-54644. (J). 1999. write for info. (*0-385-32654-8*) Doubleday.

Peter Coffee Teaches PCs. Peter Coffee. LC 98-85044. 1998. 19.99 (*0-7897-1703-4*) Que.

Peter Cooper. Rossiter W. Raymond. LC 72-1252. (Select Bibliographies Reprint Ser.). 1977. reprint ed. 15.95 (*0-8369-6835-2*) Ayer.

Peter Copani's Handbook for People in Search of Love, Money, Power, Happiness, Inspiration, Sound Health, &-or Peace of Mind. Peter Copani. LC 92-45724. 164p. (Orig.). 1993. pap. 14.95 (*1-56825-001-0*) Rainbow Bks.

Peter Corlett Sculptures: Sculptures. Patrick Hutchings. 117p. 1995. pap. 90.00 (*0-949823-23-6*, Pub. by Deakin Univ) St Mut.

Peter Cottontail. Thornton W. Burgess. LC 96-2982. (Little Activity Bks.). (Illus.). 12p. (J). 1996. pap. 1.00 (*0-486-29369-6*) Dover.

Peter Cottontail. Illus. by Karen L. Schmidt. 12p. (J). (ps). 1996. bds. 4.99 (*0-448-41086-9*, G & D) Peng Put Young Read.

Peter Cottontail. Amanda Stephens. (Illus.). 32p. (J). (ps-3). 1994. pap. 2.50 (*0-590-47761-7*, Cartwheel) Scholastic Inc.

Peter Cottontail. Pat L. Stewart. (Little Activity Bks.). (Illus.). (J). 1996. pap. 1.00 (*0-486-28882-X*) Dover.

Peter Cottontail: A Colorful Easter. Golden Books Staff. 32p. 1999. pap. text 3.99 (*0-307-09225-9*) Gldn Bks Pub Co.

Peter Cottontail Activity Book. Stewart. (Illus.). (J). pap. text 1.00 (*0-486-29922-8*) Dover.

Peter Cottontail & the Easter Bunny Impostor. Suzanne C. Smith. LC 97-218431. (Illus.). 24p. (Orig.). (J). (ps-2). 1997. pap. 3.25 (*1-57102-106-X*, Ideals Child) Hambleton-Hill.

***Peter Cottontail & the Great Mitten Hunt.** 20p. (J). 2000. write for info. (*0-307-16603-1*) Gldn Bks Pub Co.

***Peter Cottontail & the Great Mitten Hunt.** Laura P. Norton. LC 98-83006. (J). 1999. write for info. (*0-307-16007-6*, Goldn Books) Gldn Bks Pub Co.

Peter Cottontail Dot-to-Dot. Thornton W. Burgess & Pat Stewart. (Illus.). 32p. (J). 1998. pap. 1.00 (*0-486-40355-6*) Dover.

***Peter Cottontail Is on His Way.** Andrea Posner. 20p. 2000. 3.99 (*0-307-16056-4*) Gldn Bks Pub Co.

***Peter Cottontail Mazes.** Burgess & Stewart. (Little Activity Bks.). (Illus.). (J). 2000. pap. 1.00 (*0-486-40968-6*) Dover.

Peter Cottontail Play-a-Song. (J). 1995. pap. text. write for info. (*0-7853-1123-8*) Pubns Intl Ltd.

***Peter Cottontail Sticker Picture Book.** Pat L. Stewart. (Illus.). (J). 1998. pap. 3.95 (*0-486-40034-4*) Dover.

***Peter Cottontail up, up & Away!** Golden Books Staff. 2000. pap. text 2.99 (*0-307-21025-1*) Gldn Bks Pub Co.

Peter Cottontail's Easter Book. Lulu Delacre. 32p. (J). (ps-1). 1992. pap. 2.99 (*0-590-43337-7*) Scholastic Inc.

Peter Cowan: New Critical Essays. Ed. by Bruce Bennett & Susan Miller. (Orig.). pap. 9.95 (*1-875560-10-6*, Pub. by Univ of West Aust Pr) Intl Spec Bk.

***Peter Crossman 1.** J. D. Macdonald. 2001. text 23.95 (*0-312-86988-6*) St Martin.

Peter Cushing: An Autobiography. Peter Cushing. (Illus.). 320p. 1999. 55.00 (*1-887664-29-7*); pap. 20.00 (*1-887664-26-2*) Midnght Marquee Pr.

Peter Cushing: The Gentle Man of Horror & His 91 Films. Deborah Del Vecchio & Tom Johnson. LC 92-50302. (Illus.). 485p. 1992. lib. bdg. 52.50 (*0-89950-654-2*) McFarland & Co.

Peter Dale Scott. Peter S. Scott. LC 88-71998. 54p. 1989. pap. 5.00 (*0-944521-14-2*) Dia Ctr Arts.

Peter Dawnee: Story of a Spray Plane. Paul Saxton & Bill Pace. (Illus.). 24p. (Orig.). (J). (gr. k-3). 1996. pap. text 5.95 (*0-9655226-0-1*) Chapman Saxton & Pace.

Peter De Vries: A Bibliography, 1934-1977. Compiled by Edwin T. Bowden. LC 76-620049. (Tower Bibliographical Ser.: No. 14). 1978. 15.00 (*0-87959-079-3*) U of Tex H Ransom Ctr.

Peter De Vries & Surrealism. Dan Campion. LC 95-5571. 240p. 1995. 37.50 (*0-8387-5311-6*) Bucknell U Pr.

Peter Dean. Carter Ratcliff & Laurel J. Reuter. (Illus.). 68p. (Orig.). 1989. pap. 15.00 (*0-943107-02-4*) ND Mus Art.

Peter Dean: A Retrospective. Alternative Museum Staff. LC 90-55616. (Orig.). 1990. pap. 6.00 (*0-932075-31-2*) Alternative Mus.

Peter Dean's Guide to Fly-Tying. Peter Deane. 1993. pap. 24.95 (*0-88317-172-4*) Stoeger Pub Co.

Peter Decker's Catalogues of Rare Americana, 1944-1963, 3 vols. Peter Decker. 1980. 145.00 (*0-318-37954-6*, PA2-31-7179) Jenkins.

Peter des Roches: An Alien in English Politics, 1205-1238. Nicholas Vincent. (Cambridge Studies in Medieval Life & Thought: 4th Ser. No. 31). 563p. (C). 1996. text 85.00 (*0-521-55254-0*) Cambridge U Pr.

Peter Downsbrough: Photographs. (Illus.). 136p. 1990. pap. 45.00 (*90-72191-25-0*, Pub. by Imschoot) Dist Art Pubs.

Peter Downsbrough: Prospectus. (Illus.). 88p. 1991. pap. 30.00 (*90-72191-05-6*, Pub. by Imschoot) Dist Art Pubs.

***Peter Drucker.** Robert Heller. LC 99-56839. (Business Masterminds Ser.). 112p. 2000. 12.95 (*0-7894-5158-1*, D K Ink) DK Pub Inc.

***Peter Drucker--Shaping the Managerial Mind: How the World's Foremost Management Thinker Crafted the Essentials of Business Success.** John E. Flaherty. LC 99-6371. 464p. 1999. 27.00 (*0-7879-4764-4*) Jossey-Bass.

Peter Drucker in the Harvard Business Review, 1963-1989. Harvard Business Staff. 150p. 1991. pap. 19.95 (*0-07-103349-1*) McGraw.

Peter Drucker on the Profession of Management. Peter Drucker. Ed. by Nan Stone. LC 97-39984. 224p. 1998. 29.95 (*0-87584-836-2*) Harvard Busn.

Peter Drucker on the Profession of Management. Harvard Business Review Staff. 304p. 1998. 29.95 (*0-07-103720-9*) McGraw.

Peter Duck. Arthur Ransome. LC 86-46247. (Swallows & Amazons Ser.). (Illus.). 414p. 1987. reprint ed. pap. 14.95 (*0-87923-660-4*) Godine.

Peter Eisenman. Canal & Stamperia Staff. 1999. pap. write for info. (*88-86502-83-4*, Pub. by Canal & Stamperia) Antique Collect.

Peter Eisenman: Diagram Diaries. Peter Eisenman. LC 99-10846. (Illus.). 240p. 1999. pap. 25.00 (*0-7893-0264-0*, Pub. by Universe) St Martin.

Peter Elementary Algebra. Date not set. teacher ed. write for info. (*0-314-05450-2*) West Pub.

Peter Ellenshaw: Selected Works, Nineteen Twenty-Nine to Nineteen Eighty-Three. Illus. by Peter Ellenshaw. LC 83-13358. (Contemporary Realists Ser.). 72p. 1983. pap. 11.50 (*0-913060-21-6*) Norton Art.

Peter Erskine Trio Live at Jazzbaltica. 121p. 1997. pap. text 19.95 (*0-7935-7447-1*) H Leonard.

Peter Fabrizius Reader: Selected Stories, Exilia, Verses & Essays from Two Worlds. Ed. by Max Knight & Joseph Fabry. LC 93-34647. (Austrian Culture Ser.: Vol. 12). (ENG & GER.). XV, 224p. (C). 1994. text 55.95 (*0-8204-2347-5*) P Lang Pubng.

Peter Fidler: Canada's Forgotten Explorer, 1769-1822. J. G. MacGregor. 1999. pap. 9.95 (*1-894004-19-1*) Fifth Hse Publ.

Peter Fischli - David Weiss. (Parkett Art Magazine Ser.: No. 17). (Illus.). 200p. 1988. 19.50 (*3-907509-67-6*, Pub. by Parkett Verlag AG) Dist Art Pubs.

***Peter Fischli - David Weiss.** Boris Groys. 80p. 1998. pap. 44.95 (*1-880146-25-8*) M Marks.

Peter Fischli & David Weiss: In a Restless World. Elizabeth Armstrong et al. (Illus.). 128p. (Orig.). 1996. pap. 19.95 (*0-935640-51-7*) Walker Art Ctr.

Peter Fjellstedt: Missionary Mentor to Three Continents. Emmet E. Eklund. LC 83-71472. (Augustana Historical Society Publications: No. 30). 197p. 1983. 15.00 (*0-910184-30-5*) Augustana.

Peter Follows Jesus: Pencil Fun Book. Jeanne Harmon. 1989. pap. text 0.89 (*1-55513-127-1*) Chariot Victor.

Peter Forbes Architects & Associates. Oscar R. Ojeda. (Ten Houses Ser.). 1995. 19.99 (*1-56496-183-4*) Rockport Pubs.

Peter Forsberg. Meg Greene. (Ice Hockey Legends Ser.). (Illus.). 64p. (YA). (gr. 3 up). 1999. lib. bdg. 16.95 (*0-7910-5013-0*) Chelsea Hse.

Peter Frampton/Guitar Anthology: Guitar Personality Book. 100p. (Orig.). 1993. pap. 19.95 (*0-7692-0590-9*, P0984GTX) Wrner Bros.

Peter Gabriel: An Authorized Biography. 2nd rev. ed. Spencer Bright. (Illus.). 524p. 1999. 32.50 (*0-283-06187-1*, Pub. by S1 & J) Trans-Atl Phila.

Peter Geach: Philosophical Encounters. Ed. by Harry A. Lewis. (Synthese Library). (C). 1991. lib. bdg. 160.50 (*0-7923-0823-9*, Pub. by Kluwer Academic) Kluwer Academic.

Peter Green: The Biography. Martin Celmins. (Illus.). 240p. pap. 14.95 (*1-898141-13-4*, SG 00603, Pub. by Sanctuary Pubng) Music Sales.

Peter Green Founder of Fleetwood Mac: The Authorized Biography. Martin Clemens. (Illus.). 239p. 1999. pap. 19.95 (*1-86074-233-5*, SG00652, Pub. by Sanctuary Pubng) Music Sales.

Peter Greenaway. Elliot. 128p. 1997. pap. 45.95 (*0-471-97691-1*) Wiley.

Peter Greenaway. Paul Melia & Alan Woods. 160p. 1999. text 79.95 (*0-7190-5623-3*) Manchester Univ Pr.

Peter Greenaway: Architecture & Allegory. Bridget Elliot & Anthony Purdy. (Art & Design Monograph Ser.). (Illus.). 128p. (Orig.). 1997. pap. 38.00 (*1-85490-355-1*) Academy Ed UK.

Peter Greenaway: Artworks, 63-98. Paul Melia & Alan Woods. 160p. 1999. pap. 24.95 (*0-7190-5624-1*, Pub. by Manchester Univ Pr) St Martin.

Peter Greenaway: Fear of Drowning by Numbers. Peter Greenaway. (Illus.). 154p. 1989. pap. 14.95 (*2-906571-07-5*, Pub. by Editions Dis Voir) Dist Art Pubs.

***Peter Greenaway: Interviews.** Ed. by Vernon W. Gras & Marguerite Gras. LC 99-52478. (Conversations with Filmmakers Ser.). 256p. 2000. pap. 18.00 (*1-57806-255-1*) U Pr of Miss.

***Peter Greenaway: Interviews.** Ed. by Vernon W. Gras & Marguerite Gras. (Illus.). 256p. 2000. text 45.00 (*1-57806-254-3*) U Pr of Miss.

Peter Greenaway: Museums & Moving Images. David Pascoe. (Essays in Art & Culture Ser.). (Illus.). 248p. 1997. pap. 24.95 (*1-86189-005-2*, Pub. by Reaktion Bks) Consort Bk Sales.

Peter Greenaway: Papers. P. Greenaway. (Illus.). 128p. 1991. 55.00 (*2-906571-20-2*, Pub. by Editions Dis Voir) Dist Art Pubs.

Peter Grimes & Gloriana. Benjamin Britten. Ed. by Nicholas John. (English National Opera Guide Series: Bilingual Libretto, Articles: No. 24). (Illus.). 128p. (Orig.). 1984. pap. 9.95 (*0-7145-3856-6*) Riverrun NY.

Peter Grimes from the Borough. George Crabbe. 1993. 90.00 (*0-907664-07-5*, Pub. by Old Stiles) St Mut.

Peter Gzowski: An Electric Life. Marco Adria. LC 96-151097. (Illus.). 170p. 1996. pap. 14.95 (*1-55022-166-3*, Pub. by ECW) Genl Dist Srvs.

Peter Gzowski: An Electric Life. large type ed. Marco Adria. (Illus.). 170p. 1996. pap. 15.95 (*1-55022-266-X*, Pub. by ECW) Genl Dist Srvs.

Peter Hall Directs Antony & Cleopatra. Tirzah Lowen. LC 90-36644. (Illus.). 208p. 1991. pap. 16.95 (*0-87910-147-4*) Limelight Edns.

Peter Halley: Drawings, 1991-1995. Jeanne Greenberg. Ed. by Lauri Thompson. (Illus.). 40p. (Orig.). 1995. 20.00 (*0-942779-07-X*) Greenberg Van Doren.

***Peter Halley: Maintain Speed.** Peter Halley. Ed. by Cory Reynolds. (Illus.). 228p. 2000. 60.00 (*1-891024-16-7*) Dist Art Pubs.

Peter Halley: Paintings, 1989-92. I. Michael Danoff et al. LC 92-74506. (Illus.). 30p. (Orig.). 1992. pap. 20.00 (*1-879003-08-2*) Edmundson.

***Peter Hall's Diaries: The Story of a Dramatic Battle.** Peter Hall. (Oberon Bks.). 2000. pap. 25.95 (*1-84002-102-0*) Theatre Comm.

Peter Handke. Richard A. Firda. (Twayne's World Authors Ser.). 160p. 1993. 24.95 (*0-8057-8281-8*, Twyne) Mac Lib Ref.

Peter Handke & the Postmodern Transformation: The Goalie's Journey Home. Jerome Klinkowitz & James Knowlton. LC 83-6867. (Literary Frontiers Ser.). 144p. 1983. pap. 14.95 (*0-8262-0420-1*) U of Mo Pr.

***Peter Hubner - Building as a Social Process.** Peter Blundell Jones. (Illus.). 240p. 2001. 89.00 (*3-932565-02-9*) Edition A Menges.

Peter Huchel: A Literary Life in 20th-Century Germany. Stephen Parker. (British & Irish Studies in German Language & Literature: Vol. 15). 617p. 1998. 63.95 (*3-906760-55-3*) P Lang.

Peter Huchel: A Literary Life in 20th-Century Germany. Stephen Parker. LC 98-22312. (British & Irish Studies in German Language & Literature: No. 15). 617p. 1998. pap. text 63.95 (*0-8204-4202-X*) P Lang Pubng.

Peter Hujar. Max Kozloff. (Illus.). 1994. 50.00 (*1-881616-35-5*, Pub. by Scalo Pubs) Dist Art Pubs.

Peter Hurd: Insight to a Painter. James K. Ballinger & Tonia L. Horton. 84p. 1983. pap. 10.00 (*0-910407-02-9*) Phoenix Art.

Peter Huston, U. S. Marshall. Phillip E. Hauck. Ed. by William Booth & Robert A. Folchi. LC 98-73998. (Illus.). 200p. 1998. 24.95 (*0-9662228-3-0*) Dab Pub Co.

Peter Huston, U. S. Marshall. Phillip E. Hauck. Ed. by William Booth & Robert A. Folchi. LC 98-73998. (Illus.). 200p. 1998. pap. 9.95 (*0-9662228-4-9*) Dab Pub Co.

Peter Ibbetson. George L. Du Maurier. 1971. reprint ed. 69.00 (*0-403-00920-0*) Scholarly.

Peter Ibbetson. George DuMaurier. 1988. reprint ed. lib. bdg. 49.00 (*0-7812-0022-9*) Rprt Serv.

Peter Ilyich Tchaikovsky. David Nice. (Classic FM Lifelines Ser.). 112p. 1997. pap. 9.95 (*1-86205-043-0*, Pub. by Pavilion Bks Ltd) Trafalgar.

Peter in Blueberry Land. Elsa Beskow. (J). (ps-2). 1988. 15.95 (*0-86315-050-0*, 20237, Pub. by Floris Bks) Gryphon Hse.

Peter Jameson's Secret Language. Sylvan Zaft. 152p. (Orig.). 1996. pap. 9.95 (*0-9652549-0-9*, Z1) Bela Lingvo.

P

An Asterisk (*) at the beginning of an entry indicates that the title is appearing for the first time.

Peter Joins the Circus. Bolette Bonfills. LC 94-24501. (Crocodile Lift-The-Flap Bk.). (Illus.). 24p. (J). (ps-2). 1994. 9.95 (*1-56656-154-X*, Crocodile Bks) Interlink Pub.

Peter Joseph Lenne - Das Gesamtwerk des Landschaftsarchitekten und Stadteplaners. Gerhard Hinz. (GER.). 1997. 248.00 (*3-487-09210-7*) G Olms Pubs.

Peter Koch, Printer: Cowboy Surrealists, Maverick Poets & Pre-Socratic Philosophers. Robert Bringhurst & Janice Braun. (Illus.). 65p. 1995. pap. 25.00 (*0-87104-439-0*) NY Pub Lib.

Peter Kropotkin: From Prince to Rebel. George Woodcock & Ivan Avakumovic. (Illus.). 490p. (C). 1990. reprint ed. 48.99 (*0-921689-61-6*, Pub. by Black Rose); reprint ed. pap. 19.99 (*0-921689-60-8*, Pub. by Black Rose) Consort Bk Sales.

Peter L. Gluck & Partners. Oscar R. Ojeda. (Ten Houses Ser.). (Illus.). 108p. 1997. pap. 19.99 (*1-56496-314-4*) Rockport Pubs.

Peter Lanyon. Margaret Garlake. LC 99-161239. (St. Ives Artists Ser.). (Illus.). 80p. 1998. pap. 19.95 (*1-85437-226-2*, Pub. by Tate Gallery) U of Wash Pr.

Peter Lassen of California. T. Vogel-Jorgensen. Ed. by Franklyn D. Scott. LC 78-15855. (Scandinavians in America Ser.). (DAN., Illus.). 1979. reprint ed. lib. bdg. 21.95 (*0-405-11662-4*) Ayer.

Peter Leibundgutt Journal. Lois A. Mast. 118p. 1991. pap. 9.00 (*1-883294-10-X*) Masthof Pr.

Peter Lombard & the Sacramental System. Elizabeth F. Rogers. 250p. 1976. reprint ed. lib. bdg. 19.50 (*0-915172-22-4*) Richwood Pub.

*__Peter Lorre.__ Ed. by Gary J. Suehla & Susan Suehla. (Illus.). 320p. 1999. pap. 20.00 (*1-887664-30-0*) Marquee Pr.

*__Peter Lowey: The IG-Farben House.__ Photos by Peter Loewy. (Illus.). 96p. 1999. 25.00 (*3-929078-65-1*, Pub. by G Kehayoff) te Neues.

Peter MacDonald: Former Chairman of the Navajo Nation see North American Indians of Achievement

Peter Maly. Ed. by Alex Buck & Matthias Vogt. (Designer Monographs: No. 5). (ENG & GER., Illus.). 136p. 1995. 65.00 (*3-931317-01-3*, Pub. by Art Bks Intl) Partners Pubs Grp.

Peter Martyr, a Reformer in Exile, 1542-1562: A Chronology of Biblical Writings in England & Europe. Marvin W. Anderson. 607p. 1975. 125.00 (*90-6004-343-X*, Pub. by B De Graaf) Coronet Bks.

*__Peter Martyr Reader.__ Ed. by Joseph C. McLelland et al. LC 99-45360. (Illus.). 256p. 1999. pap. text 30.00 (*0-943549-75-2*) Truman St Univ.

Peter Martyr Vermigli & Predestination: The Augustinian Inheritance of an Italian Reformer. Frank A. James, III. (Oxford Theological Monographs). 304p. 1998. text 75.00 (*0-19-826969-2*) OUP.

Peter Matthiessen. William Dowie. (Twayne's United States Authors Ser.: No. 587). 152p. (C). 1991. 28.95 (*0-8057-7635-4*, Twyne) Mac Lib Ref.

Peter Matthiessen: A Bibliography, 1951-1979. Compiled by D. Nicholas. LC 80-109000. (Illus.). 63p. 1980. 15.00 (*0-938364-00-6*) Orirana Pr.

Peter Matthiessen Reader. Peter Matthiessen. Ed. & Intro. by McKay Jenkins. LC 99-35246. 359p. 2000. pap. 14.00 (*0-375-70272-5*) Vin Bks.

Peter Maurin & Other Poems. David Craig. (Cleveland Poets Ser.: No. 40). 60p. (Orig.). 1985. pap. 5.00 (*0-914946-54-4*) Cleveland St Univ Poetry Ctr.

Peter Maxwell Davies: A Bio-Bibliography, 57. Carolyn J. Smith. LC 95-21757. (Bio-Bibliographies in Music Ser.: Vol. 57). 360p. 1995. lib. bdg. 79.50 (*0-313-26831-2*, Greenwood Pr) Greenwood.

Peter McWilliams' Personal Electronics Book, 1988. Peter McWilliams. 1989. pap. 10.95 (*0-318-32500-4*) P-H.

*__Peter Monamy.__ Frank B. Cockett. (Illus.). 98p. 2000. 49.50 (*1-85149-339-5*) Antique Collect.

Peter N. Rowe: A Special Issue in His Honor: A Special Issue of the Journal Chemical Engineering Communicating. J. Garside. ii, 334p. 1987. pap. text 574.00 (*2-88124-264-2*) Gordon & Breach.

Peter 'n the Wolf: Acting Edition. rev. ed. William-Alan Landes. LC 89-69871. (Wondrawhopper Ser.). (J). (gr. 3-12). 1988. pap. 6.00 (*0-88734-106-3*) Players Pr.

Peter 'n the Wolf: Director's Guide Book. rev. ed. William-Alan Landes. LC 89-69871. (Wondrawhopper Ser.). (J). (gr. 3-12). 1988. pap., teacher ed. 30.00 (*0-88734-013-X*) Players Pr.

Peter 'n the Wolf: Music & Lyrics. rev. ed. (Wondrawhopper Ser.). (J). (gr. 3-12). 1985. pap. 15.00 (*0-88734-012-1*) Players Pr.

Peter Nadin: Recent Work & Notes on Six Series. limited ed. Peter Nadin et al. (Illus.). 72p. (Orig.). 1992. pap. 24.95 (*0-685-63223-7*) Yale Ctr Brit Art.

Peter Neagoe: L'Homme et l'Oeuvre. Denise-Claude Le Goff. (American University Studies: General Literature: Ser. XIX, Vol. 16). 423p. (C). 1988. text 51.50 (*0-8204-0658-9*) P Lang Pubng.

Peter Nevsky & the True Story of the Russian Moon Landing: A Novel. John Calvin Batchelor. 88p. 1995. pap. 15.00 (*0-8050-4667-4*, Owl) H Holt & Co.

*__Peter Norton Comp.__ Sams Staff. 1998. pap. text. write for info. (*0-672-31497-5*) Sams.

Peter Norton Inside System 7. Dan Shafer. LC 92-6741. 1991. pap. 24.95 (*0-13-656281-7*) Brady Pub.

Peter Norton's Advanced Assembly. Steven Holzner. 1991. pap. 5.00 incl. 3.5 hd (*0-13-663147-9*) Macmillan USA.

Peter Norton's Advanced Assembly. Steven Holzner & Norton. 1991. pap. 5.00 incl. 3.5 hd (*0-13-663113-4*) Macmillan USA.

Peter Norton's Advanced BASIC. Steven Holzner & Norton. 1991. pap. 5.00 incl. 3.5 hd (*0-13-663071-5*); pap. 5.00 incl. 5.25 hd (*0-13-663089-8*) Macmillan USA.

Peter Norton's Advanced DOS 5.0. Peter Norton. 1991. pap. 39.95 (*0-13-529652-8*) Brady Pub.

Peter Norton's Assembly Language Book for the IBM PC. 2nd rev. ed. Peter Norton. 512p. 1989. pap. 24.95 (*0-13-662453-7*) Brady Pub.

Peter Norton's BASIC On-Line Guide. Peter Norton. (Programming Ser.). 1989. pap. 49.95 (*0-13-662677-7*) Brady Pub.

Peter Norton's Complete Guide to DOS 6.22. 6th ed. Peter Norton. (Illus.). 1150p. (Orig.). 1994. 29.99 (*0-672-30614-X*) Sams.

Peter Norton's Complete Guide to Linux. Peter Norton. (Peter Norton (Sams) Ser.). 650p. 1999. pap. text 29.99 (*0-672-31573-4*) Sams.

Peter Norton's Complete Guide To Microsoft Office 2000. Peter Norton et al. LC 97-67998. (Peter Norton (Sams) Ser.). (Illus.). 792p. 1999. pap. 29.99 (*0-672-31174-7*) Sams.

*__Peter Norton's Complete Guide to Network Security.__ Peter Norton. 800p. 1999. pap. 39.99 (*0-672-31691-9*) Sams.

*__Peter Norton's Complete Guide to TCP/IP.__ Peter Norton. 1999. pap. 29.99 (*0-672-31695-1*) Sams.

Peter Norton's Complete Guide to Windows NT Workstation. Peter Norton. LC 95-72348. 936p. 1996. 39.99 (*0-672-30901-7*) Sams.

Peter Norton's Complete Guide to Windows NT Workstation 4. 2nd ed. Peter Norton. LC 98-85651. 1998. pap. 29.99 (*0-672-31373-1*) Sams.

Peter Norton's Complete Guide to Windows 95. Peter Norton Computing Group Staff & John Mueller. (Illus.). 848p. 1995. 29.99 (*0-672-30791-X*) Sams.

Peter Norton's Complete Guide to Windows 95. 2nd ed. Peter Norton & John Mueller. LC 96-71999. 1124p. 1997. pap. 35.00 (*0-672-31040-6*) Sams.

Peter Norton's Complete Guide to Windows 95: Primer Edition. 2nd ed. Peter Norton & John Mueller. 1997. pap. 35.00 (*0-614-28485-6*, Sams Sftwre) MCP SW Interactive.

*__Peter Norton's Complete Guide to Windows 98.__ 2nd ed. Peter Norton. 800p. 1999. pap. text 29.99 (*0-672-31693-5*) Sams.

Peter Norton's Complete Guide to Windows 98. 3rd ed. Peter Norton. LC 97-69209. 672p. 1998. 29.99 (*0-672-31230-1*) Sams.

Peter Norton's Computing Essentials. 3rd ed. Peter Norton. LC 98-39586. 1998. 18.00 (*0-02-804394-4*) Glencoe.

Peter Norton's Computing Fundamentals. Peter Norton. LC 96-32936. 1996. 30.95 (*0-02-804337-5*) Glencoe.

Peter Norton's Computing Fundamentals. 3rd ed. Peter Norton. LC 99-166725. xxxi, 461 p. 1999. write for info. (*0-02-804395-2*) Glencoe.

Peter Norton's Computing Fundamentals. 3rd ed. Peter Norton. LC 98-39530. 1998. 300.00 (*0-02-804410-X*) Glencoe.

*__Peter Norton's Computing Fundamentals.__ 4th ed. Peter Norton. LC 00-34044. (Illus.). 2000. write for info. (*0-07-822723-2*) Glencoe.

Peter Norton's DOS Guide. Peter Norton. 744p. 1994. 24.95 (*1-56686-136-5*) Sams.

*__Peter Norton's Essential Concepts.__ 4th ed. Peter Norton. LC 00-34101. (Illus.). 2000. write for info. (*0-07-822728-3*) Glencoe.

Peter Norton's Guide to Access 97 Programming. Peter Norton & Virginia Andersen. 624p. 1997. 35.00 (*0-672-31050-3*) Sams.

Peter Norton's Guide to Delphi 2. Peter Norton. LC 95-72346. 816p. 1996. 49.99 incl. disk (*0-672-30898-3*) Sams.

Peter Norton's Guide to Java: Premier Title. Peter Norton. LC 96-67206. 912p. 1996. 39.99 (*1-57521-088-6*) Sams.

Peter Norton's Guide to Linux. Peter Norton. 800p. 1997. 39.99 (*0-672-31141-0*) Macmillan.

Peter Norton's Guide to Upgrading & Repairing PCs: Premier Edition. Peter Norton & Michael Desmond. LC 97-67495. 704p. 1997. pap. 29.99 (*0-672-31140-2*) Sams.

Peter Norton's Guide to Visual Basic 6. Peter Norton. LC 96-72394. 600p. 1998. 29.99 (*0-672-31054-6*) Sams.

Peter Norton's Guide to Visual C++ 6. Peter Norton. 1000p. 1999. 34.99 (*0-672-31053-8*) Sams.

Peter Norton's Guide to Windows 95/NT 4 Programming with MFC. Peter Norton & Rob McGregor. LC 95-72339. 1200p. 1996. 49.99 (*0-672-30900-9*) Sams.

Peter Norton's Guide to Windows X.0. Peter Norton. 640p. 1995. pap. 30.00 (*0-679-75588-8*) Random.

Peter Nortons Inside the PC. Macmillan General Reference Staff. 1998. 29.99 (*0-02-865317-3*, Pub. by Macmillan) S&S Trade.

Peter Norton's Inside the PC. 6th ed. Peter Norton. 654p. 1995. 35.00 (*0-672-30624-7*) Sams.

Peter Norton's Inside the PC. 7th ed. Peter Norton et al. LC 96-72009. 752p. 1997. 29.99 (*0-672-31041-4*) Sams.

Peter Norton's Inside the PC. 8th ed. Peter Norton & Goodman John. (Peter Norton (Sams) Ser.). 816p. 1999. pap. 29.99 (*0-672-31532-7*) Sams.

Peter Norton's Inside the Sun 486i & 386i. Peter Norton. 1990. pap. 29.95 (*0-13-661612-7*) P-H.

Peter Norton's Introduction to Computers. Peter Norton. LC 93-46202. 1994. pap. 34.95 (*0-02-801318-2*) Glencoe.

Peter Norton's Introduction to Computers. Peter Norton. LC 93-46202. 1994. write for info. (*0-02-801331-X*) Glencoe.

Peter Norton's Introduction to Computers. 2nd ed. Peter Norton. LC 96-32939. 1996. write for info. (*0-02-804325-1*) Glencoe.

Peter Norton's Introduction to Computers. 3rd ed. Peter Norton. LC 98-39587. 1998. 34.00 (*0-02-804386-3*) Glencoe.

*__Peter Norton's Introduction to Computers.__ 3rd ed. Peter Norton. LC 99-474353. (Illus.). 1999. write for info. (*0-02-804389-8*); write for info. (*0-02-804412-6*) Glencoe.

*__Peter Norton's Introduction to Computers.__ 4th ed. Peter Norton. LC 00-34045. (Illus.). 2000. write for info. (*0-07-821058-5*) Glencoe.

Peter Norton's Introduction to Computers: Essential Concepts. Peter Norton. LC 94-10091. 1994. 36.25 (*0-02-802902-X*) Glencoe.

Peter Norton's Introduction to Computers: Essential Concepts. 2nd ed. Peter Norton. LC 96-29222. 1996. write for info. (*0-02-804332-4*) Glencoe.

Peter Norton's Introduction to Computers: With Microsoft Works for Windows. Peter Norton. LC 94-25920. 1994. write for info. (*0-02-802896-1*) Glencoe.

Peter Norton's OS-2 On-Line Guide. Peter Norton. (Productivity Ser.). 1989. pap. 49.95 (*0-13-662693-9*) Brady Pub.

Peter Norton's PC Resource. Peter Norton & Bill Alvernaz. (Illus.). 400p. 1987. pap. 19.95 (*0-685-18872-8*) P-H.

Peter Norton's Upgrading & Repairing PCs. 2nd ed. Peter Norton & Michael Desmond. LC 98-87673. 700p. 1999. pap. 29.99 (*0-672-31483-5*) Sams.

Peter Norton's WordPerfect On-Line Guide. Norton. 1989. pap. 5.00 incl. 3.5 hd (*0-13-660861-2*) Macmillan USA.

Peter of Ailly: Concepts & Insolubles: An Annotated Translation. Paul V. Spade. (Synthese Historical Library: No. 19). 193p. 1980. lib. bdg. 99.50 (*90-277-1079-1*) Kluwer Academic.

Peter of Ailly & the Harvest of Fourteenth Century Philosophy. Leonard A. Kennedy. LC 86-23527. (Studies in the History of Philosophy: Vol. 2). 232p. 1989. lib. bdg. 89.95 (*0-88946-307-7*) E Mellen.

Peter of Ickham: Le Livere de Reis de Brittanie e le Livere de Reis de Engleterre (From Brutus to 1274, with Two Continuations & a Translation) Ed. by John Glover. (Rolls Ser.: No. 42). 1974. reprint ed. 70.00 (*0-8115-1101-4*) Periodicals Srv.

Peter of John Olivi on the Bible: Principia Quinque in Sacram Scripturam. Ed. by David Flood & Gedeon Gal. (Text Ser.). 431p. 1997. pap. text 25.00 (*1-57659-128-X*) Franciscan Inst.

Peter of Spain: Language in Dispute: An English Translation of Peter of Spain's 'Tractatus' Called Afterwards Summulae Logicales, based by the Critical Edition by L. M. DeRijk. Francis P. Dinneen. (Studies in the History of the Language Sciences: No. 39). xl, 271p. 1990. 65.00 (*90-272-4524-X*) J Benjamins Pubng Co.

Peter of Spain Vol. 13: And Selected Anonymous Treatises. Mullally. LC 64-17335. (Medieval Philosophical Texts in Translation Ser.). 156p. 1964. 15.00 (*0-87462-213-1*) Marquette.

Peter of Spain (Petrus Hispanus Portugalensis) Syncategoreumata: First Critical Edition. L. M. De Rijk & Joke Spruyt. LC 91-39214. (Studien und Texte zur Geistesgeschichte des Mittelalters Ser.: Vol. 30). (ENG & LAT.). 619p. 1992. 186.00 (*90-04-09434-2*) Brill Academic Pubs.

Peter Oliver's "Origin & Progress of the American Rebellion" A Tory View. Peter Oliver. Ed. by Douglass Adair & John A. Schutz. xxiv, 176p. 1961. pap. 10.95 (*0-8047-0601-8*) Stanford U Pr.

Peter 1 & 2, Jude. Dana Gould. LC 97-45195. (Shepherd's Notes Ser.). 1998. 5.95 (*0-8054-9019-1*) Broadman.

Peter Owen Anthology: Forty Years of Independent Publishing. Intro. by Peter Owen. 231p. 1991. 35.00 (*0-7206-0810-4*, Pub. by P Owen Ltd) Dufour.

Peter Paladine of the Great Heart. Thomas Starling. Ed. by Richard N. Hayton. LC 92-80377. 832p. 1995. 24.95 (*0-914864-03-3*, SAN 206-3808) Spindrift.

Peter Pan. (J). 9.95 (*1-56156-305-6*) Kidsbks.

Peter Pan. (Fun-to-Read Fairy Tales Ser.). (Illus.). 24p. (J). 1992. pap. 2.50 (*1-56144-090-6*) Modern Pub NYC.

Peter Pan. (Classics Ser.). (Illus.). 96p. (J). (ps-4). 1994. 7.98 (*1-57082-046-5*, Pub. by Mouse Works) Little.

Peter Pan. (Play - a - Sound Ser.). (Illus.). 24p. (J). 1993. 12.98 (*0-7853-0132-1*) Pubns Intl Ltd.

Peter Pan. (Disney Read-Alongs Ser.). (J). 7.99 incl. audio (*1-55723-009-9*) W Disney Records.

*__Peter Pan.__ Barrie. LC 99-35540. (Illus.). 176p. 1999. pap. text 2.00 (*0-486-40783-7*) Dover.

Peter Pan. J. M. Barrie. (Illus.). 160p. (J). 1998. 24.95 (*1-85149-702-1*) Antique Collect.

Peter Pan. J. M. Barrie. 176p. (J). 1985. mass mkt. 4.95 (*0-553-21178-1*, Bantam Classics) Bantam.

Peter Pan. J. M. Barrie. LC 87-403. (Illus.). 144p. (J). (gr. 2 up). 1995. 19.95 (*0-8050-0276-6*, Bks Young Read) H Holt & Co.

Peter Pan. J. M. Barrie. (Illus.). (J). 1995. mass mkt. 8.95 (*0-340-62664-X*, Pub. by Hodder & Stought Ltd) Trafalgar.

Peter Pan. J. M. Barrie. (Illustrated Classics Ser.). (Illus.). 128p. (J). 1991. pap. 2.95 (*1-56156-029-4*) Kidsbks.

Peter Pan. J. M. Barrie. LC 92-53172. (Illus.). 224p. (J). (ps-3). 1992. 12.95 (*0-679-41792-3*, Evrymans Lib Childs) Knopf.

Peter Pan. J. M. Barrie. 1988. 2.98 (*0-671-10162-5*) PB.

Peter Pan. J. M. Barrie. LC 94-76734. (Illus.). 256p. (YA). (gr. 5-9). 1996. pap. 3.99 (*0-14-036674-1*, PuffinBks) Peng Put Young Read.

Peter Pan. J. M. Barrie. Ed. by Joshua Hanft. (Great Illustrated Classics Ser.: Vol. 46). (Illus.). 240p. (J). (gr. 3-6). 1995. 9.95 (*0-86611-997-3*) Playmore Inc.

Peter Pan. J. M. Barrie. (Folio - Junior Ser.: No. 411). (FRE., Illus.). 239p. (J). (gr. 5-10). 1988. pap. 9.95 (*2-07-033411-2*) Schoenhof.

Peter Pan. J. M. Barrie. (J). 1978. pap. 1.95 (*0-590-30054-7*) Scholastic Inc.

Peter Pan. J. M. Barrie. 208p. (J). (gr. 4-7). 1993. pap. 3.25 (*0-590-46735-2*, Apple Classics) Scholastic Inc.

*__Peter Pan.__ J. M. Barrie. (Illus.). (J). 2001. 24.95 (*1-58479-029-6*) Stewart Tabori & Chang.

Peter Pan. J. M. Barrie. Ed. by Susan Shebar. LC 87-15480. (Illus.). 48p. (J). (gr. 2-6). 1988. lib. bdg. 19.95 (*0-8167-1199-2*) Troll Communs.

Peter Pan. J. M. Barrie. Ed. by Susan Shebar. LC 87-15480. (Illus.). 48p. (J). (gr. 4-7). 1997. pap. 5.95 (*0-8167-1200-X*) Troll Communs.

Peter Pan. J. M. Barrie. (Deluxe Watermill Classic Ser.). 176p. (YA). 1998. pap. 2.95 (*0-8167-2555-1*) Troll Communs.

Peter Pan. J. M. Barrie. 1985. 9.05 (*0-606-02465-4*, Pub. by Turtleback) Demco.

Peter Pan. J. M. Barrie. (J). 1990. 15.15 (*0-606-00686-9*, Pub. by Turtleback) Demco.

Peter Pan. J. M. Barrie. (Children's Library). (gr. 4-7). 1998. pap. 3.95 (*1-85326-120-3*, 1203WW, Pub. by Wrdsworth Edits) NTC Contemp Pub Co.

Peter Pan. J. M. Barrie. LC 90-23077. (Step into Classics Ser.). (Illus.). 96p. (J). (gr. 2-7). 1991. pap. 3.99 (*0-679-81044-7*, Pub. by Random Bks Yng Read) Random.

Peter Pan. Cathy East Dubowski. LC 90-23077. (Bullseye Step into Classics Ser.). 1994. 9.09 (*0-606-06663-2*, Pub. by Turtleback) Demco.

Peter Pan. Adapted by Sarah Harris. (Comes to Life Bks.). (ENG & FRE.). 16p. (J). (ps-2). 1995. write for info. (*1-57234-044-4*); write for info. (*1-57234-035-5*) YES Ent.

Peter Pan. Michael Johnstone & J. M. Barrie. LC 98-27490. (Young Classics Ser.). (Illus.). (J). 1998. 12.95 (*0-7894-3796-1*) DK Pub Inc.

*__Peter Pan.__ Michael Johnstone et al. LC 00-20432. (Read & Listen Ser.). (Illus.). (J). 2000. pap. write for info. incl. audio (*0-7894-6199-4*) DK Pub Inc.

Peter Pan. Mouse Works Staff. LC 98-177059. (Peter Pan Ser.). (J). 1998. 3.98 (*1-57082-926-8*, Pub. by Mouse Works) Time Warner.

Peter Pan. Mousework Staff. (Illus.). (J). 1997. 7.98 (*1-57082-801-6*, Pub. by Mouse Works) Time Warner.

Peter Pan. Mouseworks Staff. (J). 1999. 4.99 (*0-7364-0045-1*, Pub. by Mouse Works) Little.

Peter Pan. Random House Value Publishing Staff. 1999. 5.99 (*0-517-20577-7*) Random Hse Value.

Peter Pan. Illus. by Roser Rius. (SPA.). 32p. (J). (ps-3). 1999. 8.95 (*0-7641-5154-1*) Barron.

Peter Pan. abr. ed. J. M. Barrie. (Children's Classics Ser.). (J). 1998. pap. 16.95 incl. audio (*1-85998-588-2*) Trafalgar.

Peter Pan. large type ed. (Classics for Children 8 & Younger Ser.). (Illus.). 48p. (J). (ps-3). 1999. write for info. (*1-85854-603-6*) Brimax Bks.

Peter Pan: A Literature Unit. Betty Burke. Ed. by Janet Cain. (Illus.). 48p. (Orig.). 1994. student ed. 7.95 (*1-55734-433-7*) Tchr Create Mat.

Peter Pan: Friends Ahoy! Disney Enterprises, Inc. Staff. (Disney's "Storytime Treasures" Library: Vol. 18). (Illus.). 44p. (J). (gr. 1-6). 1997. 3.49 (*1-57973-014-0*) Advance Pubs.

Peter Pan: My Coloring Book. (J). 1.09 (*0-307-08657-7*, 08657) Gldn Bks Pub Co.

Peter Pan: Neverland, Bk. 2. Regis Loisel. Ed. by Greg Baisden. Tr. by Mary Irwin from FRE. (Illus.). 1992. 14.95 (*1-56862-000-4*) Kitchen Sink.

Peter Pan: Off to Never Land. Illus. by Vaccaro Associates Staff. LC 94-67860. (Tiny Changing Pictures Bk.). 10p. (J). (ps-3). 1995. 4.95 (*0-7868-3016-6*, Pub. by Disney Pr) Little.

Peter Pan: Peter Pan. Illus. by Roser Rius. 32p. (J). (ps-3). 1999. 8.95 (*0-7641-5153-3*) Barron.

Peter Pan: The Story of Lost Childhood. Kathleen Kelley-Lainee. LC 97-9690. 192p. 1997. pap. 12.95 (*1-86204-009-5*, Pub. by Element MA) Penguin Putnam.

Peter Pan: U. K. English. Adapted by Sarah Harris. (Comes to Life Bks.). (J). (ps-2). 1995. write for info. (*1-57234-029-0*) YES Ent.

Peter Pan: Where Are Wendy's Brothers? Illus. by Ted Enik. LC 93-73811. (Surprise Lift-the-Flap Bk.). 18p. (J). (ps-k). 1994. 9.95 (*1-56282-625-5*, Pub. by Disney Pr) Little.

Peter Pan Bk. 1: London. Regis Loisel. Ed. by Greg S. Baisden. Tr. by Mary Irwin from FRE. (Illus.). (C). reprint ed. 14.95 (*1-879450-42-9*) Kitchen Sink.

Peter Pan & Other Plays see Works of J. M. Barrie: Peter Pan Edition

Peter Pan & Other Plays: The Admirable Crichton; Peter Pan; When Wendy Grew Up; What Ever. J. M. Barrie. Ed. by Peter Hollindale. (Oxford Drama Library). 374p. 1995. text 65.00 (*0-19-812162-8*) OUP.

Peter Pan & Other Plays: The Admirable Crichton; Peter Pan; When Wendy Grew Up; What Every Woman Knows; Mary Rose. J. M. Barrie. Ed. & Intro. by Peter Hollindale. (Oxford World's Classics Ser.). 374p. 1999. pap. 13.95 (*0-19-283919-5*) OUP.

Peter Pan & Wendy. J. M. Barrie. LC 98-31003. (Abbeville Classics Ser.). (Illus.). 176p. (J). 1999. 12.95 (*0-7892-0560-2*, Abbeville Kids); pap. 7.95 (*0-7892-0550-5*, Abbeville Kids) Abbeville Pr.

Peter Pan & Wendy. J. M. Barrie. (Illus.). 160p. (J). (gr. 3-6). 1992. pap. 17.95 (*1-85145-449-7*, Pub. by Pavilion Bks Ltd) Trafalgar.

*__Peter Pan & Wendy.__ J. M. Barrie. Ed. by Jane Carruth. (Illus.). 92p. (J). (gr. 4-6). 2000. reprint ed. 25.00 (*0-7881-9230-2*) DIANE Pub.

Peter Pan Book & Charm. J. M. Barrie. LC 99-33256. (Charming Classic Bks.). 256p. (J). (gr. 4-7). 2000. 5.95 (*0-694-01318-8*) HarpC Child Bks.

Peter Pan (Broadway) (Illus.). 32p. 1982. pap. 7.95 (*0-88188-105-8*, 00384551) H Leonard.

P

An Asterisk (*) at the beginning of an entry indicates that the title is appearing for the first time.

Peter Pan Chronicles: The Nearly 100-Year History of the "Boy Who Wouldn't Grow Up" Bruce K. Hanson. LC 92-37572. 1993. 21.95 (*1-55972-160-X*, Birch Ln Pr) Carol Pub Group.

Peter Pan in Kensington Gardens. J. M. Barrie. (J). 18.95 (*0-8488-0427-9*) Amereon Ltd.

Peter Pan in Kensington Gardens. J. M. Barrie. 150p. (J). 1980. reprint ed. lib. bdg. 16.95 (*0-89967-006-7*, Harmony Rain) Buccaneer Bks.

Peter Pan in Kensington Gardens. J. M. Barrie. 175p. (J). 1981. reprint ed. lib. bdg. 16.95 (*0-89966-328-1*) Buccaneer Bks.

Peter Pan in Kensington Gardens & Peter & Wendy. J. M. Barrie. Ed. by Peter Hollingdale. (Oxford World's Classics Ser.). (Illus.). 288p. 1999. pap. 7.95 (*0-19-283929-2*) OUP.

Peter Pan in Neverland: A Musical Fantasy in 2 Acts. J. M. Barrie. (Illus.). 58p. 1995. pap. 4.50 (*0-88680-414-0*) I E Clark.

Peter Pan: or The Boy Who Would Not Grow Up. adapted ed. J. M. Barrie. 1994. pap. 5.25 (*0-8222-1345-1*) Dramatists Play.

Peter Pan Syndrome. Dan De Kiley. 320p. 1984. mass mkt. 5.99 (*0-380-68890-5*, Avon Bks) Morrow Avon.

Peter Panini & the Search for the Menehune. Stacey S. Kaopuiki. LC 90-81734. (Peter Panini Adventure Ser.). (Illus.). 44p. (J). (ps-5). 1990. 10.95 (*1-878498-00-2*) Hawaiian Isl Concepts.

Peter Panini's Children's Guide to the Hawaiian Islands, 4 bks. Stacey S. Kaopuiki. LC 90-81735. (Illus.). (J). (ps-5). 1991. 12.95 (*1-878498-01-0*) Hawaiian Isl Concepts.

Peter Panitz - A Play Commissioned for Kadima see Kadima Advisor's Aid Series

Peter Parker & the Opening of China. Edward V. Gulick. LC 73-82628. (Harvard Studies in American-East Asian Relations: No. 3). (Illus.). 299p. reprint ed. pap. 92.70 (*0-7837-3839-0*, 204366100010) Bks Demand.

Peter Parrot, Private Eye. Sara Nickerson. LC 88-63800. (Illus.). 43p. (Orig.). (J). (gr. 3-5). 1988. pap. 9.00 (*0-935529-07-1*) Comprehen Health Educ.

Peter, Paul & Mary - Late Again. Ed. by Carol Cuellar. 36p. (Orig.). (C). 1968. pap. text 10.95 (*0-7692-0918-1*, VF0146) Wrner Bros.

Peter, Paul & Mary Songbook. Ed. by Carol Cuellar. 148p. (Orig.). (C). 1965. pap. text 16.95 (*0-943351-94-4*, VF0138) Wrner Bros.

Peter, Paul & Mary/For Guitar Tab: Guitar Personality Book. 36p. (Orig.). 1988. pap. 12.95 (*0-7692-0591-7*, GF0352) Wrner Bros.

Peter Paul Rubens. Richard McLanathan. LC 94-33330. (First Impressions Ser.). (Illus.). 92p. (J). 1995. 19.95 (*0-8109-3780-8*, Pub. by Abrams) Time Warner.

Peter Paul Rubens: Man & Artist. Christopher White. LC 86-24565. (Illus.). 320p. 1987. reprint ed. pap. 99.20 (*0-608-07853-0*, 205403000011) Bks Demand.

Peter Paul Rubens: The Pride of Life. Maria Varshavskaya. (Great Painters Ser.). (Illus.). 176p. 1996. 40.00 (*1-85995-166-X*) Parkstone Pr.

Peter Pelican's Pouch Problem. Wanda W. Hamilton. (Illus.). 22p. (Orig.). (J). (gr. k-6). 1986. pap. 3.95 (*0-935357-01-7*) CRIC Prod.

***Peter Penguin & His Chatter Beak.** Paul Flemming. (Snappy Fun Bks.). (Illus.). 12p. (J). (ps-k). 2000. bds. 4.99 (*1-57584-696-9*, Pub. by Rdrs Digest) S&S Trade.

Peter Penguin & the Polar Sea. Harry Obedin. LC 88-63171. (Illus.). 32p. (Orig.). (J). (ps-4). 1989. pap. 4.95 (*0-943990-54-8*) Parenting Pr.

Peter Peryer, Second Nature. Peter Peryer. (Illus.). 140p. 1995. pap. 39.95 (*3-905514-56-7*, Pub. by Edit Stemmle) Dist Art Pubs.

Peter Pickups Busy Day. Jen Koury. Ed. by Pat Linden & Steve Hilko. (Johnny Tractor Toybks.). (Illus.). 10p. (J). (ps-1). 1997. mass mkt. write for info. (*1-887327-10-X*) Ertl Co.

Peter Pig Likes to Dig. Roger A. Faber. (Illus.). 32p. (J). (gr. 1-2). 1998. pap. 12.00 (*1-880122-05-7*) White Stone.

Peter Pitseolak, 1902-1973: Inuit Historian of Seekooseelak: Photographs & Drawings from Cape Dorset, Baffin Island. Peter Pitseolak. Ed. by David Bellman. 1980. pap. 29.95 (*0-7735-0400-1*, Pub. by McG-Queens Univ Pr) CUP Services.

Peter Poems & Other Disgraces. Joseph Semenovich. 44p. (Orig.). 1984. pap. 4.00 (*0-916155-00-5*) Trout Creek.

Peter Porcupine in America: Pamphlets on Republicanism & Revolution. William Cobbett. LC 93-33875. (Documents in American Social History Ser.). (Illus.). 304p. 1994. text 35.00 (*0-8014-2839-4*) Cornell U Pr.

Peter Porcupine in America: The Career of William Cobbett. Mary E. Clark. (American Newspapermen 1790-1933 Ser.). v, 193p. 1974. reprint ed. 18.00 (*0-8464-0026-X*) Beekman Pubs.

Peter Porter. Peter Steele. (Australian Writers Ser.). 128p. 1993. pap. 19.95 (*0-19-553282-1*) OUP.

Peter Porter: A Bibliography, 1954-1986. J. Kaiser. 224p. 1990. text 100.00 (*0-7201-2032-2*) Continuum.

Peter Potter Teeter Totter. Bill Gillespie. (Illus.). 22p. (Orig.). (J). 1987. pap. 3.50 (*0-940859-06-8*) Snd Dollar Pub.

***Peter Pran: An Architect of Poetic Movement.** Peter Pran. 144p. 1999. 45.00 (*1-901092-08-9*) Andreas Papadakis.

***Peter Pran: An Architecture of Poetic Movement.** Peter Pran. 144p. 1999. pap. 37.50 (*1-901092-07-0*) Andreas Papadakis.

Peter Pran of Ellerbe Becket. Academy Editions Staff. (Architectural Monographs). 1993. 55.00 (*0-312-08689-X*) St Martin.

Peter Pran of Ellerbe Becket: Recent Works. Academy Editions Staff. (Architectural Monographs: No. 24). 1993. pap. 38.00 (*0-312-08690-3*) St Martin.

Peter Principle. Laurence J. Peter & Raymond Hull. Date not set. lib. bdg. 19.95 (*0-8488-2156-4*) Amereon Ltd.

Peter Principle. Laurence J. Peter & Raymond Hull. 1993. reprint ed. 29.95 (*1-56849-161-1*) Buccaneer Bks.

***Peter Principle: Why Things Always Go Wrong.** Laurence J. Peter & Raymond Hull. (Illus.). 192p. 1998. pap. 13.00 (*0-688-27544-3*, Quil) HarperTrade.

Peter Promise see No Te Dejare Hasta Que Seas Perfecto

Peter Promise: Powerful Principles from the Life of Peter. Luis Palau. LC 96-10501. Orig. Title: Walk on Water, Pete!. 128p. 1996. reprint ed. pap. 9.99 (*1-57293-011-X*) Discovery Hse Pubs.

Peter Pulpitpounder, B. D. 2nd ed. Robert E. Segerhammar. LC 94-36514. (Illus.). 56p. (Orig.). 1995. pap. 7.25 (*0-7880-0432-8*) CSS OH.

Peter Rabbit see Histoire de Pierre Lapin: Livre d'Histoires en Couleurs

Peter Rabbit see Geschichte von Peterchen Hase: Ein Buntes Marchenbuch

Peter Rabbit. (Look & Find Ser.). (Illus.). 24p. (J). 1993. 7.98 (*1-56173-417-9*); 4.98 (*1-56173-474-8*) Pubns Intl Ltd.

Peter Rabbit. Illus. by Pat Schoonover & Anita Nelson. (Classic Tales Ser.). 24p. (J). (gr. 2-4). 1992. lib. bdg. 11.95 (*1-56674-008-8*, HTS Bks) Forest Hse.

Peter Rabbit: Story Pak. Beatrix Potter. (Graphic Learning Literature Program Series: Folk Tales). (ENG & SPA., Illus.). (J). 1992. 45.00 (*0-87746-231-3*) Graphic Learning.

Peter Rabbit & Benjamin Bunny Coloring Book. Beatrix Potter. (Illus.). (J). (gr. 1 up). 1987. pap. 1.49 (*0-671-62987-5*) Litle Simon.

Peter Rabbit & Eleven Other Favorite Tales. Pat Ronson Stewart & Beatrix Potter. LC 93-14417. (Children's Thrift Classics Ser.). (Illus.). 96p. (J). 1993. reprint ed. pap. 1.00 (*0-486-27845-X*) Dover.

Peter Rabbit & Friends, 10 bks., Set, incl. stickers. Beatrix Potter & Anna Pomaska. (Illus.). (J). 1999. pap., boxed set 10.00 (*0-486-29463-3*) Dover.

Peter Rabbit & Friends: A Stand-Up Story Book. Beatrix Potter. (Illus.). 12p. (J). 1998. 14.99 (*0-7232-4343-3*, F Warne) Peng Put Young Read.

***Peter Rabbit & Friends Sticker Activity Book.** Beatrix Potter. (Illus.). (J). 2000. pap. 7.99 (*0-7232-4681-5*) F Warne Pubs.

Peter Rabbit & Friends Treasury. Beatrix Potter. (J). (ps-3). 1997. 14.99 (*0-614-29146-1*, F Warne) Peng Put Young Read.

Peter Rabbit & Friends Treasury, Vol. 1. Beatrix Potter. (Illus.). (ps-3). 1999. 19.99 (*0-7232-4576-2*, F Warne) Peng Put Young Read.

Peter Rabbit & His Friends. Beatrix Potter. (Chubby Board Bks.). (Illus.). 16p. (YA). (ps up). 1985. bds. 3.95 (*0-671-52698-7*) Litle Simon.

Peter Rabbit & His Friends. Beatrix Potter. (Illus.). 24p. (J). (ps). 1994. pap. 2.99 (*0-7232-4093-0*, F Warne) Peng Put Young Read.

Peter Rabbit & Me: Playscript. Aurand Harris. 52p. (J). 1994. 6.00 (*0-87602-326-X*) Anchorage.

Peter Rabbit & Other Stories. Beatrix Potter. (J). 1993. 4.98 (*0-89009-187-0*) Bk Sales Inc.

Peter Rabbit Bath Book: Bath Book. Beatrix Potter. (Illus.). 8p. (J). (ps-k). 1989. pap. 3.99 (*0-7232-3584-8*, F Warne) Peng Put Young Read.

Peter Rabbit Bookmarks. Anna Pomaska. (J). (ps up). 1989. pap. 3.95 (*0-486-25444-5*) Dover.

***Peter Rabbit Celebrates Christmas.** Nancy Akmon. Ed. by Roni Akmon. (Illus.). 48p. 1999. 8.95 (*1-884807-45-3*, EC745) Blushing Rose.

***Peter Rabbit Giant Shaped Board Book.** Beatrix Potter. 2001. bds. 7.99 (*0-7232-4682-3*, F Warne) Peng Put Young Read.

***Peter Rabbit Lift the Flap.** Beatrix Potter. (Illus.). (J). 2000. 9.99 (*0-7232-4639-4*) F Warne Pubs.

Peter Rabbit Nursery Book & Toy. Beatrix Potter. (Illus.). 48p. (J). (ps-k). 1997. 21.99 (*0-7232-4413-8*, F Warne) Peng Put Young Read.

Peter Rabbit Nursery Book & Toy Set. Beatrix Potter. (Illus.). (J). 1997. write for info. (*0-614-29325-1*, F Warne) Peng Put Young Read.

Peter Rabbit Plays Piano. Brian Dykstra. 46p. (Orig.). 1988. pap. text 7.95 (*0-931759-29-3*) Centerstream Pub.

Peter Rabbit Postcards in Full Color. Illus. by Susan W. LaBelle. 12p. 1984. pap. 4.50 (*0-486-24617-5*) Dover.

***Peter Rabbit Puzzle & Board Book.** Beatrix Potter. 2000. bds. 10.99 (*0-7232-4580-0*, F Warne) Peng Put Young Read.

Peter Rabbit Puzzle Play Book. Seafarer Staff. text 5.98 (*0-8289-0839-7*) Seafarer Bks.

Peter Rabbit Treasury, 12 bks. (Illus.). 24p. (J). 1993. boxed set 19.98 (*0-7853-0012-0*) Pubns Intl Ltd.

Peter Rabbit Treasury. Beatrix Potter. (J). 1997. pap. 14.98 (*0-7232-4284-4*, F Warne) Peng Put Young Read.

Peter Rabbit's ABC. Beatrix Potter. (Peter Rabbit Bks.). (Illus.). 48p. (J). (ps-1). 1987. 4.99 (*0-7232-3423-X*, F Warne) Peng Put Young Read.

Peter Rabbit's ABC 123. Beatrix Potter. (Illus.). 48p. (J). (ps-3). 1995. 10.99 (*0-7232-4188-0*, F Warne) Peng Put Young Read.

***Peter Rabbit's Board Book & Toy.** abr. ed. Beatrix Potter. (Illus.). (ps-k). 1999. 17.99 (*0-7232-8346-X*, F Warne) Peng Put Young Read.

Peter Rabbit's Christmas Activity Book. Beatrix Potter. 24p. (J). 1999. pap. 4.99 (*0-7232-4547-9*, F Warne) Peng Put Young Read.

Peter Rabbit's Counting Book. Illus. by Beatrix Potter. 20p. (YA). (ps-3). 1999. 9.99 (*0-7232-4485-5*, F Warne) Peng Put Young Read.

***Peter Rabbit's Counting Fun.** Beatrix Potter. (Illus.). (J). 2000. 3.99 (*0-7232-4594-0*, F Warne) Peng Put Young Read.

***Peter Rabbit's Finger Puppet Book.** Beatrix Potter. 2000. bds. 10.99 (*0-7232-4605-X*, F Warne) Peng Put Young Read.

***Peter Rabbit's Garden Adventure.** Beatrix Potter. (Illus.). (J). 2000. pap. 4.99 (*0-7232-4592-4*, F Warne) Peng Put Young Read.

Peter Rabbit's Little Guide to Life. Warne Frederick. (Illus.). 48p. (J). (ps up). 1998. 8.99 (*0-7232-4444-8*, F Warne) Peng Put Young Read.

Peter Rabbit's One Two Three. Beatrix Potter. (Peter Rabbit Bks.). (J). (ps-1). 1988. 4.99 (*0-7232-3424-8*, F Warne) Peng Put Young Read.

***Peter Rabbit's Puzzle Story.** Beatrix Potter. (Illus.). 6p. (J). (ps-k). 2000. 4.99 (*0-7232-4577-0*, F Warne) Peng Put Young Read.

Peter Rabbit's Second Tale. Vera Sharp. (J). 1996. write for info. (*0-9616987-1-3*) V Sharp.

***Peter Rabbit's Touch & Feel Book.** Beatrix Potter. (Illus.). (ps-3). 1999. 9.99 (*0-7232-4518-5*, F Warne) Peng Put Young Read.

Peter Rabbit's Trick. David Searcy. LC 80-5678. (Lucky Heart Bk.). 24p. 1980. reprint ed. pap. 30.00 (*0-7837-9151-8*, 204985100003) Bks Demand.

Peter Ramus's Attack on Cicero: Text & Translation of Ramus's Brutinae Quaestiones. Ed. by James J. Murphy. Tr. by Carole Newlands from LAT. 250p. (C). 1992. 24.50 (*1-880393-00-X*, Hermagoras); pap. 13.95 (*1-880393-01-8*, Hermagoras) L Erlbaum Assocs.

Peter Rice: An Engineer Imagines. Peter Rice. 1998. pap. 29.00 (*1-899858-11-3*) Watsn-Guptill.

Peter Riedmann's Hutterite Confession of Faith, Vol. 9. John J. Friesen. LC 97-77791. (Classics of the Radical Reformation Ser.). 272p. 1999. pap. 16.99 (*0-8361-3122-3*) Herald Pr.

Peter Rugg: The Missing Man. William Austin. LC 72-104409. reprint ed. lib. bdg. 22.00 (*0-8398-0071-1*) Irvington.

Peter Rugg: The Missing Man. William Austin. (C). 1988. reprint ed. pap. text 6.95 (*0-317-66458-1*) Irvington.

Peter S. Beagle's Immortal Unicorn. Ed. by Peter S. Beagle & Janet Berliner. 416p. 1998. mass mkt. 6.50 (*0-06-105480-1*, HarperPrism) HarpC.

***Peter S. Beagle's Immortal Unicorn, Vol. II.** Ed. by Peter S. Beagle & Janet Berliner. (Immortal Unicorn Ser.). 464p. 1999. mass mkt. 5.99 (*0-06-105929-3*, HarperPrism) HarpC.

Peter Schaufuss - Dancer. Craig-Dodd. 1987. 69.00 (*1-869828-00-3*, Pub. by Moonstone Bks) St Mut.

Peter Schlemihl. Adelbert Von Chamisso. Tr. by John Bowring. LC 92-26945. (GERM Ser.). (Illus.). xxxi, 122p. 1993. reprint ed. 39.95 (*1-879751-32-1*) Camden Hse.

Peter Schlemihl's Wundersame Geschichte. unabridged ed. Adelbert Von Chamisso. (World Classic Literature Ser.). (GER.). pap. 7.95 (*3-89507-020-3*, Pub. by Bookking Intl) Distribks Inc.

Peter Schlmiel: The Man Who Sold His Shadow. Adelbert Von Chamisso. Tr. & Intro. by Peter Wortsman. LC 93-2832. (Illus.). 124p. 1993. 16.95 (*0-88064-142-8*) Fromm Intl Pub.

Peter Schneider on Roses. Photos by Paul E. Jerabek. LC 94-37125. (Burpee Expert Gardener Ser.). (Illus.). 224p. 1995. 18.00 (*0-02-860038-X*) Macmillan.

Peter Schneider on Roses. Peter Schneider. 1995. 20.00 (*0-671-86589-7*) S&S Trade.

Peter Scott: Painter & Naturalist. Elspeth Huxley. (Illus.). 361p. 1995. 24.95 (*1-55591-204-4*) Fulcrum Pub.

Peter Scott: Painter & Naturalist. large type ed. Elspeth Huxley. (Large Print Ser.). (Illus.). 896p. 1996. 27.99 (*0-7089-3572-9*) Ulverscroft.

Peter Sculthorpe: A Bio-Bibliography, 50. Deborah Hayes. LC 93-56774. (Bio-Bibliographies in Music Ser.: No. 50). 328p. 1993. lib. bdg. 69.50 (*0-313-27742-7*, Greenwood Pr) Greenwood.

Peter Sekaer American Pictures. Allison Kemmerer. 1999. pap. text 20.00 (*1-879886-45-6*) Addison Gallery.

Peter Sellers: A Celebration. Compiled by Adrian Rigelsford. (Illus.). 192p. 1997. text 23.95 (*1-85227-623-1*, Pub. by Virgin Bks) London Brdge.

Peter Sellers: A Film History. Michael Starr. LC 89-43695. (Illus.). 272p. 1991. lib. bdg. 38.50 (*0-89950-512-0*) McFarland & Co.

Peter Sellers: The Authorized Biography. Alexander Walker. 429p. 1995. 24.95 (*1-85089-491-4*, Pub. by ISIS Lrg Prnt) Transaction Pubs.

Peter Shaffer: A Casebook. Ed. by Constantine J. Gianakaris. LC 91-18449. (Casebooks on Modern Dramatists Ser.: Vol. 10). 192p. 1991. text 33.00 (*0-8240-6889-0*, 291) Garland.

Peter Shaffer: Roles, Rites, & Rituals in the Theater. Gene A. Plunka. LC 87-46010. 256p. 1988. 37.50 (*0-8386-3329-3*) Fairleigh Dickinson.

Peter Shelton: Bottlesbonesandthingsgetwet. Carol S. Eliel. (Illus.). 72p. (Orig.). 1994. pap. 19.95 (*0-87587-170-4*) LA Co Art Mus.

Peter Shelton: Waxworks. Cornelia H. Butler. LC 88-70611. (Illus.). 44p. (Orig.). 1988. pap. 15.00 (*0-9614615-4-3*) Edmundson.

Peter Silten: Drawings & Paintings, a Retrospective. rev. ed. Peter R. Silten. (Illus.). 64p. 1989. write for info. (*0-9621637-0-8*) P R Silten.

Peter Simon Pallas (1741-1811) Two Teilbande: Materialien einer Biographie. Folkwart Wendland. (Veroeffentlichungen der Historischen Kommission zu Berlin, Band 67, Beitraege zu Inflation und Wiederaufbau in Deutschland und Europa 1914-1924: Bd. 80-I, Bd. 80-II). (GER.). (C). 1991. lib. bdg. 378.50 (*3-11-012997-3*, 263-91) De Gruyter.

Peter Simple. Frederick Marryat. (Heart of Oak Sea Classics Ser.). 512p. 1998. 30.00 (*0-8050-5830-3*, Owl); pap. 15.00 (*0-8050-5565-7*) H Holt & Co.

***Peter Simple's Century.** Michael Wharton. 168p. 2000. 24.95 (*1-870626-47-8*, Pub. by Claridge Pr) Paul & Co Pubs.

Peter Singer in Deutschland: Zur Gefahrdung der Diskussionsfreiheit in der Wissenschaft eine Kommentierte Dokumentation. Christoph Anstotz et al. (GER.). vii, 425p. 1997. 69.95 (*3-631-48014-8*) P Lang Pubng.

Peter Skene Ogden & the Hudson's Bay Company. Gloria G. Cline. LC 72-9266. (American Exploration & Travel Ser.). 311p. reprint ed. pap. 96.50 (*0-608-15451-2*, 202930200060) Bks Demand.

Peter Skene Ogden, Fur Trader. Archie Binns. LC 67-23627. (Illus.). 376p. 1967. 16.95 (*0-8323-0054-3*) Binford Mort.

Peter Spier's Christmas! Peter Spier. (Illus.). 40p. (J). 1996. pap. 5.99 (*0-440-41285-4*, Yearling) BDD Bks Young Read.

Peter Spier's Christmas! Peter Spier. (J). 1996. 18.95 (*0-385-44691-8*) Doubleday.

Peter Spier's Christmas! Peter Spier. 1996. 11.19 (*0-606-10283-3*, Pub. by Turtleback) Demco.

Peter Spier's Circus! Peter Spier. (Illus.). 48p. (J). (ps-4). 1995. pap. 7.50 (*0-440-40935-7*) Dell.

Peter Spier's Rain. Peter Spier. (Illus.). 40p. (J). 1997. pap. 6.99 (*0-440-41347-8*, Yearling) BDD Bks Young Read.

***Peter Squared: Peter (Math Sign for Squared)** Ken Goldberg. LC 00-103679. 189p. 2000. 22.00 (*0-9673701-1-6*) MACADAM-CAGE.

Peter Sterry Vol. 60: Select Writings. Ed. by N. I. Matar. LC 92-16212. (University of Kansas Humanistic Studies: Vol. 60). XVI, 225p. (C). 1995. text 45.95 (*0-8204-1953-2*) P Lang Pubng.

Peter Stuyvesant. Joan Banks. LC 99-24901. (Colonial Leaders Ser.). (Illus.). 80p. (J). 1999. 16.95 (*0-7910-5346-6*) Chelsea Hse.

Peter Stuyvesant. Joan Banks. (Colonial Leaders Ser.). (Illus.). 80p. (J). (gr. 3 up). 1999. pap. 8.95 (*0-7910-5689-9*) Chelsea Hse.

Peter "Sugarfoot" Cunningham's Civilized Warring: Fundamental Kickboxing Techniques. Peter S. Cunningham & Robert S. Mickey. (Illus.). 192p. (Orig.). 1996. pap. 19.95 (*0-9649331-0-1*, Ragnars Bks) Galt Pubng.

Peter Taylor. Albert J. Griffith. 192p. (C). 1990. 21.95 (*0-8057-7549-8*, Twyne) Mac Lib Ref.

Peter Taylor. James C. Robinson. (Study of the Short Fiction Ser.: No. 3). 192p. 1988. 23.95 (*0-8057-8303-2*, Twyne) Mac Lib Ref.

Peter Tchaikovsky. Mike Venezia. LC 94-9479. (Getting to Know the World's Greatest Composers Ser.). (Illus.). 48p. (J). (gr. 4 up). 1994. pap. 6.95 (*0-516-44537-5*); lib. bdg. 21.00 (*0-516-04537-7*) Childrens.

Peter Tchaikovsky - The Complete Sacred Choral Works. Peter Illich Tchaikovsky. Ed. by Vladimir Morosan. (Monuments of Russian Choral Music, Series II: Vols. 1-3). cxix, 477p. 1996. 85.00 (*0-9629460-4-4*, M-PT) Musica Russica.

Peter Testman's Account of His Experiences in North America. Ed. by Theodore C. Blegen. 60p. 1927. 5.00 (*0-87732-004-7*) Norwegian-Am Hist Assn.

Peter the Apostle. W. W. Fereday. 1996. pap. 11.99 (*0-946351-21-X*, Pub. by John Ritchie) Loizeaux.

Peter the Cruel: Don Pedro of Castille. E. Storer. 1976. lib. bdg. 69.75 (*0-8490-2426-9*) Gordon Pr.

Peter I Island 1994 Expedition. Robert W. Schmieder. (Illus.). 240p. (Orig.). 1994. pap. 20.00 (*0-9626013-5-7*) Cordell Expeditions.

Peter I, II; John I, II, III; Jude see Commentaries on the New Testament

Peter the Great. Robert K. Massie. 928p. 1981. pap. 14.00 (*0-345-29806-3*) Ballantine Pub Grp.

Peter the Great. Robert K. Massie. 960p. 1986. mass mkt. 7.99 (*0-345-33619-4*) Ballantine Pub Grp.

Peter the Great. Diane Stanley. LC 98-45250. 32p. 1999. 16.00 (*0-688-16708-X*, Wm Morrow) Morrow Avon.

Peter the Great. Diane Stanley. LC 98-45250. 1999. lib. bdg. 16.01 (*0-688-16709-8*, Wm Morrow) Morrow Avon.

Peter the Great. Eugene Schuyler. (Notable American Authors Ser.). 1999. reprint ed. lib. bdg. 125.00 (*0-7812-8881-9*) Rprt Serv.

Peter the Great, 2 vols. Kasimierz Waliszewski. LC 68-25279. (World History Ser.: No. 48). 1968. reprint ed. lib. bdg. 150.00 (*0-8383-0265-3*) M S G Haskell Hse.

Peter the Great. 2nd ed. M. S. Anderson. LC 94-44378. (Profiles in Power Ser.). 240p. (C). 1995. text 57.75 (*0-582-08412-1*, Pub. by Addison-Wesley) Longman.

Peter the Great. 2nd ed. M. S. Anderson. LC 94-44378. (Profiles in Power Ser.). 240p. (C). 1996. pap. text 22.50 (*0-582-08411-3*, Pub. by Addison-Wesley) Longman.

Peter the Great: A Life of Peter I of Russia. Stephen Graham. LC 75-138241. (Illus.). 376p. 1971. reprint ed. lib. bdg. 39.75 (*0-8371-5598-3*, GRPG, Greenwood Pr) Greenwood.

Peter the Great: The Classic Biography of Tsar Peter the Great. Vasili Klyuchevsky. Tr. by Liliana Archibald. LC 84-45072. 294p. 1984. reprint ed. pap. 17.50 (*0-8070-5647-2*, BP678) Beacon Pr.

Peter the Great & the Modernization of Russia. Richard H. Warner. (Anvil Ser.). (Orig.). 1999. pap. write for info. (*0-89464-900-0*) Krieger.

Peter the Great & Tsarist Russia. Miriam Greenblatt. LC 98-25656. (Rulers & Their Times Ser.). 80p. (YA). (gr. 4-7). 1999. lib. bdg. 28.50 (*0-7614-0914-9*, Benchmark NY) Marshall Cavendish.

Peter the Great Changes Russia. 2nd ed. Ed. by Marc Raeff. (Problems in European Civilization Ser.). 228p. (C). 1972. pap. text 18.36 (*0-669-82701-0*) HM Trade Div.

An Asterisk (*) at the beginning of an entry indicates that the title is appearing for the first time.

Peter the Great Transforms Russia. 3rd ed. Ed. by James E. Cracraft. LC 90-81300. (Problems in European Civilization Ser.). 305p. (C). 1991. pap. text 20.36 (*0-669-21674-7*) HM Trade Div.

Peter the Great's Army: Cavalry. Angus Konstam. (Men-at-Arms Ser.: No. 264). (Illus.). 48p. 1993. pap. 11.95 (*1-85532-348-6*, 9235, Pub. by Ospry) Stackpole.

Peter the Postman: Playscript. Torben Jetsmark. 37p. (J). 1988. 6.00 (*0-87602-279-4*) Anchorage.

Peter the Puppy Talks about Chemical Dependence in the Family. Teresa M. Schmidt & Thelma Spencer. (Building Trust, Making Friends Ser.). 240p. (J). (gr. k-6). 1991. pap. 65.95 (*1-56246-019-6*, 3068, HazeldenJohnson Inst) Hazelden.

Peter Third, Emperor of Russia. Robert N. Bain. 1902. 12.00 (*0-403-00465-9*) Scholarly.

Peter Third, Emperor of Russia: The Story of a Crisis & a Crime. Robert N. Bain. LC 72-156962. (BCL Ser.: No. II). reprint ed. 29.50 (*0-404-00448-2*) AMS Pr.

Peter Thornwell. Torsten Barring. (Orig.). 1993. mass mkt. 4.95 (*1-56333-149-7*, Badboy) Masquerade.

Peter Three Eight: The Pilot's Story. John C. Stamaway. LC 86-60128. (Illus.). 132p. 1986. pap. 9.95 (*0-933126-73-5*) Pictorial Hist.

Peter Ujvari's by Candlelight. Tr. by Andrew Handler. 252p. 1977. 24.50 (*0-8386-1895-2*) Fairleigh Dickinson.

Peter Underwood's Guide to Ghosts & Haunted Places. Peter Underwood. (Illus.). 256p. 1997. text 23.95 (*0-7499-1665-6*, Pub. by Piatkus Bks) London Brdge.

Peter von Artens: Paintings Portraits - Pinturas Retratos. Ed. by Iran O. Rey. Tr. by Julia Yobst. (ENG & SPA., Illus.). 80p. 1996. 36.00 (*0-9650650-1-4*) Palette Pubns.

Peter Waite. Douglas Blau. 12p. (Orig.). 1991. pap. text 5.00 (*0-914489-08-9*) Univ Miss-KC Art.

Peter Walker: Experiments in Gesture, Seriality, & Flatness. David Dillon et al. (Illus.). 72p. 1990. 20.00 (*0-614-14659-3*) Harvard Univ Graduate Schl of.

Peter Walker: Minimalist Gardens. Leah Levy. (Illus.). 210p. 1997. pap. 45.00 (*1-888931-00-0*) Spacemkr Pr.

Peter Wapnewski: Zuschreibungen. Fritz Wagner & Wolfgang Maaz. (GER.). viii, 560p. 1994. 138.00 (*3-615-00101-X*, Pub. by Weidmann) Lubrecht & Cramer.

Peter Warlock: The Life of Philip Heseltine. Barry Smith. (Illus.). 366p. 1996. pap. text 26.00 (*0-19-816606-0*) OUP.

Peter Warlock, the Composer. Brian Collins. 370p. 1996. 83.95 (*1-85928-216-4*, Pub. by Scolar Pr) Ashgate Pub Co.

Peter Weibel: On Justifying the Hypothetical Nature of Art. Peter Weibel. 186p. 1992. 24.95 (*3-88375-166-9*, Pub. by Walther Konig) Dist Art Pubs.

Peter Weir: When Cultures Collide. Marek Haltof. LC 96-2758. 1996. 33.00 (*0-8057-7843-8*); pap. 20.00 (*0-8057-9244-9*) Macmillan.

Peter Weiss in Exile: A Critical Study of His Works. Roger Ellis. 179p. 1987. pap. 59.95 (*0-7734-1988-8*) E Mellen.

Peter Whiffle. Carl Van Vechten. LC 77-78306. reprint ed. 37.50 (*0-404-15126-4*) AMS Pr.

Peter Wild. Edward Butscher. LC 92-52531. (Western Writers Ser.: No. 106). (Illus.). 53p. (Orig.). 1992. pap. 4.95 (*0-88430-105-2*) Boise St U W Writ Ser.

Peter William Butterblow. C. J. Moore. (J). pap. 14.95 (*0-86315-125-6*, 1459, Pub. by Floris Bks) Anthroposophic.

***Peter Winch.** Colin Lyas. (Philosophy Now Ser.). 2000. 57.50 (*1-902683-01-3*); pap. text 19.95 (*1-902683-02-1*) Acumen Pub.

Peter Womersley. Joseph Blackburn & Simon Green. 88p. (C). 1994. pap. 35.00 (*1-873190-19-0*, Pub. by Rutland Pr) St Mut.

Peter Zumthor: Drei Konzepte. Ed. by Architekturgalerie Luzern Staff. (Illus.). 84p. 1997. pap. 35.00 (*3-7643-5744-4*, Pub. by Birkhauser) Princeton Arch.

Peter Zumthor: Thinking Architecture. Peter Zumthor. (Illus.). 64p. 1998. 25.00 (*1-56898-144-9*) Princeton Arch.

Peter Zumthor: Three Concepts. Ed. by Architekturgalerie Luzern Staff. LC 97-39815. (Illus.). 84p. 1997. pap. 35.00 (*3-7643-5745-2*, Pub. by Birkhauser) Princeton Arch.

Peter Zumthor, Works: Buildings & Projects, 1979-1997. Peter Zumthor. (Illus.). 312p. 1998. 75.00 (*1-56898-143-0*) Princeton Arch.

***Peter Zumthor, Works: Buildings & Projects, 1979-1997.** Peter Zumthor & Helene Binet. LC 99-35918. 1999. write for info. (*3-7643-6098-4*) Birkhauser.

Peterborough: A History. Herbert F. Tebbs. (Cambridge Town, Gown & County Ser.: Vol. 24). (Illus.). 1979. 25.00 (*0-900891-30-0*) Oleander Pr.

Peterborough: History & Guide. Donald Mackreth. (History & Guide Ser.). (Illus.). 128p. 1994. pap. 13.95 (*0-7509-0235-3*, Pub. by Sutton Pub Ltd) Intl Pubs Mktg.

Peterborough in the American Revolution. Jonathan Smith. (Illus.). 423p. 1997. reprint ed. lib. bdg. 45.00 (*0-8328-6018-2*) Higginson Bk Co.

Peterborough New Hampshire in the American Revolution. large type unabridged ed. Jonathan Smith. LC 96-44047. viii, 423p. (C). 1996. reprint ed. 34.95 (*1-889881-08-2*) Old Bks Pub.

Peterborough Symposium on Cardiology. F. J. Fawcet. 1975. pap. text 30.00 (*0-7855-2852-0*) St Mut.

Peterburg V. Russkom Ocherke XIX Veka. Ed. by Collet's Holdings, Ltd. Staff. 376p. 1984. 49.00 (*0-7855-0902-X*) St Mut.

Peterkin Papers. Lucretia Hale. (J). 1992. pap. 4.95 (*0-8167-2924-7*) Troll Communs.

Peterkin Papers: The Return of the Lady from Philadelphia. Lucretia P. Hale. 256p. (J). 1994. text 10.95 (*0-312-11382-X*) St Martin.

***Peterman Rides Again: The True Story of the Real "J. Peterman" & the Unconventional Catalog Company He Built.** John Peterman. 288p. 2001. 25.00 (*0-7352-0199-4*) PH Pr.

Peters: Conrad Peters & Wife Clara Snidow: Their Descendants & Ancestry. O. E. Peters. (Illus.). 229p. 1991. reprint ed. pap. 35.00 (*0-8328-1885-2*); reprint ed. lib. bdg. 45.00 (*0-8328-1884-4*) Higginson Bk Co.

Peters & Their Allied Families, of Flat Rock, Michigan. Janet Egler. (Illus.). 182p. 1999. pap. 27.00 (*0-8328-9805-8*); lib. bdg. 37.00 (*0-8328-9804-X*) Higginson Bk Co.

Peter's Angry Toys: I Am Special Children's Story Books. Carol T. Plum. (Illus.). 30p. (J). (ps-3). 1989. pap. text 3.95 (*0-87973-012-9*, 12) Our Sunday Visitor.

Peter's Angry Toys: I Am Special Children's Story Books. Carol T. Plum. (Illus.). 30p. (J). (ps-3). 1989. lib. bdg. 6.95 (*0-87973-015-3*, 15) Our Sunday Visitor.

Peter's Bridge: Engineering. Frank Kubic. LC 97-658330. 20p. (YA). (gr. 8-12). 1997. pap. 4.50 (*1-888958-02-2*) Nuggets Wisdom.

Peter's Building Blocks for the Church. Wilma M. Jones. 300p. (Orig.). 1994. pap. text 20.95 (*0-930401-70-0*) Artex Pub.

Peter's Cat. Steve English. (Illus.). 126p. 1996. pap. text 9.99 (*1-900507-17-X*, Pub. by Solway) Eisenbrauns.

Peter's Chair. Ezra Jack Keats. (Picture Puffin Ser.). (Illus.). 1998. 11.19 (*0-606-13701-7*, Pub. by Turtleback) Demco.

Peter's Chair. Ezra Jack Keats. LC 97-48302. (Illus.). 40p. (J). (ps-3). 1998. 15.99 (*0-670-88064-7*) Viking Penguin.

Peter's Choice. Joseph Orbi. 1998. text 24.00 (*0-9661619-0-4*) Rom Pub.

Peter's Christmas. Bolette Bonfils. LC 94-24500. (Crocodile Life-the-Flap Bk.). (Illus.). 24p. (J). (ps-2). 1994. 9.95 (*1-56656-162-0*, Crocodile Bks) Interlink Pub.

Peter's Dream. Joan Hoffman. (Start to Read! Ser.). (Illus.). 16p. (J). (gr. k-2). 1992. pap. 2.29 (*0-88743-264-6*, 06031) Sch Zone Pub Co.

Peter's Dream. Joan Hoffman. (Start to Read! Ser.). (Illus.). 32p. (J). (ps-3). 1993. pap. 3.99 (*0-88743-425-8*, 06077) Sch Zone Pub Co.

Peter's First Easter. Walter Wangerin. LC 99-11590. 48p. 2000. 15.99 (*0-310-22217-6*) Zondervan.

Peter's Gate. Sherwood. 156p. 1992. pap. 9.95 (*0-85207-259-7*, Pub. by C W Daniel) Natl Bk Netwk.

Peter's Gate: A Book for the Elderly. Jane Sherwood. 96p. (Orig.). pap. 14.95 (*0-8464-4270-1*) Beekman Pubs.

Peter's House see Casa de Pedro

Peter's Journey: A Young Man's Search for the True Purpose of Life. Maurice Scott. LC 99-187292. 176p. 1998. pap. 16.95 (*1-85756-358-1*, Pub. by Janus Pubng) Paul & Co Pubs.

Peters of New England: A Genealogy & Family History. E. Peters. (Illus.). 470p. 1989. reprint ed. pap. 70.00 (*0-8328-0959-4*); reprint ed. lib. bdg. 78.00 (*0-8328-0958-6*) Higginson Bk Co.

Peter's Old House. unabridged ed. Elsa Beskow. Orig. Title: Herr Peter. (Illus.). 26p. (J). (ps-1). 15.95 (*0-86315-102-7*, 25986, Pub. by Floris Bks) Gryphon Hse.

Peter's Package. Bolette Bonfils. LC 94-24492. (Crocodile Lift-The-Flap Bk.). (Illus.). 24p. (J). (ps-2). 1994. 9.95 (*1-56656-155-8*, Crocodile Bks) Interlink Pub.

Peter's Painting. Sally Moss. LC 95-8704. (Illus.). 24p. (J). (ps-2). 1995. 13.95 (*1-57255-013-9*) Mondo Pubng.

Peter's Patchwork Dream. Illus. by Willemien Min. 32p. (J). (ps-1). 1999. 15.95 (*1-902283-45-7*) Barefoot Bks NY.

Peter's Pentecost Discourse: Tradition & Lukan Reinterpretation in Peter's Speeches of Acts 2 & 3. Richard F. Zehnle. LC 72-148063. (Society of Biblical Literature, Ser.: No. 15). 144p. reprint ed. pap. 44.70 (*0-7837-5403-5*, 204516700005) Bks Demand.

***Peter's Picture.** Valeri Gorbachev. (Illus.). 32p. (J). (ps-1). 2000. lib. bdg. 15.88 (*1-55858-966-X*, Pub. by North-South Bks NYC) Chronicle Bks.

Peter's Pip. John Smith. (C). 1989. text 35.00 (*0-948929-04-9*) St Mut.

Peter's Place. Sally Grindley. LC 95-5820. (Illus.). 36p. (J). (ps-2). 1996. 15.00 (*0-15-200916-7*, Gulliver Bks) Harcourt.

Peter's Pockets. Lenore Morgan. LC 65-27622. (Illus.). 32p. (J). (gr. k-2). 1968. lib. bdg. 9.95 (*0-87783-029-0*) Oddo.

Peter's Pockets. Lenore Morgan. (Illus.). (J). (gr. k-2). 1978. pap. 1.25 (*0-89508-063-X*) Rainbow Bks.

Peter's Present. (Ready Readers Series II Stage I). (Illus.). 32p. (J). (ps-1). 1996. pap. write for info. (*1-56144-949-0*, Honey Bear Bks) Modern Pub NYC.

Peter's Prince Edward Island Reports, 1850-1872. 1986. 42.00 (*1-57588-349-X*, 302680) W S Hein.

Peter's Quotations: Ideas for Our Time. Laurence J. Peter. 1993. pap. 12.00 (*0-688-11909-3*, Quil) HarperTrade.

***Peter's Redemption: A Novel about Power, Political Intrigue & Change in the Catholic Church of the 21st Century.** J. F. David. 307p. 1999. pap. 15.95 (*0-9668228-1-1*) Caritas Commns.

Peter's Song. Carol P. Saul. (Illus.). 40p. (ps-1). 1994. lib. bdg. 4.95 (*0-671-89283-5*, Half Moon Paper) S&S Childrens.

Peters Third Black & Blue Guide to Literary Journals. 3rd ed. Robert Peters. 164p. 1987. pap. 5.95 (*0-916685-03-9*) Dustbooks.

Peter's Trucks. Sallie Wolf. Ed. by Abby Levine. LC 91-19251. (Illus.). 24p. (J). (ps-1). 1992. lib. bdg. 14.95 (*0-8075-6519-9*) A Whitman.

Petersburg. Andrei Bely. Tr. by Robert A. Maguire & John E. Malmstad from RUS. LC 77-74442. 384p. 1979. pap. 15.95 (*0-253-20219-1*, MB 219) Ind U Pr.

Petersburg. Andrei Bely. Tr. by David McDuff. LC Png UK. 624p. 1996. pap. 15.95 (*0-14-018696-4*, Penguin Classics) Viking Penguin.

Petersburg. unabridged ed. Bely. (World Classic Literature Ser.). (RUS.). pap. 8.95 (*2-87714-266-3*, Pub. by Bookking Intl) Distribks Inc.

Petersburg: Crucible of Cultural Revolution. Katerina Clark. LC 95-17161. 368p. (C). 1995. 44.00 (*0-674-66335-7*) HUP.

Petersburg: Crucible of Cultural Revolution. Katerina Clark. 384p. 1998. pap. text 18.95 (*0-674-66336-5*) HUP.

Petersburg: Out of the Trenches. James W. Wensyel. LC 98-35166. 169p. 1998. 24.95 (*1-57249-139-6*, Burd St Pr) White Mane Pub.

Petersburg & Paris Period, 2 vols. Mihail Chemiakin. Incl. Vol. II. Transformation: New York Period. 286p. 1986. (Illus.). 504p. 1986. Set boxed set 250.00 (*0-317-56275-4*, Pub. by Mosaic Pr) Empire Pub Srvs.

***Petersburg Campaign: June, 1864-April, 1865.** John Horn. 1999. pap. 18.95 (*1-58097-024-9*, 970249) Combined Pub.

Petersburg Campaign: The Destruction of the Weldon Railroad. John Horn. (Virginia Civil War Battles & Leaders Ser.). (Illus.). 270p. 1991. 19.95 (*1-56190-010-9*) H E Howard.

Petersburg Campaign: Wasted Valor June 15-18, 1864. Thomas J. Howe. (Virginia Civil War Battles & Leaders Ser.). (Illus.). 192p. 1988. 19.95 (*0-930919-54-8*) H E Howard.

Petersburg Campaign Abraham Lincoln at City Point, March 20-April 9, 1865. Donald C. Pfanz. (Virginia Civil War Battles & Leaders Ser.). (Illus.). 12.95 (*0-930919-76-9*) H E Howard.

Petersburg Campaign the Battle of Old Men & Young Boys June 9, 1864. William G. Robertson. (Virginia Civil War Battles & Leaders Ser.). (Illus.). 143p. 1989. 19.95 (*0-930919-70-X*) H E Howard.

Petersburg Campaign the Battle of the Crater, "the Horrid Pit," June 25-August 6, 1864. Michael A. Cavanaush & William Marvel. (Virginia Civil War Battles & Leaders Ser.). (Illus.). 1989. 19.95 (*0-930919-77-7*) H E Howard.

Petersburg in the Civil War. William D. Henderson. (Virginia Civil War Battles & Leaders Ser.). (Illus.). 185p. 1998. 25.00 (*1-56190-110-5*) H E Howard.

Petersburg's Story: A History. James G. Scott & Edward A. Wyatt. (Illus.). 414p. 1998. reprint ed. 29.95 (*0-87517-104-4*) Dietz.

Petersburgskii Period Georgiia Ivanova. Vadim Kreid. LC 88-34791. (Russian Ser.). (Orig.). 1989. pap. 14.50 (*0-938920-93-6*) Hermitage Pubs.

Petersen Graph Theory. Derek A. Holton & J. Sheehan. (Australian Mathematical Society Lecture Ser.: No. 7). (Illus.). 363p. (C). 1993. pap. text 49.95 (*0-521-43594-3*) Cambridge U Pr.

Petersen's Complete Book of Toyota. Al Hall & Petersen Publishing Company Staff. LC 75-325246. 192p. 1975. write for info. (*0-8227-0115-4*) Petersen Pub.

Petersen's Complete Book of Toyota. 2nd rev. ed. Al Hall & Petersen Publishing Company Staff. LC 77-150790. 192p. 1977. write for info. (*0-8227-5009-0*) Petersen Pub.

Petersfield: A Pictorial Past. Sean Street. (C). 1989. 39.00 (*1-85455-028-4*, Pub. by Ensign Pubns & Print) St Mut.

Peterson & Peterson Family. W. H. Peterson et al. 372p. 1991. reprint ed. pap. 59.00 (*0-8328-2073-3*); reprint ed. lib. bdg. 69.00 (*0-8328-2072-5*) Higginson Bk Co.

Peterson Field Guide to Western Bird Songs, Vol. 2. Cornell Laboratory of Ornithology & Interactive Audio Staff. (Peterson Field Guide Ser.). 32p. 1992. pap. 35.00 incl. audio (*0-395-51746-X*, 684732) HM.

Peterson First Guide to Birds of North America. Roger T. Peterson. 1986. 10.05 (*0-606-04504-X*, Pub. by Turtleback) Demco.

Peterson First Guide to Dinosaurs. John C. Kricher. 1990. 10.05 (*0-606-04505-8*, Pub. by Turtleback) Demco.

Peterson First Guide to Fishes of North America. Michael Filisky. 1989. 10.05 (*0-606-04506-6*, Pub. by Turtleback) Demco.

Peterson First Guide to Insects of North America. Christopher Leahy. 1987. 10.05 (*0-606-04507-4*, Pub. by Turtleback) Demco.

Peterson First Guide to Mammals of North America. Peter Alden. 1987. 10.05 (*0-606-04508-2*, Pub. by Turtleback) Demco.

Peterson First Guide to Reptiles & Amphibians. Roger Conant. (J). 1992. 10.05 (*0-606-05537-1*, Pub. by Turtleback) Demco.

Peterson First Guide to Rocks & Minerals. Frederick H. Pough. (Peterson Field Guide Ser.). (Illus.). 128p. 1991. pap. 5.95 (*0-395-56275-9*) HM.

Peterson First Guide to Seashores. John C. Kricher. (J). 1992. 10.05 (*0-606-05538-X*, Pub. by Turtleback) Demco.

Peterson First Guide to Shells of North America. Jackie L. Douglass. 1989. 10.05 (*0-606-04509-0*, Pub. by Turtleback) Demco.

Peterson First Guide to Trees. George A. Petrides. LC 92-36586. (Illus.). 128p. (J). 1993. pap. 4.95 (*0-395-65972-8*) HM.

Peterson First Guide to Trees. George A. Petrides. (J). 1993. 10.05 (*0-606-05539-8*, Pub. by Turtleback) Demco.

Peterson 1st Urban Wildlife. Sarah Landry. LC 93-31279. 1998. pap. 5.95 (*0-395-93544-X*) HM.

Peterson Flashguides: Atlantic Coastal Birds. Roger T. Peterson. (Illus.). 24p. 1996. pap. 7.95 (*0-395-79286-X*) HM.

Peterson Flashguides: Backyard Birds. Roger T. Peterson. (Illus.). 24p. 1996. pap. 7.95 (*0-395-79290-8*) HM.

Peterson Flashguides: Birds of the Midwest. Peterson Staff. (Illus.). 24p. 1997. pap. 8.95 (*0-395-86733-9*) HM.

Peterson Flashguides: Eastern Mountain Birds. Roger T. Peterson. (Illus.). 24p. 1996. pap. 7.95 (*0-395-79288-6*) HM.

Peterson Flashguides: Freshwater Fish. Peterson Staff. (Illus.). 24p. 1997. pap. 7.95 (*0-395-86713-4*) HM.

Peterson Flashguides: Hawks. Roger T. Peterson. (Illus.). 24p. 1996. pap. 7.95 (*0-395-79291-6*) HM.

Peterson Flashguides: Pacific Coastal Birds. Roger T. Peterson. (Illus.). 24p. 1996. pap. 7.95 (*0-395-79287-8*) HM.

Peterson Flashguides: Waterfowl. Peterson Staff. (Illus.). 24p. 1997. pap. 8.95 (*0-395-86734-7*) HM.

Peterson Flashguides: Western Mountain Birds. Roger T. Peterson. (Illus.). 24p. 1996. pap. 7.95 (*0-395-79289-4*) HM.

Peterson Guide to Birds, Vol. 2. 1996. 38.47 (*0-395-84843-1*) HM.

Peterson Guide to Wildflowers. Storey Publishing Staff. 1997. pap. 18.00 (*0-676-57075-5*) Random.

Peterson Psychology Book & Study Guide. A. Peterson. 1997. write for info. (*0-201-36272-4*) Addison-Wesley.

Peterson Rocks & Minerals. F. H. Pough. Vol. 19. 1998. pap. 5.95 (*0-395-93543-1*) HM.

Peterson's ACT English Flash. American Bookworks Staff & Peterson's Guides Staff. Ed. by Mark Moscowitz. LC 97-11301. (Peterson's Guides Ser.). 208p. (Orig.). (YA). 1997. pap. 8.95 (*1-56079-767-3*) Petersons.

Peterson's ACT Math Flash. American Bookworks Staff & Peterson's Guides Staff. Ed. by Mark Moscowitz. LC 97-12094. (Peterson's Guides Ser.). 208p. (Orig.). (YA). 1997. pap. 8.95 (*1-56079-766-5*) Petersons.

Peterson's Black Colleges & Universities. Peterson's Guides Staff. (Peterson's Guides). 1998. pap. text 12.95 (*0-7689-0145-6*) Petersons.

***Peterson's CLEP Success 2001.** 2nd ed. Peterson's Guides Staff. 363p. 2000. pap. 16.95 (*0-7689-0407-2*) Petersons.

Peterson's College & University Almanac. 2nd ed. Peterson's Guides Staff. 512p. 1998. pap. text 9.95 (*0-7689-0035-2*) Petersons.

Peterson's College Money Handbook, 1997. 14th rev. ed. Ed. by Peterson's Guides Staff. 726p. 1996. pap. 26.95 (*1-56079-697-9*) Petersons.

Peterson's Colleges & Universities in the U. S. A., 1998: A Handbook for International Students. Ed. by Jon Latimer. 1997. pap. 24.95 (*1-56079-758-4*) Petersons.

Peterson's Competitive Colleges. 17th ed. Peterson's Guides Staff. 444p. 1998. pap. text 18.95 (*1-56079-988-9*) Petersons.

Peterson's Competitive Colleges: Top Colleges & Universities in the US for the World's Best St. 18th ed. Petersons. 480p. 1999. pap. 18.95 (*0-7689-0213-4*) Petersons.

***Peterson's Competitive Colleges 2000-2001.** 19th ed. Peterson's Guides Staff. 2000. pap. 18.95 (*0-7689-0385-8*) Petersons.

Peterson's Computer Science & Electrical Engineering Programs. Ed. by Peterson's Guides Staff. 900p. (Orig.). 1996. pap. 24.95 (*1-56079-663-4*) Petersons.

Peterson's Culinary Schools: The Most Comprehensive Guide to U. S. Culinary Schools & Apprenticeship Programs. Peterson's Guides Staff. 300p. 1998. pap. text 21.95 (*1-56079-943-9*) Petersons.

Peterson's Culinary Schools: Where the Art of Cooking Becomes a Career 1999. 2nd ed. Peterson's Staff. 303p. 1998. pap. text 21.95 (*0-7689-0127-8*) Petersons.

Peterson's Edible Wild Plants. Lee Allen Peterson. 1998. pap. 18.00 (*0-676-57324-X*) Random.

Peterson's English Learning Programs: A Guide to Short-Term Study Worldwide. Peterson's Guides Staff. 576p. 1998. pap. text 21.95 (*1-56079-999-4*) Petersons.

Petersons First Guide to Birds. Storey Publishers Staff. 1997. pap. 4.95 (*0-676-57074-7*) Random.

***Peterson's Four-Year Colleges 2001.** 31st ed. 3264p. 2000. pap. 26.95 (*0-7689-0377-7*) Petersons.

***Peterson's Game Plan for Getting into Business Schools.** Peterson's Guides Staff. 200p. 2000. pap. 14.95 (*0-7689-0392-0*) Petersons.

***Peterson's Game Plan for Getting into College.** Patricia K. Aviezer. LC 99-88974. 200p. 2000. pap. 14.95 (*0-7689-0390-4*) Petersons.

***Peterson's Game Plan for Getting into Graduate School.** Peterson's Guides Staff. 200p. 2000. pap. 14.95 (*0-7689-0391-2*) Petersons.

***Peterson's Game Plan for Getting into Law School.** William G. Weaver. LC 99-58761. 208p. 1999. 14.95 (*0-7689-0394-7*) Petersons.

***Peterson's Game Plan for Getting into Medical School.** Peterson's Guides Staff. LC 99-87860. 2000. pap. 14.95 (*0-7689-0393-9*) Petersons.

***Peterson's Game Plan for Getting into Private School.** Lila Lohr. LC 99-89009. 200p. 2000. 14.95 (*0-7689-0387-4*) Petersons.

Peterson's Golf Schools & Resorts. James M. Lane. LC 95-7991. 226p. (Orig.). 1995. pap. 13.95 (*1-56079-476-3*) Petersons.

Peterson's Graduate & Professional Programs: An Overview. Ed. by Jon Latimer. (Graduate & Professional Programs Ser.). 1412p. 1997. pap. 29.95 (*1-56079-791-6*) Petersons.

Peterson's Graduate & Professional Programs, 1996: An Overview, Bk. 1. 30th ed. Peterson's Guides Staff. 1204p. 1995. pap. 25.95 (*1-56079-501-8*) Petersons.

Peterson's Graduate Guides. 1998. 495.25 (*0-7689-0154-5*) Petersons.

Peterson's Graduate Programs in Biological Sciences, 1998. Ed. by Jon Latimer. (Graduate & Professional Programs Ser.). 2924p. 1997. pap. 46.95 (*1-56079-793-2*) Petersons.

P

Peterson's Graduate Programs in Business, Education, Health, Information Studies, Law & Social Work 1998. Ed. by Jon Latimer. (Graduate & Professional Programs Ser.). 1986p. 1997. pap. 29.95 (*1-56079-796-7*) Petersons.

Peterson's Graduate Programs in Engineering & Applied Sciences, 1998. Ed. by Jon Latimer. (Graduate & Professional Programs Ser.). 1714p. 1997. pap. 39.95 (*1-56079-795-9*) Petersons.

Peterson's Graduate Programs in Humanities, Arts & Social Sciences, 1998. Ed. by Jon Latimer. (Graduate & Professional Programs Ser.). 1575p. 1997. pap. 39.95 (*1-56079-792-4*) Petersons.

Peterson's Graduate Programs in the Humanities, Arts, & Social Sciences 1996, Bk. 2. 30th ed. Peterson's Guides Staff. 1514p. 1995. pap. 34.95 (*1-56079-502-6*) Petersons.

Peterson's Graduate Programs in the Physical Sciences & Mathematics, 1996, Bk. 4. 30th ed. Peterson's Guides Staff. 818p. 1995. pap. 32.95 (*1-56079-504-2*) Petersons.

Peterson's Graduate Programs in the Physical Sciences, Mathematics & Agricultural Sciences, 1998. Ed. by Jon Latimer. (Graduate & Professional Programs Ser.). 1038p. 1997. pap. 36.95 (*1-56079-794-0*) Petersons.

Peterson's Graduate Schools in the U. S. & Canada. Ed. by Jon Latimer. 800p. 1997. pap. 24.95 (*1-56079-765-7*) Petersons.

Peterson's Grants for Graduate & Postdoctoral Study. 4th ed. 526p. 1994. 89.95 (*1-56079-401-1*) Petersons.

Peterson's Grants for Graduate & Postdoctoral Study. 5th ed. Peterson's Guides Staff. 528p. 1998. pap. text 32.95 (*0-7689-0019-0*) Petersons.

Peterson's Guide to Adult Learning Opportunities. Ed. by Jon Latimer. 600p. 1997. pap. 21.95 (*1-56079-807-6*) Petersons.

***Peterson's Guide to College Visits 2001.** 3rd ed. Peterson's Guides Staff. 512p. 2000. pap. 24.95 (*0-7689-0400-5*) Petersons.

Peterson's Guide to Colleges for Careers in Allied Health. Peterson's Guides Staff. 1996. pap. 67.80 (*1-56079-531-X*) Intl School Servs.

Peterson's Guide to Colleges for Careers in Computing. (Tech Prep Ser.). 208p. (C). 1996. pap. 16.95 (*1-56079-527-1*) Thomson Learn.

Peterson's Guide to Colleges in New England, 1997, 6 vols. 13th rev. ed. Peterson's Guides Staff. (Regional College Guides Ser.). 143p. 1996. pap. 16.95 (*1-56079-623-5*) Petersons.

Peterson's Guide to Colleges in New York, 1997, 6 vols. 13th ed. Peterson's Guides Staff. (Regional College Guides Ser.). 142p. 1996. pap. 16.95 (*1-56079-622-7*) Petersons.

Petersons Guide to Colleges in New York, 1999: New York State, Including New York City. 15th ed. Peterson's Guides Staff. (Peterson's Guide to Colleges in New York Ser.). 345p. pap. 17.95 (*0-7689-0033-6*, 870092Q) Petersons.

Peterson's Guide to Colleges in the Middle Atlantic States, 1996: Delaware, the District of Columbia, Maryland . . . 12th ed. Peterson's Guides Staff. (Regional College Guides Ser.). 218p. (YA). (gr. 11-12). 1995. pap. 14.95 (*1-56079-492-5*, Petersons Pacesetter) Petersons.

Peterson's Guide to Colleges in the Middle Atlantic States, 1997, 6 vols. 13th ed. Peterson's Guides Staff. (Regional College Guides Ser.). 221p. 1996. pap. 16.95 (*1-56079-626-X*) Petersons.

Peterson's Guide to Colleges in the Midwest, 1996: Illinois, Indiana, Iowa, Kansas, Michigan... 12th ed. Peterson's Guides Staff. (Regional College Guides Ser.). 345p. (YA). (gr. 11-12). 1995. pap. 14.95 (*1-56079-489-5*) Petersons.

Peterson's Guide to Colleges in the Midwest, 1997, 6 vols. 13th rev. ed. Peterson's Guides Staff. (Regional College Guides Ser.). 363p. 1996. pap. 16.95 (*1-56079-624-3*) Petersons.

Peterson's Guide to Colleges in the South, 1996: Alabama, Arkansas, Florida, Georgia, Kentucky... 11th ed. Peterson's Guides Staff. (Regional College Guides Ser.). 288p. (YA). (gr. 11-12). 1995. pap. 14.95 (*1-56079-490-9*) Petersons.

Peterson's Guide to Colleges in the South, 1997. Peterson's Guides Staff. (Regional College Guides Ser.). 288p. 1996. pap. text 16.95 (*1-56079-625-1*) Petersons.

Peterson's Guide to Colleges in the South, 1997, 6 vols. 12th rev. ed. Peterson's Guides Staff. (Regional College Guides Ser.). 308p. 1996. pap. 16.95 (*1-56069-625-7*) Petersons.

Peterson's Guide to Colleges in the West, 1996: Alaska, Arizona, California, Colorado, Hawaii, Idaho... 10th ed. Peterson's Guides Staff. (Regional College Guides Ser.). 195p. (C). 1995. pap. 14.95 (*1-56079-491-7*) Petersons.

Peterson's Guide to Colleges in the West, 1997, 6 vols. 11th rev. ed. Peterson's Guides Staff. (Regional College Guides Ser.). 195p. 1996. pap. 16.95 (*1-56079-627-8*) Petersons.

Peterson's Guide to Colleges with Programs for Students with Learning Disabilities. 4th ed. Charles T. Mangrum & Stephen S. Strichart. LC 94-4760. 684p. (C). 1994. 32.95 (*1-56079-400-3*) Petersons.

Peterson's Guide to Distance Learning Programs. 2nd rev. ed. Peterson's Guides Staff. Orig. Title: Electronic University. (Illus.). 504p. (Orig.). 1996. pap. 24.95 (*1-56079-664-2*) Petersons.

***Peterson's Guide to Distance Learning Programs 2000.** 5th ed. 702p. 2000. pap. 26.95 (*0-7689-0403-X*) Petersons.

Peterson's Guide to Four-Year Colleges, 1997, 27th rev. ed. Peterson's Guides Staff. 3180p. 1996. pap. 24.95 (*1-56079-604-9*) Petersons.

Peterson's Guide to Graduate & Professional Programs: An Overview, 1997, Vol. 1. 31st rev. ed. Ed. by Peterson's Guides Staff. 1264p. 1996. pap. 27.95 (*1-56079-651-0*) Petersons.

Peterson's Guide to Graduate Computer Science & Electrical Engineering Programs. 2nd ed. Ed. by Jon Latimer. 800p. 1997. pap. 24.95 (*1-56079-874-2*) Petersons.

Peterson's Guide to Graduate Programs in Business, Education, Health, Information Studies, Law & Social Work 1997, Vol. 6. 31st rev. ed. Ed. by Peterson's Guides Staff. 1718p. 1996. pap. 27.95 (*1-56079-656-1*) Petersons.

Peterson's Guide to Graduate Programs in Engineering & Applied Sciences 1997, Vol. 5. 31st rev. ed. Ed. by Peterson's Guides Staff. 1567p. 1996. pap. 37.95 (*1-56079-655-3*) Petersons.

Peterson's Guide to Graduate Programs in the Biological Sciences, 1997, Vol. 3. 31st rev. ed. Ed. by Peterson's Staff. 2672p. 1996. pap. 44.95 (*1-56079-653-7*) Petersons.

Peterson's Guide to Graduate Programs in the Humanities, Arts & Social Sciences 1997, Vol. 2. 31st rev. ed. Ed. by Peterson's Guides Staff. 1427p. 1996. pap. 37.95 (*1-56079-652-9*) Petersons.

Peterson's Guide to Graduate Programs in the Physical Sciences, Mathematics & Agricultural Sciences, Vol. 4. 31st rev. ed. Ed. by Peterson's Guides Staff. 978p. 1996. pap. 34.95 (*1-56079-654-5*) Petersons.

Peterson's Guide to MBA Programs. 1000p. (Orig.). 1995. pap. 19.95 (*1-56079-366-X*) Petersons.

Peterson's Guide to MBA Programs, 1997. Peterson. 1084p. 1996. pap. text 21.95 (*1-56079-643-X*) Petersons.

Peterson's Guide to MBA Programs, 1998. 4th ed. Ed. by Jon Latimer. 1220p. 1997. pap. 24.95 (*1-56079-862-9*) Petersons.

Peterson's Guide to Medical Schools in the U. S. & Canada: M. D. & M. D. - Ph. D. Programs at Nearly 150 U. S. & Canadian Schools. 2nd ed. Peterson's Guides Staff. Ed. by Jon Latimer. 1000p. (C). 1997. pap. 21.95 (*1-56079-631-6*) Petersons.

Peterson's Guide to New York Colleges, 1996: New York State Including New York City. 12th rev. ed. Peterson's Guides Staff. (Regional College Guides Ser.). 138p. (YA). (gr. 11-12). 1995. pap. 14.95 (*1-56079-487-9*) Petersons.

Peterson's Guide to Nursing Programs: Baccalaureate & Graduate Nursing Education in the U. S. & Canada. 2nd ed. 688p. 1996. reprint ed. 24.95 (*1-56079-565-4*) Petersons.

***Peterson's Guide To Nursing Programs, 5th 1999 Ed.** 5th ed. Petersons. 672p. 1999. pap. 26.95 (*0-7689-0216-9*) Petersons.

Peterson's Guide to Scholarships, Grants & Prizes, 1997. Ed. by Peterson's Guides Staff. 511p. (Orig.). 1996. pap. 24.95 (*1-56079-696-0*) Petersons.

Peterson's Guide to Two-Year Colleges, 1996. 26th ed. Peterson's Guides Staff. 752p. (C). 1995. pap. 17.95 (*1-56079-482-8*) Petersons.

Peterson's Guide to Two-Year Colleges, 1997. 27th rev. ed. Peterson's Guides Staff. (Illus.). 842p. 1996. pap. 21.95 (*1-56079-605-7*) Petersons.

Peterson's Guide to Vocational & Technical Schools & Programs East, 1996. 2nd ed. 644p. 1995. pap. 34.95 (*1-56079-484-4*) Petersons.

Peterson's Guide to Vocational & Technical Schools & Programs West, 1996. 2nd ed. 437p. 1995. pap. 34.95 (*1-56079-485-2*) Petersons.

Peterson's Honors Programs, 1998. Joan Digby. Ed. by Jon Latimer. LC 97-216918. 600p. 1997. pap. 21.95 (*1-56079-851-3*) Petersons.

Peterson's International Directory of Summer Opportunities for Kids & Teenagers. 2nd ed. 110p. 1995. pap. 29.95 (*1-56079-515-8*) Petersons.

Peterson's International Directory of University-Preparatory Boarding Schools in the United States & Canada. 3rd ed. 256p. (C). 1995. pap. 34.95 (*1-56079-516-6*) Petersons.

Peterson's Law Schools. Petersons Staff. 384p. 1998. pap. text 24.95 incl. cd-rom (*0-7689-0011-5*) Petersons.

Peterson's Law Schools, 1998: A Comprehensive Guide to All Accredited U. S. Law Schools. Peterson's Guides Staff. Ed. by Jon Latimer. (Peterson's Guide Ser.). 416p. 1997. pap. 24.95 (*1-56079-630-8*) Petersons.

Peterson's Learning Adventures Around the World, 1997. Ed. by Peterson's Guides Staff. 800p. (Orig.). 1996. pap. 24.95 (*1-56079-701-0*) Petersons.

Peterson's Learning Adventures Around the World, 1998. 2nd ed. Ed. by Peter Greenberg & Ellen Beal. 960p. 1997. pap. 26.95 (*1-56079-860-2*) Petersons.

Peterson's Learning Adventures U. S. A. Peter S. Greenberg. 320p. 1998. pap. text 18.95 (*1-56079-870-X*) Petersons.

Peterson's Learning Adventures U. S. A., 1997. 800p. 1997. pap. 24.95 (*1-56079-759-2*) Petersons.

***Peterson's Math Review for the GRE, GMAT & MCAT.** Peterson's Guides Staff. 300p. 2000. pap. 16.95 (*0-7689-0232-0*) Petersons.

***Peterson's MBA Programs: U. S., Canadian & International Business Schools 1999.** 5th ed. Peterson's Guides Staff. 1275p. 1998. pap. text 26.95 (*0-7689-0046-8*) Petersons.

Peterson's MCAT Success. Peterson's Guides Staff. (Peterson's Guides Ser.). 356p. 1997. pap. text 14.95 incl. cd-rom (*1-56079-929-3*) Petersons.

Peterson's Nursing Programs. 4th ed. Peterson's Guides Staff. 632p. 1998. pap. text 26.95 (*1-56079-998-6*) Petersons.

***Peterson's Nursing Programs 2000-2001.** 6th ed. Peterson's Guides Staff. (Nursing Programs Ser.). 672p. 2000. pap. text 26.95 (*0-7689-0396-3*) Petersons.

Peterson's Panic Plan for the ACT. American Bookworks Staff & Peterson's Guides Staff. Ed. by Mark Moscowitz. LC 97-19985. (Peterson's Guides Ser.). 256p. (Orig.). (YA). 1997. pap. 9.95 (*1-56079-769-X*) Petersons.

Peterson's Patterns for Civil War Era Ladies. 2nd ed. 60p. 1994. reprint ed. pap. 13.00 (*1-885133-01-4*) Pioneer Prntwrk.

Peterson's Paying Less for College, 1996. 13th ed. 696p. 1995. pap. 26.95 (*1-56079-520-4*) Petersons.

Peterson's Private Secondary Schools, 1996-97. 17th rev. ed. Peterson's Guides Staff. 1370p. 1996. pap. 29.95 (*1-56079-586-7*) Petersons.

***Peterson's Private Secondary Schools 2000-2001.** 21st ed. Peterson's Guides Staff. 1460p. 2000. pap. 29.95 (*0-7689-0370-X*) Petersons.

***Peterson's Private Secondary Schools 2001.** 21st ed. Petersons. 2000. pap. 29.95 (*0-7689-0569-9*) Petersons.

Peterson's Professional Degree Programs in the Visual & Performing Arts 1996. 2nd ed. 618p. 1995. pap. 21.95 (*1-56079-536-0*) Petersons.

Peterson's Professional Degree Programs in the Visual & Performing Arts 1997. 3rd rev. ed. Ed. by Peterson's Guides Staff. 534p. 1996. pap. 24.95 (*1-56079-661-8*) Petersons.

***Peterson's PSAT Success 2001.** Peterson's Guides Staff. 300p. 2000. pap. 14.95 (*0-7689-0395-5*) Petersons.

Petersons Quick & Concise Guides to Graduate & Professional Degrees Graduate Studies in Engineer. Peterson's Guides Staff. 653p. 1998. pap. 24.95 (*0-7689-0005-0*) Petersons.

***Peterson's Regional College Guides 2000.** 15th ed. Petersons. (Peterson's Colleges in the Middle Atlantic States Ser.). 139-357p. 1999. pap. 17.95 (*0-7689-0248-7*) Petersons.

Peterson's Register of Higher Education, 1998. 11th ed. Ed. by Jon Latimer. 1160p. 1997. pap. 49.95 (*1-56079-872-6*) Petersons.

Peterson's SAT Math Flash: The Quick & Easy Way to Learn & Apply Math Skills. 2nd rev. ed. Michael R. Crystal. Ed. by Mark Moscowitz. LC 97-9127. 208p. (YA). 1997. pap. 8.95 (*1-56079-849-1*) Petersons.

Peterson's SAT Word Flash: Build Your Vocabulary in 30 Quick & Easy Lessons. 2nd rev. ed. Joan D. Carris. Ed. by Mark Moscowitz. LC 97-8917. 208p. (YA). 1997. pap. 8.95 (*1-56079-850-5*) Petersons.

Peterson's Scholarship Almanac: Including the 500 Largest Scholarships to Help Pay for College. Peterson's Guides Staff. (Peterson's Guides). 400p. 1998. pap. text 9.95 (*0-7689-0151-0*) Petersons.

Peterson's Scholarships for Study in the U. S. A. & Canada. 2nd ed. Peterson's Guides Staff. (Peterson's Guides). 429p. 1998. pap. text 21.95 (*0-7689-0142-1*) Petersons.

Peterson's Scholarships, Grants & Prizes. 3rd ed. Peterson's Guides Staff. 550p. 1998. pap. text 26.95 (*0-7689-0034-4*) Petersons.

Peterson's Sports Scholarships & College Athletic Programs. 2nd ed. 864p. 1995. pap. 24.95 (*1-56079-483-6*) Petersons.

Peterson's Sports Scholarships & College Athletic Programs, 1998. 3rd ed. Ed. by Jon Latimer. 864p. 1997. pap. 24.95 (*1-56079-830-0*) Petersons.

Peterson's Stress Concentration Factors. 2nd ed. Walter D. Pilkey et al. LC 96-27514. 544p. 1997. 125.00 (*0-471-53849-3*) Wiley.

Peterson's Study Abroad, 1998. 5th ed. Ed. by Ellen Beal. 1000p. 1997. pap. 26.95 (*1-56079-861-0*) Petersons.

Peterson's Study Abroad, 1997: Semester, Summer & Year Abroad Academic Programs. 4th rev. ed. Ed. by Peterson's Guides Staff. 1000p. 1996. pap. 26.95 (*1-56079-659-6*) Petersons.

Peterson's Study Abroad, 1996: Semester, Year Abroad, & Summer Academic Programs. 3rd ed. Peterson's Guides Staff. (Illus.). 1000p. (C). 1995. pap. 26.95 (*1-56079-537-9*) Petersons.

Peterson's Summer Opportunities for Kids & Teenagers, 1996. 13th ed. 1300p. (J). (gr. 2 up). 1995. pap. 24.95 (*1-56079-496-8*) Petersons.

Peterson's Summer Opportunities for Kids & Teenagers, 1998. 15th ed. Ed. by Ellen Beal. 1248p. 1997. pap. 26.95 (*1-56079-852-1*) Petersons.

Peterson's Summer Study Abroad. 576p. (Orig.). 1995. pap. 18.95 (*1-56079-444-5*) Petersons.

Peterson's Tennis Camps & Clinics. Joanie S. Brown & Shirley A. Thompson. LC 95-5038. 276p. 1995. pap. 13.95 (*1-56079-445-3*) Petersons.

***Peterson's the Gold Standard MCAT 2000.** 2nd ed. Peterson's Guides Staff. 800p. 2000. pap. 44.95 (*0-7689-0493-5*) Petersons.

***Peterson's 2000: Core Library Set, 15 vols.** 1999. 379.94 (*0-7689-0306-8*) Petersons.

Peterson's Two-Year Colleges: The Only Guide to More Than 1500 Community & Junior Colleges. 29th ed. Peterson's Guides Staff. 848p. 1998. pap. text 24.95 (*1-56079-993-5*) Petersons.

***Peterson's Two-Year Colleges 2001.** 31st ed. 800p. 2000. pap. 24.95 (*0-7689-0378-5*) Petersons.

Peterson's Vocational & Technical Schools & Programs - East: Accredited Institutions Offering Career Training Programs. 3rd ed. Ed. by Jon Latimer. 660p. 1997. pap. 34.95 (*1-56079-864-5*) Petersons.

Peterson's Vocational & Technical Schools & Programs - West: Accredited Institutions Offering Career Training Programs. 3rd ed. Ed. by Jon Latimer. 660p. 1997. pap. 34.95 (*1-56079-865-3*) Petersons.

Pete's a Pizza. William Steig. LC 97-78384. (Illus.). 32p. (J). (ps-3). 1998. lib. bdg. 14.89 (*0-06-205158-X*) HarpC.

Pete's a Pizza. 62nd ed. William Steig. LC 97-78384. (Illus.). 32p. (J). (ps-3). 1998. 14.95 (*0-06-205157-1*) HarpC.

Pete's Angel - A Story of Self-Love. Hunter D. Darden. LC 98-90400. (Illus.). 40p. (J). (gr. k-7). 1998. 19.95 (*0-9653729-1-X*) Sunfleur.

Pete's Chicken. Harriet Ziefert. LC 93-37314. (Illus.). 36p. (J). 1997. pap. 4.95 (*0-688-15483-2*, Wm Morrow) Morrow Avon.

Pete's Chicken. Harriet Ziefert. 1997. 10.15 (*0-606-11739-3*, Pub. by Turtleback) Demco.

Pete's Chicken. Harriet Ziefert. 40p. 1999. pap. 4.99 (*0-14-056314-8*) Viking Penguin.

Pete's Dragon. Lindsay Longford. (Romance Ser.: No. 854). 1992. per. 2.69 (*0-373-08854-X*, 5-08854-7) Silhouette.

Pete's Dragon: Vocal Selections. (Illus.). 44p. 1985. pap. 7.95 (*0-7935-0036-2*, 00360822) H Leonard.

Pete's Lost. Kate Cavanaugh. (Illus.). 24p. (Orig.). (J). 1991. pap. 4.95 (*0-9622353-2-6*) KAC.

Pete's Puddles. Hannah Roche. LC 98-60350. (My First Weather Bks.). (J). (ps-2). 1998. 8.95 (*1-84089-031-2*) Zero to Ten.

Pete's Street Beat, Vol. 2913. Margaret Allen. Ed. by Joel Kupperstein. (Dr. Maggie's Phonics Readers Ser.). (Illus.). 16p. (J). 1999. pap. 2.99 (*1-57471-588-7*) Creat Teach Pr.

Pete's Teeth. (Fisher-Price Phonics Storybooks Ser.: Vol. 1). (Illus.). (J). 1998. pap. write for info. (*0-7666-0175-7*, Honey Bear Bks) Modern Pub NYC.

***Pete's Wicked Book.** Pete Takeda. 2000. pap. 14.95 (*1-893682-05-6*) Climb Mag.

Petet Livre de Cuisine de la Nouvelle Orleans: French Edition of the Little New Orleans Cookbook. Gwen McKee. (FRE.). 1996. 10.95 (*0-937552-60-7*) Quail Ridge.

Petey. Ben Mikaelsen. 256p. (J). 1998. lib. bdg. 16.49 (*0-7868-2376-3*, Pub. by Disney Pr) Little.

Petey. Ben Mikaelsen. LC 98-10183. 256p. (YA). (gr. 7 up). 1998. 15.95 (*0-7868-0426-2*, Pub. by Disney Pr) Time Warner.

***Petey.** Ben Mikaelsen. LC 98-10183. 256p. (YA). (gr. 5-9). 2000. pap. 5.99 (*0-7868-1336-9*, Pub. by Hyprn Child) Time Warner.

Petey & Miss Magic. N. B. Dorman. LC 92-11265. (Illus.). 99p. (J). (gr. 2-6). 1992. lib. bdg. 16.00 (*0-208-02345-3*, Linnet Bks) Shoe String.

***Petey Putt-Putt & His Friends.** Robert D. Bruce. Ed. by Britta Bruce. (Illus.). 20p. 1999. 5.95 (*0-9664248-9-1*) Sloane Prtlnd ME.

Petey's Bedtime Story. Beverly Cleary. LC 92-6184. (Illus.). 32p. (J). (gr. k up). 1993. 15.00 (*0-688-10660-9*, Wm Morrow) Morrow Avon.

Petey's Bedtime Story. Beverly Cleary. LC 92-6184. (Illus.). 32p. (J). (gr. k up). 1993. lib. bdg. 14.89 (*0-688-10661-7*, Wm Morrow) Morrow Avon.

Petey's Bedtime Story. Beverly Cleary. LC 92-6184. (Illus.). 32p. (J). (ps-3). 1995. pap. 4.95 (*0-688-14390-3*, Wm Morrow) Morrow Avon.

Petey's Bedtime Story. Beverly Cleary. (J). 1995. 10.15 (*0-606-08011-2*, Pub. by Turtleback) Demco.

Pethouses of Keatley Creek. Brian Hayden. LC 96-76629. 158p. (C). 1996. pap. text 23.50 (*0-15-503837-0*) Harcourt Coll Pubs.

Petiole Anatomy of the Guttiferae & Related Families. E. K. Schofield. (Memoirs Ser.: Vol. 18 (1)). (Illus.). 55p. 1968. pap. 7.50 (*0-89327-061-X*) NY Botanical.

Petit Arpent du Bon Dieu. Erskine Caldwell. (FRE.). 1983. pap. 10.95 (*0-7859-1751-9*, 2070364194) Fr & Eur.

Petit Atlas des Champignons, 2 vols., Vols. 1 & 2. Henri Romagnesi. (Illus.). 1964. 50.00 (*0-934454-91-4*) Lubrecht & Cramer.

Petit Basset Griffon Vendeen. Jeffrey Pepper. (KW Ser.). (Illus.). 192p. 1993. text 9.95 (*0-86622-578-1*, KW-208) TFH Pubns.

Petit Basset Griffon Vendeen (PBGV) A Definitive Breed Study. Valerie Link & Linda Skerritt. Ed. by Mark Anderson. LC 99-60315. (Pure Breds Ser.). (Illus.). 286p. 2000. 26.95 (*0-944875-58-0*) Doral Pub.

Petit Cesar. William R. Burnett. (FRE.). 256p. 1987. pap. 11.95 (*0-7859-2068-4*, 2070378527) Fr & Eur.

***Petit Chaperon Rouge.** (FRE.). 1999. pap. 7.95 (*88-8148-239-8*) Europ Lang Inst.

Petit Chaperon Rouge. Tr. by Emanuel Calamaro.Tr. of Little Red-Riding-Hood. (FRE., Illus.). 20p. (Orig.). (J). (gr. 1-2). 1989. pap. 2.95 (*0-922852-02-2*, E007) Another Lang Pr.

Petit Chaperon Rouge. adapted ed. Charles Perrault. LC 95-941620. (Best-Sellers Ser.).Tr. of Little Red Riding Hood. (FRE., Illus.). (J). (ps-2). 2000. pap. 9.95 incl. audio (*2-921997-00-2*) Coffragants.

Petit Chose. Alphonse Daudet. (FRE.). 447p. 1977. pap. 11.95 (*0-7859-2213-X*, 207036979X) Fr & Eur.

Petit Chose. Alphonse Daudet. (FRE.). 347p. 1989. pap. 10.95 (*0-7859-4666-7*) Fr & Eur.

Petit Chose. Alphonse Daudet. (Folio Ser.: No. 979). (FRE.). 420p. 1948. pap. 10.95 (*2-07-036979-X*) Schoenhof.

Petit Chose. unabridged ed. Daudet. (FRE.). pap. 7.95 (*2-87714-195-0*, Pub. by Bookking Intl) Distribks Inc.

Petit Dejeuner Chez Tiffany. Truman Capote. (FRE.). 192p. 1973. pap. 10.95 (*0-7859-1741-1*, 2070363643) Fr & Eur.

Petit Dictionary Licencieux des Bretons. P. Camby. (FRE.). 208p. 1996. 45.00 (*0-320-00902-5*) Fr & Eur.

Petit Dictionary Parlanje Vendeen. (FRE.). 77p. 1997. 27.95 (*0-320-00885-1*) Fr & Eur.

Petit Dictionnaire Bambara-Francais, Francais-Bambara. Charles Bailleul. (BAM & FRE.). 340p. 1994. pap. 105.00 (*0-7859-8594-8*, 086127220x) Fr & Eur.

Petit Dictionnaire Bantou du Gabon: Francais-Ndjabi, Ndjabi-Francais. Jean-Marc Muroni. (FRE.). 207p. 1989. pap. 55.00 (*0-7859-8014-8*, 2738402658) Fr & Eur.

An Asterisk (*) at the beginning of an entry indicates that the title is appearing for the first time.

Petit Dictionnaire d'Anatomiem d'Embryologie et Histologie. Pierre Kamina. (FRE.). 775p. 1990. pap. 125.00 (*0-7859-7821-6*, 2224019009) Fr & Eur.

Petit Dictionnaire de Droit Canonique: Francias et Latin. Jean Werckmeister. (FRE & LAT.). 235p. 1993. 49.95 (*0-7859-3021-3*) Fr & Eur.

Petit Dictionnaire de la Bible. Centre Informatique et Bible Staff. (FRE.). 949p. 1992. pap. 125.00 (*0-7859-7904-2*, 2503502466) Fr & Eur.

Petit Dictionnaire de la Catechese. Jean P. Bagot. (FRE.). 96p. 1990. pap. 15.95 (*0-7859-7794-5*, 222031306) Fr & Eur.

Petit Dictionnaire de la Hypocrisie. D. Habrekorn. (FRE.). 1998. 27.95 (*0-320-00231-4*) Fr & Eur.

Petit Dictionnaire de la Micro: Avec un Glossaire Francais, Anglais, Allemand. Daniel Sillescu. (ENG, FRE & GER.). 362p. 1992. pap. 38.95 (*0-7859-7996-4*, 2736110331) Fr & Eur.

Petit Dictionnaire de la Science et de la Technique Francais-Chinois. Commercial Press Staff. (CHI & FRE.). 407p. 1990. 10.95 (*0-7859-8574-3*, 7100008395) Fr & Eur.

Petit Dictionnaire de l'Architecture. Jacqueline Martin-Bagnaudez. (FRE.). 139p. 1990. pap. 22.95 (*0-7859-8629-4*, 222003139x) Fr & Eur.

Petit Dictionnaire de L'Euro. Daniel Cohn-Bendit. (FRE., Illus.). 1998. 39.95 (*0-320-00282-9*) Fr & Eur.

Petit Dictionnaire de Mythologie Allemande. Claude Lecouteux. (FRE.). 286p. 1991. pap. 49.95 (*0-7859-7971-9*, 2726601014) Fr & Eur.

Petit Dictionnaire de Mythologie Celtique. Jean Markale. (FRE.). 224p. 1986. pap. 36.95 (*0-7859-7970-0*, 2726600778) Fr & Eur.

Petit Dictionnaire de Mythologie Egyptienne. Isabelle Franco. (FRE.). 1993. pap. 59.95 (*0-7859-7972-7*, 2726601049) Fr & Eur.

Petit Dictionnaire de Mythologies Basque et Pyreneene. Olivier De Marliave. (FRE.). 295p. 1993. pap. 55.00 (*0-7859-7973-5*, 2726601103) Fr & Eur.

Petit Dictionnaire de Theologie Catholique. Karl Rahner. (FRE.). 512p. 1970. 85.00 (*0-7859-7622-1*, 2020032392) Fr & Eur.

Petit Dictionnaire des Rues de Blaye. Arlette Cotton de Bennetot. (FRE.). 160p. 1983. 32.95 (*0-7859-8075-X*, 2852760185) Fr & Eur.

Petit Dictionnaire d'Ethique. 2nd ed. Ottfried Hoffe. (FRE.). 371p. 1993. pap. 65.00 (*0-7859-7766-X*, 2204048704) Fr & Eur.

Petit Dictionnaire Droit des Malades. C. Evin. (FRE.). 1998. 37.95 (*0-320-00389-2*) Fr & Eur.

Petit Dictionnaire du Parler de Touraine. Jacques-Marie Rouge. (FRE.). 91p. 1991. pap. 32.95 (*0-7859-8094-6*, 2854432258) Fr & Eur.

Petit Dictionnaire Francais-Anglais: French/English. (ENG & FRE.). 1999. 22.95 (*2-03-401761-7*) LKC.

Petit Dictionnaire Francais-Chinois: A Small French-Chinese Dictionary. Commercial Press Staff. (CHI & FRE.). 177p. 1978. pap. 9.95 (*0-8288-5261-8*, M9280) Fr & Eur.

Petit Dictionnaire Francais-Grec Moderne et Grec Moderne-Francais: Small Modern Greek - French, French - Modern Greek Dictionary. Andre Mirambel. (FRE & GRE.). 486p. 1969. 49.95 (*0-8288-6610-4*, M-6413) Fr & Eur.

Petit Dictionnaire Francais-Occitan (Bearn) Per Noste Staff. (FRE.). 134p. 1984. pap. 19.95 (*0-7859-8163-2*, 2868660002) Fr & Eur.

Petit Dictionnaire Francais-Portugais/Portugais-Francais. Ed. by Larousse. (FRE & POR.). 912p. 1997. 34.95 (*0-7859-9508-0*) Fr & Eur.

Petit Dictionnaire Francais-Russe, Russe-Francais. 15th ed. K. Vygodskaia. (FRE & RUS.). 678p. 1992. 24.95 (*0-7859-8099-7*, 2855360226) Fr & Eur.

Petit Dictionnaire Franco-Belge, Belgo-Francais: Mots et Expressions Usuels. Jacques Mercier. (FRE.). 286p. 1990. 49.95 (*0-7859-8175-6*, 2871760098) Fr & Eur.

Petit Dictionnaire Larousse de la Langue Francaise. Jean Dubois. (FRE.). 1095p. 1993. pap. 32.95 (*0-7859-7679-5*, 2037102216) Fr & Eur.

Petit Dictionnaire Medical. 4th ed. Alexandre Manuila. (FRE.). 566p. 1985. pap. 49.95 (*0-7859-4942-9*) Fr & Eur.

Petit Dictionnaire Philosophique. Marilyn S. Rosenthal & P. Ioudine. (FRE.). 638p. 1977. pap. 29.95 (*0-8288-5507-2*, M6446) Fr & Eur.

Petit Dictionnaire Provencal-Francais. Emil Levy. (FRE & PRO.). 387p. 1990. pap. 59.95 (*0-7859-8169-1*, 2869712790) Fr & Eur.

Petit Dictionnaire Rameau. Jean Malignon. (FRE.). 280p. 1983. pap. 26.95 (*0-7859-7912-3*, 2700703146) Fr & Eur.

Petit Dictionnaire Universel Hachette. Hachette Staff. (FRE.). 759p. 1993. 24.95 (*0-7859-7620-5*, 010209281) Fr & Eur.

Petit et le Grand Testament: Avec; Ballades en Jargon, Poesies du Cercle de Villon. Francois Villon. 210p. 40.00 (*0-686-55726-3*) Fr & Eur.

Petit Fleurus Premier Dictionary Enfants (5-8 Ans) Claude Kannas & Garagnoux. (FRE.). 1998. 49.95 (*0-320-00376-0*) Fr & Eur.

Petit Frere pour Billy. Carla Cassidy. (Horizon Ser.: Vol.502). (FRE.). 1999. mass mkt. 3.50 (*0-373-39502-7*, 1-39502-9) Harlequin Bks.

Petit Fute: Country Guide New York, in French. D. Auzias & J. P. Labourdette. (FRE.). 302p. 1994. pap. 33.95 (*0-7859-9034-8*) Fr & Eur.

Petit Garcon. Philippe Labro. Tr. by Linda Coverdale. 320p. 1992. text 23.00 (*0-374-18448-8*) FS&G.

Petit Garcon. Philippe Labro. (Folio Ser.: No. 2389). (FRE.). pap. 9.95 (*2-07-038526-4*) Schoenhof.

Petit Garcon Qui Avait Peur de Tout et de Rien. Stanley Pean & Stephane Poulin. 24p. (*2-89021-320-X*) La Courte Ech.

Petit Glossaire des Termes en Texte. A. Gervais. (FRE.). 1998. 49.95 (*0-320-00162-8*) Fr & Eur.

Petit Glossaire pour Servir l'Intelligence des Auteurs. Jacques Plowert. Ed. by Patrick McGuinness. (Exeter French Texts Ser.). (FRE.). 150p. 1998. pap. text 23.95 (*0-85989-594-7*) Univ Exeter Pr.

Petit Guide Pratique de la Formation des Membres de Bureaux de Vote. Linda Trudel et al. (FRE., Illus.). iii, 113p. 1997. pap. text. write for info. (*1-879720-49-3*) Intl Fndt Elect.

Petit Guide Spirituel. Dick Sutphen. 1994. 8.95 (*2-920083-84-8*) Edns Roseau.

Petit-Jean des Villes. Beatrix Potter.Tr. of Tale of Johnny Town-Mouse. (FRE., Illus.). 58p. (J). 1990. 9.95 (*0-7859-3632-7*, 2070560953) Fr & Eur.

Petit Larousse. (FRE.). 1896p. 1989. 59.95 (*0-686-57074-X*, M-6447) Fr & Eur.

Petit Larousse de la Medecine. Jacques Bourneuf. Ed. by Andre Domart. (FRE.). 852p. 1976. 85.00 (*0-8288-5750-4*, F12060) Fr & Eur.

Petit Larousse de la Medecine, Vol. 1. Herve Negre. (FRE.). 975p. 1988. pap. 19.95 (*0-7859-4845-7*) Fr & Eur.

Petit Larousse en Couleurs. Larousse Staff. 95.00 (*0-317-45760-8*) Fr & Eur.

Petit Larousse en Couleurs, 1996: Grand Format. 1996. 175.00 (*0-7859-9864-0*) Fr & Eur.

Petit Larousse Grand Format, 1996. Ed. by Larousse Staff. 1872p. 1996. 175.00 (*0-7859-9893-4*) Fr & Eur.

***Petit Larousse Grand Format, 1999.** large type ed. (FRE.). 1872p. 1999. 125.00 (*0-320-00692-1*) Fr & Eur.

Petit Larousse Illustre. Larousse Staff. (Illus.). 1872p. write for info. (*0-7859-3734-X*) Fr & Eur.

Petit Larousse Illustre. Larousse Staff. 39.95 (*0-317-45763-2*) Fr & Eur.

Petit Larousse Illustre en Couleurs, 1996. Ed. by Larousse Staff. 1784p. 1996. 95.00 (*0-7859-9894-2*) Fr & Eur.

Petit Larousse Illustre, 1995. Ed. by Larousse Staff. 1784p. 1994. 95.00 (*0-7859-8753-3*) Fr & Eur.

Petit Larousse Illustre, 1994. Ed. by Larousse Staff. (Illus.). 59.95 (*0-685-74790-5*) Schoenhof.

***Petit Larousse Illustre 2000.** International Book Dist. Staff. (FRE., Illus.). 1999. 69.95 (*2-03-301200-X*, Larousse LKC) LKC.

***Petit Larousse Illustre 2000 Grand Format.** (FRE.). 2000. 150.00 (*0-320-01591-2*) Fr & Eur.

Petit Larousse 1998. (FRE.). 1998. 95.00 (*0-7859-9490-4*) Fr & Eur.

Petit Larousse 1998. Ed. by Larousse Staff. (FRE.). 1998. 95.00 incl. audio compact disk (*0-7859-9537-4*) Fr & Eur.

Petit Larousse 1999. Ed. by Larousse. (FRE.). 1998. 95.00 (*0-7859-9724-5*) Fr & Eur.

Petit Larousse, 1997. Ed. by Larousse Staff. (FRE.). 1997. 95.00 (*0-7859-9308-8*) Fr & Eur.

Petit Larousse, 1996. (FRE.). 1996. 95.00 (*0-7859-9868-3*) Fr & Eur.

***Petit Larousse 2000.** annuals Ed. by Larousse Editorial Staff. (FRE.). 1999. 95.00 (*0-320-03690-1*) Fr & Eur.

Petit Lexique de la France Contemporaine: A Concise Dictionary of Contemporary France. Claudie Cox. LC 87-18226. 117p. 1988. pap. 13.00 (*0-85496-534-3*) Berg Pubs.

Petit Lexique de la Manutentio Anglais-Francais (Small English-French Lexicon of Storage) F. Bacon. Ed. by P. Chartrand. (ENG & FRE.). 37p. 1974. pap. 9.95 (*0-8288-6205-2*, M9226) Fr & Eur.

Petit Lexique de la Photographie. G. Mora. (FRE.). 1998. 59.95 (*0-320-00153-9*) Fr & Eur.

Petit Lexique du Creole Haitien. Emmanuel W. Vedrine. (CRP.). 87p. (Orig.). (YA). (gr. 9-12). 1996. pap. 7.95 (*1-885566-11-5*) Oresjozef.

Petit Lexique du Soudage, Anglais-Francais (Small English-French Dictionary of Welch Dictionary of Welding) A. Fortin. Ed. by P. Chartrand. (ENG & FRE.). 47p. 1974. pap. 9.95 (*0-8288-6206-0*, M-9227) Fr & Eur.

Petit Livre de la Vie: Manuel d'Instructions, Vol. 1. H. Jackson Brown, Jr. Tr. by Denis Ouellet. LC 92-97170.Tr. of Life's Little Instruction Book. (ENG & FRE.). 1992. 8.95 (*2-920083-66-X*) Edns Roseau.

Petit Livre de la Vie: Manuel d'Instructions, Vol. 2. H. Jackson Brown, Jr. Tr. by Denis Ouellet. LC 92-97170.Tr. of Life's Little Instruction Book. (ENG & FRE.). 1993. 8.95 (*2-920083-74-0*) Edns Roseau.

Petit Livre de la Vie: Manuel d'Instructions, Vol. 3. H. Jackson Brown, Jr. Tr. by Denis Ouellet. LC 92-97170.Tr. of Life's Little Instruction Book. (ENG & FRE.). 1996. 8.95 (*2-89466-002-2*) Edns Roseau.

Petit-Maitre Corrige. Pierre Carlet de Chamblain de Marivaux. (FRE.). 206p. 1955. 9.95 (*0-8288-9605-4*, F48050) Fr & Eur.

Petit Moure: Dictionnaire de L'Histoire. M. Moure. (FRE.). 1998. 125.00 (*0-320-00280-2*) Fr & Eur.

Petit Mourre: Dictionnaire de l'Histoire. Michel Mourre. (FRE.). 1990. lib. bdg. 125.00 (*0-7859-3953-9*) Fr & Eur.

Petit Nicolas. Goscinny. (J). Date not set. pap. text. write for info. (*0-582-36071-4*, Pub. by Addison-Wesley) Longman.

Petit Nicolas. Jean-Jacques Sempe & R. Goscinny. (Folio Ser.: No. 423). (FRE.). 156p. (J). 1991. pap. 9.95 (*2-07-036423-2*) Schoenhof.

Petit Nicolas et les Copains. 12th ed. Sempe. (FRE.). 1997. pap. 13.95 (*2-07-051342-4*) Gallimard Edns.

Petit Ours Brun Vent des Histoires see Little Brown Bear Wants to Be Read To

Petit Pierre: Avec La Vie en Fleur. Anatole France, pseud. 1961. 14.95 (*0-686-55873-1*) Fr & Eur.

Petit Prince. Antoine de Saint-Exupery. (FRE.). (J). (gr. 3-8). write for info. (*0-318-63576-3*) Fr & Eur.

Petit Prince. Antoine de Saint-Exupery. (Folio - Junior Ser.). (FRE.). 93p. (J). (gr. 5-10). 1988. pap. 29.95 incl. audio (*2-07-032267-X*) Schoenhof.

***Petit Prince.** Antoine de Saint-Exupery.Tr. of The Little Prince. 2000. pap., boxed set 16.95 incl. audio (*2-921997-42-8*, Pub. by Coffragants) Penton Overseas.

Petit Prince. Antoine de Saint-Exupery. LC 43-5812.Tr. of The Little Prince. (FRE., Illus.). 91p. (J). (gr. 3-7). 1943. 17.00 (*0-15-243818-1*, Harcourt Child Bks) Harcourt.

Petit Prince. Antoine de Saint-Exupery.Tr. of The Little Prince. (FRE.). 96p. (C). pap., student ed. 9.95 (*0-8442-1727-1*, VF1727-1) NTC Contemp Pub Co.

Petit Prince. Antoine de Saint-Exupery.Tr. of The Little Prince. (FRE., Illus.). 64p. (J). pap. 12.95 incl. audio (*2-921997-41-X*) Penton Overseas.

Petit Prince. Antoine de Saint-Exupery. (Folio - Junior Ser.: No. 453).Tr. of The Little Prince. (FRE.). 123p. (J). (gr. 5-10). 1987. pap. 9.95 (*2-07-033453-8*) Schoenhof.

Petit Prince: Avec Dessins Par L'Auteur. Antoine de Saint-Exupery. LC 43-5812. (FRE., Illus.). 113p. (J). (gr. 4-7). 1969. pap. 7.00 (*0-15-650300-X*) Harcourt.

Petit Purr Finds a Home, Vols. 3 & 4. Violet Trouern-Trend. Ed. by Katherine Slama. LC 96-71707. (Adventures of Petit Purr Ser.: Vol. 2500). (Illus.). 34p. (J). (gr. k-4). 1996. boxed set 10.95 (*1-888145-00-5*) Puddleboots.

Petit Robert. M. Legrain. (FRE.). 2551p. 1996. 70.00 (*2-85036-506-8*, Pub. by Robert) IBD Ltd.

Petit Robert de la Langue Francaise. Robert. (FRE.). 2551p. 1997. 150.00 (*0-320-00418-X*) Fr & Eur.

Petit Robert des Enfants: Dictionnaire de la Langue Francaise. Josette Rey-Debove. (FRE.). 1187p. 1990. 95.00 (*0-7859-9225-1*) Fr & Eur.

Petit Robert des Noms Propres Dictionnaire: Universel Illustre en Couleurs Alphabetique Analogique. Alain Rey. (FRE.). 2259p. 1995. 175.00 (*0-7859-9195-6*) Fr & Eur.

***Petit Robert Illustre des Noms Propres.** Distribooks Incorporated, Staff. (FRE., Illus.). 1999. 99.95 (*2-85036-413-4*) Robert.

Petit Robert Langue Francaise - Grand Format. large type ed. Robert. (FRE.). 2592p. 1997. 195.00 (*0-320-00447-3*) Fr & Eur.

***Petit Robert Noms Propres Grand Format.** large type ed. Robert. (FRE.). 1998. write for info. (*0-320-00390-6*) Fr & Eur.

Petit Ruisseau et le Don des Animaux. C. J. Taylor. LC 97-930060. (FRE., Illus.). 24p. (J). (ps up). 1997. reprint ed. pap. 6.95 (*0-88776-406-1*) Tundra Bks.

Petit Vianney Dictionnaire Medical Savant et Sympathetique. Yves-Marie Vianney. (FRE.). 70p. 1991. pap. 19.95 (*0-7859-8246-9*, 2908614049) Fr & Eur.

Petit Vocabulaire du Var. M. Abbonen. (FRE.). 90p. 1993. 34.95 (*0-320-00903-3*) Fr & Eur.

Petite Amazon: A Psychic Autobiography. 2nd ed. Rosalie Gordon. (Illus.). (Orig.). 1993. pap. text 24.95 (*1-880733-01-3*) Gd Shepherd.

Petite Anthologie: Poesies Francaises. Ed. by Thomas R. Palfrey & Samuel F. Will. (FRE.). (Orig.). 1961. pap. text 7.95 (*0-89197-337-0*) Irvington.

Petite Bebe, 1883-1887, Vol. 11. Susan B. Sirkis. (Wish Booklets Ser.). 48p. 1973. pap. 5.95 (*0-913786-11-X*) Wish Bklets.

Petite Boite Babar: Le Feu, l'Eau, l'Air, la Terre. Laurent de Brunhoff. 192p. (J). (gr. k-5). 1980. 39.95 (*0-7859-8796-7*) Fr & Eur.

Petite Bourgeoisie in Europe, 1780-1914. Geoffrey Crossick & Heinz-Gerhard Haupt. LC 97-21842. 308p. (C). 1997. pap. 25.99 (*0-415-17463-5*) Routledge.

Petite Comedienne. Ruth J. Dale. (Horizon Ser.). (FRE.). 1997. pap. 3.50 (*0-373-39438-1*, 1-39438-6) Harlequin Bks.

***Petite Corruption.** Yanick Lahens. (FRE.). 123p. 1999. pap. write for info. (*1-58437-006-8*) Edit Memo.

Petite Dorrit: Conte de Deux Villes. Charles Dickens. (FRE.). 1970. 99.50 (*0-8288-3431-8*, F77450) Fr & Eur.

Petite Ecole dans l'Ecole: Origine Pietiste-Morave de l'Ecole Maternelle Francaise. Loic Chalmel. (Exploration Ser.). (FRE.). xiv, 354p. 1996. 42.95 (*3-906754-58-8*, Pub. by P Lang) P Lang Pubng.

Petite Encyclopedie Larousse. Guy Rachet. (FRE.). 1496p. 1977. 49.95 (*0-7859-0764-5*, M-6473) Fr & Eur.

Petite Fadette. George Sand. Ed. by Salomon & Mallion. (Coll. Prestige). 27.95 (*0-685-34999-3*); pap. 9.95 (*0-685-34998-5*) Fr & Eur.

Petite Fadette. George Sand. 1973. pap. 8.95 (*0-7859-3063-9*) Fr & Eur.

Petite Fadette. unabridged ed. George Sand. (FRE.). pap. 5.95 (*2-87714-227-2*, Pub. by Bookking Intl) Distribks Inc.

Petite Fille Aux Allumettes. Felicia Cavalieri. (Best-Sellers Ser.).Tr. of Little Match Girl. (FRE., Illus.). 40p. (J). (ps-2). 2000. pap. 9.95 incl. audio (*2-921997-31-2*) Coffragants.

Petite Fille aux Yeux Sombres. Marcel Pagnol. (FRE.). 1991. pap. 13.95 (*0-7859-3330-1*, 2877060713) Fr & Eur.

Petite Fille Qui Detestait l'Heure du Dodo. Marie-Francine Hebert. (Il Etait une Fois Ser.). (FRE., Illus.). 24p. (J). (ps up). 1995. pap. 6.95 (*2-89021-252-1*, Pub. by La Courte Ech) Firefly Bks Ltd.

Petite Gare et Autres Nouvelles. Iouri Kazakov. (FRE.). 1975. pap. 11.95 (*0-7859-2361-6*, 2070366812) Fr & Eur.

Petite Gavotte. Martha Mier. 4p. 1994. pap. 2.50 (*0-7390-0845-5*, 12883) Alfred Pub.

Petite Histoire de la Litterature Francaise. Henri Clouard. 332p. 1965. 19.95 (*0-8288-7404-2*) Fr & Eur.

Petite Infante de Castille. Henry De Montherlant. (FRE.). 1973. pap. 10.95 (*0-8288-3751-1*, M3792) Fr & Eur.

Petite Infante de Castille. Henry De Montherlant. (Folio Ser.: No. 370). (FRE., Illus.). pap. 6.95 (*2-07-036370-8*) Schoenhof.

Petite Maison. Le Corbusier. (Illus.). 84p. 1923. pap. 16.95 (*3-7643-5512-3*, Pub. by Birkhauser) Princeton Arch.

Petite Marieuse. Robin Nicholas. (Horizon Ser.: No. 498). (FRE.). 1999. mass mkt. 3.50 (*0-373-39498-5*, 1-39498-0) Harlequin Bks.

Petite Martinique: Traditions & Social Change. Paul C. Clement. LC 99-90330. (Illus.). 160p. (C). 1999. pap. 10.95 (*0-9670898-0-8*) Clement Inc.

Petite Menagerie. Bill McMinn. (Orig.). 1997. pap. write for info. (*1-57553-450-9*) Watermrk Pr.

Petite Pallace of Pettie, 2 vols. George Pettie. LC 72-124763. reprint ed. 74.50 (*0-404-05025-5*) AMS Pr.

Petite Princesse. Lisa K. Laurel. (FRE.). 1998. mass mkt. 3.50 (*0-373-39479-9*, 1-39479-0) Harlequin Bks.

Petite Region Dambohimanambola (Sous-Prefecture de Betafo) La Colonisation Agricole au Moyan-Quest Malgache. Jean-Yves Marchal. (Atlas des Structures Agraires au Sud de Sahara Ser.: No. 2). (FRE., Illus.). 122p. 1974. pap. text 55.40 (*90-279-7935-9*) Mouton.

Petite Rogue. Guy de Maupassant. 9.95 (*0-686-54792-6*) Fr & Eur.

Petite Rogue. Guy de Maupassant. (FRE.). 1972. pap. 10.95 (*0-7859-3109-0*) Fr & Eur.

Petite Rouge: A Cajun Twist to an Old Tale. Sheila H. Collins. LC 97-21250. (Illus.). 32p. (J). (gr. 4-7). 1997. 14.95 (*1-56554-310-6*) Pelican.

***Petite Rouge Riding Hood: The Cajun Retelling of the Classic Folktale.** Mike Artell. LC 99-87550. (Illus.). (J). 2001. write for info. (*0-8037-2514-0*, Dial Yng Read) Peng Put Young Read.

Petite Sirene. (Best-Sellers Ser.).Tr. of Little Mermaid. (FRE., Illus.). 48p. (J). pap. 9.95 incl. audio (*2-89517-042-8*, Pub. by Coffragants) Penton Overseas.

Petite Sirene (Little Mermaid) Adapted by Sarah Harris. (Comes to Life Bks.). (ENG & FRE.). 16p. (J). (ps-2). 1995. write for info. (*1-57234-038-X*) YES Ent.

Petite Soeur. Ginette Anfousse. (Jiji et Pichou Ser.). (FRE., Illus.). 24p. (J). (ps up). 1986. pap. 6.95 (*2-89021-060-X*, Pub. by La Courte Ech) Firefly Bks Ltd.

Petite Soeur pour Fenouil. Brigitte Weninger.Tr. of Will You Mind the Baby, Davy?. (FRE., Illus.). (J). (gr. k-3). 15.95 (*3-314-21063-9*, Pub. by North-South Bks NYC) Chronicle Bks.

Petite Suite: 2 Pianos, 4 Hands. Claude Debussy. 40p. 1986. pap. 4.95 (*0-7935-5111-0*, 50262320) H Leonard.

Petites Egarees. Pascal Laine. (Folio Ser.: No. 2170). (FRE.). pap. 14.95 (*2-07-038259-1*) Schoenhof.

***Petites Filles Modeles.** Sophie Comtesse De Segur.Tr. of Perfect Little Girls. (FRE.). 1998. pap., boxed set 16.95 incl. audio compact disk (*2-921997-23-1*, Pub. by Coffragants) Penton Overseas.

Petites Filles Modeles. Sophie Comtesse De Segur. (Coffragants Ser.).Tr. of Perfect Little Girls. (FRE., Illus.). 1998. boxed set 12.95 incl. audio (*2-921997-18-5*) Penton Overseas.

"Petites Grottes" de Qumran: Planches, Vol. III. Ed. by M. Baillet et al. (Discoveries in the Judaean Desert Ser.: No. III). (Illus.). 80p. 1997. text 68.00 (*0-19-826947-1*) OUP.

"Petites Grottes" de Qumran: Textes. Ed. by Jozef R. Milik et al. (Discoveries in the Judaean Desert Ser.: No. III). 336p. 1997. text 105.00 (*0-19-826946-3*) OUP.

Petites Ironies de la Vie Preced d'Une Femme Imaginative. Thomas Hardy. (FRE.). 288p. 1981. pap. 10.95 (*0-7859-2448-5*, 2070373177) Fr & Eur.

Petites Mythologies de l'Oeil et de l'Esprit: Pour une Semiotique Plastique. Jean-Marie Floch. (Actes Semiotiques Ser.: No. 1). (FRE.). 227p. 1985. pap. 50.00 (*90-272-2261-4*) J Benjamins Pubng Co.

Petites Proses. Michel Tournier. (FRE.). 1986. pap. 10.95 (*0-8288-3799-6*, F42180) Fr & Eur.

Petites Proses. Michel Tournier. (Folio Ser.: No. 1768). (FRE.). pap. 8.95 (*2-07-037768-7*) Schoenhof.

Petition Against God: The Full Story Behind RM-2493. A. W. Allworthy. LC 75-43375. (Illus.). 150p. 1976. pap. 3.95 (*0-917320-07-7*) Mho & Mho.

Petition & Remonstrance of the Governor & Company, Etc. East India Company Staff. LC 78-25744. (English Experience Ser.: No. 305). 38p. 1971. reprint ed. 20.00 (*90-221-0305-6*) Walter J Johnson.

***Petition & Response: An Epigraphic Study of Petitions to Roman Emperors, 181-249.** Tor Hauken. (Monographs from the Norwegian Institute at Athens: Vol. 2). 395p. 1998. 72.50 (*82-91626-08-1*, Pub. by P Astroms) Coronet Bks.

Petition for Redress: Real History of Early America. Rick Watts. (Illus.). 240p. (Orig.). 1995. pap. 27.50 (*0-9644163-2-8*) Sanco Genl.

Petition Histories: Revolutionary War Related Claims. Kenneth R. Bowling et al. LC 97-7834. (Documentary History of the First Federal Congress of the United States of America Ser.: Vol. 7). 636p. 1998. 75.00 (*0-8018-5565-9*) Johns Hopkins.

Petition Histories & Nonlegislative Official Documents. Kenneth R. Bowling et al. LC 97-4994. (Documentary History of the First Federal Congress of the United States of America Ser.: Vol. 8). 912p. 1997. 75.00 (*0-8018-5566-7*) Johns Hopkins.

Petition to Agitation: Bengal, 1857-1885. Manju Chattopadhyay. 1986. 22.00 (*0-8364-1621-X*, Pub. by KP Bagchi) S Asia.

Petitioner. Suzanne Paola. (Poetry Ser.). 46p. (Orig.). 1985. pap. 12.00 (*0-937669-17-2*) Owl Creek Pr.

P

Petitioning for the Impossible. Buddy Harrison. 80p. 1992. pap. 5.99 (*0-89274-900-8*, HH-900) Harrison Hse.

Petitioning Reality with Faith. Bobby Drinnon & Michael Cartwright. (Illus.). 228p. 1988. 17.95 (*0-9621995-0-8*) B Drinnon.

Petitions Celestial (1932) Hanna J. Doumette. 220p. 1998. reprint ed. pap. 19.95 (*0-7661-0326-9*) Kessinger Pub.

***Petitions for Land from the South Carolina Council Journals Vol. VI: 1766-1770.** Brent H. Holcomb. 411p. 1999. 45.00 (*0-913363-35-9*) SCMAR.

***Petitions for Land from the South Carolina Council Journals Vol. VII: 1771-1774.** Brent H. Holcomb. 418p. 1999. 45.00 (*0-913363-36-7*) SCMAR.

Petitions for Land from the South Carolina Council Journals, 1734/5-1748. Brent H. Holcomb. 341p. 1996. 40.00 (*0-913363-25-1*) SCMAR.

Petitions for Land from the South Carolina Council Journals, 1748-1752. Brent H. Holcomb. LC 96-69860. 283p. 1997. 40.00 (*0-913363-26-X*) SCMAR.

Petitions for Land from the South Carolina Council Journals, 1752-1753. Brent H. Holcomb. LC 96-69860. 1997. 40.00 (*0-913363-28-6*) SCMAR.

Petitions for Land from the South Carolina Council Journals, 1754-1756, Vol. IV. Brent H. Holcomb. LC 96-69860. 328p. 1998. 40.00 (*0-913363-29-4*) SCMAR.

Petitions for Land from the South Carolina Council Journals, 1757-1765, Vol. V. Brent H. Holcomb. 352p. 1998. 40.00 (*0-913363-32-4*) SCMAR.

Petitions for Land Grant Suspensions in North Carolina. A. B. Pruitt. (Illus.). 402p. (Orig.). 1993. pap. 39.00 (*0-944992-48-X*) ABP Abstracts.

Petitions for Name Changes in New York City, 1848-1899. Kenneth Scott. LC 84-9974. 144p. 1984. lib. bdg. 19.95 (*0-915156-53-9*) Natl Genealogical.

Petitions of the Early Inhabitants of Kentucky to the General Assembly of Virginia, 1769 to 1792. James R. Robertson. LC 74-146415. (First American Frontier Ser.). 1971. reprint ed. 31.98 (*0-405-02879-2*) Ayer.

Petitions of the Early Inhabitants of Kentucky to the General Assembly of Virginia, 1769 to 1792. James R. Robertson. 292p. 1981. reprint ed. 25.00 (*0-89308-206-6*) Southern Hist Pr.

Petitions of the Early Inhabitants of Kentucky to the General Assembly of Virginia, 1769 to 1792. James Rood Robertson. LC 97-77490. 261p. 1998. reprint ed. 25.00 (*0-8063-1553-9*) Genealog Pub.

Petits Chateaux de Boheme see Oeuvres

Petits Chateaux de Boheme. Gerard De Nerval. (Class. Garnier Ser.). write for info. Schoenhof.

Petits Chateaux de Boheme: Prose et Poesie. Gerard De Nerval. 96p. 1973. reprint ed. 32.00 (*0-686-54808-6*) Fr & Eur.

Petits Chevaux de Tarquinia. Marguerite Duras. (FRE.). 1973. pap. 10.95 (*0-7859-2195-8*, 207036187X) Fr & Eur.

Petits Chevaux de Tarquinia. Marguerite Duras. (Folio Ser.: No. 187). (FRE.). pap. 8.95 (*2-07-036187-X*) Schoenhof.

Petits Enfants du Siecle. Christiane Rochefort. 159p. 1969. 14.95 (*0-686-55224-5*); pap. 24.95 (*0-686-55225-3*) Fr & Eur.

Petits Enfants du Siecle: B Level. Rochefort. text 8.95 (*0-8219-1451-0*) EMC-Paradigm.

***Petits Fours, Chocolate, Frozen Desserts, Sugar Work.** Roland Bilheux. LC 98-158019. (French Professional Pastry Ser.). 240p. 1998. text 69.95 (*0-470-25000-3*) Halsted Pr.

Petits Fours, Chocolate, Frozen Desserts, Sugar Work. Roland Bilheux. (French Professional Pastry Ser.). 224p. 1998. 80.00 (*0-470-24410-0*) Wiley.

Petits Oiseaux. Eugene Labiche. 9.95 (*0-686-54247-9*) Fr & Eur.

Petits Poemes en Prose: Le Spleen de Paris. Charles Baudelaire. Ed. by Henri Lemaitre. (Coll. Prestige). 49.95 (*0-685-34103-8*); pap. 29.95 (*0-685-34102-X*) Fr & Eur.

Petits Poemes en Prose: Le Spleen de Paris. Charles Baudelaire. Ed. by Doris Ruff. (Coll. GF). (FRE.). 1962. pap. 10.95 (*0-8288-9064-1*) Fr & Eur.

Petits Poemes en Prose: Le Spleen de Paris. Charles Baudelaire. (Poesie Ser.). (FRE.). pap. 9.95 (*2-07-031999-7*) Schoenhof.

Petits Points de Casa Lopez. Sophie Pelletier & Bernard Magnaint-Lopez. (Illus.). 176p. 1993. 35.00 (*2-200-21331-X*, Pub. by C Armand) Lacis Pubns.

Petits Spectacles: Recueil de Sketches. Boris Vian. (FRE.). 352p. 1980. pap. 15.95 (*0-7859-1477-3*, 2264003200) Fr & Eur.

Petitt Site (Il-Ax-253), Alexander County, Illinois. Ed. by Paul A. Webb. LC 91-76754. (Center for Archaeological Investigations Research Paper Ser.: No. 58). (Illus.). xxiv, 420p. (Orig.). 1992. pap. 25.00 (*0-88104-070-3*) Center Archaeol.

Petkau Effect: The Devastating Effect of Nuclear Radiation on Human Health & the Environment. rev. ed. Ralph Graeub. LC 91-26809. (Illus.). 256p. 1994. pap. 14.95 (*1-56858-019-3*) FWEW.

Petkeeper's Guide to Hamsters & Gerbils. David Alderton. (Illus.). 118p. 1995. 10.95 (*1-56465-128-2*, 16053) Tetra Pr.

Petkeeper's Guide to Rabbits & Guinea Pigs. David Alderton. (Illus.). 120p. 1995. 10.95 (*1-56465-137-1*, 16054) Tetra Pr.

Petkeeper's Guide to Reptiles & Amphibians. David Alderton. (Illus.). 118p. 1995. 10.95 (*1-56465-156-8*, 16055) Tetra Pr.

Petmobiles. (Fisher-Price Little People Coloring & Activity Ser.). (Illus.). 48p. (J). (gr. k-2). 1997. pap. write for info. (*1-56144-957-1*, Honey Bear Bks) Modern Pub NYC.

Petook: An Easter Story. Caryll Houselander. LC 87-21228. (Illus.). 32p. (J). (ps-3). 1988. lib. bdg. 16.95 (*0-8234-0681-4*) Holiday.

Petr Chelcicky: A Radical Separatist in Hussite Bohemia. Murray L. Wagner. LC 82-21259. (Studies in Anabaptist & Mennonite History: Vol. 25). 212p. 1983. 19.99 (*0-8361-1257-1*) Herald Pr.

Petra. E. Raymond Capt. LC 87-70766. (Illus.). 128p. 1987. pap. 6.00 (*0-934666-23-7*) Artisan Pubs.

Petra. Jane Taylor. (Illus.). 80p. 1995. 29.95 (*1-85410-253-2*, Pub. by Aurum Pr) London Brdge.

Petra. Jane Taylor. 1999. pap. 19.95 (*1-85410-461-6*, Pub. by Aurum Press Ltd) London Brdge.

***Petra: Lost City of the Ancient World.** Christian Auge & Jean-Marie Dentzer. LC 99-53256. 128p. 2000. pap. 12.95 (*0-8109-2896-5*, Pub. by Abrams) Time Warner.

Petra in History & Prophecy: Petra, Israels Hiding Place for the Tribulation? Noah W. Hutchings. (Illus.). 160p. (Orig.). 1991. pap. 12.95 (*1-879366-11-8*) Hearthstone OK.

Petra Today. Noah Hutchings. (Illus.). 31p. 1998. pap. 6.95 (*1-57558-022-5*) Hearthstone OK.

Petrach: Poet & Humanist. Kenelm Foster. 226p. 1987. pap. 15.00 (*0-85224-548-3*, Pub. by Edinburgh U Pr) Col U Pr.

Petrarca Fra Medioevo e Umanesiono: L'Esperienza Letterraria della Parola. Giuseppe M. Zaccagnini. LC 91-13495. (Harvard Romance Languages Ser.). 216p. 1991. reprint ed. text 20.00 (*0-8240-0486-8*) Garland.

Petrarca y Alvar Gomez: La Traduccion del "Triunfo de Amor" Roxana Recio. (Studies in the Humanities: Vol. 28). (SPA.). VIII, 213p. (C). 1997. text 45.95 (*0-8204-3309-8*) P Lang Pubng.

Petrarch: The Canzoniere, or Rerum Vulgarium Fragmenta. Tr. & Comment by Mark Musa. LC 95-35943. (Illus.). 800p. 1999. pap. 27.95 (*0-253-21317-7*) Ind U Pr.

Petrarch: The First Modern Scholar & Man of Letters. Francesco Petrarca. Tr. & Intro. by James H. Robinson. LC 75-127999. (World History Ser.: No. 48). 1970. reprint ed. lib. bdg. 75.00 (*0-8383-1148-2*) M S G Haskell Hse.

Petrarch & Garcilaso: A Linguistic Approach to Style. Sharon Ghertman. (Monagrafias A Ser.: No. 44). 144p. (C). 1975. pap. 41.00 (*0-900411-99-6*, Pub. by Tamesis Bks Ltd) Boydell & Brewer.

Petrarch & the English Sonnet Tradition. Thomas P. Roche, Jr. LC 85-48062. (Studies in the Renaissance: No. 18). 1990. 57.50 (*0-404-62288-7*) AMS Pr.

Petrarch & the Renascence. J. H. Whitfield. LC 68-1761. (Studies in Italian Literature: No. 46). 1969. reprint ed. lib. bdg. 75.00 (*0-8383-0687-X*) M S G Haskell Hse.

Petrarch, Laura & the Triumphs. Aldo S. Bernardo. LC 74-22084. 234p. (C). 1974. text 19.50 (*0-87395-289-8*, PSU1, Pub. by State U NY Pr) Pegasus Pr.

Petrarch Selected Letters. Craig Kallendorf. (Latin Commentaries Ser.). 156p. (Orig.). (C). 1986. pap. text 7.00 (*0-929524-49-7*) Bryn Mawr Commentaries.

Petrarch the Poet: An Introduction to the Rerum Vulgarium Fragmenta. Peter Hainsworth. 256p. (C). 1988. lib. bdg. 69.50 (*0-415-00270-2*) Routledge.

Petrarch to Pirandello: Studies in Italian Literature in Honour of Beatrice Corrigan. Ed. by Julius A. Molinaro. LC 72-185725. 276p. reprint ed. pap. 85.60 (*0-608-13763-4*, 202050900018) Bks Demand.

Petrarchan Love & the Continental Renaissance. Gordon Braden. LC 98-50952. 208p. 1999. 25.00 (*0-300-07621-5*) Yale U Pr.

Petrarch's Africa. Francesco Petrarca. Tr. by Thomas G. Bergin & Alice S. Wilson. LC 77-75380. 311p. reprint ed. pap. 96.50 (*0-8357-8748-6*, 203367000087) Bks Demand.

Petrarch's Book Without a Name: A Translation of the Liber Sine Nomine. Francesco Petrarca. Tr. by Norman P. Zacour from LAT. 128p. pap. 8.00 (*0-88844-260-2*) Brill Academic Pubs.

Petrarch's Bucolicum Carmen. Francesco Petrarca. Tr. & Anno. by Thomas G. Bergin. LC 73-94049. (ENG & LAT., Illus.). 270p. reprint ed. pap. 83.70 (*0-8357-8749-4*, 203367100087) Bks Demand.

Petrarch's Eight Years in Milan. Ernest H. Wilkins. LC 58-13250. (Medieval Academy Bks.: No. 69). 1958. 20.00 (*0-910956-43-X*) Medieval Acad.

Petrarch's Genius: Pentimento & Prophecy. Marjorie O. Boyle. LC 90-19877. 224p. 1991. 48.00 (*0-520-07293-6*, Pub. by U CA Pr) Cal Prin Full Svc.

Petrarch's Later Years. Ernest H. Wilkins. LC 59-14351. (Medieval Academy Bks.: No. 70). 1959. 25.00 (*0-910956-44-8*) Medieval Acad.

Petrarch's Laurels. Sara Sturm-Maddox. 288p. 1992. 45.00 (*0-271-00822-9*) Pa St U Pr.

Petrarch's Lyric Poems. Ed. by Robert M. Durling. 624p. 1976. pap. 22.00 (*0-674-66348-9*) HUP.

Petrarch's Lyric Poems: The Rime Sparse & Other Lyrics. Francesco Petrarca. Ed. by Robert M. Durling. 624p. 1976. 46.50 (*0-674-66345-4*) HUP.

Petrarch's Remedies for Fortune Fair & Foul: A Modern English Translation of "De Remediis Utriusque Fortune," with a Commentary, 5 vols., Set. Francesco Petrarca. Tr. by Conrad H. Rawski. LC 88-46015. (ITA., Illus.). 1991. 198.00 (*0-253-34849-8*) Ind U Pr.

Petrarch's "Secretum" Its Making & Meaning. Hans Baron. LC 84-61721. (Medieval Academy Bks.: No. 94). 254p. 1985. 25.00 (*0-910956-87-1*) Medieval Acad.

Petrarch's Songbook: Rerum Vulgarium Fragmenta. A Verse Translation. Tr. by James W. Cook. (Medieval & Renaissance Texts & Studies: Vol. 151). 464p. 1995. 30.00 (*0-86698-191-8*, MR151) MRTS.

Petrarch's Songbook: Rerum Vulgarium Fragmenta. A Verse Translation, Bilingual edition. Tr. by James W. Cook. (Medieval & Renaissance Texts & Studies: Vol. 151). 464p. 1996. pap. 19.95 (*0-86698-192-6*, P32) Pegasus Pr.

Petrarquismo Peruano: Diego Davalos y Figuera y la Poesia de la Miscelanea Austral. Alicia de Colombi-Monguio. (Monagrafias A Ser.: Vol. XCIX). (SPA.). 217p. 1985. 58.00 (*0-7293-0207-5*, Pub. by Tamesis Bks Ltd) Boydell & Brewer.

Petrels: Their Ecology & Breeding Systems. John Warham. 448p. (C). 1991. text 63.00 (*0-12-735420-4*) Acad Pr.

Petretti's Coca-Cola Collectibles Price Guide: The Encyclopedia of Coca-Cola Collectibles. 10th rev. ed. Allan Petretti. (Illus.). 648p. 1997. 42.95 (*0-930625-76-5*, Antique Trader) Krause Pubns.

Petretti's Soda Pop Collectibles Price Guide: The Encyclopedia of Soda-Pop Collectibles. 2nd ed. Allan Petretti. (Illus.). 384p. 1999. 37.95 (*1-58221-026-8*, Antique Trader); pap. 32.95 (*1-58221-014-4*, Antique Trader) Krause Pubns.

Petri Andrea Matthioli Compendium. J. Szurok. (ENG, GER & HUN.). 921p. (C). 1992. boxed set 810.00 (*963-400-969-7*, Pub. by Akade Kiado) St Mut.

Petri Net Synthesis for Discrete Event Control of Manufacturing Systems. Mengchu Zhou & Frank DiCesare. LC 92-36721. (International Series in Engineering & Computer Science, VLSI, Computer Architecture, & Digital Screen Processing). 256p. 1992. text 142.50 (*0-7923-9289-2*) Kluwer Academic.

Petri Nets: A Tool for Design & Management of Manufacturing Systems. Jean-Marie Proth & Xiaolan Xie. LC 96-28024. 298p. 1997. 85.00 (*0-471-96770-X*) Wiley.

Petri Nets: Applications & Relationships to Other Models of Concurrency. Ed. by W. Brauer et al. (Lecture Notes in Computer Science Ser.: Vol. 255). x, 516p. 1987. pap. 53.00 (*0-387-17906-2*) Spr-Verlag.

***Petri Nets & Performance Models: Proceedings International Workshop Zaragoza, Spain 1998.** 228p. 1999. 110.00 (*0-7695-0331-4*) IEEE Comp Soc.

Petri Nets & Performance Models: Proceedings of the 7th International Workshop on Petri Nets & Performance Models, Saint Malo, France, 1997. LC 10-636714. 300p. 1997. pap. 110.00 (*0-8186-7931-X*) IEEE Comp Soc.

Petri Nets for Supervisory Control of Discrete Events Systems: A Structural Approach. 200p. 1998. lib. bdg. 34.00 (*981-02-2831-7*) World Scientific Pub.

Petri Nets in Flexible & Agile Automation. Ed. by MengChu Zhou. LC 94-49010. (The Kluwer International Series in Engineering & Computer Science: Vol. 310). 400p. (C). 1995. text 175.50 (*0-7923-9557-3*) Kluwer Academic.

Petrie Family - Building Colonial Brisbane. Dimity Dornan & Denis Cryle. 1992. pap. 17.95 (*0-7022-2346-8*, Pub. by Univ Queensland Pr) Intl Spec Bk.

Petrie Terrace Brisbane, 1858-1988: Sketches. Steve Woolcock & Rod Fisher. 64p. (C). 1990. 75.00 (*0-86439-050-5*, Pub. by Boolarong Pubns) St Mut.

Petrie's Naqada Excavation: A Supplement. Elise J. Baumgartel & D. Phil Koenigsberg. 1970. 60.00 (*0-85388-005-0*, Pub. by Aris & Phillips) David Brown.

***Petrified.** Lisle. (J). 2000. pap. 6.95 (*0-552-52964-8*, Pub. by Transworld Publishers Ltd) Trafalgar.

Petrified Forest. Robert E. Sherwood. 1948. pap. 5.25 (*0-8222-0889-X*) Dramatists Play.

Petrified Forest: The Story Behind the Scenery. Sidney Ash. LC 85-81283. (Illus.). 48p. (Orig.). 1986. pap. 7.95 (*0-88714-006-8*) KC Pubns.

Petrified Forest National Park. Ed. by Jeff Nicholas. (Wish You Were Here Postcard Book Ser.). (Illus.). 32p. 1995. pap. 4.95 (*0-939365-47-2*) Panorama Intl.

Petrified Forest National Park. David Petersen. LC 96-1181. (True Bk.). (Illus.). 48p. (J). 1996. lib. bdg. 21.00 (*0-516-20052-6*) Childrens.

Petrified Forest National Park: A Wilderness Bound in Time. George M. Lubick. LC 95-32549. (Illus.). 212p. 1996. 47.00 (*0-8165-1604-9*) U of Ariz Pr.

Petrified Forest National Park: A Wilderness Bound in Time. George M. Lubick. LC 95-32549. 212p. 1996. pap. 16.95 (*0-8165-1629-4*) U of Ariz Pr.

Petrified Wood: The World of Fossilized Wood, Cones, Ferns, & Cycads. Frank J. Daniels. (Illus.). vi, 170p. (YA). (gr. 9-12). 1998. 75.00 (*0-9662938-0-0*) W Colorado Publ.

Petrikivka Painting: A Ukrainian Heritage. Rose Tanasichuk. (Illus.). 48p. 1986. pap. 8.95 (*0-941284-31-X*) J Shaw Studio.

Petril Wava. Paul Collier. (Illus.). 26p. (Orig.). 1993. pap. 5.00 (*0-926935-79-8*) Runaway Spoon.

***Petrine Ministry & the Unity of the Church: Toward a Patient & Fraternal Dialogue.** Ed. & Afterword by James F. Puglisi. LC 98-33867. 211p. 1999. pap. 19.95 (*0-8146-5936-5*) Liturgical Pr.

Petrine Revolution in Russian Architecture. James E. Cracraft. (Illus.). 408p. 1988. 54.00 (*0-226-11664-6*) U Ch Pr.

Petrine Revolution in Russian Imagery. James Cracraft. LC 97-6309. 416p. 1997. 50.00 (*0-226-11665-4*) U Ch Pr.

Petrines Arpes see Frozen Harps: Poetry from the Heart

Petro & Marine Environment. 1981. text 142.00 (*0-86010-215-7*) Kluwer Academic.

Petro International Safety Rating System. LC 78-57046. Date not set. write for info. (*0-88061-082-4*) Intl Loss Cntrl.

Petro Pals - Adventure to the Top of the Earth. Robert F. Robben. Ed. by Margaret B. Robben. LC 96-92455. (Illus.). 36p. (Orig.). (J). (ps-3). 1996. pap. 5.95 (*0-9653562-0-5*, PP-101) Petro Pals.

Petro Pals - Getting Lost in Petropolis. Robert F. Robben. Ed. by Margaret B. Robben. LC 97-75953. (Illus.). 24p. (J). (ps-3). 1998. pap. 5.95 (*0-9653562-1-3*) Petro Pals.

Petro-Safe '97 see Energy Week '97

Petro-Safe '96 see Energy Week '96: Conference Proceedings

Petrochemical & Chemical Catalysts. Contrib. by J. Charles Forman. 245p. 1996. 2850.00 (*1-56965-351-8*, C-200) BCC.

Petrochemical Industry: Petrochemical Industry. (UNIDO Guide to Information Sources Ser.: No. 29). pap. 4.00 (*92-1-106164-4*, ID/199) UN.

Petrochemical Industry & the Possibilities of Its Establishment Developing Countries. Claude Mercier. (Illus.). 202p. (C). 1966. 155.00 (*2-7108-0058-6*, Pub. by Edits Technip) Enfield Pubs NH.

***Petrochemical Industry in Colombia: A Strategic Entry Report, 1999.** Compiled by Icon Group International. (Illus.). 190p. 1999. ring bd. 1900.00 incl. audio compact disk (*0-7418-1842-6*) Icon Grp.

Petrochemical Manufacturing & Marketing Guide, 2 vols. Robert B. Stobaugh, Jr. Incl. Vol. 2. Olefins, Diolefins & Acetylene. 1968. 12.95 (*0-87201-666-8*); write for info. (*0-318-52869-X*) Gulf Pub.

Petrochemical Manufacturing & Marketing Guide, Vol. 1. Robert B. Stobaugh. LC 67-24629. 253p. reprint ed. pap. 78.50 (*0-608-15546-2*, 205221800062) Bks Demand.

Petrochemical Manufacturing & Marketing Guide Vol. 2: Olefins, Diolefins, & Acetylene. Robert B. Stobaugh. LC 67-24629. (Illus.). 236p. reprint ed. pap. 73.20 (*0-608-17457-2*, 202992500002) Bks Demand.

Petrochemical Processes, Tech. & Economic Characteristics: Synthesis-Gas Derivative & Major Hydrocarbons. Alain Chauvel & Gilles Lefebvre. (Illus.). 432p. (C). 1989. 680.00 (*2-7108-0562-6*, Pub. by Edits Technip) Enfield Pubs NH.

Petrochemical Processes, Tech. & Economic Characteristics Vol. 2: Major Oxygenated, Chlorinated & Nitrated Derivatives. Alain Chauvel & Gilles Lefebvre. (Illus.). 424p. (C). 1989. 660.00 (*2-7108-0563-4*, Pub. by Edits Technip) Enfield Pubs NH.

Petrochemical Production Machinery in Canada: A Strategic Entry Report, 1998. Compiled by Icon Group International Staff. (Country Industry Report). (Illus.). 130p. 1999. ring bd. 1300.00 incl. audio compact disk (*0-7418-0442-5*) Icon Grp.

Petrochemical Projects Update in Saudi Arabia: A Strategic Entry Report, 1997. Compiled by Icon Group International Staff. (Illus.). 135p. 1999. ring bd. 1350.00 incl. audio compact disk (*0-7418-0975-3*) Icon Grp.

***Petrochemical Projects Update in Saudi Arabia: A Strategic Entry Report, 1999.** Compiled by Icon Group International. (Illus.). 135p. 1999. ring bd. 1350.00 incl. audio compact disk (*0-7418-1792-6*) Icon Grp.

Petrochemicals. P. Wiseman. LC 85-24843. (Umist Series in Science & Technology). 1986. text 47.95 (*0-470-20279-3*); pap. text 31.95 (*0-470-20284-X*) P-H.

Petrochemicals: Spring & Fall. 1999. pap. text 165.00 (*0-911299-18-1*) OPIS Directories.

Petrochemicals: The Rise of an Industry. Peter H. Spitz. LC 87-23019. 624p. 1988. 125.00 (*0-471-85985-0*) Wiley.

Petrochemicals in Nontechnical Language. 2nd ed. William L. Leffler & Donald L. Burdick. 360p. 1990. 64.95 (*0-87814-344-0*) PennWell Bks.

Petrodvorets: Palaces, Gardens, Fountains, Sculpture. Abram Raskin. 346p. 1979. 155.00 (*0-7855-1648-4*) St Mut.

Petroff Defense Cochrance Gambit. W. John Lutes. 243p. (Orig.). 1994. pap. 14.95 (*0-945470-44-4*) Chess Ent.

Petrofina. E. Peters. 1998. 28.95 (*90-6831-900-0*, Pub. by Peeters Pub) Bks Intl VA.

Petrogenesis & Experimental Petrology of Granitic Rocks. W. Johannes & F. Holtz. 1995. write for info. (*0-387-60416-2*) Spr-Verlag.

Petrogenesis & Experimental Petrology of Granitic Rocks. W. Johannes & F. Holtz. (Minerals & Rocks Ser.: Vol. 22). (Illus.). 312p. 1996. text 129.95 (*3-540-60416-2*) Spr-Verlag.

Petrogenesis & Petrophysics of Selected Sandstone Reservoirs of the Rocky Mountain Region. Ed. by Edward B. Coalson. (Illus.). 353p. 1989. 20.00 (*0-933979-12-6*) Rocky Mtn Assoc Geol.

Petrogenesis of Metamorphic Rocks. 6th ed. K. Bucher & M. Frey. (Illus.). 320p. 1994. 47.95 (*0-387-57567-7*) Spr-Verlag.

Petrogenesis of Metamorphic Rocks: Springer Study Edition. 5th ed. H. G. Winkler. LC 79-14704. (Illus.). 1985. pap. 41.00 (*0-387-90413-1*) Spr-Verlag.

Petroglyph Calendar: An Archaeoastronomy Adventure. Hubert A. Allen. LC 98-92855. (Illus.). 160p. (Orig.). 1998. pap. 18.95 (*0-9641694-5-2*) H Allen & Assocs.

Petroglyph National Monument. Susan Lamb. Ed. by Ronald J. Foreman. LC 92-62155. (Illus.). 16p. (Orig.). 1993. pap. 3.95 (*1-877856-22-3*) SW Pks Mnmts.

Petroglyph National Monument Boundary Adjustment Act; & the Bandelier National Monument Administrative Improvement & Watershed Protection Act of 1997: Hearing Before the Subcommittee on National Parks, Historic Preservation, & Recreation of the Committee on Energy & Natural Resources, United States Senate, One Hundred Fifth Congress, First Session, On S. 633 ... S. 1132 ... October 23, 1997. United States. LC 98-161321. (S. Hrg. Ser.). 88 p. 1998. write for info. (*0-16-056247-3*) USGPO.

Petroglyph of His Own Choosing. Benjamin A. Kerner. (Illus.). 88p. (Orig.). 1998. pap. 14.95 (*0-9658945-0-9*) LinCom Pr.

Petroglyphs. Lisa L. Adams. (Illus.). 32p. (Orig.). 1994. pap. 10.00 (*0-9641577-5-6*) Spiral Triangle.

Petroglyphs. Sam Hamill. LC 75-24583. (Three Rivers Poetry Ser.). (Orig.). 1976. pap. 2.95 (*0-915606-01-1*) Three Rivers Pr.

An Asterisk (*) at the beginning of an entry indicates that the title is appearing for the first time.

Petroglyphs: Ancient Language, Sacred Art. Sabra Moore. LC 98-11903. (Illus.). 192p. 1998. 19.95 (*1-57416-011-7*) Clear Light.

Petroglyphs & Pictographs of Utah, Vol. I. Kenneth B. Castleton. 1984. pap. 24.95 (*0-940378-29-9*) U of Utah Pr.

Petroglyphs & Pictographs of Utah, Vol. II. Kenneth B. Castleton. 1987. pap. 24.95 (*0-940378-30-2*) U of Utah Pr.

Petroglyphs & Pictographs of Utah, Vol. 2. Kenneth B. Castleton. (Illus.). 1980. 15.00 (*0-686-26976-4*) Utah Mus Natural Hist.

Petroglyphs & Pueblo Myths of the Rio Grande. Carol Patterson-Rudolph. LC 90-49025. (Illus.). 156p. 1990. pap. 29.95 (*0-936755-13-X*) Avanyu Pub.

Petroglyphs & Pueblo Myths of the Rio Grande. rev. ed. Carol Patterson-Rudolph. (Illus.). 174p. 1994. reprint ed. pap. 29.95 (*0-936755-22-9*) Avanyu Pub.

Petroglyphs at Wedding Rocks & Other Poems. George B. Moore. LC 96-45642. 72p. 1997. pap. 14.95 (*0-7734-2699-X*, Mellen Poetry Pr) E Mellen.

Petroglyphs of California & Adjoining States, Vol. 24:2. fac. ed. Julian H. Steward. (University of California Publications in American Archaeology & Ethnology). (Illus.). 300p. (C). 1929. reprint ed. pap. text 31.25 (*1-55567-708-8*) Coyote Press.

Petroglyphs of Hawaii. rev. ed. L. R. McBride. 1996. pap. 7.95 (*0-912180-49-8*) Petroglyph.

Petroglyphs of Southeast Colorado & the Oklahoma Panhandle. Bill McGlone et al. (Illus.). 118p. (Orig.). 1994. pap. 14.95 (*0-9641333-0-X*) Mithras.

Petroglyphs of the Southwest. Elizabeth C. Welsh. (Easy Field Guide Ser.). (Illus.). 32p. (J). 1995. pap. 1.50 (*0-935810-60-9*) R H Pub.

Petrograd Codex of the Hebrew Bible: The Latter Prophets, Prophetarum Posteriorum. rev. ed. Hermann L. Strack. (Library of Biblical Studies). 1970. 75.00 (*0-87068-111-7*) Ktav.

Petrographic & Physical Characteristics of Utah Coals. Brigitte P. Hucka et al. LC 97-135117. (Circular of the Utah Geological Survey Ser.: Vol. 94). (Illus.). 80p. 1997. pap. 7.00 (*1-55791-602-0*, C-94) Utah Geological Survey.

Petrographisch Wichtigen Mineralien und die Methoden Ihrer Untersuchung, Zwei Teile, Teil 1. Harry F. Rosenbusch. (Mikroskopische Physiographie der Mineralien und Gesteine Ser.: Band I). (Illus.). xxiv, 847p. 73.00 (*3-510-99070-6*, Pub. by E Schweizerbartsche) Balogh.

Petrographisch Wichtigen Mineralien und die Methoden Ihrer Untersuchung, Zwei Teile, Teil 2. Harry F. Rosenbusch. (Mikroskopische Physiographie der Mineralien und Gesteine Ser.: Band I). (Illus.). xv, 814p. 86.00 (*3-510-99071-4*, Pub. by E Schweizerbartsche) Balogh.

Petrography & Pictographs of Missouri. Carol Diaz-Granados. 341p. 2000. pap. text 29.95 (*0-8173-0988-8*) U of Ala Pr.

Petrography Applied to Concrete & Concrete Aggregates. Ed. by Bernard Erlin & David Stark. LC 90-1190. (Special Technical Publication Ser.: No. 1061). (Illus.). 203p. 1990. text 36.00 (*0-8031-1452-4*, STP1061) ASTM.

Petrography of Cementitious Materials, No. 1215. Ed. by Sharon M. DeHayes & David Stark. LC 94-11867. (Special Technical Publication: 1215). (Illus.). 155p. 1994. pap. 70.00 (*0-8031-1878-3*, STP1061) ASTM.

Petrography of Concrete. Poole. (C). 1996. text. write for info. (*0-582-03784-0*, Pub. by Addison-Wesley) Longman.

Petrography of Igneous & Metamorphic Rocks. Anthony R. Philpotts. 178p. (C). 1988. pap. text 41.00 (*0-13-662313-1*) P-H.

Petrography, Petrophysics, Geochemistry, & Economic Geology see Shales & Mudstones: Recent Progress in Shale Research

Petrography to Petrogenesis. Malcolm J. Hibbard. LC 93-23101. 608p. (C). 1994. 89.00 (*0-02-354145-8*, Macmillan Coll) P-H.

***Petroleo Moderno: Un Manual Basico de la Industria.** Bill D. Berger & Kenneth E. Anderson. 537p. 1999. 64.95 (*0-87814-755-1*) PennWell Bks.

Petroleum: A Resource Interpretation. Chester G. Gilbert & Joseph E. Pogue. 1980. lib. bdg. 49.95 (*0-8490-3109-5*) Gordon Pr.

Petroleum: Strategic Planning & Future Trends. Richard K. Miller & Marcia E. Rupnow. LC 90-83932. (Survey on Technology & Markets Ser.: No. 138). 50p. 1991. pap. text 200.00 (*1-55865-163-2*) Future Tech Surveys.

Petroleum Vol. 4: Exploration & Exploitation in Norway: Proceedings of the Norwegian Petroleum Society Conference, 9-11 December 1991, Stavanger, Norway. Ed. by S. Hanslien. (Norwegian Petroleum Society Special Publications: Vol. 4). 460p. 1995. 231.50 (*0-444-81596-1*) Elsevier.

Petroleum Accounting: Principles, Procedures, & Issues. Horace R. Brock et al. LC 85-60604. 1000p. 1996. text 125.00 (*0-940966-24-7*) Pro Dev Inst.

***Petroleum Accounting: Principles, Procedures & Issues.** 5th ed. Horace R. Brock et al. (Illus.). 1150p. 2000. write for info. (*0-940966-25-5*) Pro Dev Inst.

Petroleum & Basin Evolution. Donald R. Baker et al. LC 96-23073. 1996. write for info. (*0-387-61128-2*) Spr-Verlag.

Petroleum & Basin Evolution. Donald R. Baker et al. LC 96-23073. (Illus.). 530p. 1996. 129.00 (*3-540-61128-2*) Spr-Verlag.

Petroleum & Chemical Applications, 1992. 256p. 175.00 (*1-55937-248-6*, SH15545) IEEE Standards.

Petroleum & Coal. Pradip K. Das & Hrishikesh Baruah. 139p. 1997. pap. 120.00 (*81-7533-042-2*, Pub. by Print Hse) St Mut.

Petroleum & Marine Technology Information Guide: A Bibliographic Sourcebook & Directory of Services. 4th ed. A. Myers et al. LC 95-24320. (Illus.). 405p. (C). 1993. 325.00 (*0-419-18210-1*, E & FN Spon) Routledge.

Petroleum & Medicine: Scientific Subject Index with Research Bibliography. American Health Research Institute Staff. LC 88-47604. 150p. 1988. 47.50 (*0-88164-742-X*); pap. 44.50 (*0-88164-743-8*) ABBE Pubs Assn.

Petroleum & Mining Taxation: Handbook on a Method for Equitable Sharing of Profits & Risk. Christopher Goss. 86p. 1986. text 61.95 (*0-566-05269-5*, Pub. by Dartmth Pub) Ashgate Pub Co.

Petroleum & National Development in the Middle East: The Case of Saudi Arabia. 1979. 6.00 (*0-317-56399-8*) UM Ctr MENAS.

Petroleum & Organic Chemicals, 8 vols., Vol. 4. Intro. by John J. McKetta, Jr. (Illus.). 792p. 1972. 68.50 (*0-06-491105-5*) B&N Imports.

Petroleum & Structural Change in a Developing Country: The Case of Nigeria. Peter O. Olayiwola. LC 86-21216. 225p. 1986. 59.95 (*0-275-92115-8*, C2115, Praeger Pubs) Greenwood.

Petroleum & Tectonics in Mobile Belts: 4th IFP Exploration & Production Research Conference, Bordeaux, 1988. Ed. by J. Letouzey. (Illus.). 224p. (C). 1990. 370.00 (*2-7108-0579-0*, Pub. by Edits Technip) Enfield Pubs NH.

Petroleum Applications, Vol. 2. Frwd. by C. Fairhurst. LC 98-132948. 704p. 1997. pap. 420.00 (*2-7108-0586-3*, Pub. by Edits Technip) Enfield Pubs NH.

Petroleum Basin Studies. P. M. Shannon & D. Naylor. (C). 1990. lib. bdg. 241.50 (*0-86010-780-9*, Pub. by Graham & Trotman) Kluwer Academic.

Petroleum Basins of South America. Ed. by A. J. Tankard et al. (AAPG Memoir Ser.: No. 62). (Illus.). xiii, 792p. 1995. 89.00 (*0-89181-341-1*, 531) AAPG.

Petroleum Bioventing. J. Van Eyk. (Illus.). 324p. (C). 1997. text 97.00 (*90-5410-686-7*, Pub. by A A Balkema) Ashgate Pub Co.

Petroleum Careers. Gretchen D. Krueger. LC 98-17650. (Opportunities in... Ser.). 160p. 1998. 14.95 (*0-8442-6549-7*, 65497); pap. 11.95 (*0-8442-6550-0*, 65500) NTC Contemp Pub Co.

Petroleum Catalysis in Nontechnical Language. J. S. Magee & Geoffrey E. Dolbear. LC 98-12063. 1998. 64.95 (*0-87814-661-X*) PennWell Bks.

Petroleum Chemistry & Refining. LC 97-17306. 350p. 1997. 80.00 (*1-56032-587-9*) Hemisp Pub.

Petroleum Collectibles. Rick Pease. LC 96-70896. (Illus.). 160p. 1997. pap. 29.95 (*0-7643-0202-7*) Schiffer.

Petroleum Company Operations & Agreements in the Developing Countries. Raymond F. Mikesell. LC 83-43265. 148p. 1984. pap. text 20.00 (*0-915707-07-1*) Resources Future.

Petroleum Conservation in the United States: An Economic Analysis. Stephen L. McDonald. LC 71-149242. (Resources for the Future Ser.). (Illus.). 279p. 1971. 22.50 (*0-8018-1261-5*, Pub. by Resources Future) Johns Hopkins.

Petroleum Contaminated Soils: Remediation Techniques, Environmental Fate & Risk Assessment, Vol. I. Ed. by Paul T. Kostecki & Edward J. Calabrese. (Illus.). 368p. 1988. lib. bdg. 99.95 (*0-87371-135-1*, L135) Lewis Pubs.

Petroleum Contaminated Soils: Remediation Techniques, Environmental Fate & Risk Assessment, Vol. II. Ed. by Edward J. Calabrese & Paul T. Kostecki. (Illus.). 532p. 1989. lib. bdg. 99.95 (*0-87371-226-9*, L226) Lewis Pubs.

Petroleum Contaminated Soils: Remediation Techniques, Environmental Fate, & Risk Assessment, Vol. III. Ed. by Paul T. Kostecki & Edward J. Calabrese. (Illus.). 440p. 1990. lib. bdg. 99.95 (*0-87371-380-X*, L380) Lewis Pubs.

Petroleum Derivatives, 2 vols. Incl. Vol. 1. William R. Jones. 1976. text 34.50 (*0-8422-7291-7*); Vol. 2. John G. Ditman. 1976. text 34.50 (*0-8422-7292-5*); (Energy Ser.). 1976. text. write for info. (*0-318-53723-0*) Irvington.

Petroleum-Derived Carbons. Ed. by John D. Bacha et al. LC 86-7894. (ACS Symposium Ser.: No. 303). (Illus.). x, 416p. 1986. 82.95 (*0-8412-0964-2*, PA 410) Am Chemical.

Petroleum-Derived Carbons. Ed. by John D. Bacha et al. LC 86-7894. (ACS Symposium Ser.: Vol. 303). 416p. 1986. reprint ed. pap. 129.00 (*0-608-03849-0*, 206429600008) Bks Demand.

Petroleum Development Geology. 3rd ed. Parke A. Dickey. LC 81-11943. 544p. 1986. 25.00 (*0-87814-307-6*) PennWell Bks.

Petroleum Dictionary: Dictionnaire du Petrole. Georges Ayache. (FRE.). 256p. 1981. 35.00 (*0-8288-2291-3*, M14189) Fr & Eur.

Petroleum Divestiture & the Use & Misuse of Business Segment Financial Statistics. Bernell K. Stone. (LEC Occasional Paper). 1978. pap. 2.50 (*0-916770-07-9*) Law & Econ U Miami.

Petroleum Economics. 4th ed. Jean Masseron. 536p. 1990. 370.00 (*2-7108-0597-9*, Pub. by Edits Technip) Enfield Pubs NH.

Petroleum Economics: Issues & Strategies of Oil & Natural Gas Production. Rognvaldur Hannesson. LC 98-6837. 176p. 1998. 59.95 (*1-56720-220-9*, Quorum Bks) Greenwood.

Petroleum Economics & Engineering. 2nd ed. Ed. by H. K. Abdel-Aal et al. (Illus.). 456p. 1992. text 210.00 (*0-8247-8428-6*) Dekker.

Petroleum Economics & Engineering: An Introduction. Hussein K. Abdel-Aal & Robert Schmelzlee. LC 75-213. (Chemical Processing & Engineering Ser.: No. 6). (Illus.). 431p. reprint ed. pap. 133.70 (*0-7837-0917-X*, 204122200019) Bks Demand.

Petroleum Engineering: Principles & Practice. John S. Archer & Colin G. Wall. (Illus.). 350p. 1986. pap. text 85.50 (*0-86010-715-9*) G & T Inc.

Petroleum Engineering: Principles & Practice. John S. Archer & Colin G. Wall. (Illus.). 350p. 1986. lib. bdg. 152.00 (*0-86010-665-9*) G & T Inc.

Petroleum Engineering Handbook for the Practicing Engineer. M. A. Mian. 627p. 1992. 99.95 (*0-87814-370-X*, P4445) PennWell Bks.

Petroleum Engineering Handbook for the Practicing Engineer, Vol. 2. M. A. Mian. 688p. 1992. 109.95 (*0-87814-379-3*, P4510) PennWell Bks.

Petroleum Equipment Institute Safe Practices, a Compilation, 1984-1994. Ed. by Petroleum Equipment Institute Staff. 92p. 1995. pap. 30.00 (*0-9642638-1-5*) Petrol Equip.

Petroleum Equipment Institute Safety Letters, a Compilation, 1980-1994. Ed. by Petroleum Equipment Institute Staff. 96p. (Orig.). 1995. pap. 30.00 (*0-9642638-0-7*) Petrol Equip.

Petroleum Equipment Lexicon: Terms Used in Petroleum Marketing Operations. Howard Upton. Ed. by Robert N. Renkes. 140p. (Orig.). 1995. pap. 40.00 (*0-9642638-2-3*) Petrol Equip.

Petroleum Exploration. Ray L. Sengbush. 1986. text 226.50 (*90-277-2133-5*) Kluwer Academic.

Petroleum Exploration & Exploitation Practices. Bhagwan Sahay. (C). 1994. 82.00 (*81-7023-162-0*, Pub. by Allied Pubs) S Asia.

Petroleum Exploration Opportunities in Africa & Countries Beyond. D. Keith Patton. LC 95-3072. 1995. 25.00 (*0-87814-440-4*) PennWell Bks.

Petroleum Exploration Opportunities in the Former Soviet Union. Joseph P. Riva. LC 94-201. 316p. 1994. 25.00 (*0-87814-414-5*, P4524) PennWell Bks.

Petroleum Exploration Strategies in Developing Countries. 300p. 1982. lib. bdg. 84.50 (*0-86010-346-3*) G & T Inc.

Petroleum Formation & Occurrence. enl. rev. ed. B. P. Tissot & Dietrich H. Welte. (Illus.). 610p. 1992. 156.95 (*0-387-13281-3*) Spr-Verlag.

Petroleum Fundamentals Glossary. 120p. 1990. pap. text 20.00 (*0-88698-149-2*, 1.30130) PETEX.

Petroleum Generation & Occurrence in the Miocene Monterey Formation, California. Ed. by Caroline M. Isaacs & Robert E. Garrison. (Illus.). 228p. (Orig.). 1983. pap. 8.00 (*1-878861-39-5*) Pac Section SEPM.

Petroleum Geochemistry & Basin Evaluation. Ed. by Gerard Demaison & Roelef J. Murris. LC 84-70675. (AAPG Memoir Ser.: No. 35). (Illus.). 436p. reprint ed. pap. 135.20 (*0-7837-5231-8*, 204496400005) Bks Demand.

Petroleum Geochemistry & Exploration in the Afro-Asian Region: Proceedings of the International Conference, Dehra Dun , India, 1st, 25-27 November 1985. Ed. by Ruby K. Kumar et al. 558p. (C). 1987. text 246.00 (*90-6191-791-3*, Pub. by A A Balkema) Ashgate Pub Co.

Petroleum Geochemistry & Geology. 2nd ed. John M. Hunt. LC 79-1281. 743p. (C). 1995. pap. text 73.95 (*0-7167-2441-3*) W H Freeman.

Petroleum Geochemistry & Source Rock Potential of Carbonate Rocks. Ed. by James G. Palacas. LC 84-45746. (AAPG Studies in Geology: Vol. 18). 216p. 1984. reprint ed. pap. 67.00 (*0-608-03019-8*, 206346900006) Bks Demand.

Petroleum Geochemistry in Exploration of the Norwegian Shelf: Proceedings of a Norwegian Petroleum Society Conference held in Stavanger, 22-24 October 1984. Ed. by Bruce M. Thomas. (Illus.). 500p. 1986. lib. bdg. 179.00 (*0-86010-706-X*) G & T Inc.

Petroleum Geology. F. K. North. (Illus.). 620p. (C). (gr. 13). pap. text 69.50 (*0-412-53830-X*, Chap & Hall NY) Chapman & Hall.

Petroleum Geology. F. K. North. (Illus.). 750p. 1985. text 95.00 (*0-04-553003-3*); pap. text 59.95 (*0-04-553004-1*) Routledge.

Petroleum Geology, Pt. 15. M. J. Salem et al. 1624p. 752.00 (*0-444-88844-6*) Elsevier.

Petroleum Geology & Reservoirs: Oil Well Servicing & Workover, Lesson 2. 2nd ed. Jeff Morris. (Illus.). 116p. (Orig.). 1992. pap. text 16.00 (*0-88698-156-5*, 3.70220) PETEX.

Petroleum Geology for Geophysicists & Engineers. Richard C. Selley. 439p. 1988. pap. 24.00 (*0-685-26605-2*) P-H.

Petroleum Geology Handbook. Ed. by N. A. Eremenko & George V. Chilingarian. LC 90-27091. (Translations Series in Petroleum Sciences). (ENG & RUS., Illus.). 616p. (Orig.). 1991. text 98.00 (*0-911575-69-3*) Optimization Soft.

Petroleum Geology of Ireland's Offshore Basins. Ed. by P. F. Croker & P. M. Shannon. (Geological Society Special Publication Ser.: No. 93). (Illus.). 504p. 1995. 117.00 (*1-897799-34-9*, 335, Pub. by Geol Soc Pub Hse) AAPG.

Petroleum Geology of North Africa. Ed. by D. S. Macgregor et al. (Geological Society Special Publication Ser.: No. 132). 448p. 1998. 142.00 (*1-86239-004-5*, Pub. by Geol Soc Pub Hse) AAPG.

Petroleum Geology of Northwest Europe: Proceedings of the 4th Conference. Ed. by J. R. Parker. (Illus.). 1600p. (C). 1993. 250.00 (*0-903317-85-0*, 294, Pub. by Geol Soc Pub Hse) AAPG.

***Petroleum Geology of Northwest Europe: Proceedings of the 5th Conference.** Ed. by A. J. Fleet & S. A. Boldy. 1408p. 1999. 250.00 (*1-86239-039-8*, Pub. by Geol Soc Pub Hse) AAPG.

Petroleum Geology of Northwestern Europe. Ed. by J. Brooks & K. W. Glennie. (C). 1988. lib. bdg. 535.50 (*0-86010-703-5*, Pub. by Graham & Trotman) Kluwer Academic.

Petroleum Geology of Southeast Asia. Ed. by A. J. Fraser et al. (Geological Society Special Publication Ser.: No. 126). (Illus.). 384p. 1997. 125.00 (*1-897799-91-8*, Pub. by Geol Soc Pub Hse) AAPG.

Petroleum Geology of the Devonian & Mississippian Black Shale of North America. Ed. by J. B. Roen & R. C. Kepferle. (Illus.). 358p. (Orig.). (C). 1994. pap. text 95.00 (*0-7881-0354-7*) DIANE Pub.

Petroleum Geology of the Irish Sea & Adjacent Areas. Ed. by N. Meadows et al. (Geological Society Special Publication Ser.: No. 124). (Illus.). 408p. 1997. 125.00 (*1-897799-84-5*, Pub. by Geol Soc Pub Hse) AAPG.

Petroleum Geology of the Mid-Continent. Ed. by Bailey Rascoe, Jr. & Norman J. Hyne. (Illus.). 162p. (C). 1988. 35.00 (*0-945087-00-4*) Tulsa Geol Soc.

Petroleum Geology of the North European. Norwegian Petroleum Society Staff. 444p. 1984. lib. bdg. 192.50 (*0-86010-486-9*) G & T Inc.

***Petroleum Geology of the North Sea: Basic Concepts & Recent Advances.** 4th ed. K. W. Glennie. LC 97-29316. (Illus.). 636p. 1998. pap. 85.00 (*0-632-03845-4*) Blackwell Sci.

Petroleum Geology of the Southern North Sea: Future Potential. Ed. by K. Ziegler et al. (Geological Society Special Publication Ser.: No. 123). (Illus.). 216p. 1997. 99.00 (*1-897799-82-9*, Pub. by Geol Soc Pub Hse) AAPG.

Petroleum Handbook. 6th rev. ed. Royal Dutch-Shell Group of Companies Staff. 710p. 1983. 303.25 (*0-444-42118-1*) Elsevier.

Petroleum Hydrocarbon Contamination: Legal & Technical Considerations. Robert Morrison et al. 332p. 1998. pap. 99.73 (*1-890501-02-6*) Argent Commns.

Petroleum in the Marine Environment. Ed. by Leon Petrakis & F. T. Weiss. LC 79-25524. (ACS Advances in Chemistry Ser.: No. 185). 1980. 60.95 (*0-8412-0475-6*) Am Chemical.

Petroleum in the Marine Environment. Ed. by Leonidas Petrakis & Fred T. Weiss. LC 79-25524. (Advances in Chemistry Ser.: Vol. 185). 382p. 1980. reprint ed. pap. 118.50 (*0-608-03857-1*, 206430400008) Bks Demand.

***Petroleum Industry: A Nontechnical Guide.** Charles F. Conaway. LC 99-45825. 1999. write for info. (*0-87814-777-2*) PennWell Bks.

***Petroleum, Industry & Governments - An Introduction to Petroleum Regulation, Economics.** Bernard G. Taverne. 456p. 2000. 156.00 (*90-411-9747-8*) Kluwer Law Intl.

Petroleum Industry & the Future Petroleum Province in Pennsylvania. 3rd ed. Dana R. Kelley et al. (Mineral Resource Reports: No. 65). (Illus.). 39p. 1983. reprint ed. pap. 2.85 (*0-8182-0037-5*) Commonweal PA.

Petroleum Industry Dictionary: Russian-English. D. E. Stoliarov. 432p. 1982. lib. bdg. 75.00 (*0-8288-2494-0*) Fr & Eur.

Petroleum Industry in the United Kingdom: Proceedings of the Joint Meeting of the Institute of Petroleum & the Deutsche Gesellschaft fur Mineralolwissenschaft und the Kohlechemie e V., London, 11-12 November, 1965. Ed. by Peter Hepple. LC 66-6024. 198p. reprint ed. pap. 61.40 (*0-608-13882-7*, 202369700033) Bks Demand.

Petroleum Law Guide, 1985. W. P. Winston. 160p. 1985. 57.75 (*0-85334-331-4*) Elsevier.

Petroleum Liquids: Fire & Energy Control. Edward Hawthorne. (Illus.). 112p. 1986. pap. text 36.00 (*0-89303-769-9*) P-H.

Petroleum Marketing. Jack Humbert et al. (Career Competencies in Marketing Ser.). (Illus.). (YA). (gr. 11-12). 1979. text 12.04 (*0-07-031206-0*) McGraw.

Petroleum Marketing & Transportation - New Ideas, New Methods, New Developments: Proceedings of the Institute on Marketing & Transportation in the Petroleum Industry, 1963, Dallas. LC 64-18180. 224p. reprint ed. pap. 69.50 (*0-608-18165-X*, 203287000081) Bks Demand.

Petroleum Marketing Annual, 2 vols. 1994. lib. bdg. 495.00 (*0-8490-5756-6*) Gordon Pr.

Petroleum Marketing Annual, 2 vols., Set. 1995. lib. bdg. 600.00 (*0-8490-6500-3*) Gordon Pr.

Petroleum Marketing Annual (1993) (Illus.). 412p. (Orig.). (C). 1995. pap. text 95.00 (*0-7881-1857-9*) DIANE Pub.

Petroleum Marketing Annual (1992) (Illus.). 428p. (Orig.). (C). 1994. pap. text 95.00 (*0-7881-0501-9*) DIANE Pub.

Petroleum Marketing in Africa: Issues in Pricing, Taxation & Investment. M. R. Bhagavan. (Illus.). 192p. 1999. pap. 25.00 (*1-85649-666-X*); text 59.95 (*1-85649-665-1*) St Martin.

Petroleum Marketing Monthly. Government Printing Office Staff. 1983. pap. text 101.00 (*0-16-012592-8*) USGPO.

Petroleum Mechanical Engineering Conference & Workshop: Presented at the 1979 Petroleum Mechanical Engineering Conference & Workshop, Tulsa, Oklahoma, October 28-30, 1979. Petroleum Mechanical Engineering Conference & Work. Ed. by S. L. Collier. LC 79-54866. (Illus.). 120p. reprint ed. pap. 37.20 (*0-8357-2892-7*, 203912800011) Bks Demand.

Petroleum Migration. Ed. by W. A. England & A. J. Fleet. (Geological Society Special Publications Classic: Vol. 59). (Illus.). 280p. 1996. 34.00 (*1-897799-50-0*, 261, Pub. by Geol Soc Pub Hse) AAPG.

Petroleum 1996: Issues & Trends. 163p. 1997. per. 15.00 (*0-16-063494-6*) USGPO.

Petroleum Panorama. Simon Miron. 2000. write for info. (*1-57524-096-3*) Krieger.

***Petroleum Panorama.** Simon Miron. 2000. pap. write for info. (*1-57524-102-1*) Krieger.

P

Petroleum Pipelines & Public Policy, 1906-1959. Arthur M. Johnson. LC 67-27087. (Studies in Business History: No. 24). (Illus.). 588p. reprint ed. pap. 182.30 (*0-8357-9173-4*, 201673100005) Bks Demand.

Petroleum Politics & the Texas Railroad Commission. David F. Prindle. LC 81-7535. (Elma Dill Russell Spencer Foundation Ser.: No. 12). (Illus.). 240p. (C). 1984. pap. 10.95 (*0-292-76489-8*) U of Tex Pr.

Petroleum Potential of the Palo Duro Basin, Texas Panhandle. S. P. Dutton et al. (Reports of Investigations: RI 123). (Illus.). 87p. 1982. pap. 5.00 (*0-318-03264-3*) Bur Econ Geology.

Petroleum Prices: Past, Present & Prospective. William Brown. 135p. 1987. pap. text 10.00 (*1-55813-003-9*) Hudson Instit IN.

Petroleum Processing Handbook. John J. McKetta. (Illus.). 792p. 1992. text 299.00 (*0-8247-8681-5*) Dekker.

Petroleum Processing Handbook. Ed. by William F. Bland & Robert L. Davidson. LC 64-66366. (Illus.). 1114p. reprint ed. pap. 200.00 (*0-8357-3610-5*, AU0039500003) Bks Demand.

Petroleum Production in Nontechnical Language. 2nd rev. ed. Forest Gray. LC 95-30721. 1995. 64.95 (*0-87814-450-1*) PennWell Bks.

Petroleum Production Operations. Lewis W. Hall. Ed. by Jodie Leecraft. (Illus.). 159p. (Orig.). 1986. pap. text 25.00 (*0-88698-124-7*, 3.90210) PETEX.

Petroleum Production Systems. Michael J. Economides et al. LC 93-36626. 624p. (C). 1993. 105.00 (*0-13-658683-X*) P-H.

Petroleum Products: Instability & Incompatibility. George W. Mushrush & James G. Speight. 300p. 1995. 95.00 (*1-56032-297-7*) Taylor & Francis.

***Petroleum Refinery Equipment in India: A Strategic Entry Report, 1998.** Compiled by Icon Group International Staff. (Country Industry Report). (Illus.). 191p. 1999. ring bd. 1910.00 incl. audio compact disk (*0-7418-0279-1*) Icon Grp.

Petroleum Refinery Process Economics. Robert E. Maples. LC 92-37931. 384p. 1993. 89.95 (*0-87814-384-X*, P4488) PennWell Bks.

***Petroleum Refinery Process Economics.** 2nd ed. Robert E. Maples. LC 00-39188. 2000. pap. write for info. (*0-87814-779-9*) PennWell Bks.

Petroleum Refining: Technology & Economics. 3rd expanded rev. ed. James H. Gary & Glenn E. Handwerk. LC 93-6361. (Illus.). 488p. 1993. text 69.75 (*0-8247-9157-6*) Dekker.

Petroleum Refining Vol. 1: Crude Oil, Petroleum Products, Process Flowsheets. J. P. Waquier. 468p. 1996. 145.00 (*2-7108-0685-1*, 06851) Gulf Pub.

Petroleum Refining for the Nontechnical Person. 2nd ed. William L. Leffler. 184p. 1985. 64.95 (*0-87814-280-0*) PennWell Bks.

Petroleum Refining in Africa: Origin, Growth & Prospects. Adeyinka Orimalade. (C). 1989. 22.00 (*81-7023-211-2*, Pub. by Allied Pubs) S Asia.

***Petroleum Refining in Nontechnical Language.** 3rd ed. William L. Leffler. LC 00-21021. 2000. write for info. (*0-87814-776-4*) PennWell Bks.

Petroleum Refining Process Handbook. 2nd ed. Ed. by Robert A. Meyers. LC 96-26991. (Illus.). 848p. 1996. 105.00 (*0-07-041796-2*) McGraw.

Petroleum Related Rock Mechanics. E. Fjaer et al. (Developments in Petroleum Science Ser.: Vol. 33). xiv,338p. 1992. 159.00 (*0-444-88913-2*) Elsevier.

Petroleum Research & Venezuela's Intevep: The Clash of the Giants. Emma Brossard. LC 93-13661. 250p. 1993. 25.00 (*0-87814-399-8*) PennWell Bks.

Petroleum Reserve Responsiveness in the United States: A Comparison of Alternate Forecasting Methods. J. Reeves Ferry. LC 92-37544. (Government & the Economy Ser.). 184p. 1993. text 10.00 (*0-8153-1223-7*) Garland.

Petroleum Reservoir Engineering Physical Properties. James W. Amyx et al. (C). 1960. 116.25 (*0-07-001600-3*) McGraw.

Petroleum Resources of the Paradox Basin, 1984. Keith M. Clem & Karl W. Brown. (Bulletin of the Utah Geological Survey Ser.: No. 119). (Illus.). 162p. (Orig.). 1984. pap. 15.00 (*1-55791-086-3*, B-119) Utah Geological Survey.

Petroleum Resources on the Norwegian Continental Shelf. Norwegian Petroleum Directorate Staff. 1997. pap. 75.00 (*82-7257-512-4*, Pub. by Oljedirektoratet) St Mut.

Petroleum Retailing: Europe & the U. K.: Papers Presented at an Energy Economics Group Conference on 20-21 May 1987. Institute of Petroleum, London Staff. Ed. by T. S. Radford. LC HD9560.9. 104p. reprint ed. pap. 32.30 (*0-7837-6844-3*, 204667300003) Bks Demand.

Petroleum Secretary's Handbook. 2nd ed. Willene J. Lilly. LC 84-27384. 352p. 1985. 25.00 (*0-87814-278-9*, P4369) PennWell Bks.

Petroleum Sector Guide in Lebanon. Adel Nodawar. (ARA., Illus.). 216p. 1996. pap. 8.00 (*1-886604-01-0*) Lebanese Ctr.

Petroleum Sedimentology. Winfried Zimmerle. 424p. (C). 1995. pap. text 63.50 (*0-7923-3419-1*); lib. bdg. 169.00 (*0-7923-3418-3*) Kluwer Academic.

Petroleum Shipping Industry. Michael D. Tusiani. LC 96-39044. 1996. 64.95 (*0-87814-670-9*) PennWell Bks.

Petroleum Shipping Industry, Vol. 2. Michael D. Tusiani. 1996. 69.95 (*0-87814-671-7*) PennWell Bks.

Petroleum Source Rocks. Barry J. Katz. LC 94-28601. (Casebooks in Earth Sciences Ser.). 1995. 152.95 (*0-387-57864-1*) Spr-Verlag.

Petroleum Supply & Demand: Report of the Summer Meeting of the Institute of Petroleum held at Brighton, 1965. Ed. by Peter Hepple. LC 66-5547. 152p. reprint ed. pap. 47.20 (*0-608-13885-1*, 202369800033) Bks Demand.

Petroleum Supply Annual, 3 vols. 1995. lib. bdg. 899.99 (*0-8490-6501-1*) Gordon Pr.

Petroleum Supply Annual, 1996, Vol. 1. 181p. 1997. per. 18.00 (*0-16-063485-7*) USGPO.

Petroleum Supply Annual, 1996, Vol. 2. 607p. 1997. per. 52.00 (*0-16-063486-5*) USGPO.

***Petroleum Supply Annual, 1997, Vol. 1.** 143p. 1998. per. 12.00 (*0-16-063532-2*) USGPO.

***Petroleum Supply Annual, 1997, Vol. 2.** 607p. 1998. per. 54.00 (*0-16-063533-0*) USGPO.

Petroleum Supply Monthly. Government Printing Office Staff. pap. text 87.00 (*0-16-012599-5*) USGPO.

Petroleum System: From Source to Trap. Ed. by Leslie B. Magoon & Wallace G. Dow. LC 94-240285. (AAPG Memoir Ser.: No. 60). (Illus.). 655p. 1994. 114.00 (*0-89181-338-1*, 588) AAPG.

Petroleum Well Construction. Michael J. Economides & B. N. Murali. LC 97-31698. 640p. 1998. 350.00 (*0-471-96938-9*) Wiley.

***Petrolia: The Landscape of America's First Oil Boom.** Brian Black. LC 99-42473. (Creating the North American Landscape Ser.). 248p. 2000. 42.50 (*0-8018-6317-1*) Johns Hopkins.

Petrological Study of the Sambagawa Metamorphic Rocks: The Kanto Mountains, Central Japan. Mitsuhiro Toriumi. LC 76-365163. 117p. reprint ed. pap. 36.30 (*0-608-01561-X*, 206197700001) Bks Demand.

Petrology: Igneous & Metamorphic Rocks: Proceedings of the 27th International Geological Congress, Vol. 9. International Geological Congress Staff. 614p. 1984. lib. bdg. 147.00 (*90-6764-018-2*, Pub. by VSP) Coronet Bks.

Petrology: Igneous, Sedimentary, & Metamorphic. Ernest G. Ehlers & Harvey Blatt. LC 81-12517. (Illus.). 732p. (C). 1982. pap. text 69.95 (*0-7167-1279-2*) W H Freeman.

***Petrology: Igneous Sedimentary & Metamorphic.** 3rd ed. Blatt & Tracy. 2000. pap. text. write for info. (*0-7167-3743-4*) W H Freeman.

Petrology: The Study of Igneous, Sedimentary & Metamorphic Rocks. Loren A. Raymon. 240p. (C). 1995. student ed., spiral bd. write for info. (*0-697-05976-6*, WCB McGr Hill) McGrw-H Hghr Educ.

Petrology: The Study of Igneous, Sedimentary & Metamorphic Rocks. Loren A. Raymond. 672p. (C). 1994. text. write for info. (*0-697-00190-3*, WCB McGr Hill) McGrw-H Hghr Educ.

Petrology, Age, Geochemistry & Correlation of the Tertiary Volcanic Rocks of the Awapa Plateau, Garfield, Piute & Wayne Counties, Utah. Stephen R. Mattox. (Miscellaneous Publication Ser.: Vol. 91-5). (Illus.). 46p. 1991. pap. 6.25 (*1-55791-314-5*, MP-91-5) Utah Geological Survey.

Petrology & Genesis of Leucite-Bearing Rocks. A. Gupta & Kunio Yagi. (Minerals & Rocks Ser.: Vol. 14). (Illus.). 250p. 1980. 56.95 (*0-387-09864-X*) Spr-Verlag.

Petrology & Geochemistry of Continental Rifts. Ed. by Else-Ragnhild Neumann & Ivar B. Ramberg. (NATO Advanced Study Institutes Series C: No. 36). 1978. text 177.50 (*90-277-0866-5*) Kluwer Academic.

Petrology & Reservoir Characteristics of the Lower Silurian Medina Group Sandstones, Athens & Geneva Fields, Crawford County Pennsylvania. Christopher D. Laughrey. (Mineral Resource Reports: No. 85). (Illus.). 126p. 1984. pap. 6.35 (*0-8182-0054-5*) Commonweal PA.

Petrology & Structure of Gneiss Anticlines near Baltimore, Maryland. 1989. 13.00 (*0-87590-585-4*) Am Geophysical.

Petrology, Geochemistry & Economic Geology of the Qaquarssuk Carbonatite Complex, Southern West Greenland. Christian Knudsen. (Monograph Series on Mineral Deposits: No. 29). (Illus.). iv, 110p. 1991. 79.00 (*3-443-12029-6*, Pub. by Gebruder Borntraeger) Balogh.

Petrology of Archaeological Artifacts. Ed. by D. R. Kempe & Anthony P. Harvey. (Illus.). 390p. 1983. text 69.00 (*0-19-854418-9*) OUP.

Petrology of Igneous & Metamorphic Rocks. 2nd ed. Donald W. Hyndman. 720p. (C). 1984. text 78.74 (*0-07-031658-9*) McGraw.

Petrology of Lamproites. R. H. Mitchell & S. C. Bergman. (Illus.). 440p. (C). 1991. 95.00 (*0-306-43556-X*, Plenum Trade) Perseus Pubng.

Petrology of Laterities & Tropical Soils. Yves Tardy. (Illus.). 408p. (C). 1997. text 88.00 (*90-5410-678-6*, Pub. by A A Balkema) Ashgate Pub Co.

Petrology of Sedimentary Rocks. Sam Boggs, Jr. (Illus.). 720p. (C). 1991. text 63.80 (*0-02-311790-7*, Macmillan Coll) P-H.

Petrology of Sedimentary Rocks. 4th ed. Robert L. Folk. LC 80-83557. (Illus.). (C). 1980. 17.95 (*0-914696-14-9*) Hemphill.

Petrology of the Duke Island Ultramafic Complex, Southeastern Alaska. T. N. Irvine. LC 73-87233. (Geological Society of America, Memoir Ser.: No. 138). 310p. reprint ed. pap. 96.10 (*0-608-13874-6*, 202373600033) Bks Demand.

Petrology of the Metamorphic Rocks. R. Mason. (Textbook of Petrology Ser.). (Illus.). 1978. pap. text 24.95 (*0-04-552014-3*) Routledge.

Petrology of the Metamorphic Rocks. 2nd ed. Mason. (Illus.). 240p. (C). 1990. text 90.50 (*0-04-552027-5*) Routledge.

Petrology of the Metamorphic Rocks. 2nd ed. Mason. (Illus.). 240p. (C). 1990. pap. text 37.95 (*0-04-552028-3*) Thomson Learn.

Petrology of the Sedimentary Rocks. 7th ed. J. T. Greensmith. (Illus.). 288p. 1988. text 55.00 (*0-04-552029-1*) Routledge.

Petrology of the Sedimentary Rocks. 7th ed. J. T. Greensmith. (Illus.). 288p. 1989. 42.95 (*0-04-552030-5*) Thomson Learn.

Petrology, Sedimentology & Stratigraphic Implications of the Rock Canyon Conglomerate, Southwestern Utah. R. LaRell Nielson. (Miscellaneous Publication Ser.: Vol. 91-7). (Illus.). 65p. 1991. pap. 6.00 (*1-55791-316-1*, MP-91-7) Utah Geological Survey.

Petrology, Structure, & Geologic History of the Catalina Schist Terrain, Southern California. John P. Platt. LC 74-22941. (University of California Publications in Social Welfare: Vol. 112). (Illus.). 141p. reprint ed. pap. 43.80 (*0-608-18017-3*, 201496200017) Bks Demand.

***Petronella.** Jay Williams. (Illus.). 32p. (J). (gr. 3-7). 2000. 15.95 (*0-9677929-1-6*) Moon Mt Pubng Inc.

Petronii. 4th ed. Ed. by Muller. (LAT.). 1995. pap. 29.95 (*3-519-01580-3*, T1580, Pub. by B G Teubner) U of Mich Pr.

Petronius: Cena Trimalchionis. rev. ed. Petronius Arbiter. Ed. by Thomas Cutt. LC 73-105090. (Wayne State University Classical Texts Ser.). 135p. reprint ed. pap. 41.90 (*0-7837-3644-4*, 204351300009) Bks Demand.

Petronius: Selections from the Satyricon. Ed. by Gilbert Lawall. (Textbook Ser.). (Illus.). 260p. (Orig.). 1995. pap. text 18.00 (*0-86516-288-3*) Bolchazy-Carducci.

Petronius - Concordantia Petroniana. Ed. by Matthias Korn & Stefan Reitzer. (Alpha-Omega, Reihe A Ser.: Bd. LXXI). (GER.). 252p. 1986. write for info. (*3-487-07695-0*) G Olms Pubs.

Petronius the Poet: Verse & Literary Traditions in the Satyricon. Catherine Connors. LC 97-6743. 180p. (C). 1998. text 54.95 (*0-521-59231-3*) Cambridge U Pr.

***Petronov Plan.** large type ed. James Pattinson. 312p. 2000. pap. 18.99 (*0-7089-5674-2*, Linford) Ulverscroft.

Petrophysics: Theory & Practice of Measuring Reservoir Rock & Fluid Properties. Djebbar Tiab & Erle C. Donaldson. LC 96-23132. (Illus.). 608p. 1996. 145.00 (*0-88415-634-6*, 5634); pap., student ed. 75.00 (*0-88415-636-2*, 5636) Gulf Pub.

Petrophysics: Theory & Practice of Measuring Reservoir Rock & Fluid Properties, Solutions Manual. Djebbar Tlab & Erle C. Donaldson. (Illus.). 50p. 1996. pap., teacher ed. 20.00 (*0-88415-635-4*, 5635) Gulf Pub.

Petroplyphs of South-Eastern Anatolia. Muvaffak Uyanik. LC 76-371373. (Monographs & Documentations). (ENG, FRE, ITA & TUR., Illus.). 107p. 1974. write for info. (*3-201-00880-X*) Akademische Druck-und.

Petroquimica y Sociedad. Susana C. Pangtay. (Ciencia para Todos Ser.). (SPA.). pap. 6.99 (*968-16-2669-9*, Pub. by Fondo) Continental Bk.

Petrouchka. Vivian Werner. 1999. pap. 3.95 (*0-14-054333-3*) NAL.

Petrouchka: A Ballet Cut-Out Book. Leonard Marcus. (Illus.). 16p. (J). (gr. 3-6). 1983. pap. 12.95 (*0-87923-469-5*) Godine.

Petrouchka: Stravinsky. 12p. (Orig.). (YA). 1994. pap. 17.00 (*0-89898-795-4*, BMR05095) Wrner Bros.

Petrouchka's Cry: A Biography. Charles Payne. 1992. write for info. (*0-679-40045-1*) McKay.

Petrucciani Artist Transcriptions. 1992. 17.95 (*0-7935-1512-2*, 00673226) H Leonard.

Petrucci's Harmonice Musices Odhecaton A. Ed. by Helen Hewitt. LC 77-25989. (Music Reprint Ser.). 1978. reprint ed. lib. bdg. 55.00 (*0-306-77562-X*) Da Capo.

Petruchio. Mark Dunster. 20p. (Orig.). 1995. pap. 5.00 (*0-89642-267-4*) Linden Pubs.

Petrukian. Jay O'Callahan. (YA). (gr. 2 up). 1994. 10.00 incl. audio (*1-877954-11-X*) Artana Prodns.

Petrus Alfonsi & His Medieval Readers. John V. Tolan. LC 93-7947. (Illus.). 256p. 1993. 49.95 (*0-8130-1238-4*); pap. 18.95 (*0-8130-1239-2*) U Press Fla.

Petrus Christus: His Place in Fifteenth-Century Flemish Painting. Joel M. Upton. LC 88-43440. (Illus.). 256p. 1990. lib. bdg. 50.00 (*0-271-00672-2*) Pa St U Pr.

Petrus Christus: Renaissance Master of Bruges. Maryan W. Ainsworth. LC 93-47600. (Illus.). 232p. 1994. pap. 35.00 (*0-87099-695-9*) Metro Mus Art.

Petrus Lotichius Secundus (1528-1560) Neo-Latin Poet. Stephen Zon. (American University Studies: Germanic Languages & Literature: Ser. I, Vol. 13). 420p. (C). 1983. pap. text 39.45 (*0-8204-0020-3*) P Lang Pubng.

Petrus Thomae, O. F. M. Quodlibet. M. Rachel Hooper. Ed. by Elgius M. Buytaert. xiv, 242p. 1957. pap. 11.00 (*1-57659-055-0*) Franciscan Inst.

Petrus und der Lieblingsjunger Im Johannesevangelium: Amt und Autoritat. Lutz Simon. (Europaische Hochschulschriften Ser.: Reihe 23, Bc. 498). (GER.). XLIII, 290p. 1994. 55.95 (*3-631-46433-9*) P Lang Pubng.

Petrushka see Little Box of Ballet Stories

Petrushka Igor Stravinsky. 1999. pap. 4.95 (*0-486-40870-1*) Dover.

Petrushka: Sources & Contexts. Andrew Wachtel. LC 98-12189. 176p. 1998. 35.00 (*0-8101-1566-2*) Northwestern U Pr.

Petrushka & the Dancer: The Diaries of John Cowper Powys, 1929-1939. John Cowper Powys. Ed. by Morine Krissdottir. LC 95-17084. (Illus.). xxvii, 340p. 1995. text 45.00 (*0-312-12770-7*) St Martin.

Petrushka in Full Score: Original Version. Igor Stravinsky. 160p. 1988. pap. 9.95 (*0-486-25680-4*) Dover.

Petrushka Stavinsky. Igor Stravinsky. Ed. by Charles Hamm. (Illus.). (Orig.). (C). 1967. pap. text 16.75 (*0-393-09770-6*) Norton.

Pets see Child's First Library of Learning

Pets. (Giant Step Picture Library). (Illus.). 16p. (J). (gr. k up). 1990. 9.95 (*0-88679-904-X*) Educ Insights.

***Pets!** Marion Adler et al. 70p. 1999. pap. 5.95 (*0-87129-934-8*, P87) Dramatic Pub.

Pets. Sandy Bigg. 1995. 3.95 (*1-55708-484-X*, MCT1015) McDonald Pub Co.

Pets. Boy Scouts of America. (Illus.). 64p. (YA). (gr. 6-12). 1984. pap. 2.90 (*0-8395-3281-4*, 33281) BSA.

***Pets.** Ed. by Brighter Vision Staff. (Little Books to Make & Read). (Illus.). 2000. pap. 1.49 (*1-55254-066-9*) Brighter Vision.

"Pets!" Melrose Cooper. LC 97-16173. (Illus.). 32p. (J). (ps-2). 1998. text 15.95 (*0-8050-3893-0*) St Martin.

Pets. Lorenz Staff. (Let's Look Ser.). 1998. 4.95 (*1-85967-761-4*) Anness Pub.

Pets. Macmillan Children's Book Staff. (Illus.). 12p. (J). (ps-3). 1997. 12.00 (*0-679-88421-1*, Pub. by Knopf Bks Yng Read) Random.

Pets. Terry Nutkins & Marshall Corwin. (Illus.). 48p. (J). (gr. 7-9). 1992. pap. 8.95 (*0-563-34524-1*, BBC-Parkwest) Parkwest Pubns.

Pets. Tony Ross. LC 94-36609. (Little Princess Board Bks.). (Illus.). 14p. (J). (ps). 1995. pap. 6.00 (*0-15-200318-5*, Red Wagon Bks) Harcourt.

Pets. Angela Royston. LC 97-19349. (Inside & Out Ser.). (Illus.). 24p. (J). 1998. write for info. (*1-57572-177-5*) Heinemann Lib.

***Pets.** Running Press Staff. (Fit-A-Shape Ser.). 1999. 5.95 (*0-7624-0608-9*) Running Pr.

Pets. Stewart. (Illus.). 32p. (J). pap. 1.00 (*0-486-29955-4*) Dover.

***Pets.** rev. ed. Claire Watts. (First Look at Animals Ser.). (Illus.). (J). 2000. pap. 3.95 (*1-58728-864-8*) Two Can Pub.

Pets: A Comprehensive Handbook for Kids. 4th rev. ed. Frances N. Chrystie. Ed. by Margery Facklam. LC 94-41229. (Illus.). 256p. (J). 1994. pap. 8.95 (*0-316-14281-6*) Little.

Pets: Alphabet Dot to Dot: Educational Activity-Coloring Book. Peter M. Spizzirri. Ed. by Linda Spizzirri. (Illus.). 32p. (J). (gr. k-3). 1992. pap. 1.25 (*0-86545-209-1*) Spizzirri.

Pets: Never Dance with a Tree Frog Anita Higman. LC 98-177607. (Cover-To-Cover Bks.). 56 p. 1997. write for info. (*0-7807-6136-7*, Covercraft) Perfection Learn.

Pets: Part of the Family: The Total Care Guide for All the Pets in Your Life. Mark Bricklin & Editors of Pets: Part of the Family Magazine. (Illus.). 1999. 27.95 (*1-57954-125-9*) Rodale Pr Inc.

Pets: Part of the Family: The Total Care Guide for All the Pets in Your Life. Mark Bricklin & Pets: Part of the Family Magazine Editors. LC 98-32094. (Illus.). 1999. pap. 16.95 (*1-57954-136-4*) Rodale Pr Inc.

Pets: Wacky Words. Greg Lee. LC 92-43964. (Little Jokester Ser.). (J). (gr. 3 up). 1993. 9.50 (*0-685-66291-8*) Rourke Corp.

Pets: Wacky Words. Greg Lee. LC 92-43964. (Little Jokester Ser.). 24p. (J). (gr. k-4). 1996. lib. bdg. 10.95 (*0-86593-266-2*) Rourke Corp.

Pets & Allergiees. 192p. 1999. 17.95 (*0-87605-019-4*) Howell Bks.

Pets & Domestic Animals: Index of Modern Information. Sally S. Wismar. LC 88-47609. 150p. 1988. 47.50 (*0-88164-800-0*); pap. 44.50 (*0-88164-801-9*) ABBE Pubs Assn.

Pets & Farm Animals. Ed. by Christine J. Dillon. (My First Report Ser.). (Illus.). 52p. (J). (gr. 1-3). 1995. ring bd. 5.95 (*1-57896-016-9*, 2170) Hewitt Res Fnd.

Pets & Farm Animals. Linda Losito et al. (Encyclopedia of the Animal World Ser.). (Illus.). 96p. (J). (gr. 4-9). 1990. 19.95 (*0-8160-1969-X*) Facts on File.

Pets & Mental Health. Intro. by Odean Cusack. LC 88-9671. 241p. 1988. text 39.95 (*0-86656-652-X*); pap. text 14.95 (*0-86656-801-8*) Haworth Pr.

Pets & People, Level 5. E. Evertts. (J). 1983. 16.00 (*0-03-061386-8*) Harcourt Schl Pubs.

Pets & People: The Psychology of Pet Ownership. Barrie Gunter. 1999. pap. 29.95 (*1-86156-116-4*) Whurr Pub.

Pets & Plums. Alan M. Hofmeister et al. (Reading for All Learners Ser.). (Illus.). (J). pap. write for info. (*1-56861-196-X*) Swift Lrn Res.

Pets & the Elderly: The Therapeutic Bond. Ed. by Odean Cusack & Elaine Smith. LC 83-26409. (Activities, Adaptation & Aging Ser.: Vol. 4, Nos. 2 & 3). (Illus.). 257p. 1984. text 49.95 (*0-86656-259-1*, B259) Haworth Pr.

Pets & the Family. Ed. by Marvin B. Sussman. LC 85-8410. (Marriage & Family Review Ser.: Vol. 8, Nos. 3-4). 238p. 1985. text 49.95 (*0-86656-358-X*); pap. text 19.95 (*0-86656-360-1*) Haworth Pr.

Pets, Animals & Creatures. Stanley H. Collins. (Beginning Sign Language Ser.). (Illus.). 29p. (J). (ps up). 1997. pap. 4.95 (*0-931993-89-X*, GP-089) Garlic Pr OR.

***Pets, Children & Spirit Maturity: Reflections on the Inner Journey.** Gene W. Marshall. 42p. 2000. pap. 8.00 (*1-890945-04-8*) Realistic Living.

Pets for Fun & Profit. large type ed. Julie A. Rach. (For Fun & Profit Ser.). (Illus.). 300p. Date not set. pap. 24.95 (*1-56559-912-8*) HGI-Over Fifty.

Pets in a Jar: Collecting & Caring for Small Animals. Seymour Simon. (Storybooks Ser.). (Illus.). (J). (gr. 4-8). 1979. pap. 5.99 (*0-14-049186-4*, PuffinBks) Peng Put Young Read.

Pets in a Jar: Collecting & Caring for Small Wild Animals. Seymour Simon. (Puffin Science Bks.). (J). 1979. 11.19 (*0-606-02224-4*, Pub. by Turtleback) Demco.

Pets in Paradise: Keeping Your Dog & Cat Healthy & Happy in Hawaii. Toni Polancy. (Illus.). 96p. 1999. pap. 12.95 (*0-9666253-1-5*, Pub. by Barefoot Pub) Booklines Hawaii.

Pets in Therapy. Ed. by Margaret Abdill & Denise Juppe. LC 97-16973. (Illus.). 214p. 1997. pap. 15.00 (*1-882883-29-2*, 312) Idyll Arbor.

Pets in Trumpets & Other Word-Play Riddles. Bernard Most. LC 90-23873. (Illus.). 32p. (J). (ps-3). 1991. 12.95 (*0-15-261210-6*, Harcourt Child Bks) Harcourt.

Pets Letters to God BRICKLIN. pap. 49.75 (*1-57954-223-9*) Rodale Pr Inc.

P

An Asterisk (*) at the beginning of an entry indicates that the title is appearing for the first time.

***Pets Letters to God.** Mark Bricklin. LC 99-35543. 96p. 1999. 9.95 (*1-57954-208-5*) Rodale Pr Inc.

***Pets Living with Cancer: A Pet Owner's Resource Guide.** Robin Downing. 144p. 2000. pap. 19.95 (*1-58326-022-6*, AAHA Pr) Am Animal Hosp Assoc.

Pets Need Scrapbooks Too! A Start-to-Finish Guide for Creating a Lasting Memory of Your Family Pet. Amber Russell. (Illus.). 80p. 1999. pap. 15.95 (*0-9666639-1-8*, Pub. by Ambers Albums) Partners Pubs Grp.

Pets on Parade. Abbie Dee & Annie Scott. (Emergent Reader Ser.). 14p. (J). (ps-1). 1991. pap. text 4.25 (*1-56843-075-2*) EMG Networks.

Pets on Parade: Big Book. Abbie Dee & Annie Scott. (Emergent Reader Ser.). 14p. (J). (ps-1). 1991. pap. text 21.00 (*1-56843-027-2*) EMG Networks.

Pets' Peeves: Dogs Speak Out! Anita L. Pace. (Illus.). 104p. (Orig.). 1997. pap. 6.95 (*0-9631666-5-4*) Baby Steps Pr.

Pets, People, & Prayer: For Pet Lovers of All Ages. Illus. by Diane Allison. LC 97-224304. 48p. 1997. pap. 11.95 (*0-87510-326-X*, G61360) Writings of Mary Baker.

Pets-R-Permitted Hotel, Motel & Kennel Directory: The Travel Resource for Pet Owners Who Travel. Annenberg Communications Staff. Ed. by M. E. Nelson. 222p. 1992. pap. 9.95 (*1-56471-777-1*) Annenberg.

Pets-R-Permitted Hotel, Motel, Kennel & Petsitter Directory: Over 10,000 Petcare Options When You Travel. 5th rev. ed. Ed. by M. E. Nelson. (Illus.). 320p. (Orig.). 1995. pap. 10.95 (*1-56471-795-X*) Annenberg.

Pets-R-Permitted Hotel, Motel, Kennel & Petsitter Directory: Petcare Options When You Travel. Ed. by M. E. Nelson. 288p. (Orig.). 1993. pap. 9.95 (*1-56471-779-8*) Annenberg.

Pets Silhouettes. Sandbeck. 1998. pap. 1.00 (*0-486-27943-X*) Dover.

Pets Sticker Book. Nina Barbaresi. (Little Activity Bks.). (Illus.). (J). 1991. pap. 1.00 (*0-486-26389-4*) Dover.

Pets, Vets, & Marty Howard. Joan Carris. LC 84-47635. (Illus.). 192p. (J). (gr. 5 up). 1984. lib. bdg. 12.89 (*0-397-32093-0*) HarpC Child Bks.

Pets Welcome: A Guide to Hotels, Inns & Resorts That Welcome You & Your Pet. Dreamer Dawg. 1997. pap. text 14.95 (*1-888820-05-5*) Millennium Calif.

Pets Welcome: America's South. Kathleen D. Fish & Robert Fish. Ed. by Judy Marks. LC 97-71561. (Illus.). 224p. 1997. pap. text 15.95 (*1-883214-17-3*) Bon Vivant Pr.

Pets Welcome: California. Kathleen D. Fish & Robert Fish. Ed. by Judy Marks. LC 97-71559. (Illus.). 204p. 1997. pap. text 15.95 (*1-883214-12-2*) Bon Vivant Pr.

Pets Welcome: National Edition. Kathleen D. Fish & Robert Fish. Ed. by Judy Marks. LC 97-71370. (Illus.). 480p. 1998. pap. 19.95 (*1-883214-27-0*) Bon Vivant Pr.

Pets Welcome: New England. Kathleen D. Fish & Robert Fish. Ed. by Judy Marks. (Illus.). 224p. 1998. pap. text 15.95 (*1-883214-21-1*) Bon Vivant Pr.

Pets Welcome: Pacific Northwest Edition. Kathleen D. Fish & Robert Fish. Ed. by Judy Marks. (Illus.). 1998. pap. 15.95 (*1-883214-25-4*) Bon Vivant Pr.

Pets Welcome: Southwest. Kathleen D. Fish & Robert Fish. (Illus.). 224p. (Orig.). 1999. pap. 15.95 (*1-883214-26-2*) Bon Vivant Pr.

Pets Welcome TM: Mid - Atlantic & Chesapeake Edition. Kathleen Devanna Fish et al. (Pets Welcome Ser.). (Illus.). 224p. 1999. pap. 15.95 (*1-883214-29-7*) Bon Vivant Pr.

Pets You Love see Books for Young Explorers

Petsamo-Kirkenes Operation: Soviet Breakthrough & Pursuit in the Arctic, October 1944. James F. Gebhardt. 201p. 1990. per. 12.00 (*0-16-020527-1*) USGPO.

Petsitter's Mix. Barron's Educational Editors. 1999. pap. text 11.85 (*0-7641-7316-2*) Barron.

***Petspeak: Communication Breakthroughs for Closer Companionship with You.** Ed. by Editors of Pets: Part of the Family Magazine. (Illus.). 496p. 2000. pap. 16.95 (*1-57954-077-5*) Rodale Pr Inc.

***Petspeak: You're Closer Than You Think to a Great Relationship with Your Dog or Cat!** Pets Part of the Family Firm Staff. LC 00-9290. (Illus.). 496p. 2000. 16.95 (*1-57954-337-5*) Rodale Pr Inc.

Petted by the Light: The Most Profound & Complete Feline Near-Death Experiences Ever. Patrick R. Tobin & Christine R. Doley. (Illus.). 117p. 1995. 9.95 (*1-55972-314-9*, Birch Ln Pr) Carol Pub Group.

Pettibone's Law. John Keene. (Bluejacket Paperback Ser.). 368p. 1994. pap. 15.95 (*1-55750-454-7*) Naval Inst Pr.

***Petticoat Affair: Manners, Mutiny & Sex in Andrew Jackson's White House.** John F. Marszalek. (Illus.). 312p. 2000. pap. 16.95 (*0-8071-2634-9*) La State U Pr.

Petticoat Affair: Manners, Sex, & Mutiny in Andrew Jackson's White House. John F. Marszalek. LC 97-16099. (Illus.). 304p. 1998. 24.50 (*0-684-82801-4*) Free Pr.

Petticoat Dominant: or Woman's Revenge: Anon. Intro. by Michael R. Goss. LC 95-193918. 96p. 1994. 34.95 (*1-897767-02-1*, Pub. by Delectus Bks) Xclusiv Distrib.

Petticoat Loose. M. J. Molloy. (Irish Play Ser.). 1982. pap. 3.95 (*0-912262-76-1*) Proscenium.

Petticoat Mamas. Julie A. Waterman. 7p. (Orig.). 1982. pap. 1.25 (*0-943334-03-9*) Carmonelle Pubns.

***Petticoat Prisoners of Old Wyoming.** Larry K. Brown. LC 00-33460. 2000. pap. write for info. (*0-931271-56-8*) High Plains.

Petticoat Surgeon. Bertha Van Hoosen. Ed. by Annette K. Baxter. LC 79-8820. (Signal Lives Ser.). 1980. reprint ed. lib. bdg. 37.95 (*0-405-12864-9*) Ayer.

Petticoat Surgeon. Bertha Van Hoosen. (American Autobiography Ser.). 324p. 1995. reprint ed. lib. bdg. 89.00 (*0-7812-8656-5*) Rprt Serv.

Petticoat Whalers: Whaling Wives at Sea, 1820-1920. Joan Druett. (Illus.): 214p. 1992. 25.00 (*1-86950-043-1*, Pub. by HarpC) HarpC.

Petticoats & Pistols (Lou Polk) Mary H. Hendry. (Illus.). 79p. 1992. pap. 12.00 (*0-9611656-2-6*) Hendry Pubns.

Petticoats & Prejudice: Women & Law in 19th Century Canada. Constance Backhouse. 470p. pap. 20.95 (*0-88961-161-0*, Pub. by Womens Pr) LPC InBook.

Petticoats & White Feathers: Gender Conformity, Race, the Progressive Peace Movement & the Debate over War, 1895-1919, 160. Erika A. Kuhlman. LC 97-2225. (Contributions in Women's Studies: Vol. 160). 160p. 1997. 55.00 (*0-313-30341-X*, Greenwood Pr) Greenwood.

Petticoats, Politics, & Pirouettes: Oklahoma Women from 1900 to 1950. Glenda Carlile. Ed. by Carol Welsh. LC 95-92460. (Illus.). 120p. 1995. pap. 12.95 (*0-9628214-4-6*) Sthrn Hills Pub.

Pettigrew Papers, 1819-1843, Vol. 2. Ed. & Intro. by Sarah M. Lemmon. (Pettigrew Papers). (Illus.). xlv, 631p. 1988. 45.00 (*0-86526-069-9*) NC Archives.

***Petting Farm: With Pull Tabs, Touch & Feel, & Lift Flaps.** Des. by Salina Yoon. (Illus.). (J). 2000. 6.95 (*1-58117-066-1*, Piggy Toes Pr) Intervisual Bks.

Petting Zoo. Jack Hanna. 18p. (J). (ps). 1992. 10.95 (*0-385-41694-6*) Doubleday.

Petting Zoo Sticker Activity Book. Cathy Beylon. (J). pap. text 1.00 (*0-486-40098-0*) Dover.

Pettingell Genealogy. Charles H. Pope & J. M. Pettengell. (Illus.). 596p. 1989. reprint ed. pap. 89.00 (*0-8328-0961-6*); reprint ed. lib. bdg. 97.00 (*0-8328-0960-8*) Higginson Bk Co.

Pettis County, Missouri: A Pictorial History. William B. Claycomb & Ed Brummet. LC 98-29022. (Illus.). 1998. 30.00 (*1-57864-043-1*) Donning Co.

Pettis Integral & Measure Theory. Michel Talagrand. LC 84-14614. (Memoirs of the American Mathematical Society Ser.: No. 51/307). 224p. 1986. reprint ed. pap. 27.00 (*0-8218-2307-8*, MEMO/51/307) Am Math.

Pettranella. Betty Waterton. (Illus.). 32p. (J). 1991. pap. 4.95 (*0-88899-108-8*) Publishers Group.

Pettus Family: In England & Virginia. Pocahontas H. Stacy. Ed. by A. B. Rudd. (Illus.). 67p. 1995. reprint ed. pap. 14.00 (*0-8328-4934-0*); reprint ed. lib. bdg. 24.00 (*0-8328-4933-2*) Higginson Bk Co.

Petty Classic Pin-Up Art. Reid S. Austin. 1997. 40.00 (*0-517-18840-6*) Random Hse Value.

Petty Crimes. Gary Soto. LC 97-37114. 157p. (J). (gr. 4-7). 1998. 16.00 (*0-15-201658-9*, Harcourt Child Bks) Harcourt.

Petty Demon. Fedor Sologub, pseud. Tr. by Samuel D. Cioran from RUS. 400p. 1983. pap. 13.95 (*0-88233-808-0*) Ardis Pubs.

Petty Demon. unabridged ed. Fedor Sologub, pseud. (World Classic Literature Ser.). (RUS.). pap. 8.95 (*2-87714-271-X*, Pub. by Bookking Intl) Distribks Inc.

Petty Frogs on the Potomac. unabridged ed. David Hedges. LC 97-67658. 72p. 1997. pap. 10.00 (*0-9658601-0-8*) Sweetbriar Co.

Petty Power. (Hot Wheels Coloring & Activity Book Ser.). (Illus.). (J). (ps-1). 1998. pap. write for info. (*0-7666-0098-X*, Honey Bear Bks) Modern Pub NYC.

Petty, the Origins of Political Economy. Alessandro Roncaglia. Tr. by Isabella Cherubini. LC 84-23549. 128p. 1985. reprint ed. pap. 39.70 (*0-7837-9939-X*, 206066600006) Bks Demand.

Petty Trading in the Third World: The Case of Calcutta. Nandini Dasgupta. 374p. 1992. 82.95 (*1-85628-270-8*, Pub. by Avebry) Ashgate Pub Co.

Petucha und Setuma: Untersuchungen Zu Einer Uberlieferten Gliederung Im Hebraeischen Texten des Alten Testaments. Josef M. Oesch. (Orbis Biblicus et Orientalis Ser.: Vol. 27). 1979. text 82.50 (*3-7278-0212-X*, Pub. by Ed Univ Fri) Eisenbrauns.

Petulant Children. Baxter Hathaway. LC 78-14869. 36p. 1978. 3.50 (*0-87886-099-1*, Greenfld Rev Pr) Greenfld Rev Lit.

Petunia. anniversary ed. Roger Duvoisin. (Illus.). (J). 1962. 15.95 (*0-394-80865-7*) Knopf Bks Yng Read.

PetVet: Dog First Aid. Sandra C. Mays & Michael P. Driscoll. (Illus.). 105p. (Orig.). 1995. pap. 16.95 (*1-878117-05-X*) Lagumo Corp.

Peu de Soleil dans l'Eau Froide. Francoise Sagan. 14.95 (*0-685-37083-6*) Fr & Eur.

Peugeot 205 1983-1995. Chilton Automotive Editorial Staff. (Porter Manuals Ser.). (Illus.). 128p. (C). 1998. pap. 24.95 (*1-899238-17-4*, Pub. by Porter Pub) Nichols Pub.

Peuplades de la Senegambie: Histoire, Ethnographie, Moeurs et Coutumes, Legendes, etc. Laurent J. Berenger-Feraud. (B. E. Ser.: No. 169). (FRE.). 1879. 50.00 (*0-8115-3081-7*) Periodicals Srv.

Peuple de France Aujourd'hui. Claire Laudet & Richard Cox. (FRE., Illus.). 200p. 1995. text 19.95 (*0-7190-4216-X*) Manchester Univ Pr.

Peuple et L'Histoire. Paul Sebillot. (FRE.). 240p. 1986. pap. 32.95 (*0-7859-1573-7*, 2902702310) Fr & Eur.

Peuples et Langues de France. Audrey Gaquin. (Illus.). 626p. (Orig.). (C). 1995. pap. text 34.50 (*0-7618-0136-7*); lib. bdg. 69.50 (*0-7618-0135-9*) U Pr of Amer.

Peuples et les Civilisations du Proche-Orient: Essai d'une Histoire Comparee, des Origines a nos Jours, Tomes II-V. Jawad Boulos. Incl. Proche-Orient Ottoman (1517-1918) et Postottoman (1918-1930) 300p. 1968. pap. text 28.00 Tome II. De 1600 a 64 Avant J.-C. 430p. 1962. pap. text 36.00 (*3-11-000018-0*); Tome III. De la Conquete Romaine a l'Expansion Arabo-Islamique (64 av. J.-C. to 640 ap. J.-C.) 400p. 1964. pap. text 21.60 Tome IV. De l'Expansion Arabo-Islamique a la Conquete Turco-Ottomane (640-1517) 550p. 1964. pap. text 45.35 Set pap. 32.75 (*0-685-03445-3*) Mouton.

Peut Bergere. Georges Simenon. (FRE.). 1966. pap. 11.95 (*0-7859-3964-4*) Fr & Eur.

Peut-On Eduquer l'Intelligence? L'Evaluation d'Une Methode d'Education Cognitive. Even Loarer et al. (Exploration Ser.). (FRE.). x, 216p. 1995. 36.95 (*3-906754-01-4*, Pub. by P Lang) P Lang Pubng.

Peux-tu Attraper Josephine? Stephane Poulin. LC 87-50375. (FRE., Illus.). 24p. (J). (gr. k-4). 1988. 12.95 (*0-88776-199-2*) Tundra Bks.

Peveril of the Peak see Works of Sir Walter Scott

Pevets Misha Raitzin. Arthur Shtilman. LC 92-10305. (RUS., Illus.). 96p. 1992. pap. 8.00 (*1-55779-050-7*) Hermitage Pubs.

***Pew Bible.** PEW Staff. 1999. 15.99 (*0-529-11019-9*) World Bible.

***Pew Bible.** large type ed. PEW Staff. 1999. 15.99 (*0-529-11018-0*) World Bible.

Pew Prompters. Lawrence G. Enscoe & Andrea J. Enscoe. 136p. 1990. 15.99 (*0-8341-9245-4*, MP-662) Lillenas.

Pewabic: Deadly Waters. Francis F. Reynolds. LC 99-188045. 170p. 1998. pap. 11.95 (*0-9618116-4-1*) Sarge Pubns.

Pewter. Charles Hull. (Album Ser.: No. 280). (Illus.). 32p. 1989. pap. 25.00 (*0-7478-0152-5*, Pub. by Shire Pubns) Parkwest Pubns.

Pewter. Anthony North. 1999. 65.00 (*1-85177-223-5*) V&A Ent.

Pewter & the Revival of Its Use. Arthur L. Liberty. (Shorey Lost Arts Ser.). (Illus.). 44p. 1904. reprint ed. pap. 10.00 (*0-8466-6007-5*, U-7) Shoreys Bkstore.

Pewter of the Western World, 1600-1850. R. G. Hornsby. LC 83-61251. (Illus.). 381p. 1983. 60.00 (*0-916838-83-8*) Schiffer.

Pewter Wares from Sheffield. Jack L. Scott. LC 80-68670. (Illus.). 260p. 1980. 28.00 (*0-937864-00-5*) Antiquary Pr.

Pewter Wheel. Susan Bright. 1982. 3.00 (*0-911051-04-X*); VHS. write for info. (*0-318-56961-2*) Plain View.

Pewter Wings, Golden Horns, Stone Veils: Wedding in a Dark Plum Room. John Hejduk & Kim Shkapich. LC 97-28078. 304p. 1997. 40.00 (*1-885254-71-7*, Pub. by Monacelli Pr) Penguin Putnam.

Pewter-Working: Instructions & Projects. Burl N. Osburn & Gordon O. Wilber. LC 78-74121. (Illus.). 160p. 1979. reprint ed. pap. 7.95 (*0-486-23786-9*) Dover.

Peynet Collections. Andre Renaudo. (ENG & FRE., Illus.). 108p. 55.00 (*0-903685-60-4*, Pub. by R Dennis) Antique Collect.

Peyote. Nancy Ross-Flanigan. LC 96-40105. (Drug Library Ser.). (Illus.). 112p. (YA). (gr. 6 up). 1997. lib. bdg. 20.95 (*0-89490-851-0*) Enslow Pubs.

Peyote: The Divine Cactus. 2nd rev. ed. Edward F. Anderson. LC 95-50224. (Illus.). 272p. 1996. pap. 19.95 (*0-8165-1654-5*) U of Ariz Pr.

Peyote & Magic Mushrooms see Drug Abuse Prevention Library: Drugs & Your Life

Peyote & Mescaline. rev. ed. Jennifer James. 1999. pap. 0.50 (*0-89230-210-0*) Do It Now.

Peyote & Other Psychoactive Cacti. 2nd ed. Adam Gottlieb. Ed. by Derek Westlund. (Illus.). 96p. (Orig.). 1997. pap. 9.95 (*0-914171-95-X*) Ronin Pub.

Peyote At Last: A Peyote Beadwork Primer. Barbara Grainger. (Illus.). ii, 70p. 1993. 19.95 (*0-9679833-0-4*, Pub. by B L Grainger) Helby Import.

Peyote Book: A Study of Native Medicine. 3rd ed. Compiled by Guy Mount. 144p. 1993. per. 9.95 (*0-9604462-3-0*) Sweetlight.

Peyote Cult. 5th ed. Weston La Barre. LC 89-40225. (Illus.). 352p. 1989. pap. 18.95 (*0-8061-2214-5*) U of Okla Pr.

Peyote Design Techniques. Barbara Grainger. (Illus.). vi, 88p. 1996. 24.95 (*0-9679833-1-2*, Pub. by B L Grainger) Helby Import.

Peyote Hunt: The Sacred Journey of the Huichol Indians. Barbara G. Myerhoff. LC 73-16923. (Symbol, Myth & Ritual Ser.). (Illus.). 288p. 1976. pap. text 12.95 (*0-8014-9137-1*) Cornell U Pr.

Peyote in Sanskrit. Jon Wright. LC 94-92225. 98p. (Orig.). (C). 1994. pap., per. 4.95 (*0-9643358-0-8*) Naked Bums.

Peyote Religion. Omer C. Stewart. LC 87-5941. (Civilization of the American Indian Ser.: Vol. 181). (Illus.). 464p. 1987. 37.95 (*0-8061-2068-1*) U of Okla Pr.

Peyote Religion: A History. Omer C. Stewart. LC 87-5941. 1993. pap. 17.95 (*0-8061-2457-1*) U of Okla Pr.

Peyote Religion among the Navaho. 2nd ed. David F. Aberle. LC 91-50310. (Illus.). 468p. 1991. reprint ed. pap. 24.95 (*0-8061-2382-6*) U of Okla Pr.

Peyote Religious Art: Symbols of Faith & Belief. Daniel C. Swan. LC 98-37426. (Folk Art & Artists Ser.). (Illus.). 112p. 1999. lib. bdg. 35.00 (*1-57806-096-6*) U Pr of Miss.

Peyote 2nd: The Divine Cactus. 2nd ed. Anderson. LC 95-50224. (Illus.). 272p. 1996. 50.00 (*0-8165-1653-7*) U of Ariz Pr.

***Peyotism & the Native American Church: Annotated Bibliography.** Phillip M. White. Vol. 45. 2000. lib. bdg. write for info. (*0-313-31626-0*) Greenwood.

***Peyresq Lectures on Nonlinear Phenomena.** Ed. by Robin Kaiser & James Montaldi. 300p. 2000. 68.00 (*981-02-4315-4*) World Scientific Pub.

Peyronie's Disease: Induratio Penis Plastica. Ed. by A. Kelami & J. P. Pryor. (Progress in Reproductive Biology & Medicine Ser.: Vol. 9). (Illus.). viii, 116p. 1983. 98.50 (*3-8055-3513-9*) S Karger.

***Peyton Manning: Passing Legacy.** Joe Frisaro. (SuperStar Series: Vol. 3). 96p. (J). 1999. pap. 4.95 (*1-58261-164-5*, Pub. by Sprts Pubng) Partners-West.

Peyton Manning: Primed & Ready. Jimmy Hyams. LC 98-35609. (Illus.). 240p. 1998. pap. 14.95 (*1-886110-61-1*) Addax Pubng.

***Peyton Manning: Rising Son.** Mark Stewart. LC 99-35043. (Football's New Wave Ser.). 5p. (J). 2000. pap. 6.95 (*0-7613-1332-X*) Millbrook Pr.

***Peyton Manning: Rising Son.** Mark Stewart. LC 99-35043. (Football's New Wave Ser.). 48p. (J). (gr. 4). 2000. 19.90 (*0-7613-1517-9*) Millbrook Pr.

Peyton Place. Grace Metalious. LC 98-53350. 384p. 1999. pap. 14.95 (*1-55553-400-7*) NE U Pr.

Peyton Place. Grace Metalious. 300p. 1991. reprint ed. lib. bdg. 38.95 (*0-89966-861-5*) Buccaneer Bks.

Peyton Place: And Return to Peyton Place. Grace Metalious. LC 99-20443. (Illus.). 640p. 1999. 10.99 (*0-517-20477-0*) Random Hse Value.

Peyton Randolph, 1721-1775: One Who Presided. John J. Reardon. LC 81-70431. (Illus.). 112p. 1982. lib. bdg. 12.95 (*0-89089-201-6*) Carolina Acad Pr.

Pez Arco Iris. Marcus Pfister. LC 94-30500. (Rainbow Fish Ser.). Orig. Title: Der Regenbogenfisch. (SPA., Illus.). 32p. (J). (ps-3). 1994. 18.95 (*1-55858-361-0*, Pub. by North-South Bks NYC); 25.00 (*1-55858-440-4*, Pub. by North-South Bks NYC); lib. bdg. 16.88 (*1-55858-362-9*, Pub. by North-South Bks NYC) Chronicle Bks.

Pez Arco Iris. Marcus Pfister. (Rainbow Fish Ser.). Orig. Title: Der Regenbogenfisch. (SPA., Illus.). 12p. (J). (ps-3). 1996. bds. 9.95 (*1-55858-559-1*, Pub. by North-South Bks NYC) Chronicle Bks.

Pez Arco Iris Al Rescate! Marcus Pfister. Tr. by Guillermo Gutierrez from GER. LC 97-42155. (Rainbow Fish Ser.). Orig. Title: Regenbogenfisch, Komm Hilf Mir!. (SPA., Illus.). 32p. (J). (ps-3). 1996. 18.95 (*1-55858-558-3*, Pub. by North-South Bks NYC) Chronicle Bks.

Pez Arco Iris Al Rescate! Marcus Pfister. Tr. by Guillermo Gutierrez from GER. (Rainbow Fish Ser.). Orig. Title: Regenbogenfisch, Komm Hilf Mir!. (SPA., Illus.). 32p. (J). (ps-3). 1997. 25.00 (*1-55858-815-9*, Pub. by North-South Bks NYC) Chronicle Bks.

Pez Arco Iris Al Rescate! Marcus Pfister. (Rainbow Fish Ser.). Orig. Title: Regenbogenfisch, Komm Hilf Mir!. (SPA., Illus.). 12p. (J). (ps-3). 1998. bds. 9.95 (*1-55858-885-X*, Pub. by North-South Bks NYC) Chronicle Bks.

Pez Arco Iris y la Ballena Azul. Marcus Pfister. (Rainbow Fish Ser.). Orig. Title: Regenbogenfisch und Grosser Blauer Wal. (SPA., Illus.). 32p. (J). (ps-3). 1998. 18.95 (*0-7358-1002-8*, Pub. by North-South Bks NYC) Chronicle Bks.

***Pez Arco Iris y la Ballena Azul.** Marcus Pfister. (Rainbow Fish Ser.). Orig. Title: Regenbogenfisch und Grosser Blauer Wal. (SPA., Illus.). 32p. (J). (ps-3). 1999. pap. 25.00 (*0-7358-1215-2*, Pub. by North-South Bks NYC) Chronicle Bks.

Pez Collectibles. 3rd rev. ed. Ed. by Richard Geary. LC 98-88346. (Illus.). 112p. 1999. pap. 19.95 (*0-7643-0713-4*) Schiffer.

***Pez Collectibles.** 4th ed. Richard Geary. (Illus.). 112p. 2000. pap. 19.95 (*0-7643-1095-X*) Schiffer.

Pez Collectibles: With Up-to-Date Prices. 2nd expanded rev. ed. Richard Geary. (Schiffer Book for Collectors Ser.). (Illus.). 120p. 1997. pap. 19.95 (*0-7643-0315-5*) Schiffer.

Pez de Vidrio. Mayra S. Febles. LC 96-85785. 96p. 1996. pap. 9.25 (*0-929157-41-9*) Ediciones Huracan.

Pfadfinder: Luftwaffe Pathfinder Operations over Britain, 1940-44. Ken Wakefield. (Military History Ser.). (Illus.). 272p. 1999. 34.99 (*0-7524-1692-8*, Tempus Publng) Arcadia Publng.

***Pfaffian Systems, K-Symplectic Systems.** Azzouz Awane & Michel Goze. LC 00-33049. 2000. write for info. (*0-7923-6373-6*) Kluwer Academic.

Pfaff's Problem & Its Generalizations. Jan A. Schouten & W. Van Der Kulk. LC 75-77140. 1969. reprint ed. 29.50 (*0-8284-0221-3*) Chelsea Pub.

***Pfandbrief: A European Perspective.** Phillip Moore. 2000. pap. text 225.00 (*1-85564-755-9*, Pub. by Euromoney) Am Educ Systs.

Pfander-Studien. Herbert Spiegelberg & E. Ave-Lallemant. 400p. 1982. lib. bdg. 226.00 (*90-247-2490-2*, Pub. by M Nijhoff) Kluwer Academic.

PFC Programmar's Reference Manual. Richard Brooks. LC 98-3861. 368p. 1998. pap. 37.95 (*1-884777-55-4*) Manning Pubns.

PFD Manual. American Floral Services, Inc. Staff. Ed. by Jim Morley. (SPA.). 80p. (C). 1994. text. write for info. (*0-944074-03-0*) AFS Education.

PFD Manual. American Floral Services Staff. Ed. by Jim Morley. (POR.). 80p. (C). 1994. text. write for info. (*0-944074-04-9*) AFS Education.

PFD Sympathy Design Manual. American Floral Services Staff. Ed. by Jim Morley. (Illus.). 104p. 1995. text 29.95 (*0-944074-05-7*) AFS Education.

PFD Wedding Design Manual. Ed. by Jim Morley. (Illus.). 104p. (C). 1993. text 30.95 (*0-944074-02-2*) AFS Education.

Pfeiffer & Company Library Guide - Index, Vol. 28. Intro. by J. William Pfeiffer. LC 93-86725. (Illus.). 1994. ring bd. 119.00 (*0-88390-432-2*, Pfffr & Co) Jossey-Bass.

Pfeiffer & Company Library of Experiential Learning Activities: Communication, Vol. 4. Intro. by J. William Pfeiffer. LC 93-86698. (Illus.). 1994. ring bd. 119.00 (*0-88390-388-1*) Jossey-Bass.

Pfeiffer & Company Library of Experiential Learning Activities: Consulting & Facilitating. Intro. by J. William Pfeiffer. LC 93-86708. (Illus.). 1994. ring bd. 119.00 (*0-88390-394-6*, Pfffr & Co) Jossey-Bass.

Pfeiffer & Company Library of Experiential Learning Activities: Groups, Vol. 10. Intro. by J. William Pfeiffer. LC 93-86711. (Illus.). 1994. ring bd. 119.00 (*0-88390-391-1*) Jossey-Bass.

Pfeiffer & Company Library of Experiential Learning Activities Vol. 1: Individual Development. Intro. by J. William Pfeiffer. LC 93-86699. (Illus.). 1994. ring bd. 119.00 (*0-88390-389-X*) Jossey-Bass.

P

Pfeiffer & Company Library of Experiential Learning Activities Vol. 11: Teams. Intro. by J. William Pfeiffer. LC 93-86710. (Illus.). 1994. ring bd. 119.00 (*0-88390-392-X*) Jossey-Bass.

Pfeiffer & Company Library of Experiential Learning Activities Vol. 18: Leadership. Intro. by J. William Pfeiffer. LC 93-86709. (Illus.). 1994. ring bd. 119.00 (*0-88390-393-8*) Jossey-Bass.

Pfeiffer & Company Library of Experiential Learning Activities Vol. 21: Training Technologies. Intro. by J. William Pfeiffer. LC 93-86700. (Illus.). 1994. ring bd. 119.00 (*0-88390-425-X*, Pfffr & Co) Jossey-Bass.

Pfeiffer & Company Library of Inventories, Questionnaires, & Surveys: Groups & Teams. Intro. by J. William Pfeiffer. LC 93-86704. (Illus.). 1994. ring bd. 119.00 (*0-88390-398-9*, Pfffr & Co) Jossey-Bass.

Pfeiffer & Company Library of Inventories, Questionnaires, & Surveys Vol. 2: Individual Development. Intro. by J. William Pfeiffer. LC 93-86701. (Illus.). 1994. ring bd. 119.00 (*0-88390-396-2*) Jossey-Bass.

Pfeiffer & Company Library of Inventories, Questionnaires, & Surveys Vol. 5: Communication. Intro. by J. William Pfeiffer. LC 93-86702. (Illus.). 1994. ring bd. 119.00 (*0-88390-395-4*) Jossey-Bass.

Pfeiffer & Company Library of Inventories, Questionnaires, & Surveys Vol. 8: Problem Solving. Intro. by J. William Pfeiffer. LC 93-86703. (Illus.). 1994. ring bd. 119.00 (*0-88390-397-0*) Jossey-Bass.

Pfeiffer & Company Library of Inventories, Questionnaires, & Surveys Vol. 15: Consulting & Facilitating. Intro. by J. William Pfeiffer. LC 93-86706. (Illus.). 1994. ring bd. 119.00 (*0-88390-400-4*) Jossey-Bass.

Pfeiffer & Company Library of Inventories, Questionnaires, & Surveys Vol. 19: Leadership. Intro. by J. William Pfeiffer. LC 93-86705. (Illus.). 1994. ring bd. 119.00 (*0-88390-399-7*) Jossey-Bass.

Pfeiffer & Company Library of Inventories, Questionnaires, & Surveys Vol. 22: Training Technologies. Intro. by J. William Pfeiffer. LC 93-86707. (Illus.). 1994. ring bd. 119.00 (*0-88390-426-8*, Pfffr & Co) Jossey-Bass.

Pfeiffer & Company Library of Presentation & Discussion Resources: Consulting. Intro. by J. William Pfeiffer. LC 93-86718. (Illus.). 1994. ring bd. 119.00 (*0-88390-406-3*, Pfffr & Co) Jossey-Bass.

Pfeiffer & Company Library of Presentation & Discussion Resources Vol. 3: Individual Development. Intro. by J. William Pfeiffer. LC 93-86713. (Illus.). 1994. ring bd. 119.00 (*0-88390-402-0*) Jossey-Bass.

Pfeiffer & Company Library of Presentation & Discussion Resources Vol. 6: Communication. Intro. by J. William Pfeiffer. LC 93-86714. (Illus.). 1994. ring bd. 119.00 (*0-88390-401-2*) Jossey-Bass.

Pfeiffer & Company Library of Presentation & Discussion Resources Vol. 9: Problem Solving. Intro. by J. William Pfeiffer. LC 93-86715. (Illus.). 1994. ring bd. 119.00 (*0-88390-403-9*) Jossey-Bass.

Pfeiffer & Company Library of Presentation & Discussion Resources Vol. 13: Groups & Teams. Intro. by J. William Pfeiffer. LC 93-86716. (Illus.). 1994. ring bd. 119.00 (*0-88390-404-7*) Jossey-Bass.

Pfeiffer & Company Library of Presentation & Discussion Resources Vol. 17: Facilitating. Intro. by J. William Pfeiffer. LC 93-86719. (Illus.). 1994. ring bd. 119.00 (*0-88390-407-1*) Jossey-Bass.

Pfeiffer & Company Library of Presentation & Discussion Resources Vol. 20: Leadership. Intro. by J. William Pfeiffer. LC 93-86717. (Illus.). 1994. ring bd. 119.00 (*0-88390-405-5*) Jossey-Bass.

Pfeiffer & Company Library of Presentation & Discussion Resources Vol. 23: Training Technologies. Intro. by J. William Pfeiffer. LC 93-86720. (Illus.). 1994. ring bd. 119.00 (*0-88390-427-6*, Pfffr & Co) Jossey-Bass.

Pfeiffer & Company Library of Theories & Models Vol. 24: Individual. Intro. by J. William Pfeiffer. LC 93-86721. (Illus.). 1994. ring bd. 119.00 (*0-88390-428-4*, Pfffr & Co) Jossey-Bass.

Pfeiffer & Company Library of Theories & Models Vol. 25: Group. Intro. by J. William Pfeiffer. LC 93-86722. (Illus.). 1994. ring bd. 119.00 (*0-88390-429-2*, Pfffr & Co) Jossey-Bass.

Pfeiffer & Company Library of Theories & Models Vol. 26: Management. Intro. by J. William Pfeiffer. LC 93-86723. (Illus.). 1994. ring bd. 119.00 (*0-88390-430-6*, Pfffr & Co) Jossey-Bass.

Pfeiffer & Company Library of Theories & Models Vol. 27: Organization. Intro. by J. William Pfeiffer. LC 93-86724. (Illus.). 1994. ring bd. 119.00 (*0-88390-431-4*, Pfffr & Co) Jossey-Bass.

Pferd Bei Den Arabern. Joseph F. Hammer-Purgstall. (Documenta Hippologica Ser.). (Illus.). 95p. 1981. reprint ed. write for info. (*3-487-08225-X*) G Olms Pubs.

Pferd im alten Orient. Valentin Horn. (GER., Illus.). 256p. 1994. write for info. (*3-487-08352-3*) G Olms Pubs.

Pferd und Fahrer. Theodor Heinze. xiv, 472p. 1989. write for info. (*3-487-08298-5*) G Olms Pubs.

Pferd und Reiter Im Orient. Marit Kretschmar. (Illus.). 564p. 1980. write for info. (*3-487-08214-4*) G Olms Pubs.

Pferde, Horses, Chevaux, Photographien. Peter Thomann. (ENG, FRE & GER., Illus.). 63p. 1993. lib. bdg. 49.95 (*3-487-08337-X*) G Olms Pubs.

Pferde, und Jagdbilder in der Englischen Kunst. Gerhard C. Rump. (GER., Illus.). 396p. 1983. write for info. (*3-487-07425-7*) G Olms Pubs.

Pferdebeurteilung. Gustav Rau & Ulrich J. Duerst. (Documenta Hippologica Ser.). (GER., Illus.). 62p. 1996. reprint ed. write for info. (*3-487-08210-1*) G Olms Pubs.

Pferdepassion: Von Pferdezucht und Pferdeschonheit. Ernst Bilke. (Documenta Hippologica Ser.). (Illus.). 321p. 1976. 105.00 (*3-487-08111-3*) G Olms Pubs.

Pfiesteria: Crossing Dark Water: The True Story Behind the Public Health Menace That Now Threatens the Nation's Tidal Waters: By the Maryland "Family Doc" Who Blew the Whistle-- Ritchie C. Shoemaker. LC 99-164805. x, 350p. 1998. write for info. (*0-9665535-0-0*) R C Shoemaker.

Pfitz. Andrew Crumey. LC 97-15517. 176p. 1997. text 20.00 (*0-312-16964-7*) St Martin.

Pfitz. Andrew Crumey. 192p. 1998. pap. 12.00 (*0-312-19550-8*, Picador USA) St Martin.

P(5) Compounds see Organophosphorous Stereochemistry

***Pfizer Atlas of Veterinary Clinical Parasitology.** Ed. by Byron L. Blagburn & Michael W. Dryden. (Illus.). 48p. 2000. write for info. (*0-9678005-3-6*) Gloyd Grp Inc.

Pfizer Focuses on High Growth Markets: Innovative Product Introductions Give Company Competitive Edge. 216p. 1992. 995.00 (*1-56753-022-2*) Frost & Sullivan.

Pflanzenernaehrung in Stichworten, Band 1. 5th ed. Arnold Finck. (Hirt's Stichwortbuecher Ser.). (GER., Illus.). 200p. 1991. 19.00 (*3-443-03100-5*, Pub. by Gebruder Borntraeger) Balogh.

Pflanzengesellschaften der Mehrschuerigen Wiesen (Molino-Arrhenatheretea) Nordbayerns. Karin Hauser. (Dissertationes Botanicae Ser.: Band 128). (GER., Illus.). vi, 156p. 1988. pap. 65.00 (*3-443-64040-0*, Pub. by Gebruder Borntraeger) Balogh.

Pflanzengesellschaften der Torfstiche Nordniedersaechsischer Moore und die Abhaengigkeit Dieser Vegetationseinheiten Von der Wasserqualitaet. Rainer Bertram. (Dissertationes Botanicae Ser.: Band 126). (GER., Illus.). xii, 192p. 1988. pap. 48.00 (*3-443-64038-9*, Pub. by Gebruder Borntraeger) Balogh.

Pflanzengesellschaften der Westpannonischen Zwergstrauchheiden und Azidophilen Trockenrasen. Von Milan Chytry et al. (Dissertationes Botanicae Ser.: Band 277). (Illus.). 108p. 1997. pap. 53.00 (*3-443-64189-X*, Pub. by Gebruder Borntraeger) Balogh.

Pflanzengesellschaften Nord Westdeutschlands (H. N. C. 85) Reinhold Tuexen. 1970. reprint ed. 15.00 (*3-7682-0702-1*) Lubrecht & Cramer.

Pflanzengesellschaften Nordostdeutschlands Vol. I: Hydro- und Therophytosa. Harro Passarge. (Botanical Bks.). (GER., Illus.). xiv, 298p. 1996. text 29.00 (*3-443-50020-X*, Pub. by Gebruder Borntraeger) Balogh.

Pflanzengesellschaften und Vegetations - Komplexe der Moore Des Westlichen Bodenseegebietes. Astrid Gruettner. (Dissertationes Botanicae Ser.: Band 157). (GER., Illus.). iv, 330p. 1990. pap. 106.00 (*3-443-64069-9*, Pub. by Gebruder Borntraeger) Balogh.

Pflanzengesellschaften und Vegetations Mosaike Im Noerdlichen Oberfranken. Wmfried Turk. (Dissertationes Botanicae Ser.: Band 207). (Illus.). xiv, 290p. 1993. pap. 89.00 (*3-443-64119-9*, Pub. by Gebruder Borntraeger) Balogh.

Pflanzenlexikon: Plant Lexicon, 5 vols. W. Baumeister. (GER.). 1280p. 1969. pap. 99.95 (*0-8288-6611-2*, M7580) Fr & Eur.

***Pflanzenmedizin in einer Dorfgemeinschaft Im Sudwesten Madagaskars.** Christine Paulsen. (Europaische Hochschulschriften Ser.: Bd. 52). 202p. 1999. 37.95 (*3-631-35389-X*) P Lang Pubng.

Pflanzenoekologische und Bodenkundliche Untersuchungen an Quellwaldstandorten in Bochum. Uwe Peters. (Dissertationes Botanicae Ser.: Band 122). (GER., Illus.). 211p. 1988. pap. 48.00 (*3-443-64034-6*, Pub. by Gebruder Borntraeger) Balogh.

Pflanzenoekologische Untersuchungen an Wild- und Kulturpflanzen In der Extremwueste Suedaegyptens. Ulrich Schneider. (Dissertationes Botanicae Ser.: Band 153). (GER., Illus.). 292p. 1990. pap. 65.00 (*3-443-64065-6*, Pub. by Gebruder Borntraeger) Balogh.

Pflanzenoekologische Untersuchungen In Den Subalpinen Dornpolsterfluren Kretas. Johannes Hager. (Dissertationes Botanicae Ser.: Band 89). (Illus.). viii, 196p. 1985. pap. 36.00 (*3-7682-1449-4*) Balogh.

Pflanzensociologische Studien in Chile. E. Oberdorfer. (Illus.). 1960. 48.00 (*3-7682-0011-6*) Lubrecht & Cramer.

Pflanzensystematik (Plant Systematics) 6th ed. F. Weberling. (GER., Illus.). 432p. 1992. 22.00 (*3-8001-2647-8*, Pub. by Eugen Ulmer) Balogh.

Pflegemanagement Als Gestaltungsauftrag. Ed. by Ricarda Klein & Gabriele M. Borsi. (Illus.). 256p. 1997. pap. 51.95 (*3-631-30784-5*) P Lang Pubng.

Pflegeversicherung Vol. XXI: Allokative, Meritorische und Distributive Aspekte Staatlicher Eingriffsmoglichkeiten. Oliver Sievering. (GER., Illus.). XXI, 299p. 1996. pap. 57.95 (*3-631-30862-0*) P Lang Pubng.

Pfortaderhochdruck. Ed. by K. J. Paquet & J. Schoelmerich. (GER., Illus.). x, 702p. 1994. 181.75 (*3-8055-5659-4*) S Karger.

PFS: First Choice - Applications Made Easy. Paul Dlug. (Illus.). 220p. 1987. pap. 15.95 (*0-8306-2913-0*, 2913P) McGraw-Hill Prof.

PFS: First Choice, Version 3.1. D. Michael Werner & S. Elvon Warner. (C). 1991. text 38.00 incl. 5.25 hd (*0-673-46710-4*) Addson-Wesley Educ.

PFS: First Choice Workbook. John C. Day. (C). 1989. text 31.50 (*0-673-38780-1*) Addson-Wesley Educ.

PFS: First Choice Workbook & User's Guide. Software Publishing Corp. Staff & John C. Day. (C). 1990. pap. text 45.00 (*0-673-46034-7*, Scott Frsmn) Addson-Wesley Educ.

PG: He's Having Her Baby. Carole Marsh. 1998. 19.95 (*1-877755-01-X*) Six Hse.

PGA Championship Annual 1998. Tim Rosaforte et al. Ed. by Bev Norwood. (Illus.). 80p. 1998. write for info. (*1-878843-22-2*) Intl Merc OH.

PGA Championships Annual, 1995. Bob Green et al. Ed. by Bev Norwood. (Illus.). 96p. 1995. write for info. (*1-878843-14-1*) Intl Merc OH.

PGA Championships Annual, 1997. Tim Rosaforte et al. Ed. by Bev Norwood. (Illus.). 96p. 1997. write for info. (*1-878843-21-4*) Intl Merc OH.

***PGA Championships Annual, 1999.** Tim Rosaforte et al. Ed. by Bev Norwood. (Illus.). 96p. 1999. write for info. (*1-878843-26-5*) Intl Merc OH.

PGA Manual of Golf: The Professional's Way to Play Better Golf. PGA Staff & Gary Wiren. (Illus.). 480p. 1991. 39.95 (*0-02-599291-0*) Macmillan.

PGA Manual of Golf: The Professional's Way to Play Better Golf. Gary Wiren. 452p. 1997. pap. text 21.95 (*0-02-861682-0*) Macmillan.

PGA Tour Complete Book of Golf: Wisdom & Advice from The Best Players in The Game. Michael Corcoran. LC 99-10390. (Illus.). 416p. 1999. 45.00 (*0-8050-5768-4*) H Holt & Co.

***Pga Tour Ultimate Book of Golf.** Corcoran. 1999. pap. 25.00 (*0-8050-5769-2*) St Martin.

PGC Case Graphics Software Users Handbook with IBM 3.5. Pacific Gold Coast Staff. (C). 1995. text 154.50 (*0-256-21525-1*, Irwn McGrw-H) McGrw-H Hghr Educ.

PGE Chef's Night Out Cookbook. PGE Chef's Night Out Committee. Ed. by Bridget Otto et al. 95p. (Orig.). 1991. pap. 14.95 (*0-9629263-0-2*) PGE Chefs.

PGP 5.5.5 Macintosh Documentation. Ed. by Gail Haspert et al. 238p. 1998. spiral bd. write for info. (*1-891064-12-6*) Warthman Assocs.

PGP 5.5.5 Windows Documentation. Ed. by Gail Haspert et al. 248p. 1998. spiral bd. write for info. (*1-891064-11-8*) Warthman Assocs.

PGP Lotus Notes Plugin 1.0.1. 528p. 1999. spiral bd. write for info. (*1-58368-013-6*) Network Assocs.

PGP-Pretty Good Privacy: Encryption for Everyone. Simson Garfinkel. Ed. by Deborah Russell. (Illus.). 430p. (Orig.). 1994. reprint ed. pap. write for info. (*1-56592-098-8*) Thomson Learn.

***PGP 6.5.1 Macintosh-Specific Source Code, 9 vols.** 4274p. 1999. spiral bd. write for info. (*1-58368-016-0*) Network Assocs.

***PGP 6.5.1 Macintosh-Specific Documentation.** 547p. 1999. spiral bd. write for info. (*1-58368-019-5*) Network Assocs.

***PGP 6.5.1 Platform-Independent Source Code, 18 vols.** 8104p. 1999. spiral bd. write for info. (*1-58368-015-2*) Network Assocs.

***PGP 6.5.1 Platform-Independent Documentation.** 260p. 1999. spiral bd. write for info. (*1-58368-018-7*) Network Assocs.

***PGP 6.5.1 Windows-Specific Source Code.** 6246p. 1999. spiral bd. write for info. (*1-58368-017-9*) Network Assocs.

***PGP 6.5.1 Windows-Specific Documentation.** 572p. 1999. spiral bd. write for info. (*1-58368-020-9*) Network Assocs.

PGP 6. 0. 2. Source Code Update, 4 vols. 1735p. 1998. spiral bd. write for info. (*1-58368-012-8*) Network Assocs.

***PGP 6.0.2 Macintosh-Specific Documentation.** 1998. spiral bd. write for info. (*1-58368-009-8*) Network Assocs.

***PGP 6.0.2 Macintosh-Specific Source Code.** 3574p. 1998. spiral bd. write for info. (*1-58368-007-1*) Network Assocs.

***PGP 6.0.2 Platform-Independent Source Code.** 3762p. 1998. spiral bd. write for info. (*1-58368-006-3*) Network Assocs.

***PGP 6.0.2 Platform-Independent Documentation: PGP Installation Guide, an Introduction to Cryptography, Administration's Guide.** 1998. spiral bd. write for info. (*1-58368-011-X*) Network Assocs.

***PGP 6.0.2 Windows-Specific Documentation.** 1998. spiral bd. write for info. (*1-58368-010-1*) Network Assocs.

***PGP 6.0.2 Windows-Specific Source Code.** 4336p. 1998. spiral bd. write for info. (*1-58368-008-X*) Network Assocs.

PGPdisk 1.0 for Windows 95 User's Guide. Dave Heller et al. 34p. 1998. spiral bd. write for info. (*1-891064-15-0*) Warthman Assocs.

PGPdisk 1.0 for Windows 95, Vol. 1. Dave Heller et al. 1176p. 1998. spiral bd. write for info. (*1-891064-13-4*) Warthman Assocs.

PGPdisk 1.0.2 for Macintosh, Vol. 1. Dave Heller et al. 1055p. 1998. spiral bd. write for info. (*1-891064-14-2*) Warthman Assocs.

PGPdisk 1.0.2 for Macintosh User's Guide. Dave Heller et al. (Illus.). 34p. 1998. spiral bd. write for info. (*1-891064-16-9*) Warthman Assocs.

PGS Style Guide for Master's Theses & D. Min Project Reports. Roberta Hamburger & Philips University Graduate Seminary Staff. LC 94-24169. 1994. 5.00 (*0-912832-29-0*) Seminary Pr.

PH, Acids, & Bases. H. Anthony Neidig & James N. Spencer. (Modular Laboratory Program in Chemistry Ser.). 11p. 1992. pap. text 1.50 (*0-87540-397-2*, EQUL 397-2) Chem Educ Res.

PH & Blood Gas. ring bd. 200.00 (*1-56238-247-0*, SC5-L) NCCLS.

PH & Brain Function. Ed. by Kai Kaila & Bruce R. Ransom. LC 97-40568. 688p. 1998. 225.00 (*0-471-11838-9*, Wiley-Liss) Wiley.

PH & Buffer Theory: A New Approach. H. Rilbe. LC 96-11033. 212p. 1996. 145.00 (*0-471-96735-1*) Wiley.

PH & Pion Control in Process & Waste Streams. F. Greg Shinskey. LC 73-7853. (Environmental Science & Technology Ser.). 279p. reprint ed. pap. 86.50 (*0-7837-2805-0*, 205766700006) Bks Demand.

***PH Custom Test college Accounting: Practice Approach.** 7th ed. 1999. write for info. (*0-13-083249-9*, Prentice Hall) P-H.

PH Elementary ESL Teach Composition 123. 1995. pap. text 11.40 (*0-13-373903-1*) P-H.

PH Lit. Gold. 3rd ed. Prentice-Hall Staff. (Prentice-Hall Literature). 1994. text. write for info. (*0-13-722505-9*, Prentice Hall) P-H.

***PH Literature: Tvtt 5e Mini/anthology Appalachian Writers Gr 9-12 00c.** (gr. 9-12). 1999. write for info. (*0-13-009974-0*) P-H.

PH Measurement: Fundamentals, Methods, Applications, Instrumentation. Helmuth Galster. (Illus.). 356p. 1991. 185.00 (*3-527-28237-8*, Wiley-VCH) Wiley.

PH Measurement & Control. 2nd ed. Gregory K. McMillan. LC 84-29976. (Independent Learning Module Ser.). 304p. 1994. 60.00 (*1-55617-483-7*, A483-7) ISA.

PH of Plant Cells. J. Small. (Protoplasmatologia Ser.: Vol. 2B, Pt. 2c). (Illus.). iv, 172p. 1955. 40.20 (*0-387-80386-6*) Spr-Verlag.

PH Periodic Table. Ph. 1997. pap. text 3.00 (*0-13-956764-X*) P-H.

PH Professor: A Classroom Presentation on Powerpoint. 3rd ed. (C). 1997. write for info. (*0-13-755356-0*, Macmillan Coll) P-H.

PH Reader Quiz Book. 4th ed. Miller. 1995. pap. text. write for info. (*0-13-164906-X*) Allyn.

***PH Test Manager for Griffin/ebert/starke Business.** 3rd rev. ed. 586p. 1999. write for info. (*0-13-017991-4*) P-H.

PH Training Handbook. Cummings. 1994. text 69.95 (*0-13-030578-2*) S&S Trade.

***PH You Potential for Health.** 2nd rev. ed. M. Ted Morter, Jr. 1999. pap. 5.00 (*0-944994-13-X*) Morris Pubng.

Phacodynamics: Mastering the Tools & Techniques of Phacoemulsification Surgery. 3rd ed. Barry Seibel. LC 98-29336. (Illus.). 304p. 1998. text 125.00 (*1-55642-388-8*, 63888) SLACK Inc.

***Phacodynamics: Mastering the Tools & Techniques of Phacoemulsifications Surgery.** Barry Seibel. (SPA., Illus.). 304p. 1999. 125.00 (*1-55642-447-7*) SLACK Inc.

Phacoemulsification: Principles & Techniques. Lucio Buratto. LC 97-34823. (Illus.). 544p. 1997. text 195.00 (*1-55642-360-8*, 63608) SLACK Inc.

Phacoemulsification in Difficult & Challenging Cases. Luisw Lu & Howard I. Fine. LC 98-4055. 1998. write for info. (*3-13-114671-0*) Thieme Med Pubs.

Phacoemulsification in Difficult & Challenging Cases. Luisw Lu & Howard I. Fine. LC 98-4055. (Illus.). 200p. 1998. 99.00 (*0-86577-791-8*) Thieme Med Pubs.

Phacoemulsification Surgery. Ed. by T. M. Devine & William Banko. (Illus.). 144p. 1991. 125.00 (*0-08-036840-9*) McGraw.

Phacomatoses see Handbook of Clinical Neurology

Phacomatosis in Japan: Epidemiology, Clinical Picture & Molecular Biology. Ed. by M. Niimura et al. (Gann Monograph on Cancer Research Ser.: Vol. 46). (Illus.). viii, 230p. 1999. 243.50 (*3-8055-6838-X*) S Karger.

Phadaeng Nang Ai: A Translation of a Thai-Isan Folk Epic in Verse. Ed. & Tr. by Wajuppa Tossa. LC 87-46436. (Illus.). 176p. 1990. 38.50 (*0-8387-5139-3*) Bucknell U Pr.

Phaedo. Plato. Ed. by R. Hackforth. 200p. (C). 1972. pap. 15.95 (*0-521-09702-9*) Cambridge U Pr.

Phaedo. Plato. Tr. & Notes by David Gallop. (Clarendon Plato Ser). 254p. 1977. pap. text 24.95 (*0-19-872049-1*) OUP.

***Phaedo.** Plato. Ed. by David Gallop. (Oxford World's Classics Ser.). 136p. 1999. pap. 8.95 (*0-19-283953-5*) OUP.

Phaedo. C. J. Rowe. LC 92-33958. (Greek & Latin Classics Ser.). 313p. (C). 1993. pap. text 24.95 (*0-521-31318-X*) Cambridge U Pr.

Phaedo. Plato. Ed. by John Burnet. 218p. 1979. reprint ed. pap. text 19.95 (*0-19-814014-2*) OUP.

Phaedo: A Platonic Labyrinth. Ronna Burger. LC 99-19016. 310p. (C). 2000. reprint ed. pap. 25.00 (*1-890318-58-2*) St Augustines Pr.

Phaedo Church Plato. F. J. Church. 96p. (C). 1951. pap. text 4.60 (*0-02-322400-2*, Macmillan Coll) P-H.

Phaedo of Plato. Plato. LC 72-9280. (Philosophy of Plato & Aristotle Ser.). 1977. reprint ed. 22.95 (*0-405-04831-9*) Ayer.

Phaedon: or The Death of Socrates. Moses Mendelssohn. LC 73-2219. (Jewish People; History, Religion, Literature Ser.). 1973. reprint ed. 24.95 (*0-405-05282-0*) Ayer.

Phaedra see Seventeenth Century French Drama

Phaedra. Matthew Maguire. (American Theatre in Literature Program Ser.). 80p. (Orig.). 1996. pap. 9.95 (*1-55713-242-9*) Sun & Moon CA.

***Phaedra.** Jean Racine. Tr. by Edwin Morgan. 128p. 2000. 18.95 (*1-85754-464-1*, Pub. by Carcanet Pr) Paul & Co Pubs.

Phaedra. Jean Racine. Tr. by Richard Wilbur. 1986. pap. 5.25 (*0-8222-0890-3*) Dramatists Play.

Phaedra. Jean Racine. (FRE., Illus.). 208p. 1990. pap. 10.95 (*0-685-73320-3*, 2038714088) Fr & Eur.

Phaedra. Jean Racine. Tr. by Richard Wilbur. (Illus.). 132p. (C). 1987. pap. 10.00 (*0-15-675780-X*, Harvest Bks) Harcourt.

Phaedra. Jean Racine. Ed. & Tr. by Oreste F. Pucciani. (Crofts Classics). 96p. 1959. pap. text 4.95 (*0-88295-069-X*) Harlan Davidson.

Phaedra. Jean Racine. Ed. by William-Alan Landes. Tr. by Robert B. Boswell. LC 93-16950. 1993. pap. 7.00 (*0-88734-266-3*) Players Pr.

Phaedra. Jean Racine. Tr. by Margaret Rawlings. (ENG & FRE.). 192p. 1992. pap. 11.95 (*0-14-044591-9*, Penguin Classics) Viking Penguin.

An Asterisk (*) at the beginning of an entry indicates that the title is appearing for the first time.

Phaedra. Lucius Annaeus Seneca. Tr. & Intro. by Frederick Ahl. (Masters of Latin Literature Ser.). 128p. 1986. pap. text 8.95 (*0-8014-9433-8*) Cornell U Pr.

Phaedra. Lucius Annaeus Seneca. LC 60-6496. (Rinehart Editions Ser.). 1960. write for info. (*0-318-53472-X*) Harcourt Coll Pubs.

Phaedra. Lucius Annaeus Seneca et al. 229p. (C). 1990. text 65.00 (*0-521-20085-7*); pap. text 22.95 (*0-521-33713-5*) Cambridge U Pr.

Phaedra: One-Act Adaptation. Jean Racine. (Illus.). 35p. 1966. pap. 3.25 (*0-88680-151-6*) I E Clark.

Phaedra: One-Act Adaptation (Director's Script) Jean Racine. (Illus.). 35p. 1966. pap. 10.00 (*0-88680-152-4*) I E Clark.

Phaedra of Seneca. Gilbert Lawall & Gerde Kindel. 238p. 1989. pap. text 16.00 (*0-86516-016-3*) Bolchazy-Carducci.

Phaedrus. Plato. Tr. by Alexander Nehamas & Paul Woodruff from GRE. LC 94-46613. (HPC Classics Ser.). 240p. (C). 1995. text 27.95 (*0-87220-221-6*); pap. text 6.95 (*0-87220-220-8*) Hackett Pub.

Phaedrus. Plato. Ed. by R. Hackforth. 172p. (C). 1972. pap. text 15.95 (*0-521-09703-7*) Cambridge U Pr.

***Phaedrus.** Plato. Tr. & Intro. by James H. Nichols, Jr. LC 98-27372. (Agora Editions Ser.). 224p. 1998. pap. text 9.95 (*0-8014-8532-0*) Cornell U Pr.

Phaedrus - Lexicon Phaedrianum. Ed. by Carolus A. Cremona. (Alpha-Omega, Reihe A Ser.: Bd. XV). xxxiv, 663p. 1980. 150.00 (*3-487-06970-9*) G Olms Pubs.

Phaedrus, & The Seventh & Eighth Letters. Plato. Tr. & Intro. by Walter Hamilton. (Classics Ser.). 160p. (Orig.). 1973. pap. 13.99 (*0-14-044275-8*, Penguin Classics) Viking Penguin.

Phaedrus of Plato. Plato & W. H. Thompson. LC 72-9307. (Philosophy of Plato & Aristotle Ser.). (ENG & GRE.). 1977. reprint ed. 18.95 (*0-405-04866-1*) Ayer.

Phaenomen der Sowjetischen Archaeologie: Geschichte, Schulen, Protagonisten aus dem Russischen von D. Schorkowitz unter Mitwirkung von V. Kulik. Lev S. Klejn. (Gesellschaften und Staaten im Epochenwandel Ser.: Band 6). (GER., Illus.). 411p. 1997. pap. 76.95 (*3-631-30646-6*) P Lang Pubng.

Phaenomena. Aratus. Ed. & Tr. by Douglas Kidd. LC 96-44962. (Classical Texts & Commentaries Ser.: Vol. 34). 614p. (C). 1997. text 100.00 (*0-521-58230-X*) Cambridge U Pr.

Phaenomena. Aratus. Ed. by Ernst Maass. xxvi, 100p. 1964. 36.00 (*3-296-10500-X*) G Olms Pubs.

Phaenomenologie und Psychotheraprutische Praxis Vol. 12, Nos. 1-4, 1995: Journal: Daseinsanalyse. Ed. by G. Condrau. (Journal Ser.: Vol. 12, No. 1-4, 1995). (Illus.). 250p. 1995. pap. 73.25 (*3-8055-6230-6*) S Karger.

Phaethon see Greek Mythology

Phaeton see Chefs-d'Oeuvre Classiques de l'Opera Francais

Phage & the Origins of Molecular Biology. Ed. by John Cairns et al. LC 92-15934. 384p. 1992. 40.00 (*0-87969-407-6*) Cold Spring Harbor.

***Phage Display: A Laboratory Manual.** Carlos F. Barbas. LC 00-30834. (Illus.). 2000. pap. write for info. (*0-87969-545-5*) Cold Spring Harbor.

Phage Display of Peptides & Proteins: A Laboratory Manual. Ed. by Brian K. Kay et al. (Illus.). 344p. 1996. boxed set 47.00 (*0-12-402380-0*) Acad Pr.

Phage Mu. Ed. by Neville Symonds et al. LC 87-15102. 374p. Date not set. reprint ed. pap. 116.00 (*0-608-20709-8*, 207180700002) Bks Demand.

Phagocyte Function for Research & Clinical Evaluation. J. Paul Robinson. LC 98-12095. 400p. 1998. 109.95 (*0-471-12364-1*) Wiley.

Phagocytes: Biology, Physiology, Pathology, & Pharmacotherapeutics. Ed. by Rodolfo Paolenti et al. LC 97-43318. (Annals of the New York Academy of Sciences Ser.: No. 832). 450p. 1997. 110.00 (*1-57331-102-2*); pap. 110.00 (*1-57331-103-0*) NY Acad Sci.

Phagocytes & Cellular Immunity. Hans H. Gadebusch. 176p. 1979. 103.00 (*0-8493-5349-1*, QR185, CRC Reprint) Franklin.

Phagocytes & Disease. Ed. by M. S. Klempner et al. (Immunology & Medicine Ser.). (C). 1988. lib. bdg. 75.00 (*0-7462-0086-2*) Kluwer Academic.

Phagocytic Engulfment & Cell Adhesiveness As Cellular Surface Phenomena. Carel J. Van Oss et al. LC 75-34756. (Microorganisms & Infectious Diseases Ser.: No. 2). (Illus.). 172p. reprint ed. pap. 53.40 (*0-8357-6259-9*, 203457200090) Bks Demand.

Phaidon Architecture Guide: Docklands, London. Stephanie Williams. (Phaidon Architecture Guides Ser.). 160p. (Orig.). 1996. pap. 14.95 (*0-7148-2789-4*, Pub. by Phaidon Press) Phaidon Pr.

Phaidon Architecture Guide: Glasgow. Frank Walker. (Illus.). 192p. (C). 1994. pap. 14.95 (*1-85454-301-6*, Pub. by Phaidon Press) Phaidon Pr.

Phaidon Guide to Antique Weapons & Armour. Robert Wilkinson-Latham. write for info. (*0-318-58215-5*) P-H.

Phaistos Disc: An Interpretation of Astronomical Symbols. Leon Pomerance. (Studies in Mediterranean Archaeology: No. 6). (Illus.). 76p. (Orig.). 1976. pap. 22.50 (*91-85058-67-X*, Pub. by P Astroms) Coronet Bks.

Phakmatoses. Pierre J. Vinken & George W. Bruyn. (Handbook of Clinical Neurology Ser.: Vol. 14). 824p. 1972. 445.00 (*0-7204-7214-8*) Elsevier.

Phala Deepika. Mantreswara. Tr. by Gouri S. Kapoor. (C). 1991. 17.00 (*0-8364-2769-6*, Pub. by Ranjan Pubs) S Asia.

Phalaenopsis. O. Gruss & M. Wolff. (GER., Illus.). 190p. 1995. 59.00 (*3-8001-6551-1*, Pub. by Eugen Ulmer) Balogh.

Phalante. Galaut. Ed. by Alan Howe. (Exeter French Texts Ser.: No. 94). (FRE.). 84p. 1996. pap. text 19.95 (*0-85989-488-6*, Pub. by Univ Exeter Pr) Northwestern U Pr.

Phalanx, Vol. 1, Nos. 1-23. reprint ed. lib. bdg. 72.50 (*0-404-19539-3*) AMS Pr.

Phalanx Dragon. Timothy Rizzi. 480p. 2000. reprint ed. mass mkt. 5.99 (*0-8439-3885-4*, Leisure Bks) Dorchester Pub Co.

Phallic Quest. James Wyly. (Illus.). 128p. 1995. pap. 16.00 (*0-919123-37-6*, Pub. by Inner City Bks) BookWorld.

Phallicism: Celestial & Terrestrial; Heathen & Christian & Its Connection with the Rosicrucians & the Gnostics & Its Foundation in Buddhism. Hargrave Jennings. 325p. 1996. reprint ed. pap. 17.50 (*1-56459-648-6*) Kessinger Pub.

Phallicism, Celestrial & Terrestrial, Heathen & Christian. Hargrave Jennings. 298p. 1996. reprint ed. spiral bd. 18.50 (*0-7873-0471-9*) Hlth Research.

Phallos. Eugene A. Monick. (Illus.). 144p. 1995. pap. 16.00 (*0-919123-26-0*, Pub. by Inner City Bks) BookWorld.

Phallos: A Symbol & Its History in the Male World. Thorkil Vanggaard. LC 72-80553. (Illus.). 266p. 1972. pap. 24.95 (*0-8236-8192-0*, 24135) Intl Univs Pr.

Phallus: Sacred Symbol of Male Creative Power. Alain Danielou. LC 95-220292. (Illus.). 128p. 1995. pap. 19.95 (*0-89281-556-6*) Inner Tradit.

Phan Boi Chau & the Dong-Du Movement. Ed. by Vinh Sinh. LC 88-72217. (Lac-Viet Ser.: No. 8). viii, 215p. 1988. pap. 10.00 (*0-938692-36-4*) Yale U SE Asia.

Phanerogams. Ed. by A. R. Goerts-Van-Rijn. (Flora of the Guianas Ser.: Series A, Fascicle 15). (Illus.). 126p. 1994. pap. 110.50 (*1-878762-47-8*, 056671, Pub. by Koeltz Sci Bks) Lubrecht & Cramer.

Phanerogams: Bromeliaceae, Subfamily Tillandsiodeae. Eric J. Gouda. Ed. by A. R. A. Goerts-van-Rijn. (Flora of the Guianas Ser.: Series A, Fascicle 3). (Illus.). 112p. 1987. pap. 75.00 (*3-87429-273-8*, 029922, Pub. by Koeltz Sci Bks) Lubrecht & Cramer.

Phanerogams: Burmanniaceae. H. Maas-van de Kamer & Paul J. Maas. Ed. by A. R. A. Goerts-van-Rijn. (Flora of the Guianas Ser.: Series A, Fascicle 6). (Illus.). 45p. 1989. pap. 35.00 (*3-87429-290-8*, 036458, Pub. by Koeltz Sci Bks) Lubrecht & Cramer.

Phanerogams: Caesalpiniaceae. R. S. Cowan & J. C. Lindeman. Ed. by A. R. A. Goerts-van-Rijn. (Flora of the Guianas Ser.: Series A, Fascicle 7). (Illus.). 166p. 1989. pap. 66.00 (*3-87429-287-8*, 036890, Pub. by Koeltz Sci Bks) Lubrecht & Cramer.

Phanerogams: Chrysobalanaceae Including Wood & Timber. Ghillean T. Prance & B. J. Ter Welle. Ed. by A. R. A. Goerts-van-Rijn. (Flora of the Guianas Ser.: Series A, No. 85). (Illus.). 40p. 1986. pap. 80.00 (*3-87429-266-5*, 025647, Pub. by Koeltz Sci Bks) Lubrecht & Cramer.

Phanerogams: Gymnosperms: Cycadaceae. D. Stevenson & T. Zanoni. Ed. by A. R. A. Goerts-van-Rijn. (Flora of the Guianas Ser.: Series A, Fascicle 9). (Illus.). 40p. 1991. pap. 70.00 (*3-87429-326-2*, 045639, Pub. by Koeltz Sci Bks) Lubrecht & Cramer.

Phanerogams: Hippocrateaceae Including Wood & Timber; Icacinaceae (Including Wood & Timber) Ed. by A. R. A. Goerts-van-Rijn. (Flora of the Guianas Ser.: Series A, Fascicle 16). (Illus.). 157p. 1994. pap. 80.00 (*3-87429-365-3*, Pub. by Koeltz Sci Bks) Lubrecht & Cramer.

Phanerogams: Judziewicz Poaceae (Gramineae) E. J. Judziewicz. Ed. by A. R. A. Goerts-van-Rijn. (Flora of the Guianas Ser.: Series A, Fascicle 8). (Illus.). 114p. 1990. 210.00 (*3-87429-320-3*, 042576, Pub. by Koeltz Sci Bks) Lubrecht & Cramer.

Phanerogams: Lecythidaceae. Ed. by A. R. A. Goerts-van-Rijn. (Flora of the Guianas Ser.: Series A, Fascicle 12). (Illus.). 134p. 1993. pap. 145.00 (*3-87429-340-8*, Pub. by Koeltz Sci Bks) Lubrecht & Cramer.

Phanerogams: Melastomataceae; Memocyloideae Including Wood & Timber. Ed. by A. R. A. Goerts-van-Rijn. (Flora of the Guianas Ser.: Series A, Fascicle 13). (Illus.). 424p. 1993. pap. 157.50 (*3-87429-345-9*, Pub. by Koeltz Sci Bks) Lubrecht & Cramer.

Phanerogams: Olacaceae 103: Opiliaceae. Ed. by A. R. A. Goerts-van-Rijn. (Flora of the Guianas Ser.: Series A, Fascicle 14). (Illus.). 80p. 1993. pap. 49.95 (*3-87429-343-2*, Pub. by Koeltz Sci Bks) Lubrecht & Cramer.

Phanerogams: Onagraceae. E. M. Zardini & P. H. Raven. Ed. by A. R. A. Goerts-van-Rijn. (Flora of the Guianas Ser.: Series A, Fascicle 10). (Illus.). 45p. 1991. pap. 70.00 (*3-87429-327-0*, 045640, Pub. by Koeltz Sci Bks) Lubrecht & Cramer.

Phanerogams: Tiliaceae; Dipterocarpaceae; Wood & Timber. Ed. by A. R. A. Goerts-van-Rijn. (Flora of the Guianas Ser.: Series A, Fascicle 17). (Illus.). 15p. 1995. pap. 50.00 (*3-87429-374-2*, 053592, Pub. by Koeltz Sci Bks) Lubrecht & Cramer.

Phanerogams: Truridacea. H. Maas-van de Kamer & Paul J. Maas. Ed. by A. R. A. Goerts-van-Rijn. (Flora of the Guianas Ser.: Series A, Fascicle 5, No. 174). (Illus.). 18p. 1989. pap. 30.00 (*3-87429-289-4*, 036456, Pub. by Koeltz Sci Bks) Lubrecht & Cramer.

Phanerogams: Ulmaceae, Moraceae, Cecropiaceae, Urticaceae, Casurinaceae Including Wood & Timber. Ed. by A. R. A. Goerts-van-Rijn. (Flora of the Guianas Ser.: Series A, Fascicle 11). (Illus.). 222p. 1991. pap. 98.00 (*3-87429-330-0*, Pub. by Koeltz Sci Bks) Lubrecht & Cramer.

Phanerogams: Verbenaceae, Including Wood & Timber. Marion J. Jansen-Jacobs. Ed. by A. R. A. Goerts-van-Rijn. (Flora of the Guianas Ser.: Series A, Fascicle 4). (Illus.). 114p. 1988. pap. 45.00 (*3-87429-279-7*, 032658, Pub. by Koeltz Sci Bks) Lubrecht & Cramer.

Phanerogams: Xyridaceae & Pontederiaceae & Haemodoraceae. Ed. by A. R. A. Goerts-van-Rijn. (Flora of the Guianas Ser.: Series A, Fascicle 15). (Illus.). 126p. 1994. pap. 110.00 (*3-87429-350-5*, Pub. by Koeltz Sci Bks) Lubrecht & Cramer.

Phanerogams Fascicle 12: Lecythidaceae with Wood & Timber. Ghillean T. Prance et al. Ed. by A. R. Goerts-Van-Rijn. (Flora of the Guianas Ser.: Series A, No. 17). (Illus.). 45p. 1992. pap. 125.80 (*1-878762-33-8*, 047883, Pub. by Koeltz Sci Bks) Lubrecht & Cramer.

Phanerogams Fascicle 13: Melastomataceae, Including Wood & Timber. John J. Wurdack et al. Ed. by A. R. Goerts-Van-Rijn. (Flora of the Guianas Ser.: Series A, Fascicle 13). (Illus.). 425p. 1993. pap. 178.50 (*1-878762-41-9*, 053647, Pub. by Koeltz Sci Bks) Lubrecht & Cramer.

Phanerogams Fascicle 14: Phanerogamae: Olacaceae, Opiliaceae - Balanophoraceae. B. Hansen & P. Hiepko. Ed. by A. R. Goerts-Van-Rijn. (Flora of the Guianas Ser.: Series A, Fascicle 14). (Illus.). 80p. 1993. pap. 55.25 (*1-878762-39-7*, 053648, Pub. by Koeltz Sci Bks) Lubrecht & Cramer.

Phanerogams Fascicle 16: Phanerogamae: Hippocrateaceae & Icacinaceae; Including Wood & Timber. P. Detienne et al. Ed. by A. R. Goerts-Van-Rijn. (Flora of the Guianas Ser.: Series A, Fascicle 16). (Illus.). 157p. 1995. pap. 68.00 (*1-878762-63-X*, 056670, Pub. by Koeltz Sci Bks) Lubrecht & Cramer.

Phanerozoic Diversity Patterns: Profiles in Macroevolution. Ed. by James W. Valentine. LC 84-42905. (Princeton Series in Geology & Paleontology). (Illus.). 452p. 1985. reprint ed. pap. 140.20 (*0-608-07655-4*, 205997500010) Bks Demand.

Phanerozoic Earth History of Australia. J. J. Veevers. (Oxford Monographs on Geology & Geophysics: No. 2). (Illus.). 432p. 1987. pap. text 59.00 (*0-19-854488-X*) OUP.

Phanerozoic Faunal & Floral Realms of the Earth: The Intercalary Relations of the Malvinokaffric & Gondwana Faunal Realms with the Tethyan Faunal Realm. Ed. by Arthur A. Meyerhoff et al. (Memoir Ser.: No. 189). (Illus.). 69p. 1996. 40.00 (*0-8137-1189-4*) Geol Soc.

Phanerozoic Geology of Northwest China. Ed. by Zhou Zhiyi & W. T. Dean. (Illus.). 336p. 1996. 122.50 (*90-6764-228-2*, Pub. by VSP) Coronet Bks.

Phanerozoic Geology of the World, Vol. I. M. Moullade & Alan E. Nairn. (Palaeozoic Ser.: Pt. A). 430p. 1991. 255.75 (*0-444-87384-8*) Elsevier.

Phanerozoic Geology of the World: The Mesozoic, Vol. 2A. Ed. by M. Moullade & Alan E. Nairn. 530p. 1978. 273.00 (*0-444-41671-4*) Elsevier.

Phanerozoic Geology of the World: The Mesozoic, Vol. 2B. Ed. by M. Moullade & Alan E. Nairn. 450p. 1983. 264.25 (*0-444-41672-2*, I-343-83) Elsevier.

Phanerozoic Geology of the World Vol. IB: The Paleozoic. Ed. by Alan E. Nairn & M. Moullade. 704p. 1995. 293.25 (*0-444-82090-6*) Elsevier.

Phanerozoic Ironstones. Ed. by T. P. Young & W. E. Taylor. (Geological Society Special Publications: No. 46). (Illus.). 280p. 1989. 48.00 (*0-903317-43-5*, 234, Pub. by Geol Soc Pub Hse) AAPG.

Phanerozoic Phosphorite Depositional Systems: A Dynamic Model for a Sedimentary Resource System. J. Trappe. Ed. by S. Bhattacharji et al. LC 98-29394. (Lecture Notes in Earth Sciences Ser.: Vol. 76). (Illus.). xii, 316p. 1998. pap. 98.00 (*3-540-63581-5*) Spr-Verlag.

Phanerozoic Sea-Level Changes. Anthony Hallam. (Perspectives in Paleobiology & Earth History Ser.). 224p. 1992. text 58.50 (*0-231-07424-7*); pap. text 28.00 (*0-231-07425-5*) Col U Pr.

Phanerozoic Stromatolites II. Ed. by Janine Bertrand-Sarfati & Claude Monty. LC 94-4221. 496p. (C). 1994. text 272.50 (*0-7923-2747-0*) Kluwer Academic.

Phanologische Entwicklungsstadien Monotyler, Dikotyler Pflanzen: English/French/German/Spanish. Bundesanstalt fur Arbeitsschutz Staff. (ENG, FRE, GER & SPA.). 590p. 1997. 150.00 (*0-320-00449-X*) Fr & Eur.

Phanomelogie Heute. Ed. by W. Biemel. (Phaenomenologica Ser.: No. 51). 228p. 1972. lib. bdg. 73.50 (*90-247-1336-6*, Pub. by M Nijhoff) Kluwer Academic.

Phanomen des "Ekels Vor Dem Leben" Bei Pierre Teilhard de Chardin. Peter Modler. (Europaische Hochschulschriften Ser.: Reihe 23, Bd. 394). (GER.). 185p. 1990. 43.80 (*3-631-42907-X*) P Lang Pubng.

Phanomen Zeit Bei Jan Vermeer van Delft. Irene Netta. (Studien Zur Kunstgeschichte Ser.: Bd. 105). (GER., Illus.). 270p. 1996. write for info. (*3-487-10160-2*) G Olms Pubs.

Phanomenologie der Assoziation. E. Holenstein. (Phaenomenologica Ser.: No. 44). 396p. 1972. lib. bdg. 202.00 (*90-247-1175-4*, Pub. by M Nijhoff) Kluwer Academic.

Phanomenologie der Mathematik: Elemente Einer Phanomenologischen Aufklarung der Mathematischen Erkenntnis Nach Husserl. Dieter Lohmar. (Phaenomenologica Ser.: No. 114). 252p. 1989. lib. bdg. 171.00 (*0-7923-0187-0*, Pub. by Kluwer Academic) Kluwer Academic.

Phanomenologie des Alltaglichen: Vom Aspekt der Leiblichkeit des Menschen Her. Shin-ichi Yuasa. (Illus.). VIII, 161p. 1998. 34.95 (*3-631-31008-0*) P Lang Pubng.

Phanomenologie und das Problem der Grundlegung der Ethik an Hand des Versuchs von Max Scheler. Elichi Shimomisse. (GER.). 153p. 1971. pap. text 57.00 (*90-247-5062-8*, Pub. by M Nijhoff) Kluwer Academic.

Phanomenologische Feldbegriff Bei Aron Gurwitsch. Zaeshick Choi. (Europaische Hochschulschriften Ser.: Reihe 20, Bd. 519). (GER.). 293p. 1996. 57.95 (*3-631-48021-0*) P Lang Pubng.

Phanomenologische Psychologie. 2nd ed. Edmund Husserl. (Husserliana Collected Works: No. 9). 677p. 1968. lib. bdg. 206.50 (*90-247-0226-7*, Pub. by M Nijhoff) Kluwer Academic.

Phanoregamia see United States Exploring Expedition During the Years 1838-1842 under the Command of Charles Wilkes: Botanical Section

Phantasie. Sybille Pearson. 1989. pap. 6.95 (*0-88145-079-0*) Broadway Play.

Phantasie, Bildbewusstsein, Erinnerung: Zur Phanomenologie der Anschaulichen Vergegenwartigungen. Edmund Husserl. Tr. by Eduard Marbach. (Husserliana Collected Works: Vol. 23). (GER.). 770p. 1980. lib. bdg. 361.00 (*90-247-2119-9*, Pub. by M Nijhoff) Kluwer Academic.

Phantasie und Wirklichkeit: Benedikte Naubert Im Spiegel Ihrer Spaten Romane und Erzahlungen (1802-1820) Victoria Scheibler. (GER.). XIV, 218p. 1997. 44.95 (*3-631-45595-X*) P Lang Pubng.

Phantasies of a Love-Thief: The Caurapancasika Attributed to Bilhana. Tr. by Barbara S. Miller. LC 77-122947. (Studies in Oriental Culture: No. 6). 233p. 1971. text 57.50 (*0-231-03451-2*) Col U Pr.

Phantasies of Gay Sex: Drawings & Water Colour. Ed Cervone. 1998. 79.95 (*3-925443-69-X*) Janvid Pubs.

Phantasmagoria. Evelyn Douglas. Ed. by Ian Fletcher & John Stokes. LC 82-49104. (Degeneration & Regeneration Ser.). 150p. 1984. lib. bdg. 25.00 (*0-8240-5567-5*) Garland.

Phantasmagoria. Lewis Carroll, pseud. (Literary Classics Ser.). (Illus.). 70p. 1998. reprint ed. pap. 5.95 (*1-57392-252-8*) Prometheus Bks.

Phantasmagoria, Bk. 1. Kenneth Smith. (Illus.). 64p. 1990. pap. 9.95 (*1-56097-026-X*) Fantagraph Bks.

Phantasmagoria: A Book of Poems. Altan Ogniedou. Ed. by Ian E. Probstein. (Illus.). 80p. 1993. pap. text 6.00 (*0-9635200-0-8*) R E M Pr.

Phantasmagoria: An Original Anthology. Ed. by R. Reginald & Douglas A. Menville. LC 75-46292. (Supernatural & Occult Fiction Ser.). 1976. lib. bdg. 34.95 (*0-405-08152-9*) Ayer.

Phantasmagoria: The Sociology of Opera. Ed. by David T. Evans. LC 97-46174. (Popular Culture Studies). 460p. 1998. pap. 43.95 (*1-85742-209-0*, ML1700.E92, Pub. by Ashgate Pub); text 56.95 (*1-85742-205-8*, ML1700.E92, Pub. by Ashgate Pub) Ashgate Pub Co.

Phantasmagoria Puzzle of Flesh: The Official Strategy Guide. Rick Barba. LC 96-70079. 192p. 1996. pap., per. 19.99 (*0-7615-0877-5*) Prima Pub.

Phantasmagoria Sexualis. Eric Felderman. (Illus.). 1994. 54.00 (*0-945942-48-6*); pap. 39.95 (*0-945942-49-4*) Portmanteau Editions.

Phantasmagoric Accounting, Vol. 14. Robert E. Jensen. (Studies in Accounting Research). 209p. 1976. 12.00 (*0-86539-001-0*) Am Accounting.

Phantasmatic Indochina: French Colonial Ideology in Architecture, Film, & Literature. Panivong Norindr. LC 95-50856. (Asia-Pacific Ser.). 240p. 1996. pap. text 16.95 (*0-8223-1787-7*); lib. bdg. 44.95 (*0-8223-1778-8*) Duke.

Phantasmatic Radio. Allen S. Weiss. LC 95-4120. 144p. 1995. text 39.95 (*0-8223-1652-8*); pap. text 15.95 (*0-8223-1664-1*) Duke.

Phantasmion. Sara Coleridge. LC 93-46493. (Revolution & Romanticism, 1789-1834 Ser.). 1994. 65.00 (*1-85477-166-3*) Continuum.

Phantasms of the Living, 2 Vols. Edmund Gurney. LC 71-119868. (History of Psychology Ser.). 1970. reprint ed. 150.00 (*0-8201-1075-2*) Schol Facsimiles.

Phantasms of the Living: Cases of Telepathy Printed in the Journal of the Society for Psychical Research During Thirty-Five Years, 2 vols. Eleanor M. Sidgwick et al. LC 75-7403. (Perspectives in Psychical Research Ser.). 1975. reprint ed. 81.95 (*0-405-06991-X*) Ayer.

Phantastes. George MacDonald. 1981. pap. 8.00 (*0-8028-6060-5*) Eerdmans.

Phantastes. George MacDonald. (George MacDonald Original Works Ser.: Series IV). (Illus.). 324p. 1998. reprint ed. 22.00 (*1-881084-22-1*) Johannesen.

Phantastic Painted Desert & the Phenomenal Petrified Forest. Carole Marsh. (Interactive Multimedia Titles Ser.). (J). (gr. 2-9). 1996. 29.95 (*0-7933-7608-4*, C Marsh); pap. 19.95 (*0-7933-7609-2*, C Marsh); pap., teacher ed. 19.95 (*0-7933-7845-1*, C Marsh) Gallopade Intl.

Phantastica: A Classic Survey on the Use & Abuse of Mind-Altering Plants. Louis Levin. Tr. by P. H. Wirth. LC 98-9484. 320p. 1998. pap. 16.95 (*0-89281-783-6*, Inner Trad) Inner Tradit.

***Phantastische Bei E. T. A. Hoffmann.** Kenneth B. Woodgate. 274p. 1999. 48.95 (*3-631-34453-8*) P Lang Pubng.

***Phantastische Elemente im Postmodernen Roman: Formen und Funktionen Non-Mimetischer Darstellungsweisen in Ausgewahlten Werken der Englischsprachigen Literatur.** Anke S. Herling. 160p. 1999. 32.00 (*3-631-34441-4*) P Lang Pubng.

Phantasy in Everyday Life: A Psychoanalytical Approach to Understanding Ourselves. J. Segal. 234p. 1995. pap. 25.50 (*1-85575-120-8*, Pub. by H Karnac Bks Ltd) Other Pr LLC.

P

An Asterisk (*) at the beginning of an entry indicates that the title is appearing for the first time.

Phantasy in Everyday Life: A Psychoanalytical Approach to Understanding Ourselves. Ed. by Julia Segal. LC 95-33577. 238p. 1995. pap. 45.00 (*1-56821-753-6*) Aronson.

Phantom. (YA). 1996. pap. text 5.99 (*0-934551-10-3*) Starlog Grp Inc.

Phantom. Rob MacGregor. 1996. mass mkt. 5.99 (*0-380-78887-X*, Avon Bks) Morrow Avon.

Phantom. Barbara Steiner. 176p. (YA). (gr. 7-9). 1993. pap. 3.50 (*0-590-46425-6*) Scholastic Inc.

Phantom: Spirit in the Skies. Ed. by Jon Lake. 232p. 1993. 34.95 (*1-880588-04-8*) AIRtime Pub.

Phantom: The Last Vampire. Christopher Pike, pseud. (YA). (gr. 9 up). 1996. mass mkt. 3.99 (*0-671-55030-6*) PB.

Phantom - The American Musical Sensation. Ed. by Milton Okun. pap. 12.95 (*0-89524-727-5*, Pub. by Cherry Lane) H Leonard.

Phantom Affair. Jo A. Ferguson. 224p. 1996. mass mkt. 4.50 (*0-8217-5428-9*, Zebra Kensgtn) Kensgtn Pub Corp.

Phantom Affair. Michael A. Stackpole et al. (Star Wars: No. 1). 112p. (YA). (gr. 8-12). 1998. pap. text 12.95 (*1-56971-251-4*) Dark Horse Comics.

***Phantom & the Abyss: The Gothic Fiction in America & Aesthetics of the Sublime, 1798-1856.** Marek Wilczynski. (Polish Studies in English Language & Literature). 285p. 1999. pap. 42.95 (*3-631-35321-9*) P Lang Pubng.

Phantom Animals. Daniel Cohen. (J). 1991. 8.09 (*0-606-05541-X*, Pub. by Turtleback) Demco.

Phantom Animals. Daniel Cohen. Ed. by Ruth Ashby. 112p. (J). (gr. 4-7). 1993. reprint ed. pap. 2.99 (*0-671-75930-2*, Minstrel Bks) PB.

Phantom Army of the Civil War: And Other Southern Ghost Stories. Frank Spaeth. LC 97-9237. 256p. 1999. pap. 9.95 (*1-56718-297-6*) Llewellyn Pubns.

Phantom Chapters of the Quijote. Raymond S. Willis, Jr. 128p. 1953. 2.00 (*0-318-14299-6*) Hispanic Inst.

Phantom Church & Other Short Stories from Romania. Georgiana Farnoaga et al. LC 96-25237. (Russian & East European Studies). 240p. 1997. pap. 19.95 (*0-8229-5608-X*); text 44.95 (*0-8229-3951-7*) U of Pittsburgh Pr.

***Phantom Coach: Collected Ghost Stories.** Amelia B. Edwards. Ed. by Richard Dalby. xviii, 312p. 1999. 42.50 (*1-899562-82-6*) Ash-Tree.

Phantom Communities: The Simulacrum & the Limits of Postmodernism. Scott Durham. LC 97-43145. 1998. 49.50 (*0-8047-3071-7*); pap. 18.95 (*0-8047-3336-8*) Stanford U Pr.

Phantom Custodian. Mark Littleton. (Get a Clue Mystery Puzzles Ser.). 16p. (J). (gr. 4-7). 1997. 12.99 (*0-7847-0731-6*, 04111) Standard Pub.

Phantom Deer. Joseph W. Lippincott. (Illus.). (YA). (gr. 7-9). 1954. 11.95 (*0-397-30278-9*) HarpC Child Bks.

Phantom Doors: Screenplay. Jorn K. Bramann. LC 95-70027. (Upper Potomacs Ser.). (Illus.). 120p. (Orig.). 1996. pap. 5.00 (*0-945073-19-4*) Nightsun MD.

Phantom Empire: Movies in the Mind of the Twentieth Century. Geoffrey O'Brien. (Illus.). 288p. 1995. pap. 12.00 (*0-393-31296-8*, Norton Paperbks) Norton.

Phantom Empires: The Novels of Alexander Lernet-Holenia & the Question of Postimperial Austrian Identity. Robert Dassanowsky. (Studies in Austrian Literature, Culture, & Thought). 223p. 1996. 49.50 (*1-57241-030-2*) Ariadne CA.

Phantom Encounters. (Mysteries of the Unknown Ser.). (Illus.). 160p. 1988. lib. bdg. 23.27 (*0-8094-6329-6*) Time-Life.

Phantom Encounters. Time-Life Books Editors. (Mysteries of the Unknown Ser.). (Illus.). 144p. 1988. 14.95 (*0-8094-6328-8*) Time-Life.

Phantom Fair. Lael J. Littke. LC 96-26246. (Bee There Ser.: Bk. 7). 156p. (J). (gr. 3-7). 1996. pap. 6.95 (*1-57345-200-9*, Cinnamon Tree) Deseret Bk.

Phantom Falcon. Anne Schraff. Ed. by Liz Parker. (Take Ten Bks.). (Illus.). 51p. (YA). (gr. 6-12). 1993. pap. text 3.95 (*1-56254-092-0*) Saddleback Pubns.

***Phantom Falcon.** rev. ed. Anne Schraff. (Take Ten Ser.). (Illus.). 51p. (YA). (gr. 4-12). 1999. pap. 3.95 (*1-58659-031-6*) Artesian.

Phantom Father: A Memoir. Barry Gifford. LC 96-48109. (Illus.). 256p. (C). 1997. 23.00 (*0-15-100250-9*) Harcourt.

Phantom Form: The Experiences in Earth & Spirit Life. Nettie P. Fox. 169p. 1996. reprint ed. spiral bd. 13.00 (*0-7873-0332-1*) Hlth Research.

Phantom Formations: Aesthetic Ideology & the Bildungsroman. Marc Redfield. LC 96-17186. (Illus.). 256p. 1996. text 37.50 (*0-8014-3236-7*) Cornell U Pr.

Phantom Fortress. Bruce Lancaster. 1976. reprint ed. lib. bdg. 24.95 (*0-88411-683-2*) Amereon Ltd.

Phantom Freighter. rev. ed. Franklin W. Dixon. LC 75-115957. (Hardy Boys Mystery Stories Ser.: No. 26). (Illus.). 180p. (J). (gr. 4-7). 1947. 5.95 (*0-448-08926-2*, G & D) Peng Put Young Read.

Phantom from the Past. Jarrold Printing Staff. (Ghost Ser.). (Illus.). 118p. 1993. pap. 7.95 (*0-7117-0358-2*, Pub. by JARR UK) Seven Hills Bk.

Phantom Garden. large type ed. Sheila Bishop. (Historical Romance Ser.). 320p. 1992. 27.99 (*0-7089-2619-3*) Ulverscroft.

Phantom Gardener, Vol. 3. Mary C. Reid. (Backpack Mystery Ser.). 8p. (J). (gr. 2-5). 1997. pap. 3.99 (*1-55661-717-8*) Bethany Hse.

Phantom Ghost of Harriet Lou: And Other Elk Stories. Roland Cheek. Ed. by Robert Elman. Tr. by Laura Donavan. LC 98-201551. (Illus.). 352p. 1998. pap. 19.95 (*0-918981-04-2*) Skyline Pub.

Phantom Gringo Boat: Shamanic Discourse & Development in Panama. Stephanie C. Kane. LC 93-45976. (Series in Ethnographic Inquiry). (Illus.). 288p. 1994. pap. text 19.95 (*1-56098-360-4*) Smithsonian.

Phantom Guardians: The F-4 in the Air National Guard. Daniel Soulaine. (Osprey Colour Library). (Illus.). 128p. 1992. pap. 15.95 (*1-85532-198-X*, Pub. by Ospry) Motorbooks Intl.

Phantom Hitchhiker: And Other Ghost Stories. Daniel Cohen & Elsie Lennox. LC 94-42549. (Illus.). 64p. (J). (gr. 2-7). 1995. pap. 3.95 (*1-85697-572-X*) LKC.

Phantom Homology. Melvin Hochster & Craig L. Huneke. LC 92-463. (Memoirs of the American Mathematical Society Ser.: No. 490). 91p. 1993. pap. 29.00 (*0-8218-2556-9*, MEMO/103/490) Am Math.

Phantom Horse. Bonnie Bryant. (Saddle Club Ser.: No. 59). (J). (gr. 4-6). 1997. 9.09 (*0-606-10915-3*, Pub. by Turtleback) Demco.

Phantom Horse of Collister's Fields. Gail E. Johnson. (Indian Culture Ser.). (J). (gr. 4-12). 1974. pap. 3.95 (*0-89992-062-4*) Coun India Ed.

Phantom Horseman. Gordon Snell. 124p. 1997. pap. 8.95 (*1-85371-797-5*, Pub. by Poolbeg Pr) Dufour.

Phantom Hour & Other Stories. Sri Aurobindo. 44p. 1995. pap. 0.50 (*81-7058-434-5*, Pub. by SAA) E-W Cultural Ctr.

Phantom Husband. Alana Clayton. (Zebra Regency Romance Ser.). 256p. 1998. mass mkt. 4.99 (*0-8217-6063-7*, Zebra Kensgtn) Kensgtn Pub Corp.

Phantom Illness. Carla Cantor. 368p. 1997. pap. 15.00 (*0-395-85992-1*) HM.

***Phantom Illness: Shattering the Myth of Hypochondria.** Carla Cantor & Brian A. Fallon. 351p. 2000. reprint ed. text 23.00 (*0-7881-9269-8*) DIANE Pub.

Phantom in Combat. Walter Boyne. LC 84-52013. (Illus.). 192p. 1994. 35.00 (*0-88740-599-1*) Schiffer.

***Phantom in the Bedchamber.** Ed Okonowicz. (Spirits Between the Bays Ser.: Vol. 9). (Illus.). 112p. 2000. pap. 9.95 (*1-890690-05-8*) Myst & Lace.

Phantom in the Mirror. John R. Erickson. LC 99-19583. (Hank the Cowdog Ser.: No. 20). (Illus.). 144p. (J). (gr. 2-5). 1998. pap. 4.99 (*0-14-130396-4*, PuffinBks) Peng Put Young Read.

Phantom in the Mirror. John R. Erickson. (Hank the Cowdog Ser.: No. 20). (Illus.). (J). (gr. 2-5). 1993. 12.05 (*0-606-05329-8*, Pub. by Turtleback) Demco.

***Phantom in the Mirror.** John R. Erickson. (Hank the Cowdog Ser.: No. 20). (Illus.). (J). (gr. 2-5). 2000. 14.99 (*0-670-88427-8*) Viking Penguin.

Phantom Islands of the Atlantic. Donald S. Johnson. 1998. pap. 12.00 (*0-380-73078-2*, Avon Bks) Morrow Avon.

Phantom Islands of the Atlantic: The Legends of Seven Lands That Never Were. rev. ed. Donald S. Johnson. LC 96-26067. (Illus.). 240p. 1996. 22.95 (*0-8027-1320-3*) Walker & Co.

Phantom Journal & Other Essays & Diversions. Edward V. Lucas. LC 75-111844. (Essay Index Reprint Ser.). 1977. 20.95 (*0-8369-1615-8*) Ayer.

Phantom Lady. Matt Baker. 64p. 1994. pap. 9.95 (*1-885730-02-0*) Verotik.

Phantom Lady. William Irish. 292p. 1994. 35.00 (*1-883402-73-5*) S&S Trade.

Phantom Leader. Mark Berent. 448p. 1992. mass mkt. 5.99 (*0-515-10785-9*, Jove) Berkley Pub.

Phantom Love. Sonya T. Pelton. (Orig.). 1982. mass mkt. 3.50 (*0-89083-950-6*, Zebra Kensgtn) Kensgtn Pub Corp.

Phantom Lover. Susan Napier. (Presents Ser.). 1994. per. 2.99 (*0-373-11707-8*, 1-11707-6) Harlequin Bks.

Phantom Lover. large type ed. Susan Napier. (Harlequin Ser.). 1995. lib. bdg. 18.95 (*0-263-13938-7*) Thorndike Pr.

Phantom Menace, Vol.1. George Lucas. (Star Wars Ser.). (Illus.). 112p. 1999. pap. 12.95 (*1-56971-359-6*) Dark Horse Comics.

***Phantom Menace: Star Wars Art of Epic One.** Ballantine Books Publishing Staff. (Art of Star Wars Ser.). (Illus.). (J). 2000. pap. 22.95 (*0-345-43109-X*, Del Rey) Ballantine Pub Grp.

Phantom Menace Coloring Book. (J). 2000. pap. 2.99 (*0-375-80511-7*, Pub. by Random Bks Yng Read) Random.

***Phantom Menace: Episode One.** 1999. 7.98 incl. audio (*1-56826-996-X*); 11.98 incl. audio compact disk Rhino Enter.

***Phantom Menace: Episode 1: The Art of Star Wars.** Jonathan Bresman. (Star Wars). (Illus.). 1999. 39.95 (*0-345-43108-1*, Del Rey) Ballantine Pub Grp.

Phantom of Devil's Bridge & the Tale of Buffalo Castle. Ed. by Karel B. Asolon. (Moravian Tales, Legends, Myths Ser.). (Illus.). 41p. (Orig.). (J). (gr. 4). 1985. pap. 12.00 (*0-930329-04-X*) Kabel Pubs.

Phantom of Fact: A Guide to Nabokov's PNIN. Gennady Barabtarlo. 1989. 37.95 (*0-87501-060-1*) Ardis Pubs.

Phantom of Five Chimneys. Betty R. Wright. 128p. (J). (gr. 3-7). 1998. pap. 3.95 (*0-8167-4525-0*) Troll Communs.

Phantom of Harley Grange. Jane Percy. (C). 1989. 42.00 (*0-7223-2308-5*, Pub. by A H S Ltd) St Mut.

***Phantom of Manhattan.** Frederick Forsyth. LC 99-15882. 192p. 1999. 19.95 (*0-312-24656-0*, Thomas Dunne) St Martin.

***Phantom of Manhattan.** Frederick Forsyth. 2000. mass mkt. 6.50 (*0-312-97585-6*) St Martin.

Phantom of Phys Ed. Fred E. Katz. LC 97-24441. (SpineChillers Mysteries Ser.: No. 5). 144p. (J). (gr. 3-7). 1997. pap. 5.99 (*0-8499-4060-5*) Tommy Nelson.

Phantom of Pine Hill. Carolyn Keene. (Nancy Drew Mystery Stories Ser.: No. 42). (Illus.). 180p. (J). (gr. 4-7). 1964. 5.99 (*0-448-09542-4*, G & D) Peng Put Young Read.

Phantom of Pueblo, No. 3. Jerry Jerman. (Journeys of Jessie Land Ser.). 132p. (J). 1995. pap. 5.99 (*1-56476-466-4*, 6-3466, Victor Bks) Chariot Victor.

Phantom of the Auditorium. R. L. Stine, pseud. (Goosebumps Ser.: No. 24). 160p. (J). (gr. 4-6). 1994. pap. 3.99 (*0-590-48354-4*) Scholastic Inc.

Phantom of the Auditorium. R. L. Stine, pseud. (Goosebumps Ser.: No. 24). 1994. 9.09 (*0-606-06664-0*, Pub. by Turtleback) Demco.

Phantom of the Cinema: Character in Modern Film. Lloyd Michaels. LC 97-11383. (Cultural Studies in Cinema - Video). (Illus.). 191p. (C). 1997. pap. text 19.95 (*0-7914-3568-7*) State U NY Pr.

Phantom of the Cinema: Character in Modern Film. Lloyd Michaels. LC 97-11383. (Cultural Studies in Cinema - Video). (Illus.). 191p. (C). 1997. text 59.50 (*0-7914-3567-9*) State U NY Pr.

***Phantom of the Haunted Church.** Bill Myers. LC 97-45451. (Bloodhounds, Inc. Ser.). (Illus.). 124p. (J). (gr. 4-8). 1998. pap. 5.99 (*1-55661-892-1*) Bethany Hse.

Phantom of the Lunch Wagon. Daniel Pinkwater. LC 92-3051. (Illus.). 32p. (J). (gr. k up). 1992. lib. bdg. 13.95 (*0-02-774641-0*, Mac Bks Young Read) S&S Childrens.

***Phantom of the Movies' Videoscope: The Ultimate Guide to the Latest, Greatest & Weirdest Genre Videos.** Joe Kane. 2000. pap. 25.00 (*0-8129-3149-1*, Times Bks) Crown Pub Group.

Phantom of the Music Hall. Judith Prior. 55p. 1996. pap. 10.00 (*0-88734-017-2*) Players Pr.

Phantom of the Night. Ed. by Martin H. Greenberg. 1996. pap. 5.99 (*0-88677-696-1*, Pub. by DAW Bks) Penguin Putnam.

Phantom of the Night: Overcome Sleep Apnea Syndrome - Win Your Hidden Struggle to Breathe, Sleep & Live. 3rd rev. ed. T. Scott Johnson et al. (Illus.). 192p. (Orig.). 1999. pap. 29.95 (*1-882431-05-7*) New Technology.

Sleep apnea disrupts the lives of millions - their sleep is repeatedly disturbed by snoring, by choking halts in breathing & by gasping efforts to breathe. Their struggle causes poor sleep, a major cause of daytime sleepiness, accidents, poor health, lost years of productivity & happiness & even death. Doctors & a patient guide people with obstructive sleep apnea & their families to take advantage of dramatically effective medical treatment. They explain snoring & sleep apnea; how to identify apnea, obtain a diagnosis, get treatment, overcome social, physical, or emotional obstacles to recovery. They review treatment options: CPAP, bi-level & intelligent positive pressure treatment devices, the role of surgery & oral devices. Coverage of practical issues in CPAP treatment, travel precautions for surgery & other health care contexts, equipment, bibliography, internet resources, organizations & manufacturers. Broughton, the medical director of the ASDA-accrediated University of Alabama Knowlwood Sleep Disorders Center updates current advances in understanding, diagnosing & treating sleep apnea. "The disease had extraordinary impact upon my life, affecting my personality, relationships, family & career. You bring a profound message of hope that the disease can be controlled & resurrect one's life."--Lawrence Larsen, Software Engineer, treated for sleep apnea. "More scientific, clinical & practical information for the health-care professional than is provided in all but a small percentage of medical, respiratory & nursing schools."--Respiratory Care. In USA, send $29.95 (MA residents add sales tax) per copy (includes Priority Mall delivery) to New Technology Publishing, Inc., POB 1737, Onset MA 02558-1737. 508-291-1111, or 1-800-67-APNEA (1-800-672-7632) Fax: 1-800-45-APNEA (1-800-452-7632) Distribution: Unique, Quality, Baker & Taylor, or direct by STOP order. <http://www.newtechpub.com>. E-mail: <apnea@newtechpub.com> e-mail: <phantom@newtechpub.com>. *Publisher Paid Annotation.*

Phantom of the Night: Overcome Sleep Apnea Syndrome--Win Your Hidden Struggle to Breathe, Sleep & Live. rev. ed. T. Scott Johnson & Jerry Halberstadt. (Illus.). 192p. (Orig.). 1996. pap. 29.95 (*1-882431-02-2*) New Technology.

Phantom of the Old Opera House: Comedy - Mystery in 3-Acts. Joseph G. Caruso. 48p. (J). (gr. 4 up). 1982. pap. 4.00 (*0-88680-153-2*) I E Clark.

Phantom of the Opera see Fantome De l'Opera

***Phantom of the Opera.** 16p. 1998. pap. 5.95 (*0-7935-9664-5*) H Leonard.

Phantom of the Opera. Jennifer Bassett. (Illus.). 48p. 1993. pap. text 5.95 (*0-19-422707-3*) OUP.

Phantom of the Opera. Gaston Leroux. Date not set. lib. bdg. 26.95 (*0-8488-1652-8*) Amereon Ltd.

Phantom of the Opera. Gaston Leroux. 288p. 1990. mass mkt. 4.95 (*0-553-21376-8*) Bantam.

Phantom of the Opera. Gaston Leroux. 1975. lib. bdg. 28.95 (*0-89966-136-X*) Buccaneer Bks.

Phantom of the Opera. Gaston Leroux. (Signet Classics Ser.). 1989. mass mkt. 4.95 (*0-451-52482-9*, Sig Classics) NAL.

Phantom of the Opera. Gaston Leroux. (Classics for Young Readers Ser.). (Illus.). 352p. (YA). (gr. 5 up). 1994. pap. 3.99 (*0-14-036813-2*, PuffinBks) Peng Put Young Read.

Phantom of the Opera. Gaston Leroux. LC 88-34079. (Bullseye Chillers Ser.). (Illus.). 96p. (J). (gr. 3-7). 1989. pap. 3.99 (*0-394-83847-5*, Pub. by Random Bks Yng Read) Random.

Phantom of the Opera. Gaston Leroux. 1938. 10.60 (*0-606-03258-4*, Pub. by Turtleback) Demco.

Phantom of the Opera. Gaston Leroux. 1995. mass mkt. 5.95 (*0-352-31716-7*, Pub. by Virgin Bks) London Brdge.

Phantom of the Opera. Gaston Leroux. 272p. 1986. mass mkt. 5.99 (*0-446-30120-5*) Warner Bks.

Phantom of the Opera. Gaston Leroux. (Classics Library). 224p. 1998. pap. 3.95 (*1-85326-273-0*, 2730WW, Pub. by Wrdsworth Edits) NTC Contemp Pub Co.

Phantom of the Opera. abr. ed. Gaston Leroux. Tr. by Lowell Bair. LC 98-8845. 336p. (YA). 1998. mass mkt. 3.99 (*0-440-22774-7*) BDD Bks Young Read.

Phantom of the Opera. large type ed. Gaston Leroux. (Large Print Heritage Ser.). 420p. (J). (gr. 7-12). 1999. lib. bdg. 35.95 (*1-58118-043-8*, 22512) LRS.

***Phantom of the Opera: Abraham,&F. Murray, Set.** abr. ed. Gaston Leroux. 1998. audio 18.00 (*0-89845-776-9*, CPN 2108) HarperAudio.

Phantom of the Opera: Intermediate Piano Solos. Andrew Lloyd Webber. 56p. 1993. pap. 12.95 (*0-7935-1655-2*, 00290386) H Leonard.

Phantom of the Opera: Piano Solos. Andrew Lloyd Webber. 48p. 1993. pap. 12.95 (*0-7935-1657-9*, 00292005) H Leonard.

Phantom of the Opera: The Original Novel. Gaston Leroux. LC 87-45635. 368p. 1988. reprint ed. mass mkt. 7.00 (*0-06-080924-8*, PL-7140, Perennial) HarperTrade.

Phantom of the Opera: The Original Shooting Script. Riley Philip J. Ed. by John Conforti. LC 90-61040. (Universal Filmscript Series: Classic Horror Films). (Illus.). 1999. pap. text 24.95 (*1-882127-33-1*) Magicimage Filmbooks.

Most people think that they are watching the original Phantom of the Opera on home video or in revival houses. The existing print of the film is actually a silent version of a 1929 dubbed sound reissue, which is missing at least 35 minutes of development scenes, opera scenes, titles & some of the best atmospheric photography & set designs in motion picture history. The present unmasking scene is pale compared to the original. In this comprehensive history of this landmark horror film, author Phil Riley presents the complete, complex production of this amazing film. The 320 page book includes: the complete shooting script, the complete press book, rare behind the scenes photos, & recreations of lost scenes. Contributions by Mary Philbin ("Christine"), cinematographer Charles van Enger, Ray Bradbury, Ron Chaney & more! *Publisher Paid Annotation.*

Phantom of the Opera Musical: Based upon the novel by Gaston Leroux. Joseph Robinette & Robert Chauls. 1992. pap. 5.95 (*0-87129-173-8*, P08) Dramatic Pub.

***Phantom of the Opera Piano Duets.** 64p. 1998. pap. 10.95 (*0-7935-5836-0*) H Leonard.

Phantom of the Opera, the Play. Gaston Leroux. 1979. pap. 5.50 (*0-87129-363-3*, P45) Dramatic Pub.

Phantom of the Pines: More Tales of the Jersey Devil. James F. McCloy & Ray Miller, Jr. LC 98-13684. 1998. pap. 11.95 (*0-912608-95-1*) Mid Atlantic.

Phantom of the Poles. William Reed. 1996. reprint ed. spiral bd. 23.00 (*0-7873-0711-4*) Hlth Research.

Phantom of the Poles: Mysteries of the Polar Regions & the Interior of the Earth. William Reed. 1991. lib. bdg. 79.95 (*0-8490-4966-0*) Gordon Pr.

Phantom of the Temple. Robert H. Van Gulik. LC 95-24390. (Illus.). 205p. 1995. pap. 8.95 (*0-226-84877-9*) U Ch Pr.

Phantom of the Video Store see Wishbone Mysteries

Phantom of Venice. Carolyn Keene. Ed. by Wendy Barish & Suzanne LeVert. (Nancy Drew Mystery Stories Ser.: No. 78). Orig. Title: Ghost in the Gondola. 160p. (J). (gr. 3-6). 1985. write for info. (*0-318-59378-5*) S&S Trade.

Phantom of Video Store. Leticia Gantt. Ed. by Kevin Ryan. (Wishbone Mysteries Ser.: No. 18). (Illus.). 144p. (J). (gr. 3-6). 1999. mass mkt. 3.99 (*1-57064-587-6*, Big Red) Lyrick Pub.

***Phantom on His Wheel.** Thomas Rosenberg. 2000. 24.50 (*0-88739-278-4*) Creat Arts Bk.

Phantom on His Wheel. Thomas Rosenberg. LC 98-83261. 256p. 2000. pap. 14.95 (*0-88739-253-9*) Creat Arts Bk.

Phantom Outlaw at Wolf Creek. Sigmund Brouwer. (Accidental Detective Ser.). 132p. (J). (gr. 3-7). 1990. pap. text 4.99 (*0-89693-013-0*, Victor Bks) Chariot Victor.

Phantom over Vietnam: Fighter Pilot, USMC. John Trotti. LC 83-22985. (Illus.). 272p. 1996. pap. 14.95 (*0-89141-599-8*) Presidio Pr.

An Asterisk (*) at the beginning of an entry indicates that the title is appearing for the first time.

Phantom Pain. Richard A. Sherman. LC 96-40883. (Series in Behavioral Psychophysiology & Medicine). (Illus.). 276p. 1996. 54.00 (0-306-45339-8, Kluwer Plenum) Kluwer Academic.

Phantom Pain. Alfred Van Loen. (Occasional Bks.). (Illus.). (Orig.). Date not set. pap. 9.95 (0-913057-19-3) Confrontation.

Phantom Pen-Pal. Susan Saunders. (Black Cat Club Ser.). 1997. 9.15 (0-606-11139-5, Pub. by Turtleback) Demco.

Phantom Pen Pal. Susan Saunders. LC 97-18059. (Black Cat Club Ser.: No. 6). (Illus.). 80p. (J). (gr. 1-5). 1997. pap. 3.95 (0-06-442066-3, HarpTrophy) HarpC Child Bks.

***Phantom Perfumes & Other Shades: Memories of Ghost Stories Magazine.** Ed. by Mike Ashley. xxxvi, 250p. 2000. pap. 42.50 (1-899562-89-3) Ash-Tree.

Phantom Public: Library of Conservative Thought. rev. ed. Walter Lippmann. LC 92-41593. 225p. (C). 1993. pap. text 24.95 (1-56000-677-3) Transaction Pubs.

Phantom Public Sphere. Ed. by Bruce Robbins. LC 92-28619. (Cultural Politics Ser.: Vol. 5). 336p. (C). 1993. pap. 19.95 (0-8166-2126-8); text 49.95 (0-8166-2124-1) U. of Minn Pr.

Phantom Respondents: Opinion Surveys & Political Representation. John Brehm. LC 92-40475. (Michigan Studies in Political Analysis). 280p. (C). 1993. text 44.50 (0-472-09523-4, 09523) U of Mich Pr.

Phantom Rider, No. 3. Janni L. Simner. 1996. pap. 3.50 (0-590-67315-7) Scholastic Inc.

Phantom Risk: Scientific Inference & the Law. Ed. by Kenneth R. Foster et al. LC 92-36137. 469p. 1993. 45.00 (0-262-06156-2) MIT Pr.

Phantom Risk: Scientific Inference & the Law. Kenneth R. Foster. (Illus.). 472p. 1999. pap. text 22.00 (0-262-56119-0) MIT Pr.

***Phantom Ship.** Frederick Marryat. (Classics of Nautical Fiction Ser.). 352p. 2000. pap. 14.95 (0-935526-85-4) McBooks Pr.

Phantom Ship, 3 vols., 1 bk. Frederick Marryat. LC 79-8168. reprint ed. 44.50 (0-404-62026-4) AMS Pr.

***Phantom Ship of Memories.** Betty Halverson. 1999. pap. write for info. (1-58235-193-7) Watermrk Pr.

Phantom Silver. limited ed. William Kittredge. (Illus.). 26p. (Orig.). 1987. pap. 25.00 (0-937459-02-X) Kutenai Pr.

Phantom Spur. large type ed. Norman A. Fox. LC 93-21811. 1993. pap. 15.95 (1-56054-549-6) Thorndike Pr.

***Phantom Stethoscope: A Field Manual for Finding an Optimistic Future in Medicine.** Ed. by Stephen E. Klasko & Gregory P. Shea. LC 99-62184. 272p. 1999. 24.95 (1-57736-144-X, Hillsboro Pr) Providence Hse.

Phantom Story. Anthony M. Thornborough. (Illus.). 288p. 1997. pap. 24.95 (1-85409-416-5, Pub. by Arms & Armour) Sterling.

Phantom Sugar Trade. James E. Byrne. iii, 223p. 1995. pap. 45.00 (1-888870-05-2) Inst Intl Bnking.

***Phantom Table: Woolf, Fry, Russell & the Epistemology of Modernism.** Ann Banfield. LC 99-51626. (Illus.). 420p. (C). 2000. text 49.95 (0-521-77347-4) Cambridge U Pr.

Phantom Time. Patricia Triton. LC 96-85744. 400p. (Orig.). 1996. pap. 15.95 (0-9654042-0-X) Fifth Dimension.

Phantom Tollbooth. Emily Hutchinson. (Golden Leaf Classics). 48p. 1993. student ed. 9.95 (1-56872-004-1) Incent Lrning.

Phantom Tollbooth. Norton Juster. 1976. 22.95 (0-8488-0759-6) Amereon Ltd.

***Phantom Tollbooth.** Norton Juster. (Illus.). 272p. (J). (gr. 4-7). 2000. mass mkt. 2.99 (0-375-80670-9, Pub. by Random Bks Yng Read) Random.

Phantom Tollbooth. Norton Juster. 1972. 10.09 (0-606-00940-X, Pub. by Turtleback) Demco.

***Phantom Tollbooth.** Gloria Levine. 32p. 1999. 9.95 (1-56137-290-0) Novel Units.

Phantom Tollbooth. 35th anniversary ed. Norton Juster. LC 97-184037. (J). (gr. 5 up). 1961. 19.95 (0-394-81500-9, Pub. by Knopf Bks Yng Read) Random.

Phantom Tollbooth. 35th ed. Norton Juster. LC 61-13202. (Illus.). 256p. (J). (gr. 3-7). 1988. reprint ed. pap. 4.99 (0-394-82037-1, Pub. by Knopf Bks Yng Read) Random.

Phantom Tollbooth: A Study Guide. Vicki Dobrow. (Novel-Ties Ser.). (J). (gr. 4-6). 1986. pap. text, teacher ed., student ed. 15.95 (0-88122-089-2) Lrn Links.

Phantom Tollbooth: Literature Unit. Kathleen L. Bulloch. (Illus.). 48p. (Orig.). 1994. pap., student ed. 7.95 (1-55734-431-0) Tchr Create Mat.

Phantom Toolbooth. Norton Juster. 256p. pap. 4.99 (0-8072-1400-0) Listening Lib.

Phantom Train: And Other Ghostly Legends of Colorado. F. Dean Sneed. Ed. by Sandra Talkington. (Illus.). 100p. (Orig.). (C). 1992. pap. 15.95 (0-922863-04-0) Dream Wvrs Pub Co.

Phantom Trucker. Jason K. Friedman. (Bullseye Chillers Ser.). (J). 1996. 9.09 (0-606-11745-8, Pub. by Turtleback) Demco.

Phantom Valley: The Headless Ghost. Lynn Beach. Ed. by Patricia McDonald. 128p. (Orig.). (J). (gr. 3-6). 1992. pap. 2.99 (0-671-75926-4, Minstrel Bks) PB.

Phantom Victory. Pamela F. Service. LC 93-37904. 128p. (J). (gr. 5-7). 1994. mass mkt. 16.00 (0-684-19441-4) Scribner.

Phantom Virus: A Bomber Hanson Mystery. David Champion. LC 98-48992. 275p. 1999. 23.00 (1-888310-93-6) A A Knoll Pubs.

Phantom Voices in Tibet. June Calender. LC 98-83085. 256p. 2000. pap. 14.95 (0-88739-240-7) Creat Arts Bk.

Phantom Warriors: LRRPs, LRPs & Rangers in Vietnam. Gary A. Linderer. 2000. mass mkt. 7.50 (0-8041-1601-6) Ivy Books.

Phantom Waters: Northwest Legends of Rivers, Lakes & Shores. Jessica A. Salmonson. 240p. (Orig.). 1995. pap. 14.95 (1-57061-018-5) Sasquatch Bks.

Phantom Wires. Arthur Stringer. 1976. lib. bdg. 14.35 (0-89968-120-4, Lghtyr Pr) Buccaneer Bks.

Phantoms. Dean Koontz. 432p. 1986. mass mkt. 7.50 (0-425-10145-2) Berkley Pub.

Phantoms. Dean Koontz. 1997. pap. text 7.50 (0-425-16202-8) Berkley Pub.

Phantoms. Dean Koontz. 1983. 12.60 (0-606-03685-7, Pub. by Turtleback) Demco.

Phantoms: Poetry. James Laughlin. LC 94-79649. (Illus.). 64p. 1995. 19.95 (0-89381-613-2) Aperture.

Phantoms Afoot: Helping the Spirits among Us. Mary S. Rain. 336p. 1993. pap. 12.95 (1-878901-64-8) Hampton Roads Pub Co.

Phantoms & Computational Models in Therapy, Diagnosis, & Protection. LC 92-1526. (ICRU Reports: No. 48). 194p. 1992. pap. text 70.00 (0-913394-45-9) Intl Comm Rad Meas.

Phantoms & Other Stories. Ivan Sergeevich Turgenev. Tr. by Isabel F. Hapgood from RUS. LC 79-169566. (Short Story Index Reprint Ser.). 321p. 1977. reprint ed. 20.95 (0-8369-4029-6) Ayer.

***Phantom's Dark Force.** Moody Adams. 230p. 1999. pap. 12.99 (0-937422-47-9, 1042, Olive Pr SC) Midnight Call.

Phantoms Don't Drive Sports Cars. Debbie Dadey & Marcia Thornton Jones. (Adventures of the Bailey School Kids Ser.: No. 32). (Illus.). 76p. (J). (gr. 2-5). 1998. pap. 3.99 (0-590-18982-4, Pub. by Scholastic Inc) Penguin Putnam.

Phantoms Don't Drive Sports Cars. Debbie Dadey & Marcia Thornton Jones. (Adventures of the Bailey School Kids Ser.: No. 32). (J). (gr. 2-4). 1998. 8.60 (0-606-13702-5, Pub. by Turtleback) Demco.

Phantoms for Performance Evaluation & Quality Assurance of CT Scanners. P. F. Purdy et al. (AAPM Reports: No. 1). 23p. (Orig.). 1977. pap. 10.00 (1-888340-04-5) AAPM.

Phantoms in the Brain: Probing the Mysteries of the Human Mind. V. S. Ramachandran & Sandra Blakeslee. LC 98-3953. (Illus.). 320p. 1998. 27.00 (0-688-15247-3, Wm Morrow) Morrow Avon.

Phantoms in the Brain: Probing the Mysteries of the Human Mind. V. S. Ramachandran & Sandra Blakeslee. 352p. 1999. reprint ed. pap. 16.00 (0-688-17217-2, Quil) HarperTrade.

Phantoms in the Night: A Western Story. Les Savage, Jr. LC 98-29042. 208p. 1998. 18.95 (0-7862-1161-X) Mac Lib Ref.

Phantoms of Divinity: The Collapse of Traditional Faith. Edith Carlson. LC 92-6724. 150p. (C). 1992. 24.95 (0-87975-718-3) Prometheus Bks.

Phantoms of Remembrance: Memory & Oblivion at the End of the First Millennium. Patrick J. Geary. 272p. 1995. text 39.50 (0-691-03422-2, Pub. by Princeton U Pr); pap. text 16.95 (0-691-02603-3, Pub. by Princeton U Pr) Cal Prin Full Svc.

Phantoms of the Foot-Bridge & Other Stories. Mary N. Murfree. (Notable American Authors Ser.). 1999. reprint ed. lib. bdg. 125.00 (0-7812-4600-8) Rprt Serv.

Phantoms of the Footbridge & Other Stories. Mary N. Murfree. (C). 1973. reprint ed. lib. bdg. 32.50 (0-8422-8100-2) Irvington.

Phantoms of the Footbridge & Other Stories. Mary N. Murfree. (C). 1986. reprint ed. pap. text 9.50 (0-8290-1942-1) Irvington.

Phantoms of the Hudson Valley: The Glorious Estates of a Lost Era. Monica Randall. (Illus.). 224p. 1997. 55.00 (0-87951-617-8, Pub. by Overlook Pr) Penguin Putnam.

Phantoms of the Plains: Tales of West Texas Ghosts. Docia S. Williams. LC 95-24493. 208p. 1995. pap. 16.95 (1-55622-397-8, Rep of TX Pr) Wordware Pub.

Phantoms of the Rich & Famous. Stuart A. Kallen. LC 91-73064. (Ghastly Ghost Stories Ser.). (Illus.). (J). (gr. 3-8). 1991. lib. bdg. 13.98 (1-56239-037-6) ABDO Pub Co.

Phanxico Trmong Buu Diep Ong la Ai? J. B. Hanh. 300p. Date not set. pap. text 5.00 (0-614-09373-2) Du-Sinh St Joseph.

Pharao Als Gott: In Den Unterweltsbuchern des Neuen Reiches. Friedrich Abitz. (Orbis Biblicus et Orientalis Ser.: Vol. 146). (GER.). 219p. 1995. text 47.75 (3-7278-1040-8, Pub. by Presses Univ Fribourg) Eisenbrauns.

Pharaoh. Prima. 240p. 1999. pap. 19.99 (0-7615-2146-1) Prima Pub.

***Pharaoh - Ancient Israel - 'Ich' Thoughts about an Historical Process.** Wolfgang D. Schmidt. LC 99-91600. 1999. 25.00 (0-7388-0930-6); pap. 18.00 (0-7388-0931-4) Xlibris Corp.

Pharaoh Hound Champions, 1983-1986. Camino E. E. & Bk. Co. Staff & Dorothy L. Johnson. (Illus.). 36p. 1987. pap. 24.95 (0-940808-39-0) Camino E E & Bk.

Pharaoh Hounds. Sue M. Sefscik. 1990. pap. 9.95 (0-7938-2321-8, KW-182S) TFH Pubns.

Pharaoh, Pharaoh. Claudia E. Andrews. LC 97-7077. (Southern Messenger Poets Ser.). 72p. 1997. pap. 15.95 (0-8071-2159-2) La State U Pr.

***Pharaohs.** Aude Gros de Beler. (Illus.). 136p. 2000. 29.95 (2-907670-31-X, Pub. by La Maison) IPG Chicago.

Pharaohs. Salima Ikram. (In Ancient Egypt Ser.). (Illus.). 32p. (Orig.). (J). (gr. 2-8). 1997. pap. 6.95 (977-5325-60-9, Pub. by Hoopoe Bks) AMIDEAST.

Pharaohs: Treasures of Egyptian Art from the Louvre. Lawrence M. Berman & Bernadette Letellier. LC 95-45358. (Illus.). 1996. write for info. (0-940717-31-X); pap. write for info. (0-940717-32-8) Cleveland Mus Art.

Pharaohs & Kings. David Rohl. 1997. pap. 24.00 (0-609-80130-9) Random Hse Value.

***Pharaohs & Priests.** Jane Shuter. LC 98-9471. (Ancient Egypt Ser.). 32p. (J). 1999. write for info. (1-57572-731-5) Heinemann Lib.

Pharaohs & Pyramids. Tony Allan. (Time Travelers Bks.). (J). (gr. 4-9). 1977. pap. 6.95 (0-86020-084-1, Usborne) EDC.

Pharaohs & Pyramids. Tony Allan & Philippa Wingate. (Time Traveller Ser.). (Illus.). 32p. (J). (gr. 3-6). 1998. lib. bdg. 14.95 (0-88110-978-9, Usborne) EDC.

Pharaohs & Pyramids. T. Allen. (Time Travelers Bks.). (J). (gr. 4-9). 1977. lib. bdg. 14.95 (0-88110-103-6, Usborne) EDC.

Pharaohs & Pyramids. rev. ed. Tony Allan & Philippa Wingate. (Time Traveller Ser.). (Illus.). 32p. (J). (gr. 3-6). 1998. pap. 6.95 (0-7460-3069-X, Usborne) EDC.

Pharaoh's Boat at the Carnegie. Diana C. Patch & Cheryl W. Haldane. LC 89-85819. (Illus.). 52p. (Orig.). (C). 1990. pap. text 7.95 (0-911239-22-7) Carnegie Mus.

Pharaoh's Dagger: Playscript. William Hezlep. LC 92-53871. 70p. (Orig.). (J). (gr. 3-12). 1992. reprint ed. pap. 5.00 (0-88734-404-6) Players Pr.

Pharaoh's Daughter. rev. ed. Nuala N. Dhomhnaill. LC 92-51046. 160p. 1993. pap. 10.95 (0-916390-53-5) Wake Forest.

***Pharaoh's Daughter: A Novel of Ancient Egypt.** Julius Lester. LC 99-6403. (Illus.). 192p. (YA). (gr. 7 up). 2000. 17.00 (0-15-201826-3) Harcourt.

Pharaoh's Falcon. Ramzi Najm. Ed. by G. G. Thomson. LC 97-66343. (ARA & ENG., Illus.). 60p. (Orig.). (C). 1997. pap. text 18.95 (1-887003-47-9) Dancng Jester.

***Pharaoh's Gateway to Eternity: The Hawara Labyrinth.** Eric P. Uphill. (Studies in Egyptology Ser.). (Illus.). 150p. 1999. 212.50 (0-7103-0627-X, Pub. by Edinburgh U Pr) Col U Pr.

Pharaohs of Ancient Egypt. Barron's Educational Editors. (Megascope Ser.). (Illus.). 64p. (J). (gr. 5). 1998. 6.95 (0-7641-5096-0) Barron.

Pharaohs of Ancient Egypt. Elizabeth Payne. LC 80-21392. (Landmark Books Ser.). (Illus.). 192p. (J). (gr. 5-9). 1998. pap. 5.99 (0-394-84699-0, Pub. by Knopf Bks Yng Read) Random.

Pharaohs of Ancient Egypt. Elizabeth Ann Payne. (Landmark Bks.). (J). 1964. 10.09 (0-606-02225-2, Pub. by Turtleback) Demco.

Pharaohs of the Bondage & the Exodus (1887) Charles S. Robinson. 150p. 1998. reprint ed. pap. 14.95 (0-7661-0129-0) Kessinger Pub.

Pharaohs of the Sun: Akhenaten, Nefertiti & Tutankhamen. Rita E. Freed et al. (Illus.). 320p. 1999. 60.00 (0-8212-2620-7, Pub. by Bulfinch Pr) Little.

Pharaoh's People: Scenes from Life in Imperial Egypt. T. G. James. LC 84-2482. (Illus.). 286p. (C). 1984. 20.00 (0-226-39193-0) U Ch Pr.

Pharaoh's People: Scenes from Life in Imperial Egypt. T. G. James. LC 84-2482. (Illus.). 286p. (C). 1994. pap. 12.95 (0-226-39194-9) U Ch Pr.

Pharaoh's Son. Michael J. Dahl. LC 98-73040. 262p. 1998. pap. 12.95 (0-9667244-0-2, 217) Astabora Publ.

Pharaoh's Tomb. Jim Pipe. LC 96-50172. (Mystery History Ser.). (Illus.). 32p. (YA). (gr. 3 up). 1997. lib. bdg. 23.90 (0-7613-0600-5, Copper Beech Bks) Millbrook Pr.

Pharaoh's Tomb. Jim Pipe. LC 96-50172. (Mystery History Ser.). (Illus.). 32p. (J). (gr. 3 up). 1997. 9.95 (0-7613-0591-2, Copper Beech Bks) Millbrook Pr.

Pharaoh's Workers: The Villagers of Deir el Medina. Ed. by Leonard H. Lesko. (Illus.). 212p. 1994. text 37.50 (0-8014-2915-3); pap. text 15.95 (0-8014-8143-0) Cornell U Pr.

Pharaonic Egyptian Clothing. Gillian Vogelsang-Eastwood. LC 92-40593. (Studies in Textile & Costume History: Vol. 2). (Illus.). xxii, 195p. 1993. 106.00 (90-04-09744-9) Brill Academic Pubs.

Phare du Bout du Monde. Jules Verne. 8.95 (0-686-55940-1) Fr & Eur.

Phare du Bout du Monde: Avec le Chancellor. Jules Verne. (FRE.). 1978. pap. 23.95 (0-685-73319-X) Fr & Eur.

Pharisaic Judaism in Transition. Ben Z. Bokser. LC 73-2189. (Jewish People; History, Religion, Literature Ser.). 1979. reprint ed. 20.95 (0-405-05255-3) Ayer.

Pharisee among Philistines: The Diary of Judge Matthew P. Deady, 1871-1892, 2 vols. Matthew P. Deady. LC 74-75363. (Illus.). 702p. 1975. boxed set 30.00 (0-87595-046-9) Oregon Hist.

***Pharisees.** Frieda Clark Hyman. LC 00-26438. 2000. write for info. (965-229-245-1, Pub. by Gefen Pub Hse) Gefen Bks.

Pharisees: Rabbinic Perspectives. Jacob Neusner. LC 85-5783. (Studies in Ancient Judaism). 300p. (Orig.). 1985. pap. text 19.95 (0-88125-067-8) Ktav.

***Pharisees & Jesus: The Stone Lectures for 1915-1916.** A. T. Robertson. 202p. 1999. pap. 18.00 (1-57910-289-1) Wipf & Stock.

Pharisees & Sadducees. 1996. pap. 6.99 (1-85078-222-9, Pub. by Sheffield Acad) CUP Services.

Pharisees, Scribes & Sadducees. Saldarini. 1997. 49.95 (0-567-09530-4, Pub. by T & T Clark) Bks Intl VA.

Pharisienne. Francois Mauriac. pap. 9.95 (0-686-55475-2) Fr & Eur.

Pharisienne. Francois Mauriac. (FRE.). 1985. pap. 19.95 (0-7859-3047-7) Fr & Eur.

Pharma Industry Directory, 1999-2000. Ed. by CTB Directories Group Staff. 1999. spiral bd. 188.00 (1-887566-13-9) CTB Intl.

Pharmaceutical Advertising: A Survey of Existing Legislation. rev. ed. (International Digest of Health Legislation Ser: Vol. 19, No. 3). 1968. pap. text 14.00 (92-4-169193-X, 1956802) World Health.

Pharmaceutical Aerosol: A Drug Delivery System in Transition. Myron J. Lover. 215p. 1994. ring bd. 99.95 (1-56676-200-6) Technomic.

Pharmaceutical Analysis: Modern Methods, Pt. B. Ed. by James W. Munson. LC 81-15171. (Drugs & the Pharmaceutical Sciences Ser.: No. 11). 512p. 1984. reprint ed. pap. 158.80 (0-7837-2772-0, 204316300002) Bks Demand.

Pharmaceutical Analysis Pt. A: Modern Methods. Ed. by James W. Munson. LC 81-15171. (Drugs & the Pharmaceutical Sciences Ser.: No. 11, Pt. A). (Illus.). 501p. 1981. reprint ed. pap. 155.40 (0-608-04432-6, 204316300001) Bks Demand.

Pharmaceutical & Biomedical Analysis: Development & Validation of Analytical Methods. Ed. by Christopher M. Riley & Thomas W. Rosanske. LC 96-33800. (Progress in Pharmaceutical & Biomedical Analysis Ser.: No. 3). 352p. 1996. 86.50 (0-08-042792-8, Pergamon Pr) Elsevier.

Pharmaceutical & Biomedical Applications of Capillary Electrophoresis. Susan M. Lunte & Donna M. Radzik. (Progress in Pharmaceutical & Biomedical Analysis Ser.: Vol. 2). 502p. 1996. text 133.50 (0-08-042014-1, Pergamon Pr) Elsevier.

Pharmaceutical & Biomedical Applications of Liquid Chromatography. Christopher M. Riley. Ed. by W. John Lough et al. LC 94-20192. (Progress in Pharmacology & Clinical Pharmacology Ser.: No. 1). 380p. 1994. 155.00 (0-08-041009-X, Pergamon Pr) Elsevier.

Pharmaceutical & Clinical Calculations. Mansoor A. Kahn & Indra K. Reddy. LC 96-60934. 360p. 1996. text 79.95 (1-56676-431-9) Technomic.

***Pharmaceutical & Clinical Calculations.** 2nd ed. Mansoor A. Khan & Indra K. Reddy. LC 99-69344. 416p. 2000. text 84.95 (1-56676-812-8) Technomic.

Pharmaceutical Annual Register Pharm Chemists. 1990. 145.50 (0-85369-232-7, Pub. by Pharmaceutical Pr) Rittenhouse.

Pharmaceutical Annual Register Pharm Chemists, 1991. 1991. 169.00 (0-85369-248-3, Pub. by Pharmaceutical Pr) Rittenhouse.

Pharmaceutical Applications in the European Union: A Guide Through the Registration Maze. Cheng Y. Lowe. LC 97-43310. (Illus.). 278p. 1998. 179.00 (1-57491-064-7) Interpharm.

Pharmaceutical Applications of Cell & Tissue Culture to Drug Transport. G. Wilson et al. (NATO ASI Ser.: Vol. 218). (Illus.). 398p. (C). 1992. text 135.00 (0-306-44082-2, Kluwer Plenum) Kluwer Academic.

Pharmaceutical Applications of Membrane Sensors. Vaslie V. Casofret. 448p. 1992. lib. bdg. 129.00 (0-8493-4406-9, R857) CRC Pr.

Pharmaceutical Aspects of Cancer Care. Ed. by J. M. Vaeth. (Frontiers of Radiation Therapy & Oncology Ser.: Vol. 15). (Illus.). viii, 184p. 1981. 113.25 (3-8055-1512-X) S Karger.

***Pharmaceutical Aspects of Oligonucleotides** Patrick Couvreur & Claude Malvy. LC 99-34210. (Series in Pharmaceutical Sciences). 2000. write for info. (0-7484-0841-X, Pub. by Tay Francis Ltd) Taylor & Francis.

Pharmaceutical Bioequivalence. Ed. by Peter G. Welling et al. (Drugs & the Pharmaceutical Sciences Ser.: Vol. 48). (Illus.). 488p. 1991. text 210.00 (0-8247-8484-7) Dekker.

Pharmaceutical Biotechnology: A Programmed Text. Ed. by S. William Zito. LC 92-53592. 175p. 1992. pap. text 29.95 (0-87762-911-0) Technomic.

Pharmaceutical Biotechnology: A Programmed Text. 2nd ed. Ed. by S. William Zito. LC 97-60885. 276p. 1997. pap. text 41.95 (1-56676-519-6) Technomic.

Pharmaceutical Biotechnology: An Introduction for Pharmacists & Pharmaceutical Scientists. 400p. 1997. text 110.00 (90-5702-248-6, Harwood Acad Pubs); pap. text 45.00 (90-5702-249-4, Harwood Acad Pubs) Gordon & Breach.

Pharmaceutical Biotechnology: Fundamentals & Essentials. Ed. by Melvin E. Klegerman & Michael J. Groves. 295p. 1992. 107.00 (0-935184-37-6) Interpharm.

Pharmaceutical Botany. S. W. Youngken. 692p. (C). 1986. pap. 250.00 (81-7089-051-9, Pub. by Intl Bk Distr) St Mut.

Pharmaceutical Calculations. 3rd ed. Joel L. Zatz. 354p. 1994. pap. 49.95 (0-471-10623-2) Wiley.

Pharmaceutical Calculations. 9th ed. Mitchell J. Stoklosa & Howard C. Ansel. LC 90-13622. (Illus.). 387p. 1991. text 40.00 (0-8121-1384-5) Lppncott W & W.

Pharmaceutical Calculations. 10th ed. Mitchell J. Stoklosa & Howard C. Ansel. LC 95-36483. 425p. 1996. 43.00 (0-683-08001-6) Lppncott W & W.

Pharmaceutical Calculations: A Self-Instructional Text. rev. ed. Werner Lowenthal. LC 74-9564. 460p. 1978. reprint ed. pap. 27.50 (0-88275-573-0) Krieger.

Pharmaceutical Care. Ed. by David H. Knowlton & Richard P. Penna. LC 95-14254. 350p. 1996. pap. text 45.00 (0-412-06981-4, Pub. by E A) OUP.

Pharmaceutical Care Practice. Robert J. Cipolle et al. LC 97-52763. (Illus.). 384p. 1998. pap. text 42.00 (0-07-012046-3) McGraw-Hill HPD.

Pharmaceutical Chartbook. Ed. by Abraham G. Hartzema & Jean P. Gagnon. (Illus.). 344p. 1990. lib. bdg. 91.00 (0-87371-173-4, L173) Lewis Pubs.

Pharmaceutical Chartbook. 2nd ed. Abraham G. Hartzema & C. Daniel Mullins. LC 95-11616. (Illus.). 221p. (C). 1995. lib. bdg. 39.95 (1-56024-956-0) Haworth Pr.

Pharmaceutical Chemicals in Perspective. Harold A. Wittcoff. LC 88-36857. 518p. 1989. 170.00 (0-471-84363-6) Wiley.

Pharmaceutical Chemistry: Drug Synthesis, Vol. 1. H. J. Roth & A. K. Kleeman. 328p. 1988. text 62.95 (0-470-21037-0) P-H.

Pharmaceutical Chemistry: Instrumental Techniques, Vol. 2. Ed. by Leslie G. Chatten. LC 66-11286. 789p. 1969. pap. 200.00 (0-608-08302-X, 205506300002) Bks Demand.

Pharmaceutical Chemistry: Theory & Application, Vol. 1. Leslie G. Chatten. LC 66-11286. 520p. 1966. pap. 161.20 (0-608-08301-1, 205506300001) Bks Demand.

P

An Asterisk (*) at the beginning of an entry indicates that the title is appearing for the first time.

Pharmaceutical Chemistry of Adrenergic & Cholinergic Drugs. Ed. by Gyorgy D. Szasz. 192p. 1985. 92.00 (*0-8493-5158-8*, RS341, CRC Reprint) Franklin.

Pharmaceutical Chemistry of Antihypertensive Agents. Gyorgy Szasz & ZsuZsanna Budvari-Barany. 288p. 1990. lib. bdg. 202.00 (*0-8493-4724-6*, RS431) CRC Pr.

Pharmaceutical Corporate Presence in Developing Countries. Ed. by Lee A. Tavis & Oliver F. Williams. LC 92-56864. (Multinational Managers & Developing Country Concerns Ser.). (C). 1993. text 40.50 (*0-268-01511-2*) U of Notre Dame Pr.

Pharmaceutical Dictionary: English, French, German, Italian. Graa. (FRE, GER & SPA.). 124p. 1964. 45.00 (*0-7859-7497-0*) Fr & Eur.

Pharmaceutical Dissolution Testing. Umesh V. Banakar. (Drugs & the Pharmaceutical Sciences Ser.: Vol. 49). (Illus.). 454p. 1991. text 199.00 (*0-8247-8567-3*) Dekker.

Pharmaceutical Dosage Forms: Disperse Systems, Vol. 1. 2nd ed. Ed. by Herbert A. Lieberman et al. LC 96-15604. (Illus.). 552p. 1996. text 175.00 (*0-8247-9387-0*) Dekker.

Pharmaceutical Dosage Forms: Disperse Systems, Vol. 3. 2nd ed. Ed. by Lieberman et al. (Illus.). 584p. 1998. text 165.00 (*0-8247-9842-2*) Dekker.

Pharmaceutical Dosage Forms: Parenteral Medication, Vol. 3. 2nd expanded rev. ed. Kenneth E. Avis et al. Ed. by Leon Lieberman. (Illus.). 592p. 1993. text 199.00 (*0-8247-9020-0*) Dekker.

Pharmaceutical Dosage Forms: Parenteral Medications, Vol. 2. 2nd ed. Kenneth E. Avis et al. Ed. by Leon Liberman. (Illus.). 616p. 1992. text 199.00 (*0-8247-8771-4*) Dekker.

Pharmaceutical Dosage Forms: Tablets, Vol. 1. 2nd ed. H. A. Lieberman et al. (Illus.). 576p. 1989. text 175.00 (*0-8247-8044-2*) Dekker.

Pharmaceutical Dosage Forms: Tablets, Vol. 2. 2nd ed. Lieberman et al. (Illus.). 640p. 1990. text 167.50 (*0-8247-8289-5*) Dekker.

Pharmaceutical Dosage Forms Vol. 1: Parental Medications, Vol. 1. 2nd expanded rev. ed. Ed. by Kenneth E. Avis et al. (Illus.). 689p. 1991. text 199.00 (*0-8247-8576-2*) Dekker.

Pharmaceutical Dosage Forms Vol. 2: Disperse Systems, Vol. 2. 2nd ed. Ed. by Lieberman et al. (Illus.). 528p. 1996. text 175.00 (*0-8247-9713-2*) Dekker.

Pharmaceutical Dosage Forms Vol. 3: Tablets. 2nd ed. Herbert A. Lieberman et al. (Illus.). 584p. 1990. text 165.00 (*0-8247-8300-X*) Dekker.

Pharmaceutical Dosage Forms & Drug Delivery Systems. 6th ed. Howard C. Ansel et al. LC 94-22471. 1994. write for info. (*0-683-01930-9*) Lppncott W & W.

Pharmaceutical Dosage Forms & Drug Delivery Systems. 6th ed. Howard Ansel et al. (Illus.). 530p. 1995. (*0-683-00193-0*) Lppncott W & W.

Pharmaceutical Dosage Forms & Drug Delivery Systems. 7th ed. Howard Ansel et al. LC 99-17498. 676p. 1999. 48.00 (*0-683-30572-7*) Lppncott W & W.

Pharmaceutical Drugs. (IARC Monographs on the Evaluation of Carcinogenic Risks to Humans: Vol. 50). 415p. 1990. pap. text 83.00 (*92-832-1250-9*, 1720050) World Health.

Pharmaceutical Economics & Policy. Stuart O. Schweitzer. (Illus.). 256p. 1997. text 44.00 (*0-19-510524-9*) OUP.

Pharmaceutical Emulsions: Seminar Notes - June, 1992. 1992. ring bd. 144.95 (*0-87762-890-4*) Technomic.

***Pharmaceutical Emulsions & Suspensions.** Franpcoise Nielloud & Gilberte Marti-Mestres. LC 99-87827. (Drugs & the Pharmaceutical Sciences Ser.). 2000. 0.00 (*0-8247-0304-9*) Dekker.

Pharmaceutical Enzymes. Albert Lauwers & Simon Scharpe. LC 97-15723. (Drugs & the Pharmaceutical Sciences Ser.: Vol. 84). (Illus.). 408p. 1997. text 165.00 (*0-8247-9375-7*) Dekker.

Pharmaceutical Equipment Validation: The Ultimate Qualification Guidebook. Phillip A. Cloud. LC 98-28032. v, 443 p. 1998. 229.00 (*1-57491-079-5*) Interpharm.

Pharmaceutical Equities: Evaluation & Trading. Andrew Porter. (International Equities Ser.). 208p. 1993. 180.00 (*1-85573-090-1*, Pub. by Woodhead Pubng) Am Educ Systs.

Pharmaceutical Ethics. Salek. text. write for info. (*0-471-49057-1*) Wiley.

Pharmaceutical Examiner. Jack Rudman. (Career Examination Ser.: C-1839). 1994. pap. 39.95 (*0-8373-1839-4*) Nat Learn.

Pharmaceutical Excipients: Characterization by IR & NMR Spectroscopy. David E. Bugay & W. Paul Findlay. LC 98-56652. (Drugs & the Pharmaceutical Sciences Ser.). (Illus.). 680p. 1999. text 250.00 (*0-8247-9373-0*) Dekker.

Pharmaceutical Excipients: Towards the Twenty-First Century. Christianah Adeyeye et al. 264p. 1995. ring bd. 159.95 (*1-56676-349-5*) Technomic.

Pharmaceutical Experimental Design. Gareth Lewis & Didier Mathieu. LC 98-37068. (Drugs & the Pharmaceutical Sciences Ser.). (Illus.). 552p. 1998. text 175.00 (*0-8247-9860-0*) Dekker.

Pharmaceutical Experimental Design & Interpretation. N. A. Armstrongand & K. C. James. LC 97-131175. 300p. 1996. 125.00 (*0-7484-0436-8*) Taylor & Francis.

Pharmaceutical Industry. Ed. by Australian Industry Commission. 912p. 1996. pap. 45.50 (*0-644-36257-X*, Pub. by Aust Gov Pub) Accents Pubns.

Pharmaceutical Industry. Steven N. Wiggins. Ed. by Steve Pejovich & Henry Dethloff. (Series on Public Issues: No. 18). 19p. 1985. pap. 2.00 (*0-86599-054-9*) PERC.

Pharmaceutical Industry: Guide to Pollution Prevention. (Illus.). 74p. (Orig.). (C). 1994. pap. text 30.00 (*1-56806-082-3*) DIANE Pub.

Pharmaceutical Industry & Dependency in the Third World. Gary Gereffi. LC 83-42560. 306p. reprint ed. pap. 94.90 (*0-608-06376-2*, 206673700008) Bks Demand.

Pharmaceutical Industry Guide: Drug Companies, Biotech Firms & CRO's. 2nd ed. Institute for Biotechnology Information Staff. 103p. 1997. pap. text 49.95 (*1-886041-12-1*) Inst Biotech Info.

***Pharmaceutical Industry in Brazil: A Strategic Entry Report, 1999.** Compiled by Icon Group International. (Illus.). 156p. 1999. ring bd. 1560.00 incl. audio compact disk (*0-7418-1813-2*) Icon Grp.

Pharmaceutical Industry in India & Hungary: Policies, Institutions, & Technological Development. Greg Felker et al. LC 97-47006. (Technical Paper Ser.: No. 392). 56p. 1997. pap. 22.00 (*0-8213-4071-9*, 14071) World Bank.

Pharmaceutical Industry to 2000 No. R211: Reinventing the Pharmaceutical Company. 1994. 725.00 (*0-85058-829-4*) Economist Intell.

Pharmaceutical Inhalation Aerosol Technology. Ed. by Anthony J. Hickey. (Drugs & the Pharmaceutical Sciences Ser.: Vol. 54). (Illus.). 384p. 1992. text 195.00 (*0-8247-8464-2*) Dekker.

***Pharmaceutical Innovation: Revolutionizing Health Care.** Ralph Landau et al. LC 99-52121. 1999. write for info. (*0-941901-21-1*) Chem Heritage Fnd.

Pharmaceutical Labeling, Advertising & Promotion: Meeting FDA Regulations. Leonard Hyman. 529p. 1994. ring bd. 249.95 (*1-56676-225-1*) Technomic.

Pharmaceutical Manufacturing Change Control. Ed. by Simon Turner. LC 99-10444. 1999. 179.00 (*1-57491-096-5*) Interpharm.

Pharmaceutical Manufacturers: An International Directory. David B. Braun. LC 95-21383. 290p. 1995. 109.00 (*0-8155-1384-4*) Noyes.

Pharmaceutical Manufacturing Encyclopedia, 2 vols. 2nd ed. Marshall Sittig. LC 87-31547. (Illus.). 1756p. 1988. 285.00 (*0-8155-1144-2*) Noyes.

***Pharmaceutical Market in Russia: A Strategic Entry Report, 1996.** Compiled by Icon Group International Staff. (Illus.). 153p. 1999. ring bd. 1530.00 incl. audio compact disk (*0-7418-1166-9*) Icon Grp.

***Pharmaceutical Market in Russia: A Strategic Entry Report, 1998.** Compiled by Icon Group International Staff. (Illus.). 148p. 1999. ring bd. 1480.00 incl. audio compact disk (*0-7418-1531-1*) Icon Grp.

Pharmaceutical Market Outlook. Market Intelligence Staff. 53p. 1994. 695.00 (*0-7889-0065-X*) Frost & Sullivan.

Pharmaceutical Marketing: Strategy & Cases. Mickey C. Smith. LC 91-8047. (Illus.). 430p. (Orig.). 1991. pap. text 24.95 (*1-56024-110-1*); lib. bdg. 49.95 (*0-86656-861-1*) Haworth Pr.

Pharmaceutical Marketing in the 21st Century. Ed. by Mickey C. Smith. LC 95-26641. (Journal of Pharmaceutical Marketing & Management: Vol. 10, Nos. 2/3/4). 292p. (C). 1996. 49.95 (*1-56024-795-9*, Pharmctl Prods) Haworth Pr.

Pharmaceutical Marketing in the 21st Century. Ed. by Mickey C. Smith. LC 95-26641. (Journal of Pharmaceutical Marketing & Management Ser.: Vol. 10, Nos. 2/3/4). 292p. (C). 1997. pap. 19.95 (*0-7890-0207-8*, Pharmctl Prods) Haworth Pr.

Pharmaceutical Markets: A Detailed Database on a 94 Billion Dollar Market. Market Intelligence Staff. 270p. 1992. 995.00 (*1-56753-083-4*) Frost & Sullivan.

Pharmaceutical Mass Spectra. Ed. by Ardrey. 1985. 100.00 (*0-85369-172-X*, Pub. by Pharmaceutical Pr) Rittenhouse.

Pharmaceutical Medicine. 2nd ed. Ed. by D. M. Burley et al. 384p. 1993. text 80.00 (*0-340-52517-7*, Pub. by E A) OUP.

Pharmaceutical Medicines, Ethics, & Practice, No. 3. 1990. pap. 11.00 (*0-85369-224-6*, Pub. by Pharmaceutical Pr) Rittenhouse.

Pharmaceutical Medicines, Ethics, & Practice, No. 4. 1990. pap. 11.00 (*0-85369-236-X*, Pub. by Pharmaceutical Pr) Rittenhouse.

Pharmaceutical Medicines, Ethics, & Practice, No. 5. 1991. 11.00 (*0-85369-239-4*, Pub. by Pharmaceutical Pr) Rittenhouse.

Pharmaceutical Medicines, Ethics, & Practice, No. 6. 1991. pap. 13.00 (*0-85369-261-0*, Pub. by Pharmaceutical Pr) Rittenhouse.

Pharmaceutical Microbiology. 5th ed. W. B. Hugo & A. D. Russell. (Illus.). 544p. 1992. pap. 75.00 (*0-632-03428-9*) Blackwell Sci.

Pharmaceutical Microbiology. 6th ed. W. B. Hugo & A. D. Russell. LC 97-31976. (Illus.). 510p. 1998. pap. 99.95 (*0-632-04196-X*) Blackwell Sci.

Pharmaceutical Nation: An Obsessive Study of Pill Marketing, Art, History & Culture from Flintstones Vitamins to Prozac. Jim Hogshire. LC 95-48083. (Illus.). 256p. 1996. pap. 15.95 (*0-8065-1791-3*, Citadel Pr) Carol Pub Group.

Pharmaceutical Packaging Technologies & Materials Seminar: TAPPI Notes, Adam's Mark, Philadelphia, PA, June 10-11, 1986. Technical Association of the Pulp & Paper Industry. LC TS0195.2.P42. 39p. pap. 30.00 (*0-608-15245-5*, 202917400059) Bks Demand.

Pharmaceutical Particulate Carriers: Therapeutic Applications. Ed. by Alain Rolland. (Drugs & the Pharmaceutical Sciences Ser.: Vol. 61). (Illus.). 448p. 1993. text 215.00 (*0-8247-9016-2*) Dekker.

Pharmaceutical Particulate Matter: Analysis & Control. Thomas Barber. (Illus.). 531p. 1993. 126.75 (*0-935184-29-5*) Interpharm.

***Pharmaceutical Patent Issues: Interpreting Gatt: Congressional Hearings.** Orrin G. Hatch. (Illus.). 291p. (C). 2000. reprint ed. pap. text 35.00 (*0-7881-8775-9*) DIANE Pub.

***Pharmaceutical Patents in Europe.** Bengt Domeij. LC 00-35748. (Stockholm Studies in Law). 2000. write for info. (*90-411-1348-7*) Kluwer Law Intl.

Pharmaceutical Pelletization Technology. Ghebre-Sellassie. (Drugs & the Pharmaceutical Sciences Ser.: Vol. 37). (Illus.). 296p. 1989. text 165.00 (*0-8247-8085-X*) Dekker.

Pharmaceutical Philately. George Griffenhagen. (Illus.). 92p. 1990. pap. 9.00 (*0-935991-07-7*) Am Topical Assn.

Pharmaceutical Powder Compaction Technology. Ed. by Christer Nystrom & Goran Alderborn. (Drugs & the Pharmaceutical Sciences Ser.: Vol. 71). (Illus.). 624p. 1995. text 195.00 (*0-8247-9376-5*) Dekker.

***Pharmaceutical Practice.** 2nd ed. Ed. by A. J. Winfield & R. M. Richards. (Illus.). 544p. 1998. pap. write for info. (*0-443-05729-X*) Church.

Pharmaceutical Preformulation. J.T. Carstensen. 320p. 1998. 104.95 (*1-56676-690-7*) Technomic.

Pharmaceutical Principles of Solid Dosage Forms. Jens T. Carstensen. LC 92-64420. 255p. 1992. 99.95 (*0-87762-955-2*) Technomic.

Pharmaceutical Process Validation. 2nd ed. Ira A. Berry & Robert A. Nash. (Drugs & the Pharmaceutical Sciences Ser.: Vol. 57). (Illus.). 648p. 1993. text 150.00 (*0-8247-8777-3*) Dekker.

Pharmaceutical Production Facilities: Design & Applications. 2nd ed. Graham C. Cole. LC 98-130223. 334p. 1998. 165.00 (*0-7484-0438-4*, Pub. by Tay Francis Ltd) Taylor & Francis.

Pharmaceutical Products, Vol. I-2. Mike Burstall. (Single Market Review Ser.). 1998. 70.00 (*0-7494-2306-4*) Kogan Page Ltd.

Pharmaceutical Project Management. Tony Kennedy. LC 97-31537. (Drugs & the Pharmaceutical Sciences Ser.). (Illus.). 304p. 1997. text 135.00 (*0-8247-0111-9*) Dekker.

***Pharmaceutical Quality Systems.** Oliver Schmidt. LC 99-89315. 2000. write for info. (*1-57491-109-0*) Interpharm.

Pharmaceutical R&D: Costs, Risks & Rewards. (Illus.). 364p. (Orig.). (C). 1994. pap. text 50.00 (*0-7881-0468-3*) DIANE Pub.

Pharmaceutical Reformulation. James I. Wells. (Pharmaceutical Technology Ser.). 240p. 1988. text 62.95 (*0-470-21114-8*) P-H.

Pharmaceutical Research & Development. 1995. lib. bdg. 275.99 (*0-8490-7581-5*) Gordon Pr.

***Pharmaceutical Sales Management in a Changeable Market Place.** Vincent F. Peters & Thomas B. Yeats. (Illus.). v, 220p. 2000. pap. 49.95 (*0-9656231-2-2*) Black Dog Pub.

Pharmaceutical Sector: Coordinated Sector Position on 31.12.1994. European Communities Staff. 363p. 1995. pap. text, lib. bdg. 70.00 (*92-827-0020-8*, Pub. by Comm Europ Commun) Bernan Associates.

***Pharmaceutical Sector in China A Strategic Entry Report, 1996.** Compiled by Icon Group International Staff. (Illus.). 204p. 1999. ring bd. 2040.00 incl. audio compact disk (*0-7418-1164-2*) Icon Grp.

Pharmaceutical Statistics: Practical & Clinical Applications. 3rd ed. Sanford Bolton. LC 96-49907. (Drugs & the Pharmaceutical Sciences Ser.). (Illus.). 768p. 1997. text 150.00 (*0-8247-9812-0*) Dekker.

Pharmaceutical Substances. Kleemann. LC 98-51303. (Illus.). 2304p. 1999. 375.00 (*0-86577-817-5*) Thieme Med Pubs.

Pharmaceutical Substances. Kleemann. 1999. 949.00 incl. cd-rom (*0-86577-819-1*) Thieme Med Pubs.

Pharmaceutical Tech: Control. Rubinstein. 1990. boxed set. write for info. (*0-318-68276-1*) P-H.

Pharmaceutical Technology see Elsevier's Dictionary of Pharmaceutical Science & Techniques

Pharmaceutical Technology: Controlled Drug Release. M. H. Rubinstein. LC 87-2847. (Pharmaceutical Technology Ser.). 126p. 1987. text 65.95 (*0-470-20881-3*) P-H.

Pharmaceutical Technology: Drug Stability. Ed. by M. H. Rubinstein. 1989. text 69.95 (*0-470-21411-2*) P-H.

Pharmaceutical Technology: Introduction to Pharmaceutical Systems II. Kenneth Alexander. (C). 1994. pap. text 15.00 (*1-57074-140-9*) Greyden Pr.

Pharmaceutical Technology: Tableting Technology, Vol. 1. Michael Rubinstein. 200p. 1988. text 62.95 (*0-470-21001-X*) P-H.

Pharmaceutical Technology Lab Manual. Kenneth Alexander. 226p. (C). 1994. pap. text 15.00 (*1-57074-107-7*) Greyden Pr.

Pharmaceutical Thermal Analysis: Techniques & Applications. J. L. Ford & P. Timmins. 1989. text 99.95 (*0-470-21219-5*) P-H.

Pharmaceutical Unit Operations: Coating. Ed. by Kenneth E. Avis et al. LC 98-27219. (Drug Manufacturing Technology Ser.: Vol. 3). 1998. 189.00 (*1-57491-082-5*) Interpharm.

Pharmaceutical Water: System Design, Operation, & Validation. William V. Collentro. (Illus.). 682p. 1997. 229.00 (*1-57491-027-2*) Interpharm.

Pharmaceutical Water Systems. Theodore H. Meltzer. 865p. 1996. 145.00 (*0-927188-06-6*) Tall Oaks Pub.

Pharmaceuticals & Cosmetics Manufacturing Expo: Proceedings of Technical Program May 13-15, 1980, Rosemont, Illinois. Pharmaceuticals & Cosmetics Manufacturing Expo Sta. LC TP0983.. 318p. reprint ed. pap. 98.60 (*0-608-14598-X*, 202083300019) Bks Demand.

Pharmaceuticals & Health Policy: International Perspectives on Provision & Control of Medicines. Ed. by Blum et al. LC 80-26498. 387p. 1981. 44.50 (*0-8419-0682-3*) Holmes & Meier.

Pharmaceuticals in France: A Strategic Entry Report, 1997. Compiled by Icon Group International Staff. (Illus.). 130p. 1999. ring bd. 1300.00 incl. audio compact disk (*0-7418-0809-9*) Icon Grp.

Pharmaceuticals in Hong Kong: A Strategic Entry Report, 1997. Compiled by Icon Group International Staff. (Illus.). 124p. 1999. ring bd. 1240.00 incl. audio compact disk (*0-7418-0810-2*) Icon Grp.

Pharmaceuticals in Italy: A Strategic Entry Report, 1997. Compiled by Icon Group International Staff. (Illus.). 123p. 1999. ring bd. 1230.00 incl. audio compact disk (*0-7418-0811-0*) Icon Grp.

***Pharmaceuticals in Japan: A Strategic Entry Report, 1997.** Compiled by Icon Group International Staff. (Illus.). 154p. 1999. ring bd. 1540.00 incl. audio compact disk (*0-7418-0999-0*) Icon Grp.

Pharmaceuticals in Saudi Arabia: A Strategic Entry Report, 1997. Compiled by Icon Group International Staff. (Illus.). 139p. 1999. ring bd. 1390.00 incl. audio compact disk (*0-7418-0812-9*) Icon Grp.

Pharmaceuticals Market Outlook: U. S. Edition. Frost & Sullivan Staff. 53p. Date not set. write for info. (*0-7889-0416-7*, 2723-52) Frost & Sullivan.

Pharmaceuticals/Biotechnology Market Sourcebook - 1995 Edition. Ed. by Frost & Sullivan Staff. 1995. spiral bd. 1295.00 (*0-7889-0238-5*, 2724-59) Frost & Sullivan.

Pharmaceutics: The Science of Dosage Form Design. Michael E. Aulton. (Illus.). 774p. 1988. text 59.95 (*0-443-03643-8*) Church.

Pharmacie Bei Den Alten Culturvolkern. Julius Berendes. xxii, 528p. 1989. reprint ed. 120.00 (*3-487-00902-1*) G Olms Pubs.

Pharmacist. Jack Rudman. (Career Examination Ser.: C-580). 1994. pap. 29.95 (*0-8373-0580-2*) Nat Learn.

Pharmacist & the Challenge of New Social Trends. 1997. 15.00 (*92-871-3317-4*, Pub. by Council of Europe) Manhattan Pub Co.

Pharmacist I. Jack Rudman. (Career Examination Ser.: C-1836). 1994. pap. 29.95 (*0-8373-1836-X*) Nat Learn.

Pharmacist III. Jack Rudman. (Career Examination Ser.: C-1838). 1994. pap. 34.95 (*0-8373-1838-6*) Nat Learn.

Pharmacist Trainee. Jack Rudman. (Career Examination Ser.: C-649). 1994. pap. 23.95 (*0-8373-0649-3*) Nat Learn.

Pharmacist II. Jack Rudman. (Career Examination Ser.: C-1837). 1994. pap. 34.95 (*0-8373-1837-8*) Nat Learn.

Pharmacists see Farmeceuticos

***Pharmacists.** Karen Bush Gibson. (Community Helpers Ser.). 24p. (J). (ps-3). 2000. lib. bdg. 15.93 (*0-7368-0624-5*, Bridgestone Bks) Capstone Pr.

Pharmacists. Robert James. LC 95-18939. (People Who Care for Our Health Discovery Library). 24p. (J). (gr. k-4). 1995. lib. bdg. 15.93 (*1-55916-171-X*) Rourke Bk Co.

Pharmacist's Controlled Substances Regulatory Guide & Compliance Manual: A Complete Prescription Department Guide for Practicing Pharmacists. Ronald W. Buzzeo et al. 130p. 1995. 130.00 (*0-9648291-0-X*) Regulatory Info Ctr.

Pharmacist's Guide to Over-the-Counter & Natural Remedies: A Guide to Finding Quick & Safe Relief from the Symptoms of Common Disorders. Robert Garrison & Michael Mannion. 320p. 1998. mass mkt. 6.95 (*0-89529-850-3*, Avery) Penguin Putnam.

Pharmacist's Guide to Providing Veterinary Prescription Services. 2nd rev. ed. D. S. Chan. (Illus.). 256p. (C). 2000. pap. 45.99 (*0-9663353-1-7*) Gratefuldeb.

***Pharmacist's Guide to Schools Offering Nontraditional Doctor of Pharmacy Degrees.** D. S. Chan. 144p. (C). 2000. pap. 24.99 (*0-9663353-2-5*) Gratefuldeb.

Pharmacist's Guide to the Most Misused & Abused Drugs in America: Prescription Drugs - Over-the-Counter Drugs - Designer Drugs. Ken Liska. 1988. 23.99 (*0-02-572970-5*) Macmillan.

Pharmacist's Managed Care Manual. Ed. by David B. Nash. (Illus.). 250p. (Orig.). 1997. spiral bd. 54.95 (*1-890045-04-7*) T L C Med Pub.

Pharmacist's Prescription: Your Complete Guide to the Over-the-Counter Remedies that Work Best. F. James Grogan. 384p. 1988. mass mkt. 4.95 (*0-380-70550-8*, Avon Bks) Morrow Avon.

***Pharmacists Smart Guide to the Top 50 Herbs.** Art Presser. LC 99-66309. (Smart Guide Ser.). (Illus.). 128p. 2000. pap. 9.95 (*1-890572-09-8*, Pub. by Smart Pubns CA) Publishers Group.

Pharmacists Talking with Patients: A Guide to Patient Couseling. Melanie J. Rantucci. LC 96-15264. (Illus.). 280p. 1997. 28.95 (*0-683-07127-0*) Lppncott W & W.

Pharmacoangiography in the Diagnosis of Tumours. G. Y. Vargha. 252p. (C). 1981. 96.00 (*963-05-2912-2*, Pub. by Akade Kiado) St Mut.

Pharmacodynamic Models of Selected Toxic Chemicals in Man. A. D. Smith & M. C. Thorne. 1986. text 268.50 (*0-85200-953-4*) Kluwer Academic.

Pharmacodynamics: Perspectives in Clinical Pharmacology. Ed. by Neal R. Cutler & John J. Sramek. LC 94-6103. 508p. 1994. 334.95 (*0-471-95052-1*) Wiley.

Pharmacoeconomics: Unique Perspectives on Cost, Outcomes & Value. Fred M. Cox & Barbara L. Hesslegrave. (Illus.). 225p. 1998. 55.00 (*0-07-013404-9*) McGraw.

Pharmacoeconomics in Perspective: A Primer on Research, Techniques & Information. Robert J. Bonk. LC 98-47909. (Illus.). 116p. 1999. lib. bdg. 49.95 (*0-7890-0561-1*, Pharmctl Prods) Haworth Pr.

Pharmacoepidemiology. Ed. by Brian L. Strom. (Illus.). 424p. 1989. text 113.00 (*0-443-08675-3*) Church.

Pharmacoepidemiology. 2nd ed. Ed. by Brian L. Strom. 762p. 1994. 280.00 (*0-471-94058-5*) Wiley.

Pharmacoepidemiology. 3rd ed. Strom. 1969. text. write for info. (*0-471-89925-9*) Wiley.

Pharmacoepidemiology, Vol. I. Ed. by Stanley A. Edlavitch. (Illus.). 360p. 1989. lib. bdg. 110.00 (*0-87371-129-7*, L129) Lewis Pubs.

P

An Asterisk (*) at the beginning of an entry indicates that the title is appearing for the first time.

Pharmacoepidemiology: An Introduction. 3rd ed. Ed. by Abraham C. Hartzema et al. LC 97-34219. 688p. 1998. pap. text 85.00 (*0-929375-18-1*) H W Bks.

***Pharmacoepidemiology: Principles & Practice.** Brenda Waning. (Essentials of Medical Imaging Ser.). (Illus.). 384p. 2000. pap. text 44.95 (*0-07-135507-3*) McGraw-Hill Prof.

Pharmacogenetics. Wendell W. Weber. (Oxford Monographs on Medical Genetics: No. 32). (Illus.). 360p. 1997. text 59.50 (*0-19-506878-5*) OUP.

Pharmacogenetics: Bridging the Gap Between Basic Science & Clinical. Ed. by Wendy Hori & Johanna Schlegel. (Biomedical Library). 1996. pap. 795.00 (*1-57936-021-1*) IBC USA.

Pharmacogenetics: Proceedings of the WHO Scientific Group, Geneva, 1972. WHO Staff. (Technical Reports: No. 524). 1973. pap. text 4.00 (*92-4-120524-5*, 1100524) World Health.

***Pharmacogenetics & Pharmacogenomics: Recent Conceptual & Technical Advances.** E.S. Vesell. ('Pharmacology': 61). (Illus.). 90p. 2000. pap. 34.00 (*3-8055-7128-3*) S Karger.

Pharmacogenetics of Drug Metabolism. Werner Kalow. (International Encyclopedia of Pharmacology & Therapeutics Ser.: Vol. 137). 930p. 1992. 428.50 (*0-08-041175-4*, Pergamon Pr) Elsevier.

***Pharmacognosy: Phytochemistry, Medicinal Plant.** 2nd ed. J. Bruneton. (Illus.). 1136p. 1999. 218.00 (*1-898298-63-7*, Pub. by Intercept UK) Spr-Verlag.

Pharmacognosy & Pharmacobiotechnolgy. James E. Robbers et al. LC 95-48963. 1996. write for info. (*0-614-11710-0*) Lppncott W & W.

Pharmacognosy & Pharmacobiotechnology. James E. Robbers et al. (Illus.). 352p. 1996. 36.95 (*0-683-08500-X*) Lppncott W & W.

Pharmacognosy, Phytochemistry, Medicinal Plants. Jean Bruneton. 196.50 (*1-898298-13-0*) Spr-Verlag.

Pharmacographia: A History of the Principle Drugs of Vegetables Origin. F. A. Fluchiger. 704p. 1986. pap. 1250.00 (*81-7089-048-9*, Pub. by Intl Bk Distr) St Mut.

Pharmacographia Indica, Vols. 1-3. W. Dymock. (C). 1988. 410.00 (*0-7855-2266-2*, Pub. by Scientific) St Mut.

Pharmacokinetic Analysis: A Practical Approach. I-Der Lee & Gordon L. Amidon. LC 96-60272. 562p. 1996. text 179.95 (*1-56676-425-4*) Technomic.

Pharmacokinetic Profiles of Drugs. J. P. Labaune. (Pharmaceutical Sciences Ser.). 500p. 1996. 125.00 (*0-7484-0559-3*) Taylor & Francis.

Pharmacokinetic/Pharmacodynamic Analysis: Accelerating Drug Discovery & Development. Ed. by Johanna Schlegel. (Biomedical Library). 314p. 1996. pap. 795.00 (*1-57936-011-4*) IBC USA.

Pharmacokinetic/Pharmacodynamic Analysis II. Ed. by Wendy Mori. (Illus.). (Orig.). 1997. pap. write for info. (*1-57936-045-9*) IBC USA.

Pharmacokinetics. Ed. by H. Schoenfeld et al. (Antibiotics & Chemotherapy Ser.: Vol. 25). (Illus.). 1978. 138.50 (*3-8055-2752-7*) S Karger.

Pharmacokinetics. 2nd ed. M. Gibaldi & Donald Perrier. (Drugs & the Pharmaceutical Sciences Ser.: Vol. 15). (Illus.). 504p. 1982. text 59.75 (*0-8247-1042-8*) Dekker.

Pharmacokinetics: A Modern View. Leslie Z. Benet et al. Ed. by Gerhard Levy & B. L. Ferraiolo. LC 84-15011. 548p. 1984. 95.00 (*0-306-41810-X*, Plenum Trade) Perseus Pubng.

Pharmacokinetics: Classic & Modern. Ed. by J. H. Van Rossum & A. A. Maes. (Illus.). 63p. 1986. pap. 20.00 (*0-89573-542-3*, Wiley-VCH) Wiley.

Pharmacokinetics: Mathematical & Statistical Approaches. Ed. by A. Pecile & A. Rescigno. LC 87-36043. (NATO ASI Series A, Life Sciences: Vol. 145). (Illus.). 358p. 1988. 105.00 (*0-306-42806-7*, Plenum Trade) Perseus Pubng.

Pharmacokinetics: Processes & Mathematics. Peter G. Welling. LC 86-20644. (ACS Monograph: No. 185). (Illus.). xiv, 268p. 1986. 59.95 (*0-8412-0967-7*) Am Chemical.

Pharmacokinetics: Processes, Mathematics, & Applications. 2nd ed. Peter G. Welling. LC 97-12306. (Professional Reference Book Ser.). 400p. 1997. text 105.00 (*0-8412-3481-7*, Pub. by Am Chemical) OUP.

Pharmacokinetics: Regulatory - Industrial - Academic Perspectives. 2nd expanded rev. ed. Ed. by Peter G. Welling & Francis L. Tse. (Drugs & the Pharmaceutical Sciences Ser.: Vol. 67). (Illus.). 528p. 1995. text 185.00 (*0-8247-9378-1*) Dekker.

Pharmacokinetics & Cancer Chemotherapy. Ed. by P. Workman & M. A. Graham. (Cancer Surveys Ser.: Vol. 17). (Illus.). 235p. (C). 1993. text 69.00 (*0-87969-390-8*) Cold Spring Harbor.

Pharmacokinetics & Clinical Pharmacology of Beta-Blockers in Hypertension. Ed. by P. M. Galletti. (Cardiology Ser.: Vol. 64, Suppl. 1). (Illus.). 1979. pap. 28.75 (*3-8055-3061-7*) S Karger.

Pharmacokinetics & Clinical Pharmacology of Cardiac Clyscosides. Ed. by K. Greeff. (Handbook of Experimental Pharmacology Ser.: Vol. 56). (Illus.). 394p. 1981. 216.00 (*0-387-10918-8*) Spr-Verlag.

Pharmacokinetics & Pharmacodynamics Vol. 1: Research Design & Analysis. Ed. by Randall B. Smith et al. LC 86-50775. (Illus.). viii, 104p. (Orig.). 1986. pap. text 2.00 (*0-9606488-4-4*) H W Bks.

Pharmacokinetics & Therapeutic Monitoring of Psychiatric Drugs. Ed. by Mahmoud N. Musa. LC 92-48220. (Illus.). 226p. 1993. pap. 36.95 (*0-398-06301-X*); text 52.95 (*0-398-05841-5*) C C Thomas.

Pharmacokinetics, Biodistribution & Mode of Action of Apomorphine: An In Vitro Study at Cellular Level & In Vivo Study Using Microdialysis. Exaud E. Sam. (Acta Biomedica Lovaniensia Ser.: No. 156). (Illus.). 182p. 1997. pap. 45.00 (*90-6186-838-6*, Pub. by Almqvist Wiksell) Coronet Bks.

Pharmacokinetics for the Non-Mathematical. David W. Bourne et al. 1986. text 119.00 (*0-85200-712-4*) Kluwer Academic.

Pharmacokinetics for the Pharmaceutical Scientist. John Wagner. LC 93-60366. 200p. 1993. 116.95 (*1-56676-032-1*) Technomic.

Pharmacokinetics in Teratogenesis, 2 vols., Set. H. Nau & W. M. Scott, Jr. 1987. reprint ed. 298.00 (*0-8493-6872-3*, CRC Reprint) Franklin.

Pharmacokinetics Made Easy. Donald J. Birkett. 119p. 1998. pap. write for info. (*0-07-470609-8*) McGraw-Hill HPD.

Pharmacokinetics of Drugs. Ed. by Peter G. Welling & Luc P. Balant. LC 93-43145. (Handbook of Experimental Pharmacology Ser.: Vol. 110). (Illus.). 552p. 1994. 465.95 (*0-387-57506-5*) Spr-Verlag.

Pharmacokinetics of Psychoactive Drugs: Further Studies. Ed. by Louis Gottschalk. LC 79-9430. 140p. 1979. text 35.00 (*0-88331-176-3*) R B Luce.

Pharmacokinetics of Psychotropic Drugs in the Elderly. David A. Smith. (Geriatric Psychopharmacology Ser.). 52p. (Orig.). 1995. pap. 39.95 (*1-884937-27-6*) Manisses Communs.

Pharmacokinetics of Selected Antibacterial Agents. Axel Dalhoff. LC 97-33565. (Antibiotics & Chemotherapy Ser.: No. 49). (Illus.). vi, 148p. 1997. 148.00 (*3-8055-6576-3*) S Karger.

Pharmacokinetics of Sulfonamides Revisited. T. B. Vree et al. (Antibiotics & Chemotherapy Ser.: Vol. 34). (Illus.). x, 220p. 1985. 148.00 (*3-8055-3949-5*) S Karger.

Pharmacokinetics II. Ed. by H. Schoenfeld. (Antibiotics & Chemotherapy Ser.: Vol. 31). (Illus.). xiv, 226p. 1981. 128.75 (*3-8055-2448-X*) S Karger.

Pharmacokinetics/Teratogenesis. H. Nau. 280p. 1987. 157.00 (*0-8493-6873-1*, CRC Reprint) Franklin.

Pharmacokinetics/Teratogenesis, Vol. II. H. Nau. 248p. 1987. 141.00 (*0-8493-6874-X*, CRC Reprint) Franklin.

Pharmacologic Analysis of Drug-Receptor Interaction. 3rd ed. Terry Kenakin. LC 97-12942. 617p. 1997. text 104.00 (*0-397-51815-3*) Lppncott W & W.

Pharmacologic Approach to Gastrointestinal Disorders. James H. Lewis. LC 93-13185. (Illus.). 667p. 1994. 85.00 (*0-683-04970-4*) Lppncott W & W.

Pharmacologic Approach to the Critically Ill Patient. 3rd ed. Bart Chernow. (Illus.). 1248p. 1994. 169.00 (*0-683-01524-9*) Lppncott W & W.

Pharmacologic Basis of Nursing Practice. 5th ed. Julia F. Clark & Sherry F. Queener. 96p. (C). (gr. 13). 1996. pap. text, student ed. 14.95 (*0-8151-1510-5*, 28264) Mosby Inc.

Pharmacologic Basis of Nursing Practice. 5th ed. Julia F. Clark et al. teacher ed., suppl. ed. write for info. (*0-8151-2124-5*) Mosby Inc.

Pharmacologic Basis of Nursing Practice. 5th ed. Julia F. Clark et al. (C). 1997. text. write for info. (*0-323-00701-5*) Mosby Inc.

***Pharmacologic Basis of Nursing Practice.** 6th ed. Julia F. Clark et al. (Illus.). (C). 1999. teacher ed. write for info. (*0-323-00722-8*); pap. text 52.00 (*0-323-00684-1*) Mosby Inc.

Pharmacologic Basis of Nursing Practice: Text & Student Learning Guide Package, Set. 5th ed. Julia F. Clark et al. (C). 1997. text, student ed. write for info. (*0-8151-1511-3*) Mosby Inc.

Pharmacologic Basis of Patient Care. 5th ed. Mary K. Asperheim. (Illus.). 620p. 1985. teacher ed. write for info. (*0-7216-2004-3*, W B Saunders Co) Harcrt Hlth Sci Grp.

Pharmacologic Basis of Patient Care. 5th ed. Mary K. Asperheim. (Illus.). 620p. 1985. text 65.00 (*0-7216-1229-6*, W B Saunders Co) Harcrt Hlth Sci Grp.

Pharmacologic Basis of Psychotherapeutics: An Introduction for Psychologists. Louis A. Pagliaro & Ann M. Pagliaro. LC 97-19994. 1997. pap. write for info. (*1-56032-678-6*); boxed set. write for info. (*1-56032-677-8*) Hemisp Pub.

Pharmacologic Intervention in the Treatment of AIDS. Kirk R. Ryan. 1992. pap. 9.00 (*0-9623535-4-X*) Remco Inc.

Pharmacologic Management of Heart Disease. Ed. by Joel Kupersmith & Prakash Deedwania. LC 96-326. (Illus.). 608p. 1996. pap. 39.95 (*0-683-04796-5*) Lppncott W & W.

***Pharmacologic Treatment of Schizophrenia.** Robert Conley & Deanna Kelly. 200p. 2000. pap. text 19.95 (*1-884735-56-8*) Prof Comms.

Pharmacological Adjuncts in Smoking Cessation. 1992. lib. bdg. 89.95 (*0-8490-5497-4*) Gordon Pr.

Pharmacological & Chemical Synonyms. 9th ed. Compiled by E. E. Marler. 500p. 1990. reprint ed. 275.50 (*0-444-90487-5*) Elsevier.

Pharmacological & Chemical Synonyms: A Collection of Names of Drugs, Pesticides & Other Compounds Drawn from the Medical Literature of the World. 10th ed. Ed. by E. E. Marler. 602p. 1994. 292.00 (*0-444-82081-7*) Elsevier.

Pharmacological & Therapeutic Aspects of Hypertension, Vol. 1. Ardis Walker. 224p. 1980. 130.00 (*0-8493-5385-8*, RC685, CRC Reprint) Franklin.

Pharmacological & Therapeutic Aspects of Hypertension, Vol. 2. Ardis Walker. 256p. 1980. 143.00 (*0-8493-5386-6*, CRC Reprint) Franklin.

Pharmacological Approach to the Study of the Formation & Resorption Mechanism of Hard Tissues. Hideaki Ogura. (Illus.). 192p. 1994. 55.00 (*1-56386-021-X*, Ishiyaku EuroAmerica) Med Dent Media.

Pharmacological Approaches to the Treatment of Brain & Spinal Cord Injury. Ed. by D. G. Stein & B. A. Sabel. LC 88-5942. (Illus.). 408p. 1988. 105.00 (*0-306-42732-X*, Plenum Trade) Perseus Pubng.

Pharmacological Approaches to the Treatment of Chronic Pain: New Concepts & Critical Issues. Ed. by Howard L. Fields & J. C. Liebeskind. LC 93-80786. (Progress in Pain Research & Management Ser.: Vol. 1). (Illus.). 326p. 1994. 36.00 (*0-931092-04-3*, PPRM1) Intl Assn Study Pain.

Pharmacological Aspect of Nursing Care. 6th ed. Reiss-Evans. (Nursing Education Ser.). (C). 2001. pap. text 35.95 (*0-7668-0502-6*) Delmar.

Pharmacological Aspects & Neurological Potentials of Calcium Entry Blockers. Ed. by A. Hartmann & Pieter A. Van Zwieten. (Journal: European Neurology: Vol. 25, Suppl. 1, 1986). 128p. 1986. pap. 40.00 (*3-8055-4365-4*) S Karger.

Pharmacological Aspects of Drug Dependence: Toward an Integrated Neurobehavioral Approach. Ed. by Charles R. Schuster et al. LC 95-36826. (Handbook of Experimental Pharmacology Ser.: Vol. 118). 765p. 1996. 450.00 (*3-540-58989-9*) Spr-Verlag.

Pharmacological Aspects of Heart Disease. Ed. by Naranjan S. Dhalla et al. (Developments in Cardiovascular Medicine Ser.). 1987. text 176.50 (*0-89838-867-8*) Kluwer Academic.

Pharmacological Aspects of Nursing Care. 4th ed. Barry S. Reiss & Mary E. Evans. LC 92-49601. 766p. 1993. pap. 44.95 (*0-8273-4846-0*) Delmar.

Pharmacological Aspects of Nursing Care. 5th ed. Barry S. Reiss. (Nursing Education Ser.). 112p. 1996. teacher ed. 10.50 (*0-8273-7669-3*) Delmar.

Pharmacological Aspects of Nursing Care. 5th ed. Barry S. Reiss & Mary E. Evans. (Nursing Education Ser.). 816p. (C). 1995. mass mkt. 63.95 (*0-8273-6662-0*) Delmar.

Pharmacological Aspects of Nursing Care: Computerized Testmaker & Testbank for DOS Compatible Computers. 4th ed. Barry S. Reiss & Mary E. Evans. 1993. 49.95 (*0-685-70404-1*) Delmar.

Pharmacological Aspects of Nursing Care: Instructor's Guide. 4th ed. Barry S. Reiss & Mary E. Evans. 139p. 1993. pap. 16.95 (*0-8273-5447-9*) Delmar.

Pharmacological Basis of Anesthesiology: Basic Science & Practical Applications. T. Andrew Bowdle. 1994. text 120.00 (*0-443-08878-0*) Church.

Pharmacological Basis of Anesthesiology: Clinical Pharmacology of New Analgesics & Anesthetics. Ed. by Mario Tiengo & Michael J. Cousins. LC 83-9676. (Progress in Anesthesiology Ser.: Vol. 3). 352p. 1983. reprint ed. pap. 109.20 (*0-608-00387-5*, 206110100007) Bks Demand.

Pharmacological Calculations for Nurses. 2nd ed. Peggy H. Batastini. 187p. (C). 1991. pap. 26.50 (*0-8273-4727-8*) Delmar.

Pharmacological Calculations for Nurses: A Worktext. Peggy H. Batastini & Judy K. Davidson. 202p. 1989. pap. text 24.95 (*0-8273-4202-0*) Delmar.

Pharmacological Calculus for Nursing. 3rd ed. Batastini & Davidson. LC 98-46290. (C). 1999. 21.95 (*0-7668-0166-7*) Delmar.

Pharmacological Control of Calcium & Potassium Homeostasis: Biological, Therapeutical, & Clinical Aspects. Ed. by T. Godfraind et al. LC 95-19895. (Medical Science Symposia Ser.: Vol. 9). 292p. (C). 1995. text 125.00 (*0-7923-3604-6*) Kluwer Academic.

Pharmacological Denervation & Glaucoma. Philip F. Hoyng. 1981. text 127.50 (*90-6193-802-3*) Kluwer Academic.

Pharmacological Dictionary. Latin-Russian, Russian-Latin. (LAT & RUS.). 463p. 1977. 39.95 (*0-7859-0787-4*, M-9078) Fr & Eur.

Pharmacological Effects of Ethanol on the Nervous System. Ed. by Richard A. Deitrich et al. LC 95-9425. (Pharmacology & Toxicology Ser.). 480p. 1995. boxed set 139.95 (*0-8493-8389-7*, 8389) CRC Pr.

Pharmacological Effects of Lipids. Ed. by Jon J. Kabara. 228p. 1978. 40.00 (*0-935315-02-0*) Am Oil Chemists.

Pharmacological Effects of Lipids, Vol. II. Ed. by Jon J. Kabara. 366p. 1985. 40.00 (*0-935315-10-1*) Am Oil Chemists.

Pharmacological Effects of Lipids III. Ed. by Jon J. Kabara. 366p. (C). 1990. 40.00 (*0-935315-28-4*) Am Oil Chemists.

Pharmacological Interventions on Central Cholinergic Mechanisms in Senile Dementia: Alzheimer's Disease. Ed. by H. Kewitz et al. (Clinical Pharmacology Ser.: Vol. 2). (Illus.). 328p. 1989. text 55.00 (*3-88603-362-7*, Pub. by W Zuckschwerdt) Scholium Intl.

Pharmacological Issues in Alcohol & Substance Abuse. Ed. by Barry Stimmel. LC 87-36672. (Advances in Alcohol & Substance Abuse Ser.: Vol. 7, No. 1). (Illus.). 79p. 1988. text 39.95 (*0-86656-717-8*) Haworth Pr.

Pharmacological Management of Neurological & Psychiatric Disorders. Sam J. Enna & Joe Coyle. LC 98-16368. (Illus.). 746p. 1998. text 75.00 (*0-07-021764-5*) McGraw-Hill HPD.

Pharmacological Methods in Phytotherapy Research, Vol. 1. Elizabeth M. Williamson et al. LC 95-46352. 238p. 1996. 178.00 (*0-471-94216-2*); pap. 78.00 (*0-471-94217-0*) Wiley.

Pharmacological Methods in Toxicology. Ed. by F. Gross & Gerhard Zbinden. 1979. 80.00 (*0-08-021544-0*, Pub. by Pergamon Repr) Franklin.

Pharmacological Modulation of Steroid Action. fac. ed. Ed. by Enrico Genazzani et al. LC 79-5219. (Illus.). 311p. pap. 96.50 (*0-7837-7299-8*, 204700700005) Bks Demand.

Pharmacological Nutrition Immune Nutrition. L. Cynober et al. (Illus.). 147p. 1995. pap. text 45.00 (*3-88603-543-3*, Pub. by W Zuckschwerdt) Scholium Intl.

Pharmacological Regulation of Gene Expression in the CNS: Towards An Understanding of Basal Ganglial Functions. Kalpana M. Merchant. LC 96-18410. (Pharmacology & Toxicology: Basic & Clinical Aspects Ser.). 224p. 1996. boxed set 139.95 (*0-8493-8550-4*) CRC Pr.

***Pharmacological Research on Traditional Herbal Medicines.** Hiroshi Watanabe. 248p. 1999. text 90.00 (*90-5702-054-8*, Harwood Acad Pubs) Gordon & Breach.

Pharmacological Sciences: Perspectives for Research & Theraphy in the Late 1990s. Ed. by A. Claudio Cuello & Brian Collier. LC 95-17107. 1995. 159.00 (*0-8176-5072-5*) Birkhauser.

Pharmacological Sciences: Perspectives for Research & Therapy in the Late 1990s. Ed. by A. C. Cuello & B. Collier. xxi, 519p. 1995. 159.00 (*3-7643-5072-5*) Birkhauser.

Pharmacological Stress. Elias H. Botvinick. LC 98-26415. (Nuclear Medicine Self-Study Program III Ser.: Vol. 2). 195p. 1998. pap. text 45.00 (*0-932004-60-1*) Soc Nuclear Med.

Pharmacological Therapies for Drug & Alcohol Addictions. Ed. by Norman S. Miller & Mark S. Gold. LC 94-3755. (Illus.). 480p. 1994. text 165.00 (*0-8247-8979-2*) Dekker.

Pharmacological Treatment of Alzheimer's Disease: Molecular & Neurobiological Foundations. Ed. by Jorge D. Brioni & Micahel W. Decker. LC 96-30137. 549p. 1997. 119.95 (*0-471-16758-4*) Wiley.

Pharmacological Treatment of Endocrinopathies. Ed. by Charles Y. Pak. (Progress in Basic & Clinical Pharmacology Ser.: Vol. 5). (Illus.). x, 142p. 1991. 126.25 (*3-8055-5214-9*) S Karger.

Pharmacologie Clinique des Inhibiteurs Selectifs du Recaptage de la Serotonine. Sheldon H. Preskorn.Tr. of Clinical Pharmacology of Selective Serotonin Reuptake Inhibitors. (FRE.). 253p. 1996. pap. text 19.95 (*1-884735-16-9*) Prof Comms.

Pharmacologist. Jack Rudman. (Career Examination Ser.: C-581). 1994. pap. 39.95 (*0-8373-0581-0*) Nat Learn.

Pharmacology. Ahrens. (National Veterinary Medical Ser.). 360p. 1996. pap. text 27.95 (*0-683-00085-3*) Lppncott W & W.

Pharmacology. Daniel E. Becker. (C). 1993. student ed. 20.39 (*1-56870-094-6*) RonJon Pub.

Pharmacology. Brenner. Date not set. pap. text. write for info. (*0-7216-7757-6*, W B Saunders Co) Harcrt Hlth Sci Grp.

Pharmacology. Center for Emergency Medicine Staff. 96p. (gr. 13). 1996. pap. text 9.95 (*0-8151-7951-0*) Mosby Inc.

Pharmacology. Choca. 1996. write for info. (*0-7216-4579-8*, W B Saunders Co) Harcrt Hlth Sci Grp.

Pharmacology. Charles D. Ciccone. 158p. 1995. pap. 21.00 (*1-887759-00-X*, P-115) Am Phys Therapy Assn.

Pharmacology. Richard M. Kostrzewa. 380p. 1995. pap. 19.99 (*0-945819-48-X*) Sulzburger & Graham Pub.

Pharmacology. Ed. by J. I. Moore. (Oklahoma Notes Ser.). xi, 247p. (C). 1988. pap. 14.95 (*0-387-96332-4*) Spr-Verlag.

Pharmacology. Ed. by J. I. Moore. (Oklahoma Notes Ser.). xi, 251p. 1991. pap. 15.95 (*0-387-97194-7*) Spr-Verlag.

Pharmacology. Catherine Paradiso. LC 97-35555. (Lippincott's Review Ser.). 352p. 1997. pap. text 21.95 (*0-397-55327-7*) Lppncott W & W.

Pharmacology. Robert B. Raffa. 1999. pap. text 19.95 (*1-889325-38-4*) Fence Crk Pubng.

Pharmacology. Margaret A. Reilly. LC 97-3055. (Rypins' Intensive Reviews Ser.). (Illus.). 200p. 1997. pap. text 19.95 (*0-397-51550-2*) Lppncott W & W.

Pharmacology. Smolin. 1993. 39.00 (*0-316-80269-7*, Little Brwn Med Div) Lppncott W & W.

***Pharmacology.** Webster. (Quick Look Veterinary Ser.). 2000. 23.95 (*1-889325-47-3*, Pub. by Fence Crk Pubng) Blackwell Sci.

Pharmacology. Winstanley. 1996. pap. text 22.95 (*0-443-04948-3*, W B Saunders Co) Harcrt Hlth Sci Grp.

Pharmacology. 2nd ed. Joyce L. Kee. 1997. pap. text 61.00 (*0-7216-7573-5*, W B Saunders Co) Harcrt Hlth Sci Grp.

***Pharmacology.** 2nd ed. Mary Mycek. (Illustrated Reviews Ser.). (Illus.). 1999. pap. 32.95 (*0-7817-2413-9*, Lippnctt) Lppncott W & W.

Pharmacology. 2nd ed. H. P. Rang & M. M. Dale. (Illus.). 955p. 1991. pap. text 55.00 (*0-443-04110-5*) Church.

Pharmacology. 3rd ed. (National Medical Ser.). 1991. 25.00 (*0-685-75182-1*) Lppncott W & W.

Pharmacology. 3rd ed. J. I. Moore. (Oklahoma Notes Ser.). (Illus.). 280p. 1992. 17.95 (*0-387-97779-1*) Spr-Verlag.

Pharmacology. 3rd ed. H. P. Rang et al. LC 94-47182. 1995. pap. text 38.00 (*0-443-07560-3*) Church.

Pharmacology. 3rd ed. Gary C. Rosenfeld & David S. Loose-Mitchell. LC 97-25644. (Board Review Ser.). (Illus.). 370p. 1997. pap. 22.95 (*0-683-18050-9*) Lppncott W & W.

Pharmacology. 4th ed. Leonard S. Jacob. (National Medical Series for Independent Study). (Illus.). 385p. 1996. write for info. (*0-683-06251-4*) Lppncott W & W.

Pharmacology. 4th ed. Ed. by Joanne I. Moore. LC 94-43678. (Oklahoma Notes Ser.). 235p. 1995. 17.95 (*0-387-94394-3*) Spr-Verlag.

Pharmacology. 4th ed. H. P. Rang. LC 98-31756. 1999. write for info. (*0-443-05974-8*) Church.

Pharmacology. 9th ed. John Gaddum. Ed. by J. F. Mitchell & A. S. Burgen. (Illus.). 1985. 17.95 (*0-19-261423-1*) OUP.

Pharmacology. 9th ed. Ed. by Arnold Stern. (Basic Sciences: Pretest Self Assessment & Review Ser.). (Illus.). 1998. pap. text 18.95 (*0-07-052694-X*) McGraw-Hill HPD.

P

An Asterisk (*) at the beginning of an entry indicates that the title is appearing for the first time.

Pharmacology: A Nursing Process Approach. Ed. by Joyce L. Kee & Evelyn R. Hayes. (Illus.). 1993. pap., teacher ed. write for info. (*0-7216-3661-6*, W B Saunders Co); pap., student ed. write for info. (*0-7216-4613-1*, W B Saunders Co) Harcrt Hlth Sci Grp.

Pharmacology: A Nursing Process Approach. 2nd ed. Joyce L. Kee & Evelyn R. Hayes. Ed. by Maura Connor. LC 96-46545. 848p. 1996. pap. text 47.00 (*0-7216-6057-6*, W B Saunders Co) Harcrt Hlth Sci Grp.

Pharmacology: A Nursing Process Approach. 2nd rev. ed. Ed. by Joyce L. Kee & Evelyn R. Hayes. (Illus.). 1997. pap., teacher ed. write for info. (*0-7216-6058-4*, W B Saunders Co) Harcrt Hlth Sci Grp.

Pharmacology: A Nursing Process Approach. 3rd ed. Joyce L. Kee & Evelyn R. Hayes. Ed. by Maura Conner. LC 98-50608. (Illus.). 895p. 1999. text. write for info. (*0-7216-8299-5*, W B Saunders Co) Harcrt Hlth Sci Grp.

***Pharmacology: A Physiological Approach.** Leilani Grajeda-Higley. LC 99-73102. (Illus.). 256p. (C). 1999. pap. text 19.95 (*0-8385-8136-6*, A-8136-2) Appleton & Lange.

Pharmacology: An Illustrated Review with Questions & Explanations. 3rd ed. Manuchair Ebadi. LC 95-43991. (Illus.). 326p. 1996. pap. text 31.00 (*0-316-19957-5*, Little Brwn Med Div) Lppncott W & W.

Pharmacology: An Introductory Text. 8th ed. Mary K. Asperheim. (Illus.). 1996. pap., teacher ed. write for info. (*0-7216-6039-8*, W B Saunders Co) Harcrt Hlth Sci Grp.

Pharmacology: An Introductory Text. 8th ed. Mary K. Asperheim. Ed. by Ilza Rader. LC 95-36451. (Illus.). 275p. 1996. pap. text 24.95 (*0-7216-6038-X*, W B Saunders Co) Harcrt Hlth Sci Grp.

Pharmacology: Drug Actions & Reactions. 3rd ed. Ruth R. Levine. (Illus.). 1983. 24.50 (*0-316-52222-8*, Little Brwn Med Div) Lppncott W & W.

Pharmacology: Drug Actions & Reactions. 5th ed. Ruth R. Levine et al. LC 96-29172. (Illus.). 586p. 1996. pap. text 44.95 (*1-85070-780-4*) Prthnon Pub.

***Pharmacology: Drug Actions & Reactions.** 6th ed. Ruth R. Levine & Carol T. Walsh. (Illus.). 590p. 2000. pap. 51.45 (*1-85070-497-X*) Prthnon Pub.

Pharmacology: Exam & Board Review. 6th ed. Katzung. (C). 2001. 32.95 (*0-8385-8147-1*) Appleton & Lange.

Pharmacology: Examination & Board Review. 4th ed. Bertram G. Katzung. (Illus.). 480p. (C). 1995. pap. text 29.95 (*0-8385-8067-X*, A8067-9) Appleton & Lange.

Pharmacology: Examination & Board Review. 5th ed. Katzung. (Illus.). 560p. (C). 1998. pap. 34.95 (*0-8385-7708-3*, Apple Lange Med) McGraw.

Pharmacology: MedCharts, Tables & Summaries for Review. Kevin P. Rosenbach. LC 92-49118. 1993. pap. 14.95 (*1-882531-00-0*) ILOC.

Pharmacology: Modern Medical. Frederick A. Raffa. 2001. text 65.00 (*0-07-135444-1*) McGraw.

Pharmacology: PreTest Self-Assessment & Review. 5th ed. Joseph R. Dipalma. 1988. pap. text 15.95 (*0-07-051966-8*) McGraw.

Pharmacology: Review for New National Boards. Melvin L. Billingsley. LC 95-75271. (Illus.). 186p. 1995. pap. 25.00 (*0-9632873-7-0*) J & S Pub VA.

Pharmacology set: Modern Medicine. Frederick A. Raffa. 2001. text. write for info. (*0-07-135445-X*) McGraw.

Pharmacology & Applications of Chinese Materia Medica, Vol. 1. Ed. by H. M. Chang & P. P-H. But. 780p. 1986. text 114.00 (*9971-5-0121-X*) World Scientific Pub.

Pharmacology & Applications of Chinese Materia Medica, Vol. 2. Ed. by H. M. Chang & P. P-H. But. Tr. by L. L. Wang & S. C. Yeung. 556p. 1987. text 99.00 (*9971-5-0167-8*) World Scientific Pub.

Pharmacology & Clinical Usefulness of Carisoprodol: A Symposium Sponsored by Wayne State University College of Medicine & the University of Michigan Medical School, Department of Postgraduate Medicine, held in Detroit, Michigan, July 1, 1959. James G. Miller. LC 59-15115. 192p. reprint ed. pap. 59.60 (*0-7837-3656-8*, 204352700009) Bks Demand.

Pharmacology & Drug Administration for Imaging Techniques. Jensen & Peppers. (gr. 13). 1997. teacher ed. write for info. (*0-8151-4938-7*) Mosby Inc.

Pharmacology & Drug Administration for Imaging Technologists. Jensen & Peppers. (Illus.). 192p. (gr. 13). 1998. pap. text 26.00 (*0-8151-4894-1*, 28605) Mosby Inc.

Pharmacology & Drug Management for Nurses. George Downie et al. LC 94-8716. 1995. pap. text 30.00 (*0-443-04477-5*) Church.

Pharmacology & Drug Management for Nurses. 2nd ed. Downie. (C). 1999. pap. text 30.00 (*0-443-05968-3*, W B Saunders Co) Harcrt Hlth Sci Grp.

Pharmacology & Natural Medicine Exam Review. 4th ed. Bertram G. Katzung. (C). 1996. pap. text 15.99 (*0-8385-8102-1*) P-H.

Pharmacology & Pharmacotherapeutics. R. S. Saroskar & S. D. Bhandarkar. 1989. 30.00 (*0-86132-177-4*, Pub. by Popular Prakashan) S Asia.

Pharmacology & Physiology in Anesthetic Practice. 3rd ed. Robert K. Stoelting. LC 98-29288. 976p. 1998. text 95.00 (*0-7817-1621-7*) Lppncott W & W.

Pharmacology & Physiology in Anesthetic Practice. 2nd ed. Robert K. Stoelting. (Illus.). 872p. 1991. text 99.00 (*0-397-51129-9*) Lppncott W & W.

Pharmacology & the Future of Man: Proceedings of the International Congress on Pharmacology, 5th, San Francisco, 1972, 5 vols, Set. Incl. Vol. 1. Drug Abuse & Contraception. Ed. by J. Cochin. 252p. 1973. 62.75 (*3-8055-1470-0*); Vol. 2. Toxicological Problems. Ed. by Ted A. Loomis. 204p. 1973. 51.50 (*3-8055-1471-9*); Vol. 3. Problems of Therapy. Ed. by G. T. Okita & G. H. Acheson. 400p. 1973. 101.00 (*3-8055-1472-7*); Vol. 4. Brain, Nerves & Synapses. Ed. by Floyd E. Bloom & G. H. Acheson. 430p. 1973. 95.00 (*3-8055-1473-5*); Vol. 5. Cellular Mechanisms. Ed. by R. A. Maxwell & G. H. Acheson. 380p. 1973. 90.50 (*3-8055-1474-3*); 1973. 310.50 (*3-8055-1387-9*) S Karger.

Pharmacology & the Nursing Process. Linda Lane Lilley et al. (Illus.). teacher ed. write for info. (*0-8151-5664-2*) Mosby Inc.

Pharmacology & the Nursing Process. Linda Lane Lilley et al. (Illus.). 1996. text, student ed. 13.95 (*0-8016-8116-2*) Mosby Inc.

Pharmacology & the Nursing Process. 2nd ed. Linda L. Lilley & Robert S. Aucker. LC 98-26135. (Illus.). 816p. 1998. pap. text 45.00 (*1-55664-492-2*) Mosby Inc.

***Pharmacology & the Nursing Process.** 2nd ed. Linda L. Lilley & Robert S. Aucker. (Illus.). 1998. student ed. write for info. (*1-55664-495-7*) Mosby Inc.

Pharmacology & the Nursing Process. 3rd ed. Gordon E. Johnson et al. (Illus.). 799p. 1992. pap. write for info. (*0-920513-08-5*, W B Saunders Co) Harcrt Hlth Sci Grp.

Pharmacology & the Nursing Process. 3rd ed. Gordon E. Johnson et al. (Illus.). 1992. teacher ed. write for info. (*0-920513-10-7*, Pub. by Saulnders) Saunders.

***Pharmacology & the Nursing Process, Includes Testbank.** 2nd ed. Linda L. Lilley & Robert S. Aucker. 1998. teacher ed. write for info. (*1-55664-493-0*) Mosby Inc.

***Pharmacology & the Nursing Process: Text & Student Learning Guide Package, Set.** 2nd ed. Linda L. Lilley & Robert S. Aucker. (C). 1998. text, student ed. write for info. (*1-55664-494-9*) Mosby Inc.

Pharmacology & Therapeutics, Vol. 12, No. 1. Ed. by W. C. Bowman. LC 77-25743. (Illus.). 283p. 1981. pap. 73.00 (*0-08-026854-4*, Pergamon Pr) Elsevier.

Pharmacology & Therapeutics, Vol. 12, No. 2. Ed. by W. C. Bowman. (Illus.). 190p. 1981. pap. 73.00 (*0-08-026855-2*, Pergamon Pr) Elsevier.

Pharmacology & Therapeutics for Dentistry, No. 4. 4th ed. Yagiela Hargreaves & Enid A. Neidle. LC 98-229020. (Illus.). 752p. (C). (gr. 13). 1997. text 62.00 (*0-8016-7962-1*, 07962) Mosby Inc.

Pharmacology & Therapeutics in Respiratory Care. Theodore J. Witek, Jr. & E. Neil Schachter. LC 92-48875. (Illus.). 448p. 1993. text 49.00 (*0-7216-3483-4*, W B Saunders Co) Harcrt Hlth Sci Grp.

Pharmacology & Toxicology of Amphetamine & Related Designer Drugs. 1991. lib. bdg. 250.00 (*0-8490-4372-7*) Gordon Pr.

Pharmacology & Toxicology of Amphetamine & Related Designer Drugs. 1993. lib. bdg. 261.95 (*0-8490-8913-1*) Gordon Pr.

Pharmacology & Toxicology of Naturally Occurring Toxins, 2 vols. Ed. by H. Raskova. LC 77-130797. 1971. 323.00 (*0-08-016797-7*, Pub. by Pergamon Repr) Franklin.

***Pharmacology at the Millennium: Past, Present & Future.** R. J. Huxtable et al. vi, 76p. (C). 1999. pap. write for info. (*1-930061-00-5*) West Pharm Soc.

Pharmacology Companion. Gary L. Gallia et al. 250p. (Orig.). (C). Date not set. pap. 25.95 (*0-9640124-3-X*) Alert & Oriented.

Pharmacology Essentials. Ed. by Jody A. Eckler & Judy M. Fair. (Illus.). 1996. pap., teacher ed. write for info. (*0-7216-6811-9*, W B Saunders Co) Harcrt Hlth Sci Grp.

Pharmacology Essentials. Jody A. Eckler & Judy M. Fair. Ed. by Ilze Rader. (Illus.). 464p. 1996. pap. text 31.50 (*0-7216-6486-5*, W B Saunders Co) Harcrt Hlth Sci Grp.

Pharmacology Field Reference Guide. Richard K. Beck. LC 95-50500. (Illus.). 122p. (C). 1996. pap. 20.95 (*0-8036-0133-6*) Thomson Learn.

Pharmacology for Anaesthetists. Noel Cass & Linda Cass. LC 93-7322. 208p. 1995. pap. text 25.00 (*0-443-04639-5*) Church.

Pharmacology for Athletic Trainers: Performance Enhancement & Social Drugs. Human Kinetics Staff. (Illus.). 96p. 1997. spiral bd. 69.00 (*0-88011-760-5*, COPS0760) Human Kinetics.

Pharmacology for Chemists. Joseph Cannon. LC 98-25069. (ACS Professional Reference Book Ser.). (Illus.). 288p. 1998. text 60.00 (*0-8412-3524-4*, Pub. by Am Chemical) OUP.

Pharmacology for Dental Hygiene Practice. Elena B. Haveles. LC 96-17639. (Dental Assisting Procedures Ser.). 352p. (C). 1996. mass mkt. 62.95 (*0-8273-6602-7*) Delmar.

Pharmacology for Dental Hygiene Practice - IML. Haveles. 1996. teacher ed. write for info. (*0-8273-8438-6*) Delmar.

Pharmacology for Health in Asia: Proceedings of Asian Congress of Pharmacology. Ed. by B. N. Dhawan. (C). 1988. 55.00 (*0-8364-2336-4*, Pub. by Allied Pubs) S Asia.

Pharmacology for Health Professionals. Evelyn Salerno. (Illus.). 816p. (C). (gr. 13). 1999. pap. text 39.00 (*0-8151-2711-1*, 31383) Mosby Inc.

***Pharmacology for Health Professionals: Includes Testbank.** Evelyn Salerno. (Illus.). 1998. teacher ed. write for info. (*0-323-00257-9*) Mosby Inc.

Pharmacology for Medical Assistants. E. A. Watts. 100p. 1986. pap. text 12.95 (*0-935920-28-5*, Ntl Pubs Blck) P-H.

Pharmacology for Nurses. 5th ed. James Connechen. 1983. text 17.00 (*0-7216-0803-5*, W B Saunders Co) Harcrt Hlth Sci Grp.

Pharmacology for Nurses. 5th ed. James Connechen et al. 384p. 1983. pap. text 17.95 (*0-7020-0868-0*) Bailliere Tindall.

Pharmacology for Nursing Care. 2nd ed. Richard A. Lehne. (Illus.). 1994. teacher ed. write for info. (*0-7216-5167-4*, W B Saunders Co) Harcrt Hlth Sci Grp.

Pharmacology for Nursing Care. 3rd ed. Richard A. Lehne. (Illus.). 1180p. 1998. teacher ed. write for info. (*0-7216-7151-9*, W B Saunders Co) Harcrt Hlth Sci Grp.

Pharmacology for Nursing Care. 3rd ed. Richard A. Lehne. Ed. by Maura Connor. LC 97-39758. (Illus.). 1184p. 1998. pap. text 55.95 (*0-7216-7150-0*, W B Saunders Co) Harcrt Hlth Sci Grp.

Pharmacology for Nursing Care. 3rd ed. Richard A. Lehne. (C). 1998. pap. text, student ed. 17.95 (*0-7216-7069-5*, W B Saunders Co) Harcrt Hlth Sci Grp.

Pharmacology for Prehospital Emergency Care. 2nd ed. Richard K. Beck. Ed. by James R. Vance. LC 93-33629. 307p. (C). 1994. pap. 23.95 (*0-8036-0692-3*) Thomson Learn.

Pharmacology for Respiratory Care Practitioners. Gregory P. Cottrell. LC 94-41358. 414p. 1995. 37.95 (*0-8036-1989-8*) Davis Co.

Pharmacology for Surgical Technologists. Chris Keegan & Katherine Synder. Ed. by Maureen Pfeiffer et al. (Illus.). 255p. (C). 1998. pap. text 25.00 (*0-7216-6321-4*, W B Saunders Co) Harcrt Hlth Sci Grp.

Pharmacology for Technicians. Don A. Ballington & Mary M. Laughlin. LC 98-11383. 1998. write for info. (*0-7638-0096-1*) Paradigm MN.

Pharmacology for Technicians: Instructor's Guide. Don A. Ballington & Mary M. Laughlin. text 14.00 (*0-7638-0097-X*) EMC-Paradigm.

Pharmacology for the Dental Hygienist: For Students & Practitioners. Fred F. Cowan. LC 77-17477. (Illus.). 419p. reprint ed. pap. 129.90 (*0-8357-7643-3*, 205696800096) Bks Demand.

Pharmacology for the Medical Assistant. Watts. 84p. 1993. pap. 28.80 (*0-13-662602-5*) P-H.

Pharmacology for the Primary Care Practitioner. Marilyn W. Edmunds. (Illus.). 1100p. (C). (gr. 13). 1999. text 84.95 (*0-8151-3092-9*, 28005) Mosby Inc.

Pharmacology for the Surgical Technologist. Slagle. 1996. pap. write for info. (*0-7216-4225-X*, W B Saunders Co) Harcrt Hlth Sci Grp.

Pharmacology for Veterinary Technicians. 2nd ed. Robert Bill. LC 97-11. (Illus.). 352p. (C). (gr. 13). 1997. pap. text 29.00 (*0-8151-0902-4*, 28335) Mosby Inc.

Pharmacology in Exercise & Sports. Ed. by Satu M. Somani & Mannfred Hollenger. LC 95-35490. (CRC Pharmacology & Toxicology). 384p. 1995. boxed set 139.95 (*0-8493-8540-7*, 8540) CRC Pr.

Pharmacology in Medicine: Principles & Practice. Ed. by Sachin N. Pradhan et al. 1100p. (C). 1986. text 55.00 (*0-9617129-0-2*) SP Press Intl.

Pharmacology in Rehabilitation. 2nd ed. Charles D. Ciccone. LC 95-22130. (Contemporary Perspectives in Rehabilitation Ser.). (Illus.). 642p. (C). 1995. text 49.95 (*0-8036-0030-5*) Davis Co.

Pharmacology in the Practice of Anaesthesia. Ed. by Leon Kaufman & Peter Taberner. LC 96-4707. (Arnold Publication). (Illus.). 704p. 1996. pap. text 135.00 (*0-340-55171-2*) OUP.

Pharmacology Is Murder: A Novel. Dirk Wyle. LC 97-40637. 388p. 1998. pap. 16.95 (*1-56825-038-X*, 038X) Rainbow Books.

Pharmacology Made Easy for NCLEX-PN. Linda L. Waide & Berta C. Roland. 242p. (C). 1998. pap. 23.95 (*0-9659975-0-2*) Learn Made.

Pharmacology Made Easy for NCLEX-RN. Linda L. Waide & Berta C. Roland. 242p. (Orig.). (C). 1998. pap. text 23.95 (*0-9659975-1-0*) Learn Made.

Pharmacology Math. 3rd ed. Hocking Technical College Staff. 128p. 1994. spiral bd. 16.95 (*0-8403-8868-3*) Kendall-Hunt.

Pharmacology Math. 4th ed. Hocking Technical College Staff. 120p. (C). 1996. spiral bd. 20.95 (*0-7872-2251-8*, 41225101) Kendall-Hunt.

Pharmacology Mathematics: A Unit Analysis Approach. Jerome Hart. 122p. (C). 1998. spiral bd. 24.95 (*0-7872-5178-X*) Kendall-Hunt.

Pharmacology, 1995: Digging up the Bones, Vol. 1. Medical Review Staff. (Medical Review Ser.). (Illus.). 99p. 1997. pap. 18.95 (*0-07-038214-X*) McGraw-Hill HPD.

Pharmacology Nursing. Marshal Shlafer. Ed. by Debra Hunter. 1432p. (C). 1989. pap. text 9.95 (*0-201-17839-7*) Addison-Wesley.

Pharmacology of Aging Processes: Methods of Assessment & Potential Interventions. Ed. by Denham Harman et al. LC 94-15312. (Annals Ser.: Vol. 717). 1994. write for info. (*0-89766-880-4*); pap. 105.00 (*0-89766-881-2*) NY Acad Sci.

Pharmacology of Alcohol Abuse. R. F. Anton. Ed. by Henry R. Kranzler. LC 94-28586. (Handbook of Experimental Pharmacology Ser.: 114). 1994. 471.95 (*0-387-57125-6*) Spr-Verlag.

Pharmacology of Alcohol & Alcohol Dependence. Ed. by Henri Begleiter & Benjamin Kissin. (Alcohol & Alcoholism Ser.: No. 2). (Illus.). 536p. (C). 1996. text 99.50 (*0-19-510094-8*) OUP.

Pharmacology of Alcohol & Drugs of Abuse & Addiction. N. S. Miller. (Illus.). 312p. 1990. 99.00 (*0-387-97383-4*) Spr-Verlag.

Pharmacology of Antihypertensive Therapeutics. Ed. by D. Ganten & P. J Mulrow. (Handbook of Experimental Pharmacology Ser.: Vol. 93). (Illus.). 928p. 1990. 432.00 (*0-387-50427-3*) Spr-Verlag.

Pharmacology of Antimuscarinic Agents. Laszlo Gyermek. LC 97-24422. (Pharmacology & Toxicology Ser.). 1997. lib. bdg. 129.95 (*0-8493-8559-8*) CRC Pr.

Pharmacology of Anxiolytic Drugs. rev. ed. Luca Steardo et al. LC 96-3287. (WHO Expert Series on Neuroscience: Vol. 3). (Illus.). 144p. 1997. text 29.50 (*0-88937-088-5*) Hogrefe & Huber Pubs.

Pharmacology of Asthma. Ed. by John Morley & Kim D. Rainsford. (Agents & Actions Supplements Ser.: Vol. 13). 228p. 1983. 87.50 (*0-8176-1503-2*) Birkhauser.

Pharmacology of Asthma. Ed. by C. P. Page et al. (Handbook of Experimental Pharmacology Ser.: No. 98). (Illus.). 352p. 1991. 276.95 (*0-387-52839-3*) Spr-Verlag.

Pharmacology of Ayurvedic Medicinal Plants. C. R. Karnick. 1996. 12.00 (*81-7030-482-2*, Pub. by Sri Satguru Pubns) S Asia.

Pharmacology of Benzopyrone Derivatives & Related Compounds. Ed. by M. Gabor. 1988. pap. 145.00 (*963-05-4944-1*, Pub. by Akade Kiado) St Mut.

Pharmacology of Benzopyrone Derivatives & Related Compounds. Miklos Gabor. (Illus.). 253p. 1986. 110.00 (*963-05-4124-6*, Pub. by Akade Kiado) St Mut.

Pharmacology of Cardiac & Vascular Remodelling: Antiproliferative Drugs. Ed. by J. G. De Mey et al. 200p. 1991. 47.95 (*0-387-91391-2*) Spr-Verlag.

Pharmacology of Cerebral Circulation. Ed. by Amilcare Carpi. LC 70-182263. 370p. (C). 1972. 172.00 (*0-08-016209-6*, Pub. by Pergamon Repr) Franklin.

Pharmacology of Cerebral Ischemia. Gunter K. Krieglstein. 1989. 99.00 (*3-8047-1036-0*) CRC Pr.

Pharmacology of Chinese Herbs. Huang. Ed. by Kee Chang. 416p. 1992. boxed set 187.95 (*0-8493-4915-X*, RM666) CRC Pr.

Pharmacology of Chinese Herbs. 2nd ed. Kee C. Huang & Walter M. Williams. LC 98-13930. 544p. 1998. boxed set 149.95 (*0-8493-1665-0*) CRC Pr.

***Pharmacology of Cytokines.** Alberto Mantovani et al. (Illus.). 336p. 2000. text 110.00 (*0-19-850043-2*); pap. text 50.00 (*0-19-850042-4*) OUP.

Pharmacology of Diabetes: Present Practice & Future Perspectives. Ed. by C. E. Mogensen & E. Standl. (Illus.). xii, 374p. (C). 1991. pap. text 98.50 (*3-11-012636-2*) De Gruyter.

Pharmacology of Eating Disorders: Theoretical & Clinical Developments. Ed. by Michele O. Carruba & John E. Blundell. LC 85-32329. 192p. 1986. reprint ed. pap. 59.60 (*0-608-03394-4*, 206409100008) Bks Demand.

Pharmacology of Endogenous Neurotoxins. Andreas Moser. LC 97-12361. 1997. 120.00 (*0-8176-3993-4*) Birkhauser.

Pharmacology of Endogenous Neurotoxins. Andreas Moser. LC 97-12361. (Illus.). 328p. 1997. 99.95 (*3-7643-3993-4*) Spr-Verlag.

Pharmacology of Extrapyramidal Movement Disorders. Ed. by Harold L. Klawans, Jr. (Monographs in Neural Sciences: Vol. 2). 1972. 42.75 (*3-8055-1421-2*) S Karger.

Pharmacology of Fluorides, Pt. 1. Ed. by F. A. Smith. (Handbook of Experimental Pharmacology Ser.: Vol. 20). (Illus.). 1966. 140.00 (*0-387-03537-0*) Spr-Verlag.

Pharmacology of Fluorides, Pt. 2. Ed. by F. A. Smith. (Handbook of Experimental Pharmacology Ser.: Vol. 20). (Illus.). 1970. 131.00 (*0-387-04846-4*) Spr-Verlag.

Pharmacology of Ganglionic Transmission. Ed. by D. A. Kharkevich. LC 79-9406. (Handbook of Experimental Pharmacology Ser.: Vol. 53). (Illus.). 1979. 216.00 (*0-387-09592-6*) Spr-Verlag.

Pharmacology of Glaucoma. Stephen M. Drance et al. (Illus.). 356p. 1992. 125.00 (*0-683-02655-0*) Lppncott W & W.

***Pharmacology of Ionic Channel Function: Activators & Inhibitors.** Ed. by M. Endo et al. (Handbook of Experimental Pharmacology Ser.: Vol. 147). (Illus.). xx, 650p. 2000. 369.00 (*3-540-66127-1*) Spr-Verlag.

Pharmacology of Lymphocytes. Ed. by M. A. Bray & J. Morley. (Handbook of Experimental Pharmacology Ser.: Vol. 85). (Illus.). 700p. 1988. 494.95 (*0-387-18609-3*) Spr-Verlag.

Pharmacology of Marihuana: Proceedings, Vol. 2. Ed. by Monique C. Braude & Stephen Szara. LC 75-14562. 424p. 1976. reprint ed. pap. 131.50 (*0-608-00380-8*, 206109400002) Bks Demand.

Pharmacology of Monoclonal Antibodies. Ed. by Martin Rosenberg & Gordon P. Moore. LC 93-44948. (Handbook of Experimental Pharmacology Ser.: Vol. 113). (Illus.). 460p. 1994. 379.95 (*0-387-57123-X*) Spr-Verlag.

Pharmacology of Opioid Peptides. Ed. by Leon F. Tseng. xiv, 524p. 1995. text 165.00 (*3-7186-5632-9*, Harwood Acad Pubs) Gordon & Breach.

Pharmacology of Pain. Ed. by A. H. Dickenson et al. LC 97-23531. (Handbook of Experimental Pharmacology Ser.: No. 130). (Illus.). 450p. 1997. 325.00 (*3-540-62785-5*) Spr-Verlag.

Pharmacology of Peptic Ulcer Disease: With Contributions by Numerous Experts. Ed. by M. J. Collen & S. B. Benjamin. (Handbook of Experimental Pharmacology Ser.: Vol. 99). xxii, 464p. 1991. 357.00 (*0-387-52840-7*) Spr-Verlag.

Pharmacology of Respiratory Therapy Medications. Michael J. Strauch. LC 79-10787. (Illus.). 261p. reprint ed. pap. 81.00 (*0-8357-7632-8*, 205695500096) Bks Demand.

Pharmacology of Retinoids in the Skin: 8th CIRD Symposium on Advances in Skin Pharmacology, Cannes, September 1988. Ed. by U. Reichert & B. Shroot. (Pharmacology & the Skin Ser.: Vol. 3). (Illus.). x, 282p. 1989. 207.00 (*3-8055-4909-1*) S Karger.

Pharmacology of Sexual Function & Dysfunction. Ed. by J. Bancroft. LC 95-7067. (International Congress Ser.: Vol. 1075). 366p. 1995. 212.50 (*0-444-82040-X*, Excerpta Medica) Elsevier.

Pharmacology of Sexual Function & Dysfunction: Proceedings of the Esteve Foundation Symposium VI, Son Vida, Mallorca, 9-12 October 1994. John Bancroft. LC 95-7067. (International Congress Ser.: No. 1075). 1995. write for info. (*0-614-32277-4*, Excerpta Medica) Elsevier.

Pharmacology of Sleep. Ed. by Anthony Kales. (Handbook of Experimental Pharmacology Ser.: Vol. 116). 560p. 1995. 482.95 (*3-540-58961-9*) Spr-Verlag.

Pharmacology of Smooth Muscle. Ed. by Julius Gy. Papp & Laszlo Szekeres. LC 94-17635. (Handbook of Experimental Pharmacology Ser.: Vol. 111). 1994. 465.95 (*0-387-57888-9*) Spr-Verlag.

Pharmacology of the Contraceptive Steroids. Ed. by Joseph W. Goldzieher & Kenneth Fotherby. 464p. 1993. text 108.00 (*0-7817-0097-3*) Lppncott W & W.

Pharmacology of the Endocrine System & Related Drugs: Progesterone Progestational Drugs & Antifertility Agents. M. Tausk & L. Bengtsson. (International Encyclopedia of Pharmacology & Therapeutics Ser.: Vol. 1, Sect. 48). 1971. 848.00 (*0-08-015745-9*, Pub. by Pergamon Repr) Franklin.

Pharmacology of the Eye. Ed. by M. L. Sears. (Handbook of Experimental Pharmacology Ser.: Vol. 69). 784p. 1983. 392.00 (*0-387-12578-7*) Spr-Verlag.

Pharmacology of the Respiratory Tract: Experimental & Clinical Research. Ed. by K. Fan Chung & Peter J. Barnes. (Lung Biology in Health & Disease Ser.: Vol. 67). (Illus.). 848p. 1993. text 245.00 (*0-8247-8847-8*) Dekker.

Pharmacology of the Skin. Hasan Mukhtar. (Illus.). 448p. 1991. boxed set 125.00 (*0-8493-7292-5*, RL801) CRC Pr.

Pharmacology of the Skin I. Ed. by S. Shuster & M. W. Greaves. (Handbook of Experimental Pharmacology Ser.: Vol. 87/1). (Illus.). 520p. 1988. 336.00 (*0-387-19403-7*) Spr-Verlag.

Pharmacology of the Skin II. Ed. by M. W. Greaves & S. Shuster. (Handbook of Experimental Pharmacology Ser.: Vol. 87-II). (Illus.). 650p. 1989. 407.00 (*0-387-50277-7*) Spr-Verlag.

Pharmacology of the States of Alertness: Proceedings of the Satellite Symposium to the International Congress of Pharmacology, 7th, Paris, 1978. International Congress of Pharmacology Staff. Ed. by P. Passcuant & I. Oswald. (Illus.). 271p. 1979. 63.00 (*0-08-023753-3*, Pergamon Pr) Elsevier.

Pharmacology of the Urinary Tract: Clinical Practice in Urology. Ed. by M. Caine. (Illus.). 180p. 1984. 111.00 (*0-387-13238-4*) Spr-Verlag.

Pharmacology of Therapeutic Agents Used in Anesthesia: An Introduction. Robert I. Katz et al. LC 98-19098. 300p. 1994. 68.00 (*0-9631310-2-8*) Plexus Pub.

Pharmacology of Thermoregulation: Proceedings of a Satellite Symposium on the International Congress on Pharmacology, 5th, San Francisco, 1972. International Congress on Pharmacology Staff. Ed. by E. Schoenbaum & P. Lomax. 300p. 1973. 163.50 (*3-8055-1391-7*) S Karger.

Pharmacology of Topical Retinoids. U. Reichert. Ed. by H. Schaefer et al. (Journal: Skin Pharmacology: Vol. 6, Suppl. 1, 1993). (Illus.). vi, 84p. 1994. pap. 38.50 (*3-8055-5922-4*) S Karger.

Pharmacology of Vascular Smooth Muscle. Ed. by C. J. Garland & J. A. Angus. (Illus.). 448p. (C). 1996. text 125.00 (*0-19-262387-7*) OUP.

***Pharmacology Patient Teaching Guides.** McKenry. 1999. pap. text 139.00 incl. cd-rom (*0-8151-2934-3*) Mosby Inc.

Pharmacology Recall. Ramachandran. LC 99-20847. 1999. 24.95 (*0-683-30285-X*) Lppncott W & W.

***Pharmacology Review.** Pazdernik. 1999. text 29.95 (*0-323-00838-0*) Harcourt.

Pharmacology Review. rev. ed. George M. Brenner. 255p. 1996. pap. text. write for info. (*0-7216-4604-2*, W B Saunders Co) Harcrt Hlth Sci Grp.

Pharmacology Review Notes. Nikheel S. Kolatkar. 128p. (C). 1997. spiral bd. 19.95 (*0-9665627-0-4*) IatroSoft Corp.

Pharmacophilia: or The Natural Paradises. Jonathan Ott. LC 98-163754. (Illus.). 192p. 1997. 36.00 (*1-888755-00-8*); pap. 18.00 (*1-888755-01-6*) Natural Prod.

Pharmacophore Perception, Development & Use in Drug Design. Ed. by Osman F. Guner. LC 99-88143. (Biotechnology Ser.). (Illus.). 537p. (C). 1999. 109.95 (*0-9636817-6-1*) Intl Univ Line.

Pharmacopoeia of the People's Republic of China 1992. (CHI.). 1993. 505.00 incl. cd-rom (*0-614-11851-4*, Pub. by HUWEI Cnslts) Am Overseas Bk Co.

Pharmacopoeia of the People's Republic of China, 1992. 1100p. 1993. 405.00 (*7-5359-0945-0*, Pub. by HUWEI Cnslts) Am Overseas Bk Co.

Pharmacopoeia of Tibetan Medicine. Vaidya B. Dash. LC 93-908824. (C). 1994. 34.00 (*81-7030-388-5*, Pub. by Sri Satguru Pubns) S Asia.

Pharmacopoeial Standards of Herbal Plants, Set, Vols. 1 & 2. C. R. Karnick. (C). 1994. text 68.00 (*81-7030-413-X*, Pub. by Sri Satguru Pubns) S Asia.

Pharmacopoeit India. K. C. Bose. 300p. (C). 1984. 65.00 (*0-7855-3301-X*, Pub. by Scientific) St Mut.

Pharmacotheon: Entheogenic Drugs, Their Plant Sources & History. rev. ed. Jonathan Ott & Albert Hofmann. 640p. 1997. pap. 40.00 (*0-9614234-9-8*); boxed set 100.00 (*0-9614234-8-X*) Natural Prod.

Pharmacotheon - Entheogenic Drugs, Their Plant Sources & History. Jonathan Ott. 640p. 1993. 70.00 (*0-9614234-2-0*) Natural Prod.

Pharmacotherapeutics: A Nursing Process Approach. 4th ed. Merrily Kuhn. (Illus.). 1093p. (C). 1997. text 59.95 (*0-8036-0283-9*) Davis Co.

Pharmacotherapeutics: A Primary Care Clinical Guide. Ellis Quinn Youngkin. LC 98-26172. (C). 1998. pap. text 75.00 (*0-8385-7681-8*) Appleton & Lange.

Pharmacotherapeutics & Advanced Nursing Practice. Ed. by Laurel A. Eisenhauer & Margaret A. Murphy. LC 97-35644. (Illus.). 360p. 1998. text 38.00 (*0-07-105485-5*) McGraw-Hill HPD.

Pharmacotherapeutics for Advanced Practice. Virginia Poole Arcangelo & Andrew Petersen. 992p. pap. text. write for info. (*0-7817-1876-7*) Lppncott W & W.

Pharmacotherapeutics for Nurses: Clinical Decision-Making in Nursing. Kathleen Gutierrez. Ed. by Maura Connor. LC 98-12900. (Illus.). 1435p. (C). 1999. text. write for info. (*0-7216-5405-3*, W B Saunders Co) Harcrt Hlth Sci Grp.

Pharmacotherapeutics of the Thyroid Gland. J. W. Barlow. Ed. by Anthony P. Weetman et al. (Handbook of Experimental Pharmacology Ser.: No. 128). (Illus.). 400p. 1997. 321.00 (*3-540-62499-6*) Spr-Verlag.

Pharmacotherapy. 3rd ed. Joseph T. DiPiro. 1998. text 175.00 (*0-8385-7686-9*) Appleton & Lange.

Pharmacotherapy: A Pathophysiologic Approach. 3rd ed. Joseph T. DiPiro. LC 95-25685. (C). 1996. pap. text 150.00 (*0-8385-7892-6*, A7892-1) Appleton & Lange.

Pharmacotherapy: A Patient Focused Approach. Terry Schwinghammer. (C). 1996. pap. text, teacher ed. 24.95 (*0-8385-8115-3*, A8115-6, Apple Lange Med) McGraw.

Pharmacotherapy: A Patient Focused Approach. Terry Schwinghammer. 416p. (C). 1996. pap. text 39.95 (*0-8385-8107-2*, A8107-3, Apple Lange Med) McGraw.

Pharmacotherapy & Management of Hypertension. John E. Bennett. 1994. text 99.00 (*0-443-08896-9*) Church.

***Pharmacotherapy Casebook: Patient Focused Approach.** 2nd ed. Schwinghamme. LC 99-28107. 353p. (C). 1999. pap. 39.95 (*0-8385-8154-4*, Apple Lange Med) McGraw.

Pharmacotherapy Casebook: Patient Focused Approach. 2nd ed. Schwinghammer & Dipiro. 1999. pap. text, teacher ed. 25.00 (*0-8385-8155-2*, Apple Lange Med) McGraw.

Pharmacotherapy for Child & Adolescent Psychiatric Disorders: An Updated Pocket Guide. Samuel Gershon et al. 1997. write for info. (*0-87630-842-6*) Brunner-Mazel.

***Pharmacotherapy for Mood, Anxiety & Cognitive Disorders.** Ed. by Uriel Halbreich & Stuart A. Montgomery. LC 99-13399. 976p. 2000. 79.00 (*0-88048-885-9*) Am Psychiatric.

Pharmacotherapy Handbook. 2nd ed. Wells & Dipiro. LC 99-73195. 1038p. 1999. pap. 44.95 (*0-8385-8165-X*, Apple Lange Med) McGraw.

***Pharmacotherapy Interim Value Pak.** Dipiro. 1999. 175.00 (*0-8385-8183-8*, Apple Lange Med) McGraw.

***Pharmacotherapy of Common Functional Syndromes: Evidence-Based Guidelines for Primary Care Practice.** Peter Manu. LC 00-20078. (Illus.). 308 p. 2000. pap. text 39.95 (*0-7890-0589-1*, Hawrth Medical); lib. bdg. 69.95 (*0-7890-0588-3*, Hawrth Medical) Haworth Pr.

Pharmacotherapy of Depression: Application for the Outpatient Practitioner. Jay D. Amsterdam. (Illus.). 496p. 1990. text 145.00 (*0-8247-8209-7*) Dekker.

Pharmacotherapy of Renal Disease & Hypertension. fac. ed. Ed. by William M. Bennett & David A. McCarron. LC 87-11649. (Contemporary Issues in Nephrology Ser.: No. 17). (Illus.). 429p. 1987. reprint ed. pap. 133.00 (*0-7837-7896-1*, 204765200008) Bks Demand.

Pharmacotherapy Pathology Approach. 4th ed. Dipiro. 2912p. (C). 1999. 150.00 (*0-8385-7691-5*, Apple Lange Med) McGraw.

Pharmacotherapy Self-Assessment Program, 8 vols. 2nd ed. LC 94-72072. 2000p. 1995. pap. 395.00 (*1-880401-13-4*) Amer Coll of Clin.

Pharmacotherapy Self-Assessment Program, 11 vols. 3rd rev. ed. LC 97-71255. 2800p. 1998. pap. 480.00 (*1-880401-30-4*) Amer Coll of Clin.

Pharmacotherapy Self-Assessment Program, Module 3. LC 97-71255. 182p. 1998. pap. 150.00 (*1-880401-35-5*) Amer Coll of Clin.

Pharmacotherapy Self-Assessment Program: Cardiovascular Modules A & B. LC 97-71255. 1998. pap. write for info. (*1-880401-32-0*) Amer Coll of Clin.

Pharmacotherapy Self-Assessment Program: Cardiovascular Modules A & B. 3rd rev. ed. LC 97-71255. 260p. (C). 1998. pap. 150.00 (*1-880401-31-2*) Amer Coll of Clin.

Pharmacotherapy Self-Assessment Program Vol. 1: Cardiovascular Modules A & B. rev. ed. LC 94-72072. 1995. pap., student ed. Not sold separately (*1-880401-15-0*) Amer Coll of Clin.

Pharmacotherapy Self-Assessment Program Vol. 1: Cardiovascular Modules A & B. 2nd rev. ed. LC 94-72072. 277p. 1995. pap. 150.00 (*1-880401-14-2*) Amer Coll of Clin.

Pharmacotherapy Self-Assessment Program Vol. 2: Critical Care Modules A & B. rev. ed. LC 94-72072. 1995. pap., student ed. Not sold separately (*1-880401-17-7*) Amer Coll of Clin.

Pharmacotherapy Self-Assessment Program Vol. 2: Critical Care Modules A & B. 2nd rev. ed. LC 94-72072. 317p. 1995. pap. 150.00 (*1-880401-16-9*) Amer Coll of Clin.

Pharmacotherapy Self-Assessment Program Vol. 3: Infectious Diseases Modules A & B. rev. ed. LC 94-72072. 1995. pap., student ed. Not sold separately (*1-880401-19-3*) Amer Coll of Clin.

Pharmacotherapy Self-Assessment Program Vol. 3: Infectious Diseases Modules A & B. 2nd rev. ed. LC 94-72072. 169p. 1995. pap. 150.00 (*1-880401-18-5*) Amer Coll of Clin.

Pharmacotherapy Self-Assessment Program Vol. 4: Neurology/Psychiatry Modules A & B. rev. ed. 1995. pap., student ed. Not sold separately (*1-880401-21-5*) Amer Coll of Clin.

Pharmacotherapy Self-Assessment Program Vol. 4: Neurology/Psychiatry Modules A & B. 2nd rev. ed. 195p. 1995. pap. 150.00 (*1-880401-20-7*) Amer Coll of Clin.

Pharmacotherapy Self-Assessment Program Vol. 5: Modules A & B. rev. ed. LC 94-72072. 1996. pap., teacher ed. write for info. (*1-880401-23-1*) Amer Coll of Clin.

Pharmacotherapy Self-Assessment Program Vol. 5: Modules A & B. 2nd rev. ed. LC 94-72072. 142p. 1996. pap. 150.00 (*1-880401-22-3*) Amer Coll of Clin.

Pharmacotherapy Self-Assessment Program Vol. 6: Respiratory/Nephrology/Gastro A & B. rev. ed. LC 94-72072. 1996. pap., student ed. Not sold separately (*1-880401-25-8*) Amer Coll of Clin.

Pharmacotherapy Self-Assessment Program Vol. 6: Respiratory/Nephrology/Gastro A & B. 2nd rev. ed. LC 94-72072. 323p. 1996. pap. 150.00 (*1-880401-24-X*) Amer Coll of Clin.

Pharmacotherapy Self-Assessment Program Vol. 7: Endocrinology/Immunology A & B. rev. ed. LC 94-72072. 1996. pap., student ed. Not sold separately (*1-880401-27-4*) Amer Coll of Clin.

Pharmacotherapy Self-Assessment Program Vol. 7: Endocrinology/Immunology A & B. 2nd rev. ed. LC 94-72072. 295p. 1996. pap. 150.00 (*1-880401-26-6*) Amer Coll of Clin.

Pharmacotherapy Self-Assessment Program Vol. 8: Nutrition/Oncology A & B. rev. ed. LC 94-7072. 1996. pap., student ed. Not sold separately (*1-880401-29-0*) Amer Coll of Clin.

Pharmacotherapy Self-Assessment Program Vol. 8: Nutrition/Oncology A & B. 2nd rev. ed. LC 94-7072. 236p. 1996. pap. 150.00 (*1-880401-28-2*) Amer Coll of Clin.

Pharmacotherapy Self-Assessment Program. Critical Care A & B, Module 2. 3rd ed. LC 97-71255. 190p. 1998. pap. 150.00 (*1-880401-33-9*) Amer Coll of Clin.

Pharmacotherapy Self-Assessment Program. Critical Care A & B: Answer Book. 3rd ed. LC 97-71255. 1998. write for info. (*1-880401-34-7*) Amer Coll of Clin.

Pharmacy: An Illustrated History. David L. Cowen & William H. Helfand. (Illus.). 272p. (gr. 13). 1990. 85.00 (*0-8109-1498-0*) Mosby Inc.

Pharmacy Aide. Jack Rudman. (Career Examination Ser.: C-2576). 1994. pap. 23.95 (*0-8373-2576-5*) Nat Learn.

Pharmacy & Medicine on the Air. Mickey C. Smith. (Illus.). 175p. 1989. 26.50 (*0-8108-2279-2*) Scarecrow.

Pharmacy & Pharmacotherapy of Asthma. Ed. by Patrick F. D'Arcy & James C. McElnay. 1989. text 99.95 (*0-470-21522-4*) P-H.

***Pharmacy & Socioeconomics.** (C). 1999. text. write for info. (*0-536-60693-5*) Pearson Custom.

Pharmacy & the Law. 2nd ed. Carl DeMarco. LC 84-2991. 464p. 1984. 93.00 (*0-89443-591-4*) Aspen Pub.

Pharmacy & the U. S. Health Care System. Ed. by Jack E. Fincham & Albert I. Wertheimer. LC 90-5092. (Pharmaceutical Sciences Ser.). (Illus.). 336p. 1991. text 59.95 (*0-86656-849-2*); pap. text 29.95 (*1-56024-097-0*) Haworth Pr.

Pharmacy & the U. S. Health Care System. 2nd ed. Ed. by Jack E. Fincham & Albert I. Wertheimer. LC 97-33692. (Illus.). 557p. (C). 1997. 69.95 (*1-56024-998-6*, Pharmctl Prods); pap. 39.95 (*1-56024-999-4*, Pharmctl Prods) Haworth Pr.

Pharmacy Assistant. Jack Rudman. (Career Examination Ser.: C-1388). 1994. pap. 23.95 (*0-8373-1388-0*) Nat Learn.

Pharmacy Assistant II. Jack Rudman. (Career Examination Ser.: C-2943). 1994. pap. 27.95 (*0-8373-2943-4*) Nat Learn.

Pharmacy Assisting for the Technician. 2nd ed. Durgin & Hanan. LC 98-54627. (Allied Health Ser.). 464p. (C). 1999. pap. 49.95 (*0-7668-0458-5*) Delmar.

***Pharmacy Assisting for the Technician, IML.** 2nd ed. Durgin & Hanan. 80p. 1999. teacher ed. 17.95 (*0-7668-0464-X*) Delmar.

Pharmacy Benefit Managers: Early Results on Ventures with Drug Manufacturers. (Illus.). 30p. 1996. reprint ed. pap. text 20.00 (*0-7881-3209-1*) DIANE Pub.

Pharmacy Benefits Management. Norrie Thomas et al. Ed. by Mary E. Brennan. LC 95-81607. 144p. 1996. pap. 40.00 (*0-89154-494-1*) Intl Found Employ.

Pharmacy College Admission Test. Jack Rudman. (Admission Test Ser.: ATS-52). 1994. pap. 23.95 (*0-8373-5052-2*) Nat Learn.

Pharmacy College Admission Test (PCAT) Jack Rudman. (Admission Test Ser.: Vol. 52). 43.95 (*0-8373-5152-9*) Nat Learn.

Pharmacy College Admission Test Student Guide. David M. Tarlow. (Illus.). 1993. pap. 16.95 (*0-931572-05-3*) Datar Pub.

Pharmacy College Admissions Test - Core Content. David M. Tarlow. (Medical Examinations Ser.). 575p. (Orig.). (C). 1996. pap. 49.95 (*1-57774-003-3*) Educ Tsting Cnslts.

***Pharmacy Department Compliance Manual.** 256p. 1999. 99.00 (*0-8342-1372-9*) Aspen Pub.

***Pharmacy Department Compliance Manual.** 2nd ed. HLCC Staff. 2000. pap. 100.00 (*0-8342-1772-4*) Aspen Pub.

Pharmacy Drug Cards. 13th ed. Jeffrey D. Sigler. Ed. by Brent E. Flanders. 308p. (C). 1997. student ed., ring bd. 39.95 (*1-880579-28-6*) Sigler & Flanders.

Pharmacy, Drugs & Medical Care. 5th ed. Mickey C. Smith & David A. Knapp. (Illus.). 300p. 1992. pap. 30.00 (*0-683-07763-5*) Lppncott W & W.

Pharmacy Ethics. Ed. by Mickey C. Smith et al. LC 90-5011. (Pharmaceutical Sciences Ser.: Vol. 2). (Illus.). 297p. (C). 1991. pap. 29.95 (*1-56024-172-1*); text 69.95 (*0-86656-898-0*) Haworth Pr.

Pharmacy History: Pictoral. Tallis. (Illus.). 1991. pap. 19.95 (*0-85369-241-6*, Pub. by Pharmaceutical Pr) Rittenhouse.

Pharmacy in Philately Album. George Griffenhagen. (Illus.). 88p. 1988. ring bd. 25.00 (*0-614-06186-5*) Am Inst Hist Pharm.

Pharmacy In The Forest. Fred Powledge. LC 97-6938. 47p. (J). (gr. 5-8). 1998. 17.00 (*0-689-80863-1*) S&S Childrens.

Pharmacy Information Systems: Justifying, Evaluating, & Implementing a System. Ed. by ASHP Special Projects Division Staff. 136p. (Orig.). 1993. pap. 30.00 (*1-879907-39-9*) Am Soc Hlth-Syst.

Pharmacy Inspector. Jack Rudman. (Career Examination Ser.: C-2536). 1994. pap. 34.95 (*0-8373-2536-6*) Nat Learn.

Pharmacy Law. Helen Wetherbee & Bruce D. White. LC 80-14608. (Paralegal). 592p. (C). 1980. mass mkt. 54.00 (*0-8299-2091-9*) West Pub.

Pharmacy Law: State/Federal for Massachusetts. Robert C. Pavlan. LC 98-96264. 1998. write for info. (*0-9664725-0-0*) Belmont Publ.

Pharmacy Law & Practice. J. Merrills & J. Fisher. 384p. 1995. pap. 39.95 (*0-632-03232-4*, Pub. by Blckwll Scitfc UK) Blackwell Sci.

Pharmacy Law & Practice. 2nd ed. Jonathan Merrills & Jonathan Fisher. LC 97-25805. 1997. pap. 55.00 (*0-632-04809-3*) Blackwell Sci.

Pharmacy Law Digest. Fink. 59.50 (*0-03-268650-1*) Lppncott W & W.

Pharmacy Law Digest. 27th rev. ed. Facts & Comparisons Staff. Ed. by Larry M. Simonsmeier & Joseph L. Fink. (C). Date not set. ring bd. 110.00 (*0-932686-50-8*) Facts & Comparisons.

***Pharmacy Laws & Legislative Rules of West Virginia: 1999 Edition.** 143p. 1999. pap. 20.00 (*0-327-09210-6*, 3648712) LEXIS Pub.

Pharmacy Legislation & Regulations, 1992. rev. ed. Intro. by American Society of Consultant Pharmacists Staff. 134p. 1992. pap. text 43.00 (*0-934322-09-0*) Am Soc Consult Phar.

Pharmacy Llp's Law & Medicine Report. 65.00 (*0-327-12284-6*) LEXIS Pub.

***Pharmacy Malpractice: Law & Regulations, 1.** 2nd ed. David B. Brushwood. LC 98-158259. 408p. 1998. boxed set 160.00 (*1-56706-848-0*) Panel Pubs.

Pharmacy Math for Technicians. Don A. Ballington & Mary M. Laughlin. LC 98-9872. 1998. 27.44 (*0-7638-0101-1*) Paradigm MN.

Pharmacy Math for Technicians: Instructor's Guide. Don A. Ballington & Mary M. Laughlin. text, teacher ed. 14.00 (*0-7638-0102-X*) EMC-Paradigm.

Pharmacy Museums & Collections in the United States & Canada. rev. ed. George Griffenhagen & Ernst W. Stieb. 92p. 1988. pap. 9.00 (*0-931292-20-4*) Am Inst Hist Pharm.

Pharmacy Policy & Procedure Manual, 1992. Kathy D'Achilli. 350p. 1992. ring bd. 93.00 incl. disk (*0-934322-12-0*) Am Soc Consult Phar.

Pharmacy Practice: Social & Behavioral Aspects. 3rd ed. Albert I. Wertheimer & Mickey C. Smith. (Illus.). 472p. 1989. pap. text 39.95 (*0-683-08932-3*) Lppncott W & W.

Pharmacy Practice & the Law. Richard R. Abood & David B. Brushwood. 370p. 1994. 53.00 (*0-8342-0321-9*, 20321) Aspen Pub.

Pharmacy Practice & the Law. 2nd ed. Richard R. Abood & David B. Brushwood. LC 97-18903. 448p. 1997. 49.00 (*0-8342-0915-2*, 20915) Aspen Pub.

***Pharmacy Practice & the Law / 3rd ed.** Richard R. Abood & David B. Brushwood. LC 00-33162. 2000. write for info. (*0-8342-1880-1*) Aspen Pub.

Pharmacy Practice for Technicians. Don A. Ballington. LC 98-27634. 377p. 1998. 27.95 (*0-7638-0099-6*); teacher ed. write for info. (*0-7638-0100-3*); wbk. ed. write for info. (*0-7638-0098-8*) Paradigm MN.

Pharmacy Practice for Technicians. Ed. by Jane Durgin & Zachary Hanan. LC 92-48679. 478p. (C). 1993. mass mkt. 33.50 (*0-8273-4660-3*) Delmar.

Pharmacy Practice for Technicians: Instructor's Guide. Jane Durgin & Zachary Hanan. 96p. 1994. 16.00 (*0-8273-5905-5*) Delmar.

***Pharmacy Practice Handbook of Medication Facts.** Harold L. Kirschenbaum & Michelle K. Bazil. LC 99-67719. 688p. 1999. text 64.95 (*1-56676-762-8*) Technomic.

Pharmacy Practice Management: Forms, Checklists & Guidelines on CD-ROM. Aspen Reference Group Staff & Dwayne E. Eutsey. LC 98-30817. 400p. 1999. ring bd. 199.00 (*0-8342-1079-7*, S518) Aspen Pub.

***Pharmacy Student Companion: Your Road Map to Pharmacy Education & Careers.** 3rd rev. ed. Daniel H. Albrant & Linda R. Harteker. Ed. by Vicki L. Meade. 157p. (C). 1999. pap. 20.00 (*0-917330-94-3*) Am Pharm Assn.

Pharmacy Tech: Basic Pharmacology & Calculations. Robert Reilly et al. (Illus.). 140p. (C). 1994. per. 29.95 (*1-56930-005-4*) Skidmore Roth Pub.

***Pharmacy Technician.** 384p. 1998. text. write for info. (*0-89582-472-8*); text, wbk. ed. write for info. (*0-89582-485-X*) Morton Pub.

Pharmacy Technician. Jack Rudman. (Career Examination Ser.: Vol. C-3822). 1997. pap. 23.95 (*0-8373-3822-0*) Nat Learn.

Pharmacy Technician. 2nd ed. Marvin M. Stoogenke. LC 97-13705. 416p. 1997. pap. 55.00 (*0-8359-5153-7*) P-H.

Pharmacy Technician. 2nd ed. Marvin M. Stoogenke. 1997. pap., teacher ed. 17.67 (*0-8359-5154-5*) P-H.

Pharmacy Technician Certification Quick-Study Guide. 2nd ed. Susan Moss Marks & William A. Hopkins, Jr. 125p. 1999. pap. text 25.00 (*1-58212-000-5*) Am Pharm Assn.

Pharmacy Technician Certification Review & Practice Exam. LC 99-166176. 152p. 1998. 38.00 (*1-879907-80-1*) Am Soc Hlth-Syst.

Pharmacy Technician Companion: Your Road Map to Techinician Training & Careers. Linda R. Harteker. LC 98-23840. (Illus.). 102p. 1998. pap. text 20.00 (*0-917330-87-0*) Am Pharm Assn.

Pharmacy Technician Review & Test Preparation. Marvin M. Stoogenke. LC 98-11720. 224p. 1998. pap. 33.60 (*0-8359-5328-9*) Globe Fearon.

P

***Pharmacy Technician's Pocket Drug Reference.** Joyce A. Generali. 200p. 2000. pap. 15.00 (*1-58212-020-X*) Am Pharm Assn.

Pharmacy Technology. Messler. 1999. pap. text. write for info. (*0-7216-7432-1*, W B Saunders Co) Harcrt Hlth Sci Grp.

Pharmacy-Thermomechanics-Elastomers-Telechelics. K. Dusek. (Advances in Polymer Science Ser.: Vol. 76). (Illus.). 200p. 1986. 77.00 (*0-387-15830-8*) Spr-Verlag.

Pharmako/Gnosis: Plant Teachers & the Poison Path. Dale Pendell. (Illus.). 304p. 1999. pap. 19.95 (*1-56279-104-4*, Pub. by Mercury Hse Inc) Consort Bk Sales.

Pharmako/Poeia: Plant Powers, Poisons & Herbcraft. Dale Pendell. 304p. 1995. pap. 19.95 (*1-56279-069-2*) Mercury Hse Inc.

Pharmakotherapie der Depression: Bedeutung von Serotonin und Melatonin. Ed. by P. Kielholz & B. Muller-Oerlinghausen. (Advances in Pharmacotherapy Ser.: Band 3). (Illus.). x, 150p. 1987. 121.00 (*3-8055-4539-8*) S Karger.

***PharmaSim: Administrator's Guide.** Stuart James et al. 72p. (C). 1998. pap. text 95.00 incl. disk (*1-885837-08-9*) Interpret Sftware.

PharmaSim: Windows Version. Stuart James et al. 128p. 1994. pap. text 95.00 (*1-885837-04-6*) Interpret Sftware.

Pharmasource, '94. Market Intelligence Staff. 311p. 1994. 595.00 (*1-56753-985-8*) Frost & Sullivan.

Pharmatecture: Minimizing Medications to Maximize Results. 2nd ed. Gideon Bosker. LC 99-205326. (Illus.). 704p. (Orig.). 1999. pap. text 59.95 (*1-57439-047-3*) Facts & Comparisons.

Pharmazeutisches Medizinisches Terminologi. 3rd ed. Beyer. (GER.). 188p. 1990. 39.95 (*0-7859-7439-3*, 3804711197) Fr & Eur.

Pharmcards: Review Cards for Medical Students. Eric C. Johannsen & Marc S. Sabatine. (Illus.). 200p. 1995. 26.95 (*0-316-46549-6*) Lppncott W & W.

Pharmeceutical Skin Penetration Enhancement. Kenneth A. Walters & Jonathan Hadgraft. LC 92-48507. (Drugs & the Pharmaceutical Sciences Ser.: Vol. 59). (Illus.). 448p. 1993. text 199.00 (*0-8247-9017-0*) Dekker.

Pharmeis Almanac Vol. 4: The Unofficial Guide to Phish. Ed. by Andy Bernstein et al. (Pharmer's Almanac Ser.). (Illus.). 276p. 1997. pap. 15.95 (*1-890200-03-4*) Melting Media.

Pharmer's Almanac: The Unofficial Guide to Phish. Andy Bernstein. LC 98-220842. 272p. 1998. pap. text 15.95 (*0-425-16356-3*) Berkley Pub.

Pharmer's Almanac II. rev. ed. Anthony Radcliff et al. (Illus.). 1993. pap. 12.95 (*0-910223-19-X*) MAC Pub.

Pharmex Family Guide to Prescription Drugs. Pharmex Staff. 310p. Date not set. pap. text 5.95 (*0-89529-715-9*, Avery) Penguin Putnam.

PharmFacts for Nurses. Springhouse Publishing Company Staff. (Illus.). 736p. 1995. pap. 36.95 (*0-87434-803-X*) Springhouse Corp.

Pharmicist's Pick: The Non-Prescription Choices of a Pharmacist at Your Fingertips! Scott W. Holden. 101p. 1997. pap. 9.95 (*1-890622-07-9*) Leathers Pub.

Pharo Village. John P. Marwitt. (Utah Anthropological Papers: No. 91). reprint ed. 20.00 (*0-404-60691-1*) AMS Pr.

***Pharoah's Dream: The Secret Life of Stories.** Robert Harbison. 220p. 1999. reprint ed. text 25.00 (*0-7881-6389-2*) DIANE Pub.

***Pharoahs of the Sun: Akhenaten, Nefertiti, & Tutankhamen.** Ed. by Rita E. Freed et al. LC 99-60199. (Illus.). 318p. 1999. pap. 29.95 (*0-87846-470-0*, 00821) Mus Fine Arts Boston.

Pharohs, Fellahs & Explorers. rev. ed. Amelia Edwards. (Original Sources in Exploration Ser.). (Illus.). 325p. 1996. reprint ed. 11.95 (*1-887954-03-1*) Athena FL.

Pharos the Egyptian. Guy Boothby. 390p. 1999. pap. text 7.95 (*1-902058-19-4*, Pub. by Pulp Fictions) Seven Hills Bk.

Pharos, the Egyptian. Guy Boothby. Ed. by R. Reginald & Douglas A. Menville. LC 75-46256. (Supernatural & Occult Fiction Ser.). (Illus.). 1976. reprint ed. lib. bdg. 33.95 (*0-405-08115-4*) Ayer.

Pharsalia. Tr. by Jane Wilson Joyce. (Masters of Latin Literature Ser.). 368p. 1993. text 45.00 (*0-8014-2907-2*); pap. text 18.95 (*0-8014-8137-6*) Cornell U Pr.

Phase & Flow Behavior in Petroleum Production. E. J. Hoffman. LC 81-68122. (Illus.). 915p. 1981. 225.00 (*0-9601552-3-6*) Energon Co.

Phase & Phase-Difference Modulation in Digital Communications. Yuri Okunev. LC 97-21324. (Signal Processing Technology Ser.). 392p. 1997. 109.00 (*0-89006-937-9*) Artech Hse.

Phase Behavior. (SPE Reprint Ser.). 304p. 1981. pap. 8.00 (*0-317-36509-6*, FERPT015) Soc Petrol Engineers.

Phase Change Heat Transfer, 1993. Ed. by J. E. O'Brien & R. J. Dallman. LC 91-55579. 109p. 1993. pap. 40.00 (*0-7918-1008-9*) ASME.

Phase Conjugation of Laser Emission. Ed. by N. G. Basov. (Proceedings of the Lebedev Physics Institute Ser.: Vol. 172). 240p. (C). 1987. text 165.00 (*0-941743-07-1*) Nova Sci Pubs.

Phase Diagrams Supplement 1: A Literature Source Book. J. Wisniak. (Physical Sciences Data Ser.: No. 27). 1035p. 1986. 483.75 (*0-444-42613-2*) Elsevier.

Phase Diagrams & Microstructures: A Computer Aided Learning Guide. John Pilling. 100p. 1992. 192.00 (*0-901716-11-1*, Pub. by Inst Materials) Ashgate Pub Co.

Phase Diagrams & Physical Properties of Nonequilibrium Alloys: A Nonequilibrium Phase Diagrams of Ternary Amorphous Alloys, Vol. 37. W. Martienssen. 295p. 1997. 1372.00 (*3-540-60507-X*) Spr-Verlag.

Phase Diagrams & Thermodynamic Properties of Ternary Copper-Metal Systems. University of Wisconsin, Milwaukee Staff. (INCRA Monographs). 701p. 1979. 30.00 (*0-317-42806-3*) Intl Copper.

Phase Diagrams & Thermodynamic Properties of Ternary Copper-Sulfur-Metal Systems. University of Wisconsin, Milwaukee Staff. (INCRA Monographs). 191p. 1979. 30.00 (*0-317-42814-4*) Intl Copper.

Phase Diagrams for Ceramists Vol. 1: Oxides & Salts, Vol. 1. Ed. by Ernest M. Levin et al. (Illus.). 602p. 1964. 150.00 (*0-916094-04-9*, PH01) Am Ceramic.

Phase Diagrams for Ceramists Vol. II: Oxides & Salts. Ed. by Ernest M. Levin et al. 626p. 1969. 150.00 (*0-916094-05-7*, PH02) Am Ceramic.

Phase Diagrams for Ceramists Vol. III: Oxides & Salts. Ed. by Ernest M. Levin & Howard F. McMurdie. 514p. 1975. 150.00 (*0-916094-06-5*, PH03) Am Ceramic.

Phase Diagrams for Ceramists Vol. IV: Oxides. Ed. by R. S. Roth et al. (Illus.). 330p. 1981. 150.00 (*0-916094-40-5*, PH04) Am Ceramic.

Phase Diagrams for Ceramists Vol. V: Salts. Ed. by R. S. Roth et al. 404p. 1983. 150.00 (*0-916094-47-2*, PH05) Am Ceramic.

Phase Diagrams for Ceramists Vol. VI: Oxides. Ed. by Robert S. Roth et al. 550p. 1987. 150.00 (*0-916094-90-1*, PH06) Am Ceramic.

Phase Diagrams for Ceramists Vol. VII: Salts. Ed. by L. P. Cook & Howard F. McMurdie. 592p. 1989. 150.00 (*0-944904-04-1*, PH07) Am Ceramic.

Phase Diagrams for Ceramists Vol. VIII: High-Pressure Systems. Ed. by B. O. Mysen. 416p. 1990. 150.00 (*0-944904-23-8*, PH08) Am Ceramic.

Phase Diagrams for Ceramists Vol. IX: Semiconductors & Chalcogenides. Ed. by Gerald B. Stringfellow. 400p. 1992. 150.00 (*0-944904-50-5*, PH09) Am Ceramic.

Phase Diagrams for Ceramists Vol. X: Borides, Carbides & Nitrides. Ed. by Anna E. McHale et al. 475p. 1994. 150.00 (*0-944904-74-2*, PH10) Am Ceramic.

Phase Diagrams for Ceramists Vol. 11: Oxides. Ed. by Robert S. Roth et al. (Phase Equilibria Diagrams Ser.: Vol. XI). (Illus.). 487p. 1995. 150.00 (*0-944904-90-4*, PH11) Am Ceramic.

Phase Diagrams for High TC Superconductors. John D. Whitler. Ed. by Robert S. Roth. 175p. 1991. pap. 63.00 (*0-944904-41-6*, PHT01) Am Ceramic.

Phase Diagrams for High Tc Superconductors, No. II. Ed. by T. A. Vanderan et al. (Illus.). 275p. 1997. pap. 63.00 (*1-57498-040-8*, PHT02) Am Ceramic.

Phase Diagrams for Zirconium & Zirconia Systems. Ed. by H. M. Ondik & H. F. McMurdie. (Illus.). 750p. 1998. 150.00 (*1-57498-055-6*, PhZr) Am Ceramic.

Phase Diagrams in Advanced Ceramics. Ed. by Allen M. Alper. (Treatise on Materials Science & Technology Ser.). (Illus.). 237p. 1995. text 95.00 (*0-12-341834-8*) Acad Pr.

Phase Diagrams of Binary Actinide Alloys. Ed. by M. E. Kassner & D. E. Peterson. (Binary Alloy Phase Diagram Monograph Ser.: Vol. 11). (Illus.). 489p. 1995. 326.00 (*0-87170-553-2*, 57757G) ASM.

Phase Diagrams of Binary Beryllium Alloys. Ed. by L. E. Tanner & H. Okamoto. (Monograph Series on Alloy Phase Diagrams). (Illus.). 229p. (C). 1987. reprint ed. text 131.00 (*0-87170-303-3*, 57705G) ASM.

Phase Diagrams of Binary Copper Alloys. Ed. by P. R. Subramanian et al. (Monograph Series on Alloy Phase Diagrams: No. 10). (Illus.). 512p. 1994. text 326.00 (*0-87170-484-6*, 57714G) ASM.

Phase Diagrams of Binary Gold Alloys. Frwd. & Intro. by T. B. Massalski. (Monograph Series on Alloy Phase Diagrams). (Illus.). 343p. (C). 1987. text 156.00 (*0-87170-249-5*, 57703G) ASM.

Phase Diagrams of Binary Iron Alloys. Ed. by Hiroaki Okamoto. LC 93-70331. (Monograph Series on Alloy Phase Diagrams). (Illus.). 472p. 1993. 326.00 (*0-87170-469-2*, 57733G) ASM.

Phase Diagrams of Binary Nickel Alloys. Ed. by Peter Nash. (Monograph Series on Alloy Phase Diagrams). (Illus.). 394p. (C). 1991. text 326.00 (*0-87170-365-3*, 57712G) ASM.

Phase Diagrams of Binary Titanium Alloys. Intro. by J. L. Murray. (Monograph Series on Alloy Phase Diagrams). (Illus.). 345p. (C). 1987. reprint ed. text 156.00 (*0-87170-248-7*, 57704G) ASM.

Phase Diagrams of Binary Vanadium Alloys. Frwd. by T. B. Massalski. (Monograph Series on Alloy Phase Diagrams). (Illus.). 375p. (C). 1989. text 156.00 (*0-87170-354-8*, 57708G) ASM.

Phase Diagrams of Indium Alloys & Their Engineering Applications. Ed. by Hiroaki Okamoto & C. E. White. (Monograph Series on Alloy Phase Diagrams: No. 8). (Illus.). 338p. 1991. text 297.00 (*0-87170-438-2*, 57727G) ASM.

Phase Diagrams of Ternary Boron Nitride & Silicon Nitride Systems. Ed. by P. Rogl & J. C. Schuster. 289p. 1992. 252.00 (*0-87170-445-5*, 57743G) ASM.

Phase Diagrams of Ternary Copper-Oxygen-Metal Systems. Ed. by K-C. Hsieh. (Monograph Series on Alloy Phase Diagrams). (Illus.). 150p. (C). 1989. text 131.00 (*0-87170-355-6*, 57711G) ASM.

Phase Diagrams of Ternary Gold Alloys. Evans. 1990. 250.00 (*0-904357-50-3*) Institute of Management Consultants.

Phase Diagrams of Ternary Iron Alloys. Raghavan. 1989. 145.00 (*81-85307-04-0*) Institute of Management Consultants.

Phase Diagrams of Ternary Iron Alloys, Pt. 1. Ed. & Pref. by V. Raghavan. (Monograph Series on Alloy Phase Diagrams). (Illus.). 219p. (C). 1987. reprint ed. text 197.00 (*0-87170-230-4*, 57702G) ASM.

Phase Diagrams of the Elements. David A. Young. LC 90-25978. (Illus.). 280p. 1991. 50.00 (*0-520-07483-1*, Pub. by U CA Pr) Cal Prin Full Svc.

Phase Equilibria & Crystal Chemistry in Portions of the System SRO-CAO-Bi203-CuO. B. P. Burton et al. (Illus.). 49p. (Orig.). (C). 1994. pap. text 30.00 (*0-7881-0375-X*) DIANE Pub.

Phase Equilibria & Fluid Properties in the Chemical Industry: Estimation & Correlation. Ed. by Truman S. Storvick & Stanley I. Sandler. LC 77-13804. (ACS Symposium Ser.: No. 60). 1977. 54.95 (*0-8412-0393-8*) Am Chemical.

Phase Equilibria & Fluid Properties in the Chemical Industry: Estimation & Correlation. Ed. by Truman S. Storvick & Stanley I. Sandler. LC 77-13804. (ACS Symposium Ser.: Vol. 60). 551p. 1977. reprint ed. pap. 170.90 (*0-608-03941-1*, 206438800009) Bks Demand.

Phase Equilibria & Fluid Properties in the Chemical Industry: Proceedings of the International Conference, 2nd, Berlin, 1980, Pts. 1 & 2. European Federation of Chemical Engineering Staff. (EFCE Publications: No. 11). 1012p. 1980. text 150.00 (*3-921567-35-1*, Pub. by Dechema) Scholium Intl.

Phase Equilibria & Other Physicochemical Aspects of Interest for Enzymatic Reactions in Near-Critical Carbon Dioxide. Rob M. Stevens. (Illus.). 224p. 1997. pap. 57.50 (*90-407-1553-X*, Pub. by Delft U Pr) Coronet Bks.

Phase Equilibria & Phase Diagrams of Electrolytes. Hans Engels. Ed. by Dieter Behrens & Reiner Eckermann. LC 98-137053. (Dechema Chemistry Data Ser.: Vol. 11, Pt. 1). (Illus.). 154p. 1991. text 170.00 (*3-926959-17-7*, Pub. by Dechema) Scholium Intl.

Phase Equilibria, Crystallographic & Thermodynamic Data of Binary Alloys, Vol. 5, Subvol. b: B-Ba - C-Zr. B. Predel. (Illus.). xxviii, 403p. 1992. 1165.00 (*0-387-55115-8*) Spr-Verlag.

Phase Equilibria, Crystallographic Data & Values of Thermodynamic Properties of Binary Alloys. Ed. by Otfried Madelung. (Numerical Data & Functional Relationships in Science & Technology Ser.: Vol. 5). 385p. 1994. 1540.95 (*0-387-56073-4*) Spr-Verlag.

Phase Equilibria, Crystallographic Data & Values of Thermodynamic Properties of Binary Alloys, Subvol. E, Phase Equilibria, Crystallographic & Thermodynamic Data of Binary Alloys see Macroscopic & Technical Properties of Matter: Group IV

Phase Equilibria Diagrams: Phase Diagrams for Ceramists: Annual 93. American Ceramic Society Staff. Ed. by Anna E. Mchale. LC 93-658073. 235p. 1993. reprint ed. pap. 72.90 (*0-608-00725-0*, 206150000009) Bks Demand.

Phase Equilibria Diagrams Annual, 1993. Ed. by Anna E. McHale. 227p. 1993. pap. 63.00 (*0-944904-62-9*, PHAN93) Am Ceramic.

Phase Equilibria Diagrams Cumulative Index, 1998. Ed. by Mary A. Clevinger & Christine L. Cedeno. (Illus.). 285p. 1998. pap. 15.00 (*1-57498-087-4*, PHIN98) Am Ceramic.

Phase Equilibria Diagrams, 1996 Cumulative Indexes. Ed. by Mary A. Clevenger et al. 246p. (Orig.). 1996. pap. 15.00 (*1-57498-015-7*, PHIN96) Am Ceramic.

Phase Equilibria Diagrams XII: Oxides, Vol. 12. Ed. by Anna E. McHale & Robert S. Roth. (Illus.). 398p. 1996. 150.00 (*1-57498-014-9*, PH12) Am Ceramic.

Phase Equilibria in Binary Halides. V. I. Posypaiko & E. A. Alekseeva. LC 87-29267. (Illus.). 496p. (C). 1988. text 145.00 (*0-306-65211-0*, Kluwer Plenum) Kluwer Academic.

Phase Equilibria in Chemical Engineering. Stanley M. Walas. (Illus.). 671p. (C). 1984. text 99.95 (*0-7506-9313-4*) Buttrwrth-Heinemann.

Phase Equilibria in Iron Ternary Alloys. Rivlin. 1988. 199.00 (*0-901462-34-9*) Institute of Management Consultants.

Phase Equilibria in Metamorphic Rocks: Thermodynamic Background & Petrological Applications. T. M. Will. LC 98-13004. (Lecture Notes in Earth Sciences: Vol. 71). (Illus.). xiv, 315p. 1998. pap. 79.95 (*3-540-64154-8*) Spr-Verlag.

Phase Equilibria, Phase Diagrams & Phase Transformations: A Thermodynamic Basis. Mats Hillert. LC 97-12280. (Illus.). 554p. (C). 1998. text 110.00 (*0-521-56270-8*); pap. text 44.95 (*0-521-56584-7*) Cambridge U Pr.

Phase Formation & Modification by Beam-Solid Interactions. Ed. by Gary S. Was et al. (Symposium Proceedings Ser.: Vol. 235). 911p. 1992. text 17.50 (*1-55899-129-8*) Materials Res.

Phase in Optics. Ed. by Vlasta Perinova et al. LC 98-28356. 330p. 1997. text 58.00 (*981-02-3208-X*) World Scientific Pub.

Phase-Integral Method: With Comparison Equation Technique Incorporated. Nanny Froman & Per O. Froman. LC 95-12919. (Tracts in Natural Philosophy Ser.: Vol. 40). 1995. 97.95 (*0-387-94520-2*) Spr-Verlag.

Phase Language. Lee Ballentine. 80p. (Orig.). 1995. pap. 8.95 (*1-880766-07-8*) Pantograph Pr.

Phase Language. deluxe limited ed. Lee Ballentine. LC 94-36984. 96p. (Orig.). 1995. 59.95 (*0-938075-62-4*) Ocean View Bks.

***Phase Li Evaluation Findings.** Highway Innovative Technology Evaluation Center Staff. LC 00-44767. (Technical Evaluation Reports). 2000. write for info. (*0-7844-0524-7*) Am Soc Civil Eng.

Phase Line Green: Battle for Hue, 1968. Nicholas Warr. 1999. mass mkt. 6.99 (*0-8041-1869-8*) Ivy Books.

Phase Line Green: The Battle for Hue, 1968. Nicholas Warr. LC 96-47181. (Illus.). 272p. 1997. 29.95 (*1-55750-911-5*) Naval Inst Pr.

Phase-Lock Basics. William F. Egan. LC 97-38471. 520p. 1998. 98.95 (*0-471-24261-6*, Wiley-Interscience) Wiley.

Phase-Locked Loop Circuit. Dan H. Wolaver. 272p. 1991. 84.00 (*0-13-662743-9*, 330213) P-H.

Phase-Locked Loops. rev. ed. Heath Company Staff. (Electronics Technology Ser.). (Illus.). 268p. (C). 1979. reprint ed. teacher ed. 9.95 (*0-87119-024-9*); reprint ed. pap. text 18.95 (*0-87119-023-0*); reprint ed. ring bd. 49.95 (*0-87119-025-7*) Heathkit-Zenith Ed.

Phase-Locked Loops. 4th ed. Best. LC 99-32414. (Professional Engineering Ser.). 408p. 1999. 65.00 (*0-07-134903-0*); 65.00 (*0-07-134904-9*) McGraw.

Phase-Locked Loops: Theory & Applications. John L. Stensby. LC 96-50402. 400p. 1997. boxed set 89.95 (*0-8493-9471-6*) CRC Pr.

Phase-Locked Loops: Theory, Design, & Applications. 3rd ed. Roland E. Best. (Illus.). 365p. 1996. text 60.00 incl. disk (*0-07-006051-7*) McGraw.

***Phase-Locked Loops & Synchronization Systems: Matlab-Based Simulation Laboratory.** William H. Tranter et al. 200p. 2000. pap. 24.00 (*0-13-095102-1*, Prentice Hall) P-H.

Phase-Locked Loops for Wireless Communications: Digital & Analog Implementation. Donald R. Stephens. LC 98-20256. 379p. 1998. write for info. (*0-7923-8204-8*) Kluwer Academic.

Phase Noise Analysis in Radar Systems: Using Personal Computers. Stanley J. Goldman. LC 88-23575. 518p. 1989. 175.00 (*0-471-61894-2*) Wiley.

Phase Noise in Signal Sources: Theory & Applications. rev. ed. W. P. Robins. (Telecommunications Ser.: No. 9). 336p. 1984. pap. 69.00 (*0-86341-026-X*, TE009) INSPEC Inc.

Phase of Darkness. Robin Moore & Al Dempsey. LC 73-92799. 1974. 30.00 (*0-89388-136-8*) Okpaku Communications.

Phase I Environmental Site Assessments: The State of the Practice. Ed. by P. H. Collin et al. 288p. 25.00 (*0-614-05192-4*, PIESAO4943.5M) ASFE.

Phase Portraits of Control Dynamical Systems. Anatoliy G. Butkovskiy. (Mathematics & Its Applications, Soviet Ser.). 184p. (C). 1991. text 139.00 (*0-7923-1057-8*) Kluwer Academic.

Phase Resetting in Medicine & Biology: Stochastic Modelling & Data Analysis. Peter A. Tass. LC 99-25203. (Springer Series in Synergetics). 331p. 1999. 99.00 (*3-540-65697-9*) Spr-Verlag.

Phase Retrieval & Zero Crossings: Mathematical Methods in Image Reconstruction. Norman E. Hurt. (C). 1989. text 171.00 (*0-7923-0210-9*) Kluwer Academic.

Phase Separation in Cuprate Superconductors. E. Sigmund & K. A. Muller. 401p. 1994. 111.95 (*0-387-57681-9*) Spr-Verlag.

Phase Separation in Cuprate Superconductors: Proceedings of the 2nd International Workshop on "Phase Separation in Cuprate Superconductors," September 4-10, 1993, Cottbus, Germany. E. Sigmund. Ed. by K A. Muller. LC 94-25887. 1994. write for info. (*3-540-57681-9*) Spr-Verlag.

Phase Separation in Cuprate Superconductors: Proceedings of the 3rd Workshop. K. A. Mueller & G. Benedek. 392p. 1993. text 109.00 (*981-02-1274-7*) World Scientific Pub.

Phase Space Approach to Nuclear Dynamics: Proceedings to the Topical Meeting on Phase Space Approach to Nuclear Dynamics, Sept. 3-Oct. 4, 1985, Trieste, Italy. Ed. by M. Di Toro et al. 812p. 1986. text 175.00 (*9971-5-0015-9*) World Scientific Pub.

Phase Space Picture of Quantum Mechanics: Group Theoretical Approach. Y. S. Kim & Marilyn E. Noz. 352p. 1991. text 53.00 (*981-02-0360-8*); pap. text 36.00 (*981-02-0361-6*) World Scientific Pub.

Phase Stability & Phase Transformations. Ed. by R. Krishnan. (Materials Science Forum Ser.: Vol. 3). 474p. (C). 1985. pap. text 183.00 (*0-87849-535-5*, Pub. by Trans T Pub) Enfield Pubs NH.

Phase Stability During Irradiation: Proceedings of a Symposium Sponsored by the Nuclear Metallurgy Committee at the Fall Meeting of the Metallurgical Society of AIME, Pittsburgh, PA, October 5-9, 1980. Metallurgical Society of AIME Staff. Ed. by J. R. Holland et al. LC 81-82941. (Conference Proceedings Ser.). 629p. reprint ed. pap. 195.00 (*0-8357-2513-8*, 205239300013) Bks Demand.

Phase Stability under Irradiation. K. C. Russell. (Illus.). 206p. 1985. pap. 83.00 (*0-08-032722-2*, Pergamon Pr) Elsevier.

Phase State Transition in Foods: Chemical, Structural & Rheological Changes. M. A. Rao & Richard W. Hartel. LC 98-16714. (IFT Basic Symposium Ser.). (Illus.). 416p. 1998. text 165.00 (*0-8247-0179-8*) Dekker.

Phase Structure of Strongly Interacting Matter: Proceedings of a Summer School on Theoretical Physics Held at the University of Cape Town, South Africa January 8-19, 1990. Ed. by J. Cleymans. (Illus.). 480p. 1991. 79.95 (*0-387-53138-6*) Spr-Verlag.

Phase Transfer Catalysis. 3rd enl. rev. ed. E. V. Dehmlow & S. S. Dehmlow. LC 93-13338. 512p. 1993. 235.00 (*3-527-28408-7*, Wiley-VCH) Wiley.

Phase-Transfer Catalysis: Mechanisms & Syntheses, Vol. 659. Ed. by Marc E. Halpern. LC 96-49775. (Symposium Ser.: No. 659). (Illus.). 328p. 1997. text 105.00 (*0-8412-3491-4*, Pub. by Am Chemical) OUP.

Phase-Transfer Catalysis: New Chemistry, Catalysts, & Applications. Ed. by Charles M. Starks. LC 86-25957. (ACS Symposium Ser.: No. 326). (Illus.). ix, 184p. 1986. 36.95 (*0-8412-1007-1*) Am Chemical.

Phase-Transfer Catalysis: New Chemistry, Catalysts, & Applications. Ed. by Charles M. Starks. LC 86-25957. (ACS Symposium Ser.: Vol. 326). 208p. 1987. reprint ed. pap. 64.50 (*0-608-03540-8*, 206425900008) Bks Demand.

Phase Transfer Catalysis: Selected Problems & Applications. Yuri Goldberg. LC 92-16359. 488p. 1992. text 250.00 (*2-88124-870-5*) Gordon & Breach.

An Asterisk (*) at the beginning of an entry indicates that the title is appearing for the first time.

Phase Transfer Catalysts. Giora Agam. LC 98-143423. 130p. 1998. 3450.00 (*1-56965-388-7*, C-207) BCC.

Phase Transformation Kinetics in Thin Films Vol. 230: Materials Research Society Symposium Proceedings. Ed. by M. Chen et al. 365p. 1992. text 30.00 (*1-55899-124-7*) Materials Res.

Phase Transformations & Ablation in Laser-Treated Soils. Emil N. Sobol. 332p. 1995. 95.95 (*0-471-59899-2*) Wiley.

Phase Transformations & Evolution in Materials. Ed. by P. E. A. Turchi & A. Gonis. (Illus.). 420p. 104.00 (*0-87339-468-2*) Minerals Metals.

Phase Transformations & Related Phenomena in Steels: Papers Presented at the E. C. Bain Seminar of the American Society for Metals. American Society for Metals Staff. LC 72-95849. 98p. reprint ed. pap. 30.40 (*0-608-13091-5*, 201949600013) Bks Demand.

Phase Transformations & Rock Genesis. M. V. Abdulov. Ed. by A. K. Chatterjee. Tr. by Sankar Ghose from RUS. (Russian Translation Ser.: No. 107). 152p. (C). 1994. text 71.00 (*90-5410-218-7*, Pub. by A A Balkema) Ashgate Pub Co.

Phase Transformations & Systems Driven Far from Equilibrium Vol. 481: Materials Research Society Symposium Proceedings. Ed. by E. Ma et al. LC 98-19423. 686p. 1998. text 80.00 (*1-55899-386-X*) Materials Res.

Phase Transformations in Ferrous Alloys: Proceedings of an International Conference Held October 4-6, 1983, in Philadelphia, PA. International Conference on Phase Transformations. Ed. by A. R. Marder. LC 84-61582. 419p. reprint ed. pap. 129.90 (*0-8357-2514-6*, 205239400013) Bks Demand.

Phase Transformations in Metal. 2nd ed. D. A. Porter. 1992. pap. 44.95 (*0-412-45030-5*, Chap & Hall NY) Chapman & Hall.

Phase Transformations in Metals & Alloys. D. A. Porter & K. E. Easterling. LC 92-13376. 1992. write for info. (*0-442-31638-0*) Chapman & Hall.

***Phase Transformations in Steel: A Neutron Depolarization Study.** Suzanne G. E. te Velthuis. (Illus.). 168p. 1999. pap. 43.50 (*90-407-1866-0*, Pub. by Delft U Pr) Coronet Bks.

Phase Transformations in Thin Films: Thermodynamics & Kinetics. Ed. by M. Atzmon et al. (Symposium Proceedings Ser.: Vol. 311). 399p. 1993. text 72.00 (*1-55899-207-3*) Materials Res.

Phase Transformations in Titanium & Zicronium-Based Alloys. S. Banerjee & P. Mukhopadhyay. (Pergamon Materials Ser.: Vol. 5). 1999. write for info. (*0-08-042145-8*, Pergamon Pr) Elsevier.

***Phase Transition Approach to High Temperature Superconductivity.** T. Schneider & J. M. Singer. 450p. 2000. 78.00 (*1-86094-241-5*, Pub. by Imperial College) World Scientific Pub.

Phase Transitions: Mathematics, Physics, Biology . . . Proceedings of the Conference. R. Kotecky. 250p. 1993. text 81.00 (*981-02-1502-9*) World Scientific Pub.

Phase Transitions & Adsorbate Restructuring at Metal Surfaces. Ed. by D. A. King & D. P. Woodruff. LC 94-17626. (Chemical Physics of Solid Surfaces Ser.: Vol. 7). 658p. 1994. 311.25 (*0-444-81924-X*) Elsevier.

Phase Transitions & Critical Diffusive Systems Vol. 17: Statistical Mechancis of Driven Diffusive Systems. Ed. by B. Schmittmann & R. K. Zia. (Illus.). 256p. 1995. text 111.00 (*0-12-220317-8*) Acad Pr.

***Phase Transitions & Critical Phenomena.** Ed. by C. Domb. (Phase Transitions & Critical Phenomena Ser.: Vol. 19). 576p. 2000. 145.00 (*0-12-220319-4*) Acad Pr.

Phase Transitions & Critical Phenomena, Vol. 10. Ed. by Cyril M. Domb & Joel L. Lebowitz. 363p. 1987. text 184.00 (*0-12-220310-0*) Acad Pr.

Phase Transitions & Critical Phenomena, Vol. 11. Ed. by Cyril M. Domb & Joel L. Lebowitz. 240p. 1987. text 147.00 (*0-12-220311-9*) Acad Pr.

Phase Transitions & Critical Phenomena, Vol. 14. Ed. by Cyril M. Domb & Joel L. Lebowitz. (Illus.). 376p. 1991. text 186.00 (*0-12-220314-3*) Acad Pr.

Phase Transitions & Critical Phenomena, Vol. 15. Ed. by Cyril M. Domb & Joel L. Lebowitz. (Illus.). 245p. 1992. text 138.00 (*0-12-220315-1*) Acad Pr.

***Phase Transitions & Critical Phenomena, Vol. 18.** C. Domb. 350p. 2000. 125.00 (*0-12-220318-6*) Acad Pr.

Phase Transitions & Critical Phenomena Vol. 16: Self-Assembling Amphiphilic Systems. Ed. by Martin J. Schick & G. Gompper. (Illus.). 181p. 1994. text 92.00 (*0-12-220316-X*) Acad Pr.

Phase Transitions & Crystal Symmetry. Y. A. Izyumov & V. N. Syromatnikov. (C). 1990. text 330.00 (*0-7923-0542-6*) Kluwer Academic.

Phase Transitions & Hysteresis. Ed. by Martin Brokate & Augusto Visintin. LC 94-22894. (Lecture Notes in Mathematics Ser.). 1994. 62.00 (*0-387-58386-6*) Spr-Verlag.

Phase Transitions & Hysteresis. Martin Brokate et al. Ed. by Augusto Visintin. LC 94-22894. (Lecture Notes in Mathematics Ser.: Vol. 1584). 1994. 52.95 (*3-540-58386-6*) Spr-Verlag.

Phase Transitions & Relaxation in Systems with Competing Energy Scales: Proceedings of the NATO Advance Study Institute, Geilo, Norway, 13-23 April 1993. Ed. by Tormod Riste. LC 93-31136. (NATO Advanced Science Institutes Series C: Mathematical & Physical Sciences). 464p. (C). 1993. text 259.00 (*0-7923-2504-4*) Kluwer Academic.

Phase Transitions in Colloidal Suspensions. B. J. Ackerson. 250p. 1990. text 530.00 (*0-677-26090-3*) Gordon & Breach.

Phase Transitions in Complex Fluids. Ed. by Pierre Toledano & A. M. Neto. LC 99-172214. 500p. 1998. 68.00 (*981-02-3260-8*) World Scientific Pub.

Phase Transitions in Condensed Systems - Experiments & Theory, Vol. 57. Ed. by G. S. Cargill, III et al. (Materials Research Society Symposium Proceedings Ser.). 1987. text 17.50 (*0-931837-22-7*) Materials Res.

Phase Transitions in Ferroelastic & Co-Elastic Crystals. rev. ed. E. K. Salje. (Topics in Mineral Physics & Chemistry Ser.: No. 1). (Illus.). 382p. (C). 1991. text 100.00 (*0-521-38449-4*) Cambridge U Pr.

Phase Transitions in Ferroelastic & Co-Elastic Crystals. rev. ed. E. K. Salje. (Topics in Mineral Physics & Chemistry Ser.: No. 1). (Illus.). 296p. (C). 1993. pap. text 42.95 (*0-521-42936-6*) Cambridge U Pr.

Phase Transitions in Foods. Yrjo Roos. LC 95-5987. (Food Science & Technology International Ser.). (Illus.). 360p. 1995. text 94.00 (*0-12-595340-2*) Acad Pr.

Phase Transitions in Liquid Crystals. S. Martellucci & A. N. Chester. (NATO ASI Ser.: Vol. 290). (Illus.). 520p. (C). 1992. text 145.00 (*0-306-44213-2*, Kluwer Plenum) Kluwer Academic.

Phase Transitions in Materials: A Special Issue of the Journal Phase Transitions. C. Boulesteix & J. R. Gavarri. Ed. by A. M. Glazer. 328p. 1989. pap. text 663.00 (*0-677-25780-5*) Gordon & Breach.

Phase Transitions in Molecular Solids. University of Exeter Staff & Chemical Society (Great Britain) Staff. LC 81-168774. 298 p. 1980. write for info. (*0-85186-748-0*) Royal Soc Chem.

Phase Transitions in Particle Physics: The Phase Structure of QCD. Hildegard Meyer-Ortmanns & Thomas Reisz. 200p. 1999. 28.00 (*981-02-3441-4*) World Scientific Pub.

Phase Transitions in Soft Condensed Matter. Ed. by D. Sherrington & Tormod Riste. (NATO ASI Ser.: Vol. 211). (Illus.). 402p. (C). 1990. text 156.00 (*0-306-43394-X*, Kluwer Plenum) Kluwer Academic.

Phase Transitions in Solids. K. Kawasaki. 304p. 1990. pap. text 621.00 (*2-88124-784-9*) Gordon & Breach.

Phase Transitions in Surface Films 2. Ed. by Herbert Taub et al. (NATO ASI Ser.: Vol. 267). (Illus.). 518p. (C). 1991. text 174.00 (*0-306-44005-9*, Kluwer Plenum) Kluwer Academic.

Phase Transitions in the Presence of Small Concentrations of Defects: A Special Issue of the Journal Phase Transitions. Ed. by J. C. Toledano. 371p. 1988. pap. text 533.00 (*0-677-25660-4*) Gordon & Breach.

Phase Transitions of Interacting Particle Systems. Norio Konno. 244p. 1995. text 59.00 (*981-02-2076-6*) World Scientific Pub.

Phase Transitions of the Second Order: Collective Variables Method. I. R. Yukhnovs'kii. 340p. 1987. text 72.00 (*9971-5-0087-6*) World Scientific Pub.

Phase II in Review: The Price Commission Experience. Robert F. Lanzillotti et al. LC 75-5164. (Brookings INstitution Studies in Wage-Price Policy). 223p. reprint ed. pap. 69.20 (*0-608-12712-4*, 202538700043) Bks Demand.

Phase World. Kevin Siembieda & C. J. Carella. Ed. by James Osten et al. (Rifts Dimension Bk.: Bk. 2). (Illus.). 208p. (Orig.). 1994. pap. 20.95 (*0-916211-73-8*, 816) Palladium Bks.

Phase World Sourcebook. Vince Martin & Alex Marciniszyn. (Rifts Dimension Bk.: No. 3). (Illus.). 112p. (Orig.). 1995. pap. 12.95 (*0-916211-79-7*) Palladium Bks.

Phased - Array Wavelength Demultiplenes & Their Integration with Photodetectors. M. R. Amersfoort. 108p. 1994. pap. 57.50 (*90-407-1041-4*, Pub. by Delft U Pr) Coronet Bks.

Phased Array - Based Systems & Applications. Nicholas Fourikis. LC 95-49567. (Microwave & Optical Engineering Ser.). 426p. 1997. 98.00 (*0-471-01212-2*) Wiley.

Phased Array Antenna Handbook. Robert J. Mailloux. (Antenna Ser.). 534p. 1993. text 137.00 (*0-89006-502-0*) Artech Hse.

Phased Array Antennas. R. C. Hansen. LC 97-23708. (Series in Microwave & Optical Engineering). 504p. 1998. 105.00 (*0-471-53076-X*, Wiley-Interscience) Wiley.

Phased Array Antennas: Proceedings of the 1970 Phased Array Antenna Symposium. Phased Array Antenna Symposium (1970: Polytechnic. Ed. by Arthur A. Oliner. LC TK6590.A6P45. (Modern Frontiers in Applied Science Ser.). 393p. reprint ed. pap. 121.90 (*0-608-16258-2*, 202716200054) Bks Demand.

Phased-Locked Loop Principles & Practices. P. V. Brennan. (Illus.). 204p. 1996. 50.00 (*0-07-007568-9*) McGraw.

Phaselock Techniques. 2nd ed. Floyd M. Gardner. LC 78-20777. 304p. 1979. 99.95 (*0-471-04294-3*) Wiley.

Phaseolus SPP. Bean Science. R. K. Maiti. (Illus.). 554p. (C). 1997. 79.00 (*1-57808-007-X*, V07X) Science Pubs.

Phaseplane, Version 3.0. Bard Ermentrout. LC 89-22305. 200p. (C). 1990. mass mkt. 18.25 (*0-534-12897-1*) PWS Pubs.

Phaseplane, Version 3.0. Bard Ermentrout. LC 89-22305. 200p. (C). 1990. 485.95 (*0-534-12895-5*) PWS Pubs.

Phases. Elizabeth Moon. 1997. per. 5.99 (*0-671-87855-7*) Baen Bks.

Phases: The Spiritual Rhythms of Adult Life. 4th ed. Bernard Lievegoed. Tr. by H. S. Lake from GER. 1993. pap. 16.95 (*1-85584-056-1*, 388, Pub. by R Steiner Pr) Anthroposophic.

Phases of American Culture. Jesuit Philosophical Association of the Eastern St. LC 69-17579. (Essay Index Reprint Ser.). 1977. 17.95 (*0-8369-0021-9*) Ayer.

Phases of an Inferior Planet. Ellen Glasgow. (Collected Works of Ellen Glasgow). 324p. 1998. reprint ed. lib. bdg. 98.00 (*1-58201-639-9*) Classic Bks.

Phases of Burnout: Developments in Concepts & Applications. Robert T. Golembiewski & Robert F. Munzenrider. LC 87-38491. 292p. 1988. 69.50 (*0-275-92980-9*, C2980, Praeger Pubs) Greenwood.

Phases of Childhood: Growing in Body Soul & Spirit. 2nd ed. Bernard Lievegoed. (Illus.). 204p. 1997. pap. 15.95 (*0-88010-446-5*, 644) Anthroposophic.

Phases of Dickens: The Man, His Message & His Mission. John C. Walters. LC 73-176491. (Studies in Dickens: No. 52). 1971. reprint ed. lib. bdg. 75.00 (*0-8383-1358-2*) M S G Haskell Hse.

Phases of Economic Growth, 1850-1973: Kondratieff Waves & Kuznets Swings. Solomos Solomou. (Illus.). 213p. (C). 1990. pap. text 20.95 (*0-521-38904-6*) Cambridge U Pr.

Phases of Life: Observations on Modern Life. H. Woodrow Bradley. LC 93-73425. 236p. (Orig.). 1993. pap. text 9.95 (*0-9639246-0-5*) Dream Pubng.

Phases of Modern Music. Lawrence Gilman. LC 68-22915. (Essay Index Reprint Ser.). 1977. 18.95 (*0-8369-0476-1*) Ayer.

Phases of Pre-Pagan Burma: Languages & History, 2 vols. G. H. Luce. (Illus.). 1986. 155.00 (*0-19-713595-1*) OUP.

Phases of Rilke. Norbert Fuerst. LC 72-6786. (Studies in German Literature: No. 13). 1972. reprint ed. lib. bdg. 75.00 (*0-8383-1663-8*) M S G Haskell Hse.

Phases of Silica. Robert B. Sosman. LC 65-19405. 400p. reprint ed. pap. 124.00 (*0-608-11467-7*, 205031100061) Bks Demand.

Phases of the Moon. Marilyn Busteed & Dorothy Wergin. LC 82-73123. 219p. 1996. 18.95 (*0-86690-345-3*, W2644-014) Am Fed Astrologers.

Phases of the Moon. Tiffany Busteed. 1974. mass mkt. 7.95 (*0-394-49518-7*) Random.

Phases of the Moon. Lynn Kozma. LC 94-2577. 104p. 1994. 12.00 (*0-918949-48-3*); pap. 8.00 (*0-918949-47-5*) Martz.

Phases of the Moon. James Magorian. LC 77-82560. (Illus.). 40p. 1978. 6.00 (*0-930674-01-4*) Black Oak.

Phases of the Moon. Julia Watts. LC 97-10809. 240p. (Orig.). 1997. pap. 11.95 (*1-56280-176-7*) Naiad Pr.

Phases of the Moon: Flowers from the Garden of Hel. David Porter. (Illus.). 64p. (Orig.). 1997. pap. 5.95 (*0-9641606-9-2*) Easy Break.

Phasestar Astrology & Natural Phenomena. Aniruddha. Ed. by G. R. Somayajulu. LC 98-100484. (Illus.). 64p. (Orig.). 1995. pap. 6.95 (*0-911837-02-7*) Indus Bks.

Phasic Events & Dynamic Organization of Sleep. Ed. by Mario G. Terzano et al. LC 90-9234. (L. E. R. S. Monograph Ser.: Vol. 7). 224p. 1991. reprint ed. pap. 69.50 (*0-608-04674-4*, 206539500004) Bks Demand.

Phasing & Recoverability. rev. ed. Daniel D. Silverman. LC 97-12242. (Outstanding Dissertations in Linguistics Ser.). 256p. 1997. text 62.00 (*0-8153-2876-1*) Garland.

***Phasing into Successful Science - Chemistry & Physics.** Lisa Duvall. (C). 1999. pap. text 26.95 (*1-56870-371-6*) RonJon Pub.

***Phasing into Successful Science - Earth & Science.** Lisa Duvall. 1999. pap. text 26.95 (*1-56870-370-8*) RonJon Pub.

***Phasing into Successful Science-Life.** Lisa Duvall. 1999. pap. text 26.95 (*1-56870-369-4*) RonJon Pub.

Phasing Out Lead from Gasoline: Worldwide Experience & Policy Implications. Magda Lovei. LC 97-32833. (Technical Paper Ser.: No. 397). 36p. 1998. pap. 22.00 (*0-8213-4157-X*, 14157) World Bank.

Phasing Out Lead from Gasoline in Central & Eastern Europe: Health Issues, Feasibility, & Policies. Ed. by Magda Lovei. LC 97-12022. 94p. 1997. pap. 22.00 (*0-8213-3915-X*, 13915) World Bank.

Phaze Doubt. Piers Anthony. 1991. mass mkt. 5.99 (*0-441-66263-3*) Ace Bks.

Phaze Doubt. Piers Anthony. (Illus.). 1991. write for info. (*0-450-54814-7*, Pub. by New Eng Lib); pap. write for info. (*0-450-54815-5*, Pub. by New Eng Lib) Trafalgar.

PHC & Refugees. Ed. by Anke Van der Kwaak. (Primary Health Care Publications: No. 9). 160p. 1995. pap. 13.00 (*90-5383-333-1*, Pub. by VU Univ Pr) Paul & Co Pubs.

***Phcc: Dr S. R. Williams.** 149p. (C). 2000. 32.00 (*0-13-007347-4*); student ed. 32.00 (*0-13-007346-6*) P-H.

***Phcc: George M. Sheppard.** 16p. (C). 2000. student ed. write for info. (*0-13-007348-2*) P-H.

Phcc: Qchung Stud Editn. Elam. 1999. pap. text 16.00 (*0-13-007304-0*, Pub. by P-H) S&S Trade.

Ph.D. Experience: A Woman's Point of View. Ed. by Sue Vartuli. LC 81-17797. 144p. 1982. 35.00 (*0-275-90919-0*, C0919, Praeger Pubs) Greenwood.

Ph.D. Experience: Multidisciplinary Perspectives. D. Barry Lumsden. 1997. pap. text 24.95 (*1-56032-538-0*) Hemisp Pub.

Ph.D.* Guide for Travel Photography (Push Here Dummy)* Professional Techniques the National Geographic Way. Erika Fabian & Albert Moldvay. (Illus.). 106p. 1996. pap., spiral bd. 14.00 (*0-9638417-4-2*) Eriako Assocs.

Ph.D. Is Not Enough: A Guide to Survival in Science. Peter J. Feibelman. (C). 1993. pap. 12.95 (*0-201-62663-2*) Addison-Wesley.

Ph.D. Process: A Student's Guide to Graduate School in the Sciences. Dale F. Bloom et al. LC 97-37159. 224p. 1999. pap. 16.95 (*0-19-511900-2*); text 35.00 (*0-19-511889-8*) OUP.

Ph.D.'s & the Academic Labor Market. Allan Cartter. LC 75-38700. 280p. reprint ed. pap. 86.80 (*0-608-13900-9*, 202088400020) Bks Demand.

Pheasant. P. A. Robertson. (Natural History Ser.: No. 29). (Illus.). 24p. 1989. pap. 5.25 (*0-85263-950-3*, Pub. by Shire Pubns) Parkwest Pubns.

Pheasant & Kingfisher: An Aboriginal Tale - Originally Told by Nganalgindja in the Gunwinggu Language. Catherine H. Berndt. LC 94-29581. (Illus.). 24p. (J). (gr. 1-5). 1994. pap. 4.95 (*1-879531-64-X*); lib. bdg. 9.95 (*1-879531-65-8*) Mondo Pubng.

Pheasant & Quail. S. G. B. Tennant, Jr. LC 98-39317. (Game & Fish Mastery Library). (Illus.). 96p. 1998. 19.50 (*1-57223-181-5*) Willow Creek Pr.

Pheasant Breeding & Care. Jean Delacour. (Illus.). 192p. 1978. 29.95 (*0-87666-969-0*, AP-6450) TFH Pubns.

Pheasant Cap Master (He Guan Zi) A Rhetorical Reading. Carine Defoort. LC 95-43325. (SUNY Series in Chinese Philosophy & Culture). (Illus.). 376p. (C). 1996. text 75.50 (*0-7914-3073-1*); pap. text 25.95 (*0-7914-3074-X*) State U NY Pr.

Pheasant Days. Chris Dorsey. (Illus.). 240p. 1994. pap. 9.95 (*0-89658-259-0*) Voyageur Pr.

Pheasant Jungles. William Beebe. (Illus.). 248p. 1995. reprint ed. pap. 29.95 (*0-88839-373-3*) Hancock House.

Pheasant Tales: Original Stories about America's Favorite Game Bird. Ed. by Doug Truax. LC 95-20962. 204p. 1995. 39.00 (*0-924357-55-X*, 11170-A) Countrysport Pr.

Pheasant Tales: Original Stories about America's Favorite Game Bird. limited ed. Ed. by Doug Traux. LC 95-20962. 204p. 1995. lthr. 95.00 (*0-924357-56-8*, 11170-B) Countrysport Pr.

Pheasants. Peter Robertson. LC 97-1859. (Illus.). 160p. 1997. 29.95 (*0-89658-361-9*) Voyageur Pr.

Pheasants of the Mind. Datus Proper. 154p. 1994. 25.00 (*1-885106-07-6*) Wild Adven Pr.

Pheasants of the Mind: A Hunter's Search for a Mythic Bird. limited ed. Datus Proper. (Illus.). 166p. 1995. lthr. 95.00 (*1-885106-08-4*) Wild Adven Pr.

Pheasants of the World. limited ed. Keith Howman. (Illus.). 256p. 1993. 70.00 (*0-88839-280-X*) Hancock House.

Pheasants of the World: Biology & Natural History. Paul Johnsgard. LC 98-53497. (Illus.). 384p. 1999. 50.00 (*1-56098-839-8*) Smithsonian.

Phebus Fission Product Project: Presentation of the Experimental Programme & Test Facility. Ed. by W. Krischer & M. C. Rubinstein. (Illus.). 340p. (C). (gr. 13). 1992. text 200.00 (*1-85166-765-2*) Elsevier Applied Sci.

Phebus Lane. Alec Bond. 89p. 1987. pap. 5.95 (*0-317-69927-X*) Spoon Riv Poetry.

***Phedre.** Jean Racine. Tr. by Ted Hughes from FRE. 96p. 2000. pap. 12.00 (*0-374-52616-8*) FS&G.

Phedre. Jean Racine. (FRE.). (C). 1963. pap. 7.95 (*0-8442-1994-0*, VF1994-0) NTC Contemp Pub Co.

***Phedre.** Jean Racine. 1999. pap. 7.95 (*1-85459-094-4*, Pub. by Theatre Comm) Consort Bk Sales.

Phedre et Hippolyte. Pradon. Ed. by Classe. (Exeter French Texts Ser.: Vol. 62). (FRE.). 142p. Date not set. pap. text 19.95 (*0-85989-297-2*, Pub. by Univ Exeter Pr) Northwestern U Pr.

Phedre on Stage. John D. Mitchell. LC 87-61041. 294p. 1987. 25.00 (*0-87359-047-3*); pap. 17.50 (*0-685-25024-5*) Northwood Univ.

Phelge's Stones. James Phelge. 350p. 1998. pap. 20.00 (*0-9664338-0-7*) B A Bks.

Phellinus (Hymenochaetaceae) A Survey of the World Taxa, 1990. M. J. Larsen & L. A. Cobb-Poulle. (Synopsis Fungorum Ser.: No. 3). 206p. 1990. pap. text 60.00 (*82-90724-07-1*, Pub. by Fungi-Flora) Lubrecht & Cramer.

Phelon's Discount-Jobbing Trade. 15th ed. 1999. pap. 175.00 (*0-942239-18-0*) P S & M Inc.

Phelon's Womens Apparel & Accessory Shops. 11th ed. 1999. pap. 175.00 (*0-942239-11-3*) P S & M Inc.

Phelps & Gizzi: VAT for Solicitors. 2nd ed. John Phelps & Julian Gizzi. 94p. 1993. pap. 36.00 (*0-406-02008-6*, U.K., MICHIE) LEXIS Pub.

Phelps County Marriage Books One & Two, 2 vols. Phelps County Genealogical Society Staff. Date not set. pap. 22.00 (*1-893474-14-3*) Phelps Cnty Gene.

Phelps County Marriage Sep 4, 1857-Feb 17, 1867, Bk. A. Phelps County Genealogical Society Staff. 27p. 1994. pap. 10.00 (*1-893474-15-1*) Phelps Cnty Gene.

***Phelps County (MD) Marriages, 1857-1910.** Robert M. Doerr. iv, 248p. 2000. write for info. (*1-893474-19-4*) Phelps Cnty Gene.

Phelps County Missouri Heritage, Vol. 1. Phelps County Genealogical Society Staff. (Illus.). 528p. 1992. 90.00 (*1-893474-01-1*) Phelps Cnty Gene.

Phelps County Missouri Heritage, Vol. 2. Phelps County Genealogical Society Staff. (Illus.). 342p. 1994. 73.50 (*1-893474-02-X*) Phelps Cnty Gene.

Phelps County Missouri Probate Records Index 1857-1969. Phelps County Genealogical Society Staff. 66p. 1997. pap. 30.00 (*1-893474-04-6*) Phelps Cnty Gene.

Phelps County Missouri Will Books, 1857-1924. Compiled & Contrib. by Robert M. Doerr. ii, 74p. 1998. pap. 32.00 (*1-893474-00-3*) Phelps Cnty Gene.

Phelps Family of America & Their English Ancestry, 2 vols. in 1. Phelps & Servin. (Illus.). 1865p. 1989. reprint ed. pap. 259.00 (*0-8328-0963-2*); reprint ed. lib. bdg. 267.00 (*0-8328-0962-4*) Higginson Bk Co.

Phelps. The William A. Phelps Family: Life of William Addison Phelps & Mary Jane Lippitt Phelps - Their Ancestors - Their Descendants. L. L. Krug. (Illus.). 191p. 1995. reprint ed. pap. 27.00 (*0-8328-4820-4*); reprint ed. lib. bdg. 37.00 (*0-8328-4819-0*) Higginson Bk Co.

Phencyclidine & Related Arylcyclohexylamines: Present & Future Applications. Ed. by J. M. Kamenka et al. LC 83-61728. (Illus.). 690p. 1983. 50.00 (*0-916182-04-5*) NPP Bks.

Phenetic Variation in the Avian Subfamily Cardinalinae. Jenna J. Hellack. (Occasional Papers: No. 57). 22p. 1976. pap. 1.00 (*0-317-04589-X*) U KS Nat Hist Mus.

P

An Asterisk (*) at the beginning of an entry indicates that the title is appearing for the first time.

Phenetics: Evolution, Population, Trait. A. V. Yablokov. Tr. by Marie J. Hall from RUS. LC 85-31420. 171p. 1986. text 46.00 (*0-231-05990-6*) Col U Pr.

Phenetics & Ecology of Hybridization in Buckeye Butterflies: Lepidoptera: Nymphalidae. John E. Hafernik. LC 81-13069. (University of California Publications in Entomology: No. 96). 119p. 1982. pap. 36.90 (*0-7837-7485-0*, 204920700010) Bks Demand.

Phenix: or A Revival of Scarce & Valuable Tracts, 2 vols. Ed. by Gerald M. Straka. LC 72-83168. (English Studies). 1972. reprint ed. lib. bdg. 81.00 (*0-8420-1425-X*) Scholarly Res Inc.

Phenol. (Environmental Health Criteria Ser.: No. 161). (ENG, FRE & SPA.). 151p. 1994. pap. text 30.00 (*92-4-157161-6*, 1160161) World Health.

Phenol Health & Safety Guide. (Health & Safety Guides Ser.: No. 88). 31p. 1994. pap. text 5.00 (*92-4-151088-9*, 1860088) World Health.

Phenolic Compounds in Food & Their Effects on Health I: Analysis, Occurrence & Chemistry. Ed. by Chi-Tang Ho et al. LC 92-23283. (ACS Symposium Ser.: No. 506). (Illus.). 338p. 1992. text 85.00 (*0-8412-2475-7*, Pub. by Am Chemical) OUP.

Phenolic Compounds in Food & Their Effects on Health II: Antioxidants & Cancer Prevention. Ed. by Mou-Tuan Huang et al. LC 92-23283. (ACS Symposium Ser.: No. 507). (Illus.). 402p. 1992. text 95.00 (*0-8412-2476-5*, Pub. by Am Chemical) OUP.

Phenolic Liquid Resin Hand Lay-Up Techniques. 2nd rev. ed. John A. Wills. (Illus.). 215p. 1998. 39.00 (*0-9667133-2-X*) John A Wills.

Phenolic Metabolism in Plants. H. A. Stafford & R. K. Ibrahim. (Recent Advances in Phytochemistry Ser.: Vol. 26). (Illus.). 432p. (C). 1992. text 125.00 (*0-306-44231-0*, Kluwer Plenum) Kluwer Academic.

Phenolic Resins. A. Knop & Louis A. Pilato. (Illus.). 350p. 1995. 148.00 (*0-387-15039-0*) Spr-Verlag.

***Phenolic Resins: Chemistry, Applications, Standardization, Safety & Ecology.** 2nd rev. ed. A. Gardziella et al. LC 99-39048. (Illus.). 420p. 1999. 169.00 (*3-540-65517-4*) Spr-Verlag.

Phenolic, Sulfur, & Nitrogen Compounds in Food Flavors. Ed. by George Charalambous & Ira Katz. LC 76-16544. (ACS Symposium Ser.: Vol. 26). 223p. 1976. reprint ed. pap. 69.20 (*0-608-03554-8*, 206427300008) Bks Demand.

Phenologie, Croissance et Production Vegetales dans Quelques Savanes d'Afrique de L'Ouest: Variation Selon un Gradient Climatique. A. Fournier.Tr. of Phenology, Plant Growth & Production in Several West African Savannas. (FRE.). 312p. 1991. pap. 28.00 (*2-7099-1052-7*, Pub. by LInstitut Francais) Balogh.

Phenologies. Richard Dauenhauer. (Orig.). 1988. pap. 6.00 (*0-914476-90-4*) Thorp Springs.

Phenology, Plant Growth & Production in Several West African Savannas see Phenologie, Croissance et Production Vegetales dans Quelques Savanes d'Afrique de L'Ouest: Variation Selon un Gradient Climatique

Phenols & Medicine: Subject, Reference & Research Guidebook. rev. ed. Mary S. Fayette. LC 87-47653. 149p. 1994. 47.50 (*0-7883-0668-5*); pap. 44.50 (*0-7883-0669-3*) ABBE Pubs Assn.

Phenomena. Henry Billings & Melissa Billings. (Illus.). 160p. (J). (gr. 6-8). 1984. pap. text 12.64 (*0-89061-363-X*, 762, Jamestwn Pub) NTC Contemp Pub Co.

***Phenomena.** 3rd ed. Carrieri. 2001. text. write for info. (*0-7216-8453-X*, W B Saunders Co) Harcrt Hlth Sci Grp.

Phenomena: Poems. Cathryn Hankla. LC 82-11013. (Breakthrough Bks.: No. 40). 80p. (Orig.). 1983. pap. 12.95 (*0-8262-0386-8*) U of Mo Pr.

Phenomena Identification & Ranking Tables for Westinghouse AP600 Small Break Loss of Coolant Accident, Main Steam Line Break & Steam Generator Tube Rupture Scenarios. G. E. Wilson. 248p. 1997. per. 23.00 (*0-16-062854-7*) USGPO.

Phenomena in Atmospheric & Environmental Electricity. Russell J. Reiter. LC 92-5574. (Developments in Atmospheric Science Ser.: Vol. 20). 542p. 1992. 219.75 (*0-444-89286-9*) Elsevier.

Phenomena in Ionized Gases: XXII ICPIG. Kurt H. Becker et al. (AIP Press Conference Proceedings Ser.: No. 363). (Illus.). 400p. 1996. 130.00 (*1-56396-550-X*, CP 363, AIP Pr) Spr-Verlag.

Phenomena in Mixed Surfactant Systems. Ed. by John F. Scamehorn. LC 86-8062. (ACS Symposium Ser.: No. 311). (Illus.). ix, 349p. 1986. 73.95 (*0-8412-0975-8*) Am Chemical.

Phenomena in Mixed Surfactant Systems. Ed. by John F. Scamehorn. LC 86-8062. (ACS Symposium Ser.: Vol. 311). 360p. 1986. reprint ed. pap. 111.60 (*0-608-03517-3*, 206423600008) Bks Demand.

Phenomena of Fluid Motions. Robert S. Brodkey. LC 95-2346. (Illus.). 752p. 1995. pap. text 21.95 (*0-486-68605-1*) Dover.

Phenomena of Life. Ed. by Mystic Jhamon Publishers Staff. (Conversations with a Mystic Ser.: No. 4). (Illus.). 1986. pap. write for info. (*0-933961-09-X*) Mystic Jhamom.

Phenomena of Life: An Interpretation of Oxidation, Energy & Electricity. 1991. lib. bdg. 88.95 (*0-8490-4932-6*) Gordon Pr.

Phenomena of Life Illustrations Booklet: Supplement. Ed. by Mystic Jhamon Publishers Staff. (Conversations with a Mystic Ser.: No. 4). (Illus.). 24p. 1986. pap. write for info. (*0-933961-10-3*) Mystic Jhamom.

Phenomena of Materialisation. Douglas M. Baker. 1978. pap. 11.00 (*0-906006-62-7*, Pub. by Baker Pubns) New Leaf Dist.

Phenomena of Materialisation. Baron V. Notzing. 340p. 1996. reprint ed. spiral bd. 31.00 (*0-7873-0638-X*) Hlth Research.

Phenomena of Materialisation: A Contribution to the Investigation of Mediumistic Teleplastics. A. Von Schrenck Notzing. LC 75-7408. (Perspectives in Psychical Research Ser.). (Illus.). 1975. reprint ed. 52.95 (*0-405-06995-2*) Ayer.

Phenomena of Pentecost. James A. Stewart. pap. 1.99 (*1-56632-058-5*) Revival Lit.

***Phenomenal Consciousness: A Naturalistic Theory.** Peter Carruthers. (Illus.). 358p. 2000. write for info. (*0-521-78173-6*) Cambridge U Pr.

Phenomenal Woman. Maya Angelou. LC 94-27042. 32p. 1995. 10.00 (*0-679-43924-2*) Random.

***Phenomenal Woman.** Maya Angelou. LC 99-39134. 2000. 19.95 (*0-375-50406-0*) Random.

Phenomenal Woman: Feminist Transitions & Metaphysical Traditions. Christine Battersby. LC 97-32058. 256p. (C). 1998. 75.00 (*0-415-92035-3*); pap. 18.99 (*0-415-92036-1*) Routledge.

***Phenomenal Women - That's Us! A Book of Power, Personal Strength, Inner Beauty & Radiant.** Madeleine Singer et al. LC 99-67450. 256p. 2000. pap. 16.95 (*1-56184-145-5*) New Falcon Pubns.

Phenomene de Construction et de Destruction Dans le Songe de du Bellay. Maksoud N. Feghali. LC 91-12281. (Scripta Humanistica Ser.: No. 83). 1991. write for info. (*0-916379-89-2*) Scripta.

Phenomene Humain. Pierre Teilhard De Chardin. 15.95 (*0-685-36581-6*) Fr & Eur.

Phenomene Humain. Pierre Teilhard De Chardin. (Coll. Points). (FRE.). 1955. pap. 34.95 (*0-7859-1241-X*, 2020028581) Fr & Eur.

***Phenomeno-Logic of the I: Essays on Self-Consciousness.** Hector-Neri Castaneda. Ed. by James G. Hart & Tomis Kapitan. LC 98-50153. (Illus.). 384p. 1999. text 45.00 (*0-253-33506-X*) Ind U Pr.

***Phenomenological Approaches to Popular Culture.** Ed. by Michael Thomas Carroll & Eddie Tafoya. LC 99-45937. 2000. 51.95 (*0-87972-809-4*); pap. 25.95 (*0-87972-810-8*) Bowling Green Univ Popular Press.

Phenomenological Aspects of Superstring Theories: Past '97 ICTP, Trieste, Italy 2-4 October, 1997. Ed. by G. Senjanovie & A. Smirnov. LC 98-51621. 287p. 1998. 98.00 (*981-02-3478-3*) World Scientific Pub.

Phenomenological Aspects of Supersymmetry: Proceedings of a Series of Seminars Held at the Max-Planck-Institut Fur Physik, Munich, FRG, May to November 1991. Ed. by W. Hollik et al. LC 92-28843. (Lecture Notes in Physics Ser.: Vol. 405). vii, 329p. 1992. 70.95 (*0-387-55761-X*) Spr-Verlag.

Phenomenological Aspects of Wittgenstein's Philosophy. Byong-Chul Park. LC 97-34899. (Synthese Library). 249p. 1997. text 120.50 (*0-7923-4813-3*) Kluwer Academic.

Phenomenological Epistemology. Henry Pietersma. LC 99-20502. 224p. 2000. text 45.00 (*0-19-513190-8*) OUP.

Phenomenological Explanations. Alphonso Lingis. (Phaenomenologica Ser.: Vol. 96). 122p. 1986. lib. bdg. 73.00 (*90-247-3332-4*, Pub. by M Nijhoff) Kluwer Academic.

Phenomenological Hermeneutics & the Study of Literature. Mario J. Valdes. LC 88-127047. (University of Toronto Romance Ser.: No. 56). 157p. reprint ed. pap. 48.70 (*0-8357-3785-3*, 203651500003) Bks Demand.

***Phenomenological Inquiry in Psychology: Existential & Transpersonal Dimensions.** R. Valle. LC 97-38473. (Illus.). 405p. (C). 1998. 75.00 (*0-306-45542-0*, Plenum Trade) Perseus Pubng.

***Phenomenological Inquiry in Psychology: Existential & Transpersonal Dimensions.** Ed. by Ron Valle. LC 97-38473. (Illus.). 464p. (C). 1998. pap. 42.50 (*0-306-45543-9*, Plenum Trade) Perseus Pubng.

Phenomenological Interpretation of Kant's Critique of Pure Reason. Martin Heidegger. Tr. by Parvis Emad & Kenneth Maly. LC 96-44479. (Studies in Continental Thought). 1997. 35.00 (*0-253-33258-3*) Ind U Pr.

Phenomenological Method: Theory & Practice. Fred Kersten. 446p. (C). 1989. lib. bdg. 186.00 (*0-7923-0094-7*, Pub. by Kluwer Academic) Kluwer Academic.

Phenomenological Movement. 3rd enl. rev. ed. Herbert Spiegelberg. (Phaenomenologica Ser.). 788p. 1981. lib. bdg. 230.00 (*90-247-2577-1*, Pub. by M Nijhoff) Kluwer Academic.

Phenomenological Movement: An Historical Introduction. 3rd enl. ed. Ed. by Herbert Spiegelberg. 832p. 1981. 84.50 (*90-247-2393-0*) Kluwer Academic.

Phenomenological Perspectives: Historical & Systematic Essays in Honor of Herbert Spiegelberg. Ed. by P. J. Bossert. (Phaenomenologica Ser.: No. 62). 290p. 1975. lib. bdg. 126.50 (*90-247-1701-9*, Pub. by M Nijhoff) Kluwer Academic.

Phenomenological Psychology. Ed. by Joseph J. Kockelmans. 266p. (C). 1987. lib. bdg. 155.50 (*90-247-3501-7*, Pub. by M Nijhoff) Kluwer Academic.

Phenomenological Psychology: A Text for Beginners. Eugene M. DeRobertis. LC 96-33420. 88p. 1996. pap. text 17.50 (*0-7618-0500-1*) U Pr of Amer.

Phenomenological Psychology: An Introduction. Raymond J. McCall. LC 83-47764. 136p. 1983. pap. 13.95 (*0-299-09414-6*) U of Wis Pr.

Phenomenological Realism of the Possible Worlds: Analecta Husserliana - The Yearbook Phenomenological Research, Vol. 3. Ed. by Anna-Teresa Tymieniecka. LC 78-25369. 394p. 1974. text 162.50 (*90-277-0426-0*, D Reidel) Kluwer Academic.

Phenomenological Research Methods. Clark Moustakas. LC 94-7355. 240p. 1994. 52.00 (*0-8039-5798-X*); pap. 24.00 (*0-8039-5799-8*) Sage.

Phenomenological Sociology: Issues & Applications. George Psathas. LC 73-2805. 384p. reprint ed. pap. 119.10 (*0-608-14030-9*, 205551500023) Bks Demand.

Phenomenological Theory of Linear Viscoelastic Behavior: An Introduction - Solutions. N. W. Tschoegl. (Illus.). 765p. 1989. 136.95 (*0-387-19173-9*) Spr-Verlag.

Phenomenologie & Materialisme Dialectique. Tran D. Thao. (Reimpressions G & B Ser.). (FRE.). 372p. 1972. pap. text 65.00 (*0-677-50615-5*) Gordon & Breach.

Phenomenologie & Ontology. Jitendra N. Mohanty. (Phaenomenologica Ser.: No. 37). 228p. 1970. lib. bdg. 81.00 (*90-247-5053-9*, Pub. by M Nijhoff) Kluwer Academic.

Phenomenologie de la Perception. Maurice Merleau-Ponty. (FRE.). 1976. pap. 28.95 (*0-7859-2747-6*) Fr & Eur.

Phenomenologie de la Perception. Maurice Merleau-Ponty. (Tel Ser.). (FRE.). 531p. 1945. pap. 23.95 (*2-07-029337-8*) Schoenhof.

Phenomenologie De L'experience Esthetique see Phenomenology of Aesthetic Experience

Phenomenology. Jean-Francois Lyotard. Tr. by Brian Beakley from FRE. LC 90-19828. (SUNY Series in Contemporary Continental Philosophy). 153p. (C). 1991. pap. text 19.95 (*0-7914-0806-X*) State U NY Pr.

Phenomenology. Jean-Francois Lyotard. Tr. by Brian Beakley from FRE. LC 90-19828. (SUNY Series in Contemporary Continental Philosophy). 153p. (C). 1991. text 59.50 (*0-7914-0805-1*) State U NY Pr.

Phenomenology: Between Essentialism & Transcendental Philosophy. Jitendranath Mohanty. LC 97-6392. (Studies in Phenomenology & Existential Philosophy). 1997. 59.95 (*0-8101-1401-1*); pap. 19.95 (*0-8101-1402-X*) Northwestern U Pr.

Phenomenology: Continuation & Criticism. Ed. by Fred Kersten & Richard M. Zaner. (Phaenomenologica Ser.: No. 50). 278p. 1973. lib. bdg. 112.50 (*90-247-1302-1*, Pub. by M Nijhoff) Kluwer Academic.

Phenomenology: Japanese & American Perspectives. Burt C. Hopkins. LC 98-37502. (Contributions to Phenomenology Ser.). 1p. 1998. write for info. (*0-7923-5336-6*) Kluwer Academic.

Phenomenology - East & West: Essays in Honor of J. N. Mohanty. Ed. by Frank M. Kirkland & Debiprasad Chattopadhyaya. LC 92-41533. (Contributions to Phenomenology Ser.). 340p. (C). 1993. text 174.50 (*0-7923-2087-5*) Kluwer Academic.

Phenomenology & Aesthetics: Approaches to Comparative Literature & the Other Arts. Ed. by Marlies Kronegger. 288p. (C). 1990. lib. bdg. 166.50 (*0-7923-0738-0*, Pub. by Kluwer Academic) Kluwer Academic.

Phenomenology & Beyond: The Self & Its Language. Ed. by Harold A. Durfee & David F. Rodier. 182p. (C). 1989. lib. bdg. 138.50 (*0-7923-0511-6*, Pub. by Kluwer Academic) Kluwer Academic.

Phenomenology & Deconstruction: Method & Imagination, Vol. 2. Robert D. Cumming. 404p. 1992. pap. text 28.00 (*0-226-12369-3*) U Ch Pr.

Phenomenology & Deconstruction: Method & Imagination, Vol. 2. Robert D. Cumming. 404p. 1992. lib. bdg. 61.00 (*0-226-12368-5*) U Ch Pr.

Phenomenology & Deconstruction Vol. 1: The Dream Is Over. Robert D. Cumming. LC 91-12696. 268p. 1991. lib. bdg. 60.00 (*0-226-12366-9*) U Ch Pr.

Phenomenology & Deconstruction Vol. 1: The Dream Is Over. Robert D. Cumming. LC 91-12696. 268p. 1991. pap. text 21.00 (*0-226-12367-7*) U Ch Pr.

Phenomenology & Dialectical Materialism. Tran D. Thao et al. (Boston Studies in the Philosophy of Science: No. 49). 280p. 1985. text 140.50 (*90-277-0737-5*) Kluwer Academic.

Phenomenology & Existentialism. Ed. by Edward N. Lee & Maurice Mandelbaum. LC 67-15598. (Johns Hopkins Paperbacks Ser.: Vol. JH-57). 279p. 1969. reprint ed. pap. 86.50 (*0-608-03714-1*, 206453900009) Bks Demand.

Phenomenology & Existentialism. Ed. by Robert C. Solomon. 546p. (C). 1991. reprint ed. pap. text 24.95 (*0-8226-3012-5*) Rowman.

Phenomenology & Existentialism: An Introduction. Reinhardt Grossman. 256p. 1984. 35.00 (*0-7102-0270-9*, Routledge Thoemms) Routledge.

Phenomenology & Existentialism: An Introduction. Reinhardt S. Grossman. 256p. 1984. pap. 14.95 (*0-7102-0291-1*, Routledge Thoemms) Routledge.

Phenomenology & Indian Philosophy. Ed. by D. P. Chattopadhyay et al. (C). 1992. 30.00 (*81-208-0770-7*, Pub. by Motilal Bnarsidass) S Asia.

Phenomenology & Indian Philosophy. Ed. by Debiprasad Chattopadhyaya et al. LC 90-42910. 376p. 1992. text 54.50 (*0-7914-0662-8*) State U NY Pr.

Phenomenology & Lattice QCD - Proceedings of the 1993 Uehling Summer School. G. Kilcup & S. Sharpe. LC 96-146974. 400p. 1995. text 99.00 (*981-02-2225-4*) World Scientific Pub.

Phenomenology & Marxism. Ed. by Bernhard Waldenfels et al. Tr. by J. Claude Evans, Jr. (International Library of Phenomenology & Moral Sciences). 256p. (Orig.). 1985. 45.00 (*0-7100-9854-5*, Routledge Thoemms) Routledge.

Phenomenology & Nursing Research. M. Crotty. 208p. 1996. pap. write for info. (*0-443-05432-0*) Church.

Phenomenology & Psychological Research. Amedeo Giorgi. LC 84-21168. 216p. 1985. pap. text 19.00 (*0-8207-0174-2*) Duquesne.

Phenomenology & Science in Contemporary European Thought. Anna-Teresa Tymieniecka. 198p. 1962. 5.00 (*0-940962-22-5*) Polish Inst Art & Sci.

Phenomenology & Skepticism: Essays in Honor of James M. Edie. Brice R. Wachterhauser. LC 96-25587. (Northwestern University Studies in Phenomenology & Existential Philosophy). 288p. 1996. 69.95 (*0-8101-1387-2*); pap. 22.50 (*0-8101-1388-0*) Northwestern U Pr.

Phenomenology & the Formal Sciences. Ed. by Thomas M. Seebohm et al. (Contributions to Phenomenology Ser.: No. 8). 272p. 1991. text 146.50 (*0-7923-1499-9*) Kluwer Academic.

Phenomenology & the Making of the World. Dag Hedin. (Studia Philosophiae Religionis: No. 19). 134p. 1997. pap. 43.50 (*91-22-01771-2*, Pub. by Almqvist Wiksell) Coronet Bks.

Phenomenology & the Metaphysics of Presence. W. W. Fuchs. (Phaenomenologica Ser.: No. 69). 104p. 1976. pap. text 81.00 (*90-247-1822-8*, Pub. by M Nijhoff) Kluwer Academic.

Phenomenology & the Natural Sciences: Essays & Translations. Ed. by Joseph J. Kockelmans & Theodore J. Kisiel. (Studies in Phenomenology & Existential Philosophy). 520p. 1970. pap. 29.95 (*0-8101-0613-2*) Northwestern U Pr.

Phenomenology & the Social Sciences, I. Ed. by Maurice A. Natanson. LC 79-91001. (Studies in Phenomenology & Existential Philosophy). 1066p. (C). 1973. pap. 19.95 (*0-8101-0616-7*) Northwestern U Pr.

***Phenomenology & the Theological Turn: The French Debate.** Dominique Janicaud & Jean Courtine. (Perspectives in Continental Philosophy Ser.). 2000. 34.95 (*0-8232-2052-4*); pap. 19.95 (*0-8232-2053-2*) Fordham.

Phenomenology & the Theory of Science. Aron Gurwitsch. Ed. by Lester Embree. LC 73-91997. (Studies in Phenomenology & Existential Philosophy). 272p. 1974. pap. 19.95 (*0-8101-0544-6*) Northwestern U Pr.

Phenomenology & Treatment of Alcoholism. Ed. by William E. Fann et al. LC 79-23224. (Illus.). 350p. 1980. text 40.00 (*0-88331-177-1*) R B Luce.

Phenomenology & Treatment of Anxiety. Ed. by William E. Fann et al. LC 78-32092. (Illus.). 455p. 1979. 40.00 (*0-88331-178-X*) R B Luce.

Phenomenology, Geometry & Vision: Merleau Ponty's Critique of Classical Theories of Vision. Aurora Plomer. 110p. 1991. text 72.95 (*1-85628-218-X*, Pub. by Avebry) Ashgate Pub Co.

Phenomenology in a Pluralistic Context. Ed. by William L. McBride & Calvin O. Schrag. LC 82-19609. (Selected Studies in Phenomenology & Existential Philosophy: No. 9). 317p. (C). 1984. text 74.50 (*0-87395-730-X*); pap. text 24.95 (*0-87395-731-8*) State U NY Pr.

Phenomenology in Japan Anthony J. Steinbock. LC 99-164697. 111p. 1998. write for info. (*0-7923-5291-2*) Kluwer Academic.

Phenomenology in Practice & Theory: Essays for Herbert Spiegelberg. Ed. by William S. Hamrick. (Phaenomenologica Ser.). 1988. pap. text 14.95 (*90-247-3197-6*) Kluwer Academic.

Phenomenology in Practice & Theory: Essays for Herbert Spiegelberg. Ed. by William S. Hamrick. (Phaenomenologica Ser.). 282p. 1985. lib. bdg. 101.50 (*90-247-2926-2*, Pub. by M Nijhoff) Kluwer Academic.

Phenomenology in Psychology & Psychiatry. Herbert Spiegelberg. LC 74-154833. (Studies in Phenomenology & Existential Philosophy). 411p. 1972. pap. 22.95 (*0-8101-0624-8*) Northwestern U Pr.

Phenomenology, Interpretation, & Community. Ed. by Lenore Langsdorf et al. LC 95-19602. (Selected Studies in Phenomenology & Existential Philosophy: Vol. 19). 295p. (C). 1996. text 59.50 (*0-7914-2865-6*); pap. text 19.95 (*0-7914-2866-4*) State U NY Pr.

Phenomenology, Language, & Schizophrenia. Ed. by Manfred Spitzer et al. LC 92-48781. (Illus.). 389p. 1993. 71.95 (*0-387-97950-6*) Spr-Verlag.

Phenomenology of Aesthetic Experience. Mikel Dufrenne. Tr. by Edward S. Casey et al from FRE. LC 73-76806. (Studies in Phenomenology & Existential Philosophy).Tr. of Phenomenologie De L'experience Esthetique. 578p. (C). 1973. pap. 19.95 (*0-8101-0591-8*) Northwestern U Pr.

Phenomenology of Charles S. Pierce: From the Doctrine of Categories to Phaneroscopy. William L. Rosensohn. ix, 109p. 1974. pap. 24.00 (*90-6032-024-7*, Pub. by B R Gruner) Humanities.

***Phenomenology of Chicana Experience: Communication & Transformation in Praxis.** Jacqueline M. Martinez. LC 00-24819. (New Critical Theory Ser.). 2000. pap. 17.95 (*0-7425-0701-7*) Rowman.

Phenomenology of Civilization: Reason as a Regulative Principle in Collingwood & Husserl. Maurice M. Eisenstein. LC 99-19887. 192p. 1999. 49.00 (*0-7618-1369-1*); pap. 27.50 (*0-7618-1370-5*) U Pr of Amer.

Phenomenology of Communication. Richard L. Lanigan. LC 87-24587. 288p. 1988. text 19.50 (*0-8207-0185-8*) Duquesne.

Phenomenology of Dance. Maxine Sheets-Johnstone. LC 79-7779. (Dance Ser.). 1980. reprint ed. lib. bdg. 23.95 (*0-8369-9304-7*) Ayer.

Phenomenology of Depressive Illness. Ed. by J. John Mann. (Depressive Illness Ser.: Vol. 1). 263p. 1988. 42.95 (*0-89885-369-9*, Kluwer Plenum) Kluwer Academic.

Phenomenology of Everyday Life: Empirical Investigations of Human Experience. Howard R. Pollio et al. LC 96-40020. (Illus.). 410p. (C). 1997. text 54.95 (*0-521-46205-3*) Cambridge U Pr.

Phenomenology of Henry James. Paul B. Armstrong. LC 82-24713. 256p. reprint ed. pap. 79.40 (*0-7837-2465-9*, 204261800005) Bks Demand.

An Asterisk (*) at the beginning of an entry indicates that the title is appearing for the first time.

Phenomenology of Internal Time-Consciousness. Edmund Husserl. Ed. by Martin Heidegger. Tr. by James S. Churchill. LC 64-10829. (Midland Bks.: No. 97). 188p. reprint ed. 58.30 (*0-8357-9230-7*, 201545900094) Bks Demand.

Phenomenology of Landscape: Places, Paths & Monuments. Christopher Tilley. Ed. by John Gledhill et al. (Explorations in Anthropology Ser.). (Illus.). 224p. 1994. 49.50 (*0-85496-919-5*, Pub. by Berg Pubs); pap. 19.50 (*1-85973-076-0*, Pub. by Berg Pubs) NYU Pr.

Phenomenology of Life & the Human Creative Condition. Ed. by Anna-Teresa Tymieniecka & World Institute for Advanced Phenomenological Rese. LC 97-2276. (Analecta Husserliana Ser.). 400p. 1998. lib. bdg. 180.00 (*0-7923-4545-2*) Kluwer Academic.

Phenomenology of Life & the Human Creative Condition Bk. 1: Laying down the Cornerstones of the Field. Ed. by Anna-Teresa Tymieniecka. LC 97-2276. (Analecta Husserliana Ser.). 555p. 1998. text 247.50 (*0-7923-4445-6*) Kluwer Academic.

Phenomenology of Life in a Dialogue Between Chinese & Occidental Philosophy. Anna-Teresa Tymieniecka. 378p. 1984. text 185.50 (*90-277-1620-X*, D Reidel) Kluwer Academic.

Phenomenology of Man & the Human Condition, Part II. Ed. by Anna-Teresa Tymieniecka. 420p. 1986. text 206.50 (*90-277-2185-8*, D Reidel) Kluwer Academic.

Phenomenology of Man & the Human Condition, Pt. I. Anna-Teresa Tymieniecka. 500p. 1982. text 226.00 (*90-277-1447-9*, D Reidel) Kluwer Academic.

Phenomenology of Merleau-Ponty: A Search for the Limits of Consciousness. G. B. Madison. LC 84-5080. (Series in Continental Thought : Vol. 3). 377p. 1981. pap. text 17.95 (*0-8214-0644-2*) Ohio U Pr.

Phenomenology of Mind. Georg Wilhelm Friedrich Hegel. LC 31-25066. (Muirhead Library of Philosophy). 814p. reprint ed. pap. 200.00 (*0-608-11934-2*, 202331500032) Bks Demand.

Phenomenology of Modern Legal Discourse: The Juridical Production & the Disclosure of Suffering. William E. Conklin. LC 97-40987. (Applied Legal Philosophy Ser.). 285p. 1998. 77.95 (*1-84014-071-2*, K213.C657, Pub. by Ashgate Pub) Ashgate Pub Co.

Phenomenology of Moods in Kierkegaard. Vincent A. McCarthy. 1978. pap. text 64.50 (*90-247-2008-7*) Kluwer Academic.

Phenomenology of Moral Experience. Maurice Mandelbaum. LC 72-13895. (Johns Hopkins Paperbacks Ser.: No. 65). 336p. reprint ed. pap. 104.20 (*0-8357-6745-0*, 203540000095) Bks Demand.

Phenomenology of Natural Science. Ed. by Lee Hardy & Lester Embree. (Contributions to Phenomenology Ser.). 320p. (C). 1991. lib. bdg. 160.50 (*0-7923-1541-3*, Pub. by Kluwer Academic) Kluwer Academic.

Phenomenology of Perception. Maurice Merleau-Ponty. Tr. by Colin J. Smith. (C). 1981. pap. 32.50 (*0-391-02551-1*) Routledge.

Phenomenology of Perception: An Introduction. Maurice Merleau-Ponty. 256p. (C). 1995. pap. 20.99 (*0-415-04556-8*, C0559) Routledge.

*__Phenomenology of Spirit.__ G. W. F. Hegel. 1998. 38.00 (*81-208-1473-8*, Pub. by Motilal Bnarsidass) S Asia.

Phenomenology of Spirit Reader: Critical & Interpretive Essays. Ed. by Jon Stewart. LC 96-54245. (SUNY Series in Hegelian Studies). 524p. (C). 1997. pap. text 25.95 (*0-7914-3536-9*) State U NY Pr.

Phenomenology of Spirit Reader: Critical & Interpretive Essays. Ed. by Jon Stewart. LC 96-54245. (SUNY Series in Hegelian Studies). 524p. (C). 1998. text 73.50 (*0-7914-3535-0*) State U NY Pr.

Phenomenology of the Cultural Disciplines. Ed. by Mano Daniel & Lester Embree. (Contributions to Phenomenology Ser.). 352p. (C). 1994. lib. bdg. 148.50 (*0-7923-2792-6*, Pub. by Kluwer Academic) Kluwer Academic.

Phenomenology of the Noema. Ed. by John J. Drummond & Lester Embree. LC 92-30372. (Contributions to Phenomenology Ser.: Vol. 10). 264p. (C). 1992. lib. bdg. 138.00 (*0-7923-1980-X*, Pub. by Kluwer Academic) Kluwer Academic.

Phenomenology of the Social World. Alfred Schutz. Tr. by George Walsh & Frederick Lehnert. (Studies in Phenomenology & Existential Philosophy). 255p. 1967. pap. 19.95 (*0-8101-0390-7*) Northwestern U Pr.

Phenomenology of the Standard Model & Beyond: Workshop on Hep. Phenomenology. D. P. Roy & P. Roy. 728p. 1989. text 130.00 (*9971-5-0909-1*) World Scientific Pub.

Phenomenology of the Truth Proper to Religion. Ed. by Daniel Guerriere. LC 89-4300. (SUNY Series in Philosophy). 323p. (C). 1990. pap. text 21.95 (*0-7914-0171-5*) State U NY Pr.

Phenomenology of Unification from Present to Future. C. Cosmelli & G. Diambrini-Palazzi. 508p. 1995. text 106.00 (*981-02-2106-1*) World Scientific Pub.

Phenomenology of Unification from Present to Future. G. Diambrini-Palazzi. (High Energy Physics Conference Proceedings Ser.). 1998. 78.00 (*981-02-3591-7*) World Scientific Pub.

Phenomenology of Unified Theories: Proceedings of the Topical Conference on Phenomenology of Unified Theories-from Standard Model to Supersymmetries - Dubrovnik, Yugoslavia May 22-28, 1983. Ed. by H. Gilie et al. 550p. 1984. 89.00 (*9971-966-12-3*) World Scientific Pub.

Phenomenology of Values & Valuing. James G. Hart & Lester E. Embree. LC 97-2847. (Contributions to Phenomenology Ser.). 1997. text 133.50 (*0-7923-4491-X*) Kluwer Academic.

*__Phenomenology of Working Class Experience.__ Simon J. Charlesworth. (Cambridge Cultural Social Studies). 324p. (C). 2000. text 64.95 (*0-521-65066-6*); pap. text 24.95 (*0-521-65915-9*) Cambridge U Pr.

*__Phenomenology on Kant, German Idealism, Hermeneutics & Logic: Philosophical Essays in Honor of Thomas M. Seebohm.__ Olav K. Wiegand & Thomas M. Seebohm. LC 00-37087. (Contributions to Phenomenology Ser.). 2000. write for info. (*0-7923-6290-X*, Kluwer Plenum) Kluwer Academic.

Phenomenology, Structuralism, Semilogy. Ed. by Harry R. Garvin & Patrick Brady. LC 75-29734. (Bucknell Review Ser.: Vol. 22, No. 1). 230p. 1975. 22.00 (*0-8387-1880-9*) Bucknell U Pr.

Phenomenon: Forty Years of Flying Saucers. Ed. by John Spencer & Hilary Evans. 416p. 1989. mass mkt. 4.95 (*0-380-70654-7*, Avon Bks) Morrow Avon.

Phenomenon Based Physics Vols. 1-3: Grades 6, 7, 8. Manfred Von Mackinsen. Ed. by David Mitchell. Ed. & Tr. by John Petering. (Illus.). 66p. 1997. pap. 7.00 (*0-9623978-6-5*) Assn Waldorf Schls.

Phenomenon of Commonsense Reasoning: Nonmonoticity, Action & Information. Dimitrios Thanassas. LC 92-36330. (Ellis Horwood Series in Artificial Intelligence). 1992. 68.50 (*0-13-663634-9*, Pub. by Tavistock-E Horwood) Routldge.

Phenomenon of Community: Selected Writings see Zjawisko Wspolnoty: Wybor Tekstow

Phenomenon of Language Tabula Latina. David Florian. 1990. teacher ed. 8.04 (*0-8013-0395-8*, 78174); student ed. 12.81 (*0-8013-0396-6*, 78175) Longman.

Phenomenon of Life: Toward a Philosophical Biology. Hans Jonas. LC 82-13437. xii, 304p. (C). 1994. pap. text 8.95 (*0-226-40595-8*) U Ch Pr.

Phenomenon of Literature. Bennison Gray. LC 74-77353. (De Proprietatibus Litterarum, Ser. Major: No. 36). 594p. 1975. pap. text 92.35 (*90-279-3469-X*) Mouton.

Phenomenon of Man. Pierre Teilhard De Chardin. LC 59-5154. 320p. 1976. pap. 14.50 (*0-06-090495-X*, CN495, Perennial) HarperTrade.

Phenomenon of Nehru. K. P. Karunakaran. 219p. 1979. 19.95 (*0-318-36643-6*) Asia Bk Corp.

Phenomenon of Pentecost. rev. ed. Frank J. Ewart. LC 91-37191. 150p. 2000. reprint ed. pap. 5.95 (*0-932581-91-9*) Word Aflame.

Phenomenon of Religion: A Thematic Approach. Moojan Momen. 1998. pap. 23.95 (*1-85168-161-2*, Pub. by Element MA) Penguin Putnam.

Phenomenon of Teilhard: Prophet for a New Age. David Lane. 192p. 1996. text 21.95 (*0-86554-498-0*, MUP/P131) Mercer Univ Pr.

Phenomenon of the Grotesque in Modern Southern Fiction: Some Aspects of Its Form & Function. Maria Haar. (Umea Studies in the Humanities: No. 51). 222p. (Orig.). 1983. pap. 30.00 (*91-7174-119-4*) Coronet Bks.

Phenonenological Interpretation of the I Ching see Giai Thich Hien Tuong Hoc ve Kinh Dich

Phenothiazines & Structurally Related Drugs. fac. ed. International Symposium on Phenothiazines & Structurally Related Drugs Staff. Ed. by Irene S. Forrest et al. LC 73-88571. (Advances in Biochemical Psychopharmacology Ser.: No. 9). (Illus.). 842p. pap. 200.00 (*0-7837-7438-9*, 204723200006) Bks Demand.

Phenotypic Evolution: A Reaction Norm Perspective. Carl D. Schlichting & Massimo Pigliucci. LC 98-7457. (C). 1998. pap. text 41.95 (*0-87893-799-4*) Sinauer Assocs.

Phenotypic Expression in Pigment Cells: Proceedings of the 11th International Pigment Cell Conference, Sendai, Japan, 1980. International Pigment Cell Conference Staff. Ed. by Makoto Seiji. LC 82-212512. 698p. 1981. reprint ed. pap. 200.00 (*0-608-01549-0*, 206195800001) Bks Demand.

Phenotypic Mapping of Down Syndrome & Other Aneuploid Conditions: Proceedings of the National Down Syndrome Society Conference on the Phenotypic Mapping of Down Syndrome & Other Aneuploid Conditions, Held in New York, January 14 & 15, 1993. Ed. by Charles J. Epstein. (Progress in Clinical & Biological Research Ser.: Vol. 384). 254p. 1993. 225.00 (*0-471-30449-2*, Wiley-Interscience) Wiley.

Phenotypic Variation in Populations: Relevance to Risk Assessment. Ed. by Avril D. Woodhead et al. LC 87-35795. (Basic Life Sciences Ser.: Vol. 43). (Illus.). 316p. 1988. 75.00 (*0-306-42794-X*, Plenum Trade) Perseus Pubng.

Phenoxyalkanoic Herbicides: Chemistry, Analysis & Environmental Pollution, Vol. I. Shane S. Que Hee & Ronald G. Sutherland. 321p. 1981. 187.00 (*0-8493-5851-5*, SB952, CRC Reprint) Franklin.

Phenylpropanolamine: A Review. Louis Lasagna. LC 86-28963. 458p. reprint ed. pap. 142.00 (*0-7837-2818-2*, 205765400006) Bks Demand.

Phenylpropanolamine: Risks, Benefits & Controversies, 5. Ed. by John P. Morgan & Doreen V. Kagan. LC 85-6590. (Clinical Pharmacology & Therapeutics Ser.: Vol. 5). 448p. 1985. 85.00 (*0-275-91336-8*, C1336, Praeger Pubs) Greenwood.

*__Phenytoin (Dilantin, Diphenylhydantoin) - Therapy & Clinical Uses: Index of New Information with Authors, Subjects & References.__ rev. ed. American Health Research Institute Staff. 150p. 1999. 47.50 (*0-7883-2182-X*); pap. 44.50 (*0-7883-2183-8*) ABBE Pubs Assn.

Phenytoin (Dilantin, Diphenylhydantoin) & Its Adverse Effects in the Human Body. American Health Research Institute Staff. LC 89-18673. 201p. 1990. 47.50 (*1-55914-120-4*); pap. 44.50 (*1-55914-121-2*) ABBE Pubs Assn.

Pheochromocytoma: A Clinical & Experimental Overview. 2nd ed. Ed. by William M. Manger. 700p. (C). 1995. write for info. (*0-393-71028-9*) Norton.

Pheonix Cafe. Jones Staff. 1998. pap. 14.95 (*0-312-86834-0*) St Martin.

Phep La Cua Su Tinh Thuc (The Miracle of Mindfulness) Cam Nang Tu Thien. 11th ed. Thich Nhat Hahn. (VIE.). 193p. 1997. reprint ed. pap. 11.00 (*1-891667-41-6*) La Boi Soc.

Pherekydes of Syros. H. S. Schibli. (Illus.). 224p. 1990. text 70.00 (*0-19-814383-4*) OUP.

Pheremone Factor. Lewis Kornfield. LC 98-89011. 325p. 1998. 25.00 (*0-7388-0179-8*); pap. 15.00 (*0-7388-0180-1*) Xlibris Corp.

Pheromone Communication in Social Insects: Ants, Wasps, Bees & Termites. Michael D. Breed. Ed. by Robert K. Vander Meer. LC 97-29921. (Westview Studies in Insect Biology). 384p. (C). 1997. text 85.00 (*0-8133-8976-3*, Pub. by Westview) HarpC.

Pheromones: Current Research, 2 vols., Vol. 2. U. Eugene Brady et al. 157p. 1974. text 31.50 (*0-8422-7212-7*) Irvington.

Pheromones: Current Research, 2 vols., Vol. 1, Vol. 1. D. L. Struble et al. 176p. 1974. text 31.50 (*0-8422-7211-9*) Irvington.

*__Pheromones of Non-Lepidopteran Insects Associated with Agricultural Plants.__ Jim Hardie & A. K. Minks. LC 99-17681. 480p. 1999. text 140.00 (*0-85199-345-1*) OUP.

Pheromones of Social Bees. John B. Free. 125.50 (*0-412-24740-2*) Chapman & Hall.

Pheromones of Social Bees. John B. Free. LC 86-47969. (Illus.). 192p. 1987. text 42.50 (*0-8014-2004-0*) Cornell U Pr.

Pherozeshah Mehta: Socio-Political Ideology. S. R. Bakshi. (C). 1991. 37.50 (*81-7041-427-X*, Pub. by Anmol) S Asia.

Phewal Lake Conservation Action Plan. Krishna Prasad Oli. 1997. pap. 22.00 (*0-7855-7472-7*, Pub. by Ratna Pustak Bhandar) St Mut.

Phi Sigma Omega, 1991-1992. Jim Ciano. (Illus.). 145p. (Orig.). 1994. pap. 25.00 (*1-888672-00-5*) J Ciano Pubng.

Phic Guide to the Environment, 1993. New York Public Library Staff. 392p. 1994. 175.00 (*0-7838-2082-8*, G K Hall & Co) Mac Lib Ref.

PHIGS by Example. W. A. Gaman & W. A. Giovinazzo. (Illus.). 248p. 1991. 48.95 (*0-387-97555-1*) Spr-Verlag.

PHIGS Programming Manual. Tom Gaskins. (X Window System Ser.). (Illus.). 968p. (Orig.). 1993. pap. 42.95 (*0-937175-85-4*) Thomson Learn.

Phil & Religion of Sri Caitanya. O. B. Kapoor. (C). 1994. 24.00 (*81-215-0275-6*, Pub. by M Manoharial) Coronet Bks.

Phil Collins. Toby Goldstein. (Orig.). 1987. mass mkt. 2.95 (*0-345-33884-7*) Ballantine Pub Grp.

Phil Collins: The Definitive Biography. Ray Coleman. (Illus.). 288p. 1999. 23.50 (*0-684-86830-X*) S&S Trade.

Phil Collins Anthology. Ed. by Carol Cuellar. 152p. (Orig.). (C). 1986. pap. text 18.95 (*0-7692-0273-X*, VF1273) Wrner Bros.

Phil Collins/Both Sides. Ed. by Carol Cuellar. (Personality - Piano-Vocal Ser.). 76p. (Orig.). (C). 1993. pap. text 19.95 (*0-89724-148-7*, VF2095) Wrner Bros.

Phil Collins/Serious Hits . . . Live! Ed. by Carol Cuellar. 88p. (Orig.). (C). 1991. pap. text 16.95 (*0-7692-0274-8*, VF1705) Wrner Bros.

Phil Dike. Janice Lovoos & Gordon McClelland. (Illus.). 64p. 1989. 27.50 (*0-914589-03-2*) Hillcrest Pr.

Phil Duse Versus the Tyranny of DOD: (Intelligence & Investigative Agencies) Phillip M. Duse. LC 99-172589. 140p. 1998. 35.00 (*0-9666309-0-4*); 30.00 (*0-9666309-1-2*) Debtors Arbitration.

Phil Hart: The Conscience of the Senate. Michael O'Brien. 250p. 1996. 29.95 (*0-87013-407-8*) Mich St U Pr.

Phil Hill: Yankee Champion: First American to Win the Driving Championship of the World. 2nd rev. ed. William F. Nolan. LC 96-32029. (Illus.). 280p. 1996. 39.50 (*1-888978-10-4*) Brown Fox Bks.

Phil Keaggy: Acoustic Solos. Ed. by John Schroeter. 80p. 1995. pap. 18.95 (*0-7866-1434-X*, MB95651) Mel Bay.

Phil Lynott: The Rocker. Mark Putterford. (Illus.). 288p. 1998. pap. 19.95 (*0-7119-6972-8*, OP48089) Omnibus NY.

*__Phil Ochs: A Bio-bibliography, 74.__ Compiled by David Cohen. LC 99-31634. Vol. 74. 336p. 1999. lib. bdg. 65.00 (*0-313-31029-7*) Greenwood.

Phil Rice's Correct Method for the Banjo. Phil. Rice. Ed. by Joseph W. Ayers. (Illus.). 64p. 1997. pap. 18.00 (*0-9633593-3-9*) Tuckahoe Music.

*__Phil Sheridan & His Army.__ Paul A. Hutton. LC 99-28700. 496p. 1999. pap. write for info. (*0-8061-3188-8*) U of Okla Pr.

Phil Simms on Passing: Fundamentals of Throwing the Football. Phil Simms. 1996. 25.00 (*0-614-97021-0*, Wm Morrow) Morrow Avon.

*__Phil Simms on Passing: Fundamentals of Throwing the Football.__ Phil Simms & Rick Meier. (Illus.). 224p. 1998. pap. 14.00 (*0-688-16108-1*, Quil) HarperTrade.

Phil Spector: Back to Mono. Ed. by Carol Cuellar. (Illus.). 308p. 1994. 39.95 (*0-89898-718-0*, P0966SMH) Wrner Bros.

Phil Spector Back to Mono. CPP Belwin Staff. 1993. pap. 24.95 (*0-89898-564-1*, P0966SMX) Wrner Bros.

Phil Swing & Boulder Dam. Beverly B. Moeller. LC 71-633550. (Illus.). 217p. reprint ed. pap. 67.30 (*0-608-18501-9*, 203150800075) Bks Demand.

Phil the Fiddler. Horatio Alger, Jr. (Works of Horatio Alger Jr.). 1989. reprint ed. lib. bdg. 79.00 (*0-685-44741-3*) Rprt Serv.

Phil the Fidler: or The Story of a Young Street Musician: Or, the Story of a Young Street Musician. Horatio Alger. 1976. reprint ed. lib. bdg. 22.95 (*0-88411-815-0*) Amereon Ltd.

*__Phil Upchurch: Twelve by Twelve.__ Phil Upchurch. 24p. 1998. pap. 14.95 (*0-7866-3476-6*, 95272BCD) Mel Bay.

Phil Weyerhaeuser: Lumberman. Charles E. Twining. LC 84-40663. (Illus.). 420p. 1985. 25.00 (*0-295-96218-6*) U of Wash Pr.

Phila Campbell: A Story of 1909. Jaquelyn Loveall. 120p. 1994. 14.95 (*1-878208-39-X*) Guild Pr IN.

*__Phila-Nipponica: An Historic Guide to Philadelphia & Japan.__ Felice Fischer. (JPN & ENG., Illus.). 94p. (Orig.). 1999. pap. 20.00 (*0-9672505-0-1*) Japan America.

Philadelphia. Bernadette Balcer & Fran O'Byrne-Pelham. LC 88-20198. (Downtown America Ser.). (Illus.). 60p. (J). (gr. 3 up). 1988. pap. 7.95 (*0-382-24795-7*, Dillon Silver Burdett); lib. bdg. 13.95 (*0-87518-388-3*, Dillon Silver Burdett) Silver Burdett Pr.

Philadelphia. Frank Burd. (Illus.). 64p. (Orig.). 1989. write for info. (*0-318-64677-3*) Phil Post Card.

Philadelphia. Carol M. Highsmith & Ted Landphair. LC 97-39858. (A Photographic Tour Ser.). (Illus.). 128p. 1998. 14.99 (*0-517-18615-2*) Crown Pub Group.

Philadelphia. Nancy Loewen. (Great Cities of the U. S. A. Ser.). (Illus.). 48p. (YA). (gr. 5 up). 1989. lib. bdg. 23.93 (*0-86592-542-9*) Rourke Enter.

Philadelphia. Rand McNally Staff. LC 98-689710. 1997. 5.95 (*0-528-96527-1*) Rand McNally.

Philadelphia. 2nd ed. Insight Guides Staff. (Insight Guides). 1998. pap. text 21.95 (*0-88729-739-0*) Langenscheidt.

Philadelphia. 3rd ed. Access Press Staff. (Illus.). 192p. 1998. pap. 20.00 (*0-06-277230-9*, Access Trvl) HarpInfo.

*__Philadelphia.__ 11th ed. Ed. by Fodors Travel Publications, Inc. Staff. 256p. 2000. pap. 14.50 (*0-679-00399-1*, Pub. by Random Bks Yng Read) Random.

Philadelphia: A Guide to the Nation's Birthplace. Federal Writers' Project Staff. LC 39-4271. (American Guidebook Ser.). 1982. reprint ed. 95.00 (*0-403-02204-5*) Somerset Pub.

Philadelphia: A Guide to the Nation's Birthplace. Federal Writers' Project Staff & Writers Program-WPA Staff. (American Guide Ser.). 1989. reprint ed. lib. bdg. 89.00 (*0-7812-1058-5*, 1058) Rprt Serv.

Philadelphia: A New Urban Direction. Jonathan A. Saidel et al. LC 98-54767. 1999. pap. 21.95 (*0-916101-28-2*) St Joseph.

*__Philadelphia: A Photographic Celebration.__ Running Press Staff. (Illus.). 128p. 2000. 13.98 (*0-7624-0683-6*, Courage) Running Pr.

Philadelphia: A Pictorial Souvenier. Carol Highsmith. LC 98-38557. 1999. 7.99 (*0-517-20488-6*) Random Hse Value.

Philadelphia: A Three Hundred Year History. Ed. by Russell F. Weigley et al. (Barra Bks.). (Illus.). 1982. 27.50 (*0-393-01610-2*) Norton.

Philadelphia: Neighborhoods, Division & Conflict in a Postindustrial City. Carolyn Adams et al. (Comparative American Cities Ser.). 272p. (C). 1991. 49.95 (*0-87722-842-6*) Temple U Pr.

Philadelphia: Neighborhoods, Division, & Conflict in a Postindustrial City. Carolyn Adams et al. (Comparative American Cities Ser.). 272p. 1993. pap. 16.95 (*1-56639-078-8*) Temple U Pr.

*__Philadelphia: Neighborhoods, Division, & Conflict in a Postindustrial City.__ Carolyn Adams. (Illus.). 210p. 1999. reprint ed. pap. text 17.00 (*0-7881-6747-2*) DIANE Pub.

Philadelphia: Port of History, 1609-1837. Charles L. Chandler et al. (Illus.). 82p. 1976. pap. 2.00 (*0-913346-02-0*) Indep Seaport.

Philadelphia: Portrait of an American City. Edwin Wolf, II. LC 90-2306. (Illus.). 367p. 1990. 39.95 (*0-940159-09-0*) Camino Bks.

Philadelphia: Three Centuries of American Art. Philadelphia Museum of Art Staff. LC 76-3170. (Illus.). 666p. 1990. reprint ed. pap. 42.00 (*0-87633-016-2*) Phila Mus Art.

Philadelphia: Three Centuries of American Art. Philadelphia Museum of Art Staff. (Illus.). 666p. 1990. reprint ed. 68.00 (*0-87633-113-4*) Phila Mus Art.

Philadelphia: 1870 Census Index, 2 vols. Ed. by Bradley W. Steuart. 2192p. 1989. lib. bdg. 250.00 (*1-877677-03-5*) Herit Quest.

Philadelphia, a History of the City & Its People, 4 vols. Ellsi P. Oberholtzer. 1993. reprint ed. lib. bdg. 300.00 (*0-7812-5499-X*) Rprt Serv.

Philadelphia Adventure. Lloyd Alexander. 160p. (J). (gr. 4-7). 1992. pap. 3.99 (*0-440-40605-6*) Dell.

Philadelphia Adventure. Lloyd Alexander. 1990. 9.09 (*0-606-00924-8*, Pub. by Turtleback) Demco.

Philadelphia All the Time. Charles Hardy, III. 50p. 1992. 13.95 incl. audio (*0-9635344-0-8*, SD-1231) Spinning Disc.

Philadelphia & Erie Railroad: Its Place in American Economic History. Homer T. Rosenberger & Harry C. Shriver. LC 74-75110. (Illus.). 748p. 1975. lib. bdg. 22.50 (*0-914932-02-0*) Rose Hill.

Philadelphia & Her Merchants, As Constituted Fifty to Seventy Years Ago, As Illustrated by Diagrams of the River Front & Portraits of Some of Its Prominent Occupants, Together with Sketches of Character & Incidents & Anecdotes of the Day. Abraham Ritter. (Illus.). 223p. 1998. reprint ed. lib. bdg. 32.00 (*0-8328-9625-X*) Higginson Bk Co.

Philadelphia & Its Countryside. Ruth H. Seitz. LC 94-92129. (Pennsylvania's Cultural & Natural Heritage Ser.: Vol. 3). (Illus.). 144p. 1994. 29.95 (*1-879441-94-2*) RB Bks.

Philadelphia & Its Manufactures: A Handbook Exhibiting the Development, Variety & Statistics of the Manufacturing Industry of Philadelphia in 1857. Edwin T. Freedley. (Illus.). 504p. 1998. reprint ed. lib. bdg. 52.50 (*0-8328-9624-1*) Higginson Bk Co.

P

An Asterisk (*) at the beginning of an entry indicates that the title is appearing for the first time.

Philadelphia & the China Trade, 1682-1846: Commercial, Cultural, & Attitudinal Effects. Jonathan Goldstein. LC 77-1638. (Illus.). 1978. 30.00 (*0-271-00512-2*) Pa St U Pr.

Philadelphia Architecture: A Guide to the City. 2nd ed. Ed. by John A. Gallery. (Illus.). 188p. 1994. pap. 18.95 (*0-9622908-1-5*) Fndtn Architecture.

Philadelphia Art Now: Artists Choose Artists. Julie Courtney et al. (Illus.). 126p. 1991. pap. 15.00 (*0-88454-075-8*) U of Pa Contemp Art.

Philadelphia-Baltimore Trade Rivalry, 1780-1860. James W. Livingood. LC 70-112557. (Rise of Urban America Ser.). (Illus.). 1976. reprint ed. 21.95 (*0-405-02463-0*) Ayer.

Philadelphia Baptist Tradition of Church & Church Authority, 1707-1814: An Ecumenical Analysis & Theological Interpretation. Francis W. Sacks. LC 89-48402. (Studies in American Religion: Vol. 48). 800p. 1990. lib. bdg. 139.95 (*0-88946-642-4*) E Mellen.

Philadelphia Baseball. Historical Briefs, Inc. Staff. Ed. by Thomas Antonucci & Michael Antonucci. 200p. 1991. pap. 19.95 (*0-89677-046-X*) Hist Briefs.

Philadelphia Big 5: Basketball History. Donald Hunt. (Illus.). 200p. 1996. 19.95 (*1-57167-070-X*) Sports Pub.

***Philadelphia Birds.** James Kavanagh. (Pocket Naturalist Ser.). (Illus.). 12p. (YA). 1999. pap. 5.95 (*1-58355-013-5*, Pub. by Waterford WA) Falcon Pub Inc.

Philadelphia Brand Cream Cheese First Recipe Collection. (Illus.). 224p. 1993. 19.98 (*1-56173-547-7*) Pubns Intl Ltd.

Philadelphia Campaign, 1777-1778. Gregory T. Edgar. 235p. 1998. pap. 24.00 (*0-7884-0921-2*, E121) Heritage Bk.

***Philadelphia Catholic in King James's Court.** Martin de Porres Kennedy. 300p. 1999. pap. 12.95 (*0-9671492-1-5*) Lilyfield Pr.

Philadelphia Church. 27p. (Orig.). pap. 0.95 (*0-937408-19-0*) GMI Pubns Inc.

Philadelphia City & County, Pennsylvania Taxpayers, 1779. T.L.C. Genealogy Staff. LC 92-60092. 144p. (Orig.). 1991. pap., spiral bd. 12.00 (*1-886633-38-X*) TLC Genealogy.

Philadelphia Collects: Art since 1940. Mark Rosenthal. (Illus.). 128p. 1986. 59.95 (*0-8122-7955-7*) U of Pa Pr.

Philadelphia Collects: Art since 1940. Mark Rosenthal & Ann Percy. LC 86-22490. (Illus.). 128p. 1986. pap. 20.00 (*0-87633-066-9*) Phila Mus Art.

Philadelphia Confession. 1998. reprint ed. pap. 4.49 (*0-87377-121-4*) GAM Pubns.

Philadelphia Confession of Faith: Being the London Confession of 1689. 1994. mass mkt. 4.00 (*1-56186-526-5*) Pilgrim Pubns.

Philadelphia County (PA) Court Rules. Ed. by Thomas Davies. 664p. (Orig.). 1996. pap., per. 52.50 (*1-57786-012-8*) Legal Communs.

Philadelphia Creative Directory. Contrib. by Michele Corban et al. 334p. 1998. write for info. (*1-885512-04-X*) Phila Creat.

Philadelphia Creative Directory, Vol. 3. Photos by Michael Furman. (Illus.). 416p. 1995. 50.00 (*1-885512-02-3*) Phila Creat.

Philadelphia Creative Directory, Vol. 4. Ed. by Kathy Kuhl. (Illus.). 450p. (Orig.). 1997. pap. 50.00 (*1-885512-03-1*) Phila Creat.

Philadelphia Dialect Dictionary. Claudio R. Salvucci. 1996. 34.00 (*0-9644234-2-1*) Evol Pubng & Manuf.

Philadelphia Dine-a-Mate. 320p. 1994. pap. 30.00 (*1-57393-016-4*) Dine-A-Mate.

Philadelphia Dine-a-Mate. 224p. 1996. pap. text 30.00 (*1-57393-067-9*) Dine-A-Mate.

Philadelphia Discovery Practice. 1996. 99.00 incl. audio PA Bar Inst.

Philadelphia Eagles. Bob Italia. LC 95-30599. (Illus.). 32p. (gr. 3-8). 1996. lib. bdg. 15.98 (*1-56239-528-9*) ABDO Pub Co.

***Philadelphia Eagles.** 3rd rev. ed. Julie Nelson. (Pro Football Today Ser.). (Illus.). 32p. (YA). (gr. 3-12). 2000. lib. bdg. 22.60 (*1-58341-055-4*, Creat Educ) Creative Co.

***Philadelphia East Entertainment, 2000.** (Illus.). 774p. 1999. pap. 30.00 (*1-880248-57-3*, 0031) Enter Pubns.

Philadelphia Experiment. William Moore. 1987. mass mkt. 5.99 (*0-449-21471-0*) Fawcett.

Philadelphia Experiment Chronicles: Exploring the Strange Case of Alfred Bielek & Dr. M. K. Jessup. Ed. by Commander X. 15.00 (*0-938294-00-8*) Inner Light.

Philadelphia Experiment Murder. Alexandra Bruce. Ed. by Peter Moon. 260p. 1999. pap. 19.95 (*0-9631889-5-X*) Sky Bks NY.

Philadelphia Family: The Houstons & Woodwards of Chestnut Hill. David R. Contosta. LC 88-21596. (Illus.). 226p. (C). 1988. 25.95 (*0-8122-8136-5*); pap. 15.95 (*0-8122-1406-4*) U of Pa Pr.

***Philadelphia Fels, 1880-1920: A Social Portrait.** Evelyn Bodek Rosen. LC 99-31740. (Illus.). 232p. 2000. 28.00 (*0-8386-3823-6*) Fairleigh Dickinson.

Philadelphia Fire. John Edgar Wideman. LC 91-50219. (Vintage Contemporaries Ser.). 208p. 1991. pap. 12.00 (*0-679-73650-6*) Vin Bks.

***Philadelphia Flavor: Restaurant Recipes from the City & the Suburbs.** Connie Correia Fisher. Ed. by Joanne Correia. (Illus.). 320p. 2000. pap. 15.95 (*0-9661200-5-1*) Small Potatoes.

Philadelphia Flowers: Poetry. Roberta H. Whiteman. (Illus.). 128p. (Orig.). 1996. pap. 10.95 (*0-930100-64-6*) Holy Cow.

Philadelphia Flyers see NHL Today

Philadelphia Flyers. Jim Stevens. LC 98-19165. (Inside the NHL Ser.). (J). 1999. 14.95 (*1-57765-052-2*) ABDO Pub Co.

***Philadelphia Flyers Hockey Team.** Glen Macnow. LC 99-12581. (Great Sports Teams Ser.). (Illus.). 48p. (gr. 4-10). 2000. lib. bdg. 18.95 (*0-7660-1279-4*) Enslow Pubs.

Philadelphia Food Companion: The Finest Food Shops in Greater Philadelphia. Alonna F. Smith & Rosita B. Derstine. (Illus.). 174p. (Orig.). 1995. pap. 13.95 (*0-9644975-0-6*) Food Compan Pr.

Philadelphia Garden Book: A Gardener's Guide for the Delaware Valley. Liz Ball. LC 99-18614. (Illus.). 440p. 1999. pap. 24.95 (*1-888608-46-3*) Cool Springs Pr.

Philadelphia Gentlemen: The Making of a National Upper Class. E. Digby Baltzell. LC 89-4362. (Illus.). 476p. 1989. pap. 24.95 (*0-88738-789-6*) Transaction Pubs.

***Philadelphia Ghost Stories.** Charles J. Adams. 1998. pap. text 11.95 (*1-880683-12-1*) Exeter Hse.

***Philadelphia Ghost Stories.** Charles J. Adams. 1998. pap. 11.95 (*0-88068-312-0*) Profesores Universitarios Pro-Divulgacion Academica.

Philadelphia Homestyle Cookbook. Norwood-Fontbonne Home & School Association Staff. Ed. by Wimmer Brothers Books Staff. (Illus.). 288p. 1985. 12.95 (*0-9614938-0-1*) Norwood-Fontbonne.

Philadelphia Images: Philadelphia People, Places & Pastimes by Artists from the University of the Arts. Ed. by James Merlihan. LC 90-71312. (Illus.). 184p. 1990. 40.00 (*0-9627916-0-1*) Univ of Arts Pr.

Philadelphia in Early Picture Postcards, 1900-1930. Philip Jamison, III. LC 90-12843. (Illus.). 128p. (Orig.). 1990. pap. 11.95 (*0-911572-89-9*, Vestal Pr) Madison Bks UPA.

Philadelphia in the Civil War. Frank H. Taylor. (Illus.). 360p. 1992. reprint ed. 25.00 (*0-9631314-0-0*) J M S Civil War.

Philadelphia in Transition: A Demographic History of the City & Its Occupational Groups, 1720-1830. Susan E. Klepp. (Studies in Historical Demography). 368p. 1990. reprint ed. text 25.00 (*0-8240-4164-X*) Garland.

Philadelphia Inquirer Map & Guide to Center City Philadelphia & Surrounding Area. Bill Marsh. Ed. by Ken Bookman. (Illus.). 52p. (Orig.). 1993. pap. 7.99 (*0-9634709-2-2*); write for info. (*0-9634709-3-0*) Phila Newspapers.

***Philadelphia Inquirer's Guide to Historic Philadelphia.** Edward Colimore. (Illus.). 220p. 2000. pap. 14.95 (*0-940159-67-8*) Camino Bks.

***Philadelphia Italian Market Cookbook: The Tastes of South Ninth Street.** Celeste A. Morello. LC 99-96482. (Illus.). 140p. 1999. pap. 24.95 (*0-9677334-0-5*) J & M.

***Philadelphia JobBank, 2000 (Metro)** Adams Media Corporation Staff. 464p. 1999. pap. 16.95 (*1-58062-242-9*) Adams Media.

***Philadelphia JobBank, 2001 (Metro)** (JobBank Ser.). 464p. 2000. pap. 16.95 (*1-58062-449-9*) Adams Media.

Philadelphia Lawyer: A History, 1735-1945. Robert R. Bell. LC 91-50194. (Illus.). 328p. 1992. 49.50 (*0-945636-26-1*) Susquehanna U Pr.

Philadelphia Lawyer in the London Courts. Thomas Leaming. (Illus.). xiii, 199p. 1987. reprint ed. 38.00 (*0-8377-2408-2*, Rothman) W S Hein.

Philadelphia Lawyer in the London Courts. 2nd rev. ed. Thomas Leaming. xv, 199p. 1997. reprint ed. 65.00 (*1-56169-252-2*) Gaunt.

Philadelphia Lawyers on Trial, Vol. 1. Emerita T. Gueson. Ed. by Laurie McBrinn. 200p. 1998. pap. 20.00 (*0-9653861-6-3*) Theresevision.

Philadelphia Magazines & Their Contributors, 1741-1850. Albert H. Smyth. LC 70-119944. (Select Bibliographies Reprint Ser.). 1977. 21.95 (*0-8369-5387-8*) Ayer.

Philadelphia Magazines Guide to Healthcare in the Delaware Valley, 1994-1995. Carol Saline. 1994. pap. 6.95 (*0-9635666-2-8*) Phila Mag.

Philadelphia Main Line Classics II: Cooking up a Little History. Friends & Family of JSC Members & Members of JSC. Ed. by Junior Saturday Club of Wayne Staff. LC 96-83136. (Illus.). 1996. 18.95 (*0-9650818-0-X*) Jr Saturday Clb.

Philadelphia Maritime Museum, 1961-1986. John W. Jackson. (Illus.). 79p. (Orig.). 1987. pap. 10.00 (*0-913346-13-6*) Indep Seaport.

Philadelphia Methodist Church, Putnam County, Georgia, 1860-1890: Register of Members & Notes. Margaret G. Ehrlich & Philadelphia Methodist Church (Putnam County, GA) Staff. LC 98-66680. 47 p. 1998. write for info. (*0-9638026-2-3*) Testing & Tech.

Philadelphia Museum of Art: Handbook of the Collections. Philadelphia Museum of Art Staff. LC 95-23944. 1995. pap. 16.95 (*0-87633-096-0*) Phila Mus Art.

Philadelphia Museum of Art: Handbook of the Collections. Philadelphia Museum of Art Staff. (Illus.). 360p. 1995. text 26.95 (*0-87633-098-7*) Phila Mus Art.

Philadelphia Naval Shipyard. Joseph James Ahearn. (Images of America Ser.). 1999. pap. 14.99 (*0-7524-0873-9*) Arcadia Publng.

***Philadelphia Navy Yard: An Illustrated History.** Jeffrey M. Dorwart. 2000. 45.00 (*0-8122-3575-4*) U of Pa Pr.

Philadelphia Negro. W. E. B. Du Bois. 540p. 1972. 18.95 (*0-405-18100-0*) Ayer.

***Philadelphia Negro.** DuBois. 1999. pap. text 16.95 (*0-8122-1690-3*) U of Pa Pr.

Philadelphia Negro: A Social Study. W. E. B. Du Bois. 560p. 1995. pap. 16.95 (*0-8122-1573-7*) U of Pa Pr.

Philadelphia Orchestra: A Century of Music. Philadelphia Orchestra Association Staff. Ed. by John Ardoin. LC 99-10969. (Illus.). 240p. 1999. 75.00 (*1-56639-712-X*) Temple U Pr.

Philadelphia Orchestra: The Search for a Home. Irvin R. Glazer. LC 95-19769. (Illus.). 160p. 1995. pap. 19.95 (*0-915010-39-9*) Sutter House.

Philadelphia Orchestra Cookbook. Ed. by Anne M. Krout & Doris L. Roberts. (Illus.). 400p. 1980. 16.00 (*0-9607586-0-7*) W Phila Comm.

Philadelphia, PA WW II. Historical Briefs, Inc. Staff. Ed. by Thomas Antonucci & Michael Antonucci. 176p. 1991. pap. 19.95 (*0-89677-026-5*) Hist Briefs.

Philadelphia Phillies. Chris W. Sehnert. LC 96-7598. (America's Game Ser.). (Illus.). 32p. (J). (gr. 3-8). 1997. lib. bdg. 16.48 (*1-56239-664-1*) ABDO Pub Co.

Philadelphia Photographers, 1840-1900. William Brey & Marie Brey. 180p. (Orig.). 1992. pap. text 14.95 (*0-9613955-1-6*) Willowdale Pr.

Philadelphia Plus One: A Traveler's Guide. Nancy Sokoloff. (Illus.). 309p. (Orig.). 1987. pap. 10.95 (*0-943495-00-8*) WhyNot Pr.

Philadelphia Police Department Annual Audit, Fiscal, 1994. Ed. by Donald R. Shopland et al. (Illus.). 564p. (Orig.). 1998. pap. text 50.00 (*0-7881-2843-4*) DIANE Pub.

Philadelphia Police, Past & Present. Howard O. Sprogle. LC 77-156032. reprint ed. 59.50 (*0-404-09134-2*) AMS Pr.

Philadelphia Police, Past & Present. Howard O. Sprogle. LC 72-154590. (Police in America Ser.). (Illus.). 1971. reprint ed. 39.95 (*0-405-03387-7*) Ayer.

Philadelphia Politics from the Bottom Up: The Life of Irishman William McMullen, 1824-1901. Harry C. Silcox. LC 88-70766. (Illus.). 176p. 1989. 32.50 (*0-944190-01-4*) Balch IES Pr.

***Philadelphia Postcards.** Lynn Homan & Thomas Reilly. (Images of America Ser.). 128p. 1999. pap. 18.99 (*0-7385-0238-3*) Arcadia Publng.

Philadelphia Preserved: Catalog of the Historic American Building Survey. Richard J. Webster. 272p. 1981. pap. 22.95 (*0-87722-215-0*) Temple U Pr.

***Philadelphia Presidential Conventions.** R. Craig Sautter. LC 99-75049. (Illus.). 360p. 2000. pap. 19.95 (*0-913204-37-4*, Pub. by December Pr) IPG Chicago.

Philadelphia Quakers in the Industrial Age, 1865-1920. Philip S. Benjamin. LC 76-22967. 301p. 1976. reprint ed. 6.00 (*0-87722-086-7*) Phila Yrly Mtg RSOF.

Philadelphia Quakers, 1681-1981: A Tercentenary Family Album. Robert H. Wilson. (Illus.). 132p. (Orig.). 1981. 11.50 (*0-916838-45-5*) Phila Yrly Mtg RSOF.

Philadelphia Rebel: The Education of a Bourgeoise. Clara Jaeger. LC 87-182089. 237p. 1988. pap. 7.95 (*1-85239-502-8*) Grosvenor USA.

Philadelphia Retirement & Relocation Guide. (Retirement & Relocation Guides Ser.). (Illus.). 350p. 1998. pap. 19.95 (*1-56559-121-6*) HGI-Over Fifty.

Philadelphia Revisions: The Print Department Collects. Kenneth Finkel. LC 85-221841. (Illus.). 50p. 1983. pap. 5.00 (*0-914076-71-X*) Lib Co Phila.

Philadelphia Riots of 1844: A Study of Ethnic Conflict, 43. Michael Feldberg. LC 75-65. (Contributions in American History Ser.: No. 43). (Illus.). 209p. 1975. 55.00 (*0-8371-7876-2*, FGC/, Greenwood Pr) Greenwood.

Philadelphia 76ers see Pro Basketball Today

Philadelphia 76ers. Paul Joseph. LC 96-39609. (Inside the NBA Ser.). (Illus.). 32p. (J). (gr. 3-8). 1997. lib. bdg. 16.95 (*1-56239-769-9*) ABDO Pub Co.

Philadelphia 76ers Basketball Team. Glen Macnow. LC 97-20378. (Great Sports Teams Ser.). (Illus.). 48p. (YA). (gr. 4-10). 1998. lib. bdg. 18.95 (*0-7660-1063-5*) Enslow Pubs.

***Philadelphia 76ers Basketball Team.** Glen Macnow. LC 97-20378. (Great Sports Teams Ser.). (Illus.). 48p. (YA). (gr. 4-10). 1998. pap. 9.95 (*0-7660-1751-6*) Enslow Pubs.

Philadelphia Shakespeare Story: Horace Howard Furness & the Variorum Shakespeare. James M. Gibson. LC 87-45801. (Studies in the Renaissance: No. 23). viii, 308 p. 1990. 42.50 (*0-404-62293-3*) AMS Pr.

***Philadelphia Sports Century.** Philadelphia Daily News Staff. (Illus.). 192p. 2000. 29.95 (*1-58382-059-0*) Sports Pub.

Philadelphia Sports Quiz: Phillies, Athletics, Eagles, 76ers, Warriors, Flyers. Brenda C. Alesii & Daniel Locche. LC 92-38084. 1993. 9.95 (*0-8065-1416-7*, Citadel Pr) Carol Pub Group.

Philadelphia Stories: A Photographic History, 1920-1960. Fredric M. Miller et al. (Illus.). 336p. (C). 1988. 27.95 (*0-87722-551-6*) Temple U Pr.

Philadelphia Story see Best Plays of the Modern American Theatre: Second Series, 1939-1946

Philadelphia Story: A Comedy in Three Acts. Philip Barry. LC 83-45700. reprint ed. 42.50 (*0-404-20018-4*) AMS Pr.

Philadelphia Ten: A Women's Artist Group 1917-1945. Page Talbott & Patricia T. Sydney. LC 98-88685. (Illus.). 175p. 1998. pap. 34.95 (*1-58442-000-6*); pap. 49.95 (*1-58442-047-2*) Galleries at Moore.

Philadelphia, the Place & Its People. Agnes Repplier. 1993. reprint ed. lib. bdg. 89.00 (*0-7812-5823-5*) Rprt Serv.

Philadelphia Theaters: A Pictorial Architectural History. Irvin R. Glazer. (Illus.). 138p. (Orig.). 1993. pap. text 11.95 (*0-486-27833-6*) Dover.

Philadelphia Theatres A-Z: A Comprehensive, Descriptive Record of 813 Theatres Constructed Since 1724. Irvin R. Glazer. LC 85-27131. (Illus.). 290p. 1986. lib. bdg. 69.50 (*0-313-24054-X*, GPT/, Greenwood Pr) Greenwood.

Philadelphia Then & Now. Kenneth Finkel. (Illus.). 128p. 1988. pap. 9.95 (*0-486-25790-8*) Dover.

Philadelphia 200, Performance Audit. Jonathan A. Saidel. (Illus.). 86p. (C). 1998. pap. text 25.00 (*0-7881-7436-3*) DIANE Pub.

***Philadelphia 2001.** Ed. by Zagat Publishers Staff. (Illus.). 2000. pap. 10.95 (*1-57006-236-6*) Zagat.

Philadelphia Victorian: The Building of the Athenaeum. Roger W. Moss. LC 98-10906. (Illus.). 169p. 1998. pap. 35.00 (*0-916530-16-7*) Athenaeum Phila.

Philadelphia Victorian: The Building of the Athenaeum. limited ed. Roger W. Moss. LC 98-10906. (Illus.). 169p. 1998. 75.00 (*0-916530-15-9*) Athenaeum Phila.

***Philadelphia West Entertainment, 2000.** (Illus.). 774p. 1999. pap. 30.00 (*1-880248-58-1*, 0079) Enter Pubns.

***Philadelphia with Children: A Guide to the Delaware Valley, Inlcuding Lancaster & Hershey.** 4th ed. Elizabeth S. Gephart. LC 96-5985. (Illus.). 276p. 2000. pap. 14.95 (*0-940159-62-7*) Camino Bks.

Philadelphia's Best Buildings: In (or Near) Center City. John A. Gallery. (Illus.). 39p. (Orig.). 1995. pap. text 7.95 (*0-9622908-2-3*) Fndtn Architecture.

Philadelphia's Black Elite: Activism, Accommodation, & the Struggle for Autonomy, 1787-1848. Julie Winch. 248p. 1988. 39.95 (*0-87722-515-X*) Temple U Pr.

Philadelphia's Black Elite: Activism, Accommodation, & the Struggle for Autonomy, 1787-1848. Julie Winch. 248p. 1993. pap. 22.95 (*1-56639-088-5*) Temple U Pr.

***Philadelphia's Cultural Landscape: The Sartain Family Legacy.** Ed. by Katharine A. Martinez & Page Talbott. (Illus.). 240p. 2000. 49.50 (*1-56639-791-X*) Temple U Pr.

***Philadelphia's Enlightenment, 1740-1800: Kingdom of Christ, Empire of Reason, Vol. 81.** Nina Reid-Maroney. (Contributions to the Study of World History Ser.: Vol. 81). 2000. write for info. (*0-313-31472-1*, Greenwood Pr) Greenwood.

Philadelphia's First Baptists: A Brief Baptist History of the First Baptist Church of Philadelphia. William D. Thompson. (Illus.). (Orig.). 1989. pap. text 5.00 (*0-9623555-0-X*) First Bptst Ch Phila.

Philadelphia's First Fuel Crisis: Jacob Cist & the Developing Market for Pennsylvania Anthracite. H. Benjamin Powell. LC 77-88471. (Illus.). 1978. 30.00 (*0-271-00533-5*) Pa St U Pr.

Philadelphia's Magazine's Guide to Good Health, 1997. 320p. 1996. 6.95 (*0-9635666-3-6*) Phila Mag.

Philadelphia's Old Ballparks. Rich Westcott. (Baseball in America Ser.). (Illus.). 200p. (C). 1996. 29.95 (*1-56639-454-6*) Temple U Pr.

Philadelphia's Outdoor Art: A Walking Tour. 2nd ed. Roslyn F. Brenner. LC 86-19989. (Illus.). 128p. (Orig.). 1987. pap. 9.95 (*0-940159-00-7*) Camino Bks.

Philadelphia's Philosopher Mechanics: A History of the Franklin Institute, 1824-1865. Bruce A. Sinclair. LC 74-6843. (Illus.). 367p. reprint ed. pap. 113.80 (*0-8357-8267-0*, 203414200088) Bks Demand.

Philadelphia's Progressive Orphanage: The Carson Valley School. David R. Contosta. LC 97-6406. 1997. 34.95 (*0-271-01714-7*) Pa St U Pr.

Philadelphia Experiment & Other Conspiracies. Brad Steiger. 160p. 1990. pap. 15.00 (*0-938294-97-0*) Inner Light.

Philanderer. George Bernard Shaw. Ed. by Julius Novick. LC 79-56700. (Bernard Shaw Early Texts: Play Manuscripts in Facsimile). 470p. 1981. text 20.00 (*0-8240-4576-9*) Garland.

Philanderer. George Bernard Shaw. LC 90-53569. 1991. pap. 7.00 (*0-88734-227-2*) Players Pr.

Philanthropic Foundations: New Scholarship, New Possibilities. Ed. by Ellen C. Lagemann. LC 98-55922. (Philanthropic Studies). (Illus.). 464p. 1999. text 35.00 (*0-253-33500-0*) Ind U Pr.

Philanthropic Foundations & Resources for Health: An Anthology of Sources. Ed. by Rosenkrantz & Barbara S. Gutmann. (Medical Care in the United States Ser.: Vol. 14). 200p. 1990. text 15.00 (*0-8240-8343-1*) Garland.

Philanthropic Foundations in Latin America. Ed. by Ann H. Stromberg. LC 68-54409. 223p. 1956. 29.95 (*0-87154-837-2*) Russell Sage.

***Philanthropic Foundations In the Twentieth Century, 72.** Joseph C. Kiger. LC 99-16097. (Contributions to the Study of World History Ser.: Vol. 72). 232p. 2000. 55.00 (*0-313-31223-0*) Greenwood.

Philanthropic Giving. F. Emerson Andrews. LC 56-5824. 318p. 1950. 45.00 (*0-87154-022-3*) Russell Sage.

Philanthropic Work of Josephine Shaw Lowell, Containing a Biographical Sketch of Her Life Together with a Selection of Her Public Papers & Private Letters. William R. Stewart. LC 71-172576. (Criminology, Law Enforcement, & Social Problems Ser.: No. 163). (Illus.). 1974. reprint ed. 28.00 (*0-87585-163-0*) Patterson Smith.

Philanthropist. Mason L. Weems. (Notable American Authors Ser.). 1999. reprint ed. lib. bdg. 125.00 (*0-7812-9919-5*) Rprt Serv.

Philanthropists & Their Legacies. Carol G. Traub. LC 96-6520. (Profiles Ser.). (Illus.). 160p. (YA). (gr. 5-12). 1997. lib. bdg. 18.95 (*1-881508-42-0*) Oliver Pr MN.

Philanthropists, Therapists & Activists. Gerald C. Rothman. LC 84-23514. 179p. 1985. 19.95 (*0-87073-521-7*); pap. 14.95 (*0-87073-524-1*) Schenkman Bks Inc.

Philanthropy: Four Views. Michael Novak et al. 100p. (Orig.). 1988. 32.95 (*0-912051-20-5*); pap. 21.95 (*0-912051-21-3*) Transaction Pubs.

Philanthropy: Private Means, Public Ends. Ed. by Kenneth W. Thompson. (Exxon Education Foundation Series on Rhetoric & Political Discourse: Vol. 4). 176p. (Orig.). (C). 1987. lib. bdg. 41.50 (*0-8191-5816-X*, Pub. by White Miller Center) U Pr of Amer.

Philanthropy & Cultural Context: Western Philanthropy in South, East & Southeast Asia in the 20th Century. Ed. by Soma Hewa & Philo Hove. LC 97-24849. 352p. 1997. 57.50 (*0-7618-0792-6*) U Pr of Amer.

Philanthropy & Culture: The International Foundation Perspective. Kathleen D. McCarthy. LC 84-2356. 190p. 1984. pap. 22.95 (*0-8122-1173-1*) U of Pa Pr.

P

An Asterisk (*) at the beginning of an entry indicates that the title is appearing for the first time.

Philanthropy & Economic Development, 162. Richard F. America. LC 94-30933. (Contributions in Economics & Economic History Ser.: Vol. 162). 248p. 1995. 62.95 (*0-313-28809-7*, Greenwood Pr) Greenwood.

Philanthropy & Gerontology: The Role of American Foundations, 12. Ann H. Sontz. LC 89-1679. (Contributions to the Study of Aging Ser.: No. 12). 159p. 1989. 49.95 (*0-313-26097-4*, SZF/, Greenwood Pr) Greenwood.

Philanthropy & Jim Crow in American Social Science, 82. John H. Stanfield. LC 84-8995. (Contributions in Afro-American & African Studies: No. 82). (Illus.). 216p. 1985. 57.95 (*0-313-23894-4*, SNE/, Greenwood Pr) Greenwood.

Philanthropy & Law in Asia: A Publication of the Asia Pacific Philanthropy Consortium. Thomas Silk. LC 98-32336. 1999. 39.95 (*0-7879-4510-2*) Jossey-Bass.

Philanthropy & Learning with Other Papers. Frederick P. Keppel. LC 36-14158. reprint ed. 20.00 (*0-404-03660-0*) AMS Pr.

Philanthropy & Marketing: New Strategies for Fund Raising. James G. Lord. LC 81-50197. 203p. (C). 1981. lib. bdg. write for info. (*0-939120-00-3*); ring bd. 65.00 (*0-939120-01-1*) Third Sector.

Philanthropy & Peace. Francis Neilson. 1979. lib. bdg. 79.95 (*0-685-96634-8*) Revisionist Pr.

Philanthropy & Public Policy. Ed. by Frank G. Dickinson. (Fiscal Studies Ser.: No. 7). 159p. 1962. reprint ed. 41.40 (*0-87014-468-5*) Natl Bur Econ Res.

Philanthropy & Social Progress: Seven Essays. Jane Addams et al. LC 75-108221. (Criminology, Law Enforcement, & Social Problems Ser.: No. 104). 1970. reprint ed. 15.00 (*0-87585-104-5*) Patterson Smith.

Philanthropy & Social Progress: Seven Essays by Jane Addams, Robert A. Woods, Father J. O. S. Huntington, Prof. Franklin H. Giddings, & Bernard Bosanquet, Delivered Before the School of Applied Ethics at Plymouth, Mass. During the Session of 1892. Jane Addams et al. LC 79-95059. (Select Bibliographies Reprint Ser.). 1977. 21.95 (*0-8369-5061-5*) Ayer.

Philanthropy & the Business Corporation. Marion R. Fremont-Smith. LC 72-83835. 110p. (C). 1972. pap. 14.95 (*0-87154-279-X*) Russell Sage.

Philanthropy & the Dynamics of Change in East & Southeast Asia. Ed. by Barnett F. Baron. LC 91-71259. (Occasional Papers of the East Asian Institute). 181p. (Orig.). 1991. pap. 12.00 (*0-913418-05-6*) Columbia U E Asian Inst.

Philanthropy & the Hospitals of London: The King's Fund, 1897-1990. F. K. Prochaska. (Illus.). 320p. 1992. text 75.00 (*0-19-820266-0*) OUP.

Philanthropy & the Nonprofit Sector in a Changing America. Ed. by Charles Clotfelter & Thomas Ehrlich. LC 98-31856. (Illus.). 544p. 1999. text 35.00 (*0-253-33521-3*) Ind U Pr.

Philanthropy & Voluntarism: An Annotated Bibliography. Daphne N. Layton. LC 87-12032. 308p. 1987. 18.50 (*0-87954-198-9*) Foundation Ctr.

Philanthropy at Independent Schools. Helen A. Colson. 1996. pap. 30.00 (*0-934338-83-3*) NAIS.

Philanthropy in Communities of Color: Sharing & Helping in Eight Communities of Color. Ed. by Bradford Smith et al. LC 98-27909. (Philanthropic Studies). 186p. 1999. text 29.95 (*0-253-33493-4*) Ind U Pr.

Philanthropy in England, 1480-1660: A Study of the Changing Pattern of English Social Aspirations. Wilbur K. Jordon. LC 78-5651. (Illus.). 410p. 1978. reprint ed. lib. bdg. 35.00 (*0-313-20467-5*, JOPH, Greenwood Pr) Greenwood.

Philanthropy in the Americas: New Directions & Partnerships. Ed. by Bruce E. Henderson. LC 92-41396. 168p. (C). 1992. pap. 18.95 (*1-56000-680-3*, Pub. by U Miami N-S Ctr) L Rienner.

Philanthropy in the History of American Higher Education. Jesse B. Sears. 137p. 1989. 32.95 (*0-88738-314-9*) Transaction Pubs.

Philanthropy in the World's Traditions. Ed. by Warren Ilchman et al. LC 97-51241. (Philanthropic Studies). 400p. 1998. 35.00 (*0-253-33392-X*) Ind U Pr.

***Philanthropy, Nationalism & the Growth of Civil Society in Romania.** Maria Bucur. (Working Papers of the Johns Hopkins Comparative Nonprofit Sector Project: Vol. 31). (Illus.). 32p. 1998. pap. text 6.00 (*1-886333-36-X*) JH Univ Inst Pol Studies.

Philanthropy's Role in Civilization: Its Contribution to Human Freedom. Arnaud C. Martz. 206p. (C). 1991. 39.95 (*0-88738-405-6*) Transaction Pubs.

Philaster - By Beaumont & Fletcher. Francis Beaumont. Ed. by Dora J. Ashe. LC 75-127980. (Regents Renaissance Drama Ser.). 184p. reprint ed. pap. 57.10 (*0-8357-4103-6*, 203686900005) Bks Demand.

Philatelic Commemoration of Emancipation 150 - 1848-1998. Robert V. Vaughn. (Illus.). 18p. 1998. spiral bd. 15.00 (*1-890985-07-4*) Aye-Aye Arts.

***Philatelic Fantasies of British North America (1860-1910)** David F. Sessions. (Illus.). 156p. 1999. pap. text 29.50 (*0-9652431-3-3*) C G Firby.

Philatelic Forgers: Their Lives & Works. rev. ed. Varro Tyler. 1991. 30.00 (*0-940403-38-2*); pap. 14.95 (*0-940403-37-4*) Linns Stamp News.

Philatelic Gems, No. 2. Donna O'Keefe. (Illus.). 168p. 1985. reprint ed. pap. 9.95 (*0-940403-03-X*) Linns Stamp News.

Philatelic Gems, No. 3. Donna O'Keefe. (Illus.). 168p. 1987. pap. 9.95 (*0-940403-02-1*) Linns Stamp News.

Philatelic Gems, No. 3. Donna O'Keefe. (Illus.). 168p. 1987. reprint ed. pap. 9.95 (*0-940403-04-8*) Linns Stamp News.

Philatelic Gems, No. 4. Donna O'Keefe. (Illus.). 168p. 1989. 30.00 (*0-940403-17-X*) Linns Stamp News.

Philatelic Gems, No. 5. Donna O'Keefe. (Illus.). 168p. 1991. 30.00 (*0-940403-45-5*); pap. 9.95 (*0-940403-44-7*) Linns Stamp News.

Philatelic Gems, Set. Donna O'Keefe. 1989. pap. 55.00 (*0-940403-16-1*) Linns Stamp News.

Philatelic History of Space Exploration Pt. I: The Pioneer Years, 1904-1960. Ed. by Lester E. Winick. 1986. write for info. (*0-9616382-0-6*) R&W Ent.

Philatelic Horses & Horse Relatives. Ruth Y. Wetmore. (Illus.). 212p. 1990. pap. 16.00 (*0-935991-09-3*) Am Topical Assn.

Philatelic Periodicals of the United States & Canada. Gary A. Van Cott. (Illus.). 126p. (Orig.). 1991. pap. 19.95 (*0-9630793-0-1*) Van Cott Info.

Philatelic Ramble Through Chemistry. E. Heilbronner & F. A. Miller. 278p. 1998. 225.00 (*3-906390-17-9*) Wiley.

Philatelie a la Francaise. Martin F. Stempien, Jr. et al. Ed. by Harlan F. Stone. (Seminar Textbook Ser.). (Illus.). vii, 101p. (Orig.). 1991. pap. 14.95 (*0-911989-23-4*) Philatelic Found.

Philately: The Catalog of the Collectors Club Library. Collectors Club Library Staff. 1974. 160.00 (*0-8161-1538-9*, G K Hall & Co) Mac Lib Ref.

Philately of the Third Reich: Postage & Propaganda. Alf Harper. LC 99-209886. 360p. 1998. 55.00 (*1-885184-01-8*) Album Pubng.

***Philbrook: The Perfect Setting, 2000.** Ed. by Anne Burlingame & Barbara Horn. 128p. 1999. 16.95 (*0-86659-019-6*) Philbrook Mus Art.

Philbrook Museum of Art: A Guide to the Villa & Its Gardens. James J. Yoch. LC 91-62151. (Illus.). 89p. (Orig.). 1991. pap. 11.95 (*0-86659-033-1*) Philbrook Mus Art.

Philbrook Museum of Art: A Handbook to the Collection. Joan C. Troccoli et al. LC 91-62150. (Illus.). 246p. (Orig.). 1991. pap. 15.95 (*0-86659-034-X*) Philbrook Mus Art.

Philby of Arabia. Elizabeth Monroe. 1998. pap. 21.95 (*0-86372-239-3*, Pub. by Garnet-Ithaca) LPC InBook.

Philby of Arabia. Elizabeth Monroe. 7.95 (*0-7043-3346-5*, Pub. by Quartet) Charles River Bks.

Philco Radio, 1928-1942. Ron Ramirez & Michael Prosise. LC 93-85275. (Illus.). 160p. 1993. pap. 29.95 (*0-88740-547-9*) Schiffer.

Philebus. Plato. Tr. & Intro. by Dorothea Frede. LC 93-587. 150p. 1993. pap. text 9.95 (*0-87220-170-8*); lib. bdg. 32.95 (*0-87220-171-6*) Hackett Pub.

Philebus. Plato. Tr. by Robin A. Waterfield from GRE. LC 83-164424. 160p. 1983. pap. 9.95 (*0-14-044395-9*, Penguin Classics) Viking Penguin.

Philebus of Plato. Plato. Ed. by Robert G. Bury. LC 72-9284. (Philosophy of Plato & Aristotle Ser.). (ENG & GRE.). 1977. reprint ed. 25.95 (*0-405-04834-3*) Ayer.

***Philegatia: Living a Vision, Leaving a Legacy.** Glenn E. Young-Preston. Ed. by Cynthia L. Young-Preston. (Illus.). 132p. 2000. pap. 24.95 (*0-9675972-0-X*) Young-Preston.

Philemon: Real Friendships in an Unreal World. Jeff Adams. Date not set. 14.95 (*0-9643021-9-5*) Reality Living.

Philemon 2, Peter - Jude: Portraits of the Christian Experience see Filemon 2, Pedro - Judas: Cuadros de la Experiencia Cristiana

Philemon's Problem. James T. Burthchaell. LC 98-35615. 334p. 1998. pap. 18.00 (*0-8028-4549-5*) Eerdmans.

Philharmonic Gets Dressed. Karla Kuskin. LC 81-48658. (Charlotte Zolotow Bk.). (Illus.). 48p. (J). (ps-3). 1982. 15.95 (*0-06-023622-1*) HarpC Child Bks.

Philharmonic Gets Dressed. Karla Kuskin. LC 81-48658. (Trophy Picture Bk.). (Illus.). 48p. (J). (ps-3). 1986. pap. 5.95 (*0-06-443124-X*, HarpTrophy) HarpC Child Bks.

Philharmonic Gets Dressed. Karla Kuskin. (J). 1986. 11.15 (*0-606-03257-6*, Pub. by Turtleback) Demco.

Philharmonic Society of New York: A Memorial see Early Histories of the New York Philharmonic

Philharmonic Society of New York: Its First Hundred Years see Early Histories of the New York Philharmonic

Philharmonic Society of New York & Its Seventy-Fifth Anniversary: A Retrospective see Early Histories of the New York Philharmonic

Philhellenes. C. M. Woodhouse. LC 78-149828. (Illus.). 192p. 1975. 28.50 (*0-8386-7912-9*) Fairleigh Dickinson.

Philidor Countergambit. James West. 55p. (Orig.). 1994. pap. 6.50 (*0-945470-42-8*) Chess Ent.

Philinte de Molire. P. Fabre D'Eglantine. Ed. by Judith K. Proud. (Exeter French Texts Ser.: No. 97). (FRE.). 100p. 1996. pap. 19.95 (*0-85989-496-7*, Pub. by Univ Exeter Pr) Northwestern U Pr.

Philip see Complete Works of William Makepeace Thackeray

Philip Aaberg: Piano Solos. 112p. 1995. otabind 14.95 (*0-7935-3788-6*, 00308262) H Leonard.

Philip & Alexander: The Unification of Greece. LC 96-39463. (Nations & Their Leaders Ser.). 1998. lib. bdg. write for info. (*0-531-11362-0*) Watts.

Philip & Alexander of Macedon. David G. Hogarth. 1984. lib. bdg. 90.00 (*0-8490-3239-3*) Gordon Pr.

Philip & Alexander of Macedon. David G. Hogarth. LC 75-154154. (Select Bibliographies Reprint Ser.). 1977. reprint ed. 25.95 (*0-8369-5770-9*) Ayer.

Philip & Alex's Guide to Web Publishing. rev. ed. Philip Greenspun. LC 99-21939. (Illus.). 450p. (C). 1999. pap. 44.95 (*1-55860-534-7*) Morgan Kaufmann.

Philip Augustus: King of France, 1180-1223. Jim Bradbury. LC 97-45566. (C). 1998. pap. 73.13 (*0-582-06058-3*, Pub. by Addison-Wesley) Longman.

Philip Boileau: Painter of Fair Women. Dorothy Ryan. (Illus.). (Orig.). 1980. pap. 9.95 (*0-910664-47-1*) Gotham.

Philip C. Jessup International Law Moot Court Competition, 44 bks., Set. Philip C. Jessup. Ed. by Association of Student International Law Societies & American Society of International Law Staff. LC 80-85091. 1981. 3400.00 (*0-89941-094-4*, 300730) W S Hein.

Philip Crosby's Reflections on Quality: 295 Inspirations from the World's Foremost Quality Guru. Philip B. Crosby. LC 95-37400. 144p. 1995. pap. 10.95 (*0-07-014525-3*) McGraw.

Philip Dru: Administrator. E. M. House. 1991. lib. bdg. 79.95 (*0-8490-4617-3*) Gordon Pr.

Philip Eulenberg: The Kaiser's Friend, 2 Vols. Johannes Haller. Tr. by Ethel C. Mayne. LC 72-148883. (Select Bibliographies Reprint Ser.). 1977. reprint ed. 54.95 (*0-8369-5651-6*) Ayer.

Philip Farkas: Legacy of a Master. M. Dee Stewart. 1992. 18.00 (*0-317-02838-3*) Instrumental.

Philip Farkas & His Horn: A Happy Worthwhile Life. Nancy J. Fako. LC 98-70105. (Illus.). 320p. 1998. 30.00 (*0-9662587-0-3*) Crescent Pk Mus.

Philip Farkas & His Horn: A Happy, Worthwhile Life. Nancy J. Fako. (Illus.). 320p. 1998. pap. 25.00 (*0-9662587-1-1*) Crescent Pk Mus.

Philip Freneau: The Poet of the Revolution. Mary Austin. 285p. 1993. reprint ed. lib. bdg. 79.00 (*0-7812-5266-0*) Rprt Serv.

Philip Freneau, the Poet of the Revolution. Mary H. Austin. (Collected Works of Mary Hunter Austin). 285p. 1998. reprint ed. lib. bdg. 88.00 (*1-58201-529-5*) Classic Bks.

Philip Glass: Solo Piano. (Illus.). 60p. 1991. pap. 17.95 (*0-8256-1297-7*, AM82181) Music Sales.

Philip Glass: Songs from Liquid Days. (Illus.). 132p. 1990. pap. 24.95 (*0-8256-2587-4*, AM76605) Music Sales.

Philip Grausman: Sculptures & Drawings. Howard E. Wooden. (Illus.). 16p. (Orig.). 1988. pap. 5.00 (*0-939324-33-4*) Wichita Art Mus.

Philip Guston. Robert Storr. (Modern Masters Ser.). 1986. pap. 22.95 (*0-89659-656-7*) Abbeville Pr.

Philip Guston. Robert Storr. LC 86-1030. (Modern Masters Ser.). (Illus.). 128p. 1986. 35.00 (*0-89659-665-6*); pap. 14.95 (*1-55859-250-4*) Abbeville Pr.

***Philip Guston: A New Alphabet, the Late Transition.** Philip Guston et al. LC 00-36669. 2000. write for info. (*0-89467-085-9*) Yale Art Gallery.

***Philip Guston: Paintings, 1947-1979.** Philip Guston. (Illus.). 2000. 45.00 (*3-7757-0896-0*) Gerd Hatje.

Philip Guston's Late Work: A Memoir. William Corbett. LC 94-14571. (Illus.). 128p. 1994. 17.50 (*0-944072-43-7*) Zoland Bks.

***Philip Gustons Poor Richard.** Debra Bricker Balken. 1999. pap. 17.00 (*0-226-03622-7*); lib. bdg. 55.00 (*0-226-03621-9*) U Ch Pr.

Philip Hall Likes Me, I Reckon. Bette Greene. (J). 1996. 10.09 (*0-606-00443-2*, Pub. by Turtleback) Demco.

Philip Hall Likes Me, I Reckon, Maybe. Bette Greene. (Illus.). 144p. (J). 1975. pap. 4.99 (*0-440-45755-6*, YB BDD) BDD Bks Young Read.

Philip Hall Likes Me, I Reckon Maybe: A Study Guide. Carol Klitzner. Ed. by J. Friedland & R. Kessler. (Novel-Ties Ser.). (J). (gr. 4-6). 1992. pap. text, student ed. 15.95 (*0-88122-730-7*) Lrn Links.

Philip Hooker. Edward Root. 242p. 1993. reprint ed. lib. bdg. 79.00 (*0-7812-5305-5*) Rprt Serv.

Philip II. Geoffrey Woodward. 135p. (C). 1995. pap. 15.93 (*0-582-07232-8*) Longman.

***Philip II & Alexander the Great Unify Greece in World History.** Don Nardo. LC 99-37004. (In World History Ser.). (Illus.). 112p. (gr. 5 up). 2000. lib. bdg. 20.95 (*0-7660-1399-5*) Enslow Pubs.

Philip Johnson. Peter Blake. LC 96-195790. (Studio Paperback Ser.). (Illus.). 256p. 1996. pap. 29.95 (*3-7643-5393-7*, Pub. by Birkhauser) Princeton Arch.

Philip Johnson: La Casa Di Cristallo. Kipris & Whitney. (ITA., Illus.). 160p. 1997. pap. 49.95 (*88-435-5895-1*, Pub. by Art Bks Intl) Partners Pubs Grp.

Philip Johnson: Life & Work. Franz Schulze. LC 95-43299. (Illus.). 478p. (C). 1996. pap. 16.95 (*0-226-74058-7*) U Ch Pr.

Philip Johnson: Recent Works. Jeff Kipnis. LC 97-175532. (Illus.). 129p. 1996. pap. 38.00 (*1-85490-284-9*, Pub. by Wiley) Wiley.

Philip Johnson: The Architect in His Own Words. Hilary Lewis & John O'Connor. LC 94-16057. (Illus.). 208p. 1994. 50.00 (*0-8478-1823-3*, Pub. by Rizzoli Intl) St Martin.

Philip Johnson: Turning Point. Ed. by P. Noever. (Illus.). 72p. 1997. pap. 28.00 (*3-211-82958-X*, Pub. by Birkhauser) Princeton Arch.

Philip Johnson - John Burgee: Architecture, 1979-1985. Ed. by Carleton Knight, III. LC 85-43063. (Illus.). 200p. 1990. 50.00 (*0-8478-0658-8*, Pub. by Rizzoli Intl) St Martin.

***Philip Johnson & Texas.** Frank D. Welch. LC 99-53829. 2000. 39.95 (*0-292-79134-8*) U of Tex Pr.

Philip Johnson & the Museum of Modern Art. Ed. by John Elderfield. (Studies in Modern Art: Vol. 6). (Illus.). 160p. 1997. pap. 19.95 (*0-8109-6182-2*, Pub. by Abrams) Time Warner.

Philip Johnson & the Museum of Modern Art. Ed. by John Elderfield. (Studies in Modern Art: Vol. 6). (Illus.). 160p. 1998. pap. 19.95 (*0-87070-117-7*, 0-8109-6182-2, Pub. by Mus of Modern Art) Abrams.

Philip Johnson in New Canaan. Ed. by Joseph C. Sweet. (Illus.). 74p. 1986. pap. 6.00 (*0-939958-02-3*) New Canaan.

Philip Johnston & the Navajo Code Talkers. 2nd ed. Syble Lagerquest. (Indian Culture Ser.). (Illus.). 32p. 1996. reprint ed. pap. 4.95 (*0-89992-139-6*) Coun India Ed.

Philip Jose Farmer. Mary T. Brizzi. Ed. by Roger C. Schlobin. LC 79-17691. (Starmont Reader's Guide Ser.: Vol. 3). (Illus.). ii, 80p. 1980. pap. 15.00 (*0-916732-05-3*) Millefleurs.

Philip Jose Farmer: The Complete Riverworld Novels, 5 bks. Incl. Dark Design. Fabulous Riverboat. Philip Jose Farmer. Magic Labyrinth. Riverworld. Philip Jose Farmer. 1982. To Your Scattered Bodies Go. Philip Jose Farmer. 1982. 1982. Set pap. 13.25 (*0-425-05835-2*) Berkley Pub.

Philip K. Dick. Douglas A. Mackey. (United States Authors Ser.). 168p. 1988. 22.95 (*0-8057-7515-3*, Twyne) Mac Lib Ref.

Philip K. Dick: Contemporary Critical Interpretations, 63. Ed. by Samuel J. Umland. LC 94-29271. (Contributions to the Study of Science Fiction & Fantasy Ser.: No. 63). 240p. 1995. 59.95 (*0-313-29295-7*, Greenwood Pr) Greenwood.

Philip K. Dick: Forty Articles on Philip K. Dick from Science-Fiction Studies. Ed. by R. D. Mullen et al. 320p. 1992. pap. 14.95 (*0-9633169-1-5*) SF-TH.

Philip K. Dick: The Dream Connection. 2nd ed. Ed. by D. Scott Apel. LC 87-60689. reprint ed. pap. 14.95 (*1-886404-03-8*, 1886404038) Permanent San Jose.

Philip K. Dick Is Dead, Alas. Michael Bishop. 352p. 1993. pap. 12.95 (*0-312-89002-8*) Orb NYC.

Philip K. Dick Reader. Philip K. Dick. LC 96-52695. 410p. 1997. pap. 14.95 (*0-8065-1856-1*, Citadel Pr) Carol Pub Group.

Philip Larkin. Laurence Lerner. (Writers & Their Work Ser.). 80p. (Orig.). 1997. pap. 17.00 (*0-7463-0838-8*, Pub. by Northcote House) U Pr of Miss.

Philip Larkin. Stephen Regan. LC 97-911. 240p. 1997. pap. 18.95 (*0-312-17349-0*); text 45.00 (*0-312-17348-2*) St Martin.

Philip Larkin: A Writer's Life. Andrew Motion. LC 93-71731. 570p. 1993. 35.00 (*0-374-23168-0*) FS&G.

Philip Larkin: A Writer's Life. Andrew Motion. 574p. 1994. pap. 13.00 (*0-374-52407-6*) FS&G.

Philip Larkin: His Life's Work. Janice Rossen. LC 89-51283. 176p. (C). 1990. text 25.95 (*0-87745-271-7*) U of Iowa Pr.

Philip-Lorca Dicorcia. Peter Galassi. (Illus.). 80p. 1995. 24.95 (*0-87070-145-2*, 0-8109-6151-2, Pub. by Mus of Modern Art) Abrams.

Philip Lynott: Songs for While I'm Away. Philip Lynott. (Illus.). 96p. 1996. pap. 17.99 (*1-886894-82-5*, MBS Paperbk) Mus Bk Servs.

Philip Lynott: The Ballad of the Thin Man. Stuart Bailie. (Illus.). 256p. 1996. text 25.99 (*1-886894-83-3*, MBS Paperbk) Mus Bk Servs.

Philip Maliavin. Ed. by A. Korobtsova. (Illus.). (C). 1988. text 50.00 (*0-569-09143-8*, Pub. by Collets) St Mut.

***Philip Marlowe.** Raymond Chandler. (Illus.). 397p. 1999. per. 16.00 (*0-671-03890-7*) PB.

Philip Marlowe Private Eye. Simon & Schuster Staff. 1996. 28.41 (*0-671-56825-6*) Simon & Schuster.

Philip Massinger, 2 vols. Philip Massinger. (BCL1-PR English Literature Ser.). 1992. reprint ed. lib. bdg. 150.00 (*0-7812-7251-3*) Rprt Serv.

Philip Massinger, 2 vols., Vols. 1 - 2. Philip Massinger. Ed. by Arthur Symons. (BCL1-PR English Literature Ser.). 1992. reprint ed. lib. bdg. 150.00 (*0-7812-7262-9*) Rprt Serv.

Philip Massinger: Roman Actor, Maid of Honour, New Way to Pay Old Debts, Believe As You List. Philip Massinger. (BCL1-PR English Literature Ser.). 416p. 1992. reprint ed. lib. bdg. 99.00 (*0-7812-7263-7*) Rprt Serv.

Philip Massinger: The Roman Actor, the Maid of Honor, a New Way to Pay Old Debts, Believe As You List. Philip Massinger. (BCL1-PR English Literature Ser.). 416p. 1992. reprint ed. lib. bdg. 99.00 (*0-7812-7252-1*) Rprt Serv.

Philip Massinger & John Fletcher: A Comparison. Henri J. Makkink. LC 68-1145. (Studies in Drama: No. 39). 1969. reprint ed. lib. bdg. 75.00 (*0-8383-0669-1*) M S G Haskell Hse.

Philip Massinger, 1887-1889. Philip Massinger. LC 72-108511. 59.00 (*0-403-03683-6*) Scholarly.

Philip Mazzei: Jefferson's "Zealous Whig" Ed. & Tr. by Margherita Marchione from FRE. LC 75-29945. 352p. 1975. 9.95 (*0-916322-01-7*); pap. 17.50 (*0-916322-02-5*) Am Inst Ital Stud.

Philip Mazzei: My Life & Wanderings. unabridged ed. Ed. by Margherita Marchione. Tr. by S. Eugene Scalia from ITA. LC 80-69637.Tr. of Memorie della vita e delle peregrinazioni del fiorentino Filippo Mazzei. (Illus.). 438p. (Orig.). (C). 1980. 20.00 (*0-916322-03-3*); pap. 10.00 (*0-916322-04-1*) Am Inst Ital Stud.

Philip Mazzei: World Citizen (Jefferson's "Zealous Whig") Margherita Marchione. 158p. (C). 1994. 36.50 (*0-8191-9698-3*) U Pr of Amer.

Philip McCracken. Philip McCracken. Ed. by Tacoma Art Museum Staff. LC 80-51071. (Illus.). 136p. 1980. 20.00 (*0-295-95771-9*) U of Wash Pr.

Philip Melanchthon: Orations on Philosophy & Education. Philip Melanchthon. Ed. by Sachiko Kusukawa. Tr. by Christine F. Salazar. LC 98-8077. (Texts in the History of Philosophy Ser.). 320p. (C). 1999. text 59.95 (*0-521-58350-0*); pap. text 22.95 (*0-521-58677-1*) Cambridge U Pr.

Philip Melanchthon (1497-1560) & the Commentary. Ed. by Timothy J. Wengert & M. Patrick Graham. (SAP Title Ser.). 304p. 1997. 85.00 (*1-85075-684-8*, Pub. by Sheffield Acad) CUP Services.

Philip Melanchthon's Rhetorical Construal of Biblical Authority: Oratio Sacra. John R. Schneider. LC 90-45963. (Texts & Studies in Religion: Vol. 51). 292p. 1990. lib. bdg. 89.95 (*0-88946-794-3*) E Mellen.

P

Philip Morris & the Arts: A Thirty-Year Celebration. Jere Herzenberg & Marilynn Donini. 116p. (Orig.). 1990. pap. text. write for info. (0-934037-04-3) P Morris.

Philip Morris & the Arts: Thirty-Five Year Report. Karen Brosius & Lisa Walker. 128p. (Orig.). 1993. pap. text. write for info. (0-934037-07-8) P Morris.

Philip Morris Companies, Inc. A Report on the Company's Environmental Policies & Practices. (Illus.). 29p. (C). 1994. reprint ed. pap. text 40.00 (0-7881-0989-8, Coun on Econ) DIANE Pub.

***Philip Morsberger: Paintings & Drawings from the Sixties.** J. Richard Gruber. (Illus.). 12p. 2000. pap. 9.95 (1-890021-10-5) Morris Mus Art.

Philip Neri: The Fire of Joy. Paul Turks. Tr. by Daniel Utrecht. (GER.). 187p. (Orig.). 1995. 12.50 (0-8189-0748-7) Alba.

Philip Noel-Baker (1889-1982) David J. Whittaker. 418p. 1999. pap. 23.00 (1-85072-056-8, Pub. by W Sessions) St Mut.

Philip Nolan & Texas. 1988. 16.95 (0-87244-079-6) Texian.

Philip Nolan's Friends: or Show Your Passports. Edward E. Hale. LC 70-104470. (Illus.). 401p. reprint ed. lib. bdg. 22.50 (0-8398-0751-1) Irvington.

Philip Nolan's Friends: or Show Your Passports. Edward E. Hale. (Illus.). 401p. (C). 1986. reprint ed. pap. text 7.95 (0-8290-1879-4) Irvington.

Philip of Leyden - A Fourteenth Century Jurist: A Study of His Life & Treatise de Cura Republicae et Sorte Principantis. Ed. by P. Leupen. (Rechtshistorische Studies: No. 7). xviii, 300p. 1992. pap. 68.00 (90-271-1678-4, Pub. by Egbert Forsten) Hodlder & Stoughton.

Philip of Macedon. Manolis Andronicos et al. Ed. by Miltiades B. Hatzopoulos & Louisa D. Loukopoulos. (Illus.). 254p. 1980. 60.00 (0-89241-330-1) Caratzas.

Philip of Macedon. Nicholas G. Hammond. LC 94-1067. 1994. text 45.00 (0-8018-4927-6) Johns Hopkins.

Philip of Spain. Henry Kamen. LC 96-52421. (Illus.). 448p. 1997. 40.00 (0-300-07081-0) Yale U Pr.

Philip of Spain. Henry Kamen. (Illus.). 404p. 1999. pap. text 17.95 (0-300-07800-5) Yale U Pr.

Philip One. Marilyn R. Rosenberg. 55p. 1980. pap. 8.00 (0-913615-01-3) Marilyn R Rosenberg.

Philip Pearlstein: Painting to Watercolors. Daniel E. Stetson & Sanford S. Shamen. Ed. by Kevin Boatright. LC 83-51373. (Illus.). 48p. (Orig.). 1983. pap. text 6.00 (0-932660-08-8) U of NI Dept Art.

Philip Pearlstein: Paintings & Watercolors. Michael Auping. LC 81-51324. (Illus.). 16p. 1981. pap. 4.95 (0-916758-05-2) Ringling Mus Art.

Philip Randolph: Labor Leader. James Neyland. (Black American Ser.). (Illus.). 192p. (YA). 1994. mass mkt. 3.95 (0-87067-777-2, Melrose Sq) Holloway.

Philip Roth & the Jews. Alan Cooper. LC 95-19591. (SUNY Series in Modern Jewish Literature & Culture). 319p. (C). 1996. pap. text 19.95 (0-7914-2910-5) State U NY Pr.

Philip Roth Revisited. Jay L. Halio. LC 92-12173. (Twayne's United States Authors Ser.: No. 611). 160p. 1992. 22.95 (0-8057-3962-9, Twyne) Mac Lib Ref.

Philip Schaff (1819-1893) Portrait of an Immigrant Theologian. Gary K. Pranger. LC 96-39549. (Swiss American Historical Society Ser.: Vol. 11). 305p. (C). 1997. text 45.95 (0-8204-2847-7) P Lang Pubng.

Philip Second. W. T. Walsh. 1972. lib. bdg. 59.95 (0-8490-0823-9) Gordon Pr.

Philip Second of Spain. Martin Hume. LC 68-25245. (World History Ser.: No. 48). (Illus.). 1968. reprint ed. lib. bdg. 75.00 (0-8383-0206-8) M S G Haskell Hse.

Philip Simon Miller: Butcher, Banker & Benefactor: His Life & Legacy in Douglas County, Colorado. Debbie Buboltz-Bodle. LC 98-46446. 1998. write for info. (0-929526-84-8) Double B Pubns.

***Philip Taaffe: Composite Nature: A Conversation with Stan Brakhage.** Philip Taaffe & Stan Brakhage. (Illus.). 160p. 1998. 75.00 (0-935875-16-6) P Blum Edit.

Philip Taaffe: New Paintings. Contrib. by Philip Taaffe. 1991. 5.00 (0-685-62540-0) Gagosian Gallery.

***Philip Taaffe: Recent Paintings.** Rene Ricard. Ed. by Raymond Foye. (Illus.). 20p. 1999. pap. 40.00 (1-880154-31-5) Gagosian Gallery.

P

Philip Thaxter: A Novel. Charles A. Washburn. LC 79-164578. (American Fiction Reprint Ser.). 1977. reprint ed. 28.95 (0-8369-7055-1) Ayer.

Philip the Fair & Boniface VIII: State vs. Papacy. 2nd ed. C. T. Wood. LC 76-23207. (European Problem Studies). 124p. 1976. reprint ed. pap. 11.50 (0-88275-454-8) Krieger.

Philip the Fair & the Ecclesiastical Assemblies of 1294-95. J. H. Denton. LC 90-56108. (Transactions Ser.: Vol. 81, Pt. 1). 83p. (Orig.). (C). 1991. pap. 18.00 (0-87169-811-0, T811-DEJ) Am Philos.

Philip IV & the Decoration of the Alcazar of Madrid. Steven N. Orso. LC 85-19442. (Illus.). 330p. 1986. reprint ed. pap. 102.30 (0-608-07163-3, 206738800009) Bks Demand.

Philip the Fox. Doris L. Voss-Bark. LC 66-10511. (Illus.). (J). (gr. 3-6). 1967. 14.95 (0-8023-1105-9) Dufour.

Philip II. William T. Walsh. LC 87-51071. 770p. 1989. reprint ed. 37.50 (0-89555-327-9) TAN Bks Pubs.

Philip II. 3rd ed. Geoffrey Parker. 264p. 1995. pap. 16.95 (0-8126-9279-9) Open Court.

Philip the Second & the Sacred War. John Buckler. (Supplements to Mnemosyne Ser.: No. 109). (Illus.). xvi, 224p. (Orig.). 1989. pap. text 75.50 (90-04-09095-9) Brill Academic Pubs.

Philip the Second of Macedon: A Life from the Ancient Sources. Compiled by Alfred S. Bradford. LC 92-235. 224p. 1992. 47.95 (0-275-94250-3, C4250, Praeger Pubs) Greenwood.

Philip II, the First Modern King. Jean H. Mariejol. 1977. 22.95 (0-8369-6948-0, 7829) Ayer.

***Philip III & the Pax Hispanica, 1598-1621: The Failure of Grand Strategy.** Paul C. Allen. LC 99-40557. (Historical Publications). (Illus.). 333p. 2000. 35.00 (0-300-07682-7) Yale U Pr.

Philip Towle, Hampton, New Hampshire: His English Origins & Some American Descendants. William H. Jones. 101p. (Orig.). 1995. pap. text 12.00 (0-7884-0190-4) Heritage Bk.

Philip II. Marilyn R. Rosenberg. 70p. 1980. pap. 8.00 (0-913615-02-1) Marilyn R Rosenberg.

***Philip Vera Cruz: A Personal History of Filipino Immigrants & the Farmworkers Movement.** 3rd ed. Craig Scharlin & Lilia V. Villanueva. LC 00-29902. (Illus.). 208p. 2000. pap. 16.95 (0-295-97984-4) U of Wash Pr.

Philip Webb. Kirk. text 84.00 (0-471-98708-5) Wiley.

Philip William Otterbein. Lynn W. Turner. 19p. 1976. pap. 1.00 (1-880927-06-3) Gen Comm Arch.

Philip Wilson Steer. Ysanne Holt. (Illus.). 143p. 1993. 32.00 (1-85411-073-X, Pub. by Seren Bks); pap. 15.95 (1-85411-074-8, Pub. by Seren Bks) Dufour.

Philipino (Tagalog)-German, German-Philipino (Tagalog) Dictionary: Worterbuch Filipino-Deutsch-Filipino. Heinrich Kelz & H. Smason. (GER & TAG.). 157p. 1986. 45.00 (0-8288-1109-1, F14152) Fr & Eur.

***Philipok.** Ann Keay Beneduce et al. LC 99-55298. (Illus.). 32p. (J). (ps-1). 2000. 16.99 (0-399-23482-9, Philomel) Peng Put Young Read.

Philipp Brothers: The Rise & Fall of a Trading Giant. Helmut Waskis. 1992. 55.00 (0-947671-60-9) Metal Bulletin.

***Philipp Franz von Siebold & His Era: Prerequisites, Developments, Consequences & Perspectives.** Ed. by Arnulf Thiede et al. LC 99-39683. (Illus.). 150p. 1999. 58.00 (3-540-64185-8) Spr-Verlag.

Philipp Jakob Spener. K. J. Stein. 1986. pap. 9.95 (0-910452-65-2) Covenant.

Philipp Jakob Spener und Seine Pia Desideria: Die Weiterfuhrung der Reformvorschlage der Pia Desideria in Seinem Spateren Schrifttum. Hyeong-Eun Chi. (Europaische Hochschulschriften Ser.: Reihe 23, Bd. 562). (GER., Illus.). 208p. 1997. 42.95 (3-631-49393-2) P Lang Pubng.

Philipp Melanchthon: Annotations on the First Epistle to the Corinthians. Ed. & Tr. by John P. Donnelly from LAT. (Reformation Texts with Translation Ser.: No. 2). 178p. (C). 1995. pap. 20.00 (0-87462-701-X) Marquette.

Philipp Reis: Inventor of the Telephone. Silvanus P. Thompson. LC 74-4696. (Telecommunications Ser.). (Illus.). 200p. 1979. reprint ed. 18.95 (0-405-06060-2) Ayer.

Philipp II: Von Makedonien und Griechenland in den Jahren von 346 bis 338. Fritz R. Wust. LC 72-7910. (Greek History Ser.). (GER.). 1973. reprint ed. 28.95 (0-405-04806-8) Ayer.

Philipp von Zesen-Samtliche Werke Vol. 16, Band 7. Ed. by Ferdinand Van Ingen et al. (Ausgaben Deutscher Literatur des XV bis XVIII Jahrhunderts Ser.). iv, 626p. (C). 1990. lib. bdg. 383.10 (3-11-012127-1) De Gruyter.

Philippe, Duc D'Orleans: Regent of France. Christine Pevitt. LC 97-27581. 384p. 1997. 30.00 (0-87113-695-3, Atlntc Mnthly) Grove-Atltic.

Philippe, Duke of Orleans: Regent of France, 1715-1723. J. H. Shennan. (Illus.). 1979. 16.95 (0-500-87009-8, Pub. by Thames Hudson) Norton.

Philippe Halsman: A Retrospective: Photographs from the Halsman Family Collection. Philippe Halsman. Ed. by Jane H. Bello & Steve Bello. LC 98-15245. (Illus.). 212p. (gr. 8). 1998. 75.00 (0-8212-2373-9) Little.

Philippe in Monet's Garden. Lisa Carmack. (J). (ps-1). 1998. 10.95 (0-87846-456-5) Mus Fine Arts Boston.

Philippe Petain und Pierre Laval: Das Bild Zweier Kollaborateure Im Franzosischen Gedachtnis. Christiane Florin. 447p. 1997. 63.95 (3-631-31882-0) P Lang Pubng.

Philippe Pinel et Son Oeuvre au Point de Vue de la Medecine Mentale. Rene Semelaigne. LC 75-16733. (Classics in Psychiatry Ser.). (FRE.). 1976. reprint ed. 17.95 (0-405-07454-9) Ayer.

Philippe Rogier: Eleven Motets. Philippe Rogier & Lavern J. Wagner. (Recent Researches in Music of the Renaissance Ser.: Vol. RRR2). (Illus.). 111p. 1966. pap. 35.00 (0-89579-003-3) A-R Eds.

Philippe Samyn: Architecture & Engineering, 1900-2000. Marc Dubois. LC 99-26856. 1999. write for info. (0-8176-6067-4) Birkhauser.

***Philippe Samyn: Architecture & Engineering 1900-2000.** Marc Dubois. LC 99-26856. (Illus.). 128p. 1999. pap. 49.95 (3-7643-6067-4) Birkhauser.

***Philippe Starck.** Judith Carmel Arthur. 1999. text 14.95 (1-85868-738-1, Pub. by Carlton Bks Ltd) Natl Bk Netwk.

Philippe Starck. Christine Colin. (Illus.). 128p. 1997. pap. 23.50 (2-906571-63-6) Dist Art Pubs.

Philippe Starck. Conway L. Morgan. LC 98-48499. (Illus.). 240p. 1999. pap. 25.00 (0-7893-0227-6, Pub. by Universe) St Martin.

Philippe Starck: Intuition & Invention. Watson Guptill Staff. (Cutting Edge Ser.). 1998. 16.95 (0-8230-1200-X) Watsn-Guptill.

Philippe Verdelot: Madrigals for Four & Five Voices, Vol. 2. Jessie A. Owens. LC 88-32982. (Italian Madrigal Sixteenth Century Ser.: Vol. 29). 1989. text 30.00 (0-8240-5531-4) Garland.

Philippe Verdelot: Madrigals for Four & Five Voices, Vol. 3. Jessie A. Owens. LC 88-32982. (Italian Madrigal Sixteenth Century Ser.: Vol. 30). 148p. 1989. text 30.00 (0-8240-5532-2) Garland.

Philippe Verdelot Vol. 1: Madrigals for Four & Five Voices. Ed. by Jessie A. Owens. LC 88-32982. (16th Century Madrigal Ser.: Vol. 28). 152p. 1989. text 30.00 (0-8240-5530-6) Garland.

Philippi at the Time of Paul & after His Death. Ed. by Charalambos Bakirtzis & Helmut Koester. LC 98-39837. 128p. 1998. pap. 16.00 (1-56338-263-6) TPI PA.

Philippian & Philemon. G. Getty. 1989. pap. 25.00 (0-86217-021-4, Pub. by Veritas Pubns) St Mut.

Philippian Fragment: Chinese Edition. Calvin Miller. Tr. by May-Chun Kam. (CHI.). 139p. 1985. pap. 6.50 (1-56582-080-0) Christ Renew Min.

Philippians. Don Baker. (LifeGuide Bible Studies). 60p. (Orig.). 1985. pap., wbk. ed. 4.99 (0-8308-1013-7, 1013) InterVarsity.

Philippians. Keith L. Brooks. (Teach Yourself the Bible Ser.). 1964. pap. 5.99 (0-8024-6506-4) Moody.

Philippians. F. F. Bruce. (New International Biblical Commentary Ser.). 184p. 1989. pap. 11.95 (0-943575-15-X) Hendrickson MA.

Philippians. Gordon H. Clark. 100p. 1996. pap. 8.95 (0-940931-47-8) Trinity Found.

Philippians. Fred B. Craddock. LC 84-47797. (Interpretation: A Bible Commentary for Teaching & Preaching Ser.). 96p. 1987. 20.00 (0-8042-3140-0) Westminster John Knox.

Philippians. Gordon D. Fee. LC 99-21884. (New Testament Commentary Ser.). 192p. 1999. 16.99 (0-8308-1811-1, 1811) InterVarsity.

Philippians. Gerald F. Hawthorne. (Biblical Commentary Ser.: Vol. 43). 1983. 29.99 (0-8499-0242-8) Word Pub.

Philippians. Henry A. Ironside. LC 96-44163. (The Ironside Commentaries Ser.). 1996. pap. 9.99 (0-87213-413-X) Loizeaux.

Philippians. H. Jones. (Focus on the Bible Commentary Ser.). 8.50 (1-85792-046-5, Pub. by Christian Focus) Spring Arbor Dist.

Philippians. J. B. Lightfoot. LC 94-18837. (Crossway Classic Commentaries Ser.). 224p. 1994. pap. 15.99 (0-89107-800-2) Crossway Bks.

Philippians. John MacArthur, Jr. 2000. 12.99 (0-8024-5262-0) Moody.

Philippians. Navigator Staff. (LifeChange Ser.). 113p. (Orig.). 1986. pap. 7.00 (0-89109-072-X) NavPress.

Philippians. Frank Thielman. (NIV Application Commentary Ser.). 256p. 1995. 22.99 (0-310-49300-5) Zondervan.

Philippians. Geoffrey B. Wilson. 109p. (Orig.). 1983. pap. 7.99 (0-85151-363-8) Banner of Truth.

***Philippians.** rev. ed. Donald Baker. (Orig.). 1999. pap. 4.99 (0-8308-3013-8) InterVarsity.

Philippians: A Message of Encouragement. rev. ed. Marilyn Kunz & Catherine Schell. (Neighborhood Bible Studies). 48p. 1994. pap. 5.99 (1-880266-12-1) Neighborhood Bible.

Philippians: A Study in Joy! Bob Yandian. 155p. 1997. 29.95 (1-885600-02-X) B Yandian Minist.

Philippians: A Translation with Notes. R. Paul Caudill. LC 80-70403. (Orig.). 1981. pap. 2.25 (0-938980-00-9) Blue Ridge.

***Philippians: An Expositional Commentary.** James M. Boice. LC 99-59700. 320p. 2000. 25.99 (0-8010-1190-6) Baker Bks.

Philippians: An Expositional Commentary. James M. Boice. 320p. 1982. reprint ed. mass mkt. 19.99 (0-310-21501-3, 10310P) Zondervan.

Philippians: God's Guide to Joy. Ronald Klug. (Fisherman Bible Studyguide Ser.). 40p. 1981. pap. 4.99 (0-87788-680-6, H Shaw Pubs) Waterbrook Pr.

Philippians: Joy under Pressure. Tim Stafford. (Great Books of the Bible). 64p. 1995. pap. 5.99 (0-310-49811-2) Zondervan.

Philippians: Joy Under Stress. Serendipty House Staff. (301 Depth Bible Study Ser.). 1998. pap. text 5.99 (1-57494-101-1) Serendipty Hse.

Philippians: Rejoice in the Lord Always. (God's Word for Today Ser.). 1997. pap. 5.50 (0-570-09515-8, 20-2662) Concordia.

***Philippians: Running the Race.** Bill Hybels. 96p. 1999. pap. 6.99 (0-310-23314-3) Zondervan.

Philippians: Where Life Advances. Roy L. Laurin. LC 86-7177. (Life Commentary Ser.). 208p. 1987. reprint ed. pap. 10.99 (0-8254-3134-4) Kregel.

Philippians/Colossians. J. Vernon McGee. (Thru the Bible Commentary Ser.: Vol. 48). 1997. pap. 6.97 (0-7852-0783-X) Nelson.

Philippians - Colossians - Philemon. Harlyn J. Kuschel. (People's Bible Commentary Ser.). 228p. (Orig.). 1992. pap. 9.99 (0-570-04588-6, 12-8006) Concordia.

Philippians & Colossians. (Life Application Bible Study Guide Ser.). 96p. 1990. pap. 5.99 (0-8423-2733-9, 022733-9) Tyndale Hse.

Philippians & Philemon. Mary Ann Getty. (Sacra Pagina Ser.). Date not set. write for info. (0-8146-5820-2, M Glazier) Liturgical Pr.

Philippians & Philemon. Carolyn Osiek. LC 99-40978. (New Testament Commentaries Ser.). 160p. 2000. pap. 19.95 (0-687-05822-8) Abingdon.

Philippians & Philemon: Critical & Exegetical Commentary. Marvin R. Vincent. Ed. by Samuel R. Driver & Charles A. Briggs. (International Critical Commentary Ser.). 248p. 1897. 39.95 (0-567-05031-9, Pub. by T & T Clark) Bks Intl VA.

Philippians Check. Scott Wright. (Illus.). 98p. (YA). 1999. pap. 8.95 (0-7392-0102-6, PO2993) Morris Pubng.

Philippians, Colossians, & Philemon. Bruce B. Barton et al. LC 95-6670. (Life Application Bible Commentary Ser.). 275p. 1995. pap. 14.99 (0-8423-2974-9) Tyndale Hse.

Philippians, Colossians, & Philemon. Bible Staff. LC 97-25920. (Shepherd's Notes). 1997. pap. text 5.95 (1-55819-689-7) Broadman.

Philippians-Colossians & Philemon. Harlyn J. Kuschel. Ed. by William E. Fischer. (The People's Bible Ser.). 48p. 1987. pap. text, student ed. 5.00 (0-938272-57-8, 22-2198) WELS Board.

Philippians, Colossians, & Thessalonians. William Barclay. 240p. 1993. pap. 21.00 (0-7152-0280-4, Pub. by St Andrew) St Mut.

Philippians, Colossians, Philemon. John A. Knight. Ed. by William H. Greathouse. (Bible Exposition Ser.: Vol. 9). 300p. 1985. 14.99 (0-8341-0320-6) Beacon Hill.

Philippians, Colossians, Philemon. Harlyn J. Kuschel. LC 86-60431. (People's Bible Ser.). 228p. (Orig.). 1986. pap. 10.99 (0-8100-0241-8, 15N0425) Northwest Pub.

Philippians, Colossians, Philemon. Richard R. Melick, Jr. (New American Commentary Ser.: Vol. 32). 416p. 1991. 27.99 (0-8054-0132-6) Broadman.

Philippians IV. Barry Rush. (Inter Acta Logos Ser.). (Illus.). 2p. (C). 1994. student ed., ring bd. 2.75 (1-885702-68-X, 741-058s, Inter Acta) WSN Pr.

Philippians IV, 4 bks., Set. Barry Rush. (Inter Acta Logos Ser.). (Illus.). 2p. (C). 1994. teacher ed., ring bd. 3.50 (1-885702-69-8, 741-055t, Inter Acta) WSN Pr.

Philippians I. Barry Rush. (Inter Acta Logos Ser.). (Illus.). 2p. (C). 1994. student ed., ring bd. 2.75 (1-885702-36-1, 741-055s, Inter Acta) WSN Pr.

Philippians I, 4 bks., Set. Barry Rush. (Inter Acta Logos Ser.). (Illus.). 2p. (C). 1994. teacher ed., ring bd. 3.50 (1-885702-37-X, 741-055t, Inter Acta) WSN Pr.

Philippians III. Barry Rush. (Inter Acta Logos Ser.). (Illus.). 2p. (C). 1994. teacher ed., ring bd. 3.50 (1-885702-67-1, 741-055t, Inter Acta); student ed., ring bd. 2.75 (1-885702-66-3, 741-057s, Inter Acta) WSN Pr.

Philippians: Triumph in Christ (Everyman's Bible Commentary) see Filipenses: Triunfo en Cristo

Philippians II. Barry Rush. (Inter Acta Logos Ser.). (Illus.). 2p. (C). 1994. student ed., ring bd. 2.75 (1-885702-62-0, 741-056s, Inter Acta) WSN Pr.

Philippians II, 4 bks., Set. Barry Rush. (Inter Acta Logos Ser.). (Illus.). 2p. (C). 1994. teacher ed., ring bd. 3.50 (1-885702-63-9, Inter Acta) WSN Pr.

Philippics. Marcus Tullius Cicero. (Loeb Classical Library: No. 189). 670p. 1926. 18.95 (0-674-99208-3) HUP.

Philippies of Desmosthenes. Frank B. Tarbell. (Notable American Authors). 1999. reprint ed. lib. bdg. 125.00 (0-7812-8978-5) Rprt Serv.

Philippine-American Relations: A Guide to Manuscript Sources in the United States. Ed. by Shiro Saito. LC 82-12140. 256p. 1982. lib. bdg. 95.00 (0-313-23632-1, SPH/, Greenwood Pr) Greenwood.

Philippine Bases: U. S. Security at Risk. A. James Gregor & Virgilio Aganon. LC 87-8910. 146p. (Orig.). (C). 1987. pap. text 15.50 (0-89633-111-3) Ethics & Public Policy.

Philippine Birds. John E. DuPont. 490p. 1971. 60.00 (0-913176-03-6, Delaware Estuary) Weidner & Sons.

Philippine Brittlestars: Echinodermata: Ophiuroidea, Described by R. Koehler (1922): A Corrected & Annotated List of Type Specimens. Cynthia Ahearn. LC 92-23874. (Smithsonian Contributions to Zoology Ser.: No. 537). 19p. reprint ed. pap. 30.00 (0-7837-4381-5, 204412100012) Bks Demand.

Philippine Colonial Democracy. Ed. by Ruby R. Paredes. LC 87-51575. (Monographs: No. 32). (Illus.). 166p. 1989. pap. 15.00 (0-938692-34-8) Yale U SE Asia.

Philippine Communication: An Introduction. Ed. by Crispin C. Maslog. 399p. (Orig.). (C). 1989. pap. 16.50 (971-11-0061-4, Pub. by New Day Pub) Cellar.

Philippine Cookbook. Reynaldo Alejandro. (Illus.). 256p. 1985. reprint ed. pap. 14.95 (0-399-51144-X, Perigee Bks) Berkley Pub.

Philippine Cookery & Household Hints. H. Villacorta-Alvarez. (Illus.). 256p. 1977. 8.95 (0-318-36298-8) Asia Bk Corp.

Philippine Cooking in America. M. R. Doanto. 134p. 1991. 15.95 (0-318-36299-6) Asia Bk Corp.

Philippine Debt & Poverty. Rosalinda Pineda-Ofreneo. 120p. (C). 1991. text 80.00 (0-85598-049-4, Pub. by Oxfam Pubns); pap. text 28.00 (0-85598-050-8, Pub. by Oxfam Pubns) St Mut.

Philippine Defender: A Fighter Pilot's Diary, 1941-1942. David L. Obert. LC 92-71109. 175p. (Orig.). 1992. pap. 12.95 (0-927562-12-X) Levite Apache.

Philippine Diary: A Journal of Life As a Japanese Prisoner of War. Robert A. Barker. Ed. by Paul Barker & Harry Gordon. (Illus.). 180p. 1990. 27.50 (0-9624999-1-9) R A Barker Found.

Philippine Economy & the United States: Studies in Past & Present Interactions. Ed. by Norman G. Owen. LC 82-74314. (Michigan Papers on South & Southeast Asia: No. 22). xvi, 208p. (Orig.). 1984. pap. 16.95 (0-89148-025-0); text 16.95 (0-89148-024-2) Ctr S&SE Asian.

Philippine Folk Fiction & Tales. Teresita V. Pil. 1977. pap. 7.50 (971-10-0300-7, Pub. by New Day Pub) Cellar.

Philippine Folk Literature: The Myths. Ed. by Damiana L. Eugenio. (Philippine Folk Literature Ser.: No. 2). 512p. 1994. pap. text 38.00 (971-542-019-2, Pub. by U of Philippines Pr) UH Pr.

Philippine Folk Literature: The Riddles. Ed. by Damiana L. Eugenio. LC 94-945531. (Philippine Folk Literature Ser.: No. 5). 876p. (Orig.). 1995. pap. text 50.00 (971-542-035-4) U of Philippines Pr.

Philippine Folk Tales. Mabel Cole. LC 78-67699. (Folktale Ser.). (Illus.). reprint ed. 37.50 (0-404-16073-5) AMS Pr.

Philippine Food Adventures for Children. Violeta A. Noriega. (Illus.). (Orig.). (J). (gr. 1-9). 1996. pap. 15.95 (0-9636557-3-6) Paperworks.

Philippine Foreign Policy Toward the U. S., 1972-1980: Reorientation? Virginia S. Capulong-Hallenberg. (Stockholm Studies in Politics: No. 33). 292p. (Orig.). 1987. pap. 83.00 (91-7146-478-6, Pub. by Stockholms Universitet) Coronet Bks.

Philippine Gay Culture: The Last Thirty Years: Binabe to Bakla, Silahis to MSM. J. Neil Garcia. LC 96-946369. 418 p. 1996. write for info. (971-542-090-7) UH Pr.

An Asterisk (*) at the beginning of an entry indicates that the title is appearing for the first time.

Philippine Higher Education: Toward the 21st Century. E. Nelson Swinerton. LC 90-48693. 208p. 1991. 55.00 (*0-275-93807-7*, C3807, Praeger Pubs) Greenwood.

Philippine Holdings in the Library of Congress, 1960-1987: A Bibliography. Compiled by A. Kohar Rony. LC 92-3438. 702p. 1993. 46.00 (*0-8444-0744-5*) Lib Congress.

Philippine Hospitality: A Gracious Tradition of the East. Lily G. O'Boyle & Reynaldo Alejandro. Ed. by Sonia Ner & Lyn Almario. 224p. 1988. 55.00 (*0-944863-00-0*) Acacia Corp.

Philippine Hoya Species. Dale Kloppenburg. 101p. (C). 1991. student ed. 14.95 (*0-9630489-0-2*) Orca Pub.

Philippine Independence: Motives, Problems & Prospects. Grayson L. Kirk. LC 72-2377. (FDR & the Era of the New Deal Ser.). 278p. 1974. reprint ed. lib. bdg. 37.50 (*0-306-70486-2*) Da Capo.

Philippine Industrialization: Foreign & Domestic Capital. Kunio Yoshihara. 190p. 1986. pap. 18.95 (*0-19-582620-5*) OUP.

Philippine Islands: The United States Army Campaigns of World War 2. Jennifer Bailey. 23p. 1992. pap. 1.00 (*0-16-035879-5*) USGPO.

Philippine Justice System: The Independence & Impartiality of the Judiciary & Human Rights from 1986 till 1997. Jan W. Bakker. LC 98-164482. 234p. Date not set. reprint ed. pap. 72.60 (*0-608-20633-4*, 207206900003) Bks Demand.

Philippine Law Journal, 1914-1931, 10 vols. 1914. 350.00 (*0-8377-9198-7*, Rothman) W S Hein.

Philippine Left on the Eve of World War II. 2nd ed. James S. Allen. LC 92-4722. (Studies in Marxism: Vol. 29). 167p. 1993. 32.95 (*0-930656-67-9*); pap. 14.95 (*0-930656-68-7*) MEP Pubns.

Philippine Literature in English. L. Y. Yabes. 1972. lib. bdg. 250.00 (*0-87968-568-9*) Krishna Pr.

Philippine Localities & Global Perspectives: Essays on Society & Culture. Raul Pertierra. LC 95-943873. 228p. 1997. pap. text 20.00 (*971-550-148-6*, Pub. by Ateneo de Manila Univ Pr) UH Pr.

Philippine Migration: The Settlement of the Digos-Padada Valley, Davao Province. Paul D. Simkins & Frederick L. Wernstedt. LC 73-154010. (Monographs: No. 16). (Illus.). 147p. 1970. 8.50 (*0-938692-13-5*) Yale U SE Asia.

Philippine Municipal Fisheries: A Review of Resources Technology & Socioeconomics. Ian R. Smith et al. (Illus.). 87p. 1983. pap. text 12.00 (*0-89955-388-5*, Pub. by ICLARM) Intl Spec Bk.

Philippine Pagans: The Autobiographies of Three Ifugaos. Roy F. Barton. LC 76-44686. reprint ed. 49.50 (*0-404-15903-6*) AMS Pr.

Philippine Policy Toward Sabah: A Claim to Independence. Lela G. Noble. (Monographs: No. 33). viii, 267p. 1977. 24.00 (*0-8165-0598-5*) Assn Asian Studies.

*__Philippine Politics & Society in the Twentieth Century: Colonial Legacies, Post-Colonial Trajectories.__ Eva-Lotta E. Hedman & John T Sidel. LC 00-28445. (Politics in Asia Ser.). 2000. write for info. (*0-415-14791-3*) Routledge.

Philippine Portrait. Photos by Lam Kam Chuen. (Illus.). 160p. 1999. 35.00 (*0-8478-2169-2*, Pub. by Rizzoli Intl) St Martin.

Philippine Recipes Made Easy, Vol. 1. Violeta A. Noriega. LC 93-84175. (Illus.). (Orig.). 1993. pap. text 12.95 (*0-9636557-0-1*) Paperworks.

Philippine Republic. Leandro H. Fernandez. LC 68-57571. (Columbia University. Studies in the Social Sciences: No. 268). reprint ed. 20.00 (*0-404-51268-2*) AMS Pr.

Philippine Revolution: The Leader's View. Jose M. Sison & Rainer Werning. 200p. 1989. 35.00 (*0-685-26888-8*); pap. 14.50 (*0-685-26889-6*) Taylor & Francis.

Philippine Revolution, 1986: Model of Nonviolent Change. Douglas J. Elwood. (Illus.). vi, 60p. (Orig.). 1986. pap. 7.50 (*971-10-0303-1*, Pub. by New Day Pub) Cellar.

Philippine Short Stories, 1925-1940. Ed. by Leopoldo Y. Yabes. LC 97-948417. 596p. 1999. reprint ed. pap. text 55.00 (*971-542-083-4*) UH Pr.

Philippine Society & the Individual: Selected Essays of Frank Lynch, 1949-1976. Ed. by Aram A. Yengoyan & Perla Q. Makil. LC 82-72447. (Michigan Papers on South & Southeast Asia: No. 24). xvii, 469p. 1984. pap. 15.95 (*0-89148-029-3*) Ctr S&SE Asian.

Philippine State & the Marcos Regime: The Politics of Export. Gary Hawes. LC 86-29218. (Cornell Studies in Political Economy). (Illus.). 200p. 1987. 35.00 (*0-8014-2012-1*) Cornell U Pr.

Philippine State & the Marcos Regime: The Politics of Export. Gary Hawes. LC 86-29237. (Cornell Studies in Political Economy). 197p. reprint ed. pap. 61.10 (*0-608-20899-X*, 207199800003) Bks Demand.

Philippine Temptation: Dialectics of Philippines - U. S. Literary Relations. E. San Juan, Jr. LC 95-47191. (Asian American History & Culture Ser.). 256p. (C). 1996. pap. 22.95 (*1-56639-418-X*); lib. bdg. 59.95 (*1-56639-417-1*) Temple U Pr.

Philippine Tilapia Economics. Ed. by I. R. Smith et al. 261p. 1985. pap. 21.00 (*971-10-2218-4*, Pub. by ICLARM) Intl Spec Bk.

Philippine War, 1899-1902. Brian McAllister Linn. LC 99-33549. (Modern War Studies). (Illus.). 424p. 2000. 39.95 (*0-7006-0990-3*) U Pr of KS.

Philippine Woman in America. Cecilia M. Brainard. 113p. (Orig.). 1991. pap. 12.50 (*971-10-0424-0*, Pub. by New Day Pub) Cellar.

Philippine Writing: An Anthology. Ed. by T. D. Agcaoili. LC 76-98742. 351p. 1971. reprint ed. lib. bdg. 69.50 (*0-8371-3063-8*, AGPW, Greenwood Pr) Greenwood.

Philippines see Markets of Asia-Pacific

Philippines see Festivals of the World

*__Philippines.__ Bernan Press Staff & World Trade Organization Staff. (Trade Policy Review Ser.). 2000. 50.00 (*0-89059-200-4*) Bernan Pr.

Philippines. Lucile Davis. LC 98-3487. (Countries of the World Ser.). (J). 1998. 14.00 (*0-7368-0071-9*) Bridgeview.

Philippines. Lucile Davis. (Countries of the World Ser.). (J). 1998. 14.00 (*0-516-21352-0*) Childrens.

*__Philippines.__ Walter G. Oleksy. LC 99-13701. (Enchantment of the World Ser.). 2000. 32.00 (*0-516-21010-6*) Childrens.

Philippines. Jim Richardson. LC 90-156552. (World Bibliographical Ser.: Vol. 106). 404p. 1989. lib. bdg. 65.00 (*1-85109-077-0*) ABC-CLIO.

*__Philippines.__ Elma Schemenauer. LC 98-45682. (Illus.). 32p. (J). 1999. lib. bdg. 22.79 (*1-56766-601-9*) Childs World.

*__Philippines.__ Anne E. Schraff. LC 99-50691. (Globe-Trotter Club Ser.). (Illus.). 48p. (J). (gr. 4-7). 2000. lib. bdg. 22.60 (*1-57505-124-9*, Carolrhoda) Lerner Pub.

*__Philippines.__ Anne E. Schraff. LC 99-36876. (Ticket to Ser.). (Illus.). 48p. (J). (ps-3). 2000. lib. bdg. 22.50 (*1-57505-149-4*, Carolrhoda) Lerner Pub.

Philippines. Robert E. Baldwin. LC 74-82373. (Foreign Trade Regimes & Economic Development Ser.: No. 5). 187p. reprint ed. pap. 58.00 (*0-8357-7581-X*, 205690200096) Bks Demand.

Philippines. Robert E. Baldwin. (Special Conference Series on Foreign Trade Regimes & Economic Development: No. 5). 187p. 1975. reprint ed. 48.70 (*0-87014-505-3*) Natl Bur Econ Res.

Philippines see Enchantment of the World Series

Philippines see Cultures of the World - Group 3

Philippines. 2nd rev. ed. Nelles Verlag Staff. (Nelles Guides Ser.). (Illus.). 256p. 1999. pap. 15.95 (*3-88618-106-5*) Hunter NJ.

Philippines. 3rd ed. Evelyn Peplow. LC 98-53867. (Odyssey Passport Ser.). (Illus.). 360p. 1999. pap. 19.95 (*962-217-614-3*) Norton.

Philippines. 11th ed. Insight Guides Staff. (Insight Guides). 1998. pap. text 22.95 (*0-88729-482-0*) Langenscheidt.

Philippines see Value of Children: A Cross-National Study

Philippines: A Country Study. Ronald E. Dolan. 418p. 1993. boxed set 35.00 (*0-16-061152-0*) USGPO.

*__Philippines: A Country Study.__ Global Investment & Business Center, Inc. Staff. (World Country Study Guides Library: Vol. 136). (Illus.). 350p. 2000. pap. 59.00 (*0-7397-2434-7*) Intl Business Pubns.

Philippines: A Country Study. 4th ed. Ed. by Ronald E. Dolan. LC 92-39812. (Area Handbook Ser.). 1993. write for info. (*0-8444-0748-8*) Lib Congress.

Philippines A Journey Through the Archipelago. Jonathan W. Best. 1997. 39.95 (*981-3018-99-2*) Tuttle Pubng.

Philippines: A Nation in the Making. Felix M. Keesing. LC 71-179211. reprint ed. 31.50 (*0-404-54839-3*) AMS Pr.

Philippines: A Singular & a Plural Place. David J. Steinberg. LC 82-8407. (Illus.). 160p. (C). 1982. text 31.00 (*0-89158-990-2*) Westview.

Philippines: A Singular & a Plural Place. 3rd ed. David J. Steinberg. 228p. (C). 1994. pap. 26.00 (*0-8133-2038-0*, Pub. by Westview) HarpC.

*__Philippines: A Singular & a Plural Place.__ 4th ed. David J. Steinberg. LC 99-89498. (Nations of the Modern World Ser). 2000. pap. write for info. (*0-8133-3755-0*) Westview.

Philippines: A Study in National Development. Joseph R. Hayden. LC 72-4276. (World Affairs Ser.: National & International Viewpoints). (Illus.). 1050p. 1972. reprint ed. 62.95 (*0-405-04570-0*) Ayer.

Philippines: A Treasure & a Problem. Nicholas Roosevelt. LC 71-100510. reprint ed. 39.50 (*0-404-00618-3*) AMS Pr.

Philippines: An Oxfam Country Profile. Charlie Pye-Smith. LC 98-131254. (Oxfam Country Profiles Ser.). (Illus.). 64p. (C). 1997. pap. 9.95 (*0-85598-367-1*, Pub. by Oxfam Pub) Stylus Pub VA.

Philippines: Colonialism, Collaboration, & Resistance. William J. Pomeroy. Ed. by Betty Smith. LC 92-35454. vi, 352p. (Orig.). 1993. pap. 9.95 (*0-7178-0692-8*) Intl Pubs Co.

Philippines: Debt & Poverty. Rosalinda Pineda Ofreneo. (Trade, Aid & Debt Ser.). (Illus.). 120p. (C). 1991. pap. 11.95 (*0-85598-150-4*, Pub. by Oxfam Pub) Stylus Pub VA.

Philippines: Democracy in Asia. Salvador R. Gonzales. LC 87-63563. 186p. 1987. pap. 8.50 (*0-945197-00-4*) Burgos & Burgos Ltd.

Philippines: From Crisis to Opportunity. World Bank Staff. LC 99-12535. (Operations Evaluation Study Ser.). 76p. 1999. pap. 22.00 (*0-8213-4294-0*, 14294) World Bank.

Philippines: Human Rights after Martial Law: Report of a Mission. fac. ed. Virginia A. Leary. LC 85-207205. (Illus.). 126p. 1984. reprint ed. pap. 39.10 (*0-608-00956-3*, 206180200011) Bks Demand.

Philippines: Major World Nations. Jessie Wee. LC 98-4314. (Major World Nations Ser.). (Illus.). 144p. (YA). (gr. 5 up). 1999. lib. bdg. 19.95 (*0-7910-4984-1*) Chelsea Hse.

Philippines: Pacific Crossroads. Margaret Sullivan. LC 97-7547. (Discovering Our Heritage Ser.). (Illus.). 128p. (J). (gr. 4 up). 1993. lib. bdg. 14.95 (*0-87518-548-7*, Dillon Silver Burdett) Silver Burdett Pr.

Philippines: Pacific Crossroads. Margaret W. Sullivan. LC 97-7547. (Taking Part Ser.). (J). 1998. lib. bdg. 19.95 (*0-382-39813-0*, Dillon Silver Burdett) Silver Burdett Pr.

Philippines: Priorities & Prospects for Development: Report of a Mission Sent to the Philippines by the World Bank. International Bank for Reconstruction & Development Staff. LC 76-17243. (World Bank Country Economic Report). 593p. reprint ed. pap. 183.90 (*0-7837-4462-5*, 204392100001) Bks Demand.

Philippines: The Land of Broken Promises. James R. Goodno. LC 90-27479. 320p. (C). 1991. text 25.00 (*0-86232-862-4*) St Martin.

Philippines: The Next Asian Tiger. Jose Galang. (Euromoney Country Guide Ser.). x, 191p. 1996. 170.00 (*1-85564-457-6*, Pub. by Euromoney) Am Educ Systs.

Philippines: The Political Economy of Growth & Impoverishment in the Marcos Era. James K. Boyce. LC 92-26934. 400p. 1993. text 28.00 (*0-8248-1521-1*); pap. text 15.75 (*0-8248-1522-X*) UH Pr.

Philippines: Tropical Paradise. Evelyn Peplow. (Asian Guides Ser.). (Illus.). 316p. 1994. pap. 15.95 (*0-8442-9690-2*, Passprt Bks) NTC Contemp Pub Co.

Philippines: Tropical Paradise. 2nd ed. Evelyn Peplow. (Asia Guides Ser.). (Illus.). 316p. 1997. pap. 17.95 (*0-8442-4854-1*, 48541, Passprt Bks) NTC Contemp Pub Co.

Philippines: U. S. Policy During the Marcos Years, 1965-1986, Guide & Index, 3 vols. National Security Archive Staff & Chadwyck-Healey Staff. Ed. by Craig Nelson et al. (Making of U. S. Policy Ser.). (Illus.). 1990. write for info. (*0-89887-077-1*) Chadwyck-Healey.

Philippines: Unlawful Killings by Military & Paramilitary Squads. Amnesty International Staff. (SPA.). 66p. (Orig.). 1988. pap. 6.00 (*0-939994-36-4*, Pub. by Amnesty Intl Pubns) Science Pubs.

Philippines: Violations of the Laws of War by Both Sides. Asia Watch Staff. 148p. 1990. pap. 9.00 (*0-929692-52-7*, Asia Watch) Hum Rts Watch.

Philippines - A Country Study Guide: Basic Information for Research & Pleasure. Global Investment Center, USA Staff. (World Country Study Guide Library: Vol. 136). (Illus.). 350p. 1999. pap. 59.00 (*0-7397-1533-X*) Intl Business Pubns.

Philippines Business: The Portable Encyclopedia for Doing Business with the Philippines. Edward G. Hinkelman. LC 95-37479. (Country Business Guide Ser.). (Illus.). 342p. (Orig.). 1995. pap. 24.95 (*1-885073-08-9*) Wrld Trade Pr.

*__Philippines Business Intelligence Report, 190 vols.__ Global Investment & Business Center, Inc. Staff. (World Business Intelligence Library: Vol. 136). (Illus.). 350p. 2000. pap. 99.95 (*0-7397-2634-X*) Intl Business Pubns.

*__Philippines Business Law Handbook.__ Global Investment & Business Center, Inc. Staff. (Global Business Law Handbooks Library: Vol. 136). (Illus.). 2000. pap. 99.95 (*0-7397-2034-1*) Intl Business Pubns.

*__Philippines Business Opportunity Yearbook.__ Global Investment & Business Center, Inc. Staff. (Global Business Opportunity Yearbooks Library: Vol. 136). (Illus.). 2000. pap. 99.95 (*0-7397-2234-4*) Intl Business Pubns.

*__Philippines Business Opportunity Yearbook: Export-Import, Investment & Business Opportunities.__ International Business Publications, U. S. A. Staff & Global Investment Center, U. S. A. Staff. (Global Business Opportunity Yearbooks Library: Vol. 136). (Illus.). 350p. 1999. pap. 99.95 (*0-7397-1334-5*) Intl Business Pubns.

*__Philippines Country Review 2000.__ Robert C. Kelly et al. (Illus.). 60p. 1999. pap. 39.95 (*1-58310-560-3*) CountryWatch.

Philippines Country Studies: Area Handbook. 1995. 8.95 (*0-87511-672-8*) Claitors.

Philippines Earthquake of July 16, 1990, Reconnaissance Report. Ed. by Anshel J. Schiff. (Illus.). 150p. 1991. pap. 15.00 (*0-943198-73-9*, 91-01) Earthquake Eng.

*__Philippines Foreign Policy & Government Guide.__ Contrib. by Global Investment & Business Center, Inc. Staff. (World Foreign Policy & Government Library: Vol. 130). (Illus.). 350p. 1999. pap. 99.00 (*0-7397-3628-0*) Intl Business Pubns.

*__Philippines Foreign Policy & Government Guide.__ Global Investment & Business Center, Inc. Staff. (World Foreign Policy & Government Library: Vol. 130). (Illus.). 350p. 2000. 99.95 (*0-7397-3834-8*) Intl Business Pubns.

*__Philippines Guide.__ 2nd ed. Villa Jill Gale De. 2000. pap. text 18.95 (*1-892975-26-2*) Open Rd Pub.

Philippines, Human Rights Violations & the Labour Movement. 50p. 1991. 4.00 (*0-685-50863-3*, ASA 35-16-91) Amnesty Intl USA.

Philippines in Crisis. W. Scott Thompson. 224p. 1992. text 39.95 (*0-312-05593-5*) St Martin.

Philippines in Pictures. Ed. by Lerner Publications, Department of Geography Staff. (Visual Geography Ser.). (Illus.). 64p. (YA). (gr. 5 up). 1995. lib. bdg. 19.95 (*0-8225-1863-5*, Lerner Publctns) Lerner Pub.

Philippines in World War II, 1941-1945: A Chronology & Select Annotated Bibliography Of Books & Articles in English, 12. Walter F. Bell. LC 99-30327. 12. 280p. 1999. lib. bdg. 69.50 (*0-313-30614-1*) Greenwood.

*__Philippines into the 21st Century: Future Scenarios for Governance, Democracy & Development, 1998-2025 (Ang Pilipinas Tungo Sa Ika-21 Dantaon: Pangkinabukasang Mga Senaryo para sa Pamamahala, Democracy, & Development, 1998-2025.__ Ed. by Jose V. Abueva et al. LC 98-947827. (TAG & ENG.). 242p. 1999. pap. text 38.00 (*971-542-210-1*, Pub. by U of Philippines Pr) UH Pr.

*__Philippines Investment & Business Guide.__ Global Investment & Business Center, Inc. Staff. (Global Investment & Business Guide Library: Vol. 136). (Illus.). 2000. pap. 99.95 (*0-7397-1834-7*) Intl Business Pubns.

Philippines Investment & Business Guide: Economy, Export-Import, Business & Investment Climate, Business Contacts. Contrib. by Russian Information & Business Center, Inc. Staff. (Russia, NIS & Emerging Markets Investment & Business Library-98). (Illus.). 350p. 1998. pap. 99.00 (*1-57751-875-6*) Intl Business Pubns.

*__Philippines Investment & Business Guide: Export-Import, Investment & Business Opportunities.__ International Business Publications, USA Staff & Global Investment Center, USA Staff. (World Investment & Business Guide Library-99: Vol. 136). (Illus.). 350p. 1999. pap. 99.95 (*0-7397-0331-5*) Intl Business Pubns.

Philippines Investment Manual. Asia Law & Practice Staff. 268p. 1997. pap. 225.00 (*962-360-012-7*, Pub. by Asia Law & Practice) Am Educ Systs.

Philippines Is in the Heart: A Collection of Short Stories. Carlos Bulosan, Jr. & E. San Juan. (Illus.). 1979. pap. 15.00 (*971-10-0306-6*, Pub. by New Day Pub) Cellar.

Philippines 1998. Kirsten Ellis. (Traveler's Companion Ser.). (Illus.). 272p. 1998. pap. text 22.95 (*0-7627-0237-0*) Globe Pequot.

Philippines Reader: A History of Colonialism, Neocolonialism, Dictatorship, & Resistance. Ed. by Daniel B. Schirmer & Stephen R. Shalom. LC 86-14637. 428p. 1987. 40.00 (*0-89608-276-8*) South End Pr.

Philippines, the Silenced Democracy. Raul S. Manglapus. LC 75-3342. 221p. reprint ed. pap. 68.60 (*0-8357-8982-9*, 203352300086) Bks Demand.

Philippines to the End of the Commission Government: A Study in Tropical Democracy. Charles B. Elliott. LC 69-10088. 541p. 1969. reprint ed. lib. bdg. 85.00 (*0-8371-0406-8*, ELPH, Greenwood Pr) Greenwood.

Philippines Today: The Challen. David G. Timberman. 1996. text 22.50 (*0-8133-0652-3*) Westview.

Philippines under Aquino: Five Papers. Ed. by R. W. Vokes. (University of Kent at Canterbury, England, Occasional Paper Ser.: No. 11). 84p. (Orig.). (C). 1989. pap. text 12.50 (*0-317-02739-5*, Pub. by CSEAS) Cellar.

*__Philippines with Map.__ (Illus.). 128p. 2000. pap. 14.95 (*1-85974-432-X*) New5 Holland.

Philippines Yesterday, Today & Tomorrow: Political & Socio-Economic Developments. Daniel L. Lacson, Jr. (Institute for Policy Studies Regional Speakers Lecture Ser.). 40p. 1991. 5.50 (*981-210-004-0*, Pub. by Times Academic) Intl Spec Bk.

Philips Family. Joy Haney. 1993. pap. 6.00 (*1-880969-12-2*) Schl Prophet.

Philips Family Record, 1978. George O. Philips. (Illus.). 520p. (Orig.). 1979. pap. 17.50 (*0-940846-00-4*) Hastings Bks.

Philip's Phoenix: Mary Sidney, Countess of Pembroke. Margaret P. Hannay. (Illus.). 346p. 1990. text 60.00 (*0-19-505779-1*) OUP.

Philips Stirling Engine. C. M. Hargreaves. 458p. 1991. 128.50 (*0-444-88463-7*) Elsevier.

Philosophical Thought of Mahatma Gandhi. S. K. Kim. (C). 1996. 36.00 (*81-259-0221-X*, Pub. by Vikas) S Asia.

Philistia in Transition: A History of the Philistines from ca. 1000-730 B. C. E. Carl S. Ehrlich. LC 96-39015. xii, 235p. 1996. 69.50 (*90-04-10426-7*) Brill Academic Pubs.

Philistine, 8 vols. unabridged ed. Elbert Hubbard. 1536p. 1997. reprint ed. 150.00 (*0-936128-68-2*) De Young Pr.

Philistine & Palestinian. Matityahu Glazerson. 182p. 1995. 16.95 (*1-58330-112-7*) Feldheim.

Philistines. Arlo Bates. LC 74-104412. 442p. reprint ed. lib. bdg. 32.00 (*0-8398-0154-8*) Irvington.

Philistines. Arlo Bates. 442p. (C). 1986. reprint ed. pap. text 8.95 (*0-8290-1880-8*) Irvington.

Philistines: Their History & Civilization. Robert A. Macalister. (British Academy, London, Schweich Lectures on Biblical Archaeology Series, 1930). 1974. reprint ed. pap. 25.00 (*0-8115-1253-3*) Periodicals Srv.

Philistines & Their Material Culture. Trude K. Dothan. LC 80-22060. (Illus.). 332p. reprint ed. pap. 94.70 (*0-7837-2501-9*, 2080202) Bks Demand.

Philistines at the Hedgerow: Passion & Property in the Hamptons. Steven S. Gaines. LC 98-11029. 336p. (gr. 8). 1998. 26.95 (*0-316-30941-9*) Little.

Philistines at the Hedgerow: Passion & Property in the Hamptons. Steven S. Gaines. 352p. 1999. pap. 14.95 (*0-316-30907-9*, Back Bay) Little.

Philistines at the Hedgerow: Passion & Property in the Hamptons. Steven S. Gaines. 1999. pap. write for info. (*0-316-30923-0*); pap. write for info. (*0-316-30927-3*) Little.

*__Philistines at the Hedgerow: Passion & Property in the Hamptons.__ Steven S. Gaines. 1999. pap. write for info. (*0-316-30916-8*) Little.

*__Philistines at the Hedgerow: Passion & Property in the Hamptons.__ large type ed. Steven S. Gaines. LC 98-47274. 1998. 26.95 (*1-56895-683-5*) Wheeler Pub.

*__Phillies.__ Matt Silverman. (Total Baseball Companions Ser.). 96p. 2000. mass mkt. 2.50 (*1-892129-69-8*) Total Sprts.

Phillies, '93. Rich Westcott. LC 94-5488. (Illus.). 208p. 1994. pap. 19.95 (*1-56639-231-4*) Temple U Pr.

Phillies Reader. Ed. by Richard Orodenker. LC 96-26884. 256p. 1996. 24.95 (*1-56639-503-8*) Temple U Pr.

Phillies Wit: Words of Wisdom from the Wild, Wacky, Wonderful '93 Phillies. Andrew K. Merz. Ed. by Anne E. Broussard. (Orig.). 1993. pap. 5.95 (*0-9640033-0-9*) Wit Press.

Phillip Blanc in San Francisco. Steve Brooks. (Illus.). 20p. 1972. pap. 3.00 (*0-915572-12-5*) Panjandrum.

Phillip Keller: Inspirational Writings, 4 vols. in 1. Phillip W. Keller. 576p. 1993. 14.99 (*0-88486-086-8*) Arrowood Pr.

Phillip of Australia: An Account of the Settlement at Sydney Cove 1788-92. M. Barnard Eldershaw. LC 73-168974. 366p. 1972. write for info. (*0-207-12514-7*, Pub. by Angus & Roberts) HarpC.

*__Phillip Pullman__ 1999. teacher ed. write for info. (*0-676-78242-6*) Knopf.

P

An Asterisk (*) at the beginning of an entry indicates that the title is appearing for the first time.

Phillipe De Caron: Oeuvres Completes, Pt. 1. Ed. by James Thomson. (Gesamtausgaben - Collected Works: Vol. VI). (ENG & GER.). 120p. 1970. lib. bdg. 4.00 (*0-912024-66-6*) Inst Mediaeval Mus.

Phillipe De Caron: Oeuvres Completes, Pt. 2. Ed. by James Thomson. (Gesamtausgaben - Collected Works: Vol. VI). (ENG & GER.). 130p. 1970. lib. bdg. 4.00 (*0-912024-67-4*) Inst Mediaeval Mus.

Philipians: Joy in Christ see Filipenses: Gozo en Cristo

***Philipine Chase.** Harold R. Miller. LC 99-62090. 400p. 1998. mass mkt. write for info. (*1-893181-02-2*, Simon & Northrop) Le Gesse Stevens.

Philippians & Colossians. (Life Applications Bible Studies). 90p. Date not set. student ed. 5.99 (*0-8423-3406-8*) Tyndale Hse.

Philippians: Commentary see Filipenses: Un Comentario Exegetico y Practico

Philippines Business & Investment Opportunities Yearbook-98: Business, Investment, Export-Import. Contrib. by Russian Information & Business Center, Inc. Staff. (Business & Investment Opportunity Library-98). (Illus.). 350p. 1998. pap. 99.00 (*1-57751-980-9*) Intl Business Pubns.

Philips: Brief History of the Phillips Family, Beginning with the Emigration from Wales & a Detailed Genealogy of the Descendants of John & Benjamin Philips, Pioneer Citizens of Wilson Co. TN. Harry Phillips. (Illus.). 261p. 1994. reprint ed. pap. 42.00 (*0-8328-4371-7*); reprint ed. lib. bdg. 52.00 (*0-8328-4370-9*) Higginson Bk Co.

Phillips: Professional Ethics for Scottish Solicitors. Alfred Phillips. 232p. 1990. pap. 40.00 (*0-406-12890-1*, MICHIE) LEXIS Pub.

Phillips Academy - Andover, Massachusetts: An Illustrated History of the Property. Robert A. Domingue. (Illus.). 202p. (Orig.). 1990. pap. 17.95 (*0-9620726-2-1*) RAD Pub.

***Phillips Academy, Andover: Campus Guide.** Roger C. Reeds & Susan J. Montgomery. (Illus.). 144p. 2000. pap. 24.95 (*1-56898-230-5*) Princeton Arch.

Phillip's Book of Great Thoughts & Funny Sayings. Bob Phillips. LC 92-37072. 345p. 1993. 9.99 (*0-8423-5035-7*) Tyndale Hse.

***Phillips Brooks: Pulpit Eloquence.** David B. Chesebrough. 2000. lib. bdg. write for info. (*0-313-31374-1*) Greenwood.

Phillips Collection, Vol. 1. Stacy Phillips. 1994. pap. 29.95 (*1-56222-582-0*, 94711) Mel Bay.

Phillips Collection, Vol. 2. Stacy Phillips. 392p. 1995. spiral bd. 29.95 (*1-56222-914-1*, 95078) Mel Bay.

Phillips Collection: A Summary Catalogue. Phillips Collection Staff. Ed. by Erika D. Passantino. LC 85-9575. 300p. 1985. pap. 20.00 (*0-943044-05-7*) Phillips Coll.

***Phillips, Craig & Dean: Favorite Songs of All.** 104p. 1999. otabind 16.95 (*0-634-00151-5*) H Leonard.

***Phillips, Craig & Dean D: Restoration.** 88p. 2000. otabind 14.95 (*0-634-01539-7*) H Leonard.

Phillip's Daffodil. Willis F. Cox & Rosemary C. Cox. (Orig.). (J). (gr. k-8). 1987. pap. 2.95 (*0-9610758-4-8*) W F Cox.

Phillip's Dream World: A Coloring Book. Chris Newman. (Illus.). 52p. (Orig.). (J). 1992. pap. 5.95 (*0-9635004-3-0*) Flying Heart.

Phillip's Elite Directory, 1881-1882. J. W. Hartz. 514p. 1994. reprint ed. lib. bdg. 52.50 (*0-8328-3802-0*) Higginson Bk Co.

Phillips Family: Our History, Our Heritage. Shirley P. Friel. (Illus.). 1180p. 1988. 55.00 (*0-9620911-0-3*) S P Friel.

Phillips M. Simkin. Harriett Senie & Diane Karp. (Illus.). 40p. (Orig.). 1987. pap. 10.00 (*0-939351-01-3*) Temple U Tyler Gal.

***Phillips' Maps & Atlases of World War I.** Ed. by Philip Lee Phillips. (C). 2000. reprint ed. 25.00 (*0-7881-9419-4*) DIANE Pub.

***Phillips 1999 Cable Industry Directory.** 6th rev. ed. xvi, 306p. 1999. per. 295.00 (*1-58271-014-7*) Phillips Business.

***Phillips 1999 GPS Directory: Summer 1999.** 14th rev. ed. (Illus.). 334p. 1999. per. write for info. (*1-58271-016-3*) Phillips Business.

***Phillips 1999 GPS Directory: Winter 1999.** 13th rev. ed. 292p. 1999. per. write for info. (*1-58271-009-0*) Phillips Business.

***Phillips 1999 Regional Airline Directory.** 8th rev. ed. xxv, 633p. 1999. per. write for info. (*1-58271-010-4*) Phillips Business.

***Phillips 1999 Satellite Industry Directory.** 21st rev. ed. xxiv, 736p. 1999. per. 295.00 (*1-58271-007-4*) Phillips Business.

***Phillips 1999 Telephone Industry Directory.** rev. ed. 350p. 1999. per. 295.00 (*1-58271-015-5*) Phillips Business.

Phillips Petroleum Co. A Report on the Company's Environmental Policies & Practices. (Illus.). 22p. (C). 1994. reprint ed. pap. text 40.00 (*0-7881-0982-0*, Coun on Econ) DIANE Pub.

***Phillips Satellite Transponder Guide: North American Edition, August-September 1999.** rev. ed. iv, 64p. 1999. per. write for info. (*1-58271-019-8*) Phillips Business.

***Phillips Satellite Transponder Guide: North American Edition, December-January 1999.** rev. ed. iv, 64p. 1998. per. write for info. (*1-58271-006-6*) Phillips Business.

***Phillips Satellite Transponder Guide: North American Edition, February-March 1999.** rev. ed. iv, 64p. 1999. per. write for info. (*1-58271-008-2*) Phillips Business.

***Phillips Satellite Transponder Guide: North American Edition, October-November 1998.** rev. ed. iv, 64p. 1998. write for info. (*1-58271-000-7*) Phillips Business.

Phillip's Science of Dental Mat. 10th ed. Anusavice. 656p. 1996. text 61.95 (*0-7216-5741-9*, W B Saunders Co) Harcrt Hlth Sci Grp.

Phillips 66 1945-1954 Photo Archive: Photographs from the Phillips Petroleum Company Corporate Archives. Ed. by M. Kirn. LC 95-82096. (Photo Archive Ser.). (Illus.). 128p. 1996. pap. 29.95 (*1-882256-42-5*) Iconografix.

Phillips Thygeson, MD: External Eye Disease & the Proctor Foundation. Phillips Thygeson. (Ophthalmology Oral History Ser.). (Illus.). xxvi, 321p. (Orig.). (C). 1988. pap. 45.00 (*0-926866-01-X*) FAAO.

Phillis Wheatley see Women of Achievement

Phillis Wheatley. Levernier. 1998. 22.95 (*0-8057-4019-8*) Macmillan.

Phillis Wheatley. Darlene E. Resling & Lisa Lindel. (Our Changing Lives Ser.). (Illus.). 64p. (YA). (gr. 4-12). 1997. pap. text 7.95 (*1-55596-171-1*, LW2070) Learning Well.

Phillis Wheatley: First African-American Poet. Carol Greene. (Rookie Biographies Ser.). (Illus.). 48p. (J). (gr. k-3). 1995. pap. 4.95 (*0-516-44269-4*) Childrens.

***Phillis Wheatley: Legendary African-American Poet.** Cynthia Salisbury. LC 00-8882. 2001. write for info. (*0-7660-1394-4*) Enslow Pubs.

Phillis Wheatley: Negro Slave. Marilyn Jensen. 242p. (YA). (gr. 5-9). 1987. lib. bdg. 21.95 (*0-87460-326-9*) Lion Bks.

Phillis Wheatley: Poet see Women of Achievement

Phillis Wheatley: Poet. Victoria Sherrow. LC 91-12767. (Junior Black Americans of Achievement Ser.). (Illus.). 76p. (J). (gr. 3-6). 1992. lib. bdg. 15.95 (*0-7910-1753-2*) Chelsea Hse.

Phillis Wheatley: Poet. Victoria Sherrow. (Junior Black Americans of Achievement Ser.). (Illus.). 76p. (J). (gr. 3-6). 1993. pap. 4.95 (*0-7910-2036-3*) Chelsea Hse.

Phillis Wheatley, Poet. Garnet N. Jackson. LC 92-28778. (Beginning Biographies Ser.). (Illus.). (J). (gr. 1-4). 1992. pap. 5.25 (*0-8136-5706-7*); lib. bdg. 10.55 (*0-8136-5233-2*) Modern Curr.

Philly & the Playboy. Linda Turner. (Desire Ser.: No. 701). 1992. pap. 2.89 (*0-373-05701-6*, 5-05701-3) Harlequin Bks.

Philly Firsts: The Famous, Infamous, & Quirky of the City of Brotherly Love. Janice L. Booker. LC 98-56026. (Illus.). 224p. 1999. pap. 9.95 (*0-940159-44-9*) Camino Bks.

Philly Fun-ics: Now Yuze Can Talk Like Us. Michael L. Ellis, III. LC 88-50184. (Illus.). (Orig.). 1993. pap. text 3.50 (*0-929178-17-3*) Valley Forge Pub.

Philly Nite Life: 40 Friendly Philly Nitespots. Ruth B. Harvey. (Illus.). 65p. (Orig.). 1996. pap. 9.95 (*0-9643708-1-6*) R B Harvey.

Philly Stakes. Gillian Roberts. 1990. mass mkt. 5.99 (*0-345-36266-7*) Ballantine Pub Grp.

Philly's Best Bars. Jim Anderson & Lisa Anderson. LC 90-84771. (Illus.). (Orig.). 1990. pap. 8.95 (*0-9628362-0-6*) Black Tooth Pr.

Philly's Best Bars. 2nd ed. Jim Anderson & Lisa Anderson. LC 90-84771. (Illus.). (Orig.). 1991. pap. 8.95 (*0-9628362-1-4*) Black Tooth Pr.

Philly's Favorites Recipe Collection: Delectable Recipes from Philadelphia's Finest Restaurants. Shari Faden Donahue. 196p. 1992. 16.95 (*0-9634287-0-5*) Arimax.

Phillywood, Vol I, Pt. 3. large type ed. Scott D. Martin. LC 96-96210. (Daylight Ser.: No. 2). (Illus.). 100p. (Orig.). 1996. pap. 7.95 (*0-9632177-2-0*, Daylight Bks) Bronx Orig Bks.

Philmont: A History of New Mexico's Cimarron Country. 2nd ed. Lawrence R. Murphy. LC 72-76828. (Illus.). 315p. 1976. reprint ed. pap. 97.70 (*0-608-04133-5*, 206486600011) Bks Demand.

Philmont Story: A Short History of Scouting's Paradise. Stephen Zimmer. (Illus.). 36p. 2000. pap. 0.00 (*0-86534-293-8*) Sunstone Pr.

Philo: Foundations of Religious Philosophy in Judaism, Christianity & Islam, 2 vols., Set. rev. ed. Harry A. Wolfson. LC 47-30635. 1023p. 1962. 65.00 (*0-674-66450-7*) HUP.

Philo: Semitism & the Readmission of the Jews to England, 1603-1655. Rubinstein. LC 98-52706. 1999. text 59.95 (*0-312-22205-X*) St Martin.

Philo & Paul among the Sophists. Bruce W. Winter. (Society for New Testament Studies Monograph Ser.: Vol. 96). 306p. (C). 1997. text 59.95 (*0-521-59108-2*) Cambridge U Pr.

Philo des 19. Jahrhunderts: Studien Zu Salomon Ludwig Steinheim. Ed. by J. H. Schoeps et al. (Haskala - Wissenschaftliche Abhandlungen Ser.: Vol. 4). (GER.). 303p. 1993. write for info. (*3-487-09718-4*) G Olms Pubs.

Philo Fortune's Awesome Journey to His Comfort Zone. Julian F. Thompson. LC 94-24550. 208p. (J). (gr. 7 up). 1995. 16.95 (*0-7868-0067-4*, Pub. by Hyprn Child) Little.

Philo in Early Christian Literature: A Survey. David T. Runia. LC 93-28608. (Compendia Rerum Iudaicarum ad Novum Testamentum Ser.: Vol. 3). 320p. 1993. 50.00 (*0-8006-2828-4*, Fortress Pr) Augsburg Fortress.

***Philo Index.** Peder Borgen et al. LC 99-46459. (GRE & ENG.). 1999. pap. write for info. (*0-8028-4681-5*) Eerdmans.

***Philo Index: A Complete Greek Word Index to the Writings of Philo of Alexandria.** Peder Borgen et al. 384p. 1999. 55.00 (*90-04-11477-7*) Brill Academic Pubs.

***Philo Index: A Complete Greek Word Index to the Writings of Philo of Alexandria.** Peder Borgen et al. LC 99-58967. 383p. 2000. 55.00 (*0-8028-3883-9*) Eerdmans.

Philo Judaeus: His Universe of Discourse. Naomi C. Cohen. LC 95-173093. 381p. 1995. 57.95 (*3-8204-1650-1*) P Lang Pubng.

Philo Marshall Everett: Father of Michigan's Iron Industry & Founder of the City of Marquette. Frank B. Stone. (Illus.). 178p. 1997. 24.00 (*0-9655955-0-1*) F B Stone.

Philo of Alexandria: An Annotated Bibliography, 1937-1986. Roberto Radice & David T. Runia. LC 88-26242. (Supplements to Vigiliae Christianae Ser.: Vol. 8). (Illus.). xli, 469p. 1992. reprint ed. 160.00 (*90-04-08986-1*) Brill Academic Pubs.

Philo of Alexandria: An Exegete for His Time. Peder Borgen. LC 97-29997. (Novum Testamentum, Supplements Ser.: No. 86). x, 322p. 1997. 112.50 (*90-04-10388-0*) Brill Academic Pubs.

Philo of Alexandria: The Contemplative Life, Giants & Selections. Tr. by David Winston. LC 80-84499. (Classics of Western Spirituality Ser.). 448p. 1985. pap. 24.95 (*0-8091-2333-9*) Paulist Pr.

Philo of Alexandria & the Church Fathers: A Collection of Papers. David T. Runia. (Vigiliae Christianae Ser.: No. 32). 300p. 1995. 110.00 (*90-04-10355-4*) Brill Academic Pubs.

Philo of Alexandria & the Timaeus of Plato. D. T. Runia. xii, 617p. 1986. 171.00 (*90-04-07477-5*, PHA, 44) Brill Academic Pubs.

Philo of Byblos: The Phoenician History. Harold W. Attridge & Robert A. Oden, Jr. Ed. by Bruce Vawter. LC 80-25781. (Catholic Biblical Quarterly Monographs: No. 9). x, 110p. 1981. pap. 3.50 (*0-915170-08-6*) Catholic Bibl Assn.

***Philo of Larissa: The Last of the Academic Sceptics.** Charles Brittain. (Oxford Classical Monographs). 280p. 2001. text 70.00 (*0-19-815298-1*) OUP.

Philo-Semitic & Anti-Jewish Attitudes in Post-Holocaust Poland. Marian Mushkat. LC 92-37136. (Symposium Ser.: Vol. 33). 456p. 1992. text 109.95 (*0-7734-9176-7*) E Mellen.

Philo-Sophos. Evelyn M. Huber. 1998. pap. write for info. (*1-57553-735-4*) Watermrk Pr.

Philo White's Narrative of a Cruise in the Pacific to South America & California on the U. S. Sloop of War "Dale", 1841-43. limited ed. Philo White. Ed. by C. L. Camp. (Illus.). 1965. 40.00 (*0-912094-06-0*) Old West.

Philocalia of Origen. Origen. LC 80-2359. reprint ed. 39.50 (*0-404-18911-3*) AMS Pr.

Philocalies sur les Sottises des Mortels: Documents Casanoviens. Giacomo Casanova & Chevalier De Seingalt. Ed. & Pref. by Tom Vitelli. LC 93-71713. (Cahier Ser.: No. 3). (FRE.). 71p. 1993. lib. bdg. 25.00 (*1-883696-00-3*) EveryWare Bks.

Philoctetes see Electra & Other Plays

Philoctetes see Sophocles Two

Philoctetes see Ten Greek Plays in Contemporary Translations

Philoctetes. Sohocles. Ed. by R. G. Ussher. (Classical Texts Ser.). 1990. 59.99 (*0-85668-459-7*, Pub. by Aris & Phillips) David Brown.

Philoctetes. Sophocles. Ed. by R. G. Ussher. (Classical Texts Ser.). 1990. pap. 28.00 (*0-85668-460-0*, Pub. by Aris & Phillips) David Brown.

Philoctetes. Sophocles. Ed. by T. B. Webster. 186p. 1974. pap. text 21.95 (*0-521-09890-4*) Cambridge U Pr.

***Philoctetes.** Sophocles. Ed. by William-Alan Landes. Tr. by Thomas Francklin from GEC. LC 99-47942. 41p. 1999. pap. 7.00 (*0-88734-813-0*) Players Pr.

Philoctetes. Sophocles. Tr. by Keith Dewhurst. 96p. 1999. pap. 13.95 (*1-870259-93-9*, Pub. by Theatre Comm) Consort Bk Sales.

Philoctetes & the Fall of Troy: Plays, Documents, Iconography, Interpretations. Oscar Mandel. LC 80-28524. (Illus.). 287p. 1981. reprint ed. pap. 81.80 (*0-7837-6021-3*, 2045833) Bks Demand.

Philoctetes of Sophocles. Sophocles. Tr. by Thomas Sheridan from GRE. LC 75-158291. (Augustan Translators Ser.). reprint ed. 49.50 (*0-404-54139-9*) AMS Pr.

Philodemus & Poetry: Poetic Theory & Practice in Lucretius, Philodemus & Horace. Ed. by Dirk Obbink. 336p. 1995. text 60.00 (*0-19-508815-8*) OUP.

Philodemus in Italy: The Books from Herculaneum. Marcello Gigante. Tr. by Dirk Obbink. (Body in Theory: Histories of Cultural Materialism Ser.). (Illus.). 184p. 1995. text 34.50 (*0-472-10569-8*, 10569) U of Mich Pr.

Philodemus on Piety Pt. 1: Critical Text with Commentary, Pt. 1. Philodemus. Ed. & Tr. by Dirk Obbink. (Illus.). 688p. 1997. text 145.00 (*0-19-815008-3*) OUP.

***Philodemus: On Poems Bk. 1: Edited with Introduction, Translation, & Commentary.** Philodemus. Ed. by Richard Janko. LC 99-88853. 700p. 2000. text 130.00 (*0-19-815041-5*) OUP.

***Philogelos.** R. D. Dawe. 2000. 34.50 (*3-519-01595-1*) B G Teubner.

Philogelos: or Laughter Lover. Barry Baldwin. (London Studies in Classical Philology: Vol. 10). xii, 134p. (C). 1983. 44.00 (*90-70265-45-1*, Pub. by Gieben) J Benjamins Pubng Co.

***Philogos.org - Tabula Rasa.** Somos, pseud. LC 00-90239. 2000. 15.00 (*0-533-13484-6*) Vantage.

Philography Joins Philately. George Sanders et al. (Illus.). 96p. 1998. pap. 9.95 (*1-56664-149-7*) WorldComm.

Philokalia see Dobrotoljubije, Tom Four

Philokalia see Dobrotoljubije, Tom Five

Philokalia see Dobrotoljubije, Tom Four

Philokalia, Vol. 3. G. E. Palmer. 1986. pap. 16.95 (*0-571-17525-2*) Faber & Faber.

Philokalia: The Bible of Orthodox Spirituality. Anthony M. Coniaris. LC 98-92036. 302 p. 1998. pap. 15.95 (*1-880971-38-0*) Light&Life Pub Co MN.

Philokalia Vol. 1: The Complete Text Compiled by St. Nikodimos of the Holy Mountain & St. Markarios of Corinth. Tr. by Philip Sherrard et al. 384p. (C). 1983. pap. 18.95 (*0-571-13013-5*) Faber & Faber.

Philokalia Vol. 2: The Complete Text. G. E. Palmer. 1982. pap. 19.95 (*0-571-15466-2*) Faber & Faber.

Philokalia Vol. 4: The Complete Text. Ed. by G. E. Palmer et al. Tr. by Philip Sherrard et al from GRE. 340p. 1999. pap. 17.95 (*0-571-19382-X*, Pub. by Faber & Faber) Penguin Books.

Philolakon: Lakonian Studies in Honour of Hector Catling. Ed. by Jan Motyka-Sanders. (Illus.). 334p. 1992. 68.00 (*0-904887-10-3*, Pub. by Brit Sch Athens) David Brown.

Philolaus of Croton - Pythagorean & Presocratic: A Commentary on the Fragments & Testimonia with Interpretive Essays. Carl A. Huffman. LC 92-11194. 464p. (C). 1993. text 105.00 (*0-521-41525-X*) Cambridge U Pr.

Philological & Documentary Studies, Vol. II. Incl. Hasinai Indians of East Texas As Seen by Europeans, 1687-1772. William J. Griffith. 128p. 1953. 15.00 Identification of Lienzo A: A Tracing in the Latin American Library of Tulane University. Ros Paramenter. 1970. 2.00 Interpretation of Bishop Diego de Landa's Maya Alphabet. Marshall E. Durbin. 1969. 4.00 Ordenanza del Senor Cuauhtemoc: Paleografia Traduccion, & Noticia Introdutoria. Silvia Rendon. 1952. 4.00 Palaeographic Guide for Spanish Manuscripts, Fifteenth-Seventeenth Centuries: Roman Numerals. Salo K. Lowe. 1943. 2.50 Personal Archive of Francisco Morazan. William J. Griffith. 90p. 1977. 15.00 (Publications: No. 12). 286p. 1977. 35.00 (*0-939238-13-6*) Tulane MARI.

Philological & Historical: Commentary on Ammianus Marcellinus XIX. P. De Jonge. Tr. by P. De Waard-Dekking from DUT. (Ammianus Marcellinus Ser.). ix, 279p. 1982. 47.00 (*90-6088-072-2*, Pub. by Boumas Boekhuis) Gen Publ ON.

Philological & Historical Commentary on Ammianus Marcellinus XV. P. De Jonge. 82p. 1972. 30.00 (*0-318-41852-5*, Pub. by Egbert Forsten) Hod1der & Stoughton.

Philological & Historical Commentary on Ammianus Marcellinus XVI. P. De Jonge. (Ammianus Marcellinus Ser.). xi, 304p. 1972. 60.00 (*90-6088-035-8*, Pub. by Boumas Boekhuis) Gen Publ ON.

Philological & Historical Commentary on Ammianus Marcellinus XVII. P. De Jonge. (Ammianus Marcellinus Ser.). xi, 404p. 1977. 61.50 (*90-6088-052-8*, Pub. by Boumas Boekhuis) Gen Publ ON.

Philological & Historical Commentary on Ammianus Marcellinus XVIII. P. De Jonge. (Ammianus Marcellinus Ser.). xii, 308p. 1980. 49.50 (*90-6088-065-X*, Pub. by Boumas Boekhuis) Gen Publ ON.

Philological & Historical Commentary on Ammianus Marcellinus XX. Ed. by J. Den Boeft et al. xv, 338p. (C). 1987. 63.00 (*90-6980-012-8*, Pub. by Egbert Forsten) Hod1der & Stoughton.

Philological & Historical Commentary on Ammianus Marcellinus XXI. J. Den Boeft et al. xiv, 310p. 1991. 63.00 (*90-6980-044-6*, Pub. by Egbert Forsten) Hod1der & Stoughton.

Philological & Historical Commentary on Ammianus Marcellinus XXII. J. Den Boeft et al. xiv, 392p. 1996. lib. bdg. 82.00 (*90-6980-086-1*, Pub. by Egbert Forsten) Hod1der & Stoughton.

Philological Essay Concerning the Pygmies of the Ancients. Edward Tyson. LC 72-5732. (Black Heritage Library Collection). 1977. reprint ed. 20.95 (*0-8369-9150-8*) Ayer.

Philologie, Histoire, Philosophie de L'Histoire. Benedetto Bravo. (Veroffentlichung des Comite des Sciences de la Culture Antique-Academie Polonaise des Sciences Ser.). 410p. 1988. reprint ed. 90.00 (*3-487-09041-4*) G Olms Pubs.

Philologie Im Wunderland: Medienkultur Im Deutschunterricht. Ralph Kohnen. (GER., Illus.). 168p. 1998. 28.95 (*3-631-32852-4*) P Lang Pubng.

Philologische Notizen zu Hiob 21-27. Markus Witte. (Beiheft zur Zeitschrift fur die Alttestamentliche Wissenschaft Ser.: No. 234). (GER.). 212p. (C). 1995. lib. bdg. 98.50 (*3-11-014656-8*) De Gruyter.

Philologische Untersuchungen Heft 2: Zu Augusteischen Dichtern. Friedrich Leo & Adolf Kiessling. 122p. write for info. (*0-318-70816-7*) G Olms Pubs.

Philologische Untersuchungen Heft 3: De Biographis Graecis Quaestiones Selectae. Ernst Maas. 169p. write for info. (*0-318-70817-5*) G Olms Pubs.

Philologische Untersuchungen Heft 4: Antigonos von Karystos. Ulrich Von Wilamowitz-Moellendorff. viii, 356p. 1965. write for info. (*3-296-16000-0*) G Olms Pubs.

Philologische Untersuchungen Heft 7: Homerische Untersuchungen. Ulrich Von Wilamowitz-Moellendorff. x, 426p. 1991. write for info. (*3-296-10001-6*) G Olms Pubs.

Philologische Untersuchungen Heft 8: Quaestiones Phaetonteae. Knaack. iv, 81p. write for info. (*0-318-70818-3*) G Olms Pubs.

Philologische Untersuchungen Heft 27: De Boethii Consolatione Philosophiae. Friedrich Klingner. v, 120p. 1966. write for info. (*3-296-13950-8*) G Olms Pubs.

Philologische Untersuchungen Heft 29: Die Ausdrucke fur den Begriff des Wissens in der Vorplatonischen Philosophie. Bruno Snell. viii, 100p. 1992. write for info. (*3-615-00073-0*) G Olms Pubs.

Philologische Untersuchungen Heft 30: Chronologie der Altattischen Komodie. Paul Geissler. xx, 88p. 1979. write for info. (*3-296-12740-2*) G Olms Pubs.

Philologisches Schriftsteller Lexikon. 2nd ed. Wilhelm Poekel. 1974. 95.00 (*0-7859-0844-7*, M-7582) Fr & Eur.

An Asterisk (*) at the beginning of an entry indicates that the title is appearing for the first time.

Philology & Confrontation: Paul Hacker on Traditional & Modern Vedanta. Ed. by Wilhelm Halbfass. LC 95-19393. 369p. (C). 1995. text 59.50 (*0-7914-2581-9*); pap. text 19.95 (*0-7914-2582-7*) State U NY Pr.

Philology & Philosophy: The Letters of Hermann Diels to Theodor & Heinrich Gomperz (1871-1922) Ed. by Maximilian Braun et al. xx, 202p. 1995. 68.00 (*3-615-00172-9*, Pub. by Weidmann) Lubrecht & Cramer.

Philomathic Debating Club. Ralph A. Raimi. xii, 153p. (Orig.). 1991. pap. 25.00 (*0-9609370-1-3*) Raimi.

Philomedidae of the Continental Shelf of Eastern North America & the Northern Gulf of Mexico: Ostracoda: Myodocopina. Louis S. Kornicker. LC 83-600497. (Smithsonian Contributions to Zoology Ser.: No. 393). 82p. reprint ed. pap. 30.00 (*0-608-12016-2*, 202284700030) Bks Demand.

***Philomel Anthology of Humorous Verse.** Philomel Books Staff. LC 99-89398. (Illus.). (J). 2001. write for info. (*0-399-23567-1*, Philomel) Peng Put Young Read.

Philomel Foundation. James Gollin. 208p. 1985. pap. 4.95 (*0-930330-40-4*) Intl Polygonics.

Philomena: Conte Raconte d'Apres Ovide. Chretien de Troyes & C. De Boer. (FRE.). 315p. 1974. 95.00 (*0-685-73321-1*) Fr & Eur.

Philon & Heron: Artillery & Siegecraft in Antiquity. Ed. by James G. DeVoto. LC 96-209336. 1996. pap. 15.00 (*0-89005-561-0*) Ares.

Philonis Alexandrini in Flaccum. Philo. Ed. by W. R. Connor. LC 78-18570. (Greek Texts & Commentaries Ser.). 1979. reprint ed. lib. bdg. 25.95 (*0-405-11414-1*) Ayer.

Philons Griechische und Judiscshe Bildung. Isaak Heinemann. 606p. 1973. reprint ed. write for info. (*3-487-00284-1*) G Olms Pubs.

Philos: A Designation for the Jesus-Disciple Relationship, an Exegetico-Theological Investigation of the Term in the Fourth Gospel. Eldho Puthenkandathil. LC 93-3470. XXIV, 379p. 1993. 61.00 (*3-631-45841-X*) P Lang Pubng.

Philo's Alexandria. Dorothy I. Sly. LC 95-14841. (Illus.). 224p. (C). (gr. 13). 1996. 70.00 (*0-415-09679-0*) Routledge.

Philos of Physics. Lawrence Sklar. 2000. pap. 27.00 (*0-8133-9132-6*) HarpC.

Philsohical Foundations of Education. 6th ed. Howard Ozmon. LC 98-3812. 448p. 1998. pap. text 49.00 (*0-13-624560-9*) P-H.

Philosophaster. Robert Burton. 310p. 1992. reprint ed. pap. 30.00 (*1-56459-227-8*) Kessinger Pub.

Philosophe in the Age of Revolution: Destutt de Tracy & the Origins of "Ideology" Emmet Kennedy. LC 78-56704. (American Philosophical Society, Memoirs Ser.: No. 129). 400p. reprint ed. pap. 124.00 (*0-8357-7917-3*, 203634500002) Bks Demand.

Philosophe in the French Drama of the Eighteenth Century. Ira O. Wade. (Elliott Monographs: Vol. 18). 1926. 25.00 (*0-527-02621-2*) Periodicals Srv.

Philosophen Lexikon: Lexicon of Philosophy. 2nd ed. Rudolf Eisler. (GER.). 1972. 295.00 (*0-8288-6417-9*, M-7583) Fr & Eur.

Philosopher - Kings: The Argument of Plato's "Republic" C. D. Reeve. (Illus.). 400p. 1989. reprint ed. pap. text 19.95 (*0-691-02094-9*, Pub. by Princeton U Pr) Cal Prin Full Svc.

Philosopher & Prophet: Judah Halevi, the Kuzari, & the Evolution of His Thought. Yochanan Silman. LC 94-42398. (SUNY Series in Judaica: Hermeneutics, Mysticism, & Religion). 370p. (C). 1995. text 57.50 (*0-7914-2461-8*); pap. text 18.95 (*0-7914-2462-6*) State U NY Pr.

Philosopher & the Provocateur: The Correspondence of Jacques Maritain & Saul Alinsky. Ed. by Bernard Doering. LC 93-23924. (C). 1994. text 30.00 (*0-268-03802-3*) U of Notre Dame Pr.

Philosopher As Teacher. Ed. by George F. McLean. LC 74-166186. (Proceedings of the American Catholic Philosophical Association Ser.: Vol. 47). 1973. pap. 20.00 (*0-918090-07-5*) Am Cath Philo.

Philosopher As Writer: The Eighteenth Century. Ed. by Robert Ginsberg. LC 85-63555. 248p. 1987. 42.50 (*0-941664-25-2*) Susquehanna U Pr.

Philosopher at the Keyboard: Glenn Gould. Elizabeth Angilette. LC 91-42986. 244p. 1992. 35.00 (*0-8108-2467-1*) Scarecrow.

Philosopher at Work. Yves R. Simon. Ed. by Anthony O. Simon. LC 98-37836. 240p. 1999. 58.00 (*0-8476-9238-8*); pap. 22.95 (*0-8476-9239-6*) Rowman.

Philosopher in the Community: Essays in Memory of Bertram Morris. Ed. by Berel Lang et al. LC 84-13224. (Illus.). 190p. (Orig.). 1984. pap. text 20.50 (*0-8191-4188-7*); lib. bdg. 48.00 (*0-8191-4187-9*) U Pr of Amer.

Philosopher Looks at Science. Alfred North Whitehead. (Reprints in Philosophy Ser.). reprint ed. pap. 9.95 (*0-89197-883-6*); reprint ed. lib. bdg. 32.50 (*0-697-00211-X*) Irvington.

Philosopher of Free Religion: Francis Ellingwood Abbot, 1836-1903. Creighton Peden. LC 91-31769. (American University Studies: Philosophy: Ser. V, Vol. 133). 207p. (C). 1992. text 39.95 (*0-8204-1747-5*) P Lang Pubng.

Philosopher of Mount Parnassus: Miscellanea from the Pen of Charles Browne White. Charles B. White. LC 71-38331. (Biography Index Reprint Ser.). 1977. reprint ed. 20.95 (*0-8369-8131-6*) Ayer.

Philosopher of Revelation: The Life & Thought of S. L. Steinheim. Joshua O. Haberman. 348p. 1989. 44.95 (*0-8276-0353-3*) JPS Phila.

Philosopher of the Common Man: Essays in Honor of John Dewey to Celebrate His Eightieth Birthday. LC 68-19267. 228p. 1968. reprint ed. lib. bdg. 35.00 (*0-8371-0059-3*, DEPC, Greenwood Pr) Greenwood.

Philosopher on Dover Beach: Essays. Roger Scruton. LC 97-37676. 350p. 1997. 45.00 (*1-890318-60-4*) St Augustines Pr.

Philosopher or Dog? Joaquim Maria Machado de Assis. Tr. by Clotilde Wilson. 288p. 1992. pap. 12.00 (*0-374-52328-2*) FS&G.

Philosopher or Dog? Joaquim Maria Machado de Assis. 288p. 1982. pap. 3.95 (*0-380-58982-6*, 58982-6, Avon Bks) Morrow Avon.

Philosopher, Teacher, Musician: Perspectives on Music Education. Ed. by Estelle R. Jorgensen. LC 93-3328. 280p. 1993. pap. 10.95 (*0-252-06349-X*) U of Ill Pr.

Philosopher's. Steven S. Aspenson. LC 97-16070. 144p. (C). (gr. 13). 1998. pap. text 18.95 (*0-7656-0218-0*) M E Sharpe.

Philosophers. Photos by Steve Pyke. (Illus.). 168p. 1995. 50.00 (*0-9518371-8-4*) Dist Art Pubs.

Philosophers. Photos by Steve Pyke. (Illus.). 168p. 1995. reprint ed. pap. 27.50 (*0-9518371-7-6*) Dist Art Pubs.

Philosophers: Introducing Great Western Thinkers. Ed. by Ted Honderich. LC 98-54768. (Illus.). 294p. 1999. 24.00 (*0-19-823861-4*) OUP.

Philosophers: Their Lives & the Nature of Their Thought. Ben-Ami Scharfstein. 496p. 1980. text 39.95 (*0-19-520137-X*) OUP.

Philosophers: Their Lives & the Nature of Their Thought. Ben-Ami Scharfstein. 496p. 1989. reprint ed. pap. 17.95 (*0-19-505927-1*) OUP.

Philosopher's Address: Writing & the Perception of Philosophy. Jeffrey A. Mason. LC 99-16347. 224p. 1999. 60.00 (*0-7391-0071-8*) Lxngtn Bks.

Philosophers & Kings: Education for Leadership in Twentieth-Century England. Gary McCulloch. 173p. (C). 1991. text 59.95 (*0-521-39175-X*) Cambridge U Pr.

Philosophers & Machines. Ed. by Otto Mayr. LC 75-39528. 1975. pap. text 6.95 (*0-685-52444-2*) Watson Pub Intl.

Philosophers & Religious Leaders. Moschovitis Group, Inc. Staff. Ed. by Christian Von Dehsen. LC 99-45394. (Lives & Legacies Ser.: Vol. 2). (Illus.). 246p. 1999. boxed set 69.95 (*1-57356-152-5*) Oryx Pr.

Philosophers & Their Language. Yvon Belaval. Tr. by Norbert Guterman. LC 66-18481. 157p. reprint ed. pap. 48.70 (*0-608-10097-8*, 200523000052) Bks Demand.

Philosopher's Annual, 1980, Vol. III. Ed. by David L. Boyer et al. xii, 225p. (Orig.). (C). 1980. lib. bdg. 32.00 (*0-917930-38-X*) Ridgeview.

Philosopher's Annual, 1980, Vol. III. John T. Sanders. Ed. by David L. Boyer et al. xii, 225p. (Orig.). (C). 1980. pap. text 10.00 (*0-917930-18-5*) Ridgeview.

Philosopher's Annual, 1988, Vol. XI. Ed. by Patrick Grim. vi, 188p. (Orig.). 1990. pap. text 10.00 (*0-917930-73-8*); lib. bdg. 32.00 (*0-917930-93-2*) Ridgeview.

Philosopher's Annual, 1985, Vol. VIII. Ed. by C. J. Martin et al. vi, 1976p. 1987. pap. text 10.00 (*0-917930-70-3*); lib. bdg. 32.00 (*0-917930-90-8*) Ridgeview.

Philosopher's Annual, 1984, Vol. VII. Ed. by Patrick Grim et al. vi, 264p. 1986. pap. text 10.00 (*0-917930-69-X*); lib. bdg. 32.00 (*0-917930-83-5*) Ridgeview.

Philosopher's Annual, 1989, Vol. XII. Ed. by P. Williams et al. vii, 288p. (Orig.). 1991. pap. text 10.00 (*0-924922-02-8*); lib. bdg. 32.00 (*0-924922-52-4*) Ridgeview.

Philosopher's Annual, 1981, Vol. IV. Ed. by David L. Boyer et al. xii, 250p. (Orig.). (C). 1981. pap. text 10.00 (*0-917930-61-4*); lib. bdg. 32.00 (*0-917930-75-4*) Ridgeview.

Philosopher's Annual, 1987, Vol. X. Ed. by Patrick Grim et al. vi, 242p. (Orig.). 1989. pap. text 10.00 (*0-917930-72-X*); lib. bdg. 32.00 (*0-917930-92-4*) Ridgeview.

Philosopher's Annual, 1986, Vol. IX. Ed. by P. Athay et al. vi, 253p. (Orig.). 1988. pap. text 10.00 (*0-917930-71-1*); lib. bdg. 32.00 (*0-917930-91-6*) Ridgeview.

Philosopher's Annual, 1983, Vol. VI. Ed. by P. Athay et al. xi, 171p. (Orig.). 1985. pap. text 10.00 (*0-917930-68-1*); lib. bdg. 32.00 (*0-917930-82-7*) Ridgeview.

Philosopher's Annual, 1982, Vol. V. Ed. by David L. Boyer et al. xi, 250p. (Orig.). (C). 1982. lib. bdg. 32.00 (*0-917930-77-0*) Ridgeview.

Philosopher's Annual, 1990, Vol. XIII. Ed. by P. Williams et al. vii, 310p. 1992. pap. text 10.00 (*0-924922-07-9*); lib. bdg. 32.00 (*0-924922-57-5*) Ridgeview.

Philosopher's Annual, 1995, Vol. XVIII. Ed. by P. Grim et al. x, 342p. 1997. pap. text 10.00 (*0-924922-29-X*); lib. bdg. 32.00 (*0-924922-79-6*) Ridgeview.

Philosopher's Annual, 1994, Vol. XVII. Ed. by P. Grim et al. x, 262p. 1996. pap. text 10.00 (*0-924922-26-5*); lib. bdg. 32.00 (*0-924922-76-1*) Ridgeview.

Philosopher's Annual, 1991, Vol. XIV. Ed. by Patrick Grim et al. viii, 276p. (Orig.). 1993. pap. text 10.00 (*0-924922-12-5*); lib. bdg. 32.00 (*0-924922-62-1*) Ridgeview.

Philosopher's Annual, 1996, Vol. XIX. Ed. by P. Grim et al. x, 278p. 1998. pap. 10.00 (*0-924922-31-1*); lib. bdg. 32.00 (*0-924922-81-8*) Ridgeview.

Philosopher's Annual, 1993, Vol. XVI. Ed. by P. Williams et al. x, 222p. (Orig.). (C). 1995. pap. text 10.00 (*0-924922-21-4*); lib. bdg. 32.00 (*0-924922-71-0*) Ridgeview.

Philosopher's Annual, 1992, Vol. XV. Ed. by P. Williams et al. (Orig.). 1994. pap. text 10.00 (*0-924922-18-4*); lib. bdg. 32.00 (*0-924922-68-0*) Ridgeview.

Philosopher's Annual, 1979, Vol. 1. David L. Boyer. Ed. by Patrick Grim et al. 231p. 1979. 38.50 (*0-8476-6105-9*) Rowman.

Philosopher's Annual, 1979, Vol. 2. Ed. by David L. Boyer et al. 231p. 1979. 38.50 (*0-8476-6202-0*) Rowman.

Philosophers at Work. Cohen. 1997. 41.00 (*0-15-504453-2*, Pub. by Harcourt Coll Pubs) Harcourt.

Philosophers at Work. 2nd ed. Cohen. (C). 1999. text 45.00 (*0-15-505599-2*, Pub. by Harcourt Coll Pubs) Harcourt.

Philosophers at Work: An Introduction to the Issues & Practical Uses of Philosophy. Ed. by Elliot P. Cohen. LC 88-22984. 480p. (C). 1989. pap. text 26.75 (*0-03-013234-7*) Harcourt Coll Pubs.

Philosopher's Child: Critical Perspectives in the Western Tradition. Ed. by Susan M. Turner & Gareth B. Matthews. LC 98-16003. 248p. 1998. 65.00 (*1-58046-021-6*) Univ Rochester Pr.

Philosopher's Club. Kim Addonizio. LC 93-74021. (New Poets of America Ser.). 70p. 1994. pap. 10.00 (*1-880238-03-9*) BOA Edns.

Philosopher's Club. Kim Addonizio. LC 93-74021. (New Poets of America Ser.: Vol. 14). 70p. 1994. 20.00 (*1-880238-02-0*) BOA Edns.

***Philosopher's Compass.** Jacobs. (C). 2000. pap. text. write for info. (*0-15-507543-8*, Pub. by Harcourt Coll Pubs) Harcourt.

Philosopher's Demise: Learning French. Richard A. Watson. LC 94-42803. 144p. (C). 1995. text 22.50 (*0-8262-1003-1*) U of Mo Pr.

Philosopher's Dictionary. 2nd ed. Robert M. Martin. 253p. 1994. pap. 9.95 (*1-55111-044-X*) Broadview Pr.

Philosopher's Diet: How to Lose Weight & Change the World. Richard Watson. LC 98-35759. (Nonpareil Bks.). 128p. 1998. pap. 14.95 (*1-56792-084-5*) Godine.

***Philosopher's Gaze: Modernity in the Shadows of Enlightenment** David M. Levin. LC 99-43812. 412p. 1999. 50.00 (*0-520-21780-2*, Pub. by U CA Pr) Cal Prin Full Svc.

Philosopher's Harvest: The Philosophical Papers of Isaac Franck. William Gerber. LC 88-4704. 256p. reprint ed. pap. 79.40 (*0-7837-6321-2*, 204603600010) Bks Demand.

***Philosophers House.** Joan Marysmith. 2000. pap. 10.95 (*0-552-99812-5*, Pub. by Transworld Publishers Ltd) Trafalgar.

Philosophers in Trouble: A Volume of Stories. Lawrence P. Jacks. LC 77-125224. (Short Story Index Reprint Ser.). 1977. 17.95 (*0-8369-3591-8*) Ayer.

Philosopher's Index: A Retrospective Index to Non-U. S. English Language Publications from 1940, 3 vols., Set. Ed. by Richard H. Lineback. 1265p. 1980. 375.00 (*0-912632-12-7*) Philosophers Info Ctr.

Philosopher's Index: A Retrospective to U. S. Publications from 1940, 3 vols. Ed. by Richard H. Lineback. 1619p. 1978. 395.00 (*0-912632-09-7*) Philosophers Info Ctr.

Philosopher's Index: Cumulative Edition, 1987, Vol. XXI. Ed. by Richard H. Lineback. 672p. 1988. 130.00 (*0-912632-22-4*) Philosophers Info Ctr.

Philosopher's Index: Cumulative Edition, 1988, Vol. XXII. Ed. by Richard H. Lineback. 649p. 1989. 140.00 (*0-912632-24-0*) Philosophers Info Ctr.

Philosopher's Index: Cumulative Edition, 1989, Vol. XXIII. Ed. by Richard H. Lineback. 695p. 1990. 140.00 (*0-912632-51-8*) Philosophers Info Ctr.

Philosopher's Index: Cumulative Edition, 1990, Vol. 24. Ed. by Richard H. Lineback. 774p. 1991. 150.00 (*0-912632-52-6*) Philosophers Info Ctr.

Philosopher's Index: Cumulative Edition, 1991, Vol. 25. Ed. by Richard H. Lineback. 750p. 1992. 155.00 (*0-912632-53-4*) Philosophers Info Ctr.

Philosopher's Index: Cumulative Edition, 1992, Vol. 26. Ed. by Richard H. Lineback. 534p. 1993. 162.00 (*0-912632-54-2*) Philosophers Info Ctr.

Philosopher's Index: Cumulative Edition, 1993, Vol. 27. Ed. by Richard H. Lineback. 779p. 1994. 172.00 (*0-912632-55-0*) Philosophers Info Ctr.

Philosopher's Index: Cumulative Edition 1998, Vol. 32. Ed. by Richard H. Lineback. 1075p. 1999. 239.00 (*0-9656743-3-9*) Philosophers Info Ctr.

Philosopher's Index Vol. 28: Cumulative Edition, 1994, Vol. 28. Ed. by Richard H. Lineback. 791p. 1995. 181.00 (*0-912632-56-9*) Philosophers Info Ctr.

***Philosopher's Index Vol. 33: 1999 Cumulative Edition.** Ed. by Richard H. Lineback. 1075p. (C). 2000. lib. bdg. 249.00 (*0-9656743-4-7*) Philosophers Info Ctr.

Philosopher's Index Thesaurus. 2nd rev. ed. Rev. by Kelly M. Broughton. 105p. 1998. pap. 26.00 (*0-912632-67-4*) Philos Document.

Philosopher's Index, 1996: Cumulative Edition, Vol. 30. Ed. by Richard H. Lineback. 1019p. 1997. 205.00 (*0-9656743-0-4*) Philosophers Info Ctr.

Philosopher's Index, 1997: Cumulative Edition, Vol. 31. Ed. by Richard H. Lineback. 1000p. 1998. 225.00 (*0-9656743-2-0*) Philosophers Info Ctr.

Philosopher's Joke: Essays in Form & Content. Richard A. Watson. LC 90-38430. 122p. (Orig.). (C). 1990. pap. 19.95 (*0-87975-601-2*) Prometheus Bks.

Philosophers Lead Sheltered Lives: A First Volume of Memoirs. James K. Feibleman. LC 75-3141. reprint ed. 41.50 (*0-404-59150-7*) AMS Pr.

Philosophers Look at Science Fiction. Nicholas D. Smith. LC 82-7977. 300p. (C). 1982. text 35.95 (*0-88229-740-6*) Burnham Inc.

Philosophers of China. Clarence B. Day. 1978. pap. 5.95 (*0-8065-0622-9*, Citadel Pr) Carol Pub Group.

Philosophers of East & West: The Quest for the Meaning of Existence in Eastern & Western Thought. Eric Walter Frederick Tomlin. 528p. (C). 1988. 48.00 (*81-202-0197-3*, Pub. by Ajanta) S Asia.

Philosophers of Greece. Robert S. Brumbaugh. LC 81-9120. (Illus.). 274p. (C). 1981. reprint ed. pap. text 16.95 (*0-87395-551-X*) State U NY Pr.

Philosophers of Progress. 2nd ed. Ed. by Douglas Browning & William T. Myers. LC 98-25568. xlv, 449p. 1998. 35.00 (*0-8232-1878-3*); pap. 19.95 (*0-8232-1879-1*) Fordham.

Philosophers of the Enlightenment. Ed. by Peter Gilmour. 196p. 1994. pap. 22.00 (*0-7486-0147-3*, Pub. by Edinburgh U Pr) Col U Pr.

Philosophers of the Enlightenment. Ed. by Peter Gilmour. 208p. (C). 1990. lib. bdg. 58.50 (*0-389-20910-4*) Rowman.

Philosophers of the Enlightenment: Locke, Hume & Berkeley Revisited. Gerard Hanratty. 96p. 1995. pap. 15.00 (*1-85182-201-1*, Pub. by Four Cts Pr) Intl Spec Bk.

Philosophers on Education. Amelie Rorty. LC 98-4865. 496p. 1998. pap. 35.00 (*0-415-19131-9*) Routledge.

Philosophers on Education. Amelie Rorty. LC 98-4865. 496p. (C). 1998. 99.99 (*0-415-19130-0*) Routledge.

Philosophers on Their Own Work, 11 vols., 10. Ed. by Maja Svilar & Andre Mercier. VI, 309p. 1983. 21.00 (*3-261-05090-X*) P Lang Pubng.

Philosopher's Phone Book, 1998. rev. ed. 262p. 1998. spiral bd. 19.95 (*0-912632-63-1*) Philos Document.

Philosopher's Pilgrimage. Alban G. Widgery. 1961. 59.50 (*0-614-01812-9*) Elliots Bks.

Philosophers Speak for Themselves, Vol. 1. 2nd ed. Ed. by Thomas V. Smith & Marjorie Grene. LC B 0108.S6. 406p. pap. 125.90 (*0-8357-8983-7*, 205676600085) Bks Demand.

Philosophers Speak for Themselves: Berkeley, Hume, & Kant. 2nd ed. Ed. by Thomas V. Smith & Marjorie Grene. LC 57-7905. 382p. 1957. pap. text 15.95 (*0-226-76482-6*, P18) U Ch Pr.

Philosophers Speak for Themselves: From Descartes to Locke. 2nd ed. Ed. by Thomas V. Smith & Marjorie Grene. LC 57-7905. 487p. 1956. pap. text 15.95 (*0-226-76481-8*, P17) U Ch Pr.

Philosophers Speak for Themselves: From Descartes to Locke. 2nd ed. Ed. by Thomas V. Smith & Marjorie Grene. LC 57-7905. 1957. lib. bdg. 25.00 (*0-226-76478-8*) U Ch Pr.

Philosophers Speak of God. Charles Hartshorne & William L. Reese. LC 53-10041. (Midway Reprint Ser.). 1994. pap. text 29.00 (*0-226-31862-1*) U Ch Pr.

***Philosophers Speak of God.** Ed. by Charles Hartshorne & William L. Reese. LC 99-57642. 535p. 2000. pap. 26.95 (*1-57392-815-1*, Humanity Bks) Prometheus Bks.

Philosopher's Stone: A Modern Comparative Approach to Alchemy from the Psychological & Magical Points of View. Israel Regardie. 204p. 1993. reprint ed. pap. 17.95 (*1-56459-282-0*) Kessinger Pub.

Philosopher's Stone: Michio Kushi's Guide to Alchemy, Transmutation, & the New Science. Michio Kushi. LC 95-100337. (Illus.). 96p. (Orig.). 1994. pap. text 9.95 (*1-882984-07-2*) One Peaceful World.

Philosopher's Stones: Let the Magic of Alchemy Transform Your Life. M. E. Warlick. (Illus.). 96p. 1997. boxed set 26.95 (*1-885203-50-0*) Jrny Editions.

***Philosopher's Story.** Morton White. LC 98-39334. 304p. 1999. 45.00 (*0-271-01874-7*) Pa St U Pr.

Philosopher's Tool Kit. Steven Scott Aspenson. LC 97-16070. 144p. (C). (gr. 13). 1998. text 55.95 (*0-7656-0217-2*) M E Sharpe.

Philosopher's Tree: A Selection of Michael Faraday's Writings. Michael Faraday. LC 98-54683. 1998. pap. text 29.00 (*0-7503-0571-1*) IOP Pub.

***Philosopher's Tree: A Selection of Michael Faraday's Writings.** Michael Faraday. LC 98-54683. 1998. 75.00 (*0-7503-0570-3*) IOP Pub.

Philosopher's Understanding of Quantum Mechanics: Possibilities & Impossibilities of a Model Interpretation. Pieter E. Vermaas. LC 99-14416. 270p. (C). 2000. 69.95 (*0-521-65108-5*) Cambridge U Pr.

Philosophers Who Believe: The Spiritual Journeys of Eleven Leading Thinkers. Ed. by Kelly J. Clark. 284p. 1997. reprint ed. pap. 17.99 (*0-8308-1543-0*, 1543) InterVarsity.

Philosopher's Window & Other Poems. Allen Grossman. LC 95-6257. 112p. (Orig.). 1995. pap. 12.95 (*0-8112-1300-5*, NDP807, Pub. by New Directions) Norton.

Philosopher's World Model, 12. Archie J. Bahm. LC 78-67569. (Contributions in Philosophy Ser.: No. 12). (Illus.). 295p. 1979. 59.95 (*0-313-21198-1*, BPW/, Greenwood Pr) Greenwood.

Philosophes - Geometres de la Grece: Platon & Ses & Predecesseurs. Gaston Milhaud. LC 75-13280. (History of Ideas in Ancient Greece Ser.). (FRE.). 1976. reprint ed. 26.95 (*0-405-07323-2*) Ayer.

Philosophetics: Getting Ahead? Oh, Yes You Can!! Wendell Holst. LC 95-94016. 102p. 1995. 3.00 (*1-883901-13-8*) Gethmo Pubns.

Philosophia: The Thought of Rosa Luxemburg, Simone Weil, & Hannah Arendt. Andrea Nye. LC 93-10223. 256p. (C). 1994. pap. 19.99 (*0-415-90831-0*, B2303) Routledge.

Philosophia Botanica. Carl Linnaeus. (Illus.). 1966. reprint ed. 97.50 (*3-7682-0350-6*) Lubrecht & Cramer.

Philosophia Civilis Sive Politica Bd. 47. Michael C. Hanov. 2806p. 1998. reprint ed. text. write for info. (*3-487-10630-2*) G Olms Pubs.

Philosophia Crucis: Heideggers Beschaftigung Mit Dem Apostel Paulus. Jaromir Brejdak. (Daedalus - Europaisches Denken in Deutscher Philosophie Ser.: Bd. 8). (GER.). 233p. 1996. 51.95 (*3-631-30706-3*) P Lang Pubng.

Philosophia Fundamentalis, Vol. 33. Gottlieb Canz. (GER.). 608p. 1997. reprint ed. 180.00 (*3-487-10153-X*) G Olms Pubs.

Philosophia Hermetica: A Course of Ten Lessons, Being an Introduction to the Philosophy of Alchemy. A. S. Raleigh. 127p. 1996. reprint ed. pap. 16.95 (*1-56459-521-8*) Kessinger Pub.

Philosophia Naturalis Sive Physica Dogmatica, 4 vols. Christian Wolff & Michael C. Hanov. (Gesammelte Werke Ser.: Series III, Bd. 40). (GER.). 40p. 1997. reprint ed. 975.00 (*3-487-10390-7*) G Olms Pubs.

P

Philosophia Paradoxae: Introduction to the Paradoxist Philosophy. Florentin Smarandache. Ed. by R. Muller. (Illus.). 100p. (C). 1995. pap. 9.99 (1-879585-39-1) Erhus Univ Pr.

Philosophia Pia: or A Discourse of the Religious Temper, & Tendencies of the Experimental Philosophy, Which Is Profest by the Royal Society. Joseph Glanvill. Ed. by Bernhard Fabian. (Collected Works: Vol. V). 237p. 1970. reprint ed. 45.37 (3-487-02691-0) G Olms Pubs.

Philosophia Togata: Essays on Philosophy & Roman Society. Ed. by Miriam D. Griffin & Jonathan Barnes. (Illus.). 312p. 1989. 85.00 (0-19-814884-4) OUP.

Philosophia Togata I Vol. 1: Essays on Philosophy & Roman Society, Vol. I. Ed. by Jonathan Barnes & Miriam D. Griffin. (Illus.). 316p. 1997. reprint ed. pap. text 35.00 (0-19-815085-7) OUP.

***Philosophia Togata 2: Plato & Aristotle At Rome.** Ed. by Jonathan Barnes & Miriam D. Griffin. 310p. 1999. pap. text 29.95 (0-19-815222-1) OUP.

Philosophiae Moralis Institutio Compendiaria, Libris III: Ethics et Jurisprudentiae Naturalis Elementa Continens. Editio Altera Auctior et Emendatior. Francis Hutcheson. Ed. by Bernhard Fabian. (Collected Works: Vol. III). vi, 355p. 1990. reprint ed. 63.70 (3-487-02254-0) G Olms Pubs.

***Philosophic Classics.** 3rd ed. Forrest E. Baird. (Illus.). 526p. 1999. pap. text 34.00 (0-13-021315-2) P-H.

***Philosophic Classics: From Plato to Derrida.** 3rd ed. Forrest E. Baird. LC 98-50173. 1198p. (C). 1999. pap. text 37.80 (0-13-021532-5) P-H.

***Philosophic Classics Vol. 1: Ancient Philosophy.** 3rd ed. Forrest E. Baird. (Illus.). 552p. (C). 1999. pap. text 33.60 (0-13-021314-4) P-H.

***Philosophic Classics Vol. 3: Modern Philosophy.** 3rd ed. Forrest E. Baird. (Illus.). 646p. (C). 1999. pap. text 33.60 (0-13-021316-0) P-H.

***Philosophic Classics Vol. 4: Nineteenth - Century Philosophy.** 2nd ed. Forrest E. Baird. LC 98-32332. 499p. (C). 1999. pap. text 34.00 (0-13-021533-3) P-H.

***Philosophic Classics Vol.5: Twentieth Century Philosophy, Vol. 5.** 2nd ed. Ed. by Forrest E. Baird & Walter Kaufmann. 439p. (C). 1999. pap. text 33.60 (0-13-021534-1) P-H.

Philosophic Fire: Unifying the Fragments of Heraclitus. Robert Jones. 1998. pap. 6.95 (1-55818-409-0) Holmes Pub.

Philosophic Foundations of American Education. Don-chean Chu. LC 70-150045. 392p. 1971. pap. 7.00 (0-913973-08-4) Inst Sino-Amer.

Philosophic Foundations of Quantum Mechanics. unabridged ed. Hans Reichenbach. LC 98-40052. 192p. 1998. pap. 8.95 (0-486-40459-5) Dover.

Philosophic Inquiry in Nursing. Ed. by June F. Kikuchi & Helen Simmons. 128p. (C). 1992. text 44.00 (0-8039-4460-8); pap. text 18.95 (0-8039-4461-6) Sage.

Philosophic Inquiry in Sport. 2nd rev. ed. William J. Morgan & Klaus V. Meier. LC 95-10920. (Illus.). 456p. 1995. pap. text 47.00 (0-87322-716-6, BMOR0716) Human Kinetics.

Philosophic Interpretation of Existence & Evolution. 224p. (C). 1988. 49.00 (0-7212-0758-8, Pub. by Regency Pr GBR) St Mut.

Philosophic Moment of Marxist-Humanism. Raya Dunayevskaya. xii, 52p. 1989. pap. 3.00 (0-914441-38-8) News & Letters.

Philosophic Nights in Paris. Remy De Gourmont. Tr. by Irving D. Goldberg. LC 68-8465. (Essay Index Reprint Ser.). 1977. 19.95 (0-8369-1293-4) Ayer.

Philosophic Problems of Nuclear Science see **Philosophical Problems of Quantum Physics**

Philosophic Process in Physical Education. 3rd ed. William A. Harper. LC 76-10373. 352p. reprint ed. pap. 109.20 (0-608-16679-0, 205618800055) Bks Demand.

***Philosophic Roots of Modern Ideology.** 3rd ed. Ingersoll. 350p. 2000. pap. 40.00 (0-13-109075-5) P-H.

Philosophic Solitude. William Livingston. (Notable American Authors Ser.). 1999. reprint ed. lib. bdg. 125.00 (0-7812-3797-1) Rprt Serv.

Philosophic Thought in France & the United States: Essays Representing Major Trends in Contemporary French & American Philosophy. Ed. by Marvin Farber. LC B 2421.P45. 825p. reprint ed. pap. 200.00 (0-608-10191-5, 201010700068) Bks Demand.

Philosophic Thought of Ayn Rand. Intro. by Douglas J. Den Uyl & Douglas B. Rasmussen. LC 83-5844. 248p. 1984. text 24.95 (0-252-01033-7); pap. text 14.95 (0-252-01407-3) U of Ill Pr.

***Philosophical Allegories & Mystical Treatises.** Tr. by Wheeler M. Thackston, Jr. from ARA. LC 99-32684. (Bibliotheca Iranica Ser.: Vol. 2). 280p. 1999. pap. text 25.00 (1-56859-091-1) Mazda Pubs.

Philosophical Analysis: A Collection of Essays. Ed. by Max Black. LC 78-152158. (Essay Index Reprint Ser.). 1980. reprint ed. 30.95 (0-8369-2214-X) Ayer.

Philosophical Analysis: A Collection of Essays. Ed. by Max Black. LC 78-152158. (Essay Index Reprint Ser.). 405p. reprint ed. lib. bdg. 52.00 (0-8290-0796-2) Irvington.

Philosophical Analysis: A Defense by Example. Ed. by David F. Austin. 365p. (C). 1988. lib. bdg. 173.50 (90-277-2674-4, Pub. by Kluwer Academic) Kluwer Academic.

Philosophical Analysis: An Introduction to Its Language & Techniques. 3rd ed. Samuel Gorovitz et al. LC 78-5661. 223p. (C). 1979. pap. 24.69 (0-07-553595-5) McGraw.

Philosophical Analysis & Human Welfare. Dickinson S. Miller. Ed. by Loyd D. Easton. LC 75-4832. (Philosophical Studies: No. 3). 343p. 1975. text 171.00 (90-277-0566-6, D Reidel) Kluwer Academic.

Philosophical Analysis & Illustration of Some of Shakespeare's Remarkable Characters. rev. ed. William Richardson. LC 17-30453. 36.00 (0-404-05309-2) AMS Pr.

Philosophical Analysis in Latin America. Ed. by Jorge J. Garcia et al. 443p. 1984. text 192.50 (90-277-1749-4, D Reidel) Kluwer Academic.

Philosophical & Critical Observations on the Nature, Characters, & Various Species of Composition, 2 vols. John Ogilvie. (Anglistica & Americana Ser.: No. 27). 1968. reprint ed. 128.70 (0-685-66497-X, 05102142) G Olms Pubs.

Philosophical & Critical Works, 4 vols., Set. James Beattie. Ed. by Bernhard Fabian. (Anglistica & Americana Ser.: No. 104). 1975. 720.00 (3-487-05160-5) G Olms Pubs.

Philosophical & Critical Works: Elements of Moral Science, Edinburgh, 1790-1793, Vol. III & IV. James Beattie. (GER.). xxii, 1126p. 1974. reprint ed. write for info. (3-487-05163-X) G Olms Pubs.

Philosophical & Critical Works Vol. 1: On the Nature & Immutability of Truth. James Beattie. (Anglistica & Americana Ser.: No. 104a). 1975. reprint ed. 225.00 (3-487-05161-3) G Olms Pubs.

Philosophical & Critical Works Vol. 2: Dissertations Moral & Critical. James Beattie. Ed. by Bernhard Fabian. (Anglistica & Americana Ser.: No. 104b). xvi, 677p. 1974. reprint ed. 200.00 (3-487-05162-1) G Olms Pubs.

Philosophical & Critical Works Vol. 4: Elements of Moral Science. James Beattie. Ed. by Bernhard Fabian. (Anglistica & Americana Ser.: No. 4). xxii, 1126p. 1974. reprint ed. 160.00 (3-487-05164-8) G Olms Pubs.

***Philosophical & Cultural Values: Applying Ethics in Schools.** George Crawford & Janice Nicklaus. LC 99-47167. 2000. 29.95 (1-883001-82-X) Eye On Educ.

***Philosophical & Ethical Problems in Mental Handicap.** Peter Byrne. LC 00-27830. 2000. write for info. (0-312-23460-0) St Martin.

Philosophical & Foundational Issues in Measurement Theory. Ed. by Wade Savage & Philip Ehrlich. 248p. 1992. text 49.95 (0-8058-0726-8) L Erlbaum Assocs.

Philosophical & Historical Roots of Occupational Therapy. Ed. by Karen Diasio Serrett. LC 85-8838. (Occupational Therapy in Mental Health Ser.: Vol. 5, No. 3). 113p. 1985. text 39.95 (0-86656-456-X); pap. text 14.95 (0-86656-527-2) Haworth Pr.

Philosophical & Ideological Perspectives on Education. 2nd ed. Gerald L. Gutek. LC 96-7676. 340p. 1996. 59.00 (0-205-26106-X) Allyn.

Philosophical & Legal Concept of War. Frank Przetacznik. LC 93-16073. 680p. 1994. text 129.95 (0-7734-9256-9) E Mellen.

Philosophical & Literary Commentary on Martianus Capella's de Nuptiis Philologiae Et Mercurii, Vol. Bk. 1. Danuta Shanzer. (UC Publications in Classical Studies: Vol. 32). 1987. pap. 45.00 (0-520-09716-5, Pub. by U CA Pr) Cal Prin Full Svc.

Philosophical & Literary Pieces. Samuel Alexander. LC 70-93313. (Essay Index Reprint Ser.). 1977. 26.95 (0-8369-1269-1) Ayer.

Philosophical & Mathematical Correspondence. Gottlob Frege. Ed. by Brian McGuinness. Tr. by Hans Kaal. LC 79-23199. 1980. lib. bdg. 31.00 (0-226-26197-2) U Ch Pr.

***Philosophical & Modular Nature of Economics.** unabridged ed. Chris Angle. 1999. pap. 14.99 (0-9661126-3-6) Philosophy.

Philosophical & Religious Thought in China. H. J. Hsia. (East-West Communication Ser.). 252p. 1993. 28.95 (1-881673-06-5); pap. 9.95 (1-881673-07-3) Amer Assoc Pub.

Philosophical & Theological Foundations of Ethics: An Introduction to Moral Theory & Its Relation to Religious Belief. Peter Byrne. LC 91-44846. 192p. 1992. text 49.95 (0-312-07937-0) St Martin.

Philosophical & Theological Foundations of Ethics: An Introduction to Moral Threory & Its Relation to Religious Belief. 2nd ed. Peter Byrne. LC 98-43030. 200p. 1999. pap. 19.95 (0-312-22000-6) St Martin.

Philosophical & Theological Foundations of Ethics; An Introduction to Moral Theory & Its Rel. 2nd ed. Peter Byrne. LC 98-43030. 200p. 1999. text 59.95 (0-312-21999-7) St Martin.

Philosophical & Theological Papers, 1958-1964. Bernard Lonergan. Ed. by Robert C. Croken et al. 304p. 1996. text 60.00 (0-8020-3473-X) U of Toronto Pr.

Philosophical & Theological Papers, 1958-1964. Bernard Lonergan. Ed. by Robert C. Croken et al. (Collected Works of Bernard Lonergan: Vol. 6). 304p. 1996. pap. text 19.95 (0-8020-3474-8) U of Toronto Pr.

***Philosophical & Theological Writings.** Franz Rosenzweig et al. LC 00-32028. 2000. write for info. (0-87220-472-3) Hackett Pub.

Philosophical & Theoretical Perspective for Advanced Nursing Practice. Janet W. Kenney. (Nursing Ser.). 408p. (C). 1995. pap. 48.75 (0-86720-735-3) Jones & Bartlett.

Philosophical & Theoretical Perspectives for Avanced Nursing Practice. 2nd ed. Janet W. Kenney. LC 98-43152. 353p. 1999. 42.95 (0-7637-0917-4) Jones & Bartlett.

Philosophical Anthropology in Saiva Siddhanta, with Special Reference to Sivagrayogin Jayandra Soni. (C). 1989. 37.50 (81-208-0632-8) S Asia.

Philosophical Applications of Cognitive Science. Alvin I. Goldman. (Focus Ser.). 182p. (C). 1993. pap. 20.00 (0-8133-8040-5, Pub. by Westview) HarpC.

Philosophical Apprenticeships. Hans-Georg Gadamer. Tr. by Robert R. Sullivan from GER. (Studies in Contemporary German Social Thought). 205p. 1985. 27.50 (0-262-07092-8) MIT Pr.

Philosophical Apprenticeships. Hans-Georg Gadamer. Tr. by Robert R. Sullivan from GER. (Studies in Contemporary German Social Thought). 205p. 1987. pap. text 10.95 (0-262-57066-1) MIT Pr.

Philosophical Approaches to Literature: New Essays on Nineteenth & Twentieth Century Texts. Ed. by William E. Cain. LC 82-48652. 256p. 1984. 38.50 (0-8387-5055-9) Bucknell U Pr.

***Philosophical Approaches to the Study of Literature.** Patrick Colm Hogan. 384p. 2000. 49.95 (0-8130-1764-5) U Press Fla.

Philosophical Arguments. Charles Taylor. LC 94-36548. 352p. 1995. text 41.00 (0-674-66476-0, TAYPHI) HUP.

Philosophical Arguments. Charles Taylor. (Illus.). 336p. 1997. pap. text 19.50 (0-674-66477-9) HUP.

Philosophical Artwork & Other Writings. Richard Schain. LC 83-81441. 170p. (Orig.). 1983. pap. 6.00 (0-9609922-1-9) Garric Pr.

Philosophical Aspects of Information Systems. Russel L. Winder. 256p. 1997. 89.95 (0-7484-0758-8) Taylor & Francis.

Philosophical Aspects of Modern Science. Cyril E. Joad. (Select Bibliographies Reprint Ser.). 1977. reprint ed. 23.95 (0-8369-6886-7) Ayer.

Philosophical Aspects of Sufism. Marietta Stepaniants. (C). 1989. 17.00 (81-202-0265-1, Pub. by Ajanta) S Asia.

Philosophical Aspects of Thanatology, Vol. 1. Florence M. Hetzler & Austin H. Kutscher. 1979. 20.95 (0-405-12515-1) Ayer.

Philosophical Aspects of Thanatology, Vol. 2. Florence M. Hetzler & Austin H. Kutscher. 1979. 20.95 (0-405-12516-X) Ayer.

Philosophical Aspects of the Mind-Body Problem: Proceedings. Conference on the Philosophy of Mind & Psychology. LC 75-17914. 232p. reprint ed. pap. 72.00 (0-8357-6260-2, 203463600090) Bks Demand.

Philosophical Assessment of Theology: Essays in Honour of Frederick C. Copleston. fac. ed. Frederick C. Copleston. Ed. by Gerard J. Hughes. LC 87-94. 227p. pap. 70.40 (0-7837-7394-3, 204689600006) Bks Demand.

Philosophical Bases of Theism. George D. Hicks. LC 77-27142. (Hibbert Lectures: 1931). reprint ed. 40.00 (0-404-60427-7) AMS Pr.

Philosophical Canon in the Seventeenth & Eighteenth Centuries: Essays in Honor of John W. Yolton. Ed. by G. A. Rogers & Sylvana Tomaselli. LC 96-16388. 240p. (C). 1996. 65.00 (1-878822-64-0) Univ Rochester Pr.

***Philosophical Challenge of Religious Diversity.** Philip L. Quinn & Kevin Meeker. LC 98-33341. 256p. (C). 1999. text 45.00 (0-19-512154-6); pap. text 24.95 (0-19-512155-4) OUP.

Philosophical Challenges & Opportunities of Globalization. Oliva Blanchette et al. LC 99-37510. (Cultural Heritage & Contemporary Change Ser.). Date not set. pap. write for info. (1-56518-129-8) Coun Res Values.

Philosophical Commentary on the Politics of Aristotle. Peter L. Phillips Simpson. LC 97-16515. 512p. (C). (gr. 13). 1998. 55.00 (0-8078-2380-5) U of NC Pr.

Philosophical Companion to First Order Logic. Ed. by R. I. Hughes. LC 93-14456. 288p. (Orig.). (C). 1993. pap. text 16.95 (0-87220-181-3); lib. bdg. 37.95 (0-87220-182-1) Hackett Pub.

***Philosophical Computer: Exploratory Essays in Philosophical Computer Modeling.** Patrick Grim et al. LC 97-39498. (Illus.). 333p. 1998. 50.00 (0-262-07185-1, Bradford Bks) MIT Pr.

Philosophical Concepts in Physics: The Historical Relation Between Philosophy & Scientific Theories. James T. Cushing. (Illus.). 500p. (C). 1998. text 74.95 (0-521-57071-9); pap. text 30.95 (0-521-57823-X) Cambridge U Pr.

Philosophical Consequences of Quantum Theory: Reflections on Bell's Theorem. Ed. by James T. Cushing & Ernan McMullin. LC 89-40014. (Studies in Science & the Humanities from the Reilly Center for Science, Technology, & Values: Vol. II). 336p. (C). 1989. pap. text 23.00 (0-268-01579-1) U of Notre Dame Pr.

Philosophical Conversations with God. Dimitrius Vlahakis. 1993. write for info. (0-9633000-1-6) D Vlahakis.

Philosophical Correspondence, 1759-99. Immanuel Kant. Ed. by Arnulf Zweig. x, 270p. 1986. pap. text 23.00 (0-226-42361-1, Midway Reprint) U Ch Pr.

Philosophical Correspondence, 1759-99. Immanuel Kent. Ed. by Arnulf Zweig. LC 66-23705. 270p. reprint ed. pap. 83.70 (0-608-30592-8, 202250300027) Bks Demand.

***Philosophical Counseling: Theory & Practice.** Peter B. Raabe. 240p. 2000. 59.00 (0-275-97056-6, Praeger Pubs) Greenwood.

Philosophical Criticism: Essays & Reviews. Jasper Hopkins. LC 93-74285. xii, 297p. (C). 1994. text 20.00 (0-938060-44-9) Banning Pr.

Philosophical Critiques of Policy Analysis: Lindblom, Habermas, & the Great Society. Lance deHaven-Smith. LC 88-12038. 168p. 1988. 49.95 (0-8130-0907-3) U Press Fla.

Philosophical Darwinism: On the Origin of Knowledge by Means of Natural Selection. Peter Munz. LC 92-19364. 272p. (C). (gr. 13). 1993. 75.00 (0-415-08602-7, B0295) Routledge.

Philosophical Daybook: Post-Critical Investigations. William H. Poteat. LC 90-34577. 144p. 1990. text 25.00 (0-8262-0748-0) U of Mo Pr.

Philosophical Defense of Affirmative Action. Engelbert Ssekasozi. LC 98-48614. (Symposium Ser.: Vol. 50). 236p. 1999. 89.95 (0-7734-8263-6, Mellen Poetry Pr) E Mellen.

***Philosophical Designs for a Socio-Cultural Transformation: Beyond Violence & the Modern Era.** Tetsunao Yamamori. 1999. pap. 38.50 (0-8476-9538-7) Rowman.

Philosophical Dialogue in the British Enlightenment: Theology, Aesthetics, & the Novel. Michael B. Prince. (Studies in Eighteenth-Century English Literature & Thought: No. 31). 296p. (C). 1997. text 59.95 (0-521-55062-9) Cambridge U Pr.

Philosophical Dialogues: Arne Naess & the Progress of Philosophy. Ed. by Nina Witoszek & Andrew Brennan. LC 98-24368. 496p. 1999. 70.00 (0-8476-8928-X); pap. 26.95 (0-8476-8929-8) Rowman.

Philosophical Dialogues: Dawes Hicks Lectures on Philosophy. T. J. Smiley. (Proceedings of the British Academy Ser.: Vol. 85). 94p. 1995. text 15.95 (0-19-726153-1) OUP.

***Philosophical Dictionary.** Besterman. 2000. pap. write for info. (0-13-028130-1) P-H.

Philosophical Dictionary. Voltaire. (Classics Ser.). 400p. 1984. pap. 13.95 (0-14-044257-X, Penguin Classics) Viking Penguin.

Philosophical Dilemma: Building a World View. Phil Washburn. 416p. (C). 1996. pap. text 31.95 (0-19-510693-8) OUP.

***Philosophical Dilemmas: A Pro & Con Introduction to the Major Questions.** 2nd ed. Phil Washburn. 528p. (C). 2000. pap. text 38.95 (0-19-513496-6) OUP.

Philosophical Dimensions of Personal Construct Psychology. William Warren. LC 98-17308. 208p. 1998. 75.00 (0-415-16850-3) Routledge.

Philosophical Dimensions of the Neuro-Medical Sciences. Stuart F. Spicker & H. Tristram Engelhardt. LC 76-1204. (Philosophy & Medicine Ser.: Vol. 2). 280p. 1976. text 98.50 (90-277-0672-7, D Reidel) Kluwer Academic.

Philosophical Discourse Concerning Speech. Geraud De Cordemoy. LC 78-147961. reprint ed. 15.00 (0-404-08211-4) AMS Pr.

Philosophical Discourse Concerning Speech (1668) & a Discourse Written to a Learned Frier (1670) Geraud de Cordemoy. LC 72-6400. (History of Psychology Ser.). 232p. 1972. reprint ed. 50.00 (0-8201-1106-6) Schol Facsimiles.

Philosophical Discourse of Modernity: Twelve Lectures. Jurgen Habermas. Tr. by Frederick G. Lawrence from GER. (Studies in Contemporary German Social Thought). 450p. 1990. reprint ed. pap. text 22.00 (0-262-58102-7) MIT Pr.

Philosophical Disease: Bioethics Culture & Identity. Carl Elliot. LC 98-7053. (Reflective Bioethics Ser.). 256p. (C). (gr. 13). 1998. 75.00 (0-415-91939-8) Routledge.

Philosophical Disease: Bioethics, Culture, & Identity. Carl Elliot. LC 98-7053. 256p. (C). 1998. pap. 19.99 (0-415-91940-1) Routledge.

Philosophical Disenfranchisement of Art. Arthur C. Danto. LC 86-2260. 1988. pap. text 20.00 (0-231-06365-2) Col U Pr.

Philosophical Dissertations: 1782 Edition. James Balfour. 240p. 1996. reprint ed. 68.00 (1-85506-323-9) Bks Intl VA.

Philosophical Documents in Education. Ron Reed. (C). 1995. pap. text. write for info. (0-8013-1725-8) Addison-Wesley.

***Philosophical Documents in Education.** 2nd ed. Ronald F. Reed. LC 99-12144. 301p. (C). 1999. pap. text 33.53 (0-8013-3316-4) Longman.

Philosophical Ecologies: Essays in Philosophy, Ecology, & Human Life. A. Pablo Iannone. LC 97-26791. 472p. 1998. 55.00 (0-391-04050-2) Humanities.

Philosophical Ecologies: Essays in Philosophy, Ecology, & Human Life. A. Pablo Iannone. LC 99-24179. 272p. 1999. 54.95 (1-57392-660-4, Humanity Bks) Prometheus Bks.

***Philosophical Entrees: Classic & Contemporary Readings in Philosophy.** Dale Jacquette. LC 00-22611. 768p. 2000. pap. 40.31 (0-07-365933-9) McGraw.

Philosophical Epigrams, 1939. J. H. Tilden. 50p. 1996. reprint ed. pap. 9.95 (1-56459-965-5) Kessinger Pub.

Philosophical Essay: Declaring the Probable Causes Whence Stones Are Produced in the Greater World. Thomas Sherley. Ed. by Claude C. Albritton, Jr. LC 77-6541. (History of Geology Ser.). 1978. reprint ed. lib. bdg. 19.95 (0-405-10460-X) Ayer.

Philosophical Essay on Probabilities. unabridged ed. Pierre Simon & Marquis De Laplace. 208p. 1996. reprint ed. pap. text 7.95 (0-486-28875-7) Dover.

Philosophical Essays. Richard Cartwright. 312p. 1987. 30.00 (0-262-03130-2) MIT Pr.

Philosophical Essays. Antony Flew. Ed. by John Shosky. LC 97-27642. 224p. 1997. pap. 22.95 (0-8476-8579-9) Rowman.

Philosophical Essays. Antony Flew. Ed. by John Shosky. LC 97-27642. 224p. 1998. 58.00 (0-8476-8578-0) Rowman.

***Philosophical Essays.** Carl Hasler. 144p. (C). 1999. per. 38.95 (0-7872-6230-7, 41623001) Kendall-Hunt.

Philosophical Essays. Gottfried Wilhelm Leibniz. Ed. & Tr. by Roger Ariew & Daniel Garber from FRE. LC 88-38259. (HPC Classics Ser.). 386p. (C). 1989. 37.95 (0-87220-063-9); pap. text 12.95 (0-87220-062-0) Hackett Pub.

Philosophical Essays. Alfred Jules Ayer. LC 79-24852. 289p. 1980. reprint ed. lib. bdg. 35.00 (0-313-20902-2, AYPE, Greenwood Pr) Greenwood.

Philosophical Essays. Surendranath Dasgupta. 1990. reprint ed. 29.00 (81-208-0750-2, Pub. by Motilal Bnarsidass) S Asia.

Philosophical Essays. Bertrand Russell. LC 94-5628. 160p. (C). 1994. reprint ed. pap. 19.99 (0-415-10579-X) Routledge.

An Asterisk (*) at the beginning of an entry indicates that the title is appearing for the first time.

Philosophical Essays: Concerning Human Understanding. David Hume. 256p. 1986. reprint ed. lib. bdg. 48.10 (*3-487-07709-4*) G Olms Pubs.

Philosophical Essays: From Ancient Creed to Technological Man. Hans Jonas. 1993. pap. text 19.95 (*0-226-40591-5*, Midway Reprint) U Ch Pr.

Philosophical Essays: From Ancient Creed to Technological Man. Hans Jonas. LC 80-17190. (Midway Reprint Ser.). 367p. reprint ed. pap. 113.80 (*0-608-09413-7*, 205421300004) Bks Demand.

Philosophical Essays - Descartes. Laurence J. Lafleur. (Library of Liberal Arts: No. 99). 264p. (C). 1964. pap. text 10.00 (*0-02-367240-4*, Macmillan Coll) P-H.

***Philosophical Essays & Correspondence.** Rene Descartes. Ed. by Roger Ariew. LC 99-49303. 320p. (C). 2000. pap. 14.95 (*0-87220-502-9*); lib. bdg. 37.95 (*0-87220-503-7*) Hackett Pub.

Philosophical Essays in Honor of James Edwin Creighton. Ed. by George H. Sabine. LC 67-23258. (Essay Index Reprint Ser.). 1977. 23.95 (*0-8369-0789-2*) Ayer.

Philosophical Essays in Memory of Edmund Husserl. Ed. by Marvin Farber. LC 68-19270. 332p. 1968. reprint ed. lib. bdg. 35.00 (*0-8371-0071-2*, FAPE, Greenwood Pr) Greenwood.

Philosophical Essays in Pragmatic Naturalism. Paul Kurtz. LC 89-49060. 265p. (C). 1990. 26.95 (*0-87975-592-X*) Prometheus Bks.

Philosophical Essays in the Honor of Edgar Arthur Singer, Jr. F. P. Clarke & Milton C. Nahm. LC 78-80394. (Essay Index Reprint Ser.). 1977. 26.95 (*0-8369-1062-1*) Ayer.

Philosophical Essays on Probabilities, 13. Marquis Pierre Simon De Laplace. Ed. by G. J. Toomer. Tr. by Andrew I. Dale. LC 94-25497. 270p. 1994. 79.95 (*0-387-94349-8*) Spr-Verlag.

Philosophical Essays on the Ideas of a Good Society, No. 1. Ed. by Yeager Hudson & Creighton Peden. LC 87-31358. (Studies in Social & Political Theory: Vol. 2). 354p. 1988. lib. bdg. 99.95 (*0-88946-102-3*) E Mellen.

Philosophical Essays Presented to John Watson. Queen's University Faculty of the Arts Staff. LC 70-156704. (Essay Index Reprint Ser.). 1977. reprint ed. 23.95 (*0-8369-2291-3*) Ayer.

Philosophical Ethics: An Historical & Contemporary Introduction. Stehpen Darwall. LC 97-40578. (Dimensions of Philosophy Ser.). (C). 1997. pap. 27.00 (*0-8133-7860-5*, Pub. by Westview) HarpC.

Philosophical Ethics: An Introduction to Moral Philosophy. 2nd ed. Thomas L. Beauchamp. 448p. (C). 1991. pap. 43.44 (*0-07-004256-X*) McGraw.

***Philosophical Ethics: An Introduction to Moral Philosophy.** 3rd ed. Tom L. Beauchamp. LC 99-47187. 2001. write for info. (*0-07-229721-2*) McGrw-H Hghr Educ.

Philosophical Etymology of Hobbit. Stanley V. McDaniel. 24p. (Orig.). 1995. pap. 3.50 (*1-881799-10-7*) Am Tolkien Soc.

Philosophical Events: Essays of the Eighties. John Rajchman. 192p. 1990. text 39.50 (*0-231-07210-4*) Col U Pr.

Philosophical Examination of the History & Values of Western Medicine. Paul W. Sharkey. LC 92-49051. 200p. 1993. text 79.95 (*0-7734-9210-0*) E Mellen.

Philosophical Experiments & Observations. Robert Hooke. Ed. by W. Derham. (Illus.). 398p. 1967. 35.00 (*0-7146-1115-8*, Pub. by F Cass Pubs) Intl Spec Bk.

Philosophical Explanations. Robert Nozick. LC 81-1369. 777p. 1981. 42.50 (*0-674-66448-5*) Belknap Pr.

Philosophical Explanations. Robert Nozick. 777p. 1983. pap. text 22.00 (*0-674-66479-5*) Belknap Pr.

Philosophical Finesse: Studies in the Art of Rational Persuasion. Martin Warner. (Illus.). 412p. 1989. text 69.00 (*0-19-824455-X*) OUP.

Philosophical Foundation of Miki Kiyoshi's Concept of Humanism. Shigenori Nagatomo. LC 94-39460. (Studies in Asian Thought & Religion: Vol. 15). 130p. 1995. text 69.95 (*0-7734-9145-7*) E Mellen.

Philosophical Foundations for Moral Education & Character Development: Act & Agent. 2nd ed. Ed. by George F. McLean & Frederick Ellrod. LC 91-30829. (Cultural Heritage & Contemporary Change Series VI: Foundations of Moral Education,: Vol. I). 366p. (Orig.). 1992. 45.00 (*1-56518-001-1*, BJ1012.A26); pap. 17.50 (*1-56518-000-3*) Coun Res Values.

Philosophical Foundations of Adult Education. 2nd ed. John L. Elias & Sharon B. Merriam. LC 94-33663. 266p. (C). 1994. lib. bdg. 29.50 (*0-89464-918-3*) Krieger.

Philosophical Foundations of Cybernetics, Vol. 1. F. H. George. (Illus.). x, 158p. 1979. text 106.00 (*0-85626-163-7*) Gordon & Breach.

Philosophical Foundations of Economic Doctrines. 3rd ed. Nicholas L. Chirovsky & Vincent Mott. 1981. pap. 5.95 (*0-912598-20-4*) Florham.

Philosophical Foundations of Education see Classic & Contemporary Readings in the Philosophy of Education

Philosophical Foundations of Faith. Marion J. Bradshaw. LC 78-99248. reprint ed. 20.00 (*0-404-00968-9*) AMS Pr.

Philosophical Foundations of Gerontology. Ed. by Patrick L. McKee. LC 81-2922. 352p. 1982. 43.95 (*0-89885-040-1*, Kluwer Acad Hman Sci); pap. 24.95 (*0-89885-041-X*, Kluwer Acad Hman Sci) Kluwer Academic.

Philosophical Foundations of Historical Knowledge. Murray G. Murphey. LC 93-5321. 344p. (C). 1994. text 74.50 (*0-7914-1919-3*); pap. text 24.95 (*0-7914-1920-7*) State U NY Pr.

Philosophical Foundations of Humboldt's Linguistic Doctrines. Martin L. Manchester. LC 85-9209. (Studies in the History of the Language Sciences: No. 32). xii, 216p. 1985. 48.00 (*90-272-4514-2*) J Benjamins Pubng Co.

Philosophical Foundations of Paranormal Phenomena. Harry Settanni. LC 92-23295. 96p. (Orig.). (C). 1992. pap. text 14.50 (*0-8191-8867-0*) U Pr of Amer.

Philosophical Foundations of Probability Theory. Roy Weatherford. (International Library of Philosophy). 304p. 1982. 32.50 (*0-7100-9002-1*, Routledge Thoemms) Routledge.

Philosophical Foundations of Quantum Field Theory. Ed. by Harvey R. Brown & Rom Harre. (Illus.). 196p. 1990. reprint ed. pap. text 29.95 (*0-19-824289-1*) OUP.

Philosophical Foundations of Social Work. Frederic G. Reamer. 219p. 1995. pap. 20.50 (*0-231-07127-2*) Col U Pr.

Philosophical Foundations of Soviet Aesthetics. Ed. by Edward M. Swiderski. (Sovietica Ser.: No. 42). 1979. lib. bdg. 106.00 (*90-277-0980-7*) Kluwer Academic.

Philosophical Foundations of the Social Sciences: Analyzing Controversies in Social Research. Harold Kincaid. (Illus.). 301p. (C). 1995. text 59.95 (*0-521-48268-2*); pap. text 18.95 (*0-521-55891-3*) Cambridge U Pr.

Philosophical Foundations of Tort Law. Ed. by David G. Owen. 526p. 1996. text 75.00 (*0-19-825847-X*, Clarendon Pr) OUP.

Philosophical Foundations of Tort Law. Ed. by David G. Owen. 526p. 1997. reprint ed. pap. text 26.00 (*0-19-826579-4*) OUP.

Philosophical Fragments. Friedrich von Schlegel. Tr. by Peter Firchow from GER. 144p. (C). 1991. pap. 12.95 (*0-8166-1901-8*) U of Minn Pr.

Philosophical Fragments & Johannes Climacus. Ed. by Robert L. Perkins. LC 93-48223. (International Kierkegaard Commentary Ser.: No. 7). (C). 1994. 24.95 (*0-86554-440-9*, MUP-H351) Mercer Univ Pr.

Philosophical Fragments, or a Fragment of Philosophy-Johannes Climacus, or De Omnibus Dubitandum Est, 2 bks. in 1 vol. Soren Kierkegaard. Ed. by Howard V. Hong & Edna H. Hong. LC 85-3420. (New French Thought Ser.: No. VII). 386p. 1985. pap. text 17.95 (*0-691-02036-1*, Pub. by Princeton U Pr) Cal Prin Full Svc.

Philosophical Geometry. Andre Vanden Broeck. 168p. (Orig.). 1987. pap. 12.95 (*0-89281-116-1*) Inner Tradit.

Philosophical Grammar. Ludwig Josef Johann Wittgenstein. Tr. by A. J. Kenny. 1974. pap. 16.95 (*0-520-03725-1*, Pub. by U CA Pr) Cal Prin Full Svc.

Philosophical Grounds. Thomas Molnar. LC 91-10918. (American University Studies: Philosophy: Ser. V, Vol. 114). 162p. (C). 1991. text 32.95 (*0-8204-1485-9*) P Lang Pubng.

Philosophical Health: Wittgenstein's Method in Philosophical Investigations. Richard Gilmore. LC 98-44820. 288p. 1998. 58.00 (*0-7391-0009-2*) Lxngtn Bks.

Philosophical Hermeneutics. Hans-Georg Gadamer. LC 74-30519. 1976. pap. 18.95 (*0-520-03475-9*, Pub. by U CA Pr) Cal Prin Full Svc.

Philosophical Hermenutics & Literary Theory. Joel C. Weinsheimer. 192p. (C). 1991. 30.00 (*0-300-04785-1*) Yale U Pr.

Philosophical Historicism & the Betrayal of First Philosophy. Carl Page. 256p. 1995. 38.50 (*0-271-01330-3*) Pa St U Pr.

Philosophical Humanism & Contemporary India. V. P. Varma. 1979. 10.50 (*0-89684-054-9*, Pub. by Motilal Bnarsidass) S Asia.

Philosophical Idealism. Alan P. Sell. LC 95-17944. 272p. 1995. text 55.00 (*0-312-12746-4*) St Martin.

Philosophical Idealism & Christian Belief. Alan P. Sell. 272p. 1996. 65.00 (*0-7083-1310-8*, Pub. by Univ Wales Pr) Paul & Co Pubs.

Philosophical Imaginary. Michele Le Doeuff. Tr. by Colin Gordon. LC 88-63325. 222p. 1990. 35.00 (*0-8047-1619-6*) Stanford U Pr.

Philosophical Imagination & Cultural Memory: Appropriating Historical Traditions. Ed. by Patricia Cook. LC 92-34703. (Illus.). 257p. 1993. text 49.95 (*0-8223-1307-3*); pap. text 18.95 (*0-8223-1322-7*) Duke.

Philosophical Import of Gandhism. M. Kirti Singh. (C). 1995. 32.00 (*81-7433-009-7*) South Asia Pubns.

Philosophical Inquiry: Instructional Manual to Accompany Harry Stottlemeier's Discovery. 2nd ed. Matthew Lipman et al. LC 76-9315. 1979. spiral bd. 45.00 (*0-916834-12-3*, TX467-188) Inst Advncmnt Philos Child.

Philosophical Interactions with Parapsychology: The Major Writings of H. H. Price on Parapsychology & Survival. Ed. by Frank B. Dilley. LC 95-8229. 270p. 1995. text 65.00 (*0-312-12607-7*) St Martin.

Philosophical Interpretation of History. Abdul H. Siddiqui. 1996. 14.95 (*0-933511-99-X*) Kazi Pubns.

Philosophical Interpretations. Robert J. Fogelin. (Illus.). 272p. 1992. text 60.00 (*0-19-507162-X*) OUP.

Philosophical Interventions in the Unfinished Project of Enlightment. Ed. by Axel Honneth et al. 368p. 1992. pap. text 20.00 (*0-262-58109-4*) MIT Pr.

Philosophical Interventions in the Unfinished Project of Enlightment. Ed. by Axel Honneth et al. 368p. 1992. 40.00 (*0-262-08208-X*) MIT Pr.

Philosophical Introduction to Set Theory. Stephen Pollard. LC 89-40391. (C). 1990. text 34.50 (*0-268-01584-8*); pap. text 18.50 (*0-268-01585-6*) U of Notre Dame Pr.

Philosophical Investigation. Philip Kerr. 384p. 1995. pap. 8.99 (*0-7704-2592-5*) Bantam.

Philosophical Investigation. Philip Kerr. LC 93-27543. 1994. pap. 12.95 (*0-452-27140-1*, Plume) Dutton Plume.

Philosophical Investigation. Philip Kerr. 1993. 20.00 (*0-374-23176-1*) FS&G.

Philosophical Investigations. 2nd ed. Ludwig Josef Johann Wittgenstein. Tr. by G. E. Anscombe. LC 96-37331. 1998. pap. 29.95 (*0-631-20569-1*) Blackwell Pubs.

Philosophical Investigations. 3rd ed. Ludwig Josef Johann Wittgenstein. (C). 1973. pap. text 36.00 (*0-02-428810-1*, Macmillan Coll) P-H.

Philosophical Investigations in the U. S. S. R. F. J. Adelmann. (Boston College Studies in Philosophy: No. 4). 146p. 1975. pap. text 71.50 (*90-247-1724-8*) Kluwer Academic.

Philosophical Investment. Philip Kerr. 320p. 1994. pap. 12.95 (*0-385-25456-3*) Doubleday.

Philosophical Irony of Laurence Sterne. Helene Moglen. LC 75-4574. 172p. 1975. 49.95 (*0-8130-0363-6*) U Press Fla.

Philosophical Issues & Problems. Bien & Bon. 672p. (C). 1998. pap. text 51.75 (*0-536-01337-3*) Pearson Custom.

Philosophical Issues in Adventure Education. 2nd ed. Scott D. Wurdinger. 128p. 1995. pap., per. 21.95 (*0-7872-0434-X*) Kendall-Hunt.

Philosophical Issues in Adventure Education. 3rd ed. Scott Wurdinger. LC 97-73192. 128p. (C). 1997. per. 27.95 (*0-7872-3623-3*, 41362301) Kendall-Hunt.

Philosophical Issues in Art. Patricia H. Werhane. (Illus.). 608p. (C). 1983. text 47.20 (*0-13-662288-7*) P-H.

Philosophical Issues in Education. C. M. Hamm. 200p. 1989. 49.95 (*1-85000-598-2*, Falmer Pr); pap. 34.95 (*1-85000-599-0*, Falmer Pr) Taylor & Francis.

Philosophical Issues in Journalism. Elliot D. Cohen. 288p. (C). 1992. pap. text 23.95 (*0-19-506898-X*) OUP.

Philosophical Issues in the Education of Adults. K. H. Lawson. 150p. 1997. 29.95 (*1-85041-085-2*, Pub. by U of Nottingham) St Mut.

Philosophical Issues in the Psychology of C. G. Jung. Marilyn Nagy. LC 89-26319. 252p. (C). 1991. text 21.50 (*0-7914-0451-X*) State U NY Pr.

***Philosophical Journey: A Field Manual for Explorers.** William F. Lawhead. LC 99-37468. 1999. text 52.95 (*0-7674-0218-9*) Mayfield Pub.

Philosophical Knowledge. Ed. by John B. Brough. LC 80-69505. (Proceedings of the American Catholic Philosophical Association Ser.: Vol. 54). 250p. (Orig.). 1980. pap. 20.00 (*0-918090-14-8*) Am Cath Philo.

Philosophical Law: Authority, Equality, Adjudication, Privacy, 2. Ed. by Richard Bronaugh. LC 77-18106. (Contributions in Legal Studies: No. 2). 208p. 1978. 55.00 (*0-8371-9809-7*, BPL/, Greenwood Pr) Greenwood.

Philosophical Legacy of Behaviorism Bruce A. Thyer. LC 99-22918. (Studies in Cognitive Systems). 1999. write for info. (*0-7923-5736-1*) Kluwer Academic.

Philosophical Letters & Apology of a Madman. Peter Y. Chaadaev. LC 79-88186. 219p. reprint ed. pap. 67.90 (*0-608-30623-1*, 201967500014) Bks Demand.

Philosophical Life: An Introduction. Harris. (C). 1998. pap. text. write for info. (*0-15-503728-5*) Harcourt Coll Pubs.

Philosophical Logic. 161p. 1968. pap. text 107.00 (*90-247-0290-9*) Kluwer Academic.

Philosophical Logic. Ed. by T. J. Smiley. LC 99-236289. (Proceedings of the British Academy Ser.: No. 95). 168p. 1999. text 35.00 (*0-19-726182-5*) OUP.

Philosophical Logic: An Introduction. Sybil Wolfram. 288p. (C). 1989. pap. 24.99 (*0-415-02318-1*) Routledge.

Philosophical Logic: An Introduction. Sybil Wolfram. 288p. 1989. 55.00 (*0-415-02317-3*) Routledge.

Philosophical Logic: Philosophical Papers, Vol. 2. George H. Von Wright. LC 83-71774. 192p. 1983. text 39.95 (*0-8014-1674-4*) Cornell U Pr.

Philosophical Logic & Artificial Intelligence. Ed. by Richmond H. Thomason. 228p. (C). 1989. lib. bdg. 101.50 (*0-7923-0415-2*, Pub. by Kluwer Academic) Kluwer Academic.

Philosophical Logic & Logical Philosophy: Essays in Honour of Vladimir A. Smirnov. Ed. by Peter I. Bystrov. LC 96-36289. (Synthese Library SYLI: No. 257). 288p. (C). 1996. text 133.50 (*0-7923-4270-4*) Kluwer Academic.

Philosophical Logic in Poland. Ed. by Jan Wolenski. LC 93-15478. (Synthese Library: Vol. 228). 372p. (C). 1994. lib. bdg. 219.00 (*0-7923-2293-2*, Pub. by Kluwer Academic) Kluwer Academic.

Philosophical Medical Ethics. Raanan Gillon. LC 86-15749. 200p. 1986. pap. 74.95 (*0-471-91222-0*) Wiley.

Philosophical Medical Ethics: Its Nature & Significance. Ed. by Stuart F. Spicker & H. Tristram Englehardt, Jr. (Philosophy & Medicine Ser.: No. 3). 258p. 1977. text 96.00 (*90-277-0772-3*, D Reidel) Kluwer Academic.

Philosophical Meditations on Zen Buddhism. Dale S. Wright. LC 97-38793. (Cambridge Studies in Religious Traditions: No. 13). 243p. (C). 1998. text 54.95 (*0-521-59010-8*) Cambridge U Pr.

***Philosophical Meditations on Zen Buddhism.** Dale S. Wright. (Cambridge Studies in Religious Traditions: Vol. 13). 244p. 2000. pap. write for info. (*0-521-78984-2*) Cambridge U Pr.

Philosophical Melancholy & Delirium: Hume's Pathology of Philosophy. Donald W. Livingston. LC 97-35175. 456p. 1998. pap. text 25.00 (*0-226-48717-2*); lib. bdg. 68.00 (*0-226-48716-4*) U Ch Pr.

Philosophical Midwifery: A New Paradigm for Understanding Human Problems with Its Validation. Pierre Grimes & Regina L. Uliana. 323p. (C). 1998. pap. 19.95 (*0-9648191-1-2*, 0-9648191-1-2) Hyparxis Pr.

***Philosophical Midwifery: A New Paradigm for Understanding Human Problems with Its Validation.** Pierre Grimes & Regina L. Uliana. LC 97-73816. (Illus.). 323p. 1998. 29.95 (*0-9648191-2-0*) Hyparxis Pr.

Philosophical Mutterings about Things of Some Importance. Roberta Mendel. (Sketchbook Ser.). (Illus.). 24p. 1980. reprint ed. pap. 10.00 (*0-936424-05-2*, 004) Pin Prick.

Philosophical Mysteries. Stephen D. Ross. LC 80-26837. (SUNY Series in Systematic Philosophy). 151p. 1981. text 19.50 (*0-87395-524-2*) State U NY Pr.

Philosophical Naturalism. Ed. by Peter A. French et al. LC 94-15939. (Midwest Studies in Philosophy: Vol. 19). (C). 1995. text 61.00 (*0-268-01410-8*); pap. text 31.00 (*0-268-01411-6*) U of Notre Dame Pr.

***Philosophical Nature: A Book of Haiku Poetry by Redenta Soprano.** Redenta Soprano. (Illus.). 54p. 1999. 8.00 (*0-9674603-0-1*) Ceres.

Philosophical Notebook, 2 vols., Set. John Henry Newman. Ed. by E. Sillem. Incl. Vol. 1. General Introduction. 257p. 1970. text Vol. 2. Text. v, 218p. 1970. text 1970. 105.00 (*0-912116-13-7*) Learned Pubns.

Philosophical Notes to My Friends. John Elias. LC 97-78145. (Essay Ser.: Vol. 41). 190p. 1998. pap. 18.00 (*1-55071-084-2*) Guernica Editions.

Philosophical Novelist: George Santayana & the Last Puritan. H. T. Kirby-Smith. LC 96-43073. 1997. 39.95 (*0-8093-2113-0*) S Ill U Pr.

Philosophical Occasions, 1912-1951. Ludwig Josef Johann Wittgenstein. Ed. by James Klagge & Alfred Nordmann. LC 92-38232. 448p. (Orig.). (C). 1993. pap. text 24.95 (*0-87220-154-6*); lib. bdg. 49.95 (*0-87220-155-4*) Hackett Pub.

Philosophical Orations of Thomas Reid Delivered at Graduation Ceremonies in King's College, Aberdeen, 1753, 1756, 1759, 1762. Ed. by D. D. Todd. Tr. by Shirley D. Sullivan. LC 88-21133. (Journal of the History of Philosophy Monograph Ser.). 96p. (C). 1989. pap. 14.95 (*0-8093-1468-1*) S Ill U Pr.

Philosophical Origins of Austrian Economics. David Gordon. 68p. (Orig.). 1996. pap. text 6.95 (*0-945466-14-5*) Ludwig von Mises.

Philosophical Origins of Entropy Minimax. R. Christensen. LC 81-202346. (Entropy Minimax Sourcebook Ser.: Vol. 2). x, 218p. 1980. 29.95 (*0-938876-04-X*) Entropy Ltd.

Philosophical Origins of Modern Contract Doctrine. James Gordley. (Clarendon Law Ser.). 272p. (C). 1993. reprint ed. pap. 24.95 (*0-19-825830-5*) OUP.

Philosophical Papers, 2 vols. Hilary Putnam. Incl. Vol. 2. Mind, Language & Reality. 474p. 1979. pap. text 35.95 (*0-521-29551-3*); 1975. write for info. (*0-318-51290-4*) Cambridge U Pr.

Philosophical Papers. 3rd ed. J. L. Austin. Ed. by J. O. Urmson & Geoffrey J. Warnock. 316p. 1990. pap. text 24.95 (*0-19-283021-X*) OUP.

Philosophical Papers, Set. Hilary Putman. 1986. pap. 85.00 (*0-521-31020-2*) Cambridge U Pr.

Philosophical Papers, 2 vols., Vol. 1: Human Agency & Language. Charles Taylor. 304p. 1985. pap. text 27.95 (*0-521-31750-9*) Cambridge U Pr.

Philosophical Papers, 2 vols., Vol. 2: Philosophy & the Human Sciences. Charles Taylor. 352p. 1985. pap. text 27.95 (*0-521-31749-5*) Cambridge U Pr.

Philosophical Papers: Betwixt & Between. Calvin O. Schrag. LC 93-12750. (SUNY Series in Contemporary Continental Philosophy). 318p. (C). 1994. text 59.50 (*0-7914-1829-4*); pap. text 19.95 (*0-7914-1830-8*) State U NY Pr.

Philosophical Papers: Mathematics, Science & Epistemology, Vol. 2. Imre Lakatos. Ed. by J. Worrall & Gregory Currie. LC 77-14374. 295p. 1980. pap. text 35.95 (*0-521-28030-3*) Cambridge U Pr.

Philosophical Papers: The Methodology of Scientific Research Programmes, Vol. 1. Imre Lakatos. Ed. by J. Worrall & Gregory Currie. LC 77-71415. 258p. 1980. pap. text 35.95 (*0-521-28031-1*) Cambridge U Pr.

Philosophical Papers Vol. 1: Mathematics, Matter & Method. 2nd ed. Hilary Putman. (Illus.). 374p. 1979. pap. text 35.95 (*0-521-29550-5*) Cambridge U Pr.

Philosophical Papers Vol. 1: Realism, Rationalism & Scientific Method. Paul K. Feyerabend. 368p. 1985. pap. text 33.95 (*0-521-31642-1*) Cambridge U Pr.

Philosophical Papers Vol. 2: Language & Reality. Hilary Putman. (Illus.). 457p. 1975. 47.50 (*0-317-66588-X*); pap. 18.95 (*0-317-66589-8*) Cambridge U Pr.

Philosophical Papers Vol. 2: Problems of Empiricism. Paul K. Feyerabend. 268p. 1985. pap. text 35.95 (*0-521-31641-3*) Cambridge U Pr.

Philosophical Papers Vol. 3: Reason, Truth & History. Hilary Putman. (Illus.). 312p. 1985. pap. text 26.95 (*0-521-31394-5*) Cambridge U Pr.

Philosophical Papers Vol. 3: Reason, Truth & History. Hilary Putman. LC 81-6126. 224p. 1981. pap. text 21.95 (*0-521-29776-1*) Cambridge U Pr.

Philosophical Papers, 1896-99. Bertrand Russell. Ed. by Nicholas Griffin. (The Collected Papers of Bertrand Russell: Vol. 2). 672p. (C). 1990. 175.00 (*0-415-09863-7*) Routledge.

Philosophical Papers, 1913-1946. Otto Neurath. Ed. by Robert S. Cohen & Maria Neurath. 280p. 1983. text 211.50 (*90-277-1483-5*, D Reidel) Kluwer Academic.

Philosophical Papers of Alan Donagan Vol. 1: Historical Understanding & the History of Philosophy. Alan Donagan. Ed. by J. E. Malpas. 298p. 1994. 39.95 (*0-226-15570-6*) U Ch Pr.

Philosophical Papers of Alan Donagan Vol. 2: Action, Reason & Value. Alan Donagan. Ed. by J. E. Malpas. 314p. 1994. 39.95 (*0-226-15571-4*) U Ch Pr.

Philosophical Passages: Wittgenstein, Emerson, Austen, Derrida. Stanley Cavell. LC 94-15838. (Bucknell Lectures in Literary Theory Ser.: Vol. 12). 208p. 1995. pap. 26.95 (*0-631-19271-9*) Blackwell Pubs.

Philosophical Perspectives. James E. Tomberlin. 1996. pap. text 34.95 (*1-57718-116-6*) Blackwell Pubs.

Philosophical Perspectives. James E. Tomberlin. 1997. text 58.95 (*1-57718-115-8*) Blackwell Pubs.

P

Philosophical Perspectives, Vol. 12. James E. Tomberlin. 540p. 1998. 54.95 (0-631-21206-X) Blackwell Pubs.

*__Philosophical Perspectives: Epistemology.__ James E. Tomberlin. 540p. 1999. pap. 34.95 (0-631-21826-2) Blackwell Pubs.

Philosophical Perspectives: History of Philosophy. Wilfrid Sellars. (C). 1976. reprint ed. pap. text 12.00 (0-917930-04-5); reprint ed. lib. bdg. 27.00 (0-917930-24-X) Ridgeview.

Philosophical Perspectives: Metaphysics & Epistemology. Wilfrid Sellars. (C). 1977. reprint ed. pap. text 12.00 (0-917930-05-3); reprint ed. lib. bdg. 27.00 (0-917930-25-8) Ridgeview.

Philosophical Perspectives: Mind, Causation & World. Ed. by James E. Tomberlin. (Philosophical Perspectives Ser.: No. 11). 480p. 1998. 58.95 (0-631-20793-7); pap. 34.95 (0-631-20794-5) Blackwell Pubs.

Philosophical Perspectives Vol. 1: Metaphysics, 1987. Ed. by James E. Tomberlin. x, 534p. (Orig.). 1987. pap. text 31.00 (0-917930-46-0); lib. bdg. 53.00 (0-917930-86-X) Ridgeview.

Philosophical Perspectives Vol. 2: Epistemology, 1988. Ed. by James E. Tomberlin. x, 476p. (Orig.). 1988. pap. text 31.00 (0-917930-47-9); lib. bdg. 53.00 (0-917930-87-8) Ridgeview.

Philosophical Perspectives Vol. 3: Philosophy of Mind & Action Theory, 1989. Ed. by James E. Tomberlin. x, 600p. (Orig.). 1989. pap. text 31.00 (0-917930-48-7); lib. bdg. 53.00 (0-917930-88-6) Ridgeview.

Philosophical Perspectives Vol. 4: Action Theory & Philosophy of Mind, 1990. Ed. by James E. Tomberlin. x, 582p. (Orig.). 1990. pap. text 31.00 (0-917930-49-5); lib. bdg. 53.00 (0-917930-89-4) Ridgeview.

Philosophical Perspectives Vol. 5: Philosophy of Religion, 1991. Ed. by James E. Tomberlin. x, 646p. (Orig.). 1991. pap. text 31.00 (0-924922-03-6); lib. bdg. 53.00 (0-924922-53-2) Ridgeview.

Philosophical Perspectives Vol. 7: Language & Logic, 1993. Ed. by James E. Tomberlin. x, 534p. (Orig.). 1993. pap. text 31.00 (0-924922-15-X); lib. bdg. 53.00 (0-924922-65-6) Ridgeview.

Philosophical Perspectives Vol. 8: Logic & Language, 1994. Ed. by James E. Tomberlin. x, 470p. (Orig.). 1994. pap. text 31.00 (0-924922-16-8); lib. bdg. 53.00 (0-924922-66-4) Ridgeview.

Philosophical Perspectives Vol. 9: AI, Connectionism & Philosophical Psychology, 1995. Ed. by James E. Tomberlin. 520p. (Orig.). (C). 1995. pap. text 31.00 (0-924922-23-0); lib. bdg. 53.00 (0-924922-73-7) Ridgeview.

*__Philosophical Perspectives Vol. 13: Epistemology.__ Ed. by James E. Tomberlin. 540p. 1999. 64.95 (0-631-21825-4) Blackwell Pubs.

Philosophical Perspectives Ethics, 1992 Vol. 6. Ed. by James E. Tomberlin. x, 575p. (Orig.). 1992. pap. text 31.00 (0-924922-08-7); lib. bdg. 53.00 (0-924922-58-3) Ridgeview.

Philosophical Perspectives of Sikhism. Avtar Singh & Guraneama Kaura. LC 98-915211. xviii, 254p. 1998. write for info. (81-7380-467-2) Pubn Bureau.

Philosophical Perspectives on Accounting: Essays in Honor of Edward Stamp. M. J. Mumford. LC 92-18454. 256p. (C). (gr. 13). 1992. pap. 85.95 (0-415-08093-2, A9718) Thomson Learn.

Philosophical Perspectives on Bioethics. Ed. by L. W. Sumner & Joseph Boyle. (Toronto Studies in Philosophy). 368p. 1996. text 55.00 (0-8020-0771-6); pap. text 19.95 (0-8020-7139-2) U of Toronto Pr.

Philosophical Perspectives on Computer-Mediated Communication. Ed. & Intro. by Charles Ess. LC 95-12668. (SUNY Series in Computer-Mediated Communication). 327p. (C). 1996. text 59.50 (0-7914-2871-0); pap. text 19.95 (0-7914-2872-9) State U NY Pr.

Philosophical Perspectives on God & Religion: Descartes, Lock, Leibniz & Hume, Vol. 1. Wayne P. Pomerleau. LC 92-19362. 325p. (C). 1995. text 37.50 (0-89341-706-8) Hollowbrook.

Philosophical Perspectives on God & Religion: Kant, Hegel, Kierkegaard & James, Vol. 2. Wayne P. Pomerleau. LC 92-19362. 325p. (C). 1995. text 37.50 (0-89341-713-0) Hollowbrook.

Philosophical Perspectives on Language. Robert J. Stainton. 244p. 1996. pap. 19.95 (1-55111-086-5) Broadview Pr.

Philosophical Perspectives on Law & Politics: Readings from Plato to Derrida. Ed. by Patrick Hayden. LC 98-44607. (Teaching Texts in Law & Politics Ser.: Vol. 8). VIII, 364p. (C). 1999. pap. text 29.95 (0-8204-4282-8) P Lang Pubng.

Philosophical Perspectives on Metaphor. Ed. by Mark Johnson. LC 81-872. 377p. reprint ed. pap. 116.90 (0-8357-3332-7, 203955700013) Bks Demand.

Philosophical Perspectives on Music. Wayne D. Bowman. 496p. (C). 1998. text 47.95 (0-19-511296-2) OUP.

Philosophical Perspectives on Newtonian Science. Ed. by Phillip Bricker & R. I. Hughes. LC 89-29465. (Johns Hopkins Series on the History & Philosophy of Science). 250p. 1990. 37.50 (0-262-02301-6, Bradford Bks) MIT Pr.

Philosophical Perspectives on Peace: An Anthology of Classical & Modern Sources. Ed. by Howard P. Kainz. LC 86-12836. 325p. 1986. text 39.95 (0-8214-0849-6); pap. text 19.95 (0-8214-0850-X) Ohio U Pr.

Philosophical Perspectives on Psychiatric Diagnostic Classification. Ed. by John Z. Sadler et al. LC 93-15949. (Series in Psychiatry & Neuroscience). 448p. (C). 1994. text 69.50 (0-8018-4637-4); pap. text 29.95 (0-8018-4770-2) Johns Hopkins.

Philosophical Perspectives on Punishment. Ed. by Gertrude Ezorsky. LC 72-37999. 377p. (C). 1972. text 49.50 (0-87395-212-X); pap. text 24.95 (0-87395-213-8) State U NY Pr.

Philosophical Perspectives on Sex & Love. Robert M. Stewart. 352p. (C). 1995. pap. text 33.95 (0-19-508031-9) OUP.

Philosophical Perspectives on the Israeli/Palestinian Conflict. Ed. by Tomis Kapitan. LC 96-44649. 392p. (gr. 13). 1997. pap. text 32.95 (1-56324-878-6) M E Sharpe.

Philosophical Perspectives on the Israeli/Palestinian Conflict. Ed. by Tomis Kapitan. LC 96-44649. 392p. (C). (gr. 13). 1997. text 76.95 (1-56324-877-8) M E Sharpe.

Philosophical Perspectives 12. James E. Tomberlin. (Philosophical Perspectives Ser.: No. 12). 540p. 1998. pap. 32.95 (0-631-21207-8) Blackwell Pubs.

*__Philosophical Poems.__ E. M. Johnson. Ed. by Elizabeth Coons. (Illus.). 106p. 1999. pap. 11.95 (1-886028-41-9, Pub. by Savage Pr) Bookmen Inc.

Philosophical-Political Profiles. Jurgen Habermas. Tr. by Frederick Lawrence. (Studies in Contemporary German Social Thought). (ENG & GER.). 304p. 1983. 27.50 (0-262-08133-4) MIT Pr.

Philosophical Political Profiles. Jurgen Habermas. Tr. by Frederick G. Lawrence from GER. (Studies in Contemporary German Social Thought). 240p. 1985. reprint ed. pap. text 17.00 (0-262-58071-3) MIT Pr.

Philosophical Problems: God, Free Will, & Determinism. Ron Yezzi. LC 93-79450. ii, 155p. 1993. pap. text 10.00 (0-9619368-5-1) G Bruno.

Philosophical Problems: Selected Readings. 4th ed. Samuel E. Stumpf. LC 93-29947. 432p. (C). 1993. pap. 43.44 (0-07-062177-2) McGraw.

Philosophical Problems: The Good Life. Ron Yezzi. LC 94-70175. iv, 205p. (C). 1994. pap. 13.50 (0-9619368-6-X) G Bruno.

Philosophical Problems & Arguments: An Introduction. rev. ed. James W. Cornman et al. 384p. (C). 1992. pap. text 18.95 (0-87220-124-4) Hackett Pub.

Philosophical Problems & Arguments: An Introduction. 4th rev. ed. James W. Cornman et al. 384p. (C). 1992. lib. bdg. 37.95 (0-87220-125-2) Hackett Pub.

Philosophical Problems in Health Care. Ed. by David Greaves & Hugh Upton. (Avebury Series in Philosophy). 215p. 1996. 78.95 (1-85972-222-9, Pub. by Avebury) Ashgate Pub Co.

Philosophical Problems in Logic: Some Recent Developments. Ed. by Karel Lambert. (Synthese Library: No. 29). 183p. 1970. text 94.00 (90-277-0079-6, D Reidel) Kluwer Academic.

Philosophical Problems in Physical Science. rev. ed. Herbert Hoerz et al. Tr. by Salomea Genin from GER. LC 80-13042. (Studies in Marxism: Vol. 7). Orig. Title: Philosophische Probleme der Physik. 190p. 1980. 19.95 (0-930656-14-8); pap. 9.95 (0-930656-13-X) MEP Pubns.

*__Philosophical Problems in the Law.__ 3rd ed. Adams. LC 99-19935. 608p. 1999. pap. 64.95 (0-534-51903-2) Thomson Learn.

Philosophical Problems of Many-Valued Logic. rev. ed. A. A. Zinoviev et al. Ed. & Tr. by Guido Kung & David Comey from RUS. (Synthese Library: No. 7). 169p. 1972. text 78.50 (90-277-0091-5, D Reidel) Kluwer Academic.

Philosophical Problems of Modern Physics. Peter Mittelstaedt. Ed. by R. S. Cohen. LC 72-92534. (Boston Studies in the Philosophy of Science: No. 18). 211p. 1975. pap. 17.50 (0-685-02827-5); lib. bdg. 78.00 (90-277-0285-3, D Reidel) Kluwer Academic.

Philosophical Problems of Psychology. Edward H. Madden. LC 72-11481. 149p. 1973. reprint ed. lib. bdg. 38.50 (0-8371-6668-3, MAPH, Greenwood Pr) Greenwood.

Philosophical Problems of Quantum Physics. Werner Heisenberg. LC 79-89842. Orig. Title: Philosophic Problems of Nuclear Science. 1979. reprint ed. 26.00 (0-918024-14-5); reprint ed. pap. 14.00 (0-918024-15-3) Ox Bow.

Philosophical Problems of Statistical Inference. Teddy Seidenfeld. (Theory & Decision Library: No. 22). 1979. lib. bdg. 121.50 (90-277-0965-3) Kluwer Academic.

Philosophical Problems of the Internal & External Worlds: Essays on the Philosophy of Adolf Grunbaum. Ed. by John Earman et al. LC 92-27354. (Pittsburgh-Konstanz Series in Philosophy & History of Science). 648p. (C). 1993. text 75.00 (0-8229-3738-7) U of Pittsburgh Pr.

Philosophical Problems Today, Vol. 1. Willard V. Quine. Ed. by Guttorm Flistad. LC 93-38219. 224p. (C). 1994. lib. bdg. 166.50 (0-7923-2564-8, Pub. by Kluwer Academic) Kluwer Academic.

Philosophical Profiles: Essays in a Pragmatic Mode. Richard J. Bernstein. LC 85-16431. 328p. (C). 1986. 41.95 (0-8122-7995-6) U of Pa Pr.

Philosophical Programmer. Daniel Kohanski. LC 98-9792. 256p. 1998. text 22.95 (0-312-18650-9) St Martin.

Philosophical Propositions: An Introduction to Philosophy. Jonathan Westphal. LC 97-33483. (Illus.). 192p. (C). 1998. 60.00 (0-415-17052-4); pap. 18.99 (0-415-17053-2) Routledge.

Philosophical Psychology & Interpretating Wittgenstein: How to Look at Words As Instruments. J. F. Hunter. 192p. (C). 1990. lib. bdg. 63.00 (0-389-20920-1) Rowman.

Philosophical Psychopathology. Ed. by George Graham & G. Lynn Stephens. LC 94-31921. 344p. 1995. 41.50 (0-262-07159-2, Bradford Bks) MIT Pr.

Philosophical Quest: A Cross Cultural Reader. Ed. by Gail M. Presbey et al. LC 94-33149. (C). 1994. pap. text 36.25 (0-07-062547-6) McGraw.

*__Philosophical Quest: A Cross-Cultural Reader__ 2nd ed. Gail M. Presbey et al. LC 99-35392. 2000. write for info. (0-07-289867-4) McGrw-H Intl.

*__Philosophical Questions: East & West.__ Ed. by Bina Gupta & J. N. Mohanty. LC 99-42372. 432p. 1999. 65.95 (0-8476-9284-1); pap. 26.95 (0-8476-9285-X) Rowman.

Philosophical Readings from the Arabic Tradition. Lenn Goodman. (Arabic Thought & Culture Ser.). 240p. (C). 1998. 65.00 (0-415-08142-4); pap. 18.99 (0-415-08143-2) Routledge.

Philosophical Reflection of Man in Literature. Anna-Teresa Tymieniecka. 498p. 1982. text 199.50 (90-277-1312-X, D Reidel) Kluwer Academic.

Philosophical Reflections. G. C. Nayak. (C). 1987. 11.50 (81-208-0421-X, Pub. by Motilal Bnarsidass) S Asia.

Philosophical Reflections on the Changes in Eastern Europe. William L. McBride. (Philosophy & the Global Context Ser.). 160p. 1998. 57.95 (0-8476-8797-X) Rowman.

Philosophical Reflections on the Changes in Eastern Europe. William L. McBride & Yvanka Raynova. LC 98-35373. (Philosophy & the Global Context Ser.). 160p. 1998. pap. 16.95 (0-8476-8798-8) Rowman.

Philosophical Reflections on the United States Constitution: A Collection of Bicentennial Essays. Ed. by Christopher B. Gray. LC 88-8862. (Studies in Social & Political Theory: Vol. 4). 210p. 1989. lib. bdg. 89.95 (0-88946-104-X) E Mellen.

Philosophical Relativity. Peter K. Unger. LC 83-6593. 142p. reprint ed. pap. 44.10 (0-7837-2911-1, 205754300006) Bks Demand.

Philosophical Remarks. Ludwig Josef Johann Wittgenstein. Ed. by Rush Rhees et al. LC 80-14296. 360p. 1980. pap. text 16.95 (0-226-90431-8, P912) U Ch Pr.

Philosophical Rhetoric: The Function of Indirection in Philosophical Writings. Jeff Mason. 192p. 1989. 45.00 (0-415-03043-9); pap. 13.95 (0-415-03044-7) Routledge.

Philosophical Roots of Anthropology. William Adams. LC 98-26003. (Lecture Notes Ser.: No. 86). 350p. (C). 1998. pap. 19.95 (1-57586-128-3) CSLI.

Philosophical Roots of Anthropology. William Adams. LC 98-26003. (CSLI Lecture Notes Ser.: Vol. 86). 450p. (C). 1998. text 59.95 (1-57586-129-1) CSLI.

Philosophical Selections: From the Search after Truth, Dialogue on Metaphysics, Treatise on Nature & Grace. Nicolas Malebranche. Ed. by Steven Nadler. Tr. by Thomas M. Lennon et al from FRE. LC 92-19801. 288p. (C). 1992. 37.95 (0-87220-153-8); pap. text 14.95 (0-87220-152-X) Hackett Pub.

Philosophical Skepticism & Ordinary-Language Analysis. Garrett L. Vander Veer. LC 78-1940. x, 278p. 1978. 29.95 (0-7006-0174-0) U Pr of KS.

Philosophical Sketches. Susanne K. Langer. 1979. 21.95 (0-405-10610-6) Ayer.

Philosophical Sketches of the Principles of Society & Government. William Drummond. LC 86-17791. 192p. 1986. reprint ed. 50.00 (0-8201-1418-9) Schol Facsimiles.

Philosophical Sovietology. Thomas J. Blakeley. 282p. (C). 1987. text 155.50 (90-277-2637-X, D Reidel) Kluwer Academic.

Philosophical Standardism: An Empiricist Approach to Philosophical Methodology. Nicholas Rescher. 224p. (C). 1994. text 49.95 (0-8229-3790-5) U of Pittsburgh Pr.

*__Philosophical Standardism: An Empiricist Approach to Philosophical Methodology.__ Nicholas Rescher. (Philosophy Ser.). 224p. 2000. pap. 19.95 (0-8229-5739-6) U of Pittsburgh Pr.

Philosophical Streets: New Approaches to Urbanism. Intro. by Dennis Crow. LC NA9095.P48. (Critical Studies in Community Development & Architecture: Vol. 1). (Illus.). 171p. (Orig.). (C). 1990. pap. text 13.95 (0-944624-09-X); lib. bdg. 26.95 (0-944624-08-1) Maisonneuve Pr.

Philosophical Studies. John McTaggart Ellis & S. V. Keeling. LC 99-56430. (Key Texts Ser.). Date not set. pap. text. write for info. (1-890318-66-3) St Augustines Pr.

Philosophical Studies. J. E. McTaggart. Ed. & Intro. by S. V. Keeling. Intro. by Gerald Rochelle. (Key Texts Ser.). 300p. 1996. pap. 22.00 (1-85506-479-0) Bks Intl VA.

Philosophical Studies. John M. McTaggart. Ed. by S. V. Keeling. LC 67-22104. (Essay Index Reprint Ser.). 1977. 20.95 (0-8369-0660-8) Ayer.

Philosophical Studies. Alfred E. Taylor. LC 75-13298. (History of Ideas in Ancient Greece Ser.). 1976. reprint ed. 29.95 (0-405-07342-9) Ayer.

Philosophical Studies. Alfred E. Taylor. LC 68-26480. (Essay Index Reprint Ser.). 1977. reprint ed. 31.95 (0-8369-0926-7) Ayer.

Philosophical Studies c.1611-c.1619: Phaenomena universi; De fluxu et refluxu maris; Descriptio globi intellectualis; Thema coeli; De principiis atque originibus; De vijs mortis, Vol. 6. Francis Bacon. Ed. by Graham Rees. (Oxford Francis Bacon Ser.: Vol. 5). (Illus.). 620p. (C). 1996. text 140.00 (0-19-812290-X) OUP.

Philosophical Study of T. S. Eliot's "Four Quartets" Martin Warner. LC 98-54765. 148p. 1999. text 69.95 (0-7734-8176-1) E Mellen.

Philosophical Study of the Concept of Vinsu in the Puranas. Koshlesh Bharadwaja. 416p. (C). 1998. 195.00 (81-209-0162-2, Pub. by Pitambar Pub); 250.00 (81-209-0737-X, Pub. by Pitambar Pub) St Mut.

Philosophical Study of the Criteria for Responsibility Ascriptions: Responsibility & Personal Interactions. Henry B. Tam. LC 90-28180. (Problems in Contemporary Philosophy Ser.: Vol. 28). 248p. 1990. lib. bdg. 89.95 (0-88946-786-2) E Mellen.

*__Philosophical Style, 1 Vol.__ B. Blanshard. 70p. 1999. pap. 18.95 (1-85506-598-3) Thoemmes Pr.

Philosophical Systems: A Categorical Analysis. Everett W. Hall. LC 60-11824. 1994. lib. bdg. 12.50 (0-226-31321-2) U Ch Pr.

Philosophical Systems: A Categorical Analysis. Everett W. Hall. LC 60-11824. 181p. reprint ed. pap. 56.20 (0-608-09324-6, 205419800004) Bks Demand.

Philosophical Teachings in the Upanisats. Mohan L. Sandal. LC 73-3831. (Sacred Books of the Hindus: Extra Vol. 5). reprint ed. 17.00 (0-404-57849-7) AMS Pr.

Philosophical Terms in the Moreh Nebukim. Israel I. Efros. LC 73-164764. (Columbia University. Oriental Studies: No. 22). reprint ed. 29.50 (0-404-50512-0) AMS Pr.

Philosophical Testament. Marjorie Grene. 193p. 1995. pap. text 18.95 (0-8126-9287-X) Open Court.

Philosophical Texts. Gottfried Wilhelm Leibniz. Tr. by R. S. Woolhouse & Richard Francks. (Oxford Philosophical Texts Ser.). 320p. (C). 1998. pap. text 11.95 (0-19-875153-2) OUP.

Philosophical Theology. James F. Ross. 366p. 1982. 49.50 (0-8290-0335-5) Irvington.

Philosophical Theology. James F. Ross. LC 68-17707. (C). 1969. write for info. (0-672-60721-2, Bobbs) Macmillan.

Philosophical Theology of John Duns Scotus. Allan B. Wolter. Ed. by Marilyn M. Adams. LC 89-46162. 352p. 1990. text 52.50 (0-8014-2385-6) Cornell U Pr.

Philosophical Theories. M. Lazerowitz & A. Ambrose. 1976. text 42.35 (90-279-7501-9) Mouton.

Philosophical Theories of Education. F. Raymond McKenna. LC 95-12676. 340p. (Orig.). (C). 1995. 59.50 (0-8191-9976-1) U Pr of Amer.

*__Philosophical Theories of Probability.__ Donald Gillies. LC 00-29113. 2000. pap. write for info. (0-415-18276-X) Routledge.

Philosophical Theory & Social Reality. Ed. by Ravinder Kumar. 200p. 1984. 22.95 (0-8364-1171-4, Pub. by Allied Pubs) S Asia.

Philosophical Theory & Social Reality. Ed. by Ravinder Kumar. 201p. 1984. 16.95 (0-318-37029-8) Asia Bk Corp.

Philosophical Theory of the State. Bernard Bosanquet. (Modern Revivals in Philosophy Ser.). 328p. 1993. 74.95 (0-7512-0204-5, Pub. by Gregg Revivals) Ashgate Pub Co.

Philosophical Theory of the State. 2nd ed. Bernard Bosanquet. 1986. reprint ed. pap. 28.95 (0-935005-20-X); reprint ed. lib. bdg. 45.95 (0-935005-19-6) Lincoln-Rembrandt.

Philosophical Theory of the State & Related Essays. Bernard Bosanquet. Ed. by Gerald F. Gaus & William Sweet. (Key Texts Ser.). 360p. 1999. pap. 22.95 (1-85506-584-3) Thoemmes Pr.

*__Philosophical Theory of the State & Related Essays.__ Bernard Bosanquet et al. LC 99-45575. 2000. pap. text 25.00 (1-890318-65-5) St Augustines Pr.

Philosophical Thinkers: A Compendium of Primary Texts. Daniel Rieger. 620p. (C). 1997. per. 68.95 (0-7872-2680-7) Kendall-Hunt.

Philosophical Thinking in Educational Practice. Robert D. Heslep. LC 96-53935. 200p. 1997. 55.00 (0-275-95495-1, Praeger Pubs) Greenwood.

Philosophical Thinking in Educational Practice. Robert D. Heslep. LC 96-53935. 200p. 1997. pap. 20.95 (0-275-95496-X, Praeger Pubs) Greenwood.

Philosophical Thought in America, 3 vols. Incl. Vol. 1. Panorama of Ideas in Latin America. 24p. 1971. pap. 1.00 (0-8270-5860-8); Vol. 2. Thinkers of Latin America - Andres Bello, Domingo Faustino Sarmiento, Silvio Romero. 16p. 1972. pap. 1.00 (0-8270-5865-9); Vol. 3. Inter-American Idea in the United States. 1976. pap. 3.00 (0-8270-5885-3); write for info. (0-318-54740-6) OAS.

Philosophical Traditions: A Text with Readings. Louis P. Pojman. LC 97-15855. (Philosophy Ser.). 465p. (C). 1997. 62.95 (0-534-26286-4) Wadsworth Pub.

Philosophical Traditions: A Text with Readings. 2nd ed. Louis P. Pojman. (Philosophy Ser.). Date not set. 38.50 (0-534-57042-9) Wadsworth Pub.

Philosophical Traditions of India. P. T. Raju. 256p. (C). 1992. 19.95 (1-881338-18-5) Nataraj Bks.

Philosophical Trends in the Contemporary World. Michele F. Sciacca. Tr. by Attilio M. Salerno. LC 64-20845. 1964. reprint ed. 52.50 (0-268-00210-X) Irvington.

Philosophical View of the Great Perfection in the Tibetan Bon Religion. Donatella Rossi. LC 99-57690. (ENG & TIB.). 315p. 2000. pap. 21.95 (1-55939-129-4) Snow Lion Pubns.

Philosophical Works. Incl. Vol. 1. Tr. by G. H. Whitaker & F. H. Colson. 19.95 (0-674-99249-0); Vol. 2. Tr. by G. H. Whitaker & F. H. Colson. 19.95 (0-674-99250-4); Vol. 3. Tr. by G. H. Whitaker & F. H. Colson. 19.95 (0-674-99272-5); Vol. 4. Tr. by F. H. Colson. 19.95 (0-674-99287-3); Vol. 5. Philo. 19.95 (0-674-99303-9); Vol. 6. Tr. by F. H. Colson. 19.95 (0-674-99319-5); Vol. 7. Tr. by F. H. Colson. 19.95 (0-674-99353-5); Vol. 8. Tr. by F. H. Colson. 19.95 (0-674-99376-4); Vol. 9. Tr. by F. H. Colson. 19.95 (0-674-99400-0); Vol. 10. Ed. by J. W. Earp. Tr. by F. H. Colson. 19.95 (0-674-99417-5); Suppl. 1. Tr. by Ralph Marcus. 19.95 (0-674-99418-3); Suppl. 2. Tr. by Ralph Marcus. 19.95 (0-674-99442-6); (Loeb Classical Library). write for info. (0-318-53136-4) HUP.

Philosophical Works, 4 vols., 1. Sextus Empiricus. (Loeb Classical Library: No. 273, 291, 311, 382). 560p. 1933. 18.95 (0-674-99301-2) HUP.

Philosophical Works, 4 vols., 2. Sextus Empiricus. (Loeb Classical Library: No. 273, 291, 311, 382). 498p. 1935. 18.95 (0-674-99321-7) HUP.

Philosophical Works, 4 vols., 3. Sextus Empiricus. (Loeb Classical Library: No. 273, 291, 311, 382). 564p. 1936. 18.95 (0-674-99344-6) HUP.

P

An Asterisk (*) at the beginning of an entry indicates that the title is appearing for the first time.

Philosophical Works, 4 vols., 4. Sextus Empiricus. (Loeb Classical Library: No. 273, 291, 311, 382). 418p. 1949. 18.95 (*0-674-99420-5*) HUP.

Philosophical Works, 4 Vols, Set. deluxe ed. David Hume. Ed. by Hill Green & H. Hodge Grose. reprint ed. 530.00 (*3-511-01210-4*) Adlers Foreign Bks.

***Philosophical Works: Claude-Adrien Helvetius, 3 vols.** 1460p. 2000. 400.00 (*1-85506-832-X*) Thoemmes Pr.

Philosophical Works: Including the Works on Vision. George Berkeley. Ed. by M. R. Ayers. 358p. 1993. pap. 8.95 (*0-460-87343-1*, Everyman's Classic Lib) Tuttle Pubng.

Philosophical Works: On the Relation of Philosophy to Theology. Peter M. Vermigli. Ed. & Tr. by Joseph C. McLelland from LAT. LC 96-44882. (Peter Martyr Library, Series 1: Vol. 4). 353p. 1996. 40.00 (*0-940474-41-7*, 0949474, SCJP) Truman St Univ.

Philosophical Works: With Notes & Supplementary Dissertations by Sir William Hamilton, 2 vols., Set. 8th ed. Thomas Reid. 1983. reprint ed. 154.70 (*3-487-01617-6*) G Olms Pubs.

Philosophical Works of David Hume, 1854, 4 vols., Set. 2178p. 1996. 375.00 (*1-85506-477-4*) Bks Intl VA.

Philosophical Works of Descartes, Vol. 1. Rene Descartes & G. R. Ross. Ed. by Elizabeth S. Haldane. 460p. reprint ed. pap. 131.10 (*0-608-12050-2*, 2024470) Bks Demand.

Philosophical Works of Etienne Bonnot, Abbe de Condillac, Vol. 1. F. Phillip & Harlan Lane. Tr. by Franklin Philip. 448p. (C). 1982. text 89.95 (*0-89859-181-3*) L Erlbaum Assocs.

Philosophical Works of Etienne Bonnot, Abbe de Condillac, Vol. II. Tr. by Franklin Philip & Harlan Lane from FRE. 192p. 1986. text 49.95 (*0-89859-616-5*) L Erlbaum Assocs.

Philosophical Works of Francis Bacon. Francis Bacon. LC 70-119952. (Select Bibliographies Reprint Ser.). 1977. 41.95 (*0-8369-5395-9*) Ayer.

Philosophical Works of Peter Chaadaev. Ed. by R. T. McNally. (C). 1991. lib. bdg. 180.50 (*0-7923-1285-6*, Pub. by M Nijhoff) Kluwer Academic.

Philosophical Writing: Locke, Berkeley, Hume. John J. Richetti. 304p. (C). 1983. 43.50 (*0-674-66482-5*) HUP.

Philosophical Writings. Francis Hutcheson. 336p. 1994. 8.50 (*0-460-87504-3*, Everyman's Classic Lib) Tuttle Pubng.

Philosophical Writings. Immanuel Kant. Ed. by Volkmar Sander. LC 74-78443. (German Library: Vol. 13). 316p. 1986. pap. 19.95 (*0-8264-0299-2*) Continuum.

Philosophical Writings. Immanuel Kant. Ed. by Volkmar Sander. LC 78-20935. (German Library: Vol. 13). 316p. (C). 1986. 39.50 (*0-8264-0298-4*) Continuum.

Philosophical Writings. Friedrich Wilhelm Nietzsche. Ed. by Reinhold Grimm & Caroline Molina y Vedia. LC 81-70120. (German Library). 324p. 1995. 39.50 (*0-8264-0278-X*) Continuum.

Philosophical Writings. Friedrich Wilhelm Nietzsche. Ed. by Reinhold Grimm. LC 81-70120. (German Library). 324p. 1995. pap. 19.95 (*0-8264-0279-8*) Continuum.

Philosophical Writings. Arthur Schopenhauer. Ed. by Wolfgang Schirmacher. LC 81-40469. (German Library). 324p. 1994. pap. 19.95 (*0-8264-0729-3*) Continuum.

Philosophical Writings. Arthur Schopenhauer. Ed. by Wolfgang Schirmacher. LC 81-40469. (German Library). 320p. (C). 1994. 39.50 (*0-8264-0728-5*) Continuum.

Philosophical Writings. William of Ockman. Tr. by Philotheus Boehner. LC 64-16710. pap. 4.95 (*0-672-60431-0*, LLA193, Bobbs) Macmillan.

Philosophical Writings. George Berkeley. Ed. by T. E. Jessop. LC 69-13823. 278p. 1969. reprint ed. lib. bdg. 65.00 (*0-8371-1056-4*, BEPW, Greenwood Pr) Greenwood.

Philosophical Writings. rev. ed. Gottfried Wilhelm Leibniz. Ed. by George H. Parkinson. 296p. 1995. pap. 7.50 (*0-460-87546-9*, Everyman's Classic Lib) Tuttle Pubng.

Philosophical Writings, 1. Rene Descartes et al. Tr. by John G. Cottingham & Dugald Murdoch. 432p. 1985. pap. text 29.95 (*0-521-28807-X*) Cambridge U Pr.

Philosophical Writings, 2. Rene Descartes et al. Tr. by John G. Cottingham & Dugald Murdoch. 448p. 1985. pap. text 24.95 (*0-521-28808-8*) Cambridge U Pr.

Philosophical Writings: A Selection. John D. Scotus. LC 87-11990. (HPC Classics Ser.). 400p. (C). 1987. pap. text 16.95 (*0-87220-018-3*); lib. bdg. 37.95 (*0-87220-019-1*) Hackett Pub.

Philosophical Writings: A Selection. rev. ed. William of Ockham. Tr. & Intro. by Philotheus Boehner. LC 89-48587. (ENG & LAT.). 315p. (C). 1990. reprint ed. pap. text 16.95 (*0-87220-078-7*) Hackett Pub.

Philosophical Writings: A Selection. 2nd rev. ed. William of Ockham. Tr. & Intro. by Philotheus Boehner. LC 89-48587. (ENG & LAT.). 315p. (C). 1990. reprint ed. lib. bdg. 37.95 (*0-87220-079-5*) Hackett Pub.

Philosophical Writings: Descartes. Elizabeth Anscombe et al. 368p. (C). 1971. pap. text 10.00 (*0-02-303600-1*, Macmillan Coll) P-H.

Philosophical Writings Vol. 3: The Correspondence. Rene Descartes. Ed. by John E. Cottingham et al. 430p. (C). 1991. text 69.95 (*0-521-40323-5*) Cambridge U Pr.

Philosophical Writings of Henry More. Henry More. Ed. by Flora I. MacKinnon. LC 78-95151. reprint ed. 42.50 (*0-404-04409-3*) AMS Pr.

Philosophical Writings of Peirce. Charles Sanders Peirce. Ed. by Justus Buchler. 386p. 1940. pap. 9.95 (*0-486-20217-8*) Dover.

Philosophical Writings of Percy William Bridgman: An Original Anthology, 2 vols. Percy Williams Bridgman. Ed. by I. Bernard Cohen. LC 79-7952. (Three Centuries of Science in America Ser.). 1980. lib. bdg. 21.95 (*0-405-12532-1*) Ayer.

Philosophiches Woerterbuch. 6th ed. Max Apel & Peter Luds. (Sammlung Goeschen Ser.: No. 2202). (GER.). (C). 1980. pap. 12.95 (*3-11-006729-3*) De Gruyter.

Philosophick Essay Concerning Ideas According to Dr. Sherlock's Principles. Intro. by James G. Buickerood. (Augustan Reprints Ser.: No. 270 (1991)). reprint ed. 14.50 (*0-404-70270-8*) AMS Pr.

Philosophie - Erziehung - Universitat: Zu Karl Jaspers' Bildungs- und Erziehungsphilosophie. Kurt Salamun. (GER.). 205p. 1995. 42.95 (*3-631-49041-0*) P Lang Pubng.

Philosophie & Exegese Dans le Jardin de la Metaphore de Moise Ibn Ezra, Philosophe & Poete Andalou Du XIIe Siecle. Paul B. Fenton. 460p. 1996. 165.50 (*90-04-10598-0*) Brill Academic Pubs.

Philosophie & Logik: Frege-Kolloquien Jena, 1989-1991. Ed. by Werner Stelzner. (Perspektiven der Analytischen Philosophie Ser.: Band 3). (GER.). xii, 422p. (C). 1993. lib. bdg. 125.35 (*3-11-014069-1*) Mouton.

Philosophie Bei den Arabern Im X. Jh. n. Chr. Gesamtdarstellung und Quellenwerke, 14 vols., Set. Friedrich Dieterici. cxlii, 3174p. 1969. reprint ed. write for info. (*0-318-71500-7*) G Olms Pubs.

Philosophie Contemporaine, 1850 a Nos Jours see Histoire de la Philosophie

Philosophie dans le Boudoir. Marquis De Sade, pseud. (Folio Ser.: No. 800). (FRE.). pap. 9.95 (*2-07-036800-9*) Schoenhof.

Philosophie dans le Boudoir. unabridged ed. Marquis De Sade, pseud. (FRE.). 1997. pap. 6.95 (*2-87714-214-0*, Pub. by Bookking Intl) Distribks Inc.

Philosophie dans le Boudoir: Les Instituteurs Amoureaux. Marquis De Sade, pseud. (FRE.). 1976. pap. 10.95 (*0-7859-1372-6*, 2070368009) Fr & Eur.

Philosophie de Gassendi: Nominalisme, Materialisme & Metaphysique. O. R. Bloch. (International Archives of the History of Ideas Ser.: No. 38). 555p. 1971. lib. bdg. 141.50 (*90-247-5035-0*) Kluwer Academic.

Philosophie de Leibniz. B. Russell. (Reimpressions G & B Ser.). 250p. 1971. pap. 72.00 (*0-685-47123-3*) Gordon & Breach.

Philosophie de Pascal, 3 vols. Emile Baudin. Incl. Pascal et Descartes. 358p. 1976. pap. 45.00 (*0-7859-5233-0*, F40735); Pascal et la Casuistique. 246p. 1947. pap. 45.00 (*0-7859-5235-7*, F40737); Vol. 2. Pascal, les Libertins et les Jansenites. 412p. 1947. pap. 45.00 (*0-7859-5234-9*, F40736); (Coll. Etre et Penser). (FRE.). pap. write for info. (*0-318-52002-8*) Fr & Eur.

Philosophie de Saint Thomas d'Aquin, 2 vols., 1. Charles Jourdain. (Reprints in Philosophy Ser.). (FRE.). reprint ed. lib. bdg. 52.00 (*0-697-00009-5*) Irvington.

Philosophie de Saint Thomas d'Aquin, 2 vols., 2. Charles Jourdain. (Reprints in Philosophy Ser.). (FRE.). reprint ed. lib. bdg. 52.00 (*0-697-00010-9*) Irvington.

Philosophie de Saint Thomas d'Aquin, 2 vols., Set. Charles Jourdain. (Reprints in Philosophy Ser.). (FRE.). reprint ed. lib. bdg. 98.00 (*0-89197-885-2*) Irvington.

Philosophie der Arithmetik. Edmund Husserl. (Husserliana Collected Works: No. 12). 616p. 1970. lib. bdg. 148.50 (*90-247-0230-5*, Pub. by M Nijhoff) Kluwer Academic.

Philosophie der Erleuchtung Nach Suhrawardi. Max Horten. (Abhandlungen Zur Philosophie und Ihrer Geschichte Ser.: No. 38). xi, 83p. 1981. reprint ed. write for info. (*3-487-06788-9*) G Olms Pubs.

Philosophie der Geschichte Als Soziologie, Band 1. Paul Barth. (GER.). xi, 870p. 1971. reprint ed. write for info. (*3-487-04069-7*) G Olms Pubs.

Philosophie der Griechen in Ihrer Geschichtlichen Entwicklung, 3 vols. in 6. Eduard Zeller. Ed. by F. Lortzing et al. (GER.). 1990. reprint ed. write for info. (*0-318-70432-3*) G Olms Pubs.

Philosophie der Griechen in Ihrer Geschichtlichen Entwicklung, 6 vols., Set. Eduard Zeller. Ed. by F. Lortzing et al. 1990. reprint ed. write for info. (*3-487-09103-8*) G Olms Pubs.

Philosophie der Krise see Crisis Consciousness in Contemporary Philosophy

Philosophie der Kunst see Philosophy of Art

Philosophie der Mittleren Stoa. August Schmekel. viii, 483p. 1989. write for info. (*3-615-00051-X*) G Olms Pubs.

Philosophie der Musik von Kant Bis Eduard von Hartmann. Paul Moos. (GER.). 666p. 1992. reprint ed. write for info. (*3-487-05605-4*) G Olms Pubs.

Philosophie des Deutschen Idealismus. 3rd ed. Nicolai Hartmann. (GER.). vi, 575p. (C). 1972. 146.15 (*3-11-004878-7*) De Gruyter.

Philosophie des Jungen Leibniz. Willy Kabitz. (GER.). 1997. reprint ed. 49.80 (*3-487-05175-3*) G Olms Pubs.

Philosophie des Konstruktivismus Auf Dem Hintergrund des Konstruktionsbegriffs. Mechtild Jaeger. (Studien und Materialien Zur Geschichte der Philosophie Ser.: Bd. 49). (GER.). 304p. 1998. write for info. (*3-487-10652-3*) G Olms Pubs.

***Philosophie Des Rechts: Nachschrift der Vorlesung von 1822/23 von Karl Wilhelm Ludwig Heyse Herausgegeben und Eingeleitet von Erich Schilbach.** G. W. F. Hegel. (Hegeliana. Studien und Quellen Zu Hegel und Zum Hegelianismus Ser.). XXVI, 89p. 1999. 24.95 (*3-631-34947-5*) P Lang Pubng.

Philosophie des Salomon Ibn Gabirol (Avicebron) Dargestellt und Erlautert. Jacob Guttmann. (GER.). iv, 272p. 1979. reprint ed. write for info. (*3-487-06709-9*) G Olms Pubs.

Philosophie des Thomas von Aquino see Redemption of Thinking: A Study in the Philosophy of Thomas Aquinas

Philosophie des Unbewubten. Eduard Von Hartmann. (GER.). iv, 678p. 1989. reprint ed. write for info. (*3-487-09010-4*) G Olms Pubs.

Philosophie des Zeichens. Josef Simon. x, 320p. (C). 1989. pap. text 36.95 (*3-11-012345-2*); lib. bdg. 70.80 (*3-11-011441-0*) De Gruyter.

Philosophie du Non. 3rd ed. Gaston Bachelard. (FRE.). 160p. 1988. pap. 20.95 (*0-7859-3010-8*) Fr & Eur.

Philosophie d'un Anti-Philosophe: Paul Valery. Jacques Bouveresse. 32p. 1994. pap. text 8.95 (*0-19-815196-9*) OUP.

Philosophie et les Experiences Naturelles. A. De Waelhens. (Phaenomenologica Ser.: No. 9). 220p. 1967. pap. text 81.00 (*90-247-0243-7*, Pub. by M Nijhoff) Kluwer Academic.

Philosophie Europeene Antique et Medievale see Histoire de la Philosophie

Philosophie Fichte's Nach Dem Gesammtergebnisse Ihrer Entwicklung und in Ihrem Verhaeltnisse Zu Kant und Spinoza. Johann H. Loewe. (Fichteana Ser.). (GER.). 340p. 1976. reprint ed. write for info. (*3-487-05974-6*) G Olms Pubs.

Philosophie Geschichtliches Lexikon. 2nd ed. Ludwig Noack. (GER.). 1968. 195.00 (*0-8288-6658-9*, M-7585) Fr & Eur.

Philosophie Hugo Dinglers. Wilhelm Krampf. (GER.). 71p. 1955. write for info. (*3-487-07636-5*) G Olms Pubs.

Philosophie Moderne, de la Renaissance a 1850 see Histoire de la Philosophie

Philosophie Morale: Examen Historique et Critique des Grandes Systemes. Jacques Maritain. (FRE.). 592p. 1960. 39.95 (*0-8288-9852-9*, F111820) Fr & Eur.

Philosophie und Metaphysik. Juergen-Eckardt Pleines Staff. (Studien und & Materialien Zur Geschichte der Philosophie: Bd. 46). (GER.). iv, 456p. 1997. write for info. (*3-487-10485-7*) G Olms Pubs.

Philosophie und Mythos. Hans Poser. (C). 1979. text 93.10 (*3-11-007601-2*) De Gruyter.

Philosophie und Naturwissenschaften, 2 vols. 3rd ed. Herbert Hoerz. (GER.). 1120p. 1991. 150.00 (*0-7859-8293-0*, 3320014609) Fr & Eur.

Philosophie und Politik Bei Nietzsche Vol. 2: Durchgesehene & Um ein Vorwort Erweiterte Auflage. Henning Ottmann. 444p. 1997. 124.00 (*3-11-014770-X*) De Gruyter.

***Philosophie und Theologie des ausgehenden Mittelalters: Marsilius von Inghen und das Denken seiner Zeit.** Ed. by Maarten J.F. M. Hoenen & Paul J. J. M. Bakker. 375p. 2000. 375.00 (*90-04-10912-9*) Brill Academic Pubs.

Philosophie und Wissenschaften: Formen und prozesse Ihrer Interaktion. Hans J. Sandkuhler. (Philosophie und Geschichte der Wissenschaften, Studien und Quellen: Bd. 36). (GER.). 365p. 1997. 57.95 (*3-631-32034-5*) P Lang Pubng.

Philosophie und Wissenschaften, Kuenste see Aufstieg und Niedergang der romischen Welt: Section 1, von den Anfangen Roms bis zum Ausgang der Republik

Philosophie Zoologique, 2 vols. in 1. Jean Baptiste Lamarck. 1960. reprint ed. 75.00 (*3-7682-0028-0*) Lubrecht & Cramer.

Philosophies see Cultural Heritage of India

Philosophies & Cultures. Frederick J. Copleston. 1980. 26.00 (*0-19-213960-6*) OUP.

Philosophies & Religions of India. Yogi Ramacharaka. 212p. 1980. 7.95 (*0-318-37149-9*) Asia Bk Corp.

Philosophies & Religions of India. Ramacharaka. 360p. 1998. reprint ed. pap. 24.95 (*0-7661-0364-1*) Kessinger Pub.

Philosophies & Religions of India. Yogi Ramacharaka. reprint ed. 15.00 (*0-911662-05-7*) Yoga.

Philosophies in Modern Fiction. Patrick Braybrooke. LC 67-22077. (Essay Index Reprint Ser.). 1977. 17.95 (*0-8369-1322-1*) Ayer.

Philosophies Men Live By. 2nd ed. Robert Franklin Davidson. 442p. (C). 1974. text 40.00 (*0-03-011851-4*) Harcourt Coll Pubs.

Philosophies, Missions, Goals. Otto C. Rudley & Marcia M. Rudley. 82p. (C). 1990. pap. text 19.95 (*0-9626259-0-6*) Con Mar Pub.

Philosophies of Administration Current in the Deanship of the Liberal Arts College. Merle S. Ward. LC 79-177661. (Columbia University. Teachers College. Contributions to Education Ser.: No. 632). reprint ed. 37.50 (*0-404-55632-9*) AMS Pr.

***Philosophies of Art & Beauty: Introducing Aesthetics.** Hugh Bredin & Liberato Santoro-Brienza. 240p. 2000. pap. text 23.00 (*0-7486-1191-6*) Col U Pr.

Philosophies of Art & Beauty: Selected Readings in Aesthetics from Plato to Heidegger. Ed. by Albert Hofstadter & Richard Kuhns. 728p. 1976. reprint ed. pap. text 22.00 (*0-226-34812-1*, P685) U Ch Pr.

Philosophies of Arts: An Essay in Differences. Peter Kivy. 254p. (C). 1997. text 59.95 (*0-521-59178-3*); pap. text 19.95 (*0-521-59829-X*) Cambridge U Pr.

Philosophies of Asia. Alan Watts. 1999. pap. 10.00 (*0-8048-3198-X*) Tuttle Pubng.

Philosophies of Asia: The Complete Edited Transcripts. Alan Watts. 114p. (Orig.). 1995. pap. 16.95 (*0-8048-3051-7*) Tuttle Pubng.

Philosophies of Beauty, from Socrates to Robert Bridges. Ed. by Edgar F. Carritt. LC 76-5885. 334p. 1976. reprint ed. lib. bdg. 60.00 (*0-8371-8812-1*, CAPB, Greenwood Pr) Greenwood.

Philosophies of Being & Mind: Ancient & Medieval. Ed. by James T. Martin. LC 91-27076. 240p. 1992. 50.00 (*0-88206-076-7*) Caravan Bks.

Philosophies of Education from the Standpoint of the Philosophy of Experimentalism. John P. Wynne. LC 77-97338. 427p. 1970. reprint ed. lib. bdg. 75.00 (*0-8371-2793-9*, WYPE, Greenwood Pr) Greenwood.

Philosophies of Existence: Ancient & Medieval. Ed. by Parviz Morewedge. LC 81-66643. 352p. reprint ed. pap. 109.20 (*0-7837-5613-5*, 204551900005) Bks Demand.

***Philosophies of History: From Enlightenment to Post-Modernity.** Robert Burns & Hugh Rayment-Pickard. LC 99-56272. 352p. 2000. text 64.95 (*0-631-21236-1*); pap. text 32.95 (*0-631-21237-X*) Blackwell Pubs.

Philosophies of India. Heinrich R. Zimmer. Ed. by Joseph Campbell. (Bollingen Ser.: Vol. 26). (Illus.). 724p. 1951. pap. text 24.95 (*0-691-01758-1*, Pub. by Princeton U Pr) Cal Prin Full Svc.

Philosophies of India: A New Approach. Frederick L. Kumar. LC 89-29648. (Studies in Asian Thought & Religion: Vol. 14). 562p. 1990. lib. bdg. 119.95 (*0-88946-063-9*) E Mellen.

Philosophies of Love. Ed. by David L. Norton & Mary F. Kille. (Helix Bks.: No. 376). 296p. (C). 1983. reprint ed. pap. 20.00 (*0-8226-0376-4*) Littlefield.

Philosophies of Music in Medieval Islam. Fadlou Shehadi. (Brill's Studies in Intellectual History: No. 67). 250p. 1995. 71.00 (*90-04-10128-4*) Brill Academic Pubs.

Philosophies of Music in Medieval Islam. Fadlou Shehadi. 184p. 1996. 64.75 (*0-614-21586-2*, 1414) Kazi Pubns.

Philosophies of Nature: The Human Dimension. Ed. by Robert S. Cohen & Alfred I. Tauber. LC 97-16262. (Boston College Studies in Philosophy of Science 95). 352p. 1998. 140.00 (*0-7923-4579-7*) Kluwer Academic.

Philosophies of Reference Service. Ed. by Celia H. Mabry. LC 97-36870. 246p. 1997. 49.95 (*0-7890-0371-6*) Haworth Pr.

Philosophies of Religion. William S. Sahakian. 486p. 1965. pap. 18.95 (*0-87073-510-1*) Schenkman Bks Inc.

Philosophies of Science. Jennifer McErlean. LC 99-41580. (Philosophy Ser.). 243p. 1999. pap. text 55.95 (*0-534-55163-7*) Wadsworth Pub.

Philosophies of Science: An Introductory Survey. 2nd ed. Rom Harre. 210p. 1985. pap. text 18.95 (*0-19-289201-0*) OUP.

Philosophies of Science & Feminist Theories. Jane Duran. LC 98-102367. 224p. (C). 1997. pap. text 25.00 (*0-8133-3325-3*, Pub. by Westview) HarpC.

***Philosophisch-Anthropologische Diskurs im Dreizehnten Jahrhundert.** Theodor W. Kohler. (Studien und Texte Zur Geistesgeschichte des Mittelalters). 832p. 2000. 121.00 (*90-04-11623-0*) Brill Academic Pubs.

Philosophische Anthropologie: Menschliche Selbstdeutung in Geschichte und Gegenwart. 5th ed. Michael Landmann. (Sammlung Goeschen Ser.: Vol. 2201). 228p. (C). 1976. pap. 12.95 (*3-11-008997-1*) De Gruyter.

Philosophische Bemerkungen. Rudolf Kurth. (American University Studies: Philosophy: Ser. V, Vol. 93). 224p. 1990. text 47.50 (*0-8204-1273-2*) P Lang Pubng.

Philosophische Bemerkungen, 1. M. Nedo. (Ludwig Wittgenstein, Wiener Ausgabe Ser.). 196p. 1994. 98.00 (*0-387-82499-5*) Spr-Verlag.

Philosophische Betrachtungen, 2. M. Nedo. (Ludwig Wittengenstien, Wiener Ausgabe Ser.). 333p. 1994. 125.00 (*0-387-82502-9*) Spr-Verlag.

Philosophische Bibliothek, 2. Georg Heinrich Feder. 195.00 (*1-85506-228-3*) Thoemmes Pr.

Philosophische Gehalt des Wolff-Manteuffelschen Briefwechsels. Heinrich Ostertag. (Materialien und Dokumente Ser.: Bd. 14). (GER.). 189p. 1980. reprint ed. write for info. (*3-487-06967-9*) G Olms Pubs.

***Philosophische Gotteserkenntnis Bei Suarez und Descartes: Im Zusammenhang mit der Niederlandischen reformierten Theologie und Philosophie des 17, Jahrhunderts.** Aza Goudriaan. (GER.). 400p. 1999. 95.50 (*90-04-11627-3*) Brill Academic Pubs.

Philosophische Grundlegung zu Einer Enzyklopaedie des Glaudens. Guenther Keil. (GER.). 1975. 115.00 (*0-8288-5943-4*, M7093) Fr & Eur.

Philosophische Probleme der Physik see Philosophical Problems in Physical Science

Philosophische Psychologie des Peter von Ailly. Olaf Pluta. (Beitrag zur Geschichte der Philosophie des Spaten Mittelalters Bochumer Studien zur Philosophie: Vol. 6). 366p. (C). 1987. 56.00 (*90-6032-275-4*, Pub. by B R Gruner) Humanities.

Philosophische Schriften: Band I Werttheorie, 4 Vols. Christian Von Ehrenfels. Ed. by Reinhard Fabian. (Philosophia Resources Library). (GER.). 615p. 1983. 199.00 (*3-88405-033-8*); 199.00 (*0-685-73797-7*); 199.00 (*0-685-73798-5*); 199.00 (*0-685-73799-3*) Philosophia Pr.

Philosophische Schriften: Band II, Asthetik, 4 Vols. Christian Von Ehrenfels. Ed. by Reinhard Fabian. (Philosophia Resources Library). (GER.). viii, 502p. 1986. 132.00 (*3-88405-032-X*) Philosophia Pr.

Philosophische Schriften: Band III Psychologie, Ethik, Erkenntnistheorie. Christian Von Ehrenfels. Ed. by Reinhard Fabian. (Philosophia Resources Library). (GER.). vi, 521p. 1988. 152.00 (*3-88405-034-6*) Philosophia Pr.

Philosophische Schriften: Band IV, Metaphysik. Christian Von Ehrenfels. Ed. by Reinhard Fabian. (Philosophia Resources Library). (GER.). vi, 476p. (C). 1990. 134.00 (*3-88405-052-4*) Philosophia Pr.

Philosophische Schriften: Band IV, Metaphysik, 4 vols., Set. Christian Von Ehrenfels. Ed. by Reinhard Fabian. (Philosophia Resources Library). (GER.). vi, 476p. (C). 1990. 597.00 (*0-685-27218-4*) Philosophia Pr.

Philosophische Theologie im Schatten des Nihilismus. Wilhelm Weischedel et al. Ed. by Jorg Salaquarda. (C). 1971. pap. 18.50 (*3-11-001604-4*) De Gruyter.

Philosophische und Politische Versuche. Isaak Iselin. (GER.). xv, 402p. 1978. reprint ed. write for info. (*3-487-06569-X*) G Olms Pubs.

Philosophischen Analysen zur Kunst der Gegenwart. W. Biemel. (Phaenomenologica Ser.: No. 28). 272p. 1969. pap. text 55.00 (*90-247-0262-3*, Pub. by M Nijhoff) Kluwer Academic.

P

An Asterisk (*) at the beginning of an entry indicates that the title is appearing for the first time.

Philosophischen Lehren in Leibnizens Theodicee. Adelheid Thoenes. (Abhandlungen Zur Philosophie und Ihrer Geschichte Ser.: Bd. 28). (GER.). 79p. 1980. reprint ed. write for info. (*3-487-06784-6*) G Olms Pubs.

Philosophischen Schriften, 7 vols., Set. Gottfried Wilhelm Leibniz. 4040p. 1978. reprint ed. write for info. (*3-487-00064-4*); reprint ed. pap. write for info. (*3-487-00926-9*) G Olms Pubs.

Philosophischer Phoenix, Rettung des Phoenix, Teutsche Hauptsprache, Adelicher Hausvatter see Saemtliche Werke

Philosophisches Denken - Politisches Wirken. (Philosophische Texte und Studien: Vol. 35). (GER.). 269p. 1993. write for info. (*3-487-09750-8*) G Olms Pubs.

Philosophisches Woerterbuch. Max Muller. (GER.). 39.95 (*0-7859-8369-4*, 3451041510) Fr & Eur.

Philosophisches Woerterbuch. Voltaire. (GER.). 1994. 19.95 (*0-7859-8379-1*, 3458325557) Fr & Eur.

Philosophizing Art: Selected Essays. Arthur C. Danto. LC 98-38834. 285p. 1999. 35.00 (*0-520-21283-5*, Pub. by U CA Pr) Cal Prin Full Svc.

Philosophy. (Quick Study Academic Ser.). 4p. pap. 2.95 (*1-57222-070-8*) Barcharts.

Philosophy. (Adaptable Courseware-Softside Ser.). Date not set. pap. 32.00 (*0-534-15902-8*) Wadsworth Pub.

Philosophy. Mahoney & Price. (Philosophy Ser.). 2000. pap. text 35.00 (*0-534-55857-7*) Thomson Learn.

Philosophy. Jack Rudman. (Graduate Record Examination (GRE) Ser.: Vol. 14). 43.95 (*0-8373-5264-9*) Nat Learn.

Philosophy. Jack Rudman. (Undergraduate Program Field Tests (UPFT) Ser.: Vol. 17). 43.95 (*0-8373-6067-6*) Nat Learn.

Philosophy. Jack Rudman. (Graduate Record Examination Ser.: GRE-14). 1994. pap. 23.95 (*0-8373-5214-2*) Nat Learn.

Philosophy. Jack Rudman. (Undergraduate Program Field Tests (UPFT) Ser.: Vol. UPFT-17). 1994. pap. 23.95 (*0-8373-6017-X*) Nat Learn.

Philosophy. Mel Thompson. 160p. 1995. pap., student ed. 8.95 (*0-8442-3683-7*, Teach Yrslf) NTC Contemp Pub Co.

Philosophy. 6th ed. Christian. (C). 1994. pap. text, teacher ed. 33.75 (*0-15-500612-6*) Harcourt Coll Pubs.

Philosophy, 3 vols., Vol. 1. Karl Jaspers. Tr. by E. B. Ashton. LC 69-19922. 1969. 19.00 (*0-226-39489-1*) U Ch Pr.

Philosophy, 3 vols., Vol. 2. Karl Jaspers. Tr. by E. B. Ashton. LC 69-19922. 1993. 21.00 (*0-226-39491-3*) U Ch Pr.

Philosophy, 3 vols., Vol. 3. 1971st ed. Karl Jaspers. Tr. by E. B. Ashton. LC 69-19922. 224p. 1998. 16.95 (*0-226-39494-8*) U Ch Pr.

Philosophy: A Beginner's Guide. 2nd ed. Jenny Teichman & Katterine C. Evans. 301p. (C). 1995. pap. text 24.95 (*0-631-19617-X*) Blackwell Pubs.

Philosophy: A Beginner's Guide. 3rd ed. Jenny Teichman & Katherine C. Evans. LC 99-19756. 256p. 1999. text 54.95 (*0-631-21320-1*); pap. text 24.95 (*0-631-21321-X*) Blackwell Pubs.

Philosophy: A Guide to Reference Literature. 2nd ed. BHans E. Bynagle. LC 96-31379. (Reference Sources in the Humanities Ser.). 233p. 1996. lib. bdg. 38.50 (*1-56308-376-0*) Libs Unl.

Philosophy: A Literary & Conceptual Approach. 2nd ed. Burton F. Porter. 496p. (C). 1980. pap. text 41.50 (*0-15-570553-9*, Pub. by Harcourt Coll Pubs) Harcourt.

Philosophy: A Select, Classified Bibliography of Ethics, Economics, Law, Politics, Sociology. Sebastian A. Matczak. LC 72-80678. (Philosophical Questions Ser.: No. 3). 1970. 75.00 (*0-912116-02-1*) Learned Pubns.

Philosophy: A Text with Readings. Barry. (Philosophy Ser.). 1980. pap. 17.75 (*0-534-00767-8*) Wadsworth Pub.

Philosophy: A Text with Readings. 2nd ed. Vincent E. Barry. 544p. (C). 1983. pap. write for info. (*0-534-01216-7*) Wadsworth Pub.

Philosophy: A Text with Readings. 3rd ed. Velasquez. (Philosophy Ser.). 1988. pap., teacher ed. write for info. (*0-534-08527-X*) Wadsworth Pub.

Philosophy: A Text with Readings. 3rd ed. Manuel Velasquez & Vincent E. Barry. 454p. (C). 1988. pap. write for info. (*0-534-08526-1*) Wadsworth Pub.

Philosophy: A Text with Readings. 4th ed. Velasquez. (Philosophy Ser.). 1991. mass mkt., teacher ed. write for info. (*0-534-14995-2*) Wadsworth Pub.

Philosophy: A Text with Readings. 4th ed. Manuel Velasquez. 574p. (C). 1990. pap. 42.95 (*0-534-14994-4*) Wadsworth Pub.

Philosophy: A Text with Readings. 5th ed. Manuel Velasquez. 624p. 1993. mass mkt. 43.25 (*0-534-20796-0*) Wadsworth Pub.

Philosophy: A Text with Readings. 7th ed. Velasquez. LC 98-28138. (Philosophy). 1998. pap. 68.95 (*0-534-55211-0*) Wadsworth Pub.

***Philosophy: A Text with Readings.** 8th ed. Velasquez. (Philosophy Ser.). (C). 2001. text 49.00 (*0-534-56181-0*) Wadsworth Pub.

Philosophy: An Introduction. Antony Flew. LC 79-93076. 202p. (C). 1980. pap. text 17.95 (*0-87975-127-4*) Prometheus Bks.

Philosophy: An Introduction Through Literature. Lowell Kleiman & Stephen Lewis. 512p. (C). 1992. reprint ed. pap. text 22.95 (*1-55778-539-2*) Paragon Hse.

Philosophy: An Introduction Through Original Fiction, Discussion & Readings. 3rd ed. Thomas D. Davis. 256p. (C). 1993. pap. 27.50 (*0-07-015933-5*) McGraw.

Philosophy: An Introduction to the Art of Wondering. 6th ed. James L. Christian. 650p. (C). 1994. text 71.00 (*0-15-500373-9*) Harcourt Coll Pubs.

Philosophy: An Orthodox Christian Understanding. Apostolos Makrakis. Ed. by Orthodox Christian Educational Society Staff. Tr. by Denver Cummings. (Logos & Holy Spirit in the Unity of Christian Thought Ser.: Vol. 5). 279p. 1977. reprint ed. pap. 5.00 (*0-938366-02-5*) Orthodox Chr.

Philosophy: (And Fitness) Dale J. Pritchard. 112p. (Orig.). 1997. pap., wbk. ed. 19.95 (*0-9649856-6-7*) Christina Pub.

Philosophy: Basic Judaism. (Home Study Program Ser.: No. 601). 5.00 (*0-686-96129-3*) USCJE.

Philosophy: Commonsense & Action in Educational Administration. Ed. by John Codd. 117p. (C). 1984. 60.00 (*0-7300-0014-1*, Pub. by Deakin Univ) St Mut.

Philosophy: Contemporary Perspectives on Perennial Issues. 4th ed. E. D. Klemke et al. 626p. 1993. pap. text 40.95 (*0-312-08478-1*) St Martin.

Philosophy: Discipline Analysis, Vol. 7L. Andrea Nye. (Women in the Curriculum Ser.). 22p. (Orig.). 1997. pap. 7.00 (*1-885303-23-8*) Towson St Univ.

Philosophy: East & West. Ed. by Charles A. Moore. LC 72-119008. (Essay Index Reprint Ser.). 1977. 26.95 (*0-8369-1677-8*) Ayer.

Philosophy: History & Problems. 5th ed. Samuel E. Stumpf. 976p. (C). 1994. 65.31 (*0-07-062518-2*) McGraw.

Philosophy: Its Nature, Methods & Basic Sources. Sebastian A. Matczak. LC 70-183043. (Philosophical Questions Ser.: No. 4). 300p. 1976. 50.00 (*0-912116-09-9*) Learned Pubns.

Philosophy: Literary & Conceptual. 3rd ed. Porter. (C). 1995. pap. text 41.50 (*0-15-501862-0*, Pub. by Harcourt Coll Pubs) Harcourt.

Philosophy: Love of Wisdom. 4th ed. 234p. (C). 1997. text 29.50 (*0-536-00132-4*) Pearson Custom.

Philosophy: Modern Encounter Custom Edition. 408p. (C). 1995. text 53.00 (*0-536-59183-0*) Pearson Custom.

Philosophy: Paradox & Discovery. 4th ed. Ed. by Arthur J. Minton & Thomas A. Shipka. LC 95-36201. 528p. (C). 1995. pap. 40.63 (*0-07-042525-6*) McGraw.

***Philosophy: Practice of Psychology.** Barker. 1999. pap. text 31.95 (*0-443-06004-5*) Mosby Inc.

Philosophy: Ritual-Shabbat & Kashrut. (Home Study Program Ser.: No. 602). 6.00 (*0-686-96133-1*) USCJE.

Philosophy: The Basic Readings. Nigel Warburton. LC 98-41074. 1999. 65.00 (*0-415-18719-2*); pap. 20.99 (*0-415-18720-6*) Routledge.

Philosophy: The Basics. 3rd ed. Nigel Warburton. 1999. 60.00 (*0-415-14693-3*); pap. 14.99 (*0-415-14694-1*) Routledge.

Philosophy: The Classics. Nigel Warburton. LC 97-18308. 240p. 1998. pap. 12.99 (*0-415-14692-5*) Routledge.

Philosophy: The Classics. Nigel Warburton. LC 97-18308. 240p. (C). 1998. 45.00 (*0-415-14691-7*) Routledge.

Philosophy: The Concept & Its Manifestations. Nathan Rotenstreich. LC 72-77878. 267p. 1972. pap. text 59.50 (*90-277-0284-5*); lib. bdg. 104.50 (*90-277-0236-5*) Kluwer Academic.

Philosophy: The Power of Ideas. 4th rev. ed. Brooke Noel Moore & Kenneth Bruder. LC 98-10285. xxii, 586p. 1998. text 53.95 (*1-55934-988-3*, 988-3) Mayfield Pub.

Philosophy: The Power of Ideas, Brief. 2nd abr. ed. Brooke N. Moore & Kenneth Bruder. LC 94-37688. 422p. 1995. pap. text 42.95 (*1-55934-435-0*, 1435) Mayfield Pub.

Philosophy: The Pursuit of Wisdom. Louis P. Pojman. 395p. 1993. mass mkt. 31.95 (*0-534-17982-7*) Wadsworth Pub.

Philosophy: The Pursuit of Wisdom. 2nd ed. Louis P. Pojman. LC 97-15857. (Philosophy Ser.). (C). 1997. pap. 43.95 (*0-534-52668-3*) Wadsworth Pub.

Philosophy: The Pursuit of Wisdom. 3rd ed. Pojman. (Philosophy Ser.). 2000. pap. 27.50 (*0-534-55818-6*) Wadsworth Pub.

Philosophy: The Quest for Truth. Ed. by Louis P. Pojman. 477p. (C). 1989. pap. write for info. (*0-534-10176-3*) Wadsworth Pub.

Philosophy: The Quest for Truth. 2nd ed. Ed. by Louis P. Pojman. 531p. (C). 1991. pap. 33.75 (*0-534-16530-3*) Wadsworth Pub.

Philosophy: The Quest for Truth. 3rd ed. Louis P. Pojman. LC 94-44144. 600p. (C). 1995. pap. 40.50 (*0-534-25452-7*) Wadsworth Pub.

Philosophy: The Quest for Truth. 4th ed. Louis P. Pojman. LC 98-34494. (Philosophy Ser.). 1998. 60.95 (*0-534-55187-4*) Wadsworth Pub.

***Philosophy: The Question for Truth.** 5th ed. Pojman. (Philosophy Ser.). 2002. 43.75 (*0-534-52105-3*) Wadsworth Pub.

Philosophy: The Workbook on Life. Dale J. Pritchard. 1998. 19.96 (*0-9649856-1-6*) Christina Pub.

Philosophy: Who Needs It? Ayn Rand. LC 82-4320. 288p. 1984. write for info. (*0-672-52725-1*); pap. write for info. (*0-672-52795-2*) Macmillan.

Philosophy: Who Needs It? Ayn Rand. 1984. pap. 4.99 (*0-451-17394-5*, Sig); mass mkt. 7.99 (*0-451-13893-7*, Sig) NAL.

Philosophy - Love of Wisdom: Selections & Study Questions. 3rd ed. Gary L. Baran. 230p. (C). 1994. text 30.80 (*0-536-58730-2*) S&S Trade.

Philosophy: A Text With Readings. 6th ed. Manuel Velasquez. LC 96-3065. (Philosophy). 1996. pap. 45.75 (*0-534-50662-3*) Wadsworth Pub.

Philosophy after Darwin: Chapters for the Career of Philosophy & Other Essays, Vol. 3. John H. Randall, Jr. Ed. by Beth J. Singer. LC 62-10454. 1977. text 64.50 (*0-231-04114-4*) Col U Pr.

Philosophy after F. H. Bradley. Ed. by James Bradley & Peter Johnson. (Idealism Ser.: No. 3). 390p. 1996. 75.00 (*1-85506-484-7*); pap. 27.00 (*1-85506-485-5*) Bks Intl VA.

Philosophy after Objectivity: Making Sense in Perspective. Paul K. Moser. LC 92-38864. 280p. 1993. text 65.00 (*0-19-508109-9*) OUP.

Philosophy after Objectivity: Making Sense in Perspective. Paul K. Moser. 280p. 1999. pap. 19.95 (*0-19-513094-4*) OUP.

Philosophy & Aesthetics of Music. Contrib. by Edward A. Lippman. LC 98-43967. 1999. text 60.00 (*0-8032-2912-7*); pap. text 25.00 (*0-8032-7984-1*) U of Nebr Pr.

Philosophy & AI: Essays at the Interface. Ed. by Robert Cummins & John Pollack. (Illus.). 320p. 1991. 40.00 (*0-262-03180-9*, Bradford Bks) MIT Pr.

Philosophy & AI: Essays at the Interface. Ed. by Robert Cummins & John Pollock. (Bradford Bk.). 1995. pap. text 17.50 (*0-262-53135-6*, Bradford Bks) MIT Pr.

Philosophy & Archaeology. Merrilee H. Salmon. (Studies in Archaeology Ser.). 1982. text 55.00 (*0-12-615650-6*) Acad Pr.

Philosophy & Argument in Late Vedanta. Phyllis Granoff. (Studies of Classical India: No. 1). 305p. 1978. text 171.00 (*90-277-0878-9*, D Reidel) Kluwer Academic.

Philosophy & Art. Ed. by Daniel O. Dahlstrom. LC 89-77750. (Studies in Philosophy & the History of Philosophy: Vol. 23). 266p. 1991. text 44.95 (*0-8132-0724-X*) Cath U Pr.

Philosophy & Atheism. Kai Nielsen. LC 84-63084. (Skeptic's Bookshelf Ser.). 231p. 1985. 32.95 (*0-87975-289-0*) Prometheus Bks.

Philosophy & Biblical Interpretation: A Study in Nineteenth Century Conflict. Peter Addinall. 342p. (C). 1991. text 75.00 (*0-521-40423-1*) Cambridge U Pr.

Philosophy & Care of the Mentally Retarded: A Worldwide Status Report. Johnny L. Matson. 120p. 1983. pap. 15.25 (*0-08-028093-5*, Pergamon Pr) Elsevier.

Philosophy & Choice: Selected Readings from Around the World. K. Richard Christensen. LC 98-8246. 1998. pap. text 45.95 (*1-55934-964-6*, 1964) Mayfield Pub.

Philosophy & Choice Instructor's Manual. Kit Richard Christensen. 1998. pap. text, teacher ed. write for info. (*0-7674-0600-1*, 0600-1) Mayfield Pub.

Philosophy & Christian Theology. Ed. by George F. McLean & Jude P. Dougherty. (Proceedings of the American Catholic Philosophical Association Ser.: Vol. 44). 1970. pap. 20.00 (*0-918090-04-0*) Am Cath Philo.

Philosophy & Civil Law. Ed. by George F. McLean. LC 76-150281. (Proceedings of the American Catholic Philosophical Association Ser.: Vol. 49). 1975. pap. 20.00 (*0-918090-09-1*) Am Cath Philo.

Philosophy & Civilization in the Middle Ages. Maurice M. De Wulf. LC 70-88977. 312p. 1970. reprint ed. lib. bdg. 65.00 (*0-8371-2521-9*, WUMA, Greenwood Pr) Greenwood.

Philosophy & Cognitive Science. 2nd rev. ed. James H. Fetzer. LC 95-24133. (Issues in Philosophy Ser.). 191p. 1996. pap. 16.95 (*1-55778-739-5*) Paragon Hse.

Philosophy & Cognitive Science: Categories, Consciousness, & Reasoning: Proceedings of the Second International Colloquium on Cognitive Science. Andy L. Clark & Jesus Ezquerro. LC 96-1802. (Philosophical Studies). 1996. text 140.00 (*0-7923-4068-X*) Kluwer Academic.

Philosophy & Computer Science. Timothy R. Colburn. LC 99-28936. (Explorations in Philosophy Ser.). 256p. 1999. text 58.95 (*1-56324-990-1*); pap. text 22.95 (*1-56324-991-X*) M E Sharpe.

Philosophy & Computing: An Introduction Luciano Floridi. LC 98-47915. 1999. pap. 24.99 (*0-415-18025-2*) Routledge.

Philosophy & Computing: An Introduction. Luciano Floridi. LC 98-47915. 232p. 1999. 75.00 (*0-415-18024-4*) Routledge.

Philosophy & Conceptual History of Science in Taiwan. Ed. by Cheng-hung Lin & Daiwie Fu. LC 92-12852. (Boston Studies in the Philosophy of Science: Vol. 141). 284p. (C). 1993. lib. bdg. 175.00 (*0-7923-1766-1*, Pub. by Kluwer Academic) Kluwer Academic.

Philosophy & Connectionist Theory. Ed. by William Ramsey et al. 336p. (C). 1991. pap. 36.00 (*0-8058-0883-3*); text 69.95 (*0-8058-0592-3*) L Erlbaum Assocs.

Philosophy & Contemporary Issues. 7th ed. Ed. by John R. Burr & Milton Goldinger. LC 95-16787. 576p. (C). 1995. pap. text 47.00 (*0-02-317430-7*, Macmillan Coll) P-H.

***Philosophy & Contemporary Issues.** 8th ed. John R. Burr & Milton Goldinger. LC 99-26270. 548p. 1999. pap. text 45.00 (*0-13-020993-7*) P-H.

Philosophy & Critique. S. Z. Hasan. 1990. 22.50 (*1-56744-186-6*) Kazi Pubns.

***Philosophy & Desire.** Hugh J. Silverman. LC 98-50356. 1999. pap. 22.99 (*0-415-91957-6*); text. write for info. (*0-415-91956-8*) Routledge.

Philosophy & Development of Religion, 2 vols., Set. Otto Pfleiderer. LC 77-27229. (Gifford Lectures: 1894). reprint ed. 84.50 (*0-404-60470-6*) AMS Pr.

Philosophy & Economics: The Origins & Development of Economic Theory. Piero V. Mini. LC 74-7122. 305p. 1974. 49.95 (*0-8130-0381-4*) U Press Fla.

Philosophy & Economics of J. M. Keynes. Ed. by Bill Gerrard & John Hillard. 272p. 1992. 95.00 (*1-85278-400-8*) E Elgar.

Philosophy & Economics of Market Socialism: A Critical Study. N. Scott Arnold. LC 93-31714. (Illus.). 320p. 1994. text 70.00 (*0-19-508827-1*) OUP.

Philosophy & Education. Jonas F. Soltis. LC 80-83743. (National Society for the Study of Education Publication Ser.: No. 80, Pt I). 288p. (C). 1994. lib. bdg. 17.50 (*0-226-60130-7*) U Ch Pr.

Philosophy & Education: Accepting Wittgenstein's Challenge. Ed. by Paul Smeyers & James D. Marshall. (Philosophy & Education Ser.: Vol. 6). 1995. reprint ed. text 81.00 (*0-7923-3715-8*) Kluwer Academic.

Philosophy & Education: An Introduction in Christian Perspective. 3rd ed. George R. Knight. LC 98-72676. (Illus.). 266p. 1998. pap. text 19.99 (*1-883925-20-7*) Andrews Univ Pr.

***Philosophy & Ethics.** Donald M. Borchert. LC 99-25219. (Macmillan Compendium Ser.). 1999. 173.75 (*0-02-865366-1*) Mac Bks.

***Philosophy & Everyday Life.** Ed. by Laura Duhan Kaplan. 320p. 2000. pap. text 26.95 (*1-889119-53-9*) Seven Bridges.

Philosophy & Faith of Sikhism. Kartar S. Duggal. LC 88-213598. 99p. (Orig.). 1988. pap. 10.95 (*0-89389-109-6*) Himalayan Inst.

Philosophy & Feminism at the Border. Andrea Nye. (Impact of Feminism on the Arts & Sciences Ser.). 180p. 1995. 33.00 (*0-8057-9763-7*, Twyne); pap. 20.00 (*0-8057-9778-5*, Twyne) Mac Lib Ref.

Philosophy & Feminist Criticism. Eve B. Cole. LC 92-10720. (Issues in Philosophy Ser.). 144p. 1993. pap. 16.95 (*1-55778-457-4*) Paragon Hse.

Philosophy & Feminist Thinking. Jean Grimshaw. LC 86-6993. 288p. (Orig.). 1986. pap. 18.95 (*0-8166-1546-2*) U of Minn Pr.

Philosophy & Film. Ed. by Cynthia A. Freeland & Thomas E. Wartenberg. LC 94-37854. 288p. (C). 1995. pap. 21.99 (*0-415-90921-X*, B3854) Routledge.

***Philosophy & Freedom: Derrida, Rorty, Habermas, Foucault.** John McCumber. LC 99-43396. (Studies in Continental Thought). 256p. 2000. pap. 18.95 (*0-253-21363-0*); lib. bdg. 39.95 (*0-253-33697-X*) Ind U Pr.

Philosophy & Geography III: Philosophies of Place. Ed. by Andrew Light & Jonathan M. Smith. LC 98-34655. (Philosophy & Geography Ser.: No. 98). 320p. 1998. 68.00 (*0-8476-9094-6*); pap. 25.95 (*0-8476-9095-4*) Rowman.

Philosophy & Geography II: The Production of Public Space. Ed. by Andrew Light & Jonathan Smith. LC 97-27911. (Philosophy & Geography Ser.). 255p. 1997. 61.00 (*0-8476-8809-7*); pap. 24.95 (*0-8476-8810-0*) Rowman.

Philosophy & Government, 1572-1651. Richard Tuck. LC 92-16033. (Ideas in Context Ser.: No. 26). 404p. (C). 1993. pap. text 23.95 (*0-521-43885-3*) Cambridge U Pr.

Philosophy & Government, 1572-1651. Richard Tuck. LC 92-16033. (Ideas in Context Ser.: No. 26). 404p. (C). 1993. text 64.95 (*0-521-36000-5*) Cambridge U Pr.

Philosophy & Grammar. Ed. by Stig Kanger & Sven Ohman. (Synthese Library: No. 143). 165p. 1980. text 88.00 (*90-277-1091-0*, D Reidel) Kluwer Academic.

Philosophy & Health Care. Michael A. Menlown. 237p. 1992. 82.95 (*1-85628-325-9*, Pub. by Avebry) Ashgate Pub Co.

Philosophy & History of Molecular Biology: New Perspectives. Ed. by Sahotra Sarkar. (Boston Studies in the Philosophy of Science: Vol. 183). 264p. (C). 1996. text 130.50 (*0-7923-3947-9*) Kluwer Academic.

Philosophy & Homosexuality. Ed. by Noretta Koertge. LC 84-22470. (Journal of Homosexuality Ser.: Vol. 6, No. 4). 98p. 1985. pap. text 9.95 (*0-918393-12-4*, Harrington Park) Haworth Pr.

Philosophy & Human Development. Ed. by Anand Amaladass. 333p. 1986. 19.95 (*0-318-37037-9*) Asia Bk Corp.

Philosophy & Ideology: The Development of Philosophy & Marxism-Leninism in Poland Since the Second World War. Z. A. Jordan. (Sovietica Ser.: No. 12). 600p. 1963. lib. bdg. 237.50 (*90-277-0054-0*) Kluwer Academic.

Philosophy & Its Development in the Nikayas & Abhidhamma. Fumimaro Watanabe. (C). 1983. 20.00 (*81-208-1181-X*, Pub. by Motilal Bnarsidass) S Asia.

***Philosophy & Its Epistemic Neuroses.** Michael Hymers. LC 99-37918. 240p. 1999. 60.00 (*0-8133-9137-7*) Westview.

Philosophy & Its History: Issues in Philosophical Historiography. Jorge J. Gracia. LC 90-24213. (SUNY Series in Philosophy). 409p. (C). 1991. text 19.50 (*0-7914-0817-5*) State U NY Pr.

Philosophy & Its Others: Ways of Being & Mind. William Desmond. LC 89-37872. (SUNY Series in Systematic Philosophy). 396p. (C). 1990. text 59.50 (*0-7914-0307-6*); pap. text 21.95 (*0-7914-0308-4*) State U NY Pr.

Philosophy & Its Place in Our Culture. J. O. Wisdom. (Current Topics of Contemporary Thought Ser.: Vol. 13). xii, 270p. 1975. text 117.00 (*0-677-05150-6*) Gordon & Breach.

Philosophy & Knowledge: A Commentary on Plato's Theaetetus. Ronald M. Polansky. LC 90-56167. 264p. 1992. 38.50 (*0-8387-5215-2*) Bucknell U Pr.

Philosophy & Law: Contributions to the Understanding of Maimonides & His Predecessors. Leo Strauss. Tr. by Eve Adler. LC 93-34046. (SUNY Series in the Jewish Writings of Leo Strauss). 157p. (C). 1995. reprint ed. pap. text 14.95 (*0-7914-1976-2*) State U NY Pr.

Philosophy & Law: Contributions to the Understanding of Maimonides & His Predecessors. Leo Strauss. Tr. & Intro. by Eve Adler. LC 93-34046. (SUNY Series in the Jewish Writings of Leo Strauss). 157p. (C). 1995. reprint ed. text 44.50 (*0-7914-1975-4*) State U NY Pr.

Philosophy & Life. Ed. by Ilham Dilman. LC 84-14685. 356p. 1984. text 185.50 (*90-247-2996-3*) Kluwer Academic.

Philosophy & Linguistics. Kimiko Murasugi & Robert J. Stainton. LC 99-158487. (Philosophy of Language Ser.). 296p. (C). 1998. text 75.00 (*0-8133-9085-0*, Pub. by Westview) HarpC.

Philosophy & Literature. C. Bolling. 210p. 1986. 65.00 (*0-930586-22-0*) Haven Pubns.

An Asterisk (*) at the beginning of an entry indicates that the title is appearing for the first time.

Philosophy & Literature in Latin America: A Critical Assessment of the Current Situation. Ed. by Jorge J. Gracia & Mireye Camurati. LC 88-31670. 279p. (C). 1989. pap. text 21.95 (*0-7914-0039-5*) State U NY Pr.

Philosophy & Logic in Central Europe from Bolzano to Tarski: Selected Essays. Peter Simons. 456p. (C). 1992. lib. bdg. 218.00 (*0-7923-1621-5*, Pub. by Kluwer Academic) Kluwer Academic.

Philosophy & Logic of Chemical Engineering. Howard F. Rase. LC 61-18166. (Illus.). 176p. reprint ed. pap. 54.60 (*0-608-18172-2*, 203288200081) Bks Demand.

Philosophy & Logical Syntax. Rudolf Carnap. (Key Texts Ser.). 99p. 1996. pap. 14.95 (*1-85506-428-6*) Bks Intl VA.

Philosophy & Logical Syntax. Rudolf Carnap. LC 75-41050. (BCL Ser. II). reprint ed. 21.50 (*0-404-14518-3*) AMS Pr.

Philosophy & Medical Welfare. Ed. by J. M. Bell & Susan Mendus. (Royal Institute of Philosophy Lectures: No. 23). 140p. (C). 1989. pap. text 19.95 (*0-521-36856-1*) Cambridge U Pr.

Philosophy & Medicine. E. K. Ledermann. (Avebury Series in the Philosophy of Science). 196p. 1986. text 78.95 (*0-566-05062-5*, Pub. by Avebry) Ashgate Pub Co.

Philosophy & Medicine in Ancient Greece. W. H. Jones. 100p. 1980. pap. 15.00 (*0-89005-286-7*) Ares.

Philosophy & Medicine in Ancient Greece: With an Edition of Peri Archaiees Ieetrikees. William H. Jones. 1979. 15.95 (*0-405-10606-8*) Ayer.

Philosophy & Memory Traces: Descartes to Connectionism. John Sutton. LC 97-8909. (Illus.). 382p. (C). 1998. text 69.95 (*0-521-59194-5*) Cambridge U Pr.

Philosophy & Methodology of Economics, 3 vols. Ed. by Bruce J. Caldwell. (International Library of Critical Writings in Economics). 1512p. 1993. 510.00 (*1-85278-385-0*) E Elgar.

Philosophy & Miracle: The Contemporary Debate. David Basinger & Randall Basinger. LC 86-12766. (Problems in Contemporary Philosophy Ser.: Vol. 2). 130p. 1986. lib. bdg. 69.95 (*0-88946-327-1*) E Mellen.

Philosophy & Modernization in China. Ed. by Fangtong Liu et al. LC 97-19303. (Cultural Heritage & Contemporary Change Series III: Vol. 13). 220p. 1997. pap. 17.50 (*1-56518-066-6*) Coun Res Values.

Philosophy & Mystification. Guy Robinson. LC 97-18223. 312p. (C). 1998. 75.00 (*0-415-17851-7*) Routledge.

***Philosophy & Myth in Marx.** 3rd ed. Robert C. Tucker. 248p. 2000. pap. 24.95 (*0-7658-0644-4*) Transaction Pubs.

Philosophy & Non-Philosophy since Merleau-Ponty. Hugh J. Silverman. LC 97-12824. 1997. 17.95 (*0-8101-1498-4*) Northwestern U Pr.

Philosophy & Non-Philosophy since Merleau-Ponty. Ed. by Hugh J. Silverman. 320p. 1988. text 49.50 (*0-415-00178-1*) Routledge.

Philosophy & Opinions of Marcus Garvey. Ed. by Amy Jacques-Garvey. 448p. 1992. reprint ed. pap. 16.00 (*0-689-70819-X*) Atheneum Yung Read.

Philosophy & Opinions of Marcus Garvey, Vol. 2. Ed. by Amy Jacques-Garvey. LC 69-19115. (American Negro: His History & Literature. Series 2). 1978. reprint ed. 17.95 (*0-405-01873-8*) Ayer.

Philosophy & Opinions of Marcus Garvey: Or Africa for the Africans. Marcus Garvey. (New Marcus Garvey Library: No. 9). (Illus.). xxxii, 600p. 1986. reprint ed. pap. text 14.95 (*0-912469-24-2*) Majority Pr.

Philosophy & Opinions of Marcus Garvey: or Africa for the Africans, 2 vols. in 1. rev. ed. Ed. by Amy Jacques-Garvey. (Illus.). 412p. 1977. pap. 25.00 (*0-7146-2120-X*, Pub. by F Cass Pubs) Intl Spec Bk.

Philosophy & Ordinary Language. Charles E. Caton. LC 63-7250. 260p. reprint ed. pap. 80.60 (*0-608-10774-3*, 202086000020) Bks Demand.

***Philosophy & Ordinary Language: Bent & Genius of Our Tongue.** Oswald Hanfling. LC 99-39028. (Studies in Twentieth-Century Philosophy Ser.). 264p. 2000. 85.00 (*0-415-21779-2*) Routledge.

Philosophy & Philosophers. Lois F. Roets. 50p. (J). (gr. 5-12). 1994. pap., teacher ed. 10.00 (*0-911943-37-4*) Leadership Pub.

Philosophy & Philosophers: An Introduction to Western Philosophy. John Shand. 330p. 1993. 60.00 (*0-7735-1139-3*, Pub. by McG-Queens Univ Pr) CUP Services.

Philosophy & Philosophical Authors of the Jews: A Historical Sketch with Explanatory Notes. S. Munk. Tr. by Isidor Kalisch. (Reprints in Philosophy Ser.). reprint ed. lib. bdg. 29.50 (*0-697-00012-5*) Irvington.

Philosophy & Pluralism. Ed. by David Archard. (Royal Institute of Philosophy Supplements Ser.: No. 40). 219p. (C). 1996. pap. text 22.95 (*0-521-56750-5*) Cambridge U Pr.

Philosophy & Poetics of Gaston Bachelard. Ed. by Mary McAllester. LC 89-33901. (Current Continental Research Ser.: No. 011). 192p. (C). 1989. lib. bdg. 42.00 (*0-8191-7471-8*) U Pr of Amer.

Philosophy & Policies of Woodrow Wilson. Ed. by Earl Latham. LC 58-5620. (Midway Reprint Ser.: No. 15). 284p. reprint ed. pap. 88.10 (*0-608-09461-7*, 205426100005) Bks Demand.

Philosophy & Political Change in Eastern Europe. Ed. by Barry Smith. 1993. pap. 19.95 (*0-914417-06-1*) Hegeler Inst.

Philosophy & Political Economy. James Bonar. 420p. (C). 1991. text 49.95 (*0-88738-438-2*) Transaction Pubs.

Philosophy & Political Economy, 1909. James Bonar. 452p. 1996. reprint ed. 68.00 (*1-85506-149-X*) Bks Intl VA.

Philosophy & Politics. Ed. by G. M. Hunt. (Royal Institute of Philosophy Supplements Ser.: No. 26). 153p. (C). 1990. pap. text 21.95 (*0-521-39597-6*) Cambridge U Pr.

Philosophy & Politics. Adriaan T. Peperzak. 150p. 1986. pap. text 59.00 (*90-247-3338-3*, Pub. by M Nijhoff) Kluwer Academic.

Philosophy & Politics. Adriaan T. Peperzak. 150p. 1987. lib. bdg. 87.00 (*90-247-3337-5*, Pub. by M Nijhoff) Kluwer Academic.

Philosophy & Politics in China: The Controversy over Dialectical Materialism in the 1930's. Werner Meissner. LC 89-51664. 230p. 1990. 42.50 (*0-8047-1772-9*) Stanford U Pr.

***Philosophy & Politics of Abstract Expressionism.** Nancy Jachec. LC 99-40256. 2000. write for info. (*0-521-65154-9*) Cambridge U Pr.

***Philosophy & Politics of Czech Dissidence from Patocka to Havel.** Aviezer Tucker. 226p. 2000. pap. 19.95 (*0-8229-5728-0*); text 45.00 (*0-8229-4124-4*) U of Pittsburgh Pr.

Philosophy & Politics of Freedom. Richard E. Flathman. LC 86-16128. (Illus.). x, 370p. (C). 1996. pap. text 22.00 (*0-226-25317-1*); lib. bdg. 51.00 (*0-226-25316-3*) U Ch Pr.

Philosophy & Practice. Ed. by A. Phillips Griffiths. (Royal Institute of Philosophy Lectures: No. 18). 298p. 1985. pap. text 22.95 (*0-521-31231-0*) Cambridge U Pr.

Philosophy & Practice of Corrections. Ed. by Marilyn McShane & Williams. LC 96-45337. (Criminal Justice Ser.: Vol. 4). 392p. 1997. text 76.00 (*0-8153-2510-X*) Garland.

Philosophy & Practice of Wildlife Management. 2nd ed. Frederick F. Gilbert & Donald G. Dodds. LC 90-45215. 326p. (C). 1992. lib. bdg. 39.50 (*0-89464-438-6*) Krieger.

***Philosophy & Practice of Wildlife Management.** 3rd ed. Frederick F. Gilbert & Donald G. Dodds. LC 00-41216. (Illus.). 2000. write for info. (*1-57524-051-3*) Krieger.

Philosophy & Psycholinguistics. Edmund L. Erde. LC 72-94464. (Janua Linguarum, Series Minor: No. 160). 1973. pap. 77.70 (*90-279-2444-9*) Mouton.

Philosophy & Psychology in the Abhidharma. Herbert V. Guenther. 270p. (C). 1999. pap. 19.50 (*81-208-0773-1*, Pub. by Motilal Bnarsidass) St Mut.

Philosophy & Psychology of Pietro Pomponazzi. Andrew H. Douglas. Ed. by C. Douglas & R. P. Hardie. x, 318p. 1974. reprint ed. 57.20 (*3-487-05323-3*) G Olms Pubs.

Philosophy & Psychopathology. Ed. by Brendan A. Maher & Manfred Spitzer. xii, 247p. 1990. 63.95 (*0-387-97303-6*) Spr-Verlag.

Philosophy & Psychotherapy: Razing the Troubles of the Brain. Edward Erwin. (Perspectives on Psychotherapy Ser.: Vol. 1). 192p. (C). 1997. 69.95 (*0-8039-7520-1*, 75201); pap. 23.95 (*0-8039-7521-X*, 7521X) Sage.

Philosophy & Public Policy. Sidney Hook. LC 79-16825. 296p. 1981. pap. 16.95 (*0-8093-1041-4*) S Ill U Pr.

Philosophy & Religion, 32. 1973. write for info. (*0-8357-0111-5*) Univ Microfilms.

Philosophy & Religion: Six Lectures Delivered at Cambridge. Hastings Rashdall. LC 79-98791. 1970. lib. bdg. 39.75 (*0-8371-3025-5*, RAPR, Greenwood Pr) Greenwood.

Philosophy & Religion: Some Contemporary Perspectives. Jerry H. Gill. LC 68-54894. 382p. reprint ed. pap. 118.50 (*0-608-10096-X*, 200345900029) Bks Demand.

Philosophy & Religion in Colonial America. Claude M. Newlin. LC 68-23317. 212p. 1968. reprint ed. lib. bdg. 59.50 (*0-8371-0184-0*, NEPR, Greenwood Pr) Greenwood.

Philosophy & Revolutionary Theory, Vol. 1. Ed. by Dale Riepe et al. (Philosophical Currents Ser.: Vol. 32). 253p. (Orig.). (C). 1989. pap. write for info. (*90-6032-278-9*) B R Gruner.

Philosophy & Rhetoric: Essays on Aristotle's Rhetoric. Ed. by David J. Furley & Alexander Nehamas. LC 93-26050. 344p. (C). 1994. text 49.50 (*0-691-03232-7*, Pub. by Princeton U Pr) Cal Prin Full Svc.

Philosophy & Romantic Nationalism: The Case of Poland. Andrzej Walicki. (C). 1994. pap. text 22.00 (*0-268-03806-6*) U of Notre Dame Pr.

Philosophy & Science: The Wide Range of Interaction. F. Mosedale. (C). 1979. pap. text 43.60 (*0-13-662577-0*) P-H.

Philosophy & Science As Modes of Knowing: Selected Essays. Ed. by Alden L. Fisher & George B. Murray. LC 69-18680. (Orig.). (C). 1969. pap. text 22.95 (*0-89197-340-0*) Irvington.

Philosophy & Science Fiction. Ed. by Michael Philips. LC 83-62874. 400p. 1984. pap. 24.95 (*0-87975-248-3*) Prometheus Bks.

***Philosophy & Science in the 17th & 18th Century.** Ed. by Maurizio Falyhera & Cristina Giocometti. (Audio Anthology of Italian Literature Ser.). (ITA.). 1999. 29.95 incl. audio compact disk (*1-58214-110-X*) Mltilingl Bks.

***Philosophy & Science in the 17th & 18th Century, Vol. 6.** Ed. by Maurizio Falyhera & Cristina Giocometti. (Audio Anthology of Italian Literature Ser.). (ITA.). 1999. 19.95 incl. audio compact disk (*1-58214-109-6*) Mltilingl Bks.

Philosophy & Sex. 3rd ed. Robert B. Baker. LC 97-46446. 671p. 1998. pap. text 24.95 (*1-57392-184-X*) Prometheus Bks.

Philosophy & Social Change. Ed. by Dharmendra Goel. 1989. 29.50 (*81-202-0236-8*, Pub. by Ajanta) S Asia.

***Philosophy & Social Hope.** Richard Rorty. 320p. 2000. pap. 13.95 (*0-14-026288-1*) Viking Penguin.

Philosophy & Teacher Education: A Reinterpretation of Donald A. Schon's Epistemology of Reflective Practice. Stephen Newman. LC LB1707.N49 1999. (Series in Philosophy). 262p. 1999. text 69.95 (*1-84014-891-8*) Ashgate Pub Co.

Philosophy & Technology. Ed. by Paul T. Durbin & Friedrich Rapp. 357p. 1983. text 214.50 (*90-277-1576-9*, D Reidel) Kluwer Academic.

Philosophy & Technology. Ed. by Roger Fellows. (Royal Institute of Philosophy Supplements Ser.: No. 38). 211p. (C). 1996. pap. text 22.95 (*0-521-55816-6*) Cambridge U Pr.

Philosophy & Technology: Readings in the Philosophical Problems of Technology. Ed. by Carl Mitcham & Robert Mackey. LC 82-19818. 416p. (C). 1983. reprint ed. pap. 18.95 (*0-02-921430-0*) Free Pr.

Philosophy & Technology II. Ed. by Carl Mitcham & Alois Huning. 374p. 1986. text 175.00 (*90-277-1975-6*, D Reidel) Kluwer Academic.

Philosophy & the Absolute: The Modes of Hegel's Speculation. Robert Grant McRae. 1985. lib. bdg. 118.00 (*90-247-3151-8*) Kluwer Academic.

Philosophy & the American School: An Introduction to the Philosophy of Education. 2nd ed. Van Cleave Morris & Young Pai. LC 93-4902. 490p. 1994. pap. 41.00 (*0-8191-9005-5*) U Pr of Amer.

Philosophy & the Analysis of Music: Bridges to Musical Sound, Form & Reference. Lawrence Ferrara. LC 91-20169. 388p. 1994. pap. text 24.00 (*0-935016-66-X*, Pub. by Zinn Pub Grp) Empire Pub Srvs.

Philosophy & the Analysis of Music: Bridges to Musical Sound, Form, & Reference, 24. Lawrence Ferrara. LC 91-26022. (Contributions to the Study of Music & Dance Ser.: No. 24). 392p. 1991. 59.95 (*0-313-28345-1*, FLZ/, Greenwood Pr) Greenwood.

Philosophy & the Art of Writing: Studies in Philosophical & Literary Style. Berel Lang. LC 81-65865. 248p. 1983. 35.00 (*0-8387-5030-3*) Bucknell U Pr.

Philosophy & the Arts. Ed. by Peter A. French et al. LC 91-50574. (Midwest Studies in Philosophy: Vol. XVI). (C). 1991. text 57.50 (*0-268-01391-8*); pap. text 25.50 (*0-268-01392-6*) U of Notre Dame Pr.

Philosophy & the Arts. Andrew Harrison. (Bristol Introductions Ser.: No. 4). 180p. 1996. 45.00 (*1-85506-499-5*); pap. 19.00 (*1-85506-500-2*) Bks Intl VA.

***Philosophy & the Arts in Central Europe, 1500-1700: Teaching & Texts at Schools & Universities.** Joseph S. Freedman. LC 99-66857. (Variorum Collected Studies: Vol. 626). (Illus.). 374p. 2000. text 111.95 (*0-86078-780-X*, Pub. by Ashgate Pub) Ashgate Pub Co.

Philosophy & the Belief in a Life after Death. R. W. Paterson. LC 95-23638. 204p. 1996. text 59.95 (*0-312-12838-X*) St Martin.

Philosophy & the Christian Faith. Colin Brown. LC 68-58083. 320p. (Orig.). 1969. pap. 18.99 (*0-87784-712-6*, 712) InterVarsity.

Philosophy & the Christian Faith. Ed. by Thomas V. Morris. LC 87-40618. (Studies in Philosophy of Religion: No. 5). 336p. (C). 1990. text 37.00 (*0-268-01570-8*); pap. text 17.50 (*0-268-01571-6*) U of Notre Dame Pr.

Philosophy & the Community of Speech. Donald Stoll. LC 87-25252. (Social Philosophy Research Institute Bks.: No. 6). 84p. (Orig.). (C). 1988. pap. text 13.50 (*0-8191-6684-7*); lib. bdg. 29.50 (*0-8191-6683-9*) U Pr of Amer.

Philosophy & the Criminal Law: Principle & Critique. Ed. by R. A. Duff. LC 97-25899. (Studies in Philosophy & Law). 272p. (C). 1998. text 54.95 (*0-521-55044-0*) Cambridge U Pr.

Philosophy & the Darwinian Legacy. Suzanne Cunningham. 272p. (C). 1996. 55.00 (*1-878822-61-6*) Univ Rochester Pr.

Philosophy & the Future of Man. Ed. by George F. McLean. (Proceedings of the American Catholic Philosophical Association Ser.: Vol. 42). 1968. pap. 20.00 (*0-918090-02-4*) Am Cath Philo.

Philosophy & the Good Life: Reason & the Passions in Greek, Cartesian & Psychoanalytic Ethics. John Cottingham. LC 97-27898. (Illus.). 172p. (C). 1998. pap. 17.95 (*0-521-47890-1*); text 54.95 (*0-521-47310-1*) Cambridge U Pr.

Philosophy & the Grammar of Religious Belief. Ed. by Timothy Tessin & Mario Von Der Ruhr. LC 94-31776. 362p. 1995. text 65.00 (*0-312-12394-9*) St Martin.

Philosophy & the Human Condition. 2nd ed. Thomas L. Beauchamp et al. 656p. (C). 1988. text 50.25 (*0-13-662537-1*) P-H.

Philosophy & the Liberal Arts. Edward G. Ballard. (C). 1989. lib. bdg. 160.00 (*0-7923-0241-9*) Kluwer Academic.

Philosophy & the Many Faces of Science. Ed. by Dionysios Anapolitanos et al. (CPS Publications in Philosophy of Science). 272p. (C). 1998. pap. text 23.95 (*0-8476-8175-0*); lib. bdg. 62.50 (*0-8476-8174-2*) Rowman.

Philosophy & the Maternal Body: Reading Silence. Michelle B. Walker. 248p. (C). 1998. 75.00 (*0-415-16857-0*); pap. 22.99 (*0-415-16858-9*) Routledge.

Philosophy & the Mirror of Nature. Richard McKay Rorty. LC 79-84013. 401p. 1979. pap. text 17.95 (*0-691-02016-7*, Pub. by Princeton U Pr) Cal Prin Full Svc.

Philosophy & the Nature of Language, 14. David E. Cooper. LC 86-29423. (Longman Linguistics Library). 233p. 1987. reprint ed. lib. bdg. 59.50 (*0-313-25641-1*, COPN, Greenwood Pr) Greenwood.

Philosophy & the New Physics. Powers. 208p. (C). 1982. pap. 18.95 (*0-415-07584-X*) Routledge.

Philosophy & the New Physics. Jonathan Powers. (Methuens Ideas Ser.). (Illus.). 150p. 1982. pap. 12.95 (*0-416-73480-4*, NO. 3795) Routledge.

Philosophy & the New Right. Ted Benton. (Pluto Perspectives Ser.). (C). 1996. text 45.00 (*0-7453-0503-2*); pap. text 16.95 (*0-7453-0504-0*) Westview.

Philosophy & the Origin & Evolution of the Universe. Ed. by E. Agazzi & Alberto Cordero. (Synthese Library: No. 217). 480p. 1991. text 185.50 (*0-7923-1322-4*) Kluwer Academic.

Philosophy & the Reconstruction of Culture: Pragmatic Essays after Dewey. Ed. by John J. Stuhr. LC 92-25799. 295p. (C). 1993. text 59.50 (*0-7914-1529-5*); pap. text 19.95 (*0-7914-1530-9*) State U NY Pr.

Philosophy & the Return to Self-Knowledge. Donald Phillip Verene. LC 97-7881. 336p. 1997. 35.00 (*0-300-06999-5*) Yale U Pr.

Philosophy & the Science of Behavior, Including Psychology & the Philosophy of Science. Merle B. Turner. LC 66-25267. (Century Psychology Ser.). (Illus.). 1967. 52.50 (*0-89197-341-9*); pap. text 12.95 (*0-89197-342-7*) Irvington.

Philosophy & the Self: East & West. Troy W. Organ. LC 86-62506. 240p. 1987. 42.50 (*0-941664-80-5*) Susquehanna U Pr.

Philosophy & the Turn to Religion. Hent De Vries. LC 99-10359. 1999. 55.00 (*0-8018-5994-8*); pap. 24.95 (*0-8018-5995-6*) Johns Hopkins.

Philosophy & the Visual Arts. Ed. by Andrew Harrison. 366p. (C). 1987. text 188.50 (*90-277-2468-7*) Kluwer Academic.

Philosophy & the World. Karl Jaspers. Tr. by E. B. Ashton from GER. LC 88-32675. 288p. 1989. reprint ed. pap. 10.95 (*0-89526-757-8*) Regnery Pub.

Philosophy & the Young Child. Gareth B. Matthews. LC 80-14494. 123p. 1980. 23.95 (*0-674-66605-4*) HUP.

Philosophy & the Young Child. Gareth B. Matthews. 123p. 1982. pap. text 9.50 (*0-674-66606-2*) HUP.

Philosophy & Theistic Mysticism of the Alvars. S. M. Srinivasa Chari. LC 97-913693. xx, 263p. 1997. write for info. (*81-208-1342-1*) Motilal Bnarsidass.

Philosophy & Theological Discourse. Stephen T. Davis. LC 97-3926. (Claremont Studies in the Philosophy of Religion). 260p. 1997. text 59.95 (*0-312-15837-8*) St Martin.

Philosophy & Theology. James H. Stirling. LC 77-27233. (Gifford Lectures: 1890). 1978. reprint ed. 49.50 (*0-404-60451-X*) AMS Pr.

Philosophy & Theology, 1890. James H. Stirling. 432p. 1996. reprint ed. 95.00 (*1-85506-200-3*) Bks Intl VA.

Philosophy & Theology in the Middle Ages. G. R. Evans. LC 92-14375. 152p. (C). 1993. pap. 18.99 (*0-415-08909-3*, A9931) Routledge.

Philosophy & Theology of Love: According to St. Francis de Sales. James S. Langelaan. LC 94-13278. (Toronto Studies in Theology: Vol. 67). 234p. 1994. text 89.95 (*0-7734-9100-7*) E Mellen.

***Philosophy & Tragedy.** Ed. by Miguel de Beistegui & Simon Sparks. (Warwick Studies in European Philosophy Ser.). 256p. (C). 2000. text 85.00 (*0-415-19141-6*) Routledge.

Philosophy & Tragedy. Simon Sparks & Miguel De Beistegui. LC 99-28329. (Warwick Studies in European Philosophy Ser.). 1999. pap. 24.99 (*0-415-19142-4*) Routledge.

Philosophy & Truth: Selections from Nietzsche's Notebooks of the Early 1870s. Friedrich Wilhelm Nietzsche. Ed. & Tr. by Daniel Breazeale. LC 76-53746. (Humanities Paperback Library). 232p. (C). 1990. pap. 15.95 (*0-391-03671-8*) Humanities.

Philosophy & Truth: Selections from Nietzsches Notebooks of the Early 1870s. Friedrich Wilhelm Nietzsche. (Humanities Paperback Library). 1990. pap. 16.95 (*1-57392-532-2*) Prometheus Bks.

Philosophy & Unified Science. George Talbott. 1472p. 1982. reprint ed. 36.50 (*0-941524-18-3*) Lotus Pr.

Philosophy Applied to Education: Nuturing a Democratic Community in the Class. Barbara J. Thayer-Bacon & Charles S. Bacon. LC 97-8914. 236p. 1997. pap. text 38.00 (*0-13-242413-4*) P-H.

Philosophy Arch Space, Vol. 1. Academy. 1992. pap. 25.00 (*0-312-07895-1*) St Martin.

Philosophy As a Way of Life: Spiritual Exercises from Socrates to Foucault. Pierre Hadot. Ed. by Arnold Davidson. Tr. by Michael Chase from FRE. LC 94-28788. Orig. Title: Excercises Spirituels et Philosophie Antique. 1995. 64.95 (*0-631-18032-X*) Blackwell Pubs.

Philosophy As a Way of Life: Sprirituel Exercises from Socrates to Foucault. Pierre Hadot. Ed. by Arnold Davidson. Tr. by Michael Chase from FRE. LC 94-28788. Orig. Title: Excercises Spirituels et Philosophie Antique. 1995. pap. text 29.95 (*0-631-18033-8*) Blackwell Pubs.

Philosophy As Diplomacy: Essays in Ethics & Policy Making. A. Pablo Iannone. LC 92-39814. (Illus.). 288p. (C). 1993. text 49.95 (*0-391-03808-7*) Humanities.

Philosophy As Dramatic Theory. Julian Marias. Tr. by James Parsons. LC 72-84669. 1970. 32.50 (*0-271-00100-3*) Pa St U Pr.

Philosophy As Higher Enlightenment: Paradigms Toward a New Worldview form the Perspective of Dialectical Realism. Ash Gobar. LC 93-34536. (American University Studies, V, Philosophy: Vol. 160). XII, 303p. (C). 1994. text 51.95 (*0-8204-2392-0*) P Lang Pubng.

Philosophy As Metanoetics. Hajime Tanabe. (Nanzan Studies in Religion & Culture: No. 2). 224p. (C). 1987. pap. 17.95 (*0-520-06978-1*, Pub. by U CA Pr) Cal Prin Full Svc.

Philosophy As Method & Process. Charles E. Rouse. 104p. (Orig.). 1990. pap. 10.00 (*0-9626282-0-4*) C E Rouse.

Philosophy As Passion: The Thinking of Simone de Beauvoir. Karen Vintges. LC 95-51748. (Illus.). 224p. 1996. 39.95 (*0-253-33059-9*); pap. 19.95 (*0-253-21070-4*) Ind U Pr.

P

An Asterisk (*) at the beginning of an entry indicates that the title is appearing for the first time.

Philosophy As Scientia Scientiarum: A History of Classifications of the Sciences. Robert Flint. LC 74-26261. (History, Philosophy & Sociology of Science Ser.). 1975. reprint ed. 28.95 (*0-405-06589-2*) Ayer.

Philosophy As Social Expression. Albert W. Levi. LC 73-84191. xii, 328p. 1992. pap. text 4.25 (*0-226-47390-2*, P668) U Ch Pr.

Philosophy As Therapy: An Interpretation & Defense of Wittgenstein's Later Philosophical Project. James F. Peterman. LC 91-18277. (SUNY Series in Philosophy & Psychotherapy). 158p. (C). 1992. text 24.50 (*0-7914-0981-3*) State U NY Pr.

***Philosophy at the Boundary of Reason: Ethics & Postmodernity.** Patrick L. Bourgeois. LC 00-26525. (C). 2000. pap. text 24.95 (*0-7914-4822-3*) State U NY Pr.

***Philosophy at the Boundary of Reason: Ethics & Postmodernity.** Patrick L. Bourgeois. LC 00-26525. (C). 2001. text 73.50 (*0-7914-4821-5*) State U NY Pr.

Philosophy at the Crossroads. Edward G Ballard. LC 72-130663. 317p. 1971. pap. 98.30 (*0-7837-8501-1*, 204930900011) Bks Demand.

Philosophy at 33 1-3 RPM: Themes of Classic Rock Music. James F. Harris. LC 93-6390. 304p. 1993. 34.95 (*0-8126-9240-3*); pap. 17.95 (*0-8126-9241-1*) Open Court.

Philosophy, B-BJ. Ed. by James Larrabee. (LC Cumulative Classification Ser.). 300p. 1985. ring bd. 38.00 (*0-933949-14-6*); fiche 13.00 (*0-933949-18-9*) Livia Pr.

Philosophy Before Socrates see Classical Philosophy: Collected Papers

Philosophy Before Socrates: An Introduction with Texts & Commentary. Richard D. McKirahan, Jr. LC 93-46837. 448p. (Orig.). (C). 1994. pap. text 16.95 (*0-87220-175-9*); lib. bdg. 39.95 (*0-87220-176-7*) Hackett Pub.

Philosophy Behind Physics. T. A. Brody. Ed. by L. De la Pena & P. E. Hodgson. (Illus.). 368p. 1994. 39.95 (*0-387-57952-4*) Spr-Verlag.

Philosophy Behind Physics. Thomas A. Brody. Ed. by P. E. Hodgson & L. De La Pena. LC 93-17950. (Illus.). 350p. 1994. 59.00 (*0-387-55914-0*) Spr-Verlag.

Philosophy Beside Itself: On Deconstruction & Modernism. Stephen W. Melville. LC 85-14025. (Theory & History of Literature Ser.: No. 27). (Illus.). 219p. (Orig.). 1986. reprint ed. pap. 67.90 (*0-608-00839-7*, 206163000010) Bks Demand.

Philosophy by Way of the Sciences: An Introductory Textbook. Ray H. Dotterer. (Select Bibliographies Reprint Ser.). 1977. reprint ed. 29.95 (*0-8369-6642-2*) Ayer.

Philosophy by Way of the Sciences: An Introductory Textbook. Ray H. Dotterer. 484p. reprint ed. lib. bdg. 26.50 (*0-8290-0823-3*) Irvington.

Philosophy, Cosmology & Religion: Ten Lectures. Rudolf Steiner. Ed. by Stewart C. Easton et al. 180p. (Orig.). 1984. pap. 9.95 (*0-88010-110-5*) Anthroposophic.

Philosophy, Dogma & the Impact of Greek Thought in Islam. Majid Fakhry. (Collected Studies: No. CS466). 320p. 1994. 106.95 (*0-86078-447-9*, Pub. by Variorum) Ashgate Pub Co.

Philosophy Enquiry into the Origin of Our Ideas of the Sublime & Beautiful. Edmund Burke. Ed. & Intro. by Adam Phillips. (Oxford World's Classics Ser.). 202p. 1998. pap. 9.95 (*0-19-283580-7*) OUP.

***Philosophy Football: Eleven Great Thinks Play It Deep.** Mark Perryman. 144p. 1998. pap. 13.95 (*0-14-026843-X*, Pub. by Pnguin Bks Ltd) Trafalgar.

Philosophy for a Changing Society. Ed. by Creighton Peden. (Orig.). (C). 1985. pap. text 13.95 (*0-89894-003-6*) Advocate Pub Group.

Philosophy for a Fair Society. Michael Hudson et al. LC 95-131077. (Georgist Paradigm Ser.). 182p. 1994. pap. 18.95 (*0-85683-159-X*, Pub. by Shepheard-Walwyn Pubs) Paul & Co Pubs.

Philosophy for a New Generation. 4th ed. Arthur K. Bierman & James A. Gould. 576p. (C). 1980. pap. text 39.73 (*0-02-309640-3*, Macmillan Coll) P-H.

Philosophy for Adults. Thomas O. Buford. LC 80-5524. 639p. 1980. pap. text 36.00 (*0-8191-1118-X*) U Pr of Amer.

Philosophy for Africa. Augustine Shutte. (Studies in Philosophy: No. 5). 184p. (Orig.). (C). 1996. pap. 20.00 (*0-87462-608-0*) Marquette.

Philosophy for Beginners. 2nd ed. Richard Osborne. (Illus.). 186p. (Orig.). 1992. pap. 11.95 (*0-86316-157-X*) Writers & Readers.

Philosophy for Democratic Convergence: Marxism Transcended. W. F. Whitehouse. (Avebury Series in Philosophy). 274p. 1994. 71.95 (*1-85628-551-0*, Pub. by Avebry) Ashgate Pub Co.

Philosophy for Dummies. Tom Morris. (For Dummies Ser.). 384p. 1999. pap. 19.99 (*0-7645-5153-1*, Dummies Trade Pr) IDG Bks.

***Philosophy for Linguists: An Introductory Textbook.** Siobhan Chapman. LC 99-462292. 2000. pap. write for info. (*0-415-20659-6*) Routledge.

Philosophy for Living: A Sketch of Aquinate Philosophy. Johnemery Konecsni. 184p. 1977. pap. text 20.00 (*0-8191-0138-9*) U Pr of Amer.

Philosophy for Nursing. Jan Reed & Ian Ground. (Illus.). 192p. (Orig.). 1996. pap. 45.00 (*1-56593-757-0*, 1472) Singular Publishing.

Philosophy for the Left Hand. Troy W. Organ. (Revisioning Philosophy Ser.: Vol. 3). 398p. (C). 1991. text 54.95 (*0-8204-1308-9*) P Lang Pubng.

Philosophy for the Sick. Manly P. Hall. pap. 4.95 (*0-89314-340-5*) Philos Res.

Philosophy for Understanding Theology. Diogenes Allen. LC 84-48510. 252p. 1985. pap. 24.95 (*0-8042-0688-0*) Westminster John Knox.

Philosophy for Young Thinkers see Philosophy for Young Thinkers Program

Philosophy for Young Thinkers Program. Joseph Hester & Philip Vincent. Incl. About Me: Kindergarten. (J). (gr. k). 1989. pap. 25.00 (*0-89824-651-2*); Beat Him If He Sneezes: Eighth Grade. (J). (gr. 8). 1989. pap. 9.99 (*0-89824-661-X*); But, I'm Different: Third Grade Student Book. (J). 1989. pap. 9.99 (*0-89824-654-7*); Global Village: Sixth Grade Student Book. 1989. pap. 9.99 (*0-89824-658-X*); Great Experiment: Fifth Grade Student Book. 1989. pap. 9.99 (*0-89824-657-1*); Human Community: Fourth Grade Student Book. 1989. pap. 7.99 (*0-89824-656-3*); Human Configurations: Seventh Grade. (J). (gr. 7). 1989. pap. 9.99 (*0-89824-660-1*); Living Together: First Grade Student Book. 1989. pap. 9.99 (*0-89824-652-0*); My Expanding World: Second Grade Student Book. 1989. pap. 9.99 (*0-89824-653-9*); Philosophy for Young Thinkers. 1989. pap. 15.00 (*0-89824-075-1*); Teachers Manual: Grades K-3. 1989. pap. 10.00 (*0-89824-650-4*); Teachers Manual: Grades 4-6. 1989. pap. 10.00 (*0-89824-655-5*); Teachers Manual: Grades 7-9. 1989. pap. 10.00 (*0-89824-659-8*); Wrong Think - Non Think: Ninth Grade. (YA). (gr. 9). 1989. pap. 9.99 (*0-89824-662-8*); (J). (gr. k-12). 1989. pap. write for info. (*0-318-64449-5*) Trillium Pr.

***Philosophy from the Inside.** Colin McGinn. 2000. 26.00 (*0-06-019792-7*); pap. 15.00 (*0-06-095760-3*) HarpC.

Philosophy Goes to School. Matthew Lipman. LC 87-18071. 250p. (C). 1988. 34.95 (*0-87722-537-0*); pap. 19.95 (*0-87722-555-9*) Temple U Pr.

Philosophy Gone Wild: Essays in Environmental Ethics. 2nd ed. Holmes Rolston, III. LC 86-60106. 269p. (C). 1989. pap. 19.95 (*0-87975-556-3*) Prometheus Bks.

Philosophy Guidebook: Complete with Maps. David W. Felder. 55p. 1996. pap. text 10.00 (*0-910959-05-6*, B&G 05) Wellington Pr.

Philosophy, History & Politics. Nathan Rotenstreich. (Melbourne International Philosophy Ser.: No. 1). 166p. 1976. pap. text 82.00 (*90-247-1743-4*) Kluwer Academic.

Philosophy, History & Social Action: Essays in Honor of Lewis Feuer with an Autobiographic Essay by Lewis Feuer. Ed. by Sidney Hook et al. (Boston Studies in the Philosophy of Science Ser.: No. 107). 494p. 1988. text 237.50 (*90-277-2644-2*) Kluwer Academic.

Philosophy, Humanity & Ecology Vol. 1: Philosophy of Nature & Environmental Ethics. Ed. by J. Odera Oruka. 367p. (Orig.). (C). 1996. pap. text 55.00 (*0-7881-2676-8*) DIANE Pub.

Philosophy in a Feminist Voice: Critiques & Reconstructions. Janet A. Kourany. LC 97-22817. 344p. 1998. text 55.00 (*0-691-03313-7*, Pub. by Princeton U Pr); pap. text 17.95 (*0-691-01936-3*, Pub. by Princeton U Pr) Cal Prin Full Svc.

Philosophy in a New Key: A Study in the Symbolism of Reason, Rite & Art. 3rd ed. Susanne K. Langer. LC 57-1386. (Illus.). 330p. 1957. pap. text 15.50 (*0-674-66503-1*) HUP.

Philosophy in a Time of Lost Spirit: Essays on Contemporary Theory. Ronald Beiner. LC 97-228621. 192p. 1997. pap. text 24.95 (*0-8020-8067-7*) U of Toronto Pr.

Philosophy in a Time of Lost Spirit: Essays on Contemporary Theory. Ronald Beiner. LC 97-228621. 192p. 1997. text 50.00 (*0-8020-4210-4*) U of Toronto Pr.

Philosophy in America, 204 vols., Set. (AMS Press Reprint Ser.). reprint ed. write for info. (*0-404-59000-4*) AMS Pr.

Philosophy in & Out of Europe. Ed. by Marjorie Grene. (Current Continental Research Ser.: No. 804). 182p. (Orig.). 1987. pap. text 19.50 (*0-8191-6324-4*) U Pr of Amer.

Philosophy in Christian Antiquity. Christopher Stead. LC 94-5960. 273p. (C). 1995. pap. text 22.95 (*0-521-46955-4*) Cambridge U Pr.

Philosophy in Classroom Teaching. Jacobsen. LC 98-26488. 1998. pap. text 42.00 (*0-02-360123-X*) Macmillan.

***Philosophy in Crisis: The Need for Reconstruction.** Mario Bunge. 250p. 2001. 33.00 (*1-57392-843-7*) Prometheus Bks.

***Philosophy in Cyberspace: A Guide to Philosophy-Related Resources on the Internet.** 2nd ed. Ed. by Dey Alexander. 404p. (Orig.). (C). 1998. pap. 25.00 (*1-889680-00-1*) Philos Document.

Philosophy in Economics. Ed. by Joseph C. Pitt. 217p. 1981. text 94.00 (*90-277-1210-7*, D Reidel) Kluwer Academic.

Philosophy in Epidemiology & Public Health. Dale R. Tavris. 229p. (C). 1997. lib. bdg. 75.00 (*1-56072-426-9*) Nova Sci Pubs.

Philosophy in Experience: American Philosophy in Transition. Ed. by Richard E. Hart & Douglas R. Anderson. LC 96-33512. (American Philosophy Ser.: No. 5). xi, 281p. 1996. 30.00 (*0-8232-1630-6*); pap. 18.00 (*0-8232-1631-4*) Fordham.

Philosophy in France Today. Ed. by Alan Montefiore. LC 82-9730. 223p. 1983. pap. text 22.95 (*0-521-29673-0*) Cambridge U Pr.

Philosophy in Geography. Ed. by Stephen Gale & Gunnar Olsson. (Theory & Decision Library: No. 20). 1979. lib. bdg. 126.50 (*90-277-0948-3*) Kluwer Academic.

Philosophy in History: Essays in the Historiography of Philosophy. Ed. by Richard McKay Rorty et al. (Ideas in Context Ser.). 414p. 1984. pap. text 21.95 (*0-521-27330-7*) Cambridge U Pr.

Philosophy in India: Traditions, Teaching & Research. K. Satchidanada Mutry. 237p. (C). 1991. reprint ed. 16.00 (*81-208-0002-8*, Pub. by Motilal Bnarsidass) S Asia.

Philosophy in Literature, 2 vols. Charles W. Johnson. LC 92-22574. (Illus.). 744p. 1992. pap. 59.95 (*0-7734-9915-6*) E Mellen.

Philosophy in Literature. H. P. Rickman. LC 96-3741. 1996. 36.50 (*0-8386-3652-7*) Fairleigh Dickinson.

Philosophy in Literature: Shakespeare, Voltaire, Tolstoy & Proust. Morris Weitz. LC 63-7173. (Wayne Bks.: No. 14). 125p. reprint ed. pap. 38.80 (*0-7837-3808-0*, 204362800010) Bks Demand.

Philosophy in Medicine, Science & Health: Subject Analysis Index with Reference Bibliography. Rocco Z. De Forto. LC 84-47864. 150p. 1987. 47.50 (*0-88164-402-1*); pap. 44.50 (*0-88164-403-X*) ABBE Pubs Assn.

Philosophy in Mind: The Place of Philosophy in the Study of Mind. Ed. by Michaelis Michael. (Philosophical Studies). 332p. (C). 1994. lib. bdg. 140.00 (*0-7923-3143-5*, Pub. by Kluwer Academic) Kluwer Academic.

Philosophy in Pakistan. Ahmad Naeem. LC 97-26581. (Cultural Heritage & Contemporary Change Series IIA). 1997. pap. 17.50 (*1-56518-108-5*) Coun Res Values.

Philosophy in Play: Three Dialogues. Ermanno Bencivenga. LC 93-47030. 224p. (Orig.). (C). 1994. pap. text 12.95 (*0-87220-237-2*); lib. bdg. 34.95 (*0-87220-238-0*) Hackett Pub.

Philosophy in Poetry. Elias H. Sneath. LC 79-119965. (Select Bibliographies Reprint Ser.). 1977. 21.95 (*0-8369-5408-4*) Ayer.

Philosophy in Poetry: A Study of Sir John Davies' Poem "Nosce Teipsum" Elias H. Sneath. LC 69-14084. 319p. 1970. reprint ed. lib. bdg. 65.00 (*0-8371-1934-0*, SNPP, Greenwood Pr) Greenwood.

Philosophy in Poetry: A Study of Sir John Davies' Poem "Nosce Teipsum" Elias H. Sneath. (BCL1-PR English Literature Ser.). 319p. 1992. reprint ed. pap. text 69.00 (*0-685-52796-4*); reprint ed. lib. bdg. 89.00 (*0-7812-7198-3*) Rprt Serv.

Philosophy in Practice: An Introduction to the Main Question. Adam Morton. (Illus.). 500p. (C). 1996. 87.95 (*0-631-18864-9*); pap. 36.95 (*0-631-18865-7*) Blackwell Pubs.

Philosophy in Practice: Understanding Value Debate. R. Eric Barnes. 261p. (YA). (gr. 9-12). 1996. pap. text 20.00 (*0-931054-41-9*) Clark Pub.

Philosophy in Process, Vol. 10. Paul Weiss. LC 63-14293. (SUNY Series in Philosophy). 393p. (C). 1987. text 22.50 (*0-88706-497-3*) State U NY Pr.

Philosophy in Process, Vol. 11. Paul Weiss. LC 63-14293. (SUNY Series in Philosophy). 401p. (C). 1988. text 76.50 (*0-88706-762-X*); pap. text 24.95 (*0-88706-767-0*) State U NY Pr.

Philosophy in Question: Essays on a Pyrrhonian Theme. David R. Hiley. 218p. 1996. 29.95 (*0-226-33433-3*) U Ch Pr.

Philosophy in Russia: From Herzen to Lenin to Berdyaev. Frederick C. Copleston. 480p. 1994. 75.00 (*0-85532-577-1*, Pub. by Srch Pr) St Mut.

Philosophy in Science, Vol. 1. Ed. by M. Heller et al. 191p. 1983. pap. 28.00 (*0-88126-631-0*) Pachart Pub Hse.

Philosophy in Science, Vol. 2. Ed. by M. Heller et al. 1986. pap. 28.00 (*0-88126-632-9*) Pachart Pub Hse.

Philosophy in Science, Vol. 3. Ed. by M. Heller et al. 1989. pap. 28.00 (*0-88126-633-7*) Pachart Pub Hse.

Philosophy in Science, Vol. 4. Ed. by M. Heller et al. 1990. pap. 48.00 (*0-88126-634-5*) Pachart Pub Hse.

Philosophy in Science, Vol. 5. Ed. by M. Heller et al. 1993. pap. 48.00 (*0-88126-635-3*) Pachart Pub Hse.

Philosophy in Science, Vol. 6. Ed. by M. Heller et al. 1995. pap. 48.00 (*0-88126-636-1*) Pachart Pub Hse.

Philosophy in Science, Vol. 7. Ed. by M. Heller et al. 1997. pap. 48.00 (*0-88126-637-X*) Pachart Pub Hse.

Philosophy in Science, Vol. 8. Ed. by W. R. Stoeger. 1999. pap. 48.00 (*0-88126-638-8*) Pachart Pub Hse.

Philosophy in Six Lessons & a Quarter. Witold Gombrowicz. Ed. by Simona Draghici. LC 98-54346.Tr. of Cours de Philosophie en Six Heures Un Quart. 102p. 1999. pap. text 6.95 (*0-943045-15-0*) Plutarch Pr OR.

***Philosophy in the Boudior.** Marquis De Sade. 2000. reprint ed. pap. 13.95 (*1-84068-012-1*, Pub. by Creation Bks) Subterranean Co.

Philosophy in the Boudoir. 3rd ed. Marquis De Sade, pseud. (Velvet Ser.: Vol. 1). 160p. 1996. reprint ed. pap. 12.95 (*1-871592-09-7*) Creation Books.

Philosophy in the Classroom. 2nd ed. Matthew Lipman et al. 248p. 1980. pap. 22.95 (*0-87722-183-9*) Temple U Pr.

Philosophy in the Development of Law. Pierre De Tourtoulon. Ed. by Morris R. Cohen. Tr. by M. M. Read. 1977. lib. bdg. 59.95 (*0-8490-2428-5*) Gordon Pr.

Philosophy in the Development of Law. Pierre De Tourtoulon. (Modern Legal Philosophy Ser.: Vol. 13). lxi, 653p. 1998. reprint ed. 178.00 (*1-56169-392-8*) Gaunt.

Philosophy in the Development of Law. Pierre De Tourtoulon. Tr. by Martha M. Read. (Modern Legal Philosophy Ser.: Vol. 13). lxii, 654p. 1969. reprint ed. 55.00 (*0-8377-2626-3*, Rothman) W S Hein.

Philosophy in the Flesh: The Embodied Mind & Its Challenge to Western Thought. George Lakoff & Mark Johnson. LC 98-37113. 826p. 1999. 32.00 (*0-465-05673-3*, Pub. by Basic) HarpC.

***Philosophy in the Flesh: The Embodied Mind & Its Challenge to Western Thought.** George Lakoff & Mark Johnson. 550p. 1999. pap. 20.00 (*0-465-05674-1*) HarpC.

Philosophy in the Mass Age. George Grant. Ed. & Intro. by William C. Christian. 160p. 1995. text 35.00 (*0-8020-0438-5*); pap. text 16.95 (*0-8020-7228-3*) U of Toronto Pr.

Philosophy in the Middle Ages: The Christian, Islamic & Jewish Traditions. 2nd ed. Ed. by Arthur Hyman & James J. Walsh. LC 82-23337. 816p. (Orig.). (C). 1983. reprint ed. pap. text 26.95 (*0-915145-80-4*); reprint ed. lib. bdg. 49.95 (*0-915145-81-2*) Hackett Pub.

Philosophy in the Open. Godfrey N. Vesey. 144p. 1974. pap. 21.00 (*0-335-00909-3*) OpUniv Pr.

***Philosophy in the Sixteenth & Seventeenth Centuries: Conversations with Aristotle.** Constance Blackwell & Sachiko Kusukawa. LC 99-15647. 1999. 110.95 (*0-86078-668-4*, Pub. by Ashgate Pub) Ashgate Pub Co.

Philosophy in the Soviet Union: A Survey of the Mid-Sixties. Ed. by Ervin Laszlo. (Sovietica Ser.: No.25). 208p. 1967. lib. bdg. 68.50 (*90-277-0057-5*) Kluwer Academic.

Philosophy in the Tragic Age of the Greeks. Friedrich Wilhelm Nietzsche. 117p. 1996. pap. 9.95 (*0-89526-710-1*, Gateway Editions) Regnery Pub.

Philosophy Is Not a Trivial Pursuit: A Self-Guided Introduction to Philosophy. Paul T. Sagal & Richard J. Ketchum. 230p. (Orig.). 1997. pap. text 15.95 (*0-87563-711-6*) Stipes.

Philosophy Issues in Info Systems. Winder. 256p. 1996. 79.95 (*1-85728-592-1*, Pub. by UCL Pr Ltd) Taylor & Francis.

Philosophy, Its History & Historiography. Ed. by A. J. Holland. 336p. 1985. lib. bdg. 167.00 (*90-277-1945-4*, D Reidel) Kluwer Academic.

***Philosophy, Its Scope & Relations, 1902 Edition.** Henry Sidgwick. (Key Texts Ser.). 270p. 1998. pap. 20.00 (*1-85506-559-2*) Thoemmes Pr.

Philosophy Journals & Serials: An Analytical Guide, 2. Compiled by Douglas H. Ruben. LC 84-29021. (Annotated Bibliographies of Serials: A Subject Approach Ser.: No. 2). 147p. 1985. lib. bdg. 55.00 (*0-313-23958-4*, RPJ/, Greenwood Pr) Greenwood.

Philosophy, Language, & Artificial Intelligence. Ed. by Jack Kulas et al. (C). 1988. lib. bdg. 175.00 (*1-55608-073-5*) Kluwer Academic.

Philosophy Looks at the Arts: Contemporary Readings in Aesthetics. 3rd ed. Joseph Margolis. LC 88-12303. 592p. (C). 1987. pap. 27.95 (*0-87722-440-4*) Temple U Pr.

Philosophy Looks to the Future: Confrontation, Commitment & Utopia. 2nd ed. Peyton E. Richter & Walter L. Fogg. 576p. (C). 1985. reprint ed. pap. text 31.95 (*0-88133-185-6*) Waveland Pr.

Philosophy Love of Wisdom: Selections & Study Questions. Gary L. Baran. (C). 1991. text 25.80 (*0-536-57920-2*) Pearson Custom.

Philosophy Made Simple. 2nd rev. ed. Richard H. Popkin & Avrum Stroll. LC 92-34537. 336p. 1993. pap. 12.95 (*0-385-42533-3*) Doubleday.

Philosophy Mathematics & Modern Physics: A Dialogue. Ed. by Enno Rudolph & Ion-Opimpiu Stamatescu. LC 94-8282. (Illus.). 242p. 1995. 53.95 (*0-387-57683-5*) Spr-Verlag.

Philosophy, Mind, & Cognitive Inquiry: Resources for Understanding Mental Processes. Ed. by David J. Cole et al. (Studies in Cognitive Systems). 462p. (C). 1990. lib. bdg. 186.00 (*0-7923-0427-6*, Pub. by Kluwer Academic) Kluwer Academic.

Philosophy Natural Therapeutics, Vol. I. Henry Lindlahr. (Natural Therapeutics Ser.). 327p. 1975. pap. 24.00 (*0-85207-159-0*, Pub. by C W Daniel) Natl Bk Netwk.

Philosophy Nuggets: Ideas for Building a Better World. Samoht Givotangi. LC 94-75120. (Illus.). 1994. lib. bdg. 25.00 (*0-9640470-8-X*) Givotangi.

Philosophy of A. J. Ayer. Ed. by Lewis E. Hahn. LC 92-6249. (Library of Living Philosophers: Vol. XXI). 716p. (C). 1992. 59.95 (*0-8126-9172-5*) Open Court.

Philosophy of A. J. Ayer. Ed. by Lewis E. Hahn. LC 92-6249. (Library of Living Philosophers: Vol. XXI). 716p. (C). 1992. pap. 36.95 (*0-8126-9173-3*) Open Court.

Philosophy of Abraham Shalom: A Fifteenth-Century Exposition & Defense of Maimonides. Herbert A. Davidson. LC 65-63470. (University of California Publications, Near Eastern Studies: Vol. 5). 119p. reprint ed. pap. 36.90 (*0-608-10009-9*, 201482000090) Bks Demand.

Philosophy of Accounts. Charles E. Sprague. LC 72-81869. 1972. reprint ed. text 30.00 (*0-914348-09-4*) Scholars Bk.

Philosophy of Action. Ed. by Guttorm Floistad. 1986. pap. text 23.50 (*90-247-3299-9*) Kluwer Academic.

Philosophy of Action. Ed. by Alfred R. Mele. LC 96-8682. (Oxford Readings in Philosophy). 320p. (C). 1997. text 71.00 (*0-19-875174-5*); pap. text 21.95 (*0-19-875175-3*) OUP.

Philosophy of Action. Carlos J. Moya. 1990. pap. 26.95 (*0-7456-0747-0*) Blackwell Pubs.

***Philosophy of Aikido.** John Stevens. 2001. 28.00 (*4-7700-2534-3*) Kodansha.

Philosophy of Air Power. James T. Lowe. LC 84-5254. 474p. (Orig.). (C). 1984. pap. text 34.00 (*0-8191-3954-8*); lib. bdg. 62.00 (*0-8191-3953-X*) U Pr of Amer.

Philosophy of Alain Locke: The Harlem Renaissance & Beyond. Ed. by Leonard Harris. 344p. 1991. pap. 22.95 (*0-87722-829-9*) Temple U Pr.

Philosophy of Alfred North Whitehead. 2nd ed. Ed. by Paul Arthur Schilpp. 816p. 1941. pap. 37.95 (*0-8126-9132-6*) Open Court.

Philosophy of Alfred North Whitehead. 2nd ed. Ed. by Paul Arthur Schilpp. 816p. 1951. 59.95 (*0-87548-140-X*) Open Court.

Philosophy of Alfred Rosenberg: Origins of the National Socialist Myth. James B. Whisker. 254p. (Orig.). 1990. pap. 5.75 (*0-939482-25-8*, 0241, Noontide Pr) Legion Survival.

Philosophy of Analogy & Symbolism. S. T. Cargill. 264p. 1996. reprint ed. pap. 19.95 (*1-56459-586-2*) Kessinger Pub.

Philosophy of Andy Warhol: From A to B & Back Again. Andy Warhol. LC 76-40899. 266p. 1977. pap. 13.00 (*0-15-671720-4*, Harvest Bks) Harcourt.

An Asterisk (*) at the beginning of an entry indicates that the title is appearing for the first time.

Philosophy of Appearances. Miklos Almasi. 294p. (C). 1989. 150.00 (*963-05-4554-3*, Pub. by Akade Kiado) St Mut.

Philosophy of Appearances. Miklos Almasi. 300p. (C). 1989. text 171.00 (*90-277-2150-5*, D Reidel) Kluwer Academic.

Philosophy of Appearances. Imre-Feher Hronszky & Balazs Marta-Dajka. 440p. (C). 1988. 150.00 (*963-05-4771-6*, Pub. by Akade Kiado) St Mut.

Philosophy of Argument. Trudy Govier. Ed. by John Hoaglund. (Studies in Critical Thinking & Informal Logic: Vol. 3). 1999. pap. 21.45 (*0-916475-27-1*); lib. bdg. 48.65 (*0-916475-28-X*) Vale Pr.

Philosophy of Aristotle. Renford Bambrough. 1963. mass mkt. 6.99 (*0-451-62783-0*, Sig) NAL.

Philosophy of Art. Friedrich Wilhelm Joseph Schelling. Tr. & Intro. by Douglas W. Stott. LC 87-35397. (Theory & History of Literature Ser.: Vol. 58).Tr. of Philosophie der Kunst. 395p. 1989. pap. 21.95 (*0-8166-1684-1*) U of Minn Pr.

Philosophy of Art: Being the Second Part of Hegel's Aesthetik. Georg Wilhelm Friedrich Hegel. Tr. by William M. Bryant. 1976. lib. bdg. 59.95 (*0-8490-2429-3*) Gordon Pr.

***Philosophy of Art: Contemporary Introduction.** Noel Carroll. LC 99-25928. (Contemporary Introductions to Philosophy Ser.). 1999. pap. 18.99 (*0-415-15964-4*) Routledge.

***Philosophy of Art: Contemporary Introduction.** Noel Carroll. LC 99-25928. (Contemporary Introductions to Philosophy Ser.). 224p. (C). 1999. text. write for info. (*0-415-15963-6*) Routledge.

Philosophy of Art: Readings Ancient & Modern. Alex Neill & Aaron Ridley. LC 94-37453. 592p. (C). 1994. pap. 38.75 (*0-07-046192-9*) McGraw.

Philosophy of Art Education. Edmund B. Feldman. LC 95-15160. 130p. 1995. pap. text, boxed set 34.67 (*0-13-230830-4*) P-H.

Philosophy of Art History. Arnold Hauser. 429p. 1985. reprint ed. pap. 18.95 (*0-8101-0672-8*) Northwestern U Pr.

Philosophy of Artificial Intelligence. Ed. by Margaret A. Boden. (Oxford Readings in Philosophy Ser.). 460p. 1990. pap. text 22.00 (*0-19-824854-7*) OUP.

Philosophy of Artificial Life. Ed. by Margaret A. Boden. (Oxford Readings in Philosophy Ser.). (Illus.). 414p. 1996. text 65.00 (*0-19-875154-0*); pap. text 19.95 (*0-19-875155-9*) OUP.

Philosophy of Astrology. Manly P. Hall. LC 44-21946. (Illus.). 91p. 1971. reprint ed. pap. 9.95 (*0-89314-300-6*) Philos Res.

Philosophy of Auditing. Robert K. Mautz & Hussein A. Sharaf. (Monograph No. 6). 248p. 1961. 12.00 (*0-86539-002-9*) Am Accounting.

Philosophy of Auguste Comte. Lucien Levy-Bruhl. 1976. lib. bdg. 59.95 (*0-8490-2430-7*) Gordon Pr.

Philosophy of Being. A. Hilary Armstrong & Gerard Smith. LC 61-5281. 400p. 1961. pap. 20.00 (*0-87462-530-0*) Marquette.

Philosophy of Bertrand Russell. Ed. by Paul Arthur Schilpp. 874p. 1971. 59.95 (*0-87548-138-8*); pap. 36.95 (*0-87548-287-2*) Open Court.

Philosophy of Bhakti. Chhaganlal Lala. (C). 1989. 28.50 (*81-7018-557-2*, Pub. by BR Pub) S Asia.

Philosophy of Bhartrhari. Gaurinath Sastri. (C). 1991. 19.00 (*81-217-0099-X*, Pub. by Bharat Vidya) S Asia.

Philosophy of Biology. Ed. by David L. Hull & Michael Ruse. LC 97-36921. (Oxford Readings in Philosophy Ser.). (Illus.). 782p. 1998. text 85.00 (*0-19-875213-X*) OUP.

Philosophy of Biology. Ed. by David L. Hull & Michael Ruse. (Oxford Readings in Philosophy Ser.). (Illus.). 782p. 1998. pap. text 24.95 (*0-19-875212-1*) OUP.

Philosophy of Biology. Michael Ruse. Ed. by Paul Edwards. (Philosophical Topics Ser.). 368p. (C). 1988. pap. text 15.00 (*0-02-404492-X*, Macmillan Coll) P-H.

Philosophy of Biology. Michael Ruse. LC 97-36460. 392p. 1998. pap. text 18.95 (*1-57392-185-8*) Prometheus Bks.

Philosophy of Biology. Elliott Sober. 2000. 65.00 (*0-8133-9125-3*) HarpC.

Philosophy of Biology. Elliott Sober. (Dimensions of Philosophy Ser.). 256p. (C). 1993. pap. 27.00 (*0-8133-0824-0*, Pub. by Westview) HarpC.

Philosophy of Biology. 2nd ed. Elliott Sober. LC 99-49091. (Dimensions of Philosophy Ser.). 256p. 1999. pap. 27.00 (*0-8133-9126-1*) Westview.

Philosophy of Biology Today. Michael Ruse. LC 88-15377. (SUNY Series in Philosophy & Biology). 155p. (C). 1988. pap. text 16.95 (*0-88706-911-8*) State U NY Pr.

Philosophy of Brand Blanshard. Ed. by Paul Arthur Schilpp. (Library of Living Philosophers: Vol. XV). 1160p. 1980. 42.95 (*0-87548-349-6*) Open Court.

Philosophy of C. D. Broad. Ed. by Paul Arthur Schilpp. LC 60-12084. (Library of Living Philosophers: Vol. X). 878p. 1959. 59.95 (*0-87548-128-0*) Open Court.

Philosophy of C. I. Lewis. Ed. by Paul Arthur Schilpp. LC 67-10007. (Library of Living Philosophers: Vol. XIII). 728p. 1968. 59.95 (*0-87548-135-3*) Open Court.

***Philosophy of Carl G. Hempel: Studies in Science, Explanation, & Rationality.** Carl G. Hempel. Ed. by James H. Fetzer. 400p. 2000. pap. 24.95 (*0-19-514158-X*); text 65.00 (*0-19-512136-8*) OUP.

Philosophy of Chabad, Vol. 2. Nissan Mindel. (Philosophy of Chabad Ser.). 256p. 1973. reprint ed. 15.00 (*0-8266-0417-X*) Kehot Pubn Soc.

Philosophy of Charles Hartshorne. Ed. by Lewis E. Hahn. LC 91-10824. (Library of Living Philosophers: Vol. XX). 802p. (C). 1991. 59.95 (*0-8126-9147-4*); pap. 38.95 (*0-8126-9148-2*) Open Court.

Philosophy of Charles Hodge: A 19th Century Evangelical Approach to Reason, Knowledge & Truth. Peter Hicks. LC 97-3493. (Studies in American Religion: Vol. 65). 264p. 1997. text 89.95 (*0-7734-8657-7*) E Mellen.

Philosophy of Childhood. Gareth B. Matthews. LC 94-16178. 144p. 1994. 18.95 (*0-674-66480-9*, MATPHC) HUP.

Philosophy of Childhood. Gareth B. Matthews. LC 96-215909. 144p. 1996. pap. 12.95 (*0-674-66481-7*) HUP.

Philosophy of Christian Religious Education. Jeff Astley. LC 93-43675. 322p. (Orig.). 1994. pap. 25.95 (*0-89135-093-4*) Religious Educ.

Philosophy of Christian School Education. Ed. by Paul A. Kienel et al. (Illus.). 484p. 1995. reprint ed. pap. text 18.95 (*1-58331-017-7*) Assn Christ Sch.

Philosophy of Chrysippus. J. B. Gould. 1970. pap. 25.00 (*90-04-01729-1*, PHA, 17) Brill Academic Pubs.

Philosophy of Chrysippus. Josiah B. Gould. LC 78-112606. 222p. (C). 1970. text 24.50 (*0-87395-064-X*) State U NY Pr.

Philosophy of Chrysippus. Josiah B. Gould. LC 78-112606. 230p. reprint ed. pap. 71.30 (*0-608-10189-3*, 201010900068) Bks Demand.

Philosophy of Civilization. Albert Schweitzer. LC 87-2576. 365p. 1987. pap. 21.95 (*0-87975-403-6*) Prometheus Bks.

Philosophy of Classical Yoga. Georg Feuerstein. LC 96-14380. 152p. 1996. pap. 12.95 (*0-89281-603-1*, Inner Trad) Inner Tradit.

***Philosophy of Cognitive Science.** B. Von Eckardt. (Dimensions of Philosophy Ser.). 2000. pap. 19.95 (*0-8133-2490-4*) Westview.

Philosophy of Common Sense. Frederic Harrison. LC 68-8468. (Essay Index Reprint Ser.). 1977. reprint ed. 23.95 (*0-8369-0513-X*) Ayer.

Philosophy of Composition. E. D. Hirsch, Jr. LC 77-4944. xiv, 200p. (C). 1981. reprint ed. pap. text 12.95 (*0-226-34243-3*) U Ch Pr.

Philosophy of Conduct: A Treatise of the Facts, Principles, & Ideals of Ethics. George T. Ladd. LC 75-3222. reprint ed. 46.50 (*0-404-59218-X*) AMS Pr.

Philosophy of Conflict & Other Essays in War-Time, Second Series. Havelock Ellis. LC 70-90634. (Essay Index Reprint Ser.). 1977. 23.95 (*0-8369-1568-2*) Ayer.

Philosophy of Contract. Linzer. 59.95 (*1-85521-233-1*) Ashgate Pub Co.

Philosophy of Criminal Law. Douglas N. Husak. LC 86-31562. 280p. 1987. 58.50 (*0-8476-7550-5*) Rowman.

Philosophy of Criminal Law. Francis Wharton. LC 89-45924. 332p. 1989. reprint ed. 85.00 (*0-912004-74-6*) Gaunt.

Philosophy of Cynicism: An Annotated Bibliography, 4. Luis E. Navia. LC 95-16465. (Bibliographies & Indexes in Philosophy Ser.: No. 4). 232p. 1995. lib. bdg. 69.50 (*0-313-29249-3*, Greenwood Pr) Greenwood.

Philosophy of Daya Krishna. Ed. by Bhuvan Chandel & K. L. Sharma. 1996. 32.00 (*81-85636-20-6*, Pub. by M Manoharial) S Asia.

Philosophy of Death. Andrew J. Davis. 8p. 1993. reprint ed. spiral bd. 8.00 (*0-7873-1063-8*) Hlth Research.

Philosophy of Democratic Government. Yves R. Simon. LC 77-83869. (Midway Reprint Ser.). 1977. pap. text 18.00 (*0-226-75787-0*) U Ch Pr.

Philosophy of Democratic Government. Yves R. Simon. LC 93-22812. (C). 1993. reprint ed. pap. text 17.50 (*0-268-03803-1*) U of Notre Dame Pr.

Philosophy of Development: Reconstructing the Foundations of Human Development & Education. Ed. by Wouter Van Haaften. LC 96-48833. (Philosophy & Education PHED Ser.: Vol. 8). 302p. (C). 1996. text 120.50 (*0-7923-4319-0*) Kluwer Academic.

Philosophy of Discourse Vol. 1: The Rhetorical Turn in Twentieth-Century Thought. Ed. by Chip Sills & George H. Jensen. LC 91-14249. 270p. (C). 1992. pap. text 36.00*(*0-86709-286-6*, 0286, Pub. by Boynton Cook Pubs) Heinemann.

Philosophy of Discourse Vol. 2: The Rhetorical Turn in Twentieth-Century Thought. Chip Sills & George H. Jensen. LC 91-14249. 266p. (C). 1992. pap. text 36.00 (*0-86709-287-4*, 0287, Pub. by Boynton Cook Pubs) Heinemann.

Philosophy of Disenchantment. Edgar E. Saltus. LC 75-113270. reprint ed. 37.50 (*0-404-05503-6*) AMS Pr.

Philosophy of Divine Love see Filosofia Del Amor Divino

Philosophy of Divine Love. rev. ed. Swami P. Saraswati. (Illus.). 132p. 1982. reprint ed. pap. 10.00 (*1-881921-01-8*) Intl Soc Divine Love.

Philosophy of Don Hasdai Crescas. Meyer Waxman. LC 21-5098. (Columbia University. Oriental Studies: No. 17). reprint ed. 29.50 (*0-404-50507-4*) AMS Pr.

Philosophy of Donald Davidson. Ed. by Lewis E. Hahn. LC 99-39735. (Library of Living Philosophers: Vol. 27). 768p. 1999. 72.95 (*0-8126-9398-1*); pap. 42.95 (*0-8126-9399-X*) Open Court.

***Philosophy of Ecology: From Science to Synthesis.** David R. Keller & Frank B. Golley. LC 00-23419. 2000. write for info. (*0-8203-2220-2*) U of Ga Pr.

Philosophy of Economics. Ed. by Wolfgang Balzer & Bert Hamminga. 272p. (C). 1989. lib. bdg. 132.00 (*0-7923-0157-9*, Pub. by Kluwer Academic) Kluwer Academic.

Philosophy of Economics: A Critique of Demarcation. Raphael Sassower. 238p. (Orig.). (C). 1986. lib. bdg. 46.00 (*0-8191-5041-X*) U Pr of Amer.

Philosophy of Economics: A Treatise on Reason, Value & Economic. Subroto Roy. 256p. 1989. 37.50 (*0-415-03592-9*, A3633) Routledge.

Philosophy of Economics: An Anthology. 2nd rev. ed. Ed. by Daniel M. Hausman. LC 93-5496. 479p. (C). 1994. text 74.95 (*0-521-45311-9*); pap. text 27.95 (*0-521-45929-X*) Cambridge U Pr.

***Philosophy of Economy.** Sergefi Nikolaevich Bulgakov & Catherine Evtuhov. LC 99-55454. (Russian Literature & Thought Ser.). 300p. 2000. 35.00 (*0-300-07990-7*) Yale U Pr.

Philosophy of Edmund Burke: A Selection from His Speeches & Writings. Edmund Burke. Ed. by Louis I. Bredvold & Ralph G. Ross. 288p. 1960. pap. text 16.95 (*0-472-06121-6*, 06121, Ann Arbor Bks) U of Mich Pr.

Philosophy of Education. Nel Noddings. LC 95-8820. (Dimensions of Philosophy Ser.). (Illus.). 226p. (C). 1995. pap. 25.00 (*0-8133-8430-3*, Pub. by Westview) HarpC.

Philosophy of Education. Jack Rudman. (ACT Proficiency Examination Program (PEP) Ser.: Vol. 30). 43.95 (*0-8373-5580-X*) Nat Learn.

Philosophy of Education. Jack Rudman. (Regents College Proficiency Examination Ser.: Vol. 32). 43.95 (*0-8373-5482-X*) Nat Learn.

Philosophy of Education. Jack Rudman. (ACT Proficiency Examination Program Ser.: PEP-30). 1994. pap. 23.95 (*0-8373-5530-3*) Nat Learn.

Philosophy of Education. Jack Rudman. (Regents College Proficiency Examination Ser.: Vol. CPEP-32). 1994. reprint ed. pap. 23.95 (*0-8373-5432-3*) Nat Learn.

Philosophy of Education: An Encyclopedia. Ed. by J. J. Chambliss. LC 96-18393. 736p. 1996. text 100.00 (*0-8153-1177-X*, H1671) Garland.

Philosophy of Education: An Introduction. T. W. Moore. (International Library of the Philosophy of Education). 100p. (Orig.). 1982. pap. 13.95 (*0-7100-9192-3*, Routledge Thoemms) Routledge.

Philosophy of Education: An Organization of Topics & Selected Sources. Harry S. Broudy et al. LC 67-27774. 299p. (C). reprint ed. pap. 92.70 (*0-8357-9693-0*, 201905000010) Bks Demand.

Philosophy of Education: Classical & Contemporary. John L. Elias. LC 95-8059. 288p. (C). 1995. 32.50 (*0-89464-898-5*) Krieger.

Philosophy of Education: Critical Writings. Paul H. Hirst & Patricia White. LC 97-30748. 1712p. (C). 1998. 700.00 (*0-415-12944-3*) Routledge.

Philosophy of Education: Introductory Readings. 2nd ed. Ed. by William Hare & John P. Portelli. 336p. (Orig.). 1996. pap. text. write for info. (*1-55059-136-3*) Detselig Ents.

Philosophy of Education in Historical Perspective. 2nd ed. Adrian M. Dupuis & Robin L. Gordon. LC 96-43224. 318p. 1996. pap. text 24.50 (*0-7618-0548-6*) U Pr of Amer.

Philosophy of Education, 1986: Proceedings of the 42nd Meeting of the Philosophy of Education Society. annuals Ed. by Nicholas Barbules. 352p. 1983. 30.00 (*0-318-16177-X*) Phil Ed Soc.

Philosophy of Education, 1973-1974. Ed. by James J. Jelinek. LC 74-156779. 1974. 15.00 (*0-931702-22-4*) Far Western Phil.

Philosophy of Education, 1974-1975. Ed. by James J. Jelinek. LC 74-156779. 1975. 15.00 (*0-931702-23-2*) Far Western Phil.

Philosophy of Education, 1975-1976. Ed. by James J. Jelinek. LC 74-156779. 1976. 15.00 (*0-931702-24-0*) Far Western Phil.

Philosophy of Education, 1976-1977. Ed. by James J. Jelinek. LC 74-156779. 1977. 15.00 (*0-931702-25-9*) Far Western Phil.

Philosophy of Education since Mid-Century. Jonas F. Soltis. LC 81-780. 136p. (C). 1981. reprint ed. pap. text 12.95 (*0-8077-2651-6*) Tchrs Coll.

Philosophy of Educational Knowledge: An Introduction to the Foundations of Science of Education, Philosophy of Education & Practical Pedagogics. Wolfgang Brezinka. (Philosophy & Education Ser.). 320p. (C). 1991. lib. bdg. 145.00 (*0-7923-1522-7*, Pub. by M Nijhoff) Kluwer Academic.

Philosophy of Egoism. James L. Walker. LC 72-77200. (Libertarian Broadsides Ser.: No. 3). (Illus.). 62p. 1972. pap. 1.35 (*0-87926-014-9*) R Myles.

Philosophy of Elbert Hubbard. Elbert Hubbard. 194p. 1998. reprint ed. pap. 24.95 (*0-7661-0417-6*) Kessinger Pub.

Philosophy of Emotions. Peter French & Howard Wettstein. LC 98-40348. (Midwest Studies in Philosophy). 320p. 1999. 42.00 (*0-268-01443-4*, Pub. by U of Notre Dame Pr); pap. write for info. (*0-268-01444-2*, Pub. by U of Notre Dame Pr) Chicago Distribution Ctr.

Philosophy of English Literature. John Bascom. xiii, 318p. 1985. reprint ed. lib. bdg. 49.00 (*0-932051-94-4*) Rprt Serv.

Philosophy of Epicurus: Letters, Doctrines, & Parallel Passages from Lucretius. Epicurus. Ed. by George K. Strodach. LC 63-7787. 272p. reprint ed. pap. 84.40 (*0-608-10073-0*, 200636600058) Bks Demand.

Philosophy of Ernest Holmes, Vol. 1. Ernest Holmes. Ed. by George P. Bendall. LC 96-85603. (Holmes Papers). 172p. (Orig.). 1996. pap. 12.95 (*0-87516-697-0*) DeVorss.

Philosophy of Ernst Cassirer. Ed. by Paul Arthur Schilpp. LC 72-83947. (Library of Living Philosophers: Vol. VI). 954p. 1949. 59.95 (*0-87548-131-0*); pap. 38.95 (*0-87548-146-9*) Open Court.

Philosophy of Eros & European Art. Vyacheslav P. Shestakov. LC 95-37274. 120p. 1996. 59.95 (*0-7734-8872-3*) E Mellen.

Philosophy of (Erotic) Love. Ed. by Robert C. Solomon & Kathleen M. Higgins. LC 90-19340. xii, 524p. 1991. 45.00 (*0-7006-0479-0*); pap. 17.95 (*0-7006-0480-4*) U Pr of KS.

Philosophy of Ethics Applied to Everyday Life: A Course of Study for Gifted Students at the Secondary & Post-Secondary Levels. James Logiudice & Michael E. Walters. 1987. pap. text 10.00 (*0-910609-16-0*) Gifted Educ Pr.

***Philosophy of European Union Law.** J. M. Broekman. (On the Making of Europe Ser.). 1999. 40.00 (*90-429-0728-2*, Pub. by Peeters Pub) Bks Intl VA.

Philosophy of Existence. Karl Jaspers. Tr. by Richard F. Grabau. LC 79-133203. 126p. 1971. pap. text 17.95 (*0-8122-1010-7*) U of Pa Pr.

Philosophy of Existence. Gabriel Marcel. Tr. by Manya Harai. LC 73-80390. (Essay Index Reprint Ser.). 1977. 18.95 (*0-8369-1094-X*) Ayer.

Philosophy of Existence: Introduction to Weltanschauugslehre. Wilhelm Dilthey. LC 78-5673. 74p. 1978. reprint ed. lib. bdg. 47.50 (*0-313-20460-8*, DIPH, Greenwood Pr) Greenwood.

Philosophy of Existentialism. Gabriel Marcel. 132p. 1995. pap. 8.95 (*0-8065-0901-5*, 84, Citadel Pr) Carol Pub Group.

Philosophy of F. P. Ramsey. Nils-Eric Sahlin. (Illus.). 268p. (C). 1990. text 69.95 (*0-521-38543-1*) Cambridge U Pr.

Philosophy of Fasting. Edward Purinton. 140p. 1984. reprint ed. pap. text 15.00 (*0-87556-382-1*) Saifer.

Philosophy of Fasting. Edward E. Purinton. 130p. 1996. reprint ed. spiral bd. 15.00 (*0-7873-0686-X*) Hlth Research.

Philosophy of Fine Art, 4 vols. Georg Wilhelm Friedrich Hegel. Tr. by F. B. Osmaston. 1976. lib. bdg. 550.95 (*0-8490-2431-5*) Gordon Pr.

Philosophy of Fire: The Spiritual Light. deluxe ed. R. Swinburne Clymer. 285p. 1964. lthr. 20.00 (*0-932785-98-0*) Philos Pub.

Philosophy of Fire: The Spiritual Light. 5th ed. R. Swinburne Clymer. 285p. 1964. 10.95 (*0-932785-38-7*) Philos Pub.

Philosophy of Form: An Expanded Reprint of the Author's Introduction to His "Philosophy As a Science" Paul Carus. LC 80-12865. (Philosophy in America Ser.). reprint ed. 32.50 (*0-404-59104-3*) AMS Pr.

Philosophy of Freedom. Rudolf Steiner. 1972. reprint ed. lib. bdg. 59.95 (*0-8490-0825-5*) Gordon Pr.

***Philosophy of Freedom: The Basis for a Modern World Conception.** Rudolf Steiner. 234p. 1999. reprint ed. pap. 16.95 (*1-85584-082-0*, Pub. by R Steiner Pr) Anthroposophic.

Philosophy of Freemasonry. Roscoe Pound. (Illus.). 96p. 1997. reprint ed. pap. 15.95 (*1-887560-25-4*) M Poll Pub.

Philosophy of G. E. Moore. Ed. by Paul Arthur Schilpp. LC 68-57206. (Library of Living Philosophers: Vol. IV). 742p. 1942. 59.95 (*0-87548-136-1*); pap. 35.95 (*0-87548-285-6*) Open Court.

Philosophy of Gabriel Marcel. Ed. by Paul Arthur Schilpp et al. (Library of Living Philosophers: Vol. XVII). 644p. (C). 1984. 59.95 (*0-87548-369-0*); pap. 35.95 (*0-8126-9151-2*) Open Court.

Philosophy of Gandhi: A Study of His Basic Ideas. Glyn Richards. 192p. (C). 1996. pap. text 18.00 (*0-7007-0228-8*, Pub. by Curzon Pr Ltd) UH Pr.

Philosophy of Geometry from Riemann to Poincare. Roberto Torretti. (Episteme Ser.: No. 7). 472p. 1984. pap. text 107.50 (*90-277-1837-7*) Kluwer Academic.

Philosophy of George Henrik von Wright, 2 vols. Ed. by Lewis E. Hahn & Paul Arthur Schilpp. (Library of Living Philosophers). 960p. 1989. 99.95 (*0-87548-372-0*) Open Court.

Philosophy of George Herbert Mead. Ed. by Walter R. Corti. 1977. pap. 37.95 (*3-7873-0353-7*) Adlers Foreign Bks.

Philosophy of George Santayana. Ed. by Paul Arthur Schilpp. 714p. 1940. 59.95 (*0-87548-139-6*); pap. 34.95 (*0-8126-9131-8*) Open Court.

Philosophy of Goethe's Faust. Thomas Davidson. LC 68-24963. (Studies in German Literature: No. 13). (C). 1969. reprint ed. lib. bdg. 75.00 (*0-8383-0933-X*) M S G Haskell Hse.

Philosophy of Goodness & Mercy. Gary Minkler. 150p. (Orig.). 1991. 18.50 (*0-9621618-3-7*) Magellan Bk.

Philosophy of Gorakhnath with Goraksha-Vacana-Sangraha. Akshaya K. Banerjea. 355p. (C). 1999. 21.00 (*81-208-0534-8*, Pub. by Motilal Bnarsidass); pap. 15.50 (*81-208-0535-6*, Pub. by Motilal Bnarsidass) St Mut.

Philosophy of Grammar. Otto Jesperson. LC 92-19138. viii, 372p. 1992. reprint ed. pap. text 28.00 (*0-226-39881-1*) U Ch Pr.

***Philosophy of H. P. Lovecraft: The Route to Horror.** Timo Airaksinen. LC 98-9852. (New Studies in Aesthetics: Vol. 29). VIII, 251p. (C). 1999. text 49.95 (*0-8204-4022-1*, 40221) P Lang Pubng.

Philosophy of Hans-Georg Gadamer. Ed. by Lewis E. Hahn. LC 96-48164. (Library of Living Philosophers: Vol. XXIV). 638p. 1997. 59.95 (*0-8126-9341-8*); pap. 34.95 (*0-8126-9342-6*) Open Court.

Philosophy of Hatha Yoga. 2nd ed. Pandit U. Arya & D. Lih. LC 84-19790. 95p. 1985. pap. 8.95 (*0-89389-088-X*) Himalayan Inst.

Philosophy of Health & Beauty. Charles M. Robinson & Charles Shepherd. 100p. 1998. reprint ed. pap. 11.50 (*0-7661-0680-2*) Kessinger Pub.

Philosophy of Health Care Reader. James Lindemann & Hilde L. Nelson. LC 98-30800. 416p. (C). (gr. 13). 1999. 65.00 (*0-415-91915-0*); pap. 24.99 (*0-415-91916-9*) Routledge.

Philosophy of Hegel. Georg Wilhelm Friedrich Hegel. Ed. by Carl J. Friedrich. LC 54-13055. (Modern Library College Editions). 552p. (C). 1965. pap. 7.50 (*0-07-553655-2*, T76) McGraw.

Philosophy of Helvetius with Special Emphasis on the Educational Implications of Sensationalism. Mordecai Grossman. LC 79-176822. (Columbia University. Teachers College. Contributions to Education Ser.: No. 210). reprint ed. 37.50 (*0-404-55210-2*) AMS Pr.

Philosophy of Henry James Sr. Frederic H. Young. (Orig.). 1951. pap. 16.95 (*0-8084-0245-5*) NCUP.

P

Philosophy of Herbert Spencer. W. H. Hudson. LC 74-30102. (Studies in Philosophy: No. 40). 1974. lib. bdg. 75.00 (*0-8383-1794-4*) M S G Haskell Hse.

Philosophy of Higher Education. Louis Wildman. LC 76-360049. 1974. 10.00 (*0-939630-00-1*) Inst Qual Hum Life.

Philosophy of Hinduism - An Introduction: Universal Science-Religion. T. C. Galav. (Illus.). 200p. (Orig.). 1992. 12.00 (*0-9642377-0-9*) T C Galav.

Philosophy of History. Ed. by Patrick L. Gardiner. (Oxford Readings in Philosophy Ser.). (C). 1974. pap. text 15.95 (*0-19-875031-5*) OUP.

Philosophy of History. Georg Wilhelm Friedrich Hegel. 1990. 23.50 (*0-8446-2232-X*) Peter Smith.

Philosophy of History. Georg Wilhelm Friedrich Hegel. Tr. by J. Sibree from GER. LC 90-63047. (Great Books in Philosophy). 467p. (C). 1991. pap. 9.95 (*0-87975-631-4*) Prometheus Bks.

Philosophy of History. Friedrich von Schlegel. LC 72-144683. reprint ed. 37.50 (*0-404-05606-7*) AMS Pr.

Philosophy of History. 2nd ed. William H. Dray. LC 92-24133. 176p. (Orig.). (C). 1992. pap. text 14.20 (*0-13-012816-3*) P-H.

Philosophy of History: In a Course of Lectures, Delivered in Vienna. Friedrich von Schlegel. Tr. by James B. Robertson from GER. LC 77-145282. 1971. reprint ed. 16.00 (*0-403-01196-5*) Scholarly.

Philosophy of History & Action. Ed. by Yirmiahu Yovel. (Philosophical Studies: No. 11). 254p. 1979. text 126.50 (*90-277-0890-8*, D Reidel) Kluwer Academic.

Philosophy of History with Reflections & Aphorisms. John W. Miller. LC 80-29179. 192p. (C). 1981. reprint ed. 22.25 (*0-393-01464-9*) Norton.

Philosophy of History with Reflections & Aphorisms. John W. Miller. LC 80-29179. 192p. 1983. reprint ed. pap. 12.95 (*0-393-30060-9*) Norton.

Philosophy of Horror: Paradoxes of the Heart. Noel Carroll. 288p. (C). (gr. 13). 1990. pap. 20.99 (*0-415-90216-9*, A3860) Routledge.

Philosophy of Human Hope. Joseph J. Godfrey. 280p. (C). 1987. lib. bdg. 101.50 (*90-247-3353-7*, Pub. by M Nijhoff) Kluwer Academic.

Philosophy of Human Learning. Christopher Winch. LC 97-28095. 232p. (C). 1998. 75.00 (*0-415-16190-8*) Routledge.

Philosophy of Human Life. Isaac Jennings. 159p. 1996. reprint ed. spiral bd. 18.50 (*0-7873-1257-6*) Hlth Research.

Philosophy of Human Nature. Joseph Buchanan. Ed. by James F. Adams. 368p. 1970. 25.00 (*0-87730-005-4*) M & S Pr.

Philosophy of Human Nature. Chu Hsi. 1976. lib. bdg. 59.95 (*0-8490-2432-3*) Gordon Pr.

Philosophy of Human Nature. Joseph Buchanan. LC 71-90941. (History of Psychology Ser.). (Illus.). 360p. 1969. reprint ed. 50.00 (*0-8201-1064-7*) Schol Facsimiles.

Philosophy of Human Nature. Chu Hsi. Tr. by J. Percy Bruce. LC 73-38057. (China Classic & Contemporary Works in Reprint Ser.: No. II). reprint ed. 49.50 (*0-404-56913-7*) AMS Pr.

Philosophy of Human Rights: International Perspectives, 15. Ed. by Alan S. Rosenbaum. LC 79-6191. (Contributions in Philosophy Ser.: No. 15). 272p. 1980. 49.95 (*0-313-20985-5*, RHR/, Greenwood Pr) Greenwood.

***Philosophy of Illumination.** Shihab al-Din al-Suhrawardi. Tr. by John Walbridge & Hossein Ziai from ARA. (Islamic Translation Ser.).Tr. of Hikmat al-Ishraq. xlvii, 323p. 2000. 29.95 (*0-8425-2457-6*, Pub. by Brigham) U Ch Pr.

Philosophy of Immanuel Kant. Ed. by Richard Kennington. LC 84-23887. (Studies in Philosophy & the History of Philosophy: No. 12). 264p. reprint ed. pap. 81.90 (*0-7837-4726-8*, 204435500002) Bks Demand.

Philosophy of Immortality. R. Swinburne Clymer. 251p. 1960. 8.95 (*0-932785-39-5*) Philos Pub.

Philosophy of Indian Languages: India's Contribution to the Study of Language. Bimal K. Matilal. 198p. 1991. text 24.95 (*0-19-562515-3*) OUP.

Philosophy of Individual Freedom: The Political Thought of F. A. Hayek, 119. Calvin M. Hoy. LC 84-8973. (Contributions in Political Science Ser.: No. 119). (Illus.). 144p. 1984. 49.95 (*0-313-24361-1*, HPI/, Greenwood Pr) Greenwood.

Philosophy of Intellectual Property. Peter Drahos. LC 96-24900. (Applied Legal Philosophy Ser.). 272p. (C). 1996. text 82.95 (*1-85521-240-4*, Pub. by Dartmth Pub) Ashgate Pub Co.

Philosophy of Interior Design. Stanley Abercrombie. LC 89-45506. (Illus.). 192p. 1991. pap. 25.00 (*0-06-430194-X*, Icon Edns) HarpC.

***Philosophy of International Law.** Fernando R. Teson. LC 97-52975. (New Perspectives on Law, Culture & Society Ser.). 208p. (C). 1998. pap. text 25.00 (*0-8133-6864-2*, Pub. by Westview) HarpC.

***Philosophy of Interpretation.** Ed. by Joseph Margolis & Tom Rockmore. (Metaphilosophy Ser.: Vol. 31:1/2). 208p. 2000. pap. 24.95 (*0-631-22047-X*, Pub. by Blackwell Pubs) Blackwell Pubs.

Philosophy of Iqbal: Iqbal & Existentialism. Latif H. Kazmi. x, 130p. 1997. 23.00 (*81-7024-801-9*, Pub. by APH Pubng) Nataraj Bks.

Philosophy of Islam. Khaja Khan. 135p. (Orig.). 1985. pap. 10.50 (*1-56744-352-4*) Kazi Pubns.

Philosophy of Islamic Law & the Orientalists. Muhammad Muslehuddin. 300p. 1985. 19.95 (*1-56744-353-2*) Kazi Pubns.

Philosophy of J. Krishnamurti: A Systematic Study. R. K. Shringy. 1996. reprint ed. 30.00 (*81-215-0128-8*, Pub. by M Manoharial) Coronet Bks.

Philosophy of J. N. Mohanty. Ed. by Daya Krishna. (C). 1991. text 18.00 (*0-685-50090-X*, Pub. by M Manoharial) S Asia.

Philosophy of J. S. Mill. R. P. Anschutz. LC 85-27075. (Illus.). 196p. 1986. reprint ed. lib. bdg. 41.50 (*0-313-25040-5*, ANPM, Greenwood Pr) Greenwood.

Philosophy of Jacques Maritain. Charles A. Fecher. LC 70-90705. 361p. 1969. reprint ed. lib. bdg. 52.50 (*0-8371-2287-2*, FEJM, Greenwood Pr) Greenwood.

Philosophy of Jean-Paul Sartre. Ed. by Paul Arthur Schilpp. (Library of Living Philosophers: Vol. XVI). 766p. 1981. 59.95 (*0-87548-354-2*); pap. 34.95 (*0-8126-9150-4*) Open Court.

Philosophy of Jnanadeva. B. P. Bahirat. (C). 1993. 9.00 (*81-7154-737-0*, Pub. by Popular Prakashan) S Asia.

Philosophy of John Dewey, 2 vols. John Dewey. Ed. by John J. McDermott. LC 80-39766. xiii, 768p. 1981. pap. text 25.00 (*0-226-14401-1*) U Ch Pr.

Philosophy of John Dewey. 3rd ed. Ed. by Paul Arthur Schilpp. 764p. 1989. 59.95 (*0-87548-132-9*) Open Court.

Philosophy of John Dewey. 3rd ed. Ed. by Paul Arthur Schilpp. 764p. 1990. pap. 35.95 (*0-8126-9102-4*) Open Court.

Philosophy of John Dewey: A Critical Exposition of His Method, Metaphysics & Theory of Knowledge. R. E. Dewey. 188p. 1978. pap. text 112.00 (*90-247-1980-1*, Pub. by M Nijhoff) Kluwer Academic.

Philosophy of John Norris of Bemerton, 1657-1712. Richard Acworth. (Studien und Materialien Zur Geschichte der Philosophie Ser.: Vol. VI). 400p. 1979. 80.00 (*3-487-06884-2*) G Olms Pubs.

Philosophy of John Rawls. Richardson. 450.00 (*0-8153-2946-6*) Garland.

Philosophy of John William Miller. Ed. by Joseph P. Fell, 3rd. LC 89-43150. (Bucknell Review Ser.: Vol. 34, No. 1). (Illus.). 176p. 1990. 22.00 (*0-8387-5185-7*) Bucknell U Pr.

Philosophy of Jonathan Edwards: A Study in Divine Semiotics. Stephen H. Daniel. LC 93-50171. (Indiana Series in the Philosophy of Religion). 224p. 1994. 22.95 (*0-253-31609-X*) Ind U Pr.

Philosophy of Josiah Royce. Josiah Royce. Ed. & Intro. by John K. Roth. LC 82-2932. (HPC Classics Ser.). 429p. (C). 1982. reprint ed. pap. text 14.95 (*0-915145-41-3*); reprint ed. lib. bdg. 34.95 (*0-915145-42-1*) Hackett Pub.

Philosophy of Justice Between God & Man. Benjamin P. Blood. LC 75-3056. reprint ed. 20.50 (*0-404-59054-3*) AMS Pr.

Philosophy of K. Satchidananda Murty. Ed. by Sibajiban Bhattachryya & Ashok Vohra. 1995. 31.00 (*81-85636-18-4*, Pub. by M Manoharial) S Asia.

Philosophy of Kant. Immanuel Kant. 588p. 1993. 18.50 (*0-679-60068-X*) Modern Lib NY.

Philosophy of Kant & Our Modern World. Charles W. Hendel. LC 81-13178. 132p. 1981. reprint ed. lib. bdg. 38.50 (*0-313-23051-X*, HEPK, Greenwood Pr) Greenwood.

Philosophy of Karl Jaspers. rev. ed. Ed. by Paul Arthur Schilpp. LC 57-14578. (Library of Living Philosophers: Vol. IX). 960p. 1981. 42.95 (*0-87548-361-5*) Open Court.

Philosophy of Karl Popper, 2 vols., Set. Ed. by Paul Arthur Schilpp. LC 78-186983. (Library of Living Philosophers: Vol. XIV). 1322p. 1974. 42.95 (*0-87548-353-4*) Open Court.

Philosophy of Knowledge: An Inquiry into the Nature, Limits & Validity of Human Cognitive Faculty. George T. Ladd. LC 75-3223. reprint ed. 57.50 (*0-404-59219-8*) AMS Pr.

Philosophy of Language. Ed. by Guttorm Floistad. 414p. 1986. pap. text 23.50 (*90-247-3297-2*) Kluwer Academic.

Philosophy of Language. Alex Miller. 300p. 1998. text 60.00 (*0-7735-1708-1*, Pub. by McG-Queens Univ Pr); pap. text 19.95 (*0-7735-1709-X*, Pub. by McG-Queens Univ Pr) CUP Services.

***Philosophy of Language.** Neale. 2000. 49.95 (*0-8133-1858-0*, Pub. by Westview); pap. 17.95 (*0-8133-1859-9*, Pub. by Westview) HarpC.

Philosophy of Language. F. Von Kutschera. Tr. by Burnham Terrell. (Synthese Library: No. 71). 312p. 1975. text 162.50 (*90-277-0591-7*) Kluwer Academic.

Philosophy of Language. 3rd ed. A. P. Martinich. 592p. (C). 1996. text 47.95 (*0-19-509368-2*) OUP.

***Philosophy of Language.** 4th ed. A. P. Martinich. 624p. (C). 2000. pap. text 42.95 (*0-19-513543-1*) OUP.

***Philosophy of Language: Contemporary Introduction.** William G. Lycan. LC 99-29547. (Contemporary Introductions to Philosophy Ser.). 224p. (C). 1999. text 65.00 (*0-415-17115-6*) Routledge.

***Philosophy of Language: Contemporary Introduction.** William G. Lycan. LC 99-29547. (Contemporary Introductions to Philosophy Ser.). 224p. 2000. pap. 19.99 (*0-415-17116-4*) Routledge.

Philosophy of Language: Historical Foundations & Contemporary Issues. Borgmann. 182p. 1974. pap. text 88.00 (*90-247-1589-X*, Pub. by M Nijhoff) Kluwer Academic.

Philosophy of Language: Philosophical Logic. Ed. by Guttorm Floistad & George H. Von Wright. (Contemporary Philosophy, a New Survey Ser.: 1). 320p. 1981. lib. bdg. 171.00 (*90-247-2451-1*) Kluwer Academic.

Philosophy of Language: The Big Questions. Andrea Nye. LC 97-45209. (Philosophy Ser.). 500p. 1998. 62.95 (*0-631-20601-9*); pap. 29.95 (*0-631-20602-7*) Blackwell Pubs.

Philosophy of Language & Logical Theory: Collected Papers. Haig Khatchadourian. 374p. (Orig.). (C). pap. text 39.00 (*0-8191-9913-3*); lib. bdg. 65.00 (*0-8191-9912-5*) U Pr of Amer.

Philosophy of Language in Britain: Major Theories from Hobbes to Thomas Reid. Stephen K. Land. LC 83-45287. (Studies in the Seventeenth Century: No. 2). 1986. 39.50 (*0-404-61722-0*) AMS Pr.

Philosophy Of Late Antiquity. J. Bussanich. (History of Ancient & Medieval Philosophy Ser.). 256p. 2001. pap. 55.00 (*0-8133-2523-4*) Westview.

Philosophy of Late Antiquity. John Bussanich. 2000. pap. text 21.95 (*0-8133-2524-2*) Westview.

Philosophy of Law. Ed. by Ronald M. Dworkin. (Oxford Readings in Philosophy Ser.). 190p. 1977. pap. text 21.95 (*0-19-875022-6*) OUP.

Philosophy of Law. Martin P. Golding. (Foundation of Philosophy Ser.). 176p. (C). 1974. pap. text 13.40 (*0-13-664128-8*) P-H.

Philosophy of Law. Conrad D. Johnson. (Illus.). 684p. (Orig.). (C). 1992. text 42.80 (*0-02-360935-4*, Macmillan Coll) P-H.

Philosophy of Law. Josef Kohler. (Modern Legal Philosophy Ser.: Vol. 12). xliv, 390p. 1998. reprint ed. 130.00 (*1-56169-391-X*) Gaunt.

Philosophy of Law. Josef Kohler. Tr. by Adalbert Albrecht from GER. (Modern Legal Philosophy Ser.: Vol. 12). xliv, 390p. 1969. reprint ed. 49.50 (*0-8377-2326-4*, Rothman) W S Hein.

Philosophy of Law. Paul Sayre. 1981. reprint ed. lib. bdg. 42.00 (*0-8377-1121-5*, Rothman) W S Hein.

Philosophy of Law. 3rd ed. Ed. by Joel Feinberg & Hyman Gross. 708p. (C). 1986. pap. write for info. (*0-534-06198-2*) Wadsworth Pub.

Philosophy of Law. 4th ed. Ed. by Joel Feinberg & Hyman Gross. 788p. (C). 1990. pap. 45.95 (*0-534-15156-6*) Wadsworth Pub.

***Philosophy of Law.** 6th ed. Coleman Feinberg. LC 99-12973. (Philosophy Ser.). 700p. 1999. pap. 72.95 (*0-534-52497-4*) Wadsworth Pub.

Philosophy of Law: An Encyclopedia, 2 Vols. Ed. by Christopher B. Gray. LC 99-11065. 850p. 1999. 250.00 (*0-8153-1344-6*) Garland.

Philosophy of Law: An Exposition of the Fundamental Principles of Jurisprudence as the Science of Right. Immanuel Kant. Tr. by W. Hastie. LC 77-146882. xxxvi, 265p. 1974. reprint ed. lib. bdg. 39.50 (*0-678-01152-4*) Kelley.

Philosophy of Law: An Introduction to Jurisprudence. 2nd rev. ed. Jeffrie G. Murphy & Jules L. Coleman. 256p. (C). 1989. pap. 25.00 (*0-8133-0848-8*, Pub. by Westview) HarpC.

Philosophy of Law: Anthology of Scholarly Articles, 5 vols. Ed. by Jules L. Coleman & Anthony Sebok. LC 93-32672. 2856p. 1995. 403.00 (*0-8153-1396-9*) Garland.

Philosophy of Law: Being Notes of Lectures Delivered During Twenty-Three Years (1852-1875) in the Inner Temple Hall. Herbert Broom. xi, 338p. 1980. reprint ed. 40.00 (*0-8377-0310-7*, Rothman) W S Hein.

Philosophy of Law: Classic & Contemporary Readings with Commentary. Frederick F. Schauer & Walter Sinnott-Armstrong. LC 94-79822. 1002p. (C). 1995. text 56.00 (*0-15-500827-7*, 70403) Harcourt Legal.

***Philosophy of Law: Introduction.** Mark Tebbit. LC 99-46402. 192p. 2000. pap. 20.99 (*0-415-13525-7*) Routledge.

***Philosophy of Law & Legal Theory: An Anthology.** Ed. by Dennis Patterson. (Philosophy Anthologies Ser.). 600p. 1999. 79.95 (*0-631-20287-0*); pap. 39.95 (*0-631-20288-9*) Blackwell Pubs.

Philosophy of Law in Historical Perspective. 2nd ed. Carl J. Friedrich. LC 57-9546. 309p. 1963. pap. text 17.00 (*0-226-26466-1*, P135) U Ch Pr.

Philosophy of Legal Reasoning: A Collection of Essays by Philosophers & Legal Scholars, 5 vols. Ed. by Scott Brewer. LC 98-5169. 2048p. 1998. 375.00 (*0-8153-2654-8*) Garland.

Philosophy of Leibniz. 2nd ed. Bertrand Russell. 200p. 1989. 27.50 (*0-89341-548-0*, Longwood Academic) Hollowbrook.

Philosophy of Leibniz. 3rd ed. Bertrand Russell. 352p. (C). 1992. pap. 27.99 (*0-415-08296-X*, B0541) Routledge.

Philosophy of Leibniz: Metaphysics & Language. Benson Mates. 256p. 1989. reprint ed. pap. text 19.95 (*0-19-505946-8*) OUP.

Philosophy of Leibniz & the Modern World. Ed. by Ivor Leclerc. LC 72-1346. 322p. 1973. reprint ed. pap. 99.90 (*0-7837-9882-2*, 206060800006) Bks Demand.

Philosophy of Lev Shestov, 1866-1938: A Russian Religious Existentialist. Louis J. Shein. LC 91-23662. (Toronto Studies in Theology: Vol. 57). 120p. 1991. lib. bdg. 59.95 (*0-7734-9662-9*) E Mellen.

Philosophy of Liberation. Enrique D. Dussel. Tr. by Aquilina Martinez & Christine Morkovsky from SPA. LC 85-5103. 223p. reprint ed. pap. 69.20 (*0-608-20205-3*, 207146400012) Bks Demand.

Philosophy of Library Classification. S. R. Ranganathan. 133p. 1990. pap. 5.95 (*81-85273-33-2*, Pub. by Sarada Ranganathan Endowment for Library Science) Advent Bks Div.

Philosophy of Life & Philosophy of Language. Friedrich von Schlegel. Tr. by A. J. Morrison. LC 70-147991. reprint ed. 55.00 (*0-404-08249-1*) AMS Pr.

Philosophy of Lifelong Education. Kenneth Wain. (International Perspectives on Adult & Continuing Education Ser.). 220p. 1986. 45.00 (*0-7099-3675-3*, Pub. by C Helm) Routldge.

Philosophy of Light: An Introductory Treatise. Floyd I. Lorbeer. 259p. 1981. pap. 20.00 (*0-89540-102-9*, SB-102) Sun Pub.

Philosophy of Literary Amateurism. Naomi Lebowitz. 152p. 1994. text 29.95 (*0-8262-0970-X*) U of Mo Pr.

Philosophy of Literary Form. Kenneth Burke. 1974. reprint ed. pap. 19.95 (*0-520-02483-4*, Pub. by U CA Pr) Cal Prin Full Svc.

Philosophy of Literature. Gustar E. Mueller. LC 72-14195. (Essay Index Reprint Ser.). 1977. reprint ed. 21.95 (*0-518-10021-9*) Ayer.

Philosophy of Literature: An Anthology. Ed. by David Davies & Carl Matheson. 400p. 2000. pap. 24.95 (*1-55111-177-2*) Broadview Pr.

Philosophy of Literature: An Introduction. Christopher New. LC 98-39518. 1998. 65.00 (*0-415-14485-X*) Routledge.

Philosophy of Literature: An Introduction. Christopher New. LC 98-39518. viii, 151p. 1999. pap. write for info. (*0-415-14486-8*) Routledge.

Philosophy of Living Fire. R. Swineburne Clymer. (African Studies). reprint ed. 30.00 (*0-938818-78-3*) ECA Assoc.

Philosophy of Living Fire! (1906) R. Swinburne Clymer. 173p. 1996. reprint ed. pap. 17.95 (*1-56459-663-X*) Kessinger Pub.

Philosophy of Living: or The Way to Enjoy Life & Its Comforts. Caleb Ticknor. LC 72-180595. (Medicine & Society in America Ser.). 342p. 1972. reprint ed. 25.95 (*0-405-03977-8*) Ayer.

Philosophy of Logic. Karl D. Schick. vii, 30p. (Orig.). 1996. pap. 8.95 (*0-9653564-0-X*) Alden Pr.

Philosophy of Logic. 2nd ed. Willard V. Quine. 128p. 1986. pap. 14.50 (*0-674-66563-5*) HUP.

Philosophy of Logical Atomism & Other Essays, 1914-19. Bertrand Russell. Ed. by John G. Slater. (Collected Papers of Bertrand Russell: Vol. 8). (Illus.). 418p. (C). (gr. 13). 1988. 175.00 (*0-04-920074-7*, A9416) Routledge.

Philosophy of Logical Mechanism. Merrilee H. Salmon. 552p. (C). 1990. lib. bdg. 278.00 (*0-7923-0325-3*, Pub. by Kluwer Academic) Kluwer Academic.

Philosophy of Logics. Susan Haack. LC 77-17071. (Illus.). 292p. 1978. pap. text 29.95 (*0-521-29329-4*) Cambridge U Pr.

Philosophy of Love. Judah Abarbanel. Tr. by F. Friedeberg-Seeley & J. H. Barnes. 1977. lib. bdg. 250.00 (*0-8490-2433-1*) Gordon Pr.

Philosophy of Love, the Narada Sutras. Hari P. Shastrim. 1972. 59.95 (*0-8490-0828-X*) Gordon Pr.

***Philosophy of Maat Kemetic-Soulism Exposes: The Diabolical-System of Global European Imperialism.** deluxe ed. Maaseru Tep. (Illus.). 450p. 2000. pap. 25.00 (*1-56411-238-1*) Untd Bros & Sis.

Philosophy of Mahatma Gandhi. Dhirendra M. Datta. LC 53-9213. 168p. reprint ed. pap. 52.10 (*0-8357-4744-1*, 203766500009) Bks Demand.

Philosophy of Man: A New Introduction to Some Perennial Issues. Howard P. Kainz. LC 89-38307. 208p. (C). 1989. reprint ed. pap. text 23.00 (*0-8191-7603-6*) U Pr of Amer.

Philosophy of Man-Making. Santi L. Mukherji. (C). 1989. 40.00 (*0-89771-452-0*, Pub. by Current Dist) St Mut.

Philosophy of Management. Oliver Sheldon, Jr. Ed. by Alfred D. Chandler. LC 79-7555. (History of Management Thought & Practice Ser.). 1980. reprint ed. lib. bdg. 29.95 (*0-405-12341-8*) Ayer.

Philosophy of Manners A study of the "Little Virtues" Peter Johnson. 236p. 1999. 70.00 (*1-85506-614-9*) Thoemmes Pr.

Philosophy of Marriage, in Its Social, Moral, & Physical Relations. Michael Ryan. LC 73-20638. (Sex, Marriage & Society Ser.). 400p. 1974. reprint ed. 33.95 (*0-405-05815-2*) Ayer.

Philosophy of Martin Buber. Ed. & Intro. by Paul Arthur Schilpp. LC 65-14535. (Library of Living Philosophers: Vol. XII). 830p. 1967. 59.95 (*0-87548-129-9*) Open Court.

Philosophy of Martin Buber. Ed. by Paul Arthur Schilpp & Maurice Friedman. LC 65-14535. (Library of Living Philosophers: Vol. XII). 830p. 1967. pap. 36.95 (*0-8126-9152-0*) Open Court.

Philosophy of Marx. Etienne Balibar. Tr. by Chris Turner. 160p. (C). (gr. 13). 1995. 60.00 (*1-85984-951-2*, C0515, Pub. by Verso) Norton.

Philosophy of Marxism: An Exposition. John Somerville. LC 81-82196. (Studies in Marxism: Vol. 9). 199p. (C). 1967. pap. 9.95 (*0-930656-18-0*) MEP Pubns.

Philosophy of Mass Art. Noel Carroll. LC 97-25934. 438p. 1998. text 77.00 (*0-19-871129-8*); pap. text 18.95 (*0-19-874237-1*) OUP.

Philosophy of Material Nature: Prolegomena Bd. with Metaphysical Foundations of Natural Science. Immanuel Kant. Ed. & Tr. by James W. Ellington from GER. LC 85-889. (HPC Classics Ser.). 419p. (C). 1985. pap. 14.95 (*0-915145-88-X*); lib. bdg. 34.95 (*0-915145-87-1*) Hackett Pub.

Philosophy of Mathematics. Ed. by W. D. Hart. (Readings in Philosophy Ser.). 328p. 1996. 55.00 (*0-19-875119-2*); pap. text 19.95 (*0-19-875120-6*) OUP.

Philosophy of Mathematics. Louis O. Kattsoff. LC 73-84314. (Essay Index Reprint Ser.). 1977. 18.95 (*0-8369-1086-9*) Ayer.

Philosophy of Mathematics. Albert T. Bledsoe. LC 75-3004. (Philosophy in America Ser.). reprint ed. 49.50 (*0-404-59048-9*) AMS Pr.

Philosophy of Mathematics: An Introductory Essay. Stephan Korner. 198p. 1986. reprint ed. pap. 8.95 (*0-486-25048-2*) Dover.

Philosophy of Mathematics: Introduction to a World of Proofs & Pictures. James R. Brown. LC 98-8014. (Philosophical Issues in Science Ser.). (Illus.). 224p. (C). 1999. 75.00 (*0-415-12274-0*); pap. 24.99 (*0-415-12275-9*) Routledge.

Philosophy of Mathematics: Selected Readings. 2nd ed. Hilary Putnam. Ed. by Hilary Benacerraf. LC 85-25257. 624p. 1984. pap. text 37.95 (*0-521-29648-X*) Cambridge U Pr.

***Philosophy of Mathematics: Structure & Ontology.** Stewart Shapiro. (Illus.). 288p. 2000. pap. text 19.95 (*0-19-513930-5*) OUP.

An Asterisk (*) at the beginning of an entry indicates that the title is appearing for the first time.

Philosophy of Mathematics: The Invisible Art. W. S. Anglin. LC 96-48604. (Studies in the History of Philosophy: Vol. 43). 260p. 1997. text 89.95 (*0-7734-8706-9*) E Mellen.

Philosophy of Mathematics & Deductive Structure in Euclid's "Elements" Ian Mueller. (Illus.). 400p. (C). 1981. 55.00 (*0-262-13163-3*) MIT Pr.

Philosophy of Mathematics & Mathematical Practices in the Seventeenth Century. Paolo Mancosu. (Illus.). 288p. 1996. text 70.00 (*0-19-508463-2*) OUP.

Philosophy of Mathematics & Mathematical Practices in the Seventeenth Century. Paolo Mancosu. (Illus.). 288p. 1999. pap. 19.95 (*0-19-513244-0*) OUP.

Philosophy of Mathematics & Natural Laws: Another Copernican Revolution. Noel Curran. LC 97-73212. (Avebury Series in Philosophy). 224p. 1997. text 69.95 (*1-85972-654-2*, Pub. by Ashgate Pub) Ashgate Pub Co.

Philosophy of Mathematics Today. Ed. by Evandro Agazzi. LC 96-49528. (Episteme EPIS Ser.: No. 22). 361p. (C). 1996. text 144.00 (*0-7923-4343-3*) Kluwer Academic.

Philosophy of Mathematics Today. Ed. by Matthias Schirn. (Illus.). 650p. 1998. text 140.00 (*0-19-823654-9*) OUP.

Philosophy of Matter & Mind: A New Look at an Old Major Topic in Philosophy. Gerhard D. Wassermann. (Avebury Series in Philosophy). 309p. 1994. 87.95 (*1-85628-572-3*, Pub. by Avebry) Ashgate Pub Co.

Philosophy of Medicine: The Early Eighteenth Century. Lester S. King. LC 77-24645. 303p. 1978. reprint ed. pap. 94.00 (*0-7837-4161-8*, 205900900012) Bks Demand.

Philosophy of Medicine & Bioethicsa: Twenty-Year Retrospective & Critical Appraisal. Carson. LC 97-30020. 1997. text 117.50 (*0-7923-3545-7*) Kluwer Academic.

Philosophy of Mental Healing: A Practical Exposition of Natural Restorative Power. Leander E. Whipple. 234p. 1981. pap. 20.00 (*0-89540-110-X*, SB-110) Sun Pub.

Philosophy of Michael Dummett. Ed. by Brian McGuinness & Gianluigi Oliveri. LC 94-9709. (Synthese Library: Vol. 239). 402p. (C). 1994. lib. bdg. 166.50 (*0-7923-2804-3*, Pub. by Kluwer Academic) Kluwer Academic.

Philosophy of Mind. Ed. by Guttorm Floistad. 1986. pap. text 23.50 (*90-247-3300-6*) Kluwer Academic.

Philosophy of Mind. Paul Gilbert et al. Ed. by John Shand. 240p. 1998. 55.00 (*0-7735-1825-8*); pap. 19.95 (*0-7735-1826-6*) McG-Queens Univ Pr.

Philosophy of Mind. Georg Wilhelm Friedrich Hegel. 342p. 1971. pap. text 22.00 (*0-19-875014-5*) OUP.

Philosophy of Mind. Dale Jacquette. LC 93-26773. (Foundations of Philosophy Ser.). 176p. 1993. pap. text 14.80 (*0-13-030933-8*) P-H.

Philosophy of Mind. Jaegwon Kim. LC 96-166594. (Dimensions of Philosophy Ser.). 272p. (C). 1996. pap. 28.00 (*0-8133-0776-7*, Pub. by Westview) HarpC.

Philosophy of Mind. Ed. by V. C. Chappell. 192p. (C). 1981. reprint ed. pap. 5.95 (*0-486-24212-9*) Dover.

Philosophy of Mind. Georg Wilhelm Friedrich Hegel. Tr. by William Wallace. LC 72-4220. (Select Bibliographies Reprint Ser.). 1977. reprint ed. 20.95 (*0-8369-6884-0*) Ayer.

Philosophy of Mind. Alan R. White. LC 78-5722. 178p. 1978. reprint ed. lib. bdg. 38.50 (*0-313-20430-6*, WHPM, Greenwood Pr) Greenwood.

Philosophy of Mind: A Contemporary Introduction. John Heil. LC 97-32598. (Contemporary Introductions to Philosophy Ser.). 256p. (C). 1998. 65.00 (*0-415-13059-X*); pap. 18.99 (*0-415-13060-3*) Routledge.

Philosophy of Mind: An Essay in the Metaphysics of Psychology. George T. Ladd. LC 82-45804. 432p. reprint ed. 55.00 (*0-404-59220-1*) AMS Pr.

Philosophy of Mind: An Introduction. Peter Smith & O. R. Jones. 306p. 1986. pap. text 19.95 (*0-521-31250-7*) Cambridge U Pr.

Philosophy of Mind: An Introduction. 2nd ed. George Graham. (Introducing Philosophy Ser.). 288p. 1998. 59.95 (*0-631-21205-1*); pap. 24.95 (*0-631-20541-1*) Blackwell Pubs.

Philosophy of Mind: An Overview for Cognitive Science. William Bechtel. (Tutorials in Cognitive Science Ser.). 176p. 1988. text 36.00 (*0-8058-0218-5*); pap. text 21.50 (*0-8058-0234-7*) L Erlbaum Assocs.

Philosophy of Mind: Classical Problems - Contemporary Issues. Ed. by Brian Beakley & Peter Ludlow. (Illus.). 648p. 1992. 42.50 (*0-262-02340-7*, Bradford Bks); pap. text 28.50 (*0-262-52167-9*, Bradford Bks) MIT Pr.

Philosophy of Mind & Cognition. David Braddon-Mitchell. LC 95-53332. (Illus.). 320p. (C). 1996. 60.95 (*0-631-19167-4*); pap. 26.95 (*0-631-19168-2*) Blackwell Pubs.

Philosophy of Mind in Sixth-Century China: Paramartha's "Evolution of Consciousness" Diana Y. Paul. LC 82-42862. 280p. 1984. 39.50 (*0-8047-1187-9*) Stanford U Pr.

Philosophy of Ministry. Kirby Clements, Sr. 144p. (Orig.). 1993. pap. 8.95 (*0-917595-42-4*) Kingdom Pubns.

Philosophy of Mizvot. Gersion Appel. 1995. pap. 16.95 (*0-87068-250-4*) Ktav.

Philosophy of Modern Art. Herbert E. Read. LC 70-128294. (Essay Index Reprint Ser.). 1977. 24.95 (*0-8369-2023-6*) Ayer.

Philosophy of Modern Literary Theory. Peter V. Zima. LC 99-17830. 250p. 1999. 28.95 (*0-485-12150-6*, Pub. by Athlone Pr) Transaction Pubs.

***Philosophy of Modern Literary Theory.** Peter V. Zima. LC 99-17830. 250p. 1999. 80.00 (*0-485-11540-9*, Pub. by Athlone Pr) Humanities.

Philosophy of Money. Georg Simmel. 1986. pap. 10.95 (*0-7100-9205-9*, Routledge Thoemms) Routledge.

Philosophy of Money. 2nd ed. Georg Simmel. Tr. by Thomas B. Bottomore & David Frisby from FRE. 1982. pap. 19.95 (*0-685-04394-0*, Routledge Thoemms) Routledge.

Philosophy of Money. 2nd ed. Georg Simmel. Tr. by David Frisby & Thomas B. Bottomore. 592p. (C). 1990. pap. 29.99 (*0-415-04641-6*, A4659) Routledge.

Philosophy of Mulla Sadra. 350p. 1996. 49.95 (*0-614-21235-9*, 957) Kazi Pubns.

Philosophy of Mulla Sadra Shirazi. Fazlur Rahman. LC 75-31693. 277p. (C). 1976. text 24.50 (*0-87395-300-2*) State U NY Pr.

Philosophy of Music Education. 2nd ed. Bennett Reimer. 240p. 1988. text 45.00 (*0-13-663881-3*) P-H.

Philosophy of Mysticism, 2 vols. Carl Du Prel. 1977. lib. bdg. 250.00 (*0-8490-2434-X*) Gordon Pr.

***Philosophy of Mysticism.** Ed. by Sadhu Santideva. 2000. 62.00 (*81-7755-002-0*, Pub. by Cosmo Pubns) S Asia.

Philosophy of Mysticism, 2 vols. Carl Du Prel. Tr. by Charles C. Massey. LC 75-36838. (Occult Ser.). 1976. reprint ed. 56.95 (*0-405-07951-6*) Ayer.

Philosophy of Nagarjuna. Vincente Fatone. (C). 1991. reprint ed. 14.00 (*81-208-0797-9*, Pub. by Motilal Bnarsidass) S Asia.

Philosophy of Nationalism. Paul Gilbert. LC 98-11322. 216p. (C). 1998. pap. text 21.00 (*0-8133-3084-X*, Pub. by Westview) HarpC.

Philosophy of Nationalism. J. J. Josey. 228p. 1995. pap. 18.00 (*1-878465-10-4*) Scott-Townsend Pubs.

Philosophy of Natural Magic. Henry Cornelius Agrippa. 305p. 1996. reprint ed. spiral bd. 23.00 (*0-7873-0019-5*) Hlth Research.

Philosophy of Natural Magic. Henry Cornelius Agrippa. 307p. 1992. reprint ed. pap. 21.95 (*1-56459-160-3*) Kessinger Pub.

Philosophy of Natural Science. Carl G. Hempel. 116p. (Orig.). 1966. pap. text 25.00 (*0-13-663823-6*) P-H.

Philosophy of Nature. Ivor Leclerc. LC 85-9607. (Studies in Philosophy & the History of Philosophy: No. 14). 234p. 1986. reprint ed. pap. 72.60 (*0-7837-9112-7*, 204991400004) Bks Demand.

Philosophy of Nature of St. Thomas Aquinas: Nature, the Universe, Man. Leo Elders. 387p. 1997. pap. 57.95 (*3-631-31602-X*) P Lang Pubng.

Philosophy of Nature of St. Thomas Aquinas: Nature, the Universe, Man. Leo Elders. LC 97-16106. 387p. 1997. pap. 57.95 (*0-8204-3274-1*) P Lang Pubng.

Philosophy of Nelson Goodman: Selected Essays, 4 vols. Ed. & Intro. by Catherine Z. Elgin. Incl. Vol. 1. Nominalism, Constructivism, & Relativism in the Work of Nelson Goodman. LC 96-37567. 296p. 1997. text 77.00 (*0-8153-2609-2*); Vol. 2. Nelson Goodman's New Riddle of Induction. 312p. 1997. text 77.00 (*0-8153-2610-6*); Vol. 3. Nelson Goodman's Philosophy of Art. LC 96-37569. 384p. 1997. text 88.00 (*0-8153-2611-4*); Vol. 4. Nelson Goodman's Theory of Symbols & Its Applications. LC 96-37570. 344p. 1997. text 88.00 (*0-8153-2612-2*); 300.00 (*0-8153-2608-4*) Garland.

Philosophy of Nicholas Rescher: Discussion & Replies. Ed. by Ernest Sosa. (Philosophical Studies in Philosophy: No. 15). 247p. 1979. text 85.50 (*90-277-0962-9*, D Reidel) Kluwer Academic.

Philosophy of Niels Bohr: The Framework of Complementarity. Henry J. Folse, Jr. (North-Holland Personal Library: Vol. 4). x, 282p. 1988. reprint ed. pap. 63.00 (*0-444-86938-7*, North Holland) Elsevier.

Philosophy of Nietzsche. Friedrich Wilhelm Nietzsche. 1984. pap. 14.95 (*0-452-00699-6*, Mer) NAL.

Philosophy of Nietzsche. Ed. by Prentice Hall General Reference & Travel Staff. 1965. 4.75 (*0-671-00534-0*, Arco) Macmillan Gen Ref.

Philosophy of Nietzsche: An Exposition & Appreciation. Georges Chatterton-Hill. LC 70-152409. (Studies in German Literature: No. 13). 1971. reprint ed. lib. bdg. 75.00 (*0-8383-1232-2*) M S G Haskell Hse.

Philosophy of Nietzsche, 1915. Abraham Wolf. 120p. 1996. reprint ed. pap. 14.95 (*1-85506-353-0*) Bks Intl VA.

Philosophy of Nikunja Vihari Banerjee. Ed. by Margaret Chatterjee. 1990. 23.00 (*0-685-37829-2*, Pub. by M Manoharial) S Asia.

Philosophy of Non-Violence: Martin Luther King Mini-Play. (People of Conscience Ser.). (J). (gr. 8 up). 1978. 6.50 (*0-89550-313-1*) Stevens & Shea.

Philosophy of Nonsense: The Intuitions of Victorian Nonsense Literature. Jean-Jacques Lecercle. LC 93-5384. 288p. (C). 1994. pap. 24.99 (*0-415-07653-6*) Routledge.

Philosophy of Numbers: Their Tone & Colors. L. Dow Balliett. 165p. 1996. reprint ed. spiral bd. 15.00 (*0-7873-0067-5*) Hlth Research.

Philosophy of Numbers: Their Tone & Colors. L. Don Bennett. 168p. 1996. reprint ed. pap. 13.95 (*1-56459-652-4*) Kessinger Pub.

Philosophy of Nursing: A New Vision for Health Care. Janice M. Brencick & Glenn A. Webster. LC 99-11409. 288p. (C). 1999. text 59.50 (*0-7914-4379-5*); pap. text 19.95 (*0-7914-4380-9*) State U NY Pr.

Philosophy of Oriental Medicine: Key to Your Personal Judging Ability. George Ohsawa. Ed. by Herman Aihara & Sandy Rothman. LC 91-76486. 153p. 1991. pap. 7.95 (*0-918860-52-0*) G Ohsawa.

Philosophy of Osteopathy. Andrew T. Still. LC 74-29302. reprint ed. 34.50 (*0-404-13426-2*) AMS Pr.

Philosophy of Our Uncertainties: A Comment on the Uncertainties of Our Philosophies. Gustav E. Mueller. LC 36-17433. 251p. reprint ed. pap. 77.90 (*0-608-30644-4*, 200483400047) Bks Demand.

Philosophy of P. F. Strawson. Ed. by Lewis E. Hahn. LC 98-22805. (Library of Living Philosophers: Vol. XXVI). 446p. 1998. 72.95 (*0-8126-9377-9*); pap. 42.95 (*0-8126-9378-7*) Open Court.

Philosophy of Painting by Shih-T'ao. Earle J. Coleman. (Studies in Philosophy: No. 19). 1978. pap. text 40.80 (*90-279-7756-9*) Mouton.

Philosophy of Parapsychology: Proceedings of an International Conference, Copenhagen, Aug. 25-27, 1976. Ed. by Betty Shapin & Lisette Coly. LC 77-75663. 1977. 17.00 (*0-912328-29-0*) Parapsych Foun.

Philosophy of Patanjali. Robert L. Peck & Thelma M. Peck. 1994. 7.95 (*0-917828-04-6*) Personal Dev Ctr.

Philosophy of Paul Ricoeur. Ed. by Lewis E. Hahn. LC 94-24362. (Library of Living Philosophers). 846p. 1995. 56.95 (*0-8126-9259-4*); pap. 34.95 (*0-8126-9260-8*) Open Court.

Philosophy of Paul Weiss. Ed. by Lewis E. Hahn. (Library of Living Philosophers: Vol. 23). 724p. 1995. 59.95 (*0-8126-9299-3*) Open Court.

Philosophy of Peirce: Selected Writings. Charles Sanders Peirce. Ed. by Justus Buchler. LC 75-41210. reprint ed. 39.50 (*0-404-14694-5*) AMS Pr.

Philosophy of Person, Solidarity & Cultural Creativity: Polish Philosophical Studies I. Ed. by Jozef Tischner & Joseph M. Zycinski. LC 93-4613. (Cultural Heritage & Contemporary Change Series IVA: Vol. 1). 200p. 1994. 45.00 (*1-56518-048-8*); pap. 17.50 (*1-56518-049-6*) Coun Res Values.

Philosophy of Peter Abelard. John Marenbon. 393p. 1997. text 64.95 (*0-521-55397-0*) Cambridge U Pr.

***Philosophy of Peter Abelard.** John Marenbon. 393p. (C). 1999. pap. 24.95 (*0-521-66399-7*) Cambridge U Pr.

Philosophy of Physics. Mario Bunge. LC 72-86103. (Synthese Library: No. 45). 258p. 1972. text 152.50 (*90-277-0253-5*, D Reidel) Kluwer Academic.

Philosophy of Physics. Lawrence Sklar. (Dimensions of Philosophy Ser.). 246p. (C). 1992. pap. 27.00 (*0-8133-0625-6*, Pub. by Westview) HarpC.

Philosophy of Physics. Roberto Torretti. (Evolution of Modern Philosophy Ser.). (Illus.). 496p. (C). 1999. pap. 22.95 (*0-521-56571-5*) Cambridge U Pr.

***Philosophy of Physics.** Roberto Torretti. LC 99-42504. (Evolution of Modern Philosophy Ser.). (Illus.). 496p. (C). 1999. 64.95 (*0-521-56259-7*) Cambridge U Pr.

Philosophy of Plato & Aristotle, 26 bks., Set. Ed. by Gregory Vlastos. 1973. 777.50 (*0-405-04830-0*) Ayer.

Philosophy of Play. Luther H. Gullick. 1982. 23.95 (*0-8434-0440-X*) McGrath NH.

Philosophy of Plotinus: The Gifford Lectures at St. Andrews, 1917-1918, 2 vols., Set. 3rd ed. William R. Inge. LC 68-8740. (Illus.). 1968. reprint ed. lib. bdg. 95.00 (*0-8371-0113-1*, INPP) Greenwood.

Philosophy of Plotinus: The Gifford Lectures at St. Andrews, 1917-1918, 2 vols., Vol. 1. 3rd ed. William R. Inge. LC 68-8740. (Illus.). 1968. reprint ed. lib. bdg. 55.00 (*0-8371-1793-3*, INPA) Greenwood.

Philosophy of Plotinus: The Gifford Lectures at St. Andrews, 1917-1918, 2 vols., Vol. 2. 3rd ed. William R. Inge. LC 68-8740. (Illus.). 1968. reprint ed. lib. bdg. 55.00 (*0-8371-0877-2*, INPB) Greenwood.

Philosophy of Prediction & Capitalism. M. S. Frings. (Philosophy Library: Vol. 20). 158p. 1987. lib. bdg. 89.50 (*90-247-3542-4*, Pub. by M Nijhoff) Kluwer Academic.

Philosophy of Probability. Ed. by Jacques-Paul Dubucs. LC 93-24048. (Philosophical Studies in Philosophy: Vol. 56). 304p. 1993. lib. bdg. 169.50 (*0-7923-2385-8*, Pub. by Kluwer Academic) Kluwer Academic.

Philosophy of Proof: In Its Relation to the English Law of Judicial Evidence. J. R. Gulson. xv, 496p. 1990. reprint ed. 50.00 (*0-8377-2211-X*, Rothman) W S Hein.

***Philosophy of Pscyhoanalysis & Psychology.** Stolorow. 2000. 42.00 (*0-465-09574-7*, Pub. by Basic) HarpC.

Philosophy of Psychology. George Botterill & Peter Carruthers. LC 98-33301. (Illus.). 312p. (C). 1999. pap. 21.95 (*0-521-55915-4*) Cambridge U Pr.

Philosophy of Psychology. Mario Bunge & R. Ardila. (Illus.). 320p. 1987. text 111.95 (*0-387-96442-8*) Spr-Verlag.

Philosophy of Psychology. Peter Carruthers & George Botterill. LC 98-33301. (Illus.). 312p. (C). 1999. 57.95 (*0-521-55111-0*) Cambridge U Pr.

Philosophy of Psychology. William O'Donohue. 416p. 1996. 49.50 (*0-7619-5304-3*); pap. 17.99 (*0-7619-5305-1*) Sage.

Philosophy of Psychology. Daniel N. Robinson. 176p. 1989. pap. text 18.00 (*0-231-05923-X*) Col U Pr.

Philosophy of Psychology: Debates on Psychological Explanation. Cynthia MacDonald & Graham MacDonald. 401p. 1995. pap. 31.95 (*0-631-18542-9*) Blackwell Pubs.

***Philosophy of Psychology & the Humanities.** Edith Stein & Marianne Sawicki. LC 99-57411. 2000. write for info. (*0-935216-73-1*) ICS Pubns.

Philosophy of Punk: More Than Noise. Craig O'Hara. (Illus.). 148p. (Orig.). 1995. pap. 10.00 (*1-873176-43-0*) AK Pr Dist.

Philosophy of Punk: More Than Noise. Craig O'Hara. (Orig.). 1999. pap. text 12.00 (*1-873176-16-3*) AK Pr Dist.

Philosophy of Quantum Mechanics. D. I. Blokhintsev. LC 68-22439. 132p. 1968. text 122.00 (*90-277-0105-9*) Kluwer Academic.

Philosophy of Quantum Mechanics: An Interactive Interpretation. Richard A. Healey. (Illus.). 284p. (C). 1989. text 59.95 (*0-521-37105-8*) Cambridge U Pr.

Philosophy of Quantum Mechanics: An Interactive Interpretation. Richard A. Healey. (Illus.). 284p. (C). 1991. pap. text 19.95 (*0-521-40874-1*) Cambridge U Pr.

Philosophy of Quantum Mechanics: The Interpretations of Quantum Mechanics in Historical Perspective. Max Jammer. LC 74-13030. 550p. reprint ed. pap. 170.50 (*0-7837-2823-9*, 205764900006) Bks Demand.

Philosophy of Rabindranath Tagore: His Social, Political, Religious, & Educational Views. Chandra M. Das. (C). 1996. 30.00 (*81-7100-817-8*, Pub. by Deep & Deep Pubns) S Asia.

Philosophy of Railways: The Transcontinental Railway Idea in British North America. A. A. Den Otter. LC 97-185154. (Illus.). 292p. 1997. text 34.95 (*0-8020-4161-2*, HE2810) U of Toronto Pr.

Philosophy of Religion see Filosofía de la Religion

Philosophy of Religion. Christopher J. Bostrom. 1962. 69.50 (*0-685-69791-6*) Elliots Bks.

Philosophy of Religion. C. Stephen Evans. LC 84-25198. (Contours of Christian Philosophy Ser.). 192p. (Orig.). 1985. pap. 12.99 (*0-87784-343-0*, 343) InterVarsity.

Philosophy of Religion. Peter A. French et al. LC 97-21493. (Midwest Studies in Philosophy: Vol. 21). 336p. (C). 1998. 35.00 (*0-268-01429-9*); pap. 25.00 (*0-268-01430-2*) U of Notre Dame Pr.

Philosophy of Religion. Harald Hoffding. 1977. lib. bdg. 59.95 (*0-8490-2435-8*) Gordon Pr.

Philosophy of Religion. Yeager Hudson. LC 90-37428. xvi, 355p. (C). 1991. pap. text 35.95 (*0-87484-902-0*, 902) Mayfield Pub.

Philosophy of Religion. Ed. by Basil Mitchell. (Oxford Readings in Philosophy Ser.). 206p. (Orig.). (C). 1971. pap. text 18.95 (*0-19-875018-8*) OUP.

Philosophy of Religion. A. R. Mohapatra. 1985. 16.95 (*0-318-37030-1*) Asia Bk Corp.

Philosophy of Religion. Melville Y. Stewart. (Philosophy Ser.). (C). 1996. 44.95 (*0-534-54263-8*) Wadsworth Pub.

Philosophy of Religion. William J. Wainwright. 210p. (C). 1987. pap. 19.50 (*0-534-08868-6*) Wadsworth Pub.

Philosophy of Religion. Edgar S. Brightman. LC 72-95112. 556p. 1969. reprint ed. lib. bdg. 85.00 (*0-8371-2468-9*, BRPR, Greenwood Pr) Greenwood.

Philosophy of Religion. Harald Hoffding. Tr. by B. E. Meyer from GER. LC 71-152987. (Select Bibliographies Reprint Ser.). 1977. reprint ed. 26.95 (*0-8369-5739-3*) Ayer.

Philosophy of Religion, 2 vols. George T. Ladd. LC 75-3225. 1976. reprint ed. 82.50 (*0-404-59221-X*) AMS Pr.

***Philosophy of Religion.** 2nd ed. Stewart. (Philosophy Ser.). 2001. 32.00 (*0-534-56171-3*) Wadsworth Pub.

Philosophy of Religion. 2nd ed. William J. Wainwright. LC 98-23850. 1998. pap. 29.95 (*0-534-52753-1*) Wadsworth Pub.

Philosophy of Religion. 3rd ed. Rowe. LC 97-71995. (C). 1997. pap. text 47.50 (*0-15-503687-4*, Pub. by Harcourt Coll Pubs) Harcourt.

Philosophy of Religion. 4th ed. John Harwood Hick. 176p. (C). 1989. 25.00 (*0-13-662628-9*) P-H.

Philosophy of Religion: A Buddhist Perspective. Arvind Sharma. 224p. 1996. text 23.00 (*0-19-563346-6*) OUP.

Philosophy of Religion: A Buddhist Perspective. Arvind Sharma. 224p. 1997. pap. text 14.95 (*0-19-564272-4*) OUP.

Philosophy of Religion: A Critical Introduction. Beverly Clack & Brian R. Clack. LC 98-36041. 209p. (Orig.). 1999. pap. 22.95 (*0-7456-1738-7*) Blackwell Pubs.

Philosophy of Religion: A Critical Introduction. Beverly Clack & Scott W. Taylor. LC 98-36041. 209p. (Orig.). 1999. 54.95 (*0-7456-1737-9*) Blackwell Pubs.

***Philosophy of Religion: A Guide & Anthology.** Ed. by Brian Davies. 670p. 2000. pap. 24.95 (*0-19-875194-X*) OUP.

Philosophy of Religion: A Guide to the Subject. Brian Davies. Date not set. pap. text 32.95 (*0-225-66822-X*, Pub. by G Chapman) Bks Intl VA.

Philosophy of Religion: A Guide to the Subject. Ed. by Brian Davies. LC 98-38312. 400p. 1999. pap. text 29.95 (*0-87840-695-6*) Georgetown U Pr.

Philosophy of Religion: A Universalist Perspective. Marvin C. Sterling. LC 92-29528. 234p. (Orig.). (C). 1992. pap. text 24.50 (*0-8191-8887-5*); lib. bdg. 49.00 (*0-8191-8886-7*) U Pr of Amer.

Philosophy of Religion: An Anthology. Ed. by Louis P. Pojman. 537p. (C). 1986. mass mkt. 42.95 (*0-534-06672-0*) Wadsworth Pub.

Philosophy of Religion: An Anthology. 2nd ed. Louis P. Pojman. 578p. (C). 1993. mass mkt. 44.25 (*0-534-20532-1*) Wadsworth Pub.

Philosophy of Religion: An Anthology. 3rd ed. Louis P. Pojman. LC 97-18435. (Philosophy Ser.). (C). 1997. 69.95 (*0-534-52956-9*) Wadsworth Pub.

Philosophy of Religion: An Anthology. 4th ed. Louis P. Pojman. (Philosophy Ser.). Date not set. 44.25 (*0-534-54364-2*) Wadsworth Pub.

Philosophy of Religion: An Introduction. William L. Rowe. 207p. (C). 1978. pap. write for info. (*0-8221-0208-0*) Wadsworth Pub.

Philosophy of Religion: An Introduction. 2nd ed. William L. Rowe. 206p. (C). 1992. pap. 23.50 (*0-534-18816-8*) Wadsworth Pub.

Philosophy of Religion: An Introduction. 3rd ed. Rowe. 2000. pap. text 26.50 (*0-534-57425-4*) Thomson Learn.

***Philosophy of Religion: An Introduction with Readings.** Stuart Brown. 184p. 2000. 65.00 (*0-415-21237-5*); pap. write for info. (*0-415-21238-3*) Routledge.

Philosophy of Religion: Contemporary Introduction. Keith E. Yandell. LC 98-25908. (Routledge Contemporary Introduction to Philosophy Ser.). 1p. (C). 1999. 70.00 (*0-415-13213-4*); pap. 19.99 (*0-415-13214-2*) Routledge.

Philosophy of Religion: Or, the Rational Grounds of Religious Belief. John Bascom. LC 75-3037. reprint ed. 57.50 (*0-404-59035-7*) AMS Pr.

Philosophy of Religion: Selected Readings. Ed. by Michael Peterson et al. (Illus.). 592p. (C). 1996. pap. text 38.95 (*0-19-508909-X*) OUP.

***Philosophy of Religion: Selected Readings.** 2nd ed. Michael Peterson et al. 656p. (C). 2000. pap. text 39.95 (*0-19-513546-6*) OUP.

P

Philosophy of Religion: The Big Questions. Eleonore Stump & Michael J. Murray. LC 98-8586. (Philosophy Ser.). 500p. 1998. 62.95 (*0-631-20603-5*); pap. 29.95 (*0-631-20604-3*) Blackwell Pubs.

Philosophy of Religion & Advaita Vedanta: A Comparative Study in Religion & Reason. Arvind Sharma. LC 93-25526. (Hermeneutics, Studies in the History of Religions). 256p. 1995. 35.00 (*0-271-01032-0*) Pa St U Pr.

Philosophy of Religion & Theology, 1975: Proceedings for the Section on Philosophy of Religion & Theology, American Academy of Religion, Annual Meeting, 1975. American Academy of Religion Staff. Ed. by James W. McClendon, Jr. LC 75-26618. 233p. reprint ed. pap. 72.30 (*0-608-08840-4*, 206947900004) Bks Demand.

Philosophy of Religion, 1857-1980. Alan P. Sell. (Key Texts Ser.). 260p. 1996. pap. 20.00 (*1-85506-482-0*) Bks Intl VA.

Philosophy of Religion, 1875-1980. Alan P. Sell. 272p. 1988. lib. bdg. 72.50 (*0-415-00082-3*) Routledge.

Philosophy of Religion for Advanced Level. Anne Jordan et al. (Illus.). 160p. (YA). (gr. 11 up). 1999. pap. 35.00 (*0-7487-4339-1*, Pub. by S Thornes Pubs) Trans-Atl Phila.

Philosophy of Religion in a Global Perspective. Kessler. LC 98-27276. (Philosophy Ser.). 1998. pap. 53.95 (*0-534-50549-X*) Brooks-Cole.

Philosophy of Religion in Kierkegaard's Writings. J. Heywood Thomas. LC 92-37141. (Studies in the History of Philosophy: Vol. 30). 180p. 1993. reprint ed. text 79.95 (*0-7734-9591-6*) E Mellen.

Philosophy of Religion in Nineteenth-Century England & Beyond Samuel A. Adshead. LC 99-28275. 272p. 1999. text 65.00 (*0-312-22424-9*) St Martin.

Philosophy of Religious Language: Sign, Symbol, & Story. Dan R. Stiver. 256p. (C). 1996. 60.95 (*1-55786-581-7*); pap. 28.95 (*1-55786-582-5*) Blackwell Pubs.

Philosophy of Responsibility. Edgar Bodenheimer. x, 147p. 1980. text 18.50 (*0-8377-0309-3*, Rothman) W S Hein.

Philosophy of Rhetoric. John Bascom. LC 98-12972. 312p. 1998. write for info. (*0-8201-1508-8*) Schol Facsimiles.

Philosophy of Rhetoric. George Campbell. Ed. & Intro. by Lloyd F. Bitzer. LC 87-13108. (Landmarks in Rhetoric & Public Address Ser.). 512p. (C). 1988. text 16.95 (*0-8093-1417-7*) S Ill U Pr.

Philosophy of Rhetoric. George Campbell. LC 91-46681. 424p. 1992. 50.00 (*0-8201-1460-X*) Schol Facsimiles.

Philosophy of Right. Georg Wilhelm Friedrich Hegel. Tr. by T. M. Knox. 400p. 1967. pap. text 24.95 (*0-19-500276-8*) OUP.

Philosophy of Right. Georg Wilhelm Friedrich Hegel. Tr. by S. W. Dyde. LC 96-28485. (Great Books in Philosophy). 401p. 1996. pap. 9.95 (*1-57392-105-X*) Prometheus Bks.

Philosophy of Right & Left: Incongruent Counterparts & the Nature of Space. Ed. by James Van Cleve. 376p. (C). 1991. lib. bdg. 185.50 (*0-7923-0844-1*, Pub. by Kluwer Academic) Kluwer Academic.

Philosophy of Right & Wrong. Bernard Mayo. 176p. 1986. 25.00 (*0-7102-0851-0*, 08510, Routledge Thoemms); pap. 13.95 (*0-7102-0859-6*, 08596, Routledge Thoemms) Routledge.

***Philosophy of Robert Boyle.** Peter R. Anstey. LC 99-59382. (Studies in Seventeenth-Century Philosophy). 2000. write for info. (*0-415-22429-2*) Routledge.

Philosophy of Robert Holcot, Fourteenth-Century Skeptic. Leonard A. Kennedy. LC 93-1705. (Studies in the History of Philosophy: Vol. 27). 196p. 1993. text 79.95 (*0-7734-9306-9*) E Mellen.

Philosophy of Roderick Chisholm. Ed. by Lewis E. Hahn. LC 97-32003. (Library of Living Philosophers: Vol. 25). 756p. (C). 1997. 64.95 (*0-8126-9356-6*); pap. 36.95 (*0-8126-9357-4*) Open Court.

Philosophy of Rudolph Carnap. Ed. by Paul Arthur Schilpp. LC 62-9577. (Library of Living Philosophers: Vol. XI). 1104p. 1963. 59.95 (*0-87548-130-2*); pap. 38.95 (*0-8126-9153-9*) Open Court.

Philosophy of Sadhana: With Special Reference to the Trika Philosophy of Kashmir. Deba B. SenSharma. LC 89-27739. (SUNY Series in Tantric Studies). 196p. (C). 1990. pap. text 14.95 (*0-7914-0348-3*) State U NY Pr.

Philosophy of Saivism: An Existential Analysis of Its Underlying Experiences. Frederick L. Kumar. LC 79-56036. xii, 125p. 1980. 13.95 (*0-89386-001-8*) Acorn NC.

Philosophy of Saivism: An Existential Analysis of Its Underlying Experiences. Frederick L. Kumar. (C). 1988. reprint ed. 18.50 (*81-204-0339-8*, Pub. by Oxford IBH) S Asia.

Philosophy of Sankara. D. K. Tripathi. 172p. 1990. 15.00 (*0-685-62630-X*, Pub. by Kala Prakashan) Nataraj Bks.

Philosophy of Sartre. Robert D. Cumming. 1972. pap. 11.00 (*0-394-71808-9*, V808) Vin Bks.

Philosophy of Sarvepalli Radhakrishnan. Ed. by Paul Arthur Schilpp. 898p. 1952. 59.95 (*0-87548-137-X*); pap. 36.95 (*0-8126-9133-4*) Open Court.

Philosophy of Sarvodaya. K. S. Bharathi. (C). 1990. 26.00 (*81-85182-36-1*, Pub. by Indus Pub) S Asia.

Philosophy of Schiller in Its Historical Relations, 1912. Emil C. Wilm. 198p. 1996. reprint ed. 58.00 (*1-85506-330-1*) Bks Intl VA.

Philosophy of Schopenhauer. 2nd enl. rev. ed. Bryan Magee. LC 97-220691. 476p. 1997. pap. text 18.95 (*0-19-823722-7*) OUP.

Philosophy of Schopenhauer in Its Intellectual Context: Thinker Against the Tide. Arthur Hubscher. Tr. by Joachim T. Baer & David E. Cartwright. LC 89-12440. (Studies in German Thought & History: Vol. 11). 528p. 1990. lib. bdg. 119.95 (*0-88946-787-0*) E Mellen.

Philosophy of Science. Alexander Bird. 224p. 1998. text 55.00 (*0-7735-1772-3*, Pub. by McG-Queens Univ Pr); pap. text 19.95 (*0-7735-1773-1*, Pub. by McG-Queens Univ Pr) CUP Services.

Philosophy of Science. Ed. by Richard Boyd et al. (Illus.). 592p. 1991. pap. text 37.50 (*0-262-52156-3*, Bradford Bks) MIT Pr.

Philosophy of Science. Mario Bunge. LC 97-22359. 1028p. 1998. write for info. (*0-7658-0415-8*) Transaction Pubs.

Philosophy of Science. James H. Fetzer. 224p. 1992. pap. 16.95 (*1-55778-481-7*) Paragon Hse.

Philosophy of Science. Guttorm Floistad. 1986. pap. text 23.50 (*90-247-3298-0*) Kluwer Academic.

Philosophy of Science. Ed. by Peter A. French et al. LC 93-8496. (Midwest Studies in Philosophy: Vol. XVIII). (C). 1993. text 57.50 (*0-268-01406-X*); pap. text 26.50 (*0-268-01407-8*) U of Notre Dame Pr.

Philosophy of Science. Clark Glymour. (Dimensions of Philosophy Ser.). 224p. 1996. pap. 44.00 (*0-8133-0578-0*); pap. text 17.95 (*0-8133-0579-9*) Westview.

Philosophy of Science. Bergmann Gustav. LC 77-5439. 181p. 1982. lib. bdg. 83.50 (*0-8371-9623-X*, BEPH, Greenwood Pr) Greenwood.

Philosophy of Science. Ed. by David Papineau. (Readings in Philosophy Ser.). 346p. 1996. pap. text 17.95 (*0-19-875165-6*) OUP.

Philosophy of Science. Ed. by David Papineau. (Readings in Philosophy Ser.). 352p. 1996. text 55.00 (*0-19-875164-8*) OUP.

***Philosophy of Science.** Sklar. 2000. 60.00 (*0-8133-9107-5*, Pub. by Westview); pap. 24.00 (*0-8133-9106-7*, Pub. by Westview) HarpC.

***Philosophy of Science.** Lawrence Sklar. LC 99-40012. 1999. write for info. (*0-8153-3492-3*) Garland.

Philosophy of Science, Part 1. 2nd ed. P. Henri Van Laer. LC 63-11605. (Duquesne Studies, Philosophical Ser.: No. 6). 182p. 1963. reprint ed. pap. 56.50 (*0-608-08303-8*, 205134300096) Bks Demand.

***Philosophy of Science: A Contemporary Introduction.** Alexander Rosenberg. LC 00-26960. (Contemporary Introductions to Philosophy Ser.). 2001. pap. write for info. (*0-415-15281-X*) Routledge.

Philosophy of Science: A Study of the Division & Nature of Various Groups of Sciences, Pt. 2. P. Henri Van Laer. LC 56-14599. (Duquesne Studies, Philosophical Ser.: No. 14). 356p. 1962. reprint ed. pap. 110.40 (*0-608-08304-6*, 205134400096) Bks Demand.

Philosophy of Science: An Overview for Cognitive Science. William Bechtel. (Tutorial Essays in Cognitive Science Ser.). 152p. 1988. 36.00 (*0-89859-695-5*); pap. text 19.95 (*0-8058-0221-5*) L Erlbaum Assocs.

Philosophy of Science: Science & Objectivity. George Couvalis. 224p. 1997. 69.95 (*0-7619-5100-8*); pap. 24.95 (*0-7619-5101-6*) Sage.

Philosophy of Science: The Central Issues. Martin Curd & Jan A. Cover. LC 97-39387. 1000p. (C). 1998. pap. text 50.00 (*0-393-97175-9*) Norton.

Philosophy of Science Vol. 1: From Problem to Theory. rev. ed. Mario Bunge. LC 97-22359. 607p. 1999. pap. 39.95 (*0-7658-0413-1*) Transaction Pubs.

Philosophy of Science Vol. 2: From Explanation to Justification. rev. ed. Mario Bunge. LC 97-22359. 374p. 1998. pap. text 34.95 (*0-7658-0414-X*) Transaction Pubs.

Philosophy of Science & Belief in God. 3rd rev. ed. Gordon H. Clark. Ed. & Intro. by John W. Robbins. 138p. 1996. pap. 8.95 (*0-940931-85-0*) Trinity Found.

Philosophy of Science & Economics. Robert A. Solo. LC 91-23969. 140p. (gr. 13). 1991. text 79.95 (*0-87332-899-X*) M E Sharpe.

Philosophy of Science & Education. Ed. by Vincent Shen & Tran Van Doan. LC 94-40755. (Cultural Heritage & Contemporary Change Series III: Vol. 9). 1995. 45.00 (*1-56518-075-5*); pap. text 17.50 (*1-56518-076-3*) Coun Res Values.

Philosophy of Science & Historical Enquiry. John Losee. LC 86-23550. (Illus.). 160p. 1987. text 45.00 (*0-19-824946-2*) OUP.

Philosophy of Science & Its Discontents. 2nd ed. Steve Fuller. LC 92-38514. (Conduct of Science Ser.). 240p. 1992. reprint ed. pap. text 21.95 (*0-89862-020-1*) Guilford Pubns.

Philosophy of Science & the Occult. 2nd ed. Ed. by Patrick Grim. LC 90-9619. (SUNY Series in Philosophy). 336p. 1990. pap. text 21.95 (*0-7914-0204-5*) State U NY Pr.

Philosophy of Science, Cognitive Psychology, & Educational Theory & Practice. Ed. by Richard A. Duschl & Richard J. Hamilton. LC 91-22633. (SUNY Series in Science Education). 287p. (C). 1992. text 24.50 (*0-7914-1053-6*) State U NY Pr.

Philosophy of Science in the Twentieth Century: An Introduction. Donald Gillies. LC 92-36318. 1993. pap. 26.95 (*0-631-18358-2*) Blackwell Pubs.

***Philosophy of Self.** Albert W. J. Harper. LC 99-48646. (Problems in Contemporary Philosophy Ser.: Vol. 43). 132p. 2000. text 69.95 (*0-7734-7887-6*) E Mellen.

Philosophy of Sex: Contemporary Readings. 2nd ed. Ed. by Alan Soble. 360p. (C). 1991. pap. text 18.95 (*0-8226-3013-3*) Rowman.

Philosophy of Sex: Contemporary Readings. 3rd ed. Ed. by Alan Soble. LC 97-12412. 390p. 1997. 73.00 (*0-8476-8480-6*); pap. 19.95 (*0-8476-8481-4*) Rowman.

Philosophy of Sex & Love. Robert Trevas et al. 452p. 1996. pap. text 54.00 (*0-02-312431-8*, Macmillan Coll) P-H.

Philosophy of Sex & Love: An Introduction. Alan Soble. LC 97-13965. (Issues in Philosophy Ser.). (Illus.). 208p. (Orig.). 1998. pap. text 16.95 (*1-55778-716-6*) Paragon Hse.

Philosophy of Sexuality. Don E. Marietta, Jr. LC 96-16110. 232p. (C). (gr. 13). 1996. text 66.95 (*1-56324-933-2*) M E Sharpe.

Philosophy of Sexuality. Don E. Marietta, Jr. LC 96-16110. 232p. (C). (gr. 13). 1996. pap. text 25.95 (*1-56324-934-0*) M E Sharpe.

***Philosophy of Seyyed Hossein Nasr.** Ed. by Lewis E. Hahn. 2000. 59.95 (*0-8126-9413-9*); pap. 36.95 (*0-8126-9414-7*) Open Court.

Philosophy of Sikh Religion. Wazir Singh. 127p. 1981. 14.95 (*0-940500-09-4*, Pub. by Ess Ess Pubns) Asia Bk Corp.

Philosophy of Simone de Beauvoir: Gendered Phenomenologies, Erotic Generosities. Debra B. Bergoffen. LC 97-1516. (SUNY Series in Feminist Philosophy). 250p. (C). 1996. text 54.50 (*0-7914-3151-7*); pap. text 17.95 (*0-7914-3152-5*) State U NY Pr.

Philosophy of Small Scale Industrial Management. K. Srinivasa Iyengar. 215p. 1970. 5.00 (*0-88065-134-2*) Scholarly Pubns.

Philosophy of Social Ecology. 2nd rev. ed. Murray Bookchin. 183p. 1995. 48.99 (*1-55164-019-8*, Pub. by Black Rose); pap. 19.99 (*1-55164-018-X*, Pub. by Black Rose) Consort Bk Sales.

Philosophy of Social Ecology: Essays on Dialectical Naturalism. Murray Bookchin. LC 90-81639. 199p. (Orig.). (C). 1990. 37.95 (*0-921689-69-1*, Pub. by Black Rose) Consort Bk Sales.

***Philosophy of Social Research.** 3rd ed. J. A. Hughes & W. W. Sharrock. LC 97-28440. (Social Research Ser.). 232p. (C). 1998. pap. text 25.75 (*0-582-31105-5*) Longman.

Philosophy of Social Science. 2nd ed. Alexander Rosenberg. Ed. by Norman Daniels & Keith Lehrer. LC 95-14102. (Dimensions of Philosophy Ser.). 256p. (C). 1995. pap. text 27.00 (*0-8133-2660-5*, Pub. by Westview) HarpC.

Philosophy of Social Science, Vol.1. Wisdom. 1987. 82.95 (*0-566-05027-7*) Ashgate Pub Co.

Philosophy of Social Science: An Introduction. Martin Hollis. LC 93-47234. 278p. (C). 1994. pap. text 17.95 (*0-521-44780-1*) Cambridge U Pr.

Philosophy of Social Science: Groundwork for Social Dynamics, Vol. 3. J. O. Wisdom. 150p. 1992. 72.95 (*1-85628-389-5*, Pub. by Avebry) Ashgate Pub Co.

***Philosophy of Social Science: New Perspectives** Garry Potter. LC 99-30483. 1999. write for info. (*0-582-36974-6*) Addison-Wesley.

Philosophy of Social Science: The Methods, Ideals & Politics of Social Inquiry. Michael Root. 272p. 1993. pap. 26.95 (*0-631-19042-2*) Blackwell Pubs.

***Philosophy of Social Sciences: An Interdisciplinary Approach.** R. W. Dundon & J. L. Jainer. LC 99-43354. 1999. 34.00 (*1-56072-730-6*) Nova Sci Pubs.

Philosophy of Society. Ed. by Roger Beehler & Alan R. Drengson. 1978. pap. 15.95 (*0-416-83490-6*, NO. 2083) Routledge.

Philosophy of Socrates. Nicholas D. Smith & Thomas C. Brickhouse. LC 99-36572. (History of Ancient & Medieval Philosophy Ser.). 304p. 1999. 68.00 (*0-8133-2084-4*); pap. text 22.00 (*0-8133-2085-2*) Westview.

Philosophy of Space & Time. Hans Reichenbach. Tr. by Maria Reichenbach. 295p. 1998. pap. text 8.95 (*0-486-60443-8*) Dover.

Philosophy of Spinoza. Benedict De Spinoza. 29.95 (*0-8488-1178-X*) Amereon Ltd.

Philosophy of Spinoza: The Unity of His Thought. Richard McKeon. LC 86-28563. 345p. 1987. reprint ed. 35.00 (*0-918024-47-1*); reprint ed. pap. 17.50 (*0-918024-48-X*) Ox Bow.

Philosophy of Spinoza: Unfolding the Latent Processes of His Reasoning. Harry A. Wolfson. 872p. 1983. pap. 35.00 (*0-674-66595-3*) HUP.

Philosophy of Spiritual Activity. rev. ed. Rudolf Steiner. Ed. by Joan M. Thompson. Tr. by Rita Stebbing from GER. 195p. 1993. 27.95 (*1-85584-000-6*, Pub. by R Steiner Pr) Anthroposophic.

***Philosophy of Spiritual Activity (1922)** Rudolf Steiner. 400p. 1999. reprint ed. pap. 24.95 (*0-7661-0772-8*) Kessinger Pub.

Philosophy of Spiritual Intercourse Being an Explanation of Modern Mysteries (1853) Andrew J. Davis. 150p. 1998. reprint ed. pap. 19.95 (*0-7661-0366-8*) Kessinger Pub.

Philosophy of Sport. Drew A. Hyland. (Issues in Philosophy Ser.). 161p. (C). 1990. pap. text 16.95 (*1-55778-189-3*) Paragon Hse.

Philosophy of Sri Madhvacarya. B. N. Sharma. (C). 1991. reprint ed. text 24.00 (*81-208-0068-0*, Pub. by Motilal Bnarsidass) S Asia.

Philosophy of St. Bonaventure. Etienne Gilson. 499p. 1965. 5.00 (*0-8199-0526-7*, Frncscn Herld) Franciscan Pr.

Philosophy of St. Thomas Aquinas. Etienne Gilson. Ed. by G. A. Elrington. Tr. by Edward Bullough from FRE. LC 70-157337. (Select Bibliographies Reprint Ser.). 1979. reprint ed. 29.95 (*0-8369-5797-0*) Ayer.

Philosophy of Strategy for Breeding Tropical Forest Trees. G. Namkoong et al. 1980. 60.00 (*0-85074-034-7*) St Mut.

Philosophy of Symbolic Forms, Vol. 1, Language. Ernst Cassirer. Tr. by Ralph Manheim. Vol. 1. (C). 1965. pap. 20.00 (*0-300-00037-5*, Y146) Yale U Pr.

Philosophy of Symbolic Forms, Vol. 2, Mythical Thought. Ernst Cassirer. Tr. by Ralph Manheim. Vol. 2. (C). 1965. pap. 18.00 (*0-300-00038-3*, Y147) Yale U Pr.

Philosophy of Symbolic Forms, Vol. 3, The Phenomenology Of Knowledge. Ernst Cassirer. Tr. by Ralph Manheim. 1965. pap. 22.00 (*0-300-00039-1*, Y148) Yale U Pr.

***Philosophy of Symbolic Forms Vol. 4: The Metaphysics of Symbolic Forms.** Ernst Cassirer. Ed. & Tr. by John M. Krois. Ed. by Donald Phillip Verene. 272p. 1998. pap. 16.00 (*0-300-07433-6*) Yale U Pr.

Philosophy of Symbolic Forms Vol. 4: The Metaphysics of Symbolic Forms with an Essay On... Ernst Cassirer. LC 52-13969. 272p. 1996. 40.00 (*0-300-06278-8*) Yale U Pr.

Philosophy of T. S. Eliot: From Skepticism to a Surrealist Poetic, 1909-1927. William Skaff. LC 85-31477. 262p. reprint ed. pap. 81.30 (*0-8357-3325-4*, 203954900013) Bks Demand.

***Philosophy of Technology.** Ed. by Deborah Johnson & Joseph C. Pitt. 256p. 2000. pap. text 32.95 (*1-889119-52-0*) Seven Bridges.

Philosophy of Technology. Frederick Ferre. LC 95-10155. 1995. reprint ed. pap. text 15.00 (*0-8203-1761-6*) U of Ga Pr.

Philosophy of Technology. 2nd ed. Paul T. Durbin. 216p. (C). 1989. lib. bdg. 160.00 (*0-7923-0139-0*, Pub. by Kluwer Academic) Kluwer Academic.

Philosophy of Technology: An Introduction. Don Ihde. 160p. 1992. pap. 16.95 (*1-55778-273-3*) Paragon Hse.

Philosophy of Technology Vol. 70: Annual ACPA Proceedings, 1996. Ed. by Therese-Anne Druart. 1997. pap. 20.00 (*0-918090-30-X*) Am Cath Philo.

Philosophy of Technology in Spanish Speaking Countries. Ed. by Carl Mitcham. LC 93-39783. (Philosophy & Technology Ser.). 354p. (C). 1993. lib. bdg. 209.50 (*0-7923-2567-2*, Pub. by Kluwer Academic) Kluwer Academic.

Philosophy of the Ancients. Friedo Ricken. Tr. by Eric Watkins. LC 90-70852. 232p. (C). 1991. pap. text 17.50 (*0-268-01588-0*) U of Notre Dame Pr.

Philosophy of the Arts: An Introduction to Aesthetics. Gordon Graham. LC 97-1474. 208p. (C). 1997. pap. 20.99 (*0-415-16688-8*) Routledge.

Philosophy of the Arts: An Introduction to Aesthetics. Gordon Graham. LC 97-1474. 208p. (C). 1997. 70.00 (*0-415-16687-X*) Routledge.

***Philosophy of the Arts: An Introduction to Aesthetics.** 2nd ed. Gordon Graham. LC 00-36889. 2000. pap. write for info. (*0-415-23564-2*) Routledge.

Philosophy of the Austrian School. Raimondo Cubeddu. LC 92-46097. 288p. (C). (gr. 13). 1993. 85.00 (*0-415-08647-7*, B2386) Routledge.

Philosophy of the Buddha. 2nd rev. ed. Archie J. Bahm. LC 92-33904. 176p. 1993. pap. 12.95 (*0-87573-025-6*) Jain Pub Co.

Philosophy of the Church Fathers: Faith, Trinity, Incarnation. 3rd rev. ed. Harry A. Wolfson. LC 70-119077. 665p. 1970. 34.95 (*0-674-66551-1*) HUP.

Philosophy of the Count de Gobineau. G. M. Spring. 304p. 1995. pap. 25.00 (*1-878465-13-9*) Scott-Townsend Pubs.

Philosophy of the Curriculum. Ed. by Sidney Hook et al. LC 75-3921. 295p. (C). 1975. 29.95 (*0-87975-051-0*) Prometheus Bks.

Philosophy of the Enlightenment. Ernst Cassirer. Tr. by F. Koelin & J. Pettegrove from FRE. 384p. 1951. pap. text 18.95 (*0-691-01963-0*, Pub. by Princeton U Pr) Cal Prin Full Svc.

Philosophy of the Enlightenment: The Burgess & the Enlightenment. Lucien Goldmann. Tr. by Henry Maas from FRE. 1973. 17.50 (*0-262-07060-X*) MIT Pr.

Philosophy of the Environment. T. D. Chappell. 192p. 1998. pap. 22.00 (*0-7486-0911-3*, Pub. by Edinburgh U Pr) Col U Pr.

Philosophy of the Faqirs. Ahmed Hussain. 150p. (Orig.). 1985. pap. 5.50 (*1-56744-351-6*) Kazi Pubns.

Philosophy of the Gita. Ramesh N. Patel. LC 90-40763. (American University Studies: Philosophy: Ser. V, Vol. 105). X, 311p. (C). 1991. text 47.95 (*0-8204-1416-6*) P Lang Pubng.

Philosophy of the Good Life. Charles Gore. LC 77-27197. (Gifford Lectures: 1929-30). reprint ed. 37.50 (*0-404-60484-6*) AMS Pr.

Philosophy of the Human Person. James B. Reichman. 346p. 1985. 12.95 (*0-8294-0504-6*) Loyola Pr.

Philosophy of the Human Sciences. Ed. by Peter A. French et al. LC 90-70851. (Midwest Studies in Philosophy: Vol. XV). 480p. (C). 1990. pap. text 25.50 (*0-268-01385-3*) U of Notre Dame Pr.

***Philosophy of the I Ching** 2nd exp. ed. Carol K. Anthony. LC 99-198017. xi, 216 p. 1998. write for info. (*0-9603832-2-0*) Anthony Pub Co.

Philosophy of the Inductive Sciences, 2 vols., Set. William Whewell. 1967. reprint ed. 95.00 (*0-7146-1156-5*, BHA-01156, Pub. by F Cass Pubs) Intl Spec Bk.

Philosophy of the Inner Light. Michael Marsh. LC 76-50674. (Orig.). 1976. pap. 4.00 (*0-87574-209-2*) Pendle Hill.

Philosophy of the Kalam. Harry A. Wolfson. LC 74-78718. 890p. (C). 1976. 64.00 (*0-674-66580-5*) HUP.

Philosophy of the Limit. Ed. by Drucilla Cornell. 260p. (Orig.). (C). 1992. pap. 21.99 (*0-415-90239-8*, A4267) Routledge.

Philosophy of the Literary Symbolic. Hazard Adams. LC 82-24785. (Illus.). xiv, 466p. 1983. pap. 34.95 (*0-8130-0771-2*) U Press Fla.

Philosophy of the Living Fire (Love, God) R. Swinburne Clymer. 173p. 1996. reprint ed. spiral bd. 16.00 (*0-7873-0179-5*) Hlth Research.

Philosophy of the Marquis de Sade. Timo Airaksinen. 224p. (C). 1995. pap. 22.99 (*0-415-11229-X*, C0187) Routledge.

Philosophy of the Marquis de Sade. Timo Airaksinen. LC 94-29578. 208p. (C). (gr. 13). 1995. 80.00 (*0-415-11228-1*, C0186) Routledge.

Philosophy of the Plays of Shakspere Unfolded. Delia S. Bacon. LC 73-113547. reprint ed. 44.50 (*0-404-00443-1*) AMS Pr.

Philosophy of the Practical. Benedetto Croce. Tr. by Douglas Ainslie. LC 66-30790. 1913. 32.00 (*0-8196-0192-6*) Biblo.

An Asterisk (*) at the beginning of an entry indicates that the title is appearing for the first time.

Philosophy of the Practice of Dentistry. Lindsey D. Pankey & William J. Davis. Ed. by Veronica Sanitate. (Illus.). 323p. 1987. text 69.50 (*0-944742-01-7*); audio 127.50 (*0-944742-02-5*) Med Coll of OH Pr.

Philosophy of the Present. George Herbert Mead. Ed. by Arthur E. Murphy. LC 80-16334. 240p. 1996. pap. text 8.95 (*0-226-51670-9*, P909) U Ch Pr.

Philosophy of the Quran. H. G. Sarwar. 285p. 1993. 6.50 (*1-56744-187-4*) Kazi Pubns.

Philosophy of the Real & the Possible. Harry T. Costello. LC 72-972. reprint ed. 20.00 (*0-404-01737-1*) AMS Pr.

Philosophy of the Recent Past: An Outline of European & American Philosophy Since 1860. Ralph B. Perry. LC 75-3314. reprint ed. 37.50 (*0-404-59295-3*) AMS Pr.

Philosophy of the Sciences: or the Relations Between the Departments of Knowledge. Frederick R. Tennant. LC 78-109862. 191p. 1970. reprint ed. lib. bdg. 55.00 (*0-8371-4353-5*, TEPS, Greenwood Pr) Greenwood.

Philosophy of the Sign. Josef Simon. Tr. by George Heffernan. LC 94-22420. (SUNY Series in Contemporary Continental Philosophy). 291p. (C). 1995. text 59.50 (*0-7914-2453-7*); pap. text 19.95 (*0-7914-2454-5*) State U NY Pr.

Philosophy of the Sixteenth & Seventeenth Centuries. Richard H. Popkin. LC 66-10365. (Orig.). 1966. pap. 16.95 (*0-02-925490-6*) Free Pr.

Philosophy of the State & the Practice of Welfare: Writings of Bernard & Helen Bosanquet. Ed. by David J. Gladstone. 3200p. (C). 1996. 815.00 (*0-415-14027-7*) Routledge.

Philosophy of the State As Educator. Thomas Dubay. LC 78-6256. 237p. 1978. reprint ed. lib. bdg. 59.50 (*0-313-20416-0*, DUPH, Greenwood Pr) Greenwood.

***Philosophy of the Upanishads.** Sri Aurobindo. 73p. 1998. pap. 2.95 (*81-7058-362-4*, Pub. by SAA) E-W Cultural Ctr.

***Philosophy of the Upanishads.** Paul Deussen. 429p. 1999. pap. 120.00 (*81-208-1620-X*, Pub. by Motilal Bnarsidass) St Mut.

Philosophy of the Vedanta: A Modern Scientific Perspective. Radhey S. Kaushal. (C). 1994. text 19.50 (*81-7030-403-2*, Pub. by Sri Satguru Pubns) S Asia.

Philosophy of the Vedantasutra: Study Based on the Evaluation of the Commentaries of Samkara, Ramanuja & Madhva. S. M. Srinivasa Chari. 1998. 24.00 (*81-215-0809-6*) M Manoharial.

Philosophy of the Visual Arts. Ed. by Philip A. Alperson. (Illus.). 640p. (C). 1992. pap. text 46.00 (*0-19-505975-1*) OUP.

***Philosophy of the Young Kant: The Precritical Project.** Martin Schonfeld. LC 99-30602. 368p. 2000. write for info. (*0-19-513218-1*) OUP.

Philosophy of Theism. Alexander C. Fraser. LC 77-27228. (Gifford Lectures: 1894-95). reprint ed. 39.00 (*0-404-60453-6*) AMS Pr.

Philosophy of Theism: Second Series, Second Series. Alexander C. Fraser. LC 77-27227. (Gifford Lectures: 1895-96). reprint ed. 37.50 (*0-404-60454-4*) AMS Pr.

Philosophy of Thomas Aquinas: Introductory Readings. Aquinas, Thomas, Saint. Ed. by Christopher Martin. (Croom Helm Philosophy Ser.). 256p. (C). 1988. pap. 25.99 (*0-415-00296-6*) Routledge.

Philosophy of Thomas Reid. Ed. by Melvin Dalgarno & Eric Matthews. 463p. (C). 1989. text 171.00 (*0-7923-0190-0*) Kluwer Academic.

Philosophy of Time. Albert W. Harper. LC 97-12839. (Problems in Contemporary Philosophy Ser.). 218p. 1997. write for info. (*0-7734-8618-6*) E Mellen.

Philosophy of Time. Albert W. J. Harper. LC 97-12839. 1997. write for info. (*0-88946-325-5*) E Mellen.

Philosophy of Time. Murray MacBeath. Ed. by Robin Le Poidevin. LC 92-26125. (Readings in Philosophy Ser.). (Illus.). 236p. 1993. pap. text 19.95 (*0-19-823999-8*) OUP.

Philosophy of Tort Law. Izhak Englard. (Applied Legal Philosophy Ser.). 250p. 1993. 78.95 (*1-85521-109-2*, Pub. by Dartmth Pub) Ashgate Pub Co.

Philosophy of Universality. 2nd rev. ed. Omraam M. Aivanhov. (Izvor Collection: Vol. 206). 178p. 1988. pap. 7.95 (*2-85566-420-9*, Pub. by Prosveta) Prosveta USA.

Philosophy of Vaisnava Religion. G. N. Mallik. 1972. 59.95 (*0-8490-0829-8*) Gordon Pr.

Philosophy of Vegetarianism. Daniel A. Dombrowski. LC 83-18125. 192p. 1984. pap. 15.95 (*0-87023-431-5*) U of Mass Pr.

Philosophy of W. V. Quine. Ed. by Lewis E. Hahn & Paul Arthur Schilpp. LC 86-17980. (Library of Living Philosophers: Vol. XVIII). 728p. 1986. 59.95 (*0-8126-9010-9*) Open Court.

Philosophy of W. V. Quine. 2nd rev. ed. Ed. by Lewis E. Hahn. LC 86-17980. (Library of Living Philosophers: Vol. 18). 800p. (C). 1998. pap. 34.95 (*0-8126-9371-X*) Open Court.

Philosophy of W. V. Quine: An Expository Essay. Roger F. Gibson. 228p. 1986. pap. 19.95 (*0-8130-0855-7*) U Press Fla.

Philosophy of Welfare: Selected Writing of Richard M. Titmuss. Ed. by Brian Abel-Smith & Kay Titmuss. 240p. (C). 1987. text 49.95 (*0-04-361063-3*); pap. text 18.95 (*0-04-361064-1*) Routledge.

Philosophy of Wilfrid Sellars: Queries & Extensions. Ed. by J. C. Pitt. (Philosophical Studies in Philosophy: No. 12). 313p. 1978. text 106.00 (*90-277-0903-3*, D Reidel) Kluwer Academic.

Philosophy of Wilhelm Dilthey. Herbert A. Hodges. LC 73-13024. (International Library of Sociology & Social Reconstruction). 368p. 1974. reprint ed. lib. bdg. 35.00 (*0-8371-7112-1*, HOWD, Greenwood Pr) Greenwood.

Philosophy of William Ellery Channing. Robert L. Patterson. LC 76-153342. reprint ed. 32.50 (*0-404-04916-8*) AMS Pr.

Philosophy of William James. Ed. by W. Corti. 1977. pap. 45.95 (*3-7873-0352-9*) Adlers Foreign Bks.

Philosophy of William James. Theodore Flournoy. LC 78-99658. (Select Bibliographies Reprint Ser.). 1977. 24.95 (*0-8369-5087-9*) Ayer.

Philosophy of Witchcraft. Ian Ferguson. 220p. 1998. reprint ed. pap. 19.95 (*0-7661-0440-0*) Kessinger Pub.

Philosophy of Witchcraft. Ian Ferguson. 224p. 1993. reprint ed. pap. 27.50 (*1-872736-46-7*, Pub. by Mandrake Pr) Holmes Pub.

Philosophy of Woman: An Anthology of Classic to Current Concepts. 3rd ed. Ed. by Mary B. Mahowald. LC 94-25616. 544p. (C). 1994. pap. text 16.95 (*0-87220-261-5*); lib. bdg. 39.95 (*0-87220-262-3*) Hackett Pub.

Philosophy of Worship in Islam. F. R. Ansari. 1991. pap. 3.00 (*1-56744-188-2*) Kazi Pubns.

***Philosophy of Wu Ch'eng, a Neo-Confucian of the Yuan Dynasty.** David Gedalecia. LC 99-70016. (Oriental Ser.: Vol. VIII). 206p. 1999. 39.00 (*0-933070-44-6*) Ind U Res Inst.

***Philosophy on the Internet: 1999-2000.** Ed. by Prentice-Hall Staff. (C). 1998. text. write for info. (*0-13-022072-8*) P-H.

***Philosophy 1: A Guide Through the Subject.** A. C. Grayling. 688p. 1999. pap. text 24.95 (*0-19-875243-1*) OUP.

Philosophy, Philology & Politics in Eighteenth-Century China: Li Fu & the Lu-Wang School under the Ch'ing. Chin-shing Huang. (Cambridge Studies in Chinese History, Literature & Institutions). 224p. (C). 1995. text 52.95 (*0-521-48225-9*) Cambridge U Pr.

Philosophy, Policies & Programs for Early Adolescent Education: An Annotated Bibliography. Compiled by Dale A. Blyth & Elizabeth L. Karnes. LC 81-4237. 689p. 1981. lib. bdg. 89.50 (*0-313-22687-3*, BEA/, Greenwood Pr) Greenwood.

Philosophy, Politics & Autonomy: Essays in Political Philosophy. Cornelius Castoriadis. Ed. by David A. Curtis. (Odeon Ser.). 320p. (C). 1991. pap. text 23.95 (*0-19-506963-3*) OUP.

Philosophy, Politics & Civilization: Essays on R. G. Collingwood. Ed. by David Boucher et al. 352p. 1996. 65.00 (*0-7083-1308-6*, Pub. by Univ Wales Pr) Paul & Co Pubs.

Philosophy Practice: An Alternative to Counseling & Psychotherapy. Shlomit C. Schuster. LC 99-13432. 224p. 1999. 59.95 (*0-275-96541-4*, C6541, Praeger Pubs) Greenwood.

Philosophy, Psychiatry & Neuroscience - Three Approaches to the Mind: A Synthetic Analysis of the Varieties of Human Experience. Edward M. Hundert. (Illus.). 360p. 1991. reprint ed. pap. text 28.00 (*0-19-824896-2*) OUP.

Philosophy Psychiatry & Psychopathy. Heginbotham. 56.95 (*1-84014-864-0*) Ashgate Pub Co.

Philosophy, Psychology, & Mysticism. rev. ed. Inayat Khan. LC 79-67753. (Sufi Message of Hazrat Inayat Khan Ser.: Vol. 11). 259p. 1979. 19.00 (*90-6325-099-1*, Pub. by Sufi Mvemnt) Omega Pubns NY.

Philosophy, Psychology & Psychiatry. Ed. by A. Phillips Griffiths. (Royal Institute of Philosophy Supplements Ser.: No. 37). 249p. (C). 1995. pap. text 22.95 (*0-521-46902-3*) Cambridge U Pr.

Philosophy, Religion see Comprehensive Dissertation Index: Ten Year Cumulation, 1973-1982

Philosophy, Religion, & Contemporary Life: Essays on Perennial Problems. Ed. by Leroy S. Rouner & James R. Langford. (C). 1995. pap. text 10.95 (*0-268-03807-4*) U of Notre Dame Pr.

Philosophy, Religion, & the Coming World Civilization: Essays in Honour of William Ernst Hocking. Ed. by L. S. Rouner. 526p. 1966. lib. bdg. 126.50 (*90-247-0070-1*, Pub. by M Nijhoff) Kluwer Academic.

Philosophy, Religion, & the Question of Intolerance. Ed. by Mehdi Amin Razavi & David Ambuel. LC 96-46170. 284p. (C). 1997. text 59.50 (*0-7914-3447-8*); pap. text 19.95 (*0-7914-3448-6*) State U NY Pr.

Philosophy, Religion, & the Spiritual Life. Ed. by Michael McGhee. LC 92-5707. (Royal Institute of Philosophy Supplements Ser.: No. 32). 261p. (C). 1992. pap. text 22.95 (*0-521-42196-9*) Cambridge U Pr.

Philosophy, Religious Studies, & Myth. Ed. & Intro. by Robert A. Segal. LC 95-43178. (Theories of Myth Ser.: Vol. 3). 432p. 1995. text 85.00 (*0-8153-2257-7*) Garland.

Philosophy, Rhetoric, Literary Criticism: Inter-Views. Ed. by Gary A. Olson. LC 93-38349. 264p. (C). 1994. 26.95 (*0-8093-1908-X*) S Ill U Pr.

Philosophy Rooted in Love: The Dominant Themes in the Perennial Philosophy of St. Thomas Aquinas. Francis J. Klauder. 380p. (Orig.). 1994. pap. text 32.50 (*0-8191-9448-4*) U Pr of Amer.

Philosophy, Science, & Sense Perception: Historical & Critical Studies. Maurice Mandelbaum. LC 64-16312. 276p. reprint ed. pap. 85.60 (*0-608-06124-7*, 206645700008) Bks Demand.

Philosophy, Science & the Sociology of Knowledge. Irving L. Horowitz. LC 76-27756. 169p. 1976. reprint ed. lib. bdg. 55.00 (*0-8371-9051-7*, HOPS, Greenwood Pr) Greenwood.

Philosophy, Science, & Theology of Mission in the 19th & 20th Centuries Pt. II: A Missiological Encyclopedia: Missionary Theology. Jan A. B. Jongeneel. (Studies in the Intercultural History of Christianity: Vol. 106). XXII, 428p. (C). 1997. text 76.95 (*0-8204-3299-7*) P Lang Pubng.

Philosophy, Social Theory & the Thought of George Herbert Mead. Ed. by Mitchell Aboulafia. LC 90-30134. (SUNY Series in the Philosophy of the Social Sciences). 337p. 1991. text 21.50 (*0-7914-0359-9*) State U NY Pr.

Philosophy Student Writer's Manual. Anthony Graybosch et al. LC 97-2305. 320p. (C). 1997. pap. text, student ed. 26.40 (*0-13-237371-8*) P-H.

Philosophy, the Federalist, & the Constitution. Morton White. 288p. 1989. reprint ed. pap. text 22.00 (*0-19-505948-4*) OUP.

***Philosophy, the Good, the True & the Beautiful.** Ed. by Anthony O'Hear. 320p. 2000. pap. text 24.95 (*0-521-78511-1*) Cambridge U Pr.

Philosophy Then & Now: An Introductory Text with Classic Readings. N. Scott Arnold et al. LC 97-47396. 720p. 1998. 69.95 (*1-55786-741-0*); pap. 39.95 (*1-55786-742-9*) Blackwell Pubs.

Philosophy, Theology, & Hegel's Berlin Philosophy of Religion, 1821-1827. Philip M. Merklinger. LC 92-25807. 250p. (C). 1993. text 64.50 (*0-7914-1491-4*); pap. text 21.95 (*0-7914-1492-2*) State U NY Pr.

***Philosophy Through the Ages.** Price. LC 99-16079. (Philosophy Ser.). 400p. 1999. pap. text 54.95 (*0-534-56700-2*) Brooks-Cole.

Philosophy Today: Essays on Recent Developments in the Field of Philosophy. Ed. by Edward L. Schaub. LC 68-22944. (Essay Index Reprint Ser.). 1977. 28.95 (*0-8369-0852-X*) Ayer.

Philosophy 2: Further Through the Subject. A. C. Grayling. (Illus.). 880p. 1999. text 80.00 (*0-19-875179-6*); pap. text 19.95 (*0-19-875178-8*) OUP.

Philosophy Unmasked: A Skeptic's Critique. Laurie Calhoun. LC 97-1484. 208p. 1997. 25.00 (*0-7006-0833-8*) U Pr of KS.

Philosophy Without Ambiguity: A Logico-Linguistic Essay. Jay D. Atlas. (Clarendon Library of Logic & Philosophy). (Illus.). 198p. 1989. text 55.00 (*0-19-824454-1*) OUP.

Philosophy Without Foundations: Rethinking Hegel. William Maker. LC 93-42703. (SUNY Series in Hegelian Studies). 298p. (C). 1994. text 59.50 (*0-7914-2099-X*); pap. text 19.95 (*0-7914-2100-7*) State U NY Pr.

Philosophy's Cool Place D. Z. Phillips. LC 98-50653. 1999. 32.50 (*0-8014-3600-1*) Cornell U Pr.

Philosophy's Journey: From the Presocratics to the Present. 2nd ed. Konstantin Kolenda. (Illus.). 377p. (C). 1990. pap. text 19.95 (*0-88133-509-6*) Waveland Pr.

***Philosophy's Literature.** Andrew Benjamin. 226p. 2000. pap. 29.95 (*1-903083-09-5*, Pub. by Clinamen Pr) Paul & Co Pubs.

Philosophy's Second Revolution: Early & Recent Analytic Philosophy. D. S. Clarke. LC 97-2863. 244p. 1997. 42.95 (*0-8126-9347-7*); pap. 21.95 (*0-8126-9348-5*) Open Court.

Philospher's Index: Cumulative Edition, 1995, Vol. 29. Ed. by Richard H. Lineback. 704p. 1996. 189.00 (*0-9656743-1-2*) Philosophers Info Ctr.

Philosphical Writing: An Introduction. 2nd ed. Aloysius P. Martinich. LC 96-7632. 176p. 1996. pap. 18.95 (*0-631-20281-1*) Blackwell Pubs.

Philospy at the Limit. David Wood. 192p. (C). (gr. 13). 1990. text 55.00 (*0-04-445625-5*) Routledge.

Philospy of Science: The Historical Background. Joseph J. Kockelmans. LC 99-11434. (Science & Technology Studies). 495p. 1999. pap. 29.95 (*0-7658-0602-9*) Transaction Pubs.

Philostrati, Flavii. Ed. by De Lannoy. (GRE.). 1977. 32.50 (*3-322-00878-9*, T1592, Pub. by B G Teubner) U of Mich Pr.

Philostratus: An Index to the Lives of the Sophists of Philostratus. Ivars Avotins & Miriam M. Avotins. (Alpha-Omega, Reihe A Ser.: No. XXV). xi, 308p. 1978. 70.00 (*3-487-06540-1*) G Olms Pubs.

Philostratus: Biography & Belles-Lettres in the Third Century A. D. Graham Anderson. LC 85-28013. 352p. 1987. 57.00 (*0-7099-0575-0*, Pub. by C Helm) Routldge.

Philothea: A Romance. Lydia Maria Child. LC 72-85682. (American Fiction Reprint Ser.). Orig. Title: Philothea: A Grecian Romance. 1977. 19.95 (*0-8369-7011-X*) Ayer.

Philothea: A Grecian Romance see Philothea: A Romance

Philothea: or An Introduction to the Devout Life. St. Francis De Sales & John C. Reville. LC 94-60603. 318p. 1994. reprint ed. pap. 10.00 (*0-89555-510-7*, 1253) TAN Bks Pubs.

Philotus: A Comedy. Ed. by David Irving. LC 76-175843. (Bannatyne Club, Edinburgh. Publications: No. 50). reprint ed. 32.50 (*0-404-52760-4*) AMS Pr.

Philoxene de Mabbog: Sa Vie, Ses Ecrits, Sa Theologie. Andre De Halleux. LC 82-45812. (Orthodoxies & Heresies in the Early Church Ser.). reprint ed. 64.50 (*0-404-62387-5*) AMS Pr.

Philpin's Tree. Barbara Fisher. (Illus.). 12p. (Orig.). (J). (gr. 1-3). 1977. pap. 2.00 (*0-934830-00-2*) Ten Penny.

Phineas F. Bresee: His Life in Methodism, the Holiness Movement, & the Church of the Nazarene. Carl Bangs. LC 95-35010. 320p. 1995. kivar 36.99 (*0-8341-1621-9*) Beacon Hill.

Phineas F. Bresee: Mr. Nazarene. Emily B. Moore. 72p. 1973. kivar 6.99 (*0-8341-0157-2*) Nazarene.

Phineas Finn. Anthony Trollope. Ed. by Bill MacCormack. (Everyman Paperback Classics). 432p. 1997. pap. 6.95 (*0-460-87497-7*, Everyman's Classic Lib) Tuttle Pubng.

Phineas Finn. Anthony Trollope. Ed. & Intro. by Jacques Berthoud. (Oxford World's Classics Ser.). (Illus.). 780p. 1999. reprint ed. pap. 7.95 (*0-19-283533-5*) OUP.

Phineas Finn: The Irish Member. Anthony Trollope. (Palliser Novels Ser.). (Illus.). 323p. 1991. 21.00 (*0-19-520896-X*) OUP.

Phineas Finn: (trollope 1989) Skilton. 1989. 43.00 (*1-870587-05-7*) Ashgate Pub Co.

Phineas Fletcher. Ed. by Estelle Haan. LC 97-197732. (Supplementa Humanistica Lovaniensia Ser.: Vol. IX). 226p. (Orig.). 1996. pap. 45.00 (*90-6186-737-1*, Pub. by Leuven Univ) Coronet Bks.

Phineas Parkhurst Quimby: The Complete Writings, 3 vols., Vol. 1. Phineas P. Quimby. LC 80-70090. 436p. 1988. pap. 25.00 (*0-87516-600-8*) DeVorss.

Phineas Parkhurst Quimby: The Complete Writings, 3 vols., Vol. 2. Phineas P. Quimby. LC 80-70090. 417p. 1988. pap. 25.00 (*0-87516-601-6*) DeVorss.

Phineas Parkhurst Quimby: The Complete Writings, 3 vols., Vol. 3. Phineas P. Quimby. LC 80-70090. 436p. 1988. pap. 25.00 (*0-87516-602-4*) DeVorss.

Phineas Redux. Anthony Trollope. Ed. by John C. Whale. (Palliser Novels Ser.). (Illus.). 784p. 1991. 21.00 (*0-19-520898-6*) OUP.

Phineas Redux. Anthony Trollope. (Oxford World's Classics Ser.). (Illus.). 768p. 2000. pap. text 8.95 (*0-19-283559-9*) OUP.

Phineas Redux: (trollope 1990) Skilton. 1990. 45.00 (*1-870587-11-1*) Ashgate Pub Co.

***Phippsburg.** Elin B. Dozois. (Images of America Ser.). (Illus.). 128p. 1999. pap. 18.99 (*0-7385-0095-X*) Arcadia Publng.

***Phish: Hoist.** 72p. 1998. otabind 19.95 (*0-7935-8741-7*) H Leonard.

***Phish: The Story of the Ghost.** 96p. 1999. otabind 19.95 (*0-634-00033-0*) H Leonard.

Phish Billy Breathes - Guitar Tablature. 128p. 1997. per. 22.95 (*0-7935-7237-1*) H Leonard.

***Phish Book.** Richard Gehr & Phish. LC 98-19118. (Illus.). 192p. 1998. 29.95 (*0-375-50203-3*) Villard Books.

***Phish Book.** Richard Gehr & Phish. 1999. pap. 19.95 (*0-375-75254-4*) Villard Books.

Phish Corporation: A Managerial Accounting Practice Set. Mark Zmijewski et al. 115p. (C). 1991. text 25.31 (*0-07-016543-2*) McGraw.

Phishing Manual: A Compendium to the Music of Phish. Dean Budnick. 208p. (J). 1996. pap. 9.70 (*0-7868-8203-4*, Pub. by Hyperion) Time Warner.

Phisicall & Approved Medicines. Edmund Gardiner. LC 79-25834. (English Experience Ser.: No. 191). 116p. 1969. reprint ed. 20.00 (*90-221-0191-6*) Walter J Johnson.

Phiz: A Memoir. Frederic G. Kitton. LC 73-20467. (Studies in Dickens: No. 52). 1974. lib. bdg. 49.00 (*0-8383-1817-7*) M S G Haskell Hse.

Phiz & Dickens. Edgar Browne. LC 72-39035. (Studies in Dickens: No. 52). 320p. 1972. reprint ed. lib. bdg. 75.00 (*0-8383-1391-4*) M S G Haskell Hse.

***PHJ: Personal Health Journal.** Latrice Collins. 112p. 1999. 14.95 (*0-9660451-1-4*) Empower Press.

Phlamoudhi Vounari: A Sanctuary Site in Cyprus. Selma M. Al-Radi. (Studies in Mediterranean Archaeology: Vol. LXV). (Illus.). 136p. (Orig.). 1983. pap. 52.50 (*91-86098-10-1*, Pub. by P Astroms) Coronet Bks.

Phlebography & Sonography of the Veins. W. Hach & V. Hach-Wunderle. LC 96-13128. 288p. 1996. 225.00 (*3-540-53772-4*) Spr-Verlag.

Phlebologia Houston, 1991: Proceedings of the Intensive Practical Course in Phlebologia. Pauline Raymond-Martimbeau. 438p. 1991. write for info. (*1-880693-00-3*) P Ray-Mart.

***Phlebology: The Guide.** A. A. Ramelet & M. Robert Montilla. 448p. 1999. pap. 30.00 (*2-84299-147-8*, Pub. by ESME) Elsevier.

Phlebology, '95: Proceedings of the XII World Congress Union Internationale de Phlebologie, 2 vols. Ed. by David Negus et al. 1264p. 1996. 190.00 (*3-540-19999-3*) Spr-Verlag.

Phlebotomist Test Preparation. Cynthia M. Reed. LC 94-45960. (Test Prep Ser.). 128p. 1995. pap. 29.60 (*0-8359-4945-1*, Arco) Macmillan Gen Ref.

Phlebotomy. Kathleen Becan-McBride et al. 1993. 65.00 (*0-89189-328-8*) Am Soc Clinical.

Phlebotomy. Lynn B. Hoeltke. LC 93-46473. (Clinical Laboratory Manual Ser.). 139p. (C). 1994. mass mkt. 23.00 (*0-8273-5527-0*) Delmar.

Phlebotomy: A Client-Based Approach. Bonnie K. Davis. (Medical Lab Technician Ser.). (Illus.). 176p. (C). 1996. mass mkt. 35.95 (*0-8273-5453-3*) Delmar.

Phlebotomy & Electrocardiography. Marian Edmiston. Ed. by Kelly Gorham. (Nursing Ser.). 19p. (YA). (gr. 10 up). 1995. pap., wbk. ed. 7.00 (*0-8064-0615-1*, N20) Bergwall.

Phlebotomy Blood Collection: A & L Quick Review. 4th rev. ed. Kathleen Becon-McBride & Diane Garza. LC 97-30652. 168p. (C). 1997. 29.95 (*0-8385-0334-9*, A-0334-1) Appleton & Lange.

Phlebotomy Essentials. 2nd ed. Ruth E. McCall & Cathee M. Tankersley. LC 97-11637. 368p. 1997. pap. text 29.95 (*0-7817-9198-7*) Lppncott W & W.

Phlebotomy Exam Review. Ruth E. McCall. 240p. 1996. pap. text 29.95 (*0-397-55232-7*) Lppncott W & W.

***Phlebotomy for Nurses & Nursing Personnel: What Every Nurse & Nursing Assistant Must Know about Blood Specimen Collection, Processing & Transportation.** Dennis J. Ernst & Catherine Ernst. LC 00-103918. (Illus.). 176p. 2000. pap. 29.95 (*0-9700588-9-6*) Ctr Phlebotomy Ed.

Phlebotomy Handbook. 4th ed. Diana Garza. (C). 1996. pap. text, teacher ed. write for info. (*0-8385-8113-7*, A8113-1) Appleton & Lange.

Phlebotomy Handbook: Blood Collection Essentials. 5th ed. Garza & Becan McBride. LC 98-22074. 494p. 1999. pap. text 32.95 (*0-8385-8141-2*, Medical Exam) Appleton & Lange.

Phlebotomy Review Guide. Susan E. Phelan. LC 98-23247. 1998. 49.00 (*0-89189-433-0*) Am Soc Clinical.

Phlebotomy Techniques: A Laboratory Workbook. Susan Phelan. 1993. wbk. ed. 35.00 (*0-89189-343-1*) Am Soc Clinical.

Phlebotomy Techniques Curriculum Guide. Susan Phelan. 1993. 20.00 (*0-89189-359-8*) Am Soc Clinical.

P

Phlebotomy Workbook for the Multiskilled Healthcare Professional. Susan K. Strasinger & Marjorie Di Lorenzo. (Illus.). 382p. (C). 1995. pap. text 31.95 (0-8036-8107-0) Davis Co.

Phlegon of Tralles' Book of Marvels. Tr. & Comment by William Hansen. 256p. 1996. pap. 23.95 (0-85989-425-8, Pub. by Univ Exeter Pr) Northwestern U Pr.

Phlegraean Fields. Old Vicarage Publications Staff. 168p. (C). 1982. pap. text 45.00 (0-7855-3130-0, Pub. by Old Vicarage) St Mut.

Phloem. Katherine Esau. (Handbuch der Pflanzenanatomie Encyclopedia of Plant Anatomy - Traite d' Anatomie Vegetale Ser.: Vol. 5, Pt. 2). (Illus.). ix, 505p. 1969. 111.00 (3-443-14002-5, Pub. by Gebruder Borntraeger) Balogh.

Phloem Loading & Related Processes. Ed. by W. Eschrich & H. Lorenzen. 378p. (C). 1980. pap. text 60.00 (3-437-30319-8) Lubrecht & Cramer.

Phlyogenetic Systematics of the Drynarioideae (Polypodiaceae) M. C. Roos. (Verhandelingen der Koninklijke Nederlandse Akademie van Wetenschappen, Afd. Natuurkunde Ser.: No. 85). 318p. 1987. pap. text 59.50 (0-444-85668-4) Elsevier.

Phobia: Psychological & Pharmacological Treatment. Ed. by Matig Mavissaka & David H. Barlow. LC 80-15306. 256p. 1981. lib. bdg. 35.00 (0-89862-602-1) Guilford Pubns.

***Phobia Free.** Harold N. Levinson & Steven Carter. 304p. 1999. 7.98 (1-56731-318-3, MJF Bks) Fine Comms.

Phobia Free: A Medical Breakthrough Linking Ninety Percent of all Phobias & Panic Attacks to a Hidden Physical Problem. Harold N. Levinson & Steven Carter. LC 86-6303. 300p. 1988. pap. 15.95 (0-87131-539-4) M Evans.

Phobias. Bruce Goldberg. 1981. 12.00 incl. audio (1-885577-49-4) B Goldberg.

Phobias. Ed. by Moraitis. (Psychoanalytic Inquiry Ser.: Vol. 11, No. 3). 1995. 20.00 (0-88163-950-8) Analytic Pr.

Phobias: A Handbook of Theory, Research & Treatment. Graham Davey. LC 96-32895. 470p. 1997. 179.95 (0-471-96983-4) Wiley.

***Phobias: A Handbook of Theory, Research & Treatment.** Ed. by Graham C. L. Davey. 470p. 2000. pap. 95.00 (0-471-49220-5) Wiley.

Phobias: Everything You Wanted to Know but Were Afraid to Ask. Judy Monroe. LC 95-32931. (Issues in Focus Ser.). (Illus.). 112p. (YA). (gr. 6 up). 1996. lib. bdg. 20.95 (0-89490-723-9) Enslow Pubs.

Phobias: Stories of Deepest Fear. Martin Greenberg. 1994. mass mkt. 5.50 (0-671-79237-7) PB.

Phobias: The Crippling Fears. Arthur Henley & Marshall P. Primack. 224p. 1987. 15.95 (0-8184-0425-6) Carol Pub Group.

Phobias: The Crippling Fears. Arthur Henly. 224p. 1988. pap. 3.95 (0-380-70659-8, Avon Bks) Morrow Avon.

Phobias & Disorders: Index of Modern Information. Samuel M. Morris. LC 88-47614. 150p. 1988. 47.50 (0-88164-834-5); pap. 44.50 (0-88164-835-3) ABBE Pubs Assn.

Phobic & Obsessive-Compulsive Disorders: Theory, Research, & Practice. Paul M. Emmelkamp. (Behavior Therapy Ser.). (Illus.). 366p. (C). 1982. 96.00 (0-306-41044-3, Plenum Trade) Perseus Pubng.

***Phobic Disorders & Panic in Adults: A Guide to Assessment & Treatment.** Martin M. Antony & Richard P. Swinson. LC 00-38094. 2000. write for info. (1-55798-696-7) Am Psychol.

Phobos Lock. Lynard Barnes. 1997. pap. text 9.95 (0-9668484-0-3) Trices Co.

Phocion the Good. Lawrence A. Tritle. 272p. (C). 1988. lib. bdg. 55.00 (0-7099-4363-6) Routledge.

Phoebe. Phoebe Smith. LC 79-65732. (Orig.). 1979. pap. 3.50 (0-9602976-1-8) P Smith.

Phoebe, Vol. 1. Marilyn Kaye. LC 86-29397. (Sisters Ser.). 160p. (J). (gr. 3-7). 1987. pap. 4.95 (0-15-200431-9, Gulliver Bks) Harcourt.

Phoebe Adams: The Eye, the Mind, the Hand. Eleanor Heartney & Jim Quinn. LC 93-77827. (Illus.). 36p. (Orig.). 1993. pap. text 20.00 (1-879173-13-1) Locks Gallery.

***Phoebe & the Gypsy.** Andrea Spalding. LC 98-83010. (Young Reader Ser.). (Illus.). 96p. (J). (gr. 3-6). 1999. pap. 3.99 (1-55143-135-1) Orca Bk Pubs.

Phoebe & the Monster Maze. Caroline Castle. (Illus.). 32p. (J). (ps-2). 1998. 19.95 (0-09-176714-8, Pub. by Hutchnson) Trafalgar.

***Phoebe & the River Flute.** M. C. Helldorfer. (Illus.). 32p. (J). (gr. k-3). 2000. 15.95 (0-385-32338-7) Doubleday.

Phoebe & the Spelling Bee. Barney Saltzberg. LC 94-37547. (Illus.). 32p. (J). (gr. k-3). 1997. 14.95 (0-7868-0140-9, Pub. by Hyprn Child); lib. bdg. 14.89 (0-7868-2114-0, Pub. by Hyprn Child) Little.

Phoebe Chronicles, Vol. 1. Keith Leonard. LC 97-199837. (Illus.). 64p. 1997. pap. 9.95 (1-56163-182-5, Amerotica) NBM.

Phoebe Chronicles Vol. 2: Angels of Death. Keith Leonard. (Illus.). 64p. 1998. pap. 9.95 (1-56163-221-X, Amerotica) NBM.

Phoebe Deane. Grace Livingston Hill. reprint ed. lib. bdg. 25.95 (0-89190-044-6, Rivercity Pr) Amereon Ltd.

Phoebe Flower's Adventures: That's What Kids Are For. Barbara A. Roberts. LC 98-7706. (Phoebe Flower's Adventures Ser.). (J). 1998. 5.95 (0-9660366-2-X) Advantage Books.

Phoebe Palmer: Her Life & Thought. Harold E. Raser. LC 86-31251. (Studies in Women & Religion: Vol. 22). 392p. 1987. lib. bdg. 99.95 (0-88946-527-4) E Mellen.

Phoebe Palmer: Selected Writings. Ed. by Thomas C. Oden. (Sources of American Spirituality Ser.). 384p. 1988. 24.95 (0-8091-0405-9) Paulist Pr.

Phoebe the Spy. Judith B. Griffin. 48p. (J). (gr. 4-7). 1991. pap. 2.99 (0-590-42432-7) Scholastic Inc.

Phoebe the Spy. Judith B. Griffin. (J). 1977. 9.19 (0-606-04079-X, Pub. by Turtleback) Demco.

Phoebe the Spy. Judith B. Griffin. (J). (gr. 4-6). 1979. reprint ed. pap. 1.50 (0-590-05758-8) Scholastic Inc.

Phoebe's Fabulous Father. Louisa Campbell & Bridget S. Taylor. LC 95-34811. (Illus.). 32p. (J). 1996. 14.00 (0-15-200996-5) Harcourt.

Phoebe's Folly. Kathleen Karr. (Petticoat Party Ser.). 1997. 9.60 (0-606-11742-3, Pub. by Turtleback) Demco.

Phoebe's Fortune. Holly Warriner. LC 98-48777. (Spell Casters Ser.: No. 6). 144p. (J). (gr. 3-7). 1999. pap. 3.99 (0-689-81904-8) S&S Childrens.

Phoebe's Knee. Barbara Comfort. 220p. (Orig.). 1986. pap. 3.95 (0-9608726-3-9) Norton.

Phoebe's Knee. Barbara Comfort. LC 94-171443. (Tish McWhinny Mystery Ser.). 224p. (Orig.). 1994. pap. 7.95 (0-88150-295-2, Foul Play) Norton.

***Phoebe's Lost Treasure.** Barbara A. Roberts. LC 99-39427. (Phoebe Flower's Adventures Ser.). (Illus.). (J). 1999. write for info. (0-9660366-6-2) Advantage Books.

Phoebe's Nest: An Illustrated Collection of Poems & Stories. James S. Benedict. (Illus.). 190p. 1998. 15.00 (1-892015-00-5); pap. 10.00 (1-892015-01-3) JB Press.

Phoebe's Parade. Claudia Mills. LC 93-21861. (Illus.). 32p. (J). (gr. k-3). 1994. mass mkt. 14.95 (0-02-767012-0, Mac Bks Young Read) S&S Childrens.

Phoebe's Revolt. Natalie Babbitt. LC 68-13679. (Illus.). 40p. (J). (ps-3). 1988. pap. 3.95 (0-374-45792-1) FS&G.

Phoebe's Secret Diary: Daily Life & First Romance of a Colonial Girl, 1742. Joyce K. Blackburn. (Illus.). 56p. (Orig.). (J). (gr. 5-8). 1993. pap. 7.95 (0-930803-01-9) Fort Frederica.

Phoenicia. George Rawlinson. LC 70-39206. (Select Bibliographies Reprint Ser.). 1977. reprint ed. 30.95 (0-8369-6808-5) Ayer.

Phoenicia & Western Asia. Raymond Weill. 208p. 1992. pap. 20.00 (0-89005-348-0) Ares.

Phoenicia & Western Asia to the Macedonian Conquest. Raymond Weill. 1978. 19.95 (0-405-09140-0, 1736) Ayer.

Phoenician Bronze & Silver Bowls from Cyprus & the Mediterranean. fac. ed. Glenn Markoe. LC 83-18305. (University of California Publication, Classical Studies: No. 26). (Illus.). 392p. 1985. pap. 121.60 (0-7837-8612-3, 205916700008) Bks Demand.

***Phoenician Coins & Their Countermarks.** Mark A. McMenamin. (Illus.). 68p. 2000. pap. 20.00 (0-9651136-7-1) Meanma Pr.

Phoenician Origin of Britons Scots & Anglo-Saxons. L. A. Waddell. (Illus.). 450p. 15.00 (0-944379-31-1); pap. 10.00 (0-944379-32-X) CPA Bk Pub.

***Phoenician-Punic Grammar.** Charles R. Krahmalkov. LC 00-41424. (Handbuch der Orientalistik, Erste Abteilung, Nahe und Mittlere Osten Ser.). 2000. write for info. (90-04-11771-7) Brill Academic Pubs.

Phoenician Women see Euripides: Three Tragedies

Phoenician Women. Tr. by Peter Burian & Brian Swann. (Greek Tragedy in New Translations Ser.). 112p. 1992. pap. 7.95 (0-19-507708-3) OUP.

Phoenicians. 9.95 (0-86685-705-2, LDL60E, Pub. by Librairie du Liban) Intl Bk Ctr.

Phoenicians. Librairie du Liban Staff. (J). 1991. 9.95 (0-86685-570-X) Intl Bk Ctr.

***Phoenicians.** Glenn Markoe. 200p. 2000. 45.00 (0-520-22613-5, Pub. by U CA Pr) Cal Prin Full Svc.

Phoenicians. Ed. by Sabatino Moscati. (Illus.). 672p. 1999. pap. 35.00 (0-8478-2194-3, Pub. by Rizzoli Intl) St Martin.

Phoenicians. Pamela Odijk. (Ancient World Ser.). (Illus.). 48p. (J). (gr. 5-8). 1989. 7.95 (0-382-24266-1); teacher ed. 4.50 (0-382-24281-5); lib. bdg. 14.95 (0-382-09891-9) Silver Burdett Pr.

Phoenicians & the West: Politics, Colonies & Trade. Maria E. Aubet. (Illus.). 366p. 1996. pap. text 23.95 (0-521-56598-7) Cambridge U Pr.

***Phoenicians, Fakes & Barry Fell: Solving the Mystery of Carthaginian Coins Found in America.** Mark A. McMenamin. (Illus.). 43p. 2000. pap. 30.00 (1-893882-01-2) Meanma Pr.

Phoenissae of Euripides. Euripides. Ed. by W. R. Connor & John Powell. LC 78-18595. (Greek Texts & Commentaries Ser.). 1979. reprint ed. lib. bdg. 21.95 (0-405-11436-2) Ayer.

***Phoenix.** Clayton Anderson. (Illus.). 2000. pap. 12.95 (2-89464-386-1) Ulysses Travel.

Phoenix. Ed. by N. F. Blake. 136p. 1990. pap. text 15.00 (0-85989-342-1, Pub. by Univ Exeter Pr) Northwestern U Pr.

Phoenix. Steven Brust. 1990. mass mkt. 4.99 (0-441-66225-0) Ace Bks.

Phoenix. Caroline Gray. (Colonial Ser.: Vol. 2). 256p. 1998. 25.00 (0-7278-5378-3) Severn Hse.

Phoenix. Manly P. Hall. Date not set. pap. 24.95 (0-89314-839-3) Philos Res.

Phoenix. Kelly Marshall. Ed. by Moi Tayler. 448p. (Orig.). 1996. pap. 6.99 (0-9646250-1-6) Heathchris Bks.

Phoenix. Melissa Pritchard. LC 91-71514. 133p. (Orig.). (C). 1991. pap. text 8.95 (0-943433-08-8) Cane Hill Pr.

Phoenix. Anne Reynolds Metzger. 1998. pap. write for info. (1-57553-909-8) Watermrk Pr.

Phoenix. Barry Sadler. (Casca: No. 14). 192p. 1987. mass mkt. 3.99 (0-515-09471-4, Jove) Berkley Pub.

***Phoenix.** large type ed. Caroline Gray. 400p. 2000. 31.99 (0-7089-4182-6) Ulverscroft.

***Phoenix: A Brother's Life.** J. D. Dolan. LC 99-33608. 224p. 2000. 22.00 (0-375-40342-6) Knopf.

Phoenix: Fascism in Our Time. A. James Gregor. LC 99-20842. 223p. 1999. 32.95 (1-56000-422-3) Transaction Pubs.

Phoenix: Living with the Land. Ed. by Joan S. Isom. 80p. 1989. pap. 7.00 (0-9615355-5-5) NE St U Arts & Letters.

Phoenix: The Fall & Rise of Home Videogames. Leonard Herman. LC 94-92417. 310p. (Orig.). 1994. pap. 12.99 (0-9643848-8-4) Rolenta Pr.

Phoenix: The Fall & Rise of Videogames. 2nd rev. ed. Leonard Herman. LC 94-92417. (Illus.). 330p. 1997. pap. 19.95 (0-9643848-2-5) Rolenta Pr.

Phoenix: The History of a Southwestern Metropolis. Bradford Luckingham. LC 88-24276. 316p. 1995. pap. 12.95 (0-8165-1116-0) U of Ariz Pr.

Phoenix: Therapeutic Patterns of Milton H. Erickson. David Gordon & Maribeth Meyers-Anderson. LC 81-85263. 1981. pap. 19.95 (0-916990-10-9) META Pubns.

Phoenix - from Legend to Reality. Michel F. Sarda. LC 88-51013. (Illus.). 136p. 1988. reprint ed. 29.95 (0-942078-15-2) Bridgewood Pr.

Phoenix Agenda: Power to Transform Your Workplace. John A. Whiteside. LC 93-60675. 318p. 1993. 25.00 (0-939246-47-3) Wiley.

Phoenix Agenda: Power to Transform Your Workplace. John A. Whiteside. 336p. 1995. 29.95 (0-471-13190-3) Wiley.

Phoenix & the Ashes. Geoffrey Nash. 160p. 1985. pap. 8.25 (0-85398-199-X) G Ronald Pub.

Phoenix & the Birds of Prey: The CIA's Secret Campaign to Destroy the Viet Cong. Mark Moyar. (Illus.). 464p. 1997. 29.95 (1-55750-593-4) Naval Inst Pr.

Phoenix & the Carpet. Edith Nesbit. (Illus.). (YA). (gr. 5 up). 1996. pap. 4.99 (0-14-036739-X) Viking Penguin.

Phoenix & the Carpet. Edith Nesbit. 1999. lib. bdg. 23.95 (1-56723-170-5) Yestermorrow.

Phoenix & the Flame: Catalonia & the Counter Reformation. Henry Kamen. LC 92-41268. 528p. (C). 1993. 55.00 (0-300-05416-5) Yale U Pr.

Phoenix & Vicinity Street Guide & Directory: 1999 Edition. Thomas Bros. Maps Staff. (Illus.). 216p. 1998. pap. 14.95 (1-58174-036-0) Thomas Bros Maps.

***Phoenix Arizona.** Rand McNally Staff. 1999. pap. text 17.95 (0-528-97719-9) Rand McNally.

Phoenix, Arizona. Rand McNally Staff. 1997. 5.95 (0-528-94532-7) Rand McNally.

Phoenix Assurance & the Development of British Insurance Vol. 2: The Era of the Insurance Giants, 1870-1984. Clive Trebilcock. (Illus.). 1056p. (C). 1998. text 150.00 (0-521-25415-9) Cambridge U Pr.

Phoenix at the Fountain: Images of Woman & Eternity in Lactantius's Carmen de Ave Phoenice & the Old English Phoenix. Carol F. Heffernan. LC 86-40368. (Illus.). 176p. 1988. 30.00 (0-87413-313-0) U Delaware Pr.

Phoenix Award of the Children's Literature Association, 1985-1989, Vol. 1. Ed. by Alethea Helbig & Agnes Perkins. LC 93-12580. (Children's Literature Association Ser.). 182p. 1993. 26.00 (0-8108-2677-1) Scarecrow.

Phoenix Award of the Children's Literature Association, 1990-1994, Vol. 2. Ed. by Alethea Helbig & Agnes Perkins. LC 96-17613. (Illus.). 304p. 1996. 45.00 (0-8108-3191-0) Scarecrow.

Phoenix, AZ. (Streetfinder Ser.). (Illus.). 1995. pap. 15.95 (0-528-96928-5) Rand McNally.

Phoenix Baby Resource Guide. 2nd rev. ed. Jane R. McCauley. (Illus.). 300p. pap. 9.95 (0-9637868-1-4) AZ Baby Res.

Phoenix Baby Resource Guide, 1993-1994. Trini Newquist. (Illus.). 304p. (Orig.). (C). 1993. pap. text 9.95 (0-9637868-0-6) AZ Baby Res.

Phoenix Bird Chinaware, Bk. 1. Joan C. Oates. (Illus.). 110p. 1989. reprint ed. pap. 15.00 (0-9617047-0-5) J Oates.

Phoenix Bird Chinaware, Bk. 2. Joan C. Oates. (Illus.). 112p. 1985. pap. 14.95 (0-9617047-1-3) J Oates.

Phoenix Bird Chinaware, Bk. 3. Joan C. Oates. (Illus.). 96p. 1986. reprint ed. pap. 14.50 (0-9617047-2-1) J Oates.

Phoenix Bird Chinaware, Bk. 4. Joan C. Oates. (Illus.). 100p. 1989. pap. 15.00 (0-9617047-3-X) J Oates.

Phoenix Birds. James Kavanagh. (Pocket Naturalist Ser.). (Illus.). 1999. 5.95 (1-889903-75-2, Pub. by Waterford WA) Falcon Pub Inc.

Phoenix Cafe. Gwyneth Jones. LC 97-29862. 1997. text 24.95 (0-312-86534-1) St Martin.

Phoenix Caged. John-Allen Price. 448p. 1993. mass mkt. 4.50 (0-8217-4192-6, Zebra Kensgtn) Kensgtn Pub Corp.

Phoenix Cards: Reading & Interpreting Past-Life Influences with the Phoenix Deck, Set. Susan Sheppard. (Illus.). 260p. 1990. boxed set 29.95 (0-89281-310-5) Inner Tradit.

Phoenix Central Library: Bruder/DWL Architects. Oscar R. Ojeda. (Single Building Ser.). (Illus.). 120p. 1999. pap. 19.99 (1-56496-525-2) Rockport Pubs.

Phoenix Chefs Book. William Struns. Ed. by R. McMinn. 120p. (Orig.). 1989. pap. text 6.95 (0-935201-88-2) Affordable Adven.

***Phoenix Code.** Catherine Asaro. 2000. mass mkt. 5.99 (0-553-58154-6) Bantam.

Phoenix Concept. Trace Skeen. 320p. 1999. pap. write for info. (0-7392-0224-3, PO3260) Morris Pubng.

Phoenix Coyotes. Morgan Hughes & Paul Joseph. LC 98-13893. (Inside the NHL Ser.). (J). 1998. 16.48 (1-57765-063-8) ABDO Pub Co.

Phoenix Cuisine. Intro. by Frank Aaron. (Phoenix Cuisine Ser.: Vol. 4). 164p. 1994. pap. text 4.95 (0-9632234-5-3) R Hart Mktg.

Phoenix Cuisine, Vol. 3. rev. ed. Intro. by Frank Aaron. 150p. 1994. pap. text 4.95 (0-9632234-4-5) R Hart Mktg.

Phoenix Cuisine, Vol. 5. rev. ed. Intro. by Frani Aaron. 160p. 1995. pap. 5.95 (0-9632234-6-1) R Hart Mktg.

Phoenix Cuisine, 1997, Vol. 6. rev. ed. Intro. by Frank Aaron. (Illus.). 208p. 1996. pap. 7.95 (0-9632234-9-6) R Hart Mktg.

Phoenix Cuisine, 1993, Vol. II. Ed. by Frank Aaron. (Illus.). 120p. (Orig.). 1992. pap. 4.95 (0-9632234-2-9) R Hart Mktg.

Phoenix Cuisine, 1992. Frank Aaron. 100p. 1992. 9.95 (0-9632234-0-2) R Hart Mktg.

Phoenix Cuisine '99, Vol. 9. Frank Aaron. 1999. mass mkt. 7.95 (1-893350-51-7) R Hart Mktg.

***Phoenix Cuisine 2000.** Ed. by Frank Aaron. (Illus.). 195p. 1999. pap. 8.95 (1-893350-01-0) R Hart Mktg.

Phoenix Cuisine 1998, Vol. 7. rev. ed. Intro. by Frank Aaron. (Illus.). 194p. 1997. pap. 7.95 (0-9632234-7-X) R Hart Mktg.

Phoenix Datebook. rev. ed. Kurt W. Kretsinger. 136p. 1991. 4.77 (0-929821-03-3) Datebook Pub.

Phoenix Dimension. Kent R. Brown. 58p. 1996. pap. 5.50 (0-87129-650-0, P19) Dramatic Pub.

Phoenix Dine-a-Mate. 272p. 1994. pap. 30.00 (1-57393-017-2) Dine-A-Mate.

Phoenix Dine-a-Mate Book. 240p. 1996. pap. text 30.00 (0-614-20361-9) Dine-A-Mate.

***Phoenix Entertainment, 2000.** (Illus.). 854p. 1999. pap. 35.00 (1-58553-049-2, 0047) Enter Pubns.

Phoenix Equation. Franklin W. Dixon. Ed. by Anne Greenberg. (Hardy Boys Casefiles Ser.: No. 66). 160p. (Orig.). (YA). (gr. 6 up). 1992. pap. 3.99 (0-671-73102-5, Archway) PB.

***Phoenix Eyes & Other Stories.** Russell Charles Leong. 208p. 2000. 30.00 (0-295-97944-5); pap. 16.95 (0-295-97945-3) U of Wash Pr.

Phoenix Fire. Elizabeth Forrest. 368p. (Orig.). 1992. mass mkt. 4.99 (0-88677-515-9, Pub. by DAW Bks) Penguin Putnam.

Phoenix Flight Manual: Rising above the Ashes of Ordinary Existence. Anthony Dallmann-Jones. LC 95-196784. 209p. (Orig.). 1995. pap. 14.95 (1-881952-49-5) Three Blue Herons.

Phoenix from the Ashes: The Literature of the Remade World, 30. Ed. by Carl B. Yoke. LC 87-12035. (Contributions to the Study of Science Fiction & Fantasy Ser.: No. 30). 256p. 1987. 65.00 (0-313-24328-X, YFA/, Greenwood Pr) Greenwood.

Phoenix Generation. Henry Williamson. 1999. pap. text 14.75 (0-7509-2152-8) A Sutton.

Phoenix Gone, the Terrace Empty: Poems. Marilyn Chin. LC 93-33206. (Illus.). 104p. (Orig.). 1994. pap. 11.95 (0-915943-87-5) Milkweed Ed.

Phoenix Guards. Steven Brust. 512p. 1995. 4.99 (0-8125-0689-8, Pub. by Tor Bks) St Martin.

Phoenix in Perspective: Reflections on Developing the Desert. Grady Gammage, Jr. (Phoenix Dialogues Ser.: Vol. II). (Illus.). 190p. 1999. pap. 19.95 (1-884320-17-1) ASU Herberger Ctr.

Phoenix in the Ashes: The Rise & Fall of Koch Coalition in New York City Politics. John H. Mollenkopf. (Illus.). 280p. 1992. text 47.50 (0-691-07854-8, Pub. by Princeton U Pr) Cal Prin Full Svc.

Phoenix in the Ashes: The Rise & Fall of the Coalition in New York City Politics. John H. Mollenkopf. 280p. (C). 1992. pap. text 15.95 (0-691-03673-X, Pub. by Princeton U Pr) Cal Prin Full Svc.

Phoenix in the Labyrinth. C. B. Jones. 182p. (Orig.). 1995. pap. text 14.95 (1-882658-02-7) Human Potent Fnd.

Phoenix in the Twentieth Century: Essays in Community History. Ed. by G. Wesley Johnson, Jr. LC 92-54156. 1993. pap. 24.95 (0-8061-2468-7) U of Okla Pr.

Phoenix in the Twentieth Century: Essays in Community History. Ed. by G. Wesley Johnson, Jr. (Illus.). 288p. 1999. reprint ed. text 23.00 (0-7881-6249-7) DIANE Pub.

Phoenix Indian School: Forced Assimilation in Arizona, 1891-1935. Robert A. Trennert, Jr. LC 87-40560. (Illus.). 272p. 1988. 29.95 (0-8061-2104-1) U of Okla Pr.

Phoenix Indian School: The Second Half-Century. Dorothy R. Parker. LC 96-31381. 96p. 1996. 14.95 (0-8165-1679-0) U of Ariz Pr.

***Phoenix JobBank.** 8th ed. 320p. 1999. pap. 16.95 (1-58062-235-6) Adams Media.

Phoenix Magazine's 1998-1999 Bargain Shopper's Guide. Ed. by Robert Stieve. 128p. 1998. pap. 6.99 (1-893048-00-4) Phoenix Magazine.

Phoenix Metropolitan Street Atlas - 1999. (Illus.). 130p. 1999. ring bd. 17.95 (1-887749-15-2) Wide World Maps.

***Phoenix Metropolitan Street Atlas - 2000.** (Illus.). 136p. 2000. ring bd. 18.95 (1-887749-20-9) Wide World Maps.

Phoenix, Michigan's History. (Copper Country Local History Ser.: Vol. 34). (Illus.). 120p. 1989. 3.00 (0-942363-33-7) C J Monette.

Phoenix Mountn Bikes II. Douglas J. McQuaig. (C). 1995. pap. write for info. (0-395-77034-3) HM.

Phoenix Nest, 1593. Ed. by Hyder E. Rollins. LC 31-4893. (Illus.). 285p. 1959. 16.50 (0-674-66610-0) HUP.

Phoenix Odyssey. Richard P. Henrick. 368p. 1995. mass mkt. 4.99 (0-8217-5016-X, Zebra Kensgtn) Kensgtn Pub Corp.

Phoenix of Love. Susan Shonberg. (March Madness Ser.). 1997. per. 4.99 (0-373-28955-3, 1-28955-2) Harlequin Bks.

Phoenix of Rennes: The Life & Poetry of John of St. Samson, 1571-1636. Robert Stefanotti. LC 93-31707. (Medieval & Early Modern Mysticism Ser.: Vol. 2). IX, 201p. (C). 1994. text 43.95 (0-8204-2266-5) P Lang Pubng.

Phoenix of the Elizabeth: The Only American City to be Completely Destroyed & Rebuilt. Ed. by Calvert W. Tazewell. LC 90-80508. 125p. (Orig.). 1991. pap. 15.00 (1-878515-14-4) W S Dawson.

P

An Asterisk (*) at the beginning of an entry indicates that the title is appearing for the first time.

Phoenix-Oklahoma Poets. Ed. by Joan S. Isom. Tr. by Adela T. King. 78p. (Orig.). 1988. pap. 6.00 (*0-9615355-2-0*) NE St U Arts & Letters.

Phoenix Operator-Owner Manual. Jesus Sananda & Michael St. Germain. (Phoenix Journals). 154p. 1993. pap. 6.00 (*1-56935-018-3*) Phoenix Source.

Phoenix over the Nile: A History of Egyptian Air Power, 1932-1994. Lon O. Nordeen & David Nicolle. LC 95-30047. (Illus.). 368p. 1996. 55.00 (*1-56098-626-3*) Smithsonian.

Phoenix Papers: Twenty-Three Lawrence Poets. Ed. by Stephen Addiss & Stanley Lombardo. LC 93-83842. 140p. 1993. pap. write for info. (*0-9632475-1-4*) Penthe Pub.

Phoenix Paradox: A Study of Renewal Through Change in the "Collected Poems" & "Last Poems" of D. H. Lawrence. Gail P. Mandell. LC 83-10563. 288p. 1984. 26.95 (*0-8093-1121-6*) S Ill U Pr.

Phoenix Phenomenon. Fred Holden. (C). 1984. pap. 3.50 (*0-9621767-1-0*) Phoenix Enterps.

Phoenix Phenomenon: Rising from the Ashes of Grief. J. Jozefowski. LC 98-54401. 9200p. 1999. 40.00 (*0-7657-0209-6*) Aronson.

Phoenix Program. Douglas Valentine. 480p. 1992. pap. 12.50 (*0-380-70901-5*, Avon Bks) Morrow Avon.

Phoenix Project. H. W. Braun. 1987. pap. 3.95 (*0-685-24745-7*) Research Analysts.

Phoenix Project: An Energy Transition to Renewable Resources. Harry W. Braun, III. 272p. (Orig.). 1990. 18.95 (*0-924600-00-4*); pap. 14.95 (*0-924600-01-2*) Research Analysts.

Phoenix Renewed: The Survival & Mutation of Utopian Thought in North American Science Fiction, 1965-1982. rev. ed. Hoda M. Zaki. LC 93-30397. (I. O. Evans Studies in the Philosophy & Criticism of Literature: No. 18). 112p. 1993. pap. 17.00 (*1-55742-127-7*) Millefleurs.

Phoenix Returns: Aquarius Dawns - Liberation Begins. 4th ed. Kristina Gale-Kumar. (Illus.). 480p. 1990. pap. 14.95 (*0-9611204-0-1*) Cardinal Enter.

Phoenix Rises: The Phenomenal Growth of Eight Chinese Churches. Ed. by Leslie T. Lyall. 145p. (Orig.). 1992. pap. 5.95 (*981-3009-04-7*) OMF Bks.

Phoenix Rising. (Pathways to Critical Thinking Ser.). 32p. (YA). 1997. pap. text. write for info. (*1-58303-036-0*) Pthways Pubng.

Phoenix Rising. Karen Hesse. (YA). (gr. 6 up). 1995. write for info. (*0-8050-3108-1*) H Holt & Co.

Phoenix Rising. Karen Hesse. 192p. (YA). (gr. 6 up). 1995. pap. 4.99 (*0-14-037628-3*, PuffinBks) Peng Put Young Read.

Phoenix Rising. Karen Hesse. (YA). (gr. 6 up). 1995. 10.09 (*0-606-08012-0*, Pub. by Turtleback) Demco.

Phoenix Rising. John J. Nance. 1995. mass mkt. 6.99 (*0-449-18290-8*, GM) Fawcett.

Phoenix Rising: Impressions of Vietnam. Zoe Schramm-Evans. 207p. 1998. text 20.00 (*0-7881-5598-9*) DIANE Pub.

Phoenix Rising: Impressions of Vietnam. Zoe Schramm-Evans. 1996. 20.00 (*0-614-97028-8*) HarpC.

Phoenix Rising: Impressions of Vietnam. Zoe Schramm-Evans. 256p. 1996. 20.00 (*0-04-440960-5*) Harper SF.

Phoenix Rising: Impressions of Vietnam. Zoe Schramm-Evans. 1993. pap. 15.00 (*0-04-440965-6*, Pub. by Rivers Oram) NYU Pr.

Phoenix Rising: New Jewish Voices. Roberta Kalechofsky et al. LC 81-83902. (Echad: a Whole Global Anthology Ser.: No. 3). 270p. 1982. pap. 12.00 (*0-916288-11-0*) Micah Pubns.

Phoenix Rising: No-Eyes' Vision of the Changes to Come. Mary S. Rain. 176p. 1993. pap. 11.95 (*1-878901-62-1*) Hampton Roads Pub Co.

Phoenix Rising: Poems. Vega Press Staff. LC 95-10116. 128p. 1995. per. 10.00 (*1-880729-12-1*) Vega Pr.

Phoenix Rising V Vol. XIV: Proceedings of the 14th International Conference on the Study of Shamanism & Alternative Modes of Healing 1997, Santa Sabina Center, San Rafael, California, August 31-September 2, 1997. unabridged ed. Ed. by Ruth-Inge Heinze. LC 97-44898. (Illus.). 266p. (C). 1997. pap. text 21.75 (*0-945875-18-5*) Independent Scholars Asia Inc.

Phoenix Rising IV: Proceedings of the 13th International Conference on the Study of Shamanism & Alternate Modes of Healing Held at the Santa Sabina Center, San Rafael, California, August 31 to September 2, 1996. Ed. by Ruth-Inge Heinze. LC 96-29973. (Illus.). 392p. (C). 1996. pap. 21.75 (*0-945875-17-7*) Independent Scholars Asia Inc.

***Phoenix Rising VII: Proceedings of the 16th International Conference on the Study of Shamanism & Alternative Modes of Healing, 1999, Santa Sabina Center, San Rafael, California, September 4-6, 1999.** unabridged ed. Ed. by Ruth-Inge Heinze. (Illus.). 289p. 1999. 21.75 (*0-945875-20-7*) Independent Scholars Asia Inc.

Phoenix Rising VI: Proceedings of the 15th International Conference on the Study of Shamanism & Alternative Modes of Healing 1998, Santa Sabina Center, San Rafael, California, September 5-7, 1998. unabridged ed. Ed. by Ruth-Inge Heinze. LC 98-32306. (Proceedings of the International Conference on the Study of Shamanism & Alternative Modes of Healing: No. 15). (Illus.). 249p. (C). 1998. pap. 21.75 (*0-945875-19-3*) Independent Scholars Asia Inc.

Phoenix Rising Yoga Therapy: A Bridge from Body to Soul. Michael Lee. LC 97-29358. (Illus.). 220p. 1997. pap. 11.95 (*1-55874-513-0*) Health Comm.

Phoenix Rock II. 2nd rev. ed. Greg Opland. (Illus.). 272p. 1996. pap. 25.00 (*1-57540-023-5*) Falcon Pub Inc.

Phoenix Seduction. Cap Parlier. 1997. mass mkt. 4.99 (*1-55197-238-7*) Picasso Publ.

***Phoenix Solution.** A. Alford. 1998. text 40.00 (*0-340-69614-1*, Pub. by Hodder & Stought Ltd) Trafalgar.

Phoenix Solutions. Don Peel. 256p. 1990. per. write for info. (*0-8187-0131-5*) Harlo Press.

Phoenix Sub Zero. Michael DiMercurio. 464p. (Orig.). 1995. mass mkt. 6.99 (*0-451-40603-6*, Onyx) NAL.

Phoenix Suns see Pro Basketball Today

Phoenix Suns. Bob Italia. LC 96-40305. (Inside The NBA Ser.). (Illus.). 32p. (J). (gr. 3-8). 1997. lib. bdg. 16.95 (*1-56239-770-2*) ABDO Pub Co.

Phoenix Suns Basketball Team. David Pietrusza. LC 96-26412. (Great Sports Teams Ser.). (Illus.). 48p. (YA). (gr. 4-10). 1997. lib. bdg. 18.95 (*0-89490-795-6*) Enslow Pubs.

Phoenix Suns Basketball Team. David Pietrusza. LC 96-26412. (Great Sports Teams Ser.). (Illus.). 48p. (YA). (gr. 4-10). 1997. pap. 9.95 (*0-7660-1752-4*) Enslow Pubs.

Phoenix Too Frequent. Christopher Fry. 1952. pap. 3.25 (*0-8222-0891-1*) Dramatists Play.

Phoenix Transformed: The Reconstruction of Education in Post-War Hong Kong. LC 93-26314. (East Asian Historical Monographs). 296p. 1994. 55.00 (*0-19-585520-5*) OUP.

Phoenix Tree & Other Stories. Satoko Kizaki. Tr. by Carol A. Flath. 242p. 1990. 18.95 (*0-87011-982-6*) Kodansha.

Phoenix Tree & Other Stories. Satoko Kizaki. Tr. by Carol A. Flath. (Japan's Women Writers Ser.). 242p. 1993. pap. 9.95 (*4-7700-1790-1*) Kodansha.

Phoenix Valley of the Sun Street Guide. (Illus.). 124p. (Orig.). 1997. pap. 3.95 (*1-887749-08-X*, 97896) Wide World Maps.

***Phoenix Valley of the Sun Street Guide.** Phoenix Mapping Service Staff. 124p. 1999. pap. 3.95 (*1-887749-17-9*) Wide World Maps.

Phoenix Volunteer Fire Company of Mobile, 1838-1888. Caldwell Delaney. (Illus.). (Orig.). 1967. pap. 2.00 (*0-914334-00-X*) Museum Mobile.

Phoenix Voyage. Henry. 2000. pap. text 24.95 (*0-07-135527-8*) McGraw.

Phoenix with Fetters: Studies in 19th & Early 20th Century Hebrew Fiction. David Patterson. (Oxford Centre for Postgraduate Hebrew Studies). 200p. 1988. 55.00 (*0-8476-7564-5*) Rowman.

Phoenix Without the Ashes: Achieving Organizational Excellence Through Common Sense Management. Gary English. LC 98-16304. 256p. 1998. 34.95 (*1-57444-219-8*, SL2198) St Lucie Pr.

Phoenixiana. George H. Derby. 1992. reprint ed. lib. bdg. 75.00 (*0-7812-5025-0*) Rprt Serv.

Phoenixiana: or Sketches & Burlesques. George H. Derby. LC 72-174198. reprint ed. 42.50 (*0-404-05045-X*) AMS Pr.

***Phoenix's Hidden History: Archaeological Investigations at Blocks 72 & 73.** J. Homer Thiel. (Anthropological Papers: No. 26). (Illus.). 478p. 1998. pap. 49.95 (*1-886398-39-9*) Desert Archaeol.

Phog Allen: The Father of Basketball Coaching. Blair Kerkhoff. (Illus.). 256p. 1996. 19.95 (*1-57028-111-4*, Mstrs Pr) NTC Contemp Pub Co.

Phog Allen: The Father of Basketball Coaching. Blair Kerkhoff. (Illus.). 256p. 1998. pap. 12.00 (*1-57028-217-X*, 8217XH, Mstrs Pr) NTC Contemp Pub Co.

Pholdit. rev. ed. Steve Goldberg. (Illus.). 36p. (J). (gr. 2 up). 1977. pap. 6.50 (*0-918932-67-X*, A-1136) Activity Resources.

Pholosynthesis & Nitrogen Fixation, Pt. C. Ed. by Sidney P. Colowick & Nathan O. Kaplan. LC 54-9110. (Methods in Enzymology Ser.: Vol. 69). 1980. text 188.00 (*0-12-181969-8*) Acad Pr.

Pholosynthesis & Nitrogen Fixation see Methods in Enzymology

Phone: An Appreciation, 4 vols. Paul Clark. LC 97-35667. (Design Icons Ser.). 1997. 4.99 (*1-57145-616-3*, Laurel Glen Pub) Advantage Pubs.

***Phone Address Book.** 2000. spiral bd. 6.00 (*0-7416-2615-2*) Havoc Pub.

Phone Book. Richard A. Zarro. 1989. pap. 9.95 (*0-88268-095-1*) Station Hill Pr.

Phone Book: Instant Communication from Smoke Signals to Satellites & Beyond... unabridged ed. Elizabeth MacLeod. (Illus.). 64p. (J). (gr. 3-7). 1997. pap. 12.95 (*1-55074-220-5*, Pub. by Kids Can Pr) Genl Dist Srvs.

Phone Book: Money-Saving Guide to Installing or Replacing Telephone Equipment in Your Home or Business. 2nd ed. Gerald Luecke & James B. Allen. (Illus.). 176p. 1997. pap. 24.95 (*0-7906-1133-3*) Prompt Publns.

Phone Book: Telephone Skills for Business Success. Judith E. Fisher. LC 95-1863. 144p. (C). 1995. text 17.00 (*0-256-18744-4*, Irwn McGrw-H) McGrw-H Hghr Educ.

Phone Book: Telephone Skills for Business Success. Judith E. Fisher. 1996. teacher ed. 14.72 (*0-256-20169-2*, Irwn McGrw-H) McGrw-H Hghr Educ.

Phone Book: The Latest High-Tech Techniques & Equipment for Preventing Electronic Eavesdropping, Recording Phone Calls, Ending Harassing Calls, & Stopping Toll Fraud. M. L. Shannon. LC 98-225421. (Illus.). 208p. 1998. pap. 40.00 (*0-87364-972-9*) Paladin Pr.

Phone Book: Who Else Is Listening? M. L. Shannon. (Illus.). 202p. (Orig.). 1995. pap. text 24.97 (*1-884451-03-9*) Lysias Pr.

Phone Book for Small Hotels & Country Inns, Vol. I. Camaro Editors. (Illus.). 1987. pap. 3.95 (*0-913290-31-5*) Camaro Pub.

Phone Book for Small Hotels & Country Inns, Vol. II. Camaro Editors. (Illus.). 1987. pap. 3.95 (*0-913290-40-8*) Camaro Pub.

Phone Book System: Drum Yellow Pages. B. McAfee. (Illus.). 40p. (Orig.). 1997. pap. 10.95 (*1-57424-043-9*) Centerstream Pub.

Phone Call from a Flamingo. Devra Newberger-Speregen. (Full House Stephanie Ser.). 128p. (J). (gr. 4-6). 1993. per. 3.99 (*0-671-88004-7*, Minstrel Bks) PB.

Phone Call from a Ghost: Strange Tales from Modern America. Daniel Cohen. Ed. by Patricia MacDonald. (Illus.). 112p. (J). (gr. 5-7). 1990. pap. 3.50 (*0-671-68242-3*, Minstrel Bks) PB.

Phone Call from a Ghost: Strange Tales from Modern America. Daniel Cohen. (J). 1988. 8.60 (*0-606-04769-7*, Pub. by Turtleback) Demco.

Phone Calls see Wildfire Bestsellers

Phone Calls. R. L. Stine, pseud. 160p. (YA). (gr. 7 up). 1990. mass mkt. 3.99 (*0-671-69497-9*, Archway) PB.

Phone Calls. R. L. Stine, pseud. (J). 1990. 9.09 (*0-606-04512-0*, Pub. by Turtleback) Demco.

Phone Company Services: Working Smarter with the Right Telecom Tools. June Langhoff. LC 97-73917. (Illus.). 102p. (Orig.). 1997. pap. 9.95 (*1-890154-01-6*) Aegis Pub Grp.

Phone Fear. Christopher Pike, pseud. (Spooksville Ser.). (J). (gr. 4-6). 1998. per. 3.99 (*0-671-00271-6*, Pocket Books) PB.

Phone Fear. Christopher Pike, pseud. (Spooksville Ser.). (J). (gr. 4-6). 1998. 9.09 (*0-606-13799-8*, Pub. by Turtleback) Demco.

Phone Me, Fax Me, Beep Me! Teleconnecting Your Way to Sucess in the New Cyberspaced Workplace. Dartnell Corp. Staff. LC 97-68743. 225p. 1997. pap. 16.95 (*0-85013-311-4*) Dartnell Corp.

***Phone of Our Own: The Deaf Insurrection Against Ma Bell.** Harry G. Lang. LC 00-28147. (Illus.). 256p. 2000. 29.95 (*1-56368-090-4*) Gallaudet Univ Pr.

Phone Power see Poder del Telefono en las Ventas

Phone Power. George R. Walther. 1987. pap. 4.99 (*0-425-10485-0*) Berkley Pub.

Phone Power: An Executive's Guide to Telesales & Telemarketing. Culpepper & Associates Staff. (Illus.). 198p. 1996. pap. 295.00 (*1-58128-004-1*, LM) Culpepper.

Phone Power: Increase Your Effectiveness Every Time You're on the Phone. Doc Morey. LC 98-10417. Orig. Title: Techniques of Effective Telephone Communication. 128p. 1998. pap. 10.99 (*1-56414-366-X*) Career Pr Inc.

***Phone Shaped.** Havoc Publishing Staff. 1999. 18.00 (*1-57977-879-8*) Havoc Pub.

Phone Tactics for Instant Influence. John F. Truitt. LC 89-27747. 1990. 19.95 (*0-942637-23-2*, Dembner NY) Barricade Bks.

Phoneme: Introduction to the History & Theories of a Concept. Jiri Kramsky. 1974. 49.95 (*3-7705-0944-7*) Adlers Foreign Bks.

Phonemic Awareness. Norris. (Illus.). 112p. (J). (ps-1). 1998. pap., teacher ed. 14.95 (*1-55799-665-2*, 740) Evan-Moor Edu Pubs.

Phonemic Awareness: Playing with Sounds to Strengthen Beginning Reading Skills, Vol. 2332. Jo Fitzpatrick. Ed. by Karen P. Hall. (Illus.). 128p. (Orig.). (J). (gr. k-2). 1997. pap. 12.98 (*1-57471-231-4*) Creat Teach Pr.

Phonemic Awareness in Young Children: A Classroom Curriculum. Marilyn J. Adams et al. LC 97-21682. 208p. 1997. 24.95 (*1-55766-321-1*) P H Brookes.

***Phonemic Awareness Literature Packets Set.** Lakeshore Learning Materials Staff. 1999. pap. write for info. (*1-929255-01-2*, RR910X) Lkeshore Learn Mats.

***Phonemic Awarness: Lessons, Activities & Games - An Educator's Guide.** Victoria Groves Scott. LC 99-75869. 176p. 1999. pap. 27.95 (*1-890455-28-8*, P600) Peytral Pubns.

Phonetic Alphabet. 3rd ed. Francis A. Cartier & Martin T. Todaro. 112p. (C). 1982. text. write for info. (*0-697-04218-9*) Brown & Benchmark.

Phonetic & Tonal Structure of Kikuyu. Lilias E. Armstrong. LC 41-22752. (Illus.). 382p. reprint ed. pap. 118.50 (*0-8357-3210-X*, 205708000010) Bks Demand.

Phonetic Approach to Spelling. Art Freifeld. (Illus.). 88p. 1986. pap., student ed. 7.95 (*0-916177-03-3*) Am Eng Pubns.

Phonetic Awareness Activities for Early Reading Success. Scholastic, Inc. Staff. LC 98-137435. 64p. 1997. pap. text 9.95 (*0-590-37231-9*) Scholastic Inc.

Phonetic Basis of Perceptual Ratings of Running Speech. L. Boves. (Netherlands Phonetic Archives Ser.). xii, 188p. 1984. pap. 42.35 (*90-6765-035-8*) Mouton.

Phonetic Concordance to Daniel Jones: Phonetic Readings in English. H. Joachim Neuhaus. (Alpha-Omega, Series C: Vol. 6). 174p. 1973. pap. write for info. (*3-487-10052-5*) G Olms Pubs.

Phonetic Constituents of the Native Languages of California. fac. ed. A. L. Kroeber. (University of California Publications in American Archaeology & Ethnology: Vol. 10: 1). 12p. (C). 1911. reprint ed. pap. text 1.56 (*1-55567-187-X*) Coyote Press.

Phonetic Context Drill Book. Jerry Griffith & Lynn E. Miner. 1979. pap. 16.95 (*0-685-03889-0*) P-H.

Phonetic Description of the Ukrainian Language. Ivan Zilyns'Kyj. Tr. by Wolodymyr T. Zyla & Wendell M. Aycock from POL. LC 77-73711. (Harvard Ukrainian Research Institute Monographs). (Illus.). 221p. 1979. pap. 14.00 (*0-674-66612-7*) HUP.

Phonetic Elements of the Diegueno Language. fac. ed. A. L. Kroeber & J. P. Harrington. (University of California Publications in American Archaeology & Ethnology: Vol. 11: 2). 11p. (C). 1914. reprint ed. pap. text 1.56 (*1-55567-195-0*) Coyote Press.

Phonetic Elements of the Mojave Language. fac. ed. A. L. Kroeber. (University of California Publications in American Archaeology & Ethnology: Vol. 10: 3). 52p. (C). 1911. reprint ed. pap. text 6.56 (*1-55567-189-6*) Coyote Press.

Phonetic Music with Electronic Music. Larry Wendt & Ernest M. Robson. LC 81-90189. 1981. 19.45 (*0-934982-02-3*) Primary Pr.

Phonetic Readings of Songs & Arias: With Revised German Transcriptions. 2nd ed. Berton Coffin et al. LC 82-874. 400p. (C). 1982. pap. text 38.50 (*0-8108-1533-8*) Scarecrow.

Phonetic Science: A Program of Instruction. Samuel R. Faircloth & Marjorie A. Faircloth. (Illus.). 144p. (C). 1973. pap. text 16.95 (*0-685-03890-4*) P-H.

Phonetic Spelling for College Students. Ralph M. Williams. LC 80-24084. 180p. 1980. reprint ed. lib. bdg. 65.00 (*0-313-22650-4*, WIPS, Greenwood Pr) Greenwood.

Phonetic Symbol Guide. Geoffrey K. Pullum & William A. Ladusaw. LC 86-7036. xxx, 266p. (C). 1993. lib. bdg. 35.00 (*0-226-68531-4*) U Ch Pr.

Phonetic Symbol Guide. Geoffrey K. Pullum & William A. Ladusaw. LC 86-7036. xxx, 296p. (C). 1997. pap. text 13.95 (*0-226-68532-2*) U Ch Pr.

Phonetic Symbol Guide. 2nd ed. Geoffrey K. Pullum & William A. Ladusaw. 335p. 1996. pap. text 20.00 (*0-226-68536-5*); lib. bdg. 75.00 (*0-226-68535-7*) U Ch Pr.

Phonetic Transcription of Disordered Speech. Martin J. Ball et al. (Illus.). 224p. (Orig.). 1996. pap. text 45.00 (*1-56593-206-4*, 0529) Thomson Learn.

Phonetic Value of Certain Characters in Maya Writing. B. L. Whorf. (Harvard University Peabody Museum of Archaeology & Ethnology Papers: Vol. 13, No. 2). 1974. reprint ed. pap. 25.00 (*0-527-01229-7*) Periodicals Srv.

Phonetic Variation & Acoustic Distinctive Features. Clara N. Bush. (Janua Linguarum, Ser. Practica: No. 12). (Orig.). 1964. pap. text 47.70 (*90-279-0631-9*) Mouton.

Phonetic Writings of Robert Robinson. Ed. by E. J. Dobson. (EETS Original Ser.: Vol. 238). 1963. reprint ed. 20.00 (*0-19-722238-2*, Pub. by EETS) Boydell & Brewer.

Phonetical Study of the Eskimo Language, Based on Observations Made on a Journey in North Greenland 1900-1901. William C. Thalbitzer. LC 74-5883. (Illus.). reprint ed. 64.50 (*0-404-11692-2*) AMS Pr.

Phoneticism in Mayan Hieroglyphic Writing. Ed. by John S. Justeson & Lyle Campbell. LC 84-62430. (Monographs: No. 9). (Illus.). 389p. (Orig.). 1995. reprint ed. pap. 27.00 (*0-942041-08-9*) Univ Albany IFMS.

Phonetics. J. D. O'Connor. 1992. pap. 19.95 (*0-14-013638-X*, Pub. by Pnguin Bks Ltd) Trafalgar.

Phonetics: A Critical Analysis of Phonetic Theory & a Technic for the Practical Description of Sounds. Kenneth L. Pike. 192p. 1943. pap. text 19.95 (*0-472-08733-9*, 08733) U of Mich Pr.

Phonetics: Principles & Practices. 2nd ed. Sadanand Singh & Kala S. Singh. LC 81-13031. (Illus.). 268p. (C). 1982. pap. 31.00 (*0-89079-123-6*, 1326) PRO-ED.

***Phonetics: Principles & Practices.** 3rd ed. Singh. 2001. pap. 44.75 (*0-7693-0062-6*) Singular Publishing.

Phonetics: The Science of Speech. Martin J. Ball & Joan Rahilly. 1999. 65.00 (*0-340-70009-2*, Pub. by E A); pap. 19.95 (*0-340-70010-6*, Pub. by E A) OUP.

Phonetics - Research & Results: Index of New Information. Soren C. Ledetti. 160p. Date not set. 47.50 (*0-7883-1886-1*); pap. 44.50 (*0-7883-1887-X*) ABBE Pubs Assn.

Phonetics & Phonology of Korean Prosody: Intonational Phonology & Prosodic Structure. rev. ed. Sun-Ah Jun. Ed. by Laurence Horn. LC 96-9790. (Outstanding Dissertations in Linguistics Ser.). (Illus.). 264p. 1996. text 72.00 (*0-8153-2558-4*) Garland.

Phonetics & Phonology of Modern German: An Introduction. Wilbur A. Benware. LC 85-7683. 191p. (Orig.). 1986. reprint ed. pap. 59.30 (*0-7837-9388-X*, 206013300005) Bks Demand.

***Phonetics & Phonology of Tense & Lax Obstruents in German.** Michael Jessen. LC 98-44719. (Studies in Functional & Structural Linguistics: Vol. 44). xx, 394p. 1999. 89.00 (*1-55619-895-7*) J Benjamins Pubng Co.

Phonetics Elements of the Northern Paiute Language. fac. ed. T. T. Waterman. (University of California Publications in American Archaeology & Ethnology: Vol. 10: 2). (Illus.). 33p. (C). 1911. reprint ed. pap. text 3.75 (*1-55567-188-8*) Coyote Press.

Phonetics for Speech Pathology. Ed. by Martin J. Ball. 300p. 1989. 45.00 (*0-85066-667-8*) Taylor & Francis.

Phonetics for Speech Pathology. 2nd ed. Ball. 314p. 1993. pap. 62.25 (*1-56593-240-4*, 0560) Singular Publishing.

Phonetics of English & Dutch. Beverly Collins & Inger Mees. LC 96-11518. (DUT & ENG.). 380p. 1996. pap. 32.50 (*90-04-10340-6*) Brill Academic Pubs.

Phonetics of Fingerspelling. Sherman E. Wilcox. LC 92-8926. (Studies in Speech Pathology & Clinical Linguistics: No. 4). vi, 108p. 1992. 38.00 (*1-55619-390-4*) J Benjamins Pubng Co.

Phonetik im Fremdsprachenunterricht Deutsch. Helga Dieling. 134p. 1992. 22.50 (*3-468-49444-0*) Langenscheidt.

Phonetisch-Phonologische Untersuchungen zur Vokalentwicklung in den deutschen Dialekten, Set. Incl. Vol. 1. Langvokale im Hochdeutschen. Peter Wiesinger. (Illus.). xxx, 423p. 1970. (*3-11-001895-0*); Vol. 2. Diphtonge im Hochdeutschen. Ed. by Peter Wiesinger. (Illus.). viii, 361p. 1970. (*3-11-001896-9*); (Studia Linguistica Germanica: Vols. 1 & 2). (GER.). (C). 1970. 200.00 (*0-685-24226-9*) De Gruyter.

P

Phonewriting: A Consumer's Guide to the New World of Electronic Information Services. Samuel A. Simon & Michael J. Whalen. (Orig.). 1986. pap. text 7.00 (*0-943444-03-9*) T R A C.

Phoney-Baloney Professor. Louise Munro Foley. (Vampire Cat Ser.: No. 3). 1996. pap. text 4.50 (*0-8125-5368-3*, Pub. by Tor Bks) St Martin.

Phonic Foolers: A Creative Arts Dictionary of Homophones. Gerald B. Manus & Muriel R. Manus. LC 97-65995. 238p. 1998. pap. 14.95 (*0-88739-154-0*) Creat Arts Bk.

Phonic Patterns. Fry. 1996. pap. 8.33 (*0-8092-0879-2*) NTC Contemp Pub Co.

Phonic Remedial Reading Lessons. Samuel A. Kirk et al. 144p. 1985. spiral bd. 15.00 (*0-87879-508-1*) Acad Therapy.

Phonics. (Flashboards Ser.). (J). (ps-6). 1996. bds. 2.99 (*1-56293-598-4*, McClanahan Book) Learn Horizon.

Phonics. (Jr. Academic Ser.). (Illus.). 80p. (J). (gr. k). 1998. wbk. ed. 2.99 (*1-57768-220-3*) MG-Hill OH.

Phonics. (Jr. Academic Ser.). (Illus.). 80p. (J). (gr. 1). 1998. wbk. ed. 2.99 (*1-57768-221-1*) MG-Hill OH.

Phonics. (Jr. Academic Ser.). (Illus.). 80p. (J). (gr. 2). 1998. wbk. ed. 2.99 (*1-57768-222-X*) MG-Hill OH.

Phonics. (Fisher-Price First Grade Workbooks Ser.). (Illus.). 72p. (J). (gr. 1). 1997. pap. write for info. (*1-56144-928-8*, Honey Bear Bks) Modern Pub NYC.

Phonics. Martha C. Cheney. (Gifted & Talented Ser.). (Illus.). 64p. (J). (ps-3). 1996. pap., wbk. ed. 4.95 (*1-56565-365-3*, 03653W, Pub. by Lowell Hse Juvenile); pap., wbk. ed. 4.95 (*1-56565-366-1*, 03661W, Pub. by Lowell Hse Juvenile) NTC Contemp Pub Co.

Phonics. Kate Cole. (Step Ahead Plus Workbks.). (Illus.). 64p. (J). (gr. k-2). 1986. pap., wbk. ed. 3.49 (*0-307-03650-2*, 03650) Gldn Bks Pub Co.

Phonics. Dalmatian Press Staff. (Precious Moments Workbooks Ser.). (J). 1998. pap. 2.99 (*1-57759-114-3*) Dalmatian Pr.

***Phonics.** Susan Hill. Ed. by Philippa Stratton. 104p. 2000. pap. text 15.00 (*1-57110-326-0*) Stenhse Pubs.

Phonics. A. Porus. 1995. 6.95 (*1-55708-453-X*, MCC896) McDonald Pub Co.

Phonics. SRA Staff. (Spectrum Ser.). (Illus.). 128p. (J). (gr. k). 1997. pap., wbk. ed. 6.95 (*1-57768-120-7*) MG-Hill OH.

Phonics. SRA Staff. (Spectrum Ser.). (Illus.). 306p. (J). (gr. 1). 1997. pap., wbk. ed. 6.95 (*1-57768-121-5*) MG-Hill OH.

Phonics. SRA Staff. (Spectrum Ser.). (Illus.). 172p. (J). (gr. 2). 1997. pap., wbk. ed. 6.95 (*1-57768-122-3*) MG-Hill OH.

Phonics. SRA Staff. (Spectrum Ser.). (Illus.). 208p. (J). (gr. 3). 1997. pap., wbk. ed. 6.95 (*1-57768-123-1*) MG-Hill OH.

Phonics. SRA Staff. (Spectrum Ser.). (Illus.). 208p. (J). (gr. 4). 1997. pap., wbk. ed. 6.95 (*1-57768-124-X*) MG-Hill OH.

Phonics. SRA Staff. (Spectrum Ser.). (Illus.). 220p. (J). (gr. 5). 1997. pap., wbk. ed. 6.95 (*1-57768-125-8*) MG-Hill OH.

Phonics. SRA Staff. (Spectrum Ser.). (Illus.). 224p. (J). (gr. 6). 1997. pap., wbk. ed. 6.95 (*1-57768-126-6*) MG-Hill OH.

Phonics. Annette Taulbee. (Be Smart Bks.). (Illus.). 24p. (J). (ps). 1986. 3.98 (*0-86734-066-5*, FS-3058) Schaffer Pubns.

Phonics. Kim Thompson & Karen Hilderbrand. (Early Childhood Ser.). (J). (gr. k-6). 8.99 incl. audio (*1-882331-01-X*, TWIN 105) Twin Sisters.

Phonics. Kim Thompson et al. (Early Childhood Ser.). (Illus.). 24p. (J). (ps-3). 1993. student ed. 9.98 incl. audio (*1-882331-23-0*, TWIN 405) Twin Sisters.

Phonics, Pt. 1. (Home Workbooks Ser.). (Illus.). 64p. (J). (gr. 2). 1995. pap., wbk. ed. 2.49 (*0-88724-381-9*, CD-6817) Carson-Dellos.

Phonics, Pt. 2. (Home Workbooks Ser.). (Illus.). 64p. (J). (gr. 2). 1995. pap., wbk. ed. 2.49 (*0-88724-382-7*, CD-6818) Carson-Dellos.

Phonics, Vol. I. unabridged ed. Brad Caudle & Richard Caudle. (Rock 'N Learn Ser.). (Illus.). 16p. (J). (gr. 1-12). 1994. pap. 9.95 incl. audio (*1-878489-30-5*, RL930) Rock N Learn.

Phonics, Vol. II. unabridged ed. Brad Caudle & Richard Caudle. (Rock 'N Learn Ser.). (Illus.). 16p. (J). (gr. 1-12). 1994. pap. 9.95 incl. audio (*1-878489-31-3*, RL931) Rock N Learn.

Phonics, Vols. I & II. Brad Caudle & Richard Caudle. (Rock 'N Learn Ser.). (Illus.). 24p. (J). (gr. 1 up). 1990. pap. 15.95 incl. audio (*1-878489-00-3*, RL900) Rock N Learn.

Phonics: A Tool for Better Reading & Spelling, Bk. I. J. M. Baggiani & V. M. Tewell. (Illus.). (J). (gr. 1-2). 1982. reprint ed. teacher ed. 10.75 (*0-934329-01-X*); reprint ed. pap., student ed. 9.50 (*0-934329-00-1*) Baggiani-Tewell.

Phonics: A Tool for Better Reading & Spelling, Bk. II. J. M. Baggiani & V. M. Tewell. (Illus.). (J). (gr. 3-6). 1967. student ed. 2.00 (*0-934329-03-6*); pap. 3.50 (*0-934329-02-8*) Baggiani-Tewell.

Phonics: A Tool for Better Reading & Spelling, Bk. III. J. M. Baggiani & V. M. Tewell. (Illus.). (J). (gr. 5-12). 1984. reprint ed. student ed. 4.00 (*0-934329-05-2*); reprint ed. pap. 5.75 (*0-934329-04-4*) Baggiani-Tewell.

Phonics: Blends & Digraphs. Schaffer, Frank, Publications Staff. (Reproducible Workbooks Ser.). (Illus.). 48p. (J). (gr. 1-3). 1983. student ed. 4.98 (*0-86734-027-4*, FS-2656) Schaffer Pubns.

Phonics: Consonants. Schaffer, Frank, Publications Staff. (Help Your Child Learn Ser.). (Illus.). 24p. (J). (ps-2). 1978. student ed. 3.98 (*0-86734-003-7*, FS-3004) Schaffer Pubns.

***Phonics: Games & Learning Activities.** Sandy Turly. (Illus.). 144p. (J). 1999. pap., teacher ed. 12.95 (*1-57690-354-0*, TCM2354) Tchr Create Mat.

Phonics: Grade K. American Education Publishing Staff. (J). (ps-3). 1994. pap., student ed. 3.25 (*1-56189-357-9*) Amer Educ Pub.

Phonics: Grade 1. American Education Publishing Staff. (J). (ps-3). 1994. pap. 3.25 (*1-56189-358-7*) Amer Educ Pub.

Phonics: Grade 2. American Education Publishing Staff. (J). (ps-3). 1994. pap. 3.25 (*1-56189-359-5*) Amer Educ Pub.

***Phonics: Grades K-1.** McGraw-Hill Staff. 1999. sl. 19.95 (*1-57768-036-7*) MG-Hill OH.

***Phonics: Grades 2-3.** McGraw-Hill Staff. 1999. pap. 19.95 (*1-57768-037-5*) MG-Hill OH.

Phonics: Individual Sets. Marion W. Stuart. text. write for info. (*0-943343-15-1*) Lrn Wrap-Ups.

Phonics: Teaching the Beginner & the Illiterate to Read: An Encyclopedic Reference. 1992. lib. bdg. 450.95 (*0-8490-5395-1*) Gordon Pr.

Phonics: Vowels. Schaffer, Frank, Publications Staff. (Help Your Child Learn Ser.). (Illus.). 24p. (J). (gr. 1-3). 1978. student ed. 3.98 (*0-86734-004-5*, FS-3005) Schaffer Pubns.

Phonics: Vowels. Schaffer, Frank, Publications Staff. (Reproducible Workbooks Ser.). (Illus.). 48p. (J). (gr. 1-3). 1983. student ed. 4.98 (*0-86734-028-2*, FS-2657) Schaffer Pubns.

***Phonics Activities: Long Vowel Sounds: Grades K-2.** Lynn Backer & Debbie Cline. (Illus.). 64p. 1999. pap., teacher ed. 6.95 (*1-889369-37-3*, TI0063) Teaching Ink.

***Phonics Activities: Short Vowel Sounds: Grades K-2.** Lynn Backer & Debbie Cline. (Illus.). 64p. 1999. pap., teacher ed. 6.95 (*1-889369-36-5*, TI0062) Teaching Ink.

Phonics Activities for Reading Success. Rosella Bernstein. LC 98-145250. (Illus.). 320p. 1997. pap. text 24.95 (*0-87628-564-7*) Ctr Appl Res.

Phonics & Reading Flip-Over Series, 12 vols., Set. Kathy Knoblock. (Illus.). 48p. 1998. teacher ed. 27.00 (*1-58232-013-6*, BH 90101512) Bryan Hse.

Phonics & Spelling. (Basic Skills Preschool-Kindergarten-First Grade Workbooks Ser.). (Illus.). 320p. (J). (ps-1). 1998. pap., wbk. ed. write for info. (*0-7666-0150-1*, Honey Bear Bks) Modern Pub NYC.

Phonics & Spelling Exercises. Beverly Gold & Rhona Tabor. 118p. (Orig.). 1977. pap. text. write for info. (*0-9642767-1-2*) R & B Baltimore.

***Phonics & Vocabulary Skills Practice & Apply: Grade 4.** Myrl Shireman. (Illus.). 128p. 2000. pap. text 10.95 (*1-58037-131-0*, Pub. by M Twain Media) Carson-Dellos.

***Phonics & Vocabulary Skills Practice & Apply: Grade 5.** Myrl Shireman. (Illus.). 128p. 2000. pap. text 10.95 (*1-58037-132-9*, Pub. by M Twain Media) Carson-Dellos.

***Phonics & Vocabulary Skills Practice & Apply: Grade 6.** Myrl Shireman. (Illus.). 128p. 2000. pap. text 10.95 (*1-58037-133-7*, Pub. by M Twain Media) Carson-Dellos.

Phonics Anytime! Grades K-2. Denise Fitzsimmons et al. (Illus.). 64p. (Orig.). 1993. pap. 8.95 (*0-673-36129-2*, GoodYrBooks) Addson-Wesley Educ.

Phonics Art Projects. Marilyn Bruch. (J). (gr. 1-3). 1985. pap. 8.99 (*0-8224-5541-2*) Fearon Teacher Aids.

Phonics Basics. Patricia Pedigo & Roger DeSanti. (Kelley Wingate Ser.). (Illus.). 131p. (J). (gr. 1-3). 1996. pap. text 10.95 (*0-88724-444-0*, CD-3726) Carson-Dellos.

***Phonics Book Two.** Vicky Shiotsu. (Gifted & Talented Ser.). (Illus.). (J). 2000. pap. 4.95 (*0-7373-0499-5*) Lowell Hse Juvenile.

Phonics Charts: A Complete Phonics Curriculum on 99 Charts. Edward Fry. (Illus.). 96p. (Orig.). (J). (gr. 1-4). 1996. pap. 14.95 (*0-87673-027-6*) Tchr Create Mat.

Phonics, Consonants. McClanahan Books Staff. (J). (gr. k-1). 1997. pap. text, wbk. ed. 2.25 (*1-56293-966-1*, McClanahan Book) Learn Horizon.

Phonics-Consonants. Schaffer, Frank, Publications Staff. (Reproducible Workbooks Ser.). (Illus.). 48p. (J). (gr. 1-3). 1983. student ed. 4.98 (*0-86734-026-6*, FS-2655) Schaffer Pubns.

Phonics, Consonants & Vowels. Contrib. by Twin Sisters Productions Staff. 1997. 19.95 incl. audio compact disk (*1-57583-028-0*) Twin Sisters Pub.

Phonics-Consonants Books. Frank Schaffer Publications, Incorporated Staff. (J). 1997. pap. text 3.95 (*0-7647-0221-1*) Schaffer Pubns.

Phonics Deluxe: Blends & Review, Vol. 2332. School Zone Staff. Vol. 2332. (Illus.). 64p. (J). (gr. 2-4). 1998. pap. 3.25 (*0-88743-772-9*, 02332) Sch Zone Pub Co.

Phonics Deluxe: Short & Long Vowels, Vol. 2330. School Zone Staff. Vol. 2330. (Illus.). 64p. (J). (gr. 2-4). 1998. pap. 3.25 (*0-88743-770-2*, 02330) Sch Zone Pub Co.

Phonics Easy Readers, 4 bks. Melissa Caudle. (Rock 'N Learn Ser.). (Illus.). 40p. (J). (gr. k-2). 1997. pap. 11.95 (*1-878489-65-8*, RL965) Rock N Learn.

Phonics First, Bk. 1. Leonard C. Duncan. (Illus.). 88p. (J). (gr. 1-6). 1996. student ed., spiral bd. 20.00 (*0-941414-20-5*) LCD.

Phonics First, Bk. 2. Leonard C. Duncan. (Illus.). 76p. (J). (gr. 1-6). 1996. student ed., spiral bd. 20.00 (*0-941414-21-3*) LCD.

Phonics First Bk. 3: The Words That Phonics Can't Teach. Leonard C. Duncan. (Illus.). 82p. (J). (gr. 1-6). 1996. student ed., spiral bd. 20.00 (*0-941414-22-1*) LCD.

Phonics First Bk. 4: Introduction to Words of More Than One Syllable. Leonard C. Duncan. (Illus.). 110p. (J). (gr. 1-6). 1996. student ed., spiral bd. 20.00 (*0-941414-23-X*) LCD.

Phonics Flipper. Arranged by Tamera Bryant. 39p. (J). (gr. 3 up). 1997. 6.95 (*1-878383-35-3*) C Lee Pubns.

***Phonics for Middle-Grade Students.** Myrl Shireman. (Illus.). 112p. 1998. pap. text 11.95 (*1-58037-069-1*, Pub. by M Twain Media) Carson-Dellos.

Phonics for Teachers. Michael J. Palardy & Mary S. Rogers. (C). 1996. pap. text 14.25 (*0-07-048227-6*) McGraw.

Phonics for Teachers: Self-Instruction Methods & Activities. J. Lloyd Eldredge. LC 98-17012. 1998. pap. text 22.00 (*0-13-259425-0*, Scribners Ref) Mac Lib Ref.

Phonics for the New Reader: Step-by-Step. Harriette Fields. LC 90-70334. (Illus.). 128p. (Orig.). (J). (ps-3). 1991. 17.95 (*0-9625802-0-1*); pap. 8.95 (*0-9625802-1-X*) Words Pub CO.

Phonics for the Teacher of Reading: Programmed for Self-Instruction. 7th ed. Marion A. Hull & Barbara J. Fox. LC 97-11265. 189p. 1997. pap. 18.33 (*0-13-617820-0*, Merrill Coll) P-H.

Phonics Friendly Books: Teaching Phonics Through Children's Literature. Joyce A. Carroll. 175p. 1998. pap. text 29.95 (*1-888842-11-3*) Absey & Co.

***Phonics Friendly Families.** Illus. by Emily Elizabeth Smith. 104p. 1999. pap. 21.95 (*1-888842-13-X*) Absey & Co.

Phonics from A to Z: A Practical Guide. Wiley Blevins. 112p. 1998. 14.95 (*0-590-31510-2*) Scholastic Inc.

Phonics Fun. Patrick Marrell. LC 97-214826. (Illus.). (J). 1997. write for info. (*0-7853-2417-8*) Pubns Intl Ltd.

Phonics Fun. Patricia Pedigo & Roger DeSanti. (Kelley Wingate Ser.). (Illus.). 128p. (J). (gr. 2-3). 1996. pap. text 10.95 (*0-88724-443-2*, CD-3725) Carson-Dellos.

Phonics Fun: Consonants. (Wipe-Off Activity Bks.). (Illus.). 16p. (J). (gr. k-2). 1997. wbk. ed. 3.79 (*1-889319-18-X*) Trend Enterprises.

***Phonics Fun - Vowels.** (Wipe-Off Activity Bks.). (Illus.). 16p. (J). (ps-2). 2000. wbk. ed. 3.79 (*1-889319-81-3*) Trend Enterprises.

Phonics Fun, Grades 2-3: Decoding Activities. Troll Books Staff. (Teacher Time-Savers Ser.). 80p. (J). (gr. 2-3). 1999. pap. text 11.95 (*0-8167-3938-2*) Troll Communs.

Phonics Fundamentals. Jo Ellen Moore & Bob De Weese. Ed. by Marilyn Evans. (Partners in Learning). (Illus.). 192p. (J). (gr. 1-3). Date not set. pap., wbk. ed. 19.95 (*1-58610-143-9*) Learn Horizon.

Phonics Fundamentals, Vol. 1. Robert De Weese. (Illus.). 240p. (J). (gr. k-1). 1994. pap. text 19.95 (*1-55799-304-1*, EMC 290) Evan-Moor Edu Pubs.

Phonics Fundamentals, Vol. 2. Robert De Weese. (Illus.). 240p. (J). (gr. 1-3). 1994. pap. 19.95 (*1-55799-307-6*, EMC 297) Evan-Moor Edu Pubs.

***Phonics Games Vol. 2954: 22 Reproducible Games for Playful Phonics Practice.** Margaret Allen. Ed. by Joel Kupperstein. (Dr. Maggie's Phonics Ser.). 48p. 1999. pap. text 5.98 (*1-57471-632-8*, 2954) Creat Teach Pr.

***Phonics Games Kids Can't Resist! 25 Lively Learning Games That Make Teaching Phonics Easy & Fun.** Michelle Ramsey. (Illus.). 64p. (J). (gr. k-2). 2000. pap. 15.99 (*0-439-10796-2*) Scholastic Inc.

Phonics Grade 1, Pt. 1. (Home Workbooks Ser.). (Illus.). 64p. (Orig.). (J). (gr. 1). 1995. pap., wbk. ed. 2.49 (*0-88724-318-5*, CD6815) Carson-Dellos.

Phonics Grade 1, Pt. 2. (Home Workbooks Ser.). (Illus.). 64p. (Orig.). (J). (gr. 1). 1995. pap., wbk. ed. 2.49 (*0-88724-319-3*, CD6816) Carson-Dellos.

Phonics Handbook. Sue Lloyd. (Illus.). 218p. (J). (ps-3). 1993. pap. 22.50 (*1-870946-08-1*, Pub. by Jolly Lrning) Am Intl Dist.

Phonics in Context: Strategies for Developing Sound-Symbol Relationships. Bronwyn Tester & Sue Horoch. (Illus.). 192p. (J). (gr. k-2). 1997. pap. 14.95 (*0-673-36391-0*, GoodYrBooks) Addson-Wesley Educ.

Phonics in 90 Days: Lesson Plans for Teachers. Leonard C. Duncan. 80p. Date not set. teacher ed., spiral bd. 20.00 (*0-941414-19-1*) LCD.

Phonics in Proper Perspective. 8th ed. Arthur W. Heilman. LC 96-39449. 160p. 1997. pap. 19.00 (*0-13-614645-7*) P-H.

Phonics Interactive Learning Center. School Zone Publishing Company Staff. 1997. pap. text 34.95 incl. cd-rom (*0-88743-514-9*, 08904) Sch Zone Pub Co.

Phonics Interactive Workbook with CD-ROM, Vol. 8211. School Zone Publishing Interactive Staff. Vol. 8211. (Illus.). 80p. (J). (ps-4). 1998. pap., wbk. ed. 22.99 incl. cd-rom (*0-88743-561-0*, 08211) Sch Zone Pub Co.

Phonics Is My Way Series, 21 bks. Etrulia R. Lee. Incl. Blake the Duck. (Illus.). 24p. (J). (ps-2). 1994. pap. text (*1-884876-09-9*); Dill. (Illus.). 20p. (J). (ps-2). 1995. pap. text (*1-884876-03-X*); Footprints in the Sand. (Illus.). 32p. (J). (gr. k-2). 1994. pap. text (*1-884876-19-6*); Horse on a Porch. (Illus.). 36p. (J). (gr. k-2). 1994. pap. text (*1-884876-15-3*); I Can Jump. (Illus.). 16p. (J). (ps-2). 1994. pap. text (*1-884876-01-3*); I Like to Dream. (Illus.). 32p. (J). (gr. k-2). 1994. pap. text (*1-884876-11-0*); Jam, Ham & Yams. (Illus.). 20p. (J). (ps-2). 1994. pap. text (*1-884876-02-1*); Mel. (Illus.). 20p. (J). (ps-2). 1994. pap. text (*1-884876-07-2*); Mel Is Back. (Illus.). 32p. (J). (gr. k-2). 1994. pap. text (*1-884876-13-7*); Mel's Store. (Illus.). 36p. (J). (gr. k-2). 1994. pap. text (*1-884876-21-8*); Red Beans & Rice. (Illus.). 32p. (J). (gr. k-2). 1994. pap. text (*1-884876-20-X*); Skates & Grapes. (Illus.). 24p. (J). (gr. k-2). 1994. pap. text (*1-884876-12-9*); Space Trip. (Illus.). 24p. (J). (gr. k-2). 1994. pap. text (*1-884876-18-8*); Stuff. (Illus.). 20p. (J). (gr. k-2). 1994. pap. text (*1-884876-17-X*); Team. (Illus.). 24p. (J). (ps-2). 1994. pap. text (*1-884876-08-0*); Tiff & His Bone. (Illus.). 28p. (J). (ps-2). 1994. pap. text (*1-884876-04-8*); Train Ride. (Illus.). 20p. (J). (ps-2). 1994. pap. text (*1-884876-10-2*); Wake up Time. (Illus.). 20p. (J). (ps-2). 1994. pap. text What Would You Say? (Illus.). 24p. (J). (gr. k-2). 1994. pap. text (*1-884876-14-5*); Zip-a-Zap Zing. (Illus.). 32p. (J). (gr. k-2). 1994. pap. text (*1-884876-16-1*); 149.95 (*1-884876-00-5*) Chamike Pubs.

***Phonics Learning Centers Vol. 2956: 42 Independent Activities for Hands-On Phonics Review.** Margaret Allen. Ed. by Joel Kupperstein. (Dr. Maggie's Phonics Ser.). 48p. 1999. pap. text 5.98 (*1-57471-630-1*, 2956) Creat Teach Pr.

Phonics, Linguistics & Reading. Dolores Durkin. LC 72-87115. 100p. 1972. pap. 10.95 (*0-8077-1258-2*) Tchrs Coll.

***Phonics Magic.** Barbara Neely. (Illus.). 354p. 1999. ring bd. 79.95 (*1-929343-04-3*) Peer Tutor Pr.

***Phonics Make & Take Activity Books Vol. 2955: 24 Mini-Books for Take-Home Phonics Fun.** Margaret Allen. Ed. by Joel Kupperstein. (Dr. Maggie's Phonics Ser.). 48p. 1999. pap. text 5.98 (*1-57471-631-X*) Creat Teach Pr.

Phonics Make-&-Take Manipulatives: Dozens of Reproducible Patterns & Activities That Make Le, 1 vol. Joan Novelli. 64p. 1999. pap. 9.95 (*0-590-86716-4*) Scholastic Inc.

Phonics Mini-Books: Long Vowel Sounds: Grades K-2. Lynn Backer & Debbie Cline. (Illus.). 64p. 1997. pap., teacher ed. 6.95 (*1-889369-19-5*, TI0061) Teaching Ink.

Phonics Mini-Books: Short Vowel Sounds: Grades K-2. Lynn Backer & Debbie Cline. (Illus.). 64p. 1997. pap., teacher ed. 6.95 (*1-889369-18-7*, TI0060) Teaching Ink.

Phonics Pathways: Clear Steps to Easy Reading. 7th large type ed. Dolores G. Hiskes. LC 91-67093. (Illus.). 256p. (J). (gr. 1-12). 1996. reprint ed. pap. text 29.95 (*0-9620967-7-6*) Dorbooks.

***Phonics Pathways: Clear Steps to Easy Reading & Perfect Spelling.** 8th rev. large type ed. Dolores G. Hiskes. LC 98-93072. Orig. Title: Phonics Pathways - Clear Steps to Easy Reading. (Illus.). 256p. 2000. pap. text 32.95 (*0-9620967-3-3*) Dorbooks.

Phonics Pathways - Clear Steps to Easy Reading see Phonics Pathways: Clear Steps to Easy Reading & Perfect Spelling

Phonics Patterns: Onse & Rhyme Word Lists. 2nd ed. Edward Fry. 44p. 1994. 6.95 (*0-87673-026-8*) Tchr Create Mat.

Phonics, Phonemic Awareness, & Word Recognition Activities. Brenda Calabretta. (Phonics Ser.). 320p. 1997. pap. 24.95 (*1-57690-316-8*) Tchr Create Mat.

***Phonics Practical Book: Intermediate Collections 2000.** HB Staff. 1999. pap. text, teacher ed. 19.30 (*0-15-315215-X*) Harcourt.

***Phonics Practical Book: Intermediate Collections 2000.** HB Staff. 1999. pap. text 9.80 (*0-15-315213-3*) Harcourt Schl Pubs.

Phonics Practice Readers. Modern Curriculum Press Staff. pap. text 18.95 (*0-8136-0605-5*) Modern Curr.

Phonics Puzzles & Games. Martha C. Cheney. (Gifted & Talented Ser.). 64p. (J). Date not set. pap. 4.95 (*1-56565-568-0*, 05680W, Pub. by Lowell Hse Juvenile) NTC Contemp Pub Co.

Phonics Puzzles & Games: A Workbook for Ages 6-8. Martha Cheney. (Gifted & Talented Ser.). 64p. (J). (gr. 1-3). 1997. pap., wbk. ed. 4.95 (*1-56565-750-0*, 07500W, Pub. by Lowell Hse Juvenile) NTC Contemp Pub Co.

Phonics Research & Instruction. William Rupley. 104p. (C). 1995. pap. text, ring bd. 20.95 (*0-7872-1499-X*, 41149901) Kendall-Hunt.

Phonics Review. Arlene Henkel. Ed. by Joan Hoffman. (I Know It! Book Ser.). (Illus.). 32p. (J). (ps-3). 1980. student ed. 2.49 (*0-938256-08-4*, 02008) Sch Zone Pub Co.

Phonics Seatwork. Marilyn Burch. (J). (gr. 1-3). 1985. pap. 8.99 (*0-8224-5543-9*) Fearon Teacher Aids.

Phonics Spelling & Word Study: A Sensible Approach. Susan Mandel Glazer. 98p. 1999. pap. text 15.95 (*0-926842-82-X*) CG Pubs Inc.

Phonics Super Value Blackline Workbooks Series, 5 vols., Set. Phyllis Bass. Ed. by Kathy Knoblock. (Illus.). 320p. 1998. teacher ed., wbk. ed. 24.75 (*1-58232-002-0*, BH 8899555) Bryan Hse.

Phonics That Work. Janiel Wagstaff. LC 97-177446. 112p. (gr. k-4). 1994. pap. 14.95 (*0-590-49624-7*) Scholastic Inc.

P

An Asterisk (*) at the beginning of an entry indicates that the title is appearing for the first time.

spirit of people working together & helping each other--truly an unorthodox, confidence building, learning experience. To order contact Leach Associates, 718-335-3750. ***Publisher Paid Annotation.***

Phonics They Use. Cunningham. 170p. (C). 1997. pap. text 30.60 (*0-673-46433-4*) Addson-Wesley Educ.

Phonics They Use: Words for Reading & Writing. 2nd ed. Patricia M. Cunningham. LC 94-34943. (C). 1995. pap. 22.50 (*0-673-99087-7*) Addson-Wesley Educ.

Phonics They Use: Words for Reading & Writing. 3rd ed. Cunningham. LC 99-15343. 196p. (C). 1999. pap. text 26.00 (*0-321-02055-3*) Addson-Wesley Educ.

Phonics Through Poetry: Teaching Phonemic Awareness Using Poetry. Babs Bell Hajdusiewicz. 1998. pap. 15.95 (*0-673-36345-7*) Addison-Wesley.

Phonics 2. Kim Thompson et al. (Early Childhood Ser.). (Illus.). 24p. (J). (gr. k-3). 1995. pap. 9.98 incl. audio (*1-882331-87-7*, TWIN 419) Twin Sisters.

Phonics, Vowels. WiseBooks Staff & Arlene Block. 32p. (J). (gr. k-1). 1997. pap. text 2.25 (*1-56293-967-X*, McClanahan Book) Learn Horizon.

Phonics-Vowels Books. Frank Schaffer Publications, Incorporated Staff. (J). 1997. pap. text 3.95 (*0-7647-0222-X*) Schaffer Pubns.

Phonics with Stencils. American Education Publishing Staff. (Brighter Child Ser.). (J). (ps-3). 1993. 3.49 (*1-56189-290-4*) Amer Educ Pub.

Phono-Graphics: The Visual Paraphernalia of the Talking Machine. Arnold Schwartzman. (Illus.). 120p. 1993. 16.95 (*0-8118-0302-3*) Chronicle Bks.

Phonobuilding: Using Narratives to Facilitate Phonological Development. Jerry Vicino. LC 92-37172. (Illus.). 1993. 39.00 (*0-930599-80-2*) Thinking Pubns.

Phonogram Cards: The Writing Road to Reading. 2nd ed. Romalda B. Spalding & Walter T. Spalding. LC 82-21428. 272p. 1956. 20.00 (*0-688-15001-2*, Quil) HarperTrade.

Phonograms: For the Fun of It. Betty L. Kratoville. 112p. 1999. pap. 15.00 (*1-57128-099-5*) High Noon Bks.

Phonograms with Long Vowels. Scholastic, Inc. Staff. (Fun with Phonics Ser.). (J). 1997. pap. text 6.95 (*0-590-76700-3*) Scholastic Inc.

Phonograms with Short Vowels. Scholastic, Inc. Staff. (Fun with Phonics Ser.). (J). 1997. pap. text 6.95 (*0-590-76499-3*) Scholastic Inc.

Phonograph: Sound on Disk. Bradley Steffens. LC 92-27850. (Encyclopedia of Discovery & Invention Ser.). (Illus.). 96p. (J). (gr. 5-8). 1992. lib. bdg. 23.70 (*1-56006-222-3*) Lucent Bks.

Phonograph & Our Musical Life: Proceedings of a Centennial Conference. Ed. by H. Wiley Hitchcock. LC 80-82409. (I.S.A.M. Monographs: No. 14). 91p. 1980. pap. 10.00 (*0-914678-14-0*) Inst Am Music.

Phonogroup: A Practical Guide for Enhancing Phonological Remediation. Margot E. Kelman & Mary L. Edwards. LC 94-3456. (Illus.). 1994. pap. 42.00 (*0-930599-30-6*) Thinking Pubns.

Phonologic-Articulatory Disorders: Current Therapy of Communication Disorders, Vol. 5. Ed. by William H. Perkins. 114p. 1983. 24.00 (*0-86577-402-1*) Thieme Med Pubs.

Phonologica, 1988: Proceedings of the 6th International Phonology Meeting. Ed. by Wolfgang Dressler et al. 308p. (C). 1992. text 80.00 (*0-521-40175-5*) Cambridge U Pr.

Phonological Acquisition & Phonological Theory. Ed. by John Archibald. 224p. 1995. text 49.95 (*0-8058-1352-7*) L Erlbaum Assocs.

Phonological Analysis: A Functional Approach. 2nd ed. Donald A. Burquest. LC 98-196099. x, 314p. 1998. pap. 29.00 (*1-55671-067-4*) S I L Intl.

Phonological Analysis: Focus on American English. Walt Wolfram & Robert Johnson. 250p. (C). 1988. pap. text 25.00 (*0-13-664988-2*) P-H.

Phonological & Lexical Aspects of Colloquial Finnish, Vol. 119. Melvin J. Luthy. (Uralic & Altaic Ser.). x, 94p. 1973. pap. text 11.00 (*0-87750-173-4*) Res Inst Inner Asian Studies.

Phonological & Lexical Study of the Speech of Tuscaloosa County, Alabama. Lawrence M. Foley. (Publications of the American Dialect Society: No. 58). (Illus.). 54p. 1972. pap. text 7.45 (*0-8173-0658-7*) U of Ala Pr.

Phonological & Morphological Study of the Speech of the Negro of Memphis, Tennessee. Juanita Williamson. (Publications of the American Dialect Society: No. 50). 54p. 1968. pap. text 6.85 (*0-8173-0650-1*) U of Ala Pr.

***Phonological Awareness & Primary Phonics.** Thomas G. Gunning. (Illus.). 224p. 2000. pap. text 21.00 (*0-205-32323-5*) Allyn.

Phonological Awareness Handbook for Kindergarten & Primary Teachers. Lita Ericson & Moira Juliebo. LC 97-51292. 100p. 1998. pap. text 19.95 (*0-87207-180-4*, 180) Intl Reading.

Phonological Awareness in Reading: The Evolution of Current Perspectives. Ed. by D. J. Sawyer et al. (Language & Communication Ser.: Vol. 28). (Illus.). 304p. 1990. 79.95 (*0-387-97308-7*) Spr-Verlag.

***Phonological Awareness Training & Help for Students (PATHS)** Jane C. Webb. 116p. 2000. pap. text. write for info. (*0-937857-84-X*, 1491) Speech Bin.

***Phonological Basis for the Comparison of Japanese & Korean.** John Bradford Whitman. (Michigan Monograph Series in Japanese Studies: No. 34). 210p. 2000. 38.95 (*1-929280-02-5*, 52097, Pub. by U MI Japan) U of Mich Pr.

Phonological Development: Models, Research, Implications. Ed. by Charles A. Ferguson et al. LC 92-1152. (Communicating by Language Ser.). 693p. (C). 1992. text 74.50 (*0-912752-24-6*) York Pr.

Phonological Development: The Origins of Language in the Child. Marilyn M. Vihman. (Applied Language Studies). (Illus.). 352p. (C). 1996. pap. 28.95 (*0-631-16354-9*) Blackwell Pubs.

Phonological Development in Children 18 to 72 Months. Ed. by John V. Irwin & Seok P. Wong. LC 82-5893. 256p. 1983. 26.95 (*0-8093-1057-0*) S Ill U Pr.

Phonological Disability in Children. 2nd ed. Ed. by David Ingram. 200p. 1990. pap. 45.00 (*1-56593-535-7*, 0034) Singular Publishing.

Phonological Government in Japanese. Shohei Yoshida. LC 97-197820. (Faculty of Asian Studies Monographs: Vol. 20). (Illus.). 210p. 1997. pap. text 25.00 (*0-7315-2468-3*, Pub. by Aust Nat Univ) UH Pr.

Phonological Inventories of Tibeto-Burman Languages. Ed. by Ju Namkung. (STEDT Monograph Ser.: Vol. 3). 507p. 1996. pap. text 35.00 (*0-944613-28-4*) UC Berkeley Ctrs SE Asia.

Phonological Investigation of Aphasic Speech. Sheila E. Blumstein. (Janua Linguarum, Series Minor: No. 153). 1973. pap. text 37.70 (*90-279-2448-1*) Mouton.

Phonological Investigations. Ed. by Jacek Fisiak & Stanislaw Puppel. LC 92-3517. (Linguistic & Literary Studies in Eastern Europe: No. 38). x, 507p. 1992. 118.00 (*1-55619-263-0*) J Benjamins Pubng Co.

Phonological Issues in North Alaskan Inupiaq. Lawrence D. Kaplan. (Alaska Native Language Center Research Papers Ser.: No. 6). 368p. 1981. pap. 20.00 (*0-933769-36-9*) Alaska Native.

***Phonological Knowledge: Conceptual & Empirical Issues.** Ed. by Noel Burton-Roberts et al. (Illus.). 320p. 2000. text 80.00 (*0-19-824127-5*); pap. text 35.00 (*0-19-824129-1*) OUP.

Phonological Markedness & Distinctive Features. Arthur Brakel. LC 82-49348. (Illus.). 144p. 1983. 29.95 (*0-253-34450-6*) Ind U Pr.

Phonological Processes in Literacy: A Tribute to Isabelle Y. Liberman. Ed. by Susan Brady & Donald Shankweiler. 296p. 1991. text 59.95 (*0-8058-0501-X*) L Erlbaum Assocs.

***Phonological Relations Between Words.** Laura Benua. LC 00-37123. (Outstanding Dissertations in Linguistics Ser.). 2000. write for info. (*0-8153-3810-4*) Garland.

Phonological Representation of Suprasegmentals: Studies on African Languages Offered to J. M. Stewart on His 60th Birthday. Ed. by K. Bogers et al. (Publications in African Languages & Linguistics). x, 379p. 1986. pap. 90.80 (*90-6765-158-3*) Mouton.

Phonological Representation of the Sign: Lineatity & Non-Linearity in American Sign Language. Wendy Sandler. (PLS Ser.: No. 32). x, 220p. (C). 1989. pap. 60.00 (*90-6765-287-3*) Mouton.

Phonological Representations: Their Names, Forms & Powers. John Coleman. LC 97-1847. (Studies in Linguistics: No. 85). (Illus.). 364p. (C). 1998. text 74.95 (*0-521-47208-3*) Cambridge U Pr.

Phonological Structure & Language Processing: Cross-Linguistic Studies. Ed. by Takashi Otake & Anne Cutler. (Speech Research Ser.: Vol. 12). xii, 254p. (C). 1996. lib. bdg. 117.05 (*3-11-014967-2*) Mouton.

Phonological Structure & Phonetic Form: Papers in Laboratory Phonology III. Ed. by Patricia A. Keating. 381p. (C). 1994. text 80.00 (*0-521-45237-6*) Cambridge U Pr.

***Phonological Structure of Words: An Introduction.** Colin J. Ewen & Harry Van der Hulst. (Cambridge Textbooks in Linguistics). (Illus.). 320p. 2001. write for info. (*0-521-35019-0*); pap. write for info. (*0-521-35914-7*) Cambridge U Pr.

Phonological Studies see Selected Writings

Phonological Studies in Four Languages of Maluku. Ed. by Donald A. Burquest & Wyn D. Laidig. LC 92-80562. (Publications in Linguistics: No. 108). viii, 232p. (Orig.). 1992. pap. 17.00 (*0-88312-803-9*) S I L Intl.

Phonological Study of the Gwari Lects. Heidi J. Rosendall. LC 92-81460. (Language Data, African Ser.: No. 24). x, 128p. 1992. pap. 10.00 (*0-88312-186-7*) S I L Intl.

Phonological Study of the Indo-European Laryngeals. Allan R. Keiler. LC 72-110952. (Janua Linguarum, Ser. Practica: No. 76). (Orig.). 1970. pap. text 30.80 (*90-279-0729-3*) Mouton.

Phonological System of a Hungarian Dialect: An Introduction to Structural Dialectology. A. Laszlo Arany. LC 67-63039. (Uralic & Altaic Ser.: Vol. 85). 184p. 1967. reprint ed. pap. text 13.00 (*0-87750-034-7*) Res Inst Inner Asian Studies.

Phonological Theory: Evolution & Current Practice. Ed. by Valerie B. Makkai. LC 76-138654. xii, 711p. (C). 1978. reprint ed. pap. 35.00 (*0-933104-05-7*) Jupiter Pr.

Phonological Theory: The Essential Readings. Ed. by John A. Goldsmith. LC 98-54654. 500p. 1999. 69.95 (*0-631-20469-5*); pap. 34.95 (*0-631-20470-9*) Blackwell Pubs.

Phonological Variants & Dialect Identification in Latin American Spanish. Melvyn C. Resnick. LC 73-80498. (Janua Linguarum, Series Practica: No. 201). (Illus.). 484p. 1975. pap. text 84.65 (*90-279-3227-1*) Mouton.

Phonologie der Alltagssprache: Eine Untersuchung zur Standard-Dialekt-Variation am Beispiel der Konstanzer Stadtsprache. Peter Auer. (Studia Linguistica Germanica: Band 28). (Illus.). x, 358p. (C). 1990. lib. bdg. 126.15 (*3-11-011954-4*) De Gruyter.

Phonologie du Grec Attique. Liana Lupas. (Janua Linguarum, Series Practica: No. 164). (FRE.). 186p. (Orig.). 1972. pap. 49.25 (*90-279-2325-6*) Mouton.

Phonologie du Schwa Francais. Ed. by Paul Verluyten. LC 87-36811. (Lingvisticae Investigationes Supplementa Ser.: Vol. 16). vi, 202p. (C). 1988. 44.00 (*90-272-3125-7*) J Benjamins Pubng Co.

Phonologies of Asia & Africa: Including the Caucasus, 2 vols. Ed. by Alan S. Kaye & Peter T. Daniels. LC 97-4964. 1997. text 119.50 (*1-57506-019-1*) Eisenbrauns.

Phonologies of Asia & Africa Vol. 1: Including the Caucasus. Peter T. Daniels. Ed. by Alan S. Kaye. LC 97-4964. xxi, 1041p. 1997. text 119.50 (*1-57506-017-5*) Eisenbrauns.

Phonologies of Asia & Africa Vol. 2: Including the Caucasus. Alan S. Kaye & Peter T. Daniels. LC 97-4964. 1997. text. write for info. (*1-57506-018-3*) Eisenbrauns.

Phonology see Universals of Human Language

Phonology: A Cognitive View. Jonathan Kaye. (Tutorial Essays in Cognitive Science Ser.). 184p. (C). 1989. pap. 24.50 (*0-8058-0466-8*); text 39.95 (*0-89859-858-3*) L Erlbaum Assocs.

Phonology: An Introduction to Basic Concepts. Roger Lass. LC 83-23915. (Cambridge Textbooks in Linguistics Ser.). 384p. 1984. pap. text 27.95 (*0-521-28183-0*) Cambridge U Pr.

Phonology: Applications to Assessment & Intervention. Robert J. Lowe. (Illus.). 272p. 1994. 33.00 (*0-683-05205-5*) Lppncott W & W.

***Phonology: Critical Concepts in Linguistics.** Charles W. Kreidler. LC 00-32304. 2000. write for info. (*0-415-20344-9*) Routledge.

Phonology: Development & Disorders. Mehmet Yavas. LC 97-42817. (Illus.). 340p. 1998. pap. text 42.50 (*1-56593-702-3*, 1346) Thomson Learn.

Phonology & Morphology of Kimatuumbi. David Odden. (Phonology of the World's Languages Ser.). 328p. 1996. 80.00 (*0-19-823503-8*) OUP.

Phonology & Morphology of Panjabi. Malik A. Nath. LC 95-910300. 388p. (C). 1995. 49.50 (*81-215-0644-1*, Pub. by M Manoharial) Coronet Bks.

***Phonology & Morphology of the Ciyao Verb.** Armindo Ngunga. (Stanford Monographs in African Languages: No. 4). 250p. (C). 2000. text 42.95 (*1-57586-247-6*, Pub. by CSLI) Cambridge U Pr.

Phonology & Morphology of Ulu Muar Malay. Rufus S. Hendon. LC 65-4001. (Publications in Anthropology: No. 70). 1966. pap. 7.00 (*0-913516-04-X*) Yale U Anthro.

Phonology & Phonetic Evidence: Papers in Laboratory Phonology IV. Ed. by Bruce Connell & Amalia Arvaniti. (Papers in Laboratory Phonology: Vol. IV). 417p. (C). 1995. text 74.95 (*0-521-48259-3*); pap. text 29.95 (*0-521-48388-3*) Cambridge U Pr.

***Phonology & Phonetics in Coatzospan Mixtec.** Chip Gerfen. LC 99-55908. (Studies in Natural Language & Linguistic Theory). 312p. 1999. 128.00 (*0-7923-6034-6*) Kluwer Academic.

Phonology & Prosody of Modern English. Hans Kurath. 158p. 1964. pap. 35.00 (*3-533-01213-1*) Adlers Foreign Bks.

Phonology & Reading Disability: Solving the Reading Puzzle. Ed. by Donald Shankweiler & Isabelle Y. Liberman. LC 89-5163. (International Academy for Research in Learning Disabilities Monograph Ser.: No. 6). 184p. 1989. text 47.50 (*0-472-10133-1*, 10133) U of Mich Pr.

Phonology As Human Behavior: Theoretical Implications & Clinical Approaches. Yishai Tobin. LC 96-13941. (Sound & Meaning: The Roman Jakobson Series in Linguistics & Poetics). (Illus.). 416p. 1997. pap. text 27.95 (*0-8223-1822-9*); lib. bdg. 69.95 (*0-8223-1808-3*) Duke.

Phonology in English Language Teaching. Martha C. Pennington. LC 95-31239. (Applied Linguistics & Language Ser.). 1996. pap. text 31.49 (*0-582-22571-X*, Pub. by Addison-Wesley) Longman.

Phonology in Generative Grammar. Michael Kenstowicz. LC 92-37749. 720p. 1993. pap. text 36.95 (*1-55786-426-8*) Blackwell Pubs.

Phonology in the Twentieth Century: Theories of Rules & Theories of Representations. Stephen R. Anderson. LC 85-2773. 384p. 1985. pap. text 23.50 (*0-226-01916-0*) U Ch Pr.

Phonology, Morphology & Classified Word List for the Samish Dialect of Straits Salish. Brent D. Galloway. (Mercury Ser.: No. 116). 132p. (Orig.). 1991. pap. 13.95 (*0-660-10799-6*, Pub. by CN Mus Civilization) U of Wash Pr.

Phonology-Morphology Interface: Cycles, Levels & Words. Jolanta Szpyra. (Croom Helm Linguistic Ser.). 272p. 1989. 65.00 (*0-415-00307-5*) Routledge.

Phonology, Morphonology, Morphology. Olga Akhmanova. LC 72-159459. (Janua Linguarum, Ser. Minor: No. 101). 135p. 1971. pap. text 42.35 (*90-279-1748-5*) Mouton.

Phonology of Akkadian Syllable Structure. E. Greenstein. (Afroasiatic Linguistics Ser.). 72p. 1984. pap. 14.00 (*0-89003-156-8*) Undena Pubns.

Phonology of Armenian. Bert Vaux. LC 97-23842. (The Phonology of the World's Languages Ser.). (Illus.). 294p. 1998. text 105.00 (*0-19-823661-1*) OUP.

Phonology of Coronals. T. Alan Hall. LC 97-14273. (Current Issues in Linguistic Theory Ser.: Vol. 149). x, 176p. 1997. lib. bdg. 57.00 (*1-55619-864-7*) J Benjamins Pubng Co.

Phonology of Dutch. Geert Booij. (Phonology of the World's Languages Ser.: Vol. 2). (Illus.). 216p. 1995. text 55.00 (*0-19-824027-9*) OUP.

Phonology of Dutch. Geert Booij. (The Phonology of the World's Languages Ser.). (Illus.). 218p. 1999. pap. text 29.95 (*0-19-823869-X*) OUP.

Phonology of English: A Prosodic Optimality-Theoretic Approach. Michael Hammond. LC 98-48472. (Illus.). 384p. 1999. text 95.00 (*0-19-823797-9*) OUP.

Phonology of German. Richard Wiese. (Phonology of the World's Languages Ser.). (Illus.). 362p. 1996. text 78.00 (*0-19-824040-6*) OUP.

***Phonology of German.** Richard Wiese. (The Phonology of the World's Languages). 368p. 2000. pap. text 35.00 (*0-19-829950-8*) OUP.

***Phonology of Hungarian.** Peter Siptar & Miklos Torkenczy. (The Phonology of the World's Languages). 400p. 2000. text 105.00 (*0-19-823841-X*) OUP.

Phonology of Italian in a Generative Grammar. Mario Saltarelli. (Janua Linguarum, Ser. Practica: No. 93). (Orig.). 1970. pap. text 50.00 (*90-279-0737-4*) Mouton.

***Phonology of Norwegian.** Gjert Kristoffersen. LC 99-56301. 288p. 2000. write for info. (*0-19-823765-0*) OUP.

Phonology of Old English Stress & Metrical Structure. Piotr Gasiorowski. (University of Bamberg Studies in English Linguistic: Vol. 39). x, 131p. 1997. pap. 32.95 (*3-631-31363-2*) P Lang Pubng.

Phonology of Old English Stress & Metrical Structure. Piotr Gasiorowski. (University of Bamberg Studies in English Linguistic: Vol. 39). X, 131p. 1997. pap. 32.95 (*0-8204-3245-8*) P Lang Pubng.

Phonology of Old Mandarin. F. S. Hsueh. (Janua Linguarum, Series Practica: No. 179). (Illus.). 142p. 1975. pap. text 52.35 (*90-279-3391-X*) Mouton.

Phonology of Pennsylvania German English As Evidence of Language Maintenance & Shift. Achim Kopp. LC 98-30641. 352p. 1999. 45.00 (*1-57591-006-3*) Susquehanna U Pr.

***Phonology of Portuguese.** Maria Helena Mateus & Ernesto D'Andrade. (The Phonology of the World's Languages Ser.). (Illus.). 256p. 2000. text 74.00 (*0-19-823581-X*) OUP.

***Phonology of Standard Chinese.** San Duanmu. (The Phonology of the World's Languages Ser.). (Illus.). 300p. 2000. text 74.00 (*0-19-824120-8*) OUP.

Phonology of Tarascan. Paul Friedrich. LC 75-41327. (Studies in Anthropology, Series in Social, Cultural, & Linguistic Anthropology: No. 4). 246p. 1975. pap. 6.00 (*0-916256-03-0*) U Chi Dept Anthro.

Phonology of the Conjure Tales of Charles W. Chesnutt. Charles W. Foster. (Publications of the American Dialect Society: No. 55). (Illus.). 43p. 1971. pap. 5.25 (*0-8173-0655-2*) U of Ala Pr.

Phonology of the Hupa Language Pt. I: The Individual Sounds. fac. ed. Pliny E. Goddard. (University of California Publications in American Archaeology & Ethnology: Vol. 5: 1). (Illus.). 23p. (C). 1907. reprint ed. pap. text 2.81 (*1-55567-169-1*) Coyote Press.

Phonology of the Low German Deeds in the Oldest Registry at Riga, Latvia. Charles Goetsch. (LM Ser.: No. 15). 1934. pap. 25.00 (*0-527-00819-2*) Periodicals Srv.

Phonology of the Sicilian Dialects. Joseph W. Ducibella. LC 77-94206. (Catholic University of America. Studies in Romance Languages & Literatures: No. 10). reprint ed. 62.50 (*0-404-50310-1*) AMS Pr.

Phonology of the Uncle Remus Stories. Sumner Ives. (Publications of the American Dialect Society: No. 22). 59p. 1954. pap. text 6.05 (*0-8173-0622-6*) U of Ala Pr.

Phonology of Tone: The Representation of Tonal Register. Ed. by Keith Snider & Harry Van der Hulst. LC 92-21565. (Linguistic Models Ser.: Vol. 17). xi, 278p. (C). 1993. lib. bdg. 106.15 (*3-11-013605-8*) Mouton.

Phonology Roundup: 224 Reproducible Pictures for Phonology Practice. Beverly Foster et al. (Illus.). 96p. (J). (ps-3). 1994. spiral bd., wbk. ed. 21.95 (*1-58650-040-6*, BK-232) Super Duper.

Phonology-Syntax Connection. Ed. by Sharon Inkelas & Draga Zec. LC 89-20582. 444p. 1990. pap. text 36.00 (*0-226-38101-3*); lib. bdg. 78.00 (*0-226-38100-5*) U Ch Pr.

Phonon Dispersion Relations in Insulators. H. Bilz & W. Kress. (Solid-State Sciences Ser.: Vol. 10). (Illus.). 1979. 62.95 (*0-387-09399-0*) Spr-Verlag.

Phonon, 1985. Ed. by J. Kollar et al. 1000p. 1985. 141.00 (*9971-5-0002-7*) World Scientific Pub.

Phonon Raman Scattering in Semniconductors, Quantum Wells & Superlattices, Vol. 142. Tobias Ruf et al. Ed. by G. Hshler. LC 97-39897. (Springer Tracts in Modern Physics Ser.). (Illus.). 240p. 1997. 129.00 (*3-540-63301-4*) Spr-Verlag.

P

Phonon Scattering in Condensed Matter. A. C. Anderson. Ed. by J. P. Wolfe. (Solid-State Sciences Ser.: Vol. 68). (Illus.). 430p. 1986. 73.95 (*0-387-17057-X*) Spr-Verlag.

Phonon Scattering in Condensed Matter: Proceedings. International Conference on Phonon Scattering in C. Ed. by Humphrey J. Maris. LC 80-401. (Illus.). 501p. 1980. reprint ed. pap. 155.40 (*0-608-05454-2*, 206592300006) Bks Demand.

Phonon Scattering in Condensed Matter VII: Proceedings of the Seventh International Conference. Ed. by M. Meissner & R. O. Pohl. (Solid-State Sciences Ser.: Vol. 112). 1993. 119.95 (*0-387-56395-4*); write for info. (*3-540-56395-4*) Spr-Verlag.

Phonons: Theory & Experiments II, Experiments & Interpretation of Experimental Results. P. Bruesch. (Solid-State Sciences Ser.: Vol. 65). (Illus.). 350p. 1986. 71.95 (*0-387-16623-8*) Spr-Verlag.

Phonons: Theory & Experiments III, Phenomena Related with Phonons. P. Bruesch. (Solid-State Sciences Ser.: Vol. 66). (Illus.). 270p. 1987. 70.95 (*0-387-17223-8*) Spr-Verlag.

Phonons & Resonances in Solids. Baldassare Di Bartolo & Richard C. Powell. LC 75-35691. (Illus.). 533p. reprint ed. pap. 165.30 (*0-608-10320-9*, 201243000081) Bks Demand.

Phonons in Semiconductor Nanostructures. Ed. by Jean-Pierre Leburton et al. LC 93-17083. (NATO Advanced Study Institutes Series E, Applied Sciences: Vol. 236). 1993. text 276.50 (*0-7923-2277-0*) Kluwer Academic.

Phonons, 1989. Ed. by S. Hunglinger. 1552p. (C). 1990. text 173.00 (*981-02-0034-X*) World Scientific Pub.

Phonopragmatique. Chantal Rittaud-Hutinet. (Sciences pour la Communication Ser.: Vol. 45). (FRE.). 312p. 1995. 47.95 (*3-906754-25-1*, Pub. by P Lang) P Lang Pubng.

Phonostylistique du Francais. Christian L. Van Den Berghe. (De Proprietatibus Litterarum, Ser. Practica: No. 68). 1976. text 124.65 (*90-279-3303-0*) Mouton.

Phonosurgery. Diane M. Bless. Ed. by Charles N. Ford. (Illus.). 256p. 1991. text 108.00 (*0-88167-772-8*) Lppncott W & W.

Phonosurgery. N. Isshiki. (Illus.). xvi, 233p. 1989. 198.00 (*0-387-70037-4*) Spr-Verlag.

Phonothek. Helga Dieling et al. (GER.). 208p. 1996. wbk. ed. 23.50 (*3-324-00707-0*) Langenscheidt.

Phonurgia Nova. fac. ed. Athanasius Kircher. (Monuments of Music & Music Literature in Facsimile Ser., Series II: Vol. 44). (Illus.). 1966. lib. bdg. 60.00 (*0-8450-2244-X*) Broude.

Phony Communism Is Dead . . . Long Live Real Communism! Bob Avakian. 123p. (Orig.). 1992. pap. 5.00 (*0-89851-112-7*) RCP Pubns.

Phony Culture: Confidence & Malaise in Contemporary America. James Combs. 201p. (C). 1994. 39.95 (*0-87972-667-9*); pap. 18.95 (*0-87972-668-7*) Bowling Green Univ Popular Press.

Phony Express. Elwood Ullman & Monty Collins. LC 92-11181. 1992. lib. bdg. 12.94 (*1-56239-162-3*) ABDO Pub Co.

Phony Physician. Thomas Hischak. 48p. 1997. pap. 5.00 (*0-87440-035-X*) Bakers Plays.

Phoo Ntawv Tsis Khoom (Hmong) Barbara Saul. Tr. by Yer J. Thao. (J). (gr. k-3). 1993. 12.50 (*1-57842-106-3*) Delmas Creat.

Phooj Ntawv Qha Txug Cov Lug Ntxeev los Yog Lug Tsov (Hmong) Carl Morton. Tr. by Yer J. Thao. (J). (gr. k-3). 1995. 12.50 (*1-57842-102-0*) Delmas Creat.

Phormio see Anthology of Roman Drama

Phormio. Terence. (Loeb Classical Library: No. 23). 15.50 (*0-674-99026-9*) HUP.

Phormio. Terence. Tr. by Frank O. Copley. LC 58-9961. 1958. pap. 3.50 (*0-672-60286-5*, LLA95, Bobbs) Macmillan.

Phormio: A Comedy by Terence. Terence. Ed. by Elaine Coury. (Illus.). 224p. 1982. pap. text 16.00 (*0-86516-014-7*) Bolchazy-Carducci.

Phosgene & Related Carbonyl Halides. C. Ryan et al. LC 96-1172. (Topics in Inorganic & General Chemistry Ser.: No. 24). 978p. 1996. text 463.00 (*0-444-82445-6*) Elsevier.

Phosgene Induced Edema: Diagnosis & Therapeutic Countermeasures. Ed. by Myron A. Mehlman et al. LC 85-61949. (Toxicology & Industrial Health Ser.: Vol. 1, No. 2). (Illus.). 160p. 1985. 50.00 (*0-911131-91-4*) Specialist Journals.

Phosphagen Kinases. Sussana N. Lyzlova & Stefanv. 240p. 1990. lib. bdg. 190.00 (*0-8493-6467-1*, QP606) CRC Pr.

Phosphate & Mineral Homeostasis. Ed. by Shaul G. Massry et al. LC 86-30431. (Advances in Experimental Medicine & Biology Ser.: Vol. 208). 568p. 1986. 110.00 (*0-306-42398-7*, Plenum Trade) Perseus Pubng.

Phosphate & Mineral Metabolism. Ed. by Shaul G. Massry et al. LC 83-13450. 500p. 1984. 95.00 (*0-306-41731-6*, Plenum Trade) Perseus Pubng.

Phosphate Deposits of the World Vol. 3: Genesis of Neogene to Recent Phosphorites. Ed. by W. C. Burnett & S. R. Riggs. (World & Regional Geology Ser.). (Illus.). 480p. (C). 1990. text 175.00 (*0-521-33370-9*) Cambridge U Pr.

Phosphate Fertilizers & the Environment: A Discussion Paper. James J. Schultz et al. LC 92-30388. (Papers: No. P-16). (Illus.). 65p. (Orig.). 1993. pap. text 4.00 (*0-88090-097-0*) Intl Fertilizer.

Phosphate Fertilizers & the Environment: Proceedings of an International Workshop. Ed. by J. J. Schultz. LC 92-38623. (Special Publications: No. SP-18). (Illus.). 367p. (Orig.). 1992. pap. text 40.00 (*0-88090-100-4*) Intl Fertilizer.

Phosphate Fibers. Edward J. Griffith. (Topics in Applied Chemistry Ser.). (Illus.). 248p. (C). 1995. text 85.00 (*0-306-45145-X*, Kluwer Plenum) Kluwer Academic.

Phosphate in Microorganisms: Cellular & Molecular Biology. Ed. by Annamaria Torriani-Gorini et al. (Illus.). 424p. 1994. 89.00 (*1-55581-080-2*) ASM Pr.

Phosphate in Pediatric Health & Disease. Ed. by Uri Alon & James C. Chan. 352p. 1993. lib. bdg. 219.00 (*0-8493-6785-9*, RJ399, CRC Reprint) Franklin.

Phosphate Minerals. Ed. by Jerome O. Nriagu & P. B. Moore. (Illus.). 470p. 1984. 190.95 (*0-387-12757-7*) Spr-Verlag.

Phosphate Removal in Biological Treatment Processes: Proceedings of a Seminar Held in Pretoria, Republic of South Africa, 5-6 April, 1982, Vol. 15/3-4. Ed. by H. N. Wiechers. (Illus.). 410p. 1983. pap. 88.00 (*0-08-030436-2*, Pergamon Pr) Elsevier.

Phosphate Rock. (Metals & Minerals Ser.). 1993. lib. bdg. 250.95 (*0-8490-8977-8*) Gordon Pr.

Phosphate Rock. (Metals & Minerals Ser.). 1994. lib. bdg. 256.95 (*0-8490-9029-6*) Gordon Pr.

Phosphates: What Prospects for Growth. Ed. by E. M. Dickson & Peter W. Harben. 357p. (Orig.). 1984. pap. text 35.00 (*0-913333-03-4*) Metal Bulletin.

Phosphates & Dental Caries. B. Lilienthal. (Monographs in Oral Science: Vol. 6). (Illus.). 1977. 60.00 (*3-8055-2677-6*) S Karger.

Phosphates & Phosphoric Acid: Raw Materials, Technology, & Economics of the Wet Process. 2nd expanded rev. ed. Pierre Becker. (Fertilizer Science & Technology Ser.: No. 6). (Illus.). 760p. 1988. text 255.00 (*0-8247-7976-2*) Dekker.

Phosphates in Food. Ed. by Ricardo A. Molins. 272p. 1990. lib. bdg. 225.00 (*0-8493-4588-X*, TX553) CRC Pr.

Phosphatidate Phosphohydrolase, 2 vols., Set. N. Brindley. LC 87-20867. 1988. reprint ed. 220.00 (*0-8493-4358-5*, CRC Reprint) Franklin.

Phosphatidate Phosphohydrolase, 2 vols., Vol. I. Ed. by David N. Brindley. 160p. 1988. 85.00 (*0-8493-4359-3*, QP609, CRC Reprint) Franklin.

Phosphatidate Phosphohydrolase, 2 vols., Vol. II. Ed. by David N. Brindley. 136p. 1988. 136.00 (*0-8493-4360-7*, QP609, CRC Reprint) Franklin.

Phosphatidylcholine Metabolism. Ed. by Lipoprotein Research Group Staff & Dennis E. Vance. 248p. 1989. lib. bdg. 191.00 (*0-8493-6338-1*, QP752) CRC Pr.

Phosphatidylserine. Paris M. Kidd. LC 99-163220. (Good Health Guides Ser.). pap. 3.95 (*0-87983-755-1*, 37551K, Keats Publng) NTC Contemp Pub Co.

Phosphatidylserine (Ps) Edmund Burke & Thomas D. Fahey. (Good Health Guides Ser.). pap. 3.95 (*0-87983-979-1*, 39791K, Keats Publng) NTC Contemp Pub Co.

Phosphating of Metals. R. Rausch. 418p. 1991. 144.00 (*0-904477-11-8*, Pub. by FMJ Intl) St Mut.

Phosphine & Selected Metal Phosphides. WHO Staff. (Environmental Health Criteria Ser.: No. 73). 100p. 1988. 21.00 (*92-4-154273-X*) World Health.

Phosphine & Selected Metal Phosphides: Health & Safety Guide. WHO Staff. (Health & Safety Guides: No. 28). 36p. 1989. 5.00 (*92-4-154349-3*) World Health.

Phosphodiesterase Inhibitors. Ed. by Christian Schudt et al. (Handbook of Immunopharmacology Ser.). (Illus.). 228p. 1996. text 69.95 (*0-12-210720-9*) Acad Pr.

Phosphoinositides: Chemistry, Biochemistry, & Biomedical Applications, Vol. 718. K. S. Bruzik. LC 98-38729. (ASC Symposium Ser.). (Illus.). 312p. 1998. text 115.00 (*0-8412-3628-3*, Pub. by Am Chemical) OUP.

Phospholipase: Role & Function in Inflammation, Vol. A2. Ed. by P. Y. Wong & E. A. Dennis. (Illus.). 210p. (C). 1990. text 102.00 (*0-306-43611-6*, Kluwer Plenum) Kluwer Academic.

Phospholipase A2: Basic & Clinical Aspects in Inflammatory Diseases. Ed. by Waldemar H. Uhl et al. LC 97-261. (Progress in Surgery Ser.: Vol. 24, 1997). (Illus.). xii, 250p. 1997. 213.25 (*3-8055-6441-4*) S Karger.

Phospholipase A2 in Clinical Inflammation: Molecular Approaches to Pathophysiology. Ed. by Keith B. Glaser et al. LC 95-4489. (Pharmacology & Toxicology Ser.). 224p. 1995. boxed set 189.95 (*0-8493-8544-X*, 8544) CRC Pr.

Phospholipase C Pathway: Its Regulation & Desensitization. A. B. Tobin. LC 96-26235. (Molecular Biology Intelligence Unit Ser.). 222p. 1996. 99.00 (*1-57059-386-8*) Landes Bioscience.

Phospholipases. Ed. by John N. Abelson et al. (Methods in Enzymology Ser.: Vol. 197). (Illus.). 640p. 1991. text 115.00 (*0-12-182098-X*) Acad Pr.

Phospholipases. M. Waite. LC 87-14132. (Handbook of Lipid Research Ser.: Vol. 5). (Illus.). 348p. (C). 1987. text 95.00 (*0-306-42621-8*, Kluwer Plenum) Kluwer Academic.

Phospholipases & Prostaglandins. Ed. by Claudio Galli et al. LC 77-87457. (Advances in Prostaglandin, Thromboxane Research Ser.: No. 3). (Illus.). 216p. reprint ed. pap. 67.00 (*0-7837-7131-2*, 204696000004) Bks Demand.

Phospholipid-Binding Antibodies. E. Nigel Harris et al. (Illus.). 456p. 1991. lib. bdg. 295.00 (*0-8493-5536-2*, QP752) CRC Pr.

Phospholipid Biosynthesis. Ed. by John N. Abelson et al. (Methods in Enzymology Ser.: Vol. 209). (Illus.). 584p. 1992. text 125.00 (*0-12-182110-2*) Acad Pr.

Phospholipid Metabolism in Cellular Signaling. Jose M. Mato. 160p. 1990. lib. bdg. 142.00 (*0-8493-5978-3*, QP752) CRC Pr.

Phospholipid Research & the Nervous System. Ed. by Lloyd A. Horrocks et al. 320p. 1986. 191.00 (*0-387-96386-3*) Spr-Verlag.

Phospholipid Signaling Protocols. Ed. by Ian Bird. LC 98-3874. (Methods in Molecular Biology Ser.). (Illus.). 400p. 1998. 89.50 (*0-89603-491-7*) Humana.

Phospholipid Transfer Proteins: Emerging Roles in Vesicle Trafficking, Signal Transduction & Metabolic Regulation. Vytas A. Bankaitis. (Molecular Biology Intelligence Unit Ser.). 163p. 1995. 99.00 (*1-57059-330-2*) Landes Bioscience.

Phospholipids: Biochemical, Pharmaceutical & Analytical Considerations. I. Hanin & G. Pepeu. (Illus.). 328p. (C). 1990. text 95.00 (*0-306-43698-1*, Kluwer Plenum) Kluwer Academic.

Phospholipids: Characterization, Metabolism & Novel Biological Applications. Ed. by G. Ceve & F. Paltauf. 400p. 1995. 95.00 (*0-935315-62-4*) Am Oil Chemists.

Phospholipids & Atherosclerosis. Ed. by Pietro Avogaro et al. LC 83-9678. (Illus.). 292p. 1983. reprint ed. pap. 90.60 (*0-608-00633-5*, 206122100007) Bks Demand.

Phospholipids & Cellular Regulation, Vol. I. Ed. by Hyh-Fa Kuo. 256p. 1985. 149.00 (*0-8493-5537-0*, QH604, CRC Reprint) Franklin.

Phospholipids & Cellular Regulation, Vol. 2. J. F. Kuo. Ed. by Hyh-Fa Kuo. LC 84-28569. 256p. 1985. 147.00 (*0-8493-5538-9*, QH604, CRC Reprint) Franklin.

Phospholipids & Signal Transmission. Ed. by Raphael Massarelli et al. LC 93-16726. (NATO ASI Series H: Cell Biology: Vol. 70). 1993. 262.95 (*0-387-54610-3*) Spr-Verlag.

Phospholipids Handbook. Gregor Cevc. (Illus.). 992p. 1993. text 275.00 (*0-8247-9050-2*) Dekker.

Phospholipids in the Nervous System. Ed. by Nicolas G. Bazan et al. (FIDIA Research Ser.: Vol. 17). (Illus.). 300p. 1989. 118.00 (*0-387-96994-2*) Spr-Verlag.

Phospholipids in the Nervous System Vol. 1: Metabolism. Ed. by Lloyd A. Horrocks. LC 81-40731. 400p. 1982. reprint ed. pap. 124.00 (*0-608-00300-X*, 206029700001) Bks Demand.

Phospholipids in the Nervous System Vol. 2: Physiological Roles. Ed. by Lloyd A. Horrocks et al. LC 81-40731. (Illus.). 376p. 1985. reprint ed. pap. 116.60 (*0-7837-9548-3*, 206029700002) Bks Demand.

Phosphor: Diatomeen-Relation Fuer Alkalische Seen und Fluesse Brandenburgs und Ihre Anwendung Fuer die Palaeolimnologische Analyse Von Auensedimenten der Unteren Havel. Ilka Schonfelder. (Dissertationes Botanicae Ser.: Band 283). (Illus.). vi, 198p. 1997. pap. 53.00 (*3-443-64195-4*, Pub. by Gebruder Borntraeger) Balogh.

Phosphor Handbook. William H. Yen & Shigeo Shionoya. LC 98-15663. (Laser & Optical Science & Technology Ser.). 944p. 1998. boxed set 144.95 (*0-8493-7560-6*) CRC Pr.

Phosphor in Dreamland. Rikki Ducornet. LC 95-17888. (Illus.). 174p. 1995. pap. 12.95 (*1-56478-084-8*) Dalkey Arch.

Phosphoric Acid, Pt. 1. Ed. by Archie V. Slack. LC 68-11574. (Fertilizer Science & Technology Ser.: Vol. 1). 523p. 1968. reprint ed. pap. 162.20 (*0-608-09963-5*, 202710300001) Bks Demand.

Phosphoric Acid, Pt. 2. Ed. by Archie V. Slack. LC 68-11574. (Fertilizer Science & Technology Ser.: Vol. 1). 674p. 1968. reprint ed. pap. 200.00 (*0-608-09964-3*, 202568600045) Bks Demand.

Phosphoric Acid, Phosphates, & Phosphatic Fertilizers. 2nd ed. William H. Waggaman. LC 73-76365. (American Chemical Society Symposium Ser.: No. 34). (Illus.). 697p. reprint ed. pap. 200.00 (*0-608-11542-8*, 205070800083) Bks Demand.

Phosphorimetry: Theory, Instrumentation & Applications. Robert J. Hurtubise. 370p. 1990. 60.00 (*0-89573-749-3*, Wiley-VCH) Wiley.

Phosphorimetry: Theory, Instrumentation & Applications. Robert J. Hurtubise. 370p. 1990. 109.95 (*0-471-18733-X*) Wiley.

Phosphorite Research & Development. Ed. by A. J. Notholt & I. Jarvis. (Geological Society Special Publications: No. 52). (Illus.). 326p. 1990. 48.00 (*0-903317-53-2*, 254, Pub. by Geol Soc Pub Hse) AAPG.

***Phosphorous: The Carbon Copy - From Organophosphorous to Phospaorganic Chemistry.** K. B. Dillon et al. LC 97-29187. 376p. 1998. 265.00 (*0-471-97360-2*) Wiley.

Phosphorous & Nitrogen Removal from Municipal Wastewater. Richard I. Sedlak. 256p. 1991. lib. bdg. 59.95 (*0-87371-683-3*, L683) Lewis Pubs.

Phosphorous-31 NMR: Principles & Applications. Ed. by David G. Gorenstein. LC 83-7154. 1984. text 167.00 (*0-12-291750-2*) Acad Pr.

Phosphorous-31 NMR Spectroscopy in Stereochemical Analysis: Organic Compounds & Metal Complexes. Ed. by John G. Verkade & Louis D. Quin. LC 86-19105. (MSA Ser.: Vol. 8). (Illus.). 717p. 1987. lib. bdg. 190.00 (*0-89573-149-5*, Wiley-VCH) Wiley.

Phosphorous Trichloride & Phosphorous Oxychloride Health & Safety Guide. WHO Staff. (Health & Safety Guides: No. 35). 32p. 1989. 5.00 (*92-4-154356-6*) World Health.

Phosphorous Ylides: Chemistry & Applications in Organic Synthesis. Gurmeet Singh. LC 99-214313. 568p. 1999. 205.00 (*3-527-29531-3*) Wiley.

***Phosphorus.** Richard Beatty. LC 99-88821. (Elements Ser.). 2001. lib. bdg. 22.79 (*0-7614-0946-7*) Marshall Cavendish.

Phosphorus: An Outline of Its Chemistry, Biochemistry & Technology. 5th ed. D. E. Corbridge. LC 94-48222. (Inorganic Chemistry Ser.: Vol. 20). 1220p. 1995. 560.00 (*0-444-89307-5*) Elsevier.

Phosphorus: Properties of the Element & Some of Its Compounds. Tennessee Valley Authority Staff. LC QD0181.P1. (Tennessee Valley Authority Chemical Engineering Report Ser.: No. 8). 103p. reprint ed. pap. 32.00 (*0-608-14259-X*, 201970800014) Bks Demand.

Phosphorus Biogeochemistry in Sub-Tropical Ecosystemst. K. Ramesh Reddy. LC 98-50246. 1998. 69.95 (*1-56670-331-X*) Lewis Pubs.

Phosphorus Chemistry. Ed. by Louis D. Quin & John G. Verkade. LC 81-14956. (ACS Symposium Ser.: No. 171). (Illus.). 656p. 1981. reprint ed. pap. 200.00 (*0-608-03250-6*, 206376900007) Bks Demand.

Phosphorus Chemistry: Developments in American Science. Ed. by Edward N. Walsh et al. LC 92-5966. (Symposium Ser.: No. 486). (Illus.). 285p. 1992. text 85.00 (*0-8412-2213-4*, Pub. by Am Chemical) OUP.

Phosphorus Chemistry: Proceedings of the International Conference, 1981. Ed. by Louis D. Quin & John G. Verkade. LC 81-14956. (ACS Symposium Ser.: No. 171). 1981. 65.95 (*0-8412-0663-5*) Am Chemical.

Phosphorus Chemistry in Everyday Living. 2nd ed. Arthur D. Toy & Edward N. Walsh. LC 86-32240. (Illus.). 376p. 1987. reprint ed. pap. 116.60 (*0-608-05659-6*, 205971300007) Bks Demand.

Phosphorus in Freshwater Ecosystems. Ed. by Gunnar Persson & Mats Jansson. (Developments in Hydrobiology Ser.). (C). 1989. text 292.50 (*90-6193-657-8*) Kluwer Academic.

Phosphorus in Sewage Sludge & Animal Waste Slurries. T. W. Hucker & G. Catroux. 1981. text 106.00 (*90-277-0317-5*) Kluwer Academic.

Phosphorus in the Environment: Its Chemistry & Biochemistry. CIBA Foundation Staff. LC 78-4289. (CIBA Foundation Symposium: New Ser.: No. 57). 330p. reprint ed. pap. 102.30 (*0-608-14304-9*, 202218200024) Bks Demand.

Phosphorus in the Global Environment: Transfers, Cycles & Management. Ed. by Holm Tiessen. (SCOPE Ser.: Vol. 54). 476p. 1995. 200.00 (*0-471-95691-0*) Wiley.

Phosphorus Loss from Soil to Water. Ed. by H. Tunney et al. LC 97-13060. (Illus.). 480p. 1997. text 120.00 (*0-85199-156-4*) OUP.

Phosphorus NMR in Biology. C. Tyler Burt. 248p. 1987. 141.00 (*0-8493-5842-6*, CRC Reprint) Franklin.

Phosphorus Research & Production in the U. S. S. R. Alexander Prutkovsky. Ed. by Andrew A. Michta. 118p. (Orig.). 1987. pap. text 75.00 (*1-55831-037-1*) Delphic Associates.

Phosphorus 31 NMR Spectral Properties in Compound Characterization & Structural Analysis. Ed. by Louis D. Quin & John G. Verkade. LC 94-13378. (Methods in Stereochemical Analysis Ser.). 455p. 1994. 150.00 (*1-56081-637-6*, Wiley-VCH) Wiley.

Phosphorus-31 NMR Spectral Properties in Compund: Charaterization & Structural Analysis. Ed. by L. D. Quin & J. G. Verkade. (Methods in Stereochemical Analysis Ser.). 472p. 1994. 199.00 (*0-471-18587-6*, Wiley-VCH) Wiley.

Phosphorus-32: Practical Radiation Protection. P. E. Ballance et al. (Handbook Ser.: No. 9). 82p. (C). 1992. 130.00 (*0-948237-08-2*, Pub. by H&H Sci Cnslts) St Mut.

***Phosphorus 2000: Chemistry, Biochemistry & Technology.** D. E. C. Corbridge. LC 00-28838. 2000. write for info. (*0-444-82550-9*) Elsevier.

Phosphorylation & Dephosphorylation of the Ecto-nucleotide Pyrophosphatase PC-1 from Rat Liver. M. Uriarte. No. 95. 108p. (Orig.). 1994. pap. 33.50 (*90-6186-641-3*, Pub. by Leuven Univ) Coronet Bks.

Photii Patriarchae Constantinopolitani Vol. IV: Amphilochiorum Pars Prima. Ed. by Laourdas & Westerink. (GRE.). 1986. 53.50 (*3-322-00277-2*, T1510, Pub. by B G Teubner) U of Mich Pr.

Photii Patriarchae Constantinopolitani Vol. V: Amphilochiorum Pars Altera. Ed. by Laourdas & Westerink. (GRE.). 1986. 59.50 (*3-322-00333-7*, T1511, Pub. by B G Teubner) U of Mich Pr.

Photii Patriarchae Constantinopolitani Vol. VI, Fascicule 1: Amphilochiorum Pars Tertia. Ed. by Laourdas & Westerink. (GRE.). 1987. 34.50 (*3-322-00361-2*, T1512, Pub. by B G Teubner) U of Mich Pr.

Photii Patriarchae Constantinopolitani Vol. VI, Fascicule 2: Indices. Ed. by Laourdas & Westerink. (GRE.). 1988. 37.50 (*3-322-00510-0*, T1513, Pub. by B G Teubner) U of Mich Pr.

Photismi de Lumine of Maurolycus: A Chapter in Late Medieval Optics. Tr. by Henry Crew from LAT. 1940. 30.00 (*0-686-30225-7*) R S Barnes.

Photo: Grannis-Surfing's Golden Age, 1960-1969. Ed. by Brad Barrett & Steve Pezman. (Illus.). 223p. 1998. 60.00 (*0-9663771-0-9*) Surfer Jour CA.

Photo Album. (Illus.). 15.00 (*0-9614548-3-0*) Intl Assn Trichologists.

Photo Album. Umberto Benedetti. 60p. 1993. pap. 10.00 (*0-9630506-1-3*) U Benedetti.

Photo Album: Fifty Favorite Photos from the Betsy-Tacy Companion. Compiled by Sharla S. Whalen. (Illus.). 50p. (Orig.). 1995. pap., per. 11.95 (*0-9630783-3-X*) Portalington.

***Photo Album & Collectibles: Elementary Photo Album & Collectibles, Vols. 1-6.** Ricky Riggs & Angela Wolfe. (Illus.). (J). (gr. k-5). 1999. mass mkt. 179.94 (*1-930141-06-8*) Priceless Bks.

***Photo Album & Collectibles: Fifth Grade Photo Album & Collectibles, Vol. 6.** Ricky Riggs & Angela Wolfe. (Illus.). 22p. (J). (gr. 5). 1999. mass mkt. 29.99 (*1-930141-05-X*) Priceless Bks.

***Photo Album & Collectibles: First Grade Photo Album & Collectibles, Vol. 2.** Ricky Riggs & Angela Wolfe. (Illus.). 22p. (J). (gr. 1). 1999. mass mkt. 29.99 (*1-930141-01-7*) Priceless Bks.

***Photo Album & Collectibles: Fourth Grade Photo Album & Collectibles, Vol. 5.** Ricky Riggs & Angela Wolfe. (Illus.). 22p. (J). (gr. 4). 1999. mass mkt. 29.99 (*1-930141-04-1*) Priceless Bks.

***Photo Album & Collectibles: Kindergarten Photo Album & Collectibles, Vol. 1.** Ricky Riggs & Angela Wolfe. (Illus.). 22p. (J). (gr. k). 1999. mass mkt. 29.99 (*1-930141-00-9*) Priceless Bks.

***Photo Album & Collectibles: Second Grade Photo Album & Collectibles, Vol. 3.** Ricky Riggs & Angela Wolfe. (Illus.). 22p. (J). (gr. 2). 1999. mass mkt. 29.99 (*1-930141-02-5*) Priceless Bks.

***Photo Album & Collectibles: Third Grade Photo Album & Collectibles, Vol. 4.** Ricky Riggs & Angela Wolfe. (Illus.). 22p. (J). (gr. 3). 1999. mass mkt. 29.99 (*1-930141-03-3*) Priceless Bks.

Photo Album of Ohio's Canal Era, 1825-1913. rev. ed. Jack Gieck. LC 92-22597. (Illus.). 329p. 1992. 47.00 (*0-87338-353-2*) Kent St U Pr.

Photo Album of St. Therese of Lisieux. Ed. by Francois De Saint-Marie. Tr. by Peter-Thomas Rohrback. LC 62-10909. (Illus.). 226p. 1962. pap. 24.95 (*0-87061-177-1*) Chr Classics.

Photo & Word. David Robertson. LC 97-70324. (Western Writers Ser.: Vol. 128). (Illus.). 1997. pap. 4.95 (*0-88430-127-3*) Boise St U W Writ Ser.

Photo Ann Leibovitz. Photos by Annie Leibovitz. LC 90-56384. (Illus.). 232p. 1993. pap. 40.00 (*0-06-092346-6*, Perennial) HarperTrade.

***Photo Annual 1999.** Ed. by B. Martin Pedersen. (Illus.). 256p. 1999. text 70.00 (*1-888001-65-8*) Graphis US.

Photo Archive of Famous Places of the World. 4th ed. Donald M. Witte. LC 92-32419. (Pictorial Archive Ser.). (Illus.). 128p. 1993. 10.95 (*0-486-27496-9*) Dover.

An Asterisk (*) at the beginning of an entry indicates that the title is appearing for the first time.

Photo Art Therapy: A Jungian Perspective. Jerry L. Fryrear & Irene E. Corbit. (Illus.). 220p. 1992. pap. 34.95 (*0-398-06137-8*) C C Thomas.

Photo Art Therapy: A Jungian Perspective. Jerry L. Fryrear & Irene E. Corbit. (Illus.). 220p. (C). 1992. text 49.95 (*0-398-05802-4*) C C Thomas.

Photo-Atlas Athletic-Cultural Archaeological Sites in the Greco-Roman World: Europe, North Africa & the Middle East. Russell L. Sturzebecker. LC 84-91342. (Illus.). 528p. 1985. lib. bdg. 80.00 (*0-9600466-2-3*) Sturzebecker.

Photo Atlas for Anatomy & Physiology. David Morton. LC 97-202725. (Biology Ser.). 1997. pap. 33.95 (*0-534-51716-1*) Wadsworth Pub.

Photo Atlas for Biology. David Morton & James W. Perry. (Biology Ser.). 1995. 20.95 (*0-534-23556-5*) Wadsworth Pub.

Photo Atlas for Botany. Perry. LC 98-121287. 1998. 35.95 (*0-534-52938-0*) Brooks-Cole.

Photo Atlas General Biology. Craig K. Strete. 2001. 19.25 (*0-07-234855-0*) McGraw.

***Photo Barre Chord Book.** Gene Kerr. 48p. 1999. pap. 7.95 (*0-7866-4351-X*, 97519) Mel Bay.

Photo-Based 3D Graphics in C++ Compositing, Warping, Morphing & Other Digital Special Effects. Tim Wittenburg. LC 95-3200. 346p. 1995. pap. 44.95 incl. disk (*0-471-04972-7*) Wiley.

Photo Book. Ed. by Ian Jeffrey. (Illus.). 512p. 1997. 39.95 (*0-7148-3634-6*) Phaidon Pr.

***Photo Bridge 2000.** (Illus.). 48p. 2000. pap. 15.00 (*1-886028-47-8*, Pub. by Savage Pr) Bookmen Inc.

Photo CD: Quality Photographs at Your Fingertips. John J. Larish. 256p. 1994. pap. 27.95 (*0-941845-09-5*) Micro Pub Pr.

Photo CD Book. Verbum Magazine Editors. (Illus.). 64p. 1994. pap. 14.95 (*1-882305-01-9*) Verbum.

Photo Chicago. Photos by Robert Holmes et al. (Illus.). 80p. pap. 9.95 (*1-56313-902-2*) BrownTrout Pubs Inc.

Photo-Computer Image Processing & the Crime of the Century: A New Forensic Technique Using Photographic Evidence in the Kennedy Assassination. Ralph D. Thomas. 75p. 1992. pap. 25.00 (*0-918487-62-5*) Thomas Investigative.

Photo Correlation & Scattering. LC 95-72778. (Nineteen Ninety-Six Technical Digest Ser.: No. 14). 1996. pap. 66.00 (*1-55752-457-2*) Optical Soc.

Photo Craft: 50 Creative Ideas for Using Photographs. Susie Johns. (Illus.). 128p. 1998. pap. text 19.95 (*0-8174-5428-4*) Watsn-Guptill.

Photo Creations. Elaine Hopkins. 10p. (J). (gr. k-9). 1995. pap. text 5.99 (*1-887291-06-7*) Sun Sales.

Photo du Colonel. Eugene Ionesco. (FRE.). 1962. pap. 14.95 (*0-8288-9828-6*, F105970) Fr & Eur.

Photo DX, 4 vols., 3. G. S. J. Chessell. (C). (gr. 13). 1985. 16.00 (*0-8151-1655-1*, 09050) Mosby Inc.

Photo DX, 4 vols., 4. G. S. J. Chessell. (C). (gr. 13). 1985. 16.00 (*0-8151-1656-X*, 09052) Mosby Inc.

Photo-Electric Cells & Their Application. L. R. Koller. (Technical Papers: Vol. P75). (Illus.). 16p. 1930. pap. text 30.00 (*1-55589-439-9*) AGMA.

Photo Encyclopedia of Cacheted First Day Covers, 1901-1939, Vol. 1. Michael Mellone. (Illus.). 110p. 1994. pap. 17.97 (*0-89794-051-2*) FDC Pub.

Photo Encyclopedia of Cacheted First Day Covers, 1901-1939, Vol. 2. Michael Mellone. (Illus.). 110p. 1994. pap. 17.97 (*0-89794-052-0*) FDC Pub.

Photo Encyclopedia of Cacheted First Day Covers, 1901-1939, Vol. 3. Michael Mellone. (Illus.). 110p. 1995. pap. 17.97 (*0-89794-053-9*) FDC Pub.

Photo Encyclopedia of Cacheted First Day Covers, 1901-1939, Vol. 4. Michael Mellone. (Illus.). 110p. 1995. pap. 17.97 (*0-89794-054-7*) FDC Pub.

Photo Encyclopedia of Cacheted First Day Covers, 1901-1939, Vol. 5. Michael Mellone. (Illus.). 110p. 1996. pap. 17.97 (*0-89794-055-5*) FDC Pub.

Photo Encyclopedia of Cacheted First Day Covers, 1901-1939, Vol. 6. Michael Mellone. (Illus.). 110p. (C). 1996. pap. 17.97 (*0-89794-056-3*) FDC Pub.

Photo Encyclopedia of Cacheted First Day Covers, 1901-1939, Vol. 7. Michael Mellone. (Illus.). 110p. 1997. pap. 17.97 (*0-89794-057-1*) FDC Pub.

Photo Encyclopedia of Cacheted First Day Covers, 1901-1939, Vol. 8. Michael Mellone. (Illus.). 110p. 1997. pap. 17.97 (*0-89794-058-X*) FDC Pub.

***Photo Encyclopedia of Cacheted First Day Covers, 1901-1939, Vol. 9.** Michael Mellone. (Illus.). 110p. 1999. pap. 17.97 (*0-89794-059-8*) FDC Pub.

***Photo Encyclopedia of Cacheted First Day Covers, 1901-1939, Vol. 10.** Michael Mellone. (Illus.). 110p. 1999. pap. 17.97 (*0-89794-060-1*) FDC Pub.

***Photo Encyclopedia of Cacheted First Day Covers, 1901-1939, Vol. 11.** Michael Mellone. (Illus.). 110p. 2000. pap. 17.97 (*0-89794-061-X*) FDC Pub.

***Photo Encyclopedia of Cacheted First Day Covers, 1901-1939, Vol. 12.** Michael Mellone. (Illus.). 110p. 2000. pap. 17.97 (*0-89794-062-8*) FDC Pub.

Photo-Enolisation. P. G. Sammes. 1976. pap. 15.50 (*0-08-020475-9*, Pergamon Pr) Elsevier.

Photo Essay: Photographs by Mary Ellen Mark. Ed. by Constance Sullivan. (Photographers at Work Ser.). (Illus.). 64p. 1990. pap. 16.95 (*1-56098-003-6*) Smithsonian.

Photo Essay: This Land Is Home to Me: A Pastoral Letter on Powerlessness in Appalachia by the Catholic Bishops of the Region. Ed. & Photos by Edwin G. Daschbach. (Illus.). 160p. 1998. pap. 13.00 (*0-9664525-0-X*) Soc of Divine Word.

Photo Fakery: The History & Techniques of Photographic Deception & Manipulation. Dino A. Brugioni. LC 99-36376. (Illus.). 227p. 1999. 32.95 (*1-57488-166-3*) Brasseys.

Photo-Fashion. Ed. by Wolfgang Hageney. (ENG, FRE, GER, ITA & SPA., Illus.). 208p. 1982. pap. 44.95 (*88-7070-013-5*) Belvedere USA.

Photo-Fiends. Patrick Smith. (Moon Bks.: No. 37). (Illus.). 36p. (Orig.). 1977. pap. text 5.00 (*0-942908-00-7*) Pancake Pr.

Photo Finish. Bonnie Bryant. (Saddle Club Ser.: No. 43). (J). (gr. 4-6). 1995. 8.60 (*0-606-08116-X*) Turtleback.

Photo Finish. Ngaio Marsh. 1976. 21.95 (*0-8488-0580-1*) Amereon Ltd.

***Photo Finish.** Ngaio Marsh. 224p. 2000. mass mkt. 5.99 (*0-312-97301-2*, St Martins Paperbacks) St Martin.

***Photo Finish.** Gayle Trent. 150p. 1999. pap. 6.99 (*1-893108-40-6*) Neighbrhd Pr Pubng.

Photo Finish. large type ed. Glenis Wilson. 1995. 27.99 (*0-7089-3402-1*) Ulverscroft.

Photo Finish: A Play. Peter Ustinov. LC 63-14953. (Illus.). 179p. 1963. 16.95 (*0-910278-52-0*) Boulevard.

Photo Frame Lights. Alex Spatz. (Illus.). 35p. (Orig.). 1997. pap. 9.95 (*0-9641597-3-2*) Cliffside Studio.

Photo Gallery & Workshop Handbook. Jeff Cason. 192p. 1991. pap. 19.95 (*0-929667-08-5*, 10251) Images NY.

Photo Guide for Appraising Surface Fuels in East Texas. Hershel C. Reeves. (Illus.). 89p. (Orig.). 1988. 10.00 (*0-938361-04-X*) Austin Univ Forestry.

Photo-Guide to the Constellations: A Self-Teaching Guide to Finding Your Way Around the Heavens. C. R. Kitchin. LC 97-29324. 1997. pap. write for info. (*3-540-76203-5*) Spr-Verlag.

Photo Habsburg: The Private Life of an Archduke. V. Heiszler et al. (Illus.). 171p. (C). 1989. text 180.00 (*0-569-09190-X*, Pub. by Collets) St Mut.

Photo-Hadron Interactions. Richard Phillips Feynman. (C). 1995. pap. 34.95 (*0-201-48410-2*) Addison-Wesley.

Photo History Activities: Civil Rights Events. Linda Milliken. Ed. by Kathy Rogers. (Illus.). 8p. 1996. 6.95 (*1-56472-094-2*) Edupress Inc.

Photo History Activities: Civil Rights Profiles. Linda Milliken. Ed. by Kathy Rogers. (Illus.). 8p. 1996. 6.95 (*1-56472-095-0*) Edupress Inc.

Photo History Activities: Civil War Events. Linda Milliken. (Illus.). 8p. 1996. 6.95 (*1-56472-098-5*) Edupress Inc.

Photo History Activities: Civil War Profiles. Linda Milliken. (Illus.). 8p. 1996. 6.95 (*1-56472-099-3*) Edupress Inc.

Photo History Activities: Revolutionary War Events. Linda Milliken. Ed. by Kathy Rogers. (Illus.). 8p. 1996. 6.95 (*1-56472-096-9*) Edupress Inc.

Photo History Activities: Revolutionary War Profiles. Linda Milliken. Ed. by Kathy Rogers. (Illus.). 8p. 1996. 6.95 (*1-56472-097-7*) Edupress Inc.

Photo History Activities: World War II. Linda Milliken. (Illus.). 8p. 1996. 6.95 (*1-56472-104-3*) Edupress Inc.

Photo History Activities: World War II Events. Linda Milliken. (Illus.). 8p. 1996. 6.95 (*1-56472-100-0*) Edupress Inc.

Photo-Illustrated Biographies. (Illus.). 672p. 392.00 (*0-7368-0303-3*) Capstone Pr.

Photo-Induced Defects in Semiconductors. David Redfield & Richard H. Bube. (Studies in Semiconductor Physics & Microelectronic Engineering: No. 4). (Illus.). 229p. (C). 1996. text 59.95 (*0-521-46196-0*) Cambridge U Pr.

Photo-Induced Space Charge Effects in Semiconductors: Electro-Optics, Photoconductivity & the Photorefractive Effect. Ed. by K. W. Goossen et al. (Materials Research Society Symposium Proceedings Ser.: Vol. 261). 267p. 1992. text 68.00 (*1-55899-156-5*) Materials Res.

Photo-Initiation for Polymerization: UV & EB at the Millenium. D. C. Neckers. LC 99-184625. (Chemistry & Technology of UV & EB Formations for Coatings, Inks & Paints Ser.). 410p. 1999. 185.00 (*0-471-98235-0*) Wiley.

Photo-Journal Guide to Comic Books, Vol. 1. Ernst W. Gerber. (Illus.). 452p. 1990. 75.00 (*0-9623328-0-1*) Gerber Pub Co.

Photo-Journal Guide to Comic Books, Vol. 2. Ernst W. Gerber. (Illus.). 452p. 1990. 75.00 (*0-9623328-2-8*) Gerber Pub Co.

Photo-Journal Guide to Marvel Comics, 2 vols., Vol. 3: AJ. Ernst W. Gerber. (Illus.). 176p. 1991. 29.95 (*0-9623328-4-4*) Gerber Pub Co.

Photo-Journal Guide to Marvel Comics, 2 vols., Vol. 4: KZ. Ernst W. Gerber. (Illus.). 176p. 1991. pap. 29.95 (*0-9623328-5-2*) Gerber Pub Co.

Photo Journaling: Telling the Story. Jill A. Rinner. 1998. pap. 3.95 (*1-891520-28-8*) Red Pt Publ.

Photo Journey to Central Florida. American Automobile Association Staff. (Illus.). 472p. 1992. per. 12.95 (*1-56251-013-4*) S&S Trade.

Photo Journey to New York City. American Automobile Association Staff. (Illus.). 472p. 1992. per. 12.95 (*1-56251-012-6*) S&S Trade.

Photo Journey to San Francisco. American Automobile Association Staff. (Illus.). 472p. 1992. per. 12.95 (*1-56251-014-2*) S&S Trade.

Photo Journey to Washington, D.C. American Automobile Association Staff. (Illus.). 472p. 1992. per. 12.95 (*1-56251-011-8*) S&S Trade.

Photo-Lab Index. 40th ed. Ed. by Liliane DeCock. LC 40-847. 1400p. (C). 1985. ring bd. 69.00 (*0-87100-051-2*, 2051) Morgan.

Photo Laboratory Technician. Jack Rudman. (Career Examination Ser.: C-1389). 1994. pap. 27.95 (*0-8373-1389-9*) Nat Learn.

Photo League, 1936-1951. Anne W. Tucker. (Illus.). 52p. 1987. 15.00 (*0-934483-08-6*) Gal Assn NY.

Photo Machine Operator. Jack Rudman. (Career Examination Ser.: C-1390). 1994. pap. 19.95 (*0-8373-1390-2*) Nat Learn.

Photo Manual & Dissection Guide of the Cat: With Sheep Heart, Brain, Eye. 2nd ed. Fred Bohensky. (Illus.). 176p. 1979. student ed. 10.95 (*0-89529-019-7*, Avery) Penguin Putnam.

Photo Manual & Dissection Guide of the Fetal Pig: With Sheep Heart, Brain, Eye. Fred Bohensky. (Illus.). 128p. 1978. student ed. 10.95 (*0-89529-058-8*, Avery) Penguin Putnam.

Photo Manual & Dissection Guide of the Frog. Fred Bohensky. (Avery's Anatomy Ser.). (Illus.). 88p. (C). 1982. student ed. 10.95 (*0-89529-162-2*, Avery) Penguin Putnam.

Photo Manual & Dissection Guide of the Rat: With Sheep Eye. Fred Bohensky. (Avery's Anatomy Ser.). (Illus.). 154p. (C). 1986. student ed. 10.95 (*0-89529-213-0*, Avery) Penguin Putnam.

Photo Manual & Dissection Guide of the Shark. Fred Bohensky. (Avery's Anatomy Ser.). (Illus.). 120p. (Orig.). (C). 1981. pap. text 10.95 (*0-89529-140-1*, Avery) Penguin Putnam.

Photo Marketing Handbook. Jeffrey Cason. Ed. by Peter Lawrence. 200p. (Orig.). 1988. pap. 18.95 (*0-317-91257-7*) Images NY.

Photo Marketing Handbook. 3rd ed. Jeff Cason. (Orig.). 1992. pap. 21.95 (*0-929667-11-5*) Images NY.

***Photo Marriage: Novel.** 403p. 2000. pap. 12.95 (*0-9637101-7-6*); lib. bdg. 195.00 (*0-9637101-9-2*) Cndlelght Pr.

Photo Masters for Diamond Grading. Gary Roskin. 94p. 1994. 75.00 (*0-9641733-0-1*) Gemwrld Intl.

Photo Memories: Design Originals. 1998. pap. 19.95 (*1-57486-108-5*, 15839) Leisure AR.

Photo-Micrography, 1899. Edmund Spitta. (Illus.). 163p. 1985. pap. 35.00 (*0-87556-580-8*) Saifer.

Photo Offset Fundamentals. 5th ed. John E. Cogoli. 1986. pap. 32.97 (*0-02-675590-4*) Macmillan.

Photo-Offset Fundamentals: Teacher's Resource Guide. 5th ed. John E. Cogoli. (Illus.). 80p. 1999. teacher ed. 13.82 (*0-02-675610-2*) Glencoe.

Photo Oil Painting. Veronica C. Weiss. 32p. 1986. 12.95 (*0-935333-01-0*) VC Pub.

Photo One. 2nd ed. Kenneth Muse. (Illus.). 240p. (C). 1987. pap. text 35.20 (*0-13-665340-5*) P-H.

***Photo Oops: 101 Photo Opportunities Gone Horribly Awry.** Hal Buell. (Illus.). 96p. 2000. pap. 9.95 (*1-57912-155-1*) Blck Dog & Leventhal.

Photo Op. David H. Kennerly. (Illus.). 168p. 1995. 29.95 (*0-292-74323-8*) U of Tex Pr.

Photo Op! (Spanish) Images of World Culture. Heinle & Heinle Staff et al. (Illus.). 75.95 (*0-8384-1024-3*, Pub. by Heinle & Heinle) Thomson Learn.

Photo-Optical Instrumentation Applications & Theory: 14th Annual Technical Symposium. Society of Photo-Optical Instrumentation Engineers. LC 73-19674. (SPIE Ser.: Vol. 2). (Illus.). 550p. reprint ed. pap. 170.50 (*0-608-14782-6*, 202564700045) Bks Demand.

Photo-Oxidants, Acidification & Tools: Policy Applications of Eurotrac Result: The Report of the Eurotrac Application Project. Peter Borrell & P. Builtjes. LC 96-45984. (Transport & Chemical Transformation of Pollutants in the Troposphere Ser.: Vol. 10). (Illus.). 209p. 1997. 99.95 (*3-540-61783-3*) Spr-Verlag.

Photo Pag. Dawn A. Lombard. 1994. ring bd. 249.00 (*0-929321-22-7*) WEKA Pub.

Photo Poems. Edward Scott. 36p. (Orig.). 1985. pap. 5.95 (*0-937067-06-7*) Insti Study Aware.

Photo-Reactive Materials for Ultrahigh Density Optical Memory: MITI Research & Development Program on Basic Technologies for Future Industries. Ed. by Masahiro Irie. LC 94-42436. 248p. 1994. 162.50 (*0-444-81936-3*) Elsevier.

Photo-Realist Statement: Recent Paintings by Robert Cottingham. Howard D. Spencer. LC 83-51541. (Illus.). 5p. 1983. pap. 3.00 (*0-939324-12-1*) Wichita Art Mus.

Photo Retouching with Adobe Photoshop. Gwen Lute. (Illus.). 120p. 1999. pap. 29.95 (*0-936262-91-5*, Pub. by Amherst Media) IPG Chicago.

Photo ROM. Dawn A. Lombard. 1994. ring bd. 249.00 (*0-929321-09-X*) WEKA Pub.

Photo Scriber's Memory Binder. Denis Ledoux. Ed. by Martha Blowen. 90p. 1999. ring bd. 21.95 (*0-9619373-6-X*) Soleil Pr.

Photo Script. Paul Weinman. (Illus.). 52p. (Orig.). 1990. pap. 3.00 (*0-926935-43-7*) Runaway Spoon.

Photo Shop: A Designer's Guide. Hiroyuki Hayakawa. (Illus.). 160p. 1994. pap. 59.95 (*4-7661-0768-3*, Pub. by Graphic-Sha) Bks Nippan.

Photo Speaks II: 76 Photographers on their Art. Ed. by Brooks Johnson. LC 95-78822. (Illus.). 176p. 1995. pap. 29.95 (*0-89381-652-3*) Aperture.

Photo Specialist. Jack Rudman. (Career Examination Ser.: C-1391). 1994. pap. 23.95 (*0-8373-1391-0*) Nat Learn.

Photo Story: Selected Letters & Photographs of Lewis W. Hine. Ed. by Daile Kaplan. LC 91-37951. (Illus.). 256p. 1992. text 34.95 (*1-56098-169-5*) Smithsonian.

Photo Techniques. 2nd ed. Wayne Braith. 144p. (C). 1995. pap., per. 19.95 (*0-7872-1569-4*) Kendall-Hunt.

Photo Technology. Marshall La Cour & Irvin T. Lathrop. (Illus.). 320p. (YA). (gr. 9-12). 1992. 34.64 (*0-87006-899-7*) Goodheart.

Photo Text-Text Photo: The Synthesis of Photography & Text in Contemporary Art. Peter Weiermair. LC 97-160880. (Illus.). 144p. 1997. 39.95 (*3-908162-48-3*) Dist Art Pubs.

Photo-Textualities: Reading Photographs & Literature. Ed. by Marsha Bryant. LC 95-44280. 168p. 1996. 45.00 (*0-87413-551-6*) U Delaware Pr.

Photo Tinting: Artist's Library. Edward Krebs. 1999. pap. text 7.95 (*1-56010-299-3*) W Foster Pub.

Photo Tour of San Diego. Andrew Hudson. (Photo Tours from PhotoSecrets Ser.). (Illus.). 64p. 1999. 22.95 (*0-9653087-7-4*) Photosecrets.

Photo Tour of San Diego. Andrew Hudson. (Photo Tours from PhotoSecrets Ser.). (Illus.). 64p. 1999. pap. 15.95 (*0-9653087-8-2*) Photosecrets.

***Photo Tour of San Francisco & Northern California.** Andrew Hudson. 72p. 2000. 22.95 (*0-9653087-4-X*) Photosecrets.

Photo Tour of San Francisco & Northern California. Andrew Hudson. (Photo Tours from PhotoSecrets Ser.). (Illus.). 72p. 2000. pap. 15.95 (*0-9653087-2-3*) Photosecrets.

***Photo Transfer Handbook: Snap It, Print It, Stitch It!** Jean R. Laury. Ed. by Liz Aneloski & Vera Tobin. LC 98-38813. (Illus.). 80p. 1999. pap. text 21.95 (*1-57120-064-9*, 10189) C & T Pub.

Photo UK: A Guide for Photographers. 200p. 1998. pap. 19.95 (*1-899235-75-2*, 811022, Pub. by Dewi Lewis) Dist Art Pubs.

Photoacoustic & Photothermal Phenomena. Ed. by P. Hess & J. Pelzl. (Optical Sciences Ser.: Vol. 58). (Illus.). 560p. 1988. 92.95 (*0-387-18782-0*) Spr-Verlag.

Photoacoustic & Photothermal Phenomena: 10th International Conference. Ed. by F. Scudieri. LC 99-60278. (AIP Conference Proceedings Ser.). (Illus.). 714p. 1999. 195.00 (*1-56396-805-3*) Am Inst Physics.

Photoacoustic & Photothermal Phenomena III: Proceedings of the International Topical Meeting, 7th, Doorwerth, the Netherlands, August 26-30, 1991. Ed. by D. D. Bicanic. LC 92-21891. (Optical Sciences Ser.: Vol. 69). xxviii, 731p. 1992. 132.00 (*3-540-55669-9*); 132.00 (*0-387-55669-9*) Spr-Verlag.

Photoacoustic & Photothermal Phenomena II. Ed. by J. C. Murphy et al. (Optical Sciences Ser.: Vol. 62). (Illus.). 544p. 1990. 93.95 (*0-387-52367-7*) Spr-Verlag.

Photoacoustic & Thermal Wave Phenomena in Semiconductors. Ed. by Andreas Mandelis. 480p. 1987. 91.00 (*0-444-01226-5*) P-H.

Photoacoustic, Photothermal & Photochemical Processes at Surface & in Thin Films. Ed. by P. Hess. (Topics in Current Physics Ser.: Vol. 47). (Illus.). 392p. 1990. 86.95 (*0-387-51703-0*) Spr-Verlag.

Photoacoustic, Photothermal & Photochemical Processes in Gases. Ed. by P. Hess. (Topics in Current Physics Ser.: Vol. 46). (Illus.). xiv, 252p. 1989. 66.95 (*0-387-51392-2*) Spr-Verlag.

Photoacoustic Spectroscopy in Materials Chemistry. Marek W. Urban. 1998. 65.00 (*0-8493-4413-1*) CRC Pr.

Photoacoustics & Photoacoustic Spectroscopy. Allan Rosencwaig. 320p. 1990. 69.50 (*0-89464-450-5*) Krieger.

Photoactive Organic Materials: Science & Applications: Proceedings of the NATO Advanced Research Workshop, Avignon, France, June 25-30, 1995. Ed. by F. Kajzar et al. LC 96-243. (NATO Advanced Science Institutes Ser.: No. 3). 584p. (C). 1996. text 291.00 (*0-7923-3973-8*) Kluwer Academic.

Photoassimilate Distribution of Plants & Crops: Source-Sink Relationships. Ed. by Eli Zamski & Arthur A. Schaffer. (Books in Soils, Plants & the Environment: Vol. 48). (Illus.). 928p. 1996. text 275.00 (*0-8247-9440-0*) Dekker.

Photoatlas of Inclusions in Gemstones. E. J. Gubelin & J. I. Koivula. 1986. 234.95 (*3-85504-095-8*) Gemological.

Photobiological Safety for Lamps - Risk Group Classification & Labeling - ANSI Approved: RP-27.3-96. IESNA Staff. (Illus.). 16p. 1996. pap. 32.00 (*0-87995-140-0*, RP-27.3-96) Illum Eng.

***Photobiological Safety for Lamps & Lamp Systems: Measurement Systems.** (Illus.). 25p. 2000. pap. text 32.00 (*0-87995-164-8*, RP-27.2-00) Illum Eng.

Photobiological Safety for Lamps & Lamp Systems - General Resuirements - ANSI Approved: RP-27.1-96. IESNA Staff. (Illus.). 26p. 1996. pap. 32.00 (*0-87995-139-7*, RP-27.1-96) Illum Eng.

Photobiological Techniques. D. P. Valenzeno et al. (Illus.). 400p. (C). 1992. text 79.50 (*0-306-43778-3*, Kluwer Plenum) Kluwer Academic.

Photobiological Techniques, No. 216. D. P. Valenzeno et al. (NATO ASI Series A, Life Sciences: Vol. 216). (Illus.). 400p. (C). 1992. 125.00 (*0-306-44057-1*, Plenum Trade) Perseus Pubng.

Photobiology. Elli Kohen et al. (Illus.). 506p. 1995. text 74.00 (*0-12-417755-7*) Acad Pr.

Photobiology: The Science & Its Applications. Ed. by Emmanuel Riklis & Rijuyo-Sha Staff. (Basic Life Sciences Ser.). (Illus.). 1100p. (C). 1991. text 258.00 (*0-306-43830-5*, Kluwer Plenum) Kluwer Academic.

Photobiology in Medicine. G. Jori et al. LC 94-24010. (NATO ASI Ser.: Vol. 272). (Illus.). 200p. (C). 1994. text 85.00 (*0-306-44900-5*, Kluwer Plenum) Kluwer Academic.

Photobiology, 1984. Ed. by James W. Longworth et al. LC 85-604. 202p. 1985. 59.95 (*0-275-90189-0*, C0189, Praeger Pubs) Greenwood.

Photobiology of Low-Power Laser Therapy. T. I. Karu. (Laser Science & Technology Ser.: Vol. 8). xii, 190p. 1989. pap. text 192.00 (*3-7186-4970-5*) Gordon & Breach.

Photobiology of the Skin & Eye. Edward M. Jackson. LC 86-8835. (Drug & Chemical Toxicology Ser.: Vol. 5). (Illus.). 166p. reprint ed. pap. 51.50 (*0-608-08941-9*, 206957600005) Bks Demand.

Photobleaching Kinetics of Fluorescein in Quantitative Fluorescence Microscopy. Loling Song. (Illus.). 108p. (Orig.). 1996. pap. 57.50 (*90-407-1222-0*, Pub. by Delft U Pr) Coronet Bks.

Photocabulary. Johnson. (Illus.). (J). (gr. 3-9). pap. 2.79 (*0-87783-075-4*) Oddo.

Photocatalysis: Fundamentals & Applications. Nick Serpone & Ezio Pelizzetti. LC 88-33979. 650p. 1989. 199.00 (*0-471-62603-1*) Wiley.

P

Photocatalysis & Environment: Trends & Applications. Ed. by Mario Schiavello. (C). 1988. text 325.00 (*90-277-2760-0*) Kluwer Academic.

Photocatalytical Purification & Treatment of Water & Air: Proceedings of the First International Conference on TiO2 Photocatalyical Purification & Treatment of Water & Air, London, Ontario, Canada, 8-13 November, 1992. Ed. by David F. Ollis & Hussain Al-Ekabi. LC 93-20734. (Trace Metals in the Environment Ser.: Vol. 3). 836p. 1993. 307.00 (*0-444-89855-7*) Elsevier.

Photochemical & Photobiological Reviews, Vol. 6. Ed. by Kendric C. Smith. LC 75-43689. 214p. 1981. 65.00 (*0-306-40662-4*, Plenum Trade) Perseus Pubng.

Photochemical & Photobiological Reviews, Vol. 7. Ed. by Kendric C. Smith. LC 75-43689. 384p. 1983. 95.00 (*0-306-41289-6*, Plenum Trade) Perseus Pubng.

Photochemical & Transport Processes in the Upper Atmosphere. Ed. by L. Thomas & H. Rishbeth. LC 76-26741. 1977. pap. 33.00 (*0-08-021312-X*, Pergamon Pr) Elsevier.

Photochemical Conversion & Storage of Solar Energy. Ed. by Ezio Pelizzetti & Mario Schiavello. (C). 1991. text 316.50 (*0-7923-1194-9*) Kluwer Academic.

Photochemical Key Steps in Organic Synthesis: An Experimental Course Book. Ed. by J. Mattay & A. Griesbeck. LC 95-158496. (Illus.). 350p. 1994. pap. 94.95 (*3-527-29214-4*, Wiley-VCH) Wiley.

Photochemical Lasers. V. S. Zuev. (Laser Science & Technology Ser.). 103p. 1991. pap. text 104.00 (*3-7186-5062-2*, Harwood Acad Pubs) Gordon & Breach.

Photochemical Oxidants. (Environmental Health Criteria Ser.: No. 7). 110p. 1978. pap. text 16.00 (*92-4-154067-2*, 1160007) World Health.

Photochemical, Photoelectrochemical & Photobiological Processes. Ed. by D. O. Hall et al. 1983. text 148.50 (*90-277-1614-5*) Kluwer Academic.

Photochemical, Photoelectrochemical & Photobiological Processes. Ed. by D. O. Hall & Wolfgang Palz. 1982. text 106.00 (*90-277-1371-5*) Kluwer Academic.

Photochemical Probes in Biochemistry. Ed. by Peter E. Nielsen. (C). 1989. text 171.00 (*0-7923-0171-4*) Kluwer Academic.

Photochemical Processing of Electronic Materials. Ed. by I. W. Boyd & R. B. Jackman. (Illus.). 531p. 1991. text 205.00 (*0-12-121740-X*) Acad Pr.

Photochemical Stability of Drugs & Drug Formulations. Ed. by H. H. Tonnesen. 380p. 1996. 160.00 (*0-7484-0449-X*) Taylor & Francis.

Photochemical Synthesis. I. Ninomiya & T. Naito. (Best Synthetic Methods Ser.). 350p. 1989. text 132.00 (*0-12-519490-0*) Acad Pr.

Photochemical Technology. Andre M. Braun et al. LC 90-46482. 580p. 1991. 475.00 (*0-471-92652-3*) Wiley.

Photochemical Vapor Deposition. J. G. Eden. LC 92-24564. (Chemical Analysis: A Series of Monographs on Analytical Chemistry & Its Applications: Vol. 122). 208p. 1992. 105.00 (*0-471-55083-3*) Wiley.

Photochemicals. Frost & Sullivan Staff. 427p. 1996. spiral bd. 3950.00 (*0-7889-0543-0*, 3217-39) Frost & Sullivan.

Photochemistry. Carol E. Wayne & Richard P. Wayne. (Oxford Chemistry Primers Ser.: No. 39). (Illus.). 96p. (C). 1996. pap. text 12.95 (*0-19-855886-4*) OUP.

Photochemistry, Vol. 11. D. Bryce-Smith. 1989. 274.00 (*0-85186-095-8*) CRC Pr.

Photochemistry, Vol. 12. D. Bryce-Smith. 1989. 274.00 (*0-85186-105-9*) CRC Pr.

Photochemistry, Vol. 13. D. Bryce-Smith. 1989. 296.00 (*0-85186-115-6*) CRC Pr.

Photochemistry, Vol. 14. D. Bryce-Smith. 1988. 286.00 (*0-85186-125-3*) CRC Pr.

Photochemistry, Vol. 15. D. Bryce-Smith. 1988. 330.00 (*0-85186-135-0*) CRC Pr.

Photochemistry, Vol. 16. D. Bryce-Smith. 1988. 362.00 (*0-85186-145-8*) CRC Pr.

Photochemistry, Vol. 19. D. Bryce-Smith. 1988. 296.00 (*0-85186-175-X*) CRC Pr.

Photochemistry, Vol. 20. D. Bryce-Smith. 1989. 330.00 (*0-85186-185-7*) CRC Pr.

Photochemistry, Vol. 21. D. Bryce-Smith & A. Gilbert. 1990. 318.00 (*0-85186-195-4*) CRC Pr.

Photochemistry, Vol. 22. D. Bryce-Smith & A. Gilbert. 1991. 325.00 (*0-85186-205-5*) CRC Pr.

Photochemistry, Vol. 24. Ed. by D. Bryce-Smith & A. Gilbert. 560p. 1993. 294.00 (*0-85186-225-X*, Q) CRC Pr.

Photochemistry, Vol. 25. Ed. by D. Bryce-Smith. (Specialist Periodical Reports). 620p. 1994. 293.00 (*0-85186-481-3*, R6481) CRC Pr.

Photochemistry, Vols. 1-10. D. Bryce-Smith. LC 73-17909. write for info. (*0-318-50480-4*) Am Chemical.

Photochemistry & Photobiology, Vol. 2. Ed. by Ahmed H. Zewail. xLviii, 668p. 1983. text 350.00 (*3-7186-0179-6*) Gordon & Breach.

Photochemistry & Photobiology, 2 vols., Vol. 2. Ed. by Ahmed H. Zewail. LC 83-12618. xciv, 1005p. 1984. text 561.00 (*3-7186-0205-9*) Gordon & Breach.

Photochemistry & Photobiology: Laser Chemistry Applications, Vol. 1. Ed. by Ahmed H. Zewail. Lvi, 738p. 1983. text 382.00 (*3-7186-0173-7*) Gordon & Breach.

Photochemistry & Photophysics, Vol. I. Ed. by Jan F. Rabek & Gary W. Scott. 208p. 1989. lib. bdg. 179.00 (*0-8493-4041-1*, QD714) CRC Pr.

Photochemistry & Photophysics, Vol. II. Ed. by Jan F. Rabek & Gary W. Scott. 192p. 1989. lib. bdg. 180.00 (*0-8493-4042-X*, QD714) CRC Pr.

Photochemistry & Photophysics, Vol. III. 216p. 1991. lib. bdg. 180.00 (*0-8493-4043-8*, QD714) CRC Pr.

Photochemistry & Photophysics, Vol. IV. Jan F. Rabek. 320p. 1991. lib. bdg. 218.00 (*0-8493-4044-6*, QD714) CRC Pr.

Photochemistry & Photophysics of Coordination Compounds. H. Yerson & A. Vogler. (Illus.). xii, 344p. 1987. 75.95 (*0-387-17808-2*) Spr-Verlag.

Photochemistry & Photophysics of Metal Complexes. D. M. Roundhill. (Modern Inorganic Chemistry Ser.). (Illus.). 368p. (C). 1994. text 95.00 (*0-306-44694-4*, Kluwer Plenum) Kluwer Academic.

Photochemistry & Radiation Chemistry. Ed. by James F. Wishart & Daniel G. Nocera. (Advances in Chemistry Ser.: No. 254). (Illus.). 448p. 1998. text 140.00 (*0-8412-3499-X*) OUP.

Photochemistry & Reaction Kinetics. Ed. by Philip G. Ashmore et al. LC 67-105417. 394p. reprint ed. pap. 112.30 (*0-608-12315-3*, 2024403) Bks Demand.

Photochemistry in Organized & Constrained Media. V. Ramamurthy. 875p. 1991. 210.00 (*0-471-18744-5*, Wiley-VCH) Wiley.

Photochemistry in Organized & Constrained Media. Ed. by Vaidhyanathan Ramamurthy. 526p. 1991. 135.00 (*0-89573-775-2*, Wiley-VCH) Wiley.

***Photochemistry of Carotenoids.** Harry A. Frank. LC 99-45979. (Advances in Photosynthesis Ser.). 1999. write for info. (*0-7923-5942-9*) Kluwer Academic.

Photochemistry of Environmental Aquatic Systems. Ed. by Rod G. Zika & William J. Cooper. LC 86-26489. (ACS Symposium Ser.: No. 327). (Illus.). vii, 280p. 1986. 60.95 (*0-8412-1008-X*) Am Chemical.

Photochemistry of Environmental Aquatic Systems. Ed. by Rod G. Zika & William J. Cooper. LC 86-26489. (ACS Symposium Ser.: Vol. 327). 296p. 1987. reprint ed. pap. 91.80 (*0-608-03541-6*, 206426000008) Bks Demand.

Photochemistry of Lignocellulosic Materials: Developed from a Symposium Sponsored by the Division of Cellulose, Paper, & Textile of the American Chemical Society at the 203rd Meeting, San Francisco, California, April 5-10, 1992. Ed. by Cyril Heitner & Juan C. Scaiano. LC 93-1551. (ACS Symposium Ser.: No. 531). (Illus.). 223p. 1993. text 72.00 (*0-8412-2692-X*, Pub. by Am Chemical) OUP.

Photochemistry of Planetary Atmospheres. Yuk L. Yung & William B. DeMore. (Illus.). 480p. 1998. text 70.00 (*0-19-510501-X*) OUP.

Photochemistry of Small Molecules. Hideo Okabe. LC 78-6704. (Illus.). 447p. reprint ed. pap. 138.60 (*0-608-17420-3*, 205645500067) Bks Demand.

Photochemotherapy: Photodynamic Therapy & Other Modalities II. Ed. by Stanley B. Brown et al. (Europto Ser.: Vol. 2924). 342p. 1996. 94.00 (*0-8194-2326-2*) SPIE.

Photochemotherapy: Photodynamic Therapy & Other Modalities III. Ed. by Kristian Berg et al. LC 98-164537. (Europto Ser.: Vol. 3191). 380p. 1997. 107.00 (*0-8194-2623-7*) SPIE.

Photochemotherapy in Dermatology. Elizabeth A. Abel. LC 91-7109. (Illus.). 352p. 1992. text 90.00 (*0-89640-186-3*) Igaku-Shoin.

Photochemotherapy of Cancer. Ed. by Benjamin Ehrenberg & Kristian Berg. (Europto Ser.: Vol. 3563). 1998. 89.00 (*0-8194-3025-0*) SPIE.

Photocommunication see Photo/Imaging: How to Communicate with Camera & Computer

Photoconducting Polymers & Metal-Containing Polymers. V. Mylnikov et al. (Advances in Polymer Science Ser.: Vol. 115). (Illus.). 145p. 1994. 114.95 (*0-387-57476-X*) Spr-Verlag.

Photoconductivity: Art, Science, & Technology. Joshi. (Optical Engineering Ser.: Vol. 25). (Illus.). 304p. 1990. text 155.00 (*0-8247-8321-2*) Dekker.

***Photoconversion: Clean Electricity from Photovoltaics.** Ed. by Mary D. Archer & R. Hill. (Series on Photoconversion of Solar Energy: Vol. 2). 670p. 1999. 98.00 (*1-86094-161-3*) Imperial College.

***Photocopied Joining Together: Group Theory & Group Skills.** 6th ed. 628p. 1999. write for info. (*0-13-003410-X*) P-H.

Photocopier Maintenance & Repair Made Easy. Eric Kuaimoku. 1993. pap. text 14.95 (*0-8306-4299-4*) McGraw-Hill Prof.

Photocopiers & Fax Machines in United Kingdom: A Strategic Entry Report, 1997. abr. ed. Compiled by Icon Group International Staff. (Illus.). 104p. 1999. ring bd. 1040.00 incl. audio compact disk (*0-7418-0781-5*) Icon Grp.

Photocopies. John Berger. LC 96-11650. 192p. 1996. 3.99 (*0-679-43525-5*) Pantheon.

Photocopies. John Berger. 1998. pap. 12.00 (*0-679-75517-9*) Vin Bks.

Photocopies. aut. ed. John Berger. 1996. 22.00 (*0-676-52053-7*) Random.

Photocopy Machine Operator. Jack Rudman. (Career Examination Ser.: C-2971). 1994. pap. 19.95 (*0-8373-2971-X*) Nat Learn.

Photocopy of LSJ, Vol. I, No. 1. 1989. 10.00 (*0-317-93940-8*) Arden Assocs.

Photocrafts Book of Guides, Vol. 2. Mark Baczynsky. LC 78-70581. (Illus.). 104p. 1980. pap. 21.95 (*0-89816-002-2*) Embee Pr.

Photodamage. Ed. by Barbara A. Gilchrest. LC 95-20981. 496p. 1995. 99.95 (*0-86542-343-1*) Blackwell Sci.

***Photodamaged Skin: Clinical Signs, Causes & Management.** Jean-Paul Ortonne & Ronald Marks. 149p. 1999. 89.95 (*1-85317-345-2*, Pub. by Martin Dunitz) Mosby Inc.

Photodegradation & Photostabilization of Coatings. Ed. by S. Peter Pappas & F. H. Winslow. LC 81-467. (ACS Symposium Ser.: No. 151). 1981. 43.95 (*0-8412-0611-2*) Am Chemical.

Photodegradation & Photostabilization of Coatings: Based on a Symposium. Ed. by S. Peter Pappas & F. H. Winslow. LC 81-467. (ACS Symposium Ser.: Vol. 151). 317p. 1981. reprint ed. pap. 98.30 (*0-608-03037-6*, 206349000007) Bks Demand.

Photodegradation of Polymers: Physical Characteristics & Applications. J. F. Rabek. LC 96-19743. 250p. 1996. 117.00 (*3-540-60716-1*) Spr-Verlag.

Photodegradation of Water Pollutants. Martin M. Halmann. 320p. 1995. boxed set 94.95 (*0-8493-2459-9*, 2459) CRC Pr.

Photodegradation, Photo-Oxidation, & Photostabilization of Polymers: Principles & Applications. Bengt G. Ranby & J. F. Rabek. LC 74-2498. 585p. reprint ed. pap. 181.40 (*0-608-10152-4*, 201618300001) Bks Demand.

Photodeluxe for Macintosh: Visual Quickstart Guide. Elaine Weinmann. 1996. pap. write for info. (*0-201-88673-1*) Addison-Wesley.

***PhotoDeluxe Home Edition 4 for Windows: Visual QuickStart Guide.** 2nd ed. Ted Alspach & Jen Alspach. 224p. (C). 2000. pap. 17.99 (*0-201-35479-9*) Adobe Pr.

PhotoDeluxe Two for Windows & Macintosh: Visual QuickStart Guide. Ted Alspach & Jen Alspach. LC 98-132816. 208p. (C). 1997. pap. text 16.95 (*0-201-69670-3*) Addison-Wesley.

Photodermatology. Ed. by J. L. M. Hawk. (Illus.). 320p. 1999. text 98.50 (*0-340-74094-9*, Pub. by E A) OUP.

Photodetectors. P. N. Dennis. (Updates in Applied Physics & Electrical Technology Ser.). (Illus.). 200p. (C). 1986. text 95.00 (*0-306-42217-4*, Kluwer Plenum) Kluwer Academic.

Photodetectors: Devices, Circuits & Applications. Silvano Silvano. LC 99-39804. 432p. (C). 1999. 70.00 (*0-13-020337-8*) P-H.

Photodetectors Vol. 2999: Materials & Devices II. Ed. by Gail J. Brown & Manijeh Razeghi. LC 97-193061. 458p. 1997. 89.00 (*0-8194-2410-2*) SPIE.

***Photodetectors Vol. 3287: Materials & Devices III.** Ed. by Gail J. Brown. LC 98-172295. 368p. 1998. 89.00 (*0-8194-2726-8*) SPIE.

Photodiode Amplifiers: Op Amp Solutions. Jerald G. Graeme. LC 95-42800. 252p. 1995. 55.00 (*0-07-024247-X*) McGraw.

PhotoDisc Starter Kit 98.1. Photo Disk Inc. Staff. (Illus.). 253p. 1998. pap. 19.95 (*0-9665538-0-2*) PhotoDisc Inc.

Photodisintegration of the Deuteron: A Review of Theory & Experiment. H. Arenhovel & M. Sanzone. (Few-Body Systems Ser.: Suppl. 3). 192p. 1991. 100.95 (*0-387-82276-3*) Spr-Verlag.

Photodissociation Dynamics: Spectroscopy & Fragmentation of Small Polyatomic Molecules. Reinhard Schinke. (Monographs on Atomic, Molecular, & Chemical Physics: No. 1). (Illus.). 433p. (C). 1995. pap. text 44.95 (*0-521-48414-6*) Cambridge U Pr.

Photodrama. Henry A. Phillips. LC 70-124032. (Literature of Cinema, Ser. 1). 1970. reprint ed. 12.95 (*0-405-01632-8*) Ayer.

Photodrama: Its Place among the Fine Arts. W. H. Hannon. 1972. 59.95 (*0-8490-0830-1*) Gordon Pr.

***Photodraw-Illustrated Essentials.** Fisher. (Illustrated Ser.). (C). 2000. pap. 9.95 (*0-619-01735-X*) Course Tech.

***PhotoDraw 2000: Module 2.** Kathleen DeFilippo. Ed. by Stephanie Savage & Mary Millhollon. 205p. (YA). 1999. pap. write for info. (*0-7423-0350-0*) ComputerPREP.

***Photodraw 2000 Fast & Easy.** Molly W. Joss. (Short Order Ser.). 300p. 2000. pap. 19.99 (*0-7897-2048-5*) Que.

***Photodraw 2000 Fast & Easy.** Coletta Witherspoon. LC 98-68771. (Fast & Easy Ser.). (Illus.). 325p. 1999. pap. 16.99 (*0-7615-2034-1*) Prima Pub.

Photodynamic Therapy, No. 271. C. J. Gomer. (Photochemistry & Photobiology Ser.: Vol. 46). 391p. 1988. 35.00 (*0-08-036081-5*, Pergamon Pr) Elsevier.

Photodynamic Therapy: Basic Principles & Clinical Applications. Ed. by Barbara W. Henderson & Thomas J. Dougherty. LC 92-14636. (Illus.). 480p. 1992. text 210.00 (*0-8247-8680-7*) Dekker.

***Photodynamic Therapy for Macular Degeneration.** Carmen A. Puliafito. 250p. (C). 2000. text 190.00 (*1-55642-490-6*) SLACK Inc.

Photodynamic Therapy of Neoplastic Disease, Vol. I. David Kessel. 352p. 1990. lib. bdg. 159.00 (*0-8493-5816-7*, RC271) CRC Pr.

Photodynamic Therapy of Neoplastic Disease, Vol. II. David Kessel. 280p. 1990. lib. bdg. 159.00 (*0-8493-5817-5*, RC271) CRC Pr.

Photodynamic Tumor Therapy: 2nd & 3rd Generation Photosensitizers. Ed. by Jorg G. Moser. (Illus.). 240p. 1998. text 49.00 (*90-5699-139-6*, ECU63, Harwood Acad Pubs) Gordon & Breach.

Photoeffects at Semiconductor-Electrolyte Interfaces. Ed. by Arthur J. Nozik. LC 80-27773. (Symposium Ser.: No. 146). 1981. 49.95 (*0-8412-0604-X*) Am Chemical.

Photoeffects at Semiconductor-Electrolyte Interfaces. Ed. by Arthur J. Nozik. LC 80-27773. (ACS Symposium Ser.: No. 146). (Illus.). 426p. 1981. reprint ed. pap. 132.10 (*0-608-03275-1*, 206379300007) Bks Demand.

Photoelastic & Electro-Optic Properties of Crystals. T. S. Narasimhamurty. LC 79-409. (Illus.). 544p. 1981. 110.00 (*0-306-31101-1*, Plenum Trade) Perseus Pubng.

Photoelastic Coatings. Felix Zandman et al. LC 76-46984. (Society for Experimental Stress Analysis Ser.: No. 3). 189p. reprint ed. pap. 58.60 (*0-608-16384-8*, 202669700051) Bks Demand.

Photoelastic Effect & Its Applications: Proceedings of the International Union of Theoretical & Applied Mechanics, Brussels, Belgium, 1973. International Union of Theoretical & Applied Mecha. Ed. by J. Kestens. (Illus.). 650p. 1975. 103.95 (*0-387-07278-0*) Spr-Verlag.

Photoelastic Stress Analysis. Albrecht Kuske & George Robertson. LC 73-2788. (Illus.). 533p. reprint ed. pap. 165.30 (*0-608-18494-2*, 203149600075) Bks Demand.

Photoelastic Study of Contact Stresses in Gears. R. V. Baud. (Technical Papers: Vol. P76). (Illus.). 19p. 1931. pap. text 30.00 (*1-55589-235-3*) AGMA.

Photoelastic Study of the Stresses in Gear Tooth Fillets. T. J. Dolan & E. L. Broghamer. (Technical Papers: Vol. P224). (Illus.). 31p. 1941. pap. text 30.00 (*1-55589-269-8*) AGMA.

Photoelasticity, Vol. 2. Max M. Frocht. LC 41-15664. (Illus.). 523p. reprint ed. pap. 162.20 (*0-608-30346-1*, 201783300002) Bks Demand.

Photoelasticity & Its Relation to Gear Wheels. A. L. Kimball. (Technical Papers: Vol. P77). (Illus.). 9p. 1925. pap. text 30.00 (*1-55589-236-1*) AGMA.

Photoelasticity for Designers. R. B. Heywood. (International Series in Mechanical Engineering: Vol. 2). 1969. 203.00 (*0-08-013005-4*, Pub. by Pergamon Repr) Franklin.

Photoelasticity in Theory & Practice: Proceedings of CISM, Department for Mechanics of Defable Bodies, 1970. CISM (International Center for Mechanical Sciences. Ed. by V. Brcic. (CISM International Centre for Mechanical Sciences Ser.: No. 59). (Illus.). 242p. 1975. 41.95 (*0-387-81081-1*) Spr-Verlag.

Photoelasticity of Glass. H. Aben & C. Guillemet. LC 93-10032. 1993. 131.95 (*0-387-54841-6*) Spr-Verlag.

Photoelectric Photometry of Variable Stars. 2nd rev. ed. Hall & Russell M. Genet. 1989. 24.95 (*0-943396-19-0*) Willmann-Bell.

***Photoelectric Properties & Applications of Low-Mobility Semiconductors.** Rolf Khonenkamp. LC 99-45236. (Tracts in Modern Physics Ser.). (Illus.). 2000. write for info. (*3-540-66699-0*) Spr-Verlag.

Photoelectric Sensors & Controls. 2nd ed. G. Brickell & P. Mathews. (Mechanical Engineering Ser.). Date not set. write for info. (*0-8247-9919-4*) Dekker.

Photoelectric Sensors & Controls: Selection & Applications. Scott M. Juds. (Mechanical Engineering Ser.: Vol. 63). (Illus.). 400p. 1988. text 175.00 (*0-8247-7886-3*) Dekker.

Photoelectrochemical Solar Cells. Suresh Chandra. (Electrocomponent Science Monographs: Vol. 5). xiv, 270p. 1985. text 195.00 (*2-88124-014-3*) Gordon & Breach.

Photoelectrochemistry. Ed. by K. Rajeshwar et al. LC 97-211116. (Proceedings Ser.: Vol. 97-20). 420p. 1997. 85.00 (*1-56677-148-X*) Electrochem Soc.

Photoelectrochemistry. Iurii I. Gurevich et al. Ed. by B. E. Conway. Tr. by Halina S. Wroblowa from RUS. LC 78-21541. (Illus.). 255p. 1980. reprint ed. pap. 79.10 (*0-608-05412-7*, 206588100006) Bks Demand.

Photoelectrochemistry & Photovoltaics of Layered Semiconductors. Ed. by A. Aruchamy. (C). 1992. text 185.00 (*0-7923-1556-1*) Kluwer Academic.

Photoelectrochemistry, Photocatalysis & Photoreactors Fundamentals & Developments. Mario Schiavello. 1985. text 274.00 (*90-277-1946-2*) Kluwer Academic.

Photoelectron Diffraction & Fermi Surface Mapping. Jurg Osterwalder & Philipp Aebi. 200p. 1997. pap. text 26.00 (*981-02-3207-1*) World Scientific Pub.

Photoelectron Spectra of Nonmetallic Solids & Consequences for Quantum Chemistry see Photoelectron Spectrometry

Photoelectron Spectrometry. Incl. Fractional Prentage Methods for Ionisation of Open Shells of D & F Electrons. P. A. Cox. 1975. Photoelectron Spectra of Nonmetallic Solids & Consequences for Quantum Chemistry. C. K. Jrgensen. 1975. Ultraviolet Photoelectron Spectroscopy of Gases Absorbed on Metal Surfaces. A. M. Bradshaw. 1975. X-Ray Photoelectron Spectroscopy: Application to Metals & Alloys. R. E. Watson & M. L. Perlman. 1975. (Structure & Bonding Ser.: Vol. 24). (Illus.). iv, 170p. 1975. 45.00 (*0-387-07364-7*) Spr-Verlag.

Photoelectron Spectroscopy: Principle & Application. Stefan Hufner. LC 94-7803. (Solid-State Sciences Ser.: Vol. 82). 1994. write for info. (*3-540-19108-9*) Spr-Verlag.

Photoelectron Spectroscopy: Principle & Application. Stefan Hufner. LC 94-7803. (Solid-State Sciences Ser.: Vol. 82). 1994. 99.00 (*0-387-19108-9*) Spr-Verlag.

Photoelectron Spectroscopy: Principles & Applications. 2nd ed. Stefan Hufner. LC 96-6908. (Springer Series in Solid-State Sciences: Vol. 82). (Illus.). xiv, 520p. 1996. 79.95 (*3-540-60875-3*) Spr-Verlag.

Photoelectron Spectroscopy of Solids & Surfaces. Kevin C. Prince. (Synchrotron Radiation Techniques & Applications Ser.). 300p. 1997. text 55.00 (*981-02-2164-9*) World Scientific Pub.

Photoelectronic Image Devices: Proceedings of the 10th Symposium on Photoelectronic Image Devices, "The McGee Symposium" Held 6 September 1991 at Imperial College. Ed. by B. Morgan. (Institute of Physics Conference Ser.: No. 121). (Illus.). 456p. 1992. 182.00 (*0-85498-411-9*) IOP Pub.

Photoelectronic Imaging Devices, 2 vols. Ed. by Sol Nudelman. Incl. Devices & Their Evaluation. Des. by L. M. Biberman. LC 74-120029. 584p. 1971. 125.00 (*0-306-37082-4*, Kluwer Plenum); Physical Processes & Methods of Analysis. Ed. by L. M. Biberman. LC 74-120029. 430p. 1971. 115.00 (*0-306-37081-6*, Kluwer Plenum); LC 74-120029. (Optical Physics & Engineering Ser.). 1971. write for info. (*0-318-55334-1*, Plenum Trade) Perseus Pubng.

Photoelectronic Processes & a Search for Exciton Mobility in Pure & Doped Alkali Halides. Steven W. Duckett. LC 79-135074. 145p. 1969. 25.00 (*0-403-04496-0*) Scholarly.

Photoelectronic Properties of Semiconductors. Richard H. Bube. (Illus.). 336p. (C). 1992. pap. text 42.95 (*0-521-40681-1*) Cambridge U Pr.

An Asterisk (*) at the beginning of an entry indicates that the title is appearing for the first time.

Photoelectronic Statistics: With Applications to Spectroscopy & Optical Communication. Bahaa E. Saleh. LC 77-9936. (Optical Sciences Ser.: Vol. 6). (Illus.). 1977. 50.95 (*0-387-08295-6*) Spr-Verlag.

***Photoelectronics & Night Vision Devices.** Ed. by Anatoly M. Filachev. 224p. 1999. pap. text 62.00 (*0-8194-3305-5*) SPIE.

Photoemission & the Electronic Properties of Surfaces. Ed. by Berndt Feuerbacher et al. LC 77-2761. (Illus.). 558p. reprint ed. pap. 173.00 (*0-608-18777-1*, 202979800065) Bks Demand.

Photoemission in Solids II: Case Studies. Ed. by L. Ley & M. Cardona. LC 78-2503. (Topics in Applied Physics Ser.: Vol. 27). (Illus.). 1979. 89.95 (*0-387-09202-1*) Spr-Verlag.

Photoemission Studies of High-Temperature Superconductors. David W. Lynch & Clifford G. Olson. LC 98-7169. (Cambridge Studies in Low Temperature Physics: No. 5). (Illus.). 450p. (C). 1998. 110.00 (*0-521-55189-7*) Cambridge U Pr.

Photoemissive Materials. A. H. Sommer. LC 79-9461. 280p. 1980. reprint ed. lib. bdg. 31.00 (*0-89874-009-6*) Krieger.

Photofinishing Hazardous Materials Employee Training Manual. Mike Rager. (Illus.). (Orig.). (C). 1989. pap. write for info. (*0-318-65932-8*) Amer Hazmat.

***Photofolio Down in the Garden.** Anne Geddes. (Illus.). 2000. pap. 19.95 (*0-7683-2180-8*) CEDCO Pub.

***Photofolio until Now.** Anne Geddes. (Illus.). 22p. 2000. pap. text 19.95 (*0-7683-2179-4*) CEDCO Pub.

***Photofunctional Zeolites: Synthesis, Characterization, Photocatalytic Reactions, Light Harvesting.** Masakazu Anpo. LC 00-27502. 248p. 2000. lib. bdg. 79.00 (*1-56072-801-9*) Nova Sci Pubs.

Photogeneration of Reactive Species for U. V. Curing. C. Roffey. LC 96-49972. 1002p. 1997. 425.00 (*0-471-94177-8*) Wiley.

Photogenic Drawings by William Henry Fox Talbot: Sun Pictures Catalogue Seven. Larry J. Schaaf. (Illus.). 52p. 1995. pap. 30.00 (*0-9621096-5-7*) H P Kraus Jr.

Photogenic Manipulation. Robert J. Bingham. LC 72-9182. (Literature of Photography Ser.). (Illus.). 1973. reprint ed. 15.95 (*0-405-04893-9*) Ayer.

***Photogenic Painting: Gerard Fromanger.** Gilles Deleuze & Michel Foucault. 160p. 1999. pap. 29.95 (*1-901033-56-2*, Pub. by Black Dog Pubg) RAM Publications.

Photogeology: Remote Sensing Applications in Earth Sciences. Bruno Marcolongo & Franco Mantovani. 200p. (C). 1996. lib. bdg. 45.00 (*1-886106-74-6*) Science Pubs.

Photogeology & Photogeomorphology. Ed. by Edward A. Beaumont. (Treatise of Petroleum Geology Reprint Ser.: No. 18). (Illus.). 555p. 1992. 15.00 (*0-89181-417-5*, 540); pap. 10.00 (*0-685-61029-2*, 539) AAPG.

Photograde: A Photographic Grading Encyclopedia for United States Coins. rev. ed. James F. Ruddy. (Illus.). 208p. 1988. pap. 9.95 (*0-943161-04-5*) Bowers & Merena.

Photograde: A Photographic Grading Encyclopedia for United States Coins. 17th rev. ed. James F. Ruddy. (Illus.). 208p. 1988. 19.95 (*0-943161-09-6*) Bowers & Merena.

Photogrammetric Mapping. U. S. Army Corps of Engineers Staff. LC 95-47824. (Technical Engineering & Design Guides Ser.: No. 14). 336p. 1996. 56.00 (*0-7844-0143-8*) Am Soc Civil Eng.

Photograph. Donna E. Couch. (Illus.). 40p. (J). (gr. 1-6). 1992. 10.00 (*0-9634359-0-6*) Seabright Pr.

Photograph. Joe Porcelli. Ed. by Charles L. Wyrick, Jr. 346p. 1995. 22.95 (*0-941711-30-7*) Wyrick & Co.

Photograph: A Strange, Confined Space. Mary Price. 1997. pap. text 14.95 (*0-8047-2964-6*) Stanford U Pr.

Photograph: A Strange, Confined Space. Mary Price. LC 93-31698. xiv, 204p. 1994. 32.50 (*0-8047-2308-7*) Stanford U Pr.

Photograph: A Visual & Cultural History. Graham Clarke. LC 96-47645. (Oxford History of Art Ser.). (Illus.). 246p. 1997. pap. 16.95 (*0-19-284200-5*) OUP.

Photograph: A Visual & Cultural History. Graham Clarke. (Oxford History of Art Ser.). (Illus.). 248p. (C). 1997. 39.95 (*0-19-284248-X*) OUP.

Photograph Analysis. Arlene H. Eakle. (Illus.). 63p. 1976. pap. 18.00 (*0-940764-01-6*) Genealog Inst.

Photograph & the American Indian. Alfred L. Bush & Lee C. Mitchell. LC 94-12178. 352p. 1994. text 85.00 (*0-691-03489-3*, Pub. by Princeton U Pr) Cal Prin Full Svc.

Photograph Manual. 8th ed. N. G. Burgess. LC 72-9186. (Literature of Photography Ser.). 1973. reprint ed. 24.95 (*0-405-04897-1*) Ayer.

Photographe. Pierre Boulle. 188p. 1974. pap. 3.95 (*0-686-54109-X*) Fr & Eur.

Photographed Portraits of an American Home. Carol Stratman Shea. Ed. by Bruce Arant. LC 95-174337. 160p. 1996. pap. 14.95 (*0-9647658-4-5*) Design Basics.

***Photographer.** Kathryn A. Quinian. LC 98-45192. (Careers Without College Ser.). (Illus.). 48p. (YA). (gr. 4-7). 1999. 21.26 (*0-7368-0176-6*) Capstone Pr.

***Photographer.** Kathryn A. Quinlan. 1999. 19.93 (*0-516-21774-7*) Capstone Pr.

Photographer. Jack Rudman. (Career Examination Ser.: C-582). 1994. pap. 29.95 (*0-8373-0582-9*) Nat Learn.

Photographer. Barbara Steiner. 144p. (J). 1989. pap. 3.50 (*0-380-75758-3*, Avon Bks) Morrow Avon.

***Photographer Frantisek Drtikol.** Frantisek Drtikol. (Illus.). 200p. 2000. 45.00 (*80-86217-20-5*, Pub. by Kant) Dist Art Pubs.

Photographer in the Kingdom: Christian J. Hedemann's Early Images of Hawai'i. Lynn A. Davis & Nelson Foster. 1988. 25.00 (*0-930897-36-6*) Bishop Mus.

Photographer of the World: A Biography of Herbert Ponting. H. J. Arnold. LC 75-156270. (Illus.). 176p. 1975. 18.50 (*0-8386-7959-5*) Fairleigh Dickinson.

Photographer on an Army Mule. Maurice Frink & Casey E. Barthelmess. LC 65-24202. (Illus.). 296p. 1989. pap. 15.95 (*0-8061-2182-3*) U of Okla Pr.

Photographer 2: The Dark Room. Barbara Steiner. 176p. (Orig.). (YA). 1993. pap. 3.50 (*0-380-77064-4*, Avon Bks) Morrow Avon.

Photographers: History & Culture Through the Camera. Nancy Jackson. LC 95-31386. (Illus.). 144p. (YA). (gr. 5-12). 1997. 19.95 (*0-8160-3358-7*) Facts on File.

Photographer's: Paris & U . K . Editions. Patrick Deedes-Vincke. 1992. write for info. (*0-316-88892-3*) Little.

Photographers & Authors: Portraits of Twentieth Century Writers from the Carleton College Collection. Maria Morris Hambourg. (Illus.). 60p. 1984. pap. text 12.50 (*0-9613911-0-3*) Carleton Coll.

Photographer's Assistant. John Kieffer. LC 91-77927. (Illus.). 208p. 1992. pap. 16.95 (*0-9607118-9-9*) Allworth Pr.

***Photographer's Assistant.** rev. ed. John Kieffer. (Illus.). 256p. 2000. pap. 19.95 (*1-58115-080-6*, Pub. by Allworth Pr) Watsn-Guptill.

***Photographer's Assistant Handbook.** Matt Proulx. LC 99-87666. (Illus.). 176p. 2000. pap. 29.95 (*0-240-80413-9*, Focal) Buttrwrth-Heinemann.

Photographers Business & Legal Handbook. Leonard D. DuBoff. 116p. 1989. pap. 18.95 (*0-929667-02-6*, 10255) Images NY.

Photographer's Digital Studio: Transferring Your Photos into Pixels. Joe Farace. LC 96-159345. (Illus.). 384p. (C). 1996. pap. text 24.95 (*0-201-88400-3*) Peachpit Pr.

Photographer's Guide to Exposure. Jack Neubart. (Illus.). 144p. 1988. pap. 18.95 (*0-8174-5424-1*, Amphoto) Watsn-Guptill.

Photographer's Guide to Getting & Having a Successful Exhibition. Robert S. Persky & Susan P. Levy. 124p. (Orig.). 1987. pap. 24.95 (*0-913069-10-8*) Consultant Pr.

Photographer's Guide to Marketing & Self-Promotion. 2nd ed. Maria Piscopo. LC 95-75285. (Illus.). 176p. 1995. pap. 18.95 (*1-880559-24-2*) Allworth Pr.

Photographer's Guide to Polaroid Transfer. Christopher Grey. 120p. 1999. pap. 29.95 (*0-936262-89-3*, Pub. by Amherst Media) IPG Chicago.

Photographer's Guide to Shooting Model & Actor Portfolios. C. J. Elfont et al. (Illus.). 128p. 1999. pap. 29.95 (*1-58428-005-0*, Pub. by Amherst Media) IPG Chicago.

***Photographer's Guide to the Grand Canyon & Northern Arizona.** Joseph K. Lange. LC 00-39491. (Illus.). 2001. pap. 14.95 (*0-8117-2901-X*) Stackpole.

Photographer's Guide to Using Filters. Joseph Meehan. (Illus.). 144p. 1992. pap. 22.50 (*0-8174-5449-7*, Amphoto) Watsn-Guptill.

Photographer's Guide to Using Filters. rev. ed. Joseph Meehan. LC 98-11624. 144p. 1998. pap. 24.95 (*0-8174-5452-7*) Watsn-Guptill.

Photographer's Guide to Using Light. Ted Schwarz & Brian Stoppee. (Illus.). 144p. 1986. pap. 18.95 (*0-8174-5422-5*, Amphoto) Watsn-Guptill.

***Photographer's Guide to Yellowstone & the Tetons.** Joseph K. Lange. LC 99-43766. (Illus.). 128p. 2000. pap. 14.95 (*0-8117-2895-1*) Stackpole.

Photographer's Handbook. 3rd rev. ed. John Hedgecoe. LC 92-52957. (Illus.). 352p. 1992. pap. 24.95 (*0-679-74204-2*) Knopf.

Photographers in Arizona, 1850-1920: A History & Directory. limited ed. Jeremy Rowe. (Illus.). 136p. 1997. boxed set 125.00 (*1-887694-06-4*) C Mautz Pubng.

Photographers in Arizona 1950-1920: A History & Directory. Jeremy Rowe. Ed. by Rosemarie Mossinger & Cathie Leavitt. (Illus.). 136p. (Orig.). 1997. 35.00 (*1-887694-05-6*) C Mautz Pubng.

Photographers in Ohio, 1839-1900: History & Directory. Diane Van Skiver Gagel. (Illus.). 128p. 1998. 35.00 (*1-887694-07-2*) C Mautz Pubng.

Photographer's Internet Handbook. Joe Farace. LC 96-84657. (Illus.). 208p. (Orig.). 1997. pap. 18.95 (*1-880559-62-5*) Allworth Pr.

***Photographer's Market: 2,000 Places to Sell Your Photographs.** Ed. by Donna Poehner. 640p. 2000. pap. 24.99 (*0-89879-978-3*) F & W Pubns Inc.

Photographer's Market Guide to Photo Submission & Portfolio Formats. Michael Willins. LC 97-25182. (Illus.). 160p. 1997. pap. 18.99 (*0-89879-758-6*, Wrtrs Digest Bks) F & W Pubns Inc.

Photographer's Master Printing Course. Tim Rudman. (Illus.). 160p. 1998. text 29.95 (*0-240-80324-8*, Focal) Buttrwrth-Heinemann.

Photographers on Disc. 1996. 495.00 (*0-7838-1551-4*, G K Hall & Co) Mac Lib Ref.

Photographers on Photographers: Aperture 151. Helen Levitt. (Illus.). 80p. 1998. pap. 27.95 (*0-89381-773-2*) Aperture.

Photographer's Organizer. Michal Heron. 32p. 1992. pap. 8.95 (*1-880559-02-1*) Allworth Pr.

Photographer's Publishing Handbook. Harold Davis. 182p. (Orig.). 1991. pap. 19.95 (*0-929667-07-7*, 10253) Images NY.

Photographer's Resource: The Watson-Guptill Guide to Workshops, Conferences, Artists' Colonies. Stuart Cohen. LC 97-60100. (Getting Your Act Together Ser.). (Illus.). 224p. 1997. pap. text 19.95 (*0-8230-7654-7*) Watsn-Guptill.

Photographers Scenic Photo Marketing Guide: A Guide to Making Money from Scenic Photographs for Amateur & Professional Photographers. Douglas Edwards. (Illus.). 115p. 1988. 22.95 (*0-923613-00-5*) Beaver Graphics Inc.

Photographer's Studio Manual. rev. ed. Michael Freeman. (Illus.). 256p. 1991. pap. 24.95 (*0-8174-5464-0*, Amphoto) Watsn-Guptill.

Photographer's Sweethearts. Diana Hartog. LC 95-34135. 288p. 1996. 22.95 (*0-87951-646-1*, Pub. by Overlook Pr) Penguin Putnam.

Photographer's Sweethearts. Diana Hartog. 240p. 1997. pap. 13.95 (*0-87951-796-4*, Pub. by Overlook Pr) Penguin Putnam.

Photographer's Troubleshooter: How to Turn Photographic Problems into Good Pictures. Michael Freeman. 192p. 1985. 12.95 (*0-88191-035-X*) Freundlich.

Photographer's Wife. Robert Sole. Tr. by John Brownjohn. 320p. 1999. 26.00 (*1-86046-549-8*, Pub. by Harvill Press) FS&G.

***Photographer's Wife.** Robert Sole. (Illus.). 2000. pap. 12.00 (*1-86046-699-0*) Harvill Press.

Photographes du Mali. Erika Nimis. (Illus.). 1998. pap. text 14.95 (*2-909571-21-1*, Pub. by Revue Noire) Dist Art Pubs.

Photographic Amusements Including Tricks & Unusual or Novel Effects Obtainable with the Camera. 10th ed. Frank R. Fraprie. LC 72-9199. (Literature of Photography Ser.). 1979. reprint ed. 27.95 (*0-405-04908-0*) Ayer.

Photographic Anatomy of the Human Body. 3rd ed. Chihiro Yokochi & Johannes W. Rohen. LC 89-2047. (Illus.). 150p. 1989. 39.50 (*0-89640-160-X*) Igaku-Shoin.

Photographic Art: Colombian Contemporary Photography, Pt. II. Ana Sokoloff. (Illus.). 16p. 1992. pap. text. write for info. (*1-883592-03-8*) Perm Mission.

Photographic Art: Media & Disclosure. Norman Peterson. LC 83-18127. (Studies in Photography: No. 4). (Illus.). 147p. reprint ed. pap. 45.60 (*0-8357-1529-9*, 207056900001) Bks Demand.

Photographic Art of Hoyningen-Huene. William A. Ewing. LC 97-61348. (Illus.). 248p. 1998. pap. 34.95 (*0-500-28035-5*, Pub. by Thames Hudson) Norton.

***Photographic Art of William Henry Fox Talbot.** Larry J. Schaaf & William Henry Fox Talbot. LC 00-32618. (Illus.). 256p. 2000. 75.00 (*0-691-05000-7*) Princeton U Pr.

Photographic Arts. John Wood. LC 96-32933. (Illus.). 206p. 1997. 65.00 (*0-87745-573-2*) U of Iowa Pr.

Photographic Assignments: The Expert Approach. Michael Busselle. (Illus.). 192p. 1997. pap. 19.95 (*0-7153-0179-9*) Sterling.

Photographic Atlas for Human Anatomy & Physiology. Gerard J. Tortora. LC 99-32135. 240p. (C). 1999. pap. text 26.00 (*0-8053-5105-1*) Benjamin-Cummings.

Photographic Atlas for the Anatomy & Physiology Laboratory. 3rd ed. Kent Van de Graaff & John Crawley. (Illus.). 192p. (C). 1999. pap. text 17.95 (*0-89582-313-6*) Morton Pub.

Photographic Atlas for the Anatomy & Physiology Laboratory. 4th ed. Kent M. Van De Graaff & John L. Crawley. (Illus.). 192p. (C). 1999. pap. text 18.95 (*0-89582-497-3*) Morton Pub.

Photographic Atlas for the Biology Laboratory. 3rd ed. Kent Van de Graaff & John Crawley. (Illus.). 224p. (C). 1996. pap. text 18.95 (*0-89582-314-4*) Morton Pub.

Photographic Atlas for the Botany Laboratory. 3rd ed. Kent M. Van De Graaff et al. 192p. 1997. pap. text, lab manual ed. 17.95 (*0-89582-383-7*) Morton Pub.

Photographic Atlas for the Microbiology Laboratory. Michael Leboffe & Burton Pierce. (Illus.). 144p. (C). 1999. pap. text 15.95 (*0-89582-308-X*) Morton Pub.

Photographic Atlas for the Microbiology Laboratory. 2nd ed. Michael LeBuffe & Burton Pierce. (Illus.). 192p. 1998. pap. text 17.95 (*0-89582-461-2*) Morton Pub.

***Photographic Atlas for the Molecular Biology Laboratory.** Patrick Guilforce. (Illus.). 64p. (C). 1999. pap. text 16.95 (*0-89582-513-9*) Morton Pub.

Photographic Atlas for the Zoology Laboratory. 3rd ed. Kent M. Van De Graaff & John L. Crawley. 192p. 1997. pap. text, lab manual ed. 17.95 (*0-89582-382-9*) Morton Pub.

Photographic Atlas of an Accretionary Prism: Geologic Structures of the Shimanto Belt, Japan. A. Taira et al. (Illus.). 150p. 1992. 163.95 (*0-387-55344-4*) Spr-Verlag.

Photographic Atlas of Cat Anatomy: With Sheep Heart, Brain, Eye, Kidney Dissection. 3rd rev. ed. Michael J. Timmons. LC 97-62351. (Illus.). 81p. 1998. 14.95 (*0-9627559-2-3*) Spyglass Pubns.

Photographic Atlas of Civil War Injuries: Photographs of Surgical Cases & Specimens. Bradley P. Bengtson et al. LC 96-75434. (Illus.). 480p. 1996. 125.00 (*0-9635861-8-1*) Med Staff Pr.

Photographic Atlas of Civil War Injuries: Photographs of Surgical Cases & Specimens. deluxe ed. Bradley P. Bengtson et al. (Illus.). 480p. 1996. lthr. 200.00 (*0-9653101-0-8*) Med Staff Pr.

Photographic Atlas of Practical Anatomy I: Abdomen, Lower Limb, 2 vols., Set. W. Thiel. Tr. by T. Telger. LC 97-7231. (Illus.). 860p. 1997. 298.00 (*3-540-61195-9*) Spr-Verlag.

Photographic Atlas of Practical Anatomy II: Neck, Head, Back, Chest, Upper Extremeties. W. Thiel. Tr. by T. C. Telger. LC 97-7231. (Illus.). 430p. 1998. 299.00 (*3-540-62239-X*) Spr-Verlag.

Photographic Atlas of Shark Anatomy: The Gross Morphology of Squalas Acanthias. Carl Gans & Thomas S. Parsons. LC 80-24528. (Illus.). 106p. 1981. pap. text 16.00 (*0-226-28120-5*) U Ch Pr.

***Photographic Atlas of the Human Body.** Tortora. 256p. 1999. pap. 36.95 (*0-471-37487-3*) Wiley.

Photographic Atlas of the Rat Brain: The Cell & Fiber Architecture Illustrated in Three Planes with Stereotaxic Coordinates. Lawrence Kruger et al. LC 94-11371. (Illus.). 317p. (C). 1995. text 130.00 (*0-521-41342-7*); spiral bd. 74.95 (*0-521-42403-8*) Cambridge U Pr.

***Photographic Atlas of the Stars.** H. J. P. Arnold et al. LC 97-162455. (Illus.). 220p. 1999. 31.95 (*0-7503-0654-8*) IOP Pub.

Photographic Atlas of the Stars. unabridged ed. H. J. Arnold et al. (Illus.). 224p. 1997. 59.95 (*0-913135-31-3*, 18549) Kalmbach.

Photographic Atlas of the Stars: The Whole Sky in 50 Plates & Maps. Ed. by H. J. Arnold et al. (Illus.). 224p. 1996. 63.00 (*0-7503-0378-6*) IOP Pub.

Photographic Case Studies in Cardiopulmonary Disease: Diagnostic Tests for the Practitioner. Stuart W. McCalley & Francis J. Neeson. (Photographic Case Studies). 1993. pap. text. write for info. (*0-9633775-6-6*) Clinical Comms.

Photographic Case Studies in Gastroenterology: Diagnostic Tests for the Practitioner. Richard Rothstein et al. (Photographic Case Studies). 104p. 1992. pap. text. write for info. (*0-9633775-0-7*) Clinical Comms.

Photographic Case Studies in General Medicine: Diagnostic Tests for the Practitioner. Thomas P. Habif & Felice R. Zwas. (Photographic Case Studies). 64p. 1992. pap. text. write for info. (*0-9633775-1-5*) Clinical Comms.

Photographic Case Studies in Neurology: Diagnostic Tests for the Practitioner. David J. Coffey et al. (Photographic Case Studies). 96p. 1993. text. write for info. (*0-9633775-2-3*); pap. text. write for info. (*0-9633775-3-1*) Clinical Comms.

Photographic Case Studies in Skin & Skin Structure Disease: Diagnostic Tests for the Practitioner. Thomas P. Habif. (Photographic Case Studies). 40p. 1993. pap. text. write for info. (*0-9633775-5-8*) Clinical Comms.

Photographic Case Studies in Surgical Oncology: Diagnostic Tests for the Practitioner. James J. Vredenburgh. (Photographic Case Studies). 40p. 1993. pap. text. write for info. (*0-9633775-4-X*) Clinical Comms.

Photographic Catalog of Killer Whales, Orcinus Orca, from the Central Gulf of Alaska to the Southeastern Bering Sea. Marilyn E. Dahlheim. (Illus.). 64p. 1998. 13.00 (*0-89904-779-3*, Seascape Res Alliance); spiral bd. 8.00 (*0-89904-780-7*, Seascape Res Alliance) Crumb Elbow Pub.

Photographic Collections in Texas: A Union Guide. Compiled by Richard Pearce-Moses. LC 87-9979. (Union Guide Published for Texas Historical Foundation). 400p. 1987. pap. 29.50 (*0-89096-351-7*) Tex A&M Univ Pr.

Photographic Color Printing: Theory & Technique. Ira Current. (Illus.). 296p. 1987. text 52.95 (*0-240-51787-3*, Focal) Buttrwrth-Heinemann.

Photographic Composition. Tom Grill & Mark Scanlon. (Illus.). 144p. 1990. pap. 19.95 (*0-8174-5427-6*, Amphoto) Watsn-Guptill.

***Photographic Encyclopedia of Roses.** Peter Harkness. 1999. 19.99 (*0-86283-860-6*) Quadrillion Pubng.

***Photographic Encyclopedia of Wildflowers.** Teresa Farino. 1999. 19.99 (*0-86283-918-1*) Quadrillion Pubng.

Photographic Enforcement of High-Occupancy Vehicle (HOV) Lanes. (Illus.). 100p. (Orig.). (C). 1994. pap. text 25.00 (*1-56806-148-X*) DIANE Pub.

Photographic Equipment, UL 122. 4th ed. (C). 1999. pap. text 95.00 (*1-55989-435-0*) Underwrtrs Labs.

Photographic Essay of a Capitola Cat. Photos by Minna Hertel. (Illus.). 64p. 1993. pap. 9.95 (*1-881569-01-2*) Hertel Bks.

P

Photographic Evidence, 3 vols. 2nd ed. Charles C. Scott. suppl. ed. write for info. (*0-318-57511-6*) West Pub.

Photographic Experience: Exhibition Catalogue. Heinz K. Henisch & Bridget A. Henisch. (Illus.). 194p. 1988. pap. 17.00 (*0-911209-38-7*) Palmer Mus Art.

Photographic Experience, 1839-1914: Images & Attitudes. Heinz K. Henisch & Bridget A. Henisch. LC 92-36781. (Illus.). 472p. (C). 1994. 99.50 (*0-271-00930-6*) Pa St U Pr.

Photographic Eye: Learning to See with a Camera. rev. ed. Michael F. O'Brien & Norman Sibley. LC 93-74644. (Illus.). 228p. (YA). (gr. 9-12). 1995. text 28.60 (*0-87192-283-5*) Davis Mass.

Photographic Eye of Ben Shahn. Ben Shahn. 141p. 1975. text 24.45 (*0-674-66615-1*) HUP.

Photographic Filters. Leslie Stroebel. LC 72-83109. 144p. 1974. pap. 16.95 (*0-87100-028-8*, 2028) Morgan.

Photographic Global Notes, 2 vols., Vol. I & II. Tim Mantoani. (Illus.). 308p. (C). 1998. pap. 29.95 (*1-883403-23-5*, H 707, Silver Pixel Pr) Saunders Photo.

Photographic Grant Sources. 1986. 4.95 (*0-89816-074-X*) Embee Pr.

Photographic Guide to Birds of India & Nepal: Also Bangladesh, Pakistan, Sri Lanka. Bikram Grewal. (Eco-Travel Guides Ser.). (Illus.). 144p. 1998. pap. 15.95 (*0-88359-034-4*, RCB-0344P, Pub. by R Curtis Pubng) Chelsea Green Pub.

*__Photographic Guide to Birds of Israel & the Middle East.__ David M. Cottridge. (Illus.). 144p. 2000. pap. 15.95 (*0-88359-055-7*, RCB-0557, R Curtis Bk) R Curtis Pubng.

*__Photographic Guide to Birds of Java, Sumatra & Bali.__ Tony Tilford. (Illus.). 136p. 2000. pap. 15.95 (*0-88359-049-2*, R Curtis Bk) R Curtis Pubng.

Photographic Guide to Birds of Namibia. Ian Sinclair. (Eco-Travel Guides Ser.). (Illus.). 144p. 1998. pap. 15.95 (*0-88359-037-9*, RCB-0379P, Pub. by R Curtis Pubng) Chelsea Green Pub.

Photographic Guide to Birds of Peninsular Malaysia & Singapore. G. W. Davison & Chew Yen Fook. (Eco-Travel Guides Ser.). (Illus.). 144p. 1998. pap. 15.95 (*0-88359-036-0*, Pub. by R Curtis Pubng) Chelsea Green Pub.

Photographic Guide to Birds of Thailand. Michael Webster. (Eco-Travel Guides Ser.). (Illus.). 144p. (Orig.). 1999. pap. 15.95 (*0-88359-041-7*, RCB-0417P, Pub. by R Curtis Pubng) Chelsea Green Pub.

Photographic Guide to Birds of Thailand Michael Webster & Yen Fook Chew. LC 97-942774. 144 p. 1997. write for info. (*1-85368-594-1*, Pub. by New5 Holland) Sterling.

Photographic Guide to Birds of the Himalayas. Bieram Grewal & Otto Pfister. (Photographic Wildlife Pocket Guides Ser.). (Illus.). 144p. 1998. pap. 15.95 (*0-88359-045-X*, Pub. by R Curtis Pubng) Chelsea Green Pub.

*__Photographic Guide to Birds of the Philippines.__ Timothy Fisher. (Illus.). 2000. pap. 15.95 (*0-88359-051-4*, RCB-0514, R Curtis Bk) R Curtis Pubng.

*__Photographic Guide to Birds of the West Indies.__ G. Michael Flieg. (Illus.). 144p. 2000. pap. 15.95 (*0-88359-050-6*, RCB-0506, R Curtis Bk) R Curtis Pubng.

Photographic Guide to Buying & Selling Horses. Vanessa Britton. LC 97-214688. (Illus.). 160p. 1997. 29.95 (*0-7153-0377-5*) Sterling.

Photographic Guide to Conformation. Robert Oliver & Bob Langrish. 250p. 1990. 68.00 (*0-85131-522-4*, Pub. by J A Allen) Trafalgar.

Photographic Guide to Mammals of Australia. Peter Rowland. (Eco-Travel Guides Ser.). (Illus.). 144p. 1998. pap. 15.95 (*0-88359-032-8*, Pub. by R Curtis Pubng) Chelsea Green Pub.

Photographic Guide to North American Raptors. Ed. by William S. Clerk & Brian K. Wheeler. (Illus.). 198p. 1995. text 32.00 (*0-12-745530-2*) Acad Pr.

Photographic Guide to North American Raptors. Brian K. Wheeler & William S. Clark. (Natural World Ser.). (Illus.). 198p. 1999. pap. 19.95 (*0-12-745531-0*) Acad Pr.

Photographic Guide to Snakes & Other Reptiles of Australia. Gerry Swan. (Eco-Travel Guides Ser.). (Illus.). 144p. 1998. pap. 15.95 (*0-88359-033-6*, Pub. by R Curtis Pubng) Chelsea Green Pub.

Photographic Guide to Snakes & Other Reptiles of Thailand, Singapore & Peninsular Malaysia. M. Jerel Cox et al. (Photographic Wildlife Pocket Guide Ser.). (Illus.). 144p. 1998. pap. 15.95 (*0-88359-043-3*, Pub. by R Curtis Pubng) Chelsea Green Pub.

*__Photographic Guide to the Birds of East Africa.__ 2nd ed. David Richards. (Photographic Wildlife Pocket Guides Ser.). (Illus.). 144p. 2000. pap. 15.95 (*0-88359-054-9*, RCB-0549, R Curtis Bk) R Curtis Pubng.

Photographic Guide to the Ethnographic North American Indian Basket Collection: Peabody Museum of Archaeology & Ethnology, Vol. 1. Ed. by Madeleine W. Fang & Marilyn R. Binder. (Museum Press Ser.). (Illus.). 498p. 1990. 55.00 (*0-87365-819-1*, PRBAS1) Peabody Harvard.

Photographic Guide to the Ethnographic North American Indian Basket Collection Vol. 2: Peabody Museum of Archaeology & Ethnology. Ed. by Susan H. Haskell. (Peabody Museum Press Ser.). (Illus.). 108p. 1998. 20.00 (*0-87365-827-2*, PRBAS2) Peabody Harvard.

Photographic Guide to the Evaluation of Hazard Trees in Urban Areas. 2nd ed. Nelda Matheny & James Clark. 85p. 1993. pap. text 45.00 (*1-881956-04-0*) Int Soc Arboricult.

Photographic Guide to the Shorebirds of the World. David Rosair & David Cottridge. LC 95-2502. (Illus.). 176p. 1995. 29.95 (*0-8160-3309-9*) Facts on File.

Photographic Handbook of the Wildfowl of the World. Malcolm A. Ogilvie. 1999. 49.95 (*1-85368-625-5*) Sterling.

Photographic Heritage of the Middle East: An Exhibition of Early Photographs of Egypt, Palestine, Syria, Turkey, Greece, & Iran, 1849-1893. Paul E. Chevedden. (Occasional Papers on the Near East: Vol. 1, Fascicle 3). (Illus.). 40p. (Orig.). 1981. pap. text 9.00 (*0-89003-096-0*) Undena Pubns.

Photographic History of the Civil War, Vol. II. Theo F. Rodenbough. (Illus.). 750p. 1987. 14.98 (*1-55521-199-2*) Bk Sales Inc.

Photographic History of the Civil War, Vol. 3. Theo F. Rodenbough. 750p. 1987. 15.98 (*1-55521-203-4*) Bk Sales Inc.

Photographic History of the Civil War, Vol. IV. Theo F. Rodenbough. (Illus.). 750p. 1987. 14.98 (*1-55521-201-8*) Bk Sales Inc.

Photographic History of the Civil War: Forts & Artillery - The Navies, Vol. 3. Theo F. Rodenbough. 322p. 1987. 14.98 (*1-55521-200-X*) Bk Sales Inc.

Photographic History of the Civil War: The Armies & Leaders - Poetry & Eloquence, Vol. 5. Theo F. Rodenbough. (Illus.). 750p. 1987. 14.98 (*1-55521-202-6*) Bk Sales Inc.

Photographic History of the Civil War: The Opening Battles - Two Years of Grim War. Theo F. Rodenbough. (Illus.). 750p. 1987. 14.98 (*1-55521-174-7*) Bk Sales Inc.

Photographic Image in Digital Culture. Martin Lister. LC 94-38082. (Comedia Ser.). (Illus.). 256p. (C). 1995. pap. 22.99 (*0-415-12157-4*, C0590) Routledge.

Photographic Image in Digital Culture. Ed. by Martin Lister. LC 94-38082. (Comedia Ser.). (Illus.). 256p. (C). (gr. 13). 1995. 80.00 (*0-415-12156-6*, C0589) Routledge.

Photographic Images of the Klamath National Forest in Siskiyou & Humboldt Counties - a Historical Journey. Ed. by Gilbert W. Davies & Florice M. Frank. LC 94-75404. (Illus.). 132p. (C). 1994. pap. 14.95 (*0-9634413-5-3*) HiSt ink Bks.

Photographic Imaging Techniques in C++ for Windows3 & Windows NT. Craig A. Lindley. LC 94-49718. 432p. 1995. pap. 44.95 incl. disk (*0-471-11568-1*) Wiley.

Photographic Imaging with Photoshop. James L. Pomeroy. (Illus.). 220p. 1997. pap. text 30.00 (*0-9625017-8-6*) Palms & Rhodes Pub.

Photographic Impressionists of Spain: A History of the Aesthetics & Technique of Pictorial Photography. S. Carl King. LC 88-36517. (Studies in Art & Religious Interpretation: Vol. 12). 302p. 1989. lib. bdg. 99.95 (*0-88946-564-9*) E Mellen.

Photographic Interpretation. Andre Page. (Illus.). 128p. 1973. 12.00 (*0-7207-0633-5*) Transatl Arts.

Photographic Journey Through Colorado. Carolyn Wangaard et al. (Illus.). 80p. 1997. pap. 12.00 (*1-892717-00-X*, MISB106) Sanborn Ltd.

Photographic Journey Through the Roaring Fork Valley. Karin Gamba. 50p. (Orig.). 1995. 14.95 (*0-9645444-0-7*) Sage Press.

Photographic Lens: Media Manual. 2nd ed. Sidney F. Ray. (Illus.). 355p. 2000. pap. text 37.95 (*0-240-51329-0*, Focal) Buttrwrth-Heinemann.

Photographic Lighting. John Child. 148p. 2000. pap. text 29.95 (*0-240-51549-8*, Focal) Buttrwrth-Heinemann.

Photographic Literature: An International Bibliographic Guide to General & Specialized Literature on Photographic Processes. Ed. by Albert Boni. 346p. 1996. reprint ed. 50.00 (*1-888262-39-7*) Martino Pubng.

Photographic Manual for Woody Landscape Plants. Michael A. Dirr. (Illus.). 1978. text 29.80 (*0-87563-156-8*); pap. text 19.80 (*0-87563-153-3*) Stipes.

Photographic Manual of Regional Orthopaedic & Neurological Testing. 3rd ed. Joseph J. Cipriano et al. LC 96-43896. (Illus.). 456p. 1997. 65.00 (*0-683-18100-9*) Lppncott W & W.

Photographic Manual of Regional Orthopaedics & Neurological Testing. 2nd ed. Joseph J. Cipriano. (Illus.). 346p. 1991. 60.00 (*0-683-01701-2*) Lppncott W & W.

Photographic Memories: Images of China & Vietnam. Ed. by Ruth Silverman. (Illus.). 108p. 1999. 300.00 (*1-881529-39-8*); 40.00 (*1-881529-40-1*) Custom & Limited.

Photographic Memories: The Autobiography of Jack Delano. Jack Delano. LC 96-44181. 240p. 1997. 29.95 (*1-56098-741-3*) Smithsonian.

*__Photographic Memory.__ William Claxton. 2000. 65.00 (*1-57687-085-5*, pwerHse Bks) pwerHse Cultrl.

Photographic Memory: The Kennedy Assassination November 22, 1963. Richard B. Trask. Ed. by Marian A. Montgomery. (Illus.). 65p. (Orig.). 1996. pap. 6.95 (*0-9648131-2-2*, Sixth Flr Mus) Dallas Cty Hist Foun.

Photographic Mind: Holographic Memory System. Dane Spotts. LC 99-60649. 220p. 1999. pap. 29.95 (*1-892805-24-3*) LifeQuest Pubg.

Photographic Notes: Everything Is Important - Nothing Is Important. Dick Joyce. (Illus.). 208p. 1998. 49.95 (*3-908161-05-3*, Pub. by Edit Stemmle) Abbeville Pr.

Photographic Optics. Desire Van Monckhoven. Ed. by Peter C. Bunnell & Robert A. Sobieszek. LC 76-23060. (Sources of Modern Photography Ser.). (Illus.). 1979. reprint ed. lib. bdg. 20.95 (*0-405-09624-0*) Ayer.

Photographic Portraits of American Ocean Steamships, 1850-1870. Ed. by William D. Thomas. (Illus.). 123p. 1986. 39.50 (*0-913423-07-6*) Steamship Hist Soc.

Photographic Possibilities. Robert Hirsch. (Illus.). 304p. 1991. pap. 46.95 (*0-240-80047-8*, Focal) Buttrwrth-Heinemann.

*__Photographic Possibilities.__ 2nd ed. Hirsch & Valentino. 272p. 2000. pap. 36.95 (*0-240-80362-0*, Focal) Buttrwrth-Heinemann.

Photographic Pot-Pourri of Calloway County, Kentucky. Calloway County Library Volunteers Staff. LC 87-71192. 200p. 1988. 49.95 (*0-938021-22-2*) Turner Pub KY.

Photographic Principles: Developing & Printing. (Illus.). 1981. 4.38 (*0-9601006-5-2*) G T Yeamans.

Photographic Principles: Taking Pictures. (Illus.). 1980. 4.38 (*0-9601006-4-4*) G T Yeamans.

Photographic Printing. Gene Nocon. (Illus.). 160p. 1995. pap. text 19.95 (*0-86369-653-8*, Pub. by Virgin Bks) London Brdge.

Photographic Printing Methods: A Practical Guide to the Professional & Amateur Worker. 3rd ed. W. H. Burbank. LC 72-9185. (Literature of Photography Ser.). 1978. reprint ed. 20.95 (*0-405-04896-3*) Ayer.

Photographic Record. Tyndale House Publishers Staff. (Two Become One Ser.). 1999. 12.99 (*0-8423-3542-0*) Tyndale Hse.

Photographic Retouching. Vilia Reed. LC 87-81377. (Illus.). 116p. (Orig.). (C). 1998. pap. 24.95 (*0-87985-474-X*, E-97, Kodak) Saunders Photo.

Photographic Sensitivity: Theory & Mechanisms. Tadaaki Tani. (Oxford Series on Optical & Imaging Sciences: No. 8). (Illus.). 264p. 1995. text 90.00 (*0-19-507240-5*) OUP.

Photographic Sensitometry. Hollis N. Todd & Richard D. Zakia. LC 75-82445. 312p. 1981. pap. 19.95 (*0-87100-000-8*, 2000) Morgan.

Photographic Specialist I. Jack Rudman. (Career Examination Ser.: C-1870). 1994. pap. 23.95 (*0-8373-1870-X*) Nat Learn.

Photographic Specialist II. Jack Rudman. (Career Examination Ser.: C-1871). 1994. pap. 23.95 (*0-8373-1871-8*) Nat Learn.

Photographic Studies of Old Virginia Homes & Gardens. Meredith Dietz. 1953. 3.00 (*0-87517-029-3*) Dietz.

Photographic Studios of Europe. H. Baden Pritchard. LC 72-9226. (Literature of Photography Ser.). 1973. reprint ed. 23.95 (*0-405-04932-3*) Ayer.

Photographic Study Guide for Oriental Rugs. Thomas R. Myerscough. LC 84-90640. 1983. 45.00 (*0-318-04446-3*) Persian Rug Ctr.

Photographic Supplement of Confederate Swords. William A. Albaugh, III. (William Albaugh Collection). (Illus.). 235p. 1993. reprint ed. 35.00 (*1-56837-266-3*) Broadfoot.

Photographic Systems for Engineers. 2nd ed. Ed. by Fordyce M. Brown et al. LC 77-378304. (Illus.). 278p. reprint ed. pap. 86.20 (*0-8357-8648-X*, 203508900092) Bks Demand.

Photographic Technician. Jack Rudman. (Career Examination Ser.: C-1872). 1994. pap. 23.95 (*0-8373-1872-6*) Nat Learn.

Photographic Techniques for Accident Investigation. 22p. 1984. 10.00 (*0-939874-60-1*) ASSE.

Photographic Tour of the Universe. rev. ed. Gabriele Vanin. (Illus.). 144p. 1999. pap. 24.95 (*1-55209-345-X*) Firefly Bks Ltd.

Photographic Tour of Virginia. Carol M. Highsmith & Ted Landphai. LC 97-8027. (Photographic Tour Ser.). (Illus.). 128p. 1997. 14.99 (*0-517-18614-4*) Random Hse Value.

Photographic Utilization Guide for Key Riparian Graminoids. John W. Kinney & Warren P. Clary. (Illus.). 18p. 1997. reprint ed. 9.00 (*0-89904-583-9*, Bear Meadows Resrch Grp); reprint ed. pap. 3.00 (*0-89904-584-7*, Bear Meadows Resrch Grp) Crumb Elbow Pub.

Photographic Views of Sherman's Campaign. George N. Barnard. LC 76-45964. (Illus.). 80p. 1977. reprint ed. pap. 8.95 (*0-486-23445-2*) North South Trader.

Photographic Vision in Proust. Stephen C. Infantino. LC 91-34355. (Currents in Comparative Romance Languages & Literatures Ser.: Vol. 6). 83p. (C). 1993. text 35.95 (*0-8204-1716-5*) P Lang Pubng.

Photographic Whitewash: Suppressed Kennedy Assassination Pictures. Harold Weisberg. (Illus.). 1967. per. 14.00 (*0-911606-03-3*) Weisberg.

Photographic Works, 1969-1976. William Wegman. 1994. pap. 49.95 (*2-908257-12-2*, Pub. by F R A C) Dist Art Pubs.

Photographic Works, 1969-1980. Robert Cumming. 180p. 1995. pap. 35.00 (*2-908257-15-7*, Pub. by F R A C) Dist Art Pubs.

Photographica: A Subject Catalog of Books on Photography. 1983. 175.00 (*0-8161-1447-1*, G K Hall & Co) Mac Lib Ref.

*__Photographica; the Fascination with Classic Cameras.__ Rudolf Hillebrand & Gunther Kadlubek. (Illus.). 160p. 2000. pap. 19.95 (*0-7643-1174-3*) Schiffer.

Photographie, 2 vols. A. Davanne. Ed. by Peter C. Bunnell & Robert A. Sobieszek. LC 76-23052. (Sources of Modern Photography Ser.). (FRE., Illus.). 1979. lib. bdg. 53.95 (*0-405-09615-1*) Ayer.

Photographie. L. D. Evrard-Blanquart. Ed. by Peter C. Bunnell & Robert A. Sobieszek. LC 76-23042. (Sources of Modern Photography Ser.). 1979. reprint ed. lib. bdg. 7.50 (*0-405-09604-6*) Ayer.

Photographie au Salon de 1859 et "La Photographie" et Le Stereoscope", 2 vols. Louis Figuier. Ed. by Peter C. Bunnell & Robert A. Sobieszek. LC 76-24661. (Sources of Modern Photography Ser.). (FRE., Illus.). 1979. reprint ed. lib. bdg. 27.95 (*0-405-09639-9*) Ayer.

Photographie Consideree Comme Art et Comme Industrie. Pierson & J. P. Mayer. Ed. by Peter C. Bunnell & Robert A. Sobieszek. LC 76-24666. (Sources of Modern Photography Ser.). (FRE.). 1979. reprint ed. lib. bdg. 18.95 (*0-405-09643-7*) Ayer.

Photographie Farbiger Gegenstande in Den Richtigen Tonverhaltnissen. Hermann Vogel. Ed. by Peter C. Bunnell & Robert A. Sobieszek. LC 78-19590. (Sources of Modern Photography Ser.). (GER., Illus.). 1979. reprint ed. lib. bdg. 12.95 (*0-405-09663-1*) Ayer.

Photographie Instantanee. Josef-Maria Eder. Ed. by Peter C. Bunnell & Robert A. Sobieszek. LC 76-23056. (Sources of Modern Photography Ser.). (FRE., Illus.). 1979. reprint ed. lib. bdg. 18.95 (*0-405-09619-4*) Ayer.

*__Photographien, 1950-1980.__ Herber Tobias. 1998. 59.95 (*3-925443-40-1*) Janssen.

Photographing Airplanes. Steve Mansfield. LC 91-70476. (Illus.). 160p. 1991. pap. 24.95 (*0-943231-43-4*) Howell Pr VA.

Photographing Animals & Pets. Hilton. 1998. 35.00 (*2-88046-350-5*, Rotovision) Watsn-Guptill.

Photographing Animals in the Wild. Andy Rouse. (Illus.). 1998. 19.95 (*0-86343-362-6*, Pub. by Hove Foto) Watsn-Guptill.

*__Photographing Architecture & Interiors.__ Julius Shulman. (Illus.). 180p. 2000. reprint ed. 39.95 (*1-890449-07-5*) Balcony Pr.

Photographing Arizona: Practical Techniques to Improve Your Pictures. Lawrence W. Cheek. 96p. 1992. pap. 12.95 (*0-916179-36-2*) Ariz Hwy.

Photographing Buildings Inside & Out. 2nd enl. rev. ed. Norman McGrath. LC 92-42306. (Illus.). 208p. 1993. text 27.50 (*0-8230-4016-X*, Whitney Lib) Watsn-Guptill.

Photographing Children. Liz Walker. LC 95-1418. (Point & Shoot Ser.). (Illus.). 96p. 1995. pap. 11.95 (*0-8174-5486-1*, Amphoto) Watsn-Guptill.

*__Photographing Children in Black & White.__ Helen T. Boursier. (Illus.). 128p. 2000. pap. 29.95 (*1-58428-014-X*) Amherst Media.

Photographing in the Studio: Tools & Techniques. White Paw Press Staff. 256p. (C). 1993. text. write for info. (*0-697-13189-0*) Brown & Benchmark.

Photographing Jerusalem: The Image of the City in Nineteenth-Century Photography. Issam Nassar. LC 97-61665. (Illus.). 225p. 1997. lib. bdg. 31.50 (*0-88033-379-0*, 482, Pub. by East Eur Monographs) Col U Pr.

Photographing Medicine: Images & Power in Britain & America Since Eighteen Forty, 21. Daniel M. Fox & Christopher J. Lawrence. LC 87-25088. (Contributions in Medical Studies: No. 21). (Illus.). 357p. 1988. 85.00 (*0-313-23719-0*, FMC/) Greenwood.

Photographing Minerals, Fossils, & Lapidary Arts. Jeffrey A. Scovil. (Illus.). 240p. 1996. 40.00 (*0-945005-21-0*) Geoscience Pr.

*__Photographing Montana, 1894-1928: The Life & Work of Evelyn Cameron.__ Donna M. Lucey. (Illus.). 268p. 2000. reprint ed. 60.00 (*0-87842-426-1*); reprint ed. pap. 35.00 (*0-87842-425-3*) Mountain Pr.

Photographing on Safari: A Field Guide to Wildlife Photography in East Africa. Joe McDonald. LC 96-17751. (Illus.). 144p. 1996. pap. 19.95 (*0-8174-5440-3*, Amphoto) Watsn-Guptill.

Photographing Oregon with Professional Results. Photos & Text by Bryan F. Peterson. LC 84-80434. (Illus.). 96p. (Orig.). 1984. pap. 9.95 (*0-912856-90-4*) Gr Arts Ctr Pub.

Photographing People. Michael Busselle. (Better Picture Guide Ser.). (Illus.). 128p. 1999. pap. 19.95 (*2-88046-393-9*, Rotovision) Watsn-Guptill.

Photographing Plants & Gardens. Clive Nichols. (Illus.). 160p. 1998. pap. 19.95 (*0-7153-0715-0*, Pub. by D & C Pub) Sterling.

Photographing Special Occasions. Liz Walker. LC 95-12913. (Point & Shoot Ser.). (Illus.). 8p. 1995. pap. 11.95 (*0-8174-5488-8*, Amphoto) Watsn-Guptill.

Photographing the Invisible. James Coates. LC 72-9189. (Literature of Photography Ser.). 1973. reprint ed. 34.95 (*0-405-04899-8*) Ayer.

Photographing the L. A. Art Scene, 1955-1975. Intro. by Craig Krull. (Illus.). 86p. 1996. pap. 25.00 (*1-889195-02-2*, Pub. by Smart Art Pr) RAM Publications.

Photographing the Landscape: The Art of Seeing. John Fielder. (Illus.). 192p. 1997. pap. 29.95 (*1-56579-228-9*) Westcliffe Pubs.

Photographing the Natural World. Heather Angel. LC 93-48089. (Illus.). 160p. 1994. 24.95 (*0-8069-0714-2*) Sterling.

Photographing the Natural World. Heather Angel. (Illus.). 160p. 1996. pap. 17.95 (*0-8069-0715-0*) Sterling.

Photographing the Patterns of Nature. Gary Braasch. LC 99-26661. (Illus.). 144p. 1999. pap. text 24.95 (*0-8174-5441-1*) Watsn-Guptill.

Photographing the Second Gold Rush: Dorothea Lange & the Bay Area at War 1941-1945. Intro. by Charles Wollenberg. (Illus.). 88p. (Orig.). 1995. pap. 14.95 (*0-930588-78-9*) Heyday Bks.

Photographing the Self: Methods of Observing Personal Orientations. Robert C. Ziller. (Illus.). 160p. (C). 1990. 34.00 (*0-8039-3497-1*) Sage.

Photographing the Spirit World. Permutt. 1988. 12.95 (*0-85030-762-7*, Pub. by Aqrn Pr) Harper SF.

Photographing the World Around You: A Visual Design Workshop. Freeman Patterson. (Illus.). 168p. 1994. pap. 18.95 (*1-55013-590-2*) Firefly Bks Ltd.

Photographing Wild Texas. Erwin A. Bauer & Peggy Bauer. (Illus.). 112p. 1985. pap. 16.95 (*0-292-76497-9*) U of Tex Pr.

Photographing Wildflowers: Techniques for the Advanced Amateur & Professional. Craig Blacklock & Nadine Blacklock. (Illus.). 64p. 1990. reprint ed. pap. 12.95 (*0-89658-069-5*) Voyageur Pr.

Photographing Wildlife. Patricia Caulfield. LC 87-31929. (Illus.). 144p. 1988. pap. 18.95 (*0-8174-5443-8*, Amphoto) Watsn-Guptill.

An Asterisk (*) at the beginning of an entry indicates that the title is appearing for the first time.

Photographing Wildlife & Nature. Sean Hargrave. (Point & Shoot Ser.). (Illus.). 96p. 1995. pap. 11.95 (*0-8174-5541-8*, Amphoto) Watsn-Guptill.

***Photographing Your Artwork: A Step-by-Step Guide to Taking High Quality Slides at an Affordable Price.** 3rd ed. Russell Hart. (Illus.). 128p. 2000. pap. 29.95 (*1-58428-028-X*) Amherst Media.

Photographing Your Baby: Tips for Taking Better Pictures. Eastman Kodak Company Editors. LC 84-16788. 1984. pap. 9.57 (*0-201-11698-7*) Addison-Wesley.

Photographing Your Church's History. John Hack. Ed. by Charles W. Deweese. (Resource Kit for Your Church's History Ser.). 8p. 1984. pap. 0.60 (*0-939804-18-2*) Hist Comm S Baptist.

Photographing Your Craftwork: A Hands-On Guide for Craftspeople. 2nd ed. Steve Meltzer. 136p. (Orig.). 1993. reprint ed. pap. 12.95 (*0-934026-81-5*) Interweave.

Photographing Your Heritage. rev. ed. Wilma S. Shull. LC 88-70335. (Illus.). 128p. 1988. pap. 9.95 (*0-916489-31-0*, 231) Ancestry.

Photographische Industrie Deutschland. Willy Kuhn. Ed. by Peter C. Bunnell & Robert A. Sobieszek. LC 78-67657. (Sources of Modern Photography Ser.). (GER.). 1979. reprint ed. lib. bdg. 15.95 (*0-405-09899-5*) Ayer.

Photographs. (Illus.). 96p. 1998. pap. 25.00 (*84-89698-86-4*, Pub. by Actar) Dist Art Pubs.

Photographs. Paul Himmel. 192p. 65.00 (*2-84323-153-1*, Pub. by Assouline) Rizzoli Intl.

Photographs. Jeffrey Silverthorne. (Illus.). 40p. 1994. pap. 24.95 (*1-881616-14-2*) Dist Art Pubs.

***Photographs.** Erika Stone. (Illus.). 96p. 2000. 35.00 (*3-934296-01-7*) G Kehayoff.

Photographs. Juergen Teller. (Illus.). 176p. 1998. 45.00 (*3-931141-94-2*, Pub. by Scalo Pubs) Dist Art Pubs.

***Photographs.** Raymond Vino. (Illus.). 2000. 29.95 (*3-86187-165-3*) B Gmunder.

Photographs. Albert Wendt. 92p. 1995. pap. 12.95 (*1-86940-122-0*, Pub. by Auckland Univ) Paul & Co Pubs.

Photographs. large type ed. Jeffrey O. Rath. 58p. 1999. pap. 4.99 (*1-893151-12-3*) Weavers Old.

Photographs. Eudora Welty. LC 89-35218. (Illus.). 200p. 1993. reprint ed. pap. 30.00 (*0-87805-529-0*) U Pr of Miss.

***Photographs: Eastman.** Taschen America Staff. 1999. pap. (*3-8228-6603-2*) Taschen Amer.

***Photographs: George Eastman House, Rochester, Ny.** Ed. by Therese Mulligan. (Illus.). 768p. 1999. pap. text 29.99 (*3-8228-7073-0*) Benedikt Taschen.

***Photographs & Memories.** Joseph A. Tunzi. LC 97-95120. (Illus.). 112p. 1998. pap. 48.50 (*1-888464-03-8*) JAT Pub.

***Photographs & Memories, Vol. 6.** Michael Lizza. (Illus.). 134p. 1998. 20.00 (*1-929326-56-4*) Hal Bar Pubg.

Photographs & Photographers of York, 1844-1879. Hugh Murray. (C). 1988. pap. 21.00 (*0-9503519-4-6*, Pub. by W Sessions) St Mut.

Photographs & Words. Wright Morris. Ed. by James Alinder. LC 82-82471. (Illus.). 120p. 1982. 50.00 (*0-933286-28-7*) Frnds Photography.

Photographs at the Frontier: Aby Warburg in America, 1895-1896. Peter Burke. (Illus.). 160p. 1998. 45.00 (*1-85894-067-2*) U of Wash Pr.

Photographs by Barbara Hershey: A Retrospective. Ed. by Nancy Koehler et al. (Illus.). 64p. (Orig.). (C). 1995. 20.00 (*0-940784-16-5*) Miami Univ Art.

Photographs by Horatio Ross. Chris Titterington. LC 93-60991. (Illus.). 31p. 1993. pap. 7.95 (*0-930606-70-1*) Yale Ctr Brit Art.

Photographs by Man Ray, 1920-1934. Man Ray. LC 79-50461. (Illus.). 128p. 1980. reprint ed. pap. 11.95 (*0-486-23842-3*) Dover.

***Photographs by Snowdon: A Retrospective.** Contrib. by Drusilla Beyfus et al. (Illus.). 240p. 2000. 75.00 (*0-8109-4479-0*, Pub. by Abrams) Time Warner.

Photographs from the Collection of Floyd & Josephine Segel. Verna P. Curtis. LC 82-80088. (Illus.). 36p. (Orig.). 1982. pap. 4.00 (*0-944110-22-3*) Milwauk Art Mus.

Photographs from the Real World. Photos by Lee Friedlander et al. (Illus.). 224p. 1995. 85.00 (*82-525-2664-0*) Dist Art Pubs.

Photographs from the William Merritt Chase Archives. Ronald G. Pisano & Alicia G. Longwell. LC 92-85286. (Illus.). 118p. 1992. pap. 18.00 (*0-943526-22-1*) Parrish Art.

Photographs Jazz. Ole Brask. 120p. 1995. 65.00 (*3-926048-63-8*) Dist Art Pubs.

Photographs, 1973-1983. John Mckee. (Illus.). 1984. pap. 7.50 (*0-916606-06-6*) Bowdoin Coll.

Photographs, 1973-1980. Christopher Rauschenberg. LC 82-81916. (Illus.). 139p. (Orig.). 1982. pap. 10.00 (*0-943446-00-7*) Pair O Dice.

Photographs of a Lifetime. Dorothea Lange. (Illus.). 182p. 1996. 50.00 (*0-89381-657-4*) Aperture.

Photographs of Alvan S. Harper: Tallahassee, 1885-1910. Ed. by Joan P. Morris & Lee H. Warner. LC 82-24765. (Illus.). 152p. 1983. 39.95 (*0-8130-0737-2*) U Press Fla.

Photographs of American Civil War Cavalry. Christopher Nelson et al. (Illus.). 100p. (Orig.). 1988. pap. 9.95 (*0-317-91045-0*) Guidon Pr.

Photographs of Dorothea Lange. Keith F. Davis. (Illus.). 132p. 1996. 35.00 (*0-8109-6315-9*, Pub. by Abrams) Time Warner.

Photographs of Edouard Baldus. Malcolm Daniel. LC 94-19297. (Illus.). 1994. 65.00 (*0-87099-714-9*); pap. write for info. (*0-87099-715-7*) Abrams.

***Photographs of Frederick C. Marcham.** Frederick George Marcham & John Marcham. LC 00-31497. (Illus.). 112p. 2000. pap. 21.95 (*0-942690-44-3*) DeWitt Hist.

***Photographs of Frederick C. Marcham.** John Mercham. LC 00-31497. 112p. 2000. 29.95 (*0-942690-45-1*) DeWitt Hist.

Photographs of Herbie Knott: One Hundred Photographs Reproduced in Superb Duotone. Ed. by Boxtree Ltd. Staff. 128p. (C). 1990. 100.00 (*1-85283-283-5*, Pub. by Boxtree) St Mut.

Photographs of Lyle Bonge. Lyle Bonge. 1982. 32.50 (*0-912330-53-8*) Jargon Soc.

Photographs of Manuel Alvarez Bravo: His Life's Work. Aperture Foundation Staff. 1997. 53.00 (*0-89381-721-X*) Aperture.

Photographs of Mary Todd Lincoln. Lloyd Ostendorf. 64p. 1989. reprint ed. pap. text 5.00 (*0-942579-05-4*) IHPA.

***Photographs of Men.** Bill Emrich. (Illus.). 1998. 39.95 (*3-925443-17-7*) Janssen.

Photographs of Mexico. Paul Strand. write for info. (*0-89381-787-2*) Aperture.

Photographs of New Mexico. Ed. by Arnold Vigil. LC 96-72248. (Illus.). 176p. 1997. 49.95 (*0-937206-50-4*) New Mexico Mag.

Photographs of the Ivory Coast. August C. Azaglo. (Soleil Ser.). (Illus.). 1997. pap. 18.00 (*0-614-25351-9*) Dist Art Pubs.

Photographs of the Jungle. Jon F. Glade. Ed. by Michael Hathaway. 48p. (Orig.). 1990. pap. 10.00 (*0-943795-10-9*) Chiron Rev.

Photographs of the Southwest. Ansel Adams. LC 76-10034. (Illus.). 1994. 50.00 (*0-8212-0699-0*, Pub. by Bulfinch Pr) Little.

Photographs of the Work see Architect Sigurd Lewerentz

Photographs of Union & Confederate Officers in the Civil War in America. (Illus.). 84p. 1996. 350.00 (*0-9651697-0-7*) Civil War Library.

Photographs Then & Now. National Geographic Society (U. S.) Staff. LC 98-23421. 1998. 50.00 (*0-7922-7203-X*) Natl Geog.

***Photographs Then & Now.** National Geographic Staff. Ed. by Leah Bendavid-Val. LC 98-23421. (Illus.). 304p. (YA). (gr. 5 up). 1998. per. 50.00 (*0-7922-7202-1*) Natl Geog.

Photographs Underwater. Bob Kendall. LC 76-15705. (Illus.). 104p. 1976. 24.50 (*0-914704-02-8*) ICER Pr.

Photography. (Make it Work Ser.). 42p. (J). (gr. 4-8). pap. write for info. (*1-882210-43-3*) Action Pub.

Photography. (C). 1996. write for info. (*0-13-017928-0*) Addison-Wesley.

***Photography.** 2000. write for info. (*0-13-975517-9*) P-H.

***Photography.** 2000. teacher ed. write for info. (*0-13-975491-1*) P-H.

Photography. W. Baatz. Tr. by Sally Schreiber. LC 97-71965. (Crash Course Ser.). (Illus.). 192p. 1997. pap. 13.95 (*0-7641-0243-5*) Barron.

Photography. Boy Scouts of America. (Illus.). 56p. (YA). (gr. 6-12). 1983. pap. 2.90 (*0-8395-3340-3*) BSA.

Photography. Deni Bown. (101 Essential Tips Ser.). (Illus.). 72p. 1995. pap. 4.95 (*0-7894-0174-6*, 6-70495) DK Pub Inc.

Photography. Robert V. Bullough, Sr. Ed. by James E. Duane. LC 80-21333. (Instructional Media Library: Vol. 11). (Illus.). 104p. 1981. 27.95 (*0-87778-171-0*) Educ Tech Pubns.

Photography. John Freeman. 1996. pap. 14.00 (*0-00-412786-2*) Collins.

Photography. Gregory. Date not set. pap. text. write for info. (*0-582-23503-0*, Pub. by Addison-Wesley) Longman.

***Photography.** Andrew Haslam et al. LC 00-25669. (Make it Work Ser.). (Illus.). (J). 2000. pap. write for info. (*1-58728-358-1*) Two Can Pub.

***Photography.** Horenstein. 144p. 2000. pap., wbk. ed., lab manual ed. 20.00 (*0-13-975509-8*) P-H.

Photography. S. Peach & M. Butterfield. (Practical Guides Ser.). (Illus.). 48p. (J). (gr. 6 up). 1987. pap. 8.95 (*0-7460-0107-X*, Usborne) EDC.

Photography. S. Peach & M. Butterfield. (Practical Guides Ser.). (Illus.). 48p. (J). (gr. 6 up). 1999. lib. bdg. 16.95 (*0-88110-292-X*, Usborne) EDC.

***Photography.** Ed. by Scott & Daughters Publishing Staff. (Stock Workbook Ser.: Vol. 13). (Illus.). 2000. 15.00 (*1-887528-53-9*) Scott & Daughters.

Photography. Kathryn Senior et al. (Make It Work! Ser.). (Illus.). 48p. (J). 16.99 (*0-590-24912-6*); pap. 7.99 (*0-590-24913-4*) Scholastic Inc.

***Photography.** Two Can Publishing Ltd. Staff. (Illus.). (J). 2000. 12.95 (*1-58728-372-7*) Two Can Pub.

Photography. Sue Vander Hook. LC 98-20887. (Making Contact Ser.). (Illus.). 32p. (YA). (gr. 4 up). 1999. lib. bdg. 21.30 (*1-887068-62-7*) Smart Apple.

Photography. Warren. Date not set. pap. text, teacher ed. write for info. (*0-314-00425-4*) West Pub.

Photography. Bruce Warren. Ed. by Baxter. (Illus.). 450p. (C). 1992. mass mkt. 46.75 (*0-314-92914-2*) West Pub.

Photography. Barrie Watts. LC 94-6389. (First Guide Ser.). (Illus.). 96p. (J). (gr. 3-6). 1994. lib. bdg. 23.90 (*1-56294-398-7*) Millbrook Pr.

Photography. 2nd ed. Swedlund. (C). 2000. pap. text. write for info. (*0-15-508378-3*) Harcourt Coll Pubs.

***Photography.** 2nd ed. Warren. (Student Material TV Ser.). (C). 2000. pap. 45.75 (*0-7668-1777-6*) Delmar.

Photography. 4th ed. Barbara L. Upton & John Upton. (C). 1989. pap. 45.25 (*0-673-39842-0*) Addison-Wesley Educ.

Photography. 6th ed. (C). 1997. pap. text. write for info. (*0-321-40872-1*) Addison-Wesley.

Photography. 6th ed. Ed. by Barbara London. LC 97-20714. 408p. (C). 1997. pap. 69.00 (*0-321-01108-2*, Prentice Hall) P-H.

Photography. 7th ed. Philip Davis. 448p. (C). 1994. text. write for info. (*0-697-12514-9*) Brown & Benchmark.

Photography: A Concise History. Ian Jeffrey. (World of Art Ser.). (Illus.). 248p. 1985. pap. 14.95 (*0-500-20187-0*, Pub. by Thames Hudson) Norton.

Photography: A Concise History. Ian Jeffrey. (World of Art Ser.). (Illus.). 248p. 1985. 19.95 (*0-500-18187-X*, Pub. by Thames Hudson) Norton.

***Photography: A Crash Course.** David Yorath. (Illus.). 144p. 2000. 14.95 (*0-8230-0986-6*) Watsn-Guptill.

Photography: A Critical Introduction. Liz Wells. LC 96-17229. (Illus.). 328p. (C). 1996. 85.00 (*0-415-12558-8*); pap. 25.99 (*0-415-12559-6*) Routledge.

Photography: A Handbook of History, Materials & Processes. 2nd ed. Charles Swedlund. 410p. (C). 1981. pap. text 68.00 (*0-03-056699-1*, Pub. by Harcourt Coll Pubs) Harcourt.

Photography: A Manual for Shutterbugs. Eugene Kohn. (Illus.). (J). (gr. 3-7). 1965. pap. 1.25 (*0-685-03891-2*) P-H.

Photography: A Middle-Brow Art. Pierre Bourdieu. Tr. by Shaun Whiteside. LC 89-62321. 230p. (Orig.). 1996. pap. 14.95 (*0-8047-2689-2*) Stanford U Pr.

Photography: A Middle-Brow Art. Pierre Bourdieu et al. Tr. by Shaun Whiteside from FRE. LC 89-62321. 288p. (Orig.). 1990. 35.00 (*0-8047-1760-5*) Stanford U Pr.

Photography: An Independent Art, Photographs from the Victoria & Albert Museum, 1839-1996. Mark Haworth-Booth. LC 97-65306. (Illus.). 208p. 1997. 39.50 (*0-691-01742-5*, Pub. by Princeton U Pr) Cal Prin Full Svc.

Photography: Beyond Simple Truths: An Advanced Workbook for Teachers & Students. Philip Krejcarek. 1984. pap. 10.00 (*0-317-00907-9*); sl. 28.00 (*0-318-03706-8*) P Krejcarek.

***Photography: Critical Introduction.** 2nd ed. Ed. by Liz Wells. LC 99-16503. 416p. (C). 2000. text. write for info. (*0-415-19057-6*) Routledge.

***Photography: Critical Introduction.** 2nd ed. Liz Wells. LC 99-16503. 416p. 2000. pap. write for info. (*0-415-19058-4*) Routledge.

Photography: Discovery & Invention. Getty, J. Paul Museum Staff. LC 90-5023. (Illus.). 144p. 1990. pap. 49.95 (*0-89236-177-8*, Pub. by J P Getty Trust) OUP.

Photography: Electronic Workshop. Steven R. Gilmore. (Electronic Workshop Ser.). (Illus.). 160p. 1999. pap. 37.50 (*2-88046-422-6*) Watsn-Guptill.

Photography: Foundations for Art & Design. Mark Galer. LC 95-38357. (Illus.). 120p. 1995. pap. text 32.95 (*0-240-51438-6*, Focal) Buttrwrth-Heinemann.

Photography: From Theory to Practice. 2nd ed. Michael E. Leary. (Illus.). 176p. (C). 1988. pap. 34.95 (*0-89863-124-6*) Star Pub CA.

Photography: Materials & Methods. John Hedgecoe & Michael J. Langford. (Oxford Paperbacks Handbooks for Artists). (Illus.). 1971. pap. 10.95 (*0-19-289909-0*) OUP.

Photography: Preserving the Past. Bradley Steffens. LC 91-15570. (Encyclopedia of Discovery & Invention Ser.). (Illus.). 96p. (J). (gr. 5-8). 1991. lib. bdg. 23.70 (*1-56006-212-6*) Lucent Bks.

Photography: Simple Truths: A Workbook for Teachers & Students. Philip Krejcarek. 1978. pap. 10.00 (*0-686-15968-3*) P Krejcarek.

Photography: Take Your Best Shot. Terri Morgan. (Illus.). 72p. (YA). (gr. 5 up). 1991. pap. 8.95 (*0-8225-9605-9*, Lerner Publctns) Lerner Pub.

Photography: Take Your Best Shot. Terri Morgan & Shmuel Thaler. (Media Workshop Ser.). 80p. (YA). (gr. 5 up). 1991. lib. bdg. 21.27 (*0-8225-2302-7*, Lerner Publctns) Lerner Pub.

Photography: The U. K. Photographic Market. 65p. 1985. 170.00 (*0-7855-7252-X*) St Mut.

***Photography - Foundations for Art & Design: A Guide to Creative Photography.** 2nd ed. Mark Galer. (Illus.). 200p. 2000. pap. 34.95 (*0-240-51600-1*, Focal) Buttrwrth-Heinemann.

Photography A-V Program Directory. A. D. Coleman et al. LC 80-83469. (Illus.). 224p. 1980. 28.00 (*0-936524-00-6*) PMI Inc.

Photography after Photography: Memory & Representation in the Digital Age. Ed. by Hubertus Von Amelunxen et al. (Illus.). 324p. 1997. text 59.95 (*90-5701-101-8*) Gordon & Breach.

Photography & Architecture: Eighteen Thirty-Nine to Nineteen Thirty-Nine. Richard Pare. (Illus.). 282p. 1985. reprint ed. 80.00 (*0-262-16101-X*) MIT Pr.

Photography & Art History. Ed. by H. Roberts. ix, 290p. 1990. text 30.00 (*2-88124-459-9*) Gordon & Breach.

Photography & Beyond in Japan: Space, Time & Memory. Robert Stearns et al. LC 97-190376. (Illus.). 184p. 1995. 39.95 (*0-8109-3519-8*, Pub. by Abrams) Time Warner.

Photography & Its Critics: A Cultural History, 1839-1900. Mary W. Marien. (Perspectives on Photography Ser.). (Illus.). 238p. 1997. text 55.00 (*0-521-55043-2*) Cambridge U Pr.

Photography & Language. Ed. & Intro. by Lew Thomas. LC 76-43622. (Illus.). 1979. pap. 25.00 (*0-917986-01-6*) NFS Pr.

Photography & Literature: An International Bibliography of Monographs. Eric Lambrechts & Luc Salu. LC 91-34752. 320p. 1992. text 120.00 (*0-7201-2113-2*, Z1023) Continuum.

***Photography & Painting in the Work of Gerard Richter.** Gerard Richter. (Illus.). 2000. pap. 22.00 (*84-89771-91-X*) Actar.

Photography & Philosophy of Wynn Bullock. Clyde H. Dilley. LC 81-65881. (Illus.). 129p. 1984. 35.00 (*0-87982-042-X*) Art Alliance.

Photography & Poetry of Cynlos. Ed. by Cynthia M. Potter. (Illus.). 80p. Date not set. 16.95 (*0-9700165-9-X*) Twin Rivers NC.

***Photography & Politics in America: From the New Deal into the Cold War.** Lili Corbus Bezner. LC 99-23281. (Illus.). 336p. 1999. 39.95 (*0-8018-6187-X*) Johns Hopkins.

Photography & Reform: Lewis Hine & the National Child Labor Committee. Verna P. Curtis & Stanley Mallach. Ed. by Rosalie Goldstein. LC 81-85989. (Illus.). 87p. (Orig.). 1981. pap. 10.00 (*0-944110-45-2*) Milwauk Art Mus.

Photography & the American Scene. Robert Taft. (Illus.). 54p. 1989. pap. 13.95 (*0-486-26202-2*) Dover.

Photography & the American Scene. Robert Taft. (Illus.). 1991. 25.75 (*0-8446-3046-2*) Peter Smith.

Photography & the Art of Seeing. rev. ed. Freeman Patterson. LC 89-93254. (Illus.). 156p. 1985. pap. 17.95 (*1-55013-099-4*) Firefly Bks Ltd.

Photography & the Book. Beaumont Newhall. 1983. pap. 10.00 (*0-89073-066-0*, 290) Boston Public Lib.

Photography & the Performing Arts. Gerry Kopelow. (Illus.). 194p. 1994. pap. text 36.95 (*0-240-80168-7*, Focal) Buttrwrth-Heinemann.

***Photography Annual, 2001.** Ed. by B. Martin Pedersen. (Illus.). 256p. 2000. 70.00 (*1-888001-90-9*, Pub. by Graphis US) Watsn-Guptill.

Photography As a Hobby. Alfred E. Williamson. 40p. (Orig.). 1985. pap. 9.95 (*0-934033-04-8*) Williamson Ad Agcy.

Photography As a Hobby. rev. ed. Alfred E. Williamson. (Illus.). 43p. (Orig.). 1990. pap. 9.95 (*0-318-50077-9*) Williamson Ad Agcy.

Photography at Princeton: Celebrating Twenty-Five Years of Collecting & Teaching the History of Photography. Peter C. Bunnell et al. Ed. by Jill Guthrie. LC 98-86438. (Illus.). (Orig.). Date not set. pap. text 30.00 (*0-943012-26-0*, 98-86438) Prince U Art.

Photography at the Dock: Essays on Photographic History, Institutions, & Practices. Abigail Solomon-Godeau. (Media & Society Ser.: Vol. 4). (Illus.). 1994. pap. 24.95 (*0-8166-1914-X*) U of Minn Pr.

Photography Between Covers. Thomas Dugan. 1979. 15.00 (*0-87992-012-2*) Visual Studies.

Photography Blaster! Terry Moss. LC 94-77896. (Nutshell Ser.). 52p. 1994. pap. 4.95 (*1-885962-51-7*) Lincoln Lrning.

Photography Book. Edward Stokes. (J). (gr. 4-7). 1992. 5.95 (*0-590-45257-6*) Scholastic Inc.

***Photography Book: Miniature Edition.** Ian Jeffrey. (Illus.). 520p. 2000. pap. 9.95 (*0-7148-3937-X*) Phaidon Pr.

Photography Books Index: A Subject Guide to Photo Anthologies, Vol. 1. Martha Moss. LC 79-26938. 298p. 1980. lib. bdg. 26.50 (*0-8108-1283-5*) Scarecrow.

Photography Books Index: A Subject Guide to Photo Anthologies, Vol. II. Martha Moss. LC 84-23652. 276p. 1985. 25.00 (*0-8108-1773-X*) Scarecrow.

Photography Careers. Bervin Johnson. LC 98-22684. (Opportunities in... Ser.). 160p. 1998. 14.95 (*0-8442-6551-9*, 65519); pap. 7.95 (*0-8442-6553-5*, 65535) NTC Contemp Pub Co.

Photography Careers. Robert E. Mayer et al. (Opportunities in...Ser.). (Illus.). 160p. 1988. 13.95 (*0-8442-6180-7*, VGM Career) NTC Contemp Pub Co.

***Photography Encyclopedia.** Timothy S. McDarrah. 1998. 80.00 (*0-02-865025-5*, Schirmer Books) Mac Lib Ref.

***Photography Encyclopedia - Paperback.** 1999. per. 39.95 (*0-02-865483-8*) Macmillan Gen Ref.

Photography for Artists. Hector Maclean. LC 72-9218. (Literature of Photography Ser.). 1979. reprint ed. 15.95 (*0-405-04925-0*) Ayer.

Photography for Dummies: A Reference for the Rest of Us! Russell Hart. LC 98-85431. (For Dummies Ser.). (Illus.). 464p. 1998. pap. 19.99 (*0-7645-5065-9*) IDG Bks.

Photography for Student Publications. Carl Vandermeulen. LC 79-89332. (YA). (gr. 7 up). 1979. pap. 12.95 (*0-931940-01-X*) Middleburg Pr.

Photography for the Archivist. Ken Lawrence. Ed. by Rowland P. Gill. (Collegiate Guide to Archival Science Ser.). 56p. (C). 1999. 7.95 (*0-910653-10-0*, 8334K, Red River Pr) Archival Servs.

Photography for the Joy of It. rev. ed. Freeman Patterson. (Illus.). 168p. 1986. pap. 17.95 (*1-55013-095-1*) Firefly Bks Ltd.

Photography for Writers: Using Photography to Increase Your Writing Income. Michael Havelin. LC 97-72220. (Illus.). 224p. 1998. pap. 18.95 (*1-880559-86-2*) Allworth Pr.

Photography Handbook. Terence Wright. LC 98-29625. (Media Practice Ser.). 1999. 75.00 (*0-415-11593-0*); pap. 24.99 (*0-415-11594-9*) Routledge.

Photography Illinois. Debora D. Donato & Terry Suhre. (Illus.). 26p. 1989. pap. 5.00 (*0-89792-122-4*) Ill St Museum.

Photography Imaging. Henry Horenstein. 444p. (C). 2000. pap. 52.67 (*0-13-617580-5*, Macmillan Coll) P-H.

Photography in Archaeology & Conservation. 2nd ed. Peter G. Dorrell. (Cambridge Manuals in Archaeology Ser.). (Illus.). 282p. (C). 1994. pap. text 24.95 (*0-521-45554-5*) Cambridge U Pr.

Photography in Archaeology & Conservation. 2nd ed. Peter G. Dorrell. (Cambridge Manuals in Archaeology Ser.). (Illus.). 282p. (C). 1995. text 65.00 (*0-521-45534-0*) Cambridge U Pr.

Photography in Books for Young People. Ed. by Martha E. Ward & Dorothy. A. Marquardt. LC 85-19682. 107p. 1985. 21.00 (*0-8108-1854-X*) Scarecrow.

***Photography in Boston, 1955-1985.** Ed. by Rachel Rosenfield Lafo & Gillian Nagler. (Illus.). 204p. 2000. 39.95 (*0-262-12229-4*) MIT Pr.

P

Photography in Brazil, 1840-1900. Gilberto Ferrez. Tr. by Stella De Sa Rego. LC 90-11903. (Illus.). 263p. 1990. reprint ed. pap. 81.60 (*0-608-04134-3*, 206486700011) Bks Demand.

Photography in Focus. Mark Jacobs. 1989. 19.95 (*0-8442-5483-5*, Natl Textbk Co) NTC Contemp Pub Co.

Photography in Focus. Mark Jacobs. 1994. pap. 16.95 (*0-8442-5484-3*, Natl Textbk Co) NTC Contemp Pub Co.

Photography in Focus. 4th ed. Mark Jacobs & Ken Kokrda. (Illus.). 248p. 1994. pap. 18.95 (*0-8442-5301-4*, Passprt Bks) NTC Contemp Pub Co.

Photography in Focus. 4th ed. Mark Jacobs & Ken Kokrda. (Illus.). 248p. 1994. 21.95 (*0-8442-5300-6*, Passprt Bks) NTC Contemp Pub Co.

Photography in Focus. 5th ed. Jerry Burchfield et al. (Illus.). 448p. 1996. pap. 30.95 (*0-8442-5782-6*, 57826) NTC Contemp Pub Co.

Photography in Focus. 5th rev. ed. Jerry Burchfield et al. LC 94-68802. (Illus.). 448p. (C). 1996. text 27.95 (*0-8442-5781-8*, 57818) NTC Contemp Pub Co.

Photography in Japan: Desire & Void. Gerald Matt. (Illus.). 176p. 1997. 49.95 (*3-908162-70-X*) Dist Art Pubs.

Photography in Life Sciences: Index of Modern Authors & Subjects with Guide for Rapid Research. Raymond L. Reitz. LC 90-56305. 160p. 1991. 47.50 (*1-55914-396-7*); pap. 44.50 (*1-55914-397-5*) ABBE Pubs Assn.

Photography in Modern Prague, 1900-1925. Joef Kroutvor. Ed. by Monika Faber. 120p. 1995. 40.00 (*3-7231-0432-0*) Dist Art Pubs.

Photography in Ophthalmology: Proceedings of the International Symposium, Miami, 1970. International Symposium on Photography in Ophthalmology Staff. Ed. by O. Ferrer. (Modern Problems in Ophthalmology Ser.: Vol. 9). 1971. 59.75 (*3-8055-1165-5*) S Karger.

Photography in Print: Writings from 1816 to Present. Goldberg. LC 88-14299. 570p. 1988. reprint ed. pap. 18.95 (*0-8263-1091-5*) U of NM Pr.

Photography in the American Grain: Discovering a Native American Aesthetic 1923-1941. Photos by Edward Weston et al. (Illus.). 48p. 10.00 (*0-938262-16-5*) Ctr Creat Photog.

Photography in the Collection of the Seattle Art Museum. Rod Slemmons. LC 90-52618. (Illus.). 32p. (Orig.). 1990. pap. 4.95 (*0-932216-34-X*) Seattle Art.

Photography in the Modern Era: European Documents & Critical Writings, 1913-1940. Christopher Phillips. (Illus.). 368p. 1989. pap. 19.95 (*0-89381-407-5*) Aperture.

Photography in the Modern Era: European Documents & Critical Writings, 1913-1940. Ed. by Christopher Phillips. (Illus.). 368p. 1989. 60.00 (*0-89381-406-7*) Aperture.

Photography in the Twentieth Century. Cologne Museum Ludwig Staff. (Illus.). 756p. 1996. pap. 29.99 (*3-8228-8648-3*) Taschen Amer.

Photography in the West. Peter Barney. LC 99-60989. (Illus.). 100p. 1999. 30.00 (*1-888106-91-3*) Agreka Bks.

Photography in the West. Ed. by Peter E. Palmquist. (Illus.). 116p. 1987. pap. 15.00 (*0-89745-102-3*) Sunflower U Pr.

Photography in the West II. Ed. by Peter Palmquist. (Illus.). 132p. 1989. pap. 15.00 (*0-89745-084-1*) Sunflower U Pr.

Photography Index: A Guide to Reproductions. Compiled by Pamela J. Parry. LC 78-26897. 372p. 1979. lib. bdg. 42.95 (*0-313-20700-3*, PPI/, Greenwood Pr) Greenwood.

Photography Is a Language. John R. Whiting. Ed. by Robert A. Sobieszek & Peter C. Bunnell. LC 76-24680. (Sources of Modern Photography Ser.). (Illus.). 1979. reprint ed. lib. bdg. 19.95 (*0-405-09658-5*) Ayer.

Photography, 1900. Ed. by Julie Lawson & Ray McKenzie. (Illus.). 111p. 1992. pap. text 22.50 (*0-903598-45-0*, 8450, Pub. by Ashmolean Mus) A Schwartz & Co.

Photography, 1900 to the Present. Diana E. Hulick & Joseph Marshall. LC 97-13651. 363p. 1997. pap. text 45.00 (*0-13-254095-9*) P-H.

***Photography of Alfred Stieglitz: Georgia O'Keeffe's Enduring Legacy.** Therese Mulligan. (Illus.). 2000. 29.95 (*0-935398-23-6*, Pub. by G Eastman Hse) U of NM Pr.

Photography of Architecture: Twelve Views. Akiko Busch. (Illus.). 233p. 1993. pap. 29.95 (*0-471-29369-5*, VNR) Wiley.

Photography of Gustave le Gray. Eugenia P. Janis. Ed. by Sarah C. Mollman. LC 87-13919. (Illus.). 184p. 1987. 120.00 (*0-226-39210-4*) U Ch Pr.

Photography of Invention: American Pictures of the 1980s. Joshua P. Smith. (Illus.). 208p. 1989. 39.95 (*0-262-19280-2*) MIT Pr.

***Photography of John Gutmann: Culture Shock.** Sandra B. Phillips. (Illus.). 144p. 2000. 35.00 (*1-85894-097-4*) Merrell Holberton.

Photography of Natural Things. Freeman Patterson. (Illus.). 168p. 1989. pap. 17.95 (*1-55013-097-8*) Firefly Bks Ltd.

Photography of O. G. Rejlander, 2 Selections: Orginal Anthology. Ed. by Robert A. Sobieszek & Peter C. Bunnell. LC 76-24658. (Illus.). 1979. lib. bdg. 12.95 (*0-405-09637-2*) Ayer.

Photography of the Nude: An Annotated Bibliography. Frank H. Wallis. LC 93-86015. 1993. 47.95 (*0-9638332-9-4*) Source Pub CT.

Photography of the 20th Century. 1996. pap. 5.99 (*3-8228-8867-2*) Taschen Amer.

***Photography on the Internet.** 104p. 2000. write for info. (*0-13-026990-5*) P-H.

Photography Outdoors: A Field Guide for Travel & Adventure Photographers. Art Wolfe & Mark Gardner. (Illus.). 112p. 1995. pap. 12.95 (*0-89886-430-5*) Mountaineers.

Photography Paintings: Werner Pawlok. Thomas Buchsteiner & Klaus Honnef. 72p. 1995. 40.00 (*3-7231-0014-7*) Dist Art Pubs.

Photography Politics: 2 Photography Workshops. Ed. by Patricia Holland et al. (Illus.). 200p. 1987. pap. 22.00 (*0-906890-89-6*, Pub. by Comedia) Routldge.

Photography Portfolio. 1999. 70.00 (*1-887528-42-3*) Scott & Daughters.

***Photography Portfolio: East & South, 2 vols.** Ed. by Scott & Daughters Publishing Staff. (Workbook Ser.). (Illus.). 2000. 35.00 (*1-887528-56-3*) Scott & Daughters.

***Photography Portfolio: Midwest & West, 2 vols.** Ed. by Scott & Daughters Publishing Staff. (Workbook Ser.). (Illus.). 2000. 35.00 (*1-887528-64-4*) Scott & Daughters.

Photography Portfolio - Workbook #20. Scott & Daughters Publishing Staff. 1998. pap. 70.00 (*1-887528-28-8*) Scott & Daughters.

Photography Remembered: A Selective View from the Robert W. Lisle Collection. Robert Lisle. LC 90-84178. 66p. 1990. pap. 19.95 (*0-940744-61-9*) Chrysler Museum.

Photography Show 99: 1999 Membership Directory & Illustrated Catalogue. (Illus.). 1999. pap. 25.00 (*1-893590-00-3*) Assoc Internat Photography Art.

Photography Speaks: Sixty-Nine Photographers on Their Act. Ed. by Brooks Johnson. (Illus.). 144p. 1989. 44.95 (*0-89381-354-0*) Aperture.

Photography Through the Microscope. 9th ed. Eastman Kodak Company Staff. LC 87-83471. (Illus.). 104p. (C). 1998. pap. 24.95 (*0-87985-362-X*, P-2, Kodak) Saunders Photo.

Photography to Plastics Processing see Ullmann's Encyclopedia of Industrial Chemistry

Photography until Now. John Szarkowski. (Illus.). 344p. 1989. 60.00 (*0-87070-573-3*) Mus of Modern Art.

Photography, Vision, & the Production of Modern Bodies. Suren Lalvani. LC 95-36567. (SUNY Series, Interruptions). (Illus.). 265p. (C). 1995. pap. text 17.95 (*0-7914-2718-8*) State U NY Pr.

***Photography with a Microscope.** F. W. D. Rost & Ronald Jowett Oldfield. 304p. (C). 2000. text 90.00 (*0-521-77096-3*) Cambridge U Pr.

Photography Workbook, Vol. 15. 50.00 (*0-911113-60-6*) Scott & Daughters.

Photography Yearbook, 1987-88. 1224p. 1988. 34.50 (*0-86343-093-7*) Taylor & Francis.

Photography Yearbook, 1999. Ed. by Chris Hinterobermaier & Joe Meehan. (Illus.). 1998. 39.95 (*0-86343-377-4*, Pub. by Hove Foto) Watsn-Guptill.

***Photography Your Way: A Career Guide to Satisfaction & Success.** Chuck DeLaney. (Illus.). 282p. 2000. pap. text 18.95 (*1-58115-024-5*) Allworth Pr.

Photography's Multiple Roles: Art, Document, Market, Science. Mihaly Csikszentmihalyi et al. Ed. by Terry A. Neff. LC 98-26380. (Illus.). 272p. 1998. write for info. (*0-9658887-1-1*) Mus Contemp Photo.

***Photography's Multiple Roles: Art, Document, Market, Science.** Ed Paschke et al. Ed. by Terry A. Neff. LC 98-26380. (Illus.). 256p. 1998. pap. 40.00 (*0-9658887-2-X*) Mus Contemp Photo.

Photogravure: A Process Handbook. Gary P. Kolb. LC 85-14447. 202p. (Orig.). (C). 1986. pap. text 31.95 (*0-8093-1252-2*) S Ill U Pr.

Photoguide of Common Skin Disorders: Diagnosis & Management. Herbert P. Goodheart. LC 98-26292. (Illus.). 469p. 1998. 69.00 (*0-683-30257-4*) Lppncott W & W.

***PhotoHistorica, Landmarks in Photography: Rare Images from the Collection of the Royal Photographic Society.** Pam Roberts. LC 00-38615. (Illus.). 336p. 2000. 60.00 (*1-57965-169-0*, 85169) Artisan.

Photohistory of World War One. Philip J. Haythornthwaite. (Illus.). 240p. 1995. pap. 16.95 (*1-85409-284-7*, Pub. by Arms & Armour) Sterling.

Photoimage--Printmaking, 60s to 90s: Museum of Fine Arts, Boston, July 7-September 27, 1998 & Des Moines Art Center, March 5-May 9, 1999. Clifford S. Ackley. LC 98-66291. 52 p. 1998. 14.95 (*0-87846-463-8*) Mus Fine Arts Boston.

Photo/Imaging: How to Communicate with Camera & Computer. 4th rev. ed. David H. Curl. LC 97-4064. Orig. Title: Photocommunication. (Illus.). 288p. (Orig.). (C). 1997. pap. text 30.00 (*0-88196-009-8*) Oak Woods Media.

Photoimmunology. Ed. by Jean Krutmann & Craig A. Elmets. LC 94-43729. (Illus.). 500p. 1995. 135.00 (*0-86542-826-3*) Blackwell Sci.

Photoimmunology. Ed. by John A. Parrish et al. LC 83-4216. 320p. 1983. 85.00 (*0-306-41280-2*, Plenum Trade) Perseus Pubng.

Photoinduced Electron Transfer, 4 pts. Ed. by M. A. Fox & M. Chanon. 1989. 1089.50 (*0-444-87121-7*) Elsevier.

Photoinduced Electron Transfer, Vol. II. (Topics in Current Chemistry Ser.: Vol. 158). (Illus.). 204p. 1990. 118.95 (*0-387-52568-8*) Spr-Verlag.

Photoinduced Electron Transfer: Photoinduced Electron Transfer Reactions - Inorganic Substrates & Applications. Ed. by M. A. Fox & M. Chanon. 790p. 1988. 224.00 (*0-318-40166-5*) Elsevier.

Photoinduced Electron Transfer V. Ed. by J. Mattay. (Topics in Current Chemistry Ser.: Vol. 168). (Illus.). 290p. 1993. 189.95 (*0-387-56746-1*) Spr-Verlag.

Photoinduced Electron Transfer IV. Ed. by J. Mattay. (Topics in Current Chemistry Ser.: Vol. 163). (Illus.). xiii, 250p. 1992. 142.95 (*0-387-55117-4*) Spr-Verlag.

Photoinduced Electron Transfer I. Ed. by J. Mattay. (Topics in Current Chemistry Ser.: Vol. 156). 256p. 1990. 135.95 (*0-387-52379-0*) Spr-Verlag.

Photoinduced Electron Transfer III. Ed. by J. Mattay. (Topics in Current Chemistry Ser.: Vol. 159). (Illus.). xii, 259p. 1991. 111.95 (*0-387-53257-9*) Spr-Verlag.

Photoinhibition of Photosynthesis: From Molecular Mechanisms to the Field. Ed. by N. R. Baker & J. R. Bowyer. 500p. 1994. 177.50 (*1-872748-03-1*, Pub. by Bios Sci) Coronet Bks.

Photoinitiation, Photopolymerization & Photocuring: Fundamentals & Applications. Jean-Pierre Fouassier. 388p. 1995. 140.00 (*1-56990-146-5*) Hanser-Gardner.

***Photoinitiators for Free Radical Cationic & Anionic Photopolymerisation, Vol. 3.** J. V. Crivello & K. K. Dietliker. Ed. by G. Bradley. 600p. 1999. 189.95 (*0-471-97892-2*) Wiley.

***Photoionization & Photodetachment, Vol. 10.** Cheuk-Yiu Ng. LC 99-57907. (Advanced Series in Physical Chemistry). 1999. 170.00 (*981-02-3892-4*) World Scientific Pub.

Photojournalism. 2nd ed. Lewis. 1994. teacher ed. 11.87 (*0-697-14630-8*, WCB McGr Hill) McGrw-H Hghr Educ.

Photojournalism: An Introduction. Fred Parrish. 420p. 2000. pap. 43.25 (*0-314-04564-3*) West Pub.

Photojournalism: Content & Technique. 2nd ed. D. Gregory Lewis. 352p. (C). 1994. text. write for info. (*0-697-14629-4*) Brown & Benchmark.

Photojournalism: The Professionals' Approach. 4th ed. Ken Kobre. (Illus.). 360p. 2000. pap. text 49.95 (*0-240-80240-3*, Focal) Buttrwrth-Heinemann.

***Photojournalism: The Professionals' Approach.** 4th rev. ed. Kenneth Kobre & Betsy Brill. LC 99-59412. (Illus.). 384p. 2000. pap. 49.95 (*0-240-80415-5*, Focal) Buttrwrth-Heinemann.

Photojournalism & Foreign Policy: Icons of Outrage in International Crises. David D. Perlmutter. LC 98-16908. (Praeger Series in Political Communication). 192p. 1998. 55.00 (*0-275-95812-4*, Praeger Pubs); pap. 17.95 (*0-275-96362-4*, Praeger Pubs) Greenwood.

Photojournalism Basics: An Introduction to Photography for Publication. 2nd ed. Harris Smith & John Robaton. LC 93-93528. (Illus.). 128p. (Orig.). (C). 1996. pap. text 17.95 (*0-9630699-2-6*) Upper River.

***Photojournalist.** Art Giberson. 200p. 2000. mass mkt. 14.95 (*1-891118-33-1*, Wind Canyon Bks) Wind Canyon.

Photojournalist: In the Middle of Disaster. Keith E. Greenberg. Ed. by Bruce Glassman. LC 95-22683. (Risky Business Ser.). (Illus.). 32p. (J). (gr. 2-5). 1995. lib. bdg. 16.95 (*1-56711-157-2*) Blackbirch.

Photojournalist: The Career of Jimmy Hare. Lewis L. Gould & Richard Greffe. (Illus.). 179p. 1977. 22.95 (*0-292-74004-2*) U of Tex Pr.

Photojournalist: The Career of Jimmy Hare. Lewis L. Gould & Richard Greffe. LC 76-52920. (Illus.). 169p. 1977. reprint ed. pap. 52.40 (*0-7837-8940-8*, 204965000002) Bks Demand.

***Photojournalist's Guide to Making Money.** Michael Sedge. (Illus.). 224p. 2000. pap. 18.95 (*1-58115-076-8*, Pub. by Allworth Pr) Watsn-Guptill.

Photokinetics: Theoretical Fundamentals & Applications. H. Mauser & G. Gauglitz. LC 98-26516. (Chemical Kinetics Ser.). 556p. 1998. 362.00 (*0-444-82536-3*) Elsevier.

Photolab Design for Professionals. 59th ed. Eastman Kodak Company Staff. LC 90-80577. (Illus.). 64p. (Orig.). (C). 1998. pap. 9.95 (*0-87985-659-9*, K-13, Kodak) Saunders Photo.

***Photolanguage: How Photos Reveal the Fascinating Stories of Our Lives & Relationships.** Robert Akeret. (Illus.). 240p. 2000. 29.95 (*0-393-04968-X*) Norton.

Photolithography. TEEX Staff. (Illus.). xi, 278p. 1997. spiral bd. 69.95 (*1-58257-010-8*, 8050B) TX Eng Extsn Servs.

Photolithography Overview. TEEX Staff. (Illus.). vii, 99p. 1997. spiral bd. 39.95 (*1-58257-007-8*, 8124B) TX Eng Extsn Servs.

PhotoMagic with Adobe PhotoDeluxe. Daniel Grotta. LC 96-75412. 336p. 1996. pap. 24.99 (*1-56884-883-8*) IDG Bks.

***Photomaps: Crow Wing County.** Photomaps, Inc. Staff. (Illus.). 80p. 1999. pap. write for info. (*0-9661599-2-6*, 99-1) Evergrn Pr.

Photomarketing Handbook. Jeff Cason & Peter Lawrence. 156p. 1989. pap. 19.95 (*0-929667-05-0*) Images NY.

Photomask & X-Ray Mask Technology IV, Vol. 3096. Ed. by Naoaki Aizaki. LC 98-122044. 518p. 1997. 99.00 (*0-8194-2516-8*) SPIE.

***Photomask & X-Ray Mask Technology VI.** Ed. by Hiroaki Morimoto. 642p. 1999. pap. text 120.00 (*0-8194-3230-X*) SPIE.

Photomask & X-Ray Mask Technology V. Ed. by Naoaki Aizaki. LC 98-227293. (Proceedings of SPIE Ser.: Vol. 3412). 630p. 1998. 116.00 (*0-8194-2864-7*) SPIE.

***Photomask Technology & Management.** Ed. by Frank E. Abboud & Brian J. Grenon. 1999. pap. text 145.00 (*0-8194-3468-X*) SPIE.

Photomasks, Scales & Gratings. Douglas F. Horne. LC 83-237518. 218p. reprint ed. pap. 67.60 (*0-7837-3240-6*, 204325900007) Bks Demand.

Photomath. Piersel. (J). (gr. 3-9). teacher ed. 0.29 (*0-87783-201-3*); pap. 1.99 (*0-87783-076-2*) Oddo.

Photomechanic Art: Colombian Contemporary Photography, Pt. I. Miguel Gonzalez & Ana Sokoloff. (Illus.). 20p. 1992. pap. text. write for info. (*1-883592-02-X*) Perm Mission.

***Photomechanics.** Ed. by Pramod K. Rastogi. (Topics in Applied Physics Ser.: Vol. 77). (Illus.). 438p. 1999. 165.00 (*3-540-65990-0*) Spr-Verlag.

Photomechanics '95: 11-14 September, 1995, Novosibirsk, Russia. M. K. Akhmetzyanov et al. LC 96-68789. vii, 176p. 1996. pap. write for info. (*0-8194-2177-4*) SPIE.

Photomedicine, 3 vols. Ed. by Ehud Ben-Hur & Ionel Rosenthal. LC 86-34293. 1987. 361.00 (*0-8493-4673-8*, RM837, CRC Reprint) Franklin.

Photomedicine, 3 vols., Vol. 1. Ed. by Ehud Ben-Hur & Ionel Rosenthal. 224p. 1987. 116.00 (*0-8493-4674-6*, CRC Reprint) Franklin.

Photomedicine, 3 vols., Vol. 2. Ed. by Ehud Ben-Hur & Ionel Rosenthal. 256p. 1987. 125.00 (*0-8493-4675-4*, CRC Reprint) Franklin.

Photomedicine, 3 vols., Vol. 3. Ed. by Ehud Ben-Hur & Ionel Rosenthal. 240p. 1987. 122.00 (*0-8493-4676-2*, CRC Reprint) Franklin.

***Photomedicine in Gynecology & Reproduction.** Ed. by P. Wyss et al. (Illus.). viii, 384p. 2000. 233.25 (*3-8055-6905-X*) S Karger.

Photomesic & Photonuclear Reactions & Investigation Methods with Synchrotrons. Ed. by D. V. Skobel'tsyn. Tr. by Joachim R. Buchner from RUS. LC 73-79424. (Proceedings of the P. N. Lebedev Physics Institute Ser.: No. 54). (Illus.). 260p. 1974. reprint ed. pap. 80.60 (*0-608-05515-8*, 206598300006) Bks Demand.

Photometric & Fluorometric Methods of Analysis: Nonmetals. Foster D. Snell. LC 80-20546. (Illus.). 832p. reprint ed. pap. 200.00 (*0-8357-7517-8*, 203601200097) Bks Demand.

Photometric & Fluorometric Methods of Analysis Metals, Vol. 1. Foster D. Snell. LC 77-25039. (Illus.). 1015p. reprint ed. pap. 200.00 (*0-7837-3117-5*, 205766900001) Bks Demand.

Photometric & Fluorometric Methods of Analysis Metals, Vol. 2. Foster D. Snell. LC 77-25039. (Illus.). 1174p. reprint ed. pap. 200.00 (*0-7837-3118-3*, 205766900002) Bks Demand.

Photometric & Spectroscopic Binary Systems. Ed. by E. B. Carling & Zdenek Kopal. xii, 546p. 1981. text 247.50 (*90-277-1281-6*) Kluwer Academic.

Photometric Atlas of Northern Bright Galaxies. Ed. by Keiichi Kodaira et al. (Illus.). 240p. 1990. 180.00 (*0-86008-461-2*, Pub. by U of Tokyo) Col U Pr.

Photometric Determination of Traces of Metals, Vol. 1 Set. 4th ed. Hiroshi Onishi. 1733p. 1989. 599.00 (*0-471-52748-3*) Wiley.

Photometric Determination of Traces of Metals: Individual Metals, Aluminum to Lithium, Vol. 1, Pt. 2A, Individual Metals, Aluminum to Lit. 4th ed. Hiroshi Onishi. 885p. 1986. 375.00 (*0-471-86139-1*) Wiley.

Photometric Determination of Traces of Metals: Individual Metals Magnesium, Vol. 1, Pt. 2B, Individual Metals Magnesium to Zik. 4th ed. Hiroshi Ohishi. 848p. 1989. 425.00 (*0-471-84694-5*) Wiley.

Photometric Determination of Traces of Metals Pt. 1: General Aspects. 4th ed. Ernest B. Sandell & Hiroshi Onishi. LC 77-18937. (Illus.). 1097p. reprint ed. pap. 200.00 (*0-608-17422-X*, 205645800067) Bks Demand.

Photometric Engineering of Sources & Systems. Ed. by Angelo V. Arecchi. 24p. 1997. pap. 59.00 (*0-8194-2562-1*) SPIE.

***Photometric Evaluation of Vehicle Traffic Control Signal Heads.** (Illus.). 7p. 2000. pap. text 18.00 (*0-87995-169-9*, LM-68-00) Illum Eng.

Photometric Evaluation of Vehicle Traffic Control Signal Heads: LM-68-95. IESNA Staff. (Illus.). 7p. 1995. pap. 18.00 (*0-87995-114-1*, LM-68-95) Illum Eng.

***Photometric Measurement of Roadway Lighting Installations: LM-50-99.** rev. ed. IESNA Staff. (Illus.). 4p. 1999. pap. 18.00 (*0-87995-158-3*, LM-50-99) Illum Eng.

Photometric Measurement of Tunnel Lighting Installations: LM-71-96. IESNA Staff. (Illus.). 4p. 1996. pap. 12.00 (*0-87995-136-2*, LM-71-96) Illum Eng.

Photometric Measurements Area & Sport Lighting: LM-5-96. (Lighting Measurements Ser.). (Illus.). 12p. 1996. pap. 20.00 (*0-87995-123-0*, LM-5-96) Illum Eng.

Photometric Measurements of Parking Areas: LM-64-91. (Lighting Measurements Ser.). (Illus.). 5p. 1991. pap. 15.00 (*0-87995-061-7*, LM-64-91) Illum Eng.

***Photometric Measurements of Roadway Sign Installations: LM-52-98.** IESNA Staff. (Illus.). 10p. 1998. pap. 20.00 (*0-87995-151-6*, LM-52-98) Illum Eng.

Photometric Methods in Inorganic Trace Analysis. Gyula I. Svehla et al. 404p. 1985. 281.00 (*0-444-99588-9*) Elsevier.

Photometric Methods in Inorganic Trace Analysis. Gyula I. Svehla et al. (Wilson & Wilson's Comprehensive Analytical Chemistry Ser.: Vol. 20). 1985. 253.25 (*0-685-09935-0*) Elsevier.

***Photometric Modeling for Computer Vision & Graphics: Proceedings of the IEEE Workshop on Photometric Modeling for Computer Vision & Graphics Held in Fort Collins, Colorado, 1999.** LC 99-62809. 73p. 1999. pap. 100.00 (*0-7695-0271-7*) IEEE Comp Soc.

Photometric Organic Analysis: Basic Principles with Applications. Eugene Sawicki. LC 70-116768. (Chemical Analysis Ser.: Vol. 31). 695p. pap. 200.00 (*0-608-10029-3*, 200649100059) Bks Demand.

***Photometric Redshifts & High Redshift Galaxies.** Ed. by Ray Weymann et al. (Conference Series Proceedings: Vol. 191). 376p. 1999. text 52.00 (*1-58381-017-X*) Astron Soc Pacific.

Photometric Researches. Charles Pierce. (Notable American Authors Ser.). 1999. reprint ed. lib. bdg. 125.00 (*0-7812-8737-5*) Rprt Serv.

Photometric Systems & Standard Stars. Ed. by Vytas Straizys & A. G. Davis Philip. (Illus.). (Orig.). (C). 1996. pap. 40.00 (*0-933485-20-4*) L Davis Pr.

***Photometric Testing of Flood Lights Using High Intensity Discharge or Incandescent Filament Lamps: LM-35.** IESNA Staff. (Illus.). 17p. 1999. pap. 23.00 (*0-87995-157-5*, LM-35-99) Illum Eng.

Photometric Testing of Flood Lights Using High Intensity Discharge or Incandescent Filament Lamps: LM-35-89. 12.00 (*0-87995-075-7*) Illum Eng.

***Photometric Testing of Indoor Flourescent Luminaries: LM-41-98.** IESNA Staff. (Illus.). 9p. 1998. pap. 20.00 (*0-87995-146-X*, LM-41-98) Illum Eng.

P

An Asterisk (*) at the beginning of an entry indicates that the title is appearing for the first time.

*__Photometric Testing of Indoor Luminaires Using High Intensity Discharge or Incandescent Filament Lamps: LM-46-98.__ IESNA Staff. (Illus.). 9p. 1998. pap. 16.00 (*0-87995-153-2*, LM-46-98) Illum Eng.

Photometric Testing of Outdoor Fluorescent Luminaires: LM-10-96. IESNA Staff. (Illus.). 23p. 1996. pap. 25.00 (*0-87995-138-9*, LM-10-96) Illum Eng.

Photometric Testing of Roadway Luminaries Using Incandescent Filament & High Density Discharge Lamps: LM-31-95. IESNA Staff. (Illus.). 9p. 1995. pap. 20.00 (*0-87995-120-6*, LM-31-95) Illum Eng.

Photometric Testing of Search Lights: LM-11-97. IESNA Staff. (Illus.). 23p. 1997. pap. 15.00 (*0-87995-142-7*, LM-11-97) Illum Eng.

Photometrics Handbook. 2nd rev. ed. Robert C. Mumm. (Illus.). 275p. (Orig.). (C). 1997. pap. 20.00 (*0-911747-37-0*) Broadway Pr.

Photomicrography: A Comprehensive Treatise, 2 vols. Roger P. Loveland. LC 80-12428. 1070p. 1981. reprint ed. lib. bdg. 119.50 (*0-89874-392-3*) Krieger.

Photomontage. rev. ed. Dawn Ades. LC 86-50313. (World of Art Ser.). (Illus.). 180p. 1986. reprint ed. pap. 14.95 (*0-500-20208-7*, Pub. by Thames Hudson) Norton.

Photomontage: A Step-by-Step Guide to Building Pictures. Stephen Golding. (Illus.). 144p. 1997. 29.99 (*1-56496-289-X*) Rockport Pubs.

Photomontage: An Artist's Guide to Building Pictures. Stephen Golding. (Illus.). 144p. 1997. text. write for info. (*90-5703-981-8*, Harwood Acad Pubs) Gordon & Breach.

Photomontage: Barbara Morgan. Ed. by Barbara Morgan. LC 80-81142. 64p. (Orig.). 1980. pap. 15.00 (*0-87100-171-3*) Morgan.

Photomontages of Hannah Hoch. Peter Boswell et al. (Illus.). 224p. 1996. pap. 35.00 (*0-935640-53-3*) Walker Art Ctr.

Photomontages of Hannah Hoch. Photos by Hannah Hoch. LC 96-31460. (Illus.). 224p. 1996. 55.00 (*0-935640-52-5*, 620151) Walker Art Ctr.

Photomorphogenesis. Hans Mohr. Ed. by Walter Shrosphire, Jr. (Encyclopedia of Plant Physiology Ser.: Vol. 16, Pts. A & B). (Illus.). 900p. 1983. 398.95 (*0-387-12143-9*) Spr-Verlag.

Photomorphogenesis in Plants. Ed. by R. E. Kendrick & G. H. Kronenberg. 1986. pap. text 100.50 (*90-247-3317-0*); lib. bdg. 314.00 (*90-247-3316-2*) Kluwer Academic.

Photomorphogenesis in Plants. 2nd ed. Ed. by R. E. Kendrick. LC 93-32993. 864p. (C). 1993. pap. text 116.00 (*0-7923-2551-6*) Kluwer Academic.

Photomorphogenesis in Plants. 2nd ed. Ed. by R. E. Kendrick. LC 93-32993. 864p. (C). 1993. lib. bdg. 395.50 (*0-7923-2550-8*) Kluwer Academic.

Photomosaics. Robert Silvers. Ed. by Michael Hawley. LC 97-8721. 96p. 1997. pap. 19.95 (*0-8050-5170-8*, Owl) H Holt & Co.

Photomosaics. Robert Silvers. Ed. by Michael Hawley. (Illus.). 96p. 1997. 39.95 (*0-8050-5795-1*) H Holt & Co.

*__Photomosiac Portraits.__ Robert Silvers. (Illus.). 96p. 2000. 26.95 (*0-670-89348-X*, Viking) Viking Penguin.

*__Photon: Old Problems in Lighter New Ideas.__ Ed. by Valerie V. Droeglazov. 278p. 2000. lib. bdg. 98.00 (*1-56072-810-8*) Nova Sci Pubs.

Photon Activation Analysis. Christian Segebade et al. 705p. (C). 1987. lib. bdg. 242.35 (*3-11-007250-5*) De Gruyter.

Photon & Electron Collisions with Atoms & Molecules: Proceedings of the Second European Study Conference Held in Belfast, Northern Ireland, July 23-26, 1996. P. G. Burke & C. J. Joachain. LC 97-29100. (Physics of Atoms & Molecules Ser.). 378p. (C). 1997. text 125.00 (*0-306-45692-3*, Kluwer Plenum) Kluwer Academic.

Photon & Particle Interactions with Surfaces in Space: Proceedings of the ESLAB Symposium, 6th, Noordwijk The Netherlands, Sept., 1972. ESLAB-ESRIN Symposium Staff. Ed. by R. J. Grard. LC 73-83561. (Astrophysics & Space Science Library: No. 37). 600p. 1973. text 261.50 (*90-277-0381-7*) Kluwer Academic.

*__Photon & Poincare Group.__ Valeri V. Dvoeglazov. (Contemporary Fundamental Physics Ser.). 356p. 1999. lib. bdg. 135.00 (*1-56072-718-7*) Nova Sci Pubs.

Photon-Assisted Collisions & Related Topics. Ed. by N. K. Rahman & C. Guidotti. 355p. 1982. text 274.00 (*3-7186-0130-3*) Gordon & Breach.

Photon-Assisted Processing of Surfaces & Thin Films: Proceedings of Symposium B on Photon-Assisted Processing of Surfaces & Thin Films of the 1994 E-MRS Spring Conference, Strasbourg, France, 24-27 May, 1994. Ed. by J. Dieleman et al. (European Materials Research Society Symposia Proceedings Ser.: Vol. 47). 648p. 1995. 314.00 (*0-444-82162-7*, North Holland) Elsevier.

Photon, Beam & Plasma Stimulated Chemical Processes at Surfaces. Ed. by V. M. Donnelly et al. (MRS Symposium Proceedings Ser.: Vol. 75). 1987. text 17.50 (*0-931837-41-3*) Materials Res.

Photon Correlation & Scattering. LC 92-80638. (Technical Digest Series, 1992: Vol. 20). 250p. (Orig.). 1992. lib. bdg. 66.00 (*1-55752-252-9*) Optical Soc.

Photon Correlation Techniques & Applications. LC 87-62778. (Proceedings Ser.: Vol. 1). 69p. (Orig.). 1988. pap. 75.00 (*1-55752-035-6*) Optical Soc.

Photon Correlation Techniques in Fluid Mechanics: Kiel-Damp, FRG 1982, Proceedings. (Optical Sciences Ser.: Vol. 38). (Illus.). 339p. 1983. 68.95 (*0-387-11796-2*) Spr-Verlag.

Photon Counting & Photon Statistics see Progress in Quantum Electronics

Photon Defined: Special Relativity Refuted Electron Self-Field Stabilized. John F. Johnson. (Illus.). 128p. (Orig.). (C). 1989. pap. text 50.00 (*0-931571-05-7*) RP Pubng.

Photon Detectors. Ed. by J. Schanda & I. Ungvari. (Illus.). 407p. (C). 1987. pap. text 195.00 (*0-941743-35-7*) Nova Sci Pubs.

Photon Echo & Coherent Spectroscopy, Vol. 3239. Ed. by Vitali V. Samartsev. LC 98-122573. 504p. 1997. 99.00 (*0-8194-2677-6*) SPIE.

Photon, Electron, & Ion Probes of Polymer Structure & Properties. Ed. by David W. Dwight et al. LC 81-10816. (ACS Symposium Ser.: No. 162). 1981. 49.95 (*0-8412-0639-2*) Am Chemical.

Photon, Electron, & Ion Probes of Polymer Structure & Properties. Ed. by David W. Dwight et al. LC 81-10816. (ACS Symposium Ser.: Vol. 162). 453p. 1981. reprint ed. pap. 140.50 (*0-608-03048-1*, 206350100007) Bks Demand.

Photon, Electron, Proton & Neutron Interaction Data for Body Tissues, No. 46. International Commission on Radiation Units & Meas. LC 91-20902. 1992. 60.00 incl. disk (*0-913394-41-6*) Intl Comm Rad Meas.

Photon Emission from Biological Systems-Theory & Practice: Proceedings of the International Symposium on Photon Emission from Biological Systems, Wroclaw, Poland, January 24-26, 1986. Ed. by B. Jezowska-Trzebiatowska et al. 272p. 1987. text 75.00 (*9971-5-0151-1*) World Scientific Pub.

Photon-Hadron Interactions. Richard Phillips Feynman. 1998. pap. 35.00 (*0-201-36074-8*) Addison-Wesley.

Photon Migration in Tissues. B. Chance. LC 90-7293. (Illus.). 206p. 1990. 79.50 (*0-306-43522-5*, Kluwer Plenum) Kluwer Academic.

Photon, '95: Gamma-Gamma Collisions: Proceedings of the IXth International Workshop. Ed. by David J. Miller et al. LC 95-41305. 470p. 1995. 112.00 (*981-02-2473-7*) World Scientific Pub.

Photon-Photon Collision: Proceedings of the VII International Workshop, Paris, France 1-5 April 1986. Ed. by A. Courau & P. Kessler. 500p. 1987. text 114.00 (*9971-5-0138-4*) World Scientific Pub.

Photon-Photon Collisions: Proceedings of the VIII International Workshop on Photon-Photon Collisions. Ed. by U. Karshon. 512p. (C). 1988. text 139.00 (*9971-5-0586-X*) World Scientific Pub.

Photon-Photon Collisions, 1992: 9th International Workshop. D. O. Caldwell & H. P. Paar. 532p. 1992. text 106.00 (*981-02-1053-1*) World Scientific Pub.

Photon-Photon Interactions: Proceedings of the International Colloquium, 4th, Paris, France, April 6-9, 1981. Ed. by G. W. London. 538p. 1981. text 76.00 (*9971-83-091-4*) World Scientific Pub.

Photon Physics: The Cutting Edge. Ed. by G. K. Horton & A. A. Maradudin. (Dynamical Properties of Solids Ser.: Vol. 7). 544p. 1995. 256.25 (*0-444-82262-3*, North Holland) Elsevier.

Photon Propagation in Tissues II. Ed. by David A. Benaron et al. (Europto Ser.: Vol. 2925). 312p. 1996. 66.00 (*0-8194-2327-0*) SPIE.

Photon Propagation in Tissues IV. Ed. by David A. Benaron et al. LC 99-200353. (Europto Ser.: Vol. 3566). 1998. 80.00 (*0-8194-3028-5*) SPIE.

Photon Propagation in Tissues III. Ed. by David A. Benaron et al. (Europto Ser.: Vol. 3194). 546p. 1998. 107.00 (*0-8194-2626-1*) SPIE.

Photon-Vegetation Interactions: Applications in Optical Remote Sensing & Plant Ecology. Ed. by R. B. Myneni & J. Ross. (Illus.). 560p. 1991. 262.95 (*0-387-52108-9*) Spr-Verlag.

Photon '97: Proceedings of the Conference on the Structure & Interactions of the Photon Egmond Aan Zee, The Netherlands 10-15 May, 1997. Ed. by A. Buijs & F. C. Erne. LC 97-52725. 500p. 1998. 96.00 (*981-02-3244-6*) World Scientific Pub.

Photonic & Optoelectronic Polymers: Developed from a Symposium Sponsored by the Pacific Polymer Federation at the Pacific Polymer Conference, Kauai, Hawaii, December 12-16, 1995, Vol. 672. Samson A. Jenekhe et al. LC 97-22245. (ACS Symposium Ser.). (Illus.). 580p. 1997. text 150.00 (*0-8412-3519-8*, Pub. by Am Chemical) OUP.

Photonic Aspects of Modern Radar. Ed. by Henry Zmuda & Edward N. Toughlian. LC 94-2362. 550p. 1994. 47.00 (*0-89006-670-1*) Artech Hse.

Photonic Band Gap Materials: Proceedings of the NATO Advanced Study Institute on Photonic Band Gap Materials, Elounda, Crete, Greece, June 18-30, 1995. Ed. by Costas M. Soukoulis. LC 96-10838. (NATO ASI Series E, Applied Sciences: No. 315). 729p. 1996. text 320.50 (*0-7923-3991-6*) Kluwer Academic.

Photonic Band Gaps & Localization. C. M. Soukoulis. (NATO ASI Ser.: Vol. 308). (Illus.). 530p. (C). 1993. text 139.50 (*0-306-44494-1*, Kluwer Plenum) Kluwer Academic.

Photonic Component Engineering & Applications: 8-9 April, 1996, Orlando, Florida. Andrew R. Pirich & SPIE Staff. LC 95-73019. (Proceedings Ser.). ix, 230p. 1996. pap. write for info. (*0-8194-2130-8*) SPIE.

Photonic Crystals: Molding the Flow of Light. John D. Joannopoulos et al. LC 94-12372. 184p. 1995. text 39.50 (*0-691-03744-2*, Pub. by Princeton U Pr) Cal Prin Full Svc.

Photonic Devices & Systems. R. G. Hunsperger. (Optical Engineering Ser.: Vol. 45). (Illus.). 448p. 1994. text 165.00 (*0-8247-9243-2*) Dekker.

Photonic Devices for Telecommunications: How to Model & Measure. George Guekos. LC 98-44450. (Illus.). xxxiii, 404p. 1999. 99.00 (*3-540-64318-4*) Spr-Verlag.

Photonic, Electronic & Atomic Collisions: Invited Papers of the 20th International Conference on the Physics of Electronic & Atomic Collisions, Vienna, Austria, 23-29 July 1997. Ed. by Friedrich Aumayr & Hannspeter Winter. LC 98-215271. 800p. 1998. 132.00 (*981-02-3425-2*) World Scientific Pub.

Photonic Networks. Giancarlo Prati. LC 96-29971. 1997. 109.00 (*3-540-76143-8*) Spr-Verlag.

Photonic Networks, Components & Applications. Jacek Chrostowski & J. Terry. (Series in Optics & Photonics: Vol. 2). 464p. 1991. text 118.00 (*981-02-0483-3*) World Scientific Pub.

Photonic Polymer Systems. Ed. by Wise et al. LC 98-24469. (Illus.). 968p. 1998. text 250.00 (*0-8247-0152-6*) Dekker.

Photonic Probes of Surfaces Vol. 2: Electromagnetic Waves: Recent Developments in Research. Ed. by P. Halevi. LC 95-49214. (Electromagnetic Waves Ser.: Vol. 2). 580p. 1995. 355.00 (*0-444-82198-8*, North Holland) Elsevier.

Photonic Processing Technology & Applications. Ed. by Andrew R. Pirich & Raymond K. Boncek. LC 98-111053. 26p. 1997. pap. 59.00 (*0-8194-2490-0*) SPIE.

Photonic Processing Technology & Applications II. Ed. by Andrew R. Pirich & Michael A. Parker. LC 98-227292. (Proceedings of SPIE Ser.: Vol. 3384). 220p. 1998. 59.00 (*0-8194-2833-7*) SPIE.

Photonic Quantum Computing. Ed. by Steven P. Hotaling & Andrew R. Pirich. LC 98-111054. 27p. 1997. pap. 59.00 (*0-8194-2491-9*) SPIE.

Photonic Quantum Computing II. Ed. by Steven P. Hotaling & Andrew R. Pirich. LC 98-226758. (Proceedings of SPIE Ser.: Vol. 3385). 150p. 1998. 59.00 (*0-8194-2834-5*) SPIE.

Photonic Switching. Ed. by T. K. Gustafson & P. W. Smith. (Electronics & Photonics Ser.: Vol. 25). (Illus.). 220p. 1988. 64.95 (*0-387-18866-5*) Spr-Verlag.

Photonic Switching No. II: Proceedings of the International Meeting Kobe, Japan, April 12-14, 1990. Ed. by K. Tada & H. Scott Hinton. (Electronics & Photonics Ser.: Vol. 29). (Illus.). xiii, 396p. 1991. 88.95 (*0-387-53067-3*) Spr-Verlag.

Photonic Switching & Interconnects. 1996. 195.00 (*0-614-18419-3*) Info Gatekeepers.

Photonic Switching Technology: Systems & Networks. Hussein T. Mouftah & Jaafar M. H. Elmirghani. LC 98-7873. 612p. 1998. 99.95 (*0-7803-4707-2*) Inst Electrical.

*__Photonic Systems & Applications in Defense & Manufacturing.__ Ed. by Yee L. Lam et al. 1999. pap. text 103.00 (*0-8194-3500-7*) SPIE.

Photonic Technology & Industrial Policy: U. S. Responses to Technological Change. Ernest Sternberg. LC 91-34657. 311p. (C). 1992. pap. text 21.95 (*0-7914-1182-6*) State U NY Pr.

Photonics: Maintaining Competitiveness in the Information Era. National Research Council Staff. 112p. 1988. pap. text 14.95 (*0-309-03940-1*) Natl Acad Pr.

Photonics: Nonlinear Optics & Ultrafast Phenomena. Ed. by R. R. Alfano & L. Rothberg. 182p. (C). 1991. text 175.00 (*0-941743-93-4*) Nova Sci Pubs.

*__Photonics: Using Laser Light as a Tool.__ Ralf Menzel. LC 00-38820. (Advanced Texts in Physics Ser.). (Illus.). 2000. pap. write for info. (*3-540-67074-2*) Spr-Verlag.

Photonics & Radio Frequecy II, Vol. 3463. Ed. by Gregory J. Zagar et al. LC 99-211209. 1998. 69.00 (*0-8194-2918-X*) SPIE.

Photonics & Radio Frequency, Vol. 2844. Ed. by Brian M. Hendrickson. 338p. 1996. 76.00 (*0-8194-2232-0*) SPIE.

*__Photonics Center.__ Mathias Sauerbruch. (Illus.). 2000. 29.95 (*84-95273-18-7*) Actar.

Photonics for Fiber & Integrated Optics. Keigo Lizuka. LC 98-15244. (Pure & Applied Optics Ser.). 1168p. 1998. 175.00 (*0-471-83938-8*, Wiley-Interscience) Wiley.

*__Photonics for Space & Radiation Environments.__ Ed. by Edward W. Taylor & Francis Berghmans. 1999. pap. text 62.00 (*0-8194-3467-1*) SPIE.

Photonics for Space Environments IV, Vol. 2811. Ed. by Edward W. Taylor. 322p. 1996. 66.00 (*0-8194-2199-5*) SPIE.

Photonics for Space Environments IV, Vol. 3440. Ed. by Edward W. Taylor. 1998. 69.00 (*0-8194-2895-7*) SPIE.

Photonics for Space Environments V. Ed. by Edward W. Taylor. vii, 132 p. 1997. pap. 59.00 (*0-8194-2546-X*) SPIE.

Photonics for Space Environments V, Vol. 3124. Ed. by Edward W. Taylor. 154p. 1997. 59.00 (*0-8194-2646-6*) SPIE.

Photonics in Switching. LC 95-67800. (1995 Technical Digest Ser.: Vol. 12). 177p. 1995. pap. 75.00 (*1-55752-394-0*) Optical Soc.

Photonics in Switching, 2 vols. Ed. by John E. Midwinter. LC 92-38764. (Quantum Electronics - Principles & Applications Ser.). (Illus.). 674p. 1993. text 164.00 (*0-12-496050-2*) Acad Pr.

Photonics in Switching, 2 vols., Vol. 1. Ed. by John E. Midwinter. LC 92-38764. (Quantum Electronics - Principles & Applications Ser.). (Illus.). 322p. 1993. text 82.00 (*0-12-496051-0*) Acad Pr.

Photonics in Switching, 2 vols., Vol. 2. Ed. by John E. Midwinter. LC 92-38764. (Quantum Electronics - Principles & Applications Ser.). (Illus.). 352p. 1993. text 82.00 (*0-12-496052-9*) Acad Pr.

Photonics Rules of Thumb: Optics, Electro-Optics, Fiber Optics, & Lasers. John Lester Miller & Ed Friedman. (Illus.). 423p. 1996. 55.00 (*0-07-044329-7*) McGraw.

Photonics Technology, Vol. 1. Savage. 221p. pap. write for info. (*0-471-34626-8*) Wiley.

*__Photonics Technology into the 21st Century.__ Ed. by Seng T. Ho et al. 1999. pap. text 120.00 (*0-8194-3501-5*) SPIE.

Photonoc Networks, Optical Technology & Infrastructure. LC 97-72895. 356p. (gr. 12). 1997. pap. 78.00 (*90-5199-341-2*) IOS Press.

Photons & Atoms: Introduction to Quantum Electrodynamics. Claude Cohen-Tannoudji et al. LC 88-37845. 468p. 1989. 135.00 (*0-471-84526-4*) Wiley.

Photons & Atoms: Introduction to Quantum Electrodynamics. Claude Cohen-Tannoudji et al. LC 88-37845. 496p. 1997. pap. 59.95 (*0-471-18433-0*, Wiley-Interscience) Wiley.

Photons & Local Probes: Proceedings of the NATO Advanced Research Workshop, Reichenau, Germany, September 11-17, 1994. Ed. by Othmar Marti & Rolf Moller. LC 95-37543. (NATO ASI Ser.: Vol. 300). 372p. (C). 1995. text 191.50 (*0-7923-3709-3*) Kluwer Academic.

Photons & Low Energy Particles in Surface Processing. Ed. by C. Ashby et al. (Symposium Proceedings Ser.: Vol. 236). 549p. 1992. text 58.00 (*1-55899-130-1*) Materials Res.

Photons & Non-Linear Optics. D. N. Klyshko. xxii, 416p. 1988. text 663.00 (*2-88124-669-9*) Gordon & Breach.

Photons & Quantum Fluctuations. Hans-Otto Walther. (Malvern Physics Ser.). (Illus.). 232p. 1988. 110.00 (*0-85274-240-1*) IOP Pub.

Photon's Magnetic Field: Optical NMR Spectroscopy. M. Evans. (Contemporary Chemical Physics Ser.: No. 1). 264p. 1993. text 46.00 (*981-02-1265-8*) World Scientific Pub.

Photonuclear & Photomesic Processes. Ed. by D. V. Skobel'tsyn. Tr. by Joachim R. Buchner from RUS. LC 76-12546. (Proceedings of the P. N. Lebedev Physics Institute Ser.: No. 71). (Illus.). 224p. 1976. reprint ed. pap. 69.50 (*0-608-05530-1*, 206599800006) Bks Demand.

Photopass: The Rock & Roll Photography of Randy Bachman. Joel Selvin. LC 94-24775. (Illus.). 128p. (Orig.). 1995. pap. 15.00 (*0-943389-17-8*) Snow Lion-SLG Bks.

Photoperiodism in Plants. 2nd ed. Ed. by Brian Thomas & Daphne Vince-Prue. (Illus.). 448p. 1996. text 75.00 (*0-12-688490-0*) Morgan Kaufmann.

Photophonics I. Piersel. (Illus.). (J). (gr. 1-5). 1968. teacher ed. 0.29 (*0-685-03702-9*); pap. 1.99 (*0-87783-073-8*) Oddo.

Photophonics II. Piersel. (Illus.). (J). (gr. 1-5). 1968. teacher ed. 0.29 (*0-685-03703-7*); pap. 2.39 (*0-87783-074-6*) Oddo.

Photophysical & Photochemical Properties: Aromatic Compounds. A. Y. Malkin. 448p. 1992. lib. bdg. 245.00 (*0-8493-6802-2*) CRC Pr.

Photophysical & Photochemical Tools in Polymer Science. Ed. by Mitchell A. Winnik. 1986. text 289.00 (*90-277-2307-9*) Kluwer Academic.

Photophysics of Polymers. Ed. by Charles E. Hoyle & John M. Torkelson. LC 87-27303. (Symposium Ser.: No. 358). (Illus.). xi, 531p. 1987. 104.95 (*0-8412-1439-5*, Pub. by Am Chemical) OUP.

Photophysics of Polymers. Ed. by Charles E. Hoyle & John M. Torkelson. LC 87-27307. (ACS Symposium Ser.: Vol. 358). 544p. 1987. reprint ed. pap. 168.70 (*0-608-03881-4*, 206432800008) Bks Demand.

Photophysiology. Incl. Vol. 1. General Principles - Action of Light on Plants. Ed. by Arthur C. Giese. 1964. 67.50 (*0-12-282601-9*); Vol. 2. Action of Light on Animals & Microorganisms, Photobiochemical Mechanisms, Bioluminescence. Ed. by Arthur C. Giese. 1964. 67.50 (*0-12-282602-7*); Vol. 3. Current Topics. Ed. by Arthur C. Giese. 1968. 67.50 (*0-12-282603-5*); Vol. 5. Current Topics in Photobiology & Photochemistry. Ed. by Arthur C. Giese. 1970. 67.50 (*0-12-282605-1*); Vol. 6. Current Topics in Photobiology & Photochemistry. Ed. by Arthur C. Giese. 1971. 64.50 (*0-12-282606-X*); Vol. 7. Current Topics in Photobiology & Photochemistry. Ed. by Arthur C. Giese. 1972. 67.50 (*0-12-282607-8*); 1973. 67.50 (*0-12-282608-6*); write for info. (*0-318-50328-X*) Acad Pr.

Photoplay: A Psychological Study. Hugo Munsterberg. LC 79-124021. (Literature of Cinema, Ser. 1). 1970. reprint ed. 14.95 (*0-405-01628-X*) Ayer.

Photoplay: Works from the Chase Manhattan Collection. Lisa Phillips. Ed. by Emily Russell. Tr. by Rita Guibert & Clifford Landers. (Illus.). 200p. 1992. 42.00 (*0-9635340-1-7*); pap. text 28.50 (*0-9635340-0-9*) Chase Manhattan.

Photopolymer Device Physics, Chemistry & Applications III, Vol. 2851. Ed. by Roger A. Lessard. 168p. 1996. 56.00 (*0-8194-2239-8*) SPIE.

*__Photopolymer Device Physics, Chemistry & Applications IV, No. 3417.__ Ed. by Roger A. Lessard. LC 99-170361. 1998. 69.00 (*0-8194-2871-X*) SPIE.

Photopolymerization: Fundamentals & Applications, Vol. 673. Alec B. Scranton et al. LC 97-30337. (ASC Symposium Ser.). 262p. 1997. text 99.95 (*0-8412-3520-1*, Pub. by Am Chemical) OUP.

Photopolymerization of Surface Coatings. C. G. Roffey. LC 81-12916. (Wiley-Interscience Publications). 371p. reprint ed. pap. 115.10 (*0-7837-1880-2*, 204208100001) Bks Demand.

Photopolymers: Principles, Processes & Materials: Ninth International Technical Conference on Photopolymers, October 28-30, 1991, the Nevele Country Club, Ellenville, NY. Society of Plastics Engineers Staff. LC QD0381.8.S62. 426p. pap. 132.10 (*0-7837-2151-X*, 204243700004) Bks Demand.

Photopolymers: Principles, Processes & Materials: (Technical Papers), Regional Technical Conference October 30-November 2, 1988, The Nevele Country Club, Ellenville, New York - Sponsored by the Mid-Hudson Section, SPE. Society of Plastics Engineers Staff. LC QD0381.8.S62. 451p. pap. 139.90 (*0-608-18509-4*, 203418200089) Bks Demand.

Photopolymers: Principles, Processses & Materials: Technical Papers, Regional Technical Conference, Nevele Country Club, Ellenville, New York, October

An Asterisk (*) at the beginning of an entry indicates that the title is appearing for the first time.

28-30, 1985. Society of Plastics Engineers Staff. LC TP0156.P6. 389p. reprint ed. pap. 120.60 (*0-8357-6261-0*, 202769300056) Bks Demand.

Photoprocesses in Transition Metal Complexes, Biosystems, & Other Molecules: Experiment & Theory. Ed. by Elise Kochanski. LC 92-27727. (NATO Advanced Study Institutes Series C, Mathematical & Physical Sciences). 464p. (C). 1992. text 269.50 (*0-7923-1936-2*) Kluwer Academic.

Photoprocessing Industry: Guide to Pollution Prevention. (Illus.). 61p. (Orig.). (C). 1994. pap. text 25.00 (*1-56806-083-1*) DIANE Pub.

Photoproduction of Elementary Particles see Nuclear Particles & Physics: Group I

Photoproduction of Pions in Nucleons & Nuclei. Ed. by A. A. Komar. Tr. by Al Peabody from RUS. (Proceedings of the Lebedev Physics Institute Ser.: Vol. 186). 350p. (C). 1990. text 175.00 (*0-941743-77-2*) Nova Sci Pubs.

PhotoReading Whole Mind System. 2nd ed. Paul R. Scheele. LC 93-79859. (Illus.). 156p. (Orig.). (C). 1993. pap. 14.95 (*0-925480-52-5*) Learn Strategies.

*__Photoreading Whole Mind System: Read with Speed, Comprehension & Enjoyment.__ 3rd ed. Paul R. Scheele. 166p. 1999. pap. 16.95 (*0-925480-53-3*, Pub. by Learn Strategies) ACCESS Pubs Network.

Photoreal FX. Alan Chan. (Illus.). 292p. (Orig.). 1996. pap. 44.95 (*0-9655313-0-9*) Lghtspeed.

Photorealism. Louis K. Meiser. (Illus.). 448p. 1989. pap. 39.98 (*0-8109-8092-4*, Pub. by Abrams) Time Warner.

Photorealism & Ray Tracing in C. Christopher Watkins et al. (Illus.). 450p. 1995. 44.95 incl. disk (*1-55851-247-0*, M&T Bks) IDG Bks.

Photorealism in Computer Graphics: Eurographic Seminars. Ed. by K. Bouatouch et al. (Illus.). 256p. 1992. 111.95 (*0-387-54265-5*) Spr-Verlag.

Photorealism since 1980. Selected by Louis K. Meisel. LC 92-21997. (Illus.). 368p. 1993. 95.00 (*0-8109-3720-4*, Pub. by Abrams) Time Warner.

*__PhotoRealistic Character Animation.__ Sanford Kennedy. (Illus.). 450p. 2000. pap. 54.95 incl. cd-rom (*1-58450-040-9*) Chrles River Media.

Photorealistic Painting. Illus. by Daniel K. Tennant. (Artist's Library). 64p. (Orig.). 1997. pap. 7.95 (*1-56010-146-6*, AL26) W Foster Pub.

Photorealistic Rendering in Computer Science: Proceedings of the 2nd Eurographics Workshop on Rendering. Ed. by P. Brunet et al. (Focus on Computer Graphics Ser.). x, 281p. 1994. 107.95 (*0-387-56449-7*) Spr-Verlag.

Photorealistic Rendering Techniques. G. Sakas & P. Shirley. Ed. by S. C. Muller et al. LC 95-23397. (Focus on Computer Graphics Ser.). 1995. 139.00 (*3-540-58475-7*) Spr-Verlag.

Photoreceptor Evolution & Function. Ed. by Martin G. Holmes. (Illus.). 360p. 1991. text 125.00 (*0-12-353390-2*) Acad Pr.

Photoreceptors: Their Role in Vision. Alan Fein & Ete Z. Szuts. LC 81-24209. (International Union of Pure & Applied Physics Biophysics Ser.: No. 5). (Illus.). 224p. 1982. pap. text 30.95 (*0-521-28684-0*) Cambridge U Pr.

Photorefractive Crystals in Coherent Optical Systems. M. P. Petrov et al. (Optical Sciences Ser.: Vol. 9). (Illus.). 320p. 1991. 101.95 (*0-387-52603-X*) Spr-Verlag.

Photorefractive Effects & Materials. Ed. by David D. Nolte. LC 95-11662. (International Series in Engineering & Computer Science). 504p. (C). 1995. text 181.50 (*0-7923-9560-3*) Kluwer Academic.

Photorefractive Fiber & Crystal Devices: Materials, Optical Properties, & Applications III. Ed. by Francis T. S. Yu & Shizhuo Yin. LC 98-200467. 45p. 1997. pap. 89.00 (*0-8194-2559-1*) SPIE.

Photorefractive Fiber & Crystal Devices Vol. 2849: Materials, Optical Properties & Applications II. Ed. by Francis T. Yu & Shizhuo Yin. 318p. 1996. 66.00 (*0-8194-2237-1*) SPIE.

Photorefractive Fiber & Crystal Devices Vol. 3470: Materials, Optical Properties, & Applications IV. Ed. by Francis T. Yu & Shizhuo Yin. 1998. 80.00 (*0-8194-2925-2*) SPIE.

Photorefractive Materials, Vol. 2896. Ed. by Ratnakar R. Neurgaonkar et al. 282p. 1996. 85.00 (*0-8194-2297-5*) SPIE.

Photorefractive Materials: Phenomena & Related Applications II. Ed. by Peixian Ye et al. LC 99-170350. (Proceedings of SPIE Ser.: Vol. 3554). 272p. 1998. 80.00 (*0-8194-3015-3*) SPIE.

Photorefractive Materials: Proceedings of Symposium C of the 1994 E-MRS Spring Conference, Strasbourg, France, 24-27 May, 1994. Ed. by G. Roosen et al. (European Materials Research Society Symposia Proceedings Ser.: Vol. 48). 300p. 1995. 191.50 (*0-444-82167-8*, North Holland) Elsevier.

Photorefractive Materials & Their Applications, Vol. I. Ed. by P. Gunter Eth & J. P. Huignard. (Topics in Applied Physics Ser.: Vol. 61). (Illus.). 310p. 1988. 80.00 (*0-387-18332-9*) Spr-Verlag.

Photorefractive Materials & Their Applications II. P. Guenther & J. P. Huignard. (Topics in Applied Physics Ser.: Vol. 62). (Illus.). 360p. 1989. 91.95 (*0-387-19202-6*) Spr-Verlag.

Photorefractive Materials, Effects, & Applications: Proceedings of a Conference Held 11-12 July 1993, San Diego, California. Ed. by Pochi Yeh. LC 93-47389. (Critical Reviews of Optical Science & Technology Ser.: Vol. CR48). 1993. 30.00 (*0-8194-1290-2*); 30.00 (*0-8194-1289-9*) SPIE.

Photorefractive Nonlinear Optics. Pochi Yeh. 400p. 1995. text 86.00 (*981-02-1443-X*) World Scientific Pub.

*__Photorefractive Optics: Materials, Properties & Applications.__ Francis T. S. Yu. 500p. 1999. 79.95 (*0-12-774810-5*) Acad Pr.

Photoresponsive Materials No. IMAM-12: Materials Research Society International Symposium Proceedings. Ed. by S. Tazuke. 381p. 1989. text 17.50 (*1-55899-041-0*, IMAM-12) Materials Res.

Photos & Memories of Lewis Grizzard: 'Bout 40 Miles South of Atlanta. Nancy G. Jones & Camilla S. Stevens. 52p. 1994. pap. text. write for info. (*0-9642687-0-1*) Plato Commun.

Photos at the Archives. Charles E. Magoon. 274p. (Orig.). 1981. pap. write for info. (*0-318-54244-7*) Macmillan.

Photos from the Collection: Erie Canal Museum. Erie Canal Museum Staff. (Illus.). 83p. 1989. pap. 9.95 (*1-883582-05-9*) Erie Canal Mus.

Photos from the Front Lines of Punk. V. Vale. (Illus.). 128p. Date not set. pap. 14.99 (*1-889307-04-1*) RE Search.

Photos on CD: The Ultimate Search Tool for Finding Just the Right Photo on CD-ROM. Open House Staff. 1995. pap. 49.95 incl. cd-rom (*1-56609-173-X*) Peachpit Pr.

*__Photos That Changed the World.__ Ed. by Peter Stepan. (Illus.). 192p. 2000. 29.95 (*3-7913-2395-4*) Prestel Pub NY.

Photos That Made U. S. History: From the Cold War to the Space Age, Vol. I. Edward Wakin & Daniel Wakin. (Illus.). 64p. (J). (gr. 4-7). 1993. 12.95 (*0-8027-8230-2*); lib. bdg. 13.85 (*0-8027-8231-0*) Walker & Co.

Photos That Made U. S. History: From the Cold War to the Space Age, Vol. II. Edward Wakin & Daniel Wakin. (Illus.). 59p. (J). (gr. 4-7). 1993. 12.95 (*0-8027-8270-1*); lib. bdg. 13.85 (*0-8027-8272-8*) Walker & Co.

PhotoSecrets Balboa Park: The Best Sights & How to Photograph Them. Andrew Hudson & Richard Amero. (Photosecrets Guidebks.). (Illus.). 72p. 1999. pap. 10.95 (*0-9653087-5-8*, PhotoSecrets Guidebks) Photosecrets.

PhotoSecrets San Diego: The Best Sights & How to Photograph Them. Andrew Hudson. LC 98-65786. (Photosecrets Guidebks.). (Illus.). 336p. 1998. pap. 18.95 (*0-9653087-3-1*) Photosecrets.

Photosecrets San Francisco & Northern California: The Best Sights & How to Photograph Them. Andrew Hudson. LC 96-92366. (Photosecrets Guidebks.). (Illus.). 352p. (Orig.). 1997. pap. 16.95 (*0-9653087-1-5*) Photosecrets.

Photosecrets Yosemite: The Best Sights & How to Photograph Them. Andrew Hudson. LC 97-91459. (Photosecrets Guidebks.). (Illus.). 72p. 1997. pap. 7.95 (*0-9653087-0-7*) Photosecrets.

Photosensitisation. Ed. by T. G. Truscott et al. (NATO ASI Series H: Vol. 15). 521p. 1988. 189.95 (*0-387-18554-2*) Spr-Verlag.

Photosensitive Epilepsy. 2nd expanded ed. 192p. 1995. 59.95 (*1-898683-02-6*, Pub. by Mc Keith Pr) Cambridge U Pr.

Photosensitive Epilepsy. 2nd expanded ed. Graham F. A. Harding & Peter M. Jeavons. (Clinics in Developmental Medicine Ser.: No. 133). (Illus.). 182p. 1995. 59.95 (*0-521-68302-5*) Cambridge U Pr.

Photosensitive Metal-Organic Systems: Mechanistic Principles & Applications. Ed. by Charles Kutal & Nick Serpone. LC 93-22823. (Advances in Chemistry Ser.: Vol. 238). 450p. 1993. text 120.00 (*0-8412-2527-3*, Pub. by Am Chemical) OUP.

Photosensitive Optical Materials & Devices, Vol. 2998. Ed. by Mark P. Andrews. LC 97-207734. 364p. 1997. 80.00 (*0-8194-2409-9*) SPIE.

Photosensitive Optical Materials & Devices II. Ed. by Mark P. Andrews. LC 98-227281. (Proceedings of SPIE Ser.: Vol. 3282). 134p. 1998. 59.00 (*0-8194-2721-7*) SPIE.

Photosensitive Polyimides: Fundamentals & Applications. Ed. by Kazuyuki Horie & Takashi Yamashita. LC 95-61230. 340p. 1995. 174.95 (*1-56676-297-9*) Technomic.

Photosensitive Proteins in Bioelectronics & Biocomputing. N. Vsevolodov. Ed. by D. Kaplan. LC 97-12277. (Bioengineering of Materials Ser.). (Illus.). 380p. 1997. 69.50 (*0-8176-3852-0*) Birkhauser.

Photosensitivity & Quadratic Nonlinearity in Glass Waveguides. LC 95-68691. (Nineteen Ninety-Five Technical Digest Ser.: Vol. 22). 315p. 1995. pap. 75.00 (*1-55752-414-9*) Optical Soc.

Photosensitization & Photocatalysis Using Inorganic & Organometallic Compounds. Ed. by K. Kalyanasundaram & M. Gratzel. LC 93-895. (Catalysis by Metal Complexes Ser.: Vol. 14). 484p. (C). 1993. text 294.00 (*0-7923-2261-4*) Kluwer Academic.

Photoshop & Illustrator Synergy. Jennifer Alspach. LC 97-78213. (Illus.). 288p. 1998. pap. 49.99 (*0-7645-3134-4*) IDG Bks.

Photoshop B&W Scanners, & Curves. Jim Rich. 16p. 1996. 9.00 (*0-9647627-2-2*) Rich & Assocs.

Photoshop Channel Chops. Nathan Moody et al. LC 97-80800. 320p. 1997. pap. 45.00 (*1-56205-723-5*) New Riders Pub.

*__PhotoShop 5 Facil en Espanol/Spanish con CD ROM (para PC y Mac) en Colores: El Retoque Fotografico sin Secretos Incluyendo un CD ROM.__ Maria Dolores Turro. (Manuales PC Users Ser.). (SPA.). 286p. 1999. pap. 24.90 incl. cd-rom (*987-9131-89-4*, Pub. by MP Ediciones) Am Wholesale.

Photoshop Collage Techniques. Gregory C. Haun. LC 96-78989. 259p. 1997. 45.00 (*1-56830-349-1*) Hayden.

Photoshop Color: Your Personal Consultant. Peter Fink. 1995. pap. text 29.95 (*1-56276-305-9*, Ziff-Davis Pr) Que.

Photoshop Effects Magic. Rhoda Grossman. 264p. 1997. 39.99 (*1-56830-344-0*) Hayden.

Photoshop Filter Swatch Book. Gregory C. Haun. 1997. 39.99 (*1-56830-436-6*) Hayden.

Photoshop 5. David Xenakis. LC 98-8325. 957p. 1998. pap. 59.99 (*1-57610-293-9*) Coriolis Grp.

Photoshop 5 for Macs for Dummies. Deke McClelland. (For Dummies Ser.). (Illus.). 400p. 1998. pap. 19.99 (*0-7645-0391-X*) IDG Bks.

Photoshop 5 for Windows & Macintosh: Visual QuickStart Guide. Elaine Weinmann & Peter Lourekas. LC 99-161102. (Visual QuickStart Guides Ser.). 400p. (C). 2000. pap. text 19.95 (*0-201-35352-0*, Pub. by Peachpit Pr) Addison-Wesley.

Photoshop 5 for Windows for Dummies. Deke McClelland. LC 98-85679. (For Dummies Ser.). (Illus.). 400p. 1998. pap. 19.99 (*0-7645-0392-8*) IDG Bks.

*__Photoshop 5 Interactive Course.__ Sherry London. LC 98-66765. 1998. 49.99 (*1-57169-158-8*) Sams.

*__Photoshop 5.5.__ ENI Publishing Ltd. Staff. (By Example Ser.). (Illus.). 2000. pap. 28.95 (*2-7460-0985-4*) ENI Publng.

*__Photoshop 5.5.__ ENI Publishing Ltd. Staff. (On Your Side Ser.). (Illus.). 2000. pap. 15.95 (*2-7460-0977-3*); pap. 7.95 (*2-7460-0970-6*) ENI Publng.

*__Photoshop 5.5 for Windows & Macintosh: Visual QuickStart Guide.__ 2nd ed. Elaine Weinmann & Peter Lourekas. LC 99-461882. (Visual QuickStart Guide Ser.). 400p. 1999. pap. 19.99 (*0-201-69957-5*) Peachpit Pr.

*__Photoshop 5.5 Professional Results.__ Ken Milburn. (Illus.). 2000. pap. 29.99 (*0-07-212299-4*) McGrw-H Intl.

*__Photoshop Five Point Five to Go.__ Jason Miletsky. 320p. 2000. pap. 34.99 (*0-13-027018-0*) P-H.

*__Photoshop 5.5/ImageReady 2 Hands-On Training.__ Lynda Weinman. (Illus.). 472p. 2000. pap. 49.99 incl. cd-rom (*0-201-35467-5*) Peachpit Pr.

Photoshop 5.0 Productivity Kit. Adobe Creative Team Staff. 192p. 1999. pap. text 39.99 (*1-56830-464-1*, Pub. by Adobe Pr) Peachpit Pr.

Photoshop 5.0/5.5 Wow! Book. Linnea Dayton & Jack Davis. 368p. 1999. pap. write for info. incl. cd-rom (*0-201-35371-7*, Pub. by Peachpit Pr) Addison-Wesley.

Photoshop for the Web. 2nd ed. Mikkel Aaland. Ed. by Richard Koman. (Illus.). 250p. (Orig.). 1999. pap. 29.95 (*1-56592-641-2*) OReilly & Assocs.

Photoshop 4 Answers! Certified Tech Support. David Busch. LC 98-141854. 398p. pap. text 24.99 (*0-07-882456-7*) Osborne-McGraw.

Photoshop Four for Macintosh: Visual QuickStart Guide. Elaine Weinmann & Peter Lourekas. LC 97-182566. 352p. (C). 1997. pap. text 19.95 (*0-201-68841-7*) Peachpit Pr.

Photoshop 4 for Macintosh: Windows Edition. Linnea Dayton & Jack Davis. 336p. 1997. pap. text 44.95 (*0-201-68857-3*) Peachpit Pr.

Photoshop 4 for Macs for Dummies. 2nd ed. Deke McClelland. LC 96-77699. 384p. 1996. pap. 19.99 (*0-7645-0039-2*) IDG Bks.

Photoshop 4 Windows: Visual QuickStart Guide. Elaine Weinmann & Peter Lourekas. LC 97-201650. 352p. (C). 1997. pap. text 19.95 (*0-201-68842-5*) Peachpit Pr.

Photoshop 4 for Windows for Dummies. Deke McClelland. LC 96-80227. (Illus.). 384p. 1997. pap. 19.99 (*0-7645-0102-X*) IDG Bks.

Photoshop 4 for Windows 95 Bible. Deke McClelland. 912p. 1997. pap. 49.99 (*0-7645-4032-7*) IDG Bks.

Photoshop 4 Interactive Course. Sherry London. LC 96-37574. 884p. 1997. 49.99 (*1-57169-036-0*) Sams.

Photoshop 4 One Step at a Time. Ted Padova. (New Tutorial Ser.). 400p. 1999. pap. 29.99 (*0-7645-3127-1*) IDG Bks.

Photoshop 4.0 Complete. Hayden Development Group Staff. LC 96-78097. 1088p. 1997. 49.99 incl. cd-rom (*1-56830-323-8*) Hayden.

Photoshop 4 Studio Secrets. Deke McClelland. LC 97-74339. 256p. 1997. pap. 49.99 (*0-7645-4028-9*) IDG Bks.

Photoshop 4 Wow! Macintosh Edition. Linnea Dayton & Jack Davis. LC 98-136922. 336p. 1997. pap. text 44.95 (*0-201-68856-5*) Peachpit Pr.

Adobe Photoshop 4.0: Advanced Digital Images. LC 97-52004. (Against the Clock Ser.). 368p. (C). 1998. pap. text. write for info. (*0-13-095821-2*) P-H.

Adobe Photoshop 4.0: An Introduction to Digital Images. LC 97-52003. (Against the Clock Ser.). 328p. (C). 1998. pap. text. write for info. (*0-13-095810-7*) P-H.

Photoshop Glows & Shadows Magic. Andrew Devigal. 1997. 39.99 (*1-56830-384-X*) Hayden.

*__Photoshop Grayscale Book.__ Jim Rich. 2000. pap. 25.00 (*0-9647627-3-0*) Rich & Assocs.

Photoshop Image Magic. Andrew Devigal. Date not set. 39.99 (*1-56830-449-8*) Hayden.

Photoshop in a Nutshell. 2nd ed. Donnie O'Quinn. Ed. by Troy S. Mott. (In a Nutshell Ser.). (Illus.). 656p. 1999. pap. 24.95 (*1-56592-565-3*) OReilly & Assocs.

Photoshop in Black & White. 2nd ed. Sandy Bozek & Jim Rich. 48p. (C). 1995. pap. 18.00 (*1-56609-189-6*, Pub. by Peachpit Pr) Addison-Wesley.

Photoshop in 4 Colors. 2nd ed. Mattias Nyman. (Illus.). 80p. (C). 1995. pap. text 22.95 (*0-201-88424-0*) Peachpit Pr.

Photoshop IQ: Imaging Effects for Mac & PC. D. Frobish et al. Tr. by Hayley Ohlig from GER. (Illus.). 204p. (Orig.). (C). 1998. pap. 29.95 (*1-883403-25-1*, H 720, Silver Pixel Pr) Saunders Photo.

Photoshop Magic: Expert Edition. Brendon Perkins. LC 97-72156. 344p. 1997. 45.00 (*1-56830-416-1*) Hayden.

Photoshop Magic: Premier Collection. Greg Simsic et al. 1997. pap. text 149.99 (*1-56830-442-0*) Hayden.

Photoshop Masters: The Artistic Creations of Twenty Adobe Photoshop Experts. AGOSTO, Inc. Staff. (Illus.). 144p. 1998. pap. 29.99 (*1-56496-502-3*) Rockport Pubs.

*__Photoshop Power Shortcuts.__ Michael Ninness. 250p. 1999. pap. text 17.99 (*0-7897-2172-4*) Que.

Photoshop-Praxis. 1994. 64.95 (*0-387-56838-7*) Spr-Verlag.

Photoshop Quadtones: Process Quadtones, Tritones, & Duotones. Brady Peery. (Illus.). 192p. 1996. pap. 109.95 (*0-9651388-3-6*) PickerBook.

*__Photoshop Retouching Handbook.__ Carol Braverman. (Illus.). 256p. 1998. 49.99 incl. cd-rom (*1-55828-599-7*, MIS Pr) IDG Bks.

Photoshop Retouching Techniques. 320p. 1900. 45.00 (*0-7897-2318-2*) Que.

PhotoShop Starter Kit, 2 CD-ROMs. Greg Simsic et al. 1997. pap. text 99.99 incl. cd-rom (*1-56830-431-5*) Hayden.

*__Photoshop Studio Secrets.__ 2nd ed. McClelland. LC 98-75152. (Illus.). 368p. 1999. pap. 49.99 (*0-7645-3271-5*) IDG Bks.

Photoshop Studio Skills. 4th ed. Steve Moniz. LC 96-80340. 338p. 1997. 35.00 (*1-56830-356-4*) Hayden.

Photoshop Tech Support. Ken Oyer & Dawn Erdos. LC 96-76252. 296p. 1997. pap. 29.99 (*0-7645-4000-9*) IDG Bks.

Photoshop Textures Magic. Sherry London. 288p. 1997. 39.99 (*1-56830-368-8*) Hayden.

Photoshop 3: Training on CD. Quay2 Multimedia Staff. 1995. pap. 99.95 incl. cd-rom (*0-201-88409-7*) Peachpit Pr.

Photoshp 3 COM HYB. 1996. 28.50 (*1-56205-518-6*) New Riders Pub.

Photoshop 3 Filters & Effects. New Riders Development Group Staff. (Illus.). 432p. (Orig.). 1995. pap. text 45.00 (*1-56205-448-1*) New Riders Pub.

Photoshop 3 for Macs for Dummies. Deke McClelland. 376p. 1995. pap. 19.99 (*1-56884-208-2*) IDG Bks.

Photoshop 3 Training Combo for Macintosh. Elaine Weinmann & Peter Lowrekas. (C). 1996. pap. 69.95 (*0-201-88681-2*) Peachpit Pr.

Photoshop 3.0. Suzanne S. Thomas. 224p. 1994. mass mkt. 49.95 (*0-8273-7193-4*) Delmar.

Photoshop Type Magic. David Lai & Greg Simsic. LC 95-77739. (Illus.). 240p. 1995. 35.00 (*1-56830-220-7*, Alpha Ref) Macmillan Gen Ref.

Photoshop Type Magic, Vol. 2. 2nd ed. David Lai. LC 96-77856. 272p. 1996. pap. text 39.99 incl. cd-rom (*1-56830-329-7*) Hayden.

Photoshop Type Magic, Vol. 3. Greg Simsic. 1997. 49.99 (*1-56830-438-2*) Hayden.

Photoshop Unleashed. 1997. 59.99 (*1-56830-439-0*) Hayden.

Photoshop Web Magic. Ted Schulman & Renee LeWinter. LC 96-77851. 288p. 1996. 45.00 (*1-56830-314-9*) Hayden.

Photoshop Web Magic, Vol. 2. 2nd ed. Jeff Foster. LC 97-219700. 226p. 1997. pap. text 45.00 (*1-56830-392-0*) Hayden.

Photoshop Web Techniques. J. Scott Hamlin. LC 97-4198. 288p. 1997. 50.00 (*1-56205-733-2*) New Riders Pub.

Photoshop X Artistry. Barry Haynes. LC 98-84425. 1998. 55.00 (*1-56205-895-9*, New Riders Sftwre) MCP SW Interactive.

*__Photoshop "X" for Dummies.__ Deke McClelland. (For Dummies Ser.). (Illus.). 424p. 2000. pap. 19.99 (*0-7645-0704-4*) IDG Bks.

Photoshop X for Windows Bible. Deke McClelland. (Bible Ser.). (Illus.). 960p. 1998. pap. text 49.99 incl. cd-rom (*0-7645-3232-4*) IDG Bks.

*__Photoshop X Power Shortcuts.__ Michael Ninness. 350p. 2000. pap. 17.99 (*0-7897-2426-X*) Que.

*__Photoshop X Visual Insight.__ Ramona Pruitt. (Illus.). 280p. 2000. pap. 24.99 (*1-57610-747-7*) Coriolis Grp.

Photoshop 4 Type Magic 1. David Lai. LC 97-71008. 264p. 1997. 39.99 (*1-56830-380-7*) Hayden.

*__Photoshop 5 Bible: Gold Edition.__ Deke McClelland. (Bible Ser.). 1024p. 1999. pap. 59.99 (*0-7645-3372-X*) IDG Bks.

Photoshop 5 Filters F/X & Design. T. Michael Clark. LC 98-26354. 377p. 1998. pap. 49.99 (*1-57610-300-5*) Coriolis Grp.

Photoshop 5 Type Magic. Greg Simsic. 1998. pap. 39.99 (*1-56830-465-X*) Hayden.

*__Photoshop 5 3D Textures F/X & Design.__ Bill Fleming. LC 98-26403. (Illus.). xxi, 277p. 1999. pap. 49.99 incl. cd-rom (*1-57610-274-2*) Coriolis Grp.

Photoshop 5.0. (Quick Study Computer Ser.). 4p. pap. 3.95 (*1-57222-331-6*) Barcharts.

*__Photoshop 5.5 Artistry.__ Barry Haynes. 450p. 2000. pap. text 55.00 (*0-7357-0994-7*) New Riders Pub.

Photoshop:a Hands On Introduction. Suzanne S. Thomas. LC 93-43388. (Student Material TV). (C). 1994. mass mkt. 31.00 (*0-8273-6444-X*) Delmar.

Photospeak: A Guide to the Ideas, Movements, & Techniques of Photography, 1839 to the Present. Gilles Mora. (Illus.). 212p. 1998. 29.95 (*0-7892-0370-7*); pap. 19.95 (*0-7892-0068-6*) Abbeville Pr.

Photostat Operator. Jack Rudman. (Career Examination Ser.: C-1878). 1994. pap. 19.95 (*0-8373-1878-5*) Nat Learn.

Photostatis & Related Phenomena. Ed. by Theodore P. Williams & Anne B. Thistle. LC 97-52808. (Illus.). 238p. (C). 1998. text 89.50 (*0-306-45806-3*, Kluwer Plenum) Kluwer Academic.

PhotoStory. Chip Brunk. 1998. 24.95 (*0-9636796-7-8*, PS) Chimeric.

Photosynthesis. Abramoff. Date not set. 1.50 (*0-7167-9089-0*) W H Freeman.

*__Photosynthesis.__ Robert E. Blankenship. (Illus.). 2000. pap. 39.95 (*0-632-04321-0*) Blackwell Sci.

Photosynthesis. Evert. 1998. 1.50 (*0-7167-9355-5*) W H Freeman.

Photosynthesis. Helms. 1997. 1.50 (*0-7167-9315-6*) W H Freeman.

P

Photosynthesis. Alvin Silverstein & Virginia B. Silverstein. LC 98-9279. (Science Concepts Ser.). 64p. (J). (gr. 5-8). 1998. 23.40 (0-7613-3000-3) Millbrook Pr.

Photosynthesis. Christine H. Foyer. LC 83-21764. (Wiley Series on Cell Biology: Vol. 1). 239p. reprint ed. pap. 74.10 (0-7837-2395-4, 2040080006) Bks Demand.

Photosynthesis. 6th ed. David O. Hall & Krishna Rao. LC 98-47979. (Studies in Biology). (Illus.). 232p. (C). 1999. 54.95 (0-521-64257-4); pap. 19.95 (0-521-64497-6) Cambridge U Pr.

Photosynthesis see Methods in Enzymology

Photosynthesis, Vol. 1. Mathis. 1995. lib. bdg. write for info. (0-7923-3857-X) Kluwer Academic.

Photosynthesis: A Comprehensive Treatise. Ed. by A. S. Raghavendra. LC 97-4035. (Illus.). 394p. (C). 1998. text 120.00 (0-521-57000-X) Cambridge U Pr.

***Photosynthesis: A Comprehensive Treatise.** Ed. by A. S. Raghavendra. (Illus.). 394p. (C). 2000. pap. text 49.95 (0-521-78444-1) Cambridge U Pr.

Photosynthesis: Light into Life. (YA). (gr. 8-12). 1997. pap., teacher ed. 189.00 incl. VHS (1-55548-394-1, SG-256-VSD) Human Rel Media.

Photosynthesis: Mechanisms & Effects. G. Garab. LC 98-32288. 16p. 1999. pap. write for info. (0-7923-5547-4) Kluwer Academic.

Photosynthesis: Photoreactions to Plant Productivity. Ed. by Yash P. Abrol et al. LC 92-34817. 1993. text 308.00 (0-7923-1943-5) Kluwer Academic.

Photosynthesis - From Light to Biosphere: Proceedings of the 10th International Congress, Montpellier, France, 20-25 August 1995, Set. Ed. by Paul Mathis. 5168p. (C). 1996. text 1618.00 (0-7923-3862-6) Kluwer Academic.

Photosynthesis & Plant Development. Ed. by R. Marcelle et al. 1979. text 206.50 (90-6193-595-4) Kluwer Academic.

Photosynthesis & Respiration in White Spruce & Balsam Fir, No. 85. 1961. 0.65 (0-686-20697-5) SUNY Environ.

Photosynthesis & the Environment. Ed. by Neil R. Baker. LC 96-49526. (Advances in Photosynthesis Ser.). 508p. (C). 1996. lib. bdg. 292.50 (0-7923-4316-6) Kluwer Academic.

Photosynthesis Bibliography: Publications 1974, References No. 18421-21504 ABD-ZYL & Cumulative Indexes to Volumes 2-5, Vol. 5. Ed. by Z. Sestak & J. Catsky. 1979. pap. text 211.50 (90-6193-044-8) Kluwer Academic.

Photosynthesis in Relation to Plant Production in Terrestrial Environments. C. L. Beadle et al. (Illus.). 162p. 1985. text 105.00 (1-85148-003-X, Tycooly Pub) Weidner & Sons.

Photosynthesis I: Photosynthetic Electron Transport & Photophosphorylation. Ed. by A. Trebst & M. Avron. (Encyclopedia of Plant Physiology Ser.: Vol. 5). 1977. 230.95 (0-387-07962-9) Spr-Verlag.

Photosynthesis, Productivity & Growth: The Physiological Ecology of Phytoplankton. G. P. Harris. (Ergebnisse der Limnologie Ser.: No. 10). (Illus.). 171p. 1978. pap. text 38.00 (0-685-20001-9) Lubrecht & Cramer.

Photosynthesis, Productivity & Growth: The Physiological Ecology of Phytoplankton. Graham P. Harris. (Advances in Limnology Ser.: Vol. 103). (GER., Illus.). iv, 171p. (Orig.). 1978. pap. 35.00 (3-510-47008-7, Pub. by E Schweizerbartsche) Balogh.

Photosynthesis III. Ed. by C. J. Arntzen & L. Andrew Staehelin. (Encyclopedia of Plant Physiology Ser.: Vol. 19). (Illus.). 810p. 1986. 415.95 (0-387-16140-6) Spr-Verlag.

Photosynthetic Bacterial Reaction Center: Structure & Dynamics. Jacques Breton. Ed. by Andre Vermeglio. LC 88-12581. (NATO ASI Series A, Life Sciences: Vol. 149). (Illus.). 456p. 1988. 115.00 (0-306-42917-9, Plenum Trade) Perseus Pubng.

Photosynthetic Bacterial Reaction Center II Vol. 2: Structure, Spectroscopy & Dynamics. J. Breton & A. Vermeglio. LC 92-36001. (NATO ASI Ser.: Vol. 237). (Illus.). 440p. (C). 1993. text 156.00 (0-306-44354-6, Kluwer Plenum) Kluwer Academic.

Photosynthetic Excitons. R. Van Grondelle et al. 400p. 1997. 68.00 (981-02-3280-2) World Scientific Pub.

Photosynthetic Light-Harvesting Systems Organization & Function: Proceedings of an International Workshop, October 12-16 1987, Freising, Federal Republic of Germany. Ed. by Hugo Scheer & Siegfried Schneider. 636p. (C). 1988. lib. bdg. 234.65 (3-11-011531-X) De Gruyter.

Photosynthetic Prokaryotes. N. H. Mann & N. G. Carr. (Biotechnology Handbooks Ser.: Vol. 6). (Illus.). 296p. (C). 1991. text 95.00 (0-306-43879-8, Kluwer Plenum) Kluwer Academic.

Photosynthetic Reaction Center, 2 vols. Johann Deisenhofer & James R. Norris. (Illus.). 1993. text 199.00 (0-12-208660-0) Acad Pr.

Photosynthetic Reaction Center, Vol. 1. Johann Deisenhofer & James R. Norris. (Illus.). 490p. 1993. text 100.00 (0-12-208661-9) Acad Pr.

Photosynthetic Reaction Center, Vol. 2. Johann Deisenhofer & James R. Norris. (Illus.). 574p. 1993. text 100.00 (0-12-208662-7) Acad Pr.

Photosynthetic Unit & Photosystems: History of Research & Current View (Relationship of Structure & Function) Aloysius Wild & Raphael Ball. (Illus.). 219p. 1997. pap. 56.00 (90-73348-70-6, Pub. by Backhuys Pubs) Balogh.

Phototherapy & Photochemotherapy of Skin Disease. 2nd ed. Warwick L. Morison. 304p. 1990. text 89.00 (0-88167-723-X) Lppncott W & W.

Phototherapy in Mental Health. David A. Krauss & Jerry L. Fryrear. (Illus.). 260p. 1983. pap. 34.95 (0-398-06214-5); text 49.95 (0-398-04785-5) C C Thomas.

Phototherapy of Cancer. Ed. by George Morstyn & A. H. Kaye. x, 224p. 1990. text 198.00 (3-7186-0510-4) Gordon & Breach.

***Phototherapy Techniques: Exploring the Secrets of Personal Snapshops & Family Albums.** Judy Weiser & PhotoTherapy Centre Staff. 1999. 24.95 (0-9685619-0-X) PT Centre.

Phototherapy Treatment Protocols: For Psoriasis & Other Phototherapy Responsive Dermatoses. M. D. Zanolli et al. 150p. 1999. 39.95 (1-85070-992-0) Prthnon Pub.

Photothermal Spectroscopy Methods for Chemical Analysis. Stephen E. Bialkowski. LC 95-34049. (Chemical Analysis Ser.). 584p. 1995. 110.00 (0-471-57467-8, Wiley-Interscience) Wiley.

Photothermal Therapies in Medicine. Ed. by Gaetano Bandieramonte et al. LC 98-164978. (Europto Ser.: Vol. 3193). 196p. 1998. 89.00 (0-8194-2625-3) SPIE.

Phototonic Switching & Interconnects. Abdellatif Marrakchi. (Optical Engineering Ser.: Vol. 40). (Illus.). 464p. 1993. text 199.00 (0-8247-8931-8) Dekker.

Phototrophic Prokaryotes: Proceedings of the 9th International Symposium Held in Vienna, Austria, September 6-12, 1997. Ed. by Gunter A. Peschek et al. LC 98-35189. (Illus.). 852p. (C). 1999. text 130.00 (0-306-45923-X, Kluwer Plenum) Kluwer Academic.

Phototropic Woman. Annabel Thomas. LC 81-10469. (Iowa Short Fiction Award Ser.). 168p. 1981. 5.00 (0-87745-113-3) U of Iowa Pr.

Phototypography & Graphic Art. Jozef Bruyninckx. LC 74-115394. (Illus.). 155p. reprint ed. 29.50 (0-911126-03-1) Perfect Graphic.

Photovisions. Sarah R. Lafferty. (Illus.). 1987. 9.95 (0-917562-48-8) Contemp Arts.

Photovolatic Advanced Research & Development. Rommel Noufi. (AIP Conference Proceedings Ser.: No. 268). 560p. 1992. 125.00 (1-56396-056-7) Am Inst Physics.

Photovoltaic & Photorefractive Effects in Noncentrosymmetric Materials. Boris I. Sturman & Vladimir M. Fridkin. LC 91-14294. (Ferroelectricity & Related Phenomena Ser.: Vol. 8). 264p. 1991. text 174.00 (2-88124-498-X, QC715) Gordon & Breach.

Photovoltaic Applications in Rural Areas of the Developing World. Gerald Foley. LC 95-36268. (Technical Papers: No. 304). 84p. 1995. pap. 22.00 (0-8213-3461-1) World Bank.

Photovoltaic Concentration: A Special Issue of International Journal of Solar Energy, Vol. 6, No. 6. Ed. by Antonio Luque & Wolfgang Palz. 84p. 1988. pap. text 106.00 (3-7186-4861-X) Gordon & Breach.

Photovoltaic Conversion of Concentrated Sunlight. V. M. Andreev et al. LC 97-3769. 308p. 1997. 159.95 (0-471-96765-3) Wiley.

Photovoltaic Conversion of Sol. Antonio Luque. text. write for info. (0-471-49196-9) Wiley.

Photovoltaic Engineering Handbook. F. Lasnier & T. Ang. (Illus.). 568p. 1990. 238.00 (0-85274-311-4) IOP Pub.

Photovoltaic Materials. Richard H. Bube. LC 97-36334. 300p. 1997. text 46.00 (1-86094-065-X) World Scientific Pub.

***Photovoltaic Materials: An Analysis of Emerging Technology & Markets.** John Wiley. 150p. 1999. pap. 1995.00 (0-471-38465-8) Wiley.

Photovoltaic Power for Europe. Michael R. Starr & Wolfgang Palz. 1983. text 106.00 (90-277-1556-4) Kluwer Academic.

Photovoltaic Power Generation. Wolfgang Palz. 1982. text 171.00 (90-277-1386-3) Kluwer Academic.

Photovoltaic Power Generation. Ed. by Wolfgang Palz. 1984. text 141.50 (90-277-1725-7) Kluwer Academic.

Photovoltaic Power Generation. Ed. by R. J. Van OverStraeten. 1983. text 148.50 (90-277-1585-8) Kluwer Academic.

Photovoltaic Power Generation. R. J. Van Overstraeten & G. Caratti. (C). 1988. text 177.50 (90-277-2691-4) Kluwer Academic.

Photovoltaic Power Generation. Ed. by G. Willeke & G. Grassi. (C). 1987. text 132.50 (90-277-2448-2) Kluwer Academic.

Photovoltaic Safety. Ed. by Werner Luft. LC 88-42854. (AIP Conference Proceedings Ser.: No. 166). 264p. 1988. lib. bdg. 60.00 (0-88318-366-8) Am Inst Physics.

Photovoltaic Solar Energy Conference. Ed. by Albert S. Strub. 1978. text 226.00 (90-277-0889-4) Kluwer Academic.

Photovoltaic Solar Energy Conference, 5th E. C. Ed. by Wolfgang Palz & F. Fittipaldi. 1984. text 426.00 (90-277-1724-9) Kluwer Academic.

Photovoltaic Solar Energy Conference, 2nd E. C. Proceedings of the International Conference, West Berlin, April 23-26, 1979. Ed. by R. J. Van OverStraeten & Wolfgang Palz. 1979. text 211.50 (90-277-1021-X) Kluwer Academic.

Photovoltaic System Technology: A European Handbook. M. Imamura. 566p. 1992. pap. text 387.00 (0-9510271-9-0) Gordon & Breach.

Photovoltaics. Richard K. Miller & Christy H. Gunter. (Market Research Survey Ser.: No. 335). 50p. 1997. pap. 200.00 (1-55865-354-6) Future Tech Surveys.

Photovoltaics. Richard K. Miller & Marcia E. Rupnow. LC 89-85417. (Survey on Technology & Markets Ser.: No. 109). 50p. 1991. pap. text 200.00 (1-55865-132-2) Future Tech Surveys.

Photovoltaics: Basic Design Principles & Components. 8p. 1997. pap. 1.25 (0-16-063434-2) USGPO.

Photovoltaics - World Markets, Technologies, & Opportunities: 1998-2010 Analysis & Forecasts. Dipen Kapasi. 100p. 1998. pap. text 2700.00 (1-878218-89-1) World Info Tech.

Photovoltaics - World Markets, Technologies, & Opportunities in Solar Cells & Modules: 1992-2000 Analysis. Stuart Hirschhorn. (Illus.). 150p. 1992. pap. text 1795.00 (1-878218-31-X) World Info Tech.

***Photovoltaics for the 21st Century.** Ed. by V. K. Kapur et al. 304p. 1999. 47.00 (1-56677-233-8, PV 99-11) Electrochem Soc.

Photovoltaics in Architecture: The Integration of Photovoltaic Cells in Building Envelopoes. Othmar Humm & Peter Toggweiler. (Illus.). 120p. 1994. pap. 40.00 (3-7643-2891-6, Pub. by Birkhauser) Princeton Arch.

Photovoltaics in 2010, Vols. 1-4. EPIA Staff. (Illus.). 540p. 1996. pap. 105.00 (92-827-5347-6, Pub. by Comm Europ Commun) Bernan Associates.

Photovoltaics Technical Information Guide. (Solar Energy Ser.). 1992. lib. bdg. 88.95 (0-8490-5541-5) Gordon Pr.

Photoxidation of Organosulfur Compounds, Vol. 1. W. Ando. (Sulfur Reports). 80p. 1981. pap. text 87.00 (3-7186-0073-0) Gordon & Breach.

***PHP Developer's Encyclopedia.** 600p. 2000. 39.99 (0-672-31924-1) Sams.

***PHP Essentials.** Julie Meloni. 400p. 2000. pap. 39.99 (0-7615-2729-X, Prima Tech) Prima Pub.

***PHP 4 Bible.** Tim Converse. (Bible Ser.). (Illus.). 750p. 2000. pap. text 39.99 (0-7645-4716-X) IDG Bks.

***PHP4 in 24 Hours.** Brian Schaffner. (Teach Yourself... in 24 Hours Ser.). (Illus.). 408p. 2000. pap. 24.99 incl. cd-rom (0-672-31804-0) Sams.

***PHP Pocket Reference.** Rasmus Lerdorf. Ed. by Paula Ferguson. LC 99-86930. (Illus.). 120p. 2000. pap. 9.95 (1-56592-769-9) OReilly & Assocs.

***PHP3 & PHP4 Functions Essential Reference.** Landon Bradshaw et al. (Essential Reference Ser.). 2000. 52.95 (0-7357-0970-X) New Riders Pub.

PHP3: Programming Browser-Based Applications. Dave Medinets. 448p. 1999. pap. 39.99 (0-07-135342-9) McGraw.

PHR ESL Newcomer Program, Grades 3-6. Haynes. 256p. (C). 1997. pap. 32.40 (0-13-863036-4) P-H.

Phra the Phoenician. Edwin P. Arnold. 1976. lib. bdg. 12.95 (0-89968-174-3, Lghtyr Pr) Buccaneer Bks.

Phragmosporous Species of Nectria & Related Genera. Ed. by A. Y. Rossman. (Mycological Papers: No. 150). 162p. (C). 1983. pap. 36.00 (0-00-000078-7) C A B Intl.

Phrasal Movement & Its Kin. David Michael Pesetsky. (Linguistic Inquiry Monographs: No. 37). (Illus.). 144p. (C). Date not set. 45.00 (0-262-16196-6) MIT Pr.

***Phrasal Movement & Its Kin.** David Michael Pesetsky. LC 00-38695. (Linguistic Inquiry Monographs: No. 37). (Illus.). 144p. (C). 2000. pap. 18.00 (0-262-66166-7) MIT Pr.

Phrasal Verbs. Mortimer. Date not set. pap. text. write for info. (0-582-52217-X, Pub. by Addison-Wesley) Longman.

Phrase-a-Day English for Young Children. Judith White. (Umbrella Parade Ser.). (Illus.). 100p. (J). (gr. k-6). 1993. pap. 24.95 incl. audio (0-88432-500-8, BEN850) Audio-Forum.

Phrase-a-Day French for Young Children. Foreign Language for Young Children Staff & Judith White. 98p. (J). (gr. k-6). 1989. pap. 24.95 incl. audio (0-88432-284-X; SFR850) Audio-Forum.

Phrase-a-Day Spanish for Young Children, Set 2. Foreign Language for Young Children Staff & Judith White. 98p. (J). (gr. k-6). 1989. 22.95 incl. audio (0-88432-283-1, SSP850) Audio-Forum.

Phrase Book. Jo Shapcott. 64p. (Orig.). 1992. pap. 10.95 (0-19-282951-3) OUP.

Phrase Book: English, Amharic, Tigrina & Arabic. 2nd rev. ed. Aklile G. Giorgis. 128p. 1998. pap. text 10.00 (0-9663080-0-X) G Daniel.

Phrase Book from the Poetic & Dramatic Works of Robert Browning. Marie A. Molineux. 1972. 59.95 (0-8490-0831-X) Gordon Pr.

Phrase by Phrase: Pronunciation & Listening in American English. Marsha Chan. (Illus.). 176p. (C). 1987. pap. text 27.93 (0-13-665852-0) P-H.

Phrase Rhythm in Tonal Music. William Rothstein. 349p. 1990. 45.00 (0-02-872191-8, Schirmer Books) Mac Lib Ref.

***Phrase Structure: From GB to Minimalism.** Robert A. Chametzky. (Generative Syntax Ser.). 176p. 2000. 64.95 (0-631-20158-0); pap. 29.95 (0-631-20159-9) Blackwell Pubs.

Phrase Structure & Grammatical Relations in Tagalog. Paul Kroeger. LC 92-6979. 258p. (C). 1993. 49.95 (0-937073-87-3); pap. 19.95 (0-937073-86-5) CSLI.

Phrase Structure & the Lexicon. Ed. by Johan Rooryck & Laurie Zaring. LC 95-37660. (Studies in Natural Language & Linguistic Theory: Vol. 33). 308p. (C). 1995. text 132.50 (0-7923-3745-X) Kluwer Academic.

Phrase Structure Grammar. (C). Date not set. write for info. (0-415-06045-1); pap. write for info. (0-415-06046-X) Routledge.

Phrase Structure in Natural Language. Margaret J. Speas. (C). 1990. text 171.00 (0-7923-0755-0) Kluwer Academic.

Phrase Structures in Competition: Variation & Change in Old English Word Order. Susan Pintzuk. LC 98-51954. (Outstanding Dissertations in Linguistics Ser.). 285p. 1999. 63.00 (0-8153-3269-6) Garland.

Phraseological Dictionary. Delfin C. Basset. (ENG & SPA.). 383p. 1995. 49.95 (0-320-02839-9) Fr & Eur.

Phraseological Dictionary of Economics & & Business Terms French-Italian--Italian-French. Annie Le Bris. (FRE & ITA.). 1152p. 125.00 (0-7859-8864-5) Fr & Eur.

Phraseological Dictionary of the Serbian & Croatian Languages: Frazeoloski Rjecnik Hrvatskog Ili Srpskog Jezika. Josip Maresic. 808p. 1982. 49.95 (0-8288-1998-X, F78630) Fr & Eur.

Phraseological Synonym & Antonym Dictionary of Equivalences, Analogous & Contrary Terms: Sinonimi e Contrari Dizionario Fraseologico delle Parole Equivalenti Analoghe e Contrarie. Giuseppe Pittano. (ITA.). 864p. 1987. lib. bdg. 95.00 (0-8288-3337-0, F120160); lib. bdg. 85.00 (0-685-58982-X) Fr & Eur.

Phraseologie und Uebersetzen: Eine Untersuchung der Uebersetzbarkeit Kreativ-Innovativ Gebrauchter "Wiederholter Rede" Anhand von Beispielen aus der Polnichen und Deutschen Gegenwartsliteratur. Ewa Labno-Falecka. (Europaische Hochschulschriften Ser.: Reihe 21, Band 148). (GER.). X, 542p. 1994. pap. 79.95 (3-631-48182-9) P Lang Pubng.

Phraseologisches Woerterbuch Polnisch-Deutsch. Erika Ehegoetz. (GER & POL.). 299p. 1990. 39.95 (0-7859-8310-4, 3324005000) Fr & Eur.

Phraseology: Theory, Analysis, & Applications. A. P. Cowie. 272p. 1998. text 82.00 (0-19-829425-5) OUP.

Phrases & Fragments. E. K. Wilson. 136p. 1980. 11.00 (0-86690-176-0, W1531-014) Am Fed Astrologers.

Phrases & Idioms: A Practical Guide to American English Expressions. Richard A. Spears. LC 98-5735. 320p. 1999. pap. 10.95 (0-8442-0342-4, 03424) NTC Contemp Pub Co.

Phrases & Passages of a Salutary Song. Mario Luzi. Tr. by Luigi Bonaffini. 150p. 1999. pap. write for info. (1-77051-077-X) Guerilla Poetics.

Phrases & Passages of a Salutary Song. Mario Luzi. Tr. by Luigi Bonaffini from ITA. LC 98-74234. (Essential Poets Ser.: No. 84). 150p. 1999. pap. 15.00 (1-55071-077-X) Guernica Editions.

Phrases That Sell. Edward Werz & Sally Germain. LC 97-43790. (...That Sell Ser.). 60p. 1998. pap. 12.95 (0-8092-2977-3, 297730, Contemporary Bks) NTC Contemp Pub Co.

Phrasikleia: An Anthropology of Reading in Ancient Greece. Jesper Svenbro. Tr. by Janet Lloyd. LC 92-52773. (Myth & Poetics Ser.). (Illus.). 240p. 1992. text 39.95 (0-8014-2519-0); pap. text 15.95 (0-8014-9752-3) Cornell U Pr.

Phratries of Attica. S. D. Lambert. LC 92-41140. (Monographs in Classical Antiquity). (Illus.). 440p. (C). 1994. text 77.50 (0-472-10388-1, 10388) U of Mich Pr.

Phratries of Attica. S. D. Lambert. 440p. (C). 1998. pap. text 34.50 (0-472-08399-6, 08399) U of Mich Pr.

Phreaking Caller ID & ANI. John J. Williams. Ed. by Clifford Williams. (Illus.). 30p. (Orig.). 1997. pap. 29.00 (0-934274-47-9) Consumertronics.

Phrenogarten Experience: A Supplemental Preschool Curriculum. Janet Tubbs. (Illus.). 60p. 1992. teacher ed. 39.95 (1-881185-01-X) Arcadia AZ.

Phrenological Dictionary of Nineteenth-Century Americans. Compiled by Madeleine B. Stern. LC 82-991. (Documentary Reference Collections). (Illus.). 430p. 1982. lib. bdg. 105.00 (0-313-23286-5, STN/, Greenwood Pr) Greenwood.

Phrenologist Amongst the Todas or the Study of a Primitive Tribe in South India: History, Character, Customs, Religion, Infantcide, Polyandry, Language. William E. Marshall. (C). 1995. 34.00 (81-206-0899-2, Pub. by Asian Educ Servs) S Asia.

Phrenology: The First Science of Man. David Turnbull. (C). 1982. 50.00 (0-86828-140-9, Pub. by Deakin Univ) St Mut.

Phrenology in the British Isles: An Annotated, Historical Biobibliography & Index. Roger Cooter. LC 88-31828. 449p. 1989. 52.00 (0-8108-2165-6) Scarecrow.

PHRF Handicaps, 1995. 122p. 1994. pap. 40.00 (1-882502-25-6) US Sail Assn.

PHRF Handicaps, 1994. 122p. 1994. pap. text 40.00 (1-882502-11-6) US Sail Assn.

Phronsie Pepper. Margaret Sidney. 250p. (J). 1992. reprint ed. lib. bdg. 25.95 (0-89966-967-0) Buccaneer Bks.

Phrygian. I. M. Diakonov & V. P. Neroznak. LC 85-453. (Anatolian & Caucasian Studies). 176p. 1986. 50.00 (0-88206-042-2) Caravan Bks.

Phrynichi Eclogae Nominum et Verborum Atticorum. C. August Lobeck. lxxx, 841p. 1965. reprint ed. write for info. (0-318-70969-4) G Olms Pubs.

Phrynichi Eclogae Nominum et Verborum Atticorum. Christian A. Lobeck. lxxx, 841p. 1965. reprint ed. write for info. (0-318-72045-0) G Olms Pubs.

Phrynichus (Arabius) The New Phrynichus Being a Revised Text of the Ecloga of the Grammarian Phrynichus. Comment & Intro. by William G. Rutherford. xii, 539p. 1968. reprint ed. write for info. (0-318-72064-7) G Olms Pubs.

PHS: Market & Technology Study. 1996. pap. 2995.00 (1-56851-146-9, IGIC21) Info Gatekeepers.

PH's Complete Guide to T & E Deductions & Business Car Writeoffs. Ed. by Kenneth Soderman & Robert R. Trinz. 250p. (Orig.). 1989. pap. text 35.00 (0-13-705899-3, Busn) P-H.

PH's Pension Handbook. Robert C. Wilkie & Prentice-Hall Staff. 1100p. 1989. pap. text 39.50 (0-13-656075-X, Busn) P-H.

Phthalate Esters: Toxicity & Metabolism, Vol. I. Kevin N. Woodward. LC 87-13893. 192p. 1988. 115.00 (0-8493-6692-5, CRC Reprint) Franklin.

Phthalate Esters: Toxicity & Metabolism, Vol. II. Kevin N. Woodward. LC 87-13893. 192p. 1988. 176.00 (0-8493-6693-3, CRC Reprint) Franklin.

Phthalocyanine Materials: Synthesis, Structure & Function. Neil B. McKeown. LC 97-28288. (Chemistry of Solid State Materials Ser.: Vol. 6). (Illus.). 212p. (C). 1998. text 74.95 (0-521-49623-3) Cambridge U Pr.

Phthalocyanine Research & Application. Arthur L. Thomas. 336p. 1990. lib. bdg. 259.00 (0-8493-4624-X, QD441) CRC Pr.

Phthalocyanines, Vol. I. Frank H. Moser & Arthur L. Thomas. 248p. 1983. 137.00 (0-8493-5677-6, QD441, CRC Reprint) Franklin.

P

Phthalocyanines, Vol. II. Frank H. Moser & Arthur L. Thomas. 184p. 1983. 100.00 (*0-8493-5678-4*, CRC Reprint) Franklin.

Phthalocyanines: Properties & Applications, 4 vols., Set. Ed. by Clifford C. Leznoff & A. Phillip Lever. (Illus.). vii, 1046p. 1996. 499.00 (*1-56081-951-0*, Wiley-VCH) Wiley.

Phthalocyanines: Properties & Applications, Vol. 1. Ed. by A. B. Lever & Clifford C. Leznoff. 448p. 1989. 195.00 (*0-471-18720-8*) Wiley.

Phthalocyanines: Properties & Applications, Vol. 1. Ed. by Clifford C. Leznoff & Phillip Lever. LC 89-16518. 436p. 1989. 165.00 (*0-89573-753-1*, Wiley-VCH) Wiley.

Phthalocyanines: Properties & Applications, Vol. 2. Ed. by A. B. Lever & Clifford C. Leznoff. 305p. 1992. 195.00 (*0-471-18828-X*) Wiley.

Phthalocyanines: Properties & Applications, Vol. 2. Ed. by Clifford C. Leznoff & A. B. Lever. (Illus.). 640p. 1993. text 150.00 (*1-56081-544-2*, Wiley-VCH) Wiley.

Phthalocyanines: Properties & Applications, Vol. 3. Ed. by A. B. Lever & Clifford C. Leznoff. (Illus.). xi, 303p. 1993. 150.00 (*1-56081-638-4*, Wiley-VCH) Wiley.

Phthalocyanines: Properties & Applications, Vol. 3. Ed. by A. B. Lever & Clifford C. Leznoff. 303p. 1993. 195.00 (*0-471-18863-8*) Wiley.

Phthalocyanines: Properties & Applications, Vol. 4. Ed. by A. B. Lever & Clifford C. Leznoff. (Illus.). 550p. 1996. 150.00 (*1-56081-916-2*, Wiley-VCH) Wiley.

Phthalocyanines: Properties & Applications, Vol. 4. Ed. by A. B. Lever & Clifford C. Leznoff. 524p. 1996. 195.00 (*0-471-18629-5*) Wiley.

Phuket. William Warren. LC 90-63328. (Thailand Guides Ser.). (Illus.). 144p. 1992. reprint ed. pap. 14.95 (*0-8442-9919-7*, Passprt Bks) NTC Contemp Pub Co.

***Phuket.** 2nd ed. New Holland Publishing Staff. (Globetrotter Travel Maps Ser.). 2000. pap. 8.95 (*1-85974-205-X*) New5 Holland.

Phuket. 3rd ed. Insight Guides Staff. (Insight Guides). 1998. pap. text 12.95 (*0-88729-436-7*) Langenscheidt.

***Phule & His Money.** Robert L. Asprin & Peter J. Heck. (Phule's Company: 3). 1999. mass mkt. 6.99 (*0-441-00658-2*) Ace Bks.

Phule's Company. Robert L. Asprin. (Phule's Company: 1). 1990. mass mkt. 5.50 (*0-441-66251-X*) Ace Bks.

Phule's Paradise. Robert L. Asprin. (Phule's Company: 2). 1992. mass mkt. 5.50 (*0-441-66253-6*) Ace Bks.

***Phulippines Government & Business Contacts Handbook: Strategic Government & Business Contacts for Conducting Business, Export-Import & Investment Activity.** International Business Publications, USA Staff & Global Investment Center, USA Staff. (World Export-Import & Business Library: 133). (Illus.). 250p. 2000. pap. 99.95 (*0-7397-6148-X*) Intl Business Pubns.

Phunny Pharm. C. Ty Reidhead. LC 96-29285. (Illus.). 225p. (Orig.). 1996. pap. text 21.00 (*1-56053-114-2*) Hanley & Belfus.

Phunny Phonics: Reading & Phonics Is What You Learn at Phunny Phonics. R. Ann Walker. (Illus.). 26p. (J). (ps-2). 1996. pap. text 19.95 incl. audio (*0-9667874-0-4*) AnnFranklin.

Phurst One. Vicki Northcutt. 1998. pap. write for info. (*1-58235-009-4*) Watermrk Pr.

***Physicians' Desk Reference, 2001. 55th rev. ed. 2000. 86.95 (*1-56363-376-0*, PDR) Med Econ.**
Completely revised & updated, the 2001 PDR provides-approved drug information on more than 4,000 prescription drugs, over 2,100 full-color, actual size photos of medicines for instant identification & important data on over 250 drug manufacturers. New Medicines, new drug interaction data, the most recent side effects findings & certain drugs now removed from the market make it absolutely critical that medical & healthcrare professionals keep up-to-date with the very latest prescription drug information. The 2001 PDR contains: the newest drugs--which drugs are indicated for the diagnosed condition; how different drugs interact; latest findings on side effects caused by the prescribed drug; recommended dosages; clinical pharmacology; pediatric use; contraindications; FDA use-in-pregnancy ratings & more. Hundreds of new drugs added. New larger trim size allows dramatically improved readability. 3,000+pages. Available: November 2000 *Publisher Paid Annotation.*

Phya Khankhaak, the Toad King: A Translation of an Isan Fertility Myth in Verse. Tr. by Wajuppa Tossa from THA. LC 95-23905. 176p. 1996. 29.50 (*0-8387-5306-X*) Bucknell U Pr.

Phychic Explorer: A Down-to-Earth Guide to Six Magical Arts. Jonathan Cainer. 1998. pap. text 16.95 (*0-7499-1685-0*, Pub. by Piatkus Bks) London Brdge.

***Phychotherapies for Black & Multicultured Communities.** Sonia Stephen. 224p. 2000. pap. text 32.00 (*0-7506-4313-7*) Buttrwrth-Heinemann.

Phycial Science. Louis Krause. 83p. lab manual ed. 10.00 (*1-886855-36-6*, PHSC 107) Tavenner Pub.

Phycobiliproteins. R. Maccoll & D. Guard-Friar. LC 85-32567. 224p. 1986. 132.00 (*0-8493-5525-7*, CRC Reprint) Franklin.

Phycologia Latino-Americana, Vol. 1. Ed. by Cesar O. Acleto et al. (SPA., Illus.). 186p. 1981. text 45.00 (*3-7682-1297-1*) Lubrecht & Cramer.

Phycologia Latino-Americana, Vol. 2. Ed. by Carlos E. Bicudo et al. 213p. 1984. text 60.00 (*3-7682-1410-9*) Lubrecht & Cramer.

Phycologia Ochotiensis: Tange des Ochotskischen Meeres (From Middendorff's Sibirische Reise) F. J. Ruprecht. (Illus.). 1978. reprint ed. lib. bdg. 120.00 (*3-7682-1184-3*) Lubrecht & Cramer.

Phycological Studies: Some Soil Algae from Enchanted Rock & Related Algae Species. Ed. by Harry W. Bischoff & Harold C. Bold. (Phycological Studies Ser.: Vol. 4). 195p. 1975. pap. 38.00 (*3-87429-099-9*, Pub. by Koeltz Sci Bks) Lubrecht & Cramer.

Phycological Studies Vol. 1: Studies of Texas Soil Algae. Temd R. Deason & Harold C. Bold. (University Texas Publication: No. 6022). (Illus.). 70p. 1975. reprint ed. pap. 37.40 (*3-87429-096-4*, 007820, Pub. by Koeltz Sci Bks) Lubrecht & Cramer.

Phycological Studies Vol. 2: Some Algae from Arid Soils. S. Chantanachat & Harold C. Bold. (University Texas Publication: No. 6218). (Illus.). 74p. 1975. reprint ed. pap. 37.40 (*3-87429-097-2*, 007821, Pub. by Koeltz Sci Bks) Lubrecht & Cramer.

Phycological Studies Vol. 3: The Taxonomy of Certain Ulotrichacean Algae. Karl R. Mattox & Harold C. Bold. (University Texas Publication: No. 6222). (Illus.). 66p. 1975. reprint ed. pap. 37.40 (*3-87429-098-0*, 007822, Pub. by Koeltz Sci Bks) Lubrecht & Cramer.

Phycological Studies Vol. 7: Taxonomic Investigations of Stigeoclonium. Elenor R. Cox & Harold C. Bold. (University Texas Publication: No. 6618). (Illus.). 167p. 1977. reprint ed. pap. 52.70 (*3-87429-130-8*, 007825, Pub. by Koeltz Sci Bks) Lubrecht & Cramer.

Phycology. 2nd ed. Robert E. Lee. (Illus.). 661p. (C). 1989. text 125.00 (*0-521-36502-3*); pap. text 44.95 (*0-521-36744-1*) Cambridge U Pr.

***Phycology.** 3rd ed. Robert E. Lee. LC 98-53255. (Illus.). 600p. (C). 1999. 100.00 (*0-521-63090-8*); pap. 44.95 (*0-521-63883-6*) Cambridge U Pr.

Phycomyces. Ed. by Enrique Cerda-Olmedo & Edward D. Lipson. LC 86-30982. (Illus.). 420p. 1987. text 88.00 (*0-87969-199-9*) Cold Spring Harbor.

Phylaster: or Love Lyes a Bleeding. Francis Beaumont & John Fletcher. LC 68-54617. (English Experience Ser.: No. 18). 66p. 1968. reprint ed. 20.00 (*90-221-0018-9*) Walter J Johnson.

Phyletic Analysis of 50 Characters of Advanced Snakes. Hymen Marx & George B. Rabb. LC 72-85480. (Field Museum of Natural History, Publication 1153, Zoology Ser.: No. 63). 329p. 1972. reprint ed. pap. 102.00 (*0-608-02113-X*, 206276200004) Bks Demand.

***Phyllida.** large type ed. Irene Northan. 360p. 1999. 31.99 (*0-7089-4125-7*, Linford) Ulverscroft.

Phyllis B. Steckler & the Oryx Press. Ed. by Gordon A. Sabine. (Illus.). 104p. (Orig.). 1993. pap. text. write for info. (*1-879286-05-X*) AZ Bd Regents.

Phyllis Berman: Paintings. (Illus.). 8p. (Orig.). 1990. pap. 10.00 (*0-9623799-4-8*) Locks Gallery.

Phyllis Bramson, 1973-1986. Phyllis Bramson. (Illus.). 28p. 1986. pap. 15.00 (*0-941548-10-4*) Ren Soc U Chi.

Phyllis Damon's Magic Lacing Chronicles: Gimpgoes Ballistic David Hall. LC 99-192387. 15p. 1996. write for info. (*0-9651273-2-X*) P Damon Assocs.

Phyllis J. Walsh: From Lorgnettes to Lariats: in Loving Recollection of the S Bar S Ranch, Where Work Hardened Our Hands While Visitors Lightened Our Hearts. Intro. by Mary E. Glass. 149p. 1973. lib. bdg. 36.50 (*1-56475-136-8*); fiche. write for info. (*1-56475-137-6*) U NV Oral Hist.

***Phyllis Nagy Plays.** P. Nagy. 2000. pap. 14.95 (*0-413-72370-4*) Methn.

Phyllis, Phallus, Genghis Cohen & Other Creatures I Have Known. Fredric L. Frye. LC 94-43399. (Illus.). 164p. (C). 1995. reprint ed. 16.50 (*0-89464-932-9*) Krieger.

Phyllis Shand Allfrey: A Caribbean Life. Lizabeth Paravisini-Gebert. LC 95-33061. (Illus.). 300p. (C). 1996. text 50.00 (*0-8135-2264-1*); pap. text 18.95 (*0-8135-2265-X*) Rutgers U Pr.

***Phyllis the Forest Ranger.** large type ed. Beth Esh Smith. (LB Ser.). (Illus.). 8p. (J). (ps-k). 2000. pap. text 10.95 (*1-57332-164-8*); pap. text 10.95 (*1-57332-163-X*) HighReach Lrning.

Phyllis Webb & Her Works. John F. Hulcoop. (Canadian Author Studies). 68p. (C). 1990. pap. 9.95 (*1-55022-059-4*, Pub. by ECW) Genl Dist Srvs.

Phyllis's Unique Fun & Games for Baby or Bridal Showers. Phyllis A. Wilcox. Ed. by Beach Printing Advertising, Inc. Staff. LC 98-91028. (Illus.). 51p. 1999. 15.00 (*0-9666568-0-6*) P A Wilcox.

Phyllo: Easy Recipes for Sweet & Savory Treats. Jill O'Connor. LC 96-11107. (Illus.). 96p. 1996. 14.95 (*0-8118-1019-4*) Chronicle Bks.

Phyllom Morphogenese bei Allium und Juncus unter besonderer Beruecksichtigung der Morphogenese. W. Kraehenbuehl. (Dissertationes Botanicae Ser.: No. 67). (GER., Illus.). 320p. 1983. pap. text 65.00 (*3-7682-1358-7*) Lubrecht & Cramer.

Phyllopsora: Bacidiaceae. Lois Brako. (Flora Neotropica Monographs: No. 55). (Illus.). 76p. 1991. pap. 16.00 (*0-89327-364-3*) NY Botanical.

Phyllotaxis: A Systemic Study in Plant Morphogenesis. Roger V. Jean. (Illus.). 400p. (C). 1994. text 80.00 (*0-521-40482-7*) Cambridge U Pr.

Phylloxera "A Treatise" Pierre Galet. 1997. 34.95 (*0-614-18973-X*) Wine Appreciation.

***Phylogenesis.** Alan Dean Foster. 2000. mass mkt. 6.99 (*0-345-41861-1*) Ballantine Pub Grp.

Phylogenesis of Connective Tissue: Morphological Aspects & Biosynthesis of Sponge Intercellular Matrix. R. Garrone. Ed. by L. Robert. (Frontiers of Matrix Biology Ser.: Vol. 5). (Illus.). 1978. 135.00 (*3-8055-2767-5*) S Karger.

Phylogenesis of Immune Functions. Gregory W. Warr & Cohen. 344p. 1990. lib. bdg. 239.00 (*0-8493-6434-5*, QR184) CRC Pr.

Phylogenetic Analysis & Taxonomy of Iguanian Lizards: Reptilia: Squamata. Darrel R. Frost & Richard Etheridge. (Miscellaneous Publications: No. 81). (Illus.). 65p. (C). 1989. pap. 4.00 (*0-89338-033-4*) U KS Nat Hist Mus.

Phylogenetic Analysis of DNA Sequences. Ed. by Michael M. Miyamoto & Joel Cracraft. (Illus.). 368p. 1991. text 65.00 (*0-19-506698-7*) OUP.

***Phylogenetic Analysis of Morphological Data.** Ed. by John J. Wiens. (Illus.). 272p. 2000. 49.95 (*1-56098-841-X*); pap. 26.95 (*1-56098-816-9*) Smithsonian.

Phylogenetic Analysis of the Major Lineages of the Crambinae & of the Genera of Crambini of North America (Lepidoptera: Pyralidae), Vol. 1. Bernard Landry. Ed. by Virendra K. Gupta. (Memoirs on Entomology, International Ser.). (Illus.). 248p. 1995. 45.00 (*1-56665-056-9*) Assoc Pubs FL.

Phylogenetic Analysis of the Orchidaceae. Pamela Burns-Balogh & V. A. Funk. LC 85-600315. (Smithsonian Contributions to Botany Ser.: No. 13). 83p. reprint ed. pap. 30.00 (*0-608-16203-5*, 202713800054) Bks Demand.

Phylogenetic Fantasy: An Overview of the Transference Neuroses. Sigmund Freud. Ed. by Ilse Grubrich-Simitis. Tr. by Axel Hoffer & Peter T. Hoffer from GER. LC 86-26468. (Illus.). 160p. 1987. 30.00 (*0-674-66635-6*) Belknap Pr.

Phylogenetic Models in Functional Coupling of the CNS & the Cardiovascular System. Ed. by R. B. Hill et al. LC 92-20252. (Comparative Physiology Ser.: Vol. 11). (Illus.). xiv, 256p. 1992. 278.50 (*3-8055-5570-9*) S Karger.

Phylogenetic Relationships among Advanced Snakes: A Molecular Perspective. John E. Cadle. (Publications in Zoology: Vol. 119). 88p. (Orig.). (C). 1988. pap. 19.95 (*0-520-09956-7*, Pub. by U CA Pr) Cal Prin Full Svc.

Phylogenetic Relationships among Gerrhonotine Lizards: An Analysis of External Morphology. David A. Good. (Publications in Zoology: Vol. 121). 1988. pap. 24.00 (*0-520-09744-0*, Pub. by U CA Pr) Cal Prin Full Svc.

Phylogenetic Relationships of the Colubrid Snakes of the Genus Adelphicos in the Highlands of Middle America. Jonathan A. Campbell & Linda S. Ford. (Occasional Papers: No. 100). 22p. 1982. 1.00 (*0-317-04838-4*) U KS Nat Hist Mus.

Phylogenetic Relationships of the Lizard Families: Essays Commemorating Charles L. Camp. Ed. by Richard Estes & Gregory Pregill. LC 87-21290. (Illus.). 648p. 1988. 85.00 (*0-8047-1435-5*) Stanford U Pr.

Phylogenetic Revision of the Fish Families Luvaridae & Kushlukiidae (Acanthuroidei), with a New Genus & Two New Species of Eocene Luvarids. Aleksandr F. Bannikov & James C. Tyler. LC 95-1795. (Smithsonian Contributions to Paleobiology Ser.: Vol. 81). 49p. 1995. reprint ed. pap. 30.00 (*0-608-00513-4*, 206133400008) Bks Demand.

Phylogenetic Significance of Vocal Sac Structure in Hylid Frogs. Michael J. Tyler. (Museum Ser.: Vol. 19, No. 4). 42p. 1971. pap. 1.75 (*0-686-80388-4*) U KS Nat Hist Mus.

Phylogenetic Studies of North American Minnows, with Emphasis on the Genus Cyprinella: Teleostei: Cypiniformes. Richard L. Mayden. (Miscellaneous Publications: No. 80). (Illus.). 189p. 1989. pap. text 15.00 (*0-89338-029-6*) U KS Nat Hist Mus.

Phylogenetic System: The Systematization of Organisms on the Basis of Their Phylogenesis. Peter Ax. Tr. by R. P. Jeffries. LC 86-16002. (Wiley-Interscience Publications). (Illus.). 354p. reprint ed. pap. 109.80 (*0-7837-3412-3*, 204337900008) Bks Demand.

***Phylogenetic Systematics.** Willi Hennig. 280p. 1999. pap. text 35.00 (*0-252-06814-9*) U of Ill Pr.

Phylogenetic Systematics. Willi Hennig. Tr. by Davis & Zangerl. LC 78-31969. 280p. 1979. reprint ed. 32.50 (*0-252-00745-X*) U of Ill Pr.

Phylogenetic Systematics & Biogeography of the Tribe Robinieae (Leguminosae) Matt Lavin & Mario Sousa. Ed. by Christiane Anderson. (Systematic Botany Monographs: Vol. 45). (Illus.). 165p. 1995. pap. 22.00 (*0-912861-45-2*) Am Soc Plant.

Phylogenetic Systematics of Iguanine Lizards: A Comparative Osteological Study. Kevin De Queiroz. LC 87-24594. (University of California Publications in Zoology: Vol. 118). 215p. reprint ed. pap. 66.70 (*0-608-00715-3*, 206148900009) Bks Demand.

Phylogenetics: Theory & Practice of Phylogenetic Systematics. Edward O. Wiley. LC 81-5080. 456p. 1981. 185.00 (*0-471-05975-7*) Wiley.

Phylogenetics & Ecology. Ed. by Paul Eggleton & Richard I. Vane-Wright. (Linnean Society Symposium Ser.: No. 17). (Illus.). 376p. 1994. text 79.00 (*0-12-232990-2*) Acad Pr.

Phylogenies & the Comparative Method in Animal Behavior. Ed. by Emilia P. Martins. (Illus.). 432p. (C). 1996. text 65.00 (*0-19-509210-4*) OUP.

Phylogeny & Classification of Birds: A Study in Molecular Evolution. Charles G. Sibley & Jon E. Ahlquist. (Illus.). 1008p. (C). 1991. 130.00 (*0-300-04085-7*) Yale U Pr.

Phylogeny & Classification of the Orchid Family. Robert L. Dressler. LC 92-24390. (Illus.). 332p. 1993. 49.95 (*0-931146-24-0*, Dioscorides) Timber.

Phylogeny & Development of Catecholamine Systems in the CNS of Vertebrates. Ed. by Wilhelmus J. Smeets & Anton Reiner. (Illus.). 504p. (C). 1995. text 165.00 (*0-521-44251-6*) Cambridge U Pr.

Phylogeny & Form in the Plant Kingdom. Howard J. Dittmer. (Illus.). 1974. reprint ed. text 17.50 (*0-88275-167-0*) Lubrecht & Cramer.

Phylogeny & Ontogeny. Piaget, Jean, Foundation Archives, Geneva Staff. (Human Development Ser.: Vol. 27, No. 5). (Illus.). vi, 134p. 1984. pap. 34.00 (*3-8055-3904-5*) S Karger.

Phylogeny & Systematics of the Fundulus Nottii Species Group: Teleostei: Cyprinodontidae. E. O. Wiley. (Occasional Papers: No. 66). 31p. 1977. pap. 1.00 (*0-686-79833-3*) U KS Nat Hist Mus.

Phylogeny, Ecology, & Behavior: A Research Program in Comparative Biology. Daniel R. Brooks & Deborah A. McLennan. (Illus.). xii, 392p. 1990. pap. text 23.95 (*0-226-07572-9*); lib. bdg. 54.00 (*0-226-07571-0*) U Ch Pr.

Phylogeny of an Acquired Characteristic: Proceedings of American Philosophical Society, Vol. 143. Alpheus Hyatt. Ed. by Stephen Jay Gould. LC 79-8333. (History of Paleontology Ser.). (Illus.). 1980. reprint ed. lib. bdg. 35.95 (*0-405-12714-6*) Ayer.

Phylogeny of Anguinomorph Lizards. Oliver C. Rieppel. 88p. 1980. 55.50 (*0-8176-1224-6*) Birkhauser.

Phylogeny of Pleurodema: Anura: Leptodactylidae, a Biogeographic Model. William E. Duellman & Alberto Veloso. (Occasional Papers: No. 64). 46p. 1977. pap. 1.00 (*0-686-80351-5*) U KS Nat Hist Mus.

Phylogeny of South African Variants of the Australopithecinae: Some Taxonomic Considerations. Brian A. Fields. Ed. by Don Y. Lee. LC 85-80476. 172p. (C). 1985. 38.50 (*0-939758-11-3*) Eastern Pr.

Phylogeny of the Fissiculate Blastoids. A. Breimar & D. B. Macurda. (Verhandelingen der Koninklijke Nederlandse Akademie van Wetenschappen, Afd. Natuurkunde Ser.: No. 26(3)). 390p. 1972. pap. text 46.50 (*0-7204-8232-1*) Elsevier.

Phylogeny, Speciation, & Palaeoecology of the Early Carboniferous, Mississippian, Conodont Genus Mestognathus. Peter H. Von Bitter et al. (Illus.). 115p. pap. 29.71 (*0-88854-319-0*) Brill Academic Pubs.

Phylogeography: The History & Formation of Species. John C. Avise. LC 99-19648. (Illus.). 447p. 1999. 49.95 (*0-674-66638-0*) HUP.

Phylogeography & Systematics of the Slender Mouse Opossum Marmosops (Marsupialia, Didelphidae) Meika A. Mustrangi & James L. Patton. LC 96-36518. 1997. pap. 15.00 (*0-520-09815-3*, Pub. by U CA Pr) Cal Prin Full Svc.

Phylomem. William Wayne. 414p. (Orig.). 1993. pap. 5.99 (*0-9623979-2-X*) Atlan Pub Hse.

Phylum Monsters. Hayford Peirce. 1989. pap. 3.95 (*0-8125-4894-9*, Pub. by Tor Bks) St Martin.

Phynodderree & Other Legends of the Isle of Man. Edward Callow. LC 75-174441. (Illus.). 134p. 1972. reprint ed. 23.95 (*0-405-08336-X*, Pub. by Blom Pubns) Ayer.

Phyrrus, King of Epirus. Petros Garoufalias. (Illus.). 492p. (C). 1978. 19.95 (*0-905743-13-X*, Pub. by Stacey Intl) Intl Bk Ctr.

Phys Des Of Cmos Integr Circ W/ledit-int'l Ed. Uyemura. 1994. pap. text 50.00 (*0-534-94327-6*) PWS Pubs.

Physalacriaceae du Globe: Hymenomacetales, Clavariodes. J. Berthier. (Bibliotheca Mycologica Ser.: No. 98). (Illus.). 128p. 1985. pap. text 40.00 (*3-7682-1424-9*) Lubrecht & Cramer.

Physiatric Procedures in Clinical Practice. Ed. by Ted A. Lennard. (Illus.). 400p. 1995. text 76.00 (*1-56053-069-3*) Hanley & Belfus.

Physic Meet & Metaphysic. Ed. by Yann Lovelock. 157p. pap. write for info. (*3-7052-0636-2*, Pub. by Poetry Salzburg) Intl Spec Bk.

Physic Point: Memories of Hyannis (1914-1929) Alvah W. Bearse. (Illus.). 100p. 1976. pap. 14.95 (*0-85699-203-8*) Chatham Pr.

Physica. Ed. by David W. Ross. (Oxford Classical Texts Ser). 214p. 1951. text 27.00 (*0-19-814514-4*) OUP.

Physica Plinii Bambergensis. C. Plinius Secundus. Ed. by Alf Onnerfors. (Bibliotheca Graeca Et Latina Ser.: Vol. II). 174p. 1975. write for info. (*3-487-05873-1*) G Olms Pubs.

Physical Science 101-102. 3rd ed. Peter Busher & Millard Baublitz. 162p. (C). 1995. text, lab manual ed. 35.60 (*0-536-59094-X*) Pearson Custom.

Physical Geography: Science & Systems of the Human Environment. Strahler. 437p. 1997. pap. text, teacher ed. 50.00 (*0-471-18288-5*) Wiley.

Physical Abuse What Is It? An Informational Book for People Who Are Deaf or Hard of Hearing. Jackie Niemand. (Illus.). 51p. (Orig.). (J). (ps-12). 1994. pap. text 9.00 (*0-9629302-2-9*) Ramsey Found.

Physical Acoustics, Vol. 25. Thurston. (C). 1998. text 160.00 (*0-12-477924-7*) Acad Pr.

Physical Acoustics: Fundamentals & Applications. Ed. by O. Leroy & M. A. Breazeale. (Illus.). 724p. (C). 1991. text 198.00 (*0-306-43883-6*, Kluwer Plenum) Kluwer Academic.

Physical Acoustics Vol. 19: Ultrasonic Measurement Methods. Ed. by Robert N. Thurston & Allan D. Pierce. 384p. 1990. text 150.00 (*0-12-477919-0*) Acad Pr.

Physical Acoustics Vol. 23: Ultrasonic Instruments & Devices I. Ed. by R. N. Thurston et al. (Illus.). 482p. (C). 1998. boxed set 170.00 (*0-12-477923-9*) Acad Pr.

Physical Acoustics Vol. 24: Ultrasonic Instruments & Devices II. Ed. by R. N. Thurston et al. (Illus.). 372p. (C). 1998. boxed set 145.00 (*0-12-477945-X*) Acad Pr.

Physical Acoustics & Metrology of Fluids. J. P. Trusler. (Measurement Science & Technology Ser.). (Illus.). 268p. 1991. 132.00 (*0-7503-0113-9*) IOP Pub.

Physical Acoustics & Optics: Molecular Scattering of Light; Propagation of Hypersound; Metal Optics. Ed. by D. V. Skobel'tsyn. Tr. by Frank L. Sinclair from

P

An Asterisk (*) at the beginning of an entry indicates that the title is appearing for the first time.

RUS. LC 75-33201. (Proceedings of the P. N. Lebedev Physics Institute Ser.: No. 72). (Illus.). 220p. 1975. reprint ed. pap. 68.20 (*0-608-05531-X*, 20659990006) Bks Demand.

***Physical Activities & Sport in the Lives of Girls.** 2000. per. 12.00 (*0-16-061412-0*) USGPO.

***Physical Activities for Improving Children's Learning & Behavior: A Guide to Sensory Motor Development.** Billye Ann Cheatum & Allison A. Hammond. LC 99-41127. (Illus.). 360p. (C). 2000. pap. 19.95 (*0-88011-874-1*) Human Kinetics.

Physical Activity, Aging & Sports Vol. I: Scientific & Medical Research. Ed. by Raymond Harris & Sara Harris. (Illus.). 424p. (C). 1989. text 39.95 (*0-937829-03-X*) Ctr Study Aging.

Physical Activity, Aging & Sports Vol. II: Practice, Program & Policy. Ed. by Raymond Harris et al. (Illus.). 410p. 1992. text 39.95 (*0-937829-04-8*) Ctr Study Aging.

Physical Activity, Aging & Sports Vol. III: Physiological & Biomedical Aspects Toward Health Aging-International Perspectives, Pt. 1. Ed. by Sara Harris et al. (Illus.). 320p. 1994. text 39.95 (*0-937829-06-4*) Ctr Study Aging.

Physical Activity, Aging & Sports Vol. IV: Psychology, Motivation & Programs Toward Health Aging-International Perspectives, Pt. 2. Ed. by Sara Harris et al. (Illus.). 400p. 1995. text 39.95 (*0-937829-07-2*) Ctr Study Aging.

Physical Activity, Aging & Sports Series, 4 vols., Vols. I-IV. Ed. by Raymond Harris et al. 1554p. 1994. 159.80 (*0-937829-05-6*) Ctr Study Aging.

Physical Activity & Behavioral Medicine. James F. Sallis & Neville Owen. LC 98-25362. 1998. pap. write for info. (*0-8039-5997-4*) Sage.

Physical Activity & Behavioral Medicine. James F. Sallis & Neville Owen. LC 98-25362. (Behavioral Medicine & Health Psychology Ser.: 3). 210p. 1998. 67.50 (*0-8039-5996-6*) Sage.

Physical Activity & Cancer. Laurie Hoffman-Goetz. (Exercise Physiology Ser.). 2000. 99.95 (*0-8493-8712-4*, 8712) CRC Pr.

Physical Activity & Cardiovascular Health: A National Consensus. Ed. by Arthur S. Leon. LC 96-50955. (Illus.). 288p. (Orig.). (C). 1997. pap. text 22.00 (*0-88011-610-2*, BLEO0610) Human Kinetics.

Physical Activity & Cardiovascular Health: Bibliography: January 1990 Through September 1995. Ed. by Jennie P. Hunt et al. 74p. 1999. reprint ed. pap. text 20.00 (*0-7881-8032-0*) DIANE Pub.

Physical Activity & Coronary Heart Disease: Proceedings of the Paavo Nurmi Symposium, 2nd, Helsinki, 1975. Paavo Nurmi Symposium Staff. Ed. by V. Manninen. (Advances in Cardiology Ser.: Vol. 18). (Illus.). 240p. 1976. 104.50 (*3-8055-2356-4*) S Karger.

Physical Activity & Health. 1997. lib. bdg. 253.99 (*0-8490-6259-4*) Gordon Pr.

Physical Activity & Health. Ed. by N. G. Norgan. (Society for the Study of Human Biology Symposium Ser.: No. 34). (Illus.). 263p. (C). 1993. text 74.95 (*0-521-41551-9*) Cambridge U Pr.

Physical Activity & Health: A Report of the Surgeon General. Audrey F. Manley. (Illus.). 278p. (Orig.). (C). 1996. pap. text 40.00 (*0-7881-3496-5*) DIANE Pub.

Physical Activity & Health: A Report of the Surgeon General. U. S. Department of Health & Human Services & Centers for Disease Control & Prevention Staff. 278p. (Orig.). 1996. pap. 17.00 (*1-883205-31-X*) Intl Med Pub.

Physical Activity & Health: Report of the Surgeon General. 298p. 1996. per. 22.00 (*0-16-061501-1*) USGPO.

Physical Activity & Mental Health. Ed. by William P. Morgan. LC 96-20373. (Series in Health Psychology & Behavioral Medicine). 288p. 1996. 59.95 (*1-56032-365-5*) Taylor & Francis.

***Physical Activity & Obesity.** Ed. by Claude Bouchard. LC 99-88071. (Illus.). 408p. 2000. 48.00 (*0-88011-909-8*) Human Kinetics.

***Physical Activity & Psychological Well-Being.** Stuart Biddle et al. LC 00-28617. 2000. pap. write for info. (*0-415-23439-5*) Routledge.

Physical Activity & Sport for the Secondary School Student. 4th rev. ed. Ed. by Neil J. Dougherty. (Illus.). 394p. (Orig.). 1993. pap. text 28.00 (*0-88314-526-X*, A526X) AAHPERD.

Physical Activity & the Older Adult: A Knowledge Base for Managing Exercise Programs. Devin Govindasamy & B. Donald Paterson. Ed. by Earle F. Zeigler. (Monograph Series on Sport & Physical Education Management). 73p. (Orig.). (C). 1994. pap. text 5.80 (*0-87563-493-1*) Stipes.

Physical Activity & the Social Sciences. Neil W. Widmeyer. 400p. 1983. pap. 34.95 (*0-932392-13-X*) Mouvement Pubns.

Physical Activity & Well Being. 1986. 30.00 (*0-88314-335-6*) AAHPERD.

Physical Activity & Youth Sports: Social & Moral Issues. Branta et al. (Peace & Conflict Ser.: Vol. 2, No. 4). 1997. pap. 20.00 (*0-8058-9879-4*) L Erlbaum Assocs.

Physical Activity Book: A Guide to Getting More Active. Joyce Hanna. (Illus.). 46p. 1998. pap. 4.00 (*1-879552-17-5*) SCRDP.

Physical Activity, Fitness, & Health: International Proceedings & Consensus Statement. Ed. by Claude Bouchard et al. LC 93-38996. (Illus.). 1080p. 1994. text 79.00 (*0-87322-522-8*, BBOU0522) Human Kinetics.

Physical Activity for Health & Fitness. Allen W. Jackson et al. LC 98-43165. (Illus.). 376p. 1999. pap. text 25.00 (*0-88011-599-8*, BJAC0599) Human Kinetics.

Physical Activity for Individuals with Mental Retardation. Carl B. Eichstaedt & Barry W. Lavay. LC 91-42283. (Illus.). 480p. (C). 1992. text 33.00 (*0-87322-361-6*, BEIC0361) Human Kinetics.

Physical Activity for Life East & West, South & North. pap. text 34.00 (*3-89124-321-9*) Meyer & Meyer.

Physical Activity Ideas for Action: Elementary Level. Ed. by Lynn Allen. LC 96-32497. 152p. (Orig.). 1996. pap. text 16.00 (*0-88011-554-8*, BALL0554) Human Kinetics.

Physical Activity Ideas for Action: Secondary Level. Ed. by Lynn Allen. LC 96-32474. 200p. (Orig.). 1996. pap. text 16.00 (*0-88011-555-6*, BALL0555) Human Kinetics.

Physical Activity in Health & Disease. Per-Olof Astrand & Gunnar Grimby. (Acta Medica Scandinavica Symposium Ser.: No. 2). (Illus.). 228p. 1986. 87.50 (*91-22-00817-9*) Coronet Bks.

Physical Activity in Human Experience: Interdisciplinary Perspectives. Ed. by James E. Curtis & Storm J. Russell. LC 96-8065. (Illus.). 304p. 1996. text 35.00 (*0-87322-765-4*, BCUR0765) Human Kinetics.

Physical Activity in the Social Sciences. Ed. by Neil W. Widmeyer. 398p. 1979. pap. text 19.50 (*0-8422-0532-2*) Irvington.

Physical Activity Sciences. Ed. by Claude Bouchard et al. LC 91-2011. (Illus.). 280p. (Orig.). (C). 1991. text 24.00 (*0-87322-334-9*, BBOU0334) Human Kinetics.

Physical Adjustments in a Changing Landscape: The Singapore Story. Ed. by Avijit Gupta & John Pitts. 442p. (Orig.). 1993. pap. 49.50 (*9971-69-172-8*, Pub. by Sngapore Univ Pr) Coronet Bks.

Physical Adsorption: Experiment, Theory, & Applications. Jacques P. Fraissard. LC 97-13933. (NATO ASI Series, Mathematical & Physical Sciences: Series C). 1997. text 301.00 (*0-7923-4547-9*) Kluwer Academic.

Physical Adsorption: Forces & Phenomena. L. W. Bruch et al. LC 97-164754. (International Series of Monotraphs on Chemistry: No. 33). (Illus.). 352p. 1997. text 85.00 (*0-19-855638-1*) OUP.

Physical Adsorption on Heterogeneuous Solids. M. Jaroniec & R. Madey. (Studies in Physical & Theoretical Chemistry: No. 59). 354p. 1988. 226.00 (*0-444-87117-9*) Elsevier.

Physical Agent Modalities: Theory & Application for the Occupational Therapist. Alfred Bracciano. 176p. 2000. pap. 35.00 (*1-55642-376-4*, 33764) SLACK Inc.

Physical Agents: A Comprehensive Text for Physical Therapists. Bernadette Hecox et al. (Illus.). 500p. (C). 1994. pap. text 47.50 (*0-8385-8040-8*, A8040-6) Appleton & Lange.

Physical Agents: A Comprehensive Text for Physical Therapists. 2nd ed. Bernadette Hecox. (C). 2000. 45.00 (*0-8385-8132-3*) Appleton & Lange.

Physical Agents: Theory & Practice for the Physical Therapist Assistant. Barbara J. Behrens & Susan L. Michlovitz. LC 95-26022. (Illus.). 438p. (C). 1996. text 39.95 (*0-8036-0111-5*) Davis Co.

Physical Agents for Physical Therapists. 3rd ed. James E. Griffin & Terence C. Karselis. (Illus.). 458p. 1988. 62.95 (*0-398-05384-7*); pap. 44.95 (*0-398-06363-X*) C C Thomas.

Physical Agents in Rehabilitation: From Research to Practice. Michelle H. Cameron. Ed. by Shirley Kuhn. LC 98-21395. (Illus.). 480p. (C). 1998. pap. text 39.00 (*0-7216-6244-7*, W B Saunders Co) Harcrt Hlth Sci Grp.

Physical Agents Laboratory Manual. Barbara Behrens. (Illus.). 172p. 1997. pap. text 21.95 (*0-8036-0275-8*) Davis Co.

Physical Analysis for Tribology. T. F. Quinn. (Illus.). 506p. (C). 1991. text 150.00 (*0-521-32602-8*) Cambridge U Pr.

Physical Analysis of Nine Indian Mounds of the Lower Sacramento Valley. fac. ed. R. F. Heizer & S. F. Cook. Ed. by Gifford et al. (University of California Publications in American Archaeology & Ethnology: No. 40:7). 35p. (C). 1951. reprint ed. pap. 4.06 (*1-55567-317-1*) Coyote Press.

Physical & Analytical Modeling of Contact Fatigue Pits from Rolling/Sliding Tests. Dale H. Breen. (Nineteen Eighty-Seven Fall Technical Meeting Ser.: Vol. 87FTM8). (Illus.). 18p. 1987. pap. text 30.00 (*1-55589-484-4*) AGMA.

Physical & Biogeochemical Processes in Antarctic Lakes. Ed. by William J. Green & E. Imre Friedmann. LC 93-7383. (Antarctic Research Ser.: Vol. 59). 1993. 55.00 (*0-87590-830-6*) Am Geophysical.

Physical & Biological Bases of Life Stability: Man, Biota, Environment. V. G. Gorshkov. LC 94-21157. xi, 340p. 1994. 118.95 (*0-387-57049-7*) Spr-Verlag.

Physical & Biological Hazards of the World. Peter H. Wald & Gregg M. Stave. 516p. 1994. text 92.95 (*0-442-01677-8*, VNR) Wiley.

Physical & Biological Hazards of Workplace. Peter H. Wald & Gregg M. Stave. (Industrial Health & Safety Ser.). 516p. 1994. 110.00 (*0-471-28595-1*) Wiley.

Physical & Biological Processing of Images: London, England, 1982, Proceedings. Ed. by O. J. Braddick & A. C. Sleigh. (Information Sciences Ser.: Vol. 11). (Illus.). 403p. 1983. 78.95 (*0-387-12108-0*) Spr-Verlag.

Physical & Chemical Analysis of Sedimentary from 4-MNT-85 Montery County, California. Sally A. Dean. 161p. (C). 1979. pap. text 17.50 (*1-55567-065-2*) Coyote Press.

Physical & Chemical Aspects of Combustion: A Tribute to Irvin Glassman. Ed. by Frederick L. Dryer & Robert F. Sawyer. (Combustion Science & Technology Ser.). 520p. 1997. text 69.00 (*90-5699-584-7*) Gordon & Breach.

Physical & Chemical Changes in Matter. Frank Schaffer Publications, Inc. Staff. (Science Notes Ser.). (Illus.). 8p. 1996. 2.49 (*0-86734-892-5*, FS-62029) Schaffer Pubns.

Physical & Chemical Characteristics of Oils, Fats, & Waxes. 2nd ed. Ed. by David Firestone. 150.00 incl. cd-rom (*1-893997-04-9*) Am Oil Chemists.

Physical & Chemical Characterization of Individual Airbourne Particles. K. R. Spurny. (Analytical Chemistry Ser.). 1986. text 105.00 (*0-470-20316-1*) P-H.

Physical & Chemical Essays, 3 vols. Torbern O. Bergman. 1979. lib. bdg. 350.00 (*0-8490-2438-2*) Gordon Pr.

Physical & Chemical Hydrogeology. 2nd ed. Patrick A. Domenico & Franklin W. Schwartz. LC 97-21776. 528p. 1997. text 109.95 (*0-471-59762-7*) Wiley.

Physical & Chemical Mechanisms in Molecular Radiation Biology. W. A. Glass & M. N. Varma. (Basic Life Sciences Ser.: Vol. 58). (Illus.). 528p. (C). 1992. text 145.00 (*0-306-44110-1*, Kluwer Plenum) Kluwer Academic.

Physical & Chemical Processes: Transport & Transformation: Oceanic Processes in Marine Pollution, Vol. 6. Ed. by D. J. Baumgartner & Iver W. Duedall. LC 89-2526. 262p. (C). 1990. 64.50 (*0-89874-964-6*) Krieger.

Physical & Chemical Processing see Proceedings of the XIX International Mineral Processing Congress

Physical & Chemical Properties of Oils, Fats, Waxes, Section I. Ed. by David Firestone. 1996. ring bd. 150.00 (*0-935315-89-6*, PC SECT) Am Oil Chemists.

Physical & Chemical Properties of Thin Metal Overlayers & Alloy Surfaces. Ed. by D. M. Zehner & D. W. Goodman. (MRS Symposium Proceedings Ser.: Vol. 83). 1987. text 17.50 (*0-931837-48-0*) Materials Res.

Physical & Chemical Techniques for Discharge Studies Pt. 1: Basics of Recharge & Discharge. Ed. by R. B. Salama. (Illus.). 52p. 1996. pap. 24.95 (*0-643-05879-6*, Pub. by CSIRO) Accents Pubns.

Physical & Chemical Weathering in Geochemical Cycles. Ed. by A. Lerman & M. Meybeck. (C). 1988. text 201.00 (*90-277-2821-6*) Kluwer Academic.

Physical & Computational Aspects of Convective Heat Transfer. T. Cebeci & P. Bradshaw. (Illus.). 345p. 1984. 82.50 (*0-387-12097-1*) Spr-Verlag.

Physical & Computational Aspects of Convective Heat Transfer: Springer Study Edition. T. Cebeci & P. Bradshaw. (Illus.). xii, 487p. 1991. 79.95 (*0-387-96821-0*) Spr-Verlag.

Physical & Elastic Characterisation. Ed. by M. McLean. (Characterisation of High-Temperature Materials Ser.: No. IV). vi, 226p. 1989. text 52.50 (*0-901462-66-7*, Pub. by Inst Materials) Ashgate Pub Co.

Physical & Emotional Abuse & Neglect see Child Abuse: A Multidisciplinary Survey

***Physical & Emotional Hazards of a Performing Career, Vol. 2.** Ed. by Basil Tschaikov. 88p. 2000. 21.00 (*90-5755-138-1*, Harwood Acad Pubs) Gordon & Breach.

Physical & Information Sciences & Engineering: Report of the Project 2061 Phase I Physical & Info Sciences & Engineering Panel. George Bugliarello. 42p. 1989. 8.00 (*0-87168-345-8*, 89-04S) AAAS.

Physical & Material Properties of High Temperature Superconductors. Ed. by S. K. Malik & S. S. Shah. (Illus.). 711p. (C). 1994. lib. bdg. 195.00 (*1-56072-114-6*) Nova Sci Pubs.

Physical & Mathematical Modeling of Tundish Operations. Julian Szekely & O. J. Ilegbusi. (Materials Research & Engineering Ser.). (Illus.). xi, 116p. 1989. 66.00 (*0-387-96858-X*) Spr-Verlag.

Physical & Mechanical Problems. Peter J. May. 1999. 15.95 (*1-85279-099-7*) TFH Pubns.

Physical & Mental Growth of Girls & Boys Age Six to Nineteen in Relation to Age at Maximum Growth. Frank K. Shuttleworth. (SRCD M Ser.: Vol. 4, No. 3). 1939. 25.00 (*0-527-01510-5*) Periodicals Srv.

***Physical & Mental Issues in Aging Sourcebook: Basic Consumer Health Information.** Ed. by Jenifer Swanson. LC 99-15540. (Health Reference Ser.). 625p. 1999. 78.00 (*0-7808-0233-0*) Omnigraphics Inc.

Physical & Metaphysical Works of Lord Bacon, Including the Advancement of Learning & Novum Organum. Francis Bacon. 1976. reprint ed. 95.00 (*0-403-06143-1*, Regency) Scholarly.

Physical & Motor Development in Persons with Mental Retardation. Ed. by A. Vermeer & W. E. Davis. (Medicine & Sport Science Ser.: Vol. 40). (Illus.). xii, 210p. 1995. 207.00 (*3-8055-6118-0*) S Karger.

Physical & Non-Physical Methods of Solving Crystal Structures. Michael Woolfson & Fan Hai-fu. (Illus.). 288p. (C). 1995. text 95.00 (*0-521-41299-4*) Cambridge U Pr.

Physical & Nonstandard Gauges: Proceedings of a Workshop Organized at the Institute for Theoretical Physics of the Technical University, Vienna, Austria, September 19-23, 1989. Ed. by P. Gaigg et al. (Lecture Notes in Physics Ser.). ix, 310p. 1990. 47.95 (*0-387-52815-6*) Spr-Verlag.

Physical & Occupational Therapists' Job Search Handbook: Your Complete Job Search Strategy: How to Hire; How to Be Hired. Lynda Peringian. LC 89-50592. (Illus.). 160p. (C). 1989. text 25.00 (*0-9622773-0-4*) Peringian & Assocs.

Physical & Psychological Effects of Meditation: A Review of Contemporary Meditation Research with a Comprehensive Bibliography, 1931-1988. Michael Murphy & Steven Donovan. 187p. (Orig.). (C). 1988. pap. 17.95 (*0-9621232-0-X*) Esalen Inst.

Physical & Psychological Effects of Meditation: A Review of Contemporary Research with a Comprehensive Bibliography 1931-1996. 2nd ed. Michael Murphy et al. LC 96-46701. 1996. write for info. (*0-943951-36-4*) Inst Noetic Sci.

Physical & Related Properties of 145 Timbers: Information for Practice. Jan F. Rijsdijk & Peter B. Laming. LC 94-12287. 392p. (C). 1994. text 145.50 (*0-7923-2875-2*) Kluwer Academic.

Physical & Sexual Abuse of Children: Causes & Treatment. David R. Walters. LC 75-1940. 204p. reprint ed. pap. 63.30 (*0-8357-6687-X*, 205686700094) Bks Demand.

Physical & Technical Aspects of Fire & Arson Investigation. John R. Carroll. (Illus.). 470p. 1982. pap. 56.95 (*0-398-06047-9*) C C Thomas.

Physical & Technical Aspects of Fire & Arson Investigation. fac. ed. John R. Carroll. (Illus.). 470p. 1982. 71.95 (*0-398-03785-X*) C C Thomas.

Physical & Technical Problems of SOI Structures & Devices: Proceedings of the NATO Advanced Research Workshop, Gurzuf, Ukraine, November 1-4, 1994. Ed. by J. P. Colinge. (NATO ASI - Partnership Sub-Series 3). 300p. (C). 1995. text 166.00 (*0-7923-3600-3*) Kluwer Academic.

Physical & the Moral: Anthropology, Physiology, & Philosophical Medicine in France, 1750-1850. Elizabeth A. Williams. (Cambridge History of Medicine Ser.). (Illus.). 300p. (C). 1994. text 69.95 (*0-521-43067-4*) Cambridge U Pr.

***Physical & Thermal Technologies: Remediation of Chlorinated & Recalcitrant Compounds (C2-5)** Ed. by Godage B. Wickramanayake & Arun R. Gavaskar. 332p. 2000. 74.95 (*1-57477-099-3*) Battelle.

Physical & Thermodynamic Properties of Ammonia-Water Mixtures. R. A. Macriss et al. (Research Bulletin Ser.: No. 34). iv, 42p. 1964. pap. 25.00 (*1-58222-033-6*) Inst Gas Tech.

Physical & Thermodynamic Properties of Pure Chemicals, No. 6. T. E. Daubert & R. P. Danner. 600p. 1996. ring bd. 175.00 (*1-56032-491-0*) Taylor & Francis.

Physical & Thermodynamic Properties of Pure Chemicals, Suppl. 1. T. E. Daubert & R. P. Danner. 416p. 1991. ring bd. 155.00 (*1-56032-155-5*) Hemisp Pub.

Physical & Thermodynamic Properties of Pure Chemicals, Suppl. 3. T. E. Daubert & R. P. Danner. 1993. ring bd. 175.00 (*1-56032-281-0*) Hemisp Pub.

Physical & Thermodynamic Properties of Pure Chemicals, Suppl. 4. T. E. Daubert & R. P. Danner. 1994. ring bd. 175.00 (*1-56032-307-8*) Hemisp Pub.

Physical & Thermodynamic Properties of Pure Chemicals, Suppl. 5. T. E. Daubert & R. P. Danner. 440p. 1995. ring bd. 175.00 (*1-56032-333-7*) Hemisp Pub.

Physical & Thermodynamic Properties of Pure Chemicals, Supplement 2. T. E. Daubert & R. P. Danner. 736p. 1992. ring bd. 175.00 (*1-56032-270-5*) Hemisp Pub.

Physical & Thermodynamic Properties of Pure Chemicals, Supplement 7. 1997. ring bd. 175.00 (*1-56032-647-6*) Hemisp Pub.

Physical & Thermodynamic Properties of Pure Chemicals: Data Compilation, 4 vols. Ed. by T. E. Daubert & Diane Foster. 1100p. 1989. 412.00 (*0-89116-948-2*) Hemisp Pub.

***Physical Anthropolgy 2000-2001.** 9th ed. Elvio Angeloni. (Annual Editions Ser.). 240p. (C). 1999. pap. 16.56 (*0-07-236398-3*) McGrw-H Hghr Educ.

Physical Anthropology. 1997. write for info. (*0-13-645904-8*) P-H.

Physical Anthropology. Roger Pearson. (Illus.). 164p. 2000. pap. 20.00 (*1-878465-31-7*) Scott-Townsend Pubs.

Physical Anthropology. 3rd ed. Angeloni. 1994. text 12.74 (*1-56134-285-8*) McGraw.

Physical Anthropology. 3rd ed. Diane L. France. 215p. (C). 1997. wbk. ed., lab manual ed. 25.50 (*0-314-07337-X*) West Pub.

Physical Anthropology. 4th ed. Angeloni. 1995. 12.74 (*1-56134-367-6*) McGraw.

Physical Anthropology. 5th ed. Philip L. Stein & Bruce M. Rowe. LC 92-20045. (C). 1993. pap. text 47.50 (*0-07-061184-X*) McGraw.

Physical Anthropology. 6th ed. Philip L. Stein & Bruce M. Rowe. LC 95-39797. (C). 1995. pap. text 44.74 (*0-07-061252-8*) McGraw.

Physical Anthropology. 6th ed. Philip L. Stein & Bruce M. Rowe. (C). 1996. pap., student ed. 14.69 (*0-07-061253-6*) McGraw.

Physical Anthropology. 7th ed. Stein. LC 99-15559. 531p. 1999. pap. 44.69 (*0-07-228229-0*) McGraw.

Physical Anthropology: Human Evolution. Ivan G. Pawson. LC 77-2412. (Self-Teaching Guides Ser.). 256p. reprint ed. 79.40 (*0-8357-9954-9*, 201187700079) Bks Demand.

Physical Anthropology: The Core. Philip L. Stein. LC 94-25552. (C). 1994. text 37.74 (*0-07-061249-8*) McGraw.

Physical Anthropology: The Core. Philip L. Stein & Bruce M. Rowe. (C). 1994. pap. text 13.12 (*0-07-061250-1*) McGraw.

Physical Anthropology: The Core. 2nd ed. Philip L. Stein & Bruce M. Rowe. LC 97-12510. 368p. (C). 1997. pap. 46.56 (*0-07-061493-8*) McGraw.

Physical Anthropology: 1999-2000 Edition. 8th ed. Angeloni. 1999. pap., student ed. 16.56 (*0-07-040107-1*) McGraw.

Physical Anthropology & Archaeology. 4th ed. Clifford Jolly & Fred Plog. 496p. (C). 1987. text. write for info. (*0-318-60766-2*) Random.

Physical Anthropology & Archaeology. 5th ed. Clifford J. Jolly & Randall White. LC 94-21196. 524p. (C). 1995. 65.63 (*0-07-032764-5*) McGraw.

Physical Anthropology & Prehistory An Introduction. 4th ed. Abraham Gruber. 132p. (C). 1990. pap. 35.60 (*0-536-57888-5*) Pearson Custom.

P

Physical Anthropology Core. 2nd ed. Stein. 144p. 1997. pap., student ed. 13.44 (*0-07-061459-8*) McGraw.

Physical Anthropology, 1996-1997. annuals 5th ed. Elvio Angeloni. 256p. (C). 1996. text. write for info. (*0-697-31527-4*) Brown & Benchmark.

Physical Anthropology, 98-99. 7th ed. Elvio Angeloni. (Annual Ser.). (Illus.). 240p. 1998. pap. text 12.25 (*0-697-39174-4*, Dshkn McG-Hill) McGrw-H Hghr Educ.

Physical Anthropology of a Mexican Population in Texas: A Study in Race-Mixture. Arthur R. Kelly. (Publications: No. 13). (Illus.). 118p. 1947. 10.00 (*0-939238-15-2*) Tulane MARI.

Physical Anthropology of Central California Pt. I: Osteometric Data. fac. ed. Gary S. Breschini & Trudy Haversat. 110p. (C). 1980. reprint ed. pap. text 12.19 (*1-55567-511-5*) Coyote Press.

Physical Anthropology of European Populations. Ed. by Ilse Schwidetzky et al. (World Anthropology Ser.). xii, 440p. 1980. text 70.80 (*90-279-7900-6*) Mouton.

Physical Anthropology of Ireland, 2 vols. E. A. Hooton & C. Wesley Dupertius. (Harvard University Peabody Museum of Archaeology & Ethnology Papers: Vol. 30). 1955. 115.00 (*0-527-01275-0*) Periodicals Srv.

Physical Anthropology of the Lenape Or Delawares, & of the Eastern Indians in General. Ed. by Ales Hrdlicka. (Bureau of American Ethnology Bulletins Ser.). 130p. 1995. lib. bdg. 79.00 (*0-7812-4062-X*) Rprt Serv.

Physical Anthropology 1996/97. 5th annot. ed. Angeloni. 1996. teacher ed. 13.12 (*0-697-31528-2*, WCB McGr Hill) McGrw-H Hghr Educ.

Physical Appearance & Gender: Sociobiological & Sociocultural Perspectives. Linda A. Jackson. LC 90-22724. (SUNY Series, The Psychology of Women). 326p. (C). 1992. text 64.50 (*0-7914-0823-X*); pap. text 21.95 (*0-7914-0824-8*) State U NY Pr.

Physical Appearance, Stigma, & Social Behavior Vol. III: The Ontario Symposium on Personality & Social Psychology Bol. Ed. by E. Troy Higgins et al. 336p. (C). 1986. text 69.95 (*0-89859-638-6*) L Erlbaum Assocs.

Physical Applications & Mathematical Aspects of Geometry, 2 vols. LC 97-22218. 1350p. 1997. text 103.00 (*981-02-3135-0*) World Scientific Pub.

Physical Approach to Color Image Understanding. Gudrun J. Klinker. LC 92-14994. (Illus.). 192p. (C). 1993. text 49.00 (*1-56881-013-X*) AK Peters.

***Physical Approach to Playing the Trumpet: Using the Body's Reflexes to Enhance Trumpet Performance.** Lynn K. Asper. Ed. by Renee D. Asper. LC 98-94064. (Illus.). 104p. 1999. pap. 16.95 (*0-9668847-0-1*) WaveSong.

Physical Approaches to Biological Evolution. Ed. by Michael V. Volkenstein. Tr. by A. Beknazarov. LC 94-6894. 1994. write for info. (*3-540-57652-5*) Spr-Verlag.

Physical Approaches to Biological Evolution. Ed. by Michael V. Volkenstein. Tr. by A. Beknazarov. LC 94-6894. (Illus.). 700p. 1994. 86.95 (*0-387-57652-5*) Spr-Verlag.

Physical Aspect of the Living Cell: Proceedings of the Eugene Ernst Memorial Symposium Held in Pecs, Hungary, July 3-5, 1986. Ed. by J. Tigyi et al. (Illus.). 382p. (C). 1991. 129.00 (*963-05-5926-9*, Pub. by Akade Kiado) St Mut.

Physical Aspects of Brachytherapy. T. J. Godden. (Medical Physics Handbook Ser.: No. 19). (Illus.). 304p. 1988. 21.00 (*0-85274-511-7*) IOP Pub.

Physical Aspects of Diagnostic Radiology. Michel M. Ter-Pogossian. LC 66-19240. 448p. reprint ed. pap. 138.90 (*0-608-14438-X*, 205185300010) Bks Demand.

Physical Aspects of Electron Microscopy & Microbeam Analysis. Ed. by Benjamin M. Siegel & D. R. Beaman. LC 74-22483. (Illus.). 488p. 1975. reprint ed. pap. 151.30 (*0-7837-3470-0*, 205780100008) Bks Demand.

Physical Aspects of Hyperthermia: Proceedings of the AAPM Summer School Held at Dartmouth College, Hanover, New Hampshire, August 3-7, 1981. Ed. by Gilbert H. Nussbaum. (American Association of Physicists in Medicine Symposium Ser.: No. 8). 650p. 1982. 50.00 (*0-88318-414-1*, Pub. by Am Inst Physics) Med Physics Pub.

Physical Aspects of Irradiation. 1964. 20.00 (*0-913394-02-5*, 10B) Intl Comm Rad Meas.

Physical Aspects of Medical Imaging: Proceedings of a Meeting Held at the University of Manchester, June 25-27, 1980. Ed. by B. M. Moores et al. LC 82-116267. (Illus.). 354p. reprint ed. pap. 109.80 (*0-8357-8622-6*, 203504500091) Bks Demand.

Physical Aspects of Stereotactic Radiosurgery. Ed. by M. H. Phillips. (Illus.). 312p. (C). 1993. text 75.00 (*0-306-44535-2*, Kluwer Plenum) Kluwer Academic.

Physical Assessment: A Guide for Evaluating Drug Therapy. R. Leon Longe & John C. Calvert. Ed. by Lloyd Y. Young. LC 94-76859. 486p. (Orig.). (C). 1994. pap. text 44.50 (*0-915486-20-2*) Applied Therapeutics.

Physical Assessment of the Newborn. 2nd rev. ed. Ellen P. Tappero & Mary E. Honeyfield. LC 96-9065. (Illus.). 250p. 1996. pap. text 39.95 (*1-887571-00-0*) NICU Ink.

Physical Attractiveness. Gerald Adams & Sharyn Crossman. LC 78-56850. 1979. 7.95 (*0-87212-122-4*) Libra.

Physical Attractiveness & the Theory of Sexual Selection: Results from 5 Populations. Doug Jones. (Anthropological Papers Ser.: Vol. 90). 1996. pap. 24.00 (*0-915703-40-8*) U Mich Mus Anthro.

Physical Attractiveness Phenomena. Gordon L. Patzer. LC 85-6593. (Perspectives in Social Psychology Ser.). (Illus.). 320p. (C). 1985. 83.00 (*0-306-41783-9*, Plenum Trade) Perseus Pubng.

***Physical Bases of Voice.** Callaghan. LC 99-40616. 1999. pap. 57.95 (*0-7693-0044-8*) Thomson Learn.

Physical Basis of Biochemistry: The Foundations of Molecular Biophysics. P. R. Bergethon. LC 97-26975. (Illus.). 650p. 1998. text 69.95 (*0-387-98262-0*) Spr-Verlag.

Physical Basis of Cell-Cell Adhesion. Ed. by Pierre Bongrand. 280p. 1988. 158.00 (*0-8493-6554-6*, QH623, CRC Reprint) Franklin.

Physical Basis of Chemistry. Warren S. Warren. LC 93-29740. (Illus.). 168p. 1993. pap. text 27.00 (*0-12-735850-1*) Acad Pr.

***Physical Basis of Chemistry.** 2nd ed. Warren S. Warren. 1999. 34.95 (*0-12-735855-2*) Morgan Kaufmann.

Physical Basis of Computed Tomography. Christopher Marshall. 171p. 1982. 37.50 (*0-87527-314-9*) Green.

Physical Basis of Mind see Problems of Life & Mind

Physical Basis of Mind. George Henry Lewes. 511p. 120.00 (*1-85506-666-1*) Thoemmes Pr.

Physical Basis of Musical Sound. Joseph Morgan. LC 78-5508. (Illus.). 168p. (Orig.). 1980. lib. bdg. 18.50 (*0-88275-656-7*) Krieger.

Physical Basis of Organic Chemistry. Howard Maskill. (Illus.). 504p. (C). 1986. pap. text 44.95 (*0-19-855199-1*) OUP.

Physical Basis of Predication. Andrew Newman. (Studies in Philosophy). 285p. (C). 1992. text 69.95 (*0-521-41131-9*) Cambridge U Pr.

Physical Basis of Rime: An Essay on the Aesthetics of Sound. Henry Lanz. LC 69-10115. (Illus.). 365p. 1969. reprint ed. lib. bdg. 69.50 (*0-8371-0136-0*, LABR, Greenwood Pr) Greenwood.

Physical Basis of the Direction of Time. Heinz D. Zeh. 1989. pap. 39.00 (*0-387-50930-5*) Spr-Verlag.

Physical Basis of the Direction of Time. 2nd ed. Heinz D. Zeh. (Illus.). x, 188p. 1993. 43.95 (*0-387-54884-X*) Spr-Verlag.

Physical Basis of the Direction of Time. 3rd ed. H. D. Zeh. LC 99-14727. (Illus.). xvii, 228p. 1999. pap. 64.00 (*3-540-64865-8*) Spr-Verlag.

Physical Basis of Ultrahigh Vacuum. P. A. Redhead et al. LC 92-46643. (AVS Classics of Vacuum Science & Technology Ser.). 1993. write for info. (*1-56396-122-9*) Am Inst Physics.

Physical Behaviour of Macromolecules with Biological Functions. S. P. Spragg. LC 80-40280. (Monographs in Molecular Biophysics & Biochemistry). 218p. reprint ed. pap. 67.60 (*0-608-17602-8*, 203045200069) Bks Demand.

Physical Best Activity Guide for Elementary Level. AAHPERD Staff. (Physical Best Ser.). (Illus.). 248p. 1998. pap. text 24.00 (*0-88011-962-4*, BAAH0962) Human Kinetics.

Physical Best Activity Guide for Secondary Level. Physical Best (Program) Staff & American Alliance for Health, Physical Education, Recreation & Dance Staff. LC 98-40311. 240p. 1999. 24.00 (*0-88011-971-3*) Human Kinetics.

Physical Best & Individuals with Disabilities: A Handbook for Inclusion in Fitness Programs. (Orig.). 1995. pap. text 26.00 (*0-88314-569-3*, A5693) AAHPERD.

Physical Biochemistry. 2nd ed. David M. Freifelder. LC 81-19521. (Illus.). 624p. (C). 1982. pap. text 70.95 (*0-7167-1444-2*) W H Freeman.

Physical Capacities Evaluation. Susan L. Smith & Patricia Baxter-Petralia. 130p. (C). 1992. pap. text 29.95 (*0-935273-02-6*) Chess Pub.

***Physical Causation.** Phil Dowe. (Cambridge Studies in Probability, Induction & Decision Theory). (Illus.). 248p. 2000. 54.95 (*0-521-78049-7*) Cambridge U Pr.

Physical Ceramics: Principles for Ceramics Science & Engineering. Yet-Ming Chiang et al. LC 95-32997. (MIT Series in Materials Science & Engineering). 544p. 1996. text 103.95 (*0-471-59873-9*) Wiley.

Physical Ceramics for Engineers. Lawrence H. Van Vlack. (Illus.). 1964. write for info. (*0-201-08068-0*) Addison-Wesley.

Physical Change & Aging: A Guide for the Helping Professions. 3rd rev. ed. Sue V. Saxon & Mary J. Etten. (Illus.). 448p. (Orig.). 1994. pap. text 24.90 (*0-913292-47-8*) Tiresias Pr.

Physical Characteristics & Critical Temperature of HTSC. Ed. by M. M. Sushchinskiy et al. (Proceedings of the Lebedev Physics Institute Ser.: Vol. 195). 227p. (C). 1991. pap. 175.00 (*1-56072-039-5*) Nova Sci Pubs.

Physical Characterization of Pharmaceutical Solids. Harry G. Brittain. (Drugs & the Pharmaceutical Sciences Ser.: Vol. 70). (Illus.). 440p. 1995. text 175.00 (*0-8247-9372-2*) Dekker.

Physical Characters of the Cook Islanders. H. L. Shapiro & P. H. Buck. (BMB Ser.: Vol. 11, No. 4). 1974. reprint ed. pap. 25.00 (*0-527-01669-1*) Periodicals Srv.

Physical Characters of the Indians of Southern Mexico. Frederick Starr. LC 74-9008. (Illus.). reprint ed. 39.50 (*0-404-11906-9*) AMS Pr.

Physical Chem: Methods, Tech, 2nd ed. Sime. (C). 2000. text 65.00 (*0-03-005937-2*) Harcourt Coll Pubs.

Physical, Chemical, & Biological Properties of Radiocerium Relevant to Radiation Protection Guidelines. LC 79-84485. (Report Ser.: No. 60). 115p. 1978. pap. text 35.00 (*0-913392-44-8*) NCRP Pubns.

Physical, Chemical & Biological Properties of Stable Water Clusters: Proceedings of the 1st International Symposium. Ed. by S-Y Lo & B. Bonavida. LC 98-222277. 224p. 1998. 36.00 (*981-02-3509-7*) World Scientific Pub.

Physical, Chemical & Biological Properties of Stable Water Clusters: Proceedings of the 1st International Symposium. Ed. by S-Y Lo & B. Bonavida. LC 98-222277. 224p. 1998. pap. 18.00 (*981-02-3515-1*) World Scientific Pub.

Physical, Chemical, & Thermal Technologies: Remediation of Chlorinated & Recalcitrant Compounds. Godage B. Wickramanayake & Robert E. Hinchee. LC 98-25125. 1998. 79.95 (*1-57477-060-8*) Battelle.

Physical-Chemical Aspects see Singlet 02 Series

Physical, Chemical, Biochemical & Biological Techniques & Processes. K. E. Carr et al. Ed. by Guenther Kraft. (Advances in Space Research Ser.: Vol. 18). 352p. 1995. pap. 194.50 (*0-08-042664-6*, Pergamon Pr) Elsevier.

Physical-Chemical Processes. Ed. by Harry M. Freeman. LC 90-70257. (Innovative Hazardous Waste Treatment Technology Ser.: Vol. 2). 250p. 1990. pap. 24.95 (*0-87762-617-0*) Technomic.

Physical, Chemical Properties of Drugs. Ed. by Samuel H. Yalkowsky et al. LC 80-22598. (Medicinal Research Ser.: No. 10). 379p. 1980. reprint ed. pap. 117.50 (*0-608-09965-1*, 202595100047) Bks Demand.

Physical-Chemical Properties of Ethane-Nitrogen Mixtures. B. E. Eakin et al. (Research Bulletin Ser.: No. 26). iv, 40p. 1955. pap. 25.00 (*1-58222-034-4*) Inst Gas Tech.

Physical-Chemical Properties of Methane-Ethane Mixtures. O. T. Bloomer et al. (Research Bulletin Ser.: No. 22). iv, 39p. 1953. pap. 25.00 (*1-58222-035-2*) Inst Gas Tech.

Physical-Chemical Properties of Methane-Nitrogen Mixtures. O. T. Bloomer. (Research Bulletin Ser.: No. 17). iv, 35p. 1952. pap. 25.00 (*1-58222-036-0*) Inst Gas Tech.

Physical Chemical Techniques see Physical Techniques in Biological Research

Physical Chemical Treatment of Hazardous Waste. S. Bhattacharyas. 1992. pap. write for info. (*0-442-00941-0*, VNR) Wiley.

Physical Chemistry. Abruna. (C). pap. text, lab manual ed. write for info. (*0-7167-2668-8*) W H Freeman.

Physical Chemistry. Atkins. 1998. write for info. incl. cd-rom (*0-7167-3166-5*) W H Freeman.

Physical Chemistry. Peter W. Atkins. LC 85-7048. (C). text, teacher ed. write for info. (*0-7167-2562-2*) W H Freeman.

Physical Chemistry, 2 vols. V. Kireev. Tr. by Mir Publishers Staff from RUS. (Illus.). 640p. (C). 1975. 54.95 (*0-8464-0716-7*) Beekman Pubs.

Physical Chemistry. Keith J. Laidler. (C). 1995. text 81.16 (*0-395-64153-5*) HM.

Physical Chemistry. Keith J. Laidler. (C). 1995. pap., student ed. 25.96 (*0-395-72410-4*) HM.

Physical Chemistry. Meiser & Keith J. Laider. LC 96-1823. (Illus.). xvi, 919p. 1982. text 49.50 (*0-8053-5682-7*) Benjamin-Cummings.

Physical Chemistry. Metz. (C). 1999. text. write for info. (*0-03-022372-5*) Harcourt Coll Pubs.

Physical Chemistry. Clyde R. Metz. 896p. (C). 1999. text 87.50 (*0-03-097864-5*) SCP.

Physical Chemistry. W. J. Moore. 1972. pap. 37.95 (*0-582-44234-6*, Pub. by Addison-Wesley) Longman.

Physical Chemistry. Slowinski. (C). 1912. text 34.50 (*0-03-058462-0*) Harcourt Coll Pubs.

Physical Chemistry. Krishna G. Vemulapalli. 960p. (C). 1992. text 63.80 (*0-13-673120-1*) P-H.

Physical Chemistry. J. Edmund White. (College Outline Ser.). 486p. (C). 1987. pap. text 13.25 (*0-15-601657-5*) Harcourt Coll Pubs.

Physical Chemistry. John S. Winn. 1146p. (C). 1997. 110.00 (*0-06-047148-4*) Addson-Wesley Educ.

Physical Chemistry. Woodbury. (Miscellaneous/Catalogs Ser.). 1997. mass mkt., student ed. 18.25 (*0-534-34572-7*) Course Tech.

Physical Chemistry. George Woodbury. LC 96-8657. (Chem 3100 Ser.). 950p. (C). 1997. mass mkt. 114.95 (*0-534-34567-0*) Brooks-Cole.

Physical Chemistry. 2nd ed. Alberty. 384p. 1996. pap. 36.95 (*0-471-16028-8*) Wiley.

Physical Chemistry. 2nd ed. Robert A. Alberty & Robert J. Silbey. LC 96-4841. 960p. 1996. text 106.95 (*0-471-10428-0*) Wiley.

***Physical Chemistry.** 2nd ed. R. Stephen Berry et al. (Illus.). 1216p. (C). 2000. text 98.50 (*0-19-510589-3*) OUP.

Physical Chemistry. 2nd ed. J. Philip Bromberg. (C). 1983. teacher ed. 10.00 (*0-685-07781-0*, H80203) P-H.

***Physical Chemistry.** 2nd ed. Robert G. Mortimer. 960p. 2000. 89.95 (*0-12-508345-9*) Acad Pr.

Physical Chemistry. 2nd rev. ed. E. A. Moelwyn-Hughes. 1961. text 587.00 (*0-08-010846-6*, Pub. by Pergamon Repr) Franklin.

***Physical Chemistry.** 3rd ed. Robert A. Alberty & Robert J. Silbey. 980p. (C). 2000. text 111.95 (*0-471-38311-2*) Wiley.

Physical Chemistry. 3rd ed. Brown. Date not set. pap. text. write for info. (*0-582-35365-3*, Pub. by Addison-Wesley) Longman.

Physical Chemistry. 3rd ed. Gilbert W. Castellan. LC 82-22754. (Chemistry Ser.). (Illus.). 1040p. (C). 1983. text 69.00 (*0-201-10386-9*) Addison-Wesley.

Physical Chemistry. 3rd ed. Keith J. Laidler & John H. Meiser. LC 98-72056. xvii, 1019p. 1999. text 69.87 (*0-395-91848-0*) HM.

Physical Chemistry. 3rd ed. Noggle. 416p. (C). 1997. pap. text, student ed. 37.00 (*0-673-52343-8*) Addson-Wesley Educ.

Physical Chemistry. 3rd ed. Joseph H. Noggle. LC 95-10742. 1035p. (C). 1997. 115.00 (*0-673-52341-1*) Addson-Wesley Educ.

Physical Chemistry. 3rd ed. Tinoco. 1995. pap. text, student ed. 12.00 (*0-13-435850-3*) P-H.

Physical Chemistry. 3rd rev. ed. Ira N. Levine. 920p. (C). 1988. text 73.50 (*0-07-037474-0*) McGraw.

Physical Chemistry. 4th ed. Peter W. Atkins. LC 85-7048. (C). 1990. text 45.60 (*0-7167-2073-6*) W H Freeman.

Physical Chemistry. 4th ed. Ira N. Levine. LC 93-48561. 920p. (C). 1994. 95.94 (*0-07-037528-3*) McGraw.

Physical Chemistry. 5th ed. Levine. 2000. 65.25 (*0-07-231808-2*) McGraw.

***Physical Chemistry.** 6th ed. Atkins. 1998. pap. text, student ed. 25.95 (*0-7167-3167-3*) W H Freeman.

Physical Chemistry. 6th ed. P. W. Atkins. LC 97-34485. (Illus.). 1140p. 1997. text 89.95 (*0-7167-2871-0*) W H Freeman.

Physical Chemistry. 6th ed. Peter Atkins. 1998. 23.90 incl. cd-rom (*0-7167-3168-1*) W H Freeman.

Physical Chemistry. 6th ed. Gordon M. Barrow. (Illus.). 910p. (C). 1996. 102.19 (*0-07-005111-9*) McGraw.

Physical Chemistry. 6th ed. Gordon M. Barrow. (C). 1996. student ed. 33.75 (*0-07-005113-5*) McGraw.

Physical Chemistry. 7th ed. Shoemaker. 2001. lab manual ed. 54.50 (*0-07-231821-X*) McGraw.

Physical Chemistry, Vol. I. S. Pahari. (C). 1989. 150.00 (*0-89771-408-3*, Pub. by Current Dist) St Mut.

Physical Chemistry: A Molecular Approach. Donald A. McQuarrie & John D. Simon. LC 97-142. (Illus.). 1200p. 1997. text 92.00 (*0-935702-99-7*) Univ Sci Bks.

***Physical Chemistry: A Short Course.** Wayne E. Wentworth. LC 99-16543. (Illus.). 1999. 59.95 (*0-632-04329-6*) Blackwell Sci.

Physical Chemistry: A Solution Manual. Meiser & Keith J. Laidler. (C). 1982. pap. text, teacher ed. 16.25 (*0-8053-5683-5*) Benjamin-Cummings.

Physical Chemistry: A Step-by-Step Approach. Marwin K. Kemp. LC 79-791. (Undergraduate Chemistry Ser.: No. 6). 1060p. reprint ed. pap. 200.00 (*0-7837-2640-6*, 204299300006) Bks Demand.

Physical Chemistry: Developing a Dynamic Curriculum. Ed. by Robert J. Moore & Richard W. Schwenz. LC 92-35619. (Illus.). 488p. 1993. pap. text 55.00 (*0-8412-2503-6*, Pub. by Am Chemical) OUP.

Physical Chemistry: Methods/Techniques/Experiments. Rodney J. Sime. 720p. (C). 1990. text 86.00 (*0-03-009499-2*) SCP.

Physical Chemistry: Modern Introduction. Dykstra. (C). 1997. teacher ed. write for info. (*0-13-633017-7*, Macmillan Coll) P-H.

Physical Chemistry: Principles & Applications in Biological Sciences. Ignacio Tinoco, Jr. et al. LC 77-25417. 1978. teacher ed. 9.95 (*0-685-03892-0*) P-H.

Physical Chemistry: Principles & Applications in Biological Sciences. 3rd ed. James C. Wang et al. LC 94-37619. 736p. 1995. 96.00 (*0-13-186545-5*) P-H.

***Physical Chemistry: Principles & Applications of Biological Sciences.** 4th ed. (C). 2002. text. write for info. (*0-13-026607-8*) P-H.

Physical Chemistry: With Applications to the Life Sciences. David S. Eisenberg & Donald M. Crothers. 912p. (C). 1979. text 59.06 (*0-8053-2402-X*) Benjamin-Cummings.

Physical Chemistry Vol. 5: Phase Equilibria, Crystallographic Data & Values of Thermodynamic Properties of Binary Alloys. Landolt-Bornstein. Ed. by W. Martienssen et al. (Numerical Data & Functional Relationships in Science & Technology Ser.: Group IV). (Illus.). xxx, 428p. 1997. text 1822.00 (*3-540-61433-8*) Spr-Verlag.

***Physical Chemistry & Industrial Application of Gellan Gum.** Ed. by K. Nishinari. (Progress in Colloid & Polymer Science Ser.: Vol. 114). (Illus.). 200p. 2000. 89.95 (*3-540-66389-4*) Spr-Verlag.

Physical Chemistry & Mineralogy of Soils Vol. 1: Soil Materials. C. Edmund Marshall. LC 75-22180. 398p. 1975. reprint ed. 32.50 (*0-88275-351-7*) Krieger.

Physical Chemistry & SG. 6th ed. Barrow. 1997. 88.00 (*0-07-561219-4*) McGraw.

Physical Chemistry for Students of Pharmacy & Biology. 3rd rev. ed. Stephen C. Wallwork & D. J. Grant. LC 73-94321. (Illus.). 621p. reprint ed. pap. 192.60 (*0-8357-6262-9*, 203443500090) Bks Demand.

Physical Chemistry for the Biomedical Sciences. S. R. Logan. 250p. 1998. 89.00 (*0-7484-0709-X*, Pub. by Tay Francis Ltd); pap. 29.95 (*0-7484-0710-3*, Pub. by Tay Francis Ltd) Taylor & Francis.

Physical Chemistry for the Chemical & Biological Sciences. 3rd ed. Raymond Chang. LC 99-55696. (Illus.). 960p. (C). 2000. text 86.50 (*1-891389-06-8*, 1-891389-06-8) Univ Sci Bks.

Physical Chemistry for the Life Sciences. 2nd ed. Gordon M. Barrow. (Illus.). 448p. (C). 1981. text 65.00 (*0-07-003858-9*) McGraw.

Physical Chemistry from Ostwald to Pauling: The Making of a Science in America. John W. Servos. (Illus.). 725p. 1990. text 65.00 (*0-691-08566-8*, Pub. by Princeton U Pr) Cal Prin Full Svc.

Physical Chemistry Laboratory Manual. 2nd ed. L. Gold. (C). 1997. pap. 47.50 (*0-07-290269-8*) McGrw-H Hghr Educ.

Physical Chemistry of Aqueous Systems: Meeting the Needs of Industry. Proceedings of the 12th International Conference on the Properties of Water & Steam. Ed. by H. J. White, Jr. et al. LC 95-24607. 875p. 1995. 125.00 (*1-56700-034-7*) Begell Hse.

Physical Chemistry of Biopolymer Solutions: Lecture & Course Notes in Chemistry, Vol. 4. Robert F. Steiner & L. C. Garone. 248p. 1991. text 48.00 (*981-02-0451-5*); pap. text 23.00 (*981-02-0452-3*) World Scientific Pub.

Physical Chemistry of Colloids & Interfaces in Oil Production: Proceedings of the 6th IFP Exploration & Production Res. Conference, Held in Saint-Raphael, Sept. 4-6, 1991. Ed. by H. Toulhoat & J. Lecourtier. (Colloques & Seminaires Ser.: Vol. 50). (Illus.). 392p. (C). 1992. 1000.00 (*2-7108-0618-5*, Pub. by Edits Technip) Enfield Pubs NH.

An Asterisk (*) at the beginning of an entry indicates that the title is appearing for the first time.

Physical Chemistry of Electrolyte Solutions: Modern Aspects. J. M. Barthel et al. Ed. by Hellmut Baumgartel et al. LC 98-188809. (Topics in Physical Chemistry Ser.: Vol. 5). 440p. 1998. 109.00 (*3-7985-1076-8*, Pub. by D Steinkopff) Spr-Verlag.

Physical Chemistry of Extractive Metallurgy: Proceedings of an International Symposium. Ed. by Val Kudryk & Y. Kris Rao. LC 84-29561. (Illus.). 509p. reprint ed. pap. 157.80 (*0-608-17841-1*, 203260300080) Bks Demand.

Physical Chemistry of Foods. Ed. by Henry G. Schwartzberg & Richard W. Hartel. (IFT Basic Symposium Ser.: Vol. 7). (Illus.). 764p. 1992. text 125.00 (*0-8247-8693-9*) Dekker.

Physical Chemistry of Foods. P. Walstra. (Food Science & Technology Ser.). Date not set. write for info. (*0-8247-9355-2*) Dekker.

Physical Chemistry of, in & on Silicon. G. F. Cerofolini & L. Meda. (Materials Science Ser.: Vol. 8). (Illus.). 135p. 1989. 37.95 (*0-387-19049-X*) Spr-Verlag.

Physical Chemistry of Inorganic Crystalline Solids. H. F. Franzen. (Illus.). 160p. 1986. 86.95 (*0-387-16580-0*) Spr-Verlag.

Physical Chemistry of Leather Making. Krzysztof J. Bienkiewicz. LC 88-7699. 556p. 1983. 66.50 (*0-89874-304-4*) Krieger.

Physical Chemistry of Lipids: From Alkanes to Phospholipids. D. M. Small. LC 85-19420. (Handbook of Lipid Research Ser.: Vol. 4). (Illus.). 682p. (C). 1986. text 145.00 (*0-306-41763-4*, Kluwer Plenum) Kluwer Academic.

Physical Chemistry of Macromolecules. G. D. Patterson. (Illus.). Date not set. text. write for info. (*0-8247-9467-2*) Dekker.

Physical Chemistry of Macromolecules. Charles Tanford. LC 61-11511. (Illus.). 724p. reprint ed. pap. 200.00 (*0-608-18197-8*, 205660000078) Bks Demand.

Physical Chemistry of Macromolecules: Basic Principles & Issues. S. F. Sun. 496p. 1994. 79.95 (*0-471-59788-0*) Wiley.

Physical Chemistry of Magmas. Ed. by L. L. Perchuk & I. Kushiro. (Advances in Physical Geochemistry Ser.: Vol. 9). (Illus.). x, 341p. 1991. 118.95 (*0-387-97500-4*) Spr-Verlag.

Physical Chemistry of Membranes: An Introduction to the Structure & Dynamics of Biological Membranes. Brian L. Silver. (Illus.). 432p. (C). 1985. text 110.00 (*0-04-574028-3*) Routledge.

Physical Chemistry of Non-Aqueous Solutions of Cellulose & Its Derivatives. Myasoedova. LC 99-40221. 2000. 120.00 (*0-471-95924-3*) Wiley.

Physical Chemistry of 1,2-Dithiole Compounds: The Question of Aromaticity, Vol.1. Carl T. Pedersen. (Sulfur Reports). 96p. 1980. pap. text 142.00 (*3-7186-0031-5*) Gordon & Breach.

Physical Chemistry of Powder Metals Production & Processing: Proceedings of an International Symposium on Physical Chemistry of Powder Metals Production & Processing, Sponsored by the TMS Physical Chemistry Committee, & Held October 16-18, 1989, in St. Marys, PA. International Symposium on Physical Chemistry of P. Ed. by W. Murray Small. LC 89-61035. 553p. 1989. reprint ed. pap. 171.50 (*0-608-00781-1*, 206157900010) Bks Demand.

Physical Chemistry of Solid State Materials: REMCES VI. Ed. by J. Aride et al. (Advanced Materials Research Ser.: Vols. 1-2). (Illus.). 694p. (C). 1995. 216.00 (*3-908450-05-5*, Pub. by Scitec Pubns) Enfield Pubs NH.

Physical Chemistry of Solids. Richard J. Borg & G. J. Dienes. (Illus.). 584p. (C). 1991. text 59.00 (*0-12-118420-X*) Acad Pr.

Physical Chemistry of Solids: Basic Principles of Symmetry & Stability of Crystalline Solids. H. F. Franzen. Ed. by C. Y. Ng. LC 93-45345. (Advanced Series in Physical Chemistry: Vol. 1). 296p. 1994. text 74.00 (*981-02-1153-8*); pap. text 40.00 (*981-02-1154-6*) World Scientific Pub.

Physical Chemistry of Surfaces. 4th ed. Arthur W. Adamson. LC 82-2711. (Illus.). 684p. reprint ed. pap. 200.00 (*0-7837-3525-1*, 205786000008) Bks Demand.

Physical Chemistry of Surfaces. 6th ed. Arthur W. Adamson & Alice P. Gast. LC 97-5929. 808p. 1997. 89.95 (*0-471-14873-3*) Wiley.

Physical Chemistry Problem Solver. rev. ed. Research & Education Association Staff. LC 81-522778. (Illus.). 800p. 1997. pap. text 29.95 (*0-87891-532-X*) Res & Educ.

Physical Chemistry Source Book. Sybil P. Parker. (Science Reference Ser.). (Illus.). 416p. 1988. 49.50 (*0-07-045504-X*) McGraw.

Physical Chemistry Using Mathcad. Joseph H. Noggle. LC 97-163201. (Illus.). 224p. 1997. pap. text 20.00 (*0-9655849-0-9*) Pike Creek Pub.

Physical Chemistry with Applications to the Life Sciences. David S. Eisenberg & Donald M. Crothers. 912p. 1979. teacher ed., student ed. 10.75 (*0-8053-2403-8*) Benjamin-Cummings.

Physical Chemistry/Life Science. 2nd ed. Barrow. 1981. student ed. 23.12 (*0-07-003859-7*) McGraw.

Physical Chemistryon. 4th ed. Ira N. Levine. (C). 1994. pap. text, student ed. 35.00 (*0-07-037686-7*) McGraw.

Physical City: Public Space & the Infrastructure. Ed. & Intro. by Neil L. Shumsky. LC 95-38499. (American Cities Ser.: Vol. 2). 432p. 1995. reprint ed. text 83.00 (*0-8153-2187-2*) Garland.

Physical Cleaning of Coal: Present & Developing Methods. Y. A. Liu. (Energy, Power & Environment Ser.: Vol. 15). (Illus.). 576p. 1982. text 215.00 (*0-8247-1862-3*) Dekker.

Physical Climatology. William D. Sellers. LC 65-24983. 1993. lib. bdg. 22.00 (*0-226-74699-2*) U Ch Pr.

Physical Climatology for Solar & Wind Energy. Ed. by R. Guzzi & C. G. Justus. 1096p. (C). 1988. text 137.00 (*9971-5-0551-7*) World Scientific Pub.

*__Physical Combinatorics.__ Ed. by M. Kashiwara & T. Miwa. (Progress in Mathematics Ser.: Vol. 191). (Illus.). 184p. 2000. 69.95 (*0-8176-4175-0*) Birkhauser.

*__Physical Combinatorics.__ Masaki Kashiwara et al. LC 00-37945. (Progress in Mathematics Ser.). 2000. write for info. (*3-7643-4175-0*) Birkhauser.

Physical Comedy Handbook. Davis Rider Robinson. LC 99-19681. 1999. pap. text 16.95 (*0-325-00114-6*) Heinemann.

Physical Complaints, Service Use & Social Functioning of Residents with Psychiatric Disorders Report 5: OPCS Surveys of Psychiatric Morbidity in Great Britain. Howard Meltzer. xviii, 55p. 1996. 30.00 (*0-11-691662-1*, Pub. by Statnry Office) Balogh.

Physical Complaints, Service Use & Treatment of Adults with Psychiatric Disorders Report 2: OPCS Surveys of Psychiatric Morbidity in Great Britain. Howard Meltzer. xvi, 81p. 1996. 24.00 (*0-11-691651-6*, Pub. by Statnry Office) Balogh.

Physical Conditions & Public Service. (Metropolitan America Ser.: Vol. 10). 216p. 1974. 27.95 (*0-405-05423-8*) Ayer.

Physical Constants. 9th ed. W. H. Childs. 1972. pap. 7.95 (*0-412-21050-9*, NO. 6057) Chapman & Hall.

Physical Constants of Hydrocarbon & Non-Hydrocarbon Compounds, DS 4B. LC 91-12453. (ASTM Data Series Publication). 184p. 1991. pap. text 40.00 (*0-8031-1428-1*, DS4B) ASTM.

Physical Constants of Hydrocarbons CO to CON. American Society for Testing & Materials Staff. LC 79-170766. (ASTM Data Ser.: No. DS 4A). 76p. reprint ed. pap. 30.00 (*0-8357-4126-5*, 205706100005) Bks Demand.

Physical Control of Risk. Shaun Wilkinson. 180p. (C). 1992. 210.00 (*1-85609-037-X*, Pub. by Witherby & Co) St Mut.

Physical Control of the Mind: Toward a Psychocivilized Society. Jose M. Delgado. Ed. by Ruth N. Anshen. (Illus.). 280p. (C). 1971. 29.50 (*0-8290-0574-9*); pap. text 12.95 (*0-8290-1765-8*) Irvington.

Physical Culture. Richard Friedman. LC 79-14604. 1979. pap. 3.00 (*0-916328-14-7*) Yellow Pr.

Physical Culture & the Body Beautiful: An Examination of the Role of Purposive Exercise in the Lives of American Women, 1800-1870. Jan Todd. LC 97-42876. (Illus.). (C). 1998. text 39.95 (*0-86554-561-8*, MUP/H436) Mercer Univ Pr.

Physical Damage & Human Loss: The Economic Impact of Earthquake Mitigation Measures. Robert Litan et al. LC 92-28616. (Insurance & Society Ser.). 98p. (Orig.). 1992. pap. 15.00 (*0-932387-35-7*) Insur Info.

Physical Data Acquisition for Digital Processing: Components, Parameter & Specifications. Gayle F. Miner & David J. Comer. 480p. 1992. text 75.00 (*0-13-209958-6*) P-H.

Physical Data Base Record Design. Jon Clark & Jeffrey A. Hoffer. LC 79-113431. (QED Monograph Series. Data Base Management: No. 7). 118p. reprint ed. pap. 36.60 (*0-608-15622-1*, 203175100076) Bks Demand.

Physical Demands Job Analysis: A New Approach. Robert B. Lytel & Karl F. Botterbusch. (Illus.). 166p. (Orig.). 1981. pap. write for info. (*0-916671-34-8*) TRR.

Physical Design Automation of VLSI Systems. Ed. by Bryan Preas & Michael Lorenzetti. (Illus.). 510p. (C). 1988. text 59.25 (*0-8053-0142-9*) Benjamin-Cummings.

Physical Design for Multichip Modules. Mysore Sriram & S. M. Kang. LC 94-1108. (International Series in Engineering & Computer Science, VLSI, Computer Architecture, & Digital Screen Processing: Vol. VSECS 267). 216p. (C). 1994. text 133.50 (*0-7923-9450-X*) Kluwer Academic.

Physical Design of CMOS Integrated Circuits Using L-Edit. John P. Uyemura. LC 94-28799. 256p. 1994. mass mkt. 81.95 incl. disk (*0-534-94326-8*) PWS Pubs.

Physical Design of Yagi Antennas. 1992. 20.00 (*0-87259-381-9*) Am Radio.

Physical Development of Natural & Criminal Fires. C. Detienne. (Illus.). 176p. (C). 1994. text 57.95 (*0-398-05902-0*) C C Thomas.

*__Physical Development 116.__ (C). 2000. 22.95 (*0-536-60884-9*) Pearson Custom.

Physical Diagnosis. McGee. 2001. pap. text Price not set. (*0-7216-8693-1*, W B Saunders Co) Harcrt Hlth Sci Grp.

Physical Diagnosis: Bedside Evaluation of Diagnosis & Function. Janice L. Willms et al. LC 93-4344. (Illus.). 832p. 1994. 48.00 (*0-683-09110-7*) Lppncott W & W.

Physical Diagnosis: Pretest Self-Assessment & Review. 3rd ed. Ed. by Tyson K. Cobb. LC 97-10550. (Pretest Clinical Science Ser.). (Illus.). 200p. 1997. pap. text 18.95 (*0-07-052531-5*) McGraw-Hill HPD.

Physical Diagnosis in Neonatology. Mary A. Fletcher. LC 97-940. 352p. 1997. text 82.50 (*0-397-51386-0*) Lppncott W & W.

Physical Diagnosis Secrets. Ed. by Salvatore Mangione. LC 98-43417. (Secrets Ser.). (Illus.). 350p. (Orig.). 1999. pap. text 38.00 (*1-56053-164-9*) Hanley & Belfus.

*__Physical Dimensions: High School Physical Education Curriculum.__ 3rd ed. Kathy Ermler & Joella Mehrhof. 500p. 2000. pap. 100.00 (*1-930359-02-0*) Mirror KS.

Physical Dimensions of Aging. Waneen W. Spirduso. LC 94-43969. (Illus.). 448p. 1995. text 55.00 (*0-87322-323-3*, BSPI0323) Human Kinetics.

Physical Disability. 134p. 1994. pap. 21.00 (*0-912452-95-1*, P-109) Am Phys Therapy Assn.

Physical Disability: A Psychosocial Approach. 2nd ed. Beatrice A. Wright. 544p. (C). 1997. pap. text 80.00 (*0-06-047241-3*) Addson-Wesley Educ.

Physical Disability: An Annotated Literature Guide. Ed. by Phyllis C. Self. LC 84-7101. (Books in Library & Information Science: No. 44). 488p. reprint ed. pap. 151.30 (*0-7837-3359-3*, 204331700008) Bks Demand.

Physical Disability & Social Policy. Jerome E. Bickenbach. LC 92-95724. 327p. 1993. text 60.00 (*0-8020-2914-0*) U of Toronto Pr.

Physical Disability & Social Policy. Jerome E. Bickenbach. LC 93-215336. 327p. 1994. pap. text 24.95 (*0-8020-7419-7*) U of Toronto Pr.

Physical Disability in Childhood. Ed. by Gillian T. McCarthy. (Interdisciplinary Approach to Management Ser.). (Illus.). 594p. 1992. text 64.95 (*0-443-04288-8*) Church.

Physical Distribution in Agribusiness: Activity Guide. Ronald Brown & John W. Oren. Ed. by Jasper S. Lee. (Career Preparation for Agriculture-Agribusiness Ser.). 1980. text 19.96 (*0-07-008181-6*) McGraw.

Physical Distribution Management. Didactic Systems Staff. (Simulation Game Ser.). (POR.). 1970. pap. 35.00 (*0-89401-119-7*) Didactic Syst.

Physical Distribution Management. Didactic Systems Staff. (Simulation Game Ser.). 1970. pap. 26.25 (*0-89401-071-9*) Didactic Syst.

Physical Distribution Systems. Alan McKinnon. 256p. 1989. 67.50 (*0-415-00438-1*) Routledge.

Physical Dysfunction Practice Skills for the Occupational Therapy Assistant. Early. LC 97-16858. (Illus.). 672p. (C). (gr. 13). 1997. text 49.95 (*0-8151-3091-0*, 27067) Mosby Inc.

*__Physical Dysfunction Practice Skills for the Occupational Therapy Assistant.__ Mary B. Early. 1998. teacher ed. write for info. (*0-8151-2932-7*) Mosby Inc.

Physical Education. Jack Rudman. (Undergraduate Program Field Tests (UPFT) Ser.: Vol. 18). 43.95 (*0-8373-6068-4*) Nat Learn.

Physical Education. Jack Rudman. (Graduate Record Examination (GRE) Ser.: Vol. 20). 43.95 (*0-8373-5270-3*) Nat Learn.

Physical Education. Jack Rudman. (National Teacher Examination Ser.: NT-9). 1994. pap. 23.95 (*0-8373-8419-2*) Nat Learn.

Physical Education. Jack Rudman. (Graduate Record Examination (GRE) Ser.: Vol. GRE-20). 1994. pap. 23.95 (*0-8373-5220-7*) Nat Learn.

Physical Education. Jack Rudman. (Undergraduate Program Field Tests (UPFT) Ser.: Vol. UPFT-18). 1994. pap. 23.95 (*0-8373-6018-8*) Nat Learn.

Physical Education. 5th ed. Lumpkin. 2001. pap. text 37.60 (*0-07-232901-7*) McGraw.

Physical Education: A Contemporary Introduction. Angela Lumpkin. 1993. write for info. (*0-8016-7821-8*) Mosby Inc.

Physical Education: A Reader. Ken Green. 1998. pap. text 29.00 (*3-89124-463-0*) Meyer & Meyer.

Physical Education: For Teachers & Coordinators & Key Stages 1 & 2. Sue Chedzoy. LC 96-219386. 112p. 1996. pap. 24.95 (*1-85346-410-4*, Pub. by David Fulton) Taylor & Francis.

Physical Education: From Intent to Action. G. S. Morris & Jim Stiehl. 464p. (C). 1985. 54.00 (*0-675-20115-2*, Merrill Coll) P-H.

Physical Education: Perspectives, Inquiry, Applications. 3rd ed. Robert E. Gensemer. 304p. (C). 1994. text. write for info. (*0-697-15243-X*) Brown & Benchmark.

Physical Education: Teachers' Lives & Careers. Kathleen R. Armour. LC 98-185973. 1998. 79.00 (*0-7507-0818-2*, Falmer Pr); pap. 25.95 (*0-7507-0817-4*, Falmer Pr) Taylor & Francis.

Physical Education: Teaching & Curriculum Strategies for Grades 5-12. Daryl Siedentop et al. LC 85-62623. xx, 443p. (C). 1986. text 49.95 (*0-87484-592-0*, 592) Mayfield Pub.

Physical Education Activities Handbook. 3rd rev. ed. Ed. by Betty M. Edgley & George H. Oberle. 334p. 1995. pap. text 31.95 (*0-88725-250-8*) Hunter Textbks.

Physical Education & Health: Selected Works of James H. Humphrey, 2 vols. Ed. by Joy N. Humphrey & James H. Humphrey. LC 86-47843. (Studies in Education: No. 8). 75.00 (*0-404-12669-3*) AMS Pr.

Physical Education & Health: Selected Works of James H. Humphrey, 2 vols., Vol. 1. Ed. by Joy N. Humphrey & James H. Humphrey. LC 86-47843. (Studies in Education: No. 8). 37.50 (*0-404-12670-7*) AMS Pr.

Physical Education & Health: Selected Works of James H. Humphrey, 2 vols., Vol. 2. Ed. by Joy N. Humphrey & James H. Humphrey. LC 86-47843. (Studies in Education: No. 8). 37.50 (*0-404-12671-5*) AMS Pr.

Physical Education & Kinesiology in North America: Professional & Scholarly Foundations. Ed. by Earle F. Zeigler. (Illus.). 415p. (Orig.). (C). 1994. pap. text 23.80 (*0-87563-495-8*) Stipes.

Physical Education & Sport: An Introduction. Ed. by Earle F. Zeigler. LC 81-8287. (Illus.). 317p. reprint ed. pap. 98.30 (*0-608-15992-1*, 205674300084) Bks Demand.

Physical Education & Sport Changes & Challenges. Meyer & Meyer Verlag Staff. pap. 29.00 (*3-89124-320-0*) Meyer & Meyer.

Physical Education & Sport for Exceptional Students. Michael A. Horvat. 336p. (C). 1990. text. write for info. (*0-697-06353-4*) Brown & Benchmark.

Physical Education & Sport in a Changing Society. 5th ed. William H. Freeman. LC 96-20812. 352p. 1996. pap. text 58.00 (*0-205-26392-5*) Allyn.

Physical Education & Sport in a Changing Society. 5th ed. William H. Freeman. 352p. (C). 1996. pap., teacher ed. write for info. (*0-205-26592-8*, T6592-4) Allyn.

*__Physical Education & Sport in a Changing Society.__ 6th ed. William H. Freeman. 384p. 2000. pap. 53.00 (*0-205-32039-2*) Allyn.

Physical Education & Sport Philosophy. Earle F. Zeigler. 1977. text 17.95 (*0-685-03893-9*) P-H.

Physical Education & the Study of Sport. 2nd ed. Bob Davis. 448p. (C). 1994. text 26.95 (*0-7234-1972-8*) Mosby Inc.

Physical Education by Muscular Exercise. Luther H. Gulick. (Physical Education Reprint Ser.). (Illus.). reprint ed. lib. bdg. 37.50 (*0-697-00102-4*) Irvington.

Physical Education Curriculum. 5th ed. Jim L. Stillwell & Carl E. Willgoose. LC 96-27820. 352p. 1996. 69.00 (*0-13-296997-1*) P-H.

Physical Education Curriculum Activities Kit for Grades K-6. Kenneth B. Wheeler & Otto H. Spilker. 256p. (C). 1991. pap. text 28.95 (*0-13-647033-5*) P-H.

Physical Education Curriculum & Culture. David Kirk. 1990. pap. 39.95 (*1-85000-675-X*, Falmer Pr) Taylor & Francis.

Physical Education Curriculum in Second School. Gordon L. Underwood. 1983. 33.00 (*0-685-37921-3*, Falmer Pr); pap. 18.00 (*0-685-37922-1*, Falmer Pr) Taylor & Francis.

Physical Education Facilities for the Public Accredited High Schools of Alabama. Jackson R. Sharman. LC 75-177790. (Columbia University. Teachers College. Contributions to Education Ser.: No. 408). reprint ed. 37.50 (*0-404-55408-3*) AMS Pr.

Physical Education for All: Developing Physical Education in the Curriculum for Pupils with Special Difficulties. Helen Wright. 1999. pap. text 26.95 (*1-85346-490-2*) David Fulton.

Physical Education for Children: A Focus on the Teaching Process. 2nd ed. Bette Logsdon. LC 83-11964. (Illus.). 476p. reprint ed. pap. 147.60 (*0-8357-7648-4*, 205697400096) Bks Demand.

*__Physical Education for Children: Daily Lesson Plans for Elementary School.__ Katherine T. Thomas et al. LC 99-45026. (Illus.). 1192p. 2000. 49.00 (*0-87322-681-X*) Human Kinetics.

*__Physical Education for Children: Daily Lesson Plans for Middle School.__ 2nd ed. Amelia M. Lee et al. LC 99-44613. (Illus.). 368p. 2000. 29.00 (*0-87322-683-6*) Human Kinetics.

Physical Education for Children: Instructor's Manual. Jerry R. Thomas et al. LC 87-37826. (Illus.). 69p. reprint ed. pap., teacher ed. 30.00 (*0-608-20837-X*, 207193600003) Bks Demand.

Physical Education for Elementary School Children. 9th ed. Glenn Kirchner & Graham Fishburne. 640p. (C). 1994. text. write for info. (*0-697-15248-0*) Brown & Benchmark.

Physical Education for Elementary School Children. 10th ed. Glenn Kirchner & Graham Fishburne. LC 97-20122. 672p. (C). 1997. text. write for info. (*0-697-29486-2*) Irvington.

Physical Education for Exceptional Students: Theory to Practice. Douglas C. Wiseman. LC 93-8387. 598p. (C). 1994. pap. 48.00 (*0-8273-5296-4*) Delmar.

Physical Education for Exceptional Students: Theory to Practice. Douglas C. Wiseman. 80p. 1994. teacher ed. 16.95 (*0-8273-5297-2*) Delmar.

Physical Education for Homeschoolers: An Easy to Use, Low Equipment Cost Program for Homeschooling Families. L. S. McClaine. (Illus.). 153p. (Orig.). 1994. pap. text 12.95 (*1-890537-00-4*) Nutmeg Pubns.

Physical Education for Lifelong Fitness: The Physical Best Teacher's Guide. AAHPERD Staff. LC 99-22701. (Physical Best Ser.). (Illus.). 408p. 1999. pap. 39.00 (*0-88011-983-7*) Human Kinetics.

Physical Education for Pre-School & Primary Grades. 2nd ed. Noeline T. Kelly & Brian J. Kelly. LC 96-40932. (Illus.). 256p. 1997. pap. text, spiral bd. 39.95 (*0-398-06739-2*) C C Thomas.

*__Physical Education for the Elementary Classroom Teacher.__ Carol E. Plimpton & Victoria J. Sweeney. (Illus.). 396p. 2000. pap. write for info. (*0-9671766-3-8*) Huron Valley.

Physical Education for the Elementary School. James H. Humphrey. LC 94-2060. (Illus.). 292p. 1994. pap. 35.95 (*0-398-06167-X*) C C Thomas.

Physical Education for the Elementary School. James H. Humphrey. LC 94-2060. (Illus.). 292p. (C). 1994. text 49.95 (*0-398-05906-3*) C C Thomas.

Physical Education for the Handicapped. Ruth H. Wheeler & Agnes M. Hooley. LC 75-22477. (Health Education, Physical Education, & Recreation Ser.). 393p. reprint ed. pap. 121.90 (*0-608-12696-9*, 205600900043) Bks Demand.

Physical Education for the Mentally Retarded. John N. Drowatzky. LC 70-157467. (Health Education, Physical Education, & Recreation Ser.). (Illus.). 201p. reprint ed. pap. 62.40 (*0-608-10889-8*, 205541900022) Bks Demand.

Physical Education for the Middle School. Brian J. Kelly & Noeline T. Kelly. (Illus.). 338p. (C). 1990. pap. text 48.95 (*0-398-05641-2*) C C Thomas.

Physical Education Framework for California Public Schools, K-12. California Department of Education Staff. LC 94-621237. (Illus.). 104p. 1994. pap. 7.75 (*0-8011-1065-3*) Calif Education.

Physical Education Guidebook. Ed. by University of California Regents. (Catch: Go for Health Ser.). (Illus.). 48p. (J). (gr. k-2). 1998. pap., teacher ed. 12.00 (*1-58000-036-3*) Griffin CA.

Physical Education Guidebook. Ed. by University of California Regents. (Catch: Go for Health Ser.). (Illus.). 112p. (J). (gr. 3-5). 1998. pap., teacher ed. 12.00 (*1-58000-038-X*) Griffin CA.

Physical Education Handbook. 9th ed. Neil Schmottlach & Jerre Mcmanama. LC 96-36214. 432p. 1996. pap. text 51.00 (*0-205-26343-7*) Allyn.

P

Physical Education Handbook. 9th ed. Neil Schmottlach & Jerre McManama. 480p. (C). 1997. pap., teacher ed. write for info. (*0-205-26645-2*, T6645-0) Allyn.

Physical Education in Primary Schools: Access for All. Elizabeth Knight & Sue Chedzoy. LC 98-149252. 96p. 1997. pap. 24.95 (*1-85346-491-0*, Pub. by David Fulton) Taylor & Francis.

Physical Education in the Colleges of the United Lutheran Church of America: A Survey & Program. Carl P. Schott. (Columbia University. Teachers College. Contributions to Education Ser.: No. 379). reprint ed. 37.50 (*0-404-55379-6*) AMS Pr.

Physical Education in the Early Years. Pauline Wetton. LC 96-52979. (Teaching & Learning in the First Three Years of School Ser.). 192p. (C). 1997. pap. 18.99 (*0-415-13529-X*) Routledge.

Physical Education Methods for Classroom Teachers. Human Kinetics Staff. LC 98-41469. (Illus.). 360p. 1999. pap. text 25.00 (*0-88011-842-3*, BHKP0842) Human Kinetics.

Physical Education Model Curriculum Standards, Grades 9-12. California Department of Education Staff. (Illus.). 40p. 1991. pap. 6.50 (*0-8011-0845-4*) Calif Education.

Physical Education Sourcebook. Ed. by Betty Hennessy. LC 95-38833. (Illus.). 216p. (Orig.). 1996. pap. text, teacher ed. 24.00 (*0-87322-863-4*, BHEN0863) Human Kinetics.

Physical Education, Sport & Schooling: Studies in the Sociology of Physical Education. John Evans. 260p. 1987. 59.95 (*1-85000-116-2*, Falmer Pr); pap. 34.95 (*1-85000-117-0*, Falmer Pr) Taylor & Francis.

*__Physical Education, Sport & Wellness: As We Look to Ourselves & to God.__ Ed. by Tom Visker. 251p. 1999. pap. 13.25 (*0-932914-43-8*) Dordt Coll Pr.

Physical Education Unit Plans for Grades 1-2. 2nd ed. Bette Logsdon et al. LC 96-38313. (Illus.). 184p. (Orig.). 1997. pap. text 18.00 (*0-87322-782-4*, BLOG0782) Human Kinetics.

Physical Education Unit Plans for Grades 3-4. 2nd ed. Bette Logsdon et al. LC 96-35915. (Illus.). 184p. (Orig.). 1997. pap. text 18.00 (*0-87322-783-2*, BLOG0783) Human Kinetics.

Physical Education Unit Plans for Grades 5-6. 2nd ed. Bette Logsdon et al. LC 96-43908. (Illus.). 184p. (Orig.). 1997. pap. text 18.00 (*0-87322-784-0*, BLOG0784) Human Kinetics.

Physical Education Unit Plans for Preschool-Kindergarten. Bette Logsdon et al. LC 96-38312. (Illus.). 184p. (Orig.). 1997. pap. text 18.00 (*0-87322-781-6*, BLOG0781) Human Kinetics.

Physical Education Unit Plans for Preschool-Kindergarten, for Grades 1-2, for Grades 3-4, for Grades 5-6, 4 vols. Bette J. Logsdon et al. LC 96-38312. (Illus.). 649p. 1997. pap. text 59.00 (*0-88011-697-8*, BLOG0697) Human Kinetics.

Physical Educator's Guide to Portfolios. (Illus.). 40p. (Orig.). 1997. pap. 12.95 (*0-9633582-1-9*) Pacific Sunset.

Physical Effects in the Gravitational Field of Black Holes. Ed. by M. A. Markov. (Proceedings of the Lebedev Physics Institute Ser.: Vol. 169). 262p. (C). 1987. text 175.00 (*0-941743-04-7*) Nova Sci Pubs.

Physical Efficiency of Teachers: An Analytical Study of Some Factors Affecting the Health & Physical Efficiency of Public School Teachers. George E. Carrothers. LC 76-176631. (Columbia University. Teachers College. Contributions to Education Ser.: No. 155). reprint ed. 37.50 (*0-404-55155-6*) AMS Pr.

Physical Electrochemistry: Science & Technology. Ed. by Israel Rubinstein. (Monographs in Electroanalytical Chemistry & Electrochemistry: Vol. 7). (Illus.). 608p. 1995. text 150.00 (*0-8247-9452-4*) Dekker.

Physical Electronics: A Guide to the Study of Paper 344 of the CEI Examinations. Kenneth G. Nichols. LC QC0030.N5. (PPL Study Guide Ser.: No. 4). 52p. reprint ed. pap. 30.00 (*0-608-30914-1*, 201148800080) Bks Demand.

P

Physical Eloquence & the Biology of Writing. Robert S. Ochsner. LC 89-38062. (SUNY Series, Literacy, Culture, & Learning). 223p. 1990. pap. text 21.95 (*0-7914-0314-9*) State U NY Pr.

Physical Endurance: Index of Modern Information. Barry R. Gonsalves. LC 88-47871. 150p. 1988. 47.50 (*0-88164-914-7*); pap. 44.50 (*0-88164-915-5*) ABBE Pubs Assn.

*__Physical Environment: Laboratory Exercises for Geo 111l.__ C. Mark Cowell et al. 116p. (C). 1999. per. 18.95 (*0-7872-6097-5*, 41609701) Kendall-Hunt.

Physical Environment & Behavior: An Annotated Bibliography & Guide to the Literature. J. F. Wohlwill & Gerald D. Weisman. LC 81-4840. 484p. 1981. 95.00 (*0-306-40739-6*, Plenum Trade) Perseus Pubng.

Physical Environment & the Learning Process: A Survey of Recent Research: A Report. Jonathan King et al. LC 79-64605. (Institute for Social Research, Research Report). 91p. reprint ed. pap. 30.00 (*0-7837-5256-3*; 204499300005) Bks Demand.

Physical Environment at Work. Ed. by David J. Oborne & Michael M. Gruneberg. LC 82-23743. (Wiley Series in Psychology & Productivity at Work). 252p. reprint ed. pap. 78.20 (*0-7837-6389-1*, 204610200010) Bks Demand.

Physical Environment of Canada & the Evolution of Settlement Patterns. Robinson. (NFS Canada Ser.). 1993. pap. 8.95 (*0-88922-203-7*) Genl Dist Srvs.

Physical Environment of the Faeroe Islands. G. K. Rutherford. 1982. text 135.00 (*90-6193-099-5*) Kluwer Academic.

Physical Environmental Global Environmental. Olav Slaymaker. (Global Environmental Change Ser.). 1p. (C). 1998. pap. text 22.50 (*0-582-29829-6*, Pub. by Addison-Wesley) Longman.

Physical Evidence. Desmond. LC 99-18914. 1994. pap. 20.00 (*0-226-14376-7*) U Ch Pr.

Physical Evidence. Desmond. LC 99-18914. 1999. 30.00 (*0-226-14375-9*) U Ch Pr.

*__Physical Evidence in Forensic Science.__ Henry C. Lee & Howard A. Harris. 297p. 2000. 70.00 (*1-930056-00-1*, 5564-N); pap. 45.00 (*1-930056-01-X*, 5563-N) Lawyers & Judges.

Physical Exam of the Neurologic System. Mosby Staff. 1995. 595.00 (*0-8151-6135-2*) Mosby Inc.

Physical Examination & Health Assessment. 2nd ed. Carolyn Jarvis. Ed. by Barbara N. Cullen. LC 95-3462. (Illus.). 954p. 1995. text 54.00 (*0-7216-5922-5*, W B Saunders Co) Harcrt Hlth Sci Grp.

Physical Examination & Health Assessment. 2nd ed. Ed. by Carolyn Jarvis. (Illus.). 1996. teacher ed. write for info. (*0-7216-6446-6*, W B Saunders Co) Harcrt Hlth Sci Grp.

Physical Examination & Health Assessment. 2nd ed. Ed. by Carolyn Jarvis. (Illus.). 1996. pap. text, student ed. 17.95 (*0-7216-5986-1*, W B Saunders Co) Harcrt Hlth Sci Grp.

Physical Examination & Health Assessment. 3rd ed. Carolyn Jarvis. LC 99-17267. (Illus.). 955p. 1999. text 57.00 (*0-7216-8424-6*, W B Saunders Co) Harcrt Hlth Sci Grp.

Physical Examination for the Spine & Extremities. Stanley Hoppenfeld. 288p. (C). 1992. pap. 12.15 (*0-8385-7867-5*) Appleton & Lange.

Physical Examination of the Heart & Circulation. 2nd ed. Joseph K. Perloff. (Illus.). 304p. 1989. pap. text 39.00 (*0-7216-7189-6*, W B Saunders Co) Harcrt Hlth Sci Grp.

*__Physical Examination of the Heart & Circulation.__ 3rd ed. Joseph K. Perloff. LC 99-49763. (Illus.). 300p. 2000. pap. text. write for info. (*0-7216-8321-5*, W B Saunders Co) Harcrt Hlth Sci Grp.

*__Physical Examination of the Spine.__ Todd J. Albert & Alexander R. Vaccaro. (Illus.). 232p. 2001. pap. 39.95 (*0-86577-916-3*) Thieme Med Pubs.

Physical Examination of the Spine & Extremities. Stanley Hoppenfeld. (Illus.). 276p. (C). 1976. pap. text 49.95 (*0-8385-7853-5*, A7853-3) Appleton & Lange.

Physical Examinations--Infants to Old Age & Body Parts: Index of New Information. Stanley B. Luray. (Illus.). 163p. 1999. 47.50 (*0-7883-1888-8*); pap. 44.50 (*0-7883-1889-6*) ABBE Pubs Assn.

Physical Exercise, Nutrition & Stress. Mary F. Asterita. LC 85-12261. 216p. 1985. 67.95 (*0-275-90044-4*, C0044, Praeger Pubs) Greenwood.

Physical Factors in Growth & Development: A Manual for Educators, Nurses, & Social Workers. Joseph H. Di Leo. LC 75-106235. (TC Series in Special Education). 64p. reprint ed. pap. 30.00 (*0-608-17725-3*, 203014700067) Bks Demand.

*__Physical Fitness.__ 5th ed. Getchell & Mikesky. LC 97-50489. 300p. 1998. pap. text 24.00 (*0-205-19874-0*) P-H.

Physical Fitness: A Guide for Individuals with Lower Limb Loss. Ernest M. Burgess & Albert Rappoport. (Illus.). 245p. (Orig.). (C). 1993. pap. text 40.00 (*1-56806-432-2*) DIANE Pub.

Physical Fitness: A Guide for Individuals with Spinal Cord Injury. David F. Apple, Jr. (Illus.). 110p. (Orig.). 1996. pap. text 30.00 (*0-7881-3364-0*) DIANE Pub.

Physical Fitness: A Way of Life. 4th ed. Bud Getchell. 258p. (C). 1992. pap., teacher ed. 6.00 (*0-02-341631-9*, U2545-4, Macmillan Coll) P-H.

Physical Fitness: Test Item File. Corbin & Lindsey. 1996. teacher ed. 21.87 (*0-697-31432-4*, WCB McGr Hill) McGrw-H Hghr Educ.

Physical Fitness: The Hub of the Wellness Wheel. 2nd ed. Bradley Cardinal. 256p. (C). 1994. spiral bd. 21.95 (*0-8403-9360-1*) Kendall-Hunt.

Physical Fitness: The Pathway to Healthful Ling. 2nd ed. Robert V. Hockey. LC 72-87646. ix, 194p. 1973. write for info. (*0-8016-2214-X*) Mosby Inc.

Physical Fitness: The Pathway to Healthful Living. Robert V. Hockey. LC 71-112753. x, 173 p. 1970. write for info. (*0-8403-0164-2*) Kendall-Hunt.

Physical Fitness & Athletic Performance: A Guide for Students, Athletes & Coaches. 2nd ed. A. W. Watson. LC 94-44802. 1995. pap. text. write for info. (*0-582-09110-1*, Pub. by Addison-Wesley) Longman.

Physical Fitness & Christian. 2nd ed. Pamela Johnson & L. Delyte Morris. 216p. (C). 1996. pap. text, per. 26.95 (*0-7872-1116-8*) Kendall-Hunt.

Physical Fitness & Nutrition During Growth: Studies in Children & Youth in Different Environments. Ed. by Jana Parizkova & Andrew Hills. LC 98-25054. (Medicine & Sport Science Ser.: Vol. 43, 1998). (Illus.). viii, 1672p. 1998. 169.75 (*3-8055-6679-4*) S Karger.

Physical Fitness & Wellness. 2nd ed. (C). 1998. text. write for info. (*0-205-29682-3*, Longwood Div) Allyn.

Physical Fitness & Wellness. 2nd ed. Greenberg & Dintiman. LC 97-44656. 436p. 1997. pap. text 40.00 (*0-205-27521-4*) P-H.

Physical Fitness Concepts: Toward Active Lifestyles. Charles B. Corbin & Ruth Lindsey. 600p. (C). 1995. text. write for info. (*0-697-27842-5*) Brown & Benchmark.

Physical Fitness for Adults. Bob Sharp & Danielle Kidder. (Illus.). 192p. (Orig.). 1995. pap. 12.95 (*1-886622-01-9*) Bayrock.

Physical Fitness in the Elementary School. Robert P. Pangrazi & Douglas N. Hastad. 110p. (Orig.). 1989. pap. 8.00 (*0-88314-426-3*, A4263) AAHPERD.

Physical Fitness-Sports Medicine Bibliography. 1994. lib. bdg. 260.95 (*0-8490-6431-7*) Gordon Pr.

Physical Fluid Dynamics. 2nd ed. D. J. Tritton. (Illus.). 536p. 1988. pap. text 41.95 (*0-19-854493-6*) OUP.

*__Physical Focus - 8th Grade.__ Kathy Ermler et al. 500p. 1999. 75.00 (*1-930359-05-5*) Mirror KS.

*__Physical Focus - 7th Grade.__ Kathy Ermler et al. 500p. 1999. pap. 75.00 (*1-930359-04-7*) Mirror KS.

*__Physical Focus - 6th Grade.__ Kathy Ermler et al. 500p. 1999. pap. 75.00 (*1-930359-03-9*) Mirror KS.

Physical Forces see Understanding Science & Nature Series

Physical Forces & the Mammalian Cell. John Frangos. (Illus.). 400p. 1993. text 79.00 (*0-12-265330-0*) Acad Pr.

Physical Foundations of Radiology. Paul H. Goodwin & Edith Hinkley. LC 70-106337. 409p. reprint ed. pap. 126.80 (*0-608-30364-X*, 200625200056) Bks Demand.

Physical Foundations of Technical Acoustics. I. Malecki & I. Bellert. LC 64-17267. 1969. 332.00 (*0-08-011097-5*, Pub. by Pergamon Repr) Franklin.

Physical Foundations of the Millimeter & Submillimeter Waves Technique Pt. 1: Open Structures. V. P. Shestopalov. (Illus.). 222p. 1996. 115.00 (*90-6764-215-0*, Pub. by VSP) Coronet Bks.

Physical Foundations of the Millimeter & Submillimeter Waves Technique Vol. 2: Sources, Element Base, Radio Systems - Novel Scientific Trends. V. P. Shestopalov. (Illus.). 254p. 1997. 122.50 (*90-6764-252-5*, Pub. by VSP) Coronet Bks.

Physical Foundations of the Psyche. Charles M. Fair. LC 63-8861. 299p. 1963. reprint ed. pap. 92.70 (*0-608-04799-6*, 205666500080) Bks Demand.

Physical Functions of Hydrocolloids: A Collection of Papers of the Symposium, Atlantic City, NJ, 1956. American Chemical Society, Physical Functions of H. LC 62-3026. (American Chemical Society Advances in Chemistry Ser.: No. 25). 107p. reprint ed. pap. 33.20 (*0-608-30689-4*, 205018400080) Bks Demand.

Physical Fundamentals of Remote Sensing. E. Schanda. 200p. 1986. 48.95 (*0-387-16236-4*) Spr-Verlag.

Physical Geodesy. Weikko A. Heiskanen & Helmut Moritz. LC 66-24950. (Series of Books in Geology). 376p. reprint ed. pap. 116.60 (*0-608-30923-0*, 205554600028) Bks Demand.

Physical Geography. Michael Bradshaw & Ruth Weaver. 640p. (C). 1992. text. write for info. (*0-697-24085-1*, WCB McGr Hill) McGrw-H Hghr Educ.

Physical Geography. Michael Bradshaw et al. 176p. (C). 1993. text, student ed. 21.87 (*0-697-25081-4*, WCB McGr Hill) McGrw-H Hghr Educ.

Physical Geography. Conte. 1997. pap. text, student ed. 14.00 (*0-697-38532-9*) McGraw.

Physical Geography. Greer. 576p. 1996. pap. 36.75 (*0-8016-6806-9*) Mosby Inc.

Physical Geography. Haiman. Date not set. pap. text, lab manual ed. 15.75 (*0-314-54035-0*) West Pub.

Physical Geography. F. Ted Wieden. 96p. (C). 1995. spiral bd. 15.75 (*0-7872-1019-6*) Kendall-Hunt.

Physical Geography. F. Ted Wieden. 88p. (C). 1997. spiral bd. 18.95 (*0-7872-4556-9*) Kendall-Hunt.

Physical Geography. 2nd ed. (C). 1988. 16.60 (*0-8087-9089-7*) Pearson Custom.

Physical Geography. 5th ed. Hess. 1996. pap. text, student ed. 30.60 (*0-13-443375-0*) P-H.

Physical Geography. 5th ed. Michael P. McIntyre et al. LC 90-49420. 536p. 1991. pap. 78.95 (*0-471-62017-3*) Wiley.

Physical Geography. 6th ed. Hess. (C). 1998. pap. text, student ed. write for info. (*0-13-095523-X*) P-H.

Physical Geography. 6th ed. Hess. 236p. (C). 1998. pap. text, lab manual ed. 33.00 (*0-13-095521-3*, Pub. by P-H) S&S Trade.

Physical Geography: A Laboratory Manual. 4th ed. John J. Hidore & Michael C. Roberts. 251p. (C). 1990. pap. text, lab manual ed. 46.00 (*0-02-354511-9*, Macmillan Coll) P-H.

Physical Geography: A Landscape Appreciation. 6th ed. Tom L. McKnight. LC 98-16286. 624p. (C). 1998. text 66.00 (*0-13-950445-1*) P-H.

*__Physical Geography: A Landscape Appreciation (virtual Fieldtrip Edition)__ 6th ed. Tom McKnight & Darrel Hess. 604p. (C). 1999. text 78.00 incl. audio compact disk (*0-13-020263-0*) P-H.

Physical Geography: Its Nature & Methods. Roy H. Haines-Young & James R. Petch. 248p. (C). 1986. pap. 50.00 (*0-06-318327-7*, Pub. by P Chapman) St Mut.

*__Physical Geography: Laboratory Manual.__ Darrell Roberts. 92p. (C). 1999. spiral bd., lab manual ed. 18.95 (*0-7872-6484-9*, 41648401) Kendall-Hunt.

Physical Geography: Science & Systems of the Human Environment. Strahler. 437p. 1997. pap., student ed. 31.95 (*0-471-18216-8*) Wiley.

Physical Geography: Science & Systems of the Human Environment. Alan H. Strahler & Arthur N. Strahler. LC 96-18934. 656p. 1996. text 84.95 (*0-471-11299-2*) Wiley.

Physical Geography & People. Peter Webber & Neil Punnett. (Places & Cases Ser.). (Illus.). 96p. (YA). (gr. 9-11). 1999. pap. 17.95 (*0-7487-4303-0*, Pub. by S Thornes Pubs) Trans-Atl Phila.

Physical Geography in Diagrams. 4th ed. Bunnett. Date not set. pap. text. write for info. (*0-582-22507-8*, Pub. by Addison-Wesley) Longman.

Physical Geography Lab Manual. 4th ed. Karen Eichstadt. 104p. (C). 1998. spiral bd., lab manual ed. 26.95 (*0-7872-5368-5*, 41536801) Kendall-Hunt.

Physical Geography Lab Manual. 5th ed. Erhart & Fraser. 120p. (C). 1998. spiral bd., lab manual ed. 23.95 (*0-7872-5326-X*) Kendall-Hunt.

*__Physical Geography Lab Manual.__ 5th ed. University of Idaho Staff. 116p. (C). 2000. spiral bd. 26.95 (*0-7872-7343-0*) Kendall-Hunt.

Physical Geography Lab Manual: Exercises in Atmospheric. 2nd ed. David Shankman. 208p. (C). 1998. spiral bd. 33.95 (*0-7872-4899-1*, 41489901) Kendall-Hunt.

Physical Geography Laboratory Manual. David Shankman. 176p. (C). 1997. pap. text, spiral bd. 30.39 (*0-8403-9733-X*) Kendall-Hunt.

Physical Geography Laboratory Manual. 3rd ed. University of Idaho Staff. 96p. (C). 1996. pap. text, spiral bd. 20.95 (*0-7872-2701-3*) Kendall-Hunt.

Physical Geography Manual. 4th ed. John Corbet. 425p. 1998. 36.95 (*0-7872-4908-4*, 41490801) Kendall-Hunt.

Physical Geography of Africa. Ed. by William Adams et al. (Regional Environments Ser.). (Illus.). 452p. 1999. pap. text 35.00 (*0-19-823406-6*) OUP.

Physical Geography of Africa. Antony R. Orme. Ed. by William M. Adams & Andrew S. Goudie. LC 96-232432. (Illus.). 452p. (C). 1996. text 85.00 (*0-19-828875-1*) OUP.

Physical Geography of Asiatic Russia. Sergefi P. Suslov. Ed. by Joseph E. Wiliams. Tr. by Noah D. Gershevsky. LC 61-5762. 608p. reprint ed. pap. 188.50 (*0-608-14001-5*, 205554300028) Bks Demand.

Physical Geography of China. Ed. by Sonegiao Zhao. LC 85-15574. 200p. (C). 1986. text 67.95 (*0-471-09597-4*) Wiley.

Physical Geography of New York State. Ralph S. Tarr. 397p. 1993. reprint ed. lib. bdg. 89.00 (*0-7812-5152-4*) Rprt Serv.

Physical Geography of the Global Environment. 2nd ed. H. J. De Bli. 664p. 1997. pap. text 77.95 (*0-471-24779-0*) Wiley.

Physical Geography of the Global Environment. 2nd ed. Peter O. Muller & Harm J. De Blij. 368p. 1995. pap., student ed. 31.95 (*0-471-11636-X*) Wiley.

Physical Geography of the Global Environment & Goode World Atlas. 2nd ed. Deblij. 599p. 1995. pap. text 62.00 (*0-471-13434-1*) Wiley.

Physical Geography of the Holy Land. Edward Robinson. (Notable American Authors Ser.). 1999. reprint ed. lib. bdg. 125.00 (*0-7812-8795-2*) Rprt Serv.

Physical Geography of the Mississippi Valley. Charles Ellet. (Notable American Authors Ser.). 1992. reprint ed. lib. bdg. 75.00 (*0-7812-2793-3*) Rprt Serv.

Physical Geography of Western Tibet. H. Strachey. (C). 1995. reprint ed. 10.00 (*81-206-1044-X*, Pub. by Asian Educ Servs) S Asia.

Physical Geography Science & Systems of the Human Enviroment & Visualization CD-ROM. Alan Strahler & Arthur Strahler. 656p. 1997. text 102.95 (*0-471-25246-8*) Wiley.

Physical Geography Science & Systems of the Human Environment & Goode's World Atlas to Accompany Geography: Realms Regions & Concepts, & Visualization CD-ROM. Arthur Strahler. 1028p. 1997. 130.95 incl. cd-rom (*0-471-29002-5*) Wiley.

Physical Geography Study Guide. 3rd ed. Gregory Lee & Darren Leaver. 176p. 1996. pap. text, per. 21.95 (*0-7872-2777-3*, 41277701) Kendall-Hunt.

Physical Geography Study Tips. Scotts. 1996. pap. 12.00 (*0-314-08919-5*) West Pub.

Physical Geography Today. Ed. by Oberlander. (C). 1998. pap., lab manual ed. write for info. (*0-321-40138-7*) Addison-Wesley.

Physical Geography Today. Ed. by Theodore M. Oberlander. (C). 1998. text. write for info. (*0-321-01204-6*); pap. text, student ed. write for info. (*0-321-01205-4*) Addson-Wesley Educ.

Physical Geography Today. 3rd ed. Robert A. Muller & Theodore M. Oberlander. 591p. (C). 1984. 84.38 (*0-07-554435-0*) McGraw.

Physical Geology. (C). 1988. lab manual ed. 8.80 (*0-8087-5218-9*) Pearson Custom.

Physical Geology. American Geological Institute Staff et al. 560p. 1995. pap. 38.95 (*0-8016-7872-2*) Mosby Inc.

Physical Geology. Bloss. 1999. 33.74 (*0-697-21689-6*) McGraw.

Physical Geology. F. Donald Bloss. (Illus.). 640p. 1991. 37.95 (*0-8016-0787-6*) Mosby Inc.

*__Physical Geology.__ Bucke. (Earth Science Ser.). 2002. 47.00 (*0-534-53685-9*) Wadsworth Pub.

Physical Geology. David P. Bucke. 208p. (C). 1995. student ed. write for info. (*0-697-14381-3*, WCB McGr Hill); pap. write for info. (*0-697-17426-3*, WCB McGr Hill); student ed., spiral bd. write for info. (*0-697-25681-2*, WCB McGr Hill) McGrw-H Hghr Educ.

Physical Geology. John J. Chiment. (C). 2000. pap. text. write for info. (*0-8053-4424-1*) Addison-Wesley.

Physical Geology. Anatole Dolgoff. (C). 1996. text, teacher ed. 2.66 (*0-669-33912-1*); pap. text 56.36 (*0-669-41685-1*) HM Trade Div.

Physical Geology. Anatole Dolgoff. (C). 1996. pap. text, student ed. 23.56 (*0-669-33911-3*) HM Trade Div.

Physical Geology. George Gorshkov & Alexandra Yakushova. (Illus.). 596p. (C). 1975. 29.95 (*0-8464-0718-3*) Beekman Pubs.

Physical Geology. Vicki Harder. (C). 1995. text. write for info. (*0-697-24472-5*, WCB McGr Hill); text, student ed. write for info. (*0-697-23726-5*, WCB McGr Hill) McGrw-H Hghr Educ.

Physical Geology. Jones Staff. 1995. teacher ed., lab manual ed. 13.75 (*0-697-21725-6*, WCB McGr Hill) McGrw-H Hghr Educ.

Physical Geology. Lemon. 608p. 1995. 37.95 (*0-8016-2571-8*) Mosby Inc.

Physical Geology. Ludman. 1992. lab manual ed. 67.50 (*0-697-14708-8*, WCB McGr Hill) McGrw-H Hghr Educ.

Physical Geology. Ludman. 1993. teacher ed., lab manual ed. 20.00 (*0-697-14707-X*, WCB McGr Hill) McGrw-H Hghr Educ.

An Asterisk (*) at the beginning of an entry indicates that the title is appearing for the first time.

*Physical Geology. Dorobek Mazzullo. (Earth Science Ser.). 2002. 55.00 (0-534-37731-9) Brooks-Cole.
*Physical Geology. Murphy/Nance. 2000. pap. 54.00 (0-534-37866-8) Thomson Learn.
Physical Geology. Stephen C. Porter & Brian J. Skinner. LC 86-32533. 750p. 1987. text 93.95 (0-471-05668-5) Wiley.
Physical Geology. John Renton. Date not set. pap. text, teacher ed. write for info. (0-314-03403-X) West Pub.
Physical Geology. Ross. (Earth Science Ser.). 2002. pap., lab manual ed. 29.00 (0-534-55666-3) Wadsworth Pub.
Physical Geology. Jack Rudman. (ACT Proficiency Examination Program Ser.: No. PEP-56). 1994. 39.95 (0-8373-5931-7) Nat Learn.
Physical Geology. Jack Rudman. (ACT Proficiency Examination Program Ser.: PEP-56). 1994. pap. 23.95 (0-8373-5906-6) Nat Learn.
Physical Geology. Edgar W. Spencer. (Biology Ser.). (Illus.). 656p. (C). 1983. text. write for info. (0-201-06423-5); student ed. write for info. (0-318-56791-1) Addison-Wesley.
Physical Geology. 2nd ed. Norris W. Jones. 320p. (C). 1997. text, lab manual ed. write for info. (0-697-37451-3, WCB McGr Hill) McGrw-H Hghr Educ.
*Physical Geology. 2nd ed. Sheldon Judson. 250p. 1999. spiral bd., lab manual ed. 34.67 (0-13-624586-2) P-H.
Physical Geology. 2nd ed. Turk. (C). 1991. pap. text, teacher ed. 34.00 (0-03-025399-3) Harcourt Coll Pubs.
*Physical Geology. 3rd ed. Norris W. Jones. 320p. (C). 2000. pap., lab manual ed. 45.31 (0-07-366192-9) McGrw-H Hghr Educ.
Physical Geology. 3rd ed. Mcgeary. 1997. 47.50 (0-697-38185-4, WCB McGr Hill) McGrw-H Hghr Educ.
Physical Geology. 3rd ed. James S. Monroe. 1998. student ed. 17.25 (0-534-53776-6) Brooks-Cole.
Physical Geology. 3rd ed. Montgomery. 1992. teacher ed. 13.43 (0-697-12329-4) McGraw.
Physical Geology. 3rd ed. Carla W. Montgomery & Kenneth F. Griffin. 192p. (C). 1992. text, student ed. 23.75 (0-697-12330-8, WCB McGr Hill) McGrw-H Hghr Educ.
Physical Geology. 4th ed. James S. Monroe. (Earth Science Ser.). 2000. 49.50 (0-534-57222-7) Wadsworth Pub.
Physical Geology. 4th ed. James S. Monroe & Reed Wicander. (Earth Science Ser.). 2000. student ed. 19.95 (0-534-37520-0) Thomson Learn.
Physical Geology. 5th ed. American Geological Institute Staff. 285p. 1999. pap. text, lab manual ed. 48.00 incl. audio compact disk (0-13-011630-0) P-H.
Physical Geology. 6th ed. Charles C. Plummer & David McGeary. 560p. (C). 1993. text 56.55 (0-697-13806-2, WCB McGr Hill); text. write for info. (0-697-13807-0, WCB McGr Hill) McGrw-H Hghr Educ.
Physical Geology. 6th ed. Charles C. Plummer & David McGeary. 560p. (C). 1994. text, student ed. 21.87 (0-697-13811-9, WCB McGr Hill) McGrw-H Hghr Educ.
Physical Geology. 7th ed. Plummer. 1995. 58.00 (0-697-32865-1, WCB McGr Hill) McGrw-H Hghr Educ.
Physical Geology. 7th ed. Plummer-Mcgeary. 1995. 318.75 (0-697-26679-6, WCB McGr Hill) McGrw-H Hghr Educ.
Physical Geology. 7th ed. Plummer-Mcgeary. 1996. lab manual ed. 8.75 (0-697-31280-1, WCB McGr Hill) McGrw-H Hghr Educ.
Physical Geology. 9th ed. Zumberge. 1995. lab manual ed. 13.75 (0-697-13831-3, WCB McGr Hill) McGrw-H Hghr Educ.
Physical Geology. 9th ed. Zumberge. 1995. lab manual ed. 11.25 (0-697-13830-5, WCB McGr Hill) McGrw-H Hghr Educ.
Physical Geology. 10th ed. Zumberge. 288p. 1998. spiral bd., lab manual ed. 47.19 (0-697-34407-X) McGraw.
*Physical Geology. 10th ed. James H. Zumberge et al. 288p. (C). 2000. spiral bd., lab manual ed. 47.19 (0-07-366179-1) McGrw-H Hghr Educ.
Physical Geology. 21st ed. James S. Monroe. (Earth Science Ser.). 1994. write for info. (0-314-05663-7) Wadsworth Pub.
Physical Geology: Earth Revealed. 2nd ed. David McGeary & Charles C. Plummer. 540p. (C). 1994. text 40.00 (0-697-24675-2, WCB McGr Hill) McGrw-H Hghr Educ.
Physical Geology: Earth Revealed. 3rd ed. David McGeary & Charles C. Plummer. LC 97-11483. 560p. (C). 1997. per. write for info. (0-697-37649-4, WCB McGr Hill) McGrw-H Hghr Educ.
*Physical Geology: Earth Revealed. 4th ed. David McGeary et al. LC 00-33937. 2001. write for info. (0-07-366183-X) McGraw.
Physical Geology: Exploring the Earth. James S. Monroe & Reed Wicander. Ed. by Westby. 639p. (C). 1992. text 58.75 (0-314-92195-8) West Pub.
Physical Geology: Exploring the Earth. 2nd ed. James S. Monroe. (Earth Science Ser.). 1995. pap., student ed. 18.00 (0-314-05444-8) Wadsworth Pub.
Physical Geology: Exploring the Earth. 2nd ed. Reed Wicander & James S. Monroe. LC 94-26808. 672p. (C). 1995. pap. 48.00 (0-314-04273-3) West Pub.
Physical Geology: Exploring the Earth. 3rd ed. James S. Monroe & Reed Wicander. LC 97-30966. (C). 1997. pap. 51.95 (0-534-53775-8) Wadsworth Pub.
Physical Geology: Exploring the Earth with InfoTrac. 3rd ed. James S. Monroe. (Earth Science Ser.). 1997. 49.50 (0-534-53782-0) Wadsworth Pub.
*Physical Geology: International Version. 4th ed. James S. Monroe & Reed Wicander. 2000. pap. 55.00 (0-534-37788-2) Thomson Learn.
Physical Geology: Principles & Perspectives. A. Lee McAlester & Edward A. Hay. (Illus.). 448p. 1975. 26.95 (0-685-03894-7) P-H.
Physical Geology: Test Index File. 7th ed. Plummer & McGeary. 1995. teacher ed. 18.75 (0-697-26677-X, WCB McGr Hill) McGrw-H Hghr Educ.
Physical Geology: Testbank. John Renton. Date not set. pap. text, suppl. ed. write for info. (0-314-03228-2) West Pub.
Physical Geology Booknews. 10th ed. Zumberge. 1998. pap. 7.95 (0-07-039632-9) McGraw.
Physical Geology Customs. 2nd ed. Robinson. 1999. pap. 12.80 (0-07-235581-6) McGraw.
Physical Geology Experiments. 2nd ed. (C). 1983. write for info. (0-8087-3015-0) Pearson Custom.
Physical Geology Laboratory Course. 2nd ed. C. M. Gilbert & M. N. Christensen. (C). 1967. text 47.00 (0-07-023206-7) McGraw.
Physical Geology Laboratory Manual. Linda Hanson. 65p. (C). 1993. student ed. 16.43 (1-56870-055-5) RonJon Pub.
Physical Geology Laboratory Manual. Ruth Kalamarides. 176p. (C). 1994. pap. text, spiral bd. 17.95 (0-8403-9781-X, 40978101) Kendall-Hunt.
Physical Geology Laboratory Manual. Karen Woods. 128p. (C). 1994. pap. text, spiral bd. 31.95 (0-8403-9401-2) Kendall-Hunt.
Physical Geology Laboratory Manual. 2nd ed. Karen Woods. 156p. (C). 1997. spiral bd., lab manual ed. 34.95 (0-7872-3655-1, 41365501) Kendall-Hunt.
Physical Geology Northridge Ea. 6th ed. Plummer-Mcgeary. 1994. 50.00 (0-697-25607-3, WCB McGr Hill) McGrw-H Hghr Educ.
Physical Geology Quick Review. Mark J. Crawford. LC 98-216148. (Cliffs Quick Reviews Ser.). (Illus.). 242p. 1998. pap. text 9.95 (0-8220-5335-7, Cliff) IDG Bks.
Physical Geology Study Guide. Lemon. 192p. 1994. pap. 16.95 (0-8016-2556-4) Mosby Inc.
Physical Geology, Study Guide. Stephen C. Porter & Brian J. Skinner. 236p. 1987. pap., student ed. 43.95 (0-471-62946-4) Wiley.
Physical Geology Study Guide. Steven G. Spear. 1995. ring bd. 10.00 (0-88252-173-X) Paladin Hse.
Physical Geology with Interactive Plate Tectonics. 7th ed. David McGeary & Charles C. Plummer. 560p. (C). 1995. pap., per. write for info. incl. cd-rom (0-697-26676-1, WCB McGr Hill); text, student ed. write for info. (0-697-28732-7, WCB McGr Hill) McGrw-H Hghr Educ.
Physical Geology with Interactive Plate Tectonics. 7th ed. David McGeary & Charles C. Plummer. 240p. (C). 1995. text, student ed. 21.87 (0-697-26678-8, WCB McGr Hill) McGrw-H Hghr Educ.
Physical Geology with Interactive Plate Tectonics. 7th ed. Robert H. Rutford & Charles C. Plummer. 224p. (C). 1996. text, lab manual ed. write for info. (0-697-29324-6, WCB McGr Hill) McGrw-H Hghr Educ.
Physical Golf: The Golfer's Guide to Peak Conditioning & Performance. Neil Wolkodoff. LC 97-73250. (Illus.). 296p. 1997. pap. 29.95 (0-9657863-0-7) KickPoint.
Physical Growth of Children: An Appraisal of Studies. Wilton M. Krogman. (SRCD M Ser.: Vol. 20, No. 1). 1955. pap. 25.00 (0-527-01563-6) Periodicals Srv.
Physical Growth of White Children. H. V. Meredith. (SRCD M Ser.: Vol. 1, No. 2). 1936. pap. 25.00 (0-527-01487-7) Periodicals Srv.
*Physical Hazards of the Workplace. Larry R. Collins. (Occupational Safety & Health Guide Ser.). 290p. 1999. 59.95 (1-56670-339-5) Lewis Pubs.
*Physical Hydrodynamics. Etienne Guyon et al. (Illus.). 448p. 2000. text 100.00 (0-19-851746-7); pap. text 50.00 (0-19-851745-9) OUP.
Physical Hydrology. Lawrence Dingman. LC 93-3301. 575p. (C). 1993. text 98.00 incl. disk (0-02-329745-X, Macmillan Coll) P-H.
Physical Immortality. Leonard D. Orr. (YA). (gr. 7 up). 1988. pap. 11.00 (0-945793-01-4) Inspir Univ.
Physical Immortality for Christians. Leonard D. Orr. (YA). (gr. 7 up). 1986. 22.00 (0-945793-03-0) Inspir Univ.
*Physical Inorganic Chemistry. S. F. A. Kettle. (Illus.). 496p. 2000. pap. text 45.00 (0-19-850404-7) OUP.
Physical Inorganic Chemistry, Vol. 1. Kettle. Date not set. write for info. (0-7167-4554-2) W H Freeman.
Physical Inorganic Chemistry: A Coordination Chemistry Approach. S. F. Kettle. LC 95-44747. (Illus.). 512p. (C). 1998. text 82.00 (0-19-850405-5) OUP.
Physical Inorganic Chemistry: A Coordination Chemistry Approach. Sidney F. Kettle. LC 95-44747. (C). 1996. pap. text. write for info. (0-7167-4514-3) W H Freeman.
*Physical Introduction to Fluid Mechanics. Alexander J. Smits. LC 99-16027. 544p. 1999. text 104.95 (0-471-25349-9) Wiley.
Physical Kinetics & Transfer Processes in Phase Transitions. N. V. Pavlyukevich et al. 177p. 1996. 75.00 (1-56700-044-4) Begell Hse.
Physical Knowledge in Preschool Education: Implications of Piaget's Theory. rev. ed. Constance Kamii & Rheta DeVries. (Early Childhood Education Ser.). (Illus.). 336p. (C). 1993. reprint ed. pap. text 19.95 (0-8077-3254-0) Tchrs Coll.
Physical Level Interfaces & Protocols. 2nd ed. Ulysses D. Black. LC 94-47597. 232p. 1995. 58.00 (0-8186-5697-2, BP05697) IEEE Comp Soc.
Physical Limitations to Photovoltaic Energy Conversion. Ed. by Antonio Luque & G. L. Araujo. (Illus.). 192p. 1990. 105.00 (0-7503-0030-2) IOP Pub.
Physical Logistics Management. Grant M. Davis & John E. Dillard, Jr. LC 83-10300. (Illus.). 566p. (C). 1983. lib. bdg. 74.50 (0-8191-3342-6) U Pr of Amer.
Physical Management for the Quadriplegic Patient. 2nd ed. Jack R. Ford & Bridget Duckworth. LC 87-479. (Illus.). 661p. 1987. text 59.00 (0-8036-3676-8) Davis Co.
Physical Management of Students Who Have Sustained a Traumatic Brain Injury: Guidelines & Strategies for School Personnel. Kathleen Q. Specht. 57p. (Orig.). 1996. teacher ed., spiral bd. 16.50 (1-882855-45-0) HDI Pubs.
Physical Manifestations & Philosophy of Christ. deluxe ed. Thomson J. Hudson. 1978. reprint ed. pap. 4.50 (0-87852-003-1) Inst Human Growth.
Physical Mathematics & Nonlinear Partial Differential Equations. Lightbourne & Rankin. (Lecture Notes in Pure & Applied Mathematics Ser.: Vol. 102). (Illus.). 280p. 1985. pap. text 135.00 (0-8247-7343-8) Dekker.
Physical Measurements & Signatures in Remote Sensing. Ed. by Gerard Guyot. (Remote Sensing Reviews Ser.). 342p. 1997. pap. text 174.00 (90-5702-118-8, Harwood Acad Pubs) Gordon & Breach.
Physical Measurements & Signatures in Remote Sensing: Proceedings of the 7th International Symposium, Courchevel, France, 7-11 April, 1997. Ed. by Gerard Guyot & Thierry Phulpin. (Illus.). 902p. (C). 1998. text 146.00 (90-5410-917-3, Pub. by A A Balkema) Ashgate Pub Co.
Physical Measurements in Gas Dynamics & Combustion. Ed. by R. W. Ladenburg et al. LC 54-13127. 606p. reprint ed. pap. 187.90 (0-608-10245-8, 200009700025) Bks Demand.
Physical Mechanisms in Radiation Biology: Proceedings. AEC Technical Information Center Staff. Ed. by Robert W. Wood & Raymond D. Cooper. LC 74-600124. 333p. 1974. pap. 16.25 (0-685-01481-9, CONF-721001); fiche 9.00 (0-87079-303-9, CONF-721001) DOE.
Physical Medicine & Rehabilitation. Randall L. Braddom. LC 95-11493. 1168p. 1995. text 180.00 (0-7216-5243-3, W B Saunders Co) Harcrt Hlth Sci Grp.
Physical Medicine & Rehabilitation. 2nd ed. Randall L. Braddom. 1275p. Date not set. text. write for info. (0-7216-8076-3, W B Saunders Co) Harcrt Hlth Sci Grp.
Physical Medicine & Rehabilitation Secrets. Ed. by Mark Young & Bryan O'Young. LC 96-32242. (Secrets Ser.). (Illus.). 650p. (Orig.). 1996. pap. text 39.00 (1-56053-155-X) Hanley & Belfus.
*Physical Medicine Rehabilitation: The Complete Approach. Martin Grabois et al. LC 98-17785. (Illus.). 1999. 199.00 (0-86542-536-1) Blackwell Sci.
Physical Mesomechanics of Heterogeneous Media & Computer-Aided Design of Materials. Ed. by V. E. Panin. 450p. 1995. boxed set 130.00 (1-898326-19-3, Pub. by CISP) Balogh.
Physical Metallurgy. Bruce Chalmers. LC 59-14983. (Wiley Series on the Science & Technology of Materials). 468p. reprint ed. pap. 145.10 (0-608-11262-3, 205514000008) Bks Demand.
Physical Metallurgy. 3rd ed. Paul Haasen. (Illus.). 436p. 1996. text 140.00 (0-521-55092-0) Cambridge U Pr.
Physical Metallurgy. 3rd ed. Paul Haasen. (Illus.). 436p. (C). 1996. pap. text 49.95 (0-521-55925-1) Cambridge U Pr.
Physical Metallurgy of Cast Iron V. Ed. by G. Lesoult & J. Lacaze. LC 99-515148. (Advanced Materials Research Ser.: Vols. 4-5). (Illus.). 600p. (C). 1998. text 215.00 (3-908450-28-4, Pub. by Scitec Pubns) Enfield Pubs NH.
Physical Metallurgy of Cast Iron IV. Eisuke Niyama. Ed. by Goro Ohira et al. (Conference Proceedings Ser.: Vol. PMC4). 1990. text 17.50 (1-55899-090-9) Materials Res.
Physical Metallurgy of Controlled Expansion Invar-Type Alloys: Proceedings of an International Conference Sponsored by the TMS Ferrous Metallurgy Committee & Held at the TMS Annual Meeting, February 27-March 3, 1989, Las Vegas NV. Minerals, Metals & Materials Society Staff. Ed. by Kenneth C. Russell & Darrell F. Smith. LC 89-61033. (Illus.). 331p. 1990. reprint ed. pap. 102.70 (0-608-00877-X, 206167100010) Bks Demand.
Physical Metallurgy of Direct-Quenched Steels: Proceedings of a Symposium Sponsored by the Ferrous Metallurgy Committee of TMS & the Phase Transformations Committee of ASM International, Held at Materials Week '92 in Chicago, IL, November 2-4, 1992. Minerals, Metals & Materials Society Staff. Ed. by K. A. Taylor et al. LC 93-79177. (Illus.). 479p. 1993. reprint ed. pap. 148.50 (0-608-05686-3, 206620100007) Bks Demand.
Physical Metallurgy of Metal Joining: Proceedings of a Symposium. Metallurgical Society of AIME Staff. Ed. by Ram Kossowsky & M. E. Glicksman. LC 80-82303. 278p. reprint ed. pap. 86.20 (0-608-12290-4, 202377200034) Bks Demand.
Physical Metallurgy of Microalloyed Steels. T. Gladman. (Illus.). 376p. 1997. pap. text 80.00 (0-901716-81-2, Pub. by Inst Materials) Ashgate Pub Co.
Physical Metallurgy of Platinum Metals. Evgeny M. Savitsky et al. 1979. 183.00 (0-08-023259-0, Pub. by Pergamon Repr) Franklin.
Physical Metallurgy of Steels. William C. Leslie. (Illus.). 408p. (C). 1991. reprint ed. 88.00 (1-878907-25-5) TechBooks.
Physical Metallurgy of Stress Corrosion Fracture. Ed. by Thor N. Rhodin. LC 59-14890. (Metallurgical Society Conference Ser.: Vol. 4). 409p. reprint ed. pap. 126.80 (0-608-11559-2, 200066700038) Bks Demand.
Physical Metallurgy of Thermomechanical Treatment of Structural Steels. K. Mazanec & E. Mazancova. 130p. 1996. pap. 70.00 (1-898326-43-6, Pub. by CISP) Balogh.
Physical Metallurgy of Zinc Coated Steel: Proceedings of an International Conference Sponsored by the Ferrous Metallurgy Committee of TMS/AIME Held at the TMS Annual Meeting in San Francisco, CA, February 27-March 3, 1994. Minerals, Metals & Materials Society Staff. Ed. by A. R. Marder. LC 93-80903. (Illus.). 343p. 1993. reprint ed. pap. 106.40 (0-608-05691-X, 206620600007) Bks Demand.
Physical Metallurgy Principles. 3rd ed. Robert E. Reed-Hill & Reza Abbaschian. (C). 1991. 82.00 (0-534-92173-6) PWS Pubs.
Physical Metallurgy 4th Revised & Enhanced Edition, 3 vols. 4th rev. ed. Ed. by Robert W. Cahn & Peter Haasen. 2888p. 1996. 883.50 (0-444-89875-1, North Holland) Elsevier.
Physical Meteorology. Herny G. Houghton. (Illus.). 450p. 1985. 47.50 (0-262-08146-6) MIT Pr.
Physical Methods for Fossil Fuels Characterization, Coal Gasification, Pyrolysis & Biomass: Presented at Miami Beach, FL, April 28-May 3, 1985, Vol. 7. American Chemical Society, Division of Fuel Chemis. LC TP0321.. (American Chemical Society Division of Fuel Chemistry, Preprints of Papers Ser.: Vol. 30, No. 1). 435p. reprint ed. pap. 134.90 (0-608-13336-1, 202556400044) Bks Demand.
Physical Methods for Inorganic Biochemistry, Vol. 5. John R. Wright et al. (Biochemistry of the Elements Ser.). (Illus.). 400p. (C). 1986. text 150.00 (0-306-42049-X, Kluwer Plenum) Kluwer Academic.
Physical Methods for Materials Characterisation. P. E. Flewitt & R. K. Wild. (Graduate Student Series in Materials Science & Engineering). (Illus.). 518p. 1994. 185.00 (0-7503-0203-8); pap. 64.00 (0-7503-0320-4) IOP Pub.
Physical Methods for Microorganisms Detection. Wilfred H. Nelson. 176p. 1991. lib. bdg. 149.00 (0-8493-4140-X, QR69) CRC Pr.
Physical Methods in Bioinorganic Chemistry: Spectroscopy & Magnetism. Ed. by Lawrence Que, Jr. LC 99-51651. (Illus.). 504p. (C). 2000. text 72.00 (1-891389-02-5) Univ Sci Bks.
Physical Methods in Chemistry. Ed. by V. A. Afanasiev & G. E. Zaikov. 182p. 1993. text 165.00 (1-56072-063-8) Nova Sci Pubs.
Physical Methods in Macromolecular Chemistry, 1. Ed. by Benjamin Carroll. LC 69-12679. 397p. 1969. reprint ed. pap. 123.10 (0-608-08305-4, 202710400001) Bks Demand.
Physical Methods in Macromolecular Chemistry, 2. Ed. by Benjamin Carroll. LC 69-12679. 381p. 1972. reprint ed. pap. 118.20 (0-608-08306-2, 202710400002) Bks Demand.
Physical Methods in Plant Sciences. Ed. by H. F. Linskens & J. F. Jackson. (Modern Methods of Plant Analysis Ser.: Vol. 11). (Illus.). 320p. 1990. 206.95 (0-387-50332-3) Spr-Verlag.
Physical Methods of Chemistry, 3 vols., Vol. 1. 2nd ed. Bryant W. Rossiter & John F. Hamilton. LC 85-6386. (Techniques of Chemistry Ser.). 834p. 1986. 315.00 (0-471-08034-9) Wiley.
Physical Methods of Chemistry, 3 vols., Vol. 2. 2nd ed. Bryant W. Rossiter & John F. Hamilton. LC 85-6386. (Techniques of Chemistry Ser.). 928p. 1986. 315.00 (0-471-08027-6) Wiley.
Physical Methods of Chemistry, 3 vols., Vol. 3, Pt. B, Determination of Chemical Compositi. 2nd ed. Bryant W. Rossiter & John F. Hamilton. (Techniques of Chemistry Ser.). 992p. 1989. 299.00 (0-471-85051-9) Wiley.
Physical Methods of Chemistry, 12 vols., Vol. 12. 2nd ed. Ed. by Bryant W. Rossiter & Roger C. Baetzold. 7840p. 1993. 2875.00 (0-471-02577-1) Wiley.
Physical Methods of Chemistry: Determination of Thermodynamic Properties, Vol. 6. 2nd ed. Ed. by Bryant W. Rossiter & John F. Hamilton. LC 85-6386. 760p. 1992. 375.00 (0-471-57087-7) Wiley.
Physical Methods of Chemistry: Investigations of Surfaces & Interfaces, Vol. 9, Pt. A, Investigations of Surfaces and Inte. 2nd ed. Ed. by Bryant W. Rossiter & Roger C. Baetzold. LC 91-39605. 528p. 1992. 230.00 (0-471-54406-X) Wiley.
Physical Methods of Chemistry: Investigations of Surfaces & Interfaces, Vol. 9, Pt. B, Investigations of Surfaces and Inte. 2nd ed. Bryant W. Rossiter & Roger C. Baetzold. LC 92-24513. 768p. 1993. 379.00 (0-471-54405-1) Wiley.
Physical Methods of Chemistry: Supplement & Cumulative Index, Vol. 10. 2nd ed. Ed. by Roger C. Baetzold. LC 92-24512. 416p. 1993. 299.00 (0-471-57086-9) Wiley.
Physical Methods of Chemistry Pt. A: Part A: Determination of Chemical Composition & Molecular Structure, Vol. 3, Pt. A, Determination of Chemical Compositi. 2nd ed. Ed. by Bryant W. Rossiter & John F. Hamilton. 624p. 1987. 299.00 (0-471-85041-1) Wiley.
Physical Methods of Chemistry Vol. 4: Microscopy, Vol. 4. 2nd ed. Ed. by Bryant W. Rossiter & John F. Hamilton. LC 90-24799. 560p. 1991. 299.00 (0-471-08026-8) Wiley.
Physical Methods of Chemistry Vol. 5: Determination of Structural Features of Crystalline & Amorphous Solids, Vol. 5. 2nd ed. Ed. by Bryant W. Rossiter & John F. Hamilton. LC 85-6386. 618p. 1990. 299.00 (0-471-52509-X) Wiley.
Physical Methods of Chemistry Vol. 7: Determination of Elastic & Mechanical Properties, Vol. 7, Determination of Elastic and Mechanical Pr. 2nd ed. Ed. by Bryant W. Rossiter et al. LC 90-13009. 313p. 1991. 189.00 (0-471-53438-2) Wiley.
Physical Methods of Chemistry, 2E, Vol. 8, Determination of Electronic & Optical Properties, Vol. 8, Determination of Electronic and Optical Pr. 2nd ed. Ed. by Bryant W. Rossiter & Roger C. Baetzold. LC 92-24323. 544p. 1993. 215.00 (0-471-54407-8) Wiley.

An Asterisk (*) at the beginning of an entry indicates that the title is appearing for the first time.

Physical Methods of Investigating Textiles. Ed. by R. Meredith & John W. Hearle. LC 59-13795. (Illus.). 441p. reprint ed. pap. 136.80 (*0-608-11497-9*, 201195500080) Bks Demand.

Physical Methods to Characterize Pharmaceutical Proteins. Ed. by James N. Herron et al. LC 95-37641. (Pharmaceutical Biotechnology Ser.: Vol. 7). (Illus.). 380p. (C). 1995. text 89.50 (*0-306-45026-7*, Kluwer Plenum) Kluwer Academic.

***Physical Milestones for One-Year-Old.** Ed. by Parents Magazine Staff. (I Can Do It Ser.). (Illus.). 24p. (J). 2000. pap. 9.95 (*0-312-25360-5*, St Martin Griffin) St Martin.

***Physical Milestones for 1 Year Olds.** (I Can Do It Ser.). 2000. text 9.95 (*0-307-44033-8*) Gldn Bks Pub Co.

***Physical Milestones for the First 12 Months.** Golden Books Staff. (I Can Do It Ser.). 2000. text 9.95 (*0-307-44032-X*) Gldn Bks Pub Co.

***Physical Milestones for the First 12 Months.** Ed. by Parents Magazine Staff. (I Can Do It Ser.). (Illus.). 24p. 2000. pap. 9.95 (*0-312-25359-1*) St Martin.

Physical Milestones for Three & Four Years Olds. Golden Books Staff. (I Can Do It Ser.). 24p. 2000. text 9.95 (*0-307-44035-4*) Gldn Bks Pub Co.

***Physical Milestones for Three & Four-Year-Old.** Ed. by Parents Magazine Staff. (I Can Do It Ser.). (Illus.). 24p. (J). 2000. pap. 9.95 (*0-312-25363-X*, St Martin Griffin) St Martin.

***Physical Milestones for Two-Year-Old.** Ed. by Parents Magazine Staff. (I Can Do It Ser.). (Illus.). 24p. (J). 2000. pap. 9.95 (*0-312-25362-1*, St Martin Griffin) St Martin.

Physical Milestones for Two-Year-Olds. (I Can Do It Ser.). 2000. text 9.95 (*0-307-44034-6*) Gldn Bks Pub Co.

Physical Modalities: A Primer for Chiropractic. Paul D. Hooper. (Illus.). 329p. 1996. 52.00 (*0-683-04143-6*) Lppncott W & W.

Physical Modeling of Metalworking Processes: Proceedings of a Symposium Sponsored by the TMS-AIME Shaping & Forming Committee, Held at the TMS Annual Meeting in Denver, Colorado, February 24-27, 1987. Metallurgical Society of AIME Staff. Ed. by S. L. Semiatin & E. Erman. LC 87-73245. 271p. reprint ed. pap. 84.10 (*0-7837-1452-1*, 205242800018) Bks Demand.

Physical Modelling in Coastal Engineering: Proceedings of an International Conference, Newark, Delaware, August 1981. Ed. by R. A. Dalrymple. 320p. (C). 1984. text 123.00 (*90-6191-516-3*, Pub. by A A Balkema) Ashgate Pub Co.

Physical Models & Equilibrium Methods in Programming & Economics. B. S. Razumikhin. (Mathematics & Its Applications, Soviet Ser.). 372p. 1984. text 200.00 (*90-277-1644-7*) Kluwer Academic.

Physical Models & Laboratory Techniques in Coastal Engineering. Steven A. Hughes. (Advanced Series in Ocean Engineering). 550p. 1993. text 97.00 (*981-02-1540-1*); pap. text 48.00 (*981-02-1541-X*) World Scientific Pub.

Physical Models of Neural Workshops. Ed. by T. Geszti. 152p. (C). 1990. text 48.00 (*981-02-0012-9*) World Scientific Pub.

Physical Models of Semiconductor Quantum Devices. Ying Fu & M. Willander. LC 99-11907. (Electronic Materials Ser.). 1999. write for info. (*0-7923-8457-1*) Kluwer Academic.

Physical Nature of the Skin. Ed. by R. M. Marks et al. (C). 1988. text 144.00 (*0-85200-977-1*) Kluwer Academic.

Physical Nonequilibrium in Soils: Modeling & Application. Ed. by H. Magdi Selim & Liwang Ma. LC 97-48516. (Illus.). 492p. (C). 1998. lib. bdg. 79.95 (*1-57504-049-2*) CRC Pr.

Physical Oceanographic Processes of the Great Barrier Reef. Erick Wolanski. LC 93-31280. (Marine Science Ser.). 208p. 1994. boxed set 104.95 (*0-8493-8047-2*, GC862) CRC Pr.

Physical Oceanography, 2 vols. A. Defant. 1961. 584.00 (*0-08-009453-8*, Pub. by Pergamon Repr) Franklin.

Physical Oceanography of Coastal & Shelf Seas. Ed. by B. Johns. 470p. 1983. 219.75 (*0-444-42153-X*, I-419-83) Elsevier.

Physical Oceanography of Coastal Waters. K. F. Bowden. 302p. 1984. text 94.95 (*0-470-27505-7*) P-H.

Physical Oceanography of Sea Straits. Ed. by L. J. Pratt. (C). 1990. text 299.50 (*0-7923-0905-7*) Kluwer Academic.

Physical Optics. S. A. Akhmanov & S. Y. Nikitin. LC 96-48892. (Illus.). 502p. 1997. text 115.00 (*0-19-851795-5*) OUP.

Physical Optics. Alan R. Mickelson. (Illus.). 320p. 1992. text 64.95 (*0-442-00614-4*, VNR) Wiley.

Physical Optics. 3rd ed. Robert W. Wood. 1989. reprint ed. pap. 41.25 (*1-55752-063-1*) Optical Soc.

Physical Optics of Dynamic Phenomena & Processes in Macromolecular Systems: Proceedings of the 27th Microsymposium on Macromolecules, Prague, Czechoslovakia, July 16-19, 1984. Ed. by Blahoslav Sedlacek. (Illus.). xv, 555p. 1985. 161.55 (*3-11-010234-X*) De Gruyter.

Physical Organic Chemistry. Ed. by M. J. Dewar et al. (Topics in Current Chemistry Ser.: Vol. 146). (Illus.). 270p. 1988. 128.95 (*0-387-18541-0*) Spr-Verlag.

Physical Organic Chemistry. 2nd ed. Neil S. Isaacs. LC 94-32137. (C). 1995. pap. text 67.50 (*0-582-21863-2*, Pub. by Addison-Wesley) Longman.

Physical Organic Chemistry: The Fundamental Concepts. 2nd expanded rev. ed. C. A. Ritchie. (Illus.). 376p. 1989. text 59.75 (*0-8247-8307-7*, 8307-7) Dekker.

Physical Organic Chemistry Through Solved Problems. Joseph B. Lambert. 1978. pap. text 26.95 (*0-8162-4921-0*) Holden-Day.

Physical Origin of Homochirality in Life. Ed. by David B. Cline. (AIP Conference Proceedings Ser.: No. 379). 283p. 1996. 125.00 (*1-56396-507-0*, AIP Pr) Spr-Verlag.

Physical Paradoxes & Sophisms. V. N. Lange. 232p. (C). 1987. 25.00 (*0-7855-4969-2*, Pub. by Collets) St Mut.

Physical Pharmacy. 4th ed. Alfred Martin et al. (Illus.). 622p. 1993. text 59.50 (*0-8121-1438-8*) Lppncott W & W.

Physical Pharmacy: Text & Solutions Manual Set. 4th ed. Alfred Martin. 1993. write for info. (*0-8121-1688-7*) Lppncott W & W.

Physical Pharmacy (book) Amiji. 2001. write for info. (*0-07-135076-4*) McGraw.

Physical Pharmacy (set 2) Amiji. 2001. 59.00 (*0-07-135075-6*) McGraw.

***Physical Phenomena at High Magnetic Fields.** Zachary Fisk. LC 99-37082. 800p. 1999. 128.00 (*981-02-3656-5*) World Scientific Pub.

Physical Phenomena at High Magnetic Fields: Proceedings. Efstratios Manousakis. (C). 1991. 64.00 (*0-201-57869-7*) Addison-Wesley.

Physical Phenomena at High Magnetic Fields II: Tallahassee, FL, U. S. A. May 1995. Ed. by Zachary Fisk et al. LC 96-11990. 850p. 1996. text 148.00 (*981-02-2463-X*, Pc-P2934) World Scientific Pub.

Physical Phenomena in Granular Materials, Vol. 195. Ed. by G. D. Cody et al. (Symposium Proceedings Ser.). 679p. 1990. text 17.50 (*1-55899-084-4*) Materials Res.

Physical Phenomena of Spiritualism Fraudulent & Genuine (1920) Hereward Carrington. 462p. 1998. reprint ed. pap. 29.95 (*0-7661-0512-1*) Kessinger Pub.

Physical Planning & Environmental Policy in the Netherlands: A Guide to English-Language Publications. Barrie Needham. LC 92-5721. (CPL Bibliographies Ser.: No. 280). (Illus.). 1992. 10.00 (*0-86602-280-5*, Sage Prdcls Pr) Sage.

Physical Planning Prospects in Israel During 50 Years of Statehood. Elisha Efrat. (Mobility & Norm Change Ser.: Vol. 1). (Illus.). 175p. 1998. 52.00 (*3-931397-17-3*) Galda & Wilch.

Physical Plant Operations Handbook. K. L. Petrocelly. (Illus.). 216p. 1991. 69.00 (*0-88173-054-8*, 0180) Fairmont Pr.

Physical Principles Chemical Engineering, 1. Peter Grassman. 1989. write for info. (*0-89116-800-1*) CRC Pr.

Physical Principles Chemical Engineering, 2. Peter Grassman. 1989. write for info. (*0-89116-801-X*) CRC Pr.

Physical Principles in Chemoreception. F. W. Wiegel. Ed. by S. A. Levin. (Lecture Notes in Biomathematics Ser.: Vol. 91). ix, 185p. 1991. 31.95 (*0-387-54319-8*) Spr-Verlag.

***Physical Principles in the Theory of Economic Growth.** Vladimir N. Pokrovski. 176p. 1999. text 61.95 (*0-7546-1118-3*, Pub. by Ashgate Pub) Ashgate Pub Co.

Physical Principles of Chemical Engineering. Grassman. Date not set. write for info. (*0-8493-9352-3*) CRC Pr.

Physical Principles of Computed Tomography. William R. Hendee. 1983. 37.50 (*0-316-35594-1*, Little Brwn Med Div) Lppncott W & W.

Physical Principles of Infrared Irradiation of Foodstuffs: Revised, Augmented & Updated Edition. rev. ed. S. G. Il'yasov & V. V. Krasnikov. 416p. 1990. 176.00 (*0-89116-958-X*) Hemisp Pub.

Physical Principles of Magneto-Optical Recording. Masud Mansuripur. LC 93-48553. (Illus.). 776p. (C). 1995. text 115.00 (*0-521-46124-3*) Cambridge U Pr.

Physical Principles of Magneto-Optical Recording. Masud Mansuripur. (Illus.). 776p. (C). 1998. pap. text 54.95 (*0-521-63418-0*) Cambridge U Pr.

Physical Principles of Medical Imaging. 2nd ed. Perry Sprawls, Jr. LC 95-14209. 656p. 1995. 69.95 (*0-944838-54-5*) Med Physics Pub.

Physical Principles of Sedimentology. Kenneth J. Hsu. (Illus.). 210p. 1989. 40.95 (*0-387-51268-3*) Spr-Verlag.

Physical Principles of Semiconductor Devices. Harry E. Talley & Don G. Daugherty. LC 75-45182. 383p. reprint ed. pap. 118.80 (*0-608-15517-9*, 202969700063) Bks Demand.

Physical Principles of STM & AFM Operation. G. Doyen & D. Drakova. (Illus.). 250p. 1996. 80.00 (*3-05-501616-5*, Pub. by Akademie Verlag) Wiley.

***Physical Principles of STM & AFM Operation.** Gerold Doyen. 350p. 2000. 124.95 (*3-527-40037-0*) Wiley.

Physical Principles of the Plant Biosystem. George E. Merva. LC 95-79226. (Illus.). 272p. 1995. text 54.00 (*0-614-10659-1*, MO895) Am Soc Ag Eng.

Physical Principles of the Quantum Theory. Werner Heisenberg. 184p. 1930. pap. text 7.95 (*0-486-60113-7*) Dover.

Physical Problems in Microelectronics: Proceedings of the 5th International School. Ed. by J. Kassabov. 556p. (C). 1987. text 156.00 (*9971-5-0380-8*) World Scientific Pub.

Physical Problems in Microelectronics: Proceedings of the 6th International School. Ed. by J. Kassabov. 542p. (C). 1989. text 130.00 (*9971-5-0976-8*) World Scientific Pub.

Physical Problems of Microelectronics: Proceedings of the 4th International School, Varna, Bulgaria, May 20-26, 1985. J. Kassabov. 650p. 1986. text 124.00 (*9971-5-0017-5*) World Scientific Pub.

Physical Process in Inorganic Scintillators. Piotr A. Rodnyi. LC 96-29773. 240p. 1997. boxed set 149.95 (*0-8493-3788-7*) CRC Pr.

Physical Processes & Chemical Reactions in Liquid Flows. Ed. by F. S. Rys & A. Gyr. LC 99-496414. (IAHR Monograph Ser.). (Illus.). 244p. (C). 1998. text 95.00 (*90-5410-700-6*, Pub. by A A Balkema) Ashgate Pub Co.

Physical Processes & Methods of Analysis see Photoelectronic Imaging Devices

Physical Processes in Astrophysics: Proceedings of a Meeting in Honour of Evry Schatzman Held in Paris, France, 22-24 September 1993, Vol. XII. Ed. by Ian W. Roxburgh et al. LC 95-37623. (Lecture Notes in Physics Ser.: Vol. 458). 249p. 1995. 80.95 (*3-540-60259-3*) Spr-Verlag.

Physical Processes in Comets, Star & Active Galaxies. Ed. by W. Hillebrandt et al. (Illus.). 200p. 1987. 56.95 (*0-387-17766-3*) Spr-Verlag.

Physical Processes in Fragmentation & Star Formation. Ed. by Roberto Capuzzo-Dolcetta et al. (C). 1990. text 236.50 (*0-7923-0769-0*) Kluwer Academic.

Physical Processes in Hot Cosmic Plasmas. Ed. by Wolfgang Brinkmann et al. (C). 1990. text 226.50 (*0-7923-0665-1*) Kluwer Academic.

Physical Processes in Interstellar Clouds. Ed. by G. E. Moffill & M. Scholer. (C). 1987. text 256.00 (*90-277-2563-2*) Kluwer Academic.

Physical Processes in Lakes & Oceans. Ed. by Jorg Imberger. LC 98-41142. (Coastal & Estuarine Ser.: Vol. 54). 662p. 1998. 65.00 (*0-87590-268-5*) Am Geophysical.

Physical Processes in Lasers. Ed. by D. V. Skobel'tsyn. Tr. by James S. Wood from RUS. LC 72-94826. (Proceedings of the P. N. Lebedev Physics Institute Ser.: No. 56). (Illus.). 191p. 1973. reprint ed. pap. 59.30 (*0-608-05516-6*, 206598400006) Bks Demand.

Physical Processes in Low-Temperature Gas-Dynamic Lasers. Ed. by V. K. Konyukhov. (Proceedings of the Institute of General Physics of the Academy of Sciences of the U. S. S. R. Ser.: Vol. 12). (Illus.). 225p. (C). 1991. text 165.00 (*0-941743-90-X*) Nova Sci Pubs.

Physical Processes in Red Giants. Alvio Renzini. Ed. by Icko Iben, Jr. xviii, 488p. 1981. text 176.50 (*90-277-1284-0*) Kluwer Academic.

Physical Processes in Solar Flares. Boris V. Somov. (C). 1992. text 175.00 (*0-7923-1261-9*) Kluwer Academic.

Physical Processes in the Coastal Zone: Computer Modelling & Remote Sensing. A. Cracknell. (Scottish Universities Summer School in Physics Ser.: No. 49). 389p. 1998. 240.00 (*0-7503-0563-0*) IOP Pub.

Physical Processes in the Interstellar Medium. Lyman Spitzer. 318p. 1998. pap. 44.95 (*0-471-29335-0*) Wiley.

Physical Processes of Lake Biwa, Japan. Ed. by Setsuo Okuda et al. LC 95-1870. (Coastal & Estuarine Studies: Vol. 48). 216p. 1995. 45.00 (*0-87590-262-6*) Am Geophysical.

Physical Processes of the Interaction of Fusion Plasma with Solids. Ed. by Wolfgang O. Hofer & Joachim Roth. LC 95-30892. (Plasma-Materials Interaction Ser.). (Illus.). 389p. 1996. text 120.00 (*0-12-351530-0*) Acad Pr.

Physical Properites of High Temperature Superconductors V. Ed. by Donald M. Ginsberg. 600p. 1996. text 98.00 (*981-02-2464-8*, Pc-PB2935) World Scientific Pub.

Physical Properties see Apollo Eleven Lunar Science Conference, Jan., 1970: Proceedings

Physical Properties & Thermodynamic Behaviour of Minerals. Ed. by Ekhard K. Salje. (C). 1988. text 315.50 (*90-277-2656-6*) Kluwer Academic.

Physical Properties of Amorphous Materials. Ed. by David A Adler et al. (Illus.). 456p. (C). 1985. text 132.00 (*0-306-41907-6*, Kluwer Plenum) Kluwer Academic.

Physical Properties of Asphalt Cement Binders. Ed. by John C. Hardin. LC 95-20815. (STP Ser.: Vol. 1241). 231p. 1995. 59.00 (*0-8031-1988-7*, STP1241) ASTM.

Physical Properties of Biological Membranes & Their Functional Implications. C. Hidalgo. LC 87-36111. (Centro de Estudios Cientificos de Santiago Ser.). (Illus.). 248p. (C). 1988. text 89.50 (*0-306-42748-6*, Kluwer Plenum) Kluwer Academic.

Physical Properties of Chemical Compounds, 3 vols. Incl. Vol. 1. Ed. by Robert R. Dreisbach. LC 55-2887. 536p. 1955. incl. fiche (*0-8412-0016-5*); Vol. 2. Robert R. Dreisbach. LC 55-2887. 491p. 1959. 41.95 (*0-8412-0023-8*); Vol. 3. Robert R. Dreisbach. LC 55-2887. 489p. 1961. 49.95 (*0-8412-0030-0*); LC 55-2887. (Advances in Chemistry Ser.: Nos. 15, 22, 29). write for info. (*0-318-50481-2*) Am Chemical.

Physical Properties of Chemical Compounds - II: A Systematic Tabular Presentation of Accurate Data on the Physical Properties of 476 Organic Straight-Chain Compounds. Robert R. Dreisbach. LC QD0001.A355. (Advances in Chemistry Ser.: No. 22). 495p. 1959. reprint ed. pap. 153.50 (*0-608-03268-9*, 206378700007) Bks Demand.

Physical Properties of Chemical Compounds - III. Robert R. Dreisbach. LC QD0001.A355. (Advances in Chemistry Ser.: No. 29). 495p. 1961. reprint ed. pap. 153.50 (*0-608-03270-0*, 206378900007) Bks Demand.

Physical Properties of Crystals: Their Representation by Tensors & Matrices. J. F. Nye. (Illus.). 352p. 1985. pap. text 45.00 (*0-19-851165-5*) OUP.

***Physical Properties of Fats, Oils & Emulsifiers.** Neil Widlak. LC 00-21575. 272p. 2000. 115.00 (*0-935315-95-0*) Am Oil Chemists.

Physical Properties of Food & Agricultural Materials: A Teaching Manual. Nuri N. Mohsenin. x, 147p. (C). 1989. text 102.00 (*0-677-05630-3*) Gordon & Breach.

Physical Properties of Foods & Food Processing Systems. Michael J. Lewis. 465p. 1987. reprint ed. pap. text 74.95 (*1-85573-272-6*) Technomic.

Physical Properties of High Temperature Superconductors. Ed. by Yu I. Koptev. 235p. 1993. lib. bdg. 175.00 (*1-56072-099-9*) Nova Sci Pubs.

Physical Properties of High Temperature Superconductors, No. II. Ed. by Donald M. Ginsberg. 712p. (C). 1990. text 99.00 (*981-02-0124-9*); pap. text 48.00 (*981-02-0190-7*) World Scientific Pub.

Physical Properties of High Temperature Superconductors, Vol. 4. 584p. 1994. text 44.00 (*981-02-1638-6*) World Scientific Pub.

Physical Properties of High Temperature Superconductors I. Ed. by Donald M. Ginsberg. 528p. (C). 1989. text 106.00 (*9971-5-0683-1*); pap. text 55.00 (*9971-5-0894-X*) World Scientific Pub.

Physical Properties of High Temperature Superconductors III. Donald M. Ginsberg. 500p. 1992. text 109.00 (*981-02-0874-X*); pap. text 53.00 (*981-02-0875-8*) World Scientific Pub.

Physical Properties of High Temperature Superconductors IV. Donald M. Ginsberg. 584p. 1994. text 121.00 (*981-02-1637-8*) World Scientific Pub.

Physical Properties of Hydrocarbons, Vol. 1. Robert W. Gallant. LC 68-9302. (Illus.). 231p. 1984. reprint ed. pap. 71.70 (*0-608-15547-0*, 205221900062) Bks Demand.

Physical Properties of Hydrocarbons, Vol. 1. 2nd ed. Robert W. Gallant & Carl L. Yaws. LC 83-22604. (Library of Physico-Chemical Property Data). 257p. 1992. 85.00 (*0-88415-067-4*, 5067) Gulf Pub.

Physical Properties of Hydrocarbons, Vol. 2. 2nd fac. ed. Robert W. Gallant & Jay M. Railey. LC 83-22604. (Illus.). 219p. 1984. reprint ed. pap. 67.90 (*0-608-01023-5*, 206188100002) Bks Demand.

Physical Properties of Hydrocarbons, Vol. 2. 3rd ed. Robert W. Gallant & Carl L. Yaws. LC 92-45600. (Library of Physico-Chemical Property Data). 240p. 1993. 85.00 (*0-88415-175-1*, 5175) Gulf Pub.

Physical Properties of Liquid Crystalline Materials. W. H. De Jeu. x, 134p. 1980. text 209.00 (*0-677-04040-7*) Gordon & Breach.

Physical Properties of Liquid Crystals. Dietrich Demus. LC 99-202912. 524p. 1999. 135.00 (*3-527-29747-2*) Wiley.

Physical Properties of Materials for Engineers. D. Pollock. LC 81-839. 1982. 127.00 (*0-8493-6200-8*, CRC Reprint) Franklin.

Physical Properties of Materials for Engineers. 2nd ed. 608p. 1993. boxed set 115.95 (*0-8493-4237-6*, QC176) CRC Pr.

Physical Properties of Materials for Engineers, Vol. I. Ed. by Daniel D. Pollock. 224p. 1981. 144.00 (*0-8493-6201-6*, QC176) CRC Pr.

Physical Properties of Materials for Engineers, Vol. II. Ed. by Daniel D. Pollock. 208p. 1981. 118.00 (*0-8493-6202-4*, QC176, CRC Reprint) Franklin.

Physical Properties of Materials for Engineers, Vol. III. Ed. by Daniel D. Pollock. 312p. 1982. 119.00 (*0-8493-6203-2*, QC176) CRC Pr.

Physical Properties of Plant & Animal Materials. Nuri N. Mohsenin. 758p. 1970. 150.00 (*0-677-02300-6*) Gordon & Breach.

Physical Properties of Plant & Animal Materials. 2nd ed. Nuri N. Mohsenin. xviii, 892p. 1986. text 283.00 (*0-677-21370-0*) Gordon & Breach.

Physical Properties of Polymeric Gels. Ed. by J. P. Cohen-Addad. 324p. 1996. 235.00 (*0-471-93971-4*) Wiley.

Physical Properties of Polymers. (Advances in Polymer Science Ser.: Vol. 120). 242p. 1995. 180.95 (*3-540-58704-7*) Spr-Verlag.

Physical Properties of Polymers. 2nd ed. James E. Mark et al. LC 92-35330. (Illus.). 300p. 1993. text 75.00 (*0-8412-2505-2*, Pub. by Am Chemical) OUP.

Physical Properties of Polymers. 2nd ed. James E. Mark et al. LC 92-35330. (Illus.). 409p. 1993. pap. 44.95 (*0-8412-2506-0*) Am Chemical.

Physical Properties of Polymers: Prediction & Control. A. A. Askadskii. (Polymer Science & Engineering Monographs). 208p. 1996. text 51.00 (*2-88449-155-4*); pap. text 27.00 (*2-88449-220-8*) Gordon & Breach.

Physical Properties of Polymers Handbook. Ed. by James E. Mark. (Polymers & Complex Materials Ser.). (Illus.). 744p. 1996. text 120.00 (*1-56396-295-0*) Spr-Verlag.

Physical Properties of Polymers Handbook. Ed. by James E. Mark. 1996. text 189.00 (*1-56396-599-2*) Spr-Verlag.

***Physical Properties of Quasicrystals.** Zbigniew Stadnik. LC 98-45459. (Solid-State Sciences Ser.). 438p. 1998. 134.00 (*3-540-65188-8*) Spr-Verlag.

Physical Properties of Rocks. J. H. Schon. (Handbook of Geophysical Exploration Ser.). (Illus.). 592p. 1995. write for info. (*0-08-041008-1*, Pergamon Pr) Elsevier.

Physical Properties of Rocks see Geophysics & Space Research: Group V

Physical Properties of Rocks & Minerals. Ed. by Y. S. Touloukian et al. (CINDAS Data Series on Material Properties: Vol. II-2). 548p. 1981. reprint ed. 154.00 (*0-89116-883-4*) Hemisp Pub.

Physical Properties of Textile Fibres. W. E. Morton. 660p. 1975. 125.00 (*0-7855-7212-0*) St Mut.

Physical Properties of Textile Fibres. 3rd ed. W. E. Morton & John W. Hearle. 1997. 250.00 (*1-870812-41-7*, Pub. by Textile Inst) St Mut.

Physical Properties of III-V Semiconductor Compounds: InP, InAs, GaAs, GaP, InGaAs, & InGaAsP. Sadao Adachi. LC 92-7286. 336p. 1992. 140.00 (*0-471-57329-9*) Wiley.

Physical Properties of Tissue: A Comprehensive Reference Work. Francis A. Duck. (Illus.). 336p. 1990. text 94.00 (*0-12-222800-6*) Acad Pr.

Physical Properties of Wool Fibres & Fabrics. Ed. by Wira Staff. 1955. 75.00 (*0-7855-1015-X*) St Mut.

Physical Property Data for the Design Engineer. Ed. by C. F. Beaton & Geoffrey F. Hewitt. 500p. 1988. 94.95 (*0-89116-739-0*) Hemisp Pub.

***Physical Protection Documents Published by the NRC.** B. T. Miller. 61p. 1998. pap. 5.00 (*0-16-063008-8*) USGPO.

P

An Asterisk (*) at the beginning of an entry indicates that the title is appearing for the first time.

Physical Protection of Nuclear Materials: Experience in Regulation & Implementation. IAEA Staff. LC 98-475000. 527p. 1998. 155.00 (*92-0-101398-1*, STI/PUB/1037, Pub. by IAEA) Bernan Associates.

Physical Quantities & the Units of the International System (SI) Kuzman Raznjevic. 252p. 1996. 65.00 (*1-56700-047-9*) Begell Hse.

Physical Readiness Training. 1991. lib. bdg. 79.95 (*0-8490-4085-X*) Gordon Pr.

Physical Reality & Mathematical Description: Dedicated to Josef Maria Jauch on the Occasion of His Sixtieth Birthday. Ed. by Charles P. Enz & Jagdish Mehra. LC 74-81937. xxiii, 552p. 1974. lib. bdg. 171.00 (*90-277-0513-5*) Kluwer Academic.

Physical Rehabilitation: Assessment & Treatment. 4th ed. Susan B. O'Sullivan & Thomas J. Schmitz. (Illus.). 1296p. 2000. text 65.00 (*0-8036-0533-1*) Davis Co.

Physical Rehabilitation Laboratory Manual: Focus on Functional Training. Susan B. O'Sullivan & Thomas J. Schmitz. LC 98-205026. (Illus.). 388p. 1998. pap. 24.95 (*0-8036-0257-X*) Davis Co.

Physical Rehabilitation of the Injured Athlete. 2nd ed. James R. Andrews & Gary L. Harrelson. Ed. by Richard Lampert. LC 97-9769. (Illus.). 608p. 1997. text 75.00 (*0-7216-6549-7*, W B Saunders Co) Harcrt Hlth Sci Grp.

Physical Religion. Friedrich M. Mueller. LC 73-18811. (Gifford Lectures: 1890). reprint ed. 44.50 (*0-404-11451-2*) AMS Pr.

Physical Requirement Guidelines for Sensory Evaluation Laboratories. Ed. by Jean Eggert & Katherine Zook. LC 86-14150. (Special Technical Publication Ser.: No. 913). (Illus.). 55p. 1986. pap. 19.00 (*0-8031-0479-0*, 04-913001-36); ring bd. 25.00 (*0-8031-0924-5*, STP913) ASTM.

Physical Resource Inventory of the Communal Lands of Zimbabwe: An Overview. I. Anderson et al. (Illus.). 186p. 1993. pap. 60.00 (*0-85954-340-4*, Pub. by Nat Res Inst) St Mut.

Physical Review. Patricia B. Whitten. LC 91-12966. 50p. 1991. pap. 7.95 (*0-89924-039-9*) Lynx Hse.

Physical Review: The First Hundred Years - Version 2.0. H. Henry Stroke. LC 94-49713. 1266p. 1999. 100.00 incl. cd-rom (*1-56396-188-1*) Am Inst Physics.

Physical Science see Ideas & Investigations in Science: Earth Science

Physical Science. Frederick J. Bueche. LC 73-182927. (Illus.). 1972. text 54.95 (*0-87901-019-3*) Worth.

Physical Science. Louis Krause. 134p. 12.00 (*1-886855-37-4*, PHCS 108) Tavenner Pub.

Physical Science. Jack Rudman. (Dantes Subject Standardized Tests (DANTES) Ser.: Vol. 30). 43.95 (*0-8373-6530-9*) Nat Learn.

Physical Science. Jack Rudman. (Dantes Subject Standardized Tests Ser.: DANTES-30). 1994. pap. 23.95 (*0-8373-6630-5*) Nat Learn.

Physical Science. Myrl Shireman. (Illus.). 80p. (YA). (gr. 5-8). 1997. pap. text 9.95 (*1-58037-023-3*, Pub. by M Twain Media) Carson-Dellos.

*__Physical Science.__ Time-Life Books Editors. Ed. by Jean Crawford & Karin Kinney. LC 99-57136. (Student Library: Vol. 10). 128p. (J). (gr. 3). 2000. write for info. (*0-7835-1359-3*) Time-Life.

Physical Science. Frank White. 96p. teacher ed. 11.99 (*0-86653-725-2*, GA1444) Good Apple.

Physical Science. 2nd ed. Jerry S. Faughn. LC 94-66359. (C). 1995. pap. text 76.00 (*0-03-001112-4*, Pub. by Harcourt Coll Pubs); pap. text, teacher ed. 28.00 (*0-03-001113-2*); pap. text, student ed. 28.00 (*0-03-001114-0*, Pub. by Harcourt Coll Pubs) Harcourt.

Physical Science. 2nd ed. Jerry S. Faughn. (C). 1995. 276.50 (*0-03-001247-3*, Pub. by Harcourt Coll Pubs) Harcourt.

Physical Science. 2nd ed. Bill W. Tillery. 624p. (C). 1992. text. write for info. (*0-697-17218-X*) Brown & Benchmark.

Physical Science. 2nd ed. Bill W. Tillery. 624p. (C). 1992. text. write for info. (*0-697-17219-8*) Brown & Benchmark.

Physical Science. 2nd ed. Bill W. Tillery. 624p. (C). 1992. text. write for info. (*0-697-17216-3*) Brown & Benchmark.

Physical Science. 2nd ed. George A. Williams et al. Ed. by Irwin Siegelman. (Challenges to Science Ser.). (YA). (gr. 9-12). 1978. text 32.24 (*0-07-070415-5*) McGraw.

Physical Science. 3rd ed. Tillery. 1995. 43.75 (*0-697-23131-3*, WCB McGr Hill) McGrw-H Hghr Educ.

Physical Science. 3rd ed. Tillery. 1995. teacher ed., lab manual ed. 36.00 (*0-697-23129-1*, WCB McGr Hill) McGrw-H Hghr Educ.

Physical Science. 3rd ed. Tillery. 1995. teacher ed. 31.25 (*0-697-23127-5*, WCB McGr Hill) McGrw-H Hghr Educ.

Physical Science. 3rd ed. Bill W. Tillery. 416p. (C). 1995. text, student ed. write for info. (*0-697-23130-5*, WCB McGr Hill); per. 63.80 (*0-697-23121-6*, WCB McGr Hill) McGrw-H Hghr Educ.

Physical Science. 3rd ed. Bill W. Tillery. 238p. (C). 1995. text, student ed. 23.75 (*0-697-23128-3*, WCB McGr Hill); text, student ed. write for info. (*0-697-28918-4*, WCB McGr Hill) McGrw-H Hghr Educ.

Physical Science. 4th ed. Merken. (C). 1989. pap. text, teacher ed. 28.00 (*0-03-023322-4*) Harcourt Coll Pubs.

Physical Science. 4th ed. Bill W. Tillery. LC 98-18179. 1998. 70.13 (*0-697-35803-8*) McGraw.

*__Physical Science.__ 4th ed. Bill W. Tillery. 1999. 52.24 (*0-07-236087-9*) McGraw.

Physical Science. 6th ed. Payne. 1991. 18.12 (*0-697-09821-4*, WCB McGr Hill) McGrw-H Hghr Educ.

Physical Science. 6th ed. Payne. 1992. 103.12 (*0-697-09822-2*, WCB McGr Hill) McGrw-H Hghr Educ.

*__Physical Science.__ 7th ed. Payne. 1999. 44.00 (*0-697-15821-7*, WCB McGr Hill) McGrw-H Hghr Educ.

Physical Science, Incl. testbank. Jerry S. Faughn. (C). 1991. pap. text, teacher ed., suppl. ed. 34.00 (*0-03-054649-4*) Harcourt Coll Pubs.

Physical Science , Vol. 1. Vancleave. 1999. pap. text 39.95 (*0-471-34942-9*) Wiley.

*__Physical Science , Vol. 2.__ Vancleave. 1999. pap. text 27.00 (*0-471-34943-7*) Wiley.

Physical Science, Vols. 101-102. 2nd ed. Peter Busher & Millard Baublitz. 152p. (C). 1996. text, lab manual ed. 32.80 (*0-536-58601-2*) Pearson Custom.

Physical Science: A Laboratory Approach. I. J. Aluka. 200p. 1996. spiral bd. 31.95 (*0-8403-5371-5*) Kendall-Hunt.

Physical Science: A Unified Approach. Jerry Schad. 680p. 1995. mass mkt. 88.95 (*0-534-19248-3*) Brooks-Cole.

Physical Science: A Unified Approach. Jerry Schad. 1995. mass mkt., teacher ed. write for info. (*0-534-33885-2*) Brooks-Cole.

Physical Science: An Inquiry Approach. Bonnie Jackson & James S. Monroe. LC 76-51749. 623p. reprint ed. pap. 193.20 (*0-608-13392-2*, 202250700027) Bks Demand.

Physical Science: An Integrated Approach Laboratory Manual. 2nd ed. Russell A. Roy. 117p. (C). 1990. pap. text 18.95 (*0-89892-071-X*) Contemp Pub Co of Raleigh.

Physical Science: Astronomy: Foundations Split 3. 3rd ed. Bill W. Tillery. 640p. (C). 1995. text. write for info. (*0-697-23124-0*, WCB McGr Hill) McGrw-H Hghr Educ.

Physical Science: Big Book Set. Ed. by Susan Evento. (Ranger Rick Ser.). (J). (gr. 2-5). 1997. pap. text 84.00 (*1-56784-461-8*) Newbridge Educ.

Physical Science: Complete Program. Ed. by Susan Evento. (Ranger Rick Ser.). (Illus.). (J). (gr. 2-5). 1997. pap. text 179.00 (*1-56784-460-X*) Newbridge Educ.

Physical Science: Earth Science: Foundations Split 4. 3rd ed. Bill W. Tillery. 640p. (C). 1995. text. write for info. (*0-697-23125-9*, WCB McGr Hill) McGrw-H Hghr Educ.

Physical Science: Matter & Motion. Edward Shevick. Ed. by Judy Mitchell. (Illus.). 64p. (J). (gr. 4-8). 1998. pap., teacher ed. 8.95 (*1-57310-144-3*) Teachng & Lrning Co.

Physical Science: Physics: Foundations Split 1. 3rd ed. Bill W. Tillery. 640p. (C). 1995. text. write for info. (*0-697-23122-4*, WCB McGr Hill) McGrw-H Hghr Educ.

Physical Science: Principles & Applications. 6th ed. Charles A. Payne et al. 688p. (C). 1991. text. write for info. (*0-697-09818-4*, WCB McGr Hill) McGrw-H Hghr Educ.

Physical Science: Principles & Applications. 6th ed. Charles A. Payne et al. 688p. (C). 1992. text. write for info. (*0-697-13929-8*, WCB McGr Hill) McGrw-H Hghr Educ.

Physical Science: Student Book Set. Ed. by Susan Evento. (Ranger Rick Ser.). (J). (gr. 2-5). 1997. pap. text 99.00 (*1-56784-462-6*) Newbridge Educ.

Physical Science Aide. Jack Rudman. (Career Examination Ser.: C-583). 1994. pap. 27.95 (*0-8373-0583-7*) Nat Learn.

Physical Science & Creation: An Introduction. Don B. DeYoung. Ed. by Robert L. Goette. (Reader Ser.: Vol. 2). (Illus.). 81p. 1997. pap. 5.00 (*0-940384-19-1*) Creation Research.

Physical Science & Engineering, Vol. 1. 4th ed. Serway. (C). 1995. 441.50 (*0-03-018059-7*) Harcourt.

Physical Science & Engineering, Vol. II. 4th ed. Serway. (C). 1995. 441.50 (*0-03-018058-9*) Harcourt.

Physical Science & English, Vol. 1 & 2. 4th ed. Serway. (C). 1995. 129.50 (*0-03-016488-5*) Harcourt.

Physical Science & English with Mod & Pg 96. 4th ed. Serway. (C). 1995. 123.00 (*0-03-016512-1*) Harcourt.

Physical Science Applications in Agriculture. Philip Buriak & Edward W. Osborne. 500p. 1996. text 58.75 (*0-8134-3013-5*); text, teacher ed. 9.95 (*0-8134-3014-3*) Interstate.

Physical Science Applications in Agriculture I Teacher's Guide. Philip Buriak & Edward W. Osborne. 1998. teacher ed. 40.00 (*0-8134-3037-2*, 3037) Interstate.

Physical Science Applications in Agriculture II Teacher's Guide. Philip Buriak & Edward W. Osborne. 1998. teacher ed. 40.00 (*0-8134-3038-0*, 3038) Interstate.

Physical Science Big Books Set. Melvin Berger. Ed. by Susan Evento. (Macmillan Early Science Big Bks.). (Illus.). (J). (ps-2). 1995. pap. write for info. (*1-56784-166-X*) Newbridge Educ.

Physical Science College Edition. Donn Carlson et al. (Invitation to Inquiry a Comprehensive Program of Inquiry Activities in Physical Science Ser.). (Illus.). 156p. (C). 1995. ring bd. 33.00 (*1-878276-22-0*) Educ Systs Assocs Inc.

Physical Science Curriculum Set. (Macmillan Early Science Activities Ser.). (Illus.). 384p. (J). (ps-2). 1997. pap. text 115.00 (*1-56784-699-8*) Newbridge Educ.

Physical Science Electricity/Electronics Instructor's Manual. Donn Carlson & Roger Carlson. (Invitation to Inquiry a Comprehensive Program of Inquiry Activities in Physical Science Ser.). (Illus.). 98p. (YA). (gr. 6-12). 1990. 20.00 (*1-878276-16-6*) Educ Systs Assocs Inc.

Physical Science Electricity/Electronics Student Activity Packet. Donn Carlson & Roger Carlson. (Invitation to Inquiry a Comprehensive Program of Inquiry Activities in Physical Science Ser.). (Illus.). 85p. (YA). (gr. 6-12). 1990. ring bd. 8.00 (*1-878276-09-3*) Educ Systs Assocs Inc.

Physical Science for ESL. M. Christison & Sharron Bassano. (Science Through Active Reading Ser.). 128p. 1991. teacher ed. 11.21 (*0-685-59057-7*, 79277) Longman.

Physical Science Homework. 1996. pap. 2.95 (*1-56822-145-2*) Instruct Fair.

Physical Science in the Laboratory: An STS Approach. 3rd ed. Stephen P. Cook. (Illus.). 128p. (C). 1993. pap. 7.50 (*0-9627349-2-6*) Parthenon Bks.

Physical Science in the Laboratory: An STS Approach. 4th rev. ed. Stephen P. Cook. Ed. by Pamela J. Cook. (Illus.). 144p. (C). 1995. pap. 9.25 (*0-9627349-3-4*) Parthenon Bks.

Physical Science in the Middle Ages. E. Grant. LC 77-8393. (Cambridge History of Science Ser.). (Illus.). 128p. 1978. pap. text 17.95 (*0-521-29294-8*) Cambridge U Pr.

Physical Science Lab Manual. 2nd ed. George Caviris & Sophie Moore. 320p. 1995. pap. text, ring bd. 31.95 (*0-7872-1389-6*) Kendall-Hunt.

Physical Science Laboratory: How Do You Get Someone to Agree or Disagree with Your View of the Natural World. Patrick Kenealy. 480p. (C). 1995. pap. text, spiral bd. 34.95 (*0-8403-9784-4*) Kendall-Hunt.

*__Physical Science Laboratory Manual.__ Jannie Trautwein & Ann Ross. 86p. (C). 1999. spiral bd., lab manual ed. 19.95 (*0-7872-6448-2*, 41644801) Kendall-Hunt.

Physical Science Light/Computer Instructor's Manual. Donn Carlson & Roger Carlson. (Invitation to Inquiry a Comprehensive Program of Inquiry Activities in Physical Science Ser.). (Illus.). 124p. (YA). (gr. 6-12). 1990. 20.00 (*1-878276-18-2*) Educ Systs Assocs Inc.

Physical Science Light/Computer Labs Student Activity Packet. Donn Carlson & Roger Carlson. (Invitation to Inquiry a Comprehensive Program of Inquiry Activities in Physical Science Ser.). (Illus.). 102p. (YA). (gr. 6-12). 1990. ring bd. 8.00 (*1-878276-11-5*) Educ Systs Assocs Inc.

Physical Science Magnetism Instructor's Manual. Donn Carlson & Roger Carlson. (Invitation to Inquiry a Comprehensive Program of Inquiry Activities in Physical Science Ser.). (Illus.). 80p. (YA). (gr. 6-12). 1990. 15.00 (*1-878276-17-4*) Educ Systs Assocs Inc.

Physical Science Magnetism Student Activity Packet. Donn Carlson & Roger Carlson. (Invitation to Inquiry a Comprehensive Program of Inquiry Activities in Physical Science Ser.). (Illus.). 66p. (YA). (gr. 6-12). 1990. ring bd. 6.00 (*1-878276-10-7*) Educ Systs Assocs Inc.

Physical Science Matter: Building Blocks. 2nd ed. PH Inc. Staff. text. write for info. (*0-13-225418-2*) P-H.

Physical Science Measurement Instructor's Manual. Donn Carlson & Roger Carlson. (Invitation to Inquiry a Comprehensive Program of Inquiry Activities in Physical Science Ser.). (Illus.). 77p. (YA). (gr. 6-12). 1990. 15.00 (*1-878276-13-1*) Educ Systs Assocs Inc.

Physical Science Measurement Student Activity Packet. Donn Carlson & Roger Carlson. (Invitation to Inquiry a Comprehensive Program of Inquiry Activities in Physical Science Ser.). (Illus.). 77p. (YA). (gr. 6-12). 1990. ring bd. 6.00 (*1-878276-12-3*) Educ Systs Assocs Inc.

Physical Science Mechanics/Computer Labs Instructor's Manual. Donn Carlson & Roger Carlson. (Invitation to Inquiry a Comprehensive Program of Inquiry Activities in Physical Science Ser.). (Illus.). 114p. (YA). (gr. 6-12). 1990. 20.00 (*1-878276-15-8*) Educ Systs Assocs Inc.

Physical Science Mechanics/Computer Labs Student Activity Packet. Donn Carlson & Roger Carlson. (Invitation to Inquiry a Comprehensive Program of Inquiry Activities in Physical Science Ser.). (Illus.). 102p. (YA). (gr. 6-12). 1990. ring bd. 8.00 (*1-878276-08-5*) Educ Systs Assocs Inc.

Physical Science Microchemistry Instructor's Manual: A New Concept in Teaching Chemistry. Donn A. Carlson & Roger L. Carlson. (Invitation to Inquiry a Comprehensive Program of Inquiry Activities in Physical Science for Middle Through Secondary Schools Ser.). (Illus.). 167p. (Orig.). 1990. 25.00 (*1-878276-19-0*) Educ Systs Assocs Inc.

Physical Science Microchemistry Student Activity Packet. Donn Carlson & Roger Carlson. (Invitation to Inquiry a Comprehensive Program of Inquiry Activities in Physical Science Ser.). (Illus.). 136p. (YA). (gr. 6-12). 1990. ring bd. 10.00 (*1-878276-06-9*) Educ Systs Assocs Inc.

Physical Science Middle School Instructor's Manual. Donn A. Carlson & Roger L. Carlson. (Science: Invitation to Inquiry Ser.). (Illus.). 279p. 1990. teacher ed. 40.00 (*1-878276-20-4*) Educ Systs Assocs Inc.

Physical Science Middle School Student Activity Packet. Donn Carlson & Roger Carlson. (Invitation to Inquiry a Comprehensive Program of Inquiry Activities in Physical Science Ser.). (Illus.). 290p. (YA). (gr. 6-12). 1990. ring bd. 16.00 (*1-878276-21-2*) Educ Systs Assocs Inc.

Physical Science, 1988. Ramsey. 1987. 52.50 (*0-03-014394-2*) H Holt & Co.

Physical Science, 1989. Watkins. 1989. teacher ed. 55.50 (*0-15-364305-6*) H Holt & Co.

Physical Science, 1989: Records of the District of West Augusta & Ohio & Yohogania Counties, Virginia 1775-1780. Lamb. 542p. 1989. reprint ed. pap. 53.75 (*0-614-09954-4*, 1260) H Holt & Co.

Physical Science, 1994. Lamb. 1994. text, teacher ed. 105.75 (*0-03-097539-5*) H Holt & Co.

Physical Science I. UNT, Physics Department Staff. 82p. (C). 1994. 21.39 (*1-56870-159-4*) RonJon Pub.

Physical Science 110. 4th ed. Richard Bady. 160p. (C). 1998. spiral bd., lab manual ed. 26.95 (*0-7872-1152-4*, 41115201) Kendall-Hunt.

Physical Science 110. Eastern Michigan University Staff. (C). 1993. student ed. 10.00 (*1-881592-07-3*) Hayden-McNeil.

Physical Science Projects for Integration & Cooperative Learning. Ira Hickman. 140p. 1996. pap. text, spiral bd. 19.95 (*0-7872-3306-4*) Kendall-Hunt.

Physical Science Resource Manual: A Comprehensive Program of Inquiry Activities in Physical Science for Middle Through Secondary School. Donn A. Carlson & Roger L. Carlson. (Science: Invitation to Inquiry a Comprehensive Program of Inquiry Activities in Physical Science for Middle Through Secondary Schools Ser.). (Illus.). 712p. (Orig.). 1990. teacher ed. 75.00 (*1-878276-05-0*) Educ Systs Assocs Inc.

Physical Science Set. Melvin Berger. Ed. by Susan Evento. (Macmillan Early Science Big Bks.). (Illus.). (J). (ps-2). 1995. pap. write for info. (*1-56784-165-1*) Newbridge Educ.

*__Physical Science Syllabus & Tests.__ 18p. (YA). 1999. ring bd. 2.50 (*1-57896-056-8*, 1540, Hewitt Homeschl Res) Hewitt Res Fnd.

Physical Science Technician. Jack Rudman. (Career Examination Ser.: C-584). 1994. pap. 27.95 (*0-8373-0584-5*) Nat Learn.

Physical Science 1014. Steven D. Kamm. 1996. pap. text 10.37 (*1-56870-232-9*) RonJon Pub.

Physical Science Today: Environmental Applications. 2nd ed. Arthur W. Wiggins. Ed. by Gary L. Dennison. (Illus.). 305p. (C). 1987. pap. text 20.00 (*0-923231-04-8*) Mohican Pub.

Physical Science Two. Newton College of the Sacred Heart Staff. (C). 1972. text 21.32 (*0-13-671354-8*); pap. text 11.00 (*0-13-671339-4*); 46.00 (*0-13-671156-1*) P-H.

Physical Science II. UNT Physics Dept. University of North Texas Staff. (C). 1995. 21.39 (*1-56870-202-7*) RonJon Pub.

Physical Science Variables Instructor's Manual. Donn Carlson & Roger Carlson. (Invitation to Inquiry a Comprehensive Program of Inquiry Activities in Physical Science Ser.). (Illus.). 38p. (YA). (gr. 6-12). 1990. 8.00 (*1-878276-14-X*) Educ Systs Assocs Inc.

Physical Science Variables Student Activity Packet. Donn Carlson & Roger Carlson. (Invitation to Inquiry a Comprehensive Program of Inquiry Activities in Physical Science Ser.). (Illus.). 36p. (YA). (gr. 6-12). 1990. ring bd. 4.00 (*1-878276-07-7*) Educ Systs Assocs Inc.

Physical Science with Environment. 2nd ed. Faughn. (C). 1994. 82.50 (*0-03-015517-7*) Harcourt.

Physical Science with Modular Applications. 5th ed. Melvin Merken. (C). 1993. pap. text 66.50 (*0-03-096010-X*, Pub. by Harcourt Coll Pubs) Harcourt.

Physical Science 110L Lab Manual. 3rd ed. Richard J. Bady. 164p. (C). 1996. pap. text 16.95 (*0-7872-2379-4*) Kendall-Hunt.

Physical Sciences. Hazen. 174p. 1996. pap. 31.95 (*0-471-01545-8*) Wiley.

Physical Sciences, Level I. David R. Browning. LC 77-27083. (Longman Technician Ser.). 249p. reprint ed. pap. 77.20 (*0-608-11600-9*, 201960700013) Bks Demand.

Physical Sciences: A Primary Teacher's Guide. Kevin Carlton & Eric Parkinson. (Illus.). 192p. 1994. pap. 35.95 (*0-304-32766-2*) Continuum.

Physical Sciences: An Integrated Approach. Robert M. Hazen & James S. Trefil. LC 95-40786. 768p. 1995. pap. 86.95 (*0-471-00249-6*) Wiley.

Physical Sciences: An Integrated Approach. Robert M. Hazen & James S. Trefil. 768p. 1996. text 90.95 (*0-471-15440-7*) Wiley.

Physical Sciences - Area Examination. Jack Rudman. (Graduate Record Examination Ser.: GRE-43). 1994. pap. 23.95 (*0-8373-5243-6*) Nat Learn.

Physical Sciences & the History of Physics. Robert S. Cohen & Marx W. Wartofsky. 272p. 1983. text 148.50 (*90-277-1615-3*, D Reidel) Kluwer Academic.

Physical Sciences, Mathematics, Agricultural Sciences, the Environment & Natural Resources see Graduate & Professional Programs 2000

Physical Sciences, Mathematics, Agricultural Sciences, the Environment & Natural Resources, 1999, Bk. 4. Guide Patersons Staff. (Peterson's Graduate & Professional Program Ser.). 1040p. 1998. 39.95 (*1-56079-984-6*) Intl School Servs.

Physical Sciences on File. Diagram Group Staff. (Illus.). 300p. 1989. ring bd. 165.00 (*0-8160-2068-X*) Facts on File.

Physical Sciences on File. rev. ed. Diagram Group Staff & Catherine Riches. LC 98-55737. (Illus.). 318p. 1999. ring bd. 165.00 (*0-8160-3874-0*, Checkmark) Facts on File.

Physical Security. 1991. lib. bdg. 88.95 (*0-8490-4568-1*) Gordon Pr.

Physical Security: Practices & Technology. Charles Schnabolk. 388p. 1983. 34.95 (*0-409-95067-X*) Buttrwrth-Heinemann.

*__Physical Security: 150 Things You Should Know.__ Louis A. Tyska & Lawrence J. Fennelly. LC 99-55139. (Illus.). 224p. 2000. pap. 29.95 (*0-7506-7255-2*) Buttrwrth-Heinemann.

Physical Security & the Inspection Process. Carl A. Roper. LC 96-43147. 290p. 1996. 56.95 (*0-7506-9712-1*) Buttrwrth-Heinemann.

Physical Security Standard for Construction of Sensitive Compartmented Information Facilities. 281p. (Orig.). (C). 1994. pap. text 50.00 (*0-941375-87-0*) DIANE Pub.

Physical Self: From Motivation to Well-Being. Ed. by Kenneth R. Fox. LC 97-128. (Illus.). 344p. 1997. text 38.00 (*0-87322-689-5*, BFOX0689) Human Kinetics.

Physical Sensors for Biomedical Applications. Ed. by Michael R. Neuman et al. 168p. 1980. 101.00 (*0-8493-5975-9*, R857, CRC Reprint) Franklin.

Physical Separation & Recovery of Metals from Wastes. Terry J. Veasey et al. LC 93-14593. (Process Engineering for the Chemical Ser.: Vol. 1). 201p. 1993. text 94.00 (*2-88124-916-7*) Gordon & Breach.

P

Physical Side of Learning: A Parent-Teacher's Guide of Physical Activities Kids Need to Be Successful in School. Leela C. Zion. Ed. by Frank Alexander. (Illus.). 87p. (Orig.). 1994. pap. 8.00 (0-915256-41-X, 103) Front Row.

Physical Signatures of Magnetospheric Boundary Layer Processes: Proceedings of the NATO Advanced Research Workshop, Honefoss, Norway, May 9-14, 1993. Ed. by Jan A. Holtet & Alv Egeland. LC 94-8299. (NATO ASI Series C: Mathematical & Physical Sciences: Vol. 425). 480p. (C). 1994. text 229.00 (0-7923-2763-2) Kluwer Academic.

Physical Signs in Child Abuse. Hobbs. 1995. text 89.00 (0-7020-1778-7, W B Saunders Co) Harcrt Hlth Sci Grp.

Physical Signs in Orthopaedics. Ed. by L. Klenerman. 104p. (Orig.). 1994. pap. text 19.00 (0-7279-0845-6, Pub. by BMJ Pub) Login Brothers Bk Co.

Physical Status - The Use & Interpretation of Anthropometry: Report of a WHO Expert Committee. LC 96-145907. (Technical Report Ser.: Vol. 854). (FRE & SPA.). 452p. (C). 1995. pap. 71.00 (92-4-120854-6, 1100854) World Health.

Physical Stresses in Plants: Genes & Their Products for Tolerance. Ed. by S. Grillo & A. Leone. LC 96-22127. 288p. 1996. 149.50 (3-540-61347-1) Spr-Verlag.

Physical Structure. LC 96-44174. (Handbook of Surface Science Ser.). 900p. 1996. 372.00 (0-444-89036-X) Elsevier.

Physical Structure in Modelling: Proceedings of the Bond Graph Workshop Held at the Twente University of Technology, Enschede, The Netherlands, 1983. Ed. by Jan J. Van Dixhoorn & Dean C. Karnopp. 150p. 1985. pap. 48.00 (0-08-032593-9, Pergamon Pr) Elsevier.

Physical Structure of Olympic Athletes. Ed. by J. E. Carter. (Medicine & Sport Science Ser.: Vol. 18). (Illus.). viii, 248p. 1984. 136.75 (3-8055-3871-5) S Karger.

Physical Structure of Solid Surfaces. Ed. by W.N. Unertl. 1996. write for info. (0-614-17905-X, North Holland) Elsevier.

Physical Structure of the Amorphous State. Ed. by Geoffrey Allen & S. E. Petrie. LC 76-53665. 312p. reprint ed. pap. 96.80 (0-608-16967-6, 202710500054) Bks Demand.

Physical Studies of Water-Formed Corrosion Products on Copper & Proposals for an Alternative Mechanism of Pitting Corrosion. British Non-Ferrous Metals Research Association St. 73p. 10.95 (0-317-34539-7, 34) Intl Copper.

Physical Supramolecular Chemistry: Proceedings of the NATO Advanced Research Workshop, Miami, U. S. A., Jan. 7-10, 1996. Angel E. Kaifer. Ed. by Luis Echegoyen. LC 96-28466. (NATO ASI Series C: Mathematical & Physical Sciences). 492p. (C). 1996. text 268.50 (0-7923-4181-3) Kluwer Academic.

Physical Surveillance Training Manual. Ralph D. Thomas. 65p. 1984. pap. text 19.95 (0-918487-11-0) Thomas Investigative.

Physical Synthesis. 2nd ed. Silverman. (C). 1998. pap. text 24.00 (0-471-32522-8) Wiley.

Physical Techniques in Biochemistry. Sheehan. pap. text 49.95 (0-471-98663-1) Wiley.

Physical Techniques in Biological Research. Incl. Cells & Tissues., **3 prts.** Ed. by Arthur W. Pollister. 1969. 74.50 (0-12-560953-1); Cells & Tissues., **3 prts.** 2nd ed. Ed. by Arthur W. Pollister. 1966. 74.50 (0-12-560903-5); 2A. Physical Chemical Techniques. 2nd ed. Ed. by Dan H. Moore. 74.50 (0-12-505552-8); Vol. 2B. Physical Chemical Techniques. Ed. by Dan H. Moore. 1969. 74.50 (0-12-505554-4); Vol. 3, Pt. B. Cells & Tissues., **3 pts.** 2nd ed. Ed. by Arthur W. Pollister. 1966. 74.50 (0-12-560943-4); write for info. (0-318-50332-8) Acad Pr.

Physical Techniques in Cardiological Imaging: Proceedings of the Meeting on Physical Techniques in Cardiological Imaging Held at the Medical & Biological Sciences Building, University of Southampton, 8-9 July 1982. fac. ed. Meeting on Physical Techniques in Cardiological Im. Ed. by M. D. Short et al. LC 83-20768. (Illus.). 221p. 1983. reprint ed. pap. 68.60 (0-7837-8014-1, 204777000008) Bks Demand.

P

Physical Techniques in Medicine, 2 vols., 1. John T. McMullan. LC 76-30281. (Illus.). reprint ed. pap. 85.30 (0-608-15573-X, 2029636) Bks Demand.

Physical Techniques in Medicine, 2 vols., 2. John T. McMullan. LC 76-30281. (Illus.). reprint ed. pap. 43.70 (0-608-15574-8) Bks Demand.

Physical Testing & Quality Control. H. Weston. 150p. 1974. 95.00 (0-7855-7211-2) St Mut.

Physical Testing of Plastics - STP 736. Ed. by R. Evans. 125p. 1984. 24.00 (0-8031-0768-4, STP736) ASTM.

Physical Testing of Textiles. Saville. LC 99-219979. 350p. 1999. ring bd. 159.95 (0-8493-0568-3) CRC Pr.

Physical Testing of Textiles. B. P. Saville. LC 99-219979. 350p. 1999. boxed set 170.00 (1-85573-367-6, Pub. by Woodhead Pubng) Am Educ Systs.

Physical, the Mental, the Spiritual. Joel Jessen. 185p. 1978. pap. 14.00 (0-942958-05-5) Kappeler Inst Pub.

Physical Theory As Logico-Operational Structure. Ed. by Clifford A. Hooker. (Western Ontario Ser.: No. 7). 351p. 1978. text 155.50 (90-277-0711-1, D Reidel) Kluwer Academic.

Physical Theory in Biology: Foundations & Explorations. Charles J. Lumsden et al. LC 97-7676. (Studies of Nonlinear Phenomena in Life Sciences). 1997. write for info. (981-02-3082-6); pap. write for info. (981-02-3121-0) World Scientific Pub.

Physical Theory of Kalam: Atoms, Space & Void in Basrian Mutazili Cosmology. Alnoor Dhanani. LC 93-35729. (Islamic Philosophy, Theology & Science, Studies & Texts Ser.: Vol. 14). 1993. 72.00 (90-04-09831-3) Brill Academic Pubs.

Physical Theory of Neutron Chain Reactors. Alvin M. Weinberg & Eugene K. Wigner. LC 58-8507. (Illus.). 800p. reprint ed. pap. 200.00 (0-608-09595-8, 205439900006) Bks Demand.

Physical Therapist. Jack Rudman. (Career Examination Ser.: C-585). 1994. pap. 29.95 (0-8373-0585-3) Nat Learn.

Physical Therapist Assistant. (Career Examination Ser.). 1997. pap. 27.95 (0-8373-3791-7, C3791) Nat Learn.

Physical Therapist Assistant. Kathryn A. Quinlan. (Careers Without College Ser.). (Illus.). 48p. (J). (gr. 3-7). 1998. 19.00 (0-516-21286-9) Childrens.

Physical Therapists see Fisioterpeutas

Physical Therapists. Robert James. LC 95-18937. (People Who Care for Our Health Discovery Library). 24p. (J). (gr. k-4). 1995. lib. bdg. 15.93 (1-55916-170-1) Rourke Bk Co.

***Physical Therapist's Clinical Companion.** Springhouse Corporation Staff. LC 99-52570. 2000. 39.95 (1-58255-004-2) Springhouse Corp.

Physical Therapists Facing Changing Organizational Structures. Contrib. by APTA Staff. 165p. 1996. pap. 18.50 (1-887759-43-3, P-126) Am Phys Therapy Assn.

Physical Therapist's Guide to Health Care. Kathleen Curtis. LC 98-46544. (Illus.). 320p. 1999. pap. 28.00 (1-55642-378-0, 43780) SLACK Inc.

***Physical Therapist's Guide to Health Care, Instructor's Manual.** Kathleen Curtis. 80p. (C). 1999. pap. text, teacher ed. write for info. (1-55642-458-2) SLACK Inc.

Physical Therapy. Bernice Krumhansl. (Opportunities in...Ser.). (Illus.). 160p. 1989. 13.95 (0-8442-6158-0, Passprt Bks) NTC Contemp Pub Co.

Physical Therapy. Bernice Krumhansl. (Opportunities in...Ser.). (Illus.). 160p. 1993. pap. 10.95 (0-8442-6159-9, Passprt Bks) NTC Contemp Pub Co.

Physical Therapy. Crispian Scully & Marylou R. Barnes. (Illus.). 1319p. 1989. text 58.00 (0-397-50798-4) Lppncott W & W.

Physical Therapy. John S. Coulter. LC 75-23658. (Clio Medica Ser.: 8). (Illus.). reprint ed. 29.50 (0-404-58908-1) AMS Pr.

Physical Therapy after Amputation: The Treatment of the Unilateral Lower-Extremity Amputee. Margaret Bryce. LC 54-6930. (Illus.). 103p. reprint ed. pap. 32.00 (0-8357-6799-X, 203547800095) Bks Demand.

Physical Therapy Aide: A Worktext. Roberta C. Weiss. LC 92-23403. 368p. (C). 1993. pap. 34.50 (0-8273-5110-0) Delmar.

Physical Therapy Aide: A Worktext. 2nd ed. Weiss. LC 98-29790. 320p. (C). 1998. text 49.95 (0-7668-0294-9) Delmar.

Physical Therapy Aide: A Worktext Instructor's Guide. Roberta C. Weiss. 45p. 1993. pap., teacher ed. 16.00 (0-8273-5111-9) Delmar.

Physical Therapy & Massage for the Horse: A Comprehensive Approach to Equine Kinesiology. Jean-Marie Denoux & Jean-Pierre Pailloux. LC 94-61970. (Illus.). 200p. 1996. 29.95 (1-57076-021-7, Trafalgar Sq Pub) Trafalgar.

Physical Therapy & Occupational Therapy in Schools Vol. 2: A Related Service. Bonnie Blossom et al. (Illus.). 317p. (C). 1996. pap. text 65.00 (0-9630294-1-X) Rehab P & T.

Physical Therapy & the Arthritis Patient: Clinical Aspects & Approaches to Management. Ed. by Eleanor F. Branch & Mary Singleton. LC 88-563. (Physical Therapy in Health Care Ser.: Vol. 2, Nos. 1-2). (Illus.). 78p. 1988. text 39.95 (0-86656-728-3) Haworth Pr.

Physical Therapy & the Pulmonary Patient: Aspects of Evaluation & Treatment. Ed. by Mary C. Singleton & Eleanor F. Branch. LC 87-21224. (Physical Therapy in Health Care Ser.: Vol. 1, Nos. 2-3). 99p. 1987. text 39.95 (0-86656-705-4) Haworth Pr.

Physical Therapy & the Stroke Patient: Pathologic Aspects & Clinical Management. Ed. by Eleanor F. Branch & Mary C. Singleton. LC 87-26668. (Physical Therapy in Health Care Ser.: Vol. 1, No. 4). 73p. 1987. text 39.95 (0-86656-740-2) Haworth Pr.

Physical Therapy Assistant. Quinlan. LC 97-32102. (Careers Without College Ser.). (YA). 1998. 19.00 (1-56065-707-3) Capstone Pr.

Physical Therapy Assistant License Exam. Rothman. (Physical Therapy Ser.). (C). 2000. 29.95 (0-8273-8082-8) Delmar.

Physical Therapy Clinical Performance Instruments. 96p. 1998. pap. 140.00 (1-887759-13-1, E-42) Am Phys Therapy Assn.

Physical Therapy Evaluation in Early Infancy. Ed. by Irma J. Wilhelm. (Clinics in Physical Therapy Ser.). (Illus.). 316p. 1992. text 60.00 (0-443-08815-2) Church.

Physical Therapy for Children. Suzann K. Campbell. Ed. by Robert Palisono & Darl W. Vander Linden. LC 94-10990. (Illus.). 880p. 1994. text. write for info. (0-7216-6503-9, W B Saunders Co) Harcrt Hlth Sci Grp.

Physical Therapy for Children. 2nd ed. Ed. by Suzann Cambell et al. (Illus.). 1055p. Date not set. text. write for info. (0-7216-8316-9, W B Saunders Co) Harcrt Hlth Sci Grp.

Physical Therapy for Sports. 2nd ed. Werner Kuprian. Tr. by Todd Konjte & Lynn Braunsdorf. LC 94-7651. (Illus.). 464p. 1995. text 58.00 (0-7216-3758-2, W B Saunders Co) Harcrt Hlth Sci Grp.

Physical Therapy for the Cancer Patient. Ed. by Charles L. McGarvey, III. (Clinics in Physical Therapy Ser.). (Illus.). 188p. 1990. text 49.95 (0-443-08667-2) Church.

Physical Therapy for the Cancer Patient. Charles L. McGarvey, III. LC 90-32270. (Clinics in Physical Therapy Ser.). (Illus.). 202p. 1990. reprint ed. pap. 62.70 (0-7837-9592-0, 206034800005) Bks Demand.

Physical Therapy for Traumatic Head Injury. Jacqueline Montgomery. 1994. text 69.00 (0-443-08908-6) Church.

Physical Therapy in Arthritis. Joan M. Walker & Antoine Helewa. Ed. by Margaret Biblis. (Illus.). 384p. 1996. text 58.00 (0-7216-4999-8, W B Saunders Co) Harcrt Hlth Sci Grp.

Physical Therapy in Craniomadibular Disorders. Tore L. Hansson et al. LC 92-1717. (Illus.). 80p. 1992. text 36.00 (0-86715-192-7) Quint Pub Co.

Physical Therapy in Public Schools Vol. 1: A Related Service. Bonnie Blossom & Fran Ford. LC 91-62293. (Illus.). 182p. (Orig.). (C). 1991. pap. text 45.00 (0-9630294-0-1) Rehab P & T.

Physical Therapy in the Paddock: Techniques for Treating Common Soft-Tissue Injuries of the Horse. Lyn P. Taylor. Ed. by Richard McDonald. (Illus.). 101p. 1995. pap. 20.00 (0-942558-01-4) BATI.

Physical Therapy Licensure Examination Guide: Pretest Self-Assessment & Review. Theresa Nalty. 208p. 1999. pap. write for info. (0-07-134723-2) McGraw-Hill HPD.

Physical Therapy Management of Arthritis, No. 16. Ed. by Barbara F. Banwell & Victoria Gall. (Clinics in Physical Therapy Ser.: Vol. 16). (Illus.). 212p. 1987. pap. text 50.00 (0-443-08438-6) Church.

Physical Therapy Markets. (Market Research Reports: No. 420). (Illus.). 153p. 1994. 795.00 (0-614-01238-4) Theta Corp.

Physical Therapy of the Cervical & Thoracic Spine. Ed. by Ruth Grant. (Clinics in Physical Therapy Ser.: Vol. 17). (Illus.). 338p. 1988. text 47.50 (0-443-08507-2) Church.

Physical Therapy of the Cervical & Thoracic Spine. 2nd ed. Ruth Grant. LC 94-12194. (Clinics in Physical Therapy Ser.). 1994. reprint ed. text 67.00 (0-443-08918-3) Church.

Physical Therapy of the Foot & Ankle. Ed. by Gary C. Hunt. LC 87-24235. (Clinics in Physical Therapy Ser.: No. 15). (Illus.). 350p. reprint ed. pap. 108.50 (0-7837-3406-9, 204336600008) Bks Demand.

Physical Therapy of the Foot & Ankle. 2nd ed. Thomas G. McPoil. Ed. by Gary C. Hunt. LC 95-7870. (Clinics in Physical Therapy Ser.). 1995. pap. text 49.00 (0-443-08925-6) Church.

Physical Therapy of the Geriatric Patient. 2nd ed. Ed. by Osa L. Jackson. (Clinics in Physical Therapy Ser.: Vol. 21). (Illus.). 292p. 1989. text 49.95 (0-443-08619-2) Church.

Physical Therapy of the Hip. Ed. by John L. Echternach. (Clinics in Physical Therapy Ser.). (Illus.). 221p. 1990. text 59.95 (0-443-08650-8) Church.

Physical Therapy of the Knee. Ed. by Robert E. Mangine. LC 87-24284. (Clinics in Physical Therapy Ser.: Vol. 19). (Illus.). 264p. reprint ed. pap. 81.90 (0-7837-1611-7, 204190300024) Bks Demand.

Physical Therapy of the Knee. 2nd ed. Ed. by Robert E. Mangine. LC 95-12053. (Clinics in Physical Therapy Ser.). 1995. pap. text 44.00 (0-443-08916-7) Church.

Physical Therapy of the Low Back. Ed. by Lance T. Twomey & James R. Taylor. (Clinics in Physical Therapy Ser.: Vol. 13). (Illus.). 328p. 1987. text 42.95 (0-443-08493-9) Church.

Physical Therapy of the Low Back. fac. ed. Ed. by Lance T. Twomey & James R. Taylor. LC 87-11654. (Clinics in Physical Therapy Ser.: No. 13). (Illus.). 344p. 1987. reprint ed. pap. 106.70 (0-7837-7880-5, 204763700007) Bks Demand.

Physical Therapy of the Low Back. 2nd ed. Ed. by Lance T. Twomey & J. R. Taylor. (Clinics in Physical Therapy Ser.). (Illus.). 384p. 1994. text 73.00 (0-443-08894-2) Church.

***Physical Therapy of the Low Back.** 3rd ed. Lance T. Twomey & James R. Taylor. (Illus.). 430p. 2000. text. write for info. (0-443-06552-7, W B Saunders Co) Harcrt Hlth Sci Grp.

Physical Therapy of the Shoulder. Ed. by Robert Donatelli. LC 86-20722. (Clinics in Physical Therapy Ser.: No. 11). (Illus.). 333p. reprint ed. pap. 103.30 (0-8357-3068-9, 203932400012) Bks Demand.

Physical Therapy of the Shoulder. 3rd ed. Robert Donatelli. LC 96-29475. (Clinics in Physical Therapy Ser.). 1996. pap. text 69.00 (0-443-07591-3) Church.

Physical Therapy of the Thorax. Sandra Rusnak-Smith & Marilyn Moffat. (Illus.). 256p. 1999. spiral bd. 34.95 (0-397-55272-6) Lppncott W & W.

Physical Therapy Pharmacology. Lynne Eddy. (Illus.). 208p. (gr. 13). 1991. pap. text 33.95 (0-8151-3076-7, 20946) Mosby Inc.

Physical Therapy Procedures: Selected Techniques. 5th ed. Ann H. Downer. LC 95-35460. (Illus.). 406p. (C). 1996. pap. text 49.95 (0-398-06556-X) C C Thomas.

Physical Therapy Protocols: Guidelines for Rehabilitation. Ed. by Janet Bezner. (Illus.). 232p. (C). 1991. pap. text 49.00 (0-7616-4221-8) Commun Skill.

Physical Therapy Research: Principles & Applications. Elizabeth Domholdt. LC 92-13390. (Illus.). 464p. 1992. pap. text 43.00 (0-7216-3611-X, W B Saunders Co) Harcrt Hlth Sci Grp.

Physical Therapy Research: Principles & Applications. 2nd ed. Elizabeth Domholdt. LC 99-47086. (Illus.). 479p. 1998. pap. text. write for info. (0-7216-6963-8, W B Saunders Co) Harcrt Hlth Sci Grp.

Physical Training, Conditioning & Building Endurance: Index of New Information. Steve K. Turko. 160p. Date not set. 47.50 (0-7883-1890-X); pap. 44.50 (0-7883-1891-8) ABBE Pubs Assn.

Physical Universe. Frank H. Shu. LC 81-51271. (Astronomy Ser.). (Illus.). 584p. (C). 1982. text 72.00 (0-935702-05-9) Univ Sci Bks.

Physical Universe. 6th ed. Ron Samec. 267p. (C). 1991. lab manual ed. 33.75 (0-07-035714-5) McGraw.

Physical Universe. 7th ed. Konrad B. Krauskopf & Arthur Beiser. LC 92-15742. 1993. 43.95 (0-07-035861-3) McGraw.

Physical Universe. 7th ed. Konrad B. Krauskopf et al. (C). 1993. text 51.25 (0-07-911502-0); pap. text, student ed. 41.87 (0-07-035862-1) McGraw.

Physical Universe. 8th ed. Konrad B. Krauskopf & Arthur Beiser. 1996. pap., student ed. 8.44 (0-07-036171-1) McGraw.

Physical Universe. 8th ed. Konrad B. Krauskopf & Arthur Beiser. 359p. (C). 1996. 68.13 (0-07-913011-9) McGraw.

Physical Universe. 8th ed. Konrad Bates Krauskopf & Arthur Beiser. LC 96-20187. (Schaum's Outline Series In Science). 1996. pap. write for info. (0-07-036170-3) McGraw.

Physical Universe. 9th ed. Krauskopf. LC 99-14627. 1999. 56.74 (0-07-228414-5) McGraw.

Physical Universe: The Interface Between Cosmology, Astrophysics & Particle Physics: Proceedings of the XII Autumn School of Physics, Lisbon, Portugal, October 1-5, 1990 Particle Physics. Ed. by John D. Barrow et al. (Lecture Notes in Physics Ser.: Vol. 383). viii, 312p. 1991. 50.95 (0-387-54293-0) Spr-Verlag.

Physical Vapor Deposition. Business Communications Co., Inc. Staff. 179p. 1990. 2850.00 (0-89336-746-X, GB-133) BCC.

Physical Vapor Deposition of Thin Films. Mahan. LC 99-21926. 312p. 2000. 84.95 (0-471-33001-9) Wiley.

Physical Violence in American Families: Risk Factors & Adaptations to Violence in 8,145 Families. Richard J. Gelles & Murray A. Straus. LC 88-27549. 623p. 1995. pap. 29.95 (1-56000-828-8) Transaction Pubs.

Physical Violence in American Families: Risk Factors & Adaptations to Violence in 8,145 Families. Murray A. Straus & Richard J. Gelles. 623p. 1995. 39.95 (0-88738-263-0) Transaction Pubs.

Physical Wisdom. Yogi Bhajan. Ed. & Illus. by Hari J. Khalsa. 50p. (Orig.). 1995. pap. 14.95 (0-9639847-1-3) KRI.

Physical Wisdom: Kundalini Yoga As Taught by Yogi Bhajan. Yogi Bhajan. (Illus.). x, 50p. 1997. reprint ed. spiral bd. write for info. (0-9639991-2-5) KRI.

Physical Work Capacity in Organ Transplantation. Ed. by Michel Rieu. LC 97-51463. (Medicine & Sport Science Ser.: Vol. 42, 1998). (Illus.). viii, 188p. 1998. 194.00 (3-8055-6610-7) S Karger.

Physical World. Holman. (UK - Science Ser.). 1992. mass mkt. 31.95 (0-17-438409-2) S-W Pub.

Physical World. Ed. by Scott Morris. LC 92-22285. (Using & Understanding Maps Ser.). (Illus.). 48p. (YA). (gr. 5 up). 1993. lib. bdg. 17.95 (0-7910-1801-6) Chelsea Hse.

Physical World: Big Book Set. Ed. by Susan Evento. (Early Science Ser.). (J). (ps-2). 1997. pap. text 84.00 (1-56784-397-2) Newbridge Educ.

Physical World: Student Book Set. Ed. by Susan Evento. (Early Science Ser.). (J). (ps-2). 1997. pap. text 94.00 (1-56784-398-0) Newbridge Educ.

Physical World Set. Ed. by Susan Evento. (Early Science Ser.). (Illus.). (J). (ps-2). 1997. pap. text 245.00 (1-56784-396-4) Newbridge Educ.

Physicalism: The Philosophical Foundations. Jeffrey Poland. 392p. 1994. text 65.00 (0-19-824980-2) OUP.

Physicalism in Mathematics. Ed. by A. D. Irvine. 392p. (C). 1989. lib. bdg. 171.00 (0-7923-0513-2, Pub. by Kluwer Academic) Kluwer Academic.

Physicalizing FE Principle. Bette Patterson. 44p. 1994. pap. text, per. 9.95 (0-9643532-0-2) Teel & Co.

Physically-Based Modeling for Computer Graphics: A Structured Approach. Ronen Barzel. (Illus.). 334p. 1992. text 48.00 (0-12-079880-8) Acad Pr.

Physically-Based Modelling & Simulation of Climate & Climatic Change, 2 vols. Ed. by M. E. Schlesinger. (C). 1900. text 260.00 (90-277-2787-2) Kluwer Academic.

Physically Based Modelling in Graphics & Animation. Avron Barr. (C). 1999. 52.95 (0-201-18366-8) Addison-Wesley.

Physically Challenged Can-Do: Anthology. large type ed. Ed. by Marilyn R. Riddle. 84p. (Orig.). 1989. pap., per. 10.00 (0-9603748-6-8) Sandpiper OR.

Physically Handicapped in India: Policy & Programme. Mani Rama. 223p. (C). 1988. 26.50 (81-7024-164-2, Pub. by Ashish Pub Hse) S Asia.

Physically Handicapped in Society Series, 39 bks. Ed. by William R. Phillips & Janet Rosenberg. 1980. lib. bdg. 965.00 (0-405-13100-3) Ayer.

Physically Speaking: A Dictionary of Quotations on Physics & Astronomy. Carl C. Gaither & Alma E. Cavazos-Gaither. LC 97-33282. (Illus.). 367p. 1997. pap. 39.00 (0-7503-0470-7) Institute of Personal Magnetism.

Physican & the Mental Health of the Child, 2 vols. Incl. Vol. 1. Assessing Development & Treating Disorders Within a Family. (0-89970-120-5, OP-006); Vol. 2. Psychological Concomitants of Illness. 155p. pap. (0-89970-008-X, OP-079); Vol. 3. Issues & Skills in Relating Primary Medical Care to the Other Human Services. pap. (0-89970-108-6, OP-118); Set pap. 8.00 (0-318-59522-2) AMA.

Physician. Noah Gordon. 640p. 1987. mass mkt. 6.99 (0-449-21426-5, Crest) Fawcett.

Physician. Jack Rudman. (Career Examination Ser.: C-1392). 1994. pap. 44.95 (0-8373-1392-9) Nat Learn.

***Physician: Medicine & the Unsuspected Battle for Human Freedom.** Richard Leviton. 480p. 2000. pap. 16.95 (1-57174-168-2) Hampton Roads Pub Co.

Physician & Child-Rearing: Two Guides, 1809-1894. William Buchan & L. Emmett Holt, Jr. 1974. 18.95 (0-405-03965-4, 15717) Ayer.

Physician & Hospice Care: Roles, Attitudes, & Issues. Ed. by Wilma Bulkin et al. LC 92-49811. (Loss, Grief & Care Ser.: Vol. 6, Nos. 2 & 3). (Illus.). 200p. 1993. lib. bdg. 39.95 (1-56024-320-1) Haworth Pr.

An Asterisk (*) at the beginning of an entry indicates that the title is appearing for the first time.

Physician & Nurse Migration Analysis & Policy Implications. A. Mejia & H. Pizurki. 476p. 1979. 64.00 (92-4-156059-2) World Health.

Physician & Patient or a Practical View of the Mutual Duties, Relations & Interests of the Medical Profession & the Community. Worthington Hooker. LC 75-180577. (Medicine & Society in America Ser.). 456p. 1972. reprint ed. 28.95 (0-405-03954-9) Ayer.

Physician & Sexuality in Victorian America. John S. Haller, Jr. & Robin M. Haller. LC 94-47384. 352p. (C). 1995. pap. 20.95 (0-8093-2009-6) S Ill U Pr.

Physician & the Slave Trade: John Kirk, the Livingstone Expeditions & the Crusade Against Slavery in East Africa. Daniel Liebowitz. (Illus.). 375p. 1998. pap. text 27.95 (0-7167-3098-7) W H Freeman.

Physician As Captain of the Ship: A Critical Appraisal. Ed. by Nancy M. King et al. 269p. 1988. text 153.00 (1-55608-044-1, D Reidel) Kluwer Academic.

Physician as Manager. 2nd ed. J. J. Aluise. (Illus.). xvi, 260p. 1986. 80.00 (0-387-96381-2) Spr-Verlag.

Physician Assistant: A Guide to Clinical Practice. Ed. by Ruth Ballweg et al. LC 93-12579. 1994. pap. text. write for info. (0-7216-4586-0, W B Saunders Co) Harcrt Hlth Sci Grp.

***Physician Assistant: A Guide to Clinical Practice.** 2nd ed. Ruth Ballweg et al. Ed. by Edward M. Sullivan & Shirley Kuhn. LC 98-24848. (Illus.). 860p. (C). 1999. text 69.00 (0-7216-7653-7) Harcourt.

Physician Assistant Legal Handbook. Aspen Health Law Center Staff. LC 97-16412. 320p. 1997. 59.00 (0-8342-0925-X, 20925) Aspen Pub.

Physician Assistant Medical Handbook. James B. Labus. LC 94-17891. (Illus.). 752p. 1995. pap. text 41.00 (0-7216-5169-0, W B Saunders Co) Harcrt Hlth Sci Grp.

Physician Assistant Pearls of Wisdom. Gillian Lewke et al. (Pearls of Wisdom Ser.). 1998. pap. 32.00 (1-890369-05-5) Boston Medical.

Physician Assistant Protocols. Matthew M. Cohen & Anni Lanigan. 264p. 1994. pap. 55.00 (0-924381-15-9); ring bd. 85.00 (0-924381-17-5); disk. write for info. (0-924381-16-7) Sunbelt Med Pubs.

Physician Assistant Surgical Handbook. James B. Labus. Ed. by Andrew Allen. LC 96-49868. (Illus.). 480p. 1997. pap. text 39.95 (0-7216-6815-1, W B Saunders Co) Harcrt Hlth Sci Grp.

Physician Assistants: Their Contribution to Health Care. Henry B. Perry & Bina Breitner. LC 81-6260. 331p. 1982. 45.95 (0-89885-066-5, Kluwer Acad Hman Sci) Kluwer Academic.

***Physician Assistant's Clinical Companion.** Springhouse Corporation Staff. LC 99-52569. 2000. 39.95 (1-58255-005-0) Springhouse Corp.

Physician Assistant's Drug Handbook. 1248p. 1999. 39.95 (0-87434-975-3) Springhouse Corp.

Physician Assistant's Emergency Medicine Handbook. Steven W. Salyer. Ed. by Lisa Biello. 656p. 1996. pap. text 41.00 (0-7216-5869-5, W B Saunders Co) Harcrt Hlth Sci Grp.

Physician Assistants in American Medicine. Roderick S. Hooker et al. LC 97-8216. 1997. pap. text 29.95 (0-443-05731-1) Church.

Physician-Assisted Death. Ed. by James M. Humber et al. LC 84-640015. (Biomedical Ethics Reviews Ser.: No. 1993). 165p. 1994. 49.50 (0-89603-265-5) Humana.

Physician-Assisted Suicide. Ed. by Daniel Leone. LC 97-27792. (At Issue Ser.). 107p. (YA). (gr. 5-12). 1997. 18.70 (1-56510-019-0); pap. 11.20 (1-56510-018-2) Greenhaven.

Physician-Assisted Suicide. Ed. by Robert F. Weir. LC 96-49417. (Medical Ethics Ser.). 1997. 29.95 (0-253-33282-6) Ind U Pr.

Physician Assisted Suicide: Expanding the Debate. M. Pabst Battin et al. LC 97-52070. 320p. (C). 1998. 75.00 (0-415-92002-7) Routledge.

Physician Assisted Suicide: Expanding the Debate. Ed. by Margaret P. Battin et al. 320p. 1998. pap. 21.99 (0-415-92003-5) Routledge.

***Physician-Assisted Suicide: Pro & Con.** David Mayo. (Point/Counterpoint Ser.). 2000. 53.00 (0-8476-8815-1) Rowman.

***Physician-Assisted Suicide & Euthanasia.** Lisa Yount. (Library in a Book). 256p. 2000. lib. bdg. 39.95 (0-8160-4021-4) Facts on File.

Physician Bonding: Developing a Successful Hospital Program. Ed. by Steven T. Valentine. 230p. 1990. 70.00 (0-8342-0105-4) Aspen Pub.

Physician Capitation Strategies: Real-Life Physician Case Studies. 100p. 79.95 (0-614-19661-2, OP046796WE) AMA.

Physician Characteristics & Distribution in the U. S. 350p. 1999. pap. 149.95 (0-89970-964-8) AMA.

***Physician Characteristics & Distribution in the U. S. 2000.** 350p. 1999. 160.00 (1-57947-015-7) AMA.

Physician Compensation Arrangements: Management & Legal Trends Dan Zismer. LC 99-30382. 228p. 1999. 64.00 (0-8342-0993-4) Aspen Pub.

Physician Compensation Systems. Max Reiboldt. Ed. by Kay Stanley. 1998. 44.95 (0-89970-910-9) AMA.

Physician-Computer Connection: A Practical Guide to Physician Involvement in Health Care Information Systems. rev. ed. William F. Bria & Richard L. Rydell. LC 96-26417. 124p. 1996. pap. 42.50 (1-55648-166-7, 093106) AHPI.

Physician Documentation for Reimbursement. Gabrielle M. Kotoski & Melinda Stegman. LC 94-7576. 254p. 1994. 53.00 (0-8342-0534-3) Aspen Pub.

***Physician Empowerment Through Capitation.** Frank. 2000. pap. 59.00 (0-8342-1212-9) Aspen Pub.

Physician Equity Groups & Other Emerging Entities: Competitive Organizational Choices for Physicians. Fred McCall-Perez. LC 97-16015. 1997. write for info. (0-7863-0960-1, Irwn Prfssnl) McGraw-Hill Prof.

Physician Equity Model. Keith M. Korenchuk. 229p. 1996. 45.00 (1-56829-077-2, 4908) Med Group Mgmt.

Physician Executive Compensation Report: A 1998-99 Survey of Physician Leadership. David R. Kirschman & Jennifer R. Grebenschikoff. 101p. (C). 1999. pap. text 150.00 (1-881310-09-4) Phys Exec Mgmt.

Physician Executives & the Law: Issues & Trends in Liability. Ed. by Todd Sagin. LC 95-80572. 165p. (Orig.). 1996. pap. 48.00 (0-924674-39-3) Am Coll Phys Execs.

Physician Executives' Guide to Patient Management for the '90s & Beyond. Raymond J. Fabius. LC 95-76633. 107p. 1995. pap. 48.00 (0-924674-33-4) Am Coll Phys Execs.

Physician Extraordinary: Dr. Richard Bright (1789-1858) R. M. Kark. LC 86-62925. (Illus.). (Orig.). 1986. pap. text 5.00 (0-9614070-1-8) Horn Moon Ent.

Physician Fees, 1998. annuals rev. ed. 410p. 1998. pap. text 99.95 (1-57066-080-8, 9835) Practice Mgmt Info.

Physician Financial Planning in a Changing Environment. Russ A. Prince et al. 300p. (Orig.). 1996. reprint ed. pap. text 44.95 (1-57066-104-9, ME115) Practice Mgmt Info.

Physician, Heal Thyself. John Allegro. LC 85-43081. 93p. 1985. 25.95 (0-87975-305-6) Prometheus Bks.

Physician, Heal Thyself: A Doctor's Dietary Recovery from Incurable Cancer. Hugh Faulkner. 112p. 1993. pap. 7.95 (0-9628528-6-4) One Peaceful World.

Physician Heal Thyself: Medical Practitioner of Eighteenth-Century New York. Marynita A. Nolosco. LC 94-13012. (American University Studies, Series IX: History: Vol. 170). 1994. write for info. (0-8204-2580-X) P Lang Pubng.

Physician Heal Thyself: What Every Practitioner Should Know about Alternative Medicine. Richard Sarnat. LC 95-77514. 112p. 1995. pap. 10.95 (0-9639297-2-0) Herbal Free.

***Physician, Health System Partnerships: Models for the Next Generation.** Craig E. Holm. LC 99-89952. 2000. pap. write for info. (1-56793-124-3) Health Admin Pr.

Physician Himself & What He Should Add to His Scientific Acquirements. 2nd ed. D. W. Cathell. LC 70-180562. (Medicine & Society in America Ser.). 216p. 1972. reprint ed. 18.95 (0-405-03941-7) Ayer.

Physician Hospital Organizations. Keith M. Korenchuk. 209p. 1994. 45.00 (1-56829-033-0, 4541) Med Group Mgmt.

Physician Hospital Organizations: Cases & Analysis. Thomas M. Gorey et al. LC 97-20196. 121p. 1997. pap. 18.20 (1-56793-063-8) Health Admin Pr.

Physician Hospital Transactions. James J. Unland. 1994. text 125.00 (1-55738-612-9, Irwn Prfssnl) McGraw-Hill Prof.

Physician ICD 9 CM: 1999 Edition. Medicode, Med-Index Division Staff. (C). 1999. pap. 69.95 (1-56337-283-5) Thomson Learn.

Physician in Industry. William P. Shepard. Ed. by Leon Stein. LC 77-70532. 1977. reprint ed. lib. bdg. 33.95 (0-405-10200-3) Ayer.

Physician Interaction Style & Medication Management: Abstract, Executive Summary & Final Report. Betsy Sleath. (Illus.). 90p. (C). 1998. reprint ed. pap. text 25.00 (0-7881-4502-9) DIANE Pub.

Physician Interaction Systems Manual. M. Johnson. 32p. (C). 1993. pap., student ed. write for info. (0-933195-63-X) CA College Health Sci.

Physician Investigator Handbook: GCP Tools & Techniques. Deborah Rosenbaum & Fred O. Smith. LC 96-48071. (Practical Clinical Trials Ser.: Vol. 2). (Illus.). 300p. 1997. 145.00 (1-57491-040-X) Interpharm.

Physician Leader's Guide. Ed. by Jonathan T. Lord. 200p. 1992. pap. text 20.00 (0-915910-10-8, TPLG) Capitol Publns.

Physician-Legislators of France: Medicine & Politics in the Early Third Republic, 1870-1914. Jack D. Ellis. (Cambridge History of Medicine Ser.). (Illus.). 317p. (C). 1990. text 69.95 (0-521-38208-4) Cambridge U Pr.

Physician-Manager Alliance: Building the Healthy Health Care Organization. Stephen M. Davidson et al. (Health Ser.). 288p. 1996. 36.95 (0-7879-0215-2) Jossey-Bass.

Physician Manager in Group Practice. John W. Pollard. 142p. 1994. pap. 36.00 (1-56829-005-5, 3931) Med Group Mgmt.

Physician Manager's Handbook: Essential Skills for Succeeding in Health Care. 2nd ed. Robert J. Solomon. LC 96-24308. (Illus.). 464p. 79.00 (0-8342-0768-0) Aspen Pub.

***Physician Medical Group Acquisition Report, 2000.** 5th ed. Irving Levin Associates, Inc. Staff. (Illus.). v, 104p. 2000. pap. 395.00 (1-930625-08-1) I Levin.

Physician Networks: Strategy, Start-Up, & Operation. Richard Krohn. LC 98-21935. 1998. 46.00 (1-56793-089-1) Health Admin Pr.

Physician of His Honour. Pedro Calderon de la Barca. Ed. & Tr. by Dian Fox & Donald Hindley from SPA.Tr. of Medico de su Honra. 1996. 59.95 (0-85668-639-5, Pub. by Aris & Phillips); pap. 25.00 (0-85668-640-9, Pub. by Aris & Phillips) David Brown.

Physician of the Dance of Death: A Historical Study of the Evolution of the Dance of Death Mythus in Art. Alfred S. Warthin. Ed. by Robert J. Kastenbaum. LC 76-19592. (Death & Dying Ser.). (Illus.). 1977. reprint ed. lib. bdg. 19.95 (0-405-09587-2) Ayer.

***Physician of the Soul: A Modern Kabbalistic Approach to Health & Healing.** Joseph H. Gelberman & Lesley Sussman. LC 99-58581. 170p. 2000. pap. 16.95 (1-58091-061-0, Pub. by Crossing Pr) Publishers Group.

Physician Office Health Records see Documentation & Reimbursement for Physician Offices

***Physician Office Letters 2000.** Joan Damsey. 2000. pap. 60.00 (1-57947-081-5) AMA.

Physician Organizations: Cases & Analysis. Thomas M. Gorey. LC 97-20193. 1997. pap. 18.20 (1-56793-064-6) Health Admin Pr.

Physician Organizations & Medical Staff: Contracts, Rights & Liabilities, 2 vols. Aspen Health Law Center Staff. 1996. 249.00 (0-8342-0792-3, S287) Aspen Pub.

Physician Participation in Medicaid Managed Care. Sunday E. Ubokudom. LC 97-25938. (Health Care Policy in the United States Ser.). (Illus.). 224p. 1997. text 65.00 (0-8153-2905-9) Garland.

***Physician-Patient Communication Skills for Improving Patient Relations.** 80p. 1999. 27.95 (0-89970-973-7) AMA.

Physician-Patient Decision-Making: A Study in Medical Ethics, 27. Douglas N. Walton. LC 85-5412. (Contributions in Philosophy Ser.: No. 27). (Illus.). 265p. 1985. 59.95 (0-313-24888-5, WPH/, Greenwood Pr) Greenwood.

Physician-Patient Relations: Subject, Reference & Research Guidebook. Wayne C. Heier. LC 87-47637. 160p. 1987. 47.50 (0-88164-576-1); pap. 44.50 (0-88164-577-X) ABBE Pubs Assn.

Physician-Patient Relationships: An Annotated Bibliography. Michael Glasser. LC 90-14126. (Applied Social Science Bibliographies Ser.: Vol. 4). 102p. 1991. text 28.00 (0-8240-0688-7, SS580) Garland.

Physician Payment Reform: Its Impact on Payers & Providers. Ed. by Richard Lauve. LC 92-81837. (Orig.). (C). 1992. pap. text 25.95 (0-924674-15-6) Am Coll Phys Execs.

Physician Performance Management: Tool for Survival & Success. Christine N. Micklitsch & Theresa A. Ryan-Mitlyng. (Illus.). 122p. (Orig.). 1996. pap. 75.00 (1-56829-078-0, 4928) Med Group Mgmt.

Physician Practice Acquisition Resource Book. William O. Cleverley et al. (Illus.). 221p. 1995. pap. 995.00 (1-882733-06-1) Ctr Hlthcare IPS.

Physician Productivity: A Productivity Handbook for Practitioners. Marshall O. Zaslove. LC 98-4368. 300p. 1998. 29.00 (0-8342-1098-3, 10983) Aspen Pub.

Physician Profiling: A Source Book for Health Care Administrators. Neill F. Piland. LC 99-11319. (Jossey-Bass Health Ser.). 1999. 42.95 (0-7879-4601-X) Jossey-Bass.

***Physician Profiling: Background & Practical Experience.** Ed. by Kenneth J. Pechman. 2000. 55.00 (0-924674-74-1) Am Coll Phys Execs.

Physician Profiling & Risk Adjustment. Norbert Goldfield & Peter Boland. 416p. 1996. 89.00 (0-8342-0743-5, 20743) Aspen Pub.

Physician Profiling & Risk Adjustment. 2nd ed. Norbert Goldfield. LC 98-37565. 672p. 1999. 69.00 (0-8342-1169-6, 11696) Aspen Pub.

Physician Salary Survey Report, 1992. Hospital Compensation Service Staff. 1992. pap. 250.00 (0-939326-68-X) Hosp & Hlthcare.

***Physician Socioeconomic Statistics Text 2000-2001.** Ed. by AMA Staff. (Illus.). 2000. pap. 495.00 (1-57947-088-2) AMA.

Physician Staffing for the VA, Vol. I. Ed. by Joseph Lipscomb. 432p. 1991. pap. text 39.95 (0-309-04549-5) Natl Acad Pr.

Physician to the World: The Life of General William C. Gorgas. John M. Gibson. LC 89-33463. (Library of Alabama Classics). (Illus.). 352p. 1989. reprint ed. pap. text 19.95 (0-8173-0457-6) U of Ala Pr.

***Physician Within.** Ed. by Gross. 232p. 1999. text 26.00 (0-536-02687-4) P-H.

Physician Within: A Step-by-Step Guide to Living Well with Chronic Illness. 2nd ed. Catherine Feste. LC 95-15194. 1995. pap. 12.95 (0-8050-3951-1, Owl) H Holt & Co.

Physician Within You: Alternative Medicine for the Millennium. Gladys T. McGarey. LC 96-29513. 250p. 1997. pap. 12.95 (1-55874-454-1) Health Comm.

***Physician Within You: Medicine for the Millenium.** Gladys Taylor McCarey & Jess Stearn. 295p. 2000. pap. 14.95 (0-9658158-5-4) Inkwell Prods.

Physicians & Hospitals: The Great Partnership at the Crossroads. Ed. by Duncan Yaggy & Patricia Hodgson. LC 84-25928. (Duke Press Policy Studies). xxiii, 202p. 1985. text 39.95 (0-8223-0639-5) Duke.

Physicians & Management in Health Care. Ed. by Montague Brown. (Health Care Management Review Ser.). 244p. 1992. 41.00 (0-8342-0300-6, 20300) Aspen Pub.

***Physicians & Surgeons Directory, 2000 Edition.** rev. ed. American Business Directories Staff. 2920p. 1999. boxed set 695.00 incl. cd-rom (0-7687-0203-8) Am Busn Direct.

Physicians & Surgeons of Color: Real Image Models for Youth & Adults. Robert E. Greene. LC 96-90518. 360p. 1996. pap. 24.95 (0-945733-14-3) R E Greene.

Physicians & the Peace Movement. Nick Lewer. 140p. 1992. text 29.50 (0-7146-3438-7, Pub. by F Cass Pubs) Intl Spec Bk.

***Physician's Art: Representations of Art & Medicine.** Julie V. Hansen & Suzanne Porter. LC 99-74558. (Illus.). 144p. 1999. 54.95 (0-9672946-0-6, Pub. by Duke Univ Med); 29.95 (0-9672946-1-4, Pub. by Duke Univ Med) Duke.

Physicians As Employees. Aspen Staff. LC 98-9397. (Current Issue Ser.). 160p. 1998. 39.00 (0-8342-1157-2, 11572) Aspen Pub.

Physicians As Employees: Aspen Health Law Center Current Issues. Aspen Health Law Center Staff. LC 98-9397. 160p. 1998. pap. 39.00 (0-8342-1121-1) Aspen Pub.

Physician's Assistant. Jack Rudman. (Career Examination Ser.: C-2557). 1994. pap. 29.95 (0-8373-2557-9) Nat Learn.

Physician's Assistant, No. 1210-1211. Diane V. Lloyd & Marta B. Stavrou. 1977. 10.00 (0-686-19685-6, Sage Prdcls Pr) Sage.

Physicians Assistants: Present & Future Models of Utilization. Ed. by Sarah F. Zarbock & Kenneth Harbert. LC 85-25664. 152p. 1986. 57.95 (0-275-92065-8, C2065, Praeger Pubs) Greenwood.

Physicians at Teaching Hospitals (path) Audits: Hearing Before a Subcommittee of the Committee on Appropriations, United States Senate, One Hundred Fifth Congress, First Session, Special Hearing. United States. LC 98-160487. iii, 48p. 1998. write for info. (0-16-056304-6) USGPO.

Physicians' Attitudes Toward Elder Suicide. Lori M. Secouler. LC 97-32973. (Studies on the Elderly in America). 100p. 1998. text 35.00 (0-8153-3005-7) Garland.

Physician's Book Compendium, 1969-1970: The Medical Book Reference for Physicians. Ed. by Max Celnik. LC Z 6658.. 872p. reprint ed. pap. 200.00 (0-608-16971-4, 202710600054) Bks Demand.

Physicians' Book of Days. Marcia O. Levin. (Illus.). 128p. 1992. 10.95 (0-88363-392-2) H L Levin.

Physicians, Colonial Racism & Diaspora in West Africa. Adell Patton. LC 95-45070. 296p. (C). 1996. 49.95 (0-8130-1432-8) U Press Fla.

***Physician's Compass: A Navigation Guide to the Internet.** Kevin W. Fergusson. 80p. 2000. pap. 7.00 (0-615-11516-0) DrPEN.

***Physician's Compensation: Measurement, Benchmarking & Implementation.** Lucy R. Carter & Sara S. Lankford. 20p. 2000. 75.00 (0-471-32361-6) Wiley.

***Physician's Covenant: Images of the Healer in Medical Ethics.** 2nd ed. William F. May. 232p. 2000. pap. 19.95 (0-664-22274-9) Westminster John Knox.

Physicians' Dentists' & Druggists' Directing for 1890 of Minnesota & Wisconsin. 1997. reprint ed. pap. 12.00 (0-915709-56-2) Pk Geneal Bk.

Physician's Desk Reference (Diccionario de Especialidades Farmaceuticas), 1990. 36th ed. (SPA.). 1990. pap. 150.00 (0-685-60775-5) Fr & Eur.

Physician's Desk Reference (Dictionnaire Vidal), 1990. 66th ed. (FRE.). 2296p. 1990. 225.00 (0-685-60776-3) Fr & Eur.

Physicians Disciplined for Sex-Related Offenses. Christine E. Dehlendorf & Sidney M. Wolfe. LC 98-162160. viii, 194 p. 1997. write for info. (0-937188-60-3) Pub Citizen.

Physician's Drug Handbook. 7th ed. Springhouse Corporation Staff. (Illus.). 1232p. 1997. 39.95 (0-87434-899-4) Springhouse Corp.

Physicians Drug Handbook. 8th ed. 1312p. 1999. 39.95 (0-87434-987-7) Springhouse Corp.

***Physicians' Drug Manual: 2001 Edition.** rev. ed. Michael Safani & Paul D. Chan. (Current Clinical Strategies Ser.). 90p. 2000. pap. 9.95 (1-881528-96-0) Current Clin Strat.

***Physicians' Drug Manual: 2001 Edition.** rev. ed. Michael Safani. (Current Clinical Strategies Ser.). 90p. 2000. pap. 28.95 incl. cd-rom (1-881528-97-9) Current Clin Strat.

Physicians' Drug Resource, 1999 Edition: Current Clinical Strategies. rev. ed. Ed. by Michael Safani. (Current Clinical Strategies Ser.). 98p. 1998. pap. 9.95 (1-881528-73-1) Current Clin Strat.

Physician's Essential MBA: What Every Physician Leader Needs to Know. Ed. by Michael J. Stahl & Peter J. Dean. LC 98-54872. 322p. 1999. pap. 35.00 (0-8342-1244-7) Aspen Pub.

Physician's Eye. John Naish. LC 97-4009. (Mellen Lives Ser.: Vol. 6). (Illus.). 172p. 1997. text 79.95 (0-7734-8662-3) E Mellen.

Physicians' Fee Reference, 1999. 16th ed. Yale Wasserman, D.M.D. Medical Publishers, Limited. 1999. per. 129.00 (1-881072-33-9) Y W DMD Med.

Physicians' Fee Reference, 2000. 17th ed. Yale Wasserman, D.M.D. Medical Publishers, Limited. 2000. per. 129.00 (1-881072-37-1) Y W DMD Med.

Physician's Financial Sourcebook Vol. 1: Investment, Risk Management & Retirement Tools for a Balanced Life. Paul H. Sutherland. Ed. by Matthew F. Sutherland. LC 97-95333. (Illus.). 250p. 1998. pap. 29.95 (0-9661060-0-8) Finan Srcebk Pub.

Physicians for the 21st Century. Lawrence E. Stevens. vi, 171p. 1997. 14.95 (0-9661514-0-2, 1) White Bush Pub.

Physicians' Generix: The Official Drug Reference of FDA Prescribing Information & Therapeutic Equivalents, 1992. 2700p. 1992. 68.00 (1-880891-02-6) Work-Loss Data.

Physicians' Generix, 1993: The Official Drug Reference of FDA Prescribing Information & Therapeutic Equivalents. Ed. by Jonathan A. Epner. 2600p. 1993. 77.00 (1-880891-03-4) Work-Loss Data.

Physicians Genrix, 1995: The Complete Drug Reference of FDA Prescribing Information &... Philip L. Denniston. 1995. 77.00 (1-880891-07-7) Work-Loss Data.

Physicians GenRx 1997 Book Update, No. 1. rev. ed. Physicians GenRx Staff Corporation. 1997. write for info. (0-8151-7222-2) Mosby Inc.

Physicians GenRx 1997 Book Update, No. 2. 2nd rev. ed. Physicians GenRx Staff Corporation. 1997. write for info. (0-8151-7223-0) Mosby Inc.

Physician's Guide for Expert Witnessing. Reda A. Abdel-Fattah. 175p. 1993. 105.00 (1-883865-01-8) Biomed Pr.

Physician's Guide for the Collection of Bacteriological & Viral Specimens. Stephen J. Cavalleri & Gilles R. G. Monif. (Illus.). 52p. 1995. pap. 6.95 (1-880906-41-4) IDI Pub.

Physician's Guide for the Collection of Bacteriological & Viral Specimens. Gilles R. Monif. 55p. 7.95 (1-880906-73-2) IDI Pub.

P

An Asterisk (*) at the beginning of an entry indicates that the title is appearing for the first time.

Physician's Guide for the Handling of Gynecologic & Obstetric Tissue Specimens. Chhandra Bewtra. (Illus.). 69p. (Orig.). 1996. pap. 9.95 (1-880906-15-5) IDI Pub.

Physician's Guide to Advance Medical Directives. Alan D. Lieberson. Ed. by Melanie C. Karaffa. LC 92-48385. 350p. 1993. 69.95 (1-878487-52-3, ME223) Practice Mgmt Info.

Physician's Guide to Arthropods of Medical Importance. Jerome Goddard. 352p. 1993. lib. bdg. 126.95 (0-8493-5160-X, RA641) CRC Pr.

Physician's Guide to Arthropods of Medical Importance. 2nd ed. Jerome Goddard. LC 96-28904. 400p. 1996. lib. bdg. 139.00 (0-8493-2662-1) CRC Pr.

***Physician's Guide to Arthropods of Medical Importance.** 3rd ed. Jerome Goddard. 422p. 1999. boxed set 149.95 (0-8493-1186-1) CRC Pr.

Physician's Guide to Cancer Care Complications: Prevention & Management. Ed. by John Laszlo. LC 85-29361. (Fundamentals of Cancer Management Ser.: No. 2). 359p. 1986. reprint ed. pap. 111.30 (0-608-01296-3, 206204200001) Bks Demand.

***Physician's Guide to Caring for Children with Disabilities & Chronic Conditions.** Robert E. Nickel & Larry W. Desch. LC 99-35344. 2000. 125.00 (1-55766-446-3) P H Brookes.

***Physician's Guide to Chronic Illness in Pediatrics.** (Hazelden Chronic Illness Ser.). (Illus.). 320p. 2000. 39.95 (0-07-134720-8) McGraw-Hill Prof.

***Physician's Guide to Clinical Forensic Medicine.** Ed. by Margaret M. Stark. (Forensic Science & Medicine Ser.). 352p. 2000. 89.50 (0-89603-742-8) Humana.

Physician's Guide to Disease Management: Patient-Centered Care for the 21st Century. James B. Couch. LC 97-18244. 368p. 1997. pap. 49.00 (0-8342-1003-7) Aspen Pub.

Physician's Guide to Diving Medicine. C. W. Shilling et al. LC 84-14817. (Illus.). 768p. 1984. 165.00 (0-306-41428-7, Kluwer Plenum) Kluwer Academic.

Physician's Guide to Domestic Violence: How to Ask the Right Questions & Recognize Abuse. Patricia R. Salber & Ellen Taliaferro. LC 94-23000. 114p. 1995. pap. 10.95 (1-884244-04-1) Volcano Pr.

Physicians' Guide to Drug Eruptions. Jerome Z. Litt. LC 97-36824. 278p. 1997. 68.00 (1-85070-003-6) Prthnon Pub.

Physician's Guide to Eye Care. Jonathan D. Trobe. LC 93-9068. 200p. 1993. pap. 59.95 (1-56055-073-2) Am Acad Ophthal.

Physicians' Guide to Free Radicals, Immunity & Aging. Lee-Benner. 1986. lib. bdg. 125.00 (0-944213-00-6) World Hlth Found.

Physician's Guide to Free Radicals, Immunity & Aging. deluxe ed. Lord Lee-Benner. LC 90-71564. (Illus.). 301p. (C). 1991. write for info. (0-944213-27-8) World Hlth Found.

Physician's Guide to Free Radicals, Immunity & Aging. rev. ed. Lord Lee-Benner. LC 90-71564. (Illus.). 301p. (C). 1991. lib. bdg. 150.00 (0-944213-26-X) World Hlth Found.

Physician's Guide to Free Radicals, Immunity & Aging. 2nd rev. ed. Lord Lee-Benner. LC 90-71564. (Illus.). 301p. (C). 1991. 125.00 (0-944213-25-1) World Hlth Found.

Physician's Guide to Herbal Wellness: Safe & Effective Remedies for Achieving & Maintaining Health. John Cammarata. LC 96-12822. (Illus.). 192p. (Orig.). 1996. pap. 14.95 (1-55652-273-8) Chicago Review.

Physician's Guide to Internet Explorer. American Medical Association. 1999. 29.95 (0-89970-934-6) AMA.

Physician's Guide to Managed Care. Ed. by David B. Nash. 272p. 1994. 67.00 (0-8342-0393-6, 20393) Aspen Pub.

Physicians Guide to Managed Care. 2nd ed. James R. Lyle & Hoyt W. Torras. 1995. pap. 49.95 (1-879249-17-0) HlthCare Consult.

Physician's Guide to Mental Illness. Hazelden. 1999. 34.95 (0-07-134716-X) McGraw.

Physician's Guide to Natural Remedies. D. Paul Barney. 1998. pap. text 19.95 (1-885670-84-2) Woodland UT.

Physicians' Guide to Nutriceuticals. Douglas L. Ringer. 290p. 1998. 39.99 (0-9665665-0-5) Nutrtnl Data Resces.

***Physician's Guide to Pain & Symptom Management in Cancer Patients** J. Abrahm. LC 99-37061. 2000. 26.00 (0-8018-6246-9) Johns Hopkins.

Physician's Guide to Psychoactive Drugs. Richard Seymour & David E. Smith. LC 87-354. 186p. 1987. text 5.95 (0-86656-382-2) Haworth Pr.

Physicians' Guide to Rare Diseases. Ed. by Doris C. Smith. (Illus.). 1224p. 1992. 69.50 (0-9628716-0-5) Dowden Pub.

Physician's Guide to Rare Diseases: 1995 Edition. 2nd ed. Ed. & Intro. by Jess G. Thoene. (Illus.). 1200p. 1995. 129.99 (0-9628716-1-3) Dowden Pub.

Physician's Guide to Spirituality in the Treatment of Chronic Illness. Hazelden. (Hazelden Chronic Illness Ser.). 320p. 1999. 34.95 (0-07-134717-8) McGraw-Hill Prof.

Physician's Guide to Street Drugs. Hazelden. 1999. 34.95 (0-07-134719-4) McGraw.

Physician's Guide to Substance Abuse. Hazelden. 1999. 34.95 (0-07-134713-5) McGraw.

Physician's Guide to Sunscreens. Nicholas Lowe. (Illus.). 232p. 1990. text 110.00 (0-8247-8496-0) Dekker.

Physician's Guide to the Laboratory Diagnosis of Inherited Metabolic Diseases. N. Blail et al. (Arnold Publication Ser.). (Illus.). 544p. 1996. text 69.00 (0-412-57560-4) OUP.

***Physician's Guide to Thriving in the New Managed Care Environment: Selecting the Right Strategy for Your Practice.** Richard V. Stenson. LC 99-22237. 320p. 2000. 49.95 (1-58151-030-6, Pub. by BookPartners) Midpt Trade.

Physician's Guide to Transgendered Medicine. Sheila Kirk. Date not set. pap. 10.00 (1-887796-03-7) Together Lifeworks.

Physician's Guide to 12 Step Principles. Hazelden. 1999. 34.95 (0-07-134718-6) McGraw.

Physicians' Guides to Healing: Treating Asthma, Allergies, & Food Sensitivities. Alan Pressman et al. 224p. 1997. mass mkt. 5.99 (0-425-15669-9) Berkley Pub.

Physicians' Guides to Healing No. 3: Treating Hypertension, & Other Cardiovascular Conditions. Alan Pressman et al. LC 97-168749. 224p. 1997. mass mkt. 5.99 (0-425-15853-5) Berkley Pub.

Physicians' Guides to Healing No. 4: Treating Gynecological Conditions. Alan Pressman & Herbert D. Goodman. LC 97-178492. (Physicians Guides to Healing Ser.). 192p. 1997. mass mkt. 5.99 (0-425-15908-6) Berkley Pub.

Physicians' Guides to Healing No. 5: Treating Digestive Conditions. Alan Pressman et al. LC 97-225152. (The Physicians' Guide to Healing Ser.). 272p. 1997. mass mkt. 6.50 (0-425-15940-X) Berkley Pub.

Physician's Hand. Barbara Melosh. (C). 1982. pap. text 22.95 (0-87722-290-8) Temple U Pr.

Physician's Handbook. 20th ed. Marcus A. Krupp. pap. text 12.00 (0-87041-023-7) Appleton & Lange.

Physicians Handbook of Clinical Nutrition. Henry Osiecki. 252p. (C). 1990. pap. 65.00 (1-875239-03-0, Pub. by Bio Concepts) St Mut.

Physician's Handbook of Clinical Photography. Lawrence B. Stack et al. LC 98-41939. (Illus.). 350p. 2000. text 45.00 (1-56053-213-0) Hanley & Belfus.

Physicians in Bureaucracy: A Case Study of Professional Pressures on Organizational Roles. Mary E. Goss. Ed. by Harriet Zuckerman & Robert K. Merton. LC 79-9002. (Dissertations on Sociology Ser.). 1980. lib. bdg. 19.95 (0-405-12971-8) Ayer.

Physicians in Corporations: Medicine As Management. Diana C. Walsh. LC 87-6096. 272p. 1987. 42.50 (0-300-03902-6) Yale U Pr.

Physicians in Managed Care: A Career Guide. Ed. by Mark Bloomberg & Steven Mohlie. LC 94-70991. 152p. (Orig.). 1994. pap. text 25.00 (0-924674-25-3) Am Coll Phys Execs.

Physicians in the Academic Marketplace, 53. Dolores L. Burke. LC 91-28327. (Contributions to the Study of Education Ser.: No. 53). 184p. 1991. 52.95 (0-313-27850-4, BYE/, Greenwood Pr) Greenwood.

Physicians in the Making. Davis G. Johnson. LC 83-48159. (Jossey-Bass Higher Education Ser.). 327p. reprint ed. pap. 101.40 (0-8357-4950-9, 203788100009) Bks Demand.

Physicians Insurance Reference, 1999. 10th ed. Yale Wasserman, D.M.D. Medical Publishers, Limited. 1999. per. 69.00 (1-881072-35-5) Y W DMD Med.

Physicians Insurance Reference, 2000. 11th ed. Yale Wasserman, D.M.D. Medical Publishers, Limited. 2000. per. 69.00 (1-881072-39-8) Y W DMD Med.

Physician's Job-Search Rx: Marketing Yourself for the Position You Want. Javad H. Kashani et al. 229p. 1998. pap. 16.95 (0-471-19336-4) Wiley.

Physicians of Tomorrow: A Colloquium to Advance Medical Education in Alcohol & Other Drug Dependencies. 1989. pap. 4.00 (0-911290-20-6) Rutgers Ctr Alcohol.

Physicians of Western Medicine. Ed. by Robert A. Hahn & Atwood D. Gaines. 1984. pap. text 64.50 (90-277-1881-4); lib. bdg. 153.50 (90-277-1790-7) Kluwer Academic.

Physician's Office. Leif C. Beck. LC 77-87555. (Illus.). 1977. 14.95 (90-219-0346-6) Excerpta Princeton.

Physician's Office & Ambulatory Surgery: Detailed Survey Data of Value to Medical, Insurance & High Tech Industries. 277p. 1986. 1350.00 (0-931634-63-6) FIND-SVP.

Physician's Office in Vitro Diagnostic Testing Markets. (Market Research Reports: No. 140). (Illus.). 123p. 1991. 295.00 (0-317-04148-7) Theta Corp.

Physicians Office Information Systems. (Market Research Reports: No. 153). (Illus.). 167p. 1991. 295.00 (0-317-05004-4) Theta Corp.

Physician's Office Laboratory. 2nd ed. Bernard D. Statland et al. 468p. 1993. pap. 49.95 (1-878487-49-3, ME200) Practice Mgmt Info.

Physician's Office Laboratory Guidelines, Procedure Manual: Tentative Guideline. 3rd ed. NCCLS Staff. 200p. 1995. pap. text 150.00 (1-56238-159-8, POL1/2-T3) NCCLS.

Physicians Office 97: Coding Workbook. 4th ed. Covell. (Medical Assisting Ser.). (C). 1997. text 17.50 (0-7668-0081-4) Delmar.

Physician's Perspective on Medical Law, Vol. I. Ed. by Howard H. Kaufman & Jeffrey L. Lewin. (Neurosurgical Topics Ser.: Vol. 28). (Illus.). 202p. 1997. 95.00 (1-879284-44-8) Am Assn Neuro.

Physician's Perspective on Medical Law, Vol. II. Ed. by Howard H. Kaufman & Jeffrey L. Lewin. (Neurosurgical Topics Ser.: Vol. 28B). 238p. 1997. 95.00 (1-879284-53-7) Am Assn Neuro.

Physicians Posy. Dorothy Shepard. 109p. 1934. pap. 15.95 (0-85207-272-4, Pub. by C W Daniel) Natl Bk Netwk.

Physician's Posy. Dorothy Shepherd. 256p. (Orig.). 1993. pap. 19.95 (0-8464-4177-2) Beekman Pubs.

Physician's Practice. Ed. by John M. Eisenberg & Sankey V. Williams. LC 80-13691. 288p. 1984. reprint ed. 32.50 (0-471-05469-0) Krieger.

Physician's Prescription for the Soul. Douglas J. Engelbrecht. 55p. (Orig.). 1987. pap. 5.00 (0-8100-0265-5, 22N0804) Northwest Pub.

Physician's Primer on Workers' Compensation. Committee on Occupational Health Staff. 79p. 1992. pap. 25.00 (0-89203-073-9) Amer Acad Ortho Surg.

Physician's Reference Guide to Cardiology. Ed. by Dennis S. Reison. 935p. 1992. write for info. (1-878212-00-1) Prof & Tech Pub.

Physician's Reference Guide to Medical Literature, Dermatology: A Compendium of Medical Books, Abstracts of Journal Articles, Educational Software, Audio & Video Cassettes. Ed. by American Academy of Dermatology Staff. 1995. write for info. (0-614-06028-1) Prof & Tech Pub.

Physician's Risk Management Desk Reference. Ed. by Grena G. Porto. xi, 176p. 1997. pap. 15.00 (0-9629192-0-9) V H A.

Physician's Role in Home Health Care. Peter Boling. LC 97-13704. 328p. 1997. 46.95 (0-8261-9700-0) Springer Pub.

Physician's RX Shorthand. Stanley Jablonski. LC 97-102931. 100p. 1996. text 9.95 (1-56053-167-3) Hanley & Belfus.

Physician's Slimming Guide: For Permanent Weight Control. Neal D. Barnard. LC 92-9631. (Illus.). 80p. 1992. pap. 5.95 (0-913990-91-4) Book Pub Co.

Physician's Socioeconomic Statistics, 1999-2000 Edition. American Medical Association. 1999. 495.00 (0-89970-974-5) AMA.

Physician's Survival Guide to Business of Medicine. Robert W. Katz. LC 93-33907. 192p. 1994. 107.00 (0-8342-0532-7) Aspen Pub.

Physician's Survival Guide to the Business of Medicine. 2nd ed. Robert W. Katz. 250p. 1998. 49.00 (0-8342-1024-X, 20124) Aspen Pub.

Physician's Tale. Geoffrey Chaucer. Ed. by Helen S. Corsa. LC 79-33146. (Variorum Edition of the Works of Geoffrey Chaucer, The Canterbury Tales Ser.: Vol. 2, Pt. 17). (Illus.). 208p. 1987. 49.95 (0-8061-2038-X) U of Okla Pr.

***Physician's Tale.** David Aaron Goldstein. 344p. 2000. 24.95 (0-9656635-5-8) July Blue.

***Physicians/Surgeons Directory 2001.** American Business Directory Staff. 2000. 595.00 (0-7687-0326-3) Am Busn Direct.

Physicist. Jack Rudman. (Career Examination Ser.: C-586). 1994. pap. 34.95 (0-8373-0586-1) Nat Learn.

Physicist at the Mall. Janet Holmes. Ed. by Donna J. Long. LC 93-74406. (Anhinga Prize for Poetry Ser.). 64p. (Orig.). (C). 1994. pap. 10.00 (0-938078-37-2) Anhinga Pr.

Physicist Looks at Biology: Sesquicentennial Celebration Proceedings, Pt. II. Max Delbruck. (Connecticut Academy of Arts & Sciences Ser., Trans.: Vol. 38). 1949. pap. 29.50 (0-685-22900-9) Elliots Bks.

Physicist on Madison Avenue. Tony Rothman. LC 90-44941. (Illus.). 162p. 1991. reprint ed. pap. 50.30 (0-608-02503-8, 206314700004) Bks Demand.

Physicists. Friedrich Durrenmatt. Tr. by James Kirkup from GER. LC 91-20775. 96p. 1964. pap. 10.00 (0-8021-5088-8, Grove) Grove-Atltic.

Physicists: The History of a Scientific Community in Modern America. Daniel J. Kevles. LC 94-23708. 544p. 1995. pap. 17.95 (0-674-66656-9, KEVPHY) HUP.

Physicist's ABC on Plasma. L. A. Artsimovich. 124p. 1985. 39.75 (0-7855-1183-0, Pub. by Collets); pap. 30.00 (0-7855-2959-4, Pub. by Collets) St Mut.

Physicist's ABC on Plasma. L. A. Artsimovich. 124p. (C). 1978. 40.00 (0-7855-4968-4, Pub. by Collets) St Mut.

Physicist's Conception of Nature. Ed. by Jagdish Mehra. LC 73-75765. 1973. lib. bdg. 299.00 (90-277-0345-0) Kluwer Academic.

Physicist's Conception of Nature. Werner Heisenberg. Tr. by Arnold J. Pomerans. LC 72-90526. 192p. 1970. reprint ed. lib. bdg. 38.50 (0-8371-3107-3, HECN, Greenwood Pr) Greenwood.

***Physicist's Desk Reference.** 3rd ed. Contrib. by E. Richard Cohen et al. LC 99-59693. 400p. 2000. 59.95 (0-387-98973-0, AIP Pr) Spr-Verlag.

Physicist's Desk Reference: Physics Vade Mecum. 2nd ed. Ed. by Herbert L. Anderson. 356p. 1989. 70.00 (0-88318-629-2); pap. 45.00 (0-88318-610-1) Am Inst Physics.

Physicist's Guide to Mathematica. Patrick Tam. LC 96-9900. (Illus.). 506p. 1997. pap. 59.00 (0-12-683190-4) Morgan Kaufmann.

Physicist's Guide to Skepticism. Milton A. Rothman. LC 88-4077. (Illus.). 247p. 1988. 29.95 (0-87975-440-0) Prometheus Bks.

Physicists in Conflict. N. A. Porter. LC 98-8669. (Illus.). 367p. 1998. 39.50 (0-7503-0509-6) IOP Pub.

Physicists' Inaugural Lectures in History. Martin J. Klein. 32p. (Orig.). (C). 1994. pap. 12.95 (90-5356-057-2, Pub. by Amsterdam U Pr) U of Mich Pr.

Physicists Look Back: Studies in the History of Physics. Ed. by J. Roche. LC 91-148368. (Illus.). 404p. 1990. 143.00 (0-85274-001-8) IOP Pub.

Physicist's Outlook on New Materials. Ed. by E. Bonnetti et al. 200p. 1991. text 100.00 (0-87849-615-7, Pub. by Trans T Pub) Enfield Pubs NH.

Physick for the Sickness, Commonly Called the Plague. Stephen Bradwell. LC 77-6859. (English Experience Ser.: No. 852). 1977. reprint ed. lib. bdg. 15.00 (90-221-0852-X) Walter J Johnson.

Physicke Against Fortune. Francesco Petrarca. Tr. by Thomas Twyne. LC 80-22768. 728p. 1980. reprint ed. 90.00 (0-8201-1359-X) Schol Facsimiles.

Physico-Chemical & Theoretical Studies see Biomolecular Structure, Conformation, Function & Evolution

Physico-Chemical Applications of NMR: A Practical Guide. LC 97-109494. 372p. 1996. 31.00 (981-02-2540-7) World Scientific Pub.

Physico-Chemical Aspects of Soil & Related Materials. Ed. by Keith B. Hoddinott & Robert O. Lamb. LC 90-37460. (Special Technical Publication (STP) Ser.: No. 1095). (Illus.). 200p. 1990. text 48.00 (0-8031-1396-X, STP1095) ASTM.

Physico-Chemical Behaviour of Atmospheric Pollutants. Ed. by G. Angeletti & Giambattista Restelli. (C). 1987. text 357.00 (90-277-2464-4) Kluwer Academic.

Physico-Chemical Behaviour of Atmospheric Pollutants. Ed. by G. Angeletti & Giambattista Restelli. (C). 1990. text 375.00 (0-7923-0700-3) Kluwer Academic.

Physico-Chemical Behaviour of Atmospheric Pollutants. Ed. by V. Versino & G. Angeletti. 1984. text 303.50 (90-277-1873-3) Kluwer Academic.

Physico-Chemical Behaviour of Atmospheric Pollution. Ed. by B. Versino & H. Ott. 1982. text 255.50 (90-277-1349-9) Kluwer Academic.

Physico-Chemical Constituents & Engineering Properties of Food Crop. R. P. Kachru et al. 1994. pap. 90.00 (81-7233-083-9, Pub. by Scientific Pubs) St Mut.

Physico-Chemical Factors of Biological Evolution. S. E. Shnol. (Soviet Scientific Reviews, Biology Reviews Supplement Ser.: Vol. 1). xvi, 280p. 1981. text 368.00 (3-7186-0044-7) Gordon & Breach.

Physico-Chemical Methodologies in Psychiatric Research. fac. ed. Ed. by Israel Hanin & Stephen H. Koslow. LC 80-13575. (Illus.). 277p. pap. 85.90 (0-7837-7204-1, 204709500005) Bks Demand.

Physico-Chemical Principles for Processing of Oligomeric Blends. Semjon M. Mezhikovskii. (Polymer Science & Engineering Monographs, a State-of-the-Art Tutorial Ser.: Vol. 4). 224p. 1998. text 90.00 (90-5699-661-4) Gordon & Breach.

Physico-Chemical Principles of Color Chemistry. Harold Freeman. Ed. by Arnold T. Peters. 312p. 1996. write for info. (0-7514-0245-1) Kluwer Academic.

Physico-Chemical Processes & Nonequilibrium Flow: Proceedings of the 19th International Symposium on Shock Waves, Held at Marseille, France, July 1993. Ed. by R. Brun & L. Z. Dumitrescu. LC 95-14593. (Shock Waves at Marseilles Ser.: No. 2). 1995. write for info. (3-540-57711-4) Spr-Verlag.

Physico-Chemical Properties of Matter. 1993. write for info. (0-8493-7724-2) CRC Pr.

Physico-Chemical Properties of Selected Anionic, Cationic, & Nonionic Surfactants. N. M. Van Os et al. LC 93-15051. 608p. 1993. 298.25 (0-444-89691-0) Elsevier.

Physico-Chemistry of Elastomer Heat-Shielding Materials. Donskoi. LC 98-203914. 211p. 1998. 115.00 (1-56072-558-3) Nova Sci Pubs.

Physico Physiological Researches on the Dynamics. 2nd ed. Charles Von Reichenbach. 456p. 1996. pap. 35.00 (0-7873-0914-1) Hlth Research.

Physico-Theology: A Demonstration of the Being & Attributes of God, from His Works of Creation. William Derham. Ed. by Frank N. Egerton. 3rd. LC 77-74212. (History of Ecology Ser.). 1978. reprint ed. lib. bdg. 41.95 (0-405-10383-2) Ayer.

Physico-Theology: or A Demonstration of the Being & Attributes of God, from His Works of Creation. William Derham. (Anglistica & Americana Ser.: No. 162). xiv, 482p. 1976. reprint ed. 76.70 (3-487-05924-X) G Olms Pubs.

Physicochemical & Environmental Plant Physiology. 2nd ed. Park S. Nobel. LC 98-88525. (Illus.). 512p. 1999. 59.95 (0-12-520025-0) Acad Pr.

Physicochemical Anthropology Pt. I: Human Behavioral Structure. N. R. Joseph. (Illus.). 1978. 68.00 (3-8055-2793-4) S Karger.

Physicochemical Anthropology Pt. II: Comparative Morphology & Behavior. N. R. Joseph. 1979. 85.25 (3-8055-2951-1) S Karger.

Physicochemical Aspects of Medicine Reviews, Vol. 8. Ed. by Isaac M. Khalatnikov. xiv, 608p. 1987. text 822.00 (3-7186-0215-6) Gordon & Breach.

Physicochemical Aspects of Medicine Reviews: Affinity Chromatography in Artificial Detoxification Systems; Hemosorption in the Management of Atherosclerosis; Fertility Alpha2-Microglobulin (FAMG), Vol. 2. I. P. Andrianov et al. (Soviet Medical Reviews Ser.: Vol. 2, Pt. 1). ii, 84p. 1989. pap. text 63.00 (3-7186-4966-7) Gordon & Breach.

Physicochemical Aspects of Medicine Reviews: Electrochemical Methods of Detoxification for Medical Use, Vol. 2. V. I. Sergienko & Y. B. Vasiliev. (Soviet Medical Reviews Ser.: Vol. 2, Pt. 2). iv, 60p. 1989. pap. text 70.00 (3-7186-4967-5) Gordon & Breach.

Physicochemical Aspects of Medicine Reviews: The Rate of Myocardial Necrotization As a Major Criterion of Infarction Severity; Automated Analysis of Chromatin Structures in Interphase Cell Nuclei, Vol. 2. A. V. Vinogradov et al. (Soviet Medical Reviews Ser.: Vol. 2, Pt. 4.1 & Pt. 4.2). iv, 84p. 1989. pap. text 62.00 (3-7186-4968-3) Gordon & Breach.

Physicochemical Aspects of Medicine Reviews: Thymic Peptides As Immunoregulators, with Special Reference to T-Activin, Vol. 2. V. Y. Arion. (Soviet Medical Reviews Ser.: Vol. 2, Pt. 3). iv, 64p. 1989. pap. text 69.00 (3-7186-4965-9) Gordon & Breach.

Physicochemical Aspects of Medicine Reviews Vol. 2, Pt. 5.4: Life As the Existence & Reproduction of Ordered Nucleotide & Amino-Acid Sequences, Vol. 2. N. N. Butusova. (Soviet Medical Reviews Ser.: Section B). 145p. 1991. text 128.00 (3-7186-5175-0, Harwood Acad Pubs) Gordon & Breach.

An Asterisk (*) at the beginning of an entry indicates that the title is appearing for the first time.

Physicochemical Aspects of Medicine Reviews Vol. 3, Pt. 1.3: Methods for Evaluating Crystalline Lens Transparency, & Some Approaches to the Early Detection, Vol. 3. V. E. Formazyuk. (Soviet Medical Reviews Ser.: Section B). 528p. 1991. pap. text 177.00 (*3-7186-5231-5*, Harwood Acad Pubs) Gordon & Breach.

Physicochemical Aspects of Medicine Reviews Vol. 3, Pt. 2: Hydromechanics of the Eye, Vol. 3. A. Nesterov. (Soviet Medical Reviews Ser.: Section B). 68p. 1992. pap. text 71.00 (*3-7186-5256-0*, Harwood Acad Pubs) Gordon & Breach.

Physicochemical Aspects of Medicine Reviews Vol. 3, Pt. 3: Peroxidation of Blood Lipoproteins & the Development of Atherosclerosis, Vol. 3. O. Panosenko. (Soviet Medical Reviews Ser.: Section B). 76p. 1992. pap. text 92.00 (*3-7186-5290-0*, Harwood Acad Pubs) Gordon & Breach.

Physicochemical Aspects of Medicine Reviews Vol. 3, Pt. 4: The Skin & Atherosclerosis, a Three-Drop Test, Vol. 3. Y. M. Lopukhin. (Soviet Medical Reviews Ser.: Section B). 124p. 1992. pap. text 147.00 (*3-7186-5291-9*, Harwood Acad Pubs) Gordon & Breach.

Physicochemical Aspects of Polymer Surfaces, Vol. 1. Ed. by K. L. Mittal. 610p. 1983. 125.00 (*0-306-41189-X*, Plenum Trade) Perseus Pubng.

Physicochemical Aspects of Polymer Surfaces, Vol. 2. Ed. by K. L. Mittal. 652p. 1983. 125.00 (*0-306-41190-3*, Plenum Trade) Perseus Pubng.

Physicochemical Biology: Restriction-Modification Enzymes; Cell-Model Membrane Interactions, Vol. 9. E. G. Malygin et al. Ed. by V. P. Skulachev. (Soviet Scientific Reviews Ser.: Vol. 9, Pt. 2). 196p. 1989. text 87.00 (*3-7186-4917-9*) Gordon & Breach.

Physicochemical Biology Reviews, Vol. 4. Ed. by V. P. Skulachev. (Soviet Scientific Reviews Ser.: Section D). xii, 334p. 1984. text 552.00 (*3-7186-0140-0*) Gordon & Breach.

Physicochemical Biology Reviews, Vol. 5. V. P. Skulachev. (Soviet Scientific Reviews Ser.: Section D). xiv, 406p. 1984. text 503.00 (*3-7186-0219-9*) Gordon & Breach.

Physicochemical Biology Reviews, Vol. 6. Ed. by V. P. Skulachev. (Soviet Scientific Reviews Ser.: Section D). xi, 266p. 1986. text 503.00 (*3-7186-0268-7*) Gordon & Breach.

Physicochemical Biology Reviews, Vol. 7. Ed. by V. P. Skulachev. (Soviet Scientific Reviews Ser., Section D). xii, 252p. 1987. text 557.00 (*3-7186-0411-6*) Gordon & Breach.

Physicochemical Biology Reviews: Mechanisms of Enzyme Action, Vol. 9. O. I. Lavrik. Ed. by V. P. Skulachev. (Soviet Scientific Reviews Ser.: Vol. 9, Pt. 1). ii, 92p. 1989. text 87.00 (*3-7186-4918-7*) Gordon & Breach.

Physicochemical Hydrodynamics. Ronald F. Probstein. 353p. 1989. text 89.95 (*0-7506-9401-7*) Buttrwrth-Heinemann.

Physicochemical Hydrodynamics: Interfacial Phenomena. Ed. by M. G. Verlarde. LC 88-9899. (NATO ASI Series B, Physics: Vol. 174). (Illus.). 1128p. 1988. 195.00 (*0-306-42905-5*, Plenum Trade) Perseus Pubng.

Physicochemical Hydrodynamics of Capillary Systems. V. V. Krotov. 1999. 88.00 (*1-86094-160-5*) World Scientific Pub.

Physicochemical Measurement by Gas Chromatography. John R. Conder & C. L. Young. LC 78-9899. (Illus.). 652p. reprint ed. pap. 200.00 (*0-8357-8984-5*, 203333200085) Bks Demand.

Physicochemical Measurements at High Temperatures. Ed. by John O. Bockris & J. L. White. LC QD0515.P54. 402p. reprint ed. pap. 124.70 (*0-608-10166-4*, 205133200001) Bks Demand.

Physicochemical Principles of Pharmacy. 3rd ed. A. T. Florence & D. Attwood. (Illus.). 564p. (C). 1998. pap. text 45.00 (*0-333-69081-8*, Pub. by Macmillan Ed) Scholium Intl.

Physicochemical Processes & Wastes in the Ocean: Oceanic Processes in Marine Pollution, Vol. 2. Ed. by Thomas P. O'Connor et al. LC 84-29746. 252p. (C). 1987. lib. bdg. 54.50 (*0-89874-811-9*) Krieger.

Physicochemical Processes for Water Quality Control. Walter J. Weber, Jr. (Environmental Science & Technology Ser.). 672p. 1972. 200.00 (*0-471-92435-0*) Wiley.

Physics. (Quick Study Academic Ser.). 4p. pap. 3.95 (*1-57222-126-7*) Barcharts.

Physics. (College Board SAT II Subject Test Ser.). 1997. pap. 23.95 (*0-8373-6313-6*, SATII-13) Nat Learn.

Physics. Marcello Alonso. 1138p. (C). 1992. pap. text 65.00 (*0-201-56518-8*) Addison-Wesley.

Physics. Peter Alonso. (World Student Ser.: Bk. 3). (C). 1969. pap. text 14.33 (*0-201-00262-0*) Addison-Wesley.

Physics. Aristotle. 166p. 1998. pap. 13.95 (*0-9665678-3-8*) Buy Books.

Physics. Aristotle. Ed. by W. David Ross. 1936. 135.00 (*0-19-814109-2*) OUP.

Physics. Aristotle. 382p. 1999. pap. 9.95 (*0-19-283586-6*) OUP.

Physics. Bob Bonnet. LC 99-33938. 1999. 17.95 (*0-8069-0707-X*) Strlng Pub CA.

Physics. C. Boyle. 290p. 1987. 60.00 (*1-85313-001-X*, Pub. by Checkmate Pubns) St Mut.

Physics. Coletta. 1995. pap., student ed. 26.88 (*0-8151-9165-0*) McGraw.

Physics. Coletta. 1996. 294.68 (*0-8151-1940-2*) Mosby Inc.

Physics. Robert W. Deutsch & J. W. Whitney. (Academic Program for Nuclear Power Plant Personnel Ser., BWR Version: Vol. II). (Illus.). 532p. 1972. teacher ed., ring bd. 195.00 (*0-87683-154-4*); teacher ed., ring bd. 35.00 (*0-87683-161-7*); teacher ed., ring bd. 25.00 (*0-87683-168-4*); ring bd. 39.50 (*0-87683-147-1*, A 373978) GP Courseware.

Physics. Alonso Finn. (C). 1994. pap. text. write for info. (*0-201-59183-9*) Addison-Wesley.

Physics. Hecht. (Physics Ser.). Date not set. student ed. 66.50 (*0-534-32064-3*); 69.25 (*0-534-32065-1*) Brooks-Cole.

Physics. Amanda Kent. (Introductions Ser.). (Illus.). 48p. (gr. 6 up). 1984. pap. 7.95 (*0-86020-711-0*) EDC.

Physics. David P. Lawrence. (Graphing Calculator Approach Ser.). 64p. (YA). (gr. 9 up). 1995. pap. text, lab manual ed. 12.95 (*1-881641-25-2*) Pencil Point.

Physics. Reese. 1999. mass mkt., student ed. 35.95 (*0-534-35234-0*) Brooks-Cole.

Physics. Reese. LC 98-41666. (Physics Ser.). 1999. 74.00 (*0-534-24655-9*) Brooks-Cole.

Physics. Jack Rudman. (Graduate Record Examination (GRE) Ser.: Vol. 15). 43.95 (*0-8373-5265-7*) Nat Learn.

Physics. Jack Rudman. (Undergraduate Program Field Tests (UPFT) Ser.: Vol. 19). 43.95 (*0-8373-6069-2*) Nat Learn.

Physics. Jack Rudman. (DANTES Ser.). 1994. 39.95 (*0-8373-6531-7*) Nat Learn.

Physics. Jack Rudman. (Graduate Record Examination Ser.: GRE-15). 1994. pap. 23.95 (*0-8373-5215-0*) Nat Learn.

Physics. Jack Rudman. (Undergraduate Program Field Tests Ser.: UPFT-19). 1994. pap. 23.95 (*0-8373-6019-6*) Nat Learn.

Physics. Jack Rudman. (Dantes Subject Standardized Tests (DANTES) Ser.: Vol. DANTES-31). 1994. pap. 23.95 (*0-8373-6631-3*) Nat Learn.

Physics. Snow. Date not set. pap. text, teacher ed. write for info. (*0-314-97155-6*) West Pub.

***Physics.** VanDenburgh. 2000. pap. 16.00 (*1-58243-100-0*, Pub. by Counterpt DC) HarpC.

Physics. Walker. 1991. 14.60 (*0-87901-541-1*) Worth.

Physics. Western. 1994. 21.25 (*0-697-11205-5*) McGraw.

Physics. J. Wolff. (Barron's College Review Ser.). 1996. pap. 13.95 (*0-8120-9522-7*) Barron.

Physics. Aristotle. Tr. by Richard Hope. LC 61-5498. (Illus.). 256p. reprint ed. pap. 79.40 (*0-8357-6443-5*, 203581400097) Bks Demand.

Physics. Aristotle. Ed. by Hippocrates G. Apostle. LC 80-80037. (Apostle Translations of Aristotle's Works: Vol. 2). 386p. 1980. reprint ed. pap. text 18.00 (*0-9602870-3-5*) Peripatetic.

Physics. rev. ed. Peter Alonso. (C). 1996. pap. text. write for info. (*0-201-40349-8*) Addison-Wesley.

***Physics.** 2nd ed. 1998. text 5.00 (*0-471-32931-2*) Wiley.

Physics. 2nd ed. Alonso. (World Student Ser.: Bk. 2). (C). 1983. pap. text 15.33 (*0-201-00162-4*) Addison-Wesley.

Physics. 2nd ed. Hobson. LC 98-14593. 536p. 1998. pap. text 65.33 (*0-13-095381-4*) S&S Trade.

Physics. 2nd ed. Frederick J. Keller et al. LC 92-38761. 1072p. (C). 1992. 104.06 (*0-07-023461-2*) McGraw.

Physics. 2nd ed. Loyd. (C). 1997. pap. text, teacher ed., lab manual ed. 31.50 (*0-03-025106-0*) Harcourt Coll Pubs.

Physics. 2nd ed. Hans O'Hanian. (C). 1990. text 70.00 (*0-393-96038-2*) Norton.

Physics. 2nd ed. Richard T. Weidner. 945p. (C). 1988. 10.00 (*0-685-18773-X*, H11570) P-H.

Physics. 3rd ed. (C). 1994. lab manual ed. 19.00 (*0-8087-1479-1*) Pearson Custom.

Physics. 3rd ed. Boleman. 1995. pap. text, teacher ed. write for info. (*0-13-164121-2*) Allyn.

Physics. 3rd ed. Michael Steffancin. 1995. pap. text, student ed. 26.00 (*0-13-400052-8*) P-H.

Physics. 3rd ed. N. Wilson. 1999. text 84.00 (*0-13-632951-9*) P-H.

Physics 4th ed. Cutnell. 1997. text, student ed. 76.00 (*0-471-29147-1*) Wiley.

Physics. 4th ed. John D. Cutnell. 640p. 1997. pap. 37.95 (*0-471-16411-9*) Wiley.

Physics. 4th ed. John D. Cutnell & Kenneth W. Johnson. 1984p. 1997. text, student ed. 177.85 (*0-471-25254-9*) Wiley.

Physics, 2 vols. 4th ed. David Halliday et al. 688p. 1992. pap., student ed. 42.95 (*0-471-51873-5*) Wiley.

Physics, 2 vols. 4th ed. David Halliday et al. 392p. 1992. pap., student ed. 42.95 (*0-471-51860-3*) Wiley.

Physics. 5th ed. Giancoli. 1997. pap. text, student ed. 29.33 (*0-13-627944-9*) P-H.

Physics. 5th ed. Giancoli. LC 97-28516. 1096p. 1997. 106.67 (*0-13-611971-9*) P-H.

Physics. 5th ed. Paul E. Tippens. LC 94-17806. 1994. text 45.95 (*0-02-806502-6*) Glencoe.

***Physics.** 6th ed. Paul E. Tippens. LC 99-52055. 1999. write for info. (*0-07-820340-6*) McGraw.

***Physics.** 10th ed. Young. 2000. pap., student ed., suppl. ed. 18.00 (*0-201-64394-4*) Benjamin-Cummings.

***Physics.** 10th ed. Young. 2000. pap., teacher ed. 26.00 (*0-201-61836-2*) Benjamin-Cummings.

Physics, 2. 2nd ed. Hans C. Ohanian. (C). 1989. 97.25 (*0-393-95750-0*) Norton.

Physics, Bk. 8. Aristotle. Tr. & Comment by Daniel W. Graham. LC 98-49448. 227p. 1999. pap. text 24.95 (*0-19-824092-9*) OUP.

Physics, Bk. 8. Aristotle. Tr. & Comment by Daniel W. Graham. LC 98-49448. Bk. VIII. 229p. 1999. text 70.00 (*0-19-824091-0*) OUP.

Physics, Bks. 1 & 2. Ed. by W. Charlton. (Clarendon Aristotle Ser.). 184p. 1984. pap. text 29.95 (*0-19-872026-2*) OUP.

Physics, Bks. III & IV. Aristotle. Tr. & Notes by Edward Hussey. (Clarendon Aristotle Ser.). (Illus.). 274p. 1983. pap. text 29.95 (*0-19-872069-6*, Clarendon Pr) OUP.

***Physics, 2 vols., Set.** 5th ed. John D. Cutnell & Kenneth W. Johnson. (C). 2000. write for info. (*0-471-39377-0*) Wiley.

Physics, Vol. 1. Lawrence S. Lerner. LC 96-9427. 1996. pap. 48.75 (*0-86720-491-5*) Jones & Bartlett.

Physics, Vol. 1. 2nd ed. Hans C. Ohanian. (C). 1989. 47.00 (*0-393-95748-9*) Norton.

Physics, Vol. 1. 4th ed. Cutnell. 1999. pap. text, student ed. 48.00 (*0-471-37750-3*) Wiley.

Physics, Vol. 1. 4th ed. John D. Cutnell & Kenneth W. Johnson. LC 97-21746. 584p. 1997. pap. 70.95 (*0-471-19112-4*) Wiley.

Physics, Vol. 1. 5th ed. John D. Cutnell & Kenneth W. Johnson. 584p. (C). write for info. (*0-471-38717-7*) Wiley.

Physics, Vol. 2. Lawrence Lerner. 656p. Date not set. pap. 43.75 (*0-86720-492-3*) Jones & Bartlett.

Physics, Vol. 2. 2nd ed. Hecht. (Physics Ser.). 1998. pap. 46.25 (*0-534-36576-0*) Brooks-Cole.

Physics, Vol. 2. 2nd ed. Hans C. Ohanian. (C). 1989. 65.50 (*0-393-95786-1*) Norton.

Physics, Vol. 2. 4th ed. John D. Cutnell & Kenneth W. Johnson. LC 97-21746. 544p. 1997. pap. 67.95 (*0-471-19113-2*); pap. text 80.00 (*0-471-19768-8*) Wiley.

Physics, 2 vols., Vol. 2. 4th ed. Robert E. Resnick et al. 1136p. (C). 1992. text 59.50 (*0-471-56898-8*) Wiley.

Physics, Vol. 2. 5th ed. Cutnell. 1999. pap. text, student ed. 46.00 (*0-471-37751-1*) Wiley.

***Physics, Vol. 2.** 5th ed. John D. Cutnell & Kenneth W. Johnson. 544p. (C). 2000. write for info. (*0-471-38718-5*) Wiley.

Physics, 2 vols., Vol. 2, Bks. 5-8. Tr. by P. H. Wicksteed & F. M. Cornford. LC 61-5498. (Loeb Classical Library: No. 255). 452p. 1934. 18.95 (*0-674-99281-4*) HUP.

Physics, Vol. 2, Chapters 23-39. Lawrence Lerner. 536p. 1997. pap. 46.25 (*0-7637-0460-1*) Jones & Bartlett.

***Physics, Vol.1&2.** 4th ed. Cutnell. 1998. text 78.00 (*0-471-31871-X*) Wiley.

Physics, Vols. 1-3. 4th ed. Tipler. LC 98-60168. 1160p. 1998. pap. text 80.00 (*1-57259-615-5*) Worth.

Physics, 2 vols., Vols. 1 & 2. Wolfson. (C). 1995. student ed. write for info. (*0-201-34636-2*); text. write for info. (*0-201-34635-4*) Addison-Wesley.

Physics, Vols. I & II. Hans C. Ohanian. (C). 1989. student ed. write for info. incl. trans. (*0-393-95763-2*) Norton.

Physics, Vols. I & II. Hans C. Ohanian. (C). 1990. pap. text, teacher ed., student ed. write for info. (*0-393-95754-3*) Norton.

Physics, Vols. I & II. 2nd ed. Hans C. Ohanian. (C). 1989. 87.00 (*0-393-95746-2*) Norton.

Physics, Vols. I & II. 2nd ed. Hans C. Ohanian et al. (C). 1989. pap., student ed. 32.00 (*0-393-95752-7*) Norton.

Physics: A Basic Course, High School Sophomore Level (Grade 10) Dale Crane. LC 86-22225. (ABC (A Basic Course) Ser.). (Illus.). (Orig.). (C). 1986. pap. text 12.95 (*0-914565-23-0*) Capstan Pubns.

***Physics: A Contemporary Perspective.** 1999. write for info. (*0-201-38422-1*) P-H.

Physics: A Contemporary Perspective Workbook, Vol. 1. Randall D. Knight. Ed. by Julie Berrisford. 177p. (C). 1996. pap. text, student ed. 18.00 (*0-201-43166-1*) Addison-Wesley.

Physics: A General Introduction. Van. (C). 1999. write for info. (*0-673-39914-1*) Addison-Wesley.

Physics: A Laboratory Approach. Harold D. Tiller. (Illus.). 300p. (C). 1995. lab manual ed. 31.95 (*0-89892-124-4*) Contemp Pub Co of Raleigh.

Physics: A Practical & Conceptual Approach. 4th ed. Wilson. (C). 1999. pap. text 55.50 (*0-03-006224-1*) Harcourt.

Physics: A Refresher Course. B. M. Yavorsky & Y. A. Seleznev. 654p. (C). 1979. 65.00 (*0-7855-4966-8*, Pub. by Collets) St Mut.

Physics: A Student Solution Manual, Vol. 1 & 2. 3rd ed. Tipler. 1997. student ed. 72.00 (*1-57259-612-0*) Worth.

Physics . A World View. Kirkpatric. (C). 1992. pap. text, teacher ed. 34.00 (*0-03-075131-4*) Harcourt Coll Pubs.

Physics: A World View. 2nd ed. Kirkpatric. (C). 1994. pap. text, teacher ed. 33.75 (*0-03-000603-1*) Harcourt Coll Pubs.

Physics: A World View. 3rd ed. Kirkpatric. (C). 1997. pap. text 31.00 (*0-03-024391-2*, Pub. by Harcourt Coll Pubs) Harcourt.

Physics: A World View. 3rd ed. Kirkpatrick. (Illus.). 768p. (C). 1997. text 82.50 (*0-03-020052-0*, Pub. by SCP) Harcourt.

Physics: A World View, Numerical. 3rd ed. Kirkpatrick. 200p. (C). 1997. pap. text, suppl. ed. 10.00 (*0-03-024394-7*) SCP.

Physics: Algebra/Trigonometry. Eugene Hecht. 1996. mass mkt., teacher ed. write for info. (*0-534-09115-6*) Brooks-Cole.

Physics: Algebra/Trigonometry. 2nd ed. Eugene Hecht. 1998. mass mkt. 19.00 (*0-534-35244-8*) Brooks-Cole.

***Physics: Algebra/Trigonometry.** 2nd ed. Eugene Hecht. (Physics Ser.). 2000. pap. 78.00 (*0-534-37503-0*) Brooks-Cole.

***Physics: Algebra/Trigonometry.** 2nd rev. ed. Eugene Hecht. (Physics Ser.). 1999. pap. 39.50 incl. cd-rom (*0-534-37504-9*) Brooks-Cole.

Physics: Algebra/Trigonometry, Vol. I. Eugene Hecht. (Physics Ser.: Vol. 1, Chapters 1-16). 1994. mass mkt. 40.00 (*0-534-09130-X*) Brooks-Cole.

Physics: Algebra/Trigonometry, Vol. 1. 2nd ed. Hecht. (Physics). 1998. pap. 46.25 (*0-534-36575-2*) Brooks-Cole.

Physics: Algebra/Trigonometry, Vol I, Chapters 17-33. Eugene Hecht. (Physics Ser.: Vol. 2, Chapters 17-33). 1994. mass mkt. 34.00 (*0-534-09131-8*) Brooks-Cole.

***Physics: Algebra/Trigonometry, Vol. 2.** 2nd rev. ed. Eugene Hecht. (Physics Ser.). 1999. pap. 38.00 (*0-534-37505-7*) Brooks-Cole.

Physics: An Incremental Development. John H. Saxon. (YA). (gr. 9-12). 1993. student ed. 45.00 (*1-56577-005-6*); student ed. 20.00 (*1-56577-009-9*); teacher ed. 17.00 (*1-56577-007-2*); 39.00 (*1-56577-006-4*) Saxon Pubs OK.

Physics: Answer Key. David P. Lawrence. (Graphing Calculator Approach Ser.). 4p. (YA). (gr. 9 up). 1995. pap. text 1.50 (*1-881641-34-1*) Pencil Point.

Physics: Answers to Problems, Vols. I & II. 2nd ed. Hans C. Ohanian. (Orig.). (C). 1990. pap. text, student ed. 6.25 (*0-393-95756-X*) Norton.

Physics: Calculus. Eugene Hecht. (Physics Ser.). 1264p. 1996. 72.75 (*0-534-33985-9*) Brooks-Cole.

Physics: Calculus. Eugene Hecht. 1996. mass mkt., teacher ed. write for info. (*0-534-33989-1*) Brooks-Cole.

***Physics: Calculus.** 2nd ed. Eugene Hecht. (Physics Ser.). 1856p. 2000. mass mkt. 104.95 (*0-534-36270-2*) Brooks-Cole.

Physics: Calculus, Vol. 2. Eugene Hecht. (Physics Ser.: Vol. 2, Chapters 17-33). 1996. mass mkt. 42.50 (*0-534-34157-8*) Brooks-Cole.

Physics: Calculus, Vol. 2, Chapters 17-33. Eugene Hecht. 1996. mass mkt. 42.50 (*0-534-34156-X*) Brooks-Cole.

***Physics: Calculus with Infotrac & CD , Vol.2.** 2nd ed. Hecht. 1999. text 56.95 incl. cd-rom (*0-534-37084-5*) Brooks-Cole.

Physics: Chapters 1-5. 4th ed. Cutnell. 1998. pap. text 15.00 (*0-471-32456-6*) Wiley.

Physics: Concept & Model. 2nd ed. Wenham. Date not set. pap. text. write for info. (*0-582-35580-X*, Pub. by Addison-Wesley) Longman.

***Physics: Concepts & Connections.** 104p. (C). 1999. 11.00 (*0-536-02699-8*) Pearson Custom.

Physics: Concepts & Consequences. R. L. Murray & G. C. Cobb. (American Nuclear Society Textbook Ser.). 710p. 1970. text 19.00 (*0-13-672501-5*, 350004) Am Nuclear Soc.

***Physics: Contemporary Approach Vl 1 Preliminary Ed, Vol. 1.** 157p. (C). 1998. pap. text 27.40 (*0-201-38029-3*) Addison-Wesley.

Physics: Electricity. 3rd ed. George Carney. 228p. (C). 1995. pap. text, ring bd. 32.95 (*0-7872-0947-3*) Kendall-Hunt.

Physics: Extended Version, 2 vols., Vol. 2. 4th ed. Robert E. Resnick et al. 1344p. (C). 1992. text 61.00 (*0-471-56897-X*) Wiley.

Physics: Extended Version, 2 vols., Vol. 2 Extended. 4th ed. Robert E. Resnick et al. LC 92-24917. 688p. (C). 1992. text 81.95 (*0-471-54804-9*) Wiley.

Physics: For Athletes & Other Serious Students. Joseph E. Finck. Ed. by T. E. Dennison. (Illus.). 159p. (Orig.). (C). 1988. pap. text 16.00 (*0-923231-10-2*) Mohican Pub.

Physics: For Scientists & Engineers, Vol. 1. 4th ed. Gene Mosca & Ronald Gautreau. 2000. student ed. write for info. (*1-57259-511-6*) Worth.

Physics: For Scientists & Engineers - Instructor's Resource Manual. 4th ed. Robert D. Allen & Vicki S. Williams. 2000. teacher ed. write for info. (*1-57259-516-7*) Worth.

Physics: For Scientists & Engineers - Solutions, Vol. 1. 4th ed. Frank J. Blatt. 1998. pap. write for info. (*1-57259-514-0*) Worth.

Physics: For Scientists & Engineers - Test Bank, Vol. 1. 4th ed. David Mills. 1998. write for info. (*1-57259-517-5*) Worth.

Physics: For Scientists & Engineers - Test Bank, Vol. 2. 4th ed. David Mills. 1998. write for info. (*1-57259-518-3*) Worth.

Physics: Imagination & Reality. Ed. by P. R. Wallace. 592p. (C). 1991. text 74.00 (*9971-5-0929-6*); pap. text 41.00 (*9971-5-0930-X*) World Scientific Pub.

Physics: Lab Experiments & Correlated Computer Aids. Herbert H. Gottlieb. 1981. 10.50 (*0-318-01172-7*) Microphys Prog.

Physics: Mastery Learning Approach to Laboratory Exercises. Dwight F. Decker. 287p. (C). 1993. spiral bd. 25.95 (*0-8403-9109-9*) Kendall-Hunt.

Physics MCAT Student Survey. 4th ed. Cutnell. 1999. text 93.00 (*0-471-37020-7*) Wiley.

Physics Parts 4 & 5 5th ed. Halliday. 1997. pap. text 32.00 (*0-471-24033-8*) Wiley.

Physics: Practical Concept Approach. 3rd ed. Wilson. (C). 1993. pap. text 99.50 (*0-03-096035-5*, Pub. by Harcourt Coll Pubs) Harcourt.

Physics: Principles & Applications. 5th ed. Norman C. Harris et al. (C). 1989. text 60.30 (*0-07-026851-7*) McGraw.

***Physics: Principles & Problems, Teacher's Wraparound Edition.** Zitzewitz & Murphy. 1999. teacher ed. 68.34 (*0-02-825474-0*) Glencoe.

***Physics: Principles & Problems, 1999.** 1999. teacher ed., student ed. 22.67 (*0-02-825494-5*); teacher ed., lab manual ed. 18.06 (*0-02-825484-8*) Glencoe.

Physics: Principles with Applications. (C). 1998. text 45.00 (*0-536-01803-0*) Pearson Custom.

Physics: Principles with Applications. 3rd ed. (C). 1991. 20.00 (*0-13-672999-1*, Macmillan Coll) P-H.

Physics: Principles with Applications, Vol. 1. 5th ed. Giancoli. 576p. (C). 1997. pap. text 64.67 (*0-13-679754-7*) P-H.

Physics: Selected Chapters. 4th ed. Cutnell. 1998. pap. text 21.75 (*0-471-32240-7*) Wiley.

Physics: Student Solutions Manual, Vol. 1. 4th ed. Paul Tipler. (C). 2000. pap. text 21.80 (*1-57259-513-2*) Worth.

Physics: Student Solutions Manual, Vol. 2. 4th ed. Paul Tipler. (C). 1998. pap. text 21.80 (*1-57259-524-8*) Worth.

Physics: Student Study Guide. Lawrence Lerner & French. 136p. 1996. pap. 22.50 (0-7637-0204-8) Jones & Bartlett.

Physics: Take Note, vol. 2. 4th ed. Cutnell. pap. text 46.00 (0-471-38069-5) Wiley.

Physics: Take Notes Ideas. 4th ed. Cutnell. text 78.00 (0-471-38068-7) Wiley.

Physics: The Nature of Things. Lea. (Physics Ser.). 1997. student ed. 18.50 (0-314-20731-7) Brooks-Cole.

Physics: The Nature of Things. Lea. LC 99-194107. (Physics Ser.). 1997. mass mkt., student ed. 25.95 (0-314-20933-6) Wadsworth Pub.

Physics: The Nature of Things. Lea & Burke. 1100p. 1997. write for info. (0-314-07012-5) West Pub.

Physics: The Nature of Things. Susan M. Lea & John R. Burke. LC 96-13354. (C). 1996. mass mkt. 116.95 (0-314-05273-9) West Pub.

Physics: The Nature of Things, Vol. 1. Lea. (Physics Ser.). 1997. 68.95 (0-534-35734-2) Brooks-Cole.

Physics: The Nature of Things, Vol. 2. Lea. (Physics Ser.). 1997. 58.95 (0-534-35735-0) Brooks-Cole.

Physics: Using the CBL. James Ealy. (Graphing Calculator Approach Ser.). (Illus.). 24p. 1996. pap. text, teacher ed., suppl. ed. 7.45 (1-881641-52-X) Pencil Point.

Physics: With Tanner Interactive Learningware, MAC, Pt. 2. 4th expanded ed. Robert E. Resnick et al. 688p. 1994. text 41.00 incl. disk (0-471-11107-4) Wiley.

Physics: With Tanner Interactive Learningware, Vol. 1. 4th ed. Robert E. Resnick et al. 656p. 1994. text 41.00 incl. disk (0-471-11108-2) Wiley.

Physics: With Tanner Interactive Learningware-IBM, Part 2. 4th expanded ed. Robert E. Resnick et al. 688p. 1994. text 41.00 incl. disk (0-471-11109-0) Wiley.

***Physics Chapters 1-35 & 39.** 4th ed. Tipler. 1999. pap. text 103.95 (0-7167-3821-X) W H Freeman.

***Physics Chapters 1-41.** 4th ed. Tipler. 1999. pap. text 108.95 (0-7167-3822-8) W H Freeman.

Physics Preliminary Edition: A Contemporary Approach, Vol. I. Randall D. Knight. Ed. by Karen Guardino. 606p. (C). 1996. pap. text 49.00 (0-201-43164-5) Addison-Wesley.

Physics Pt. 1: Literature, 1997. Ed. by Astronomisches Rechen-Institut ARI, Heidelberg, Ge. (Astronomy & Astrophysics Abstracts Ser.: Vol. 67). viii, 1904p. 1998. 350.00 (3-540-63954-3) Spr-Verlag.

Physics Vol. 1. 4th ed. John D. Cutnell & Kenneth W. Johnson. LC 97-21746. 1064p. 1997. text 114.95 (0-471-15519-5) Wiley.

Physics Vol. 1, 2 vols., Vol. 1, Bks. 1-4. Tr. by P. H. Wicksteed & F. M. Cornford. LC 61-5498. (Loeb Classical Library: No. 228). 522p. 1929. 18.95 (0-674-99251-2) HUP.

Physics Vol. 2: Student Study Guide. Lawrence Lerner & French. 144p. 1996. pap. 22.50 (0-7637-0340-0) Jones & Bartlett.

***Physics - The Big Problem - Solve!: or Merging QED & General Relativity.** W. S. Oakley. LC 99-98155. 2000. pap. 8.95 (0-533-13451-X) Vantage.

Physics - The Root Science with Applications: Suggestions for the Teacher. 3rd rev. ed. Wallace C. Caldwell et al. (Illus.). vii, 404p. (YA). (gr. 10-13). 1996. text. write for info. (0-9663589-0-2) Archimedies Pubns.

Physics - The Root Science with Applications Suppl. 1: Problem Solution Manual. 3rd rev. ed. Wallace C. Caldwell et al. (Illus.). 84p. (YA). (gr. 10-12). 1996. pap. write for info. (0-9663589-1-0) Archimedies Pubns.

Physics, Algebra & Trigonometry with InfoTrac. 2nd ed. Hecht. (Health Sciences Ser.). 1998. pap. 72.00 incl. cd-rom (0-534-36344-X) Brooks-Cole.

Physics: Algebra/trig. Eugene Hecht. LC 93-43106. (Physics). 1164p. 1994. mass mkt. 72.50 (0-534-09114-8) Brooks-Cole.

Physics & Applications of Amorphous Semiconductors. Arun Madan & Melvin P. Shaw. 545p. 1988. text 123.00 (0-12-464960-2) Acad Pr.

Physics & Applications of Amorphous Semiconductors: Proceedings of the 1st International Symposium Workshop, Torino, Villa Gualino, Italy. Ed. by F. Demichelis. 424p. (C). 1988. text 99.00 (9971-5-0550-9) World Scientific Pub.

Physics & Applications of Amorphous Semiconductors: 2nd International Workshop, 1988. Ed. by F. Demichelis et al. 252p. (C). 1989. text 92.00 (9971-5-0879-6) World Scientific Pub.

Physics & Applications of Defects in Advanced Semincoductors. Ed. by M. Lannoo et al. LC 94-1533. (Materials Research Society Symposium Proceedings Ser.: Vol. 325). 523p. 1994. text 71.00 (1-55899-224-3) Materials Res.

Physics & Applications of Non-Crystalline Semiconductors in Optoelectronics. Mario Bertolotti & A. M. Andriesh. LC 97-20563. (NATO ASI Series: Partnership Sub-Series 3). 1997. text 251.00 (0-7923-4623-8) Kluwer Academic.

Physics & Applications of Optical Solitons in Fibres, '95: Proceedings of the Symposium Held in Kyoto, November 14-17, 1995. Ed. by Akira Hasegawa. LC 96-28674. (Solid-State Science & Technology Library Ser.). 416p. (C). 1996. text 217.50 (0-7923-4155-4) Kluwer Academic.

Physics & Applications of Photorefractive Materials. L. Solymar et al. (Oxford Series on Optical & Imaging Sciences: No. 11). (Illus.). 504p. 1996. text 145.00 (0-19-856501-1) OUP.

Physics & Applications of Pseudosparks. Ed. by M. A. Gundersen & G. Schaefer. (NATO ASI Series B, Physics: Vol. 219). (Illus.). 372p. (C). 1990. 144.00 (0-306-43539-X, Plenum Trade) Perseus Pubng.

Physics & Applications of Quantum Wells & Superlattices. Ed. by E. E. Mendez & K. Von Klitzing. (NATO ASI Series B, Physics: Vol. 170). (Illus.). 442p. 1988. 125.00 (0-306-42823-7, Plenum Trade) Perseus Pubng.

Physics & Applications of Resonant Tunnelling Diodes. Hiroshi Mizuta & Tomonori Tanoue. (Studies in Semiconductor Physics & Microelectronic Engineering: Vol. 2). (Illus.). 253p. (C). 1995. text 64.95 (0-521-43218-9) Cambridge U Pr.

***Physics & Applications of Semiconductor Microstructures.** Jong-Chun Woo. 1999. 130.00 (0-7503-0637-8) IOP Pub.

Physics & Applications of the Josephson Effect. Antonio Barone & Gianfranco Paterno. LC 81-7554. (Wiley-Interscience Publications). 551p. reprint ed. pap. 170.90 (0-7837-2372-5, 204005800006) Bks Demand.

Physics & Astrophysics from a Lunar Base. Ed. by A. E. Potter & T. L. Wilson. LC 90-55073. (AIP Conference Proceedings Ser.: No. 202). (Illus.). 344p. 1990. 70.00 (0-88318-646-2) Am Inst Physics.

Physics & Astrophysics in Quark-Gluon Plasma: Proceedings. B. Sinha et al. 536p. 1994. text 109.00 (981-02-1660-2) World Scientific Pub.

Physics & Astrophysics of Neutrinos. Ed. by M. Fukugita & A. Suzuki. LC 94-3134. 1995. 194.00 (0-387-70136-2) Spr-Verlag.

Physics & Astrophysics of Quark-Gluon Plasma: Proceedings of the International Conference. Bikas K. Sinha & S. Raha. 716p. 1989. pap. 59.00 (9971-5-0555-X); text 135.00 (9971-5-0553-3) World Scientific Pub.

Physics & Chabay's Electric & Magnetic Interactions Set, 1-2. 4th ed. David Halliday et al. 2016p. 1996. text 194.85 (0-471-16981-1) Wiley.

Physics & Chance: Philosophical Issues in the Foundations of Statistical Mechanics. Lawrence Sklar. 453p. 1995. pap. text 25.95 (0-521-55881-6) Cambridge U Pr.

Physics & Chemistry at Oxid Surfaces. Claudine Noguera. (Illus.). 238p. (C). 1996. text 69.95 (0-521-47214-8) Cambridge U Pr.

Physics & Chemistry at Upper Atmospheres: Proceedings of the Summer Advanced Study Institute Symposium, University of Orleans, France, July 31-Aug 11, 1972. Summer Advanced Study Institute Staff. Ed. by Billy M. McCormac. LC 72-92533. (Astrophysics & Space Science Library: No. 35). 385p. 1973. lib. bdg. 152.00 (90-277-0283-7) Kluwer Academic.

Physics & Chemistry of Aqueous Ionic Solutions. M. C. Bellisent-Funel & G. W. Neilson. (C). 1987. text 234.00 (90-277-2534-9) Kluwer Academic.

Physics & Chemistry of Carbides: Nitrides & Borides. Ed. by Robert Freer. (C). 1990. text 346.00 (0-7923-0870-0) Kluwer Academic.

Physics & Chemistry of Color: The 15 Causes of Color. Kurt Nassau. LC 83-10580. (Pure & Applied Optics Ser.). 480p. 1983. 170.00 (0-471-86776-4, 1-349) Wiley.

Physics & Chemistry of Comets. Ed. by W. F. Huebner et al. (Astronomy & Astrophysics Library). (Illus.). 384p. 1990. 69.95 (0-387-51228-4) Spr-Verlag.

Physics & Chemistry of Crystalline Lithium Niobate. A. M. Prokhorov & Yu S. Kuz'minov. (Optics & Optoelectronics Ser.). (Illus.). 392p. 1990. 208.00 (0-85274-002-6) IOP Pub.

Physics & Chemistry of Dykes: Proceedings: International Dyke Conference (3d: 1995: Jerusalem, Israel) Ed. by G. Baer & A. Heimann. (Illus.). 350p. (C). 1995. text 162.00 (90-5410-551-8, QE511, Pub. by A A Balkema) Ashgate Pub Co.

Physics & Chemistry of Earth, Vol. 8. L. H. Ahrens. 1971. 115.00 (0-08-012630-8, Pergamon Pr) Elsevier.

Physics & Chemistry of Earth Materials. Alexandra Navrotsky. LC 93-43135. (Cambridge Topics in Mineral Physics & Chemistry Ser.: No. 6). (Illus.). 431p. (C). 1994. text 90.00 (0-521-35378-5); pap. text 39.95 (0-521-35894-9) Cambridge U Pr.

Physics & Chemistry of Electrons & Ionsin Condensed Matter. Ed. by J. V. Acrivos. 768p. 1984. text 315.50 (90-277-1799-0) Kluwer Academic.

Physics & Chemistry of Finite Systems - From Clusters to Crystals. Ed. by P. Jena et al. LC 92-16307. (NATO Advanced Study Institutes Series C, Mathematical & Physical Sciences: Vol. 374). 1992. lib. bdg. write for info. (0-7923-1816-1) Kluwer Academic.

Physics & Chemistry of Finite Systems - From Clusters to Crystals: Proceedings of the NATO Advanced Research Workshop, Richmond, VA, U. S. A., October 8-12, 1992, 2 vols. P. Jena. 1468p. (C). 1992. text 544.00 (0-7923-1818-8) Kluwer Academic.

Physics & Chemistry of Fission. Ed. by H. Marten & D. Seelinger. 405p. (C). 1992. text 195.00 (1-56072-023-9) Nova Sci Pubs.

Physics & Chemistry of Fullerenes. P. W. Stephens. 256p. 1993. text 95.00 (981-02-1116-3); pap. text 45.00 (981-02-1117-1) World Scientific Pub.

Physics & Chemistry of Fullerenes & Derivatives: Proceedings of the Winter School. J. Fink et al. LC 95-232395. 608p. 1995. text 108.00 (981-02-2380-3) World Scientific Pub.

Physics & Chemistry of Interstellar Molecular Clouds: Proceedings of the 2nd Cologne-Zermatt Symposium Held at Zermatt, Switzerland, 21-24 September 1993. Ed. by G. Winnewisser & G. C. Pelz. (Lecture Notes in Physics Ser.: Vol. 459). 393p. 1995. 101.95 (3-540-60482-0) Spr-Verlag.

Physics & Chemistry of Interstellar Molecular Clouds mm & Sub-mm Observations in Astrophysics. Ed. by G. Winnewisser & J. T. Armstrong. (Lecture Notes in Physics Ser.: Vol. 331). xviii, 463p. 1989. 70.95 (0-387-51297-7) Spr-Verlag.

Physics & Chemistry of Lakes. 2nd ed. L. M. Chou. Ed. by Abraham Lerman et al. LC 95-6098. 1995. write for info. (3-540-57891-9) Spr-Verlag.

Physics & Chemistry of Lakes. 2nd ed. Ed. by Abraham Lerman et al. (Illus.). 351p. 1995. 97.95 (0-387-57891-9) Spr-Verlag.

Physics & Chemistry of Liquid Crystal Devices. Symposium on the Physics & Chemistry of Interfaces. Ed. by Gerald J. Sprokel. LC 80-12097. (IBM Research Symposia Ser.). (Illus.). 360p. 1980. reprint ed. pap. 111.60 (0-608-05444-5, 206591300006) Bks Demand.

Physics & Chemistry of Low-Dimensional Inorganic Conductors: Proceedings of a NATO ASI Held in Les Houches, France, June 13-23, 1995, Vol. 354. C. Schlenker et al. (NATO ASI Ser.: No. 354). (Illus.). 474p. (C). 1996. text 150.00 (0-306-45304-5, Kluwer Plenum) Kluwer Academic.

Physics & Chemistry of Low Dimensional Solids. Ed. by Luis Alcacer. (NATO Advanced Study Institutes Series C, Mathematical & Physical Sciences: No. 56). 436p. 1980. text 148.50 (90-277-1144-5) Kluwer Academic.

***Physics & Chemistry of Luminescent Materials: 7th International Symposium.** International Symposium on Physics and Chemistry of Luminescent Materials & Electrochemical Society. Luminescent and Display Materials Division. Ed. by Charles W. Struck et al. LC 99-201831. (Illus.). 362p. 1999. 82.00 (1-56677-218-4, PV 98-24) Electrochem Soc.

Physics & Chemistry of Materials. Gersten. 1500p. write for info. (0-471-05794-0) Wiley.

Physics & Chemistry of Mercury Cadmium Telluride & Novel IR Detector Materials. D. G. Seiler. (AIP Conference Proceedings Ser.: Vol. 235). 320p. 1991. 95.00 (0-88318-931-3) Am Inst Physics.

Physics & Chemistry of Metal Cluster Compounds: Model Systems for Small Metal Particles. Ed. by L. J. De Jongh. LC 93-49928. (Physics & Chemistry of Materials with Low-Dimensional Structures Ser.: Vol.18). 320p. (C). 1994. text 204.50 (0-7923-2715-2) Kluwer Academic.

Physics & Chemistry of Mineral Surfaces. Ed. by Patrick V. Brady. LC 95-47556. (Chemistry & Physics of Surfaces & Interfaces Ser.). 384p. 1996. boxed set 139.95 (0-8493-8351-X) CRC Pr.

Physics & Chemistry of Minerals & Rocks. NATO Advanced Study Institute (1974: Newcastle upo. Ed. by R. G. Strens. LC 75-6930. (Illus.). 715p. reprint ed. pap. 200.00 (0-608-17618-4, 203047100069) Bks Demand.

***Physics & Chemistry of Nano-Structured Materials.** Ping Sheng & Shihe Yang. LC 99-35581. 241p. 1999. write for info. (0-7484-0873-8, Pub. by Tay Francis Ltd) Taylor & Francis.

Physics & Chemistry of Organic Superconductors: Proceedings of the ISSP International Symposium, Tokyo, Japan, August 28-30, 1989. Ed. by G. Saito & S. Kagoshima. (Proceedings in Physics Ser.: Vol. 51). 440p. 1990. 78.00 (0-387-52157-7) Spr-Verlag.

Physics & Chemistry of Oxide Superconductors: Proceedings of the Second ISSP International Symposium Tokyo, Japan, January 16-18, 1991. Ed. by Y. Iye & H. Yasuoka. (Proceedings in Physics Ser.: Vol. 60). (Illus.). xxi, 578p. 1992. 103.95 (0-387-54914-5) Spr-Verlag.

Physics & Chemistry of Porous Media: Schlumberger-Doll Research, 1983. Ed. by D. L. Johnson & P. N. Sen. LC 83-73640. (AIP Conference Proceedings Ser.: No. 107). 223p. 1984. lib. bdg. 37.50 (0-88318-306-4) Am Inst Physics.

Physics & Chemistry of Porous Media II. Ed. by Jayanth R. Banavar et al. LC 83-73640. (AIP Conference Proceedings Ser.: No. 154). 336p. 1987. lib. bdg. 65.00 (0-88318-354-4) Am Inst Physics.

Physics & Chemistry of Protective Coatings. Ed. by W. D. Sproul et al. LC 86-72019. (AIP Conference Proceedings Ser.: No. 149). 192p. 1986. lib. bdg. 55.00 (0-88318-348-X) Am Inst Physics.

Physics & Chemistry of SiO2 & the Si-SiO2 Interface, Vol. 1. C. R. Helms & B. E. Deal. (Illus.). 570p. (C). 1988. text 145.00 (0-306-43032-0, Kluwer Plenum) Kluwer Academic.

Physics & Chemistry of SiO2 & the Si-SiO2 Interface, Vol. 2. C. R. Helms & B. E. Deal. LC 93-14058. (Illus.). 520p. (C). 1993. text 135.00 (0-306-44419-4, Kluwer Plenum) Kluwer Academic.

Physics & Chemistry of SiO2 & the Si-SiO2 Interface: 3rd International Symposium. Ed. by H. Z. Massoud et al. (Proceedings Ser.: Vol. 96-1). (Illus.). 780p. 1996. 98.00 (1-56677-151-X) Electrochem Soc.

Physics & Chemistry of Small Clusters. Ed. by P. Jena et al. LC 87-14199. (NATO ASI Series B, Physics: Vol. 158). (Illus.). 972p. 1987. 165.00 (0-306-42606-4, Plenum Trade) Perseus Pubng.

***Physics & Chemistry of Solids.** Elliott. 794p. 1998. 84.95 (0-471-98194-X) Wiley.

***Physics & Chemistry of Solids.** Stephen Elliott & John Wiley & Sons Publishing Staff. 794p. 1998. pap. 49.95 (0-471-98195-8) Wiley.

Physics & Chemistry of the Earth, Vol. 3. L. H. Ahrens. 1959. 200.00 (0-08-009157-1, Pergamon Pr) Elsevier.

Physics & Chemistry of the Earth, Vol. 4. L. H. Ahrens. 1961. 200.00 (0-08-009455-4, Pergamon Pr) Elsevier.

Physics & Chemistry of the Earth, Vol. 5. L. H. Ahrens. 1964. 200.00 (0-08-010191-7, Pergamon Pr) Elsevier.

Physics & Chemistry of the Earth, Vol. 6. L. H. Ahrens. 1965. 175.00 (0-08-010426-6, Pergamon Pr) Elsevier.

Physics & Chemistry of the Earth, Vol. 7. L. H. Ahrens. 1966. 200.00 (0-08-011765-1, Pergamon Pr) Elsevier.

Physics & Chemistry of the Earth, Vol. 9. L. H. Ahrens. 1975. 165.00 (0-08-018017-5) Elsevier.

Physics & Chemistry of the Earth, Vol. 10. L. H. Ahrens. (Illus.). 270p. 1980. 115.00 (0-08-020287-X, Pergamon Pr) Elsevier.

Physics & Chemistry of the Fullerenes: Proceedings of the NATO Advanced Research Workshop, Aghia Pelaghia, Greece, June 7-13, 1993. Ed. by Kosmas Prassides. (NATO Advanced Science Institutes Series C: 444). 352p. (C). 1994. text 204.50 (0-7923-3109-5) Kluwer Academic.

Physics & Chemistry of the Inorganic Azides see Energetic Materials

Physics & Chemistry of the Solar System. rev. ed. 56p. 1998. write for info. (0-12-446743-1) Acad Pr.

Physics & Chemistry of the Solar System. 2nd rev. ed. Ed. by John S. Lewis. LC 97-207375. (Illus.). 591p. 1997. pap. text 69.95 (0-12-446742-3) Morgan Kaufmann.

Physics & Chemistry of III-V Compound Semiconductor Interfaces. Ed. by Carl W. Wilmsen. LC 85-6598. 480p. 1985. 125.00 (0-306-41769-3, Plenum Trade) Perseus Pubng.

Physics & Chemistry of Transition Metal Oxides: Proceedings of the 20th Taniguchi Symposium, Kashikojima, Japan, May 24-30, 1998. Taniguchi International Symposium on the Theory of Condensed Matter Staff et al. LC 99-17768. (Series in Solid-State Sciences). xviii, 304p. 1999. 92.00 (3-540-65187-X) Spr-Verlag.

Physics & Chemistry of II-VI Luminescent Semiconductors. Ed. by D. R. Vij & N. Singh. 389p. (C). 1997. lib. bdg. 125.00 (1-56072-433-1) Nova Sci Pubs.

Physics & Chemistry of Wavepackets. Yeazell. LC 99-22019. 341p. 1999. 89.95 (0-471-24684-0) Wiley.

Physics & Contemporary Needs, Vol. 20. Ed. by S. A. Ansari et al. 377p. (C). 1997. lib. bdg. 145.00 (1-56072-435-8) Nova Sci Pubs.

Physics & Contemporary Needs: Proceedings of the International Nathiagali Summer College, Islamabad, August 1982, Vol. 7. Ed. by M. N. Qazi. 312p. (C). 1985. 75.00 (9971-966-83-2) World Scientific Pub.

Physics & Dosimetry of Therapy Electron Beams. Stanley C. Klevenhagen. LC 93-33161. 479p. 1993. pap. text 29.95 (0-944838-35-9) Med Physics Pub.

Physics & Dynamics of Planetary Nebulae. G. G. Gurzadyan. LC 96-35762. (Illus.). 490p. 1997. 69.95 (3-540-60965-2) Spr-Verlag.

Physics & Engineering Applications of Magnetism. Ed. by Y. Ishikawa et al. (Solid-State Sciences Ser.: Vol. 92). (Illus.). 336p. 1991. 88.95 (0-387-52420-7) Spr-Verlag.

Physics & Engineering of Medical Imaging. Ed. by Riccardo Guzzardi. 1987. text 529.00 (90-247-3454-1) Kluwer Academic.

Physics & Everyday Phenomenas. Griffith. 1992. 193.12 (0-697-06466-2, WCB McGr Hill) McGrw-H Hghr Educ.

Physics & Evolution of the Earth's Interior, 6 vols. 1994. 843.00 (0-444-81750-6) Elsevier.

Physics & Experiments with Linear Colliders. F. A. Harris et al. 980p. 1993. text 206.00 (981-02-1569-X) World Scientific Pub.

Physics & Experiments with Linear Colliders: LCWS '95, 2 vols. LC 97-106719. 832p. 1996. lib. bdg. 174.00 (981-02-2701-9) World Scientific Pub.

Physics & Experiments with Linear Colliders: Saariselk A, Finland, 9-14 September 1991, 2 vols. P. Eerola et al. LC 92-34980. 872p. 1992. text 190.00 (981-02-1054-X) World Scientific Pub.

Physics & Fabrication of Microstructures & Microdevices. Ed. by Claude Weisbuch & M. J. Kelly. (Proceedings in Physics Ser.: Vol. 13). (Illus.). 480p. 1986. 91.95 (0-387-16898-2) Spr-Verlag.

Physics & Fractal Structures. J. Gouyet. LC 96-160809. (Partially Ordered Systems Ser.). 248p. 1996. pap. 39.00 (3-540-94153-3) Spr-Verlag.

Physics & Fractal Structures. Jean-Francois Gouyet. LC 96-160809. (Illus.). 234p. 1996. 39.00 (0-387-94153-3) Spr-Verlag.

***Physics & Fuel Performance of Reactor-Based Plutonium Disposition.** OECD Staff. (OECD Proceedings Ser.). 236p. (Orig.). 1999. pap. 70.00 (92-64-17050-2, 66 1999 07 1 P, Pub. by Org for Econ) OECD.

Physics & General Science. (National Teacher Examination Ser.: NT-7B). 1994. pap. 23.95 (0-8373-8410-9) Nat Learn.

Physics & General Science, Sr. H. S. Jack Rudman. (Teachers License Examination Ser.: T-46). 1994. pap. 27.95 (0-8373-8046-4) Nat Learn.

Physics & Heat Technology of Reactors. Consultants Bureau Staff. LC 59-958. (Soviet Journal of Atomic Energy: No. 1, 1958). 180p. reprint ed. pap. 55.80 (0-608-30740-8, 202065400018) Bks Demand.

Physics & Human Affairs. Art Hobson. LC 81-11407. 94p. (C). 1982. pap. text 7.50 (0-471-09706-3) Wiley.

Physics & Industrial Development. 500p. 1997. 68.00 (981-02-3014-1) World Scientific Pub.

Physics & Industry: Proceedings of Academic Session of the XXI General Assembly of the International Union of Pure & Applied Physics Held at Nara, Japan, 22 & 23 September 1993. Ed. by E. Maruyama & H. Watanabe. LC 94-30559. (Lecture Notes in Physics Ser.: Vol. 435). 1994. 59.95 (3-540-58376-9) Spr-Verlag.

Physics & Industry: Proceedings of Academic Session of the XXI General Assembly of the International Union of Pure & Applied Physics Held at Nara, Japan, 22 & 23 September 1993, 435. Ed. by E. Maruyama & H. Watanabe. LC 94-30559. (Lecture Notes in Physics Ser.). 1994. write for info. (0-387-58376-9) Spr-Verlag.

Physics & Instrumentation of Diagnostic Medical Ultrasound. John Fish. 260p. 1990. pap. 139.95 (0-471-92651-5) Wiley.

Physics & Its 5th Dimension: Society. Dietrich Schroeer. LC 75-184158. (C). 1972. text 32.25 (0-201-06767-6) Addison-Wesley.

An Asterisk (*) at the beginning of an entry indicates that the title is appearing for the first time.

Physics & Materials Science of High Temperature Superconductors. Ed. by Ram Kossowsky et al. (C). 1990. text 361.00 (*0-7923-0735-6*) Kluwer Academic.

Physics & Materials Science of High Temperature Superconductors: Proceedings of the Fourth NATO Advanced Research Workshop on Physics & Materials Science of High Temperature Superconductors, Held in the Slovak Republic, 1996. Kossowsky. LC 97-12279. (NATO ASI Ser.: No. 3, Vol. 26). 360p. 1997. text 197.50 (*0-7923-4501-0*) Kluwer Academic.

Physics & Materials Science of High Temperature Superconductors, II: Proceedings of the NATO Advanced Study Institute, Porto Carras, Greece 18-31 August 1991. Ed. by Ram Kossowsky et al. 832p. (C). 1992. text 359.50 (*0-7923-1619-3*) Kluwer Academic.

Physics & Materials Science of Vortex States, Flux Pinning & Dynamics. Ram Kossowsky & North Atlantic Treaty Organization Staff. LC 99-14206. (NATO ASI Series: Series E: Applied Sciences). 1999. write for info. (*0-7923-5663-2*) Kluwer Academic.

Physics & Mathematics of Anyons: Proceedings of the TCSUH Workshop, Houston, Texas, 1-2 February 1991. Ed. by Shiing-Shen Chern et al. 340p. (C). 1991. pap. 32.00 (*981-02-0722-0*); text 118.00 (*981-02-0650-X*) World Scientific Pub.

Physics & Mathematics of Strings. Ed. by L. Brink et al. 608p. (C). 1990. text 86.00 (*9971-5-0980-6*); pap. text 40.00 (*9971-5-0981-4*) World Scientific Pub.

Physics & Mechanics of Amorphous Polymers. Jo Perez. LC 99-227348. (Illus.). 324p. (C). 1998. text 87.00 (*90-5410-766-9*, Pub. by A A Balkema) Ashgate Pub Co.

Physics & Mechanics of Ice: Proceedings of the Copenhagen, Technical University of Denmark, August 6-10, 1979. Symposium Copenhagen, Technical University of Denm. Ed. by P. Tryde. (International Union of Theoretical & Applied Mechanics Symposia Ser.). (Illus.). 378p. 1980. 43.70 (*3-540-09906-9*) Spr-Verlag.

Physics & Mechanics of Soil Liquidification: Proceedings of the International Workshop, Baltimore, MD, USA, 10-11 September 11. Ed. by Poul V. Lade & Jerry A. Yamamuro. (Illus.). 385p. (C). 1999. 98.00 (*90-5809-038-8*, TA710, Pub. by A A Balkema) Ashgate Pub Co.

Physics & Metaphysics: Theories of Space & Time. Jennifer Trusted. LC 94-16273. 224p. (C). 1994. pap. 18.99 (*0-415-05949-6*, A5472) Routledge.

Physics & Methods in Criticality Safety, Nashville, TN, September 19-23, 1993. 260p. 1994. 83.00 (*0-89448-183-5*, 700186) Am Nuclear Soc.

Physics & National Socialism, Vol. 18. Ed. by E. Hiebert & H. Wussing. 610p. 1996. 139.50 (*3-7643-5312-0*) Spr-Verlag.

Physics & National Socialism: An Anthology of Primary Sources. Ed. by Klaus Hentschel & Ann M. Hentschel. LC 96-3347. (Science Networks Historical Studies: Vol. 18). 406p. 1996. write for info. (*0-8176-5312-0*) Birkhauser.

Physics & Nuclear Arms Today. Ed. by David Hafemeister. 336p. 1991. 119.95 (*0-88318-626-8*); pap. 59.95 (*0-88318-640-3*) Spr-Verlag.

Physics & Our View of the World. Ed. by Jan Hilgevoord. LC 93-46713. (Illus.). 314p. (C). 1994. pap. text 27.95 (*0-521-47680-1*) Cambridge U Pr.

Physics & Our View of the World. Ed. by Jan Hilgevoord. LC 93-46713. (Illus.). 314p. (C). 1995. text 69.95 (*0-521-45372-0*) Cambridge U Pr.

Physics & Our World: A Symposium in Honor of Victor F. Weisskopf MIT 1974. Ed. by Kerson Huang. LC 76-7207. (AIP Conference Proceedings Ser.: No. 28). 164p. 1976. 15.00 (*0-88318-127-4*) Am Inst Physics.

Physics & Parameterization of Moist Atmospheric. Ed. by Roger K. Smith. LC 97-43108. 512p. 1998. text 291.00 (*0-7923-4868-0*) Kluwer Academic.

Physics & Philosophy. James Jeans. 244p. 1981. reprint ed. pap. 7.95 (*0-486-24117-3*) Dover.

Physics & Philosophy: Selected Essays. Henry Margenau. (Episteme Ser.: No. 6). 441p. 1978. text 126.50 (*90-277-0901-7*, D Reidel) Kluwer Academic.

Physics & Philosophy: The Revolution in Modern Science. Werner Heisenberg. LC 99-10404. (Great Minds Ser.). 220p. 1999. pap. 11.95 (*1-57392-694-9*) Prometheus Bks.

Physics & Physical Chemistry of Water see Water: A Comprehensive Treatise

Physics & Physical Technology, Pt. 1, Physics see Science & Civilisation in China

Physics & Physical Technology, Pt. 2, Mechanical Engineering see Science & Civilisation in China

Physics & Physical Technology, Pt. 3, Civil Engineering & Nautics see Science & Civilisation in China

Physics & Politics. Walter Bagehot. LC 99-19271. 256p. 1999. pap. 14.95 (*1-56663-221-8*, Elephant Paperbacks) I R Dee.

Physics & Politics in Revolutionary Russia. Paul Josephson. (California Studies in the History of Science: No. 9). (Illus.). 330p. 1991. 50.00 (*0-520-07482-3*, Pub. by U CA Pr) Cal Prin Full Svc.

Physics & Psychics: The Search for a World Beyond the Senses. Victor J. Stenger. LC 90-60256. (Illus.). 323p. (C). 1990. 29.95 (*0-87975-575-X*) Prometheus Bks.

Physics & Psychophysics of Music. 3rd ed. Juan G. Roederer. (Illus.). 219p. 1994. 29.95 (*0-387-94366-8*) Spr-Verlag.

Physics & Psychophysics of Music: An Introduction. 3rd ed. Juan G. Roederer. LC 94-16447. (Illus.). 219p. 1994. 64.95 (*0-387-94298-X*) Spr-Verlag.

Physics & Radiobiology of Fast Neutron Beams. D. K. Bewley. (Medical Science Ser.). (Illus.). 164p. 1989. 104.00 (*0-85274-093-X*) IOP Pub.

***Physics & Radiobiology of Nuclear Medicine.** 2nd ed. G. B. Saha. (Illus.). 212p. 2000. 65.00 (*0-387-95021-4*) Spr-Verlag.

Physics & Radiobiology of Nuclear Medicine, Vol. XIV. rev. ed. Gopal B. Saha. LC 93-635. (Illus.). 208p. 1995. 59.00 (*0-387-94036-7*) Spr-Verlag.

Physics & Simulation of Optoelectronic Devices V, Vol. 2994. Ed. by Marek Osinski & Weng W. Chow. 890p. 1997. 132.00 (*0-8194-2405-6*) SPIE.

Physics & Simulation of Optoelectronic Devices VI. Ed. by Marek Osinski et al. (Proceedings of SPIE Ser.: Vol. 3283). 1037p. 1998. 149.00 (*0-8194-2722-5*) SPIE.

***Physics & Simulation of Optoelectronic Devices VII.** Ed. by Peter Blood et al. 840p. 1999. pap. text 136.00 (*0-8194-3095-1*) SPIE.

Physics & Student Workbook: A Contemporary Approach, 2 bks. 2nd ed. Randall Knight. (C). 1997. text, student ed. 47.40 (*0-201-69441-7*) Addison-Wesley.

Physics & Technology for the Liberal Arts. 2nd ed. Robert Dixon. 208p. (C). 1998. per. 37.95 (*0-7872-4634-4*) Kendall-Hunt.

Physics & Technology of Amorphous SiO2. Ed. by R. A. B. Devine. LC 88-17464. (Illus.). 592p. 1988. 125.00 (*0-306-42929-2*, Plenum Trade) Perseus Pubng.

Physics & Technology of Heterojunction Devices. Ed. by D. V. Morgan & R. H. Williams. (Materials & Devices Ser.: No. 8). 326p. 1991. 99.00 (*0-86341-204-1*, ED008Z) INSPEC Inc.

Physics & Technology of Hyperthermia. Ed. by Stanley B. Field & Cafiero Franconi. (C). 1987. text 306.50 (*90-247-3509-2*) Kluwer Academic.

Physics & Technology of Ion Sources. Ed. by Ian G. Brown. LC 88-20507. 444p. 1989. 173.50 (*0-471-85708-4*) Wiley.

Physics & Technology of Laser Resonators. Ed. by D. Hall & P. Jackson. 272p. 1990. 80.00 (*0-85274-117-0*) IOP Pub.

Physics & Technology of Semiconductor Quantum Devices: Proceedings of the International School Held in Mesagne, Brindisi, Italy, 21-26 September 1992. Ed. by K. H. Ploog & L. Tapfer. (Lecture Notes in Physics Ser.: Vol. 419). (Illus.). viii, 212p. 1993. 73.95 (*0-387-56989-8*) Spr-Verlag.

Physics & Technology of Submicron Structures. Ed. by H. Heinrich et al. (Solid-State Sciences Ser.: Vol. 83). (Illus.). 305p. 1988. 73.95 (*0-387-19109-7*) Spr-Verlag.

Physics & Technology of Xerographic Processes. rev. ed. Edgar M. Williams. LC 92-20095. 302p. (C). 1993. reprint ed. lib. bdg. 64.50 (*0-89464-772-5*) Krieger.

Physics & Technology Semi Cond. Andrew S. Grove. 388p. 1967. text 99.95 (*0-471-32998-3*) Wiley.

Physics & the Circulation. fac. ed. J. O. Rowan. LC 81-12790. (Medical Physics Handbks.: No. 9). (Illus.). 132p. 1981. reprint ed. pap. 41.00 (*0-7837-7999-2*, 204775500008) Bks Demand.

Physics & the Rise of Scientific Research in Canada. Yves Gingras. Tr. by Peter Keating from FRE. 224p. (C). 1991. text 65.00 (*0-7735-0823-6*, Pub. by McG-Queens Univ Pr) CUP Services.

Physics & the Sound of Music. 2nd ed. John S. Rigden. LC 84-10401. 368p. 1985. text 89.95 (*0-471-87412-4*) Wiley.

Physics & the Ultimate Significance of Time: Bohm, Prigogine, & Process Philosophy. Ed. by David R. Griffin. LC 85-2782. 322p. (C). 1985. pap. text 19.95 (*0-88706-115-X*) State U NY Pr.

Physics & the Ultimate Significance of Time: Bohm, Prigogine, & Process Philosophy. Ed. by David R. Griffin. LC 85-2782. 322p. (C). 1985. text 59.50 (*0-88706-113-3*) State U NY Pr.

Physics ANS Supplement Problems. Hans C. Ohanian. pap. text 0.00 (*0-393-95684-9*) Norton.

Physics Around You. Long. (Physics Ser.). 1980. pap., teacher ed. write for info. (*0-534-01974-9*) Wadsworth Pub.

Physics As a Calling: Discipline & Practice in the Konigsberg Seminar for Physics. Kathryn M. Olesko. LC 90-55717. (History of Science Ser.). (Illus.). 496p. 1991. text 52.50 (*0-8014-2248-5*) Cornell U Pr.

Physics As a Career. 6th ed. Rao. 1998. pap. text, lab manual ed. 24.67 (*0-13-957606-1*) P-H.

Physics As Natural Philosophy: Essays in Honor of Laszlo Tisza. Ed. by Abner Shimony & Herman Feshbach. 350p. 1982. 60.00 (*0-262-19208-X*) MIT Pr.

Physics As Science: International Meeting on Empiricalli Correct Science Held in Cologne, Germany (Aug. 25-30, 1997) Ed. by George Galeczki et al. (Illus.). 16p. (C). 1998. pap. text 75.00 (*1-57485-031-8*) Hadronic Pr Inc.

Physics at Fermilab in the 1990's. Ed. by H. Lubatti & D. Green. 576p. (C). 1990. text 113.00 (*981-02-0103-6*) World Scientific Pub.

Physics at KAON: Hadron Spectroscopy, Strangeness, Rare Decays; Proceedings of the International Meeting, Bad Honnef, 7-9 June, 1989. Ed. by D. Frekers et al. vii, 204p. 1990. 93.95 (*0-387-52241-7*) Spr-Verlag.

Physics at LEAR with Low Energy Antiprotons, Vol. 14. C. Amsler et al. xviii, 828p. 1988. text 312.00 (*3-7186-4814-8*) Gordon & Breach.

Physics at LEP: Seventeenth International Meeting on Fundamental Physics. M. Aguilar-Benitez & M. Cerrada. 460p. (C). 1990. text 113.00 (*981-02-0227-X*) World Scientific Pub.

Physics at Surfaces. A. Zangwill. (Illus.). 480p. 1988. pap. text 44.95 (*0-521-34752-1*) Cambridge U Pr.

Physics at Tandem: Proceedings of the Beijing International Symposium, China, May 26-30, 1986. Ed. by C. L. Jiang. 628p. 1987. text 124.00 (*9971-5-0129-5*) World Scientific Pub.

Physics at the Highest Energy & Luminosity: To Understand the Origin of Mass. A. Zichichi. LC 92-26658. (Subnuclear Ser.: Vol. 29). (Illus.). 430p. (C). 1992. 145.00 (*0-306-44301-5*, Plenum Trade) Perseus Pubng.

Physics at the Planck Scale: Proceedings of the Workshop, Puri, India 12 - 21 December 1994. Ed. by J. Maharana et al. 500p. 1997. text 112.00 (*981-02-2470-2*, PhMaPma-P2941) World Scientific Pub.

Physics at Work Set. (C). 1993. pap. text 615.93 (*0-07-009597-3*) McGraw.

Physics B. Jack Rudman. (Advanced Placement Test (AP) Ser.: Vol. AP-16). 1997. pap. 23.95 (*0-8373-6216-4*) Nat Learn.

Physics-Based Deformable Models: Applications to Computer Vision, Graphics & Medical Imaging. Dimitris N. Metaxas. LC 96-49366. 328p. (C). 1996. text 157.50 (*0-7923-9840-8*) Kluwer Academic.

Physics-Based Modeling of Lakes, Reservoirs & Impoundments. Ed. by William G. Gray. 308p. 1986. 44.00 (*0-87262-531-1*) Am Soc Civil Eng.

Physics-Based Technologies for the Detection of Contraband, Vol. 2936. Ed. by Lyle O. Malotky & John J. Pennella. LC 96-69886. 238p. 1997. 56.00 (*0-8194-2338-6*) SPIE.

Physics-Based Vision, Principles & Practice Vol. 1: Radiometry. Ed. by Lawrence B. Wolff et al. LC 92-13368. (Illus.). 424p. (C). 1992. text 86.00 (*0-86720-294-7*) AK Peters.

Physics-Based Vision, Principles & Practice Vol. 2: Color. Ed. by Steven A. Shafer et al. LC 92-13370. (Illus.). 432p. (C). 1992. text 86.00 (*0-86720-295-5*) AK Peters.

Physics-Based Vision, Principles & Practice Vol. 3: Shape Recovery. Ed. by Lawrence B. Wolff et al. LC 92-13369. (Illus.). 544p. (C). 1992. text 86.00 (*0-86720-296-3*) AK Peters.

Physics Basic Facts. E. Deeson. (Collins Gem Ser.). 1996. pap. 8.00 (*0-00-470908-X*) Collins.

Physics Begins with Another "M"...Mysteries, Magic, Myth, & Modern Physics. John H. Jewett. 496p. (C). 1995. pap. text 33.00 (*0-205-17406-X*) P-H.

Physics Beyond the Standard Model: Proceedings of the Fifth International Wein Symposium Santa F. Peter Herczeg. 900p. 1999. 128.00 (*981-02-3857-6*) World Scientific Pub.

Physics Builder for Standardized Tests. Research & Education Association Staff. 544p. 1995. pap. text 12.95 (*0-87891-941-4*) Res & Educ.

Physics by Example: Two Hundred Problems & Solutions. W. G. Rees. LC 93-34300. (Illus.). 388p. (C). 1994. pap. text 30.95 (*0-521-44975-8*) Cambridge U Pr.

Physics by Inquiry: An Introduction to Physics & the Physical Sciences see Physics by Inquiry: An Introduction to Physics & the Physical Sciences

Physics by Inquiry: An Introduction to Physics & the Physical Sciences, 2 vols., Vol. 2. Lillian C. McDermott & Physics Education Group Staff. Incl. Vol. 1. Physics by Inquiry: An Introduction to Physics & the Physical Sciences. LC 95-40316. 400p. 1995. pap. 40.95 (*0-471-14440-1*); Vol. 2. Physics by Inquiry: An Introduction to Physics & the Physical Sciences. LC 95-40316. 464p. 1995. pap. 40.95 (*0-471-14441-X*, Wiley-Interscience); LC 95-40316. 1995. Set pap. text 52.95 (*0-471-54870-7*) Wiley.

Physics C (Electricity & Magnetism) Jack Rudman. (Advanced Placement Test (AP) Ser.: Vol. AP-18). 1997. pap. 23.95 (*0-8373-6218-0*) Nat Learn.

Physics C (Mechanics) Jack Rudman. (Advanced Placement Test (AP) Ser.: Vol. AP-17). 1997. pap. 23.95 (*0-8373-6217-2*) Nat Learn.

Physics Careers, Employment & Education. Ed. by Martin L. Perl. LC 77-9403. (AIP Conference Proceedings Ser.: No. 39). (Illus.). 1978. lib. bdg. 18.50 (*0-88318-138-X*) Am Inst Physics.

***Physics, Chemistry & Application of Nanostructures: Reviews & Short Notes to Nanomeeting 99.** V E Borisenko. 1999. 122.00 (*981-02-3889-4*) WSC Inst MA Studies.

Physics, Chemistry & Application of Nanostructures, Reviews & Short Notes to "Nanomeeting '97" LC 97-166188. 400p. 1997. text 64.00 (*981-02-3113-X*) World Scientific Pub.

Physics, Chemistry & Dynamics of Interplanetary Dust Vol. 104: Iau Colloquium 150. Ed. by B. A. Bustafson & Martin S. Hanner. (ASP Conference Series Proceedings). 538p. 1996. 34.00 (*1-886733-24-4*) Astron Soc Pacific.

Physics, Chemistry, & Technology of Solid State Gas Sensor Devices. Andreas Mandelis & Constantinos Christofides. (Chemical Analysis Ser.: Vol. 125). 352p. 1993. 98.00 (*0-471-55885-0*) Wiley.

***Physics-Chemistry of the Process of Diffusion Bonding of Porous-Monolithic Titanium-Based Metal-Ceramic Products, Vol. 9.** V. Kireev et al. 108p. 1998. pap. text 64.00 (*90-5702-302-4*, Harwood Acad Pubs) Gordon & Breach.

***Physics Circa Nineteen Hundred.** Richard Staley. 1999. 38.00 (*0-226-77056-7*) U Ch Pr.

Physics, Classical & Modern. 2nd ed. W. Edward Gettys et al. LC 92-27894. (C). 1992. text 81.50 (*0-07-023460-4*) McGraw.

Physics, Classics, & the Bible: Elements of the Secular & the Sacred in Barthold Heinrich Brockes' Irdisches Vergnugen in Gott. Harold P. Fry. Ed. by Charlotte Craig. LC 89-13062. (Enlightenment: German & Interdisciplinary Studies: Vol. 2). XVI, 351p. 1990. text 59.95 (*0-8204-1166-3*) P Lang Pubng.

***Physics Coloring Book.** Concepts Coloring Staff. (Illus.). 128p. 2000. 17.95 (*0-06-273719-8*) HarpC.

Physics Contemporay Perspective Chapter 11A - 11B. (C). 1998. text 6.00 (*0-201-38421-3*) S&S Trade.

Physics, Cosmology & Astronomy, 1300-1799: Tension & Accommodation. Ed. by Sabetai Unguru. (Boston Studies in the Philosophy of Science). 352p. 1991. lib. bdg. 171.00 (*0-7923-1022-5*, Pub. by Kluwer Academic) Kluwer Academic.

Physics, Dance & the Pas de Deux. Kenneth Laws & Cynthia Harvey. (Illus.). 224p. 1994. 22.00 (*0-02-871326-5*, Schirmer Books) Mac Lib Ref.

Physics, Dance & the Pas de Deux. Kenneth Laws & Cynthia Harvey. 1994. 35.00 incl. VHS (*0-02-871327-3*, Schirmer Books) Mac Lib Ref.

Physics, Dance & the Pas de Deux. Kenneth Laws & Cynthia Harvey. (Illus.). 227p. 1994. text 50.00 incl. VHS (*0-02-871329-X*, Schirmer Books) Mac Lib Ref.

Physics Demonstrations. Shoma Kutasov. (Illus.). 300p. (YA). (gr. 7-12). 1996. pap. 14.95 (*0-9662191-0-4*) Penn Co.

Physics Dictionary: Dictionnaire de Physique. J. P. Sarmant. (FRE.). 312p. 1982. 55.00 (*0-8288-2236-0*, M14211) Fr & Eur.

Physics Dictionary: Dictionnaire de Physique. 3rd rev. ed. J. Mathieu & P. Fleury. (FRE.). 567p. 1991. 135.00 (*0-8288-2233-6*, F23760) Fr & Eur.

Physics Dictionary: Worterbuch Physik, 3 vols. 2nd ed. Ralf Sube et al. (ENG, FRE, GER & RUS.). 2895p. 1984. 495.00 (*0-8288-2247-6*, M6909) Fr & Eur.

Physics 1120 Laboratory Manual. University of Wyoming Staff. 116p. 1995. spiral bd. 14.64 (*0-8403-8378-9*) Kendall-Hunt.

Physics Engineers & Scientists. Carmony & Blais. Date not set. text 45.00 (*0-697-11137-7*) McGraw.

Physics Engineers & Scientists. Carmony & Blais. 1999. pap. text, student ed. 15.00 (*0-697-11139-3*) McGraw.

Physics Everyday Phenomenon. 2nd ed. Griffith. 1997. student ed. 19.74 (*0-697-15803-9*, McGrw-H College) McGrw-H Hghr Educ.

Physics Exam III File: Electricity & Magnetism. Ed. by M. Frank Anderson. LC 85-25306. (Exam File Ser.). 346p. 1986. pap. 19.50 (*0-910554-56-0*) Engineering.

Physics Experiments & Projects, Vol. 3. C. Isenberg & S. Chomet. 250p. 1996. pap. 47.95 (*1-56032-280-2*) Hemisp Pub.

Physics Experiments & Projects for Students, 2 vols., 1. C. Isenberg & S. Chomet. (Illus.). 1988. pap. 36.95 (*0-89116-732-3*) Hemisp Pub.

Physics Experiments & Projects for Students, 2 vols., 2. C. Isenberg & S. Chomet. (Illus.). 1988. pap. 36.95 (*0-89116-270-4*) Hemisp Pub.

Physics Experiments for Children. Muriel Mandell. LC 68-9308. Orig. Title: Science for Children. (Illus.). 96p. (J). (gr. 3-10). 1968. reprint ed. pap. 3.50 (*0-486-22033-8*) Dover.

Physics Experiments Using PC's: A Guide for Instructors & Students. Hans M. Staudenmaier. (Illus.). 312p. 1995. pap. text 39.95 (*0-387-58801-9*) Spr-Verlag.

Physics Experiments Using PC's: A Guide for Instructors & Students. Ed. by Hans M. Staudenmaier. LC 94-47309. 1995. 43.95 (*3-540-58801-9*) Spr-Verlag.

Physics Exploration. Jane Davis. 172p. (C). 1995. 20.95 (*0-7872-1205-9*) Kendall-Hunt.

Physics, Fabrication, & Applications of Multilayered Structures. Ed. by Claude Weisbuch & P. Dhez. (NATO ASI Series B, Physics: Vol. 182). (Illus.). 404p. 1988. 120.00 (*0-306-42995-0*, Plenum Trade) Perseus Pubng.

Physics Family. Myungkark Park. (Illus.). 100p. (Orig.). 1991. pap. write for info. (*1-877974-21-8*) Prompter Pubns.

Physics Ferret: A Guide to Ferreting Out the Solution to Problems in Science, Math, &...Life. Robert H. Lieberman. (Illus.). 32p. 1994. pap. 4.95 (*0-933124-02-3*) Gamma Bks.

Physics Flipper. George Stassinopoulos. 49p. (YA). (gr. 8 up). 1990. 6.95 (*1-878383-17-5*) C Lee Pubns.

Physics for a New Century: Papers Presented at the 1904 St. Louis Congress. Katherine R. Sopka. LC 85-28623. (History of Modern Physics & Astronomy Ser.). (Illus.). 304p. 1986. reprint ed. text 39.95 (*0-88318-487-7*) Spr-Verlag.

Physics for a New Generation: Prospects for High-Energy Physics at New Accelerators; Proceedings of the XXVIII, Internationale Universitatswochen fur Kernphysik, Schladming, Austria, March 1989. Ed. by H. Mitter & Heimo Latal. (Illus.). 344p. 1990. 71.95 (*0-387-52378-2*) Spr-Verlag.

Physics for Aviation Technology. Noel Dreska & Leonard Weisenthal. LC 92-27173. (Illus.). 183p. 1992. pap. text 17.65 (*0-89100-411-4*, JS312620) Jeppesen Sanderson.

Physics for Biology & Medicine. I. W. Richardson & Ejler B. Neergaard. LC 76-180711. (Illus.). 257p. reprint ed. pap. 79.70 (*0-608-18404-7*, 203053800069) Bks Demand.

Physics for Career Education. 6th ed. Dale Ewen et al. LC 98-21698. 627p. (C). 1998. 84.00 (*0-13-692823-4*) P-H.

Physics for Computer Science Students: With Emphasis on Atomic & Semiconductor Physics. Nicholas Garcia & A. Damask. (Springer Study Edition Ser.). xvi, 528p. 1995. 39.95 (*0-387-97656-6*) Spr-Verlag.

Physics for Computer Science Students: With Emphasis on Atomic & Semiconductor Physics. 2nd ed. Narciso Garcia et al. LC 96-44234. (Illus.). 550p. 1997. pap. 49.00 (*0-387-94903-8*) Spr-Verlag.

***Physics for Diagnostic Radiology.** P. P. Dendy. LC 99-24542. 1999. 160.00 (*0-7503-0590-8*) IOP Pub.

***Physics for Diagnostic Radiology.** 2nd ed. P. P. Dendy. LC 99-24542. 1999. pap. text 49.00 (*0-7503-0591-6*) IOP Pub.

Physics for Engineering & Science. Michael Browne. LC 98-35391. (Schaum's Outline Ser.). (Illus.). 452p. 1999. pap. 15.95 (*0-07-008498-X*) McGraw.

P

An Asterisk (*) at the beginning of an entry indicates that the title is appearing for the first time.

Physics for Every Kid: One Hundred One Easy Experiments in Motion, Heat, Light, Machines & Sound. Janice P. Vancleave. (Science Editions Ser.). 256p. (J). 1991. pap. 12.95 (*0-471-52505-7*) Wiley.

Physics for Geologists. Chapman. LC 94-32051. 192p. 1994. 65.00 (*1-85728-259-0*, Pub. by UCL Pr Ltd); pap. 24.95 (*1-85728-260-4*, Pub. by UCL Pr Ltd) Taylor & Francis.

Physics for Kids: Forty-Nine Easy Experiments in Electricity & Magnetism. Robert W. Wood. 1990. pap. text 10.95 (*0-07-156616-3*) McGraw.

Physics for Kids: Forty-Nine Easy Experiments with Acoustics. Robert W. Wood. 1990. pap. 9.95 (*0-07-156359-8*); text 16.95 (*0-07-156351-2*) McGraw.

Physics for Kids: Forty-Nine Easy Experiments with Heat. Robert W. Wood. 160p. 1990. pap. 10.95 (*0-07-155138-7*) McGraw.

Physics for Kids: Forty-Nine Easy Experiments with Heat. Robert W. Wood. (Illus.). 160p. 1989. 16.95 (*0-8306-9292-4*); pap. 9.95 (*0-8306-3292-1*) McGraw-Hill Prof.

Physics for Kids: Forty-Nine Easy Experiments with Mechanics. Robert W. Wood. (Illus.). 160p. 1989. 16.95 (*0-8306-9282-7*); pap. 9.95 (*0-8306-3282-4*) McGraw-Hill Prof.

Physics for Kids: 49 Easy Experiments with Electricity. Robert W. Wood. (Illus.). 192p. (J). 1990. pap. 9.95 (*0-8306-3412-6*) McGraw-Hill Prof.

Physics For Kids: 49 Easy Experiments with Optics. Robert W. Wood. (Illus.). 176p. (J). 1990. 16.95 (*0-8306-8402-6*, 3402) McGraw-Hill Prof.

Physics for Kids: 49 Easy Experiments with Optics. Robert W. Wood. (J). 1990. 16.05 (*0-606-04513-9*, Pub. by Turtleback) Demco.

Physics for Medical Imaging. Farr. 1996. text 44.95 (*0-7020-1770-1*, W B Saunders Co) Harcrt Hlth Sci Grp.

Physics for Poets. 4th ed. Robert H. March. LC 95-18959. 282p. (C). 1995. pap. 41.88 (*0-07-040248-5*) McGraw.

Physics for Rural Development: A Sourcebook for Teachers & Extension Workers in Developing Countries. Digby G. Swift. LC 82-2748. (Illus.). 269p. reprint ed. pap. 83.40 (*0-7837-4407-2*, 204415000012) Bks Demand.

Physics for Science, Vol. 2. 4th ed. Raymond A. Serway. (C). 1995. pap. text, student ed., wbk. ed. 33.00 (*0-03-016487-7*) Harcourt.

Physics for Science & Engineering. 4th ed. Raymond A. Serway. (C). 1995. pap. text, teacher ed. 28.00 (*0-03-015663-7*) Harcourt Coll Pubs.

Physics for Science & English. 4th ed. Serway. (C). 1995. student ed. 85.00 (*0-03-018777-X*) Harcourt.

***Physics for Scientist & Engineer & Modern Physic.** 3rd ed. (C). 1999. text 24.00 (*0-321-05149-1*) S&S Trade.

Physics for Scientist & Engineers. 2nd ed. C. W. Scherr. 1995. pap. text, teacher ed. write for info. (*0-13-231614-5*) Allyn.

***Physics for Scientist & Engineers, 4 vols., Vol. 1.** 5th ed. Raymond A. Serway & Robert J. Beicher. 528p. 1999. 115.00 (*0-03-026944-X*, Pub. by SCP) Harcourt.

***Physics for Scientist & Engineers, 4 vols., Vol. 2.** 5th ed. Raymond A. Serway & Robert J. Beicher. 256p. 1999. 115.00 (*0-03-026946-6*, Pub. by SCP) Harcourt.

***Physics for Scientist & Engineers, 4 vols., Vol. 3.** 5th ed. Raymond A. Serway & Robert J. Beicher. 432p. 1999. 115.00 (*0-03-026947-4*, Pub. by SCP) Harcourt.

***Physics for Scientist & Engineers, Vol. 4.** 5th ed. Raymond A. Serway & Robert J. Beicher. 304p. 1999. 115.00 (*0-03-026948-2*, Pub. by SCP) Harcourt.

Physics for Scientist & Engineers: Learning Guide. 2nd ed. Princeton Un Staff. 1995. pap. text. write for info. (*0-13-231705-2*) Allyn.

Physics for Scientist & Engineers with Modern Physics. 3rd ed. Ed. by Prentice-Hall Staff. 1184p. (C). 2000. 116.00 (*0-13-021517-1*) P-H.

***Physics for Scientists & Engineer.** 5th ed. Raymond A. Serway & Robert J. Beicher. 1408p. (C). 1999. text 81.00 (*0-03-022654-6*, Pub. by SCP) Harcourt.

Physics for Scientists & Engineers. Rodney Cole. 1216p. (C). 2000. text 76.00 (*0-03-097362-7*) SCP.

Physics for Scientists & Engineers. Lawrence Lerner. (Physics Ser.). 1168p. (C). 1996. text 83.75 (*0-86720-479-6*) Jones & Bartlett.

Physics for Scientists & Engineers. Lawrence S. Lerner. LC 96-9427. Date not set. 80.00 (*0-7637-0253-6*) Jones & Bartlett.

Physics for Scientists & Engineers. 2nd ed. Fishbane. 1996. text. write for info. (*0-13-231606-4*) Allyn.

Physics for Scientists & Engineers. 2nd ed. Miller. 1996. pap. text, student ed. 25.20 (*0-13-231697-8*) P-H.

Physics for Scientists & Engineers. 2nd ed. Shelden Radin & Robert Folk. 832p. (C). 1992. pap. text 93.00 (*0-536-58178-9*) Pearson Custom.

***Physics for Scientists & Engineers.** 3rd ed. Douglas C. Giancoli. 411p. 2000. pap. 26.67 (*0-13-029094-7*); pap. 26.67 (*0-13-029095-5*) P-H.

Physics for Scientists & Engineers. 3rd ed. Douglas C. Giancoli. 1152p. (C). 2000. 112.00 (*0-13-243106-8*, Macmillan Coll) P-H.

Physics for Scientists & Engineers. 4th ed. Raymond A. Serway. (C). 1996. pap. text 44.50 (*0-03-015667-X*) Harcourt.

Physics for Scientists & Engineers. 4th ed. Raymond A. Serway. (C). 1995. pap. text, teacher ed. 30.00 (*0-03-015662-9*) Harcourt Coll Pubs.

Physics for Scientists & Engineers. 4th ed. Raymond A. Serway. (C). 1995. text 111.50 (*0-03-005932-1*, Pub. by Harcourt Coll Pubs) Harcourt.

***Physics for Scientists & Engineers** 4th ed. Paul A. Tipler. LC 98-60168. 1999. write for info. (*1-57259-814-X*) Worth.

***Physics for Scientists & Engineers.** 4th ed. Paul Allen Tipler. LC 98-60168. (Illus.). 1998. write for info. (*1-57259-812-3*); pap. text. write for info. (*1-57259-813-1*) Worth.

Physics for Scientists & Engineers, Chs. 1-35. 3rd ed. Paul A. Tipler. Ed. by Valerie Neal & Steve Tenney. (Illus.). 1171p. (C). 1991. text 74.95 (*0-87901-430-X*) Worth.

Physics for Scientists & Engineers, Chs. 1-42. 3rd ed. Paul A. Tipler. Ed. by Valerie Neal & Steve Tenney. (Illus.). 1425p. (C). 1991. text 77.95 (*0-87901-432-6*) Worth.

Physics for Scientists & Engineers, Vol. 1. 2nd expanded ed. Paul M. Fishbane et al. LC 95-25229. 619p. 1995. 69.00 (*0-13-231150-X*) P-H.

***Physics for Scientists & Engineers, Vol. 1.** 3rd ed. Ed. by Prentice-Hall Staff. LC 99-40008. 576p. (C). 1999. 69.00 (*0-13-021518-X*) P-H.

Physics for Scientists & Engineers, Vol. 1. 3rd ed. Paul A. Tipler. Ed. by Valerie Neal & Steve Tenney. (Illus.). (C). 1991. pap. text, student ed. 14.95 (*0-87901-431-8*) Worth.

Physics for Scientists & Engineers, Vol. 1. 4th ed. Seerway. (C). 1995. text 67.00 (*0-03-015657-2*, Pub. by Harcourt Coll Pubs) Harcourt.

Physics for Scientists & Engineers, Vol. 1. 4th ed. Raymond A. Serway. (C). 1995. pap. text, student ed. 26.50 (*0-03-015664-5*, Pub. by Harcourt Coll Pubs) Harcourt.

Physics for Scientists & Engineers, Vol. 1 & 2. 4th ed. Tipler. LC 98-60168. 1998. pap. text 72.00 (*1-57259-614-7*) Worth.

Physics for Scientists & Engineers, Vol. 1, Chapters 1-21. 4th ed. Tipler. LC 98-60168. 2000. pap. text 39.00 (*1-57259-491-8*) Worth.

Physics for Scientists & Engineers, Vol. 1, Chs. 1-17. 3rd ed. Paul A. Tipler. Ed. by Valerie Neal & Steve Tenney. (Illus.). 595p. (C). 1990. text 46.95 (*0-87901-433-4*) Worth.

Physics for Scientists & Engineers, Vol. 2. Jerry B. Marion. (C). 1983. pap. text, teacher ed. 27.50 (*0-03-058362-4*) Harcourt Coll Pubs.

Physics for Scientists & Engineers, Vol. 2. 3rd ed. Ed. by Prentice-Hall Staff. 468p. (C). 2000. 70.67 (*0-13-021519-8*) P-H.

Physics for Scientists & Engineers, Vol. 2. 3rd ed. Paul A. Tipler. Ed. by Valerie Neal & Steve Tenney. (Illus.). (C). 1992. pap. text, student ed. 14.95 (*0-87901-429-6*) Worth.

Physics for Scientists & Engineers, Vol. II. 4th ed. Raymond A. Serway. (C). 1995. text 62.50 (*0-03-015658-0*, Pub. by Harcourt Coll Pubs) Harcourt.

Physics, for Scientists & Engineers, Vol. 2, Chapters 22-35. 4th ed. Paul Tipler. LC 98-60168. (Illus.). (C). 1998. pap. text 39.00 (*1-57259-492-6*) Worth.

Physics for Scientists & Engineers, Vol. 2, Chs. 18-42. 3rd ed. Paul A. Tipler. Ed. by Valerie Neal & Steve Tenney. (Illus.). 830p. (C). 1991. text 48.95 (*0-87901-434-2*) Worth.

***Physics for Scientists & Engineers, Vol. 3.** 3rd ed. Douglas C. Giancoli. 344p. 2000. pap. 26.67 (*0-13-029096-3*) P-H.

Physics for Scientists & Engineers, Vol. 3, Chapters 36-41. 4th ed. Tipler. LC 98-60168. 2000. pap. text 20.00 (*1-57259-490-X*) Worth.

***Physics for Scientists & Engineers, Vol. 4.** 3rd ed. Douglas C. Giancoli. 218p. 2000. pap. 24.00 (*0-13-029097-1*) P-H.

***Physics for Scientists & Engineers, Vol. 5.** 3rd ed. Douglas C. Giancoli. 288p. 2000. pap. 24.00 (*0-13-029098-X*) P-H.

Physics for Scientists & Engineers, Vol. 5. 4th ed. Serway. (C). 1996. 116.00 (*0-03-023968-0*) Harcourt.

***Physics for Scientists & Engineers: Doing Physics with Spreadsheets.** 3rd ed. Aubrecht. 304p. 2000. pap. 26.00 incl. disk (*0-13-021474-4*) P-H.

Physics, for Scientists & Engineers: International Edition. 4th ed. Paul Tipler. (Illus.). (C). 1998. text 72.00 (*1-57259-673-2*) Worth.

Physics for Scientists & Engineers: Pocket Guide. 4th ed. Raymond A. Serway. (C). 1995. pap. text 21.50 (*0-03-015659-9*, Pub. by Harcourt Coll Pubs) Harcourt.

***Physics for Scientists & Engineers Extended.** 3rd ed. (C). 1999. pap. text 177.00 (*0-321-03577-1*, Celebration); pap. text 24.00 (*0-321-03578-X*, Celebration); pap. text 24.00 (*0-321-03590-9*, Celebration) Addson-Wesley Educ.

***Physics for Scientists & Engineers Extended.** 3rd ed. 432p. (C). 1999. pap. text 35.00 (*0-321-05148-3*, Celebration) Addson-Wesley Educ.

Physics for Scientists & Engineers with Modern. 4th ed. Serway. LC 95-69620. (C). 1995. text 117.00 (*0-03-015654-8*) Harcourt Coll Pubs.

Physics for Scientists & English, Vol. I. 4th ed. Raymond A. Serway. (C). 1995. 99.75 (*0-03-015674-2*) Harcourt Coll Pubs.

Physics for Technicians - A Systems Approach. Center for Occupational Research & Development Staff. (Illus.). 997p. 1988. text 45.00 (*1-55502-272-3*) CORD Commns.

Physics for Technicians - A Systems Approach. Center for Occupational Research & Development Staff. (Illus.). 1993. write for info. (*1-55502-516-1*) CORD Commns.

Physics for Technicians - A Systems Approach: Instructor's Manual. Center for Occupational Research & Development Staff. (Illus.). 103p. 1988. pap. text 15.00 (*1-55502-462-9*) CORD Commns.

Physics for Technicians - A Systems Approach: Laboratory Exercises. Center for Occupational Research & Development Staff. 366p. 1989. pap. text 28.00 (*1-55502-362-2*) CORD Commns.

Physics for Technology Lab Manual. 4th ed. James F. Sullivan & James F. Marquardt, Sr. (Illus.). 150p. (C). 1995. 15.95 (*0-9626661-7-3*) Gilmar Pub.

***Physics for the Allied Health Services.** Anne Johnson. 1999. pap. text 18.49 (*1-56870-353-8*) RonJon Pub.

Physics for the Health Sciences. 3rd ed. Carl R. Nave & Brenda C. Nave. (Illus.). 1985. pap., teacher ed. write for info. (*0-7216-2043-4*, W B Saunders Co) Harcrt Hlth Sci Grp.

Physics for the Health Sciences. 3rd ed. Carl R. Nave & Brenda C. Nave. (Illus.). 432p. (C). 1985. pap. text 46.00 (*0-7216-1309-8*, Pub. by SCP) Harcourt.

Physics for the Heart. Dale Pendell. 20p. 1986. 5.00 (*1-882623-01-0*) Exiled-Am Pr.

Physics for the Life Sciences. 2nd ed. Alan Cromer. (C). 1994. text 52.50 (*0-07-014440-0*) McGraw.

Physics for the Rest of Us. Roger S. Jones. 384p. 1993. pap. 18.95 (*0-8092-3716-4*, 371640, Contemporary Bks) NTC Contemp Pub Co.

Physics for the Rest of Us: The Ten Basic Ideas of Twentieth-Century Physics that Everyone Should Know...& How They Have Shaped Our Culture & Consciousness. Roger S. Jones. LC 92-20232. (Illus.), 368p. 1992. 21.95 (*0-8092-3939-6*) NTC Contemp Pub Co.

Physics for the Utterly Confused. Robert Oman & Daniel Oman. LC 98-25808. (Illus.). 208p. 1998. pap. 15.95 (*0-07-048262-4*) McGraw.

Physics for You: National Curriculum Edition for GCSE. 3rd rev. ed. Keith Johnson. 384p. (C). 1996. pap. 34.50 (*0-7478-0565-2*, Pub. by S Thornes Pubs) Trans-Atl Phila.

Physics for You: New National Curriculum Edition for GCSE. 3rd ed. Keith Johnson. (Illus.). 384p. 1998. pap., student ed. 34.50 (*0-7487-2761-2*, Pub. by S Thornes Pubs) Trans-Atl Phila.

Physics for You: New National Curriculum Edition, Teacher's Support Pack. Keith Johnson. 368p. 1998. pap., teacher ed. 195.00 (*0-7487-2755-8*) St Mut.

Physics 1440. UNT Physics Department Staff. (C). 1997. pap. text 21.39 (*1-56870-280-9*) RonJon Pub.

Physics 1401-2475: Lab Experiments. Anahita F. Sidhwa. (Orig.). (C). 1995. pap. text 20.23 (*1-56870-183-7*) RonJon Pub.

Physics 1470 Lab Experiments. Anahita F. Sidhwa. (Orig.). (C). 1995. pap. text 19.90 (*1-56870-216-7*) RonJon Pub.

Physics 1430. UNT Physics Department Staff. (C). 1997. pap. text 21.39 (*1-56870-279-5*) RonJon Pub.

Physics from Fisher Information: A Unification. B. Roy Frieden. LC 98-20461. (Illus.). 230p. (C). 1999. 64.95 (*0-521-63167-X*) Cambridge U Pr.

Physics from Planck Scale to Electroweak Scale. P. Nath et al. 508p. 1995. text 124.00 (*981-02-2184-3*) World Scientific Pub.

Physics from the Junk Drawer & Counter Top Chemistry. Science House Staff. 120p. (C). 1997. spiral bd. 28.95 (*0-7872-3415-X*, 41341501) Kendall-Hunt.

Physics, Geometry & Topology. Ed. by Henry C. Lee. (NATO ASI Ser.: Vol. 232). (Illus.). 690p. (C). 1990. text 198.00 (*0-306-43693-0*, Kluwer Plenum) Kluwer Academic.

Physics Graduate Education for Diverse Career Options. Ed. by Judy R. Franz. 84p. 1995. pap. 6.00 (*0-917853-60-1*, DC-01) Am Assn Physics.

***Physics Handbook: Fundamentals & Key Equations.** Charles P. Poole. 493p. 1999. pap. 64.95 (*0-471-31460-9*) Wiley.

Physics History from AAPT Journals. Ed. by Melba Phillips. 240p. 1985. per. 23.00 (*0-917853-14-8*, OP-54) Am Assn Physics.

Physics History from AAPT Journals II. Ed. by A. P. French & Thomas B. Greenslade, Jr. (Illus.). 238p. (C). 1995. pap. 16.00 (*0-917853-58-X*) Am Assn Physics.

***Physics I & II Laboratory Manual.** 2nd ed. Terry Bradfield. 214p. (C). 1999. pap. text, wbk. ed. 36.95 (*0-7872-6298-6*, 41629801) Kendall-Hunt.

Physics in a Technological World: From a Joint Meeting of the International Union of Pure & Applied Physics & the American Institute of Physics Corporate Associates, Washington D. C., October 1987. Ed. by Anthony French. 320p. 1988. 27.50 (*0-88318-591-1*) Am Inst Physics.

Physics in Collision. 540p. 1997. 75.00 (*981-02-3027-3*) World Scientific Pub.

Physics in Collision: Proceedings of the Seventh International Conference (EF - Promote Only in Asia) Koichiro Takahashi & T. Kondo. 1988. text 164.00 (*9971-5-0471-5*) World Scientific Pub.

Physics in Collision: Proceedings of the XVII International Conference Bristol, England 25-27 June, 1997. Ed. by Helen F. Heath. 500p. 1998. 92.00 (*981-02-3378-7*) World Scientific Pub.

Physics in Collision: Proceedings of the 6th International Conference, Chicago, Illinois, September, 3-5, 1986. Ed. by M. Derrick. 552p. 1987. pap. 47.00 (*9971-5-0282-8*); text 144.00 (*9971-5-0281-X*) World Scientific Pub.

Physics in Environmental & Biomedical Research: Rome, Italy, November 26-29, 1985. Ed. by S. Onori & E. Tabet. 608p. 1986. text 144.00 (*9971-5-0110-4*) World Scientific Pub.

Physics in Everyday Life. Dittman. 1979. teacher ed. 26.87 (*0-07-017057-6*) McGraw.

Physics in Everyday Life. Richard Dittman & Glenn Schmieg. Ed. by Janice L. Rogers & C. Robert Zappa. LC 78-13381. (Schaum's Outline Ser.). (Illus.). 512p. (C). 1979. 40.63 (*0-07-017056-8*) McGraw.

Physics in Higher Dimensions: Proceedings of the 2nd Jerusalem Winter School on Theoretical Physics Jerusalem, Israel, December 27-January 4, 1985. Ed. by S. Weinberg & T. Piran. 248p. 1986. text 64.00 (*9971-5-0154-6*); pap. text 37.00 (*9971-5-0155-4*) World Scientific Pub.

Physics in Living Matter. Ed. by D. Baeriswyl et al. (Lecture Notes in Physics Ser.: Vol. 284). v, 180p. 1987. 34.95 (*0-387-18192-X*) Spr-Verlag.

Physics in Medicine & Biology, 2 vols., Vol. 1-2. T. F. McAinsh. 1986. 185.00 (*0-08-033930-1*, Pergamon Pr); 135.00 (*0-08-033931-X*, Pergamon Pr) Elsevier.

Physics in Medicine & Biology Encyclopedia, 2 vols., Set. Ed. by T. F. McAinsh. (Illus.). 650p. 1986. 447.00 (*0-08-026497-2*, Pub. by Pergamon Repr) Franklin.

Physics in Modern World. 2nd ed. Jerry B. Marion. (C). 1990. pap. text, teacher ed. 34.00 (*0-15-570603-9*) Harcourt Coll Pubs.

Physics in My Generation. 2nd rev. ed. M. Born. LC 68-59281. (Heidelberg Science Library: Vol. 7). (Illus.). 1989. 29.95 (*0-387-90008-X*) Spr-Verlag.

Physics in Nuclear Medicine. 2nd ed. Ed. by James A. Sorenson & Michael E. Phelps. 608p. 1986. text 89.00 (*0-8089-1804-4*, 794189, Grune & Strat) Harcrt Hlth Sci Grp.

Physics in Quantum Electron Devices. Ed. by F. Capasso. (Electronics & Photonics Ser.: Vol. 28). (Illus.). 425p. 1990. 74.50 (*0-387-51128-8*) Spr-Verlag.

Physics in the Automotive Industry: APS-AAPT Topical Conference. Ed. by F. E. Jamerson. LC 80-70987. (AIP Conference Proceedings Ser.: No. 66). 174p. 1981. lib. bdg. 26.50 (*0-88318-165-7*) Am Inst Physics.

Physics in the Life Sciences. 2nd ed. G. Duncan. 1990. pap. 39.95 (*0-632-01778-3*) Blackwell Sci.

Physics in the Making: Essays on Developments in 20th Century Physics; In Honour of H. B. G. Casimir on the Occasion of His 80th Birthday. Ed. by A. Sarlemijn & M. J. Sparnaay. (North-Holland Personal Library). xvi, 362p. 1989. pap. 77.25 (*0-444-88019-4*, North Holland) Elsevier.

Physics in the Nineteenth Century. Robert D. Purrington. LC 96-49115. 320p. (C). 1997. text 55.00 (*0-8135-2441-5*); pap. text 22.00 (*0-8135-2442-3*) Rutgers U Pr.

Physics in the Real World. Keith Lockett. 208p. (C). 1990. pap. text 23.95 (*0-521-36690-9*) Cambridge U Pr.

Physics in the Real World. Jasper McKee. (Illus.). 91p. 1999. write for info. (*0-7541-0816-3*, Pub. by Minerva Pr) Unity Dist.

Physics in the Steel Industry: APS-AISI, Lehigh University, 1981. American Institute of Physics. Ed. by Fred C. Schwerer. LC 82-72033. (AIP Conference Proceedings Ser.: No. 84). 409p. 1982. lib. bdg. 36.00 (*0-88318-183-5*) Am Inst Physics.

Physics in the 20th Century. Curt Suplee. Ed. by Judith R. Franz & John S. Rigden. LC 98-41306. (Illus.). 224p. (YA). 1999. 49.50 (*0-8109-4364-6*, Pub. by Abrams) Time Warner.

Physics in the 21st Century. 250p. 1997. text 40.00 (*981-02-3088-5*) World Scientific Pub.

***Physics in the 20th Century.** Abrams Staff. 1999. pap. 6.30 (*0-8109-2919-8*, Pub. by Abrams) Time Warner.

Physics in 2 Plus 1 Dimension: Proceedings of the Second Winter School on Mathematical Physics. Y. M. Cho. 368p. 1992. text 105.00 (*981-02-1111-2*) World Scientific Pub.

Physics in Welding. William J. Harris. (Monticello Bks.). 62p. 1970. pap. 4.50 (*0-686-12002-7*) Jefferson Pubns.

Physics Is Fundamental. Michael H. Suckley. 240p. (Orig.). (C). 1996. pap. text 32.65 (*0-88252-203-5*) Paladin Hse.

Physics Lab Experiments, 5 vols. 5th ed. Wilson. (C). 1998. pap. text 47.56 (*0-395-87466-1*) HM.

Physics Lab Experiments & Correlated Computer Aids see **Experiments for Physics Labs**

Physics Lab Experiments & Correlated Computer Aids see **Experiments for Physics Labs: Teacher's Edition**

Physics Lab in a Hardware Store. Bob Friedhoffer. (Physical Science Labs Ser.). 112p. (J). 1997. pap. 6.95 (*0-531-15823-3*) Watts.

Physics Lab in a Hardware Store. Robert Friedhoffer. LC 96-15828. (Physical Science Labs Ser.). (Illus.). (J). (gr. 5-8). 1996. lib. bdg. 24.00 (*0-531-11292-6*) Watts.

Physics Lab in a Housewares Store. Bob Friedhoffer. LC 95-49012. (Physical Science Labs Ser.). (J). 1996. lib. bdg. 24.00 (*0-531-11293-4*) Watts.

Physics Lab in a Housewares Store. Bob Friedhoffer. (Physical Science Labs Ser.). 96p. (J). 1997. pap. 6.95 (*0-531-15824-1*) Watts.

Physics Lab in a Supermarket. Robert Friedhoffer. LC 96-37285. (Physical Science Labs Ser.). (Illus.). (J). 1997. 24.00 (*0-531-11335-3*) Watts.

Physics Lab in the Home. Bob Friedhoffer. (Physical Science Labs Ser.). 1998. pap. 6.95 (*0-531-15845-4*) Watts.

Physics Lab in the Home. Robert Friedhoffer. LC 96-36802. (Physical Science Labs Ser.). (Illus.). (J). 1997. lib. bdg. 24.00 (*0-531-11323-X*) Watts.

Physics Lab Manual. Patrick Briggs. 114p. (C). 1997. lab manual ed. 20.00 (*1-886855-79-X*) Tavenner Pub.

Physics Lab Manual No. I: Mechanics, Waves & Heat. 3rd ed. Earl Oxford. 154p. 1998. spiral bd. 28.95 (*0-7872-4892-4*, 41489201) Kendall-Hunt.

Physics Lab Manual Vol. II: Electricity, Magnetism & Light. 2nd ed. Earl Oxford. 180p. (C). 1998. spiral bd. 28.95 (*0-7872-5177-1*, 41517701) Kendall-Hunt.

Physics Lab Manual 2/E. 2nd ed. Loyd. LC 97-2566. 576p. (C). 1997. pap. text, lab manual ed. 54.50 (*0-03-024561-3*) SCP.

Physics Lab Transitions, 5 vols. Wilson. (C). Date not set. pap. 11.96 (*0-395-89745-9*) HM.

Physics Laboratory. Angelo Ferrari & Russell A. Roy. (Illus.). 400p. (C). 1997. lab manual ed. 37.95 (*0-89892-157-0*) Contemp Pub Co of Raleigh.

Physics Laboratory Experiments. 3rd ed. Jerry D. Wilson. 627p. (C). 1990. teacher ed. 2.66 (*0-669-18908-1*) HM Trade Div.

P

An Asterisk (*) at the beginning of an entry indicates that the title is appearing for the first time.

Physics Laboratory Experiments. 4th ed. Jerry D. Wilson. 582p. (C). 1994. pap. text 47.56 (0-669-35074-5); pap. text, teacher ed. 2.66 (0-669-35075-3) HM Trade Div.
Physics Laboratory Experiments, 1990. Michael J. Longo. (Illus.). 244p. 1990. student ed. 7.50 (0-9621002-2-6) ML Pub MI.
Physics Laboratory Manual. 3rd ed. Ralph Alexander. 80p. (C). 1994. spiral bd. 16.95 (0-8403-9438-1) Kendall-Hunt.
Physics Made Simple. Ira M. Freeman. 208p. 1989. pap. 12.95 (0-385-24228-X) Doubleday.
Physics, Materials & Applications of High Temperature Superconductors. LC 96-51107. 700p. 1996. lib. bdg. 61.00 (981-02-2715-9) World Scientific Pub.
Physics Media Activity: Conversion Guide. 4th ed. Raymond A. Serway. (C). 1996. pap. text, teacher ed. 13.50 (0-03-018057-0) Harcourt Coll Pubs.
***Physics Meets Mineralogy: Condensed Matter Physics in Geosciences.** Ed. by Hideo Aoki et al. LC 99-86299. (Illus.). 432p. 2000. write for info. (0-521-64342-2) Cambridge U Pr.
***Physics Meets Philosophy at the Planck Scale: Contemporary Theories in Quantum Gravity.** Ed. by Craig Callender & Nick Huggett. (Illus.). 340p. 2001. write for info. (0-521-66280-X); pap. write for info. (0-521-66445-4) Cambridge U Pr.
***Physics of Absolute Motion.** Text & Pref. by Ken H. Seto. Orig. Title: Model Mechanics: A New Interpretation of Nature. (Illus.). v, 191p. 2000. pap. 13.00 (0-9647136-1-6) KHS Pubng.
Physics of Accretion onto Compact Objects. Ed. by K. O. Mason et al. (Lecture Notes in Physics Ser.: Vol. 266). viii, 421p. 1986. 59.95 (0-387-17195-9) Spr-Verlag.
Physics of Actinide Compounds. Paul Erdos & John M. Robinson. (Physics of Solids & Liquids Ser.). 226p. 1983. 69.50 (0-306-41150-4, Plenum Trade) Perseus Pubng.
Physics of Active Galactic Nuclei: Proceedings of the International Conference, Heidelberg, 3-7 June 1991. Ed. by S. J. Wagner & W. J. Duschl. LC 92-20770. (Illus.). 720p. 1992. 158.95 (0-387-55554-4) Spr-Verlag.
Physics of Amorphous Semiconductors. K. Morigaki. 300p. 1997. text 55.00 (981-02-1381-6) World Scientific Pub.
***Physics of Amorphous Solids.** Richard Zallen. (Wiley Classics Library). 304p. 1998. pap. 49.50 (0-471-29941-3) Wiley.
Physics of Amphiphilic Layers. J. Meunier. Ed. by D. Langevin & Nino Boccara. (Proceedings in Physics Ser.: Vol. 21). (Illus.). 410p. 1987. 78.95 (0-387-18255-1) Spr-Verlag.
Physics of Angels: Exploring the Realm Where Science & Spirit Meet. Matthew Fox & Rupert Sheldrake. LC 96-12696. 240p. 1996. 16.00 (0-06-062864-2, Pub. by Harper SF) HarpC.
Physics of Astrophysics Vol. I: Radiation Processes. Frank H. Shu. (Illus.). 429p. (C). 1991. text 52.00 (0-935702-64-4) Univ Sci Bks.
Physics of Astrophysics Vol. II: Gas Dynamics. Frank H. Shu. LC 91-65165. 476p. (C). 1992. text 54.00 (0-935702-65-2) Univ Sci Bks.
Physics of Atomic Collisions. Ed. by D. V. Skobel'tsyn. Tr. by Paul Robeson from RUS. LC 79-157934. (Proceedings of the P. N. Lebedev Physics Institute Ser.: No. 51). (Illus.). 194p. 1971. reprint ed. pap. 60.20 (0-608-05514-X, 20659820006) Bks Demand.
Physics of Atoms & Molecules, 1. A. Bransden. 1996. 84.33 (0-582-44401-2) Addison-Wesley.
Physics of Atoms & Molecules: An Introduction to the Structure of Matter. Ugo Fano & L. Fano. LC 76-184808. 606p. 1973. lib. bdg. 42.00 (0-226-23782-6) U Ch Pr.
Physics of Atoms & Quanta: Introduction to Experiments & Theory. 3rd ed. Hermann Haken & Hans C. Wolf. Tr. by William D. Brewer from GER.Tr. of Atom- und Quantenphysik. (Illus.). 462p. 1993. 49.00 (0-387-56312-1) Spr-Verlag.
Physics of Atoms & Quanta: Introduction to Experiments & Theory. 4th ed. Hermann Haken et al. Tr. by William D. Brewer from GER. LC 94-12049.Tr. of Atom- und Quantenphysik. (Illus.). 467p. 1994. 54.95 (0-387-57874-9) Spr-Verlag.
Physics of Atoms & Quanta: Introduction to Experiments & Theory. 5th ed. H. Haken & H. C. Wolf. LC 96-29219. 467p. 1996. 64.50 (3-540-61555-5) Spr-Verlag.
***Physics of Atoms & Quanta: Introduction to Experiments & Theory.** 6th rev. enl. ed. H. Haken & H. C. Wolf. Tr. by W. D. Brewer from GER. LC 00-38826. (Advanced Texts in Physics Ser.). (Illus.). xviii, 490p. 2000. 68.00 (3-540-67274-5) Spr-Verlag.
Physics of Auroral Arc Formation. Ed. by S. I. Akasofu & J. R. Kan. (Geophysical Monograph Ser.: Vol. 25). 465p. 1981. 32.00 (0-87590-050-X) Am Geophysical.
Physics of Baseball. Robert K. Adair. LC 89-45623. (Illus.). 128p. (Orig.). 1990. pap. 7.95 (0-00-001526-1, Perennial) HarperTrade.
Physics of Baseball: 2nd Edition, Revised, Updated, & Enlarged. 2nd rev. ed. Robert K. Adair. (Illus.). 160p. 1994. pap. 12.00 (0-06-095047-1, Perennial) HarperTrade.
Physics of Beams: Andrew Sessler Symposium, Los Angeles, CA December 5-6, 1993. W. Barletta. (CP Ser.: No. 351). (Illus.). 144p. 1995. 120.00 (1-56396-376-0) Am Inst Physics.
Physics of Big Sample Instrumental Neutron Activation Analysis. R. M. Overwater. (Delft Studies in Integrated Water Management: No. 5). 192p. 1994. pap. 57.50 (90-407-1048-1, Pub. by Delft U Pr) Coronet Bks.
Physics of Bioenergetics Processes. L. A. Blumenfeld. Ed. by H. Haken. (Springer Series in Energetics: Vol. 16). (Illus.). 150p. 1983. 57.95 (0-387-11417-3) Spr-Verlag.
Physics of Biological Systems: From Molecules to Species, Vol. 480. Henrik Flyvbjerg. LC 96-54730. (Lecture Notes in Physics Ser.). 1997. 89.95 (3-540-62475-9) Spr-Verlag.
Physics of Biomaterials - Fluctuations, Self-Assembly & Evolution: Proceedings of the NATO Advanced Study Institute, Geilo, Norway, March 27-April 6, 1995. D. C. Sherrington. Ed. by Tormod Riste. LC 96-26729. (NATO Advanced Science Institutes Series C). 400p. (C). 1996. text 209.50 (0-7923-4131-7) Kluwer Academic.
Physics of Biomolecules. Hans Frauenfelder & Debrunner. 608p. (C). 1999. write for info. (0-201-15671-7) Addison-Wesley.
***Physics of Black Holes.** G. Gorini. Ed. by Pietro Fre' et al. LC 99-43057. (Studies in High Energy Physics, Cosmology & Gravitation). (Illus.). 424p. 1999. 128.00 (0-7503-0627-0) IOP Pub.
Physics of Black Holes. Igor D. Novikov & Valery P. Frolov. (C). 1989. text 234.50 (90-277-2685-X) Kluwer Academic.
Physics of Block Copolymers. Ian Hamley. LC 99-206499. (Illus.). 432p. 1999. text 150.00 (0-19-850218-4) OUP.
Physics of Carbon Nanotube. R. Saito et al. 200p. 1998. 44.00 (1-86094-093-5, Pub. by Imperial College) World Scientific Pub.
Physics of Caribou Creek: A Story of Love. Carl Forest. LC 90-81922. 352p. (Orig.). 1991. 14.95 (1-878987-01-1) Fir Pub IN.
Physics of Caribou Creek: A Story of Love. deluxe ed. Carl Forest. LC 90-81922. 352p. (Orig.). 1991. 18.95 (1-878987-00-3) Fir Pub IN.
Physics of Cerebrovascular Diseases: Biophysical Mechanisms of Development, Diagnosis & Therapy. George J. Hademenos & Tarik F. Massoud. LC 97-30653. (Biological Physics Ser.: Vol. 2). (Illus.). 311p. 1997. 69.00 (1-56396-558-5, AIP Pr) Spr-Verlag.
Physics of Chance: From Blaise Pascal to Niels Bohr. Charles Ruhia. Tr. by Gabriel Barton. (Illus.). 240p. 1992. text 65.00 (0-19-853960-6); pap. text 38.00 (0-19-853977-0) OUP.
Physics of Chaos in Hamiltonian Systems. LC 98-23901. 250p. 1998. text 30.00 (1-86094-052-8); text 30.00 (981-02-3104-0) World Scientific Pub.
Physics of Charged-Particle Beams. 2nd ed. Jimmie D. Lawson. (International Series of Monographs on Physics: No. 75). (Illus.). 472p. 1988. 135.00 (0-19-851719-X) OUP.
Physics of Christmas: From the Aerodynamics of Reindeer to the Thermodynamics of Turkey. Roger Highfield. LC 98-20072. 1998. write for info. (0-316-36605-6) Little.
Physics of Christmas: From the Aerodynamics of Reindeer to the Thermodynamics of Turkey. Roger Highfield. LC 98-20072. (Illus.). 320p. (gr. 8). 1998. 20.00 (0-316-36611-0, Back Bay) Little.
***Physics of Christmas: From the Aerodynamics of Reindeer to the Thermodynamics of Turkey.** Roger Highfield. 320p. 1999. pap. 12.95 (0-316-36695-1, Back Bay) Little.
Physics of Classical Novae: Proceedings of Colloquium No. 122 of the International Astronomical Union Held in Madrid, Spain, on 27-30 June 1989. Ed. by A. Cassatella & Roberto Viotti. (Lecture Notes in Physics Ser.: Vol. 369). xii, 462p. 1991. 67.95 (0-387-53500-4) Spr-Verlag.
Physics of Climate. J. P. Peixoto et al. 560p. 1992. 97.00 (0-88318-711-6); pap. 49.95 (0-88318-712-4) Spr-Verlag.
Physics of Clusters. Ed. by V. D. Lakhno & G. N. Chuev. 360p. 1998. 68.00 (981-02-3307-8) World Scientific Pub.
Physics of Clusters & Nanophase Materials. M. S. Multani. 850p. 1990. text 1571.00 (0-677-26120-9) Gordon & Breach.
Physics of Cognitive Processes: Proceedings of the International Symposium. Ed. by E. R. Caianiello. 480p. (C). 1987. pap. 46.00 (9971-5-0327-1); text 148.00 (9971-5-0255-0) World Scientific Pub.
Physics of Collective Beam Instabilities in High Energy Accelerators. Alexander W. Chao. LC 92-39599. (Beam Physics & Accelerator Technology Ser.). 384p. 1993. 110.00 (0-471-55184-8) Wiley.
Physics of Collisionless Shocks. Ed. by C. T. Russell. (Advances in Space Research (RJ) Ser.: Vol. 15). 542p. 1995. pap. 194.50 (0-08-042558-5, Pergamon Pr) Elsevier.
Physics of Comets. LC 97-7970. 300p. 1997. lib. bdg. 26.00 (981-02-2632-2) World Scientific Pub.
Physics of Comets. Swamy K. Krishna. 273p. 1986. text 41.00 (9971-978-18-0) World Scientific Pub.
Physics of Compact Objects: Proceedings of the COSPAR - IAU Symposium Held in Sofia, Bulgaria, 13-18 July, 1987. Ed. by N. E. White & L. G. Filipov. LC 83-645550. (Advances in Space Research Ser.: Vol. 8). (Illus.). 724p. 1988. pap. 120.00 (0-08-036866-2, Pergamon Pr) Elsevier.
Physics of Complex & Supermolecular Fluids. Ed. by Samuel A. Safran & Noel A. Clark. 736p. (C). 1987. reprint ed. text 69.50 (0-471-85081-0) Krieger.
Physics of Complex Liquids: Proceedings of the International Symposium Nagoya, Japan 10-12 November 1997. Ed. by Fumiko Yonezawa et al. 350p. 1998. 94.00 (981-02-3631-X) World Scientific Pub.
Physics of Complex Systems. Ed. by F. Mallamace & H. E. Stanley. LC 97-75045. (International School of Physics Enrico Fermi Ser.: Vol. 134). 750p. Date not set. 145.00 (90-5199-351-X, 351-X) IOS Press.
Physics of Composite Superconductors. Alexander V. Gurevich et al. Tr. by S. Chomet from RUS. 1995. write for info. (0-8493-9903-3) Begell Hse.
Physics of Composite Superconductors. Alexander V. Gurevich et al. LC 96-37924. 350p. 1997. 112.50 (1-56700-066-5) Begell Hse.
Physics of Conformal Radiotherapy: Advances in Technology. S. Webb. (Medical Science Ser.). (Illus.). 272p. 1997. text 179.00 (0-7503-0396-4); pap. text 53.00 (0-7503-0397-2) IOP Pub.
***Physics of Consciousness: The Quantum Mind & the Meaning of Life.** Evan H. Walker. (Illus.). 320p. 2000. text 27.50 (0-7382-0234-7, Pub. by Perseus Pubng) HarpC.
Physics of Continuous Media. G. E. Vekstein. (Illus.). 204p. 1992. 130.00 (0-7503-0140-6); pap. 43.00 (0-7503-0141-4) IOP Pub.
Physics of Cosmic X-Ray, Gamma-Ray & Particle Sources. 2nd ed. Kenneth Greisen. Ed. by A. G. W. Cameron & G. B. Field. LC 78-135063. (Topics in Astrophysics & Space Physics Ser.). (Illus.). 124p. 1971. pap. text 58.00 (0-685-73338-6) Gordon & Breach.
Physics of Cosmic X-Ray, Gamma-Ray & Particle Sources. 2nd ed. Kenneth Greisen. Ed. by A. G. W. Cameron & G. B. Field. LC 78-135063. (Topics in Astrophysics & Space Physics Ser.). (Illus.). viii, 116p. 1971. text 142.00 (0-677-03380-X) Gordon & Breach.
Physics of Creep & Creep-Resistant Alloys. F. R. Nabarro & H. Filmer. LC 95-215798. 200p. 1993. 110.00 (0-85066-852-2) Taylor & Francis.
Physics of Critical Fluctuations. Y. M. Ivanchenko & A. A. Lisyansky. (Graduate Texts in Contemporary Physics Ser.). (Illus.). xii, 382p. 1995. 59.95 (0-387-94414-1) Spr-Verlag.
Physics of Cryocrystals. Ed. by Vadim G. Manzhelii & Yuri A. Freiman. LC 96-34042. (Illus.). 765p. 1996. text 135.00 (1-56396-537-2) Spr-Verlag.
Physics of Crystal Growth. Alberto Pimpinelli & Jacques Villain. (Collection Alea - Saclay Ser.: Vol. 4). (Illus.). 398p. (C). 1999. text 90.00 (0-521-55198-6); pap. text 44.95 (0-521-55855-7) Cambridge U Pr.
Physics of Dendrites: Computational Experiments. P. K. Galenko & V. A. Zhuravlev. LC 94-40113. 212p. 1995. text 53.00 (981-02-2062-6) World Scientific Pub.
Physics of Dense Matter. Y. C. Leung. 280p. 1985. text 61.00 (9971-978-10-5) World Scientific Pub.
Physics of Dense Matter: Proceedings of the International Astronomical Union Symposium, 53rd, Boulder, Aug. 21-26, 1972. Interntional Astronomical Union Symposium Staff. Ed. by Carl J. Hansen. LC 73-91431. (I.A.U. Symposia Ser.: No. 53). 1974. lib. bdg. 141.50 (90-277-0406-6) Kluwer Academic.
Physics of Desertification. Ed. by Farouk El-Baz & M. H. Hassan. 1986. text 209.50 (90-247-3292-1) Kluwer Academic.
Physics of Diagnostic Imaging. D. Dowsett & P. Kennedy. (Illus.). 520p. 1997. text 52.50 (0-412-46060-2, Pub. by E A) OUP.
Physics of Diamonds. Ed. by A. Paoletti & A. Tucciarone. (International School of Physics Enrico Fermi Ser.: Vol. 135). 630p. 1997. write for info. (90-5199-352-8) IOS Press.
Physics of Disordered Materials. Ed. by David A Adler et al. (Institute for Amorphous Studies). 868p. 1985. 165.00 (0-306-42074-0, Plenum Trade) Perseus Pubng.
Physics of Dry Granular Media. Hans J. Herrmann et al. LC 98-20259. (NATO ASI Series E, Applied Sciences). 1998. 324.00 (0-7923-5102-9) Kluwer Academic.
Physics of Duns Scotus: The Scientific Context of a Theological Vision. Richard Cross. 320p. 1999. text 80.00 (0-19-826974-9) OUP.
Physics of Dusty Plasmas: Proceedings of the 6th Workshop. 252p. 1996. lib. bdg. 41.00 (981-02-2644-6) World Scientific Pub.
Physics of Dusty Plasmas: Seventh Workshop. Ed. by M. Horanyi et al. LC 98-87500. (Conference Proceedings Ser.: Vol. 446). (Illus.). 330p. 1998. 98.00 (1-56396-809-6) Am Inst Physics.
Physics of DX Centers in GaAs Alloys. J. C. Bourgoin. 310p. 1990. 116.00 (3-908044-05-7, Pub. by Trans T Pub) Enfield Pubs NH.
Physics of Electrolytes, 2 vols. Ed. by J. Hladik. Incl. Vol. 1. Transport Processes in Solid Electrolytes. 1972. 89.50 (0-12-349801-5); 1972. write for info. (0-318-50334-4) Acad Pr.
Physics of Electromagnetic Masses, Including the Derivation of E=mc2 from a Point Source. 3rd rev. ed. John W. Carr. Ed. & Photos by Helen Carr. (Illus.). 294p. 1998. pap. 35.00 (0-9666831-5-3) H Carr.
Physics of Electron Beam Therapy. S. C. Klevenhagen. (Medical Physics Handbook Ser.: No. 13). (Illus.). 214p. 1985. 19.00 (0-85274-781-0) IOP Pub.
Physics of Electronic & Atomic Collisions. Ed. by A. Dalgarno et al. LC 90-53183. (AIP Conference Proceedings Ser.: No. 205). 696p. 1990. lib. bdg. 99.00 (0-88318-390-0) Am Inst Physics.
Physics of Electronic & Atomic Collisions: Invited Lectures, Review Papers & Progress Reports of the Ninth International Conference on the Physics of Electronic & Atomic Collisions. Ed. by John S. Risley & Ronald Geballe. LC 75-39962. 916p. 1976. 50.00 (0-295-95455-8) U of Wash Pr.
Physics of Electronic & Atomic Collisions: Proceedings of ICPEAC XVII Brisbane, 10-16 July 1991. Ed. by W. R. MacGillivray et al. (Illus.). 720p. 1992. 326.00 (0-7503-0167-8) IOP Pub.
Physics of Electronic & Atomic Collisions: XVIII International Conference. Ed. by T. Andersen et al. (AIP Conference Proceedings Ser.: No. 295). 1300p. 1993. text 834.00 (1-56396-290-X) Am Inst Physics.
***Physics of Electronic & Atomic Collisions: XXI International Conference.** Ed. by Yukikazu Itikawa et al. LC 99-69861. (AIP Conference Proceedings: Vol. 500). (Illus.). xvi, 728p. 2000. (1-56396-777-4) Am Inst Physics.
Physics of Electronic & Atomic Collissions: XIX International Conference, Whistler, Canada 1995. Louis J. Dube et al. (AIP Press Conference Proceedings Ser.: No. 360). (Illus.). 928p. 1996. 175.00 (1-56396-440-6, CP 360, AIP Pr) Spr-Verlag.
Physics of Electronic Ceramics, Pt. B. Ed. by L. Hench & D. Dove. (Ceramics & Glass, Science & Technology Ser.: Vol. 2). (Illus.). 584p. 1972. text 195.00 (0-8247-1314-1) Dekker.
Physics of Elementary Excitations. S. Nakajima. (Solid-State Sciences Ser.: Vol. 12). (Illus.). 340p. 1980. 82.95 (0-387-09921-2) Spr-Verlag.
Physics of Elementary Interactions. A. Ajduk et al. 544p. 1991. text 137.00 (981-02-0508-2) World Scientific Pub.
Physics of Elementary Particles. L. J. Tassie. LC 73-175761. (Longman Text Ser.). 267p. 1973. reprint ed. pap. 82.80 (0-608-10310-1, 201356600087) Bks Demand.
***Physics of Estuaries & Coastal Areas: Proceedings of an International Conference, 9-12 September 1996.** Ed. by J. Dronkers & M. B. Scheffers. 432p. (C). 1998. text 87.00 (90-5410-965-3, Pub. by A A Balkema) Ashgate Pub Co.
Physics of Everyday Phenomena: A Conceptual Introduction to Physics. W. Thomas Griffith. 512p. (C). 1992. text. write for info. (0-697-06463-8, WCB McGr Hill) McGrw-H Hghr Educ.
Physics of Everyday Phenomena: A Conceptual Introduction to Physics. W. Thomas Griffith & Joseph A. Schaefer. 160p. (C). 1992. text, student ed. 22.50 (0-697-06465-4, WCB McGr Hill) McGrw-H Hghr Educ.
Physics of Everyday Phenomena: A Conceptual Introduction to Physics. 2nd ed. W. Thomas Griffith. LC 96-79882. 480p. (C). 1997. text. write for info. (0-697-15801-2, WCB McGr Hill) McGrw-H Hghr Educ.
Physics of Everyday Phenomena: A Conceptual Introduction to Physics. 3rd ed. W. Thomas Griffith. 2000. 50.00 (0-07-232837-1) McGraw.
Physics of Ferromagnetism. 2nd ed. Soshin Chikazumi. Tr. by C. D. Graham. LC 96-27148. (The International Series of Monographs on Physics: No. 94). (Illus.). 668p. 1997. text 225.00 (0-19-851776-9) OUP.
Physics of Flow Through Porous Media. 3rd ed. Adrian E. Scheidegger. LC 74-185869. 369p. reprint ed. pap. 114.40 (0-608-16341-4, 202654300050) Bks Demand.
Physics of Fluid Turbulence. W. D. McComb. (Oxford Engineering Science Ser.: No. 25). (Illus.). 600p. 1992. reprint ed. pap. text 65.00 (0-19-856256-X) OUP.
Physics of Fluids & Plasmas: An Introduction for Astrophysicists. Arnab R. Choudhuri. LC 97-31092. (Illus.). 446p. (C). 1998. text 74.95 (0-521-55487-X); pap. text 29.95 (0-521-55543-4) Cambridge U Pr.
Physics of Fluids in Hierarchical Porous Media: Angstroms to Miles. John H. Cushman. LC 97-13423. (Theory & Applications of Transport in Porous Media Ser.: No. 10). 467p. 1997. text 220.50 (0-7923-4742-0) Kluwer Academic.
Physics of Foams. Denis Weaire & Stefan Hutzler. LC 99-33466. (Illus.). 272p. 2000. 80.00 (0-19-850551-5) OUP.
Physics of Formation of FeII Lines Outside LTE. Ed. by Roberto Viotti et al. (C). 1987. text 175.00 (90-277-2626-4) Kluwer Academic.
***Physics of Free Electron Lasers.** E. L. Saldin et al. LC 99-39000. (Illus.). x, 478p. 1999. 79.00 (3-540-66266-9) Spr-Verlag.
***Physics of Fullerene-Based & Fullerene-Related Materials.** Wanda Andreoni. 464p. 2000. 199.00 (0-7923-6234-9) Kluwer Academic.
Physics of Galactic Halos. Ed. by Harald Lesch et al. 324p. 1997. 175.00 (3-527-40111-3) Wiley.
Physics of Galactic Halos: Proceedings of the 156th WE-Heraeus Seminar, Bad Honnef, Germany, February 1996. Ed. by Harald Lesch & Ralf J. Dettmar. LC 97-175783. 324p. 1997. 125.00 (3-05-501752-8, Wiley-VCH) Wiley.
Physics of Glaciers. W. S. Paterson. (Illus.). vii, 380p. 1981. pap. text 27.00 (0-08-024004-6, Pergamon Pr) Elsevier.
Physics of Glaciers. 2nd ed. W. S. Paterson. (Illus.). vii, 380p. 1981. text 96.00 (0-08-024005-4, Pergamon Pr) Elsevier.
***Physics of Glaciers.** 3rd ed. Paterson. 496p. 1999. text 125.00 (0-7506-4406-0) Buttrwrth-Heinemann.
Physics of Glaciers. 3rd ed. W. S. Paterson. LC 94-30918. 380p. 1995. text 169.00 (0-08-037945-1, Prgamon Press) Buttrwrth-Heinemann.
Physics of Glaciers. 3rd ed. W. S. B. Paterson. (Illus.). 380p. 1995. pap. 49.95 (0-08-037944-3, Prgamon Press) Buttrwrth-Heinemann.
***Physics of Glasses: Structure & Dynamics.** Ed. by Philippe Jund & Remi Jullien. LC 99-67179. (Conference Proceedings Ser.: Vol. 489). (Illus.). 284p. 1999. 90.00 (1-56396-903-3, Pub. by Am Inst Physics) Spr-Verlag.
Physics of Glassy Polymers. 2nd ed. Chapman & Hall Staff. text 159.50 (0-412-62460-5) Chapman & Hall.
Physics of Golf. 2nd ed. Theodore P. Jorgensen. LC 98-32112. (Illus.). 176p. 1999. pap. 24.95 (0-387-98691-X) Spr-Verlag.
Physics of Golf. 7th ed. Theodore P. Jorgensen. LC 93-30146. (Illus.). 155p. 1997. reprint ed. pap. 27.00 (0-88318-955-0) Am Inst Physics.
Physics of Granular Materials. Jacques Duran. Tr. by A. Reisinger. LC 98-31321. (Partially Ordered Systems Ser.). (Illus.). 314p. 1999. 59.95 (0-387-98656-1) Spr-Verlag.
Physics of Granular Media. Ed. by D. Bideau & J. A. Dodds. 435p. 1992. text 175.00 (1-56072-034-4) Nova Sci Pubs.

P

An Asterisk (*) at the beginning of an entry indicates that the title is appearing for the first time.

Physics of Gravitating Systems Vol. 1: Vol. 1 - Equilibrium & Stability of Gravitating Systems. A. M. Fridman & V. I. Polyachenko. Tr. by A. B. Aries & I. N. Poliakoff from RUS. (Illus.). 480p. 1984. 179.00 (*0-387-11045-3*) Spr-Verlag.

Physics of Gravitating Systems Vol. 2: Vol. 2 - The Nonlinear Theory of Collective Processes in a Gravitating Medium: Astrophysical Application. A. M. Fridman & V. L. Polyachenko. Tr. by A. B. Aries & I. N. Poliakoff from RUS. (Illus.). 385p. 1984. 171.00 (*0-387-13103-5*) Spr-Verlag.

Physics of Hadrons & QCD. Hiroyuki Yabu. 300p. 1999. 96.00 (*981-02-3935-1*) World Scientific Pub.

Physics of High - Density Z - Pinch Plasmas. M. Liberman et al. 350p. 1998. 79.00 (*0-387-98568-9*) Spr-Verlag.

Physics of High Energy Particle Accelerators: BNL-SUNY Summer School. Ed. by Melvin Month et al. LC 85-70057. (AIP Conference Proceedings Ser.: No. 127). 970p. 1985. lib. bdg. 65.00 (*0-88318-326-9*) Am Inst Physics.

Physics of High Energy Particle Accelerators: Fermilab School. American Institue of Physics Staff. Ed. by M. Month et al. LC 82-72421. (AIP Conference Proceedings Ser.: No. 87). 960p. 1982. lib. bdg. 48.00 (*0-88318-186-X*) Am Inst Physics.

Physics of High Energy Particle Accelerators: SLAC Summer School, 1982. Melvin Month. LC 83-72986. (AIP Conference Proceedings Ser.: No. 105). 1102p. 1983. lib. bdg. 55.50 (*0-88318-304-8*) Am Inst Physics.

Physics of High Energy Particle in Toroidal Systems. Ed. by T. Tajima & M. Okamoto. (AIP Conference Proceedings Ser.: No. 311). 352p. 1994. text 135.00 (*1-56396-364-7*) Am Inst Physics.

Physics of High Power Laser Matter Interactions. H. Takabe. 468p. 1993. text 137.00 (*981-02-1137-6*) World Scientific Pub.

Physics of High-Speed Transistors. J. Pozela. (Microdevices: Physics & Fabrication Technologies Ser.). (Illus.). 355p. (C). 1993. text 95.00 (*0-306-44619-7*, Kluwer Plenum) Kluwer Academic.

Physics of Highly Charged Ions. Ed. by Martin Stockli & Patrick Richard. (AIP Conference Proceedings Ser.: No. 274). (Illus.). 700p. 1993. text 175.00 (*1-56396-102-4*, AIP Pr) Spr-Verlag.

Physics of Highly Excited Atoms & Ions. V. S. Lebedev et al. LC 98-35427. (Springer Series on Atoms & Plasmas: Vol. 22). (Illus.). 370p. 1998. 99.00 (*3-540-64234-X*) Spr-Verlag.

Physics of Hot Electron Transport in Semiconductors. C. S. Ting. 320p. 1992. text 95.00 (*981-02-1008-6*) World Scientific Pub.

Physics of Human. (C). 1984. write for info. (*0-8087-4317-1*) Pearson Custom.

Physics of Hydrogenated Amorphous Silicon I. Ed. by John D. Joannopoulos & G. Lucovsky. (Topics in Applied Physics Ser.: Vol. 55). (Illus.). 320p. 1984. 91.95 (*0-387-12807-7*) Spr-Verlag.

Physics of Hydrogenated Amorphous Silicon II. Ed. by John D. Joannopoulos & G. Lucovsky. (Topics in Applied Physics Ser.: Vol. 56). (Illus.). 385p. 1984. 91.95 (*0-387-12808-5*) Spr-Verlag.

Physics of Ice. Victor F. Petrenko & Robert W. Whitworth. LC 99-19984. (Illus.). 390p. 1999. text 130.00 (*0-19-851895-1*) OUP.

Physics of Ice. E. Pounder. LC 65-21141. 1965. 78.00 (*0-08-011148-3*, Pub. by Pergamon Repr) Franklin.

Physics of Immortality: Modern Cosmology, God & the Resurrection of the Dead. Frank J. Tipler. LC 95-9881. 560p. 1997. pap. 16.95 (*0-385-46799-0*, Anchor NY) Doubleday.

***Physics of Information Technology.** Neil Gershenfeld. (Illus.). 375p. 2000. write for info. (*0-521-58044-7*) Cambridge U Pr.

Physics of Instabilities in Solid State Electron Devices. M. P. Shaw et al. (Illus.). 480p. (C). 1991. text 110.00 (*0-306-43788-0*, Kluwer Plenum) Kluwer Academic.

Physics of Intense Beams & Storage Rings. Dmitri Pestrikov & Nikolai Dikansky. LC 93-19889.Tr. of Fizika Intensivnykh Puchkov v Nakopiteliakh. 1994. 79.95 (*1-56396-107-5*) Spr-Verlag.

Physics of Intense Beams in Plasmas. Mikhail V. Nezlin. (Plasma Physics Ser.). (Illus.). 344p. 1993. 176.00 (*0-7503-0186-4*) IOP Pub.

Physics of Interacting Electrons in Disordered Systems. Hiroshi Kamimura & Hideo Aoki. (International Series of Monographs on Physics: No. 76). (Illus.). 272p. 1990. text 75.00 (*0-19-852023-9*) OUP.

Physics of Intermediate & High Energy Heavy-Ion Reactions: Proceedings of the Workshop. Ed. by Michael Kutschers & M. Plossajcsak. 264p. 1988. text 89.00 (*9971-5-0498-7*) World Scientific Pub.

Physics of Ion Impact Phenomena. Ed. by D. Mathur. (Chemical Physics Ser.: Vol. 54). (Illus.). 304p. 1991. 79.95 (*0-387-53429-6*) Spr-Verlag.

Physics of Ionized Gases. Ed. by L. Tanovic et al. 728p. 1989. text 295.00 (*0-941743-59-4*) Nova Sci Pubs.

Physics of Ionized Gases. Ed. by D. Veza. 607p. (C). 1994. lib. bdg. 195.00 (*1-56072-151-0*) Nova Sci Pubs.

Physics of Ionized Gases: Proceeding of the XII International Symposium on the Physics of Ionized Gases (SPIG) 84 Yugoslavia, Sept. 1984. Ed. by M. M. Popovic et al. 1060p. 1985. 143.00 (*9971-5-0001-9*) World Scientific Pub.

Physics of Ionized Gases: Proceedings of the XIII Symposium on Sibenik, Yugoslavia, September 1-5, 1986. Ed. by J. Puric & D. Belic. 528p. 1987. text 148.00 (*9971-5-0292-5*) World Scientific Pub.

Physics of Irradiation Effects in Metals. Ed. by G. Szenes. 820p. 1992. text 275.00 (*0-87849-641-6*, Pub. by Trans T Pub) Enfield Pubs NH.

Physics of Laser-Atom Interactions. Dieter Suter. LC 96-52448. (Cambridge Studies in Modern Optics). 544p. 1997. text 100.00 (*0-521-46239-8*) Cambridge U Pr.

Physics of Laser Plasma. Ed. by A. Rubenchik & S. Witkowski. (Handbook of Plasma Physics Ser.: Vol. 3). x, 654p. 1991. 300.00 (*0-444-87426-7*) Elsevier.

Physics of Laser Plasma Interactions. William L. Kruer. (Frontiers in Physics Ser.: Vol. 73). 208p. 1988. text 40.95 (*0-201-15672-5*) Addison-Wesley.

Physics of Latent Image Formation in Silver Halides: Proceedings of the 3rd Symposium, Trieste Italy, 1983. Ed. by A. Baldereschi. 313p. 1984. 46.00 (*9971-966-34-4*) World Scientific Pub.

Physics of Liners, Vol. 103. Ed. by M. Eracleous et al. (ASP Conference Series Proceedings). 256p. 1996. 34.00 (*1-886733-23-6*) Astron Soc Pacific.

Physics of Liquid Crystalline Materials. Ed. by Iam-Choon Khoo. xx, 549p. 1991. text 267.00 (*2-88124-481-5*) Gordon & Breach.

Physics of Liquid Crystals. 2nd ed. P. E. DeGennes & J. Prost. (International Series of Monographs on Physics: No. 83). (Illus.). 614p. 1995. reprint ed. pap. text 55.00 (*0-19-851785-8*) OUP.

Physics of Liquids & Boiling: Heat Makes Molecules Shake & Liquids Boil. Professor Ima Kook. LC 98-96235. (As Dreamed by Itsy Ser.: Vol. 3). (Illus.). 26p. (J). (gr. k-3). 2000. 14.95 (*1-892298-05-8*) Abique.

Physics of Love: The Ultimate Universal Laws. Dale Pond et al. LC 95-81524. (Illus.). 152p. (Orig.). 1996. pap. 15.95 (*1-57282-002-0*, D20020) Message NM.

Physics of Low-Dimensional Semiconductor Structures. P. Butcher et al. (Physics of Solids & Liquids Ser.). (Illus.). 606p. (C). 1992. text 130.00 (*0-306-44170-5*, Kluwer Plenum) Kluwer Academic.

Physics of Low-Dimensional Semiconductors: An Introduction. John H. Davies. LC 97-88. (Illus.). 456p. 1998. pap. text 44.95 (*0-521-48491-X*) Cambridge U Pr.

Physics of Low-Dimensional Semiconductors: An Introduction. John H. Davies. LC 97-88. (Illus.). 456p. (C). 1998. text 100.00 (*0-521-48148-1*) Cambridge U Pr.

Physics of Luminous Blue Variables. Ed. by Kris Davidson et al. (C). 1989. text 186.00 (*0-7923-0443-8*) Kluwer Academic.

Physics of Magmatic Processes. Ed. by R. B. Hargraves. LC 80-7525. (Illus.). 800p. 1980. pap. text 39.50 (*0-691-08261-8*, Pub. by Princeton U Pr) Cal Prin Full Svc.

Physics of Magnetic Flux Ropes. Ed. by C. T. Russell. (Geophysical Monograph Ser.: Vol. 58). 752p. 1990. 60.00 (*0-87590-026-7*) Am Geophysical.

Physics of Magnetic Materials: Proceedings of the International Symposium on Physics of Magnetic Materials. Ed. by S. Maekawa. 620p. (C). 1987. text 153.00 (*9971-5-0358-1*) World Scientific Pub.

Physics of Magnetic Materials: Proceedings of the Third International Conference on Physics of Magnetic Materials, Szczyrk-Bila, Poland 9-14 September 1986. Ed. by Waldemar Gorzkowski et al. 600p. 1987. text 156.00 (*9971-5-0188-0*) World Scientific Pub.

Physics of Magnetic Materials: Proceedings of the 2nd International Conference. Ed. by J. Rauluszkiewicz et al. 592p. 1985. 100.00 (*9971-978-34-2*) World Scientific Pub.

Physics of Magnetic Materials: Proceedings of the 4th International Conference. Ed. by Waldemar Gorzkowski et al. 660p. 1989. text 131.00 (*9971-5-0696-3*) World Scientific Pub.

Physics of Magnetic Materials: Proceedings of the 5th International Conference. Ed. by Waldemar Gorzkowski et al. 456p. (C). 1991. text 113.00 (*981-02-0529-5*) World Scientific Pub.

Physics of Magnetic Recording. C. Dennis Mee. (North-Holland Personal Library). xviii, 270p. 1986. reprint ed. pap. 56.75 (*0-444-87043-1*, North Holland) Elsevier.

Physics of Magnetospheric Substorms. Syun-Ichi Akasofu. (Astrophysics & Space Science Library: No. 47). 1977. lib. bdg. 245.50 (*90-277-0748-0*) Kluwer Academic.

***Physics of Manganites.** T. A. Kaplan & S. D. Mahanti. LC 99-30037. (Fundamental Materials Research Ser.). x, 296p. (C). 1999. text. write for info. (*0-306-46132-3*, Kluwer Plenum) Kluwer Academic.

***Physics of Mass.** Behram N. Kursunoglu et al. LC 98-42065. 1998. write for info. (*0-306-46029-7*, Kluwer Plenum) Kluwer Academic.

Physics of Massive Neutrinos. B. Kayser & F. Perrier. (Lecture Notes in Physics Ser.: Vol. 25). 128p. 1989. text 36.00 (*9971-5-0661-0*); pap. text 23.00 (*9971-5-0662-9*) World Scientific Pub.

Physics of Massive Neutrinos. 2nd ed. F. Boehm & Paul Vogel. (Illus.). 259p. (C). 1992. text 99.95 (*0-521-41824-0*); pap. text 37.95 (*0-521-42849-1*) Cambridge U Pr.

Physics of Materials. Y. Quere. 496p. 1998. text 38.00 (*90-5699-118-3*, ECU55, Harwood Acad Pubs); pap. text 16.00 (*90-5699-119-1*, ECU22, Harwood Acad Pubs) Gordon & Breach.

Physics of Materials. R. J. Weiss. 1990. 76.95 (*0-89116-968-7*) Hemisp Pub.

Physics of Materials: Proceedings of the Fourth & Fifth International Courses. Ed. by S. Radhakrishna & K. Srinivasan. 476p. (C). 1988. text 117.00 (*9971-5-0398-0*) World Scientific Pub.

***Physics of Medical Imaging.** Ed. by John M. Boone & James T. Dobbins. 1032p. 1999. pap. text 145.00 (*0-8194-3131-1*) SPIE.

Physics of Medical Imaging. Ed. by Steve Webb. LC 88-4487. (Medical Science Ser.). (Illus.). 633p. 1988. pap. 61.00 (*0-85274-349-1*) IOP Pub.

Physics of Medical Imaging. Ed. by Steve Webb. (Medical Science Ser.). (Illus.). 633p. 1988. 258.00 (*0-85274-361-0*) IOP Pub.

Physics of Metal Cutting. E. M. Martelloti & H. Ernst. (Technical Papers: Vol. P226). (Illus.). 66p. 1942. pap. text 30.00 (*1-55589-214-0*) AGMA.

Physics of Metals. Ed. by S. Giuliano & C. Rizzuto. 548p. (C). 1988. text 125.00 (*9971-5-0628-9*) World Scientific Pub.

Physics of Metaphysics: Everything You Wanted to Know about the Universe & Your Place in It, but Did Not Know What to Ask. Donna H. Lloyd. (Illus.). 300p. (C). 1993. pap. 13.95 (*0-9627291-3-2*) Deltaran Pub.

Physics of Microfabrication. Ivor Brodie & Julius J. Muray. LC 82-3835. (Illus.). 522p. (C). 1982. 144.00 (*0-306-40863-5*, Plenum Trade) Perseus Pubng.

Physics of Micro/Nano-Fabrication. I. Brodie & Julius J. Muray. (Microdevices: Physics & Fabrication Technologies Ser.). (Illus.). 670p. (C). 1993. text 110.00 (*0-306-44146-2*, Kluwer Plenum) Kluwer Academic.

Physics of Microwave Discharges: Artificially Ionized Regions in the Atmosphere. A. V. Gurevich et al. 208p. 1997. text 49.00 (*90-5699-008-X*) Gordon & Breach.

Physics of Moire Metrology. Oded Kafri & Ilana Glatt. LC 89-32480. (Series in Pure & Applied Optics). 194p. 1990. 109.00 (*0-471-50967-1*) Wiley.

Physics of Monsoons. R. N. Keshavamurty. (C). 1992. 18.00 (*81-7023-325-9*, Pub. by Allied Pubs) S Asia.

Physics of Musical Instruments. Neville H. Fletcher & Thomas D. Rossing. LC 93-27442. (Illus.). 620p. 1993. 49.95 (*0-387-94151-7*) Spr-Verlag.

Physics of Musical Instruments. Thomas D. Rossing & N. H. Flechter. (Illus.). xvii, 620p. 1991. 69.00 (*0-387-96947-0*) Spr-Verlag.

Physics of Musical Instruments. 2nd ed. N. H. Fletcher & T. D. Rossing. LC 97-35360. (Illus.). 580p. 1998. pap. 49.95 (*0-387-98375-9*) Spr-Verlag.

Physics of Musical Instruments. 2nd ed. Neville H. Fletcher & Thomas D. Rossing. LC 97-35360. (Illus.). 580p. 1998. 79.00 (*0-387-98374-0*) Spr-Verlag.

Physics of Nanostructures. Ed. by J. H. Davies & A. R. Long. (Scottish Universities Summer School in Physics, a NATO Advanced Study Institute Ser.: No. 38). (Illus.). 356p. 1993. pap. 50.00 (*0-7503-0169-4*) IOP Pub.

Physics of Neutron Stars. Ed. by A. M. Kaminker. (Illus.). 207p. (C). 1994. lib. bdg. 110.00 (*1-56072-164-2*) Nova Sci Pubs.

Physics of New Materials. Ed. by Francisco E. Fujita. LC 93-29420. (Materials Science Ser.: Vol. 27). 1994. 79.00 (*0-387-56851-4*) Spr-Verlag.

Physics of New Materials. 2nd ed. F. E. Fujita & R. W. Cahn. LC 98-26048. (Series in Materials Science: Vol. 27). (Illus.). 320p. 1998. 99.00 (*3-540-64143-2*) Spr-Verlag.

Physics of New Methods of Charged Particle Acceleration. A. G. Bonch-Osmolovsky. 156p. 1994. text 61.00 (*981-02-1238-0*) World Scientific Pub.

Physics of Non-Conventional Energy Sources & Material Science for Energy: Proceedings of the International Workshop. Ed. by G. Furlan et al. 608p. 1987. pap. 60.00 (*9971-5-0346-8*); text 144.00 (*9971-5-0252-6*) World Scientific Pub.

Physics of Non-Crystalline Solids. Ed. by David L. Pye et al. 900p. 1992. 135.00 (*0-7484-0050-8*, Pub. by Tay Francis Ltd) Taylor & Francis.

Physics of Non-Equilibrium Plasmas. V. M. Lelevkin et al. LC 92-44398. xviii, 418p. 1992. 166.75 (*0-444-89533-7*, North Holland) Elsevier.

Physics of Non-Neutral Plasmas. Ronald Davidson. (C). 1992. pap. 49.95 (*0-201-57830-1*) Addison-Wesley.

Physics of Non-Thermal Radio Sources: Proceedings of the NATO Advanced Study Institute, Urbino, 1975. NATO Advanced Study Institute Staff. Ed. by Giancarlo Setti. (Mathematical & Physical Sciences Ser.: No. 28). 1976. lib. bdg. 88.00 (*90-277-0753-7*) Kluwer Academic.

Physics of Nonideal Plasma. V. E. Fortov & I. T. Iakubov. 325p. 1989. 176.00 (*0-89116-604-1*) Hemisp Pub.

Physics of Nonlinear Optics. Guang S. He & Song H. Liu. LC 99-39800. 500p. 1998. 68.00 (*981-02-3319-1*) World Scientific Pub.

Physics of Novel Materials. Mukunda P. Das. 1998. 48.00 (*981-02-3552-6*) World Scientific Pub.

Physics of Nuclear Medicine: Recent Advances: Proceedings of the AAPM 1983 Summer School Held at Farleigh Dickinson University, Madison, New Jersey, July 24-29, 1983. Ed. by Dandamudi V. Rao et al. (American Association of Physicists in Medicine Symposium Ser.: No. 10). 570p. 1984. 60.00 (*0-88318-440-0*, Pub. by Am Inst Physics) Med Physics Pub.

Physics of Optical Recording. Kurt Schwartz. LC 93-14006. (Illus.). 250p. 1994. 99.95 (*0-387-52237-9*) Spr-Verlag.

Physics of Optoelectronic Devices. Shun L. Chuang. LC 94-24701. (Series in Pure & Applied Optics). 736p. 1995. 110.00 (*0-471-10939-8*) Wiley.

Physics of Oscillations & Waves: With Applications in Electricity & Mechanics. I. Bloch. LC 97-15933. 328p. (C). 1997. text 89.50 (*0-306-45721-0*, Kluwer Plenum) Kluwer Academic.

Physics of Particle Accelerators, 2 vols. Melvin Month & Margaret Dienes. LC 87-70103. (AIP Conference Proceedings Ser.: No. 153). 1748p. 1987. lib. bdg. 175.00 (*0-88318-353-6*) Am Inst Physics.

Physics of Particle Accelerators. Ed. by Melvin Month & Margaret Dienes. LC 89-83575. (AIP Conference Proceedings Ser.: No. 184). 2376p. 1990. lib. bdg. 199.00 (*0-88318-384-6*) Am Inst Physics.

Physics of Particle Accelerators Vols. 1 & 2: AIP Conference Proceedings, 2 vols. Ed. by Melvin Month et al. LC 92-52843. (AIP Conference Proceedings Ser.). (Illus.). 220p. (C). 1992. 245.00 (*0-88318-789-2*) Am Inst Physics.

***Physics of Particle Detectors.** Dan Green. (Cambridge Monographs on Particle Physics, Nuclear Physics & Cosmology: Vol. 12). (Illus.). 288p. 2000. 100.00 (*0-521-66226-5*) Cambridge U Pr.

Physics of Phase Space. Ed. by Y. S. Kim & W. W. Zachary. (Lecture Notes in Physics Ser.: Vol. 278). ix, 449p. 1987. 64.95 (*0-387-17894-5*) Spr-Verlag.

Physics of Phonons. Ed. by T. Paszkiewicz. (Lecture Notes in Physics Ser.: Vol. 285). x, 486p. 1987. 64.95 (*0-387-18244-6*) Spr-Verlag.

Physics of Phonons. G. P. Srivastava. (Illus.). 440p. 1990. 200.00 (*0-85274-153-7*) IOP Pub.

Physics of Planetary Interiors. V. N. Zharkov et al. Ed. by W. B. Hubbard. (Astronomy & Astrophysics Ser.: Vol. 6). 399p. 1978. pap. text 24.00 (*0-912918-15-2*, 0015) Pachart Pub Hse.

Physics of Planetary Magnetospheres. Ed. by K. Knott. (Advances in Space Research Ser.: Vol. 1, Pt. 1). (Illus.). 390p. 1981. pap. 56.00 (*0-08-027151-0*, Pergamon Pr) Elsevier.

Physics of Planetary Rings: Celestial Mechanics of Continuous Media. A. M. Fridman & N. N. Gor'kavyi. Ed. by I. Appenzeller et al. Tr. by D. Haar from RUS. LC 99-19567. xxii, 436p. 1999. 89.95 (*3-540-64864-X*) Spr-Verlag.

Physics of Plasma-Wall Interactions in Controlled Fusion. Ed. by D. E. Post & R. Behrisch. (NATO ASI Series B, Physics: Vol. 131). 1196p. 1986. 175.00 (*0-306-42097-X*, Plenum Trade) Perseus Pubng.

Physics of Plastics: Processing, Properties & Materials Engineering. Arthur W. Birley et al. 549p. 1992. 95.00 (*1-56990-003-5*); pap. 59.95 (*1-56990-004-3*) Hanser-Gardner.

Physics of Plutonium Recycling Vol. I: Issues & Perspectives. OECD Staff & NEA Staff. LC 96-123706. 190p. (Orig.). 1995. pap. 39.00 (*92-64-14538-9*, Pub. by Org for Econ) OECD.

Physics of Plutonium Recycling Vol. II: Plutonium Recycling in Pressurized-Water Reactors. OECD/NEA Staff. LC 96-123706. 176p. (Orig.). 1995. pap. 35.00 (*92-64-14590-7*, Pub. by Org for Econ) OECD.

Physics of Plutonium Recycling Vol. III: Void Reactivity Effect in Pressurized-Water Reactors. OECD/NEA Staff. LC 96-123706. 132p. (Orig.). 1995. pap. 27.00 (*92-64-14591-5*, Pub. by Org for Econ) OECD.

Physics of Plutonium Recycling Vol. IV: Fast Plutonium-Burner Reactors: Beginning of Life. OECD (Nuclear Energy Agency) Staff. LC 96-123706. (ENG & FRE.). 66p. (Orig.). 1996. pap. 16.00 (*92-64-14703-9*, Pub. by Org for Econ) OECD.

Physics of Plutonium Recycling Vol. V: Plutonium Recycling in Fast Reactors. OECD (Nuclear Energy Agency) Staff. LC 96-123706. (ENG & FRE.). 156p. (Orig.). 1996. pap. 37.00 (*92-64-14704-7*, Pub. by Org for Econ) OECD.

Physics of Pocket Billiards. Wayland C. Harlow. 1995. pap. 36.00 (*0-9645370-0-1*) MAST FL.

Physics of Polymer Networks. Ed. by S. Wartewig et al. (Advances in Pharmacological Sciences Ser.: Vol. 90). viii, 250p. 1992. 132.95 (*0-387-91411-0*) Spr-Verlag.

Physics of Polymer Surfaces & Interfaces. Isaac Sanchez. 336p. 1992. text 84.95 (*0-7506-9214-6*) Buttrwrth-Heinemann.

Physics of Polymers: Concepts for Understanding Their Structures & Behavior. Gert R. Strobl. LC 96-14078. (Illus.). 500p. 1996. pap. text 39.95 (*3-540-60768-4*) Spr-Verlag.

Physics of Polymers: Concepts for Understanding Their Structures & Behavior. 2nd ed. Gert R. Strobl. LC 97-28362. (Illus.). xii, 439p. (C). pap. 39.00 (*3-540-63203-4*) Spr-Verlag.

Physics of Pulsars. Allen M. Lenchek. (Topics in Astrophysics & Space Physics Ser.). x, 174p. (C). 1972. text 252.00 (*0-677-14290-0*) Gordon & Breach.

***Physics of Pulsatile Flow.** M. Zamir. Ed. by E. Greenbau. LC 99-42457. (Biological Physics Ser.: Vol. 3). (Illus.). 440p. 2000. 59.95 (*0-387-98925-0*) Spr-Verlag.

***Physics of Quantum Fields.** Michael Stone. LC 99-39802. (Graduate Texts in Contemporary Physics Ser.). (Illus.). 280p. 1999. 49.00 (*0-387-98909-9*) Spr-Verlag.

***Physics of Quantum Information: Quantum Cryptography, Quantum Teleportation, Quantum Computation.** Ed. by Dik Bouwmeester et al. (Illus.). xvi, 316p. 2000. 54.00 (*3-540-66778-4*) Spr-Verlag.

Physics of Quasicrystals. Ed. by P. Steinhardt & S. Ostlund. 788p. 1987. text 116.00 (*9971-5-0226-7*); pap. text 55.00 (*9971-5-0227-5*) World Scientific Pub.

Physics of Radiation Protection. James E. Martin. LC 99-38913. 832p. 2000. text 185.00 (*0-471-35373-6*, Wiley-Interscience) Wiley.

Physics of Radiation Therapy. 2nd ed. Faiz M. Khan. LC 92-18111. (Illus.). 632p. 1994. 87.00 (*0-683-04502-4*) Lppncott W & W.

Physics of Radiology. Anthony B. Wolbarst. (Illus.). 576p. (C). 1993. pap. text 75.00 (*0-8385-5769-4*, A5769-3) Appleton & Lange.

***Physics of Radiology.** Anthony Brinton Wolbarst. 478p. 2000. pap. text 65.95 (*0-944838-95-2*) Med Physics Pub.

Physics of Radiology. 4th ed. Harold E. Johns & John R. Cunningham. (Illus.). 816p. (C). 1983. 78.95 (*0-398-04669-7*) C C Thomas.

Physics of Radiotherapy X-Rays from Linear Accelerators. Peter Metcalfe et al. LC 96-51445. (Illus.). 493p. 1997. text 119.95 (*0-944838-75-8*); pap. text 98.95 (*0-944838-76-6*) Med Physics Pub.

Physics of Rainclouds. Neville H. Fletcher. 404p. reprint ed. pap. 115.20 (*0-608-10072-2*, 2051499) Bks Demand.

Physics of Rare Earth Solids. K. N. R. Taylor & M. I. Darby. LC 72-188984. xii, 308 p. 1972. write for info. (*0-412-10160-2*) Chapman & Hall.

An Asterisk (*) at the beginning of an entry indicates that the title is appearing for the first time.

Physics of Sediment Transport by Wind & Water: A Collection of Hallmark Papers. Ralph A. Bagnold. Ed. by Colin R. Thorne et al. 376p. 1988. 49.00 (*0-87262-665-2*) Am Soc Civil Eng.

Physics of Semiconductor Devices. Michael Shur. 638p. 1989. boxed set 52.00 (*0-685-27166-8*) P-H.

Physics of Semiconductor Devices. Michael Shur. (C). 1990. text 63.00 (*0-13-666496-2*) P-H.

Physics of Semiconductor Devices. 2nd ed. Simon M. Sze. 880p. 1981. 98.95 (*0-471-05661-8*) Wiley.

Physics of Semiconductor Devices, Vol. 3316. Ed. by Vikram Kumar & S. K. Agarwal. 1382p. 1998. 116.00 (*0-8194-2756-X*) SPIE.

Physics of Semiconductor Devices: Proceedings of the IV International Workshop, Madras, India. Ed. by S. C. Jain & S. Radhakrishna. 544p. (C). 1987. pap. 70.00 (*9971-5-0532-0*); text 159.00 (*9971-5-0531-2*) World Scientific Pub.

Physics of Semiconductor Devices: Proceedings of the Third International Workshop on Physics of Semiconductor Devices, Madras, India, Nov 27 - Dec 2, 1985. Ed. by S. Radhakrishna & S. C. Jain. 500p. 1985. 78.00 (*9971-5-0082-5*) World Scientific Pub.

Physics of Semiconductor Failures. 4th rev. ed. Howard K. Dicken. (Illus.). 270p. 1998. ring bd. 395.00 (*1-878266-00-4*) DM Data.

Physics of Semiconductor Lasers. B. Mroziewicz et al. 474p. 1991. 210.00 (*0-444-98737-1*, North Holland) Elsevier.

Physics of Semiconductor Nanostructures. 400p. 1998. 48.00 (*981-02-2525-3*) World Scientific Pub.

Physics of Semiconductors. B. Sapoval & C. Hermann. LC 93-286.Tr. of Physique des Semi-Conducteurs. 1993. 87.95 (*0-387-94023-5*) Spr-Verlag.

Physics of Semiconductors. B. Sapoval & C. Hermann.Tr. of Physique des Semi-Conducteurs. (Illus.). 304p. 1994. 49.95 (*0-387-94024-3*) Spr-Verlag.

Physics of Semiconductors: Proceedings of the International Conference, 18th, Stockholm, Sweden, August 11-15, 1986, 2 vols. Ed. by O. Engstrom. 1964p. 1987. pap. 115.00 (*9971-5-0198-8*); text 334.00 (*9971-5-0197-X*) World Scientific Pub.

Physics of Semiconductors: Proceedings of the 21st International Conference, 3 vols. Xide D. Xie & Kun Huang. 2148p. 1993. text 455.00 (*981-02-1156-2*) World Scientific Pub.

Physics of Semiconductors: Proceedings of the 22nd International Conference, 3 vols. D. Lockwood. 2852p. 1995. text 446.00 (*981-02-2021-9*) World Scientific Pub.

Physics of Semiconductors: Proceedings of the 23rd International Conference, 3 vols. 3800p. 1996. lib. bdg. 370.00 (*981-02-2777-9*) World Scientific Pub.

Physics of Semiconductors: Proceedings of the 24th International Conference Jerusalem, Israel, 2-7 August 1998. Ed. by David Gershoni. 600p. 1998. 168.00 (*981-02-3613-1*) World Scientific Pub.

Physics of Semiconductors: With Applications to Optoelectronic Devices. Kevin F. Brennan. LC 98-29503. (Illus.). 784p. (C). 1999. text 120.00 (*0-521-59350-6*) Cambridge U Pr.

Physics of Semiconductors: With Applications to Optoelectronic Devices. Kevin F. Brennan. (Studies in Semiconductor Physics & Microelectronic Engineering). (Illus.). 784p. (C). 1999. pap. text 54.95 (*0-521-59662-9*) Cambridge U Pr.

Physics of Semiconductors: 20th International Conference, 3 vols. John D. Joannopoulos & E. Anastassakis. 2764p. 1990. text 469.00 (*981-02-0539-2*) World Scientific Pub.

Physics of Semiconductors & Their Heterostructures. Jasprit Singh. LC 92-30339. (Series in Electrical & Computer Engineering). 864p. (C). 1992. 93.75 (*0-07-057607-6*) McGraw.

Physics of Shallow Estuaries & Bays. Ed. by J. Van de Kreeke. (Lecture Notes on Coastal & Estuarine Studies: Vol. 16). ix, 280p. 1986. pap. 41.00 (*0-387-96328-6*) Spr-Verlag.

Physics of Shock Waves in Gases & Plasmas. M. A. Liberman & A. L. Velikovich. (Electrophysics Ser.: Vol. 19). (Illus.). 400p. 1986. 102.95 (*0-387-15605-4*) Spr-Verlag.

Physics of Skiing: Skiing at the Triple Point. David A. Lind & Scott P. Sanders. (Illus.). 300p. 1997. pap. 24.95 (*1-56396-319-1*) Spr-Verlag.

Physics of Sliding Friction: Proceedings of the NATO Advanced Research Workshop & Adriatico Research Conference, Miramare, Trieste, Italy, June 20-23, 1995. Ed. by B. N. Persson & E. Tosatti. (NATO ASI Series E: Applied Sciences: Series E, Vol. 311). 472p. (C). 1996. text 247.00 (*0-7923-3935-5*) Kluwer Academic.

Physics of Solar, ser. vol. 6. Jager. (Advances in Space Research Ser.). 1988. pap. 56.00 (*0-08-036641-4*, Pergamon Pr) Elsevier.

Physics of Solar & Stellar Coronae - G. S. Vaiana Memorial Symposium: Proceedings of a Conference Held in Palermo, Italy, 22-26 June 1992. Ed. by Jeffrey L. Linsky & Salvatore Serio. LC 93-17752. (Astrophysics & Space Science Library: Vol. 183). 1993. text 353.00 (*0-7923-2346-7*) Kluwer Academic.

Physics of Solar System Plasmas. Thomas E. Cravens. LC 96-48929. (Atmospheric & Space Science Ser.). (Illus.). 493p. (C). 1997. text 90.00 (*0-521-35280-0*) Cambridge U Pr.

Physics of Solid-State Laser Materials. Richard C. Powell. LC 97-27736. (Atomic, Molecular & Optical Physics Ser.: Vol. 1). (Illus.). 336p. 1998. 59.95 (*1-56396-658-1*) Spr-Verlag.

Physics of Solid State Lasers. V. V. Antsiferov & G. I. Smirnov. 250p. 1995. pap. 111.00 (*1-898326-17-7*, Pub. by CISP) Balogh.

Physics of Solid Surfaces. Ed. by G. F. Chiarotti. 370p. 1993. 1105.95 (*0-387-56069-6*) Spr-Verlag.

Physics of Solid Surfaces: Electronic & Vibrational Properties. Ed. by G. F. Chiarotti et al. 270p. 1994. 1919.95 (*0-387-56070-X*) Spr-Verlag.

Physics of Solid Surfaces, Subvol. C, Interaction of Charged Particles & Atoms with Surfaces see Crystal & Solid State Physics: Group III

***Physics of Solids.** Richard John Turton. 352p. (C). 2000. pap. text 36.95 (*0-19-850352-0*) OUP.

Physics of Solids. 2nd ed. Charles A. Wert & Robb W. Thomson. LC 77-98055. (Materials Science & Engineering Ser.). 544p. (C). 1970. 114.06 (*0-07-069435-4*) McGraw.

Physics of Sound. 2nd ed. Richard E. Berg & David G. Stork. LC 94-20877. 416p. (C). 1994. 76.00 (*0-13-183047-3*) P-H.

Physics of Sound in the Sea. LC 88-62268. 577p. 1989. reprint ed. 39.95 (*0-932146-24-2*) Peninsula CA.

Physics of Sound in the Sea, 4 pts., Vol. 4. Ed. by E. Gerjuoy et al. Incl. Vol. 2. Reverberation: Reflection of Sound from Submarines & Surface Vessels. xii, 208p. 1968. text 176.00 (*0-677-01900-9*); (Documents on Modern Physics Ser.). 616p. 1969. Set text 292.00 (*0-677-01920-3*) Gordon & Breach.

Physics of Space Plasmas: An Introduction. George Parks. (C). 1991. pap. 65.00 (*0-201-48987-2*) Addison-Wesley.

Physics of Speech. Dennis B. Fry. LC 78-56752. (Textbooks in Linguistics Ser.). (Illus.). 160p. 1979. pap. text 20.95 (*0-521-29379-0*) Cambridge U Pr.

Physics of Sports. Ed. by Angelo Armenti, Jr. 360p. 1992. 35.00 (*0-88318-946-1*) Am Inst Physics.

Physics of Sports: Basketball. P. Chinnappa Reddy. (C). 1992. text 20.00 (*81-7024-511-7*, Pub. by Ashish Pub Hse) S Asia.

Physics of Sports: Selected Reprints. Ed. by C. Frohlich. (Reprint Bks.). (Illus.). 124p. (Orig.). (C). 1986. per. 26.00 (*0-917853-24-5*, RB-48) Am Assn Physics.

Physics of Star Formation & Early Stellar Evolution. Ed. by Nikolaos D. Kylafis & Charles J. Lada. (C). 1991. pap. text 92.50 (*0-7923-1367-4*); lib. bdg. 283.00 (*0-7923-1349-6*) Kluwer Academic.

Physics of Star Trek. Lawrence M. Krauss. LC 95-33266. 208p. 1996. pap. 12.00 (*0-06-097710-8*) HarpC.

Physics of Stellar Evolution & Cosmology. Howard S. Goldberg & Michael D. Scadron. xiv, 390p. 1982. text 201.00 (*0-677-05540-4*); pap. text 82.00 (*0-677-21740-4*) Gordon & Breach.

Physics of Stereo - Quad Sound. Joseph G. Traylor. LC 77-21768. (Illus.). 198p. 1977. reprint ed. pap. 61.40 (*0-608-00011-6*, 206077700006) Bks Demand.

Physics of Strained Quantum Well Lasers. John P. Loehr. LC 97-38984. 272p. 1998. text 121.00 (*0-7923-8098-3*) Kluwer Academic.

Physics of Strong Fields. Ed. by Walter Greiner. (NATO ASI Series B, Physics: Vol. 153). (Illus.). 1003p. 1987. 165.00 (*0-306-42577-7*, Plenum Trade) Perseus Pubng.

Physics of Strongly Coupled Plasma: Proceedings of International Conference. T. Bornath et al. 550p. 1996. text 128.00 (*981-02-2348-X*) World Scientific Pub.

Physics of Structural Phase Transitions. Minoru Fujimoto. LC 96-33166. (Illus.). 247p. 1997. 69.00 (*0-387-94856-2*) Spr-Verlag.

Physics of Structurally Disordered Matter: An Introduction. N. E. Cusack. (Graduate Student Series in Physics). (Illus.). 424p. 1987. 210.00 (*0-85274-591-5*); pap. 62.00 (*0-85274-829-9*) IOP Pub.

Physics of Structure Formation: Theory & Simulation. Ed. by W. Guttinger & G. Dangelmayr. (Synergetics Ser.: Vol. 37). (Illus.). 450p. 1987. 80.95 (*0-387-18383-3*) Spr-Verlag.

Physics of Submicron Devices. D. K. Ferry & R. O. Grondin. (Microdevices: Physics & Fabrication Technologies Ser.). (Illus.). 416p. (C). 1991. text 110.00 (*0-306-43843-7*, Kluwer Plenum) Kluwer Academic.

Physics of Submicron Lithography. K. A. Valiev. (Microdevices: Physics & Fabrication Technologies Ser.). (Illus.). 510p. (C). 1992. text 110.00 (*0-306-43578-0*, Kluwer Plenum) Kluwer Academic.

Physics of Submicron Semiconductor Devices. Ed. by Harold L. Grubin et al. LC 88-19713. (NATO ASI Series B, Physics: Vol. 180). (Illus.). 744p. 1988. 145.00 (*0-306-42986-1*, Plenum Trade) Perseus Pubng.

Physics of Sunset. Jane Vandenburgh. LC 98-49031. 320p. 1999. 24.00 (*0-679-42483-0*) Pantheon.

***Physics of Sunset.** large type ed. Jane Vandenburgh. LC 99-50318. 485p. 1999. write for info. (*0-7862-2298-0*) Thorndike Pr.

Physics of Superconductors: Introduction to Fundamentals & Applications. Paul Muller. Tr. by Irina V. Grigorieva. LC 97-8371. 224p. 1997. text 59.95 (*3-540-61243-2*) Spr-Verlag.

Physics of Superlattice & Quantum Wells. Ed. by C. H. Tsai et al. 394p. (C). 1989. text 106.00 (*9971-5-0764-1*) World Scientific Pub.

Physics of Tachyons. Ernst L. Wall. (Hadronic Press Monographs in Theoretical Physics). 234p. (C). 1995. pap. 60.00 (*1-57485-001-6*) Hadronic Pr Inc.

Physics of the Atom. 4th ed. M. Russell Wehr et al. LC 83-7072. (Illus.). 536p. (C). 1984. 101.00 (*0-201-08878-9*) Addison-Wesley.

Physics of the Aurora & Airglow. Joseph W. Chamberlain. LC 95-25022. 1995. pap. 55.00 (*0-87590-857-8*) Am Geophysical.

Physics of the Blue Sack. M. K. Park. Ed. by Myungkark Park. 100p. (C). 1989. pap. write for info. (*1-877974-00-5*) Prompter Pubns.

***Physics of the Body.** 2nd ed. John Cameron et al. LC 99-26114. (Illus.). 410p. 1999. text 53.95 (*0-944838-90-1*); pap. text 45.95 (*0-944838-91-X*) Med Physics Pub.

Physics of the Early Universe: Proceedings of the Thirty Sixth Scottish Universities Summer School in Physics, Edinburgh, July 24-August 11, 1989. Ed. by J. A. Peacock et al. (Scottish Universities Summer School in Physics, a NATO Advanced Study Institute Ser.: No. 36). (Illus.). 502p. 1990. 189.00 (*0-905945-19-0*) IOP Pub.

Physics of the Earth & the Solar System: Dynamics & Evolution, Space Navigation, Space-Time Structure. Bruno Bertotti & Paolo Farinella. (C). 1990. text 236.50 (*0-7923-0535-3*) Kluwer Academic.

Physics of the Earthquake Focus. M. A. Sadovski. (C). 1985. 33.00 (*81-205-0033-4*, Pub. by Oxford IBH) S Asia.

Physics of the Earthquake Focus. Ed. by M. A. Sodovksii. Tr. by S. Guha from RUS. 262p. (C). 1986. text 123.00 (*90-6191-462-0*, Pub. by A A Balkema) Ashgate Pub Co.

Physics of the Electron Solid. Ed. by S. T. Chui. (Series in Applied Physics). 258p. 1994. 42.00 (*1-57146-106-X*) Intl Pr Boston.

Physics of the Environment & Climate. G. Guyot. LC 96-32859. 642p. 1998. 135.00 (*0-471-96828-5*); pap. 64.95 (*0-471-96818-8*) Wiley.

Physics of the Galaxy & Interstellar Matter. H. Scheffler & H. Elsasser. (Astronomy & Astrophysics Library). (Illus.). 150p. 1987. 69.50 (*0-387-17314-5*) Spr-Verlag.

Physics of the Galaxy & Interstellar Matter. H. Scheffler & H. Elsasser. (Astronomy & Astrophysics Library). (Illus.). xi, 492p. 1988. 69.95 (*0-387-17315-3*) Spr-Verlag.

Physics of the Green-Back Dollar. M. K. Park. 100p. (Orig.). (C). 1990. pap. write for info. (*1-877974-01-3*) Prompter Pubns.

Physics of the Inner Heliosphere I: Large-Scale Phenomena. Ed. by R. Schwenn et al. (Physics & Chemistry in Space Ser.: Vol. 20). 288p. 1990. 94.95 (*0-387-52081-3*) Spr-Verlag.

Physics of the Inner Heliosphere II: Particles, Waves & Turbulence. Ed. by R. Schwenn et al. (Physics & Chemistry in Space, Space & Solar Physics Ser.: Vol. 21). (Illus.). xi, 352p. 1991. 119.00 (*0-387-52083-X*) Spr-Verlag.

Physics of the Interstellar Medium. 2nd ed. J. E. Dyson & D. A. Williams. LC 97-16359. (Graduate Series in Astronomy). 1997. 137.00 (*0-7503-0306-9*); pap. 40.00 (*0-7503-0460-X*) IOP Pub.

Physics of the Living State. T. Musha & Y. Sawada. LC 93-80960. 289p. (gr. 12). 1994. 70.00 (*90-5199-147-9*, Pub. by IOS Pr) IOS Press.

Physics of the Magnetopause. Ed. by Paul Song et al. LC 95-22170. (Geophysical Monograph Ser.: Vol. 90). 447p. 1995. 80.00 (*0-87590-047-X*) Am Geophysical.

Physics of the Magnetosphere: Proceedings. Conference on Physics of the Magnetosphere, Boston. Ed. by R. L. Carovillano et al. (Astrophysics & Space Science Library: No.10). 686p. 1968. lib. bdg. 175.00 (*90-277-0111-3*) Kluwer Academic.

Physics of the Moon (AAS/AAAS Symposium), Dec. 29, 1966, Washington, D.C. AAS/AAAS Symposium, Washington, D. C., Dec. 29, 1966. Ed. by S. Fred Singer. (Science & Technology Ser.: Vol. 13). 260p. 1967. 25.00 (*0-87703-041-3*, Am Astronaut Soc) Univelt Inc.

Physics of the Outer Heliosphere: Proceedings of the 1st COSPAR Colloquium Held in Warsaw, Poland, 19-22 September 1989. Ed. by S. Grzedzielski & D. E. Page. (COSPAR Colloquia Ser.: Vol. 1). (Illus.). 420p. 1990. 125.00 (*0-08-040780-3*, Pergamon Pr); 40.00 (*0-08-040781-1*, Pergamon Pr) Elsevier.

Physics of the Planets: Their Origin, Evolution & Structure. Ed. by S. K. Runcorn. LC 87-10465. 468p. reprint ed. pap. 145.10 (*0-8357-6944-5*, 203900300009) Bks Demand.

Physics of the Plasma Universe. Anthony L. Peratt. (Illus.). 250p. 1991. 79.00 (*0-387-97575-6*) Spr-Verlag.

Physics of the Plasmapause. Kaiser. 1977. pap. 33.00 (*0-08-021311-1*) Elsevier.

Physics of the Pulsar Magnetosphere. V. S. Beskin et al. Tr. by M. V. Tsaplina from RUS. LC 92-18417. (Illus.). 432p. (C). 1993. text 140.00 (*0-521-41746-5*) Cambridge U Pr.

Physics of the Quark-Gluon Plasma. B. Muller. (Lecture Notes in Physics Ser.: Vol. 225). vii, 142p. 1985. 18.95 (*0-387-15211-3*) Spr-Verlag.

Physics of the Quark-Gluon Plasma: Proceedings of the IX Autumn School of Physics, Lisbon. Ed. by S. Costa Ramos & J. Dias de Deus. 332p. (C). 1988. text 84.00 (*9971-5-0570-3*) World Scientific Pub.

Physics of the Secret Doctrine. William Kingsland. 154p. 1996. reprint ed. spiral bd. 16.00 (*0-7873-0500-6*) Hlth Research.

Physics of the Secret Doctrine. William Kingsland. 160p. 1992. reprint ed. pap. 14.95 (*1-56459-253-7*) Kessinger Pub.

Physics of the Seoul Guy. M. K. Park. (Illus.). 100p. (Orig.). 1990. pap. write for info. (*1-877974-02-1*) Prompter Pubns.

Physics of the Solar Corona: Proceedings of the NATO Advanced Study Institute on Physics of the Solar Corona, Cavouri-Vouliagmeni, Athens, 1970. NATO Advanced Study Institute Staff. Ed. by C. J. Macris. LC 76-154741. (Astrophysics & Space Science Library: No. 27). 345p. 1971. text 178.50 (*90-277-0204-7*) Kluwer Academic.

***Physics of the Solar Corona & Transition Region.** Carolus J. Schriver & Neale E. Hurlburt. LC 00-42411. 2000. write for info. (*0-7923-6357-4*) Plenum.

***Physics of the Solar System: A Companion to Introductory Astronomy Textbooks.** Loris Magnani & Theodore LaRosa. (Physics of the Solor System). 210p. (C). 1998. per. 28.95 (*0-7872-4890-8*, 41489001) Kendall-Hunt.

Physics of the Space Environment. Tamas I. Gombosi. LC 97-51318. (Atmospheric & Space Science Ser.). (Illus.). 350p. (C). 1998. 80.00 (*0-521-59264-X*) Cambridge U Pr.

Physics of the Stars. 2nd ed. Phillips. LC 99-20530. 262p. (C). 1999. 145.00 (*0-471-98797-2*) Wiley.

***Physics of the Stars.** 2nd ed. Phillips. LC 99-20530. 262p. (C). 1999. pap. 65.00 (*0-471-98798-0*) Wiley.

Physics of the Sun. 3rd ed. Peter A. Sturrock. (Geophysics & Astrophysics Monographs). 1987. text 37.50 (*90-277-1823-7*) Kluwer Academic.

Physics of the Sun: Astrophysics & Solar-Terrestrial Relations, Vol. 3. Ed. by Peter A. Sturrock. 1985. lib. bdg. 129.50 (*90-277-1862-8*) Kluwer Academic.

Physics of the Sun: The Solar Atmosphere, Vol. 2. Ed. by Peter A. Sturrock. 1985. lib. bdg. 167.00 (*90-277-1861-X*) Kluwer Academic.

Physics of the Sun: The Solar Interior, Vol. 1. Ed. by Peter A. Sturrock. 1985. lib. bdg. 118.50 (*90-277-1860-1*) Kluwer Academic.

Physics of the Twentieth Century: History & Outlook. E. P. Velikhov. 342p. (C). 1987. 80.00 (*0-7855-4967-6*, Pub. by Collets) St Mut.

Physics of the 2-Dimensional Electron Gas. Ed. by J. T. Devresse & F. M. Peeters. LC 87-13983. (NATO ASI Series B, Physics: Vol. 157). (Illus.). 452p. 1987. 105.00 (*0-306-42605-6*, Plenum Trade) Perseus Pubng.

Physics of the Violin. Lothar Cremer. Tr. by John S. Allen from GER. 472p. 1984. 55.00 (*0-262-03102-7*) MIT Pr.

Physics of Therman Gaseous Nebulae: Physical Processes in Gaseous Nebulae. Lawrence H. Aller. 1984. lib. bdg. 133.00 (*90-277-1814-8*) Kluwer Academic.

Physics of Thin Films. 2nd ed. L. Eckertova. (Illus.). 340p. (C). 1986. text 75.00 (*0-306-41798-7*, Kluwer Plenum) Kluwer Academic.

Physics of Thin Films: Mechanical & Dielectric Properties of Thin Films & Smart Materials, Vol. 17. Ed. by Maurice H. Francombe & John Vossen. (Illus.). 397p. 1993. text 128.00 (*0-12-533017-0*) Acad Pr.

Physics of Thin Films Vol. 15: Thin Films for Advanced Electronic Devices. Ed. by Maurice H. Francombe & John Vossen. (Illus.). 331p. (C). 1991. text 136.00 (*0-12-533015-4*) Acad Pr.

Physics of Thin Films Vol. 16: Thin Film for Emerging Applications. Ed. by Maurice H. Francombe & John Vossen. (Illus.). 367p. 1992. text 111.00 (*0-12-533016-2*) Acad Pr.

Physics of Thin Films Vol. 18: Advances in Research & Development. Ed. by Maurice H. Francombe & John Vossen. (Illus.). 328p. 1994. text. write for info. (*0-12-533018-9*) Acad Pr.

Physics of Thin Films Vol. 19: Optical Characterization of Real Surfaces & Films. Ed. by K. Vedam et al. (Illus.). 328p. 1994. text. write for info. (*0-12-533019-7*) Acad Pr.

Physics of Three Dimensional Radiation Therapy: Conformal Radiotherapy, Radiosurgery, & Treatment Planning. Steve Webb. (Medical Science Ser.). (Illus.). 373p. (C). 1993. 188.00 (*0-7503-0247-X*); pap. 48.00 (*0-7503-0254-2*) IOP Pub.

Physics of Time Reversal. Robert G. Sachs. LC 87-5826. (Illus.). 324p. (C). 1987. pap. text 28.00 (*0-226-73331-9*) U Ch Pr.

Physics of Time Reversal. Robert G. Sachs. LC 87-5826. (Illus.). 312p. (C). 1994. lib. bdg. 55.00 (*0-226-73330-0*) U Ch Pr.

Physics of Transition Metals, 1980: Invited & Contributed Papers from the International Conference on the Physics of Transition Metals Held at the University of Leeds, 18-22 August 1980. International Conference on the Physics of Transit. Ed. by P. Rhodes. LC 81-154161. (Conference Ser.: No. 55). 710p. reprint ed. pap. 200.00 (*0-7837-3253-8*, 204327200007) Bks Demand.

Physics of Transition Metals, 1992: Proceedings of the International Conference. J. Kubler & P. M. Oppeneer. 1080p. 1993. text 192.00 (*981-02-1158-9*) World Scientific Pub.

Physics of Ultracold Neutrons. V. K. Ignatovich. Tr. by G. B. Pontecorvo. (Oxford Series on Neutron Scattering in Condensed Matter: No. 5). (Illus.). 410p. 1990. text 110.00 (*0-19-851015-2*) OUP.

Physics of Unstable Nuclear Beams. LC 97-166094. 450p. 1997. 61.00 (*981-02-2926-7*) World Scientific Pub.

Physics of Vibrations & Waves. 3rd ed. Herbert J. Pain. LC 86-1597. (Illus.). 432p. reprint ed. pap. 134.00 (*0-7837-1876-4*, 204207700001) Bks Demand.

Physics of Vibrations & Waves. 5th ed. Pain. LC 98-36212. 576p. (C). 1999. 140.00 (*0-471-98542-2*) Wiley.

***Physics of Vibrations & Waves.** 5th ed. Pain. LC 98-36212. 576p. (C). 1999. pap. 69.95 (*0-471-98543-0*) Wiley.

Physics of VLSI: AIP Conference Proceedings, No. 122. Ed. by John C. Knights. LC 84-72729. 292p. 1984. lib. bdg. 39.75 (*0-88318-321-8*) Am Inst Physics.

Physics of Waves. Howard Georgi. LC 92-27348. 432p. (C). 1992. 60.00 (*0-13-665621-8*) P-H.

Physics of Waves. William C. Elmore & Mark A. Heald. 477p. 1985. reprint ed. pap. 13.95 (*0-486-64926-1*) Dover.

Physics of Weather Modification. James E. Jiusto. (Illus.). 56p. 1984. pap. 15.00 (*0-917853-03-2*, IO-3) Am Assn Physics.

Physics of Welding. Ed. by International Institute of Welding Staff. 1984. text 61.00 (*0-08-030554-7*, Pergamon Pr); pap. text 28.00 (*0-08-030555-5*, Pergamon Pr) Elsevier.

Physics of Welding. 2nd ed. Ed. by International Institute of Welding Staff. (International Series of Monographs on Materials Science & Technology). 362p. 1986. text 160.00 (*0-08-034076-8*, A110, A145) Franklin.

Physics of X-Ray Multilayer Structures. LC 92-80502. (Nineteen Ninety-Two Technical Digest Ser.: Vol. 7). 250p. 1992. pap. 66.00 (*1-55752-228-6*) Optical Soc.

P

An Asterisk (*) at the beginning of an entry indicates that the title is appearing for the first time.

Physics of X-Ray Multilayer Structures. LC 93-87343. (Nineteen Ninety-Four Technical Digest Ser.: Vol. 6). 200p. 1994. pap. 66.00 (*1-55752-335-5*) Optical Soc.

Physics of X-Ray Multilayer Structures, 1994. LC 93-87344. (Technical Digest Ser.: Vol. 6). 200p. (Orig.). 1994. pap. text 43.00 (*1-55752-334-7*) Optical Soc.

Physics Olympics Handbook. Ed. by Susan Agruso et al. 26p. 1984. 14.00 (*0-917853-00-8*, OP-51) Am Assn Physics.

***Physics on All Fours: Nick Herbert: Selected Verse 1995-2000.** Nick Herbert. (Illus.). v, 83p. 2000. pap. 12.00 (*0-615-11361-3*) Sea Creature Pr.

Physics on Manifolds: Proceedings of the International Colloquim in Honour of Yvonne Choquet-Bruhat, Paris, June 3-5, 1992. Ed. by Moshe Flato & Robert J. Kerner. LC 93-31133. (Mathematical Physics Studies). (FRE.). 384p. (C). 1993. text 214.50 (*0-7923-2500-1*) Kluwer Academic.

Physics on the Internet 1997-1998. (C). 1997. write for info. (*0-13-890153-8*, Macmillan Coll) P-H.

Physics I. M. Azad Islam. (Test Yourself Ser.). 1997. pap. 12.95 (*0-614-27612-8*) NTC Contemp Pub Co.

Physics 1 Exam File: Mechanics. Ed. by Arthur B. Western. LC 85-25306. (Exam File Ser.). 346p. 1986. pap. 18.50 (*0-910554-54-4*) Engineering.

Physics 115. Russell Palma. (C). 1995. pap. text 15.37 (*1-56870-196-9*) RonJon Pub.

Physics 151. 3rd ed. Nathan Goldstein. 190p. (C). 1996. text 28.40 (*0-536-59559-3*) Pearson Custom.

Physics 132. Bob Erickson. (C). 1994. pap. text, lab manual ed. 15.47 (*1-56870-127-6*) RonJon Pub.

Physics 120. Don Duncan. (C). 1997. pap. text 19.88 (*1-56870-275-2*) RonJon Pub.

Physics 121. Don Duncan. (C). 1997. text 22.17 (*1-56870-274-4*) RonJon Pub.

Physics 1003 Laboratory Manual. Miriam Sidran. 112p. (C). 1994. spiral bd. 17.95 (*0-8403-8940-X*) Kendall-Hunt.

Physics 128 & 241: Lab Manual. Fred Becchetti. (C). 1993. 30.00 (*1-881592-12-X*) Hayden-McNeil.

Physics 127 & 141: Lab Manual. Fred Becchetti. (C). 1993. 30.00 (*1-881592-13-8*) Hayden-McNeil.

Physics 123 Laboratory. Robert Whitaker. 128p. (C). 1995. 20.95 (*0-7872-0960-0*) Kendall-Hunt.

Physics or Metaphysics: Einstein & Hawking Locked in a Time Warp - Like Two Flies Caught in a Spider's Web. Gerhard Kraus. 128p. 1998. pap. 15.95 (*1-85756-338-7*, Pub. by Janus Pubng) Paul & Co Pubs.

Physics over Easy. Leonid V. Azaroff. LC 96-200777. 250p. 1996. text 48.00 (*981-02-2357-9*); pap. text 26.00 (*981-02-2367-6*) World Scientific Pub.

Physics, Philosophy & Psychoanalysis. Robert S. Cohen et al. 356p. 1983. text 191.50 (*90-277-1533-5*, D Reidel) Kluwer Academic.

Physics, Philosophy, & the Scientific Community: Essays in the Philosophy & History of the Natural Sciences & Mathematics in Honor of Robert S. Cohen. Ed. by Kostas Gavroglu et al. LC 94-22250. (Boston Studies in the Philosophy of Science: Vol. 163). 1994. write for info. (*0-7923-2991-0*, Pub. by Kluwer Academic) Kluwer Academic.

Physics, Philosophy, & the Scientific Community: Essays in the Philosophy & History of the Natural Sciences & Mathematics in Honor of Robert S. Cohen. Ed. by Kostas Gavroglu & John J. Stachel. LC 94-22250. (Boston Studies in the Philosophy of Science: Vol. 163). 411p. 1994. lib. bdg. 186.50 (*0-7923-2988-0*, Pub. by Kluwer Academic) Kluwer Academic.

Physics Potential & Development of Mu-Mu Colliders: Fourth International Conference. Ed. by David B. Cline. LC 98-86574. (Conference Proceedings Ser.: Vol. 441). (Illus.). 400p. 1998. 105.00 (*1-56396-723-5*) Am Inst Physics.

Physics Power Pack. Barron's Educational Editors. 1996. pap. text 15.95 (*0-8120-8471-3*) Barron.

Physics Principles with Applications, Vol. 2. 5th ed. Giancoli. 620p. (C). 1997. pap. text 61.33 (*0-13-679762-8*) P-H.

Physics Problem. Kathleen Atkins. 32p. 1984. pap. 12.00 (*0-930513-00-2*) Blackwells Pr.

Physics Problem Solver. rev. ed. Research & Education Association Staff. LC 76-332. (Illus.). 1200p. (C). 2000. pap. text 23.95 (*0-87891-507-9*) Res & Educ.

Physics Problems: Electricity, Magnetism, & Optics. Robert L. Gray. LC 73-20445. (Wiley Self-Teaching Guides Ser.). 174p. reprint ed. pap. 54.00 (*0-608-10311-X*, 201261900082) Bks Demand.

Physics Programs: Optics. Alan D. Boardman. LC 80-40123. 131p. reprint ed. pap. 40.70 (*0-608-12335-8*, 202437500037) Bks Demand.

Physics Projects for Young Scientists. Richard Adams & Peter Goodwin. LC 98-40401. (Projects For Young Scientists Ser.). (YA). (gr. 9-12). 2000. 25.00 (*0-531-11667-0*) Watts.

***Physics Projects for Young Scientists.** rev. ed. Richard Adams. (Projects for Young Scientists Ser.). (Illus.). (J). 2000. pap. 6.95 (*0-531-16461-6*) Watts.

Physics Quick Reference. Coletta. 1995. (*0-8151-1909-7*) Mosby Inc.

Physics Quick Reference Guide. E. Richard Cohen. 209p. 1995. pap. 30.00 (*1-56396-143-1*) Spr-Verlag.

***Physics Quick Reference Guide.** 2nd ed. Richard E. Cohen. (Illus.). 2000. pap. text 29.95 (*0-387-98986-2*) Spr-Verlag.

Physics Quick Review. Linda Huetinck. (Cliffs Quick Reviews Ser.). 184p. 1994. pap. text 7.95 (*0-8220-5337-3*, Cliff) IDG Bks.

Physics Reference Guide. Longman. Date not set. pap. text. write for info. (*0-582-05794-9*, Pub. by Addison-Wesley) Longman.

Physics Research Activities: Teacher's Edition (with Answers) Eugene Kutscher. (Illus.). 1988. teacher ed. write for info. (*0-318-64022-8*); student ed. write for info. (*0-318-64023-6*) Alpha Pub MD.

Physics Reviews. Isaac M. Khalatnikov. (Soviet Scientific Reviews Ser.: Vol. 3). x, 594p. 1981. text 691.00 (*3-7186-0068-4*) Gordon & Breach.

Physics Reviews, Vol. 1. Ed. by Isaac M. Khalatnikov. (Soviet Scientific Reviews Ser.: Section A). xv, 305p. 1979. text 691.00 (*3-7186-0004-8*) Gordon & Breach.

Physics Reviews, Vol. 4. Ed. by Isaac M. Khalatnikov. (Soviet Scientific Reviews Ser.: Section A). x, 286p. 1982. text 691.00 (*3-7186-0106-0*) Gordon & Breach.

Physics Reviews, Vol. 5. Ed. by Isaac M. Khalatnikov & L. D. Landau. (Soviet Scientific Reviews Ser.: Section A). xiv, 508p. 1984. text 627.00 (*3-7186-0138-9*) Gordon & Breach.

Physics Reviews, Vol. 6. Isaac M. Khalatnikov. (Soviet Scientific Reviews Ser.: Section A). xiv, 514p. 1985. text 627.00 (*3-7186-0150-8*) Gordon & Breach.

Physics Reviews, Vol. 7. Ed. by Isaac M. Khalatnikov. (Soviet Scientific Reviews Ser.: Section A, Vol. 7). xii, 312p. 1986. text 527.00 (*3-7186-0204-0*) Gordon & Breach.

Physics Reviews, Vol. 9. Ed. by Isaac M. Khalatnikov. xiv, 562p. 1987. text 1001.00 (*3-7186-0456-6*) Gordon & Breach.

Physics Reviews, Vol. 10. Isaac M. Khalatnikov. (Soviet Scientific Reviews Ser.: Section A, Vol. 10). 96p. 1989. pap. text 79.00 (*3-7186-4849-0*) Gordon & Breach.

Physics Reviews, Vol. 10. Isaac M. Khalatnikov. (Soviet Scientific Reviews Ser.: Section A, Vol. 10). viii, 88p. 1989. pap. text 90.00 (*3-7186-4848-2*) Gordon & Breach.

Physics Reviews: Excitons Bound to Impurities of 3rd Elements in II-VI Compounds, Vol. 12. V. I. Sokolov & K. A. Kikoin. Ed. by V. I. Gol'danskii et al. (Soviet Scientific Reviews Ser.: Vol. 12, Pt. 3). ii, 146p. 1989. pap. text 171.00 (*3-7186-4931-4*) Gordon & Breach.

Physics Reviews: Non-centrosymmetric Langmuir-Blodgett Films, Vol. 12. L. M. Blinv. Ed. by V. I. Gol'danskii et al. (Soviet Scientific Reviews Ser.: Vol. 12, Pt. 1). ii, 90p. 1989. pap. text 96.00 (*3-7186-4906-3*) Gordon & Breach.

Physics Reviews: Optics of Chiral Liquid Crystals, Vol. 13. V. A. Belyakov & V. E. Dmitrienko. Ed. by V. I. Gol'danskii et al. (Soviet Scientific Reviews Ser.: Vol. 13, Pt. 1). ii, 222p. 1989. pap. text 249.00 (*3-7186-4950-0*) Gordon & Breach.

Physics Reviews: The Dynamics of Planetary Rings & the Prediction of New Uranian Satellites; Theory of Photothermal & Photoacoustic Diagnostics of Semiconductor Structures, Vol. 12. A. M. Fridman et al. Ed. by V. I. Gol'danskii et al. (Soviet Scientific Reviews Ser.: Vol. 12, Pt. 4). ii, 92p. 1989. pap. text 83.00 (*3-7186-4930-6*) Gordon & Breach.

Physics Reviews: X-Ray Diffraction Study of Nematic, Smectic A & C Liquid Crystals, Vol. 12. B. I. Ostrovskii. Ed. by V. I. Gol'danskii et al. (Soviet Scientific Reviews Ser.: Vol. 12, Pt. 2). ii, 68p. 1989. pap. text 74.00 (*3-7186-4907-1*) Gordon & Breach.

Physics Reviews Section A, Vol. 2. Ed. by Isaac M. Khalatnikov. (Soviet Scientific Reviews Ser.). x, 484p. 1980. text 552.00 (*3-7186-0017-X*, Harwood Acad Pubs) Gordon & Breach.

Physics Reviews Vol. 13, Pt. 2: Non-Linear Dynamics & Acceleration of Ions When a Plasma Expands into a Plasma, Vol. 13. A. V. Gurevich. Ed. by V. I. Gol'danskii et al. (Soviet Scientific Reviews Ser.). ii, 74p. 1989. pap. text 75.00 (*3-7186-4977-2*) Gordon & Breach.

Physics Reviews Vol. 13, Pt. 3: An Experimental Study of Quasi-Particles in Antiferromagnetic Materials, Vol. 13. B. Y. Kotyuzhanskii & L. A. Prozorova. Ed. by V. I. Gol'danskii et al. (Soviet Scientific Reviews Ser.). ii, 132p. 1990. pap. text 145.00 (*3-7186-4988-8*) Gordon & Breach.

Physics Reviews Vol. 14, Pt. 1: Magnetic Resonance & Relaxation in Dielectric Crystals of Rare Earth Compounds, Vol. 14. L. K. Aminov. (Soviet Scientific Reviews Ser.: Section A). 159p. 1991. text 157.00 (*3-7186-4991-8*, Harwood Acad Pubs) Gordon & Breach.

Physics Reviews Vol. 14, Pt. 2: Electron Liquid in Disordered Conductors, Vol. 14. A. M. Finkelstein. (Soviet Scientific Reviews Ser.: Section A). 101p. 1991. text 110.00 (*3-7186-4990-X*, Harwood Acad Pubs) Gordon & Breach.

Physics Reviews Vol. 14, Pt. 3: The Theory of Quantum Nondegenerate Liquids, Vol. 14. A. M. Dyugaev. (Soviet Scientific Reviews Ser.: Section.A). 177p. 1991. text 192.00 (*3-7186-5040-1*, Harwood Acad Pubs) Gordon & Breach.

Physics Reviews Vol. 15, Pt. 1: Spin Glasses & Related Problems, Vol. 15. V. S. Dotsenko. (Soviet Scientific Reviews Ser.: Section A). 250p. 1991. text 269.00 (*3-7186-5039-8*, Harwood Acad Pubs) Gordon & Breach.

Physics Reviews Vol. 15, Pt. 2: Additional Symmetries & Exactly Solvable Models in Two Dimensional Conformal Field Theory, Vol. 15. S. L. Lukyanov. (Soviet Scientific Reviews Ser.: Section A). 117p. 1991. text 121.00 (*3-7186-5047-9*, Harwood Acad Pubs) Gordon & Breach.

Physics Reviews Vol. 15, Pt. 3: Spin Super-Current & Magnetic Relaxation in Helium-3, Vol. 15. A. S. Borovik-Romanov. (Soviet Scientific Reviews Ser.: Section A). 57p. 1990. text 69.00 (*3-7186-5050-9*, Harwood Acad Pubs) Gordon & Breach.

Physics Reviews Vol. 16, Pt. 1: Kinetic Size Effects in Metals in a Magnetic Field, Vol. 16. V. G. Peschansky. (Soviet Scientific Reviews Ser.: Section A). 111p. 1991. text 110.00 (*3-7186-5170-X*, Harwood Acad Pubs) Gordon & Breach.

Physics Reviews Vol. 16, Pt. 2.1: Non-Homogeneous Liquids Near the Critical Point & the Boundary of Stability, Vol. 16. A. V. Chalyi. (Soviet Scientific Reviews Ser.: Section A). 125p. 1992. pap. text 136.00 (*3-7186-5219-6*, Harwood Acad Pubs) Gordon & Breach.

Physics Reviews Vol. 16, Pt. 3: Solitons & Thermodynamics of Low-Dimensions Magnets, Vol. 16. V. Bar'yakhtar. (Soviet Scientific Reviews Ser.: Section A). 253p. 1992. pap. text 319.00 (*3-7186-5383-4*, Harwood Acad Pubs) Gordon & Breach.

Physics Reviews Vol. 17, No. 3: Theory of Diffusive Decomposition of Solid Solutions, Vol. 17. Ed. by Isaac M. Khalatnikov. (Physics Reviews Ser.). 200p. 1995. pap. text 77.00 (*3-7186-5815-1*) Gordon & Breach.

Physics Reviews Vol. 17, Pt. 2: Secondary Hadron Production at High Energies, Vol. 17. Isaac M. Khalatnikov. (Soviet Scientific Reviews Ser.). 80p. 1995. pap. text 123.00 (*3-7186-5629-9*, Harwood Acad Pubs) Gordon & Breach.

Physics, Science & Engineering. Dean Lee & Lawrence Lerner. (Physics Ser.). 272p. 1996. pap. 50.00 (*0-7637-0205-6*) Jones & Bartlett.

Physics Science & Engineering. 2nd ed. Paul M. Fishbane et al. 1329p. 1995. 112.00 (*0-13-231176-3*) P-H.

Physics, Science & Engineering, 4 vols. 4th ed. Serway. (C). 1996. pap. text 94.00 (*0-03-020057-1*, Pub. by Harcourt Coll Pubs) Harcourt.

Physics, Science & Engineering, Vol. 2. Lerner & Lee. (Physics Ser.). 312p. 1996. pap., teacher ed. 50.00 (*0-7637-0206-4*) Jones & Bartlett.

Physics Science & Engineering, Vol. 2. 2nd expanded ed. Paul M. Fishbane & Stephen Gasiorowicz. 1329p. 1995. 72.00 (*0-13-231168-2*) P-H.

Physics, Science & English Ninety-Six. 4th ed. Serway. (C). 1995. 115.50 (*0-03-016509-1*) Harcourt.

Physics, Science & English 96, Vol. One. 4th ed. Serway. (C). 1995. 71.00 (*0-03-016492-3*) Harcourt.

Physics-Scientists & Engineers. Sokol. Date not set. pap. text. write for info. (*1-57259-188-9*) W H Freeman.

Physics Simulations at High Energy: Proceedings of the Workshop Sponsored by the Institute for Elementary Particle Physics Research Madison, Wisconsin, 5-16 May 1986. Ed. by V. Barger et al. 668p. 1987. text 144.00 (*9971-5-0181-3*) World Scientific Pub.

Physics since Parity Symmetry Breaking: In Memory of Professor C. S. Wu Nanjing, People's Republic of China 16-18 August, 1997. Ed. by Tingyang Chen et al. 500p. 1998. 86.00 (*981-02-3475-9*) World Scientific Pub.

Physics Study-Aid. 1966. pap. 2.50 (*0-87738-041-4*) Youth Ed.

Physics Study Companion. (C). 1998. 16.00 (*0-536-02220-8*) Pearson Custom.

Physics Study Guide. 5th ed. Arthur Beiser. 368p. (C). 1991. pap. text 28.00 (*0-201-50320-4*) Addison-Wesley.

Physics Study Guide Set. 4th ed. Cutnell. 1997. text 76.00 (*0-471-28381-9*) Wiley.

***Physics Syllabus & Tests.** 24p. 1999. ring bd. 2.50 (*1-57896-059-2*, 2419, Hewitt Homeschl Res) Hewitt Res Fnd.

Physics Teacher 18-Year Cumulative Index. 125p. 1982. 16.00 (*0-917853-79-2*, OP-28) Am Assn Physics.

Physics Teaching in Schools. Ed. by G. Delacote. 404p. 1978. pap. 55.00 (*0-85066-136-6*) Taylor & Francis.

Physics, Technology & the Nuclear Arms Race (APS Baltimore, 1983) Ed. by D. W. Hafemeister & Dietrich Schroeer. LC 83-72533. (AIP Conference Proceedings Ser.: No. 104). 384p. 1983. lib. bdg. 36.75 (*0-88318-203-3*) Am Inst Physics.

Physics, Technology & Use of Photovoltaics. R. J. Van OverStraeten & R. P. Mertens. (Modern Energy Studies). (Illus.). 288p. 1986. 158.00 (*0-85274-487-0*) IOP Pub.

Physics Tells Why: An Explanation of Some Common Physical Phenomena. 2nd ed. Overton Luhr. LC 51-30387. (Illus.). 397p. reprint ed. pap. 123.10 (*0-608-10329-2*, 201236300081) Bks Demand.

Physics Terminology. Andreas Jesse. (ENG, FRE & GER.). 129p. 1980. pap. 49.95 (*0-8288-2244-1*, M9310) Fr & Eur.

Physics the Easy Way. 3rd ed. Robert L. Lehrman. LC 97-35217. 400p. 1998. pap. 12.95 (*0-7641-0236-2*) Barron.

Physics 1350. Dan Wilkins. 1998. text 13.02 (*1-56870-324-4*) RonJon Pub.

Physics 3030. UNT, Physics Department Staff. 1996. pap. text, lab manual ed. 21.39 (*1-56870-244-2*) RonJon Pub.

Physics 1210 - 1310 Laboratory Manual. University of Wyoming Staff. 132p. 1996. spiral bd. 12.95 (*0-8403-7918-8*) Kendall-Hunt.

Physics 2425. Paul Johnson. (C). 1998. pap. text 22.54 (*1-56870-290-6*) RonJon Pub.

Physics 2426. Paul Johnson. (C). 1998. pap. text 22.54 (*1-56870-291-4*) RonJon Pub.

Physics II. Robert M. Dixon. 128p. (C). 1995. spiral bd. 19.95 (*0-8403-8200-6*) Kendall-Hunt.

Physics 211L, General Physics I. New Mexico State University Staff. 158p. (C). 1997. spiral bd., lab manual ed. 13.95 (*0-7872-4168-7*) Kendall-Hunt.

Physics 214-218. Wayne State University Staff. (C). 1993. student ed. 10.00 (*1-881592-04-9*) Hayden-McNeil.

Physics 291. Ramsier. 284p. (C). 1998. pap. text 35.75 (*0-536-01493-0*) Pearson Custom.

Physics 292. 531p. (C). 1998. pap. text 38.20 (*0-536-01492-2*) Pearson Custom.

Physics 213-217. Wayne State University Staff. (C). 1993. student ed. 10.00 (*1-881592-03-0*) Hayden-McNeil.

Physics 2000. John M. Charap. (Bowerdean Briefings Ser.). (Illus.). 144p. 1997. pap. text 14.95 (*0-906097-79-7*, Pub. by Bowerdean Pub) Capital VA.

***Physics 2000-2001.** 2nd ed. Princeton Review Publishing Staff. 2000. pap. 19.00 (*0-375-75492-X*, Pub. by PRP NY) Random.

Physics 221-223: Lab Manual. Diane Jacobs. (C). 1993. 10.00 (*1-881592-17-0*) Hayden-McNeil.

Physics 222-224: Lab Manual. Diane Jacobs. (C). 1993. 9.00 (*1-881592-19-7*) Hayden-McNeil.

Physics 208-219 Lab Manual. 5th ed. 232p. (C). 1996. text 13.60 (*0-8087-6758-5*) Pearson Custom.

Physics up to 200. Ed. by Antonio L. Zichichi. (Subnuclear Ser.: Vol. 28). (Illus.). 488p. (C). 1991. 162.00 (*0-306-43935-2*, Plenum Trade) Perseus Pubng.

Physics Vade Mecum. Ed. by Herbert L. Anderson. LC 81-69849. 340p. 1981. 25.00 (*0-88318-289-0*) Am Inst Physics.

Physics, Vol. 1, Vol. 1. 4th ed. David Halliday et al. LC 91-35885. 656p. 1991. text 81.95 (*0-471-80458-4*) Wiley.

Physics, Vol. 2, Vol. 2. 4th ed. David Halliday et al. 480p. 1992. text 81.95 (*0-471-80457-6*) Wiley.

***Physics with a High Luminosity Polarized Electron-Ion Collider.** Ed. by L. C. Bland et al. 450p. 1999. 88.00 (*981-02-4052-X*) World Scientific Pub.

Physics with Answers: 500 Problems & Solutions. A. R. King & O. Regev. 328p. 1997. text 80.00 (*0-521-48270-4*); pap. text 32.95 (*0-521-48369-7*) Cambridge U Pr.

Physics with Applications. 218p. (C). 1998. text 21.96 (*0-536-01151-6*) Pearson Custom.

Physics with Applications. Keefer. 512p. (C). 2001. 67.00 (*0-02-362201-6*, Macmillan Coll) P-H.

Physics with Calculus: Electricity & Magnetism. (Dantes Subject Standardized Tests (DANTES) Ser.: Vol. DANTES-57). 1997. pap. 23.95 (*0-8373-6657-7*) Nat Learn.

Physics with Calculus: Mechanics. (Dantes Subject Standardized Tests (DANTES) Ser.: Vol. DANTES-56). pap. 23.95 (*0-8373-6656-9*) Nat Learn.

Physics with GeV-Particle Beams: Proceedings of the International Conference. Hartmut Machner & Knornel Sistemich. 550p. 1995. text 128.00 (*981-02-2279-3*) World Scientific Pub.

Physics with Health Science Applications. Paul P. Urone. 512p. 1985. pap. 84.95 (*0-471-60389-9*) Wiley.

Physics with High Energy Colliders. S. Yamada & T. Koryu Ishii. 488p. 1995. text 99.00 (*981-02-2205-X*) World Scientific Pub.

Physics with High-Intensity Hadron Accelerators: Eighteenth Ins. International Symposium. T. Nomura & S. Kunobo. 516p. 1990. text 130.00 (*981-02-0261-X*) World Scientific Pub.

***Physics with Illustrative Examples from Medicine & Biology, 3 vols.** 2nd rev. ed. Incl. Vol. 1. Physics with Illustrative Examples from Medicine & Biology: Volume 1. 2nd ed. George Bernard Benedek & Felix Villars. LC 99-33040. (Illus.). 520p. 2000. 69.95 (*0-387-98769-X*, AIP Pr); Vol. 2. Statistical Physics. 2nd ed. (Illus.). 552p. 2000. 69.95 (*0-387-98754-1*); Vol. 3. Electricity & Magnetism. 2nd ed. (Illus.). 304p. 2000. 49.95 (*0-387-98770-3*, AIP Pr); LC 99-52754. (Biological Physics Ser.). (Illus.). 2000. 129.00 (*0-387-98952-8*, AIP Pr) Spr-Verlag.

Physics with Illustrative Examples from Medicine & Biology, 2 vols., Vol. 1. G. B. Benedek & F. M. Villars. 1973. 30.25 (*0-685-00008-7*) Addison-Wesley.

Physics with Illustrative Examples from Medicine & Biology, 2 vols., Vol. 2. G. B. Benedek & F. M. Villars. 1974. 30.25 (*0-201-00551-4*) Addison-Wesley.

Physics with Illustrative Examples from Medicine & Biology, 2 vols., Vol. 3. G. B. Benedek & F. M. Villars. 1979. 30.25 (*0-685-00009-5*) Addison-Wesley.

Physics with Illustrative Examples from Medicine & Biology, Vol. 3. G. B. Benedek & F. M. Villars. 1979. pap. text 32.25 (*0-201-00559-X*) Addison-Wesley.

Physics with Illustrative Examples from Medicine & Biology: Volume 1 see Physics with Illustrative Examples from Medicine & Biology

Physics with Modern Physics for Scientists & Engineers. 3rd ed. Jeffrey Braun. (C). 1999. pap. text, student ed. write for info. (*0-321-03576-3*) Addison-Wesley.

Physics with Modern Physics for Scientists & Engineers. 3rd ed. Richard Wolfson. 1073p. (C). 1999. 112.00 (*0-321-03571-2*) Addson-Wesley Educ.

Physics with Modern Physics for Scientists & Engineers. 3rd expanded ed. Richard Wolfson. LC 98-45595. (C). 1999. text 99.38 (*0-321-03572-0*) Addson-Wesley Educ.

Physics with Modern Physics for Scientists & Engineers, Vol. 1. 3rd ed. Richard Wolfson. LC 98-45595. (C). 1999. pap. text 59.06 (*0-321-03573-9*) Addson-Wesley Educ.

Physics with Modern Physics for Scientists & Engineers, Vol. 2. 3rd ed. Richard Wolfson. LC 98-45595. (C). 1999. pap. text 59.06 (*0-321-03574-7*) Addson-Wesley Educ.

Physics with Modern Physics for Scientists & Engineers, Vol. 3. 3rd ed. Richard Wolfson. (C). 1999. pap. text. write for info. (*0-321-03581-X*) Addson-Wesley Educ.

Physics with Modern Physics for Scientists & Engineers, Vol. 4. 3rd ed. Richard Wolfson. (C). 1999. pap. text. write for info. (*0-321-03582-8*) Addson-Wesley Educ.

Physics with Multiply Charged Ions: Proceedings of a NATO ASI Held in Cargese, France, July 18-30, 1994, Vol. 348. Ed. by Dieter Liesen. (NATO ASI Ser.: Vol. 349). (Illus.). 376p. (C). 1995. text 125.00 (*0-306-45114-X*, Kluwer Plenum) Kluwer Academic.

P

An Asterisk (*) at the beginning of an entry indicates that the title is appearing for the first time.

Physics with Polarized Beams on Polarized Targets. Ed. by J. Sowinski & Steven E. Vigdor. 424p. (C). 1990. text 130.00 (*981-02-0156-7*) World Scientific Pub.

***Physics with tau-Leptons.** Achim Stahl. LC 99-47498. (Tracts in Modern Physics Ser.: Vol. 160). (Illus.). viii, 313p. 2000. 169.00 (*3-540-66267-7*) Spr-Verlag.

Physics with the Computer. Douglas Shawhan. (Orig.). (C). teacher ed. 24.95 (*0-87567-037-7*); student ed. 14.95 (*0-685-01562-9*) Entelek.

Physics Without Math: A Descriptive Introduction. Gilbert Shapiro. (C). 1994. pap. text 42.74 (*0-07-057173-2*) McGraw.

Physics 1: A Computer-Based Approach. 3rd ed. WYU (Physics) Staff. 124p. (C). 1997. spiral bd., lab manual ed. 21.95 (*0-7872-4337-X*, 41433701) Kendall-Hunt.

***Physics 202** Samarth. 1999. pap. text, lab manual ed. 14.00 (*0-471-37282-X*) Wiley.

Physics 4, Vol. 2 & 3. Tipler. 1998. teacher ed. 21.80 (*1-57259-515-9*); student ed. 15.00 (*1-57259-512-4*) Worth.

Physics:Calculus: 2E w/CD (Intl Version), Vol.1. 2nd ed. Hecht. (Physics). 1999. pap. text 38.00 incl. cd-rom (*0-534-37391-7*) Brooks-Cole.

Physics:Calculus: 2E W/infotrac & CD, Vol.1. 2nd ed. Hecht. LC 99-32079. (Physics). 1999. pap. text 38.00 incl. cd-rom (*0-534-37350-X*) Brooks-Cole.

Physik: Band 4: Atome, Festkorper, Kerne, Teilchen. Herbert Daniel. 350p. 1998. 80.00 (*3-11-016221-0*); pap. 61.00 (*3-11-014631-2*) De Gruyter.

Physik Theorie/Experiment/Didautik. Herbert Druxes. (GER.). (C). 1991. text. write for info. (*0-201-55946-3*) Addison-Wesley.

Physik und Chemie des Zellkerns. Petr F. Milovidov. (Handbuch der Pflanzenanatomie Encyclopedia of Plant Anatomy - Traite d' Anatomie Vegetale Ser.: Teils 1 & 2). (Illus.). xiv, 529p. 1949. 103.00 (*3-443-39017-X*, Pub. by Gebruder Borntraeger) Balogh.

Physik und Chemie des Zellkerns. Petr F. Milovidov. (Handbuch der Pflanzenanatomie Encyclopedia of Plant Anatomy - Traite d' Anatomie Vegetale Ser.: Teils 1 & 2). (Illus.). viii, 479p. 1954. 103.00 (*3-443-39018-8*, Pub. by Gebruder Borntraeger) Balogh.

Physik und Physikotheologie des Jungen Kant: Die Vorgeschichte seiner Allgemeinen Naturgeschichte und Theorie des Himmels. Hans-Joachim Waschkies. (Bochumer Studien zur Philosophie Ser.: Vol. 8). (GER.). 711p. (C). 1987. write for info. (*90-6032-273-8*) B R Gruner.

Physikalisch-Mathematische Monographien. W. V. Ignatowsky. LC 66-23758. (AMS/Chelsea Ser.). 232p. 1997. text 29.00 (*0-8284-0201-9*) Am Math.

Physikalisch-Okonomische Bibliothek, 23 vols. Johann Beckmann. write for info. (*0-318-71736-0*) G Olms Pubs.

Physikalische Chemie. 3rd ed. Walter J. Moore. (GER.). 1236p. 1983. 75.40 (*3-11-008554-2*) De Gruyter.

Physiker. Friedrich Durrenmatt. Ed. by Robert E. Helbling. (GER., Illus.). 188p. (Orig.). 1965. text 18.95 (*0-19-500908-8*) OUP.

Physiklernen: Eine Herausforderung Fur Unterrichtsforschung: Arbeiten zur Lernprozebforschung Im Physikunterricht. Hans E. Fischer. Ed. by D. Nachtigall. (Didaktik und Naturwissenschaft Ser.: Bd. 3). (GER.). IV, 245p. 1994. 46.95 (*3-631-47899-2*) P Lang Pubng.

Physio-Synthesis: Inner Muscle Balancing. Ida M. Thomas. Ed. by James R. Thomas & Rose Rosenthal. (Illus.). 250p. 1998. ring bd. 38.50 (*0-9622726-3-9*, 5231844) Thomas CA.

Physio-Synthesis: Structural Balance Training. Ida M. Thomas. (Illus.). 269p. (C). 1989. lib. bdg. 35.50 (*0-9622726-0-4*) Thomas CA.

Physiochemical & Environmental Plant Physiology. Park S. Nobel. 635p. (C). 1991. pap. text 48.00 (*0-12-520021-8*) Acad Pr.

Physiochemical Aspects of Medicine Reviews, Vol. 1. Yu. M. Lopukhin. xiii, 426p. 1987. text 500.00 (*3-7186-0316-0*) Gordon & Breach.

Physiochemical Hydrodynamics. 2nd ed. Ronald F. Probstein. 400p. 1994. 89.95 (*0-471-01011-1*) Wiley.

Physiochemical Hydrodynamics: An Introduction. 2nd ed. Ronald F. Probstein. 133p. 1995. teacher ed. write for info. (*0-471-11703-X*) Wiley.

Physiochemical Methods for Water & Wastewater Treatment. Ed. by L. Pawlowski. (Studies in Environmental Science: Vol. 19). 394p. 1982. 203.75 (*0-444-42067-3*) Elsevier.

Physiocrats: Six Lectures on the French Economistes of the Eighteenth Century. Henry Higgs. LC 87-17066. (Reprints of Economic Classics Ser.). x, 158p. 1989. reprint ed. 35.00 (*0-678-00398-X*) Kelley.

Physiocrats: 6 Lecture on the French Economistes of the 18th Century (1897 Edition) Henry Higgs. 176p. 1996. reprint ed. 58.00 (*1-85506-235-6*) Bks Intl VA.

***Physioeconomics: The Basis for Long-Run Economic Growth.** Philip Parker. LC 00-21973. (Illus.). 252p. 2000. 29.95 (*0-262-16194-X*) MIT Pr.

Physiofinder: Investigative Modules in Physiology/Book & Disk. P. George Simone. 112p. (C). 1997. cd-rom 58.00 (*0-673-46933-6*) Addson-Wesley Educ.

Physiognomie & Pathognomie: Zur Literarischen Darstellung Von Individualitaet Festschrift Fuer Karl Pestalozzi Zum 65. Geburtstag. Ed. by Wolfram Groddeck & Ulrich Stadler. (GER.). xiii, 450p. (C). 1994. lib. bdg. 161.55 (*3-11-013716-X*) De Gruyter.

Physiognomy. Jeffrey Ford. LC 97-11961. 224p. 1997. pap. 12.00 (*0-380-79331-8*, Avon Bks) Morrow Avon.

Physiognomy. Jeffrey Ford. LC 97-11961. 244p. 2000. mass mkt. 3.99 (*0-380-79332-6*, Eos) Morrow Avon.

Physiognomy: The Mark Seliger Photographs. Photos by Mark Seliger. (Illus.). 224p. 1999. 75.00 (*0-8212-2598-7*, Pub. by Bulfinch Pr) Little.

Physiognomy of Capital in Charles Dickens: An Essay in Dialectical Criticism. Hye-Joon Yoon. LC 98-5505. 364p. 1998. 74.95 (*1-57309-219-3*); pap. 54.95 (*1-57309-218-5*) Intl Scholars.

Physiognomy of Mental Diseases. 2nd ed. Alexander Morison. LC 75-16723. (Classics in Psychiatry Ser.). (Illus.). 1976. reprint ed. 23.95 (*0-405-07447-6*) Ayer.

Physiography of Arctic Canada, with Special Reference to the Area South of Perry Channel. John B. Bird. LC 67-16232. 427p. reprint ed. pap. 132.40 (*0-608-11893-1*, 202308300032) Bks Demand.

Physiography of Burma. Harbans L. Chhibber. LC 72-179178. (Illus.). reprint ed. 39.50 (*0-404-54808-3*) AMS Pr.

Physiography of the Rio Grande Valley, New Mexico in Relation to Pueblo Culture. Edgar L. Hewett. (Bureau of American Ethnology Bulletins Ser.). 76p. 1995. lib. bdg. 79.00 (*0-7812-4054-9*) Rprt Serv.

Physiolgcl Animal Ecolgy. Gideon N. Louw. 288p. (C). 1992. pap. text 54.50 (*0-582-05922-4*, Pub. by Addison-Wesley) Longman.

Physiologia: Natural Philosophy in Late Aristotelian & Cartesian Thought. Dennis Des Chene. (Illus.). 456p. 1996. text 45.00 (*0-8014-3072-0*) Cornell U Pr.

Physiologic & Chemical Basis for Metal Toxicity see Metal Toxicity in Mammals

Physiologic & Pharmacologic Bases of Anesthesia. Ed. by Vincent J. Collins. LC 95-14786. (Illus.). 890p. 1996. 89.00 (*0-683-02011-0*) Lppncott W & W.

Physiologic Basis of Obstetrics & Gynecology. David B. Seifer et al. 600p. text 79.00 (*0-683-30249-3*) Lppncott W & W.

Physiologic Basis of Surgery. Patrick J. O'Leary. Ed. by Lea R. Capote. LC 93-17306. (Illus.). 672p. 1993. 95.00 (*0-683-06634-X*) Lppncott W & W.

Physiologic Basis of Surgery. 2nd ed. Ed. by J. Patrick O'Leary & Lea R. Capote. LC 96-4702. (Illus.). 752p. 1996. write for info. (*0-683-06616-1*) Lppncott W & W.

Physiologic Foundations of Perinatal Care. Ed. by Leo Stern et al. LC 84-24813. 398p. 1984. 75.00 (*0-275-91454-2*, C14541, Praeger Pubs) Greenwood.

Physiological Acoustics. Ernest G. Wever & Merle Lawrence. LC 53-6389. 474p. 1954. reprint ed. pap. 147.00 (*0-7837-9370-7*, 206011300004) Bks Demand.

Physiological Activity of the Speech Organs: An Analysis of the Speech-Organs During the Phonation of Sung, Spoken, & Whispered Czech Vowels on the Basis of X-Ray Methods. Jana Ondrackova. Tr. by D. Short from DUT. LC 72-94494. (Illus.). 105p. 1973. text 46.15 (*90-279-2374-4*) Mouton.

Physiological Adaptability & Nutritional Status of the Japanese, Pt. 1. Japanese Committee for the International Biologica. LC 79-319071. (JIBP Synthesis Ser.: No. 3-4). 288p. 1975. pap. 89.30 (*0-608-01583-0*, 206200400001) Bks Demand.

Physiological Adaptability & Nutritional Status of the Japanese, Pt. 2. Japanese Committee for the International Biologica. LC 79-319071. (JIBP Synthesis Ser.: No. 3-4). 260p. 1975. pap. 80.60 (*0-608-01584-9*, 206200400002) Bks Demand.

Physiological Adaptability & Nutritional Status of the Japanese B, Vol. 4. Ed. by Asahina & R. Shigiya. (Japan International Biological Program Synthesis Ser.). 250p. 1975. 50.00 (*0-86008-214-8*, Pub. by U of Tokyo) Col U Pr.

Physiological Adaptations in Vertebrates: Respiration, Circulation & Metabolism. Ed. by Stephen C. Wood et al. (Lung Biology in Health & Disease Ser.: Vol. 56). (Illus.). 432p. 1991. text 230.00 (*0-8247-8558-4*) Dekker.

Physiological & Behavioral Effects of Food Constituents. Ed. by Richard J. Wurtman & Judith J. Wurtman. LC 83-9690. (Nutrition & the Brain Ser.: Vol. 6). 292p. reprint ed. pap. 90.60 (*0-608-04738-4*, 206545900004) Bks Demand.

Physiological & Biochemical Basis for Perinatal Medicine. Ed. by A. Minkowski & M. Monset-Couchard. (Illus.). xiv, 370p. 1981. 135.75 (*3-8055-1283-X*) S Karger.

Physiological & Biochemical Foundations of Therapeutics. Shirley D. Kraus. LC 80-67378. (Illus.). 259p. (Orig.). (C). 1982. pap. text 35.95 (*0-932126-33-2*) Graceway.

Physiological & Clinical Anatomy of the Domestic Mammals, Vol. 1, Central Nervous System. A. S. King. (Illus.). 212p. 1987. pap. 27.95 (*0-19-854187-2*) OUP.

Physiological & Clinical Aspects of Short Chain Fatty Acids. Ed. by J. H. Cummings et al. (Illus.). 595p. (C). 1995. text 150.00 (*0-521-44048-3*) Cambridge U Pr.

***Physiological & Ethological Responses of Pigs During Simulation of Transport.** Sabine Perremans. (Acta Biomedica Lovaniensia Ser.: No. 201). (Illus.). 156p. 1999. pap. 46.50 (*90-6186-974-9*, Pub. by Leuven Univ) Coronet Bks.

Physiological & Medical Observations among the Indians of Southwestern United States & Northern Mexico. Ales Hrdlicka. (Bureau of American Ethnology Bulletins Ser.). 460p. 1995. lib. bdg. 109.00 (*0-7812-4034-4*) Rprt Serv.

Physiological & Morphological Adaption & Evolution. Ed. by William A. Stini. (World Anthropology Ser.). xiv, 526p. 1979. text 72.35 (*90-279-7710-0*) Mouton.

Physiological & Pathological Aspects of Eye Movements. A. Roucoux & M. Crommelinck. 1982. text 249.00 (*90-6193-730-2*) Kluwer Academic.

Physiological & Pharmacological Aspects of the Reticulo-rumen. Ed. by L. A. Ooms & A. D. Degryse. (Current Topics in Veterinary Medicine & Animal Science Ser.). (C). 1987. text 218.00 (*0-89838-878-3*) Kluwer Academic.

Physiological & Psychological Considerations in the Management of Stroke. Arnold Brown. LC 72-7682. 160p. 1976. 12.50 (*0-87527-094-8*) Green.

Physiological & Psychophysiological Bases for Jungian Concepts: An Annotated Bibliography. Katherine Benziger. (Illus.). 45p. 1996. pap. 15.00 (*1-880931-08-7*) KBA Pub.

Physiological Aspects of Crop Yield. Ed. by J. D. Eastin. (Illus.). 396p. 1969. 5.60 (*0-89118-004-4*) Am Soc Agron.

Physiological Aspects of Deep Sea Biology. Alister G. MacDonald. LC 73-90652. (Physiological Society Monographs: No. 31). 464p. reprint ed. pap. 132.30 (*0-608-15748-1*, 2031685) Bks Demand.

Physiological Aspects of Digestion & Metabolism in Ruminants: Proceedings of the Seventh International Symposium on Ruminant Physiology. Ed. by T. Tsuda et al. (Illus.). 779p. (C). 1991. text 121.00 (*0-12-702290-2*) Acad Pr.

Physiological Aspects of Flight. Robert J. Del Vecchio. LC 77-82675. 1977. pap. 10.00 (*0-917428-05-6*, Dowling College) Global Pubns.

Physiological Aspects of Photosynthesis. O. V. Heath. 320p. 1969. 42.50 (*0-8047-0745-6*) Stanford U Pr.

Physiological Aspects of the Liquor Problem, 2 Vols. John S. Billings & Wilbur O. Atwater. 1977. 40.95 (*0-8369-6965-0*, 7846) Ayer.

Physiological Assessment of Human Fitness. Ed. by Peter J. Maud & Carl Foster. LC 94-40072. (Illus.). 304p. 1995. text 50.00 (*0-87322-776-X*, BMAU0776) Human Kinetics.

***Physiological Bases for Maize Improvement.** Ed. by Maria Elena Otegui & Gustavo A. Slafer. LC 00-22372. (Illus.). 265p. (C). 2000. lib. bdg. 69.95 (*1-56022-889-X*, Food Products) Haworth Pr.

Physiological Basis for Crop Growth & Development. Ed. by M. B. Tesar. 341p. 1984. 20.00 (*0-89118-037-0*) Am Soc Agron.

Physiological Basis for Exercise & Sport. 5th ed. Edward L. Fox et al. 736p. (C). 1993. text. write for info. (*0-697-12626-9*) Brown & Benchmark.

Physiological Basis for Exercise & Sport. 6th ed. Ann Fox et al. LC 97-13902. 720p. (C). 1997. text. write for info. (*0-697-25904-8*, WCB McGr Hill) McGrw-H Hghr Educ.

Physiological Basis Musculoskeletal Therapy. David J. Magee. 1997. text. write for info. (*0-7216-5982-9*, W B Saunders Co) Harcrt Hlth Sci Grp.

Physiological Basis of Aging & Geriatrics. 2nd rev. ed. Ed. by Paola S. Timiras. LC 93-44066. Orig. Title: Physiological Basis of Geriatrics. 336p. 1994. boxed set 104.95 (*0-8493-8979-8*) CRC Pr.

Physiological Basis of Anxiety. (Journal: Psychopathology: Vol. 17, Suppl. 1). (Illus.). 120p. 1984. pap. 31.50 (*3-8055-3812-X*) S Karger.

Physiological Basis of Behaviour: Neural & Hormonal Processes. Kevin Silber. LC 98-33671. (Modular Psychology Ser.). 1999. 50.00 (*0-415-18653-6*); pap. 12.99 (*0-415-18654-4*) Routledge.

Physiological Basis of Geriatrics see Physiological Basis of Aging & Geriatrics

Physiological Basis of Geriatrics. Paola S. Timiras. 448p. 1988. 62.95 (*0-02-420810-8*, Macmillan Coll) P-H.

Physiological Basis of Health Standards for Dwellings. M. S. Goromosov. (Public Health Papers: No. 33). 99p. 1968. pap. text 5.00 (*92-4-130033-7*, 1110033) World Health.

Physiological Basis of Occupational Health: Stressful Environments. Ed. by Keizo Shiraki et al. LC 97-107047. (Progress in Biometeorology Ser.: Vol. 11). (Illus.). 280p. 1996. 105.00 (*90-5103-127-0*, Pub. by SPB Acad Pub) Balogh.

Physiological Basis of Primary Care. rev. ed. Patrick Eggena. (Illus.). 734p. 1998. pap. text 59.95 (*0-9663441-0-3*) Novateur Med.

Physiological Basis of Rehabilitation Medicine. 2nd ed. Ed. by John A. Downey et al. LC 93-37020. (Illus.). 766p. 1994. text 140.00 (*1-56372-080-9*) Buttrwrth-Heinemann.

Physiological Basis of Starling's Law of the Heart. CIBA Foundation Staff. LC 74-77177. (CIBA Foundation Symposium: New Ser.: No. 24). 308p. reprint ed. pap. 95.50 (*0-608-13985-8*, 202215300024) Bks Demand.

Physiological Basis of Ventilatory Support. Ed. by John J. Marini & Arthur S. Slutsky. LC 98-4262. (Lung Biology in Health & Disease Ser.). (Illus.). 1480p. 1998. text 295.00 (*0-8247-9861-9*) Dekker.

Physiological Chemistry of Domestic Animals. Rudolf Clarenburg. (Illus.). 448p. (gr. 13). 1992. pap. text 56.00 (*0-8016-6953-7*, 06953) Mosby Inc.

Physiological Chemistry of Exercise & Training. Ed. by P. E. Di Prampero & J. R. Poortmans. (Medicine & Sport Science Ser.: Vol. 13). (Illus.). viii, 216p. 1981. 85.25 (*3-8055-2028-X*) S Karger.

Physiological Chemistry of Training & Detraining. Ed. by J. R. Poortmans & P. Marconnet. (Medicine & Sport Science Ser.: Vol. 17). (Illus.). xii, 264p. 1984. 172.25 (*3-8055-3764-6*) S Karger.

Physiological-comparative, perception, learning, cognitive, & developmental see Handbook of Demonstrations & Activities in Teaching of Psychology

Physiological Concept of Love in the Elizabethan & Early Stuart Drama. L. Babb. 1972. 59.95 (*0-8490-0833-6*) Gordon Pr.

Physiological Control of Mammalian Vocalization. Ed. by J. D. Newman. (Illus.). 438p. 1988. 105.00 (*0-306-43003-7*, Plenum Trade) Perseus Pubng.

***Physiological Control Systems.** Michael C. Khoo. LC 99-27107. (Series in Biomedical Engineering). 1999. 89.95 (*0-7803-3408-6*) IEEE Standards.

Physiological Correlates of Human Behaviour, Vol. 3. Ed. by Anthony Gale & John A. Edwards. 308p. 1986. pap. text 55.00 (*0-12-273906-X*) Acad Pr.

Physiological Correlates of Human Behaviour Vol. 1: Basic Issues. John A. Edwards. 350p. 1986. pap. text 56.00 (*0-12-273904-3*) Acad Pr.

Physiological Correlates of Psychological Disorder: Proceedings of an Interdisciplinary Research Conference Sponsored by the Wisconsin Psychiatric Institute & the Dept. of Psychiatry of the University of Wisconsin Medical Center, August 29-31, 1961. Ed. by Robert Roessler & Norman S. Greenfield. LC 62-15990. 294p. reprint ed. pap. 91.20 (*0-608-14474-6*, 202114500021) Bks Demand.

Physiological Correspondences. John Worcester. (Illus.). 432p. 1987. reprint ed. 16.95 (*0-915221-64-0*) Swedenborg Sci Assn.

***Physiological Diversity & Its Ecological Implications.** John I. Spicer & Kevin J. Gaston. LC 99-16986. (Illus.). 2000. pap. 59.95 (*0-632-05452-2*) Blackwell Sci.

Physiological Ecology of Harmful Algal Blooms. Ed. by D. M. Anderson et al. LC 98-5063. (NATO ASI Ser.: Series G, Vol. 41). (Illus.). xix, 662p. 1998. 275.00 (*3-540-64117-3*) Spr-Verlag.

Physiological Ecology of North American Desert Plants. Stanley D. Smith et al. LC 96-27909. (Adaptations of Desert Organisms Ser.). 200p. 1996. 179.50 (*3-540-53113-0*) Spr-Verlag.

Physiological Ecology of the Alpine Timberline. W. Tranquillini. (Ecological Studies: Vol. 31). (Illus.). 1979. 45.00 (*0-387-09065-7*) Spr-Verlag.

Physiological Ecology of Tropical Plants. Ulrich Luttge. LC 96-52359. 392p. 1997. 45.95 (*3-540-61161-4*) Spr-Verlag.

Physiological Ecology of Woody Plants. Theodore T. Kozlowski et al. (Physiological Ecology Ser.). 657p. 1990. text 84.00 (*0-12-424160-3*) Acad Pr.

Physiological Engineering Aspects of Penicillium Chrysogenum. 250p. 1997. lib. bdg. 34.00 (*981-02-2765-5*) World Scientific Pub.

Physiological Enigma of Woman: The Mystery of Menstruation. Raymond W. Bernard. 183p. 1996. reprint ed. spiral bd. 16.00 (*0-7873-1214-2*) Hlth Research.

Physiological Fluid Dynamics Vol. 3: Papers of the 3rd International Conference of Physiological Fluid. Ed. by N. V. Swamy & Madan G. Singh. (Illus.). xii, 378p. 1993. 101.00 (*0-387-54266-3*) Spr-Verlag.

Physiological Function in Special Environments. Ed. by C. V. Paganelli & Leon E. Farhi. (Illus.). 240p. 1989. 141.00 (*0-387-96833-4*) Spr-Verlag.

Physiological Genetics of Agricultural Crops. Andor Balint. 166p. (C). 1984. 50.00 (*963-05-3288-3*, Pub. by Akade Kiado) St Mut.

Physiological Limitations & the Genetic Improvement of Symbiotic Nitrogen Fixation. Ed. by F. O. Gara et al. (Advances in Agricultural Biotechnology Ser.). (C). 1988. text 107.50 (*90-247-3692-7*) Kluwer Academic.

Physiological Limitations to Human Exercise Tolerance. Ed. by B. J. Whipp. (Studies in Physiology: Vol. 4). (Illus.). 192p. (C). Date not set. pap. text 37.40 (*1-85578-026-7*, Pub. by Portland Pr Ltd) Ashgate Pub Co.

Physiological Mammalogy, 2 vols. Ed. by William V. Mayer & R. G. Van Gelder. Incl. Vol. 1. 1964. 63.00 (*0-12-481001-2*); Vol. 2. 1964. 63.00 (*0-12-481002-0*); 1964. write for info. (*0-318-50336-0*) Acad Pr.

Physiological Measurements with Radionuclides in Clinical Practice. A. M. Peters & M. J. Myers. LC 97-21585. (Illus.). 318p. 1998. text 73.00 (*0-19-261994-2*) OUP.

Physiological Mechanisms of Piano Technique. Otto Ortmann. LC 80-26521. (Music Ser.). (Illus.). xvi, 396p. 1981. reprint ed. lib. bdg. 52.50 (*0-306-76058-4*) Da Capo.

***Physiological Medicine.** Vishwanath R. Lingappa. (Illus.). 550p. 1999. pap. text. write for info. (*0-07-038128-3*) McGraw-Hill HPD.

Physiological Models in Microbiology, 2 vols., Set. Michael J. Bazin & James I. Prosser. LC 87-18330. 1988. reprint ed. 184.00 (*0-8493-5953-8*, CRC Reprint) Franklin.

Physiological Models in Microbiology, 2 vols., Vol. I. Ed. by Michael J. Bazin & James I. Prosser. 160p. 1988. 90.00 (*0-8493-5954-6*, QR84, CRC Reprint) Franklin.

Physiological Models in Microbiology, 2 vols., Vol. II. Ed. by Michael J. Bazin & James I. Prosser. 160p. 1988. 95.00 (*0-8493-5955-4*, QR84, CRC Reprint) Franklin.

Physiological Monitoring & Instrument Diagnosis in Perinatal & Neonatal Medicine. Ed. by Yves W. Brans & William W. Hay, Jr. (Illus.). 407p. (C). 1995. text 145.00 (*0-521-41951-4*) Cambridge U Pr.

Physiological Optics. Y. LeGrand & S. G. El Hage. (Optical Sciences Ser.: Vol. 13). (Illus.). 350p. 1980. 73.95 (*0-387-09919-0*) Spr-Verlag.

Physiological Origins of Heart Sounds & Murmurs CD-ROM. J. Michael Criley. 1995. 149.95 (*0-316-16154-3*, Little Brwn Med Div) Lppncott W & W.

Physiological-Pathological Interactions Affecting Seed Deterioration. Ed. by S. H. West. (Special Publication Ser.: Vol. 12). 95p. 1986. 15.00 (*0-89118-524-0*) Crop Sci Soc Am.

Physiological Peptides & New Trends in Radioimmunology. Ed. by C. A. Bizollon. 370p. 1984. 136.25 (*0-444-80358-0*) Elsevier.

Physiological Pharmaceutics. Clive G. Wilson & Neena Washington. 1989. text 69.95 (*0-470-21545-3*) P-H.

Physiological Plant Anatomy. G. Haberlandt. 777p. 1979. reprint ed. 20.00 (*0-88065-098-2*) Scholarly Pubns.

Physiological Plant Anatomy. 4th ed. G. Haberlandt. Tr. by M. Drummond from GER. 398p. 1979. reprint ed. lib. bdg. 17.50 (*0-934454-89-2*) Lubrecht & Cramer.

P

An Asterisk (*) at the beginning of an entry indicates that the title is appearing for the first time.

Physiological Plant Anatomy. 4th ed. G. Haberlandt. Tr. by Montagu Drummond from GER. 777p. 1990. reprint ed. text 35.00 (*0-945454-89-9*, Pub. by Today Tomorrow) Lubrecht & Cramer.

Physiological Plant Biology IV: Ecosystems Processes - Mineral Cycling, Productivity, & Man's Influence. Ed. by O. L. Lange et al. (Encyclopedia of Plant Physiology Ser.: Vol. 12 D). (Illus.). 690p. 1983. 362.95 (*0-387-10908-0*) Spr-Verlag.

Physiological Plant Ecology. rev. ed. Tr. by M. A. Biederman-Thorson. LC 79-26396. (Illus.). 304p. 1980. 34.00 (*3-540-09795-3*) Spr-Verlag.

Physiological Plant Ecology: Ecophysiology & Stress Physiology of Function Groups. 3rd ed. Walter Larcher. LC 94-24405.Tr. of Okophysiologie der Pflanzen. 506p. 1995. 47.95 (*0-387-58116-2*) Spr-Verlag.

Physiological Plant Ecology: Ecophysiology & Stress Physiology of Functional Groups. 3rd ed. Walter Larcher. 1997. 53.95 (*3-540-58116-2*) Spr-Verlag.

***Physiological Plant Ecology: The 39th Symposium of the British Ecological Society, Held at the University of York, 7-9 September 1998.** British Ecological Society Staff et al. LC 99-29393. (British Ecological Society Symposium Ser.: Vol. 39). (Illus.). 2000. pap. 49.95 (*0-632-05491-3*) Blackwell Sci.

Physiological Plant Ecology I: Responses to the Physical Environment. Ed. by O. L. Lange et al. (Encyclopedia of Plant Physiology Ser.: Vol. 12 A). (Illus.). 625p. 1981. 294.95 (*0-387-10763-0*) Spr-Verlag.

Physiological Plant Ecology III: Responses to the Chemical & Biological Environment. Ed. by O. L. Lange et al. (Encyclopedia of Plant Physiology Ser.: Vol. 12C). (Illus.). 850p. 1983. 362.95 (*0-387-10907-2*) Spr-Verlag.

Physiological Plant Ecology II: Water Relations & Carbon Assimilation. O. L. Lange et al. (Encyclopedia of Plant Physiology Ser.: Vol. 12 B). (Illus.). 153p. 1982. 362.95 (*0-387-10906-4*) Spr-Verlag.

Physiological Plant Pathology. Ed. by Rudolph Heitefuss & P. H. Willaims. (Encyclopedia of Plant Physiology Ser.: Vol. 4). 1976. 269.95 (*0-387-07557-7*) Spr-Verlag.

Physiological Potential of Yield Improvement of Annual Oil & Protein Crops. Wulf Diepenbrock & Heiko Becker. 291p. 1995. pap. 43.00 (*3-8263-3020-X*, Pub. by Blckwell Wissenschafts) Balogh.

Physiological Programmatics of the Nineteenth Century. Ed. by William Coleman & I. Bernard Cohen. LC 80-2107. (Development of Science Ser.). (Illus.). 1981. lib. bdg. 55.95 (*0-405-13872-5*) Ayer.

Physiological Psychology. Smock. 1998. pap. text, student ed. 17.70 (*0-13-095802-6*) P-H.

Physiological Psychology. 2nd ed. Marvin Schwartz. LC 77-17438. (Century Psychology Ser.). (Illus.). 1978. 27.95 (*0-685-03895-5*) P-H.

Physiological Psychology: A Neuroscience Approach. Smock. LC 98-26733. 511p. 1998. 86.00 (*0-13-673112-0*) P-H.

***Physiological Psychology: Neuroscience Approach.** 1998. write for info. (*0-13-020570-2*) P-H.

Physiological Psychology: Study Guide. Robert B. Graham. (Psychology Ser.). 1990. mass mkt., student ed. 19.50 (*0-534-10105-4*) Brooks-Cole.

Physiological Psychology Dictionary: A Reference Guide for Students & Professionals. George S. Grosser & Carol S. Spafford. LC 94-18010. 368p. (C). 1994. pap. 16.88 (*0-07-059860-6*) McGraw.

Physiological Researches on Life & Death. Marie F. Bichat. Ed. by Robert J. Kastenbaum. Tr. by F. Gold et al. LC 76-19561. (Death & Dying Ser.). 1977. reprint ed. lib. bdg. 33.95 (*0-405-09557-0*) Ayer.

Physiological Researches on Life & Death, 2. Xavier Bichat. Tr. by F. Gold from FRE. LC 77-72191. (Contributions to the History of Psychology Ser.: Vol. II, Pt. E, Physiological Psychology). 302p. 1978. reprint ed. lib. bdg. 89.50 (*0-313-26950-5*, U6950, Greenwood Pr) Greenwood.

Physiological Signal Processing, Modelling & System Implementation in Cardiography, Speech & Hearing. R. H. Mitchell. 201p. 1994. pap. text 196.00 (*2-88124-991-4*) Gordon & Breach.

Physiological Strategies for Gas Exchange & Metabolism. Ed. by A. J. Woakes et al. (Society for Experimental Biology Seminar Ser.: No. 41). (Illus.). 281p. (C). 1991. text 95.00 (*0-521-36602-X*) Cambridge U Pr.

Physiological Studies of Consciousness. Robert E. Ornstein. 20p. 1973. pap. 6.00 (*0-904674-00-2*, Pub. by Octagon Pr) ISHK.

Physiological Testing of the High-Performance Athlete. 2nd ed. Ed. by J. Duncan MacDougall et al. LC 90-35488. 448p. (C). 1990. text 46.00 (*0-87322-300-4*, BMAC0300) Human Kinetics.

***Physiological Tests for Elite Athletes.** Australian Sports Commission. LC 99-88959. (Illus.). 480p. 2000. 69.00 (*0-7360-0326-6*) Human Kinetics.

Physiological Theory & the Doctrine of the Mean in Plato & Aristotle. Theodore J. Tracy. LC 68-23201. (Loyola University Studies in Philosophy: No. 17). 398p. reprint ed. 123.40 (*0-8357-9430-X*, 201702200006) Bks Demand.

Physiological Tremor, Pathological Tremor & Clonus. Ed. by J. E. Desmedt. (Progress in Clinical Neurophysiology Ser.: Vol. 5). (Illus.). 1978. 85.25 (*3-8055-2713-6*) S Karger.

Physiological Variation & Its Genetic Basis. Ed. by J. S. Weiner. (Symposia of the Society for the Study of Human Biology Ser.: Vol. 17). 180p. 1977. 36.00 (*0-85066-108-0*) Taylor & Francis.

Physiologie. Maurice Fontaine. (Methodique Ser.). 1956p. 52.50 (*0-686-56432-4*) Fr & Eur.

Physiologie de la Reproduction des Bovins Trypanotolerants: Synthese des Connaissances Actuelles. (FRE.). 156p. 1993. 15.00 (*92-5-203372-6*, FF3726, Pub. by FAO) Bernan Associates.

Physiologie des Lumieres: Empirisme, Modeles et Theories. Francois Duchesneau. 640p. 1982. lib. bdg. 287.50 (*90-247-2500-3*) Kluwer Academic.

Physiologie du Mariage. Honore de Balzac. (FRE.). 448p. 1987. pap. 11.95 (*0-7859-2063-3*, 2070378322) Fr & Eur.

Physiologie du Mariage. Honore de Balzac. (Folio Ser.: No. 1832). (FRE.). pap. 7.95 (*2-07-037809-8*) Schoenhof.

Physiologie du Mariage. Honore de Balzac. Ed. by Maurice Regard. (Folio Ser.: No. 1832). (FRE.). 320p. 1968. 9.95 (*2-07-037832-2*) Schoenhof.

Physiologoe des Scherzes: Bedeutung und Rechtfertigung der Ars Jocandi Im 16. Heinz G. Schmitz. (Deutsche Volksbucher in Faksimiledrucken Ser.: Reihe B, Bd. 2). (GER.). vii, 290p. 1972. write for info. (*3-487-04246-0*) G Olms Pubs.

Physiologus. Ed. by Francesco Sbordone. cxviii, 322p. 1991. reprint ed. write for info. (*3-487-06033-7*) G Olms Pubs.

Physiology. (C). 1988. lab manual ed. write for info. (*0-8087-5801-2*) Pearson Custom.

Physiology. Costanzo. (Board Review Ser.). 1994. 19.95 (*0-685-75156-2*) Lppncott W & W.

Physiology. Linda S. Costanzo. Ed. by William Schmitt. LC 97-28809. (Text & Review Ser.). (Illus.). 416p. 1998. pap. text 29.95 (*0-7216-6611-6*, W B Saunders Co) Harcrt Hlth Sci Grp.

Physiology. McGeown. 1996. pap. text 22.95 (*0-443-05196-8*, W B Saunders Co) Harcrt Hlth Sci Grp.

Physiology. Montani. 1997. pap. text. write for info. (*0-7216-5058-9*, W B Saunders Co) Harcrt Hlth Sci Grp.

Physiology. Ed. by R. Theis & Robert J. Person. (Oklahoma Notes Ser.). viii, 263p. 1991. pap. 17.95 (*0-387-97039-8*) Spr-Verlag.

Physiology. Ed. by R. Thies & Robert J. Person. (Oklahoma Notes Ser.). x, 237p. (C). 1988. pap. 15.95 (*0-387-96340-5*) Spr-Verlag.

Physiology. John F. Fulton. LC 75-23655. (Clio Medica Ser.: 5). (Illus.). reprint ed. 34.50 (*0-404-58905-7*) AMS Pr.

Physiology. rev. ed. Paulev. 1996. pap. text, student ed. 26.00 (*0-7020-2043-5*, W B Saunders Co) Harcrt Hlth Sci Grp.

Physiology. 2nd ed. (National Medical Ser.). 1991. 25.00 (*0-685-75183-X*) Lppncott W & W.

Physiology. 2nd ed. J. Bullock et al. (National Medical Ser.). (Illus.). 501p. 1991. 25.00 (*0-683-06258-1*) Lppncott W & W.

***Physiology.** 2nd ed. Linda S. Costanzo. LC 98-7540. (Board Review Ser.). 326p. 1998. 24.95 (*0-683-30396-1*) Lppncott W & W.

Physiology. 3rd ed. (National Medical Ser.). 1994. 25.00 (*0-685-75184-8*) Lppncott W & W.

Physiology. 3rd ed. John Bullock et al. LC 93-23683. (National Medical Series for Independent Study). (Illus.). 648p. 1995. 25.00 (*0-683-06259-X*) Lppncott W & W.

Physiology. 3rd ed. R. Scott Thies. (Oklahoma Notes Ser.). (Illus.). 280p. 1994. 17.95 (*0-387-97778-3*) Spr-Verlag.

Physiology. 4th ed. Robert M. Berne & Levy. LC 97-38215. (Illus.). 1232p. (C). (gr. 13). 1998. text 60.00 (*0-8151-0952-0*, 31012) Mosby Inc.

Physiology. 4th ed. Roger Thies. LC 94-45261. (Oklahoma Notes Ser.). 280p. 1995. 17.95 (*0-387-94397-8*) Spr-Verlag.

***Physiology.** 5th ed. (C). 2000. lab manual ed. 20.00 (*0-8087-0589-X*) Pearson Custom.

Physiology. 5th ed. Ewald E. Selkurt. 691p. 1984. 34.00 (*0-316-78038-3*, Little Brwn Med Div) Lppncott W & W.

Physiology. 9th ed. Ed. by James P. Ryan & Ronald F. Tuma. (Basic Sciences: Pretest Self Assessment & Review Ser.). (Illus.). 291p. 1998. pap. 18.95 (*0-07-052691-5*) McGraw-Hill HPD.

Physiology see Nephrology: Proceedings of the International Congress, 5th, Mexico, 1972

Physiology: An Illustrated Review with Questions & Explanations. 2nd ed. Charles H. Tadlock et al. LC 95-10424. (Illus.). 344p. 1995. pap. text 32.00 (*0-316-82764-9*) Lppncott W & W.

Physiology: Digging up the Bones, Vol. 8. Nikos M. Linardakis. LC 98-10208. (Digging Up the Bones Medical Review Ser.). (Illus.). 1998. pap. 18.95 (*0-07-038221-2*) McGraw-Hill HPD.

Physiology: MEPC. 9th ed. David G. Penney. (Illus.). 255p. (C). 1996. pap. text 21.95 (*0-8385-6222-1*, A6222-2, Apple Lange Med) McGraw.

Physiology: Pretest Self-Assessment & Review. 4th ed. Craig A. Dise. LC 85-12839. vii, 201p. 1985. write for info. (*0-07-051946-3*) McGraw-Hill HPD.

Physiology: Pretest Self-Assessment & Review. 5th ed. Craig Dise. 1988. pap. text 15.95 (*0-07-051967-6*) McGraw.

Physiology: Pretest Self-Assessment & Review. 6th ed. Eileen M. Mulligan. LC 90-5599. vii, 195 p. 1991. write for info. (*0-07-051978-1*) McGraw-Hill HPD.

Physiology: Renal Filtration. Tortora. (C). 1993. pap., teacher ed. 44.33 (*0-06-502197-5*) HarpC.

Physiology: Review for New National Boards. Emma R. Jakoi & Ronald C. Bohn. LC 94-75277. (Illus.). 230p. 1994. pap. 25.00 (*0-9632873-4-6*) J & S Pub VA.

Physiology: Scientific Basis Physics. Bovell. 1995. pap. text 41.50 (*0-7020-1936-4*, W B Saunders Co) Harcrt Hlth Sci Grp.

Physiology: Ssr Section F, Vol. 10, No. 2. 62p. 1997. pap. text 31.00 (*3-7186-5767-8*, Harwood Acad Pubs) Gordon & Breach.

Physiology: Ssr Section F, Vol. 10, No. 4. 58p. 1997. pap. text 29.00 (*3-7186-5769-4*, Harwood Acad Pubs) Gordon & Breach.

***Physiology: The Basis of Clinical Practice.** Glenn Irion. (Illus.). 432p. 2000. text 35.00 (*1-55642-380-2*) SLACK Inc.

***Physiology: The Basis of Clinical Practice Instructor's Manual.** Glenn Irion. 96p. 2000. pap. text, teacher ed. write for info. (*1-55642-424-8*) SLACK Inc.

***Physiology: 2000 Multiple-Choice Questions & Answers.** 298p. 1999. spiral bd. 25.95 (*1-893720-02-0*) Biotest.

Physiology & Anatomy. write for info. (*0-340-63190-2*, Pub. by E A) Routldge.

Physiology & Anatomy: A Basis for Nursing & Health Care. Sigrid Rutishauser. LC 94-27137. (C). 1994. pap. text 39.95 (*0-443-04151-2*) Church.

Physiology & Anatomy: A Homeostatic Approach. John Clancy & Andrew McVicar. (Illus.). 736p. (Orig.). 1995. pap. text 47.99 (*1-56593-614-0*, 1274) Singular Publishing.

***Physiology & Applied Anatomy for Veterinary Nurses.** College of Animal Welfare Staff. (Illus.). 500p. 2001. pap. 49.50 (*0-7506-4802-3*) Buttrwrth-Heinemann.

Physiology & Behavior Therapy: Conceptual Guidelines for the Clinician. J. G. Hollandsworth, Jr. (Behavioral Psychophysiology Ser.). (Illus.). 256p. (C). 1986. 49.50 (*0-306-42180-1*, Plenum Trade) Perseus Pubng.

Physiology & Biochemistry of Auxins in Plants. M. Kutacek et al. 428p. 1988. 150.00 (*90-5103-010-X*, Pub. by SPB Acad Pub) Balogh.

Physiology & Biochemistry of Cestodes. Donald P. McManus & James D. Smyth. (Illus.). 416p. (C). 1989. text 120.00 (*0-521-35557-5*) Cambridge U Pr.

Physiology & Biochemistry of Cytokinins in Plants. Ed. by M. Kaminek et al. (Illus.). xii, 485p. 1991. 137.50 (*90-5103-066-5*, Pub. by SPB Acad Pub) Balogh.

Physiology & Biochemistry of Exercise. Roy J. Shephard. LC 84-24862. 560p. 1982. 95.00 (*0-275-91380-5*, C1380, Praeger Pubs) Greenwood.

Physiology & Biochemistry of Free-Living & Plant-Parasitic Nematodes. Roland N. Perry & Denise J. Wright. LC 98-23906. (Illus.). 464p. 1998. text 120.00 (*0-85199-231-5*) OUP.

Physiology & Biochemistry of Muscle As a Food, Vol. 1. Ed. by Ernest J. Briskey et al. LC 66-22849. (Illus.). 453p. reprint ed. pap. 140.50 (*0-7837-7020-0*, 204683600001) Bks Demand.

Physiology & Biochemistry of Muscle As a Food, Vol. 2. Ed. by Ernest J. Briskey et al. LC 66-22849. (Illus.). 859p. reprint ed. pap. 200.00 (*0-7837-7021-9*, 204683600002) Bks Demand.

Physiology & Biochemistry of Plant Cell Walls. C. T. Brett & K. Waldron. (Topics in Plant Physiology Ser.). 240p. 1989. 49.95 (*0-04-581034-6*) Routledge.

Physiology & Biochemistry of Plant Cell Walls. C. T. Brett & K. Waldron. (Topics in Plant Physiology Ser.). 240p. (C). 1989. pap. text 24.95 (*0-04-581035-4*) Routledge.

Physiology & Biochemistry of Plant Cell Walls. C. T. Brett & K. W. Waldron. 1996. text. write for info. (*0-412-72020-5*) Kluwer Academic.

Physiology & Biochemistry of Plant Cell Walls. 2nd ed. C. T. Brett & K. W. Waldron. (Topics in Plant Functional Biology Ser.). (Illus.). 256p. 1995. pap. write for info. (*0-412-58060-8*) Kluwer Academic.

Physiology & Biochemistry of Plant-Microbial Interactions: Proceedings of the Eleventh Annual Symposium on Plant Physiology. Ed. by Noel T. Keen et al. LC 88-70333. 106p. 1988. pap. text 20.00 (*0-943088-12-7*) Am Soc of Plan.

Physiology & Biochemistry of Plant-Pathogen Interactions. I. J. Misaghi. LC 82-18594. 304p. (C). 1982. 65.00 (*0-306-41059-1*, Plenum Trade) Perseus Pubng.

Physiology & Biochemistry of Prokaryotes. 2nd ed. David White. LC 98-38420. (Illus.). 600p. (C). 1999. text 59.95 (*0-19-512579-7*) OUP.

Physiology & Biochemistry of Seeds in Relation to Germination: Viability, Dormancy, & Environmental Control, Vol. 2. M. Black & J. D. Bewley. (Illus.). 380p. 1983. 163.95 (*0-387-11656-7*) Spr-Verlag.

Physiology & Biochemistry of Sterols. Ed. by Glenn W. Patterson & W. David Nes. 395p. (C). 1992. 85.00 (*0-935315-38-1*) Am Oil Chemists.

Physiology & Biochemistry of the Domestic Fowl, Vol. 4. Ed. by B. M. Freeman. 1983. text 157.00 (*0-12-267104-X*) Acad Pr.

Physiology & Biochemistry of the Uterus in Pregnancy & Labor. Ed. by Gabor Huszar. 328p. 1985. 187.00 (*0-8493-5997-X*, RG558, CRC Reprint) Franklin.

Physiology & Biophysics of the Circulation: An Introductory Text. 2nd ed. Alan C. Burton. LC 70-182003. (Physiology Ser.). 240p. reprint ed. pap. 74.40 (*0-608-13466-X*, 202273200029) Bks Demand.

Physiology & Determination of Crop Yield. Ed. by K. J. Boote et al. LC 94-12436. 601p. 1994. 66.00 (*0-89118-122-9*) Am Soc Agron.

Physiology & Form of Fish Circulation. Geoffrey H. Satchell. (Illus.). 253p. (C). 1991. text 74.95 (*0-521-39519-4*) Cambridge U Pr.

***Physiology & Function from Multidimensional Images.** Ed. by Chin T. Chen & Anne V. Clough. 524p. 1999. pap. text 103.00 (*0-8194-3132-X*) SPIE.

Physiology & General Biology: Reviews, Vol. 1, Part A. T. M. Turpaev et al. xiv, 410p. 1987. text 814.00 (*3-7186-0312-8*) Gordon & Breach.

Physiology & General Biology: Reviews, Vol. 2. T. M. Turpaev et al. xvi, 376p. 1988. text 711.00 (*3-7186-0458-2*) Gordon & Breach.

Physiology & General Biology: Reviews, Vol. 2. rev. ed. T. M. Turpaev et al. xii, 354p. 1988. text 697.00 (*3-7186-0457-4*) Gordon & Breach.

Physiology & General Biology Review Pt. 1: Part 1: Neurohormonal Regulation of the Gonad Function in Mammals, Vol. 6. O. N. Savchenko & O. A. Danilova. (Soviet Scientific Reviews Ser.). 78p. 1993. pap. text 96.00 (*3-7186-5379-6*, Harwood Acad Pubs) Gordon & Breach.

Physiology & General Biology Reviews, Vol. 6. T. M. Turpaev. (Soviet Scientific Reviews Ser.: Section F). 82p. 1993. pap. text 123.00 (*3-7186-5455-5*) Gordon & Breach.

Physiology & General Biology Reviews: Developmental Biology, Vol. 1, Part B. T. M. Turpaev & N. G. Khrushchov. (Soviet Scientific Reviews Ser.: Vol. 1, Pt. B). xv, 370p. 1987. text 677.00 (*3-7186-0407-8*) Gordon & Breach.

Physiology & General Biology Reviews: Part 5, Pt. 5. T. M. Turpaev. (Soviet Scientific Reviews Ser). 96p. 1992. pap. text 107.00 (*3-7186-5323-0*, Harwood Acad Pubs) Gordon & Breach.

Physiology & General Biology Reviews: Physiology & General Biology Reviews : Philopatry of Migratory Birds, Vol. 11, Pt. 2. L. V. Sokolov. (Soviet Scientific Reviews Ser.). 58p. 1997. pap. text 22.00 (*90-5702-231-1*, Harwood Acad Pubs) Gordon & Breach.

Physiology & General Biology Reviews No. 2: No. 2: Effect of Radioactive Contamination (Chernobyl Nuclear Power Plant), Vol. 8. T. M. Turpaev. (Soviet Scientific Reviews Ser). 174p. 1994. pap. text 95.00 (*3-7186-5607-8*, Harwood Acad Pubs) Gordon & Breach.

Physiology & General Biology Reviews No. 3: No. 3: Ion Transport Across Erythrocyte Membrane, Vol. 8. E. T. Turpaev. (Soviet Scientific Reviews Ser). 48p. 1994. pap. text 72.00 (*3-7186-5666-3*, Harwood Acad Pubs) Gordon & Breach.

Physiology & General Biology Reviews No. 4: No. 4: The APUD System in Normal & Pathological States, Vol. 8. E. T. Turpaev. (Soviet Scientific Reviews Ser). 44p. 1994. pap. text 65.00 (*3-7186-5667-1*, Harwood Acad Pubs) Gordon & Breach.

Physiology & General Biology Reviews Pt. 1: Energetics & Avian Behavior, Vol. 11. V M. Gavrilov. (Soviet Scientific Reviews Ser.). 225p. 1997. pap. text 87.00 (*90-5702-255-9*, Harwood Acad Pubs) Gordon & Breach.

Physiology & General Biology Reviews Pt. 2: Bird Comparitive Ethology, Vol. 12. 2nd ed. E. N. Panov. (Soviet Scientific Reviews Ser.). 125p. 1997. pap. text 48.00 (*90-5702-234-6*, Harwood Acad Pubs) Gordon & Breach.

Physiology & General Biology Reviews Pt. 5: Haematopoiesis During Chronic Irradiation, Vol. 10. V. G. Tyazhelova. (Soviet Scientific Reviews Ser.). 52p. 1997. pap. text 17.00 (*3-7186-5830-5*, Harwood Acad Pubs) Gordon & Breach.

Physiology & General Biology Reviews Vol. 3, Pt. 5.2: Progress & Problems in Population Biology, Vol. 3. A. V. Yablokov. (Soviet Scientific Reviews Ser.: Section F). 176p. 1989. pap. text 91.00 (*3-7186-4978-0*, Harwood Acad Pubs) Gordon & Breach.

Physiology & General Biology Reviews Vol. 5, Pt. 1: Problems of Internal Inhibitions - the Dominant & the Conditioned Reflex, Vol. 5. V. G. Gassanov. (Soviet Scientific Reviews Ser.: Section F). iv, 71p. 1991. text 75.00 (*3-7186-5160-2*, Harwood Acad Pubs) Gordon & Breach.

Physiology & General Biology Reviews Vol. 5, Pt. 2: Relay Functions of Hippocampal Monoamines in Acquired & Inborn Forms of Behavior - Physiological, Vol. 5. G. G. Gasanov. (Soviet Scientific Reviews Ser.: Section F). 79p. 1991. text 77.00 (*3-7186-5161-0*, Harwood Acad Pubs) Gordon & Breach.

Physiology & General Biology Reviews Vol. 5, Pt. 3: A New Ideology of Studies of the Neurophysiological Correlates to Mental Activity, Vol. 5. S. V. Medvedev. (Soviet Scientific Reviews Ser.: Section F). 50p. 1991. text 52.00 (*3-7186-5177-7*, Harwood Acad Pubs) Gordon & Breach.

Physiology & General Biology Reviews Vol. 5, Pt. 4: The Neural Mechanisms of Conscious & Unconcious Perception, Vol. 5. E. A. Kostandov. (Soviet Scientific Reviews Ser.: Section F). iv, 51p. 1991. text 52.00 (*3-7186-5176-9*, Harwood Acad Pubs) Gordon & Breach.

Physiology & General Biology Reviews Vol. 6, No. 3: Possible Mechanisms of the Neostriatum in Regulation of Voluntary Movement, Vol. 6. T. M. Turpaev. (Soviet Scientific Reviews Ser.: Section F). 85p. 1994. pap. text 99.00 (*3-7186-5475-X*, Harwood Acad Pubs) Gordon & Breach.

Physiology & General Biology Reviews Vol. 6, No. 4: Vitamins A & D in the Exchange of Divalent Cations, Vol. 6. T. M. Turpaev. (Soviet Scientific Reviews Ser.: Section F). 56p. 1994. pap. text 65.00 (*3-7186-5474-1*, Harwood Acad Pubs) Gordon & Breach.

Physiology & General Biology Reviews Vol. 6, No. 5: Neurophysiology of Mammalian Locomotion, Vol. 6. T. M. Turpaev. (Soviet Scientific Reviews Ser.: Section F). 50p. 1994. pap. text 73.00 (*3-7186-5531-4*) Gordon & Breach.

Physiology & General Biology Reviews Vol. 7, No. 4: Hormone-Transmitter Imprinting in the Neuroendocrine Control, Vol. 7. T. M. Turpaev. (Soviet Scientific Reviews Ser.: Section F). 50p. 1994. pap. text 73.00 (*3-7186-5542-X*) Gordon & Breach.

Physiology & General Biology Reviews Vol. 7, No. 5: Contractile Properties of Skeletal Muscle & Movement Control, Vol. 7. T. M. Turpaev. (Soviet Scientific Reviews Ser.: Section F). 90p. 1994. pap. text 134.00 (*3-7186-5540-3*) Gordon & Breach.

P

An Asterisk (*) at the beginning of an entry indicates that the title is appearing for the first time.

Physiology & General Biology Reviews Vol. 7, Nos. 1-3: Water-Electrolyte Metabolism & Its Regulations under Space Flight, Vol. 7. T. M. Turpaev. (Soviet Scientific Reviews Ser.: Section F). 226p. 1994. pap. text 336.00 (*3-7186-5541-1*) Gordon & Breach.

Physiology & General Biology Reviews Vol. 8, No. 1: Hypothalmic Pathway of Endocrine Pancreas Regulation: Histopathological Aspects, Vol. 8. T. M. Turpaev. (Soviet Scientific Reviews Ser.: Section F). 70p. 1994. pap. text 112.00 (*3-7186-5543-8*) Gordon & Breach.

Physiology & Growth see Prenatal & Perinatal Biology & Medicine

Physiology & Management of Mangroves. Ed. by H. J. Teas. (Tasks for Vegetation Science Ser.). 1984. text 129.50 (*90-6193-949-6*) Kluwer Academic.

Physiology & Medicine of Diving. Peter B. Bennett & David H. Elliott. (Illus.). 613p. (C). 1993. pap. 84.00 (*0-941332-02-0*, D088) Best Pub Co.

Physiology & Medicine of Diving. 4th ed. Ed. by Peter B. Bennett & David H. Elliott. (Illus.). 624p. 1993. text 147.00 (*0-7020-1589-X*, Pub. by W B Saunders) Saunders.

Physiology & Metabolism see Bile Acids: Chemistry, Physiology & Metabolism

Physiology & Pathobiology of Axons. fac. ed. Ed. by Stephen G. Waxman. LC 77-17751. (Illus.). 462p. pap. 143.30 (*0-7837-7228-9*, 204707000005) Bks Demand.

Physiology & Pathological Physiology see Encyclopedia of Urology

Physiology & Pathology of Dendrites. fac. ed. Ed. by Georg W. Kreutzberg. LC 74-14474. (Advances in Neurology Ser.: No. 12). (Illus.). 523p. pap. 162.20 (*0-7837-7542-3*, 204696200005) Bks Demand.

Physiology & Pathology of Interferon System. Ed. by L. Borecky & V. Lackovic. (Beitraege Zur Onkologie, Contributions to Oncology Ser.: Vol. 20). (Illus.). x, 390p. 1984. 68.75 (*3-8055-3839-1*) S Karger.

Physiology & Pathology of Mind, 2 vols. 3rd enl. rev. ed. Henry Maudsley. LC 78-72810. reprint ed. 75.00 (*0-404-60878-7*) AMS Pr.

Physiology & Pathology of the Cerebellum. Robert Dow & Giuseppe Moruzzi. LC 58-8343. 689p. reprint ed. pap. 200.00 (*0-608-13261-6*, 205585700039) Bks Demand.

Physiology & Pathology of the Mind, 4. Henry Maudsley. LC 77-72191. (Contributions to the History of Psychology Ser.: Pt. C, Vol. IV, Medical Psychology). 442p. 1977. reprint ed. lib. bdg. 79.50 (*0-313-26943-2*, U6943, Greenwood Pr) Greenwood.

Physiology & Pathology of the Mucociliary System: Special Regards to Mucociliary Transport in Malignant Lesions of the Human Larynx. T. Deitmer. (Advances in OtoRhinoLaryngology Ser.: Vol. 43). (Illus.). x, 136p. 1989. 115.00 (*3-8055-4944-X*) S Karger.

Physiology & Pathology of the Newborn. A. N. Antonov. (SRCD M Ser.: Vol. 10, No. 2). 1945. 25.00 (*0-527-01535-0*) Periodicals Srv.

Physiology & Pathophysiology of Exercise Tolerance: Proceedings of an International Symposium Held in Ulm, Germany, September 21-24, 1994. Ed. by Jurgen M. Steinacker & Susan A. Ward. LC 96-39630. 346p. (C). 1997. text 95.00 (*0-306-45492-0*, Kluwer Plenum) Kluwer Academic.

Physiology & Pathophysiology of Leukcoyte Adhesion. Ed. by D. Neil Granger & Geert W. Schmid-Schonbein. LC 93-44619. (Illus.). 560p. 1995. text 89.50 (*0-19-508102-1*) OUP.

Physiology & Pathophysiology of Temperature Regulation. Ed. by Clark M. Blatteis. 120p. 1998. 18.00 (*981-02-3172-5*) World Scientific Pub.

Physiology & Pathophysiology of the Endothelium: 15th Annual Meeting of the German Society for Clinical Microcirculation & Hemorheology, Dortmund, October 1996. Ed. by G. Siegel & Rolf K. Kinne. (International Journal of Microcirculation Ser.: Vol. 17, No. 5, 1997). (Illus.). 72p. 1997. pap. 38.25 (*3-8055-6607-7*) S Karger.

Physiology & Pathophysiology of the Heart. Ed. by Nicholas Sperelakis. (Developments in Cardiovascular Medicine Ser.). 1984. text 427.50 (*0-89838-615-2*) Kluwer Academic.

Physiology & Pathophysiology of the Heart. 2nd ed. Ed. by Nicholas Sperelakis. (Developments in Cardiovascular Medicine Ser.). 1040p. (C). 1988. text 427.50 (*0-89838-388-9*) Kluwer Academic.

Physiology & Pathophysiology of the Islets of Langerhans: Proceedings of the 1st International Meeting of the Pancreatic Islet Study Group Held in Alicante, Spain, November, 25-28, 1994. Ed. by Bernat Soria. LC 97-27991. (Advances in Experimental Medicine & Biology Ser.: Vol. 426). (Illus.). 468p. 1998. 150.00 (*0-306-45702-4*, Kluwer Plenum) Kluwer Academic.

Physiology & Pharmacology for the Anaesthetist. Kumar. pap. text. write for info. (*0-340-56758-9*, Pub. by E A) Routldge.

Physiology & Pharmacology of Biological Rhythms. F. Andreotti et al. LC 96-2935. (Handbook of Experimental Pharmacology Ser.). (Illus.). 600p. 1997. 445.00 (*3-540-61525-3*) Spr-Verlag.

Physiology & Pharmacology of Bone. Ed. by Gregory R. Mundy & T. John Martin. LC 92-42565. (Handbook of Experimental Pharmacology Ser.: Vol. 107). 1993. 500.00 (*0-387-56293-1*) Spr-Verlag.

Physiology & Pharmacology of Cardio-Respiratory Control. Albert Dahan & Johannes H. Van Beek. Ed. by Luc Teppema. LC 98-22537. 1998. 59.00 (*0-7923-5135-5*) Kluwer Academic.

Physiology & Pharmacology of Epileptogenic Phenomena. fac. ed. Ed. by Manfred R. Klee et al. LC 80-83271. (Illus.). 432p. pap. 134.00 (*0-7837-7294-7*, 204701200005) Bks Demand.

Physiology & Pharmacology of the Airways. Ed. by Jay A. Nadel. LC 80-16046. (Lung Biology in Health & Disease Ser.: No. 15). (Illus.). 371p. reprint ed. pap. 115.10 (*0-7837-0863-7*, 204117100019) Bks Demand.

Physiology & Pharmacology of the Blood-Brain Barrier. Ed. by W. B. Bradury et al. LC 92-2227. (Handbook of Experimental Pharmacology Ser.: Vol. 103). (Illus.). 520p. 1992. 345.00 (*3-540-54492-5*) Spr-Verlag.

Physiology & Pharmacology of the Heart. Hilary F. Brown & Roland Kozlowski. (Illus.). 126p. 1997. pap. text 30.95 (*0-86542-722-4*) Blackwell Sci.

Physiology & Social Nutrition & Nutritional Education. Ed. by Geoffrey H. Bourne. (World Review of Nutrition & Dietetics Ser.: Vol. 38). (Illus.). x, 230p. 1982. 141.75 (*3-8055-3048-X*) S Karger.

Physiology & Technology of Reproduction in Female Domestic Animals. R. H. Hunter. 1981. text 178.00 (*0-12-361950-5*) Acad Pr.

Physiology & the Enteric Nervous System in the Gastric Antrum of the Guinea-Pig. J. Tack. No. 53. 145p. (Orig.). 1992. pap. 33.50 (*90-6186-497-6*, Pub. by Leuven Univ) Coronet Bks.

Physiology & Therapeutics. Rudolf Steiner. Tr. by Alice Wulsin & Gerald F. Karnow from GER. (Illus.). 65p. (Orig.). 1986. pap. 8.50 (*0-936132-79-5*) Merc Pr NY.

Physiology & Treatment of Peptic Ulcer. Ed. by J. Garrott Allen. LC 59-10421. 246p. reprint ed. pap. 76.30 (*0-608-12489-3*, 202410900035) Bks Demand.

Physiology, Biochemistry, & Genetics of Nongreen Plastids: Fourth Annual Penn State Symposium in Plant Physiology. Ed. by Charles D. Boyer et al. LC 89-80455. 300p. (Orig.). (C). 1989. pap. text 20.00 (*0-943088-15-1*) Am Soc of Plan.

Physiology, Biochemistry & Molecular Biology of Plant Lipids. Ed. by John P. Williams. LC 96-52352. 440p. (C). 1997. text 244.50 (*0-7923-4379-4*) Kluwer Academic.

Physiology by Numbers: An Encouragement to Quantitative Thinking. Richard F. Burton. LC 93-37134. (Illus.). 201p. (C). 1994. text 64.95 (*0-521-42067-9*); pap. text 22.95 (*0-521-42138-1*) Cambridge U Pr.

***Physiology by Numbers: An Encouragement to Quantitative Thinking.** 2nd ed. Richard F. Burton. (Illus.). 200p. (C). 2000. text 64.95 (*0-521-77200-1*); pap. text 24.95 (*0-521-77703-8*) Cambridge U Pr.

Physiology Coloring Book. Kenneth Axen & Kathleen Axen. 1997. pap. 18.00 (*0-679-77850-0*) Random.

Physiology Coloring Book. 2nd ed. Wynn Kapit. (Illus.). 320p. (C). 1999. pap. text 19.99 (*0-321-03663-8*) Addson-Wesley Educ.

Physiology Concepts & Connections German. (C). 2001. 94.00 (*0-8053-6056-5*) Benjamin-Cummings.

Physiology, Emotion & Psychosomatic Illness. CIBA Foundation Staff. LC 72-93253. (CIBA Foundation Symposium: New Ser.: No. 8). 430p. reprint ed. pap. 133.30 (*0-608-13508-9*, 202214000024) Bks Demand.

Physiology for Health Care Students. Judy L. Hubbard & Derek J. Mechan. LC 86-23312. (Illus.). 344p. (Orig.). (C). 1987. pap. text 24.95 (*0-443-02123-6*) Church.

Physiology for Nursing Practitioners. 2nd ed. Hinchliff. 1996. pap. text 44.00 (*0-7020-1638-1*, W B Saunders Co) Harcrt Hlth Sci Grp.

Physiology for Sportspeople: A Serious User's Guide to the Body. Peter G. Bursztyn. LC 90-3608. (Illus.). 292p. 1991. text 19.95 (*0-7190-3087-0*, Pub. by Manchester Univ Pr) St Martin.

Physiology, Growth, & Development of Plants in Culture. Ed. by P. J. Lumsden et al. LC 93-20900. 430p. (C). 1994. text 298.50 (*0-7923-2516-8*) Kluwer Academic.

Physiology in Bicycling. G. Sjogaard et al. 1985. pap. 24.95 (*0-932392-21-0*) Mouvement Pubns.

Physiology in Childbearing. Dot Stables. LC 98-54877. 1999. write for info. (*0-7020-2135-0*, Pub. by W B Saunders) Saunders.

Physiology in Industry: Eval. Ind. Stresses Physiological Reactions of the Worker, Vol. 4. 2nd ed. L. Brouha & J. Zapp. LC 60-8058. (International Series of Monographs on Pure & Applied Mathematics). 1960. 79.00 (*0-08-011703-1*, Pub. by Pergamon Repr) Franklin.

Physiology in Surgical Practice. text. write for info. (*0-7131-4558-7*, Pub. by E A) Routldge.

Physiology in the American Context, 1850-1940. Ed. by Gerald L. Geison. (American Physiological Society Book). (Illus.). 411p. 1988. text 55.00 (*0-19-520698-3*) OUP.

***Physiology Laboratory Book.** Russell Di Fiori & Paul Jarrell. 94p. (C). 1999. spiral bd., lab manual ed. 28.95 (*0-7872-6523-3*) Kendall-Hunt.

Physiology Monitor & Therapy of the Critically Ill Patient: Proceedings of the International Symposium on Acute Care, 5th, Rio de Janeiro, Sao Paulo, November, 1976. International Symposium on Acute Care Staff. Ed. by W. C. Shoemaker & B. M. Tavares. (Current Topics in Critical Care Medicine Ser.: Vol. 3). (Illus.). 1977. 49.75 (*3-8055-2652-0*) S Karger.

Physiology of Adrenocortical Secretion. T. Suzuki. (Frontiers of Hormone Research Ser.: Vol. 11). (Illus.). viii, 216p. 1983. 115.00 (*3-8055-3644-5*) S Karger.

Physiology of ALS & Related Diseases. Jun Kimura & Ryuji Kaji. LC 97-2859. 252p. 1997. 184.50 (*0-444-82557-6*); pap. 106.25 (*0-444-82668-8*) Elsevier.

Physiology of Behavior. 6th ed. (C). 1997. write for info. (*0-205-28196-6*, Macmillan Coll) P-H.

Physiology of Behavior. 6th ed. Carlson. 1998. pap. text, student ed. 21.00 (*0-205-27435-8*) P-H.

Physiology of Behavior. 6th ed. Neil R. Carlson. 144p. (C). 1997. text, teacher ed. write for info. (*0-205-27432-3*, T7432-2) Allyn.

Physiology of Behavior. 6th ed. Neil R. Carlson. LC 97-41384. 736p. 1997. 83.00 (*0-205-27340-8*) P-H.

***Physiology of Behavior.** 7th ed. 2000. teacher ed. write for info. (*0-205-32586-6*) Allyn.

***Physiology of Behavior.** 7th ed. Neil R. Carlson. LC 00-38093. 720p. 2000. pap. 80.00 (*0-205-30840-6*) Allyn.

***Physiology of Behavior: Study Guide.** 7th ed. 2000. write for info. (*0-205-32588-2*) Allyn.

Physiology of Behaviour. Seller. (Biology Ser.). 2000. text 34.00 (*0-412-44340-6*) Chapman & Hall.

Physiology of Biodegradative Microorganisms. Ed. by Colin Ratledge. 142p. 1991. text 171.00 (*0-7923-1132-9*) Kluwer Academic.

Physiology of Blood & Lymph Vessels: Proceedings of the Symposia Angiologica Santoriana, 3rd International Symposium, Fribourg, 1970, 2 pts. Symposia Angiologica Santoriana Staff. Ed. by M. Comel & L. Lastz. 1972. 67.50 (*3-8055-1263-5*) S Karger.

Physiology of Blood & Lymph Vessels: Proceedings of the Symposia Angiologica Santoriana, 3rd International Symposium, Fribourg, 1970 see Physiology of Blood & Lymph Vessels: Proceedings of the Symposia Angiologica Santoriana, 3rd International Symposium, Fribourg, 1970

Physiology of Blood & Lymph Vessels: Proceedings of the Symposia Angiologica Santoriana, 3rd International Symposium, Fribourg, 1970, 2 pts., Set. Symposia Angiologica Santoriana Staff. Ed. by M. Comel & L. Lastz. Incl. Pt. 1. Physiology of Blood & Lymph Vessels: Proceedings of the Symposia Angiologica Santoriana, 3rd International Symposium, Fribourg, 1970., **2 pts.** 1972. pap. text 52.75 (*3-8055-2472-2*); Pt. 2. Physiology of Blood & Lymph Vessels: Proceedings of the Symposia Angiologica Santoriana, 3rd International Symposium, Fribourg, 1970., **2 pts.** 1972. pap. text 35.75 (*3-8055-1289-9*); 1972. Set pap. text 67.50 (*3-8055-1726-2*) S Karger.

Physiology of Bone. 3rd ed. Janet M. Vaughan. (Illus.). 286p. 1981. 60.00 (*0-19-857584-X*) OUP.

Physiology of Cell Aging. Ed. by V. V. Frolkis. (Interdisciplinary Topics in Gerontology Ser.: Vol. 18). (Illus.). viii, 208p. 1984. 142.75 (*3-8055-3866-9*) S Karger.

Physiology of Cell Expansion During Plant Growth: Proceedings of the Second Annual Penn State Symposium in Plant Physiology. Ed. by Daniel J. Cosgrove & Daniel P. Knievel. LC 87-72933. (Illus.). 329p. (C). 1987. pap. 20.00 (*0-943088-11-9*) Am Soc of Plan.

Physiology of Cephalopod Mollusc: Lifestyle & Performance Adaptations. Ed. by Hans O. Portner et al. 214p. 1995. text 104.00 (*2-88449-027-2*) Gordon & Breach.

Physiology of Cerebral Circulation. M. J. Purves. LC 70-169577. (Monographs of the Physiological Society: No. 28). 436p. reprint ed. pap. 124.30 (*0-608-15770-8*, 2031716) Bks Demand.

Physiology of Circulation. Helms. 1997. 1.50 (*0-7167-9341-5*) W H Freeman.

Physiology of Cold Adaptation in Birds. Ed. by C. Bech & R. E. Reinertsen. (NATO ASI Series A, Life Sciences: Vol. 173). (Illus.). 394p. 1989. 120.00 (*0-306-43237-4*, Plenum Trade) Perseus Pubng.

Physiology of Consciousness. Robert K. Wallace. LC 93-7553. (Orig.). 1993. 15.00 (*0-923569-02-2*, E-02) Maharishi U Mgmt Pr.

Physiology of Consciousness: How Maharishi's Vedic Physiology & Its Practical Application, Maharishi Ayur-Ved, Can Solve the Problems of Individual & Collective Health & Raise Life to a New Level of Fulfillment. Robert K. Wallace. (Illus.). 311p. (Orig.). 1993. pap. 15.00 (*0-923569-26-X*, E 02) Maharishi U Mgmt Pr.

Physiology of Crop Plants. Frank P. Gardner et al. LC 84-15667. (Illus.). 328p. (C). 1984. text 44.95 (*0-8138-1376-X*) Iowa St U Pr.

Physiology of Crop Plants-Re-Printed in India. P. Gardner Franklin. (C). 1988. pap. 60.00 (*81-85046-71-9*, Pub. by Scientific Pubs) St Mut.

Physiology of Crustacea, 2 vols. Ed. by T. H. Waterman. write for info. (*0-686-76924-4*) Acad Pr.

Physiology of Disease Resistance in Plants, Vol. 1. P. Vishyasekaran. LC 87-18416. 160p. 1988. 95.00 (*0-8493-4532-4*, SB750, CRC Reprint) Franklin.

Physiology of Disease Resistance in Plants, Vol. II. P. Vidhyasekaran. 160p. 1988. 84.00 (*0-8493-4533-2*, CRC Reprint) Franklin.

Physiology of Diuretic Action. Ed. by F. P. Lang. (Journal: Renal Physiology & Biochemistry: Vol. 10, No. 3, 1987). 92p. 1988. pap. 49.75 (*3-8055-4769-2*) S Karger.

Physiology of Domestic Animals. William O. Reece. LC 90-5543. (Illus.). 372p. 1990. pap. text 39.50 (*0-8121-1307-1*) Lppncott W & W.

Physiology of Domestic Animals. 2nd ed. William O. Reece. LC 96-18088. (Illus.). 464p. 1997. 44.95 (*0-683-07240-4*) Lppncott W & W.

Physiology of Earthworms. M. S. Laverack & G. A. Kerkut. (International Series of Monographs on Pure & Applied Mathematics: Vol. 15). 1963. 99.00 (*0-08-009812-6*, Pub. by Pergamon Repr) Franklin.

Physiology of Excitable Cells. 4th rev. ed. David J. Aidley. LC 97-46773. (Illus.). 550p. (C). 1998. text 90.00 (*0-521-57415-3*); pap. text 47.95 (*0-521-57421-8*) Cambridge U Pr.

Physiology of Exercise. (C). 1992. write for info. (*0-8087-9375-6*) Pearson Custom.

Physiology of Exercise & Sport, No. 2. Noble. (Illus.). 608p. 1991. 37.95 (*0-8016-3342-7*) Mosby Inc.

Physiology of Exercise for Physical Education, Athletics & Excerise Science. Herbert A. Devries et al. (C). 1995. text, student ed. write for info. (*0-697-28495-6*) Brown & Benchmark.

Physiology of Exercise for Physical Education, Athletics & Exercise Science. 5th ed. Herbert A. Devries & Terry J. Housh. 112p. (C). 1995. text, student ed. 10.00 (*0-697-29080-8*) Brown & Benchmark.

Physiology of Exercise for Physical Education, Athletics & Exercise Science. 5th ed. Herbert A. DeVries & Terry J. Housh. 640p. (C). 1993. text. write for info. (*0-697-10097-9*) Brown & Benchmark.

Physiology of Fish in Intensive Culture Systems. Gary A. Wedemeyer. LC 96-5252. 232p. (gr. 13). 1997. write for info. (*0-412-07801-5*) Kluwer Academic.

Physiology of Fishes. David H. Evans. LC 93-18071. (Series on Marine Science). 608p. 1993. boxed set 110.00 (*0-8493-8042-1*, QL639) CRC Pr.

Physiology of Fishes. 2nd ed. David H. Evans. LC 97-7964. (Marine Science Ser.). 544p. (C). 1997. boxed set 99.95 (*0-8493-8427-3*) CRC Pr.

Physiology of Flower Bulbs: A Comprehensive Treatise on the Physiology & Utilization of Ornamental Flowering Bulbous & Tuberous Plants. Ed. by A. De Hertogh & M. Le Nard. 812p. 1992. 307.00 (*0-444-87498-4*) Elsevier.

Physiology of Flowering, 3 vols., III. Ed. by Georges Bernier. 288p. 1985. 162.00 (*0-8493-5711-X*, CRC Reprint) Franklin.

Physiology of Flowering, 3 vols., Vol. I. Ed. by Georges Bernier. 168p. 1981. 95.00 (*0-8493-5709-8*, QK830, CRC Reprint) Franklin.

Physiology of Flowering, 3 vols., Vol. II. Ed. by Georges Bernier. 248p. 1981. 139.00 (*0-8493-5710-1*, CRC Reprint) Franklin.

Physiology of French Consonant Changes. Ernest F. Haden. (LD Ser.: No. 26). 1938. 25.00 (*0-527-00772-2*) Periodicals Srv.

Physiology of Fungal Nutrition. D. H. Jennings. LC 93-45578. (Illus.). 638p. (C). 1995. text 160.00 (*0-521-35524-9*) Cambridge U Pr.

Physiology of Growth & Nutrition. Ed. by Miloslav Rechcigl, Jr. (Comparative Animal Nutrition Ser.: Vol. 4). (Illus.). xii, 344p. 1981. pap. 216.75 (*3-8055-1199-X*) S Karger.

***Physiology of Health & Illness: With Related Anatomy.** L. Hubbard & D. J. Mechan. 704p. 1999. pap. text (*0-7487-3173-3*) S Thornes Pubs.

Physiology of Health & Illness with Related Anatomy. D. J. Hubbard & Derek J. Mechan. (Illus.). 452p. (Orig.). (C). 1997. pap. text 47.75 (*1-56593-335-4*, 0665) Singular Publishing.

Physiology of Hemostasis. Derek Ogston. (Illus.). 390p. (C). 1983. 49.95 (*0-674-66660-7*) HUP.

Physiology of Human Growth. Ed. by James M. Tanner & M. A. Preece. (Society for the Study of Human Biology Symposium Ser.: No. 29). (Illus.). 232p. 1989. text 69.95 (*0-521-34410-7*) Cambridge U Pr.

Physiology of Human Placenta. Page. 192p. 1993. 75.00 (*1-85728-065-2*, Pub. by UCL Pr Ltd); pap. 29.50 (*1-85728-066-0*, Pub. by UCL Pr Ltd) Taylor & Francis.

Physiology of Immunity. Ed. by James A. Marsh & Marion D. Kendall. 464p. 1996. boxed set 139.95 (*0-8493-8033-2*) CRC Pr.

Physiology of Industry: Being an Exposure of Certain Fallacies in Existing Theories of Economics. A. F. Mummery & John A. Hobson. LC 87-17943. (Reprints of Economic Classics Ser.). xvii, 215p. 1989. reprint ed. 35.00 (*0-678-00673-3*) Kelley.

***Physiology of Inflammation.** Ed. by Klaus Ley. (Methods in Physiology Ser.). (Illus.). 496p. 2000. text 95.00 (*0-19-512829-X*) OUP.

Physiology of Joints see Physiology of the Joints

Physiology of Lactation. T. B. Mepham. 224p. 1991. 255.00 (*0-471-93246-9*, Wiley-Liss) Wiley.

Physiology of Mammary Glands. Lewis G. Sheffield. 1999. 60.00 (*0-8493-8760-4*) CRC Pr.

Physiology of Marriage. William A. Alcott. LC 79-180551. (Medicine & Society in America Ser.). 266p. 1972. reprint ed. 20.95 (*0-405-03931-X*) Ayer.

Physiology of Marriage. Honore de Balzac. LC 97-1641. 358p. (C). 1997. reprint ed. pap. text 15.95 (*0-8018-5550-0*) Johns Hopkins.

Physiology of Membrane Disorders. 2nd ed. Ed. by Thomas E. Andreoli et al. LC 85-19367. (Illus.). 1094p. 1986. 234.00 (*0-306-41774-X*, Kluwer Plenum) Kluwer Academic.

Physiology of Membrane Fluidity, 2 vols. Meir Shinitzky. 208p. 1984. 120.00 (*0-8493-6141-9*, QH601, CRC Reprint) Franklin.

Physiology of Membrane Fluidity, 2 vols., Vol. II. Meir Shinitzky. 144p. 1985. 88.00 (*0-8493-6142-7*, CRC Reprint) Franklin.

Physiology of Movements. Ed. by W. Haupt & M. E. Feinleib. (Encyclopedia of Plant Physiology Ser.: Vol. 7). (Illus.). 1979. 186.00 (*0-387-08776-1*) Spr-Verlag.

Physiology of Nerve Cells. John C. Eccles. LC 68-9181. (Johns Hopkins Paperback Ser.: Vol. JH-47). 282p. 1968. reprint ed. pap. 87.50 (*0-608-03682-X*, 206450800009) Bks Demand.

Physiology of Oral Tissues. Ed. by Yojiro Kawamura. (Frontiers of Oral Physiology Ser.: Vol. 2). (Illus.). 350p. 1976. 101.00 (*3-8055-1360-7*) S Karger.

Physiology of Parasitism: Proceedings of the All India Symposium, Jabalpur, Feb. 24-27, 1978. All India Symposium Staff. Ed. by G. P. Agarwal & K. S. Bilgrami. (Current Trends in Life Sciences Ser.: Vol. 7). vi, 478p. 1979. 50.00 (*0-88065-004-4*) Scholarly Pubns.

Physiology of Physical Stress: A Selective Bibliography, 1500-1964. Carl B. Chapman & Elinor C. Reinmiller. LC 74-15565. 376p. 1974. 49.95 (*0-674-66670-4*) HUP.

P

An Asterisk (*) at the beginning of an entry indicates that the title is appearing for the first time.

***Physiology of Plants under Stress: Soil & Biotic Factors.** David M. Orcutt & Erik T. Nilsen. 550p. 2000. text 125.00 (*0-471-17008-9*) Wiley.

Physiology of Plants under Stress Vol. 1: Abiotic Factors, Vol. 1. 2nd ed. Erik T. Nilsen & David M. Orcutt. LC 96-5443. 704p. 1996. 175.00 (*0-471-03152-6*) Wiley.

Physiology of Polyamines, 2 vols., Vol. I. Ed. by Uriel Bachrach & Yair M. Heimer. 384p. 1989. lib. bdg. 259.00 (*0-8493-6808-1*, QP801) CRC Pr.

Physiology of Polyamines, 2 vols., Vol. II. Ed. by Uriel Bachrach & Yair M. Heimer. 336p. 1989. lib. bdg. 249.00 (*0-8493-6809-X*) CRC Pr.

Physiology of Psychological Disorders: Schizophrenia, Depression, Anxiety, & Substance Abuse. J. G. Hollandsworth, Jr. LC 89-26559. (Behavioral Psychophysiology & Medicine Ser.). (Illus.). 336p. (C). 1990. 49.50 (*0-306-43353-2*, Plenum Trade) Perseus Pubng.

Physiology of Reproduction, 2 vols., Vols. 1 - 2. 2nd ed. Ed. by Ernst Knobil et al. LC 93-853. 3312p. 1993. text 394.00 (*0-7817-0086-8*) Lppncott W & W.

Physiology of Respiration. Michael P. Hlastala & Albert J. Berger. (Illus.). 320p. (C). 1996. text 49.95 (*0-19-504434-7*); pap. text 28.50 (*0-19-504435-5*) OUP.

Physiology of Rubber Tree Latex, 2 vols. Ed. by J. D'Auzac et al. 488p. 1988. 265.00 (*0-8493-4893-5*, SB291, CRC Reprint) Franklin.

Physiology of Seeds: An Introduction to the Study of Seed & Germination Problems. W. Crocker & L. V. Barton. (Illus.). 267p. 1990. reprint ed. text 45.00 (*0-685-41268-7*, Pub. by Mahendra Pal Singh) Lubrecht & Cramer.

Physiology of Smooth Muscle. fac. ed. Ed. by Edith Bulbring & M. F. Shuba. LC 75-14566. (Illus.). 448p. pap. 138.90 (*0-7837-7539-3*, 204696500005) Bks Demand.

Physiology of Spinal Anesthesia. 4th ed. Nicholas M. Greene & Sorin J. Brull. LC 92-5578. (Illus.). 387p. 1993. 78.00 (*0-683-03555-X*) Lppncott W & W.

Physiology of Sport & Exercise. 2nd rev. ed. Jack H. Wilmore & David L. Costill. LC 98-30309. (Illus.). 728p. 1999. text 59.00 (*0-7360-0084-4*, BWIL0084) Human Kinetics.

Physiology of Sport & Exercise Study Guide. 2nd ed. Christine M. Drews & Jack H. Wilmore. LC 99-22719. 1999. 16.00 (*0-7360-0090-9*) Human Kinetics.

Physiology of Sports. Ed. by T. Reilly et al. (Illus.). 320p. 1990. 63.00 (*0-419-13580-4*, A4403, E & FN Spon) Routledge.

Physiology of Sports. Ed. by T. Reilly et al. (Illus.). 512p. (C). 1990. pap. 45.00 (*0-419-13590-1*, A4407, E & FN Spon) Routledge.

Physiology of Stress: With Special Reference to the Neuroendocrine System. Mary F. Asterita. 240p. (C). 1984. pap. 22.95 (*0-89885-187-4*, Kluwer Acad Hman Sci); text 42.95 (*0-89885-176-9*, Kluwer Acad Hman Sci) Kluwer Academic.

Physiology of Synapses. John C. Eccles. (Illus.). 1964. reprint ed. 61.95 (*0-387-03112-X*) Spr-Verlag.

***Physiology of Taste.** Jean Anthelme Brillat-Savarin. Tr. by M. F. K. Fisher. 2000. pap. 23.00 (*1-58243-103-5*, Pub. by Counterpt DC) HarpC.

Physiology of Taste: Or, Meditations on Transcendental Gastronomy. Jean Anthelme Brillat-Savarin. Tr. by M. F. K. Fisher from FRE. (Illus.). 376p. 1995. 55.00 (*1-887178-09-0*, Pub. by Counterpt DC) HarpC.

Physiology of Taste: Or, Meditations on Transcendental Gastronomy. Jean Anthelme Brillat-Savarin. Tr. & Pref. by M. F. K. Fisher. LC TX637.B8613 1999. 464p. 1999. text 35.00 (*1-58243-008-X*, Pub. by Counterpt DC) HarpC.

Physiology of Taste: Or, Meditations on Transcendental Gastronomy. Jean Anthelme Brillat-Savarin. Tr. & Intro. by Anne Drayton. 384p. 1994. pap. 13.95 (*0-14-044614-1*, Penguin Classics) Viking Penguin.

Physiology of Taste: Or, Meditations on Transcendental Gastronomy. Jean Anthelme Brillat-Savarin. (Illus.). 350p. 1982. reprint ed. pap. 9.95 (*0-918172-11-X*) Leetes Isl.

Physiology of the Cerebrospinal Fluids & Blood-Brain Barriers. Ed. by Hugh Davson & Malcolm B. Segal. LC 95-8041. (Illus.). 832p. 1995. boxed set 314.95 (*0-8493-4472-7*, 4472) CRC Pr.

Physiology of the Digestive Tract. 5th ed. Horace W. Davenport. (Illus.). 1982. 32.95 (*0-8151-2330-2*) Mosby Inc.

Physiology of the Ear. Ed. by Anthony F. Jahn & Joseph Santos-Sacchi. LC 88-12198. (Illus.). 551p. 1988. reprint ed. pap. 170.90 (*0-608-07211-7*, 206743600009) Bks Demand.

***Physiology of the Ear.** 2nd ed. Jahn. 2000. pap. 89.95 (*1-56593-994-8*) Singular Publishing.

Physiology of the Eye. 5th ed. H. Davson. (Illus.). 750p. 1990. 85.00 (*0-08-037907-9*, Pub. by PPI) McGraw.

Physiology of the Fetal & Neonatal Lung. Ed. by D. V. Walters et al. 1987. text 200.50 (*0-85200-948-8*) Kluwer Academic.

Physiology of the Gastro-Intestinal Lymphatic System. J. A. Barrowman. LC 77-22823. (Monographs of the Physiological Society: No. 33). 340p. reprint ed. pap. 96.90 (*0-608-17040-2*, 2027280) Bks Demand.

Physiology of the Gastrointestinal Tract, 2 vols. 3rd ed. Ed. by Leonard R. Johnson et al. LC 93-6429. 2320p. 1994. text 376.00 (*0-7817-0132-5*) Lppncott W & W.

Physiology of the Heart. 2nd ed. Arnold M. Katz. 704p. 1991. text 71.00 (*0-88167-838-4*) Lppncott W & W.

Physiology of the Heart. 3rd ed. Arnold M. Katz. 688p. text 75.00 (*0-7817-1548-2*) Lppncott W & W.

Physiology of the Human Body. 6th ed. Guyton. (C). 1984. pap. text, teacher ed. 34.00 (*0-03-058341-1*) Harcourt Coll Pubs.

Physiology of the Hypothalamus. Ed. by Peter J. Morgane & Jaak Panksepp. LC 80-17602. (Handbook of the Hypothalamus Ser.: No. 2). 700p. 1980. reprint ed. pap. 200.00 (*0-608-01324-2*, 206206700001) Bks Demand.

Physiology of the Intestinal Circulation. Ed. by A. P. Shepherd & D. N. Granger. LC 84-9858. (Illus.). 440p. 1984. reprint ed. pap. 136.40 (*0-7837-9531-9*, 206028000005) Bks Demand.

Physiology of the Joints, 3 vols. Incl. Vol. 1. Physiology of Joints. 5th ed. Matthew J. Kandel & Kapandji. 208p. 1982. pap. text 45.00 (*0-443-02504-5*); Vol. 2. Lower Limb. 5th ed. Matthew J. Kandel & Kapandji. (Illus.). 242p. (C). 1988. pap. text 45.00 (*0-443-03618-7*); Vol. 3. Physiology of Joints. 2nd ed. I. A. Kapandji. Tr. by L. H. Honore. 256p. 1974. pap. text 45.00 (*0-443-01209-1*); (Illus.). write for info. (*0-318-51368-4*) Church.

Physiology of the Lower Urinary Tract. Ed. by M. J. Torrens & J. F. Morrison. (Illus.). 255p. 1987. 249.00 (*0-387-17486-9*) Spr-Verlag.

Physiology of the Opera by Scrici (Philadelphia) Willis P. Hazard, 1852. Intro. by Donald W. Krummel. LC 81-81546. (I.S.A.M. Special Publications: No. 2). 125p. 1981. pap. 8.00 (*0-914678-16-7*) Inst Am Music.

Physiology of the Plant Root System. Ed. by J. Kolek. (Developments in Plant & Soil Sciences Ser.). 374p. (C). 1992. text 199.50 (*0-7923-1205-8*) Kluwer Academic.

Physiology of Thirst & Sodium Appetite. Ed. by G. De Caro et al. LC 86-4982. (NATO ASI Series A, Life Sciences: Vol. 105). 586p. 1986. 125.00 (*0-306-42265-4*, Plenum Trade) Perseus Pubng.

Physiology of Trees. A. S. Raghavendra. LC 91-7494. 528p. 1991. 220.00 (*0-471-50110-7*) Wiley.

Physiology of Trematodes. 2nd ed. James D. Smyth & D. W. Halton. LC 82-12961. (Illus.). 460p. reprint ed. pap. 131.10 (*0-608-17528-5*, 2030621) Bks Demand.

Physiology of Tropical Crop Production. G. R. Squire. (Illus.). 256p. (Orig.). 1990. pap. text 40.00 (*0-85198-677-3*) OUP.

Physiology of Tropical Field Crops. Ed. by Peter R. Goldsworthy & N. M. Fisher. LC 83-21624. 682p. reprint ed. pap. 200.00 (*0-7837-4009-3*, 204383900011) Bks Demand.

Physiology of Tropical Orchids in Relation to the Industry. LC 97-18872. 200p. 1997. lib. bdg. 23.00 (*981-02-2855-4*) World Scientific Pub.

Physiology of Tropical Orchids in Relation to the Industry. Choy S. Hew & J. W. Yong. LC 97-18872. 1997. pap. write for info. (*981-02-3193-8*) World Scientific Pub.

Physiology of Vegetable Crops. Ed. by H. C. Wien. LC 97-12577. 672p. 1997. text 150.00 (*0-85199-146-7*) OUP.

Physiology of Violin Playing. Mihaly Nemessuri & O. Szende. 202p. (C). 1988. 75.00 (*0-569-06196-2*, Pub. by Collets) St Mut.

Physiology of Virus Infected Plants. P. Sreenivasulu et al. (C). 1989. 22.00 (*81-7003-101-X*, Pub. by S Asia Pubs) S Asia.

Physiology of Woody Plants. 2nd ed. Ed. by Theodore T. Kozlowski & Stephen G. Pallardy. (Illus.). 411p. 1996. text 69.95 (*0-12-424162-X*) Acad Pr.

Physiology of Work. Ed. by Kaare Rodahl. 250p. 1989. 110.00 (*0-85066-478-0*) Taylor & Francis.

Physiology, Pharmacology & Development of Epileptogenic Phenomena. Ed. by M. R. Klee et al. (Experimental Brain Research Ser.: Vol. 20). (Illus.). 288p. 1991. 79.95 (*0-387-53664-7*) Spr-Verlag.

Physiology Phil's True Life Lab Experiences. 2nd ed. J. Timothy Lightfoot. LC 95-71158. (Illus.). 76p. (C). 1995. pap. 13.95 (*0-9629526-2-1*) Presyncopal.

***Physiology, Promiscuity & Prophecy at the Millennium: A Tale of Tails.** Bruce J. West. (Studies of Nonlinear Phenomena in Life Sciences: Vol. 9). 400p. 1999. pap. 48.00 (*981-02-3836-3*) World Scientific Pub.

Physiology, Promiscuity & Prophecy at the Millennium: A Tale of Tails, Vol. 9. Bruce J. West. LC 99-35349. (Studies of Nonlinear Phenomena in Life Sciences). 400p. 1999. 88.00 (*981-02-3835-5*) World Scientific Pub.

Physiology Review Book. Montoni. Date not set. pap. text. write for info. (*0-7216-5177-1*, W B Saunders Co) Harcrt Hlth Sci Grp.

Physiology Secrets. Hershel Raff. LC 98-29331. (Secrets Ser.). (Illus.). 350p. 1998. pap. text 35.00 (*1-56053-255-6*) Hanley & Belfus.

Physiology, Stress & Malnutrition: Functional Correlates, Nutritional Intervention. John M. Kinney & Hugh N. Tucker. LC 96-51070. 656p. 1997. text 68.00 (*0-397-58763-5*) Lppncott W & W.

Physiology Through Questions. Trevor Morgan. 200p. 1996. pap. text 25.00 (*0-07-470196-7*) McGraw-Hill HPD.

Physiology 250: A Study Guide. Patrick Dillon. (C). 1993. student ed. 12.00 (*1-881592-46-4*) Hayden-McNeil.

Physiology 431 Study Guide. 4th ed. Adams. 332p. (C). 1997. spiral bd. 23.95 (*0-7872-2829-X*) Kendall-Hunt.

Physiology 431 Study Guide. 4th ed. Thomas Adams et al. 336p. (C). 1997. student ed., spiral bd. 29.95 (*0-7872-4403-1*) Kendall-Hunt.

Physiology 432 Study Guide. Thomas Adams. 154p. (C). 1997. pap. text, spiral bd. 22.95 (*0-7872-3396-X*) Kendall-Hunt.

Physiology 432 Study Guide. 5th ed. Thomas Adams. 298p. (C). 1998. spiral bd. 38.95 (*0-7872-4655-7*, 41465501) Kendall-Hunt.

Physiopathological Processes of Aging: Towards a Multicasual Interpretation. Ed. by Nicola Fabris et al. LC 92-48196. (Annals Ser.: Vol. 673). 1992. write for info. (*0-89766-743-3*); pap. 90.00 (*0-89766-744-1*) NY Acad Sci.

Physiopathology of Cancer Vol. 2: Diagnosis, Treatment, Prevention. Ed. by H. Hamburger. 1976. 50.50 (*3-8055-1623-1*) S Karger.

Physiopathology of Illicit Drugs: Cannabis, Cocaine, Opiates. Gabriel G. Nahas & C. Latour. (Advances in the Biosciences Ser.: Vol. 80). 346p. 1991. 181.50 (*0-08-041146-0*, Pergamon Pr) Elsevier.

Physiopathology of the Cardiovascular System. Joseph S. Alpert. 348p. 1984. 31.95 (*0-316-03504-1*, Little Brwn Med Div) Lppncott W & W.

Physiotherapy: A Psychosocial Approach. 2nd ed. Sally French. LC 96-37310. 464p. 1997. pap. text 45.00 (*0-7506-2608-9*) Buttrwrth-Heinemann.

Physiotherapy: Controlled Trials & Facts. Ed. by P. Schlapbach & N. Gerber. (Rheumatology, the Interdisciplinary Concept Ser.: Vol. 14). (Illus.). x, 252p. 1991. 85.25 (*3-8055-5234-3*) S Karger.

Physiotherapy & the Growing Child. Ed. by Yvonne R. Burns & Julie MacDonald. (Illus.). 529p. 1996. text 68.00 (*0-7020-1942-9*, Pub. by W B Saunders) Saunders.

Physiotherapy Assessment. 2nd ed. Anne Parry. LC 85-4615. 168p. (Orig.). 1985. pap. 17.95 (*0-7099-4009-2*, Pub. by C Helm) Routldge.

Physiotherapy for Amputees: The Roehampton Approach. 3rd ed. Engstrom. (C). 1999. text 49.00 (*0-443-05975-6*) Church.

***Physiotherapy for Respiratory & Cardiac Problems.** 2nd ed. Ed. by J. A. Pryor & B. A. Webber. (Illus.). 556p. 1998. pap. write for info. (*0-443-05841-5*) Church.

Physiotherapy in Paediatrics. 3rd ed. Roberta B. Shepherd. (Illus.). 420p. 1995. pap. text 50.00 (*0-7506-0620-7*) Buttrwrth-Heinemann.

Physiotherapy in Respiratory Care: A Problem-Solving Approach to Respiratory & Cardiac Management. Hough. 250p. 1992. pap. 39.95 (*1-56593-011-8*, 0252) Thomson Learn.

Physiotherapy in Respiratory Care: A Problem-Solving Approach to Respiratory & Cardiac Management. 2nd ed. Alexandra Hough. 352p. 1995. pap. 45.00 (*1-56593-131-9*, 1241) Singular Publishing.

***Physiotherapy in Respiratory Care: A Problem-Solving Approach to Respiratory & Cardiac Management.** 3rd ed. A. Hough. (Illus.). 400p. 2000. pap. 33.00 (*0-7487-4037-6*, Pub. by S Thornes Pubs) Trans-Atl Phila.

Physiotherapy with Older People. Pickles. 1995. pap. text 62.00 (*0-7020-1931-3*, W B Saunders Co) Harcrt Hlth Sci Grp.

Physique: An Intimate Portrait of the Female Fitness Athlete. Paul B. Goode. LC 96-40384. (Illus.). 128p. 1997. pap. 22.95 (*1-56025-145-X*, Thunders Mouth) Avalon NY.

Physique: The Life of John S. Barrington. Rupert Smith. (Illus.). 240p. (Orig.). 1996. pap. 24.99 (*1-85242-374-9*) Serpents Tail.

Physique & Intellect. Donald G. Paterson. LC 73-98866. 304p. 1970. reprint ed. lib. bdg. 65.00 (*0-8371-2886-2*, PAPI, Greenwood Pr) Greenwood.

Physique Atomique et Connaissance Humaine. Niels Bohr. (FRE.). 641p. 1991. pap. 18.95 (*0-7859-1676-8*, 2070326195) Fr & Eur.

Physique des Semi-Conducteurs see Physics of Semiconductors

Physique et Physiciens en France, 1918-1940. 2nd ed. D. Pestre. (FRE.). xvi, 356p. 1992. pap. text 60.00 (*2-903928-08-8*) Gordon & Breach.

***Physique, Fitness & Performance.** Thomas Battinelli. (Calvin P. Horn Lectures). 2000. 99.95 (*0-8493-0231-5*) CRC Pr.

Physique III. 3rd ed. Serway. (C). 1992. pap. write for info. (*0-276-07054-2*) Harcourt Coll Pubs.

Physique, Personality & Scholarship. N. R. Sanford et al. (Society for Research in Child Development Monographs: Vol. 8, No. 1). 1974. reprint ed. 65.00 (*0-527-01526-1*) Periodicals Srv.

Physis und Psyche see Austrian Expressionism: The Formative Years

Physisorption Kinetics. H. J. Kreuzer & Z. W. Gortel. (Surface Sciences Ser.: Vol. 1). (Illus.). 335p. 1986. 71.95 (*0-387-16176-7*) Spr-Verlag.

Physoelectric Transducers: Surface Acoustic Wave Devices. Aerospace Abstracts Database Staff. 1996. 85.00 (*0-614-18490-8*, 135P27) Info Gatekeepers.

***Physologia: Natural Philosophy in Late Aristotelian & Cartesian Thought.** Dennis Des Chene. 2000. reprint ed. pap. 19.95 (*0-8014-8687-4*) Cornell U Pr.

Physostegia: Poems from Hollywood. Mark Dunster. 24p. (Orig.). (YA). (gr. 9-12). 1997. pap. 5.00 (*0-89642-362-X*) Linden Pubs.

Physyke of the Soule. Thomas Becon. LC 74-28831. (English Experience Ser.: No. 713). 1975. reprint ed. 20.00 (*90-221-0713-2*) Walter J Johnson.

Phytates in Cereals & Legumes. Ed. by N. R. Reddy. 160p. 1989. lib. bdg. 153.00 (*0-8493-6108-7*, QP801) CRC Pr.

Phyto Nutrients: Medicinal Nutrients Found in Foods. Beth M. Ley. 40p. 1998. pap. 3.95 (*0-9642703-9-0*) B L Pubns.

Phyto Paper No. 32: Status of Eutypa Lata as a Pathogen. M. V. Carter. (Illus.). 70p. (C). 1991. pap. text 38.00 (*0-85198-695-1*) C A B Intl.

Phytochemical Adaptations to Stress. Ed. by Barbara N. Timmermann et al. (Recent Advances in Phytochemistry Ser.: Vol. 18). 334p. 1984. 75.00 (*0-306-41720-0*, Plenum Trade) Perseus Pubng.

Phytochemical Dictionary: A Handbook of Bioactive Compounds from Plants. Ed. by Jeffrey B. Harborne et al. LC 92-26366. 700p. 1993. 395.00 (*0-85066-736-4*) Taylor & Francis.

Phytochemical Dictionary: A Handbook of Bioactive Compounds from Plants. 2nd ed. Jeffrey B. Harborne. LC 99-195675. 1998. 450.00 (*0-7484-0620-4*) Taylor & Francis.

Phytochemical Diversity: A Source of New Industrial Products. Ed. by S. Wrigley et al. (Special Publication Ser.: No. 200). xii, 254p. 1997. 135.00 (*0-85404-717-4*) Am Chemical.

Phytochemical Diversity & Redundancy in Ecological Interactions: Proceedings of the 35th Annual Meeting of the Phytochemical Society of North America Held in Sault St. Marie, Ontario, Canada, August 12-16, 1995. Ed. by John T. Romeo et al. LC 96-47605. (Recent Advances in Phytochemistry Ser.: Vol. 30). (Illus.). 327p. (C). 1996. text 107.00 (*0-306-45500-5*, Kluwer Plenum) Kluwer Academic.

Phytochemical Effects of Environmental Compounds. Ed. by J. A. Saunders et al. LC 87-18659. (Recent Advances in Phytochemistry Ser.: Vol. 21). (Illus.). 278p. 1987. 75.00 (*0-306-42675-7*, Plenum Trade) Perseus Pubng.

Phytochemical Induction by Herbivores. Ed. by Douglas W. Tallamy & Michael J. Raupp. LC 90-24394. 431p. 1991. 190.00 (*0-471-63241-4*) Wiley.

Phytochemical Methods: A Guide to Modern Techniques of Plant Analysis. 2nd ed. Jeffrey B. Harborne. 288p. 1988. pap. 39.50 (*0-412-34330-4*) Chapman & Hall.

***Phytochemical Methods: A Guide to Modern Techniques of Plant Analysis.** 3rd ed. HARBORNE. 1999. pap. write for info. (*0-412-57270-2*) Kluwer Academic.

Phytochemical Potential of Tropical Plants. K. R. Downum et al. (Recent Advances in Phytochemistry Ser.: Vol. 27). (Illus.). 308p. (C). 1993. text 95.00 (*0-306-44527-1*, Kluwer Plenum) Kluwer Academic.

Phytochemical Resources for Medicine & Agriculture. H. N. Nigg & D. Seigler. LC 92-20152. (Illus.). 454p. (C). 1992. text 135.00 (*0-306-44245-0*, Kluwer Plenum) Kluwer Academic.

Phytochemical Signals & Plant-Microbe Interactions: Proceedings of a Joint Meeting of the Phytochemical Society of North America & the Phytochemical Society of Europe Held in Noondwijkerhout, the Netherlands, April 20-23, 1997. Ed. by John T. Romeo. LC 98-19421. (Recent Advances in Phytochemistry Ser.). (Illus.). 264p. 1998. 95.00 (*0-306-45917-5*, Kluwer Plenum) Kluwer Academic.

Phytochemicals: A New Paradigm. Ed. by Wayne R. Bidlack et al. LC 98-86874. 200p. 1998. 104.95 (*1-56676-684-2*) Technomic.

***Phytochemicals & Phytopharmaceuticals.** Fereidoon Shahidi & Chi-Tang Ho. LC 99-56987. 1999. 135.00 (*1-893997-05-7*) Am Oil Chemists.

***Phytochemicals As Bioactive Agents.** Ed. by Wayne R. Bidlack et al. LC 99-69881. 296p. 2000. text 99.95 (*1-56676-788-1*) Technomic.

Phytochemicals for Pest Control, Vol. 658. American Chemical Society Staff. Ed. by Paul A. Hedin et al. LC 96-52457. (Symposium Ser.: No. 658). (Illus.). 356p. 1997. text 115.00 (*0-8412-3488-4*, Pub. by Am Chemical) OUP.

***Phytochemicals in Human Health Protection, Nutrition & Plant Defense.** John T. Romeo. LC 99-37365. (Recent Advances in Phytochemistry Ser.). (C). 1999. text. write for info. (*0-306-46203-6*, Kluwer Plenum) Kluwer Academic.

Phytochemische Analyse Seltener Digitalisarten (Wie Digitalis Subalpina Br.-Bl.) und Reziproker Digitaliskreuzungen. Johannes J. Lichius. (Dissertationes Botanicae Ser.: Band 172). (GER., Illus.). 298p. 1991. pap. 71.00 (*3-443-64084-2*, Pub. by Gebruder Borntraeger) Balogh.

Phytochemistry & Agriculture. Ed. by T. A. Van Beek & H. Breteler. LC 93-4235. (Proceedings of the Phytochemical Society of Europe Ser.: No. 34). 416p. (C). 1994. 95.00 (*0-19-857762-1*, Clarendon Pr) OUP.

Phytochemistry & Angiosperm Phylogeny. Ed. by David A. Young & David S. Seigler. LC 81-8603. 295p. 1981. 69.50 (*0-275-90746-5*, C0746, Praeger Pubs) Greenwood.

Phytochemistry & Chemotaxonomy of Lichenized Ascomycetes: A Festschrift in Honour of Siegfried Huneck. Ed. by Guido B. Feige et al. (Bibliotheca Lichenologica: Vol. 53). (GER., Illus.), xiv, 288p. 1993. pap. 83.00 (*3-443-58032-7*, Pub. by Gebruder Borntraeger) Balogh.

Phytochemistry of Fruits & Vegetables. Ed. by F. A. Tomas-Barberan & R. J. Robins. (Proceedings of the Phytochemical Society of Europe Ser.: No. 41). (Illus.). 398p. 1997. text 140.00 (*0-19-857790-7*) OUP.

Phytochemistry of Medicinal Plants: Proceedings of the Thirty-Fourth Annual Meeting of the Phytochemical Society of North America Held in Mexico City, Mexico, August 15-19, 1994, Vol. 29. Ed. by John T. Arnason et al. LC 95-39616. (Recent Advances in Phytochemistry Ser.: Vol. 29). (Illus.). 372p. 1995. 105.00 (*0-306-45181-6*, Kluwer Plenum) Kluwer Academic.

Phytochemistry of Plants Used in Traditional Medicine. Ed. by K. Hostettmann et al. (Proceedings of the Phytochemical Society of Europe Ser.: No. 37). (Illus.). 422p. 1995. text 145.00 (*0-19-857775-3*) OUP.

Phytochrome Properties & Biological Action. Ed. by B. Thomas & C. B. Johnson. (NATO ASI Series H: Cell Biology: Vol. 50). x, 337p. 1991. 177.95 (*0-387-51770-7*) Spr-Verlag.

***Phytodiversification & Human Welfare: Dedicated to Late Prof. K. S. Bilgrami, FNA (1933-96)** Ed. by A. K. Roy et al. LC 99-931560. 329 p. 1998. pap. 200.00 (*81-7533-077-5*, Pub. by Print Hse) St Mut.

Phytodynamique et Biogeographie Historique des Forets: Bailleul, 1991. Ed. by Jean-Marie Gehu. (Illus.). xx, 436p. 1993. 124.00 (*3-443-70009-8*, Pub. by Gebruder Borntraeger) Balogh.

P

An Asterisk (*) at the beginning of an entry indicates that the title is appearing for the first time.

Phytogeographic Literature on the Central African Savannas see Documents Phytogeographiques sur les Savanes Centrafricaines (Phytogeographic Literature on the Central African Savannas)

Phytogeographic Survey of North America: A Consideration of the Phytogeography of the North American Continent, Including Mexico, Central America & the West Indies, Together with the Evolution of North American Plant Distribution. J. W. Harshberger. (Illus.). 1958. reprint ed. 75.00 (*3-7682-0003-5*) Lubrecht & Cramer.

Phytogeographie Tropicale (Tropical Phytogeography) Realites et Perspectives (Reality & Perspectives), Vol. XXXVII. Ed. by J. L. Guillaumet et al. (ENG & FRE.). 388p. 1996. pap. 25.00 (*2-7099-1356-9*, Pub. by LInstitut Francais) Balogh.

Phytogeography & Vegetation Ecology of Cuba. A. Borhidi. 752p. 1995. 550.00 (*963-05-6956-6*, Pub. by Akade Kiado) St Mut.

Phytogeography & Vegetation Ecology of Cuba. Attila Borhidi. LC 97-200394. 857p. (C). 1991. 222.00 (*963-05-5295-7*, Pub. by Akade Kiado) St Mut.

Phytogeography of Nebraska: General Survey. rev. ed. Roscoe Pound & Frederic E. Clements. Ed. by Frank N. Egerton, 3rd. LC 77-74248. (History of Ecology Ser.). (Illus.). 1978. reprint ed. lib. bdg. 39.95 (*0-405-10417-0*) Ayer.

Phytogeography of Northern Europe: British Isles, Fennoscandia, & Adjacent Areas. Eilif Dahl. LC 96-37970. (Illus.). 310p. (C). 1998. text 95.00 (*0-521-38358-7*) Cambridge U Pr.

Phytohormones in Soils: Microbial Production & Function. Ed. by W. T. Frankenberger & Muhammed Arshad. (Books in Soils, Plants & the Environment Ser.: Vol. 43). (Illus.). 520p. 1995. text 199.00 (*0-8247-9442-7*) Dekker.

Phytolacca Dodecandra (Endod) Aklilu Lemma et al. 332p. 1984. pap. 40.00 (*0-907567-85-1*, Tycooly Pub); text 60.00 (*0-907567-84-3*, Tycooly Pub) Weidner & Sons.

Phytolith Analysis: An Archaeological & Geological Perspective. Dolores R. Piperno. 280p. 1987. text 89.95 (*0-12-557175-5*) Acad Pr.

Phytolith Systematics: Emerging Issues. G. Rapp, Jr. & S. C. Mulholland. (Advances in Archaeological & Museum Science Ser.: Vol. 1). (Illus.). 376p. (C). 1992. 75.00 (*0-306-44208-6*, Plenum Trade) Perseus Pubng.

Phytomedicine, a Treatise on Plant Diseases. N. Nema. (C). 1988. 197.50 (*81-7136-009-2*, Pub. by Periodical Expert) St Mut.

Phytomedicines of Europe: Chemistry & Biological Activity. Ed. by Larry D. Lawson & Rudloph Bauer. (ACS Symposium Ser.: No. 691). (Illus.). 336p. 1998. text 125.00 (*0-8412-3559-7*) OUP.

Phytonematology Study Guide. rev. ed. Michael McKenry. (Illus.). 64p. 1985. reprint ed. pap. text 5.00 (*0-931876-51-6*, 4045) ANR Pubns CA.

Phytopathogehen Grosspilze Deutschlands (Basidiomycetes mit Ausschluss der Rost-und Brandpilze) H. Kreisel. (Illus.). 1979. reprint ed. lib. bdg. 40.00 (*3-7682-1228-9*) Lubrecht & Cramer.

Phytopathogenic Bacteria: Selections from the "The Prokaryotes-A Handbook on Habitats, Isolation, & Identification of Bacteria" Ed. by M. P. Starr. (Illus.). 168p. 1983. 101.00 (*0-387-90880-3*) Spr-Verlag.

Phytopathological Classics of the Eighteenth Century: An Original Anthology. Ed. by Frank N. Egerton, 3rd. LC 77-74247. (History of Ecology Ser.). (Illus.). 1978. lib. bdg. 52.95 (*0-405-10416-2*) Ayer.

Phytopathological Classics of the Nineteenth Century: An Original Anthology. Ed. by Frank N. Egerton, 3rd. LC 77-74246. (History of Ecology Ser.). (Illus.). 1978. lib. bdg. 37.95 (*0-405-10415-4*) Ayer.

Phytopathological Paper No. 33: Vascular-Streak Dieback of Cocoa, No. 33. P. J. Keane & C. Prior. 40p. 1991. pap. 32.50 (*0-85198-733-8*) C A B Intl.

Phytopharmaceutical Technology. P. H. List & P. C. Schmidt. 1990. 105.00 (*0-8493-7709-9*) CRC Pr.

Phytophthora. Ed. by J. D. Lucas et al. (British Mycological Society Symposium Ser.: No. 17). 461p. (C). 1991. text 125.00 (*0-521-40080-5*) Cambridge U Pr.

Phytophthora: Its Biology, Taxonomy, Ecology & Pathology. Ed. by D. C. Erwin et al. 392p. 1988. pap. 53.00 (*0-89054-084-5*) Am Phytopathol Soc.

Phytophthora Disease of Cocoa. Ed. by Philip H. Gregory. LC 73-85686. 372p. reprint ed. pap. 115.40 (*0-608-14472-X*, 202097900020) Bks Demand.

Phytophthora Diseases of Forest Trees. Ed. by E. M. Hansen & W. Sutton. Date not set. write for info. (*0-87437-002-7*) Forest Research Laboratory.

Phytophthora Diseases Worldwide. D. C. Erwin & O. K. Ribeiro. LC 95-83805. (Illus.). 550p. (C). 1996. text 159.00 (*0-89054-212-0*) Am Phytopathol Soc.

Phytopia Cookbook: A World of Plant-Centered Cuisine. Barbara Gollman & Kim Pierce. LC 97-95067. (Illus.). 192p. 1998. pap. 17.95 (*0-9661875-4-7*) Phytopia Pr.

Phytoplankton & Trophic Gradients, Vol. 129. M. Alvarez-Cobelas & International Association of Phytoplankton Taxonom. LC 98-24597. (Developments in Hydrobiology Ser.). 372p. 1998. write for info. (*0-7923-5171-1*) Kluwer Academic.

Phytoplankton des Suesswassers. Systematik und Biologie, Band XVI. Gottfried Huber-Pestalozzi. (Binnengewaesser Ser.: Teil 2, 2). (GER., Illus.). x, 183p. 1975. 35.00 (*3-510-40018-6*, Pub. by E Schweizerbartsche) Balogh.

Phytoplankton des Suesswassers. Systematik und Biologie: Freilebende Copepoda - Freeliving Stages of Freshwater Parasitic Copepoda, Band XVI. Friedrich Kiefer & Geoffrey Fryer. (Binnengewaesser Ser.: Teil II). (ENG & GER., Illus.). viii, 380p. 1978. 64.00 (*3-510-40036-4*, Pub. by E Schweizerbartsche) Balogh.

Phytoplankton des Susswasers, Systematik und Biologie: Chrysophyceen, Farblose Flagellaten, Heterokonten, Band XVI. Gottfried Huber-Pestalozzi. (Binnengewaesser Ser.: Teil 2, 1). (GER., Illus.). v, 365p. 1941. 58.00 (*3-510-40017-8*, Pub. by E Schweizerbartsche) Balogh.

Phytoplankton des Susswasers, Systematik und Biologie Teil 7, 1: Chlorophyceae (Gruenalgen), Ordung Chlorococcales Von Jiri Komarek und Bohuslav Fott. Gottfried Huber-Pestalozzi. (Binnengewaesser Ser.: Band XVI). (GER., Illus.). viii, 543p. 1982. 176.00 (*3-510-40024-0*, Pub. by E Schweizerbartsche) Balogh.

Phytoplankton des Susswassers - Systematik und Biologie, Band XVI. Gottfried Huber-Pestalozzi. (Binnengewaesser Ser.: Teil 6). (GER., Illus.). x, 116p. 1972. 33.00 (*3-510-40022-4*, Pub. by E Schweizerbartsche) Balogh.

Phytoplankton des Susswassers - Systematik und Biologie, Band XVI. Gottfried Huber-Pestalozzi. (Binnengewaesser Ser.: Teil 7, 1). (GER., Illus.). x, 1044p. 1983. 176.00 (*3-510-40023-2*, Pub. by Gebruder Borntraeger) Balogh.

Phytoplankton des Susswassers, Systematik und Biologie Teil 5: Chlorophyceae (Gruenalgen), Ordnung Volvacales. Gottfried Huber-Pestalozzi. (Binnengewaesser Ser.: Band XVI). (GER., Illus.). xii, 744p. 1974. 135.00 (*3-510-40021-6*, Pub. by E Schweizerbartsche) Balogh.

Phytoplankton Dynamics in the North American Great Lakes Vol. 1: Lakes Ontario, Erie, St. Clair. M. Munawar et al. 275p. 1997. 110.00 (*90-5103-115-7*, Pub. by SPB Acad Pub) Balogh.

Phytoplankton Dynamics in the North American Great Lakes Vol. 2: Lakes Huron, Superior & Michigan. M. Munawar. 275p. 1998. 110.00 (*0-614-23637-1*, Pub. by SPB Acad Pub) Balogh.

Phytoplankton in Turbid Environments - Rivers & Shallow Lakes: Proceedings of the 9th Workshop of the International Association of Phytoplankton Taxonomy & Ecology (IAP) Held in Mont Rigi (Belgium), 10-18 July 1993. Ed. by J. P. Descy et al. LC 94-32312. (Developments in Hydrobiology Ser.: Vol. 100). 240p. (C). 1994. text 213.00 (*0-7923-3111-7*) Kluwer Academic.

Phytoplankton of Lac St-Jean, Quebec. H. Contant & H. C. Duthie. (Bibliotheca Phycologica Ser.: No. 40). (Illus.). 1978. pap. text 40.00 (*3-7682-1198-3*) Lubrecht & Cramer.

Phytoplankton of the Gulf of Mexico: Taxonomy of Calcareous Nannoplankton. R. W. Pierce & G. F. Hart. (Geoscience & Man Ser.: Vol. 20). (Illus.). 106p. 1979. pap. 12.00 (*0-938909-19-3*) Geosci Pubns LSU.

Phytoplankton of the Inland Lakes of Wisconsin, 2 vols. in one. G. M. Smith. 1977. reprint ed. 120.00 (*3-7682-1134-7*) Lubrecht & Cramer.

Phytoplankton, Zooplankton, & Ichthyoplankton in Resurrection Bay. A. J. Paul et al. (Alaska Sea Grant Report: No. 91-02). 22p. 1991. pap. 4.00 (*1-56612-002-0*) AK Sea Grant CP.

***Phytoremediation & Innovative Strategies for Specialized Remedial Applications.** Ed. by Bruce C. Alleman & Andrea Leeson. LC 99-23328. (Situ & On-Site Bioremediation Symposium Ser.). 314p. 1999. 65.00 (*1-57477-079-9*) Battelle.

***Phytoremediation of Contaminated Soil & Groundwater.** Norman Terry. (Illus.). 300p. 1999. text 69.95 (*0-8493-4113-2*) CRC Pr.

Phytoremediation of Contaminated Soil & Water. Norman Terry & Gary Banuelos. LC 99-30741. 389p. 1999. ring bd. 69.95 (*1-56670-450-2*) Lewis Pubs.

***Phytoremediation of Hydrocarbon Contaminiated Soils.** Stephanie Fiorenza et al. 192p. 1999. boxed set 64.95 (*1-56670-463-4*) Lewis Pubs.

Phytoremediation of Soil & Water Contaminants. Ed. by Ellen L. Kruger et al. LC 97-5740. (Symposium Ser.: No. 664). (Illus.). 328p. 1997. text 109.95 (*0-8412-3503-1*, Pub. by Am Chemical) OUP.

***Phytoremediation of Toxic Metals: Plants to Clean up the Environment, 1.** Ilya Raskin & Burt D. Ensley. LC 99-43427. 304p. 1999. 89.95 (*0-471-19254-6*) Wiley.

Phytoserologische Untersuchungen Zur Systematik der Euphorbiaceae: Beitraege zur intrafamiliaeren Gliederung und zu Beziehungen im Extrafamiliaeren Bereich. Christina Vogel. (Dissertationes Botanicae Ser.: Band 98). (GER., Illus.). iv, 124p. 1986. pap. 24.00 (*3-443-64010-9*, Pub. by Gebruder Borntraeger) Balogh.

Phytosociological Study of the Upper Orange River Valley. M. J. Werger. (Memoirs of the Botanical Survey of South Africa Ser.: No. 46). (Illus.). 98p. 1980. 15.00 (*0-621-05308-2*, Pub. by Natl Botanical Inst) Balogh.

Phytosociologie et Conservation de la Nature. Ed. by Jean-Marie Gehu. (Colloque Phytosociologiques Ser.: Vol. XV). (FRE., Illus.). v, 790p. 1988. 130.00 (*3-443-70004-7*, Pub. by Gebruder Borntraeger) Balogh.

Phytosociologie et Foresterie. Ed. by Jean-Marie Gehu. (Colloque Phytosociologiques Ser.: Vol. XIV). (FRE., Illus.). viii, 813p. 1988. 130.00 (*3-443-70003-9*, Pub. by Gebruder Borntraeger) Balogh.

Phytosociologie et Pastoralisme. Ed. by Jean-Marie Gehu. (Colloque Phytosociologiques Ser.: Vol. XVI). (ENG, FRE & SPA., Illus.). vii, 859p. 1988. 165.00 (*3-443-70005-5*, Pub. by Gebruder Borntraeger) Balogh.

Phytosociologie et Paysage: Versailles, 1988. Ed. by Jean-Marie Gehu. (Colloque Phytosociologiques Ser.). (Illus.). xiv, 519p. 1991. 165.00 (*3-443-70006-3*, Pub. by Gebruder Borntraeger) Balogh.

Phytosociologie Littorale et Taxonomie. Ed. by Jean-Marie Gehu. (Colloque Phytosociologiques Ser.: Vol. XVIII). (FRE., Illus.). xvi, 350p. 1989. 89.00 (*3-443-70007-1*, Pub. by Gebruder Borntraeger) Balogh.

Phytotelmata: Terrestrial Plants As Hosts of Aquatic Insect Communities. Ed. by J. H. Frank & L. P. Lounibus. 293p. 1983. pap. 24.95 (*0-937548-05-7*) Plexus Pub.

Phytotherapy in Paediatrics: Handbook for Physicians & Pharmacists. 2nd rev. ed. Heinz Schilcher. Tr. by A. R. Meuss from GER. 181p. (C). 1997. pap. text 35.00 (*3-88763-026-2*, Pub. by Medpharm Scientific Pubs) Medicina Bio.

***Phytotherapy of Chronic Fatigue Syndrome: Evidence-Based & Potentially Useful Botanicals in the Treatment of CFS.** Roberto Patarca-Montero. LC 00-33544. 2000. write for info. (*0-7890-0909-9*, Hawrth Medical) Haworth Pr.

Phyzzics for Kids. Carole Marsh. (Quantum Leap Ser.). (J). (gr. 4-9). 1994. 29.95 (*1-55609-258-X*); pap. 19.95 (*1-55609-245-8*); disk 29.95 (*1-55609-340-3*) Gallopade Intl.

PI. Darren Aronofsky. (Illus.). 160p. 1999. pap. 14.00 (*0-571-20042-7*) Faber & Faber.

PI: A Hodge-Podge of the Letters, Papers, & Addresses Written During the Last Sixty Years. Bruce Rogers. LC 79-167407. (Essay Index Reprint Ser.). 1977. reprint ed. 20.95 (*0-8369-2669-2*) Ayer.

PI: A Self-Study Guide on Becoming a Private Detective. Roger Willard. 128p. 1997. pap. 18.00 (*0-87364-954-0*) Paladin Pr.

***PI: A Source Book.** 2nd ed. Lennart Berggren et al. LC 99-46584. 752p. 1999. 64.95 (*0-387-98946-3*) Spr-Verlag.

PI - 101. Greg Hauser. 1997. spiral bd. 35.00 (*1-882852-02-8*) Marinelli Publishing.

***Pi - Unleashed.** Jorg Arndt. 250p. 2000. pap. text 39.95 (*3-540-66572-2*) Spr-Verlag.

***PI & the AGM: A Study in Analytic Number Theory & Computational Complexity, Vol. 1.** Jonathan M. Borwein & Peter B. Borwein. (Canadian Mathematical Society Series & Advanced Texts). 432p. 1998. pap. 64.95 (*0-471-31515-X*) Wiley.

Pi in the Sky: A Revelation of the Ancient Celtic Wisdom Tradition. Michael Poynder & George Trevelyan. 192p. 1998. pap. 29.95 (*1-898256-33-0*, Pub. by Collins Press) Dufour.

Pi-Pi Scattering, 1973, No. 13. American Institute of Physics. Ed. by D. K. Williams & V. Hagopian. LC 73-81704. (AIP Conference Proceedings Ser.). 361p. 1973. 14.00 (*0-88318-112-6*) Am Inst Physics.

***Pi, the Reciprocal of Seven & Trigono/MetriX.** Charles William Johnson. (Science in Ancient Artwork Ser.). (Illus.). 80p. 1999. pap. 30.00 (*1-58616-178-4*, 178-4) Earth Matrix.

PIA Desideria. Philip J. Spener. Ed. & Tr. by Theodore G. Tappert. LC 64-12995. 136p. 1964. pap. 14.00 (*0-8006-1953-6*, 1-1953, Fortress Pr) Augsburg Fortress.

***PIA Productivity Benchmarks: Sheetfed Printers' Production Characteristics.** PIA Staff. (Illus.). 50p. 2000. pap. text 129.00 (*0-88362-310-2*) GATFPress.

PIA Ratios, 14 vols. 995.00 (*0-614-25528-7*, 00FM44263) Print Indus Am.

PIA Safety Manual. VHS 190.00 (*0-614-25593-7*, 00ES25161); VHS 80.00 (*0-614-25594-5*, 00ES5193) Print Indus Am.

***PIA Survey of Printing Management & Administrative Compensation: 1999-2000 Edition.** PIA Staff. 145p. (C). 2000. pap. text 250.00 (*0-88362-296-3*) GATFPress.

***PIA Survey of Sales Compensation: 1999-2000 Edition.** PIA Staff. 222p. (C). 2000. pap. text 250.00 (*0-88362-295-5*) GATFPress.

***PIA Technology Benchmarks: Printes' Awareness, Use & Assessment of New Graphic Communications Technology, 1999 Edition.** PIA Staff. (Illus.). 56p. (C). 1999. pap. text 129.00 (*0-88362-263-7*) GATFPress.

***PIA Toya: A Goshute Indian Legend.** (Illus.). 48p. 2000. 11.95 (*0-87480-661-5*) U of Utah Pr.

Piadosas. Federico Andahazi.Tr. of Pious. 219p. 1999. pap. 12.95 (*0-553-06099-6*) Bantam.

Piaf. Margaret Crosland. LC 87-74. (Illus.). 240p. 1987. reprint ed. pap. 8.95 (*0-88064-069-3*) Fromm Intl Pub.

***Piaf: A Passionate Life.** David Bret. 282p. 1999. 30.95 (*1-86105-218-9*) Robson.

***Piaf in Context.** Margaret Crosland. 2000. pap. 14.95 (*1-900850-50-8*) Arcadia Bks.

Piaffer & Passage. Decarpentry. LC 98-22033. (Masters of Horsemanship Ser.). 1998. 26.95 (*0-939481-51-0*) Half Halt Pr.

Piaget: Watches & Wonders since 1874. Franco Cologni et al. (Illus.). 264p. 1996. 85.00 (*0-7892-0078-3*); 39.98 (*0-89660-097-1*, Artabras) Abbeville Pr.

Piaget: A Handbook for Parents & Teachers in the Age of Discovery see Piaget Handbook for Teachers & Parents: Children in the Age of Discovery, Preschool to 3rd Grade

Piaget & Knowledge: Theoretical Foundations. Hans G. Furth. LC 80-26284. 302p. 1995. pap. text 9.00 (*0-226-27420-9*) U Ch Pr.

Piaget & Knowledge: Theoretical Foundations. 2nd ed. Hans G. Furth. LC 80-26284. (Illus.). 324p. reprint ed. pap. 100.50 (*0-608-09305-X*, 205417900004) Bks Demand.

Piaget & the Foundations of Knowledge. Ed. by Lynn Liben. 272p. 1984. text 59.95 (*0-89859-248-8*) L Erlbaum Assocs.

Piaget as a Visionary Thinker. Mary V. Goot. LC 89-40378. 67p. (C). 1989. text 32.00 (*1-55605-078-X*); pap. text 16.00 (*0-932269-24-9*) Wyndham Hall.

Piaget Before Piaget. Fernando Vidal. LC 93-43068. 448p. 1994. 51.95 (*0-674-66716-6*) HUP.

Piaget, Evolution, & Development. Ed. by Jonas Langer & Melanie Killen. LC 98-12663. (Jean Piaget Symposia Ser.). 270p. 1998. write for info. (*0-8058-2210-0*) L Erlbaum Assocs.

***Piaget for Beginners.** Adriana Serulnicov. (Illus.). 192p. 1999. pap. 11.95 (*0-86316-288-6*) Writers & Readers.

Piaget for Educators. 2nd ed. Rodger W. Bybee & Robert B. Sund. (Illus.). 318p. (C). 1990. reprint ed. pap. text 24.95 (*0-88133-516-9*) Waveland Pr.

Piaget Handbook for Teachers & Parents: Children in the Age of Discovery, Preschool to 3rd Grade. Rosemary Peterson & Victoria Felton-Collins. (Early Childhood Education Ser.). Orig. Title: Piaget: A Handbook for Parents & Teachers in the Age of Discovery. 80p. (C). 1986. pap. text 11.95 (*0-8077-2841-1*) Tchrs Coll.

Piaget or the Advance of Knowledge: An Overview & Glossary. Jacques Montangero & Danielle Maurice-Naville. LC 97-12995. 192p. 1997. pap. 22.50 (*0-8058-2568-1*) L Erlbaum Assocs.

Piaget or the Advance of Knowledge: An Overview & Glossary. Jacques Montangero & Danielle Maurice-Naville. LC 97-12995. 192p. 1997. 45.00 (*0-8058-2567-3*) L Erlbaum Assocs.

Piaget, Philosophy & the Human Sciences. Hugh J. Silverman. LC 97-2643. 1997. pap. 16.95 (*0-8101-1497-6*) Northwestern U Pr.

Piaget Primer: How a Child Thinks. rev. ed. Dorothy G. Singer & Tracey A. Revenson. LC 97-6225. 1997. 27.95 (*0-8236-4134-1*) Intl Univs Pr.

Piaget Primer: How a Child Thinks. variorum ed. Dorothy G. Singer & Tracey A. Revenson. 160p. (C). 1996. pap. 12.95 (*0-452-27565-2*) NAL.

Piaget Sampler: An Introduction to Jean Piaget Through His Own Words. Jean Piaget. Ed. by Sarah F. Campbell. LC 75-34129. 168p. reprint ed. pap. 52.10 (*0-608-30711-4*, 202059400018) Bks Demand.

Piaget Systematized. Gilbert Voyat. (Illus.). 240p. 1982. text 49.95 (*0-89859-026-4*) L Erlbaum Assocs.

Piaget Theory of Intellectual Development. 3rd ed. Herbert Ginsbury & Sylvia Opper. 272p. 1987. pap. text 51.00 (*0-13-675158-X*) P-H.

Piaget-Vygotsky: The Social Genesis of Thought. Anastasia Tryphon & Jacques Voneche. Ed. by Jean P. Archives. 224p. 1996. pap. 24.95 (*0-86377-414-8*) Psychol Pr.

Piaget Vygotsky & Beyond. Ed. by Leslie Smith & Julie Dockrell. LC 98-107787. (Illus.). 280p. (C). 1997. 100.00 (*0-415-14743-3*) Routledge.

Piagetian Activities: A Diagnostic & Developmental Approach. Richard Copeland. 225p. 1988. spiral bd. 35.00 (*0-930599-17-9*) Thinking Pubns.

Piagetian Dimensions of Clinical Relevance. Hugh Rosen. LC 85-2608. 320p. 1985. text 64.50 (*0-231-06076-9*) Col U Pr.

Piagetian Epistemology of William Wordsworth: A Reconsideration of the Poet's Genius. Ronald L. Terranella. LC 98-22007. (Salzburg Romantic Reassessment Ser.: Vol. 150). 112p. 1998. text 59.95 (*0-7734-8294-6*) E Mellen.

Piagetian Model of Character Structure. Abraham J. Malerstein & Mary Ahern. 252p. (C). 1993. text 22.50 (*0-9644089-0-2*) Cole Valley Pr.

Piaget's Babies: The First Two Years of Life: Child Development for the Intellectual. Joanne Burnett. 200p. (Orig.). 1995. pap. 21.95 (*0-9647389-0-2*) J Burnett.

Piaget's Conception of Evolution: Beyond Darwin & Lamarck. John G. Masserly. 184p. 1996. pap. text 23.95 (*0-8476-8243-9*) Rowman.

Piaget's Conception of Evolution: Beyond Darwin & Lamarck. John G. Masserly. 184p. 1996. lib. bdg. 55.50 (*0-8476-8242-0*) Rowman.

Piaget's Construction of the Child's Reality. Susan Sugarman. (Illus.). 328p. 1987. text 59.95 (*0-521-34164-7*) Cambridge U Pr.

Piaget's Construction of the Child's Reality. Susan Sugarman. (Illus.). 266p. (C). 1990. pap. text 20.95 (*0-521-37967-9*) Cambridge U Pr.

Piaget's Theory: A Primer. John L. Phillips, Jr. LC 80-20800. (Psychology Ser.). (Illus.). (C). 1981. pap. text 11.20 (*0-7167-1236-9*) W H Freeman.

Piaget's Theory: Prospects & Possibilities. Ed. by Harry Beilin & Peter Pufall. (Jean Piaget Symposia Ser.). 360p. 1992. text 79.95 (*0-8058-1050-1*) L Erlbaum Assocs.

Piaget's Theory of Cognitive & Affective Development. 5th ed. Barry J. Wadsworth. 176p. (C). 1995. pap. text. write for info. (*0-8013-1698-7*) Addison-Wesley.

Piaget's Theory of Cognitive & Affective Development: Foundations of Constructivism. 5th ed. Barry J. Wadsworth. LC 95-14394. 195p. (C). 1995. pap. 49.00 (*0-8013-0773-2*) Longman.

Piaget's Theory of Intellectual Development. 3rd ed. Herbert P. Ginsburg & Sylvia Opper. (Illus.). 272p. 1988. pap. text 13.50 (*0-317-63001-6*) P-H.

PIALA '98: Libraries, Archives & Museums - What's in Them for Us? Ed. by Arlene Cohen. LC 99-462607. 1999. pap. text 25.00 (*1-892485-05-2*) Pacfc Islds Assn.

Piala '95: Preservation of Culture Through Archives & Libraries. Ed. by Arlene Cohen. vii, 125p. 1996. pap. text 20.00 (*1-892485-02-8*) Pacfc Islds Assn.

Piala '94 - Pacific Information Liberation: The Wave of the Future. Ed. by Arlene Cohen. vi, 114p. 1995. pap. text 13.50 (*1-892485-01-X*) Pacfc Islds Assn.

Piala '97 Wasahn Kamarain: Place of Enlightenment. Ed. by Arlene Cohen. LC 99-179475. 1998. pap. text 25.00 (*1-892485-04-4*) Pacfc Islds Assn.

Piala '96: Jaketo Jaketak Kobban Alele Eo: Identifying, Using & Sharing Local Resources. Ed. by Arlene Cohen. vii, 125p. 1997. pap. text 25.00 (*1-892485-03-6*) Pacfc Islds Assn.

***Pian.** Mathew Lee. 2000. text. write for info. (*0-312-24228-X*) St Martin.

PIA/NAPL Printing Professionals Compensation Survey. 195.00 (*0-614-25524-4*, OOHR44535); 195.00 (*0-614-25556-2*, 00HR44535) Print Indus Am.

P

***Pianist.** Wladyslaw Szpilman. LC 99-36033. 240p. 1999. text 23.00 (0-312-24415-0, Picador USA) St Martin.

***Pianist: The Extraordinary Story of One Man's Survival in Warsaw, 1939-1945.** large type ed. Wladyslaw Szpilman. LC 99-87901. (General Ser.). (Illus.). 2000. pap. 23.95 (0-7862-2420-7) Thorndike Pr.

***Pianist: The Extraordinary True Story of One Man's Survival in Warsaw, 1939-1945.** Wladyslaw Szpilman. (Illus.). 224p. 2000. pap. 13.00 (0-312-26376-7, Picador USA) St Martin.

Pianist As Orator: Beethoven & the Transformation of Keyboard Style. George Barth. LC 92-52743. (Illus.). 200p. 1992. text 37.50 (0-8014-2411-9) Cornell U Pr.

Pianist Who Liked Ayn Rand: A Novella & 13 Stories. Gene H. Bell-Villada. LC 98-71489. 256p. 1999. pap. 14.00 (0-938513-24-9) Amador Pubs.

Pianista Virtuoso: En Sesenta Ejercicios Piano. C. Hanon. (SPA.). 120p. 1986. per. 9.95 (0-7935-3914-5) H Leonard.

Pianist's Bookshelf: A Practical Guide to Books, Videos, & Other Resources. Maurice Hinson. LC 97-47307. 352p. 1998. 35.00 (0-253-33332-6); pap. 18.95 (0-253-21145-X) Ind U Pr.

Pianist's Chord Manual, EFS150. (Illus.). 48p. 1972. pap. 8.95 (0-8256-2150-X, AM40668) Music Sales.

Pianist's Guide to Blues, Jazz, & Melodic Imp. Herb Drury. 104p. 1994. spiral bd. 11.95 (1-56222-905-2, 95080) Mel Bay.

Pianist's Guide to Pedaling. Joseph Banowetz. LC 84-47534. (Illus.). 320p. 1992. reprint ed. pap. 15.95 (0-253-20732-0) Ind U Pr.

Pianists' Guide to Progressive Finger Fitness. Richard Bobo & Jana Bobo. 1994. 24.95 (0-9633819-5-4) Prescott Pub.

Pianists Guide to Standard Literature. Magrath. 1995. pap. 29.95 (0-88284-655-8) Alfred Pub.

Pianist's Landscape. Carol Montparker. LC 97-49643. (Illus.). 297p. 1998. 24.95 (1-57467-039-5, Amadeus Pr) Timber.

Pianists on Playing: Interviews with 12 Concert Pianists. Linda J. Noyle. LC 86-29810. (Illus.). 187p. 1987. 24.00 (0-8108-1953-8) Scarecrow.

Pianist's Picture Chords. Roger Day. (Illus.). 32p. 1978. pap. 8.95 (0-86001-528-9, AM21429) Music Sales.

Pianist's Problems. 4th ed. William S. Newman. (Quality Paperbacks Ser.). (Illus.). x, 208p. 1986. reprint ed. pap. 11.95 (0-306-80269-4) Da Capo.

Pianist's Reference Guide: A Bibliographical Survey. Maurice Hinson. 352p. (Orig.). 1987. pap. 14.95 (0-88284-358-3, 1400) Alfred Pub.

Pianist's Talent. Harold Taylor. pap. 8.15 (0-912483-65-2, T081) Pro-Am Music.

Pianist's Treasury: One Hundred Pieces from Across the Centuries. (Kevin Mayhew Ser.). 300p. 1995. 35.00 (0-7866-1881-7, MB95799) Mel Bay.

Pi(ankh)y in Egypt: A Study of the Pi(ankh)y Stela. Hans Goedicke. LC 98-38763. 239p. 1998. pap. 40.00 (1-892840-00-6) Halgo Inc.

Pianna. Mary L. Ray. LC 91-14609. (Illus.). 32p. (J). (ps-3). 1994. 14.95 (0-15-261357-9, Harcourt Child Bks) Harcourt.

Piano. 32p. 1981. pap. 0.95 (0-87166-551-4, 93750) Mel Bay.

Piano. Philip Belt. (New Grove Ser.). 1997. pap. 14.95 (0-393-30518-X) Norton.

Piano. Phillip R. Belt. Ed. by Stanley Sadie. (New Grove Musical Instrument Ser.). (Illus.). 1988. 22.50 (0-393-02553-5) Norton.

Piano. Fred Bock. (Bock's Best Ser.: Vol. 2). 1997. pap. 24.95 (0-7935-9394-8) H Leonard.

Piano. Jane Campion. (Illus.). 160p. (J). 1993. pap. 9.50 (1-56282-703-0, Pub. by Hyperion) Time Warner.

Piano. Ed. by Tricia Hedge. (Illus.). 48p. 1989. pap. text 5.95 (0-19-421630-6) OUP.

Piano. Louis Kentner. (Illus.). 1976. write for info. (0-318-54245-5); pap. 9.95 (0-685-03272-8) Macmillan.

***Piano.** William Miller. LC 99-38004. (Illus.). 32p. (J). (ps-7). 2000. 15.95 (1-880000-98-9, Pub. by Lee & Low Bks) Publishers Group.

Piano. Jeremy Siepmann. LC 97-217293. 1997. 47.50 (0-375-40022-2) Random.

Piano. large type ed. Jane Campion & Kate Pullinger. (Charnwood Large Print Ser.). 1995. 27.99 (0-7089-8833-4, Charnwood) Ulverscroft.

Piano, Bk. 3. pap. 6.50 (0-685-69121-7, Chester Music) Music Sales.

Piano: A History. 2nd rev. ed. Cyril Ehrlich. (Illus.). 262p. 1990. pap. text 24.95 (0-19-816171-9) OUP.

Piano: A Novel. Jane Campion & Kate Pullinger. 218p. (J). 1995. pap. 12.45 (0-7868-8096-1, Pub. by Hyperion) Time Warner.

Piano: A Photographic History of the World's Most Celebrated Instrument. David Crombie. (Illus.). 112p. 1995. 35.00 (0-87930-372-7) Miller Freeman.

Piano: A Piano Technician's Guide for the Piano Owner. Philip Gurlik, Jr. 40p. (Orig.). 1986. pap. 2.95 (0-918464-66-8) Bookman Hse.

Piano: Music from the Film. 1997. 12.95 (0-7119-3322-7, CH 60871) Omnibus NY.

***Piano: The Complete Illustrated Guide to the World's Most Popular Musical Instrument.** Jeremy Siepmann. 1998. pap. text 19.95 (0-7935-9976-8) H Leonard.

Piano - Beds & Music by Steam: An Index with Abstracts to Music-Related United States Patent Records, 1790-1874. Jean M. Bonin. LC 92-93191. (Reference Books in Music: No. 24). xxii, 236p. 1993. 39.50 (0-914913-17-4, Fallen Lef Pr) Scarecrow.

Piano - Guitar. (Standard of Excellence Ser.: Bk. 1). 1993. 6.45 (0-8497-5947-1, W21PG) Kjos.

Piano - Guitar. (Standard of Excellence Ser.: Bk. 2). 1994. 6.45 (0-8497-5972-2, W22PG) Kjos.

Piano - Guitar. Bruce Pearson. (Standard of Excellence Ser.: Bk. 3). 1996. 6.45 (0-8497-5993-5, W23PG) Kjos.

Piano Accompaniments, Bk. 1. Peter Davey. 64p. (J). 1998. pap. 10.95 (0-7136-3728-5, Pub. by A & C Blk) Midpt Trade.

Piano Accompaniment, Bk. 1. Jacquelyn Dillon et al. (Strictly Strings Ser.). (Illus.). 64p. (J). (gr. 4-6). 1992. pap. 11.95 (0-88284-535-7, 5298) Alfred Pub.

Piano Adventures Christmas Book: A Basic Piano Method, Level 1. Nancy Faber & Randall Faber. Ed. by Victoria McArthur. (Illus.). 20p. (Orig.). (J). (gr. 1). 1996. pap. 4.95 (1-56939-036-3, FF1138) FJH Music Co Inc.

Piano Adventures Christmas Book: A Basic Piano Method, Level 2B. Nancy Faber & Randall Faber. Ed. by Victoria McArthur. (Piano Adventures Library). (Illus.). 20p. (Orig.). (J). (gr. 2). 1996. pap. 4.95 (1-56939-037-1, FF1139) FJH Music Co Inc.

Piano Adventures Christmas Book: A Basic Piano Method, Level 2B. Nancy Faber & Randall Faber. Ed. by Victoria McArthur & Carol Matz. (Piano Adventures Library). (Illus.). 24p. (Orig.). (J). (gr. 2). 1996. pap. 4.95 (1-56939-042-8, FF1140) FJH Music Co Inc.

Piano Adventures Christmas Book: A Basic Piano Method, Level 3. Nancy Faber & Randall Faber. Ed. by Victoria McArthur & Carol Matz. (Piano Adventures Library). (Illus.). 28p. (Orig.). (J). (gr. 3). 1996. pap. 5.50 (1-56939-040-1, FF1141) FJH Music Co Inc.

Piano Adventures Christmas Book: A Basic Piano Method, Level 4. Nancy Faber & Randall Faber. Ed. by Victoria McArthur & Carol Matz. (Piano Adventures Library). (Illus.). 32p. (Orig.). (J). (gr. 4). 1996. pap. 5.50 (1-56939-047-9, FF1142) FJH Music Co Inc.

Piano Adventures Christmas Book: A Basic Piano Method, Primer Level. Nancy Faber & Randall Faber. Ed. by Victoria McArthur. (Piano Adventures Library). (Illus.). 16p. (Orig.). (J). (gr. k). 1996. pap. 3.95 (1-56939-035-5, FF1137) FJH Music Co Inc.

Piano Adventures Lesson Book: A Basic Piano Method, Level 1. Nancy Faber & Randall Faber. Ed. by Victoria McArthur & Edwin McLean. (Piano Adventures Library). (Illus.). 56p. (Orig.). (J). (gr. 1). 1993. pap. 6.50 (0-929666-59-3) FJH Music Co Inc.

Piano Adventures Lesson Book: A Basic Piano Method, Level 2A. Nancy Faber & Randall Faber. Ed. by Victoria McArthur & Edwin McLean. (Piano Adventures Library). (Illus.). 48p. (Orig.). (J). (gr. 2). 1993. pap. 6.50 (0-929666-62-3) FJH Music Co Inc.

Piano Adventures Lesson Book: A Basic Piano Method, Level 2B. Nancy Faber & Randall Faber. Ed. by Victoria McArthur & Edwin McLean. (Piano Adventures Library). (Illus.). 56p. (Orig.). (J). (gr. 2). 1994. pap. 6.50 (0-929666-66-6, FF1084) FJH Music Co Inc.

Piano Adventures Lesson Book: A Basic Piano Method, Level 3. Nancy Faber & Randall Faber. Ed. by Victoria McArthur & Edwin McLean. (Piano Adventures Library). (Illus.). 48p. (Orig.). (J). (gr. 3). 1994. pap. 5.95 (0-929666-69-0, FF1087) FJH Music Co Inc.

Piano Adventures Lesson Book: A Basic Piano Method, Level 4. Nancy Faber & Randall Faber. Ed. by Victoria McArthur & Edwin McLean. (Piano Adventures Library). (Illus.). 48p. (Orig.). (J). (gr. 4). 1995. pap. 5.95 (0-929666-87-9, FF1090) FJH Music Co Inc.

Piano Adventures Lesson Book: A Basic Piano Method, Primer Level. Nancy Faber & Randall Faber. Ed. by Victoria McArthur & Edwin McLean. (Piano Adventures Library). (Illus.). 64p. (Orig.). (J). (gr. k). 1993. pap. 6.50 (0-929666-54-2) FJH Music Co Inc.

Piano Adventures Performance Book: A Basic Piano Method, Level 1. Nancy Faber & Randall Faber. Ed. by Victoria McArthur & Edwin McLean. (Piano Adventures Library). (Illus.). 32p. (Orig.). (J). (gr. 1). 1993. pap. 5.50 (0-929666-61-5) FJH Music Co Inc.

Piano Adventures Performance Book: A Basic Piano Method, Level 2A. Nancy Faber & Randall Faber. Ed. by Victoria McArthur & Edwin McLean. (Piano Adventures Library). (Illus.). 32p. (Orig.). (J). (gr. 2). 1993. pap. 5.50 (0-929666-65-8) FJH Music Co Inc.

Piano Adventures Performance Book: A Basic Piano Method, Level 2B. Nancy Faber & Randall Faber. Ed. by Victoria McArthur & Edwin McLean. (Piano Adventures Library). (Illus.). 32p. (Orig.). (J). (gr. 2). 1994. pap. 5.50 (0-929666-68-2, FF1086) FJH Music Co Inc.

Piano Adventures Performance Book: A Basic Piano Method, Level 3. Nancy Faber & Randall Faber. Ed. by Victoria McArthur & Edwin McLean. (Piano Adventures Library). (Illus.). 32p. (Orig.). (J). (gr. 3). 1994. pap. 5.50 (0-929666-84-4, FF1089) FJH Music Co Inc.

Piano Adventures Performance Book: A Basic Piano Method, Level 4. Nancy Faber & Randall Faber. Ed. by Victoria McArthur & Edwin McLean. (Piano Adventures Library). (Illus.). 32p. (Orig.). (J). (gr. 4). 1995. pap. 5.50 (0-929666-92-5, FF1092) FJH Music Co Inc.

Piano Adventures Performance Book: A Basic Piano Method, Primer Level. Nancy Faber & Randall Faber. Ed. by Victoria McArthur & Edwin McLean. (Piano Adventures Library). (Illus.). 32p. (Orig.). (J). (gr. k). 1993. pap. 5.50 (0-929666-56-9) FJH Music Co Inc.

Piano Adventures Technique & Artistry Book: A Basic Piano Method, Level 1. Nancy Faber et al. (Piano Adventures Library). (Illus.). 40p. (Orig.). (J). (gr. 1). 1996. pap. 5.50 (1-56939-039-8, FF1097) FJH Music Co Inc.

Piano Adventures Techniques & Artistry Book: A Basic Piano Method, Primer Level. Nancy Faber et al. (Piano Adventures Library). (Illus.). 32p. (Orig.). (J). (gr. k). 1995. pap. 5.50 (0-929666-85-2) FJH Music Co Inc.

Piano Adventures Theory Book: A Basic Piano Method, Level 1. Nancy Faber et al. Ed. by Edwin McLean. (Piano Adventures Library). (Illus.). 40p. (Orig.). (J). (gr. 1). 1993. pap. 5.50 (0-929666-07-0) FJH Music Co Inc.

Piano Adventures Theory Book: A Basic Piano Method, Level 2A. Nancy Faber et al. Ed. by Edwin McLean. (Piano Adventures Library). (Illus.). 32p. (Orig.). (J). (gr. 2). 1993. pap. 5.50 (0-929666-64-X) FJH Music Co Inc.

Piano Adventures Theory Book: A Basic Piano Method, Level 2B. Nancy Faber et al. Ed. by Edwin McLean. (Piano Adventures Library). (Illus.). 40p. (Orig.). (J). (gr. 2). 1994. pap. 5.50 (0-929666-67-4, FF1085) FJH Music Co Inc.

Piano Adventures Theory Book: A Basic Piano Method, Level 3. Nancy Faber et al. Ed. by Edwin McLean. (Piano Adventures Library). (Illus.). 40p. (Orig.). (J). (gr. 3). 1994. pap. 5.50 (0-929666-83-6, FF1088) FJH Music Co Inc.

Piano Adventures Theory Book: A Basic Piano Method, Level 4. Nancy Faber et al. Ed. by Edwin McLean. (Piano Adventures Library). (Illus.). 32p. (Orig.). (J). (gr. 4). 1995. pap. 5.50 (0-929666-91-7, FF1091) FJH Music Co Inc.

Piano Adventures Theory Book: A Basic Piano Method, Primer Level. Nancy Faber et al. Ed. by Edwin McLean. (Piano Adventures Library). (Illus.). 48p. (Orig.). (J). (gr. k). 1993. pap. 5.95 (0-929666-55-0) FJH Music Co Inc.

Piano Album. L. Hoiby. 72p. 1993. pap. 12.95 (0-7935-0919-X) H Leonard.

Piano & Its Music 1770-1850. Carew. 76.95 (0-85967-969-1) Ashgate Pub Co.

Piano & Keyboard Blue Book, 1998. rev. ed. 1997. lib. bdg. 200.00 (0-932089-56-9) Orion Res.

Piano & Keyboards. King Palmer. LC 97-76229. (Teach Yourself Ser.). (Illus.). 192p. 1998. pap. 10.95 (0-8442-0040-9, 00409, Teach Yrslf) NTC Contemp Pub Co.

Piano & Keyboards. King Palmer. (Teach Yourself Ser.). 192p. 1999. pap. 17.95 incl. audio (0-8442-1082-X, 1082X, Teach Yrslf) NTC Contemp Pub Co.

Piano & Organ Without a Teacher, Bk. 1. Vladislav Celik. LC 92-80239. (Music Instructional Ser.). (Illus.). 80p. pap. text 9.95 (0-9624062-3-6) Music Inst CA.

Piano & Organ Without a Teacher One. Vladislav Celik. (Music Instructional Ser.). (Illus.). 80p. pap. 12.95 incl. audio (0-9624062-4-4) Music Inst CA.

Piano & Player Piano: Buyer's Guide of 1926. AMI\Rowe International Company Staff. 176p. 1984. reprint ed. spiral bd. 27.50 (0-913599-42-5, R-64) A M C Corp.

Piano & Song (Didactic & Polemical) The Collected Writings of Clara Schumann's Father & Only Teacher. Friedrich Wieck. Ed. by Henry Pleasants. LC 85-28445. (Monographs in Musicology: No. 9). 250p. 1988. lib. bdg. 51.00 (0-918728-62-2) Pendragon NY.

Piano Bar. Date not set. pap. 34.95 (0-7692-1043-0, 01020691) Wrner Bros.

Piano Basics IV. Kone Music Inc. Staff. (Illus.). 1999. 7.95 (963-9155-18-7) Kone Music.

Piano Basics I. Abr. by Kone Music Inc. Staff. (Illus.). 1999. 7.95 (963-9155-15-2) Kone Music.

Piano Basics III. Kone Music Inc. Staff. 1999. 7.95 (963-9155-17-9) Kone Music.

Piano Basics II, 1. Kone Music Inc. Staff. 1999. 7.95 (963-9155-16-0) Kone Music.

***Piano Bench of Classical Music.** Ed. by Amy Appleby. 399p. 1999. pap. text 27.95 (0-8256-1769-3, AM961510) Music Sales.

***Piano Book.** 4th ed. Larry Fine. 200p. 2000. 27.95 (1-929145-02-0, Pub. by Brookside Pr MA) IPG Chicago.

Piano Book: Buying & Owning a New Or Used Piano. 3rd ed. Larry Fine. LC 94-71153. (Illus.). 176p. 1994. pap. 16.95 (0-9617512-4-X) Brookside Pr MA.

***Piano Book: Buying & Owning a New or Used Piano.** 4th ed. Larry Fine. 200p. 2000. pap. 19.95 (1-929145-01-2, Pub. by Brookside Pr MA) IPG Chicago.

***Piano Book: 2000-01 Annual Supplement.** Larry Fine. 200p. 2000. pap. 14.95 (1-929145-03-9, Pub. by Brookside Pr MA) IPG Chicago.

***Piano Camp, Bk. 3.** June Montgomery. 48p. 1999. pap. 6.95 (0-7390-0593-6, 14595) Alfred Pub.

Piano Camp Primer. June Montgomery. Date not set. write for info. (0-7390-0649-5, 14655) Alfred Pub.

Piano Chord Dictionary. Morton Manus. (Alfred Handy Guide Ser.). 48p. 1978. 5.50 (0-88284-154-8, 285) Alfred Pub.

Piano Chords Pocketbook. L. Dean Bye. 32p. 1981. pap. 0.95 (0-87166-552-2, 93749) Mel Bay.

***Piano Classics.** 256p. 2000. per. 14.95 (0-634-01265-7) H Leonard.

Piano Classics Adult. 64p. 1990. pap. 7.95 (0-7935-0244-6, 00001022) H Leonard.

Piano Classics (Blue) C. Phipps & Philip Hawthorne. (Learn to Play Ser.). (Illus.). 128p. (J). (gr. 4-7). 1994. pap. 17.95 (0-7460-1967-X, Usborne) EDC.

Piano Collection. Illus. by Kathy Parsons. (New Voices Ser.). 57p. 1999. 14.95 (0-9671341-0-2) Solo Piano Pubns.

Piano Companion: A Comprehensive, Accelerated Approach to Learning How to Play the Piano by Note, Chord Symbol & Ear. Dave Clark. (Illus.). 244p. (Orig.). 1996. pap. 19.95 (0-941072-18-5) Southern Herit.

***Piano Complete.** Modest Mussorgsky. (Music Scores Ser.). (Illus.). 1998. pap. text 7.98 (963-8303-77-8) Kone Music.

Piano Complete Works Mily Balakirev. (Music Scores Ser.). 1998. pap. text 7.98 (963-8303-76-X) Kone Music.

Piano Complete Works IV, 1. Mily Balakirev. 1998. pap. text 7.95 (963-9059-62-5) Konemann.

***Piano Complete Works III.** Mily Balakirev. (Music Scores Ser.). 1998. pap. 7.98 (963-9059-61-7) Kone Music.

Piano Concerti in Full Score. Franz Liszt. 144p. 1987. pap. 8.95 (0-486-25221-3) Dover.

Piano Concerto: Score. E. Carter. 1986. 45.00 (0-7935-1130-5) H Leonard.

Piano Concerto: 2 Pianos, 4 Hands. S. Barber. 88p. 1987. pap. 17.95 (0-7935-3812-2, 50289380) H Leonard.

Piano Concerto in F Minor, Op. 16 Two-Piano Score. Adolf Henselt. LC 70-159114. (Illus.). (Orig.). 1971. pap. 7.50 (0-912028-04-1) Music Treasure.

Piano Concerto in Full Score. Edvard Grieg. 96p. pap. text 8.95 (0-486-27931-6) Dover.

Piano Concerto No. 1 in B-Flat Minor, Op. 32 Two Piano Score. Xaver Scharwenka. LC 74-159115. (Illus.). (Orig.). 1971. pap. 10.00 (0-912028-06-8) Music Treasure.

Piano Concerto No. 1 in D Minor: The Composer's Original Arrngement for Piano Four-Hands. Johannes Brahms. 80p. 1996. pap. 8.95 (0-486-29336-X) Dover.

Piano Concerto No. 3 in G Minor, Op. 58 Two-Piano Score. Ignaz Moscheles & Hans Kann. LC 79-155179. (Illus.). (Orig.). 1971. pap. 6.50 (0-912028-03-3) Music Treasure.

Piano Concerto No. 26 in D Major ("Coronation"), K.537: The Autograph Score. Wolfgang Amadeus Mozart. 128p. 1991. pap. 12.95 (0-486-26747-4) Dover.

Piano Concerto Nos. 20, 21 & 22: With Orchestral Reduction for Second Piano. Wolfgang Amadeus Mozart. 208p. 1995. pap. text 12.95 (0-486-28435-2) Dover.

***Piano Concerto No. 5 in E-Flat Major, Op. 73.** unabridged ed. Ludwig van Beethoven. 96p. 1999. pap. 3.95 (0-486-40636-9) Dover.

Piano Concerto Opus 38: Study Score. S. Barber. 144p. 1986. per. 35.00 (0-7935-3946-3, 50339520) H Leonard.

Piano Concertos, No. 1, 2 & 3. Sergey Rachmaninoff. 400p. 1990. pap. 18.95 (0-486-26350-9) Dover.

Piano Concertos Arranged for 2 Pianos. Frederic Chopin. 208p. 1993. pap. 11.95 (0-486-27498-5) Dover.

Piano Concertos in Full Score. Frederic Chopin. 176p. 1989. pap. 10.95 (0-486-25835-1) Dover.

Piano Concertos No. 1 & No. 2. Franz Liszt. 112p. 1996. pap. 10.95 (0-486-29238-X) Dover.

Piano Concertos Nos. 11-16 in Full Score. Wolfgang Amadeus Mozart. 256p. 1987. pap. 12.95 (0-486-25468-2) Dover.

Piano Concertos Nos. 4 & 5 ("Emperor") With Orchestral Reduction for Second Piano. Ludwig van Beethoven. 160p. pap. 10.95 (0-486-28442-5) Dover.

Piano Concertos, Nos. 17-22. Wolfgang Amadeus Mozart. 370p. 1978. pap. 16.95 (0-486-23599-8) Dover.

Piano Concertos, Nos. 23-27. Wolfgang Amadeus Mozart. 310p. 1978. pap. 13.95 (0-486-23600-5) Dover.

Piano Concertos Nos. 2 & 4 in Full Score. Camille Saint-Saens. 288p. pap. text 15.95 (0-486-28723-8) Dover.

Piano Concertos Nos. 1 & 2: With Orchestral Reduction for Second Piano. Johannes Brahms. 192p. Date not set. pap. 14.95 (0-486-40625-3) Dover.

***Piano Concertos Nos. 7-10 in Full Score: With Mozart's Cadenzas for Nos. 7 & 9.** Wolfgang Amadeus Mozart. 2000. pap. 16.95 (0-486-41165-6) Dover.

Piano Course, Bk. 1. K. Elliott & Kathy Gemmell. (Piano Courses Ser.). (Illus.). 32p. (J). (gr. k up). 1995. lib. bdg. 14.95 (0-88110-738-7, Usborne) EDC.

Piano Course, Bk. 1. K. Elliott & Kathy Gemmell. (Piano Courses Ser.: Vol. 1). (Illus.). 32p. (J). (gr. k-3). 1995. text 6.95 (0-7460-2000-7, Usborne) EDC.

Piano Course, Bk. 2. K. Elliott & K. Gemmell. (Piano Courses Ser.: Vol. 2). (Illus.). 32p. (J). (gr. k-3). 1995. text 6.95 (0-7460-2002-3, Usborne) EDC.

Piano Course, Bk. 2. K. Elliott & Kathy Gemmell. (Piano Courses Ser.). (Illus.). 32p. (J). (gr. k up). 1995. lib. bdg. 14.95 (0-88110-748-4, Usborne) EDC.

Piano Course, Bk. 2. H. Kasschau. 64p. 1987. pap. 5.95 (0-7935-5302-4) H Leonard.

Piano dans l'Herbe. Francoise Sagan. 12.95 (0-685-37084-4) Fr & Eur.

Piano dans l'Herbe. Francoise Sagan. (FRE.). 184p. 1970. 8.95 (0-7859-1413-7, 2080605038) Fr & Eur.

Piano de Cristal. Luis I. Larcada. Ed. by Editorial Arcos, Inc., Staff. LC 86-80617. (Coleccion Narrativa y Ensayo). (Illus.). 117p. (Orig.). 1986. 7.50 (0-937509-00-0) Edit Arcos.

***Piano di Dio per "La Chiesa" Uno Studio Sulla Natura e l'Intento della Chiesa del Nuovo Testamento.** Eddie Cloer. Orig. Title: Design of God for "the Church". 254p. 1998. pap. 2.50 (0-945441-28-2) Res Pubns AR.

Piano Duet. Ernest Lubin. LC 76-10328. (Quality Paperbacks Ser.). (Illus.). 240p. 1976. pap. 5.95 (0-306-80045-4) Da Capo.

Piano Duet: A Learning Guide. Weekly & Nancy Arganbright. 1996. 8.95 (0-8497-9598-2, WP381) Kjos.

Piano Duet Repertoire: Music Originally Written for 1 Piano, Four Hands. Cameron McGraw. LC 80-8097. 384p. 1981. 49.95 (0-253-14766-2) Ind U Pr.

Piano Duets, EFS7. (Illus.). 160p. 1962. pap. 14.95 (0-8256-2007-4, AM40064) Music Sales.

Piano Duets of Andrew Lloyd Webber: 1 Piano, 4 Hands. Andrew Lloyd Webber. 64p. 1991. pap. 9.95 (0-7935-0638-7, 00290332) H Leonard.

***Piano Ensemble: Hl Student Piano Library, Vol. 3.** 40p. 1998. pap. 5.95 (0-7935-9216-X) H Leonard.

***Piano Ensembles: Hal Leonard Student Piano Library, Vol. 2.** 32p. 1998. pap. 5.95 (0-7935-9215-1) H Leonard.

***Piano Ensembles: Hl Student Piano Library, Vol. 1.** 32p. 1998. pap. 5.95 (0-7935-9214-3) H Leonard.

***Piano Ensembles: Hl Student Piano Library, Vol. 4.** 8p. 1998. pap. 5.95 (0-7935-9217-8) H Leonard.

***Piano Ensembles Orchestrated Arrangements: Hal Leonard Student Piano Library Level 5.** 40p. 1999. pap. 5.95 (0-634-00244-9) H Leonard.

P

An Asterisk (*) at the beginning of an entry indicates that the title is appearing for the first time.

Piano Etudes: For the Development of Musical Fingers, Bk. 1. Frances Clark et al. 24p. 1990. pap. 4.95 (*0-913277-24-X*) Summy-Birchard.

Piano Etudes: For the Development of Musical Fingers, Bk. 2. Frances Clark et al. 24p. 1990. pap. 4.95 (*0-913277-25-8*) Summy-Birchard.

Piano Etudes: For the Development of Musical Fingers, Bk. 3. Frances Clark et al. 24p. 1990. pap. 4.95 (*0-913277-26-6*) Summy-Birchard.

Piano Etudes: For the Development of Musical Fingers, Bk. 4. Frances Clark et al. 32p. 1990. pap. 5.95 (*0-913277-27-4*) Summy-Birchard.

***Piano Exercises I - Partita.** Johann Sebastian Bach. 1998. pap. text 7.98 (*963-8303-91-3*) Kone Music.

Piano Favorites. (In Classical Mood Ser.: Vol. 34). (Illus.). 1998. write for info. incl. cd-rom (*1-886614-60-1*) Intl Masters Pub.

Piano for Adults, Bk. 1. M. Nevin. 64p. 1984. pap. 6.95 (*0-7935-0702-2*, 00009295) H Leonard.

Piano for Dummies: A Reference for the Rest of Us! Mark Phillips & Jon Chappell. (For Dummies Ser.). 368p. 1998. pap. 24.99 incl. audio compact disk (*0-7645-5105-1*) IDG Bks.

Piano for Pleasure. 2nd ed. Martha Hilley & Lynn F. Olson. Ed. by Baxter. 348p. (C). 1992. pap. 37.75 (*0-314-93369-7*) West Pub.

Piano for Pleasure. 3rd ed. Martha Hilley & Lynn F. Olson. (Music Ser.). (C). 1997. 52.95 (*0-314-12690-2*) Wadsworth Pub.

Piano for Pleasure. 4th ed. Hilley. (Music Ser.). 2001. 32.25 (*0-534-51962-8*) Wadsworth Pub.

Piano for the Developing Musician. 5th ed. Hilley. (Music Ser.). 2001. 34.25 (*0-534-51778-1*) Wadsworth Pub.

Piano for the Developing Musician, Vol. 1. 4th ed. Hilley. 1997. 55.95 (*0-314-20415-6*) Wadsworth Pub.

Piano for the Developing Musician: Comprehensive Edition. Martha Hilley & Lynn F. Olson. (C). 1997. pap. text. write for info. (*0-314-12689-9*) Wadsworth Pub.

Piano-Forte. Rosamond E. Harding. LC 69-15634. (Music Ser.). 1973. reprint ed. lib. bdg. 49.50 (*0-306-71084-6*) Da Capo.

Piano-Forte. Rosamond E. Harding. 1988. reprint ed. lib. bdg. 75.00 (*0-7812-0384-8*) Rprt Serv.

Piano-Forte: Its History Traced to the Great Exhibition of 1851. Rosamond E. Harding. LC 71-181171. 1933. reprint ed. 69.00 (*0-403-01574-X*) Scholarly.

Piano Fun! (Pooh Songbook Ser.). (Illus.). 274p. 1998. pap. 19.95 (*0-7935-9376-X*, HL00824131) H Leonard.

Piano Fun! (Disney Collection). (Illus.). 274p. 1998. pap. 19.95 (*0-7935-9373-5*, HL00824129) H Leonard.

Piano Games, OP 42. Jaroslaw Golembiowski. (Illus.). 52p. 1996. 8.95 (*0-9652399-0-X*) J Golembiowski.

Piano Garden. Bonnie Worth. (Illus.). 16p. (J). (ps-k). 1996. 4.99 (*0-689-80428-8*) Litle Simon.

Piano Goes to the Movies. 128p. (Orig.). 1995. pap. 12.95 (*0-7692-1146-1*, AF9543) Wrner Bros.

Piano Hammer: A Detailed Investigation into an Important Facet of Piano Mfg. Walter Pfeifer. Tr. by J. Englehardt from GER. (Illus.). 120p. 1978. pap. 54.95 (*0-933224-33-8*, I131) Bold Strummer Ltd.

Piano Hymn Favorites: Songs of Eternal Faith, Songs of Everlasting Joy, Songs of Inspiration, 3 bks., Set. Lynn S. Lund. 1994. pap. 29.98 (*0-88290-492-2*) Horizon Utah.

Piano Hymns. Transcribed by Paul Howard. 64p. 1997. pap. 22.96 incl. audio compact disk (*0-7866-3221-6*, 96648CDP) Mel Bay.

Piano Hymns. Stan Whitmire. 64p. 1997. pap. 7.95 (*0-7866-3185-6*, 96648) Mel Bay.

Piano Hymns of Faith. Contrib. by Marilyn White. 1991. 8.99 (*0-685-68275-7*, MB-621) Lillenas.

Piano Improvising. Wilfred Adler. 128p. 1977. spiral bd. 11.95 (*0-87166-529-8*, 93410) Mel Bay.

Piano Improvs for Keyboards. 1997. pap. 9.99 (*0-8341-9627-1*) Lillenas.

Piano in America, 1890-1940. Craig H. Roell. LC 88-14326. (Illus.). 416p. 1989. reprint ed. pap. 129.00 (*0-608-03181-X*, 206363400007) Bks Demand.

Piano in Chamber Ensemble: An Annotated Guide. Maurice Hinson. LC 77-9862. 608p. 1978. 52.50 (*0-253-34493-X*) Ind U Pr.

Piano in Chamber Ensemble: An Annotated Guide. annot. ed. Maurice Hinson. 608p. 1996. pap. 22.50 (*0-253-21055-0*) Ind U Pr.

Piano in the Rhythm Section. Tom Rainer. Ed. by Debbie Cavalier. (Contemporary Rhythm Section Ser.). 36p. (Orig.). (YA). 1997. pap. text 24.95 (*1-57623-994-2*, 0051B) Wrner Bros.

Piano Interpretations of the Seventeenth, Eighteenth & Nineteenth Centuries: A Study of Theory & Practice Using Original Documents. Elena Letnanova. LC 91-52596. (Illus.). 196p. 1991. lib. bdg. 39.95 (*0-89950-616-X*) McFarland & Co.

Piano Jubilation. Contrib. by Teresa Wilhelmi. 40p. 1986. 9.99 (*0-8341-9114-8*, MB-563) Lillenas.

Piano Keys & White Paper. Wayne Oakley. 64p. 1993. pap. 12.95 (*1-55082-091-5*, Pub. by Quarry Pr) LPC InBook.

Piano Lesson. August Wilson. 112p. 1990. pap. 9.95 (*0-452-26534-7*, Plume) Dutton Plume.

Piano Lessons. Leonard, Hal, Corporation Staff. (Student Piano Library). 1p. 1996. pap. text 10.95 incl. audio compact disk (*0-7935-6263-5*) H Leonard.

Piano Lessons. Perf. by Leonard, Hal, Corporation Staff. (Student Piano Library). 1p. 1996. pap. text 10.95 incl. audio compact disk (*0-7935-6268-6*) H Leonard.

Piano Lessons. Leonard, Hal, Corporation Staff. (Student Piano Library: Bk. 1). 64p. 1996. pap. 5.95 (*0-7935-6260-0*) H Leonard.

Piano Lessons, Bk. 2. Leonard, Hal, Corporation Staff. (Student Piano Library). 48p. 1996. pap. 5.95 (*0-7935-6265-1*) H Leonard.

Piano Lessons, Bk. 3. Leonard, Hal, Corporation Staff. (Student Piano Library). 48p. 1996. pap. 5.95 (*0-7935-6270-8*) H Leonard.

Piano Lessons: Approaches to "The Piano" Ed. by Felicity O'Brien & Suzanne Gemmell. 1999. pap. 19.95 (*1-86462-035-8*) Ind U Pr.

Piano Lessons: General MIDI. Leonard, Hal, Corporation Staff. (Student Piano Library). 1p. 1996. pap. text 14.95 incl. disk (*0-7935-6269-4*) H Leonard.

Piano Lessons: General MIDI, Bk. 3. Leonard, Hal, Corporation Staff. (Student Piano Library). 1p. 1996. pap. text 14.95 (*0-7935-6274-0*) H Leonard.

***Piano Lessons: Hl Student Piano Library, Vol. 5.** 56p. 1998. pap. 6.50 (*0-7935-9286-0*) H Leonard.

Piano Lessons: Music, Love & True Adventures. Noah Adams. 272p. 1997. pap. 12.95 (*0-385-31821-9*, Delta Trade) Dell.

Piano Lessons Can Be Murder. R. L. Stine, pseud. LC 94-155308. (Goosebumps Ser.: No. 13). 160p. (J). (gr. 3-7). 1993. pap. 3.99 (*0-590-49448-1*) Scholastic Inc.

Piano Lessons Can Be Murder. R. L. Stine, pseud. (Goosebumps Ser.: No. 13). (J). 1993. 9.09 (*0-606-05971-7*, Pub. by Turtleback) Demco.

***Piano Lessons International: Hl Student Piano Library.** 56p. 1998. pap. 5.95 (*0-7935-9897-4*) H Leonard.

Piano Literature of the 17th, 18th, & 19th Centuries, Bk. 1. Frances Clark & Louise Goss. (Frances Clark Library for Piano Students). 32p. 1964. pap. text 5.95 (*0-87487-125-5*) Summy-Birchard.

Piano Literature of the 17th, 18th, & 19th Centuries, Bk. 2. Frances Clark & Louise Goss. (Frances Clark Library for Piano Students). (Illus.). 32p. 1954. pap. text 5.95 (*0-87487-126-3*) Summy-Birchard.

Piano Literature of the 17th, 18th, & 19th Centuries, Bk. 5B. Frances Clark & Louise Goss. (Frances Clark Library for Piano Students). (Illus.). 48p. 1957. pap. text 7.95 (*0-87487-129-8*) Summy-Birchard.

Piano Literature of the 17th, 18th, & 19th Centuries, Bk. 6B. Frances Clark. (Frances Clark Library for Piano Students). (Illus.). 64p. 1956. pap. text 9.95 (*0-87487-130-1*) Summy-Birchard.

Piano Literature of the 17th, 18th, & 19th Centuries, Bks. 3, 4A & 4B. Frances Clark & Louise Goss. (Frances Clark Library for Piano Students). (Illus.). 64p. 1957. pap. text 9.95 (*0-87487-127-1*) Summy-Birchard.

Piano Literature of the 17th, 18th, & 19th Centuries, Bks. 5A & 6A. Frances Clark & Louise Goss. (Frances Clark Library for Piano Students). (Illus.). 48p. 1974. pap. text 7.95 (*0-87487-128-X*) Summy-Birchard.

Piano Magic. John Brimhall. 9.95 (*0-7692-9204-6*) Warner Bros.

Piano Magic: Pro-Line Piano. 56p. (Orig.). 1992. pap. 8.95 (*0-7692-1012-0*, BMP504) Wrner Bros.

Piano Magic: 18 Great Standards. Ed. by Tony Esposito. 80p. (YA). 1995. pap. text 10.95 (*0-89724-745-0*, AF9535) Wrner Bros.

Piano Magic: 21 Jazz Standards. Ed. by Tony Esposito. 80p. (YA). 1995. pap. text 10.95 (*0-89724-733-7*, AF9529) Wrner Bros.

Piano Majesty: Seasonal Solos for the Advanced Pianist. Arranged by Marilyn Ham. 44p. 1988. pap. 9.99 (*0-8341-9301-9*) Lillenas.

Piano Man. Debbi Chocolate. LC 97-22668. (Illus.). 32p. (J). (gr. k-3). 1998. 15.95 (*0-8027-8646-4*); lib. bdg. 16.85 (*0-8027-8647-2*) Walker & Co.

***Piano Man.** Debbi Chocolate. 32p. (J). (gr. k-3). 2000. pap. 7.95 (*0-8027-7578-0*) Walker & Co.

Piano Man. Joyce Sweeney. 1992. 18.95 (*0-385-30724-1*) Doubleday.

Piano Master Classes of Franz Liszt, 1884-1886: Diary Notes of August Gollerich. Ed. by Wilhelm Jerger. Tr. by Richard L. Zimdars. LC 96-4010. (Illus.). xii, 209p. 1996. text 35.00 (*0-253-33223-0*) Ind U Pr.

Piano Masterpieces of Maurice Ravel. Maurice Ravel. 128p. 1986. pap. 8.95 (*0-486-25137-3*) Dover.

Piano Method Book 2. Andrew Scott. (Progressive Ser.). (Illus.). 1997. pap. text 11.95 incl. cd-rom (*1-875726-27-6*) Koala Pubns.

Piano Method for Young Beginners, Bk. 3. Andrew Scott. (Progressive Ser.). (Illus.). 1997. pap. text 8.95 incl. cd-rom (*0-947183-28-0*) Koala Pubns.

Piano Method for Young Beginners Supplementary Songbook A. Andrew Scott. (Progressive Ser.). 1997. pap. text 8.95 (*0-947183-95-7*) Koala Pubns.

Piano Method for Young Beginners Supplementary Songbook B. Andrew Scott. (Progressive Ser.). 1997. pap. 8.95 incl. audio compact disk (*0-947183-96-5*) Koala Pubns.

Piano Method for Young Beginners Supplementary Songbook C. Andrew Scott. (Progressive Ser.). (Illus.). 1997. pap. text 8.95 (*0-947183-97-3*) Koala Pubns.

***Piano Music.** Jean Sibelius. 2000. pap. 12.95 (*0-486-41162-1*) Dover.

Piano Music. Heitor Villa-Lobos. 208p. 1999. 10.95 (*0-486-29384-X*, 278797Q) Dover.

Piano Music by Black Women Composers: A Catalog of Solo & Ensemble Works, 35. Helen Walker-Hill. LC 91-38146. (Music Reference Collection: No. 35). 160p. 1992. lib. bdg. 45.00 (*0-313-28141-6*, WPK, Greenwood Pr) Greenwood.

Piano Music, 1888-1905. 5th ed. Claude Debussy. 175p. 1974. pap. 7.95 (*0-486-22771-5*) Dover.

***Piano Music for Four Hands.** Roger Grenier. Tr. by Alice Kaplan. 2001. pap. 15.00 (*0-8032-7087-9*) U of Nebr Pr.

***Piano Music for Four Hands.** Roger Grenier. Tr. & Pref. by Alice Kaplan. 2001. text 45.00 (*0-8032-2181-9*) U of Nebr Pr.

Piano Music for One Hand. 136p. 1986. pap. 13.95 (*0-7935-5268-0*, 50331590) H Leonard.

Piano Music for One Hand. Theodore Edel. LC 94-5139. 176p. 1994. 19.95 (*0-253-31905-6*) Ind U Pr.

Piano Music of Bela Bartok, Series I. Bela Bartok. 167p. 1982. pap. 11.95 (*0-486-24108-4*) Dover.

Piano Music of Bella Bartok, Series II. Bela Bartok. 192p. 1982. pap. 11.95 (*0-486-24109-2*) Dover.

Piano Music of Heitor Villa-Lobos, MFM62. (Illus.). 168p. 1988. pap. 15.95 (*0-8256-4062-8*, AM41732) Music Sales.

Piano Music of Louis Moreau Gottschalk: 26 Complete Pieces from Original Editions. Louis M. Gottschalk. Ed. by Richard Jackson. LC 73-75872. 301p. (Orig.). 1973. pap. 13.95 (*0-486-21683-7*) Dover.

Piano Music of Robert Schumann. Robert Schumann. Incl. Series I. 274p. 1972. pap. 13.95 (*0-486-21459-1*); Series 2. 272p. 1972. pap. 13.95 (*0-486-21461-3*); 1972. pap. write for info. (*0-318-51770-1*) Dover.

Piano Music of Robert Schumann, Series III. Robert Schumann. Ed. by Clara (Wieck) Schumann. 224p. 1980. reprint ed. 11.95 (*0-486-23906-3*) Dover.

Piano Music of 6 Great Composers. Donald N. Ferguson. LC 73-111830. (Essay Index Reprint Ser.). 1977. 26.95 (*0-8369-1652-2*) Ayer.

Piano Noel. 1997. pap. 7.99 (*0-8341-9623-9*) Lillenas.

Piano Nomenclature: Deutch, English, Francais, Italiano, Norsk, Espanol. N. Schimmel. Ed. by H. K. Herzog. 130p. 1983. pap. text 59.95 (*0-933224-34-6*, 59.95) Bold Strummer Ltd.

***Piano 101: An Exciting Group Course for Adults, Bk. 1.** E. L. Lancaster & Kenon D. Renfrow. 160p. 1999. spiral bd. 24.95 (*0-7390-0255-4*, 14588) Alfred Pub.

***Piano 101: An Exciting Group Course for Adults, Bk. 2.** E. L. Lancaster & Kenon D. Renfrow. 152p. 1999. spiral bd. 24.95 (*0-7390-0257-0*, 4591) Alfred Pub.

***Piano 101, the Short Course.** E. L. Lancaster & Kenon D. Renfrow. 56p. 1999. 8.95 (*0-7390-0343-7*, 17176) Alfred Pub.

***Piano 101, the Short Course.** E. L. Lancaster & Kenon D. Renfrow. 1999. 19.95 incl. audio compact disk (*0-7390-0607-X*, 17179) Alfred Pub.

Piano-Owner's Guide. Carl D. Schmeckel. LC 74-7362. (Illus.). 120p. 1974. 7.95 (*0-684-13869-7*) S&S Trade.

Piano Pieces. Russell Sherman. LC 95-25707. 224p. 1996. 22.00 (*0-374-23206-7*) FS&G.

Piano Pieces. Russell Sherman. 256p. 1997. pap. text 12.00 (*0-374-52500-5*) N Point Pr.

Piano Pieces & Children Songs: Piano. 47p. (Orig.). 1995. pap. 5.95 (*0-89724-883-X*, BP3343A) Wrner Bros.

Piano Pieces for Children, EFS-3. (Illus.). 192p. 1951. pap. 11.95 (*0-8256-2003-1*, AM40023) Music Sales.

Piano Pieces for the Adult Student, EFS4. Maxwell Eckstein. (Illus.). 192p. 1958. pap. 11.95 (*0-8256-2004-X*, AM40031) Music Sales.

***Piano Pieces I: Phantasies.** Franz Schubert. (Music Scores Ser.). 1998. pap. 7.98 (*963-8303-85-9*) Kone Music.

***Piano Pieces II: Intermezzi, Caprici.** Johannes Brahms. (Music Scores Series). 1998. pap. text 7.98 (*963-9059-30-7*) Kone Music.

Piano Pieces, Opus 51, 55, 61, 62. Edward MacDowell. LC 70-170391. (Earlier American Music Ser.: No. 8). 144p. 1972. reprint ed. lib. bdg. 32.50 (*0-306-77308-2*) Da Capo.

Piano Pieces the Whole World Plays, WW2. Ed. by Albert E. Weir. (Illus.). 224p. pap. 19.95 (*0-8256-1000-1*, AM42524) Music Sales.

***Piano Pieces II: Impromptus.** Franz Schubert. (Music Scores Ser.). 1998. pap. 7.98 (*963-8303-37-9*) Kone Music.

Piano Pieces-4 Hand I, 1. Konemann Music Staff. 1998. pap. text 7.95 (*963-9059-42-0*) Konemann.

Piano Pieces-4 Hand II, 1. Konemann Music Staff. 1998. pap. text 7.95 (*963-9059-35-8*) Konemann.

Piano Pieces-4 Hand III, 1. Koneman Music Staff. 1999. pap. text 7.95 (*963-9059-02-1*) Konemann.

Piano Plain & Simple. 144p. 1997. pap. 14.95 (*0-7935-4695-8*, 00372364) H Leonard.

Piano Players. Anthony Burgess. 22.95 (*0-8488-1332-4*) Amereon Ltd.

***Piano Playing: A Handbook for the Advanced Student.** Richard S. Collins. Orig. Title: Piano Playing: A Positive Approach. (Illus.). 70p. 2000. pap. 22.50 (*0-9678421-0-7*) R S Collins.

Piano Playing: A Positive Approach see Piano Playing: A Handbook for the Advanced Student

Piano Playing Made Easy. Consumer Guide Editors. (Illus.). 64p. 1993. spiral bd. 5.98 (*1-56173-737-2*, 3615000) Pubns Intl Ltd.

Piano Playing with Piano Questions Answered. Josef Hofmann. (Illus.). 272p. 1976. reprint ed. pap. 7.95 (*0-486-23362-6*) Dover.

***Piano Power: A Breakthrough Approach to Improving Your Technique.** unabridged ed. Richard Prokop. Ed. by Jean Newton. LC 99-65769. (Illus.). 115p. 1999. pap. 34.95 (*1-929583-00-1*) Greenacres Pr.

***Piano Power Exercises: For Large Hands.** unabridged ed. Richard Prokop. 74p. 1999. pap. 12.95 (*1-929583-03-6*) Greenacres Pr.

***Piano Power Exercises: For Medium Hands.** unabridged ed. Richard Prokop. 74p. 1999. pap. 12.95 (*1-929583-02-8*) Greenacres Pr.

***Piano Power Exercises: For Small Hands.** unabridged ed. Richard Prokop. 74p. 1999. pap. 12.95 (*1-929583-01-X*) Greenacres Pr.

***Piano Practice Games, Vol. 4.** 40p. 1999. pap. 5.50 (*0-7935-7691-1*) H Leonard.

Piano Practice Games, Bk. 1. Leonard, Hal, Corporation Staff. (Student Piano Library). 48p. 1996. pap. 5.50 (*0-7935-6261-9*) H Leonard.

Piano Practice Games, Bk. 2. Leonard, Hal, Corporation Staff. (Student Piano Library). 40p. 1996. pap. 5.50 (*0-7935-6266-X*) H Leonard.

Piano Practice Games, Bk. 3. (Student Piano Library). 40p. 1997. pap. 5.50 (*0-7935-6271-6*) H Leonard.

Piano Praise & Worship. Arranged by Fred Bock. (Piano Collection Ser.). 1997. pap. 10.95 (*0-7935-9990-3*) H Leonard.

Piano Praise & Worship. Arranged by Fred Bock. (Piano Collection Ser.: No. 3). 1997. pap. 10.95 (*0-7935-9991-1*) H Leonard.

Piano Prayer & Praises. Contrib. by Johnie Dean. 1987. 8.99 (*0-685-68292-7*, MB-582) Lillenas.

Piano Preludes. M. Valenti. 32p. 1986. pap. 9.95 (*0-7935-3626-X*) H Leonard.

Piano Pro. Dick Hyman. 1993. 24.95 (*0-943748-61-5*) Ekay Music.

Piano Professor, Vol. 1. (YA). 1992. pap. 19.95 (*0-943748-58-5*, PF0800) Wrner Bros.

Piano Progress - Primary Book. June Davison & Ardella Schaub. Ed. by Leo Podolsky. 1982. 5.50 (*0-913650-42-0*, V032PMBP) Wrner Bros.

Piano Progress for the Partially Sighted. large type ed. Incl. Bks. 1A-2B. 1972. 4.00 Bks. 1A-2B. 1972. Bks. 1A-2B. 1972. Bks. 1A-2B. 1972. Bks. 1A-2B. 1972. (*0-89898-339-8*); Bks. 3A & 3B. 1974. 6.00 Bks. 3A & 3B. 1974. Bks. 3A & 3B. 1974. write for info. (*0-318-66012-1*) Wrner Bros.

Piano Progress for the Partially Sighted, Bk. 2A. June Davison & Ardella Schaub. Ed. by Leo Podolsky. 1967. 5.00 (*0-913650-15-3*) Wrner Bros.

Piano Progress for the Partially Sighted, Bk. 2B. June Davison & Ardella Schaub. Ed. by Leo Podolsky. 1967. 4.00 (*0-913650-16-1*) Wrner Bros.

Piano Progress for the Partially Sighted, Bk. 3A. June Davison & Ardella Schaub. Ed. by Leo Podolsky. 1974. 6.00 (*0-913650-17-X*) Wrner Bros.

Piano Progress for the Partially Sighted, Bk. 3B. June Davison & Ardella Schaub. Ed. by Leo Podolsky. 1974. 6.95 (*0-913650-18-8*) Wrner Bros.

Piano Progress for the Partially Sighted, Bk. IA. June Davison & Ardella Schaub. Ed. by Leo Podolsky. 1972. 5.00 (*0-913650-13-7*) Wrner Bros.

Piano Progress for the Partially Sighted, Bk. IB. June Davison & Ardella Schaub. Ed. by Leo Podolsky. 1972. 5.00 (*0-913650-14-5*) Wrner Bros.

Piano Quartet & Quintet: Style, Structure, & Scoring. Basil Smallman. (Illus.). 208p. 1994. 45.00 (*0-19-816374-6*) OUP.

Piano Quartet & Quintet: Style, Structure & Scoring. Basil Smallman. LC 96-17389. (Illus.). 208p. 1996. reprint ed. pap. text 21.00 (*0-19-816640-0*, Clarendon Pr) OUP.

Piano Quartets, Nos. 1 & 2 & Piano Quintet No. 1. Gabriel Faure. 256p. 1995. pap. text 14.95 (*0-486-28606-1*) Dover.

Piano Quintet. J. Harbison. 1993. per. 35.00 (*0-7935-3087-3*) H Leonard.

***Piano Quintet in a Major, D667, Trout String Quintet in C Major, D956.** Franz Schubert. 96p. (Orig.). 1999. pap. text 3.95 (*0-486-40643-1*) Dover.

Piano Recital. Richard L. Baldwin. LC 98-229708. (Illus.). 24p. 1999. pap. 6.95 (*0-9660685-1-3*) Buttonwood.

Piano Reductions of Orchestral Works. Ed. by Joel Sachs. LC 89-754035. (J. N. Hummel: The Complete Works for Piano Ser.: Vol. 6). 312p. 1990. text 45.00 (*0-8240-3791-X*) Garland.

Piano Repertoire. Bloeh & Isacoff. 1999. 40.00 (*0-02-864748-3*, Schirmer Books) Mac Lib Ref.

Piano Repertoire, Level 5. 32p. (YA). 1985. pap. 5.95 (*0-7692-1237-9*, FDL 00467) Wrner Bros.

Piano Roles: Three Hundred Years of Life with the Piano. James Parakilas et al. LC 99-29430. (Illus.). 462p. 2000. 39.95 (*0-300-08055-7*) Yale U Pr.

Piano Selections. 160p. (YA). 1993. pap. 12.95 (*0-7692-1470-3*, WFM00009) Wrner Bros.

Piano Selections from E. T. John Williams. 32p. 1985. pap. 9.95 (*0-7935-1721-4*, 00120574) H Leonard.

Piano Servicing, Tuning, & Rebuilding: For the Professional, the Student, the Hobbyist. 2nd ed. Arthur A. Reblitz. LC 92-13175. (Illus.). 340p. 1993. 39.95 (*1-879511-02-9*, Vestal Pr); pap. 29.95 (*1-879511-03-7*, Vestal Pr) Madison Bks UPA.

Piano Solo Favorites. 72p. 1994. pap. 12.95 (*0-7935-3563-8*, 00292068) H Leonard.

Piano Solos, Bk. 1. Leonard, Hal, Corporation Staff. (Student Piano Library). 32p. 1996. pap. 4.95 (*0-7935-6262-7*) H Leonard.

Piano Solos, Bk. 2. 1p. 1997. pap. text 10.95 incl. audio compact disk (*0-7935-7683-0*) H Leonard.

Piano Solos, Bk. 2. Leonard, Hal, Corporation Staff. (Student Piano Library). 32p. 1996. pap. 4.95 (*0-7935-6267-8*) H Leonard.

Piano Solos, Bk. 3. Leonard, Hal, Corporation Staff. (Student Piano Library). 32p. 1996. pap. 4.95 (*0-7935-6272-4*) H Leonard.

Piano Solos: Elementary. David W. Faust & Edith W. Faust. (Sound Drops Ser.). 14p. (Orig.). Date not set. pap. 5.95 (*1-891162-00-4*) EDF Music.

Piano Solos: Instrumental Accompaniments, Bk. 1. 1p. 1997. pap. text 10.95 incl. audio compact disk (*0-7935-7678-4*) H Leonard.

Piano Solos: Intermediate. David W. Faust & Edith W. Faust. (Sound Drops Ser.). 28p. (Orig.). Date not set. pap. 6.95 (*1-891162-01-2*) EDF Music.

Piano Solos - Young Adult. 164p. (YA). 1995. pap. 8.95 (*0-7692-1457-6*, AF9541) Wrner Bros.

Piano Solos for Kids. expanded rev. ed. 63p. (J). 1994. pap. 8.95 (*0-7692-1013-9*, F2331PFC) Wrner Bros.

Piano Solos of Richard Clayderman: Anthology. (Illus.). 144p. 1985. pap. 21.95 (*0-8256-1055-9*, AM61441) Music Sales.

Piano Sonata, No. 1. Harold Zabrack. 1978. pap. 7.50 (*0-934286-06-X*) Kenyon.

P

Piano Sonata, No. 2. Harold Zabrack. 1981. pap. 7.50 (*0-934286-61-2*) Kenyon.

Piano Sonata No. 1. J. Harbison. 24p. 1994. pap. 12.95 (*0-7935-3008-3*) H Leonard.

Piano Sonata No. I in Db. Albert De Vito. (Orig.). 1979. pap. 7.50 (*0-934286-12-4*) Kenyon.

Piano Sonatas. Muzio Clementi. 272p. 1992. pap. text 10.95 (*0-486-27310-5*) Dover.

Piano Sonatas: Centennial Edition. Alexander Scriabin. 216p. 1994. pap. 12.95 (*0-7935-3011-3*) H Leonard.

Piano Sonatas of Carl Loewe (1796-1869) John Salmon. LC 92-34418. (American University Studies: Series XX: Vol. 7). X, 247p. (C). 1996. text 44.95 (*0-8204-1890-0*) P Lang Pubng.

Piano Sonatina. Albert De Vito. (Illus.). 16p. (Orig.). 1985. pap. 7.50 (*0-934286-65-5*) Kenyon.

***Piano Song Book.** Sanduik Bokforlag. (Illus.). 1998. pap. 9.99 (*1-58048-026-8*) Sandvik Pub.

Piano Sonority of Claude Debussy. Virginia Raad. LC 93-50847. (Studies in the History & Interpretation of Music: Vol. 34). 92p. 1993. 49.95 (*0-7734-9138-4*) E Mellen.

***Piano Standards: Classic Jazz Masters.** 72p. 1998. pap. 14.95 (*0-7935-6550-2*) H Leonard.

Piano Stool: Footnotes. Simon Cutts. 1982. pap. 12.50 (*0-912330-55-4*) Jargon Soc.

Piano Stories. Felisberto Hernandez. Tr. by Luis Harss from SPA. LC 92-82646. 360p. 1993. pap. 18.00 (*0-941419-54-1*, Eridanos Library) Marsilio Pubs.

Piano Student, Level 1. 48p. (YA). 1985. pap. 5.95 (*0-7692-1236-0*, FDL00315) Wrner Bros.

Piano Teacher. Elfriede Jelinek. 1999. pap. 12.00 (*1-85242-725-6*, Pub. by Serpents Tail) Consort Bk Sales.

Piano Teacher's Art (Guideline for Successful Piano Teaching) Isabelle Y. Byman. Ed. by Albert K. De Vito. LC 79-88361. 1979. pap. 15.95 (*0-934286-13-2*) Kenyon.

Piano Teacher's Words of Wisdom. Bertha F. Lang. LC 97-67138. 124p. (Orig.). 1998. pap. 10.95 (*1-57197-078-9*) Pentland Pr.

Piano Technic, Bk. 1. Frances Clark & Louise Goss. (Frances Clark Library for Piano Students). 48p. 1954. pap. text 7.95 (*0-87487-131-X*) Summy-Birchard.

Piano Technic, Bk. 2. Frances Clark & Louise Goss. (Frances Clark Library for Piano Students). 40p. 1954. pap. text 7.95 (*0-87487-132-8*) Summy-Birchard.

Piano Technic, Bk. 3. Frances Clark & Louise Goss. (Frances Clark Library for Piano Students). 40p. 1954. pap. text 7.95 (*0-87487-133-6*) Summy-Birchard.

Piano Technic, Bk. 4. Frances Clark & Louise Goss. (Frances Clark Library for Piano Students). 40p. 1960. pap. text 7.95 (*0-87487-134-4*) Summy-Birchard.

Piano Technic, Bk. 5. Frances Clark & Louise Goss. (Frances Clark Library for Piano Students). 40p. 1960. pap. text 7.95 (*0-87487-135-2*) Summy-Birchard.

Piano Technic, Bk. 6. Frances Clark & Louise Goss. (Frances Clark Library for Piano Students). 40p. 1960. pap. text 7.95 (*0-87487-136-0*) Summy-Birchard.

Piano Technique. Walter Gieseking & Karl Leimer. (Illus.). 140p. 1972. reprint ed. pap. 5.95 (*0-486-22867-3*) Dover.

Piano Technique: Tone, Touch, Phrasing & Dynamics. Lillie H. Philipp. (Illus.). 90p. (J). (gr. 7 up). 1982. reprint ed. pap. 6.95 (*0-486-24272-2*) Dover.

***Piano Technique BK.1.** 32p. 1999. pap. 4.95 (*0-634-00426-3*) H Leonard.

***Piano Technique BK.2: Hal Leonard Student Piano Library.** 40p. 2000. pap. 4.95 (*0-634-00427-1*) H Leonard.

Piano Technique Book: Division I. Ronald Shinn. Date not set. wbk. ed. write for info. (*1-886096-03-1*) Priceless Prnting.

Piano Technique Book: Division II. Ronald Shinn. Date not set. wbk. ed. write for info. (*1-886096-04-X*) Priceless Prnting.

Piano Technique Book: Division III. Ronald Shinn. Date not set. wbk. ed. write for info. (*1-886096-02-3*) Priceless Prnting.

Piano Themes from Grand Opera: Intermediate Piano. 14.95 (*1-56922-021-2*, 07-2021) Creat Cncpts.

Piano Theory: Piano Library Hl, Vol. 2. 40p. 1997. pap., wbk. ed. 5.50 (*0-7935-7688-1*) H Leonard.

***Piano Theory Workbook, Vols. 4.** 40p. 1998. pap. 5.50 (*0-7935-9891-5*) H Leonard.

Piano Theory Workbook. Ed. by Leonard, Hal, Corporation Staff. (Hal Leonard Student Piano Library). 40p. 1997. pap. 5.50 (*0-7935-7689-X*) H Leonard.

Piano Transcriptions from French & Italian Operas. Franz Liszt. (Illus.). 247p. 1982. pap. 13.95 (*0-486-24273-0*) Dover.

Piano Trio: Its History, Technique, & Repertoire. Basil Smallman. (Illus.). 238p. 1992. reprint ed. pap. text 24.00 (*0-19-816304-5*) OUP.

Piano Tuner. Peter Meinke. LC 85-28864. (Flannery O'Connor Award for Short Fiction Ser.). 168p. 1994. pap. 12.95 (*0-8203-1645-8*) U of Ga Pr.

Piano Tuning: A Simple & Accurate Method for Amateurs. J. Cree Fischer. LC 75-14759. (Illus.). 201p. 1975. reprint ed. pap. 6.95 (*0-486-23267-0*) Dover.

Piano Tuning for Musicians & Teachers. Donald W. Stauffer. (Illus.). 135p. 1989. pap. 19.95 (*1-929263-03-1*) Stauffer Pr.

***Piano II.** Joseph Haydn. (Music Scores Ser.). (Illus.). 1998. pap. text 7.95 (*963-9059-27-7*) Kone Music.

Piano Variations. Harold Zabrack. 1981. pap. 7.50 (*0-934286-60-4*) Kenyon.

Piano Variations Bk. 1: Piano. Ludwig van Beethoven. 152p. 1986. per. 13.95 (*0-7935-3580-8*) H Leonard.

Piano Violin Viola Cello Score & Parts, November 19, 1828. J. Harbison. 48p. 1992. pap. 40.00 (*0-7935-1488-6*) H Leonard.

Piano Vocal Manuscript Book. 64p. 1994. pap. 5.95 (*0-7866-0009-8*, 95158) Mel Bay.

Piano Works. Gabriel Faure. 19.95 (*0-7935-4075-5*, 50482370) H Leonard.

Piano Works, Vol. 2. J. Brahms. 160p. 1986. per. 14.95 (*0-7935-5233-8*, 50261470) H Leonard.

Piano Works: Woodland Sketches, Complete Sonatas & Other Pieces. Edward MacDowell. 224p. 1990. pap. 12.95 (*0-486-26293-6*) Dover.

Piano Works of Claude Debussy. Elie R. Schmitz. (Illus.). 234p. 1966. pap. 6.95 (*0-486-21567-9*) Dover.

Piano Works of Claude Debussy. E. Robert Schmitz. LC 82-23642. (Music Reprint Ser.). 238p. 1983. reprint ed. lib. bdg. 29.50 (*0-306-76199-8*) Da Capo.

Piano Works of Louis Moreau Gottschalk, 5 vols. Vera B. Lawrence. 1970. 247.95 (*0-405-02401-0*) Ayer.

Piano Works of Serge Prokofiev. Stephen C. Fiess. LC 94-13606. (Illus.). 265p. 1994. 40.00 (*0-8108-2901-0*) Scarecrow.

Piano Worship: Arrangements for the Advanced Pianist. Arranged by Marilyn Thompson. 52p. 1991. pap. 9.99 (*0-8341-9856-8*) Lillenas.

***Piano 101: Teacher's Handbook, Bks. 1 & 2.** E. L. Lancaster & Kenon D. Renfrow. 64p. 1999. pap., teacher ed. 8.95 (*0-7390-0254-6*, 14594) Alfred Pub.

Pianoforte: A Social History of the Piano. Dieter Hildebrandt. Tr. by Harriet Goodman from GER. LC 88-4314. 224p. 1988. 19.95 (*0-8076-1182-4*) Braziller.

Pianoforte: A Social History of the Piano. Dieter Hildebrandt. Tr. by Harriet Goodman from GER. LC 88-4314. 212p. 1999. pap. 17.95 (*0-8076-1458-0*, Pub. by Braziller) Norton.

Pianoforte in the Classical Era. Michael Cole. (Illus.). 412p. 1998. text 75.00 (*0-19-816634-6*) OUP.

Pianoforte Sonata: Its Origin & Development. 2nd ed. J. S. Shedlock. LC 64-18993. (Music Ser.). 1964. reprint ed. lib. bdg. 29.50 (*0-306-70900-7*) Da Capo.

Pianola: The History of the Self-Playing Piano. Arthur W. Ord-Hume. (Illus.). 360p. 1984. 70.00 (*0-04-789009-6*) Routledge.

PianoLab: An Introduction to Class Piano. Carolynn A. Lindeman. 292p. (C). 1983. pap. write for info. (*0-534-01305-8*) Wadsworth Pub.

PianoLab: An Introduction to Class Piano. 3rd ed. Carolynn A. Lindeman. LC 95-23956. (C). 1995. 32.75 (*0-534-25140-4*) Wadsworth Pub.

***PianoLab: An Introduction to Classic Piano.** 4th ed. Lindeman. LC 99-27834. (Music Ser.). 1999. pap. 51.95 (*0-534-53434-1*) Wadsworth Pub.

Pianoplayers. Anthony Burgess. 1987. reprint ed. pap. 4.95 (*0-685-19178-8*, WSP) PB.

***Pianos.** Pamela K. Harris. LC 99-59950. (Illus.). (J). 2000. lib. bdg. write for info. (*1-56766-682-5*) Childs World.

Pianos & Player Pianos: An Informative Guide for Owners & Prospective Buyers. Adrian Bezdechi. LC 79-318082. (Illus.). 63p. (Orig.). 1979. pap. 10.95 (*0-9604092-0-3*) Interstate Piano.

Pianos & Police. Alan M. Hofmeister et al. (Reading for All Learners Ser.). (Illus.). (J). pap. write for info. (*1-56861-212-5*) Swift Lrn Res.

Pianos & Politics in China: Middle-Class Ambitions & the Struggle over Western Music. Richard C. Kraus. (Illus.). 308p. 1989. text 65.00 (*0-19-505836-4*) OUP.

Pianos & Their Makers. Alfred Dolge. (Illus.). 581p. 1972. reprint ed. pap. 11.95 (*0-486-22856-8*) Dover.

***Pianos Around the Cape.** Glenna Luschei. 105p. 1999. pap. 10.00 (*0-9648562-2-0*) Aspermont.

Pianos, Piano-Tuners & Their Problems. George W. Booth. 320p. 1996. 39.95 (*1-85756-215-1*, Pub. by Janus Pubng) Paul & Co Pubs.

Pi'a'pa: Alphabet. Wren & Maile. (Keiki's First Bks.). (ENG & HAW., Illus.). 10p. (J). (ps). 1992. bds. 4.95 (*1-880188-30-9*) Bess Pr.

Piasah. Joy Steele. 49p. 2000. 7.00 (*0-8059-4692-6*) Dorrance.

Piast Poland. Pawel Jasienica. Tr. by Alexander Jordan. LC 92-81179. (Illus.). 266p. 1992. reprint ed. 25.00 (*1-881284-00-X*) Am Inst Polish.

Piat' Dram. Fedor Sologub, pseud. (RUS.). 264p. (C). 1989. reprint ed. pap. 16.00 (*0-933884-72-9*) Berkeley Slavic.

***Piave, Boito, Pirandello: From Romantic Realism to Modernism.** Deidre O'Grady. LC 00-33872. (Studies in Italian Literature). 2000. write for info. (*0-7734-7703-9*) E Mellen.

***Piazza.** New York Daily News Staff. (Illus.). 128p. 2000. 24.95 (*1-58261-262-5*) Sports Pub.

Piazza Armerina. R. J. Wilson. (Illus.). 124p. 1983. 12.50 (*0-292-76472-3*) U of Tex Pr.

Piazza Armerina Imperial Villa. Old Vicarage Publications Staff. 92p. (C). 1982. pap. text 65.00 (*0-7855-3133-5*, Pub. by Old Vicarage) St Mut.

Piazza Tales see Piazza Tales

Piazza Tales. Herman Melville. 21.95 (*0-89190-877-3*) Amereon Ltd.

Piazza Tales. Herman Melville. LC 95-53225. 1996. 14.50 (*0-679-60198-8*) Modern Lib NY.

Piazza Tales. Herman Melville. Ed. by Daniel Reagan. (Masterworks of Literature Ser.). 1994. 14.95 (*0-8084-0443-1*) NCUP.

Piazza Tales. Herman Melville & Harrison Hayford. LC 96-34027. 187p. 1996. 14.95 (*0-8101-1467-4*) Northwestern U Pr.

Piazza Tales. annot. ed. Incl. Bartleby. Herman Melville. Ed. by Egbert S. Oliver. 1962. Bell-Tower. Herman Melville. Ed. by Egbert S. Oliver. 1962. Benito Cereno. Encantadas. Herman Melville. Ed. by Egbert S. Oliver. 1962. Lightning-Rod Man. Herman Melville. Ed. by Egbert S. Oliver. 1962. Piazza Tales. Herman Melville. Ed. by Egbert S. Oliver. 1962. (Complete Works of Herman Melville Ser.). 268p. 1962. 24.95 (*0-87532-005-8*) Hendricks House.

Piazza Tales. Herman Melville. (BCL1-PS American Literature Ser.). 250p. 1993. reprint ed. lib. bdg. 79.00 (*0-7812-6989-X*) Rprt Serv.

Piazza Tales & Other Prose Pieces, 1839-60. Herman Melville. Ed. by Hershel Parker & G. Thomas Tanselle. (Northwestern-Newberry Edition of the Writings of Herman Melville: Vol. 9). (Illus.). 847p. (C). 1987. 89.95 (*0-8101-0550-0*); pap. text 29.95 (*0-8101-0551-9*) Northwestern U Pr.

Piazzetta: A Tercentenary Exhibition of Drawings, Prints, & Books. Ed. by George Knox. LC 83-17484. 258p. 1984. 99.95 (*0-521-26431-6*) Cambridge U Pr.

***PIC: Your Personal Introductory Course.** John Morton. 384p. 2001. pap. 26.95 (*0-7506-5038-9*, Newnes) Buttrwrth-Heinemann.

Pic-Jour Math: A Guide for Parents & Teachers Using Manipulatives, Pictures, Words, & Numbers to Help Children in Grades 3-8 Understand Mathematics. Andi Stix. 316p. 1994. pap. text 29.95 (*0-936386-67-3*) Creative Learning.

Pic Microcontroller Project Book. John Iovine. (Illus.). 324p. 2000. pap. 29.95 (*0-07-135479-4*) McGraw-Hill Prof.

Pic-Nic - Eltriciclo - El Laberinto. Fernando Arrabal. (SPA.). 269p. 1985. 14.95 (*0-8288-7047-0*, S31240) Fr & Eur.

Pic Puzzles. Ken A. Russell. (MENSA Ser.). 224p. 1995. pap. 7.95 (*0-572-01889-4*, Pub. by Foulsham UK) Assoc Pubs Grp.

Pica Gallo: Estampas Humoristicas. Emilio Santana. LC 89-82407. (Coleccion Caniqui). (SPA.). 256p. (Orig.). 1990. pap. 12.00 (*0-89729-504-8*) Ediciones.

Pica, Pica Varicela: Itchy, Itchy Chicken Pox. Grace Maccarone. (Hola Lector! Ser.).Tr. of Itchy, Itchy Chicken Pox. 1996. 8.70 (*0-606-08844-X*, Pub. by Turtleback) Demco.

Pica, Pica Varicela (Itchy, Itchy Chicken Pox) Grace Maccarone. Tr. by Yolanda Noda. LC 97-102383.Tr. of Itchy, Itchy Chicken Pox. (SPA., Illus.). 30p. (J). (ps-3). 1996. mass mkt. 3.50 (*0-590-69817-6*) Scholastic Inc.

Pica Roma Type in Elizabethan England. W. Craig Ferguson. 234p. 1989. text 131.95 (*0-85967-718-4*, Pub. by Scolar Pr) Ashgate Pub Co.

Picabia. Maria L. Borras. (Grandes Monografias). (SPA., Illus.). 552p. 1993. 350.00 (*84-343-0414-7*) Elliots Bks.

Picabo Sreet: Downhill Dynamo. Joel Dippold. LC 98-28467. (J). 1998. 5.95 (*0-8225-9839-6*) Lerner Pub.

Picabo Street: Downhill Dynamo. Joel Dippold. LC 97-8848. (J). 1997. lib. bdg. 19.95 (*0-8225-3659-5*, Lerner Publctns) Lerner Pub.

Picabo Street: Downhill Dynamo. Joel Dippold. LC 97-8848. (Illus.). 64p. (J). 1997. pap. 5.95 (*0-8225-9808-6*, Lerner Publctns) Lerner Pub.

Picacho: Life & Death of a Great Gold Mining Camp. Peter R. Odens. (Illus.). 44p. 1982. reprint ed. lib. bdg. 3.50 (*0-9609484-4-9*) P R Odens.

Picacho Gold. Jack Metzler. Ed. by Gillian Eaton. 336p. (Orig.). (YA). 1995. pap. 8.95 (*1-888445-00-9*) Sonstar Pubns.

Picador New Writing Helen Daniel & Robert Dessaix. LC 93-216482. xiii, 294 p. 1993. write for info. (*0-330-27397-3*) Trans-Atl Phila.

Picara: From Hera to Fantasy Heroine. Anne K. Kaler. LC 90-86056. 200p. (C). 1991. 39.95 (*0-87972-515-X*); pap. 18.95 (*0-87972-516-8*) Bowling Green Univ Popular Press.

Picara y la Dama: La Imagen de las Nujeres en las Novelas Picaresco Cortesanas de Maria de Zayas y Sotomayor. Mireya Perez-Erdelyi. LC 78-74597. (SPA., Illus.). 128p. 1979. pap. 10.00 (*0-89729-216-2*) Ediciones.

Picaresque: A Symposium on the Rogue's Tale. Ed. by Carmen Benito-Vessels & Michael Zappala. LC 91-51136. 1994. 35.00 (*0-87413-458-7*) U Delaware Pr.

Picaresque: Tradition & Displacement. Ed. by Giancarlo Maiorino. (Hispanic Issues Ser.: Vol. 12). 1996. pap. 21.95 (*0-8166-2723-1*); text 54.95 (*0-8166-2722-3*) U of Minn Pr.

Picaresque Hero in European Fiction. Richard Bjornson. LC 76-11312. (Illus.). 319p. 1977. reprint ed. pap. 98.90 (*0-608-07465-9*, 206769200009) Bks Demand.

Picaresque Narrative, Picaresque Fictions: A Theory & Research Guide. Ulrich Wicks. LC 88-15493. 383p. 1989. lib. bdg. 85.00 (*0-313-24934-2*, WPI/, Greenwood Pr) Greenwood.

Picaroons. Richard Hill. LC 77-37306. (Black Heritage Library Collection). 1977. reprint ed. 15.95 (*0-8369-8943-0*) Ayer.

***Picasso.** Matilde Battistini. LC 00-27067. (Illus.). (J). 2000. write for info. (*0-7894-6123-4*) DK Pub Inc.

***Picasso.** Mila Boutan. (Art Activity Ser.). (Illus.). (J). (gr. k-7). 1998. pap. 9.95 (*0-8118-2029-7*) Chronicle Bks.

Picasso. Chelsea House Publishing Staff. (World's Greatest Artists Ser.). 1997. 17.95 (*1-85813-606-7*) Chelsea Hse.

Picasso. Pierre Daix. (Illus.). 160p. 1995. 35.00 (*0-8050-1792-5*) H Holt & Co.

Picasso. Josep P. Fabre. LC 85-42962. (Illus.). 128p. 1990. 27.50 (*0-8478-0652-9*, Pub. by Rizzoli Intl) St Martin.

Picasso. Ed. by Jose M. Faerna. (Great Modern Masters Ser.). (Illus.). 64p. 1995. pap. 11.98 (*0-8109-4690-4*, Pub. by Abrams) Time Warner.

Picasso. Nathaniel Harris. 80p. (YA). (gr. 7 up). 1997. 17.95 (*1-85813-666-0*) Chelsea Hse.

Picasso. Tony Hart. LC 93-8750. (Famous Children Ser.). (Illus.). 24p. (J). (ps-3). 1994. pap. 5.95 (*0-8120-1826-5*) Barron.

Picasso. Timothy Hilton. (World of Art Ser.). (Illus.). 288p. 1985. pap. 14.95 (*0-500-20144-7*, Pub. by Thames Hudson) Norton.

Picasso. David Hockney. (Illus.). 86p. (Orig.). 1990. pap. 5.95 (*0-937815-33-0*) Hanuman Bks.

Picasso. Arianna S. Huffington. 1996. pap. 15.00 (*0-380-72947-4*, Avon Bks) Morrow Avon.

Picasso. Hans L. Jaffe. (Masters of Art Ser.). (Illus.). 128p. 1983. 24.95 (*0-8109-1480-8*, Pub. by Abrams) Time Warner.

Picasso. Stefano Loria. LC 95-31830. (Masters of Art Ser.). (Illus.). 64p. (J). (gr. 4-7). 1995. lib. bdg. 22.50 (*0-87226-318-5*, 63185B, P Bedrick Books) NTC Contemp Pub Co.

Picasso. Antony Mason. (Famous Artists Ser.). (Illus.). 32p. (YA). (gr. 5 up). 1995. 10.95 (*0-8120-6496-8*); pap. 6.95 (*0-8120-9175-2*) Barron.

Picasso. Antony Mason. (Famous Artists Ser.). 1994. 12.15 (*0-606-08845-8*, Pub. by Turtleback) Demco.

***Picasso.** Pablo Picasso. (Illus.). 2000. pap. 1.00 (*0-486-41076-5*) Dover.

Picasso. Gabriel Potter. 1992. 5.98 (*1-55521-764-8*) Bk Sales Inc.

Picasso. Gertrude Stein. (Illus.). 128p. 1984. pap. 5.95 (*0-486-24715-5*) Dover.

Picasso. Mike Venezia. LC 87-33023. (Getting to Know the World's Greatest Artists Ser.). (Illus.). 32p. (J). (ps-4). 1988. pap. 6.95 (*0-516-42271-5*); lib. bdg. 21.00 (*0-516-02271-7*) Childrens.

Picasso, 11 vols. Ingo F. Walther. (Thunder Bay Artists Ser.). (Illus.). 96p. 1997. pap. 4.99 (*1-57145-130-7*, Thunder Bay) Advantage Pubs.

Picasso. Ingo F. Walther. (SPA.). 1996. pap. 9.99 (*3-8228-0104-6*) Taschen Amer.

***Picasso.** Carsten P. Warncke. (Illus.). 1998. 24.99 (*3-8228-7370-5*) Benedikt Taschen.

Picasso. Carsten P. Warncke. (Big Art Ser.). 1998. 19.99 (*3-8228-7221-0*) Taschen Amer.

Picasso. C.P. Warncke. 1997. 49.99 (*3-8228-8267-4*) Taschen Amer.

Picasso. Hans L. Jaffe. (Illus.). 160p. 1996. reprint ed. pap. 19.98 (*0-8109-8142-4*, Pub. by Abrams) Time Warner.

Picasso. Lorraine Levy. (Illus.). 160p. 1998. reprint ed. 19.95 (*1-56852-172-3*, Konecky & Konecky) W S Konecky Assocs.

Picasso. Roland Penrose. (Color Library). (Illus.). 128p. (C). 1994. reprint ed. pap. 14.95 (*0-7148-2708-8*, Pub. by Phaidon Press) Phaidon Pr.

Picasso: A Biography. Patrick O'Brian. 520p. 1994. pap. 18.95 (*0-393-31107-4*) Norton.

Picasso: A Day in His Studio see Art for Children

***Picasso: A Dialogue with Ceramics.** Kosme de Baranano. LC 99-192323. (Illus.). 234p. 1998. pap. 60.00 (*84-89413-36-3*, Pub. by Fundacion Bancaja) U of Wash Pr.

Picasso: Art As Autobiography. Mary M. Gedo. LC 80-11126. (Illus.). 288p. 1999. pap. text 24.00 (*0-226-28483-2*) U Ch Pr.

***Picasso: Artist of the Century.** Pablo Picasso. LC 99-209122. (ENG & DUT.). 143p. 1999. pap. write for info. (*90-400-9357-1*) Waandrs.

Picasso: Breaking the Rules of Art. David Spence. (Illus.). 32p. 1997. pap. 5.95 (*0-7641-0293-1*) Barron.

Picasso: Collected Writings. Pref. by Michel Leiris. (Illus.). 456p. 1989. 70.00 (*1-55859-045-5*) Abbeville Pr.

Picasso: Drawings, 1966-1967. Pablo Picasso. (FRE., Illus.). 74p. 1968. pap. 25.00 (*1-55660-273-1*) A Wofsy Fine Arts.

Picasso: Drawings, 1969-1971. Pablo Picasso. (FRE., Illus.). 110p. 1971. pap. 30.00 (*1-55660-274-X*) A Wofsy Fine Arts.

Picasso: Figures. Raymond Cogniat. (Rhythem & Color One Ser.). 1970. 9.95 (*0-8288-9502-3*) Fr & Eur.

***Picasso: From Ballet to Drama.** Konemann Inc. Staff. (Illus.). 140p. 2000. 99.95 (*3-8290-3111-4*) Konemann.

Picasso: Graphic Magician. Clinton Adams. 1998. 48.00 (*0-85667-494-X*) P Wilson Serv.

Picasso: Graphic Magician - Prints from the Norton Simon Museum. Betsy G. Fryberger et al. 176p. Date not set. pap. write for info. (*0-937031-13-5*); text. write for info. (*0-937031-12-7*) Stanford Art.

Picasso: His Life & Work. 3rd ed. Roland Penrose. (Illus.). 550p. 1981. pap. 17.95 (*0-520-04207-7*, Pub. by U CA Pr) Cal Prin Full Svc.

Picasso: Inside the Image. Aldo Crommelynck et al. LC 94-62008. (Illus.). 128p. 1995. 27.50 (*0-500-09251-6*, Pub. by Thames Hudson) Norton.

Picasso: Inside the Image: Prints from the Ludwig Museum, Cologne. Janie Cohen et al. (Illus.). 136p. (Orig.). 1995. pap. 19.95 (*0-934658-06-4*) R H Flem Mus.

Picasso: Last Etchings, 1968-72. Pablo Picasso. (FRE., Illus.). 216p. 1973. pap. 40.00 (*1-55660-266-9*) A Wofsy Fine Arts.

Picasso: Les Demoiselles de Avignon - Album de Dibujos. Brigitte Leal. (Ediciones Especiales y de Bibliofilo Ser.). (SPA., Illus.). 116p. 1993. 375.00 (*84-343-0533-X*) Elliots Bks.

Picasso: Master of the New Idea. Marie-Laure Bernadac & Paule Du Bouchet. Tr. by Carey Lovelace. (Discoveries Ser.). (Illus.). 200p. 1993. pap. 12.95 (*0-8109-2802-7*, Pub. by Abrams) Time Warner.

Picasso: Masterpieces of the Blue Period. Text by Laszlo Glozer. (Schirmer's Visual Library). (Illus.). 120p. 1993. pap. 10.95 (*0-393-30894-4*) Norton.

Picasso: Midi Double. Carsten C. Warncke. (SPA.). 1996. 29.99 (*3-8228-8843-5*) Taschen Amer.

Picasso: Painter & Sculptor in Clay. Pablo Picasso. LC 98-73227. (Illus.). 264p. 1999. 60.00 (*0-8109-4353-0*, Pub. by Abrams) Time Warner.

P

An Asterisk (*) at the beginning of an entry indicates that the title is appearing for the first time.

Picasso: Spanish. Taschen Staff. (SPA.). Date not set. 19.99 (*3-8228-8015-9*, Pub. by Benedikt Taschen) Bks Nippan.

***Picasso: The Art of the Poster, Catalogue Raisonne.** Marc Gundel. (Illus.). 2000. 39.95 (*3-7913-2277-X*) Prestel Pub NY.

Picasso: The Early Years, 1881-1907. Josep Palau i Fabre. (Illus.). 560p. 1985. boxed set 225.00 (*1-55660-166-2*) A Wofsy Fine Arts.

Picasso: The Early Years, 1892-1906. Ed. by Marilyn McCully. 1997. 60.00 (*0-614-28054-0*) Yale U Pr.

Picasso: The Early Years, 1892-1906. Ed. by Marilyn McCully. (Illus.). 430p. 1997. 65.00 (*0-300-07166-3*) Yale U Pr.

Picasso: The Ludwig Collection. Ed. by Evelyn Weiss et al. (Illus.). 280p. 1992. 65.00 (*3-7913-1250-2*, Pub. by Prestel) te Neues.

Picasso: Works from the Rue des Grands-Augustins Studio, 1939-47. Contrib. by Richard Stone. (Illus.). 1995. 9.95 (*1-880146-12-6*) M Marks.

Picasso--The Early Years, 1892-1906. Pablo Picasso et al. LC 96-49663. (Illus.). 1997. 60.00 (*0-89468-268-7*) Natl Gallery Art.

Picasso & Braque: A Symposium. William S. Rubin. (Illus.). 360p. 1992. 35.00 (*0-8109-6115-6*, Pub. by Abrams); pap. 19.95 (*0-8109-6117-2*, Pub. by Abrams) Time Warner.

Picasso & Braque: A Symposium. Ed. by Lynn Zelevansky. (Illus.). 360p. 1992. 35.00 (*0-87070-677-2*, 0-8109-6115-6, Pub. by Mus of Modern Art); pap. 19.95 (*0-87070-678-0*, 0-8109-6117-2, Pub. by Mus of Modern Art) Abrams.

Picasso & Braque: Pioneering Cubism. William Rubin. (Illus.). 464p. 1989. 70.00 (*0-87070-675-6*, 0-8109-6065-6, Pub. by Mus of Modern Art) Abrams.

Picasso & Braque: Pioneering Cubism. William S. Rubin. (Illus.). 1990. 70.00 (*0-8109-6065-6*, Pub. by Abrams); pap. 34.95 (*0-685-58430-5*, 0-8109-6120-2) Abrams.

Picasso & Cubism. Kay Hyman. (Illus.). 64p. 1994. write for info. (*0-9640034-5-7*) World Pubns.

Picasso & Dora: A Memoir. James Lord. 1993. 35.00 (*0-374-23208-3*) FS&G.

Picasso & Dora: A Personal Memoir. James Lord. LC 94-23057. (Illus.). 352p. 1994. pap. 16.95 (*0-88064-162-2*) Fromm Intl Pub.

Picasso & Drawing. Contrib. by Bernice Rose. (Illus.). 120p. (Orig.). 1995. pap. write for info. (*1-878283-50-2*) PaceWildenstein.

Picasso & His Times. Daniele Giraudy & Patrick De Maupeou. (W5 Who, What, Where, When, & Why Ser.). 96p. (YA). (gr. 6 up). 1999. 19.95 (*0-8050-5061-2*) H Holt & Co.

Picasso & Photography: The Dark Mirror. Anne Baldassari. Tr. by Deke Dusinberre. LC 97-34000. (Illus.). 256p. 1997. 55.00 (*2-08-013646-1*, Pub. by Flammarion) Abbeville Pr.

Picasso & Photography: The Dark Mirror. Anne Baldassari. LC 97-34000. (Illus.). 256p. 1998. pap. 39.95 (*2-08-013649-6*) Tex A&M Univ Pr.

Picasso & Portraiture: Representation & Transformation. Ed. by William Rubin. (Illus.). 496p. 1999. text 50.00 (*0-7881-6076-1*) DIANE Pub.

Picasso & Portraiture: Representation & Transformation. William S. Rubin. (Illus.). 496p. 1996. 75.00 (*0-87070-143-6*, 0-8109-6140-1); pap. 35.00 (*0-87070-142-8*) Mus of Modern Art.

Picasso & Printmaking in Paris. Stephen Coppel. (Illus.). 128p. 1999. pap. 29.95 (*1-85332-180-X*, Pub. by U CA Pr) Cal Prin Full Svc.

Picasso & the Age of Iron. Carmen Gimenez. 1993. 59.95 (*0-89207-103-6*) S R Guggenheim.

Picasso & the Age of Iron. Carmen Gimenez et al. (Illus.). 320p. 1995. pap. 39.95 (*0-8109-6882-7*) Abrams.

Picasso & the Girl with a Ponytail. Laurence Anholt. LC 98-14005. (SPA., Illus.). 32p. (J). (ps-2). 1998. 13.95 (*0-7641-5031-6*) Barron.

Picasso & the Spanish Tradition. Ed. by Jonathan Brown. LC 96-60716. (Illus.). 224p. 1996. 45.00 (*0-300-06475-6*) Yale U Pr.

Picasso & the War Years, 1937-1945. Ed. by Steven A. Nash. LC 98-60335. (Illus.). 256p. 1998. 50.00 (*0-500-09274-5*, Pub. by Thames Hudson) Norton.

Picasso Anthology: Documents, Criticism, Reminiscences. Ed. by Marilyn McCully. LC 82-47632. (Illus.). 288p. 1982. pap. 16.95 (*0-691-00348-3*, Pub. by Princeton U Pr) Cal Prin Full Svc.

Picasso at the Bellagio. Libby O. Lumpkin & Stephen A. Wynn. Ed. by Kathleen M. Clewell. (Illus.). 42p. 1999. pap. 16.95 (*0-9666625-1-2*) Mirage Resorts.

Picasso at the Lapin Agile & Other Plays. Steve Martin. 160p. 1997. pap. 12.00 (*0-8021-3523-4*, Grove) Grove-Atltic.

Picasso at the Lapin Agile & Other Plays: Picasso at the Lapin Agile; WASP; The Zig-Zag Woman; Patter for a Floating Lady. Steve Martin. LC 96-13222. 160p. 1996. 20.00 (*0-8021-1595-0*, Grove) Grove-Atltic.

Picasso Braque L'Eger & the Cubist Spirit, 1919-1939. Kenneth Wayne et al. LC 96-68506. (Illus.). 64p. 1996. pap. text 14.95 (*0-916857-08-5*, N6848) Port Mus Art.

Picasso Catalogue of the Printed Graphic Work, 4 vols. George Bloch. (Illus.). 1971. 795.00 (*0-8150-0026-X*) Wittenborn Art.

Picasso Catalogue of the Printed Graphic Work, Vol. 1, 1904-1967. George Bloch. (Illus.). 1971. 175.00 (*0-8150-0467-2*) Wittenborn Art.

Picasso Catalogue of the Printed Graphic Work, Vol. 2, 1967-1969. George Bloch. (Catalogue of the Printed Graphic Work Ser.: Vols. 1 & 2). (Illus.). 1971. 175.00 (*0-8150-0468-0*) Wittenborn Art.

Picasso Catalogue of the Printed Graphic Work, Vol. 4, 1970-1972. George Bloch. (ENG, FRE & GER., Illus.). 253p. 1979. 175.00 (*3-85773-009-9*) Wittenborn Art.

Picasso Ceramics. George Bloch. (Catalogue of the Printed Graphic Work Ser.: Vol. 3, Ceramiques 1949-1971). (Illus.). 1972. 195.00 (*0-8150-0646-2*) Wittenborn Art.

Picasso, Dessins. Rene Char & Charles Feld. 256p. 1969. 65.00 (*0-7859-0686-X*, F93300) Fr & Eur.

Picasso Drawings & Watercolors, 1899-1907 in the Collection of the Baltimore Museum of Art. Victor I. Carlson. LC 76-41022. 1977. 25.00 (*0-912298-43-X*); pap. 17.50 (*0-912298-42-1*) Baltimore Mus.

Picasso, 50 Years of His Art. Alfred H. Barr, Jr. LC 66-26126. (Museum of Modern Art Publications in Reprint). 1967. reprint ed. 28.95 (*0-405-01519-4*) Ayer.

Picasso for Kids. LC 95-80614. (Great Art for Kids Ser.). (Illus.). 12p. (J). (ps). 1996. 12.95 (*1-888108-06-1*) Budding Artists.

Picasso I. 1994. pap. 8.99 (*3-8228-9344-7*) Taschen Amer.

Picasso II. 1994. pap. 8.99 (*3-8228-9446-X*) Taschen Amer.

Picasso Line Drawings & Prints. Pablo Picasso. (Art Library). (Illus.). 48p. (Orig.). 1982. pap. 4.95 (*0-486-24196-3*) Dover.

Picasso Linoleum Cuts: The Mr. & Mrs. Charles Kramer Collection in the Metropolitan Museum of Art. Ed. by L. Donald McVinney. 1985. 60.00 (*0-394-54692-X*) Random.

Picasso Lithographs: 61 Works. Pablo Picasso. (Art Library). (Illus.). 64p. (Orig.). 1980. pap. 3.95 (*0-486-23949-7*) Dover.

Picasso Museum, Paris: The Masterpieces. 2nd ed. Marie-Laure Bernadac et al. (Illus.). 224p. 1991. 45.00 (*3-7913-1118-2*, Pub. by Prestel) te Neues.

Picasso on Art: A Selection of Views. Ed. by Dore Ashton. (Quality Paperbacks Ser.). (Illus.). 220p. 1988. reprint ed. pap. 13.95 (*0-306-80330-5*) Da Capo.

***Picasso Paints a Portrait.** David Douglas-Duncan. (Illus.). 62p. 2000. reprint ed. text 30.00 (*0-7881-9009-1*) DIANE Pub.

Picasso Papers. Rosalind E. Krauss. LC 97-16471. (Illus.). 272p. 1998. 25.00 (*0-374-23209-1*) FS&G.

Picasso Papers. Rosalind E. Krauss. LC 98-39139. (Illus.). 288p. 1999. pap. text 15.00 (*0-262-61142-2*) MIT Pr.

Picasso Postcard Book. Pablo Picasso. 1997. pap. 5.99 (*3-8228-7917-7*) Taschen Amer.

Picasso Scam. Stuart Pawson. 320p. 1997. mass mkt. 9.95 (*0-7472-4977-6*, Pub. by Headline Bk Pub) Trafalgar.

Picasso the Engraver, 1900-1942. Brigitte Baer. LC 97-60543. (Illus.). 112p. 1997. 34.95 (*0-500-09269-9*, Pub. by Thames Hudson) Norton.

Picasso 2 Posterbook. Taschen, Benedikt Staff. (SPA.). Date not set. pap. 8.99 (*3-8228-0774-5*) Taschen Amer.

Picasso, Vollard Suite. Angel G. Garcia. 1994. pap. 29.95 (*0-295-97349-8*) U of Wash Pr.

***Picasso Working on Paper.** Anne Baldassari. 2000. 45.00 (*1-85894-107-5*) Merrell Holberton.

Picasso, World of Children: Postcard Book. Prestel Staff. 1997. 8.95 (*3-7913-1499-8*, Pub. by Prestel) te Neues.

Picasso's Complete Ceramics. Alain Ramie. (Illus.). 315p. 1988. 325.00 (*1-55660-067-4*) A Wofsy Fine Arts.

Picasso's Complete Sculpture. Werner Spies. (GER., Illus.). 424p. 1988. pap. 125.00 (*1-55660-006-2*) A Wofsy Fine Arts.

Picasso's Complete Work, 33 Vols. Christian Zervos. (Illus.). 1984. 6500.00 (*0-915346-84-2*) A Wofsy Fine Arts.

Picasso's Cubist Paintings, 1907-16: Catalogue Raisonne. Pierre Daix & Joan Rosselet. (FRE., Illus.). 378p. 1979. 225.00 (*1-55660-101-8*) A Wofsy Fine Arts.

Picasso's Guernica. Alice D. Tankard. LC 81-65876. (Illus.). 160p. 1984. 35.00 (*0-87982-044-6*) Art Alliance.

Picasso's Guernica: Images Within Images. 2nd rev. ed. Melvin E. Becraft. LC 85-73564. (Illus.). 146p. 1987. 23.95 (*0-9615981-0-7*) M E Becraft.

Picasso's Illustrated Books: Catalogue Raisonne. Sebastian Goeppert et al. (Catalogue Raisonne Ser.). (Illus.). 380p. 1983. 295.00 (*1-55660-057-7*) A Wofsy Fine Arts.

***Picasso's Ladies: Jewellery by Wendy Ramshaw.** Arnoldsche. 1999. 75.00 (*3-925369-80-5*) Arnoldsche Art Pubs.

Picasso's Ladies: Jewelry by Wendy Ramshaw. Marina Vaizey et al. (Illus.). 136p. 1998. 29.95 (*1-85894-065-6*, Pub. by Merrell Holberton) U of Wash Pr.

Picasso's Mask. annot. ed. Andre Malraux. Tr. & Anno. by June Guicharnaud. LC 94-34604.Tr. of Tete d'Obsidienne. (Illus.). 285p. 1995. pap. 13.95 (*0-306-80629-0*) Da Capo.

Picasso's One-Liners. Pablo Picasso. LC 97-3776. (Illus.). 80p. 1997. 14.95 (*1-885183-78-X*) Artisan.

Picasso's Paintings, 1900-1906. Pierre Daix & Georges Boudaille. (FRE., Illus.). 360p. 1989. 200.00 (*1-55660-048-8*) A Wofsy Fine Arts.

Picasso's Paintings, Watercolors, Drawings & Sculpture: Surrealism, 1930-1936. Picasso Project Staff. (Illus.). 336p. 1997. 150.00 (*1-55660-234-0*) A Wofsy Fine Arts.

Picasso's Paintings, Watercolors, Drawings & Sculpture - A Comprehensive Illustrated Catalogue: Europe at War, 1939-1940. Picasso Project Staff et al. (Illus.). 233p. 1998. 150.00 (*1-55660-235-9*) A Wofsy Fine Arts.

Picasso's Paintings, Watercolors, Drawings & Sculpture - A Comprehensive Illustrated Catalogue: From Cubism to Neoclassicism, 1917-1919. Picasso Project Staff. (Illus.). 320p. 1995. 150.00 (*1-55660-230-8*) A Wofsy Fine Arts.

Picasso's Paintings, Watercolors, Drawings & Sculpture - A Comprehensive Illustrated Catalogue: Liberation & Post-War Years, 1944-1949. Picasso Project Staff. (Illus.). 288p. 1999. 150.00 (*1-55660-237-5*) A Wofsy Fine Arts.

Picasso's Paintings, Watercolors, Drawings & Sculpture - A Comprehensive Illustrated Catalogue: Nazi Occupation, 1940-1944. Picasso Project Staff. (Illus.). 400p. 1999. 150.00 (*1-55660-236-7*) A Wofsy Fine Arts.

Picasso's Paintings, Watercolors, Drawings & Sculpture - A Comprehensive Illustrated Catalogue: Neoclassicism I, 1920-21. Picasso Project Staff. (Illus.). 304p. 1995. 150.00 (*1-55660-231-6*) A Wofsy Fine Arts.

Picasso's Paintings, Watercolors, Drawings & Sculpture - A Comprehensive Illustrated Catalogue: Neoclassicism II, 1922-1924. Picasso Project Staff. (Illus.). 288p. 1996. 150.00 (*1-55660-232-4*) A Wofsy Fine Arts.

Picasso's Paintings, Watercolors, Drawings & Sculpture - A Comprehensive Illustrated Catalogue: Spanish Civil War, 1937-1939. Picasso Project Staff. (Illus.). 288p. 1997. 150.00 (*1-55660-262-6*) A Wofsy Fine Arts.

Picasso's Paintings, Watercolors, Drawings & Sculpture - A Comprehensive Illustrated Catalogue: Toward Surrealism, 1925-1929. Picasso Project Staff. (Illus.). 288p. 1996. 150.00 (*1-55660-233-2*) A Wofsy Fine Arts.

Picasso's Parade: From Page to Stage. Deborah M. Rothschild. (Illus.). 280p. 1991. 90.00 (*0-85667-392-7*, Pub. by P Wilson) Scala Books.

Picasso's Paris: Walking Tours of the Artist's Life in the City. Ellen Williams. LC 98-67311. 144p. 1998. 19.95 (*0-9641262-7-3*) Little Bkrm.

Picasso's Variations on the Masters: Confrontations with the Past. Susan G. Galassi. (Illus.). 240p. 1996. 39.95 (*0-8109-3741-7*, Pub. by Abrams) Time Warner.

Picasso's Vollard Suite. Intro. by Hans Bolliger. LC 85-50441. (Illus.). 120p. 1994. reprint ed. pap. 15.95 (*0-500-27100-3*, Pub. by Thames Hudson) Norton.

***Picasso's Weeping Woman: The Life & Art of Dora Maar.** Mary Ann Caws. (Illus.). 224p. 2000. 50.00 (*0-8212-2693-2*) Bulfinch Pr.

Picasso's Woman: A Breast Cancer Story. Rosalind MacPhee. Ed. by Deborah Baker. LC 95-42781. 288p. 1996. 20.00 (*1-56836-138-6*) Kodansha.

Picasso's Women: Eight Monologues. Brian Mcavera. 144p. 1998. pap. 16.95 (*1-870259-86-6*, Pub. by Oberon Bks Ltd) Consort Bk Sales.

Picasso's World of Children. Werner Spies. (Illus.). 256p. 1996. 65.00 (*3-7913-1608-7*, Pub. by Prestel) te Neues.

Picasso's World of Children. Werner Spies et al. LC 96-118158. (Pegasus Library). (Illus.). 128p. 1994. 25.00 (*3-7913-1375-4*, Pub. by Prestel) te Neues.

***Picathartes to Oxpeckers, Vol. 6.** Brown. (Birds of Africa Ser.). 600p. 2000. write for info. (*0-12-137306-1*) Acad Pr.

***Picatinny Arsenal.** John Rae. (Images of America Ser.). 128p. 1999. pap. 18.99 (*0-7385-0196-4*) Arcadia Publng.

Picayune Creole Cookbook. Picayune Staff. (Cookbook Ser.). 1971. pap. 9.95 (*0-486-22678-6*) Dover.

Piccadilly. large type ed. Claire Rayner. (General Fiction Ser.). 560p. 1992. 27.99 (*0-7089-2776-9*) Ulverscroft.

Piccadilly. Arnold Bennett. LC 74-17299. (Collected Works of Arnold Bennett: Vol. 65). 1977. reprint ed. 22.95 (*0-518-19146-X*) Ayer.

Piccadilly Jim. P. G. Wodehouse. 240p. 1984. pap. 14.95 (*0-14-003039-5*, Penguin Bks) Viking Penguin.

Piccapu. Giuseppe A. Sbrocchi. (Creative Writing Ser.). 142p. 1993. pap. 10.00 (*0-921252-31-5*) LEGAS.

Piccola Guida al Messale see Introduction to the Liturgical Year

Piccolo. James Baddock. 252p. 1992. 19.95 (*0-8027-1201-0*) Walker & Co.

Piccolo. Jennifer E. Martin. (Orig.). Date not set. pap. write for info. (*0-9643049-1-0*) Cayuse Press.

Piccolo. large type ed. James Baddock. LC 92-33397. 402p. 1993. reprint ed. lib. bdg. 18.95 (*1-56054-589-5*) Thorndike Pr.

Piccolo Santo. Roberto Bracco. Ed. by Vincent Luciani. (ITA.). (C). 1961. pap. 7.95 (*0-913298-23-9*) S F Vanni.

Picelj: Ivan Picelj, An Exhibition of Sculptures, Paintings, & Prints. Intro. by Eldon N. Van Liere. (Illus.). 16p. (Orig.). 1985. pap. 4.00 (*1-879147-06-8*) Kresge Art Mus.

Pichardo's Treatise on the Limits of Louisiana & Texas, 4 vols. Ed. by Charles W. Hackett. LC 72-157340. (Select Bibliographies Reprint Ser.). 1977. reprint ed. 145.95 (*0-8369-5800-4*) Ayer.

Pichia Protocols. Ed. by David R. Higgins & James Cregg. LC 98-6428. (Methods in Molecular Biology Ser.: Vol. 103). (Illus.). 284p. 1998. 84.50 (*0-89603-421-6*) Humana.

Pichifkes: Stories Heard on the Road & along the Way. Hanoch Teller. 246p. 1989. 15.95 (*0-9614772-7-X*) NYC Pub Co.

Pichka Harawikuna: Five Quechua Poets. Ed. by J. Noriega Bernuy. Tr. by Maureen Ahern. LC 98-37802. (ENG, QUE & SPA.). 160p. 1998. pap. 14.95 (*0-935480-98-6*) Lat Am Lit Rev Pr.

Pick: The Easy Way: Database & Word Processing for the New User, Vol. 1. Matthew H. Stern & Betsy Pollack. (Illus.). 412p. (Orig.). (C). 1986. pap. 26.95 (*0-936477-01-6*) Comp Info Sci.

Pick: The Easy Way: Expanded Theory & Operation, Vol. II. Matthew H. Stern. LC 86-2586. (Illus.). 312p. (Orig.). (C). 1986. pap. 23.95 (*0-936477-02-4*) Comp Info Sci.

Pick a Better Country: An Unassuming Colored Guy Speaks His Mind about America. Ken Hamblin. 256p. 1996. 23.00 (*0-684-80755-6*) S&S Trade.

Pick a Better Country: An Unassuming Colored Guy Speaks His Mind about America. Ken Hamblin. (Illus.). 256p. 1997. per. 12.00 (*0-684-84318-8*, Touchstone) S&S Trade Pap.

Pick a Card. Betsy Sholl. 32p. (Orig.). 1991. pap. 6.95 (*0-913341-14-2*) Coyote Love.

Pick a Card, Any Card: Card Tricks for Beginners. Harry Baron. LC 94-6125. (Illus.). 128p. 1994. pap. 9.95 (*1-55958-493-9*) Prima Pub.

***Pick a New Dream.** Lenora Mattingly Weber. (Beany Malone Ser.). 301p. (J). 1999. reprint ed. pap. 12.95 (*1-930009-03-8*) Image Cascade.

Pick a Pack of Praise. (J). (gr. 3-6). 1988. 6.99 (*0-685-68211-0*, MB-594); 3.99 (*0-685-68212-9*, MB-594A) Lillenas.

Pick a Pack of Praise. (J). (gr. 3-6). 1988. audio 12.99 (*0-685-68213-7*, TA-9100C) Lillenas.

Pick a Pack of Praise: Songbook Edition. 102p. 1988. pap. 7.99 (*0-8341-9335-3*) Lillenas.

Pick a Party. Patti Sachs. 204p. 1997. 9.00 (*0-671-52123-3*) S&S Trade.

Pick a Party: The Big Book of Party Themes. Patty Sachs. LC 97-20080. 1997. 9.00 (*0-88166-280-1*) Meadowbrook.

Pick-a-Party Cookbook. Sachs. LC 98-4415. 264p. 1998. pap. 11.00 (*0-671-02386-1*) S&S Trade.

Pick-a-Party Cookbook. Patty Sachs. LC 98-4415. 1998. 11.00 (*0-88166-310-7*) Meadowbrook.

Pick a Pet. Shelley Rotner et al. LC 98-33752. (Illus.). 32p. (J). (ps-k). 1999. 15.95 (*0-531-30147-8*); lib. bdg. 16.99 (*0-531-33147-4*) Orchard Bks Watts.

Pick-a-Pick a Partner Music Tape, Bk. 1. large type ed. Charlene Wrighton et al. (SPA., Illus.). 36p. (J). (ps up). 1997. pap. text, student ed. 16.95 incl. audio (*1-886441-04-9*, SR 131-761) Zoo-phonics.

Pick a Plum: An Insider's View of the Finest Antiques, Specialty Shops & Unique Talent in the Valley of the Sun. Lenore Wadsworth. (Illus.). 112p. 1997. pap. 8.50 (*0-9662175-0-0*) Word Play.

Pick-a-Prayer for Bedtime. Illus. by Suzy-Jane Tanner. 12p. (ps-1). 1999. 4.99 (*0-8054-2085-1*) Broadman.

***Pick-a-Prayer for Every Day.** Illus. by Suzy-Jane Tanner. 12p. (J). (ps-1). 1999. 4.99 (*0-8054-2086-X*) Broadman.

Pick-a-Prayer for Special Days. Illus. by Suzy-Jane Tanner. 12p. (J). (ps-1). 1999. 4.99 (*0-8054-2087-8*) Broadman.

Pick-a-Prayer to Say Thank You. Illus. by Suzy-Jane Tanner. 12p. (J). (ps-1). 1999. 4.99 (*0-8054-2088-6*) Broadman.

Pick a Pretty Indian Name for Your Baby. Meenal A. Pandya & Rashmee P. Bhanot. (Illus.). 256p. 1991. 19.95 (*0-9635539-0-9*) Meera Pubns.

Pick a Word: Poems by Frank Fagan. Frank Fagan. LC 92-71183. (Orig.). 1992. pap. 8.95 (*0-9632732-0-5*) Dendron Pr.

Pick & Choose: Program Ideas for Youth Ministry. Group Publishing Staff. 1993. boxed set 19.99 (*1-55945-199-8*) Group Pub.

Pick & Choose: Program Ideas for Youth Ministry see Escoja y Seleccione: Ideas Dinamicas para Reuniones de Jovenes

Pick & Grin Patterns for Guitar. Ron Middlebrook. 4p. 1995. pap. text 2.00 (*1-57424-005-6*) Centerstream Pub.

Pick & Shop Marketplace. Ron Van Der Meer. (Illus.). (J). 1996. 19.99 (*0-614-19348-6*) Random.

***Pick-&-Shovel Poet: The Journeys of Pascal D'Angelo.** Jim Murphy. (Illus.). 176p. (J). (gr. 4-7). 2000. 20.00 (*0-395-77610-4*, Clarion Bks) HM.

Pick Basic: A System Programmer's Guide. Jonathan E. Sisk. 224p. (Orig.). 1987. 36.95 (*0-8306-2845-2*) McGraw-Hill Prof.

Pick for Humans. Newman Binney. 1991. 29.95 (*0-8306-1800-7*) McGraw-Hill Prof.

Pick for Professionals: Advanced Methods & Techniques. Harvey E. Rodstein. 368p. 1990. 34.95 (*0-07-156991-X*) McGraw.

Pick for Professionals: Advanced Methods & Techniques. Harvey E. Rodstein. (Pick Library). (Illus.). 256p. 1989. 34.95 (*0-8306-0125-2*) McGraw-Hill Prof.

Pick Guns: Lock Picking for Spies, Cops & Locksmiths. John Minnery. (Illus.). 128p. 1989. pap. 18.00 (*0-87364-510-3*) Paladin Pr.

PICK in the PC Environment. John W. Winters & Dale E. Winters. (Pick Library). (Illus.). 256p. 1988. 29.95 (*0-8306-3152-6*, 3152) McGraw-Hill Prof.

***Pick It & Stick It Book.** Golden Books Staff. (Between the Lions Ser.). (Illus.). (J). 2000. pap. 3.99 (*0-307-28327-5*, Goldn Books) Gldn Bks Pub Co.

Pick Me Ups Reading. Ed. by Scholastic, Inc. Staff. 1982. pap. 2.95 (*0-590-49054-0*, Scholastic Hardcover) Scholastic Inc.

Pick of the Crop. 2nd ed. North Sunflower Academy Staff. (Illus.). 18.95 (*0-9664025-0-2*) Sthborough Grdnrs.

Pick of the Crop Vol. 2: Favorites from the Mississippi Delta. 2nd ed. North Sunflower PTA Staff. (Illus.). 320p. 1998. 18.95 (*0-9666954-0-2*) North Sunflower Academy.

Pick of the Litter. Bill Tarrant. LC 94-34323. (Illus.). 184p. 1995. 22.95 (*1-55821-345-7*) Lyons Pr.

***Pick of the Pack Patience Games.** 2nd ed. Jacqueline Harrod. (Illus.). 128p. 2001. pap. 6.95 (*0-7160-2077-7*, Pub. by Elliot RW Bks) Midpt Trade.

Pick of the Season: The Best of British Football Writing, 1995-96. Ed. by Stephen F. Kelly. 352p. 1997. pap. 22.95 (*1-85158-891-4*, Pub. by Mainstream Pubng) Trafalgar.

Pick One: A User-Friendly Guide to Religion. John W. Friesen. (Illus.). 256p. (Orig.). 1995. pap. write for info. (*1-55059-112-6*) Detselig Ents.

Pick Pocket Guide. 5th rev. ed. Jonathan E. Sisk. (Pick Library). 319p. 1991. pap. 24.95 (*0-8306-3827-X*, 3827) McGraw-Hill Prof.

Pick Programming Language: BASIC. Malcolm Bull. LC 93-673. (Computing Ser.). 456p. 1994. mass mkt. 64.95 (*0-412-46660-0*) Chapman & Hall.

Pick the Brighter Tulip: There Is an Alternative to Calvinism. Alger Fitch. 65p. 1997. pap. 4.99 (*0-89900-622-1*) College Pr Pub.

***Pick the Right Guitar: The Guitar Buyer's Handbook.** unabridged ed. Vern Juran. Ed. by Jean A. Verch. 96p. 1999. pap. 14.95 (*0-9675609-0-X*) J-V Pubg.

***Pick the Right Plant.** Ed. by Time-Life Books Editors. 2000. spiral bd. 24.95 (*0-7370-0621-8*) T-L Custom Pub.

P

An Asterisk (*) at the beginning of an entry indicates that the title is appearing for the first time.

Pick the Right Plant: A Sun & Shade Guide to Successful Plant Selection. Time-Life Books Editors. LC 97-44631. (Illus.). 384p. (YA). (gr. 11). 1999. 24.95 (*0-7835-5293-9*) Time-Life.

Pick-Up. Charles Willeford. LC 90-50254. (Vintage Crime - Black Lizard Ser.). 176p. 1990. pap. 9.00 (*0-679-73253-5*) Vin Bks.

Pick up Ax. Anthony Clarvoe. 1991. pap. 6.95 (*0-88145-103-7*) Broadway Play.

***Pick-Up Games: The Rules, the Players, the Equipment.** D. W. Crisfield. (Illus.). 192p. (gr. 5-10). 1999. pap. text 13.00 (*0-7881-6481-3*) DIANE Pub.

***Pick-Up Games: The Rules, the Players, the Equipment.** D. W. Crisfield. 208p. 1999. 22.95 (*0-7351-0196-5*) Replica Bks.

Pick-Up Games: The Rules, the Players, the Equipment. Deborah Crisfield. LC 92-16296. 208p. 1993. reprint ed. pap. 64.50 (*0-608-02833-9*, 206390000007) Bks Demand.

Pick-Up Lines: The Best & Worst on Planet Earth. Ed. by Buzz Boxx. LC 96-84514. 144p. (Orig.). 1996. pap. 7.95 (*1-885174-02-0*) Andrews & McMeel.

Pick-Up Man. Pamela Bauer. (American Romance Ser.). 1997. per. 3.75 (*0-373-16668-0*, 1-16668-5) Harlequin Bks.

Pick up on Noon Street. Raymond Chandler. 200p. 1993. reprint ed. lib. bdg. 16.95 (*1-56849-008-9*) Buccaneer Bks.

Pick-Up Sticks. Sarah Ellis. LC 91-26585. 128p. (YA). (gr. 7 up). 1992. lib. bdg. 15.00 (*0-689-50550-7*) McElderry Bks.

Pick up the House. Anselm Hollo. LC 86-4143. (Illus.). 112p. (Orig.). 1986. pap. 8.95 (*0-918273-18-8*) Coffee Hse.

Pick up Your Couch & Walk! How to Take Back Control of Your Life. Peter M. Kalellis. 144p. (Orig.). 1994. pap. 14.95 (*0-8245-1378-9*) Crossroad NY.

Pick up Your Ears, Henry. Patricia B. Demuth. LC 91-27162. (Illus.). 32p. (J). (ps-1). 1992. lib. bdg. 13.95 (*0-02-728465-4*, Mac Bks Young Read) S&S Childrens.

Pick up Your Socks... And Other Skills Growing Children Need! A Practical Guide to Raising Responsible Children. Elizabeth Crary. LC 89-62656. (Illus.). 112p. 1990. pap. 14.95 (*0-943990-52-1*); lib. bdg. 19.95 (*0-943990-53-X*) Parenting Pr.

Pick Ups. William Seitz. LC 96-220253. 192p. 1996. 39.95 (*0-679-44946-9*) Random.

Pick Your Job & Land It. Sidney Edlund & Mary Edlund. 1973. 10.00 (*0-686-17213-2*) Sandollar Pr.

Pick Your Numbers: Easy Ways to Play the Lottery. Signet Staff. 160p. 1996. pap., mass mkt. 4.99 (*0-451-18879-9*, Sig) NAL.

Pick Your Own Apples, Oranges, & Pear Locations: A How to Find or Locate Workbook. Center for Self Sufficiency, Research Division Sta. 50p. 1985. ring bd. 24.95 (*0-910811-48-2*) Ctr Self Suff.

Pick Your Own Blueberries, Raspberries & Other Berries Locations: A How to Find or Locate Workbook. Center for Self-Sufficiency, Research Division Sta. 50p. 1985. ring bd. 24.95 (*0-910811-50-4*) Ctr Self Suff.

Pick-Your-Own Farms: A Comprehensive Guide to Over 3,000 Farms Where You Can "Pick-Your-Own" Fruits & Vegetables. Nicholas A. Roes & Monique E. DuBacher. 242p. (Orig.). 1990. pap. 24.95 (*0-89780-011-7*) NAR Pubns.

Pick Your Own Fruits & Vegetables & More: A How to Find or Locate Workbook. Frieda Carrol. LC 80-70861. 1981. ring bd. 25.95 (*0-939476-11-8*) Prosperity & Profits.

Pick Your Own Peaches, Melons & Grapes Locations: A How to Find or Locate Workbook. Center for Self Sufficiency, Research Division Sta. 50p. 1985. ring bd. 24.95 (*0-910811-60-1*) Ctr Self Suff.

Pick Your Own Strawberries. Evelyn Marie. (Illus.). 32p. (J). (gr. k-3). 1998. reprint ed. pap. 3.50 (*0-9614746-3-7*) Berry Bks.

Pick Your Own Tomatoes, Plums & Avocadoes Locations: A How to Find or Locate Workbook. Center for Self-Sufficiency, Research Division Sta. 50p. 1985. ring bd. 24.95 (*0-910811-57-1*) Ctr Self Suff.

Pick Your Score!! SAT Prep. Diane Shih. (Illus.). 810p. (YA). 1999. spiral bd. 15.99 (*1-58379-021-7*, PYST2000-1) Delancey Pl Pr.

Pickaberry Pig. Tom Davis. LC 95-70168. (Illus.). 32p. (J). 1995. pap. text 6.95 (*1-884778-10-0*) Old Mountain.

Pickard Operative Dentistry. 4th ed. 1976. 15.50 (*0-19-267004-2*) OUP.

Pickard's Manual of Operative Dentistry. 6th ed. E. A. Kidd et al. (Illus.). 208p. 1990. pap. text 56.95 (*0-19-261808-3*) OUP.

Pickard's Manual of Operative Dentistry. 7th ed. E. A. Kidd & B. G. Smith. (Illus.). 208p. (C). 1996. text 124.50 (*0-19-262610-8*); pap. text 59.50 (*0-19-262609-4*) OUP.

Pickens County, Alabama, 1841-1861. Marilyn D. Barefield & Carr B. Barefield. 120p. 1984. pap. 15.00 (*0-89308-533-2*) Southern Hist Pr.

Pickens Sentinel Favorite Newspaper of Pickens County: Pickens Court House, South Carolina 1872-1893 Historical & Genealogical Abstracts. Compiled by Peggy B. Rich & Marion A. Whitehurst. (Illus.). 755p. (Orig.). 1994. pap. text 70.00 (*1-55613-985-3*) Heritage Bk.

Picker McClikker. Allen Johnson, Jr. LC 96-68190. (Illus.). 48p. (J). (ps-3). 1996. pap. 6.95 (*1-887654-14-3*) Premium Pr TN.

***Picker of the Kingdom: Sharon's Life, Dreams & Odyssey in N. Y.** David Howard. 360p. 1999. pap. 12.95 (*1-57087-410-7*) Prof Pr NC.

Pickers Is a Thief: A Story about Shoplifting. Gary D. Antilla. LC 96-79868. (Illus.). 16p. (J). (gr. 3-6). 1997. pap. 5.95 (*1-57543-027-4*) Mar Co Prods.

Pickets & Pastimes, Vol. I. Jim King. 52p. 1995. pap. 10.50 (*1-56770-329-1*) S Scheewe Pubns.

Pickets & Pastimes Feathered Inns. Marie King & Jim King. 1997. pap. 10.50 (*1-56770-385-2*) S Scheewe Pubns.

Pickett or Pedigrew? An Historical Essay. W. R. Bond. 25.00 (*0-8488-0919-X*) Amereon Ltd.

Pickett's Charge: A Microhistory of the Final Attack at Gettysburg, July 3, 1863. George R. Stewart. (Illus.). 384p. 1991. pap. 15.00 (*0-395-59772-2*) HM.

Pickett's Charge: A Microhistory of the Final Attack on Gettysburg. George R. Stewart. 1994. 27.50 (*0-8446-6730-7*) Peter Smith.

Pickett's Charge: Eyewitness Accounts. Ed. by Richard Rollins. xxxi, 376p. 1994. 35.00 (*0-9638993-1-7*); pap. 18.00 (*0-9638993-0-9*) Rank & File.

Pickett's Charge in History & Memory. Carol Reardon. LC 97-10965. (Civil War America Ser.). (Illus.). 296p. (gr. 13). 1997. 29.95 (*0-8078-2379-1*) U of NC Pr.

***Pickett's History of Alabama: And Incidentally of Georgia & Mississippi from the Earliest.** Albert J. Pickett. (Illus.). 686p. 1999. pap. 23.95 (*1-880216-67-1*, Black Belt) Black Belt Communs.

Pickett's Men: A Fragment of War History. Walter H. Harrison. 1976. 31.00 (*0-8488-1043-0*) Amereon Ltd.

***Pickett's Men: A Fragment of War History.** Walter H. Harrison. (Illus.). 224p. 2000. pap. 15.95 (*0-8071-2598-9*) La State U Pr.

Pickett's Men: A Fragment of War History. Walter H. Harrison. 220p. 1988. reprint ed. 25.00 (*0-942211-61-8*) Olde Soldier Bks.

***Pickford: The Woman Who Made Hollywood.** Eileen Whitfield. (Illus.). 456p. 2000. pap. 16.00 (*0-571-19980-1*) Faber & Faber.

Pickford: The Woman Who Made Hollywood. Eileen Whitfield. LC 97-29312. (Illus.). xiv, 441 p. (C). 1997. 27.50 (*0-8131-2045-4*) U Pr of Ky.

Pickfords Guide to Business Removals. Bligh & Woodgate. 1977. 25.00 (*0-85941-047-1*) St Mut.

***Pickin' 'n' Squintin' A Collection of 12 Fingerstyle Guitar Solos.** Adrian Legg. 88p. 2000. otabind 19.95 (*1-57560-255-5*, Pub. by Cherry Lane) H Leonard.

Pickin' on Peachtree: A History of Country Music in Atlanta, Georgia. Wayne W. Daniel. (Music in American Life Ser.). (Illus.). 328p. 1990. text 32.50 (*0-252-01687-4*) U of Ill Pr.

Pickin' Peas. Illus. by Pat Cummings. LC 95-26133. 32p. (J). (ps-3). 1998. 15.95 (*0-06-027235-X*) HarpC.

Pickin' Peas. Margaret R. MacDonald. LC 95-26133. (Illus.). 32p. (J). (ps-3). 1998. lib. bdg. 15.89 (*0-06-027970-2*) HarpC.

Pickin' Peter. (Little Monsters Ser.). (J). 1997. write for info. (*0-614-21782-2*, Pub. by Splash) Assoc Pubs Grp.

Picking & Choosing: Essays on Prose. Carolyn Kizer. LC 95-33603. 172p. 1996. 25.00 (*0-910055-25-4*) East Wash Univ.

Picking Apples see Apples Series

Picking Apples. Gail Saunders-Smith. (J). 1998. 13.25 (*0-516-21245-1*) Childrens.

Picking Apples & Pumpkins. Amy Hutchings & Richard Hutchings. LC 94-233656. (Read with Me Paperback Ser.). (Illus.). 32p. (J). (ps-3). 1994. pap. 2.50 (*0-590-48456-7*, Cartwheel) Scholastic Inc.

Picking Federal Judges: Lower Court Selection from Roosevelt Through Reagan. Sheldon Goldman. LC 97-7129. 410p. 1997. 55.00 (*0-300-06962-6*) Yale U Pr.

***Picking Federal Judges: Lower Court Selection from Roosevelt Through Reagan.** Sheldon Goldman. LC 97-7129. (Illus.). 488p. 1999. 18.00 (*0-300-08073-5*) Yale U Pr.

Picking Guru. Bill Hartman. (Guitar Guru Ser.). (Illus.). 20p. 1997. spiral bd. 5.99 (*1-891052-20-9*) Guru Books.

Picking Raspberries. Ruth Maassen. (Chapbook Ser.: No. 4). 40p. (Orig.). 1997. pap. 8.95 (*0-9649463-3-5*) Folly Cove.

Picking Time. Glenn McKee. (Illus.). 26p. 1994. 5.00 (*0-9636689-1-9*) White Wave ME.

Picking Uncle Sam's Pocket: A Comprehensive Guide to 50 Best Federal Education Grant Sources. Ed. by Shari G. Kleiner. 278p. 1995. pap. 86.00 (*1-56925-039-1*, SAM) Capitol Publns.

Picking up a Pin for the Lord. Naylor. 1994. pap. 15.99 (*0-946462-25-9*, Pub. by Evangelical Pr) P & R Pubng.

Picking up Airs: Hearing the Music in Joyce's Text. Ed. by Ruth H. Bauerle. LC 92-23294. 216p. (C). 1993. text 34.95 (*0-252-01984-9*) U of Ill Pr.

***Picking up Cowboys: Duet.** Lori Soard. 200p. 1999. pap. write for info. (*1-58365-039-3*, Timeless Romance) BT Pub.

Picking up Gold & Silver: Stories. Rudyard Kipling. 288p. 23.95 (*0-8488-2624-8*) Amereon Ltd.

Picking up the Linen Threads: Life in Ulster's Mills. Betty Messenger. 265p. 1988. pap. 13.95 (*0-85640-415-2*, Pub. by Blackstaff Pr) Dufour.

Picking up the Pieces. 9.95 (*0-317-69755-2*) IAQC Pr.

Picking up the Pieces. Patricia Calvert. 176p. (J). 1999. per. 4.50 (*0-689-82451-3*) S&S Childrens.

Picking up the Pieces. Patricia Calvert. LC 92-27909. 192p. (YA). (gr. 7 up). 1993. 15.00 (*0-684-19558-5*) Scribner.

Picking up the Pieces. Luis Gonzalez Palma. Ed. by Kisha Gunter et al. 386p. 1998. pap. 13.95 (*0-9667331-0-X*) Celestial Sun.

Picking up the Pieces. Mary Sheepshanks. LC 98-33243. 304p. 1998. text 23.95 (*0-312-19997-X*) St Martin.

Picking Up the Pieces. Mary Sheepshanks. 336p. 1999. pap. 5.99 (*0-312-97037-4*, St Martins Paperbacks) St Martin.

Picking up the Pieces: Restoring Rural Housing & Communities after a Disaster. Housing Assistance Council Staff. 53p. 1997. 5.00 (*1-58064-004-4*) Housing Assist.

Picking up the Pieces: Restoring Rural Housing & Communities after Tornadoes in Kansas, Missouri, Oklahoma, Tennessee & Texas. Housing Assistance Council Staff. 54p. 1999. 5.00 (*1-58064-094-X*) Housing Assist.

Picking up the Pieces: Two Accounts of a Psychoanalytic Journey. Fayek Nakhla & Grace Jackson. LC 93-1304. 192p. 1993. 23.00 (*0-300-05653-2*) Yale U Pr.

Picking up the Pieces: Words of Comfort. Jarrold Printing Staff. (Illus.). 64p. 1993. 6.95 (*0-7117-0524-0*, Pub. by JARR UK) Seven Hills Bk.

Picking Up the Tab: The Life & Movies of Martin Ritt. Carlton Jackson. (Illus.). 272p. 1995. 45.95 (*0-87972-671-7*); pap. 25.95 (*0-87972-672-5*) Bowling Green Univ Popular Press.

Picking Winners: A Horse Player's Guide. Andrew Beyer. 240p. 1994. pap. 14.00 (*0-395-70132-5*) HM.

***Picking Winners: A Total Hiring System for Spotting Exceptional Performers & Getting Them on Board.** Steve Kneeland. (Pathways Ser.: No. 3). 208p. 2000. pap. 15.95 (*1-85703-460-0*, Pub. by How To Bks) Midpt Trade.

Picking Winners at the Harness Races. Paul Goodwin. 32p. 1997. pap. 7.95 (*0-934650-12-8*) Sunnyside.

Picking Your Kids Dog. Walter Meadley. Ed. by Milton Adams. (Illus.). 160p. 1997. pap. 12.95 (*1-890676-08-X*) Beavers Pond.

Picking Your Perfect Partner: A Guide to Compatibility in Relationships. Mary Coleman. LC 96-34671. (Illus.). 224p. (Orig.). 1996. pap. 12.00 (*0-916360-61-X*) CRCS Pubns CA.

Picking Your Shots & Other Stories of Dogs & Birds & Guns & Days Afield. Steve Smith. LC 86-5789. 155p. 1986. reprint ed. pap. 48.10 (*0-608-00480-4*, 206129900007) Bks Demand.

Pickingill Papers: The Origin of the Gardnerian Craft. W. E. Liddell & M. Howard. 1994. pap. 22.95 (*1-898307-10-5*, Pub. by Capall Bann Pubng) Holmes Pub.

Pickle & the Ball. Lynn Breeze. LC 97-76652. (Illus.). (J). 1998. 4.95 (*0-7534-5148-4*, Kingfisher) LKC.

Pickle & the Blanket. Lynn Breeze. LC 97-76650. (Illus.). (J). 1998. 4.95 (*0-7534-5149-2*) LKC.

Pickle & the Blocks. Lynn Breeze. LC 97-76468. (J). 1998. 4.95 (*0-7534-5151-4*) LKC.

Pickle & the Box. Lynn Breeze. LC 97-76651. (Illus.). (J). 1998. 4.95 (*0-7534-5150-6*) LKC.

Pickle Handbook: Pickle Eligibility Determination. 119p. 1987. 15.00 (*0-685-30152-4*, 43,275) NCLS Inc.

Pickle in the Middle. Nora M. Braun. 1997. 9.09 (*0-606-11746-6*, Pub. by Turtleback) Demco.

Pickle in the Middle & Other Easy Snacks. Frances W. Zweifel. LC 78-19478. (I Can Read Bks.). (Illus.). 64p. (J). (ps-3). 1979. 11.95 (*0-06-027072-1*) HarpC Child Bks.

Pickle Packet for Elementary Counselors. Patricia T. Kienzle. (Illus.). 112p. (Orig.). 1987. pap. 21.95 (*1-890798-00-2*) P T Kienzle.

Pickle, Pepper, & Tip-in-Too: 275 Sports-Derived Games & Activities for Kids. Kevin Nelson. (Illus.). 208p. 1994. pap. 15.00 (*0-671-87956-1*, Fireside) S&S Trade Pap.

Pickle Pizza. Beverly Lewis. (Cul-de-Sac Kids Ser.). 80p. (J). (gr. 2-5). 1996. pap. 3.99 (*1-55661-728-3*) Bethany Hse.

Pickle Puss. Patricia Reilly Giff. (Kids of the Polk Street School Ser.: No. 12). 80p. (J). (gr. k-3). 1986. pap. 3.99 (*0-440-46844-2*, YB BDD) BDD Bks Young Read.

Pickle Puss. Patricia Reilly Giff. 69p. (J). (gr. 1-2). pap. 3.99 (*0-8072-1261-X*) Listening Lib.

Pickle Puss. Patricia Reilly Giff. (Kids of the Polk Street School Ser.). (J). 1986. 8.45 (*0-606-02424-7*, Pub. by Turtleback) Demco.

Pickle Stew. Wendy Lord. LC 93-19018. (Tabitha Sarah Bigbee Book). 96p. (J). 1994. pap. 4.99 (*0-7814-0886-5*, Chariot Bks) Chariot Victor.

Pickle the Spy. Andrew Lang. LC 72-110132. reprint ed. 37.50 (*0-404-03853-0*) AMS Pr.

Pickles. Brian Crane. LC 98-66374. (Illus.). 96p. 1998. pap. 7.95 (*1-56352-510-0*) Longstreet.

Pickles & Chutney Markets. Market Intelligence Staff. 263p. 1993. 1200.00 (*1-56753-553-4*) Frost & Sullivan.

Pickles & Peanuts. Martha M. Ivery. (Illus.). 80p. 1996. reprint ed. pap. 5.99 (*1-57532-051-7*) Press-Tige Pub.

Pickles & Peanuts Meet Sandpiper the Wonder Horse. Martha M. Ivery. 125p. (Orig.). (J). 1998. pap. 5.95 (*1-57532-020-7*) Press-Tige Pub.

Pickles & Preserves. 1992. pap. 3.95 (*0-919433-88-X*) Lone Pine.

Pickles & Preserves. Bridgewater Book Co. (Victorian Kitchen Ser.). 41p. 1995. write for info. (*1-57215-049-1*) World Pubns.

Pickles & Relishes: One Hundred Fifty Recipes - Apples to Zucchini. 2nd rev. ed. Andrea Chesman. Ed. by Louise Lloyd & Kim Foster. LC 91-10887. (Illus.). 152p. 1991. pap. 12.95 (*0-88266-744-0*, Garden Way Pub) Storey Bks.

Pickles & Relishes: One Hundred Fifty Recipes, Apples to Zucchini. Andrea Chesman. LC 83-1460. (Illus.). 160p. (Orig.). 1983. pap. 6.95 (*0-88266-321-6*, Garden Way Pub) Storey Bks.

Pickle's Book. Thoru Yamamoto. (Illus.). 30p. (J). (gr. k-6). 1997. 34.95 incl. cd-rom (*0-9661632-0-6*) Soft Material.

Pickles in My Soup. Mary Pearson. LC 99-22470. (Rookie Readers Ser.). 32p. (J). (gr. 1-2). 1999. 17.50 (*0-516-21636-8*) Childrens.

***Pickles in My Soup.** Mary Pearson. (Rookie Readers Ser.). (J). 2000. pap. text 4.95 (*0-516-26550-4*) Childrens.

***Pickles Mixed Counter Display.** Brian Crane. 1999. pap. text 95.40 (*1-56352-591-7*) Longstreet.

Pickles, Peaches & Chocolate: Easy, Elegant Gifts from Your Kitchen. Karen L. Ward. LC 98-91753. (Illus.). 144p. 1999. 18.95 (*0-9666580-0-0*) C&K Entrprs.

Pickles, Relishes, & Chuntneys. Orla Broderick. 128p. 1995. 14.98 (*0-7858-0352-1*) Bk Sales Inc.

***Pickles the Frog: A Picture-It Storybook - A Reader Illustrated Storybook.** Julia Kalin. (Illus.). 12p. (J). (ps-6). 1999. pap. 12.95 (*0-9672430-6-8*) Stay Play.

***Pickles to Pittsburgh.** Judi Barrett. (J). (gr. k-6). 1999. 24.95 incl. audio (*0-87499-538-8*) Live Oak Media.

Pickles to Pittsburgh: The Sequel to Cloudy with a Chance of Meatballs. Judith Barrett. LC 95-40510. (Illus.). 32p. (J). (ps-3). 1997. 16.00 (*0-689-80104-1*) Atheneum Yung Read.

***Pickles, Too: The Older I Get, the Better I Was.** Brian Crane. LC 99-61758. (Illus.). 96p. 1999. pap. 7.95 (*1-56352-583-6*) Longstreet.

Picks! pap. 12.95 (*0-7935-5618-X*, 00330183) H Leonard.

Picks! The Colorful Saga of Vintage Celluloid Guitar Plectrums. Will Hoover. (Illus.). 107p. 1995. pap. 12.95 (*0-87930-377-8*) Miller Freeman.

Pick's Disease & Pick Complex. Andrew Kertesz & David G. Munoz. LC 97-34191. 301p. 1998. 99.95 (*0-471-17792-X*) Wiley.

Pickup Artists: Street Basketball in America. Lars Anderson. LC 98-17460. 240p. 1998. 25.00 (*1-85984-235-6*, Pub. by Verso) Norton.

***Pickup Artists: Street Basketball in America.** Lars Anderson. 1999. pap. text 15.00 (*1-85984-243-7*, Pub. by Verso) Norton.

Pickup Sticks. Klutz Press Staff. 18p. 1993. pap. 8.95 (*1-878257-49-8*) Klutz.

Pickup Trucks see Rollin'

***Pickup Trucks.** Ariel. 80p. 1999. 4.95 (*0-7407-0075-8*) Andrews & McMeel.

***Pickup Trucks.** John Carroll. LC 97-62276. (Illus.). 112p. 1998. 14.98 (*0-7651-9124-5*) Smithmark.

Pickup Trucks see Encyclopedia of Custom & Classic Transportation

***Pickup Trucks: A Heavy-Duty History of the Great American Vehicle.** Justin Lukach. (Illus.). 112p. (YA). (gr. 7 up). 1999. 24.98 (*1-57912-011-3*) Blck Dog & Leventhal.

Pickups. Rob Wagner. LC 97-37165. 1998. 17.98 (*1-56799-616-7*) M Friedman Pub Grp Inc.

Pickups: Classic American Trucks. Photos by William B. Seitz. (Illus.). Date not set. write for info. (*0-614-25314-4*) Random.

Pickups: Trucking in Style. P. Quarto. 192p. 1996. 19.98 (*0-7858-0615-6*) Bk Sales Inc.

Pickwells Binocular Vision Anomalies: Investigation & Treatment. 3rd ed. Bruce J. W. Evans. LC 96-24277. 280p. 1997. text 70.00 (*0-7506-2062-5*) Buttrwrth-Heinemann.

Pickwick Ladle, & Other Collector's Stories. Winfield S. Moody. LC 70-37556. (Short Story Index Reprint Ser.). 1977. reprint ed. 21.95 (*0-8369-4115-2*) Ayer.

Pickwick Papers. Charles Dickens. 784p. 1983. mass mkt. 5.95 (*0-553-21123-4*, Bantam Classics) Bantam.

Pickwick Papers. Charles Dickens. 1964. mass mkt. 6.95 (*0-451-51756-3*, CE1756, Sig Classics) NAL.

Pickwick Papers. Charles Dickens. Ed. by James Kinsley. (Clarendon Dickens Ser.). (Illus.). 600p. 1986. 149.00 (*0-19-812631-X*) OUP.

Pickwick Papers. Charles Dickens. Ed. & Intro. by James Kinsley. (Oxford World's Classics Ser.). (Illus.). 772p. 1998. pap. 8.95 (*0-19-283457-6*) OUP.

Pickwick Papers. Charles Dickens. 960p. (YA). (gr. 7 up). 1998. mass mkt. 5.99 (*0-8125-6719-6*, Pub. by Tor Bks) St Martin.

Pickwick Papers. Charles Dickens. 1964. 11.05 (*0-606-00941-8*, Pub. by Turtleback) Demco.

Pickwick Papers. Charles Dickens. Ed. by Malcolm Andrews. (Everyman Paperback Classics). (Illus.). 960p. 1997. pap. 5.95 (*0-460-87664-3*, Everyman's Classic Lib) Tuttle Pubng.

Pickwick Papers. Charles Dickens. Ed. by Robert L. Patten. LC 73-154771. (English Library). (Illus.). 960p. 1973. pap. 9.95 (*0-14-043078-4*, Penguin Classics) Viking Penguin.

Pickwick Papers. Charles Dickens. (Classics Library). 720p. pap. 3.95 (*1-85326-052-5*, 8525WW, Pub. by Wrdsworth Edits) NTC Contemp Pub Co.

Pickwick Papers. D. H. Howe. (Illus.). 94p. 1995. pap. text 5.95 (*0-19-586308-9*) OUP.

Pickwick Papers. abr. ed. Charles Dickens. LC 66-1746. 1972. audio 14.00 (*0-694-50091-7*, SWC 1121, Caedmon) HarperAudio.

Pickwick Papers. Charles Dickens. 495p. 1983. reprint ed. lib. bdg. 49.95 (*0-89966-314-1*) Buccaneer Bks.

Pickwick Papers, Vol. 1. large type ed. Charles Dickens. (Isis Clear Type Classic Ser.). 450p. 1991. 24.95 (*1-85089-464-7*, Pub. by ISIS Lrg Prnt) Transaction Pubs.

Pickwick Papers, Vol. 2. large type ed. Charles Dickens. (Isis Clear Type Classic Ser.). 540p. 1991. 24.95 (*1-85089-514-7*, Pub. by ISIS Lrg Prnt) Transaction Pubs.

Pickwick Papers: An Annotated Bibliography. Elliot D. Engel. LC 89-71396. (Dickens Bibliographies Ser.: Vol. 7). 350p. 1990. text 20.00 (*0-8240-8766-6*, 568) Garland.

Pickwick Papers Notes. James Weigel, Jr. (Cliffs Notes Ser.). 104p. 1970. pap. 4.95 (*0-8220-1021-6*, Cliff) IDG Bks.

Pickwickian & Other Stories of Intensive Care: Medical & Ethical Challenges in the ICU. Lawrence Martin. LC 91-61828. 247p. 1991. pap. 10.95 (*1-879653-04-4*) Lakeside Pr.

Pickwickian Dictionary & Cyclopaedia. Percy H. Fitzgerald. LC 71-148777. reprint ed. 52.50 (*0-404-08778-7*) AMS Pr.

P

An Asterisk (*) at the beginning of an entry indicates that the title is appearing for the first time.

Pickwickian Manners & Customs. Percy H. Fitzgerald. LC 73-21619. (Studies in Dickens: No. 52). 1974. lib. bdg. 75.00 (0-8383-1822-3) M S G Haskell Hse.

Picky Ali. 2nd ed. Nancy N. Bijan. (First Ser.). (PER., Illus.). 15p. (J). (ps-6). 1998. pap. 5.95 (1-880710-08-0) Monterey Pacific.

***Picky Mrs. Pickle.** Christine M. Schneider. LC 99-26025. (Illus.). 32p. (J). (gr. k-3). 1999. 15.95 (0-8027-8702-9); lib. bdg. 16.85 (0-8027-8703-7) Walker & Co.

Picky Nicky. Cathy E. Dubowski & Mark Dubowski. (All Aboard Reading Picture Readers Ser.). (Illus.). 32p. (J). (ps-1). 1996. pap. text 3.95 (0-448-41295-0, G & D) Peng Put Young Read.

Picky Pig. Carol B. Kaplan. Ed. by Janet L. Bolinske. LC 87-62998. (Animal Tales Ser.). (Illus.). 24p. (Orig.). (J). (ps). 1988. pap. 4.95 (0-88335-078-5) Milliken Pub Co.

Picky Vicki & the Magical Squirrel. Vicki G. Baggett. (Illus.). 16p. (Orig.). (J). (gr. 3-6). 1995. pap. text 4.50 (0-9644795-0-8) Baggett Bks.

Picky Vicki, Myrtle the Turtle & the Freckled Blues. Vicki Gandy-Baggett. (Illus.). 16p. (Orig.). (J). (gr. 1-6). 1995. pap. 4.50 (0-9644795-1-6) Baggett Bks.

PICMET 97 Portland International Conference on Management of Engineering & Technology. IEEE (Engineering Management Society) Staff. Ed. by IEEE (Institute of Electrical & Electronics Engine. LC 97-68438. 1000p. 1997. lib. bdg. write for info. (0-7803-3574-0, 97CB35982) Inst Electrical.

PICMET 97 Portland International Conference on Management of Engineering & Technology. IEEE (Engineering Management Society) Staff & IEEE, Oregon Section, Engineering Management Socie. Ed. by IEEE (Institute of Electrical & Electronics Engine. LC 97-68438. 1000p. 1997. fiche. write for info. (0-7803-3566-X, 97CM35982) Inst Electrical.

PICMET 97 Portland International Conference on Management of Engineering & Technology. IEEE, Oregon Section, Engineering Management Socie. Ed. by Institute of Electrical & Electronics Engineers, I. LC 97-68438. 1600p. 1997. pap. write for info. (1-890843-00-8, 97CB35982) Inst Electrical.

***Picmicro Pocket Reference.** Myke Predko. (Pocket References Ser.). (Illus.). 450p. 2000. pap. text 29.95 (0-07-136175-8) McGraw.

PIC'n Techniques Vol. 1: PIC Microcontroller Applications Guide. David Benson. (Illus.). 275p. 1999. pap. 34.95 (0-9654162-3-2) Sq One Elect.

PIC'n up the Pace Vol. 1: An Intermediate Guide to Using PIC16/17 Microcontrollers from Square 1. David Benson. (Illus.). 272p. 1997. pap. 34.95 (0-9654162-1-6) Sq One Elect.

Picnic see Best American Plays: Fourth Series, 1952-1957

Picnic see Four Plays

Picnic see Summer Brave

Picnic. Chris Baines. LC 89-77746. (Ecology Story Book Ser.). (Illus.). 24p. (J). (ps-3). 1990. 7.95 (0-940793-54-7, Crocodile Bks) Interlink Pub.

Picnic. Caroljean Ellis. (Tales of Little Angels: Bk. 4). (Illus.). 40p. (Orig.). (J). (gr. k-4). 1996. pap. 8.95 (1-889383-03-1) Angel Publns NJ.

Picnic. European Language Institute Staff. (Tell & Sing a Story Ser.). (Illus.). 27p. (J). (gr. k-2). 1992. pap. 19.95 (88-85148-61-1, Pub. by Europ Lang Inst) Midwest European Pubns.

Picnic. William Inge. 1955. pap. 5.25 (0-8222-0892-X) Dramatists Play.

Picnic. Emily Arnold McCully. (Illus.). (J). (ps-1). 1984. 12.95 (0-06-024099-7, 622997); lib. bdg. 16.89 (0-06-024100-4) HarpC Child Bks.

Picnic. Linda Parry. (Honey-Bear Farm Ser.). (Illus.). 28p. 1998. pap. 4.99 (0-8054-1789-3) Broadman.

Picnic! Recipes & Menus for Outdoor Enjoyment. Edith Stovel. Ed. by Constance Oxley. LC 89-46014. (Illus.). 176p. (Orig.). 1990. pap. 12.95 (0-88266-586-3, Garden Way Pub) Storey Bks.

Picnic! Recipes & Menus for Outdoor Enjoyment. Edith Stovel. Ed. by Constance Oxley. LC 89-46014. (Illus.). 176p. (Orig.). 1990. 16.95 (0-88266-587-1, Garden Way Pub) Storey Bks.

Picnic at Bull Run. Betty McPherson. (Pocket Tales Ser.: Bk. 3). (Illus.). 40p. (J). (ps-1). 1991. 6.00 (0-918823-05-6) Boyce-Pubns.

Picnic at Hanging Rock. Joan Lindsay. 1976. 18.95 (0-8488-1415-0) Amereon Ltd.

Picnic at Hanging Rock. Joan Lindsay. 1988. pap. 5.50 (0-87129-248-3, P62) Dramatic Pub.

Picnic at Hanging Rock. Joan Lindsay. 192p. 1999. reprint ed. 29.95 (0-89966-560-8) Buccaneer Bks.

***Picnic at Jigsaw Farm.** Jennie Maizels. 14p. (J). 1999. 10.95 (1-86233-068-9) Levinson Bks.

Picnic at Mudsock Meadow. Patricia Polacco. LC 91-7374. (Illus.). 32p. (J). (ps-3). 1992. 15.95 (0-399-21811-4, Philomel) Peng Put Young Read.

Picnic at Mudsock Meadow. Patricia Polacco. LC 91-7374. (J). 1997. 11.15 (0-606-11747-4, Pub. by Turtleback) Demco.

Picnic Basket. Jane Pinel. LC 83-90332. (Illus.). 96p. 1983. pap. 5.00 (0-915909-00-6) Ruggles Pub.

Picnic Colors. Eugenie Fernandes. (Toddler Bks.: No. 905-1). (J). 1990. pap. 3.95 (0-7214-5270-1, Ladybrd) Penguin Putnam.

Picnic Farm. Christine Morton. LC 97-10880. (Illus.). 32p. (J). 1998. lib. bdg. 15.95 (0-8234-1332-2) Holiday.

Picnic in October. Eve Bunting. LC 98-20044. (Illus.). 32p. (J). (gr. k-5). 1999. 16.00 (0-15-201656-2, Harcourt Child Bks) Harcourt.

***Picnic in October.** Raintree Steck-Vaughn Publishing Staff. 2000. 24.26 (0-7398-1367-6) Raintree Steck-V.

Picnic, Lightning. Billy Collins. LC 97-33955. (Pitt Poetry Ser.). 103p. 1998. pap. 12.95 (0-8229-5670-5) U of Pittsburgh Pr.

Picnic, Lightning. Billy Collins. LC 97-33955. (Pitt Poetry Ser.). 104p. 1998. text 25.00 (0-8229-4066-3) U of Pittsburgh Pr.

Picnic on a Cloud. Created by Mark Icanberry. (Look, Learn & Do Ser.). (Illus.). 48p. (J). 1999. 14.95 (1-893327-00-0) Look-Learn-Do Pubns.

Picnic on the Battlefield see Guernica & Other Plays

Picnic on the Moon: Poems by Charles Coe. Charles Coe. LC 98-32361. 82p. 1999. pap. 12.95 (0-9654578-2-6, Pub. by Leapfrog Pr) Consort Bk Sales.

Picnic Suite: Solo Flute. C. Bolling. 1990. 7.00 (0-685-32121-5, SIL41) Hansen Ed Mus.

Picnic Suite for Flute, Guitar, & Jazz Piano Trio. C. Bolling. 1991. pap. text 40.00 (0-7935-0842-8, 00673218) H Leonard.

Picnic with Piggins. Jane Yolen. LC 87-13564. (Illus.). 32p. (J). (ps-3). 1988. 14.95 (0-15-261534-2) Harcourt.

Picnic with Piggins. Jane Yolen. LC 87-13564. (Illus.). 32p. (J). (ps-3). 1993. pap. 4.95 (0-15-261535-0) Harcourt.

Picnics. Louise Pickford. 112p. 1996. write for info. (1-57215-191-9) World Pubns.

Picnics. Joan C. Taylor. LC 79-64872. (Illus.). 88p. 1979. 4.95 (0-685-04237-5) Random.

Picnics: Country Garden Cookbook. Ed. by Heidi H. Cusick et al. LC 94-21598. (Illus.). 96p. 1995. 9.95 (0-00-255484-4, Pub. by Harper SF) HarpC.

Picnics: Elegant Recipes for Alfresco Dining. Barbara Scott-Goodman. LC 98-30314. (Illus.). 72p. 1999. 12.95 (0-8118-2078-5) Chronicle Bks.

Picnics: Picnic Recipes from Summer Music Festivals, Classic Ragtime Music. Sharon O'Connor. LC 94-75888. (Sharon O'Connor's Menus & Music Ser.). (Illus.). 248p. 1994. 24.95 incl. audio compact disk (1-883914-08-6) Menus & Music.

Picnics & Barbecues. Maflower Culinary Editors. LC 98-134052. (The Everyday Chef Ser.). 64p. 1997. pap. text 5.99 (1-58029-012-4, Everywhere) Hambleton-Hill.

***Picnics & Barbecues: In the Kitchen with Bob.** Bob Bowersox. (Illus.). 2000. 24.00 (1-928998-02-X) Q V C Pubg.

***Picnics & Porch Supplement.** Hearst Books Staff. LC 98-2565. (Illus.). 192p. 1998. 29.95 (0-688-15101-9, Hearst) Hearst Commns.

Picnics & Tailgates: Good Food for the Great Outdoors. Williams-Sonoma Staff. LC 97-28367. (Williams-Sonoma Outdoors Ser.). (Illus.). 108p. (gr. 7). 1999. pap. 14.95 (0-7835-4619-X) Time-Life.

Picnics in Paradise: The Owl Bay Guide to Miami Hurricanes Tailgating. Taylor Littleton. (Illus.). 128p. 1994. pap. 8.95 (1-885623-03-8) Owl Bay Pubs.

Picnics of New England: Recipes to Inspire & Paintings to Enchant. Gisela Voss. LC 97-184247. (Illus.). (ps-3). 1998. 14.95 (0-87846-408-5) Mus Fine Arts Boston.

Picnics of Tuscany: Italian Country-Style Picnics to Enjoy at Home of Abroad. Craig Pyes. LC 93-34448. 64p. 1994. 14.00 (0-671-87015-7) S&S Trade.

Picnics on the Plains: The Owl Bay Guide to Auburn Tiger Tailgating. Lucy Littleton. (Illus.). 128p. 1994. pap. 8.95 (0-9638568-3-9) Owl Bay Pubs.

Picnics, Potlucks & Prize Winners: Celebrating Indiana Hospitality with 4-H Family & Friends. (Illus.). 208p. 1999. 18.95 (0-9669065-0-0) Indiana FourH.

Pico: The White Paper Act. John A. Abatecola. LC 99-185553. 350p. 1998. text 24.50 (0-9659628-0-6) Tadone Publ.

Pico de Orizaba: or Citlaltepetl: Geology, Archaeology, History, Natural History, & Mountaineering Routes: With Additional Material on the High Mexican Volcanoes. Winston Crausaz. LC 93-80607. (Illus.). xiv, 594p. 1993. 125.00 (1-884681-50-6) Geopress Intl.

Pico Della Mirandola: Of Being & Unity. Giovanni Pico Della Mirandola. Tr. by Victor M. Hamm. (Medieval Philosophical Texts in Translation Ser.). 1943. pap. 10.00 (0-87462-203-4) Marquette.

Pico Della Mirandola's Encounter with Jewish Mysticism. Chaim Wirszubski. LC 87-24515. (Illus.). 304p. 1988. 49.95 (0-674-66730-1) HUP.

Pico Street Stories. Kingsley Tufts. LC 97-37646. 208p. 1998. pap. 12.00 (1-880284-27-8) J Daniel.

Picolinis. Anne G. Eastern. 160p. (Orig.). (J). (gr. 2-5). 1988. pap. 2.75 (0-553-15566-0, Skylark BDD) BDD Bks Young Read.

Picolinis & the Haunted House. Anne G. Estern. (Illus.). 115p. (J). (gr. 3-5). 1989. pap. 2.95 (0-553-15771-X, Skylark BDD) BDD Bks Young Read.

Picosecond Electronics & Optoelectronics II. Ed. by F. J. Leonberger et al. (Electronics & Photonics Ser.: Vol. 24). (Illus.). 280p. 1987. 75.95 (0-387-18329-9) Spr-Verlag.

Picosecond Phenomena III, Garmisch Partenkirchen, FRG, 1982: Proceedings. Ed. by Kenneth B. Eisenthal et al. (Chemical Physics Ser.: Vol. 23). (Illus.). 401p. 1982. 49.95 (0-387-11912-4) Spr-Verlag.

Picosecond Phenomena II: Proceedings. Ed. by R. M. Hochstrasser et al. (Chemical Physics Ser.: Vol. 14). (Illus.). 382p. 1980. 51.95 (0-387-10403-8) Spr-Verlag.

Picosescond Electronics & Optoelectronics. Ed. by G. A. Mourou et al. (Electrophysics Ser.: Vol. 21). (Illus.). x, 258p. 1988. text 59.40 (0-387-15884-7) Spr-Verlag.

Picot Lace Designs I: More Innovative Beadwork. Sandy Forrington. (Illus.). 65p. 1996. spiral bd. 12.00 (0-9642395-1-5) Picot Press.

Picot Lace Designs II: More New Lights on Tatting & New Twists on Beading. Sandy Forrington. (Illus.). 71p. (Orig.). 1996. pap., spiral bd. 12.00 (0-9642395-2-3) Picot Press.

Picot Lace Innovative Beadwork: A New Light on Tatting - A New Twist on Beading. Sandy Forrington. LC 94-67245. (Illus.). 160p. (Orig.). 1994. spiral bd. 22.00 (0-9642395-0-7) Picot Press.

***Picotee: The Polka Dotted Llama.** (Illus.). 24p. (J). (ps-5). 1999. pap. 8.00 (0-9669355-4-3) L Chiappini.

PICSYMS Categorical Dictionary. Faith Carlson. 186p. 1995. reprint ed. pap. 35.00 (1-886498-02-4, 8-0006) Poppin & Co.

***Pict O Graph Beatitudes.** (Illus.). 2000. pap. 10.99 (0-7847-1001-5) Standard Pub.

***Pict-O-Graph, Creation to Abram, Old Testament: Eight Stories Including Creation, Adam & Eve.** (Illus.). 2000. pap. 10.99 (0-7847-1034-1) Standard Pub.

***Pict O Graph Tabernacle.** 2000. pap. 10.99 (0-7847-1018-X) Standard Pub.

Picti. Robert C. Wallace. (Mons Graupius Ser.: Vol. 4). (Illus.). 748p. 1998. pap. 14.00 (1-892276-00-3) Pretani.

Pictionary Fictionary: Selected Writings of Gunther Brus. Gunther Brus. Ed. by Denise Spampinato. 150p. 2000. pap. 25.00 (1-889195-34-0) Smart Art Pr.

Pictish & Norse Finds from the Brough of Birsay. C. Curle. (Illus.). 141p. 1982. pap. 19.98 (0-903903-01-6) David Brown.

***Pictish Child.** Jane Yolen. LC 99-6303. (Tartan Magic Ser.). 135p. (J). (gr. 3-6). 1999. 16.00 (0-15-202261-9, Harcourt Child Bks) Harcourt.

Pictish Colouring Book. Joy-Elizabeth Mitchell. (Illus.). 36p. (J). 1998. pap. 9.95 (1-900428-26-1) Dufour.

Pictish Guide. Elizabeth Sutherland. LC 97-135215. (Illus.). 154p. pap. 15.95 (1-874744-66-1, Pub. by Birlinn Ltd) Dufour.

Pictish Symbol Stones. John Stevenson. (Illus.). 32p. 1998. pap. 9.95 (0-11-495837-8, Pub. by Statnry Office) Seven Hills Bk.

Pictograms: Graphing Pictures for a Reusable Classroom Grid. Laura D. Choate. 56p. 1997. pap. text 9.95 (0-86651-487-2) Seymour Pubns.

Pictographic Score Notation: A Compendium. Gardner Read. LC 97-49480. 296p. 1998. lib. bdg. 65.00 (0-313-30469-6, Greenwood Pr) Greenwood.

Pictographs. Bill Keith. (Illus.). 48p. (Orig.). 1996. pap. 9.00 (1-880516-20-9) Left Hand Bks.

Pictographs & Petroglyphs of the Oregon Country, Set, Pts. 1 & 2. 2nd ed. J. Malcolm Loring & Louise Loring. LC 96-3832. (UCLA Institute of Archaeology Publications: Nos. 21/23). (Illus.). 292p. 1996. pap. 48.00 (0-917956-86-9) UCLA Arch.

Pictographs of Adolph Gottlieb. Sanford Hirsch et al. LC 94-21579. (Illus.). 144p. 1995. 45.00 (1-55595-114-7) Hudson Hills.

Pictographs of the Coso Region: Analysis & Interpretation of the Coso Painted Style. fac. ed. Ed. by Robert A. Schiffman. (Bakersfield College Publications in Archaeology: No. 2). (Illus.). 115p. 1982. reprint ed. pap. text 13.13 (1-55567-553-0) Coyote Press.

Pictoral Laboratory Guide for Anatomy & Physiology. Dennis Strete. LC 96-45953. 256p. (C). 1997. pap. text 27.20 (0-673-99225-X, GoodYrBooks) Addson-Wesley Educ.

Pictoral Library of the Landscape Plants, Vol. I. 5th ed. M. Jane Helmer. LC 81-82113. (Northern Hardiness Zones Ser.: No. 1-5). (Illus.). 343p. 1992. reprint ed. text 95.00 (0-89484-027-4) Merchants Pub Co.

Pictorial Anatomy of the Cat. rev. ed. Stephen G. Gilbert. LC 67-21200. (Illus.). 128p. (C). 1975. pap. 20.00 (0-295-95454-X) U of Wash Pr.

Pictorial & Descriptive View of All Religions: Stories on the History of Connecticut. Charles A. Goodrich. (Notable American Authors Ser.). 1992. reprint ed. lib. bdg. 75.00 (0-7812-2932-4) Rprt Serv.

Pictorial & Genealogical Record of Green County: With 1932 Index by J.R. Moll. (Illus.). 434p. 1997. reprint ed. lib. bdg. 42.00 (0-8328-6836-1) Higginson Bk Co.

Pictorial Approach to Molecular Bonding. John G. Verkade. (Illus.). 280p. 1986. 79.00 (0-387-96271-9) Spr-Verlag.

Pictorial Approach to Molecular Bonding & Vibrations. 2nd ed. John G. Verkade. LC 96-19135. 367p. 1997. 59.95 (0-387-94811-2) Spr-Verlag.

Pictorial Approach to Molecular Structure & Reactivity. Robert F. Hout et al. LC 83-16914. (Wiley-Interscience Publications). 415p. reprint ed. pap. 128.70 (0-7837-2398-9, 204008300006) Bks Demand.

Pictorial Archive of Decorative & Illustrative Mortised Cuts: 551 Eye-Catching Designs for Advertising & Other Uses. Ed. by Carol B. Grafton. (Pictorial Archive Ser.). 112p. (Orig.). 1984. pap. 8.95 (0-486-24540-3) Dover.

Pictorial Archive of Decorative Frames & Labels: 550 Copyright-Free Designs. 81st ed. Ed. by Carol B. Grafton. (Illus.). 128p. 1982. pap. 8.95 (0-486-24277-3) Dover.

Pictorial Archive of Geometric Designs. Wil Stegenga. 128p. 1992. pap. 7.95 (0-486-27148-X) Dover.

Pictorial Archive of Printer's Ornaments from the Renaissance to the 20th Century. Ed. by Carol B. Grafton. (Pictorial Archive Ser.). (Illus.). 128p. (Orig.). 1980. pap. 8.95 (0-486-23944-6) Dover.

Pictorial Archives of Lace Designs. Carol B. Grafton. (Illus.). 96p. 1989. pap. 6.95 (0-486-26112-3) Dover.

Pictorial Arts of the West, 800-1200. C. R. Dodwell. LC 92-32502. (Pelican History of Art Ser.). (Illus.). 494p. (C). 1993. 65.00 (0-300-05348-7) Yale U Pr.

Pictorial Arts of the West, 800-1200. C. R. Dodwell. 1995. pap. 35.00 (0-300-06493-4) Yale U Pr.

Pictorial Atlas of North American Wines. Thomas K. Hardy. 1989. 39.95 (0-932664-63-6) Wine Appreciation.

Pictorial Atlas of Soil & Seed Fungi: Morphologies of Cultured Fingi & Key to Species. Tsuneo Watanabe. LC 94-11111.Tr. of Dojo Shijokin. 432p. 1994. lib. bdg. 95.00 (1-56670-072-8, L1072) Lewis Pubs.

Pictorial Atlas of the U. S. & Canada. Kathie B. Smith. (Illus.). 324p. 1998. 24.99 (1-888777-07-9) Trident Pr Intl.

Pictorial Atlas to Homer's Iliad & Odyssey. R. Engelmann. (Illus.). 90p. 1998. reprint ed. pap. text 35.00 (0-87556-869-6) Saifer.

Pictorial Beauty on the Screen. Victor O. Freeburg. 1972. 15.95 (0-405-08533-8, 1482) Ayer.

Pictorial Beauty on the Screen. Victor O. Freeburg. LC 76-124007. (Literature of Cinema, Ser. 1). 1970. reprint ed. 15.95 (0-405-01613-1) Ayer.

Pictorial Biography of C. H. Spurgeon. Bob L. Ross. 1974. pap. 7.00 (1-56186-205-3) Pilgrim Pubns.

Pictorial Biography of M. Bulgakov - Fotobiografiia M. Bulgakova. Ed. by Ellendea C. Proffer. 140p. 1984. pap. 15.00 (0-88233-813-7) Ardis Pubs.

Pictorial Biography of the Venerable Hsu Yun see Pictorial Biography of the Venerable Master Hsu Yun

Pictorial Biography of the Venerable Master Hsu Yun, 2 vols. Hsuan Hua. Tr. by Buddhist Text Translation Society Staff. Incl. Vol. 1. Pictorial Biography of the Venerable Hsu Yun., **2 vols.** (Illus.). 208p. 1983. pap. Not sold separately (0-88139-008-9); Vol. 2. Pictorial Biography of the Venerable Hsu Yun., **2 vols.** (Illus.). 208p. 1985. pap. Not sold separately (0-88139-116-6); Set pap. 16.00 (0-917512-40-5) Buddhist Text.

Pictorial Biography of Toyotomi Hideyoshi: The Unifier of Japan. Ichiyusai Kuniyoshi & W. M. Hawley. (Illus.). 620p. 1986. reprint ed. 110.00 (0-910704-68-6) Hawley.

Pictorial Bookbindings. Miriam Foot. LC 86-21620. 1986. pap. 13.95 (0-7123-0099-6, Pub. by B23tish Library) U of Toronto Pr.

Pictorial Calligraphy & Ornamentation. Edmund V. Gillon, Jr. (Illus.). 96p. (Orig.). 1972. pap. 5.95 (0-486-22788-X) Dover.

Pictorial Chinese Sayings: 1 to 10,000, 8 vols., Vol. 1. Andre Loo. Tr. by Esther Dent-Young. LC 97-61702. (Illus.). vi, 95p. 1997. pap. 8.95 (1-890807-00-1, L001) Silk Rd Pr.

Pictorial Chinese Sayings Vol. 2: The Animal World. Andre Loo. Tr. by Esther Dent-Young. LC 97-61702. (Illus.). viii, 95p. 1997. pap. 8.95 (1-890807-01-X, L002) Silk Rd Pr.

Pictorial Chinese Sayings Vol. 3: The Plant World. Andre Loo. Tr. by Adrienne Lam. LC 97-61702. (Illus.). viii, 102p. 1997. pap. 8.95 (1-890807-02-8, L003) Silk Rd Pr.

Pictorial Chinese Sayings Vol. 4: Towards Nature. Andre Loo. Tr. by Adrienne Lam. LC 97-61702. (Illus.). vi, 104p. 1997. pap. 8.95 (1-890807-03-6, L004) Silk Rd Pr.

Pictorial Chinese Sayings Vol. 5: The Physical Self. Andre Loo. Tr. by Adrienne Lam. LC 97-61702. (Illus.). v, 104p. 1997. pap. 8.95 (1-890807-04-4, L005) Silk Rd Pr.

Pictorial Chinese Sayings Vol. 6, Pt. I: A Tale to Tell. Andre Loo. Tr. by Esther Dent-Young. LC 97-61702. (Illus.). viii, 104p. 1997. pap. 8.95 (1-890807-05-2, L006) Silk Rd Pr.

Pictorial Chinese Sayings Vol. 7, Pt. II: A Tale to Tell. Andre Loo. Tr. by Adrienne Lam. LC 97-61702. (Illus.). viii, 95p. 1997. pap. 8.95 (1-890807-06-0, L007) Silk Rd Pr.

Pictorial Chinese Sayings Vol. 8, Pt. III: A Tale to Tell. Andre Loo. Tr. by Adrienne Lam. LC 97-61702. (Illus.). viii, 95p. (Orig.). 1997. pap. 8.95 (1-890807-07-9, L008) Silk Rd Pr.

Pictorial Chronology of Events in the Life of Thomas Alva Edison 1847-1931. Lawrence Frost. 1985. 39.95 (0-89190-406-9, J M C & Co) Amereon Ltd.

Pictorial Communication in Virtual & Real Environments. Ed. by Stephen R. Ellis et al. 603p. 1991. 95.00 (0-7484-0008-7, Pub. by Tay Francis Ltd) Taylor & Francis.

Pictorial Communication in Virtual & Real Environments. 2nd ed. Ed. by Stephen R. Ellis & Arthur J. Grunwald. 604p. 1993. pap. 49.95 (0-7484-0082-6) Taylor & Francis.

Pictorial Compositions & the Critical Judgment of Pictures. Henry R. Poore. Ed. by Robert A. Sobieszek & Peter C. Bunnell. LC 76-24676. (Sources of Modern Photography Ser.). (Illus.). 1979. reprint ed. lib. bdg. 20.95 (0-405-09652-6) Ayer.

Pictorial Connecticut. Lawrence F. Willard & Alvin V. Sizer. 1962. 25.95 (0-8084-0246-3) NCUP.

Pictorial Data Analysis. Ed. by Robert M. Haralick. (NATO ASI Series F: Computer & Systems Sciences, Special Programme AET: Vol. 4). 480p. 1983. 93.95 (0-387-12288-5) Spr-Verlag.

Pictorial Dictionary. 39.99 (0-310-48380-8) Zondervan.

Pictorial Dictionary of British 18th Century Furniture Design. Elizabeth White, pseud. (Illus.). 700p. 1992. 89.50 (1-85149-105-8) Antique Collect.

Pictorial Dictionary of British 19th Century Furniture Design. Intro. by Edward Joy. (Illus.). 632p. 1977. 89.50 (0-902028-47-2) Antique Collect.

Pictorial Dogfish, Anatomy. S. Gilbert. LC 74-152331. (Illus.). 66p. (Orig.). (C). 1973. pap. 20.00 (0-295-95148-6) U of Wash Pr.

Pictorial Effect Naturalistic Vision: The Photographs & Theories of Henry Peach Robinson & Peter Henry Emerson. Ellen Handy. LC 94-70204. (Illus.). 87p. 1994. pap. 20.00 (0-940744-66-X) Chrysler Museum.

Pictorial Encyclopedia of Civil War Medical Instruments & Equipment, 3 vols., Vol. 1. Gordon Dammann. LC 83-80357. (Illus.). 104p. 1983. 8.95 (0-933126-32-8) Pictorial Hist.

Pictorial Encyclopedia of Civil War Medical Instruments & Equipment, Vol. II. Gordon Dammann. LC 88-60472. (Illus.). 96p. 1988. pap. 8.95 (0-933126-94-8) Pictorial Hist.

Pictorial Encyclopedia of Civil War Medical Instruments & Equipment, Vol. III. Gordon Dammann. LC 83-80357. (Illus.). 132p. 1998. pap. text 9.95 (1-57510-034-7) Pictorial Hist.

P

Pictorial Encyclopedia of Historic Architectural Plans, Details & Elements. John T. Haneman. (Architecture, Interior Design, Period Style Ser.). 141p. 1984. reprint ed. pap. 9.95 (*0-486-24605-1*) Dover.

Pictorial Encyclopedia of Ocean Liners, 1860-1993: 402 Photographs. 93rd ed. William H. Miller, Jr. (Illus.). 192p. (Orig.). 1995. pap. 16.95 (*0-486-28137-X*) Dover.

Pictorial Encyclopedia of Oncidium. Ed. by Mark Chase. LC 98-131602. (Illus.). 152p. 185.00 (*0-9661344-0-0*) ZAI Pubns.

Pictorial English-Haitian-Creole Dictionary. Henock Vilsaint & Maude Heurtelou. LC 95-8289. 1995. write for info. (*1-881839-11-7*) Educa Vision.

Pictorial English-Japanese Dictionary. Ed. by Intercultural Group Staff. (ENG & JPN., Illus.). 288p. 1992. pap. 22.95 (*1-881267-02-4*) Intercultural.

Pictorial Essay of Harley Owners. Philippe Vermes. Ed. by Clyde Fessler. (Illus.). 96p. (Orig.). 1991. 49.95 (*0-925965-06-5*); pap. 29.95 (*0-925965-04-9*) Iris Pubns.

Pictorial Expression in Psychiatry: Psychiatric & Artistic Analysis. enl. ed. Irene Jakab. LC 98-224181. 204p. 1998. 58.00 (*963-05-7492-6*) Intl Spec Bk.

Pictorial Family Tree of Brass Instruments in Europe Since the Early Middle Ages. Emilie Mende. (ENG, FRE & GER., Illus.). 1978. 20.00 (*2-88039-003-6*) Brass Pr.

Pictorial Fetal Pig Anatomy. 2nd rev. ed. S. Gilbert. LC 63-10797. (Illus.). 96p. (C). 1966. pap. 20.00 (*0-295-73877-4*) U of Wash Pr.

Pictorial Field-Book of the Civil War, Vol. 1. Benson J. Lossing. LC 97-12445. Vol. 1. (Illus.). 722p. 1997. reprint ed. pap. 24.95 (*0-8018-5669-8*) Johns Hopkins.

Pictorial Field-Book of the Civil War, Vol. 2. Benson J. Lossing. LC 97-12445. Vol. 2. (Illus.). 712p. 1997. reprint ed. pap. 24.95 (*0-8018-5671-X*) Johns Hopkins.

Pictorial Field-Book of the Civil War, Vol. 3. Benson J. Lossing. LC 97-12445. Vol. 3. (Illus.). 730p. 1997. reprint ed. pap. 24.95 (*0-8018-5672-8*) Johns Hopkins.

Pictorial Field Book of the Revolution, 2 vols. Benson J. Lossing. 1993. reprint ed. lib. bdg. 150.00 (*0-7812-5112-5*) Rprt Serv.

Pictorial Field-Book of the Revolution: or Illustrations, by Pen & Pencil, of the History, Biography, Scenery, Relics & Traditions of the War for Independence, 2 Vols. Benson J. Lossing. LC 72-85457. (Select Bibliographies Reprint Ser.). 1977. 90.95 (*0-8369-5029-1*) Ayer.

Pictorial Field Book of the War of 1812. Benson J. Lossing. 108p. 1993. reprint ed. lib. bdg. 119.00 (*0-7812-5113-3*) Rprt Serv.

Pictorial Folk History of Jefferson City, Missouri, 1890-1990. rev. ed. Joseph S. Summers, Jr. 100p. (Orig.). 1984. pap. 9.95 (*0-916109-00-3*) Summers Pub.

Pictorial Guide Vol. 1. 2nd rev. ed. Pabloo Tepoot. Ed. by Ian Tepoot. (Illus.). 206p. 1995. 49.00 (*0-9645058-0-0*) New Life Exotic Fish.

Pictorial Guide Vol. 2. Pabloo Tepoot. Ed. by Ian Tepoot et al. (Illus.). 311p. 1996. 59.00 (*0-9645058-1-9*, New Life Press) New Life Exotic Fish.

Pictorial Guide to Bible Prophecy. Paul L. Tan. 413p. (C). 1991. 29.95 (*0-932940-07-2*) Bible Coms.

Pictorial Guide to Fossils. Gerard R. Case. 528p. (C). 1992. reprint ed. 62.50 (*0-89464-678-8*); reprint ed. pap. 45.50 (*0-89464-713-X*) Krieger.

Pictorial Guide to House Plants. M. Jane Helmer & Karla S. Hodge. LC 93-78210. (Illus.). 136p. 1992. text 21.95 (*0-89484-052-5*); pap. text 14.95 (*0-89484-053-3*) Merchants Pub Co.

Pictorial Guide to Perennials. rev. ed. M. Jane Helmer & Karla S. Hodge. LC 90-91896. (Illus.). 136p. (Orig.). 1996. reprint ed. pap. text 13.95 (*0-89484-051-7*) Merchants Pub Co.

Pictorial Guide to the Birds of the Indian Subcontinent. 2nd ed. Salim Ali & S. Dillon Ripley. LC 97-145281. (Illus.), 170p. 1996. text 28.00 (*0-19-563732-1*) OUP.

Pictorial Guide to the Florida Keys. Stephen Frink. (Illus.). 32p. (Orig.). (C). 1992. pap. 4.95 (*0-9625409-1-9*) Blue Water FL.

Pictorial Guide to the Living Primates. Noel Rowe. (Illus.). 272p. 1996. 79.95 (*0-9648825-0-7*); pap. 59.95 (*0-9648825-1-5*) Pogonias Pr.

Pictorial Guide to the Verbal Suffixes of TlhIngan Hol. Ed. by Lawrence M. Schoen. (Illus.). 20p. 1995. 5.00 (*0-9644345-0-4*) Klingon Lang Inst.

Pictorial Guide to West Virginia's Civil War Sites & Related Information. Stan B. Cohen. LC 90-60031. (Illus.). 124p. (Orig.). 1990. pap. text 9.95 (*0-929521-34-X*) Pictorial Hist.

Pictorial Guide to Yosemite see Guide Illustre de Yosemite

Pictorial Guide to Yosemite see Guia Ilustrada de Yosemite

Pictorial Guide to Yosemite. Maryann Olsen & Henry Berrey.Tr. of Bildfuhrer fur Yosemite. (Illus.). 22p. 1981. pap. 2.95 (*0-939666-37-5*) Yosemite Assn.

Pictorial Guide to Yosemite. Maryann Olsen & Henry Berrey. Tr. by Edith Stock from GER.Tr. of Bildfuhrer fur Yosemite. (Illus.). 22p. 1981. pap. 2.95 (*0-939666-35-9*) Yosemite Assn.

Pictorial Guide to Yosemite: Japanese. (JPN., Illus.). 22p. 1979. pap. 2.95 (*0-939666-09-X*) Yosemite Assn.

Pictorial Handbook of Anatomy & Physiology. James Bevan. (Illus.). 96p. 1994. pap. text 17.50 (*1-85732-392-0*) Buttrwrth-Heinemann.

Pictorial Handbook of Creative Graphic Design. Ed. by Wolfgang Hageney. (Illus.). 264p. 1986. 49.95 (*88-7070-071-2*) Belvedere USA.

Pictorial Handbook of Technical Devices. Paul Grafstein & Otto M. Schwarz. (Illus.). 1971. 70.00 (*0-8206-0234-5*) Chem Pub.

***Pictorial Historic Presidents of the United States.** Random House Value Publishing Staff. 128p. 2001. 12.99 (*0-517-16160-5*) Random Hse Value.

Pictorial History, 8 vols. R. J. Unstead. Incl. Vol. 1. Invaded Island. 1972. (*0-382-06063-6*); Vol. 2. Kings, Barons, & Serfs. 1972. (*0-382-06064-4*); Vol. 3. Years of the Sword. 1972. (*0-382-06065-2*); Vol. 4. Struggle for Power. 1972. (*0-382-06066-0*); Vol. 5. Emerging Empire. 1972. (*0-382-06067-9*); Vol. 6. Freedom & Revolution. 1972. (*0-382-06068-7*); Vol. 7. Age of Machines. 1973. (*0-382-06069-5*); Vol. 8. Incredible Century. 1975. (*0-382-06070-9*); (Illus.). (gr. 4 up). 11.96 (*0-685-36802-5*) Silver Burdett Pr.

Pictorial History, 1846-1966: School of Medicine & Biomedical Sciences, University at Buffalo. Ronald E. Batt et al. LC 95-47775. 1996. write for info. (*0-89865-963-9*) Donning Co.

Pictorial History of Adolf Hitler. Nigel Blundell. (Illus.). 96p. 1995. write for info. (*1-57215-137-4*) World Pubns.

Pictorial History of American Trucks. Niels Janssen. (Illus.). 151p. 1994. 19.95 (*1-870979-56-7*, Bay View Bks) MBI Pubg.

***Pictorial History of America's Railroads.** Mike Del Vecchio. LC 99-52134. (Illus.). 224p. 1999. pap. 19.95 (*0-7603-0829-2*, 129614AP, Pub. by MBI Pubg) Motorbooks Intl.

Pictorial History of Ancient Japanese Weapons, Armour, & Artifacts. M. Suenaga. (Illus.). 100p. 1983. pap. 25.00 (*0-87556-582-4*) Saifer.

Pictorial History of Ancient Japanese Weapons, Armour & Artifacts. M. Suenaga. 100p. pap. 20.00 (*0-87556-702-9*) Saifer.

Pictorial History of Arkansas: From Earliest Times to the Year 1890: Full & Complete Account...; Also an Extended History of Each County... & of the Principal Cities & Towns; Together with Biographical Notices of Distinguished & Prominent Citizens. Fay Hempstead. (Illus.). 1240p. 1997. reprint ed. lib. bdg. 119.00 (*0-8328-6599-0*) Higginson Bk Co.

Pictorial History of Arkansas from Earliest Times to 1890. Fay Hempstead. 1256p. 1978. reprint ed. 40.00 (*0-89308-074-8*) Southern Hist Pr.

Pictorial History of Arran. Andrew Boyle. 1980. pap. 40.00 (*0-907526-57-8*, Pub. by Alloway Publ) St Mut.

Pictorial History of Astoria, Oregon: The Early Years. (Illus.). 128p. 1997. 39.95 (*1-891395-01-7*) Pediment Grp.

***Pictorial History of Austin, Minnesota, Vol. II.** 128p. 1998. 39.95 (*1-891395-19-X*) Pediment Grp.

Pictorial History of Austin, Minnesota: The Early Years. (Illus.). 128p. 1997. 39.95 (*1-891395-05-X*) Pediment Grp.

Pictorial History of Ayr. Dane Love. 1980. pap. 40.00 (*0-907526-58-6*, Pub. by Alloway Publ) St Mut.

Pictorial History of Blood Practices & Transfusion. A. Matthew Gottlieb. (Illus.). 399p. 1994. 99.00 (*0-9641510-0-6*) Arcane Publns.

***Pictorial History of Butler County, Alabama.** 128p. 1999. 39.95 (*1-891395-22-X*) Pediment Grp.

***Pictorial History of Chevrolet, 1955-1957.** John Robertson. (Illus.). 288p. 1999. 24.95 (*1-880524-35-X*, 128442AP) Cars & Parts.

Pictorial History of Chevrolet, 1940-1954. John D. Robertson. (Illus.). 256p. 1998. boxed set 24.95 (*1-880524-29-5*) Cars & Parts.

Pictorial History of Chevrolet, 1929-1939, Vol. 1. John D. Robertson. (Illus.). 270p. 1998. boxed set 24.95 (*1-880524-25-2*) Cars & Parts.

Pictorial History of Civil War Era Musical Instruments & Military Bands. Robert Garofalo & Mark Elrod. LC 85-60321. (Illus.). 1985. pap. 12.95 (*0-933126-60-3*) Pictorial Hist.

***Pictorial History of College Basketball (to 1988)** Bill Gutman. (Illus.). 192p. 1999. reprint ed. text 30.00 (*0-7881-6834-7*) DIANE Pub.

Pictorial History of Costume. Wolfgang Bruhn & Max Tilke. (Illus.). 200p. 1992. 60.00 (*3-8030-5008-1*, Pub. by E J Wasmuth) Empire Pub Srvs.

Pictorial History of Costume. Ed. by Pepin Press Design Book Staff. (Illus.). 224p. 1998. pap. 29.95 (*0-89676-227-0*, Costume & Fashion Pr) QSMG Ltd.

Pictorial History of Costume: A Survey of Costume of All Periods & Peoples from Antiquity to Modern Times Including National Costume in Europe & Non-European Countries. Wolfgang Bruhn & Max Tilke. LC 95-19731. (Illus.). 200p. 1995. 60.00 (*0-88734-920-X*) Empire Pub Srvs.

Pictorial History of Cripple Creek. Leland Feitz. (Illus.). 48p. (Orig.). 1990. pap. 5.95 (*0-936564-37-7*) Little London.

Pictorial History of Cumnock. Dane Love. 1980. pap. 30.00 (*0-907526-54-3*, Pub. by Alloway Publ) St Mut.

Pictorial History of Darvel. J. Mair. (C). 1989. pap. 50.00 (*0-907526-40-3*, Pub. by Alloway Pub) St Mut.

Pictorial History of Delta State University. Jack W. Gunn & Gladys C. Castle. LC 80-19085. (Illus.). 223p. reprint ed. pap. 69.20 (*0-7837-1072-0*, 204159600021) Bks Demand.

Pictorial History of Diving. Ed. by Barbara M. Desiderati et al. 150p. 1988. 97.00 (*0-941332-09-8*, D270) Best Pub Co.

Pictorial History of Dundonald. R. Kirk. (C). 1988. pap. 50.00 (*0-907526-39-X*, Pub. by Alloway Pub) St Mut.

***Pictorial History of East Multnomah County.** (Illus.). 144p. 1998. 39.95 (*1-891395-18-1*) Pediment Grp.

Pictorial History of European Medicine & Pharmaceutics. J. Antall. 1981. 55.00 (*0-7855-1605-0*) St Mut.

Pictorial History of Fayetteville & Lincoln County, Tennessee. Patricia E. Lindquist. LC 94-22425. (Illus.). 1994. write for info. (*0-89865-926-4*) Donning Co.

Pictorial History of Franklin Delano Roosevelt. Nigel Blundell. (Illus.). 96p. 1996. 10.99 (*1-57215-139-0*, JG1138) World Pubns.

***Pictorial History of Freeborn County, Minnesota, Vol. II.** (Illus.). 136p. 1998. pap. write for info. (*1-891395-21-1*) Pediment Grp.

Pictorial History of Freeborn County, Minnesota: The Early Years. (Illus.). 128p. 1997. 39.95 (*1-891395-02-5*) Pediment Grp.

Pictorial History of Galston. J. Mair. (C). 1988. pap. 50.00 (*0-907526-37-3*, Pub. by Alloway Pub) St Mut.

***Pictorial History of Hendricks County, Indiana** Linda Balough & Betty Bartley. LC 99-29868. (Illus.). 1999. write for info. (*1-57864-074-1*) Donning Co.

***Pictorial History of Hoover Dam.** Ed. by Patty Sullivan. (Illus.). 46p. 1999. pap. 20.00 (*0-9665540-1-9*) Draco Pubg.

***Pictorial History of Hungarian Art.** Jozsef Vadas. (Illus.). 110p. 1999. 32.00 (*963-13-4532-7*, Pub. by Corvina Bks) St Mut.

Pictorial History of Indiana. Dwight W. Hoover. 304p. 1998. 49.95 (*0-253-33482-9*); pap. 29.95 (*0-253-21235-9*) Ind U Pr.

Pictorial History of Japanese Motorcycles. Cornelis Vanderheuvel. LC 97-35971. (Illus.). 168p. 1997. 29.95 (*0-7603-0410-6*) MBI Pubg.

Pictorial History of Joseph Stalin. Nigel Blundell. (Illus.). 96p. 1996. write for info. (*1-57215-138-2*) World Pubns.

***Pictorial History of Josephine County.** (Illus.). 128p. 1998. 39.95 (*1-891395-10-6*) Pediment Grp.

Pictorial History of LaGrange County, Indiana. Sandra Yoder. LC 95-44051. 1995. write for info. (*0-89865-958-2*) Donning Co.

***Pictorial History of Lawrence County.** (Illus.). 144p. 1998. 49.95 (*1-891395-14-9*) Pediment Grp.

Pictorial History of Medicine. Otto L. Bettmann. (Illus.). 336p. 1979. 48.95 (*0-398-00149-9*); pap., spiral bd. 36.95 (*0-398-06019-3*) C C Thomas.

Pictorial History of Montgomery County: One Hundred & Seventy-Five Years, 1818-1993. William J. Auchly et al. LC 93-29511. (Illus.). 1993. write for info. (*0-89865-878-0*) Donning Co.

Pictorial History of New Earswick. J. F. Murphy. (C). 1988. 58.00 (*0-7855-5034-8*, Pub. by W Sessions) St Mut.

Pictorial History of New Earswick. Ed. by J. F. Murphy. (C). 1990. 65.00 (*0-7855-5100-X*, Pub. by W Sessions) St Mut.

Pictorial History of New Earswick. J. F. Murphy. (Illus.). 1999. pap. 21.00 (*1-85072-098-3*, Pub. by W Sessions) St Mut.

Pictorial History of Newmilns. J. Mair. (C). 1988. pap. 50.00 (*0-907526-34-9*, Pub. by Alloway Pub) St Mut.

Pictorial History of Old Duncan: Duncan, South Carolina. Nell Hughes & Frederick Tucker. LC 98-209295. x, 85 p. 1998. 25.00 (*1-884416-23-3*) A Press.

Pictorial History of Old Lewis County: The Crossroads of Central West Virginia. Joy G. Gilchrist & Charles H. Gilchrist. LC 93-19357. 224 p. 1993. write for info. (*0-89865-867-5*) Donning Co.

Pictorial History of Our English Bible. David Beale. (Illus.). 79p. (Orig.). 1982. pap. 7.00 (*0-89084-149-7*, 018044) Bob Jones Univ.

Pictorial History of Paisley. David Rowand. 1980. pap. 40.00 (*0-907526-55-1*, Pub. by Alloway Publ) St Mut.

Pictorial History of Palestine & Anderson County, Texas. Ed. by Museum for East Texas Culture Staff. (Illus.). 128p. 1999. 40.00 (*0-9667999-1-7*) Landmark Publ.

Pictorial History of Psychology. Ed. by Wolfgang G. Bringmann et al. LC 96-24728. (Illus.). 656p. 1997. 78.00 (*0-86715-292-3*); pap. 38.95 (*0-86715-330-X*) Quint Pub Co.

Pictorial History of Roseburg, Oregon: Commemorating the City's 125th Anniversary. (Illus.). 128p. 1997. 39.95 (*1-891395-00-9*) Pediment Grp.

Pictorial History of St. Paul's Anglican Church, Halifax, Nova Scotia. J. Philip McAleer. LC 92-98603. (Illus.). 160p. 1993. pap. 16.95 (*0-929112-19-9*, Pub. by Tuns Pr) Baker & Taylor.

Pictorial History of Science Fiction Films. Jeff Rovin. (Illus.). 1976. pap. 12.95 (*0-8065-0537-0*, Citadel Pr) Carol Pub Group.

***Pictorial History of Seaside & Gearhart.** (Illus.). 112p. 1998. 39.95 (*1-891395-12-2*) Pediment Grp.

Pictorial History of Shakespearean Production in England, 1576-1946. Arts Council Of Great Britain. Ed. by M. St. Clare Byrne. LC 70-109640. (Select Bibliographies Reprint Ser.). 1977. 13.95 (*0-8369-5249-9*) Ayer.

Pictorial History of Smoke Jumping. Stan B. Cohen. LC 83-62751. (Illus.). 180p. 1983. pap. 12.95 (*0-933126-40-9*) Pictorial Hist.

Pictorial History of St. Paul's School. Ed. by Jose A. Ordonez y Montalvo. 242p. 1991. 155.00 (*0-9630522-0-9*) St Pauls Sch.

Pictorial History of Sumner County, Tennessee, 1786-1986. Walter T. Durham & James W. Thomas. LC 86-62487. (Illus.). 152p. 1986. 24.95 (*0-9644297-0-5*) Sumner Cnty Hist.

Pictorial History of Texas. Homer Thrall. 1993. reprint ed. lib. bdg. 75.00 (*0-7812-5908-8*) Rprt Serv.

Pictorial History of the Battle of Gettysburg. (Illus.). 73p. 1996. pap. 5.00 (*1-890541-04-4*) Americana Souvenirs & Gifts.

***Pictorial History of the Brewton Area.** 112p. 1998. 39.95 (*1-891395-17-3*) Pediment Grp.

Pictorial History of the Carousel. Frederick Fried. (Illus.). 234p. 1983. 34.95 (*0-911572-29-5*, Vestal Pr) Madison Bks UPA.

Pictorial History of the Civil War. Benson J. Lossing. (Notable American Authors Ser.). 1999. reprint ed. lib. bdg. 125.00 (*0-7812-3861-7*) Rprt Serv.

Pictorial History of the Fire Engine. Matthew Lee. 320p. 1997. 39.95 (*0-9630472-1-3*) Lee & Sons.

Pictorial History of the Flying Tigers. Larry M. Pistole & Stephen W. Sylvia. LC 81-84192. (Illus.). 261p. 1981. 29.95 (*0-943522-05-6*) North South Trader.

Pictorial History of the Saint Lucy Filippini Chapel: Edizioni del Palazzo, Prato. Margherita Marchione. 130p. 1992. 40.00 (*0-614-10146-8*) Am Inst Ital Stud.

Pictorial History of the Sea War, 1939-1945. Paul J. Kemp. LC 95-71396. (Illus.). 192p. 1996. 39.95 (*1-55750-674-4*) Naval Inst Pr.

***Pictorial History of the University of Georgia.** 2nd ed. F. N. Boney. LC 99-49011. (Illus.). 2000. 34.95 (*0-8203-2198-2*) U of Ga Pr.

Pictorial History of the University of Iowa. John C. Gerber. LC 87-30769. (Illus.). 288p. 1988. 29.95 (*0-87745-189-3*) U of Iowa Pr.

Pictorial History of the Willamette Valley. (Illus.). 1997. 39.95 (*1-891395-07-6*) Pediment Grp.

Pictorial History of the 7th Bombardment Group/Wing 1918-1995, Vol. 1. Wilbur W. Mayhew. LC 97-61932. (Illus.). 328p. 1998. 50.00 (*0-9660462-0-X*) Seventh Bomb Gp.

Pictorial History of W. E. B. Du Bois. Shirley G. Du Bois. LC 77-16696. 174p. 14.95 (*0-87485-076-2*) Johnson Chicago.

Pictorial History of Waco. Roger Conger. (Illus.). 292p. 1969. 24.95 (*0-87244-026-5*) Texian.

Pictorial History of Wayne County, Indiana. Carolyn Lafever. LC 98-10951. 1998. write for info. (*1-57864-029-6*) Donning Co.

***Pictorial History of Wells County: Towns & Townships.** Wells County Historical Society Staff. LC 99-49185. (Illus.). 1999. write for info. (*1-57864-091-1*) Donning Co.

Pictorial History of Winston Churchill. Nigel Blundell. (Illus.). 96p. 1996. 10.99 (*1-57215-140-4*, JG1139) World Pubns.

Pictorial History of World War II. Charles Messenger. (Illus.). 256p. 19.99 (*1-57215-244-3*, JG2443) World Pubns.

Pictorial in Modernist Fiction from Stephen Crane to Ernest Hemingway. Deborah Schnitzer. Ed. by A. Walton Litz. LC 88-11091. (Studies in Modern Literature: No. 93). 298p. 1988. reprint ed. pap. 92.40 (*0-8357-1876-X*, 207062900009) Bks Demand.

Pictorial Information Systems in Medicine. Ed. by K. H. Hohne. (NATO ASI Series F: Computer & Systems Sciences, Special Programme AET: Vol. 19). xii, 525p. 1986. 216.95 (*0-387-13921-4*) Spr-Verlag.

Pictorial Introduction to the Bible. William S. Deal. 436p. 1997. reprint ed. 19.95 (*1-56563-296-6*) Hendrickson MA.

Pictorial Journalism. Laura Vitray et al. LC 72-9241. (Literature of Photography Ser.). 1973. reprint ed. 31.95 (*0-405-04945-5*) Ayer.

Pictorial Journey Through Edwardian Gower. David Gwynn & Peter Muxworthy. 130p. (C). 1989. text 35.00 (*0-86383-422-1*, Pub. by Gomer Pr) St Mut.

Pictorial Key to the Hawkmoths (Lepidotera: Sphingidae) of Eastern United States (Except Florida) Charles L. Selman. (Biological Notes Ser.: No. 9). 1975. pap. text 5.00 (*0-86727-079-9*) Ohio Bio Survey.

Pictorial Key to the Tarot. Arthur E. Waite. (Illus.). 1979. pap. 11.95 (*0-8065-0715-2*, Citadel Pr) Carol Pub Group.

Pictorial Key to the Tarot. Arthur E. Waite. (Illus.). 352p. 1987. pap. 10.95 (*0-89345-231-9*, Steinerbks) Garber Comm.

Pictorial Key to the Tarot. Arthur E. Waite. 340p. 1996. reprint ed. spiral bd. 18.50 (*0-7873-1067-0*) Hlth Research.

Pictorial Key to the Tarot. Arthur E. Waite. (Illus.). 352p. 1973. reprint ed. pap. 6.95 (*0-87728-218-8*) Weiser.

Pictorial Key to the Tarot, Vol. 1. Arthur E. Waite. (Illus.). 340p. 1977. pap. 6.95 (*0-913866-08-3*, BK18) US Games Syst.

Pictorial Library of Landscape Plants Southern Hardiness Zones Six to Ten, Vol. II. Ruth F. Woods. LC 81-82113. (Illus.). 344p. 1989. text 95.00 (*0-89484-095-9*) Merchants Pub Co.

Pictorial Logging Butte Falls Oregon. (Illus.). 50p. 1996. pap. 6.00 (*1-884728-01-4*) B Hegne.

Pictorial Memoir. Sylvia R. Miller. LC 80-81146. (Illus.). 120p. 1980. 20.00 (*0-913504-57-2*) Lowell Pr.

Pictorial Metaphor in Advertising. Charles Forceville. (Illus.). 248p. (C). 1998. pap. 29.99 (*0-415-18676-5*) Routledge.

Pictorial Narrative in Ancient Greek Art. Mark Stansbury-O'Donnell. LC 98-38137. (Studies in Classical Art & Iconography). (Illus.). 256p. (C). 1999. 75.00 (*0-521-64000-8*) Cambridge U Pr.

Pictorial Narrative in Antiquity & the Middle Ages. Ed. by Herbert L. Kessler & Marianna S. Simpson. 1996. 35.00 (*0-300-07516-2*) Yale U Pr.

Pictorial New Zealand, 1895. Pref. by W. B. Perceval. 316p. (C). 1986. 85.00 (*0-85091-239-3*) St Mut.

Pictorial Nominalism: On Marcel Duchamp's Passage from Painting to the Readymade, Vol. 51. Thierry De Duve. Tr. by Dana B. Polan. (Theory & History of Literature Ser.). (FRE., Illus.). 244p. (Orig.). 1991. pap. 17.95 (*0-8166-1565-9*) U of Minn Pr.

Pictorial of Life Photo Album. Date not set. write for info. (*1-888185-64-3*) Davis Pubng LA.

***Pictorial Outline of Cat Anatomy.** abr. ed. Stephen G. Gilbert & Cheralea Gilbert. (Illus.). 96p. 1999. pap. text 14.95 (*0-8020-8308-0*) U of Toronto Pr.

Pictorial Photography in Philadelphia: The Pennsylvania Academy's Salons, 1898-1901. William I. Homer. (Illus.). 57p. (Orig.). 1984. pap. 9.95 (*0-614-30569-1*) Penn Acad Art.

Pictorial Pilgrim's Progress. John Bunyan. (J). (gr. 2-7). 1960. pap. 5.99 (*0-8024-0019-1*, 554) Moody.

P

An Asterisk (*) at the beginning of an entry indicates that the title is appearing for the first time.

Pictorial Pottery of Eleventh Century B. C. Cyprus. Maria Iacovou. (Studies in Mediterranean Archaeology: Vol. LXXVIII). (Illus.). 122p. (Orig.). 1988. pap. 65.00 (*91-86098-59-4*, Pub. by P Astroms) Coronet Bks.

Pictorial Price Guide to American Antiques, 1992-1993. 13th ed. Dorothy Hammond. (Illus.). 224p. 1992. pap. 16.00 (*0-525-48595-3*, Dutton Studio) Studio Bks.

Pictorial Price Guide to American Antiques, 1993-1994. 14th ed. Dorothy Hammond. (Illus.). 224p. (Orig.). 1993. pap. 16.00 (*0-525-48608-9*, Dutton Studio) Studio Bks.

Pictorial Price Guide to American Antiques, 1994-1995. 15th ed. Dorothy Hammond. (Illus.). 224p. 1994. pap. 16.95 (*0-525-48620-8*) Studio Bks.

***Pictorial Price Guide to American Antiques 2000-2001.** 21st ed. Dorothy Hammond. (Illus.). 224p. 1999. pap. 19.95 (*0-14-028529-6*, Viking Studio) Studio Bks.

Pictorial Price Guide to Metal Lunch Boxes & Thermoses. rev. ed. Larry Aikins. (Illus.). 218p. 1999. reprint ed. pap. 19.95 (*0-89538-007-2*) L-W Inc.

Pictorial Primer: Easy Lessons for Little Ones at Home. LC 97-47658. 1998. 10.00 (*1-57683-091-8*) NavPress.

***Pictorial Quilting.** Maggi McCormick Gordon. (Illus.). 128p. 2000. pap. write for info. (*0-8230-4475-0*) Watsn-Guptill.

Pictorial Record of Great Western Absorbed Engines. J. H. Russell. 288p. 1986. 65.00 (*0-902888-74-9*) St Mut.

Pictorial Review of Pediatrics: Acute Care & Emergency Medicine. Gary R. Fleisher et al. LC 97-28142. (Illus.). 512p. 1997. pap. 69.00 (*0-683-30267-1*) Lppncott W & W.

Pictorial Review of the African American Experience. Donald C. Wilson & Jane Y. Wilson. (Illus.). 375p. 1997. 49.95 (*0-9648805-1-2*, 002) DCW Pubng.

Pictorial Sino-Korean Characters: Fun with Hancha. Jacob C. Kim. 367p. 1998. 29.95 (*0-930878-58-2*) Hollym Intl.

Pictorial Story of the Oregon/California Trail. 1995. pap. 19.95 (*0-9650703-0-1*) Heritge Assocs Pubs.

Pictorial Surface Preparation Standards for Painting Steel Surfaces - D 2200. 56p. 1989. 250.00 (*0-685-53336-0*, ADJD2200) ASTM.

Pictorial Toledo, Oregon: Then & Now. Evelyn P. Parry. LC 83-81298. (Illus.). 97p. (Orig.). 1983. pap. 9.95 (*0-911443-01-0*) Lincoln Coun Hist.

Pictorial Tour of Unarius. Unarius Publications Staff. (Illus.). 164p. 1982. pap. 10.00 (*0-932642-68-3*) Unarius Acad Sci.

Pictorial Weavings of the Navajos. Nancy N. Schiffer. LC 91-60955. (Illus.). 64p. 1991. pap. 12.95 (*0-88740-318-2*) Schiffer.

Pictorial Workbook of the Code, Vol. 1. Tom Henry. (Illus.). 182p. (C). 1993. pap. text 25.00 (*0-945495-34-X*) T Henrys CECB.

Pictorial Workbook of the Code, Vol. 2. Tom Henry. (Illus.). 218p. (C). 1993. pap. text 25.00 (*0-945495-38-2*) T Henrys CECB.

Pictorialism in California: Photographs, 1900-1940. Michael G. Wilson & Dennis Reed. LC 94-14039. (Illus.). 160p. 1994. pap. 30.00 (*0-89236-313-4*, Pub. by J P Getty Trust) OUP.

Pictorialism in the Fictional Miniatures of Albert Paris Guttersloh. Ingrid E. Laue. (Austrian Culture Ser.: Vol. 22). XIV, 186p. (C). 1996. text 47.95 (*0-8204-3003-X*) P Lang Pubng.

Pictor's Metamorphoses & Other Fantasies. Hermann Hesse. Tr. by Rika Lesser from GER. (Illus.). 208p. 1983. pap. 12.00 (*0-374-51723-1*) FS&G.

PicTrix Vol. 1: The Original Book of Picture Tricks. Paul J. Gruen. (Illus.). 96p. (Orig.). 1991. pap. 5.95 (*0-9630521-0-1*) PicTrix Pub.

Picts: An Introduction to the Life of the Picts & the Carved Stones in the Care of the Secretary of State for Scotland. Anna Ritchie. Ed. by Christopher Tabraham. (Historic Scotland Ser.). (Illus.). 64p. 1989. pap. 15.00 (*0-11-493491-6*, Pub. by Statnry Office) Seven Hills Bk.

Picts & the Scots. Lloyd Robert Laing. 1997. pap. text 19.95 (*0-7509-0677-4*, Pub. by Sutton Pub Ltd) Intl Pubs Mktg.

Picts & the Scots. Lloyd Robert Laing & Jennifer Laing. (Illus.). 172p. 1999. reprint ed. text 30.00 (*0-7881-6124-5*) DIANE Pub.

Picts & Their Symbols. W. A. Cummins. 1999. 34.95 (*0-7509-2207-9*, Pub. by Sutton Publng) Intl Pubs Mktg.

Picture see Hunger & Thirst & Other Plays

Picture. Lillian Ross. LC 82-49210. (Cinema Classics Ser.). 264p. 1985. lib. bdg. 16.00 (*0-8240-5775-9*) Garland.

Picture. Lillian Ross. LC 96-34440. 1997. 16.50 (*0-679-60254-2*) Modern Lib NY.

Picture: Penguin Readers Level 4. Oscar Wilde. 1998. pap. 7.00 (*0-14-081572-4*) Viking Penguin.

Picture - Animal - Crisscross. Oliver Hailey. 1970. pap. 3.25 (*0-8222-0893-8*) Dramatists Play.

Picture a Country. Henry Pluckrose. 1998. 144.00 (*0-531-19435-3*) Watts.

Picture America: States & Capitals. Derek Lancaster. Ed. by Stevens Anderson. (Illus.). 136p. (YA). (gr. 5). 1991. pap. 4.95 (*1-880184-02-8*) Compact Classics.

Picture & Text see Works of Henry James Jr.: Collected Works

Picture Archiving & Communication Systems in Medical Imaging. H. K. Huang. LC 95-38928. (Illus.). 400p. 1995. 146.00 (*1-56081-685-6*, Wiley-VCH) Wiley.

Picture Archiving & Communication Systems (PACS) in Medicine. Ed. by H. K. Huang et al. (NATO ASI Series F: Computer & Systems Sciences, Special Programme AET: Vol. 74). xii, 438p. 1991. 114.95 (*0-387-53916-6*) Spr-Verlag.

Picture Atlas of Our Fifty States. Ed. by Margaret Sedeen. (Illus.). 1991. 19.95 (*0-87044-860-9*) Natl Geog.

Picture Atlas of the World. Illus. by Brian Delf. LC 92-37056. (J). 1992. 19.95 (*0-528-83564-5*) Rand McNally.

Picture Atlas of the World. Illus. by John Dillow. (SL Twenty One Ser.). 45p. (J). 1993. text 11.95 (*0-7214-5354-6*, Ladybrd) Penguin Putnam.

Picture-Based Approach for the World of Work, Bk. 1. Contemporary Books Staff. 150p. 1991. pap., teacher ed. 8.45 (*0-8092-4167-6*) NTC Contemp Pub Co.

Picture Beaded Earrings for Beginners. Starr Steil. Ed. by Denise Knight. LC 95-61188. (Illus.). 64p. (Orig.). 1996. pap. 9.95 (*0-943604-50-8*, BOO/39) Eagles View.

Picture Bible. (Illus.). 256p. (J). 1991. write for info. (*1-55513-542-0*, Chariot Bks) Chariot Victor.

Picture Bible. Iva Hoth. LC 98-215778. 1998. pap. text 16.99 (*0-7814-3058-5*) Chariot Victor.

Picture Bible. Iva Hoth. LC 98-215778. (Illus.). 1998. 19.99 (*0-7814-3055-0*) Chariot Victor.

Picture Bible. deluxe ed. Iva Hoth. LC 98-215778. (Illus.). 1998. 21.99 (*0-7814-3057-7*) Chariot Victor.

***Picture Bible Devotions.** Jeannie Harmon. 1998. pap. text 11.99 (*0-7814-3067-4*) Chariot Victor.

Picture Bible New Testament. 256p. (J). 1997. 8.99 (*0-7814-0211-5*, Chariot Bks) Chariot Victor.

Picture Bible New Testament Recover. Iva Hoth. 256p. (J). (gr. 2 up). 1997. 8.99 (*0-7814-0200-X*) Chariot Victor.

Picture Bidding. Alvin Roth. 317p. 1991. 24.95 (*0-940257-11-4*) Granovetter Bks.

Picture Book. Frances A. Cannon. Ed. by Rita K. Petz. (Illus.). (J). (gr. 4-6). write for info. (*0-318-62234-3*) RAPCOM Enter.

***Picture Book.** Tana Hoban. (J). 2001. 15.95 (*0-688-17193-1*, Grenwillow Bks); lib. bdg. 15.89 (*0-688-17194-X*, Grenwillow Bks) HarpC Child Bks.

***Picture Book.** Pat Hutchins. (J). 2001. 15.95 (*0-688-16799-3*, Grenwillow Bks); lib. bdg. 15.89 (*0-688-16800-0*, Grenwillow Bks) HarpC Child Bks.

***Picture Book.** Susannah Keating. 256p. 2000. 20.00 (*0-688-17888-X*, Wm Morrow) Morrow Avon.

Picture Book No. 1. Scholastic, Inc. Staff. (Godzilla Ser.). 32p. (J). (gr. k-3). 1998. pap. text 3.50 (*0-590-57212-1*) Scholastic Inc.

***Picture Book & Price Guide to Antique American Quilts.** large type ed. Craig Ambrose. (Illus.). 200p. 2000. pap. text 25.00 (*0-9679834-0-1*) C Ambrose.

Picture Book Comes of Age: Looking at Childhood Through the Art of Illustration. Joseph Schwarcz & Chava Schwarcz. LC 90-37809. 217p. (C). 1990. pap. text 17.00 (*0-8389-0543-9*, 0543-9) ALA.

Picture Book Companion, Bk. III. Clifford J. Kramer. 96p. 1993. pap. text 12.95 (*0-944459-64-1*) ECS Lrn Systs.

Picture Book Companion, No. I. Clifford J. Kramer. 96p. 1992. pap. text 12.95 (*0-944459-58-7*) ECS Lrn Systs.

Picture Book Companion, No. II. Clifford J. Kramer. 96p. 1992. pap. text 12.95 (*0-944459-59-5*) ECS Lrn Systs.

Picture Book for Baby. Ladybird Books Staff. (First Picture Bks.: No. 832-1). (Illus.). (J). (ps). pap. 3.50 (*0-7214-0749-8*, Ladybrd) Penguin Putnam.

Picture Book for Zone Cooks. Carolyn Brooks & Darlene Kvist. (Illus.). 94p. 1997. pap. 18.95 (*0-9661630-8-7*) Nutrit Weight.

Picture Book of Abraham Lincoln. David A. Adler. LC 88-16393. (Illus.). 32p. (J). (gr. k-3). 1989. lib. bdg. 16.95 (*0-8234-0731-4*) Holiday.

Picture Book of Abraham Lincoln. David A. Adler. LC 88-16393. (Picture Book Biography Ser.). (Illus.). 26p. (J). (ps-3). 1990. pap. 6.95 (*0-8234-0801-9*) Holiday.

Picture Book of Abraham Lincoln. unabridged ed. David A. Adler. (Illus.). (J). (gr. 2-4). 1990. 24.95 incl. audio (*0-87499-159-5*); pap. 15.95 incl. audio (*0-87499-158-7*) Live Oak Media.

Picture Book of Abraham Lincoln, 4 bks., Set. unabridged ed. David A. Adler. (Illus.). (J). (gr. 2-4). 1990. pap. 37.95 incl. audio (*0-87499-160-9*) Live Oak Media.

Picture Book of Amelia Earhart. David A. Adler. LC 96-54854. (Picture Book Biography Ser.). (Illus.). 32p. (J). (gr. 2-5). 1998. lib. bdg. 16.95 (*0-8234-1315-2*) Holiday.

***Picture Book of Amelia Earhart.** David A. Adler. (Illus.). (J). 1998. pap. 6.95 (*0-8234-1517-1*) Holiday.

Picture Book of Ancient British Art. Stuart Piggott & Glyn E. Daniel. LC 53-3905. (Illus.). 85p. reprint ed. pap. 25.00 (*0-608-11301-8*, 2051470) Bks Demand.

Picture Book of Animal Opposites. Grace Mabie. LC 91-33596. (Picture Book of...Ser.). (Illus.). 24p. (J). (gr. 1-4). 1992. pap. 2.95 (*0-8167-2439-3*); text 14.50 (*0-8167-2438-5*) Troll Communs.

Picture Book of Anne Frank. David A. Adler. LC 92-17283. (Illus.). 32p. (J). (gr. k-3). 1993. lib. bdg. 16.95 (*0-8234-1003-X*) Holiday.

Picture Book of Anne Frank. David A. Adler. (Illus.). 32p. (J). (ps-3). 1994. pap. 6.95 (*0-8234-1078-1*) Holiday.

Picture Book of Anne Frank. unabridged ed. David A. Adler. (Illus.). (J). (gr. 2-4). 1995. 24.95 incl. audio (*0-87499-347-4*); pap. 15.95 incl. audio (*0-87499-346-6*) Live Oak Media.

Picture Book of Anne Frank, 4 bks., Set. David A. Adler. (Illus.). (J). (gr. 2-4). pap., teacher ed. 37.95 incl. audio (*0-87499-348-2*) Live Oak Media.

Picture Book of Arctic Animals. Kellie Conforth. LC 90-44896. (Picture Book of...Ser.). (Illus.). 24p. (J). (gr. 1-4). 1991. lib. bdg. 14.50 (*0-8167-2144-0*) Troll Communs.

Picture Book of Arctic Animals. Kellie Conforth. LC 90-44896. (Picture Book of...Ser.). (Illus.). 24p. (J). (gr. 1-4). 1996. pap. 2.95 (*0-8167-2145-9*) Troll Communs.

Picture Book of Armenian Miniatures. Ed. by Zabel Der Bedrosian & Robert Der Bedrosian. LC 68-59356. (Illus.). 63p. (Orig.). 1968. pap. 4.95 (*0-935411-03-8*) Natl Assn Arm.

Picture Book of Australian Animals. Kellie Conforth. LC 91-18706. (Picture Book of...Ser.). (Illus.). 24p. (J). (gr. 1-4). 1992. pap. 2.95 (*0-8167-2471-7*); lib. bdg. 14.50 (*0-8167-2470-9*) Troll Communs.

Picture Book of Baby Animals. Grace Mabie. LC 92-26264. (Picture Book of...Ser.). (Illus.). 24p. (J). (gr. 1-4). 1992. lib. bdg. 14.50 (*0-8167-2468-7*) Troll Communs.

Picture Book of Baby Animals. Grace Mabie. LC 92-26264. (Picture Book of...Ser.). (Illus.). 24p. (J). (gr. 1-4). 1997. pap. 2.95 (*0-8167-2469-5*) Troll Communs.

Picture Book of Benjamin Franklin. David A. Adler. LC 89-20059. (Illus.). 32p. (J). (gr. k-3). 1990. lib. bdg. 16.95 (*0-8234-0792-6*) Holiday.

Picture Book of Benjamin Franklin. David A. Adler. LC 89-20059. (Illus.). 32p. (J). (ps-3). 1991. pap. 6.95 (*0-8234-0882-5*) Holiday.

Picture Book of Birds. Joanne Gise. LC 89-37328. (Picture Book of...Ser.). (Illus.). 24p. (J). (gr. 1-4). 1990. lib. bdg. 14.50 (*0-8167-1898-9*) Troll Communs.

Picture Book of Birds. Joanne Gise. LC 89-37328. (Picture Book of...Ser.). (Illus.). 24p. (J). (gr. 1-4). 1997. pap. 2.95 (*0-8167-1899-7*) Troll Communs.

Picture Book of Butterflies & Moths. Joanne Mattern. LC 92-5225. (Picture Book of...Ser.). (Illus.). 24p. (J). (gr. 1-4). 1992. lib. bdg. 9.95 (*0-8167-2796-1*, BP089) Troll Communs.

Picture Book of Butterflies & Moths. Joanne Mattern. LC 92-5225. (Picture Book of...Ser.). (Illus.). 24p. (J). (gr. 1-4). 1996. pap. 2.95 (*0-8167-2797-X*) Troll Communs.

Picture Book of Cats. Joanne Mattern. LC 90-42548. (Picture Book of...Ser.). (Illus.). 24p. (J). (gr. 1-4). 1991. lib. bdg. 14.50 (*0-8167-2146-7*) Troll Communs.

Picture Book of Cats. Joanne Mattern. LC 90-42548. (Picture Book of...Ser.). (Illus.). 24p. (J). (gr. 4-7). 1991. pap. 2.95 (*0-8167-2147-5*) Troll Communs.

Picture Book of Christopher Columbus. David A. Adler. LC 90-39211. (Illus.). 32p. (J). (gr. k-3). 1991. lib. bdg. 16.95 (*0-8234-0857-4*) Holiday.

Picture Book of Christopher Columbus. David A. Adler. (Illus.). (J). (gr. k-3). 1992. reprint ed. pap. 6.95 (*0-8234-0949-X*) Holiday.

Picture Book of Christopher Columbus. unabridged ed. David A. Adler. (Illus.). (J). (gr. 2-4). 1992. 24.95 incl. audio (*0-87499-263-X*); pap. 15.95 incl. audio (*0-87499-262-1*) Live Oak Media.

Picture Book of Christopher Columbus, 4 bks., Set. unabridged ed. David A. Adler. (Illus.). (J). (gr. 2-4). 1992. pap., teacher ed. 37.95 incl. audio (*0-87499-264-8*) Live Oak Media.

Picture Book of Davy Crockett. David A. Adler. (Illus.). 32p. (J). (ps-3). 1996. 16.95 (*0-8234-1212-1*); pap. 6.95 (*0-8234-1343-8*) Holiday.

Picture Book of Desert Animals. Joanne Gise. LC 90-40436. (Picture Book of...Ser.). (Illus.). 24p. (J). (gr. 1-4). 1991. lib. bdg. 14.50 (*0-8167-2148-3*) Troll Communs.

Picture Book of Devils, Demons, & Witchcraft. Ernst Lehner & Johanna Lehner. LC 72-137002. 174p. 1971. pap. 9.95 (*0-486-22751-0*) Dover.

Picture Book of Dinosaurs. Claire Nemes. LC 89-37331. (Picture Book of...Ser.). (Illus.). 24p. (J). (gr. 1-4). 1990. lib. bdg. 14.50 (*0-8167-1900-4*) Troll Communs.

Picture Book of Dinosaurs. Claire Nemes. LC 89-37331. (Picture Book of...Ser.). (Illus.). 24p. (J). (gr. 1-4). 1996. pap. 2.95 (*0-8167-1901-2*) Troll Communs.

Picture Book of Dinosaurs. Claire Nemes. (Illus.). (J). 1990. 8.15 (*0-606-04514-7*, Pub. by Turtleback) Demco.

Picture Book of Dogs. Joanne Gise. LC 89-39430. (Picture Book of...Ser.). (Illus.). 24p. (J). (gr. 1-4). 1990. lib. bdg. 14.50 (*0-8167-1902-0*) Troll Communs.

Picture Book of Dogs. Joanne Gise. LC 89-39430. (Picture Book of...Ser.). (Illus.). 24p. (J). (gr. 1-4). 1997. pap. 2.95 (*0-8167-1903-9*) Troll Communs.

Picture Book of Eleanor Roosevelt. David A. Adler. LC 90-39212. (Illus.). 32p. (J). (gr. k-3). 1991. lib. bdg. 16.95 (*0-8234-0856-6*) Holiday.

Picture Book of Eleanor Roosevelt. David A. Adler. (Illus.). 32p. (J). (ps-3). 1991. pap. 6.95 (*0-8234-1157-5*) Holiday.

Picture Book of Eleanor Roosevelt. unabridged ed. David A. Adler. (J). (gr. 1-6). 1997. 24.95 incl. audio (*0-87499-400-4*) Live Oak Media.

Picture Book of Eleanor Roosevelt. unabridged ed. David A. Adler. (J). (gr. 3-5). 1997. pap. 15.95 incl. audio (*0-87499-399-7*) Live Oak Media.

Picture Book of Eleanor Roosevelt, 4 bks., Set. David A. Adler. (J). (gr. 3-5). 1997. pap., teacher ed. 37.95 incl. audio (*0-87499-401-2*) Live Oak Media.

Picture Book of Farm Animals. Mary Scott. LC 90-44888. (Picture Book of...Ser.). (Illus.). 24p. (J). (gr. 1-4). 1991. lib. bdg. 14.50 (*0-8167-2150-5*) Troll Communs.

Picture Book of Farm Animals. Mary Scott. LC 90-44888. (Picture Book of...Ser.). (Illus.). 24p. (J). (gr. 1-4). 1997. pap. 2.95 (*0-8167-2151-3*) Troll Communs.

Picture Book of Florence Nightingale. David A. Adler. LC 91-43388. (Illus.). 32p. (J). (gr. k-2). 1992. lib. bdg. 16.95 (*0-8234-0965-1*) Holiday.

Picture Book of Florence Nightingale. David A. Adler. (Illus.). (J). (gr. k-3). 1993. reprint ed. pap. text 6.95 (*0-8234-1284-9*) Holiday.

Picture Book of Flowers. Theresa Grace. LC 92-8716. (Picture Book of...Ser.). (Illus.). 24p. (J). (gr. 1-4). 1992. lib. bdg. 9.95 (*0-8167-2836-4*, BP088) Troll Communs.

Picture Book of Forest Animals. Joanne Gise. LC 89-37329. (Picture Bks.). (Illus.). 24p. (J). (gr. 1-4). 1990. lib. bdg. 14.50 (*0-8167-1904-7*) Troll Communs.

Picture Book of Frederick Douglass. David A. Adler. LC 92-17378. (Illus.). 32p. (J). (gr. k-3). 1993. lib. bdg. 16.95 (*0-8234-1002-1*) Holiday.

Picture Book of Frederick Douglass. David A. Adler. (Illus.). 32p. (J). (gr. k-3). 1993. pap. 6.95 (*0-8234-1205-9*) Holiday.

Picture Book of George Washington. David A. Adler. LC 88-16384. (Illus.). 32p. (J). (gr. k-3). 1989. lib. bdg. 16.95 (*0-8234-0732-2*) Holiday.

Picture Book of George Washington. David A. Adler. LC 88-16384. (Illus.). 30p. (J). (ps-3). 1990. pap. 6.95 (*0-8234-0800-0*) Holiday.

Picture Book of George Washington. unabridged ed. David A. Adler. LC 88-16384. (Illus.). (J). (gr. 2-4). 1990. 24.95 incl. audio (*0-87499-162-5*); pap. 15.95 incl. audio (*0-87499-161-7*) Live Oak Media.

Picture Book of George Washington, 4 bks., Set. David A. Adler. LC 88-16384. (Illus.). (J). (gr. 2-4). 1990. pap., teacher ed. 37.95 incl. audio (*0-87499-163-3*) Live Oak Media.

Picture Book of George Washington Carver. David A. Adler. LC 98-20261. (Illus.). (J). (ps-3). 1999. lib. bdg. 15.95 (*0-8234-1429-9*) Holiday.

***Picture Book of George Washington Carver.** David A. Adler. (Illus.). (J). (gr. 4-7). 2000. 6.95 (*0-8234-1633-X*) Holiday.

Picture Book of Greenwich Village. R. Bruce Gaylord. 1991. pap. 16.95 (*0-8065-1236-9*, Citadel Pr) Carol Pub Group.

Picture-Book of Happiness: In Each Face, a Discovery Awaits You. Kazunori Shimamoto. Tr. by Juliet Winters Carpenter. (JPN & ENG., Illus.). 60p. 1999. 8.95 (*4-7700-2343-X*, Pub. by Kodansha Intl) Kodansha.

Picture Book of Harriet Tubman. David A. Adler. LC 91-19628. (Illus.). 32p. (J). (ps-3). 1992. lib. bdg. 16.95 (*0-8234-0926-0*) Holiday.

Picture Book of Harriet Tubman. David A. Adler. 29p. (J). (ps-3). 1993. pap. 6.95 (*0-8234-1065-X*) Holiday.

Picture Book of Helen Keller. David A. Adler. LC 89-77510. (Illus.). 32p. (J). (gr. k-3). 1990. lib. bdg. 16.95 (*0-8234-0818-3*) Holiday.

Picture Book of Helen Keller. David A. Adler. LC 89-77510. (Illus.). (J). (gr. k-3). 1990. reprint ed. pap. 6.95 (*0-8234-0950-3*) Holiday.

Picture Book of Horses. Joanne Gise. LC 90-40437. (Picture Book of...Ser.). (Illus.). 24p. (J). (gr. 1-4). 1991. pap. 2.95 (*0-8167-2153-X*) Troll Communs.

Picture Book of Insects. Joanne Mattern. LC 90-11211. (Picture Book of...Ser.). (Illus.). 24p. (J). (gr. 1-4). 1991. lib. bdg. 14.50 (*0-8167-2154-8*) Troll Communs.

Picture Book of Insects. Joanne Mattern. LC 90-11211. (Picture Book of...Ser.). (Illus.). 24p. (J). (gr. 1-4). 1997. pap. 2.95 (*0-8167-2155-6*) Troll Communs.

Picture Book of Jackie Robinson. David A. Adler. LC 93-27224. (Illus.). 32p. (J). (gr. k-3). 1994. lib. bdg. 16.95 (*0-8234-1122-2*) Holiday.

Picture Book of Jackie Robinson. David A. Adler. LC 93-27224. (Illus.). 29p. (J). (gr. 1-4). 1994. reprint ed. pap. text 6.95 (*0-8234-1304-7*) Holiday.

Picture Book of Jesse Owens. David A. Adler. (J). (gr. k-3). 1992. pap. text 6.95 (*0-8234-1066-8*) Holiday.

Picture Book of Jesse Owens. David A. Adler. LC 91-44735. (Illus.). 32p. (J). (gr. k-3). 1992. lib. bdg. 16.95 (*0-8234-0966-X*) Holiday.

Picture Book of John F. Kennedy. David A. Adler. LC 90-23589. (Illus.). 32p. (J). (gr. k-3). 1991. lib. bdg. 16.95 (*0-8234-0884-1*) Holiday.

Picture Book of John F. Kennedy. David A. Adler. LC 90-23589. (Illus.). 32p. (J). (ps-3). 1992. pap. 6.95 (*0-8234-0976-7*) Holiday.

Picture Book of Kids' Crafts & Activities. Roxanne Henderson. LC 97-50344. (Illus.). 272p. (gr. k-7). 1998. pap. 14.95 (*0-8092-2968-4*, 296840, Contemporary Bks) NTC Contemp Pub Co.

Picture Book of Louis Braille. David A. Adler. LC 96-38453. (Illus.). 34p. (J). 1997. 16.95 (*0-8234-1291-1*) Holiday.

Picture Book of Louis Braille. David A. Adler. (Illus.). (J). (ps-3). 1997. pap. text 6.95 (*0-8234-1413-2*) Holiday.

Picture Book of Martin Luther King, Jr. see Libro Ilustrado Sobre Martin Luther King, Hijo

Picture Book of Martin Luther King, Jr. unabridged rev. ed. David Adler. (Illus.). (J). (gr. 2-4). 1998. 24.95 incl. audio (*0-87499-166-8*) Live Oak Media.

***Picture Book of Martin Luther King, Jr.; Un Libro Illustrado Sobe Martin Luther King, Hijo, 2 bks., Set.** unabridged ed. David Adler. Tr. by Teresa Mlawer. (J). 1999. pap. 29.95 incl. audio (*0-87499-569-8*) Live Oak Media.

Picture Book of Martin Luther King, Jr. David A. Adler. LC 89-1930. (Illus.). 32p. (J). (ps-3). 1989. lib. bdg. 16.95 (*0-8234-0770-5*) Holiday.

Picture Book of Martin Luther King, Jr. David A. Adler. LC 89-1930. (Illus.). 32p. (J). (ps-3). 1990. pap. 6.95 (*0-8234-0847-7*) Holiday.

Picture Book of Martin Luther King, Jr. unabridged rev. ed. David A. Adler. (Illus.). (J). (gr. 2-4). 1998. pap. 15.95 incl. audio (*0-87499-165-X*) Live Oak Media.

Picture Book of Martin Luther King, Jr., Set unabridged ed. David A. Adler. (Illus.). (J). (gr. 2-4). 1998. pap., teacher ed. 37.95 incl. audio (*0-87499-167-6*) Live Oak Media.

Picture Book of Niagara Falls. Pierre Berton. (Illus.). 160p. 1998. text 20.00 (*0-7881-5401-X*) DIANE Pub.

Picture Book of Night-Time Animals. Grace Mabie. LC 91-33597. (Picture Book of...Ser.). (Illus.). 24p. (J). (gr. 1-4). 1992. lib. bdg. 14.50 (*0-8167-2432-6*) Troll Communs.

Picture Book of Night-Time Animals. Grace Mabie. LC 91-33597. (Picture Book of...Ser.). (Illus.). 24p. (J). (gr. 1-4). 1997. pap. 2.95 (*0-8167-2433-4*) Troll Communs.

Picture Book of Old Massachusetts. Sam Tuttle, pseud. LC 91-46064. (Illus.). 143p. (Orig.). 1992. pap. 14.95 (*0-914166-24-7*) Americana Rev.

Picture Book of Patrick Henry. David A. Adler. LC 94-43849. (Illus.). 32p. (J). (gr. k-3). 1995. lib. bdg. 16.95 (*0-8234-1187-7*) Holiday.

P

Picture Book of Paul Revere. David A. Adler. LC 94-9783. (Illus.). 32p. (J). (gr. k-3). 1995. lib. bdg. 16.95 (*0-8234-1144-3*) Holiday.

Picture Book of Paul Revere. David A. Adler. (Illus.). (J). (gr. k-3). 1995. reprint ed. pap. text 6.95 (*0-8234-1294-6*) Holiday.

Picture Book of Prayers. Lawrence G. Lovasik. LC 97-221272. (Illus.). (J). 1994. 5.95 (*0-89942-265-9*, 265/22) Catholic Bk Pub.

Picture Book of Quantum Mechanics. 2nd ed. Siegmund Brandt & Hans D. Dahmen. LC 94-30916. (Illus.). 423p. 1995. 49.95 (*0-387-94380-3*) Spr-Verlag.

Picture Book of Reptiles & Amphibians. Mary Scott. LC 92-19054. (Picture Book of...Ser.). (Illus.). 24p. (J). (gr. 1-4). 1992. lib. bdg. 14.50 (*0-8167-2838-0*, BP090) Troll Communs.

Picture Book of Reptiles & Amphibians. Mary Scott. LC 92-19054. (Picture Book of...Ser.). (Illus.). 24p. (J). (gr. 1-4). 1996. pap. 2.95 (*0-8167-2839-9*) Troll Communs.

Picture Book of Robert E. Lee. David A. Adler. (Illus.). (J). 1994. pap. 6.95 (*0-8234-1366-7*) Holiday.

Picture Book of Robert E. Lee. David A. Adler. LC 93-22998. (Illus.). 32p. (J). (gr. k-3). 1994. lib. bdg. 16.95 (*0-8234-1111-7*) Holiday.

Picture Book of Rosa Parks. David A. Adler. LC 92-41826. (Illus.). 32p. (J). (ps-3). 1993. pap. 6.95 (*0-8234-1177-X*) Holiday.

Picture Book of Rosa Parks. David A. Adler. LC 92-41826. (Illus.). 32p. (J). (gr. k-3). 1993. lib. bdg. 16.95 (*0-8234-1041-2*) Holiday.

Picture Book of Rosa Parks. unabridged ed. David A. Adler. (J). (ps-2). 1997. 24.95 incl. audio (*0-87499-397-0*); pap. 15.95 incl. audio (*0-87499-396-2*) Live Oak Media.

Picture Book of Rosa Parks, 4 bks., Set. unabridged ed. David A. Adler. (J). (ps-2). 1997. pap., teacher ed. 37.95 incl. audio (*0-87499-398-9*) Live Oak Media.

***Picture Book of Sacagawea.** Illus. by David A. Adler & Dan Brown. LC 99-37135. (Picture Book Biography Ser.). 32p. (J). (gr. k-3). 2000. 16.95 (*0-8234-1485-X*) Holiday.

Picture Book of Saints. Lawrence G. Lovasik. (Illus.). (J). 1988. 7.95 (*0-89942-235-7*, 235/22) Catholic Bk Pub.

Picture Book of San Antonio. David Bowen. (Illus.). 32p. (J). 1978. pap. 6.95 (*0-931722-02-0*) Corona Pub.

Picture Book of Simon Bolivar. David A. Adler. LC 91-19419. (Illus.). 32p. (J). (ps-3). 1992. lib. bdg. 16.95 (*0-8234-0927-9*) Holiday.

Picture Book of Sojourner Truth. David A. Adler. LC 93-7478. (Illus.). 32p. (J). (gr. k-3). 1994. lib. bdg. 16.95 (*0-8234-1072-2*) Holiday.

Picture Book of Sojourner Truth. David A. Adler. (Illus.). 32p. (J). (ps-3). 1994. pap. 6.95 (*0-8234-1262-8*) Holiday.

Picture Book of Swamp & Marsh Animals. Theresa Grace. LC 91-16034. (Picture Book of...Ser.). (Illus.). 24p. (J). (gr. 1-4). 1992. lib. bdg. 14.50 (*0-8167-2434-2*) Troll Communs.

Picture Book of Swamp & Marsh Animals. Theresa Grace. LC 91-16034. (Picture Book of...Ser.). (Illus.). 24p. (J). (gr. 1-4). 1996. pap. 2.95 (*0-8167-2435-0*) Troll Communs.

Picture Book of the Graphic Arts: Thirty-Five Hundred Woodcuts, Etchings, & Engravings by the Masters 1500-1800, 6 vols. Georg Hirth. Tr. by Elena Tanasescu. LC 68-56472. (Illus.). 1972. reprint ed. 399.95 (*0-405-08624-5*, Pub. by Blom Pubns) Ayer.

Picture Book of the Graphic Arts: Thirty-Five Hundred Woodcuts, Etchings, & Engravings by the Masters 1500-1800, 6 vols., 1. Georg Hirth. Tr. by Elena Tanasescu. LC 68-56472. (Illus.). 1972. reprint ed. 72.95 (*0-405-08625-3*, Pub. by Blom Pubns) Ayer.

Picture Book of the Graphic Arts: Thirty-Five Hundred Woodcuts, Etchings, & Engravings by the Masters 1500-1800, 6 vols., Vol. 2. Georg Hirth. Tr. by Elena Tanasescu. LC 68-56472. (Illus.). 1972. reprint ed. 72.95 (*0-405-08626-1*, Pub. by Blom Pubns) Ayer.

Picture Book of the Graphic Arts: Thirty-Five Hundred Woodcuts, Etchings, & Engravings by the Masters 1500-1800, 6 vols., Vol. 3. Georg Hirth. Tr. by Elena Tanasescu. LC 68-56472. (Illus.). 1972. reprint ed. 72.95 (*0-405-08627-X*, Pub. by Blom Pubns) Ayer.

Picture Book of the Graphic Arts: Thirty-Five Hundred Woodcuts, Etchings, & Engravings by the Masters 1500-1800, 6 vols., Vol. 4. Georg Hirth. Tr. by Elena Tanasescu. LC 68-56472. (Illus.). 1972. reprint ed. 72.95 (*0-405-08628-8*, Pub. by Blom Pubns) Ayer.

Picture Book of the Graphic Arts: Thirty-Five Hundred Woodcuts, Etchings, & Engravings by the Masters 1500-1800, 6 vols., Vol. 5. Georg Hirth. Tr. by Elena Tanasescu. LC 68-56472. (Illus.). 1972. reprint ed. 72.95 (*0-405-08629-6*, Pub. by Blom Pubns) Ayer.

Picture Book of the Graphic Arts: Thirty-Five Hundred Woodcuts, Etchings, & Engravings by the Masters 1500-1800, 6 vols., Vol. 6. Georg Hirth. Tr. by Elena Tanasescu. LC 68-56472. (Illus.). 1972. reprint ed. 72.95 (*0-405-08630-X*, Pub. by Blom Pubns) Ayer.

Picture Book of the Revolution's Privateers see Pirates & Patriots of the Revolution: An Illustrated Encyclopedia of Colonial Seamanship

Picture Book of Thomas Alva Edison. David A. Adler. LC 95-42533. (Illus.). (ps-3). 1996. pap. 6.95 (*0-8234-1414-0*) Holiday.

Picture Book of Thomas Jefferson. David A. Adler. LC 89-20076. (Illus.). 32p. (J). (gr. k-3). 1990. lib. bdg. 16.95 (*0-8234-0791-8*) Holiday.

Picture Book of Thomas Jefferson. David A. Adler. LC 89-20076. (Illus.). 32p. (J). (ps-3). 1991. pap. 6.95 (*0-8234-0881-7*) Holiday.

Picture Book of Thurgood Marshall. David A. Adler. LC 96-37248. (Illus.). (ps-3). 1997. pap. 6.95 (*0-8234-1506-6*) Holiday.

Picture Book of Thurgood Marshall. David A. Adler. LC 96-37248. (Picture Book Biographies Ser.). (Illus.). 32p. (J). (gr. k-3). 1997. lib. bdg. 16.95 (*0-8234-1308-X*) Holiday.

Picture Book of Underwater Life. Theresa Grace. LC 89-37330. (Picture Book of...Ser.). (Illus.). 24p. (J). (gr. 1-4). 1990. lib. bdg. 14.50 (*0-8167-1906-3*) Troll Communs.

Picture Book of Underwater Life. Theresa Grace. LC 89-37330. (Picture Book of...Ser.). (Illus.). 24p. (J). (gr. 1-4). 1996. pap. 2.95 (*0-8167-1907-1*) Troll Communs.

Picture Book of Unseen Things. Ernest Young. LC 95-206570. (Illus.). 96p. (Orig.). (C). 1995. 15.00 (*1-883893-10-0*) WinePress Pub.

Picture Book of Vaseline Glass. Sue C. Davis. LC 98-83237. (Illus.). 160p. 1999. 29.95 (*0-7643-0830-0*) Schiffer.

Picture Book of Water Birds. Grace Mabie. LC 91-34129. (Picture Book of...Ser.). (Illus.). 24p. (J). (gr. 1-4). 1992. lib. bdg. 14.50 (*0-8167-2436-9*) Troll Communs.

Picture Book of Wild Animals. Joanne Gise. LC 89-37334. (Picture Book of...Ser.). (Illus.). 24p. (J). (gr. 1-4). 1990. lib. bdg. 14.50 (*0-8167-1908-X*) Troll Communs.

Picture Book of Wild Animals. Joanne Gise. LC 89-37334. (Picture Book of...Ser.). (Illus.). 24p. (J). (gr. 1-4). 1996. pap. 2.95 (*0-8167-1909-8*) Troll Communs.

Picture Book of Wild Cats. Mary Scott. LC 91-16500. (Picture Book of...Ser.). (Illus.). 24p. (J). (gr. 1-4). 1992. lib. bdg. 14.50 (*0-8167-2430-X*) Troll Communs.

Picture Book of Wild Cats. Mary Scott. LC 91-16500. (Picture Book of...Ser.). (Illus.). 24p. (J). (gr. 1-4). 1997. pap. 2.95 (*0-8167-2431-8*) Troll Communs.

Picture Book Story Hours: From Birthdays to Bears. Paula G. Sitarz. LC 86-21439. xii, 190p. 1986. pap. text 18.50 (*0-87287-556-3*) Libs Unl.

Picture-Book Two in Arabic. (Ladybird Stories Ser.). (ARA., Illus.). 52p. (J). (gr. 1-3). 1987. 4.95 (*0-86685-215-8*) Intl Bk Ctr.

Picture Books for Children. 4th ed. Patricia J. Cianciolo. LC 96-51538. (Illus.). 288p. 1997. 40.00 (*0-8389-0701-6*) ALA.

Picture Books for Looking & Learning: Awakening Visual Perceptions Through the Art of Children's Books. Sylvia S. Marantz. LC 92-14953. 216p. 1992. pap. 26.50 (*0-89774-716-X*) Oryx Pr.

***Picture Books for the Literacy Hour: Activities for Primary Teachers.** Guy Merchant. (Illus.). 1999. pap. 27.95 (*1-85346-627-1*) David Fulton.

Picture Books in the Primary School Classroom. Stuart Marriott. 160p. 1991. pap. 27.00 (*1-85396-144-2*, Pub. by P Chapman) Taylor & Francis.

Picture Books Strategies for a Balanced Reading Program K-3. Nancy Polette. (Illus.). 112p. 1998. pap. 13.95 (*1-880505-40-1*, CLC0224) Pieces of Lrning.

Picture Books to Enhance the Curriculum. Jeanne M. Harms & Lucille Lettow. LC 94-42653. 522p. 1996. lib. bdg. 38.00 (*0-8242-0867-6*) Wilson.

Picture Bride. Cathy Song. LC 82-48910. (Younger Poets Ser.: No. 78). 89p. 1983. pap. 12.00 (*0-300-02969-1*) Yale U Pr.

Picture Bride. Yoshiko Uchida. LC 97-3. 222p. 1997. reprint ed. pap. 14.95 (*0-295-97616-0*) U of Wash Pr.

Picture Cape Town: Landmarks of a New Generation. Getty Conservation Institute Staff. LC 96-27589. (Getty Trust Publications). (Illus.). 120p. (Orig.). 1997. pap. 19.95 (*0-89236-444-0*, Pub. by J P Getty Trust) OUP.

Picture Catechism Explained. Theodore Hartwig. (Illus.). 98p. (Orig.). 1994. pap. 4.95 (*1-890600-00-8*) M L College.

***Picture Chord Encyclopedia: Photos & Diagrams for 2,600 Guitar Chords!** 272p. 2000. otabind 19.95 (*0-7935-8491-4*) H Leonard.

Picture Chords for Guitar. 2nd ed. Harry Reser. Ed. by Aaron Stang. 60p. (Orig.). (C). 1981. pap. text 7.95 (*0-7692-1345-6*, GF0195) Wrner Bros.

Picture Collections in Mexico: A Guide to Picture Sources in the United Mexican States. Martha Davidson. LC 87-28475. (Illus.). 346p. 1988. 70.00 (*0-8108-2074-9*) Scarecrow.

Picture Communication Symbols, Bk. 1. 5th ed. Roxanna M. Johnson. (Illus.). 108p. 1982. ring bd. 45.00 (*0-9609160-0-8*) Mayer-Johnson.

Picture Communication Symbols, Bk. III. Roxanna M. Johnson. (Illus.). 184p. 1992. ring bd. 49.00 (*0-9609160-7-5*) Mayer-Johnson.

Picture Communication Symbols Book, Bk. II. Roxanna M. Johnson. (Illus.). 142p. 1985. ring bd. 49.00 (*0-9609160-1-6*) Mayer-Johnson.

Picture Communication Symbols Combination Book. Roxanna M. Johnson. (Illus.). 1994. ring bd. 119.00 (*1-884135-12-9*) Mayer-Johnson.

Picture Communication Symbols Combination Book: Wordless Edition. Roxanna M. Johnson. (Illus.). 378p. 1995. spiral bd. 99.00 (*1-884135-14-5*) Mayer-Johnson.

Picture Communication Symbols Guide. Roxanna M. Johnson. (Illus.). 60p. (Orig.). 1995. pap. 9.00 (*1-884135-15-3*) Mayer-Johnson.

Picture Communication Symbols "Wordless Edition" Roxanna M. Johnson. (Illus.). 240p. 1989. spiral bd. 60.00 (*0-9609160-4-0*) Mayer-Johnson.

Picture Composition: French. Edward S. Jenkins & Barbara Whelpton. 1989. pap. text 7.65 (*0-582-22461-6*, 70937) Longman.

Picture Composition for Film & Television. Peter Ward. (Illus.). 192p. 1995. pap. 44.95 (*0-240-51421-1*, Focal) Buttrwrth-Heinemann.

Picture Compression with JPEG. Ronald Boucher. (C). 1995. text. write for info. (*0-201-52885-1*) Addison-Wesley.

Picture Control: The Electron Microscope & the Transformation of Biology in America, 1940-1960. Nicolas Rasmussen. LC 97-1230. (Writing Science Ser.). 424p. 1997. 55.00 (*0-8047-2837-2*) Stanford U Pr.

***Picture Control: The Electron Microscope & the Transformation of Biology in America, 1940-1960.** Nicolas Rasmussen. 1999. 24.95 (*0-8047-3850-5*) Stanford U Pr.

***Picture Crossword Puzzles.** Deb T. Bunnell. (Illus.). (J). 1999. pap. 2.95 (*0-486-40798-5*) Dover.

Picture Crosswords: An Educational Activity-Coloring Book. Spizzirri Publishing Co. Staff. Ed. by Linda Spizzirr. (Illus.). 32p. (J). (gr. 1-8). 1986. pap. 1.99 (*0-86545-081-1*) Spizzirri.

Picture Crosswords: Early Learning Workbooks. Peter M. Spizzirri. Ed. by Linda Spizzirri. (Illus.). 32p. (J). (ps-2). 1997. pap. 2.95 (*0-86545-238-5*) Spizzirri.

Picture Descriptions in Russian. Elfimov Gennadi & Brian Lehmann. (RUS., Illus.). 64p. (Orig.). (YA). (gr. 7 up). 1993. pap. 39.00 (*0-939990-88-1*) Intl Linguistics.

Picture Dictionary: An Educational Coloring Book. Spizzirri Publishing Co. Staff. Ed. by Linda Spizzirri. (Illus.). 32p. (J). (gr. 1-8). 1982. pap. 1.99 (*0-86545-049-8*) Spizzirri.

Picture Dictionary: Early Learning Workbooks. Peter M. Spizzirri. Ed. by Linda Spizzirri. (Illus.). 32p. (J). (ps-2). 1997. pap. 2.95 (*0-86545-239-3*) Spizzirri.

Picture Dictionary: More Than 35 Real-life Scene; More than 650 every-day words. Ed. by Scholastic, Inc. Staff. (Illus.). 96p. (ps-2). 1999. pap. text 6.95 (*0-590-03547-9*) Scholastic Inc.

***Picture Dictionary: More Than 35 Real-Life Scenes: More Than 650 Every-Day Words.** Scholastic, Inc. Staff. (Hello, Reader! Ser.). (Illus.). (J). 1999. 12.30 (*0-606-18558-5*) Turtleback.

Picture Dictionary & Guide for Tutors see Shared Umbrella Series: Set 1

Picture Dictionary English/Spanish. Berlitz Kids Editors. (Berlitz Kids Ser.). (SPA., Illus.). 128p. 1998. pap. text 16.95 (*2-8315-6253-8*) Berlitz.

Picture Dictionary for Young Learners. Wright. (Illus.). 1991. pap. text. write for info. (*0-17-556879-0*) Addison-Wesley.

Picture Dictionary French/English. Berlitz Kids Editors. LC 98-221215. (Berlitz Kids Ser.). (FRE., Illus.). 128p. 1998. pap. text 16.95 (*2-8315-6254-6*) Berlitz.

Picture Dictionary German/English. Berlitz Kids Editors. LC 98-221213. (Berlitz Kids Ser.). (GER., Illus.). 128p. 1998. pap. text 16.95 (*2-8315-6255-4*) Berlitz.

Picture Dictionary in Six Languages Vol. I: Cantonese, English, Korean, Russian, Spanish, Vietnamese. Claudia Schwalm. (Picture Dictionary Ser.). 89p. (J). (gr. k-6). 1994. 65.00 incl. audio (*0-9636629-8-8*) Cultural Cnnect.

Picture Dictionary in Six Languages Vol. II: Cambodian, English, French, Hmong, Japanese, Tagalog. Claudia Schwalm. (Picture Dictionary Ser.). 89p. (J). (gr. k-6). 1994. vinyl bd. 65.00 incl. audio (*0-9636629-9-6*) Cultural Cnnect.

Picture Dictionary Italian/English. Berlitz Kids Editors. (Berlitz Kids Ser.). (ITA., Illus.). 128p. 1998. pap. text 16.95 (*2-8315-6256-2*) Berlitz.

Picture Dictionary Skills Book. Kelly. 64p. 1986. spiral bd. 10.07 (*0-201-09601-3*) Addison-Wesley.

Picture Dictionary Spanish/English. Berlitz Kids Editors. LC 97-36273. (Berlitz Kids Ser.). (SPA., Illus.). 128p. 1998. pap. text 16.95 (*2-8315-6257-0*) Berlitz.

***Picture Dorian Gray.** (Penguin Readers Ser.: Level 4). (C). 2000. pap. 7.00 (*0-582-41808-9*) Pearson Educ.

***Picture Editing.** 2nd ed. Tom Ang. (Illus.). 288p. 2000. pap. 47.95 (*0-240-51618-4*, Focal) Buttrwrth-Heinemann.

Picture Editing. 2nd ed. Tom Ang. LC 97-944. (Illus.). 240p. 2000. pap. text 36.95 (*0-240-51469-6*, Focal) Buttrwrth-Heinemann.

Picture Editing & Layout: A Guide to Better Visual Communication. Angus McDougall & Veita J. Hampton. LC 89-51942. (Illus.). 300p. 1990. text 27.50 (*0-9625137-0-9*) Viscom Pr.

Picture Engineering. Ed. by K. S. Fu & Toshiyasu L. Kunii. (Information Sciences Ser.: Vol. 6). (Illus.). 320p. 1982. 72.95 (*0-387-11822-5*) Spr-Verlag.

Picture Folk-Tales. Valery Carick. Orig. Title: Valery Carick's Picture Folk-Tales. (Illus.). vi, 90p. (J). 1992. reprint ed. pap. 1.00 (*0-486-27083-1*) Dover.

Picture for Harold's Room. Crockett Johnson. (I Can Read Bks.). (Illus.). (J). (ps-1). 1960. 6.93 (*0-06-023005-3*, 495817) HarpC.

Picture for Harold's Room. Crockett Johnson. LC 60-6372. (I Can Read Bks.). (Illus.). (J). (gr. k-3). 1960. lib. bdg. 15.89 (*0-06-023006-1*) HarpC Child Bks.

Picture for Harold's Room. Crockett Johnson. LC 60-6372. (I Can Read Bks.). (Illus.). 64p. (J). (ps-3). 1985. pap. 3.95 (*0-06-444085-0*, HarpTrophy) HarpC Child Bks.

Picture for Harold's Room. Crockett Johnson. (I Can Read Bks.). (J). (ps-1). 1985. 8.95 (*0-606-00383-5*, Pub. by Turtleback) Demco.

Picture for Patti. Linda K. Garvey. (Doug Chronicles: No. 3). (Illus.). 64p. (J). (gr. 2-4). 1998. pap. 3.99 (*0-7868-4236-9*, Pub. by Disney Pr) Time Warner.

***Picture Frame & Other Stories.** Robert Drake. 208p. 2000. 23.00 (*0-86554-689-4*) Mercer Univ Pr.

Picture Frames. Thyra S. Winslow. LC 73-145379. 1971. reprint ed. 19.00 (*0-403-01282-1*) Scholarly.

Picture Frames in an Afternoon. Kaye Evans. LC 98-52818. (Illus.). 112p. 1999. 22.95 (*0-8069-3947-8*) Sterling.

Picture Framing. Fay Boon. 1995. 7.98 (*0-7858-0316-5*) Bk Sales Inc.

Picture Framing. Moyra Byford. 96p. 1996. pap. text 11.95 (*1-56799-262-5*, Friedman-Fairfax) M Friedman Pub Grp Inc.

Picture Framing. Rian Kanduth. (New Crafts Collection). 1999. 16.95 (*0-7548-0189-6*, Lorenz Bks) Anness Pub.

Picture Framing. Ilona Sherratt. LC 96-1556. (Bulletin Ser.: No. A-153). 1996. pap. 2.95 (*0-88266-512-X*, Storey Pub) Storey Bks.

Picture Framing. rev. ed. Vivian C. Kistler. LC 86-72676. (Library of Professional Picture Framing: Vol. 1). (Illus.). 96p. 1998. pap. text 19.00 (*0-938655-11-6*) Columba Pub.

Picture Framing: A Manual of Techniques. David Scholes. (Illus.). 160p. 1996. 35.00 (*1-85223-879-8*, Pub. by Cro1wood) Trafalgar.

Picture Framing: A Practical Guide. Robert Self. (Illus.). 120p. 1987. 15.95 (*0-900873-42-6*, Pub. by Bishopsgte Pr); pap. 11.95 (*0-900873-43-4*, Pub. by Bishopsgte Pr) Intl Spec Bk.

Picture Framing Basics. Hugh Foster. LC 96-37955. (Illus.). 128p. 1997. pap. 10.95 (*0-8069-0646-4*) Sterling.

Picture Framing Course. Pete Bingham. 1997. 24.95 (*0-8117-1246-X*) Stackpole.

Picture Framing Made Easy. Penelope Stokes. (Illus.). 128p. 1996. 27.95 (*0-304-34523-7*, Pub. by Cassell) Sterling.

Picture Framing Made Easy. Penelope Stokes. (Illus.). 128p. 1998. pap. 16.95 (*0-304-34952-6*, Pub. by Cassell) Sterling.

Picture Framing Techniques. 1995. 5.98 (*0-7858-0401-3*) Bk Sales Inc.

Picture Guide to Chess. Paul Langfield. LC 75-46637. (J). (gr. 5-9). 1977. 11.50 (*0-397-31681-X*) HarpC Child Bks.

Picture Guide to Rock 'n Roll Drums. Joel Rothman. (Illus.). 32p. 1980. pap. 8.95 (*0-86001-739-7*, AM26337) Music Sales.

***Picture History.** Miller. (Illus.). 2000. pap. 14.95 (*0-486-40967-8*) Dover.

Picture History of Aviation on Long Island, 1908-1938. 38th ed. George C. Dade. (Illus.). 160p. 1998. pap. 13.95 (*0-486-26008-9*) Dover.

Picture History of Early Aviation, 1903-1913. Joshua Stoff. (Illus.). 128p. (Orig.). 1996. pap. text 12.95 (*0-486-28836-6*) Dover.

Picture History of Great Inventors. Gillian Clements. LC 93-21705. (J). 1994. pap. 13.00 (*0-679-84787-1*, Pub. by Knopf Bks Yng Read) Random.

Picture History of the America's Cup. John Rousmaniere et al. 1989. 39.95 (*0-393-02819-4*) Norton.

Picture History of the Boston Celtics. George A. Sullivan. LC 82-4129. (Illus.). 1982. pap. 14.95 (*0-672-52728-6*) Sams.

Picture History of the Brooklyn Bridge. Mary J. Shapiro. LC 82-9506. (New York City Ser.). (Illus.). 96p. (Orig.). 1983. pap. 9.95 (*0-486-24403-2*) Dover.

Picture History of the Cunard Line, 1840-1990, Vol. 199. Frank O. Braynard. (Illus.). 144p. 1991. pap. 14.95 (*0-486-26550-1*) Dover.

Picture History of the French Line. William H. Miller, Jr. LC 97-5791. (Illus.). 128p. (Orig.). 1997. pap. text 13.95 (*0-486-29443-9*) Dover.

Picture History of the Italian Line, 1932-1977. William H. Miller, Jr. LC 99-33035. (Illus.). 128p. 1999. pap. text 14.95 (*0-486-40489-7*) Dover.

Picture History of the "Normandie" Frank O. Braynard. (Illus.). 144p. 1987. pap. 12.95 (*0-486-25257-4*) Dover.

Picture History of World War II & American Aircraft Production. Joshua Stoff. LC 93-15726. (Illus.). 160p. (Orig.). 1993. pap. 13.95 (*0-486-27618-X*) Dover.

Picture House in East Anglia. Stephen Pearl. 192p. (C). 1988. 60.00 (*0-900963-56-5*, Pub. by T Dalton) St Mut.

Picture, Image & Experience: A Philosophical Inquiry. Robert Hopkins. LC 98-4543. (Illus.). 215p. (C). 1999. text 59.95 (*0-521-58259-8*) Cambridge U Pr.

Picture in Question. Taylor. LC 98-34761. 1999. pap. text 12.00 (*0-226-79129-7*); lib. bdg. 30.00 (*0-226-79128-9*) U Ch Pr.

Picture Interpretation: A Symbolic Approach, Vol. 20. Z. Q. Liu & T. Caelli. LC 96-113789. (Series in Machine Perception & Artificial Intelligence). 152p. 1995. text 28.00 (*981-02-2402-8*) World Scientific Pub.

Picture Is Worth a Thousand Words. 216p. (C). 1995. pap. text 18.95 (*0-9647437-6-0*) RFT Pubng.

Picture Is Worth 62 Words. Illus. by Joie Cook & Redo. 36p. 1998. pap. 4.95 (*1-893084-04-3*) Benway Inst.

Picture It. Ed. by John Dumicich. (Illus.). 208p. (YA). (gr. 10-12). 1987. pap. text 19.40 (*0-13-676149-6*, 18677) Prentice ESL.

Picture It in Cross-Stitch. Jo Verso. (Illus.). 128p. 1989. pap. 14.95 (*0-7153-9485-1*, Pub. by D & C Pub) Sterling.

Picture-Journey along the Pennsylvania Main Line Canal. Ed. by William H. Shank & Philip J. Hoffman. (Illus.). 80p. 1993. pap. 15.00 (*0-933788-84-3*) Am Canal & Transport.

Picture Journeys in Alaska's Wrangell-St. Elias: America's Largest National Park. George Herben. LC F912.W74 H47 1997. (Illus.). 128p. 1997. 35.95 (*0-88240-496-2*, Alaska NW Bks) Gr Arts Ctr Pub.

Picture L. A. Landmarks of a New Generation. Jeffrey Levin. LC 94-31176. (Illus.). 120p. (Orig.). 1994. pap. 19.95 (*0-89236-305-3*, Pub. by J P Getty Trust) OUP.

***Picture Letters: Using Visual Links to Remember Letter Names.** Betty LaPointe. Ed. by Kristy Shine & Don LaPointe. (Illus.). 30p. (C). 1999. pap. 25.00 (*0-9674918-1-9*) Litracy Links CT.

Picture Librarianship. Ed. by Helen P. Harrison. LC 81-149552. (Handbooks on Library Practice). 554p. reprint ed. pap. 171.80 (*0-7837-5322-5*, 204506100005) Bks Demand.

Picture Makers. large type ed. Emily Ellison. (General Ser.). 362p. 1991. lib. bdg. 20.95 (*0-8161-5166-0*, G K Hall Lrg Type) Mac Lib Ref.

An Asterisk (*) at the beginning of an entry indicates that the title is appearing for the first time.

Picture Making. Philip Brown. 1989. pap. 39.00 (*1-873812-00-0*, Pub. by Icon Pr) St Mut.

Picture-Making by Photography. 5th ed. Henry P. Robinson. LC 72-9230. (Literature of Photography Ser.). 1973. reprint ed. 18.95 (*0-405-04936-6*) Ayer.

Picture Man: Photographs by Paul Buchanan. Ed. by Ann Hawthorne. LC 93-7368. (Illus.). xxiv, 126p. 1993. pap. 14.95 (*0-8078-4431-4*) U of NC Pr.

Picture Math: Drawing to Solve Problems. (Wipe-Off Activity Bks.). (Illus.). 16p. (J). (gr. k-2). 1997. wbk. ed. 3.79 (*1-889319-21-X*) Trend Enterprises.

***Picture Me As a Ballerina.** rev. ed. Deborah D'Andrea. (Illus.). 10p. (J). (ps-1). 2000. bds. 5.99 (*1-57151-575-5*) Picture Me Bks.

***Picture Me As a Bunny.** rev. ed. Deborah D'Andrea. (Illus.). 10p. (J). (ps-1). 2000. bds. 5.99 (*1-57151-577-1*) Picture Me Bks.

***Picture Me As a Firefighter.** rev. ed. Deborah D'Andrea. (Illus.). 10p. (J). (ps-1). 2000. bds. 5.99 (*1-57151-583-6*) Picture Me Bks.

***Picture Me As a Pirate.** rev. ed. Deborah D'Andrea. (Illus.). 10p. (J). (ps-1). 2000. bds. 5.99 (*1-57151-578-X*) Picture Me Bks.

***Picture Me As a Reindeer.** Deborah D'Andrea. (Illus.). 10p. (J). (ps-1). 1999. bds. 5.99 (*1-57151-580-1*) Picture Me Bks.

Picture Me As Goldilocks. Dandi. LC 97-229323. (Fairy Tale Ser.). (Illus.). 8p. (Orig.). (J). (ps-1). 1997. bds. 6.99 (*1-57151-529-1*, 1-57151-529-1) Picture Me Bks.

Picture Me As Jack & the Beanstalk. Dandi. LC 97-229317. (Fairy Tale Ser.). (Illus.). 8p. (Orig.). (J). (ps-1). 1997. bds. 6.99 (*1-57151-531-3*, 1-57151-531-3) Picture Me Bks.

Picture Me As Little Bo Peep & Other Nursery Rhymes. Illus. by Wendy Rasmussen. 8p. (Orig.). (J). (ps-2). 1999. bds. 6.99 (*1-57151-543-7*) Picture Me Bks.

Picture Me As Little Red Riding Hood. Dandi. LC 97-229320. (Fairy Tale Ser.). (Illus.). 8p. (Orig.). (J). (ps-1). 1997. bds. 6.99 (*1-57151-530-5*, 1-57151-530-5) Picture Me Bks.

Picture Me As Yankee Doodle Dandy & Other Nursery Rhymes. Illus. by Wendy Rasmussen. 8p. (Orig.). (J). (ps-2). 1999. bds. 6.99 (*1-57151-544-5*) Picture Me Bks.

Picture Me at My Party with Mickey & Friends. Catherine McCafferty. (Picture Me Disney Ser.). (Illus.). 8p. (J). (ps-3). 1997. bds. 6.99 (*1-57151-540-2*) Picture Me Bks.

Picture Me at the First Christmas. Dandi. (Inspirational Picture Me Ser.). (Illus.). 8p. (J). (ps-k). 1997. bds. 6.99 (*1-57151-534-8*) Picture Me Bks.

***Picture Me Counting 1 - 2 - 3.** rev. ed. Deborah D'Andrea. (Illus.). 10p. (J). (ps-1). 2000. bds. 5.99 (*1-57151-581-X*) Picture Me Bks.

Picture Me Cute As Can Bee. Ed. by J. Thompson & R. McGovern. (Illus.). 10p. (J). (ps-k). 1998. bds. 6.99 (*1-57151-546-1*) Picture Me Bks.

Picture Me Dancing with Minnie Mouse. Catherine McCafferty. (Picture Me Disney Ser.). (Illus.). 8p. (J). (ps-k). 1997. bds. 6.99 (*1-57151-538-0*) Picture Me Bks.

Picture Me Famous. Lisa Simon & Peter Landesman. (Full House Stephanie Ser.). 144p. (J). (gr. 4-6). 1995. per. 3.99 (*0-671-52276-0*) PB.

***Picture Me Grown-Up.** Ed. by Jennifer Thompson. (Illus.). 10p. (J). (ps-3). 1999. bds. 7.99 (*1-57151-576-3*) Picture Me Bks.

Picture Me Having Trick or Treat Fun. Ed. by Roxanne McGovern. (Illus.). 8p. (J). (ps-k). 1998. bds. 6.99 (*1-57151-548-8*) Picture Me Bks.

Picture Me in a Poem: Poetry by Jeanette Adams. 2nd ed. Jeanette Adams. (Illus.). 20p. (gr. k-8). 1980. pap. 5.00 (*0-9627018-1-5*) J Adams Pubns.

***Picture Me in the Circus.** Ed. by Jennifer Thompson. (Illus.). 10p. (J). (ps-3). 2000. bds. 6.99 (*1-57151-586-0*) Picture Me Bks.

***Picture Me in the Future.** Craig Strasshofer. (Illus.). 10p. (J). (ps-3). 2000. bds. 7.99 (*1-57151-585-2*) Picture Me Bks.

***Picture Me Learning Letters A, B, C.** rev. ed. Deborah D'Andrea. (Illus.). 10p. (J). (ps-1). 2000. bds. 5.99 (*1-57151-582-8*) Picture Me Bks.

Picture Me Married? A Personalized of Nuptial Bliss. Aaron Sutherland. LC 96-163819. (Illus.). 24p. 1995. pap. 7.95 (*1-57151-502-X*) Picture Me Bks.

Picture Me on Halloween. Dandi. (Picture Me Holiday Ser.). (Illus.). 8p. (J). (ps-3). 1997. bds. 6.99 (*1-57151-536-4*) Picture Me Bks.

Picture Me on Noah's Ark. Dandi. (Illus.). 8p. (J). (ps-k). 1997. bds. 6.99 (*1-57151-532-1*) Picture Me Bks.

Picture Me on Santa's Knee. Dandi. (Picture Me Holiday Ser.). (Illus.). 8p. (J). (ps-k). 1997. bds. 6.99 (*1-57151-537-2*) Picture Me Bks.

Picture Me on Vacation with Mickey Mouse. Catherine McCafferty. (Picture Me Disney Ser.). (Illus.). 8p. (J). (ps-k). 1997. bds. 6.99 (*1-57151-539-9*) Picture Me Bks.

***Picture Me Playing Baseball.** rev. ed. Joseph D'Andrea. (Illus.). 10p. (J). (ps-1). 2000. bds. 5.99 (*1-57151-584-4*) Picture Me Bks.

Picture Me Pregnant? A Personalized Tale of Impending Motherhood. Aaron Sutherland. LC 96-163802. (Illus.). 24p. 1995. pap. 7.95 (*1-57151-500-3*) Picture Me Bks.

Picture Me Telephone Book see My 9-1-1 Telephone Book

Picture Me under the Christmas Tree. Ed. by J. Thompson. (Illus.). 8p. (J). (ps-k). 1998. bds. 6.99 (*1-57151-547-X*) Picture Me Bks.

Picture Me with Grandma. Joseph C. D'Andrea. (Illus.). 8p. (Orig.). (J). (ps-2). 1998. bds. 6.99 (*1-57151-545-3*) Picture Me Bks.

Picture Me with Jonah & the Whale. Dandi. (Inspirational Picture Me Ser.). (Illus.). 8p. (J). (ps-k). 1997. bds. 6.99 (*1-57151-533-X*) Picture Me Bks.

Picture Me with My Friend Jesus: Boy Version. Dandi. (Illus.). 8p. (Orig.). (J). (ps-2). 1998. bds. 6.99 (*1-57151-541-0*) Picture Me Bks.

Picture Me with My Friend Jesus: Girl Version. Dandi. (Illus.). 8p. (Orig.). (J). (ps-2). 1998. bds. 6.99 (*1-57151-542-9*) Picture Me Bks.

***Picture Me with My Grandpa.** Catherine McCafferty. (Illus.). 10p. (J). (ps-1). 2000. bds. 6.99 (*1-57151-579-8*) Picture Me Bks.

Picture Me with the Easter Bunny. Dandi. (Picture Me Holiday Ser.). (Illus.). 8p. (J). (ps-k). 1997. bds. 6.99 (*1-57151-535-6*) Picture Me Bks.

Picture Me Working? A Personalized Tale of Postgraduate Semi-Employment. Aaron Sutherland. LC 96-163827. (Illus.). 24p. 1995. pap. 7.95 (*1-57151-501-1*) Picture Me Bks.

Picture Mexico City. LC 97-18231. 128p. 1997. pap. text 19.95 (*0-89236-490-4*, Pub. by J P Getty Trust) OUP.

Picture Mumbai: Landmarks of a New Generation. Getty Conservation Institute. LC 96-48666. (Illus.). 120p. (Orig.). 1997. pap. 19.95 (*0-89236-464-5*, Pub. by J P Getty Trust) OUP.

Picture Nouns: Word & Picture Flash Cards for Beginning Readers & ESL. Edward Fry. (Illus.). 48p. (Orig.). (J). (gr. k-2). 1996. pap. 5.95 (*0-87673-035-7*) Tchr Create Mat.

Picture of a Papist: Whereunto Is Annexed a Certain Treatise, Intituled Pagano-Papismus. Oliver Ormerod. LC 74-28878. (English Experience Ser.: No. 756). 1975. reprint ed. 35.00 (*90-221-0756-6*) Walter J Johnson.

Picture of a Puritane: or a Relation of the Opinions - of the Anabaptists in Germanie & of the Puritanes in England. Oliver Ormerod. LC 74-28879. (English Experience Ser.: No. 757). 1975. reprint ed. 35.00 (*90-221-0757-4*) Walter J Johnson.

***Picture of Dorian Gray.** Cliffs Notes Staff. (Cliffs Notes Ser.). 85p. 1999. 4.95 (*0-7645-8506-1*) IDG Bks.

Picture of Dorian Gray. Estelle Kleinman. Ed. by Joyce Friedland & Rikki Kessler. (Novel-Ties Ser.). (YA). (gr. 9-12). 1993. pap. text, student ed. 15.95 (*0-88122-123-6*) Lrn Links.

Picture of Dorian Gray. Oscar Wilde. 172p. 1964. pap. 44.95 (*3-418-00018-5*) Adlers Foreign Bks.

Picture of Dorian Gray. Oscar Wilde. Ed. by Norman Page. 279p. 1998. pap. 9.95 (*1-55111-126-8*) Broadview Pr.

Picture of Dorian Gray. Oscar Wilde. 240p. 1998. 7.95 (*3-89508-098-5*) Konemann.

Picture of Dorian Gray. Oscar Wilde. LC 98-5466. 1998. pap. 7.95 (*0-375-75151-3*) Modern Lib NY.

Picture of Dorian Gray. Oscar Wilde. 1997. pap. 2.95 (*0-89375-995-3*) NAL.

Picture of Dorian Gray. Oscar Wilde. (Illus.). 64p. 1990. pap. text 5.95 (*0-19-421652-7*) OUP.

Picture of Dorian Gray. Oscar Wilde. Ed. & Intro. by Isobel M. Murray. (Oxford World's Classics Ser.). 260p. 1998. pap. 6.95 (*0-19-283365-0*) OUP.

Picture of Dorian Gray. Oscar Wilde. LC 99-462503. (Oxford World's Classics Hardcovers Ser.). 238p. 1999. 13.50 (*0-19-210031-9*) OUP.

Picture of Dorian Gray. Oscar Wilde. Ed. by Joshua Hanft. (Great Illustrated Classics Ser.: Vol. 47). (Illus.). 240p. (J). (gr. 3-6). 1995. 9.95 (*0-86611-998-1*) Playmore Inc.

***Picture of Dorian Gray.** Oscar Wilde. 1999. pap. 10.95 (*1-84002-103-9*, Pub. by Theatre Comm) Consort Bk Sales.

Picture of Dorian Gray. Oscar Wilde. Ed. by Peter Faulkener. 186p. 1993. pap. 4.95 (*0-460-87364-4*, Everyman's Classic Lib) Tuttle Pubng.

Picture of Dorian Gray. Oscar Wilde. Ed. & Intro. by Peter Ackroyd. (Classics Ser.). 272p. 1986. pap. 7.95 (*0-14-043187-X*, Penguin Classics) Viking Penguin.

Picture of Dorian Gray. Oscar Wilde. (Classics Library). 320p. pap. 3.95 (*1-85326-015-0*, 0150WW, Pub. by Wrdsworth Edits) NTC Contemp Pub Co.

Picture of Dorian Gray. large type ed. Oscar Wilde. Ed. by Peter Ackroyd. 324 p. 1995. 22.95 (*0-7838-1547-6*, G K Hall Lrg Type) Mac Lib Ref.

Picture of Dorian Gray. large type ed. Oscar Wilde. 380p. 1995. lib. bdg. 24.00 (*0-939495-80-5*) North Bks.

Picture of Dorian Gray, 2 vols. large type ed. Oscar Wilde. (YA). (gr. 10 up). reprint ed. 10.00 (*0-89064-049-1*) NAVH.

Picture of Dorian Gray see Works of Oscar Wilde

Picture of Dorian Gray. Oscar Wilde. 1990. reprint ed. lib. bdg. 21.95 (*0-89966-654-X*) Buccaneer Bks.

Picture of Dorian Gray. Oscar Wilde. LC 93-24484. 165p. 1993. reprint ed. pap. text 1.00 (*0-486-27807-7*) Dover.

Picture of Dorian Gray. Oscar Wilde. 245p. 1998. reprint ed. lib. bdg. 24.00 (*1-58287-056-X*) North Bks.

Picture of Dorian Gray. Oscar Wilde. (BCL1-PR English Literature Ser.). 255p. 1992. reprint ed. lib. bdg. 79.00 (*0-7812-7603-9*) Rprt Serv.

Picture of Dorian Gray. 19th ed. Oscar Wilde. LC 92-11593. 254p. 1992. 14.50 (*0-679-60001-9*) Modern Lib NY.

Picture of Dorian Gray: And Other Short Stories. Oscar Wilde. 305p. 1995. mass mkt. 4.95 (*0-451-52601-5*, Sig Classics) NAL.

Picture of Dorian Gray: Authoritative Texts, Backgrounds, Reviews, Reactions, & Criticism. Oscar Wilde. Ed. by Donald L. Lawler. LC 86-12330. (Critical Editions Ser.). 462p. (C). 1988. pap. text 14.75 (*0-393-95568-0*) Norton.

***Picture of Dorian Gray: Reproducible Teaching Unit.** James Scott. 68p. (Orig.). (YA). (gr. 7-12). 2000. pap. 29.50 (*1-58049-196-0*, TU135) Prestwick Hse.

Picture of Dorian Gray: "What the World Thinks of Me" Michael P. Gillespie. LC 95-7086. (Twayne's Masterwork Studies: No. 145). 1995. 29.00 (*0-8057-8375-X*, Twyne); pap. 13.95 (*0-8057-8595-7*, Twyne) Mac Lib Ref.

Picture of Dorian Gray & Dr. Jekyll & Mr. Hyde: Curriculum Unit. Center for Learning Network Staff et al. (Novel Ser.). 83p. (YA). (gr. 9-12). 1992. spiral bd. 18.95 (*1-56077-211-5*) Ctr Learning.

Picture of Dorian Gray & Other Stories. Oscar Wilde. 318p. 1988. 31.95 (*0-86225-014-5*) Queens Hse-Focus Serv.

Picture of Dorian Gray & Other Stories. Oscar Wilde. reprint ed. lib. bdg. 22.95 (*0-88411-893-2*) Amereon Ltd.

Picture of Dorian Gray & Other Writings. Oscar Wilde. Ed. by Richard Ellmann. (Bantam Classics Ser.). 512p. (gr. 9-12). 1982. mass mkt. 4.95 (*0-553-21254-0*) Bantam.

***Picture of Dorian Gray & Selected Stories, Vol. 1.** Oscar Wilde. 1999. mass mkt. 3.99 (*0-8125-6711-0*, Pub. by Forge NYC) St Martin.

Picture of Dorian Gray & Selected Stories. Oscar Wilde. 1962. pap. 1.95 (*0-317-00253-8*, Ment) NAL.

Picture of Edgewood. Donald G. Mitchell. (Notable American Authors Ser.). 1999. reprint ed. lib. bdg. 125.00 (*0-7812-4567-2*) Rprt Serv.

Picture of Freedom: The Diary of Clotee, a Slave Girl, Belmont Plantation, Virginia, 1859. Patricia McKissack. (Dear America Ser.). 132p. (YA). (gr. 4-9). 1997. 9.95 (*0-614-25386-1*) Scholastic Inc.

Picture of Freedom: The Diary of Clotee, a Slave Girl, Belmont Plantation, Virginia, 1859. Patricia C. McKissack. LC 96-25673. (Dear America Ser.). (Illus.). 195p. (YA). (gr. 4-7). 1997. 9.95 (*0-590-25988-1*) Scholastic Inc.

Picture of God. Barry Bailey. 108p. 1994. pap. 2.69 (*0-687-31019-9*) Abingdon.

Picture of Guilt. Carolyn Keene. Ed. by Ruth Ashby. (Nancy Drew Files: No. 101). 160p. (YA). (gr. 6 up). 1994. mass mkt. 3.99 (*0-671-88192-2*, Archway) PB.

Picture of Guilt. Carolyn Keene. (Nancy Drew Files: No. 101). (YA). (gr. 6 up). 1994. 9.09 (*0-606-07052-4*, Pub. by Turtleback) Demco.

Picture of Happiness. Alfred LaCaze, Jr. LC 96-67039. 76p. 1996. pap. 9.95 (*1-57197-015-0*) Pentland Pr.

Picture of Health? A Review & Annotated Bibliography of the Health of Young People in Developing Countries, WHO/FHE/ADH/95.14. 81p. (Orig.). 1995. 18.00 (*0-614-19512-8*, 1930087) World Health.

Picture of Health: Healing Your Life with Art. 2nd ed. Lucia Capacchione. (Illus.). 176p. (Orig.). 1996. pap. 12.95 (*0-87877-231-6*) Newcastle Pub.

Picture of Her Tombstone. Thomas Lipinski. (Carroll Dorsey Mystery Ser.: 2). 224p. 1998. mass mkt. 5.99 (*0-380-73024-3*, Avon Bks) Morrow Avon.

Picture of Hostility: A Reconsideration of Some Aspects on the Origins of the American Revolution. Jack P. Green & William G. McLoughlin. 69p. 1977. pap. 5.00 (*0-944026-83-4*) Am Antiquarian.

***Picture of Innocence.** Jill McGown. LC 97-45816. 336p. 1998. 22.00 (*0-449-00250-0*) Fawcett.

Picture of Innocence. Jill McGown. 1999. mass mkt. 6.99 (*0-449-00251-9*, Crest) Fawcett.

Picture of Innocence. large type ed. Jill McGown. Date not set. 30.00 (*0-7862-1670-0*) Thorndike Pr.

Picture of Lycoming County. Pennsylvania Writers' Project Staff. 1993. reprint ed. lib. bdg. 89.00 (*0-7812-5818-9*) Rprt Serv.

Picture of Philadelphia. James Mease. LC 75-112561. (Rise of Urban America Ser.). (Illus.). 1970. reprint ed. 23.95 (*0-405-02466-5*) Ayer.

Picture of St. John. Bayard Taylor. (Notable American Authors). 1999. reprint ed. lib. bdg. 125.00 (*0-7812-8987-4*) Rprt Serv.

Picture of Slavery in the United States. George Bourne. LC 74-92420. (Illus.). 228p. 1972. reprint ed. 29.00 (*0-403-00179-X*) Scholarly.

Picture of Subsidized Households in 1997: United States: Totals & Agencies with over 500 Units. Paul Burke. (Illus.). 109p. 1998. pap. text 25.00 (*0-7881-7389-8*) DIANE Pub.

Picture of the Picture of the Image in the Glass. Craig Watson. 48p. 1992. pap. 8.00 (*1-882022-10-6*) O Bks.

Picture of the Royal Academy. Constance-Anne Parker. 80p. (C). 1989. 110.00 (*0-903696-33-9*, Pub. by Hurtwood Pr Ltd); pap. 70.00 (*0-903696-34-7*, Pub. by Hurtwood Pr Ltd) St Mut.

Picture of the Year. large type ed. Clive Egleton. 512p. 1988. 27.99 (*0-7089-1758-5*) Ulverscroft.

Picture Oregon: Portraits of the University of Oregon. James McChesney. (Illus.). 1994. 59.95 (*0-87114-287-2*) U of Oreg Bks.

Picture Painting Self Taught. D. M. Campana. 16.95 (*0-939608-28-6*) Campana Art.

Picture Palace. Paul Theroux. LC 99-462494. 368p. 1999. pap. 13.95 (*0-14-005072-8*, Viking) Viking Penguin.

Picture Parade of Jewish History. Morris Epstein. 1977. pap. 8.95 (*0-8197-0024-X*) Bloch.

Picture Paris: Landmarks of a New Generation. LC 98-9668. (Illus.). 120p. 1998. pap. 19.95 (*0-89236-503-X*, Pub. by J P Getty Trust) OUP.

Picture Patterns, Set 1 & 2. Arthur J. Wiebe. (Illus.). 24p. (J). (gr. k-4). 1985. 8.95 (*1-878669-32-X*, CTA-4752) Crea Tea Assocs.

Picture Patterns Duplicating, Bk. 1. Arthur J. Wiebe. 24p. (J). (gr. k-4). 1982. student ed. 6.95 (*1-878669-33-8*, CTA-4752) Crea Tea Assocs.

Picture Patterns Duplicating, Bk. 2. Arthur J. Wiebe. 24p. (J). (gr. k-4). 1985. student ed. 6.95 (*1-878669-34-6*, CTA-4755) Crea Tea Assocs.

***Picture Perfect.** Sandra Byrd. (Secret Sisters Ser.: Vol. 11). 112p. (J). (gr. 3-7). 2000. pap. 4.95 (*1-57856-063-2*) Waterbrook Pr.

***Picture Perfect.** Reon Carter. 2000. pap. 8.95 (*1-58571-004-0*, Pub. by Genesis Press) BookWorld.

Picture Perfect. Sukey S. Gross. LC 92-70597. 144p. 1992. 13.95 (*1-56062-107-9*); pap. 10.95 (*1-56062-108-7*) CIS Comm.

Picture Perfect. Kate Hanford. 1999. mass mkt. 4.99 (*0-8217-5105-0*) NAL.

Picture Perfect. Yvonne Lehman. LC 96-45909. (White Dove Romance Ser.: No. 4). 176p. (YA). (gr. 7-10). 1997. mass mkt. 4.99 (*1-55661-708-9*) Bethany Hse.

Picture Perfect. Fern Michaels. (Illus.). 256p. 25.00 (*0-7278-5515-8*) Severn Hse.

***Picture Perfect.** Melanie Stewart. 128p. 1999. mass mkt. 3.99 (*0-307-23454-1*, Goldn Books) Gldn Bks Pub Co.

***Picture Perfect.** Herbert L. Strock. LC 00-41987. (Filmmakers Ser.). (Illus.). 2000. write for info. (*0-8108-3815-X*) Scarecrow.

Picture Perfect. Jodi Picoult. 432p. 1996. reprint ed. mass mkt. 6.50 (*0-425-15411-4*) Berkley Pub.

***Picture Perfect: The Art & Artifice of Public Image Making.** Kiku Adatto. 200p. 1999. reprint ed. pap. text 12.00 (*0-7881-6243-8*) DIANE Pub.

***Picture Perfect: The Powerpuff Girls.** Golden Books Staff. (Illus.). (J). 2000. 5.99 (*0-307-10146-0*, Goldn Books) Gldn Bks Pub Co.

Picture-Perfect Crime. Jahnna N. Malcolm. (Clue Ser.: No. 7). 112p. (J). (gr. 3-6). 1994. pap. 3.25 (*0-590-48735-3*) Scholastic Inc.

Picture-Perfect Crime. Jahnna N. Malcolm. (Clue Ser.: No. 7). (J). (gr. 3-6). 1994. 9.09 (*0-606-09748-1*, Pub. by Turtleback) Demco.

***Picture Perfect Framing: Making, Matting, Mounting, Embellishing, Displaying, & More.** Katie DuMont. LC 00-28227. (Illus.). 128p. 2000. write for info. (*1-57990-165-4*, Pub. by Lark Books) Sterling.

Picture Perfect Golf. rev. ed. Gary Wiren & Dawson Taylor. LC 97-42183. (Illus.). 160p. 1998. pap. 14.95 (*0-8092-2918-8*, 291880, Contemporary Bks) NTC Contemp Pub Co.

Picture-Perfect Golf: The 100 Most Common Golf Mistakes & How to Correct Them. rev. ed. Gary Wiren & Dawson Taylor. (Illus.). 176p. (Orig.). 1998. pap. 14.95 (*0-8092-5104-3*) NTC Contemp Pub Co.

Picture Perfect Memory: With Camera. Fun Works Staff. (Barbie Ser.). 16p. (J). 1997. 9.98 (*1-57082-719-2*, Pub. by Mouse Works) Time Warner.

Picture Perfect Mystery. Carolyn Keene. (Nancy Drew Mystery Stories Ser.: No. 94). 160p. (J). (gr. 3-6). 1990. per. 3.99 (*0-671-66319-4*, Minstrel Bks) PB.

Picture Perfect Mystery. Carolyn Keene. (Nancy Drew Mystery Stories Ser.: No. 94). (J). (gr. 3-6). 1990. 9.09 (*0-606-05941-5*, Pub. by Turtleback) Demco.

Picture Perfect 1: Reproducible Stories & Worksheets for Articulation Practice. Monica Gustafson. 350p. 1987. pap. text 37.00 (*0-7616-7368-7*) Commun Skill.

Picture Perfect Patchwork. Naomi Norman. (Illus.). 88p. 1996. pap. text 8.95 (*0-486-29469-2*) Dover.

Picture-Perfect Planet see Time-Life Early Learning Program Series

Picture-Perfect Planet. LC 92-20831. (Early Learning Program Ser.). (J). 1992. lib. bdg. write for info. (*0-8094-9320-9*) Time-Life.

Picture-Perfect Prom? Created by Francine Pascal. (Sweet Valley High Ser.: No. 141). 208p. (YA). (gr. 7-12). 1998. mass mkt. 3.99 (*0-553-49231-4*, Sweet Valley) BDD Bks Young Read.

***Picture Perfect Spanish: A Survival Guide to Speaking Spanish.** Jerry Lucas. LC 00-104324. (Illus.). 240p. 2000. pap. 21.95 (*1-930853-00-9*) Lucas Ed Systm.

Picture Perfect 2: Reproducible Worksheets for Phonological Practice. Monica Gustafson. 265p. 1987. pap. text 37.00 (*0-7616-7369-5*) Commun Skill.

Picture Perfect Walls. Home Decorating Institute Staff. LC 95-30809. (Arts & Crafts for Home Decorating Ser.). (Illus.). 128p. 1995. 18.95 (*0-86573-378-3*) Creat Pub Intl.

Picture-Perfect Worry-Free Weddings: 72 Destinations & Venues. Diane Warner. LC 97-50086. 160p. 1998. pap. 12.99 (*1-55870-479-5*, Betrwy Bks) F & W Pubns Inc.

Picture Pie No. 2: A Drawing Book & Stencil. Ed E. Emberley. (J). (gr. 1-5). 1996. pap. 9.95 (*0-614-15672-6*) Little.

***Picture Play Quilts.** Ami Simms. (Illus.). 2000. pap. write for info. (*0-943079-07-1*) Mallery Pr.

Picture Plus Dictionary. Virginia McKinney. (Illus.). 576p. (J). 1997. 49.00 (*1-884362-24-9*) Butte Pubns.

Picture Poetry Book. Gertrude P. McBrown. (Illus.). (J). 1990. 4.25 (*0-87498-007-0*) Assoc Pubs DC.

Picture Post Idols. Jon Savage. (Illus.). 160p. 1993. pap. 29.95 (*1-85585-146-6*) Trafalgar.

Picture Post Nineteen Thirty-Eight to Nineteen Fifty. Frwd. by Tom Hopkinson. (Illus.). 288p. 1985. pap. 12.95 (*0-7011-2858-5*, Pub. by Chatto & Windus) Random House.

Picture Postcard History of New York's Elmira, Corning, & Vicinity. Alfred N. Weiner. LC 88-941. (Illus.). 101p. (Orig.). 1988. pap. 9.95 (*0-930256-17-4*, Vestal Pr) Madison Bks UPA.

Picture Postcard History of Salem. Dale E. Shaffer & Maurice Sechler. (Illus.). 218p. (Orig.). 1994. pap. text 18.00 (*0-915060-30-2*) D E Shaffer.

Picture Postcard History of U. S. Aviation. Jack W. Lengenfelder. LC 88-36433. (Illus.). 100p. (Orig.). 1989. pap. 12.95 (*0-930256-19-0*, Vestal Pr) Madison Bks UPA.

Picture Postcard History of U. S. Baseball. Ron Menchine. LC 92-16270. (Illus.). 124p. 1992. pap. 14.95 (*0-930256-21-2*, Vestal Pr) Madison Bks UPA.

Picture Postcards. LeeAnn Heringer. LC 96-203620. 40p. (Orig.). 1995. pap. 3.00 (*1-888431-03-2*) ASGP.

Picture Postcards. C. W. Hill. 1989. pap. 25.00 (*0-85263-907-4*, Pub. by Shire Pubns) St Mut.

***Picture Postcards.** C. W. Hill. (Illus.). 40p. 1999. pap. 30.00 (*0-7478-0398-6*, Pub. by Shire Pubns) Parkwest Pubns.

Picture Postcards of Old Brooklyn. Spina. (Illus.). 1994. pap. text 4.95 (*0-486-24489-X*) Dover.

P

Picture Processing & Digital Filtering. T. S. Huang. LC 75-5770. (Illus.). 270p. 1979. 47.95 (0-387-09339-7) Spr-Verlag.

Picture Profits: Let Your Camera Make Money for You. 4th ed. Andrew S. Linick. 1981. pap. 7.95 (0-917098-02-1) LKA Inc.

Picture Puzzle Book. Davidson. 1995. pap. 10.95 (0-201-48008-5) Addison-Wesley.

Picture Puzzler. Kathleen Westray. LC 94-4066. (Illus.). 32p. (J). (gr. k-3). 1994. 13.95 (0-395-70130-9) Ticknor & Flds Bks Yng Read.

Picture Puzzles. Barrie Henderson. (Illus.). (J). (gr. 4-7). 1994. pap. 2.95 (0-590-20838-1) Scholastic Inc.

Picture Puzzles. Jenny Tyler. (Brain Benders Ser.). (J). (gr. 3 up). 1980. text 4.95 (0-86020-433-2, Usborne) EDC.

Picture Puzzles. Judy Tyler. (Brain Benders Ser.). (Illus.). 321p. (J). (gr. 3 up). 1999. lib. bdg. 12.95 (0-88110-049-8, Usborne) EDC.

Picture Puzzles with Cuisenaire Rods. Patricia Davidson & Jeffrey Sellon. 64p. (J). (gr. 1-6). 1979. pap. text 9.50 (0-914040-77-4) Cuisenaire.

Picture Pyramids. Art Freifeld. (Illus.). 50p. 1988. student ed. 7.95 (0-916177-34-3); 4.95 (0-916177-35-1); audio 9.95 (0-916177-36-X) Am Eng Pubns.

Picture Pyramids, Set. Art Freifeld. (Illus.). 1988. 19.95 (0-916177-37-8) Am Eng Pubns.

*__Picture Reference.__ (Illus.). 240p. (J). (gr. 2-6). 1999. write for info. (0-7166-9916-8) World Bk.

*__Picture Reference Atlas.__ Mel Pickering. (Illus.). 2000. pap. 7.95 (1-58728-651-3) Two Can Pub.

Picture Researcher's Handbook. 4th ed. Hilary Evans & Mary Evans. 464p. 1989. 72.95 (0-7476-0038-4) Chapman & Hall.

Picture Researcher's Handbook: An International Guide to Picture Sources & How to Use Them. 6th ed. Hilary Evans & Mary Evans. 672p. (C). 1996. 75.00 (0-415-15126-0) Routledge.

Picture Resources for the Remediation of Articulation & Phonological Disorders. Robert J. Lowe & Julia M. Weitz. (Illus.). 111p. (Orig.). 1992. pap. 19.95 (0-9626939-5-2) Janelle Pubns.

Picture Rulebook of Kids' Games. Roxanne Henderson. (Illus.). 256p. 1996. pap. 14.95 (0-8092-3227-8, 322780, Contemporary Bks) NTC Contemp Pub Co.

Picture Searching: Techniques & Tools. Renate V. Shaw. LC 72-13234. (SLA Bibliographies Ser.: No. 6). 75p. reprint ed. pap. 30.00 (0-608-30064-0, 201728200007) Bks Demand.

*__Picture Showmen: Insights into the Narrative Tradition in Indian Art.__ Ed. by Jyotindra Jain. LC 98-902735. 1998. 92.00 (81-85026-39-4, Pub. by Marg Publns) S Asia.

Picture Shows: The Life & Films of Peter Bogdanovich. Andrew Yule. LC 91-33290. (Illus.). 300p. (Orig.). 1992. 22.95 (0-87910-153-9) Limelight Edns.

Picture Smocking with Ellen McCarn. Ellen D. McCarn. (Illus.). 48p. 1990. pap. 10.00 (0-9618066-2-1) McCarn Enterp.

Picture Sourcebook for Collage & Decoupage. Edmund V. Gillon, Jr. LC 74-82206. (Illus.). 156p. (Orig.). 1974. pap. 11.95 (0-486-23095-3) Dover.

Picture Sources, No. 4. Special Libraries Association Staff. Ed. by Ernest H. Robl. LC 83-625. (Illus.). 192p. 1983. reprint ed. pap. 59.60 (0-608-07905-7, 206788600011) Bks Demand.

Picture Sources Three: Collections of Prints & Photographs in the U. S. & Canada. Special Libraries Association Staff. Ed. by Ann Novotny & Rosemary Eakins. LC 75-6582. 407p. reprint ed. pap. 126.20 (0-608-11036-1, 201201100081) Bks Demand.

Picture Speaks a Thousand Words. Melvia Miller. pap. 25.00 (0-685-74228-8) Mothership Pubns.

Picture Stories. 2nd ed. Sandra Heyer. 138p. 1989. pap. text 20.67 (0-13-675844-4) P-H.

Picture Stories: Language & Literacy Activities for Beginners. Fred Ligon & Elizabeth Tannenbaum. (Illus.). 1990. pap. text 16.55 (0-8013-0366-4, 78145) Longman.

Picture Stories from the Bible: The New Testament in Comic-Strip Form. M. C. Gaines. LC 80-51593. (Comic-Book Bible Ser.: Vol. 2). (Illus.). 143p. (J). (gr. 3-10). 1980. reprint ed. 14.95 (0-934386-02-1) Bloch.

Picture Stories from the Bible: The Old Testament in Full-Color Comic-Strip Form. M. C. Gaines. LC 79-66064. (Illus.). 222p. (J). (gr. 3-10). 1979. reprint ed. 12.95 (0-934386-01-3) Scarf Pr.

Picture Story Approach to Infant Teaching. L. Gostelow. LC 68-141022. 96p. 1968. write for info. (0-237-28007-8) EVN1 UK.

Picture Story Bible ABC Book. rev. ed. Elsie E. Egermeier. (Illus.). (J). (ps-1). 1963. 9.95 (0-87162-262-9, D1703) Warner Pr.

Picture Tales from Mexico. Dan Storm. LC 95-32329. (Illus.). 122p. (J). (gr. 2 up). 1995. pap. 9.95 (0-88415-670-2, 5670) Gulf Pub.

Picture Talk. (Illus.). 31p. 1999. pap. 5.95 (0-88729-191-0) Langenscheidt.

Picture Test in Ophthalmology. 2nd ed. Jack J. Kanski. 1997. pap. text 16.95 (0-443-06037-1, W B Saunders Co) Harcrt Hlth Sci Grp.

Picture Tests & Short Cases for the MRCP. Debra King. (Illus.). 315p. 1996. pap. text 34.00 (0-7020-1815-5, Pub. by W B Saunders) Saunders.

Picture Tests for the MRCP (Paediatrics) Adam Craig & Keith Brownlee. (Illus.). 235p. 1997. pap. text 45.00 (0-7020-2163-6, Pub. by W B Saunders) Saunders.

Picture Tests in Anatomy. Robert M. McMinn et al. (Illus.). 128p. (C). (gr. 13). 1986. 15.95 (0-8151-5836-X, 09146) Mosby Inc.

Picture Tests in Haematology. Barbara J. Bain. LC 98-10014. (Colour Guide Ser.). 1999. pap. text 19.95 (0-443-05943-8) Church.

Picture Tests in Obstetrics. Rymer. 1994. pap. text 16.95 (0-443-04950-5, W B Saunders Co) Harcrt Hlth Sci Grp.

Picture Tests in Surgery. Rhodes. 1996. pap. text 16.95 (0-443-05187-9, W B Saunders Co) Harcrt Hlth Sci Grp.

Picture That! Bible Storybook. Tracy Harrast. 160p. (J). 1998. 11.99 (0-310-92600-9) Zondervan.

Picture That Came Alive. Hugh Lewin. (Junior African Writers Ser.). (Illus.). 80p. (J). (gr. 3 up). 1992. pap. 4.95 (0-7910-2912-3) Chelsea Hse.

Picture That Mom Drew. Bruce McMillan & Kathy Mallat. LC 96-30165. (Illus.). 24p. (J). (ps-3). 1997. 14.95 (0-8027-8617-0); lib. bdg. 15.85 (0-8027-8618-9) Walker & Co.

Picture the Blues. Susan Antone. (Illus.). 1990. pap. 22.95 (0-932117-13-9) Osborne Enterps.

*__Picture the Girl: Young Women Speak Their Minds.__ Audrey Shehyn. LC 99-59211. 128p. 2000. pap. 14.95 (0-7868-8567-X, Pub. by Hyperion) Time Warner.

Picture the Middle Ages. Linda Honan. (Illus.). 162p. 26.00 (1-56696-025-8) Jackdaw.

Picture the Past: Art Ideas to Recreate History for Children Ages 5-11. Joan Chambers. (Kids' Stuff Ser.). (Illus.). (J). 1995. 15.95 (0-947882-22-7) Belair Pubns Ltd.

Picture the Universe Vol. 1: Images from the Hubble Space Telescope. Ed. by Stephen P. Maran. (Illus.). 228p. 1997. 34.95 (0-9655136-2-9) ReedDrabick.

Picture Theory. Nicole Brossard. 186p. pap. 12.00 (0-920717-22-5) Guernica Editions.

Picture Theory. Nicole Brossard. Tr. by Barbara Goddard. LC 90-63921. (Roof Bks.). (Illus.). 160p. 1991. pap. text 75.00 (0-937804-40-1) Segue NYC.

Picture Theory: Essays on Verbal & Visual Representation. W. J. Mitchell. (Illus.). xvi, 462p. 1995. pap. text 18.00 (0-226-53232-1) U Ch Pr.

Picture This. Philip Hayward. 1998. write for info. (1-86020-518-6) U of Luton Pr.

Picture This. Joseph Heller. 352p. 1989. mass mkt. 5.99 (0-345-35886-4) Ballantine Pub Grp.

Picture This. Joseph Heller. LC 99-56107. 352p. 2000. per. 13.00 (0-684-86819-9) S&S Trade.

*__Picture This...__ Alison Jay. (Illus.). 40p. (J). (ps-k). 2000. 15.99 (0-525-46380-1, Dutton Child) Peng Put Young Read.

*__Picture This.__ David Peal. LC 99-40521. 1999. write for info. (1-891556-58-4) Amer Online.

*__Picture This!__ Edward Willett. LC 99-38967. 1999. write for info. (1-891556-56-8) Amer Online.

*__Picture This.__ Lisa Williams. (Illus.). 32p. 1998. 7.99 (1-58050-065-X, 40-6195) Provo Craft.

Picture This: A Guide to Over Three Hundred Environmentally, Socially, & Politically Relevant Films & Videos. Sky Hiatt. LC 91-50642. 389p. 1991. pap. 12.95 (1-879360-05-5) Noble Pr.

Picture This! A Science-by- Mail Challenge about Imaging. Science-by-Mail Staff. 1997. pap. text 54.00 (0-7872-4324-8) Kendall-Hunt.

Picture This! A Vocabulary Puzzle Book - Blackline Master. Blaine Kirn. (Illus.). 52p. 1991. pap. text 16.50 (0-9627878-0-9) Authors Editors.

Picture This: An Illustrated Guide to Complete Dinners. Susan Bachner. (Illus.). 72p. 1984. 27.50 (0-9613439-0-7) Spec Addns.

*__Picture This: Digital & Instant Photography Activities for Early Childhood Learning.__ Susan Entz & Sheri Lyn Galarza. (Illus.). 223p. (C). 1999. 67.95 (0-8039-6886-8); pap. 30.95 (0-8039-6887-6) Corwin Pr.

*__Picture This: How Pictures Work.__ Molly Bang. (Illus.). 2000. 19.95 (1-58717-029-9) SeaStar.

*__Picture This: How Pictures Work.__ Molly Bang. LC 00-24402. (Illus.). (J). 2000. pap. 12.95 (1-58717-030-2) SeaStar.

Picture This: Picture Books for Use with Young Adults a Curriculum-Related Annotated Bibliography. Denise I. Matulka. LC 97-2234. 296p. 1997. 39.95 (0-313-30182-4, Greenwood Pr) Greenwood.

Picture This, Too! A Vocabulary Puzzle Book - Blackline Masters. Elaine Kirn. (Illus.). 52p. 1991. pap. text 16.50 (0-9627878-1-7) Authors Editors.

Picture Tour of the Smithsonian. Smithsonian Press Staff. 64p. 1990. 6.98 (0-87474-899-2) Smithsonian.

Picture-Tube Imperialism? The Impact of U. S. Television on Latin America. Alan Wells. LC 70-190165. (Illus.). 213p. reprint ed. pap. 66.10 (0-8357-8985-3, 203357200086) Bks Demand.

*__Picture Wagon.__ Donna Getzinger. 156p. (J). (gr. 4-7). 2000. pap. 8.95 (0-87714-481-8) Denlingers.

Picture Window: A Carol Lynn Pearson Collection. Carol Lynn Pearson. Ed. by Jennifer Utley. LC 96-5449. (Illus.). 201p. 1996. 16.95 (1-882723-27-9, Pub. by Gold Leaf Pr) Origin Bk Sales.

Picture Windows. Elizabeth Ewen. 2001. pap. 15.00 (0-465-07013-2, Pub. by Basic) HarpC.

Picture Windows: How the Suburbs Happened. Elizabeth Ewen & Rosalyn F. Baxandall. 320p. 2000. 26.00 (0-465-07045-0, Pub. by Basic) HarpC.

Picture Windows on the Christ. Charles C. Wise, Jr. LC 78-69928. (Illus.). 354p. 1979. 11.95 (0-917023-03-X); pap. 5.95 (0-917023-04-8) Magian Pr.

Picture with Patience. Jorg Immendorff. 1997. 49.95 (3-89322-844-6, Pub. by Edition Cantz) Dist Art Pubs.

Picture Within a Picture: An Illustrated Guide to the Origins of Chinese Characters. Shi Zhengyu. (CHI & ENG., Illus.). 544p. 1997. pap. 25.95 (7-80005-332-6, Pub. by New World Pr) China Bks.

Picture Women Late Medieval Art. Grossinger. LC 96-36815. (Manchester Medieval Sources Ser.). 200p. 1997. 69.95 (0-7190-4109-0, Pub. by Manchester Univ Pr) St Martin.

Picture Word Book Four. Illus. by Joanna Williams. 28p. (J). (ps). 1991. pap. 3.50 (0-7214-1437-0, 916-4, Ladybrd) Penguin Putnam.

Picture Word Book One. Illus. by Joanna Williams. 28p. (J). (ps). 1991. pap. 3.50 (0-7214-1434-6, 916-1, Ladybrd) Penguin Putnam.

Picture Word Book Three. Illus. by Peter Stevenson. 28p. (J). (ps). 1991. pap. 3.50 (0-7214-1436-2, 916-3, Ladybrd) Penguin Putnam.

Picture Word Book Two. Illus. by Peter Stevenson. 28p. (J). (ps). 1991. pap. 3.50 (0-7214-1435-4, 916-2, Ladybrd) Penguin Putnam.

Picture Word Cards. William Murray. (Read with Me Key Words to Reading Ser.). (J). (ps-2). 1991. pap. 9.95 (0-7214-3232-8, 9113, Ladybrd) Penguin Putnam.

Picture Word Prayers & Bible Stories. Mary E. Erickson. 48p. 1999. 7.99 (0-88486-260-7) Galahad Bks.

*__Picture Words.__ Contrib. by P. Thorburn & S. Cobb. (Illus.). (J). (ps-2). 1999. pap. 24.00 (0-7217-0658-4, Pub. by Schofield) St Mut.

*__Picture Words: Using Visual Links to Remember Early Sight Words.__ Betty LaPointe. Ed. by Kristy Shine et al. (Illus.). 30p. (C). 1999. pap. 25.00 (0-9674918-0-0) Litracy Links CT.

Picture-Writing of the American Indians. Garrick Mallery. 1972. 79.95 (0-8490-0836-0) Gordon Pr.

Picture-Writing of the American Indians, 2 vols., 1. Garrick Mallery. (Illus.). 822p. 1972. reprint ed. pap. 14.95 (0-486-22842-8) Dover.

Picture-Writing of the American Indians, 2 vols., 2. Garrick Mallery. (Illus.). 822p. 1972. reprint ed. pap. 12.95 (0-486-22843-6) Dover.

Picture-Writings & Other Documents by Nele, Paramount Chief of the Cuna Indians, & Ruben Perez Kantule, His Secretary, 2 pts. in 1 vol. Erland Nordenskiold. LC 75-46061. (Comparative Ethnographical Studies: Vol. 7). reprint ed. 55.00 (0-404-15147-7) AMS Pr.

Picture Yourself: A Casebook for Reading & Writing. Louis Molina & Michel DeBenedictis. 222p. (C). 1994. pap. text, per. 34.95 (0-8403-9613-9) Kendall-Hunt.

Picture Yourself More Independent. Deorsey E. McGruder. Ed. by Vera E. McGruder. (Illus.). 46p. (Orig.). 1996. pap. 14.95 (0-9658837-0-1) Windchime.

Pictureback Gang Printing 1998. 1998. pap. write for info. (0-679-88326-6) Random.

Picturebook: Source & Resource for Art Education. Kenneth A. Marantz et al. 85p. (Orig.). 1994. pap. 18.00 (0-937652-68-7, 211) Natl Art Ed.

Picturebook 99: Directory of Illustration. Ed. by Amy Gary & Cyd Moore. (Illus.). 1999. pap. 19.95 (1-882077-99-7, Pub. by WaterMark Inc) Menasha Ridge.

Picturebook 99: The Directory of Children's Book Illustration. Ed. by Amy Gary & Cyd Moore. (Illus.). 156p. (Orig.). 1999. pap. 29.95 (0-929077-15-6) Menasha Ridge.

*__Picturebook 2K: The Directory of Children's Illustration.__ Ed. by Cyd Moore & Amy Gary. (Illus.). 328p. 2000. pap. 29.95 (1-882077-92-X) WaterMark Inc.

Picturecology: A Picture Book for "Living Lightly on the Earth" 3rd ed. High Moon. Tr. by Maura Hurley-Basu & Anne Hill from JPN. (Illus.). 96p. 1998. pap. text 25.00 (0-7881-7377-4) DIANE Pub.

Pictured in My Mind: Contemporary American Self-Taught Art. Ed. by Gail A. Trechsel. (Illus.). 372p. (C). 1996. 55.00 (0-87805-877-X); pap. 30.00 (0-87805-878-8) U Pr of Miss.

Picturegoers Who's Who & Encyclopedia of the Screen. G. Arliss. 608p. 1976. lib. bdg. 300.00 (0-8490-0837-9) Gordon Pr.

*__Pictures: Oasis in Japan, 1995.__ Dennis Morris. (Illus.). 2000. pap. 14.95 (1-902588-03-7) Glitter Bks.

*__Pictures: Oasis 1995.__ Dennis Morris. 72p. 1999. pap. 14.95 (1-902588-04-5, Pub. by Glitter Bks) Subterranean Co.

Pictures & Biographies of Brigham Young & His Wives. 1992. lib. bdg. 250.95 (0-8490-5419-2) Gordon Pr.

Pictures & Biographies of Brigham Young & His Wives. J. H. Crockwell. 1980. lib. bdg. 59.95 (0-8490-3158-3) Gordon Pr.

Pictures & Fictions: Visual Modernism & Pre-War Novels of D. H. Lawrence. Nancy Kushigian. LC 89-13640. VIII, 178p. (C). 1990. text 48.95 (0-8204-1208-2) P Lang Pubng.

*__Pictures & Passions: A History of Homosexuality in the Visual Arts.__ James M. Saslow. LC 99-19960. 1999. 39.95 (0-670-85953-2) Viking Penguin.

Pictures & Patterns. Prod. by Zobeida Perez. (Illus.). 16p. (Orig.). (J). 1994. pap. 17.00 (0-89898-745-8, BMR05066) Wrner Bros.

Pictures & Plans. rev. ed. Philip Sauvain. (Practical Geography Ser.: Bk. 1). (Illus.). 100p. 1969. 13.95 (0-7175-0485-9) Dufour.

Pictures & Poetry: Activities for Creating. Janis Bunchman & Stephanie B. Briggs. LC 93-72681. (Illus.). 64p. (J). (gr. 3-7). 1994. text 18.65 (0-87192-273-8) Davis Mass.

Pictures & Reality: Monumental Frescoes & Mosaics in Rome around 1300. Jens T. Wollesen. LC 97-22342. (Hermeneutics of Art Ser.: Vol. 8). (Illus.). XXV, 432p. (C). 1998. 64.95 (0-8204-3846-4) P Lang Pubng.

Pictures & Stories from Forgotten Children's Books. Arnold Arnold. (Illus.). 170p. (Orig.). (J). (gr. k-6). 1969. pap. 11.95 (0-486-22041-9) Dover.

Pictures & Texts: Henry James, A. L. Coburn, & New Ways of Seeing in Literary Culture. Ralph F. Bogardus. LC 84-8844. (Studies in Photography: No. 2). (Illus.). 265p. reprint ed. pap. 82.20 (0-8357-1471-3, 207049500097) Bks Demand.

Pictures & Their Stories. Ashkan Sahihi. LC 92-16654. (Illus.). 208p. 1993. 48.00 (0-88064-141-X) Fromm Intl Pub.

Pictures & Visuality in Early Modern China. Craig Clunas. LC 97-22449. 248p. 1998. text 39.50 (0-691-05761-3, Pub. by Princeton U Pr) Cal Prin Full Svc.

Pictures & Words, 10 bks. Incl. Baby Animals: A Very First Picture Book. Nicola Tuxworth. LC 98-48808. (Illus.). 24p. (J). (ps up). 1999. lib. bdg. 19.93 (0-8368-2379-6); Farm Animals: A Very First Picture Book. Nicola Tuxworth. LC 98-31773. (Illus.). 24p. (J). (ps up). 1999. lib. bdg. 19.93 (0-8368-2271-4); Food: A Very First Picture Book. Nicola Tuxworth. LC 99-19214. (Illus.). 24p. (J). (ps up). 1999. lib. bdg. 19.93 (0-8368-2430-X); Funny Faces: A Very First Picture Book. Nicola Tuxworth. LC 98-47412. (Illus.). 24p. (J). (ps up). 1999. lib. bdg. 19.93 (0-8368-2272-2); Hop, Skip, Jump: A Very First Picture Book. Nicola Tuxworth. LC 99-13436. (Illus.). 24p. (J). (ps up). 1999. lib. bdg. 19.93 (0-8368-2431-8); Kittens: A Very First Picture Book. Nicola Tuxworth. LC 98-31776. (Illus.). 24p. (J). (ps up). 1999. lib. bdg. 19.93 (0-8368-2273-0); Machines at Work: A Very First Picture Book. Nicola Tuxworth. LC 99-19213. (Illus.). 24p. (J). (ps up). 1999. lib. bdg. 19.93 (0-8368-2432-6); Puppies: A Very First Picture Book. Gareth Stevens Publishing. LC 98-49302. (Illus.). 24p. (J). (ps up). 1999. lib. bdg. 19.93 (0-8368-2380-X); Splish, Splash: A Very First Picture Book. Nicola Tuxworth. LC 99-13422. (Illus.). 24p. (J). (ps up). 1999. lib. bdg. 19.93 (0-8368-2433-4); Wild Animals: A Very First Picture Book. Nicola Tuxworth. LC 98-31775. (Illus.). 24p. (J). (ps up). 1999. lib. bdg. 19.93 (0-8368-2274-9); (Illus.). (YA). (ps up). 1999. Set lib. bdg. 199.70 (0-8368-2456-3) Gareth Stevens Inc.

*__Pictures & Words: Animals.__ Carolyn Jackson. (Reference Collection Ser.). (Illus.). (J). 2000. pap. 19.95 (0-531-16437-3) Watts.

Pictures & Words New Releases: Incl. Baby Animals; Food; Hop, Skip, Jump; Machines at Work; Puppies; Splish, Splash, 6 bks. Nicola Tuxworth. (Pictures & Words Ser.). (Illus.). 24p. (J). (ps up). lib. bdg. 119.60 (0-8368-2429-6) Gareth Stevens Inc.

Pictures Are Fun to Look At. (Shorewood Art Programs for Education Ser.). 8p. 1974. teacher ed. 107.00 (0-88185-002-0); 143.00 (0-685-07203-7) Shorewood Fine Art.

Pictures at an Execution. Wendy Lesser. LC 93-7336. 288p. 1993. 25.95 (0-674-66735-2) HUP.

Pictures at an Execution: An Inquiry into the Subject of Murder. Wendy Lesser. (Illus.). 288p. (Orig.). (C). 1995. pap. 14.95 (0-674-66736-0) HUP.

Pictures at an Exhibition. D. M. Thomas. 278p. 1994. mass mkt. 10.95 (0-7867-0147-1) Carroll & Graf.

Pictures at an Exhibition: Piano 1874 Centennial Edition. Modest Mussorgsky. 56p. 1986. pap. 9.95 (0-7935-3889-0, 50335140) H Leonard.

Pictures at an Exhibition: Poems. Julian Palley. 88p. (Orig.). 1989. pap. 6.00 (0-9624205-0-6) Inevitable Pr.

Pictures at an Exhibition: Selected Essays on Art & Art Therapy. Ed. by Andrea Gilroy & Tessa Dalley. 240p. 1989. 48.00 (0-415-00136-6, A3500) Routledge.

Pictures at an Exhibition & Other Works for Piano. Modest P. Moussorgsky. 224p. 1990. pap. 12.95 (0-486-26515-3) Dover.

Pictures at Play or Dialogues of the Galleries. Andrew Lang & W. E. Henley. LC 70-112940. (Illus.). reprint ed. 37.50 (0-404-03829-8) AMS Pr.

Pictures at the Abbey: The Collection of the Irish National Theatre. M. Ohaodha & Lennox Robinson. (Illus.). 64p. 1983. 21.00 (0-85105-418-8, Pub. by Smyth); pap. 11.95 (0-85105-399-8, Pub. by Smyth) Dufour.

Pictures, Dreams & Visits: A True Story. Linda Graham & Betty Graham-Freiling. (Illus.). 135p. 1997. mass mkt. 15.95 (0-9659122-0-5) Gramus Publ.

Pictures for Conversation. Pam Fedie. (Illus.). 40p. 1991. pap. 8.00 (0-942017-05-6) Amer Assn Teach German.

Pictures for Language Learning. Andrew Wright. (Cambridge Handbooks for Language Teachers Ser.). (Illus.). 230p. (C). 1990. pap. text 20.95 (0-521-35800-0) Cambridge U Pr.

Pictures for Miss Josie. Sandra Belton. 1924. write for info. (0-688-17480-9, Grenwillow Bks) HarpC Child Bks.

Pictures for Writing Book 2. Stephens. 1997. pap. write for info. (0-582-22973-1) Addison-Wesley.

Pictures from a Wax Museum. David Southwood-Smith. 27p. (Orig.). 1989. pap. 5.00 (0-932662-80-3) St Andrews NC.

Pictures from an Expedition: Early Views of the American West. Martha A. Sandweiss. (Illus.). 1978. pap. 7.00 (0-89467-006-9) Yale Art Gallery.

Pictures from an Institution: A Comedy. Randall Jarrell. LC 85-20965. (Phoenix Fiction Ser.). viii, 286p. 1986. reprint ed. pap. 15.00 (0-226-39374-7) U Ch Pr.

Pictures from Brueghel: Collected Poems, 1950-1962. William Carlos Williams. LC 62-10410. 1967. reprint ed. pap. 9.95 (0-8112-0234-8, NDP118, Pub. by New Directions) Norton.

Pictures from Italy. Charles Dickens. Ed. & Intro. by Kate Flint. LC 98-164810. xxxvii, 220p. 1998. pap. 11.95 (0-14-043431-3) Viking Penguin.

Pictures from No-Man's Land. Photos by David Williams. LC 85-20215. (Illus.). 112p. 1986. 24.95 (0-915269-03-1); pap. 12.95 (0-915269-04-X) Windgate Pr.

Pictures from Northwest History. Glenn N. Ranck. (Shorey Historical Ser.). (Illus.). 36p. 1982. reprint ed. pap. 10.00 (0-8466-0115-X, S-115) Shoreys Bkstore.

Pictures from Pilgrim's Progress. Charles H. Spurgeon. 1992. pap. 10.00 (1-56186-201-0) Pilgrim Pubns.

Pictures from the Douglas M. Duncan Collection. Frances Barwick. LC 74-75587. 160p. reprint ed. pap. 49.60 (0-608-12795-7, 202349100033) Bks Demand.

Pictures from the Past. Ruth Geller. LC 80-82075. 205p. 1980. pap. 7.95 (0-9603008-1-3) Imp Pr.

Pictures from the Past: A Schenectady Album. Larry Hart. (Illus.). 159p. (Orig.). 1992. pap. text 15.00 (0-932035-13-2) Old Dorp Bks.

P

An Asterisk (*) at the beginning of an entry indicates that the title is appearing for the first time.

Pictures from the Word. Marlene J. Cahse. LC 98-70855. (Illus.). 240p. 1998. pap. 6.00 (0-9657601-3-8, Crest Books) SANP.

Pictures, Images & Conceptual Change: An Analysis of Wilfrid Sellars' Philosophy of Science. Joseph C. Pitt. (Synthese Library: No. 151). 175p. 1981. pap. text 51.50 (90-277-1277-8) Kluwer Academic.

Pictures, Images & Conceptual Change: Wilfrid Sellars & the Philosophy of Science. Joseph C. Pitt. 175p. 1981. lib. bdg. 78.00 (90-277-1276-X, D Reidel) Kluwer Academic.

Pictures in Action. Herbert Puchta & Gunter Gerngross. 160p. (C). 1992. pap. 18.75 (0-13-675182-2) P-H.

Pictures in My Head. Gabriel Byrne. (Illus.). 168p. 1995. 19.95 (1-57098-046-2) Roberts Rinehart.

Pictures in My Head. Gabriel Byrne. (Illus.). 168p. 1997. pap. 12.95 (1-57098-152-3) Roberts Rinehart.

Pictures in Needlework: Twenty Miniature Designs for All Occasions. Shelley F. Lazar. (Illus.). 96p. 1990. text 15.95 (0-02-569510-X) Macmillan.

Pictures in Poetry. Barbara J. Hall. 64p. 1994. pap. write for info. (0-9642649-0-0) Nanas Wrld.

Pictures in Provence. large type ed. Lorna McKenzie. (Linford Romance Library). 240p. 1994. pap. 16.99 (0-7089-7513-5, Linford) Ulverscroft.

Pictures in the Air: The Story of the National Theatre of the Deaf. Stephen C. Baldwin. (Illus.). 176p. 1994. 24.95 (1-56368-025-4) Gallaudet Univ Pr.

Pictures in the Dark. Gillian Cross. LC 96-7660. 208p. (J). (gr. 7-12). 1996. 16.95 (0-8234-1267-9) Holiday.

Pictures in the Dark. Gillian Cross. 1998. 10.09 (0-606-13703-3, Pub. by Turtleback) Demco.

Pictures in the Fire. Charles Lounsbury. (Illus.). 48p. 1993. 18.95 (0-9621131-9-0) Laughing Elephant.

Pictures in the Hallway, Vol. 2. Sean O'Casey. LC 72-181386. (His Autobiography Ser.). 240p. 1971. write for info. (0-330-02717-4) Pan.

Pictures in the Post: The Story of the Picture Postcard. Richard Carline. LC 70-190038. 128p. 1971. pap. 7.95 (0-913782-04-1); pap. 7.95 (0-685-08357-8) Deltiologists Am.

Pictures, Moving. James Thomas. LC 85-4334. 192p. 1985. 16.00 (0-937872-22-9); pap. 8.00 (0-937872-23-7) Dragon Gate.

Pictures, 1918. Jeanette Ingold. Ed. by Diane D'Andrade. LC 98-5229. 155p. (J). (gr. 7 up). 1998. lib. bdg. 16.00 (0-15-201809-3) Harcourt.

***Pictures, 1918.** Jeanette Ingold. LC 99-27763. 2000. pap. 5.99 (0-14-130695-5) Peng Put Young Read.

Pictures of a Childhood: Sixty-Six Watercolours & an Essay. rev. ed. Alice Miller. Tr. by Hildegarde Hannum. (Illus.). 178p. 1999. pap. text 15.00 (0-7881-6200-4) DIANE Pub.

Pictures of a Dying Man. Agymah Kamau. LC 99-35461. 240p. 1999. 23.95 (1-56689-087-X, Pub. by Coffee Hse) SPD-Small Pr Dist.

Pictures of Buddhist Ceylon & Other Papers F. L. Woodward & Asian Educational Services Staff. LC 99-932491. 63 p. 1999. write for info. (81-206-1387-2, Pub. by Asian Educ Servs) S Asia.

Pictures of Health: A Photographic History of Health Care in Philadelphia, 1860-1945. Janet Golden & Charles E. Rosenberg. LC 90-22745. (Studies in Health, Illness, & Caregiving). (Illus.). 224p. (C). 1991. pap. 32.95 (0-8122-1311-4); text 52.50 (0-8122-8237-X) U of Pa Pr.

Pictures of Initiation in Greek Mythology. Leo Heirman. 1987. pap. 17.95 (0-935690-03-4) Schaumburg Pubns.

Pictures of Innocence: The History & Crisis of Ideal Childhood. Anne Higonnet. LC 97-61994. (Interplay Ser.). (Illus.). 232p. 1998. pap. 24.95 (0-500-28048-7, Pub. by Thames Hudson) Norton.

Pictures of Jesus. Daniel Barratt. (C). 1989. 45.00 (0-907839-45-2, Pub. by Brynmill Pr Ltd) St Mut.

Pictures of Messiah (In the Holy Scriptures) Ruth Lascelle. LC 97-71130. (Illus.). 255p. (Orig.). 1997. pap. text 13.00 (0-9654519-8-4) Bedrock Pub.

Pictures of Paradise: Elements of Garden Architecture. Pierre Zoelly. (Illus.). 104p. 1994. 50.00 (3-7643-2986-6, Pub. by Birkhauser) Princeton Arch.

Pictures of Patriarchy. Batya Weinbaum. LC 82-61150. 148p. 1983. 30.00 (0-89608-162-1); pap. 7.00 (0-89608-161-3) South End Pr.

Pictures of People: Alice Neel's American Portrait Gallery. Pamela Allara. LC 97-18403. (Illus.). 358p. 1998. 45.00 (0-87451-837-7) U Pr of New Eng.

***Pictures of People: Alice Neel's American Portrait Gallery.** Pamela Allara. LC 97-18403. (Illus.). 358p. 1998. 22.95 (1-58465-036-2) U Pr of New Eng.

Pictures of Perfection. Reginald Hill. 352p. 1995. mass mkt. 6.50 (0-440-21800-4) Dell.

Pictures of Perfection. large type ed. Reginald Hill. (Charnwood Large Print Ser.). 432p. 1995. 27.99 (0-7089-8845-8, Charnwood) Ulverscroft.

Pictures of Practice Vol. 1: Community Social Work in Scotland. David Stevenson et al. (C). 1988. 40.00 (0-7855-4022-9, Pub. by Natl Inst Soc Work) St Mut.

Pictures of Practice Vol. 1: Community Social Work in Scotland. David Stevenson et al. Ed. by W. Bennett & Gerald G. Smale. (C). 1989. 49.00 (0-7855-6305-9, Pub. by Natl Inst Soc Work) St Mut.

Pictures of Romance: Form Against Context in Painting & Literature. Wendy Steiner. LC 87-19023. (Illus.). 230p. 1987. 33.95 (0-226-77229-2) U Ch Pr.

Pictures of Romance: Form Against Context in Painting & Literature. Wendy Steiner. (Illus.). 230p. 1991. pap. text 16.50 (0-226-77230-6) U Ch Pr.

Pictures of Russian History & Russian Literature. Serge Wolkonsky. 1977. lib. bdg. 59.95 (0-8490-2442-0) Gordon Pr.

Pictures of Slavery & Anti-Slavery. John B. Robinson. LC 70-83875. (Black Heritage Library Collection). 1977. 20.95 (0-8369-8646-6) Ayer.

Pictures of the Bible: The New Testament & the Apocrypha. Illus. by Gustave Dore. LC 87-83047. 102p. (Orig.). 1988. 23.95 (0-945171-02-1); pap. 16.95 (0-945171-03-X) Harbour Pr.

Pictures of the Bible: The Old Testament & the Books of Maccabees: New Special Jewish Edition! Dore's Classical Pictures in the First Edition Especially Designed for the Jewish Reader. Illus. by Gustave Dore. LC 87-83046. (ENG & HEB.). 174p. (Orig.). 1988. pap. 18.95 (0-945171-01-3) Harbour Pr.

Pictures of the Body: Pain & Metamorphosis. James Elkins. LC 99-27632. (Illus.). 320p. 1999. 65.00 (0-8047-3023-7); pap. 24.95 (0-8047-3024-5) Stanford U Pr.

Pictures of the Crucifixion. Jerome Rothenberg. (Illus.). 30p. 1996. 375.00 (1-887123-07-5) Granary Bks.

Pictures of the Floating World. Amy Lowell. LC 78-64045. (Des Imagistes: Literature of the Imagist Movement Ser.). reprint ed. 42.50 (0-404-17128-1) AMS Pr.

Pictures of the Floating World. Amy Lowell. (Collected Works of Amy Lowell). 257p. 1999. reprint ed. lib. bdg. 88.00 (1-58201-759-X, c0759) Classic Bks.

Pictures of the Gone World. 2nd enl. ed. Lawrence Ferlinghetti. LC 95-5423. (Pocket Poets Ser.: Vol. 1). 1995. pap. 6.95 (0-87286-303-4) City Lights.

Pictures of the Heart: The Hyakunin Isshu in Word & Image. Joshua S. Mostow. LC 95-30185. (Illus.). 640p. 1996. text 48.00 (0-8248-1705-2) UH Pr.

Pictures of the Night. Geras Adele. (Egerton Hall Trilogy). 1998. 11.10 (0-606-13704-1, Pub. by Turtleback) Demco.

Pictures of the Night. Adele Geras. LC 92-27425. 192p. (YA). (gr. 7 up). 1993. 16.95 (0-15-261588-1) Harcourt.

Pictures of the Night. Adele Geras. Ed. by Michael Stearns. (Illus.). 1998. pap. 6.00 (0-15-201519-1) Harcourt.

Pictures of the Pain: Photography & the Assassination of President Kennedy. Richard B. Trask. LC 93-61324. (Illus.). 640p. 1994. 35.00 (0-9638595-0-1) Yeoman Pr.

Pictures of the Palace: Travellers' Accounts of the Brunei of Sultan Abdul Momin & Sultan Hashim Between 1881 & 1906 Simon Francis. LC 97-153897. 1993. write for info. (0-85958-829-7) Univ of Hull Pr.

Pictures of the Past, 4 bks. Denise Allard. Incl. Egyptians. LC 96-46378. 32p. (J). (gr. 2 up). 1997. lib. bdg. 21.27 (0-8368-1714-1); Greeks. LC 96-44372. 32p. (J). (gr. 2 up). 1997. lib. bdg. 21.27 (0-8368-1715-X); Romans. LC 96-46230. (Illus.). 32p. (J). (gr. 2 up). 1997. lib. bdg. 21.27 (0-8368-1716-8); Vikings. LC 96-46231. (Illus.). 32p. (J). (gr. 2 up). 1997. lib. bdg. 21.27 (0-8368-1717-6); (J). Set lib. bdg. 85.07 (0-8368-1713-3) Gareth Stevens Inc.

Pictures of the Times: A Century of Photography from the New York Times. Ed. by Peter Galassi & Susan Kismaric. (Illus.). 192p. 1996. 39.95 (0-87070-115-0, 0-8109-6167-9, Pub. by Mus of Modern Art); pap. 24.95 (0-87070-116-9, 0-8109-6176-8, Pub. by Mus of Modern Art) Abrams.

Pictures of the Times: A Century of Photography from the New York Times. Contrib. by William Safire & Peter Galassi. (Illus.). 192p. 1996. 39.95 (0-8109-6167-9, Pub. by Abrams) Time Warner.

Pictures of Travel: Heinrich Heine's Travels In Europe. Heinrich Heine. 1999. 27.95 (1-56886-100-1, Pub. by Marsilio Pubs) Consort Bk Sales.

Pictures on the Piano: A Family Chronicle of World War II. Alex Stewart. (Illus.). 381p. 1999. pap. 23.95 (0-89745-239-9) Sunflower U Pr.

Pictures, Please! An Articulation Supplement. Marcia S. Abbate & Nancy B. LaChappelle. 290p. 1984. ring bd. 55.00 (0-7616-2091-5) Commun Skill.

Pictures, Quotations, & Distinctions: Fourteen Essays in Phenomenology. Robert Sokolowski. LC 91-50575. (C). 1992. text 38.00 (0-268-01592-9) U of Notre Dame Pr.

***Pictures Tell the Story: Ernest C. Withers Reflections in History.** F. Jack Hurley et al. LC 99-76174. (Illus.). 191p. 2000. 38.00 (0-940744-68-6) Chrysler Museum.

Pictures, Their Preservation & Restoration. Carl D. Clarke. (Illus.). 250p. 1959. 40.00 (0-911426-06-X) Standard Arts.

Pictures to Print: The Nineteenth-Century Engraving Trade. Anthony Dyson. (Illus.). 234p. 1985. 35.00 (0-916271-02-1) BkPr Ltd.

Pictures to Print: The Nineteenth-Century Engraving Trade. deluxe ed. Anthony Dyson. (Illus.). 234p. 1985. 115.00 (0-916271-03-X) BkPr Ltd.

Pictures Will Talk: The Life & Films of Joseph L. Mankiewicz. Kenneth Geist. LC 82-23659. (Quality Paperbacks Ser.). (Illus.). 458p. 1983. reprint ed. pap. 9.95 (0-306-80188-4) Da Capo.

Pictures, Words, Threes & Other Numbers. Keith Shein. 1977. pap. 4.00 (0-917588-02-9) Trike.

Picture's Worth. Bruce Balan. (Cyber.Kdz Ser.). 1997. 9.09 (0-606-11231-6, Pub. by Turtleback) Demco.

Picture's Worth a Thousand Words: A Vocabulary Book. Kim Sanabria. (Illus.). 128p. (C). 1988. pap. text 18.20 (0-13-672213-X) P-H.

Picture's Worth 1,000 Words: A Workbook for Visual Communications. Jean Westcott & Jennifer H. Landau. (Illus.). 80p. 1996. pap. 29.95 (0-7879-0352-3, Pfffr & Co) Jossey-Bass.

***Pictures Your Heart Remembers: Building Lasting Memories of Love & Acceptance in Your Family.** John Trent. 256p. 2000. pap. 12.95 (1-57856-253-8) Waterbrook Pr.

Picturesque & the Sublime: A Poetic of the Canadian Landscape. Susan Glickman. 208p. 1998. text 55.00 (0-7735-1732-4, Pub. by McG-Queens Univ Pr) CUP Services.

Picturesque Catskills 1923 Vacationland: A Summer Paradise. (Illus.). 100p. 1996. 9.95 (0-941567-61-3) J C & A L Fawcett.

Picturesque Expressions: A Thematic Dictionary. 2nd ed. Ed. by Lawrence Urdang & Walter W. Hunsinger. 770p. 1985. 95.00 (0-8103-1606-4, 004439) Gale.

Picturesque Expressions: A Thematic Dictionary. 2nd ed. Laurence Urdang et al. LC 85-25274. 770p. 1998. reprint ed. 39.95 (0-930454-07-3) Verbatim Bks.

Picturesque Expressions Dictionary. 3rd ed. Urdang Staff. 1905. 90.00 (0-8103-5474-8) Gale.

Picturesque Frontier: The Army's Fort Dalles. 2nd rev. ed. Priscilla Knuth. (Illus.). 112p. 1988. pap. 8.95 (0-87595-140-6) Oregon Hist.

Picturesque Garden & Its Influence Outside the British Isles see Colloquium on the History of Landscape Architecture

Picturesque Harford County: The Artistic Impressions of William F. Turner. William F. Turner. LC 97-77185. (Illus.). 120p. 1997. 29.00 (1-878647-48-2) APU Pub Grp.

Picturesque Hawaii: A Charming Description of Her Unique History, Strange People, Exquisite Climate, Wondrous Volcanoes, Luxurious Productions, Beautiful Cities, Corrupt Monarchy, Recent Revolution & Provisional Government. John L. Stevens & W. B. Oleson. (Illus.). 224p. 1995. pap. 14.95 (0-9643829-1-1) Blue-Green Delta.

Picturesque Hudson. Clifton Johnson. 227p. 1993. reprint ed. lib. bdg. 79.00 (0-7812-5128-1) Rprt Serv.

Picturesque Itinerary of the Hudson River & Peripheral Parts of North America. Jacques Milbert. LC 67-29606. (American Environmental Studies). 1971. reprint ed. 26.95 (0-405-02678-1) Ayer.

Picturesque Landscapes of China: Photographys by Lang Hua. Hua Lang. Ed. by Haibo Luo. (CHI., Illus.). 68p. (Orig.). 1997. pap. 12.95 (0-9644818-9-8) Waymont Intl.

Picturesque Lies & Assorted Atrocities. Wayne Thorpe. LC 90-81544. 118p. (Orig.). 1990. pap. 11.95 (0-9624708-3-X) Chesterworks Babcock.

Picturesque Nepal. Percy Brown. 1997. pap. 132.00 (0-7855-7617-7) St Mut.

Picturesque New London & Its Environs: Groton, Mystic, Montville, Waterford. (Illus.). 192p. 1992. reprint ed. lib. bdg. 30.00 (0-8328-2245-0) Higginson Bk Co.

Picturesque Prison: Evelyn Waugh & His Writing. Jeffrey M. Heath. 1983. pap. text 24.95 (0-7735-0407-9, Pub. by McG-Queens Univ Pr) CUP Services.

Picturesque Prison: Evelyn Waugh & His Writing. Jeffrey M. Heath. LC 82-211598. 352p. reprint ed. pap. 109.20 (0-7837-1156-5, 204168500022) Bks Demand.

Picturesque Scenery of the Lake District, 1752-1855: A Bibliographical Study. P. Bicknell. 1990. 40.00 (0-906795-60-5) Oak Knoll.

Picturesque Spain. K. Hielscher. 1976. lib. bdg. 59.95 (0-8490-2444-7) Gordon Pr.

Picturesque St. Lawrence. Clifton Johnson. 253p. 1993. reprint ed. lib. bdg. 79.00 (0-7812-5129-X) Rprt Serv.

Picturesque Ulster. Richard Lionel Delisser. (Illus.). 300p. 1998. reprint ed. pap. 35.00 (0-910746-01-X, PU01) Hope Farm.

Picturing a Nation: Art & Social Change in Nineteenth-Century America. David M. Lubin. LC 93-19392. (Illus.). 584p. 1994. 55.00 (0-300-05732-6) Yale U Pr.

Picturing a Nation: Art & Social Change in Nineteenth-Century America. David M. Lubin. 1996. pap. 30.00 (0-300-06637-6) Yale U Pr.

Picturing a People: A History of African Americans from 1619-1900. N. Frank Woods. 196p. (C). per. write for info. (0-7872-6755-4) Kendall-Hunt.

Picturing a People: A History of African Americans from 1619-1900. N. Frank Woods. 208p. (C). 1996. pap. text, per. 55.95 (0-7872-3246-7, 41324601) Kendall-Hunt.

Picturing Algebra, Unit IX. Michael J. Arcidiacono & Eugene Maier. (Math & the Mind's Eye Ser.). (Illus.). 88p. (C). 1993. teacher ed., ring bd. 10.00 (1-886131-21-X, ME9) Math Lrning.

Picturing an Exhibition: "The Family of Man" & 1950s America. Eric J. Sandeen. LC 94-3205. (Illus.). 227p. 1995. 19.95 (0-8263-1558-5) U of NM Pr.

Picturing Art in Antwerp, 1550-1700. Zirka Z. Filipczak. LC 87-45518. 367p. 1987. reprint ed. pap. 113.80 (0-608-04639-6, 206532600003) Bks Demand.

Picturing Asian America: A Collaborative Project Organized by Mei-ling Hom. Richard Torchia. (Illus.). 10p. 1994. pap. 5.00 (1-58442-036-7) Galleries at Moore.

Picturing Britain: Time & Place in Image & Text, 1700-1850. Katherine Haskins. LC 93-408. (Illus.). 32p. (C). 1993. pap. text 6.00 (0-943056-19-5) Univ Chi Lib.

Picturing Bushmen: The Denver African Expedition of 1925. Robert J. Gordon. LC 97-2395. (Illus.). 325p. 1997. text 44.95 (0-8214-1187-X); pap. text 24.95 (0-8214-1188-8) Ohio U Pr.

Picturing California's Other Landscape: The Great Central Valley. Ed. & Intro. by Heath Schenker. (Illus.). 192p. 1999. pap. 35.00 (1-890771-25-2) Heyday Bks.

Picturing Casablanca: Portraits of Power in a Modern City. Susan Ossman. LC 93-36561. 1994. 48.00 (0-520-08402-0, Pub. by U CA Pr); pap. 16.95 (0-520-08403-9, Pub. by U CA Pr) Cal Prin Full Svc.

Picturing Change: An Illustrated Guide to Worldwide Literacy Programs. Lynn Curtis. (Illus.). (Orig.). 1995. pap. 4.00 (0-9623561-6-6) Laubach Literacy.

Picturing Cultural Values in Postmodern America. Ed. by William G. Doty. LC 94-13361. 272p. 1995. pap. text 29.95 (0-8173-0733-8) U of Ala Pr.

***Picturing Culture: Explorations in Film & Anthropology.** Jay Ruby. 1999. pap. text 19.00 (0-226-73099-9) U Ch Pr.

***Picturing Culture: Explorations in Film & Anthropology.** Jay Ruby. (Illus.). 1999. lib. bdg. 44.00 (0-226-73098-0) U Ch Pr.

Picturing Cultures: Historical Photographs in Anthropological Inquiry, Vol. 3, Nos. 3-4. Ed. by Joanna C. Scherer. (Visual Anthropology Ser.). 235p. 1990. text 125.00 (3-7186-0523-6, Harwood Acad Pubs) Gordon & Breach.

Picturing Empire: Photography & the Visualization of the British Empire. James Ryan. LC 97-26401. 272p. 1998. 38.00 (0-226-73233-9) U Ch Pr.

***Picturing Faith: A Facsimile Edition of the Pictographic Quechua Catechism in the Huntington.** Barbara H. Jaye. 76p. 2000. 24.95 (0-8061-9949-0); pap. text 14.95 (0-8061-9948-2) U of Okla Pr.

Picturing God. Ed. by Jean Holm & John W. Bowker. LC 94-13746. (Themes in Religious Studies). 1994. 45.00 (1-85567-100-X); pap. 16.95 (1-85567-101-8) St Martin.

Picturing Health & Illness: Images of Identity & Difference. Sander L. Gilman. LC 95-75700. (Illus.). 200p. 1995. text 32.95 (0-8018-5197-1) Johns Hopkins.

Picturing Hemingway. Frederick S. Voss & Michael S. Reynolds. LC 98-52550. (Illus.). 160p. 1999. 35.00 (0-300-07926-5) Yale U Pr.

Picturing Hong Kong: Photography, 1855-1910. Roberta Wue et al. LC 97-72657. (Illus.). 144p. 1997. 40.00 (0-8076-1424-6) Braziller.

Picturing Imperial Power: Colonial Subjects in Eighteenth-Century British Painting. Beth F. Tobin. LC 98-38415. 1999. 54.95 (0-8223-2305-2); pap. 18.95 (0-8223-2338-9) Duke.

Picturing Japaneseness: Monumental Style, National Identity, Japanese Film. Darrell W. Davis. (Film & Culture Ser.). 1996. 55.00 (0-231-10230-5); pap. 19.50 (0-231-10231-3) Col U Pr.

Picturing Knowledge: Historical & Philosophical Problems Concerning the Use of Art in Science. Ed. by Brian S. Baigrie. (Toronto Studies in Philosophy). (Illus.). 400p. 1996. text 80.00 (0-8020-2985-X); pap. text 24.95 (0-8020-7439-1) U of Toronto Pr.

Picturing Learning: Artists & Writers in the Classroom. Karen Ernst. LC 93-5426. (Illus.). 174p. 1993. pap. text 24.00 (0-435-08795-9, 08795) Heinemann.

***Picturing Lincoln.** George Sullivan. (Illus.). 96p. (J). (gr. 4-7). 2000. 16.00 (0-395-91682-8, Clarion Bks) HM.

Picturing Manchester Vol. 1: A Selection of Images from the Manchester Historic Association. Betty Lessard. Ed. by Holly Babin. (Illus.). 92p. 1997. mass mkt. 19.95 (0-9660881-0-7) Manchest Hist.

Picturing Minnesota, 1936-1943: Photographs from the Farm Security Administration. Ed. by Robert L. Reid. LC 89-13104. (Illus.). viii, 200p. (Orig.). 1989. pap. 19.95 (0-87351-248-0) Minn Hist.

Picturing Modernism: Moholy-Nagy & Photography in Weimar Germany. Eleanor M. Hight. (Illus.). 312p. 1994. 42.50 (0-262-08232-2) MIT Pr.

***Picturing New York: The City fom Its Beginnings to the Year 2000.** Gloria Deak. LC 99-54832. (Illus.). 400p. 2000. 49.95 (0-231-10728-5) Col U Pr.

***Picturing Old New England: Image & Memory.** William H. Truettner. LC 98-40097. (Illus.). 272p. 1999. 45.00 (0-300-07938-9) Yale U Pr.

Picturing Old New England: Image & Memory. William H. Truettner et al. LC 98-40097. (Illus.). write for info. (0-937311-48-0) Natl Mus Amer Art.

Picturing Ourselves: Photography & Autobiography. Linda H. Rugg. LC 97-3996. 286p. 1997. pap. 17.95 (0-226-73147-2) U Ch Pr.

Picturing Ourselves: Photography & Autobiography. Linda H. Rugg. LC 97-3996. 286p. 1997. lib. bdg. 46.00 (0-226-73146-4) U Ch Pr.

Picturing Paradise: Colonial Photography of Samoa, 1875 to 1925. Elizabeth Edwards et al. Ed. by Casey Blanton. (Illus.). 149p. 1995. pap. text 40.00 (1-887040-14-5) SE Mus Photo.

Picturing Performance: The Iconography of the Performing Arts in Theory & Practice. Ed. by Thomas F. Heck. LC 99-33072. (Illus.). 256p. 1999. 49.50 (1-58046-044-5, Pub. by Univ Rochester Pr) Boydell & Brewer.

Picturing Place. Schwartz. 115.00 (0-471-98339-X); pap. 34.95 (0-471-98340-3) Wiley.

Picturing Plants: An Analytical History of Botanical Illustration. Gill Saunders. LC 95-10204. (Illus.). 160p. 1995. 34.95 (0-520-20306-2, Pub. by U CA Pr) Cal Prin Full Svc.

Picturing Polygons: 2-D Geometry. Doug Clements et al. Ed. by Catherine Anderson. (Investigations in Number, Data, & Space Ser.). (Illus.). 206p. (J). (gr. 5-6). 1996. teacher ed. 32.95 incl. disk (0-86651-996-3, DS21432) Seymour Pubns.

Picturing Polygons: 2-D Geometry. rev. ed. Doug Clements et al. Ed. by Catherine Anderson et al. (Investigations in Number, Data, & Space Ser.). (Illus.). 211p. (YA). (gr. 5 up). 1997. pap. text 32.95 (1-57232-797-9, 47044) Seymour Pubns.

***Picturing Power in the People's Republic of China: Posters of the Cultural Revolution.** Ed. by Harriet Evans & Stephanie Donald. LC 99-24279. 208p. 1999. pap. 24.95 (0-8476-9511-5); text 69.00 (0-8476-9510-7) Rowman.

Picturing Science, Producing Art. Caroline A. Jones & Peter L. Galison. LC 97-40521. 608p. (C). 1998. 85.00 (0-415-91911-8) Routledge.

Picturing Science, Producing Art. Caroline A. Jones & Peter L. Galison. LC 97-40521. (Illus.). 608p. (C). 1998. pap. 35.00 (0-415-91912-6) Routledge.

Picturing Silence: Language, Emblem, Counter-Reformation Materiality. Karen Pinkus. LC 95-50241. (Body in Theory: Histories of Cultural Materialism Ser.). 200p. (C). 1996. text 44.50 (0-472-10705-4, 10705) U of Mich Pr.

P

Picturing Texas: The FSA-OWI Photographers in the Lone Star State, 1935-1943. Robert L. Reid. LC 94-21684. (Illus.). 224p. 1995. 49.95 (*0-87611-140-1*) Tex St Hist Assn.
Picturing the Bomb: Photographs from the Secret World of the Manhattan Project. Rachel Fermi & Esther Samra. LC 94-42666. (Illus.). 232p. 1995. 39.95 (*0-8109-3735-2*, Pub. by Abrams) Time Warner.
Picturing the Century: One Hundred Years of Photography from the National Archives. Bruce I. Bustard. LC 98-44102. (Illus.). 144p. 1999. pap. 24.95 (*0-295-97772-8*) U of Wash Pr.
Picturing the City. (C). Date not set. write for info. (*0-415-08785-6*) Routledge.
***Picturing the Human: The Moral Thought of Iris Murdoch.** Maria Antonaccio. LC 99-41886. 272p. 2000. 35.00 (*0-19-513171-1*) OUP.
***Picturing the Modern Amazon.** Ed. by Joanna Frueh et al. (Illus.). 176p. 2000. text 39.95 (*0-8478-2247-8*) Rizzoli Intl.
Picturing the Passion in Late Medieval Italy: Narrative Painting, Franciscan Ideologies & the Levant. Anne Derbes. LC 95-10981. (Illus.). 286p. (C). 1996. text 80.00 (*0-521-47481-7*) Cambridge U Pr.
Picturing the Passion in Late Medieval Italy: Narrative Painting, Franciscan Ideologies, & the Levant. Anne Derbes. (Illus.). 286p. (C). 1998. reprint ed. pap. text 22.95 (*0-521-63926-3*) Cambridge U Pr.
***Picturing the Past: English History in Text & Image, 1830-1870.** Rosemary C. Mitchell. LC 99-89337. (Oxford Historical Monographs). (Illus.). 332p. 2000. text 85.00 (*0-19-820844-8*) OUP.
Picturing the Past: Media,History & Photography. Bonnie Brennen. LC 98-58009. (History of Communication Ser.). 320p. 1999. 50.00 (*0-252-02465-6*) U of Ill Pr.
Picturing the Past: Media,History & Photography. Hanno Hardt. LC 98-58009. (History of Communication Ser.). 320p. 1999. pap. text 22.50 (*0-252-06769-X*) U of Ill Pr.
Picturing the Past: The Rise & Fall of the British Costume Film. Sue Harper. (Illus.). 264p. 1994. 49.95 (*0-85170-448-4*, Pub. by British Film Inst); pap. 23.95 (*0-85170-449-2*, Pub. by British Film Inst) Ind U Pr.
Picturing the Rose: A Way of Looking at Fairy Tales. Marcia Lane. LC 93-5777. 121p. 1994. 30.00 (*0-8242-0848-X*) Wilson.
Picturing the South: 1860 to the Present; Photographers & Writers. Ellen Dugan. 216p. 1996. 55.00 (*0-8118-1323-1*); pap. 29.95 (*0-8118-1343-6*) Chronicle Bks.
***Picturing the Story: Using Picture Books in the Middle School.** 56p. 1999. pap. text 24.95 (*1-58303-075-1*) Pthways Pubng.
Picturing the Tale: Chapters in the Study of the Use of Classical Myths by Painters & Sculptors. David D. Mulroy. 92p. (C). 1995. pap. text 17.95 (*0-8403-7761-4*) Kendall-Hunt.
Picturing the World. John C. Gilmour. LC 85-17189. (SUNY Series in Philosophy). 214p. (C). 1985. pap. text 17.95 (*0-88706-093-5*) State U NY Pr.
Picturing the Wreck. large type ed. Dani Shapiro. LC 96-10393. 1996. 24.95 (*0-7862-0686-1*) Thorndike Pr.
Picturing Time: The Work of Etienne-Jules Marey, 1830-1904. Marla Braun. (Illus.). xxii, 472p. 1994. pap. text 35.00 (*0-226-07175-8*) U Ch Pr.
Picturing Time: The Work of Etienne-Jules Marey, 1830-1904. Marta Braun. 1996. 70.00 (*0-226-07173-1*) U Ch Pr.
Picturing Us: African American Identity in Photography. Ed. by Deborah Willis. (Illus.). 208p. 1996. pap. 14.00 (*1-56584-106-9*, Pub. by New Press NY) Norton.
***Picturing Utopia: Bertha Shambaugh & the Amana Photographers.** Abigail Foerstner. LC 99-47858. (Bur Oak Original Ser.). (Illus.). 166p. 2000. 34.95 (*0-87745-699-2*) U of Iowa Pr.
Picturing Will. Ann Beattie. LC 90-50167. (Vintage Contemporaries Ser.). 240p. 1991. pap. 12.00 (*0-679-73194-6*) Vin Bks.
Picturing Women in Renaissance & Baroque Italy. Ed. by Geraldine A. Johnson & Sara F. Grieco. LC 96-51101. (Illus.). 336p. (C). 1998. text 85.00 (*0-521-56276-7*) Cambridge U Pr.
Picturing Women in Renaissance & Baroque Italy. Ed. by Geraldine A. Johnson & Sara F. Grieco. LC 96-51101. (Illus.). 336p. (C). 1998. pap. text 30.95 (*0-521-56580-4*) Cambridge U Pr.
Picturpedia: The Earth. DK Publishing Staff. 1997. 12.95 (*1-56458-138-1*) DK Pub Inc.
PIC16C5X Microcontroller: A Practical Approach to Embedded Control. Terry L. Dalby & William H. Rigby. (Illus.). 100p. (C). 1997. text. write for info. (*0-9654740-0-3*) Tecksysts.
PID Controllers. Richard K. Miller & Marcia E. Rupnow. LC 89-85429. (Survey on Technology & Markets Ser.: No. 121). 50p. 1991. pap. text 200.00 (*1-55865-144-6*) Future Tech Surveys.
PID Controllers: Theory, Design, & Tuning. 2nd ed. Karl J. Astrom & Tore H. Hagglund. LC 88-3010. 343p. 1995. 60.00 (*1-55617-516-7*) ISA.
Pidgin & Creole Languages. Suzanne Romaine. (Linguistics Library). (Illus.). 376p. (C). 1989. pap. text 26.04 (*0-582-29647-1*, 71828) Longman.
Pidgin & Creole Languages: Longman Linguistics Library. Suzanne Romaine. (Linguistics Library). (Illus.). 376p. (C). 1988. pap. text 39.95 (*0-582-01474-3*, 71828) Longman.
Pidgin & Creole Linguistics. Ed. by Albert Valdman. LC 76-48496. (Illus.). 415p. reprint ed. pap. 128.70 (*0-7837-8733-2*, 205924900012) Bks Demand.
Pidgin & Creole Tense-Mood-Aspect Systems. Ed. by John V. Singler. LC 90-32192. (Creole Language Library: Vol. 6). xvi, 240p. 1990. 65.00 (*1-55619-102-2*) J Benjamins Pubng Co.
Pidgin-English Sing-Song. Charles G. Leland. LC 74-166796. 1971. reprint ed. 25.00 (*0-403-01418-2*) Scholarly.
Pidgin Phrasebook: Pidgin Language of Oceania. 2nd ed. Ernest W. Lee. 250p. 1999. pap. 5.95 (*0-86442-587-2*) Lonely Planet.
Pidgin to Da Max. Douglas Simonson et al. (Illus.). 114p. (Orig.). 1986. pap. 9.95 (*0-935848-41-X*) Bess Pr.
Pidgin to Da Max Hana Hou. Douglas Simonson et al. (Illus.). 112p. (Orig.). 1992. pap. 9.95 (*0-935848-91-6*) Bess Pr.
Pidginization & Creolization: The Case of Arabic. Kees Versteegh. LC 84-28364. (Current Issues in Linguistic Theory Ser.: Vol. 33). xiii, 194p. 1984. 71.00 (*90-272-3529-5*) J Benjamins Pubng Co.
***Pidgins & Creoles.** Ed. by Ishtla Singh. 144p. 2000. pap. 19.95 (*0-340-70095-5*); text 65.00 (*0-340-70094-7*) OUP.
Pidgins & Creoles. Loreto Todd. (Language & Society Ser.). 1974. 16.95 (*0-7100-7865-X*, Routledge Thoemms); pap. 10.95 (*0-7100-7927-3*, Routledge Thoemms) Routledge.
Pidgins & Creoles. Loreto Todd. 128p. (C). (gr. 13). 1990. pap. 22.99 (*0-415-05311-0*, A4958) Routledge.
Pidgins & Creoles: An Introduction. Ed. by Jacques Arends et al. LC 94-24286. (Creole Language Library: No. 15). xv, 412p. 1995. pap. 29.95 (*1-55619-170-7*); lib. bdg. 79.00 (*1-55619-169-3*) J Benjamins Pubng Co.
Pidgins & Creoles: Current Trends & Prospects. Georgetown University Round Table on Languages & L. Ed. by David De Camp & Ian F. Hancock. LC 74-76081. (Illus.). 143p. reprint ed. pap. 44.40 (*0-7837-6315-8*, 204603000010) Bks Demand.
Pie & Pastry Bible. Rose L. Beranbaum. (Illus.). 512p. 1998. 35.00 (*0-684-81348-3*) Scribner.
Pie & the Patty-Pan. Beatrix Potter. (Illus.). 46p. (J). 1976. reprint ed. pap. 1.95 (*0-486-23383-9*) Dover.
Pie-Biter. Ruthanne L. McCunn. Tr. by Ellen L. Yeung & Teresa Mlawer from CHI. LC 97-27586. (Illus.). 32p. (J). (gr. k-4). 1998. 15.95 (*1-885008-07-4*) Shens Bks.
Pie Book: 419 Recipes. Louis P. De Gouy. LC 73-88331. 384p. 1974. reprint ed. pap. 7.95 (*0-486-22997-1*) Dover.
Pie Every Day. Pat Willard. 1998. reprint ed. pap. 14.00 (*0-425-16436-5*) Berkley Pub.
Pie Every Day: Recipes & Slices of Life. Pat Willard. LC 96-47650. 336p. 1997. 19.95 (*1-56512-147-3*, 72147) Algonquin Bks.
Pie for Thanksgiving. Paul Evans. LC 96-27280. (J). 1997. write for info. (*1-56763-265-3*); pap. write for info. (*1-56763-266-1*) Ozark Pub.
Pie in the Sky. Bruce Balan. 1999. pap. 4.99 (*0-14-055533-1*) NAL.
Pie in the Sky. Anne Page. (Illus.). 40p. (Orig.). (J). (ps-3). 1985. pap. 4.95 (*0-9613925-2-5*) Joane Pubns.
Pie in the Sky: Profiling Portland Bakeries. Lianne Forney & James L. Forney. LC 81-81595. (Illus.). 140p. (Orig.). 1981. pap. 5.95 (*0-939930-00-5*) Hampshire Pacific.
***Pie is Cherry.** Michael Rex. 2001. text 15.95 (*0-8050-6308-0*) H Holt & Co.
Pie Lady of Winthrop: And Other Minnesota Tales. Peg Meier & Dave Wood. (Illus.). 244p. (Orig.). 1985. pap. 8.95 (*0-933387-00-8*) Neighbors Pub.
Pie Magic. Toby Forward. 112p. (J). (gr. 3 up). 1998. mass mkt. 4.95 (*0-688-15856-0*, Wm Morrow) Morrow Avon.
Pie Method for Career Success: A New Job Search Strategy. Daniel Porot. (Illus.). 218p. (Orig.). 1995. pap. 14.95 (*1-56370-182-0*, J1820) JIST Works.
Pie Powder by a Circuit Tramp. John A. Foote. Ed. by J. Myron Jacobstein. (Classics in Legal History Reprint Ser.: Vol. 1). 216p. 1967. reprint ed. lib. bdg. 42.00 (*0-89941-000-6*, 300350) W S Hein.
Pie Rats Ahoy! Richard Scarry. LC 92-50998. (Step into Reading Ser.: A Step 1 Book). (Illus.). 32p. (J). (ps-1). 1994. pap. 3.99 (*0-679-84760-X*, Pub. by Random Bks Yng Read) Random.
Pie Rats Ahoy! Richard Scarry. LC 92-50998. (Step into Reading Ser.: A Step 1 Book). (Illus.). 32p. (J). (ps-3). 1994. lib. bdg. 11.99 (*0-679-94760-4*, Pub. by Random Bks Yng Read) Random.
Pie-Rat's Revenge. Jim Davis. (Garfield's Pet Force Ser.: Vol. 2). (Illus.). (J). (gr. 3-7). 1998. pap. text 3.99 (*0-590-05909-2*) Scholastic Inc.
Pie Went By. Carolyn Dunn. LC 98-16790. 32p. (J). (ps-1). Date not set. pap. 4.95 (*0-06-443649-7*) HarpC Child Bks.
***Pie Went By.** Carolyn Dunn. LC 98-16790. 32p. (J). (ps-1). 2000. 14.95 (*0-06-028807-8*); lib. bdg. 14.89 (*0-06-028808-6*) HarpC Child Bks.
Piebald Pup. Irina Korschunow. (Illus.). (J). (gr. k-3). 1959. 9.95 (*0-8392-3026-5*) Astor-Honor.
Piebald Standard. Edith Simon. LC 76-29836. reprint ed. 40.00 (*0-404-15419-0*) AMS Pr.
Piece As a Whole: Studies in Holistic Musical Analysis. Hugh Aitken. 136p. 1997. pap. 17.95 (*0-275-96038-2*, Praeger Pubs) Greenwood.
Piece As a Whole: Studies in Holistic Musical Analysis, 45. Hugh Aitken. LC 97-2714. (Contributions to the Study of Music & Dance: Vol. 45). 136p. 1997. 49.95 (*0-313-30061-5*, Greenwood Pr) Greenwood.
Piece by Piece! Mosaics of the Ancient World. Avi Avi-Yonah. LC 93-10746. (Buried Worlds Ser.). (YA). (gr. 6 up). 1993. lib. bdg. 23.93 (*0-8225-3204-2*, Lerner Publctns) Lerner Pub.
Piece de Chambertin. Eugene Labiche. 9.95 (*0-686-54248-7*) Fr & Eur.
Piece Is Missing. Donald R. Lima. LC 98-85234. 192p. 1998. text 19.95 (*1-56167-427-3*) Noble House.
Piece of Bread. Stefan Wysznski. (C). 1988. 39.00 (*0-85439-215-7*, Pub. by St Paul Pubns) St Mut.
Piece of Cake. Jill Murphy. LC 96-26251. (Illus.). 32p. (Orig.). (J). (ps-3). 1997. pap. 4.99 (*0-7636-0111-X*) Candlewick Pr.
Piece of Cake. Jill Murphy. (Orig.). 1997. 11.19 (*0-606-12791-7*, Pub. by Turtleback) Demco.
Piece of Cake. 2nd ed. Jill Murphy. LC 96-26251. (Illus.). 32p. (J). (ps-3). 1998. 13.99 (*0-7636-0572-7*) Candlewick Pr.
***Piece of Cake: A Delectable Pop-Up Book.** David Pelham. (Illus.). (J). 2000. 12.95 (*1-929766-02-5*) Handprint.
Piece of Eight: A Women's Anthology of Verse. unabridged ed. Sara Gouldin et al. 48p. 1998. pap. 10.00 (*1-891812-02-5*, 98-003) Cedar Hill Pubns.
***Piece of Forever: Selected Prose & Poetry.** Ed. by Mary Ann Huddleston. LC 99-28649. 128p. 1999. 16.95 (*0-8298-1349-7*) Pilgrim OH.
Piece of Heaven. Jacquelyn R. Thrash. (YA). 1996. pap. 24.95 (*0-9635247-4-7*) Three Pines.
Piece of Jungle. Sarah Weeks. LC 98-54328. (Illus.). 32p. (J). (ps-3). 1999. 15.95 incl. audio (*0-06-028409-9*) HarpC Child Bks.
Piece of Mine. J. California Cooper. 144p. 1991. reprint ed. pap. 9.95 (*0-385-42087-0*, Anchor NY) Doubleday.
Piece of My Heart. Richard Ford. (Vintage Contemporaries Ser.). 1985. pap. 12.00 (*0-394-72914-5*) Vin Bks.
Piece of My Heart. Richard Ford. 1996. pap. 12.00 (*0-676-51111-2*) Vin Bks.
Piece of My Heart. Julia Watts. LC 97-52960. 240p. 1998. pap. 11.95 (*1-56280-206-2*) Naiad Pr.
Piece of My Heart: A Lesbian of Colour Anthology. Ed. by Makeda Silvera. 416p. 1995. per. 17.95 (*0-920813-65-8*) Sister Vis Pr.
Piece of My Heart: A Portrait of Janis Joplin. David Dalton. (Quality Paperbacks Ser.). (Illus.). 287p. 1991. reprint ed. pap. 14.95 (*0-306-80446-8*) Da Capo.
***Piece of My Heart: Living Through the Grief of Miscarriage, Stillbirth or Infant Death.** Molly Fumia. 200p. 2000. pap. 14.95 (*1-57324-510-0*) Conari Press.
Piece of My Heart: The Stories of 26 American Women Who Served in Vietnam. Keith Walker. LC 85-19416. (Illus.). 352p. 1997. pap. 15.95 (*0-89141-617-X*) Presidio Pr.
Piece of My Heart - Pedacito de Mi Corazon: The Art of Carmen Lomas Garza. Carmen L. Garza. 1994. pap. 12.95 (*1-56584-164-6*, Pub. by New Press NY) Norton.
Piece of My Mind. Peter Nichols. LC 88-116276. (Methuen Modern Plays Ser.). 80p. (C). 1988. pap. 10.95 (*0-413-17360-7*, A0210, Methuen Drama) Methn.
Piece of Paradise: The Story of Custer State Park. Edward Raventon. LC 96-7949. (Illus.). 104p. 1996. pap. 14.95 (*1-56044-499-1*) Falcon Pub Inc.
Piece of Peace: Kids Share Their Lives Through Poetry, Art & Photography. Ed. by Beth Krensky et al. 104p. (Orig.). (J). (gr. 3-7). 1995. pap. 17.95 (*1-883280-05-2*) Font & Ctr Pr.
Piece of String. George Mendoza. (Illus.). 1965. 10.95 (*0-8392-1160-0*) Astor-Honor.
Piece of String is a Wonderful Thing. Judy Hindley. (Read & Wonder Ser.). (J). 1995. 11.19 (*0-606-08013-9*) Turtleback.
Piece of Tape: The Watergate Story: Fact & Fiction. James W. McCord. LC 74-79864. xvi, 329 p. 1974. write for info. (*0-914286-00-5*) McCord Pubns.
Piece of the Action. Stephen Solomita. 352p. 1994. mass mkt. 4.99 (*0-380-72103-1*, Avon Bks) Morrow Avon.
Piece of the Action: How Women & Minorities Can Launch Their Own Successful Businesses. Suzanne Caplan. LC 93-42510. 160p. 1994. pap. 17.95 (*0-8144-7869-7*) AMACOM.
Piece of the Cake. Robert Colby. (Midnight Reading Ser.). 1997. pap. 4.20 (*1-55855-691-5*) Raintree Steck-V.
Piece of the Fox's Hide. Katharine Boling. LC 72-86903. 376p. 1998. reprint ed. pap. 9.95 (*0-87844-054-2*) Sandlapper Pub Co.
Piece of the Moon Is Missing. Ed. by Ruth Roston. (Illus.). 192p. (Orig.). 1985. pap. 7.00 (*0-927663-06-6*) COMPAS.
Piece of the Moon World: Paul Klee in Texas Collections. Ed. by Susan E. Davidson. LC 94-4876. 1994. pap. 14.95 (*0-939594-31-5*, Menil Collection) Menil Found.
Piece of the Mountain: The Story of Blaise Pascal. Joyce McPherson. 128p. (YA). (gr. 5-12). 1995. pap. 7.95 (*1-882514-17-3*) Greenleaf TN.
Piece of the Pie: Blacks & White Immigrants since 1880. Stanley Lieberson. (Illus.). 420p. 1980. pap. 18.95 (*0-520-04362-6*, Pub. by U CA Pr) Cal Prin Full Svc.
Piece of Tomorrow. Kate Stevenson. 1994. per. 3.50 (*0-373-07576-6*, 5-07576-7) Harlequin Bks.
Piece of Work: Five Writers Discuss Their Revisions. Ed. by Jay Woodruff. LC 92-39413. (Illus.). 285p. 1993. pap. 12.95 (*0-87745-409-4*) U of Iowa Pr.
Piece on Earth: A Little Book Made with Special Quilting. Andrews & McMeel Staff. LC 97-71548. (Little Library to Make It Special). (Illus.). 80p. 1997. 4.95 (*0-8362-3612-2*) Andrews & McMeel.
Piece Power. Peter Wells. 1995. pap. 11.95 (*0-8050-3580-X*, Pub. by Batsford Chess) H Holt & Co.
Piece Together Praise. Brian Wren. LC 96-75969. 1996. pap. 11.95 (*0-916642-62-3*, 1884) Hope Pub.
Piece Work. Miriam Packer. LC 95-81761. (Drama Ser.: No. 14). 160p. Date not set. pap. 10.00 (*1-55071-038-9*) Guernica Editions.
Pieced Border Collection. Ed. by Sandra L. Hatch. LC 95-81674. (Illus.). 160p. 1996. 19.95 (*1-882138-13-9*) Hse White Birches.
Pieced by Mother: Symposium Papers. Jeannette Lasansky et al. (Illus.). 104p. (Orig.). 1988. pap. 19.95 (*0-917127-03-X*) Oral Traditions.
Pieced Clothing. rev. ed. Yvonne Porcella. LC 86-90565. (Illus.). 60p. 1987. pap. 11.95 (*0-936589-01-9*) Porcella Studios.
***Pieced Flowers.** Ruth B. Macdowell. Ed. by Barb Kuhn & Sara MacFarland. (Illus.). 112p. 2000. pap. 24.95 (*1-57120-091-6*, 10208, Pub. by C & T Pub) Watsn-Guptill.
Pieced from Ellen's Quilt: Ellen Spaulding Reed's Letters & Story. Linda O. Lipsett. LC 91-16329. (Illus.). 224p. (Orig.). 1991. pap. 13.95 (*0-9629399-0-0*) Halstead Meadows.
***Pieced or Appliqued Flowers: From the AQS Contest Flowers on Parade.** Barbara Smith. (Illus.). 96p. 2000. pap. 19.95 (*1-57432-742-9*, Am Quilters Soc) Collector Bks.
Pieced Quilts. Caren Caraway. (International Design Library). (Illus.). 48p. (Orig.). 1981. pap. 5.95 (*0-916144-79-8*) Stemmer Hse.
***Pieced Roman Shades: Turn Your Favorite Quilt Patterns into Window Hangings.** Terrell Sundermann. Ed. by Beate Nelleman & Lynn Koolish. LC 99-6794. (Illus.). 112p. 2000. pap. 24.95 (*1-57120-094-0*, 10211) C & T Pub.
Piecemeal, Pt. 1. Guy Beining. (Illus.). 42p. (Orig.). 1988. pap. 3.00 (*0-926935-25-9*) Runaway Spoon.
Piecemeal, Pt. 2. Guy Beining. (Illus.). 44p. (Orig.). 1988. pap. 3.00 (*0-926935-26-7*) Runaway Spoon.
Piecemeal, Pt. 3. Guy Beining. (Illus.). 36p. (Orig.). 1989. pap. 3.00 (*0-926935-27-5*) Runaway Spoon.
Piecemeal, Pt. 4. Guy Beining. (Illus.). 36p. (Orig.). 1989. pap. 3.00 (*0-926935-28-3*) Runaway Spoon.
Piecemeal, Pt. 5. Guy Beining. (Illus.). 36p. (Orig.). 1989. pap. 3.00 (*0-926935-29-1*) Runaway Spoon.
Piecemeal, Pt. 6. Guy Beining. (Illus.). 36p. (Orig.). 1989. pap. 3.00 (*0-926935-30-5*) Runaway Spoon.
Piecemeal, Pt. 7. Guy Beining. (Illus.). 36p. (Orig.). 1989. pap. 3.00 (*0-926935-31-3*) Runaway Spoon.
Piecemeal, Pt. 8. Guy Beining. (Illus.). 42p. (Orig.). 1989. pap. 3.00 (*0-926935-32-1*) Runaway Spoon.
Piecemeal, Pts. 1-8. Guy Beining. (Illus.). 308p. (Orig.). 1989. pap. 20.00 (*0-926935-33-X*) Runaway Spoon.
Pieces. Barbara Clark. 72p. 1985. pap. 6.95 (*0-9612296-3-2*) Williams SC.
***Pieces.** Anna G. Hines. (J). 2001. 15.95 (*0-688-16963-5*, Grenwillow Bks); lib. bdg. 15.89 (*0-688-16964-3*, Grenwillow Bks) HarpC Child Bks.
Pieces. Francis Ponge. (FRE.). 1971. pap. 11.95 (*0-7859-2770-0*) Fr & Eur.
Pieces. Francis Ponge. (Poesie Ser.). 194p. 1971. 11.95 (*2-07-031873-7*) Schoenhof.
Pieces: Toward a Revisioning of Communication/Life. Lee Thayer. LC 96-25517. 280p. 1997. pap. 39.50 (*1-56750-271-7*); text 73.25 (*1-56750-270-9*) Ablx Pub.
Pieces - The Story of Elgin in a Quilt. Gladys J. Peterson. (Illus.). 128p. (Orig.). 1988. write for info. (*0-318-64354-5*); pap. 9.95 (*0-685-24078-9*) Amer Healthcare Ctr.
Pieces a Une et a Deux Violes (1686-1689) Marin Marais. (Instrumental Works: Vol. 1). (Illus.). 1980. lib. bdg. 150.00 (*0-8450-7201-3*) Broude.
Pieces a une et a Trois Violes, Quatrieme Livre (1717) Marin Marais. (Instrumental Works Ser.: Vol. 4). 1998. lib. bdg. 150.00 (*0-8450-7204-8*) Broude.
Pieces & Patterns: A Patchwork in Math & Science. Judith A. Hillen. (J). (gr. 5-9). 1986. 16.95 (*1-881431-03-7*, 1309) AIMS Educ Fnd.
Pieces & Places of Billings History: Local Monuments & Sites. Joyce Jensen. 124p. 1994. pap. text 8.95 (*0-9643921-0-0*) Westrn Hrtge.
Pieces & Pontifications Norman Mailer. LC 84-203538. x, 208p. 1983. write for info. (*0-450-06030-6*, Pub. by New Eng Lib) Trafalgar.
***Pieces & Stems.** Jane Elton. 473p. 1999. pap. 17.95 (*1-929481-01-2*) Zach London.
Pieces Brillantes: L'invitation au chateau, Colombe, La repetition ou L'amour puni [et] L'ecole des peres. Jean Anouilh. Incl. Cecile: Ou, L'ecole des Peres. Colombe. L'invitation au Chateau. Repetition Ou l'Amour Puni. 42.50 (*0-685-37149-2*, F81770) Fr & Eur.
Pieces Costumees: L'Alouette, Becket, la Foire d'Empoigne. Jean Anouilh. (FRE.). 42.95 (*0-685-37150-6*, F81772) Fr & Eur.
Pieces de Clavecin. fac. ed. Johann Mattheson. (Monuments of Music & Music Literature in Facsimile, I Ser.: Vol. 5). (Illus.). 1965. lib. bdg. 50.00 (*0-8450-2005-6*) Broude.
Pieces de Clavecin see Oeuvres Completes de Jean-Philippe Rameau
Pieces de Clavecin: Premier, Second, Troisieme et Quatrieme Livres. fac. ed. Francois Couperin. (Monuments of Music & Music Literature in Facsimile Ser., Series I: Vol. 9). 1974. lib. bdg. 125.00 (*0-8450-2009-9*) Broude.
Pieces de Clavecin, Livre Premier: Paris, 1689. fac. ed. Jean-Henry D'Anglebert. (Monuments of Music & Music Literature in Facsimile Ser.: Vol. 4). 1964. lib. bdg. 60.00 (*0-8450-2004-8*) Broude.
Pieces de Clavessin. fac. ed. Jacques De Chambonnieres. (Monuments of Music & Music Literature in Facsimile, I Ser.: Vol. 3). 1967. lib. bdg. 60.00 (*0-8450-2003-X*) Broude.
Pieces de Voile, Second Livre, 1701. Marin Marais. (Instrumental Works: Vol. 2). 1987. lib. bdg. 150.00 (*0-8450-7202-1*) Broude.
Pieces de Voile, Troisieme Livre (1711) Marin Marais. (Instrumental Works: Vol. 3). (Illus.). 1995. lib. bdg. 150.00 (*0-8450-7203-X*) Broude.
Pieces Detachees. Michel Tremblay. Tr. by VanMeer. 112p. 1975. pap. 11.95 (*0-88922-092-1*, Pub. by Talonbks) Genl Dist Srvs.
Pieces Diverses see Melanges
Pieces en un Acte: Avec: La Scintillante, Amedes et les Messieurs en rang. Jules Romains, pseud. (FRE.). 176p. 1930. pap. 10.95 (*0-7859-1307-6*, 2070255166) Fr & Eur.
Pieces for Children Piano. C. Griffes. 40p. 1995. pap. 5.95 (*0-7935-3539-5*, 50482204) H Leonard.

P

An Asterisk (*) at the beginning of an entry indicates that the title is appearing for the first time.

Pieces for Prize Speaking. Ed. by A. H. Craig & Binney Gunnison. LC 75-5592. (Granger Index Reprint Ser.). 1977. reprint ed. 25.95 (*0-8369-6371-7*) Ayer.

Pieces from My Crazy Quilt. Jan Keller. Ed. by Janetta Roberts & Amy Holzworth. (Illus.). 128p. Date not set. pap. 12.95 (*1-889579-00-9*) Blck Sheep Bks.

Pieces from My Heart. James W. Hamilton. 52p. (Orig.). 1991. pap. 9.95 (*1-879260-02-6*) Evanston Pub.

***Pieces from My Mind.** Carl E. Clark. LC 99-64938. 188p. 2000. pap. 13.95 (*0-88739-307-1*) Creat Arts Bk.

***Pieces from the Past.** J. J. Despain. LC 00-26549. (Illus.). 224p. 2000. pap. 16.95 (*1-58017-249-0*) Storey Bks.

Pieces Grincantes. Incl. Ardele: Ou, La Marguerite. Ed. by Jean Anouilh. Ornifle Ou le Courant d'Air. Jean Anouilh. Pauvre Bitos Ou le Diner de Tetes. Jean Anouilh. Valse des Toreadors. Jean Anouilh. 19.50 (*0-685-37151-4*, F81774) Fr & Eur.

***Pieces in Place.** Jerry Martien. 128p. 1999. pap. 10.95 (*0-942396-82-0*, Pub. by Blackberry ME) SPD-Small Pr Dist.

Pieces Noires. Incl. Eurydice. Hermine. Jean Anouilh. Sauvage. Jean Anouilh. Voyageur sans Bagage. Jean Anouilh. 42.95 (*0-685-37152-2*, F81775) Fr & Eur.

Pieces O' Six. Jackson Mac Low. (Sun & Moon Classics Ser.: No. 17). 188p. 1989. pap. 11.95 (*1-55713-060-4*) Sun & Moon CA.

Pieces of a Dream: The Ethnic Worker's Crisis with America. Michael G. Wenk. Ed. by Geno Baroni et al. LC 72-93362. (Illus.). 212p. (C). 1977. pap. 9.95 (*0-913256-08-0*) CMS.

Pieces of a Dreamer. Amaga Peyton. 66p. (J). 1999. pap. 12.95 (*1-890667-09-9*, Hand-In-Hand Bks) Introspect Bks.

Pieces of a Pattern: Lacroix by Lacroix. Christian Lacroix. Ed. by Patrick Mauries. LC 92-60343. (Illus.). 192p. 1997. pap. 34.95 (*0-500-27933-0*, Pub. by Thames Hudson) Norton.

Pieces of a Song: Selected Poems of Diane DiPrima. Diane DiPrima. 205p. (Orig.). 1989. pap. 12.95 (*0-87286-237-2*) City Lights.

Pieces of a Woman. Barbara Holley. (Illus.). 12p. 1982. pap. 2.50 (*0-943696-01-1*) Red Key Pr.

Pieces of an American Quilt: Quilts, Patterns, Photos & Behind the Scene Stories from the Movie. Patty McCormick. Ed. by Elizabeth Aneloski. LC 96-33759. (Illus.). 96p. (Orig.). 1996. pap. 19.95 (*1-57120-012-6*, 10136) C & T Pub.

Pieces of an Examined Life. Stephen Vicchio. LC 99-13695. 208p. 1999. pap. 14.95 (*1-891521-06-3*) Woodholme Hse.

Pieces of Another World: The Story of Moon Rocks. Franklyn M. Branley. LC 71-158684. (Illus.). (J). (gr. 5-8). 1972. lib. bdg. 11.89 (*0-690-62566-9*) HarpC Child Bks.

Pieces of Blue. Kainoa A. Koeninger. 98p. (Orig.). 1993. pap. text 9.95 (*0-9625767-6-X*) Chumash Pr.

Pieces of Brandon. Albert Huffstickler. 20p. (Orig.). 1989. pap. 4.00 (*0-941720-71-3*) Slough Pr TX.

Pieces of Dreams. Donna Hill. 1999. mass mkt. 4.99 (*1-58314-020-4*) BET Bks.

Pieces of Dreams. Charlotte Vale Allen. 1998. reprint ed. pap. 20.00 (*1-892738-06-6*) Isld Nation.

Pieces of Dreams. Charlotte Vale Allen. 314p. 1999. reprint ed. 23.95 (*1-892738-21-X*, Pub. by Isld Nation) Brodart.

Pieces of Earth. Kate Perry. Ed. by Lyons Graphic Designs Staff. (Illus.). 159p. (Orig.). 1994. pap. text 12.95 (*0-9626823-5-7*) Perry ME.

Pieces of Eight. Sydney J. Harris. 1985. pap. 7.95 (*0-685-09890-7*) HM.

Pieces of Eight. Charles Johnson. (Footprints in Time Ser.). (Illus.). 110p. (J). (gr. 3-6). 1989. 9.95 (*0-944770-00-2*) Discovery GA.

Pieces of Eight. Robert A. Nisbet. 145p. (C). 1982. pap. 30.00 (*0-85088-555-8*, Pub. by Spencer Pr) St Mut.

Pieces of Eight. L. B. Taylor, Jr. & Kip Wagner. (Illus.). 222p. 1998. pap. 17.95 (*0-912451-08-4*) Florida Classics.

Pieces of Gold(man) Florence Goldman. LC 94-62133. 179p. 1995. pap. 12.00 (*1-882203-03-8*) Orange Frazer.

Pieces of Home: A Family of Poems. Patricia Hammond. 110p. 1993. write for info. (*0-9639679-0-8*) P Hammond.

Pieces of Light. Adam Thorpe. 488p. 2000. 25.95 (*0-7867-0661-9*) Carroll & Graf.

Pieces of Map, Pieces of Music. Robert Bringhurst. LC 86-73199. 128p. (Orig.). 1987. reprint ed. pap. 9.00 (*1-55659-003-2*) Copper Canyon.

Pieces of Me. Susan Colgan. 1999. pap. 11.95 (*0-9656748-4-3*) Winter Again.

Pieces of Me. AnneMarie Pierce. (Illus.). (J). (gr. 1-9). write for info. (*0-9623937-3-8*) Forword MN.

Pieces of Mind: Fragmented Commentary on Domestic Blisters & Living Laughably Ever After. Marilyn Dittoe. LC 98-30175. 176p. 1998. pap. 12.95 (*1-888683-77-5*) Wooster Bk.

Pieces of Modesty. Peter O'Donnell. 1990. mass mkt. write for info. (*0-8125-0732-0*) Tor Bks.

Pieces of Modesty. Peter O'Donnell. 192p. 1986. reprint ed. 15.45 (*0-89296-172-4*, Pub. by Mysterious Pr) Little.

Pieces of Mosaic: An Essay in the Making of Makedonija. Jonathan M. Schwartz. 160p. (Orig.). (C). 1996. pap. text 24.00 (*87-89825-16-0*) Smyrna.

Pieces of My Heart. Belle N. Lipe. (Illus.). 120p. 1996. 19.95 (*1-888366-03-6*) Dixie Pr.

***Pieces of My Heart.** Nancy Ann Mattingly. 136p. 1999. 12.95 (*0-9630274-6-8*) J D Huff.

Pieces of My Mind. Andrew A. Rooney. 1985. mass mkt. 4.95 (*0-380-69885-4*, Avon Bks) Morrow Avon.

Pieces of My Mind. Edith S. Weigand. ix, 61p. 1998. pap. 7.95 (*0-9618904-4-4*) Zhera Pubns.

Pieces of Peace. W. Calvin McCain. LC 74-25235. 80p. 1983. reprint ed. pap. text 5.95 (*0-931680-01-8*) Dunbar Pub.

Pieces of Purgatory: Mental Retardation in & out of Institutions. J. David Smith. LC 94-17199. 144p. 1994. 20.95 (*0-534-25206-0*) Brooks-Cole.

Pieces of Rainbow. Elizabeth Nash. LC 93-33450. (American University Studies, XX, Fine Arts: Vol. 22). 136p. (C). 1994. text 34.95 (*0-8204-2413-7*) P Lang Pubng.

Pieces of Resistance: Selected Essays. Eugene Goodheart. 216p. 1987. text 59.95 (*0-521-34036-5*) Cambridge U Pr.

Pieces of Sky. Marianne Willman. 400p. 1986. per. 4.50 (*0-373-97022-6*) Harlequin Bks.

Pieces of Sky. Marianne Willman. (Historical Ser.). 1993. per. 3.99 (*0-373-28795-X*, 1-28795-2) Harlequin Bks.

***Pieces of Sky.** Marianne Willman. 401p. 2000. per. 5.99 (*1-55166-564-6*) Harlequin Bks.

Pieces of String & Other Stories. Tita Lacambra-Ayala. 138p. (Orig.). 1984. pap. 12.50 (*971-10-0186-1*, Pub. by New Day Pub) Cellar.

Pieces of the Bone - Text Still There. Ivan Arguelles. (Illus.). 28p. 1987. pap. 3.00 (*0-318-23467-X*) Skydog OR.

***Pieces of the Civil War: The Yankee, the Rebel & the Lighter Side.** Bobby W. Brendell. LC 99-62326. 361p. 1999. pap. 15.95 (*1-884778-65-8*) Old Mountain.

Pieces of the Frame. John McPhee. 320p. 1975. 19.95 (*0-374-23281-4*) FS&G.

Pieces of the Frame. John McPhee. LC 75-4960. 320p. 1979. pap. 13.00 (*0-374-51498-4*) FS&G.

Pieces of the Heart: New Chicano Fiction. Ed. by Gary Soto. LC 92-19164. 192p. 1993. pap. 10.95 (*0-8118-0068-7*) Chronicle Bks.

Pieces of the Past. Jim Reis. (Illus.). 200p. (Orig.). 1988. pap. 9.95 (*0-9621043-0-2*) KY Post.

Pieces of the Past, Pt. II. Jim Reis. (Illus.). 190p. (Orig.). 1991. pap. 9.95 (*0-9624673-3-2*) Picture This Bks.

Pieces of the Personality Puzzle: Readings in Theory & Research. David Charles Funder & Daniel J. Ozer. LC 97-172990. (Illus.). (C). 1997. pap. text 22.00 (*0-393-97048-5*) Norton.

Pieces of the Picture. Barbara M. Joosse. LC 88-28151. 144p. (J). (gr. 5-7). 1989. 12.95 (*0-397-32342-5*); lib. bdg. 12.89 (*0-397-32343-3*) HarpC Child Bks.

Pieces of the Picture. Barbara M. Joosse. LC 88-28150. (Trophy Bk.). 144p. (J). (gr. 5-7). 1991. mass mkt. 3.50 (*0-06-440310-6*, HarpTrophy) HarpC Child Bks.

Pieces of the Piedmont, the Puzzle of One Life: A Personal Georgraphy of Virginia's Foothills & America's Historic Heart. unabridged ed. Walter Nicklin. (Illus.). 112p. 1997. pap. 19.95 (*1-885937-06-7*, Virginia Heritage) Casco Commns.

Pieces of the Tapestry. Elizabeth Bowers et al. LC 94-74245. 336p. 1994. pap. 21.95 (*0-9644473-0-4*) Adept Pubng.

Pieces of Time: The Life of James Stewart. Gary Fishgall. LC 97-10639. (Illus.). 416p. 1997. 27.00 (*0-684-82454-X*) S&S Trade.

Pieces of White Shell. Terry Tempest Williams. LC 86-24915. (Illus.). 162p. 1987. pap. 10.95 (*0-8263-0969-0*) U of NM Pr.

Pieces of Yesterday. Carol C. Otten. 1999. mass mkt. 5.99 (*0-515-12524-5*, Jove) Berkley Pub.

Pieces on the "Jew Bill" Intro. by Roy S. Wolper. LC 92-22743. (Augustan Reprints Ser.: No. 217). 1983. reprint ed. 14.50 (*0-404-70217-1*) AMS Pr.

Pieces Roses. Jean Anouilh. Incl. Bal des Voleurs. Humulus le Muet. Leocadia. Rendez-Vous de Senlis. (FRE.). 19.50 (*0-685-37153-0*, F81777) Fr & Eur.

Pieces Secretes. Jean Anouilh. Incl. Arrestation. 1977. 24.95 Scenario. 1977. Tu Etais Si Gentil Quand Tu Etais Petit. 1977. (FRE.). 384p. 1977. 39.95 (*0-8288-9015-3*, M11237) Fr & Eur.

Pieces sur l'Art see Oeuvres

Pieces sur l'Art. Paul Valery. pap. 4.95 (*0-685-36622-7*) Fr & Eur.

Pieces That Have Won Prizes: Also Many Encore Pieces; Enlarged Edition. Compiled by Frank McHale. LC 79-39381. (Granger Index Reprint Ser.). 1977. reprint ed. 21.95 (*0-8369-6346-6*) Ayer.

Piecewise Constant Orthogonal Functions & Their Application to Systems & Control. G. P. Rao. (Lecture Notes in Control & Information Sciences: Vol. 55). 254p. 1983. 35.95 (*0-387-12556-6*) Spr-Verlag.

Piecewise Linear Concordances & Isotopies. Kenneth C. Millett. LC 74-18328. (Memoirs Ser.: No. 1/153). 73p. 1974. pap. 17.00 (*0-8218-1853-8*, MEMO/1/153) Am Math.

Piecewise Linear Modeling & Analysis. Domine M. Leenaerts & Wim M. Van Bokhoven. LC 98-8186. 208p. 1998. 112.50 (*0-7923-8190-4*) Kluwer Academic.

Piecewise Regular Arrays: Application-Specific Computations. T. M. Plaks. (Parallel Processing Ser.: Vol. 1). 260p. 1998. text 45.00 (*90-5699-173-6*, ECU64, Harwood Acad Pubs) Gordon & Breach.

Piecework. Pam Rehm. 1992. pap. 5.00 (*1-879645-06-8*) o-blek editions.

***Piecework: Writings on Men & Women, Fools & Heroes, Lost Cities, Vanished Friends, Small Pleasures, Large Calamities, & How the Weather Was.** Pete Hamill. 1998. pap. 14.95 (*0-316-19127-2*, Back Bay) Little.

Piecework: Writings on Men & Women, Fools & Heroes, Lost Cities, Vanquished Friends, Small Pleasures, Large Calamities & How the Weather Was. Pete Hamill. LC 95-4738. 448p. 1997. pap. 16.00 (*0-316-34098-7*) Little.

Piecing: Expanding the Basics. Ruth B. McDowell. Ed. by Sally Lanzarotti. LC 97-43176. (Illus.). 160p. 1998. pap. 27.95 (*1-57120-041-X*, 10166) C & T Pub.

Piecing It Together: A Guide to Academic Success. Jane Jensen & Lisa D'Adamo-Weinstein. 213p. 1998. pap. 28.00 (*0-205-28195-8*, Longwood Div) Allyn.

Piecing It Together: Feminism & Nonviolence. British Feminism & Nonviolence Study Group Staff. (Illus.). 60p. 1983. 3.00 (*0-9508602-0-4*) J Tiffany.

Piecing Life Together. (Illus.). 88p. 1996. 14.95 (*0-925623-06-7*) B Boyink.

***Piecing Together Hypertension.** Anatomical Chart Company Staff. (Illus.). 9p. 2000. 24.95 (*1-889241-05-9*, 9767FC) Anatomical Chart.

***Piecing Together the Digestive System.** Anatomical Chart Company Staff. (Illus.). 9p. 2000. pap. 24.95 (*1-889241-02-4*, 9859FC) Anatomical Chart.

***Piecing Together the Heart.** Anatomical Chart Company Staff. (Illus.). 9p. 2000. pap. 24.95 (*1-889241-01-6*, 8023FC) Anatomical Chart.

Piecing Together the Prosperity Puzzle. Gregg E. Wear. 201p. 1997. pap. 10.00 (*0-9671368-1-4*) G Wear Min.

***Piecing Together the Respiratory System.** Anatomical Chart Company Staff. (Illus.). 9p. 2000. pap. 24.95 (*1-889241-03-2*, 9766FC) Anatomical Chart.

***Piecing Together the Skeletal System.** Anatomical Chart Company Staff. (Illus.). 20p. 2000. pap. 34.95 (*1-889241-04-0*, 8943FC) Anatomical Chart.

Pied. Illus. by Georges Lemoine. (Gallimard - Mes Premieres Decouvertes Ser.: No. 9). (FRE.). (J). (ps-1). 1989. 12.95 (*2-07-035701-5*) Schoenhof.

Pied dans le Crime. Eugene Labiche. 9.95 (*0-686-54249-5*) Fr & Eur.

Pied Flycatcher. Arne Lundberg & Rauno V. Alatalo. (Illus.). 267p. 1992. text 39.00 (*0-85661-072-0*, 784672) Acad Pr.

Pied Piper. Ed. by Hanna Hutchinson. Tr. by Qiu Yuzhug.Tr. of Pied Piper of Hamlin. (CHI., Illus.). 20p. (Orig.). (J). (gr. 1-2). 1992. pap. 2.95 (*0-922852-15-4*, A005) Another Lang Pr.

Pied Piper. Ed. by Hanna Hutchinson. Tr. by Kana Thurston.Tr. of Pied Piper of Hamlin. (JPN., Illus.). 20p. (Orig.). (J). (gr. 1-2). 1992. pap. 2.95 (*0-922852-14-6*) Another Lang Pr.

Pied Piper. Claire Jones & Bob Varga. 22p. (J). (gr. k-5). 1995. mass mkt. 4.00 (*1-58193-171-9*) Brown Bag Prods.

Pied Piper. Anne C. Martens. 83p. (J). (gr. 1 up). 1969. pap. 3.50 (*0-87129-784-1*, P23) Dramatic Pub.

Pied Piper. Adrian Mitchell. (Oberon Bks.). 72p. 1997. pap. 12.95 (*1-870259-09-2*) Theatre Comm.

Pied Piper. Ridley Pearson. LC 97-49709. 497p. 1998. 23.45 (*0-7868-6300-5*, Pub. by Hyperion) Time Warner.

Pied Piper. Nevil Shute. 24.95 (*0-88411-323-X*) Amereon Ltd.

***Pied Piper.** large type ed. Ridley Pearson. LC 99-59455. 2000. pap. 22.95 (*1-56895-834-X*) Wheeler Pub.

Pied Piper. Ridley Pearson. 672p. 1999. reprint ed. mass mkt. 7.99 (*0-7868-8955-1*, Pub. by Hyperion) Time Warner.

***Pied Piper/ Beyond Recognition.** Ridley Pearson. (J). 1998. write for info. (*0-7868-6433-8*) Disney Pr.

Pied Piper of Hamelin. Barbara Bartos-Hoppner. LC 87-45150.Tr. of Der/Rattenfanger von Hameln. (Illus.). 32p. (J). (gr. k-3). 1987. 9.95 (*0-397-32239-9*) HarpC Child Bks.

Pied Piper of Hamelin. Barbara Bartos-Hoppner. LC 87-45150.Tr. of Der/Rattenfanger von Hameln. (Illus.). 32p. (J). (gr. k-3). 1987. lib. bdg. 11.89 (*0-397-32240-2*) HarpC Child Bks.

Pied Piper of Hamelin. Robert Browning. (J). 1993. 12.95 (*0-679-42812-7*) Everymns Lib.

Pied Piper of Hamelin. Ed. by Sara Corrin. (Illus.). 32p. (J). (ps-5). 1989. 14.95 (*0-15-261596-2*, Harcourt Child Bks) Harcourt.

Pied Piper of Hamelin. Robert Holden. LC 97-33221. (Illus.). 32p. (J). (ps-3). 1998. 15.00 (*0-395-89918-4*) HM.

Pied Piper of Hamelin. Madge Miller. (J). 1951. 6.00 (*0-87602-174-7*) Anchorage.

Pied Piper of Hamelin. William Glennon. 49p. 1963. reprint ed. pap. 3.45 (*0-87129-056-1*, P67) Dramatic Pub.

***Pied Piper of Hamelin: Poem.** Robert Browning & Bud Peen. LC 98-43395. (Illus.). 32p. 1999. 14.95 (*0-8109-4351-4*, Pub. by Abrams) Time Warner.

Pied Piper of Hamelin in Full Color. Kate Greenaway & Robert Browning. LC 96-54625. (Illus.). 48p. (J). 1997. reprint ed. pap. text 7.95 (*0-486-29619-9*) Dover.

Pied Piper of Hamlin see Flutiste de Jamelin

Pied Piper of Hamlin see Rattenfanger von Hameln

Pied Piper of Hamlin see Flautista di Hamerline

Pied Piper of Hamlin see Pied Piper

Pied Piper of Hamlin see Salmisto de Hamlin

Pied Piper of Hamlin see Flautista de Jamelin

Pied Piper of Hamlin. Ed. by Hanna Hutchinson. Tr. by Marina Dolgin. (RUS., Illus.). 20p. (Orig.). (J). (gr. 1-2). 1992. pap. 2.95 (*0-922852-16-2*, E017) Another Lang Pr.

Pied Piper of New Orleans: Playscript. Jeff Church. (J). 1993. pap. 6.00 (*0-87602-324-3*) Anchorage.

Pied Piper Syndrome. Hunter & Stefan Czernecki. LC 91-39990. 144p. 1992. pap. 9.95 (*0-06-446130-0*) HarpC Child Bks.

Pied Piper Syndrome: And Other Essays. Mollie Hunter. LC 91-39990. (Charlotte Zolotow Bk.). 144p. (J). 1992. 21.00 (*0-06-020379-X*) HarpC Child Bks.

***Pied Piper's Poison.** Christopher Wallace. LC 00-27685. 298p. 2000. 25.95 (*1-58567-013-8*, Pub. by Overlook Pr) Penguin Putnam.

Pied Piper's Repertoire: Soprano Recorder. 1990. 6.95 (*0-685-32156-8*, M554) Hansen Ed Mus.

Pied Poets: Contemporary Verse of the Transylvanian & Danube. Robert Elsie. (Illus.). 187p. (Orig.). 1990. pap. 22.00 (*0-948259-77-9*, Pub. by Forest Bks) Dufour.

***Piedmont: Traditional Cuisine from the Piedmontese Provinces.** Ed. by Editors of Time-Life Books. 120p. (YA). 2000. 16.95 (*0-7370-0014-7*) T-L Custom Pub.

Piedmont Archaeology: Recent Research & Results, No. 10A. Ed. by J. Mark Wittkofski & Lyle E. Browning. 160p. 1983. pap. 19.00 (*1-884626-03-3*) Archeolog Soc.

Piedmont Conspiracy. James Washburn. LC 96-31200. 280p. 1996. pap. 19.95 (*1-56833-075-8*) Madison Bks UPA.

Piedmont Garden: How to Grow by the Calendar. 2nd ed. Juanita B. Garrison. LC 90-39323. (Illus.). 219p. 1990. pap. 14.95 (*0-87249-717-8*) U of SC Pr.

Piedmont Plantation: The Bennehan-Cameron Family & Lands in North Carolina. Jean B. Anderson. LC 85-81002. (Illus.). xix, 227p. 1985. 24.95 (*0-9615577-1-0*) HPS Durham.

Piedmont/Triad Dine-a-Mate Book. 264p. 1996. pap. text 30.00 (*1-57393-060-1*) Dine-A-Mate.

Piedra Abstracta see Stone & the Thread: Andean Roots of Abstract Art

***Piedra Extraordinaria.** Leo Lionni. (SPA., Illus.). (J). (ps-3). 1999. pap. 6.95 (*980-257-239-X*) Ediciones Ekare.

Piedras. Ana Andrade et al. (SPA.). 24p. 1995. pap. text 5.00 (*0-435-08856-4*, 08856) Heinemann.

***Piedras Claman.** Randall Price. (SPA.). 2000. mass mkt. 13.99 (*0-7899-0421-7*) Editorial Unilit.

Piedras Negras see Dark Stones

Piedras Negras Archaeology: Artifacts, Caches, & Burials. William R. Coe. LC 60-4422. (University Museum, University of Pennsylvania. Museum Monographs). (Illus.). 323p. reprint ed. pap. 100.20 (*0-8357-7513-5*, 203600000002) Bks Demand.

Piedras Negras Pottery. Mary Butler. LC 36-19557. (Piedras Negras Preliminary Papers: No. 4). 100p. reprint ed. pap. 31.00 (*0-608-12381-1*, 205212400037) Bks Demand.

Pieds Dans les Nuages. David Goodis. (FRE.). 246p. 1990. pap. 10.95 (*0-7859-2661-5*, 207038232X) Fr & Eur.

Piege de Charme pour un Celibataire. Miranda Lee. (Azur Ser.: No. 781). (FRE.). 1999. mass mkt. 3.99 (*0-373-34781-2*, 1-34781-4) Harlequin Bks.

Piege de Tendresse. Caroline Anderson. (Azur Ser.: No. 745). (FRE.). 1999. mass mkt. 3.50 (*0-373-34745-6*, 1-34745-9) Harlequin Bks.

Piege Dore pour une Actrice. Amanda Carpenter. (Azur Ser.: Bk. 736). 1999. mass mkt. 3.50 (*0-373-34736-7*, 1-34736-8) Harlequin Bks.

Piege pour Cendrillon. Sebastien Japrisot. (FRE.). 224p. 1972. pap. 10.95 (*0-7859-2282-2*, 2070362167) Fr & Eur.

Piege pour un Ange Gardien. Joann Ross. (Rouge Passion Ser.: Vol 504). (FRE.). 1999. mass mkt. 3.50 (*0-373-37504-2*, 1-37504-7) Harlequin Bks.

Piege pour un Milliardaire. Miranda Lee. (Azur Ser.: No. 780). (FRE.). 1999. mass mkt. 3.99 (*0-373-34780-4*, 1-34780-6) Harlequin Bks.

***Piege pour un Solitaire.** Dixie Browning. 1999. mass mkt. 3.99 (*0-373-37536-0*) Silhouette.

Piel. Arlene C. Rourke. (Buena Presencia Ser.).Tr. of Skin. (SPA.). 32p. (J). 1989. lib. bdg. 19.93 (*0-86625-294-0*) Rourke Pubns.

***Piel del Tambor.** Arturo Perez-Reverte. LC 96-125309. (SPA.). 2000. pap. 16.95 (*84-204-8201-3*) Alfaguara Ediciones.

Piel y Alergia. R. Pelta & E. Vivas. (SPA.). 211p. 1997. pap. 33.00 (*84-7978-298-6*, Pub. by Ediciones Diaz) IBD Ltd.

Pien Chih-Lin: A Study in Modern Chinese Poetry. Lloyd Halt. (Publications in Modern Chinese Language & Literature). xii, 210p. 1983. pap. 50.00 (*90-70176-92-0*) Mouton.

Piensa-Tu. 2nd ed. Susan F. Tierno. Tr. by Ana M. Alvarado. (Illus.). 96p. (J). (gr. 3-8). 1996. reprint ed. pap. 25.00 (*1-58237-034-6*) Creat Think.

***Piensa-Tu: Coleccion de Libros, 20 vols., Set.** Susan F. Tierno. Tr. by Ana M. Alvarado.Tr. of Think Kids Book Collection. (SPA., Illus.). (J). (gr. 1-4). 2000. pap. 2.95 (*1-58237-059-1*) Creat Think.

Piense en Grande. Ben Carson. 1994. pap. 10.99 (*0-88113-185-7*) Caribe Betania.

Piense Y Hagase Rico. Napoleon Hill Foundation Staff. 1997. pap. 13.98 (*970-05-0381-X*) Grijalbo Edit.

Piense y Hagase Rico - Think & Grow Rich. Napoleon Hill. (SPA.). 295p. (YA). Date not set. reprint ed. pap. 11.95 (*1-880369-01-X*) N Hill Found.

Pienza: Der Entwurf Einer Humanistischen Weltsicht. Jan Pieper. (GER., Illus.). 632p. 1997. 240.00 (*3-930698-06-4*) Edition A Menges.

***Pienza: Il Progetto Di una Visione Umanistica del Mondo.** Jan Pieper. (Illus.). 632p. 2000. 216.00 (*3-930698-07-2*) Edition A Menges.

Pienza: The Creation of a Renaissance City. Charles R. Mack. LC 86-24269. (Illus.). 256p. 1987. text 52.50 (*0-8014-1699-X*) Cornell U Pr.

Pieper Lectures Vol. 1: The Office of the Ministry. Contrib. by David Scaer et al. 1997. write for info. (*0-9659555-1-6*) Concordia Hist.

Pier Paolo Pasolini: Contemporary Perspectives. Ed. by Patrick Rumble & Bart Testa. LC 95-120658. 258p. 1993. text 50.00 (*0-8020-2966-3*) U of Toronto Pr.

Pier Paolo Pasolini: Contemporary Perspectives. Ed. by Patrick Rumble & Bart Testa. LC 95-120658. (Major Italian Authors Ser.: No. 1). 256p. 1993. pap. text 17.95 (*0-8020-7737-4*) U of Toronto Pr.

Pier Paolo Pasolini: The Poetics of Heresy. Beverly Allen. (Illus.). 144p. (Orig.). 1982. pap. 56.50 (*0-915838-11-7*) Anma Libri.

Pier Paolo Pasolini & the Theatre of the Word. William Van Watson. 150p. 1989. 69.95 (*0-7734-2002-9*) E Mellen.

P

An Asterisk (*) at the beginning of an entry indicates that the title is appearing for the first time.

Pier Paolo Vergerio & the "Paulus," a Latin Comedy. Michael Katchmer. (Studies in the Humanities: Vol. 36). 145p. (C). 1998. text 38.95 (*0-8204-3787-5*) P Lang Pubng.

Pier Queen. Emanuel Xavier. 64p. 1997. pap. 6.99 (*0-9658708-3-9*) Pier Queen.

Pier Simone Agostini (1635-1680) - Mario Savioni (1608-1685), Vol. 12. Ed. by Irving Eisley. (Italian Cantata in the Seventeenth Century Ser.). 1986. lib. bdg. 25.00 (*0-8240-8886-7*) Garland.

***Pier 21: Gateway to Hope.** Linda Granfield. (Illus.). 48p. (J). (gr. 2 up). 2000. pap. 12.99 (*0-88776-517-3*) Tundra Bks.

Pieracci & Shelley: An Italian Ur-Cenci. George Yost. 27.50 (*0-916379-33-7*) Scripta.

Pierce & Law: Issues in Pragmatism, Legal Realism & Semiotics. Ed. by Roberta Kevelson. LC 90-22202. (Semiotics & the Human Sciences Ser.: Vol. 1). X, 225p. (C). 1991. text 43.95 (*0-8204-1519-7*) P Lang Pubng.

***Pierce-Arrow.** Susan Howe. LC 98-47300. 160p. 1999. pap. 14.95 (*0-8112-1410-9*, NDP878, Pub. by New Directions) SPD-Small Pr Dist.

***Pierce Arrow Fire Apparatus, 1979-1998: Photo Archive.** Steven Hagy. LC 99-76051. (Illus.). 128p. 2000. pap. 32.95 (*1-58388-023-2*, 130003AE, Pub. by Iconografix) Motorbooks Intl.

Pierce Brosnan: The Biography. York Membery. (Illus.). 224p. 1997. mass mkt. 7.95 (*0-7535-0158-9*, Pub. by Virgin Bks) London Brdge.

***Pierce County; Street Guide & Directory, 2000 ed., Vol. 1.** Thomas Brothers Maps Staff. 1999. pap. write for info. (*1-58174-141-3*) Thomas Bros Maps.

Pierce Genealogy, Being the Record of the Posterity of Captain Michael, John, & Captain William Pierce, Who Came to This County England, No. IV. F. C. Pierce. 441p. 1989. reprint ed. pap. 66.00 (*0-8328-0967-5*); reprint ed. lib. bdg. 74.00 (*0-8328-0966-7*) Higginson Bk Co.

Pierce Genealogy, Being the Record of the Posterity of Thomas Pierce, an Early Inhabitant of Charlestown. F. B. Pierce. Ed. by F. C. Pierce. (Illus.). 369p. 1989. reprint ed. pap. 66.00 (*0-8328-0965-9*); reprint ed. lib. bdg. 74.00 (*0-8328-0964-0*) Higginson Bk Co.

Pierce Means Business: A History of Pierce Junior College, (1865-1989) Carl Fassl. 1990. write for info. (*0-614-30146-7*) Intergalactic NJ.

Pierce, Pace, Hall, Minton, & Huie Families. Pref. by Virginia C. Jantz. LC 86-80864. (Illus.). 442p. 1986. 30.00 (*0-9607170-1-3*) V C Jantz.

Pierce Penilesse. Thomas Nash. (BCL1-PR English Literature Ser.). 137p. 1992. reprint ed. lib. bdg. 69.00 (*0-7812-7217-3*) Rprt Serv.

Pierce Piano Atlas. 10th enl. rev. ed. Ed. by Bob Pierce & Larry Ashley. LC 65-2545. (Illus.). 448p. 1997. 38.95 (*0-614-30059-2*); pap. 28.95 (*0-911138-02-1*) Pierce Piano.

Pierce Seminar Papers: Essays in Semiotic Analysis. Ed. by Michael Shapiro. LC 97-51519. (Critic of Institutions Ser.: Vol. 12). 123p. (C). 1998. text 39.95 (*0-8204-3142-7*) P Lang Pubng.

Pierce with a Pin. large type ed. Kenneth Hopkins. (Mystery Ser.). 368p. 1993. 27.99 (*0-7089-2897-8*) Ulverscroft.

Pierced by a Ray of Sun: Poems about the Times We Feel Alone. Compiled by Ruth Gordon. LC 94-3757. 128p. (J). (gr. 7-12). 1995. 15.95 (*0-06-023613-2*); lib. bdg. 15.89 (*0-06-023614-0*) HarpC Child Bks.

Pierced by a Sword: A Chronicle of the Coming Tribulations. Bud Macfarlane, Jr. 592p. (Orig.). 1995. mass mkt. 3.99 (*0-9646316-0-1*) St Jude Media.

Pierced by Murugan's Lance: Ritual, Power & Moral Redemption among Malaysian Hindus. Elizabeth F. Collins. LC 96-52671. (Illus.). 230p. 1997. pap. text 22.50 (*0-87580-574-4*); lib. bdg. 35.00 (*0-87580-223-0*) N Ill U Pr.

Pierced by Sound: Stories, Sketches & Poems. 2nd rev. ed. Lawrence Pike. 83p. 1994. pap. 9.95 (*1-56439-042-X*) Ridgeway.

Pierced Heart. Robin D. Laws. Ed. by John Nephew. (Over the Edge Ser.). 207p. (Orig.). 1996. pap. 14.95 (*1-887801-54-5*) Trident MN.

Pierced Hearts & True Loves: A Century of Drawings for Tattoos. Hardy Marks. (Illus.). 128p. 1995. pap. 30.00 (*0-942324-09-9*) Drawing Ctr.

Pierce's Doctrine of Signs: Theory, Applications, & Connections. Ed. by Vincent M. Colapietro & Thomas M. Olshewsky. LC 95-37229. (Approaches to Semiotics Ser.: No. 123). xi, 463p. (C). 1995. lib. bdg. 190.80 (*3-11-014252-X*) Mouton.

Piercing Cry: Translation of Anna Banti's Un Grido Lacerante. Anna Banti. Tr. by S. Mark Lewis & Daria Valentini from ITA. LC 96-1195. XV, 119p. (C). 1997. pap. 24.95 (*0-8204-3001-3*) P Lang Pubng.

Piercing the Autumn Sky: A Guide to Discovering the Natural Freedom of Mind. Peter F. Barth. LC 93-77066. 128p. (Orig.). 1993. pap. 9.95 (*0-9635796-3-0*) Lame Turtle.

Piercing the Darkness see Penetrando la Oscuridad

Piercing the Darkness. Frank E. Peretti. LC 89-50338. 442p. 1989. pap. 12.99 (*0-89107-527-5*) Crossway Bks.

Piercing the Darkness. Karen Ramsland. 2000. pap. 14.00 (*0-06-107322-9*) HarpC.

Piercing the Darkness. large type ed. Frank E. Peretti. LC 93-16771. 771p. 1993. lib. bdg. 22.95 (*0-8161-5699-9*, G K Hall Lrg Type) Mac Lib Ref.

Piercing the Darkness: Undercover with Vampires in America Today. Karen Ramsland. 560p. 1999. mass mkt. 6.99 (*0-06-105945-5*, HarperPrism) HarpC.

Piercing the Darkness: Undercover with Vampires in America Today. Katherine M. Ramsland. LC 98-7784. (Illus.). 384p. 1998. 24.00 (*0-06-105062-8*, HarperPrism) HarpC.

Piercing the Fog: Intelligence & Army Air Forces Operations in World War II, 2 vols. 1997. lib. bdg. 600.95 (*0-8490-6248-9*) Gordon Pr.

Piercing the Fog: Intelligence & Army Air Forces Operations in World War II. John F. Kreis et al. (Illus.). 501p. 1996. 31.00 (*0-16-048187-2*) AFH & MP.

***Piercing the Future: Prophecy & the New Millennium.** William Terry James. 428p. 2000. pap. text 12.95 (*0-9670498-1-4*) N Walker Pubs.

Piercing the Heartland. Jim Miles. LC 95-50653. (Illus.). 224p. (Orig.). 1991. pap. 12.95 (*1-55853-104-1*) Cumberland Hse.

***Piercing the Heartland: A History & Tour Guide of the Fort Donelson, Shiloh & Perryville Campaigns.** Jim Miles. 176p. 1999. pap. 12.95 (*1-58182-075-5*, Cumberland Hearthside) Cumberland Hse.

Piercing the Mist: Glimpses of God in the Wonders of Life. Leo Holland. LC 93-77523. 128p. (Orig.). 1993. pap. text 7.95 (*0-89243-526-7*) Liguori Pubns.

Piercing the Paper Curtain: Gaining Access to Federal Records. 12p. 1993. pap. 3.95 (*0-918734-44-4*) Reymont.

Piercing the Shields of Justice: Inside the ATF. William J. Burgess. LC 95-45086. (Illus.). 224p. 1995. 25.00 (*1-55618-156-6*) Brunswick Pub.

Pierda Grasa Mientras Usted Duerme see Lose Fat While You Sleep: No Dieting, No Drugs, No Exercise

Pierian Spring: The True Account of the Case of John Toiro. . . Charles B. Brooks. LC 93-152071. x, 179p. 1991. pap. 17.50 (*0-9667578-0-7*) Brooks Hse.

Pierik in Vitro Culture Higher. 1997. pap. text 91.00 (*0-7923-4527-4*) Kluwer Academic.

Pierio Valeriano on the Ill-Fortune of Learned Men: A Renaissance Humanist & His World. Julia H. Gaisser. LC 99-6234. (Recentiores Ser.). 384p. 1999. text 52.50 (*0-472-11055-1*, 11055) U of Mich Pr.

Piero Della Francesca. Alessandro Angelini. (Grandes Maestros del Arte Ser.). (SPA., Illus.). 80p. 1992. pap. 12.99 (*1-878351-23-0*) Riverside NY.

Piero Della Francesca. Perry Brooks. (Rizzoli Art Ser.). 24p. 1992. pap. 7.95 (*0-8478-1513-7*, Pub. by Rizzoli Intl) St Martin.

Piero della Francesca. Maurizio Calves. (Illus.). 248p. 1998. 75.00 (*0-8478-2148-X*, Pub. by Rizzoli Intl) St Martin.

Piero Della Francesca. DK Publishing Staff. LC 99-31209. (Artbook Ser.). 144p. 1999. pap. 12.95 (*0-7894-4853-X*) DK Pub Inc.

Piero Della Francesca. Birgit Laskowski. (Masters Of Italian Art Ser.). (Illus.). 140p. 1998. 19.95 (*3-8290-0247-5*, 520534) Konemann.

Piero Della Francesca. Marilyn A. Lavin. (Masters of Art Ser.). (Illus.). 128p. 1992. 24.95 (*0-8109-3210-5*, Pub. by Abrams) Time Warner.

Piero Della Francesca. Ronald Lightbown. (Illus.). 312p. 1992. 95.00 (*1-55859-168-0*) Abbeville Pr.

***Piero della Francesca.** Roberto Longhi. Tr. & Pref. by David Tabbat. LC 00-26564. (Illus.). 256p. 2000. write for info. (*1-878818-77-5*, Pub. by Sheep Meadow) U Pr of New Eng.

Piero Della Francesca. rev. ed. Alessandro Angelini. Tr. by Lisa C. Pelletti from ITA. (Library of Great Masters). (Illus.). 80p. 1990. pap. 14.99 (*1-878351-04-4*) Riverside NY.

Piero Della Francesca: San Francesco, Arezzo. Marilyn A. Lavin. (Great Fresco Cycles of the Renaissance Ser.). (Illus.). 104p. 1994. 25.00 (*0-8076-1317-7*) Braziller.

Piero Della Francesca: The Flagellation. Marilyn A. Lavin. (Illus.). 112p. 1990. pap. 14.95 (*0-226-46958-1*) U Ch Pr.

Piero Della Francesca & His Legacy. Ed. by Marilyn A. Lavin. (Illus.). 1995. 60.00 (*0-300-07711-4*) Yale U Pr.

Piero Di Cosimo: Fiction, Invention, & Fantasia. Sharon Fermor. (Illus.). 232p. 1993. 55.00 (*0-948462-36-1*, Pub. by Reaktion Bks) Consort Bk Sales.

Piero Manzoni. Text by Germano Celant et al. LC 98-155335. (Illus.). 265p. 1998. pap. 49.95 (*88-8158-141-8*, 810921, Pub. by Charta) Dist Art Pubs.

Piero Sraffa: Critical Assessments, 4 vols., Vols. 1-4, Set. Ed. by John C. Wood. LC 94-10583. (Critical Assessments of Leading Economists Ser.). (Illus.). 1624p. (C). (gr. 13). 1995. 700.00 (*0-415-11443-8*, C0371) Routledge.

***Piero Sraffa: His Life, Thought & Cultural Heritage.** Alessandro Roncaglia. LC 00-28075. 2000. write for info. (*0-415-23480-8*) Routledge.

Piero Sraffa, 1898-1983. Ed. by Mark Blaug. (Pioneers in Economics Ser.: Vol. 44). 192p. 1992. 100.00 (*1-85278-508-X*) E Elgar.

***Piero Sraffa's Political Economy: A Centenary Estimate.** Terenzio Cozzi & Roberto Marchionatti. LC 00-30515. 2000. write for info. (*0-415-22424-1*) Routledge.

Pierpaolo Vergerio the Elder: The Humanist as Orator. John M. McManamon. LC 96-24767. (Medieval & Renaissance Texts & Studies: Vol. 163). 240p. 1996. 26.00 (*0-86698-204-3*, MR163) MRTS.

Pierpaolo Vergerio the Elder & Saint Jerome: An Edition & Translation of "Sermones Pro Sancto Hieronymo" Ed. & Tr. by John M. McManamon from LAT. LC 99-19915. (Medieval & Renaissance Texts & Studies: Vol. 177). 416p. 1999. 36.00 (*0-86698-219-1*, MR177) MRTS.

Pierpont Morgan Library Manuscript M.817: A Facsimile. Geoffrey Chaucer. Ed. by Paul G. Ruggiers. (Illus.). 265p. 1987. 125.00 (*0-937664-74-X*) Pilgrim Bks OK.

Pierre see Nutshell Library

Pierre. Mary Holman. LC 94-60875. (Illus.). 48p. (J). (gr. k-3). 1994. pap. 12.95 (*0-9641430-1-1*) Villa Press.

Pierre. Herman Melville. (Twelve-Point Ser.). 1999. lib. bdg. 24.00 (*1-58287-113-2*) North Bks.

Pierre. Herman Melville. Ed. by Harrison Hayford et al. (Northwestern-Newberry Edition of the Writings of Herman Melville: Vol. 7). 435p. 1972. 59.95 (*0-8101-0266-8*); pap. text 19.95 (*0-8101-0267-6*) Northwestern U Pr.

Pierre. Herman Melville. 435p. 1995. pap. 14.95 (*0-8101-1412-7*) Northwestern U Pr.

Pierre: A Cautionary Tale. Maurice Sendak. LC 62-13315. (Trophy Picture Bk.). (Illus.). 48p. (J). (ps-3). 1991. pap. 4.95 (*0-06-443252-1*, HarpTrophy) HarpC Child Bks.

Pierre: A Cautionary Tale in Five Chapters & a Prologue. Maurice Sendak. LC 66-992. (Illus.). 48p. (J). (gr. 2 up). 1962. lib. bdg. 15.89 (*0-06-025965-5*) HarpC Child Bks.

Pierre: A Cautionary Tale in Five Chapters & a Prologue. Maurice Sendak. (J). 1991. 10.15 (*0-606-04770-0*, Pub. by Turtleback) Demco.

Pierre: A Celebration of Landmark Style. William Weathersby. LC 98-10167. 1998. write for info. (*0-86636-648-2*) PBC Intl Inc.

Pierre: Or the Ambiguities. Herman Melville. Ed. by William C. Spengemann. LC 95-32700. (Penguin Classics Ser.). 400p. 1996. pap. 12.95 (*0-14-043484-4*, Penguin Bks) Viking Penguin.

Pierre: Or the Ambiguities. annot. ed. Herman Melville. Ed. by Henry A. Murray. (Complete Works of Herman Melville Ser.). 608p. 1962. 29.95 (*0-87532-003-1*) Hendricks House.

Pierre Albert-Birot: A Poetics in Movement. Debra Kelly. LC 96-28000. (Illus.). 440p. 1997. 55.00 (*0-8386-3625-X*) Fairleigh Dickinson.

Pierre Alechinsky: Margin & Center. Michael Gibson & Pierre Alechinsky. (Illus.). 144p. 1987. 18.00 (*0-89207-061-7*) S R Guggenheim.

Pierre & His People. Gilbert Parker. LC 74-101287. (Short Story Index Reprint Ser.). 1977. 21.95 (*0-8369-3224-2*) Ayer.

Pierre & Jean. Guy de Maupassant. 1976. 19.95 (*0-8488-0472-4*) Amereon Ltd.

Pierre & Jean. Guy de Maupassant. Tr. & Intro. by Leonard W. Tancock. (Classics Ser.). 176p. 1979. pap. 9.95 (*0-14-044358-4*, Penguin Classics) Viking Penguin.

Pierre Angulaire. Zoe Oldenbourg. (FRE.). 1972. pap. 17.95 (*0-7859-3986-5*) Fr & Eur.

Pierre August Renoir. Mike Venezia. LC 95-39666. (Getting to Know the World's Greatest Artists Ser.). (Illus.). 32p. (J). (ps-4). 1996. lib. bdg. 21.00 (*0-516-02225-3*) Childrens.

Pierre August Renoir: Getting to Know the World's Greatest Artists. Mike Venezia. LC 95-39666. (Getting to Know the World's Greatest Artists Ser.). (Illus.). 32p. (J). (ps-4). 1996. pap. 6.95 (*0-516-20068-2*) Childrens.

Pierre Auguste Renoir. Tom Parsons. LC 96-25747. (Art for Young People Ser.). (Illus.). 32p. (J). 1996. 14.95 (*0-8069-6162-7*) Sterling.

Pierre-Auguste Renoir. Susan Rayfield. LC 98-12988. (First Impressions Ser.). (Illus.). 92p. (J). (gr. k up). 1998. 19.95 (*0-8109-3795-6*, Pub. by Abrams) Time Warner.

Pierre-Auguste Renoir: La Promenade. John House. LC 97-21894. (Getty Museum Studies on Art). 94p. 1998. pap. 17.50 (*0-89236-365-7*, Pub. by J P Getty Trust) OUP.

Pierre-Auguste Renoir: La Vie et L'Oeuvre. Ambroise Vollard. (FRE., Illus.). 376p. 1999. reprint ed. 195.00 (*1-55660-294-4*) A Wofsy Fine Arts.

Pierre-Auguste Renoir: The Etchings & Lithographs. rev. ed. Loys Delteil. (ENG & FRE., Illus.). 132p. 1999. 175.00 (*1-55660-293-6*) A Wofsy Fine Arts.

Pierre-Auguste Renoir, Mon Pere. Jean Renoir. (FRE.). 1981. pap. 13.95 (*0-7859-4151-7*) Fr & Eur.

Pierre Auguste Renoir Postcard Book. 1996. pap. 5.99 (*3-8228-8591-6*) Taschen Amer.

Pierre Bayle: Reader of Travel Literature. Joy Charnley. LC 98-19237. 202p. (C). 1998. pap. text 40.95 (*0-8204-3434-5*) P Lang Pubng.

Pierre Bayle Tome I: Du Pays de Foix a la Cite d'Erasme. Elisabeth Labrousse. (International Archives of the History of Ideas Ser.: No. 1). 296p. 1985. lib. bdg. 184.00 (*90-247-3136-4*, Pub. by M Nijhoff) Kluwer Academic.

Pierre Bayle Tome II: Heterodoxie & Rigorisme. Elisabeth Labrousse. (International Archives of the History of Ideas Ser.: No. 6). 655p. 1964. lib. bdg. 250.00 (*90-247-0182-1*) Kluwer Academic.

***Pierre Bayle's Reformation: Conscience & Criticism on the Eve of the Enlightenment.** Barbara Sher Tinsley. 2001. 55.00 (*1-57591-043-8*) Susquehanna U Pr.

***Pierre Bensusan Presents Dadgad Guitar.** Pierre Bensusan. 80p. 2000. pap. 22.95 (*0-7866-5770-7*, 99238BCD) Mel Bay.

Pierre Bernac 1899-1979. Chimenes & Buckland. 51.95 (*1-85928-362-4*) Ashgate Pub Co.

Pierre Berton's Canada: The Land & the People. Pierre Berton. LC 98-226151. (Illus.). 224p. 1999. 40.00 (*0-7737-3095-8*) Genl Dist Srvs.

Pierre Berton's Canada: The Land & the People. Pierre Berton. LC 99-492061. (Illus.). 208p. 1999. 40.00 (*0-7737-3160-1*) Stoddart Publ.

Pierre Bonnard: Illustrator. Antoine Terrasse. Tr. by Jean-Marie Clarke. (Illus.). 328p. 1989. 75.00 (*0-8109-0749-6*) Abrams.

Pierre Bonnard: Landscapes. Text by Clement Greenberg et al. (Illus.). 24p. 1997. pap. 12.00 (*1-58821-006-5*) Salander OReilly.

Pierre Bonnard: Sketches of a Journey. Octave Mirbeau. (Illus.). 176p. 1989. 35.00 (*0-85667-364-1*) Sothebys Pubns.

Pierre Bonnard: The Graphic Art. Colta F. Ives et al. (Illus.). 272p. 1989. 60.00 (*0-87099-566-9*); pap. 45.00 (*0-87099-567-7*) Metro Mus Art.

Pierre Bouguer's Optical Treatise on the Gradation of Light. Pierre Bouguer. Tr. by W. E. Middleton. LC 61-19105. 264p. reprint ed. pap. 81.90 (*0-608-10077-3*, 201414000090) Bks Demand.

Pierre Boulez. Dominique Jameux. Tr. by Susan Bradshaw. LC 90-4715. 416p. 1990. 37.95 (*0-674-66740-9*) HUP.

Pierre Boulez: A World of Harmony. Lev Koblyakov. (Contemporary Music Studies). 229p. 1993. pap. text 26.00 (*3-7186-0553-8*) Gordon & Breach.

Pierre Boulle. Lucille F. Becker. LC 95-37767. (Twayne's World Authors Ser.: Vol. 859). 1996. 32.00 (*0-8057-8272-9*, Twyne) Mac Lib Ref.

Pierre Bourdieu. Richard Jenkins. (Key Sociologists Ser.). 192p. (C). (gr. 13). 1992. pap. 17.99 (*0-415-05798-1*, A9637) Routledge.

Pierre Bourdieu: A Bibliography. Ed. & Compiled by Joan Nordquist. (Social Theory: Vol. 47). 72p. (Orig.). 1997. pap. 20.00 (*0-937855-93-6*) Ref Rsch Serv.

***Pierre Bourdieu: A Critical Introduction.** Jeremy Lane. 224p. 2000. pap. 17.95 (*0-7453-1501-1*, Pub. by Pluto GBR) Stylus Pub VA.

***Pierre Bourdieu: A Critical Introduction.** Jeremy F. Lane. 2000. 59.95 (*0-7453-1506-2*) Pluto GBR.

***Pierre Bourdieu: Fieldwork in Culture.** Ed. by Nicholas Brown & Imre Szeman. LC 99-44609. 256p. 2000. pap. 24.95 (*0-8476-9389-9*); text 70.00 (*0-8476-9388-0*) Rowman.

***Pierre Bourdieu: Language, Culture & Education: Theory into Practice.** Ed. by Michael Grenfell & Michael Kelly. LC 99-37467. 333p. (C). 1999. pap. text 47.95 (*0-8204-4602-5*) P Lang Pubng.

Pierre Bourdieu & Cultural Theory: Critical Investigations. Bridget Fowler. Ed. by Mike Featherstone. LC 96-71789. (Theory, Culture & Society Ser.). 224p. 1996. 69.95 (*0-8039-7625-9*); pap. 23.95 (*0-8039-7626-7*) Sage.

Pierre Bourdieu & Literary History, Vol. 58, No. 4. Ed. by Marshall Brown. 150p. 1997. pap. 10.00 (*0-8223-6457-3*) Duke.

Pierre Cardin. Pierre Cardin. 1997. 50.00 (*2-08-013642-9*, Pub. by Flammarion) Abbeville Pr.

Pierre Chareau. Brian B. Taylor. (Big Ser.). 1998. 24.99 (*3-8228-7887-1*) Taschen Amer.

Pierre Clereau: Odes de Pierre de Ronsard. Ed. by Jane A. Bernstein. LC 88-752951. (16th Century Chanson Ser.: Vol. 7). 184p. 1989. text 30.00 (*0-8240-3106-7*) Garland.

Pierre Corneille. Claude Abraham. LC 76-186715. (Twayne's World Authors Ser.). 169p. (C). 1972. lib. bdg. 17.95 (*0-8290-1745-3*) Irvington.

Pierre Corneille Revisited. Carlin. LC 98-34788. 1998. 32.00 (*0-8057-4561-0*, Twyne) Mac Lib Ref.

Pierre Courtade: The Making of a Party Scribe. John E. Flower. (French Studies). 288p. 1995. 47.50 (*1-85973-043-4*) Berg Pubs.

Pierre Courtin. L'Oeuvre Grave, 1944-1972. Yves Riviere. 240p. 1973. 50.00 (*0-915346-18-4*) A Wofsy Fine Arts.

Pierre Crignon: Poete et Navigateur: Oeuvres en Prose et en Vers. John Nothnagle. LC 90-70299. (FRE., Illus.). 133p. 1990. lib. bdg. 27.95 (*0-917786-80-7*) Summa Pubns.

Pierre de la Folie: Poemes. Fernando Arrabal. (FRE.). 111p. 1969. pap. 15.95 (*0-7859-3181-3*, F83452) Fr & Eur.

Pierre de la Folie: Poemes. Fernando Arrabal. 1970. pap. 9.95 (*0-686-54461-7*) Fr & Eur.

Pierre de Manchicourt: Twenty-Nine Chansons. Pierre De Manchicourt. Ed. by Margery A. Baird. (Recent Researches in Music of the Renaissance Ser.: Vol. RRR11). (Illus.). xix, 88p. 1972. pap. 35.00 (*0-89579-038-6*) A-R Eds.

Pierre de Ronsard. K. R. Jones. LC 75-120502. (Twayne's World Authors Ser.). 1970. lib. bdg. 20.95 (*0-8057-2778-7*) Irvington.

***Pierre Descaves, Temoin et Pionnier de la Radio, Vol. 2.** Christopher Todd. LC 00-21156. (Studies French Civilization: Vol. 19). 396p. 2000. text 99.95 (*0-7734-7736-5*) E Mellen.

Pierre d'Horeb. Georges Duhamel. (FRE.). 248p. 1974. pap. 10.95 (*0-7859-1787-X*, 2070365948) Fr & Eur.

Pierre d'Horeb. Georges Duhamel. (Folio Ser.: No. 594). (FRE.). 286p. 1947. pap. 8.95 (*2-07-036594-8*) Schoenhof.

Pierre Dubreuil Photographs, 1896-1935. Tom Jacobson. (Illus.). 96p. 1988. pap. 25.00 (*0-9619090-0-5*) Dubroni Pr.

Pierre Duhem. R. N. Martin. LC 91-26643. 286p. (C). 1991. 44.95 (*0-8126-9159-8*); pap. 21.95 (*0-8126-9160-1*) Open Court.

Pierre Elliott Trudeau: Reason Before Passion. Kevin J. Christiano. LC 94-194904. (Illus.). 160p. 1994. pap. 9.95 (*1-55022-188-4*, Pub. by ECW) LPC InBook.

Pierre Elliott Trudeau: Reason Before Passion. large type ed. Kevin J. Christiano. (Illus.). 220p. 1995. pap. 15.95 (*1-55022-241-4*, Pub. by ECW) Genl Dist Srvs.

Pierre en Gaule Narbonnaise et les Carrieres du Bois des Lens (Nimes) Histoire, Archeologie, Ethnographie & Techniques. Jean-Claude Bessac. (JRA Supplementary Ser.: No. 16). (FRE., Illus.). 354p. 1996. lib. bdg. 89.50 (*1-887829-16-4*) Jour Roman Arch.

***Pierre et Gilles.** Dan Cameron. (Illus.). 2000. 35.00 (*1-85894-113-X*, Pub. by Merrell Holberton) Rizzoli Intl.

Pierre et Gilles. N. Currie. (Illus.). 1994. pap. 12.99 (*3-8228-9377-3*) Taschen Amer.

Pierre et Gilles. Bernhard Marcade. (Jumbo Ser.). 1997. 69.69 (*3-8228-8095-7*) Taschen Amer.

Pierre et Jean. Guy de Maupassant. (FRE.). (C). pap. 11.95 (*0-8442-1813-8*, VF1813-8) NTC Contemp Pub Co.

Pierre et Jean. Guy de Maupassant. (Folio Ser.: No. 1414). (FRE.). 1962. pap. 9.95 (*2-07-037414-9*) Schoenhof.

Pierre et Jean. unabridged ed. Guy de Maupassant. (FRE.). pap. 5.95 (*2-87714-163-2*, Pub. by Bookking Intl) Distribks Inc.

P

An Asterisk (*) at the beginning of an entry indicates that the title is appearing for the first time.

Pierre et Luce. Romain Rolland. (FRE.). 160p. 1959. pap. 15.95 (*0-7859-5457-0*) Fr & Eur.

Pierre Eugene DuSimitiere: His American Museum 200 Years After. (Illus.). 43p. (Orig.). 1985. pap. 5.00 (*0-914076-61-2*) Lib Co Phila.

Pierre Fournier: Cellist in a Landscape with Figures. Angela Hughes. LC 97-33080. (Illus.). 256p. 1998. text 69.95 (*1-85928-422-1*, Pub. by Ashgate Pub) Ashgate Pub Co.

Pierre-Francois Tubeuf & the Advent of Capitalism in France, 1770-1840. Gwynne Lewis. (Illus.). 350p. 1993. text 65.00 (*0-19-822895-3*) OUP.

Pierre Franey Cooks with His Friends. Pierre Franey & Claudia F. Jensen. LC 96-47968. (Illus.). 224p. 1997. 30.00 (*1-885183-60-7*) Artisan.

Pierre Franey's Cooking in France. Pierre Franey & Richard Flaste. LC 94-292. 320p. 1994. 32.50 (*0-679-43157-8*) Knopf.

Pierre Franey's Low-Calorie Dessert: The New York Times 60-Minute Gourmet's Lighter Approach to Classic Cuisine. Pierre Franey & Richard Flaste. 14.95 (*0-317-18179-3*, Times Bks) Crown Pub Group.

Pierre Gassendi: From Aristotelianism to a New Natural Philosophy. Harry Brundell. (Synthese Historical Library: No. 30). 268p. 1987. text 144.00 (*90-277-2428-8*) Kluwer Academic.

Pierre Gavinies: Six Sonatas for Two Violins, Opus 5. Pierre Gauinies. Ed. by Anthony F. Ginter. (Recent Researches in Music of the Classical Era Ser.: Vol. RRC54). (Illus.). x, 66p. 1999. pap. 35.00 (*0-89579-429-2*) A-R Eds.

Pierre Gavinies: Six Sonatas for Violin & Basso Continuo, Opus 1. Pierre Gavinies. Ed. by Anthony F. Ginter. (Recent Researches in Music of the Classic Era Ser.: Vol. RRC43). xvi, 84p. 1995. pap. 35.00 (*0-89579-317-2*) A-R Eds.

Pierre Gy's Sampling Theory & Sampling Practice. 2nd ed. Francis F. Pitard. 528p. 1993. boxed set 131.95 (*0-8493-8917-8*, TN560) CRC Pr.

Pierre Gy's Sampling Theory & Sampling Practice, 2 Vols., Vol. I. Francis F. Pitard. 208p. 1989. lib. bdg. 177.00 (*0-8493-6658-5*, TN560) CRC Pr.

Pierre Gy's Sampling Theory & Sampling Practice, 2 Vols., Vol. II. Francis F. Pitard. 288p. 1989. lib. bdg. 217.00 (*0-8493-6659-3*, TN560) CRC Pr.

Pierre, Israel Potter, the Confidence-Man, Tales & Billy Budd. Herman Melville. Ed. by Harrison Hayford. LC 84-11259. 1478p. 1985. 40.00 (*0-940450-24-0*, Pub. by Library of America) Penguin Putnam.

Pierre-Joseph Favrot's Education Manual for His Sons, Set. Tr. by Martha S. Gruning from FRE. LC 88-25792. (Favrot Family Papers Ser.: Separatum No. I). (Illus.). xiii, 27p. (Orig.). 1988. pap. 5.00 (*0-87409-004-0*) Tulane Univ.

Pierre-Joseph Proudhon. 2nd rev. ed. George Woodcock. 295p. 1987. 48.99 (*0-921689-09-8*, Pub. by Black Rose); pap. 19.99 (*0-921689-08-X*, Pub. by Black Rose) Consort Bk Sales.

***Pierre Klossowski: The Persistence of Name.** Ian James. (Legenda Ser.). 200p. (C). 2000. pap. 49.50 (*1-900755-34-3*, Pub. by E H R C) David Brown.

Pierre Koenig. James Steele. LC 99-215019. (Illus.). 160p. 1998. 45.00 (*0-7148-3753-9*, Pub. by Phaidon Press) Phaidon Pr.

Pierre Lalande: Special Agent. large type ed. Guido Zembsch-Schreve. (Ulverscroft Large Print Ser.). (Illus.). 432p. 1998. 29.99 (*0-7089-3888-4*) Ulverscroft.

Pierre Lalande: Special Agent: The Wartime Memoirs of Guido Zembsch-Schreve. Tr. by John Brownjohn. (Illus.). 207p. 1996. 31.95 (*0-85052-533-0*, Pub. by Leo Cooper) Trans-Atl Phila.

Pierre Lapin: Peter Rabbit. Beatrix Potter. (FRE., Illus.). 62p. (J). 1980. 9.95 (*0-7859-3624-6*, 2070560694) Fr & Eur.

Pierre Lapin: Peter Rabbit. Beatrix Potter. (Gallimard Ser.). (FRE.). 62p. (J). 1980. 10.95 (*2-07-056069-4*) Schoenhof.

Pierre Leroux & the Birth of Democratic Socialism. Jack Bakunin. 1976. lib. bdg. 250.00 (*0-87700-221-5*) Revisionist Pr.

Pierre Loti. Michael G. Lerner. LC 73-2368. (Twayne's World Authors Ser.). 172p. (C). 1974. lib. bdg. 17.95 (*0-8057-2546-6*) Irvington.

Pierre Loti: Ses Maisons. Pierre De Boisdeffre. (FRE., Illus.). 200p. 1996. pap. 54.95 (*2-86808-099-5*) Intl Scholars.

Pierre Loti's Dramatic Works. Michael G. Lerner. LC 98-45070. (Studies in French Literature). 103 p. 1998. write for info. (*0-88946-572-X*) E Mellen.

Pierre Loti's Dramatic Works. Michael G. Lerner. LC 98-45070. (Studies in French Literature: Vol. 30). 103p. 1998. text 79.95 (*0-7734-8247-4*) E Mellen.

Pierre Mendes France. Jean Lacouture. Tr. by George Holoch. LC 84-10912. (FRE.). 494p. 1984. 45.00 (*0-8419-0856-7*) Holmes & Meier.

Pierre Nicole, Jansenist & Humanist: A Study of His Thought. E. D. James. (Archives Internationales D'Histoire des Idees Ser.: No. 1). 198p. 1972. pap. text 57.00 (*90-247-1282-3*, Pub. by M Nijhoff) Kluwer Academic.

Pierre Noziere. Anatole France, pseud. (FRE.). 332p. 1948. 7.95 (*0-8288-9762-X*, F101340) Fr & Eur.

Pierre, or the Ambiguities: Kraken Edition, The. Herman Melville. Ed. by Hershel Parker. (Illus.). 560p. 1995. 16.00 (*0-06-118009-2*) HarperTrade.

Pierre Puvis de Chavannes. Aimee Brown-Price. LC 94-65750. (Illus.). 272p. 1994. 60.00 (*0-8478-1826-8*, Pub. by Rizzoli Intl) St Martin.

Pierre Raconte: Sculptures en Stiatite du Nouveau-Quibec et du Kenya. Thomas O. Eisemon et al.Tr. of Stories in Stone: Soapstone Sculptures from Northern Quebec & Kenya. (ENG & FRE., Illus.). 84p. 1988. pap. 14.95 (*0-660-50288-7*, Pub. by CN Mus Civilization) U of Wash Pr.

Pierre Santerre, the Complete Chansons: Alessandro Striggio, Touteau, Phillipe Verdelot, Johannes Verius, Antoine de Villers. Ed. by Jane A. Bernstein. LC 92-750047. (Sixteenth-Century Chanson Ser.: Vol. 22). 160p. 1992. text 72.00 (*0-8240-3121-0*) Garland.

Pierre-Simon Ballanche: Precursor of Romanticism. Albert J. George. 1945. 30.00 (*0-89366-097-3*) Ultramarine Pub.

Pierre-Simon Laplace, 1749-1827: A Life in Exact Science. Charles C. Gillispie et al. LC 97-8331. 304p. 1997. text 49.50 (*0-691-01185-0*, Pub. by Princeton U Pr) Cal Prin Full Svc.

***Pierre-Simon Laplace, 1749-1827: A Life in Exact Science.** Charles Coulston Gillespie et al. (Illus.). 336p. 2000. pap. text 19.95 (*0-691-05027-9*) Princeton U Pr.

Pierre since 1910. Harold H. Schuler. LC 98-90579. 280p. 1998. per. 15.95 (*0-9619578-1-6*) H H Schuler.

Pierre Soulages. (Illus.). 128p. 1989. 60.00 (*3-9832212-8-9*, Pub. by Edition Cantz) Dist Art Pubs.

Pierre Teilhard de Chardin. Intro. by Ursula King. LC 98-52408. (Modern Spiritual Masters Ser.). 173p. 1999. pap. 13.00 (*1-57075-248-6*) Orbis Bks.

Pierre Trudeau Speaks Out on Meech Lake. Pierre E. Trudeau. 171p. 1990. pap. 9.95 (*0-7736-7244-3*) Genl Dist Srvs.

***Pierre Turgeon: The Playmaker.** Jeff Gordon. LC 98-89349. (Sport Snaps Ser.). (Illus.). 40p. 1999. pap. 9.95 (*1-892920-03-4*) G H B Pubs.

Pierre Van Maldere: 6 Symphonies a Pie Strumenti, Opus 4. Pierre V. Maldere. Ed. by Craig Lister. (Recent Researches in Music of the Classic Era Ser.: Vol. RRC35-36). (Illus.). xxvii, 174p. 1990. pap. 60.00 (*0-89579-248-6*) A-R Eds.

Pierre Verger: The Go-Between. Pierre F. Verger. 240p. 1997. 65.00 (*1-881616-81-9*) Dist Art Pubs.

Pierre Zoelly: Elements of an Architectural Language. Ed. by Pierre Zoelly. (ENG, FRE & GER., Ilus.). 276p. 1998. 75.00 (*3-7643-5773-8*, Pub. by Birkhauser) Princeton Arch.

Pierres de Lune. Tr. of Moon Lake. (FRE.). (J). 18.95 (*3-314-20865-0*, Pub. by North-South Bks NYC) Chronicle Bks.

Pierre's Dream. Jennifer Armstrong. LC 98-36179. (Illus.). (J). 1999. lib. bdg. 15.89 (*0-8037-2460-8*, Dial Yng Read) Peng Put Young Read.

Pierre's Dream. Jennifer Armstrong. Ed. by Diane Arico. LC 98-36179. (Illus.). 32p. (J). (ps-3). 1999. 15.99 (*0-8037-1700-8*, Dial Yng Read) Peng Put Young Read.

Pierrette. Honore de Balzac & Pierre Citron. 9.95 (*0-686-53924-9*) Fr & Eur.

***Pierriche.** Louis Ritchotte. (Illus.). 143p. 2000. pap. 11.95 (*0-595-00251-X*, Writers Showcase) iUniversecom.

Pierrot: A Critical History of a Mask. Robert F. Storey. LC 78-51194. (Illus.). 272p. 1978. reprint ed. pap. 84.40 (*0-608-07497-7*, 206772000009) Bks Demand.

Pierrot, et Autres Nouvelles. Guy de Maupassant. (FRE.). 1991. pap. 16.95 (*0-7859-3162-7*, 2253055816) Fr & Eur.

Pierrot in Petrograd: Commedia dell'Arte & Balagan in Twentieth-Century Russian Theatre & Drama. J. Douglas Clayton. (Illus.). 400p. 1994. 65.00 (*0-7735-1136-9*, Pub. by McG-Queens Univ Pr) CUP Services.

Pierrot la Lune. Pierre Gripari. (FRE.). 352p. 1983. pap. 11.95 (*0-7859-2477-9*, 2070374823) Fr & Eur.

Pierrot Mon Ami. Raymond Queneau. Tr. by Barbara Wright from FRE. LC 87-72849. 160p. 1989. pap. 9.95 (*0-916583-40-6*) Dalkey Arch.

Pierrot Mon Ami. Raymond Queneau. (Folio Ser.: No. 226). (FRE.). 224p. 1972. pap. 8.95 (*2-07-036226-4*) Schoenhof.

Pierrot, Mon Ami. Raymond Queneau. (FRE.). 1989. pap. 10.95 (*0-8288-3774-0*, F120390) Fr & Eur.

Pierrot ou les Secrets de la Nuit. Michel Tournier. (Folio - Cadet Rouge Ser.: No. 205). (FRE., Illus.). 56p. (J). (gr. 3-7). 1989. pap. 8.95 (*2-07-031205-4*) Schoenhof.

Pierrots & Harlequins. (Prestel Postcard Bks.). (Illus.). 18p. 1995. pap. 8.95 (*3-7913-1458-0*, Pub. by Prestel) te Neues.

Pierrots on the Stage of Desire: 19th-Century French Literary Artists & the Comic Pantomime. Robert F. Storey. LC 84-42904. 408p. 1985. reprint ed. pap. 126.50 (*0-608-03338-3*, 206405000008) Bks Demand.

Piers Anthony. Michael R. Collings. Ed. by Roger C. Schlobin. LC 83-2466. (Starmont Reader's Guide Ser.: Vol. 20). 96p. 1983. pap. 17.00 (*0-916732-52-5*) Millefleurs.

Piers Anthony's Pretender. Piers Anthony & Frances Hall. 320p. 1993. mass mkt. 4.99 (*0-8125-2396-2*, Pub. by Tor Bks) St Martin.

Piers Gaveston: A Chapter of Early Constitutional History. Walter P. Dodge. LC 74-173161. (Illus.). 259p. 1972. reprint ed. 23.95 (*0-405-08451-X*, Pub. by Blom Pubns) Ayer.

Piers Plowman. William Langland. Ed. by Elizabeth D. Kirk & Judith H. Anderson. Tr. by E. Talbot Donaldson. (C). 1990. pap. text 14.75 (*0-393-96011-0*) Norton.

Piers Plowman: A Facsimile of Bodleian Library, Oxford, MS Douce 104. Ed. by Derek Pearsall & Kathleen Scott. (Illus.). 336p. (C). 1992. 250.00 (*0-85991-345-7*) Boydell & Brewer.

Piers Plowman: A Facsimile of the Z-Text in Bodleian Library, Oxford, MS Bodley 851. Ed. by Charlotte Brewer & A. G. Rigg. (Illus.). 52p. (C). 1994. 150.00 (*0-85991-396-1*, DS Brewer) Boydell & Brewer.

Piers Plowman: A Glossary of Legal Diction. John A. Alford. 202p. 1988. 75.00 (*0-85991-248-5*) Boydell & Brewer.

Piers Plowman: A Guide to the Quotations. Ed. by John A. Alford. (Medieval & Renaissance Texts & Studies: Vol. 77). 176p. 1992. 18.00 (*0-86698-088-1*, MR77) MRTS.

Piers Plowman: A New Translation of the B-Text. William Langland. Tr. & Intro. by A. V. Schmidt. (World's Classics Ser.). 402p. 1992. pap. 8.95 (*0-19-282587-9*) OUP.

***Piers Plowman: A New Translation of the B-Text.** William Langland. Tr. by A.V.C. Schmidt. (Oxford World's Classics Ser.). 408p. 2000. pap. 9.95 (*0-19-283646-3*) OUP.

Piers Plowman: An Edition of the C-Text. William Langland. Ed. by Derek Pearsall. 416p. 1995. pap. text 16.95 (*0-85989-429-0*, Pub. by Univ Exeter Pr) Northwestern U Pr.

Piers Plowman: An Introduction to the B-Text. James Simpson. LC 89-34272. 1990. text 56.95 (*0-582-01392-5*, Pub. by Addison-Wesley) Longman.

Piers Plowman: An Introduction to the B Text. James Simpson. LC 89-34272. (C). 1991. pap. text 22.95 (*0-582-01391-7*, Pub. by Addison-Wesley) Longman.

Piers Plowman: The A-Text - An Alliterative Verse Translation by Sister Francis Lovella. Ed. by David C. Fowler. Tr. by Francis Covella. LC 92-16912. 108p. 1992. pap. 9.95 (*0-86698-120-9*, P11) Pegasus Pr.

Piers Plowman: The C Version. Ed. by George Russell & George Kane. LC 96-45499. 1997. 155.00 (*0-520-21058-1*, Pub. by U CA Pr) Cal Prin Full Svc.

Piers Plowman: The Three Versions, Vol. "Vol. "'"Vol. I, A Vers" Ed. by George Kane. 1988. 165.00 (*0-520-06229-9*, Pub. by U CA Pr) Cal Prin Full Svc.

Piers Plowman: The Three Versions, Vol. "Vol. "'"Vol. II, B Ver" Ed. by George Kane. 1988. 165.00 (*0-520-06230-2*, Pub. by U CA Pr) Cal Prin Full Svc.

Piers Plowman: The Z Version. William Langland. Ed. by A. G. Rigg & Charlotte Brewer. x, 137p. pap. text 13.71 (*0-88844-059-6*) Brill Academic Pubs.

Piers Plowman & the Image of God. Daniel M. Murtaugh. LC 77-25544. 137p. reprint ed. pap. 42.50 (*0-7837-4909-0*, 204457400004) Bks Demand.

Piers Plowman & the Problem of Belief. Britton J. Harwood. 240p. 1992. text 60.00 (*0-8020-5799-3*) U of Toronto Pr.

Piers Plowman & the Problem of Belief. Britton J. Harwood. 237p. 1995. pap. text 22.00 (*0-8020-7655-6*) U of Toronto Pr.

Piers Plowman Glossary, Pt. 4. William Langland. Ed. by Walter W. Skeat. (EETS, OS Ser.: No. 81). 1974. reprint ed. 70.00 (*0-527-00060-4*) Periodicals Srv.

Piers Plowman Tradition. Helen Barr. 1993. pap. 12.95 (*0-460-87050-5*) J M Dent & Sons.

Piers the Ploughman. William Langland. Tr. by J. F. Goodridge. (Classics Ser.). 320p. (Orig.). 1959. pap. 10.95 (*0-14-044087-9*, Penguin Classics) Viking Penguin.

Piers the Plowman: A Critical Edition of the A-Version. William Langland. Ed. by Thomas A. Knott & David C. Fowler. LC PR2010.K65. 316p. reprint ed. pap. 98.00 (*0-608-11904-0*, 202312200032) Bks Demand.

Pierse: The Law of Road Traffic in the Republic of Ireland. Robert Pierse. 1989. boxed set 73.00 (*1-85475-055-0*, MICHIE) LEXIS Pub.

Pierson Barton Reading: Man of Destiny - Pioneer of Shasta County, California. Helen S. Giffen. Ed. by Eleanor L. Templeman. (Illus.). xiv, 164p. 1985. text 25.00 (*0-933395-00-0*); pap. text 10.00 (*0-933395-01-9*) Shasta Hist Soc.

Pierson Millenium. Richard E. Pierson & Jennifer Pierson. LC 98-107759. viii, 332p. 1997. pap. 34.50 (*0-7884-0742-2*, P319) Heritage Bk.

Pies. Robert James. LC 95-20190. (SPA.). (J). 1995. lib. bdg. 14.60 (*1-57103-114-6*) Rourke Pr.

***Pies.** Dana Meachen Rau. (Rookie Espanol Ser.). (SPA., Illus.). (J). 2000. 15.00 (*0-516-22020-9*) Childrens.

Pies. Wilma Riley. (Illus.). 32p. 1991. pap. 7.95 (*1-55050-021-X*, Pub. by Coteau) Genl Dist Srvs.

Pies. Louise Stoltzfus. LC 94-14905. (Best of Favorite Recipes from Quilters Ser.). (Illus.). 64p. 1994. 7.95 (*1-56148-115-7*) Good Bks PA.

Pies: Cook Books from Amish Kitchens. Phyllis Pellman Good & Rachel T. Pellman. (From Amish Kitchens Ser.). 32p. 1996. mass mkt. 2.95 (*1-56148-191-2*) Good Bks PA.

Pies & Tarts. John P. Carroll. Ed. by Laurie Wertz. LC 92-10315. (Williams-Sonoma Kitchen Library). (Illus.). 108p. 1992. lib. bdg. write for info. (*0-7835-0201-X*) Time-Life.

Pies & Tarts. John P. Carroll. Ed. by Laurie Wertz. LC 92-10315. (Williams-Sonoma Kitchen Library). (Illus.). 108p. (gr. 11). 1999. 18.95 (*0-7835-0200-1*) Time-Life.

Pies & Tarts. Maida Heatter. LC 97-31254. (Illus.). 288p. 1997. 19.95 (*0-8362-5075-3*, Cader Bks) Andrews & McMeel.

Pies, Classic Essential. (Mini Cook Bks.). (Illus.). 64p. 1999. pap. 1.95 (*3-8290-1594-1*) Konemann.

Pies del Dragon. Marjorie Jackson. Tr. by Alberto Romo. (Books for Young Learners).Tr. of Dragon Feet. (SPA., Illus.). 16p. (J). (gr. k-2). 1998. pap. text 5.00 (*1-57274-199-6*, A2890) R Owen Pubs.

Pie's in the Oven. Rosemary Breckler. LC 95-518. (Illus.). 32p. (J). 1996. 15.95 (*0-395-76501-3*) HM.

Pies, Pies & Pies. 96p. (Orig.). 1995. mass mkt. 12.50 (*0-9647104-0-4*) M Calcote.

Pies, Puddings & Desserts. (Mini Cook Bks.). (Illus.). 64p. 1999. pap. 1.95 (*3-8290-1616-6*) Konemann.

Piesn Niepodlegla. Ed. by Czeslaw Milosz. (Michigan Slavic Materials Ser.: No. 18).Tr. of Invincible Song. 1981. 10.00 (*0-930042-41-7*) Mich Slavic Pubns.

Piesni Wiatru: Songs of the Wind. Stanislaw Kowalski. (POL.). 52p. (Orig.). 1986. 4.00 (*0-930401-04-2*) Artex Pub.

Piesse: The Elements of Drafting. 8th ed. J. K. Aitken. xvi, 137p. 1991. pap. 25.00 (*0-455-21023-3*, Pub. by LawBk Co) Gaunt.

Piet Mondrian: Catalogue Raisonne. Joop M. Joosten & Robert P. Welsh. LC 96-12348. (Illus.). 1008p. 1996. 250.00 (*0-8109-4287-9*, Pub. by Abrams) Time Warner.

Piet Mondrian: Colour, Structure & Symbolism. Hans Locher. Tr. by Michael Latcham. (Illus.). 100p. 1995. 35.00 (*3-906127-44-3*) Dist Art Pubs.

***Pieta.** Robert Hupka. 1999. pap. 15.95 (*0-89870-771-4*) Ignatius Pr.

Pieta. Ulysses Kay. 1978. pap. 7.50 (*0-8258-0061-7*, PCB113) Fischer Inc NY.

Pieta. George Klein. (Illus.). 304p. 1994. pap. text 14.95 (*0-262-61098-1*) MIT Pr.

Pieta for the Dispossessed: The Grace of Palestinians. Aminta Marks. LC 93-80534. (Illus.). 170p. (Orig.). 1994. pap. 12.00 (*0-9626898-2-3*) Grindstone Pr.

Pieta in French Late Gothic Sculpture: Regional Variations. William H. Forsyth. LC 93-23887. (Illus.). 219p. 1995. 40.00 (*0-87099-681-9*) Metro Mus Art.

Pietas et Societas, New Trends in Reformation Social History: Essays in Memory of Harold J. Grimm. Kyle Sessions & Phillip Bebb. (Sixteenth Century Essays & Studies: Vol. 4). (Illus.). 240p. (C). 1985. 40.00 (*0-940474-04-2*, SCJP) Truman St Univ.

Pietas from Vergil to Dryden. James D. Garrison. (Illus.). 336p. 1992. text 50.00 (*0-271-00787-7*) Pa St U Pr.

Pietas in Patrian (Life of Sir William Phips) Cotton Mather. (Notable American Authors Ser.). 1999. reprint ed. lib. bdg. 125.00 (*0-7812-3955-9*) Rprt Serv.

Pieter Breughel. John Malam. LC 98-8486. (Tell Me about Ser.). (Illus.). 24p. (J). (ps-3). 1999. 19.93 (*1-57505-366-7*, Carolrhoda) Lerner Pub.

Pieter Bruegel. Mike Venezia. LC 92-4810. (Getting to Know the World's Greatest Artists Ser.). (Illus.). 32p. (J). (ps-4). 1992. lib. bdg. 21.00 (*0-516-02279-2*) Childrens.

Pieter Bruegel. Mike Venezia. LC 92-4810. (Getting to Know the World's Greatest Artists Ser.). (Illus.). 32p. (J). (ps-4). 1993. pap. 6.95 (*0-516-42279-0*) Childrens.

Pieter Bruegel: Dutch Proverbs. Juergen Mueller. (Illus.). 96p. 1999. pap. 9.99 (*3-8228-7057-9*) Taschen Amer.

Pieter Bruegel: Parables of Order & Enterprise. Ethan M. Kavaler. LC 98-29502. (Studies in Netherlandish Visual Culture). (Illus.). 403p. (C). 1999. text 80.00 (*0-521-62267-0*) Cambridge U Pr.

Pieter Bruegel the Elder: 2 Studies. Walter S. Gibson. (Franklin D. Murphy Lectures: No. 11). (Illus.). 150p. 1993. 12.00 (*0-913689-32-7*) Spencer Muse Art.

Pieter Bruegel the Elder - The Prints: Catalogue Raisonne. rev. ed. Rene Van Bastelaer. (Illus.). 320p. 1992. 150.00 (*1-55660-140-9*) A Wofsy Fine Arts.

Pieter Bruegel's Tower of Babel: The Builder with the Red Hat. Nils Jockel. LC 98-186657. (Adventures in Art Ser.). (Illus.). 30p. (J). (gr. 4-6). 1998. 14.95 (*3-7913-1941-8*) te Neues.

Pieter de Hooch, 1629-1684. Peter Sutton. LC 98-26337. (Illus.). 160p. 1998. 45.00 (*0-300-07757-2*) Yale U Pr.

Pieter de Marees: Description & Historical Account of the Gold Kingdom of Guinea (1602) Ed. by Albert Van Dantzig & Adam Jones. (Fontes Historiae Africanae, Series Varia: Vol. V). (Illus.). 300p. 1987. 89.00 (*0-19-726056-X*) OUP.

Pieter Laurens Mol: The Sanguine Surrender. (Illus.). 30p. 1989. 30.00 (*0-948274-05-0*, Pub. by Graeme Murray) Dist Art Pubs.

Pieter Saenredam: The Painter & His Time. Gary Schwartz & Marten J. Bok. (Illus.). 224p. 1990. 95.00 (*1-55859-073-0*) Abbeville Pr.

Pietermaritzburg, 1838-1988: A New Portrait of an African City. Ed. by John P. Laband & Robert Haswell. 320p. 1988. 25.00 (*0-86980-639-4*, Pub. by Univ Natal Pr) Intl Spec Bk.

***Pieter's & Anna's Trek.** Helen Denboer. LC 98-35694. (Immigrants Chronicles Ser.). (J). 1999. 5.99 (*0-7814-3083-6*) Chariot Victor.

Pietism in Petticoats & Other Comedies. Thomas Kerth & Luise Gottsched. Tr. & Intro. by John R. Russell. (GERM Ser.). xxxvi, 306p. 1994. 55.00 (*1-879751-60-7*) Camden Hse.

Pietists: Selected Writings. Ed. by Peter C. Erb. (Classics of Western Spirituality Ser.). (C). 1983. pap. 19.95 (*0-8091-2509-9*) Paulist Pr.

Pietists, Protestants, & Mysticism: The Use of Late Medieval Spiritual Texts in the Work of Gottfried Arnold 1666-1714. Peter C. Erb. LC 89-29185. (Pietist & Wesleyan Studies: No. 2). 339p. 1989. 45.00 (*0-8108-2281-4*) Scarecrow.

Pieton de Paris, D'Apres Paris. Leon-Paul Fargue. (Folio Ser.: No. 1376). (FRE.). pap. 9.95 (*2-07-037376-2*) Schoenhof.

Pieton de Paris Suivi de D'Apres Paris. Leon-Paul Fargue. (FRE.). 1982. pap. 11.95 (*0-7859-2461-2*, 2070373762) Fr & Eur.

Pietra di Luna. Tr. of Moon Lake. (ITA., Illus.). (J). (gr. k-3). 18.95 (*88-8203-054-7*, Pub. by North-South Bks NYC) Chronicle Bks.

Pietre Dure: The Uses of Hardstone Furniture & Decorations, 1588-1900. Anna M. Giusti. (Illus.). 312p. 1991. 150.00 (*0-85667-393-5*) Sothebys Pubns.

Pietro Belluschi: Modern American Architect. Meredith L. Clausen. (Illus.). 479p. 1995. 65.00 (*0-262-03220-1*) MIT Pr.

Pietro Belluschi: Modern American Architect. Meredith L. Clausen. LC 94-20789. (Illus.). 479p. 1999. reprint ed. pap. 34.50 (*0-262-53167-4*) MIT Pr.

P

Pietro Cesti - (1623-1669) - Giovanni Legrenzi (1626-1690), Vol. 6. Ed. by David Burrows & Anne Schnoebelen. (Italian Contata in the Seventeenth Century Ser.). 1986. lib. bdg. 25.00 (*0-8240-8880-8*) Garland.

Pietro da Cortona at the Pitti Palace: A Study of the Planetary Rooms & Related Projects. Malcolm Campbell. LC 76-3247. (Princeton Monographs in Art & Archaeology: Vol. 41). 426p. 1977. reprint ed. pap. 132.10 (*0-608-04637-X*, 206532400003) Bks Demand.

Pietro DiDonato, the Master Builder. Matthew Diomede. LC 94-38036. 1995. 32.50 (*0-8387-5289-6*) Assoc Univ Prs.

Pietro Perugino: Master of the Italian Renaissance. Joseph A. Becherer et al. LC 97-33981. 1997. pap. write for info. (*0-942159-20-9*) Rizzoli Intl.

Pietro Perugino: Master of the Italian Renaissance. Joseph A. Becherer et al. LC 97-33981. 317p. 1997. 60.00 (*0-8478-2076-9*, Pub. by Rizzoli Intl) St Martin.

Pietro Von Abano. Ed. by Clive Brown. (Selected Works of Louis Spohr, 1784-1859: Vol. 3). 500p. 1989. reprint ed. text 45.00 (*0-8240-1502-9*) Garland.

Pietro's Girl. Frank R. Nichols. LC 95-7905. 192p. (Orig.). 1995. pap. 12.95 (*0-923687-36-X*) Celo Valley Bks.

Piety. S. R. Bourghei et al. Tr. by Amir Tavakoli from PER. 1980. pap. 2.00 (*0-318-03827-7*) Book Dist Ctr.

Piety: Partial History of James Duncan Piety, His Forebears & Descendants, 1796-1948. W. P. Morgan. (Illus.). 150p. 1994. reprint ed. pap. 23.00 (*0-8328-4232-X*); reprint ed. lib. bdg. 33.00 (*0-8328-4231-1*) Higginson Bk Co.

Piety & Charity in Late Medieval Florence. John Henderson. (Illus.). 568p. 1994. 95.00 (*0-19-820271-7*) OUP.

Piety & Charity in Late Medieval Florence. John Henderson. LC 96-44594. 1997. pap. text 29.95 (*0-226-32688-8*) U Ch Pr.

Piety & Fanaticism: Rabbinic Criticism of Stringency. Sara E. Weinstein. LC 96-41188. 280p. 1997. 40.00 (*1-56821-976-8*) Aronson.

Piety & Humanity: Essays on Religion & Early Modern Political Philosophy. Ed. by Douglas Kries. LC 97-17196. 320p. 1997. 71.50 (*0-8476-8618-3*); pap. 26.95 (*0-8476-8619-1*) Rowman.

Piety & Intellect: The Aims & Purposes of Ante-Bellum Theological Education. Glenn T. Miller. 458p. 1990. write for info. (*1-55540-470-7*) Assn of Theol Schls.

Piety & Intellect at Amherst College, 1865-1912. Thomas Le Duc. LC 77-89196. (American Education: Its Men, Institutions, & Ideas. Series 1). 1977. reprint ed. 17.95 (*0-405-01434-1*) Ayer.

Piety & Nationalism: Lay Voluntary Associations & the Creation of an Irish-Catholic Community in Toronto, 1850-1895. Brian P. Clarke. 352p. 1993. 55.00 (*0-7735-1130-X*, Pub. by McG-Queens Univ Pr) CUP Services.

Piety & Patriotism. James W. Van Hoeven. 1976. pap. 7.00 (*0-8028-1663-0*) Eerdmans.

Piety & Perseverance: Jews from the Carpathian Mountains. Herman Dicker & Elie Wiesel. LC 80-54595. (Illus.). 252p. 1981. pap. 10.00 (*0-87203-098-9*) Hermon.

Piety & Politics: Evangelicals & Fundamentalists Confront the World. Ed. by Richard J. Neuhaus & Michael Cromartie. LC 87-19942. 434p. (Orig.). (C). 1988. pap. text 12.95 (*0-89633-108-3*) Ethics & Public Policy.

***Piety & Politics: Imaging Divine Kingship in Louis XIV's Chapel at Versailles.** Martha Mel Stumberg Edmunds. LC 00-28674. (Illus.). 2000. write for info. (*0-87413-693-8*) U Delaware Pr.

Piety & Poverty: Working-Class Religion in Berlin, London, & New York, 1870-1914. Hugh McLeod. (Europe Past & Present Ser.). 400p. (C). 1996. text 45.00 (*0-8419-1356-0*) Holmes & Meier.

Piety & Power: Muslims & Christians in West Africa. Lamin Sanneh. LC 96-43354. (Faith Meets Faith Ser.). 140p. (Orig.). 1996. pap. 20.00 (*1-57075-090-4*) Orbis Bks.

Piety & Power: The Role of Italian Parishes in the New York Metropolitan Area (1889-1930) Silvano M. Tomasi. LC 74-79913. 201p. (C). 1975. 10.00 (*0-913256-16-1*) CMS.

Piety & Power: The World of Jewish Fundamentalism. David Landau. LC 92-37540. 1992. 27.50 (*0-8090-7605-5*) Hill & Wang.

***Piety & Power in Ireland, 1760-1960: Essays in Honour of Emmet Larkin.** Ed. by Stewart J. Brown & David W. Miller. 360p. 2000. 30.00 (*0-268-03863-5*, Pub. by U of Notre Dame Pr) Chicago Distribution Ctr.

Piety & the People: Religious Printing in French, 1511-1551. Francis Higman. (St. Andrews Studies in Reformation History). 544p. 1996. 86.95 (*1-85928-350-0*, Pub. by Scolar Pr) Ashgate Pub Co.

Piety & the Professions: Sir John Coleridge & His Sons. Timothy J. Toohey. (Modern European History Ser.). 376p. 1987. text 15.00 (*0-8240-7834-9*) Garland.

Piety & Tolerance: Pennsylvania German Religion, 1700-1850. Stephen L. Longenecker. LC 93-49988. (Pietist & Wesleyan Studies: No. 6). 216p. 1994. 32.00 (*0-8108-2771-9*) Scarecrow.

***Piety, Fraternity & Power: Religious Gilds in Late Medieval Yorkshire, 1389-1547.** David J. F. Crouch. LC 99-46618. (Warfare in History Ser.). (Illus.). 288p. 2000. 75.00 (*0-9529734-4-8*, Suffolk Records Soc) Boydell & Brewer.

***Piety in Providence: Class Dimensions of Religious Experience in Antebellum Rhode Island.** Mark S. Schantz. 2000. write for info. (*0-8014-2952-8*) Cornell U Pr.

***Piety of John Witherspoon: Pew, Pulpit & Public Forum.** L. Gordon Tait. (Illus.). 350p. 2000. write for info. (*0-664-50133-8*, Pub. by Geneva Press) Presbyterian Pub.

Piety on Its Knees: Three Sufi Traditions in South Asia in Modern Times. Claudia Liebeskind. LC 98-903530. (Illus.). 356p. 1998. text 35.00 (*0-19-564309-7*) OUP.

***Piety, Peace & the Freedom to Philosophize.** Ed. by Paul J. Bagley. LC 99-47089. (New Synthese Historical Library). 304p. 1999. text 128.00 (*0-7923-5984-4*) Kluwer Academic.

Piety, Power, & Politics: Religion & Nation Formation in Guatemala, 1821-1871. Douglass Sullivan-Gonzalez. LC 97-45346. (Pittsburgh Latin American Ser.). (Illus.). 221p. 1998. text 45.00 (*0-8229-4057-4*) U of Pittsburgh Pr.

Pieza Obscura. Enrique Uhn. (SPA.). 90p. 1984. pap. 8.50 (*84-86236-08-8*, 3403) Ediciones Norte.

Piezas y Disenos - Pieces & Patterns. Judith A. Hillen. (ENG & SPA.). 160p. (J). (gr. 5-9). 1992. 16.95 (*1-881431-31-2*, 1456) AIMS Educ Fnd.

Piezo-Driven Stages for Nanopositioning with Extreme Stability: Theoretical Aspects & Practical Design Considerations. Henk Van Der Wulp. (Illus.). 173p. 1997. pap. 47.50 (*90-407-1491-6*, Pub. by Delft U Pr) Coronet Bks.

Piezoelectric Actuators & Ultrasonic Motors. Kenji Uchino. LC 96-34506. (Electronic Materials, Science & Technology Ser.). 1996. text 181.50 (*0-7923-9811-4*) Kluwer Academic.

Piezoelectric Ceramics. Bernard Jaffe et al. (Illus.). 327p. (C). 1990. reprint ed. text 90.00 (*1-878907-10-7*, RAN) TechBooks.

Piezoelectric Ceramics, Ceramic-Polymer Composites & Polymers-New Developments & Markets, No. GB-064N. LC 95-213779. 229p. 1993. 2450.00 (*1-56965-200-7*) BCC.

Piezoelectric Filters: Markets, Applications & Competitors: Quartz Crystal, SAW, Ceramic, Mechanical. Amadee Bender. (Illus.). 196p. 1988. pap. text 2400.00 (*1-878218-00-X*) World Info Tech.

***Piezoelectric Materials: Advances in Science, Technology.** Carmen Galassi et al. 420p. 2000. pap. 79.50 (*0-7923-6213-6*) Kluwer Academic.

***Piezoelectric Materials: Advances in Science, Technology & Applications.** Carmen Galassi. LC 00-22970. (NATO ASI Ser.). (Illus.). 2000. write for info. (*0-7923-6212-8*) Kluwer Academic.

Piezoelectric Resonators & Their Applications. J. Zelenka. (Studies in Electrical & Electronic Engineering: No. 24). 302p. 1986. 116.00 (*0-317-54802-6*) Elsevier.

Piezoelectric Resonators & Their Applications. J. Zelenka. (Studies in Electrical & Electronic Engineering: Vol. 24). 302p. 1986. 208.75 (*0-444-99516-1*, North Holland) Elsevier.

Piezoelectric Shells: Distributed Sensing & Control of Continua. H. S. Tzou. LC 93-9596. (Solid Mechanics & Its Applications Ser.: Vol. 19). 496p. (C). 1993. text 264.50 (*0-7923-2186-3*) Kluwer Academic.

Piezoelectricity. Ed. by J. J. Gagnepain et al. (Ferroelectrics & Related Phenomena Ser.: Vols. 40, Nos. 3-4; 41; & 42, Nos. 1-2). 788p. 1982. pap. text 1323.00 (*0-677-16415-7*) Gordon & Breach.

Piezoelectricity. Ed. by G. W. Taylor et al. (Ferroelectricity & Related Phenomena Ser.: Vol. 4). xiv, 406p. 1985. text 307.00 (*0-677-16660-5*) Gordon & Breach.

Piezoelectrcy. Ed. by C. Rosen et al. LC 90-24044. (Illus.). 552p. (C). 1992. 125.00 (*0-88318-647-0*) Spr-Verlag.

Pig see Who Am I?

***Pig.** Sally Chambers. (J). 1999. 6.95 (*1-86233-025-5*) Levinson Bks.

Pig. Andrew Cowan. LC 96-19123. 224p. 1996. 21.00 (*0-15-100218-5*) Harcourt.

Pig. Andrew Cowan. 224p. (YA). 1997. pap. 12.00 (*0-15-600545-X*, Harcourt Child Bks) Harcourt.

Pig. D K Publishing Staff. LC 99-209408. (Watch the Fun Unfold Ser.). 1999. 3.95 (*0-7894-4311-2*) DK Pub Inc.

Pig. Kwok Man-Ho. LC 93-48006. (Chinese Horoscopes Library). (Illus.). 42p. 1994. pap. 8.95 (*1-56458-605-7*) DK Pub Inc.

Pig. Mary Ling. LC 92-53487. (See How They Grow Ser.). (Illus.). 16p. (J). (ps-1). 1993. 9.95 (*1-56458-204-3*) DK Pub Inc.

Pig. Tammy Ryan. LC 98-222981. 1998. pap. 5.25 (*0-8222-1600-0*) Dramatists Play.

***Pig & Crow.** Illus. by Kay Chorao. LC 99-31776. 32p. (J). 1999. 15.95 (*0-8050-5863-X*) H Holt & Co.

***Pig & Duck Buy a Truck: A Book of Colors.** Lee Lorenz. (Illus.). (ps-3). 2000. pap. text 10.95 (*0-689-83780-1*) Litle Simon.

Pig & the Python. David Cork & Susan Lightstone. LC 97-37319. 256p. 1997. per. 14.00 (*0-7615-1275-6*) Prima Pub.

Pig & the Shrink. Pamela Todd. LC 98-37700. 192p. (YA). (gr. 5 up). 1999. 14.95 (*0-385-32657-2*) BDD Bks Young Read.

***Pig & the Shrink.** Pamela Todd. (Illus.). 192p. (J). (gr. 4-7). 2000. pap. 4.50 (*0-440-41587-X*, Yearling) BDD Bks Young Read.

***Pig & the Whale.** Bill Dahlin. (Illus.). 15p. (J). 1999. pap. 8.97 (*0-9678028-0-6*) B Dahlin.

Pig at Play: Level 1. Jon Buller & Susan Schade. (Planet Reader Picture Bks.). (Illus.). 32p. (J). (ps-1). 1998. pap. 2.95 (*0-8167-4375-4*) Troll Communs.

Pig at Work: Level 1. Jon Buller & Susan Schade. (Planet Reader Picture Bks.). (Illus.). 32p. (J). (ps-1). 1998. pap. 2.95 (*0-8167-4374-6*) Troll Communs.

Pig Barn. Marlon Davidson. (Illus.). 78p. 1997. pap. 9.95 (*0-926147-09-9*) Loonfeather.

Pig Boats & River Hogs: Further Voyages into Michigan's Past. 2nd ed. Larry B. Massie. (Illus.). 296p. 1990. pap. 12.50 (*0-9626408-0-8*) Priscilla Pr.

Pig Diseases. 6th ed. David Conrad Taylor. 300p. 1995. pap. 36.95 (*0-9506932-5-1*) Diamond Farm Bk.

Pig Earth. John Berger. LC 92-50074. 1992. pap. 12.00 (*0-679-73715-4*) Vin Bks.

***Pig Farmer's Daughter & Other Tales of American Justice: Episodes of Racism & Sexism in the Courts from 1865 to the Present.** Mary Frances Berry. 2000. pap. 13.00 (*0-375-70746-8*) Vin Bks.

Pig Gets Lost. H. Amery. (Farmyard Tales Ser.). (Illus.). 16p. (J). (ps up). 1992. pap. 4.95 (*0-7460-0590-3*) EDC.

Pig Gets Lost Sticker Book. Ed. by Heather Amery. (Farmyard Tales Sticker Bks.: Vol. 9). (Illus.). 18p. (J). (ps-3). 1999. text 6.95 (*0-7460-3514-4*, Usborne) EDC.

Pig Gets Stuck. H. Amery. (Farmyard Tales Ser.). (Illus.). 16p. (J). (ps). 1989. lib. bdg. 11.95 (*0-88110-374-8*, Usborne) EDC.

Pig Gets Stuck. H. Amery. (Farmyard Tales Ser.). (Illus.). 16p. (J). (ps-3). 1989. pap. 3.95 (*0-7460-0469-9*, Usborne) EDC.

***Pig Gets Stuck Book.** Ed. by Heather Amery. (Big Bks.). (Illus.). 16p. (J). (ps up). 1999. pap. text 14.95 (*0-7460-3488-1*, Usborne) EDC.

Pig Gets Stuck Sticker Book. Judy Tatchell. (Farmyard Tales Sticker Storybook Ser.: Vol. 4). (Illus.). 16p. (J). (ps-3). 1996. text 6.95 (*0-7460-2431-2*, Usborne) EDC.

***Pig-Heart Boy.** Blackman. (J). 2000. pap. 6.95 (*0-552-52841-2*, Pub. by Transworld Publishers Ltd) Trafalgar.

Pig in a Passage. large type ed. Anne Drysdale. 250p. 1998. 24.95 (*0-7531-5059-X*, Pub. by ISIS Lrg Prnt) Transaction Pubs.

***Pig in a Passage.** large type ed. Anne Drysdale. 1998. 25.95 (*0-7531-5829-9*) T T Beeler.

***Pig in a Passage.** large type unabridged ed. Anne Drysdale. 130p. 1999. pap. 19.95 (*0-7531-5067-0*, 150670, Pub. by ISIS Lrg Prnt) ISIS Pub.

***Pig in a Wig.** Alan MacDonald. LC 98-51318. (Illus.). 32p. (J). (ps-1). 1999. 15.95 (*1-56145-197-5*) Peachtree Pubs.

Pig in the Pond. Martin Waddell. LC 91-58751. (Illus.). (J). (ps-3). 1996. pap. 4.99 (*1-56402-604-3*) Candlewick Pr.

Pig in the Pond. Martin Waddell. LC 91-58751. (J). 1996. 11.19 (*0-606-09749-X*, Pub. by Turtleback) Demco.

Pig in the Pond, Big Book. Martin Waddell. LC 91-58751. (Illus.). (J). (ps up). 1996. 19.99 (*1-56402-671-X*) Candlewick Pr.

Pig in the Spigot. Richard Wilbur. LC 99-6296. (Illus.). 48p. (J). (ps up). 2000. 16.00 (*0-15-202019-5*, Harcourt Child Bks) Harcourt.

Pig Is Big. Douglas Florian. LC 99-53528. (Illus.). 24p. (J). (ps-3). 2000. 15.95 (*0-688-17125-7*, Grenwillow Bks); 15.89 (*0-688-17126-5*, Grenwillow Bks) HarpC Child Bks.

***Pig Is Moving In!** Claudia Fries. (Illus.). 32p. (J). (gr. k-2). 2000. 15.95 (*0-531-30307-1*); write for info. (*0-531-33307-8*) Orchard Bks Watts.

Pig Keeping on a Small Scale. Annette McFarlane. 1996. pap. 14.95 (*0-86417-790-9*, Pub. by Kangaroo Pr) Seven Hills Bk.

Pig Named Fred. Dolores Goldapp. LC 97-32470. (Illus.). (J). 1998. pap. write for info. (*1-56763-339-0*); lib. bdg. write for info. (*1-56763-338-2*) Ozark Pub.

Pig Notes & Dumb Music: Prose on Poetry. William Heyen. LC 97-72084. (American Readers Ser.: No. 2). 156p. 1998. pap. 11.95 (*1-880238-56-X*) BOA Edns.

***Pig Notes & Dumb Music: Prose on Poetry.** limited ed. William Heyen. (American Reader Ser.: Vol. 2). 189p. 1998. 35.00 (*1-880238-68-3*, Pub. by BOA Edns) Consort Bk Sales.

***Pig on a Skateboard.** Viona Tew. 2000. pap. 13.95 (*0-595-09483-X*, Writers Club Pr) iUniversecom.

Pig Out! Portia Aborio. LC 95-79285. (All Aboard Reading Picture Readers Ser.). (Illus.). 32p. (Orig.). (J). (ps-1). 1997. pap. 3.99 (*0-448-41294-2*, G & D) Peng Put Young Read.

Pig Out. Christina Hanley. 1983. pap. 5.95 (*0-8065-0843-4*, Citadel Pr) Carol Pub Group.

Pig Out: Selected Recipes from the Junior League of Waterloo-Cedar Falls. LC 85-51884. 272p. 1986. spiral bd. 17.95 (*0-9615904-0-8*) WCF Pubns.

Pig Out? 25 Reasons Why Christians May Eat Pork. James B. Jordan. 66p. 1992. pap. 7.00 (*1-883690-01-3*) Transfig Pr.

Pig Out on Kansas City Barbecue. Karen Adler & Carolyn Wells. (Illus.). 96p. (Orig.). Date not set. pap. 9.95 (*0-925175-21-8*) Pig Out Pubns.

Pig Out with Peg: Secrets from the Bundy Family Kitchen. Peg Bundy, pseud. 1990. pap. 8.95 (*0-380-76431-8*, Avon Bks) Morrow Avon.

Pig Pancakes. Laura Joffe Numeroff. (Illus.). 32p. (J). (ps-2). 12.95 (*0-06-028563-X*) HarpC Child Bks.

Pig Papers. 128p. (J). 1993. write for info. (*0-7814-0522-X*, Chariot Bks) Chariot Victor.

Pig Picnic. Patricia Hubbell. LC 98-33464. (Road to Reading Ser.). (Illus.). 32p. (J). 1999. pap. 3.99 (*0-307-26108-5*, Whitman Coin) St Martin.

***Pig Picnic.** Patricia Hubbell & Nadine B. Westcott. LC 98-33464. (Road to Reading Ser.). 32p. (J). 1999. lib. bdg. 10.99 (*0-307-46108-4*) Gldn Bks Pub Co.

Pig Pig Gets a Job. David McPhail. LC 89-25606. (Pig Pig Ser.). (Illus.). 24p. (J). (ps-3). 1990. 14.99 (*0-525-44619-2*, Dutton Child) Peng Put Young Read.

Pig Pig Grows Up. David McPhail. (Pig Pig Ser.). (J). (ps-3). 1992. pap. 5.99 (*0-14-054779-7*) NAL.

Pig Pig Grows Up. unabridged ed. David McPhail. (Pig Pig Ser.). (Illus.). (J). (ps-3). 1985. pap. 15.95 incl. audio (*0-941078-94-9*) Live Oak Media.

Pig Pig Grows Up, 4 bks., Set. unabridged ed. David McPhail. (Pig Pig Ser.). (Illus.). (J). (ps-3). 1985. pap., teacher ed. 31.95 incl. audio (*0-941078-95-7*) Live Oak Media.

Pig, Pigger, Piggest. Rick Walton. LC 96-29810. (Illus.). 32p. (J). (ps-3). 1997. 15.95 (*0-87905-806-4*) Gibbs Smith Pub.

Pig Production. M. R. Taverner. 1995. write for info. (*0-444-41836-9*) Elsevier.

Pig Production. Ed. by M. R. Taverner & A. C. Dunkin. LC 96-19107. (World Animal Science Ser.: Vol. C10). 372p. 1996. 244.00 (*0-444-88347-9*) Elsevier.

Pig Production: The Scientific & Practical Principles. Colin T. Whittemore. LC 79-42758. (Longman Handbooks in Agriculture Ser.). (Illus.). 155p. reprint ed. pap. 48.10 (*0-8357-2993-1*, 203925600011) Bks Demand.

Pig Soup. unabridged ed. Bruce Palma. LC 99-231478. xiv, 90p. 1998. pap. 10.00 (*0-9662452-0-2*) Pisix Pr.

Pig Stroller Songs. Laura Joffe Numeroff. (Illus.). (J). 10.95 (*0-694-01428-1*) HarpC.

Pig-Tail Days in Old Seattle. Sophie F. Bass. LC 72-77591. (Illus.). 200p. (J). (gr. 4-6). 1973. 12.50 (*0-8323-0206-6*) Binford Mort.

***Pig Tails 'n Breadfruit: A Culinary Memoir.** Austin Clarke. 256p. 2000. 22.95 (*1-56584-580-3*, Pub. by New Press NY) Norton.

Pig Tale. Robert Lund. 8p. 1994. pap. 5.00 (*0-941543-07-2*) Sun Dog Pr.

Pig Tale. Olivia Newton-John & Brian S. Hurst. LC 92-44116. (Illus.). 32p. (J). 1999. per. 5.99 (*0-689-82428-9*) Aladdin.

Pig Tale. Olivia Newton-John & Brian S. Hurst. LC 92-44116. (Illus.). 40p. (J). (ps-1). 1993. pap. 14.00 (*0-671-78778-0*) S&S Bks Yung.

***Pig Tales.** Kate Tym. 128p. (gr. 2). 1999. pap. 4.95 (*1-902618-50-5*, Pub. by Element Childrns) Penguin Putnam.

Pig Tales: A Novel of Lust & Transformation. Marie Darrieussecq. 1997. 18.00 (*1-56584-361-4*, Pub. by New Press NY) Norton.

Pig Tales: A Novel of Lust & Transformation. Henning Mankell. Tr. by Laurie Thompson from SWE. 1998. pap. 10.95 (*1-56584-442-4*, Pub. by New Press NY) Norton.

Pig Tales: The Adventures of Arnold the Chinese Potbelly Miniature Pig. Kujoko. (Illus.). 21p. (Orig.). (J). (ps-8). 1988. pap. 4.95 (*0-9623210-0-1*) Kiyoko & Co.

Pig That Is Not a Pig: El Cerdo Que No es Cerdo. Maria L. Retana. (SPA., Illus.). 32p. (Orig.). (J). (gr. k-2). 1997. pap. 6.95 (*0-9652920-8-8*) Hgh Desert Prods.

Pig, the Prince & the Unicorn. Karen A. Brush. 224p. 1987. pap. 2.95 (*0-380-75062-7*, Avon Bks) Morrow Avon.

***Pig War: Standoff at Griffin Bay.** Michael Vouri. LC 98-72748. (Illus.). 274p. 1999. pap. 15.95 (*0-9634562-5-3*) Griffin Bay Bk.

Pig War & Other Experiences of William A. Peck, Soldier, 1858-1862: The Journal of William A. Peck, Jr. C. Brewster Coulter & Bert Webber. LC 93-26331. (Illus.). 224p. 1993. pap. 12.95 (*0-936738-17-0*) Webb Research.

Pig War Islands: The San Juans of Northwest Washington. David B. Richardson. LC 70-149337. (Illus.). 416p. 1990. reprint ed. pap. 16.95 (*0-945742-04-5*) Orcas Pub.

***Pig Who Didn't Want to Get Dirty.** Taylor Brandon. LC 96-94848. (The World's Greatest Children's Bks.). (Illus.). 48p. (J). (gr. k-5). 1999. 14.99 (*1-889945-63-3*) Imperius.

Pig Who Ran a Red Light. Paul Brett Johnson. LC 98-36161. (Illus.). 32p. (J). (ps-2). 1999. 15.95 (*0-531-30136-2*); lib. bdg. 16.99 (*0-531-33136-9*) Orchard Bks Watts.

Pig Who Wished. Joyce Dunbar. LC 98-28832. (Toddlers Storybook Ser.). (Illus.). 32p. (J). 1999. 9.95 (*0-7894-3487-3*) DK Pub Inc.

***Pig Who Wished.** Joyce Dunbar. LC 98-28832. (Toddlers Storybook Ser.). (Illus.). 32p. (J). (ps). 2000. pap. text 5.95 (*0-7894-5748-2*, D K Ink) DK Pub Inc.

Pig William. Arlene Dubanevich. LC 85-5776. (Illus.). 32p. (J). (ps-2). 1985. lib. bdg. 14.95 (*0-02-733200-4*, Bradbury S&S) S&S Childrens.

Pig with a View. Pamela Platt. (Illus.). 80p. (J). (gr. 2-6). 1995. pap. 9.95 (*0-7022-2589-4*, Pub. by Univ Queensland Pr) Intl Spec Bk.

Piganeers Big Boars, Bk. 3. Michael Salmon. (J). 1998. 3.25 (*0-689-81213-2*) S&S Childrens.

Piganeers Captain, Bk. 2. Michael Salmon. 24p. (J). 1998. 3.25 (*0-689-81212-4*) S&S Childrens.

Piganeers Talent Night, Bk. 1. Michael Salmon. (J). 1998. pap. 3.25 (*0-689-81211-6*) S&S Childrens.

Pigboat 39: An American Sub Goes to War. Bobette Gugliotta. LC 84-15295. (Illus.). 264p. 1984. 32.00 (*0-8131-1524-8*) U Pr of Ky.

***Pigboat 39: An American Sub Goes to War.** Bobette Gugliotta. (Illus.). 240p. 2000. reprint ed. pap. 17.00 (*0-8131-0985-X*) U Pr of Ky.

Pigeon. Wendell M. Levi. 1986. reprint ed. 52.00 (*0-910876-01-0*) Levi Pub.

Pigeon: Poems. Roland Flint. LC 91-62198. 72p. 1991. 8.50 (*0-933598-30-0*) NC Wesleyan Pr.

Pigeon: Poems. deluxe limited ed. Roland Flint. LC 91-62198. 72p. 1991. 17.00 (*0-933598-31-9*) NC Wesleyan Pr.

***Pigeon Cove: Poems by Peter Tuttle.** Peter Tuttle. LC 99-93763. viii, 62p. 1999. pap. 12.95 (*0-9670981-0-6*) Tutboro Pr.

Pigeon Creek & Tidal Delta: A Field Trip Guide. Mark Boardman & Cindy Carney. (Illus.). 8p. (C). 1996. pap. text 2.00 (*0-935909-59-1*) Bahamian.

Pigeon d'Argile: The Clay Pigeon. Anne-Marie De Grazia. 104p. 1984. pap. 14.00 (*0-940268-99-X*) Metron Pubns.

Pigeon Factory. John Richards. (Illus.). (Orig.). 1987. pap. 10.95 (*0-932274-40-4*) Cadmus Eds.

Pigeon Fanciers' Handbook. J. A. Fancier. (Illus.). 350p. 1989. write for info. (*0-9622998-4-7*) WFancier Pubns.

P

*__Pigeon Feathers.__ Sherry H. Bowen. (Books for Young Learners). (Illus.). 16p. (J). (gr. k-2). 1999. pap. text 5.00 (*1-57274-279-8*, A2761) R Owen Pubs.

Pigeon Feathers. John Updike. 192p. 1986. mass mkt. 5.99 (*0-449-21132-0*, Crest) Fawcett.

Pigeon Feathers. John Updike. 1996. pap. 12.00 (*0-449-91225-6*) Fawcett.

Pigeon Feathers & Other Stories. John Updike. 1962. 19.95 (*0-394-44056-0*) Knopf.

*__Pigeon French: Almost Get by in French.__ 2000. pap. 4.95 (*0-9534360-2-0*, Pub. by Pigeon Pubns Ltd) IPG Chicago.

*__Pigeon German: Almost Get by in German.__ Ed. by Kenneth Griffiths. (ENG & GER.). 10p. 2000. pap. 4.95 (*0-9534360-8-X*, Pub. by Pigeon Pubns Ltd) IPG Chicago.

Pigeon Holes of Memory: The Life & Times of Dr. John Mackenzie (1803-1886) Ed. by Christina Byam Shaw. LC 87-63257. (Illus.). 436p. 1988. 36.00 (*0-930664-07-8*) SPOSS.

*__Pigeon Italian: Almost Get by in Italian.__ 2000. pap. 4.95 (*0-9534360-1-2*, Pub. by Pigeon Pubns Ltd) IPG Chicago.

Pigeon Pair. Elizabeth Ogilvie. reprint ed. lib. bdg. 19.95 (*0-88411-336-1*) Amereon Ltd.

Pigeon Pie. Campbell. 296p. 1998. 20.00 (*0-7862-1527-5*) Thorndike Pr.

Pigeon Pie. Robert Campbell. LC 97-48921. Vol. 27. 240p. 1998. 21.50 (*0-89296-665-3*, Pub. by Mysterious Pr) Little.

Pigeon Pie. large type ed. R. Wright Campbell. LC 98-22096. 1999. 27.95 (*0-7862-1528-3*) Thorndike Pr.

Pigeon Pie. 2nd ed. Nancy Mitford. 192p. 1999. pap. 11.95 (*0-7867-0633-3*) Carroll & Graf.

*__Pigeon Portuguese: Almost Get by in Portuguese.__ Ed. by Kenneth Griffiths. (ENG & POR.). 10p. 2000. pap. 4.95 (*0-9534360-6-3*, Pub. by Pigeon Pubns Ltd) IPG Chicago.

Pigeon Post. Arthur Ransome. (Swallows & Amazons Ser.). (Illus.). 382p. (YA). 1992. pap. 11.95 (*0-87923-864-X*) Godine.

Pigeon Racing: Science & Practice. Ernest Pawson. (Illus.). 98p. 1999. pap. 13.00 (*0-627-02217-0*, Pub. by J L Van Schaik) BHB Intl.

Pigeon Roost & Shaddox Hollow Hiking Trails. Tim Ernst. (Illus.). 28p. 1995. pap. 4.95 (*1-882906-10-1*) CLOUDLAND.

*__Pigeon Spanish: Almost Get By in Spanish.__ 2000. pap. 4.95 (*0-9534360-0-4*, Pub. by Pigeon Pubns Ltd) IPG Chicago.

Pigeon to Packhorse: The Illustrated Story of Animals in Army Communications. Ed. by Alan Harfield. 114p. (C). 1989. pap. 55.00 (*0-948251-42-5*, Pub. by Picton) St Mut.

Pigeon Toes & Colicos. N. M. Bodecker. (J). Date not set. 12.95 (*0-689-50373-3*) McElderry Bks.

*__Pigeonholed in the Land of Penguins: A Tale of Seeing Beyond Stereotypes.__ Barbara J. Hateley & Warren H. Schmidt. LC 00-22545. (Illus.). 160p. 2000. pap. 15.00 (*0-8144-7075-0*) AMACOM.

Pigeons. Carlienne Frisch. (Responsible Pet Care Ser.: Set II). (Illus.). 32p. (J). (gr. 2-5). 1989. lib. bdg. 21.27 (*0-86625-193-6*) Rourke Pubns.

Pigeons. Carl Naether. (Illus.). 96p. 1989. 9.95 (*0-87666-837-6*, KW-148) TFH Pubns.

Pigeons. Dorothy H. Patent. LC 96-42072. (Illus.). 80p. (J). (gr. 3-6). 1997. 16.00 (*0-395-69848-0*, Clarion Bks) HM.

Pigeons. Matthew M. Vriends. (Barron's Pet Owner's Manuals Ser.). 80p. 1988. pap. 6.95 (*0-8120-4044-9*) Barron.

*__Pigeons & Doves.__ David Gibbs. (Illus.). 480p. 2000. 55.00 (*0-300-07886-2*) Yale U Pr.

Pigeons & Doves. Ray Nofsinger & Jim Hargrove. LC 92-12948. (New True Books Ser.). (Illus.). 48p. (J). (ps-3). 1992. lib. bdg. 21.00 (*0-516-02196-6*) Childrens.

Pigeons & Gudgeons. Walter J. Simmons. (Boatbuilding Ser.). (Illus.). 232p. 1993. pap. 29.95 (*0-924947-08-X*) Duck Trap Pr.

Pigeons & Moles: Selected Writings. Gunter Eich. Tr. & Intro. by Michael Hamburger. (GERM Ser.: Vol. 62). (Illus.). xviii, 190p. 1991. 45.00 (*0-938100-96-3*) Camden Hse.

Pigeons for Pleasure & Profit. Charles Foy. (Illus.). 1972. pap. 6.00 (*0-911466-19-3*) Swanson.

Pigeons for Pleasure & Profit: A Complete Guide to Pigeon Raising. rev. ed. Charles Foy & Clair Hetland. Ed. by Karen Hetland. (Illus.). 112p. 1997. pap. 10.00 (*0-911466-21-5*) Swanson.

Pigeons in the Chandeliers. Judy Ray. (Illus.). 75p. (Orig.). 1993. pap. 10.00 (*0-944048-04-8*) Timberline Missouri.

*__Pigeons of the World: The Magna Illustrated Guide.__ Andrew McNeillie. (Illus.). 160p. 1999. reprint ed. text 20.00 (*0-7881-6574-7*) DIANE Pub.

Pigeons on the Grass. Wolfgang Koeppen. Tr. by David Ward. LC 88-11043. (Modern German Voices Ser.). 210p. 1988. 27.95 (*0-8419-1163-0*) Holmes & Meier.

Pigeons on the Grass. Wolfgang Koeppen. Tr. by David Ward from GER. LC 88-11043. (Portico Paperbacks Ser.). 1991. pap. 14.95 (*0-8419-1291-2*) Holmes & Meier.

Pigeons, Racing Homer Facts & Secrets. Leslie C. Swanson. 1958. pap. 3.50 (*0-911466-17-7*) Swanson.

Pigeons, Racing Homer Topics. Leslie C. Swanson. 1955. pap. 3.50 (*0-911466-18-5*) Swanson.

Pigeons That Went to War. Gordon Hayes. LC 81-90046. (Illus.). 160p. 1981. 9.95 (*0-9605880-1-9*) G H Hayes.

Piggest Show on Earth. Arlene Dubanevich. LC 88-11742. (Illus.). 32p. (J). (ps-1). 1998. pap. 6.95 (*0-531-07105-7*) Orchard Bks Watts.

Piggest Show on Earth. Arlene Dubanevich. LC 88-11742. (Illus.). 32p. (J). (ps-1). 1989. 15.95 (*0-531-30122-2*) Orchard Bks Watts.

Piggety Pig Books. Harriet Ziefert. (Illus.). 96p. (J). (ps). 1988. 2.95 (*0-316-98758-1*) Little.

Piggie Pie! Margie Palatini. LC 94-19726. (Illus.). 32p. (J). (ps-3). 1995. 15.00 (*0-395-71691-8*) HM.

Piggie Pie! Margie Palatini. (Illus.). 32p. (J). (ps-3). 1997. pap. 5.95 (*0-395-86618-9*, Clarion Bks) HM.

Piggie Pie! Margie Palatini. (J). 1997. 11.15 (*0-606-12792-5*, Pub. by Turtleback) Demco.

*__Piggie Pie.__ Margie Palatini. (Illus.). (J). (ps-3). 1998. 9.95 incl. audio (*0-395-90063-8*, Clarion Bks) HM.

Piggies... Ed. by Helen Exley. (Mini Square Ser.). (Illus.). 64p. 1998. 6.00 (*1-86187-016-7*) Exley Pubns Ltd.

Piggies. Audrey Wood & Don Wood. LC 89-24598. (Illus.). 32p. (J). (ps-1). 1991. 16.00 (*0-15-256341-5*, Harcourt Child Bks) Harcourt.

Piggies. Audrey Wood & Don Wood. (Illus.). 32p. (J). (ps-1). 1994. pap. 14.00 incl. audio (*0-15-200191-3*) Harcourt.

Piggies. Audrey Wood & Don Wood. LC 89-24598. (Illus.). 32p. (J). (ps-1). 1995. pap. 7.00 (*0-15-200217-0*, Voyager Bks) Harcourt.

Piggies. Audrey Wood & Don Wood. (Illus.). (J). (ps-1). 1997. 15.00 (*0-15-201685-6*, Harcourt Child Bks) Harcourt.

*__Piggies.__ Audrey Wood & Don Wood. (Illus.). 32p. (J). (ps-k). 2000. bds. 5.95 (*0-15-202638-X*, Harcourt Child Bks) Harcourt.

Piggies. Don Wood. (J). 1991. 12.45 (*0-606-08014-7*) Turtleback.

Piggies. limited ed. Audrey Wood & Don Wood. (Illus.). (J). (ps-1). 1991. 100.00 (*0-15-256344-X*, Harcourt Child Bks) Harcourt.

Piggies Finger Puppets. Harcourt Staff. 1998. 17.95 (*0-15-201838-7*, Red Wagon Bks) Harcourt.

Piggies Piggies Piggies. Walter Retan. (J). (gr. 3 up). 1993. pap. 15.00 (*0-671-75244-8*) S&S Bks Yung.

Piggies Scholastic Book Fair. Wood. (J). 1994. pap. 5.95 (*0-15-200291-X*, Harcourt Child Bks) Harcourt.

Piggin' Out: A Southern States Guide to Bar-B-Que Eateries. Keith Johnson. 151p. 1996. pap. 11.95 (*1-885954-01-8*) Gateway Publctns.

Pigging Out in Columbus. rev. ed. Carl Japikse. 160p. 1993. pap. 8.95 (*0-89804-812-5*, Enthea Pr) Ariel GA.

Piggins. Jane Yolen. LC 86-22915. (Illus.). 32p. (J). (ps-3). 1987. 14.95 (*0-15-261685-3*) Harcourt.

Piggins. Jane Yolen. LC 86-22915. (Illus.). 32p. (J). (ps-3). 1992. pap. 4.95 (*0-15-261686-1*) Harcourt.

Piggins & the Royal Wedding. Jane Yolen. LC 88-5399. (Illus.). 32p. (J). (ps-3). 1994. pap. 4.95 (*0-15-200078-X*, Harcourt Child Bks) Harcourt.

Piggle. Crosby N. Bonsall. (I Can Read Bks.). (Illus.). (J). (gr. 1-3). 1973. 14.89 (*0-06-020579-2*, 133490) HarpC Child Bks.

Piggle. Crosby N. Bonsall. LC 73-5478. (I Can Read Bks.). (Illus.). 64p. (J). (ps-3). 1973. lib. bdg. 15.89 (*0-06-020580-6*) HarpC Child Bks.

Piggle. Donald Woods Winnicott. LC 76-46815. 201p. 1977. 35.00 (*0-8236-4137-6*); pap. 27.95 (*0-8236-8189-0*, BN 24137) Intl Univs Pr.

Piggo & the Nosebag. Pam Ayres. (Illus.). 32p. (J). (gr. k-3). 1991. 7.95 (*0-563-20922-4*, BBC-Parkwest) Parkwest Pubns.

*__Piggy Bank: Book & Bank, 1 vol.__ Kate Simpson. (ps-3). 1999. 9.99 (*0-525-46157-4*, Dutton Child) Peng Put Young Read.

*__Piggy Christmas.__ Howard Fine. 32p. (J). 2000. lib. bdg. 15.49 (*0-7868-2505-7*, Pub. by Hyperion) Little.

*__Piggy Christmas.__ Howard Fine. 32p. (J). 2000. 14.99 (*0-7868-0587-0*, Pub. by Hyprn Child) Time Warner.

Piggy Divers Wreck Our Reefs. Joe Strykowski. 24p. 1992. pap. 3.00 (*1-882533-07-0*) Star Thrower.

Piggy Goes to Bed. Carol Thompson. LC 97-20603. 24p. (Orig.). (J). 1998. pap. 3.99 (*0-7636-0428-3*) Candlewick Pr.

Piggy in the Parlor: And Other Tales, Vol. 1. unabridged ed. Sara S. Miller. (Illus.). 53p. (J). (gr. 1-5). 1997. 19.50 (*1-57529-057-X*) Kabel Pubs.

Piggy in the Puddle. Charlotte Pomerantz. LC 73-6047. (Illus.). 32p. (J). (ps-1). 1974. lib. bdg. 15.00 (*0-02-774900-2*, Mac Bks Young Read) S&S Childrens.

Piggy in the Puddle. Charlotte Pomerantz. (J). 1989. 10.15 (*0-606-04298-9*, Pub. by Turtleback) Demco.

Piggy in the Puddle. Charlotte Pomerantz. LC 88-8368. (Illus.). 32p. (J). (ps-1). 1989. reprint ed. mass mkt. 5.99 (*0-689-71293-6*) Aladdin.

Piggy Pals Puppet & Book Set. Wood. 1998. pap. 24.95 (*0-15-202065-9*) Harcourt.

Piggy Party. Beverly Lewis. (Cul-de-Sac Kids Ser.). 80p. (J). (gr. 2-5). 1999. pap. 3.99 (*0-7642-2124-8*) Bethany Hse.

*__Piggy Pie Po.__ Audrey Wood. 2001. write for info. (*0-15-202494-8*) Harcourt.

Piggy Poems. Illus. by Diane Lilley. LC 97-35007. (J). 1998. write for info. (*0-7894-2485-1*) DK Pub Inc.

Piggy Washes Up. Carol Thompson. LC 96-26252. (Illus.). 24p. (Orig.). (J). (ps up). 1997. pap. 3.99 (*0-7636-0107-1*) Candlewick Pr.

Piggyback & Containers: A History of Rail Intermodal on America's Steel Highway. David J. DeBoer. LC 92-39181. 1992. 47.95 (*0-87095-108-4*) Gldn West Bks.

Piggyback Songs: New Song Sung to the Tunes of Childhood Favorites. Illus. by Marion H. Ekberg. LC 83-90111. (Piggyback Songs Ser.). 64p. (Orig.). (J). (ps-1). 1983. pap. 7.95 (*0-911019-01-4*, WPH 0201) Totline Pubns.

Piggyback Songs for Infants & Toddlers. Illus. by Marion H. Ekberg. LC 85-50433. (Piggyback Songs Ser.). 80p. (Orig.). (J). (ps). 1985. 8.95 (*0-911019-07-3*, WPH 0203) Totline Pubns.

Piggyback Songs for School. Ed. by Gayle Bittinger. LC 85-50433. (Piggyback Songs Ser.). (Illus.). 96p. (Orig.). (J). (ps-1). 1991. pap. 8.95 (*0-911019-44-8*, WPH 0208) Totline Pubns.

Piggyback Songs in Praise of God. Illus. by Marion H. Ekberg. (Piggyback Songs Ser.). 80p. (Orig.). (J). (ps-1). 1986. pap. 8.95 (*0-911019-10-3*, WPH 0204) Totline Pubns.

Piggyback Songs in Praise of Jesus: New Songs Sung to the Tunes of Childhood Favorites. Illus. by Marion H. Ekberg. (Piggyback Songs Ser.). 96p. (Orig.). (J). (ps-1). 1986. pap. 8.95 (*0-911019-11-1*, WPH 0205) Totline Pubns.

Piggyback Songs to Sign. Jean Warren & Susan Shroyer. LC 85-50433. (Piggyback Songs Ser.). (Illus.). 96p. (J). (ps-1). 1992. pap. 8.95 (*0-911019-53-7*, WPH 0209) Totline Pubns.

Piggybook see Libro de los Cerdos

Piggybook. Anthony Browne. (J). 1986. 13.19 (*0-606-04771-9*, Pub. by Turtleback) Demco.

Piggy's Birthday Dream. Anke De Vries. LC 97-10027. (Illus.). 32p. (J). 14.95 (*1-886910-21-9*, Front Street) Front Str.

Piggy's Luck & More Tales of Evildoing. Robert Perrin. LC 98-74578. 244p. 1998. pap. 14.95 (*0-9668151-0-6*) Claybanks Pr.

Piglet. Dorling Kindersley Staff. LC 97-136564. (Shaped Board Bks.). (Illus.). 10p. (J). 1997. bds. 3.95 (*0-7894-1542-9*) DK Pub Inc.

*__Piglet.__ A. A. Milne, pseud. (Pooh Giant Shaped Board Bks.). (Illus.). 10p. (YA). 2000. bds. 7.99 (*0-525-46334-8*, Dutton Child) Peng Put Young Read.

*__Piglet Clip & Read Book.__ abr. ed. A. A. Milne, pseud. (Illus.). 24p. (ps-3). 1999. pap. 2.99 (*0-525-46205-8*, Dutton Child) Peng Put Young Read.

Piglet Has a Bath. A. A. Milne, pseud. LC 99-172612. (Winnie-the-Pooh Collection). (J). 1998. pap. 5.99 (*0-525-46092-6*, Dutton Child) Peng Put Young Read.

Piglet in a Playpen. Lucy Daniels. (Animal Ark Ser.: No. 9). (J). (gr. 3-5). 1996. 9.05 (*0-606-11748-2*, Pub. by Turtleback) Demco.

*__Piglet in a Playpen, Vol. 9.__ Ben M. Baglio. (Animal Ark Ser.: No. 9). (J). (gr. 3-5). 1999. pap. 3.99 (*0-590-18756-2*) Scholastic Inc.

Piglet Is Entirely Surrounded by Water. A. A. Milne, pseud. (Illus.). 32p. (J). 1993. 4.99 (*0-525-45143-9*, Dutton Child) Peng Put Young Read.

Piglet Is Surrounded by Water Puzzle. A. A. Milne, pseud. (Illus.). 14p. 1999. 7.99 (*0-525-46273-2*, Dutt) Dutton Plume.

Piglet Tales. Mouse Works Staff. LC 99-159402. (Illus.). 5p. (J). 1997. 6.99 (*1-57082-691-9*, Pub. by Mouse Works) Time Warner.

Piglets. Kelly Doudna. LC 98-21702. (Baby Animals Ser.). (Illus.). 24p. (J). 2000. lib. bdg. 18.50 (*1-57765-185-5*, SndCastle) ABDO Pub Co.

Piglet's Bath. Kate Spohn. (J). (ps-4). 1998. 4.99 (*0-679-88677-X*, Pub. by Random Bks Yng Read) Random.

Piglet's up & down Day. Mouseworks Staff. LC 98-106124. (Illus.). 5p. (J). (ps). 1997. 7.98 (*1-57082-613-7*, Pub. by Mouse Works) Time Warner.

Pigling Bland. (Classic Tales Ser.). (Illus.). 24p. (J). 1993. 4.98 (*1-56173-592-2*) Pubns Intl Ltd.

Pigling Bland. Illus. by Sam Thiewes & Anita Nelson. (Classic Tales Ser.). 24p. (J). (gr. 2-4). 1992. lib. bdg. 11.95 (*1-56674-021-5*, HTS Bks) Forest Hse.

Pigman. (Assessment Packs Ser.). 15p. 1998. pap. text 15.95 (*1-58303-057-3*) Pthways Pubng.

*__Pigman.__ Gloria Levine. 40p. 1999. 9.95 (*1-56137-389-3*) Novel Units.

*__Pigman.__ Deborah Miller & Mary L. Dennis. 32p. (YA). (gr. 7-8). 1999. 11.95 (*1-56137-390-7*) Novel Units.

Pigman. Paul Zindel. 176p. (YA). 1978. mass mkt. 5.50 (*0-553-26321-8*) Bantam.

Pigman. Paul Zindel. LC 68-10784. 192p. (YA). (gr. 7 up). 1968. lib. bdg. 15.89 (*0-06-026828-X*) HarpC Child Bks.

Pigman. Paul Zindel. (J). 1978. 10.09 (*0-606-04308-X*, Pub. by Turtleback) Demco.

Pigman. adapted ed. Paul Zindel. 1975. pap. 5.25 (*0-8222-0894-6*) Dramatists Play.

Pigman: A Student Response Journal. rev. ed. James Scott. 16p. (YA). (gr. 7-12). 1998. ring bd. 19.95 (*1-58049-751-9*, RJ01R) Prestwick Hse.

Pigman: A Study Guide. Joyce Friedland & Rikki Kessler. (Novel-Ties Ser.). (J). (gr. 4-6). 1983. pap. text, teacher ed., student ed. 15.95 (*0-88122-019-1*) Lrn Links.

Pigman: A Unit Plan. Mary B. Collins. 154p. 1994. teacher ed., ring bd. 26.95 (*1-58337-015-3*) Teachers Pet Pubns.

Pigman: Reproducible Teaching Unit. rev. ed. James Scott. 29p. (YA). (gr. 7-12). 1995. teacher ed., ring bd. 29.50 (*1-58049-029-8*, TU61/U) Prestwick Hse.

Pigman & Me. Paul Zindel. 176p. (YA). 1993. mass mkt. 4.99 (*0-553-56456-0*) Bantam.

Pigman & Me. Paul Zindel. (Bantam Starfire Bks.). (J). 1993. 9.60 (*0-606-05543-6*, Pub. by Turtleback) Demco.

Pigmania. Emil Van Beest. (Illus.). 96p. pap. 7.95 (*0-85236-167-X*, Pub. by Farming Pr) Diamond Farm Bk.

Pigman's Handbook. 2nd ed. Gerry Brent. (Illus.). 256p. 1987. pap. 29.95 (*0-85236-170-X*, Pub. by Farming Pr) Diamond Farm Bk.

Pigman's Legacy. Paul Zindel. 1980. 10.09 (*0-606-02432-8*, Pub. by Turtleback) Demco.

Pigman's Legacy. Paul Zindel. 128p. (YA). (gr. 12 up). 1984. mass mkt. 5.50 (*0-553-26599-7*) Bantam.

Pigman/The Pigman's Legacy: Curriculum Unit. Center for Learning Network Staff & Paul Zindel. (Novel Ser.). 87p. (YA). (gr. 6-12). 1993. spiral bd. 18.95 (*1-56077-246-8*) Ctr Learning.

Pigment-Coated Papers: A Critical Assessment of the Processes, Technical Developments, & Economics. James P. Casey. LC 85-6836. (Series of Special Reports: No. 13). (Illus.). 115p. reprint ed. pap. 35.70 (*0-7837-0860-2*, 204116800019) Bks Demand.

*__Pigment Compendium: Optical Microscopy of Historical Pigments.__ Chris Collins et al. 288p. 2000. 250.00 (*0-7506-4553-9*) Buttrwrth-Heinemann.

Pigment Handbook, 3 vols. 3rd ed. Ed. by Peter A. Lewis. 2000p. 1988. 995.00 (*0-471-60021-0*) Wiley.

Pigment Handbook, 3 vols., Vol. 1. 2nd ed. Ed. by Peter A. Lewis. LC 87-13358. 976p. 1988. 435.00 (*0-471-82833-5*) Wiley.

Pigment Handbook: Applications & Markets, 3 vols., Vol. 2, Applications and Markets, 1st ed. Ed. by Peter A. Lewis. 464p. 1973. 365.00 (*0-471-67124-X*) Wiley.

Pigment Handbook: Characterization & Physical Relationships, 3 vols., Vol. 3, Characterization and Physical Relationship. Ed. by Peter A. Lewis. 560p. 1973. 365.00 (*0-471-67126-6*) Wiley.

Pigment of the Imagination: A History of Phytochrome Research. Linda C. Sage. (Illus.). 562p. 1992. text 125.00 (*0-12-614445-1*) Acad Pr.

Pigment the Rainbow Pig. Nicole K. Clark. (Illus.). (J). (ps-2). Date not set. write for info. (*1-892176-18-1*) PremaNations.

Pigmentary System: Physiology & Pathophysiology. Ed. by James J. Nordlund et al. LC 97-28806. (Illus.). 1106p. 1998. text 225.00 (*0-19-509861-7*) OUP.

Pigmentation: Proceedings of the International Pigment Cell Conference, 7th, Seattle, 1969. International Pigment Cell Conference Staff. Ed. by Vernon Riley. LC 77-150501. 706p. reprint ed. pap. 200.00 (*0-608-12428-1*, 205569300030) Bks Demand.

Pigmentation & Pigmentary Disorders. Norman Levine. 576p. 1993. lib. bdg. 199.00 (*0-8493-7353-0*, RL790) CRC Pr.

Pigments, Pt. 1. Ed. by Raymond R. Myers & J. S. Long. LC 67-21701. (Treatise on Coatings Ser.: No. 3). (Illus.). 590p. reprint ed. pap. 182.90 (*0-7837-0885-8*, 204119100001) Bks Demand.

Pigments & Dyes in Mexico: A Strategic Entry Report, 1997. Compiled by Icon Group International Staff. (Illus.). 144p. 1999. ring bd. 1440.00 incl. audio compact disk (*0-7418-1037-9*) Icon Grp.

Pigments, & Pigmented Coatings for Architectural & Industrial Applications see Organic Coating Technology

Pigments for Inkmakers. FMJ Intl. Publ. Ltd. Staff. (C). 1989. 295.00 (*0-7855-4924-2*, Pub. by Fuel Metallurgical Jrnl) St Mut.

Pigments for Inkmakers. Sanders. (C). 1989. 300.00 (*0-86108-151-X*, Pub. by Fuel Metallurgical Jrnl) St Mut.

Pigments for Paper. Robert W. Hagemeyer. LC 96-54592. 1997. 125.00 (*0-89852-064-9*, 0102B062) TAPPI.

Pigments for Paper: A Project of the Coating Pigments & the Papermaking Additives Committee. Technical Association of the Pulp & Paper Industry. Ed. by Robert W. Hagemeyer. LC 84-50800. 310p. reprint ed. pap. 96.10 (*0-608-14576-9*, 202492100041) Bks Demand.

Pigments in Fruits. Jeana Gross. (Food Science & Technology Ser.). 303p. 1987. text 157.00 (*0-12-304200-3*) Acad Pr.

Pigments of Your Imagination, 2. Jackie Shaw. (Illus.). (Orig.). 1978. pap. 5.95 (*0-941284-07-7*) J Shaw Studio.

*__Pignapped! A Cobtown Story.__ Julia Van Nutt. (Illus.). 32p. (J). (ps-3). 2000. 15.95 (*0-385-32559-2*) BDD Bks Young Read.

*__Pignatelli.__ Achille Bonito Oliva. 2000. pap. 29.95 (*88-8158-252-X*) Charta.

Pignic Vol. 1: An Alphabet Book in Rhyme. Anne Miranda. LC 95-78075. (Illus.). 32p. (J). (gr. k-3). 1996. 14.95 (*1-56397-558-0*) Boyds Mills Pr.

Pignight & Blow Job. Snoo Wilson. 1989. 12.95 (*0-7145-3503-6*) Riverrun NY.

Pigors Incident Process of Case Study. Paul Pigors & Faith Pigors. LC 79-23530. (Instructional Design Library). 128p. 1980. 27.95 (*0-87778-149-4*) Educ Tech Pubns.

Pigouts. Date not set. pap. 4.95 (*0-89868-400-5*) ARO Pub.

Pigouts. Janie Spaht-Gill. (Illus.). (J). (gr. k-2). Date not set. 5.95 (*0-89868-317-3*); lib. bdg. 10.95 (*0-89868-316-5*) ARO Pub.

Pigrates Clean Up. Steven Kroll. LC 92-21823. (Illus.). 32p. (J). (ps). 1995. 14.95 (*0-8050-2368-2*, Bks Young Read) H Holt & Co.

Pigs see Animals Are Not Like Us Series

Pigs see Cerdos

Pigs see Cochinos

Pigs see Farm Animals Series

Pigs. Gail Gibbons. LC 98-28807. (J). (ps-3). 1998. 16.95 (*0-8234-1441-8*) Holiday.

*__Pigs.__ Gail Gibbons. (Illus.). (J). 2000. pap. 6.95 (*0-8234-1554-6*) Holiday.

Pigs. Ann L. Hansen. LC 96-299. (J). 1998. lib. bdg. 13.95 (*1-56239-605-6*) ABDO Pub Co.

Pigs. David Holness. 150p. 1991. 9.95 (*0-333-52308-3*) Macmillan.

*__Pigs.__ Cynthia Fitterer Klingel & Robert B. Noyed. LC 99-57537. (Illus.). (J). 2000. write for info. (*1-56766-822-4*) Childs World.

Pigs. George MacLeod. 129p. 1994. pap. 19.95 (*0-85207-278-3*, Pub. by C W Daniel) Natl Bk Netwk.

*__Pigs.__ Sara S. Miller. LC 99-30129. (True Bks.). (J). 2000. 22.00 (*0-516-21579-5*) Childrens.

Pigs. Robert Munsch. (Illus.). 32p. (J). (ps-2). 1989. pap. 5.95 (*1-55037-038-3*, Pub. by Annick); lib. bdg. 15.95 (*1-55037-039-1*, Pub. by Annick) Firefly Bks Ltd.

Pigs. Robert Munsch. (Annikins Ser.: Vol. 14). (Illus.). (J). (ps-2). 1995. pap. 0.99 (*1-55037-388-9*, Pub. by Annick) Firefly Bks Ltd.

P

Pigs. Robert Munsch. (Munsch for Kids Ser.). (J). 1989. 11.15 (*0-606-04299-7*, Pub. by Turtleback) Demco.

Pigs. Peter Murray. LC 97-8363. (Nature Books Ser.). (Illus.). 32p. (J). (gr. 2-6). 1997. lib. bdg. 22.79 (*1-56766-378-8*) Childs World.

Pigs. Lynn M. Stone. (Farm Animal Discovery Library). (Illus.). 24p. (J). (gr. k-4). 1990. lib. bdg. 10.95 (*0-86593-037-6*) Rourke Corp.

Pigs. Lynn M. Stone. (Farm Animals Discovery Library). (Illus.). 24p. (J). (gr. k-5). 1990. lib. bdg. 8.95 (*0-685-36312-0*) Rourke Corp.

Pigs, Vol. 3629. Rozanne L. Williams. (Emergent Reader Bks.). 8p. 1994. pap. 1.75 (*0-916119-57-2*) Creat Teach Pr.

Pigs, Vol. 3686. Rozanne L. Williams. (Emergent Reader Big Bks.). (Illus.). 8p. (J). (gr. k-2). 1995. pap. 8.98 (*1-57471-057-5*) Creat Teach Pr.

Pigs: A Guide to Management. Neville Beynon. (Illus.). 176p. 1994. pap. 29.95 (*1-85223-754-6*, Pub. by Crolwood) Trafalgar.

***Pigs: A Guide to Wonderful Wallowing.** James Croft. LC 00-26991. (Illus.). 112p. 2000. 9.95 (*1-57145-657-0*, Laurel Glen Pub) Advantage Pubs.

Pigs: A Handbook to the Breeds of the World. Valerie Porter. (Comstock Bk.). (Illus.). 272p. 1993. text 39.95 (*0-8014-2920-X*) Cornell U Pr.

Pigs: Homoeopathic Approach to the Treatment & Prevention. George MacLeod. 1994. pap. 29.95 (*0-8464-4336-8*) Beekman Pubs.

Pigs Ahoy! David McPhail. LC 95-17753. (Illus.). 32p. (J). (ps-2). 1995. 14.99 (*0-525-45334-2*, Dutton Child) Peng Put Young Read.

Pigs Ahoy. David McPhail. 32p. (J). (gr. 3-7). 1998. pap. 5.99 (*0-14-055819-5*) Viking Penguin.

Pigs Ahoy! David M. McPhail. 1998. 11.19 (*0-606-13705-X*, Pub. by Turtleback) Demco.

Pigs & Fleas. Alan M. Hofmeister et al. (Reading for All Learners Ser.). (Illus.). pap. write for info. (*1-56861-190-0*) Swift Lrn Res.

Pigs & Other Animals. Roger Martin. LC 79-92628. 300p. (C). 1980. 10.95 (*0-936634-00-6*) Myco Pub Hse.

***Pigs & Pork.** Gabriele Roveda & Daniel Garavini. (Illus.). 183p. 1999. 12.95 (*3-8290-1463-5*, 520874) Konemann.

Pigs & Robbers. Bonnie Worth. (Babe Ser.). (Illus.). 62p. (J). (gr. k-5). 1999. lib. bdg. 11.99 (*0-679-99467-X*) Random.

Pigs & Wild Boar. Ben Sonder. 1998. 10.98 (*1-57717-081-4*) Todtri Prods.

Pigs Aplenty, Pigs Galore! see Cerdos a Montones, Cerdos a Granel!

Pigs Aplenty, Pigs Galore! David M. McPhail. (Illus.). 32p. (J). 1996. pap. 5.99 (*0-14-055313-4*) NAL.

Pigs Aplenty, Pigs Galore! David M. McPhail. LC 92-27986. (Illus.). (J). (ps-2). 1993. 15.99 (*0-525-45079-3*, Dutton Child) Peng Put Young Read.

Pigs Aplenty, Pigs Galore! David M. McPhail. (J). 1996. 11.19 (*0-606-10904-8*, Pub. by Turtleback) Demco.

Pigs Are Flying! Emily Rodda. Orig. Title: Pigs Might Fly. (Illus.). 144p. (J). (gr. 2 up). 1989. reprint ed. pap. 2.95 (*0-380-70555-9*, Avon Bks) Morrow Avon.

Pigs Don't Fly. Mary Brown. 336p. 1994. mass mkt. 6.99 (*0-671-87601-5*) Baen Bks.

Pig's Ear: Nonsense from the Pigsty. Simon Drew. (Illus.). 48p. 1994. 12.95 (*1-85149-208-9*) Antique Collect.

***Pig's Eggs.** Elizabeth Partridge. (Family Storytime Ser.). (Illus.). 32p. (J). 2000. 9.95 (*0-307-10232-7*) Gldn Bks Pub Co.

Pig's Eye Sewage Treatment Plant Rock. Al Blair. 6p. 1988. pap. 3.95 (*0-930366-49-2*) Northcountry Pub.

***Pigs for the Ancestors: Ritual in the Ecology of a New Guinea People.** Roy A. Rappaport. 501p. (C). 2000. pap. 22.95 (*1-57766-101-X*) Waveland Pr.

Pigs from A to Z, 001. Arthur Geisert. LC 86-18542. (Illus.). 64p. (J). (gr. 2 up). 1986. 17.95 (*0-395-38509-1*) HM.

Pigs from A to Z. Arthur Geisert. LC 86-18542. (Illus.). 64p. (J). (ps-3). 1996. pap. 7.95 (*0-395-77874-3*, Sandpiper) HM.

Pigs from A to Z. Arthur Geisert. LC 86-18542. (J). 1986. 13.15 (*0-606-09750-3*, Pub. by Turtleback) Demco.

Pigs from 1 to 10. Arthur Geisert. LC 92-5097. (Illus.). 32p. (J). (gr. k-3). 1992. 16.00 (*0-395-58519-8*) HM.

Pigs Go to Market: Fun with Math & Shopping. Amy Axelrod. LC 96-25566. (Illus.). 40p. (J). (ps-4). 1999. per. 5.99 (*0-689-82553-6*, 076714005990) Aladdin.

Pigs Go to Market: Fun with Math & Shopping. Amy Axelrod. LC 96-25566. (Illus.). 40p. (J). (ps-4). 1997. per. 13.00 (*0-689-81069-5*) S&S Childrens.

***Pigs Have Piglets.** Lynn M. Stone. (Animals & Their Young Ser.). (Illus.). 24p. (J). (gr. 1-3). 2000. write for info. (*0-7565-0003-6*) Compass Point.

***Pigs Have Wings.** P. G. Wodehouse. LC 00-26871. 224p. 2000. pap. 15.95 (*1-58567-059-6*, Pub. by Overlook Pr) Penguin Putnam.

Pig's Hell. Illus. by Natalie Y. 50p. (C). 1999. pap. 4.95 (*1-893084-07-8*) Benway Inst.

***Pigs in Heaven.** Barbara Kingsolver. 343p. 1999. text 22.00 (*0-7881-6057-5*) DIANE Pub.

Pigs in Heaven. Barbara Kingsolver. LC 92-54739. 352p. 1994. reprint ed. pap. 14.00 (*0-06-092253-2*, Perennial) HarperTrade.

***Pigs in Heaven: A Novel.** Barbara Kingsolver. 448p. 1999. mass mkt. 6.99 (*0-06-109868-X*) HarpC.

Pigs in Heaven: Kingsolver, & Barbara, Set. abr. ed. Barbara Kingsolver. 1993. audio 18.00 (*1-55994-722-5*, CPN 2332) HarperAudio.

Pigs in Space. Kate Foster & Larry DiFiori. LC 96-79566. (Muppet All Aboard Reading Ser.). (Illus.). 24p. (Orig.). (J). (ps-3). 1997. pap. 3.95 (*0-448-41571-2*, G & D) Peng Put Young Read.

Pigs in the Mud in the Middle of the Rud. Lynn Plourde. LC 96-23098. (Illus.). 32p. (YA). (ps-2). 1997. 15.95 (*0-590-56863-9*) Scholastic Inc.

Pigs in the Pantry: Fun with Math & Cooking. Amy Axelrod. LC 95-30021. (Illus.). 40p. (J). (ps-4). 1999. per. 5.99 (*0-689-82555-2*, 076714005990) Aladdin.

Pigs in the Pantry: Fun with Math & Cooking. Amy Axelrod. LC 95-30021. (Illus.). 40p. (J). (ps-4). 1997. 14.00 (*0-689-80665-5*) S&S Bks Yung.

Pigs in the Pantry Activity Guide. 1997. write for info. (*0-689-00322-6*) S&S Childrens.

Pigs in the Parlor see Cerdos en la Sala

Pigs in the Parlor. Frank Hammond & Ida M. Hammond. 176p. (Orig.). 1973. pap. 7.95 (*0-89228-027-1*) Impact Christian.

Pigs in the Playground. John Terry. (Illus.). 208p. (J). 1986. pap. 8.95 (*0-85236-158-0*) Diamond Farm Bk.

Pigs Is Pigs & Folks Is Folks. Raleigh Hussung. 160p. 1997. pap. 16.95 (*0-9658827-0-5*) RMH Ent.

Pigs' Meat: Selected Writings of Thomas Spence. Thomas Spence. 192p. 1982. 55.00 (*0-85124-315-0*) Dufour.

Pig's Meat: Selected Writings of Thomas Spence. Thomas Spence. 192p. 1982. pap. 14.95 (*0-85124-424-6*) Dufour.

Pigs Might Fly see Pigs Are Flying!

Pigs Might Fly. Dick King-Smith. (Illus.). 160p. (J). (gr. 4 up). 1990. pap. 4.99 (*0-14-034537-X*, PuffinBks) Peng Put Young Read.

***Pigs Might Fly.** Dick King-Smith. (J). (gr. 3-7). 2000. 19.25 (*0-8446-7146-0*) Peter Smith.

Pigs Might Fly. Dick King-Smith. 168p. (J). (gr. 3-7). 1984. pap. 2.75 (*0-590-43341-5*) Scholastic Inc.

Pigs Might Fly: A Novel. Dick King-Smith. (J). 1980. 10.09 (*0-606-04772-7*, Pub. by Turtleback) Demco.

Pigs of a Feather. Tish Rabe. LC 97-38411. (J). 1998. 0.07 (*0-679-89089-0*, Pub. by Random Bks Yng Read) Random.

Pigs of Lake Hood. Michael Prince. 64p. 1994. pap. 6.95 (*0-9642662-0-2*) Sundog Pubng.

Pigs on a Blanket. Amy Axelrod. LC 95-3677. (Illus.). (J). 1996. 15.95 (*0-02-707766-7*) S&S Bks Yung.

Pigs on a Blanket. Amy Axelrod. LC 95-3677. (Illus.). 40p. (J). (ps-4). 1996. per. 13.00 (*0-689-80505-5*) S&S Childrens.

Pigs on a Blanket: Fun with Math & Time. Amy Axelrod. LC 95-3677. (Illus.). 40p. (J). (ps-3). 1998. per. 5.99 (*0-689-82252-9*) Aladdin.

Pigs on the Ball. Amy Axelrod. LC 97-39776. (Illus.). 40p. (J). (gr. 1-3). 1998. mass mkt. 14.00 (*0-689-81565-4*) S&S Trade.

***Pigs on the Ball: Fun with Math & Sports.** Amy Axelrod. (Illus.). 40p. (J). (gr. k-3). 2000. per. 5.99 (*0-689-83537-X*) Aladdin.

Pigs on the Links: Hidden Hazards for the Woman. Alice O'Leary. LC 94-77832. (Illus.). 88p. (Orig.). 1994. pap. 11.95 (*0-936485-09-4*) Lkng Glass Pubns.

Pigs on the Move. Amy Axelrod. LC 98-19566. (Illus.). 40p. (J). 1999. 14.00 (*0-689-81070-9*) S&S Bks Yung.

Pigs over Boulder. Kerry L. Maclean. (Illus.). 32p. (Orig.). (J). (ps-k). 1996. pap. 12.95 (*0-9652998-0-5*) On the Spot.

Pigs over Colorado. Kerry L. MacLean. 1997. pap. text 14.95 (*0-9652998-1-3*) On the Spot.

***Pigs over Louisville.** Lori Winslow. (Illus.). (J). (gr. k-6). 2000. pap. 12.95 (*0-615-11566-7*) L Winslow.

Pigs, Peccaries & Hippos: An Action Plan for the Suiformes. Ed. by William Oliver. (C). 1995. pap. text 27.00 (*2-8317-0057-4*, Pub. by IUCN) Island Pr.

Pigs Peek see Cerdos Espian!

Pigs Peek. Rhonda Cox. (Books for Young Learners). (Illus.). 12p. (J). (gr. k-2). 1996. pap. text 5.00 (*1-57274-030-2*, A2180) R Owen Pubs.

Pigs Pet People. Vicki Armstrong. (Beginning Sounds Readers Ser.). (Illus.). (J). (ps-4). 1985. student ed. 5.99 (*0-933367-00-7*) See the Sounds.

Pigs, Pies, & Plenty of Problems. Cathy East Dubowski. (Full House Michelle & Friends Ser.: Vol. 28). 96p. (J). (gr. 4-7). 1999. per. 3.99 (*0-671-02152-4*) PB.

***Pigs, Plants & Other Biological Wonders: An Investigative Approach.** 2nd ed. Lynn Rivers & Sharon McDonald. 282p. (C). 1999. spiral bd. 32.95 (*0-7872-6366-4*, 41636603) Kendall-Hunt.

Pig's Ploughman. Bernard Evslin. (Monsters of Mythology Ser.). (Illus.). 104p. 1990. lib. bdg. 19.95 (*1-55546-256-1*) Chelsea Hse.

Pigs, Profits, & Rural Communities. Ed. by Kendall M. Thu & E. Paul Durrenberger. LC 97-35434. (SUNY Series in Anthropological Studies of Contemporary Issues). (Illus.). 192p. (C). 1998. text 54.50 (*0-7914-3887-2*); pap. text 17.95 (*0-7914-3888-0*) State U NY Pr.

Pigs' Wedding. Helme Heine. LC 78-57691. (Illus.). 32p. (J). (ps-3). 1986. 16.00 (*0-689-50409-8*) McElderry Bks.

Pigs' Wedding. Helme Heine. LC 90-40996. (Illus.). 32p. (J). (gr. k-3). 1991. reprint ed. mass mkt. 5.99 (*0-689-71478-5*) Aladdin.

Pigs Went Marching Out! Justin Rigamonti. Ed. by Nancy R. Thatch. LC 98-13553. (Books for Students by Students). (Illus.). 29p. (J). (gr. k-3). 1998. lib. bdg. 15.95 (*0-933849-70-2*) Landmark Edns.

Pigs Will Be Pigs. Axelrod. (J). 1998. pap. 5.99 (*0-87628-989-8*) S&S Trade.

Pigs Will Be Pigs. Amy Axelrod. LC 93-7640. (Illus.). 40p. (J). (ps-4). 1994. mass mkt. 14.00 (*0-02-765415-X*, Four Winds Pr) S&S Childrens.

Pigs Will Be Pigs. Amy Axelrod. (Fun with Math & Money Ser.). 1997. 11.19 (*0-606-13706-8*, Pub. by Turtleback) Demco.

Pigs Will be Pigs: Fun with Math & Money. Amy Axelrod. (Illus.). 1997. per. 5.99 (*0-689-81219-1*) S&S Childrens.

Pigsfoot Jelly & Persimmon Beer: Foodways from Virginia's Writer's Project. Ed. by Charles L. Perdue, Jr. LC 92-9356. (New Deal & Folk Culture Ser.). (Illus.). 128p. (Orig.). 1992. pap. 11.95 (*0-941270-74-2*) Ancient City Pr.

Pigskin: The Early Years of Pro Football. Robert W. Peterson. (Illus.). 256p. 1997. pap. 13.95 (*0-19-511913-4*) OUP.

Pigskin Pulpit: A Social History of Texas High School Football Coaches. Ty Cashion. LC 98-20976. (Illus.). 300p. 1998. 29.95 (*0-87611-168-1*) Tex St Hist Assn.

Pigskin Rabbi. Willard Manus. 304p. 1999. 23.00 (*1-891369-07-5*, Pub. by Breakaway Bks) Consort Bk Sales.

***Pigskin Rabbi.** Willard Manus. 304p. 2000. pap. 15.00 (*1-891369-23-7*, Pub. by Breakaway Bks) Consort Bk Sales.

Pigspurt. Ken Campbell. 112p. 1995. pap. write for info. (*0-413-68100-9*, A0710, Methuen Drama) Methn.

Pigsty. Mark Teague. LC 93-21179. (Illus.). 32p. (J). (gr. 1-4). 1994. 14.95 (*0-590-45915-5*) Scholastic Inc.

Pigtail War: American Involvement in the Sino-Japanese War of 1894-1895. Jeffery M. Dorwart. LC 75-8446. (Illus.). 176p. 1975. reprint ed. pap. 54.60 (*0-608-04438-5*, 206497000012) Bks Demand.

Pigtails & Flexible Hose Connectors for LP-Gas, UL 569. 7th ed. (C). 1995. pap. text 135.00 (*1-55989-827-5*) Underwrtrs Labs.

Pigtails & Froglegs: A Family Cookbook from Neiman Marcus. Ed. by Laura Rivers. (Illus.). 1993. 19.95 (*0-9629473-1-8*) Neiman-InCircle.

Pigtown. William J. Caunitz. 352p. 1996. mass mkt. 6.99 (*0-7860-0293-X*, Pinncle Kensgtn) Kensgtn Pub Corp.

Pigtown. William J. Caunitz. 1996. pap. 5.99 (*0-614-98083-6*, Onyx) NAL.

Pihkal: A Chemical Love Story. Ann Shulgin & Alexander Shulgin. (Illus.). 978p. 1990. pap. 18.95 (*0-9630096-0-5*) Transform Pr.

Piikani Blackfeet: A Culture under Siege. John C. Jackson. LC 00-27023. (Illus.). 256p. 2000. 30.00 (*0-87842-385-0*) Mountain Pr.

Piikani Blackfeet: A Culture under Siege. John C. Jackson. LC 00-27023. (Illus.). 256p. 2000. pap. 18.00 (*0-87842-386-9*) Mountain Pr.

Piine Frinta: Vin Camilele, Samson Ucide un Leu, Turnat Dintr-Un Vas in Altul. John W. Follette. Tr. by Genovieva Sfatcu Beattie. Orig. Title: Broken Bread. (RUM.). 39p. 1992. write for info. (*1-893179-06-0*) Eastern Europe Aid.

Pika Don. Al Dempsey. 384p. (Orig.). 1993. mass mkt. 4.99 (*0-8125-0939-0*) Tor Bks.

***Pikachu's Day.** Toshiuao Aoki. (Pokemon Tales Ser.: No. 4). (Illus.). 18p. (J). (ps-k). 1999. bds. 4.95 (*1-56931-386-5*, Pub. by Viz Commns Inc) Publishers Group.

***Pikachu's Hot Springs.** Yumi Tsukirino. No. 4. (Illus.). (J). 2000. pap. 4.95 (*1-56931-484-5*) Viz Commns Inc.

***Pikachu's Rescue Adventure.** Tracey West. (Pokemon Ser.). 64p. (gr. 4-7). 2000. pap. 4.50 (*0-439-19969-7*) Scholastic Inc.

***Pikachu's Unparalleled Adventure.** Junko Wada. (Pokemon Tales Movie Special Ser.: No. 2). (Illus.). (J). 2000. 4.95 (*1-56931-485-3*) Viz Commns Inc.

***Pikachu's Vacation.** Golden Books Staff. (J). 1999. pap. text 3.99 (*0-307-13271-4*, Goldn Books) Gldn Bks Pub Co.

***Pikachu's Vacation.** Scholastic, Inc. Staff. (Illus.). 65p. (gr. k-4). 1999. mass mkt. 4.50 (*0-439-15986-5*) Scholastic Inc.

Pika's Tail: A Children's Story about Mountain Wildlife. Sally Plumb. Ed. by Sharlene Milligan. (Illus.). 40p. (J). (gr. k-5). 1994. 14.95 (*0-931895-26-X*); pap. 9.95 (*0-931895-25-1*) Grand Teton NHA.

Pike. Al Lindner. LC 83-83060. 1994. pap. 11.95 (*0-929384-52-0*) In-Fisherman.

Pike: A Fortress in the Wetlands. Bertram H. Groene. (Illus.). 60p. (Orig.). 1988. pap. 10.95 (*0-945083-00-9*) SE LA Univ Pr.

Pike County. Charlotte Gibson. (Images of America Ser.). (Illus.). 128p. 1999. pap. 16.99 (*0-7524-1235-3*) Arcadia Publng.

Pike County, Alabama Cemetery Records. Ed. by Homer T. Jones. LC 99-214240. 368p. 1998. pap. 40.00 (*1-885480-25-3*) Pioneer Pubng.

Pike County, Arkansas Census, 1850. Courtney York & Gerlene York. 52p. 1969. pap. 12.00 (*0-916660-04-4*) Hse of York.

Pike County, Arkansas Census, 1860. Bobbie J. McLane. 59p. (Orig.). 1985. pap. 12.00 (*0-929604-36-9*) Arkansas Ancestors.

Pike County, Kentucky: A Pictorial History. Ed Maddox & Connie Maddox. LC 98-2624. 1998. write for info. (*1-57864-026-1*) Donning Co.

***Pike Creek Primitives.** Susan Allemand. (Illus.). 42p. 1999. pap. 10.95 (*1-57377-072-8*, 19884-2290) East Pubns.

Pike McCallister. Stephen Hahn. LC 98-85659. 253p. (YA). (gr. 6 up). 1998. pap. 14.95 (*1-888125-29-2*) Publ Consult.

Pike National Forest Recreation Guide. rev. ed. Outdoor Books & Maps, Inc. Staff. 64p. 1998. pap. 12.95 (*0-930657-11-X*) Outdr Bks & Maps.

Pike on the Fly: The Flyfishing Guide to Northerns, Tigers, & Muskies. Barry Reynolds & John Berryman. LC 93-38057. (Illus.). 160p. (Orig.). 1993. pap. 16.95 (*1-55566-113-0*, Sprng Creek Pr) Johnson Bks.

Pike on the Silverstrand. Ed. by Loretta Berner. (Illus.). 72p. 1982. pap. 11.00 (*0-9610250-3-4*) Hist Soc of Long Bch.

Pike Place Market Cookbook: Recipes, Anecdotes, & Personalities from Seattle's Renowned Public Market. Braiden Rex-Johnson. (Illus.). 272p. (Orig.). 1992. pap. 15.95 (*0-912365-52-8*) Sasquatch Bks.

Pike Place Public Market Seafood Cookbook. Braiden Rex-Johnson. LC 97-3447. (Illus.). 341p. 1997. pap. 24.95 (*0-89815-872-9*) Ten Speed Pr.

Pike's Illustrated Descriptive Catalogue of Optical, Mathematical, & Philosophical Instruments. Benjamin Pike, Jr. (Illus.). 755p. 1993. reprint ed. 125.00 (*0-930405-54-4*) Norman SF.

Pikes Peak. Potter. 1998. 76.00 (*0-323-00685-X*) Mosby Inc.

Pike's Peak: A Mining Saga. Frank Waters. LC 77-150753. 743p. 1987. 36.95 (*0-8040-0503-6*); pap. 19.95 (*0-8040-0900-7*) Swallow.

Pikes Peak: Legends of America's Mountain. James McChristal. 1999. pap. 12.00 (*0-9670867-0-1*) Sierra Grande.

Pikes Peak - Canon City, CO. 1996. 8.99 (*0-925873-91-8*) Trails Illustrated.

Pikes Peak & Garden of the Gods: Two Worlds, One Vision. Todd Caudle. (Illus.). 96p. 1997. 25.00 (*1-888845-00-7*) Skyline Pr.

Pikes Peak Backcountry: The Historic Saga of the Peak's West Slope. Celinda Reynolds Kaelin. LC 99-18189. 3p. 1999. pap. 15.95 (*0-87004-391-9*) Caxton.

Pike's Peak Country. 2nd rev. ed. Jim Scott. LC 86-82747. (Colorado Geographic Ser.). (Illus.). 101p. (Orig.). 1994. pap. 9.95 (*1-56044-249-2*) Falcon Pub Inc.

Pikes Peak Country: The Complete Guide to Natural Wonders, Historic Sites, Attractions & Outdoor Recreation. Stewart M. Green. LC 85-60701. (Illus.). 104p. (Orig.). 1985. pap. 6.95 (*0-933393-07-5*) Ponderosa Pr.

Pikes Peak Is Unser Mountain: Race to the Clouds. Stanley L. DeGeer. LC 90-62413. (Illus.). 216p. (Orig.). 1990. pap. 24.95 (*0-9626278-0-1*) Peak Pub NM.

Pikes Peak or Bust, 1916-1996: Eighty Years of Racing to the Clouds. Stanley L. DeGeer. (Illus.). 100p. (Orig.). 1996. pap. 7.95 (*0-9626278-2-8*) Peak Pub NM.

Pikes Peak Race, 1916-1990. Stanley L. DeGeer. (Illus.). 330p. 1991. pap. 14.95 (*0-9626278-1-X*) Peak Pub NM.

Pikes Peak Region: A Pictorial Guidebook. Ed. by Alice Moffet et al. (Illus.). 32p. 1998. pap. 6.00 (*1-892717-02-6*, MISB101) Sanborn Ltd.

Pikes Peak Region Atlas-Street Guide. 1995. pap. 10.95 (*0-914449-56-7*) Pierson Graph.

Pikes Peak Region Traveler. Melissa Walker. LC 97-51849. (Illus.). 144p. 1998. pap. 14.95 (*1-56579-292-0*) Westcliffe Pubs.

***Pike's Peek at the World of Sherlock Holmes.** Franklin W. Rhode & Robert W. Hahn. (Illus.). 68p. 1998. pap. 10.00 (*1-55246-108-4*) Battered Silicon.

Piki Ake! Poems 1990-92. Robert Sullivan. LC 93-187671. 58p. 1993. write for info. (*1-86940-084-4*, Pub. by Auckland Univ) Paul & Co Pubs.

Pikoi & Other Legends of the Island of Hawaii see Hawai'i Island Legends: Pikoi, Pele & Others

Pikolo: L'Arbre aux Mille Tresors (Pikolo's Night Voyage) Pierre Filion. (FRE., Illus.). 32p. (J). (ps-3). 1994. 15.95 (*1-55037-367-6*, Pub. by Annick); pap. 6.95 (*1-55037-366-8*, Pub. by Annick) Firefly Bks Ltd.

Pikolo Le Secret des Garde-Robes - Paper Nights. Gilles Tibo. (FRE., Illus.). 32p. (J). (ps-6). 1996. pap. 6.95 (*1-55037-226-2*, Pub. by Les Editions); lib. bdg. 15.95 (*1-55037-227-0*, Pub. by Les Editions) Firefly Bks Ltd.

Pikolo's Night Voyage. Pierre Filion. (Illus.). 32p. (J). (ps-3). 1994. pap. 5.95 (*1-55037-364-1*, Pub. by Annick); lib. bdg. 15.95 (*1-55037-365-X*, Pub. by Annick) Firefly Bks Ltd.

Pikovaja Dama: Barysnja Krest Janka, C Level. text 8.95 (*0-8219-1452-9*) EMC-Paradigm.

***Pilaf, Pozole, & Pad Thai: American Women & Ethnic Food.** Ed. by Sherrie A. Inness. 2001. pap. 17.95 (*1-55849-286-0*) U of Mass Pr.

Pilands of Diamond Grove: A Family History Spanning over Eight Generations. John M. Griffin. (Illus.). 70p. (Orig.). 1988. pap. 10.00 (*0-317-93030-3*) J M Griffin.

Pilar la Dura, Bk. One. H. Glenn Carson. 173p. (Orig.). 1993. pap. 9.95 (*0-941620-47-6*) Carson Ent.

***Pilates at Home: An Illustrated Guide to Achieving Balance, Shape & Fitness Without Equipment.** Eleanor McKenzie. (Illus.). 128p. 2000. pap. 16.95 (*1-56975-210-9*, Pub. by Ulysses Pr) Publishers Group.

***Pilates Body: The Ultimate at Home Guide to Strengthening, Lengthening & Toning Your Body Without Machines.** Brooke Siler. LC 99-36046. 208p. 2000. pap. 18.00 (*0-7679-0396-X*) Broadway BDD.

Pilates Method of Body Conditioning: Introduction to the Core Exercises. Sean P. Gallagher & Romana Kryzanowska. LC 98-52214. (Illus.). 208p. 1999. pap. 19.95 (*1-891696-08-4*) BainBridgeBooks.

***Pilates Powerhouse: Body Conditioning for Strength, Flexibility & the Shape You Have Always Wanted in Less Than an Hour a Day.** Mari Winsor & Mark Laska. (Illus.). 208p. 1999. pap. text 18.00 (*0-7382-0228-2*, Pub. by Perseus Pubng) HarpC.

***Pilates' Primer: The Millennium Edition: Return to Life Through Contrology & Your Health.** Joseph H. Pilates & William J. Miller. (Illus.). 2000. reprint ed. 15.95 (*1-928564-00-3*) Present Dynam.

Pilates' Return to Life Through Contrology. Joseph H. Pilates & William J. Miller. Ed. by Judd Robbins. Orig. Title: Return to Life Through Contrology. 93p. 1998. pap. 29.95 (*0-9614937-9-8*) Present Dynam.

***Pilate's Wife.** H. D., pseud. Ed. & Intro. by Joan Burke. LC 99-59104. 2000. pap. 12.95 (*0-8112-1433-8*, Pub. by New Directions) Norton.

Pilchuck: A Glass School. Tina Oldknow. LC 96-16615. (Illus.). 296p. 1996. 60.00 (*0-295-97559-8*) U of Wash Pr.

Pilchuck, the Life of a Mountain. Harry W. Higman & Earl J. Larrison. (Shorey Historical Ser.). 288p. reprint ed. 20.00 (*0-8466-2307-2*, S307); reprint ed. pap. 10.00 (*0-8466-0307-1*) Shoreys Bkstore.

P

Pile Construction. 1995. lib. bdg. 250.75 (*0-8490-6632-8*) Gordon Pr.

Pile Design & Construction. Tomlinson. 1997. 125.95 (*0-419-15770-0*, E & FN Spon) Routledge.

Pile Design & Construction Practice. 4th ed. Tomlinson. LC 94-183413. (Illus.). 432p. (C). 1994. 140.00 (*0-419-18450-3*, E & FN Spon) Routledge.

Pile Driving: Construction Guide. W. A. Dawson. 30p. 1981. 10.00 (*0-7277-0093-6*, Pub. by T Telford) RCH.

Pile Driving Engineer. Jack Rudman. (Career Examination Ser.: C-2558). 1994. pap. 34.95 (*0-8373-2558-7*) Nat Learn.

Pile Foundations. Dinesh Mohan. 178p. (C). 1988. text 60.00 (*90-6191-918-5*, Pub. by A A Balkema) Ashgate Pub Co.

Pile Foundations: Snip 2.02.03-85. Russia's Gosstroy Staff. Ed. & Tr. by Snip Register, Inc. Staff from RUS. (Building Codes of Russia Ser.). (Illus.). iv, 75p. 1998. ring bd. 399.95 (*1-57937-056-X*, S5000385) Snip Register.

Pile Foundations for Buildings & Structures in Collapsible Soils. A. A. Grigorian. (Illus.). 158p. (C). 1997. text 71.00 (*90-5410-763-4*, Pub. by A A Balkema) Ashgate Pub Co.

Pile Foundations in Engineering Practice. Shamsher Prakash & Hari D. Sharma. LC 89-31977. 768p. 1990. 150.00 (*0-471-61653-2*) Wiley.

Pile of Puppies. National Geographic Staff. (J). (ps). 1993. 4.50 (*0-7922-1834-5*) Natl Geog.

Pile of Stones: Devotions for Kids. Jessie Schut. LC 97-45747. 103p. (J). 1998. pap. 7.95 (*1-56212-332-7*, 1701-0402) CRC Pubns.

Pileated Woodpecker. Seliesa Pembleton. LC 88-20220. (Remarkable Animals Ser.). (Illus.). 60p. (J). (gr. 3 up). 1988. lib. bdg. 13.95 (*0-87518-392-1*, Dillon Silver Burdett) Silver Burdett Pr.

Piled Higher & Deeper: The Folklore of Student Life. 2nd ed. Simon J. Bronner. 246p. 1996. pap. 14.95 (*0-87483-443-0*) August Hse.

Piles & Foundations. Ed. by F. E. Young. 341p. 1981. 46.00 (*0-7277-0118-5*, Pub. by T Telford) RCH.

Piles of Pets. Judy Delton. (Pee Wee Scouts Ser.: No. 19). 96p. (J). (ps-3). 1993. pap. 3.99 (*0-440-40792-3*) Dell.

Piles of Pets. Judy Delton. (Pee Wee Scouts Ser.). (J). 1993. 9.19 (*0-606-05544-4*, Pub. by Turtleback) Demco.

Piles under Dynamic Loads: Proceedings of Sessions Sponsored by the Geotechnical Engineering Division of the American Society of Civil Engineers in Conjunction with the ASCE National Convention, New York, New York, September 13-17, 1992. Ed. by Shamsher Prakash. LC 92-27783. (Geotechnical Special Publications: No. 34). 164p. 1992. 28.00 (*0-87262-905-8*) Am Soc Civil Eng.

Pileup on Death Row. Burton H. Wolfe. LC 82-45676. (Capital Punishment Ser.). (Illus.). reprint ed. 46.50 (*0-404-62436-7*) AMS Pr.

Pilgram Marpeck: His Life & Social Theology. Stephen B. Boyd. LC 90-44076. (Duke Monographs in Medieval & Renaissance Studies). 375p. 1992. text 39.95 (*0-8223-1100-3*) Duke.

*__Pilgrim.__ 128p. 1998. otabind 19.95 (*0-7935-9423-5*) H Leonard.

Pilgrim. Richard Gere. LC 97-23614. (Illus.). 144p. 1997. 75.00 (*0-8212-2322-4*, Pub. by Bulfinch Pr) Little.

Pilgrim. Charles H. Norton. 136p. (Orig.). 1993. pap. 9.95 (*1-880451-04-2*) Rainbows End.

Pilgrim. Fred Saberhagen. 1997. per. 6.99 (*0-671-87856-5*) Baen Bks.

Pilgrim: A Biography of William Brewster. Mary B. Sherwood. LC 82-80574. 272p. 1982. 25.00 (*0-9608234-0-9*) Great Oak Pr VA.

Pilgrim: A Novel. Timothy Findley. LC 99-41348. 496p. 2000. 25.00 (*0-06-019197-X*) HarpC.

Pilgrim Adrift in the Dunes. Roger Chauvette. 121p. 1998. pap. 12.95 (*0-9666275-0-4*, 1-0001) Vital Links.

Pilgrim among the Shadows. Boris Pahor. Tr. by Michael Biggins from SLV. LC 94-20605. 1995. 20.00 (*0-15-171958-6*) Harcourt.

Pilgrim among Us. Roberta Spear. LC 91-10658. (Wesleyan Poetry Ser.). 70p. 1991. pap. 12.95 (*0-8195-1200-1*, Wesleyan Univ Pr); text 25.00 (*0-8195-2198-1*, Wesleyan Univ Pr) U Pr of New Eng.

Pilgrim & Other Tales. Edward Thomas. 198p. (Orig.). 1992. pap. 9.95 (*0-460-87083-1*, Everyman's Classic Lib) Tuttle Pubng.

Pilgrim & the Book: A Study of Dante, Langland & Chaucer. 3rd ed. Julia B. Holloway. LC 92-18571. (American University Studies: English Language & Literature: Ser. IV, Vol. 42). (Illus.). XXII, 303p. (C). 1993. text 49.95 (*0-8204-2090-5*) P Lang Pubng.

*__Pilgrim at Tinker Creek.__ Annie Dillard. 1999. 24.75 (*0-8446-6986-5*) Peter Smith.

*__Pilgrim at Tinker Creek.__ Annie Dillard. LC 99-88723. (Famous Authors Ser.). 2000. 28.95 (*0-7862-2325-1*) Thorndike Pr.

Pilgrim at Tinker Creek. anniversary ed. Annie Dillard. LC 98-29765. 304p. 1998. pap. 13.00 (*0-06-095302-0*) HarpC.

Pilgrim at Tinker Creek. Annie Dillard. 1998. reprint ed. 41.95 (*1-56849-706-7*) Buccaneer Bks.

*__Pilgrim Centre Parshuram Kund: Articulation of Indian Society, Culture & Economic Dimension.__ M. C. Behera. LC 98-908717. 1998. 24.00 (*81-7169-503-5*, Pub. by Commonwealth) S Asia.

Pilgrim Chaucer: Center Stage. Dolores Cullen. LC 99-11191. (Illus.). 208p. 1999. pap. 14.95 (*1-56474-306-3*) Fithian Pr.

Pilgrim Children Had Many Chores, Vol. 3902. Gina Lems-Tardif. Ed. by Rozanne L. Williams. (Social Studies Learn to Read Ser.). (Illus.). 8p. (J). (ps-2). 1996. pap. 1.75 (*1-57471-121-0*, 3902) Creat Teach Pr.

Pilgrim Children Had Many Chores, Vol. 3959. Gina Lems-Tardif. Ed. by Rozanne L. Williams. (Social Studies Big Bks.). (Illus.). 8p. (J). (ps-2). 1997. pap. 8.98 (*1-57471-167-9*, 3959) Creat Teach Pr.

Pilgrim Church. E. H. Broadbent. 422p. 1987. pap. 12.95 (*0-310-55171-4*, 19017P) Zondervan.

*__Pilgrim Church.__ E. H. Broadbent. 456p. 1999. 21.99 (*1-882701-53-4*, Gospel Folio Pr) Uplook Min.

Pilgrim Church: A Popular History of Catholic Christianity. William J. Bausch. LC 89-50938. 480p. 1989. 19.95 (*0-89622-395-7*) Twenty-Third.

Pilgrim Colony: A History of New Plymouth, 1620-1691. George D. Langdon. LC 66-21526. (Yale Publications in American Studies: No. 12). 268p. reprint ed. pap. 83.10 (*0-8357-8268-9*, 203379600087) Bks Demand.

Pilgrim Experience Ore Book. Carl L. Risner. 40p. 1998. pap. write for info. (*1-57502-991-X*, PO2701) Morris Pubng.

Pilgrim Experiences the World's Religions. Aaron Milavec. LC 84-9024. (Mellen Lives Ser.: Vol. 1). 96p. 1984. pap. 34.95 (*0-88946-010-8*) E Mellen.

*__Pilgrim Family Play Set & Booklet: 15 Pieces Include 5" Tall Figures, House, Accessories.__ (American Adventure Play Sets Ser.). (Illus.). 32p. (J). (gr. k-7). 1999. 28.00 (*0-9677511-0-1*) Child Light.

Pilgrim Fathers from a Dutch Point of View. Daniel Plooij. LC 71-100509. reprint ed. 20.00 (*0-404-05065-4*) AMS Pr.

Pilgrim Fathers from a Dutch Point of View. Daniel Plooij. LC 79-131801. 1970. reprint ed. 7.00 (*0-403-00688-0*) Scholarly.

*__Pilgrim Footnotes: With Humor.__ Robert Fairchild Huber. LC 99-61743. 192p. 1999. 9.95 (*0-89725-372-8*) Picton Pr.

Pilgrim God: A Biblical Journey. John Taize. 220p. 1989. pap. 24.00 (*1-85390-044-3*, Pub. by Veritas Pubns) St Mut.

Pilgrim God: A Biblical Journey. Brother John of Taize. 220p. 1985. reprint ed. pap. 13.95 (*0-912405-18-X*, Pastoral Press) OR Catholic.

Pilgrim God: A Preacher Reflects on the Story of Jesus. Donald Burt. 312p. (Orig.). 1995. pap. 15.95 (*0-8146-2246-1*) Liturgical Pr.

Pilgrim Goes Forth. John Robson. 276p. (Orig.). 1986. pap. 8.75 (*0-685-17666-5*) Lake Crest Hse.

Pilgrim Hawks see Six Great Modern Short Novels

Pilgrim Hymnal. Blue. LC 58-1015. 1958. 12.95 (*0-8298-0460-9*) Pilgrim OH.

Pilgrim Hymnal. Red. LC 58-1015. 1958. 12.95 (*0-8298-0107-3*) Pilgrim OH.

Pilgrim Hymnal: Organist's Edition. UCC Staff. LC 58-1015. 1981. 18.00 (*0-8298-0454-4*) Pilgrim OH.

Pilgrim in Aquarius. David Spangler. 256p. (Orig.). 1996. pap. 13.95 (*0-905249-83-6*, Pub. by Findhorn Pr) Words Distrib.

Pilgrim in Chinese Culture: Negotiating Religious Diversity. Judith A. Berling. LC 97-30863. (Faith Meets Faith Ser.). 160p. (Orig.). 1997. pap. 18.00 (*1-57075-152-8*) Orbis Bks.

Pilgrim in Lent: Prayer for Every Day. Donal Neary. 96p. (Orig.). 1992. pap. 4.95 (*0-8146-2123-6*) Liturgical Pr.

Pilgrim in Rome. Richard G. Roland. LC 94-92066. (Illus.). 80p. 1994. per. 18.75 (*0-9640694-0-7*) R G Roland.

Pilgrim in the Ruins: A Life of Walker Percy. Jay Tolson. LC 92-20101. 1992. 27.50 (*0-671-65707-0*) S&S Trade.

Pilgrim Journey. 208p. 1998. write for info. (*1-57502-848-4*, P02321) Morris Pubng.

*__Pilgrim Kamanita.__ unabridged ed. Karl A. Gjellerup. Orig. Title: Pilgrimen Kamanita. (Illus.). 320p. 2000. pap. 25.00 (*0-89564-084-8*) IBS Intl.

Pilgrim Law. Robert E. Rodes. LC 97-37190. 224p. 1998. pap. 18.00 (*0-268-03822-8*) U of Notre Dame Pr.

Pilgrim Must Embark: Living in Community. Adelman & Shultz. 1994. 125.00 (*1-56321-143-2*) L Erlbaum Assocs.

Pilgrim of Eternity: Byron - A Conflict. John Drinkwater. (BCL1-PR English Literature Ser.). 408p. 1992. reprint ed. lib. bdg. 99.00 (*0-7812-7477-X*) Rprt Serv.

Pilgrim of Hate. Ellis Peters. 256p. 1997. mass mkt. 5.99 (*0-446-40531-0*, Pub. by Warner Bks) Little.

*__Pilgrim of Hate: The Tenth Chronicle of Brother Cadfael.__ large type ed. Ellis Peters. LC 99-14891. 257p. 1999. pap. text 23.95 (*0-7862-1945-9*, G K Hall Lrg Type) Mac Lib Ref.

Pilgrim of the Clouds: Poems & Essays from Ming China. Yuan Hung-tao. Tr. by Jonathan Chaves from CHI. (Illus.). 136p. 1992. reprint ed. pap. 7.95 (*0-8348-0257-0*, Inklings Edits) Weatherhill.

Pilgrim of the Clouds: Poems & Essays from Ming China by Yuan Hung-Tao & His Brothers. Yuan Hung-Tao. Tr. & Intro. by Jonathan Chaves. LC 78-17455. (Illus.). 144p. 1978. pap. 6.95 (*0-8348-0134-5*) Weatherhill.

Pilgrim of the Himalayas: The Discovery of Tibetan Buddhism. Edmond B. Szekely. (Illus.). 32p. 1974. pap. 3.50 (*0-89564-061-9*) IBS Intl.

Pilgrim on a Bicycle. Barbara M. Johnson. LC 81-68637. 144p. 1982. 20.00 (*0-86693-001-9*) B M Johnson.

Pilgrim Path: Five Discipleship Dramas with Homilies & Discussion Helps. Theodore W. Schroeder. LC 97-1319. 1997. 10.99 (*0-570-04978-4*, 12-3328) Concordia.

Pilgrim Path: The First Company of Women Missionaries to Hawaii. Mary Zwiep. LC 91-15555. (Illus.). 396p. (Orig.). reprint ed. pap. 122.80 (*0-608-09934-1*, 206927200003) Bks Demand.

*__Pilgrim Pathways: Essays in Baptist History in Honour of B. R. White.__ Ed. by William H. Brackney et al. LC 99-41193. 352p. 2000. 45.00 (*0-86554-687-8*) Mercer Univ Pr.

Pilgrim Pope, 1. John Paul, II, pseud. LC 99-33238. 1999. 24.95 (*0-7407-0045-6*) Andrews & McMeel.

*__Pilgrim Prayers: Prepared by the Vatican Committee for the Jubilee Year 2000.__ Vatican Committee for the Jubilee Year 2000. LC 99-29243. (Illus.). 252p. 1999. pap. 15.95 (*0-8264-1186-X*) Continuum.

Pilgrim Progression: The Protestant Experience in California. Eldon G. Ernst & Douglas F. Anderson. Ed. by Phillip Hammond. (Religious Contours of California: Window to the World's Religions: Vol. II). 144p. (Orig.). 1993. pap. 9.95 (*1-56474-063-3*) Fithian Pr.

Pilgrim Recipes. 3rd ed. Anthony Gauquier & Beverly Gauguier. 27p. 1983. reprint ed. pap. 3.00 (*0-9609574-0-5*) A Gauquier.

Pilgrim Road. Origen et al. Tr. by Alexnder Roberts et al from GRE. 192p. (Orig.). 1991. pap. 7.95 (*0-924722-04-5*) Scroll Pub.

Pilgrim Road: Sermons on Christian Living. B. A. Gerrish. Ed. by Mary T. Stimming. LC 99-38816. 216p. 1999. pap. 14.95 (*0-664-25691-0*) Westminster John Knox.

Pilgrim Self: Traveling the Path from Life to Life. Robert S. Ellwood. LC 96-8902. 120p. 1997. pap. 12.00 (*0-8356-0739-9*, Quest) Theos Pub Hse.

Pilgrim Soul. Deborah Misenhimer. 215p. 1993. pap. 12.00 (*0-9636313-0-6*) D Misenhimer.

Pilgrim Soul. unabridged ed. Anne M. Downes. LC 97-204871. (Illus.). 288p. (Orig.). 1997. pap. 15.00 (*0-9633560-9-7*) Durand Pr.

Pilgrim Souls. Mary MacIver. 1990. text 28.00 (*0-08-037978-8*, Pergamon Pr) Elsevier.

Pilgrim Souls: A Collection of Spiritual Autobiographies. Ed. by Amy Mandelker & Elizabeth Powers. LC 98-40813. 544p. 1999. per. 17.00 (*0-684-84311-0*) S&S Trade.

Pilgrim Souvenirs & Secular Badges. Brian Spencer. (Medieval Finds from Excavations in London Ser.: No. 7). (Illus.). 349p. 1998. 100.00 (*0-11-290574-9*, Pub. by Statnry Office) Balogh.

Pilgrim, Spirit of the West. Sara Hooff. (Illus.). 36p. (Orig.). (J). (gr. 1-8). 1997. pap. 12.95 (*0-9659525-0-9*) Hooff Prints.

Pilgrim Stars. Peter Telep. 320p. (YA). 1999. mass mkt. 6.50 (*0-06-105986-2*) HarpC Child Bks.

Pilgrim Stories: On & Off the Road to Santiago, Modern Journeys Along an Ancient Way in Spain. Nancy Louise Frey. LC 98-14153. 298p. 1998. 45.00 (*0-520-21084-0*, Pub. by U CA Pr); pap. 17.95 (*0-520-21751-9*, Pub. by U CA Pr) Cal Prin Full Svc.

Pilgrim Street. Hesba Stretton. LC 96-39180. (Golden Inheritance Ser.). (J). 1996. 7.90 (*0-921100-91-4*) Inhtce Pubns.

Pilgrim Theology: Taking the Path of Theological Discovery. Michael Bauman. LC 92-13328. 1992. pap. 14.99 (*0-310-58531-7*) Zondervan.

Pilgrim to Rome. Hubert J. Richards. 216p. 1994. pap. 35.00 (*0-85597-532-6*) St Mut.

Pilgrim to the Holy Land. Hubert J. Richards. 256p. 1993. 50.00 (*0-85597-321-8*) St Mut.

Pilgrim Village Mystery. Illus. by Charles Tang. LC 95-17618. (Boxcar Children Ser.: No. 5). (J). (gr. 2-5). 1995. pap. 3.95 (*0-8075-6531-8*); lib. bdg. 13.95 (*0-8075-6530-X*) A Whitman.

Pilgrim Village Mystery. Created by Gertrude Chandler Warner. (Boxcar Children Special Ser.: No. 5). (J). (gr. 2-5). 1995. 8.85 (*0-606-08700-1*, Pub. by Turtleback) Demco.

Pilgrim Voices: Our First Year in the New World. Ed. by Connie Roop & Peter Roop. LC 95-10114. (Illus.). 48p. (J). (gr. 3-7). 1997. 16.95 (*0-8027-8314-7*); pap. 7.95 (*0-8027-7530-6*); lib. bdg. 17.85 (*0-8027-8315-5*) Walker & Co.

Pilgrim Wind. Mollie M. O'Brien. LC 85-60237. 64p. (Orig.). 1985. pap. 5.95 (*0-89390-062-1*) Resource Pubns.

Pilgrimage see Hajj & Umrah: From A to Z

Pilgrimage. 96p. 1997. pap. 8.95 (*0-9644574-3-1*) Shoeless Pub.

Pilgrimage. Ed. by Christian Duquoc et al. (Concilium Ser.). 115p. 1996. pap. 15.00 (*1-57075-073-4*) Orbis Bks.

Pilgrimage. Zenna Henderson. 1980. pap. 3.50 (*0-380-01507-2*, Avon Bks) Morrow Avon.

Pilgrimage. Ed. by Makhan Jha. (C). 1995. 36.00 (*81-210-0340-7*, Pub. by Inter-India Pubns) S Asia.

Pilgrimage. Stuart Kestenbaum. (Illus.). 42p. 1990. pap. 8.95 (*0-913341-13-4*) Coyote Love.

Pilgrimage. Ian Slater. 72p. 1999. pap. 21.00 (*1-85072-191-2*, Pub. by W Sessions) St Mut.

*__Pilgrimage: A Chronicle of Christianity Through the Churches of Rome.__ June Hager. (Illus.). 224p. 1999. 40.00 (*0-297-82517-8*) G Weidenfeld & Nicolson.

*__Pilgrimage: A Contemporary Quest for Ancient Wisdom.__ Paulo Coelho. Tr. by Alan Clarke. LC 94-45312. 272p. 2000. pap. 13.00 (*0-06-251279-X*, Pub. by Harper SF) HarpC.

Pilgrimage: A Journey Through Colorado's History & Culture. Stephen May. LC 82-76537. (Illus.). 200p. 1986. pap. 8.95 (*0-8040-0883-3*); text 18.95 (*0-8040-0882-5*) Swallow.

Pilgrimage: A Tale of Old Natchez. Louise W. Collier. LC 94-27835. 480p. 1994. 6.95 (*1-56554-064-6*) Pelican.

*__Pilgrimage: Adventures of the Spirit.__ Ed. by James O'Reilly & Sean O'Reilly. (Illus.). 344p. 2000. pap. 16.95 (*1-885211-56-2*) Trvlers Tale.

*__Pilgrimage: An Encyclopedia.__ Linda Kay Davidson. 2001. lib. bdg. 65.00 (*1-57607-004-2*) ABC-CLIO.

Pilgrimage: Hajj & Umrah from A to Z. Mamdouh N. Mohamed. (Illus.). 96p. 1996. pap. 12.95 (*0-9652877-0-X*) M N Mohamed.

Pilgrimage: Memoirs of an Adventist Administrator. Richard L. Hammill. LC 91-977161. 239p. 1992. 16.99 (*0-943872-59-6*) Andrews Univ Pr.

*__Pilgrimage: One Woman's Return to a Changing India.__ Pramila Jayapal. (Illus.). 288p. 2000. 22.95 (*1-58005-032-8*, Pub. by Seal Pr WA) Publishers Group.

Pilgrimage: Past & Present in the World Religions. Simon Coleman & John Elsner. (Illus.). 240p. (C). 1995. 29.95 (*0-674-66765-4*) HUP.

Pilgrimage: Past & Present in the World Religions. Simon Coleman & John Elsner. (Illus.). 240p. 1997. reprint ed. pap. 20.50 (*0-674-66766-2*) HUP.

Pilgrimage: Tales from the Open Road. Patrick Pfister. 1999. reprint ed. pap. 14.95 (*0-89733-472-8*) Academy Chi Pubs.

Pilgrimage: The Book of the People. Zenna Henderson. 1993. reprint ed. lib. bdg. 18.95 (*0-89968-342-8*, Lghtyr Pr) Buccaneer Bks.

*__Pilgrimage: Timothy Gabashvili's Travels to Mount Athos, Constantinople & Jerusalem, 1755-1759.__ Ed. by Mzia Ebanoidze & John Wilkinson. 288p. 2000. 80.00 (*0-7007-1264-X*, Pub. by Curzon Pr Ltd) Paul & Co Pubs.

Pilgrimage Vol. 1: Pointed Roofs, Backwater, Honeycomb. Dorothy Richardson. 496p. 1989. reprint ed. pap. 12.50 (*0-252-06076-8*) U of Ill Pr.

Pilgrimage & Exile: Mother Marianne of Molokai. Mary L. Hanley & O. A. Bushnell. LC 91-34539. (Illus.). 464p. 1992. reprint ed. pap. 19.95 (*0-8248-1387-1*) UH Pr.

Pilgrimage & Holy Space in Late Antique Egypt. David Frankfurter. LC 98-21382. (Religions in the Graeco-Roman World Ser.). 1998. write for info. (*90-04-11127-1*) Brill Academic Pubs.

Pilgrimage & Narrative in the French Renaissance: The Undiscovered Country. Wes Williams. LC 98-27486. (Illus.). 336p. 1999. text 80.00 (*0-19-815940-4*) OUP.

Pilgrimage & Service. Joseph Krimsky. Ed. by Moshe Davis. LC 77-70712. (America & the Holy Land Ser.). 1977. reprint ed. lib. bdg. 19.95 (*0-405-10261-5*) Ayer.

Pilgrimage As Rite of Passage: A Guidebook for Youth Ministry. Robert Brancatelli. LC 98-10840. 80p. 1998. pap. 11.95 (*0-8091-3798-4*, 3798-4) Paulist Pr.

*__Pilgrimage Explored.__ Ed. by Jennie Stopford. LC 98-51451. 288p. 1999. 75.00 (*0-9529734-3-X*) Boydell & Brewer.

*__Pilgrimage for Love: Essays in Early Modern Literature in Honor of Josephine A. Roberts.__ Ed. by Sigrid King. LC 99-39579. (Medieval & Renaissance Texts & Studies: Vol. 213). 304p. 1999. 30.00 (*0-86698-255-8*) MRTS.

Pilgrimage for the Elixir. Susan Y. C. Wong. 55p. 1998. mass mkt. write for info. (*0-7541-0232-7*, Pub. by Minerva Pr) Unity Dist.

Pilgrimage from Rome. rev. ed. Bartholomew F. Brewer & Alfred W. Furrell. (Illus.). 1986. pap. 11.95 (*0-89084-327-9*, 018036) Bob Jones Univ.

Pilgrimage in Faith: An Introduction to the Episcopal Church. rev. ed. Franklin C. Ferguson. LC 75-5220. 136p. (Orig.). 1990. pap. 8.95 (*0-8192-1277-6*) Morehouse Pub.

Pilgrimage in Indian Civilisation. Sabita Acharya. LC 97-906047. xv, 270p. 1997. 30.00 (*81-86562-35-4*, Pub. by Manak Pubns Pvt Ltd) Nataraj Bks.

Pilgrimage in Ireland: The Monuments & the People. Peter Harbison. LC 91-5052. (Irish Studies). (Illus.). 256p. (Orig.). 1992. 39.95 (*0-8156-0265-0*) Syracuse U Pr.

Pilgrimage in Ireland: The Monuments & the People. Peter Harbison. (Irish Studies). (Illus.). 224p. (Orig.). 1995. pap. 19.95 (*0-8156-0312-6*) Syracuse U Pr.

Pilgrimage in Latin America, 4. Ed. by N. Ross Crumrine. LC 89-11845. (Contributions to the Study of Anthropology Ser.: No. 4). 464p. 1991. 67.95 (*0-313-26110-5*, CPG/, Greenwood Pr) Greenwood.

Pilgrimage in Mission. Donald R. Jacobs. LC 83-306. 168p. 1983. pap. 6.50 (*0-8361-3324-2*) Herald Pr.

Pilgrimage in Tibet. Ed. by Alex McKay. 260p. 1998. text 45.00 (*0-7007-0992-4*, Pub. by Curzon Pr Ltd) UH Pr.

Pilgrimage Motif in the Works of the Medieval German Author Hartmann von Aue. Mary V. Mills. LC 95-43256. (Studies in Medieval Literature: Vol. 13). 1996. write for info. (*0-7734-8855-3*) E Mellen.

Pilgrimage of a Proselyte: From Auschwitz to Jerusalem. David Patterson. LC 93-13626. 207 p. 1993. 19.95 (*0-8246-0363-X*) Jonathan David.

Pilgrimage of Buddhism & a Buddhist Pilgrimage. James B. Pratt. LC 75-3325. (Philosophy America Ser.). reprint ed. 94.50 (*0-404-59320-8*) AMS Pr.

Pilgrimage of Buddhism & a Buddhist Pilgrimage, 2 vols. James B. Pratt. (C). 1993. reprint ed. 60.00 (*81-85326-47-9*, Pub. by Vintage) S Asia.

*__Pilgrimage of Dorothy Richardson.__ Joanne Winning. 2000. 57.95 (*0-299-17030-6*); pap. 22.95 (*0-299-17034-9*) U of Wis Pr.

Pilgrimage of Fa Hian. M. M. Remusat. (C). 1990. reprint ed. text 31.50 (*0-685-50087-X*, Pub. by Mittal Pubs Dist) S Asia.

Pilgrimage of Faith. J. B. Toews. (Perspectives on Mennonite Life & Thought Ser.: Vol. 8). 376p. 1993. pap. 11.95 (*0-921788-17-7*) Kindred Prods.

Pilgrimage of Faith of Tanzania Mennonite Church, 1934-83. Mahlon M. Hess. (Illus.). 176p. 1985. 5.00 (*0-9613368-2-X*) Estrn Mennonite Mssns.

Pilgrimage of Grace: A Study of the Rebel Armies of October 1536. Michael L. Bush. LC 95-1037. (Illus.). 280p. 1996. text 99.95 (*0-7190-4696-3*, Pub. by Manchester Univ Pr) St Martin.

Pilgrimage of Harriet Ransom's Son. Reverdy Ransom. (American Autobiography Ser.). 336p. 1995. reprint ed. lib. bdg. 89.00 (*0-7812-8622-0*) Rprt Serv.

Pilgrimage of Henry James. Van Wyck Brooks. (BCL1-PS American Literature Ser.). 170p. 1992. reprint ed. lib. bdg. 69.00 (*0-7812-6770-6*) Rprt Serv.

Pilgrimage of James. 3rd ed. George A. Jones. LC 76-27107. vii, 88p. 1977. pap. 3.00 (*0-917610-01-6*) Peacehaven.

P

An Asterisk (*) at the beginning of an entry indicates that the title is appearing for the first time.

Pilgrimage of Love, Book I. Shri Kripalvanandji. LC 81-82015. 86p. (Orig.). 1981. pap. 6.95 (*0-940258-02-1*) Kripalu Pubns.

Pilgrimage of Love, Book II. Shri Kripalvanandji. LC 81-82015. 416p. (Orig.). 1982. pap. 9.95 (*0-940258-05-6*) Kripalu Pubns.

Pilgrimage of Love: Premyatra, Bk. III. Shri Kripalvanandji. LC 81-82015. (Illus.). 136p. (Orig.). 1984. pap. 6.95 (*0-940258-12-9*) Kripalu Pubns.

Pilgrimage of Peace. Beatrice Hewitt. 114p. (C). 1989. text 39.00 (*0-946270-51-1*, Pub. by Pentland Pr) St Mut.

Pilgrimage of the Abbot Daniel in the Holy Land, 1106-1107 AD. Abbot Daniel. 1986. pap. 7.50 (*0-89981-070-5*) Eastern Orthodox.

Pilgrimage of the Heart: Finding Your Way Back to God. Bill Henegar. LC 94-41727. (Meditations Ser.). 1995. 9.99 (*0-89900-725-2*) College Pr Pub.

Pilgrimage of the Life of Man, Pts. 1-3. Guillaume De Deguileville. Ed. by F. J. Furnivall & K. B. Locock. (EETS, ES Ser.: Nos. 77, 83, & 92). 1974. reprint ed. 90.00 (*0-527-00279-8*) Periodicals Srv.

Pilgrimage of the Lyf of the Manhode. Guillaume de Deguilleville. Ed. by W. A. Wright. LC 78-178536.Tr. of Le/Pelerinage De Vie Humaine. (ENG.). xii, 250 p. 1975. reprint ed. 47.50 (*0-404-56613-8*) AMS Pr.

Pilgrimage of the Lyfe of the Manhode, Vol. I. Ed. by Avril Henry. (OS 288 Ser.: No. 288). (Illus.). (C). 1986. 59.00 (*0-19-722290-0*) OUP.

Pilgrimage of the Lyfe of the Manhode, Vol. II. Ed. by Avril Henry. (OS 292 Ser.: No. 292). 286p. 1989. 35.00 (*0-19-722294-3*) OUP.

*__Pilgrimage of the People of God, 3 vols., Set.__ Jose Barriuso. Tr. by Bertha Gonzales et al. LC 98-93444. 2000. pap. 30.00 (*0-936707-10-0*) Action Life Pubns.

*__Pilgrimage of the People of God, Vol. I.__ Jose Barriuso. Tr. by Bertha Gonzales et al from SPA. LC 98-93444. (Illus.). 2000. pap. 10.00 (*0-936707-02-X*) Action Life Pubns.

*__Pilgrimage of the People of God, Vol. II.__ Jose Barriuso. Tr. by Bertha Gonzales et al from SPA. LC 98-93444. 2000. pap. 10.00 (*0-936707-03-8*) Action Life Pubns.

*__Pilgrimage of the People of God, Vol. III.__ Jose Barriuso. Tr. by Bertha Gonzales et al. 2000. pap. 10.00 (*0-936707-09-7*) Action Life Pubns.

Pilgrimage of the Soul: A Critical Edition of the Middle English Dream Vision, Vol. I. Ed. by Rosemarie P. McGerr. (Medieval Texts Ser.: Vol. 16). 250p. 1990. text 20.00 (*0-8240-6617-0*) Garland.

Pilgrimage of Western Man. Stringfellow Barr. LC 73-21283. 369p. 1974. reprint ed. lib. bdg. 35.00 (*0-8371-6152-5*, BAPI, Greenwood Pr) Greenwood.

Pilgrimage on a Steel Ride: A Memoir about Men & Motorcycles. Gary Paulsen. LC 97-24799. 192p. 1997. 21.00 (*0-15-193093-7*) Harcourt.

Pilgrimage Pattern in Exodus. Mark S. Smith. (JSOTS Ser.: Vol. 239). 355p. 1997. 85.00 (*1-85075-652-X*, Pub. by Sheffield Acad) CUP Services.

*__Pilgrimage Road to Santiago.__ David M. Gitlitz. LC 99-89860. 464p. 2000. pap. 22.95 (*0-312-25416-4*) St Martin.

Pilgrimage through the Briar Patch: Fifty Years of Indiana Politics. Ted Sendak. 1997. 24.95 (*1-57860-054-5*); pap. 20.00 (*1-57860-007-3*) Guild Pr IN.

*__Pilgrimage through Universities.__ Charles E. Odegaard. LC 99-13655. (Illus.). 244p. 1999. 30.00 (*0-295-97760-4*) U of Wash Pr.

Pilgrimage to Al-Madinah & Meccah, Vol. 1. R. F. Burton. 488p. 1986. 350.00 (*1-85077-125-1*, Pub. by Darf Pubs Ltd) St Mut.

Pilgrimage to Al-Madinah & Meccah, Vol. 2. R. F. Burton. 512p. 1986. 350.00 (*1-85077-126-X*, Pub. by Darf Pubs Ltd) St Mut.

Pilgrimage to Al-Madinah & Meccah, Vols. 1 & 2. R. F. Burton. 1986. write for info. (*0-7855-2569-6*, Pub. by Darf Pubs Ltd) St Mut.

Pilgrimage to Beethoven & Other Essays. Richard Wagner. Tr. by William A. Ellis. LC 94-28468. xxii, 396p. 1994. pap. 15.00 (*0-8032-9763-7*, Bison Books) U of Nebr Pr.

Pilgrimage to Chimayo. Sam Howarth & Enrique R. Lamadrid. LC 98-42268. (Illus.). 80p. 1999. pap. 19.95 (*0-89013-374-3*) Museum NM Pr.

Pilgrimage to Compostela in the Middle Ages: A Book of Essays. Linda K. Davidson & Maryjane Dunn. LC 96-5338. (Medieval Casebooks Ser.: Vol. 17). (Illus.). 240p. 1996. text 39.00 (*0-8153-1638-0*, H1829) Garland.

Pilgrimage to Earth. Robert Sheckley. 1993. reprint ed. lib. bdg. 18.95 (*0-89968-362-2*, Lghtyr Pr) Buccaneer Bks.

Pilgrimage to Eternity. Muhammad Iqbal. Tr. by Shaikh Ahmad. 180p. 1985. 16.50 (*1-56744-354-0*) Kazi Pubns.

Pilgrimage to Hell. Jack Adrian. (Deathlands Ser.: No. 1). 384p. 1986. per. 4.99 (*0-373-63057-3*) Harlequin Bks.

Pilgrimage to Hell. James Axler. 1997. per. 5.99 (*0-373-48595-6*, 1-48595-2) Harlequin Bks.

Pilgrimage to Mecca: A Hajj Dairy. Dawud Ujamaa. (Illus.). 50p. 1980. pap. 4.00 (*1-884938-06-X*) Dawud Ujamma.

Pilgrimage to Mecca: The Indian Experience, 1500-1800. Michael N. Pearson. (World History Ser.). (Illus.). 296p. (C). 1996. text 42.95 (*1-55876-089-X*); pap. text 18.95 (*1-55876-090-3*) Wiener Pubs Inc.

Pilgrimage to Neid, 2 vols. Anne Blunt. (Illus.). 1968. reprint ed. 135.00 (*0-7146-1979-5*, Pub. by F Cass Pubs) Intl Spec Bk.

Pilgrimage to Nejd. Anne Blunt. 632p. 1984. 350.00 (*1-85077-016-6*, Pub. by Darf Pubs Ltd) St Mut.

Pilgrimage to Palestine. Harry E. Fosdick. Ed. by Moshe Davis. LC 77-70688. (America & the Holy Land Ser.). 1977. reprint ed. lib. bdg. 33.95 (*0-405-10247-X*) Ayer.

Pilgrimage to Parnassus. Incl. Pt. 1. Return from Parnassus. LC 77-133721. LC 77-133721. (Tudor Facsimile Texts. Old English Plays Ser.: No. 80). reprint ed. 49.50 (*0-404-53380-9*) AMS Pr.

Pilgrimage to Puritanism: History & Theology of the Marian Exiles at Geneva, 1555-1560. Dan G. Danner. LC 97-26602. (Studies in Church History: Vol. 9). 168p. (C). 1999. text 42.95 (*0-8204-3884-7*) P Lang Pubng.

*__Pilgrimage to Rome in the Middle Ages.__ Debra J. Birch. (Studies in the History of Medieval Religion: Vol. 0955-2480). 256p. 2000. pap. 24.95 (*0-85115-771-8*, Pub. by Camden Hse) Boydell & Brewer.

Pilgrimage to Russia: The Soviet Union & the Treatment of Foreigners, 1924-1937. Sylvia R. Margulies. LC 68-16062. 302p. 1968. reprint ed. pap. 93.70 (*0-608-01979-8*, 206263400003) Bks Demand.

Pilgrimage to Santiago de Compostela: A Comprehensive Annotated Bibliography. Maryjane Dunn & Linda K. Davidson. LC 94-8769. (Medieval Bibliographies Ser.: Vol. 18). (Illus.). 568p. 1994. text 20.00 (*0-8240-7220-0*, H1380) Garland.

Pilgrimage to Senegal & the Gambia, West Africa. unabridged ed. Jane B. McIntosh. LC 96-71572. (Illus.). 136p. (Orig.). (YA). (gr. 7-12). 1997. pap. 19.95 (*0-9655944-0-8*) Ninth Sign CA.

This is a true saga of some of the extraordinary experiences of two resolute African-American women who fulfilled their dreams of a Pilgrimage to their Motherland. The author writes that "On Saturday, July first, at one o'clock in the afternoon, Birdie & I boarded AIR AFRIQUE at JFK International Airport, New York, New York, USA. This flight would take us to Dakar, Senegal, West Africa." "As I looked around that cabin & basked in pride & glory, a voice inside me said, 'Jane, you are just about to fly on an airplane that is owned by Africa. The airline crew is African. You are at least part-African. And finally, your prayer is being answered. You are on your way to AFRICA.'" "On the large-screen TV monitor, we would chart our course & location during the entire flight. Off & on, I nodded or napped but for the most part, Birdie & I talked all the way across the Atlantic Ocean to our Motherland - AFRICA." Among their other experiences, several unfathomable incidents occurred which the author vividly depicts. With more than sixty photographs interpolated, she captivates her reader with her pervading passion to share their experiences with others. Thus emerged her literary production which she published, entitled, A PILGRIMAGE TO SENEGAL & THE GAMBIA, WEST AFRICA. To order: The Ninth Sign, Box 67 - 24470 Foothill Boulevard, Hayword, CA 94541-1061. Tel. (510) 317-7519. Fax. (510) 278-4706. *Publisher Paid Annotation.*

Pilgrimage to the Black Madonna: The Story of a Woman's Spiritual Journey. Barbara Groth-Mahrnet. 1994. pap. 14.95 (*0-9627961-0-7*) Red Rose Pubns.

Pilgrimage to the Ecstasy of Soul. Madhukar L. Wadikar. 1998. pap. write for info. (*1-57553-777-X*) Watermrk Pr.

Pilgrimage to the Heart of Man Through My Mercy Vol. 1: The Age of Two Hearts. unabridged ed. Josefina Maria. 274p. 1994. pap. 12.95 (*0-9634307-2-6*) MaxKol Communs.

Pilgrimage to the Holy Land. Alphorse De Lamartine. Ed. by Charles M. Lombard. LC 78-14368. 512p. 1978. reprint ed. 75.00 (*0-8201-1323-9*) Schol Facsimiles.

Pilgrimage to the Mother: A Woman's Journey to the Source of the Ganges. Alakananda Devi. LC 97-66228. (Pathwork Mandala Ser.: Vol. 1). (Illus.). 360p. 1999. pap. 17.95 (*0-9657559-0-8*) Prema Pr.

Pilgrimage to the Nejd, the Cradle of the Arab Race, 2 pts. in 1 vol. Lady A. Blunt. (Documenta Arabica Ser.). (Illus.). xlvi, 556p. 1983. reprint ed. 95.00 (*3-487-07407-9*) G Olms Pubs.

Pilgrimage to the Rebirth, Vol.1. Erlo Van Waveren. 1998. pap. 19.95 (*3-85630-571-8*) Continuum.

Pilgrimage to the Tree of Life. 2nd ed. Albert Steffen. 66p. 1978. 6.50 (*0-932776-01-9*) Adonis Pr.

Pilgrimage Yesterday & Today: Why? Where? How? J. G. Davies. 1988. 27.00 (*0-334-02254-1*) TPI PA.

*__Pilgrimage/Brokenville.__ Paul Goetzee & Philip Ridley. (Connections Ser.). (Illus.), 112p. (YA). 2000. pap. 17.95 (*0-7487-4292-1*, Pub. by S Thornes Pubs) Trans-Atl Phila.

Pilgrimages. Richard Barber. (Illus.). 168p. 1998. pap. 22.95 (*0-85115-471-9*, Boydell Pr) Boydell & Brewer.

Pilgrimages & Journeys. Katherine Prior. LC 93-16318. (Comparing Religions Ser.). (Illus.). 32p. (J). (gr. 4-8). 1993. lib. bdg. 22.83 (*1-56847-032-0*) Raintree Steck-V.

Pilgrimages to Rome & Beyond: A Guide to the Holy Places of Southern Europe for Today's Traveler. Paul L. Higgins, (Illus.). 156p. 1985. 17.95 (*0-13-676073-2*) P-H.

Pilgrimages to Rome & Beyond: A Guide to the Holy Places of Southern Europe for Today's Traveler. Paul L. Higgins. 1985. pap. 7.95 (*0-685-43293-9*) S&S Trade.

Pilgrimen Kamanita see **Pilgrim Kamanita**

Pilgrims John Evans. LC 99-176324. 188p. 1998. write for info. (*1-86023-070-9*, Pub. by Martello Bks) Irish Amer Bk.

Pilgrims' Daniel Gavron. LC 99-60636. 272p. 2000. pap. 15.95 (*0-88739-255-5*) Creat Arts Bk.

Pilgrims. Elizabeth Gilbert. 224p. 1998. pap. 12.00 (*0-395-92485-5*) HM.

Pilgrims. Susan Moger. (J). 1995. pap. 9.95 (*0-590-49787-1*) Scholastic Inc.

Pilgrims. R. Conrad Stein. LC 95-3292. (Cornerstones to Freedom Ser.). (Illus.). 32p. (J). (gr. 4-7). 1995. lib. bdg. 19.50 (*0-516-06628-5*) Childrens.

Pilgrims. R. Conrad Stein. (Cornerstones to Freedom Ser.). (Illus.). 32p. (J). (gr. 4-7). 1996. reprint ed. pap. 5.95 (*0-516-46628-3*) Childrens.

Pilgrims. Jean Valentine. LC 94-68943. (Classic Contemporaries Ser.). 64p. 1995. reprint ed. pap. 12.95 (*0-88748-206-6*) Carnegie-Mellon.

Pilgrims: Explorations in Life Science. C. Margaret Hall. LC 77-91663. 1978. 6.00 (*0-87212-083-X*) Libra.

*__Pilgrims: Sinners, Saints & Prophets.__ Marty Stuart. LC 99-38150. 1999. 29.95 (*1-55853-773-2*) Rutledge Hill Pr.

Pilgrims: The Hands-On Way to Build Reading Skills!, 1 vol. Scholastic, Inc. Staff. 1999. pap. text 7.95 (*0-439-09490-9*) Scholastic Inc.

Pilgrim's Account of Cyprus: Bars'kyj's Travels in Cyprus. Tr. by Alexander D. Grishin. (Sources for the History of Cyprus Ser.: Vol. III). (Illus.). vii, 114p. (Orig.). 1996. pap. 40.00 (*0-9651704-3-8*) Greece & Cyprus Res.

Pilgrim's Almanac: Reflections for Each Day of the Year. Edward Hays. LC 89-91470. (Illus.). 224p. 1989. pap. 10.95 (*0-939516-12-8*) Forest Peace.

Pilgrims & Pilgrimage in Ancient Greece. Matthew Dillon. LC 97-205641. 336p. (C). 1997. 70.00 (*0-415-12775-0*) Routledge.

Pilgrims & Pioneers: New England Women in the Arts. Ed. by Alicia Faxon & Sylvia Moore. LC 87-60021. (Regional Women Artists Ser.). (Illus.). 176p. (Orig.). 1987. pap. 12.00 (*0-9602476-6-1*) Midmarch Arts.

*__Pilgrims & Pocahontas: Rival Myths of American Origin.__ Ann U. Abrams. LC F68.A16 1999. (Illus.). 432p. 1999. 28.00 (*0-8133-3497-7*, Pub. by Westview) HarpC.

Pilgrims & Puritans, 1620-1676 see **Drama of American History: Group 1**

Pilgrims & Sacred Sites in China. Ed. by Susan Naquin & Chun-Fang Yu. LC 91-20671. (Studies on China: Vol. 15). 456p. (C). 1992. 60.00 (*0-520-07567-6*, Pub. by U CA Pr) Cal Prin Full Svc.

Pilgrims & Strangers on the Earth. Jim Carten. LC 94-78461. (Illus.). 240p. (Orig.). 1994. pap. 17.50 (*0-9643069-0-5*) Heretic Pr.

Pilgrims & Strangers on the Earth. limited ed. Jim Carten. (Illus.). 240p. (Orig.). 1994. 32.50 (*0-9643069-1-3*) Heretic Pr.

Pilgrims & Sultans: The Hajj under the Ottomans. Suraiya Faroqui. LC 95-62313. 256p. 1996. text 24.50 (*1-86064-033-8*, Pub. by I B T) St Martin.

Pilgrims & Their History. Roland G. Usher. (Illus.). 310p. 1977. reprint ed. 26.95 (*0-87928-082-4*) Corner Hse.

Pilgrims & Travelers to the Holy Land. Ed. by Bryan F. Le Beau & Menachem Mor. (Studies in Jewish Civilization: Vol. 7). xix, 284p. 1995. 30.00 (*1-881871-15-0*) Creighton U Pr.

Pilgrims at Heart: Scriptural Reflections Prayers & Poems. Elizabeth-Anne Vanek. 158p. 1993. pap. 7.95 (*0-9629585-3-0*, Liv Faith Pubns) Crtve Commns MO.

Pilgrims at Plymouth. Lucille R. Penner. 1996. lib. bdg. 14.99 (*0-679-93201-1*) McKay.

Pilgrims' Castle ('Atlit), David's Tower (Jerusalem) & Qal'at ar-Rabad ('Ajlun) C. N. Johns & Denys Pringle. LC 97-15947. (Collected Studies). 424p. (C). 1997. text 147.95 (*0-86078-627-7*, Pub. by Variorum) Ashgate Pub Co.

Pilgrim's Companion. Barnwell. 1993. pap. 13.95 (*1-85230-342-5*, Pub. by Element MA) Penguin Putnam.

Pilgrim's 1st Thanksgiving. Ann McGovern. (Illus.). 48p. (J). (gr. k-5). 1984. pap. 2.50 (*0-590-40617-5*) Scholastic Inc.

Pilgrims' First Thanksgiving. Ann McGovern. 32p. (J). (ps-3). 1993. pap. 3.95 (*0-590-46188-5*) Scholastic Inc.

Pilgrims' First Thanksgiving. Ann McGovern. 1993. 9.15 (*0-606-05973-3*, Pub. by Turtleback) Demco.

Pilgrim's Guide: A Gazetteer. Anne Shaver-Crandell et al. (Illus.). 424p. 1995. text 105.00 (*1-872501-65-6*) Gordon & Breach.

Pilgrim's Guide: A Gazetteer. Anne Shaver-Crandell et al. (Illus.), 424p. 1996. pap. text 28.00 (*1-872501-93-1*) Gordon & Breach.

Pilgrim's Guide: C. S. Lewis & the Art of Witness. Ed. by David Mills. 315p. 1999. pap. 16.00 (*0-8028-4689-0*) Eerdmans.

Pilgrim's Guide to 46 Temples. Shiro Usui. (Illus.). 366p. (Orig.). 1990. pap. 22.50 (*0-8348-0211-2*) Weatherhill.

Pilgrim's Guide to India. Krsna B. Swami. Ed. by Norman Komtols. (Illus.). 240p. (Orig.). 1988. pap. text. write for info. (*0-318-65939-5*) Prabhupada Inst.

Pilgrim's Guide to Lourdes: And the Surrounding Area. David Houseley & Peter Latham. (Pilgrim's Guide Ser.). (Illus.). 72p. 1991. pap. 10.00 (*0-905858-63-8*, Pub. by Egon Publishers Ltd) Pilgrim Bk Servs.

*__Pilgrim's Guide to Oberammergau & Its Passion Play.__ 4th rev. ed. David Houseley & Raymond Goodburn. (Pilgrim's Guides Ser.). (Illus.). 64p. 1999. pap. 9.00 (*0-9532511-1-X*) Pilgrim Bk Servs.

Pilgrim's Guide to Rome: For the Millennial Jubilee Year 2000. Barrett McGurn. LC 98-29027. (Illus.). 205p. 1999. 19.95 (*0-670-87627-5*) Viking Penguin.

Pilgrim's Guide to Rome & The Holyland: For the Third Millennium. Aurelie A. Hagstrom. 160p. 1999. pap. 14.95 (*0-88347-440-9*, Pub. by T More) BookWorld.

Pilgrim's Guide to Santiago de Compostela. William Melczer. LC 93-18623. (Historical Travel Ser.). (Illus.). 368p. (Orig.). 1993. pap. 20.00 (*0-934977-25-9*) Italica Pr.

Pilgrim's Guide to Santiago de Compostela Vol. I: A Critical Edition, 2 vols., Vols. I & II. Alison Stones et al. (Illus.). 560p. 1998. text 125.00 (*0-905203-52-6*) Gordon & Breach.

Pilgrim's Guide to the Holy Land. Werner Linz. (Illus.). 224p. 1998. text 17.95 (*0-670-87749-2*) Viking Penguin.

*__Pilgrim's Guide to the Holy Land: Israel & Jordan.__ 2nd rev. ed. David Houseley & Raymond Goodburn. (Pilgrim's Guides Ser.). (Illus.). 96p. 1998. pap. 10.00 (*0-9532511-0-1*) Pilgrim Bk Servs.

Pilgrim's Guide to the Holy Land for Orthodox Christians. Holy Nativity Convent Staff. LC 97-68989. (Illus.). 188p. 1997. pap. 22.00 (*0-913026-46-8*) St Nectarios.

Pilgrim's Harbor. Floyd Skloot. 200p. (Orig.). 1992. pap. 14.95 (*0-934257-71-X*) Story Line.

Pilgrims in a New Land. Lee M. Friedman. LC 78-26208. (Illus.). 471p. 1979. reprint ed. lib. bdg. 75.00 (*0-313-20877-8*, FRPI, Greenwood Pr) Greenwood.

Pilgrims in a Strange Land: Hausa Communities in Chad. John A. Works, Jr. LC 76-23138. 1976. text 64.50 (*0-231-03976-X*) Col U Pr.

Pilgrims in Aztlan. Miguel Mendez. Tr. by David W. Foster. LC 92-23636. 184p. 1992. 25.00 (*0-927534-22-3*); pap. 15.00 (*0-927534-23-1*) Biling Rev-Pr.

Pilgrims in Hindu Holy Land. Geoffrey Waring Maw. Ed. by Gillian M. Conacher & Marjorie Sykes. 176p. 1999. pap. 23.00 (*1-85072-190-4*, Pub. by W Sessions) St Mut.

Pilgrims in Lotus Land: Conservative Protestantism in British Columbia, 1917-1981. Robert K. Burkinshaw. LC 95-235185. (McGill-Queen's Studies in the History of Religion Ser.). 376p. 1995. 55.00 (*0-7735-1286-1*, Pub. by McG-Queens Univ Pr) CUP Services.

Pilgrims in Progress: Growing Through Groups. Jim Plueddemann & Carol Plueddemann. 176p. (Orig.). 1990. pap. 8.99 (*0-87788-647-4*, H Shaw Pubs) Waterbrook Pr.

*__Pilgrims in Rome: Prepared by the Vatican Committee for the Jubilee Year 2000.__ Vatican Committee for the Jubilee Year 2000. LC 99-29745. (Illus.). 240p. 1999. pap. 15.95 (*0-8264-1187-8*) Continuum.

*__Pilgrims in the Rough: St. Andrews Beyong the 19th Hole.__ Michael Tobert. (Illus.). 188p. 2000. pap. 14.95 (*0-946487-74-X*, Pub. by Luath Pr Ltd) Midpt Trade.

Pilgrims in Their Own Land. Martin E. Marty. 512p. 1985. pap. 15.95 (*0-14-008268-9*, Penguin Bks) Viking Penguin.

Pilgrims in This World: A Lay Spirituality. Virginia S. Finn. LC 89-78458. 320p. 1990. pap. 12.95 (*0-8091-3144-7*) Paulist Pr.

Pilgrim's Inn. Elizabeth Goudge. Orig. Title: The Herb of Grace. 352p. Date not set. 25.95 (*0-8488-2625-6*) Amereon Ltd.

Pilgrim's Journey. Loxia Hipsky. 188p. 1998. pap. 10.00 (*0-7392-0042-9*, PO2819) Morris Pubng.

Pilgrim's New Guide to the Holy Land. 2nd ed. Stephen C. Doyle. 1999. pap. text 14.95 (*0-8146-5955-1*) Liturgical Pr.

Pilgrim's Notebook: An Experience of Religious Life. David A. Fleming. LC 91-21488. 103p. reprint ed. pap. 32.00 (*0-608-20250-9*, 207150900012) Bks Demand.

Pilgrims of 48. Josephine Goldmark. LC 74-27989. (Modern Jewish Experience Ser.). (Illus.). 1975. reprint ed. 31.95 (*0-405-06716-X*) Ayer.

Pilgrims of Plimoth. Marcia Sewall. LC 86-3362. (Illus.). 48p. (J). (gr. 2 up). 1986. 15.95 (*0-689-31250-4*) Atheneum Yung Read.

Pilgrims of Plimoth. Marcia Sewall. (J). (gr. 2). 1996. mass mkt. 5.99 (*0-689-80861-5*) S&S Childrens.

Pilgrims of Plimoth. Marcia Sewall. LC 86-3362. (J). 1996. 11.19 (*0-606-10284-1*, Pub. by Turtleback) Demco.

*__Pilgrims of Plymouth__ Susan E. Goodman. LC 98-51320. 1999. write for info. (*0-7922-9424-6*) Natl Geog.

*__Pilgrims of Plymouth.__ Susan E. Goodman. LC 98-51320. 1999. write for info. (*0-7922-9429-7*) Natl Geog.

Pilgrims of the Lonely Road. Gaius G. Atkins. LC 67-28741. (Essay Index Reprint Ser.). 1977. 20.95 (*0-8369-0162-2*) Ayer.

Pilgrims of the Prairie. Andrew Dubovy. Tr. by Marie H. Bloch from UKR. write for info. (*0-318-57394-6*) Ukrainian Cult Inst.

Pilgrims of the Prairie: Pioneer Ukrainian Baptists in North Dakota. Andrew Dubovy. Ed. by Marie H. Bloch. (Illus.). 72p. (Orig.). 1983. pap. 4.50 (*0-317-00667-3*); lib. bdg. 8.50 (*0-317-00666-5*) Ukrainian Cult Inst.

Pilgrims of the Rhine (1840) Edward Bulwer Lytton. 116p. 1999. reprint ed. pap. 12.95 (*0-7661-0786-8*) Kessinger Pub.

Pilgrims of the Thames in Search of the National! Pierce Egan. LC 79-8261. reprint ed. 44.50 (*0-404-61842-1*) AMS Pr.

Pilgrims on the Ice: Robert Falcon Scott's First Antarctic Expedition. T. H. Baughman. LC 99-20685. (Illus.). 360p. 1999. text 45.00 (*0-8032-1289-5*) U of Nebr Pr.

Pilgrims on the Ohio: The River Journey & Photographs of Reuben Gold Thwaites, 1894. Robert L. Reid & Dan H. Fuller. LC 97-24067. (Illus.). vii, 105p. 1997. pap. 29.95 (*0-87195-118-5*) Ind Hist Soc.

Pilgrim's Path, 3 vols. deluxe ed. Irina Starr. 1991. 65.00 (*0-930596-08-0*) Pilgrims Path.

Pilgrim's Path, 3 vols., Vol. I. deluxe ed. Irina Starr. 240p. 1991. 25.95 (*0-930596-05-6*) Pilgrims Path.

Pilgrim's Path, 3 vols., Vol. II. deluxe ed. Irina Starr. 152p. 1991. 15.95 (*0-930596-06-4*) Pilgrims Path.

Pilgrim's Path, 3 vols., Vol. III. deluxe ed. Irina Starr. 256p. 1991. 25.95 (*0-930596-07-2*) Pilgrims Path.

Pilgrim's Path: Freemasonry & the Religious Right. John J. Robinson. LC 93-9178. 192p. 1993. 17.95 (*0-87131-732-X*) M Evans.

Pilgrim's Pride 50th Anniversary, 1946-1996: The 1st 50 Years. Dick White. (Illus.). 56p. 1996. write for info. (*0-9637402-1-0*); pap. write for info. (*0-9637402-3-7*) Brown Comm.

Pilgrim's Profession. fac. ed. Thomas Taylor. LC 94-38459. 236p. 1995. 50.00 (*0-8201-1492-8*) Schol Facsimiles.

Pilgrim's Progress see Pilgrim's Progress in Modern English

Pilgrim's Progress. John Bunyan. 384p. 1993. mass mkt. 2.49 (*1-55748-345-0*) Barbour Pub.

Pilgrim's Progress. John Bunyan. (Essential Christian Library Ser.). 432p. 1998. 9.97 (*1-57748-262-X*) Barbour Pub.

***Pilgrim's Progress.** John Bunyan. (Deluxe Christian Classics). 304p. 2000. 9.97 (*1-57748-916-0*) Barbour Pub.

Pilgrim's Progress. John Bunyan. Ed. & Intro. by N. H. Keeble. LC 99-192015. (Oxford World's Classics Ser.). 336p. 1998. pap. 7.95 (*0-19-283400-2*) OUP.

Pilgrim's Progress. John Bunyan. 400p. 1981. mass mkt. 6.99 (*0-88368-096-3*) Whitaker Hse.

Pilgrim's Progress. John Bunyan. LC 99-19873. (Nelson's Royal Classic Ser.: Vol. 1). 320p. 1999. 18.99 (*0-7852-4222-8*) Nelson.

***Pilgrim's Progress.** John Bunyan. (Classics of World Literature Ser.). 1998. pap. 5.95 (*1-85326-468-7*, 4687WW, Pub. by Wrdsworth Edits) NTC Contemp Pub Co.

Pilgrims Progress. John Bunyan. 384p. 1998. pap. 3.97 incl. audio (*0-916441-24-5*) Barbour Pub.

Pilgrim's Progress. John Bunyan. Ed. by Hal M. Helms. LC 81-85770. (Living Library). (Illus.). 268p. 1982. pap. 12.95 (*0-941478-02-5*, 930-033, Pub. by Paraclete MA) BookWorld.

Pilgrim's Progress. Cheryl Ford. 1999. pap. 13.99 (*0-8423-5145-0*) Tyndale Hse.

Pilgrims Progress. Monica Furlong. (Element Classics of World Spirituality Ser.). 304p. 1997. pap. 19.95 (*1-85230-918-0*, Pub. by Element MA) Penguin Putnam.

Pilgrim's Progress. Gary D. Schmidt. LC 94-8798. (Illus.). 88p. (YA). (gr. 5 up). 1994. 20.00 (*0-8028-5080-4*, Eerdmans Bks) Eerdmans.

Pilgrim's Progress. Mack Thomas. LC 96-15031. 64p. 1996. 14.99 (*0-88070-917-0*, Gold n Honey) Zondervan.

Pilgrim's Progress. Ralph Vaughan Williams. 1968. 2.25 (*0-19-339227-5*) OUP.

***Pilgrim's Progress.** deluxe ed. Emerald House Group Inc., Staff. 1999. 29.99 (*1-889893-41-2*) Emerald House Group Inc.

Pilgrim's Progress. unabridged ed. John Bunyan. (Illus.). 379p. 1992. pap. 9.99 (*0-907927-74-2*) Emerald House Group Inc.

Pilgrim's Progress: A Modern-Day Abridgement for Today's Reader. John Bunyan. (Little Library Ser.). 48p. 1995. pap. text 0.99 (*1-55748-648-4*) Barbour Pub.

***Pilgrim's Progress: A Spiritual Guide for the Holy Land Traveler.** Robert A. Wallace & Gwynneth Wallace. LC 99-54012. 104p. 2000. pap. 9.95 (*0-664-50127-3*, Pub. by Westminster John Knox) Presbyterian Pub.

Pilgrim's Progress: A Study of the Short Stories of Hugh Hood. Susan Copoloff-Mechanic. 161p. (C). 1988. text 25.00 (*1-55022-001-2*, Pub. by ECW); pap. text 15.00 (*1-55022-000-4*, Pub. by ECW) Genl Dist Srvs.

Pilgrim's Progress: Boston. Alan Champion. (C). 1989. text 35.00 (*0-902662-40-6*, Pub. by R K Pubns); pap. text 21.00 (*0-902662-41-4*, Pub. by R K Pubns) St Mut.

Pilgrim's Progress: John Bunyan's Immortal Allegory (Condensed & Adapted for Coloring) John Bunyan. Ed. & Intro. by Cantelon House Publishers Staff. 174p. (YA). (gr. 6-12). 1994. pap. text 19.95 (*0-9642116-0-2*) Cantelon Hse.

Pilgrims' Progress: Letters about the First Time Soupy & Huldah Confronted Europe. Franklin Jones, Sr. LC 87-32786. (Hindsight Saga Ser.). (Illus.). 160p. 1988. 29.95 (*0-915433-15-X*) Packrat WA.

Pilgrim's Progress: One Man's Search for Eternal Life - a Christian Allegory. John Bunyan. 23.95 (*0-8488-0141-5*) Amereon Ltd.

Pilgrim's Progress: One Man's Search for Eternal Life - a Christian Allegory. John Bunyan. Ed. by Dan Larsen. (Young Reader's Christian Library). (Illus.). 224p. (J). (gr. 4-8). 1989. pap. text 1.39 (*1-55748-099-0*) Barbour Pub.

Pilgrim's Progress: One Man's Search for Eternal Life - a Christian Allegory. John Bunyan. 1976. lib. bdg. 26.95 (*0-89968-156-5*, Lghtyr Pr) Buccaneer Bks.

Pilgrim's Progress: One Man's Search for Eternal Life - a Christian Allegory. John Bunyan. (Classics Ser.). mass mkt. 4.99 (*0-8024-0012-4*, 392) Moody.

Pilgrim's Progress: One Man's Search for Eternal Life - a Christian Allegory. John Bunyan. 1964. mass mkt. 5.95 (*0-451-52399-7*, CE1813, Sig Classics) NAL.

Pilgrim's Progress: One Man's Search for Eternal Life - a Christian Allegory. John Bunyan. Ed. by Roger Sharrock. 384p. 1965. pap. 7.99 (*0-14-043004-0*, Penguin Classics) Viking Penguin.

Pilgrim's Progress: One Man's Search for Eternal Life - a Christian Allegory. John Bunyan. 304p. (gr. 11). 1989. mass mkt. 5.99 (*0-8007-8609-2*, Spire) Revell.

Pilgrim's Progress: One Man's Search for Eternal Life - a Christian Allegory. large type ed. John Bunyan. 416p. 1982. 27.99 (*0-7089-8072-4*, Charnwood) Ulverscroft.

Pilgrim's Progress: One Man's Search for Eternal Life - a Christian Allegory. John Bunyan. 1979. reprint ed. 35.99 (*0-85151-259-3*) Banner of Truth.

Pilgrim's Progress: One Man's Search for Eternal Life - a Christian Allegory. John Bunyan. 256p. 1973. reprint ed. pap. 3.95 (*0-310-22142-0*, 6610S) Zondervan.

Pilgrim's Progress: The Ecclesiastical History of the Old Colony. J. M. Bumsted. (Outstanding Studies in Early American History). 407p. 1989. reprint ed. 25.00 (*0-8240-6174-8*) Garland.

Pilgrim's Progress Devotional: A Daily Journey Through the Christian Life. Cheryl V. Ford. LC 98-20709. 384p. 1998. 19.99 (*1-58134-030-3*) Crossway Bks.

Pilgrim's Progress from This World to That Which Is to Come. John Bunyan. (BCL1-PR English Literature Ser.). 352p. 1992. reprint ed. lib. bdg. 89.00 (*0-7812-7326-9*) Rprt Serv.

Pilgrim's Progress Illustrated see Progreso Del Peregrino Ilustrado

Pilgrim's Progress in Modern English. rev. ed. John Bunyan. Ed. by L. Edward Hazelbaker. LC 98-72704. Orig. Title: The Pilgrim's Progress. (Illus.). 450p. 1998. pap. 12.99 (*0-88270-757-4*, Bridge) Bridge-Logos.

Pilgrim's Progress in Today's English see Peregrino: El en un Castellano Actualizado

Pilgrim's Progress in Today's English. John Bunyan. 1964. pap. 8.99 (*0-8024-6520-X*) Moody.

Pilgrim's Progress in Today's English. John Bunyan & James H. Thomas. 1999. lib. bdg. 23.95 (*1-56723-201-9*) Yestermorrow.

***Pilgrim's Progress Journal.** (Illus.). 136p. 2000. pap. 12.99 (*1-889893-44-7*, Ambassador-Emerald) Emerald House Group Inc.

Pilgrim's Progress (1902) John Bunyan. 466p. 1998. reprint ed. pap. 29.95 (*0-7661-0600-4*) Kessinger Pub.

Pilgrim's Progress Notes. George F. Willison. (Cliffs Notes Ser.). 104p. 1968. pap. 4.95 (*0-8220-1030-5*, Cliff) IDG Bks.

***Pilgrim's Progress Primer.** large type ed. William C. Nichols & Mary Godolphin. 104p. 1999. pap. 15.95 (*1-892838-03-6*) Internat Outreach.

Pilgrim's Progress, Puritan Progress: Discourses & Contexts. Kathleen M. Swaim. 408p. (C). 1993. text 44.95 (*0-252-01894-X*) U of Ill Pr.

Pilgrim's Progress (Retold for Children) Laurence Morris. (J). (gr. 1-5). 1993. mass mkt. 5.99 (*0-87508-747-7*) Chr Lit.

Pilgrim's Progress Study Guide. Maureen L. Bradley. 128p. (Orig.). 1994. pap. 6.99 (*0-87552-108-8*) P & R Pubng.

Pilgrims Promise. Bryan Cutshall. LC 98-65572. 216p. 1998. pap. 9.99 (*0-87148-987-2*) Pathway Pr.

***Pilgrims, Puritans & Cavaliers: From Hunger to Feasting.** Patricia B. Mitchell. 1999. pap. 4.00 (*0-925117-96-X*) Mitchells.

Pilgrims Regress: An Allegorical Apology for Christianity, Reason, & Romanticism. C. S. Lewis. 219p. 1992. pap. 14.00 (*0-8028-0641-4*) Eerdmans.

Pilgrim's Rest. Patricia Wentworth. 25.95 (*0-88411-721-9*) Amereon Ltd.

Pilgrim's Road. large type ed. Bettina Selby. (Illus.). 1995. 27.99 (*0-7089-3299-1*) Ulverscroft.

Pilgrim's Song: Selected Poems to Mark the Poet's 100th Birthday. Geoffrey Dearmer. 82p. 1994. 29.95 (*0-7195-5242-7*, Pub. by John Murray) Trafalgar.

Pilgrim's Tale. Ed. by Aleksei Pentkovsky. Tr. by T. Allan Smith from RUS. LC 99-35236. (Classics of Western Spirituality Ser.: No. 90). 176p. 1999. pap. 19.95 (*0-8091-3709-7*) Paulist Pr.

Pilgrim's Tale. Ed. by Aleksei Pentkovsky. Tr. by T. Allan Smith from RUS. LC 99-35236. (Classics of Western Spirituality Ser.: No. 91). 176p. 1999. 28.95 (*0-8091-0486-5*) Paulist Pr.

Pilgrim's Testament: The Memoirs of St. Ignatius of Loyola. Tr. by Parmananda R. Divarkar from ITA. LC 95-60352. (Jesuit Primary Sources in English Translation Ser.: Vol. 13). (Illus.). xxx, 150p. (Orig.). 1995. pap. 14.25 (*1-880810-09-3*) Inst Jesuit.

Pilgrims Through Space & Time: Trends & Patterns in Scientific & Utopian Fiction. James O. Bailey. LC 76-38126. 341p. 1972. reprint ed. lib. bdg. 69.50 (*0-8371-6323-4*, BAPS, Greenwood Pr) Greenwood.

***Pilgrims to the Light: Encounters in a Shared Destiny.** Ed. by Valson Thampu. 148p. 2000. 18.00 (*81-241-0643-6*, Pub. by Har-Anand Pubns) Nataraj Bks.

Pilgrims to the Wild: Everett Ruess, Henry David Thoreau, John Muir, Clarence King, Mary Austin. John P. O'Grady. LC 92-29783. 184p. (Orig.). 1993. pap. 16.95 (*0-87480-412-4*) U of Utah Pr.

Pilgrim's Way. John Buchan. (Illus.). 352p. 1984. pap. 10.95 (*0-88184-107-2*) Carroll & Graf.

***Pilgrim's Way.** Christopher Martin. 64p. 2000. pap. 6.50 (*1-85311-251-8*) Canterbury Press Norwich.

Pilgrim's Way. Walter C. Righter. LC 97-49461. 1999. pap. 11.00 (*0-679-77655-9*) Knopf.

Pilgrim's Way. Walter C. Righter. LC 97-49461. 192p. 1998. 22.00 (*0-679-45442-X*) Knopf.

Pilgrim's Way: An Essay in Recollection. John Buchan. LC 76-6591. (BCL Ser. II). reprint ed. 41.50 (*0-404-15278-3*) AMS Pr.

***Pilgrim's Way: From Winchester to Canterbury.** Christopher Martin. 2000. pap. text. write for info. (*5-550-02611-2*) Nairi.

Pilgrim's Way from Winchester to Canterbury. Julia M. Ady. LC 71-158231. reprint ed. 34.50 (*0-404-01399-6*) AMS Pr.

Pilgrims Way Guide: A Week's Walk in Kent. Richard Hayward. (British Footpath Guides Ser.: No. 3). (Illus.). 100p. 1995. pap. 8.95 (*1-880848-13-9*) Brit Footpaths.

Pilier. Yachar Kemal. (Au-Dela de la Montagne Ser.: No. I). (FRE.). 1977. pap. 12.95 (*0-7859-2392-6*, 2070369579) Fr & Eur.

Piling: European Practice & Worldwide Trends: Proceedings of a Conference Organized by the Institution of Civil Engineers, London, England, April 7-9, 1992. Ed. by M. J. Sands. 349p. 1993. 119.00 (*0-7277-1698-0*) Am Soc Civil Eng.

Piling & Deep Foundations: Proceedings of the 3rd International Conference, London, 15-18 May 1989. Ed. by J. B. Burland & J. M. Mitchell. 700p. (C). 1989. text 304.00 (*90-6191-889-8*, Pub. by A A Balkema) Ashgate Pub Co.

Piling & Deep Foundations: Proceedings of the 4th International Conference, Stresa, Italy, April 1991, 2 vols. Ed. by R. Quieti. (Illus.). 1000p. (C). 1991. text 304.00 (*90-6191-185-0*, Pub. by A A Balkema) Ashgate Pub Co.

Piling & Deep Foundations 3rd Edition, Vol. 1. 155.00 (*90-6191-887-1*) Ashgate Pub Co.

Piling & Deep Foundations 3rd Edition, Vol. 2. 1991. 155.00 (*90-6191-888-X*) Ashgate Pub Co.

Piling & Deep Foundations 4th Edition, Vol. 1. 1989. 155.00 (*90-6191-196-6*) Ashgate Pub Co.

Piling & Deep Foundations 4th Edition, Vol. 2. Deep Foundations Ins. Staff. 1994. 155.00 (*90-6191-197-4*) Ashgate Pub Co.

Piling & Ground Treatment: Proceedings of a Conference Organized by the Institution of Civil Engineers. 297p. 1984. 67.00 (*0-7277-0185-1*, Pub. by T Telford) RCH.

Piling Engineering. 2nd ed. W. G. Fleming et al. 390p. 1991. text 149.95 (*0-470-21825-8*) Halsted Pr.

Piling in Rock. Joram M. Amir. 112p. (C). 1986. text 123.00 (*90-6191-586-4*, Pub. by A A Balkema) Ashgate Pub Co.

Piling up the Ricks: A Sequel to Beyond Affection. Peter Kavanagh. LC 88-91434. 1989. 50.00 (*0-914612-12-3*) Kavanagh.

Pilipino-English - English-Pilipino Concise Dictionary. Sam Bickford. 389p. 1989. pap. 8.95 (*0-87052-491-7*) Hippocrene Bks.

Pilipino-English - English-Pilipino Dictionary & Phrasebook. Raymond P. Barrager & Jesusa V. Salvador. (ENG & TAG.). 120p. 1996. pap. 11.95 (*0-7818-0451-5*) Hippocrene Bks.

Pilipino (Tagalog) Language Survival Kit. 2nd ed. Violetta Lorenzana. LC 99-168067. (Illus.). 200p. 1998. pap. 5.95 (*0-86442-432-9*) Lonely Planet.

Pilipino Through Self-Instruction, 4 vols. John U. Wolff et al. (Orig.). 1991. pap. text 60.00 (*0-87727-524-6*) Cornell SE Asia.

Pilipino Through Self-Instruction, 4 vols., Vol. 1. John U. Wolff et al. (Orig.). 1991. pap. text 18.00 (*0-87727-525-4*) Cornell SE Asia.

Pilipino Through Self-Instruction, 4 vols., Vol. 2. John U. Wolff et al. (Orig.). 1991. pap. text 18.00 (*0-87727-526-2*) Cornell SE Asia.

Pilipino Through Self-Instruction, 4 vols., Vol. 3. John U. Wolff et al. (Orig.). 1991. pap. text 18.00 (*0-87727-527-0*) Cornell SE Asia.

Pilipino Through Self-Instruction, 4 vols., Vol. 4. John U. Wolff et al. (Orig.). 1991. pap. text 18.00 (*0-87727-528-9*) Cornell SE Asia.

Pilkington's Royal/Ancastrian Pottery & Tiles. A. J. Cross. (Illus.). 93p. 1980. 75.00 (*0-903685-08-6*, Pub. by R Dennis) Antique Collect.

Pill. John Guillebaud. (Illus.). 1980. pap. 9.95 (*0-19-286002-X*) OUP.

***Pill & I.** Djerassi. 2000. 28.00 (*0-465-01657-X*, Pub. by Basic); pap. 14.00 (*0-465-01658-8*, Pub. by Basic) HarpC.

Pill Book. Harold M. Silverman. 1995. mass mkt. 8.99 (*0-553-85155-1*) Bantam.

Pill Book. 6th ed. Harold M. Silverman. 1995. mass mkt. 8.99 (*0-553-85146-2*) Bantam.

Pill Book. 7th ed. Harold M. Silverman. 1996. mass mkt. 8.99 (*0-553-85109-8*) Bantam.

Pill Book. 8th ed. Harold M. Silverman. 1248p. 1998. mass mkt. 25.95 (*0-553-57926-6*) Bantam.

Pill Book: The Illustrated Guide to the Most-Prescribed Drugs in the United States. 8th rev. ed. Harold Silver. LC 98-184440. (Illus.). 1248p. 1998. pap. 25.95 (*0-553-37960-7*) Bantam.

***Pill Book: The Illustrated Guide to the Most-Prescribed Drugs in the United States.** 9th expanded rev. ed. Ed. by Harold M. Silverman. (Illus.). 1248p. 2000. mass mkt. 6.99 (*0-553-57974-6*) Bantam.

***Pill Book: The Illustrated Guide to the Most-Prescribed Drugs in the United States.** 9th rev. exp. ed. Harold M. Silverman. (Illus.). 1248p. 2000. pap. 25.95 (*0-553-37964-X*, Spectra) Bantam.

Pill Book Guide to Children's Medications. 2nd rev. ed. Michael D. Mitchell. 320p. 1990. mass mkt. 6.50 (*0-553-56927-9*) Bantam.

Pill Book Guide to Medication for Your Dog & Cat. Ed. by Bantam Books Inc. Editors. LC 99-159362. 624p. 1998. mass mkt. 6.99 (*0-553-57989-4*) Bantam.

Pill Book Guide to over the Counter Medications. Robert Rapp. LC 98-105756. 1120p. 1997. mass mkt. 6.99 (*0-553-57729-8*) Bantam.

Pill Boxes on the Western Front: A Guide to the Design, Construction & Use of Concrete Pill Boxes, 1914-1918. Peter Oldham. (Illus.). 208p. 1995. 31.95 (*0-85052-418-0*, Pub. by Leo Cooper) Trans-Atl Phila.

Pill Bug's Life. John Himmelman. LC 99-30137. (Nature Upclose Ser.). 32p. (J). (gr. k-2). 1999. 24.00 (*0-516-21165-X*) Childrens.

***Pill Bug's Life.** John Himmelman. (Nature Upclose Ser.). (J). 2000. pap. text 6.95 (*0-516-26798-1*) Childrens.

Pill Hill. Samuel L. Kelly. 1995. 5.60 (*0-87129-492-3*, P35) Dramatic Pub.

Pill Mills, Medicaid Fraud & the Diversion of Pharmaceuticals. 1994. lib. bdg. 248.75 (*0-8490-5699-3*) Gordon Pr.

Pill Peddlers: Essays on the History of the Pharmaceutical Industry. Ed. by Jonathan Liebenau et al. 133p. (Orig.). (C). 1990. pap. 10.95 (*0-931292-22-0*) Am Inst Hist Pharm.

Pill, Pygmy Chimps, & Degas' Horse: The Remarkable Autobiography of the Award-Winning Scientist Who Synthesized the Pill. Carl Djerassi. LC 91-58599. (Illus.). 336p. 1993. reprint ed. pap. 16.00 (*0-465-05758-6*, Pub. by Basic) HarpC.

Pillage of the 3rd World. Pierre Jalee. LC 68-13069. 128p. 1969. pap. 10.00 (*0-85345-118-4*, Pub. by Monthly Rev) NYU Pr.

Pillaging the Empire: Piracy in the Americas, 1500-1750. Kris E. Lane. LC 97-32619. (Latin American Realities Ser.). 264p. (C). 1998. 61.95 (*0-7656-0256-3*) M E Sharpe.

Pillaging the Empire: Piracy in the Americas, 1500-1750. Kris E. Lane. LC 97-32619. (Latin American Realities Ser.). (Illus.). 264p. (gr. 13). 1998. pap. 21.95 (*0-7656-0257-1*) M E Sharpe.

Pillar & Ground of the Truth. I. P. Florenski. Tr. by Boris Jakim. LC 96-45564. 624p. 1997. text 49.50 (*0-691-03243-2*, Pub. by Princeton U Pr) Cal Prin Full Svc.

Pillar of Celestial Fire. Robert Cox. Ed. by Tom Stanley. LC 97-66694. (Illus.). 230p. 1997. pap. 18.95 (*1-887472-30-4*) Sunstar Pubng.

Pillar of Cloud. Francis Stuart. 234p. 1994. pap. 14.95 (*1-874597-09-X*) Dufour.

Pillar of Fire. Judith Tarr. 448p. 1995. 23.95 (*0-312-85542-7*) Tor Bks.

Pillar of Fire. Judith Tarr. 1997. mass mkt. 6.99 (*0-8125-3903-6*, Pub. by Tor Bks) St Martin.

Pillar of Fire. Shaindel Weinbach. 1992. 15.99 (*0-89906-847-2*) Mesorah Pubns.

Pillar of Fire. S. Wienbach. 1992. pap. 12.99 (*0-89906-848-0*) Mesorah Pubns.

Pillar of Fire: America in the King Years, 1963-65. Taylor Branch. (Illus.). 768p. 1999. pap. 17.00 (*0-684-84809-0*, Touchstone) S&S Trade Pap.

Pillar of Fire: America in the King Years, 1963-65. Taylor Branch. LC 97-46076. (Illus.). 746p. 1998. 29.50 (*0-684-80819-6*) Scribner.

***Pillar of Fire: Selected Poems.** Nikolai Gumilyov. (Orig.). 1999. pap. 23.95 (*0-85646-310-8*, Pub. by Anvil Press) Dufour.

Pillar of Fire to Follow: American Indian Dramas, 1808-1859. Priscilla F. Sears. LC 81-85523. 149p. (C). 1982. 12.95 (*0-87972-193-6*); pap. 6.95 (*0-87972-194-4*) Bowling Green Univ Popular Press.

Pillar of Salt: A Novel. Albert Memmi. LC 91-16952. 352p. 1992. reprint ed. pap. 16.00 (*0-8070-8327-5*) Beacon Pr.

Pillar of Salt: Gender, Memory, & the Perils of Looking Back. Janice Haaken. LC 97-45761. 336p. (C). 1998. 26.00 (*0-8135-2524-1*) Rutgers U Pr.

***Pillar of Salt: Gender, Memory, & the Perils of Looking Back.** Janice Haaken. 336p. 2000. pap. 22.00 (*0-8135-2837-2*) Rutgers U Pr.

***Pillar of Salt: It All Began with Mona.** Leroy B. Inman. (Illus.). 320p. 1999. pap. 14.95 (*0-9655076-2-9*) South Fork Pr.

Pillar of Sand: Can the Irrigation Miracle Last? Sandra Postel. 320p. 1999. pap. 13.95 (*0-393-31937-7*) Norton.

Pillar of the Constitution. Ed. by C. Jones. 256p. 1989. 55.00 (*1-85285-007-8*) Hambledon Press.

***Pillar of the Sky.** Cecelia Holland. 544p. 2000. pap. 14.95 (*0-312-86887-1*) Forge NYC.

Pillar Power. Ronald E. Bell & Mark Andrews. (Illus.). 14p. 1998. pap. text. write for info. (*1-892664-02-X*) Moves Pubg.

Pillar Stability in Large Underground Openings: Applications from a Case Study in Competent, Jointed Rock. J. F. Agapito. Ed. by Jon W. Raese. (Colorado School of Mines Quarterly Ser.: Vol. 81 No. 3 1986). (Illus.). 90p. 1986. pap. text 17.00 (*0-918062-70-5*) Colo Sch Mines.

Pillarization. Post. 1989. 82.95 (*0-566-07026-X*) Ashgate Pub Co.

Pillars: The Coming Crisis in Canada's Finance Industry. Michael Babad & Catherine Mulroney. 240p. 1993. 24.95 (*0-7737-2743-4*) Genl Dist Srvs.

Pillars: The 10 Commandments Still Standing after Centuries of Change. Randel Everett. LC 94-70698. 128p. 1994. 12.95 (*0-9637647-5-6*) Ardara Hse.

Pillars in Ethiopian History: The William Leo Hansberry African History Notebook, Vol. I. Ed. by Joseph E. Harris. LC 73-88970. 1981. pap. 11.95 (*0-88258-090-6*) Howard U Pr.

Pillars of Apartheid: Land Tenure, Rural Planning & the Chieftancy. Fred T. Hendricks. (Studia Sociologica Upsaliensia: No. 32). 187p. (Orig.). 1990. pap. 42.50 (*91-554-2650-6*) Coronet Bks.

Pillars of Balam. Daniel Johnson. 1998. mass mkt. 5.99 (*1-55262-008-5*) Picasso Publ.

Pillars of Catholic Social Teaching: A Brief Social Catechism. Perry J. Roets. LC 98-13910. 136p. 1999. pap. 25.50 (*1-57309-228-2*, Cath Scholar Pr) Intl Scholars.

Pillars of Christian Character: The Basic Essentials of a Living Faith. John F. MacArthur. LC 98-16146. 192p. 1998. pap. 10.99 (*0-89107-950-5*) Crossway Bks.

Pillars of Economic Understanding: Ideas & Traditions. Ed. by Mark Perlman & Charles R. McCann, Jr. LC 98-8953. 680p. 1998. text 79.50 (*0-472-10907-3*, 10907) U of Mich Pr.

***Pillars of Economic Understanding: The Factor Markets.** Mark Perlman & Charles R. McCann. LC 99-53550. (Illus.). 400p. (C). 2000. text 79.50 (*0-472-11110-8*, 11110) U of Mich Pr.

Pillars of Eternity: Time & Providence in the Faerie Queene. Ian McCabe. 256p. 1989. 14.95 (*0-7165-2428-7*, Pub. by Irish Acad Pr) Intl Spec Bk.

Pillars of Faith. Brian J. Bailey. 147p. 1995. pap. 10.00 (*0-9630837-9-1*) Zion Christ.

Pillars of Fire. Steve Shagan. Ed. by Bill Gross. 384p. 1990. reprint ed. mass mkt. 5.95 (*0-671-68938-X*) PB.

P

An Asterisk (*) at the beginning of an entry indicates that the title is appearing for the first time.

Pillars of Fire: The Battle of Messines Ridge 1917. Ian Passingham. LC 99-193844. 1999. 39.99 (*0-7509-1704-0*) Bks Intl VA.

***Pillars of Gold.** Alice Thomas Ellis. 200p. 2000. 22.95 (*1-55921-284-5*, Pub. by Moyer Bell) Publishers Group.

Pillars of Gold & Silver. Beatriz De la Garza. LC 97-22161. 260p. (YA). (gr. 5 up). 1997. pap. 9.95 (*1-55885-206-9*, Pinata Bks) Arte Publico.

Pillars of Hercules: A Grand Tour of the Mediterranean. Paul Theroux. 528p. 1996. pap. 14.00 (*0-449-91085-7*) Fawcett.

Pillars of Hindustani Music. B. R. Deodhar. 1993. 23.00 (*81-7154-555-6*, Pub. by Popular Prakashan) S Asia.

Pillars of Lace: The Anthology of Italian-Canadian Women Writers. Marisa De Franceschi. 290p. 1998. pap. 18.00 (*1-55071-055-9*) Guernica Editions.

***Pillars of Leadership.** David J. Vaughan. 224p. 2000. pap. 12.95 (*1-58182-060-7*, Cumberland Hearthside) Cumberland Hse.

Pillars of Paul's Gospel: Galatians & Romans. John F. O'Grady. LC 91-45556. 192p. 1992. pap. 9.95 (*0-8091-3327-X*) Paulist Pr.

***Pillars of Peace for the 21st Century: Study Guide.** Patricia Rumer & National Council of the Churches of Christ in the United States of America Staff. LC 99-24264. 1999. write for info. (*0-377-00329-8*) Friendship Pr.

Pillars of Salt. Fadia Faqir. LC 96-46044. (Emerging Voices Ser.). 256p. 1997. 29.95 (*1-56656-220-1*); pap. 12.95 (*1-56656-253-8*) Interlink Pub.

Pillars of Salt: An Anthology of Early American Criminal Narratives. Daniel E. Williams. (Illus.). 368p. 1994. pap. 19.95 (*0-945612-37-0*); text 36.95 (*0-945612-31-1*) Madison Hse.

Pillars of Smoke. Byron L. Sherwin. 16p. 1971. pap. 1.00 (*0-935982-08-6*, BLS-01) Spertus Coll.

Pillars of Society see Ibsen: Plays Four

Pillars of Solomon. Jon Land. LC 98-46710. 352p. 1999. 24.95 (*0-312-86819-7*, Pub. by Forge NYC) St Martin.

***Pillars of Solomon, 1.** Jon Land. LC 98-46710. 438p. 2000. mass mkt. 6.99 (*0-8125-6672-6*, Pub. by Forge NYC) St Martin.

Pillars of the Church. Theodore Maynard. LC 76-136763. (Essay Index Reprint Ser.). 1977. 21.95 (*0-8369-1940-8*) Ayer.

Pillars of the Community see Hedda Gabler & Other Plays

Pillars of the Earth. Ken Follett. 1999. pap. 17.95 (*0-452-28010-9*) NAL.

Pillars of the Earth. Ken Follett. 983p. 1990. mass mkt. 7.99 (*0-451-16689-2*, Sig) NAL.

Pillars of The House: An Anthology of Verse by Irish Women from 1690 to Present. Ed. by A. A. Kelly. 172p. 1998. pap. 12.95 (*0-86327-143-X*, Pub. by Wolfhound Press) Irish Amer Bk.

Pillars of the Kingdom: Five Features of the Kingdom of God Progressively Revealed in the Old Testament. Robert I. Vasholz. LC 97-37403. 248p. (C). 1997. pap. 31.00 (*0-7618-0918-X*) U Pr of Amer.

Pillars of Truth. A. W. Knock. 104p. 1993. reprint ed. pap. text 4.95 (*1-58572-006-2*) Ambassdor Pubns.

Pillars of Wisdom in Ireland & England. David R. Howlett. 840p. 2000. boxed set 55.00 (*1-85182-186-4*, Pub. by Four Cts Pr) Intl Spec Bk.

Pillars on Modern India, 1757-1947. Sayed J. Mahmud. 140p. 1994. 16.00 (*81-7024-586-9*, Pub. by Ashish Pub Hse) Nataraj Bks.

Pillbug Project: A Guide to Investigation. Robin Burnett. (Illus.). 110p. 1992. pap. text 16.50 (*0-87355-109-5*) Natl Sci Tchrs.

***Pillbugs: Life Cycles.** Donna Schaffer. LC 98-53029. (Life Cycles Ser.). (Illus.). 24 p. (J). (gr. 3-4). 1999. 15.93 (*0-7368-0212-6*, Bridgestone Bks) Capstone Pr.

Pillion Riders. Elisabeth Russell-Taylor et al. 165p. 1993. 29.00 (*0-7206-0890-2*, Pub. by P Owen Ltd) Dufour.

Pillow. Rosemary Allison. (Kids of Canada Ser.). (Illus.). 32p. (J). 1979. 5.95 (*0-88862-245-7*, Pub. by J Lorimer) Formac Dist Ltd.

Pillow: Exploring the Heart of Eros. Lily Pond. LC 98-11915. 112p. 1998. pap. 9.95 (*0-89087-858-7*) Celestial Arts.

Pillow Book. Retold by Peter Greenaway. (Illus.). 150p. 1996. pap. 19.95 (*2-906571-52-0*, 620451, Pub. by Editions Dis Voir) Dist Art Pubs.

Pillow Book of Carol Tinker. Carol Tinker. LC 79-57557. (Illus.). 100p. 1980. pap. 5.00 (*0-932274-08-0*) Cadmus Eds.

Pillow Book of Sei Shonagon. Tr. by Ivan Morris from JPN. 411p. 1991. pap. text 19.00 (*0-231-07337-2*) Col U Pr.

Pillow Boy of the Lady Onogoro. Ed. by Alison Fell. Tr. by Arye Blower. LC 95-13169. 256p. 1996. 22.00 (*0-15-100186-3*) Harcourt.

Pillow Boy of the Lady Onogoro. Alison Fell. Tr. by Arye Blower. 256p. 1997. pap. 12.00 (*0-15-600468-2*, Harvest Bks) Harcourt.

Pillow for My Mom. Charissa Sgouros. LC 97-36077. (Illus.). 32p. (J). 1998. 15.00 (*0-395-82280-7*) HM.

Pillow Friend. Lisa Tuttle. 336p. 1996. 21.99 (*1-56504-938-1*, 11043, Borealis) White Wolf.

Pillow Ideas. Ed. by Janet DuBane & Alexandra Kuman. (Illus.). 64p. (Orig.). 1980. pap. 2.50 (*0-918178-19-3*) Simplicity.

***Pillow in the Kitchen.** Unisa Asokan. 50p. 2000. pap. 15.00 (*1-880855-08-9*) Fifth Planet.

Pillow Lace: A Practical Handbook. Elizabeth Mincoff & Margaret S. Marriage. 1981. 22.95 (*0-903585-10-3*) Robin & Russ.

***Pillow Lace & Bobbins.** Jeff Hopewell. (Illus.). 40p. 1999. pap. 30.00 (*0-7478-0400-1*, Pub. by Shire Pubns) Parkwest Pubns.

Pillow Lace & Bobbins. Jeffery Hopewell. 1989. pap. 25.00 (*0-85263-659-8*, Pub. by Shire Pubns) St Mut.

Pillow Mountain: Notes on Inhabiting a Living Planet. Michael Bridge. LC 91-35970. (Illus.). 192p. (Orig.). 1991. pap. 10.95 (*0-87810-039-3*) Times Change.

***Pillow of Dreams.** Peter J. Honigsberg. (Illus.). 32p. (J). (gr. k-4). 1999. 17.95 (*1-57143-076-8*) RDR Bks.

Pillow of Gold. George A. Montgomery. 256p. 1985. mass mkt. 3.95 (*0-939332-13-2*) J Pohl Assocs.

Pillow of Stone. Al Lacy. LC 98-29213. (Hannah of Fort Bridger Ser.: Vol. 4). 306p. 1998. pap. 10.99 (*1-57673-234-7*, Multnomah Fiction) Multnomah Pubs.

Pillow People Plan a Party (with Keyboard) Sideline. 1989. pap. 8.99 (*0-88704-108-6*) Sight & Sound.

Pillow Problems & a Tangled Tale. Lewis Carroll, pseud. 261p. 1958. pap. 7.95 (*0-486-20493-6*) Dover.

***Pillow Pup.** (gr. k-3). 2001. per. 17.00 (*0-689-83408-X*) Litle Simon.

Pillow Talk. Roger McGough. (Illus.). 80p. (YA). (gr. 7 up). 1992. pap. 7.95 (*0-14-032504-2*, Pub. by Pnguin Bks Ltd) Trafalgar.

Pillow Talk. Paula Meehan. LC 94-217445. 74p. 1994. pap. 13.95 (*1-85235-133-0*) Dufour.

***Pillow Talk.** Hailey North. LC 98-94823. 384p. 1999. mass mkt. 5.99 (*0-380-80519-7*, Avon Bks) Morrow Avon.

Pillow Talk. Contrib. by Stanley Shapiro et al. 1959. 5.50 (*0-87129-527-X*, P24) Dramatic Pub.

Pillow Talk: Humorous Quotes on Love & Marriage. Ed. by Patrick Caton. 80p. 1997. spiral bd. 7.95 (*1-56245-292-4*) Great Quotations.

Pillow Talk: Lesbian Stories Between the Covers. Ed. by Leslea Newman. LC 98-5296. 224p. (Orig.). 1998. pap. 12.95 (*1-55583-419-1*) Alyson Pubns.

Pillow Talk: The Intimate Marriage from A to Z. Karen S. Linamen. LC 96-20791. 272p. 1998. pap. 9.99 (*0-8007-5655-X*) Revell.

Pillow Talk (Matching Moms) Kristine Rolofson. 1997. per. 3.50 (*0-373-44027-8*, 1-44027-0) Harlequin Bks.

***Pillow Talk II: More Lesbian Stories Between the Covers.** Ed. by Leslea Newman. 2000. pap. 12.95 (*1-55583-519-8*, Pub. by Alyson Pubns) Consort Bk Sales.

Pillow War. Matt Novak. LC 96-53864. (Illus.). 32p. (J). (ps-1). 1998. pap. 15.95 (*0-531-30048-X*); lib. bdg. 16.99 (*0-531-33048-6*) Orchard Bks Watts.

Pillows. Benny Andersen. LC 83-7166. 184p. 1983. pap. 8.95 (*0-915306-37-9*) Curbstone.

Pillows. Creative Publishing International Staff. LC 97-7673. (Creative Textiles Ser.). (Illus.). 112p. (Orig.). 1997. pap. 16.95 (*0-86573-410-0*) Creat Pub Intl.

Pillows: For Beginners. Cowles Creative Publishing, Inc. Staff. LC 98-18266. (Seams Sew Easy Ser.). (Illus.). 128p. 1998. 17.95 (*0-86573-324-4*) Creat Pub Intl.

Pillows, Curtains, & More: Coordinated Projects to Sew. Myra Davidson. (Illus.). 160p. 1993. 19.95 (*0-8019-8389-4*) NP-Chilton.

Pills-a-Go-Go: A Fiendish Investigation into Pill Marketing, Art, History & Consumption. Jim Hogshire. (Illus.). 220p. 1998. pap. 16.95 (*0-922915-53-9*) Feral Hse.

Pills Aren't Enough: Stories for Emotional Healing in Chronic Illness. Cody Wasner. 177p. 1997. pap. 18.50 (*1-890018-14-7*) Anadem Pubng.

Pills for Parents in Pain. Lee Ezell. LC 98-84090. (Illus.). 176p. 1998. pap. 10.00 (*1-883928-30-3*) Longwood.

Pills, Pearls & Potions. 2nd ed. Jane A. Passamonte. 114p. (Orig.). 1997. pap. 11.95 (*1-884441-02-5*) Tyler Pr.

Pills, Petticoats, & Plows: The Southern Country Store. Thomas D. Clark. LC 64-11333. (Illus.). 336p. 1989. pap. 13.95 (*0-8061-1093-7*) U of Okla Pr.

***Pills, Potions, & Poisons: How Drugs Work.** Trevor Stone & Gail Darlington. LC 99-52844. 384p. 2000. 27.50 (*0-19-850403-9*) OUP.

Pills That Work, Pills That Do. Gideon Bosker. LC 98-96386. 1998. pap. 15.95 (*0-449-91273-6*) Fawcett.

***Pills That Work, Pills That Don't.** 420p. 2000. reprint ed. 26.00 (*0-7881-6999-8*) DIANE Pub.

***Pillsbury: All Time Favorite Sweets & Treats.** Creative Publishing International Staff & Pillsbury Company Staff. LC 99-26467. (Illus.). 96p. 1999. pap. 14.95 (*0-86573-541-7*) Creat Pub Intl.

Pillsbury: Best Desserts. Pillsbury Company Staff. LC 98-9183. (Illus.). 352p. 1998. 24.95 (*0-609-60285-3*) C Potter.

Pillsbury: Best of the Bake-Off Cookbook. 1996. 24.95 (*0-614-19359-1*, Crown) Crown Pub Group.

Pillsbury: Best of the Bake-Off Cookbook. Ed. by Pillsbury Company Staff. LC 96-221257. 1996. 24.95 (*0-517-70574-5*) Random.

Pillsbury: Fast & Healthy Cookbook. Pillsbury Company Staff. LC 97-23960. 352p. 1998. 24.95 (*0-609-60085-0*) C Potter.

Pillsbury Best Assortment, 3. Random House Staff. 1999. 19.95 (*0-676-58496-9*) Random.

Pillsbury Best Cookies Cookbook: Favorite Recipes from America's Most-Trusted Kitchens. Pillsbury Company Staff. LC 97-1773. 1997. 19.95 (*0-609-60084-2*) C Potter.

Pillsbury, Best Muffins & Quick Breads Cookbook: Favorite Recipes from America's Most-Trusted Kitchens. Pillsbury Company Staff. LC 98-38176. (Pillsbury Ser.). (Illus.). 239p. 1999. 19.95 (*0-609-60283-7*) Crown Pub Group.

Pillsbury Chicken Cookbook. Pillsbury Company Staff. LC 97-184242. 1997. 19.95 (*0-517-70880-9*) C Potter.

***Pillsbury Complete Cookbook: Recipes from America's Most Trusted Kitchens.** Pillsbury Company. Ed. by Maureen Rosener. LC 99-46945. (Illus.). 544p. 2000. 26.95 (*0-609-60284-5*) C Potter.

Pillsbury Cookbook. 1995. mass mkt. 9.99 (*0-553-85098-9*) Bantam.

Pillsbury Cookbook. 1995. mass mkt. 9.99 (*0-553-85113-6*) Bantam.

Pillsbury Cookbook. Tocome. 928p. 1996. mass mkt. 7.99 (*0-553-57534-1*) Bantam.

Pillsbury Cookbook. Unknown. 1996. mass mkt. 9.99 (*0-553-85143-8*) Bantam.

Pillsbury Family; Being a History of William & Dorothy Pillsbury (or Pilsbery) of Newbury in New England, & Their Descendants to the Eleventh Generation. D. B. Pilsbury & E. A. Getchell. (Illus.). 336p. 1989. reprint ed. pap. 40.25 (*0-8328-0969-1*); reprint ed. lib. bdg. 48.25 (*0-8328-0968-3*) Higginson Bk Co.

Pillsbury Kitchens' Family Cookbook. Pillsbury Company Staff. write for info. (*0-318-58126-4*) S&S Trade.

Pillsbury One Dish Meals: More than 300 Recipes for Crock-Pot Dishes, Casseroles, Stir-Fries & More. Pillsbury Company Staff. LC 99-14444. 336p. 1999. 24.95 (*0-609-60282-9*) Crown.

Pilon, el Extraordinario Elefanton. Susan Joyce. Tr. by Aida E. Marcuse from ENG. LC 92-35437. (SPA., Illus.). 48p. (Orig.). (J). (ps-3). 1993. pap. 8.95 (*0-939217-05-8*) Peel Prod.

Pilon-Tibial Fracture: Classification, Surgical Techniques, Results. Urs F. A. Heim. (Illus.). 320p. 1995. text 210.00 (*0-7216-5658-7*, W B Saunders Co) Harcrt Hlth Sci Grp.

Pilosocereus (Cactaceae) The Genus in Brazil. D. C. Zappi. (Succulent Plant Research Ser.: Vol. 3). (Illus.). 160p. 1994. 66.00 (*0-9517234-5-6*, Pub. by Royal Botnic Grdns); pap. 36.00 (*0-9517234-4-8*, Pub. by Royal Botnic Grdns) Balogh.

Pilot. James Fenimore Cooper. Ed. by Kay Seymour-House. LC 84-8765. (Writings of James Fenimore Cooper). 479p. (C). 1986. pap. text 19.95 (*0-87395-791-1*) State U NY Pr.

Pilot. Duncan McNaughton. 64p. 1991. pap. 7.00 (*0-9631462-0-3*) Blue Millennium.

Pilot. Anita Virgil. LC 97-134906. (Illus.). 40p. 1996. pap. 10.95 (*0-9628567-9-7*) Peaks Pr.

Pilot. James Fenimore Cooper. 1990. reprint ed. lib. bdg. 27.95 (*0-89966-704-X*) Buccaneer Bks.

Pilot. James Fenimore Cooper. (Works of James Fenimore Cooper). 1990. reprint ed. lib. bdg. 79.00 (*0-7812-2372-5*) Rprt Serv.

Pilot. James Fenimore Cooper. (BCL1-PS American Literature Ser.). 339p. 1993. reprint ed. lib. bdg. 89.00 (*0-7812-6953-9*) Rprt Serv.

Pilot: A Tale of the Sea. James Fenimore Cooper. Ed. by Kay Seymour House. LC 84-8765. (Writings of James Fenimore Cooper). 479p. (C). 1986. text 59.50 (*0-87395-415-7*) State U NY Pr.

Pilot: WWII - From Hitler to Yon. unabridged ed. Lobo Blanco. LC 96-90528. (Classic American Historical Novels: Vol. 1). (Illus.). 160p. (Orig.). 1996. pap. 12.50 (*1-890492-13-2*) Univ Pr of Coppers.

Pilot - Take Charge. W. Bartlett Prince. (C). 1987. 60.00 (*0-85174-139-8*) St Mut.

Pilot Application of Risk-Informed Methods to Establish Inservice Inspection Priorities for Nuclear Components at Surry Unit 1 Nuclear Power Station. T. V. Vo. 80p. 1997. pap. 7.00 (*0-16-062813-X*) USGPO.

Pilot Bee: I'm a Book with Wheels. Rita Balducci & Reader's Digest Editors. (Pull-Back 'n Go Bks.: No. 2). (Illus.). 10p. (J). (gr. k-3). 1998. bds. 7.99 (*1-57584-212-2*, Pub. by Rdrs Digest) Random.

Pilot, Diplomat & Garage Rat. H. M. Pearson. (C). 1989. 49.00 (*0-7855-6628-7*) St Mut.

Pilot Down, Presumed Dead. Marjorie Phleger. LC 63-16244. (Trophy Bk.). 224p. (J). (gr. 4-7). 1975. pap. 5.95 (*0-06-440067-0*, HarpTrophy) HarpC Child Bks.

Pilot Down, Presumed Dead. Marjorie Phleger. 206p. (J). (gr. 5-6). pap. 5.95 (*0-8072-1426-4*) Listening Lib.

Pilot Down, Presumed Dead. Marjorie Phleger. 1963. 9.60 (*0-606-03888-4*, Pub. by Turtleback) Demco.

Pilot Error. large type ed. Bill Knox. (Linford Mystery Library). 336p. 1993. pap. 16.99 (*0-7089-7384-1*, Linford) Ulverscroft.

Pilot Error: A Professional Study of Contributory Factors. Ed. by Ronald Hurst. (Illus.). 1983. 20.00 (*0-685-04567-6*) S&S Trade.

Pilot Examiner's Handbook: FAA Order 8710.3B. Federal Aviation Administration, D. O. T. Staff. (Illus.). 196p. 1995. reprint ed. pap. 19.95 (*1-56027-284-8*, ASA-8710.3C) ASA Inc.

Pilot Handbook. 5th ed. Irvin N. Gleim. LC 95-79317. (Illus.). 408p. (C). 1995. pap. 13.95 (*0-917539-50-8*) Gleim Pubns.

Pilot Handbook. 6th ed. Irvin N. Gleim. (Illus.). 458p. (C). 1998. pap. 13.95 (*0-917539-83-4*) Gleim Pubns.

Pilot Household Survey of Perception & Use of a Large Urban Park. Robert E. Coughlin & Ursala Scherer. (Discussion Papers: No. 59). 1972. pap. 10.00 (*1-55869-093-X*) Regional Sci Res Inst.

Pilot in Command. Craig. 268p. 1999. 29.95 (*0-07-134844-1*) McGraw.

Pilot Instructional Journal. Don Gladney. 100p. (Orig.). 1989. pap. write for info. (*0-318-65365-6*) ATDI.

Pilot Judgement & Crew Resource Management. Richard S. Jensen. 324p. 1995. text 69.95 (*0-291-39804-9*, Pub. by Avebury Technical) Ashgate Pub Co.

Pilot Ladder Safety. M. C. Armstrong. (C). 1987. 50.00 (*0-85174-499-0*) St Mut.

Pilot Logbook & Journal. Dorothy Schick. (Illus.). 120p. 1996. spiral bd. 24.95 (*0-9651183-0-4*, FW2656) Flywrite Systs.

***Pilot Logbook & Journal.** 2nd rev. ed. Dorothy Schick. 120p. 2000. spiral bd. 24.95 (*0-9651183-1-2*, FW2656DB & FW2656DM) Flywrite Systs.

***Pilot Manual for B-29 Superfortress.** (Illus.). xxxi, 177p. 1999. pap. 14.95 (*0-87994-006-9*) Aviat Pub.

Pilot MIGa: Poslednii Polet Leitinanta Belenko. John Barron.Tr. of MIG Pilot - the Final Escape of Lieutenant Belenko. (RUS., Illus.). 172p. 1987. 15.00 (*0-911971-04-1*) Effect Pub.

Pilot-Operated Pressure-Control Valves for Fire-Protection Service, UL 1739. 3rd ed. (C). 1994. pap. text 330.00 (*1-55989-643-4*) Underwrtrs Labs.

Pilot Plant Catalytic Gasification of Hydrocarbons. C. H. Riesz et al. (Research Bulletin Ser.: No. 6). viii, 44p. 1953. pap. 25.00 (*1-58222-037-9*) Inst Gas Tech.

Pilot Plants & Scale-Up of Chemical Processes II. Ed. by W. Hoyle. (Special Publication Ser.: Vol. 236). 459p. 1999. 99.00 (*0-85404-719-0*) Spr-Verlag.

Pilot Project, India. Albert Mayer et al. LC 72-12332. (Illus.). 367p. 1973. reprint ed. lib. bdg. 75.00 (*0-8371-6729-9*, MAPI, Greenwood Pr) Greenwood.

***Pilot Protective Relaying.** Walter A. Elmore. LC 99-51575. (Electrical Engineering & Electronics Ser.). 165p. 1999. 99.75 (*0-8247-8195-3*) Dekker.

Pilot Reports & Flight Testing. reprint ed. 1.29 (*0-614-13205-3*, 21-16520) EAA Aviation.

Pilot Review, 1992-1997. Joseph B. Strauss. 257p. (C). 1997. text 30.00 (*1-890419-09-5*) Fnd Chiropractic Educ.

Pilot Sans Visage see Mystery Driver

Pilot Scale Evaluation of Ozone & Peroxone. 372p. 1991. 99.00 (*0-89867-577-4*, 90591) Am Water Wks Assn.

Pilot Star Elegies: Poems. Sherod Santos. LC 98-28875. 96p. 1999. 22.00 (*0-393-04704-0*) Norton.

***Pilot Star Elegies: Poems.** Sherod Santos. 104p. 2000. pap. 12.00 (*0-393-32049-9*) Norton.

Pilot Teacher - Development Program in Mathematics: Evaluation Report. Institute for Independent Education. (Illus.). 52p. 1987. pap. 3.50 (*0-941001-05-9*) Inst Indep Educ.

Pilot Training: You Can Learn to Fly. Arthur J. Sabin. LC 78-24387. (Illus.). 200p. 1979. pap. 4.95 (*0-89037-171-7*) Anderson World.

Pilot Transition Courses for Complex Single-Engine & Light Twin-Engine Airplanes. Government Printing Office Staff. 20p. 1992. pap. 3.25 (*0-16-005092-8*) USGPO.

Pilot Vision: And Other Pilot Secrets to Succeed in the Business World. John M. Magness. LC 98-27851. 128p. 1998. 17.95 (*0-944708-50-1*) Adams Hall.

Pilot Workload Vol. 5, No. 1, 1995: Contemporary Issues: A Special Issue of "The International Journal of Aviation Psychology", Vol. 5, No. 1. Ed. by Anthony D. Andre & P. A. Hancock. 136p. 1995. pap. 20.00 (*0-8058-9953-7*) L Erlbaum Assocs.

Pilote de Guerre. Antoine de Saint-Exupery. (FRE.). 221p. 1976. write for info. (*0-318-63578-X*); pap. 10.95 (*0-8288-3732-5*, F123551) Fr & Eur.

Pilote de Guerre. Antoine de Saint-Exupery. (Folio Ser.: No. 824). (FRE.). 221p. 1976. 8.95 (*2-07-036824-6*) Schoenhof.

Piloting & Dead Reckoning. 3rd ed. H. H. Shufeldt & G. D. Dunlap. (Illus.). 192p. 1991. 29.95 (*0-87021-664-3*) Naval Inst Pr.

***Piloting & Dead Reckoning.** 4th ed. H. H. Shufeldt. LC 99-30742. 1999. 29.95 (*1-55750-683-3*) Naval Inst Pr.

Piloting & General Navigation. rev. ed. George Trowbridge. (Illus.). 258p. 1996. pap. text 22.78 (*1-888116-02-1*) DG Training.

Piloting at Night. Lewis Bjork. LC 98-4236. (Practical Flying Ser.). (Illus.). 250p. 1998. 39.95 (*0-07-006698-1*); pap. 29.95 (*0-07-006697-3*) McGraw.

***Piloting Basics Handbook.** Lewis Bjork. (Illus.). 650p. 2000. 49.95 (*0-07-136104-9*) McGraw.

Piloting For Maximum Performance. Lewis Bjork. LC 96-13568. (Illus.). 295p. 1996. pap. 29.95 (*0-07-005699-4*) McGraw.

Piloting Through Chaos: Wise Leadership-Effective Negotiation for the 21st Century. Julian Gresser. LC 95-62030. 1996. pap. text 19.95 (*1-888278-00-5*) Logos Network.

Piloto de la Selva en Liberia. Abraham Guenter. Ed. by Robert Collins. (SPA.). 163p. 1996. 7.95 (*1-879892-62-6*) Editorial Bautista.

Pilots. William Russell. LC 93-45009. (J). 1994. lib. bdg. 14.60 (*1-57103-059-X*) Rourke Pr.

Pilot's Air Traffic Control Handbook. Paul E. Illman. (Practical Flying Ser.). (Illus.). 224p. (Orig.). 1989. 24.95 (*0-8306-9435-8*); pap. 16.95 (*0-8306-0435-9*) McGraw-Hill Prof.

Pilot's Air Traffic Control Handbook. 2nd ed. Paul E. Illman. LC 93-9151. (Orig.). 1993. 28.95 (*0-8306-4137-8*) McGraw-Hill Prof.

Pilot's Air Traffic Control Handbook. 3rd ed. Paul E. Illman. (Practical Flying Ser.). (Illus.). 264p. (Orig.). 1998. 34.95 (*0-07-031835-2*) McGraw.

Pilot's Air Traffic Control Handbook. 3rd ed. Paul E. Illman. (Practical Flying Ser.). (Illus.). 304p. (Orig.). 1999. pap. 29.95 (*0-07-031834-4*) McGraw.

Pilots & Aircraft Owners Legal Guide. 5th ed. Jay C. White. 125p. 1991. pap. 6.95 (*0-685-08920-7*) Pilots Pubs Inc.

Pilots & Aviation. Carter M. Ayres. (Space & Aviation Ser.). (Illus.). 72p. (J). (gr. 5 up). 1990. lib. bdg. 9.50 (*0-8225-1590-3*, Lerner Publctns) Lerner Pub.

Pilot's Avionics Survival Guide. Edward R. Maher. (Illus.). 224p. 1994. pap. 19.95 (*0-07-039622-1*) McGraw.

Pilot's Avionics Survival Guide. Edward R. Maher. LC 93-8051. 1993. pap. 18.95 (*0-8306-4204-8*) McGraw-Hill Prof.

Pilot's Bahama: Aviation Guide. Brian Strong. (Illus.). 500p. 1988. ring bd. 19.95 (*0-685-11975-0*) Pilot Pubns.

Pilot's Bahamas & Caribbean Aviation Guide, 1990. 12th rev. ed. Dale R. Cady. Ed. by Tom Jones & Brian Strong. (Illus.). 500p. 1989. pap. 24.95 (*0-938923-03-X*) Pilot Pubns.

P

An Asterisk (*) at the beginning of an entry indicates that the title is appearing for the first time.

Pilot's Bahamas & Caribbean Aviation Guide, 1991. 13th rev. ed. Dale R. Cady. Ed. by Tom Jones. (Illus.). 500p. 1990. pap. 24.95 (*0-938923-04-8*) Pilot Pubns.

Pilot's Bahamas Aviation Guide, 1988. 10th rev. ed. Dale R. Cady. Ed. by Brian Strong & Donn Pfaff. (Illus.). 500p. 1987. pap. 19.95 (*0-938923-01-3*) Pilot Pubns.

Pilot's Bill of Rights. 5.00 (*0-614-13206-1*, 21-37865) EAA Aviation.

***Pilot's Burden: Flight Safety & the Roots of Pilot Error.** Robert N. Buck. (Illus.). 252p. 2000. pap. 32.95 (*0-8138-2815-5*) Iowa St U Pr.

Pilots Database User's Guide. Fred Lerner. 254p. 1995. per. 22.00 (*0-16-062478-9*, Veterans Affairs) USGPO.

Pilots Database User's Guide: Published International Literature on Post-Traumatic Stress Disorder. 1997. lib. bdg. 250.95 (*0-8490-7644-7*) Gordon Pr.

Pilot's Daughter. Gardner McFall. 79p. (Orig.). 1996. 18.95 (*1-56809-028-5*); pap. 12.50 (*1-56809-029-3*) Time Being Bks.

Pilots Die Faster. C. W. Morton. LC 97-6271. 1997. text 21.95 (*0-312-15624-3*) St Martin.

Pilots' Directions: The Transcontinental Airway & Its History. Ed. by William M. Leary. LC 89-20479. (American Land & Life Ser.). (Illus.). 112p. 1990. reprint ed. text 19.95 (*0-87745-278-4*) U of Iowa Pr.

Pilots Fly Airplanes. Fay Robinson. LC 96-7199. (Community Helpers Ser.). (Illus.). 32p. (J). (gr. k-3). 1996. lib. bdg. 21.36 (*1-56766-308-7*) Childs World.

Pilot's Guide to Affordable Classics. 2nd ed. Bill Clarke. LC 92-41242. 1993. 26.95 (*0-8306-4106-8*); pap. 16.60 (*0-8306-4107-6*) McGraw-Hill Prof.

Pilots Guide to Affordable Classics. 2nd ed. Bill Clarke. 320p. 1993. pap. 19.95 (*0-07-011268-1*) McGraw.

***Pilot's Guide to Aircraft Icing.** Lankford. LC 99-41781. 352p. 1999. pap. 34.95 (*0-07-134139-0*) McGraw.

Pilot's Guide to Cabin Noise. Jack E. Foster. Ed. by Maryanna J. Foster. (Illus.). 99p. (Orig.). 1995. pap. 19.95 (*1-888638-01-X*) Arrow Pr WA.

Pilot's Guide to California Airports. R. Fouquet. (Illus.). 1990. spiral bd. 36.95 (*0-911721-24-X*) Aviation.

Pilot's Guide to Recreational Destinations: Eastern United States. Poldi Mikula. LC 99-90433. (Illus.). 350p. 1999. pap. 26.95 (*0-9671785-0-9*) Beyond Clouds.

Pilots Guide to Southwestern Airports. rev. ed. Richard G. Reese, Jr. & Suzanne L. Reese. (Illus.). 550p. 1982. 34.95 (*0-9622494-0-8*) RGR Pubns.

***Pilots Guide To Weather Report.** 3rd ed. Lankford. LC 99-57417. 470p. 1999. pap. 34.95 (*0-07-135456-5*) McGraw.

Pilot's Guide to Weather Reports, Forecasts & Flight Planning. 2nd ed. Terry T. Lankford. (TAB Practical Flying Series). (Illus.). 400p. 1995. 29.95 (*0-07-036426-5*) McGraw.

Pilot's Guide to Weather Reports, Forecasts & Flight Planning. 2nd ed. Terry T. Lankford. LC 95-1617. (Illus.). 416p. 1995. pap. 20.95 (*0-07-036427-3*) McGraw-Hill Prof.

Pilot's Handbook of Aeronautical Knowledge. Government Printing Office Staff. 184p. 1997. pap. 14.00 (*0-16-049161-4*) USGPO.

Pilot's Handbook of Aeronautical Knowledge. rev. ed. Paul E. Illman. (Illus.). 400p. 1990. pap. 19.95 (*0-8306-3517-3*) McGraw-Hill Prof.

Pilot's Handbook of Aeronautical Knowledge. 3rd ed. P. E. Illman. LC 95-9203. 448p. 1995. pap. 24.95 (*0-07-031782-8*) McGraw.

***Pilot's Handbook of Aeronautical Knowledge.** 4th ed. Paul E. Illman. LC 99-54046. (Illus.). 614p. 1999. 49.95 (*0-07-134519-1*) McGraw.

Pilot's Handbook of Aeronautical Knowledge, AC 61-23C: Advisory Circular 61- 23C. rev. ed. FAA Staff. (Illus.). 180p. 1997. pap. 14.95 (*1-56027-309-7*, ASA-AC61-23C) ASA Inc.

Pilots' Information File, 1944: The Authentic World War II Guidebook for Pilots & Flight Engineers. LC 94-74327. (Illus.). 268p. (Orig.). 1995. pap. 19.95 (*0-88740-780-3*) Schiffer.

***Pilots, Man Your Planes! The History of Naval Aviation.** Wilbur H. Morrison. LC 99-10941. (Illus.). 462p. 1999. 33.95 (*1-55571-466-8*) PSI Resch.

Pilot's Manual - Commercial Pilot Syllabus: A Flight & Ground Training Course for Commercial Pilot Airplane Certification Based on Trevor Thom's "Private & Commercial" Jackie Spanitz. (Pilot's Manual Series Syllabi). 46p. 1995. pap. 10.95 (*1-56027-228-7*, ASA-PM-S-C) ASA Inc.

Pilot's Manual - Private Pilot Syllabus: A Flight & Ground Training Course for Private Airplane Certification Based on Trevor Thom's "Private & Commercial" 2nd ed. Jackie Spanitz. (Illus.). 50p. 1997. pap. 10.95 (*1-56027-332-1*, ASA-PM-S-P) ASA Inc.

Pilot's Manual-Instrument Rating Syllabus: A Flight & Ground Training Course for Instrument Rating Based on Trevor Thom's "Instrument Flying" 2nd ed. Jackie Spanitz. (Pilot's Manual Series Syllabi). (Illus.). 100p. 1998. pap. 10.95 (*1-56027-362-3*, ASA-PM-S-I2) ASA Inc.

Pilots of the Panhandle: Aviation in Southeast Alaska, the Early Years, 1920-1935. Jim Ruotsala. LC 97-91980. (Illus.). 120p. 1997. pap. 29.95 (*0-9658830-0-0*) Seadrome Pr.

Pilot's Operating Instructions for Army Model B-29 Airplane. 1992. pap. 12.95 (*0-911139-07-9*) Flying Bks.

Pilot's Outline Guide to Basic Aerodynamics. William M. Jones. Ed. by Ronald G. Gallagher. (Illus.). 180p. (Orig.). (C). 1995. pap. text 12.95 (*0-9639984-2-0*) Century Creations.

Pilot's Perception & Control of Aircraft Motions. Ruud Hosman. (Illus.). 160p. (Orig.). 1996. pap. 43.50 (*90-407-1384-7*, Pub. by Delft U Pr) Coronet Bks.

Pilots, Personality, & Performance: Human Behavior & Stress in the Skies. Ed. by Sheila R. Deitz & William E. Thoms. LC 91-11427. 232p. 1991. 62.95 (*0-89930-577-6*, DPB/, Quorum Bks) Greenwood.

Pilot's Pocket Decoder. Christopher J. Abbe. LC 98-4210. 224p. 1998. pap. 14.95 (*0-07-007549-2*) McGraw.

Pilot's Point. large type ed. Leila Mackinlay. 464p. 1987. 27.99 (*0-7089-1601-5*) Ulverscroft.

Pilot's Radio Communications Handbook. 2nd ed. Paul E. Illman & Jay Pouzar. (Practical Flying Ser.). (Illus.). 240p. 1988. 22.95 (*0-8306-0265-8*); pap. 14.60 (*0-8306-2465-1*) McGraw-Hill Prof.

Pilot's Radio Communications Handbook. 4th ed. Paul E. Illman. (Illus.). 256p. 1992. 28.95 (*0-8306-4139-4*, 4233); pap. 16.95 (*0-8306-4140-8*, 4233) McGraw-Hill Prof.

Pilot's Radio Communications Handbook. 5th ed. Paul E. Illman. LC 98-12759. (Practical Flying Ser.). (Illus.). 272p. 1998. 39.95 (*0-07-031831-X*) McGraw.

Pilot's Radio Communications Handbook. 5th ed. Paul E. Illman. LC 98-12759. (Practical Flying Ser.). (Illus.). 272p. 1998. pap. 34.95 (*0-07-031832-8*) McGraw.

Pilot's Reference to ATC Procedures & Phraseology. 7th ed. Thomas S. Mills & Janet S. Archibald. (Illus.). 370p. 1999. pap. 27.95 (*0-935695-24-9*) Reavco Pub.

Pilot's Rules of Thumb: Easy Aviation Math, Handy Formulas, Quick Tips. Art Parma & Emille Lecorre. LC 99-209325. (Illus.). 48p. 1998. pap. 6.95 (*0-9631973-4-7*) Flight Time.

Pilots Tale & Other Stories. unabridged ed. Robert Steiner. 226p. 1998. pap. 14.95 (*0-9665678-1-1*) Buy Books.

Pilot's Travel & Recreation Guide: Northwest & Western Canada. Douglas S. Carmody. 1999. pap. 24.95 (*0-07-001744-1*) Osborne-McGraw.

Pilot's Travel & Recreation Guide: Southeast & the Caribbean. Douglas S. Carmody. LC 98-34944. (Illus.). 330p. 1998. pap. 24.95 (*0-07-001648-8*) McGraw.

Pilot's Travel & Recreation Guide: Southwest & Baja. Douglas S. Carmody. LC 98-34945. (Illus.). 234p. 1998. pap. 24.95 (*0-07-001647-X*) McGraw.

Pilots under Stress. S. J. Sloan & C. L. Cooper. 240p. 1987. 45.00 (*0-7102-0479-5*, 04795, Routledge Thoemms) Routledge.

Pilot's Voice. Isabel Byrum. (Illus.). 146p. pap. 3.50 (*0-686-29159-X*) Faith Pub Hse.

Pilot's Weather: A Commonsense Approach to Metereology. Brian Cosgrove. (Illus.). 192p. 1999. 34.95 (*1-882663-41-1*) Plymouth VT.

Pilot's Weight & Balance Handbook. rev. ed. Federal Aviation Administration Staff. 68p. 1977. reprint ed. pap. text 5.00 (*0-939158-22-1*) Flightshops.

Pilot's Wife: A Novel. Anita Shreve. LC 97-51647. 304p. (gr. 8). 1998. 23.95 (*0-316-78908-9*) Little.

Pilot's Wife: A Novel. Anita Shreve. LC 97-51647. 293p. 1999. pap. 13.95 (*0-316-60195-0*, Back Bay) Little.

Pilot's Wife: A Novel. Anita Shreve. 320p. 1999. pap. 13.95 (*0-316-78990-9*) Little.

***Pilot's Wife: A Novel.** Anita Shreve. 304p. 2000. pap. 7.99 (*0-316-78915-1*, Pub. by Little) Time Warner.

Pilot's Wife: A Novel. large type ed. Anita Shreve. LC 98-44853. 337p. 1998. 26.95 (*1-56895-686-X*, Compass) Wheeler Pub.

Pilots Wings of the United States: Civilian & Commercial. Philip R. Martin. Ed. by John Ritums & Dennis Guido. LC 93-90426. (Illus.). 268p. 1982. pap. 2.95 (*0-930968-01-8*) Beach Cities.

Pilpali Sahab: The Story of a Big Ego in a Small Body. Mulk-Raj Anand. (C). 1990. text 14.00 (*1-85529-059-6*, Pub. by Arnold Pubs) S Asia.

Pilsen & the West Side. William Adelman. (Illus.). 100p. 1983. pap. 7.95 (*0-685-02463-6*) Ill Labor Hist Soc.

Pilsudski: A Biography by His Wife. Alexandra Pilsudska. LC 76-135829. (Eastern Europe Collection). 1971. reprint ed. 24.95 (*0-405-02771-0*) Ayer.

Pilze Vol. 1: Lamellenpilze, Taeublinge, Milchlinge und andere Gruppen mit Lamellen. Ewald Gerhardt. (GER., Illus.). 318p. 1984. pap. 28.00 (*3-405-12927-3*) Lubrecht & Cramer.

Pilze Vol. 2: Roehrlinge, Porlinge, Bauchpilze, und Schlauchpilze und Andere. Ewald Gerhardt. (GER., Illus.). 320p. 1985. pap. 28.00 (*3-405-12965-6*) Lubrecht & Cramer.

Pilze im Garten see Mushrooms in the Garden

Pilze im Garten. 2nd ed. H. Steineck. (Illus.). 148p. 1981. lib. bdg. 16.80 (*3-8001-6122-2*, Pub. by Eugen Ulmer) Balogh.

Pilze Mitteleuropas Vol. 4: Die Gattung Phlegmacium (Schleimkoepfe) Meinhard Moser. (Illus.). 1960. 143.00 (*3-7682-0523-1*) Lubrecht & Cramer.

Pilze Mitteleuropas Vol. 5, Pt. 1: Die Roehrlinge Die Boletaceae (Ohne Boletoideae) Rolf Singer. (Illus.). 1965. 96.00 (*3-7682-0526-6*) Lubrecht & Cramer.

Pilze Mitteleuropas Vol. 6, Pt. 2: Die Roehrlinge die Boletoiceae una Strobilomycetaceae. Rolf Singer. (Illus.). 1967. 128.00 (*3-7682-0529-0*) Lubrecht & Cramer.

Pilze Mitteleuropas. Herve Chaumeton. Tr. by Ute Juelich from FRE. (GER., Illus.). 484p. 1987. lib. bdg. 50.00 (*0-318-33439-9*) Lubrecht & Cramer.

Pilze Schlesiens, 2 vols. J. Schroeter. (Illus.). 1973. reprint ed. 200.00 (*3-7682-0761-7*) Lubrecht & Cramer.

Pilzflora der Deutschen Demokratischen Republik Basidiomycetes (Gallert-Hut-und Bauchpilze) Ed. by Hans Kreisel. (GER.). 261p. 1987. lib. bdg. 40.50 (*3-334-00025-7*) Lubrecht & Cramer.

Pilzmikroskopie: Praeparation und Untersuchung von Pilzen. Bruno Erb & W. Matheis. (Illus.). 166p. 1982. lib. bdg. 50.95 (*3-440-05127-7*) Lubrecht & Cramer.

***Pim Pim the Mouse.** H. R. Coursen. 1999. text 15.95 (*0-8050-6095-2*) St Martin.

Pima & Papago Indian Agriculture. Edward F. Castetter et al. LC 76-43674. reprint ed. 42.50 (*0-404-15510-3*) AMS Pr.

Pima Bajo of Central Sonora Mexico, 2 vols., 1. Campbell W. Pennington. LC 79-89878. 430p. reprint ed. pap. 133.30 (*0-8357-8986-1*, 203336300001) Bks Demand.

Pima Bajo of Central Sonora Mexico, 2 vols., 2. Campbell W. Pennington. LC 79-89878. 159p. pap. 49.30 (*0-8357-8987-X*, 203336300002) Bks Demand.

Pima County Land Exchange Survey. Gayle H. Hartman. (Archaeological Ser.: No. 151). (Illus.). 106p. 1981. pap. 6.95 (*1-889747-28-9*) Ariz St Mus.

Pima Indian Basketry: Illustrated with Photographs from the Collection of the Heard Museum. H. Thomas Cain. LC 62-20907. (Heard Museum Research Project Ser.: No. 2). (Illus.). 40p. (Orig.). 1962. pap. 5.00 (*0-934351-17-1*) Heard Mus.

Pima Indian Legends. Anna M. Shaw. LC 68-13547. (Illus.). 111p. 1993. reprint ed. pap. 12.95 (*0-8165-0186-6*) U of Ariz Pr.

Pima Indians: Pathfinders for Health. Ed. by Jane Demouy et al. (Illus.). 37p. 1998. pap. text 15.00 (*0-7881-7358-8*) DIANE Pub.

Pima Past. Anna M. Shaw. LC 73-87716. (Illus.). 262p. 1994. reprint ed. pap. 17.95 (*0-8165-0426-1*) U of Ariz Pr.

Pima Remembers. rev. ed. George Webb. LC 59-4914. 126p. 1982. pap. 11.95 (*0-8165-0786-4*) U of Ariz Pr.

Piman & Papago Ritual Oratory. Donald Bahr. 1975. pap. 7.00 (*0-685-64956-3*) Indian Hist Pr.

Piman Shamanism & Staying Sickness. Donald M. Bahr. Ed. by Albert Alvarez. LC 72-92103. (Illus.). 144p. 1974. pap. 44.70 (*0-7837-8349-3*, 204913800010) Bks Demand.

Pime in North America: Fifty Years: Impact & Presence. Piero Gheddo. LC 97-76007. (Illus.). 191p. 1998. pap. 8.00 (*0-9642010-6-2*) Pime Wrld Pr.

***Pime in North America--Fifty Years: Presence & Impact.** Piero Gheddo. LC 97-76007. 1998. write for info. (*0-09-642016-2*) Trafalgar.

Pimle on Growing Golden. Katina Kefalos. (Illus.). 14p. 1998. pap. 4.95 (*0-9666822-3-8*) Emerald Prodns.

Pimle's Family. Katina Kefalos. (Illus.). 14p. 1998. pap. 4.95 (*0-9666822-2-X*) Emerald Prodns.

Pimle's Journey. Katina Kefalos. (Illus.), 14p. 1998. pap. 4.95 (*0-9666822-1-1*) Emerald Prodns.

Pimle's Key. Katina Kefalos. 14p. 1998. pap. 4.95 (*0-9666822-4-6*) Emerald Prodns.

Pimm's Book of Polo. John Lloyd. (Illus.). 240p. 1989. 35.00 (*0-943955-17-3*, Trafalgar Sq Pub) Trafalgar.

Pimp. Iceberg Slim & Robert Beck. 317p. 1996. mass mkt. 6.99 (*0-87067-979-1*, BH759) Holloway.

Pimp Game. Mickey Royal. Ed. by Stacie Foote. (Illus.). 96p. (YA). pap. 14.95 (*0-9700587-0-5*) Sharif Pubng.

Pimpernel & Rosemary. Emmuska Orczy. 312p. 24.95 (*0-8488-2543-8*) Amereon Ltd.

Pimpernel & Rosemary. Emmuska Orczy. 1996. 37.95 (*0-89966-462-8*) Buccaneer Bks.

Pimpernel Project. large type ed. Mary Raymond. (Linford Romance Library). 288p. 1989. pap. 16.99 (*0-7089-6654-3*, Linford) Ulverscroft.

Pimpinella. Ilse Kramer. 258p. mass mkt. 4.99 (*1-55197-003-1*) Picasso Publ.

***Pimpon.** Alma Flor Ada. (SPA., Illus.). (ps-3). 1999. pap. text 7.95 (*1-58105-401-7*) Santillana.

Pimporello: A Fable for All Ages. Marcel Marceau. 128p. 1991. 25.00 (*0-7206-0813-9*) Dufour.

Pimps, Whores & Welfare Brats. Star Parker & Lorenzo Benet. 1998. per. 14.00 (*0-671-53466-1*, PB Trade Paper) PB.

PIMS Principles: Linking Strategy to Performance. Robert D. Buzzell & Bradley T. Gale. 352p. 1987. 40.00 (*0-02-904430-8*) Free Pr.

Pimsleur Hebrew, Set. unabridged ed. Pimsleur International Staff. (HEB.). 1997. audio 295.00 (*0-671-57932-0*) S&S Audio.

Pimsleur Ojibwe, Set. unabridged ed. Pimsleur International Staff. (OJI.). 1997. audio 295.00 (*0-671-57941-X*) S&S Audio.

Pimsleur Spanish III, Set. unabridged ed. Pimsleur International Staff. (SPA.). 1997. audio 295.00 (*0-671-57952-5*) S&S Audio.

Pimsleur's Checklists of Basic American Legal Publications. Ed. by Marcia S. Zubrow. Incl. Pt. 1. Statutes. 1962. Pt. 2. Session Laws. 1962. Pt. 3. Attorneys General Opinions & Reports. 1962. Pt. 4. Judicial Councils. 1962. Pt. 5. Restatements. 1962. (AALL Publications Ser.: No. 4). Set ring bd., suppl. ed. 240.00 (*0-8377-0104-X*, Rothman) W S Hein.

Pimsleur's Checklists of Basic American Legal Publications. Ed. by Marcia S. Zubrow. (AALL Publications Ser.: No. 4). lib. bdg. 225.00 (*0-8377-9228-2*, Rothman) W S Hein.

Pin & Sleeve Configurations, UL 1686, UL1686. 2nd ed. (C). 1998. pap. text 135.00 (*1-55989-547-0*) Underwrtrs Labs.

Pin Curling. Kip Productions, Inc. Staff. (Cosmetology Ser.). 1980. 44.95 (*0-87350-457-7*) Milady Pub.

Pin Pals. Pleasant Company Staff. (gr. 9-12). 1999. pap. text 1.95 (*1-56247-740-4*) Pleasant Co.

Pin, Pin, Sarabin. Alma F. Ada. (Cuentos con Alma Ser.). (SPA., Illus.). 24p. (J). (gr. 3-9). 1993. 16.95 (*1-56492-130-1*) Laredo.

***Pin Pointer: Nashville.** (Illus.). 215p. 1999. pap. 48.50 (*1-58461-055-7*) Indust Map.

Pin Prick Press Annual Index of Serial & Chapbook Publications, 1980. Roberta Mendel. 28p. (Orig.). 1981. pap. 3.00 (*0-936424-07-9*, 008) Pin Prick.

Pin the Tail on the Donkey & Other Party Games. Joanna Cole & Stephanie Calmenson. LC 92-29786. (Illus.). 48p. (J). (ps up). 1993. pap. 6.95 (*0-688-12521-2*, Wm Morrow); lib. bdg. 14.93 (*0-688-11892-5*, Wm Morrow) Morrow Avon.

Pin Up. Mark Gabor. 1996. pap. 14.99 (*3-8228-8664-5*) Taschen Amer.

Pin-Up Poster Book: The Billy DeVorss Collection. Max Allan Collins. LC 97-66771. (Illus.). 48p. 1997. pap. 17.95 (*1-888054-11-5*, 54115) Collectors Pr.

Pin-Up Poster Book: The Edward Runci Collection. Charles G. Martinette & Louis K. Meisel. Ed. by Ann Bennett. LC 97-69357. (Edward Runci Collection). (Illus.). 48p. 1999. pap. 17.95 (*1-888054-15-8*, 54158) Collectors Pr.

Pin Ups. Taschen, Benedikt Staff. (Illus.). 64p. 1996. pap. 3.99 (*3-8228-8171-6*) Taschen Amer.

Pin-Ups & Glamour Art: The Collector's & Dealer's Price & Identification Guide. 2nd rev. ed. Denis C. Jackson. (Illus.). 52p. (Orig.). 1996. pap. 8.95 (*1-888687-02-9*) Illust Collectors.

Pinaceae: Drawings & Descriptions of the Genera Abies, Cedrus, Pseudolarix, Keteleeria, Nothotsuga, Tauga, Cathaya, Pseudotsuga, Larix & Picea. Aljos Farjon. (Regnum Vegetabile Ser.: Vol. 121). (Illus.). 340p. 1990. 245.00 (*3-87429-298-3*, 041498, Pub. by Koeltz Sci Bks) Lubrecht & Cramer.

Pinafore Palace: A Book of Rhymes for the Nursery. Ed. by Kate D. Wiggin et al. LC 72-8290. (Granger Index Reprint Ser.). (YA). (ps-1). 1977. reprint ed. 23.95 (*0-8369-6399-7*) Ayer.

Pinafores & Pelotas. Alicia Zorzoli. LC 96-152453. (Illus.). 24p. (J). (gr. 1-3). 1996. pap. text 3.99 (*1-56309-179-8*, N968104, New Hope) Womans Mission Union.

Pinal Dome Oil Company: An Adventure in Business, 1901-1917. Richard C. Schwatzman. LC 75-41782. (Companies & Men: Business Enterprises in America Ser.). 1976. 31.95 (*0-405-08097-2*) Ayer.

Pinasco. David A. Wilson. (Illus.). 16p. (Orig.). 1971. ring bd. 1.00 (*0-685-30026-9*) Cottonwood KS.

Pinata. Junior League of McAllen Inc. Staff. LC 80-82158. 435p. 1994. spiral bd. 15.95 (*0-9604548-0-2*) Jr Leag McAllen.

Pinata & More! Bilingual Songs for Children. 2nd rev. ed. Sarah Barchas. (ENG & SPA., Illus.). 36p. (J). (gr. k-6). 1997. pap. 12.95 incl. audio (*1-889686-06-9*) High Haven Mus.

Pinata & More! Bilingual Songs for Children. 2nd rev. ed. Sarah Barchas. (ENG & SPA., Illus.). 36p. (J). (gr. k-6). 1997. pap. 15.98 incl. audio compact disk (*1-889686-07-7*) High Haven Mus.

Pinata Maker. George Ancona. LC 93-2389.Tr. of El Pinatero. (Illus.). 40p. (J). 1994. pap. 9.00 (*0-15-200060-7*, Harcourt Child Bks) Harcourt.

Pinata Maker: El Pinatero. George Ancona. 1995. 15.20 (*0-606-06668-3*, Pub. by Turtleback) Demco.

***Pinata Quilt.** Jane Tenorio Coscarelli. Tr. by Nicole Coscarelli. LC 99-64894. (ENG & SPA.). 48p. (J). (gr. k-6). 1999. 13.95 (*0-9653422-5-5*, Pub. by Quarter-Inch); pap. 9.95 (*0-9653422-6-3*, Pub. by Quarter-Inch) Sunbelt Pubns.

Pinata Vacia. Alma F. Ada. (Cuentos para Todo el Ano Ser.). (SPA., Illus.). (J). (gr. k-12). pap. 7.95 (*1-56014-225-1*) Santillana.

***Pinata Vacia.** Alma Flor Ada. (Cuentos para Todo el Ano (Little Books) Ser.). (SPA., Illus.). (J). 1999. pap. 7.95 (*1-58105-188-3*) Santillana.

Pinatamaker - El Pinatero. George Ancona. LC 93-2389. (Illus.). 40p. (YA). (gr. 7 up). 1994. 17.00 (*0-15-261875-9*) Harcourt.

Pinatas & Paper Flowers (Pinatas y Flores de Papel) Holidays of the Americas in English & Spanish. Lila Perl. (ENG & SPA.). (J). 1983. 12.15 (*0-606-02983-4*, Pub. by Turtleback) Demco.

Pinatas & Paper Flowers-Pinatas y Flores de Papel: Holidays of the Americas in English & Spanish. Lila Perl & Alma F. Ada. LC 82-12211. (Illus.). 91p. (J). (gr. 3-6). 1983. pap. 7.95 (*0-89919-155-X*, Clarion Bks) HM.

Pinatas & Smiling Skeletons: Celebrating Mexican Festivals. Zoe Harris & Suzanne Williams. LC 98-27409. (Illus.). 48p. (YA). (gr. 2-8). 1998. lib. bdg. 19.95 (*1-881896-19-6*, Dragon Bks) Pacific View Pr.

Pinball. Sabine Bartels. 1994. 12.98 (*0-7858-0071-9*) Bk Sales Inc.

Pinball. Gary Flower. 1988. 12.98 (*1-55521-322-7*) Bk Sales Inc.

Pinball. Jerzy N. Kosinski. 320p. 1996. pap. 12.00 (*0-8021-3482-3*, Grove) Grove-Atltic.

Pinball: Lure of the Silver Ball. G. Flower. 128p. 1997. 12.98 (*0-7858-0784-5*) Bk Sales Inc.

Pinball Collectors Resource. 2nd ed. Robert Hawkins & Donald Mueting. 1999. 19.95 (*0-9623962-1-4*) Mueting Electronics.

Pinball Effect: How Renaissance Water Gardens Made the Carburetor Possible & Other Journeys Through Knowledge. James Lee Burke. 336p. 1997. pap. 15.95 (*0-316-11610-6*) Little.

***Pinball Machine Care & Maintenance: For Electro-Mechanical & Solid State Machines.** Bernard B. Kamoroff. LC 99-94686. (Illus.). 100p. 2000. pap. 24.95 (*0-917510-13-5*) Bell Springs Pub.

Pinball Machines. Heribert Eiden & Jurgen Lukas. 168p. 1997. 35.00 (*0-7643-0316-3*) Schiffer.

Pinball Machines. 3rd rev. ed. Heribert Eiden & Jurgen Lukas. (Illus.). 168p. 1999. 35.00 (*0-7643-0895-5*) Schiffer.

Pinball 1: Illustrated Historical Guide to Pinball Machines, Vol. 1. Richard M. Bueschel. (Illus.). 256p. (Orig.). (C). 1988. pap. text 29.95 (*0-86667-047-5*) Coin Slot Bks.

P

An Asterisk (*) at the beginning of an entry indicates that the title is appearing for the first time.

Pinball Pandemonium. Illus. by Martha Auckland. (Doodle Art Medium Tubes Ser.). (J). (gr. k up). 1997. pap. 8.95 (0-8431-6569-3, Price Stern) Peng Put Young Read.

Pinball Player. Pat M. Kuras. 1982. pap. 3.50 (0-914852-11-6) Good Gay.

Pinball Science. DK Multimedia Staff. (YA). (gr. 3 up). 1998. cd-rom 29.95 (0-7894-3260-9) DK Pub Inc.

Pinballs see Bolas Locas

***Pinballs.** (J). 1999. 9.95 (1-56137-082-7) Novel Units.

***Pinballs.** (J). 1999. 11.95 (1-56137-827-5) Novel Units.

Pinballs. Betsy C. Byars. LC 76-41518. (Illus.). 144p. (YA). (gr. 4-7). 1977. lib. bdg. 15.89 (0-06-020918-6) HarpC Child Bks.

Pinballs. Betsy C. Byars. LC 76-41518. (Trophy Bk.). 144p. (YA). (gr. 5-9). 1993. pap. 4.95 (0-06-440198-7, HarpTrophy) HarpC Child Bks.

Pinballs. Betsy C. Byars. 137p. (J). (gr. 4-6). pap. 4.95 (0-8072-1383-7); pap. 4.95 (0-8072-1356-X) Listening Lib.

Pinballs. Betsy C. Byars. (J). 1987. 10.05 (0-606-03346-7, Pub. by Turtleback) Demco.

Pinballs. unabridged ed. Betsy C. Byars. (J). (gr. 4-6). 1988. pap. 21.98 incl. audio (0-8072-8536-6, LB2SP) Listening Lib.

***Pinballs.** unabridged ed. Betsy C. Byars. (J). (gr. 4-6). 1999. pap. 15.98 incl. audio (0-8072-1800-6, JJRH100SP) Listening Lib.

Pinballs: A Study Guide. Edna Ritzenberg. (Novel-Ties Ser.). (J). (gr. 4-6). 1984. pap. text, teacher ed., student ed. 15.95 (0-88122-090-6) Lrn Links.

Pinballs: A Unit Plan. Janine Sherman. 168p. 1997. teacher ed., ring bd. 26.95 (1-58337-172-9) Teachers Pet Pubns.

Pinballs: Playscript. Aurand Harris. (YA). 1992. pap. 6.00 (0-87602-301-4) Anchorage.

Pincel en el Alba: Poemas Selectos. Marilu Capin de Aguilar. LC 92-71411. (Coleccion Espejo de Paciencia). (SPA.). 176p. (Orig.). 1992. pap. 15.00 (0-89729-641-9) Ediciones.

Pinceladas Criollas. Jorge R. Plasencia. LC 87-83348. (Coleccion Caniqui). (SPA.). 88p. (Orig.). 1988. pap. 9.95 (0-89729-472-6) Ediciones.

Pinceladas Literarias Hispanoamericanas. Gloria Bautista Gutierrez. 352p. 1999. pap. text 52.95 (0-471-29747-X) Wiley.

Pincengrain. Marcel Jouhandeau. (FRE.). 256p. 1984. pap. 11.95 (0-7859-2487-6, 2070375447) Fr & Eur.

Pincers. Philip Ward. (Dramascripts Ser.: Vol. 7). 1975. pap. 4.95 (0-902675-30-3) Oleander Pr.

Pinch of Herbs. Katy Holder. 128p. 1997. 14.98 (0-7858-0666-0) Bk Sales Inc.

Pinch of Poison. Claudia Bishop. (Hemlock Falls Mystery Ser.). 1995. mass mkt. 5.99 (0-425-15104-2) Berkley Pub.

Pinch of Poison. Frances Lockridge & Richard Lockridge. 18.95 (0-89190-917-6) Amereon Ltd.

Pinch of Salt Lake. Junior League of Salt Lake City, Inc. Staff. LC 86-81537. 272p. 1986. 19.95 (0-9616972-0-2) Jr League Salt Lake City.

Pinch of Snuff. Reginald Hill. 336p. 1984. mass mkt. 6.50 (0-440-16912-7) Dell.

Pinch of This, a Dash of That. Ed. by Gooseberry Patch Staff. (Illus.). 224p. 1998. spiral bd. 14.95 (1-888052-33-3) Gooseberry Patch.

Pinch of This & a Dash of That. Kaye Johns. (Illus.). 1989. vinyl bd. 24.95 (0-9615390-5-4) Aspen West Pub.

Pinch of This & a Handful of That: Historic Recipes of Texas, 1830-1900. Daughters of the Republic of Texas District VIII S. 200p. 1988. 16.95 (0-89015-649-2) Sunbelt Media.

***Pinch of This & a Pinch of That: The Cooking Treasures of Our Fairytale Italian Restaurant, Mama Lena's Italian Kitchen.** Salvino Madonna & Margo Madonna. (Illus.). 280p. 1999. pap. 29.95 (0-7392-0457-2, PO3762) Morris Pubng.

Pinch of Thyme: A Low Fat Cookbook Four Busy People. Robyn Webb. 125p. 1994. pap. 11.95 (0-9631345-4-X) Regal Direct.

Pinch of Thyme: Easy Lessons Toward a Leaner Life. Robyn Webb. 208p. (C). 1994. per. 15.95 (0-8403-9384-9) Kendall-Hunt.

Pinch of Thyme: Recipes from the New Hanover Regional Medical Center Auxiliary. LC 98-67393. 192p. 1998. 16.95 (0-9665428-0-0) New Han Reg Med.

***Pinch of Time: Meals in Less Than 30 Minutes.** Sandra Rudloff. (Illus.). 128p. 2000. pap. 8.95 (1-55867-251-6, Nitty Gritty Ckbks) Bristol Pub Ent CA.

Pinch Runner Memorandum. Kenzaburo Oe. Tr. by Michiko N. Wilson & Michael K. Wilson from JPN. LC 93-16114. 265p. (C). (gr. 13). 1994. text 59.95 (1-56324-183-8, East Gate Bk); pap. text 21.95 (1-56324-184-6, East Gate Bk) M E Sharpe.

Pinched Nerves. Steven Hartman. Ed. by Stanley H. Barkan. (Review Brooklyn Writers Chapbook Ser.: No. 1). 48p. 1991. 15.00 (0-89304-202-1); pap. 5.00 (0-89304-203-X) Cross-Cultrl NY.

Pinched Nerves: Mini Book. Steven Hartman. Ed. by Stanley H. Barkan. (Review Brooklyn Writers Chapbook Ser.: No. 1). 48p. 1991. 15.00 (0-89304-204-8); pap. 5.00 (0-89304-205-6) Cross-Cultrl NY.

Pincher Martin. William Golding. LC 57-10059. Orig. Title: Two Deaths of Christopher Martin. 216p. 1968. reprint ed. pap. 10.00 (0-15-671833-2, Harvest Bks) Harcourt.

Pinckney's Treaty: America's Advantage from Europe's Distress, 1783-1800. Samuel F. Bemis. LC 73-8148. (Illus.). 372p. 1973. reprint ed. lib. bdg. 65.00 (0-8371-6954-2, BEPT, Greenwood Pr) Greenwood.

Pincushion's Strawberry. Jared Carter. (Illus.). 31p. (Orig.). 1984. pap. 3.50 (0-914946-43-9) Cleveland St Univ Poetry Ctr.

Pindar, Vol. I. Ed. & Tr. by William H. Race from GRE. LC 95-42927. (Loeb Classical Library: Vol. 56 & 485). 400p. 1997. 19.95 (0-674-99564-3) HUP.

Pindar, Vol. II. Ed. & Tr. by William H. Race from GRE. (Loeb Classical Library: No. 56 & 485). 416p. 1996. 19.95 (0-674-99534-1) HUP.

Pindar: Selected Odes. Peter Pindar. Ed. & Tr. by Stephen Instone from GRE. (Classical Texts Ser.). (Illus.). 200p. 1996. 59.99 (0-85668-668-9, Pub. by Aris & Phillips); pap. text 28.00 (0-85668-669-7, Pub. by Aris & Phillips) David Brown.

Pindar: The Olympian & Pythain Odes. Pindar. 1998. reprint ed. lib. bdg. 79.00 (0-7812-4796-9) Rprt Serv.

Pindar & Homer. Frank J. Nisetich. LC 88-46123. (American Journal of Philology Monographs: No. 4). 128p. 1989. text 24.00 (0-8018-3820-7) Johns Hopkins.

Pindar, the Olympian & Pythian Odes. Peter Pindar. Ed. by Basil L. Gildersleeve. 1885. 59.00 (0-403-00331-8) Scholarly.

Pindar TV Viewer's Guide to the 1984 Olympic Games. (Illus.). 112p. 1984. pap. 6.95 (0-918223-33-4) Pindar Pr.

Pindari Pt. I: Epinicia. Ed. by Maehler & Snell. (GRE.). 1997. 29.95 (3-8154-1585-3, T1585, Pub. by B G Teubner) U of Mich Pr.

Pindari Pt. II: Fragmenta, Indices. Ed. by Maehler. (GRE.). 1989. 44.50 (3-322-00673-5, T1586, Pub. by B G Teubner) U of Mich Pr.

Pindaric Mind. T. K. Hubbard. 1985. pap. 27.00 (90-04-07303-5, MNS, 85) Brill Academic Pubs.

Pindaros. Ulrich Von Wilamowitz-Moellendorff. vii, 528p. 1985. write for info. (3-296-16130-9) G Olms Pubs.

Pindar's Homer: The Lyric Possession of an Epic Past. Gregory Nagy. LC 89-19938. 552p. 1990. text 50.00 (0-8018-3932-7) Johns Hopkins.

Pindar's Mythmaking: The Fourth Pythian Ode. Charles Segal. LC 85-43312. 196p. 1986. text 39.50 (0-691-05473-8, Pub. by Princeton U Pr) Cal Prin Full Svc.

Pindar's Mythmaking: The Fourth Pythian Ode. Charles Segal. LC 85-43312. 223p. 1986. reprint ed. pap. 69.20 (0-608-04626-4, 206531300003) Bks Demand.

Pindar's Odes. Peter Pindar. Tr. by Roy A. Swanson from GRE. 416p. reprint ed. pap. 15.95 (0-8290-0332-0) Irvington.

Pindar's Paeans: A Reading of the Fragments with a Survey of the Genre. Ian Rutherford. 544p. (C). 2000. text 110.00 (0-19-814381-8) OUP.

Pindar's Victory Songs. Frank J. Nisetich. LC 79-3739. 384p. 1980. pap. text 25.95 (0-8018-2356-0) Johns Hopkins.

Pindarus: Concordantia in Scholia Vetera in Pindarum, 2 vols. Graziano Arrighetti et al. write for info. (0-318-71986-X) G Olms Pubs.

Pindarus: Interpretatio Epiniciorum Latina Cum Commentario Perpetuo, Fragmenta et Indices. Ed. by A. Boeckh. 862p. 1963. reprint ed. 225.00 (0-318-72066-3) G Olms Pubs.

Pindarus - Concordantia et Indices in Scholia Pindarica Vetera, 2 vols. Ed. by Graziano Arrighetti et al. (Alpha-Omega, Reihe A Ser.: Bd. LXXXVII). (GER.). ix, 1376p. 1991. 475.00 (3-487-09446-0) G Olms Pubs.

***Pindelfin Collectors Handbook.** Stella Ashbrook. (Illus.). 2000. 24.95 (1-870703-83-9) Francis Jos Pubns.

Pinder Poet: Cherishing This Heritage. 66p. 1997. 9.95 (0-9659748-1-2) Center Pr Bks.

Pine & Palm. Moncure D. Conway. (Works of Moncure Daniel Conway). 1990. reprint ed. lib. bdg. 79.00 (0-7812-2338-5) Rprt Serv.

Pine & Pond: A Haiku Cycle. Jim Wilson. 50p. 1994. 10.00 (0-9677158-1-4) Hse of Ho Tei.

Pine Barrens. John McPhee. LC 67-22439. (Illus.). 157p. 1978. 27.50 (0-374-23360-8); pap. 11.00 (0-374-51442-9) FS&G.

Pine Barrens: Ecosystem & Landscape. Richard T. Forman. LC 98-26022. (Illus.). 684p. (C). 1998. pap. text 30.00 (0-8135-2593-4) Rutgers U Pr.

Pine Barrens Legends, Lore & Lies. William McMahon. (Illus.). 149p. 1986. pap. 9.95 (0-912608-19-6) Mid Atlantic.

Pine Barrens Odyssey: A Naturalist's Year in the Pine Barrens of New Jersey. Howard P. Boyd. LC 97-22070. (Illus.). 275p. 1997. pap. 19.95 (0-937548-34-0) Plexus Pub.

Pine Boat Finishes. Paul Butler & Marya Butler. 160p. 1991. pap. 18.95 (0-07-009403-9) McGraw.

Pine Cones & Holly. Marcia Leonard. 1996. pap. 2.95 (0-8167-1493-2) Troll Communs.

Pine Cones & Magnolia Blossoms. Joan W. Martin. LC 99-72740. (Illus.). 100p. 1999. pap. text 8.95 (1-58521-005-6) Bks Black Chldn.

Pine Creek Parish Hall & Other Poems. Barton Sutter. LC 85-50678. (Plains Poetry Ser.: Vol. 2). (Illus.). 72p. (Orig.). 1985. 13.00 (0-911015-06-X); pap. 6.95 (0-911015-07-8) Sandhills Pr.

Pine Forest Snow. Ansel Adams. 1997. 30.00 (0-8212-2421-2) Little.

Pine Furniture: The Country Look. Nancy N. Schiffer. LC 98-88029. (Schiffer Book for Collectors Ser.). (Illus.). 144p. (Orig.). 1999. pap. 29.95 (0-7643-0742-8) Schiffer.

Pine Furniture Making. Anthony Hontoir. (Illus.). 160p. 1994. 35.00 (1-85223-740-6, Pub. by Cro1wood) Trafalgar.

Pine Furniture of Early New England. Russell H. Kettell. (Illus.). 477p. 1949. 19.95 (0-486-20145-7) Dover.

Pine Furniture Projects for the Home. Dave Mackenzie. LC 97-198854. (Illus.). 128p. 1997. pap. text 14.95 (1-86108-035-2, Pub. by Guild Master) Sterling.

Pine Mountain Groups Network Analysis Reference Guide: The Definitive Resource for the Network Analyst. 8th rev. ed. William N. Alderson. (Illus.). 78p. 1998. pap. 65.00 (1-58392-000-5) Pine Mt.

Pine Needle Basketry: From Forest Floor to Finished Project. Judy M. Mallow. Ed. by Chris Rich. LC 96-26504. (Illus.). 120p. 1997. 18.95 (1-887374-14-0) Lark Books.

Pine Needle National Park Visitor Guide: America's Favorite Fictitious National Park. Troy Dunham. LC 90-82942. (Illus.). 112p. (Orig.). 1990. pap. 12.95 (1-877967-07-6) Cttnwd Pr.

Pine Needle Raffia Basketry. rev. ed. Jeannie McFarland. (Illus.). 48p. 1996. reprint ed. pap. 9.00 (0-9618828-0-8) Baskets & Bullets.

Pine Needles on the Grass. Kosta Kontoyiannaki. (Illus.). 20p. (J). (gr. k-3). 1995. pap. 8.95 (1-56606-034-6) Bradley Mann.

Pine Nut Chronicle: The History & Adventures of Mining in Douglas County, Nevada. Nyle N. Nation. 300p. 1991. pap. 12.95 (0-9630420-0-9) Triple N Ent.

Pine Nut Chronicle: The History & Adventures of Mining in Douglas County Nevada. 2nd ed. Nyle N. Nation. Ed. by Sue Parkhurst. 250p. 1992. reprint ed. pap. 12.95 (0-9630420-1-7) Triple N Ent.

Pine Ridge Plantation. William Drysdale. LC 75-38647. (Black Heritage Library Collection). 1977. reprint ed. 27.95 (0-8369-9005-6) Ayer.

Pine River & Lone Peak: An Anthology of 3 Choson Dynasty Poets. Tr. by Peter H. Lee from KOR. LC 90-44433. 208p. 1991. text 21.50 (0-8248-1298-0) UH Pr.

Pine Tree Legal Assistance, Inc. Annual Docket Report. 74p. 1988. 10.50 (0-317-03739-0, 44,070) NCLS Inc.

Pine Tree Parable. Liz C. Higgs. LC 97-15570. (Illus.). 32p. (J). (ps-2). 1997. 7.99 (0-8499-1480-9) Tommy Nelson.

***Pine Tree Quilts: Perfect Patchwork Piecing.** Lois Embree Arnold. (Illus.). 144p. 2000. pap. 25.95 (1-57432-749-6, Am Quilters Soc) Collector Bks.

Pine Tree Suite. Ed. by W. Strickland. 1975. 5.00 (0-913334-30-8, CM1033) Consort Music.

Pine Trees. Marcia S. Freeman. LC 98-22679. (Trees Ser.). (Illus.). 24p. (J). 1998. write for info. (0-7368-0095-6, Pebble Bks) Capstone Pr.

Pine Trees. Marcia S. Freeman. (Trees (Captstone) Ser.). (J). 1998. 13.25 (0-516-21507-8) Childrens.

Pine Trees & Cotton Fields: Reminiscences of a Childhood NE Texas-NW Louisiana 1925-1942. Janie R. Koenig. LC 90-92182. (Illus.). 352p. 1991. 35.00 (0-9628249-3-3) Piney Woods Prodns.

Pine Trees & Politics. Joseph J. Malone. Ed. by Stuart Bruchey. LC 78-53552. (Development of Public Land Law in the U. S. Ser.). 1979. reprint ed. lib. bdg. 19.95 (0-405-11380-3) Ayer.

Pine Trees & the Sky. Jean C. Stewart. 108p. 1998. pap. 21.00 (1-898218-97-8) St Mut.

Pine Vole in North Carolina. John R. Paul. (Reports of Investigations: No. 20). (Illus.). 28p. 1970. pap. 1.00 (0-89792-044-9) Ill St Museum.

Pineal & Midbrain Lesions. G. Pendl. (Illus.). 280p. 1985. 126.00 (0-387-81858-8) Spr-Verlag.

Pineal & Reproduction. Ed. by Russell J. Reiter. (Progress in Reproductive Biology & Medicine Ser.: Vol. 4). (Illus.). 1978. 103.50 (3-8055-2815-9) S Karger.

Pineal Gland. Ed. by Russell J. Reiter. LC 84-4762. (Comprehensive Endocrinology Ser.). (Illus.). 394p. 1984. reprint ed. pap. 122.20 (0-7837-9579-3, 206032800005) Bks Demand.

Pineal Gland, Vol. I. Ed. by Russell J. Reiter. 1981. 186.00 (0-8493-5714-4, QP188, CRC Reprint) Franklin.

Pineal Gland: Extra-Reproductive Effects, Vol. III. Ed. by Russel J. Rieter. 248p. 1982. 144.00 (0-8493-5717-9, QP188, CRC Reprint) Franklin.

Pineal Gland: Reproductive Effects, Vol. II. Ed. by Russell J. Reiter. 240p. 1981. 137.00 (0-8493-5716-0, QP188, CRC Reprint) Franklin.

Pineal Gland: Update 1996: From Molecular Mechanisms to Clinical Implications. Ed. by Russell J. Reiter & Susan M. Webb. LC 97-50031. 1996. 69.95 (0-915340-19-4) PJD Pubns.

***Pineal Gland & Cancer: Neuro-Imuno-Endocrine Interactions.** Christian Bartsch. LC 00-35760. 2000. write for info. (3-540-64051-7) Spr-Verlag.

Pineal Gland & Its Endocrine Aspects: Proceedings of a Symposium with the 7th International Endocrinology Congress, Canada, April 1984. Ed. by G. Brown & S. D. Wainwright. LC 85-9571. (Advances in the Biosciences Ser.: Vol. 53). (Illus.). 390p. 1985. 92.00 (0-08-031992-0, Pub. by Pergamon Repr) Franklin.

Pineal Gland & Its Hormones: Fundamentals & Clinical Perspectives: Proceedings of NATO ASI Held in Erice, Italy, June 7-13, 1994. Ed. by Russell J. Reiter et al. LC 95-33471. (NATO ASI Ser.: Series A, Vol. 277). (Illus.). 244p. (C). 1995. text 95.00 (0-306-45105-0) Plenum.

Pineal Gland Series, 3 vols. Russell J. Reiter. 465.00 (0-8493-5713-6, CRC Reprint) Franklin.

Pineal Organ. L. E. Vollrath. (Handbuch der Mikroskopischen Anatomie Des Menschen: Vol. VI-7). (Illus.). 670p. 1981. 383.00 (0-387-10313-9) Spr-Verlag.

Pineal Organ, Its Hormone Melatonin, & the Photoneuroendocrine System. H. W. Korf et al. LC 98-2791. (Advances in Anatomy, Embryology & Cell Biology Ser.: Vol. 146). (Illus.). 105p. 1998. pap. 99.95 (3-540-64135-1) Spr-Verlag.

***Pineapple?** unabridged ed. Audrey Miller. 243p. 1999. 65.00 (1-881119-02-5) Pyncheon Hse.

***Pineapple?** unabridged limited ed. Audrey Miller. 243p. 1999. 95.00 (1-881119-20-3) Pyncheon Hse.

Pineapple Air Force: Pearl Harbor to Tokyo. John W. Lambert. LC 90-60558. (Illus.). 220p. (C). 1990. 34.95 (0-9625860-0-5) Specialty Pr.

Pineapple Crochet Designs. Ed. by Rita Weiss. (Illus.). 48p. (Orig.). 1980. pap. 3.95 (0-486-23939-X) Dover.

***Pineapple Girl.** 1999. per. 3.99 (0-373-63105-7, Harlequin) Harlequin Bks.

Pineapple Gold. Joann H. Dobbins. LC 83-90001. 304p. 1983. pap. 10.95 (0-9610540-0-X) J H Dobbins.

Pineapple Quilt, a Piece of Cake. Loretta Smith. Ed. by Eleanor Burns. (Illus.). 64p. 1989. pap. 9.95 (0-922705-19-4) Quilt Day.

Pineapple Quilts: New Quilts from an Old Favorite. Ed. by Barbara Smith. LC 98-16426. 112p. 1998. pap. 16.95 (1-57432-711-9) Collector Bks.

Pineapple Story. LC 78-60645. (Illus.). 39p. (J). (gr. 3 up). 1984. 5.00 (0-916888-03-7) Inst Basic Life.

Pineapple Tart. Anne Dunlop. 263p. 1992. pap. 10.95 (1-85371-169-1) Dufour.

Pineapple White. Jon Shirota. 165p. 1972. 4.95 (0-89986-388-4) Oriental Bk Store.

Pineapples Are Never Black or White. Harry C. Goode. LC 96-50217. (Local History Ser.: Vol. 15). (Illus.). (Orig.). 1997. pap. 16.98 (0-9617352-4-4) Kellersberger Fund.

Pineapples, Penguins, & Pagodas: Traveling Around the World Through Literature, Research, & Thinking Skills. Barbara Jinkins. Ed. by Jan Keeling. (Illus.). 128p. (Orig.). (J). (gr. 3-6). 1993. pap. text 12.95 (0-86530-258-8, 258-8) Incentive Pubns.

***Pinecrest Resthaven.** Grace Cavalieri. LC 97-61901. (Capital Collection). 60p. 1998. pap. 10.00 (0-915380-39-0) Word Works.

Pinehaven. William G. Schmidt. LC 99-70329. 306p. 1999. pap. 15.95 (0-7392-0128-X, PO3042) Morris Pubng.

Pinelands. Robert Bateman. LC 98-106192. 248p. 1994. 21.95 (0-937548-27-8); pap. 12.95 (0-937548-28-6) Plexus Pub.

Pinellas County. Alejandro M. DeQuesada, Jr. & Vincent Luisi. LC 98-86768. (Images of America Ser.). (Illus.). 128p. 1998. pap. 16.99 (0-7524-1236-1) Arcadia Publng.

***Pinellas County Business Directory (2000)** American Business Directories Staff et al. 1,680p. 2000. boxed set 450.00 incl. cd-rom (0-7687-0276-3) Am Busn Direct.

Pinero: A Theatrical Life. John Dawick. (Illus.). 384p. 1993. 39.95 (0-87081-302-1) Univ Pr Colo.

Pines: Brad Davis. Ruth K. Meyer. (Illus.). 10p. (Orig.). 1984. pap. 3.00 (0-915577-04-6) Taft Museum.

Pines & Plantations. Vashti. pap. 14.95 (0-9607860-0-7) Vashti Auxiliary.

Pines Cookbook: Pines on the Severn/1992 Anniversary 1997. Noni Paradis. Ed. by Joyce Bowers. (Illus.). 214p. 1997. 12.00 (0-9659824-0-8) Pines Comm Improve.

Pines Hold Their Secrets. Jill Blee. 283p. 1998. pap. 19.95 (0-9587718-8-X, Pub. by Indra Pub) Intl Spec Bk.

Pinesnakes. W. P. Mara. (Illus.). 48p. 1995. pap. text 9.95 (0-7938-0262-8, RE119) TFH Pubns.

Pinewoods Country Scroll Patterns, Vol. 1. Ruth A. Cunningham. (Illus.). 36p. 1997. pap. 11.95 (0-9659393-0-8) Pinewoods Cntry Crafts.

Piney Woods School: An Oral History. Alferdteen Harrison. LC 82-11150. (Illus.). 193p. reprint ed. pap. 59.90 (0-8357-4343-8, 203714600007) Bks Demand.

Piney Woods Tavern: or Sam Slick in Texas. Samuel A. Hammett. LC 71-104473. 309p. reprint ed. lib. bdg. 28.00 (0-8398-0758-9) Irvington.

Piney Woods Tavern: or Sam Slick in Texas. Samuel A. Hammett. 309p. (C). 1986. reprint ed. pap. text 7.95 (0-8290-1882-4) Irvington.

Pinfire System see Systeme Lefaucheux: Continuing the Study of Pinfire Cartrige Arms

Ping. Yuki Hartman. 1984. 10.00 (0-936538-07-4) Kulchur Foun.

PING American College Golf Guide: 1994-95 Edition. Dean W. Frischknecht. (Illus.). 288p. 1994. pap. 9.95 (0-9624046-5-9) D Frischknecht Pubng.

PING American College Golf Guide: 1995-96 Edition. Dean W. Frischknecht. 1995. pap. 9.95 (0-9624046-6-7) D Frischknecht Pubng.

PING American College Golf Guide: 1996-97 Edition. 8th ed. Dean W. Frischknecht. (Illus.). 288p. (YA). (gr. 9-12). 1996. 9.95 (0-9624046-7-5) D Frischknecht Pubng.

PING American College Golf Guide: 1997-98 Edition. Dean W. Frischknecht. (Illus.). 304p. (YA). (gr. 9-12). 1997. pap. 11.95 (0-9624046-8-3) D Frischknecht Pubng.

***Ping American College Golf Guide: 1999-2000 Edition.** 11th rev. ed. Dean W. Frischknecht. (Illus.). 320p. (YA). (gr. 9-12). 1999. pap. 13.95 (1-929259-25-5) D Frischknecht Pubng.

***Ping American College Golf Guide: 2000-2001.** 12th rev. ed. Dean W. Frischknecht. (Illus.). 320p. (YA). (gr. 9-12). 2000. pap. 13.95 (1-929259-00-X) D Frischknecht Pubng.

Ping Pong Balls. Norma N. Bracy. (Illus.). (J). (ps-12). 1988. pap. text 2.50 (0-915783-06-1) Book Binder.

Ping Saves Earth. Roger S. Busse. LC 95-90113. 128p. (Orig.). 1995. pap. 10.00 (0-9629242-4-5) WKB Enterp.

Pingo the Plaid Panda. Loreen Leedy. LC 88-17005. (Illus.). 32p. (J). (gr. k-3). 1989. lib. bdg. 13.95 (0-8234-0727-6) Holiday.

Pingouin Book of Classic Knitting Patterns. Compiled by Phillipa Davis. 80p. (C). 1989. 125.00 (1-85368-018-4, Pub. by New5 Holland) St Mut.

Pinguin Pit. Tr. of Penguin Pete. (GER., Illus.). 32p. (J). (gr. k-3). 1996. 15.95 (3-314-00297-1, Pub. by North-South Bks NYC) Chronicle Bks.

Pinguino Pedro. Marcus Pfister. LC 95-36187.Tr. of Penguin Pete. (SPA., Illus.). 32p. (J). (gr. k-3). 1996. 15.95 (1-55858-564-8, Pub. by North-South Bks NYC); pap. 6.95 (1-55858-547-8, Pub. by North-South Bks NYC) Chronicle Bks.

Pinguino Pedro. Marcus Pfister.Tr. of Penguin Pete. (SPA., Illus.). 12p. (J). (ps). 1997. bds. 6.95 (1-55858-739-X, Pub. by North-South Bks NYC) Chronicle Bks.

An Asterisk (*) at the beginning of an entry indicates that the title is appearing for the first time.

Pinguino Pedro, Aprendiz de Marinero. Marcus Pfister. (SPA., Illus.). 32p. (J). (gr. k-3). 1998. 15.95 (*1-55858-919-8*, Pub. by North-South Bks NYC); pap. 6.95 (*1-55858-920-1*, Pub. by North-South Bks NYC) Chronicle Bks.

Pinguino Pedro y el Pequeno Timoteo. Marcus Pfister. LC 98-19644. (SPA., Illus.). 32p. (J). (gr. k-3). 1996. 15.95 (*1-55858-346-7*, Pub. by North-South Bks NYC) Chronicle Bks.

Pinguino Pedro y el Pequeno Timoteo. Marcus Pfister. (J). (gr. k-3). 1998. pap. 6.95 (*1-55858-347-5*, Pub. by North-South Bks NYC) Chronicle Bks.

Pinguino Pedro y Pat. Marcus Pfister. (SPA., Illus.). 32p. (J). (gr. k-3). 1998. 15.95 (*1-55858-886-8*, Pub. by North-South Bks NYC); pap. 6.95 (*1-55858-892-2*, Pub. by North-South Bks NYC) Chronicle Bks.

Pinguino Pedro y Sus Nuevos Amigos. Marcus Pfister. (SPA., Illus.). 32p. (J). (gr. k-3). 1996. 15.95 (*1-55858-641-5*, Pub. by North-South Bks NYC); pap. 6.95 (*1-55858-640-7*, Pub. by North-South Bks NYC) Chronicle Bks.

Pinguino Pedro y Sus Nuevos Amigos. Marcus Pfister. (SPA., Illus.). 12p. (J). (ps). 1997. bds. 6.95 (*1-55858-740-3*, Pub. by North-South Bks NYC) Chronicle Bks.

***Pinguino Polluelo.** Michelle McKenzie. Tr. by Bahia Translators Staff & Taro Echibuni.Tr. of Penguin Chick. (SPA., Illus.). 12p. (J). (gr. k). 2000. bds. 5.95 (*1-878244-29-9*) Monterey Bay Aquarium.

Pinguinos. Lynn M. Stone. (Aves Ser.).Tr. of Penguins. 24p. (J). (gr. k-4). 1994. lib. bdg. 10.95 (*0-86593-194-1*) Rourke Corp.

Pinguinos Son Padres Modelos. Arthur Morton. Tr. by Angelita L. Aguilar. (SPA.). (J). (gr. k-3). 1994. 12.50 (*1-57842-068-7*) Delmas Creat.

Pinhole Photographs. Ed. by Constance Sullivan. (Photographers at Work Ser.). (Illus.). 64p. 1995. pap. 16.95 (*1-56098-622-0*) Smithsonian.

Pinhole Photography: Rediscovering a Historic Technique. Eric Renner. (Illus.). 192p. 1994. pap. text 29.95 (*0-240-80231-4*, Focal) Buttrwrth-Heinemann.

***Pinhole Photography: Rediscovering a Historic Technique.** 2nd ed. Eric Renner. LC 99-25672. 228p. 1999. pap. text 32.95 (*0-240-80350-7*, Focal) Buttrwrth-Heinemann.

Pinikindu: Maternal Nurture, Paternal Substance. Brenda J. Clay. LC 76-8083. (Illus.). 1977. lib. bdg. 14.00 (*0-226-10943-7*) U Ch Pr.

***Pininfarina: Seventy Years.** Antoine Prunet. (Illus.). 308p. 2000. text 95.00 (*0-8478-2243-5*) Rizzoli Intl.

Pininfarina: Sixty Years. (Illus.). 290p. 1995. 75.00 (*88-7911-068-3*, Pub. by Giorgio Nada Editore) Howell Pr VA.

Pining Wind: A Cycle of No Plays. Tr. by Royall Tyler. LC 78-104624. (Cornell East Asia Ser.: No. 17). 204p. 1978. pap. 10.20 (*0-939657-17-1*) Cornell East Asia Pgm.

Piniqpiaranka Cangssagqt (My Favorite Things) (Cupig) large type ed. Agnes Kairaiuak et al. (ESK., Illus.). 8p. (J). (gr. k-3). 1999. pap. text 6.00 (*1-58084-162-7*) Lower Kuskokwim.

Pink. John A. Miller, Jr. 216p. mass mkt. 4.99 (*1-55197-173-9*) Picasso Publ.

Pink: A Novel. Gus Van Sant. 272p. 1998. pap. 12.95 (*0-385-49353-3*) Doubleday.

Pink - A Novel: There is No Gravity. David Wilde. 170p. 1994. pap. 20.00 (*1-882204-13-1*) Wilde Pub.

***Pink - A Novel: There is No Gravity.** David Wilde. 170p. 1999. write for info. (*1-882204-31-X*) Wilde Pub.

Pink Album. (Butterfly Bks.). (ARA., Illus.). 12.95 (*0-86685-712-5*) Intl Bk Ctr.

Pink & Blue. Gina C. Erickson & Kelli C. Foster. (Get Ready...Get Set...Read! Ser.). (Illus.). 24p. (J). (gr. k-8). 1994. pap. 3.50 (*0-8120-1921-0*) Barron.

Pink & Blue. Kelli C. Foster & Gina C. Erickson. (Get Ready...Get Set...Read! Ser.: Set 3). (Illus.). (J). 1996. lib. bdg. 11.95 (*1-56674-157-2*) Forest Hse.

Pink & Blue Baby Pages. Laurie Waldstein & Leslie Zinberg. LC 95-30763. (Illus.). 320p. 1995. pap. 12.95 (*0-8092-3396-7*, 339670, Contemporary Bks) NTC Contemp Pub Co.

Pink & Blue Toddler & Preschooler Pages. Laurie Waldstein & Leslie Zinberg. LC 99-29188. 320p. 1999. pap. 14.95 (*0-8092-2790-8*, 279080, Contemporary Bks) NTC Contemp Pub Co.

Pink & Naked in the Ultra-Violet Life. Donna Gebron. 49p. 1996. 18.00 (*1-888662-12-3*); pap. 6.00 (*1-888662-11-5*) Vinegar Hill.

Pink & Say. Patricia Polacco. LC 93-36340. (Illus.). 48p. (J). (gr. 4 up). 1994. 15.95 (*0-399-22671-0*, Philomel) Peng Put Young Read.

***Pink & the Black: Homosexuals in France since 1968.** Frederic Martel. LC 99-49932. 444p. 2000. pap. 19.95 (*0-8047-3274-4*) Stanford U Pr.

Pink & the Green with Mina de Vanghel. Stendhal, pseud. Tr. & Afterword by Richard Howard. LC 87-383210. 160p. 1988. 17.95 (*0-8112-1062-6*, Pub. by New Directions) Norton.

Pink Book. Cicely M. Barker. (Illus.). 64p. (J). 1995. 2.99 (*0-7232-0025-4*, F Warne) Peng Put Young Read.

Pink Champagne. large type ed. Anne Weale. 285p. 1992. reprint ed. 18.95 (*0-263-12814-8*) Mac Lib Ref.

Pink Chimneys: A Novel of 19th Century Maine. Ardeana H. Knowles. 320p. 1999. pap. 12.95 (*0-88448-056-9*) Tilbury Hse.

Pink Collar Blues: Work, Gender & Technology. Ed. by Belinda Probert & Bruce W. Wilson. 192p. (Orig.). 1993. pap. 19.95 (*0-522-84520-7*, Pub. by Melbourne Univ Pr) Paul & Co Pubs.

Pink Drink. S. Simeon. (Illus.). (J). 1995. 8.95 (*0-671-89833-7*) Litle Simon.

Pink Dust: Comics, 1997: 39th Parallel. J. O'Barr. LC 98-14186. 1998. 3.50 (*0-87816-585-1*) Kitchen Sink.

Pink Elephants & Other Bar Animals. Mary Jay. (Illus.). 100p. (Orig.). 1983. pap. 4.95 (*0-9612156-9-0*) M Jacobs.

Pink Fairy Book. Ed. by Andrew Lang. (Illus.). 360p. (J). (gr. 4-6). 1967. pap. 7.95 (*0-486-21792-2*) Dover.

Pink Fairy Book. Ed. by Andrew Lang. 26.95 (*0-89190-080-2*) Amereon Ltd.

Pink Fairy Book. Ed. by Andrew Lang. (Illus.). (J). (gr. 2 up). 1990. 22.75 (*0-8446-0755-X*) Peter Smith.

Pink Flamingo Murders: A Francesca Vierling Mystery. Elaine Viets. 272p. 1999. mass mkt. 5.99 (*0-440-22445-4*) Dell.

Pink Flamingoes: Splendor on the Grass. Don Featherstone. (Illus.). 96p. 1999. pap. 14.95 (*0-7643-0963-3*) Schiffer.

***Pink Flamingos.** Photos by Carol Mari. (Illus.). 208p. 2000. 55.00 (*0-7892-0668-4*) Abbeville Pr.

***Pink Flat Shoe.** Havoc Publishing Staff. 1999. 8.00 (*0-7416-1714-5*) Havoc Pub.

Pink Floyd. Andy Mabbett. (Complete Guides to the Music Of...Ser.). (Illus.). 150p. (Orig.). 1995. pap. 8.95 (*0-7119-4301-X*, OP 47735, Pub. by Omnibus Press) Omnibus NY.

Pink Floyd. Nick Mason. 1995. 40.00 (*0-684-81600-8*) Simon & Schuster.

Pink Floyd. Glenn Povey & Ian Russell. LC 99-199909. 256p. 1998. pap. 19.95 (*0-312-19175-8*) St Martin.

Pink Floyd: A Momentary Lapse of Reason. (Illus.). 108p. pap. 24.95 (*0-8256-1265-9*, AM76712) Music Sales.

Pink Floyd: A Momentary Lapse of Reason. (Illus.). 72p. 1987. pap. 19.95 (*0-7119-1340-4*, AM68834) Music Sales.

Pink Floyd: Animals. (Illus.). 88p. pap. 17.95 (*0-8256-1077-X*, AM64197) Music Sales.

Pink Floyd: Dark Side of the Moon. (Illus.). 144p. pap. 24.95 (*0-8256-2595-5*, AM 76704) Omnibus NY.

Pink Floyd: Early Classics. 1990. 12.95 (*0-7935-0277-2*, 00660118) H Leonard.

Pink Floyd: Early Classics with Notes & Tablature. 80p. 1987. pap. 19.95 (*0-7935-2463-6*, 00693800) H Leonard.

Pink Floyd: Tear-Out Photo Book. (Illus.). 22p. (Orig.). 1993. pap. 11.95 (*1-870049-51-9*, OB 11010) Oliver Bks.

Pink Floyd: The Division Bell. 1996. pap. 24.95 (*0-8256-1410-4*, AM 92091) Music Sales.

Pink Floyd: The Division Bell. Pink Floyd. 1996. pap. 29.95 (*0-8256-1409-0*, AM 92188) Music Sales.

Pink Floyd: The Final Cut. (Illus.). 72p. pap. 17.95 (*0-8256-1080-X*, AM64213) Music Sales.

Pink Floyd: The Official History. Nick Mason. 1996. 40.00 (*0-684-82238-5*) S&S Trade.

Pink Floyd: The Wall. (Illus.). 104p. 1996. pap. 21.95 (*0-8256-1076-1*, AM 64205) Music Sales.

Pink Floyd: The Wall. Roger Waters. LC 92-773381. (Illus.). 224p. 1996. pap. 27.95 (*0-8256-1267-5*, AM 76696) Music Sales.

Pink Floyd: Wish You Were Here. (Illus.). 128p. pap. 22.95 (*0-8256-1287-X*, AM80011) Omnibus NY.

Pink Floyd: Wish You Were Here. (Illus.). 88p. 1997. pap. 19.95 (*0-8256-1079-6*, AM64189) Omnibus NY.

Pink Floyd: 21st Anniversary Edition. 25th anniversary ed. Miles & Andy Mabbett. LC 95-234243. (Illus.). 156p. 1988. pap. 24.95 (*0-7119-4109-2*, OP40583) Omnibus NY.

Pink Floyd - Dark Side of the Moon: With Notes & Tablature. 64p. 1991. pap. 14.95 (*0-7935-0420-1*, 00660172) H Leonard.

Pink Floyd - Dark Side of the Moon: With Notes & Tablature. 56p. 1991. pap. 14.95 (*0-7935-0276-4*, 00660173) H Leonard.

Pink Floyd Anthology. 112p. 1986. per. 16.95 (*0-88188-445-6*, HL 00357875) H Leonard.

Pink Floyd Anthology. Ed. by Sy Feldman. 128p. (Orig.). 1994. pap. 16.95 (*0-89724-200-9*, VF0790) Wrner Bros.

***Pink Floyd Encyclopedia.** Vernon Fitch. 1998. 24.95 (*1-896522-44-0*) CN06.

Pink Floyd Through the Eyes of . . . The Band, Its Fans, Friends & Foes. Ed. by Bruno MacDonald. LC 97-5216. (Illus.). 400p. 1997. reprint ed. pap. 14.95 (*0-306-80780-7*) Da Capo.

Pink for Polar Bear. Valerie Solis. (Illus.). 32p. (J). pap. 7.95 (*0-14-038837-0*, Pub. by Pnguin Bks Ltd) Trafalgar.

Pink Glass Swan: Selected Feminist Essays on Art. Lucy R. Lippard. LC 94-23406. 352p. 1995. pap. 20.00 (*1-56584-213-8*, Pub. by New Press NY) Norton.

Pink Highways: Tales of Queer Madness on the Open Road. Michael Lane. LC 94-20515. 288p. 1995. 19.95 (*1-55972-263-0*, Birch Ln Pr) Carol Pub Group.

Pink Inside Feels Best of All. Sybil Fleming. (Illus.). (J). 1996. pap. 4.95 (*0-9681657-0-2*) A Good Val.

Pink Instrument: Poems by Max Blagg; Photographs by Ralph Gibson. Max Blagg. (Illus.). 168p. 1998. pap. 21.95 (*1-57129-054-0*) Brookline Bks.

Pink Is Perfect for Pigs. Barbara Ruiter & Cindy Ruiter. (Illus.). 32p. (Orig.). (J). 1993. pap. 5.95 (*1-56883-019-X*) Colonial Pr AL.

Pink Ladies in the Afternoon. 2nd ed. Naomi L. Madgett. LC 90-60605. 75p. (YA). (gr. 7-10). 1990. pap. 7.00 (*0-916418-78-2*) Lotus.

***Pink Lemonade & Other Delights: 12 Refreshing Quilt Projects.** Linda Johnson. (Illus.). 80p. 2001. pap. 19.95 (*1-56477-324-8*) Martingale & Co.

Pink Madonna: Selected Poems. Lucile Adler. Ed. by Chris Merrill & Ellen Kleiner. (Illus.). 112p. 1997. pap. 12.00 (*0-9659508-0-8*) Juniper Pr NM.

Pink Mat Monster. Patt Wagner. 1987. pap. 10.00 (*0-932526-71-3*) Nexus Pr.

Pink Medicine Lesson. Eric Berg. LC 93-8908. (J). (gr. 4 up). 1993. 10.00 (*1-56071-326-7*) ETR Assocs.

Pink Menace. Ritah Parrish. 36p. 1998. 3.00 (*0-9653194-9-0*) Future Tense.

Pink Milk Sea: My First Self Esteem Reader. Dee Frances. (Illus.). 32p. 1996. pap. 4.95 (*1-885519-01-X*) DDDD Pubns.

Pink Milk Sea Coloring Book. Dee Frances. (Illus.). 32p. (J). Date not set. pap. text 3.00 (*1-885519-26-5*) DDDD Pubns.

Pink Milk Sea Coloring Book. Dee Frances. (J). Date not set. 3.00 (*1-885519-58-3*) DDDD Pubns.

Pink Motel. Carol R. Brink. (J). 1993. 9.05 (*0-606-05545-2*, Pub. by Turtleback) Demco.

Pink Motel. Carol R. Brink. LC 92-17953. (Illus.). 224p. (J). (gr. 3-7). 1993. reprint ed. mass mkt. 3.95 (*0-689-71677-X*) Aladdin.

Pink Palace: Behind Closed Doors at the Beverly Hills Hotel. Sandra L. Stuart. LC 92-36512. 1993. 21.00 (*0-942637-84-4*) Barricade Bks.

Pink Palace: The Royal Hawaiian Hotel, a Sheraton Hotel in Hawaii. Stan B. Cohen. Ed. by Steve Smith. LC 86-62548. (Illus.). 100p. 1986. pap. 9.95 (*0-933126-82-4*) Pictorial Hist.

Pink Panther Strikes Again! William Gleason. 1981. 5.50 (*0-87129-384-6*, P52) Dramatic Pub.

Pink Paper Swans. Virginia L. Kroll. LC 93-41093. (Illus.). 32p. (J). (gr. k-3). 1994. 15.00 (*0-8028-5081-2*, Eerdmans Bks) Eerdmans.

Pink Parrot. Gill McBarnet. (Illus.). 40p. (J). (gr. k-2). 1986. 8.95 (*0-9615102-1-8*) Ruwanga Trad.

Pink Party. Maryann MacDonald. LC 93-20989. (Illus.). 40p. (J). (gr. k-3). 1994. lib. bdg. 10.89 (*1-56282-621-2*, Pub. by Hyprn Child) Little.

Pink Pencil. Charles Lambert. LC 96-95244. 132p. (Orig.). 1997. pap. 7.95 (*1-57502-372-5*, PO1192) Morris Pubng.

Pink Power. Cheryl Henderson. 1999. pap. text 5.95 (*1-56245-354-8*) Great Quotations.

Pink Rabbit Caper. Georgette Livingston. LC 97-97118. (Jennifer Gray Veterinarian Mystery Ser.: Bk. 11). 192p. 1998. 18.95 (*0-8034-9279-0*, Avalon Bks) Bouregy.

***Pink-Ribbon Quilts: A Book Because of Breast Cancer.** Mimi Dietrich. LC 99-40527. (Illus.). 80p. 1999. pap. 19.95 (*1-56477-279-9*, B399, That Patchwrk Pl) Martingale & Co.

Pink Ribbons: ACA Poems from My Heart. Carol A. Friges. (Illus.). 117p. 1991. pap. 10.95 (*0-9630237-0-5*) Carol Ann Ent.

Pink Ribbons for Sandy. Alex N. Holland. (Illus.). 21p. (J). (gr. k-4). 1996. pap. 11.89 (*1-56606-039-7*) Bradley Mann.

Pink Rosary. Ricardo M. Ybarra. LC 92-35442. (Discoveries Ser.). 208p. 1993. pap. 16.95 (*0-935480-59-5*) Lat Am Lit Rev Pr.

Pink Rose Bush. Bonnie Spirit. (Illus.). 64p. (J). (ps up). 1985. text 9.95 (*0-9614089-0-1*) Avitar Bks.

Pink Samurai. Nicholas Bornoff. Ed. by Bill Grose. 1992. pap. 12.00 (*0-671-74266-3*) PB.

Pink Samurai: Love, Marriage, & Sex in Contemporary Japan Nicholas Bornoff. LC 91-177895. xvi, 492p. 1991. write for info. (*0-246-13453-4*) Grfton HrprCllns.

Pink Slip. Rita Ciresi. LC 98-21130. 368p. 1998. 22.95 (*0-385-32362-X*) Dell.

***Pink Slip.** Rita Ciresi. 416p. 1999. pap. 11.95 (*0-385-32363-8*) Dell.

Pink Slippers, Bat Mitzvah Blues. Ferida Wolff. (J). (gr. 4-7). 1994. pap. 8.95 (*0-8276-0531-5*) JPS Phila.

Pink Snow: And Other Weird Weather, Level 2. Jennifer Dussling. LC 98-14336. (All Aboard Reading Ser.). (Illus.). 48p. (J). (gr. 1-3). 1998. lib. bdg. 13.89 (*0-448-41887-8*, G & D); mass mkt. 3.99 (*0-448-41858-4*, G & D) Peng Put Young Read.

Pink Stars & Angel Wings. Susan Ekberg. LC 91-91216. (Illus.). 32p. (J). (ps up). 1992. 16.95 (*0-9630419-0-8*) Spiritseeker.

Pink Swastika: Homosexualtiy in the Nazi Party. 3rd rev. ed. Scott Lively & Kevin Abrams. (Illus.). 280p. 1998. pap. 11.95 (*0-9647609-3-2*) Fndrs Pubng.

Pink Tanks & Velvet Hangovers: An American in Prague. Douglas Lytle. LC 94-41644. (Illus.). 250p. (Orig.). (C). 1995. pap. 16.95 (*1-883319-24-2*) Frog Ltd CA.

Pink Therapy: A Guide for Counsellors & Therapists Working with Lesbian, Gay, & Bisexual Clients. Ed. by Dominic Davies & Charles Neal. LC 95-26372. 256p. 1996. pap. 33.95 (*0-335-19145-2*) OpUniv Pr.

Pink Therapy: A Guide for Counsellors & Therapists Working with Lesbian, Gay, & Bisexual Clients. Ed. by Dominic Davies & Charles Neal. LC 95-26372. 256p. 1996. 97.95 (*0-335-19657-8*) OpUniv Pr.

***Pink Think.** Lynn Peril. 2000. 26.50 (*0-688-17534-1*, Wm Morrow) Morrow Avon.

Pink Topaz. Jennifer Greene. (Intimate Moments Ser.: No. 418). 1992. per. 3.29 (*0-373-07418-2*, 5-07418-2) Harlequin Bks.

Pink Triangle: The Gay Law Reform Debate in Tasmania. Miranda Morris. (Illus.). xii, 135p. 1995. pap. 26.95 (*0-86840-135-8*, Pub. by New South Wales Univ Pr) Intl Spec Bk.

Pink Triangle: The Nazi War Against Homosexuals. Richard Plant. LC 86-346. 272p. 1995. pap. 11.95 (*0-8050-0600-1*) H Holt & Co.

Pink Vodka Blues. Neal Barrett, Jr. 304p. 1997. mass mkt. 5.99 (*1-57566-237-X*, Knsington) Kensgtn Pub Corp.

Pink Vodka Blues. Neal Barrett, Jr. 320p. 1992. text 18.95 (*0-312-07766-1*) St Martin.

Pink y Say (Pink & Say) Patricia Polacco. 1997. 15.95 (*1-880507-30-7*) Lectorum Pubns.

Pink, Yellow, Black & Green What Do All the Differences Mean? Carolyn A. O'Riley. (Illus.). 36p. (J). (ps-2). 1998. spiral bd. 15.00 incl. audio (*1-891870-04-1*, 00500) Archangels Pen.

Pinkerton, Behave! Steven Kellogg. LC 78-31794. (Illus.). 32p. (J). (ps-3). 1979. 16.99 (*0-8037-6573-8*, Dial Yng Read) Peng Put Young Read.

Pinkerton, Behave! Steven Kellogg. (Illus.). 40p. (J). (ps-3). 1993. pap. 6.99 (*0-14-054687-1*, PuffinBks) Peng Put Young Read.

Pinkerton, Behave! Steven Kellogg. (J). 1982. 11.19 (*0-606-03315-7*, Pub. by Turtleback) Demco.

Pinkerton, Behave: A Study Guide. Garrett Christopher. Ed. by J. Friedland & R. Kessler. (Little Novel-Ties Ser.). (J). (gr. k-2). 1994. pap. text, student ed. 14.95 (*1-56982-082-1*) Lrn Links.

Pinkham's Notch: The Daniel Pinkham Story. Carol Hayes. LC 98-40550. (Illus.). 125p. 1998. pap. 15.00 (*0-914339-74-5*) P E Randall Pub.

***Pinkie.** Illus. by Dave Sargent & Jane Lenoir. LC 99-87655. (J). 2000. pap. write for info. (*1-56763-466-4*) Ozark Pub.

Pinkie: Alias Witches. Mark Dunster. (Holiday Ser.: Pt. 11: Halloween). 36p. (Orig.). 1990. pap. 5.00 (*0-89642-188-0*) Linden Pubs.

Pinkish, Purplish, Bluish Egg, 001. Bill Peet. (Illus.). 48p. (J). (gr. k-3). 1984. pap. 7.95 (*0-395-36172-9*) HM.

Pinkish, Purplish, Bluish Egg. Bill Peet. (J). 1963. 11.15 (*0-606-03199-5*, Pub. by Turtleback) Demco.

Pinkmount Drive. large type ed. Jan Webster. (Ulverscroft Large Print Ser.). 432p. 1997. 27.99 (*0-7089-3729-2*) Ulverscroft.

Pinktoes. Chester B. Himes. 264p. 1996. pap. 16.95 (*0-87805-887-7*) U Pr of Miss.

Pinktoes. Chester B. Himes. 264p. (C). 1996. 40.00 (*0-87805-886-9*) U Pr of Miss.

Pinkus' Guide to Dermatohistopathology. 6th ed. Amir H. Mehregan et al. (Illus.). 816p. (C). 1995. pap. text 185.00 (*0-8385-8077-7*, A8077-8, Apple Lange Med) McGraw.

Pinkwater, Bk. 2. Ed. by Simon & Schuster Children's. (J). 2000. 16.00 (*0-689-81144-6*) S&S Childrens.

Pinky. Florence A. Hasenau. (Illus.). (J). (gr. 1-6). 1975. 12.95 (*0-913042-02-1*) Holland Hse Pr.

***Pinky & Bluey Explore the Sky.** Edie Wiede. (J). (gr. k-3). 1999. pap. 6.95 (*0-533-13148-0*) Vantage.

Pinky & Rex. James Howe. LC 89-30783. (Pinky & Rex Ser.). (Illus.). 48p. (J). (gr. 1-4). 1998. pap. 3.99 (*0-689-82348-7*) Aladdin.

Pinky & Rex. James Howe. LC 89-30786. (Pinky & Rex Ser.). (Illus.). 48p. (J). (gr. 1-4). 1990. 12.95 (*0-689-31454-X*) Atheneum Yung Read.

Pinky & Rex. James Howe. (Pinky & Rex Ser.). (Illus.). 48p. (J). (gr. 1-4). 1991. pap. 3.99 (*0-380-71190-7*, Avon Bks) Morrow Avon.

Pinky & Rex & the Bully. James Howe. LC 95-22006. (Pinky & Rex Ser.). (Illus.). 48p. (J). (gr. 1-4). 1996. per. 3.99 (*0-689-80834-8*) Aladdin.

Pinky & Rex & the Bully. James Howe. LC 95-22006. (Pinky & Rex Ser.). (Illus.). 48p. (J). (gr. 1-4). 1996. 15.00 (*0-689-80021-5*) Atheneum Yung Read. •

Pinky & Rex & the Bully. James Howe. LC 95-22006. (Pinky & Rex Ser.). (Illus.). (J). (gr. 1-4). 1996. 9.19 (*0-606-09751-1*, Pub. by Turtleback) Demco.

Pinky & Rex & the Bully, unabridged ed. James Howe. (Pinky & Rex Ser.). (Illus.). (J). (gr. 1-4). 1997. 22.24 incl. audio (*0-7887-1825-8*, 40605) Recorded Bks.

Pinky & Rex & the Double-Dad Weekend. James Howe. (Pinky & Rex Ser.). (Illus.). 48p. (J). (gr. 1-4). 1996. per. 3.99 (*0-689-80835-6*) Aladdin.

***Pinky & Rex & the Double-Dad Weekend.** James Howe. (Pinky & Rex Ser.). (Illus.). (J). (gr. 1-4). 1999. pap. text 11.10 (*0-7857-9131-0*) Econo-Clad Bks.

Pinky & Rex & the Double-Dad Weekend. James Howe. LC 94-9384. (Pinky & Rex Ser.). (Illus.). 48p. (J). (gr. 1-4). 1995. 14.00 (*0-689-31871-5*) S&S Childrens.

Pinky & Rex & the Double-Dad Weekend. James Howe. LC 94-9384. (Pinky & Rex Ser.). (Illus.). (J). (gr. 1-4). 1995. 9.19 (*0-606-09752-X*, Pub. by Turtleback) Demco.

Pinky & Rex & the Double-Dad Weekend, unabridged ed. James Howe. (Pinky & Rex Ser.). (Illus.). (J). (gr. 1-4). 1997. 22.24 incl. audio (*0-7887-1824-X*, 40604) Recorded Bks.

***Pinky & Rex & the Just-Right Pet.** James Howe. LC 00-26034. (Pinky & Rex Ser.). (Illus.). (J). (gr. 1-4). 2001. write for info. (*0-689-82861-6*) Athenean.

***Pinky & Rex & the Mean Old Witch.** James Howe. (Pinky & Rex Ser.). (Illus.). 48p. (J). (gr. 1-4). 1999. pap. 3.99 (*0-689-82879-9*) Aladdin.

Pinky & Rex & the Mean Old Witch. James Howe. LC 89-78204. (Pinky & Rex Ser.). (Illus.). 48p. (J). (gr. 1-4). 1999. 12.95 (*0-689-31617-8*) Atheneum Yung Read.

Pinky & Rex & the Mean Old Witch. James Howe. (Pinky & Rex Ser.). (Illus.). 48p. (J). (gr. 1-4). 1992. pap. 3.99 (*0-380-71644-5*, Avon Bks) Morrow Avon.

Pinky & Rex & the New Baby. James Howe. (Pinky & Rex Ser.). (Illus.). 48p. (J). (gr. 1-4). 1994. pap. 3.99 (*0-380-72083-3*, Avon Bks) Morrow Avon.

***Pinky & Rex & the New Baby.** James Howe. LC 91-39801. (Pinky & Rex Ser.). (Illus.). 48p. (J). (gr. 1-4). 1999. per. 3.99 (*0-689-82548-X*) S&S Childrens.

***Pinky & Rex & the New Baby.** James Howe. (Pinky & Rex Ser.). (Illus.). (J). (gr. 1-4). 1999. 9.44 (*0-606-15941-X*, Pub. by Turtleback) Demco.

Pinky & Rex & the New Neighbors. James Howe. LC 95-42543. (Pinky & Rex Ser.). (Illus.). 48p. (J). (gr. 1-4). 1997. 15.00 (*0-689-80022-3*) Atheneum Yung Read.

Pinky & Rex & the New Neighbors. James Howe. LC 95-42543. (Pinky & Rex Ser.:). (Illus.). 48p. (J). (gr. 1-4). 1997. per. 3.99 (*0-689-81296-5*) S&S Childrens.

Pinky & Rex & the New Neighbors. James Howe. (Pinky & Rex Ser.). (Illus.). (J). (gr. 1-4). 1997. 9.44 (*0-606-11749-0*) Turtleback.

Pinky & Rex & the New Neighbors, Homework. unabridged ed. James Howe. (Pinky & Rex Ser.). (Illus.). (J). (gr. 1-4). 1997. 22.24 incl. audio (*0-7887-1826-6*, 40606) Recorded Bks.

P

Pinky & Rex & the Perfect Pumpkin. James Howe. LC 97-45020. (Pinky & Rex Ser.). (Illus.). 48p. (J). (gr. 1-4). 1998. 15.00 (*0-689-81782-7*); per. 3.99 (*0-689-81777-0*) S&S Childrens.

Pinky & Rex & the School Play. James Howe. (Pinky & Rex Ser.). (Illus.). (J). (gr. 1-4). 1998. 9.09 (*0-606-13707-6*, Pub. by Turtleback) Demco.

Pinky & Rex & the Spelling Bee. James Howe. LC 89-78305. (Pinky & Rex Ser.). (Illus.). 48p. (J). (gr. 1-4). 1991. 15.00 (*0-689-31618-6*) Atheneum Yung Read.

Pinky & Rex & the Spelling Bee. James Howe. (Pinky & Rex Ser.). (Illus.). 48p. (J). (gr. 1-4). 1992. pap. 3.99 (*0-380-71643-7*, Avon Bks) Morrow Avon.

Pinky & Rex & the Spelling Bee. James Howe. (Pinky & Rex Ser.). (Illus.). 48p. (J). (gr. 1-4). 1999. reprint ed. per. 3.99 (*0-689-82880-2*) Aladdin.

Pinky & Rex Get Married. James Howe. LC 89-406. (Pinky & Rex Ser.). (Illus.). 48p. (J). (gr. 1-4). 1990. lib. bdg. 11.95 (*0-685-58512-3*) Atheneum Yung Read.

Pinky & Rex Get Married. James Howe. (Pinky & Rex Ser.). (Illus.). 48p. (J). (gr. 1-4). 1991. pap. 3.99 (*0-380-71191-5*, Avon Bks) Morrow Avon.

Pinky & Rex Get Married. James Howe. LC 89-406. (Pinky & Rex Ser.). (Illus.). 48p. (J). (gr. 1-4). 1999. pap. 3.99 (*0-689-82526-9*, 076714003996) S&S Childrens.

Pinky & Rex Go to Camp. James Howe. LC 91-16123. (Pinky & Rex Ser.). (Illus.). 48p. (J). (gr. 1-4). 1992. 15.00 (*0-689-31718-2*) Atheneum Yung Read.

Pinky & Rex Go to Camp. James Howe. (Pinky & Rex Ser.). (Illus.). 48p. (J). (gr. 1-4). 1993. pap. 3.99 (*0-380-72082-5*, Avon Bks) Morrow Avon.

Pinky & Rex Go to Camp. James Howe. LC 91-16123. (Pinky & Rex Ser.). (Illus.). 48p. (J). (gr. 1-4). 1999. pap. 3.99 (*0-689-82588-9*, 076714003996) S&S Childrens.

Pinky & the Brain. (Look & Find Bks.). (Illus.). 24p. (J). (gr. k-5). 7.98 (*0-7853-1607-8*, PI11) Pubns Intl Ltd.

Pinky & the Brain in Bubba Bo Bob Brain. (Illus.). 32p. (J). (ps up). pap. 7.89 incl. audio (*1-56826-759-2*, KR2) Rhino Enter.

Pinky Baby, Vol. 1. Pam Munoz Ryan. Vol. 1. (Illus.). 32p. (J). (ps-2). 1999. pap. 4.95 (*0-7868-1144-7*, Pub. by Hyperion) Time Warner.

***Pinky Ball Book & the Pinky Ball.** Dina Anastasio. (Illus.). 176p. (J). (ps-3). 2000. pap. 9.95 (*0-7611-1977-9*) Workman Pub.

Pinky Extensions & Eye Gaze: Language Use in Deaf Communities. Ed. by Ceil Lucas. (Sociolinguistics in Deaf Communities Ser.: Vol. 4). 224p. 1998. text 55.00 (*1-56368-070-X*) Gallaudet Univ Pr.

Pinky Is a Baby Mouse & Other Baby Animal Names. Pam Munoz Ryan et al. LC 95-25396. (Illus.). 32p. (J). (ps-3). 1997. lib. bdg. 14.89 (*0-7868-2190-6*, Pub. by Hyprn Child) Time Warner.

***Pinky Pye.** Eleanor Estes. LC 00-23879. (Illus.). 192p. (J). (gr. 4-7). 2000. 17.00 (*0-15-202559-6*, Harcourt Child Bks); pap. 6.00 (*0-15-202565-0*, Harcourt Child Bks) Harcourt.

Pinky Pye. Eleanor Estes. LC 75-31581. (Illus.). 192p. (J). (gr. 3-7). 1976. reprint ed. pap. 4.95 (*0-15-671840-5*, Voyager Bks) Harcourt.

***Pinky Swear: The Gift of a Lifetime.** Dawn M. Chicilo. Ed. by Sid Korpi. LC 00-91460. 150p. 2000. 16.95 (*0-9678920-0-7*, PS-3858) TreeHouse Pubng Co.

Pinn Systems. H. Garcilazo & T. Mizutani. 324p. 1990. text 70.00 (*9971-5-0847-8*) World Scientific Pub.

Pinnacle. Ora N. Sylvester. LC 97-90395. 1998. pap. 8.95 (*0-533-12379-8*) Vantage.

Pinnacle Game. Mayfair Games Staff. 1986. pap. 7.00 (*0-912771-41-0*) Mayfair Games.

Pinnacle Jake. Nellie S. Yost. (Illus.). 348p. 1991. pap. 12.95 (*0-934904-28-6*) J & L Lee.

***Pinnacle Principle: How to Maximise Your Potential.** Peter Thompson. 256p. 2000. per. 12.00 (*0-684-86832-6*) S&S Trade.

Pinnacled Tower: Selected Poems. Thomas Hardy & Clare Leighton. LC 74-14836. xiii, 146p. 1975. write for info. (*0-02-742630-0*) Macmillan.

Pinnacles & Pyramids: The Art of Marsden Hartley. Jeanne Hokin. LC 92-25854. (Illus.). 226p. 1993. reprint ed. pap. 70.10 (*0-608-07282-6*, 206751000009) Bks Demand.

Pinnacles Guide: Pinnacles National Monument San Benito County, California. 2nd rev. ed. Elvin R. Johnson & Richard P. Cordone. (Illus.). 64p. 1994. pap. 5.95 (*0-9643492-0-5*) Tillicum Pr.

Pinnacles National Monument. Sandra L. Keith. Ed. by Randolph Jorgen & T. J. Priehs. LC 91-61044. (Illus.). 16p. (Orig.). 1991. pap. 3.95 (*0-911408-95-9*) SW Pks Mnmts.

Pinnell & Talifson: Last of the Great Brown Bear Men. Marvin H. Clark, Jr. (Illus.). 224p. (C). 1980. 39.95 (*0-937708-00-3*) Great Northwest.

Pinnell & Talifson: Last of the Great Brown Bear Men. Marvin H. Clark, Jr. (Illus.). 224p. 1985. reprint ed. pap. 19.95 (*0-937708-03-8*) Great Northwest.

Pinnipeds: Seals, Sea Lions, & Walruses. Marianne Riedman. (Illus.). 439p. 1991. reprint ed. pap. 27.50 (*0-520-06498-4*, Pub. by U CA Pr) Cal Prin Full Svc.

Pinnipeds & El Nino: Responses to Environmental Stress. F. Trillmich & K. A. Ono. Ed. by Hermann Remmert et al. (Ecological Studies: Vol. 88). (Illus.). 344p. 1991. 158.95 (*0-387-53634-5*) Spr-Verlag.

***Pinnipeds from Pole to Pole: Seals, Sea Lions & Walruses.** Jody Byrum. (Illus.). 75p. (YA). (gr. 4 up). 2000. pap. 10.00 (*1-893698-07-6*, SeaWorld Educ) SeaWorld Inc.

Pinnochio. (Ladybird Bks.). (ARA., Illus.). 14.95 incl. audio (*0-86685-230-1*, LDL118C, Pub. by Librairie du Liban) Intl Bk Ctr.

Pinnochio. William Glennon. 1994. 3.95 (*0-87129-486-9*, P44) Dramatic Pub.

Pinnularia: Eine Monographie der Europaeischne Taxa. Kurt Krammer. (Bibliotheca Diatomologica Ser.: Vol. 26). (GER., Illus.). iv, 353p. 1992. lib. bdg. 83.00 (*3-443-57017-8*, Pub. by Gebruder Borntraeger) Balogh.

Pinocchia. Leroi & Gibrat. (Illus.). 50p. 1996. pap. 11.95 (*1-56163-169-8*, Eurotica) NBM.

Pinocchio. 1999. pap. 7.95 (*88-8148-243-6*); pap. 7.95 (*88-8148-253-3*) Europ Lang Inst.

Pinocchio. (FRE.). (J). 6.25 (*0-685-33974-2*) Fr & Eur.

Pinocchio. (Recorder Fun! Ser.). 841p. (J). (gr. 3 up). 1992. 9.95 (*0-7935-1659-5*, 00710363) H Leonard.

Pinocchio. (Treasury of Fairy Tales Ser.). (Illus.). 24p. (J). (gr. 2-5). 1993. pap. 3.95 (*1-56144-361-1*, Honey Bear Bks) Modern Pub NYC.

Pinocchio. (J). 1997. 7.98 (*1-57082-047-3*, Pub. by Mouse Works) Time Warner.

***Pinocchio.** (Penguin Young Reader Ser.). (C). 2000. pap. 8.00 (*0-582-42864-5*) Pearson Educ.

Pinocchio. (Disney Read-Alongs Ser.). (J). 1993. 7.99 incl. audio (*1-55723-363-2*) W Disney Records.

Pinocchio. Carlo Collodi. 22.95 (*0-88411-249-7*) Amereon Ltd.

Pinocchio. Carlo Collodi. LC 97-52928. (Illus.). (J). 1998. pap. 1.00 (*0-486-40090-5*) Dover.

Pinocchio. Carlo Collodi. (FRE., Illus.). (J). (gr. 3-8). 5.95 (*0-685-11495-3*, S16273) Fr & Eur.

Pinocchio. Carlo Collodi. 1986. pap. 2.50 (*0-451-51986-8*, Sig Classics) NAL.

Pinocchio. Carlo Collodi. (Illus.). 272p. (YA). (gr. 5 up). 1996. pap. 4.99 (*0-14-036708-X*, PuffinBks) Peng Put Young Read.

Pinocchio. Carlo Collodi. LC 95-10127. (Illus.). 48p. (J). (ps-3). 1996. 18.95 (*0-399-22941-8*, Philomel) Peng Put Young Read.

Pinocchio. Carlo Collodi. (Folio - Junior Ser.: No. 283). (FRE., Illus.). 235p. (J). (gr. 5-10). 1985. pap. 10.95 (*2-07-033283-7*) Schoenhof.

Pinocchio. Carlo Collodi. (J). (gr. 4-7). 1996. mass mkt. 2.99 (*0-8125-6702-1*, Pub. by Tor Bks) St Martin.

Pinocchio. Carlo Collodi. 1996. 8.09 (*0-606-11750-4*, Pub. by Turtleback) Demco.

Pinocchio. Carlo Collodi. (Children's Library). (J). (gr. 4-7). 1998. pap. 3.95 (*1-85326-160-2*, 1602WW, Pub. by Wrdsworth Edits) NTC Contemp Pub Co.

Pinocchio. Carlo Collodi et al. LC 97-214344. (Pair-It Bks.). 32 p. 1998. write for info. (*0-8172-7290-9*) Raintree Steck-V.

***Pinocchio.** Distribooks Inc. Staff. 1999. pap. text 7.95 (*88-8148-258-4*) Midwest European Pubns.

Pinocchio. Distribooks Inc. Staff. (Lesen Leicht Germacht Ser.). (GER.). (ps up). 1999. pap. text 7.95 (*88-8148-248-7*) Midwest European Pubns.

Pinocchio. Jane Fior. LC 98-45496. (Young Classics Ser.). (J). 1999. write for info. (*0-7894-4443-7*) DK Pub Inc.

***Pinocchio.** Jane Fior et al. LC 00-27358. (Read & Listen Ser.). (Illus.). 2000. write for info. (*0-7894-6112-9*) DK Pub Inc.

Pinocchio. M. Hillert. 1985. 4.95 (*0-87895-684-0*) Modern Curr.

Pinocchio. Margaret Hillert. (Illus.). (J). (ps). 1981. pap. 5.10 (*0-8136-5603-6*, TK2173); lib. bdg. 7.95 (*0-8136-5103-4*, TK2172) Modern Curr.

Pinocchio. Linda M. Jennings. (Favorite Tales Ser.). (Illus.). 28p. (J). 1994. 2.99 (*0-7214-5449-6*, Ladybrd) Penguin Putnam.

Pinocchio. Pierre Lambert. LC 98-146716. (Illus.). 236p. 1997. 150.00 (*0-7868-6247-5*, Pub. by Hyperion) Time Warner.

Pinocchio. Madge Miller. (J). 1954. 6.00 (*0-87602-175-5*) Anchorage.

Pinocchio. Mousework Staff. (Illus.). (J). 1997. 7.98 (*1-57082-806-7*, Pub. by Mouse Works) Little.

Pinocchio. Nickel. (J). Date not set. 4.99 (*0-7214-5404-6*) Nickel Pr.

Pinocchio. Adapted by Dorothy D. Stone. 1974. 3.45 (*0-87129-266-1*, P27) Dramatic Pub.

Pinocchio. Walt Disney Company Staff. (FRE.). 96p. (J). (gr. k-5). pap. 9.95 (*0-7859-8845-9*) Fr & Eur.

Pinocchio. Walt Disney Staff. (Penguin-Disney Ser.). (Illus.). 96p. (J). (ps-3). 1992. 6.98 (*0-453-03026-2*) Viking Penguin.

Pinocchio. Catherine Daly Weir. LC 95-33455. (Bullseye Step into Classics Ser.). (J). 1996. 9.09 (*0-606-09753-8*, Pub. by Turtleback) Demco.

Pinocchio. unabridged ed. Carlo Collodi & Brian Ajhar. LC 95-8578. (Illus.). 40p. (J). (ps-3). 1996. per. 19.95 incl. audio (*0-689-80230-7*, Rabbit Ears) Litle Simon.

Pinocchio, 6 cassettes, Set. (ITA.). 202p. (YA). 1985. pap. 79.50 incl. audio (*1-57970-006-3*, SIT100) Audio-Forum.

Pinocchio, Vol. 516. rev. ed. Alfred Lipton. Ed. & Illus. by Janice Caban. (Once upon a Tale Ser.). 10p. (J). (gr. k). 1989. pap. 2.00 (*1-878501-03-8*) Ntrl Science Indus.

Pinocchio: A Play. Sam Kuglen. 1999. pap. 3.00 (*1-57514-338-0*, 1134) Encore Perform Pub.

Pinocchio: Geppetto's Surprise. Illus. by Fred Marvin. LC 92-54877. (Tiny Changing Pictures Bk.). 10p. (J). (ps). 1993. 4.95 (*1-56282-397-3*, Pub. by Disney Pr) Little.

Pinocchio: Musical Dramatization of Carlo Collodi's Tale. R. Eugene Jackson. (Illus.). 36p. (J). (gr. k-12). 1985. pap. 4.50 (*0-88680-245-8*) I E Clark.

Pinocchio: My Coloring Book. (J). 1.09 (*0-307-08675-5*, 08675) Gldn Bks Pub Co.

Pinocchio: Nose for Trouble. Disney Enterprises, Inc. Staff. (Disney's "Storytime Treasures" Library: Vol. 13). (Illus.). 44p. (J). (gr. 1-6). 1997. 3.49 (*1-57973-009-4*) Advance Pubs.

Pinocchio: Storia di un Burattino. Carlo Collodi. (ITA.). 70p. 1997. pap. text 19.50 (*1-58085-003-0*) Interlingua VA.

Pinocchio: Storia di un Burattino. Carlo Collodi. Tr. by Dick Gibson. (ENG & ITA.). 140p. 1997. pap. text 29.50 (*1-58085-004-9*) Interlingua VA.

Pinocchio - Toy Story, 2. 75th anniversary ed. Mouse Works Staff. 1998. 9.99 (*0-7364-0088-5*) Mouse Works.

Pinocchio & Geppetto see Pinocchio Series

***Pinocchio & Jack & The Beanstalk.** (Tele-Story Ser.). (SPA & ENG., Illus.). (J). (ps-1). 2000. 8.95 incl. audio (*1-886972-93-1*, Pub. by Emaginit) Penton Overseas.

Pinocchio Bath Book. Walt Disney Staff. (Penguin-Disney Ser.). (J). (ps). 1992. 5.98 (*0-453-03028-9*) Viking Penguin.

Pinocchio Catalogue: Being a Descriptive Bibliography & Printing History of English Language Translations & Other Renditions Appearing in the United States, 1892-1987, 16. Richard Wunderlich. LC 88-24650. (Bibliographies & Indexes in World Literature Ser.). 241p. 1988. lib. bdg. 69.50 (*0-313-26334-5*, WUP) Greenwood.

Pinocchio Coloring Book. Carlo Collodi. (Illus.). (J). (gr. k-3). 1994. pap. 2.95 (*0-486-28003-9*) Dover.

Pinocchio Commedia: A Commedia Dell' Arte Play. Johnny Simons. (Illus.). 30p. 1993. pap. 4.00 (*0-88680-386-1*) I E Clark.

Pinocchio Goes on Stage see Pinocchio Series

Pinocchio in Africa: Cherubini, 1911. Angelo Patri. Orig. Title: Cherubini. (Illus.). 150p. (J). 1995. pap. 25.00 (*0-87556-781-9*) Saifer.

Pinocchio in Venice. Robert Coover. LC 96-19879. 336p. 1997. reprint ed. pap. 12.00 (*0-8021-3485-8*, Grove) Grove-Atltic.

Pinocchio Little Library. Walt Disney Staff. (Penguin-Disney Ser.). (J). (ps-3). 1992. 5.98 (*0-453-03027-0*) Viking Penguin.

Pinocchio (Musical) Contrib. by Arnold Wengrow. (J). 1992. pap. 6.00 (*0-87602-298-0*) Anchorage.

Pinocchio Plays Truant see Pinocchio Series

Pinocchio Series. Virginia Parsons. Incl. Pinocchio & Geppetto. 1979. (*0-07-048531-3*); Pinocchio Goes on Stage. 1979. 4.95 (*0-07-048532-1*); Pinocchio Plays Truant. 1979. 4.95 (*0-07-048530-5*); (J). (gr. k-3). 1979. write for info. (*0-318-54173-4*) McGraw.

Pinocchio II: One Little Puppet. Michael Lancy. 68p. 1983. pap. 5.00 (*1-890298-36-0*) Centerstage Pr.

Pinocchio's Progeny: Puppets, Marionettes, Automatons, & Robots in Modernist & Avant-Garde Drama. Harold B. Segel. (PAJ Bks.). (Illus.). 424p. 1995. text 48.50 (*0-8018-5031-2*); pap. text 16.95 (*0-8018-5262-5*) Johns Hopkins.

***Pinocchio's Quest.** Robert Rogland. (Illus.). 192p. (J). (gr. 4-6). 2000. 2.95 (*1-930367-40-6*, CLP 29650); pap. 8.95 (*1-930367-39-2*, CLP 29650) Christian Liberty.

Pinoccio. Carlo Collodi. (Fairy Tales Ser.). 1998. 12.95 (*2-215-06193-6*) CE75.

Pinochet: The Politics of Power. Genaro Arriagada. 224p. 1988. 34.95 (*0-04-497061-7*); pap. 12.95 (*0-04-497062-5*) Routledge.

***Pinochet: The Politics of Torture.** Hugh O'Shaughnessy. LC 99-59431. 2000. 25.95 (*0-8147-6201-8*) NYU Pr.

***Pinochet & Me: A Chilean Anti-Memoir.** Marc Cooper. 144p. 2000. 22.00 (*1-85984-785-4*, Pub. by Verso) Norton.

***Pinochet Case: A Legal & Constitutional Analysis.** Ed. by Diane Woodhouse. 288p. 2000. 54.00 (*1-84113-102-4*, Pub. by Hart Pub) Intl Spec Bk.

***Pinochet File.** Peter Kornbluh. 2001. 25.95 (*1-56584-586-2*, Pub. by New Press NY) Norton.

***Pinochet Papers: The Case of Augusto Pinochet Ugarte in Spain & Britain.** Reed Brody & Michael Ratner. LC 00-33090. 2000. write for info. (*90-411-1404-1*) Kluwer Law Intl.

Pinochet's Economists: The Chicago School of Economics in Chile. Juan G. Valdes. (Historical Perspectives on Modern Economics Ser.). 348p. (C). 1995. text 54.95 (*0-521-45146-9*) Cambridge U Pr.

Pinochet's Shadow over NAFTA: Chile's Worker & Free Trade. Rachel Geman & Mark Hager. 42p. 1995. pap. 7.50 (*1-880103-05-2*) Intl Labor Rghts.

Pinocho: Grade 2 Well Loved Tales Series 700. Ladybird Books Staff. (Spanish Well Loved Tales Ser.: No. 700-2). (SPA.). (J). (gr. 2). 1990. boxed set 3.50 (*0-7214-1412-5*, Ladybrd) Penguin Putnam.

Pinocho Con Botas (Pinocchio with Boots) Luigi Malerba. Tr. by Fabio Morabito. (SPA., Illus.). 68p. (J). (gr. 5-6). 1992. pap. 5.99 (*968-16-3913-8*, Pub. by Fondo) Continental Bk.

Pinocho (Pinocchio) La Historia de un Muneco (Story of a Puppet) Carlo Collodi. (ENG & SPA.). 220p. (J). 1998. 29.50 (*1-58085-015-4*); pap. 19.50 (*1-58085-014-6*) Interlingua VA.

Pinon Pine: A Natural & Cultural History. Ronald M. Lanner. LC 81-119. (Illus.). 224p. 1981. 21.95 (*0-87417-065-6*); pap. 13.95 (*0-87417-066-4*) U of Nev Pr.

Pinophyta (Gymnospers) of New York State. E. A. Cope. (New York State Museum Bulletin Ser.: No. 483). (Illus.). 80p. (Orig.). 1992. pap. 8.50 (*1-55557-198-0*) NYS Museum.

***Pinot Noir: A Reference Guide to California & Oregon Pinot Noir.** 260p. 2000. pap. 24.95 (*1-891267-16-7*) Wine Appreciation.

Pinot Noir TasteTour: Queen of Red Wines see TasteTour Collection: Fine Wines of the World

Pinoy: The First Wave. Roberto V. Vallangca. LC 76-47180. (Illus.). 160p. (Orig.). 1977. pap. 9.95 (*0-89407-000-2*) Strawberry Hill.

***Pinpoint for Office 97.** 1998. cd-rom 13.33 (*1-58076-217-4*) Que Educ & Trng.

Pinpoint Guide to Alabama & Florida Civil War Sites. James J. Condra & Jeff Slaton. (Pinpoint Guides to Civil War Sites Ser.). (Illus.). 1998. pap. 7.95 (*1-57587-090-8*) Crane Hill AL.

Pinpoint Guide to Atlanta: The March to the Sea. James J. Condra & Jeff Slaton. (Pinpoint Guides to Civil War Sites Ser.). (Illus.). 1998. pap. 7.95 (*1-57587-086-X*) Crane Hill AL.

Pinpoint Guide to California Lighthouses. Ray Jones. (Pinpoint Guides Ser.). (Illus.). 1998. pap. 8.95 (*1-57587-079-7*) Crane Hill AL.

Pinpoint Guide to Eastern Great Lakes Lighthouses. Ray Jones. (Pinpoint Guides Ser.). (Illus.). 1998. pap. 8.95 (*1-57587-080-0*) Crane Hill AL.

Pinpoint Guide to Florida Lighthouses. Ray Jones. (Pinpoint Guides Ser.). (Illus.). 1998. pap. 8.95 (*1-57587-076-2*) Crane Hill AL.

Pinpoint Guide to Mid-Atlantic Lighthouses. Ray Jones. (Pinpoint Guides Ser.). (Illus.). 1998. 8.95 (*1-57587-078-9*) Crane Hill AL.

Pinpoint Guide to Mississippi Civil War Sites. James J. Condra & Jeff Slaton. (Pinpoint Guides to Civil War Sites Ser.). (Illus.). 1998. pap. 7.95 (*1-57587-089-4*) Crane Hill AL.

Pinpoint Guide to North & South Carolina Civil War Sites. James J. Condra & Jeff Slaton. (Pinpoint Guides to Civil War Sites Ser.). (Illus.). 1998. pap. 7.95 (*1-57587-085-1*) Crane Hill AL.

Pinpoint Guide to South Atlantic Lighthouses. Ray Jones. (Pinpoint Guides Ser.). (Illus.). 1998. 8.95 (*1-57587-077-0*) Crane Hill AL.

Pinpoint Guide to the Atlanta Campaign. James J. Condra & Jeff Slaton. (Pinpoint Guides to Civil War Sites Ser.). (Illus.). 1998. pap. 7.95 (*1-57587-087-8*) Crane Hill AL.

Pinpoint Guide to Virginia - From Richmond to Appomattox. James J. Condra & Jeff Slaton. (Pinpoint Guides to Civil War Sites Ser.). (Illus.). 1998. pap. 7.95 (*1-57587-088-6*) Crane Hill AL.

Pinpoint Guide to Western Great Lakes Lighthouses. Ray Jones. (Pinpoint Guides Ser.). (Illus.). 1998. 8.95 (*1-57587-081-9*) Crane Hill AL.

Pinpoint of Eternity: European Literature in Search of the All-Encompassing Moment. Peter Salm. (German Literature: Art & Thought Ser.). 156p. (Orig.). 1986. pap. text 19.50 (*0-8191-5209-9*); lib. bdg. 44.50 (*0-8191-5208-0*) U Pr of Amer.

***Pinpoint Office 97 Demo.** 1999. write for info. (*0-13-026423-7*, Prentice Hall) P-H.

PinPointer: Akron - Canton. (Illus.). 428p. 1997. pap. 54.50 (*1-58461-029-8*) Indust Map.

***PinPointer: Akron/Canton.** (Illus.). 438p. 1999. pap. write for info. (*1-58461-069-7*) Indust Map.

PinPointer: Ann Arbor. (Illus.). 120p. 1998. pap. 42.50 (*1-58461-017-4*) Indust Map.

PinPointer: Ashtabula - Geauga. (Illus.). 72p. 1997. pap. 35.50 (*1-58461-030-1*) Indust Map.

***PinPointer: Ashtabula/Geauga.** (Illus.). 77p. 1999. pap. write for info. (*1-58461-066-2*) Indust Map.

PinPointer: Berks County. (Illus.). 1998. pap. 39.50 (*1-58461-045-X*) Indust Map.

PinPointer: Bloomington - Columbus. (Illus.). 116p. 1998. pap. 42.50 (*1-58461-009-3*) Indust Map.

PinPointer: Bowling Green. (Illus.). 88p. 1997. pap. 39.50 (*1-58461-014-X*) Indust Map.

***PinPointer: Bowling Green.** (Illus.). 76p. 1999. pap. write for info. (*1-58461-065-4*) Indust Map.

PinPointer: Buffalo. (Illus.). 372p. 1997. pap. 72.50 (*1-58461-028-X*) Indust Map.

***Pinpointer: Buffalo.** (Illus.). 418p. 2000. pap. write for info. (*1-58461-070-0*) Indust Map.

PinPointer: Butler - Warren. (Illus.). 124p. 1998. pap. 37.50 (*1-58461-031-X*) Indust Map.

PinPointer: Charlotte. (Illus.). 360p. 1998. pap. 54.50 (*1-58461-027-1*) Indust Map.

***PinPointer: Charlotte.** (Illus.). 340p. 2000. pap. write for info. (*1-58461-072-7*) Indust Map.

PinPointer: Chattanooga. (Illus.). 110p. 1996. pap. 37.50 (*1-58461-046-8*) Indust Map.

PinPointer: Chicago. (Illus.). 450p. 1998. pap. 99.50 (*1-58461-011-5*) Indust Map.

PinPointer: Cleveland. (Illus.). 390p. 1997. pap. 75.50 (*1-58461-033-6*) Indust Map.

***PinPointer: Cleveland.** (Illus.). 408p. 1999. pap. write for info. (*1-58461-067-0*) Indust Map.

PinPointer: Detroit. (Illus.). 354p. 1997. pap. 79.50 (*1-58461-018-2*) Indust Map.

PinPointer: Du Page. (Illus.). 300p. 1998. pap. 61.50 (*1-58461-010-7*) Indust Map.

PinPointer: East Central. (Illus.). 146p. 1998. pap. 44.50 (*1-58461-008-5*) Indust Map.

PinPointer: Elkhart - Kosciusko. (Illus.). 180p. 1998. pap. 48.50 (*1-58461-007-7*) Indust Map.

PinPointer: Erie - New Castle. (Illus.). 1998. pap. 45.50 (*1-58461-041-7*) Indust Map.

PinPointer: Evansville - Owensboro. (Illus.). 162p. 1998. pap. 45.50 (*1-58461-006-9*) Indust Map.

PinPointer: Flint. (Illus.). 100p. 1998. pap. 37.50 (*1-58461-019-0*) Indust Map.

PinPointer: Fort Wayne. (Illus.). 1998. pap. 48.50 (*1-58461-005-0*) Indust Map.

PinPointer: Gary - La Porte. (Illus.). 120p. 1998. pap. 45.50 (*1-58461-004-2*) Indust Map.

PinPointer: Greater Asheville. (Illus.). 1988. pap. 37.50 (*1-58461-026-3*) Indust Map.

PinPointer: Greater Birmingham. (Illus.). 1999. pap. 58.50 (*1-58461-001-8*) Indust Map.

PinPointer: Greater Cincinnati. (Illus.). 1998. pap. 60.00 (*1-58461-032-8*) Indust Map.

PinPointer: Greater Columbus. (Illus.). 318p. 1998. pap. 51.50 (*1-58461-034-4*) Indust Map.

P

An Asterisk (*) at the beginning of an entry indicates that the title is appearing for the first time.

PinPointer: Greater Dallas. (Illus.). 396p. 1998. pap. 72.50 (*1-58461-051-4*) Indust Map.
PinPointer: Greater Dayton. (Illus.). 1997. pap. 51.50 (*1-58461-035-2*) Indust Map.
PinPointer: Greater Fort Worth. (Illus.). 222p. 1998. pap. 45.50 (*1-58461-052-2*) Indust Map.
PinPointer: Greater Grand Rapids. (Illus.). 1998. pap. 61.50 (*1-58461-020-4*) Indust Map.
PinPointer: Greater Indianapolis. (Illus.). 1998. pap. 54.50 (*1-58461-003-4*) Indust Map.
***PinPointer: Greater Knoxville.** (Illus.). 184p. 1999. pap. write for info. (*1-58461-060-3*) Indust Map.
***PinPointer: Greater Montgomery.** (Illus.). 84p. 2000. pap. write for info. (*1-58461-071-9*) Indust Map.
***Pinpointer: Greater Reading.** (Illus.). 188p. 2000. pap. write for info. (*1-58461-075-1*) Indust Map.
***PinPointer: Greater St. Louis.** (Illus.). 402p. 1999. pap. 75.00 (*1-58461-057-3*) Indust Map.
***PinPointer: Greater St. Louis Supplement.** 143p. 1999. pap. 30.00 (*1-58461-058-1*) Indust Map.
***PinPointer: Harrisburg, PA.** (Illus.). 159p. 1999. pap. 40.00 (*1-58461-061-1*) Indust Map.
PinPointer: Kalamazoo - Battle Creek. (Illus.). 1998. pap. 42.50 (*1-58461-021-2*) Indust Map.
PinPointer: Knoxville. (Illus.). 1997. pap. 37.50 (*1-58461-047-6*) Indust Map.
PinPointer: Lancaster. (Illus.). 158p. 1998. pap. 42.50 (*1-58461-042-5*) Indust Map.
***PinPointer: Lancaster.** 151p. 2000. pap. write for info. (*1-58461-073-5*) Indust Map.
PinPointer: Lansing. (Illus.). 122p. 1998. pap. 39.50 (*1-58461-023-9*) Indust Map.
PinPointer: Lexington. (Illus.). 166p. 1997. pap. 39.50 (*1-58461-015-8*) Indust Map.
***PinPointer: Lexington.** (Illus.). 161p. 1999. pap. write for info. (*1-58461-064-6*) Indust Map.
PinPointer: Long Beach. (Illus.). 1999. pap. 38.50 (*1-58461-000-X*) Indust Map.
PinPointer: Lorain - Medina. (Illus.). 1997. pap. 35.50 (*1-58461-036-0*) Indust Map.
***PinPointer: Lorain/Medina.** (Illus.). 98p. 1999. pap. write for info. (*1-58461-068-9*) Indust Map.
PinPointer: Louisville. (Illus.). 256p. 1997. pap. 47.50 (*1-58461-016-6*) Indust Map.
***PinPointer: Louisville.** (Illus.). 272p. 1999. pap. 49.00 (*1-58461-062-X*) Indust Map.
PinPointer: Macomb - St. Clair. (Illus.). 256p. 1998. pap. 61.50 (*1-58461-022-0*) Indust Map.
PinPointer: Memphis. (Illus.). 1997. pap. 39.50 (*1-58461-048-4*) Indust Map.
PinPointer: Nashville. (Illus.). 1997. pap. 42.50 (*1-58461-049-2*) Indust Map.
PinPointer: North Central. (Illus.). 252p. 1998. pap. 44.50 (*1-58461-037-9*) Indust Map.
PinPointer: Philadelphia. (Illus.). 492p. 1997. pap. 75.50 (*1-58461-043-3*) Indust Map.
***PinPointer: Philadelphia.** (Illus.). 523p. 2000. pap. write for info. (*1-58461-074-3*) Indust Map.
PinPointer: Pittsburgh. (Illus.). 406p. 1997. pap. 65.50 (*1-58461-044-1*) Indust Map.
PinPointer: Pontiac. (Illus.). 322p. 1998. pap. 61.50 (*1-58461-024-7*) Indust Map.
PinPointer: Saginaw. (Illus.). 1998. pap. 34.50 (*1-58461-025-5*) Indust Map.
PinPointer: Southbend. (Illus.). 110p. 1998. pap. 44.50 (*1-58461-002-6*) Indust Map.
PinPointer: Tacoma. (Illus.). 1999. pap. 37.50 (*1-58461-053-0*) Indust Map.
PinPointer: Terre Haute - Danville. (Illus.). 86p. 1998. pap. 37.50 (*1-58461-013-1*) Indust Map.
PinPointer: Toledo. (Illus.). 222p. 1997. pap. 47.50 (*1-58461-038-7*) Indust Map.
***PinPointer: Toledo.** (Illus.). 218p. 1999. pap. 50.00 (*1-58461-054-9*) Indust Map.
PinPointer: Tri-Cities. (Illus.). 1997. pap. 37.50 (*1-58461-050-6*) Indust Map.
PinPointer: Warren - Youngstown. (Illus.). 200p. 1998. pap. 47.50 (*1-58461-039-5*) Indust Map.
PinPointer: Western Ohio. (Illus.). 296p. 1997. pap. 44.50 (*1-58461-040-9*) Indust Map.
***PinPointer: Western Ohio, 1999-2001.** (Illus.). 259p. 1999. pap. 50.00 (*1-58461-059-X*) Indust Map.
***PinPointer: Williamsport.** (Illus.). 88p. 1999. pap. write for info. (*1-58461-063-8*) Indust Map.
***PinPointer, 1999-2000: Greater Dayton.** (Illus.). 264p. 1999. pap. 55.00 (*1-58461-056-5*) Indust Map.
Pinpointing: How to Detect Child or Teen Alcohol-Drug Use & What to Do about It. J. Stuart Rahrer. LC 97-92446. (New Parent Awareness Ser.: No. 3). (Illus.). 86p. (Orig.). 1997. pap. 14.95 (*1-890897-05-1*) Pharos Consult.
Pinpointing Affluence: Increasing Your Share of Major Donor Dollars. Judith E. Nichols. 293p. 1994. 40.00 (*0-944496-40-7*) Precept Pr.
Pinpointing Student Behavioral Problems. Thomas McDonnell. (Orig.). 1988. pap. 9.95 (*1-55804-950-9*) Info Res Cons.
Pinprick of Light: The Troy & Greenfield Railroad & Its Hoosac Tunnel. rev. ed. Carl R. Byron. 152p. 1995. pap. text 16.95 (*1-881535-17-7*) New Eng Pr VT.
Pins: A Novel. Jim Provenzano. LC 99-90529. 285p. 1999. pap. 14.95 (*0-9672382-0-X*, Pub. by Myrmidude Pr) Alamo Sq Dist.
Pins in the Liberal Balloon. Francis Canavan. Ed. by Maria McFadden. LC 90-62956. (Illus.). 192p. 1990. pap. 12.95 (*0-9627780-0-1*) Natl Comm of Cath Laymen.
Pinshooting: A Complete Guide. Mitchell Ota. 1991. 14.95 (*1-879356-04-X*) Wolfe Pub Co.
Pinstripe Parables: Searching Stories about Things That Matter Most to a Man. David McCasland. 144p. 1995. 12.99 (*0-929239-91-1*) Discovery Hse Pubs.
Pinstripe Prayers: Or How to Talk to God While Pursuing Mammon. John V. Chervokas. 48p. (Orig.). 1984. 2.95 (*0-86683-874-0*, 7457) Harper SF.
Pinstripes & Reds: An American Ambassador Caught Between the State Department & the Romanian Communists, 1981-85. rev. ed. David B. Funderburk. LC 87-82566. 226p. 1990. 17.95 (*0-944273-01-7*) Selous Found Pr.
Pint of Murder. Alisa Craig, pseud. 192p. 1988. mass mkt. 3.99 (*0-380-70334-3*, Avon Bks) Morrow Avon.
Pint-Sized Puppets & Poems. Cara H. Bradshaw. (Illus.). 48p. (J). (ps-2). 1994. 6.99 (*0-86653-785-6*, GA1479) Good Apple.
***Pint-Sized Secret.** Sherryl Woods. (Special Edition Ser.: Bk. 1333). 2000. mass mkt. 4.50 (*0-373-24333-2*, 1-24333-6) Silhouette.
Pinta - Pan: Spanish Take-Home Parent Pack, Set. (Take-Home Parent Packs Ser.). (SPA., Illus.). (Orig.). 1993. pap. 16.95 incl. audio (*1-56334-382-7*) Hampton-Brown.
Pinta, Pinta, Gregorita. Lada J. Kratky. (Rimas y Risas Red Ser.). (SPA., Illus.). 16p. (Orig.). (J). (gr. 1-3). 1992. pap. 36.00 (*1-56334-126-3*) Hampton-Brown.
Pinta, Pinta, Gregorita (Big Book) Lada J. Kratky. (Rimas y Risas Red Ser.). (SPA., Illus.). 16p. (Orig.). (J). (gr. k-3). 1990. pap. text 29.95 (*0-917837-53-3*) Hampton-Brown.
Pinta, Pinta, Gregorita (Small Book) Lada J. Kratky. (Rimas y Risas Red Ser.). (SPA., Illus.). 16p. (Orig.). (J). (gr. k-3). 1992. pap. text 6.00 (*1-56334-084-4*) Hampton-Brown.
Pinta Ratones. Ellen S. Walsh. Tr. by Gerardo Cabello. (Illus.). 32p. 1994. 12.99 (*968-16-3768-2*, Pub. by Fondo) Continental Bk.
Pintail 3. Lucien Thomas. 250p. 1999. pap. 21.95 (*0-9670416-1-9*) L Thomas.
Pintar con Ceras. Usborne Books Staff. 1999. 12.95 (*1-58086-213-6*) EDC.
***Pintar Con Ceras (I Can Crayon)** Ray Gibson. (Playtime Ser.). (SPA., Illus.). 32p. (J). (ps-3). 1999. pap. 4.95 (*0-7460-3670-1*, Usborne) EDC.
Pintar Con Las Manos. Usborne Books Staff. 1999. 12.95 (*1-58086-214-4*) EDC.
***Pintar Con las Manos (I Can Fingerpaint)** Ray Gibson. (Spot the Differences Ser.). (SPA., Illus.). 32p. (J). (ps up). 1999. pap. 4.95 (*0-7460-3667-1*, Usborne) EDC.
***Pintar Personajes.** Ed. by Usborne Publishing Staff. (SPA., Illus.). 32p. (ps-3). 2000. 12.95 (*1-58086-285-3*) EDC.
***Pintar Personajes (I Can Draw People)** Ed. by Ray Gibson. (Playtime Ser.). (SPA., Illus.). 32p. (J). (ps-3). 2000. pap. 4.95 (*0-7460-3871-2*, Pub. by Usbrne Pbng UK) EDC.
Pinter at Sixty. Ed. by Katherine H. Burkman & John L. Kundert-Gibbs. LC 92-35160. (Drama & Performance Studies). 240p. 1993. 36.95 (*0-253-34499-9*); pap. 15.95 (*0-253-20811-4*) Ind U Pr.
Pinter Ethic: The Erotic Aesthetic. Penelope Prentice. LC 93-7620. (Studies in Modern Drama: Vol. 3). (Illus.). 480p. 1993. text 30.00 (*0-8153-1385-3*) Garland.
Pinter in Play: Critical Strategies & the Plays of Harold Pinter. Susan H. Merritt. LC 90-31163. 367p. (C). 1995. text 49.95 (*0-8223-1040-6*) Duke.
Pinter in Play: Critical Strategies & the Plays of Harold Pinter. Susan H. Merritt. LC 90-31163. 376p. 1995. pap. text 17.95 (*0-8223-1674-9*) Duke.
Pinter Review: Annual Essays, 1990. Ed. by Francis Gillen & Steven H. Gale. ix, 124p. 1991. 25.00 (*1-879852-00-4*); pap. 15.00 (*1-879852-01-2*) Univ Tampa.
Pinter Review: Annual Essays, 1991. Ed. by Francis Gillen & Steven H. Gale. 94p. 1992. 30.00 (*0-685-57608-6*); pap. 15.00 (*1-879852-03-9*) Univ Tampa.
Pinter the Playwright. 4th ed. Martin Esslin. (Illus.). 288p. (C). 1988. pap. write for info. (*0-413-51550-8*, A0212, Methuen Drama) Methn.
Pinter's Comic Play. Elin Diamond. LC 84-45230. (Illus.). 248p. 1985. 37.50 (*0-8387-5068-0*) Bucknell U Pr.
Pinter's Female Portraits: A Study of the Female Characters in the Plays of Harold Pinter. Elizabeth Sakellaridou. LC 87-1338. 208p. 1987. 56.00 (*0-389-20747-0*, N8306) B&N Imports.
Pinter's Odd Man Out: Staging & Filming Old Times. Sidney Homan et al. LC 91-58962. 192p. 1993. 34.50 (*0-8387-5238-1*) Bucknell U Pr.
Pintlers: Majestic They Stand. Nola Imus & Charlotte McLucas. (Illus.). 176p. 1999. pap. text 12.95 (*0-9668372-0-7*) The Gilted Edge.
Pinto. Lemercier. Ed. by Perry. (Exeter French Texts Ser.: Vol. 21). (FRE.). 187p. Date not set. pap. text 19.95 (*0-85989-011-2*, Pub. by Univ Exeter Pr) Northwestern U Pr.
Pinto & Sons. Leslie Epstein. LC 91-37314. 420p. 1992. pap. 9.95 (*0-393-30846-4*) Norton.
***Pinto & Sprinto.** Grace R. Friday. (J). (ps-2). 2000. pap. 6.95 (*0-533-13487-0*) Vantage.
Pinto Basin Site. Elizabeth W. Campbell & William H. Campbell. 51p. 1963. reprint ed. pap. 5.00 (*0-916561-55-0*) Southwest Mus.
Pinto Beans & Prehistoric Pots: The Legacy of Al & Alice Lancaster. Jenny L. Adams. (Archaeological Ser.: No. 183). (Illus.). 106p. 1994. pap. 14.95 (*1-889747-48-3*) Ariz St Mus.
Pinto Horse see Learning about Horses Series
Pinto Horse. Gail B. Stewart. (Illus.). 48p. (J). (gr. 3-7). 1995. 19.00 (*0-516-35298-9*) Childrens.
Pinto Horse & the Phantom Bull. Charles E. Perkins. LC 98-36712. (Illus.). 164p. 1998. reprint ed. pap. 10.00 (*0-8032-8752-6*, PERPIX Pr) U of Nebr Pr.
Pinto Horses. Janet L. Gammie. LC 95-2240. (Horses Ser.). (Illus.). 24p. (J). (ps-4). 1995. lib. bdg. 13.98 (*1-56239-439-8*) ABDO Pub Co.
Pintor de Su Deshonra. Pedro Calderon de la Barca. (SPA.). 236p. 1969. 8.95 (*0-8288-7065-9*, S8849) Fr & Eur.
Pintor de Trenes. Jose P. Montero. (SPA.). 1996. 11.95 (*84-241-3342-0*) Lectorum Pubns.
Pintupi Country, Pintupi Self: Sentiment, Place & Politics among Western Desert Aborigines. Fred R. Myers. (Illus.). 334p. 1991. pap. 16.95 (*0-520-07411-4*, Pub. by U CA Pr) Cal Prin Full Svc.
Pintura al Oleo. (Fine Arts for Beginners Ser.). (Illus.). 172p. 1999. pap. 9.95 (*3-8290-1937-8*, 540732) Konemann.
Pintura al Pastel. (Fine Arts for Beginners Ser.). (Illus.). 172p. 1999. pap. 9.95 (*3-8290-1938-6*, 540733) Konemann.
Pintura Cristiana en los Tres Primeros Siglos. Miguel Figueroa Y Miranda. (UPREX, Humanidades Ser.: No. 12). 110p. (C). 1972. pap. 1.50 (*0-8477-0012-7*) U of PR Pr.
Pintura de la Porcelana por Placer y Provecho. (SPA.). 1977. 18.00 (*0-9624294-3-0*) Brack Pubns.
Pintura Decorativa. Cy DeCosse Staff. (SPA., Illus.). 128p. 1996. pap. text 17.95 (*0-86573-392-9*) Creat Pub Intl.
Pintura del Siglo XX. Brest J. Romero. (Breviarios Ser.). (SPA.). pap. 11.99 (*968-16-0149-1*, Pub. by Fondo) Continental Bk.
Pintura Espanola del Siglo XVII. Jose Camon Aznar. (Summa Artis Ser.: Vol. 25). 600p. 1989. 295.00 (*84-239-5225-8*) Elliots Bks.
Pintura Espanola del Siglo XVI. Jose Camon Aznar. (Summa Artis Ser.: Vol. 24). 600p. 1989. 295.00 (*84-239-5224-X*) Elliots Bks.
Pintura Facial, Incl. face paints. Klutz Editors. Orig. Title: Face Painting. (SPA., Illus.). 63p. (J). (ps up). 1997. spiral bd. 19.95 (*1-57054-059-4*) Klutz.
Pintura Gotica en Mallorca. Gabriel Llompart. (SPA., Illus.). 128p. 1993. 100.00 (*84-343-0477-5*) Elliots Bks.
Pintura Medieval Espanola. Jose Camon Aznar. (Summa Artis Ser.: Vol. 22). 600p. 1989. 295.00 (*84-239-5222-3*) Elliots Bks.
Pinus Caribaea, Vol. 1. A. F. Lamb. 1978. 50.00 (*0-85074-015-0*) St Mut.
Pinus Kesiya. F. B. Armitage & J. Burley. 1980. 50.00 (*0-85074-030-4*) St Mut.
Pinus Patula. T. J. Wormald. 1975. 50.00 (*0-85074-025-8*) St Mut.
Pinus (Pinaceae) Aljos Farjon & Brian T. Styles. (Flora Neotropica Monograph Ser.: Vol. 75). (Illus.). 286p. 1997. text 31.00 (*0-89327-411-9*, FLN 75) NY Botanical.
Pinwheel: An Exploration in Color-&-Weave Design. Margaret B. Windeknecht. (Illus.). 64p. (Orig.). 1992. pap. 9.95 (*0-9618797-2-6*) T G Windeknecht.
Pinwheels: A Collection of Pinwheel Projects to Get You Spinning. Barbara M. Siedlecki. (Illus.). 24p. 1997. pap. 12.95 (*0-9643998-2-2*, 80100) Cabin Fev Crafts.
Pinyin Chinese-English Dictionary. Beijing Language Institute Staff. Ed. by Wu Jingrong. (CHI & ENG.). 976p. 1982. pap. 59.95 (*0-471-86796-9*) Wiley.
Pinyon Jay: Behavioural Ecology of a Colonial & Cooperative Corvid. John M. Marzluff & Russell P. Balda. (Poyser Popular Bird Bks.). (Illus.). 317p. 1992. text 39.00 (*0-85661-064-X*, 784664) Acad Pr.
Pi'o: An Enquiry into the Marriage of Brothers & Sisters & Other Close Relatives in Old Hawai'i. William H. Davenport. LC 93-45520. 104p. lib. bdg. 32.50 (*0-8191-9395-X*) U Pr of Amer.
Pio Baroja's Memorias de un Humbre de Acion & the Ironic Mode: The Search for Order & Meaning. Marsha S. Collins. 1986. 69.00 (*0-7293-0252-0*, Pub. by Tamesis Bks Ltd) Boydell & Brewer.
Pio Del Pilar & Other Heroes. Orlino A. Ochosa & Frank A. Hilario. LC 97-946860. xvii, 220 p. 1997. write for info. (*971-10-1009-7*, Pub. by New Day Pub) Cellar.
Pio Pio. (Libros de Carton Con Sonido Ser.). (SPA.). 1995. bds. 4.98 (*1-85854-293-6*) Brimax Bks.
Piobaireachd & Its Interpretation. F. Richardson & Seumas Macneill. 144p. 1996. pap. 45.00 (*0-85976-440-0*, Pub. by J Donald) St Mut.
Pion-Nucleon Scattering. Robert J. Cence. LC 66-11964. (Investigations in Physics Ser.: Vol. 11). 148p. 1969. reprint ed. pap. 45.90 (*0-7837-9313-8*, 206005300004) Bks Demand.
Pion-Nucleon System. B. H. Bransden & R. Gordon Moorhouse. LC 73-39795. 548p. 1973. reprint ed. pap. 169.90 (*0-7837-9304-9*, 206004400004) Bks Demand.
Pion-Nucleus Double Charge Exchange. Ed. by W. R. Gibbs. 620p. (C). 1990. text 113.00 (*981-02-0148-6*) World Scientific Pub.
Pion-Nucleus Physics: Future Directions & New Facilities at Lampf. Ed. by R. J. Peterson & D. D. Strottman. LC 87-72961. (AIP Conference Proceedings Ser.: No. 163). 592p. 1988. lib. bdg. 75.00 (*0-88318-363-3*) Am Inst Physics.
Pion Production & Absorption in Nuclei, 1981: Indiana University Cyclatron Facility. Ed. by Robert D. Bent. LC 82-70678. (AIP Conference Proceedings Ser.: No. 79). 432p. 1982. lib. bdg. 36.00 (*0-88318-178-9*) Am Inst Physics.
Pioneer. reprint ed. lib. bdg. 270.00 (*0-404-19540-7*) AMS Pr.
Pioneer. Ed. by James Russell Lowell. LC 47-30458. 200p. 1947. reprint ed. lib. bdg. 50.00 (*0-8201-1215-1*) Schol Facsimiles.
Pioneer Aboriginal Mission. William McNair & Hilary Rumley. (Illus.). 162p. (Orig.). pap. 19.95 (*0-85564-178-9*, Pub. by Univ of West Aust Pr) Intl Spec Bk.
Pioneer Adventures. Frank Gray. (American Autobiography Ser.). 384p. 1995. reprint ed. lib. bdg. 89.00 (*0-7812-8538-0*) Rprt Serv.
Pioneer Agricultural Journalists: Brief Biographical Sketches of Some of the Early Editors in the Field of Agricultural Journalism. William E. Ogilvie. LC 72-89071. (Rural America Ser.). 1973. reprint ed. 16.00 (*0-8420-1492-6*) Scholarly Res Inc.
Pioneer Airplane Mails of the United States. Thomas J. O'Sullivan. 346p. 1986. 25.00 (*0-939429-13-6*) Am Air Mail.
Pioneer American Railroads: The Mohawk & Hudson & the Saratoga & Schenectady. F. Daniel Larkin. LC 95-41702. (Illus.). 96p. 1995. lib. bdg. 25.00 (*0-935796-71-1*) Purple Mnt Pr.
Pioneer American Synagogues - A State by State Guide. Julian H. Preisler. LC 97-211149. x, 165p. 1997. pap. 17.00 (*0-7884-0711-2*, P617) Heritage Bk.
Pioneer Ancestors of Members of the Society of Indiana Pioneers. Compiled by Ruth Dorrel. iv, 245p. 1983. pap. 20.00 (*0-87195-076-6*) Ind Hist Soc.
Pioneer & General History of Geauga Co., with Sketches of Some of the Pioneers & Prominent Men. Historical Society of Geauga Co. Staff. 861p. 1994. pap. text 48.00 (*0-7884-0102-5*) Heritage Bk.
Pioneer & General History of Geauga County. Ed. by Historical Society of Geauga County Staff. 822p. 1993. reprint ed. lib. bdg. 83.00 (*0-8328-2826-2*) Higginson Bk Co.
Pioneer & General History of Geauga County, (Ohio) Ed. by Geauga County Historical Society Staff. (Illus.). 783p. 1993. reprint ed. lib. bdg. 78.50 (*0-8328-3226-X*) Higginson Bk Co.
Pioneer & the Prairie Lawyer: Boone & Lincoln Family Historical & Biographical Heritage. Willard Mounts. Ed. by Manuscripts International Staff. LC 91-72847. (Illus.). 224p. (Orig.). 1992. pap. 14.95 (*0-9630038-0-1*) Ginwill Pub.
Pioneer & the Prairie Lawyer: Historical & Biographical - Boone & Lincoln Family Heritage. Willard Mounts. LC 91-72847. (Illus.). 224p. 1992. reprint ed. pap. 14.95 (*0-9630038-1-X*) Ginwill Pub.
Pioneer Aviator: The Remarkable Life of Lores Bonney. Terry Gwynn-Jones. (Illus.). 190p. 1988. reprint ed. pap. 16.95 (*0-7022-2118-X*, Pub. by Univ Queensland Pr) Intl Spec Bk.
Pioneer Baptist Church Records of South-Central Kentucky & the Upper Cumberland of Tennessee. C. P. Cawthorn & N. L. Warnell. 1987. reprint ed. 34.00 (*0-685-30502-3*) Church History.
Pioneer Battalions in the Great War: Organised & Intelligent Labour. Michinson. (Illus.). 1997. 35.00 (*0-85052-566-7*) Leo Cooper.
Pioneer Bear. Joan Sandin. LC 93-48023. (Step into Reading Ser.: A Step 2 Book). (Illus.). 43p. (J). (ps-3). 1995. pap. 3.99 (*0-679-86050-9*) Random.
Pioneer Bear. Joan Sandin. LC 93-48023. (Step into Reading Ser.: A Step 2 Book). (Illus.). 43p. (J). (ps-3). 1995. lib. bdg. 11.99 (*0-679-96050-3*) Random.
Pioneer Bear. Joan Sandin. (Step into Reading Ser.: A Step 2 Book). (J). (gr. 1-3). 1995. 9.19 (*0-606-08015-5*, Pub. by Turtleback) Demco.
Pioneer Book of Nature Crafts. Harlan G. Metcalf. Orig. Title: Whittlin, Whistlin & Thingama Jigs. 1977. reprint ed. pap. 4.95 (*0-8065-0568-0*, Citadel Pr) Carol Pub Group.
Pioneer Book of Washington County. Washington County Museum Association Staff. (Illus.). 392p. 1999. reprint ed. lib. bdg. 44.00 (*0-8328-9795-7*) Higginson Bk Co.
Pioneer Bush Pilot: The Story of Noel Wien see Noel Wien: Alaska Pioneer Bush Pilot
Pioneer California: Tales of Explorers, Indians, & Settlers. Margaret Roberts. LC 81-22543. (Illus.). 296p. (J). (gr. 6 up). 1982. 12.95 (*0-914598-42-2*) Bear Flag Bks.
Pioneer Camp of the Saints: The 1846 & 1847 Mormon Trail Journals of Thomas Bullock. Ed. by Will Bagley. LC 96-51745. (Kingdom in the West Ser.: Vol. 1). (Illus.). 400p. 1997. 39.50 (*0-87062-276-5*) A H Clark.
Pioneer Cat. William H. Hooks. (Stepping Stone Bks.). (J). 1988. 9.19 (*0-606-03889-2*, Pub. by Turtleback) Demco.
Pioneer Cat. William J. Hooks. LC 88-4708. (Stepping Stone Bks.). (Illus.). 64p. (Orig.). (J). (gr. 4-7). 1988. pap. 3.99 (*0-394-82038-X*, Pub. by Random Bks Yng Read) Random.
Pioneer Children of Appalachia. Joan W. Anderson. LC 86-2624. 48p. (J). (gr. 4-7). 1990. pap. 7.95 (*0-395-54792-X*, Clarion Bks) HM.
Pioneer Children on the Journey West. Emmy E. Werner. (Illus.). 202p. (C). 1996. pap. 19.00 (*0-8133-2027-5*, Pub. by Westview) HarpC.
Pioneer Church. Carolyn B. Otto. LC 95-42007. 32p. (J). (gr. k-4). 2000. 16.95 (*0-8050-2554-5*) H Holt & Co.
***Pioneer Churches: In Mercer County, West Virginia, 1840-1915.** William Sanders. LC 98-90722. (Illus.). 144p. 1998. pap. 15.00 (*0-9625273-7-8*, Pub. by W Sanders) McClain.
Pioneer Churchman: The Narrative & Journal of J. W. C. Dietrichson, 1844-1850. Ed. by Clifford A. Nelson. Tr. by Malcom Rosholt & Harris Kaasa. 265p. 1974. 20.00 (*0-87732-053-5*) Norwegian-Am Hist Assn.
Pioneer Clothing on the Oregon Trail. Christina R. May. LC 98-183244. (Illus.). 90p. 1998. pap. 10.95 (*1-57502-690-2*, PO1950) Morris Pubng.
Pioneer College: The Centennial History of Saint Leo College, Saint Leo Abbey, & Holy Name Priory. James J. Horgan. LC 89-51121. (Illus.). 648p. 1990. 24.95 (*0-945759-01-0*) St Leo Col Pr.
Pioneer Colored Christians. Harriet P. Miller. LC 73-37313. (Black Heritage Library Collection). 1977. reprint ed. 22.95 (*0-8369-8950-3*) Ayer.
Pioneer Commercial Photography: The Burgert Brothers, Tampa, Florida. Robert E. Snyder & Jack B. Moore. (Illus.). 248p. 1992. 39.95 (*0-8130-1150-7*) U Press Fla.

P

An Asterisk (*) at the beginning of an entry indicates that the title is appearing for the first time.

Pioneer Cook: A Historical View of Canadian Prairie Food, Vol. 1. Beulah M. Barss. 134p. (Orig.). 1980. pap. 7.95 (*0-920490-11-5*) Temeron Bks.

Pioneer Cookery Around Oklahoma. Linda K. Rosser. (Illus.). 250p. 1978. reprint ed. pap. 9.95 (*0-929546-01-6*) Bobwhite Pubns.

Pioneer Cooking. Kathryn S. Maxwell. (Illus.). 184p. (Orig.). 1987. pap. 4.95 (*0-940649-02-0*) Parnell Pub.

Pioneer Cooking: A Collection of Original Recipes of Yesteryear. 2nd ed. Alayne Elster. Ed. by Toby Elster. LC 93-78845. 130p. (Orig.). 1994. reprint ed. pap. 9.95 (*1-882420-02-0*) Hearth KS.

Pioneer Cooking in Ontario: Tested Recipes from Ontario's Pioneer Villages & Historic Sites. 2nd ed. Illus. by C. W. Jeffreys. 64p. (Orig.). 1988. pap. 4.95 (*1-55021-015-7*, Pub. by NC Ltd) U of Toronto Pr.

Pioneer Crafts. Barbara Greenwood. (Illus.). 40p. (Orig.). (J). (gr. 2 up). 1997. pap. 4.95 (*1-55074-359-7*, Pub. by Kids Can Pr) Genl Dist Srvs.

Pioneer Cross: Swedish Settlements along the Smoky Hill Bluffs. Thomas N. Holmquist. LC 93-80031. (Illus.). 144p. (Orig.). 1994. pap. 9.95 (*1-882420-06-3*) Hearth KS.

Pioneer Days. Mary Hayden. 68p. 1979. 17.95 (*0-87770-203-9*) Ye Galleon.

Pioneer Days. Mary Hayden. 68p. 1979. pap. 12.95 (*0-87770-685-9*) Ye Galleon.

Pioneer Days. David King. (J). 1997. write for info. (*0-614-29329-4*) Wiley.

Pioneer Days: Discover the Past with Fun Projects, Games, Activities, & Recipes. David C. King. LC 96-37495. (Kid's Life Ser.). (Illus.). 128p. (J). (gr. 3-6). 1997. pap. 12.95 (*0-471-16169-1*) Wiley.

Pioneer Days & Later Times in Corning & Vicinity, 1789-1920. Uri Mulford. (Illus.). 528p. 1997. reprint ed. lib. bdg. 55.00 (*0-8328-6125-1*) Higginson Bk Co.

Pioneer Days at Tekoa. Bertha E. Williams. (Illus.). 28p. 1986. pap. 4.95 (*0-87770-383-3*) Ye Galleon.

Pioneer Days in Arkansas. Samuel H. Chester. Ed. by Phillip A. Sperry & Joe R. Goss. (Illus.). 76p. 1993. reprint ed. 23.95 (*1-56869-024-X*); reprint ed. pap. 13.95 (*1-56869-025-8*) Oldbuck Pr.

Pioneer Days in San Francisco. John W. Palmer. Ed. by William R. Jones. (Illus.). 24p. 1977. reprint ed. pap. 2.95 (*0-89646-015-0*) Vistabooks.

*__Pioneer Days in the Black Hills: Accurate History & Facts Related by One of the Early Day Pioneers.__ John McClintock. LC 99-55842. (Illus.). 368p. 2000. pap. text 17.95 (*0-8061-3191-8*) U of Okla Pr.

Pioneer Days in the Catskill High Peaks: Tannersville & the Region Around. Leah Wiltse. Ed. by Shirley Dunn. LC 99-22550. (Illus.). 160p. 1999. pap. 15.95 (*1-883789-19-2*) Blk Dome Pr.

Pioneer Days in the Early Southwest. Grant Foreman. LC 93-45372. (Illus.). ix, 345p. 1994. reprint ed. pap. 14.95 (*0-8032-6883-1*, Bison Books) U of Nebr Pr.

Pioneer Days in Upper Canada. Edwin C. Guillet. LC 66-37656. (Canadian University Paperbooks Ser.: 30). 270p. reprint ed. pap. 83.70 (*0-608-14784-2*, 205582300038) Bks Demand.

*__Pioneer Days on Puget Sound.__ Arthur Armstrong Denny. (Illus.). 101p. 1999. pap. 14.95 (*0-87770-674-3*) Ye Galleon.

Pioneer Days on Puget Sound. rev. ed. Arthur A. Denny. 101p. 1980. 19.95 (*0-87770-226-8*) Ye Galleon.

Pioneer Dictionary from A to Z. Bobbie Kalman & Jane Lewis. LC 99-38619. (Alphabasics Ser.). (Illus.). 32p. (J). (gr. 1-4). 1999. pap. 7.95 (*0-86505-420-7*) Crabtree Pub Co.

*__Pioneer Dictionary from A to Z.__ Bobbie Kalman & Jane Lewis. LC 99-38619. (Alphabasics Ser.). (Illus.). 32p. (J). (gr. 1-4). 1999. lib. bdg. 20.60 (*0-86505-390-1*) Crabtree Pub Co.

Pioneer Doctor in the Ozarks White River Country. rev. ed. Amy J. Miller. (Illus.). 165p. 1994. pap. 15.80 (*0-9643894-0-1*) Delphi Assocs.

Pioneer Evangelists of the Church of God in the Pacific Northwest. John L. Green. 164p. pap. 3.50 (*0-686-29135-2*) Faith Pub Hse.

Pioneer Experience. Trudy R. Pederson. (Illus.). 116p. (Orig.). 1982. 10.00 (*0-686-95352-5*) Directed Media.

Pioneer Experiment Station, 1875 to 1975: A History. James G. Horsfall. Ed. by Margaret H. Schadler. (Illus.). 123p. write for info. (*0-9634039-0-7*) Antoca Pr.

Pioneer Families of Cleveland, 2 vols. Gertrude Van Rensselaer Wickham. 1993. reprint ed. lib. bdg. 69.50 (*0-8328-2921-8*) Higginson Bk Co.

Pioneer Families of Cleveland, Vol. I. Gertrude Van Rensselaer Wickham. 370p. 1993. reprint ed. lib. bdg. 39.50 (*0-8328-2920-X*) Higginson Bk Co.

Pioneer Families of Eastern & Southeastern Kentucky. William C. Kozee. LC 73-9090. 272p. 1994. reprint ed. 25.00 (*0-8063-0576-2*, 3270) Genealog Pub.

Pioneer Families of Garrett County. Garrett County Historical Society Staff. Ed. by Martha Kahl & John Grant. 656p. 1988. text 30.00 (*0-9621074-0-9*) Garrett Cnty Hist Soc.

*__Pioneer Families of the Midwest, 3 vols. in 1.__ Blanche L. Walden. LC 98-177787. 162p. 1998. reprint ed. pap. 25.00 (*0-8063-4791-0*, 9600) Clearfield Co.

Pioneer Families of the South Platte Valley: Then & Now: A History of Families in the Fort Lupton Area. Richelle Cross. LC 95-197047. (Illus.). 192p. (Orig.). 1995. pap. 12.50 (*0-9644165-0-6*) S Platte Valley.

Pioneer Family. Loren E. Jeter, Sr. Ed. & Illus. by Jeanette F. Jeter. LC 91-90623. 173p. (Orig.). 1992. pap. write for info. (*0-9623339-1-3*) L E Jeter.

Pioneer Family: Life on Florida's 20th-Century Frontier. Michel Oesterreicher. LC 95-15202. (Illus.). 192p. (Orig.). (C). 1996. pap. 24.95 (*0-8173-0783-4*) U of Ala Pr.

Pioneer Farm: Living on a Farm in the 1880s. Megan O'Hara. LC 97-31874. (Living History Ser.). (Illus.). 32p. (J). (gr. 2-3). 1998. lib. bdg. 21.00 (*1-56065-726-X*, Blue Earth Bks) Capstone Pr.

Pioneer Farm Cooking. Mary Gunderson. LC 99-24390. (Exploring History Through Simple Recipes Ser.). 32p. (J). (gr. 2-7). 2000. lib. bdg. 22.60 (*0-7368-0356-4*, Blue Earth Bks) Capstone Pr.

*__Pioneer Farm Cooking.__ Mary Gunderson. (Exploring History Through Simple Recipes Ser.). 32p. (J). (gr. 2-7). 1999. 14.60 (*0-516-21867-0*) Childrens.

*__Pioneer Farm Girl: The Diary of Sarah Gillespie, 1877-1878.__ Suzanne L. Bunkers. (Diaries, Letters & Memoirs Ser.). 32p. (J). (gr. 2-7). 1999. 21.00 (*0-516-21340-7*) Childrens.

Pioneer Farm Girl: The Diary of Sarah Gillespie, 1877-1878. Ed. by Suzanne L. Bunkers & Ann Hodgson. LC 99-15273. (Diaries, Letters & Memoirs Ser.). 32p. (J). (gr. 2-7). 2000. lib. bdg. 22.60 (*0-7368-0347-5*, Blue Earth Bks) Capstone Pr.

Pioneer Farmer & Backwoodsman, Vol. 1. Edwin C. Guillet. LC F 1058.G88. (Illus.). 371p. reprint ed. pap. 115.10 (*0-8357-3640-7*, 203636900001) Bks Demand.

Pioneer Farmer & Backwoodsman, Vol. 2. Edwin C. Guillet. LC F 1058.G88. (Illus.). 404p. reprint ed. pap. 125.30 (*0-8357-3641-5*, 203636900002) Bks Demand.

Pioneer Farming. Madge Kelly. (History of Iowa Ser.). (Illus.). 51p. (Orig.). (YA). (gr. 5 up). 1988. pap. text 1.50 (*0-924702-03-6*) Grn Valley Area.

Pioneer Flights of Garden City Estates, New York: The First U. S. Airmail Service. Robert Schoendorf. Ed. by Peter S. Lemmo. (Illus.). 75p. (Orig.). 1982. pap. 19.95 (*0-686-39388-0*) A Zimmerman.

Pioneer Folks: The Notable Band of Men & Women of Medina County Whose Early Struggles Brought Success & Prosperity. Sharon L. Kraynek. LC 95-125693. 59p. 1994. per. 6.00 (*1-55856-170-6*, 418) Closson Pr.

Pioneer Fringe. Isaiah Bowman. LC 71-160960. (Select Bibliographies Reprint Ser.). 1977. reprint ed. 42.95 (*0-8369-5828-4*) Ayer.

Pioneer Gentlewoman in British Columbia: The Recollections of Susan Allison. Ed. by Margaret Ormsby. (Pioneers of British Columbia Ser.). (Illus.). 196p. 1976. pap. 15.95 (*0-7748-0392-4*) U of Wash Pr.

*__Pioneer Ghost.__ K. L. Morgan. LC 00-103153. 110p. 2000. pap. 8.95 (*1-58308-185-2*, 81852) TriQuest.

Pioneer Ghosts of Kentucky: Rest in Peace John Jay Dickey, 5 vols. Wilma Winton. (History & Genealogy of Kentucky Families Ser.). 1987. pap. write for info. (*0-9618206-0-8*) Pearl Bullock.

Pioneer Ghosts of Kentucky: Rest in Peace John Jay Dickey. Wilma Winton. (History & Genealogy of Kentucky Families Ser.: Vol. II). 250p. 1987. pap. write for info. (*0-9618206-3-2*) Pearl Bullock.

Pioneer Ghosts of Kentucky: Rest in Peace John Jay Dickey. Wilma Winton. (History & Genealogy of Kentucku Families Ser.: Vol. III). 250p. 1987. pap. write for info. (*0-9618206-4-0*) Pearl Bullock.

Pioneer Ghosts of Kentucky: Rest in Peace John Jay Dickey. Wilma Winton. (History & Genealogy of Kentucky Families Ser.: Vol. IV). 250p. 1987. pap. write for info. (*0-9618206-5-9*) Pearl Bullock.

Pioneer Ghosts of Kentucky: Rest in Peace John Jay Dickey. rev. ed. Wilma Winton. LC 87-70773. (History & Genealogy of Kentucky Families Ser.: Vol. I). 250p. 1987. pap. write for info. (*0-9618206-2-4*) Pearl Bullock.

Pioneer Girl: Growing up on the Prairie. Andrea Warren. LC 98-4999. (Illus.). 96p. (J). (gr. 3-7). 1998. 15.95 (*0-688-15438-7*, Wm Morrow) Morrow Avon.

*__Pioneer Girl: Growing Up on the Prairie.__ Andrea Warren. LC 98-4999. (Illus.). 96p. (YA). (gr. 4-7). 2000. mass mkt. 4.95 (*0-688-17151-6*, Wm Morrow) Morrow Avon.

Pioneer Girl: The Story of Laura Ingalls Wilder. William Anderson. LC 96-31203. (Illus.). 32p. (J). (gr. 2 up). 1998. 15.95 (*0-06-027243-0*); lib. bdg. 15.89 (*0-06-027244-9*) HarpC.

*__Pioneer Girl: The Story of Laura Ingalls Wilder.__ William Anderson. (Illus.). 32p. (YA). (gr. 2 up). 2000. pap. 5.95 (*0-06-446234-X*) HarpC Child Bks.

Pioneer Heritage: The First Century of the Arizona Historical Society. Charles L. Sonnichsen. LC 83-17264. (Illus.). 240p. 1984. 15.00 (*0-910037-21-3*) AZ Hist Soc.

Pioneer Heritage Wild Game Cookbook. Jack French. LC 86-62881. (Illus.). 416p. (Orig.). 1987. pap. 14.95 (*0-685-17315-1*) Realco Pub.

Pioneer History: Being an Account of the First Examinations of the Ohio Valley, & the Early Settlement of the Northwest Territory. S. P. Hildreth. LC 79-146400. (First American Frontier Ser.). (Illus.). 1971. reprint ed. 45.95 (*0-405-02854-7*) Ayer.

Pioneer History of Becker County, Minnesota. Alvin H. Wilcox. (Illus.). 757p. 1994. reprint ed. lib. bdg. 77.50 (*0-8328-3852-7*) Higginson Bk Co.

Pioneer History of Clarksfield. F. E. Weeks. (Illus.). 175p. 1997. reprint ed. lib. bdg. 26.50 (*0-8328-6302-5*) Higginson Bk Co.

Pioneer History of Cortland Co. & the Border Wars of New York. H. C. Goodwin. LC 98-138936. 480p. 1998. pap. 33.00 (*0-7884-0829-1*, G552) Heritage Bk.

Pioneer History of Custer County. Solomon D. Butcher. 15.50 (*0-931068-05-3*); pap. 10.00 (*0-685-04190-5*) Purcells.

Pioneer History of Eaton County, Massachusetts, 1833-1866. David Strange. (Illus.). 192p. 1997. reprint ed. lib. bdg. 29.50 (*0-8328-7129-X*) Higginson Bk Co.

Pioneer History of Eaton County, Michigan. Daniel Strange. 192p. 1993. reprint ed. lib. bdg. write for info. (*0-8328-2930-7*) Higginson Bk Co.

Pioneer History of Elkhart County: With Sketches & Stories. Henry S. Bartholomew. (Illus.). 337p. 1997. reprint ed. lib. bdg. 39.50 (*0-8328-6647-4*) Higginson Bk Co.

Pioneer History of Indiana: Including Stories, Incidents & Customs of the Early Settlers. W. M. Cockrum. (Illus.). 638p. 1997. reprint ed. lib. bdg. 65.00 (*0-8328-6642-3*) Higginson Bk Co.

Pioneer History of Ingham County, Vol. I. Compiled by F. L. Adams. (Illus.). 856p. 1997. reprint ed. lib. bdg. 87.50 (*0-8328-6760-8*) Higginson Bk Co.

*__Pioneer History of Jefferson County, Pennsylvania & My First Recollections of Brookville, Pennsylvania, 1840-1843, When My Feet Were Bare & My Cheeks Were Brown.__ W. J. McKnight. (Illus.). 697p. 1999. reprint ed. (*0-7884-1216-7*, M139) Heritage Bk.

Pioneer History of Jefferson County, Pennsylvania, 1755-1844. William J. McKnight. (Illus.). 670p. 1992. reprint ed. lib. bdg. 69.50 (*0-8328-1415-6*) Higginson Bk Co.

Pioneer History of Medina County. N. B. Northrop. (Illus.). 224p. 1997. reprint ed. lib. bdg. 29.50 (*0-8328-6344-0*) Higginson Bk Co.

Pioneer History of Medina County, Ohio. N. B. Northrop. 236p. 1999. reprint ed. pap. 21.00 (*0-7884-1184-5*, N569) Heritage Bk.

Pioneer History of Meigs County, Ohio. Stillman C. Larkin. 208p. 1995. reprint ed. lib. bdg. 31.00 (*0-8328-4479-9*) Higginson Bk Co.

Pioneer History of Milwaukee. James S. Buck. (Illus.). 292p. 1994. reprint ed. lib. bdg. 32.00 (*0-8328-3877-2*) Higginson Bk Co.

Pioneer History of Milwaukee, Wisconsin, 4 vols. James S. Buck. (Illus.). 1709p. 1997. reprint ed. lib. bdg. 159.00 (*0-8328-7186-9*) Higginson Bk Co.

Pioneer History of Orleans County, New York. Arad Thomas. (Illus.). 498p. 1998. reprint ed. pap. 35.50 (*0-7884-0957-3*, T354) Heritage Bk.

Pioneer History of Pocahontas County, Iowa. Robert E. Flickinger. (Illus.). 909p. 1993. reprint ed. lib. bdg. 89.50 (*0-8328-2910-2*) Higginson Bk Co.

Pioneer History of the Champlain Valley, NY. Winslow C. Watson. 231p. 1993. reprint ed. lib. bdg. 29.50 (*0-8328-3183-2*) Higginson Bk Co.

Pioneer History of the Holland Purchase of Western New York. Orsamus Turner. 666p. 1993. reprint ed. lib. bdg. 109.00 (*0-7812-5203-2*) Rprt Serv.

Pioneer History of the Holland Purchase of Western New York . . . & a History of Pioneer Settlement . . . Orasmus Turner. (Illus.). 699p. 1991. reprint ed. pap. 40.00 (*1-55613-385-5*) Heritage Bk.

Pioneer History of the Township of Grand Blanc. Alvah Brainerd. LC 64-1263. (Local History Reprints Ser.). 73p. 1964. reprint ed. pap. 3.25 (*0-916699-00-5*) CMU Clarke Hist Lib.

Pioneer Homesteaders of the Fort Rock Valley. Raymond R. Hatton. LC 82-71119. (Illus.). 144p. 1982. 12.95 (*0-8323-0407-7*) Binford Mort.

Pioneer in Marketing: L. D. H. Weld: An Original Anthology. Ed. by Henry Assael. LC 78-283. (Century Classic Ser.). 1979. lib. bdg. 58.95 (*0-405-11157-6*) Ayer.

Pioneer in Modern Medicine: David Linn Edsall of Harvard. Joseph C. Aub & Ruth K. Hapgood. LC 78-145896. (Illus.). 384p. 1970. 22.50 (*0-674-66875-8*) HUP.

Pioneer in Northwest America, 1841-1858, 2 vols. Ed. by Nils W. Olsson. LC 60-11209. 1960. 16.00 (*0-318-03680-0*) Swedish-Am.

Pioneer in the U. S. Air Corps. George H. Beverley. (Illus.). 70p. (Orig.). 1982. pap. text 12.00 (*0-89745-029-9*) Sunflower U Pr.

Pioneer Irish in New England. Michael J. O'Brien. 325p. 1998. reprint ed. pap. 27.50 (*0-8063-4790-2*, 9321) Clearfield Co.

Pioneer Irish in New England. Michael J. O'Brien. 325p. 1988. reprint ed. pap. 18.00 (*1-55613-106-2*) Heritage Bk.

Pioneer Irish of Onondaga (about 1776-1847) Teresa Bannan. (Illus.). 333p. 1997. reprint ed. lib. bdg. 39.50 (*0-8328-6190-1*) Higginson Bk Co.

Pioneer Jesuits in Northern Mexico. Peter M. Dunner. LC 78-10566. (Illus.). 227p. 1979. reprint ed. lib. bdg. 59.75 (*0-313-20653-8*, DUPI, Greenwood Pr) Greenwood.

Pioneer Jewish Texans: Their Impact on Texas & American History for 400 Years, 1590-1990. Natalie Ornish. (Illus.). 336p. 1989. 39.95 (*0-9620755-0-7*) TX Heritage Pr.

Pioneer Jews: A New Life in the Far West. Harriet Rechlin & Fred Rechlin. (Illus.). 256p. 1986. pap. 21.95 (*0-395-42639-1*) HM.

Pioneer Jews of the California Mother Lode, 1849-1880: An Annotated Bibliography. Sara G. Cogan. (Western Jewish Americana Ser.: No. 1). 1968. 7.50 (*0-943376-01-7*) Magnes Mus.

Pioneer Journal: A Modern-Day Journey to an Unknown World. Michael Hall. LC 94-75295. (Illus.). 256p. (Orig.). 1994. pap. 10.00 (*0-9634920-3-9*) Golden Heart.

Pioneer Journeys: Drama in Museum Education. Jennifer F. Hayes & Dorothy M. Schindel. (Illus.). 152p. 1994. pap. 14.95 (*0-932720-94-3*) New Plays Inc.

Pioneer Lady of Flight Hazel Jane Raines: A Biography in Letters. Regina T. Hawkins. (Illus.). 192p. 1996. 29.95 (*0-86554-532-4*, MUP/H407) Mercer Univ Pr.

Pioneer Lady's Country Christmas. Jane W. Hopping. LC 97-47138. 384p. 1998. 9.99 (*0-517-18349-8*) Random Hse Value.

Pioneer Lady's Hearty Winter Cookbook: A Treasury of Old-Fashioned Foods & Fond Memories. Jane W. Hopping. (Illus.). 261p. 1999. text 25.00 (*0-7881-5962-3*) DIANE Pub.

Pioneer Leaders & Early Institutions in Louisiana Education. Rodney Cline. 1969. 20.00 (*0-87511-019-3*) Claitors.

*__Pioneer Lessons: 87 Things I Almost Wish We'd Known.__ Chas Ridley. (Illus.). 112p. 1999. pap. 15.00 (*1-890894-13-3*) Chas HotBooks.

Pioneer Letters: The Letter As Literature. Ed. by John Witte. LC 81-1903. (Illus.). 1981. pap. 6.95 (*0-918402-05-0*) NW Review Bks.

Pioneer Life from A to Z see Alphabasics Series

*__Pioneer Life in Dayton.__ John F. Edgar. (Illus.). 289p. 2000. reprint ed. 37.00 (*0-7404-0095-9*) Higginson Bk Co.

Pioneer Life in Dayton & Vicinity. John F. Edgar. 289p. 1993. reprint ed. lib. bdg. 35.00 (*0-8328-2791-6*) Higginson Bk Co.

*__Pioneer Life in Dayton (Ohio) & Vicinity, 1796-1840.__ John F. Edgar. (Illus.). 311p. 1999. reprint ed. pap. 24.50 (*0-7884-1276-0*) Heritage Bk.

Pioneer Life in Kentucky: A Tribute to Parenthood. Daniel Drake. Ed. by Albert N. Drake. LC 99-219026. 147p. 1999. 25.00 (*0-9668883-2-4*) Salt Pr.

Pioneer Life in Kentucky: A Tribute to Parenthood. Daniel Drake. Ed. by Albert N. Drake. LC 99-219026. 147p. 1999. pap. 15.00 (*0-9668883-3-2*) Salt Pr.

Pioneer Life in Kentucky: Series of Reminscential Letters from Daniel Dranke, M.D., of Cincinnati to His Children. Ed. by Charles D. Drake. (Ohio Valley Historical Ser.: No. VI). (Illus.). 263p. 1997. reprint ed. lib. bdg. 32.00 (*0-8328-6728-4*) Higginson Bk Co.

Pioneer Life in Kentucky, 1785-1800: American Autobiography. Daniel Drake. 257p. 1995. lib. bdg. 79.00 (*0-7812-8502-X*) Rprt Serv.

Pioneer Life in Southeast Florida. Charles W. Pierce. Ed. by Donald W. Curl. LC 70-122290. 1981. 19.95 (*0-87024-304-7*) U of Miami Pr.

Pioneer Life in Western Pennsylvania. J. E. Wright & Doris S. Corbett. LC 40-10730. (Illus.). 251p. 1968. reprint ed. pap. 15.95 (*0-8229-6044-3*) U of Pittsburgh Pr.

Pioneer Life: or 30 Years a Hunter. Philip Tome. (American Biography Ser.). 238p. 1991. reprint ed. lib. bdg. 69.00 (*0-7812-8393-0*) Rprt Serv.

Pioneer Life: or 30 Years a Hunter: Being Scenes & Adventures in the Life of Philip Tome, Fifteen Years Interpreter for Cornplanter & Gov. Blacksnake, Chiefs on the Allegheny River. Philip Tome. LC 89-7025. 186p. 1977. reprint ed. lib. bdg. 22.95 (*0-88143-108-7*) Ayer.

*__Pioneer Life Sticker Picture.__ Marty Noble. (Illus.). (J). 1999. pap. 4.50 (*0-486-40586-9*) Dover.

Pioneer Loves. large type ed. Ernest Haycox. LC 97-331. (Western Ser.). 239p. 1997. 18.95 (*0-7862-1078-8*) Thorndike Pr.

Pioneer Lutheran Ministry - L. P. Esbjorn & His Family in Andover, Illinois. Lilly Setterdahl. LC 86-80107. (Augustana College Library Occasional Papers, Wallin Lecture: No. 15). 54p. 1986. pap. 4.00 (*0-910182-42-6*) Augustana Coll.

Pioneer Merchant of St. Louis, 1810-1820. Marietta Jennings. LC 68-58594. (Columbia University. Studies in the Social Sciences: No. 462). reprint ed. 27.50 (*0-404-51462-6*) AMS Pr.

Pioneer Michigan City & Pictorial History. Edna P. Kitchell & Gwalter Calvert. (Illus.). 16p. 1969. 1.50 (*0-935549-00-5*) MI City Hist.

Pioneer Miner & the Pack Mule Express. Ernest A. Wiltsee. LC 76-4134. (Illus.). 160p. 1976. reprint ed. 40.00 (*0-88000-084-8*) Quarterman.

Pioneer Mother see Collected Works of Hamlin Garland

Pioneer Mother. Hamlin Garland. (Collected Works of Hamlin Garland). 1988. reprint ed. lib. bdg. 59.00 (*0-7812-1247-2*) Rprt Serv.

Pioneer Mothers of the West: or Daring & Heroic Deeds of American Women, Comprising Thrilling Examples of Courage, Fortitude, Devotedness & Self-Sacrifice. John Frost. LC 74-3950. (Women in America Ser.). (Illus.). 360p. 1974. reprint ed. 28.95 (*0-405-06097-1*) Ayer.

Pioneer Museum Book. 1983. 5.00 (*0-318-01715-6*) Daughters Utah.

Pioneer Naturalist on the Plains: The Diary of Elam Bartholomew, 1871-1934. David M. Bartholomew. LC 98-199500. (Illus.). 350p. 1998. pap. 24.95 (*0-89745-221-6*) Sunflower U Pr.

Pioneer Naturalists: The Discovery & Naming of North American Plants & Animals. Howard E. Evans. 1995. pap. 12.95 (*0-8050-2339-9*) H Holt & Co.

Pioneer of American Folklore: Karl Knortz & His Collections. Eleonore Schamschula. (Northwest Folklife Ser.). 366p. 1996. text 39.95 (*0-89301-185-1*) U of Idaho Pr.

Pioneer of Inner Space: The Life of Fitz Hugh Ludlow, Hasheesh Eater. Donald P. Dulcinos. (Illus.). 320p. 1998. pap. 14.00 (*1-57027-071-6*) Autonomedia.

Pioneer of the Chinese Revolution: Zhang Binglin & Confucianism. Shimada Kenji. Tr. by Joshua A. Fogel from JPN. LC 90-30377. 208p. 1990. 35.00 (*0-8047-1581-5*) Stanford U Pr.

Pioneer of the Mojave: The Life & Times of Aaron G. Lane. Richard D. Thompson & Kathryn L. Thompson. (Illus.). 210p. (C). 1995. text 34.95 (*0-938121-10-3*) Cenotto Pubns.

Pioneer of Tropical Landscape Architecture: William Lyman Phillips in Florida. Faith R. Jackson. LC 96-37166. (Illus.). 304p. 1997. 34.95 (*0-8130-1516-2*) U Press Fla.

Pioneer Ohio Newspapers: Genealogical & Historical Abstracts, 2 vols. Karen M. Green. Incl. Vol. 1. 1793-1810. LC 86-80238. 384p. 1986. lib. bdg. 27.50 (*0-932231-03-9*); Vol. 2. 1802-1818. LC 86-80238. 362p. 1988. lib. bdg. 27.50 (*0-932231-04-7*); 1986. Set lib. bdg. 55.00 (*0-932231-05-5*) Frontier Pr.

An Asterisk (*) at the beginning of an entry indicates that the title is appearing for the first time.

Pioneer Outline History of Northwestern Pennsylvania: Embracing the Counties of Tioga, Potter, McKean, Warren, Crawford, Venango, Forest, Clarion, Elk, Jefferson, Cameron, Butler, Lawrence & Mercer; Also, a Pioneer Sketch of the Cities of Allegheny, Beaver du Bois & Towanda. W. J. McKnight. (Illus.). 747p. 1997. reprint ed. lib. bdg. 76.00 (*0-8328-6380-7*) Higginson Bk Co.

Pioneer Partners: Thomas & Molly Bugbee Frontier Ranchers. large type ed. Ruth A. Jones. (Illus.). 64p. 1996. write for info. (*0-942376-24-2*) Paramount TX.

Pioneer, Patriot, & Patriarchy: Samuel Johnson & the Yoruba People. Ed. by Toyin Falola. LC 93-48612. (C). 1994. 25.00 (*0-942615-19-0*) U Wis African Stud.

Pioneer Peasant Colonization in Ceylon. Bertram H. Farmer. LC 76-8924. (Illus.). 1976. reprint ed. lib. bdg. 79.50 (*0-8371-8888-1*, FAPI, Greenwood Pr) Greenwood.

Pioneer Pentecostal Women, Vol. I. Mary H. Wallace. (Illus.). 272p. 2000. reprint ed. pap. 5.95 (*0-912315-18-0*) Word Aflame.

Pioneer Pentecostal Women, Vol. II. Mary H. Wallace. LC 85-20981. (Illus.). 288p. 2000. reprint ed. pap. 5.95 (*0-912315-19-9*) Word Aflame.

Pioneer Period of Hungarian Airmail. Victor G. Berecz, Jr. (Illus.). 244p. (Orig.). 1996. pap. 10.00 (*0-939429-16-0*) Am Air Mail.

Pioneer Perspective of Early Medina. Sharon L. Kraynek. 89p. 1995. per. 8.95 (*1-55856-186-2*, 422) Closson Pr.

***Pioneer Photographers of the Far West: A Biographical Dictionary, 1840-1865.** Peter E. Palmquist & Thomas R. Kailbourn. LC 00-40009. 2000. write for info. (*0-8047-3883-1*) Stanford U Pr.

Pioneer Pilot: Early Aviation, 1911-1931. Jo Cooper. 176p. 1993. pap. 19.95 (*0-9638147-0-2*) Converse Pubng.

Pioneer Plastic: The Making & Selling of Celluloid. Robert Friedel. LC 81-69818. (Illus.). 192p. 1983. 35.00 (*0-299-09170-8*) U of Wis Pr.

Pioneer Plastic: The Making & Selling of Celluloid. Robert Friedel. (Illus.). 153p. 1999. reprint ed. text 22.00 (*0-7881-6458-9*) DIANE Pub.

Pioneer Players: The Lives of Louis & Hilda Esson. Peter Fitzpatrick. (Illus.). 407p. (C). 1996. text 69.95 (*0-521-45010-1*) Cambridge U Pr.

Pioneer Plowmaker: A Story about John Deere. David R. Collins. (Creative Minds Ser.). (Illus.). 64p. (J). (gr. 3-6). 1990. lib. bdg. 19.95 (*0-87614-424-5*, Carolrhoda) Lerner Pub.

Pioneer Poetree Treasury: Generations of Rhyme Through Time. Darla Petersen. LC 97-92203. x, 246p. (Orig.). 1997. pap. 11.95 (*0-9658926-0-3*) Poet Tree.

Pioneer Policewomen. Mary S. Allen. Ed. by Julie H. Heyneman. LC 71-156001. reprint ed. 36.50 (*0-404-09100-8*) AMS Pr.

Pioneer Preacher: Incidents of Interest, & Experiences in the Author's Life. Sherlock Bristol. (Illus.). 240p. 1989. reprint ed. pap. text 14.95 (*0-252-06091-1*) U of Ill Pr.

Pioneer Preacher in Idaho. James A. Hedges. 87p. 1981. 9.95 (*0-87770-249-7*) Ye Galleon.

Pioneer Projects see Historic Communities Series

Pioneer Quiltmaker: The Story of Dorinda Moody Slade, 1808-1895. Carolyn O. Davis. Ed. by Margaret Rooker & Stacey Lynn. LC 90-62945. (Illus.). 80p. 1990. pap. 17.95 (*0-918080-75-4*) Treas Chest Bks.

Pioneer Radio on the Prairies. 3rd ed. William C. Hess. (Illus.). 320p. 1985. text 69.95 (*0-9603038-1-2*) W C Hess.

***Pioneer Recipes.** Bobbie Kalman et al. LC 00-34606. (Historic Communities Ser.). (Illus.). 2000. pap. write for info. (*0-86505-468-1*) Crabtree Pub Co.

Pioneer Recipes & Remedies: Enriched with Poetry : A Sesquicentennial Collection. Millie Foster Cheesman. LC 98-222646. xxiv, 402 p. 1997. write for info. (*0-9658406-0-3*) Daughters Utah.

Pioneer Record & Reminiscences of the Early Settlers & Settlement of Ross County. Isaac J. Finley & Rufus Putnam. (Illus.). 148p. 1997. reprint ed. pap. 19.00 (*0-8328-6359-9*) Higginson Bk Co.

Pioneer Records of Trinity County, California: A Century of Facts, 1850-1950. Patricia J. Hicks. LC 98-229726. 312p. 1998. pap. 46.00 (*0-7884-1028-8*, H315) Heritage Bk.

Pioneer Reminiscence. John E. Smith. LC 96-19882. 83p. 1996. pap. 4.95 (*0-87770-578-9*) Ye Galleon.

Pioneer Reminiscences of Jefferson County. Thomas J. Russell. Ed. by Bertie H. Boodry. LC 86-62792. 160p. 1987. reprint ed. 28.00 (*0-318-22096-2*); reprint ed. pap. 20.00 (*0-318-22097-0*) SE Tex G&H.

Pioneer Reminiscences of Puget Sound. Ezra Meeker. (Northwest Historical Classics Ser.). (Illus.). 199p. 1980. reprint ed. pap. 12.95 (*0-939806-01-0*) Hist Soc Seattle.

Pioneer Roads see Historic Highways of America...with Maps & Illustrations

Pioneer Sampler. Eleanor Burns. (Quilt Block Party Ser.: No. 5). (Illus.). 88p. 1993. 14.95 (*0-922705-43-7*) Quilt Day.

Pioneer Sampler: The Daily Life of a Pioneer Family in 1840. Barbara Greenwood. LC 94-12829. (Illus.). 244p. (J). (gr. 3-7). 1995. 18.95 (*0-395-71540-7*, Pub. by Ticknor & Fields) HM.

Pioneer Sampler: The Daily Life of a Pioneer Family in 1840. Barbara Greenwood. 240p. 1998. pap. 10.95 (*0-395-88393-8*) HM.

Pioneer Scrap-Book of Wood County: Many Incidents & Reminiscences of the Early History of Wood County, Together with Some of the Historic Events of the Maumee Valley. Compiled by Charles W. Evers. (Illus.). 264p. 1997. reprint ed. lib. bdg. 35.00 (*0-8328-6371-8*) Higginson Bk Co.

Pioneer Settlement. American Geographical Society of New York Staff. LC 74-90599. (Essay Index Reprint Ser.). 1977. 34.95 (*0-8369-1241-1*) Ayer.

Pioneer Settlement in Northeast Argentina. Robert C. Eidt. LC 71-138058. (Illus.). 301p. reprint ed. pap. 93.40 (*0-8357-6783-3*, 203546000095) Bks Demand.

Pioneer Settlement in the Asiatic Tropics: Studies in Land Utilization & Agricultural Colonization in Southeastern Asia, 29. Karl J. Pelzer. LC 83-1484. (American Geographical Society Ser.-Special publication). (Illus.). 288p. 1983. reprint ed. lib. bdg. 65.00 (*0-313-23853-7*, PEPI) Greenwood.

Pioneer Settlement in the Twenties: An Original Anthology. Ed. by Moshe Davis. LC 77-70699. (America & the Holy Land Ser.). 1977. lib. bdg. 23.95 (*0-405-10250-X*) Ayer.

Pioneer Sisters. Illus. by Renee Graef. LC 96-11927. (Little House Chapter Bks.: No. 2). 80p. (J). (gr. 2-5). 2000. pap. 4.25 (*0-06-442046-9*, HarpTrophy) HarpC Child Bks.

Pioneer Sisters. Illus. by Renee Graef. (Little House Chapter Bks.: No. 2). (J). (gr. k-2). 1997. 9.15 (*0-606-10905-6*, Pub. by Turtleback) Demco.

Pioneer Sisters. Illus. by Renee Graef. LC 96-11927. (Little House Chapter Bks.: No. 2). 80p. (J). (gr. 2-5). 1997. lib. bdg. 14.89 (*0-06-027132-9*) HarpC Child Bks.

Pioneer Spirit: Modern-Day Stories of Courage & Conviction. Heidi S. Swinton. LC 96-22570. 1996. 16.95 (*1-57345-192-4*) Deseret Bk.

Pioneer Squire Barker Family. rev. ed. Marjorie Phillips & Robert Phillips. LC 96-78966. (Illus.). vi, 70p. (Orig.). 1996. pap. write for info. (*0-9655473-0-2*) HARP Ent.

Pioneer Stories. fac. ed. Arthur W. Spalding. LC 94-61167. 288p. (J). 1995. reprint ed. per. 9.95 (*1-57258-042-9*) Teach Servs.

Pioneer Stories of Linn County, Oregon, Vol. 1. 115p. write for info. (*0-939509-34-2*); pap. 12.00 (*0-317-58904-0*) L Benton Geneal.

Pioneer Stories of Linn County, Oregon, Vol. 2. 115p. write for info. (*0-939509-35-0*); pap. 12.00 (*0-317-58906-7*) L Benton Geneal.

Pioneer Stories of Linn County, Oregon, Vol. 3. 115p. write for info. (*0-939509-36-9*); pap. 12.00 (*0-317-58912-1*) L Benton Geneal.

Pioneer Stories of Linn County, Oregon, Series. write for info. (*0-939509-33-4*) L Benton Geneal.

Pioneer Story: The Daily Life of a Canadian Family in 1840. Barbara Greenwood. (Illus.). 240p. (J). 1994. pap. 16.95 (*1-55074-128-4*) Kids Can Pr.

Pioneer Studio Pottery: Milner-White Collection. Sarah Riddick. (Illus.). 176p. 1990. 60.00 (*0-85331-590-6*, Pub. by Lund Humphries) Antique Collect.

Pioneer Studio Pottery: Milner-White Collection. Sarah Riddick. (Illus.). 176p. (C). 1990. pap. 35.00 (*0-85331-581-7*, Pub. by Lund Humphries) Antique Collect.

Pioneer Tales of San Bernardino County: WPA Federal Writers' Project. LC 88-34119. (West Coast Studies: No. 2). 60p. (C). 1989. reprint ed. pap. 13.00 (*0-89370-936-0*) Millefleurs.

Pioneer Teacher: Josie Grows Up. large type ed. Josephine A. Vacher & Eugene De Bac Vacher. Ed. by Eldonna Lay. (East County Childhoods Ser.: Vol. 2). (Illus.). 30p. (Orig.). (J). (gr. 3 up). 1995. pap. 2.50 (*0-9619184-5-4*) E P Lay Assocs.

Pioneer Teachers. F. H. Behncke. 114p. 1996. reprint ed. spiral bd. 11.00 (*0-7873-0087-X*) Hlth Research.

Pioneer Teachers (1920) F. H. Behncke. 114p. 1996. reprint ed. pap. 9.95 (*1-56459-887-X*) Kessinger Pub.

***Pioneer Thanksgiving: A Story of Harvest Celebrations in 1841.** Barbara Greenwood. 48p. (J). (gr. 2-7). 1999. pap. text 6.95 (*1-55074-574-3*) Kids Can Pr.

***Pioneer Thanksgiving: A Story of Harvest Celebrations in 1841.** Barbara Greenwood. (Illus.). 48p. (J). (gr. 2-7). 1999. 14.95 (*1-55074-744-4*) Kids Can Pr.

Pioneer Times in the Onandaga Country, N. Y. Carroll E. Smith. (Illus.). 413p. 1993. reprint ed. lib. bdg. 45.00 (*0-8328-2867-X*) Higginson Bk Co.

Pioneer Trails West: Great Stories of the Westering Americans & the Trails They Followed. Western Writers of America Staff. Ed. by Donald Worcester. LC 84-15592. (Illus.). 283p. 1985. 24.95 (*0-87004-304-8*) Caxton.

Pioneer Travel. Edwin C. Guillet. LC 66-4464. (Illus.). 1966. pap. 10.95 (*0-8020-6052-8*) U of Toronto Pr.

Pioneer Twins. Lucy F. Perkins. 21.95 (*0-89190-472-7*) Amereon Ltd.

Pioneer Twins. Lucy F. Perkins. 1993. reprint ed. lib. bdg. 17.95 (*1-56849-214-6*) Buccaneer Bks.

Pioneer Urbanites: A Social & Cultural History of Black San Francisco. Douglas H. Daniels. (Illus.). 248p. 1991. pap. 15.95 (*0-520-07399-1*, Pub. by U CA Pr) Cal Prin Full Svc.

Pioneer Valley Reader: Prose & Poetry from New England's Heartland. Ed. by James C. O'Connell. LC 95-8414. (Illus.). 416p. 1995. 27.95 (*0-936399-71-6*) Berkshire Hse.

Pioneer Venus: A Planet Unveiled. Richard Fimmel. (Illus.). 300p. (Orig.). (C). 1995. 40.00 (*0-9645537-0-8*); pap. 30.00 (*0-9645537-1-6*) NASA Ames Res.

Pioneer Vigilante: The Legend of John Dietz. Gunnard Landers. (Heritage Ser.). 1998. pap. 14.95 (*1-878569-53-8*, Waubesa Pr) Badger Bks Inc.

Pioneer Voices from Plymouth to Breckenridge: The Peabody Family over Eleven Generations. Cynthia Peabody Anderson. Ed. by Mary E. Gilliland. (Illus.). 237p. 1999. pap. 22.95 (*0-9666420-0-7*) Summit Books.

Pioneer Woman. Theodore Knight. LC 94-741. (How They Lived Ser.). 32p. (J). (gr. 3-8). 1994. lib. bdg. 21.27 (*1-55916-038-1*) Rourke Bk Co.

Pioneer Woman: A Canadian Character Type. Elizabeth Thompson. 208p. (C). 1991. text 60.00 (*0-7735-0832-5*, Pub. by McG-Queens Univ Pr) CUP Services.

Pioneer Woman: The Memoirs of Bert Goldstein. Bert Goldstein. 398p. 1994. 14.95 (*965-229-084-X*, Pub. by Gefen Pub Hse) Gefen Bks.

Pioneer Woman Educator: The Progressive Spirit of Annie Webb Blanton. Debbie M. Cottrell. LC 93-9375. (Centennial Series of the Association of Former Students: No. 48). (Illus.). 208p. 1993. 28.50 (*0-89096-543-9*); pap. 12.95 (*0-89096-555-2*) Tex A&M Univ Pr.

Pioneer Woman in Alaska. Emily Romig. (American Autobiography Ser.). 140p. 1995. reprint ed. lib. bdg. 69.00 (*0-7812-8628-X*) Rprt Serv.

Pioneer Woman's Memoir. Judith E. Greenberg & Helen C. McKeever. (In Their Own Words Ser.). (Illus.). 144p. (YA). (gr. 7-12). 1995. lib. bdg. 24.00 (*0-531-11211-X*) Watts.

Pioneer Women. Charles L. Convis. (True Tales of the Old West Ser.: Vol. 5). (Illus.). 62p. 1997. pap. 7.95 (*0-9651954-5-7*) Pioneer Pr NV.

Pioneer Women. Joanna Stratton, Jr. 320p. 1982. pap. 12.95 (*0-671-44748-3*, Touchstone) S&S Trade Pap.

Pioneer Women: The Lives of Women on the Frontier. Linda S. Peavy & Ursula Smith. LC 97-40684. (Illus.). 144p. 1998. pap. 17.95 (*0-8061-3054-7*) U of Okla Pr.

***Pioneer Women of California.** Linda Lewin. (California Biography Ser.). (Illus.). 48p. (J). (gr. 4-8). 1999. pap. text 14.95 (*1-884925-81-2*) Toucan Valley.

Pioneer Women of the West. Elizabeth F. Ellet. LC 72-13219. (Essay Index Reprint Ser.). 1977. reprint ed. 24.95 (*0-8369-8157-X*) Ayer.

Pioneer Women's Diaries: A Resource Guide. Jocelyn Riley. 114p. 1995. VHS 45.00 (*1-877933-07-4*) Her Own Words.

Pioneer Work in Opening the Medical Profession to Women: Autobiographical Sketches. Elizabeth Blackwell. (American Biography Ser.). 264p. 1991. reprint ed. lib. bdg. 69.00 (*0-7812-8025-7*) Rprt Serv.

Pioneer Writer. Patricia Clarke. 272p. 1991. 29.95 (*0-04-442267-9*, Pub. by Allen & Unwin Pty) Paul & Co Pubs.

***Pioneer Years in the Black Hills.** 2nd ed. Richard B. Hughes. Ed. by Agnes Wright Spring. (Illus.). 316p. 1999. 15.95 (*0-9673910-0-8*) Dakota Alpha.

Pioneering. Boy Scouts of America. (Illus.). 104p. (YA). (gr. 6-12). 1974. pap. 2.90 (*0-8395-3377-2*) BSA.

Pioneering: Poems from the Construction Site. Susan Eisenberg. LC 97-43452. 88p. 1998. pap. text 12.95 (*0-8014-8526-6*, ILR Press) Cornell U Pr.

***Pioneering a Global Vision: The Story of Baker & McKenzie.** Jon Bauman. 1999. 24.95 (*0-15-900433-0*) Harcourt.

Pioneering a Modern Small Business: Wakefield Seafoods & the Alaskan Frontier. Mansel G. Blackford. Ed. by Glenn Porter. LC 77-7794. (Industrial Development & the Social Fabric Ser.: Vol. 6). 222p. 1979. 73.25 (*0-89232-088-5*) Jai Pr.

Pioneering Adventures of Johan Edvard Lilljeholm in America, 1846-1850. Tr. by Arthur Wald. (Augustana Historical Society Publications: No. 19). xii, 53p. 1962. pap. 3.00 (*0-910184-19-4*) Augustana.

***Pioneering Ascents: The Origins of Climbing.** David Mazel. 255p. 1998. 14.00 (*0-915746-83-2*) Potomac Appalach.

Pioneering Aviation in the West. Lloyd Bungey. 328p. 1992. pap. 22.95 (*0-88839-271-0*) Hancock House.

***Pioneering Deans of Women.** Jana Nidiffer. LC 99-41290. (Athene Ser.). 208p. 2000. pap. text 26.95 (*0-8077-3914-6*) Tchrs Coll.

***Pioneering Deans of Women: More Than Wise & Pious Matrons.** Jana Nidiffer. LC 99-41290. (Athene Series in Women's Studies). 208p. 2000. write for info. (*0-8077-3915-4*) Tchrs Coll.

***Pioneering Economic Reform in China's Special Economic Zones: The Promotion of Foreign Investment & Technology Transfer in Shenzhen.** Weiping Wu. LC 98-45772. 182p. 1999. text 61.95 (*1-84014-811-X*, Pub. by Ashgate Pub) Ashgate Pub Co.

Pioneering Economic Theory, 1630-1980: A Mathematical Restatement. Hans Brems. LC 85-19819. 432p. 1986. text 65.00 (*0-8018-2667-5*) Johns Hopkins.

Pioneering for Peace: A Study of American Peace Efforts to 1846. W. Freeman Galpin. LC 73-143429. (Peace Movement in America Ser.). x, 237p. 1972. reprint ed. lib. bdg. 32.95 (*0-89198-069-5*) Ozer.

***Pioneering French Porcelain at the Saint-Cloud Manufacture, CA 1690-1766.** Bertrand Rondot. LC 99-24633. (Illus.). 368p. 1999. 75.00 (*0-300-08107-3*) Yale U Pr.

Pioneering Frozen Worlds: Polar Region Exploration. Sandra Markle. LC 95-15971. (Illus.). 48p. (J). (gr. 3-7). 1996. 17.00 (*0-689-31824-3*) Aladdin.

Pioneering Generations Vol. 1: The Utica College Story, 1946-96. John Behrens. (Illus.). 217p. 1997. 40.00 (*0-9660363-0-1*); pap. 20.00 (*0-9660363-1-X*) Utica College.

Pioneering Hematology: The Research & Treatment of Malignant Blood Disorders. William C. Maloney. LC 98-126281. xv, 196p. 1997. 24.95 (*0-88135-195-4*, Sci Hist) Watson Pub Intl.

Pioneering Ideas for the Physical & Chemical Sciences: Joseph Loschmidt's Contributions & Modern Developments in Structural Organic Chemistry, Atomistics & Statistical Mechanics. W. Fleischhacker & T. Schonfeld. LC 97-28671. 332p. (C). 1998. text 110.00 (*0-306-45684-2*, Kluwer Plenum) Kluwer Academic.

Pioneering in Delinquency Prevention: The California Experience. Barry Krisberg et al. 1978. 7.50 (*0-318-02057-2*) Natl Coun Crime.

Pioneering in Formosa. W. A. Pickering. 1993. reprint ed. 35.00 (*957-638-163-0*) Oriental Bk Store.

Pioneering in Montana: The Making of a State. Granville Stuart. (American Biography Ser.). 265p. 1991. reprint ed. lib. bdg. 69.00 (*0-7812-8371-X*) Rprt Serv.

Pioneering in Oregon's Coast Range: Surviving the Depression Years. Ione Reed. (Illus.). 140p. (Orig.). 1983. pap. 7.95 (*0-934784-31-0*) Calapooia Pubns.

Pioneering in Steel Research: A Personal Record. Edgar C. Bain. LC 74-31126. (Illus.). 297p. reprint ed. pap. 92.10 (*0-8357-6263-7*, 203307400083) Bks Demand.

Pioneering in Texas & Wyoming: Incidents in the Life of James C. Shaw see North from Texas: Incidents in the Early Life of a Range Cowman in Texas, Dakota, & Wyoming, 1852-1883

Pioneering in the Far East & Journeys to California in 1849 & to the White Sea in 1878. Ludvig V. Helms. (Illus.). 408p. 1969. 100.00 (*0-614-01828-5*) Elliots Bks.

Pioneering New Serials Frontiers: From Petroglyphs to Cyberserials. Ed. by Christine Christiansen & Cecilia Leathem. LC 97-11234. 407p. 1997. 89.95 (*0-7890-0324-4*) Haworth Pr.

Pioneering New Technologies: Management Issues & Challenges in the Third Millennium : Iemc'98 Proceedings, International Conference on Engineering & Technology Management, October 11 to 13, 1998, San Juan, Puerto Rico, Usa. IEEE International Conference on Engineering and Technology Management et al. LC 98-86887. 555 p. 1998. write for info. (*0-7803-5085-5*) IEEE Standards.

Pioneering Ocean Depths. Sandra Markle. LC 93-33555. (Illus.). 40p. (J). (gr. 3-7). 1995. 17.00 (*0-689-31823-5*) Atheneum Yung Read.

Pioneering on Social Frontiers. Graham R. Taylor. LC 75-17246. (Social Problems & Social Policy Ser.). 1976. reprint ed. 39.95 (*0-405-07517-0*) Ayer.

Pioneering on the Yukon, 1892-1917. Anna DeGraf. Ed. by Roger S. Brown. LC 92-14808. (Illus.). ix, 128p. (C). 1992. lib. bdg. 19.50 (*0-208-02362-3*, Archon Bks) Shoe String.

***Pioneering Organizations: The Convergence of Individualism, Teamwork & Leadership.** Larry Davis. LC 00-8278. 2000. 22.95 (*1-890009-84-9*) Exec Excell.

***Pioneering Perspectives in 19th Century Criminology.** David M. Horton. 412p. (C). 2000. pap. 19.95 (*1-928916-04-X*) Copperhouse.

Pioneering Plantsman: A. K. Bulley & the Great Plant Hunters. Brenda Maclean. (Illus.). 200p. 1997. pap. 58.00 (*0-11-250018-8*, Pub. by Statnry Office) Balogh.

***Pioneering Portfolio Management: An Unconventional Approach to Investment Success.** David F. Swensen. LC 99-87064. 384p. 2000. 34.50 (*0-684-86443-6*) Free Pr.

Pioneering Research in Surgical Shock & Cardiovascular Surgery: Vivien Thomas & His Work with Alfred Blalock. Vivien T. Thomas. (Illus.). 304p. 1985. 47.95 (*0-8122-7989-1*) U of Pa Pr.

Pioneering Space. Sandra Markle. LC 91-24936. (Illus.). 40p. (J). (gr. 3-7). 1992. lib. bdg. 14.95 (*0-689-31748-4*) Atheneum Yung Read.

Pioneering Spirits: The Life & Times of Remarkable Women Artists in Western History. Abby Remer. LC 96-85574. (Illus.). 160p. (YA). (gr. 9-12). 1997. 27.00 (*0-87192-317-3*) Davis Mass.

Pioneering Strategies. Ed. by Rhema Ministerial Association International Staff. 72p. 1994. pap. 9.95 (*0-89276-956-4*) Faith Lib Pubns.

Pioneering Television. K. Takayanagi. (Illus.). 1993. 25.00 (*0-911302-66-2*) San Francisco Pr.

Pioneering Television News. Lutton Staff. LC 95-219766. 1997. pap. 35.95 (*0-86196-484-5*, Pub. by J Libbey Med) Bks Intl VA.

Pioneering with Wildflowers. George D. Aiken. 1994. pap. 12.95 (*0-911469-11-7*) A C Hood.

Pioneering Women at the Catholic University of America. Ed. by Catherine Dunn & Dorothy A. Mohler. 112p. 1991. pap. 9.95 (*0-8132-0749-5*, DUPWP) Cath U Pr.

Pioneering Women of the Wild West. Jeff Savage. LC 94-32324. (Trailblazers of the Wild West Ser.). (Illus.). 48p. (J). (gr. 4-10). 1995. lib. bdg. 16.95 (*0-89490-604-6*) Enslow Pubs.

Pioneers. John Artman. (Illus.). 64p. (J). (gr. 4 up). 1987. pap. 8.99 (*0-86653-401-6*, GA 1027) Good Apple.

Pioneers. Jack Cavanaugh. LC 96-22940. (American Family Portrait Ser.). 500p. 1996. pap. 11.99 (*1-56476-587-3*) Chariot Victor.

Pioneers. James Fenimore Cooper. 346p. Date not set. 25.95 (*0-8488-2544-6*) Amereon Ltd.

Pioneers. James Fenimore Cooper. 448p. (YA). 1964. mass mkt. 5.95 (*0-451-52521-3*, Sig Classics) NAL.

Pioneers. James Fenimore Cooper. 1976. lib. bdg. 26.95 (*0-89968-157-3*, Lghtyr Pr) Buccaneer Bks.

Pioneers. James Fenimore Cooper. Ed. & Intro. by James D. Wallace. (Oxford World's Classics Ser.). (Illus.). 496p. 2000. pap. 8.95 (*0-19-283667-6*) OUP.

Pioneers. James Fenimore Cooper. Ed. by James F. Beard. LC 77-21795. (Writings of James Fenimore Cooper). 460p. (C). 1980. pap. text 18.95 (*0-87395-423-8*) State U NY Pr.

Pioneers. James Fenimore Cooper. Ed. by Robert Clark. (Illus.). 444p. 1993. pap. 6.95 (*0-460-87187-0*, Everyman's Classic Lib) Tuttle Pubng.

Pioneers. James Fenimore Cooper. Ed. & Intro. by Donald A. Ringe. LC 87-31694. 448p. 1988. pap. 9.95 (*0-14-039007-3*, Penguin Classics) Viking Penguin.

Pioneers. Dennis B. Fradin. LC 84-9418. (New True Books Ser.). (Illus.). 48p. (J). (ps-3). 1984. lib. bdg. 21.00 (*0-516-01927-9*) Childrens.

Pioneers. Janeway. (C). 1997. pap. text. write for info. (*0-321-02604-7*) Addson-Wesley Educ.

Pioneers. Laing Communications Staff. 1999. 16.99 (*0-525-67504-3*) NAL.

P

An Asterisk (*) at the beginning of an entry indicates that the title is appearing for the first time.

Pioneers. Leonard Matthews. (Wild West in American History Ser.). (Illus.). 32p. (J). (gr. 3-8). 1989. 13.50 (*0-685-73975-9*) Rourke Corp.

Pioneers. Leonard Matthews. (Wild West in American History Ser.). (Illus.). 32p. (J). (gr. 3-8). 1989. lib. bdg. 18.00 (*0-86625-362-9*) Rourke Pubns.

Pioneers. Robert Miller. (Reflections of a Black Cowboy Ser.). (Illus.). 104p. (J). (gr. 4-7). 1991. pap. 4.95 (*0-382-24086-3*) Silver Burdett Pr.

*__Pioneers.__ Martin Sandler. LC 92-47495. (Library of Congress Bk.). (Illus.). 96p. (YA). (gr. 3 up). 1999. pap. 10.95 (*0-06-446743-0*) HarpC Child Bks.

Pioneers. Martin W. Sandler & James Billington. LC 92-47495. (Library of Congress Bk.). (Illus.). 96p. (J). (gr. 4-7). 1994. 24.95 (*0-06-023023-1*) HarpC Child Bks.

Pioneers. Rick Steber. (Tales of the Wild West Ser.: Vol. 11). (Illus.). 60p. 1993. pap. 4.95 (*0-945134-11-8*); lib. bdg. 14.95 (*0-945134-89-4*) Bonanza Pub.

Pioneers. James Fenimore Cooper. (Works of James Fenimore Cooper). 1990. reprint ed. lib. bdg. 79.00 (*0-7812-2371-7*) Rprt Serv.

Pioneers, Bk. 3. Robert Miller. (Reflections of a Black Cowboy Ser.). (Illus.). 104p. (J). (gr. 4-7). 1991. lib. bdg. 12.95 (*0-382-24081-2*) Silver Burdett Pr.

Pioneers: An Educational Coloring Book. Spizzirri Publishing Co. Staff. Ed. by Linda Spizzirri. (Illus.). 32p. (J). (gr. 1-8). 1989. pap. 1.99 (*0-86545-138-9*) Spizzirri.

Pioneers: Challenges from the Past. Margot Griffin. pap. 5.95 (*0-590-73439-3*) Scholastic Inc.

Pioneers: Nature, Life & Times, & American Geography. Amanda Bennett. 141p. 1996. pap. text 13.99 (*1-888306-04-1*, Home School Pr) Holly Hall.

Pioneers: Notes from the Diaries of Judge Benjamin Hayes, 1849-1875. Benjamin Hayes. Ed. by Carlos E. Cortes. LC 76-1274. (Chicano Heritage Ser.). (Illus.). 1977. reprint ed. lib. bdg. 28.95 (*0-405-09506-6*) Ayer.

Pioneers: Novels of the American Frontier. Reader's Digest Editors. LC 85-23236. (Illus.). 640p. 1988. 19.95 (*0-89577-229-9*) RD Assn.

Pioneers: The Evolution of a Wilderness Farm into a Modern Community on the Shore of Bay Lake. Albert L. Knieff. LC 96-94602. (Illus.). 150p. 1996. pap. 14.95 (*0-9652032-0-4*) KSA Pubng.

Pioneers along the Manatawny. W. Edmunds Claussen. (Illus.). 52p. (Orig.). 1968. pap. text 5.00 (*0-9616068-4-3*) Boyertown Hist.

Pioneers & Caretakers: A Study of Nine American Women Novelists. Louis Auchincloss. LC 65-17016. 208p. reprint ed. pap. 64.50 (*0-608-16700-2*, 205619700055) Bks Demand.

Pioneers & Homemakers: Jewish Women in Pre-State Israel. Ed. by Deborah S. Bernstein. LC 91-21247. 312p. 1992. text 21.50 (*0-7914-0905-8*) State U NY Pr.

*__Pioneers & Makers of Arkansas.__ Josiah H. Shinn. LC 67-17587. 423p. 1999. reprint ed. 32.50 (*0-8063-0311-5*) Clearfield Co.

Pioneers & Preachers: Stories of the Old Frontier. Robert W. Mondy. LC 79-16906. (Illus.). 272p. 1980. text 46.95 (*0-88229-619-1*) Burnham Inc.

Pioneers & Residents of West Central Alabama Prior to the Civil War. Madge Pettit. xvi, 337p. (Orig.). 1988. pap. 27.50 (*1-55613-125-9*) Heritage Bk.

Pioneers & Their Better Halves. Honour C. Burcher. 240p. (C). 1990. 50.00 (*0-9589309-0-2*, Pub. by Boolarong Pubns) St Mut.

Pioneers & Their Homes on Upper Kanawha. Ruth W. Dayton. (Illus.). 378p. 1991. reprint ed. pap. 22.00 (*1-55613-516-5*) Heritage Bk.

Pioneers & Their Homes on Upper Kanawha [West Virginia]. Ruth W. Dayton. (Illus.). 320p. 1998. reprint ed. pap. 38.00 (*0-8063-4815-1*) Clearfield Co.

Pioneers East: The Early American Experience in the Middle East. David H. Finnie. LC 67-20875. (Harvard Middle Eastern Studies: No. 13). (Illus.). 355p. 1967. reprint ed. pap. 110.10 (*0-7837-6083-3*, 205912900007) Bks Demand.

Pioneers for Profit: Foreign Entrepreneurship & Russian Industrialization, 1885-1913. John P. McKay. LC 79-103932. 456p. 1970. lib. bdg. 36.00 (*0-226-55990-4*) U Ch Pr.

Pioneers Go West. George R. Stewart. (Landmark Bks.). (J). 1987. 11.09 (*0-606-13017-9*, Pub. by Turtleback) Demco.

Pioneers Go West. George R. Stewart. LC 87-4568. (Landmark Ser.). 160p. (J). (gr. 5-9). 1987. reprint ed. pap. 5.99 (*0-394-89180-5*, Pub. by Random Bks Yng Read) Random.

Pioneers in a Frontier Land: The Strabane Knoxes & Other Families. Daryl K. Knox. LC 78-108863. 165p. 1978. 12.00 (*0-9605790-0-1*) D Knox.

Pioneers in Adult Education. Willis D. Moreland & Erwin H. Goldenstein. (Illus.). 280p. 1985. text 38.95 (*0-8304-1082-1*) Burnham Inc.

Pioneers in American Anthropology: The Bandelier-Morgan Letters, 1873-1883, 2 vols. Adolf F. Bandelier. Ed. by Leslie Alvin White. LC 74-7921. reprint ed. 81.50 (*0-404-11806-2*) AMS Pr.

*__Pioneers in American Anthropology: The Bandelier-Morgan Letters, 1873-1883, 2 vols.__ Adolph F. Bandelier. (LC History-America-E). 1999. reprint ed. lib. bdg. 180.00 (*0-7812-4234-7*) Rprt Serv.

Pioneers in Bibliography. Ed. by Robin Myers & Michael Harris. LC 96-43082. 117p. 1996. 30.00 (*1-884718-30-2*) Oak Knoll.

Pioneers in Canada. Harry Johnston. (C). 1996. 52.00 (*81-206-1152-7*, Pub. by Asian Educ Servs) S Asia.

Pioneers in Change, 9 bks. in 11 vols. (Illus.). (J). (gr. 5-9). 1992. pap. 62.55 (*0-382-24161-4*); lib. bdg. 195.30 (*0-382-09930-3*) Silver Burdett Pr.

Pioneers in Criminology. enl. ed. Hermann Mannheim. LC 78-108238. (Criminology, Law Enforcement, & Social Problems Ser.: No. 121). (C). 1972. pap. 20.00 (*0-87585-902-X*) Patterson Smith.

Pioneers in Criminology. 2nd enl. ed. Hermann Mannheim. LC 78-108238. (Criminology, Law Enforcement, & Social Problems Ser.: No. 121). (C). 1972. 31.50 (*0-87585-121-5*) Patterson Smith.

Pioneers in Every Land. Bruce A. Van Orden et al. LC 96-80168. 1997. 14.95 (*1-57008-306-1*) Bookcraft Inc.

Pioneers in Food Science, Vol. 1. S. C. Prescott & S. A. Goldblith. 194p. 1993. pap. 25.00 (*0-917678-33-8*) Food & Nut Pr.

Pioneers in Historical Archaeology: Breaking New Ground. S. South. (Illus.). 248p. (C). 1994. 49.50 (*0-306-44821-1*, Plenum Trade) Perseus Pubng.

Pioneers in India. Harry Johnston. (Pioneers of Empire Ser.). (C). 1993. reprint ed. 44.00 (*81-206-0843-7*, Pub. by Asian Educ Servs) S Asia.

Pioneers in Invitro Fertilization: Proceedings of a Symposium Held in Oss, the Netherlands, November 5, 1993. Ed. by A. T. Alberda & Hendricus M. Vemer. LC 94-48589. (Studies in Profertility Ser.: Vol. 3). (Illus.). 122p. 1995. 65.00 (*1-85070-566-6*) Prthnon Pub.

Pioneers in Jewish Medical Ethics. Fred Rosner. LC 97-12965. 280p. 1997. 40.00 (*0-7657-9968-5*) Aronson.

Pioneers in Leisure & Recreation. Ed. by Hilmi Ibrahim. (Illus.). 250p. (Orig.). 1989. pap. 13.00 (*0-88314-423-9*, A4239) AAHPERD.

Pioneers in Medical Physics: A History of Hospital Physics. J. E. Roberts. LC 99-19619. (Illus.). 180p. 1998. 65.00 (*0-7503-0494-4*) IOP Pub.

*__Pioneers in Medicine & Their Impact on Tuberculosis.__ Thomas M. Daniel. (Illus.). 270p. 2000. 59.00 (*1-58046-067-4*, Pub. by Univ Rochester Pr) Boydell & Brewer.

Pioneers in Modern Factory Management: An Original Anthology. Ed. by Alfred D. Chandler, Jr. LC 79-7526. (History of Management Thought & Practice Ser.). 1980. lib. bdg. 21.95 (*0-405-12310-8*) Ayer.

Pioneers in Music. David Ewen. LC 72-6816. (Essay Index Reprint Ser.). 1977. reprint ed. 30.95 (*0-8369-7262-7*) Ayer.

Pioneers in Nation - Building in the Caribbean Mini-State. 1979. 12.00 (*92-1-157064-6*, E.79.XV.RS/8) UN.

Pioneers in Pediatric Oncology. Ed. by Grant Taylor. xv, 355p. 1990. text 55.00 (*2-88124-508-0*) Gordon & Breach.

Pioneers in Petticoats. Nellie McCaslin. (Illus.). 205p. 1993. 20.00 (*0-88734-625-1*) Players Pr.

Pioneers in Petticoats. Shirley Sargent. 1966. 7.95 (*0-685-29089-1*) Flying Spur Pr.

Pioneers in Policing. Ed. by Philip J. Stead. LC 75-14556. (Criminology, Law Enforcement, & Social Problems Ser.: No. 213). (Illus.). (C). 1978. 26.50 (*0-87585-213-0*) Patterson Smith.

Pioneers in Polymer Science. Ed. by Raymond B. Seymour. (C). 1989. text 160.00 (*0-7923-0300-8*) Kluwer Academic.

Pioneers in Popular Culture Studies. Ray B. Browne & Michael T. Marsden. LC 98-30244. 221p. 1998. 49.95 (*0-87972-775-6*); pap. 24.95 (*0-87972-776-4*) Bowling Green Univ Popular Press.

Pioneers in Protest. Lerone Bennett, Jr. LC 68-55366. 267p. 1968. 10.95 (*0-87485-026-6*) Johnson Chicago.

Pioneers in Quaker Education: The Story of John W. & Mary C. Woody. rev. ed. Mary Edith Hinshaw. Orig. Title: The Woody-Chawner Story. (Illus.). 119p. 1992. pap. 12.00 (*0-942727-21-5*) NC Yrly Pubns Bd.

Pioneers in the Arab World. Dorothy Van Ess. 1974. pap. 7.00 (*0-8028-1585-5*) Eerdmans.

Pioneers in the Tropics: The Political Organization of Japanese in an Immigrant Community in Brazil. Philip Staniford. (London School of Economics Monographs on Social Anthropology: No. 45). (Illus.). 201p. (C). 1973. text 36.50 (*0-485-19545-3*, Pub. by Athlone Pr) Humanities.

Pioneers in World Order. Ed. by Harriet E. Davis. LC 70-128232. (Essay Index Reprint Ser.). 1977. 21.95 (*0-8369-1913-0*) Ayer.

Pioneers of American Anthropology: The Uses of Biography. Ed. by June Helm. LC 84-45536. (American Ethnological Society Monographs: No. 43). 1988. reprint ed. 39.50 (*0-404-62941-5*) AMS Pr.

Pioneers of American Landscape Design. 1994. lib. bdg. 256.95 (*0-8490-5801-5*) Gordon Pr.

*__Pioneers of American Landscape Design.__ National Parks Service Staff. LC 00-36155. (Illus.). 352p. 2000. 59.95 (*0-07-134420-9*) McGraw-Hill Prof.

Pioneers of American Landscape Design: An Annotated Bibliography. (Illus.). 152p. (C). 1994. pap. text 35.00 (*0-7881-0467-5*) DIANE Pub.

Pioneers of American Landscape Design: An Annotated Bibliography. Charles A. Birnbaum. 148p. 1994. per. 15.00 (*0-16-041974-3*) USGPO.

Pioneers of American Landscape Design: An Annotated Bibliography, 2 vols., Set. 1995. lib. bdg. 612.95 (*0-8490-7426-6*) Gordon Pr.

Pioneers of American Landscape Design 2: An Annotated Bibliography. Charles A. Birnbaum. 186p. 1995. per. 13.00 (*0-16-048060-4*) USGPO.

Pioneers of Anglo-Irish Fiction, 1800-1850. Barry Sloan. LC 86-17438. 224p. 1986. 66.00 (*0-389-20662-8*, N8220) B&N Imports.

Pioneers of Calcasieu & Cameron Parish, Vol. III. Nola M. Ross. (Illus.). 102p. 1990. pap. 12.95 (*1-887144-04-8*) N M Ross.

Pioneers of Calcasieu Parish, Vol. II. Nola M. Ross. (Illus.). 80p. 1988. pap. 12.95 (*1-887144-03-X*) N M Ross.

Pioneers of Calcasieu Parish: Memories of Early Calcasieu, Vol. I. Nola M. Ross. (Illus.). 72p. 1987. pap. 12.95 (*1-887144-02-1*) N M Ross.

*__Pioneers of Canada.__ Alan Salman. LC 99-196687. 1998. per. 19.95 (*1-895909-65-1*) Unitrade Pr.

Pioneers of Christian Thought. Frederick D. Kershner. LC 68-57327. (Essay Index Reprint Ser.). 1977. 23.95 (*0-8369-0594-6*) Ayer.

Pioneers of Davidson County, Tennessee. Edythe R. Whitley. LC 79-50041. 84p. 1999. reprint ed. pap. 12.50 (*0-8063-0840-0*) Clearfield Co.

Pioneers of Discovery. Ed. by Richard S. Rennert. (Profiles of Great Black Americans Ser.). (Illus.). 64p. (J). (gr. 3 up). 1993. lib. bdg. 15.95 (*0-7910-2067-3*) Chelsea Hse.

Pioneers of Discovery. Richard S. Rennert. (Profiles of Great Black Americans Ser.). (Illus.). 64p. (J). (gr. 3 up). 1994. pap. 5.95 (*0-7910-2068-1*) Chelsea Hse.

Pioneers of Discovery. Richard Scott Rennert. (Profiles of Great Black Americans Ser.). (J). 1994. 11.15 (*0-606-08016-3*) Turtleback.

Pioneers of Early Childhood Education. Barbara R. Peltzman. (Source Books on Education). Date not set. text 40.00 (*0-8153-0032-8*) Garland.

Pioneers of Early Childhood Education: A Bio-Bibliographical Guide. Barbara R. Peltzman. LC 97-26907. 160p. 1998. lib. bdg. 65.00 (*0-313-30404-1*, Greenwood Pr) Greenwood.

Pioneers of Electrical Communication. Rollo Appleyard. LC 68-54322. (Essay Index Reprint Ser.). 1977. 26.95 (*0-8369-0156-8*) Ayer.

Pioneers of Evolution: From Thales to Huxley; with an Intermediate Chapter on the Causes of Arrest of the Movement. Edward Clodd. LC 74-37470. (Essay Index Reprint Ser.). 1977. reprint ed. 21.95 (*0-8369-2540-8*) Ayer.

Pioneers of Evolution from Thales to Huxley. Edward Clodd. 270p. 1997. reprint ed. pap. 19.95 (*0-7661-0086-3*) Kessinger Pub.

Pioneers of Faith. Lester Sumrall. LC 95-174791. 208p. 1995. pap. 10.99 (*0-89274-742-0*, HH-742) Harrison Hse.

Pioneers of Flight: A Documentary History. Phil Scott. LC 98-38412. (Illus.). 216p. 1999. 24.95 (*0-691-01117-6*, Pub. by Princeton U Pr) Cal Prin Full Svc.

Pioneers of France in the New World. Francis Parkman. LC 96-17586. (Illus.). xxxiv, 473p. 1996. pap. 20.00 (*0-8032-8744-5*, Bison Books) U of Nebr Pr.

*__Pioneers of France in the New World.__ Francis Parkman. (Notable American Authors Ser.). 1999. reprint ed. lib. bdg. 125.00 (*0-7812-4730-6*) Rprt Serv.

Pioneers of Freedom. McAlister Coleman. LC 68-20292. (Essay Index Reprint Ser.). 1977. reprint ed. 19.95 (*0-8369-0326-9*) Ayer.

Pioneers of Freedom & Social Change in India. Brijendra Sankhder. 1986. 18.00 (*0-8364-1905-7*, Pub. by Deep & Deep Pubns) S Asia.

Pioneers of Heavy Haulage. T. McTaggart. (C). 1988. pap. 60.00 (*0-907526-17-9*, Pub. by Alloway Pub) St Mut.

Pioneers of High, Water, & Main: Reflections of Jefferson City. R. E. Young. LC 97-61169. (Illus.). 224p. 1997. 25.00 (*0-9659631-7-9*, 19970229) Twelfth State.

Pioneers of Interpersonal Psychoanalysis. Ed. by Donnel B. Stern et al. LC 95-30973. 336p. 1995. text 59.95 (*0-88163-177-9*); pap. text 29.95 (*0-88163-216-3*) Analytic Pr.

Pioneers of Islamic Revival. Ed. by Ali Rahnema. (Studies in Islamic Society). 272p. (C). 1994. text 65.00 (*1-85649-253-2*, Pub. by Zed Books); text 25.00 (*1-85649-254-0*, Pub. by Zed Books) St Martin.

Pioneers of Lake View: A Guide to Seattle's Early Settlers & Their Cemetery. Robert L. Ferguson. Ed. by Duse F. McLean. (Illus.). 120p. 1995. pap. 12.95 (*0-9621935-5-0*) Thistle Pr.

Pioneers of Land Reform. Thomas Spence et al. 1972. 34.95 (*0-8490-0838-7*) Gordon Pr.

Pioneers of Landscape Photography: Gustave LeGray & Carleton E. Watkins. Weston J. Naef et al. (Illus.). 128p. 1993. 45.00 (*0-89236-299-5*, Pub. by J P Getty Trust) OUP.

Pioneers of Long Ago. Jessie H. Roy & Geneva C. Turner. (Illus.). (J). 1990. 12.95 (*0-87498-008-9*) Assoc Pubs DC.

Pioneers of Macedon & Other Papers of the Macedon Center Historical Society. Mary L. Eldredge. (Illus.). 190p. 1997. reprint ed. lib. bdg. 28.50 (*0-8328-6169-3*) Higginson Bk Co.

Pioneers of Madison & Hancock Counties, Indiana. Samuel Harden. (Illus.). 498p. 1990. reprint ed. pap. 27.50 (*1-55613-279-4*) Heritage Bk.

Pioneers of Magalloway Region, from 1820 to 1904. Granville P. Wilson. (Illus.). 64p. 1997. reprint ed. pap. 13.00 (*0-8328-5806-4*) Higginson Bk Co.

Pioneers of Maine & New Hampshire. Charles H. Pope. 252p. 1985. reprint ed. pap. text 5.50 (*0-935207-19-8*) Danbury Hse Bks.

Pioneers of Maine & New Hampshire, 1623-1660. Charles H. Pope. 263p. 1997. reprint ed. 26.50 (*0-8063-0278-X*, 4655) Clearfield Co.

Pioneers of Massachusetts. Charles H. Pope. 551p. 1985. reprint ed. pap. 15.00 (*0-935207-36-8*) Danbury Hse Bks.

Pioneers of Massachusetts. Charles H. Pope. 550p. 1991. reprint ed. pap. 27.50 (*1-55613-398-7*) Heritage Bk.

Pioneers of Massachusetts, 1620-1650: A Descriptive List, Drawn from Records of the Colonies, Towns & Churches. Charles H. Pope. 550p. 1998. reprint ed. 35.00 (*0-8063-0774-9*) Genealog Pub.

Pioneers of Menard & Mason Counties . . . Including Personal Reminiscences of Abraham Lincoln & Peter Cartwright. T. G. Onstot. (Illus.). 400p. 1997. reprint ed. lib. bdg. 45.00 (*0-8328-5770-X*) Higginson Bk Co.

Pioneers of Menard & Mason Counties, Illinois. T. G. Onstott. 404p. 1987. reprint ed. pap. 19.95 (*1-877869-08-2*) Mason Cnty Hist Proj.

Pioneers of Modern Craft: Twelve Essays Profiling Key Figures in the History of Contemporary Crafts. Margot Coatts. LC 96-52329. (Illus.). 128p. 1997. pap. 24.95 (*0-7190-5059-6*) St Martin.

Pioneers of Modern Economics in Britain. Ed. by D. P. O'Brien & John R. Presley. LC 79-55496. (Illus.). 292p. 1981. text 53.00 (*0-389-20181-2*, N6622) B&N Imports.

Pioneers of Modern Geography: Translations Pertaining to German Geographers of the Late Nineteenth & Early Twentieth Centuries. Robert C. West. LC 90-81472. (Geoscience & Man Ser.: Vol. 28). (Illus.). 196p. (C). 1990. pap. text 30.00 (*0-938909-52-5*) Geosci Pubns LSU.

Pioneers of Modern Typography. Herbert Spencer. (Illus.). 160p. 1983. reprint ed. pap. text 22.00 (*0-262-69081-0*) MIT Pr.

Pioneers of New France in New England. James P. Baxter. 450p. 1980. reprint ed. 25.00 (*0-917890-20-5*) Heritage Bk.

Pioneers of New France in New England (Mostly Maine), with Contemporary Letters & Documents. James P. Baxter. 450p. 1995. reprint ed. lib. bdg. 45.00 (*0-8328-4667-8*) Higginson Bk Co.

Pioneers of New York. Charles F. Hoffman. (Notable American Authors Ser.). 1992. reprint ed. lib. bdg. 75.00 (*0-7812-3137-X*) Rprt Serv.

Pioneers of NMR & Magnetic Resonance in Medicine: The Story of MRI. James S. Mattson & Merrill Simon. (Illus.). 838p. 1996. lib. bdg. 75.00 (*0-9619243-1-4*) Dean Bks.

Pioneers of Old Hopewell, with Sketches of Her Revolutionary Heroes. Ralph Ege. (Illus.). 290p. 1997. reprint ed. lib. bdg. 35.00 (*0-8328-6051-4*) Higginson Bk Co.

Pioneers of Old Monocacy: The Early Settlement of Frederick County, Maryland, 1721-1743. Grace L. Tracey & John P. Dern. LC 86-83226. (Illus.). 442p. 1998. reprint ed. 35.00 (*0-8063-1183-5*) Genealog Pub.

Pioneers of Outagamie County: Containing the Records of the Outagamie County Pioneer Association; A Biographical & Historical Sketch of Some of the Earliest Settlers of the County & Their Families, Their Children & Grandchildren. Elihu Spencer. (Illus.). 303p. 1997. reprint ed. lib. bdg. 37.00 (*0-8328-6979-1*) Higginson Bk Co.

Pioneers of Peace Research. William Eckhardt. 1983. 25.00 (*0-933061-08-0*) Lentz Peace Res.

Pioneers of Photography. William Marder & Estelle Marder. 91p. 1991. pap. 28.00 (*0-9607480-3-2*) Marder.

Pioneers of Plant Study. Ellison Hawks & George S. Boulger. LC 75-86759. (Essay Index Reprint Ser.). 1977. 21.95 (*0-8369-1139-3*) Ayer.

Pioneers of Polk County, Iowa, Vols. I & II. L. F. Andrews. (Illus.). 928p. 1993. reprint ed. lib. bdg. 105.00 (*0-8328-3465-3*) Higginson Bk Co.

Pioneers of Popular Education, 1760-1850. Hugh M. Pollard. LC 73-20922. 297p. 1975. reprint ed. lib. bdg. 35.00 (*0-8371-5871-0*, POPP, Greenwood Pr) Greenwood.

Pioneers of Prefabrication: The British Contribution in the Nineteenth Century. Gilbert Herbert. LC 76-47372. (Johns Hopkins Studies in Nineteenth-Century Architecture). (Illus.). 240p. reprint ed. pap. 74.40 (*0-8357-6613-6*, 203525800094) Bks Demand.

Pioneers of Progress: Policy Entrepreneurs & Community Development, Vol. 1. David Bollier et al. 1991. pap. 20.00 (*1-887410-53-8*) Jobs for Future.

Pioneers of Progress Vol. 2: Policy Entrepreneurs & Community Development: The Network of Pioneer Organizations. 75p. 1991. pap. 20.00 (*1-887410-78-3*) Jobs for Future.

Pioneers of Psychology. 3rd ed. Raymond E. Fancher. LC 96-6403. (C). 1996. pap. 19.25 (*0-393-96994-0*) Norton.

Pioneers of Public Health: The Story of Some Benefactors of the Human Race. M. E. Walker. LC 68-26483. (Essay Index Reprint Ser.). 1977. 23.95 (*0-8369-0965-8*) Ayer.

Pioneers of Religious Education. Tom F. Kinlock. LC 69-18929. (Essay Index Reprint Ser.). 1977. 17.95 (*0-8369-0045-6*) Ayer.

Pioneers of Representation Theory: Frobenius, Burnside, Schur & Brauer. Charles W. Curtis. LC 99-14983. (History of Mathematics Ser.). 287p. 1999. 49.00 (*0-8218-9002-6*) Am Math.

Pioneers of Rocketry. Michael Stoiko. 18.95 (*0-89190-722-X*) Amereon Ltd.

Pioneers of Science. Amelia D. Defries. LC 74-117782. (Essay Index Reprint Ser.). 1977. 19.95 (*0-8369-1646-8*) Ayer.

Pioneers of Science & Exploration. (Illus.). 104-144p. (gr. 5). 1996. 139.95 (*0-7910-3512-3*); 139.95 (*0-7910-3518-2*) Chelsea Hse.

Pioneers of Science in America: Sketches of Their Lives & Scientific Work. rev. ed. Ed. by William J. Youmans & Keir B. Sterling. LC 77-83845. (Biologists & Their World Ser.). (Illus.). 1978. reprint ed. lib. bdg. 51.95 (*0-405-10743-9*) Ayer.

Pioneers of Soviet Architecture. T. Khan-Magomedov. (C). 1990. 400.00 (*0-7855-4456-9*, Pub. by Collets) St Mut.

Pioneers of Soviet Photography. M. Shudakov. (C). 1990. 240.00 (*0-7855-4423-2*, Pub. by Collets) St Mut.

Pioneers of Space Physics, Vol. 1. 112p. 1994. pap. 14.00 (*0-87590-847-0*) Am Geophysical.

Pioneers of Superior, Wisconsin. Compiled by Ronald V. Mershart. (Orig.). 1996. pap. 24.95 (*0-915709-24-4*) Pk Geneal Bk.

Pioneers of the Air. Barron's Educational Editors. LC 98-73626. (Great Explorers Ser.). (Illus.). 32p. (YA). (gr. 5 up). 1998. pap. 5.95 (*0-7641-0633-3*) Barron.

An Asterisk (*) at the beginning of an entry indicates that the title is appearing for the first time.

Pioneers of the Black Atlantic: Five Slave Narratives from the Enlightenment: 1772-1815. Ed. by Henry Louis Gates, Jr. & William L. Andrews. LC 98-34796. 439p. 1998. pap. 19.50 (*1-887178-98-8*, Pub. by Counterpt DC) HarpC.

Pioneers of the British Film. John Barnes. (C). 1988. 90.00 (*1-85219-012-4*, Pub. by Bishopsgate Pr Ltd) St Mut.

Pioneers of the Colorado Parks: North, Middle & South Parks: From 1850 to 1900. Richard C. Barth. Ed. by Wayne Cornell. LC 97-36878. (Illus.). 288p. 1997. pap. 17.95 (*0-87004-381-1*, 038110) Caxton.

Pioneers of the Frontier. Charles W. Sundling. LC 98-6606. (Frontier Land Ser.). (Illus.). 32p. (J). 2000. lib. bdg. 19.93 (*1-57765-047-6*, ABDO & Dghtrs) ABDO Pub Co.

Pioneers of the Hardwood: Indiana & the Birth of Professional Basketball. Todd Gould. LC 97-38268. (Illus.). 320p. (C). 1998. text 35.00 (*0-253-33373-3*) Ind U Pr.

Pioneers of the Heavenly Way. T. A. Sparks. 135p. 1993. pap. text 5.70 (*1-883137-11-X*) Christ Stewards.

Pioneers of the Mono Basin. Margaret Calhoun. (Illus.). 172p. 1984. reprint ed. pap. 7.95 (*0-932347-07-X*) Artemisia Pr.

Pioneers of the Old South: A Chronicle of English Colonial Beginnings. Mary Johnston. (BCL1 - United States Local History Ser.). 260p. 1991. reprint ed. text 79.00 (*0-7812-6285-2*) Rprt Serv.

Pioneers of the Old Southwest: A Chronicle of the Dark & Bloody Ground. Constance L. Skinner. (BCL1 - United States Local History Ser.). 304p. 1991. reprint ed. text 89.00 (*0-7812-6313-1*) Rprt Serv.

***Pioneers of the Soil: California Farmers Cultivating a Healthier Future.** Susan Benson. 2000. pap. text 16.95 (*0-935028-77-3*) Inst Food & Develop.

Pioneers of the Soul: The Last Teachings of Hilda Charlton. Hilda Charlton. Ed. by Golden Quest Staff. (Golden Quest Ser.: Vol. 6). (Illus.). 204p. (Orig.). 1992. pap. 11.95 (*0-927383-12-8*) Golden Quest.

Pioneers of Unadilla Village, 1784-1840, with Reminiscences of Village Life, & of Panama & California from 1840 to 1850. Francis W. Halsey & G. L. Halsey. (Illus.). 323p. 1995. reprint ed. lib. bdg. 39.00 (*0-8328-5086-1*) Higginson Bk Co.

Pioneers of Utica, New York. M. M. Bagg. (Illus.). 665p. 1993. reprint ed. lib. bdg. 67.50 (*0-8328-2872-6*) Higginson Bk Co.

Pioneers of Utica, New York. M. M. Bagg. (Illus.). 665p. 1993. reprint ed. lib. bdg. 67.50 (*0-8328-2912-9*) Higginson Bk Co.

Pioneers of Wireless. Ellison Hawks. LC 74-4685. (Telecommunications Ser.). (Illus.). 400p. 1974. reprint ed. 29.95 (*0-405-06049-1*) Ayer.

Pioneers of Women's Education in the United States. Ed. by Willystine Goodsell. (Illus.). reprint ed. 32.50 (*0-404-02864-0*) AMS Pr.

***Pioneers of Wonder: Conversations with the Founders of Science Fiction.** Eric Leif Davin. LC 99-37717. 414p. 1999. 24.95 (*1-57392-702-3*) Prometheus Bks.

Pioneers over Jordan: The Frontier of Settlement in Transjordan, 1850-1914. Raouf S. Abujaber. 352p. 1990. text 65.00 (*1-85043-116-7*, Pub. by I B T) St Martin.

Pioneers, Passionate Ladies & Private Eyes: Dime Novels, Series Books & Paperbacks. Ed. by Larry E. Sullivan & Lydia C. Schuman. LC 96-44437. (Primary Sources & Original Works: Vol. 4, Nos. 1-4). 318p. (C). 1997. 39.95 (*0-7890-0016-4*) Haworth Pr.

Pioneers, Peddlers, & Tsadikim: The Story of the Jews in Colorado. 2nd ed. Ida L. Uchill. LC 57-57817. 327p. 1979. pap. 25.00 (*0-9604468-0-X*) Pion Pubns.

***Pioneers, Peddlers, & Tsadikim: The Story of the Jews in Colorado.** 3rd ed. Ida L. Uchill. 363p. 2000. pap. 24.95 (*0-87081-593-8*) U of Okla Pr.

Pioneer's Search for an Ideal Home. Phoebe G. Judson. LC 84-7478. iv, 314p. 1984. reprint ed. pap. 13.95 (*0-8032-7559-5*, Bison Books) U of Nebr Pr.

Pioneros de las Ciencias Nucleares. Pedro Bosch. (Ciencia para Todos Ser.). (SPA.). pap. 6.99 (*968-16-4213-9*, Pub. by Fondo) Continental Bk.

Pioniergenossenschaften: Am Beispiel der Konsumgenossenschaften in Grobbritannien, Schweden & Japan. Johann Brazda et al. (Forschungen zur Wirtschafts-, Finanz- und Sozialgeschichte Ser.: Bd. 4). (GER., Illus.). 301p. 1996. pap. 57.95 (*3-631-46488-6*) P Lang Pubng.

Pionniers. Willa Cather. Orig. Title: Oh Pioneers!. (FRE.). 310p. 1989. pap. 12.95 (*0-7859-2117-6*, 2070381382) Fr & Eur.

Pionniers de Dieu. Bernice C. Jordan. (Sentier de la Foi Ser.). (FRE.). 1989. 9.95 (*0-86508-358-4*) BCM Pubn.

Pionniers de Dieu. Bernice C. Jordan. (Sentier de la Foi Ser.). (FRE.). 1989. student ed. 2.50 (*0-86508-357-6*) BCM Pubn.

Pions in Nuclei: Proceedings of the International Workshop, Penyscola, Spain, 3-9 June 1991. Ed. by E. Oset et al. 600p. (C). 1992. text 130.00 (*981-02-0732-8*) World Scientific Pub.

Pions to Quarks: Particle Physics in the 1950's. Ed. by Laurie M. Brown et al. (Illus.). 766p. (C). 1989. text 90.00 (*0-521-30984-0*) Cambridge U Pr.

Piotr Gal'perin: A Lifetime of Searching for the Content of Psychology. Jacques Haenen. (Illus.). 267p. (C). 1994. lib. bdg. 95.00 (*1-56072-199-5*) Nova Sci Pubs.

Pious see Piadosas

Pious Bacchanal: Affinities Between the Lives & Works of John Flaxman & Aubrey Beardsley. Daniel O. Bell. LC 93-41838. (New Connections Ser.: Vol. 10). 344p. 2000. text 58.95 (*0-8204-2318-1*) P Lang Pubng.

Pious Brief Narrative in Medieval Castilian & Galician Verse: From Berceo to Alfonso X. John E. Keller. LC 77-84064. (Studies in Romance Languages: No. 21). 152p. 1978. 22.00 (*0-8131-1381-4*) U Pr of Ky.

Pious Impostures & Unproven Words: The Romance of Deconstruction in Nineteenth Century America. Steven C. Scheer. Ed. by John Deely & Brooke Williams. LC 89-32322. (Sources in Semiotics Ser.: Vol. VIII). 164p. (Orig.). (C). 1989. pap. text 19.50 (*0-8191-7468-8*); lib. bdg. 37.00 (*0-8191-7467-X*) U Pr of Amer.

Pious Passengers: The Hajj in Earlier Times. M. N. Pearson. (C). 1994. write for info. (*81-207-1601-9*) Sterling Pubs.

Pious Passion: The Emergence of Modern Fundamentalism in the United States & Iran. Martin Riesebrodt. Tr. by Don Reneau from GER. LC 92-32233. (Comparative Studies in Religion & Society: Vol. 6). 1993. 48.00 (*0-520-07463-7*, Pub. by U CA Pr) Cal Prin Full Svc.

Pious Passion: The Emergence of Modern Fundamentalism in the United States & Iran. Martin Riesebrodt. (Comparative Studies in Religion & Society). 1998. pap. text 18.95 (*0-520-07464-5*, Pub. by U CA Pr) Cal Prin Full Svc.

Pious Persuasions: Laity & Clergy in Eighteenth-Century New England. Erik R. Seeman. LC 99-15429. (Early America). 200p. 1999. 36.00 (*0-8018-6208-6*) Johns Hopkins.

Pious Prentice, or, the Prentices Piety. Abraham Jackson. LC 74-28866. (English Experience Ser.: No. 746). 1975. reprint ed. 15.00 (*90-221-0746-9*) Walter J Johnson.

Pious Secrets. Irene Dische. 1999. pap. 8.95 (*0-14-013943-5*) Viking Penguin.

Pious Sinner: Ethics & Aesthetics in Medieval Hasidic Narrative. Tamar Frizer-Alexander. (Texts & Studies in Medieval & Early Modern Judaism: No. 5). 175p. 1990. 62.50 (*3-16-145656-4*, Pub. by JCB Mohr) Coronet Bks.

***Pious Traders in Medicine: German Pharmaceutical Networks in Eighteenth-Century North America.** Renate Wilson. LC 99-86276. 2000. write for info. (*0-271-02052-0*) Pa St U Pr.

Piozzi Letters, Vol. 6. write for info. (*0-87413-395-5*) U Delaware Pr.

Piozzi Letters: Correspondence of Hester Lynch Piozzi, 1784-1791, Vol. 1. Ed. by Edward A. Bloom & Lillian D. Bloom. LC 87-40231. (Illus.). 424p. 1989. 75.00 (*0-87413-115-4*) U Delaware Pr.

Piozzi Letters: Correspondence of Hester Lynch Piozzi, 1784-1821 (Formerly Mrs. Thrale), Vol. 2: 1792-1798. Hester Lynch Piozzi. Ed. by Edward A. Bloom & Lillian D. Bloom. LC 87-40231. (Illus.). 592p. 1991. 75.00 (*0-87413-360-2*) U Delaware Pr.

Piozzi Letters: Correspondence of Hester Lynch Piozzi, 1784-1821 (Formerly Mrs. Thrale), Vol. 3: 1799-1804. Ed. by Edward A. Bloom & Lillian D. Bloom. LC 87-40231. (Illus.). 536p. 1992. 75.00 (*0-87413-392-0*) U Delaware Pr.

Piozzi Letters: Correspondence of Hester Lynch Piozzi, 1784-1821, Vol. 4: 1805-1810, Vol. 4. Edward A. Bloom & Lillian D. Bloom. LC 87-40231. (Illus.). 360p. 1996. 52.50 (*0-87413-393-9*) U Delaware Pr.

Piozzi Letters Vol. 5, 1811-1816: Correspondence of Hester Lynch Piozzi, 1784-1821 (Formerly Mrs. Thrale) Hester Lynch Piozzi. Ed. by Edward A. Bloom et al. LC 87-40231. (Illus.). 608p. 1999. 69.50 (*0-87413-394-7*) U Delaware Pr.

Pip. Mark Dunster. (Rin Ser.: Pt. 53). 1979. pap. 4.00 (*0-89642-052-3*) Linden Pubs.

Pip & Kip. Gina Clegg Erickson. (Get Ready - Get Set - Read! Ser.). 1993. 8.70 (*0-606-13708-4*, Pub. by Turtleback) Demco.

Pip & Kip. Gina Clegg Erickson & Kelli C. Foster. LC 92-29864. (Get Ready...Get Set...Read! Ser.). (Illus.). 24p. (J). (ps-2). 1993. pap. 3.50 (*0-8120-1454-5*) Barron.

Pip & Kip. Kelli C. Foster & Gina Clegg Erickson. (Get Ready...Get Set...Read! Ser.: Set 2). (Illus.). 26p. (J). 1995. lib. bdg. 11.95 (*1-56674-111-4*) Forest Hse.

***Pip Anthology of World Poetry of the 20th Century, Vol. 1.** Ed. by Douglas Messerli. Vol. 1. (Illus.). 199p. 2000. pap. 15.95 (*1-892295-47-4*, Pub. by Green Integer) SPD-Small Pr Dist.

***PIP Anthology of World Poetry of the 20th Century, Vol. 2.** Douglas Messerli. Vol. 2. (Illus.). 124p. 2000. pap. 15.95 (*1-892295-94-6*) Green Integer.

Pip Book. Keith Mossman. 128p. pap. 12.95 (*0-14-046255-4*, Pub. by Pnguin Bks Ltd) Trafalgar.

PIP College "HELPS" - Handicapped & Exceptional Learners Programs & Services. P. M. Fielding. (College Handicapped & Exceptional Programs & Services Ser.: Vol. 3). 1978. pap. 8.95 (*0-937660-04-3*) PIP.

PIP College "HELPS" - Handicapped & Exceptional Learners Programs & Services, Vol. 2. P. M. Fielding. 1977. pap. 7.95 (*0-937660-03-5*) PIP.

***Pip Gandhi.** 2000. write for info. (*0-582-31979-X*) Pearson Educ.

Pip of Weeville. Jean L. Matus. LC 88-70820. (Illus.). 16p. (J). (ps-2). 1987. lib. bdg. 11.95 (*0-945938-00-4*) Peartree.

Pipe: The Art & Love of a Great Tradition. Robin Crole. LC 99-32960. (Illus.). 144p. 1998. boxed set 25.00 (*0-7615-1507-0*) Prima Pub.

Pipe All Hands! Aylward E. Dingle. LC 74-101279. (Short Story Index Reprint Ser.). 1977. 23.95 (*0-8369-3216-1*) Ayer.

Pipe & Christ. 4th ed. William Stolzman. (Illus.). 222p. 1992. reprint ed. pap. 7.95 (*1-877976-00-8*, 406-0001) Tipi Pr.

This book is the result of a six-year dialogue between Sioux medicine men & Christian missionaries on the Rosebud Reservation in South Dakota. Fr. Stolzman presents a clear & learned comparison between Native American religion & Christianity...both parallel & different--each having an enduring, authentic place in salvation history. The author offers a word of caution. In that the things of which I speak are sacred & should not be bantered about in ordinary conversation. These visions are mine, & anyone who speaks of them speaks not from what he knows but from hearsay. The stories may fill you with wonder, desire & questioning. That is good. Real answers & satisfaction, however, come only from one's own pursuit & experience of the Sacred. It is with a great deal of pride that we recommend that unique & enlightening study. *Publisher Paid Annotation.*

Pipe & Couplings, Polyvinyl Chloride (PVC), for Underground Fire Service, UL 1285. 3rd ed. (C). 1995. pap. text 175.00 (*1-55989-807-0*) Underwrtrs Labs.

Pipe & Drum. Ed. by Rose Fyleman. (Illus.). 88p. 1977. 15.95 (*0-8369-6360-1*) Ayer.

Pipe & Excavation Contracting. Dave Roberts. 400p. (Orig.). 1987. pap. 29.00 (*0-934041-22-9*) Craftsman.

Pipe & Pouch. Ed. by Joseph Knight. LC 74-108584. (Granger Index Reprint Ser.). 1977. 19.95 (*0-8369-6112-9*) Ayer.

Pipe & Tube Bending Manual: Methods - Equipment - Reference Data. 2nd ed. John Gillanders. (Illus.). 202p. (C). 1994. pap. 50.00 (*1-881113-06-X*) Croydon Grp.

Pipe & Tube Fabrication. 1987. 60.00 (*0-85083-017-6*) St Mut.

Pipe & Tube Welding. 1989. 49.00 (*0-7855-2868-7*) St Mut.

Pipe, Bible, & Peyote among the Oglala Lakota: A Study in Religious Identity. Paul B. Steinmetz. LC 98-41348. 1998. pap. text 19.95 (*0-8156-0557-9*) Syracuse U Pr.

Pipe, Bible, & Peyote among the Oglala Lakota: A Study in Religious Identity. Paul B. Steinmetz. LC 89-33829. (Illus.). 254p. 1990. reprint ed. pap. 78.80 (*0-608-07782-8*, 206787000010) Bks Demand.

***Pipe Book.** Alfred Dunhill. 304p. 2000. 9.99 (*0-517-16187-7*) Random Hse Value.

Pipe Book. Alfred Dunhill. LC 98-46883. (Illus.). 262p. 1999. reprint ed. 25.00 (*1-55821-776-2*) Lyons Pr.

Pipe Caulker. Jack Rudman. (Career Examination Ser.: C-641). 1994. pap. 23.95 (*0-8373-0641-8*) Nat Learn.

Pipe Characteristics Handbook. Williams Natural Gas Company Staff. LC 96-3060. 1996. 79.95 (*0-87814-611-3*) PennWell Bks.

Pipe Cleaners Gone Crazy: A Complete Guide to Bending Fuzzy Sticks. Laura Torres & Michael Sherman. (Illus.). 44p. (J). (gr. 4-7). 1997. 12.95 (*1-57054-075-6*) Klutz.

***Pipe Companion.** David Wright. (Connoisseur's Guides Ser.). 2000. 24.95 (*0-7624-0323-3*) Running Pr.

Pipe Connectors for Petroleum Products & LP-Gas, UL 567. 8th ed. (C). 1996. pap. text 330.00 (*0-7629-0021-0*) Underwrtrs Labs.

Pipe de Maigret et Maigret Se Fache. Georges Simenon. (FRE.). pap. 3.95 (*0-685-11496-1*) Fr & Eur.

Pipe de Maigret, Maigret Se Fache, Maigret a New York, Lettre a Mon Juge, le Destin Des Malou. Georges Simenon. (FRE.). 1988. 49.95 (*0-7859-0476-X*, 2258020980) Fr & Eur.

Pipe Down. Clyde Bosco. Ed. by Ruth Ashby. (Nintendo Adventure Bks.: No. 5). 128p. (J). 1991. mass mkt. 3.50 (*0-671-74203-5*, Archway) PB.

Pipe Drafting & Design: Using Manual, AutoCAD, & PRO-PIPE Applications. Roy A. Parisher & Robert A. Rhea. LC 95-13984. (Illus.). 288p. 1996. text 39.95 (*0-88415-657-5*, 5657) Gulf Pub.

Pipe Drafting & Design: Using Manual, AutoCAD, & PRO-PIPE Applications. Roy A. Parisher & Robert A. Rhea. (Illus.). 56p. 1996. pap. text, teacher ed. 20.00 (*0-88415-659-1*, 5659); pap. text, wbk. ed. 16.00 (*0-88415-658-3*, 5658) Gulf Pub.

Pipe Dream. Richard Rodgers. (Vocal Score Ser.). 232p. 1981. per. 45.00 (*0-88188-045-0*, 00312321) H Leonard.

Pipe Dream: Vocal Selections. (Illus.). 32p. 1986. pap. 8.95 (*0-88188-602-5*, 00312320) H Leonard.

Pipe Dream Blues: Racism & the War on Drugs. Clarence Lusane. 293p. 1991. 30.00 (*0-89608-411-6*); pap. 14.00 (*0-89608-410-8*) South End Pr.

Pipe Dreams, Bk. 1. Stanley E. Walker. 304p. 1997. pap. 18.00 (*0-8059-4308-0*) Dorrance.

Pipe Dreams: An Anthology of Drug Experiences in Literature. Gilbert Alter-Gilbert. 1998. pap. text 16.00 (*1-57650-088-8*) Hi Jinx Pr.

Pipe Fitters & Welders Handbook. Thomas W. Frankland. (Illus.). (Orig.). 1984. pap. 12.10 (*0-02-802500-8*) Glencoe.

Pipe Fitter's Math Guide. Johnny E. Hamilton. LC 89-92081. (Illus.). 166p. (Orig.). (C). 1989. pap. 19.95 (*0-9624197-0-2*) Constrctn Trades.

Pipe Flanges & Flanged Fittings: NPS 1/2 Through NPS 24. 172p. 1996. 95.00 (*0-7918-2431-4*, M01596) ASME Pr.

Pipe Hanger Equipment for Fire Protection Service, UL 203, UL203. 8th ed. (C). 1996. pap. text 175.00 (*0-7629-8040-0*) Underwrtrs Labs.

Pipe Jointing Methods. EEMUA Staff. 1968. 125.00 (*0-85931-052-3*, Pub. by EEMUA) St Mut.

Pipe Music of the Great Plains: Highland Bagpipe Music by Midwestern & Canadian Composers. Paul Deloughery. 64p. (Orig.). 1992. pap. 9.95 (*1-880954-01-X*) Kalevala Bks.

Pipe, Rails & Wire Supply, Salvage Shortage & Surplus. William B. Sinclair. (Confusion Beyond Imagination Ser.: Bk. 3). (Illus.). 210p. 1988. 24.00 (*0-937577-04-9*); pap. 16.00 (*0-937577-05-7*) J F Whitley.

***Pipe Saddle Handbook.** Bennie Herrington. 330p. 2000. pap. 11.00 (*0-935545-24-7*) Land & Land.

Pipe Spring & the Arizona Strip see History of Arizona's Pipe Spring National Monument

Pipe Trades Pocket Manual. Thomas W. Frankland. (Illus.). (Orig.). 1969. pap. 13.16 (*0-02-802410-9*) Glencoe.

Pipe Unions for Flammable & Combustible Fluids & Fire-Protection Service, UL 860. 6th ed. (C). 1993. pap. text 95.00 (*1-55989-341-9*) Underwrtrs Labs.

Pipe Welding. Richard Hunter & Robert O'Con. (Series 911). (Orig.). 1985. pap., student ed. 7.00 (*0-8064-0389-6*) Bergwall.

Pipe Welding Procedures. Hoobasar Rampaul. LC 73-7849. (Illus.). 238p. 1973. 28.50 (*0-8311-1100-3*) Indus Pr.

Pipe Welding Techniques. 4th ed. Ivan H. Griffin et al. LC 85-1513. 128p. 1985. mass mkt. 24.50 (*0-8273-2248-8*) Delmar.

Pipe Welding Techniques. 4th ed. Ivan H. Griffin et al. LC 85-1513. 128p. 1985. teacher ed. 12.95 (*0-8273-2249-6*) Delmar.

Pipedreams: Poems. Debra Williams-Garner. LC 88-90092. (Orig.). 1988. pap. 3.50 (*0-9620332-0-0*) D Williams-Garner.

Pipefitter. Jack Rudman. (Career Examination Ser.: C-587). 1994. pap. 23.95 (*0-8373-0587-X*) Nat Learn.

Pipefitter, Level 1. (C). 1996. pap. text, student ed. 50.00 (*0-13-266446-1*, Prentice Hall) P-H.

Pipefitter: Binder, Trainee Guide, Update, Level 4. rev. ed. NCCER Staff. 1997. pap. text, student ed. 80.00 (*0-13-773011-X*, Prentice Hall) P-H.

Pipefitter: Instructor's Guide, Level 1. (C). 1996. teacher ed., per. 50.00 (*0-13-245929-9*) P-H.

Pipefitter: Instructor's Guide, Level 3. (C). 1996. teacher ed., per. 80.00 (*0-13-245960-4*) P-H.

Pipefitter: Instructor's Guide, Level 4. (C). 1996. per. 80.00 (*0-13-245986-8*) P-H.

Pipefitter: Trainee Guide, Level 1. (C). 1996. student ed., ring bd. 80.00 (*0-13-264888-1*, Prentice Hall) P-H.

Pipefitter: Trainee Guide, Level 2. (C). 1996. teacher ed., per. 80.00 (*0-13-245945-0*); per. 80.00 (*0-13-245937-X*) P-H.

Pipefitter: Trainee Guide, Level 3. NCCER Staff. 1996. student ed., ring bd. 80.00 (*0-13-265893-3*, Prentice Hall) P-H.

Pipefitter Level Three, Level 3. rev. ed. NCCER Staff. 378p. (C). 1997. pap. text 80.00 (*0-13-771353-3*) P-H.

Pipefitter Wheels, Level 1. NCCER Staff. 1996. pap. text, teacher ed. 50.00 (*0-13-265471-7*) P-H.

Pipefitter Wheels, Level 2. NCCER Staff. 1996. teacher ed., ring bd. 80.00 (*0-13-265489-X*) P-H.

Pipefitter Wheels, Level 3. NCCER Staff. 1996. teacher ed., ring bd. 80.00 (*0-13-265497-0*) P-H.

Pipefitters & Welders Pocket Manual. Charles N. McConnell. LC 96-79620. 320p. 1996. per. 14.95 (*0-02-034624-7*, Aude IN) IDG Bks.

Pipefitters Handbook. 3rd ed. Forrest Lindsey. (Illus.). 464p. 1967. 22.95 (*0-8311-3019-9*) Indus Pr.

Pipejacking & Microtunnelling. Barry S. Coller. 1991. text 99.95 (*0-442-31332-2*, VNR) Wiley.

Pipejacking & Microtunnelling. James C. Thomson. LC 93-34461. 1993. 144.95 (*0-7514-0102-1*, Pub. by B Acad & Prof) Routldge.

Pipeline. Paul Malone. (Agents Bks.: No. 02). 1991. per. 3.50 (*0-373-63802-7*) Harlequin Bks.

Pipeline: Materials & Design. American Society of Civil Engineers Staff. Ed. by B. Jay Schrock. LC 84-71894. 79p. 1984. reprint ed. pap. 30.00 (*0-608-00801-X*, 205935000011) Bks Demand.

Pipeline at Sparrow Ridge: Read-Along. Laurence. (Illus.). 32p. (J). (gr. 4-8). 1982. pap. 9.95 (*0-87386-307-0*) Jan Prods.

Pipeline Construction. Max Hosmanek. Ed. by Cinda Cyrus. (Illus.). 122p. (C). 1984. pap. text 30.00 (*0-88698-096-8*, 4.00030) PETEX.

Pipeline Corrosion & Cathodic Protection. 3rd ed. Marshall E. Parker & Edward G. Peattie. LC 83-22630. 166p. 1984. 39.00 (*0-87201-149-6*, 1149) Gulf Pub.

Pipeline Crossings. American Society of Civil Engineers Staff. LC 96-8562. (Manuals & Reports on Engineering Practice Ser.). 144p. 1996. 39.00 (*0-7844-0183-7*) Am Soc Civil Eng.

Pipeline Crossings. Ed. by Joseph P. Castronovo. LC 91-7788. 1991p. 1991. pap. text 7.00 (*0-87262-800-0*) Am Soc Civil Eng.

Pipeline Crossings: Proceedings of the Specialty Conference, Burlington, Vermont, June 16-19, 1996. American Society of Civil Engineers Staff. LC 96-19475. 520p. 1996. 54.00 (*0-7844-0180-2*) Am Soc Civil Eng.

***Pipeline Design & Construction: A Practical Approach /** Mo Mohitpour et al. LC 00-40625. 2000. write for info. (*0-7918-0156-X*) ASME Pr.

Pipeline Design & Installation. Ed. by Kenneth K. Kienow. 712p. 1990. pap. text 63.00 (*0-87262-749-7*) Am Soc Civil Eng.

Pipeline Design for Water Engineers. 3rd rev. ed. D. Stephenson. (Developments in Water Science Ser.: No. 40). 264p. 1989. 153.75 (*0-444-87373-2*) Elsevier.

Pipeline Dictionary. Herbert Bucksch & A. P. Altmeyer. (ENG, FRE & GER.). 288p. 1969. 150.00 (*0-8288-6612-0*, M7588) Fr & Eur.

P

Pipeline Engineering, 1995: Proceedings: The Energy & Environmental EXPO '95 - the Energy-Sources Technology Conference & Exhibition (1995: Houston, TX) Ed. by B. Williams et al. LC 82-74407. (PD Ser.: Vol. 69). 119p. 1995. pap. 72.00 (*0-7918-1292-8*, H00924) ASME.

Pipeline Engineering, 1994, Vol. 60. Ed. by B. S. Williams et al. 88p. 1994. pap. 32.50 (*0-7918-1188-3*) ASME.

Pipeline Engineering, 1993. Ed. by B. H. Basavaraj & B. Williams. LC 82-77407. 77p. 1993. pap. 30.00 (*0-7918-0952-8*, H00784) ASME.

Pipeline Engineering Symposium. Ed. by K. Chickering. 96p. 1983. pap. text 24.00 (*0-317-02640-2*, I00157) ASME.

Pipeline Gas from Coal by Methanation of Synthesis Gas. H. A. Dirksen & H. R. Linden. (Research Bulletin Ser.: No. 31). vi, 137p. 1963. pap. 25.00 (*1-58222-038-7*) Inst Gas Tech.

Pipeline Infrastructure. Ed. by Bruce A. Bennett. (Conference Proceedings Ser.). 536p. 1988. 52.00 (*0-87262-662-8*) Am Soc Civil Eng.

Pipeline Infrastructure: Proceedings of the International Conference, San Antonio, Texas, August 16-17, 1993. Ed. by Mark B. Pickell. LC 93-21532. 720p. 1993. 63.00 (*0-87262-923-6*) Am Soc Civil Eng.

Pipeline Installation. unabridged ed. Amster Howard. LC 95-73308. (Illus.). 280p. (Orig.). 1996. pap. 50.00 (*0-9651002-0-0*) Relativity Pub.

Pipeline Pigging Technology. 2nd ed. Ed. by J. N. Tiratsoo. 460p. 1992. 80.00 (*0-87201-426-6*, 1426) Gulf Pub.

Pipeline Politics: The Complex Political Economy of East-West Energy Trade. Bruce W. Jentleson. LC 86-47643. (Cornell Studies in Political Economy). 272p. 1986. 42.50 (*0-8014-1923-9*) Cornell U Pr.

Pipeline Politics: The Complex Political Economy of East-West Energy Trade. Bruce W. Jentleson. LC 86-47643. (Cornell Studies in Political Economy). 264p. reprint ed. pap. 81.90 (*0-608-20904-X*, 207200300003) Bks Demand.

***Pipeline Protection: Proceedings International Conference Edinburgh, Scotland, 1999.** Ed. by J. Duncan. (BHR Group Conference Ser.: No. 37). 332p. 1999. 340.00 (*1-86058-214-1*) Prof Eng Pubng.

Pipeline Research Needs: Proceedings of the Workshop on Pipeline Needs; March 28-29, 1996, Held at the Lansdowne Resort & Conventionn Center, Leesburg, Virginia. Ed. by John G. Bomba. LC 97-16680. 160p. 1997. 18.00 (*0-7844-0246-9*) Am Soc Civil Eng.

Pipeline Risk Management Manual. W. Kent Muhlbauer. LC 91-32612. (Illus.). 275p. 1992. reprint ed. pap. 85.30 (*0-608-04208-0*, 206494300011) Bks Demand.

Pipeline Risk Management Manual. 2nd ed. W. Kent Muhlbauer. (Illus.). 438p. 1996. 75.00 (*0-88415-668-0*, 5668) Gulf Pub.

Pipeline Route Selection for Rural & Cross-Country Pipelines. Nicholas B. Day & American Society of Civil Engineers Staff. LC 98-26052. (ASCE Manuals & Reports on Engineering Practice). 95p. 1998. 49.00 (*0-7844-0345-7*) Am Soc Civil Eng.

Pipeline Rules of Thumb. 4th rev. ed. E. W. McAllister. 616p. 1998. pap. 79.00 (*0-88415-671-0*, 5671) Gulf Pub.

Pipeline Rules of Thumb Handbook: A Manual of Quick, Accurate Solutions to Everyday Pipeline Problems. fac. ed. Ed. by E. W. McAllister. LC 87-24408. (Illus.). 456p. 1988. reprint ed. pap. 141.40 (*0-608-00979-2*, 206183300012) Bks Demand.

***Pipeline Safety, Reliability & Rehabilitation: Proceedings of the Group of ASCE Technical Sessions at the 1999 American Public Works Association International Public Works Congress & Exposition, September 19-22, 1999, Denver, Colorado.** Randall C. Conner et al. LC 99-26671. 320p. 1999. pap. 40.00 (*0-7844-0452-6*) Am Soc Civil Eng.

Pipeline Supervisory & Control Systems Workshop: Presented at the 5th Annual Energy-Sources Technology Conference, New Orleans, Louisiana, March 8-10, 1982. Pipeline Supervisory & Control Systems Workshop St. Ed. by E. J. Seiders. LC 82-70514. 96p. reprint ed. pap. 30.00 (*0-8357-8750-8*, 203365300087) Bks Demand.

Pipeline Symposium Vol. 5: Pipeline Symposium. Ed. by Alan F. Murray et al. LC 82-70515. (1995 Offshore Mechanics & Arctic Engineering Conference Ser.: Vol. V). 608p. 1995. 180.00 (*0-7918-1311-8*, H00943) ASME.

Pipeline Systems. E. P. Evans. 1992. text 236.00 (*0-7923-1668-1*) Kluwer Academic.

Pipeline Technology: Proceedings of the 2nd International Pipeline Technology Conference, Ostend (Belgium), September 11-14, 1995, Set. Ed. by R. Denys. LC 95-23454. (Illus.). 1376p. 1995. text 406.50 (*0-444-82197-X*) Elsevier.

Pipeline, Terminals & Storage & Processing & Refining, '97 see Energy Week '97

Pipelined Adaptive Digital Filters. Naresh R. Shanbhag & Keshab K. Parhi. LC 94-15255. (International Series in Engineering & Computer Science, VLSI, Computer Architecture, & Digital Screen Processing: No. 274). 200p. (C). 1994. text 120.00 (*0-7923-9463-1*) Kluwer Academic.

Pipelined & Parallel Computer Architectures. Sajjan G. Shiva. (Illus.). 390p. (C). 1997. 100.00 (*0-673-52093-5*) Addson-Wesley Educ.

Pipelined Lattice & Wave Digital Recursive Filters. Jin-Gyun Chung & Keshab K. Parhi. (International Series in Engineering & Computer Science, Natural Language Processing & Machine Translation: Vol. 344). 240p. (C). 1995. text 109.00 (*0-7923-9656-1*) Kluwer Academic.

Pipelines: A Study in Private Enterprise & Public Policy, 1862-1906. Arthur M. Johnson. LC 81-23728. (Illus.). 307p. 1982. reprint ed. lib. bdg. 55.00 (*0-313-23409-4*, JODEV, Greenwood Pr) Greenwood.

Pipelines & Permafrost: Science in a Cold Climate. 2nd enl. rev. ed. Peter J. Williams. (Illus.). 140p. 1988. pap. 14.95 (*0-88629-056-2*) OUP.

Pipelines in Adverse Environments, 2 vols. 562p. 1979. pap. 44.00 (*0-87262-176-6*) Am Soc Civil Eng.

Pipelines in Adverse Environments II. Ed. by Mark B. Pickell. 748p. 1983. 64.00 (*0-87262-385-8*) Am Soc Civil Eng.

Pipelines in the Constructed Environment. Joseph P. Castronovo et al. LC 98-35557. 824p. 1998. 89.00 (*0-7844-0372-4*) Am Soc Civil Eng.

Pipelines in the Ocean. 114p. 1974. pap. 3.00 (*0-87262-062-X*) Am Soc Civil Eng.

Pipelines of Progress: A Status Report on the Glass Ceiling. 41p. 1996. reprint ed. pap. text 20.00 (*0-7881-3711-5*) DIANE Pub.

Pipelines of Progress: An Update on the Glass Ceiling Initiative. Government Printing Office Staff. 45p. 1992. pap. 4.50 (*0-16-038019-7*) USGPO.

Pipelines of Progress: The Glass Ceiling Initiative. 1997. lib. bdg. 251.95 (*0-8490-6080-X*) Gordon Pr.

Pipelines, Terminals & Storage, '96 see Energy Week '96: Conference Proceedings

Pipemajor's Handbook: How to Tune, Maintain, & Set up a Band for Competition. 2nd rev. ed. R. W. Lerwick. Ed. by Joseph Croft & Ceilidh Croft. LC 98-60286. (Illus.). 144p. 1998. pap. text 19.95 (*0-9663321-2-1*) Shetland Piper.

***Piper.** John Keegan. 2001. 24.00 (*1-57962-029-9*) Permanent Pr.

Piper. Ed. by Brett Rutherford & John Robertson. 1987. 4.50 (*0-318-64157-7*) Poets Pr.

Piper Airplanes: A Legend Aloft. Edward H. Phillips. 1993. 29.95 (*0-911139-14-1*) Flying Bks.

Piper Alpha: Lessons for Life-Cycle Safety Management. Institution of Chemical Engineers Staff. (Institution of Chemical Engineers Symposium Ser.: No. 122). 183p. 1991. 94.95 (*1-56032-134-2*) Hemisp Pub.

Piper Classics. Joe Christy. (Illus.). 160p. 1988. 19.95 (*0-8306-9457-9*, 2457); pap. 13.95 (*0-8306-2457-0*) McGraw-Hill Prof.

Piper in Peace & War. C. A. Malcolm. (Illus.). 300p. 1993. boxed set 29.95 (*0-9521580-0-0*) Lancer.

Piper Indians. Bill Clarke. (Illus.). 288p. 1988. pap. 18.95 (*0-07-155369-X*) McGraw.

Piper Indians. Bill Clarke. (Illus.). 288p. 1987. 24.95 (*0-8306-0232-1*, 2432); pap. 17.95 (*0-8306-2432-5*) McGraw-Hill Prof.

Piper, John: Fifty Years of Work: Paintings & Photographs 1929-1979. Ed. by John Hoole et al. (Illus.). 1979. pap. 20.00 (*0-905836-15-4*, Pub. by Museum Modern Art) St Mut.

Piper of Laide. large type ed. Alex Stuart. 384p. 1992. 27.99 (*0-7089-2596-0*) Ulverscroft.

Piper on the Mountain: An Inspector George Felse Mystery. Ellis Peters. 208p. 1996. mass mkt. 5.99 (*0-446-40071-8*, Pub. by Warner Bks) Little.

Piper on the Mountain: An Inspector George Felse Mystery. large type ed. Ellis Peters. 342p. 1993. 27.99 (*0-7505-0584-2*, Pub. by Mgna Lrg Print) Ulverscroft.

Piper Single Engine Aircraft. Compiled by Jim Cavanagh. (Illus.). 525p. 49.95 (*0-614-13201-0*, 21-31836) EAA Aviation.

***Piper Steals the Show!** Mark Lowry & Martha Bolton. (Adventures of Piper the Hyper Mouse Ser.). (Illus.). 32p. (J). (ps-5). 2000. 14.99 (*1-58229-127-6*) Howard Pub LA.

Piperonyl Butoxide. Glynne Jones. LC 98-86854. (Illus.). 323p. 1998. text 99.95 (*0-12-286975-3*) Acad Pr.

***Pipers at the Gates of Dawn.** Lynn Stegner. LC 00-9138. (Hardscrabble Books Ser.). 2000. pap. write for info. (*1-58465-064-8*) U Pr of New Eng.

***Pipers at the Gates of dawn: A Triptych.** Lynn Stegner. 2000. 24.95 (*1-58465-063-X*) U Pr of New Eng.

Piper's Night Before Christmas. Mark Lowry & Martha Bolton. LC 98-42458. (The Adventures of Piper the Hyper Mouse Ser.). (Illus.). 24p. (J). (gr. k-3). 1998. 14.99 (*1-58229-000-8*) Howard Pub LA.

Piper's Park. (Read with Me Key Words to Reading Ser.: No. 9010-13). (Illus.). 1990. teacher ed. 3.95 (*0-317-04036-7*, Ladybrd) Penguin Putnam.

Piper's Park. Ladybird Books Staff. (Read with Me Key Words to Reading Ser.: No. 9010-13). (Illus.). 1990. 3.50 (*0-7214-1326-9*, Ladybrd) Penguin Putnam.

Piper's Ring. Michael Scott. (Illus.). 32p. (J). (gr. 1-3). 1993. 17.95 (*0-460-88130-2*, Pub. by J M Dent & Sons) Trafalgar.

Piper's Sons. Bruce C. Fergusson. LC 98-36192. 352p. 1999. 24.95 (*0-525-94431-1*) NAL.

Piper's Sons. Bruce C. Fergusson. 432p. 1999. reprint ed. mass mkt. 6.99 (*0-451-40875-6*, Sig) NAL.

Piper's Tune. large type ed. Margaret Maddocks. 384p. 1994. 27.99 (*0-7089-3097-2*) Ulverscroft.

Pipes & Mules. Alan M. Hofmeister et al. (Reading for All Learners Ser.). (Illus.). (J). pap. write for info. (*1-56861-157-9*) Swift Lrn Res.

Pipes Are Calling: Our Jaunts Through Ireland. Christine Breen & Niall Williams. LC 89-26104. 224p. 1991. pap. 11.00 (*0-939149-52-4*) Soho Press.

Pipes, Kukris & Nips. G. M. Forteath. 149p. (C). 1989. text 60.00 (*1-872795-07-2*, Pub. by Pentland Pr) St Mut.

Pipes O' Pan at Zekesbury. James Whitcomb Riley. (Notable American Authors Ser.). 1999. reprint ed. lib. bdg. 125.00 (*0-7812-8783-9*) Rprt Serv.

***Pipes of Margaree.** large type ed. Jacquelyn Aeby. LC 99-42433. (Thorndike Candlelight Romance Ser.). 1999. 19.95 (*0-7862-2199-2*) Thorndike Pr.

Pipes of Orpheus. Jane Lindskold. 256p. (Orig.). 1995. mass mkt. 4.99 (*0-380-77848-3*, Avon Bks) Morrow Avon.

Pipes of Pan: Intertextuality & Literary Filiation in the Pastoral Tradition from Theocritus to Milton. Thomas K. Hubbard. LC 98-36928. 400p. (C). 1998. text 54.50 (*0-472-10855-7*, 10855) U of Mich Pr.

Pipes That Won't Smoke: Coal That Won't Burn: Haida Sculpture in Argillite. Carol Sheehan. (Illus.). 214p. (C). 1983. pap. 19.95 (*0-919224-20-2*, 28739-4) Glenbow-Alberta Inst.

Pipil Language of El Salvador. Lyle Campbell. (Grammar Library: No. 1). xiv, 957p. 1985. 106.15 (*0-89925-040-8*) Mouton.

Piping, Vol. III, Module II. Multimedia Development Services Staff. (Plant Fundamentals Ser.). (Illus.). (Orig.). 1995. teacher ed. 49.95 (*1-57431-049-6*) Tech Trng Systs.

Piping V, Vol. III, Module II. Multimedia Development Services Staff. (Plant Fundamentals Ser.). (Illus.). 46p. (Orig.). 1995. student ed. 30.00 (*1-57431-009-7*) Tech Trng Systs.

Piping & Pipe Support Systems: Design & Engineering. 4th ed. R. P. Smith & T. Van Laan. 384p. 1987. 66.00 (*0-07-058931-3*) McGraw.

Piping Benchmark Problems for the Westinghouse AP600 Standardized Plant. P. Bezler. 327p. 1997. per. 30.00 (*0-16-062809-1*) USGPO.

Piping Components. (Principles of Steam Generation Ser.: Module 9). (Illus.). 100p. 1982. spiral bd. 35.00 (*0-87683-259-1*) GP Courseware.

Piping Design for Process Plants. Howard F. Rase. LC 89-24404. (Illus.). 312p. 1990. reprint ed. 73.00 (*0-89464-424-6*) Krieger.

Piping Design Handbook. John J. McKetta. (Illus.). 1280p. 1992. text 295.00 (*0-8247-8570-3*) Dekker.

Piping down the Valleys Wild. Nancy Larrick. (J). 1982. 10.60 (*0-606-03339-4*, Pub. by Turtleback) Demco.

Piping down the Valleys Wild: Poetry for the Young of All Ages. Nancy Larrick. 272p. (J). 1999. pap. 5.99 (*0-440-41582-9*) BDD Bks Young Read.

Piping, Flexibility & Stresses. Spiros D. Vinieratos & D. R. Zeno. LC 41-19398. 91p. reprint ed. pap. 30.00 (*0-608-30777-7*, 201525800098) Bks Demand.

Piping Guide: A Compact Reference for the Design & Drafting of Piping Systems. 2nd ed. David R. Sherwood & Dennis J. Whistance. (Illus.). 264p. 1991. 89.00 (*0-914082-19-1*) Syentek.

Piping Guide for Control Centers: ISA Standard RP60.9. 1981. pap. 25.00 (*0-87664-556-2*, RP60.9) ISA.

***Piping Handbook.** 7th ed. Mohinder L. Nayyar. 1999. pap. text 125.00 (*0-07-047106-1*, McGrw-H College) McGrw-H Hghr Educ.

Piping Practice for Refrigeration Applications. Stanley H. Aglow. LC 94-6360. 1994. pap. 14.95 (*0-912524-90-1*) Busn News.

Piping, Supports, & Structural Dynamics. Ed. by A. A. Dermenjian. (PVP Ser.: Vol. 264). 184p. 1993. 45.00 (*0-7918-0991-9*, H00823) ASME.

Piping Traditions of the North of Scotland. Bridget Mackenzie. 360p. 1998. pap. 30.00 (*0-85976-476-1*, Pub. by J Donald) St Mut.

Pippa. Betsy Brown. (Illus.). (J). (gr. 1-2). 1996. pap. write for info. (*1-888479-06-X*) Tarpley Pubng.

Pippa Mouse's House. Betty Boegehold. (J). 1998. lib. bdg. 7.99 (*0-679-99191-3*, Pub. by Random Bks Yng Read) Random.

Pippa Mouse's House. Betty Boeghold. 24p. (J). (ps-k). 1998. 1.99 (*0-679-89191-9*) Random.

Pippa on Pointe. H. Castor. (Illus.). (J). 1996. mass mkt. 7.95 (*0-340-65131-8*, Pub. by Hodder & Stought Ltd) Trafalgar.

Pippa Passes. large type ed. Rumer Godden. LC 94-41310. 229p. 1995. lib. bdg. 19.95 (*0-7862-0383-8*) Thorndike Pr.

Pippa's Puppy. Debbie MacKinnon. (Illus.). (J). (ps-k). 1997. bds. 4.99 (*0-614-28686-7*, Dial Yng Read) Peng Put Young Read.

Pippi Goes on Board. Astrid Lindgren. (Pippi Longstocking Ser.). 172p. (J). (gr. 3-5). 1980. lib. bdg. 25.95 (*0-89967-014-8*, Harmony Rain) Buccaneer Bks.

Pippi Goes on Board. Astrid Lindgren. (Pippi Longstocking Ser.). (Illus.). 144p. (J). (gr. 2-5). 1957. 14.99 (*0-670-55677-7*, Viking Child) Peng Put Young Read.

Pippi Goes on Board. Astrid Lindgren. LC 76-54740. (Pippi Longstocking Ser.). 144p. (J). (gr. 3-7). 1977. pap. 4.99 (*0-14-030959-4*, PuffinBks) Peng Put Young Read.

Pippi Goes on Board. Astrid Lindgren. (Pippi Longstocking Ser.). (J). (gr. 3-5). 1970. 9.09 (*0-606-04316-0*, Pub. by Turtleback) Demco.

Pippi Goes on Board. Astrid Lindgren. (Pippi Longstocking Ser.). 140p. (J). (gr. 3-5). pap. 3.99 (*0-8072-1401-9*) Listening Lib.

Pippi Goes to School. Astrid Lindgren. Tr. by Frances Lamborn. LC PZ7.L6585Pgf 1998. (Pippi Longstocking Ser.). (Illus.). 32p. (J). (gr. 3-5). 1998. 13.99 (*0-670-88075-2*) Viking Penguin.

***Pippi Goes to the Circus.** Astrid Lindgren. (Pippi Longstocking Ser.). (Illus.). 32p. (J). (ps-3). 2000. pap. 5.99 (*0-14-130243-7*, PuffinBks) Peng Put Young Read.

Pippi Goes to the Circus. Astrid Lindgren & Florence Lamborn. LC 98-8836. (Pippi Longstocking Ser.). (Illus.). 32p. (J). (ps-3). 1999. 13.99 (*0-670-88070-1*) Viking Penguin.

Pippi in the South Seas. Astrid Lindgren. Tr. by Gerry Bothmer. (Pippi Longstocking Ser.). (Illus.). 128p. (J). (gr. 2-5). 1959. 15.99 (*0-670-55711-0*, Viking Child) Peng Put Young Read.

Pippi in the South Seas. Astrid Lindgren. Tr. by Gerry Bothmer. LC 76-54802. (Pippi Longstocking Ser.). (Illus.). 128p. (J). (gr. 3-7). 1977. pap. 4.99 (*0-14-030958-6*, PuffinBks) Peng Put Young Read.

Pippi in the South Seas. Astrid Lindgren. (Pippi Longstocking Ser.). (J). (gr. 3-5). 1998. 18.50 (*0-8446-6974-1*) Peter Smith.

Pippi in the South Seas. Astrid Lindgren. (Pippi Longstocking Ser.). (J). (gr. 3-5). 1977. 9.09 (*0-606-04317-9*, Pub. by Turtleback) Demco.

Pippi in the South Seas. Astrid Lindgren. (Pippi Longstocking Ser.). 125p. (J). (gr. 3-5). pap. 3.99 (*0-8072-1392-6*) Listening Lib.

***Pippi Longstocking.** (Pippi Longstocking Ser.). (J). (gr. 3-5). 1999. 9.95 (*1-56137-036-3*) Novel Units.

Pippi Longstocking. Astrid Lindgren. Tr. by Florence Lamborn. LC 50-10396. (Pippi Longstocking Ser.). (Illus.). 158p. (J). (gr. 2-5). 1950. 15.99 (*0-670-55745-5*, Viking Child) Peng Put Young Read.

Pippi Longstocking. Astrid Lindgren. Tr. by Florence Lamborn. LC 77-1374. (Pippi Longstocking Ser.). (Illus.). 158p. (J). (gr. 3-7). 1977. pap. 4.99 (*0-14-030957-8*, PuffinBks) Peng Put Young Read.

Pippi Longstocking. Astrid Lindgren. (Pippi Longstocking Ser.). (J). (gr. 3-5). 1969. 9.09 (*0-606-04318-7*, Pub. by Turtleback) Demco.

Pippi Longstocking. Astrid Lindgren. (Pippi Longstocking Ser.). 160p. (J). (gr. 3-5). pap. 4.99 (*0-8072-1431-0*) Listening Lib.

Pippi Longstocking. Astrid Lindgren. (Pippi Longstocking Ser.). 192p. (J). (gr. 3-5). 1980. reprint ed. lib. bdg. 25.95 (*0-89967-013-X*, Harmony Rain) Buccaneer Bks.

Pippi Longstocking. unabridged ed. Astrid Lindgren. (Pippi Longstocking Ser.). (J). (gr. 3-5). 1990. audio 15.95 (*0-8072-7388-0*, YA 807 CXR) Listening Lib.

Pippi Longstocking: A Study Guide. Gloria Levine. (Novel-Ties Ser.). (J). (gr. 3-5). 1989. pap. text, teacher ed., student ed. 15.95 (*0-88122-050-7*) Lrn Links.

Pippi Longstocking Omnibus. Astrid Lindgren. (Pippi Longstocking Ser.). (Illus.). (J). 1997. write for info. (*0-614-29322-7*) Viking Penguin.

Pippi Longstocking's After-Christmas Party. Astrid Lindgren. (Pippi Longstocking Ser.). (Illus.). 32p. (J). (gr. k-3). 1998. pap. 5.99 (*0-14-056425-X*, PuffinBks) Peng Put Young Read.

Pippi Longstocking's After-Christmas Party. Astrid Lindgren. (Pippi Longstocking Ser.). (Illus.). 32p. (J). (gr. 3-5). 1996. 13.99 (*0-670-86790-X*) Viking Penguin.

***Pippi to the Rescue.** Astrid Lindgren. LC 99-56111. (Pippi Longstocking Ser.). (Illus.). 32p. (J). (ps-3). 2000. 13.99 (*0-670-88074-4*, Viking Child) Peng Put Young Read.

Pippin. Stephen Schwartz. 1995. pap. 13.95 (*0-89898-627-3*) Wrner Bros.

Pippin: Complete Vocal Score. Ed. by Dale Tucker. 260p. (Orig.). (C). 1988. pap. text 60.00 (*0-7692-0492-9*, EL03488) Wrner Bros.

***Pippin & the Bones.** unabridged ed. K. V. Johansen. (Pippin & Mabel Ser.). (Illus.). 32p. (J). (gr. k-2). 2000. pap. 12.95 (*1-55074-629-4*, Pub. by Kids Can Pr) Genl Dist Srvs.

Pippin Takes a Bath. K. V. Johansen & Bernice Lum. (Pippin & Mabel Ser.). 32p. (J). (gr. k-2). 1999. 12.95 (*1-55074-627-8*) Kids Can Pr.

Pippi's Extraordinary Ordinary Day. Astrid Lindgren. LC 99-26986. (Pippi Longstocking Ser.). (Illus.). 64p. (J). (ps-3). 1999. pap. 13.99 (*0-670-88073-6*, Viking Child) Peng Put Young Read.

Pippo: A Little Dog Finds a Home. Annette Langen. (Illus.). 40p. (J). (ps-3). 1995. 12.95 (*0-7892-0071-6*, Abbeville Kids) Abbeville Pr.

Pippo Gets Lost. Helen Oxenbury. (Tom & Pippo Ser.). (Illus.). 16p. (J). (ps). 1998. mass mkt. 4.99 (*0-689-81957-9*) S&S Childrens.

PIP's Freebie Guide: A Guide to Free & Inexpensive Publications, Products & Aids to Successful Completion of College or Career Training for Learning Disabled Youth. P. M. Fielding & M. E. Alexander. 1978. pap. 5.00 (*0-937660-06-X*) PIP.

Pip's Magic. Ellen S. Walsh. LC 93-34155. (Illus.). 32p. (J). (ps-3). 1994. 14.00 (*0-15-292850-2*) Harcourt.

Pip's Magic. Ellen S. Walsh. LC 93-34155. (Illus.). 32p. (J). 1999. pap. 6.00 (*0-15-201962-6*) Harcourt.

Pipsqueak! Maze School, 1. Patrick Merrell. (Read with Me Paperback Ser.). (Illus.). 32p. (ps-1). 1999. pap. text 3.25 (*0-590-03712-9*) Scholastic Inc.

Pipsqueaks! Maze Party. Patrick Merrell. 1999. pap. text 3.25 (*0-590-03713-7*) Scholastic Inc.

Pique, Vol. 2. Macmillan Staff. 1992. pap. 10.00 (*0-688-11974-3*, Wm Morrow) Morrow Avon.

Pique-Nique. European Language Institute Staff. (Raconte et Chante Ser.). (FRE., Illus.). 27p. (Orig.). (J). (gr. k-2). 1992. pap. 19.95 (*88-85148-67-0*, Pub. by Europ Lang Inst) Midwest European Pubns.

Pique-Niqueurs. (FRE.). (C). 1993. pap. 7.95 (*0-8442-1197-4*, VF1197-4) NTC Contemp Pub Co.

PIRA Guide to Wastepaper. Kate Cathie & David Guest. 134p. 1991. 65.00 (*0-902799-81-9*, Pub. by Pira Internatl) Bks Intl VA.

Pira Handbook of Statistical Sources see Marketing Information

Piracy - Days of Long Ago. 2nd rev. ed. Kenneth W. Mulder. Ed. by Sandra Mulder. (Illus.). 88p. 1998. reprint ed. per. 14.95 (*1-889034-03-7*) Mulder Ent.

Piracy & Counterfeiting: GATT TRIPS & Developing Countries, Vol. IEDL 5. Bankole Sodipo. LC 97-197520. 392p. 1997. 160.00 (*90-411-0947-1*) Kluwer Law Intl.

Piracy & Counterfeiting of Industrial Property & Copyright. Ed. by W. R. Cornish. 143p. 1983. pap. 26.00 (*0-903067-27-7*, Pub. by Brit Inst ICL) St Mut.

Piracy & Diplomacy in 17th Century North Africa: The Journal of Thomas Baker, English Consul in Tripoli, 1677-1685. Ed. by C. R. Pennell. LC 86-45999. (Illus.). 264p. 1989. 39.50 (*0-8386-3302-1*) Fairleigh Dickinson.

An Asterisk (*) at the beginning of an entry indicates that the title is appearing for the first time.

Piracy & the Decline of Venice, 1580-1615. Alberto Tenenti. LC 67-31956. (Illus.). 232p. reprint ed. pap. 72.00 (*0-608-18021-1*, 202906500058) Bks Demand.

Piracy & the English Government, 1616-1642. David D. Hebb. (Studies in Naval History). 300p. 1994. 86.95 (*0-85967-949-7*, Pub. by Scolar Pr) Ashgate Pub Co.

Piracy in the Ancient World. H. A. Ormerod. LC 96-44837. 286p. 1996. reprint ed. pap. text 15.95 (*0-8018-5505-5*) Johns Hopkins.

***Piracy in the Greeco-Roman World.** Philip De Souza. (Illus.). 292p. (C). 2000. text 59.95 (*0-521-48137-6*) Cambridge U Pr.

Piracy in the West Indies & Its Suppression. Francis B. Bradlee. (Illus.). 236p. 1990. reprint ed. pap. 12.00 (*0-87380-170-9*) Popular E Commerce.

Piracy of America: Profiteering in the Public Domain. Ed. by Judith Scherff. 278p. 1999. pap. 18.95 (*0-932863-28-0*) Clarity Pr.

Piradello: Plays. Luigi Pirandello. Tr. by Eric Bentley from ITA. LC 97-44195. (European Drama Classics Ser.). 200p. 1998. 16.95 (*0-8101-1652-9*) Northwestern U Pr.

Piraeus: From the Fifth to the First Century B. C. Robert Garland. LC 87-47596. 272p. (C). 1987. text 52.50 (*0-8014-2041-5*) Cornell U Pr.

Piramide Asesinada. Christian Jacq. 1998. pap. text 9.95 (*84-08-01996-1*) Planeta Edit.

Pirandellism & Samuel Beckett's Plays. Godwin O. Uwah. 145p. 1990. 28.00 (*0-916379-55-8*) Scripta.

Pirandello: Contemporary Perspectives. Ed. by Gian-Paolo Biasin & Manuela Gieri. (Toronto Italian Studies). 256p. 1998. text 45.00 (*0-8020-4387-9*) U of Toronto Pr.

Pirandello: Three Plays. Luigi Pirandello. 1999. pap. write for info. (*0-14-044646-X*) Viking Penguin.

Pirandello: 25 Essays on the Fiction & Plays of L. P. Jennifer Stone et al. (Review of National Literatures Ser.: Vol. 14). 1986. pap. 6.95 (*0-918680-27-1*) Griffon House.

Pirandello & Film. Nina Da Vinci Nichols & Jana O. Bazzoni. LC 94-32071. (Illus.). xxviii, 248p. 1995. text 55.00 (*0-8032-3336-1*) U of Nebr Pr.

Pirandello & His Muse: The Plays for Marta Abba. Daniela Bini. LC 97-33089. (Crosscurrents Ser.). 248p. 1998. 49.95 (*0-8130-1548-0*) U Press Fla.

Pirandello & the Crisis of Modern Consciousness. Anthony Caputi. LC 87-10801. 184p. 1988. text 24.95 (*0-252-01468-5*) U of Ill Pr.

Pirandello & the Crisis of Modern Consciousness. fac. ed. Anthony F. Caputi. LC 87-10801. 183p. 1988. pap. 56.80 (*0-7837-7610-1*, 204736200007) Bks Demand.

Pirandello & the Vagaries of Knowledge: A Reading of Il fu Mattia Pascal. Donatella Stocchi-Perucchio. (Stanford French & Italian Studies: Vol. 64). 160p. 1991. pap. 56.50 (*0-915838-82-6*) Anma Libri.

Pirandello's in Performance. Felicity Firth. (Theatre in Focus Ser.). 1990. pap. incl. sl. (*0-85964-201-1*) Chadwyck-Healey.

Pirandello's Love Letters to Marta Abba. Luigi Pirandello. Ed. & Tr. by Benito Ortolani from ENG. LC 93-38617. (ITA.). 440p. 1994. text 39.50 (*0-691-03499-0*, Pub. by Princeton U Pr) Cal Prin Full Svc.

Pirandello's Theater: The Recovery of the Modern Stage for Dramatic Art. Anne Paolucci. Ed. by Harry T. Moore. LC 73-20324. (Crosscurrents-Modern Critiques Ser.). 159p. 1974. 12.00 (*0-8093-0594-1*) Griffon House.

Piranesi. Pierre Seghers. Tr. & Intro. by Ian Higgins. (Illus.). 57p. 1993. pap. 14.95 (*1-85610-021-9*, Pub. by Forest Bks) Dufour.

Piranesi: Catalogue Raisonne of the Etchings. Henri Focillon. (FRE.). 76p. 1964. pap. 40.00 (*1-55660-162-X*) A Wofsy Fine Arts.

Piranesi: Early Architectural Fantasies: A Catalog Raisonne of the Etchings. Andrew Robison. (Illus.). x, 206p. 1996. pap. text 48.00 (*0-226-72320-8*, 72319-4) U Ch Pr.

Piranesi As Architect & Designer. John Wilton-Ely. (Illus.). 166p. 1993. 40.00 (*0-87598-099-6*) Pierpont Morgan.

Piranesi as Architect & Designer. John Wilton-Ely. (Illus.). 192p. 1993. 47.50 (*0-300-05382-7*) Yale U Pr.

Piranesi Giovanni Battista Varie Vedute di Roma 1748 & Aleune Vedute di Archi Trionfali 1765, 2 vol. in 1. fac. ed. (GER & ITA., Illus.). 136p. 1974. 95.00 (*1-55660-172-7*) A Wofsy Fine Arts.

Piranesi's Carcerci: Sources of Invention. William L. MacDonald. (Illus.). 18p. (Orig.). (C). 1979. pap. 5.00 (*1-880269-01-5*) D H Sheehan.

***Piranesi's Dream.** Gerhard Kopf. Tr. by Leslie Willson. LC 99-87741. 2000. 22.50 (*0-8076-1473-4*) Braziller.

Piranha Firing Point, 1 vols., Vol. 1. Michael Dimercurio. 1999. mass mkt. 6.99 (*0-451-40876-4*) NAL.

Piranhas. Mary Berendes. LC 97-31355. (Illus.). 32p. (J). 1998. lib. bdg. 22.79 (*1-56766-493-8*) Childs World.

Piranhas. Susan Grossman. LC 93-1772. (Remarkable Animals Ser.). (Illus.). 60p. (YA). (gr. 5 up). 1994. lib. bdg. 13.95 (*0-87518-593-2*) Silver Burdett Pr.

Piranhas. Susan Grossman. (Illus.). 60p. (J). (gr. 4-7). 1996. pap. text 5.95 (*0-382-39482-8*) Silver Burdett Pr.

Piranhas. Elaine Landau. LC 98-16117. (Animals Ser.). (Illus.). 47p. (J). 1999. 21.50 (*0-516-20673-7*) Childrens.

Piranhas. Elaine Landau. (True Bks.). (Illus.). 48p. (gr. 2-4). 1999. lib. bdg. 6.95 (*0-516-26498-2*) Childrens.

Piranhas. Emily McAuliffe. (Dangerous Animals Ser.). (Illus.). 48p. (J). (gr. 3-7). 1997. lib. bdg. 19.00 (*0-531-11471-6*, Rivr Front Bks) Capstone Pr.

Piranhas. Emily McAuliffe. LC 97-8317. (Dangerous Creatures Ser.). (Illus.). 48p. (J). 1998. lib. bdg. write for info. (*1-56065-620-4*) Capstone Pr.

Piranhas. George Myers. 128p. 11.95 (*0-87666-771-X*, M539) TFH Pubns.

Piranhas. Manolito Pinkguni. LC 98-23989. (Fish Ser.). (Illus.). 64p. (YA). (gr. 3 up). 1999. lib. bdg. 17.95 (*0-7910-5093-9*) Chelsea Hse.

Piranhas. Harold Robbins. 1986. write for info. (*0-318-60976-2*) S&S Trade.

Piranhas. Harold Robbins. 1994. per. 6.99 (*0-671-87494-2*) S&S Trade.

Piranhas: Everything about Origins, Care, Feeding, Diseases, Breeding & Behavior. David H. Schleser. LC 96-37938. (Complete Pet Owner's Manual Ser.). (Illus.). 96p. 1997. 6.95 (*0-8120-9916-8*) Barron.

Piranhas & Other Wonders of the Jungle. Querida L. Pearce. (Amazing Science Ser.). (Illus.). 64p. (J). (gr. 4-6). 1990. pap. 5.95 (*0-671-70690-X*, Julian Messner) Silver Burdett Pr.

Piranhas; Fact & Fiction. John R. Quinn. (Illus.). 128p. 1992. 23.95 (*0-86622-172-7*, TS-172) TFH Pubns.

Piranhas in the Aquarium. Wolfgang Schulte. (Illus.). 128p. 1988. lib. bdg. 17.95 (*0-86622-950-7*, TS 117) TFH Pubns.

Piranhas, Keeping & Breeding Them in Captivity: Keeping & Breeding Them in Captivity. Manolito Pinkguni. (Illus.). 64p. 1996. pap. 6.95 (*0-7938-0363-2*, RE614) TFH Pubns.

Pirate. Deni Bown. (Ultimate Sticker Books Ser.). (Illus.). 20p. (J). (gr. k-7). 1997. pap. 6.95 (*0-7894-1527-5*) DK Pub Inc.

Pirate. DK Publishing Staff. 1999. 9.95 (*0-7894-4276-0*) DK Pub Inc.

Pirate. Jayne Ann Krentz. (Mira Bks.). 1998. per. 6.99 (*1-55166-437-2*, 1-66437-4, Mira Bks) Harlequin Bks.

Pirate. Connie Mason. 400p. 1998. mass mkt. 5.99 (*0-8439-4456-0*, Leisure Bks) Dorchester Pub Co.

***Pirate.** Richard Platt. (Eyewitness Books). (Illus.). (J). (gr. 4-7). 2000. 19.99 (*0-7894-6608-2*) DK Pub Inc.

***Pirate.** Richard Platt. (Eyewitness Books). (Illus.). (J). (gr. 4-7). 2000. 15.95 (*0-7894-6024-6*) DK Pub Inc.

Pirate. Richard Platt. (Illus.). (J). 1995. 19.00 (*0-679-87255-8*) Knopf.

Pirate. Harold Robbins. 1993. per. 6.99 (*0-671-87493-4*) PB.

Pirate. Barry Sadler. (Casca: No. 15). 176p. 1987. mass mkt. 3.99 (*0-515-09599-0*, Jove) Berkley Pub.

Pirate. Sir Walter Scott. 152p. 1996. pap. 20.00 (*81-209-0027-8*, Pub. by Pitambar Pub) St Mut.

***Pirate.** rev. ed. Ivan Bulloch. (I Wish I Were Ser.). (Illus.). (J). 2000. 9.95 (*1-58728-034-5*); pap. 4.95 (*1-58728-038-8*) Two Can Pub.

Pirate see Works of Sir Walter Scott

Pirate: An I Can Read Book. Daniel Laurence. (Illus.). 64p. (J). (ps-3). 14.95 (*0-06-028956-2*); 14.89 (*0-06-028957-0*) HarpC Child Bks.

Pirate Affair. deluxe ed. Author22 Publishing Staff. LC 98-96142. 300p. 1999. pap. 19.95 (*1-892183-03-X*) DTTN.

Pirate & His Lady. Linda L. Chaikin. LC 97-147217. (Buccaneers Ser.: No. 2). 384p. 1997. pap. 11.99 (*0-8024-1072-3*, 251) Moody.

Pirate & the Pagan. Virginia Henley. 464p. 1990. mass mkt. 6.50 (*0-440-20623-5*) Dell.

Pirate & the Pig. Frank Rodgers. (Illus.). 32p. (J). pap. 9.95 (*0-14-055561-7*, Pub. by Pnguin Bks Ltd) Trafalgar.

Pirate & Treasure Dingbats Book. Carole Marsh. (Carole Marsh Dingbats Bks.). (Illus.). (J). (gr. 3-12). 1994. pap. 19.95 (*0-7933-5408-0*); lib. bdg. 29.95 (*0-7933-5407-2*); disk 29.95 (*0-7933-5409-9*) Gallopade Intl.

Pirate Bride. Elizabeth August. (Historical Ser.: No. 730). 1992. mass mkt. 3.99 (*0-373-28730-5*, 1-28730-9) Harlequin Bks.

Pirate Candy Treasure. Catherine McCafferty. (Illus.). 10p. (J). (gr. k-2). 1998. bds. 6.99 (*1-57151-607-7*, Nibble Me Bks) Picture Me Bks.

***Pirate Chase.** 2nd ed. Earl Schenck Miers. (YA). 1998. pap. 4.95 (*0-87935-203-5*) Colonial Williamsburg.

***Pirate Cookbook.** Victoria Sauers. 48p. 2000. 4.25 (*0-9666294-3-4*) Blue Bear Pr.

Pirate Galleon. Fred Finney. (Mystery History Ser.). (Illus.). 32p. (J). (gr. 4-6). 1996. 10.95 (*0-7613-0502-5*, Copper Beech Bks); lib. bdg. 23.90 (*0-7613-0496-7*, Copper Beech Bks) Millbrook Pr.

Pirate Ghost (Dreamscape) Laura Pender. (Intrigue Ser.). 1996. per. 3.75 (*0-373-22368-4*, 1-22368-4) Harlequin Bks.

Pirate in My Arms. Danelle Harmon. 416p. (Orig.). 1992. mass mkt. 4.50 (*0-380-76675-2*, Avon Bks) Morrow Avon.

***Pirate Joke & Fun Book.** Shoo Rayner. (Illus.). 96p. (J). 1999. pap. 5.95 (*0-14-037518-X*, Pub. by Pnguin Bks Ltd) Trafalgar.

***Pirate Looks at Fifty.** Jimmy Buffett. 2000. pap. 14.00 (*0-449-00586-0*) Ballantine Pub Grp.

***Pirate Looks at Fifty.** Jimmy Buffett. 420p. 1999. mass mkt. 7.99 (*0-449-22334-5*, Crest) Fawcett.

Pirate Looks at Fifty. Jimmy Buffett. LC 98-10853. 385p. 1998. 24.95 (*0-679-43527-1*) Random.

Pirate Looks at Fifty. large type ed. Jimmy Buffett. LC 97-51827. 1998. pap. 24.95 (*0-375-70288-1*) Random.

Pirate Lord. Sabrina Jeffries. 384p. 1998. mass mkt. 5.99 (*0-380-79747-X*, Avon Bks) Morrow Avon.

Pirate McGrew & His Nautical Crew. Philip Hawthorn. (Rhyming Stories Ser.). (Illus.). 24p. (J). (gr. 2-5). 1995. text 4.95 (*0-7460-1646-8*, Usborne) EDC.

Pirate McGrew & His Nautical Crew. Philip Hawthorn. (Rhyming Stories Ser.). (Illus.). 24p. (J). (gr. 2 up). 1995. lib. bdg. 12.95 (*0-88110-778-6*, Usborne) EDC.

Pirate Moon. Peg Sutherland. 1994. per. 3.50 (*0-373-70599-9*, 1-70599-5) Harlequin Bks.

Pirate Novels: Fictions of Nation-Building in Spanish America. Nina Gerassi-Navarro. LC 99-25491. 256p. 1999. pap. 17.95 (*0-8223-2393-1*) Duke.

***Pirate Novels: Fictions of Nation Building in Spanish America.** Nina Gerassi-Navarro. LC 99-25491. (Illus.). 256p. 1999. 49.95 (*0-8223-2360-5*) Duke.

Pirate of Her Own. Kinley MacGregor. 320p. 1999. mass mkt. 5.99 (*0-06-108711-4*) HarpC.

Pirate of the Plains: Adventures with Prairie Falcons in the High Desert. Bruce A. Haak. 1995. pap. 19.95 (*0-88839-306-7*) Hancock House.

Pirate of Topsail Island. Lew Wallace. LC 97-93371. 80p. (Orig.). (J). (gr. 1-6). 1997. pap. 5.95 (*1-889062-05-7*) Artel.

Pirate Prince. Gaelen Foley. 1998. mass mkt. 5.99 (*0-449-00247-0*, Crest) Fawcett.

Pirate Princess see Princesa Pirata

Pirate Princess. Suzanne Simms. 1994. per. 2.99 (*0-373-05862-4*, 5-05862-3) Harlequin Bks.

Pirate Queen. Emily Arnold McCully. LC 94-5389. (Illus.). 32p. (J). (ps-3). 1995. 16.95 (*0-399-22657-5*, G P Putnam) Peng Put Young Read.

Pirate Queen. Emily Arnold McCully. (Illus.). 32p. (J). (gr. k-3). 1998. pap. 6.99 (*0-698-11629-1*, PapStar) Peng Put Young Read.

Pirate Queen. Emily Arnold McCully. 1998. 12.19 (*0-606-13709-2*, Pub. by Turtleback) Demco.

***Pirate Radio & Video.** Newton C. Braga. 304p. 2000. pap. 29.95 (*0-7506-7331-1*, Newnes) Buttrwrth-Heinemann.

Pirate Radio Stations: Tune-in Underground Broadcasts. Andrew Yoder. (Illus.). 192p. 1989. pap. 12.95 (*0-8306-3268-9*) McGraw-Hill Prof.

Pirate Rock. David Walker. 236p. reprint ed. lib. bdg. 19.95 (*0-88411-870-3*) Amereon Ltd.

Pirate (Rogues) Kate Hoffmann. (Temptation Ser.). 1996. per. 3.50 (*0-373-25677-9*, 1-25677-5) Harlequin Bks.

Pirate School. Cathy E. Dubowski & Mark Dubowski. LC 95-23241. (All Aboard Reading Ser.: Level 2). (Illus.). 48p. (J). (gr. 1-3). 1996. pap. 3.95 (*0-448-41132-6*, G & D) Peng Put Young Read.

Pirate School. Cathy East Dubowski. (All Aboard Reading Ser.). (J). 1996. 9.15 (*0-606-11751-2*, Pub. by Turtleback) Demco.

Pirate Ship. Peter Tonkin. 608p. 1997. pap. 11.95 (*0-7472-4741-2*, Pub. by Headline Bk Pub) Trafalgar.

Pirate Ship: Black Shield. 1992. write for info. (*1-881466-29-9*) Old Ivory Coast.

Pirate Strikes Again. Lew Wallace. 80p. (J). (gr. 3-7). 1998. pap. 5.95 (*1-889062-06-5*) Artel.

Pirate the Seal. Brenda Jobling. LC 97-49356. (Animal Tales Ser.). (Illus.). 131p. (J). (gr. 3-7). 1998. pap. 3.95 (*0-7641-0601-5*) Barron.

Pirate the Seal. Brenda Jobling. (Animal Tales Ser.). 1998. 9.05 (*0-606-13710-6*, Pub. by Turtleback) Demco.

***Pirate Treasure.** Edi Brown. ii, 232p. (YA). (gr. 5-10). 2000. 5.95 (*0-9677953-0-3*) Red Fox OR.

Pirate Treasure. Kris Jamsa. (Happy & Max Ser.). 64p. 1998. 18.95 incl. cd-rom (*1-884133-88-6*, Jamsa Press) Gulf Pub.

Pirate Treasure Mazes. Dave Phillips. 48p. pap. 2.95 (*0-486-27049-1*) Dover.

Pirate Uncle. Margaret Mahy. (Illus.). 128p. (J). (gr. 3-7). 1994. 14.95 (*0-87951-555-4*, Pub. by Overlook Pr) Penguin Putnam.

Pirate Utopias: Moorish Corsairs & European Renegadoes. Peter L. Wilson. 208p. Date not set. 7.00 (*1-57027-024-4*) Autonomedia.

Pirates. Dina Anastasio. LC 96-17597. (All Aboard Bks.). (Illus.). 32p. (J). (ps-3). 1997. pap. 2.95 (*0-448-41494-5*, G & D) Peng Put Young Read.

Pirates. Dina Anastasio. LC 96-17597. (Grosset & Dunlap All Aboard Bks.). 1997. 8.15 (*0-606-11752-0*, Pub. by Turtleback) Demco.

***Pirates.** Ed. by Anness Publishing Staff. (Discovery Ser.). (Illus.). (J). 1999. 12.95 (*0-7548-0208-6*, Lorenz Bks) Anness Pub.

***Pirates.** Gary L. Blackwood. LC 99-86674. (Bad Guys Ser.). 2001. lib. bdg. write for info. (*0-7614-1019-8*, Benchmark NY) Marshall Cavendish.

Pirates. Chrystine Brouillet. (Novels in the Roman Jeunesse Ser.). (FRE.). 96p. (J). (gr. 4-7). 1992. pap. 8.95 (2-89021-180-0, Pub. by La Courte Ech) Firefly Bks Ltd.

Pirates. Daniel Defoe & Harry Knill. (Illus.). 64p. 1975. pap. 5.95 (*0-88388-027-X*) Bellerophon Bks.

Pirates. Lawrence Drechsler. LC 85-52401. (Illus.). (Orig.). (J). (gr. 6 up). pap. write for info. (*0-935143-01-7*) Treadle Pr.

Pirates. Charles Johnson. 608p. 1999. pap. 22.95 (*1-871592-36-4*, Pub. by Creation Books) Subterranean Co.

Pirates. Bobbie Kalman & Greg Nickles. LC 97-2240. (Illus.). 32p. (J). (ps-3). 1997. pap. text 5.95 (*0-86505-733-8*) Crabtree Pub Co.

Pirates. Bobbie Kalman & Greg Nickles. LC 97-2240. (Illus.). 32p. (J). (ps-3). 1997. lib. bdg. 19.96 (*0-86505-633-1*) Crabtree Pub Co.

Pirates. Lamm. LC 98-52662. 32p. (J). 2000. 10.45 (*0-7868-0392-4*, Pub. by Hyperion); lib. bdg. 15.49 (*0-7868-2343-7*, Pub. by Hyperion) Little.

Pirates, 1 vol. Sonja Lamut. (J). (ps-2). 1999. pap. text 4.99 (*0-448-41988-2*) Putnam Pub Group.

Pirates. Linda Lael Miller. 336p. 1996. per. 6.50 (*0-671-87316-4*, PB Trade Paper) PB.

Pirates. Greg Nickles. (Crabapples Ser.). 1996. 11.15 (*0-606-12793-3*, Pub. by Turtleback) Demco.

***Pirates.** Will And Ma Osborne. (J). 2001. 11.99 (*0-375-90299-6*) Random.

***Pirates.** Will And Ma Osborne. (J). 2001. mass mkt. 4.99 (*0-375-80299-1*, Pub. by Random Bks Yng Read) Random.

Pirates. Stewart Ross. LC 94-43659. (Fact or Fiction Ser.). 1995. 12.15 (*0-606-09253-6*, Pub. by Turtleback) Demco.

***Pirates.** Matt Silverman. (Total Baseball Companions Ser.). 96p. 2000. mass mkt. 2.50 (*1-892129-74-4*) Total Sprts.

***Pirates!** David Spence. (Illus.). 24p. (gr. 5-8). 1999. text. write for info. (*0-7881-6469-4*) DIANE Pub.

Pirates. Scott Steedman. LC 95-46730. (Illus.). (J). 1996. lib. bdg. 23.00 (*0-531-14403-8*) Watts.

Pirates. Scott Steedman. (Worldwise Ser.). 40p. (J). 1997. pap. 7.00 (*0-531-15297-9*) Watts.

Pirates. Philip Steele. LC 96-34542. (Illus.). 64p. (J). (gr. 3-7). 1997. 16.95 (*0-7534-5052-6*) LKC.

***Pirates.** Phillip Steele. (Illus.). 64p. (J). (gr. 3-7). 2000. pap. 10.95 (*0-7534-5298-7*, Kingfisher) LKC.

Pirates. large type ed. Linda Lael Miller. LC 95-34858. (Large Print Bks.). 1995. 24.95 (*1-56895-249-X*, Compass) Wheeler Pub.

Pirates!, 67. Osprey. 1999. pap. text 14.95 (*1-85532-837-2*) Osprey.

Pirates: Adventurers of the High Seas. David F. Marley. (Illus.). 160p. 1996. 29.95 (*1-85409-215-4*, Pub. by Arms & Armour) Sterling.

Pirates! Brigands, Buccaneers, & Privateers in Fact, Fiction & Legend. Jan Rogozinski. LC 94-12717. 432p. 1995. 50.00 (*0-8160-2761-7*) Facts on File.

Pirates! Brigands, Buccaneers, & Privateers in Fact, Fiction, & Legend - An A-Z Encyclopedia. Jan Rogozinski. LC 96-11351. (Illus.). 416p. 1996. pap. 19.95 (*0-306-80722-X*) Da Capo.

Pirates: Fact & Fiction. David Cordingly & John Falconer. (Illus.). 128p. 1993. 15.98 (*0-89660-034-3*, Artabras) Abbeville Pr.

Pirates: New Method Supplementary Series see New Method Supplementary Readers

Pirates! Puzzles, Jokes, & Things to Make & Do. Cathy Gale. (Illus.). 32p. (J). (ps-3). 1994. pap. 2.99 (*1-56402-406-7*) Candlewick Pr.

Pirates: Raiders of the High Seas. Christopher Maynard. LC 98-20850. (Eyewitness Readers). 48p. (J). (gr. 2-4). Date not set. 3.95 (*0-7894-3443-1*) DK Pub Inc.

Pirates: Raiders of the High Seas. Christopher Maynard. LC 98-20850. (Eyewitness Readers). 48p. (J). (gr. 2-4). 1998. 12.95 (*0-7894-3768-6*) DK Pub Inc.

Pirates: Robbers of the High Seas. Gail Gibbons. LC 92-18375. (Illus.). 32p. (J). (gr. k-3). 1993. 15.95 (*0-316-30975-3*) Little.

Pirates: Robbers of the High Seas. Gail Gibbons. 32p. (ps-3). 1999. pap. 4.95 (*0-316-30660-6*) Little.

Pirates: The Story of Buccaneers, Brigands, Corsairs & Their Piracy on the High Seas from the Spanish Main to the China Sea. Stewart Ross. (Fact or Fiction Ser.). (Illus.). 48p. (YA). (gr. 5 up). 1995. pap. 7.95 (*1-56294-637-4*, Copper Beech Bks) Millbrook Pr.

Pirates Ahoy! Illus. by Jim Auckland. (Doodle Art Mini Tubes Ser.). (J). (gr. k up). 1997. pap. 6.95 (*0-8431-6563-4*, Price Stern) Peng Put Young Read.

***Pirates Ahoy!** Hilary McKay. (Illus.). 32p. (J). (ps-3). 2000. 16.00 (*0-689-83114-5*) McElderry Bks.

Pirates Ahoy!, 1, 13. Franklin W. Dixon. (Hardy Boys Are: The Clues Brothers Ser.: No. 13). (Illus.). 80p. (J). (gr. 2-4). 1999. pap. 3.99 (*0-671-02786-7*) PB.

Pirates & Buccaneers Coloring Book. Peter F. Copeland. (Illus.). (J). (gr. k-3). 1977. pap. 2.95 (*0-486-23393-6*) Dover.

Pirates & Buried Treasure on Florida Islands. rev. ed. Jack Beater. LC 65-1579. (Illus.). 118p. 1959. pap. 4.95 (*0-8200-1019-7*) Great Outdoors.

Pirates & Emperors. Noam Chomsky. 206p. 1996. 48.99 (*1-895431-21-2*, Pub. by Black Rose); pap. 19.99 (*1-895431-20-4*, Pub. by Black Rose) Consort Bk Sales.

Pirates & Emperors: International Terrorism in the Real World. Noam Chomsky. 175p. (Orig.). pap. 8.95 (*0-912439-06-8*) Amana Bks.

Pirates & Patriots of the Revolution. Keith C. Wilbur. LC 96-42335. (Illustrated Living History Ser.). 112p. (YA). (gr. 5 up). 1996. lib. bdg. 19.95 (*0-7910-4530-7*) Chelsea Hse.

Pirates & Patriots of the Revolution: An Illustrated Encyclopedia of Colonial Seamanship. C. Keith Wilbur. LC 84-13776. (Illustrated Living History Ser.). Orig. Title: Picture Book of the Revolution's Privateers. (Illus.). 96p. 1984. pap. 14.95 (*0-87106-866-4*) Globe Pequot.

Pirates & Privateers. (Star Wars Ser.). 18.00 (*0-87431-294-9*, 40143) West End Games.

Pirates & Privateers: New Perspectives on the War on Trade in the Eighteenth & Nineteenth Centuries. Ed. by David J. Starkey et al. 272p. 1997. 70.00 (*0-85989-481-9*) Univ Exeter Pr.

Pirates & Privateers of the Americas: An Illustrated Encyclopedia. David F. Marley. LC 94-31348. 458p. 1994. lib. bdg. 75.00 (*0-87436-751-4*) ABC-CLIO.

Pirates & Privateers of the Caribbean. Jenifer Marx. 320p. (C). 1992. 32.50 (*0-89464-483-1*); pap. 23.50 (*0-89464-633-8*) Krieger.

Pirates & Seafaring Swashbucklers on the Hollywood Screen: Plots, Critiques, Casts & Credits for 137 Theatrical & Made-for-Television Releases. James R. Parish. LC 94-24197. 240p. 1995. lib. bdg. 43.50 (*0-89950-935-5*) McFarland & Co.

***Pirates & Treasure.** Michael Kramme. (Illus.). 80p. 1998. pap. text 9.95 (*1-58037-035-7*, Pub. by M Twain Media) Carson-Dellos.

Pirates & Treasure. Saviour Pirotta. LC 94-48746. (Remarkable World Ser.). (Illus.). 48p. (YA). (gr. 3-8). lib. bdg. 24.26 (*1-56847-366-4*) Raintree Steck-V.

Pirates & Treasure: The Remarkable World. Saviour Pirotta. 1997. 24.25 (*0-8172-4820-X*) Raintree Steck-V.

Pirate's Cookbook. Carole Marsh. (Naked Gourmet Ser.). (Orig.). 1997. 29.95 (*1-55609-002-1*) Gallopade Intl.

Pirate's Cove: Paint with Water. Disney Staff. (Walt Disney's Peter Pan Ser.). (Illus.). (J). 1998. pap. text 1.79 (*0-307-27000-9*, 27000, Goldn Books) Gldn Bks Pub Co.

Pirate's Daughter. Robert Girardi. 336p. 1997. pap. 11.95 (*0-385-31952-5*) Doubleday.

Pirate's Daughter. large type ed. Robert Girardi. (Basic Ser.). 545p. 1997. 23.95 (*0-7862-1057-5*) Thorndike Pr.

P

An Asterisk (*) at the beginning of an entry indicates that the title is appearing for the first time.

Pirates Don't Wear Pink Sunglasses. Debbie Dadey & Marcia Thornton Jones. (Adventures of the Bailey School Kids Ser.: No. 9). 80p. (J). (gr. 4-7). 1994. pap. 3.50 (*0-590-47298-4*) Scholastic Inc.

Pirates Don't Wear Pink Sunglasses. Debbie Dadey & Marcia Thornton Jones. (Adventures of the Bailey School Kids Ser.: No. 9). (J). (gr. 2-4). 1994. 8.70 (*0-606-06671-3*, Pub. by Turtleback) Demco.

Pirate's Feast. Created by Mark Icanberry. (Look, Learn & Do Ser.). (Illus.). 48p. (J). 2000. 14.95 (*1-893327-02-7*) Look-Learn-Do Pubns.

Pirate's Handbook. Margarette Lincoln. (Illus.). (J). 15.99 (*0-590-24558-9*) Scholastic Inc.

Pirate's Handbook. Margarette Lincoln. (Puffin Book Ser.). 1998. 12.19 (*0-606-13711-4*, Pub. by Turtleback) Demco.

Pirate's Hostage. Eleanor Rees. (Presents Ser.: No. 452). 1992. per. 2.89 (*0-373-11452-4*, 1-11452-9) Harlequin Bks.

Pirates in Petticoats. Terri Sprenger. (J). 1996. lib. bdg. write for info. (*0-679-97645-0*, Bullseye Bks) Random Bks Yng Read.

Pirates Island. John E. Chaparro. 170p. 2000. pap. 11.95 (*1-891929-32-1*) Four Seasons.

Pirate's Life for Me! Julie Thompson & Brownie Macintosh. (Illus.). (J). 1996. pap. 13.95 incl. audio (*0-88106-835-7*) Charlesbridge Pub.

Pirate's Life for Me! A Day Aboard a Pirate Ship. Julie Thompson & Brownie Macintosh. LC 95-36169. (Illus.). 32p. (J). (ps-3). 1996. 15.95 (*0-88106-932-9*); pap. 6.95 (*0-88106-931-0*) Charlesbridge Pub.

Pirate's Love. Johanna Lindsey. LC 96-54265. (Star-Romance Ser.). 373p. 1997. 23.95 (*0-7862-0953-4*) Five Star.

Pirate's Love. Johanna Lindsey. 384p. 1978. mass mkt. 6.99 (*0-380-40048-0*, Avon Bks) Morrow Avon.

Pirate's Love. large type ed. Johanna Lindsey. LC 96-12830. 1996. 25.95 (*0-7862-0724-8*) Thorndike Pr.

Pirates of Bat Cave Island. Burton Albert. (Illus.). 24p. (J). 1997. per. 12.95 (*0-689-81284-1*) S&S Childrens.

Pirates of Colonial North Carolina. Hugh F. Rankin. (Illus.). viii, 72p. 1998. reprint ed. pap. 8.00 (*0-86526-100-8*) NC Archives.

Pirates of Doom: A Choose-Your-Challenge Gamebook. Patrick Burston. LC 95-46002. (Candlewick Gamebks.). (Illus.). 48p. (Orig.). (J). (gr. k-3). 1996. pap. 5.99 (*1-56402-855-0*) Candlewick Pr.

Pirates of Malabar & an Englishwoman in India Two Hundred Years Ago. John Biddulph. (C). 1995. reprint ed. 34.00 (*81-206-0919-0*, Pub. by Asian Educ Servs) S Asia.

Pirates of Penzance. (Vocal Score Ser.). 1986. pap. 13.95 (*0-88188-726-9*, 50337530) H Leonard.

Pirates of Penzance: Children's Edition. Gilbert & Sullivan. 1990. 5.95 (*0-685-32070-7*, E8495) Hansen Ed Mus.

Pirates of Penzance: Vocal Score with Dialogue the Slave of Duty. A. Sullivan. 220p. 1986. per. 13.95 (*0-7935-2586-1*, 50337530) H Leonard.

Pirates of Penzance Chorus Parts. Gilbert & Sullivan. 64p. 1986. pap. 5.95 (*0-7935-5361-X*, 50337650) H Leonard.

Pirates of Penzance: or A Slave to Duty. William S. Gilbert. Ed. by William-Alan Landes. LC 97-23703. 55p. 1997. pap. 10.00 (*0-88734-729-0*) Players Pr.

Pirates of Tarutao. Paul Adirex. 246p. 1995. 24.95 (*974-89020-2-1*, Pub. by Aries Bks); pap. 17.95 (*974-88992-9-2*, Pub. by Aries Bks) Weatherhill.

***Pirates of the Carolinas.** Terrance Zepke. (Illus.). 2000. pap. write for info. (*1-56164-205-3*) Pineapple Pr.

Pirates of the New England Coast, 1630-1730. George F. Dow & John Edmonds. (Illus.). 512p. 1993. pap. 15.00 (*0-87380-179-2*) Popular E Commerce.

Pirates of the New England Coast, 1630-1730. George F. Dow & John H. Edmonds. (Illus.). 1968. reprint ed. 30.00 (*0-87266-008-7*) Argosy.

Pirates of the New England Coast, 1630-1730. unabridged ed. George F. Dow & John H. Edmonds. (Illus.). 480p. 1996. reprint ed. pap. 11.95 (*0-486-29064-6*) Dover.

Pirates of the Pacific, 1575-1742. Peter Gerhard. LC 90-33807. 274p. 1960. reprint ed. pap. 85.00 (*0-608-07997-9*, 206796200012) Bks Demand.

Pirates of the Range. large type ed. B. M. Bower. 1998. 18.95 (*1-57490-156-7*, Sagebrush LP West) T T Beeler.

Pirates of the South China Coast, 1790-1810. Dian H. Murray. LC 87-10049. (Illus.). 256p. 1987. 39.50 (*0-8047-1376-6*) Stanford U Pr.

Pirates of the Spring. Forrest Reid. LC 76-145255. 1971. reprint ed. 24.00 (*0-403-01170-1*) Scholarly.

Pirates of the Thunder. Jack L. Chalker. (Rings of the Master Ser.: Bk. 2). (Orig.). 1987. mass mkt. 5.99 (*0-345-32561-3*, Del Rey) Ballantine Pub Grp.

Pirates of the Universe. Terry Bisson. 1997. pap. 12.95 (*0-312-86295-4*) St Martin.

Pirates of the Universe. Terry Bisson. 1997. pap. 12.95 (*0-614-27318-8*) Tor Bks.

Pirates of the Virgin Islands: Mavericks in Paradise, 2 bks. in 1. Fritz Seyfarth. 80p. 9.95 (*0-944428-15-0*) F Papy Cruising Guide.

Pirates of the West Indies. Clinton Black. (Illus.). 144p. (C). 1989. pap. text 17.95 (*0-521-35818-3*) Cambridge U Pr.

Pirates on Our River. Anne Zinsser. LC 97-41988. (Illus.). (J). (gr. 3-5). 1998. pap. 5.95 (*0-933951-77-9*) Locust Hill Pr.

Pirates on the Chesapeake: Being a True History of Pirates, Picaroons, & Sea Raiders on Chesapeake Bay, 1610-1807. Donald G. Shomette. LC 85-40532. (Illus.). 352p. 1985. 22.95 (*0-87033-343-7*, Tidewtr Pubs) Cornell Maritime.

Pirates on the High Seas: Why the Unites States Cares about Global Intellectual Property Rights & What It Can Do about Them. Benedicte Callan. 1998. pap. 5.00 (*0-87609-219-9*) Coun Foreign.

Pirates' Own Book: Authentic Narratives of the Lives, Exploits, & Executions of the Most Celebrated Sea Robbers. Charles Ellms. (Illus.). 488p. 1993. pap. 15.00 (*1-873801-78-5*) Popular E Commerce.

Pirates Own Book: Authentic Narratives of the Most Celebrated Sea Robbers. Marine Research Society Staff. LC 93-12468. Orig. Title: The Pirates Own Book: or Authentic Narratives of the Lives, Exploits, & Executions of the Most Celebrated Sea Robbers. (Illus.). xv, 479p. 1993. reprint ed. pap. 9.95 (*0-486-27607-4*) Dover.

Pirates Own Book: or Authentic Narratives of the Lives, Exploits, & Executions of the Most Celebrated Sea Robbers see Pirates Own Book: Authentic Narratives of the Most Celebrated Sea Robbers

Pirate's Pantry: Treasured Recipes of Southwest Louisiana. Junior League of Lake Charles, Inc. Staff. LC 91-14651. (Illus.). 480p. 1991. reprint ed. 16.95 (*0-88289-865-5*) Pelican.

***Pirate's Parrot.** Lyn Rossiter-McFarland. LC 99-38357. (Illus.). 40p. (J). (gr. k-2). 2000. 14.95 (*1-58246-014-0*) Tricycle Pr.

Pirates Past Noon. Mary Pope Osborne. LC 93-2039. (Magic Tree House Ser.: No. 4). (Illus.). 80p. (J). (gr. k-3). 1994. pap. 3.99 (*0-679-82425-1*) Random.

Pirates Past Noon. Mary Pope Osborne. LC 93-2039. (Magic Tree House Ser.: No. 4). (Illus.). 80p. (J). (gr. k-3). 1994. lib. bdg. 11.99 (*0-679-92425-6*) Random.

Pirates Past Noon. Mary Pope Osborne. (Magic Tree House Ser.). (Illus.). 1994. 9.19 (*0-606-07068-0*, Pub. by Turtleback) Demco.

Pirates, Pirates over the Salt, Salt Sea. Patty Wolcott. LC 84-40772. (Illus.). 24p. (J). (ps-1). 1981. 8.95 (*0-201-08335-3*) HarpC Child Bks.

Pirate's Pleasure. Heather Graham. 400p. (Orig.). 1989. mass mkt. 6.50 (*0-440-20236-1*) Dell.

***Pirates, Privateers & Rebel Raiders of the Carolina Coast.** Lindley S. Butler. LC 99-86288. (Illus.). 296p. 2000. 29.95 (*0-8078-2553-0*); pap. 15.95 (*0-8078-4863-8*) U of NC Pr.

Pirate's Promise. Clyde R. Bulla. LC 58-8209. (Illus.). 96p. (J). (gr. 2-5). 1994. pap. 4.95 (*0-06-440457-9*, HarpTrophy) HarpC Child Bks.

Pirate's Promise. Clyde R. Bulla. 1995. 19.00 (*0-8446-6813-3*) Peter Smith.

Pirate's Promise. Clyde Robert Bulla. LC 58-8209. (Trophy Chapter Bks.). 1994. 9.70 (*0-606-06670-5*, Pub. by Turtleback) Demco.

Pirates, 1660-1730. Angus Konstam. (Military History Ser.). (Illus.). 96p. 1999. pap. 16.95 (*1-85532-706-6*, Pub. by Osprey) Stackpole.

Pirate's Son. Geraldine McCaughrean. LC 97-45650. 224p. (YA). (gr. 5-9). 1998. 16.95 (*0-590-20344-4*, Pub. by Scholastic) Scholastic Inc.

***Pirate's Son.** Geraldine McCaughrean. 304p. (gr. 5-9). 1999. mass mkt. 4.99 (*0-590-20348-7*) Scholastic Inc.

Pirate's Treasure. Sandra G. Garrett & Philip C. Williams. LC 93-33877. (Screech Owl Mysteries Ser.). 32p. (J). (gr. k-5). 1994. lib. bdg. 18.60 (*0-86625-506-0*) Rourke Pubns.

Pirates Who's Who. Philip Gosse. 1977. lib. bdg. 59.95 (*0-8490-2446-3*) Gordon Pr.

Pirates' Who's Who: Giving Particulars of the Lives & Deaths of the Pirates & Buccaneers. Philip Gosse. (Illus.). 344p. 1989. pap. 15.00 (*0-87380-165-2*) Popular E Commerce.

Pirate's Woman. Madeline Harper. (Temptation Ser.). 1994. per. 2.99 (*0-373-25576-4*, 1-25576-9) Harlequin Bks.

Pirate's Yo-Ho Hoax, Vol. 6. David LaRochelle. (Mad Mysteries Ser.: Vol. 6). (Illus.). 48p. (J). (gr. 2 up). 1997. pap. 2.95 (*0-8431-7958-9*, Price Stern) Peng Put Young Read.

***Pirating the Pacific: Images of Trade, Travel & Tourism.** Ed. by Ann Stephen. (Illus.). 80p. 2000. pap. 23.95 (*1-86317-042-1*) Museum Applied Arts.

Pirc Defense. Alex Chernin. 176p. 1997. pap. 17.95 (*1-880673-16-9*) Hays Pub.

Pirelli Calendar. Ed. by Mario Andreose. Tr. by Andrew Ellis. LC 97-65574. (Illus.). 396p. 1997. 70.00 (*0-8478-2032-7*, Pub. by Rizzoli Intl) St Martin.

Pirelli Calendar. Pirelli Company Staff. LC 98-67172. (Illus.). 396p. 2000. 70.00 (*0-8478-2150-1*, Pub. by Rizzoli Intl) St Martin.

Pirelli Calendar Classics: Over 100 Remarkable Images from the Legendary Pirelli Calendar. Welcome Rain Publishers Staff. (Illus.). 223p. 1997. pap. 24.95 (*1-55670-659-6*) Stewart Tabori & Chang.

Pirenne Thesis: Analysis, Criticism, & Revision. 3rd ed. Alfred F. Havighurst. (Problems in European Civilization Ser.). 195p. (C). 1976. pap. text 18.36 (*0-669-94680-X*) HM Trade Div.

Piri Audit Adverse Drug Event Auditor. Michael C. Joseph & Katherine M. Schoeffler. Ed. by Leslie Killeen & Saru Salvi. (Illus.). 55p. (Orig.). (YA). 1995. pap. write for info. (*0-9632538-1-6*) Pract Info Res.

Piri Muridi Relationship: Study of the Nizamuddin Dargah. Desiderio Pinto. (C). 1995. 38.00 (*81-7304-111-3*, Pub. by Manohar) S Asia.

Piri Reis & Turkish Mapmaking after Columbus: The Khalili Portolan Atlas. Svat Soucek. LC 94-122207. (Studies in the Khalili Collection of Islamic Art: Vol. II). (Illus.). 176p. (C). 1996. text 65.00 (*0-19-727501-X*) OUP.

***Piriphiriques M.i.n.n.e.s.o.t.a. Architectural Projects & Cultural Productions.** Alice Laguard. (Illus.). 288p. 2000. pap. 28.00 (*3-7643-6299-5*) Birkhauser.

Pirir Papers. Robert M. Hill, 3rd. Ed. by William Fowler et al. (Vanderbilt University Publications in Anthropology: No. 37). 109p. (Orig.). (C). 1989. pap. 12.95 (*0-935462-28-7*) VUPA.

Pirke Aboth: Sayings of the Fathers. deluxe ed. Tr. by Joseph H. Hertz. (Illus.). 1945. pap. 35.00 (*0-87441-420-2*) Behrman.

Pirke Aboth: Sayings of the Fathers: Drawings by Saul Raskin. Saul Raskin. 136p. 1994. 39.95 (*0-8197-0608-6*) Bloch.

Pirke & the Pearl. Jerome Rothenberg. LC 74-24550. 32p. (Orig.). 1975. pap. 12.50 (*0-686-10821-3*) Tree Bks.

Pirke Avot: A Modern Commentary on Jewish Ethics. Ed. by Leonard Kravitz & Kerry M. Olitzky. LC 92-45802. (C). 1993. pap. text 12.95 (*0-8074-0480-2*, 160502) UAHC.

Pirke Avot: Wisdom of the Jewish Sages. Chaim Stern. LC 97-2736. 1997. pap. 17.95 (*0-88125-595-5*) Ktav.

Pirke De Rabbi Eliezer: The Chapters of Rabbi Eliezer the Great. Ed. by Gerald Friedlander. LC 70-174366. 1972. reprint ed. 31.95 (*0-405-08535-4*, Pub. by Blom Pubns) Ayer.

Pirke De Rabbi Eliezer (The Chapters of Rabbi Eliezer the Great) Tr. by Gerald Friedlander from HEB. LC 80-545920. (Judaic Studies: No. SHP6). 552p. 1981. reprint ed. pap. 22.50 (*0-87203-095-4*) Hermon.

Pirkei Avos. Avie Gold. (Illus.). (J). 18.99 (*0-89906-621-6*, PIYH); pap. 15.99 (*0-89906-622-4*, PIYP) Mesorah Pubns.

Pirkei Avos, Vol. 2. Avie Gold. (Illus.). (J). pap. 12.99 (*0-89906-199-0*, PIYP) Mesorah Pubns.

Pirkei Avos: Ethics of the Fathers. Meir Zlotowitz. (ArtScroll Mesorah Ser.). 64p. 1984. 9.99 (*0-89906-205-9*); pap. 5.99 (*0-89906-206-7*) Mesorah Pubns.

Pirket Ovous: Beir Yehuda. 2nd ed. Illus. by Joseph Bernath. write for info. (*1-879515-00-8*) Beir Yehuda.

Pirkie Avot - Shemona Perakim/Thirteen Principles of Faith. Maimonides. Tr. by Eliyahu Touger from HEB. (Mishneh Torah Ser.). 184p. 1994. 20.00 (*0-940118-98-X*) Moznaim.

Pirlei Avos Treasury - Ethics of the Fathers: The Sages Guide to Living with an Anthologized Commentary & Anecdotes. M. Lieber. Ed. by Nosson Scherman. (ArtScroll Mesorah Ser.). Date not set. 54.99 (*0-89906-374-8*) Mesorah Pubns.

Pirna: Kunstgeschichtliche Wurdigung Alten Sachsischen Stadt. H. Quinger. (GER., Illus.). 64p. 1993. pap. text 7.00 (*3-364-00290-8*) Gordon & Breach.

***Pirone's Tree Maintenance.** 7th ed. John R. Hartman et al. LC 99-21143. (Illus.). 560p. 2000. 49.95 (*0-19-511991-6*) OUP.

Pirotechnia. Vannoccio Biringuccio. 507p. 1990. pap. 14.95 (*0-486-26134-4*) Dover.

Pirouette: Pierre Trudeau & Canadian Foreign Policy. Jack L. Granatstein & Robert Bothwell. 524p. 1990. text 35.00 (*0-8020-5780-2*); pap. text 19.95 (*0-8020-6873-1*) U of Toronto Pr.

Pirouette of Earth: A Novel in Verse. Ian M. Emberson. (Illus.). 172p. pap. write for info. (*3-7052-0747-4*, Pub. by Poetry Salzburg) Intl Spec Bk.

Pirouettes. Marcel Pagnol. pap. 9.95 (*0-685-37007-0*) Fr & Eur.

Pirouettes. Marcel Pagnol. (FRE.). 1991. pap. 13.95 (*0-7859-3440-5*) Fr & Eur.

Pirrie Kylsant Motorships, 1915-1932. A. S. Mallett & A. M. Bell. 1990. 50.00 (*0-9509453-0-7*, Pub. by Ship Pictorial Pubng) St Mut.

Pirsig on Minnesota Pleading, 2 vols. 5th ed. Maynard E. Pirsig. 1987. 175.00 (*0-327-00994-2*, 81880, MICHIE); boxed set 175.00 (*0-86678-554-X*, 81880, MICHIE) LEXIS Pub.

Pirsig on Minnesota Pleading, 2 vols. 5th ed. Maynard E. Pirsig. 960p. 1992. suppl. ed. 60.00 (*1-56257-835-9*, MICHIE) LEXIS Pub.

Pirsig on Minnesota Pleading, 1998 Cumulative Supplement. Pirsig. 1998. pap. text 80.00 (*0-327-00137-2*, 81883-14) LEXIS Pub.

Pirsig on Minnesota Pleading, 1999 Cumulative Supplement. Maynard E. Pirsig. 400p. 1999. pap. write for info. (*0-327-01363-X*, 8188315) LEXIS Pub.

Pirush Hamilos. Dov B. Schneuri. (HEB.). 254p. 1993. reprint ed. 25.00 (*0-8266-5494-0*) Kehot Pubn Soc.

PISA Programming System for Interactive Production of Application Software. R. Marty. (Informatik-Fachberichte Ser.). 297p. 1981. 32.00 (*0-387-10825-4*) Spr-Verlag.

Pisacah: A Place of Plenty. Lillian H. Bidal. (Illus.). 352p. 1996. 32.50 (*0-9646793-0-2*) R E McKee Fnd.

***Pisadas Firmes.** Randall Wittig. (SPA.). 176p. 1998. pap. 7.99 (*0-8254-1919-0*, Edit Portavoz) Kregel.

Pisaner Marientafel des Meisters von San Martino und die Zyklischen Darstellungen der Annenlegende in Italien von 700 bis 1350. Johann Von Behr. (Europaische Hochschulschriften, Reihe 28: Bd. 274). (GER., Illus.). 325p. 1996. 63.95 (*3-631-30252-5*) P Lang Pubng.

Piscataqua Pioneers, 1623-1775: Register of Members & Ancestors. John Scales. (Illus.). 212p. 1997. reprint ed. pap. 24.50 (*0-8328-6019-0*) Higginson Bk Co.

Piscataquis Biography & Fragments. John F. Sprague. (Illus.). 102p. 1997. reprint ed. pap. 8.00 (*0-8328-5896-X*) Higginson Bk Co.

Piscataway Story: The Legend of Kittimuquinn. Piscataway Conoy Conferency & Subtribes, Inc. Sta. Ed. by Rebecca Seib-Toup. (Illus.). 96p. (J). (gr. 4-6). 1994. 10.00 (*0-945253-09-5*) Thornsbury Bailey Brown.

Pisces. (Total Horoscopes, 1995 Ser.). 272p. 1994. pap. text 4.50 (*0-515-11422-7*, Jove) Berkley Pub.

Pisces. (Parker's Love Signs Ser.). 1996. 8.95 (*0-614-20707-X*) DK Pub Inc.

Pisces. 1995. mass mkt. 1.29 (*0-440-22119-6*) Dell.

Pisces. (Cosmopolitan a Bedside Astrologer Book Ser.). (Illus.). 24p. 1997. pap. write for info. (*1-56144-971-7*, Honey Bear Bks) Modern Pub NYC.

Pisces. Ariel Books Staff. (Tiny Tomes Ser.). 128p. 1997. 3.95 (*0-8362-2669-0*, Arie Bks) Andrews & McMeel.

Pisces. Astrology World Staff. (Super Horoscopes Ser.). 1998. pap. 7.99 (*0-425-16335-0*) Berkley Pub.

Pisces. Lucille Callard. (Astro-Pups: Your Sign, Your Dogs Ser.). (Illus.). 60p. 1991. pap. 9.95 (*1-881038-11-4*) Penzance Pr.

Pisces. Jove Publications Incorporated, Staff. (Total Horoscopes Ser.). 272p. 1997. mass mkt. 5.99 (*0-515-12119-3*, Jove) Berkley Pub.

Pisces. Jove Publications Staff. (Total Horoscopes Ser.). 1998. mass mkt. 5.99 (*0-515-12315-3*, Jove) Berkley Pub.

Pisces. Teresa Moorey. (Reach Your Potential Ser.). (Illus.). 96p. 1998. pap. 9.95 (*0-340-69720-2*, Pub. by Headway) Trafalgar.

Pisces. Derek Parker & Julia Parker. LC 92-52795. (Sun & Moon Signs Library). (Illus.). 58p. 1992. 8.95 (*1-56458-095-4*) DK Pub Inc.

Pisces. Julia Parker & Derek Parker. (Love Signs Library). 64p. 1996. 8.95 (*0-7894-1088-5*) DK Pub Inc.

Pisces: A Portrait from Life: The Awakened Feminine. Tom Eagle. (Illus.). 90p. 1977. pap. 15.00 (*1-930259-08-5*) Anabasis.

Pisces: Astro-Numerogia. Michael J. Kurban. Tr. by Loretta H. Kurban from ENG. LC 86-91278. (SPA., Illus.). (Orig.). 1992. pap. 8.00 (*0-938863-56-8*) HCI Pr.

Pisces: Astrological Horoscopes for 1999. Teri King. (Teri King Ser.). 1998. pap. 4.95 (*1-86204-274-8*, Pub. by Element MA) Penguin Putnam.

Pisces: Little Birth Sign. Ariel Books Staff. (Illus.). 80p. 1994. 4.95 (*0-8362-3076-0*, Arie Bks) Andrews & McMeel.

Pisces: Mini Edition. Ariel Books Staff. (Women's Astrology Library). 1999. 4.95 (*0-8362-7891-7*) Andrews & McMeel.

***Pisces: Secrets of the Sun Signs.** Ed. by Jennifer Fox. (Illus.). 272p. 2000. pap. 5.95 (*0-7407-1076-1*) Andrews & McMeel.

Pisces: The Fish (February 20-March 20) Sterling Publishing Staff. 1999. 4.95 (*0-8069-3141-8*) Sterling.

***Pisces: Your Personal Horoscope.** rev. ed. American Astroanalysts Institute Staff. (Astroanalysis Ser.). 2000. pap. 12.95 (*0-425-17569-3*) Berkley Pub.

Pisces: Your Sun-&-Moon Guide to Love & Life. Ariel Books Staff. 374p. (Orig.). 1997. pap. 5.95 (*0-8362-3563-0*, Arie Bks) Andrews & McMeel.

Pisces: 2000 Edition. Jove Books Publishing Staff. (Total Horoscopes Ser.). 1999. mass mkt. 5.99 (*0-515-12547-4*, Jove) Berkley Pub.

Pisces Guide to Caribbean Reef Ecology. William S. Alevizon. LC 93-2430. 128p. 1994. pap. 15.95 (*1-55992-077-7*, Pisces Books) Lonely Planet.

Pisces Guide to Shooting Underwater Video. Steve Rosenberg & John Ratterree. 256p. 1991. pap. 15.95 (*1-55992-041-6*, Pisces Books) Lonely Planet.

Pisces Guide to Venomous & Toxic Marine Life of the World. Patricia Cunningham & Paul Goetz. LC 95-34470. 152p. 1996. pap. 18.95 (*1-55992-088-2*, 2088, Pisces Books) Lonely Planet.

Pisces Guide to Watching Fishes: Understanding Coral Reef Fish Behavior. Roberta Wilson & James Q. Wilson. 288p. 1992. pap. 15.95 (*1-55992-061-0*, Pisces Books) Lonely Planet.

Pisces 1995 Purse Book. 1994. mass mkt. 0.99 (*0-440-60244-0*) Dell.

Pisces 1994 Purse Book. 1994. mass mkt. 1.25 (*0-440-60215-7*) Dell.

Pisces 1996 Purse Book. 1995. mass mkt. 1.19 (*0-440-60257-2*) Dell.

Pisces Rising. Douglas M. Baker. (Esoteric Astrology: The Rising Signs Ser.). 1981. pap. 7.50 (*0-906006-40-6*, Pub. by Baker Pubns) New Leaf Dist.

***Pisces Rising.** Martha C. Lawrence. 240p. 2000. text 23.95 (*0-312-20298-9*, Minotaur) St Martin.

Pisces Sun Sign. Douglas M. Baker. (Astrological Sun Sign Ser.). 1972. pap. 5.50 (*0-906006-28-7*, Pub. by Baker Pubns) New Leaf Dist.

***Pisces 2001.** Ed. by Jove Books Publishing Staff. (Total Horoscopes Ser.). 272p. 2000. mass mkt. 5.99 (*0-515-12826-0*, Jove) Berkley Pub.

***Pisces 2001.** Teri King. (Astrological Horoscopes Ser.). 2000. pap. 4.95 (*1-86204-777-4*, Pub. by Element MA) Penguin Putnam.

Piscinae: Artificial Fishponds in Roman Italy. James A. Higginbotham. LC 96-29229. 353p. (C). (gr. 13). 1997. 55.00 (*0-8078-2329-5*) U of NC Pr.

Piscopo Tapes. Joe Piscopo. 1987. pap. 5.95 (*0-317-56817-5*) PB.

Pisekin Noomw Noon Tonaachaw: Archeology in the Tonaachaw Historic District, Moen Island, Truk. Thomas F. King & Patricia L. Parker. LC 84-71523. (Center for Archaeological Investigations Occasional Paper Ser.: No. 3). (Illus.). xxxii, 541p. 1984. pap. 20.00 (*0-88104-018-5*) Center Archaeol.

Pisemsky: A Provincial Realist. Charles A. Moser. LC 78-78521. 283p. reprint ed. pap. 87.80 (*0-7837-5938-X*, 204573700007) Bks Demand.

Pisgah Ranger District/National Forest, North Carolina. (Illus.). 1996. 8.99 (*1-56695-037-6*) Trails Illustrated.

Pish Posh, Said Hieronymous Bosch. Nancy Willard. (Illus.). 18.95 (*0-685-53461-8*) Harcourt.

Pish Posh, Said Hieronymous Bosch. Nancy Willard & Leo Dillon. LC 86-3173. (Illus.). 32p. (J). (ps up). 1991. 22.00 (*0-15-262210-1*, Harcourt Child Bks) Harcourt.

Pishey Thompson Man of Two Worlds. Isabel Bailey. 275p. (C). 1991. 80.00 (*0-902662-96-1*, Pub. by R K Pubns) St Mut.

Pisidian Antioch: The Site & Its Monuments. Stephen Mitchell & Marc Waelkens. (Illus.). 247p. 1998. 59.50 (*0-7156-2860-7*, Pub. by Classical Pr) David Brown.

Piskei Admir Hazaken B'hilchas Issur Uneter. Schneur Zalman. Ed. by Aryenleib Kaplan & Menachem M. Kaplan. (HEB.). 210p. 1996. 13.00 (*0-8266-5512-2*) Kehot Pubn Soc.

Piskei Pri Magadim Haares Lishulchon Arukh. (HEB.). 432p. 1985. 15.00 (*0-8266-5306-5*) Kehot Pubn Soc.

Piskel Dinim-Tzemach Tzedek. Menachem M. Schneerson. (HEB.). 892p. reprint ed. 35.00 (*0-8266-5601-3*) Kehot Pubn Soc.

Piskies, Spriggans, & Other Magical Beings: Tales from the Droll-Teller. Shirley Climo. LC 79-7839. (Illus.). 128p. (J). (gr. 4-7). 1981. 11.95 (*0-690-04063-6*); lib. bdg. 11.89 (*0-690-04064-4*) HarpC Child Bks.

Pis'ma K Iu Ivasku, Etc. Marina I. Tsvetaeva & Ariadna Efron. Ed. by Alexander Sumerkin. (Marina Tsvetaeva Teksty I Materialy Ser.: No. 1). 350p. (Orig.). (C). pap. write for info. (*0-89830-103-3*); pap. write for info. (*0-89830-104-1*) Russica Pubs.

***Pis'ma k Roditeliam i Sestram.** Boris Pasternak & Leonid Pasternak. Ed. by E. B. Pasternak & E. V. Pasternak. (Stanford Slavic Studies: Vols. 18 & 19). (RUS., Illus.). 658p. 1998. pap. 70.00 (*1-57201-047-9*) Berkeley Slavic.

Pisma Startsa Anatolia Monakjhiniam see Collection of Letters to Nuns

Pisoma Tsarskoj Semji iz Zatotchenija. Ed. by E. E. Alferirff. LC 73-91829.Tr. of Letters of the Tsar's Family from Captivity. (Illus.). 544p. 1974. 25.00 (*0-317-29225-0*) Holy Trinity.

Pisot & Salem Numbers. Marie-Jose Bertin et al. LC 92-32812. xiii, 291p. 1992. 146.50 (*0-8176-2648-4*) Birkhauser.

Pissaro: Landscapes & Cities. C. Kunstler. (Rhythem & Color One Ser.). 1970. 9.95 (*0-8288-9511-2*) Fr & Eur.

Pissarro. John Rewald. (Masters of Art Ser.). (Illus.). 128p. 1989. 24.95 (*0-8109-1499-9*, Pub. by Abrams) Time Warner.

Pissarro. Christopher Lloyd. (Color Library). (Illus.). 128p. (C). 1994. reprint ed. pap. 14.95 (*0-7148-2729-0*, Pub. by Phaidon Press) Phaidon Pr.

Pissarro, Vol. 1. Metropolitan Museum of Art Staff. (Illus.). 26p. 1998. 12.95 (*0-8212-2521-9*) Little.

Pissarro & Pontoise: The Painter in a Landscape. Richard Brettell. (Illus.). 240p. (C). 1990. 65.00 (*0-300-04336-8*) Yale U Pr.

Pissarro in Essex. Nicholas Reed. 1990. pap. 29.95 (*0-9515258-4-0*, Pub. by Lilburne Pr) St Mut.

Pissarro in West London. Nicholas Reed. 1990. pap. 29.95 (*0-7855-7038-1*, Pub. by Lilburne Pr) St Mut.

Pissarro, Neo-Impressionism, & the Spaces of the Avant-Garde. Martha Ward. LC 95-6881. 368p. 1996. 85.00 (*0-226-87324-2*) U Ch Pr.

Pissarro's Art & Oeuvre: A Catalogue Raisonne, 2 vols. Ludovic-Rodo Pissarro. (FRE., Illus.). 1989. reprint ed. 295.00 (*1-55660-027-5*) A Wofsy Fine Arts.

Pisscat Songs. E. F. Dyck. 40p. 1984. pap. 7.00 (*0-919626-23-8*, Pub. by Brick Bks) Genl Dist Srvs.

Pissed-Off Poems. Johnnierenee Nelson. 48p. (Orig.). 1996. pap. 10.95 (*0-9623205-4-4*) House Nia.

Pissing in the Snow & Other Ozark Folktales. Vance Randolph. LC 76-18181. 192p. 1976. 8.95 (*0-252-01364-6*) U of Ill Pr.

Pissle & the Holy Grail. Omar Pound. LC 86-62329. 64p. 1987. 12.95 (*0-913506-18-4*) Woolmer-Brotherson.

Pistachio Peak. Noreen Wise. LC 97-74167. (Illus.). 32p. (J). 1997. pap. 5.95 (*1-890570-46-X*) Huckleberry CT.

Pistachio Prescription. Paula Danziger. LC 77-86330. 154p. (gr. 5-9). 1999. pap. 4.99 (*0-698-11690-9*) Putnam Pub Group.

Pistachio Prescription. Paula Danziger. 154p. (J). (gr. 4-6). pap. 3.99 (*0-8072-1525-2*); pap. 3.99 (*0-8072-1374-8*) Listening Lib.

Pistachio Prescription: A Student Response Journal. rev. ed. James Scott. 15p. (J). (gr. 7-12). 1998. ring bd. 19.95 (*1-58049-753-5*, RJ08R) Prestwick Hse.

Pistachios: Poems from Hollywood. Mark Dunster. 11p. 1998. pap. 5.00 (*0-89642-540-1*) Linden Pubs.

Pistis Sophia. G. R. Mead. 325p. 1992. reprint ed. pap. 24.95 (*0-922802-87-4*) Kessinger Pub.

Pistis Sophia: A Gnostic Gospel. G. R. Mead. 1991. lib. bdg. 88.75 (*0-8490-5036-7*) Gordon Pr.

Pistis Sophia: A Gnostic Gospel. G. R. Mead. 394p. 1996. reprint ed. spiral bd. 34.50 (*0-7873-1104-9*) Hlth Research.

Pistis Sophia: A Gnostic Gospel. 3rd ed. G. R. Mead. LC 83-83170. 408p. 1984. reprint ed. lib. bdg. 28.50 (*0-89345-041-3*, Spir Sci Lib) Garber Comm.

Pistol: Browning, F. N. 9mm. No. 2, Mark 1. Command of the Army Council Staff. LC 83-6127. 1992. pap. text 5.00 (*0-86663-991-8*) Ide Hse.

Pistol Law. large type ed. Paul E. Lehman. (Linford Western Library). 280p. 1985. pap. 16.99 (*0-7089-6088-X*) Ulverscroft.

Pistol Packin' Mama: Aunt Molly Jackson & the Politics of Folksong. Shelly Romalis. LC 98-19726. (Music in American Life Ser.). 264p. 1998. pap. 18.95 (*0-252-06728-2*); text 39.95 (*0-252-02421-4*) U of Ill Pr.

Pistol Passport. large type ed. Eugene Cunningham. LC 94-2967. 321p. 1994. pap. 17.95 (*0-8161-7418-0*, G K Hall Lrg Type) Mac Lib Ref.

Pistol Pete - Veteran of the Old West. Frank Eaton. LC 79-109054. (Illus.). 1979. reprint ed. text 22.00 (*0-934188-01-7*) Evans Pubns.

Pistoleer. James C. Blake. 368p. (Orig.). 1995. pap. 12.00 (*0-425-14782-7*) Berkley Pub.

Pistoleer. James C. Blake. (Orig.). 1996. mass mkt. 6.99 (*0-425-15412-2*) Berkley Pub.

Pistoleer. large type ed. James C. Blake. (Niagara Large Print Ser.). 512p. (Orig.). 1996. pap. 29.50 (*0-7089-5823-0*) Ulverscroft.

Pistolen. F. Temesvary. 496p. 1988. 180.00 (*963-05-4843-7*, Pub. by Akade Kiado) St Mut.

Pistolero. Walt Denver. 1984. mass mkt. 2.25 (*0-8217-1331-0*, Zebra Kensgtn) Kensgtn Pub Corp.

Pistoles - Paroles: Money & Language in Seventeenth-Century French Comedy. Helen L. Harrison. LC 95-36059. 201p. 1996. lib. bdg. 39.95 (*1-886365-03-2*) Rookwood Pr.

Pistolman. large type ed. Steve Frazee. 1998. 18.95 (*1-57490-161-3*, Sagebrush LP West) T T Beeler.

Pistolman. large type ed. Steve Frazee. (Linford Western Library). 320p. 1985. pap. 16.99 (*0-7089-6095-2*, Linford) Ulverscroft.

Pistols & Petticoats: 13 Female Trailblazers of the Old West. Bob L'Aloge. LC 95-90642. (Illus.). 272p. 1995. pap. 14.95 (*0-938147-99-4*, Pub. by Flying Eagle) Yucca Tree Pr.

Pistols & Politics: The Dilemma of Democracy in Louisiana's Florida Parishes, 1810-1899. Samuel C. Hyde, Jr. LC 96-24025. 312p. 1998. pap. 14.95 (*0-8071-2270-X*) La State U Pr.

Pistols & Revolvers: A Handbook. 1989. lib. bdg. 79.95 (*0-8490-3975-4*) Gordon Pr.

Pistols for Two. Georgette Heyer. 20.95 (*0-89190-638-X*) Amereon Ltd.

Pistols for Two. Georgette Heyer. 341p. 1983. reprint ed. lib. bdg. 24.95 (*0-89966-449-0*) Buccaneer Bks.

Pistols of the World. 3rd ed. Ian Hogg & John Weeks. LC 82-71370. (Illus.). 352p. 1992. pap. 20.95 (*0-87349-128-9*, POW3, DBI Bks) Krause Pubns.

Pistolsmithing. George C. Nonte, Jr. LC 74-10783. (Illus.). 560p. 1974. 29.95 (*0-8117-1265-6*) Stackpole.

Piston & the Porkers. Colene Copeland. LC 89-84652. (Illus.). 127p. (Orig.). 1989. 8.95 (*0-939810-09-3*); pap. 3.95 (*0-939810-10-7*) Jordan Valley.

Pisukti Asianik Pukugiarami (When the Fox Went Berry Picking) large type ed. Hilda Olick. (ESK., Illus.). 8p. (J). (gr. k-3). 1999. pap. text 14.50 (*1-58084-128-7*) Lower Kuskokwim.

Pit. Ab Hugh Dafydd. (Swept Away Ser.). 1996. 9.60 (*0-606-10339-2*, Pub. by Turtleback) Demco.

Pit. Dafydd Hugh. (YA). (gr. 7 up). 1996. pap. 4.50 (*0-614-15656-4*, Harp PBks) HarpC.

Pit. Mrs. Gould's 1996-97 Third Grade Class, Rochester. (WeWrite Kids! Ser.: No. 35). (Illus.). 50p. (J). (ps-4). 1997. pap. 3.95 (*1-57635-011-8*) WeWrite.

Pit. Frank Norris. 1976. lib. bdg. 19.95 (*0-89968-069-0*, Lghtyr Pr) Buccaneer Bks.

Pit: A Story of Chicago. Frank Norris. lib. bdg. 27.95 (*0-8488-1886-5*) Amereon Ltd.

Pit: A Story of Chicago. Frank Norris. 496p. 1994. pap. 13.95 (*0-14-018758-8*, Penguin Classics) Viking Penguin.

Pit: A Story of Chicago. Frank Norris. LC 70-184738. 432p. 1971. reprint ed. lib. bdg. 22.00 (*0-8376-0407-9*) Bentley Pubs.

Pit: A Story of Chicago. Frank Norris. (BCL1-PS American Literature Ser.). 421p. 1992. reprint ed. lib. bdg. 99.00 (*0-7812-6813-3*) Rprt Serv.

Pit Ahoi! Marcus Pfister.Tr. of Penguin Pete, Ahoy!. (GER., Illus.). 32p. (J). (gr. k-3). 1996. 15.95 (*3-314-00600-4*, Pub. by North-South Bks NYC) Chronicle Bks.

Pit & Fissure Sealants. Norman O. Harris & Linda S. Scheirton. 1985. 30.00 (*0-318-19100-8*) Am Dental Hygienists.

Pit-&-Groove Petroglyph Style in Southern California, No. 15. Rick Minor. (San Diego Museum of Man, Ethnic Technology Notes Ser.). (Illus.). '33p. 1975. pap. text 3.75 (*1-55567-816-5*) Coyote Press.

Pit & the Pendulum: The Pit & the Pendulum. Amarantha Knight. (The Darker Passions Ser.). 1998. mass mkt. 6.95 (*1-56333-639-1*) Masquerade.

Pit & the Pendulum. Edgar Allan Poe. (Classic Short Stories on Tape Ser.). (YA). (gr. 8-12). 1993. ring bd. 38.00 (*1-878298-11-9*) Balance Pub.

Pit & the Pendulum. Edgar Allan Poe. Ed. by Jamestown Publishers Staff. 1982. pap. 7.80 (*0-8092-0047-3*, Jamestwn Pub) NTC Contemp Pub Co.

Pit & the Pendulum. Edgar Allan Poe. Ed. by Raymond Harris. (Classics Ser.). (Illus.). 48p. (YA). (gr. 6-12). 1982. teacher ed. 7.32 (*0-89061-266-8*, 473, Jamestwn Pub); pap. text 5.99 (*0-89061-265-X*, 471, Jamestwn Pub); audio 17.96 (*0-89061-267-6*, 472, Jamestwn Pub) NTC Contemp Pub Co.

***Pit & the Pendulum.** Edgar Allan Poe. (Short Stories Ser.). 22p. 2000. pap. 3.95 (*1-86092-019-5*, Pub. by Travelman Pub) IPG Chicago.

***Pit & the Pendulum & Other Stories.** Edgar Allan Poe & James Prunier. (Illus.). 153p. (YA). (gr. 8 up). 1999. 25.99 (*0-670-88706-4*, Viking Child); pap. 17.99 (*0-670-88725-0*, Viking Child) Peng Put Young Read.

Pit & the Trap: A Chronicle of Survival. Leyb Rochman. Ed. by Sheila Friedling. Tr. by O. Kohn from YID. (Illus.). 288p. (Orig.). 1983. 11.95 (*0-89604-046-1*, Holocaust Library); pap. 6.95 (*0-89604-047-X*, Holocaust Library) US Holocaust.

Pit Bull. large type ed. Gwen Moffat. (Ulverscroft Large Print Ser.). 432p. 1997. 27.99 (*0-7089-3780-2*) Ulverscroft.

Pit Bull: Lessons from Wall Street's Champion Trader. Martin B. Schwartz et al. LC 97-49931. 294p. 1998. 27.50 (*0-88730-876-7*, HarpBusn) HarpInfo.

Pit Bull: Lessons from Wall Street's Champion Trader. Martin Schwartz et al. 306p. 1999. pap. 16.00 (*0-88730-956-9*, HarpBusn) HarpInfo.

***Pit Bull: Lessons from Wall Street's Champion Trader.** abr. ed. Martin Schwartz. 1998. audio 18.00 (*0-694-51931-6*) HarperAudio.

Pit Bull Dilemma: The Gathering Storm - 1000 Annotated Abstracts from Books, Journals, Etc. Ed. by Donald H. Clifford et al. LC 89-22176. 480p. 1990. text 65.00 (*0-914783-36-X*) Charles.

Pit Bull Sting: The Other Side of the Story. Boen Hallum. 190p. 1987. pap. 12.00 (*0-9608854-1-2*) B Hallum.

Pit Bulls & Tenacious Guard Dogs. Carl Semencic. (Illus.). 320p. 1991. text 47.95 (*0-86622-639-7*, TS141) TFH Pubns.

***Pit Bulls Terriers.** D. Caroline Coile. 1999. pap. 14.95 (*1-58245-146-X*) Howell Bks.

Pit Crew. Tara B. Mello. LC 98-19266. (Race Car Legends Ser.). (Illus.). 64p. (YA). (gr. 3 up). 1999. lib. bdg. 16.95 (*0-7910-5022-X*) Chelsea Hse.

Pit et Pat. Marcus Pfister. (FRE., Illus.). 32p. (J). (gr. k-3). 1992. 15.95 (*3-314-20657-7*, Pub. by North-South Bks NYC) Chronicle Bks.

***Pit Fighter.** Roger Hammarberg. 2000. pap. 8.50 (*0-9671005-0-X*) R Hammarberg.

Pit House, Presidio, & Privy: 1,400 Years of Archaeology & History on Block 180, Tucson, Arizona. Ed. by Richard Ciolek-Torrello & Mark T. Swanson. (Statistical Research Technical Ser.: Vol. 63). (Illus.). 762p. 1997. per. 45.00 (*1-879442-60-4*) Stats Res.

Pit il Piccolo Piguino. Marcus Pfister.Tr. of Penguin Pete. (ITA., Illus.). 32p. (J). (gr. k-3). 15.95 (*88-8203-030-X*, Pub. by North-South Bks NYC) Chronicle Bks.

Pit, le Petit Pingouin. Marcus Pfister.Tr. of Penguin Pete. (FRE., Illus.). 32p. (J). (gr. k-3). 1996. 15.95 (*3-314-20627-5*, Pub. by North-South Bks NYC) Chronicle Bks.

Pit Sense vs. the State. David J. Douglass. 112p. (Orig.). 1993. pap. 9.95 (*0-948984-26-0*, Pub. by Phoenix Pr) AK Pr Dist.

Pit Trading: Do You Have the Right Stuff? Michael K. Hoffman & Gerald Baccetti. 248p. 1999. 39.95 (*0-934380-52-X*) Traders Pr.

Pit und Pat. Marcus Pfister.Tr. of Penguin Pete & Pat. (GER., Illus.). 32p. (J). (gr. k-3). 1996. 15.95 (*3-314-00327-7*, Pub. by North-South Bks NYC) Chronicle Bks.

***Pit Vipers.** Doug Wechsler. LC 00-35981. (Really Wild Life of Snakes Ser.). (J). 2000. write for info. (*0-8239-5605-9*, PowerKids) Rosen Group.

***Pit Women: Coal Communities in Northern England in the Early Twentieth Century.** Griselda Carr. 250p. 2000. pap. 65.00 (*0-85036-495-7*, Pub. by U Wales Pr) Paul & Co Pubs.

Pita the Great. Virginia T. Habeeb. LC 85-40902. (Illus.). 176p. 1986. pap. 9.95 (*0-89480-039-6*, 1039) Workman Pub.

Pitaka Disclosure. Tr. by Ven. Nanamoli from PLI. (C). 1964. 48.00 (*0-86013-026-6*, Pub. by Pali Text) Elsevier.

Pitambar's Encyclopaedia of General Knowledge & Current Affairs. B. N. Ahuja & Ashley Burn. 1992. 60.00 (*81-209-0000-6*, Pub. by Pitambar Pub) St Mut.

Pitambar's Handbook of General Knowledge. B. N. Ahuja & Paresh Saxena. 344p. (C). 1997. pap. 60.00 (*81-209-0516-4*, Pub. by Pitambar Pub) St Mut.

Pitcaim's Island. Charles Nordhoff & James N. Hall. Date not set. lib. bdg. 23.95 (*0-8488-2153-X*) Amereon Ltd.

Pitcairn - Port of Call. Herbert Ford. (Illus.). 512p. (Orig.). 1996. pap. 19.95 (*0-9649642-0-1*) Hawser Titles.

Pitcairn Island: Life & Death in Eden. Trevor Lummis. LC 97-18806. (Illus.). 184p. 1997. text 61.95 (*1-85928-431-0*, Pub. by Scolar Pr) Ashgate Pub Co.

Pitcairn Island: The 1st 200 Years. Spencer Murray. LC 92-81932. (Illus.). 192p. 1992. pap. 19.95 (*0-9633229-0-7*) Bounty Sagas.

Pitcairn Island Register Book. Ed. by Charles Lucas. LC 75-3444. (Illus.). reprint ed. 32.50 (*0-404-14447-0*) AMS Pr.

***Pitcairn Islands: A Country Study Guide, 110 vols.** International Business Publications, USA Staff & Global Investment Center, USA Staff. (World Country Study Guides Library Ser.: Vol. 218). (Illus.). 350p. 2000. pap. 69.95 (*0-7397-1041-9*) Intl Business Pubns.

Pitcairners. Robert B. Nicolson & Brian F. Davies. LC 96-225098. (Illus.). 1997. write for info. (*0-908597-28-2*) Pasifika Pr.

Pitcairners. Robert B. Nicolson & Brian F. Davies. LC 96-35483. (Pasifika Library). (Illus.). 200p. 1997. pap. 19.95 (*0-8248-1921-7*) UH Pr.

Pitcairnioideae (Bromeliaceae) Lyman B. Smith & Robert J. Downs. LC 74-3365. (Flora Neotropica Monographs: Vol. 14, No. 1). (Illus.). 660p. 1986. reprint ed. pap. 45.00 (*0-89327-303-1*) NY Botanical.

Pitcairn's Island. Thomas Murray. LC 72-281. (World History Ser.: No. 48). 1972. reprint ed. lib. bdg. 75.00 (*0-8383-1410-4*) M S G Haskell Hse.

Pitcairn's Island, & the Islanders in 1850. 3rd ed. Walter Brodie. LC 75-3441. reprint ed. 34.50 (*0-404-14445-4*) AMS Pr.

Pitch. 2nd rev. ed. Hugh Rank. (Illus.). 160p. 1991. pap. text 14.95 (*0-943468-03-5*, HF5821.R26) Counter-Prop Pr.

Pitch Accent in Hupa. fac. ed. Pliny E. Goddard. (University of California Publications in American Archaeology & Ethnology: Vol. 23: 6). 8p. (C). 1928. reprint ed. pap. text 1.25 (*1-55567-263-9*) Coyote Press.

Pitch Analysis: Journal: Phonetica, Vol. 39, No. 4-5, 1982. Ed. by K. J. Kohler. (Illus.). viii, 156p. 1982. pap. 81.75 (*3-8055-3670-4*) S Karger.

***Pitch Black.** Frank Lauria. 1999. 143.75 (*0-312-97529-5*) St Martin.

Pitch Black, 1 Vol. Frank Lauria. 1999. mass mkt. 5.99 (*0-312-97088-9*, St Martins Paperbacks) St Martin.

Pitch Determination of Speech Signals: Algorithms & Devices. W. Hess. (Information Sciences Ser.: Vol. 3). (Illus.). 698p. 1983. 84.95 (*0-387-11933-7*) Spr-Verlag.

Pitch Invaders: The Modern Black Football Revolution. Stella Orakwue. (Illus.). 256p. 1998. pap. 22.95 (*0-575-06118-9*, Pub. by V Gollancz) Trafalgar.

Pitch of Philosophy: Autobiographical Exercises. Stanley Cavell. LC 93-47642. (Jerusalem-Harvard Lectures). 282p. (C). 1994. text 26.00 (*0-674-66980-0*) HUP.

Pitch of Philosophy: Autobiographical Exercises. Stanley Cavell. 216p. 1996. pap. 15.95 (*0-674-66981-9*) HUP.

Pitchcap & Pike. Colm Brennan. 84p. 1998. pap. 14.95 (*1-901233-18-9*, Pub. by Dedalus) Dufour.

Pitchcap & Pike. Colm Brennan. (Illus.). 84p. 1998. 24.95 (*1-901233-19-7*, Pub. by Dedalus) Dufour.

Pitcher. George A. Sullivan. (J). 1986. 10.95 (*0-690-04538-7*) HarpC Child Bks.

Pitcher - Plants of Borneo. Anthea Phillipps & Anthony Lamb. (Illus.). x, 171p. 1996. 42.00 (*983-812-009-X*, Pub. by Royal Botnic Grdns) Balogh.

Pitcher is Broken: Memorial Essays for Gosta W. Ahlstrom. Ed. by Steven W. Holloway & Lowell K. Handy. (Journal for the Study of the Old Testament Supplement Ser.: Vol. 190). 474p. 1995. 90.00 (*1-85075-525-6*, Pub. by Sheffield Acad) CUP Services.

Pitcher of Cream. Bud Robinson. 110p. 1996. reprint ed. pap. 8.99 (*0-88019-354-9*) Schmul Pub Co.

Pitcher Plants: Slippery Pits of No Escape see Bloodthirsty Plants

Pitcher Who Went Out of His Mind. Dan Gutman. (Tales from the Sandlot Ser.). (J). 1997. 9.09 (*0-606-11969-8*, Pub. by Turtleback) Demco.

Pitchers: Twenty-Seven of Baseball's Greatest. George Sullivan. LC 93-3007. (Illus.). 80p. 1999. per. 7.99 (*0-689-82454-8*) S&S Childrens.

Pitchers Bible Scorebook. Stanley Horowitz. 65p. 1993. pap. 4.00 (*0-9639660-1-4*) All Spts Pubng.

Pitchers Bible, 1994. Stanley Horowitz. 830p. 1993. pap. 25.00 (*0-9639660-0-6*) All Spts Pubng.

Pitchers Duel. Clair Bee. LC 98-50758. (Chip Hilton Sports Ser.: Vol. 7). 208p. (YA). 1999. reprint ed. pap. 5.99 (*0-8054-1989-6*) Broadman.

Pitchers of Perfection. John Marino. LC 95-23804. 80p. 1996. 11.98 (*1-56799-178-5*, MetroBooks) M Friedman Pub Grp Inc.

Pitchfork Hollow. Dean Feldmeyer. Ed. by Jane Chelius. 256p. (Orig.). 1995. mass mkt. 5.50 (*0-671-76983-9*) PB.

***Pitchfork Patrol.** Will Henry, pseud. 176p. 2000. pap. 3.99 (*0-8439-4754-3*, Leisure Bks) Dorchester Pub Co.

Pitchforks & Pearly Gates: Nagged by God & the Devil. Loy Young & Natalie. (Illus.). 94p. 1998. pap. 7.95 (*1-882888-48-0*) Aquarius Hse.

Pitchin' Man. Leroy S. Paige. (American Autobiography Ser.). 96p. 1995. reprint ed. lib. bdg. 69.00 (*0-7812-8606-9*) Rprt Serv.

Pitchin' Man: Satchel Paige's Own Story. Leroy S. Paige. (Baseball & American Society Ser.: No. 20). (Illus.). 130p. 1992. lib. bdg. 29.50 (*0-88736-836-0*) Mecklermedia.

Pitching Aces '98. Phil Erwin. 1998. spiral bd. 19.95 (*0-9663525-1-3*) Parrish Pubns.

Pitching Aces, '99. Phil Erwin. Date not set. spiral bd. 19.95 (*0-9663525-3-X*) Parrish Pubns.

***Pitching Aces 2000.** Phil Erwin. 160p. 2000. spiral bd. 22.95 (*0-9663525-5-6*) Parrish Pubns.

***Pitching Around Fidel: A Journey into the Heart of Cuban Sports.** S. L. Price. LC 00-20523. (Illus.). 288p. 2000. 24.00 (*0-06-019660-2*, Ecco Press) HarperTrade.

Pitching Clinic. (Baseball Ser.). 29.95 (*1-887209-26-3*) Spirit of St Louis.

Pitching Edge. 2nd fac. ed. Tom House. LC 99-18237. (Illus.). 168p. 1999. pap. 18.95 (*0-7360-0155-7*, PHOU0155) Human Kinetics.

Pitching from the Ground Up. Bob Bennett. 223p. 1997. pap. 20.00 (*1-57167-076-9*) Coaches Choice.

Pitching In: When Your Elderly Parents Need Help. Sandra B. Ross. 190p. 1999. pap. 12.95 (*1-881235-25-4*) Creat Opport.

Pitching in a Pinch. Christy Mathewson. 1976. 29.95 (*0-8488-1546-7*) Amereon Ltd.

Pitching in a Pinch: or Baseball from the Inside. Christy Mathewson. LC 93-42716. (Illus.). xxii, 320p. 1994. pap. 15.00 (*0-8032-8212-5*, Bison Books) U of Nebr Pr.

Pitching in a Pinch: or Baseball from the Inside. Christopher Mathewson. (American Biography Ser.). 306p. 1991. reprint ed. lib. bdg. 79.00 (*0-7812-8277-2*) Rprt Serv.

Pitching Like a Pro: A Guide for Young Pitchers & Their Coaches, Little League, Through High School. Leo Mazzone & Jim Rosenthal. LC 98-43623. (Illus.). 112p. 1999. pap. 12.95 (*0-312-19946-5*) St Martin.

Pitching the Presidency: How Presidents Depict the Office. Paul H. Zernicke. LC 94-1139. 192p. 1994. 55.00 (*0-275-94678-9*, Praeger Pubs) Greenwood.

Pitching to the Star & Other Short Plays. Donald Margulies. 1993. pap. 5.25 (*0-8222-1358-3*) Dramatists Play.

Pitchman's Melody: Shaw About Shakespeare. Jerry Lutz. LC 72-3529. 175p. 1974. 18.00 (*0-8387-1247-9*) Bucknell U Pr.

Pitfall 3D, Official Guide: Beyond the Jungle Strategy Guide. Bradygames Staff. 112p. 1998. pap. text 11.99 (*1-56686-772-X*) Brady Pub.

Pitfalls & Complications in the Diagnosis & Management of Hepatobiliary & Pancreatic Diseases. Ed. by N. J. Lygidakis et al. LC 93-11759. 1993. 259.00 (*0-86577-487-0*) Thieme Med Pubs.

Pitfalls & Potholes: A Checklist for Avoiding Common Mistakes of Beginning Teachers. Barbara A. Murray & Kenneth T. Murray. LC 97-38927. (Checklist Ser.). 56p. (Orig.). 1997. pap. 5.95 (*0-8106-2151-7*, 2151-7) NEA.

Pitfalls & Promise of Resource Recovery in Union County, New Jersey. rev. ed. Brenda A. Platt et al. LC 89-7632. 200p. 1989. pap. text 20.00 (*0-917582-36-5*) Inst Local Self Re.

Pitfalls in Development. H. McKinley Conway. LC 78-62198. 350p. 1981. pap. 11.95 (*0-910436-06-1*) Conway Data.

Pitfalls in Genealogical Research. 2nd ed. Milton Rubincam. LC 87-70105. (Illus.). 74p. 1987. reprint ed. pap. 7.95 (*0-916489-28-0*, 143) Ancestry.

P

Pitfalls in Histopathologic Diagnosis of Malignant Melanoma. rev. ed. A. Bernard Ackerman & Kerl Delmut. (Illus.). 900p. 1993. text 195.00 (*0-8121-1352-7*) Lppncott W & W.

Pitfalls in Human Research: 10 Pivotal Points. Theodore X. Barber & A. Goldstein. LC 76-13488. (General Psychology Ser.: No. 67). 128p. 1976. 64.00 (*0-08-020935-1*, BF76, Pub. by Pergamon Repr) Franklin.

Pitfalls in Preaching. Richard L. Eslinger. 167p. (Orig.). 1996. pap. 12.00 (*0-8028-0820-4*) Eerdmans.

Pitfalls in Seismic Interpretation. Paul M. Tucker & Howard J. Yorston. LC 73-84680. (Geophysical Monographs: No. 2). 56p. 1973. pap. 4.00 (*0-931830-11-7*, 142A) Soc Expl Geophys.

Pitfalls of a Minimum Wage Increase: Hearing Before the Subcommittee on National Economic Growth, Natural Resources & Regulatory Affairs of the Committee on Government Reform & Oversight, House of Representatives, One Hundred Fourth Congress, Second Session, May 14, 1996. LC 98-107157. ii, 110p. 1997. write for info. (*0-16-055541-8*) USGPO.

Pitfalls of Practice. New York State Bar Association Staff. Ed. by Joanne M. White. LC 93-86813. 348p. (Orig.). 1993. pap. text 45.00 (*0-942954-65-3*) NYS Bar.

Pitfalls of Speculation. Thomas Gibson. 151p. (C). 1994. reprint ed. pap. 13.00 (*0-87034-114-6*) Fraser Pub Co.

Pitfalls Revisited. Paul M. Tucker. (Geophysical Monographs: No. 3). 23p. 1982. pap. 3.00 (*0-931830-24-9*, 143A) Soc Expl Geophys.

Pitfalls, Variants & Artifacts in Body MR Imaging. Scott A. Mirowitz. (Illus.). 536p. (C). (gr. 13). 1996. text 155.00 (*0-8016-7670-3*, 07670) Mosby Inc.

PITFCS: The Proceedings of the Institute for Twenty-First Century Studies. Ed. by Theodore Cogswell. (Illus.). x, 374p. 1993. 40.00 (*0-911682-30-9*) Advent.

Pithole: The Vanished City. William C. Darrah. LC 72-78194. (Illus.). 260p. 1972. 8.50 (*0-913116-03-3*) W C Darrah.

Pithy Sayings from FORMAT Interviews, Vol. I. Ed. by C. L. Morrison. 1979. pap. 4.95 (*0-932508-06-5*) Seven Oaks.

Pithy Sayings from FORMAT Interviews, Vol. II. Ed. by C. L. Morrison. 1980. pap. 4.95 (*0-932508-07-3*) Seven Oaks.

Pithy Truths, 4 vols., set. unabridged ed. Ross E. Gutman. Incl. Vol. 1. 40 Pithy Truths: A Self-Analysis Test. unabridged ed. LC 96-94433. (Illus.). 96p. (Orig.). 1996. pap. 3.50 (*0-9652555-0-6*); Vol. 2. 40 More Pithy Truths: A Self-Analysis Test. unabridged ed. LC 96-94696. (Illus.). 96p. (Orig.). 1996. pap. 3.50 (*0-9652555-1-4*); Vol. 3. 40 Old Pithy Truths; A Self-Analysis Test. unabridged ed. LC 97-93069. (Illus.). 96p. (Orig.). 1997. pap. 3.50 (*0-9652555-2-2*); Vol. 4. 40 New Pithy Truths: A Self-Analysis Test to Test Thinking Skills Applying Personal Ananlysis to Varities of Pithy Truths. unabridged ed. 96p. 1999. pap. 3.50 (*0-9652555-4-9*); Set pap. 12.50 (*0-9652555-3-0*) R Gutman.

Piti Piti Plen Kay. Serge Madhere. 90p. 1987. pap. text. write for info. (*1-881686-00-0*) Madhere.

Pitia: An Archaeological Series in Northwestern Venezuela. Patrick Gallagher. LC 75-21042. (Publications in Anthropology: No. 76). 1976. pap. 12.00 (*0-913516-09-0*) Yale U Anthro.

Pitie de Dieu. Jean Cau. (FRE.). 384p. 1974. pap. 10.95 (*0-7859-1780-2*, 2070365565) Fr & Eur.

Pitie pour les Femmes. Henry De Montherlant. (Jeunes Filles Ser.: Vol. 2). (FRE.). 1972. pap. 10.95 (*0-8288-3752-X*, F115780) Fr & Eur.

Pitie pour les Femmes. Henry De Montherlant. (Folio Ser.: No. 156). (FRE.). 224p. 1972. 8.95 (*2-07-036156-X*) Schoenhof.

Pitied but Not Entitled: Single Mothers & the History of Welfare. Linda Gordon. 300p. 1994. 22.95 (*0-02-912485-9*) Free Pr.

Pitied but Not Entitled: Single Mothers & the History of Welfare. Linda Gordon. 448p. 1995. pap. 16.50 (*0-674-66982-7*) HUP.

***Pitiful Gardener's Handbook: Successful Gardening, in Spite of Yourself.** unabridged ed. Tracey Cheney & Connie Eden. LC 99-25415. (Illus.). 176p. 1999. pap. 12.95 (*1-881409-23-5*) Jhnstn Assocs.

Pitiful Life of Simon Schultz. Barbara M. Joosse. LC 90-22352. 192p. (J). (gr. 5-9). 1991. 13.95 (*0-06-022486-X*); lib. bdg. 13.89 (*0-06-022487-8*) HarpC Child Bks.

***Pitiful Plaintiffs: Child Welfare Litigation & the Federal Courts.** Susan Gluck Mezey. LC 99-50679. 288p. 2000. pap. 19.95 (*0-8229-5717-5*); text 45.00 (*0-8229-4116-3*) U of Pittsburgh Pr.

Pitiless Parodies & Other Outrageous Verse. Frank Jacobs. LC 94-472. (Dover Books on Literature & Drama). 82p. (Orig.). 1994. pap. 3.95 (*0-486-28126-4*) Dover.

Pitiless Rain: The Battle of Williamsburg, 1862. Earl C. Hastings, Jr. & David Hastings. LC 97-11269. 160p. 1997. 24.95 (*1-57249-042-X*) White Mane Pub.

***Pitiquito Trail.** large type ed. L. D. Tetlow. 264p. 2000. pap. 18.99 (*0-7089-5669-6*, Linford) Ulverscroft.

Pitirim A. Sorokin: An Intellectual Biography. Barry V. Johnston. LC 95-43645. (Illus.). 416p. 1996. 45.00 (*0-7006-0736-6*) U Pr of KS.

Pitman: History & Pedigree of the Family Pitman of Dunchideock, Exeter, & Collaterals, & of the Pitmans of Alphington, Norfolk & Edinburgh. C. E. Pitman. (Illus.). 181p. 1992. reprint ed. pap. 27.50 (*0-8328-2707-X*); reprint ed. lib. bdg. 37.50 (*0-8328-2706-1*) Higginson Bk Co.

Pitman New Era Shorthand: Anniversary Edition Workbooks, Vol. 1. Ed. by Pitman Publishing Staff. 192p. 1988. pap., student ed. 19.95 (*0-582-28863-0*, Pub. by Pitman Pub) Trans-Atl Phila.

Pitman New Era Shorthand. Facility Drills: Anniversary Edition. Julie Watson. 64p. (Orig.). 1988. pap. 19.95 (*0-273-02904-5*, Pub. by Pitman Pub) Trans-Atl Phila.

Pitman New Era Shorthand Key. anniversary ed. O'Dea & Sykes. 1992. pap. text. write for info. (*0-273-02901-0*) Addison-Wesley.

Pitman New Era Shorthand Pocket Dictionary. 2nd ed. Ed. by Pitman Publishing Ltd Staff. 221p. 1985. pap. text 24.50 (*0-582-29890-3*, Pub. by Pitman Pub) Trans-Atl Phila.

Pitman New Era Shorthand Workbook: Lessons 13-20. Ed. by Pitman Publishing Ltd. Staff. 1988. pap. text, student ed. 19.95 (*0-273-02903-7*, Pub. by Pitman Pub) Trans-Atl Phila.

Pitman Notes on U. S. Martial Small Arms & Ammunition, 1776-1933: Miscellaneous Notes, Vol. 5. John Pitman. (Illus.). 212p. (C). 1993. text 29.95 (*0-939631-35-0*) Thomas Publications.

Pitman Notes on U. S. Martial Small Arms & Ammunition, 1776-1933: U. S. Magazine Rifles & Carbines, Cal. 30, Vol. 4. John Pitman. (Illus.). 194p. (C). 1992. text 29.95 (*0-939631-34-2*) Thomas Publications.

Pitman Notes on U. S. Martial Small Arms & Ammunition, 1776-1933 Vol. 2: Revolvers & Automatic Pistols. John Pitman. (Illus.). 192p. (C). 1991. text 29.95 (*0-939631-32-6*) Thomas Publications.

Pitman Notes on U. S. Martial Small Arms & Ammunition, 1776-1933 Vol. 3: U. S. Breech-Loading Rifles & Carbines, Cal. 45. John Pitman. (Illus.). 192p. 1991. 29.95 (*0-939631-33-4*) Thomas Publications.

Pitman Office Handbook. 4th ed. Lial & Hornsby. (C). 1999. pap. text, wbk. ed. write for info. (*0-201-38887-1*) Addison-Wesley.

Pitman Shorterhand Dictionary. George A. Reid. Ed. by Marion Angus. LC 96-36410. 1930. 15.00 (*0-273-04229-7*) F T P-H.

Pitman 2000 Phrasebuilder. Coombs. 1992. pap. text. write for info. (*0-273-03822-2*) Addison-Wesley.

Pitman Two Thousand Shorthand: Rapid Review & Speed Development. Bryan Coombs. 96p. 1991. pap. 26.00 (*0-582-29170-4*, Pub. by Addison-Wesley) Trans-Atl Phila.

Pitman 2000 Shorthand Pocket Dictionary. 2nd ed. Ed. by Pitman Publishing Staff. 221p. 1996. pap. 24.50 (*0-582-28722-7*, Pub. by Addison-Wesley) Trans-Atl Phila.

Pitman's Dictionary of Industrial Administration: A Comprehensive Encyclopedia of the Organization, Administration, & Management of Modern Industry, 2 vols. Ed. by John H. Lee, Jr. & Alfred D. Chandler. LC 79-7552. (History of Management Thought & Practice Ser.). 1980. reprint ed. lib. bdg. 158.95 (*0-405-12336-1*) Ayer.

Pitman's Dictionary of Industrial Administration: A Comprehensive Encyclopedia of the Organization, Administration, & Management of Modern Industry, 2 vols., Vol. 1. Ed. by John H. Lee, Jr. & Alfred D. Chandler. LC 79-7552. (History of Management Thought & Practice Ser.). 1980. reprint ed. lib. bdg. 79.95 (*0-405-12337-X*) Ayer.

Pitman's Dictionary of Industrial Administration: A Comprehensive Encyclopedia of the Organization, Administration, & Management of Modern Industry, 2 vols., Vol. 2. Ed. by John H. Lee, Jr. & Alfred D. Chandler. LC 79-7552. (History of Management Thought & Practice Ser.). 1980. reprint ed. lib. bdg. 79.95 (*0-405-12338-8*) Ayer.

Pitman's Measure of Closeness: A Comparison of Statistical Estimations. Jerome P. Keating et al. LC 93-3059. (Miscellaneous Bks.: No. 37). xv, 226p. 1993. pap. 33.00 (*0-89871-308-0*) Soc Indus-Appl Math.

Piton: A Mechanically Verified Assembly-Level Language. J. Strother Moore. LC 95-48177. (Automated Reasoning Ser.: Vol. 3). 328p. (C). 1996. text 169.00 (*0-7923-3920-7*) Kluwer Academic.

Pitot House on Bayou St. John. Samuel Wilson, Jr. LC 92-83702. 64p. 1992. pap. 10.00 (*1-879714-04-3*) SW PF LA Land.

Pits. Lesley Howarth. LC 96-15127. 228p. (J). (gr. 4-7). 1996. 14.99 (*1-56402-903-4*) Candlewick Pr.

Pits & Pores: Formation, Properties & Significance for Advanced Luminescent Materials. Ed. by P. Schmuki et al. LC 98-110530. (Proceedings Ser.: Vol. 97-7). 538p. 1997. 78.00 (*1-56677-134-X*) Electrochem Soc.

Pits & Wells. Alan M. Hofmeister et al. (Reading for All Learners Ser.). (Illus.). (J). pap. write for info. (*1-56861-151-X*) Swift Lrn Res.

***Pit's Letter.** Sue Coe. LC 00-24391. (Illus.). 48p. 2000. 22.00 (*1-56858-163-7*, Pub. by FWEW) Publishers Group.

Pits Neue Freunde. Marcus Pfister.Tr. of Penguin Pete's New Friends. (GER., Illus.). 32p. (J). (gr. k-3). 1996. 15.95 (*3-314-00301-3*, Pub. by North-South Bks NYC) Chronicle Bks.

Pits Neue Freunde: German Edition. Marcus Pfister. 1995. 13.95 (*3-85825-301-4*) Nord-Sud Verlag AG.

Pits of Middle Texas: People of the Smoke Pits . . . & Their Barbecue. James W. Latimer. (Illus.). 144p. (Orig.). 1993. pap. 12.95 (*0-9635939-0-0*) Literary Serv.

Pitschi. Hans Fischer. LC 96-18716. (Illus.). 32p. (J). (gr. k-3). 1996. 16.95 (*1-55858-644-X*, Pub. by North-South Bks NYC); lib. bdg. 16.88 (*1-55858-645-8*, Pub. by North-South Bks NYC) Chronicle Bks.

Pitt. Archibald P. Rosebery. LC 78-106521. reprint ed. 34.00 (*0-404-05405-6*) AMS Pr.

Pitt. Archibald P. Rosebery. LC 68-25264. (English Biography Ser.: No. 31). 1969. reprint ed. lib. bdg. 75.00 (*0-8383-0236-X*) M S G Haskell Hse.

Pitt The Great Commoner. Jeremy Black. 2000. pap. text 22.95 (*0-7509-2276-1*) Sutton Pub Ltd.

Pitt & Fox. Preston W. Slosson. 1979. pap. 15.00 (*0-911586-33-4*) Wahr.

Pitt County, North Carolina: Eastern Reflections. Mary Boccaccio. LC 98-86002. (Images of America Ser.). (Illus.). 128p. 1998. pap. 14.99 (*0-7524-0974-3*) Arcadia Publng.

Pittaway & Hamerton: Professional Negligence Cases. David Pittaway & Alastair Hammerton. 1997. write for info. (*0-406-08191-3*, PHPNC, MICHIE) LEXIS Pub.

Pitter Patter Pigtail Girls: A Simpler Thyme. Ed. by Stacy Gross West. (Illus.). 50p. 1998. pap. 10.50 (*1-56770-432-8*) S Scheewe Pubns.

Pitti Palace: Guide to the Collections & Complete Catalogue of the Palatine Gallery. Marco Chianni et al. (Illus.). 128p. 1992. 21.95 (*0-8161-0606-1*, G K Hall & Co) Mac Lib Ref.

Pitti Palace: The Palace & Its Art. Marilena Mosco. (Illus.). 96p. 1997. 30.00 (*1-85759-133-X*) Antique Collect.

Pitti Palace, Florence: A Souvenir Guide to the Palace & Its Art. Marilena Mosco. (Illus.). 96p. 1997. 30.00 (*0-85667-469-9*) Scala Books.

Pitting Corrosion of Metals. LC 86-60401. (Illus.). 417p. 1986. 49.00 (*0-915567-19-9*) NACE Intl.

Pitting Resistance of Bevel & Hypoid Gear Teeth. W. Coleman. (Technical Papers: Vol. P229.05). (Illus.). 35p. 1960. pap. text 30.00 (*1-55589-273-6*) AGMA.

Pittis Genealogy: The Pittis Family in England & America, 464 Years, 16 Generations, 1480-1944, with Allied Families. Margaret B. Pittis. (Illus.). 315p. 1996. reprint ed. pap. 49.50 (*0-8328-5254-6*); reprint ed. lib. bdg. 59.50 (*0-8328-5253-8*) Higginson Bk Co.

Pittman-Robertson Program: 50 Years of Dollars & Sense for Wildlife. 20p. 1986. 1.00 (*0-318-23134-4*) Wildlife Mgmt.

Pittoresco: Marco Boschini, His Critics, & Their Critiques of Painterly Brushwork in Seventeenth- & Eighteenth-Century Italy. Philip Sohm. (Studies in the History of Art). (Illus.). 294p. (C). 1992. text 55.00 (*0-521-38256-4*) Cambridge U Pr.

Pittsburg Chefs Book. William Struns. Ed. by R. McMinn. 120p. (Orig.). 1989. pap. text 6.95 (*0-935201-86-6*) Affordable Adven.

***Pittsburgh.** Rand McNally Staff. 1998. pap. 5.95 (*0-528-94534-3*) Rand McNally.

Pittsburgh, 1. Rand McNally Staff. 1998. pap. 15.95 (*0-528-97254-5*) Rand McNally.

Pittsburgh. Ruth H. Seitz. (Pennsylvania's Cultural & Natural Heritage Ser.: Vol. 5). (Illus.). 120p. 1997. 29.95 (*1-879441-96-9*) RB Bks.

Pittsburgh. Ed. by Lubove. LC 76-3119. (Documentary History of American Cities Ser.). (C). 1976. reprint ed. pap. 6.95 (*0-531-05590-6*) Wiener Pubs Inc.

Pittsburgh: A Place in Time. Abby Mendelson. LC 98-32214. 180p. 1999. pap. 15.95 (*1-887969-08-X*) Cathedral PA.

Pittsburgh: A Portrait of Progress. Evan M. Pattak & Andrew G. Wilson. Ed. by Scott Robertson. LC 92-64401. (Illus.). 160p. 1993. text 49.95 (*0-9634100-0-8*, 08) Wyndham Pubns.

Pittsburgh: An Urban Portrait. Franklin Toker. LC 85-71786. (Illus.). 360p. 1995. pap. 19.95 (*0-8229-5434-6*) U of Pittsburgh Pr.

Pittsburgh: The Story of a City. Leland Baldwin. 1993. reprint ed. lib. bdg. 89.00 (*0-7812-5424-8*) Rprt Serv.

Pittsburgh: The Story of a City, 1750-1865. rev. ed. Leland D. Baldwin. LC 73-104172. (Illus.). 360p. 1970. reprint ed. pap. 14.95 (*0-8229-5216-5*) U of Pittsburgh Pr.

Pittsburgh: The Story of an American City. enl. ed. Stefan Lorant. LC 75-24970. (Illus.). 736p. 1988. 24.95 (*0-685-92012-7*) Authors Edn MA.

Pittsburgh: Views into the 21st Century. Photos by Joel B. Levinson & Susan L. Nega. (Illus.). 96p. (Orig.). 1996. pap. 16.50 (*0-914355-23-6*) J B Jeffers.

Pittsburgh Book of Contemporary American Poetry. Ed. by Ed Ochester & Peter Oresick. LC 92-50846. (Poetry Ser.). (Illus.). 416p. (Orig.). (C). 1993. pap. 15.95 (*0-8229-5506-7*); text 29.95 (*0-8229-3752-2*) U of Pittsburgh Pr.

Pittsburgh Business Directory. 2nd rev. ed. Jeffrey Levine. 1041p. 1997. 49.95 (*0-9650280-1-1*) Pittsbrgh Busn.

Pittsburgh District Civic Frontage, Vol. 5. Ed. by Paul U. Kellogg. LC 73-11904. (Metropolitan America Ser.). 678p. 1974. reprint ed. 46.95 (*0-405-05397-5*) Ayer.

***Pittsburgh East Entertainment, 2000.** (Illus.). 966p. 1999. pap. 33.00 (*1-880248-60-3*, 005A) Enter Pubns.

***Pittsburgh Entertainment, 2000.** (Illus.). 965p. 1999. pap. 33.00 (*1-880248-59-X*, 0007) Enter Pubns.

Pittsburgh Figured Out. Robert Firth. 1990. pap. 8.95 (*0-9628042-0-7*) Informing Design.

Pittsburgh Figured Out. 2nd ed. Robert Firth. 1991. pap. 10.95 (*0-9628042-1-5*) Informing Design.

Pittsburgh FUN-ics: Yunz Can Talk Like Pixberg. Michael L. Ellis, 3rd. (Illus.). 221p. 1993. pap. text 3.50 (*0-929178-24-6*) Valley Forge Pub.

Pittsburgh Graded Tax Plan. Percy R. Williams. 71p. 1964. pap. 1.00 (*0-911312-38-2*) Schalkenbach.

Pittsburgh in a Box: Pittsburgh Fast; Pittsburgh on Foot; Pittsburgh Happens Here, 3 bks., Set. Robert Firth. 1992. boxed set. write for info. (*0-9628042-2-3*) Informing Design.

Pittsburgh in the Year 1826. Samuel Jones. LC 70-125749. (American Environmental Studies). 1974. reprint ed. 18.95 (*0-405-02673-0*) Ayer.

Pittsburgh Job Source: Everything You Need to Know to Land the Internship, Entry-Level, or Middle Management Job of Your Choice. Mary McMahon et al. Ed. by Donna C. Hicks. 328p. (Orig.). 1996. 15.95 (*0-9635651-5-X*) Benjamin Scott.

***Pittsburgh JobBank.** 3rd ed. (JobBank Ser.). 336p. 2000. pap. 16.95 (*1-58062-444-8*) Adams Media.

Pittsburgh JobBank: 1999 Edition. 2nd ed. Ed. by Adams Media Corporation Staff. (JobBank Ser.). 304p. 1998. pap. 16.95 (*1-58062-094-9*) Adams Media.

Pittsburgh Memoranda. Haniel Long. LC 90-33956. 88p. 1990. reprint ed. text 14.95 (*0-8229-3657-7*) U of Pittsburgh Pr.

Pittsburgh Metro Recreation & Shopping Guide. Gousha, H. M., Editors. 1995. pap. 2.95 (*0-671-53571-4*, H M Gousha) Prntice Hall Bks.

Pittsburgh over 50 & Retirement Guide. large type ed. Leslie Swiantek. LC 98-30177. (Retirement & Relocation Guides Ser.). (Illus.). 350p. (Orig.). 1999. pap. 24.95 (*1-56559-109-7*) HGI-Over Fifty.

Pittsburgh, Pa. Gazette Genealogical Gleanings, 1786-1820, Vol. I. Mark H. Welchley. 81p. 1983. per. 11.00 (*0-933227-66-3*, 504) Closson Pr.

Pittsburgh Penguins see NHL Today

Pittsburgh Penguins. Morgan Hughes. LC 98-19358. (Inside the NHL Ser.). (J). 1998. write for info. (*1-57765-058-1*) ABDO Pub Co.

Pittsburgh Photography: A New Generation. John Caldwell, pseud & Annegreth Nill. (Illus.). 1987. pap. 5.00 (*0-88039-015-8*) Mus Art Carnegie.

Pittsburgh Pirates. Chris W. Sehnert. LC 96-1514. (Illus.). 32p. (J). (gr. 3-8). 1997. lib. bdg. 15.95 (*1-56239-660-9*) ABDO Pub Co.

Pittsburgh Pirates. Robert Smizik. (Illus.). 256p. 1990. 29.95 (*0-8027-1102-2*) Walker & Co.

Pittsburgh Portraits. Elizabeth Moorhead. (Orig.). 1955. pap. 1.95 (*0-910286-25-6*) Boxwood.

Pittsburgh Resource Book. 96p. (Orig.). 1996. pap. 5.95 (*0-914355-22-8*) J B Jeffers.

Pittsburgh Revealed: Photographs since 1850. Linda Benedict-Jones et al. LC 96-52218. (Illus.). 208p. (Orig.). 1997. pap. 39.95 (*0-88039-034-4*) Mus Art Carnegie.

***Pittsburgh Sports: Stories from the Steel City.** Ed. by Randy Roberts. (Sports History Ser.). (Illus.). 238p. 2000. 29.95 (*0-8229-4143-0*) U of Pittsburgh Pr.

Pittsburgh Steelers. Ed Bouchette. LC 94-16792. 1994. pap. 9.99 (*0-312-11325-0*) St Martin.

Pittsburgh Steelers. C. W. C. Sports Staff. 1998. pap. text 9.95 (*1-891613-19-7*) Innov Futures.

Pittsburgh Steelers. Bob Italia. LC 95-22314. (Inside the NFL Ser.). (Illus.). 32p. (J). (gr. 3-8). 1996. lib. bdg. 15.98 (*1-56239-526-2*) ABDO Pub Co.

Pittsburgh Steelers. Abby Mendelson. 1996. 36.95 (*0-87833-957-4*) Taylor Pub.

Pittsburgh Steelers. limited ed. Abby Mendelson. 1996. 75.00 (*0-87833-134-4*) Taylor Pub.

***Pittsburgh Steelers.** 3rd rev. ed. Julie Nelson. (Pro Football Today Ser.). (Illus.). 32p. (YA). (gr. 3-12). 2000. lib. bdg. 22.60 (*1-58341-056-2*, Creat Educ) Creative Co.

Pittsburgh Steelers Football Team. William W. Lace. LC 98-9664. (Great Sports Teams Ser.). 48p. (J). (gr. 4-10). 1999. lib. bdg. 18.95 (*0-7660-1099-6*) Enslow Pubs.

Pittsburgh Street Atlas. H. M. Gousha. 1995. 12.95 (*0-671-89550-8*) S&S Trade.

Pittsburgh Surveyed: Social Science & Social Reform in the Early Twentieth Century. Ed. by Maurine W. Greenwald & Margo J. Anderson. LC 96-10048. (Illus.). 368p. 1996. pap. 22.95 (*0-8229-5610-1*); text 49.95 (*0-8229-3956-8*) U of Pittsburgh Pr.

***Pittsburgh, the Story of an American City: The Millennium Edition.** 5th ed. Stefan Lorant et al. (Illus.). 776p. 1999. 39.95 (*0-9674103-0-4*) Esselmont Bks.

Pittsburgh Then & Now. Arthur G. Smith. LC 89-35895. (Illus.). 336p. 1990. text 37.50 (*0-8229-3830-8*) U of Pittsburgh Pr.

***Pittsburgh Trivia for Baby Boomers.** Sports Publishing Inc. Staff. (Illus.). 128p. 1999. pap. 4.95 (*1-58261-143-2*, Pub. by Sprts Pubng) Partners-West.

Pittsburgh Walking Map & Guide: Rivers Edition. rev. ed. Rosemary Parlak. 1994. pap. 3.50 (*0-944101-19-4*) New Pittsburgh.

Pittsburgh Zoo: A 100 Year History. Rachel Colker. 1998. write for info. (*1-57864-055-5*); pap. write for info. (*1-57864-076-8*) Donning Co.

Pittsburgh's Best Shopping. Maggie Setler. 50p. (Orig.). 1993. pap. 4.95 (*0-9621737-1-1*) Pittsburgh Promo.

***Pittsburgh's Bridges: Architecture & Engineering.** Walter C. Kidney. LC 99-75974. (Illus.). 252p. 1999. 49.95 (*0-916670-21-X*, Pub. by Pitt Hist & Landmks Found) United Mag Co.

Pittsburgh's Landmark Architecture: The Historic Buildings of Pittsburgh & Allegheny County. expanded rev. ed. Walter C. Kidney. Ed. by Louise Sturgess. LC 96-72583. Orig. Title: Landmark Architecture: Pittsburgh & Allegheny County (1985). (Illus.). 736p. 1997. boxed set 60.00 (*0-916670-18-X*) Pitt Hist & Landmks Found.

Pittsburgh's Vintage Firemen. Howard V. Worley, Jr. LC 97-93810. (Illus.). 96p. (Orig.). 1997. pap. 22.95 (*0-9658620-0-3*) HowDy Prods.

Pittsford's Second Century, 1872-1997. Jean S. Davies et al. (Illus.). 768p. 1999. 50.00 (*0-914659-85-5*) Phoenix Pub.

Pittsylvania Country. George Swetnam. LC 92-80815. 315p. 1993. pap. 19.95 (*0-945437-10-2*) MacDonald-Sward.

Pittsylvania County Marriages, 1767-1805. Catherine L. Knorr. 136p. 1982. reprint ed. 17.50 (*0-89308-260-0*, VA 23) Southern Hist Pr.

An Asterisk (*) at the beginning of an entry indicates that the title is appearing for the first time.

Pittsylvania County, Virginia Deed, 1774-1778, Bk. 4. T.L.C. Genealogy Staff. LC 91-65011. 114p. (Orig.). 1991. pap., spiral bd. 12.00 (*1-886633-98-3*) TLC Genealogy.

Pittsylvania County, Virginia Deeds, 1791-1794. T.L.C. Genealogy Staff. LC 91-65011. 103p. (Orig.). 1991. pap., spiral bd. 12.00 (*1-886633-99-1*) TLC Genealogy.

Pittsylvania County, Virginia, Deeds, 1778-1780. LC 98-121934. 86p. 1997. spiral bd. 10.00 (*1-57445-034-4*) TLC Genealogy.

Pittura del Cinquecento see Storia dell'Arte Italiana, 1901-1940

Pittura del Quattrocento see Storia dell'Arte Italiana, 1901-1940

Pittura del Trecento e le Sue Origini see Storia dell'Arte Italiana, 1901-1940

Pittura e Misericordia: The Oratory of S. Giovanni Decollato in Rome. Jean S. Weisz. LC 84-151. (Studies in the Fine Arts - Art Patronage: No. 2). 197p. reprint ed. pap. 61.10 (*0-8357-1461-6*, 207058600001) Bks Demand.

Pituitary. Shlomo Melmed. (Illus.). 752p. 1990. 59.95 (*0-86542-126-9*) Blackwell Sci.

Pituitary Adenoma. Ed. by Kalmon D. Post et al. LC 79-24811. (Illus.). 531p. 1980. reprint ed. pap. 164.70 (*0-608-05439-9*, 206590800006) Bks Demand.

Pituitary Adenomas. Landolt. 1995. text 215.00 (*0-443-05134-8*, W B Saunders Co) Harcrt Hlth Sci Grp.

Pituitary Adenomas. Glenn E. Sheline et al. (Oncologic Multidisciplinary Decisions in Onology Ser.). (Illus.). 248p. 1981. pap. 135.00 (*0-08-027463-3*, Pergamon Pr) Elsevier.

Pituitary Adenomas: From Basic Research to Diagnostic & Therapy, Proceedings of the 6th European Workshop on Pituitary Adenomas, Berlin, Germany, 24-27 July, 1996, Vol. 112. Klaus Von Werder & Rudolf Fahlbusch. LC 96-47748. (International Congress Ser.). 356p. 1996. 192.00 (*0-444-82425-1*) Elsevier.

Pituitary & Testis: Clinical & Experimental Studies. Ed. by David M. De Kretser et al. (Monographs on Endocrinology: Vol. 25). (Illus.). 200p. 1983. 100.00 (*0-387-11874-8*) Spr-Verlag.

Pituitary Diseases. Kalman Kovacs et al. 208p. 1980. 121.00 (*0-8493-5435-8*, RC658, CRC Reprint) Franklin.

Pituitary Function & Immunity. Ed. by Istvan Berczi. 336p. 1986. lib. bdg. 248.00 (*0-8493-6107-9*, QR182) CRC Pr.

Pituitary Gland. C. R. Kannan. (Clinical Surveys in Endocrinology Ser.: Vol. 1). (Illus.). 704p. (C). 1987. text 130.00 (*0-306-42506-8*, Kluwer Plenum) Kluwer Academic.

Pituitary Gland. 2nd ed. Ed. by Hiroo Imura. LC 94-2236. (Comprehensive Endocrinology Ser.). 544p. 1994. text 140.00 (*0-7817-0207-0*) Lppncott W & W.

Pituitary Patient Resource Guide. 2nd ed. Ed. by Shereen Ezzat. (Illus.). 300p. 1997. pap. 39.95 (*0-9660141-0-3*) Pit Tumor Netwk.

Pituitaty Disorders: Comprehensive Management. Ed. by Ali F. Krisht & George T. Tindall. LC 98-3826. 427p. 1998. 175.00 (*0-683-30143-8*) Lppncott W & W.

Pity Him Afterwards. Donald E. Westlake. 192p. 1996. mass mkt. 4.95 (*0-7867-0396-2*) Carroll & Graf.

Pity Is Not Enough. Josepine Herbst. LC 97-25830. (Radical Novel Reconsidered Ser.). 400p. 1998. 16.95 (*0-252-06652-9*) U of Ill Pr.

Pity My Simplicity. John Wilson. 1980. pap. 11.99 (*0-85234-140-7*, Pub. by Evangelical Pr) P & R Pubng.

Pity of War: Explaining World War I. Niall Ferguson. (Illus.). 608p. 1999. 24.00 (*0-465-05711-X*, Pub. by Basic) HarpC.

Pity of War: Explaining World War I. Niall Ferguson. LC 99-212497. (Illus.). 608p. 2000. pap. 17.00 (*0-465-05712-8*, Pub. by Basic) HarpC.

Pity of War: Explaining World War I. Niall Ferguson. 304p. 1998. (*0-7139-9246-8*) Viking Penguin.

Pity of War: Poems of the 1st World War. Ed. by Jill Balcon. (Illus.). 80p. 1985. 18.95 (*0-85683-083-6*, Pub. by Shepheard-Walwyn Pubs) Paul & Co Pubs.

***Pity the Bathtub Its Forced Embrace of the Human Form.** Matthea Harvey. 82p. 2000. per. 11.95 (*1-882295-26-9*, Pub. by Alice James Bks) SPD-Small Pr Dist.

Pity the Monsters: The Political Vision of Robert Lowell. Alan Williamson. LC 86-1864. 232p. 1986. reprint ed. lib. bdg. 59.50 (*0-313-25135-5*, WIPI, Greenwood Pr) Greenwood.

Pity the Puddy-Tat. Oliver Noone. LC 97-220742. (Looney Tunes Pop-up Bks.). (Illus.). 10p. (J). (ps-k). 1997. bds. 7.98 (*0-7853-2181-0*, PIL20) Pubns Intl Ltd.

Pity the Sinner. large type ed. Mark Daniel. 1995. 27.99 (*0-7505-0728-4*, Pub. by Mgna Lrg Print) Ulverscroft.

Piuma E il Conigliettо Fifone. Hans De Beer.Tr. of Little Polar Bear & the Brave Little Hare. (ITA., Illus.). (J). 15.95 (*88-8203-045-8*, Pub. by North-South Bks NYC) Chronicle Bks.

Piuma Nel Paese delle Tigri. Hans De Beer.Tr. of Little Polar Bear, Take Me Home!. (ITA., Illus.). 32p. (J). (gr. k-3). 15.95 (*88-8203-020-2*, Pub. by North-South Bks NYC) Chronicle Bks.

Pius XII: Selected Encyclicals & Addresses. Pius XII, pseud. vi, 387p. 1995. text 21.95 (*0-912141-19-0*) Roman Cath Bks.

***Pius XII & the Second World War: According to the Archives of the Vatican.** Pierre Blet. Tr. by Lawrence J. Johnson from FRE. LC 99-24020. 416p. 1999. 29.95 (*0-8091-0503-9*) Paulist Pr.

Pivot of Asia. Owen Lattimore. LC 72-4438. reprint ed. 32.50 (*0-404-10634-X*) AMS Pr.

Pivot of Civilization. Margaret Sanger. (Illus.). 284p. 1997. reprint ed. pap. text 20.00 (*1-878465-27-9*) Scott-Townsend Pubs.

Pivot of Civilization see Works

Pivot of the Universe: Nasir al-Din Shah & the Iranian Monarchy, 1831-1896. Abbas Amanat. 1998. 45.00 (*0-934211-51-5*) Mage Pubs Inc.

Pivot of the Universe: Nasir al-Din Shah & the Iranian Monarchy, 1831-1896. Abbas Amanat. LC 95-50481. (Illus.). 532p. (C). 1997. 50.00 (*0-520-08321-0*, Pub. by U CA Pr) Cal Prin Full Svc.

Pivot Patterns in the Former Prophets. Nathan Klauss. (J. S. O. T. S. Ser.: Vol. 247). 200p. 1999. 57.50 (*1-85075-912-X*, Pub. by Sheffield Acad) CUP Services.

Pivotal Catalogues in the Aeneid. Philip W. Basson. xii, 208p. (Orig.). 1975. pap. 54.00 (*90-256-0767-5*, Pub. by AM Hakkert); pap. text 40.00 (*0-317-57962-2*, Pub. by AM Hakkert) Coronet Bks.

Pivotal Conflict: A Comprehensive Chronology of the First World War, 1914-1919. Gerald Herman. LC 91-22245. 824p. 1992. lib. bdg. 145.00 (*0-313-22793-4*, HPC, Greenwood Pr) Greenwood.

Pivotal Decades: The United States, 1900-1920. John J. Cooper, Jr. 432p. 1990. pap. 16.95 (*0-393-95655-5*) Norton.

Pivotal Measures in Statistical Experiments & Sufficiency. Sakutaro Yamada. LC 93-47440. (Lecture Notes in Statistics Ser.: Vol. 84). 144p. 1994. 39.95 (*0-387-94216-5*) Spr-Verlag.

Pivotal Papers on Identification. Ed. by George H. Pollock. LC 93-9298. 508p. 1993. 72.50 (*0-8236-4130-9*) Intl Univs Pr.

Pivotal Politics. Krehbiel. LC 97-42848. (Illus.). 240p. 1998. lib. bdg. 50.00 (*0-226-45271-9*) U Ch Pr.

Pivotal Politics. Keith Krehbiel. LC 97-42848. (Illus.). 258p. 1998. pap. text 17.00 (*0-226-45272-7*) U Ch Pr.

***Pivotal States.** Robert Chase. (C). 2000. pap. text 12.50 (*0-393-97583-5*) Norton.

Pivotal States: A New Framework for U. S. Policy in the Developing World. Ed. by Robert S. Chase et al. LC 98-29490. 448p. 1998. 35.00 (*0-393-04675-3*) Norton.

Pix 1. Ed. by Flona Halberstadt. 1995. pap. 22.95 (*0-253-30017-7*) Ind U Pr.

Pix 2. Ed. by Llona Halberstadt. (Illus.). 160p. 1995. pap. 29.95 (*0-253-30019-3*) Ind U Pr.

Pixaud's Practical Grimoire. (Torg Ser.). 96p. 15.00 (*0-87431-318-X*, 20559) West End Games.

Pixel Helps Pooper Out of a Pickle. Barbara Belle. (Pixel Ser.: No. 2). (Illus.). 24p. (Orig.). (J). (gr. 1-5). 1995. pap. 3.25 (*0-935163-02-6*) Pixel Prods Pubns.

Pixel Juice. Jeff Noon. 1998. 29.95 (*0-385-40859-5*, DD Bks Yng Read) BDD Bks Young Read.

***Pixel Perfect: The New Digital Designer.** Ed. by Kathleen Ziegler & Nick Greco. (Illus.). 160p. 2000. pap. 35.00 (*0-8230-7408-0*) Watsn-Guptill.

Pixel Photography. Robert McMahan. 200p. 1993. pap. 18.95 (*1-881656-01-2*) Olive Pr.

Pixie. Matthew Lipman. LC 81-67706. (Philosophy for Children Ser.). 98p. (Orig.). (J). (gr. 3-4). 1981. pap. 10.50 (*0-916834-17-4*, TX782-682) Inst Advncmnt Philos Child.

Pixie. large type ed. Peggy O'More. (Linford Romance Library). 256p. 1995. pap. 16.99 (*0-7089-7664-6*, Linford) Ulverscroft.

Pixie Dust: Fabulous Father. Carla Cassidy. (Romance Ser.). 1993. per. 2.75 (*0-373-08958-9*, 5-08958-6) Silhouette.

Pixies - Bossanova. Ed. by Milton Okun. pap. 12.95 (*0-89524-608-2*) Cherry Lane.

***Pixiewater: The Miracle of the Pixie Pool.** Brian J. Helsaple. LC 99-93208. (Life Lessons Ser.). (J). (gr. k-5). 1999. 20.95 incl. audio (*1-928714-00-5*) Peri Tales.

Pixy. Max Andersson. 72p. 1993. pap. 11.95 (*1-56097-131-2*) Fantagraph Bks.

Pixy Junket-Comic. Pure. (Illus.). 192p. 15.95 (*1-56931-239-7*) Viz Commns Inc.

Piyaataalghiit (Going for Walk) V. Kaneshiro. (ESK.). 25p. (J). 1975. pap. 2.50 (*0-933769-74-1*) Alaska Native.

***Pizarro & the Conquest of the Incan Empire.** Richard Worth. LC 99-39107. (Illus.). 128p. (gr. 5 up). 2000. lib. bdg. 20.95 (*0-7660-1396-0*) Enslow Pubs.

Pizarro, Orellana, & the Exploration of the Amazon. Brendan Bernhard. Ed. by William H. Goetzmann. (World Explorers Ser.). (Illus.). 120p. (YA). (gr. 5 up). 1991. lib. bdg. 19.95 (*0-7910-1305-7*) Chelsea Hse.

***Pizazz: Poems from Hollywood.** Mark Dunster. 11p. 1999. pap. 5.00 (*0-89642-857-5*) Linden Pubs.

***Pizca de Sal, Vol. 1.** Xiomara J. Pages. LC 99-60997. (Coleccion Felix Varela: Vol. 7). (SPA., Illus.). 112p. 1999. pap. 12.00 (*0-89729-888-8*) Ediciones.

Pizca de Sal, Vol. II. Xiomara J. Pages. (Coleccion Felix Varela: Vol. 7). (SPA.). 111p. pap. 12.00 (*0-89729-903-5*) Ediciones.

Pizza. Lorenza De' Medici. Ed. by Laurie Wertz. LC 92-27838. (Williams-Sonoma Kitchen Library). (Illus.). 108p. 1993. lib. bdg. write for info. (*0-7835-0230-3*) Time-Life.

Pizza. Lorenza De' Medici. Ed. by Laurie Wertz. LC 92-27838. (Williams-Sonoma Kitchen Library). (Illus.). 108p. (J). (gr. 11). 1999. 18.95 (*0-7835-0229-X*) Time-Life.

Pizza! Teresa Martino. (Real Readers Ser.: Level Green). (Illus.). 32p. (J). (ps-3). 1989. lib. bdg. 21.40 (*0-8172-3533-7*) Raintree Steck-V.

Pizza. James McNair. LC 87-17381. (Illus.). 96p. 1987. 19.95 (*0-87701-481-7*); pap. 12.95 (*0-87701-448-5*) Chronicle Bks.

***Pizza!** Jean Pare. 1999. pap. 10.99 (*1-895455-52-9*) Companys Coming.

***Pizza.** Fog City Press. LC 99-88295. (Little Guides Ser.). (Illus.). 320p. 2000. reprint ed. pap. 14.95 (*1-875137-78-5*) Weldon Owen.

Pizza: A Slice of the New West. Dennis L. Rhode. LC 97-17037. (Illus.). 144p. 1997. pap. 9.95 (*0-87358-677-8*) Northland AZ.

Pizza: Any Way You Slice It. Robert Scicolone. 224p. (Orig.). 1999. reprint ed. pap. 15.00 (*0-7679-0373-0*) Broadway BDD.

***Pizza: From Its Italian Origins to the Modern Table.** Rosario Buonassisi. (Illus.). 168p. 2000. pap. 24.95 (*1-55209-321-2*) Firefly Bks Ltd.

***Pizza & Neopolitan Cookery.** Elizabetta Piazzesi. 1999. pap. text 20.95 (*88-8029-898-4*) Bonechi.

Pizza & Pasta Recipes: Appetising, Exciting & Inexpensive Italian Dishes. Renato Rudatis. (Illus.). 1991. 24.50 (*0-572-01691-3*, Pub. by W Foulsham) Trans-Atl Phila.

Pizza & Snacks - Make It Tonight: Home Library Mini-Menu Cookbooks. Home Library Editors. (Illus.). 64p. 1999. pap. 3.95 (*1-56426-204-9*, Pub. by Cole Group) ACCESS Pubs Network.

Pizza & the Art of Life Management. Maura Beatty. 236p. 1996. pap. text 14.95 (*0-7872-2142-2*) Kendall-Hunt.

Pizza Boogie Songbook. Joanne Olshansky Hammil. (Illus.). 33p. (Orig.). (J). (gr. k-6). 1990. pap. 10.00 (*0-9626239-0-3*) JHO Music.

Pizza Book. Stephen Krensky. (Illus.). 32p. (J). (gr. 1-5). 1992. pap. 2.50 (*0-590-44844-7*, 042, Cartwheel) Scholastic Inc.

Pizza Book: Everything There Is to Know about the World's Greatest Pie. Evelyn Slomon. LC 83-45926. (Illus.). 276p. 1984. 23.00 (*0-8129-1113-X*, Times Bks) Crown Pub Group.

Pizza California Style. Norman Kolpas. (Illus.). 128p. 1989. pap. 12.95 (*0-8092-4500-0*, 450000, Contemporary Bks) NTC Contemp Pub Co.

Pizza Cats. Gail Herman. (Ready to Read). (Illus.). 32p. (J). (ps-3). 1999. pap. 3.99 (*0-689-82391-6*) S&S Childrens.

***Pizza Cats.** Gail Herman. (Ready to Read). (Illus.). (J). (ps-3). 2000. per. write for info. (*0-671-77316-X*) S&S Childrens.

***Pizza Connection: Lawyers, Money, Drugs, Mafia.** Shana Alexander. (Illus.). 442p. 1999. reprint ed. text 20.00 (*0-7881-6836-3*) DIANE Pub.

Pizza Cookbook. Myra Street. 1995. 6.98 (*0-7858-0507-9*) Bk Sales Inc.

Pizza, Focaccia, Flat & Filled Breads from Your Bread Machine: Perfect Every Time. Lora A. Brody. LC 94-26833. 320p. 1995. pap. 23.00 (*0-688-13752-0*, Wm Morrow) Morrow Avon.

Pizza for Breakfast. Maryann Kovalski. (Illus.). 32p. (J). 1990. reprint ed. pap. 4.95 (*1-55074-152-7*) Kids Can Pr.

Pizza, Fries & a Slice of Pie. Moira Butterfield. LC 97-22348. (Can You Find? Ser.). (Illus.). (J). 1998. pap. write for info. (*0-382-39988-9*) Silver Burdett Pr.

Pizza, Fries & a Slice of Pie. Moira Butterfield & Jan Lewis. LC 97-22348. (Can You Find? Ser.). (Illus.). (J). 1998. lib. bdg. write for info. (*0-382-39989-7*) Silver Burdett Pr.

Pizza Fun. Judy Bastyra. LC 96-30161. (Illus.). 24p. (J). (ps-2). 1997. 11.95 (*0-7534-5061-5*, Kingfisher) LKC.

Pizza Gourmet: Simple Recipes for Spectacular Pizzas. Shea MacKenzie. LC 95-4860. (Illus.). 232p. pap. 14.95 (*0-89529-656-X*, Avery) Penguin Putnam.

Pizza Lover's Collection. (Favorite All Time Recipes Ser.). (Illus.). 96p. 1993. 7.98 (*0-7853-0194-1*, 2016803) Pubns Intl Ltd.

Pizza Lover's Cookbook: Creative & Delicious Recipes for Making the World's Favorite Food. Kirk S. Stuart & Gregory D. Boock. LC 96-22971. 144p. 1996. pap. text 15.00 (*0-7615-0448-6*) Prima Pub.

Pizza Man. Marjorie Pillar. LC 89-35526. (Illus.). 40p. (J). (gr. k-3). 1990. 11.95 (*0-690-04836-X*); lib. bdg. 11.89 (*0-690-04838-6*) HarpC Child Bks.

Pizza Mystery. Illus. by Charles Tang. LC 92-32263. (Boxcar Children Ser.: No. 33). 128p. (J). (gr. 2-5). 1993. pap. 3.95 (*0-8075-6535-0*); lib. bdg. 13.95 (*0-8075-6534-2*) A Whitman.

Pizza Mystery. Created by Gertrude Chandler Warner. (Boxcar Children Ser.: No. 33). (J). (gr. 2-5). 1992. 9.05 (*0-606-08935-7*, Pub. by Turtleback) Demco.

***Pizza Napoletana!** Pamela Sheldon Johns & Jennifer Barry. LC 99-14301. 112p. 1999. 17.95 (*1-58008-085-5*) Ten Speed Pr.

Pizza Party, 1. S. Johnston. (Illus.). 24p. (ps-3). 1998. pap. text 5.25 (*0-9681925-2-1*) Hushion Hse.

Pizza Party. Grace Maccarone. LC 93-19732. (Hello Reader! Ser.). (Illus.). 32p. (J). (ps-4). 1994. pap. 3.50 (*0-590-47563-0*, Cartwheel) Scholastic Inc.

Pizza Party! Grace Maccarone. LC 93-19732. (Hello, Reader! Ser.). 1994. 8.70 (*0-606-06672-1*, Pub. by Turtleback) Demco.

Pizza Pat. Rita G. Gelman. LC 97-44609. (Step into Reading Ser.: A Step 1 Book). (Illus.). 32p. (J). (ps-1). 1999. pap. 3.99 (*0-679-89134-X*) Random.

Pizza Pat. Rita G. Gelman. LC 97-44609. (Step into Reading Ser.: A Step 1 Book). (Illus.). 32p. (J). (gr. k-3). 1999. lib. bdg. 11.99 (*0-679-99134-4*) Random.

***Pizza Perfection.** . Southwater. 2000. 12.95 (*1-84215-143-6*) Anness Pub.

Pizza Pie Slugger. Jean Marzollo. (Stepping Stone Bks.). (J). 1989. 9.19 (*0-606-04300-4*, Pub. by Turtleback) Demco.

Pizza Pizzazz Vol. 12: Basic to Gourmet. Richard Erickson. Ed. by Jeannine Winquist. (Illus.). 64p. (Orig.). 1985. pap., per. 3.95 (*0-942320-19-0*) Am Cooking.

Pizza Plot: And a Few Other Slices from Life. John I. Ades. LC 88-37409. 160p. (Orig.). 1989. pap. 8.95 (*0-931832-22-5*) Fithian Pr.

Pizza Presto. Norman Kolpas. LC 96-11466. 176p. 1996. pap. 12.95 (*0-8092-3220-0*, 322000, Contemporary Bks) NTC Contemp Pub Co.

Pizza Primer. Cole Group Editors Staff. (Cole's Cooking Companion Ser.). 96p. 1995. pap. 7.95 (*1-56426-806-3*) Cole Group.

Pizza Problem: Democracy in Action. Maryrose Eannace. 70p. (Orig.). (J). (gr. 6-10). 1990. pap. text 8.75 (*0-936826-35-5*) PS Assocs Croton.

Pizza Puzzle. Susan Beth Pfeffer. 128p. (J). (gr. 3-7). 1997. pap. 3.99 (*0-440-41391-5*) Dell.

Pizza Puzzle. Susan Beth Pfeffer. 1996. 21.95 (*0-385-31730-1*) Doubleday.

Pizza Puzzle. Susan Beth Pfeffer. 1997. 9.09 (*0-606-11753-9*, Pub. by Turtleback) Demco.

***Pizza Puzzle.** Susan Beth Pfeffer. 119p. (YA). (gr. 7-9). 1999. reprint ed. text 16.00 (*0-7881-6640-9*) DIANE Pub.

Pizza Restaurant. 49p. 1996. pap. 5.00 (*0-16-061967-X*) USGPO.

Pizza Restaurant: Market Segment Specialization Program - Audit Technique Guide. 56p. (Orig.). 1996. pap. 17.60 (*1-57402-118-4*) Athena Info Mgt.

Pizza Tastes Great. William P. Pickett. 1995. pap. text, wbk. ed. 13.60 (*0-13-102492-2*) P-H.

Pizza Tastes Great: Dialogues & Stories. William P. Pickett. (Illus.). 176p. (C). 1987. pap. text 22.27 (*0-13-677626-4*) P-H.

Pizza That Time Forgot. William L. DeAndrea & Matthew DeAndrea. 128p. (J). (gr. 3-7). 1999. mass mkt. 3.99 (*0-380-79155-2*, Avon Bks) Morrow Avon.

Pizza the Size of the Sun. Jack Prelutsky. LC 95-35930. (Illus.). 160p. (J). (ps-3). 1996. 18.00 (*0-688-13235-9*, Grenwillow Bks) HarpC Child Bks.

Pizza the Size of the Sun. Jack Prelutsky. LC 95-35930. (Illus.). 160p. (J). (ps-3). 1996. 17.93 (*0-688-13236-7*, Grenwillow Bks) HarpC Child Bks.

Pizza Time, 1. Young & Hoidas. 1998. pap. text 5.50 (*0-9681925-0-5*) Hushion Hse.

Pizza War: Mercer Mayer's LC & The Critter Kids. Mercer Mayer. LC 94-75364. (Mini Novels Ser.: Vol. 5). (Illus.). 72p. (J). (ps-3). 1995. per. 4.69 (*0-307-15979-5*, 15979, Goldn Books) Gldn Bks Pub Co.

Pizza with Extra Creeps. Fred E. Katz. LC 97-11115. (Spinechillers Mysteries Ser.: Vol. 4). (Illus.). 144p. (J). (gr. 3-7). 1997. pap. 5.99 (*0-8499-4059-1*) Tommy Nelson.

Pizza Zombies. E. W. Leroe. LC 95-45998. (Friendly Corners Ser.: No. 2). (Illus.). 128p. (J). (gr. 4-7). 1996. pap. 3.95 (*0-7868-1096-3*, Pub. by Hyprn Ppbks) Little.

Pizzas. Better Homes & Gardens. (Cooking for Today Ser.). (Illus.). 144p. 1994. 15.95 (*0-696-02569-8*) Meredith Bks.

Pizzas & Melts. (Mini Cook Bks.). 148p. pap. 1.95 (*3-8290-0380-3*, 770241) Konemann.

PIZZAstrology: How to Interpret Your Sauce Sign for Fun & Prophet! Tom Olshefski & Jacqueline Olshefski. (Illus.). iv, 108p. 1998. pap. 14.95 (*0-9666873-0-2*) Life Enhancing Pubns.

Pizzaz for Pennies: Designer Clothes for Children. Barb Griffin. (Illus.). 148p. (Orig.). 1989. pap. 14.95 (*0-937679-04-6*) Sewing Sampler.

Pizzeria: The Best of Casual Pizza Oven Cooking. Evan Kleiman. LC 97-4090. (Casual Cuisines of the World Ser.). (Illus.). 128p. 1997. 19.95 (*0-376-02043-1*) Sunset Books.

PJ Funnybunny Beginner Book. Marilyn Sadler. LC 96-16735. (J). 1997. lib. bdg. 11.99 (*0-679-98181-0*) McKay.

Pjatidesjatnitsa. M. Skaballanovitch.Tr. of Pentacost. 176p. reprint ed. pap. 6.00 (*0-317-29163-7*) Holy Trinity.

PK: A Report on the Power of Psychokinesis, the Mental Energy to Move Matter. Michael H. Brown. LC 76-21121. (Freedeeds Library). (Illus.). 320p. 1976. 15.95 (*0-8334-0716-3*, Freedeeds Libr) Garber Comm.

PK: Helping Pastors' Kids Through Their Identity Crisis. Cameron Lee. LC 92-12684. 256p. 1992. pap. 14.99 (*0-310-58451-5*) Zondervan.

PK CHEM/CS BUILD V5.1. 6th ed. Chang. 1997. 82.75 (*0-07-561201-1*) McGraw.

***PK Man: A True Story of Mind-Over-Matter.** Jeffrey Mishlove. (Illus.). 2000. pap. 14.95 (*1-57174-183-6*) N D Walsch.

PKD: A Philip K. Dick Bibliography, 1. Daniel J. Levack. (Bibliographies on Science Fiction, Fantasy & Horror Ser.: No. 1). 160p. 1988. lib. bdg. 69.50 (*0-313-27680-3*) Greenwood.

PKD Patient's Manual: Understanding & Living with Autosomal Dominant Polycystic Kidney Disease. 2nd rev. ed. Irene Duley et al. Ed. by Wendy Rueb et al. (Illus.). 68p. 1995. teacher ed. 15.00 (*0-9614567-4-4*) PKR Foundation.

PKG:ADV SKI CO:STR SIM +(3 1/2. Efendio. (C). 1990. 22.00 incl. 3.5 hd (*0-03-033032-7*) Harcourt Coll Pubs.

Pkged with MansfieldTutor Macintosh. Edwin Mansfield. 1993. pap. 57.00 (*0-393-96438-8*) Norton.

Pkged with The Public Sector in Canada. Frances Woolley. 1994. pap. 63.00 (*0-393-96365-9*) Norton.

***PKI Essentials: Implementing & Planning Digital Certificate Systems.** Austin. 384p. 2000. pap. 44.99 (*0-471-35380-9*) Wiley.

PL-4A Construction Manual. ed. Ladislao Pazmany. (Illus.). 104p. (YA). (gr. 10 up). 1974. reprint ed. pap. 30.00 (*0-9616777-3-2*) Pazmany Aircraft.

PL-4A Exploded Views. Ladislao Pazmany. (Illus.). 45p. (YA). (gr. 10 up). 1974. pap. 30.00 (*0-9616777-4-0*) Pazmany Aircraft.

PL-1: Structured Programming & Problem Solving. Rama N. Reddy & Carol Ziegler. (Illus.). 739p. (C). 1986. mass mkt. 63.00 (*0-314-93915-6*) West Pub.

PL-1 & PL-C Workbook. David Goldberg et al. (Illus.). 176p. 1984. pap. 8.95 (*0-13-677618-3*) P-H.

PL-One Programming in Technological Applications. Gabriel F. Groner. LC 70-136713. 242p. reprint ed. 75.10 (*0-8357-9955-7*, 201258500081) Bks Demand.

PL-1 Structured Programming. 3rd ed. Joan K. Hughes. LC 86-18. 656p. 1986. text 78.95 (*0-471-83746-6*) Wiley.

P

Pl Terenti Afri Andria. Terence. Ed. by W. R. Connor. LC 78-67150. (Latin Texts & Commentaries Ser.). (ENG & LAT.). 1979. reprint ed. lib. bdg. 22.95 (*0-405-11618-7*) Ayer.

PL-8 Main Gear Design & Trade Offs. ed. Ladislao Pazmany. (Illus.). 75p. (YA). (gr. 10 up). 1980. reprint ed. pap. 25.00 (*0-9616777-7-5*) Pazmany Aircraft.

***PLA & the Kosovo Conflict.** June Teufel Dreyer. 26p. 2000. pap. write for info. (*1-58487-022-2*) SSI US Army.

Plaasarbeid - 'n Handleiding van Basiese Arbeidsreg in die Landbousektor. A. E. DeJager. 1993. pap. write for info. (*0-7021-3001-X*, Pub. by Juta & Co) Gaunt.

***Placak Report.** unabridged ed. John J. Williams. (Illus.). 1999. pap. 29.00 (*0-934274-78-9*) Consumertronics.

Place. Annie Ernaux. (FRE.). 114p. 1986. pap. 10.95 (*0-7859-2515-5*, 2070377229) Fr & Eur.

Place. Annie Ernaux. (Folio Ser.: No. 1722). (FRE.). pap. 6.95 (*2-07-037722-9*) Schoenhof.

Place: Experience & Symbol. Ed. by Miles Richardson. LC 83-83212. (Geoscience & Man Ser.: Vol. 24). (Illus.). 80p. 1984. pap. 10.00 (*0-938909-32-0*) Geosci Pubns LSU.

Place: Ten Artists View. Ed. by Claire W. Frantz & Claire Prussian. LC 93-11705. 1993. 14.00 (*0-89792-142-9*) Ill St Museum.

Place - Culture - Representation. James S. Duncan & David Ley. LC 92-37659. (Illus.). 368p. (C). 1993. pap. 25.99 (*0-415-09451-8*, B2362) Routledge.

Place - Dream & Other Poems. Robert G. Deamer. 1991. 14.95 (*0-7734-9671-8*) E Mellen.

Place - Une Femme, Ernaux: Critical Monographs in English. Loraine Day & Tony Jones. 96p. 1993. pap. 32.00 (*0-85261-262-1*, Pub. by Univ of Glasgow) St Mut.

Place against Time: Land & Environment in the Papua New Guinea Highlands. Paul Sillitoe. (Studies in Environmental Anthropology). 450p. 1996. text 49.00 (*3-7186-5925-5*, Harwood Acad Pubs) Gordon & Breach.

Place among People. Rodney Hall. 249p. 1985. pap. 16.95 (*0-7022-0963-5*, Pub. by Univ Queensland Pr) Intl Spec Bk.

Place among the Fallen. Adrian Cole. 384p. 1990. mass mkt. 4.99 (*0-380-70556-7*, Avon Bks) Morrow Avon.

Place among the Stars: The Women of the Star Trek Voyager. Na. (Star Trek Ser.). 1998. pap. 8.00 (*0-671-03455-3*) PB.

Place & Displacement in the Renaissance: Papers from the 25th Annual CEMERS Conference. Ed. by Alvin Vos. LC 94-3352. (Medieval & Renaissance Texts & Studies: Vol. 132). 320p. 1995. 25.00 (*0-86698-139-X*, MR132) MRTS.

Place & Experience: A Philosophical Topography. J. E. Malpas. LC 98-39069. 232p. (C). 1999. 54.95 (*0-521-64217-5*) Cambridge U Pr.

Place & Persistence in the Lives of Newfoundland Women. Marilyn Porter. LC 95-23148. (Illus.). 203p. 1993. 66.95 (*1-85628-444-1*, Pub. by Avebry) Ashgate Pub Co.

Place & Politics: The Geographical Mediation of State & Society. John A. Agnew. 228p. 1987. text 55.00 (*0-04-320177-6*) Routledge.

Place & the Politics of Identity. Ed. by Steve Pile & Michael Keith. LC 93-9979. 240p. (C). 1993. pap. 25.99 (*0-415-09009-1*, A9827) Routledge.

Place Apart. Paula Fox. 192p. (YA). (gr. 7 up). 1993. pap. 3.95 (*0-374-45868-5*) FS&G.

Place Apart. Paula Fox. (Aerial Fiction Ser.). (J). 1993. 9.05 (*0-606-05546-0*, Pub. by Turtleback) Demco.

Place Apart. Dervla Murphy. 1980. 15.00 (*0-8159-6516-8*) Devin.

Place Apart: A Brief History of the Early Williamson Road & North Roanoke Valley Residents & Places. Helen R. Prillaman. 187p. 1997. reprint ed. pap. 29.95 (*0-8063-4706-6*) Clearfield Co.

Place Apart: A Cape Cod Reader. Ed. by Robert Finch. LC 92-39867. 352p. 1993. 25.00 (*0-393-03480-1*) Norton.

Place Apart: An Anthropological Study of the Icelandic World. Kirsten Hastrup. LC 97-39269. (Oxford Studies in Social & Cultural Anthropology). (Illus.). 240p. 1998. text 55.00 (*0-19-823380-9*) OUP.

***Place Apart: Houses of Christian Hospitality & Prayer in Europe - Albania, Bosnia & Hercegovina, Croatia, Czech Republic, Denmark, Finland, Latvia, Lithuania, Netherlands, Norway, Poland, Romania, Russia, Slovakia, Sweden, Ukraine.** Janet Joy. Tr. by Cathy Kowalczewska et al. LC 99-96204. (Illus.). 88p. 1999. pap. 8.98 (*0-9673074-3-0*) Raphael Pubng.

***Place Apart: Houses of Christian Hospitality & Prayer in Europe - Austria - Germany - Switzerland.** Janet L. Joy. Tr. by Kate Babinsky & Agnes Murray. LC 99-93423. (Illus.). 80p. 1999. pap. 7.98 (*0-9673074-0-6*) Raphael Pubng.

***Place Apart: Houses of Christian Hospitality & Prayer in Europe - Belgium-France.** Janet L. Joy. Tr. by John McCarthy et al. LC 99-98014. (Illus.). 64p. 2000. pap. 6.98 (*0-9673074-5-7*) Raphael Pubng.

***Place Apart: Houses of Christian Hospitality & Prayer in Europe - Cyprus - Greece - Turkey.** Janet L. Joy. Tr. by Elly Pangis. LC 99-95457. (Illus.). 80p. 1999. pap. 7.98 (*0-9673074-1-4*) Raphael Pubng.

***Place Apart: Houses of Christian Hospitality & Prayer in Europe - England - Ireland - Scotland - Wales.** Janet L. Joy. Ed. by Poor Clare Nuns Staff. LC 99-96114. (Illus.). 96p. 1999. pap. 9.98 (*0-9673074-2-2*) Raphael Pubng.

***Place Apart: Houses of Christian Hospitality & Prayer in Europe - Italy - Malta - San Marino.** Janet Joy. Tr. by Joann Culver & Colomba Ghigliotti. LC 99-97805. (Illus.). 96p. 2000. pap. 9.98 (*0-9673074-4-9*) Raphael Pubng.

***Place Apart: Houses of Christian Hospitality & Prayer in Europe, Belgium & France.** Janet L. Joy. Tr. by Cecile Schossow & Natalie Curtis. LC 00-90500. (Illus.). 120p. 2000. pet. 11.98 (*0-9673074-6-5*) Raphael Pubng.

Place Apart: Houses of Prayer in the U. S. Janet Joy. LC 94-42225. (Illus.). 220p. (Orig.). 1994. pap. 10.95 (*0-940147-30-0*) Source Bks CA.

Place Apart Series 1: Monastic Prayer & Practice for Everyone. M. Basil Pennington. LC 98-11820. (Illus.). 192p. 1998. reprint ed. pap. 12.95 (*0-7648-0258-5*, Liguori Triumph) Liguori Pubns.

Place at the Lake. Paul C. Larson. LC 97-53072. (Illus.). 160p. 1998. 45.00 (*1-890434-05-1*) Afton Hist Soc.

***Place at the Table.** Simon Block. 72p. 2000. pap. 16.95 (*1-85459-488-5*) Theatre Comm.

Place at the Table. Favorite Recipes Press Staff. LC 98-60479. 173p. 1998. write for info. (*0-9662554-0-2*) P W Babies Ctr.

Place at the Table: A Study of the Statewide Nonprofit Association Movement. John Grey & Jenice L. View. 62p. (Orig.). 1992. pap. 10.00 (*1-886949-11-5*) Union Inst.

***Place at the Table: Participating in Community Building.** Kathleen de la Pedna McCook. LC 00-38050. 2000. pap. write for info. (*0-8389-0788-1*) ALA.

Place at the Table: The Gay Individual in American Society. Bruce Bawer. 1993. 21.00 (*0-671-79533-3*) S&S Trade.

Place at the Table: The Gay Individual in American Society. Bruce Bawer. 272p. 1994. per. 12.00 (*0-671-89439-0*) S&S Trade Pap.

Place Attachment. I. Altman & S. M. Low. (Human Behavior & Environment: Advances in Theory & Research Ser.: Vol. 12). (Illus.). 336p. (C). 1992. 54.50 (*0-306-44071-7*, Kluwer Plenum) Kluwer Academic.

Place au Dessineur! Essai sur la Conception Technique. Rene Loire. (FRE., Illus.). 630p. (Orig.). 1991. pap. 25.00 (*0-9611614-7-7*) A Ghosh.

***Place Between "Amen"** Russell Piliar. 2000. pap. 8.99 (*1-930027-06-0*, Pub. by Insght Pub) BookWorld.

Place by Me. Jerry Kirchner. 1996. pap. 6.99 (*1-56043-424-4*, Companion Pr) Destiny Image.

Place Called Ace. Henry W. Gurley. 1993. 12.95 (*0-938645-95-1*) In His Steps.

Place Called Antelope: The Rajneesh Story. Donna Quick. 152p. 1995. pap. text 11.50 (*0-9643118-0-1*) August Press.

***Place Called Appomattox.** William Marvel. LC 00-25593. (Civil War America Ser.). 416p. 2000. 34.95 (*0-8078-2568-9*) U of NC Pr.

Place Called Aullwood in Southwestern Ohio: Its Flowers, Woodlands & Meadows. unabridged ed. Ed. by Gail Horvath. (Illus.). 64p. 1997. 29.95 (*0-9654152-0-1*) Allan Horvath Pubns.

Place Called Community. Parker J. Palmer. LC 77-75909. (Orig.). 1977. pap. 4.00 (*0-87574-212-2*) Pendle Hill.

Place Called Freedom. Ken Follett. 1996. mass mkt. 6.99 (*0-449-22515-1*, Crest) Fawcett.

Place Called Freedom. Ken Follett. 1998. pap. 6.99 (*0-449-45861-X*) Fawcett.

Place Called Freedom. Scott Russel Sanders. LC 95-52368. (Illus.). 32p. (J). (gr. k-3). 1997. 16.00 (*0-689-80470-9*) S&S Bks Yung.

Place Called Grand Canyon: Contested Geographies. Barbara J. Morehouse. (Society, Environment, & Place Ser.). 202p. 1996. 42.00 (*0-8165-1603-0*); pap. 19.95 (*0-8165-1628-6*) U of Ariz Pr.

Place Called Heaven. Ed. by Cathy Davis. LC 98-182281. (Count Your Blessings Ser.: No. 3). 96p. 1998. 4.99 (*1-56476-692-6*, Victor Bks) Chariot Victor.

Place Called Heaven. James T. Jeremiah. LC 90-25361. 87p. (Orig.). 1991. pap. 6.99 (*0-87227-150-1*, RBP5182) Reg Baptist.

Place Called Hiroshima. Betty J. Lifton. LC 84-48127. (Illus.). 151p. 1985. 24.95 (*0-87011-649-5*) Kodansha.

Place Called Hiroshima. Betty J. Lifton. Ed. by Pockell & Ichiba. (Illus.). 152p. 1990. reprint ed. pap. 14.95 (*0-87011-961-3*) Kodansha.

Place Called Home. Cathy Davis. LC 98-182366. (Count Your Blessings Ser.: No. 1). 96p. 1998. 4.99 (*1-56476-691-8*, Victor Bks) Chariot Victor.

***Place Called Home.** Lori Wick. LC 00-32600. 2000. write for info. (*0-7862-2718-4*) Thorndike Pr.

Place Called Home. Lori Wick. (Place Called Home Ser.). 240p. 1996. reprint ed. pap. 8.99 (*1-56507-588-9*) Harvest Hse.

Place Called Home: Environmental Issues & Low Cost Housing. Merle Sowman & Penny Urquhart. (Illus.). 220p. 1998. pap. 69.95 (*1-919713-18-2*, U Pr W Africa) Intl Scholars.

***Place Called Home: Twenty Writing Women Remember.** Ed. by Mickey Pearlman. 257p. 2000. reprint ed. text. write for info. (*0-7881-9046-6*) DIANE Pub.

Place Called Hope: A Collection of Recipes by Hope Junior Auxiliary. Ed. by Cathy Sites & Bonnie Stubber. LC 92-75747. (Illus.). 240p. 1993. 14.95 (*0-9635736-0-8*) Hope Jr Auxil.

Place Called Keesler's Corners. Doris H. Masi. 137p. 1991. per. 12.00 (*0-9628208-1-4*) Canal Side Pubs.

***Place Called Milagro de la Paz.** Manlio Arguerta. Tr. by Michael B. Miller. LC 99-86710. 203p. 2000. pap. 15.95 (*1-880684-68-3*) Curbstone.

Place Called Mississippi: Mississippi Narratives. Marion Barnwell. LC 96-29607. 1997. 47.50 (*0-87805-963-6*); pap. 18.00 (*0-87805-964-4*) U Pr of Miss.

Place Called Morning. Ann Tatlock. 288p. 1998. pap. 10.99 (*1-55661-922-7*) Bethany Hse.

***Place Called Morning.** large type ed. Ann Tatlock. LC 99-16635. (G. K. Hall Inspirational Ser.). 1999. pap. 25.95 (*0-7838-8683-7*, G K Hall Lrg Type) Mac Lib Ref.

Place Called Peculiar: Stories about Unusual American Place-Names. Frank K. Gallant. LC 97-44615. (Illus.). 288p. 1998. pap. 14.95 (*0-87779-619-X*) Merriam-Webster Inc.

Place Called St. John's: The Story of John's, Edisto, Wadmalaw, Kiawah, & Seabrook Islands of South Carolina. Laylon W. Jordan & Elizabeth H. Stringfellow. LC 97-39443. 1998. 35.00 (*0-87152-513-5*) Reprint.

Place Called School. John I. Goodlad. 416p. 1984. pap. 16.95 (*0-07-023627-5*) McGraw.

Place Called Simplicity. Claire Cloninger. LC 93-7342. 1993. pap. 8.99 (*1-56507-056-9*) Harvest Hse.

Place Called Sweet Shrub. large type ed. Jane R. Wood. LC 91-7682. 428p. 1991. reprint ed. lib. bdg. 19.95 (*1-56054-156-3*) Thorndike Pr.

***Place Called Sweet Shrub.** 3rd ed. Jane Roberts Wood. LC 90-32497. (Lucy Richards Trilogy Ser.: Vol. 2). 286p. 2000. reprint ed. pap. 15.95 (*1-57441-079-2*, Pub. by UNTX Pr) Tex A&M Univ Pr.

Place Called Tackett Creek: Home of Good News Grannies & B. R. Beaver & Friends. Martha Ashcraft & Myrna Malicoat. LC 97-75782. (Illus.). 32p. 1998. pap. 9.95 (*1-57736-070-2*, Hillsboro Pr) Providence Hse.

Place Called the Light. Arlean Thornton. 210p. 1998. pap. 13.95 (*1-888672-18-8*) J Ciano Pubng.

***Place Called the Light: Soul Rescue, Remote Depossession, Exorcism, Spiritual Cleansing.** Arlean Thornton. Ed. by Robin May. 146p. 2000. pap. 12.95 (*1-893774-02-3*, Allisone Pr) Star Rising.

Place Called There see **Lugar Llamado Alli**

Place Called There. John Osteen. 32p. 1982. mass mkt. 0.75 (*0-912631-19-8*) J O Pubns.

Place Called Ugly. Avi. (J). 1995. 10.34 (*0-606-08018-X*) Turtleback.

Place Called Ugly. Avi. 144p. (YA). (gr. 7 up). 1995. mass mkt. 4.99 (*0-380-72423-5*, Avon Bks) Morrow Avon.

Place Called Waco: A Survivor's Story of Life & Death at Mt. Carmel. David Thibodeau & Leon Whiteson. LC 99-30582. (Illus.). 400p. 1999. 25.00 (*1-891620-42-8*, Pub. by PublicAffairs NY) HarpC.

Place Coding in Analog VLSI: A Neuromorphic Approach to Computation. Oliver Landolt. LC 98-9929. 216p. 1998. 110.00 (*0-7923-8194-7*) Kluwer Academic.

Place Data & Indices see **1980 U. S. Census Population & Housing Characteristics**

Place de la Concorde Suisse. John McPhee. LC 83-27466. 152p. 1984. pap. 12.00 (*0-374-51932-3*) FS&G.

Place de l'Etoile. Patrick Modiano. (Folio Ser.: No. 698). (FRE.). pap. 8.95 (*2-07-036698-7*) Schoenhof.

Place de l'Etoile. Patrick Modiano. (FRE.). 1975. pap. 10.95 (*0-7859-2882-0*) Fr & Eur.

Place de l'Homme dans la Nature. Pierre Teilhard De Chardin. 15.95 (*0-685-36584-0*) Fr & Eur.

Place de l'Homme dans la Nature. Pierre Teilhard De Chardin. (Coll. Le Monde en 10-18). (FRE.). 1963. pap. 29.95 (*0-7859-1246-0*, 2020028824) Fr & Eur.

Place des Nations, Geneve: International Competition. Birkhauser. (Illus.). 124p. 1996. pap. 34.50 (*3-7643-5358-9*, Pub. by Birkhauser) Princeton Arch.

Place Fit Only for Refuse. Norman S. Reed. (Illus.). 63p. 1985. pap. 12.95 (*0-317-53582-X*); pap. 7.95 (*0-317-53583-8*) Quill Pubns GA.

Place Fit Only for Refuse: Stories of Dump-Picking on Martha's Vineyard Island. 2nd ed. Norman S. Reed. 1986. write for info. (*0-318-61140-6*) Quill Pubns GA.

Place for All: Mental Retardation, Catechesis, & Liturgy. Mary T. Harrington. (American Essays in Liturgy Ser.). 48p. (Orig.). 1992. pap. 4.95 (*0-8146-2050-7*) Liturgical Pr.

Place for All People. Beth B. Schneider. LC 97-47137. 199p. 1998. pap. write for info. (*0-89090-084-1*) Mus Fine TX.

Place for Art: The Architecture of the National Gallery of Canada. Witold Rybczynski. (FRE & ENG., Illus.). 97p. 1993. pap. text 25.00 (*0-88884-620-7*) U Ch Pr.

Place for Baptism. Regina Kuehn. (Illus.). 137p. (Orig.). 1992. pap. 16.00 (*0-929650-00-X*, BPLACE) Liturgy Tr Pubns.

***Place for Ben.** Jeanne Titherington. 24p. (J). 1999. mass mkt. 4.95 (*0-688-17064-1*, Wm Morrow) Morrow Avon.

Place for Caring & Celebration: The School Media Center. Ralph L. Peterson. LC 78-31809. (School Media Center: Focus on Trends & Issues Ser.: No. 4). 39p. reprint ed. pap. 30.00 (*0-608-17139-5*, 202735800055) Bks Demand.

***Place for Children: Public Libraries as a Major Force in Children's Reading.** Ed. by Judith Elkin. (British Library Research & Innovation Report: Vol. 117). 198p. 2000. 75.00 (*1-85604-320-7*, Pub. by Library Association) Bernan Associates.

Place for Claire. large type ed. Dorothy M. Cray. 336p. 1985. 27.99 (*0-7089-1252-4*) Ulverscroft.

Place for Dreaming see **Lugar para Sonar: The Honeymoon House**

Place for Eagles. Laurie Paige. (Wild River Trilogy Ser.). 1993. per. 3.50 (*0-373-09839-1*, 5-09839-7) Silhouette.

Place for Everything: Organizing the Stuff of Life. Peri Wolfman & Charles Gold. LC 98-55420. 192p. 1999. pap. 25.00 (*0-609-80448-0*) Crown Pub Group.

***Place for God: A Guide to Spiritual Retreats & Retreat Centers.** Timothy K. Jones. LC 99-29733. 352p. 2000. pap. 14.95 (*0-385-49158-1*, Image Bks) Doubleday.

Place for Grace. Jean D. Okimoto. (Illus.). 32p. (J). (ps up). 1996. reprint ed. pap. 7.95 (*1-57061-069-X*) Sasquatch Bks.

Place for Human Beings. 2nd ed. Pam Rainbear Portugal. (Living on This Planet Ser.). (Illus.). 160p. 1978. pap. 6.95 (*0-9601088-5-8*) Wild Horses.

Place for Ideas: Our Theatre. Jearnine Wagner & Kitty Baker. (Illus.). 1977. pap. 28.00 (*0-87602-010-4*) Anchorage.

Place for Jeremy. Patricia Hermes. LC 86-31793. (Illus.). 160p. (J). (gr. 3-7). 1987. 13.95 (*0-15-262350-7*) Harcourt.

Place for Joe. Elizabeth Leland. (Illus.). 166p. 1997. 19.95 (*1-878086-60-X*, Pub. by Down Home NC) Blair.

Place for Kathy: A Novel. Henry Denker. LC 96-7259. 320p. 1997. 24.00 (*0-688-14963-4*, Wm Morrow) Morrow Avon.

Place for Kathy Cameron. large type ed. Henry Denker. (Charnwood Large Print Ser.). 448p. 1998. 29.99 (*0-7089-9008-8*, Charnwood) Ulverscroft.

Place for Me. Robert Westall. LC 93-33492. (J). 1994. 13.95 (*0-590-47747-1*) Scholastic Inc.

Place for Me, Level 7. E. Evertts. 1983. 3325.00 (*0-03-061388-4*); write for info. (*0-03-061389-2*) Harcourt Schl Pubs.

Place for Me, Level 7. E. Evertts. (J). 1983. pap., wbk. ed. 14.75 (*0-03-061431-7*) Harcourt Schl Pubs.

Place for Me: Including Children with Special Needs in Early Care & Education Settings. Phyllis A. Chandler. LC 94-65096. (Illus.). 96p. 1994. pap. text 6.00 (*0-935989-59-5*, 237) Natl Assn Child Ed.

Place for Me: Level 7. E. Evertts. 1986. 28.00 (*0-03-002312-2*) Harcourt Schl Pubs.

Place for Me: Level 7. E. Evertts. 1986. pap. text, wbk. ed. 13.75 (*0-03-002338-6*) Holt R&W.

Place for Our Gods: The Construction of an Edinburgh Hindu Temple Community. Malory Nye. (SOAS London Studies on South Asia: No. 8). 220p. (C). 1995. text 45.00 (*0-7007-0356-X*, Pub. by Curzon Pr Ltd) UH Pr.

Place for Owls: True Animal Stories. Katherine McKeever. (True Animal Stories Ser.). (Illus.). 96p. (YA). (gr. 3 up). 1992. pap. 7.95 (*0-920775-24-1*, Pub. by Owl Bks) Firefly Bks Ltd.

Place for Peter. Elizabeth Yates. LC 94-9147. (Pennant Ser.). (Illus.). 176p. 1994. pap. 6.49 (*0-89084-748-7*, 079830) Bob Jones Univ.

Place for Strangers: Towards a History of Australian Aboriginal Being. Tony Swain. LC 92-30379. (Illus.). 315p. (C). 1996. pap. text 22.95 (*0-521-44691-0*) Cambridge U Pr.

Place for Summer: A Narrative History of Tiger Stadium. Richard Bak. LC 98-2509. (Illus.). 512p. 1998. 34.95 (*0-8143-2512-2*, Great Lks Bks) Wayne St U Pr.

Place for Teacher Renewal: Challenging the Intellect, Creating Education Reform. Ed. by Anthony G. Rud, Jr. & Walter P. Oldendorf. 176p. (C). 1992. text 35.00 (*0-8077-3147-1*); pap. text 17.95 (*0-8077-3146-3*) Tchrs Coll.

Place for Teacher Renewal: Challenging the Intellect, Creating Educational Reform. Ed. by Anthony G. Rud, Jr. & Walter P. Oldendorf. LC 91-28670. 176p. reprint ed. pap. 54.60 (*0-608-20009-3*, 207128500010) Bks Demand.

Place for Teddy. (Teddy Ser.). (J). (gr. 1-2). 1991. pap. text 2.95 (*0-9636154-0-8*) Teddy & Frnds.

Place for the Genuine: Collections of Poems by Writers in Maryland, Virginia & the District of Columbia. Compiled & Pref. by Joseph D. Adams. (Poet's Domain Ser.: Vol. 2). xiv, 66p. (Orig.). 1990. pap. 5.95 (*1-880016-03-6*) Road Pubs.

Place for Theodore: The Murder of Dr. Theodore Parkman. L. G. Williams. LC 96-95373. (Illus.). 230p. (Orig.). 1997. pap. 9.95 (*0-9656484-0-0*, 161262) Holly Two Leaves.

Place for Truth: The Bicentennial James Henley Thornwell Lectures. David B. Calhoun. Ed. by Stephen R. Berry. 75p. 1998. pap. text 9.95 (*1-884416-16-0*) A Press.

***Place for Us: Essay on the Broadway Musical.** D. A. Miller. 160p. 2000. pap. 14.00 (*0-674-00388-8*) HUP.

Place for Us: Essay on the Broadway Musical. D. A. Miller. LC 98-15685. (Illus.). 160p. 1998. 22.00 (*0-674-66990-8*) HUP.

Place for Us: How to Make Society Civil & Democracy Strong. Benjamin R. Barber. LC 97-44914. 172p. 1998. 22.00 (*0-8090-7657-8*) Hill & Wang.

***Place for Wayfaring: The Poetry & Prose of Gary Snyder.** Patrick D. Murphy. LC 99-88384. 256p. 2000. pap. 21.95 (*0-87071-479-1*) Oreg St U Pr.

Place for Winter: Paul Tiulana's Story, (A) Vivian Senungetuk & Paul Tiulana. (Illus.). 120p. (YA). (gr. 10-12). 1989. reprint ed. 17.95 (*0-938227-02-5*) CIRI Found.

Place Geography. Tim Unwin. 273p. (C). 1996. pap. 67.00 (*0-582-05107-X*) Addison-Wesley.

Place He Made. large type ed. Edie Clark. (General Ser.). 1996. pap. 20.95 (*0-7862-0668-3*) Thorndike Pr.

Place I Call Home: What's Wrong with U. S. & What We Can Do about It. Kirsten E. Borg. (Illus.). 209p. 1987. 9.00 (*0-9617604-0-0*) Dragon Tree IA.

***Place I Work: The Adventures of a Common Man.** Romy Greer. 128p. 1998. pap. 7.95 (*0-9664868-1-1*) Rags Inc.

Place Images in the Media: A Geographic Appraisal. Ed. by Leo E. Zonn. 224p. (C). 1989. 59.50 (*0-8476-7594-7*, R7394) Rowman.

Place in Between. Kenneth W. Brewer. 44p. 1998. pap. 20.00 (*0-931659-50-7*) Limberlost Pr.

Place in Between. deluxe ed. Kenneth W. Brewer. 44p. 1998. 60.00 (*0-931659-51-5*) Limberlost Pr.

Place in El Paso: A Mexican-American Childhood. Gloria Lopez-Stafford. 222p. (C). 1996. pap. 16.95 (*0-8263-1709-X*) U of NM Pr.

Place in History: Social & Monumental Time in a Cretan Town. Michael Herzfeld. (Illus.). 274p. 1991. pap. text 22.95 (*0-691-02855-9*, Pub. by Princeton U Pr) Cal Prin Full Svc.

Place in Legal History of Sir William Shareshull. Bertha H. Putnam. LC 85-48163. (Cambridge Studies in English Legal History). 346p. 1986. reprint ed. 85.00 (*0-912004-33-9*) Gaunt.

P

An Asterisk (*) at the beginning of an entry indicates that the title is appearing for the first time.

***Place in Literature: Regions, Cultures, Communities.** Roberto M Dainotto. LC 99-38957. 2000. 35.00 (*0-8014-3683-4*) Cornell U Pr.

Place in Mind. Dulce D. Moore. LC 92-70845. 265p. 1992. 18.00 (*0-9627509-9-9*) Baskerville.

Place in Mind. Sydney Lea. LC 97-921. (Fiction Ser.). 240p. 1997. reprint ed. pap. 12.95 (*1-885266-39-1*) Story Line.

Place in Mind: A Novel. large type ed. Dulce D. Moore. LC 92-33395. 430p. 1993. reprint ed. lib. bdg. 16.95 (*1-56054-587-9*) Thorndike Pr.

Place in My Heart. Betty Brooks. 1999. mass mkt. 4.99 (*0-8217-6179-X*, Zebra Kensgtn) Kensgtn Pub Corp.

Place in Normandy. Nicholas Kilmer. 240p. 1997. pap. 12.95 (*0-8050-5532-0*) H Holt & Co.

Place in Space: Ethics, Aesthetics, & Watersheds. Gary Snyder. 272p. 1996. pap. text 15.00 (*1-887178-27-9*, Pub. by Counterpt DC) HarpC.

Place in the City. Luli Callinicos. (People's History of South Africa Ser.: Vol. 3). (Illus.). 150p. (Orig.). (C). 1993. pap. text 19.95 (*0-86975-424-6*) Ohio U Pr.

Place in the Country. John Brookes. LC 83-51677. (Illus.). 240p. 1984. 24.95 (*0-500-01327-6*, Pub. by Thames Hudson) Norton.

Place in the Country. Laura Cunningham. 2000. 24.00 (*0-06-019398-0*) HarpC.

***Place in the Country.** Laura Cunningham. LC 99-59914. 304p. 2000. 24.95 (*1-57322-157-0*, Riverhead Books) Putnam Pub Group.

Place in the Country: Matilda Wilson's Personal Guidebook to Meadow Brook Hall. Matilda Wilson. LC 98-68038. 64p. 1998. pap. 8.95 (*0-9666988-0-0*) Oakland Univ Pr.

***Place in the Heart.** Theresa Kelly. LC 99-58991. (Aloha Cove Ser.: Vol. 6). (Illus.). 269p. (J). (gr. 7-11). 2000. pap. text 5.99 (*0-570-07034-1*) Concordia.

Place in the Kingdom: Spiritual Insights from Latter-Day Saints about Same-Sex Attraction. Ed. by Garrick Hyde & Ginger Hyde. LC 97-67742. 224p. 1997. 16.95 (*0-941846-05-9*) Centry Pub.

Place in the News: From the Women's Pages to the Front Page. Kay Mills. (Illus.). 384p. 1990. pap. text 19.50 (*0-231-07417-4*) Col U Pr.

Place in the Race. William D. Day. 1998. pap. 11.27 (*1-57502-782-8*, P02165) Morris Pubng.

Place in the Rainforest: Settling the Costa Rican Frontier. Darryl Cole-Christensen. LC 96-32321. 216p. 1997. 35.00 (*0-292-71190-5*); pap. 14.95 (*0-292-71191-3*) U of Tex Pr.

Place in the Sun. David Hamilton. (Illus.). 216p. 1996. 39.95 (*1-85410-431-4*, Pub. by Aurum Pr) London Brdge.

Place in the Sun. Michael Phillips & Judith Pella. LC 91-4987. (Journals of Corrie Belle Hollister: Bk. 4). 34p. (Orig.). 1991. pap. 9.99 (*1-55661-222-2*) Bethany Hse.

Place in the Sun. Jill Rubalcaba. LC 96-38635. 96p. (J). (gr. 3-7). 1997. 13.95 (*0-395-82645-4*) HM.

Place in the Sun. Jill Rubalcaba. LC 98-16336. (Puffin Novels Ser.). 96p. (J). (gr. 3-7). 1998. pap. 4.99 (*0-14-130123-6*) Peng Put Young Read.

Place in the Sun. Evan Skolnick. (Pocahontas Ser.). (J). 1997. pap. text 4.50 (*1-57840-161-5*, Pub. by Acclaim Bks) Penguin Putnam.

Place in the Sun. Evan Skolnick. (Disney's Enchanting Stories Ser.). 1998. pap. text 4.50 (*1-57840-204-2*) Acclaim Bks.

Place in the Sun: Liberation Theology in the Third World. Theo Witvliet. Tr. by John Bowden from DUT. LC 84-27229.Tr. of Fen Plaats onder de zon Bevrijdingstheologie in de Derde Wereld. 192p. (Orig.). reprint ed. pap. 59.60 (*0-8357-8556-4*, 203490200091) Bks Demand.

Place in the Sun: The Evolution of the Real Goods Solar Living Center. Schaeffer. LC 97-31121. (Illus.). 187p. 1997. pap. 24.95 (*1-890132-01-2*) Chelsea Green Pub.

Place in the Sun: The Journals of Corrie Belle Hollister, Bk. 4. large type ed. Michael Phillips. 448p. 1996. 23.95 (*0-7838-1702-9*, G K Hall Lrg Type) Mac Lib Ref.

Place in the Sun? Women Writers in Twentieth Century Cuba. Catherine Davies. LC 97-36970. 256p. 1998. 65.00 (*1-85649-541-8*); pap. 25.00 (*1-85649-542-6*) Humanities.

Place in the Sun-history of California Labor. David F. Selvin. pap. write for info. (*0-87835-117-5*) Thomson Learn.

Place in the Woods. Helen Hoover. LC 98-51141. (The Fesler-lampert Minnesota Heritage Bks.). 1999. 15.95 (*0-8166-3129-8*) U of Minn Pr.

Place in the World: Places, Cultures & Globalization. Ed. by Doreen Massey & Pat Jess. (Shape of the World Ser.: Bk. 4). (Illus.). 256p. (C). 1996. text 56.95 (*0-19-874190-1*); pap. text 24.95 (*0-19-874191-X*) OUP.

Place in the World Called Paris. Ed. by Steven Barclay. LC 94-2089. (Illus.). 176p. 1994. 18.95 (*0-8118-0586-7*) Chronicle Bks.

Place in Time: Caregivers for Their Elderly. Tom Koch. LC 92-1754. 244p. 1993. 35.00 (*0-275-94483-2*, C4483, Praeger Pubs) Greenwood.

Place in Times: Britain, 1450-1700. Rosemary Kelly. 124p. (C). 1990. pap. 15.95 (*0-7487-0029-3*) Dufour.

***Place in Your Heart.** large type ed. Rachael Croft. 208p. 1999. pap. 18.99 (*0-7089-5527-4*, Linford) Ulverscroft.

Place Is Too Small for Us: The Israelite Prophets in Recent Scholarship. Ed. by Robert P. Gordon. LC 95-38977. (Sources for Biblical & Theological Study Ser.: Vol. 5). 640p. 1995. 37.95 (*1-57506-000-0*) Eisenbrauns.

Place I've Never Been: Stories. David Leavitt. (Contemporay American Fiction Ser.). 224p. 1991. reprint ed. pap. 12.95 (*0-14-010959-5*, Penguin Bks) Viking Penguin.

***Place Last Seen: A Novel.** Charlotte McGuinn-Freeman. LC 99-55047. 294p. 2000. text 23.00 (*0-312-24227-1*, Picador USA) St Martin.

***Place Like Any Other: Sabbath Blessings.** Molly Wolf. LC 00-27285. 256p. 2000. pap. 12.95 (*0-385-49955-8*) Doubleday.

Place Like This. Steven Herrick. (J). 1998. pap. 12.95 (*0-7022-2984-9*, Pub. by Univ Queensland Pr) Intl Spec Bk.

Place Like This: Hugh Benjamin's Peter Island. Hugh Benjamin & Richard Myers. (Illus.). 64p. (Orig.). 1994. pap. 10.95 (*0-9639905-3-5*) Two Thous-Three Assocs.

Place Makers. Ronald L. Fleming & Renata Von Tscharner. 128p. (Orig.). 1987. 29.95 (*0-15-172000-2*, Harvest Bks); pap. 14.95 (*0-15-672013-2*, Harvest Bks) Harcourt.

Place Matters: Victorian Women's Travel Books on Southeast Asia. Susan Morgan. 350p. (C). 1996. text 50.00 (*0-8135-2248-X*); pap. text 19.95 (*0-8135-2249-8*) Rutgers U Pr.

Place Me with Your Son: Ignatian Spirituality in Everyday Life. 3rd ed. James W. Skehan. LC 91-13226. 176p. 1991. pap. 8.95 (*0-87840-525-9*) Georgetown U Pr.

Place, Memory & Identity in the Vietnamese Diaspora. Mamdy Thomas. LC 99-233928. 224p. 1998. pap. 29.95 (*1-86448-862-X*, Pub. by Allen & Unwin Pty) Paul & Co Pubs.

Place, Modernity, & the Consumer's World: A Relational Framework for Geographical Analysis. Robert D. Sack. (Illus.). 352p. 1993. text 42.00 (*0-8018-4336-7*) Johns Hopkins.

Place My Words Are Looking For: What Poets Say about & Through Their Work. Paul B. Janeczko. LC 89-39331. 128p. (J). (gr. 4-8). 1990. mass mkt. 16.00 (*0-02-747671-5*, Bradbury S&S) S&S Childrens.

Place-Name Changes, 1900-1991. Compiled by Adrian Room. LC 93-5159. 322p. 1993. 45.00 (*0-8108-2600-3*) Scarecrow.

***Place Name in the Rocky Mountains Between the 49th Parallel & the Athabasca River.** James White. 34p. 2000. pap. 5.00 (*1-886560-89-7*) Quintin Pub RI.

***Place-Name Workbook & Map-Pak to Accompany Essentials of World Regional Geography.** 3rd ed. Christopher L. Salter et al. 424p. 1999. 20.00 (*0-03-030896-8*, Pub. by SCP) Harcourt.

Place Names in Alabama. Virginia O. Foscue. LC 88-828. (Illus.). 192p. (Orig.). 1988. pap. 17.95 (*0-8173-0410-X*) U of Ala Pr.

Place Names in Bucks County, Pennsylvania, Alphabetically Arranged in an Historical Narrative. Compiled by George MacReynolds. 474p. 1996. reprint ed. lib. bdg. 49.00 (*0-8328-5218-X*) Higginson Bk Co.

Place Names in Classical Mythology: Greece. Robert E. Bell. LC 88-16870. 350p. 1988. lib. bdg. 60.00 (*0-87436-507-4*) ABC-CLIO.

Place Names in Colorado. J. Frank Dawson. 1976. pap. 1.75 (*0-87315-067-8*) Golden Bell.

Place-Names in Imprints: An Index to the Latin & Other Forms Used on Title-Pages. Robert A. Peddie. 1968. reprint ed. 35.00 (*1-55888-207-3*) Omnigraphics Inc.

Place-Names in the Landscape. Margaret Gelling. (Illus.). 326p. 1993. pap. 22.95 (*0-460-86086-0*, Pub. by John Murray) Trafalgar.

***Place Names in the Midwestern United States.** Edward Callary. LC 00-33951. 208p. 2000. 89.95 (*0-7734-7723-3*) E Mellen.

Place Names of Africa, 1935-1986: A Political Gazetteer. Eugene C. Kirchherr. LC 87-20765. (Illus.). 144p. 1987. 21.00 (*0-8108-2061-7*) Scarecrow.

Place Names of America. Ed. by Donald Orth. (International Library of Names). 400p. (C). text. write for info. (*0-8290-1210-9*) Irvington.

Place Names of Atlantic Canada. William B. Hamilton. (Illus.). 456p. 1996. pap. 24.95 (*0-8020-7570-3*); text 60.00 (*0-8020-0471-7*) U of Toronto Pr.

Place Names of Boone County, Missouri. Robert L. Ramsey. (Publications of the American Dialect Society: No. 18). (Illus.). 52p. 1952. pap. text 5.35 (*0-8173-0618-8*) U of Ala Pr.

Place Names of Bourbon County, Kansas. 2nd ed. Charles E. Cory. (Illus.). 96p. 1994. reprint ed. pap. 6.95 (*1-882355-03-2*) Mostly Bks Pub.

Place-Names of Dane County, Wisconsin. F. G. Cassidy. (Publications of the American Dialect Society: No. 7). 255p. 1947. pap. text 23.50 (*0-8173-0607-2*) U of Ala Pr.

Place-Names of East Flintshire. Hywel W. Owen. LC 94-202940. xxxvi, 428p. 1994. write for info. (*0-7083-1242-X*, Pub. by Univ Wales Pr) Paul & Co Pubs.

Place Names of Hawaii. 2nd ed. Mary K. Pukui et al. LC 73-85582. 310p. 1974. pap. 10.95 (*0-8248-0524-0*) UH Pr.

Place Names of Historic Sleepy Hollow & Tarrytown. Henry Steiner. LC 99-193236. (Illus.). 223p. 1998. pap. 22.00 (*0-7884-0961-1*, S714) Heritage Bk.

Place Names of Humboldt County, California: A Compendium, 1542-1992. Dennis W. Turner. 280p. 1993. pap. 40.00 (*0-9629617-1-X*) D W Turner.

Place Names of Monroe County, Pennsylvania. Robert J. Jones. 50p. 1993. per. 6.00 (*1-55856-140-4*, 077) Closson Pr.

Place Names of New Mexico. 2nd abr. rev. ed. Robert Julyan. LC 98-25232. 385p. 1996. pap. 19.95 (*0-8263-1689-1*) U of NM Pr.

Place Names of Ontario. Alan Rayburn. LC 97-160862. 400p. 1997. pap. 21.95 (*0-8020-7207-0*) U of Toronto Pr.

Place-Names of St. Kilda: Nomina Hirtensia. Richard Coates. LC 90-6667. (Celtic Studies: Vol. 1). (Illus.). 240p. 1990. lib. bdg. 89.95 (*0-88946-077-9*) E Mellen.

Place Names of Sumter County, Alabama. Virginia O. Foscue. (Publications of the American Dialect Society: No. 65). (Illus.). 75p. 1978. pap. text 7.50 (*0-8173-0663-3*) U of Ala Pr.

Place Names of the Avalon Peninsula of the Island of Newfoundland. E. R. Seary. LC 73-151390. (Memorial University Ser.: No. 2). 404p. reprint ed. pap. 125.30 (*0-608-16649-9*, 202637200049) Bks Demand.

***Place Names of the County of Longford.** Joseph MacGivney. 224p. 2000. cd-rom 19.95 (*1-58211-235-5*) Quintin Pub RI.

***Place Names of the Greek & Roman World: A Gazetteer Arranged by One Degree Quadrants.** Richard W. Thompson. 550p. 1999. pap. 59.95 (*0-9631097-2-3*) Barriclyn.

Place Names of the Isle Royale. Smitty Parratt & Doug Welker. (Illus.). 96p. 1999. pap. 7.95 (*0-935289-10-0*) Isle Royale Hist.

Place Names of the Sierra Nevada. 2nd ed. Peter Browning. LC 84-52655. 264p. 1991. 16.95 (*0-89997-072-9*) Wilderness Pr.

***Place Names of the Smokies.** Allen R. Coggins. Ed. by Steve Kemp & Kent Cave. (Cultural History Handbooks Ser.). (Illus.). 168p. 1999. pap. 9.95 (*0-937207-23-3*) GSMNH.

Place Names of the White Mountains. rev. ed. Robert Julyan & Mary Julyan. LC 93-13606. (Illus.). 198p. 1993. pap. 11.95 (*0-87451-638-2*) U Pr of New Eng.

***Place Names of the World Vol. 1: Europe: Historical, Context, Meanings, & Changes.** John Everett-Heath. Vol. 1. (Illus.). 300p. 2000. lib. bdg. 70.00 (*1-56159-300-1*) Groves Dictionaries.

Place Names of Upper Deeside. Adam Watson & Elizabeth Allan. 256p. 1984. text 40.00 (*0-08-030403-6*, Pergamon Pr) Elsevier.

***Place Near Kolob.** 368p. 1999. pap. 14.95 (*0-9673990-0-9*, Pub. by Ross Hse Pubg) Stellar Pubg.

***Place No One Knew: Glen Canyon on the Colorado.** Eliot Porter. Ed. by David Brower. LC 99-88752. (Illus.). 192p. 2000. reprint ed. pap. 29.95 (*0-87905-971-0*) Gibbs Smith Pub.

***Place Not Forgotten: Landscapes of the South from the Morris Museum of Art.** William W. Freehling et al. LC 99-72902. (Illus.). 84p. (C). 1999. pap. 25.00 (*1-882007-17-4*) Univ KY Art Mus.

Place Not Home. unabridged ed. Eva Wiseman. 192p. (YA). (gr. 7 up). 1997. pap. 6.95 (*0-7737-5834-8*) STDK.

***Place of Angels.** J. W. Andrews & Donald D. McCall. (Illus.). 74p. 1999. pap. 14.95 (*0-9674400-0-9*) RL Fromm.

Place of Animal Behavioural Studies in Agricultural Training. R. Ewbank. 1976. 16.00 (*0-7855-1122-9*) St Mut.

***Place of Antique Early Modern Europe.** Ingrid D. Rowland. 2000. pap. 22.00 (*0-935573-28-3*) U Ch Pr.

***Place of Art.** Thomas Da Costa Kaufman. 1999. lib. bdg. 50.00 (*0-226-13311-7*) U Ch Pr.

***Place Of Art.** Thomas Da Costa Kaufman. 1999. pap. text 20.00 (*0-226-13312-5*) U Ch Pr.

Place of Art in Education. Thomas Davidson. (Notable American Authors Ser.). 1992. reprint ed. lib. bdg. 75.00 (*0-7812-2618-X*) Rprt Serv.

***Place of Beauty: The Artists & Gardens of the Cornish Colony.** Alma M. Gilbert & Judith B. Tankard. LC 00-36425. (Illus.). 144p. 2000. 29.95 (*1-58008-129-0*) Ten Speed Pr.

Place of Blessed Augustine in the Orthodox Church. Seraphim Rose. (Illus.). 143p. 1997. pap. 10.00 (*0-938635-12-3*) St Herman Pr.

Place of Bonhoeffer: Problems & Possibilities in His Thought. Ed. by Martin E. Marty. LC 79-8718. 224p. 1981. reprint ed. lib. bdg. 55.00 (*0-313-20812-3*, MAPL, Greenwood Pr) Greenwood.

Place of Christ in Liturgical Prayer. Josef Jungmann. 320p. (Orig.). 1989. pap. 14.95 (*0-8146-1916-9*) Liturgical Pr.

Place of Confluent Education in the Human Potential Movement: A Historical Perspective. Stewart B. Shapiro. LC 98-24302. 224p. 1998. 34.00 (*0-7618-1186-9*) U Pr of Amer.

Place of Connection: Expressive Counseling Techniques for Families & Individuals. Jackie S. Gerstein. (Illus.). 214p. 1998. pap. 27.95 (*1-885473-23-0*) Wood N Barnes.

Place of Creation: Six Essays. Erich Neumann. LC 88-25297. (Essays of Erich Neumann: Vol. 3). 410p. 1989. reprint ed. pap. 127.10 (*0-608-07136-6*, 206736200009) Bks Demand.

Place of Creation Vol. 3: Essays of Erich Neumann. Tr. by Hildegard Nagel et al from GER. 280p. 1989. text 65.00 (*0-691-09965-0*, Pub. by Princeton U Pr) Cal Prin Full Svc.

Place of Culture & Civilization in Foreign Language Teaching see Culture, Literature, & Articulation

Place of Dead Roads. William S. Burroughs. 320p. 1995. pap. 12.00 (*0-8050-3954-6*) H Holt & Co.

Place of Dead Roads. William S. Burroughs. 1994. reprint ed. lib. bdg. 29.95 (*1-56849-539-0*) Buccaneer Bks.

Place of Eagles. large type ed. Margaret Evans. (General Ser.). 544p. 1993. 27.99 (*0-7089-2801-3*) Ulverscroft.

***Place of Economics in Learning.** Ludwig Von Mises. 54p. 2000. pap. 1.25 (*0-945466-27-7*) Ludwig von Mises.

Place of Emotion in Argument. Douglas Walton. (Illus.). 320p. 1992. 50.00 (*0-271-00833-4*); pap. 16.95 (*0-271-00853-9*) Pa St U Pr.

***Place of Execution.** Val McDermid. 416p. 2000. 24.95 (*0-312-26632-4*, Minotaur) St Martin.

Place of Exile: The European Settlement of New South Wales. David Mackay. 184p. 1986. 29.95 (*0-19-554632-6*) OUP.

Place of Fiction in the Time of Science: A Disciplinary History of American Writing. John Limon. (Cambridge Studies in American Literature & Culture: No. 39). 230p. (C). 1990. text 54.95 (*0-521-35251-7*) Cambridge U Pr.

Place of Genre in Learning: Current Debates. Ed. by Ian Reid. 124p. (C). 1987. 50.00 (*0-7300-0247-0*, Pub. by Deakin Univ) St Mut.

Place of Gentle Waters. Jessica Maji. (Heartbeats Ser.). 112p. (YA). (gr. 7 up). 1994. pap. 5.95 (*0-7910-2933-6*) Chelsea Hse.

Place of Grammar in Writing Instruction: Past, Present, Future. Ed. by Susan Hunter & Ray Wallace. LC 94-38896. 265p. 1995. pap. text 24.50 (*0-86709-352-8*, 0352, Pub. by Boynton Cook Pubs) Heinemann.

Place of Greater Safety. Hilary Mantel. LC 98-26688. 768p. 1998. pap. 15.00 (*0-8050-5204-6*) St Martin.

Place of Help. Oswald Chambers. 1979. pap. 10.95 (*0-87508-303-X*) Chr Lit.

Place of Help: God's Provision for Our Daily Needs. Oswald Chambers. 256p. 1989. pap. 10.99 (*0-929239-18-0*) Discovery Hse Pubs.

Place of Her Own: The Story of Elizabeth Garrett. rev. ed. Ruth K. Hall. LC 83-5104. (Illus.). 171p. 1983. pap. 8.95 (*0-913270-68-7*) Sunstone Pr.

Place of Herbs in Rational Therapy. Ellen Gould Harmon White. 40p. 1993. reprint ed. spiral bd. 8.00 (*0-7873-0958-3*) Hlth Research.

Place of Home: English Domestic Environments, 1914-2000. A. Ravetz & Turkington. (Studies in History, Planning & the Environment). (Illus.). 256p. (C). 1995. 80.00 (*0-419-17980-1*, E & FN Spon) Routledge.

Place of Hope, Place of Healing. Ted Roberts. LC 99-11351. 300p. 1999. pap. 11.99 (*0-8307-2335-8*, Regal Bks) Gospel Lght.

***Place of Houses.** Charles Willard Moore et al. LC 99-43787. (Illus.). 288p. 2000. 22.50 (*0-520-22357-8*, Pub. by U CA Pr) Cal Prin Full Svc.

Place of Houses. Charles Moore et al. LC 70-182776. (Illus.). 288p. 1995. pap. 19.95 (*0-8050-1044-0*, Owl) H Holt & Co.

Place of Iceland in the History of European Institutions, Being the Lothian Prize Essay, 1877. Charles A. Conybeare. reprint ed. 34.50 (*0-404-01696-0*) AMS Pr.

Place of Lions. Campbell. 1995. pap. 5.00 (*0-15-201031-9*) Harcourt.

Place of Lions. E. Campbell. LC 91-8037. 160p. (J). (gr. 3-7). 1995. pap. 6.00 (*0-15-200371-1*) Harcourt.

Place of Lions. Eric Campbell. LC 91-8037. 160p. (J). (gr. 3 up). 1991. 17.00 (*0-15-262408-2*, Harcourt Child Bks) Harcourt.

Place of Lions. Eric Campbell. (J). 1991. 11.35 (*0-606-08019-8*) Turtleback.

Place of Magic in the Intellectual History of Europe. Lynn Thorndike. LC 70-177455. (Columbia University. Studies in the Social Sciences: No. 62). reprint ed. 29.50 (*0-404-51062-0*) AMS Pr.

Place of Marxism in History. Ernest Mandel. LC 93-12067. (Revolutionary Studies). 112p. (C). 1994. pap. 10.95 (*0-391-03814-1*) Humanities.

Place of Marxism in History. Ernest Mandel. LC 98-54283. 104p. 1999. pap. 14.95 (*1-57392-331-1*, Humanity Bks) Prometheus Bks.

Place of Mathematics in Education: 11th Yearbook. NCTM Staff. Ed. by W. D. Reeve. 258p. 1995. reprint ed. pap. 15.00 (*0-87353-400-X*) NCTM.

Place of "Measure for Measure" in Shakespeare's Universe of Comedy. William J. Martz. 150p. 1982. 12.50 (*0-87291-159-4*) Coronado Pr.

***Place of Media Power.** Nick Couldry. (Comedia Ser.). 240p. 2000. pap. 27.99 (*0-415-21315-0*); text 75.00 (*0-415-21314-2*) Routledge.

Place of Mind. Cooney. LC 99-12987. (Philosophy Ser.). 1999. mass mkt. 52.95 (*0-534-52825-2*) Wadsworth Pub.

Place of Minds in the World. William Mitchell. LC 77-27201. (Gifford Lectures: 1924-26). 400p. reprint ed. 45.00 (*0-404-60477-3*) AMS Pr.

Place of Mirrors: Lessons of the Ancient Maya. Jeeni Criscenzo. LC 96-76576. 300p. 1996. 21.95 (*0-9652318-1-X*) Jaguar Books.

Place of Mists. large type ed. Bill Knox. (Linford Mystery Library). 352p. 1996. pap. 16.99 (*0-7089-7978-5*) Ulverscroft.

Place of Music. Ed. by Andrew Leyshon et al. LC 97-46480. (Mappings). 326p. 1998. pap. 24.95 (*1-57230-314-X*, C0314) Guilford Pubns.

Place of Music. Andrew Leyshon et al. LC 97-46480. (Mappings Ser.). 326p. 1998. 43.95 (*1-57230-313-1*) Guilford Pubns.

Place of Musicology in American Institutions of Higher Learning, 2 vols. in 1. Ed. by Manfred F. Bukofzer et al. Incl. Some Aspects of Musicology. LC 77-4226. 1977. lib. bdg. LC 77-4226. (Music Reprint Ser.). 1977. reprint ed. Set lib. bdg. 27.50 (*0-306-77407-0*) Da Capo.

Place of My Own: The Education of an Amateur Builder. Michael Pollan. 336p. 1998. pap. 13.95 (*0-385-31990-8*) Delacorte.

Place of Narrative: Mural Decoration in Italian Churches, 431-1600. Marilyn A. Lavin. LC 89-49474. (Illus.). 448p. 1993. 65.00 (*0-226-46956-5*) U Ch Pr.

Place of Narrative: Mural Decoration in Italian Churches, 431-1600. Marilyn A. Lavin. (Illus.). xx, 426p. 1994. pap. text 49.95 (*0-226-46960-3*) U Ch Pr.

***Place of One's Own: Stories of Self in China, Taiwan, Hong Kong & Singapore.** Ed. by Kwok-kan Tam et al. LC 99-31643. 272p. 1999. pap. 24.95 (*0-19-591658-1*) OUP.

***Place of Passage: Contemporary Catholic Poetry.** Ed. by David Craig & Janet McCann. LC 00-27109. 288p. 2000. pap. 18.95 (*1-885266-86-3*, Pub. by Story Line) Consort Bk Sales.

Place of Peace. Beatrice Hewitt. 153p. (C). 1989. text 39.00 (*0-946270-60-0*, Pub. by Pentland Pr) St Mut.

Place of Poetry: Two Centuries of an Art in Crisis. Christopher Clausen. LC 80-5172. 160p. 1981. 20.00 (*0-8131-1429-2*) U Pr of Ky.

Place of Power. Marilyn Cunningham. Ed. by Betty Lou Kratoville. (Meridian Bks.). (Illus.). 64p. (J). (gr. 3-9). 1989. lib. bdg. 4.95 (*0-87879-651-7*) High Noon Bks.

Place of Power: Central & East Moloka'i. Faith M. Roelofs. (Exploring the Islands: Islands of Maui & Moloka'i Ser.). 36p. 1994. pap. write for info. (*1-882163-25-7*) Moanalua Grdns Fnd.

Place of Prayer in an Age of Grace. Michael Penny. 56p. 1999. pap. 4.00 (*1-880573-43-1*) Bible Search Pubns.

***Place of Quiet Rest: Finding Intimacy with God Through Daily Devotional Life.** Nancy DeMoss. 2000. 14.99 (*0-8024-7596-5*) Moody.

Place of Reason in Ethics. Stephen E. Toulmin. 256p. (C). 1993. pap. text 11.95 (*0-226-80844-0*) U Ch Pr.

Place of Reason in Ethics. Stephen E. Toulmin. 256p. (C). 1995. lib. bdg. 30.00 (*0-226-80843-2*) U Ch Pr.

***Place of Safety.** Caroline Graham. 2001. pap. write for info. (*0-312-97710-7*, St Martins Paperbacks) St Martin.

Place of Safety. large type ed. Dilys A. Gater. 1995. 27.99 (*0-7089-3412-9*) Ulverscroft.

***Place of Safety.** large type ed. Caroline Graham. (G. K. Hall Core Ser.). 2000. 29.95 (*0-7838-8968-2*, G K Hall Lrg Type) Mac Lib Ref.

Place of Safety. 2nd ed. Caroline Graham. 288p. 1999. text 23.95 (*0-312-24419-3*) St Martin.

Place of Saint Thomas More in English Literature & History. Raymond W. Chambers. LC 65-15870. (English Biography Ser.: No. 31). 1969. reprint ed. lib. bdg. 75.00 (*0-8383-0523-7*) M S G Haskell Hse.

Place of Science in Modern Civilization. Thorstein B. Veblen. 525p. 1989. pap. 24.95 (*0-88738-808-6*) Transaction Pubs.

Place of Sense: Essays in Search of the Midwest. Ed. by Michael Martone. LC 88-15058. (Bur Oak Original Ser.). (Illus.). 170p. (Orig.). 1988. pap. 12.95 (*0-87745-217-2*) U of Iowa Pr.

Place of Shelley among English Poets. R. P. Scott. LC 76-116800. (Studies in Shelley: No. 25). 1970. reprint ed. lib. bdg. 59.00 (*0-8383-1042-7*) M S G Haskell Hse.

Place of Shelter. Nolan Dennett. LC 94-28963. (New American Fiction Ser.: No. 30). 224p. 1994. 19.95 (*1-55713-130-9*) Sun & Moon CA.

Place of Social Security in Welfare Policy: An Assessment of Federal Policy Changes & Their Impact on Texas. Jurgen Schmandt. (Policy Research Project Report Ser.: No. 5). 66p. 1974. pap. 3.00 (*0-89940-602-5*) LBJ Sch Pub Aff.

Place of Songs: A History of the World Gospel Mission & the Africa Gospel Church in Kenya. Burnette C. Fish & Gerald W. Fish. (Illus.). 564p. (C). 1990. reprint ed. 25.00 (*0-9620406-3-0*) World Gospel Mission.

Place of Space & Other Themes. Jan T. Srzednicki. 190p. 1983. lib. bdg. 106.00 (*90-247-2844-4*, Pub. by M Nijhoff) Kluwer Academic.

Place of Springs. Patricia Clow et al. Ed. by Linda G. Salisbury. LC 92-61931. (Illus.). 102p. 1992. pap. 8.95 (*0-9627974-9-9*) Tabby Hse Bks.

Place of Springs. Viola G. Liddell. 192p. 1982. pap. 14.95 (*0-8173-0121-6*) U of Ala Pr.

Place of Stones. Deirdre Purcell. 448p. (Orig.). 1993. mass mkt. 5.99 (*0-451-17329-5*, Sig) NAL.

***Place of Stunted Ironwood Trees: A Year in the Lives of the Cattle-Herding Himba of Namibia.** David P. Crandall. LC 00-34065. 2000. write for info. (*0-8264-1270-X*) Continuum.

Place of Supply in European VAT. Ben J. M. Terra. LC 98-18350. 320p. 1998. 103.00 (*90-411-0750-9*) Kluwer Law Intl.

***Place of the Dead: Death & Remembrance in Late Medieval & Early Modern Europe.** Ed. by Bruce Gordon & Peter Marshall. (Illus.). 376p. (C). 2000. text 64.95 (*0-521-64256-6*); pap. text 24.95 (*0-521-64518-2*) Cambridge U Pr.

P

Place of the Elementary Calculus in the Senior High School Mathematics. Noah B. Rosenberger. LC 71-177209. (Columbia University. Teachers College. Contributions to Education Ser.: No. 117). reprint ed. 37.50 (*0-404-55117-3*) AMS Pr.

Place of the Heart: An Introduction to Orthodox Spirituality. Elisabeth Behr-Sigel. Tr. by Stephen Bigham from FRE. 192p. (Orig.). 1992. per. 8.95 (*1-879038-04-8*) Oakwood Pubns.

Place of the Heart in Lonergan's Ethics: The Role of Feelings in the Ethical Intentionality Analysis of Bernard Lonergan. Mark J. Doorley. LC 96-15003. 154p. 1996. lib. bdg. 44.50 (*0-7618-0367-X*) U Pr of Amer.

Place of the Hidden Moon: Erotic Mysticism in the Vaisnava-Sahajiya Cult of Bengal. Edward C. Dimock, Jr. LC 66-13865. xx, 332p. 1989. reprint ed. pap. text 23.00 (*0-226-15237-5*) U Ch Pr.

Place of the Humanities in Medicine. Eric J. Cassell. 1984. 7.00 (*0-916558-19-3*) Hastings Ctr.

Place of the Merchant of Venice in Shakespeare's Universe of Comedy. William J. Martz. 1976. lib. bdg. 250.00 (*0-87700-233-9*) Revisionist Pr.

Place of the New 3rd Temple. Ernest L. Martin. LC 95-194820. (Illus.). 136p. (Orig.). (C). 1994. pap. text 10.95 (*0-945657-80-3*) Acad Scriptural Knowledge.

Place of the Person in Social Life. Ed. by George F. McLean et al. (Cultural Heritage & Contemporary Change Ser.: No. 6). 398p. (Orig.). 1991. 45.00 (*1-56518-013-5*, BD450.P5477) Coun Res Values.

Place of the Person in Social Life. Ed. by George F. McLean et al. (Cultural Heritage & Contemporary Change Series VI: Foundations of Moral Education,: Vol. I, No. 6). 398p. (Orig.). 1991. pap. 17.50 (*1-56518-012-7*) Coun Res Values.

***Place of the Pike (Gnoozhekaaning) A History of the Bay Mills Indian Community.** Charles E. Cleland. (Illus.). 116p. 2000. 27.95 (*0-472-09740-7*, 09740); pap. 18.95 (*0-472-06740-0*, 06740) U of Mich Pr.

Place of the Pots in Akan Funerary Custom. James Bellis. LC 82-74220. 59p. (Orig.). 1982. pap. 5.00 (*0-941934-40-3*) Indiana Africa.

Place of the Psalms in the Intellectual Culture of the Middle Ages. Ed. by Nancy Van Deusen. LC 98-26656. (SUNY Series in Medieval Studies). (Illus.). 220p. (C). 1999. pap. text 18.95 (*0-7914-4130-X*) State U NY Pr.

Place of the Psalms in the Intellectual Culture of the Middle Ages. Ed. by Nancy Van Deusen. LC 98-26656. (SUNY Series in Medieval Studies). (Illus.). 224p. (C). 1999. text 57.50 (*0-7914-4129-6*) State U NY Pr.

Place of the Sacred: The Rhetoric of the "Satanic Verses" Affair. Joel Kuortti. LC 97-27999. 187p. 1997. 42.95 (*3-631-31995-9*) P Lang Pubng.

Place of the Sacred: The Rhetoric of the "Satanic Verses" Affair. Joel Kuortti. LC 97-27999. 187p. 1997. 42.95 (*0-8204-3294-6*) P Lang Pubng.

Place of the Stage: License, Play, & Power in Renaissance England. Steven Mullaney. LC 87-17327. 192p. (Orig.). (C). 1995. pap. text 17.95 (*0-472-08346-5*, 08346) U of Mich Pr.

Place of the Stage: License, Play, & Power in Rennaissance England. Steven Mullaney. (Illus.). 192p. 1988. 24.95 (*0-226-54760-4*) U Ch Pr.

Place of the Stage: License, Play, & Power in Rennaissance England. Steven Mullaney. (Illus.). 192p. 1994. pap. text 12.95 (*0-226-54761-2*) U Ch Pr.

Place of the Storehouses Pts. 1 & 2: Roosevelt Platform Mound Study, Report on the Schoolhouse. Owen Lindauer et al. LC 96-28094. (Anthropological Field Studies: Vol. 35). 998p. 1996. pap. 58.00 (*1-886067-06-6*) ASU Office Cultural Res.

Place of the Tempest in Shakespeare's Universe of Comedy. William J. Martz. 1978. 10.00 (*0-87291-098-9*) Coronado Pr.

Place of the Wild: A Wildlands Anthology. Ed. by David C. Burks. LC 94-29221. (Illus.). 288p. 1994. pap. 17.95 (*1-55963-342-5*); text 38.00 (*1-55963-341-7*) Island Pr.

Place of Their Own: Creating the Deaf Community in America. John V. Van Cleve & Barry A. Crouch. LC 88-26996. (Illus.). 224p. (Orig.). 1989. pap. text 16.95 (*0-930323-49-1*) Gallaudet Univ Pr.

Place of Their Own: Family Farming in Eastern Finland. Ray Abrahams. (Cambridge Studies in Social & Cultural Anthropology: No. 81). (Illus.). 222p. (C). 1991. text 80.00 (*0-521-38100-2*) Cambridge U Pr.

Place of Thought in Writing. Van E. Hillard & Julianna Smith. 406p. (C). 1995. text 51.00 (*0-536-59049-4*) Pearson Custom.

Place of Understanding: A Poem. J. W. Rivers. 72p. (Orig.). 1994. pap. 14.95 (*0-936044-06-3*) Pikestaff Pr.

Place of Value in a World of Facts. Wolfgang Kohler. 320p. 1976. reprint ed. pap. 3.95 (*0-87140-107-X*, Pub. by Liveright) Norton.

Place of Wesley in the Christian Tradition: Essays Delevered at Drew University in Celebration of the Commencement of the Publication of the Oxford Edition of the Works of John Wesley. Ed. by Kenneth E. Rowe. LC 76-27659. 168p. 1976. 26.50 (*0-8108-0981-8*) Scarecrow.

Place of Your Own: A Guide to Creating a Personal Space for Spiritual Contemplation & Meditation, with Fifty-Two Weekly Devotions to Use in Your Home. Edward Searl. LC 99-186719. 304p. 1998. pap. 13.00 (*0-425-16546-9*) Berkley Pub.

Place on Earth. rev. ed. Wendell Berry. LC 82-81478. 352p. 1982. reprint ed. pap. 13.00 (*0-86547-044-8*) N Point Pr.

***Place on Earth.** rev. ed. Wendell Berry. 2001. pap. 14.00 (*1-58243-124-8*) Counterpt DC.

Place on the Corner: Identity & Rank among Black Streetcorner Men. Elijah Anderson. LC 78-1879. (Studies of Urban Society). 1978. lib. bdg. 20.00 (*0-226-01953-5*) U Ch Pr.

Place on the Corner: Identity & Rank among Black Streetcorner Men. Elijah Anderson. LC 78-1879. (Studies of Urban Society). 248p. 1981. pap. text 10.95 (*0-226-01954-3*) U Ch Pr.

Place on the Glacial Till: Time, Land, & Nature Within an American Town. Thomas F. Sherman. (Illus.). 224p. 1996. 22.00 (*0-19-510442-0*) OUP.

Place on the Magdalena Flats. Preston Jones. 1984. pap. 5.25 (*0-8222-0895-4*) Dramatists Play.

Place on Water. Jerry Dennis. (Illus.). 240p. 1996. pap. 10.95 (*0-312-14127-0*) St Martin.

Place over Time: The Continuity of Southern Distinctiveness. Carl N. Degler. LC 97-6955. 1997. pap. 16.00 (*0-8203-1942-2*) U of Ga Pr.

Place, Power, Situation & Spectacle: A Geography of Film. Ed. by Stuart C. Aitken & Leo E. Zonn. 278p. (C). 1994. pap. text 26.95 (*0-8476-7826-1*); lib. bdg. 71.50 (*0-8476-7825-3*) Rowman.

Place, Practice & Structure: Social & Spatial Transformation in Southern Sweden, 1750-1850. Allan R. Pred. LC 85-30652. 300p. 1986. 56.00 (*0-389-20615-6*, N8173) B&N Imports.

***Place Prepared for You.** R. A. Russell. (Illus.). 10p. 1998. 1.00 (*1-56722-250-1*) Word Aflame.

Place Royale & Urban Design in the Ancien Regime. Richard L. Cleary. LC 98-3572. (Illus.). 320p. (C). 1999. text 90.00 (*0-521-57268-1*) Cambridge U Pr.

Place She Lives. Allione Tsultrim. 1999. pap. 10.95 (*0-14-019456-8*, Viking) Viking Penguin.

Place to Belong. Emily Crofford. LC 93-9289. (J). (gr. 4-7). 1993. lib. bdg. 19.95 (*0-87614-808-9*, Carolrhoda) Lerner Pub.

Place to Belong. Joan Lowery Nixon. (Orphan Train Ser.: No. 4). 160p. (J). 1996. mass mkt. 4.50 (*0-440-22696-1*) BDD Bks Young Read.

Place to Belong. Joan Lowery Nixon. (Orphan Train Quartet Ser.). (J). 1996. 9.60 (*0-606-04516-3*, Pub. by Turtleback) Demco.

Place to Belong. University of Georgia Staff. 45.00 (*0-8203-1395-5*) U of Ga Pr.

Place to Belong see Orphan Train Adventures

Place to Belong: Community Order & Everyday Space in Calvert, Newfoundland. Gerald L. Pocius. 384p. 1991. text 29.95 (*0-7735-0805-8*) McG-Queens Univ Pr.

Place to Bloom. Lorianne Siomades. LC 96-86536. (Illus.). 32p. (J). (ps-1). 1997. 7.95 (*1-56397-656-0*) Boyds Mills Pr.

Place to Call Home. Ruth Glover. LC 99-19363. (Wildrose Ser.: 6). 212p. 1999. pap. text 11.99 (*0-8341-1753-3*) Beacon Hill.

Place to Call Home. Jackie F. Koller. LC 95-7559. 208p. (YA). (gr. 7 up). 1995. 16.00 (*0-689-80024-X*) Atheneum Yung Read.

Place to Call Home. Jackie F. Koller. LC 95-7559. 208p. (YA). (gr. 7 up). 1997. per. 4.50 (*0-689-81395-3*) Atheneum Yung Read.

Place to Call Home. Jackie French Koller. LC 95-7559. (YA). 1997. 9.60 (*0-606-11754-7*, Pub. by Turtleback) Demco.

***Place to Call Home.** Susan M. Wood. (Illus.). 350p. 1999. pap. write for info. (*0-7392-0437-8*, PO3721) Morris Pubng.

Place to Call Home. large type ed. Deborah Smith. LC 98-3234. 1998. 25.95 (*1-56895-548-0*, Wheeler) Wheeler Pub.

Place to Call Home. Deborah Smith. 448p. 1998. reprint ed. mass mkt. 6.50 (*0-553-57813-8*) Bantam.

Place to Call Home: Men in Blue. Sharon Sala. (Intimate Moments Ser.: Vol. 973). 248p. 2000. mass mkt. 4.25 (*0-373-07973-7*, 1-07973-0) Silhouette.

***Place to Come Home to.** Melody Carlson. LC 99-14245. (Whispering Pine Ser.). 300p. 1999. pap. 9.99 (*0-7369-0053-5*) Harvest Hse.

***Place to Dream.** large type ed. Beryl Walthew. 256p. 1999. pap. 18.99 (*0-7089-5525-8*, Linford) Ulverscroft.

Place to Go Someday. Cleda Hedrich. 352p. 1999. pap. 14.95 (*0-9671680-5-8*) NewSouth Bks.

Place to Grow: Voices & Images of Urban Gardeners. Ed. by David Hassler & Lynn Gregor. LC 98-22405. (Illus.). 120p. 1998. pap. 23.95 (*0-8298-1295-4*) Pilgrim OH.

Place to Grow: Women in the American West. Glenda Riley. 325p. 1992. pap. text 21.95 (*0-88295-886-0*) Harlan Davidson.

Place to Grow Old: The Meaning of Environment in Old Age. Stephen M. Golant. LC 84-5042. (Columbia Studies of Social Gerontology & Aging). (Illus.). 435p. reprint ed. pap. 134.90 (*0-8357-4576-7*, 203748500008) Bks Demand.

Place to Heal: The History of National Jewish Center for Immunology & Respiratory Medicine. Mary A. Fitzharris. (Illus.). 128p. (Orig.). 1989. pap. write for info. (*0-318-65724-4*) NJCI&RM.

Place to Hide. Robert Fleshner. 356p. (Orig.). 1995. pap. 7.99 (*0-9646496-0-8*, Orville & Wilbur Pub) O & W Pub Co.

Place to Hide. Robert Westall. 208p. (YA). (gr. 7-9). 1994. 13.95 (*0-590-47748-X*, Scholastic Hardcover) Scholastic Inc.

Place to Hide see Strange Matter

Place to Hide: True Stories of Holocaust Rescues. Jayne Pettit. LC 94-219468. 176p. (J). (gr. 4-7). 1993. pap. 3.50 (*0-590-45353-X*) Scholastic Inc.

Place to Hide: True Stories of Holocaust Rescues. Jayne Pettit. (Scholastic Biography Ser.). 1993. 9.09 (*0-606-05974-1*, Pub. by Turtleback) Demco.

Place to Hold My Shaky Heart: Reflections from Life in a Community. Sue Mosteller. LC 98-72904. 128p. 1998. pap. 12.95 (*0-8245-1763-6*, Crsrd) Crossroad NY.

Place to Land. Sharon Brondos. (Superromance Ser.: No. 459). 1991. per. 3.25 (*0-373-70459-3*) Harlequin Bks.

Place to Live. Ed. by Raymond C. Cheever & Betty Garee. LC 90-80564. (Illus.). 64p. (Orig.). 1990. pap. 4.95 (*0-915708-30-2*) Cheever Pub.

Place to Live: A Study of Housing for Women. YMCA of India Staff. 136p. 1983. 4.50 (*0-318-37043-3*) Asia Bk Corp.

Place to Live: Families & Child Health in a New Neighborhood of Cairo. Belgin Tekce et al. (Illus.). 272p. 1994. 35.00 (*977-424-315-3*, Pub. by Am Univ Cairo Pr) Col U Pr.

Place to Live: Gender Research on Housing in Africa. Ed. by Ann Schlyter. LC 96-217782. 171p. (Orig.). 1996. pap. 42.50 (*91-7106-388-9*) Coronet Bks.

Place to Live & Work: The Henry Disston Saw Works & the Tacony Community of Philadelphia. Harry C. Silcox. LC 93-9923. (Illus.). 288p. (C). 1994. 40.00 (*0-271-01079-7*) Pa St U Pr.

***Place to Place: Emerging Architects in Britain & Japan.** Dennis Sharp. 1998. 40.00 (*1-875498-95-8*) Images Aust AT.

Place to Pray. Roberta C. Bondi. LC 98-35200. 208p. 1998. 18.95 (*0-687-02574-5*) Abingdon.

Place to Remember: Using History to Build Community. Robert R. Archibald. LC 99-6261. (AASLH Ser.). 200p. 1999. 59.00 (*0-7619-8942-0*); pap. 22.95 (*0-7619-8943-9*) AltaMira Pr.

Place to Shine: Bringing Special Gifts to Light. 2nd ed. Daniel S. Hanson. (Illus.). 205p. (Orig.). 1994. reprint ed. pap. 11.95 (*0-9635762-0-8*) TPG Pr.

Place to Shine: Emerging from the Shadows at Work. Daniel S. Hanson. 208p. 1996. pap. text 17.95 (*0-7506-9738-5*) Buttrwrth-Heinemann.

Place to Stand. Jimmy S. Baca. 2001. 23.00 (*0-8021-1602-7*, Grove) Grove-Atltic.

Place to Stand. Philip Holmes. Date not set. pap. 14.95 (*0-85646-034-6*, Pub. by Anvil Press) Dufour.

Place to Start: The Bible As a Guide for Today. R. T. Brooks. 120p. 1983. reprint ed. 4.95 (*0-86683-708-6*) Harper SF.

Place to Which We Belong: Wisconsin Writers on Wisconsin Landscapes. Ed. by Dennis Boyer & Justin Isherwood. (Illus.). 1998. pap. 16.95 (*0-9666359-0-6*) One Thous Friends.

Place Value: An Educator's Guide to Good Literature on Rural Lifeways, Environments, & Purposes of Education. Toni Haas & Paul Nachtigal. LC 98-21364. 79p. 1998. pap. 12.00 (*1-880785-19-6*) ERIC-CRESS.

Place Value Addition & Subtraction. Donna Burk et al. (Box It or Bag It Mathematics Ser.). (Illus.). 66p. (C). 1988. teacher ed., ring bd. 9.50 (*1-886131-10-4*, BB9) Math Lrning.

Place Value & Regrouping Games. Lee Jenkins & Marion Nordberg. (Illus.). 64p. (Orig.). (J). (gr. 1-4). 1976. pap. 8.50 (*0-918932-39-4*, A-1418) Activity Resources.

Place Value Counting. Donna Burk et al. (Box It or Bag It Mathematics Ser.). (Illus.). 57p. (C). 1988. teacher ed., ring bd. 8.00 (*1-886131-09-0*, BB8) Math Lrning.

Place Value, Grades 1-2. Marilyn Burns. (Math by All Means Ser.). (Illus.). 208p. 1994. pap. text 23.95 (*0-941355-09-8*) Math Solns Pubns.

Place Value, Multiplication & Division. Kathy Richardson. LC 98-196536. 1998. pap. 22.95 (*0-7690-0060-6*) Seymour Pubns.

Place Value to One Hundred. Earl Ockenga & Walt Rucker. (Elementary Mathematics Ser.). (Illus.). 16p. (J). (gr. 1). 1990. pap. text 1.25 (*1-56281-115-0*, M115) Extra Eds.

Place Vendome: Architecture & Social Mobility in 18th-Century Paris. Rochelle Ziskin. LC 98-25880. (Illus.). 240p. (C). 1999. text 75.00 (*0-521-59259-3*) Cambridge U Pr.

Place, Void, & Eternity. Philoponus & Simplicius. Tr. by David Furley & Christian Wildberg from GRE. (Ancient Commentators on Aristotle Ser.). 160p. 1991. text 49.95 (*0-8014-2634-0*) Cornell U Pr.

Place We Call Home. Linda Morgan. 148p. 1999. pap. write for info. (*0-7392-0097-6*, PO2982) Morris Pubng.

***Place We Call Home: Exploring the Soul's Existence after Death.** Robert J. Grant. LC 99-27934. 208p. 2000. pap. 12.95 (*0-87604-457-7*, 487) ARE Pr.

Place Where Hell Bubbled Up: A History of Yellowstone National Park. David A. Clary. LC 93-77119. (Illus.). 64p. 1993. reprint ed. pap. 8.95 (*0-943972-19-1*) Homestead WY.

Place Where Memories & Dreams Meet. Linda S. Landers. LC 96-95473. 192p. 1997. 18.95 (*0-8034-9199-9*, Avalon Bks) Bouregy.

Place Where the Eelgrass Flows. Norman S. Reed. Ed. by Vineyard Gazette Editors. (Illus.). 81p. pap. 7.95 (*0-685-18165-0*) Quill Pubns GA.

Place Where the Planes Take Off. Steven Herrick. (Illus.). (J). 1995. pap. 12.95 (*0-7022-2727-7*, Pub. by Univ Queensland Pr) Intl Spec Bk.

Place Where the Sea Remembers. Sandra Benitez. LC 93-25176. 160p. (YA). (gr. 10-12). 1993. 10.00 (*1-56689-011-X*) Coffee Hse.

Place Where the Sea Remembers. Sandra Benitez. 176p. 1995. per. 10.00 (*0-671-89267-3*) Simon & Schuster.

***Place Where We Belong.** Carol A. Fuller. LC 99-93766. 2000. pap. 13.95 (*0-533-13147-2*) Vantage.

Place Where You Are Standing Is Holy: A Jewish Theology on Human Relationships. Gershon Winkler. 1998. pap. 20.00 (*0-7657-6035-5*) Aronson.

Place Where You Are Standing Is Holy: A Jewish Theology on Human Relationships. Gershon Winkler & Lakme B. Elior. LC 94-17362. 256p. 1995. 25.00 (*1-56821-218-6*) Aronson.

***Place with Promise.** Edward Swift. 2000. pap. 14.95 (*1-930709-10-2*) HAWK Pubng Grp.

***Place Within: Portraits of the American Landscape by Contemporary Writers.** Jodi Daynard. 268p. 2000. reprint ed. text 23.00 (*0-7881-9119-5*) DIANE Pub.

Place Within: Portraits of the American Landscape by 20 Contemporary Writers. Jodi Daynard. 224p. 1996. 23.00 (*0-393-03999-4*) Norton.

Place Within: The Poetry of Pope John Paul II. John Paul, II, pseud. Tr. by Jerzy Peterkiewicz from ITA. LC 94-68389. Orig. Title: Collected Poems. (Illus.). 197p. 1994. pap. 12.00 (*0-679-76064-4*) Random.

Place Without Twilight. Peter Feibleman. LC 97-15673. (Voices of the South Ser.). 392p. 1997. pap. 14.95 (*0-8071-2225-4*) La State U Pr.

Place Your Body Is. Marjorie Edel. 98p. 1984. pap. 6.00 (*0-932136-07-9*) Petronium HI.

Placebo Effect. Gary Russell. 1998. pap. 5.95 (*0-563-40587-2*) BBC.

Placebo Effect: An Interdisciplinary Exploration. Anne Harrington. LC 97-4324. (Illus.). 256p. 1997. 39.95 (*0-674-66984-3*) HUP.

Placebo Effect: An Interdisciplinary Exploration. Anne Harrington. 1999. pap. text 19.95 (*0-674-66986-X*) HUP.

Placebo Effects: Poems. Jeanne M. Beaumont. 1997. 21.00 (*0-614-29433-9*) Norton.

Placebo Effects: Poems. Jeanne M. Beaumont. LC 97-3978. 96p. 1997. 21.00 (*0-393-04128-X*) Norton.

Placebo Effects: Poems. Jeanne M. Beaumont. 96p. 1999. pap. 11.00 (*0-393-31891-5*) Norton.

Placebo Effects in Health & Disease: Index of New Information with Authors, Subjects & References. rev. ed. Joseph J. Hartwick. 165p. 1997. 47.50 (*0-7883-1493-9*); pap. 44.50 (*0-7883-1494-7*) ABBE Pubs Assn.

Placebo or Panacea? Putting Psychiatric Drugs to the Test. Seymour Fisher & Roger P. Greenberg. LC 97-1074. 404p. 1997. 69.95 (*0-471-14848-2*) Wiley.
***Placebo Response: How You Can Release the Body's Inner Pharmacy for Better Health.** Howard Brody. 336p. 2000. 25.00 (*0-06-019493-6*, Cliff Street) HarperTrade.
Placebos & the Philosophy of Medicine: Clinical, Conceptual, & Ethical Issues. Howard Brody. LC 79-18481. 171p. Date not set. reprint ed. pap. 53.10 (*0-608-20611-3*, 205457900003) Bks Demand.
***Placebound: Australian Feminist Geographies.** Louise Johnson. (Illus.). 240p. 2000. pap. 29.95 (*0-19-553566-9*) OUP.
Placemaking: Production on Built Environment in Two Cultures. David Stea & Mete Turan. LC 93-3856. (Ethnoscapes: Current Challenges in the Environmental Social Science Ser.). 400p. 1993. reprint ed. 82.95 (*1-85628-460-3*, Pub. by Avebry) Ashgate Pub Co.
Placemaking: The Art & Practice of Building Communities. Lynda H. Schneekloth & Robert G. Shibley. LC 94-33124. 263p. 1995. 59.95 (*0-471-11026-4*) Wiley.
Placemat Pets 'n Playmates. Pam Aulson. (Illus.). 24p. (J). (gr. 6 up). 1980. pap. 3.00 (*0-9601896-2-9*) Patch As Patch.
Placement & Compaction of Asphalt Mixtures- STP 829. Ed. by F. T. Wagner. LC 83-71927. 149p. 1984. text 29.00 (*0-8031-0223-2*, STP829) ASTM.
Placement & Improvement of Soil to Support Structures: Specialty Conference Held at Cambridge, MA, August 26-28, 1968. American Society of Civil Engineers Staff. LC 72-185397. (Illus.). 446p. reprint ed. pap. 138.30 (*0-608-30749-1*, 201953500013) Bks Demand.
Placement & Routing of Electronic Modules. Ed. by Michael G. Pecht. LC 92-44796. (Electrical Engineering & Electronics Ser.: Vol. 82). (Illus.). 352p. 1993. text 175.00 (*0-8247-8916-4*) Dekker.
Placement Art: A Beginner's Guide to Feng-Shui. Penelope A. Lindsay. LC 97-51963. (Illus.). 144p. 1998. pap. 14.95 (*0-8348-0413-1*) Weatherhill.
Placement Handbook for Counseling Disabled Persons. Chrisann S. Geist & William A. Calzaretta. (Illus.). 346p. 1982. pap. 41.95 (*0-398-06146-7*) C C Thomas.
Placement Handbook for Counseling Disabled Persons. Chrisann S. Geist & William A. Calzaretta. (Illus.). 346p. (C). 1982. text 60.95 (*0-398-04592-5*) C C Thomas.
***Placement of Multiple Birth Children in School: A Guide for Educators.** 36p. 2000. pap. 3.00 (*1-880805-08-1*) Natl Org Mothers Twins.
Placement Plus & Plenty More. Pam Aulson. (Illus.). 64p. 1982. pap. 3.50 (*0-9601896-5-3*) Patch As Patch.
Placement Procedures in Bilingual Education: Education & Policy Issues. 168p. 1984. 69.00 (*0-905028-32-5*, Pub. by Multilingual Matters); pap. 24.95 (*0-905028-31-7*, Pub. by Multilingual Matters) Taylor & Francis.
Placement Representative I. Jack Rudman. (Career Examination Ser.: C-868). 1994. pap. 27.95 (*0-8373-0868-2*) Nat Learn.
Placement Representative II. Jack Rudman. (Career Examination Ser.: C-869). 1994. pap. 29.95 (*0-8373-0869-0*) Nat Learn.
Placement Services & Techniques. James T. Bowman & W. H. Graves. 1976. pap. 11.80 (*0-87563-124-X*) Stipes.
Placement Test. Steven J. Molinsky & Bill Bliss. (C). 1989. text. write for info. (*0-318-65462-8*) P-H.
Placement Test Bittinger. 5th ed. Mervin L. Keedy & Marvin L. Bittinger. (Illus.). 435p. (C). 1987. pap. text 6.25 (*0-201-15369-6*) Addison-Wesley.
Placement Test Success. Walker. 32p. 1995. 28.07 (*0-201-58890-0*) Addison-Wesley.
Placements. Arlene J. Nelson. (Teachings of the Master, Sinat Schirah, "Suggestions for Learning" Ser.). 200p. (Orig.). 1988. pap. 9.95 (*0-685-26084-4*, TXU 309-553) Loveline Prodns.
Placenames in Maryland: Their Origin & Meaning. Hamill Kenny. LC 84-60803. 368p. (Orig.). 1984. pap. 22.50 (*0-938420-28-3*) MD Hist.
Placenames of Russia & the Former Soviet Union: Origins & Meanings of the Names for over 2000 Natural Features, Towns, Regions & Countries. Adrian Room. LC 96-1916. 288p. 1996. lib. bdg. 58.50 (*0-7864-0042-0*) McFarland & Co.
Placenames of the World: Origins & Meanings of the Names for over 5,000 Natural Features, Countries, Capitals, Territories, Cities & Historic Sites. Adrian Room. LC 97-38011. 441p. 1997. lib. bdg. 65.00 (*0-7864-0172-9*) McFarland & Co.
Placenta: Basic Research for Clinical Application for the Next Decade. Ed. by Hiroaki Som. (Illus.). viii, 214p. 1992. 200.00 (*3-8055-5468-0*) S Karger.
Placenta: Human & Animal. Elizabeth M. Ramsey. LC 81-23372. 187p. 1982. 65.00 (*0-275-91378-3*, C1378, Praeger Pubs) Greenwood.
Placenta: Receptors, Pathology & Toxicology. R. K. Miller. Ed. by Henry A. Thiede. 390p. 1981. 95.00 (*0-275-91350-3*, C1350, Praeger Pubs) Greenwood.
Placenta: To Know Me Is to Love Me - A Reference Guide for Gross Placental Examination. Doris L. Schuler-Maloney & Steve S. Lee. (Illus.). xviii, 174p. 1998. pap. 69.00 (*0-9670354-0-6*) D S M.
Placenta As a Model & a Source. Ed. by O. Genbacev et al. (Illus.). 162p. 1989. 65.00 (*0-306-43238-2*, Plenum Trade) Perseus Pubng.
***Placenta from Implantation to Trophoblastic Disease Vol. 13: Apoptosis, Proliferation, Invasion & Pathology.** Ed. by Richard Miller et al. LC 99-44470. (Illus.). 548p. 1999. 120.00 (*1-58046-064-X*, Pub. by Univ Rochester Pr) Boydell & Brewer.
***Placenta in Clinical Practice.** E. Jauniaux & R. K. Miller. (Illus.). 352p. 1998. text. write for info. (*0-443-05604-8*) Church.
Placenta Transfer Methods & Interpretation. M. Young. 1981. 89.50 (*0-275-91357-0*, C1357, Praeger Pubs) Greenwood.
Placental & Endometrial Proteins: Basic & Clinical Aspects: Proceedings of the International Conference, Japan, 1987. Ed. by S. Mizutani et al. 728p. 1988. 175.00 (*90-6764-115-4*, Pub. by VSP) Coronet Bks.
***Placental & Fetal Doppler.** K. H. Nicolaides & G. Rizzo. LC 00-25526. (Diploma in Fetal Medicine Ser.). (Illus.). 224p. 2000. 65.00 (*1-85070-757-X*) Prthnon Pub.
Placental Function & Fetal Nutrition. Frederick C. Battaglia. LC 97-11147. 288p. 1997. text 74.00 (*0-7817-1406-0*) Lppncott W & W.
Placental Molecules in Hemodynamics, 2 vols., Vol. 9. Ed. by Toshio Hata et al. LC 97-28672. (Trophoblast Research Ser.: Vol. 9, Pt. 1). (Illus.). 600p. 1997. 150.00 (*1-58046-016-X*) Univ Rochester Pr.
Placental, Neonatal, & Pediatric Pathology: Based on the Proceedings of the 61st Annual Anatomic Pathology Slide Seminar of the American Society of Clinical Pathologists, New Orleans, Louisiana, September 21-22, 1995. Don B. Singer et al. LC 96-620. 1996. write for info. (*0-89189-404-7*) Am Soc Clinical.
Placental Pharmacology. B. V. Sastry. 224p. 1996. boxed set 139.95 (*0-8493-7811-7*) CRC Pr.
Placental Proteins. P. Bischof. (Contributions to Gynecology & Obstetrics Ser.: Vol. 12). (Illus.). viii, 96p. 1984. 57.50 (*3-8055-3853-7*) S Karger.
Placental Signals: Autocrine & Paracine Control of Pregnancy. Ed. by Lise Cedard & Anthony Firth. (Trophoblast Research Ser.: Vol. 6). (Illus.). 400p. (C). 1993. 90.00 (*1-878822-21-7*) Univ Rochester Pr.
Placental Toxology. Ed. by B. V. Sastry. LC 94-27711. 304p. 1995. boxed set 179.95 (*0-8493-7812-5*) CRC Pr.
Placentia, a Pleasant Place. 2nd enl. ed. Virginia L. Carpenter. LC 88-51559. (Illus.). 294p. 1988. 15.95 (*0-943480-67-1*) Friis-Pioneer Pr.
Placer Examination Principles - Practice. 1996. pap. 14.95 (*0-931913-26-8*) Met-Chem Rsch.
Placer Gold: Where to Find It. Gregory V. Stone. (Illus.). 64p. 1982. pap. 10.95 (*0-8059-2833-2*) Dorrance.
Placer Gold Deposits of Arizona. Maureen G. Johnson. LC 81-70327. 103p. 1987. pap. 7.95 (*0-935182-33-0*) Gem Guides Bk.
Placer Gold Deposits of Nevada. Maureen G. Johnson. LC 81-70326. 118p. 1987. reprint ed. pap. text 7.95 (*0-89632-010-3*) Gem Guides Bk.
Placer Gold Deposits of the Sierra Nevada. Ed. by Paul D. Morrison. LC 97-60923. (Illus.). 192p. (Orig.). 1997. pap. 10.95 (*0-935182-97-7*) Gem Guides Bk.
Placer Primitivo: Boots in the Bedroom! Alison Kelly. (Bianca Ser.: Vol. 117).Tr. of Primitive Pleasure. (SPA.). 1998. per. 3.50 (*0-373-33467-2*, 1-33467-1) Harlequin Bks.
Placer Sexual Ordenado por Dios. Ed Wheat & Gaye De Wheat.Tr. of Intended for Pleasure. 224p. 1980. 9.99 (*0-88113-320-5*) Caribe Betania.
***Placeres Prohibidos.** 2000. per. 3.50 (*0-373-33551-2*) S&S Trade.
Places see **Working Series**
Places. Hilaire Belloc. LC 78-117759. (Essay Index Reprint Ser.). 1977. 20.95 (*0-8369-2037-6*) Ayer.
Places. Robert Creeley. (Illus.). 16p. 1990. 7.50 (*0-9628035-1-0*) Shuffaloff Bks.
Places: A Directory of Public Places for Private Events & Private Places for Public Functions. 8th rev. ed. Hannelore Hahn. Ed. by Tatiana Stoumen. LC 80-50723. (Illus.). 244p. 1998. pap. 24.95 (*0-9603310-7-7*) Tenth Hse Ent.
***Places: A Travel Companion for Music & Art Lovers.** Robert Craft. LC 99-66974. (Illus.). 2000. 29.95 (*0-500-01990-8*, Pub. by Thames Hudson) Norton.
Places - Everyone. Jim Daniels. LC 85-40366. (Brittingham Prize in Poetry, 1985 Ser.). 96p. 1985. pap. 11.95 (*0-299-10354-4*) U of Wis Pr.
Places along the Way: Meditations on the Journey of Faith. Martin E. Marty. LC 94-29532. (Illus.). 112p. 1994. pap. 15.99 (*0-8066-2746-8*, 9-2746, Augsburg) Augsburg Fortress.
Places & Cases Teacher's Resource Pack: Europe. John Edwards. 64p. 1998. pap. 77.50 (*0-7487-3476-7*, Pub. by S Thornes Pubs) Trans-Atl Phila.
Places & Cases Teacher's Resource Pack: The World. Robert Prosser. 64p. 1998. pap. 77.50 (*0-7487-3477-5*, Pub. by S Thornes Pubs) Trans-Atl Phila.
Places & Elegies: Poems & Translations. Fred Beake. LC 98-213925. 1998. pap. 14.95 (*3-7052-0118-2*, Pub. by Poetry Salzburg) Intl Spec Bk.
Places & Faces. Illus. by Horst Lemke. LC 78-160446. 32p. (J). (ps). 14.95 (*0-87592-041-1*) Scroll Pr.
Places & Occasions: Poems. Betzabe M. Praeger & Frank C. Praeger. LC 91-60318. 64p. (Orig.). 1991. pap. 8.00 (*0-9628816-0-0*) Keweenaw Pr.
Places & Spaces for Preschool & Primary (Indoors) Jeanne Vergeront. LC 87-61485. 24p. 1987. pap. 2.50 (*0-935989-07-2*, NAEYC #310) Natl Assn Child Ed.
Places & Spaces for Preschool & Primary (Outdoors) Jeanne Vergeront. LC 88-62204. 1988. pap. 3.00 (*0-935989-25-0*, NAEYC #311) Natl Assn Child Ed.
Places & Stories. Kim R. Stafford. LC 86-72299. (Poetry Ser.). 1987. pap. 11.95 (*0-88748-043-8*) Carnegie-Mellon.
Places & Stories. Kim R. Stafford. LC 86-72299. (Poetry Ser.). 1987. 20.95 (*0-88748-042-X*) Carnegie-Mellon.
Places & Valuations in Noncommutative Ring Theory. Jan V. Geel. LC 81-12634. (Lecture Notes in Pure & Applied Mathematics Ser.: Vol. 71). 128p. reprint ed. pap. 39.70 (*0-608-08996-6*, 206963100005) Bks Demand.
Places & Visions Shared: The Collected Poems of Lawrence V. Jowers. 2nd ed. Lawrence V. Jowers. Ed. by John E. Westburg. 64p. 1983. pap. 10.00 (*0-87423-033-0*) Westburg.
Places Around the Bases: A Historic Tour of the Coors Field Neighborhood. Diane Bakke & Jackie Davis. (Illus.). 160p. 1995. pap. text 16.95 (*1-56579-117-7*) Westcliffe Pubs.
Places by the Sea. Jean Stone. 384p. 1997. mass mkt. 5.99 (*0-553-57424-8*, Fanfare) Bantam.
Places Far from Ellesmere. Aritha Van Herk. 144p. 1990. pap. 10.95 (*0-88995-060-1*, Pub. by Red Deer) Genl Dist Srvs.
Places for Childhoods: Making Quality Happen in the Real World. Jim Greenman. (Illus.). 196p. 1998. pap. 33.00 (*0-942702-25-5*) Child Care.
***Places for Dead Bodies.** Gary J. Hausladen. LC 99-47170. (Illus.). 208p. 2000. 40.00 (*0-292-73127-2*); pap. 18.95 (*0-292-73130-2*) U of Tex Pr.
Places for Devotion. John Buscemi. Ed. by David Philippart. (Meeting House Essays Ser.: No. 4). (Illus.). 32p. (Orig.). 1993. pap. 6.00 (*0-929650-68-9*, DEVOT) Liturgy Tr Pubns.
Places for Learning, Places for Joy: Speculations on American School Reform. Theodore R. Sizer. LC 72-86381. 181p. 1973. 25.95 (*0-674-66985-1*) HUP.
Places for Worship: A Guide to Building & Renovating. Marchita Mauck. LC 94-7252. (American Essays in Liturgy Ser.). 72p. (Orig.). 1995. pap. write for info. (*0-8146-2283-6*) Liturgical Pr.
Places I Never Meant to Be: Original Stories by Censored Writers. Ed. by Judy Blume. LC 98-30343. 208p. (YA). (gr. 7 up). 1999. per. 16.95 (*0-689-82034-8*) S&S Bks Yung.
Places in Art. National Gallery of London Staff. (Illus.). 144p. 1999. pap. 14.95 (*0-8230-0336-1*) Watsn-Guptill.
Places in Art. Anthea Peppin. (J). (gr. 4-7). 1992. pap. 6.70 (*0-395-64557-3*) HM.
Places in Art. Anthea Peppin. LC 91-34978. (Millbrook Arts Library). (Illus.). 48p. (J). (gr. 2-6). 1992. pap. 8.95 (*1-56294-819-9*); lib. bdg. 22.90 (*1-56294-172-0*) Millbrook Pr.
***Places in Mind.** Catharine Savage Brosman. LC 99-59204. 80p. 2000. 22.50 (*0-8071-2546-6*); pap. 14.95 (*0-8071-2547-4*) La State U Pr.
***Places in the Dark.** Thomas H. Cook. LC 99-89644. 256p. 2000. 23.95 (*0-553-10563-9*, Spectra) Bantam.
Places in the Primary School: Knowledge & Understanding of Places at Key Stages 1 & 2. Patrick Wiegand. 192p. 1992. 85.00 (*0-7507-0052-1*, Falmer Pr); pap. 34.95 (*0-7507-0053-X*, Falmer Pr) Taylor & Francis.
Places in the Sand. Margaret Courtney-Clarke. LC 97-28067. (Illus.). 128p. 1997. 45.00 (*1-885254-76-8*, Pub. by Monacelli Pr) Penguin Putnam.
Places in the Sun. James Fenimore Cooper. Ed. by Lew Place. (Illus.). 1989. 19.95 (*0-87026-070-7*) Westernlore.
Places in the Sun: The History & Romance of Florida Placenames. Bertha E. Bloodworth & Alton C. Morris. LC 77-13754. (University of Florida Bk.). 251p. reprint ed. pap. 77.90 (*0-7837-0594-8*, 204094200019) Bks Demand.
Places in the System: New Directions for the Vocational Education of Rural Women. Faith Dunne. 16p. 1985. 2.75 (*0-318-22167-5*, OC108) Ctr Educ Trng Employ.
***Places in the World a Person Could Walk: Family, Stories, Home, & Place in the Texas Hill Country.** David Syring. LC 00-23487. (Illus.). 233p. 2000. 40.00 (*0-292-77746-9*); pap. 18.95 (*0-292-77754-X*) U of Tex Pr.
Places in the World a Woman Could Walk. Janet Kauffman. LC 95-80426. 175p. 1996. pap. 12.00 (*1-55597-233-0*) Graywolf.
Places in Time: Prehistoric Europe. Chris Scarre. (Places in Time Ser.). (Illus.). 240p. 1999. 39.95 (*0-19-510323-8*) OUP.
Places Left Behind: Regional Development Policies in the United States & Canada, 1930-1990. Charles S. Colgan. 328p. 1996. text 50.00 (*0-8020-0433-4*); pap. text 21.95 (*0-8020-7223-2*) U of Toronto Pr.
Places Left Unfinished at the Time of Creation. John Santos. LC 99-13228. 288p. 1999. 24.95 (*0-670-86808-6*) Viking Penguin.
***Places Left Unfinished at the Time of Creation.** John P. Santos. 2000. pap. 12.95 (*0-14-029202-0*) Viking Penguin.
***Places Near the Mountain: Botetourt & Roanoke Counties, Virginia, from the Community of Amsterdam, Virginia up the Road to Catawba, on the Waters of the Catawba & Tinker Creeks, along the Carolina Road as It Approached Big Lick & Other Areas, Primarily North Roanoke.** Helen R. Prillaman. (Illus.). 397p. 1999. reprint ed. pap. 49.95 (*0-8063-4606-X*) Clearfield Co.
***Places of Commemoration: Search for Identity & Landscape Design** Joachim Wolschke-Bulmahn. LC 99-36997. 1999. write for info. (*0-88402-260-9*) Dumbarton Oaks.
Places of Delight: The Pastoral Landscape. Robert C. Cafritz et al. LC 88-18028. (Illus.). 256p. 1988. pap. 19.95 (*0-943044-12-X*) Phillips Coll.
Places of Folklore & Legend. Reader's Digest Editors. LC 96-40045. (Explore America Ser.). 1997. write for info. (*0-89577-905-6*) RD Assn.
Places of Grace. David Elias. LC 98-124783. 185p. 1997. pap. 12.95 (*1-55050-117-8*, Pub. by Coteau) Genl Dist Srvs.
Places of Grace: The Natural Landscapes of the American Midwest. Michal Strutin. LC 98-58012. (Illus.). 160p. 1999. 49.95 (*0-252-02323-4*) U of Ill Pr.
Places of History: Regionalism Revisited in Latin America. Ed. by Doris Sommer. LC 98-40998. (Illus.). 296p. 1999. 49.95 (*0-8223-2310-9*) Duke.
Places of History Vol. 47, No. 2: Regionalism Revisited in Latin America. Ed. by Doris Sommer. 275p. 1996. pap. text 12.00 (*0-8223-6436-0*) Duke.
Places of History Vol. 47, No. 2: Regionalism Revisited in Latin America. Doris Sommer. LC 98-40998. 1999. 49.95 (*0-8223-2344-3*) Duke.
Places of Inquiry: Research & Advanced Education in Modern Universities. Burton R. Clark. LC 94-25325. 1995. 48.00 (*0-520-08762-3*, Pub. by U CA Pr) Cal Prin Full Svc.
Places of Memory, Vol. 2. Pierre Nora. 1996. 39.95 (*0-226-59133-6*) U Ch Pr.
Places of Memory, Vol. 3. Pierre Nora. 1996. 39.95 (*0-226-59134-4*) U Ch Pr.
Places of Memory, Vol. 4. Pierre Nora. 1996. 39.95 (*0-226-59135-2*) U Ch Pr.
Places of Memory: Whiteman's Schools & Native American Communities. Alan Peshkin. LC 97-5612. 1997. write for info. (*0-8058-2468-5*); pap. write for info. (*0-8058-2469-3*) L Erlbaum Assocs.
***Places of Naples.** Donatella Mazzoleni. (Illus.). 312p. 2000. text 95.00 (*0-8478-2216-8*) Rizzoli Intl.
Places of Performance: The Semiotics of Theatre Architecture. Marvin Carlson. LC 88-47936. (Illus.). 224p. 1989. text 49.95 (*0-8014-2254-X*) Cornell U Pr.
Places of Performance: The Semiotics of Theatre Architecture. Marvin Carlson. LC 88-47936. (Illus.). 224p. 1993. pap. text 21.95 (*0-8014-8094-9*) Cornell U Pr.
Places of Picasso: A Biographical Guide to Spain & France. Marilyn Zolton & Raymond Zolton. LC 98-92754. (Biographical Guides Ser.: Vol. 1). (Illus.). xv, 111p. 1998. pap. 12.50 (*0-9663021-0-9*) Raymar Assocs.
Places of Power. Michael DeMunn. LC 98-127246. (Illus.). 36p. (YA). (gr. k up). 1997. 16.95 (*1-883220-64-5*); pap. 7.95 (*1-883220-65-3*) Dawn CA.
Places of Power: A Decade of Living in National Parks. Kathleen Kemsley. LC 90-50961. (Illus.). 315p. 1991. pap. 12.95 (*0-923568-20-4*) Wilderness Adventure Bks.
Places of Power: Measuring the Secret Energy of Ancient Sites. Paul Devereux. (Illus.). 224p. 1999. pap. 16.95 (*0-7137-2765-9*, Pub. by Blandford Pr) Sterling.
***Places of Power: The Aesthetics of Technology.** John Sexton. (Illus.). 128p. 2000. 60.00 (*0-9672188-1-0*) Ventana Edtns.
Places of Presence. Marlene Creates. (Illus.). 64p. 1997. pap. 12.95 (*1-895387-87-6*) Creative Bk Pub.
Places of Pride: The Work & Photography of Clara Brian. Margaret Esposito. Ed. by Tona Schenck. (Transactions of the Mclean County Historical Society Ser.). (Illus.). (Orig.). 1989. pap. 24.95 (*0-943788-05-6*) McLean County.
Places of Quiet Beauty: Parks, Preserves, & Environmentalism. Rebecca Conard. LC 96-27207. (American Land & Life Ser.). (Illus.). 400p. (Orig.). 1997. pap. 15.95 (*0-87745-558-9*) U of Iowa Pr.
Places of Silence, Journeys of Freedom: The Fiction of Paule Marshall. Eugenia C. Delamotte. LC 97-47580. (Studies in Contemporary American Fiction). 240p. 1998. 39.95 (*0-8122-3437-5*) U of Pa Pr.
Places of the Soul: Architecture & Environmental Design As Healing Art. Christopher Day. 1990. 22.95 (*0-85030-880-1*, Pub. by Aqrn Pr) Harper SF.
Places of Victory: Lessons from Psalm 23. Jean Meppelink. 135p. (Orig.). 1993. pap. 6.95 (*0-9657979-1-0*) Growing Life.
***Places of Worship, 6 bks.** Incl. Buddhist Temple. Angela Wood. LC 99-53805. (Illus.). 32p. (J). (gr. 2 up). 1999. lib. bdg. 21.27 (*0-8368-2605-1*); Christian Church. Angela Wood. LC 99-55999. 32p. (J). (gr. 2 up). 1999. lib. bdg. 21.27 (*0-8368-2606-X*); Hindu Mandir. Angela Wood. LC 99-53802. (J). (gr. 2 up). 1999. lib. bdg. 21.27 (*0-8368-2607-8*); Jewish Synagogue. Angela Wood. LC 99-53806. 32p. (J). (gr. 2 up). 1999. lib. bdg. 21.27 (*0-8368-2608-6*); Muslim Mosque. Angela Wood. LC 99-53803. 32p. (J). 1999. lib. bdg. 21.27 (*0-8368-2609-4*); Sikh Gurdwara. Kanwaljit Kaus-Singh. LC 99-53804. 32p. (J). (gr. 2 up). 1999. lib. bdg. 21.27 (*0-8368-2610-8*); (Illus.). (J). (gr. 2 up). 1999. Set lib. bdg. 127.62 (*0-8368-2604-3*) Gareth Stevens Inc.
***Places of Worship.** James Russell. (Architecture 3s Ser.). 1999. 19.95 (*0-7148-3877-2*) Phaidon Pr.
Places of Worship: Exploring Their History. James P. Wind. LC 97-38736. (American Association for State & Local History Book Ser.). 1997. pap. 17.95 (*0-7619-8978-1*) AltaMira Pr.
Places of Worship - Milwaukee. Mary E. Young & Wayne Attoe. (Publications in Architecture & Urban Planning: No. R77-1). (Illus.). viii, 112p. 1977. per. 5.00 (*0-938744-46-1*) U of Wis Ctr Arch-Urban.
Places, Paths & Passes. Jeannette G. Maino. 80p. (Orig.). 1991. write for info. (*0-941885-07-0*) Dry Creeks Bks.
Places People Dare Not Enter. Martine Bellen. 67p. (Orig.). 1991. pap. 8.00 (*0-937013-40-4*) Potes Poets.
Places, Please! Dave Brandl. 1997. pap. 2.50 (*1-57514-287-2*, 3078) Encore Perform Pub.
Places, Please - Musical. Herb Martin. 106p. (gr. 10 up). 1978. pap. 5.95 (*0-87129-855-4*, P04) Dramatic Pub.
Places Rated Almanac. 5th ed. David Savageau & Geoffrey Loftus. LC 96-79148. 448p. 1996. pap. 24.95 (*0-02-861233-7*) Macmillan USA.
Places Rated Almanac. 6th ed. David Savageau. LC 98-38078. (Illus.). 496p. 1999. pap. text 24.95 (*0-02-863447-0*) Macmillan Gen Ref.
Places Rated Almanac: Your Electronic Guide to Finding the Best Places to Live in North America. David Savageau & Richard Boyer. 448p. 1993. pap. 34.95 incl. disk (*0-671-88395-X*) S&S Trade.

P

Places Rated Almanac: Your Electronic Guide to Finding the Best Places to Live in North America. rev. ed. David Savageau & Richard Boyer. LC 93-12340. 448p. 1993. pap. 20.00 (*0-671-84947-6*) Prntice Hall Bks.

Places, Shadows, Dancing People. Thomas J. Lyon et al. LC 71-632230. (Utah State University, Monograph Ser.: Vol. 17, No. 1). 70p. reprint ed. pap. 30.00 (*0-8357-6264-5*, 203460700090) Bks Demand.

Places She Lives. Tsultrim Allione. 1999. pap. 21.95 (*0-670-84762-3*) Viking Penguin.

Places, Thoughts, & Things. Lobo Nocho. LC 97-90372. 1997. pap. 17.95 (*0-533-12376-3*) Vantage.

Places Through the Body. Heidi J. Nast & Steve Pile. LC 97-37994. (Illus.). 448p. (C). 1998. 85.00 (*0-415-17904-1*) Routledge.

Places Through the Body. Heidi J. Nast & Steve Pile. LC 97-37994. 344p. (C). 1998. pap. 27.99 (*0-415-17905-X*) Routledge.

Places to Go with Children in Miami & South Florida. rev. ed. Cheryl L. Juarez & Deborah A. Johnson. LC 93-37798. 240p. 1994. pap. 10.95 (*0-8118-0479-8*) Chronicle Bks.

Places to Hide: Pacific Coast. Thomas Preston & Elizabeth Preston. (Double Eagle Guides Ser.). (Illus.). 178p. 1999. 19.95 (*0-929760-86-7*) Discovery MT.

Places to Hide Vol. 2: Intermountain West. Thomas Preston & Elizabeth Preston. (Double Eagle Guides Ser.). (Illus.). 170p. 1999. 19.95 (*0-929760-87-5*) Discovery MT.

Places to Hide Vol. 3: Rocky Mountains. Thomas Preston & Elizabeth Preston. (Double Eagle Guides Ser.). (Illus.). 176p. 1999. 19.95 (*0-929760-88-3*) Discovery MT.

Places to Hide Vol. 4: Great Plains. Thomas Preston & Elizabeth Preston. (Double Eagle Guides Ser.). (Illus.). 174p. 1999. 19.95 (*0-929760-89-1*) Discovery MT.

Places to Play Golf in Colorado. John H. Shelton. 240p. (Orig.). 1996. pap. text 9.95 (*0-9646055-1-1*) Places to Play.

Places to Visit, Places to See: Big Book, Theme 4. large type ed. Selected by Lee B. Hopkins. (Worlds of Poetry Ser.). (Illus.). 16p. (J). (gr. k-3). 1998. pap. text 28.95 (*0-8215-0530-0*) Sadlier.

Places to Visit, Places to See: Theme Pack, Theme 4. large type ed. Selected by Lee B. Hopkins. (Worlds of Poetry Ser.). (Illus.). 16p. (J). (gr. k-3). 1998. pap. text 90.00 (*0-8215-0537-8*) Sadlier.

Places to Visit Theme Set, 10 bks. (Beginners Ser.). 1991. 100.44 (*0-8123-7217-4*); pap. 10.52 (*0-8123-6952-1*); pap. 10.52 (*0-8123-6953-X*); pap. 10.52 (*0-8123-6957-2*); pap. 10.52 (*0-8123-6963-7*); pap. 10.52 (*0-8123-6964-5*); pap. 10.52 (*0-8123-6965-3*); pap. 10.52 (*0-8123-6966-1*); pap. 10.52 (*0-8123-6971-8*); pap. 10.52 (*0-8123-6978-5*); pap. 10.52 (*0-8123-6997-1*) McDougal-Littell.

Places, Towns, & Townships. Ed. by Courtenay M. Slater & George E. Hall. (County & City Extra Companion Ser.). (Illus.). 700p. 1993. lib. bdg. 69.95 (*0-89059-014-1*) Bernan Pr.

Places, Towns & Townships, 1998. 2nd ed. Ed. by Deirdre A. Gaquin & Richard W. Dodge. 923p. 1997. 89.00 (*0-89059-072-9*, 077-43073) Bernan Pr.

Places We Save: A Guide to the Nature Conservancy's Preserves in Wisconsin. Nature Conservancy of Wisconsin Staff. LC 96-46823. (Illus.). 128p. (Orig.). 1997. pap. 16.95 (*1-55971-597-9*, NorthWord Pr) Creat Pub Intl.

Places We Save: Wisconsin Chapter of the Nature Conservancy. Mary M. Maher. (Illus.). 88p. (Orig.). 1988. pap. text 11.95 (*0-9619854-0-2*) Nat Conserv WI.

Places Where Children Succeed: A Profile of Outstanding Elementary Schools. Bruce L. Wilson & Thomas B. Corcoran. 97p. 1987. pap. 21.95 (*1-56602-014-X*) Research Better.

Places Where Teachers Are Taught. Ed. by John I. Goodlad et al. LC 90-38687. (Education-Higher Education Ser.). 460p. 1990. text 41.50 (*1-55542-276-4*) Jossey-Bass.

Places Where They Sing: Memoirs of a Church Musician. Lionel Dakers. (Illus.). 244p. 1995. lib. bdg. 24.95 (*1-85311-122-8*, 853, Pub. by Canterbury Press Norwich) Morehouse Pub.

Places Worth Keeping: Conservationists, Politics & Law in Australia. Tim Bonyhady. 208p. 1994. pap. 19.95 (*1-86373-448-1*, Pub. by Allen & Unwin Pty) Paul & Co Pubs.

Placeways: A Theory of the Human Environment. E. V. Walter. LC 87-13952. (Illus.). xvi, 254p. (C). 1988. pap. text 17.95 (*0-8078-4200-1*) U of NC Pr.

Placido Domingo. Cornelius Schnauber. Tr. by Susan H. Ray. LC 97-9669. (Illus.). 224p. 1997. text 28.95 (*1-55553-315-9*) NE U Pr.

Placido Domingo: Opera Superstar. David Goodnough. LC 96-46451. (Hispanic Biographies Ser.). (Illus.). 104p. (YA). (gr. 6 up). 1997. lib. bdg. 20.95 (*0-89490-892-8*) Enslow Pubs.

Placido Domingo: Spanish Singer. Rebecca Stefoff. (Hispanics of Achievement Ser.). (Illus.). 120p. (YA). (gr. 5 up). 1992. lib. bdg. 19.95 (*0-7910-1563-7*) Chelsea Hse.

Placido Domingo: Spanish Singer. Rebecca Stefoff. (Hispanics of Achievement Ser.). (Illus.). 120p. (YA). (gr. 5 up). 1992. pap. 8.95 (*0-7910-1692-7*) Chelsea Hse.

Placido Domingo - Bajo el Cielo Espanol. Ed. by Carol Cuellar. 84p. (Orig.). (C). 1997. pap. text 16.95 (*0-7692-0024-9*) Wrner Bros.

Placido Domingo's Tales from the Opera. Daniel S. Nowman. (Illus.). 186p. 1998. text 23.00 (*0-7881-5699-3*) DIANE Pub.

Placido, Poeta Social y Politico. Jorge Castellanos. LC 83-82303. (SPA.). 141p. (Orig.). 1984. pap. 10.00 (*0-89729-341-X*) Ediciones.

***Placido Yambao's Art of Arnis.** Placido Yanbao. Tr. by Reynaldo S. Galang. (Illus.). 112p. 1999. pap. 16.95 (*0-8048-3157-2*) Tuttle Pubng.

Placid's View. Murray Heller. LC 96-51731. 196p. 1997. 22.50 (*0-935796-81-9*) Purple Mnt Pr.

***Placing Aesthetics: Reflections on the Philosophic Tradition.** Robert E. Wood. LC 99-27142. (Series in Continental Thought : Vol.26). 406p. 1999. 55.00 (*0-8214-1280-9*) Ohio U Pr.

***Placing Aesthetics: Reflections on the Philosophic Tradition.** Robert E. Wood. LC 99-27142. (Series in Continental Thought). (Illus.). 406p. 1999. pap. 24.95 (*0-8214-1281-7*) Ohio U Pr.

Placing AIDS & HIV in Remission Vol. 1: A Guide to Aggressive Medical Therapy for People with HIV Infection. David Senechek. LC 97-91829. (Illus.). 202p. 1997. 24.95 (*0-9657466-0-7*) Senyczak Pubns.

***Placing Autobiography in Geography.** Pamela J. Moss. LC 00-38780. (Space, Place & Society Ser.). 2000. 19.95 (*0-8156-2848-X*) Syracuse U Pr.

Placing Blame: A Theory of Criminal Law. Michael Moore. LC 98-137950. 870p. (C). 1998. text 115.00 (*0-19-825417-2*) OUP.

Placing Children at Risk: Questionable Psychologists & Therapists in the Sacremanto Family Court... Karen Winner. pap. 25.00 (*0-9669126-1-6*) Justice Seekers.

Placing Concrete with Belt Conveyors. 18p. 1995. 19.50 (*0-614-11129-3*, 304495.BOW6) ACI.

Placing Elvis: A Guide to the Kingdom. Sharon C. Urquhart. Ed. by Werner A. Riefling. LC 92-63059. (Illus.). 112p. (Orig.). 1994. pap. 12.95 (*1-879706-57-1*) Paper Chase.

Placing, Finishing, & Curing. 42p. 1992. pap. 11.95 (*0-924659-51-3*, 1030) Hanley.

Placing, Finishing & Curing Concrete. Tr. by Marcos E. Rodriguez.Tr. of Colocacion, Acabado y Curado del Concreto. (SPA.). 48p. 1994. pap. 11.95 (*0-924659-65-3*, 2120) Hanley.

Placing Friendship in Context. Ed. by Rebecca G. Adams & Graham Allan. LC 98-15200. (Structural Analysis in the Social Sciences Ser.: No. 15). (Illus.). 222p. (C). 1998. text 54.95 (*0-521-58456-6*); pap. text 19.95 (*0-521-58589-9*) Cambridge U Pr.

Placing Movies: The Practice of Film Criticism. Jonathan Rosenbaum. LC 93-42954. 1995. 50.00 (*0-520-08632-5*, Pub. by U CA Pr); pap. 18.95 (*0-520-08633-3*, Pub. by U CA Pr) Cal Prin Full Svc.

Placing Nature: Culture & Landscape Ecology. Joan I. Nassauer. LC 97-14842. 215p. 1997. pap. text. write for info. (*1-55963-559-2*) Island Pr.

Placing Parties in American Politics: Organization, Electoral Settings, & Government Activity in the Twentieth Century. David R. Mayhew. LC 85-43298. 412p. 1986. reprint ed. pap. 127.80 (*0-608-06485-8*, 206678200009) Bks Demand.

Placing Shadows: The Art of Video Lighting. 2nd ed. Tom LeTourneau. 224p. 1998. pap. 39.95 (*0-240-80313-2*, Focal) Buttrwrth-Heinemann.

***Placing Shadows, Lighting Techniques for Video Production.** 2nd ed. Chuck Gloman & Tom LeTourneau. LC 99-89950. (Illus.). 222p. 2000. pap. 29.95 (*0-240-80409-0*, Focal) Buttrwrth-Heinemann.

Placing Sorrow: A Study of the Pastoral Elegy Convention from Theocritus to Milton. Ellen Z. Lambert. LC 76-23154. (Studies in Comparative Literature: No. 60). xxxiv, 231p. 1977. lib. bdg. 37.50 (*0-8078-7060-9*) U of NC Pr.

***Placing the Accents.** Truong Tran. LC 99-73275. 72p. 1999. pap. 12.95 (*0-9669937-1-3*, 02) Apogee.

Placing the Dead: Tombs, Ancestral Villages, & Kinship Organization in Madagascar. rev. ed. Maurice Bloch. (Illus.). 241p. (C). 1994. reprint ed. pap. text 12.95 (*0-88133-766-8*) Waveland Pr.

Placing the Gods: Sanctuaries & Sacred Space in Ancient Greece. Ed. by Susan E. Alcock & Robin Osborne. (Illus.). 282p. (C). 1996. pap. text 28.00 (*0-19-815060-1*) OUP.

Placing the Gods: Sanctuaries & Sacred Space in Ancient Greece. Ed. by Robin Osborne & Susan E. Alcock. (Illus.). 288p. 1994. 58.00 (*0-19-814947-6*) OUP.

Placing the Poet: Badr Shakir Al-Sayyab & Postcolonial Iraq. Terri DeYoung. LC 97-23836. 320p. (C). 1998. text 74.50 (*0-7914-3731-0*); pap. text 24.95 (*0-7914-3732-9*) State U NY Pr.

Placing Wildlife Management in Perspective. 32p. 1984. 1.00 (*0-318-23133-6*) Wildlife Mgmt.

Placing Womens' Studies. Raiskin. Date not set. write for info. (*0-07-230406-5*) McGraw.

Placita Anglo-Normannica. Melville M. Bigelow. lxiv, 328p. 1974. reprint ed. 90.00 (*3-487-05293-8*) G Olms Pubs.

Placita Anglo-Normannica: Law Cases from William I to Richard I. Melville M. Bigelow. lxiv, 328p. 1970. reprint ed. 35.00 (*0-8377-1928-3*, Rothman) W S Hein.

Placita Coram Domino Rege Apud Westmonasterium de Termino Sancte Trinitatis Anno Regni Regis Edwardii Filii Regis Henrici Vicesimo Quinto: The Pleas of the Count of Kings Bench, Trinity Team, 25 Edward I, 1297. Ed. by W. P. Phillimore. (British Record Society Index Library: Vol. 19). 1974. reprint ed. pap. 36.00 (*0-8115-1464-1*) Periodicals Srv.

Placmnt Tsts Turn Points. 2nd ed. Mario Papa. 80p. 1995. pap. text 39.73 (*0-201-53804-0*) Addison-Wesley.

Placodermi. Robert Denison. Ed. by O. Kuhn & H. P. Schultz. (Handbook of Paleoichthyology: Vol. 2). (Illus.). 128p. 1978. text 90.00 (*3-437-30265-5*) Lubrecht & Cramer.

Placrosym VI. Ed. by S. N. Potty. 476p. (C). 1987. 34.00 (*81-204-0239-1*, Pub. by Oxford IBH) S Asia.

Pladoyer Fur Eine Sozialpadagogische Schule. Norbert Hilbig. (Hildesheimer Schriftenreihe Zur Sozialpadagogik und Sozialarbeit Ser.: Vol. 2). (GER.). 170p. 1993. write for info. (*3-487-09792-3*) G Olms Pubs.

Pladoyer fuer eine Rehabilitierung der Individualethik. Hans Kraemer. (GER.). 68p. (Orig.). 1983. pap. 21.00 (*90-6032-248-7*, Pub. by B R Gruner) Humanities.

Plagas y Enfermedades de la Vid. Ed. by R. C. Pearson & A. C. Goheen.Tr. of Compendium of Grape Diseases. (SPA., Illus.). 128p. pap. 42.00 (*84-7114-607-X*) Am Phytopathol Soc.

Plagas y Enfermedades de los Citricos. Ed. by S. O. Whiteside et al.Tr. of Compendium of Citrus Diseases. (SPA., Illus.). 165p. pap. 42.00 (*84-7114-608-8*) Am Phytopathol Soc.

Plage Trop Chaude. Chrystine Brouillet. (Novels in the Roman Plus Ser.). (FRE.). 160p. (YA). (gr. 8 up). 1991. pap. 8.95 (*2-89021-148-7*, Pub. by La Courte Ech) Firefly Bks Ltd.

Plages de Thule see Beaches of Thule

***Plages du Maine.** Joel Pomerleau. LC 97-940019. (Travel Guide (French Guides) Ser.). (FRE.). 1998. pap. text 13.95 (*2-89464-110-9*) Ulysses Travel.

Plagiarism & the Culture War: The Writings of Martin Luther King, Jr. & Other Prominent American's. Theodore Pappas. LC 98-72137. 256p. 1998. pap. 16.95 (*0-87319-045-9*) Hallberg Pub Corp.

Plagiarism Book: A Student's Manual. Edward G. Rozycki & Gary K. Clabaugh. 51p. 1999. pap., student ed. 7.95 (*1-929463-00-6*) NewFound.

Plagiarism, Copyright Violation & Other Thefts of Intellectual Property: An Annotated Bibliography with a Lenghty Introduction. Judy Anderson. LC 97-44084. 212p. 1998. pap. 42.50 (*0-7864-0463-9*) McFarland & Co.

Plagiarism in Utopia. Arthur E. Morgan. 1944. pap. 1.00 (*0-910420-16-5*) Comm Serv OH.

Plagiat in der Griechischen Literatur. Eduard Stemplinger. vi, 294p. 1990. reprint ed. write for info. (*3-487-09269-7*) G Olms Pubs.

Plagioclase - Sodium, Vol. 10. Jocelyn F. Thorpe & M. A. Whiteley. LC 37-28650. 942p. reprint ed. pap. 200.00 (*0-608-08505-7*, 200454900065) Bks Demand.

Plagiotheciaceae. William R. Buck & Robert R. Ireland. (Flora Neotropica Monographs: No. 50). (Illus.). 22p. 1989. pap. text 7.00 (*0-89327-342-2*) NY Botanical.

Plagiotropis Pfitzer & Tropidoneis Cleve, a Summary Account. T. B. Paddock. (Bibliotheca Diatomologica Ser.: Vol. 16). (Illus.). 190p. 1988. pap. 65.00 (*3-443-57007-0*, Pub. by Gebruder Borntraeger) Balogh.

Plague. Albert Camus. 1948. 19.45 (*0-07-541541-0*) McGraw.

Plague. Albert Camus. Tr. by Stuart Gilbert. (Modern Library College Editions). 278p. (C). 1965. pap. 5.00 (*0-07-553649-8*, T69) McGraw.

Plague, 2 vols. Albert Camus. 20.00 (*0-614-30537-3*) NAVH.

Plague. Albert Camus. Tr. by Stuart Gilbert. LC 90-50477. (Vintage International Ser.). 308p. 1991. pap. 12.00 (*0-679-72021-9*) Vin Bks.

Plague. Albert Camus. 1948. 16.10 (*0-606-04321-7*, Pub. by Turtleback) Demco.

Plague. Katie Roden. (Illus.). 40p. (J). (gr. 4-6). 1996. pap. 6.95 (*0-7613-0516-5*, Copper Beech Bks); lib. bdg. 23.90 (*0-7613-0541-6*, Copper Beech Bks) Millbrook Pr.

Plague. Jean Ure. (J). 1993. 10.09 (*0-606-05548-7*, Pub. by Turtleback) Demco.

Plague. large type ed. Albert Camus. 400p. 1984. 27.99 (*0-7089-8192-5*, Charnwood) Ulverscroft.

Plague: Fiction & Resistance. Steven G. Kellman. (Masterwork Studies). 170p. 1993. 29.00 (*0-8057-8361-X*, Twyne); pap. 18.00 (*0-8057-8575-2*, Twyne) Mac Lib Ref.

Plague? Jesuit Accounts of Epidemic Disease in the 16th Century: Jesuit Accounts of Epidemic Diseases in the Sixteenth Century. A. Lynn Martin. LC 94-21215. (Sixteenth Century Essays & Studies: Vol. 28). 268p. 1996. 40.00 (*0-940474-30-1*, SCJP) Truman St Univ.

Plague & Fire of London. Compiled by John Langdon-Davies. 39.00 (*1-56696-079-7*) Jackdaw.

***Plague & I.** large type ed. Betty MacDonald. LC 00-39600. 314p. 2000. 23.95 (*0-7838-9106-7*, G K Hall & Co) Mac Lib Ref.

***Plague & I.** Betty MacDonald. (Common Reader Edition Ser.). 2000. reprint ed. pap. 15.95 (*1-888173-29-7*, Pub. by Akadine Pr) Trafalgar.

Plague & Other Yersinia Infections. Thomas C. Butler. LC 83-17467. (Current Topics in Infectious Disease Ser.). 232p. 1983. 59.50 (*0-306-41414-7*, Plenum Trade) Perseus Pubng.

Plague & Pestilence: A History of Infectious Disease. Linda J. Altman. LC 98-12677. (Issues in Focus Ser.). (Illus.). 128p. (YA). (gr. 6-12). 1998. lib. bdg. 20.95 (*0-89490-957-6*) Enslow Pubs.

Plague & Pestilence: Deadly Diseases That Changed the World. Margrete Lamond. (True Stories Ser.). (Illus.). 100p. (Orig.). (J). (gr. 3-8). 1997. pap. 6.95 (*1-86448-456-X*, Pub. by Allen & Unwin Pty) IPG Chicago.

Plague & Print in the Netherlands: A Short-Title Catalogue of Publications in the University Library of Amsterdam. Paul Dijstelberge & Leo Noordegraaf. LC 98-163788. 360p. 1997. pap. 60.00 (*90-5235-126-0*, Pub. by Erasmus Pub) Balogh.

Plague C. Jean Ure. LC 91-8714. 160p. (YA). (gr. 5 up). 1991. 16.95 (*0-15-262429-5*, Harcourt Child Bks) Harcourt.

Plague Doctors: Responding to the AIDS Epidemic in France & America. Jamie L. Feldman. LC 94-43601. 288p. 1995. 59.95 (*0-89789-385-9*, Bergin & Garvey) Greenwood.

Plague Dogs. Richard Adams. 480p. 1986. mass mkt. 5.95 (*0-449-21182-7*, Crest) Fawcett.

***Plague Dogs.** Richard Adams. LC 98-48270. 1999. 26.95 (*0-7838-8489-3*) Macmillan Gen Ref.

Plague in Siena. Erich W. Skwara. Tr. by Michael Roloff. (Studies in Austrian Literature, Culture, & Thought. Translation Ser.). 133p. 1994. pap. 11.95 (*0-929497-81-3*) Ariadne CA.

Plague in Sydney - The Anatomy of an Epidemic. Peter Curson & Kevin McCracken. 220p. 1990. pap. 24.95 (*0-86840-219-2*, Pub. by New South Wales Univ Pr) Intl Spec Bk.

Plague Journal: A Novel. Michael O'Brien. LC 96-75778. 1999. 19.95 (*0-89870-610-6*) Ignatius Pr.

***Plague Makers: The Secret World of Biological Warfare.** Wendy Barnaby. (Illus.). 202p. 1999. pap. 15.95 (*1-883319-85-4*) Frog Ltd CA.

***Plague Makers: The Secret World of Biological Warfare.** rev. ed. Wendy Barnaby. 2000. pap. text. write for info. (*0-8264-1258-0*) Continuum.

Plague Notes. Gary Carey. (Cliffs Notes Ser.). 80p. 1967. pap. 4.95 (*0-8220-1039-9*, Cliff) IDG Bks.

***Plague of Angels.** P. F. Chisholm. 2000. pap. 14.95 (*1-890208-43-4*) Poisoned Pen.

Plague of Angels. Sheri S. Tepper. 592p. 1994. mass mkt. 6.99 (*0-553-56873-6*) Bantam.

Plague of Dreamers: 3 Novellas. Steve Stern. LC 96-49834. (Library of Modern Jewish Literature). 267p. 1997. pap. 17.95 (*0-8156-0453-X*) Syracuse U Pr.

Plague of Fantasies. Slavoj Zizek. 288p. 1997. 65.00 (*1-85984-857-5*, Pub. by Verso) Norton.

Plague of Fantasies. Ed. by Slavoj Zizek. 288p. 1997. pap. 20.00 (*1-85984-193-7*, Pub. by Verso) Norton.

Plague of Frogs: The Horrifying True Story. William E. Souder. LC 99-49564. 304p. 2000. 23.95 (*0-7868-6360-9*, Pub. by Hyperion) Time Warner.

Plague of Gunfighters. large type ed. Tom Anson. (Linford Western Library Ser.). 256p. 1997. pap. 16.99 (*0-7089-5130-9*, Linford) Ulverscroft.

Plague of Hunger. Gene Erb. LC 90-32423. (Illus.). 149p. 1990. reprint ed. pap. 46.20 (*0-608-00121-X*, 206088600006) Bks Demand.

Plague of Insurrection: Popular Politics & Peasant Revolt in Flanders, 1323-1328. William H. TeBrake. LC 93-8222. (Middle Ages Ser.). (Illus.). 208p. (Orig.). (C). 1993. text 37.50 (*0-8122-3241-0*); pap. text 14.95 (*0-8122-1526-5*) U of Pa Pr.

Plague of Knives. James R. Silke. (Death Dealer Ser.: Vol. 4). 1990. mass mkt. 4.99 (*0-8125-2305-9*, Pub. by Tor Bks) St Martin.

Plague of Lawyers: Greed & the American Legal System. Stephen P. Magee & Frances T. Magee. 1994. write for info. (*0-446-51811-5*) Warner Bks.

Plague of Paradoxes: AIDS, Culture & Demography in Northern Tanzania. Philip W. Setel. LC 99-16509. 272p. 2000. pap. text 19.00 (*0-226-74886-3*); lib. bdg. 42.00 (*0-226-74885-5*) U Ch Pr.

Plague of Perfection. Bill McCay. (Spider-Man Super-Thriller Ser.: No. 2). 1996. mass mkt. 4.99 (*0-671-00320-8*) PB.

Plague of Sheep: Environmental Consequences of the Conquest of Mexico. Elinor G. Melville. LC 96-5374. (Studies in Environment & History). (Illus.). 219p. (C). 1994. text 69.95 (*0-521-42061-X*) Cambridge U Pr.

Plague of Sheep: Environmental Consequences of the Conquest of Mexico. Elinor G. Melville. (Illus.). 219p. 1997. pap. text 17.95 (*0-521-57448-X*) Cambridge U Pr.

Plague of Silence. large type ed. John Creasey. 1990. 12.00 (*0-85456-191-9*) Ulverscroft.

Plague of Sorcerers: A Magical Mystery. Mary Frances Zambreno. LC 95-36184. 288p. (YA). (gr. 3-7). 1996. pap. 5.95 (*0-7868-1126-9*, Pub. by Hyprn Ppbks) Little.

Plague of Sorcerers: A Magical Mystery. Mary Frances Zambreno. (YA). 1996. 11.05 (*0-606-08846-6*, Pub. by Turtleback) Demco.

Plague of Strangers: Social Groups & the Origins of City Services in Cincinnati, 1819-1870. Alan I. Marcus. LC 91-16750. (Urban Life & Urban Landscape Ser.). 311p. reprint ed. pap. 96.50 (*0-608-09854-X*, 206981900006) Bks Demand.

Plague on Both Your Houses. Susanna Gregory. LC 98-30109. (Chronicle of Matthew Bartholomew Ser.). 1998. text 24.95 (*0-312-19318-1*) St Martin.

Plague on Both Your Houses: Minor Parties in Australia. Dean Jaensch & David S. Mathieson. LC 98-213222. 256p. 1999. pap. 29.95 (*1-86448-421-7*, Pub. by Allen & Unwin Pty) Paul & Co Pubs.

***Plague on Your Houses: How New York Was Burned down & National Public Health Crumbled.** E. A. Wallis Budge et al. 2000. pap. 20.00 (*1-85984-253-4*, Pub. by Verso) Norton.

Plague on Your Houses: How New York Was Burned Down & National Public Health Crumbled. Rodrick Wallace & Deborah Wallace. (Illus.). 222p. 1999. 30.00 (*1-85984-858-3*, Pub. by Verso) Norton.

Plague Pamphlets. Thomas Dekker. (BCL1-PR English Literature Ser.). 268p. 1992. reprint ed. lib. bdg. 79.00 (*0-7812-7200-9*) Rprt Serv.

Plague Pamphlets of Thomas Dekker. Thomas Dekker. LC 73-161963. 268p. 1925. reprint ed. 39.00 (*0-403-01319-4*) Scholarly.

Plague Prevention & Politics in Manchuria, 1910-1931. Carl F. Nathan. LC 67-8500. (East Asian Monographs: No. 23). (Illus.). 111p. 1967. pap. 12.00 (*0-674-67050-7*) HUP.

Plague Ship. Frank G. Slaughter. 22.95 (*0-89190-715-7*) Amereon Ltd.

Plague Ship. large type ed. Frank G. Slaughter. 544p. 1982. 27.99 (*0-7089-0895-0*) Ulverscroft.

Plague-Sower. Gesualdo Bufalino. Tr. by Stephen Sartarelli from ITA. LC 88-80810. 186p. 1988. pap. 13.00 (*0-941419-13-4*, Eridanos Library) Marsilio Pubs.

P

Plague Stone. large type ed. Gillian White. LC 96-4335. 295 p. 1996. write for info. (0-7451-4809-3) Chivers Pr.

Plague Tales. Ann Benson. 688p. 1998. mass mkt. 6.50 (0-440-22510-8) Dell.

***Plague Time: How Stealth Infections Cause Cancers, Heart Disease & Other Deadly Ailments.** Paul W. Ewald. 272p. 2000. 24.50 (0-684-86900-4) Free Pr.

Plague Wars: The Terrifying Reality of Biological Warfare. Tom Mangold & Jeff Goldberg. LC 99-17022. (Illus.). 336p. 2000. text 27.95 (0-312-20353-5) St Martin.

Plague Wind. Don Pendleton. (Executioner Ser.). 1998. per. 3.99 (0-373-64235-0, 1-64235-4, Wrldwide Lib) Harlequin Bks.

Plague Year. Stephanie S. Tolan. 160p. (YA). 1991. mass mkt. 4.50 (0-449-70403-3, Juniper) Fawcett.

***Plague Year.** Stephanie S. Tolan. 208p. 1999. mass mkt. 4.95 (0-688-16125-1, Wm Morrow) Morrow Avon.

***Plagues: Their Origin, History & Future.** Christopher Wills. (Illus.). 324p. 1999. reprint ed. text 30.00 (0-7881-6170-9) DIANE Pub.

Plagues & People. William H. McNeill. LC 76-2798. (Illus.). 368p. 1977. pap. 14.95 (0-385-12122-9, Anchor NY) Doubleday.

Plagues & People. William H. McNeill. 1992. 25.50 (0-8446-6492-8) Peter Smith.

Plagues & Poxes: The Rise & Fall of Epidemic Disease. Alfred J. Bollet. LC 87-71319. 208p. 1987. pap. text 39.95 (0-939957-06-X) Demos Medical.

Plagues of the Mind: The New Epidemic of False Knowledge. Bruce S. Thornton. LC 99-64337. 1999. 24.95 (1-882926-34-X) ISI Books.

Plagues on the Doorstep see Outbreak Alert: Responding to the Increasing Threat of Infectious Diseases

Plagues, Products, & Politics: Emergent Public Health Hazards & National Policymaking. Christopher H. Foreman, Jr. 210p. (C). 1994. 34.95 (0-8157-2876-X); pap. 14.95 (0-8157-2875-1) Brookings.

PLAID: Practical Lessons for Apraxia with Illustrated Drills. Brenda D. Whisonant. (Illus.). 168p. (Orig.). 1996. pap. text 22.95 (0-937857-68-8, 1424) Speech Bin.

***Plaid Design: Garden Photo Album.** T. Eliot. (Illus.). 1998. text 17.95 (1-55670-840-8) Stewart Tabori & Chang.

***Plaid Tidings to You Floor Display.** Rutledge Hill Press Staff. 1999. pap. text. write for info. (1-55853-723-6) Rutledge Hill Pr.

Plaid Vest. Samantha J. Peterson. Ed. by Peggy E. Peterson. (Illus.). 24p. (Orig.). (J). (gr. k-3). 1996. pap. 5.95 (1-888860-00-6) Plaid Platypus.

Plaideurs. Jean Racine. (FRE., Illus.). 128p. 1984. pap. 10.95 (0-7859-1265-7, 2040160779) Fr & Eur.

Plaideurs. Jean Racine. (FRE.). 1987. pap. 10.95 (0-7859-3138-4) Fr & Eur.

Plaidoyer pour les Intellectuels. Jean-Paul Sartre. (FRE.). 1972. pap. 10.95 (0-7859-2842-1) Fr & Eur.

Plaidoyers Ecrits et les Plaidoyers Reelles de Ciceron. Jules Humbert. 296p. 1972. reprint ed. write for info. (3-487-04509-5) G Olms Pubs.

Plaidoyers Politiques de Demosthene, 2 vols. in 1. Demosthenes. xiii, 935p. 1974. reprint ed. write for info. (3-487-05053-6) G Olms Pubs.

Plaids: A Visual Survey of Pattern Variations. Tina Skinner. LC 97-80419. (Illus.). 112p. 1998. pap. 24.95 (0-7643-0481-X) Schiffer.

Plaids & Stripes: The Use of Directional Fabric in Quilts. Roberta M. Horton. Ed. by Sayre Van Young. LC 89-82564. (Illus.). 128p. (Orig.). 1990. pap. 21.95 (0-914881-29-9, 10039) C & T Pub.

Plain Account of Christian Perfection. John Wesley. 120p. 1966. pap. 8.99 (0-8341-0158-0) Beacon Hill.

***Plain Account of Christian Perfection.** John Wesley. (Shepherd's Notes Christian Classics). 1999. pap. 5.95 (0-8054-9216-X) Broadman.

Plain Account of Christian Perfection. John Wesley. LC 71-400150. 116p. 1952. pap. 10.00 (0-7162-0081-3) TPI PA.

Plain Air. Michael McFee. LC 83-9109. (University of Central Florida Contemporary Poetry Ser.). 65p. 1983. 14.95 (0-8130-0774-7) U Press Fla.

Plain & Accurate Style in Court Papers. Irwin M. Alterman. 179p. 1987. text 37.00 (0-8318-0563-3, B563) Am Law Inst.

Plain & Amish: An Alternative to Modern Pessimism. Bernd G. Langin. Tr. by Jack Thiessen from GER. LC 94-8324. (Illus.). 416p. 1994. pap. 16.99 (0-8361-3665-9) Herald Pr.

Plain & Compendious Method of Teaching Thorough Bass. fac. ed. John F. Lampe. (Monuments of Music & Music Literature in Facsimile Ser., Series II: Vol. 29). 1969. lib. bdg. 45.00 (0-8450-2229-6) Broude.

Plain & Easy Introduction to the Harpsichord. Ruth Nurmi. LC 86-1875. 262p. 1986. reprint ed. 31.00 (0-8108-1886-8) Scarecrow.

Plain & Elegant: A Georgia Heritage. West Georgia Medical Center Staff. 1991. 16.95 (0-9628655-0-8) W GA Med Aux.

Plain & Fancy: American Women & Their Needlework, 1650-1850. rev. ed. Susan B. Swan. (Illus.). 248p. 1995. pap. 29.95 (0-9633331-3-5) Curious Works.

Plain & Fancy: Vermont's People & Their Quilts As a Reflection of America. Richard Cleveland & Donna Bister. LC 90-28670. (Illus.). 104p. 1991. pap. 24.95 (0-8442-2630-0, Quilt Dgst Pr) NTC Contemp Pub Co.

Plain & Fancy Amish Cookie Recipes. Adrienne F. Lund. (Illus.). 69p. (Orig.). 1993. pap. 6.95 (1-886645-01-9) Jupiter Press.

Plain & Happy Living: Amish Recipes & Remedies. Emma Byler. LC 92-6121. (Illus.). 160p. 1992. pap. 9.95 (1-879863-71-5, Pub. by Goosefoot Acres) Chelsea Green Pub.

Plain & Normal: A Novel. James Wilcox. LC 98-14038. 288p. (gr. 8). 1998. 24.00 (0-316-94026-7, Back Bay) Little.

Plain & Normal: A Novel. James Wilcox. 288p. 1999. pap. 12.95 (0-316-94135-2, Back Bay) Little.

Plain & Not-So-Plain Main Meals. large type ed. pap. 8.00 (0-317-01857-4) Cath Guild Blind.

Plain & Ordinary Things: Reading Women in the Writing Classroom. Deborah A. Dooley. LC 94-21538. (SUNY Series, Feminist Theory in Education). 273p. (C). 1995. pap. text 14.95 (0-7914-2320-4) State U NY Pr.

Plain & Ordinary Things: Reading Women in the Writing Classroom. Deborah A. Dooley. LC 94-21538. (SUNY Series, Feminist Theory in Education). 273p. (C). 1995. text 44.50 (0-7914-2319-0) State U NY Pr.

Plain & Pleasant Talks about Fruits, Flowers & Farming. Henry W. Beecher. (Works of Henry Ward Beecher). 1989. reprint ed. lib. bdg. 79.00 (0-685-44727-8) Rprt Serv.

Plain & Precious: An LDS Daybook of Renewal & Joy. Beppie Harrison. LC 97-29252. x, 437p. 1997. 19.95 (1-57345-317-X) Deseret Bk.

Plain & Precious Truths Restored. Ed. by Robert L. Millet & Robert J. Matthews. LC 95-77056. 1995. 14.95 (0-88494-987-7) Bookcraft Inc.

***Plain & Simple.** Darrell Hayes. 1999. pap. write for info. (1-58235-213-5) Watermrk Pr.

Plain & Simple: A Journey to the Amish. Sue Bender. LC 89-45234. 176p. 1989. 21.00 (0-06-250058-9) HarperTrade.

Plain & Simple: A Woman's Journey to the Amish. Sue Bender. LC 90-56467. (Illus.). 176p. 1991. reprint ed. pap. 15.00 (0-06-250186-0, Pub. by Harper SF) HarpC.

Plain & Simple Family Cookbook. Ladies Auxiliary Hadar Zion Staff. 189p. 1992. spiral bd. 11.95 (0-944070-37-X, Pub. by Targum Pr) Feldheim.

Plain & Simple Fun: 59 Full-Size Designs, Ready to Cut. John A. Nelson. (Scroll Saw Pattern Bks.). (Illus.). 96p. 1995. pap. 14.95 (0-8117-3025-5) Stackpole.

Plain & Simple Journal: A Journey to the Amish. Sue Bender. (Illus.). 144p. 1991. pap. 16.00 (0-06-250129-1, Pub. by Harper SF) HarpC.

Plain & Simple Wisdom. Sue Bender. LC 94-38418. 96p. 1995. pap. 9.00 (0-06-251174-2, Pub. by Harper SF) HarpC.

Plain Anne Ellis: More about the Life of an Ordinary Woman. Anne Ellis. LC 97-28212. xvi, 265p. 1997. pap. 12.00 (0-8032-6736-3, Bison Books) U of Nebr Pr.

Plain As a Pipestem: Essays about Local History Reprinted from New York History. Carol Kammen. 160p. (Orig.). 1989. pap. 15.00 (1-55787-036-5, SR00100) Hrt of the Lakes.

***Plain Blue Caterpillar.** Mandana S. Changizi. LC 99-58817. (Illus.). 16p. (J). (ps-5). 2000. pap. 9.95 (0-9637240-9-6) Biograph Pub.

Plain Bread. Ben Kinchlow. 228p. 1993. pap. 12.99 (1-56043-754-5, Treasure Hse) Destiny Image.

Plain Buggies: Amish, Mennonite, & Brethren Horse-Drawn Transportation. rev. ed. Stephen Scott. LC 81-82208. (People's Place Book Ser.: No. 3). (Illus.). 96p. 1997. pap. 6.95 (1-56148-239-0) Good Bks PA.

Plain City. Virginia Hamilton. LC 93-19910. 176p. (J). (gr. 7-9). 1993. 13.95 (0-590-47364-6) Scholastic Inc.

Plain City. Virginia Hamilton. LC 93-19910. 176p. (YA). (gr. 4-7). 1995. mass mkt. 4.50 (0-590-47365-4, Point) Scholastic Inc.

Plain City. Virginia Hamilton. (J). 1993. 9.60 (0-606-08020-1, Pub. by Turtleback) Demco.

Plain Concise Practical Remarks, on the Treatment of Wounds & Fractures. John Jones. 1979. 18.95 (0-88143-147-8) Ayer.

Plain Concise Practical Remarks, on the Treatment of Wounds & Fractures. John Jones. LC 77-140870. (Eyewitness Accounts of the American Revolution Ser.). 1970. reprint ed. 18.00 (0-405-01222-5) Ayer.

Plain Dealer. William Ardin. 224p. 1998. 24.00 (0-7278-5288-4) Severn Hse.

Plain Dealer. William Wycherley. Ed. by James L. Smith. (New Mermaid Ser.). (C). 1980. pap. text 9.75 (0-393-90042-8) Norton.

Plain Dealer. William Wycherley. (Swan Theatre Plays Ser.). 76p. (Orig.). (C). 1988. pap. write for info. (0-413-19060-9, A0341, Methuen Drama) Methn.

Plain Dealer. large type ed. William Ardin. 352p. 31.99 (0-7089-4044-7) Ulverscroft.

Plain Dealer. William Wycherley. Ed. by Leo Hughes. LC 67-10670. (Regents Restoration Drama Ser.). 205p. reprint ed. pap. 63.60 (0-608-16277-9, 202653300053) Bks Demand.

Plain Dealings: or News from New England. Thomas Lechford. 1972. reprint ed. lib. bdg. 20.50 (0-8422-8140-1) Irvington.

Plain Directions for Obtaining Photographic Pictures by the Calotype & Energiatype, Also Upon Albumenized Paper & Glass, by Collodion & Albumen, Etc., Etc., Pts. 1[00ad]3. J. H. Croucher & Gustave Le Gray. LC 72-9191. (Literature of Photography Ser.). 1979. reprint ed. 17.95 (0-405-04901-3) Ayer.

Plain Enemies: Best True Stories of the Frontier West. Bob Scott. LC 95-4103. (Illus.). 300p. 1995. pap. 14.95 (0-87004-364-1) Caxton.

Plain English. 2nd ed. Diane Collinson et al. 128p. 1992. pap. 21.95 (0-335-15675-4) OpUniv Pr.

Plain English Approach to Business Writing. rev. ed. Edward P. Bailey, Jr. LC 96-45541. (Illus.). 144p. 1997. pap. 10.95 (0-19-511565-1) OUP.

Plain English at Work: A Guide to Writing & Speaking. Edward P. Bailey. 304p. (C). 1996. 25.00 (0-19-510449-8) OUP.

***Plain English for Cops.** Nicholas Meier & R. J. Adams. LC 99-66963. 152p. 1999. pap. 15.00 (0-89089-846-4) Carolina Acad Pr.

Plain English for Lawyers. 3rd ed. Richard C. Wydick. LC 93-73561. 160p. (C). 1994. pap. 9.95 (0-89089-561-9) Carolina Acad Pr.

Plain English for Lawyers. 4th ed. Richard C. Wydick. LC 97-77746. 184p. 1998. pap. 10.95 (0-89089-994-0) Carolina Acad Pr.

Plain English Guide to IRA Distributions. 9th rev. ed. Leo Martin. LC 97-78367. 175p. 1998. ring bd. 99.00 (0-9664421-0-5) IRA Doctor.

Plain English Guide to IRA Distributions. 10th rev. ed. Leo Martin. LC 99-71542. 175p. 1999. ring bd. 99.00 (0-9664421-1-3) IRA Doctor.

Plain English Guide to the EPA Part 503 Biosolids Rule. Contrib. by Michael B. Cook. (Illus.). 176p. (C). 1998. reprint ed. pap. text 40.00 (0-7881-4260-7) DIANE Pub.

Plain English Guide to Your PC. Alan Wallach. 80p. 1998. pap. 9.95 (1-884820-33-6) ATN Grp Pub.

Plain English 1. Longman Publishing Staff. Date not set. pap. text. write for info. (0-582-75641-3, Pub. by Addison-Wesley) Longman.

Plain English Please. 5th ed. McPherson. 1987. teacher ed. 18.12 (0-07-555049-0) McGraw.

Plain English Please. 5th ed. Elizabeth McPherson & Gregory Cowan. 480p. (C). 1986. pap. 43.75 (0-07-554227-7) McGraw.

Plain English Reference to the Book of Mormon. Timothy B. Wilson. pap. 16.95 (1-55517-401-9) CFI Dist.

Plain Facts for Old & Young: Natural History & Hygiene of Organic Life. J. H. Kellogg. LC 73-20633. (Sex, Marriage & Society Ser.). 648p. 1974. reprint ed. 47.95 (0-405-05808-X) Ayer.

Plain Folk: The Life Stories of Undistinguished Americans. Ed. by David M. Katzman & William H. Tuttle, Jr. LC 81-3026. 224p. 1982. text 24.95 (0-252-00884-7); pap. text 14.95 (0-252-00906-1) U of Ill Pr.

Plain Folk & Gentry in a Slave Society: White Liberty & Black Slavery in Augusta's Hinterlands. J. William Harris. LC 97-46686. (Illus.). 312p. 1998. pap. text 14.95 (0-8071-2265-3) La State U Pr.

Plain Folk & Gentry in a Slave Society: White Liberty & Black Slavery in Augusta's Hinterlands. J. William Harris. LC 85-7108. 293p. 1987. reprint ed. pap. 90.90 (0-608-02323-X, 206296400004) Bks Demand.

Plain Folk in the New South: Social Change & Cultural Persistence, 1880-1915. I. A. Newby. LC 88-17439. 588p. 1989. text 80.00 (0-8071-1456-1) La State U Pr.

Plain Folk of the Old South. Frank L. Owsley. LC 82-9903. (Walter Lynwood Fleming Lectures in Southern History). 234p. (C). 1982. pap. text 17.95 (0-8071-1063-9) La State U Pr.

Plain Folk of the South Revisited. Ed. by Samuel C. Hyde, Jr. LC 97-20625. (Illus.). 304p. 1997. text 55.00 (0-8071-2200-9); pap. text 16.95 (0-8071-2237-8) La State U Pr.

Plain Girl. Virginia Sorensen. LC 87-26963. (Illus.). 156p. (J). (gr. 3-7). 1988. pap. 7.00 (0-15-262437-6, Voyager Bks) Harcourt.

Plain Introduction to the Criticism of the New Testament, 2. 4th ed. Frederick Scrivener & Edward Miller. 846p. 1997. pap. 45.00 (1-57910-071-6) Wipf & Stock.

Plain Jane Gets Her Man. Robin Wells. 1997. per. 3.25 (0-373-19262-2, 1-19262-4) Silhouette.

Plain Jane Marries the Boss. Elizabeth Harbison. (Romance Ser.). 2000. per. 3.50 (0-373-19416-1, 1-19416-6) Silhouette.

Plain Jane Vanilla. Missy McConnell. (Illus.). 48p. (J). 1980. 24.00 (0-88014-018-6) Mosaic Pr OH.

***Plain Jane's Man.** Kristine Rolofson. 2000. mass mkt. 4.50 (0-373-82210-3, 1-82210-5) Harlequin Bks.

Plain Jane's Texan. Jan Hudson. (Desire Ser.: Bk. 1229). 1999. per. 3.75 (0-373-76229-1, 1-76229-3) Silhouette.

Plain Language: Principles & Practice. Ed. by Erwin R. Steinberg. LC 90-38008. (Illus.). 258p. (C). 1991. text 34.95 (0-8143-2020-1); pap. text 19.95 (0-8143-2021-X) Wayne St U Pr.

Plain Language about Shiftwork. Roger Rosa. 44p. 1997. pap. 5.00 (0-16-061560-7) USGPO.

Plain Language for Lawyers. Michele Asprey. 140p. 1991. 48.00 (1-86287-064-0, Pub. by Federation Pr); pap. 33.00 (1-86287-063-2, Pub. by Federation Pr) Gaunt.

Plain Language for Lawyers. 2nd ed. Michele Asprey. LC 96-147371. 250p. 1996. pap. 34.00 (1-86287-205-8, Pub. by Federation Pr) Gaunt.

Plain Language from Truthful James. Bret Harte. 20.95 (0-88411-593-3) Amereon Ltd.

Plain-Language Law Dictionary. 2nd ed. Robert E. Rothenberg. LC 97-113882. 464p. 1996. mass mkt. 7.99 (0-451-18408-4, Sig) NAL.

Plain Language Readings. Carol A. Wilson. 221p. (C). 1995. pap. text 29.20 (0-13-199639-8) P-H.

***Plain Life: Walking My Belief.** Scott Savage. 224p. 2000. 22.00 (0-345-43803-5) Ballantine Pub Grp.

Plain Man's Book of Prayers. William Barclay. LC 90-83632. 144p. 1959. pap. 8.95 (0-87061-180-1) Chr Classics.

Plain Man's Guide to the Glorious Revolution, 1688. Mary Howarth. 120p. (C). 1988. 35.00 (0-7212-0704-9, Pub. by Regency Pr GBR) St Mut.

Plain Man's Pathway to Heaven. Arthur Dent. 332p. 1993. reprint ed. 24.95 (1-877611-69-7) Soli Deo Gloria.

Plain Man's Talk on the Labor Question. Simon Newcomb. LC 77-89756. (American Labor, from Conspiracy to Collective Bargaining Ser., No. 1). 195p. 1978. reprint ed. 17.95 (0-405-02143-7) Ayer.

Plain Man's Talk on the Labor Question. Simon Newcomb. (Notable American Authors Ser.). 1999. reprint ed. lib. bdg. 125.00 (0-7812-4620-2) Rprt Serv.

Plain Murder. C. S. Forester. 21.95 (0-8488-0097-4) Amereon Ltd.

Plain Noodles. Betty Waterton. (Illus.). 32p. (J). 5.95 (0-88899-132-0) Publishers Group.

Plain of Smokes. Harvey Mudd. LC 82-14792. (Illus.). 98p. (Orig.). (C). 1982. 14.00 (0-87685-567-2); pap. 6.50 (0-87685-566-4) Black Sparrow.

Plain Ol' Charlie Deam: Pioneer Hoosier Botanist. Robert C. Kriebel. LC 87-2373. (Illus.). 194p. 1994. reprint ed. 29.95 (1-55753-057-2) Purdue U Pr.

Plain Old Man. Charlotte MacLeod. 224p. 1986. mass mkt. 3.99 (0-380-70148-0, Avon Bks) Morrow Avon.

***Plain Once Seen.** Virgil Hurley & Lance Hurley. 300p. 1999. pap. 14.95 (1-58275-007-6, Pub. by Black Forest Pr) Epic Bk Promo.

Plain Pathway to Plantations (1624) Richard Eburne. Ed. by Louis B. Wright. (Documents Ser.). 1978. 26.50 (0-918016-37-1) Folger Bks.

Plain People see Collected Works of E. W. Howe

Plain People. Edgar W. Howe. (American Biography Ser.). 317p. 1991. reprint ed. lib. bdg. 79.00 (0-7812-8199-7) Rprt Serv.

Plain People Look at the Beatitudes. William Barclay. (Abingdon Classics Ser.). 128p. (Orig.). 1993. pap. 4.95 (0-687-31550-6) Abingdon.

***Plain People of the Confederacy.** Bell Irvin Wiley. LC 00-28622. 128p. 2000. pap. text 12.95 (1-57003-362-5) U of SC Pr.

Plain Pictures: Images of the American Prairie. Joni L. Kinsey. LC 95-49898. 256p. 1996. pap. 36.95 (1-56098-630-1) Smithsonian.

Plain Pictures: Images of the American Prairie. Joni L. Kinsey. (Illus.). 256p. 1996. 65.00 (1-56098-688-3) Smithsonian.

Plain Pictures of Plain Doctoring: Vernacular Expression in New Deal Medicine & Photography. John D. Stoeckle. 274p. 1985. pap. text 17.50 (0-262-69138-8) MIT Pr.

Plain Pig's ABC's: A Day on Plain Pig's Amish Farm. Phyllis Pellman Good. LC 98-20868. (Illus.). 24p. (J). (ps-1). 1998. pap. 6.95 (1-56148-250-1) Good Bks PA.

Plain Pig's ABC's: A Day on Plain Pig's Amish Farm. Phyllis Pellman Good. LC 98-20868. (Illus.). 24p. (J). (ps-1). 1998. 14.95 (1-56148-251-X) Good Bks PA.

Plain Pine Box: A Return to Simple Jewish Funerals & Eternal Traditions. Arnold M. Goodman. 8.95 (0-87068-895-2) Ktav.

Plain Prayers for a Complicated World. Avery Brooke. LC 93-22817. (Illus.). 160p. 1993. pap. 10.95 (1-56101-084-7) Cowley Pubns.

Plain Prayers for a Complicated World. Avery Brooke. 1984. 6.20 (0-8164-3501-4) Harper SF.

Plain Prayers for a Complicated World. Avery Brooke. 124p. 1983. reprint ed. 5.95 (0-8164-0501-8) Harper SF.

Plain Princess: Musical. Aurand Harris. (J). 1955. 6.00 (0-87602-176-3) Anchorage.

Plain Reader: Essays on Making a Simple Life. Scott Savage. LC 98-9737. (Illus.). 272p. 1998. pap. 12.95 (0-345-41434-9) Ballantine Pub Grp.

Plain Sailing: A Masters & Green Mystery. large type ed. Douglas Clark. 384p. 1989. 27.99 (0-7089-2008-X) Ulverscroft.

Plain Seeing: A Novel. Sandra Scofield. 320p. 1998. pap. 13.00 (0-06-092945-6, Cliff Street) HarperTrade.

Plain Sense of Things: The Fate of Religion in an Age of Normal Nihilism. James D. Edwards. LC 96-48047. 1997. 45.00 (0-271-01677-9); pap. 17.95 (0-271-01678-7) Pa St U Pr.

Plain Song. Brian Meehan. 24p. 1982. pap. 10.00 (0-936576-07-3) Symposium Pr.

Plain Songs: Stories & Poems by Carleton Writers. Carleton College Faculty Staff. (Orig.). 1990. pap. 11.95 (0-9613911-5-4) Carleton Coll.

***Plain Songs II: Thirteen Carleton Writers.** Keith Harrison et al. (Illus.). 120p. 1999. pap. 16.95 (0-939394-08-1) Blck Willw Pr.

Plain Southern Eating: Reminiscences of A. L. "Tommie" Bass, Herbalist. Ed. by John K. Crellin. LC 87-31765. (Illus.). xii, 130p. 1988. text 19.95 (0-8223-0828-2) Duke.

Plain Speaking: An Oral Biography of Harry S. Truman. Merle Miller. 480p. 1986. mass mkt. 6.99 (0-425-09499-5) Berkley Pub.

Plain Style: Techniques for Simple, Concise, Emphatic Business Writing. Richard Lauchman. LC 93-4324. 144p. 1993. pap. 15.95 (0-8144-7852-2) AMACOM.

Plain Tales from the Hills. Rudyard Kipling. 1976. 23.95 (0-8488-0172-5) Amereon Ltd.

Plain Tales from the Hills. Rudyard Kipling. (Oxford World Classics Ser.). 368p. 2000. pap. 8.95 (0-19-283571-8) OUP.

Plain Tales from the Hills. Rudyard Kipling. Ed. by H. R. Woudhuysen. 288p. 1991. pap. 10.95 (0-14-018312-4, Penguin Classics) Viking Penguin.

Plain Tales from the Raj: Images of British India in the 20th Century. Charles Allen. LC 76-8693. (C). 1992. reprint ed. pap. text 10.00 (0-8364-2835-8, Pub. by Rupa) S Asia.

Plain Talk: Lessons from a Business Maverick. Ken Iverson & Tom Varian. LC 97-30126. 196p. 1997. 23.00 (0-471-15514-4) Wiley.

Plain Talk about Acupuncture. Ellinor R. Mitchell. (Illus.). 123p. (Orig.). 1987. pap. 10.95 (0-9617918-0-2) Whalehall Inc.

Plain Talk about Art see Language of Art from A to Z

Plain Talk about Art: The Language of Art from A to Z. 4th rev. ed. N. E. Lahti. LC 94-90022. 203p. 1994. pap. 11.00 (0-9620147-1-0) York Bks.

Plain Talk about Church Growth. Steve Clapp. LC 89-49600. 183p. 1990. reprint ed. pap. 56.80 (0-608-02155-5, 206282400004) Bks Demand.

Plain Talk about Churches & Money. Dean R. Hoge et al. LC 97-73982. 154p. 1997. pap. 15.75 (1-56699-185-4, AL184) Alban Inst.

P

Plain Talk about Drinking Water: Questions & Answers about the Water You Drink. 3rd ed. LC 96-54034. 1997. 6.75 (*0-89867-860-9*, 20244) Am Water Wks Assn.

*__Plain Talk about Purchasing.__ James P. Morgan. 2000. pap. 37.00 (*0-9644791-3-3*, Purchasing Mag) Cahners Business.

Plain Talk about Salvation: God's Plan & Man's Response to the Good Life Now & Here after. rev. ed. Marvin L. Smith. LC 93-70172. 120p. 1993. pap. text 7.00 (*1-882581-01-6*) Campbell Rd Pr.

Plain Talk about the Human Genome Project: A Tuskegee University Conference on Its Promise & Perils & Matters of Race. Ed. by Edward Smith & Walter Sapp. LC 97-61711. (Illus.). 292p. 1998. pap. 14.95 (*1-891196-01-4*) Tuskegee U CAENS.

Plain Talk about Using the Web. 5th ed. Arthur L. Buikema & Brian A. Ward. 96p. (C). 1998. pap. text, teacher ed. 15.00 (*0-03-022112-9*) SCP.

Plain Talk about Women in the Church. Jerry Blacklaw. (Illus.). 64p. (Orig.). 1992. pap. 8.95 (*1-881576-04-3*) Providence Hse.

*__Plain Talk & Common Sense from the Black Avenger.__ Ken Hamblin. LC 99-28017. 288p. 1999. 24.50 (*0-684-80756-4*) S&S Trade.

*__Plain Talk & Common Sense from the Black Avenger.__ Ken Hamblin. 288p. 2000. pap. 13.00 (*0-684-86556-4*, Touchstone) S&S Trade Pap.

Plain Talk Before God: The Language of Worship. Handt Hanson. 72p. 1992. ring bd. 45.00 (*0-933173-60-1*) Chging Church Forum.

Plain Talk on Dual Diagnosis. Mac Griffith. 150p. 1998. pap. 16.95 (*0-9662099-1-5*) Mariah Manage.

Plain Talk on Hebrews. Manford G. Gutzke. 160p. 1976. pap. 6.95 (*0-310-25541-4*, 9852P) Zondervan.

Plain Talk on the Epistles of John. Manford G. Gutzke. 1977. pap. 6.95 (*0-310-25631-3*, 9857P) Zondervan.

Plain Talks on Parenting. William S. Deal. 1984. pap. 3.95 (*0-318-18715-9*) Crusade Pubs.

Plain Talks on Parenting. William S. Deal. pap. 5.99 (*0-685-70973-6*) Schmul Pub Co.

Plain Talks with Husbands & Wives. Havelock Ellis & George S. Viereck. 1991. lib. bdg. 69.00 (*0-8490-4210-0*) Gordon Pr.

Plain TEX Primer. Malcolm Clark. (Illus.). 490p. 1993. pap. text 35.00 (*0-19-853724-7*) OUP.

Plain Treatise on the Peruvian Bark: The Stanitz Manuscript. Tr. & Intro. by Saul Jarcho. 116p. 1992. 19.95 (*0-88135-176-8*, Sci Hist) Watson Pub Intl.

*__Plain Truth.__ Jodi Picoult. LC 99-462185. 416p. 2000. 24.95 (*0-671-77612-6*, PB Hardcover) PB.

Plain Truth about the Plain Truth. Salem Kirban. (Illus.). 1972. pap. 4.95 (*0-912582-12-X*) Second Comng Inc.

Plain Truth & Redirection of the Cold War. rev. ed. Edward F. Haskell & Harold G. Cassidy. 170p. 1984. write for info. (*0-318-58154-X*) CURE.

Plain Truth: or Serious Considerations on the Present State of the City of Philadelphia & Province of Pennsylvania. Benjamin Franklin. (Notable American Authors Ser.). 1992. reprint ed. lib. bdg. 75.00 (*0-7812-2887-5*) Rprt Serv.

Plain Understanding. Aratis. 8p. (Orig.). 1994. pap. 2.00 (*0-938075-57-8*) Ocean View Bks.

Plain Vanilla, Toppings No. Clara L. Fentress. (Illus.). 69p. 1991. write for info. (*0-9660824-0-0*) C L Fentress.

Plain White. Heidi Lampietti. (Color Me Notebooks Ser.). 100p. 1998. pap. 4.00 (*1-892619-03-2*) RedJack.

Plain Word about Biblical Images: Growing in Our Faith Through the Scriptures. Margaret N. Ralph. 1989. pap. 10.95 (*0-8091-3045-9*) Paulist Pr.

Plain Words about AIDS: With a Glossary of Related Terms. 3rd ed. W. Hovey Smith. (Illus.). 200p. (Orig.). 1988. pap. 19.50 (*0-916565-11-4*) Whitehall Pr.

Plain Wrapper Press, 1966-1988. Elaine Smyth. (Illus.). 76p. 1993. pap. 45.00 (*0-614-10103-4*) Oak Knoll.

Plain Yarns from the Fleet: The Spirit of the Royal Navy During Its Twentieth Century Heyday. Charles Owen. LC 97-160012. (Illus.). 224p. 1997. 33.95 (*0-7509-0770-3*, Pub. by Sutton Pub Ltd) Intl Pubs Mktg.

Plainchant Tradition of Southwester Rus. Joan L. Roccasalvo. 185p. 1986. text 52.50 (*0-88033-096-1*, Pub. by East Eur Monographs) Col U Pr.

Plainclothes & Off-Duty Officer Survival: A Guide to Survival for Plainclothes Officers, Undercover Officers, & Off-Duty Police Officers. John C. Cheek & Tony Lesce. (Illus.). 202p. 1988. pap. 26.95 (*0-398-06055-X*) C C Thomas.

Plainclothes & Off-Duty Officer Survival: A Guide to Survival for Plainclothes Officers, Undercover Officers, & Off-Duty Police Officers. John C. Cheek & Tony Lesce. (Illus.). 202p. (C). 1988. text 38.95 (*0-398-05528-9*) C C Thomas.

Plaine Declaration That Our Brownists Be Full Donatists. George Gifford. LC 74-80180. (English Experience Ser.: No. 661). 1974. reprint ed. 20.00 (*90-221-0661-6*) Walter J Johnson.

Plaine Description of the Barmudas Now Called Sommer Islands: With an Addition Etc. Silvester Jourdan. LC 75-171770. (English Experience Ser.: No. 394). 52p. 1971. reprint ed. 15.00 (*90-221-0394-3*) Walter J Johnson.

Plaine Mans Path-Way to Heaven. Arthur Dent. LC 74-80173. (English Experience Ser.: No. 652). 430p. 1974. reprint ed. 45.00 (*90-221-0652-7*) Walter J Johnson.

*__Plainer Still.__ Catherine Cookson. 2000. mass mkt. 10.95 (*0-552-14384-7*, Pub. by Transworld Publishers Ltd) Trafalgar.

Plainer Translation: Joseph Smith's Translation of the Bible: A History & Commentary. Robert J. Matthews. LC 75-5937. xxvii, 468p. 1975. pap. 11.95 (*0-8425-2237-9*, Friends of the Library) Brigham.

Plainfield & North Plainfield, Embracing a Descriptive History of the Municipal, Religious, Social & Commercial Institutions, with Biographical Sketches, Profusely Illustrated. F. T. Smiley. (Illus.). 108p. 1997. reprint ed. lib. bdg. 25.00 (*0-8328-6074-3*) Higginson Bk Co.

Plainfield's African-American: From Northern Slavery to Church Freedom. Ed. by Leonard L. Bethel & Frederick A. Johnson. LC 97-25342. (Illus.). 180p. (C). 1997. text 32.50 (*0-7618-0848-5*) U Pr of Amer.

Plains Across: The Overland Emigrants & the Trans-Mississippi West, 1840-60. John D. Unruh, Jr. LC 78-9781. (Illus.). 592p. 1982. text 49.95 (*0-252-00698-4*) U of Ill Pr.

Plains Across: The Overland Emigrants & the Trans-Mississippi West, 1840-60. John D. Unruh, Jr. LC 93-13751. 592p. 1993. 21.95 (*0-252-06360-0*) U of Ill Pr.

Plains Across: The Overland Emigrants & the Trans-Mississippi West, 1840-60. abr. ed. John D. Unruh, Jr. LC 78-9781. (Illus.). 384p. 1982. pap. text 15.95 (*0-252-00968-1*) U of Ill Pr.

Plains & Peaks: A Wilderness Outfitter's Story. Tory Taylor. LC 93-81012. (Illus.). 224p. (Orig.). 1994. pap. 11.95 (*0-943972-30-2*) Homestead WY.

Plains & the Rockies. 4th ed. Henry R. Wagner. Ed. by Robert H. Becker. LC 81-86051. (Illus.). 765p. 1982. 150.00 (*0-910760-11-X*) Brick Row.

Plains Country Towns. John C. Hudson. LC 84-13049. (Illus.). 203p. 1985. reprint ed. pap. 63.00 (*0-608-00836-2*, 206162700010) Bks Demand.

Plains Cree, Vol. 37, Pt. 2. David G. Mandelbaum. LC 76-43772. reprint ed. 42.00 (*0-404-15626-6*) AMS Pr.

Plains Cree Texts. Leonard Bloomfield. LC 73-3552. (American Ethnological Society Publications: No. 16). reprint ed. 47.50 (*0-404-58166-8*) AMS Pr.

Plains Families: Exploring Sociology Through Social History. Scott G. McNall & Sally A. McNall. 384p. 1983. teacher ed. write for info. (*0-318-56959-0*) St Martin.

Plains Folk: A Commonplace of the Great Plains. Jim Hoy & Tom Isern. LC 87-5082. (Illus.). 214p. 1987. 22.95 (*0-8061-2064-9*) U of Okla Pr.

Plains Folk: North Dakota's Ethnic History. Ed. by William C. Sherman & Playford V. Thorson. LC 86-63088. (Illus.). 419p. 1986. 35.00 (*0-911042-35-0*) NDSU Inst Reg.

Plains Folk II: The Romance of the Landscape. Jim Hoy & Tom Isern. (Illus.). 216p. 1990. 19.95 (*0-8061-2272-2*) U of Okla Pr.

Plains Indian & Mountain Man Arts & Crafts: An Illustrated Guide. Charles W. Overstreet. Ed. by Monte Smith & Denise Knight. LC 93-74239. (Illus.). 160p. (Orig.). 1994. pap., per. 13.95 (*0-943604-41-9*, BOO/34) Eagles View.

Plains Indian & Mountain Man Arts & Crafts II: An Illustrated Guide, Vol. II. Charles W. Overstreet. Ed. by Denise Knight. LC 95-83908. (Illus.). 144p. (Orig.). 1996. pap., per. 12.95 (*0-943604-51-6*, BOO40) Eagles View.

Plains Indian Book. (J). (gr. 1-6). 1974. pap. 4.95 (*0-918858-02-X*) Fun Pub AZ.

Plains Indian Culture. O. J. Fargo. (Western History Ser.). (Illus.). 50p. (Orig.). (YA). (gr. 5 up). 1990. pap. 1.50 (*0-924702-29-X*) Grn Valley Area.

Plains Indian Designs. Caren Caraway. (International Design Library). (Illus.). 48p. (Orig.). 1984. pap. 5.95 (*0-88045-050-9*) Stemmer Hse.

Plains Indian Drawings, 1865-1935: Pages from a Visual History. Ed. by Janet Catherine Berlo. LC 96-5517. (Illus.). 240p. 1996. 60.00 (*0-8109-3742-5*, Pub. by Abrams) Time Warner.

Plains Indian Drawings, 1865-1935: Pages from a Visual History. Ed. by Janet Catherine Berlo. LC 96-5517. (Illus.). 1996. pap. write for info. (*1-885444-02-8*) Am Fed Arts.

Plains Indian History & Culture: Essays on Community & Change. John C. Ewers. LC 96-34648. (Illus.). 304p. 1998. pap. 14.95 (*0-8061-2943-3*) U of Okla Pr.

Plains Indian History & Culture: Essays on Continuity & Change. John C. Ewers. LC 96-34648. 296p. 1997. 29.95 (*0-8061-2862-3*) U of Okla Pr.

Plains Indian Painting: A Description of Aboriginal American Art. John C. Ewers. LC 76-43701. reprint ed. 37.50 (*0-404-15533-2*) AMS Pr.

*__Plains Indian Photographs of Edward S. Curtis.__ Photos by Edward S. Curtis. (Illus.). 219p. 2001. 50.00 (*0-8032-1512-6*) U of Nebr Pr.

Plains Indian Raiders: The Final Phases of Warfare from the Arkansas to the Red River. Wilbur S. Nye. LC 67-24624. (Illus.). 438p. 1984. pap. 21.95 (*0-8061-1175-5*) U of Okla Pr.

*__Plains Indians.__ Mir Tamim Ansary. LC 99-37137. (Illus.). 32p. 2000. lib. bdg. write for info. (*1-57572-929-6*) Heinemann Lib.

Plains Indians. Paul H. Carlson. LC 98-13697. (Elma Dill Russell Spencer Series in the West & Southwest: Vol. 19). (Illus.). 256p. 1998. 29.95 (*0-89096-828-4*); pap. 16.95 (*0-89096-817-9*) Tex A&M Univ Pr.

Plains Indians. Kate Hayden. LC 97-1601. (My World Ser.). (Illus.). 32p. (J). (gr. 2-7). 1997. write for info. (*0-7166-9410-7*) World Bk.

Plains Indians. Fiona MacDonald. (Insights Ser.). (Illus.). 60p. (J). (gr. 4 up). 1993. 15.95 (*0-8120-6376-7*) Barron.

Plains Indians. Robbins & Taylor. (Illus.). 48p. (J). (gr. 3-6). 1996. pap., teacher ed. 5.95 (*1-55799-576-1*, 545) Evan-Moor Edu Pubs.

*__Plains Indians.__ rev. ed. Kate Hayden. (My World Ser.). (Illus.). (J). 2000. 9.95 (*1-58728-070-1*); pap. 5.95 (*1-58728-064-7*) Two Can Pub.

Plains Indians: An Educational Coloring Book. Spizzirri Publishing Co. Staff. Ed. by Linda Spizzirri. (Illus.). 32p. (J). (gr. 1-8). 1981. pap. 1.99 (*0-86545-025-0*) Spizzirri.

Plains Indians, A. D. 500-1500: The Archaeological Past of Historic Groups. Ed. by Karl H. Schlesier. LC 93-46120. (Illus.). 512p. 1995. 42.95 (*0-8061-2593-4*) U of Okla Pr.

Plains Indians Coloring Book. David Rickman. (Illus.). (J). (gr. 4-7). 1983. pap. 2.95 (*0-486-24470-9*) Dover.

Plains Indians Dioramas. Matthew Kalmenoff. (Illus.). 1985. pap. 6.95 (*0-486-24919-0*) Dover.

Plains Indians of North America. Robin May. (Original People Ser.). (Illus.). 48p. (J). (gr. 4-8). 1987. lib. bdg. 16.67 (*0-86625-258-4*) Rourke Pubns.

Plains Indians of the 20th Century. Ed. & Intro. by Peter J. Iverson. LC 85-40475. (Illus.). 278p. 1985. pap. 14.95 (*0-8061-1959-4*) U of Okla Pr.

Plains Indians Punch-Out Panorama. A. G. Smith. (Illus.). (J). (gr. 4-7). 1994. pap. 3.95 (*0-486-27741-0*) Dover.

Plains Indians Wars. Sherry Marker. Ed. by John Bowman. (America at War Ser.). (Illus.). 128p. (J). (gr. 5-12). 1996. 19.95 (*0-8160-3254-8*) Facts on File.

Plains Miwok Dictionary. Catherine A. Callaghan. LC 83-18034. (University of California Publications in Linguistics: No. 105). 319p. pap. 98.90 (*0-7837-7474-5*, 204919600010) Bks Demand.

Plains of Camdeboo. large type ed. Eve Palmer. 560p. 1985. 27.99 (*0-7089-1242-7*) Ulverscroft.

*__Plains of Heaven.__ Thomas Bloom. 2000. 24.95 (*0-9659845-5-9*, Pub. by Ravenhaus Pub) Seven Hills Bk.

Plains of North America & Their Inhabitants. Richard I. Dodge. Ed. by Wayne R. Kime. LC 87-40706. (Illus.). 1989. 65.00 (*0-87413-344-0*) U Delaware Pr.

Plains of Passage. Jean M. Auel. (Earth's Children Ser.). 880p. 1991. mass mkt. 7.99 (*0-553-28941-1*) Bantam.

Plains of Passage. large type ed. Jean M. Auel. 1465p. 1992. pap. 17.95 (*1-56054-985-8*) Thorndike Pr.

Plains of Promise. Alexis Wright. LC 97-187750. (Black Australian Writers Ser.). 314p. 1998. pap. 19.95 (*0-7022-2917-2*, Pub. by Univ Queensland Pr) Intl Spec Bk.

Plains Outbreak Tornadoes: Killer Twisters. Victoria Sherrow. LC 97-39180. (American Disasters Ser.). 48p. (YA). (gr. 4-10). 1998. 18.95 (*0-7660-1059-7*) Enslow Pubs.

Plains People. Sally Hewitt. LC 95-25251. (Footsteps in Time Ser.). (Illus.). 24p. (J). (gr. k-3). 1996. lib. bdg. 17.00 (*0-516-08073-3*) Childrens.

Plains Rifle. Hanson. 35.00 (*0-88227-015-X*) Gun Room.

*__Plains Song: For Female Voices.__ Wright Morris. (Illus.). 237p. 2000. pap. 14.00 (*0-8032-8267-2*, Bison Books) U of Nebr Pr.

Plains States. Suzanne Winckler et al. LC 96-40549. (Smithsonian Guide to Historic America Ser.). 462p. 1998. 19.95 (*1-55670-643-X*) Stewart Tabori & Chang.

Plains Warrior: Chief Quanah Parker & the Comanches. Albert Marrin. (Illus.). 208p. (YA). (gr. 5 up). 1996. 18.00 (*0-689-80081-9*) Atheneum Yung Read.

Plains Woman: The Diary of Martha Farnsworth, 1882-1922. Ed. by Haskell S. Springer & Marlene Springer. LC 84-43169. (Illus.). 352p. 1988. pap. 15.95 (*0-253-20480-1*, MB-480) Ind U Pr.

Plains Women: Women in the American West. Paula Bartley & Cathy Loxton. (Women in History Ser.). (Illus.). 48p. (C). 1991. pap. 13.95 (*0-521-38616-0*) Cambridge U Pr.

Plainsmen No. 4: Black Sun: The Battle of Summit Springs, 1869. Terry C. Johnston. 1991. mass mkt. 3.99 (*0-312-92465-8*) St Martin.

Plainsmen of the Yellowstone: A History of the Yellowstone Basin. Mark H. Brown. LC 60-5262. (Illus.). 480p. 1969. pap. 17.95 (*0-8032-5026-6*, Bison Books) U of Nebr Pr.

Plainsong. David Barnett. 75p. 1990. pap. 7.95 (*0-912549-41-6*) Bread & Butter.

*__Plainsong.__ Kent Haruf. LC 99-15606. 320p. 1999. 24.00 (*0-375-40618-2*) Knopf.

*__Plainsong.__ Kent Haruf. (Contemporaries Ser.). 320p. 2000. pap. 13.00 (*0-375-70585-6*) Vin Bks.

*__Plainsong.__ large type ed. Kent Haruf. 2000. 26.95 (*1-56895-839-0*) Wheeler Pub.

Plainsong for Caitlin. Elizabeth M. Rees. (American Dreams Ser.). 176p. (Orig.). (gr. 7). 1996. mass mkt. 3.99 (*0-380-78216-2*, Avon Bks) Morrow Avon.

Plainspeaking: Interviews with Saskatchewan Writers. Doris Hillis. 320p. (YA). 1988. pap. 11.95 (*0-919926-87-8*, Pub. by Coteau); text 19.95 (*0-919926-86-X*, Pub. by Coteau) Genl Dist Srvs.

*__Plainswoman.__ Irene Bennett Brown. LC 00-41715. 2000. write for info. (*0-7862-2775-3*) Five Star.

Plainswoman. large type ed. Irene B. Brown. 508p. (Orig.). 1996. 21.95 (*0-7838-1599-9*, G K Hall Lrg Type) Mac Lib Ref.

Plainswoman: Her First Hundred Years. Kathleene West. LC 85-50677. (Plains Poetry Ser.: Vol. 1). (Illus.). 72p. (Orig.). 1985. 13.00 (*0-911015-04-3*); pap. 6.95 (*0-911015-05-1*) Sandhills Pr.

Plaint of Nature. Alan of Lille. Tr. by James J. Sheridan from LAT. viii, 256p. pap. 13.14 (*0-88844-275-0*) Brill Academic Pubs.

Plaintext. Mairs. LC 85-27043. 154p. 1992. reprint ed. pap. 14.95 (*0-8165-1337-6*) U of Ariz Pr.

Plaintiff's Case: From Voir Dire to Verdict. Jack McGehee. 1997. 85.00 (*1-891216-51-1*); pap. 65.00 (*1-891216-50-3*) TX Trial Lawyers.

Plaintiff's Personal Injury Handbook. Kathleen M. Reade. LC 94-163. (Paralegal Ser.). (C). 1995. ring bd. 52.75 (*0-87632-993-8*) Thomson Learn.

Plaintiff's Proof of a Prima Facie Case. Callaghan Editorial Staff. 1988. 130.00 (*0-685-30210-5*) West Group.

Plaintiff's Proof of a Prima Facie Case, 1982-1990. LC 82-4177. 98.00 (*0-317-12039-5*) West Group.

Plainverse: For People Who Can't Stand Obscure Poetry. Rachael Beck. LC 91-58773. 120p. 1991. 17.95 (*1-878208-11-X*) Guild Pr IN.

Plainwater: Essays & Poetry. Anne Carson. 260p. 2000. pap. 13.00 (*0-375-70842-1*) Vin Bks.

Plaire et Instruire. Scavillo. (C). 1994. pap. text 41.00 (*0-15-501133-2*) Harcourt Coll Pubs.

Plaire et Instruire: 16th & 17th-Century French Studies in Honor of George B. Daniel. Ed. by Judy Kem. LC 92-25008. (Illus.). XIV, 216p. 1994. 4.95 (*0-8204-1998-2*) P Lang Pubng.

Plaisanterie. Milan Kundera. (FRE.). 1987. pap. 13.95 (*0-8288-3700-7*) Fr & Eur.

Plaisir des Mots: Dictionnaire Poetique Illustre. Georges Jean. (Gallimard - Decouverte Cadet Ser.). 352p. (J). (gr. 4-9). 1982. 29.95 (*2-07-039499-9*) Schoenhof.

Plaisir du Texte. Roland Barthes. (FRE.). 1982. pap. 19.95 (*0-7859-3561-4*, F80575) Fr & Eur.

Plaisirs d'Aimer. Roger Pare. (Plaisirs Ser.). (FRE., Illus.). 24p. (J). (ps up). 1988. pap. 6.95 (*2-89021-087-1*, Pub. by La Courte Ech) Firefly Bks Ltd.

Plaisirs d'Amour: An Erotic Guide to the Senses. Elizabeth Nash. LC 94-23173. 192p. 1995. pap. 20.00 (*0-06-251149-1*, Pub. by Harper SF) HarpC.

Plaisirs d'Animaux. Roger Pare. (Plaisirs Ser.). (FRE., Illus.). 24p. (J). (ps up). 1990. pap. 6.95 (*2-89021-140-1*, Pub. by La Courte Ech) Firefly Bks Ltd.

Plaisirs de Chats. Roger Pare. (Plaisirs Ser.). (FRE., Illus.). 24p. (J). (ps up). 1983. pap. 6.95 (*2-89021-044-8*, Pub. by La Courte Ech) Firefly Bks Ltd.

Plaisirs de Cirque. Roger Pare. (Plaisirs Ser.). (FRE., Illus.). 24p. (J). (ps up). 1988. pap. 6.95 (*2-89021-086-3*, Pub. by La Courte Ech) Firefly Bks Ltd.

Plaisirs de Vacances. Roger Pare. (Plaisirs Ser.). (FRE., Illus.). 24p. (J). (ps up). 1995. pap. 6.95 (*2-89021-253-X*, Pub. by La Courte Ech) Firefly Bks Ltd.

Plaisirs des Creations Manuelles. Ed. by International Masters P Staff. (FRE., Illus.). 1998. write for info. (*1-892207-00-1*) Intl Masters Pub.

Plaisirs d'Ete. Roger Pare. (Plaisirs Ser.). (FRE., Illus.). 24p. (J). (ps up). 1988. pap. 6.95 (*2-89021-088-X*, Pub. by La Courte Ech) Firefly Bks Ltd.

Plaisirs d'Hiver. Roger Pare. (Plaisirs Ser.). (FRE., Illus.). 24p. (J). (ps up). 1990. pap. 6.95 (*2-89021-141-X*, Pub. by La Courte Ech) Firefly Bks Ltd.

Plaisirs et les Jours. Marcel Proust. (FRE.). 1979. pap. 17.95 (*0-7859-2743-3*) Fr & Eur.

Plaisirs et les Jours. Marcel Proust. (Imaginaire Ser.). (FRE.). 1924. reprint ed. pap. 13.95 (*2-07-028613-4*) Schoenhof.

*__Plaistow.__ Plaistow Historical Society Staff. (Images of America Ser.). 128p. 1999. pap. 18.99 (*0-7385-0071-2*) Arcadia Publng.

Plaited Glory: For Colored Girls Who've Considered Braids, Locks & Twists. Lonnice B. Bonner. (Illus.). 128p. 1996. pap. 12.00 (*0-517-88498-4*) Crown Pub Group.

Plaited Patchwork. Shari Cole. 128p. 1995. 19.95 (*0-89145-831-X*, 4513, Am Quilters Soc) Collector Bks.

Plan. Stephen J. Cannell. LC 94-35145. 1995. 23.00 (*0-688-14046-7*, Wm Morrow) Morrow Avon.

Plan. Stephen J. Cannell. 1996. mass mkt. 6.99 (*0-380-72754-4*, Avon Bks) Morrow Avon.

Plan. Susan F. Tierno. LC 98-71332. (Think-Kids Book Collection). (Illus.). 16p. (J). (gr. 1-4). 1998. pap. 2.95 (*1-58237-006-0*) Creat Think.

*__Plan.__ Susan F. Tierno. Tr. by Ana M. Alvarado. (Think-Kids Book Collection).Tr. of Plan. (SPA., Illus.). 16p. (J). 2000. pap. 2.95 (*1-58237-056-7*) Creat Think.

Plan: A Mission-Mandate Melodrama. Judy Theriault. 32p. 1999. pap. write for info. (*0-9652533-4-1*) Presby Ctr Mission.

Plan: Collected Poems & Stories of Mary Lelia Allen Smith. Marjie L. Eckhout. 170p. 1995. pap. 12.00 (*0-9645968-0-6*) R L Gaines.

Plan: To Restore the Constitution & Help Us All Get Out of Debt. Paul Fisher. (Illus.). 300p. (Orig.). 1988. pap. 10.00 (*0-9619843-0-9*) P Fisher.

Plan: Women Shall Lead the Way. Jim Wyler. LC 98-85041. xiv, 384p. 1998. pap. 24.95 (*0-9664018-0-8*) Grt Divide Pubng.

Plan - Predict - Prevent: How to Reinvest in Public Buildings. Eric Melvin. (Special Reports: No. 62). 83p. (Orig.). 1992. pap. text 50.00 (*0-917084-11-X*) Am Public Works.

Plan A: An Optimist Prepares for Y2K. Judith A. Cummings. 160p. 1998. pap. 21.95 (*0-9668348-0-1*) Rehoboth Publ.

*__Plan a Perfect Garden: Garden Design Made Simple, from Planning & Planting to Creating Special Gardens.__ Peter McHoy. (Illus.). 2000. 14.95 (*0-7548-0039-3*, Lorenz Bks) Anness Pub.

Plan Analysis: Toward Optimizing Therapy. Franz Caspar. (Illus.). 294p. 1995. text 35.00 (*0-88937-117-2*) Hogrefe & Huber Pubs.

Plan & Market: Economic Reform in Eastern Europe. Intro. by Morris Bornstein. LC 72-91289. (Yale Russian & East European Studies: No. 12). (Illus.). 424p. reprint ed. pap. 131.50 (*0-608-10716-6*, 202198200024) Bks Demand.

Plan & Market in Yugoslav Economic Thought. Deborah D. Milenkovitch. LC 78-140534. (Russian & East European Studies: No. 9). 333p. reprint ed. 103.30 (*0-8357-9440-7*, 201110400074) Bks Demand.

P

An Asterisk (*) at the beginning of an entry indicates that the title is appearing for the first time.

Plan & Market under Socialism. Ota Sik. LC 66-23896. 382p. reprint ed. pap. 118.50 (*0-608-14897-0*, 202613800048) Bks Demand.

Plan & Operation: National Nursing Home Survey Followup, 1987, 1988, 1990. Ilene B. Gottfried. LC 93-17510. (Vital & Health Statistics Ser.: Series 1, No. 30). 1993. write for info. (*0-8406-0481-5*) Natl Ctr Health Stats.

Plan & Operation of the National Employer Health Insurance Survey Abigail J. Moss. LC 99-25082. (DHHS Publication Ser.). 1999. write for info. (*0-8406-0553-6*) Natl Ctr Health Stats.

Plan & Operation of the National Hospital Ambulatory Medical Care Survey. Linda F. McCraig & Thomas McLemorel. LC 94-12448. (Vital & Health Statistics, Series 1, Programs & Collection Procedures: No. 34). 1994. 6.00 (*0-8406-0493-9*) Natl Ctr Health Stats.

Plan & Operation of the National Survey of Ambulatory Surgery. Thomas McLemore. 128p. 1997. per. 12.00 (*0-16-061478-3*) USGPO.

Plan & Operation of the National Survey of Ambulatory Surgery (NSAS) Thomas McLemore et al. LC 97-36605. (Vital & Health Statistics Ser.: Series 1, No. 37). 1997. write for info. (*0-8406-0532-3*) Natl Ctr Health Stats.

***Plan & Operation of the Nhanes II Mortality Study, 1992.** National Center for Health Statistics (U.S.) Staff. LC 99-29384. (Vital & Health Statistics, Series 1, Programs & Collection Procedures). 1999. write for info. (*0-8406-0556-0*) Natl Ctr Health Stats.

Plan & Operation of the NHANES I Epidemiologic Followup Study, 1986: PHS 90-1307. (Vital & Health Statistics Ser. 1: Programs & Collection Procedures: No. 25). 160p. 8.50 (*0-685-61581-2*, 017-022-01114-0) Natl Ctr Health Stats.

***Plan & Operation of the NHANES 2 Mortality Study, 1992.** Catherine M. Loria. 22p. 1999. pap. 2.50 (*0-16-050053-2*) USGPO.

Plan & Operation of the 1995 National Survey of Family Growth. Allen P. Duffer. LC 97-36607. (Vital & Health Statistics Ser.: Series 1, No. 37). 1997. write for info. (*0-8406-0531-5*) Natl Ctr Health Stats.

Plan & Operation of the 1995 National Survey of Family Growth. Janice E. Kelly. 95p. 1997. pap. 8.50 (*0-16-061477-5*) USGPO.

Plan & Operation of the Third National Health & Nutrition Examination Survey, 1994-1988. 413p. 1994. per. 37.00 (*0-16-045088-8*) USGPO.

Plan & Operation of the 3rd National Health & Nutrition Examination Survey, 1988-94. National Center for Health Statistics Staff. LC 94-1308. (Vital & Health Statistics Ser.: Series 1, No. 32). 407p. 25.00 (*0-614-02899-X*, 017-022-01260-0) Natl Ctr Health Stats.

Plan & Operations of the NHANES I Epidemiologic Followup Study, 1992. National Center for Health Statistics (U.S.) Staff. LC 97-53305. (Vital & Health Statistics Ser.: Series 1, No. 35). 1998. write for info. (*0-8406-0542-0*) Natl Ctr Health Stats.

Plan & Policy for a System of National Parks & Protected Areas Government of Grenada - GS-OAS. 23.00 (*0-685-60272-9*) OAS.

Plan & Section Drawing. 2nd ed. Thomas C. Wang. (Illus.). 160p. 1996. pap. 32.95 (*0-442-01765-0*, VNR) Wiley.

Plan & the Austrian Rebirth: A Journal of Literature, Art, & Culture. Ruth V. Gross. LC 81-66918. (GERM Ser.: Vol. 6). (Illus.). 158p. 1993. 29.95 (*0-938100-03-3*) Camden Hse.

Plan B. Chester B. Himes. Ed. by Michel J. Fabre & Robert E. Skinner. LC 93-13939. 250p. 1993. text 27.50 (*0-87805-645-9*) U Pr of Miss.

Plan B. Chester B. Himes. LC 93-13939. 204p. 1994. pap. 14.95 (*0-87805-751-X*) U Pr of Miss.

Plan B: A Liaden Adventure, 4 vols. Sharon Lee & Steve Miller. 336p. 1999. pap. 14.00 (*1-892065-00-2*) Meisha Merlin.

Plan B: Converting Change into Career Opportunity. rev. ed. Elwood N. Chapman. Ed. by Michael Crisp. LC 92-54603. (Fifty-Minute Ser.). 103p. 1993. reprint ed. pap. 10.95 (*1-56052-195-3*) Crisp Pubns.

***Plan B: Getting Unstuck from the Problems That Plague You.** Stephanie M. Asker. LC 99-46839. 304p. 1999. pap. 14.95 (*0-399-52566-1*, Perigee Bks) Berkley Pub.

***Plan B: Novel.** Jonathon Tropper. LC 99-56148. 384p. 2000. text 24.95 (*0-312-25253-6*) St Martin.

Plan-B, Personal Budget Planner Vol. 1: A Simple Blueprint for Success. Sandra M. Brunsmann. 23p. 1986. pap. text. write for info. (*0-9632178-2-8*) S M Brunsmann.

***Plan Book for Everyday! Ideas, Inspirations, Reminders, Remedies, Tips, Strategies & More.** Linda Karges-Bone. Ed. by Judy Mitchell. (Illus.). 144p. 2000. pap. 14.95 (*1-57310-215-6*) Teachng & Lrning Co.

Plan Book Plus, No. 3. Lee Canter. (Illus.). 104p. 1990. student ed. 6.95 (*0-939007-37-1*) Canter & Assocs.

Plan Briand d'Union Federale Europeenne (The Brand Plan of a European Federal Union : Der Briand-Plan eines Europaischen Bundessystems. Ed. by Antoine Fleury & Lubor Jilek. xvii, 610p. 1998. 58.95 (*3-906760-61-8*) P Lang.

Plan Brooklyn see Plan for New York City

Plan Care Special Practice: Ambulatory Care. Allbaugh. (Professional Reference - Nursing Ser.). 1994. pap. 20.95 (*0-8273-6121-1*) Delmar.

Plan de Accion para Ser un Mejor Papa. Gordon MacDonald. (Serie Guia de Bolsillo - Pocket Guides Ser.).Tr. of Action Plan for Great Dads. (SPA.). 2.79 (*0-7899-0010-6*, 498076) Editorial Unilit.

Plan de Accion para Ser un Mejor Papa - Action Plan for Great Dads. Gordon MacDonald. (SPA.). 1990. write for info. (*1-56063-033-7*) Editorial Unilit.

Plan de Dios para la Familia. Victor Ricardo & Gloria Ricardo. (Estudio Biblico Para Mujeres Ser.). 98p. 1992. pap. 4.00 (*1-885630-25-5*) HLM Producciones.

Plan de Dios para Su Dinero. D. S. Prince.Tr. of God's Plan for Your Money. (SPA.). 3.50 (*0-7899-0114-5*, 550081) Editorial Unilit.

Plan de la Senorita Monstruo see Monstruo

Plan de Negocios. 7th ed. David H. Bangs, Jr.Tr. of Business Planning Guide. (SPA.). 192p. 1997. pap. 19.95 (*0-7931-2696-7*, 1700-0501) Dearborn.

Plan de Paris par Arrondissement. 300p. 1995. 24.95 (*0-7859-9799-7*); pap. 24.95 (*0-7859-9182-4*) Fr & Eur.

Plan (Demon & Lesly) James E. Brown. LC 97-91124. 1998. 14.95 (*0-533-12567-7*) Vantage.

Plan Divino Perfecto Profecia Biblica. Kay Arthur.Tr. of God's Blueprint for Prophecy. (SPA.). 7.95 (*0-8297-1508-8*) Vida Pubs.

Plan Empresarial, la Guia de Ernst & Young. E. Siegel. (SPA.). 171p. 1994. pap. 23.50 (*84-7978-142-4*, Pub. by Ediciones Diaz) IBD Ltd.

***Plan Eterno de Dios.** Living Stream Ministry Staff. (SPA.). 1999. pap. write for info. (*0-7363-0415-0*) Living Stream Ministry.

Plan Examiner. Jack Rudman. (Career Examination Ser.: C-651). 1994. pap. 29.95 (*0-8373-0651-5*) Nat Learn.

Plan Execution: Problems & Issues: Papers from the Fall Symposium. Ed. by Louise Pryor. (Technical Reports). (Illus.). 155p. 1996. spiral bd. 25.00 (*1-57735-015-4*) AAAI Pr.

Plan for a Daily Reading of the 4 Standard Works. Eldin Ricks. 48p. 1997. reprint ed. pap. text 2.95 (*1-57636-036-9*) SunRise Pbl.

Plan for a Research Program on Aerosol Radiative Forcing & Climate Change. National Research Council, Panel on Aerosol Radiat. 180p. (Orig.). 1996. pap. text 34.00 (*0-309-05429-X*) Natl Acad Pr.

***Plan for Baseball.** Don Weiskopf. 1999. pap. 7.95 (*0-9674773-1-X*) Weiskopf Enter.

Plan for Developing an Uplifting Trench-Town: Making Better the Lives of Trench-Town People. Ricardo Scott. (Ras Cardo Gives a Plan to Improving Trench-Town Ser.). (Illus.). 75p. 1999. pap. write for info. (*1-58470-034-3*) Crnerstone GA.

***Plan for Estimating the Number of "Hardcore" Drug Users in the United States, Preliminary Findings, Fall 1997.** Ronald Simeone. LC 98-210432. 37p. 1998. pap. 4.00 (*0-16-049384-6*) USGPO.

Plan for Improving Female Education. Emma Willard. LC 87-32477. 44p. 1987. reprint ed. pap. 3.95 (*0-89783-044-X*) Cherokee.

Plan for It All. Barbara Bacigalupi. (Truly Human Ser.). Date not set. pap. write for info. (*1-893470-04-0*) Umano.

Plan for Life Community Encounter: Origins, History, Growth. Don P. Gelmini. Ed. by Aldo Curiotto. 192p. (C). 1996. pap. 39.95 (*0-85439-462-1*, Pub. by St Paul Pubns) St Mut.

Plan for Managing the Costs of Biomedical Research. (Illus.). 34p. (Orig.). (C). 1993. pap. text 20.00 (*1-56806-425-X*) DIANE Pub.

Plan for New York City. New York City Planning Commission. Ed. by Peter Richards. Incl. Vol. 3. Plan Brooklyn. 1970. pap. text 25.00 (*0-262-64005-8*); Set pap. 24.00 (*0-685-03388-0*) MIT Pr.

Plan for Planning: The Need for a Better Method of Assisting Underdeveloped Countries on Their Economic Policies. Gustav F. Papanek. LC 78-38759. (Harvard University. Center for International Affairs. Occasional Papers in International Affairs: No. 1). reprint ed. 27.50 (*0-404-54601-3*) AMS Pr.

Plan for Profitability! How to Write a Strategic Business Plan. Lee E. Hargrave. 300p. 1999. pap. 13.95 (*1-891929-19-4*) Four Seasons.

Plan for SoBro: A Study Sponsored by the Nashville Scene. Christine Kreyling. 64p. 1997. pap. write for info. (*0-9638616-1-1*) City Press.

Plan for Stewardship Education & Development Through the Year. David W. Gordon. LC 98-44028. 1998. pap. 11.95 (*0-8192-1803-0*) Morehouse Pub.

Plan for Success. James R. Sherman. (Do It! Success Ser.). 72p. 1988. pap. 4.95 (*0-935538-12-7*) Pathway Bks.

Plan for the Abolition of Slavery: Consistently with the Interests of All Parties Concerned. 2nd annot. ed. Moses E. Levy. Ed. by Chris Monaco. (Illus.). 64p. 1999. reprint ed. 14.95 (*0-9653864-0-6*) Wacahoota Pr.

Plan for the Dictionary of Old English. Roberta Frank. Ed. by Angus Cameron. LC 72-97152. 355p. reprint ed. pap. 110.10 (*0-8357-6398-6*, 203575500096) Bks Demand.

Plan for Women. Lawrence Naumoff. LC 97-10951. 288p. 1997. 23.00 (*0-15-100231-2*) Harcourt.

Plan for Women. Lawrence Naumoff. 259p. (C). 1999. pap. 13.00 (*0-15-600452-6*, Harvest Bks) Harcourt.

Plan for Writing. 3rd ed. Brereton. (C). 1987. pap. text, teacher ed. 27.50 (*0-03-001433-6*) Harcourt Coll Pubs.

Plan for Writing. 3rd ed. John Brereton. 264p. (C). 1987. pap. text 36.50 (*0-03-001432-8*, Pub. by Harcourt Coll Pubs) Harcourt.

Plan Graphics. 5th ed. Davis. (Landscape Architecture Ser.). 1997. pap. 39.95 (*0-442-02481-9*, VNR) Wiley.

Plan Graphics. 5th ed. David A. Davis & Theodore D. Walker. LC 98-51606. 224p. 1999. pap. 49.95 (*0-471-29221-4*) Wiley.

Plan Graphics: Drawing - Delineation - Lettering. 4th ed. Theodore D. Walker & David A. Davis. 218p. 1990. pap. 34.95 (*0-442-23779-0*, VNR) Wiley.

Plan Guide for Free Stall Systems. 2nd ed. W. G. Bickert & Richard R. Stowell. (Illus.). 1997. spiral bd. 29.95 (*0-932147-30-5*, Hoards Dairyman) Hoard & Sons Co.

Plan Implementation. John Stuart MacDonald. (Progress in Planning Ser.). 1979. pap. 35.00 (*0-08-024307-X*, Pergamon Pr) Elsevier.

Plan Infinito. Isabel Allende. LC 95-7171.Tr. of Infinite Plan. (SPA.). 336p. 1995. pap. 13.00 (*0-06-095127-3*, Harp PBks) HarpC.

Plan It Beanie. Kelly Heaps & Brittany Heaps. (Illus.). 184p. (J). (gr. 1-12). 1998. 14.95 (*1-885628-19-6*) Buckaroo Bks.

***Plan Letters: Managing Correspondence: A Records Management Handbook.** Ed. by Barry Leonard. (Illus.). 51p. 2000. reprint ed. pap. 20.00 (*0-7881-8934-4*) DIANE Pub.

Plan Maestro de la Evangelizacion. R. E. Coleman.Tr. of Master Plan of Evangelism. (SPA.). 8.99 (*0-7899-0357-1*, 498612) Editorial Unilit.

Plan Manzanares. Alonso Millan. (SPA.). 85p. 1967. 1.00 (*0-8288-7154-X*) Fr & Eur.

Plan Modelo para el Desarrollo Integrado del Eje Tabatinga-Apaporis. 12.00 (*0-8270-2885-7*) OAS.

Plan of Action for Implementing the Global Strategy for Health for All. 1982. text. write for info. (*92-4-180007-0*) World Health.

Plan of Action to Resolve Spent Nuclear Fuel Vulnerabilities, Phase 3. 250p. (Orig.). (C). 1995. pap. text 50.00 (*0-7881-1952-4*) DIANE Pub.

Plan of Chicago. Burnham & Bennett Staff. LC 93-14988. (Illus.). 268p. 1993. reprint ed. 75.00 (*1-878271-41-5*) Princeton Arch.

Plan of Chicago Prepared under the Direction of the Commercial Club During the Years 1906, 1907, 1908. Daniel H. Burnham & Edward H. Bennett. Ed. by Charles Moore. LC 71-75303. (Architecture & Decorative Art Ser.: Vol. 29). (Illus.). 1970. reprint ed. lib. bdg. 125.00 (*0-306-71261-X*) Da Capo.

Plan of Education for the Young Nobility: 1769 Edition. Thomas Sheridan. 178p. 1996. 75.00 (*1-85506-310-7*) Bks Intl VA.

Plan of Mr. Pope's Garden, As It Was Left at His Death: With a Plan & Perspective View of the Grotto. John Serle. LC 92-24239. (Augustan Reprints Ser.: No. 211). 1982. reprint ed. 14.50 (*0-404-70211-2*, SB466.G75L66) AMS Pr.

Plan of Parliamentary Reform, in the Form of a Catechism, with Reasons for Each Article. Jeremy Bentham. LC 75-41027. (BCL Ser. II). reprint ed. 39.50 (*0-404-14777-1*) AMS Pr.

Plan of Salvation. Robert J. Walker. 185p. 1994. pap. 11.95 (*0-9642553-0-8*) In His Name.

Plan of Salvation. Ostis B. Wilson. 64p. pap. 1.50 (*0-686-29160-3*) Faith Pub Hse.

Plan of Salvation. Benjamin B. Warfield. 128p. 1989. reprint ed. 11.95 (*0-9622508-0-5*) Simpson NJ.

Plan of Salvation & the Future in Prophecy. Duane S. Crowther. LC 72-173391. (Scripture Guide Ser.). 228p. 1971. pap. 12.98 (*0-88290-005-6*) Horizon Utah.

Plan of the English Commerce see Shakespeare Head Edition of the Novels & Selected Writings of Daniel Defoe

Plan or Die! 10 Keys to Organizational Success. Timothy M. Nolan et al. Ed. by JoAnn Padgett. LC 92-51082. (Illus.). 178p. 1993. 29.95 (*0-88390-377-6*, Pfffr & Co); pap. 19.95 (*0-89384-207-9*, Pfffr & Co) Jossey-Bass.

Plan or Not to Plan. Ash & Dauija. 320p. 2000. 49.00 (*0-13-095192-7*) S&S Trade.

Plan Paris. 14th ed. Michelin Staff. 1995. pap. 14.95 (*0-7859-9130-1*) Fr & Eur.

***Plan Perfecto.** Merline Lovelace. (Deseo Ser.: Bk. 206).Tr. of Perfect Plan. (SPA.). 156p. 2000. per. 3.50 (*0-373-35336-7*, 1-35336-6) Harlequin Bks.

Plan Reading & Nonstructural Plan Review BIT-101: 1988 Edition. 1988. teacher ed. 59.00 (*1-884590-13-6*, 212L88); student ed. 16.25 (*1-884590-14-4*, 212W88) Intl Conf Bldg Off.

Plan Recognition in Natural Language Dialogue. Sandra Carberry. (Bradford - ACL-MIT Press Series in Natural Language Processing). 240p. 1990. 44.00 (*0-262-03167-1*, Bradford Bks) MIT Pr.

Plan Review Manual, 1994. 200p. 1994. pap. text 32.60 (*1-884590-61-6*, 201S94) Intl Conf Bldg Off.

Plan Smart, Retire Rich! George D. Brenner. (Illus.). 230p. 1998. 24.95 (*0-07-044464-1*) McGraw.

Plan Supremo. D. Reagan.Tr. of Master Plan. (SPA.). 9.99 (*0-7899-0076-9*, 492300) Editorial Unilit.

Plan Supremo de Evangelizacion. Robert E. Coleman.Tr. of Master Plan of Evangelism. (SPA.). 1972. 4.99 (*0-311-13816-0*) Casa Bautista.

Plan Termination Answer Book, 1. annuals Pamela D. Perdue. 964p. 1999. boxed set 125.00 (*1-56706-810-3*, 68103) Panel Pubs.

***Plan the Play.** Dave Huggett. 1999. pap. text 13.95 (*0-575-06707-1*) Gollehon Pr.

Plan to Be Spiritual: The Wonderful Blessing of God's Direction & God's Power. David A. Norris. (Illus.). 31p. 1987. pap. 1.95 (*0-943177-05-7*) Heartland Pr.

Plan to Heal the World. Richard Rainbolt. 98p. (Orig.). 1989. pap. 10.00 (*0-317-93650-6*) Peace Curriculum.

Plan to Kill. Jack W. Boone. 347p. 1997. pap. 14.95 (*1-880719-02-9*, Grafco Bks) Grafco Prods.

***Plan to Retire on Full Pay: A Personal Guide to Retirement Planning.** Thomas C. Holmes. (Illus.). 184p. 2000. pap. 24.95 (*0-615-11180-7*) T C Holmes.

Plan to Strengthen Public Health in the U. S. 86p. (Orig.). (C). 1993. pap. text 25.00 (*1-56806-557-4*) DIANE Pub.

Plan to Succeed: A Guide to Strategic Planning. Steven C. Stryker. (Illus.). 330p. 1986. text 32.95 (*0-89433-251-1*) Petrocelli.

Plan to Teach: Page a Day. Carol Cummings. (Illus.). 224p. (J). (gr. k-12). 1987. pap. 5.95 (*0-685-40556-7*) Teaching WA.

Plan to Teach: 2 Pages per Week. Carol Cummings. (Illus.). 176p. (C). 1988. pap. 5.95 (*1-881660-05-2*) Teaching WA.

Plan to Win: A Definitive Guide to Business Processes. John Garside. LC 99-19791. 1999. pap. 24.95 (*1-55753-163-3*) Purdue U Pr.

Plan to Win: Success Guide for Young Athletes. Glenn Moore. LC 93-72102. (Illus.). 176p. (Orig.). 1993. pap. 12.95 (*0-9637345-0-4*) Champ Spts Pr.

Plan to Win: Turning Strategy into Success. Steve Smith. 1999. pap. text 15.95 (*0-7494-2847-3*) Kogan Page Ltd.

Plan Wholly New: Pierre Charles L'Enfant's Plan of the City of Washington. Richard W. Stephenson. LC 92-28798. 1993. write for info. (*0-8444-0699-6*) Lib Congress.

Plan Your Defense. Freddie North. Ed. by Tony Sowter. LC 98-39176. (How to Play Bridge Ser.). (Illus.). 96p. 1998. pap. 8.95 (*0-8442-0079-4*, 00794, Natl Textbk Co) NTC Contemp Pub Co.

Plan Your Estate. 3rd rev. ed. Denis Clifford & Cora Jordan. Ed. by Mary Randolph. LC 94-973. (Illus.). 416p. 1997. pap. 24.95 (*0-87337-239-5*) Nolo com.

***Plan Your Estate.** 5th ed. Denis Clifford & Cora Jordan. LC 99-87910. 2000. write for info. (*0-87337-580-7*) Nolo com.

Plan Your Estate-A Self-Study Course: Continuing Professional Education Credits-Self Study Course-Worth 12 CPE Credits. 462p. 1995. pap. 75.85 (*1-57402-323-3*) Athena Info Mgt.

***Plan Your Future.** Jim Ogg et al. (Illus.). 1999. pap. write for info. (*0-9678649-2-5*) Coole Schl.

***Plan Your Future.** 2nd ed. Lori Tate. Ed. by Jim Ogg et al. (YA). (gr. 9-12). 2000. pap. write for info. (*0-9678649-6-8*) Coole Schl.

Plan Your Home with Feng Shui. Ian Bruce. 1998. pap. 14.95 (*0-572-02395-2*, Pub. by W Foulsham) Trans-Atl Phila.

Plan Your Work - Work Your Plan: Secrets for More Productive Planning. Jim Sherman. Ed. by Tony Hicks. LC 90-83481. (Fifty-Minute Ser.). (Illus.). 71p. (Orig.). 1991. pap. 10.95 (*1-56052-078-7*) Crisp Pubns.

***Plan Z.** 212p. 1999. pap. 13.95 (*1-929741-25-1*) Carolelle.

***Plan Z by Leslie Kove.** Betsy Robinson. 2000. pap. 14.00 (*0-922811-48-2*) Mid-List.

Planar & Linear Fabrics of Deformed Rocks: A Selection of Papers Delivered at an International Conference held at ETH Zurich 30 August to 2 September 1982. Ed. by Paul L. Hancock et al. 218p. 1984. pap. 48.00 (*0-08-031428-7*, Pergamon Pr) Elsevier.

Planar Chromatography in the Life Sciences. Ed. by Joseph C. Touchstone & Sydney S. Levin. LC 89-5748. 199p. 1990. 135.00 (*0-471-50109-3*) Wiley.

Planar Circuits. Takanori Okoshi. (Electrophysics Ser.: Vol. 18). (Illus.). 220p. 1985. 86.95 (*0-387-13853-6*) Spr-Verlag.

Planar Dimension: Europe, 1912-1932. Margit Rowell. LC 78-74711. 1981. reprint ed. pap. 12.95 (*0-89207-017-X*) S R Guggenheim.

Planar Graphs. Ed. by William T. Trotter. LC 93-22339. (DIMACS Series in Discrete Mathematics & Theoretical Computer Science: Vol. 9). 152p. 1993. text 45.00 (*0-8218-6600-1*, DIMACS/9) Am Math.

Planar Lipid Bilayers: Methods & Applications. Ed. by Wolfgang Hanke & W. R. Schlue. (Biological Techniques Ser.). (Illus.). 144p. 1993. text 78.00 (*0-12-322994-4*) Acad Pr.

Planar Lipid Bilayers: Methods & Applications. Ed. by Wolfgang Hanke & W. R. Schlue. (Biological Techniques Ser.). (Illus.). 133p. 1994. 48.00 (*0-12-322995-2*) Acad Pr.

Planar Phonology & Morphology. Jennifer S. Cole. (Linguistics Ser.). 219p. 1991. text 15.00 (*0-8153-0165-0*) Garland.

Planar Powers. Robert King. 1997. pap. 5.99 (*0-7869-0532-8*, Pub. by TSR Inc) Random.

Planar Sites. TSR Staff. (AD & D Ser.). (Illus.). 96p. 1999. pap. 13.95 (*0-7869-1326-6*, Pub. by TSR Inc) Random.

Planar Transmission Line Structures. Tatsuo Itoh. LC 87-17277. 424p. 1987. 89.95 (*0-87942-232-7*, PCO2196) Inst Electrical.

Planarian Regeneration. H. Bronsted & G. A. Kerkut. LC 70-75454. (International Series of Monographs on Pure & Applied Mathematics: Vol. 42). 1969. 134.00 (*0-08-012876-9*, Pub. by Pergamon Repr) Franklin.

Plane. Monique Felix. (Mouse Bks.). (Illus.). 32p. (J). (gr. k-3). 1993. 10.60 (*1-56846-079-1*, Creat Educ) Creative Co.

Plane. Chris Oxlade. (Take It Apart Ser.). (Illus.). (J). (gr. 1-2). 1997. pap. 5.95 (*0-382-39668-5*, Silver Pr NJ); lib. bdg. 12.95 (*0-382-39667-7*, Silver Pr NJ) Silver Burdett Pr.

Plane Algebraic Curves. E. Brieskorn & Horst Knorrer. 864p. 1986. 137.00 (*0-8176-1769-8*) Birkhauser.

Plane Algebraic Curves. Morris Orzech. (Pure & Applied Mathematics Ser.: Vol. 61). (Illus.). 240p. 1981. text 135.00 (*0-8247-1159-9*) Dekker.

Plane & Coordinate Geometry Study Aid. Joseph A. Vellozi. (J). 1974. pap. 2.50 (*0-87738-040-6*) Youth Ed.

Plane & Pilot International Aircraft Directory. Plane & Pilot Magazine Staff. 1995. pap. 24.95 (*0-07-050305-2*) McGraw-Hill Prof.

Plane Answers to Complex Questions: The Theory of Linear Models. R. Christensen. LC 87-4978. (Texts in Statistics Ser.). (Illus.). 390p. (C). 1987. 49.95 (*0-387-96487-8*) Spr-Verlag.

Plane Answers to Complex Questions: The Theory of Linear Models. 2nd ed. Ronald Christensen. 452p. 1996. 57.95 (*0-387-94767-1*) Spr-Verlag.

Plane Basics. Sam Allen. LC 93-24609. (Basics Ser.). (Illus.). 128p. 1993. pap. 10.95 (*0-8069-8804-5*) Sterling.

Plane Crazy: A Celebration of Flying. Burton J. Bernstein. (Illus.). 192p. 1985. 16.95 (*0-685-11128-8*) HM.

Plane Death. Anne M. Dooley. 250p. write for info. (*1-896300-14-6*) NeWest Pubs.

P

An Asterisk (*) at the beginning of an entry indicates that the title is appearing for the first time.

Plane Ellipticity & Related Problems. Ed. by Robert P. Gilbert. LC 82-11562. (Contemporary Mathematics Ser.: Vol. 11). 245p. 1982. pap. 33.00 (*0-8218-5012-1*, CONM/11) Am Math.
***Plane Facts, Here & Now.** Barbara J. Bishop. iv, 100p. 1999. pap. 10.95 (*0-9673337-0-9*) Bar-Lor Pubng.
Plane Geometry & Other Affairs of the Heart: Stories. R. M. Berry. LC 84-8172. 189p. 1985. 15.95 (*0-914590-88-X*); pap. 7.95 (*0-914590-89-8*) Fiction Coll.
Plane of Bliss: On Earth as It Is in Heaven. Ramtha. 1997. pap. text 10.95 (*1-57873-026-0*) JZK Inc.
***Plane of Excellence: Superior Piloting, 3 vols.** Tony T. Kern. 2000. 59.95 (*0-07-137009-9*) McGraw.
***Plane of Excellence: Superior Piloting Trilogy.** Tony T. Kern. 2000. 59.95 (*0-07-136375-0*) McGraw.
***Plane Reading.** Edward L. McNeil. 224p. 2001. pap. write for info. (*1-57197-244-7*, Pub. by Pentland Pr) Assoc Pubs Grp.
***Plane Reading, Vol. II.** Edward L. McNeil. (Illus.). 368p. 2000. write for info. (*1-57197-230-7*, Pub. by Pentland Pr) Assoc Pubs Grp.
***Plane Rides.** Pam Walker. (Welcome Bks.). (Illus.). (J). 2000. 13.50 (*0-516-23102-2*) Childrens.
***Plane Rides.** Pam Walker. (Let's Go Ser.). (Illus.). 24p. (J). (ps-2). 2000. pap. 4.95 (*0-516-23027-1*) Childrens.
Plane Song. Diane Siebert. LC 92-17359. (Illus.). 32p. (J). (ps-3). 1995. pap. 6.95 (*0-06-443367-6*, HarpTrophy) HarpC Child Bks.
Plane Song. Diane Siebert. (J). 1993. 12.15 (*0-606-08021-X*) Turtleback.
Plane Strain Crack Toughness: Testing of High Strength Metallic Materials. American Society for Testing & Materials Staff. LC 66-29517. No. 410. 136p. reprint ed. pap. 38.80 (*0-317-08331-7*, 2051707) Bks Demand.
Plane Talk. Art Freifeld. 20p. (Orig.). 1990. 6.95 (*0-916177-63-7*) Am Eng Pubns.
Plane Thoughts on Parish Ministry: A Flight Plan for Being an Effective & Faithful Pastor. Jerry L. Schmalenberger. LC 93-38127. 160p. 1994. pap. 14.50 (*1-55673-599-5*, 9420) CSS OH.
Plane Tips. Bob Stevens. LC 82-70150. (Illus.). 80p. 1987. pap. 3.95 (*0-910497-00-1*) Aviation.
Plane Trigonometry. Louis Leithold. (Illus.). (C). 1989. text 48.50 (*0-201-17056-6*); student ed. 18.25 (*0-201-17058-2*) Addison-Wesley.
Plane Trigonometry. Bernard J. Rice. (Mathematics Ser.). 1995. text 12.75 (*0-534-93464-1*) Brooks-Cole.
Plane Trigonometry. Bernard J. Rice. (Mathematics Ser.). Date not set. mass mkt. 12.00 (*0-87150-540-1*) PWS Pubs.
Plane Trigonometry. Jack Rudman. (Dantes Subject Standardized Tests Ser.: DANTES-29). 1994. pap. 23.95 (*0-8373-6629-1*) Nat Learn.
Plane Trigonometry. Jack Rudman. (DANTES Ser.: No. 29). 1994. 39.95 (*0-8373-6529-5*) Nat Learn.
Plane Trigonometry. 2nd ed. David R. Gustafson. LC 84-9446. (Math). (C). 1984. mass mkt. 35.00 (*0-534-03606-6*) Brooks-Cole.
Plane Trigonometry. 2nd ed. Bernard J. Rice. (Mathematics Ser.). 1978. 15.00 (*0-87150-250-X*) PWS Pubs.
Plane Trigonometry. 3rd ed. R. David Gustafson & Peter D. Frisk. LC 88-19475. (Math). 442p. (C). 1988. mass mkt. 48.25 (*0-534-09822-3*) Brooks-Cole.
Plane Trigonometry. 3rd ed. Bernard J. Rice & Jerry D. Strange. LC 80-26108. 322p. (C). 1981. mass mkt. 27.75 (*0-87150-297-6*, 2381) PWS Pubs.
Plane Trigonometry. 4th ed. Bernard J. Rice & Jerry D. Strange. (C). 1986. mass mkt. 33.50 (*0-87150-913-X*, 33L4040) PWS Pubs.
Plane Trigonometry. 5th ed. Bernard J. Rice & Jerry D. Strange. (Math). 384p. (C). 1989. mass mkt. 39.25 (*0-534-91562-0*) PWS Pubs.
Plane Trigonometry. 6th ed. Bernard J. Rice & Strange. (Mathematics Ser.). 1992. pap., student ed. 17.50 (*0-534-93121-9*) PWS Pubs.
Plane Trigonometry. 6th ed. Bernard J. Rice & Jerry D. Strange. 400p. 1992. text 50.00 (*0-534-92894-3*) PWS Pubs.
Plane Trigonometry. 7th ed. E. Richard Heineman & J. Dalton Tarwater. LC 92-17811. 320p. (C). 1993. 69.06 (*0-07-028187-4*); pap. text, student ed. 15.00 (*0-07-028188-2*) McGraw.
Plane Trigonometry. 7th ed. Bernard J. Rice & Jerry D. Strange. (Mathematics Ser.). 1995. mass mkt. 49.00 (*0-534-94824-3*) PWS Pubs.
Plane Trigonometry. 7th ed. Bernard J. Rice et al. (Math Ser.). 1995. pap., student ed. 21.25 (*0-534-94825-1*) Brooks-Cole.
Plane Trigonometry. 7th ed. Carroll M. Schleppi. (Mathematics Ser.). 1996. pap., student ed. 18.95 (*0-534-95062-0*) Wadsworth Pub.
Plane Trigonometry & 4 Place Tables. William A. Granville. LC 52-3178. 276p. reprint ed. pap. 85.60 (*0-608-30962-1*, 200016000025) Bks Demand.
Plane Trigonometry with Practical Applications. Leonard E. Dickson. xii, 211p. 1992. text 14.95 (*0-8284-0230-2*) Chelsea Pub.
Plane Trigonometry with Tables. 7th ed. Charles S. Rees et al. (Illus.). 1977. text 23.95 (*0-685-03896-3*) P-H.
Plane Truth: Tips for Combating the Health & Safety Perils of Flying. Rikki Stevens & Ralph Luciano. 1994. pap. 12.95 (*0-88282-094-X*) New Horizon NJ.
Plane Verse: Lite Flight Entertainment from an Etheral Plane. Hunt Harris. 64p. (Orig.). 1995. pap. 6.95 (*0-9646822-0-6*) Exposures Unltd.
Plane Wave Spectrum Representation of Electromagnetic Fields. P. C. Clemmow. (Series on Electromagnetic Wave Theory). 200p. 1996. 49.95 (*0-7803-3411-6*, PC5682) Inst Electrical.
Plane Wave Spectrum Representation of Electromagnetic Fields. P. Clemmow & A. Cullen. LC 66-25066. (International Series of Monographs in Electromagnetic Waves: Vol. 12). 1966. 85.00 (*0-08-013162-X*, Pub. by Pergamon Repr) Franklin.
Plane Wave Spectrum Representation of Electromagnetic Fields. P. C. Clemmow. (IREE/OUP Series on Electromagnetic Wave Theory). (Illus.). 198p. 1996. reprint ed. text 75.00 (*0-19-859225-6*) OUP.
Plane Wave Theory of Time-Domain Fields: Applications. Arthur D. Yaghjian & Thorkild B. Hansen. LC 99-17759. 400p. 1999. 99.95 (*0-7803-3428-0*, PC5702-QOE) Inst Electrical.
Plane Weather. William Herrick. 116p. (C). 1994. spiral bd. 15.95 (*0-8403-9473-X*) Kendall-Hunt.
Plane Weather: A Programmed Study Guide & Exercise Manual. 2nd ed. William Herrick. 114p. (C). 1998. spiral bd. 20.95 (*0-7872-5157-7*) Kendall-Hunt.
Planeacion de los Requerimentos de Material. APICS Bucks-Mont. Chapter Staff.Tr. of Material Requirements Planning. (SPA.). 87p. (Orig.). 1994. pap. 40.00 (*1-55822-113-1*) Am Prod & Inventory.
Planeacion Estrategica y Subsistema Direccion, Vol. 48. (SPA.). (C). 1997. pap. 14.33 (*0-673-19302-0*) Addison-Wesley.
Planecraft. C. W. Hampton & E. Clifford. LC 79-57129. (Illus.). 1982. reprint ed. pap. 7.50 (*0-918036-00-3*) Woodcraft Supply.
Planejamento Estrategico e Conselho Diretor Na Organizacao Sem Fins Lucrativos. Dabney G. Park, Jr.Tr. of Strategic Planning & the Nonprofit Board. (POR.). 12p. (Orig.). 1996. pap. write for info. (*0-925299-69-3*) Natl Ctr Nonprofit.
Planemaker: A Magical Story with Songs. Marvin Payne & Guy Randle. Date not set. pap. 4.00 (*1-57514-182-5*) Encore Perform Pub.
Planemakers & Other Edge Tool Enterprises in New York State in the Nineteenth Century. 2nd rev. ed. Kenneth D. Roberts & Jane W. Roberts. (Illus.). 244p. 1989. reprint ed. pap. text 30.00 (*0-913602-66-3*) K Roberts.
Planen und Auswerten von Versuchen. 3rd ed. A. Linder. (Reihe der Experimentellen Biologie Ser.: No. 13). (GER., Illus.). 344p. 1980. 111.00 (*0-8176-0248-8*) Birkhauser.
Planer Operations for Machinists. 1996. lib. bdg. 250.75 (*0-8490-8344-3*) Gordon Pr.
Planes see On the Move
Planes. (Chunky Ser.). (Illus.). (J). (ps up). 1997. 2.95 (*0-614-28716-2*) DK Pub Inc.
Planes. Donna Bailey. LC 89-21737. (Facts About Ser.). (Illus.). 48p. (J). 1990. pap. 4.95 (*0-8114-6630-2*) Raintree Steck-V.
Planes. Francesca Baines. (Worldwise Ser.). (Illus.). 48p. (J). (gr. 4-6). 1994. lib. bdg. 23.00 (*0-531-14341-4*) Watts.
Planes. Francesca Baines. (Worldwise Ser.). (Illus.). 48p. (J). (gr. 4-6). 1995. pap. 7.00 (*0-531-15268-5*) Watts.
Planes. D K Publishing Staff. (FunFax Sticker Ser.). 1999. pap. text 3.95 (*0-7894-4319-8*) DK Pub Inc.
Planes. DK Publishing Staff. (What's Inside? Ser.). 1999. pap. text 3.95 (*0-7894-4296-5*) DK Pub Inc.
Planes. Clive Gifford. (Machines Board Bks.). (Illus.). 12p. (J). (ps up). 1994. bds. 4.95 (*0-7460-1978-5*, Usborne) EDC.
Planes, 56 Vols. Michael Johnstone. LC 93-46373. (What's Inside? Ser.). (Illus.). 32p. (J). (gr. 1-4). 1994. pap. 6.95 (*1-56458-520-4*) DK Pub Inc.
Planes. Neil Morris. LC 97-21773. (Traveling Through Time Ser.). 1997. 18.95 (*0-382-39791-6*) Silver Burdett Pr.
Planes. Neil Morris. LC 97-21773. (Traveling Through Time Ser.). (J). (gr. 5). 1997. pap. 8.95 (*0-382-39792-4*) Silver Burdett Pr.
***Planes.** Chris Oxlade. LC 00-27549. 2000. write for info. (*1-57572-303-4*) Heinemann Lib.
Planes. Kindersley Planes. LC 91-25688. (Eye Openers Ser.). (Illus.). 24p. (J). (ps-k). 1992. mass mkt. 8.99 (*0-689-71564-1*) Aladdin.
Planes. Anne Rockwell. (J). (ps-3). 1993. pap. 5.99 (*0-14-054782-7*, PuffinBks) Peng Put Young Read.
Planes. Snapshot Staff. LC 97-222715. (Things That Go Shaped Board Bks.). 10p. (J). 1997. 3.95 (*0-7894-2209-3*) DK Pub Inc.
Planes. Philip Steele. LC 90-41181. (Pocket Facts Ser.). (Illus.). 32p. (J). (gr. 5-6). 1991. lib. bdg. 11.95 (*0-89686-524-X*, Crstwood Hse) Silver Burdett Pr.
Planes: Ran Oron. Dore Ashton et al. (Illus.). 44p. (Orig.). 1996. pap. 7.00 (*1-884300-02-2*) HUC Jew Inst.
***Planes & Helicopters.** Nigel Hawkes. LC 99-37560. 1999. 21.90 (*0-7613-3260-X*) Millbrook Pr.
Planes & Flying Machines. (Popular Mechanics for Kids Coloring & Activity Bks.). (Illus.). 32p. (J). (gr. k-2). 1997. pap. write for info. (*1-56144-912-1*, Honey Bear Bks) Modern Pub NYC.
Planes & Helicopters. Clive Gifford. (Young Machines Ser.). (Illus.). 32p. (J). (gr. 5 up). 1994. text 6.95 (*0-7460-1658-1*, Usborne) EDC.
Planes & Helicopters. Clive Gifford. (Young Machines Ser.). (Illus.). 32p. (J). (ps-4). 1994. lib. bdg. 14.95 (*0-88110-673-9*, Usborne) EDC.
***Planes & Other Aircraft: Learn the Science - Build the Model.** Nigel Hawkes. LC 99-37560. (How Science Works Ser.). (Illus.). 32p. (J). (gr. 4-6). 1999. pap. 6.95 (*0-7613-0826-1*, Copper Beech Bks) Millbrook Pr.
Planes & Other Flying Things. Florence Temko. LC 96-4545. (Paper Magic Ser.). (Illus.). 48p. (J). (gr. 3-6). 1996. pap. 7.95 (*0-7613-0082-1*) Millbrook Pr.
Planes & Other Flying Things. Florence Temko. LC 96-4545. (Paper Magic Ser.). (Illus.). 48p. (J). (gr. 3-6). 1996. lib. bdg. 20.90 (*0-7613-0041-4*) Millbrook Pr.
Planes Board Book. Byron Barton. (Illus.). 16p. (J). (ps-k). 1998. 6.95 (*0-694-01166-5*) HarpC Child Bks.
Planes de Boda (Wedding Plans) Pamela Ingrahm. (Deseo Ser.: No. 220). (SPA.). 1998. per. 3.50 (*0-373-35220-4*) Harlequin Bks.
Planes de Seduccion - Seduction Plans, Vol. 199. Susan Crosby. (Silhouette Deseo Ser.).Tr. of Seduction Plans. (SPA.). 1997. per. 3.50 (*0-373-35199-2*, 1-35199-8) Harlequin Bks.
Planes de Seguros. Larry Burkett. (Serie Conceptos Cristianos Financieros (Christian Financial Concepts) Ser.).Tr. of Insurance Plans. (SPA.). 100p. 1995. pap. 3.29 (*0-7899-0017-3*, 497251) Editorial Unilit.
Planes, Gliders, Helicopters, & Other Flying Machines. Terry Jennings. LC 92-28422. (How Things Work Ser.). (Illus.). 40p. (J). (gr. 3-8). 1993. lib. bdg. 13.90 (*1-85697-684-X*, Kingfisher) LKC.
Planes, Gliders, Helicopters, & Other Flying Machines. Terry Jennings. LC 92-28422. (How Things Work Ser.). (Illus.). 40p. (J). (gr. 4-7). 1995. pap. 8.95 (*1-85697-869-9*, Kingfisher) LKC.
Planes, Gliders, Helicopters, & Other Flying Machines. Terry J. Jennings. (How Things Work Ser.). (J). 1993. 12.15 (*0-606-05362-X*, Pub. by Turtleback) Demco.
Planes, Jets & Helicopters. John Bringhurst. (Illus.). 160p. 1994. pap. 11.95 (*0-07-007904-8*) McGraw.
***Planes Kid Kit.** Clive Gifford. (Illus.). 12p. (J). (ps up). 1999. 16.95 (*1-58086-218-7*, Usborne) EDC.
Planes, Names & Dames. (Illus.). 9.95 (*0-614-13193-6*, 21-39911) EAA Aviation.
Planes, Names & Dames, Vol. 3. Larry Davis. (Aircraft Specials Ser.). (Illus.). 80p. 1995. pap. 14.95 (*0-89747-339-6*) Squad Sig Pubns.
Planes, Names & Dames Vol. 2: Korea Nose Art. Larry Davis. (Specials Ser.: Vol. 2). (Illus.). 80p. 1993. pap. 10.95 (*0-89747-291-8*, 6058) Squad Sig Pubns.
Planes of Chaos. Wolfgang Baur & L. W. Smith. 1994. 30.00 (*1-56076-874-6*, Pub. by TSR Inc) Random.
Planes of Conflict. 1995. 30.00 (*0-7869-0309-0*, Pub. by TSR Inc) Random.
Planes of Law. TSR Inc. Staff. (Advanced Dungeons & Dragons, 2nd Edition: Planescape Campaign World Ser.). 1995. 30.00 (*0-7869-0093-8*) TSR Inc.
***Planes of the President: An Illustrated History of Air Force One.** Bill Holder. (Illus.). 96p. 2000. pap. 19.95 (*0-7643-1187-5*) Schiffer.
Planes, Pilots & Gofer Tales of Lynchburg, Virginia's Old Preston Glenn Airport. Jim Rogers. LC 98-134005. (Illus.). 160p. 1997. pap. 15.95 (*1-883912-05-9*) Hamiltons.
Planes, Pilots & Progress. Duane Cole. 140p. 1993. pap. 14.95 (*0-916413-25-X*) Aviation.
***Planes, Rockets & Other Flying Machines.** Ian Graham. (Fast Forward Ser.). (Illus.). (J). 2000. pap. 9.95 (*0-531-16444-6*) Watts.
Planes, Trains, & Automobiles: The Transportation Revolution in Children's Picture Books. Neil Harris. LC 95-6703. 1995. pap. 8.00 (*0-943056-23-3*) Univ Chi Lib.
Planes Without Pilots: Advances in Unmanned Flight. Bill Siuru. (Illus.). 81p. 1997. reprint ed. pap. text 15.00 (*0-7881-5006-5*) DIANE Pub.
Planescape: Torment Official Strategies & Secrets. 4th ed. Chris Avellone. (Strategies & Secrets Ser.). 240p. 1999. pap. 19.99 (*0-7821-2585-9*, Strategies & Secrets) Sybex.
Planescape Campaign Setting. David J. Cook. (Advanced Dungeons & Dragons, 2nd Edition: Planescape Campaign World Ser.). 1994. 30.00 (*1-56076-834-7*, Pub. by TSR Inc) Random.
Planescape Player's Primer. TSR Inc. Staff. (Advanced Dungeons & Dragons, 2nd Edition Ser.). (Illus.). 1995. 15.00 incl. audio (*0-7869-0121-7*, Pub. by TSR Inc) Random.
Plane/Structures. Contrib. by David Pagel et al. (Illus.). 64p. 1994. pap. 18.00 (*0-911291-23-7*, Pub. by Fellows Cont Art) RAM Publications.
Planeswalker. Lynn Abbey. 1998. pap. 5.99 (*0-7869-1182-4*, Pub. by TSR Inc) Random.
Planet Ant. Planet Dexter. LC 96-210795. (Illus.). 48p. 1996. pap. 14.99 (*0-201-48985-6*) Addison-Wesley.
Planet Beyond. Steve Mudd. 224p. 1990. mass mkt. 4.50 (*0-445-21047-8*, Pub. by Warner Bks) Little.
Planet Boys: The Most Beautiful Boys on the Planet. Barry Cranwell. 1996. pap. text 30.00 (*0-9524647-1-3*, Pub. by Prowler Pr) LPC InBook.
Planet Champions: Adventures in Saving the World. Jack Yost. 1999. pap. 14.95 (*0-9623683-5-0*, New Politics) BridgeCity Bks.
Planet Colors. Photos by Charlie Price. (Illus.). 42p. 1997. pap. 25.00 (*0-9661580-0-8*) Planet Pub Intl.
Planet Dexter's Treasure Hunt. J. L. Bell. 1998. spiral bd. write for info. (*0-201-16542-2*) Addison-Wesley.
Planet Doonesbury: A Doonesbury Book. Garry B. Trudeau. LC 97-71641. (Illus.). 152p. (Orig.). 1997. pap. 12.95 (*0-8362-3686-6*) Andrews & McMeel.
Planet Dora: A Memoir of the Holocaust & the Birth of the Space Age. Yves Beon. 288p. 1998. pap. 20.00 (*0-8133-3492-6*, Pub. by Westview) HarpC.
Planet Dreams. Michaela Carlock. LC 97-75467. 336p. (Orig.). 1998. pap. 13.95 (*0-9653024-2-3*) Keswick Hse.
Planet Drum: A Celebration of Percussion & Rhythm. Mickey Hart. (Illus.). 224p. 1998. pap. 19.95 (*1-888358-20-3*) Acid Test Prodns.
Planet Earth see Understanding Science & Nature Series
Planet Earth. Ed. by Jill Bailey & Catherine Thomas. (Illus.). 160p. (J). (gr. 3-9). 1993. 40.00 (*0-19-910144-2*) OUP.
Planet Earth. Neil Curtis et al. LC 93-20103. (Visual Factfinders Ser.). (Illus.). 96p. (J). (gr. 5 up). 1993. pap. 12.95 (*1-85697-847-8*, Kingfisher) LKC.
***Planet Earth.** John Farndon. (Investigations Ser.). (Illus.). (J). 2000. 12.95 (*0-7548-0475-5*, Lorenz Bks) Anness Pub.
Planet Earth. Robin Kerrod. LC 98-53270. 1999. write for info. (*1-57505-381-0*) Lerner Pub.
Planet Earth. Robin Kerrod. LC 98-53270. (Planet Library). (Illus.). 32p. (J). (gr. 4-7). 2000. 22.60 (*0-8225-3902-0*, Lerner Publctns) Lerner Pub.
Planet Earth. Maurice Kraft. LC 98-7124. (Creative Discoveries Ser.). Orig. Title: Our Planet Earth. (Illus.). 80p. (YA). (gr. 4 up). 2000. lib. bdg. 25.30 (*0-88682-953-4*, Creat Educ) Creative Co.
Planet Earth. Peter Murray. LC 96-47043. (Our Universe Ser.). (Illus.). 32p. (J). (gr. 2-6). 1997. lib. bdg. 22.79 (*1-56766-387-7*) Childs World.
Planet Earth. David Prebenna. (Macmillan World Atlas Ser.). (Illus.). 432p. 1996. 34.95 (*0-02-861266-3*, Pub. by Macmillan) S&S Trade.
***Planet Earth.** Kathryn Senior. (Fast Forward Ser.). (Illus.). 2000. pap. 9.95 (*0-531-16445-4*) Watts.
***Planet Earth.** Kathryn Senior. (Fast Forward Ser.). (Illus.). (J). 2000. 26.50 (*0-531-11879-7*) Watts.
Planet Earth. Time-Life Books Editors. Ed. by Jean Crawford. LC 97-28566. (Student Library). (Illus.). 128p. (J). (gr. 3-8). 1999. 14.99 (*0-7835-1350-X*) Time-Life.
Planet Earth. Claudio Vita-Finzi. 10p. (J). 1989. boxed set 13.95 (*0-671-67573-7*) S&S Bks Yung.
Planet Earth. F. Watt. (Science & Experiments Ser.). (Illus.). 48p. (J). (gr. 5-11). 1991. pap. 7.95 (*0-7460-0637-3*, Usborne) EDC.
Planet Earth. F. Watt. (Science & Experiments Ser.). (Illus.). 48p. (J). (gr. 5-11). 1999. lib. bdg. 15.95 (*0-88110-510-4*, Usborne) EDC.
Planet Earth. Karl Stumpff. Tr. by Philip Wayne. LC 59-5266. (Ann Arbor Science Library). 191p. reprint ed. pap. 59.30 (*0-608-30145-0*, 205565300029) Bks Demand.
Planet Earth: Cosmology, Geology, & the Evolution of Life & the Environment. Cesare Emiliani. (Illus.). 735p. (C). 1992. pap. text 44.95 (*0-521-40949-7*) Cambridge U Pr.
***Planet Earth: Discussion Guide.** 7th ed. 120p. (C). 1999. text 11.50 (*0-536-60486-X*) Pearson Custom.
Planet Earth: Egotists & Ecosystems. Ed. by Roger Rosen & Patra McSharry. (World Issues Ser.: Vol. 4). (Illus.). 176p. (YA). (gr. 7-12). 1991. pap. 8.95 (*0-8239-1335-X*); lib. bdg. 16.95 (*0-8239-1334-1*) Rosen Group.
Planet Earth: GeoScience Twenty. Richard E. Alley & Earl K. Graham. 176p. (C). 1996. spiral bd. 16.01 (*0-7872-2007-8*) Kendall-Hunt.
Planet Earth: Introduction to Earth Systems 272p. (C). 1999. text, lab manual ed. 22.00 (*0-536-02373-5*) Pearson Custom.
Planet Earth: Macmillan World Atlas. David Prebenna. (Illus.). 1997. 34.95 (*0-02-865339-4*) Mac Lib Ref.
Planet Earth: Problems & Prospects. John H. Spencer. Ed. by James A. Leith et al. 208p. 1995. 44.95 (*0-7735-1292-6*); pap. 19.95 (*0-7735-1312-4*) U of Toronto Pr.
***Planet Earth: The Complete Guide to Our Living World.** Martyn J Bramwell. (J). 1999. 16.99 (*1-84100-264-X*) Quadrillion Pubng.
Planet Earth: The Final Chapter. Hal Lindsey. 295p. 1998. pap. 12.99 (*1-888848-25-1*) Western Front.
Planet Earth: The View from Space. D. James Baker. (Frontiers of Space Ser.). (Illus.). 192p. 1990. text 36.50 (*0-674-67070-1*) HUP.
Planet Earth: The View from Space. D. James Baker. 208p. 1993. pap. text 12.95 (*0-674-67071-X*) HUP.
Planet Earth - Inside Out. Gail Gibbons. (Illus.). 395p. (J). (gr. 1 up). 1995. lib. bdg. 14.93 (*0-614-06506-2*, Wm Morrow) Morrow Avon.
Planet Earth & the New Geoscience. 3rd ed. Schmidt-Harbert. LC 98-66442. 649p. 1998. per. 48.95 (*0-7872-4296-9*) Kendall-Hunt.
***Planet Earth Expanding & the Eocene Tectonic Event: Paradigm Shift Toward Expansion Tectonics.** Karl W. Luckert. (Illus.). 78p. 1999. pap. 9.50 (*0-9675806-0-9*) Lufa.
***Planet Earth Home.** Mel Moench. LC 94-68754. (Illus.). lxxv, 481p. 1999. 65.00 (*0-9673711-0-4*) Osprey.
Planet Earth in Jeopardy: Environmental Consequences of Nuclear War (Scope 28) Lydia Dotto. 142p. 1986. 80.00 (*0-471-99836-2*) Wiley.
Planet Earth Inside Out. Gail Gibbons. (Illus.). 32p. (J). 1998. mass mkt. 4.95 (*0-688-15849-8*, Wm Morrow) Morrow Avon.
Planet Earth, 2000 A. D. rev. ed. Hal Lindsey. LC 96-60756. 314p. 1996. pap. 12.99 (*1-888848-05-7*) Western Front.
Planet Earth with Calendar 1998. Bertelsmann Cartographic Institute Staff. 432p. 1997. 39.95 (*0-02-862012-7*) Macmillan.
Planet Earth/Inside Out. Gail Gibbons. LC 94-41926. (Illus.). 32p. (J). (gr. 1 up). 1995. 15.93 (*0-688-09681-6*, Wm Morrow) Morrow Avon.
Planet Earth/Inside Out. Gail Gibbons. 1998. 10.15 (*0-606-13712-2*, Pub. by Turtleback) Demco.
Planet Earth's Secrets Unveiled. Fred E. Rosell, Jr. (Orig.). 1996. pap. 27.00 (*0-9653323-0-6*) Mstr Prods.
Planet Evolution. large type ed. Manuel J. Flashner. LC 96-96125. (Illus.). 108p. (Orig.). 1996. pap. 12.95 (*0-9642718-1-8*) Flashners Pub Co.
Planet Fires. Thomas Babe. 1987. pap. 5.25 (*0-8222-0896-2*) Dramatists Play.
Planet Harbor. Brian Bartlett. 95p. 1989. pap. 7.95 (*0-86492-102-0*, Pub. by Goose Ln Edits) Genl Dist Srvs.
***Planet Health: An Interdisciplinary Curriculum for Teaching Middle School Nutrition & Physical Activity.** Jill Carter et al. (Illus.). 312p. 2000. pap. write for info. (*0-7360-3105-7*) Human Kinetics.

P

***Planet Hong Kong: Popular Cinema & the Art of Entertainment.** David Bordwell. LC PN1993.5.H6B63 2000. 384p. 2000. pap. 29.95 (*0-674-00214-8*) HUP.

***Planet Hong Kong: Popular Cinema & the Art of Entertainment.** David Bordwell. LC PN1993.5.H6B63 2000. (Illus.). 384p. 2000. 65.00 (*0-674-00213-X*) HUP.

Planet, Humanity & the Albino - Aryan - European World Order. Donald E. Ramsey. LC 98-91355. 266p. 1998. 18.00 (*0-9663137-0-4*) Olmec Pub.

Planet Hunters. Dennis Brindell Fradin. LC 96-29721. (Illus.). 160p. (J). (gr. 5-9). 1997. per. 19.95 (*0-689-81323-6*) S&S Childrens.

Planet in Peril: Essays in Environmental Ethics. Ed. by Fred Westphal. LC 92-83845. 224p. (C). 1994. pap. text 43.00 (*0-03-073903-9*, Pub. by Harcourt Coll Pubs) Harcourt.

Planet in the Mist. (Star Wars Ser.). 1992. 10.00 (*0-87431-122-5*, 40049) West End Games.

Planet Joe. Joe Cole. (Illus.). 140p. (Orig.). 1992. pap. 9.00 (*1-880985-09-8*) Two Thirteen Sixty-one.

Planet Law School: What You Need to Know (Before You Go) . . . But Didn't Know to Ask. Atticus Falcon. LC 97-77865. 440p. 1998. pap. 19.95 (*1-888960-02-7*) Fine Print Pr.

Planet Magick. Keith Morgan. (Orig.). 1993. pap. 7.95 (*1-872189-11-3*, Pub. by Mandrake Pr) Holmes Pub.

Planet Management. Ed. by Michael Williams. LC 92-34497. (Illustrated Encyclopedia of World Geography Ser.). (Illus.). 256p. 1993. 45.00 (*0-19-520945-1*) OUP.

Planet Management: Limits to Growth, Computer Simulation, & the Emergence of Global Spaces. Fernando I. Elichirigoity. LC 98-43942. (Media Topographies Ser.). 136p. 1999. text 64.95 (*0-8101-1587-5*); pap. text 24.95 (*0-8101-1588-3*) Northwestern U Pr.

Planet Mars: A History of Observation & Discovery. Sheehan. LC 96-4485. 270p. 1996. 45.00 (*0-8165-1640-5*) U of Ariz Pr.

Planet Mars: A History of Observation & Discovery. William Sheehan. LC 96-4485. (Illus.). 270p. 1996. pap. 19.95 (*0-8165-1641-3*) U of Ariz Pr.

Planet Medicine: From Stone Age Shamanism to Post-Industrial Healing. 5th rev. ed. Richard Grossinger. LC 82-50278. 496p. 1990. pap. 16.95 (*1-55643-093-0*) North Atlantic.

Planet Medicine Vol. I: Origins. 6th rev. ed. Richard Grossinger. LC 95-22428. (Illus.). 500p. (C). 1995. pap. 25.00 (*1-55643-179-1*) North Atlantic.

Planet Medicine Vol. II: Modalities. 6th ed. Richard Grossinger. LC 95-22428. (Illus.). 500p. 1995. pap. 25.00 (*1-55643-214-3*) North Atlantic.

***Planet Meditation Kit: How to Harness the Energy of the Planets for Good Fortune, Health, & Well-Being, Set.** Harish Johari. LC 99-33221. (Illus.). 32p. 1999. pap., boxed set 35.00 incl. audio (*0-89281-759-3*) Inner Tradit.

***Planet Melta & the People of Melta.** John C. Tibbitts. 119p. 1998. 14.95 (*1-887750-96-7*) Rutledge Bks.

Planet Monster. Heather Maisner. LC 95-47979. (Illus.). (J). 1996. write for info. (*1-56402-864-X*) Candlewick Pr.

Planet Monster: A Math-Fun Gamebook. Heather Maisner. LC 95-47979. (Gamebks.). (Illus.). 32p. (J). (gr. 1-3). 1997. reprint ed. pap. 5.99 (*0-7636-0292-2*) Candlewick Pr.

Planet Monster: A Number Puzzle Adventure. Heather Maisner. LC 95-47979. (Illus.). 32p. (J). (ps-3). 1996. 12.99 (*0-7636-0057-1*) Candlewick Pr.

Planet Musician: The World Music Sourcebook for Musicians. Julie L. Lieberman. 152p. 1998. otabind 22.95 incl. audio compact disk (*0-7935-8695-X*) H Leonard.

Planet Neptune. Patrick Moore. 1989. text 29.95 (*0-470-21366-3*) P-H.

Planet News: Poems, 1961-1964. Allen Ginsberg. LC 68-25477. (Pocket Poets Ser.: No. 23). (Orig.). 1968. pap. 8.95 (*0-87286-020-5*) City Lights.

Planet Observer's Handbook. Fred W. Price. (Illus.). 430p. (C). 1994. text 39.95 (*0-521-44257-5*) Cambridge U Pr.

Planet Observer's Handbook. Fred W. Price. (Illus.). 432p. (C). 1998. reprint ed. pap. 19.95 (*0-521-62708-7*) Cambridge U Pr.

***Planet Observer's Handbook.** 2nd ed. Fred William Price. (Illus.). 450p. 2000. pap. 24.95 (*0-521-78981-8*) Cambridge U Pr.

Planet Ocean. Brian Bett. Ed. by Fran Balkwill. (Making Sense of Science Ser.). (Illus.). 32p. (J). 1997. pap. 12.00 (*1-85578-094-1*, Pub. by Portland Pr Ltd) Ashgate Pub Co.

Planet Ocean. Ray Troll & Bradford Matsen. (Illus.). 133p. (Orig.). 1995. pap. 19.95 (*0-89815-778-1*) Ten Speed Pr.

Planet Ocean: A Story of Life, the Sea, & Dancing to the Fossil Record. Ray Troll. LC 94-5174. (Illus.). 133p. 1994. 29.95 (*0-89815-618-1*) Ten Speed Pr.

Planet of Adventure. Jack Vance. 544p. 1993. 12.95 (*0-312-85488-9*) Orb NYC.

Planet of Darkness. TSR Inc. Staff. (Adventure Ser.). 1999. 12.95 (*0-7869-1328-2*, Pub. by TSR Inc) Random.

Planet of Destiny. Kenneth Unger. 40p. 1998. pap. 8.00 (*0-8059-4402-8*) Dorrance.

***Planet of Joy.** Charles Mills. (Shadow Creek Ranch Ser.: Vol. 12). 1999. pap. 5.99 (*0-8280-1359-4*) Review & Herald.

Planet of Junior Brown. Hamilton. (J). 1998. pap. 4.50 (*0-87628-347-4*) Ctr Appl Res.

Planet of Junior Brown. Virginia Hamilton. LC 71-155264. 240p. (YA). (gr. 5-9). 1971. lib. bdg. 17.00 (*0-02-742510-X*, Mac Bks Young Read) S&S Childrens.

Planet of Junior Brown. Virginia Hamilton. (YA). 1993. 9.60 (*0-606-05975-X*, Pub. by Turtleback) Demco.

Planet of Junior Brown. 2nd ed. Virginia Hamilton. LC 92-40350. 224p. (YA). (gr. 3-7). 1993. reprint ed. mass mkt. 4.50 (*0-689-71721-0*) Aladdin.

Planet of Junior Brown. 3rd ed. Virginia Hamilton. LC 85-16651. (Illus.). 224p. (YA). (gr. 5-9). 1986. mass mkt. 3.95 (*0-02-043540-1*) Macmillan.

Planet of No Return. Harry Harrison. 256p. 1993. mass mkt. 3.99 (*0-8125-3524-3*, Pub. by Tor Bks) St Martin.

Planet of No Return. N. Vardy. LC 97-90800. 221p. 1998. pap. 15.95 (*0-533-12473-5*) Vantage.

Planet of Terror: A Choose-Your-Challenge Gamebook. Patrick Burston. LC 95-47634. (Candlewick Gamebks.). (Illus.). 48p. (Orig.). (J). (gr. k-3). 1996. pap. 5.99 (*1-56402-851-8*) Candlewick Pr.

***Planet of the Apes.** L. Boulle. LC 00-24533. (Cinema Classics Ser.). 192p. 2000. 7.99 (*0-517-20948-9*) Random Hse Value.

***Planet of the Apes.** Prima Publishing Staff. (Illus.). 96p. 2000. pap. 12.99 (*0-7615-2596-3*) Prima Pub.

Planet of the Apes. Pierre Boulle. 1993. reprint ed. lib. bdg. 25.95 (*0-89968-331-2*, Lghtyr Pr) Buccaneer Bks.

Planet of the Apes As American Myth: Race & Politics in the Films & Television Series. Eric Greene. LC 95-44163. (Illus.). 261p. 1996. lib. bdg. 35.00 (*0-7864-0087-0*) McFarland & Co.

Planet of the Apes As American Myth: Race, Politics, & Popular Culture. Eric Greene. LC 98-31193. (Illus.). 264p. 1998. reprint ed. pap. 17.95 (*0-8195-6329-3*, Wesleyan Univ Pr) U Pr of New Eng.

Planet of the Apes Collectibles: An Unauthorized Guide with Trivia & Values. Christopher Sausville. LC 97-80173. 129p. 1998. pap. 29.95 (*0-7643-0332-5*) Schiffer.

Planet of the Apes Revisited. Joe Russo et al. (Illus.). 212p. (Orig.). (YA). (gr. 9-12). 1991. pap. 12.95 (*0-9627508-2-4*) Retro Vision.

***Planet of the Apes RPG.** (Illus.). 20p. (Orig.). 1999. pap. 10.00 (*1-58265-009-8*, 00033) Orphan Press.

Planet of the Blind. Stephen Kuusisto. 208p. 1998. pap. 11.95 (*0-385-33327-7*) Dell.

Planet of the Blind. large type ed. Stephen Kuusisto. LC 98-9769. (Core Ser.). 253p. 1998. 26.95 (*0-7838-0126-2*, G K Hall Lrg Type) Mac Lib Ref.

Planet of the Damned. Harry Harrison. 1993. mass mkt. 4.50 (*0-8125-3507-3*, Pub. by Tor Bks) St Martin.

Planet of the Dinosaurs. Barbara Carr. LC 92-9287. (Illus.). 32p. (J). (gr. k-3). 1992. 16.95 (*0-89334-161-4*, 161-4) Humanics Ltd.

Planet of the Dips. Bruce Coville. LC 95-69331. (Space Brat Ser.: No. 4). (Illus.). 71p. (J). (gr. 4-7). 1995. 14.00 (*0-671-50090-2*, Minstrel Bks); pap. 3.99 (*0-671-50092-9*, Minstrel Bks) PB.

Planet of the Dips. Bruce Coville. (Space Brat Ser.: No. 4). (J). (gr. 4-7). 1995. 9.19 (*0-606-08188-7*, Pub. by Turtleback) Demco.

Planet of the Grapes: Show Biz Jokes & Riddles. Charles Keller. (Illus.). 40p. (J). (gr. 3-7). 1992. 13.95 (*0-945912-17-X*) Pippin Pr.

Planet of the Jews. Philip Graubart. LC 98-72713. 201p. 1999. pap. 13.95 (*0-88739-186-9*) Creat Arts Bk.

Planet of the Nose Pickers, No. 2. Gordon Korman. 140p. (YA). 2000. lib. bdg. 14.49 (*0-7868-2571-5*, Pub. by Hyprn Child) Little.

Planet of the Nosepickers, Vol. 2. Gordon Korman. (Illus.). 140p. (YA). (gr. 2-6). 2000. pap. 3.99 (*0-7868-1344-X*, Pub. by Hyprn Ppbks) Little.

Planet of the Perfectly Awful People. Joseph Robinette. 40p. (YA). (gr. 7 up). 1979. pap. 3.00 (*0-87129-889-9*, P46) Dramatic Pub.

Planet of Twilight. Barbara Hambly. (Star Wars Ser.). 1997. 22.95 (*0-614-27885-6*) Bantam.

Planet of Twilight. Barbara Hambly. LC 96-46341. (Star Wars Ser.). 416p. 1998. reprint ed. mass mkt. 5.99 (*0-553-57517-1*) Bantam.

Planet of Waters. Douglas Anderson. 135p. (Orig.). 1983. pap. 7.95 (*0-912549-00-9*) Bread & Butter.

Planet of Youth. Coblentz. 1952. 3.50 (*0-686-21530-3*); pap. 1.00 (*0-686-21531-1*) Fantasy Pub Co.

***Planet Omicron.** Julie Ferris & Jane Tassie. LC 99-48394. (Math for Martians Ser.). (Illus.). 32p. (J). (gr. 1-3). 2000. pap. 5.95 (*0-7534-5277-4*, Kingfisher) LKC.

Planet on the Desk: Selected & New Poems, 1960-1990. David Young. LC 90-50913. (Wesleyan Poetry Ser.). 160p. 1991. text 30.00 (*0-8195-2187-6*, Wesleyan Univ Pr) U Pr of New Eng.

Planet on the Table. Kim Stanley Robinson. 256p. 1987. reprint ed. pap. 3.50 (*0-8125-5237-7*) Tor Bks.

Planet Origami. (Illus.). 32p. (J). (gr. 3 up). 1999. lib. bdg. 17.95 (*1-56674-268-4*) Forest Hse.

Planet Origami. Steve Biddle & Megumi Biddle. (Illus.). 32p. (J). (gr. 4 up). 1998. pap. 8.95 (*0-7641-0694-5*) Barron.

***Planet Parenthood: Adapting to Your New Life Form.** Julie Tilsner. LC 99-57945. 256p. 2000. pap. 14.95 (*0-8092-2518-2*, 251820, Contemporary Bks) NTC Contemp Pub Co.

Planet Pee Wee, 34. Judy Delton. (Pee Wee Scouts Ser.). 1998. 9.09 (*0-606-13699-1*, Pub. by Turtleback) Demco.

Planet Peru. Marilyn Bridges. (Illus.). 108p. 1991. 53.00 (*0-89381-469-5*) Aperture.

Planet Pirates. Anne McCaffrey et al. 864p. (Orig.). 1993. pap. 15.00 (*0-671-72187-9*) Baen Bks.

Planet Plague. John Whitman. (Star Wars: No. 3). 144p. (J). (gr. 4-8). 1997. pap. 4.99 (*0-553-48452-4*, Skylark BDD) BDD Bks Young Read.

Planet Plague. John Whitman. (Star Wars: No. 3). (J). (gr. 4-8). 1997. mass mkt. 4.99 (*0-553-54298-2*, Skylark BDD) BDD Bks Young Read.

Planet Plague. John Whitman. (Star Wars: No. 3). (J). 1997. 10.09 (*0-606-11890-X*, Pub. by Turtleback) Demco.

Planet Plague see Galaxy of Fear Boxed Set

Planet Protection: Biodiversity, Conservation, Environmental Education & Degradation & Socio-Economic Development. Ed. by S. P. Shukla et al. xvii, 268p. 1997. 38.00 (*81-7099-628-7*, Pub. by Mittal Pubs Dist) Nataraj Bks.

***Planet Quest: The Epic Discovery of Alien Solar Systems.** Ken Croswell. (Illus.). 324p. 1999. text 25.00 (*0-7881-6047-8*) DIANE Pub.

Planet Quest: The Epic Discovery of Alien Solar Systems. Ken Croswell. LC 98-15032. (Illus.). 336p. (C). 1998. pap. 14.00 (*0-15-600612-X*, Harvest Bks) Harcourt.

Planet Quest: The Epic Discovery of Alien Solar Systems. Ken Croswell. LC 97-27751. 1997. write for info. (*0-19-850198-6*) OUP.

Planet Quest: The Epic Discovery of Alien Solar Systems. Ken Croswell. LC 97-9473. (Illus.). 336p. 1997. 24.50 (*0-684-83252-6*) S&S Trade.

Planet Racers: Life Cycle. Jim Lawson & Peter Laird. LC 99-176320. (Illus.). 300p. 1997. pap. 14.95 (*0-9661985-0-6*) Zeromayo Studios.

Planet Racers: Off-Season. Jim Lawson & Peter Laird. (Illus.). 175p. 1998. pap. 7.95 (*0-9661985-1-4*) Zeromayo Studios.

Planet Savers. Marion Zimmer Bradley. 1985. pap. 3.50 (*0-441-67026-1*) Ace Bks.

***Planet Savers: Also Including the Waterfall.** Marion Zimmer Bradley. LC 00-33492. (Illus.). 2001. write for info. (*0-7838-9065-6*, G K Hall & Co) Mac Lib Ref.

Planet Savers - Winds of Darkover. Marion Zimmer Bradley. 320p. 1995. mass mkt. 4.99 (*0-88677-630-9*, Pub. by DAW Bks) Penguin Putnam.

Planet Soup: World Fusion Music, Set, incl. 3 cass. (Illus.). 48p. 1995. pap. 44.95 incl. audio compact disk (*1-55961-311-4*); pap. 29.95 incl. audio (*1-55961-312-2*) Relaxtn Co.

Planet Squeezebox: Accordion Music from Around the World, Vol. 1. Contrib. by Michal Shapiro. 56p. 1995. 44.95 incl. audio compact disk (*1-55961-319-X*, CD3470); 34.95 incl. audio (*1-55961-320-3*, CD3470) Relaxtn Co.

Planet They Once Called Green. Worthington Elementary Staff. 32p. (J). 1994. write for info. (*0-9634087-3-9*) Silly Billys Bks.

Planet Under Stress: The Challenge of Global Change. Ed. by Constance Mungall & Digby McLaren. (Illus.). 360p. 1990. pap. text 29.95 (*0-19-540731-8*) OUP.

Planet Venus. Mikhail Y. Marov & David H. Grinspoon. Tr. by Tobias Owen et al. LC 98-10158. (Planetary Exploration Ser.). (Illus.). 464p. 1998. 65.00 (*0-300-04975-7*) Yale U Pr.

Planet Vulcan: History, Nature, Tables. L. Weston. 35p. 1941. 11.00 (*0-86690-196-5*, 1515-01) Am Fed Astrologers.

Planet Was, Vol. 1. Amy Boesky. (J). (ps-3). 1990. 14.95 (*0-316-10084-6*, Joy St Bks) Little.

Planet, with Mother, May I? Alma L. Villanueva. LC 92-46299. 136p. 1993. pap. 12.00 (*0-927534-17-7*) Biling Rev-Pr.

Planet X. Michael J. Friedman. (Star Trek: The Next Generation Ser.). (Illus.). 265p. 1998. per. 6.50 (*0-671-01916-3*) PB.

Planet Yes. Dallas Lewis & Lisa Lewis. (Illus.). 32p. (Orig.). (J). (gr. 3). 1994. 13.95 (*0-9634087-1-2*); pap. 6.95 (*0-9634087-2-0*) Silly Billys Bks.

Planeta de los Ratonejos (The Planet of the Bunnyrats) Renata S. Campo. (SPA.). 64p. (YA). 1992. pap. 5.99 (*968-16-3749-6*, Pub. by Fondo) Continental Bk.

Planeta Fraerov: Arabeski. Roman Sonynn. Ed. by Lubov Levin. LC 94-61878. (Biblioteka Bibliofila Ser.).Tr. of Friars' Planet. (RUS.). 48p. 1996. pap. 19.95 (*0-914265-54-7*) New Eng Pub MA.

Planeta Tierra: Ciencia y Experimentos. E. Watt. (SPA.). pap. 8.95 (*950-724-135-3*) Lumen ARG.

Planeta Tierra (Planet Earth) see Enciclopedia Ilustrada de Ciencia Naturaleza (Understanding Science & Nature)

Planetarium. Nathalie Sarraute. (FRE.). 1972. pap. 10.95 (*0-8288-3740-6*, F124451) Fr & Eur.

Planetarium. Nathalie Sarraute. (Folio Ser.: No. 92). (FRE.). 1972. pap. 8.95 (*2-07-036092-X*) Schoenhof.

Planetarium. Nathalie Sarraute. Tr. by Maria Jolas from FRE. (Orig.). pap. 9.95 (*0-7145-0444-0*) Riverrun NY.

Planetarium 57 - Mene Tequel Urbasin: Poesias. Rene Schneegans. LC 91-70700. (Coleccion Hispanica - Poetica: No. 1). (SPA.). 173p. (Orig.). 1991. pap. 15.00 (*0-89729-599-4*) Ediciones.

Planetarization of Consciousness. Dane Rudhyar. (Dane Rudhyar Ser.). 318p. 1977. pap. 22.95 (*0-943358-16-7*) Aurora Press.

***Planetary: All over the World & Other Stories.** Warren Ellis. (Planetary Ser.). (Illus.). 144p. (YA). 2000. pap. 14.95 (*1-56389-648-6*, Pub. by DC Comics) Time Warner.

Planetary Adventures. Moore. Ed. by Jance Sellers. 1999. per. 15.00 (*0-671-04007-3*, Pocket Books) PB.

Planetary Aeronomy & Astronomy. Ed. by S. K. Atreya & J. J. Caldwell. (Advances in Space Research Ser.: Vol. 1, No. 9). (Illus.). 216p. 1981. pap. 34.00 (*0-08-028385-3*, Pergamon Pr) Elsevier.

Planetary & Interstellar Processes Relevant to the Origins of Life. D. C. Whittet. LC 97-20235. 1997. text 129.00 (*0-7923-4597-5*) Kluwer Academic.

***Planetary & Lunar Co-ordinates, 2001-2020.** Nautical Almanac Office Staff. 70p. 2000. pap. 40.00 incl. cd-rom (*0-11-887312-1*, Pub. by Statnry Office) Balogh.

Planetary & Lunar Exploration. National Research Council Staff. (Space Science in the Twenty-First Century Ser.). 128p. (C). 1988. pap. text 14.95 (*0-309-03885-5*) Natl Acad Pr.

Planetary & Proto-Planetary Nebulae: From IRAS to ISO. Ed. by Andrea P. Martinez. (C). 1987. text 168.00 (*90-277-2517-9*) Kluwer Academic.

Planetary & Stellar Worlds: A Popular Exposition of the Great Discoveries & Theories of Modern Astronomy. Ormsby M. Mitchel. Ed. by I. Bernard Cohen. LC 79-7976. (Three Centuries of Science in America Ser.). (Illus.). 1980. reprint ed. lib. bdg. 25.95 (*0-405-12559-3*) Ayer.

Planetary Aspects: From Conflict to Cooperation. rev. ed. Tracy Marks. LC 86-26445. 225p. (Orig.). 1987. pap. 13.95 (*0-916360-32-6*) CRCS Pubns CA.

Planetary Astronomy: From Ancient Times to the Third Millennium. Ronald A. Schorn. (Illus.). 448p. 1998. 44.95 (*0-89096-787-3*) Tex A&M Univ Pr.

Planetary Astronomy from the Renaissance to the Rise of Astrophysics Pt. B: The 18th & 19th Centuries. Ed. by Rene Taton et al. (General History of Astronomy Ser.: No. 2). (Illus.). 295p. (C). 1995. text 74.95 (*0-521-35168-5*) Cambridge U Pr.

Planetary Astronomy from the Renaissance to the Rise of Astrophysics, Pt. A: Tycho Brahe to Newton. Ed. by Rene Taton & Curtis Wilson. No. 4. (Illus.). 240p. (C). 1989. write for info. (*0-318-64351-0*) Cambridge U Pr.

Planetary Atmospheres & Ionospheres & Reference Atmospheres. L. V. Zasova. (Advances in Space Research Ser.: Vol. 19). 154p. 1997. pap. 110.00 (*0-08-043284-0*, Pergamon Pr) Elsevier.

Planetary Bargain: Corporate Social Responsibility Comes of Age. Michael Hopkins. LC 98-8575. 229p. 1998. text 65.00 (*0-312-21833-8*) St Martin.

Planetary Brother. M. Moore. (I Come As a Brother Ser.: Bk. 4). 176p. (Orig.). 1991. pap. 10.95 (*0-9614010-6-0*) High Mesa Pr.

Planetary Brother. 2nd rev. ed. Bartholomew. LC 98-55705. 176p. 1999. pap. 12.95 (*1-56170-388-5*, 870) Hay House.

Planetary Containments: A Study of 990 Combinations. John Sandbach & Ronn Ballard. 336p. 1980. per. 12.95 (*0-930706-05-6*) Seek-It Pubns.

Planetary Cycles: That Get You from Beginning to End Without a Guide. Betty Lundsted. LC 84-51107. (Illus.). 194p. (Orig.). 1984. pap. 12.95 (*0-87728-630-2*) Weiser.

Planetary Dreams: The Quest to Discover Life Beyond Earth. Robert Shapiro. LC 98-35326. 273p. 1999. 27.95 (*0-471-17936-1*) Wiley.

Planetary Electrodynamics, 2 vols. Ed. by Samuel C. Coroniti & J. Hughes. (Illus.). xL, 1092p. (C). 1969. text 835.00 (*0-677-13600-5*) Gordon & Breach.

Planetary Emergencies: The Collision of an Asteroid or Comet with the Earth. Ralph Coppola. LC 96-11736. 1996. write for info. (*0-387-94669-1*) Spr-Verlag.

Planetary Emergencies: 10th International Seminar on Nuclear War. K. Goebel. (Science & Culture Ser.). 336p. 1992. text 114.00 (*981-02-1193-7*) World Scientific Pub.

Planetary Emergencies: 11th International Seminar on Nuclear War. K. Goebel. (Science & Culture Ser.). 332p. 1992. text 106.00 (*981-02-1194-5*) World Scientific Pub.

Planetary Gear. Ted Pearson. LC 91-67074. (Roof Bks.). 72p. (Orig.). 1991. pap. 8.95 (*0-937804-43-6*) Segue NYC.

Planetary Harmonics of Speculative Markets. Larry Pesavento. (Illus.). 202p. 1997. reprint ed. pap. 49.00 (*0-934380-32-5*, 336) Traders Pr.

Planetary Harmonies: An Astrological Book of Meditations. Joan Hodgson. (Illus.). 160p. 1990. reprint ed. (*0-85487-081-4*) White Eagle.

Planetary Herbology. Michael Tierra. Ed. by David Frawley. LC 88-15901. (Illus.). 490p. (Orig.). 1990. reprint ed. pap. 17.95 (*0-941524-27-2*) Lotus Pr.

Planetary Herbology Book with Windows 95 Program. Michael Tierra & Steve Blake. 490p. 1998. pap. 54.95 incl. cd-rom (*0-914955-40-3*) Lotus Pr.

Planetary Herbology Computer Book: DOS WIN 3.1. Michael Tierra & Steve Blake. 490p. 1998. pap. 65.00 incl. 3.5 hd (*0-914955-41-1*) Lotus Pr.

Planetary Heredity. Michel Gauquelin. (Illus.). 26p. (Orig.). 1988. pap. 12.95 (*0-935127-01-1*) ACS Pubns.

Planetary Influence & the Human Soul. Manly P. Hall. 32p. 1957. pap. 4.95 (*0-89314-341-3*) Philos Res.

Planetary Influences & Therapeutic Uses of Precious Stones. George F. Kunz. 63p. 1985. pap. 4.50 (*0-89540-153-3*, SB-153) Sun Pub.

Planetary Influences on Human Affairs. Bangalore V. Raman. (C). 1992. 4.50 (*81-85273-90-1*, Pub. by Ranjan Pubs) S Asia.

Planetary Influences Upon Plants: Cosmological Botany. Ernst M. Kranich. 184p. 1985. pap. 12.95 (*0-938250-20-5*) Anthroposophic.

Planetary Initiation. Rita Milios. LC 94-60531. 128p. 1995. pap. 9.95 (*0-9641657-0-8*) Tools for Transform.

Planetary Interest. Ed. by Kennedy Graham. LC 98-45307. (Illus.). 320p. (C). 1999. text 55.00 (*0-8135-2678-7*); pap. text 22.00 (*0-8135-2679-5*) Rutgers U Pr.

Planetary Interiors. Ed. by H. Stiller & R. Z. Sagdeev. (Advances in Space Research Ser.: Vol. 1, No. 7). (Illus.). 265p. 1981. pap. 41.00 (*0-08-028382-9*, Pergamon Pr) Elsevier.

Planetary Ionospheres & Magnetospheres. T. E. Cravens & Margaret G. Kivelson. (Advances in Space Research Ser.: Vol. 20). 184p. 1997. pap. 100.50 (*0-08-043297-2*, Pergamon Pr) Elsevier.

Planetary Landscapes. Ronald Greeley. (Illus.). 256p. (C). 1985. 95.00 (*0-04-551080-6*) Routledge.

Planetary Landscapes. rev. ed. Ronald Greeley. (Illus.). 288p. (C). 1987. pap. text 34.95 (*0-04-551081-4*) Routledge.

Planetary Landscapes. 2nd ed. Ronald Greeley. LC 93-6885. 1993. write for info. (*0-412-49480-9*) Chapman & Hall.

P

Planetary, Lunar & Solar Positions A. D. 2 to A. D. 1649 at 5 Day & 10 Day Intervals. Bryant Tuckerman. LC 64-14093. (Memoirs Ser.: Vol. 59). 842p. 1964. 30.00 (*0-87169-059-4*, M059-TUB) Am Philos.

Planetary, Lunar & Solar Positions 601 B. C. to A. D. 1 at 5-Day & 10-Day Intervals. Bryant Tuckerman. LC 62-14516. (Memoirs Ser.: Vol. 56). 333p. 1979. reprint ed. 20.00 (*0-87169-056-X*, M056-TUB) Am Philos.

Planetary, Lunar & Solar Positions, 1650-1805. Owen Gingerich & Barbara L. Welther. LC 83-71297. (Memoirs Ser.: Vol. 59S). 1983. 20.00 (*0-87169-590-1*, M59S-GIO) Am Philos.

Planetary Magick: A Complete System for Knowledge & Attainment. Melita Denning & Osborne Phillips. LC 82-83316. (Aurum Solis Ser.). (Illus.). 456p. (Orig.). 1989. pap. 15.00 (*0-87542-193-8*) Llewellyn Pubns.

Planetary Magnetospheric Physics I: Proceedings of Symposium 6 & of Topical Meeting of the Interdisciplinary Scientific Commission D (Meetings D2 & D4) of the COSPAR 28th Plenary Meeting Held in The Hague, The Netherlands, 25 June-6 July, 1990. Ed. by R. J. Grard et al. (Advances in Space Research Ser.: Vol. 11). 298p. 1991. pap. 147.00 (*0-08-041834-1*, Pergamon Pr) Elsevier.

Planetary Magnetospheric Physics II: Proceedings of Symposium 5 & the Topical Meetings of the COSPAR Interdisciplinary Scientific Commission B (Meetings B1 & B6) of the COSPAR 28th Plenary Meeting Held in The Hague, The Netherlands, 25 June-6 July, 1990. Ed. by Margaret G. Kivelson et al. (Advances in Space Research Ser.: Vol. 12). 414p. 1992. pap. 165.00 (*0-08-041854-6*, Pergamon Pr) Elsevier.

Planetary Mapping. Ed. by Ronald Greeley & Raymond Batson. (Cambridge Planetary Science Ser.: No. 6). (Illus.). 310p. (C). 1990. text 95.00 (*0-521-30774-0*) Cambridge U Pr.

***Planetary Materials.** J. J. Papike. LC 99-474392. (Reviews in Mineralogy Ser.: Vol. 36). (Illus.). 1056p. 1998. pap. 40.00 (*0-939950-46-4*) Mineralogical Soc.

Planetary Mind see Creating Consciousness: Science as the Language of God

Planetary Music: Understanding Astrological Rhythms. Edwin Rose. (Illus.). 445p. 1998. pap. 19.95 (*0-9661522-0-4*) Guiding Star.

Planetary Mysteries. 2nd ed. Ed. by Richard Grossinger. (Illus.). 200p. 1986. pap. 12.95 (*0-938190-90-3*) North Atlantic.

Planetary Nebulae. David R. Flower. (International Astronomical Union Symposia Ser.). 1983. pap. text 82.50 (*90-277-1558-0*) Kluwer Academic.

Planetary Nebulae. Ed. by David R. Flower. 1983. lib. bdg. 175.00 (*90-277-1557-2*) Kluwer Academic.

Planetary Nebulae. G. A. Gurzadyan. Ed. & Tr. by D. G. Hummer. LC 69-11664. 314p. 1971. text 175.50 (*90-277-0117-2*) Kluwer Academic.

Planetary Nebulae. Habing. 1997. pap. text 90.00 (*0-7923-4893-1*) Kluwer Academic.

Planetary Nebulae. Ed. by Harm J. Habing & Henny J. Lamers. LC 97-45955. 507p. 1998. lib. bdg. write for info. (*0-7923-4892-3*) Kluwer Academic.

Planetary Nebulae. Hynes. 1991. 24.95 (*0-943396-30-1*) Willmann-Bell.

Planetary Nebulae. Stuart R. Pottasch. 1983. text 162.50 (*90-277-1672-2*) Kluwer Academic.

Planetary Nebulae. Ed. by Silvia Torres-Peimbert. (C). 1988. pap. text 108.00 (*0-7923-0003-3*); lib. bdg. 220.50 (*0-7923-0002-5*) Kluwer Academic.

Planetary Nebulae: Proceedings of the I. A. U. Symposium, No. 34, Tatranska, Lomnica, Czechoslovakia, 1967. International Astronomical Union Staff. Ed. by Donald E. Osterbrock & C. R. O'Dell. (I.A.U. Symposia Ser.: No. 34). 469p. 1965. text 121.50 (*90-277-0134-2*) Kluwer Academic.

Planetary Nebulae: Proceedings of the I. A. U. Symposium, No. 78. International Astronomical Union Staff. Ed. by Yervant Terzian. 1978. pap. text 85.50 (*90-277-0873-8*) Kluwer Academic.

Planetary Nebulae: Proceedings of the I. A. U. Symposium, No. 78. International Astronomical Union Staff. Ed. by Yervant Terzian. 1978. lib. bdg. 117.50 (*90-277-0872-X*) Kluwer Academic.

Planetary Nebulae: Proceedings of the 155th Symposium of the International Astronomical Union Held in Innsbruck, Austria, July 13-17, 1992. Ed. by Weinberger. LC 93-21552. 644p. (C). 1993. pap. text 107.50 (*0-7923-2440-4*) Kluwer Academic.

Planetary Nebulae: Proceedings of the 155th Symposium of the International Astronomical Union Held in Innsbruck, Austria, July 13-17, 1992. Ed. by R. Weinberger. LC 93-21552. 644p. (C). 1993. lib. bdg. 218.50 (*0-7923-2439-0*) Kluwer Academic.

Planetary Overload: Global Environmental Change & the Health of the Human Species. A. J. McMichael. LC 92-38292. (Illus.). 368p. (C). 1993. text 64.95 (*0-521-44138-2*) Cambridge U Pr.

Planetary Overload: Global Environmental Change & the Health of the Human Species. A. J. McMichael. (Canto Book Ser.). (Illus.). 370p. (C). 1995. pap. 13.95 (*0-521-55871-9*) Cambridge U Pr.

Planetary Petrology & Geochemistry: The Lawrence A. Taylor Volume. Ed. by Gregory A. Snyder et al. LC 99-61137. (International Book Ser.: Vol. 2). (Illus.). 277p. (Orig.). 1999. pap. 89.95 (*0-9665869-1-3*, Pub. by Bellwther Pubg) Geol Soc.

Planetary Planting. Louise Riotte. LC 98-5959. 1998. pap. 16.95 (*1-58017-066-8*) Storey Bks.

Planetary Programs & Tables. Pierre Bretagnon & Jean L. Simon. LC 86-9099. 160p. 1986. pap. text 19.95 (*0-943396-08-5*) Willmann-Bell.

Planetary Progressions in the Mystic Quadrates. Thomas Morrell. (Illus.). 90p. 1997. spiral bd. 15.95 (*0-9665163-0-3*) Awakening IA.

Planetary Satellites. Ed. by Joseph A. Burns. LC 76-7475. 598p. 1977. text 47.00 (*0-8165-0552-7*) U of Ariz Pr.

Planetary Science: A Lunar Perspective. Stuart R. Taylor. LC 82-193. (Illus.). 512p. (C). 1982. 30.00 (*0-942862-00-7*) Lunar & Planet Inst.

Planetary Sciences: American & Soviet Research - Proceedings from the U. S.-U. S. S. R. Workshop on Planetary Sciences. National Academy of Science Staff. Ed. by T. M. Donahue et al. 304p. 1991. pap. text 29.00 (*0-309-04333-6*) Natl Acad Pr.

Planetary Scientist's Companion. Katharina Lodders & Bruce Fegley, Jr. (Illus.). 400p. 1998. pap. 24.95 (*0-19-511694-1*) OUP.

Planetary Service. Eugen Rosenstock-Huessy. Tr. by Mark Huessy & Freya Von Moltke from GER. LC 78-68422. 1978. pap. 13.00 (*0-912148-09-8*) Argo Bks.

Planetary Studies, ser. vol. 7. Keating. (Advances in Space Research Ser.). 1988. pap. 56.00 (*0-08-036635-X*, Pergamon Pr) Elsevier.

Planetary Studies: Proceedings of Symposium 4 & the Topical Meeting of the COSPAR Interdisciplinary Scientific Commission B (Meetings B7 & B8) of the COSPAR 28th Plenary Meeting Held in The Hague, The Netherlands, 25 June-6 July, 1990. Ed. by M. Fulchignoni et al. (Advances in Space Research Ser.: Vol. 12). 202p. 1992. pap. 176.00 (*0-08-042042-7*, Pergamon Pr) Elsevier.

***Planetary Survival Manual: A Guide for Living in a World of Diminishing Resources.** Matthew Stein. LC 00-24031. (Illus.). 256p. 2000. 24.95 (*1-57416-046-X*); pap. 14.95 (*1-57416-047-8*) Clear Light.

Planetary Symbolism in the Horoscope. Karen Hamaker-Zondag. 208p. (Orig.). 1996. pap. 12.95 (*0-87728-868-2*) Weiser.

Planetary System. 2nd ed. David Morrison & Tobias C. Owen. Ed. by Julie Berrisford. (Illus.). 570p. (C). 1992. 91.00 (*0-201-55450-X*) Addison-Wesley.

Planetary Systems - Formation, Evolution & Detection: Proceedings of the 1st International Conference, Held in Pasadena, California on December 8-10, 1992. Ed. by Bernard F. Burke et al. LC 94-20181. 1994. text 323.00 (*0-7923-2895-7*) Kluwer Academic.

***Planetary Systems from the Ancient Greeks to Kepler.** Theodor S. Jacobsen. LC 99-14605. (Illus.). 275p. 1999. 65.00 (*0-295-97821-X*) U of Wash Pr.

Planetary Theology. Tissa Balasuriya. LC 83-19339. 288p. (Orig.). reprint ed. pap. 89.30 (*0-8357-2665-7*, 204020100015) Bks Demand.

Planetary Volcanism: A Study of Volcanic Activity in the Solar System. Peter Cattermole. 1990. text 72.95 (*0-470-21602-6*) P-H.

Planetas. Joy Evans & Joellen Moore. (SPA., Illus.). 16p. (J). (gr. 1-3). 1992. pap., teacher ed. 6.95 (*1-55799-237-1*, 039) Evan-Moor Edu Pubs.

Planetas. Chris Jaeggi. (I Know about Ser.). (Illus.). (J). 1995. pap. 2.50 (*0-528-83738-9*) Rand McNally.

Planete des Fleurs see King's Garden

Planete des Singes. Pierre Boulle. 9.95 (*0-686-54110-3*, M4878) Fr & Eur.

Planetfall. Scott G. Gier. (Genellan Ser.). 472p. 1995. mass mkt. 5.99 (*0-345-39509-3*, Del Rey) Ballantine Pub Grp.

Planetfall: In Search of Floyd. Arthur B. Cover. (INFOCOM Ser.: No. 1). 304p. 1988. pap. 3.95 (*0-380-75384-7*, Avon Bks) Morrow Avon.

PlanetHood: The Key to Your Future. Benjamin B. Ferencz & Ken Keyes, Jr. LC 90-13519. 240p. 1991. pap. 7.95 (*0-915972-21-2*) Love Line Bks.

Planetoid of Amazement. Mel Gilden. LC 91-7261. 224p. (J). (gr. 5-9). 1991. lib. bdg. 14.89 (*0-06-021714-6*) HarpC Child Bks.

Planetology: Comparing Other Worlds to Our Own. Fred Schaaf. LC 96-15826. (Venture-Science Ser.). 128p. (J). 1996. lib. bdg. 24.00 (*0-531-11300-0*) Watts.

Planetology: Comparing Other Worlds to Our Own. Fred Schaaf. (Venture Bks.). 128p. (J). 1997. pap. 9.95 (*0-531-15828-4*) Watts.

Planetomachia; Penelope's Web; The Spanish Masquerado, 1585-1589 see Life & Complete Works in Prose & Verse of Robert Greene

***Planets.** (Illus.). 16p. (YA). (ps-3). 2000. 9.95 (*1-878427-79-2*) Cimino Pub Grp.

Planets. Gilda Berger. (Smart Science Ser.). (Illus.). 16p. (J). (gr. 2-5). Date not set. pap. 5.95 (*1-58273-508-5*) Newbridge Educ.

Planets. James Boylan. 1992. pap. 10.00 (*0-679-73906-8*) Vin Bks.

Planets. Mark R. Chartrand. (Golden Guide Ser.). 1990. 11.05 (*0-606-11755-5*, Pub. by Turtleback) Demco.

***Planets.** Jennifer Dussling. (All Aboard Reading Ser.). (Illus.). 48p. (J). (gr. 1-3). 2000. 13.89 (*0-448-42416-9*, Planet Dexter); pap. 3.99 (*0-448-42406-1*, Planet Dexter) Peng Put Young Read.

Planets. Gabriele. (J). 1986. pap. 1.95 (*0-911211-61-6*) Penny Lane Pubns.

Planets. Gail Gibbons. LC 92-44429. (Illus.). 32p. (J). (gr. k-3). 1993. pap. 6.95 (*0-8234-1133-8*); lib. bdg. 16.95 (*0-8234-1040-4*) Holiday.

Planets. Kim Jackson. LC 84-16451. (Illus.). 32p. (J). (gr. k-2). 1996. pap. 3.50 (*0-8167-0451-1*) Troll Communs.

Planets. David McNab & James Younger. LC 98-89995. (Illus.). 240p. 1999. 35.00 (*0-300-08044-1*) Yale U Pr.

Planets. Moore. (Illus.). 16p. (J). (gr. 1-3). 1987. pap., teacher ed. 5.95 (*1-55799-102-2*, 812) Evan-Moor Edu Pubs.

Planets. Patrick Moore. LC 94-43928. (Starry Sky Ser.). (Illus.). 24p. (J). (gr. k-3). 1996. lib. bdg. 18.90 (*1-56294-624-2*, Copper Beech Bks) Millbrook Pr.

Planets. Peter Murray. LC 92-20016. (Umbrella Bks.). (Illus.). 32p. (J). (gr. 2-6). 1993. lib. bdg. 21.36 (*0-89565-975-1*) Childs World.

Planets. Cynthia P. Nicolson. (Starting with Space Ser.). (Illus.). 40p. (J). (gr. 3-4). 1998. 1495.00 (*1-55074-512-3*, Pub. by Kids Can Pr) Genl Dist Srvs.

***Planets.** Cynthia Pratt Nicolson. (Starting with Space Ser.). (Illus.). 40p. (J). (gr. 2-6). 1999. pap. text 6.95 (*1-55074-716-9*) Kids Can Pr.

Planets. Lesley Sims. 32p. (J). (gr. 1-4). 1995. pap. text 4.95 (*0-8114-4945-9*) Raintree Steck-V.

Planets. Lynda Sorensen. LC 93-14874. (Solar System Discovery Library). 24p. (J). (gr. k-4). 1993. lib. bdg. 10.95 (*0-86593-274-3*) Rourke Corp.

Planets. Lynda Sorensen. LC 93-14874. (Solar System Ser.). (J). (ps-6). 1993. 9.50 (*0-685-66588-7*) Rourke Corp.

Planets. Jenny Tesar. LC 97-25179. (Space Observer Ser.). (J). (gr. 3-4). 1998. 19.92 (*1-57572-580-0*) Heinemann Lib.

Planets. Anne Welsbacher. LC 96-18862. (Universe Ser.). 24p. (J). (ps-4). 1997. lib. bdg. 13.95 (*1-56239-718-4*) ABDO Pub Co.

Planets: An Educational Coloring Book. Spizzirri Publishing Co. Staff. Ed. by Linda Spizzirri. (Illus.). 32p. (J). (gr. 1-8). 1982. pap. 1.99 (*0-86545-043-9*) Spizzirri.

Planets: Discover the Power of the Planets. Sasha Fenton. (Illus.). 224p. 1994. pap. 10.00 (*1-85538-352-7*, Pub. by Aqrn Pr) Harper SF.

Planets: Neighbors in Space. Jeanne Bendick. (Early Bird Astronomy Ser.). (Illus.). 32p. (J). (gr. k-2). 1991. pap. 3.80 (*1-878841-51-3*) Millbrook Pr.

Planets: Neighbors in Space. Jeanne Bendick. (Early Bird Astronomy Ser.). (Illus.). 32p. (J). (gr. k-2). 1991. lib. bdg. 19.90 (*1-878841-03-3*) Millbrook Pr.

Planets: Outer Space Sticker Atlas. C. Bloch. (Illus.). 32p. (J). (gr. k-6). 1993. reprint ed. pap. 3.95 (*1-879424-13-4*) Nickel Pr.

Planets: Portraits of New Worlds. rev. ed. Nigel Henbest. 208p. 1994. reprint ed. pap. 21.95 (*0-14-013414-X*, Penguin Bks) Viking Penguin.

Planets & Perception: Telescopic Views & Interpretations, 1609-1909. William Sheehan. LC 88-20501. 324p. 1988. 43.50 (*0-8165-1059-8*) U of Ariz Pr.

Planets & Planet Centered Astrology. Stephanie Clement. 176p. 1992. 16.00 (*0-86690-426-3*, C3344-014) Am Fed Astrologers.

***Planets & Possibilities: Explore the Worlds Beyond Your Sun Sign.** Susan Miller. 1999. 24.98 incl. audio compact disk (*1-57042-807-7*) Time Wrner AudioBks.

Planets & Possibilities: Explore the Worlds Beyond Your Sun Sign. Susan Miller. 288p. 2001. 29.95 (*0-446-52434-4*, Pub. by Warner Bks) Little.

Planets & Satellites. Robert Estalella. LC 93-18068. (Window on the Universe Ser.). (Illus.). 32p. (J). (gr. 4-7). 1993. 12.95 (*0-8120-6372-4*); pap. 7.95 (*0-8120-1737-4*) Barron.

Planets & Satellites. Ed. by Gerard P. Kuiper & Barbara M. Middlehurst. LC 54-7183. (Solar System Ser.: Vol. 3). 1993. lib. bdg. 50.00 (*0-226-45927-6*) U Ch Pr.

Planets & Stars. Chelsea House Publishing Staff. (Concise Collection). 48p. (J). (gr. 3 up). 1997. 15.95 (*1-85627-738-0*) Chelsea Hse.

Planets & Stars. Ron Marson. (Science with Simple Things Ser.: No. 41). (Illus.). 80p. 1994. teacher ed. 15.00 (*0-941008-41-X*) Tops Learning.

Planets & Their Atmospheres: Origin & Evolution (Monograph) John S. Lewis & Ronald G. Primm. LC 83-10001. (International Geophysics Ser.). 1983. pap. text 77.00 (*0-12-446582-X*) Acad Pr.

Planets & Their Moons. Audubon Society Staff. (National Audubon Society Pocket Guides Ser.). 1995. pap. 7.99 (*0-679-77997-3*) Knopf.

Planets Around Pulsars. Ed. by J. A. Phillips et al. (ASP Conference Series Proceedings: Vol. 36). 391p. 1993. 34.00 (*0-937707-55-4*) Astron Soc Pacific.

Planets Beyond the Solar System & the Next Generation of Space Missions: Proceedings of a Workshop Held at the Space Telescope Science Institute, Baltimore, Maryland, October 16-18, 1996. Ed. by David Soderblom. (ASP Conference Series Proceedings: Vol. 119). 293p. 1997. 34.00 (*1-886733-39-2*) Astron Soc Pacific.

Planets Collection. (Star Wars Ser.). 25.00 West End Games.

Planets in Aspect: Understanding Your Inner Dynamics. Robert Pelletier. LC 74-82711. (Planets Ser.). 364p. 1974. pap. 19.95 (*0-914918-20-6*, Whitford) Schiffer.

Planets in Composite: Analyzing Human Relationships. Robert Hand. LC 75-17260. (Planets Ser.). 372p. 1975. pap. 19.95 (*0-914918-22-2*, Whitford) Schiffer.

Planets in Full Score. G. Holst. 192p. 1997. pap. 11.95 (*0-486-29277-0*) Dover.

Planets in Houses: Experiencing Your Environment Planets. Robert Pelletier. Ed. by Margaret Anderson. (Planets Ser.). (Illus.). 372p. 1978. pap. 19.95 (*0-914918-27-3*, Whitford) Schiffer.

Planets in Locality. Steve Cozzi. LC 88-45190. (Modern Astrology Library). (Illus.). 320p. (Orig.). 1997. pap. 20.00 (*0-87542-098-2*) Am Fed Astrologers.

Planets in Love: Exploring Your Emotional & Sexual Needs. John Townley. (Planets Ser.). 372p. 1978. pap. 19.95 (*0-914918-21-4*) Schiffer.

Planets in Our Solar System. Franklyn M. Branley. LC 79-7894. (Let's-Read-&-Find-Out Science Bks.). (Illus.). 40p. (J). (gr. k-3). 1981. lib. bdg. 12.89 (*0-690-04026-1*) HarpC Child Bks.

Planets in Our Solar System. Franklyn M. Branley. LC 79-7894. (Trophy Let's Read-&-Find-Out Science Bk.). (Illus.). 40p. (J). (gr. k-3). 1983. pap. 3.95 (*0-06-445001-5*, HarpTrophy) HarpC Child Bks.

Planets in Our Solar System. Franklyn M. Branley. (Let's-Read-And-Find-Out Book Ser.). (J). 1987. 10.15 (*0-606-01657-0*, Pub. by Turtleback) Demco.

Planets in Our Solar System. rev. ed. Franklyn M. Branley. LC 86-45171. (Trophy Let's-Read-&-Find-Out Bk.). (Illus.). 32p. (J). (ps-3). 1987. reprint ed. pap. 4.95 (*0-06-445064-3*, HarpTrophy) HarpC Child Bks.

Planets in Our Solar System, Stage 2. Franklyn M. Branley. LC 97-1174. (Let's-Read-&-Find-Out Science Ser.). (Illus.). 32p. (J). (gr. k-4). 1998. 15.95 (*0-06-027769-6*); pap. 4.95 (*0-06-445178-X*); lib. bdg. 15.89 (*0-06-027770-X*) HarpC.

Planets in Peril: A Critical Study of C. S. Lewis's Ransom Trilogy. David C. Downing. LC 91-34369. 200p. 1995. pap. 15.95 (*0-87023-997-X*) U of Mass Pr.

Planets in Signs. Skye Alexander. Ed. by Marah Ren & Julie Lockhart. LC 87-63416. 272p. 1988. pap. 18.95 (*0-914918-79-6*, Whitford) Schiffer.

***Planets in Solar Returns: Yearly Cycles of Transformation & Growth.** rev. ed. Mary Fortier Shea. 314p. 1999. 30.00 (*0-9626626-8-2*) Twin Stars.

Planets in Synastry: Astrological Patterns of Relationships. E. W. Neville. 276p. 1990. pap. 16.95 (*0-924608-01-3*, Whitford) Schiffer.

Planets in the Signs & Houses, Vol. 2. Bepin Behari. 256p. 1990. pap. 14.95 (*1-878423-10-X*) Morson Pub.

Planets in Transit: Life Cycles for Living. Robert Hand & Charles A. Jayne. LC 76-12759. (Planets Ser.). 532p. 1980. pap. 24.95 (*0-914918-24-9*, Whitford) Schiffer.

Planets in Youth: Patterns of Early Development. Robert Hand. (Planets Ser.). 372p. 1981. pap. 19.95 (*0-914918-26-5*, Whitford) Schiffer.

Planets, Moons, & Meteors. John R. Gustafson. (J). (gr. 4-7). 1992. lib. bdg. 12.95 (*0-671-72534-3*, Julian Messner) Silver Burdett Pr.

Planets, Moons, & Meteors: The Young Stargazer's Guide to the Galaxy. John R. Gustafson. 64p. (J). (gr. 4-7). 1992. pap. 6.95 (*0-671-72535-1*, Julian Messner) Silver Burdett Pr.

***Planets of the UFP: A Guide to Federation Worlds.** Last Unicorn Games Staff. (Star Trek Next Generation Ser.). 1999. pap. 20.00 (*0-671-04006-5*) PB.

***Planets of the UFP: A Guide To Federation Worlds.** Sourcebooks Staff. 1999. pap. 20.00 (*1-889533-05-X*) Last Unicorn Games.

Planets on the Move: The Astrology of Relocation. Maritha Pottenger & Zipporah Dobyns. 320p. (Orig.). 1995. pap. 15.95 (*0-935127-23-2*) ACS Pubns.

Planets Outside the Solar System: Theory & Observations. J. M. Mariotti & D. M. Alloin. LC 99-25782. (NATO ASI Series, Series C, Mathematical & Physical Sciences). 1999. write for info. (*0-7923-5708-6*) Kluwer Academic.

Planets, Potions & Parchments: Scientifica Hebraica from the Dead Sea Scrolls to the Eighteenth Century. B. Barry Levy. (Illus.). 152p. 1990. pap. 32.95 (*0-7735-0791-4*, Pub. by McG-Queens Univ Pr) CUP Services.

Planets, Potions & Parchments: Scientifica Hebraica from the Dead Sea Scrolls to the Eighteenth Century. B. Barry Levy. (Illus.). 152p. 1990. 65.00 (*0-7735-0793-0*, Pub. by McG-Queens Univ Pr) CUP Services.

Planets, Stars & Galaxies. Anthony E. Fanning. (Illus.). 189p. 1966. pap. 6.95 (*0-486-21680-2*) Dover.

Planets, Stars & Nebulae Studied With Photopolarimetry. Ed. by T. Gehrels. LC 73-86446. 1133p. 1974. 66.00 (*0-8165-0428-8*) U of Ariz Pr.

Planets, Stars & Orbs: The Medieval Cosmology, 1200-1687. Edward Grant. (Illus.). 842p. 1996. pap. text 34.95 (*0-521-56509-X*) Cambridge U Pr.

Planets Through the Signs: Astrology for Living. Abbe Bassett. 152p. 1987. pap. 12.50 (*0-89540-170-3*, SB-170, Sun Bks) Sun Pub.

Planets Within: The Astrological Psychology of Marsilio Ficino. Thomas Moore. 240p. 1993. reprint ed. pap. 16.95 (*0-940262-28-2*, Lindisfarne) Anthroposophic.

Planets X & Pluto. William G. Hoyt. LC 79-15665. (Illus.). 316p. 1980. reprint ed. pap. 98.00 (*0-7837-9233-6*, 204998400004) Bks Demand.

Planewalker's Handbook. Monte Cook. 1996. 20.00 (*0-7869-0460-7*, Pub. by TSR Inc) Random.

Planewaves, Pseudopotentials & the LAPW Method. David J. Singh. LC 93-37706. 128p. (C). 1993. text 110.00 (*0-7923-9412-7*) Kluwer Academic.

Planificacion Familiar: Guia para Investigar el Tema. Charles Balsam & Elizabeth Balsam. LC 96-77378. (SPA.). 64p. 1997. pap. 2.95 (*0-7648-0027-2*) Liguori Pubns.

Planificacion Familiar Natural - Sistema de Cuentas see Bead System of Natural Family Planning

Planification des Naissances en Milieu Canadien-Francais. Colette Carisse. LC 66-56044. (FRE.). 228p. reprint ed. pap. 70.70 (*0-7837-6944-X*, 204677300003) Bks Demand.

Planimetria Arqueologica de Teotihuacan. Daniel Schavelon. (SPA., Illus.). 20p. 1981. pap. 1.25 (*1-877812-67-6*, UN022) UPLAAP.

Planispheric Astrolabes from the National Museum of American History. National Museum of American History Staff et al. LC 83-600270. (Smithsonian Studies in History & Technology: 45). 239p. reprint ed. pap. 74.10 (*0-608-11955-5*, 202316500032) Bks Demand.

***Planiverse: Computer Contact with a Two-Dimensional World.** A. K. Dewdney. LC 99-42454. (Illus.). 272p. 1999. pap. 20.00 (*0-387-98916-1*) Spr-Verlag.

Plank: Poems from Hollywood. Mark Dunster. 11p. 1998. pap. 5.00 (*0-89642-556-8*) Linden Pubs.

***Plank House.** Dolores A. Dyer. LC 00-25459. (Native American Homes Ser.). 2000. write for info. (*1-55916-248-1*) Rourke Pubns.

Plank-on-Frame Models & Scale Masting & Rigging, Vol. 1. Harold A. Underhill. (C). 1987. 115.00 (*0-85174-186-X*) St Mut.

P

An Asterisk (*) at the beginning of an entry indicates that the title is appearing for the first time.

Plank-on-Frame Models & Scale Masting & Rigging, Vol. 2. Harold A. Underhill. (C). 1987. 115.00 (*0-85174-174-6*) St Mut.

Plankhouse. Shelby Stephenson. LC 91-68530. (Illus.). 112p. 1993. 29.95 (*0-933598-39-4*) NC Wesleyan Pr.

Plankhouse. deluxe limited ed. Shelby Stephenson. LC 91-68530. (Illus.). 112p. 1993. 150.00 (*0-933598-40-8*) NC Wesleyan Pr.

Planking & Fastening. Peter H. Spectre. 170p. 1996. pap. 24.95 (*0-937822-41-8*) WoodenBoat Pubns.

Planking Techniques for Model Ship Builders. Donald Dressel. 144p. 1988. pap. 14.95 (*0-07-155312-6*) McGraw.

Planking Techniques for Model Ship Builders. Donald Dressel. (Illus.). 160p. 1988. pap. 10.95 (*0-8306-2868-1*) McGraw-Hill Prof.

Planks of Reason: Essays on the Horror Film. Ed. by Barry K. Grant. LC 84-10592. 442p. 1984. pap. 22.50 (*0-8108-2156-7*) Scarecrow.

Plankton & Productivity in the Oceans: Zooplankton, Vol. 2. 2nd ed. John E. Raymont. (Illus.). 700p. 1983. 368.00 (*0-08-024404-1*, Pub. by Pergamon Repr) Franklin.

***Plankton Culture Manual.** 5th rev. ed. Frank H. Hoff & Terry W. Snell. (Illus.). viii, 156p. 1999. pap. 30.00 (*0-9662960-0-1*) FL Aqua Farms.

Plankton Dynamics of the Southern California Bight. Ed. by R. W. Eppley. (Lecture Notes on Coastal & Estuarine Studies: Vol. 15). xiii, 373p. 1986. pap. 52.00 (*0-387-96320-0*) Spr-Verlag.

Plankton of the Illinois River, 1894-1899. Charles A. Kofoid. (Bibliotheca Phycologica Ser.: No. 29). 1977. reprint ed. lib. bdg. 97.50 (*3-7682-1104-5*) Lubrecht & Cramer.

Plankton of the Illinois River, 1894-1899: Quantitative Investigations & General Results, Pt.1. Charles A. Kofoid. Ed. by Frank N. Egerton, 3rd. LC 77-74235. (History of Ecology Ser.). (Illus.). 1978. reprint ed. lib. bdg. 51.95 (*0-405-10404-9*) Ayer.

Plankton Regulation Dynamics: Experiments & Models in Rotifer Continuous Cultures. Ed. by Norbert Walz. LC 92-39672. (Ecological Studies: Vol. 98). x, 308p. 1993. 207.95 (*0-387-55955-8*) Spr-Verlag.

Plankton Rotifers: Biology & Taxonomy, Band XVI. Agnes Ruttner-Kolisko. Tr. by G. Kolisko. (Binnengewaesser Ser.). (Illus.). vii, 146p. 1974. pap. text 28.00 (*3-510-40735-0*, Pub. by E Schweizerbartsche) Balogh.

Planned & Unplanned: Creative Handwoven Clothing. Pat White & Isa Vogel. 1992. 19.95 (*0-932394-17-5*) Dos Tejedoras.

Planned Approach to Community Health: Guide for the Local Coordinator. Byron Breedlove. (Illus.). 311p. (C). 1998. pap. text 50.00 (*0-7881-7262-X*) DIANE Pub.

Planned Approach to Community Health: Visual Aids. Byron Breedlove. (Illus.). 150p. (C). 1998. pap. text 25.00 (*0-7881-7261-1*) DIANE Pub.

Planned Assaults: The No Family House, Love-House, Texas Zero. Lars Lerup. (Illus.). 112p. (Orig.). 1987. 35.00 (*0-262-12123-9*) MIT Pr.

Planned Businesshood: You Can Plan & Manage Your Own Successful Small Business. Robert Wardrick. (Small Business Headstart Ser.). 32p. 1996. pap. text 5.95 (*0-9652744-0-3*); audio 5.95 (*0-9652744-1-1*) Authors Wkshp.

Planned Change Theories for Nursing: Review, Analysis, & Implications. Constance R. Tiffany & Louette R. Johnson Lutjens. LC 97-33801. 320p. 1997. 52.00 (*0-7619-0234-1*); pap. 24.95 (*0-7619-0235-X*) Sage.

Planned Chaos. Ludwig Von Mises. 90p. 1961. pap. 6.95 (*0-910614-00-8*) Foun Econ Ed.

Planned Communities: Ownership Options & Developmental Formats. LC 95-79322. (ACREL Papers: Vol. 7). 225p. 1995. pap. 89.95 (*1-57073-199-3*, 543-0369, ABA Real Prop) Amer Bar Assn.

Planned Community Living: Handbook for California Homeowners Associations. John Linford. LC 96-96606. 309p. (Orig.). 1996. pap. 19.95 (*0-9652973-0-6*) BenchMark Ent.

Planned Destruction of America. James Wardner. (Illus.). 208p. 1993. pap. 13.95 (*0-9632190-5-7*) Longwood.

Planned Economies: Confronting the Challenges of the 1980s. Ed. by John P. Hardt & Carl H. McMillan. (Illus.). 208p. 1989. text 69.95 (*0-521-34461-1*) Cambridge U Pr.

Planned Economies & International Economic Organizations. Jozef M. Van Brabant. (Soviet & East European Studies: No. 77). (Illus.). 320p. (C). 1991. text 69.95 (*0-521-38350-1*) Cambridge U Pr.

Planned Economies of Eastern Europe. Alan H. Smith. LC 83-10748. 250p. (C). 1983. 39.50 (*0-8419-0891-5*) Holmes & Meier.

***Planned Giving: A Board Member's Perspective.** Grant Thornton. 24p. 1999. pap. text 12.00 (*0-925299-98-7*) Natl Ctr Nonprofit.

Planned Giving: Management, Marketing & Law. 2nd ed. Ronald R. Jordan et al. LC 99-15334. (Nonprofit Law, Finance, & Management Ser.). 592p. 1999. 165.00 incl. disk (*0-471-35102-4*) Wiley.

Planned Giving Essentials: A Step by Step Guide to Success. Richard D. Barrett & Molly E. Ware. LC 96-48718. 165p. 1997. pap. 59.00 (*0-8342-0900-4*) Aspen Pub.

Planned Giving Simplified: The Gift, the Giver, & the Gift Planner. Robert F. Sharpe, Sr. LC 98-24360. (NSFRE-Wiley Fund Development Ser.). 240p. 1999. 34.95 (*0-471-16674-X*) Wiley.

Planned Invasion of Japan, 1945: The Siberian Weather Advantage. H. S. Yoder, Jr. LC 97-22539. (Memoirs Ser.: Vol. 223). (Illus.). 161p. 1997. 25.00 (*0-87169-223-6*, M223-yoh) Am Philos.

Planned Maintenance. Didactic Systems Staff. (Simulation Game Ser.). 1969. pap. 26.25 (*0-89401-072-7*) Didactic Syst.

Planned Maintenance & the Use of Computers. J. Armstrong. (C). 1991. pap. 60.00 (*0-86022-127-X*, Pub. by Build Servs Info Assn) St Mut.

Planned Maintenance for Productivity & Energy Conservation. 3rd ed. John W. Criswell. (Illus.). 191p. Date not set. 57.00 (*0-88173-098-X*) Fairmont Pr.

Planned Management of Forests. N. V. Brasnett. 238p. 1985. pap. 275.00 (*81-7089-024-1*, Pub. by Intl Bk Distr) St Mut.

Planned Management of Forests. N. V. Brasnett. 238p. (C). 1985. 50.00 (*0-7855-3251-X*, Pub. by Scientific) St Mut.

Planned Management of Forests. N. V. Brashett. 238p. 1985. reprint ed. 150.00 (*0-7855-3070-3*, Pub. by Intl Bk Distr) St Mut.

Planned Marketing: The Roadmap to Sales. Judith H. Pettigrew. Ed. by Judith S. Voiers et al. 58p. 1989. student ed. 19.95 (*0-9622899-1-4*) Creative Consort Inc.

Planned Markets & Public Competition: Strategic Reform in Northern European Health Systems. Richard B. Saltman & Casten Von Otter. (State of Health Ser.). 160p. 1992. 123.00 (*0-335-09729-4*); pap. 39.95 (*0-335-09728-6*) OpUniv Pr.

Planned Parenthood: Alameda-San Francisco, 1929-1994. Thomas N. Saunders. 135p. 1995. lib. bdg. 10.00 (*0-9646004-0-4*) Plan Parenthd.

Planned Press & Public Relations. 3rd ed. Frank W. Jefkins. LC 92-47028. 1993. pap. 35.95 (*0-7514-0016-5*) Thomson Learn.

Planned Residential Environments: A Report Prepared for the U. S. Department of Transportation, Bureau of Public Road. John B. Lansing et al. LC 76-632967. (Illus.). 281p. reprint ed. pap. 87.20 (*0-7837-5243-1*, 204497700005) Bks Demand.

Planned Short-Term Psychotherapy: A Clinical Handbook. 2nd ed. Bernard L. Bloom. LC 96-48082. 309p. 1997. pap. text 47.00 (*0-205-19344-7*) Allyn.

Planned Short-Term Treatment. Richard A. Wells. 288p. 1982. 35.00 (*0-02-934650-9*) Free Pr.

Planned Short-Term Treatment. 2nd ed. Richard A. Wells. LC 94-13229. 1994. 35.00 (*0-02-934655-X*) Free Pr.

Planned to Death: The Annihilation of a Place Called Howdendyke. J. Douglas Porteous. 254p. 1989. text 47.50 (*0-8020-2661-3*) U of Toronto Pr.

Planned Urban Environments: Sweden, Finland, Israel, the Netherlands, France. Ann L. Strong. LC 73-134204. (Illus.). 440p. reprint ed. pap. 136.40 (*0-7837-3388-7*, 204334600008) Bks Demand.

Planned Variation in Education: Should We Give up or Try Harder? Ed. by Alice M. Rivlin & P. Michael Timpane. LC 75-5151. (Brookings Institution Studies in Social Experimentation). 198p. reprint ed. pap. 61.40 (*0-608-12471-0*, 202540200043) Bks Demand.

Planner. Jack Rudman. (Career Examination Ser.: C-588). 1994. pap. 27.95 (*0-8373-0588-8*) Nat Learn.

Planner & Analyst Trainee. Jack Rudman. (Career Examination Ser.: C-2996). 1994. pap. 29.95 (*0-8373-2996-5*) Nat Learn.

Planner (Criminal Justice) Jack Rudman. (Career Examination Ser.: C-3020). 1994. pap. 34.95 (*0-8373-3020-3*) Nat Learn.

Planner Trainee. Jack Rudman. (Career Examination Ser.: C-2778). 1994. pap. 23.95 (*0-8373-2778-4*) Nat Learn.

Planner Youth Services. Jack Rudman. (Career Examination Ser.: C-3003). 1994. pap. 29.95 (*0-8373-3003-3*) Nat Learn.

Planners & Local Politics: Impossible Dreams. Anthony J. Catanese. LC 73-94287. (Sage Library of Social Research: No. 7). 189p. reprint ed. pap. 58.60 (*0-8357-4774-3*, 203771100009) Bks Demand.

Planners & Politicians: Liberal Politics & Social Policy, 1957-1968. P. E. Bryden. 256p. 1997. text 60.00 (*0-7735-1650-6*, Pub. by McG-Queens Univ Pr) CUP Services.

Planners & Politicians: Liberal Politics & Social Policy, 1957-1968. Penny Bryden. 1998. pap. 22.95 (*0-7735-1651-4*) McG-Queens Univ Pr.

Planners & Protesters: Airport Opposition As Social Movement. Lisa R. Peattie. (Urban Studies: No. 9). 40p. 1991. pap. text 6.00 (*0-913749-19-2*) U MD Urban Stud.

Planners & Public Expectations. Howell S. Baum. LC 82-16961. 325p. 1983. reprint ed. pap. 100.80 (*0-608-05351-1*, 206505700012) Bks Demand.

Planner's Guide for Selecting Clean-Coal Technologies for Power Plants. Karin Oskarsson et al. LC 97-38022. (World Bank Technical Papers: No. 387). 176p. 1997. pap. 22.00 (*0-8213-4065-4*, 14065) World Bank.

Planners on Planning: Leading Planners Offer Real-Life Lessons on What Works, What Doesn't & Why. Bruce W. McClendon & Anthony J. Catanese. LC 96-10091. (Public Administration Ser.). 1996. 30.95 (*0-7879-0285-3*) Jossey-Bass.

Planner's Use of Information. Ed. by Hemalata C. Dandekar. LC 88-71130. (Illus.). 224p. 1988. reprint ed. pap. 33.95 (*0-918286-56-5*, Planners Press) Am Plan Assn.

Planning. Central Office of Info. (Aspects of Britain Ser.). (Illus.). 1997. pap. 10.00 (*0-11-701723-X*, Pub. by Statnry Office) Bernan Associates.

Planning. Neil McDonald. 88p. 1995. pap. 12.00 (*0-8050-3897-3*, Pub. by Batsford Chess) H Holt & Co.

Planning: Universal Process. Melville C. Branch. LC 89-16025. 247p. 1990. 55.00 (*0-275-93160-9*, C3160, Praeger Pubs) Greenwood.

Planning - Conducting a Course: "Managing Trials Effectively" National Judicial College Staff. 273p. 1994. rng bd. 35.00 (*0-614-06247-0*) Natl Judicial Coll.

Planning a Baby? A Complete Guide to Pre-Conceptual Care. Sarah Brewer. 296p. 1996. pap. 11.95 (*0-09-181256-9*, Pub. by Optima) Trafalgar.

Planning a Baby? Complete Guide to Pre-Conceptual Care. Brewer. 1998. pap. 11.95 (*0-356-21056-1*) Trafalgar.

Planning a Better Kitchen. 2nd rev. ed. Ed. by Creative Homeowner Press Editors. LC 96-84701. (Illus.). 96p. 1996. pap. 10.95 (*1-880029-90-1*) Creative Homeowner.

Planning a Christ Centered Wedding. 1979. 5.95 (*0-918403-07-3*) Agape Ministries.

Planning a Christian Wedding. Linda R. Miller. 82p. 1992. ring bd. 12.95 (*0-940883-05-8*) Calvary Pubns.

Planning a Funeral Service. Jedediah D. Holdorph. 2nd. 48p. 1998. pap. 5.95 (*0-8192-1769-7*) Morehouse Pub.

Planning a Future. Ed. by Jerri M. Lucas. 1986. pap. 6.55 (*0-89137-816-2*) Quality Pubns.

Planning a Meaningful Cremation Funeral. Doug Manning. 32p. 1998. spiral bd. 4.95 (*1-892785-11-0*) In-Sight Bks Inc.

Planning a Mixed Region in Israel: The Political Geography of Israel's Policy in the Galilee Region. Oren Yiftachel. 250p. 1992. 82.95 (*1-85628-255-4*, Pub. by Avebry) Ashgate Pub Co.

Planning a Model Boat Regatta, 2 Vols., No. 1. Sandra E. Ciminero. (Boat Book Series: Vol. 1). (Illus.). 32p. 1999. pap. 9.95 (*0-9669513-1-X*) ArtsyKids.

Planning a New Business Venture: A Step by Step Guide to Preparing an Effective Business Plan see Planning Series

***Planning a New Career: How to Take Stock, Change Course & Secure a Better Future for Yourself.** 3rd ed. Judith Johnstone. (Illus.). 140p. (Orig.). 1999. pap. 19.95 (*1-85703-453-8*, Pub. by How To Bks) Trans-Atl Phila.

Planning a New West: The Columbia River Gorge National Scenic Area. Carl Abbott et al. LC 96-39753. (Culture & Environment in the Pacific West Ser.). (Illus.). 224p. 1997. 26.95 (*0-87071-392-2*) Oreg St U Pr.

Planning a One-Day Geriatrics Retreat. 55p. 1998. ring bd. write for info. (*1-891539-00-0*) U Chi Pritzker Schl.

Planning a Personal Program for Doctoral Education for the Physical Therapist. rev. ed. 12p. 1990. pap. 7.50 (*1-887759-24-7*, E-20) Am Phys Therapy Assn.

Planning a Pizza Party. Cindy Iutzi. (Illus.). 16p. (Orig.). (J). (gr. 5-8). 1996. pap. write for info. (*1-56490-017-7*) G Grimm Assocs.

Planning a Profitable Hydroponic - Greenhouse Business. Adam J. Savage. LC 96-205063. (Illus.). 244p. (Orig.). (C). 1996. pap., student ed. 79.95 (*0-929440-00-5*) Sovereign Univ.

Planning a Research Project. Martin Herbert. 144p. 1991. pap. text 35.00 (*0-304-31846-9*) Continuum.

Planning a Running Event: A Manual on the Administration of a Successful Running Race. Dan Newport & Joe Schultz. LC GV1061.N4. (Quest for Quality Ser.: No. 2). 50p. reprint ed. pap. 30.00 (*0-7837-1551-X*, 204184400024) Bks Demand.

Planning a Small Garden: Big Inspirations for Compact Plots. Richard Bird. LC 98-36923. (Illus.). 128p. 1998. pap. 25.00 (*1-57959-035-7*, SOMA) BB&T Inc.

Planning a Small Yard. Deni Bown. (101 Essential Tips Ser.). 72p. 1996. pap. 4.95 (*0-7894-0564-4*) DK Pub Inc.

Planning a Social Studies Program: Activities, Guidelines, Resources. rev. ed. Ed. by James E. Davis. 203p. 1997. pap. 24.95 (*0-89994-395-0*, 395-0) Soc Sci Ed.

Planning a Succesful Conference. Cynthia Winter. LC 94-15526. (Survival Skills for Scholars Ser.: Vol. 13). 124p. 1994. 37.00 (*0-8039-5524-3*); pap. 16.50 (*0-8039-5525-1*) Sage.

Planning a System of Regions. 245p. 1985. 6.00 (*92-1-129000-7*) UN.

Planning a Theme-Based Curriculum: Goals, Themes, Activities, & Planning Guides for 4's & 5's. Carla F. Berry & Gayle Mindes. (Illus.). 160p. (Orig.). 1992. pap. 12.95 (*0-673-46409-1*, GoodYrBooks) Addson-Wesley Educ.

Planning a Tradeshow from Z to A Guidebook. Cindy C. Murray. Ed. by Gretchen Lingham. 24p. (Orig.). 1995. pap. text 14.95 (*0-9645468-0-9*) Staicer & Assocs.

Planning a Tradeshow from Z to A Worksheets. Cindy C. Murray. Ed. by Gretchen Lingham. 54p. (Orig.). 1995. 14.95 (*0-9645468-1-7*) Staicer & Assocs.

Planning a Tragedy: The Americanization of the War in Vietnam. Larry Berman. 224p. 1983. reprint ed. pap. 9.95 (*0-393-95326-2*) Norton.

Planning a Vacation. Cindy Iutzi. (Illus.). 19p. (Orig.). (J). (gr. 5-8). 1996. pap. 15.95 (*1-56490-018-5*) G Grimm Assocs.

***Planning a Wedding: A Step-by-Step Guide to Preparing for a Successful Day.** 4th ed. Mary Kilborn. (Illus.). 128p. (Orig.). 1999. pap. 19.95 (*1-85703-487-2*, Pub. by How To Bks) Trans-Atl Phila.

Planning a Wedding to Remember: Special & Unique Ideas. rev. ed. Beverly Clark. (Illus.). 250p. 1989. pap. 12.95 (*0-934081-06-9*) Wlshre Pubns.

***Planning a Wedding to Remember: The Perfect Wedding Planner.** 5th rev. ed. Intro. by Beverly Clark. (Illus.). 248p. 1999. pap. 18.95 (*0-934081-17-4*) Wlshre Pubns.

Planning a Wedding When Your Parents Are Divorced. 2nd rev. ed. Cindy Moore & Tricia Windom. (Illus.). 208p. 1997. pap. 12.95 (*0-942407-35-0*) Father & Son.

Planning a Will in Colorado. 32p. 1999. pap. 9.95 (*1-883726-42-5*) Bradford Pub.

Planning Academic & Research Library Buildings. 3rd ed. Philip Leighton. LC 98-46757. 928p. 1999. 155.00 (*0-8389-0747-4*) ALA.

Planning Accessible Meetings: A Guide to ADA Compliance. Bill Scott. LC 96-40866. (Illus.). ix, 81p. 1998. pap. 34.95 (*0-88034-121-1*) Am Soc Assn Execs.

***Planning Activities for Child Care: A Curriculum Guide for Early Childhood Education.** 2nd ed. Caroline S. Rosser. LC 97-40259. (Illus.). 504p. 1998. 34.64 (*1-56637-428-6*) Goodheart.

Planning Additions to Academic Library Buildings: A Seamless Approach. Ed. by Pat Hawthorne & Ron G. Martin. LC 95-14005. (Illus.). 64p. (Orig.). 1995. spiral bd. 25.00 (*0-8389-0651-6*, 0651-6-2045) ALA.

Planning Adult Learning: Issues, Practices & Directions. W. M. Rivera. 180p. (C). 1986. 33.00 (*0-7099-4224-9*, Pub. by C Helm) Routldge.

Planning Ahead: A Positive Act of Love for Family & Friends. Beverly Peace & Philip Peace. 32p. (Orig.). 1992. pap., student ed. 4.95 (*1-881576-00-0*) Providence Hse.

Planning Aide. Jack Rudman. (Career Examination Ser.: C-2770). 1994. pap. 23.95 (*0-8373-2770-9*) Nat Learn.

Planning America's Communities. Herbert H. Smith. LC 90-82670. 262p. (Orig.). 1991. pap. 29.95 (*0-918286-71-9*, Planners Press) Am Plan Assn.

***Planning America's Security: Lessons from the National Defense Panel.** John Tedstrom & John G. McGinn. LC 99-26323. xi, 22p. 1999. pap. 7.50 (*0-8330-2736-0*, MR-1049-OSD) Rand Corp.

***Planning an Appropriate Curriculum for the under Fives.** Rosemary Rodger. 1999. pap. 26.95 (*1-85346-550-X*) David Fulton.

Planning an Aviary. R. Mathews-Danzer. (Exotic Bird Ser.). 140p. 1996. pap. 14.00 (*1-888417-81-1*) Dimefast.

Planning an Aviary: With CD-ROM. R. Mathews-Danzer & Emmett Cestero. (Exotic Bird Ser.). (Illus.). 1999. pap. write for info. incl. cd-rom (*1-888417-93-5*) Dimefast.

Planning an Endoscopy Suite for Office & Hospital. Jerome D. Waye & Martin Rich. LC 90-4105. (Illus.). 184p. 1990. 65.00 (*0-89640-173-1*) Igaku-Shoin.

Planning & Administering Early Childhood. 6th ed. Celia A. Decker & John R. Decker. 459p. (C). 1996. pap. text 48.00 (*0-02-327991-5*, Macmillan Coll) P-H.

Planning & Administering Early Childhood Programs. 6th ed. Celia A. Decker & John R. Decker. 1997. pap. 48.00 (*0-13-027991-9*) P-H.

***Planning & Administering Early Childhood Programs.** 7th ed. Celia A. Decker & John R. Decker. 476p. 2000. pap. 48.00 (*0-13-027168-3*) P-H.

Planning & Analysis of Construction Operations. Daniel W. Halpin & Leland S. Riggs. 400p. 1992. 120.00 (*0-471-55510-X*) Wiley.

Planning & Architectural Design of Integrated Services Digital Networks: Civil & Military Applications. A. Nejat Ince et al. LC 94-48207. (The Kluwer International Series in Engineering & Computer Science: Vol. 308). 512p. (C). 1995. text 187.50 (*0-7923-9554-9*) Kluwer Academic.

Planning & Architectural Design of Modern Command Control Communications & Information Systems Military & Civilian Applications. A. Nejat Ince et al. LC 97-8310. 1997. text 178.00 (*0-7923-9916-1*) Kluwer Academic.

Planning & Assessing Health Worker Activities Module 3: Facilitator's Guide. Martine Hilton. (Primary Health Care Management Advancement Programme (PHC MAP) Modules Ser.). 84p. 1993. pap. text. write for info. (*1-882839-10-2*) Aga Khan Fnd.

Planning & Assessing Health Worker Activities Module 3: User's Guide. Khatidja Husein et al. (Primary Health Care Management Advancement Programme (PHC MAP) Modules Ser.). 136p. 1993. pap. text. write for info. (*1-882839-02-1*) Aga Khan Fnd.

Planning & Assessing the Curriculum in English Language Arts. Stephen Tchudi. LC 91-26547. 122p. (Orig.). 1991. pap. 18.95 (*0-87120-185-2*, 611-91150) ASCD.

Planning & Assigning Work. Didactic Systems Staff. (Study Units Ser.). 1978. pap. 9.00 (*0-89401-121-9*) Didactic Syst.

Planning & Budgeting in Poor Countries. Naomi Caiden & Aaron Wildavsky. 371p. (Orig.). 1979. pap. text 21.95 (*0-87855-707-5*) Transaction Pubs.

Planning & Change see Progress in Planning

Planning & Community Equity. LC 94-72240. 220p. (Orig.). 1994. pap. 25.95 (*1-884829-05-8*, Planners Press); lib. bdg. 36.00 (*1-884829-04-X*, Planners Press) Am Plan Assn.

Planning & Conducting Chemical, Biological, Radiological, & Nuclear Defense Training. 1991. lib. bdg. 75.00 (*0-8490-4061-2*) Gordon Pr.

Planning & Conducting Competitive Golf Events. 94p. (Orig.). 1998. pap. 50.00 (*1-57701-054-X*, 99IP005) Natl Golf.

Planning & Conducting Family Cluster: Education for Family Wellness. Barbara Vance. LC 89-30555. (Illus.). 294p. 1989. reprint ed. pap. 91.20 (*0-608-01623-3*, 205960200003) Bks Demand.

***Planning & Conducting Family Law Discovery Pts. 1 & 2: Fall 1999 Action Guide.** Susan S. Coats & John A. DeRonde, Jr. Ed. by Julie H. Brook. 160p. 1999. pap. text 58.00 (*0-7626-0371-2*, FA-11322) Cont Ed Bar-CA.

Planning & Conducting Family Law (Dissolution) Discovery Pts. 1 & 2: Spring 1993, Action Guide. Susan S. Coats. Ed. by Elizabeth M. Johnson. 155p. 1993. pap. text 52.00 (*0-88124-620-4*, FA-11321) Cont Ed Bar-CA.

Planning & Conducting Needs Assessment: A Practical Guide. Belle R. Witkin & James W. Altschud. 320p. (C). 1995. 49.95 (*0-8039-5809-9*); pap. 24.00 (*0-8039-5810-2*) Sage.

Planning & Control. Ed. by Thomas L. Dean & Michael P. Wellman. 1991. text 53.95 (*1-55860-209-7*) Morgan Kaufmann.

Planning & Control for Food & Beverage Operations. 4th ed. Jack D. Ninemeier. LC 97-46737. 424p. 1998. pap. 68.95 (*0-86612-161-7*) Educ Inst Am Hotel.

P

An Asterisk (*) at the beginning of an entry indicates that the title is appearing for the first time.

Planning & Control for Information Technology Services. CCTA Staff. (Information Technology Infrastructure Library (ITIL)). 135p. 1994. pap. 87.00 (*0-11-330548-6*, HM5413, Pub. by Statnry Office) Sftware Mgmt Network.

Planning & Control in the Managed Forest. H. Knuchel. 380p. 1983. reprint ed. 350.00 (*81-7089-014-4*, Pub. by Intl Bk Distr) St Mut.

Planning & Control of Maintenance Systems: Modeling & Analysis. S. Duffuaa et al. LC 98-13431. 400p. 1998. 90.00 (*0-471-17981-7*) Wiley.

Planning & Control of Manufacturing Operations. John Kenworthy. 272p. 1997. text 105.00 (*1-85573-307-2*) Buttrwrth-Heinemann.

***Planning & Control of Manufacturing Operations.** John Kenworthy. 262p. 1998. 58.95 (*0-471-25339-1*) Wiley.

Planning & Control of Multinational Marketing Strategy: The Issue of Integration. Shahid Siddiqi. Ed. by Stuart Bruchey. LC 80-592. (Multinational Corporations Ser.). 1981. lib. bdg. 31.95 (*0-405-13384-7*) Ayer.

Planning & Control of Public Works. Leo Wolman. (General Ser.: No. 17). 292p. 1930. reprint ed. 76.00 (*0-87014-016-7*) Natl Bur Econ Res.

Planning & Control Systems Design: Principles & Cases for Process Manufacturing. Byron J. Finch & James F. Cox. LC 87-72179. 184p. 1987. pap. text 30.00 (*0-935406-94-8*) Am Prod & Inventory.

Planning & Controlling Construction Projects. M. J. Mawdesley. LC 97-144702. 432p. (C). 1997. 100.00 (*0-582-23409-3*) Addison-Wesley.

Planning & Controlling Land Development, 1995. 4th ed. Mandelker & Cunningham. LC 95-80658. 957p. 1995. text 54.00 (*1-55834-279-6*, 12209-11, MICHIE) LEXIS Pub.

Planning & Costing Community Care. Ed. by Chris Clark & Irvine Lapsley. (Research Highlights in Social Work Ser.: No. 27). 180p. 1996. pap. 28.95 (*1-85302-267-5*, Pub. by Jessica Kingsley) Taylor & Francis.

Planning & Creating Better Direct Mail. John D. Yeck & John T. Maguire. LC 61-11133. (McGraw-Hill Series in Marketing & Advertising). 399p. reprint ed. pap. 123.70 (*0-8357-5492-8*, AU0037900093) Bks Demand.

Planning & Creating Successful Engineered Designs. rev. ed. Sydney S. Love. (Illus.). 292p. 1986. 40.00 (*0-912907-00-2*) Adv Prof Dev.

***Planning & Cruising Guide to the Great Circle Cruise: Around the Eastern U. S. A.** G. Bickley Remmey, Jr. (Illus.). 1999. pap. 34.95 (*0-9669987-0-7*) G B Remmey.

Planning & Decision Making. Jon Sutherland. 246p. 1997. pap. 37.50 (*0-273-62510-1*) F T P-H.

Planning & Decision Making Skillbook. Educational Foundation of the National Restaurant. (Management Skills Program Ser.). 28p. (Orig.). 1993. pap. 10.95 (*0-915452-31-6*) Educ Found.

***Planning & Deploying Microsoft Exchange Server 2000.** 2nd ed. Kent Joshi. (Illus.). 600p. 2000. pap. 49.99 (*0-7897-2279-8*) Que.

***Planning & Design Guide for Secure Adult & Juvenile Facilities** Leonard R. Witke & American Correctional Association Staff. LC 99-43095. 1999. pap. write for info. (*1-56991-116-9*) Am Correctional.

Planning & Design Guidelines for Small Craft Harbor. rev. ed. American Society of Civil Engineers, Task Committe. LC 94-20810. (Manuals & Reports on Engineering Practice Ser.: No. 50). 296p. 1994. 54.00 (*0-7844-0033-4*) Am Soc Civil Eng.

Planning & Design of Airports. 4th ed. Robert Horonjeff & Francis X. McKelvey. LC 93-23138. 848p. 1991. 80.00 (*0-07-045345-4*) McGraw.

Planning & Design of Bridges. M. S. Troitsky. 318p. 1994. 110.00 (*0-471-02853-3*) Wiley.

Planning & Design of Fixed Offshore Platforms. Ed. by Bramlette McClelland & Michael Reifel. LC 84-27078. (Illus.). 1056p. 1985. text 125.95 (*0-442-25223-4*, VNR) Wiley.

Planning & Design of Information Systems. Ed. by Andre Blokdijk & Paul Blokdijk. (Illus.). 578p. 1991. pap. text 65.00 (*0-12-107071-9*) Acad Pr.

Planning & Design of Ports & Marine Terminals. Hans Agerschou et al. LC 83-7032. (Wiley-Interscience Publications). (Illus.). 330p. reprint ed. pap. 102.30 (*0-7837-3411-5*, 204337800008) Bks Demand.

Planning & Design of Roads, Airbases, & Heliports in the Theater of Operations. 1991. lib. bdg. 79.95 (*0-8490-4086-8*) Gordon Pr.

Planning & Design of Townhouses & Condominiums. Robert E. Engstrom & Marc R. Putman. LC 79-64813. 256p. reprint ed. pap. 79.40 (*0-7837-1007-0*, 204131700020) Bks Demand.

Planning & Designing Data Warehouses. Ramon Barquin & Herb Edelstein. 352p. 1996. pap. text 41.99 (*0-13-255746-0*) P-H.

***Planning & Designing Effective Web Sites.** 10th ed. Sue Conger & Mason. 160p. (C). 1998. pap. text, mass mkt. 32.95 incl. cd-rom (*0-7600-4988-2*) Course Tech.

Planning & Designing Focus Group Research from Start to Finish. David L. Morgan. (Focus Group Kit Ser.: Vol. 2). 128p. 1997. pap. 16.95 (*0-7619-0817-X*) Sage.

Planning & Designing Schools. C. William Brubaker. LC 97-35484. (Illus.). 240p. 1997. 59.95 (*0-07-049405-3*) McGraw-Hill Prof.

Planning & Designing Training Programmes. Leslie Rae. LC 97-11021. 244p. 1997. 69.95 (*0-566-07929-1*, Pub. by Gower) Ashgate Pub Co.

Planning & Developing a Library Orientation Program: Proceedings. Ed. by Mary Bolner. LC 75-676. (Library Orientation Ser.: No. 3). 1975. 25.00 (*0-87650-061-0*) Pierian.

Planning & Development in India. K. N. Dubey. 1990. 47.50 (*81-7024-268-1*, Pub. by Ashish Pub Hse) S Asia.

Planning & Development in India. Ed. by R. K. Sinha. (C). 1994. text 24.00 (*81-241-0225-2*, Pub. by Har-Anand Pubns) S Asia.

Planning & Development in Iran. George B. Baldwin. LC 67-18377. 231p. reprint ed. pap. 71.70 (*0-608-11863-X*, 202308200032) Bks Demand.

Planning & Development of Educational Programmes for Personnel in Oral Health. H. Allred & M. H. Hobdell. (WHO Offset Publications: No. 93). 101p. 1986. pap. text 16.00 (*92-4-170093-9*, 1120093) World Health.

Planning & Development of Key Sectors in India, 5 vols. Ed. by Devendra Thakur. (C). 325.00 (*81-7100-329-X*, Pub. by Anmol) S Asia.

Planning & Development of Nuclear Power Programmes. (Nuclear Power Experience Ser.: Vol. 1). 459p. 1983. pap. text 130.00 (*92-0-050083-8*, ISP627 1, Pub. by IAEA) Bernan Associates.

Planning & Directing a Wedding: Guidelines for a Bride, Mother & Director. unabridged ed. Dorothy B. Parrish. LC 86-641927. (Illus.). 65p. 1996. reprint ed. pap. 9.95 (*0-9656331-0-1*) D Parrish.

Planning & Drafting for the Generation-Skipping Transfer Tax. Jerold I. Horn. LC 90-5581. xxi, 166p. 1990. 18.00 (*0-8318-0649-4*, B649) Am Law Inst.

Planning & Drafting for the Generation-Skipping Transfer Tax. 2nd ed. Jerold I. Horn. LC 93-74943. 188p. 1994. 45.00 (*0-8318-0724-5*, B724) Am Law Inst.

Planning & Drafting of Wills & Trusts. 3rd ed. Thomas L. Shaffer & Carol A. Mooney. (Paralegal). 434p. 1998. text 31.50 (*0-88277-840-4*) Foundation Pr.

Planning & Economic Change: An Historical Perspective. Ed. by S. V. Ward. (C). 1984. 29.00 (*0-7855-3841-0*, Pub. by Oxford Polytechnic) St Mut.

Planning & Economic Policy in India: Evaluation & Lessons for the Future. Ed. by Manabendu Chattopadhyay et al. 220p. 1996. 32.00 (*0-8039-9280-7*) Sage.

Planning & Engineering Interface with a Modernized Land Data System. Ed. by G. Warren Marks. LC 80-66123. 269p. 1980. pap. 5.00 (*0-87262-243-6*) Am Soc Civil Eng.

Planning & Equipping Educational Music Facilities. Harold P. Geerdes. LC 75-15271. (Illus.). 88p. 1975. pap. 30.00 (*0-608-04835-6*, 206549200004) Bks Demand.

Planning & Equipping Music Facilities see Music Facilities: Building, Equipping, & Renovating

Planning & Evaluating Distance Education: A Collaborative Approach. Tara D. Knott. Ed. by Sandy Mayer. LC 93-33245. (Illus.). 200p. (Orig.). (C). pap. text 16.95 (*0-9638070-0-5*) Diaphera Pubns.

Planning & Evaluating Health Programs: A Primer. Charles D. Hale et al. LC 92-47070. 232p. (C). 1993. pap. 36.50 (*0-8273-5448-7*) Delmar.

Planning & Evaluating Special Education Services. Charles A. Maher & Randy E. Bennett. (Illus.). 288p. (C). 1984. text 21.75 (*0-13-679481-5*) P-H.

Planning & Evaluating Water Conservation Measures. Ed. by Richard H. Sullivan. (Special Reports: No. 48). 69p. 1981. reprint ed. pap. text 30.00 (*0-917084-14-4*) Am Public Works.

Planning & Evaluation Assistant. Jack Rudman. (Career Examination Ser.: C-549). 1994. pap. 29.95 (*0-8373-0549-7*) Nat Learn.

Planning & Evaluation of Forestry Projects. G. A. Watt. 1973. 40.00 (*0-85074-014-2*) St Mut.

Planning & Evaluation of Hallmark Events. Geoffrey J. Syme et al. 299p. 1989. text 83.95 (*0-566-05763-8*, Pub. by Avebry) Ashgate Pub Co.

Planning & Evaluation of Health Education Services: Proceedings of the WHO Expert Committee, Geneva, 1967. WHO Staff. (Technical Reports: No. 409). 1969. pap. text 6.00 (*92-4-120409-5*, 1100409) World Health.

Planning & Evaluation of Public Dental Health Services: Proceedings of the WHO Expert Committee, Geneva, 1975. WHO Staff. (Technical Reports: No. 589). 1976. pap. text 6.00 (*92-4-120589-X*, 1100589) World Health.

***Planning & Executing Successful Seminars.** Bernie Goldberg. (Illus.). 72p. 1999. pap. 12.95 (*1-879644-13-4*) Direct Mktg.

Planning & Financial Management for the School Principal. fac. ed. Howard M. Johnson. LC 82-3288. 296p. 1982. reprint ed. pap. 91.80 (*0-7837-8208-X*, 204796600009) Bks Demand.

Planning & Financing School Improvement & Construction Projects. Ed. by Edgar H. Bittle. (Monograph Ser.: Vol. 57). 160p. 1996. text 32.00 (*1-56534-093-0*) Ed Law Assn.

Planning & Financing the New Venture. Jeffry A. Timmons. LC 89-22115. 200p. 1990. 24.95 (*0-931790-92-1*); pap. 18.95 (*0-931790-93-X*) Brick Hse Pub.

Planning & Formation of Central Alabama Veterans Health Care System (CAVHCS) Field Hearing Before the Subcommittee [ON] Oversight & Investigations of the Committee on Veterans' Affairs, House of Representatives, One Hundred Fifth Congress, First Session . . . Montgomery, Alabama, July 28, 1997. USGPO Staff. LC 98-160062. iii, 63 p. 1998. 3.25 (*0-16-056244-9*) USGPO.

Planning & Goal Setting for Improved Performance. Mescon Group Staff. (GC - Principles of Management Ser.). 1995. text, teacher ed. 25.95 (*0-538-85038-8*) S-W Pub.

Planning & Hazard. Christopher Miller & Claire Fricker. (Progress in Planning Ser.: Vol. 40). 260p. 1994. 56.25 (*0-08-042474-0*, Pergamon Pr) Elsevier.

Planning & Human Survival. Melville C. Branch. LC 91-44569. 192p. 1992. 52.95 (*0-275-93826-3*, C3826, Praeger Pubs) Greenwood.

***Planning & Implementing Effective Tobacco Education & Prevention Programs.** Martin L. Forst. LC 99-34116. 288p. 1999. text 43.95 (*0-398-06990-5*) C C Thomas.

***Planning & Implementing Effective Tobacco Education & Prevention Programs.** Martin L. Forst. LC 99-34116. 288p. 1999. pap. 30.95 (*0-398-06991-3*) C C Thomas.

Planning & Implementing End-User Information. Hershey. (KK - Legal Secretary Studies). 1992. text 53.95 (*0-538-70219-2*) S-W Pub.

***Planning & Implementing Forest Operations to Achieve Sustainable Forests: Proceedings (1996)** Ed. by Charles R. Blinn & Michael A. Thompson. (Illus.). 282p. (C). 2000. reprint ed. pap. text 45.00 (*0-7881-8613-2*) DIANE Pub.

Planning & Implementing Pedestrian Facilities in Suburban & Developing Rural Areas (Research Report) (National Cooperative Highway Research Program Report Ser.: No. 294A). 92p. 1987. 10.40 (*0-309-04417-0*, NR294A) Transport Res Bd.

Planning & Implementing Pedestrian Facilities in Suburban & Developing Rural Areas (State-of-the-Art Report) (National Cooperative Highway Research Program Report Ser.: No. 294B). 165p. 1987. 12.40 (*0-309-04418-9*, NR294B) Transport Res Bd.

Planning & Implementing Programs for the Gifted. James H. Borland. (Education & Psychology of the Gifted Ser.). 272p. 1989. pap. text 20.95 (*0-8077-2966-3*) Tchrs Coll.

Planning & Implementing Sustainable Projects in Developing Countries: Theory, Practice & Economics. Audace I. Kanshahu. (Illus.). 196p. 1996. pap. 45.00 (*981-00-7687-8*, Pub. by AgBe Pub) Balogh.

Planning & Implementing Technical Services Workstations. Ed. by Michael Kaplan. LC 97-6204. 237p. 1997. 32.00 (*0-8389-0698-2*) ALA.

Planning & Implementing Your Year 2000 Strategy: A Handbook for Managers. LC 98-143351. 130p. 1997. ring bd. 895.00 (*0-945052-33-2*) Computer Econ.

Planning & Internal Control under Prospective Payment. Robert W. Broyles & Michael D. Rosko. 1986. 90.00 (*0-87189-266-9*) Aspen Pub.

Planning & Layout see Modern Power Station Practice

Planning & Learning: On to Real Applications: Papers from the 1994 Fall Symposium. Ed. by Yolanda Gil & Manuela M. Veloso. (Technical Reports). (Illus.). 165p. 1995. spiral bd. 25.00 (*0-929280-75-X*) AAAI Pr.

Planning & Learning by Analogical Reasoning. Manuela M. Veloso. LC 94-43959. (Lecture Notes in Computer Science Ser.: Vol. 886). 1994. 34.95 (*3-540-58811-6*); write for info. (*0-387-58811-6*) Spr-Verlag.

Planning & Making Crowns & Bridges. 3rd ed. Bernard G. N. Smith. 264p. (C). 1998. text. write for info. (*1-85317-314-2*, Pub. by Martin Dunitz) Mosby Inc.

Planning & Manage African Power, Vol. 1. Ranganathan. 302p. 1998. pap. text 65.00 (*1-85649-551-5*, Pub. by Zed Books); pap. text 27.50 (*1-85649-552-3*, Pub. by Zed Books) St Martin.

Planning & Management for a Changing Environment: A Handbook on Redesigning Postsecondary Education. Marvin W. Peterson et al. LC 96-50208. (Jossey-Bass Higher & Adult Education Ser.). 1997. 55.00 (*0-7879-0849-5*) Jossey-Bass.

Planning & Management for Health. (EURO Reports & Studies: No. 102). 65p. 1986. pap. text 8.00 (*92-890-1268-4*, 1330102) World Health.

Planning & Management for the Decommissioning of Research Reactors & Other Small Nuclear Facilities. IAEA Staff. (Technical Reports: No. 351). 50p. 1993. pap. 25.00 (*92-0-100693-4*, STI/DOC/351, Pub. by IAEA) Bernan Associates.

Planning & Managing Agricultural & Ecological Experiments. P. Johnstone. 128p. 1998. pap. 42.50 (*0-7487-3989-0*) St Mut.

Planning & Managing ATM Networks. Daniel Minoli. 300p. 1996. 48.00 (*0-13-262189-4*) P-H.

Planning & Managing Death Issues in the Schools: A Handbook. Robert L. Deaton & William A. Berkan. LC 94-21693. 208p. 1995. lib. bdg. 52.95 (*0-313-29525-5*) Greenwood.

Planning & Managing Dissection Laboratories. Florida Association of Science Teachers Staff. 36p. 1994. pap. text 5.95 (*0-87355-126-5*) Natl Sci Tchrs.

Planning & Managing Effective E-Mail Applications. Charles Bermant. LC 95-50848. 214p. 1996. pap. 265.00 (*1-56607-960-8*) Comput Tech Res.

Planning & Managing Foodservice Equipment: Student Manual. Educational Foundation of the National Restaurant. 76p. (Orig.). 1993. pap. write for info. (*0-915452-09-X*) Educ Found.

Planning & Managing for Greater Profit. Don A. Rice. 65p. 1989. pap., teacher ed. 14.00 (*1-881154-08-4*); pap., student ed. 14.00 (*1-881154-09-2*) Darco Pr.

Planning & Managing for Greater Profit, 2 cass., No. 1 & 2. Don A. Rice. 1989. pap. 300.00 incl. VHS (*1-881154-07-6*) Darco Pr.

Planning & Managing Higher Education Facilities. Ed. by Harvey H. Kaiser. LC 85-645339. (New Directions for Institutional Research Ser.: No. IR 61). 1989. pap. 22.00 (*1-55542-868-1*) Jossey-Bass.

Planning & Managing Housing for the Elderly. Mortimer P. Lawton. LC 74-28099. (Illus.). 350p. reprint ed. pap. 108.50 (*0-608-30696-7*, 202248800027) Bks Demand.

Planning & Managing Human Resources. William J. Rothwell & Hercules C. Kazanas. 1993. ring bd. 34.95 (*0-87425-246-6*) HRD Press.

Planning & Managing Industry-University Research Collaborations. Rudolph A. Carboni. LC 92-14724. 240p. 1992. 59.95 (*0-89930-769-8*, CHZ, Quorum Bks) Greenwood.

***Planning & Managing Interior Projects.** 2nd rev. ed. Carol E. Farren. (Illus.). 2000. 69.95 (*0-87629-537-5*, 67245A) R S Means.

Planning & Managing Regional Air Quality: Modeling & Measurement. Ed. by Paul A. Solomon & Terry A. Silver. 864p. 1994. lib. bdg. 104.95 (*1-56670-059-0*, L1059) Lewis Pubs.

Planning & Managing Reliable Urban Water Systems. Robert J. Harberg. LC 97-20477. 1997. 90.00 (*0-89867-909-5*, 20412) Am Water Wks Assn.

Planning & Managing School Facilities. Theodore J. Kowalski. LC 89-16078. 225p. 1989. 55.00 (*0-275-93279-6*, C3279, Praeger Pubs) Greenwood.

Planning & Managing the Economy of the City: Policy Guidelines for the Metropolitan Mayor. Joseph Oberman & Robert Bingham. LC 72-79544. (Special Studies in U. S. Economic, Social & Political Issues). 1972. 32.50 (*0-275-06160-4*) Irvington.

Planning & Managing Web Sites on the Macintosh: The Complete Guide to WebSTAR & MacHTTP. Jon Wiederspan & Chuck Shotton. 384p. (C). 1995. pap. 39.95 (*0-201-47957-5*) Addison-Wesley.

Planning & Market Relations: Proceedings of a Conference Held by the International Economic Association at Liblice, Czechoslovakia. Ed. by Michael C. Kaser & Richard Portes. LC 75-163474. (Illus.). 261p. 1971. text 32.50 (*0-333-12825-7*) Irvington.

Planning & Marketing Conferences & Workshops: Tips, Tools & Techniques. Robert G. Simerly. LC 89-49493. (The Management Ser.). 240p. 1990. text 32.95 (*1-55542-235-7*) Jossey-Bass.

Planning & Measurement in Your Organization of the Future. D. Scott Sink & Thomas C. Tuttle. 331p. 1989. pap. text 59.95 (*0-89806-090-7*, PLMSOF) Eng Mgmt Pr.

Planning & Operation of Low Level Waste Disposal Facilities. International Atomic Energy Agency Staff. LC 97-193750. 601p. 1997. pap. 195.00 (*92-0-104496-8*, STI/PUB/1022, Pub. by IAEA) Bernan Associates.

Planning & Organisation of National Research Programs in Information Science. Ed. by V. Slamecka & H. Borka. (Illus.). 83p. 1982. pap. 73.00 (*0-08-026472-7*, Pergamon Pr) Elsevier.

Planning & Organising Business Functions. Stuart Turner. 176p. 1983. text 54.95 (*0-566-02394-6*, Pub. by Gower) Ashgate Pub Co.

Planning & Organization of Health Laboratory Services: Proceedings of the WHO Expert Committee on Health Laboratory Services, 5th, Geneva, 1971. WHO Staff. (Technical Reports: No. 491). 1972. pap. text 4.00 (*92-4-120491-5*, 1100491) World Health.

Planning & Organizing Career Curricula. Larry J. Kenneke et al. LC 72-92619. 1975. write for info. (*0-672-97533-5*) Macmillan.

Planning & Organizing for Multicultural Instruction. 2nd ed. Gwendolyn C. Baker. 1993. pap. 20.95 (*0-201-86112-7*) Addison-Wesley.

***Planning & Organizing Personal & Professional Development.** Chris Sangster. LC 00-21822. 192p. 2000. 84.95 (*0-566-08264-0*, Pub. by Ashgate Pub) Ashgate Pub Co.

Planning & Organizing the Post-War Air Force, 1943-1947 see Struggle for Air Force Independence, 1943-1947

Planning & Organizing Work. Learning Business Staff. 1997. 26.95 (*0-7506-3150-3*) Buttrwrth-Heinemann.

Planning & Planting the Garden. Robert Smaus. (Illus.). 176p. 1990. 29.95 (*0-8109-1189-2*, Pub. by Abrams) Time Warner.

Planning & Planting Your Dwarf Fruit Orchard. Garden Way Publishing Editors. Ed. by Kim Foster & Louise Lloyd. (Illus.). 32p. 1992. 2.95 (*0-88266-758-0*, Garden Way Pub); 2.95 (*0-88266-759-9*, Garden Way Pub) Storey Bks.

Planning & Power in Iran: Ebtehaj & Economic Development under the Shah. Frances Bostock & Geoffrey Jones. (Illus.). 238p. 1989. text 47.50 (*0-7146-3338-0*, Pub. by F Cass Pubs) Intl Spec Bk.

Planning & Programming for Nursing Services. (Public Health Papers: No. 44). 1971. pap. text 7.00 (*92-4-130044-2*, 1110044) World Health.

Planning & Programming, Land Use, Public Participation, & Computer Technology in Transportation. Ed. by Naomi Kassabian. (Transportation Research Record Ser.: No. TRR 1400). (Illus.). 120p. 1993. pap. text 25.00 (*0-309-05470-2*) Transport Res Bd.

Planning & Programming the Introduction of CAD-CAM Systems: A Reference Guide for Developing Countries. 156p. 1989. 25.00 (*92-1-106236-5*, E.89.III.E.7) UN.

Planning & Public Transport in Great Britain, France, & West Germany. Barry J. Simpson. LC 87-209547. (Illus.). 381p. reprint ed. pap. 118.20 (*0-7837-4032-8*, 204386100011) Bks Demand.

Planning & Reduction Technique in Fracture Surgery. J. W. Mast et al. (Illus.). 270p. 1995. 265.00 (*0-387-16283-6*) Spr-Verlag.

Planning & Reduction Technique in Fracture Surgery. Jeffrey W. Mast et al. 254p. 1995. 265.00 (*3-540-16283-6*) Spr-Verlag.

Planning & Role Setting for Public Libraries: A Manual of Options & Procedures. Charles M. McClure et al. LC 87-11445. 140p. 1987. pap. text 25.00 (*0-8389-3341-6*) ALA.

Planning & Rural Recreation in Britain. David Groome. 351p. 1993. 79.95 (*1-85628-454-9*, Pub. by Avebry) Ashgate Pub Co.

Planning & Supplying a Hotel Bar-Lounge. Ad Wittemann. LC 88-26035. 16p. (Orig.). 1988. pap. 25.00 (*0-938481-33-9*) Camelot Consult.

An Asterisk (*) at the beginning of an entry indicates that the title is appearing for the first time.

Planning & Support for the Congenitally Deafblind. Ed. by John M. McInnes. 644p. 1999. text 60.00 (*0-8020-4242-2*) U of Toronto Pr.

Planning & the Heritage. W. Rogers. 1997. 57.95 (*0-419-15100-1*, E & FN Spon) Routledge.

Planning & the Historic Environment. (Planning Policy Guidance Note Ser.: No. 15). 66p. 1994. pap. 17.00 (*0-11-752944-3*, HM29443, Pub. by Statnry Office) Bernan Associates.

Planning & the Innovative Process see Progress in Planning

***Planning & the Political Market: Public Choice & the Politics of Government Failure.** Mark Pennington. LC 00-31308. 2000. pap. write for info. (*0-485-00606-5*, Pub. by Athlone Pr) Transaction Pubs.

Planning & the Politicians & Other Essays. Albert H. Hanson. LC 75-95618. x, 355p. 1969. lib. bdg. 39.50 (*0-678-06524-1*) Kelley.

Planning & Urban Change. Stephen V. Ward. LC 94-204028. 320p. 1994. pap. 27.50 (*1-85396-218-X*, Pub. by P Chapman) Taylor & Francis.

Planning & Urban Growth: An Anglo-American Comparison. Marion Clawson & Peter Hall. LC 72-12364. (Illus.). 314p. reprint ed. pap. 97.40 (*0-608-18084-X*, 203214600078) Bks Demand.

Planning & Urban Growth in Nordic Countries. Ed. by T. Hall. (Studies in History, Planning & the Environment). (Illus.). 288p. (C). 1991. 110.00 (*0-419-16840-0*, A6241, E & FN Spon) Routledge.

Planning & Validating QC Procedures: Workshop Manual. 2nd ed. James O. Westgard. LC 95-90953. 154p. 1996. spiral bd. 75.00 (*1-886958-04-1*) Westgard Qual.

Planning & Zoning in the United States. Beverly J. Pooley. LC 61-63301. (Michigan Legal Publications). 123p. 1982. reprint ed. lib. bdg. 37.50 (*0-89941-243-2*, 302330) W S Hein.

Planning & Zoning New York City: Yesterday, Today, & Tomorrow. Ed. by Todd W. Bressi. LC 92-30574. 278p. (C). 1993. text 19.95 (*0-88285-143-8*) Ctr Urban Pol Res.

Planning Appeals. Sasha White. 250p. 1997. pap. 63.00 (*1-85811-065-3*, Pub. by CLT Prof) Gaunt.

Planning Appeals: A Critique. Michael Purdue. (Studies in Law & Politics Ser.). 72p. 1991. pap. 25.95 (*0-335-09630-1*) OpUniv Pr.

Planning Applications: The RMJM Guide. 3rd ed. Adrian Salt & Henry Brown. LC 98-12722. 1998. pap. 85.00 (*0-632-04117-X*) Blackwell Sci.

Planning Applications & Appeals. Helen Bryan. LC 96-32860. 192p. 1997. pap. text 42.95 (*0-7506-2792-1*) Buttrwrth-Heinemann.

***Planning Armageddon: Britain, the United States & the Command of Western Nuclear Forces, 1945-1964.** Stephen R. Twigge & Len Scott. (Studies in the History of Science, Technology & Medicine: Vol. 8). 384p. 2000. 52.00 (*90-5823-006-6*, Harwood Acad Pubs) Gordon & Breach.

Planning As Control-Policy & Resistance in a Deeply Divided Society. Oren Yiftachel. (Progress in Planning Ser.: Vol. 44). 186p. 1995. 105.75 (*0-08-042656-5*, Pergamon Pr) Elsevier.

Planning at the Crossroads. Simmie. 224p. 1993. 75.00 (*1-85728-024-5*, Pub. by UCL Pr Ltd); pap. 25.00 (*1-85728-025-3*, Pub. by UCL Pr Ltd) Taylor & Francis.

Planning Basics: Everyone a Planner, Booklet I. Institute for High Performance Planners Members. (Everyone-A-Planner Series). (Illus.). 44p. (Orig.). (C). 1995. pap. 10.00 (*0-933684-15-0*) Mgmt & Indus Res Pubns.

Planning Basketball Practice. Sidney Goldstein. (N-G Ser.). 1998. per. 7.45 (*1-884357-36-9*) Golden Aura.

Planning Benefits Strategically Vol. 38: An Approach to Meeting Organizational Objectives. Victor Barocas. LC 97-229423. (Building Blocks Ser.). (Illus.). (Orig.). 1997. pap. 24.95 (*1-57963-042-1*, AO238) Am Compensation.

Planning Better Board Meetings. John Carver. LC 96-45761. (CarverGuide on Policy Governance Ser.: No. CG 05). 26p. 1996. pap. 10.95 (*0-7879-0301-9*) Jossey-Bass.

Planning Beyond 2000. Allmendinger. LC 98-49776. 318p. (C). 1999. 99.00 (*0-471-98441-8*); pap. 39.95 (*0-471-98442-6*) Wiley.

Planning Blended Worship: The Creative Mixture of Old & New. Robert Webber. LC 98-39716. 160p. 1998. pap. 15.00 (*0-687-03223-7*) Abingdon.

Planning, Building & Implementation Vol. 1: The Enterprise Data Warehouse. Eric Sperley. LC 98-44762. (Illus.). 368p. (C). 1999. 44.99 (*0-13-905845-1*, Macmillan Coll) P-H.

Planning, Building & Using the Enterprise Data Warehouse, Vol. 2. (C). 1999. 40.00 (*0-13-905852-4*, Macmillan Coll) P-H.

***Planning Buildings for a High-Rise Environment in Hong Kong: A Review of Building Appeal Decisions.** Lawrence Wai-Chung Lai & Daniel Chi-Wing Ho. (Illus.). 376p. 2000. pap. 38.00 (*962-209-505-4*, Pub. by HK Univ Pr) Coronet Bks.

Planning Bulletin Boards for Church & Synagogue Libraries. Janelle A. Paris. LC 83-7331. (Guide Ser.: No. 11). 48p. (Orig.). 1984. pap. 8.25 (*0-915324-20-2*) CSLA.

Planning by Agreement in a Berkshire District. David Henry. (C). 1982. 35.00 (*0-7855-3848-8*, Pub. by Oxford Polytechnic) St Mut.

Planning by Mathematics. S. Vajda. LC 73-330815. (Topics in Operational Research Ser.). (Illus.). 150p. reprint ed. pap. 46.50 (*0-608-11451-0*, 205191300013) Bks Demand.

Planning Challenges of the 70's in the Public Domain, 15th Annual AAS Meeting, Jun. 17-20, 1969, Denver, CO. George W. Morgenthaler. Ed. by William J. Burnsnali et al. (Science & Technology Ser.: Vol. 22). (Illus.). 504p. 1970. 40.00 (*0-87703-050-2*, Am Astronaut Soc) Univelt Inc.

Planning Challenges of the 70's in Space, 15th Annual AAS Meeting, Jun. 17-20, 1969, Denver CO. Ed. by George W. Morgenthaler & Robert G. Morra. LC 57-43769. (Advances in the Astronautical Sciences Ser.: Vol. 26). (Illus.). 470p. 1970. 35.00 (*0-87703-053-7*, Am Astronaut Soc) Univelt Inc.

Planning Christian Worship, Ser. C. 130p. (Orig.). 1994. pap. 14.99 (*0-8100-0524-7*, 03N3009) Northwest Pub.

Planning Christian Worship, Ser. A. Northwestern Publishing House Staff. LC 95-69080. 130p. 1995. pap. 14.99 (*0-8100-0569-7*, 03N3007) Northwest Pub.

Planning Christian Worship, Ser. B. Northwestern Publishing House Staff. LC 93-86632. 160p. 1993. pap. 14.99 (*0-8100-0509-3*, 03N3008) Northwest Pub.

Planning Clinical Trials in the Pharmaceutical Industry: An Introduction to the Statistical Principles in the Planning & Design of Clinical Studies. William M. Wooding. LC 00-301. (Probability & Mathematical Statistics Ser.). 560p. 1993. 134.95 (*0-471-62244-3*) Wiley.

Planning Colleges for the Community. Dorothy M. Knoell & Charles McIntyre. LC 73-10943. (Jossey-Bass Higher Education Ser.). 171p. reprint ed. pap. 53.10 (*0-608-14798-2*, 202565900045) Bks Demand.

Planning Commissioners Guide. David J. Allor. LC 83-62938. (Illus.). 186p. 1984. pap. 24.95 (*0-918286-30-1*, Planners Press) Am Plan Assn.

Planning Committee. Judith O'Connor. 20p. 1997. pap. 12.00 (*0-925299-77-4*) Natl Ctr Nonprofit.

Planning Community Mental Health Services for Women: A Multiprofessional Handbook. Ed. by Kathryn Abel et al. LC 95-38887. 280p. (C). 1996. 80.00 (*0-415-11455-1*); pap. 25.99 (*0-415-11456-X*) Routledge.

Planning Community Policing: Goal Specific Cases & Exercises. Victor G. Strecher. LC 97-205605. (Illus.). 225p. (C). 1997. pap. text 16.95 (*0-88133-930-X*) Waveland Pr.

Planning Companion: A Practical Guide for Pre-Retirement Planning (Federal Edition) R. N. Garnitz. (LifeSystems Ser.). (Illus.). 120p. 1996. pap. 13.95 (*0-927289-43-1*) LifeSpan Services.

Planning Companion: A Practical Guide for Pre-Retirement Planning (Federal Law Enforcement Edition) R. N. Garnitz. (LifeSystems Ser.). (Illus.). 120p. 1996. pap. 13.95 (*0-927289-33-4*) LifeSpan Services.

Planning Companion: Practical Guide for Pre-Retirement Planning -5-250 (Regular Edition) Life Span Editorial Staff. (LifeSystems Ser.). 1999. 13.95 (*0-927289-45-8*) LifeSpan Services.

Planning Considerations, Addressing Preparation of Documents for Image Capture: ANSI/AIIM TR15-1997. Association for Information & Image Management Staff. 20p. 1997. 52.00 (*0-89258-336-3*, TR15) Assn Inform & Image Mgmt.

Planning Control: Philosophies, Prospects & Practice. Ed. by M. L. Harrison & R. Murday. 235p. (C). 1986. 55.00 (*0-7099-3790-3*, Pub. by C Helm) Routldge.

Planning Controls & Their Enforcement. A. J. Little. 1982. pap. 180.00 (*0-7219-0492-0*, Pub. by Scientific) St Mut.

Planning Conventional Forces, 1950-80. William W. Kaufmann. LC 81-70777. (Studies in Defense Policy). 26p. 1982. 7.95 (*0-8157-4847-7*) Brookings.

Planning Conversions to Micrographic Systems. Daniel A. Brathal & Mark Langemo. 62p. 1987. pap. 15.00 (*0-933887-19-1*, A4557) ARMA Intl.

Planning Corporate Manpower. D. J. Bell. LC 73-86105. (Manpower Studies Ser.). 191p. reprint ed. pap. 59.30 (*0-608-30410-7*, 201005500071) Bks Demand.

***Planning Derry: Planning & Politics in Northern Ireland.** Gerald McSheffrey. 368p. 1999. 72.95 (*0-85323-714-2*, Pub. by Liverpool Univ Pr); pap. 45.95 (*0-85323-724-7*, Pub. by Liverpool Univ Pr); pap. 45.95 (*0-86356-724-X*, Pub. by Liverpool Univ Pr) Intl Spec Bk.

Planning, Design, & Analysis of Cellular Manufacturing Systems. Ed. by Ali K. Kamrani et al. LC 95-7223. (Manufacturing Research & Technology Ser.: Vol. 24). 400p. 1995. 227.25 (*0-444-81815-4*) Elsevier.

Planning, Design & Construction of Health Care Environments. Joint Commission on Accreditation of Healthcare Organizations. (Illus.). 174p. 1997. pap. 45.00 (*0-86688-543-9*, EC-506) Joint Comm Hlthcare.

Planning, Design & Implementation of Bicycle & Pedestrian Facilities. 610p. 1976. pap. 5.00 (*0-87262-170-7*) Am Soc Civil Eng.

Planning Director. Jack Rudman. (Career Examination Ser.: C-3401). 1994. pap. 39.95 (*0-8373-3401-2*) Nat Learn.

Planning Districts in South Dakota: An Assessment of Economic Change & Development. Mitchel J. Beville et al. 1984. 1.00 (*1-55614-077-0*) U of SD Gov Res Bur.

Planning Drain, Waste & Vent Systems. Howard C. Massey. 192p. (Orig.). 1990. pap. 19.25 (*0-934041-51-2*) Craftsman.

Planning Education Reforms in Developing Countries: The Contingency Approach. Dennis A. Rondinelli et al. LC 89-36234. 225p. (C). 1990. text 45.95 (*0-8223-0966-1*); pap. text 19.95 (*0-8223-0974-2*) Duke.

Planning Educational Facilities. Donald G. Mackenzie. LC 89-14610. 102p. (Orig.). (C). 1989. pap. text 20.00 (*0-8191-7480-7*) U Pr of Amer.

Planning Educational Facilities for Information Technology. Tweed Ross. (Illus.). 32p. 1997. pap. text 9.95 (*0-914607-52-9*, 1734) Master Tchr.

Planning Effective Curriculum for Gifted Learners. Joyce VanTassel-Baska. LC 91-77051. 402p. 1992. 44.00 (*0-89108-218-2*, S382) Love Pub Co.

Planning Efficient Arbitration Proceedings: The Law Applicable in International Arbitration. Ed. by Albert J. Van Den Berg. (ICCA Congress Ser.: No. 7). 1996. pap. 151.00 (*90-411-0224-8*) Kluwer Law Intl.

Planning Efficient Hospital Systems. Robert E. Coughlin & Walter Isard. (Discussion Papers: No. 1). 1963. pap. 10.00 (*1-55869-094-8*) Regional Sci Res Inst.

Planning Enforcement. Richard Harwood. 220p. 1996. pap. 53.00 (*1-85811-066-1*, Pub. by CLT Prof) Gaunt.

Planning, Engineering & Constructing the Superprojects. 537p. 1979. pap. 30.00 (*0-87262-178-2*) Am Soc Civil Eng.

Planning, Engineering & Construction Projects. Ed. by David C. Johnston. (Symposium Proceedings Ser.). 70p. 1986. 5.00 (*0-87262-529-X*) Am Soc Civil Eng.

Planning English Sentences. Douglas E. Appelt. (Studies in Natural Language Processing). (Illus.). 181p. (C). 1992. pap. text 19.95 (*0-521-43803-9*) Cambridge U Pr.

Planning Enjoyable Reunions. Alma Heaton. pap. 10.95 (*1-55517-386-1*) CFI Dist.

Planning Environment. Weston. (C). pap. text. write for info. (*0-582-27325-0*, Pub. by Addison-Wesley) Longman.

***Planning Environmental Communication & Education: Lessons from Asia.** Ed. by Seema Saeed et al. LC 98-190638. xiii, 79 p. 1998. write for info. (*2-8317-0415-4*, Pub. by IUCN) Island Pr.

Planning Environmental Health Programs. Sanford M. Brown. LC 86-21267. 250p. 1986. 59.95 (*0-275-92237-5*, C2237, Praeger Pubs) Greenwood.

Planning Environments for Young Children: Physical Space. 2nd ed. Sybil Kritchevsky et al. LC 75-78941. (Illus.). 56p. (Orig.). 1977. pap. text 2.50 (*0-912674-28-8*, NAEYC 115) Natl Assn Child Ed.

Planning, Estimating & Control of Chemical Construction Projects. Pablo F. Navarrete. LC 95-124. (Cost Engineering Ser.: Vol. 23). (Illus.). 344p. 1995. text 135.00 (*0-8247-9359-5*) Dekker.

Planning Estuaries. Cees-Jan Van Westen & Reinier J. Scheele. LC 96-21923. (NATO - Challenges of Modern Society Ser.: Vol. 20). (Illus.). 125p. (C). 1996. 71.00 (*0-306-45361-4*, Plenum Trade) Perseus Pubng.

Planning Ethically Responsible Research: A Guide for Social Science Students. Joan E. Sieber. (Applied Social Research Methods Ser.: Vol. 31). 160p. (C). 1992. text 42.00 (*0-8039-3963-9*); pap. text 18.95 (*0-8039-3964-7*) Sage.

Planning Ethics: A Reader in Planning Theory, Practice, & Education. Ed. by Sue Hendler. LC 94-17143. 394p. (C). 1995. pap. text 19.95 (*0-88285-151-9*) Ctr Urban Pol Res.

Planning Europe's Capital Cities. Hall. LC 97-66869. (Studies in History, Planning & the Environment). (Illus.). 408p. (C). 1997. 90.00 (*0-419-17290-4*, E & FN Spon) Routledge.

Planning Facilities for Sci-Tech Libraries. Ed. by Ellis Mount. LC 83-8570. (Science & Technology Libraries: Vol. 3, No. 4). 121p. 1983. text 29.95 (*0-86656-237-0*) Haworth Pr.

Planning Family in India Prevedic Times to Early 1950's. B. L. Raina. 1990. 42.00 (*81-7169-060-2*, Commonwealth) S Asia.

Planning Fences. (Illus.). 84p. 1980. 7.50 (*0-89606-049-7*, 404) Am Assn Voc Materials.

Planning Foodservice Facilities & Equipment Skillbook. Educational Foundation of the National Restaurant. (Management Skills Program Ser.). 52p. (Orig.). 1992. pap. 10.95 (*0-915452-44-8*) Educ Found.

Planning for a Better Living Environment in Asia. Gar-On Yeh Mee Kam. 59.95 (*1-85972-223-7*) Ashgate Pub Co.

Planning for a Change: A Citizen's Guide to Creative Planning & Program Development. Duane Dale & Nancy Mitiguy. LC 79-624733. (Illus.). (Orig.). (C). 1978. pap. 10.00 (*0-934210-01-2*) Devlp Commy.

Planning for a Movable Compact Shelving System. Franklyn F. Bright. LC 91-14261. (Library Administration & Management Association Ser.: No. 1). (Illus.). 80p. 1991. reprint ed. pap. 30.00 (*0-608-02968-8*, 206343600006) Bks Demand.

***Planning for a New Century: The Regional Agenda.** Ed. by Jonathan Barnett. (Illus.). 218p. 2000. pap. 29.95 (*1-55963-806-0*, Shearwater Bks) Island Pr.

***Planning for A New Generation of Public Library Buildings.** Gerard B. McCabe. LC 99-32004. 184p. 2000. lib. bdg. 59.95 (*0-313-30592-7*) Greenwood.

Planning for a Satisfying Retirement: Program Workbook. Ed. by Stephen D. Bruce. 72p. 1989. 9.95 (*1-55645-426-0*) Busn Legal Reports.

Planning for a Successful Career Transition: The Physician's Guide to Managing Career Change. American Medical Association. (Illus.). 65p. 1999. pap. 27.95 (*0-89970-980-X*, OP208299) AMA.

Planning for Adult Career Counseling. Robert D. Bhaerman. 64p. 1985. 6.25 (*0-318-17845-1*, IN 290) Ctr Educ Trng Employ.

Planning for Affordable Housing. J. Barlow et al. 102p. 1994. pap. 30.00 (*0-11-752969-9*, HM29699, Pub. by Statnry Office) Bernan Associates.

Planning for Aging or Incapacity, 1993: Legal & Financial Issues. (Tax Law & Estate Planning Course Handbook Ser.: Vol. 219). 506p. 1993. 70.00 (*0-685-65543-1*, D4-5237) PLI.

Planning for Agriculture Development in Nepal. Mehar M. Paudel. 1985. 75.00 (*0-7855-0250-5*, Pub. by Ratna Pustak Bhandar) St Mut.

Planning for Agriculture Development in Nepal. Ed. by Mehar M. Paudel. 216p. (C). 1985. 250.00 (*0-89771-054-1*, Pub. by Ratna Pustak Bhandar) St Mut.

Planning for Agroforestry. F. R. Steiner et al. (Developments in Landscape Management & Urban Planning Ser.: Vol. 6C). x,338p. 1990. 135.00 (*0-444-88634-6*) Elsevier.

Planning for Alcohol & Other Drug Abuse Treatment for Adults in the Criminal Justice System. Ed. by Sandra Clunies. 116p. (C). 1999. pap. text 25.00 (*0-7881-7594-7*) DIANE Pub.

Planning for an Individual Water System. Henderson & America Association for Vocational Institute Mater. 160p. 1982. 15.00 (*0-89606-097-7*, 600) Am Assn Voc Materials.

Planning for an Irrigation System. (Illus.). 120p. 1980. 6.00 (*0-914452-44-4*, 501) Am Assn Voc Materials.

Planning for ASEAN: How to Prepare for Free Trade in SE Asia after 2003. 1996. 645.00 (*0-614-25472-8*) Econ Intel.

Planning for ASEAN: How to Take Advantage of South-East Asia's Free Trade Area. 1997. 645.00 (*0-85058-919-3*) Economist Intell.

Planning for Automation: A How-to-Do-It Manual for Librarians. 2nd ed. John M. Cohn et al. LC 97-27284. (How-to-Do-It Manuals for Libraries Ser.). 148p. 1997. 55.00 (*1-55570-313-5*) Neal-Schuman.

Planning for Balanced Development: A Guide for Native American & Rural Communities. Susan Guyette. LC 94-43553. (Illus.). 328p. (C). 1995. pap. 14.95 (*0-940666-64-2*); text 24.95 (*0-940666-63-4*) Clear Light.

Planning for Basic Needs in Kenya: Performance, Policies & Prospects. Dharam P. Ghai et al. (Illus.). vii, 166p. 1981. pap. 18.00 (*92-2-102171-8*) Intl Labour Office.

Planning for Biodiversity: Issues & Examples. Sheila Peck. LC 98-10504. 256p. 1998. pap. text 27.50 (*1-55963-401-4*) Island Pr.

Planning for Business Owners & Professionals. 7th ed. Ted Kurlowicz et al. LC 98-74588. 400p. (C). 1999. text 54.00 (*1-57996-011-1*) Amer College.

Planning for Change: Industrial Policy & Japanese Economic Development 1945-1990. James Vestal. (Illus.). 256p. 1994. text 42.00 (*0-19-828808-5*) OUP.

Planning for Change: Industrial Policy & Japanese Economic Development 1945-1990. James E. Vestal. (Illus.). 256p. 1995. pap. text 26.00 (*0-19-829027-6*) OUP.

Planning for Change in Turbulent Times: The Case for Multi-Racial Primary Schools. Mike Wallace & Agnes McMahon. Ed. by David Hopkins & David Reynolds. (School Development Ser.). (Illus.). 224p. 1994. text 100.00 (*0-304-32674-7*); pap. text 33.95 (*0-304-32676-3*) Continuum.

Planning for Changing Energy Conditions. Ed. by John Byrne & Daniel Rich. (Energy Policy Studies: Vol. 4). 196p. 1987. pap. 24.95 (*0-88738-713-6*) Transaction Pubs.

Planning for Children: Dispositional Plans & Case Plans. 480p. 1988. pap. 8.50 (*0-685-30176-1*, 44,200A) NCLS Inc.

Planning for Christian Education: A Practical Guide for Your Congregation. Ed. by Carol F. Krau. LC 94-72135. 72p. 1994. pap. 9.95 (*0-88177-134-1*, DR134) Discipleship Res.

Planning for Cleanup of Large Areas Contaminated As a Result of a Nuclear Accident. IAEA Staff. (Technical Reports: No. 327). 56p. 1991. pap. 25.00 (*92-0-125691-4*, STI/DOC/327, Pub. by IAEA) Bernan Associates.

Planning for College & a Career see College Bound: A Comprehensive Guide to Optional Preparation & Decision Making

Planning for Colleges & Universities: The President's Guide. Stephan D. Hogan & Harold E. Knight. 197p. 1988. 45.00 (*0-945253-00-1*) Thornsbury Bailey Brown.

Planning for Community-Oriented Health Systems. James E. Rohrer. 168p. (Orig.). 1996. pap. 32.00 (*0-87553-230-6*) Am Pub Health.

Planning for Computer Success. Jay Weininger & Deborah Clowney. 1985. 24.95 (*0-13-679440-8*) P-H.

Planning for Computing in Higher Education: Proceedings. 240p. 25.00 (*0-318-14028-4*) EDUCOM.

Planning for Data Base Systems. Robert M. Curtice. LC 76-374222. (QED Monograph Series. Data Base Management: No. 2). 49p. reprint ed. pap. 30.00 (*0-608-15621-3*, 203175000076) Bks Demand.

Planning for Department of Defense Investment in Technology Demonstrations. Timothy Webb & Richard Pei. LC 92-14258. 1992. pap. 4.00 (*0-8330-1247-9*, R-4198-DR&E) Rand Corp.

Planning for Developing a Backward Economy. Abhimanyu Singh. 1989. text 27.95 (*0-7069-4273-6*, Pub. by Vikas) S Asia.

Planning for Developing a Backward Economy. Abhimanyu Singh. 1991. 20.00 (*0-7069-8556-7*, Pub. by Vikas) S Asia.

Planning for Disability Management: An Approach to Controlling Costs While Caring for Employees. Sheila H. Akabas & Lauren B. Gates. (Building Blocks Ser.: Vol. 25). (Illus.). 24p. (Orig.). 1995. pap. 24.95 (*1-57963-027-8*, A045) Am Compensation.

***Planning for Disaster: A Guide for School Administrators.** 2nd ed. Harmon A. Baldwin. LC 99-68091. 1999. pap. 8.00 (*0-87367-818-4*) Phi Delta Kappa.

Planning for Diversity in Rural Southwestern Schools: Practical Research & Recommendations. Max Ferguson. 144p. (Orig.). 1997. pap. write for info. (*1-57502-519-1*, P01541) Morris Pubng.

Planning for Divorcing Couples. 95th ed. Connell. 1995. pap. text 35.00 (*0-15-601700-8*) Harcourt.

Planning for Drilling in H2S Zones: An Outline of Safety & Health Procedures. 44p. 1978. pap. text 15.00 (*0-88698-129-8*, 2.75010) PETEX.

P

Planning for Early Learning: Educating Young Children. 2nd ed. Victoria Hurst. LC 97-223230. (One-Off Ser.). (Illus.). 176p. 1997. pap. (*1-85396-344-5*) Corwin Pr.

Planning for Early Learning: Education in the First Five Years. Victoria Hurst. 176p. 1991. pap. 27.00 (*1-85396-129-9*, Pub. by P Chapman) Taylor & Francis.

Planning for Earthquakes: Risk, Politics, & Policy. Philip R. Berke & Timothy Beatley. (Illus.). 240p. 1992. text 40.00 (*0-8018-4255-7*) Johns Hopkins.

Planning for Education in Pakistan: A Personal Case Study. Adam Curle. LC 66-14440. (Illus.). 230p. 1966. 24.00 (*0-674-67100-7*) HUP.

***Planning for Education in Pakistan: A Personal Case Study.** Adam Curle. 232p. 1999. 25.95 (*0-7351-0178-7*) Replica Bks.

Planning for Effective Faculty Development: Using Adult Learning Strategies. Patricia A. Lawler & Kathleen P. King. LC 00-26717. (Illus.). (C). 2000. pap. text. write for info. (*1-57524-105-6*) Krieger.

Planning for Effective Staff Development: 6 Research-Based Models - A Primer. exp. ed. Meredith D. Gall & Roseanne Vojtek. LC 94-19882. Orig. Title: Effective Staff Development for Teachers. 1994. reprint ed. pap. 6.95 (*0-86552-126-3*) U of Oreg ERIC.

Planning for Effective Technical Training: A Guide for Instructors & Trainers. Jerrold E. Kemp & George W. Cochern. LC 93-28872. 200p. 1994. pap. 39.95 (*0-87778-267-9*) Educ Tech Pubns.

Planning for Estates & Administration in Michigan, 4 vols. Hoops. LC 82-84394. 1983. 420.00 (*0-317-00654-1*) West Group.

Planning for Estates & Administration in Michigan, 4 vols. Hoops. 1993. suppl. ed. 140.00 (*0-317-03232-1*) West Group.

Planning for Estates & Administration in Michigan, Vol. 3. 2nd ed. Frederick K. Hoops. Ed. by Marcia Clifford. LC 95-81847. 1500p. 1995. text. write for info. (*0-7620-0029-5*) West Group.

Planning for Europe, 1992: Britain & the Common Internal Market. Ed. by W. M. Clarke. (Waterlow Publications). (Illus.). 240p. 1989. pap. 19.95 (*0-08-036903-0*, Pergamon Pr) Elsevier.

Planning for Executive Success: Shaping up for the Real Corporate World Walter Vieira. LC 99-11083. 1999. write for info. (*0-7619-9323-1*) Sage.

Planning for Field Safety. Ed. by Gerald O'Reilly. LC 89-83681. 197p. (Orig.). 1992. pap. text 18.75 (*0-913312-93-2*) Am Geol.

Planning for Freedom. enl. ed. Ludwig Von Mises. 296p. 1996. pap. 9.95 (*0-910884-31-5*) Libertarian Press.

Planning for Full Employment. Ed. by Bertram M. Gross et al. LC 74-84801. (Annals Ser.: No. 418). 1975. pap. 18.00 (*0-87761-187-4*) Am Acad Pol Soc Sci.

Planning for Growth. Didactic Systems Staff. (Simulation Game Ser.). 1972. pap. 26.25 (*0-89401-074-3*) Didactic Syst.

Planning for Human Systems: Essays in Honor of Russell L. Ackoff. Ed. by Jean-Marc Choukroun & Roberta M. Snow. LC 91-45087. (Illus.). 448p. (C). 1992. text 49.95 (*0-8122-3128-7*) U of Pa Pr.

Planning for Improved Campus Facilities. (Illus.). 84p. 1992. pap. 31.00 (*0-913359-70-X*) APPA VA.

Planning for Improved Enterprise Performance: A Guide for Managers & Consultants. Robert Abramson & Walter Halset. (Management Development Ser.: No. 15). (Illus.). 170p. 1992. pap. 18.00 (*92-2-102082-7*) Intl Labour Office.

Planning for Independent Schools: A Practical Guide. Stephen D. Hogan & Harold E. Knight, III. 190p. (Orig.). 1988. 45.00 (*0-945253-01-X*) Thornsbury Bailey Brown.

Planning for Information as a Corporate Resource. Alfred Collins. 118p. 83.50 (*0-08-037270-8*, Pergamon Pr) Elsevier.

Planning for Information as a Corporate Resource. Alfred Collins. (Best of Long Range Planning Ser.). 118p. 1990. pap. text 42.00 (*0-08-037409-3*, Pergamon Pr) Elsevier.

Planning for Innovation Through Dissemination & Utilization of Knowledge. Ronald G. Havelock. LC 78-634679. 579p. reprint ed. pap. 179.50 (*0-608-18491-8*, 203149300075) Bks Demand.

Planning For Instruction. Queen. 2000. pap. text 13.27 (*0-13-021996-7*) S&S Trade.

Planning for Intervention: International Cooperation in Conflict Management. Antonia H. Chayes & Abram Chayes. LC 99-11646. 200p. 1999. 65.00 (*90-411-0643-X*) Kluwer Law Intl.

***Planning for Intervention: International Cooperation in Conflict Management.** Antonia H. Chayes & Abram Chayes. LC 99-11646. ix, 224p. 1999. pap. 65.00 (*90-411-9242-5*) Kluwer Law Intl.

Planning for Large Estates: Tools & Techniques. Douglas K. Freeman. 1985. 185.00 incl. cd-rom (*0-8205-1128-5*) Bender.

Planning for Library Services: A Guide to Utilizing Planning Methods for Library Management. Ed. by Charles R. McClure. LC 82-896. (Journal of Library Administration: Vol. 2, Nos. 3-4). 250p. 1982. 49.95 (*0-917724-84-4*) Haworth Pr.

Planning for Local & National Assembly Elections: Report to the Royal Government of Cambodia, August 1996. Ronald A. Gould et al. iv, 54p. 1996. pap. 8.00 (*1-879720-73-6*) Intl Fndt Elect.

Planning for Low Cost Rural Housing: The Role of Local Authority Planners in the Solution of Problems Caused by Competition for Rural Housing - The North Cotswolds & Evesham. J. L. Greenwood. (C). 1989. 49.00 (*0-7855-3817-8*, Pub. by Oxford Polytechnic) St Mut.

Planning for Microcomputers in Higher Education Strategies for the Next Generation: Strategies for the Next Generation. Reynolds Ferrante et al. LC 89-83628. (ASHE-ERIC Higher Education Reports: No. 88-7). 170p. (Orig.). 1989. pap. text 24.00 (*0-913317-51-9*) GWU Grad Schl E&HD.

Planning for Multiple Objectives. Morris Hill. (Monographs: No. 5). 1973. 20.00 (*1-55869-095-6*) Regional Sci Res Inst.

Planning for Nature Conservation. D. R. Helliwell. 116p. (C). 1991. text 100.00 (*0-906527-09-0*, Pub. by Surrey Beatty & Sons) St Mut.

Planning for NetWare 4.2. David Doering. 416p. 1995. pap. 27.95 (*1-55851-550-X*, M&T Bks) IDG Bks.

Planning for Online Search Services in Sci-Tech Libraries. Ed. by Ellis Mount. (Science & Technology Libraries: Vol. 1, No. 1). 142p. 1981. pap. text 29.95 (*0-917724-73-9*) Haworth Pr.

Planning for Our Cultural Heritage. Ed. by H. Coccossis & P. Nijkamp. 240p. 1995. 78.95 (*1-85972-178-8*, Pub. by Avebry) Ashgate Pub Co.

Planning for Parks & Recreation Needs in Urban Areas. Elinor C. Guggenheimer. LC 68-31141. (Illus.). 261p. 1969. text 32.00 (*0-8290-0192-1*) Irvington.

Planning for People in Museum Exhibitions. Kathleen McLean. (Illus.). 196p. (C). 1993. text 35.00 (*0-944040-32-2*, 67-0) AST Ctrs.

Planning for Pharmacy Services, 1991, Level 2. 134p. 1991. ring bd. 63.00 (*1-879907-13-5*, P320) Am Soc Hlth-Syst.

Planning for Population Change. Ed. by W. T. Gould & R. Lawton. LC 85-26828. 228p. (C). 1986. 50.00 (*0-389-20606-7*, N8164) B&N Imports.

Planning for Population, Labour Force & Service Demand: A Microcomputer-Based Training Module. Geoffrey Greene. (Background Paper for Training in Population, Human Resources & Development Planning Ser.: No. 3). v, 100p. 1989. pap. 13.50 (*92-2-105622-8*) Intl Labour Office.

Planning for Pregnancy, Birth, & Beyond. American College of Obstetricians & Gynecologists. LC 95-6754. Orig. Title: ACOG Guide to Planning for Pregnancy, Birth, & Beyond. 323p. 1995. 12.95 (*0-915473-27-5*) Am Coll Obstetric.

Planning for Pregnancy, Birth, & Beyond. rev. ed. American College of Obstetricians & Gynecologists. Orig. Title: ACOG Guide to Planning for Pregnancy, Birth, & Beyond. 1997. mass mkt. 6.99 (*0-451-19175-7*, Sig) NAL.

***Planning for Pregnancy, Birth, & Beyond.** 3rd ed. American College of Obstetricians and Gynecologists. LC 99-58049. 2000. write for info. (*0-915473-56-9*) Am Coll Obstetric.

Planning for Proficiency. Magnan. (Teaching Methods Ser.). (J). 1990. mass mkt. 27.95 (*0-8384-2924-6*) Heinle & Heinle.

Planning for Profits: The Retailers Guide to Success. Anita Goldwasser. 1981. pap. 24.95 (*0-86730-001-9*) Lebhar Friedman.

Planning for Public Transport Needs. P. A. Stanley. (C). 1982. 29.00 (*0-7855-3849-6*, Pub. by Oxford Polytechnic) St Mut.

Planning for Quality, Productivity & Competitive Position, ASQC Edition. Process Management Institute Staff & Howard S. Gitlow. 172p. 1990. text 17.47 (*1-55623-466-X*, Irwn Prfssnl) McGraw-Hill Prof.

Planning for Rare Events: Nuclear Accident Preparedness & Management Proceedings, Laxenburg, Austria, August 28-31, 1980. IIASA International Workshop Staff & J. W. Lathrop. (IIASA Proceedings Ser.: Vol. 14). (Illus.). 280p. 1981. 121.00 (*0-08-028703-4*, Pub. by Pergamon Repr) Franklin.

Planning for Research: A Guide for the Helping Professions. Raymond M. Berger & Michael A. Patchner. (Human Services Guides Ser.: Vol. 50). 160p. (C). 1988. pap. text 18.95 (*0-8039-3033-X*) Sage.

Planning for Research: A Guide for the Helping Professions. Raymond M. Berger & Michael A. Patchner. LC 87-17535. (Sage Human Services Guides Ser.: Vol. 50). 160p. reprint ed. pap. 49.60 (*0-608-09791-8*, 206996500007) Bks Demand.

Planning for Results: A Public Library Transformation Process. Ethel E. Himmel et al. LC 98-5252. 328p. 1998. 20.00 (*0-8389-3488-9*); pap. 40.00 (*0-8389-3479-X*) ALA.

***Planning for Retirement Distributions: Tax, Financial, & Personal Aspects with CD-ROM.** Eric Donner. 300p. 2000. pap. 109.00 incl. cd-rom (*0-15-607232-7*) Harcourt Prof.

Planning for Retirement Needs. 3rd ed. Kenn B. Tacchino & David A. Littell. LC 98-73889. 530p. (C). 1999. text 60.00 (*1-57996-012-X*) Amer College.

Planning for Revivals in African American Contexts. J. M. Capers & J. K. Echols. 1993. pap. 8.40 (*0-8066-1383-1*, 23-1787) Augsburg Fortress.

Planning for Rural Development. R. B. Singh. (C). 1987. 11.50 (*0-8364-2171-X*) S Asia.

Planning for Rural Development Administration. Aruna Sharma & Rajagopal. (C). 1995. 22.00 (*0-614-13263-0*, Pub. by Rawat Pubns) S Asia.

Planning for Rural Development & Poverty Alleviation. B. D. Singh. (C). 1992. 16.00 (*81-7099-316-4*, Pub. by Mittal Pubs Dist) S Asia.

Planning for School Emergencies. 1988. 5.00 (*0-88314-396-8*) AAHPERD.

***Planning for Seismic Rehabilitation: Societal Issues.** Ed. by Eugene Zeller. 102p. (C). 1999. pap. text 20.00 (*0-7881-8382-6*) DIANE Pub.

Planning for Serfdom: Legal Economic Discourse & Downtown Development. Robin P. Malloy. LC 90-29188. 208p. (C). 1991. text 32.50 (*0-8122-3055-8*) U of Pa Pr.

Planning for Social & Economic Development: Essays in Honour of Professor D. M. Nanjundappa. Ed. by R. Bharadwaj & M. V. Nadkarni. LC 92-20729. (Illus.). 276p. (C). 1992. text 36.00 (*0-8039-9444-3*) Sage.

***Planning for Social Reforms: The Key to Economic Progress.** P. V. Rajeev. 1999. 20.00 (*81-7629-189-7*, Pub. by Deep & Deep Pubns) S Asia.

Planning for Software Validation, Verification & Testing. 1986. lib. bdg. 79.95 (*0-8490-3760-3*) Gordon Pr.

Planning for Strikes: Obtaining Maximum Performance with Minimum Personnel. Stephen R. Levine. 54p. 1975. pap. 25.00 (*0-941496-00-7*) Model Cities.

***Planning for Student Services: Best Practices for the 21st Century.** Ed. by Martha Beede & Darlene Burnett. (Illus.). 160p. 1999. pap. 45.00 (*0-9601608-9-2*) Soc Coll & Univ Planning.

Planning for Success: A 10-Step Process for Setting & Achieving Your Goals in Life. Ronald W. Miller. (Illus.). 120p. (Orig.). 1990. pap. write for info. (*0-9625695-0-X*) New Pers Pub.

Planning for Success: Effective Insights & Strategies for Administration of Jewish Religious Schools. Dorothy C. Herman. Ed. by Paul Flexner. 120p. (Orig.). 1992. pap. text 10.95 (*0-933873-65-4*) Torah Aura.

Planning for Success: Successful Implementation of Middle Level Reorganization. Ronald Williamson & J. Howard Johnston. 96p. (Orig.). (C). 1991. pap. 12.00 (*0-88210-242-7*) Natl Assn Principals.

Planning for Success on the Job. Rodger Busse. Ed. by Valerie Harris. LC 93-71674. (Illus.). 264p. 1993. pap. 16.95 (*0-89262-220-2*); teacher ed., ring bd. 80.00 (*0-89262-221-0*) Career Pub.

***Planning for Survival.** Gary L. Schilling. (Illus.). 24p. 1999. pap. 3.95 (*0-9676241-0-X*) G L Schilling.

Planning for Sustainability in Irrigation: Command Area Development & Indira Gandhi Canal Project. Ed. by Rakesh Hooja & P. S. Kavdia. (C). 1994. 34.00 (*81-7033-220-6*, Pub. by Rawat Pubns) S Asia.

Planning for Sustainable Development: Guidelines for Developing Countries. rev. ed. 263p. 1994. 25.00 (*92-1-104440-5*) UN.

Planning for Sustainable Development Urban Management in Nepal & South Asia. Jibgar Joshi. 1997. pap. 60.00 (*0-7855-7474-3*, Pub. by Ratna Pustak Bhandar) St Mut.

Planning for Tech Prep: A Guidebook for School Leaders. Carol Fagen & Dan Lumley. LC 95-8812. (Illus.). 160p. 1995. 29.95 (*0-590-49786-3*) Scholastic Inc.

Planning for Technology: A Guidebook for Teachers, Technology Leaders & School Administrators. Dan Lumley & Gerald Bailey. LC 98-160762. 171p. 1997. ring bd. 69.00 (*1-879639-54-8*) Natl Educ Serv.

Planning for the Archival Profession. SAA Task Force on Goals & Priorities Staff. 42p. (Orig.). 1986. pap. text 8.00 (*0-931828-34-1*) Soc Am Archivists.

Planning for the Closely Held Business. (Tax Law & Estate Planning Course Handbook Ser.). 303p. 1990. 17.50 (*0-685-69472-0*) PLI.

Planning for the Elderly. Alfred C. Clapp & William H. Mears. LC 98-184320. (Personal Financial Planning Portfolio Ser.). viii, 104p. 1996. write for info. (*0-15-601848-9*) Harcourt Legal.

Planning for the Factory of the Future. 1984. write for info. (*0-318-57947-2*) C I M Systems.

Planning for the Fiber Distributed Data Interface. William E. Burr. (Illus.). 102p. (Orig.). (C). 1995. pap. text 40.00 (*0-7881-1233-3*) DIANE Pub.

Planning for the Fire Service. Hoover. (Career Education Ser.). 1997. pap., teacher ed. 14.00 (*0-8273-7341-4*) Delmar.

Planning for the Fire Service. David H. Hoover. (Career Education Ser.). 1997. text 42.95 (*0-8273-7340-6*) Delmar.

Planning for the Future: Providing a Meaningful Life for a Child with a Disability after Your Death. L. Mark Russell et al. LC 95-187250. 430p. 1993. pap. 24.95 (*0-9635780-0-6*) Amer Pub IL.

Planning for the Future - Guidelines for Self Assessment & Service Planning. Resa Hall & Lori Hansherr. 1996. pap. 27.50 (*1-57654-006-5*, Creative Core) Creat Core.

Planning for the Information City: The U. K. Case. S. D. Graham & G. R. Dominy. (Illus.). 80p. 1991. pap. 53.25 (*0-08-041152-5*, Pergamon Pr) Elsevier.

Planning for the Lower East Side. Peter Abeles & Harry W. Schwartz. LC 72-88988. (Special Studies in U. S. Economic, Social & Political Issues). 1973. 32.00 (*0-275-28805-6*) Irvington.

Planning for the Nation's Health: A Study of 20th-Century Developments in the United States, 19. Grace Budrys. LC 86-12142. (Contributions in Medical Studies: No. 19). 168p. 1987. 45.00 (*0-313-25348-X*, BYP/, Greenwood Pr) Greenwood.

Planning for the Needs of People with Dementia: The Development of a Profile for Use in Local Services. P. Spicker & D. S. Gordon. 184p. 1997. text 59.95 (*1-85972-600-3*, Pub. by Avebry) Ashgate Pub Co.

***Planning for the Past: An Archaeological Resource Management Plan.** Bonnie L. Gums et al. (Archaeological Monograph Ser.: Vol. 5). (Illus.). vi, 143p. 1999. pap. 15.00 (*1-893955-05-2*) Univ S AL Ctr Archa.

Planning for the Rural Poor. Shahi B. Singh. (C). 1990. 35.00 (*81-7169-094-7*, Pub. by Commonwealth) S Asia.

Planning for the Times of Your Life: 45 Great Financial Planning Ideas, Practical Strategies to Help You to Take Charge of Your Finances. Ed. by Kathleen M. Rehl. LC 99-60702. (Illus.). 76p. (C). 1999. pap. 19.95 (*0-9670673-0-8*) Cambridge Advisors LLC.

Planning for the Year 2000: A Practical Guide for Conducting Legal Audits. Richard I. Werder. LC 99-227741. (Corporate Practice Ser.). 1998. 95.00 (*1-55871-372-7*) BNA.

Planning for Tomorrow. Michael J. Klein. LC 79-11308. 1979. ring bd. 35.00 (*0-07-035031-0*) McGraw.

Planning for Tourism Development: Quantitative Approaches Charles E. Gearing et al. LC 74-1731. (Special Studies in International Economics & Development). xiv, 221 p. 1976. 17.50 (*0-275-28872-2*) Greenwood.

Planning for Tourism in the Cocos Islands. 69p. 1991. pap. 35.00 (*1-882866-46-0*) Pac Asia Trvl.

Planning for Transitions. 174p. 1997. pap. 15.00 (*0-16-042716-9*) USGPO.

Planning for Urban Quality: Urban Design in Towns & Cities. Gordon Power & Michael Parfect. LC 96-41631. (Illus.). 264p. (C). 1997. 110.00 (*0-415-15967-9*); pap. 37.99 (*0-415-15968-7*) Routledge.

Planning for Vegetation in Urbanizing Areas. Lisa Rosenberger & Robert E. Coughlin. (Discussion Papers: No. 115). 1979. pap. 10.00 (*1-55869-096-4*) Regional Sci Res Inst.

Planning for War Against Russia & Serbia: Austro-Hungarian & German Military Strategies, 1871-1914. Graydon J. Tunstall, Jr. (Atlantic Studies on Society in Change: No. 78). 373p. 1993. 58.50 (*0-88033-271-9*, 374, Pub. by East Eur Monographs) Col U Pr.

Planning for Water Shortages: Water Reallocations & Transfers Drought Management. Ed. by Jerry Schaack et al. (Illus.). 273p. 1990. pap. 40.00 (*0-9618257-5-8*) US Comm Irrigation.

Planning for Water Source Protection. Philip M. Kappen. 33p. 1993. pap. 10.00 (*0-86602-299-6*, Sage Prdcls Pr) Sage.

Planning for Wellness: A Guidebook for Achieving Optimal Health. 3rd ed. Donald Ardell & Mark J. Tager. 112p. 1988. per. 16.95 (*0-8403-5031-7*) Kendall-Hunt.

Planning for Windows 2000. Eric Cone et al. LC 99-60311. (Illus.). 415p. 1999. pap. 29.99 (*0-7357-0048-6*) New Riders Pub.

Planning for Your Financial Future. Meredith G. Resnick. (Spotlight on Military Issues Ser.). (Illus.). 8p. 1997. pap. 1.25 (*1-56688-388-1*) Bur For At-Risk.

Planning Freedom, 2000. John Gliha. 200p. 2000. pap. write for info. (*0-9671019-3-X*) Due Process.

Planning from Lesson to Lesson. Seth Lindstromberg. (Pilgrims Longman Resource Bks.). 1995. pap. text 22.39 (*0-582-08959-X*, Pub. by Addison-Wesley) Longman.

Planning, Funding & Implementing a Child Abuse Prevention Project. Rebekah L. Dorman et al. LC 98-24861. 200p. 1998. pap. 18.95 (*0-87868-562-6*) Child Welfare.

Planning Future Land Uses. Ed. by Gary W. Petersen & Marvin T. Beatty. (ASA Special Publications: No. 42). 71p. (C). 1981. pap. 3.85 (*0-89118-067-2*) Am Soc Agron.

Planning Future U. S. Fighter Forces. Kevin N. Lewis. LC 93-23131. 1993. pap. 15.00 (*0-8330-1416-1*, MR-285-AF) Rand Corp.

Planning Gain. Healey. (Illus.). 304p. (C). 1995. 65.00 (*0-419-19410-X*, E & FN Spon) Routledge.

Planning Gain in Theory & Practice. Gene Bunnell. (Progress in Planning Ser.: No. 44-1). 114p. 1995. pap. 112.50 (*0-08-042646-8*, Pergamon Pr) Elsevier.

Planning Global Information Infrastructure. Ed. by Ching-Chih Chen. 548p. 1995. pap. text 39.50 (*1-56750-200-8*, Z674) Ablx Pub.

***Planning, Governance & Spatial Strategy in Britain: An Institutionalist Analysis.** Geoff Vigar. LC 99-54950. 2000. write for info. (*0-312-23125-3*) St Martin.

Planning Guide for Corporate Museums, Galleries, & Visitor Centers. Victor J. Danilov. LC 91-28085. 224p. 1991. lib. bdg. 57.95 (*0-313-27657-9*, DPG/) Greenwood.

Planning Guide for Developing Number Concepts. Kathy Richardson. 2000. pap. 14.95 (*0-201-49524-4*) Addison-Wesley.

Planning Guide for Integrated Thematic Instruction. Lauren Kirk & Lorrie Powers. (Orig.). 1996. pap., teacher ed. 9.95 (*1-878631-28-4*, Pub. by S Kovalik) Bks Educators.

Planning Guide to Office Automation. Ed. by Gower Publishing Co., Ltd. Staff. 123p. 1984. text 69.00 (*0-566-02503-5*, Pub. by Gower) Ashgate Pub Co.

Planning Guide to Successful Computer Instruction. rev. ed. G. David Peters & John M. Eddins. (C). 1995. 19.95 (*0-942132-00-9*) Electron Course.

Planning Guide to the Preschool Curriculum. rev. ed. Anne Sanford et al. 1983. pap. 29.95 (*0-88076-001-X*) Kaplan Pr.

Planning Human Activities on Protected Natural Ecosystems. W. Luisigi. (Dissertationes Botanicae Ser.: No. 48). (Illus.). 1979. pap. 24.00 (*3-7682-1214-9*) Lubrecht & Cramer.

Planning Imperative & Human Behavior. Melville C. Branch. LC 99-14381. 200p. 1999. 55.00 (*0-275-96534-1*) Greenwood.

Planning Imperatives for the 1990s: Papers Presented at an Invitational Seminar on Planning in Higher Education. Frwd. by Cameron Fincher. 78p. (Orig.). (C). 1989. pap. 6.00 (*1-880647-00-1*) U GA Inst High Educ.

Planning Implementation & Control in Product Test Assurance. Richard H. Spencer. (Illus.). 240p. 1983. text 57.00 (*0-13-679506-4*) P-H.

Planning Implementation Tools & Techniques: A Resource Book for Local Governments. Forster O. Ndubisi. (Illus.). 224p. (Orig.). 1992. pap. text 20.00 (*0-911847-04-9*) U GA Inst Community.

An Asterisk (*) at the beginning of an entry indicates that the title is appearing for the first time.

Planning, Implementing & Evaluating Critical Pathways: A Guide for Health Care Survival into the 21st Century. Ed. by Patricia C. Dykes & Kathleen Wheeler. LC 97-16500. 184p. 1997. 34.95 (*0-8261-9790-6*) Springer Pub.

Planning, Implementing & Evaluating Health. 2nd ed. James F. McKenzie & Jan L. Smeltzer. LC 96-9109. 336p. 1996. pap. text 57.00 (*0-205-20069-9*) Allyn.

Planning, Implementing, & Evaluating Targeted Communication Programs: A Manual for Business Communicators. Gary W. Selnow & William D. Crano. LC 86-30418. 300p. 1987. 72.95 (*0-89930-208-4*, SPQ/, Quorum Bks) Greenwood.

Planning in a Military Context: An Army Perspective. I. M. Datz. 1998. 38.00 (*81-259-0438-7*, Pub. by Vikas) S Asia.

Planning in Child Care. Ed. by M. Bryer. (C). 1989. 80.00 (*0-903534-76-2*, Pub. by Brit Ag for Adopt & Fost) St Mut.

Planning in Chinese Agriculture: Socialisation & the Private Sector, 1956-1962. Kenneth R. Walker. 109p. 1965. 35.00 (*0-7146-1256-1*, Pub. by F Cass Pubs) Intl Spec Bk.

Planning in Criminal Justice Organizations & Systems. John Hudzik & Gary W. Cordner. 352p. (C). 1983. text 53.20 (*0-02-475170-7*, Macmillan Coll) P-H.

Planning in Decentralized Firms. B. R. Meijboom. (Lecture Notes in Economics & Mathematical Systems Ser.: Vol. 289). x, 168p. 1987. 33.90 (*0-387-17795-7*) Spr-Verlag.

Planning in Developing Countries: Theory & Methodology. (United Nations Studies). 18.50 (*92-1-157052-2*, E.80.XV.ST/17) UN.

Planning in Government: Shaping Programs that Succeed. Melvin R. Levin. (Illus.). 257p. (Orig.). (C). 1987. pap. 24.95 (*0-918286-44-1*, Planners Press) Am Plan Assn.

Planning in India. rev. ed. Mrityunjoy Banerjee. (C). 1988. 16.00 (*81-204-0334-7*, Pub. by Oxford IBH) S Asia.

Planning in India: A Critique. R. K. Sinha. ix, 247p. (C). 1987. 18.00 (*81-7003-079-X*) S Asia.

Planning in India: The Challenge for the 90's. Arun Ghosh. 300p. (C). 1992. 32.00 (*0-8039-9419-2*) Sage.

Planning in Library Resource Sharing. A. S. Chandel. 237p. (C). 1986. 175.00 (*81-85009-24-4*, Pub. by Print Hse) St Mut.

Planning in OCLC Member Libraries. (Library, Information, & Computer Science Ser.: No. 9). 130p. (Orig.). 1988. pap. 16.00 (*1-55653-051-X*) OCLC Online Comp.

Planning in Oxford - An Historical Survey & Bibliography. Steve Hopkins. (C). 1978. 35.00 (*0-7855-3877-1*, Pub. by Oxford Polytechnic) St Mut.

***Planning in Post Modern Times.** Philip Allmendinger. LC 00-37779. (RTPI Library). 2000. pap. write for info. (*0-415-23423-9*) Routledge.

Planning in Residential Conservation Areas. A. D. Thomas. (Illus.). 88p. 1983. pap. 22.00 (*0-08-031039-7*, Pergamon Pr) Elsevier.

Planning in School Administration: A Handbook. Ward Sybouts. LC 91-18596. (Educators' Reference Collection). 344p. 1992. lib. bdg. 65.00 (*0-313-27272-7*, SYC, Greenwood Pr) Greenwood.

Planning in Soviet Union. P. Bernard. LC 66-14654. 1966. 146.00 (*0-08-013503-X*, Pub. by Pergamon Repr) Franklin.

Planning in the Face of Power. John F. Forester. 264p. 1988. pap. 17.95 (*0-520-06413-5*, Pub. by U CA Pr) Cal Prin Full Svc.

Planning in the Perspective of Development. Ed. by Anima Bhattacharya et al. 231p. 1995. pap. 150.00 (*81-85880-62-X*, Pub. by Print Hse) St Mut.

Planning in the Public Domain. John Friedmann. LC 87-3194. (Illus.). 480p. 1987. pap. text 20.95 (*0-691-02268-2*, Pub. by Princeton U Pr) Cal Prin Full Svc.

Planning in the U. S. A. Policies, Issues & Processes. J. B. Cullingworth. LC 96-33158. (Illus.). 304p. (C). 1997. pap. 32.99 (*0-415-15012-4*) Routledge.

Planning in the U. S. A. Policies, Issues & Processes. J. B. Cullingworth. LC 96-33158. (Illus.). 304p. (C). 1997. 100.00 (*0-415-15011-6*) Routledge.

Planning in the University Library, 28. Stanton F. Biddle. LC 92-8678. (New Directions in Information Management Ser.: No. 28). 238p. 1992. 55.00 (*0-313-27788-5*, BLO/, Greenwood Pr) Greenwood.

Planning in Urban India. John Van Willigen & Jacqueline Van Willigen. 1975. 5.50 (*0-686-20339-9*, 743, Sage Prdcls Pr) Sage.

Planning Integrated Curriculum: The Call to Adventure. Susan M. Drake. LC 93-9219. 1993. pap. 10.95 (*0-87120-208-5*) ASCD.

Planning Investigative Projects: A Workbook for Social Services Practitioners. Carole Addison. (C). 1988. 40.00 (*0-7855-3735-X*, Pub. by Natl Inst Soc Work); 40.00 (*0-685-40353-X*, Pub. by Natl Inst Soc Work); pap. 21.00 (*0-902789-54-6*, Pub. by Natl Inst Soc Work) St Mut.

Planning Is a Verb. Jean O'Neil. 84p. 1988. pap. 14.95 (*0-934513-44-9*, M10B) Natl Crime DC.

Planning Is the Key. Billie I. Reynolds. 1983. 10.00 (*0-915807-00-9*) Hidden Valley Bks.

Planning IT: Creating an Information Management Strategy. David J. Silk. LC 92-142706. (Illus.). 180p. 1991. reprint ed. pap. 55.80 (*0-608-08867-6*, 206950600004) Bks Demand.

Planning It Safe: How to Control Liability & Risk in Volunteer Programs. LC 99-170586. iii, 91p. 1998. pap. text 17.95 (*1-881282-00-7*) MN Ofc Citizenship.

***Planning Land 3-D Seismic Surveys.** Andreas Cordsen et al. LC 00-26159. (Geophysical Developments Ser.). 2000. write for info. (*1-56080-089-5*) Soc Expl Geophys.

Planning Landscapes. NK Lawn & Garden Co. Staff. (Step-by-Step Visual Guide Ser.). 80p. 1991. pap. 7.95 (*1-880281-02-3*) NK Lawn & Garden.

Planning Language, Planning Inequality. Tollefson. 1991. text. write for info. (*0-582-07454-1*, Pub. by Addison-Wesley) Longman.

Planning Law. Clive Brand. (C). 1990. 125.00 (*1-85431-088-7*, Pub. by Blackstone Pr) St Mut.

Planning Law. Clive Brand. (C). 1991. text 22.00 (*1-85431-128-X*, Pub. by Blackstone Pr) Gaunt.

Planning Law. Michael Theis. 88p. 1992. 33.00 (*1-85190-178-7*, Pub. by Tolley Pubng) St Mut.

Planning Law. 2nd ed. Clive Brand. (Practice Notes Ser.). 109p. 1994. pap. write for info. (*0-85121-870-9*, Pub. by Cavendish Pubng) Gaunt.

Planning Law. 3rd ed. Clive Brand. (Cavendish Practice Notes Ser.). 1996. pap. 32.00 (*1-85941-294-7*, Pub. by Cavendish Pubng) Gaunt.

***Planning Law: A Handbook for Conveyancers & Property Professionals.** 2nd ed. David Forbes. 256p. 1999. pap. 63.00 (*1-85811-190-0*, Pub. by CLT Prof) Gaunt.

***Planning Law: Principles & Procedures of Land-Use Management.** Jeannie Van Wyk. 336p. 1999. 55.00 (*0-7021-5086-X*, Pub. by Juta & Co) Gaunt.

Planning Law & Practice. James C. Blackhall. xlv, 418p. 1998. pap. 45.00 (*1-85941-391-9*, Pub. by Cavendish Pubng) Gaunt.

Planning Law for Conveyancers. David Forbes. 185p. 1994. pap. 46.50 (*1-85811-022-X*, Pub. by CLT Prof) Gaunt.

Planning LDS Weddings & Receptions. rev. ed. Lois F. Worlton & Opal D. Jasinski. LC 72-88908. (Illus.). 73p. 1972. pap. 9.98 (*0-88290-014-5*) Horizon Utah.

Planning Legislation in North Carolina. 18th ed. Compiled by David W. Owens. 386p. (C). 1996. pap. text 30.00 (*1-56011-283-2*) Institute Government.

Planning Library Buildings: A Select Bibliography. 4th ed. Compiled by Anders C. Dahlgren & Erla P. Heyns. LC 95-2767. 63p. 1995. pap. 15.00 (*0-8389-7800-2*) Library Admin.

Planning Library Buildings & Facilities (From Concept to Completion) Raymond M. Holt. LC 89-10947. (Library Administration Ser.: No. 9). (Illus.). 260p. 1990. 41.50 (*0-8108-2203-2*) Scarecrow.

Planning Library Facilities: A Selected Annotated Bibliography. Mary S. Stephenson. LC 89-70043. 259p. 1990. 35.00 (*0-8108-2285-7*) Scarecrow.

Planning Library Interiors: The Selection of Furnishings for the 21st Century. 2nd ed. Carol R. Brown. LC 94-30430. (Illus.). 176p. 1994. pap. 29.95 (*0-89774-850-6*) Oryx Pr.

Planning Local Economic Development: Theory & Practice. 2nd ed. Ed. by Edward J. Blakely. (C). 1994. text 58.00 (*0-8039-5209-0*); pap. text 26.50 (*0-8039-5210-4*) Sage.

Planning London. Simmie. 192p. 1994. 65.00 (*1-85728-057-1*, Pub. by UCL Pr Ltd); pap. 21.95 (*1-85728-058-X*, Pub. by UCL Pr Ltd) Taylor & Francis.

Planning Made Easy: A Manual for Planning Commissioners, Members of Zoning Boards of Appeal, & Trainers. Efraim Gil et al. LC 93-74202. (Illus.). 128p. 1994. 36.95 (*0-918286-89-1*, Planners Press) Am Plan Assn.

Planning, Market Private House: The Local Supply Response. Bramley et al. 192p. 1994. 65.00 (*1-85728-162-4*, Pub. by UCL Pr Ltd); pap. 24.95 (*1-85728-163-2*, Pub. by UCL Pr Ltd) Taylor & Francis.

Planning Media. William J. Donnelly. 333p. (C). 1995. 75.00 (*0-13-567858-3*) P-H.

Planning Memorial Celebrations: A Sourcebook. Rob Baker. LC 99-13085. 224p. 1999. pap. 12.00 (*0-609-80404-9*) Crown.

Planning Models for Colleges & Universities. David S. Hopkins & William F. Massy. LC 78-66176. 572p. 1981. 59.50 (*0-8047-1023-6*) Stanford U Pr.

Planning My Career. Vincent Capozziello, Jr. (YA). (gr. 7 up). 1998. student ed. 5.50 (*0-912486-82-1*) Finney Co.

Planning, Need & Scarcity: Essays on the Personal Social Services. Adrian Webb & Gerald Wistow. LC 85-14804. 276p. 1986. pap. text 21.95 (*0-04-361057-9*) Routledge.

Planning Non-Traditional Programs. Kathryn P. Cross & John R. Valley. LC 73-18505. (Josey-Bass Series in Higher Education). 279p. reprint ed. pap. 86.50 (*0-608-17055-0*, 202774900056) Bks Demand.

Planning Now for Irrigation & Drainage in the 21st Century. Ed. by DeLynn R. Hay. (Conference Proceedings Ser.). 800p. 1988. 10.00 (*0-87262-666-0*) Am Soc Civil Eng.

Planning of Experiments. David Cox. LC 92-7007. (Classics Library). 320p. 1992. pap. 64.95 (*0-471-57429-5*) Wiley.

Planning of Geothermal District Heating Systems. Alberto Piatti et al. LC 92-26787. (C). 1992. text 185.00 (*0-7923-1968-0*) Kluwer Academic.

Planning of Health Services: Studies in 8 European Countries. G. McLachlan. (EURO Nonserial Publication Ser.). 252p. 1980. 20.00 (*92-9020-195-9*, 1340002) World Health.

Planning of Investment Programs in the Steel Industry. David A. Kendrick et al. LC 83-18722. (Planning of Investment Programs Ser.: No. 3). 327p. reprint ed. pap. 101.40 (*0-7837-6191-0*, 204591300009) Bks Demand.

Planning of Medical Education Programmes: Proceedings of the WHO Expert Committee, Geneva, 1973. WHO Staff. (Technical Reports: No. 547). 1974. pap. text 4.00 (*92-4-120547-4*, 1100547) World Health.

Planning on Murder. David Williams. 1992. 13.99 (*0-00-232399-0*, Pub. by HarpC) HarpC.

Planning on Murder. David Williams. 1994. mass mkt. 4.99 (*0-00-647882-4*, Pub. by HarpC) HarpC.

Planning on Murder. large type ed. David Williams. 1996. 11.50 (*0-7505-0890-6*, Pub. by Mgna Lrg Print) Ulverscroft.

Planning, Operation, Rehabilitation & Automation of Irrigation Water Delivery Systems. Ed. by Darrell D. Zimbelman. 392p. 1987. 43.00 (*0-87262-608-3*) Am Soc Civil Eng.

Planning, Organizing & Teaching Agricultural Mechanics. rev. ed. Intro. by W. Forrest Bear & Thomas A. Hoerner. (Illus.). 224p. 1986. pap. text 24.15 (*0-913163-18-X*, 178) Hobar Pubns.

Planning Out the Coming Year. Laddie F. Hutar. 150p. 1995. ring bd. 96.00 (*0-918896-05-3*, 91930) Hutar.

Planning Outdoor Play. Henry Sanoff. LC 92-2626. (Illus.). 96p. (Orig.). 1982. lib. bdg. 24.95 (*0-89334-186-X*, 186-X) Humanics Ltd.

Planning Parks for People. John Hultsman et al. LC 86-50935. (Illus.). 314p. (C). 1987. 27.95 (*0-910251-16-9*) Venture Pub PA.

Planning Parks for People. 2nd rev. ed. John Hultsman et al. LC 98-84038. (Illus.). ix, 308p. 1998. text 39.95 (*0-910251-95-9*, PPP100) Venture Pub PA.

Planning, People & Preferences: A Role for Contingent Valuation. Richard K. O'Doherty. 192p. 1996. text 63.95 (*1-85972-176-1*, Pub. by Avebry) Ashgate Pub Co.

***Planning, Performing, & Controlling Projects.** 2nd ed. Robert B. Angus et al. LC 99-27061. (Illus.). 290p. (C). 1999. 56.00 (*0-13-099878-8*) P-H.

Planning Perspectives for Education. Ed. by A. P. Johnston & James F. McNamara. 287p. 1975. pap. text 19.50 (*0-8422-0505-5*) Irvington.

Planning Perspectives of the Central Zone. Ed. by Malcolm S. Adiseshiah. 167p. (C). 1992. text 25.00 (*81-220-0261-7*, Pub. by Konark Pubs Pvt Ltd) Advent Bks Div.

Planning Principles for Accelerated Immunization Activities: A Joint WHO-UNICEF Statement. 24p. 1985. pap. text 3.00 (*92-4-156087-8*, 1150239) World Health.

Planning Process on the Pine Ridge & Rosebud Indian Reservations. Richard E. Brown. 1969. 1.00 (*1-55614-078-9*) U of SD Gov Res Bur.

Planning Processes: An Introduction for Geographers. John Herington. (Cambridge Topics in Geography Second Ser.). (Illus.). 128p. (C). 1989. pap. text 21.95 (*0-521-31305-8*) Cambridge U Pr.

Planning Processes: An Introduction for Geographers. John Herington. (Cambridge Topics in Geography Second Ser.). (Illus.). 128p. (C). 1991. text 41.95 (*0-521-30770-8*) Cambridge U Pr.

Planning Processes & Muslim Responses to Rural Development in India. Mumtaz Ali Khan. (C). 1993. 30.00 (*81-85565-25-2*, Pub. by Uppal Pub Hse) S Asia.

Planning, Procurement, & Quality Management. (Site Investigation in Construction Ser.: No. 2). 38p. 1993. text 14.00 (*0-7277-1983-1*) Am Soc Civil Eng.

Planning, Producing & Using Instructional Media. 6th ed. Jerrold E. Kemp. (C). 1989. pap. 54.66 (*0-06-043592-5*) Addison-Wesley Educ.

Planning Professional Training Days. Bob Gough & Dave James. 128p. 1990. pap. 31.95 (*0-335-09412-0*) OpUniv Pr.

Planning, Profit & Incentives in the U. S. S. R. Vol. 1: The Liberman Discussion: A New Phase in Soviet Economic Thought. Ed. by Myron E. Sharpe. LC 66-20464. 328p. reprint ed. pap. 101.70 (*0-608-14899-7*, 202613600048) Bks Demand.

Planning Program Development & Evaluation. Thomas S. Timmreck. 240p. 1995. pap. 37.50 (*0-86720-787-6*) Jones & Bartlett.

Planning, Programming & Input-Output Models: Selected Papers on Indian Planning. A. Ghosh. LC 68-29327. (University of Cambridge, Dept. of Applied Economics, Occasional Papers: No. 15). 175p. reprint ed. pap. 49.90 (*0-608-14098-8*, 2055839) Bks Demand.

Planning-Programming-Budgeting System: Implications for Library Management. Ed. by Sul H. Lee. LC 73-78314. (Library Management Ser.: No. 1). 112p. 1973. 24.50 (*0-87650-040-8*) Pierian.

Planning-Programming-Budgeting Systems in Three Federal Agencies. Joon C. Doh. LC 74-149965. (Special Studies in U. S. Economic, Social & Political Issues). 1971. 32.00 (*0-89197-887-9*) Irvington.

Planning Programs for Adult Learners: A Practical Guide for Educators, Trainers & Staff Developers. Rosemary S. Caffarella. LC 94-21355. (Higher & Adult Education Ser.). 276p. 1994. pap. text 34.95 (*0-7879-0033-8*) Jossey-Bass.

Planning Project Construction. Intro. by William H. Hamilton & Arthur R. Mann. (Illus.). 52p. 1974. pap. text 6.60 (*0-913163-08-2*, 174) Hobar Pubns.

Planning, Proposing, & Presenting Science Effectively: A Guide for Graduate Students & Researchers in the Behavioral Sciences & Biology. Jack P. Hailman & Karen B. Strier. LC 97-6504. (Illus.). 190p. (C). 1997. text 49.95 (*0-521-56023-3*); pap. text 15.95 (*0-521-56875-7*) Cambridge U Pr.

Planning, Protectionism, & Politics in Liberal Italy: Economics & Politics in the Giolittian Age. Frank J. Coppa. LC 73-148346. 292p. reprint ed. pap. 90.60 (*0-608-17278-2*, 202952300061) Bks Demand.

Planning Pub Transport. Simpson. 1987. pap. text. write for info. (*0-582-46248-7*, Pub. by Addison-Wesley) Longman.

Planning Publications: An Annotated Bibliography & Reference Guide. Paul Matty. (CPL Bibliographies Ser.: No. 68). 100p. 1981. 10.00 (*0-86602-068-3*, Sage Prdcls Pr) Sage.

Planning Recreational Places. Jay S. Shivers & George Hjelte. LC 70-120068. 518p. 1971. 65.00 (*0-8386-7358-9*) Fairleigh Dickinson.

Planning Research & Development. U. Colombo & R. Galli. 1995. write for info. (*81-224-0708-0*, Pub. by Wiley Estrn) Franklin.

Planning Research for Resource Decisions. Carl H. Stoltenberg & Kenneth D. Ware. LC 76-103839. 191p. pap. 59.30 (*0-608-14885-7*, 202614300048) Bks Demand.

Planning Reserve Mobilization: Inferences from Operation Desert Shield. Ronald E. Sortor et al. LC 93-19704. 1993. pap. 15.00 (*0-8330-1386-6*, MR-123-A) Rand Corp.

Planning Responsibly for Adult Education: A Guide to Negotiating Power & Interests. Ronald M. Cervero & Arthur L. Wilson. LC 93-43174. (Higher & Adult Education Ser.). 228p. 1994. text 32.95 (*1-55542-628-X*) Jossey-Bass.

Planning Rules & Urban Economic Performance: The Case of Hong Kong. Samuel R. Staley. LC 97-153484. (Hong Kong Centre for Economic Research Ser.). 190p. 1997. pap. text 17.95 (*962-201-632-4*, Pub. by Chinese Univ) U of Mich Pr.

Planning School Events. Ed. by Instructional Fair Staff. 1997. pap. 7.95 (*1-56822-527-X*) Instruct Fair.

Planning Seafood Cold Storage. 2nd ed. Edward Kolbe & Donald C. Kramer. (Marine Advisory Bulletin Ser.: Vol. 46). (Illus.). 60p. 1997. pap. 9.00 (*1-56612-047-0*) AK Sea Grant CP.

***Planning Series, 3 vols.** Incl. Effective Strategic Planning: Getting Your Organization Focused & Directed. Paul Yelder & Mike Burns. 40p. 1999. pap. (*0-942901-20-7*, Pub. by Enterprise Fnd); Guide to Community Planning: An Overview of Developing & Managing Neighborhood-Planning Initiatives That Work. Moustafa Mourad & Michael Downie. 16p. 1999. pap. (*0-942901-22-3*, Pub. by Enterprise Fnd); Planning a New Business Venture: A Step by Step Guide to Preparing an Effective Business Plan. Paul Yelder & Mike Burns. 32p. 1999. pap. (*0-942901-21-5*, Pub. by Enterprise Fnd); 1999. pap. write for info. (*0-942901-19-3*, Pub. by Enterprise Fnd) BookMasters.

Planning Settlements Naturally. Stephen Owen. (Illus.). 154p. (C). 1994. text 175.00 (*1-85341-029-2*, Pub. by Surrey Beatty & Sons) St Mut.

Planning, Shortage & Transformation: Essays in Honor of Janos Kornai. Ed. by Eric S. Maskin & Andras Simonovits. LC 99-37733. (Illus.). 550p. 2000. 60.00 (*0-262-13357-1*) MIT Pr.

Planning Skills see Productive Supervisor: A Program of Practical Managerial Skills

Planning Small Town America. Kristina Ford et al. LC 89-83384. (Illus.). 179p. (Orig.). 1990. pap. 35.95 (*0-918286-61-1*, Planners Press); lib. bdg. 49.00 (*0-918286-62-X*, Planners Press) Am Plan Assn.

Planning, Staffing & Contracting for an Environmental Audit. Stephen D. Hoffman. (Environmental Audit Handbook Ser.: Vol. 4). 1989. pap. 49.95 (*1-55840-066-4*) Exec Ent Pubns.

Planning, Staffing & Contracting for an Environmental Audit. Stephen D. Hoffman. (Environmental Audit Handbook Ser.: Vol. 4). 73p. 1994. pap. 99.00 (*0-471-11254-2*) Wiley.

Planning Strategic Interaction. Charles R. Berger. LC 96-54036. (LEA's Communication Ser.). 184p. 1997. 39.95 (*0-8058-2308-5*) L Erlbaum Assocs.

Planning Strategies of Intracranial Microsurgery. Wolfgang Seeger. (Illus.). 430p. 1986. 199.00 (*0-387-81916-9*) Spr-Verlag.

Planning Strategies That Work. Ed. by Arnoldo C. Hax. (Sloan Management Review Ser.). (Illus.). 288p. 1987. text 30.00 (*0-19-504883-0*) OUP.

Planning Strategy for a Developing Region. A. K. Singh. 352p. (C). 1990. 300.00 (*81-85009-36-8*, Pub. by Print Hse) St Mut.

Planning Study - Colorado Division of Youth Services. 8.00 (*0-318-20314-6*) Natl Coun Crime.

Planning Successful Board Retreats: A Guide for Board Members & Chief Executives. Barry S. Bader. (Nonprofit Governance Ser.: No. 10). 28p. 1992. reprint ed. pap. text 12.00 (*0-925299-14-6*) Natl Ctr Nonprofit.

Planning Successful Computing. Murray Laver. 52p. (C). 1986. 70.00 (*0-86236-004-8*, Pub. by Granary) St Mut.

Planning Successful Employee Performance: A Practical Guide to Planning Individual Achievement. Karen R. Seeker & Joe B. Wilson. (Management Skills Ser.). (Illus.). 120p. 1997. pap. 12.95 (*1-883553-60-1*) R Chang Assocs.

Planning Successful Practice Transitions. David W. Griggs. LC 97-42663. 1997. 59.95 (*0-87814-617-2*) PennWell Bks.

Planning Successul Meetings & Events. Ann J. Boehme. LC 98-35089. 174p. 1998. pap. 18.95 (*0-8144-7995-2*) AMACOM.

Planning Sustainability: Implications of Sustainability for Public Planning Policy. Ed. by Michael Kenny & James Meadowcroft. LC 98-33290. (Environmental Politics Ser.). 230p. 1999. pap. 29.99 (*0-415-16477-X*) Routledge.

***Planning Sustainability: Implications of Sustainability for Publice Planning Policy.** Michael Kenny. LC 98-33290. 1999. text. write for info. (*0-415-16476-1*) Routledge.

Planning Sustainable Environment. Ed. by Andrew Blowers. 240p. (Orig.). 1992. 34.00 (*1-85383-145-X*, Pub. by Escan Pubns) Island Pr.

Planning Tax-Exempt Organizations, 2 vols. Shepard's Mcgraw-Hill Staff. Ed. by Robert J. Desiderio & Scott A. Taylor. LC 83-16168. (Tax & Estate Planning Ser.). 1983. text 210.00 (*0-07-016567-X*) Shepards.

Planning Technician. Jack Rudman. (Career Examination Ser.: C-3185). 1994. pap. 27.95 (*0-8373-3185-4*) Nat Learn.

P

An Asterisk (*) at the beginning of an entry indicates that the title is appearing for the first time.

Planning Techniques (Basic & Advanced), Advanced. Robert M. Kelley. LC 88-82282. (Illus.). 90p. (C). 1988. pap. write for info. (*0-9620832-0-8*) Kelley Comn Dev.

Planning Techniques (Basic & Advanced), Basic. Robert M. Kelley. LC 88-82281. (Illus.). 150p. (C). 1988. pap. write for info. (*0-9620832-1-6*) Kelley Comn Dev.

Planning Techniques (Basic & Advanced), Set. Robert M. Kelley. (Illus.). 240p. (C). 1988. pap. 29.95 (*0-9620832-2-4*) Kelley Comn Dev.

Planning Techniques for the Closely Held Business. (Tax Law & Estate Planning Course Handbook Ser.: Vol. 221). 304p. 1993. 70.00 (*0-685-65545-8*, D4-5238) PLI.

Planning Technological Change & Economic Development in Greece: High Technology & the Microelectronics Industry. Maria Petmesidou & Lefteris Tsoulouvis. (Progress in Planning Ser.: Vol. 33). (Illus.). 88p. 1990. pap. 41.50 (*0-08-040770-6*, Pergamon Pr) Elsevier.

Planning Telecommunication Networks. Thomas G. Robertazzi & IEEE Communications Society Staff. LC 98-38908. 208p. 1999. 79.95 (*0-7803-4702-1*) Inst Electrical.

Planning That "Perfect" Vacation: A Wheelchair Guide to an Enjoyable Vacation. deluxe ed. Patricia Smither. (Disabled Travel Ser.). 12p. 1999. 5.00 (*1-928616-02-X*) Access for Disabled.

Planning the Border's Future: An Analysis of the Mexican-U. S. Environmental Plan. Jan Gilbreath. (U. S. - Mexican Occasional Papers: No. 1). 54p. 1992. pap. 7.00 (*0-614-01232-5*) LBJ Sch Pub Aff.

Planning the Border's Future: The Mexican - U. S. Integrated Border Environmental Plan. Jan Gilbreath Rich. (U. S. - Mexican Occasional Papers: Vol. 1). 54p. (C). 1992. pap. 7.00 (*0-89940-584-3*) LBJ Sch Pub Aff.

Planning the Business Adventure. 2nd ed. Jack A. Spigarelli. (Illus.). 182p. (C). 1989. student ed. 49.95 (*0-929191-01-3*) Co Connect.

Planning the Business Venture. Jack A. Spigarelli. 182p. (C). 1988. student ed. 49.95 (*0-929191-00-5*) Co Connect.

***Planning the Campus: Process, Organization & Recommendations.** Lewis Roscoe. LC 00-191052. (Illus.). 2000. pap. 29.95 (*0-9700916-0-5*) L & A Pubns.

Planning the Canadian Environment. Ed. by L. O. Gertler. LC 68-57715. 311p. reprint ed. pap. 96.50 (*0-608-14571-8*, 202493000040) Bks Demand.

Planning the Capitalist City: The Colonial Era to the 1920s. Richard E. Foglesong. LC 85-43278. 297p. 1986. reprint ed. pap. 92.10 (*0-608-02937-8*, 206400300008) Bks Demand.

Planning the Church Year. Leonel L. Mitchell. LC 90-27365. 104p. 1991. pap. 9.95 (*0-8192-1554-6*) Morehouse Pub.

Planning the City upon a Hill: Boston since 1630. Lawrence W. Kennedy. LC 91-43645. (Illus.). 320p. (C). 1992. 35.00 (*0-87023-780-2*) U of Mass Pr.

Planning the City upon a Hill: Boston since 1630. Lawrence W. Kennedy. LC 91-43645. (Illus.). 328p. 1994. reprint ed. pap. 19.95 (*0-87023-923-6*) U of Mass Pr.

Planning the Development of Builders, Leaders, & Managers for 21st-Century Business: Curriculum Review at Columbia Business School. Noel Capon. 544p. (C). 1996. lib. bdg. 109.00 (*0-7923-9728-2*) Kluwer Academic.

Planning the Eternal City: Roman Politics & Planning Since World War II. Robert C. Fried. LC 72-91312. 366p. reprint ed. pap. 113.50 (*0-608-14184-4*, 202199800024) Bks Demand.

Planning the French Canals: Bureaucracy, Politics, & Enterprise under the Restoration. Reed G. Geiger. LC 94-7829. 1994. 43.50 (*0-87413-527-3*) U Delaware Pr.

Planning the Global Family. Jodi L. Jacobson. (Worldwatch Papers: No. 80). 54p. 1987. pap. 5.00 (*0-916468-81-X*) Worldwatch Inst.

Planning the Golf Clubhouse. (Illus.). 169p. 1986. pap. 40.00 (*1-57701-165-1*, 99GCP02) Natl Golf.

Planning the Golf Clubhouse. rev. ed. 268p. 1981. 35.00 (*0-317-35659-3*, 0608) Pro Golfers.

Planning the Great Metropolis: New York: The 1929 Regional Plan. David A. Johnson. (Illus.). 312p. (C). (gr. 13). 1995. 110.00 (*0-419-19010-4*) Chapman & Hall.

Planning the Ideal Family: The Small Family Option. Pamela Wasserman. Ed. by Dianne Sherman. LC 89-16632. (Illus.). 24p. (Orig.). (C). 1989. pap. 5.00 (*0-945219-02-4*, PLAN) Zero Pop Growth.

Planning the Impossible. Mavis Jukes. LC 98-26222. 176p. (YA). (gr. 5). 1999. 14.95 (*0-385-32243-7*) BDD Bks Young Read.

***Planning the Impossible.** Mavis Jukes. (Illus.). 176p. (J). 2000. pap. 4.50 (*0-440-41230-7*, Yearling) BDD Bks Young Read.

Planning the Interstate Highway System. Jonathan L. Gifford. LC 94-35983. 224p. (C). Date not set. pap. 54.95 (*0-8133-8873-2*) Westview.

Planning the Liturgy with Celebration Hymnal. Compiled by Stephen Dean. 120p. (C). 1988. 30.00 (*0-85597-437-0*, Pub. by McCrimmon Pub) St Mut.

Planning the Management Operation & Maintenance of Irrigation & Drainage Systems: A Guide for the Preparation of Strategies & Manuals. rev. ed. International Commission on Irrigation & Drainage,. LC 97-37307. (Technical Paper Ser.: No. 389). 136p. 1998. pap. 22.00 (*0-8213-4067-0*, 14067) World Bank.

Planning the Marketing Strategy Module, PACE Level 1: A Program for Acquiring Competence in Entrepreneurship, 3 levels. rev. ed. National Center for Research in Vocational Educati. 1983. 2.50 (*0-317-06076-7*, RD240AB6) Ctr Educ Trng Employ.

Planning the Marketing Strategy Module, PACE Level 2: A Program for Acquiring Competence in Entrepreneurship, 3 levels. rev. ed. National Center for Research in Vocational Educati. 1983. 2.50 (*0-317-06077-5*, RD240BB6) Ctr Educ Trng Employ.

Planning the Marketing Strategy Module, PACE Level 3: A Program for Acquiring Competence in Entrepreneurship, 3 levels. rev. ed. National Center for Research in Vocational Educati. 1983. 2.50 (*0-318-67180-8*, RD240CB6) Ctr Educ Trng Employ.

***Planning the Medical Response to Radiological Accidents.** International Atomic Energy Agency. (Safety Report Ser.). 31p. 1998. pap. 19.00 (*92-0-102598-X*, Pub. by IAEA) Bernan Associates.

Planning the Metropolitan Airport System. Government Printing Office Staff. 108p. 1970. pap. 7.25 (*0-16-005304-8*) USGPO.

Planning the Oregon Way: A 20-Year Evaluation. Ed. by Carl Abbott et al. LC 93-36408. (Illus.). 352p. (C). 1994. text 27.95 (*0-87071-381-7*) Oreg St U Pr.

Planning the Organic Vegetable Garden. Dick Kitto. LC 92-54761. (Illus.). 160p. (Orig.). 1993. pap. 10.95 (*1-55591-109-9*) Fulcrum Pub.

Planning the Perfect Party. 6.95 (*1-871349-39-7*, Pub. by Kensington West) Midpt Trade.

Planning the Planners, How to Control the Recovery: An Examination of the 1982 TUC-Labour Party Report on Economic Planning & Industrial Democracy. Ed. by Tony Topham. 104p. (Orig.). 1983. pap. 19.95 (*0-85124-370-3*, Pub. by Spkesman) Coronet Bks.

Planning the Quality of Education. Ross & Mahlck. 192p. 1990. text 36.50 (*0-08-041026-X*, Pergamon Pr) Elsevier.

Planning the Small Library Facility. 2nd ed. Library Administration & Management Association Pr & Anders C. Dahlgren. LC 96-16226. (Small Library Publications Ser.: 23). 55p. 1996. pap. 15.00 (*0-8389-0681-8*, 0681-8-2045) ALA.

Planning the Small Office Library. LC 93-73465. 106p. 1993. pap. 39.95 (*0-89707-926-4*, 511-0325) Amer Bar Assn.

Planning the Special Library: A Project of the New York Chapter, SLA. Blueprint for the '70s: A Seminar on Library Planning (1971: New York) Ed. by Ellis Mount. LC 72-85956. (Special Libraries Association Monographs: No. 4). 128p. reprint ed. pap. 39.70 (*0-608-16444-5*, 202675600052) Bks Demand.

Planning the State Aviation System. Government Printing Office Staff. 60p. 1989. pap. 5.25 (*0-16-005265-3*) USGPO.

Planning the Twentieth Century. Ward. text. write for info. (*0-471-49097-0*); pap. text. write for info. (*0-471-49098-9*) Wiley.

Planning the 20th-Century American City. Ed. by Mary C. Sies & Christopher Silver. (Illus.). 592p. (C). 1996. text 55.00 (*0-8018-5163-7*); pap. text 24.95 (*0-8018-5164-5*) Johns Hopkins.

***Planning the Unthinkable: How New Powers Will Use Nuclear, Biological, & Chemical Weapons.** Ed. by Peter R. Lavoy et al. LC 00-37678. (Studies in Security Affairs). 2000. pap. 45.00 (*0-8014-3776-8*); pap. 19.95 (*0-8014-8704-8*) Cornell U Pr.

Planning the Urban Region: A Comparative Study of Policies & Organizations. Peter Self. LC 81-16429. 186p. 1982. pap. 57.70 (*0-608-05155-1*, 206571600005) Bks Demand.

Planning the Use of the Earth's Surface. Ed. by A. Cendrero et al. (Lecture Notes in Earth Sciences Ser.: Vol. 42). (Illus.). ix, 556p. 1992. 131.95 (*0-387-55353-3*) Spr-Verlag.

Planning the Uses & Management of Land. Ed. by M. T. Beatty et al. (Agronomy Monograph Ser.: No. 21). (Illus.). 1028p. 1979. 30.00 (*0-89118-058-3*) Am Soc Agron.

Planning Theory. Andreas Faludi. LC 73-11236. 312p. 1984. 145.00 (*0-08-017741-7*, Pub. by Pergamon Repr) Franklin.

Planning to Care: Regulation, Procedure & Practice Under the Children Act 1989 Roger Grimshaw. LC 98-224615. xi, 267p. 1997. write for info. (*1-874579-94-6*) Natl Childrens Bur.

Planning to Finance Your Child's College Education. 4th ed. David L. Gibberman. 80p. 1997. pap. text 7.00 (*0-8080-0204-X*) CCH INC.

Planning to Live: Evaluating & Treating Suicidal Teens in Community Settings. Ed. by Mary J. Rotheram-Borus et al. (Illus.). 408p. (C). 1990. 24.95 (*1-878848-00-3*, 119) Natl Res Ctr.

Planning to Make the Arts Basic. Louise K. Stevens. 293p. 1991. write for info. (*0-9630540-0-7*) ArtsMarket.

Planning to Retire in Comfort. 3rd ed. David L. Gibberman. 80p. 1997. pap. text 7.00 (*0-8080-0205-8*) CCH INC.

***Planning to Stay: Learning to See the Physical Features in Your Neighborhood.** William R. Morrish & Catherine R. Brown. (Illus.). 120p. 2000. pap. 19.95 (*1-57131-246-3*) Milkweed Ed.

Planning to Stay: Learning to See the Physical Features of Your Neighborhood. William R. Morrish & Catherine R. Brown. LC 94-25402. (Illus.). 120p. 1994. pap. 16.95 (*1-57131-203-X*) Milkweed Ed.

Planning to Succeed in Business. David Irwin. 256p. (C). 1995. pap. 49.50 (*0-273-61086-4*, Pub. by Pitman Pub) Trans-Atl Phila.

Planning to Win Bk. 1: Effective Preparation. Roger S. Haydock & John O. Sonsteng. (C). 1994. 12.50 (*0-314-04379-9*) West Pub.

Planning Together. David Bowker et al. (Patchwork Ser.: No. 6). (Illus.). 12p. 1993. pap. 18.00 (*1-873791-65-8*) Taylor & Francis.

Planning Tourism in Nepal. Kamal Maiya Pradhan. 1997. pap. 54.00 (*0-7855-7473-5*, Pub. by Ratna Pustak Bhandar) St Mut.

Planning Transportation Services for Handicapped Persons - User's Guide. (National Cooperative Highway Research Program Report Ser.: No. 262). 74p. 1983. 8.00 (*0-309-03603-8*, NR262) Transport Res Bd.

Planning U. S. Security: Defense Policy in the '80's. Ed. by Philip S. Kronenberg. LC 81-13791. (Policy Studies on Security Affairs). 232p. 1982. text 56.00 (*0-08-028082-X*, Pergamon Pr); pap. text 17.50 (*0-08-028081-1*, Pergamon Pr) Elsevier.

Planning under Pressure: The Strategic Choice Approach. J. K. Friend & A. Hickling. (Urban Regional Planning Ser.: No. 37). (Illus.). 358p. 1987. pap. text 41.95 (*0-08-018765-X*, Prgamon Press) Buttrwrth-Heinemann.

Planning under Pressure: The Strategic Choice Approach. 2nd ed. John Friend & Allen Hickling. LC 97-7488. 368p. 1997. pap. text 32.95 (*0-7506-2955-X*) Buttrwrth-Heinemann.

Planning Urban Economics in Southern & Eastern Africa. K. H. Wekwete. 342p. 1993. 87.95 (*1-85628-563-4*, Pub. by Avebry) Ashgate Pub Co.

Planning Urban Education: New Techniques to Transform Learning in the City. Ed. by Dennis L. Roberts, 2nd. LC 73-160895. 384p. 1972. 47.95 (*0-87778-024-2*) Educ Tech Pubns.

Planning Useful Evaluations: Evaluability Assessment. Leonard Rutman. LC 79-24116. (Sage Library of Social Research: No. 96). 208p. reprint ed. pap. 64.50 (*0-7837-1131-X*, 204166100022) Bks Demand.

Planning War, Pursuing Peace: The Political Economy of American Warfare, 1920-1939. Paul A. Koistinen. LC 97-47716. (Modern War Studies). 474p. 1998. 45.00 (*0-7006-0890-7*) U Pr of KS.

Planning with Incomplete Information for Robot Problems: Papers from the 1996 Spring Symposium. Ed. by Illah Nourbakhsh. (Technical Reports). (Illus.). 143p. 1996. spiral bd. 25.00 (*1-57735-006-5*) AAAI Pr.

Planning with Linear Programming: A Practical Approach with the Program LP-TOOLS. E. Alaphia Wright. LC 99-227315. (Illus.). 180p. (C). 1996. pap., student ed. 35.00 (*90-5410-613-1*, Pub. by A A Balkema); text 65.00 (*90-5410-612-3*, Pub. by A A Balkema) Ashgate Pub Co.

***Planning with Multiple Criteria: Investigation, Communication & Choice.** 2nd ed. Peter Bogetoft. LC 98-115551. 1999. 38.00 (*87-16-13386-2*) Mksgaard.

Planning with Neighborhoods. William M. Rohe & Lauren B. Gates. LC 84-17221. (Urban & Regional Policy & Development Studies). xi, 238p. (C). 1985. pap. text 22.50 (*0-8078-4133-1*) U of NC Pr.

Planning with the Small Computer: An Applications Reader. Ed. by Mathew E. MacIver & Jan Schreiber. LC 86-8462. (Lincoln Institute of Land Policy Bk.). 182p. reprint ed. pap. 56.50 (*0-7837-3270-8*, 204328900007) Bks Demand.

Planning Worship Services see Como Planificar los Cultos de Adoracion

Planning Your Addition. Jerry Germer. Ed. by Lynn Elliott & Davide Schiff. LC 97-75262. (Illus.). 192p. 1998. pap. 14.95 (*1-880029-99-5*) Creative Homeowner.

***Planning Your Capital Campaign.** Marilyn Bancel. (Excellence in Fund Raising Workbooks Ser.). 2000. pap. 25.95 (*0-7879-5247-8*) Jossey-Bass.

Planning Your Career: A Business Decision Guide for the Ob-Gyn Resident. 2nd ed. Ed. by Mark Dowden & Maria Kassberg. 244p. 1995. pap. text. write for info. (*0-9628716-2-1*) Dowden Pub.

Planning Your Career: A Workshop Series for Women. Carole M. Davis & Dorothy Graham. 138p. (Orig.). 1981. pap., teacher ed. 12.00 (*1-55719-106-9*); pap., student ed. 9.50 (*1-55719-102-6*) U NE CPAR.

Planning Your Career Change. Kent B. Banning & Ardelle Friday. 1995. pap. 6.95 (*0-8442-6688-4*, Passprt Bks) NTC Contemp Pub Co.

Planning Your Career in Alternative Medicine: A Guide to Degree & Certificate Programs in Alternative Health Care. Dianne J. Lyons. LC 98-108399. 444p. 1997. pap. 19.95 (*0-89529-802-3*, Avery) Penguin Putnam.

Planning Your Career of Tomorrow. Adrian A. Paradis. (Illus.). 160p. 1993. pap. 6.95 (*0-8442-6678-7*, Passprt Bks) NTC Contemp Pub Co.

Planning Your College Education. William A. Rubinfeld. 160p. 1994. pap. 6.95 (*0-8442-6673-6*, Passprt Bks) NTC Contemp Pub Co.

Planning Your Cosmetology Career. Mary Murphy-Martin. LC 93-28878. 108p. (C). 1993. pap. text 13.00 (*0-13-605999-6*) P-H.

Planning Your Family: How to Decide What's Best for You. Peter DeJong & William Smit. 208p. 1987. pap. 7.95 (*0-310-37961-X*, 12500P) Zondervan.

Planning Your Financial Future. Boone. (C). 1996. pap. text, teacher ed. 42.00 (*0-03-018419-3*) Harcourt Coll Pubs.

Planning Your Financial Future. Louis E. Boone. 1997. pap. text 60.00 (*0-03-024084-0*, Pub. by Harcourt Coll Pubs) Harcourt.

Planning Your Financial Future. 2nd ed. Boone. LC 99-72431. (C). 1999. text. write for info. (*0-03-021042-9*) Harcourt Coll Pubs.

Planning Your Financial Future. 2nd ed. Louis E. Boone et al. LC 95-83880. 718p. (C). 1996. pap. text 61.50 incl. disk (*0-03-098844-6*) Dryden Pr.

Planning Your Future. Credit Research Foundation Staff. 64p. 1963. 40.00 (*0-939050-36-6*) Credit Res NYS.

***Planning Your Future: A Guide for Professional Women.** Janet L. Skarbek. LC 00-134096. (Illus.). 2001. pap. 19.95 (*0-9702344-7-3*) Prof Womens.

Planning Your Future: Resources on Careers & Higher Education. Juleann Fallgatter et al. Orig. Title: Guide to Educational Advising Resources. 352p. 1995. pap. 29.95 (*0-913957-13-5*) AMIDEAST.

***Planning Your Gap Year: How to Have the Time of Your Life Working, Studying or Travelling.** 2nd ed. Mark Hempshell. (Illus.). 128p. 1998. pap. 19.95 (*1-85703-387-6*) How To Bks.

***Planning Your Garden: A Practical Guide to Designing & Planting Your Garden.** 2000. pap. 12.95 (*0-7548-0118-7*, Lorenz Bks) Anness Pub.

***Planning Your Herbal Wedding: From Saying "Yes" to Preserving Your Bouquet.** 4th rev. ed. Betsy Williams. (Illus.). 80p. 2000. pap. write for info. (*0-9701611-0-7*) Proper Season.

Planning Your Manpower. IPM Staff. (C). 1988. pap. 30.00 (*0-85171-054-9*, Pub. by IPM Hse) St Mut.

Planning Your Marriage Service: With Traditional & Contemporary Readings. Christopher L. Webber & Margaret Webber. LC 92-15257. 72p. 1992. pap. 6.95 (*0-8192-1590-2*) Morehouse Pub.

Planning Your Military Career. Robert McKay. 160p. 1992. pap. 6.95 (*0-8442-6672-8*, NTC Business Bks) NTC Contemp Pub Co.

Planning Your Rare Coin Retirement: How to Select a $10,000 Rare Coin Portfolio Full of Growth Potential. David L. Ganz. LC 98-17193. (Illus.). 227p. 1998. pap. 13.95 (*1-56625-098-6*) Bonus Books.

***Planning Your Retirement.** Michael Perry. (Cliffs Notes Ser.). 128p. 1999. pap. text 8.99 (*0-7645-8542-8*) IDG Bks.

Planning Your School PR Investment. (Public Relations Professional Development Ser.). 1987. 24.95 (*0-317-59089-8*, 411-13372) Natl Sch PR.

Planning Your Vacation in Florida: Miami & Dade County, Including Miami Beach & Coral Gables. Writers Program, Florida Staff. LC 73-3603. reprint ed. 13.50 (*0-404-57907-8*) AMS Pr.

Planning Your Veterinary Career. Ed. by John McCarthy. 115p. 1987. 15.00 (*0-941451-00-3*) Am Animal Hosp Assoc.

Planning Your Wedding Ceremony. Bishops' Committee for Pastoral Research Staff & Practices National Conference of Catholic Bishops. (Marriage Is a Sacrament Ser.). 48p. (Orig.). (C). 1990. pap. 2.95 (*1-55586-354-X*) US Catholic.

Planning Your Will with Your Family in Mind: How Your Estate Planning Decisions Will Affect the Ones You Love. Ian McPhail. LC 93-17734. 320p. 1993. pap. 14.95 (*1-55958-364-9*) Prima Pub.

Planning Your Young Child's Education. J. Robert Parkinson. 1986. pap. 6.95 (*0-8442-6683-3*, Passprt Bks) NTC Contemp Pub Co.

Planning, Zoning & Building Safety Laws of Ohio. 672p. (Orig.). 1994. pap. 45.00 (*1-884669-01-8*) Conway Greene.

Plannning & Conducting Agency Based Research Projects: For Social Work Students in Field Placements. Alexander H. Westerfelt. 192p. (C). 1996. pap., wbk. ed. 33.00 (*0-8013-1855-6*) Addison-Wesley.

Plano: An Illustrated Chronicle. Vicki Northcutt. Ed. by Lori Fairchild. (Illus.). 128p. 1999. 39.95 (*0-9654999-5-2*) Hist Pub Network.

Plano Diet. Max Morales, Jr. (Illus.). 87p. (Orig.). 1984. pap. 6.95 (*0-934157-00-6*) Morales Pubns.

Plano Seasons. Bonney J. Rousseau. iv, 147p. (YA). (gr. 7-12). 1999. pap. 11.00 (*0-9667395-4-X*) In the BAG.

Plano, Texas: The Early Years. Mozelle J. Campbell et al. (Illus.). ix, 402p. 1986. 32.00 (*0-9651841-0-2*) Frnds Plano Public Lbry.

Plano, Texas: The Early Years. Mozelle J. Campbell et al. (Illus.). 402p. 1986. reprint ed. lthr. 100.00 (*0-9651841-1-0*) Frnds Plano Public Lbry.

Planos from Piedmont: A Plano Family History. George E. Bell. Ed. & Illus. by Jean P. Bell. LC 94-61997. 450p. (C). 1995. text. write for info. (*0-9623275-4-9*) Wayne Ridge.

Planpak Number 83131: Model Rocket Launch Panel. Howard A. Goodman. (Illus.). 24p. (Orig.). 1984. pap. text 5.95 (*0-914465-00-7*, 83131) H A Goodman & Assocs.

Plans & Patters for Preschool. Ideal Instructional Fair Staff. 1998. pap. 21.95 (*0-513-02057-8*) Instruct Fair.

Plans & Policies for Technology in Education: A Compendium. Anne Wujcik et al. Ed. by Anne Ward. 250p. (Orig.). 1995. pap. 35.00 (*0-88364-192-5*, 03-133) Natl Sch Boards.

Plans & Provisions for the Mentally Handicapped. M. Bone et al. 1972. 50.00 (*0-7855-0582-2*, Pub. by Natl Inst Soc Work) St Mut.

Plans & Recommendations for Linking Automated Systems in Long Island Libraries. RMG Consultants, Inc. Staff. 84p. 1991. pap. 10.00 (*0-938435-21-3*) LI Lib Resources.

Plans & Section Drawing. 2nd ed. Thomas C. Wang. (Landscape Architecture Ser.). 144p. 1996. pap. 39.95 (*0-471-28608-7*, VNR) Wiley.

Plans & the Structure of Behavior. George A. Miller et al. (Illus.). 226p. (C). 1986. reprint ed. text 24.95 (*0-937431-00-1*) Adams Bannister Cox.

Plans for Children & Communities. Eugene M. Schwartz. 1992. pap. 14.95 (*0-945803-23-0*) R Steiner Col.

Plans for City Police Jails & Village Lockups. Hastings H. Hart. (Russell Sage Foundation Reprint Ser.). (Illus.). reprint ed. lib. bdg. 37.50 (*0-697-00203-9*) Irvington.

Plans for Global War: Rainbow-5 & the Victory Program, 1941. Ed. by Steven T. Ross. LC 92-20669. (American War Plans, 1919-1941 Ser.: Vol. 5). 328p. 1992. text 50.00 (*0-8153-0693-8*) Garland.

Plans for Peace: Negotiation & the Arab-Israeli Conflict. Karen A. Feste. LC 91-38251. 224p. 1991. pap. 18.95 (*0-275-94227-9*, Praeger Pubs) Greenwood.

An Asterisk (*) at the beginning of an entry indicates that the title is appearing for the first time.

Plans for Peace: Negotiation & the Arab-Israeli Conflict, 284. Karen A. Feste. LC 91-18597. (Contributions in Political Science Ser.: No. 284). 216p. 1991. 57.95 (*0-313-26361-2*, FAI, Greenwood Pr) Greenwood.

***Plans for Stalin's War Machine: Tukhachevskii & Military-Economy.** Lennart Samuelson. LC 99-14622. 267p. 2000. text 65.00 (*0-312-22527-X*) St Martin.

***Plans for the Future: A Study on Future Trends.** Lawrence George Lux. LC 99-91913. 187p. 2000. 25.00 (*0-7388-1294-3*); pap. 18.00 (*0-7388-1295-1*) Xlibris Corp.

Plans for the Future: The Best Service Shop Layouts Published by Electrical Apparatus. Kevin N. Jones. (Illus.). 76p. (Orig.). 1992. pap. text 24.95 (*0-943876-05-2*) Barks Pubns.

Plans for War against the British Empire & Japan: The Red, Orange, & Red-Orange Plans, 1923-1938. Ed. by Steven T. Ross. LC 92-20669. (American War Plans, 1919-1941 Ser.: Vol. 2). 440p. 1992. text 60.00 (*0-8153-0690-3*) Garland.

Plans, Pragmatism & People: The Failure of Soviet City Planning. R. A. French. LC 95-12855. (Pitt Series in Russian & East European). (Illus.). 233p. (C). 1996. pap. 19.95 (*0-8229-6106-7*) U of Pittsburgh Pr.

Plans, Purposes & Pursuits. Kenneth E. Hagin. 1988. pap. 7.95 (*0-89276-512-7*) Faith Lib Pubns.

Plans to Meet the Axis Threat, 1939-1940, Vol. 3. Intro. by Steven T. Ross. LC 92-20669. 376p. 1992. text 60.00 (*0-8153-0691-1*) Garland.

Planson: Nature. (Rhythm & Color One Ser.). 1970. 9.95 (*0-8288-9513-9*) Fr & Eur.

***Plansprache und Phraseologie: Empirische Untersuchungen Zu Reproduziertem Sprachmaterial im Esperanto.** Sabine Fiedler. 444p. 1999. 52.95 (*3-631-34088-5*) P Lang Pubng.

***Plant.** David Burnie. (Eyewitness Books). (Illus.). (J). (gr. 4-7). 2000. 19.99 (*0-7894-6563-9*) DK Pub Inc.

***Plant.** David Burnie. (Eyewitness Books). (J). (gr. 4-7). 2000. 15.95 (*0-7894-5812-8*) DK Pub Inc.

Plant: The House of Plant of Macon, Ga. G. S. Dickerman. (Illus.). 259p. 1990. reprint ed. pap. 39.50 (*0-8328-1519-5*); reprint ed. lib. bdg. 47.50 (*0-8328-1518-7*) Higginson Bk Co.

Plant Vol. I: A Guide to Understanding Its Nature. 2nd ed. Gerbert Grohmann. Tr. by K. Castelliz & B. Saunders-Davies from GER.Tr. of Die Pflanze Band I. (Illus.). 210p. 1989. reprint ed. pap. text 12.75 (*0-938250-23-X*) Bio-Dynamic Farm.

Plant Vol. II: Flowering Plants. Gerbert Grohmann. Tr. by K. Castelliz & B. Saunders-Davies from GER.Tr. of Die Pflanze Band II. (Illus.). 210p. (Orig.). 1989. pap. text 12.75 (*0-938250-24-8*) Bio-Dynamic Farm.

Plant - Microbe Interactions, Vol. 4. Ed. by Gary Stacey & Noel T. Keen. LC 95-10088. (Illus.). 296p. 1999. 64.00 (*0-89054-228-7*) Am Phytopathol Soc.

Plant a Garden in Your Sneaker! Fun & Outrageous Planting Projects for All Seasons. Diane L. Burns & Jill A. Burns. LC 98-182178. (Illus.). 64p. (J). (gr. 2 up). 1998. pap. 10.95 (*0-07-009228-1*) McGraw.

Plant a Garden the Lazy Way. MacMillan Lifestyles Group Staff. (Lazy Way Ser.). (Illus.). 304p. 1999. pap. 12.95 (*0-02-863161-7*) Glencoe.

***Plant a Page.** Somerville House Staff. 2000. pap. 55.92 (*1-58184-084-5*) Somerville Hse.

Plant a Seed . . . Read! 101 Activities to Motivate Children to Read! Gwendolyn R. Lewis. (Illus.). 112p. (Orig.). 1995. pap., spiral bd. write for info. (*0-9649216-0-X*) Hold on to your Dreams.

Plant a Tree: Choosing, Planting, & Maintaining This Precious Resource. Michael Weiner. LC 92-6220. 304p. 1992. pap. 18.95 (*0-471-57104-0*) Wiley.

Plant Accounting Regulations of the Federal Power Commission: A Critical Analysis. Sydney Davidson. Ed. by Richard P. Brief. LC 77-87296. (Development of Contemporary Accounting Thought Ser.). 1978. reprint ed. lib. bdg. 23.95 (*0-405-10936-9*) Ayer.

Plant Adaptation & Crop Improvement. Ed. by M. Cooper & G. L. Hammer. LC 97-142325. (CAB International Publication). (Illus.). 656p. 1997. text 130.00 (*0-85199-108-4*) OUP.

Plant Aging: Basic & Applied Approaches. Ed. by R. Rodriguez et al. LC 90-6996. (NATO ASI Ser.: Vol. 186). (Illus.). 462p. (C). 1990. text 162.00 (*0-306-43518-7*, Kluwer Plenum) Kluwer Academic.

Plant Alkaloids: A Guide to Their Discovery & Distribution. Robert F. Raffauf. LC 96-5319. 298p. 1996. 69.95 (*1-56022-860-1*) Haworth Pr.

Plant Allometry: The Scaling of Form & Process. Karl J. Niklas. LC 94-2418. 412p. 1994. pap. text 24.95 (*0-226-58081-4*); lib. bdg. 62.50 (*0-226-58080-6*) U Ch Pr.

Plant Amino Acids: Biochemistry & Biotechnology. Ed. by Bijay K. Singh. LC 98-44485. (Books in Soils, Plants & the Environment). (Illus.). 648p. 1998. text 195.00 (*0-8247-0204-2*) Dekker.

Plant Analysis. Ed. by J. Benton Jones, Jr. 1994. lib. bdg. 104.95 incl. VHS (*1-884015-29-8*) St Lucie Pr.

Plant Analysis: An Interpretation Manual. 2nd rev. ed. Ed. by D. J. Reuter & J. B. Robinson. (Illus.). 572p. 1997. 89.95 (*0-643-05938-5*, Pub. by CSIRO) Accents Pubns.

Plant Analysis Handbook II: A Practical Sampling, Preparation, Analysis & Interpretation Guide. Harry A. Mills & J. Benton Jones, Jr. (Illus.). 1996. 79.95 (*1-878148-05-2*) Micro-Macro Pub.

Plant Analysis Manual. Ed. by I. Walinga et al. LC 94-35634. 272p. 1995. lib. bdg. 97.50 (*0-7923-3182-6*) Kluwer Academic.

Plant Anatomy. James D. Mauseth. 600p. (C). 1988. text 63.95 (*0-8053-4570-1*) Benjamin-Cummings.

Plant Anatomy. 3rd ed. A. Fahn. LC 81-13813. (Illus.). 528p. 1982. text 105.00 (*0-08-028030-7*, Pergamon Pr); pap. text 43.00 (*0-08-028029-3*, Pergamon Pr) Elsevier.

Plant Anatomy. 4th ed. A. Fahn. 1990. pap. 62.95 (*0-7506-2843-X*) Buttrwrth-Heinemann.

Plant & Animal Alphabet Coloring Book. Leslie Tillett. (Illus.). (J). (gr. k-3). 1979. pap. 2.95 (*0-486-23898-9*) Dover.

Plant & Animal Biology, Vol. 1. 4th ed. Vines. Date not set. pap. text. write for info. (*0-582-35598-2*, Pub. by Addison-Wesley) Longman.

Plant & Animal Biology, Vol. 2. 4th ed. Vines. Date not set. pap. text. write for info. (*0-582-35599-0*, Pub. by Addison-Wesley) Longman.

***Plant & Animal Physiology.** 4th ed. (C). 2000. lab manual ed. write for info. (*0-8087-6798-4*) Pearson Custom.

Plant & Animal Populations: Methods in Demography. Thomas A. Ebert. LC 98-86238. (Illus.). 312p. (C). 1998. boxed set 69.95 (*0-12-228740-1*) Acad Pr.

Plant & Animal Ways see Child Horizons

***Plant & Crop Modelling: A Mathematical Approach to Plant & Crop Physiology.** John H. M. Thornley & Ian R. Johnson. 667p. 2000. reprint ed. 97.95 (*1-930665-05-9*) Blackburn Pr.

Plant & Floral Woodcuts for Designers & Craftsmen. Carolus Clusius. Ed. by Theodore Menten. LC 74-77539. (Illus.). 184p. 1974. pap. 10.95 (*0-486-20722-6*) Dover.

Plant-&-Grow Project Book. Ulla Dietl. LC 93-24788. (Illus.). 48p. (J). (gr. 2-10). 1993. 14.95 (*0-8069-0456-9*) Sterling.

Plant & Grow Project Book. Storey Publishing Staff. 1997. pap. 6.95 (*0-676-57208-1*) Random.

Plant & Insect Nematodes. fac. ed. Ed. by William R. Nickle. LC 84-4937. (Illus.). 943p. 1984. pap. 200.00 (*0-7837-7715-9*, 204747700007) Bks Demand.

Plant & Maintenance Manager's Desk Book. W. H. Weiss. LC 97-16067. 512p. 1997. 60.00 (*0-8144-0329-8*) AMACOM.

Plant & Process Ventilation. 2nd ed. Wesley C. Hemeon. LC 63-3486. 493p. reprint ed. pap. 152.90 (*0-608-15175-0*, 205607500046) Bks Demand.

Plant & Service Tours in Operations Management. 5th ed. Roger W. Schmenner. LC 97-34761. 254p. 1997. pap. text 38.20 (*0-13-257247-8*) P-H.

Plant & Soil - Interfaces & Interactions: Proceedings of the International Symposium Plant & Soil, Wageningen, the Netherlands, August 6-8, 1986. (Developments in Plant & Soil Sciences Ser.). (C). 1987. text 251.50 (*90-247-3535-1*) Kluwer Academic.

Plant-Animal-I. Terry L. Persun. Ed. by Robert Bixby. 26p. 1994. pap. text 6.00 (*1-882983-17-3*) March Street Pr.

Plant Animal Interactions. Wilcock. write for info. (*0-412-00961-7*) Thomson Learn.

Plant-Animal Interactions: Evolutionary Ecology in Tropical & Temperate Regions. Ed. by Peter W. Price et al. LC 90-39766. 639p. 1991. 200.00 (*0-471-50937-X*) Wiley.

Plant-Animal Interactions in Mediterranean-Type Ecosystems. Ed. by Margarita Arianoutsou. LC 93-6345. (Tasks for Vegetation Science Ser.). 184p. (C). 1994. text 156.00 (*0-7923-2470-6*) Kluwer Academic.

Plant-Animal Interactions in the Marine Benthos. Ed. by David M. John et al. (Systematics Association Special Volume Ser.: Vol. 46). (Illus.). 592p. 1992. text 150.00 (*0-19-857754-0*) OUP.

Plant-Associated Toxins: Agricultural, Phytochemical & Ecological Aspects. Ed. by S. M. Colegate & P. R. Dorling. (Illus.). 596p. 1994. text 150.00 (*0-85198-909-8*) OUP.

Plant Based Specialty Products & Biopolymers: Tema Nord 1997:606. (Tema Nord Ser.). 222p. 1998. pap. 17.00 (*92-893-0121-X*, NC121X, Pub. by Nordic Coun Minsters) Bernan Associates.

Plant Basics: A Manual for the Care of Indoor Plants. Susan McCollum & Teena Risley. 86p. 1994. pap. 14.95 (*0-9644264-0-4*) McCollum Risley.

Plant Biochemical Regulators. Ed. by Harold W. Gausman. (Books in Soils, Plants & the Environment: Vol. 21). (Illus.). 368p. 1991. text 195.00 (*0-8247-8536-3*) Dekker.

Plant Biochemistry. P. M. Dey & Jeffrey B. Harborne. (Illus.). 576p. 1997. text 74.95 (*0-12-214674-3*) Acad Pr.

Plant Biochemistry. 3rd ed. Ed. by James Bonner & Joseph Varner. 1976. text 94.00 (*0-12-114860-2*) Acad Pr.

Plant Biochemistry & Molecular Biology. Hans-Walter Heldt. (Illus.). 546p. (C). 1998. text 132.00 (*0-19-850180-3*); pap. text 59.95 (*0-19-850179-X*) OUP.

Plant Biochemistry & Molecular Biology. 2nd ed. Peter J. Lea & Richard C. Leegood. LC 98-29156. 384p. 1999. pap. 54.95 (*0-471-97683-0*) Wiley.

***Plant Biochemistry & Molecular Biology.** 2nd ed. Peter J. Lea & Richard C. Leegood. LC 98-29156. 384p. 1999. 129.95 (*0-471-97682-2*) Wiley.

Plant Biology. David Bruck. 1998. pap., lab manual ed. 25.95 (*0-7872-5268-9*) Kendall-Hunt.

***Plant Biology.** Ed. by Cliffs Notes Staff. (Cliffs Quick Reviews Ser.). (Illus.). 80p. 2000. pap. 9.99 (*0-7645-8560-6*) IDG Bks.

***Plant Biology.** Carolyn Dunn. 128p. (C). 1999. spiral bd. 31.95 (*0-7872-6310-9*, 41631001) Kendall-Hunt.

Plant Biology. Don Smith & Camelia Maier. 176p. (C). 1995. spiral bd. 25.95 (*0-7872-1279-2*, 41127901) Kendall-Hunt.

Plant Biology Laboratory Manual. 3rd ed. Roland Dute & Curt Peterson. 212p. (C). 1996. spiral bd. 21.99 (*0-8403-9336-9*) Kendall-Hunt.

Plant Biology Laboratory Manual for Biology I. David Bruck. 156p. (C). 1996. pap. text, spiral bd. 19.95 (*0-7872-2809-5*) Kendall-Hunt.

Plant Biology of the Basin & Range. Ed. by George M. Hidy et al. (Ecological Studies: Vol. 80). 384p. 1990. 83.00 (*0-387-51219-5*) Spr-Verlag.

Plant Biology Research & Training for the 21st Century. National Research Council Staff. 80p. (C). 1992. pap. text 19.00 (*0-309-04679-3*) Natl Acad Pr.

Plant Biology Science Projects. David R. Hershey. (Best Science Projects for Young Adults Ser.). 176p. (J). 1995. pap. 12.95 (*0-471-04983-2*) Wiley.

Plant Biomechanics: An Engineering Approach to Plant Form & Function. Karl J. Niklas. (Illus.). 622p. 1992. pap. text 32.95 (*0-226-58631-6*); lib. bdg. 82.50 (*0-226-58630-8*) U Ch Pr.

Plant Biotechnolgy & in Vitro Biology in the 21st Century: Proceedings of the 21st International Congress of the International Association of Plant Tissue Culture & Biotechnology, Jerusalem, Israel, 14-19 June 1998. Congress of the International Association of Plant Tissue Culture & Biotechnology Staff et al. LC 99-33164. 1999. write for info. (*0-7923-5826-0*) Kluwer Academic.

Plant Biotechnology. Ed. by M. W. Fowler et al. (Comprehensive Biotechnology Supplement Ser.: No. 2). 373p. 1992. 181.50 (*0-08-034731-2*, Pergamon Pr) Elsevier.

Plant Biotechnology. S. Ignacimuthu. 308p. 1997. 39.00 (*1-886106-30-4*) Science Pubs.

Plant Biotechnology: A Laboratory Course. Robert Lebowitz. 160p. (C). 1994. text. write for info. (*0-697-15119-0*, WCB McGr Hill) McGrw-H Hghr Educ.

Plant Biotechnology: Commercial Prospects & Problems. J. Prakash & T. Pierik. 300p. 1993. text 79.00 (*1-881570-31-2*) Science Pubs.

Plant Biotechnology: New Products & Applications. Ed. by J. Hammond et al. (Current Topics in Microbiology & Immunology Ser.: Vol. 240). (Illus.). 180p. 1999. 119.00 (*3-540-65104-7*) Spr-Verlag.

***Plant Biotechnology: New Products & Applications.** J. Hammond et al. LC 99-45293. (Illus.). xii, 200p. 1999. pap. 54.00 (*3-540-66265-0*) Spr-Verlag.

Plant Biotechnology & Development. Ed. by Peter M. Gresshoff. 192p. 1992. boxed set 94.95 (*0-8493-8261-0*, QK728) CRC Pr.

Plant Biotechnology & Plant Genetic Resources for Sustainability & Productivity. Watanabe & Pehu. 247p. 1997. 74.00 (*0-12-737145-1*) Acad Pr.

Plant Biotechnology in Agriculture. Lindsey. 1991. pap. text 101.00 (*0-471-93238-8*) Wiley.

Plant Biotechnology Transfer to Developing Countries. Ed. by David W. Altman & Kazuo N. Watanabe. (Biotechnology Intelligence Unit Ser.). (Illus.). 300p. 1995. text 74.00 (*0-12-054505-5*) Acad Pr.

Plant Blossoms see Look Once, Look Again

Plant Blossoms, Vol. 3038. David M. Schwartz. (Look Once, Look Again! Ser.: Vol. 11). (Illus.). 16p. (J). (gr. 1-3). 1998. pap. 2.99 (*1-57471-329-9*, 3038) Creat Teach Pr.

Plant-Book: A Portable Dictionary of the Vascular Plants. 2nd ed. D. J. Mabberley. LC 96-30091. 874p. (C). 1997. text 52.95 (*0-521-41421-0*) Cambridge U Pr.

Plant Breeding. Ed. by V. L. Chopra. (C). 1988. 34.00 (*81-204-0388-6*, Pub. by Oxford IBH) S Asia.

Plant Breeding, Vol. 17. Janick. 352p. 1999. 180.00 (*0-471-33373-5*) Wiley.

Plant Breeding: A Symposium, Iowa State University, 1965. Plant Breeding Symposium Staff. Ed. by Kenneth J. Frey. LC 66-21642. 438p. reprint ed. pap. 135.80 (*0-608-14570-X*, 202493200040) Bks Demand.

Plant Breeding & Whole-System Crop Physiology: Improving Adaptation, Maturity & Yield. D. H. Wallace & Weikai Yan. LC 98-6441. (Illus.). 416p. 1998. text 100.00 (*0-85199-265-X*) OUP.

Plant Breeding for Stress Environments. Abraham Blum. LC 87-23855. 208p. 1988. 135.00 (*0-8493-6388-8*, SB123, CRC Reprint) Franklin.

Plant Breeding in the 1990's. Ed. by H. T. Stalker & J. P. Murphy. (Illus.). 540p. 1992. text 140.00 (*0-85198-717-6*) OUP.

Plant Breeding Methodology. Neal F. Jensen. LC 88-2663. 676p. 1988. 140.00 (*0-471-60190-X*) Wiley.

Plant Breeding Perspective. J. Sneep. 435p. (C). 1979. reprint ed. pap. 375.00 (*81-7089-052-7*, Pub. by Intl Bk Distr) St Mut.

Plant Breeding Reviews, Vol. 9. Jules Janick. LC 83-641963. 416p. 1992. 180.00 (*0-471-57498-8*) Wiley.

Plant Breeding Reviews, Vol. 10. Jules Janick. 392p. 1992. 180.00 (*0-471-57347-7*) Wiley.

Plant Breeding Reviews, Vol. 12. Jules Janick. 315p. 1994. 180.00 (*0-471-57344-2*) Wiley.

Plant Breeding Reviews, Vol. 13. Ed. by Jules Janick. 400p. 1995. 180.00 (*0-471-57343-4*) Wiley.

Plant Breeding Reviews, Vol. 14. Ed. by Jules Janick. LC 83-641963. (Plant Breeding Reviews Ser.). 400p. 1996. 180.00 (*0-471-57342-6*) Wiley.

Plant Breeding Reviews, Vol. 15. Jules Janick. LC 83-641963. 395p. 1997. 180.00 (*0-471-18904-9*) Wiley.

***Plant Breeding Reviews, Vol. 16.** Ed. by Jules Janick. 352p. 1998. 180.00 (*0-471-25446-0*) Wiley.

***Plant Breeding Reviews, Vol. 18, Vol. 18.** Janick. 336p. 1999. 180.00 (*0-471-35567-4*) Wiley.

Plant Breeding Systems in Seed Plants. A. J. Richards. (Illus.). 320p. (C). 1986. text 100.00 (*0-04-581020-6*); pap. text 44.95 (*0-04-581021-4*) Routledge.

Plant Breeding II. Plant Breeding Symposium Staff. Ed. by Kenneth J. Frey. LC 80-28879. (Illus.). 507p. 1981. reprint ed. pap. 157.20 (*0-608-00051-5*, 206081700006) Bks Demand.

Plant Bugs of the World (Insecta: Heteroptera: Miraidae) Systematic Catalog, Distributions, Host List & Bibliography. Randall T. Schuh. LC 95-17046. 1995. write for info. (*0-913424-15-3*) Am Mus Natl Hist.

Plant by Numbers: A Step-by-Step Planting Guide. Nigel Colborn. (Illus.). 160p. 1998. 30.00 (*1-57959-032-2*, SOMA) BB&T Inc.

Plant Canopies: Their Growth, Form & Function. Ed. by Graham Russell et al. (Society for Experimental Biology Seminar Ser.: No. 31). 188p. (C). 1990. pap. text 29.95 (*0-521-39563-1*) Cambridge U Pr.

Plant Carbohydrates I: Intracellular Carbohydrates. Ed. by F. A. Loewus & W. Tanner. (Encyclopedia of Plant Physiology Ser.: Vol. 13 a). (Illus.). 880p. 1982. 318.95 (*0-387-11060-7*) Spr-Verlag.

Plant Carbohydrates II: Extracellular Carbohydrates. Ed. by W. Tanner & F. A. Loewus. (Encyclopedia of Plant Physiology Ser.: Vol. 13 B). (Illus.). 800p. 1981. 318.95 (*0-387-11007-0*) Spr-Verlag.

Plant Cast Precast & Prestressed Concrete a Design Guide. 560p. pap. 24.00 (*0-937040-17-7*, MNL-125-80) P-PCI.

Plant Cell - Cell Interactions. Ed. by Ian M. Sussex et al. LC 86-213910. (Current Communications in Molecular Biology Ser.). 163p. 1985. reprint ed. pap. 50.60 (*0-608-01804-X*, 206245700003) Bks Demand.

Plant Cell & Tissue Culture. Ed. by Indra K. Vasil & Trevor A. Thorpe. LC 93-30125. 550p. (C). 1994. text 306.50 (*0-7923-2493-5*) Kluwer Academic.

Plant Cell & Tissue Culture. Ed. by John M. Walker & Jeffrey W. Pollard. LC 84-15696. (Methods in Molecular Biology Ser.: Vol. 6). (Illus.). 609p. 1990. 69.50 (*0-89603-161-6*) Humana.

Plant Cell & Tissue Culture for the Production of Food Ingredients. Tong-Jen Fu et al. LC 99-11915. 1999. write for info. (*0-306-46100-5*) Kluwer Academic.

Plant Cell & Tissue Culture in Liquid Systems. G. Payne et al. 368p. 1993. 120.00 (*0-471-03726-5*) Wiley.

Plant Cell Biology. Brian E. Gunning & Martin W. Steer. (Life Science Ser.). 542p. (C). 1996. text 58.75 (*0-86720-509-1*) Jones & Bartlett.

Plant Cell Biology: A Practical Approach. Ed. by N. Harris & K. J. Oparka. LC 93-46555. (Practical Approach Ser.: Vol. 139). (Illus.). 358p. 1994. pap. text 58.00 (*0-19-963399-1*) OUP.

Plant Cell Biology: Structure Function. Brian E. Gunning & Martin W. Steer. LC 95-37693. (Life Science Ser.). 144p. (C). 1996. pap. text 37.50 (*0-86720-504-0*) Jones & Bartlett.

Plant Cell Biotechnology. Ed. by Ferda Mavituna et al. (NATO ASI Series H: Vol. 18). (Illus.). xx, 500p. 1988. 207.00 (*0-387-18556-9*) Spr-Verlag.

Plant Cell Culture. (Advances in Biochemical Engineering-Biotechnology Ser.: Vol. 31). (Illus.). 140p. 1985. 72.95 (*0-387-15489-2*) Spr-Verlag.

Plant Cell Culture. S. Edwards & H. A. Collin. (Introduction to Biotechniques Ser.). 160p. 1996. pap. text 34.95 (*1-872748-47-3*, Pub. by Bios Sci) Bks Intl VA.

Plant Cell Culture. S. Edwards & H. A. Collin. LC 98-15351. (Introduction to Biotechniques Ser.). (illus.). 176p. 1997. pap. 34.95 (*0-387-91508-7*) Spr-Verlag.

Plant Cell Culture: A Practical Approach. Ed. by Richard A. Dixon & Robert A. Gonzales. (The Practical Approach Ser.: No. 145). (Illus.). 256p. 1995. ring bd. 85.00 (*0-19-963403-3*) OUP.

Plant Cell Culture: A Practical Approach. 2nd ed. Ed. by Richard A. Dixon & Robert A. Gonzales. (The Practical Approach Ser.: No. 145). (Illus.). 250p. 1995. pap. text 55.00 (*0-19-963402-5*) OUP.

Plant Cell Culture Protocols. Robert D. Hall. (Methods in Molecular Biology Ser.: Vol. 111). (Illus.). 440p. 1999. 89.50 (*0-89603-549-2*) Humana.

***Plant Cell Cycle & Its Interfaces.** D. Francis. LC 00-36826. (Sheffield Biological Sciences Ser.). 2000. write for info. (*0-8493-0504-7*) CRC Pr.

Plant Cell Division. Ed. by D. Francis et al. (Portland Press Research Monograph Ser.: Vol. 10). (Illus.). 384p. (C). 1997. text 128.00 (*1-85578-089-5*, Pub. by Portland Pr Ltd) Ashgate Pub Co.

Plant Cell Electroporation & Electrofusion Protocols. Ed. by Jac A. Nickoloff. LC 95-358. (Methods in Molecular Biology Ser.: Vol. 55). 220p. 1995. 79.50 (*0-89603-328-7*) Humana.

Plant Cell Membranes. Ed. by Sidney P. Colowick et al. (Methods in Enzymology Ser.: Vol. 148). 762p. 1987. text 157.00 (*0-12-182048-3*) Acad Pr.

Plant Cell Proliferation & Its Regulation in Growth & Development. J. A. Bryant & Donato Chiatante. LC 97-14886. 224p. 1998. 137.95 (*0-471-97267-3*) Wiley.

Plant Cell, Tissue & Organ Culture: Fundamental Methods. Ed. by O. L. Gamborg & G. C. Phillips. (Illus.). 358p. 1995. 97.95 (*0-387-58068-9*) Spr-Verlag.

Plant Cell, Tissue & Organ Culture: Fundamental Methods. Ed. by O. L. Gamborg & G. C. Phillps. LC 95-10062. (Lab Manuals Ser.). 1995. write for info. (*3-540-58068-9*) Spr-Verlag.

Plant Cell Wall. 3rd rev. ed. Albert Frey-Wyssling. (Handbuch der Pflanzenanatomie Encyclopedia of Plant Anatomy - Traite d' Anatomie Vegetale Ser.: Vol. 3, Pt. 4). (Illus.). xi, 294p. 1976. 104.00 (*3-443-14009-2*, Pub. by Gebruder Borntraeger) Balogh.

Plant Cell Wall Analysis. Ed. by H. F. Linskens & J. F. Jackson. (Modern Methods of Plant Analysis Ser.: Vol. 17). (Illus.). 224p. 1996. 179.00 (*3-540-59406-X*) Spr-Verlag.

Plant Cell Wall Polymers: Biogenesis & Biodegradation. Ed. by Norman G. Lewis & Michael G. Paice. LC 89-6926. (Symposium Ser.: No. 399). (Illus.). xi, 664p. 1989. 119.95 (*0-8412-1658-4*) Am Chemical.

Plant Cell Wall Polymers: Biogenesis & Biodegradation. Ed. by Norman G. Lewis & Michael G. Paice. LC 89-17541. (ACS Symposium Ser.: No. 399). (Illus.). 688p. 1989. reprint ed. pap. 200.00 (*0-608-03199-2*, 206371800007) Bks Demand.

Plant Chemosystematics. Jeffrey B. Harborne & Billie L. Turner. 1984. text 209.00 (*0-12-324640-7*) Acad Pr.

Plant Chimeras. Richard A. Tilney-Bassett. LC 86-232382. 1986. pap. 29.95 (*0-7131-2936-0*) St Martin.

P

Plant Chromosomes. A. Love & D. Love. 1975. 25.00 (*3-7682-0966-0*) Lubrecht & Cramer.

*****Plant Chromosomes: Analysis, Manipulation & Engineering.** Ed. by Arun K. Sharma & Archana Sharma. (Illus.). 408p. 1999. text 80.00 (*90-5702-387-3*, Harwood Acad Pubs) Gordon & Breach.

Plant Chromosomes: Laboratory Methods. Ed. by Kiichi Fukui & Shigeki Nakayama. LC 97-100811. 288p. 1996. spiral bd. 84.95 (*0-8493-8919-4*) CRC Pr.

Plant Clinic: A Training System for Decision-Making & Resource Management in Plant Disease Diagnostics. Rhonda M. Black et al. 1995. pap. 39.00 (*0-85954-396-X*, Pub. by Nat Res Inst) St Mut.

Plant Clinic Handbook. J. M. Waller et al. LC 97-43255. (IMI Technical Handbks. Ser.: No. 3). (Illus.). 104p. 1998. spiral bd. 28.00 (*0-85198-918-7*) OUP.

Plant Closings: International Context & Social Costs. Robert Perrucci et al. (Social Institutions & Social Change Ser.). 203p. 1988. lib. bdg. 48.95 (*0-202-30338-1*) Aldine de Gruyter.

Plant Closings: International Context & Social Costs. Robert Perrucci et al. (Social Institutions & Social Change Ser.). 203p. (C). 1988. pap. text 25.95 (*0-202-30339-X*) Aldine de Gruyter.

Plant Closings: Myths, Power, Politics. Lawrence E. Rothstein. LC 85-23025. 216p. 1986. 57.95 (*0-86569-121-5*, Auburn Hse) Greenwood.

Plant Closings: Public or Private Choices? Ed. by Richard McKenzie. LC 84-14957. 326p. 1984. pap. 3.00 (*0-932790-42-9*) Cato Inst.

Plant Closings: Worker Rights, Management Rights, & the Law. Francis A. O'Connell. (Studies in Social Philosophy & Policy: No. 7). 313p. 1987. 34.95 (*0-912051-07-8*); pap. 21.95 (*0-912051-08-6*) Transaction Pubs.

Plant Closings & Economic Dislocation. Jeanne P. Gordus et al. LC 81-16188. 170p. 1981. text 22.00 (*0-911558-89-6*); pap. text 12.00 (*0-911558-90-X*) W E Upjohn.

Plant Closings & Employment Loss in Manufacturing: The Role of Local Economic Conditions. rev. ed. Elizabeth P. Patch. LC 95-18534. (Garland Studies in the History of American Labor). 144p. 1995. text 20.00 (*0-8153-2028-0*) Garland.

Plant Closings & Labor Rights see Fermetures d'Usines et Droits en Matiere de Travail

Plant Closings & Labor Rights: The Effects of Sudden Plant Closings on Freedom of Association & the Right to Organize in Canada, Mexico, & the United States. Labor Secretariat of the Commission. (SPA.). 240p. 1998. pap. 27.50 (*0-89059-079-6*) Bernan Pr.

Plant Closings & Worker Displacement: The Regional Issues. Marie Howland. LC 88-17032. 172p. 1988. pap. 13.00 (*0-88099-062-7*); text 32.00 (*0-88099-063-5*) W E Upjohn.

Plant Closings in the U. S. A Guide to Information Sources. Paul Haschak et al. Ed. by Wahib Nasrallah. (Research & Information Guides in Business, Industry, & Economic Institutions Ser.). 300p. Date not set. text 45.00 (*0-8153-1295-4*) Garland.

Plant Closure Literature, 1980-1994. Ralph E. Thayer & John S. Bishop, Jr. LC 95-40593. (CPL Bibliographies Ser.: Vol. 326). 50p. 1995. pap. 10.00 (*0-86602-326-7*, Sage Prdcls Pr) Sage.

Plant Closure Policy Dilemma: Labor, Law & Bargaining. Wayne R. Wendling. LC 84-10387. 166p. 1984. pap. text 12.00 (*0-88099-020-1*) W E Upjohn.

Plant Closure, Regulation, & Liberalism: The Limits to Liberal Public Philosophy. Oren M. Levin-Waldman. LC 92-16876. 200p. (C). 1992. lib. bdg. 49.50 (*0-8191-8760-7*) U Pr of Amer.

Plant Closure, Regulation, & Liberalism: The Limits to Liberal Public Philosophy. Oren M. Levin-Waldman. LC 92-16876. 200p. (C). 1992. pap. text 26.00 (*0-8191-8761-5*) U Pr of Amer.

Plant Closures: Myths, Realities & Responses. Gilda Haas. LC 85-27925. (Institute for New Communications Pamphlet Ser.). (Illus.). 64p. (Orig.). 1985. per. 5.00 (*0-89608-212-1*) South End Pr.

Plant Closures & Community Recovery. Ed. by John Lynch. 208p. (Orig.). 1990. pap. 39.50 (*0-317-04839-2*) Natl Coun Econ Dev.

Plant Cold Hardiness: Molecular Biology, Biochemistry & Physiology: Proceedings of the 5th International Seminar Held in Corvallis, Oregon, August 4-8, 1996. Ed. by Paul H. Li & Tony H. Chen. LC 97-28663. (Illus.). 380p. (C). 1998. text 150.00 (*0-306-45712-1*, Kluwer Plenum) Kluwer Academic.

Plant Collecting. 1970. 0.35 (*0-686-20732-7*) SUNY Environ.

Plant Collecting & Documentation Field Notebook. Michael G. Simpson. (Illus.). x, 112p. 1997. pap. write for info. (*0-9658975-1-6*) S D S U Herb.

Plant Collectors in Madagascar & the Comoro Islands. Laurence Dorr. (Illus.). 524p. 1997. 116.00 (*1-900347-18-0*, Pub. by Royal Botnic Grdns) Balogh.

Plant Collector's Notebook. rev. ed. Betty B. Mackey. 150p. 1996. pap. 7.95 (*0-9616338-5-9*) B B Mackey Bks.

*****Plant Communities in Australia: The Dynamics of Structure, Growth & Biodiversity.** Raymond L. Specht & Alison Specht. 464p. 2000. text 60.00 (*0-19-553705-X*) OUP.

Plant Communities of Marin County, California. W. David Shuford & Irene C. Timossi. (Illus.). 32p. (Orig.). 1989. pap. write for info. (*0-943460-15-8*) Calif Native.

Plant Communities of New Jersey: A Study in Landscape Diversity. rev. ed. Beryl R. Collins & Karl H. Anderson. LC 93-36695. Orig. Title: Vegetation of New Jersey. (Illus.). 280p. (C). 1994. text 47.00 (*0-8135-2070-3*); pap. text 20.00 (*0-8135-2071-1*) Rutgers U Pr.

Plant Communities of Southern Illinois. John W. Voigt & Robert H. Mohlenbrock. LC 64-11168. (Illus.). 220p. 1964. 14.95 (*0-8093-0132-6*) S Ill U Pr.

Plant Communities of the Mono Basin. Helen Constantine. (Mono Lake Committee Field Guide Ser.). (Illus.). 50p. 1993. pap. text 3.95 (*0-939716-04-6*) Mono Lake Comm.

Plant Competition: An Analysis of Community Functions. Frederic E. Clements, 3rd. Ed. by Frank N. Egerton. LC 77-74209. (History of Ecology Ser.). (Illus.). 1978. reprint ed. lib. bdg. 41.95 (*0-405-10380-8*) Ayer.

Plant Competition in Forest Stands. Clarence F. Korstian & Theodore S. Coile. LC 39-15396. (Duke University, School of Forestry Bulletin Ser.: No. 3). 140p. reprint ed. pap. 43.40 (*0-7837-6053-1*, 204586600008) Bks Demand.

Plant Conservation. David W. Ehrenfeld. LC 94-46718. (Readings from Conservation Biology Ser.). 221p. 1995. pap. 24.95 (*0-86542-450-0*) Blackwell Sci.

Plant Conservation in the Mediterranean Area. Ed. by C. Gomez-Campo. (Geobotany Ser.). 1985. text 264.50 (*90-6193-523-7*) Kluwer Academic.

Plant Contamination: Modeling & Simulation of Organic Chemical Processes. Ed. by Stefan Trapp & Craig McFarlane. LC 94-9734. 272p. 1994. lib. bdg. 95.00 (*1-56670-078-7*, L1078) Lewis Pubs.

Plant Corrosion: Prediction of Materials & Perfromance. Ed. by J. E. Strutt & J. R. Nicholls. LC 87-22602. (Corrosion & Its Prevention Ser.). 332p. 1987. text 78.95 (*0-470-20906-2*) P-H.

Plant Cuticles: An Integrated Functional Approach. G. Kirstiens. (Environmental Plant Biology Ser.). (Illus.). 250p. 1996. text 130.00 (*1-85996-130-4*, Pub. by Bios Sci) Bks Intl VA.

Plant Cytogenetics. Ram J. Singh. 416p. 1993. boxed set 131.95 (*0-8493-8656-X*, QK981) CRC Pr.

Plant Defenses Against Mammalian Herbivory. R. Thomas Palo & Charles T. Robbins. 192p. 1991. lib. bdg. 139.00 (*0-8493-6550-3*, SB292) CRC Pr.

Plant Demography in Vegetation Succession. Krystyna Falinska. (Tasks for Vegetation Science Ser.). 220p. 1991. text 208.50 (*0-7923-1060-8*) Kluwer Academic.

Plant-Derived Chemicals, No. C-102. Business Communications Co., Inc. Staff. 176p. 1990. 2850.00 (*0-89336-639-0*) BCC.

Plant-Derived Drugs: Products, Technologies, Applications. Philip Rotheim. 324p. 1998. 3450.00 (*1-56965-392-5*, B-121) BCC.

Plant Design & Economics for Chemical Engineers. 4th ed. Max S. Peters & Klaus D. Timmerhaus. 992p. (C). 1990. 101.56 (*0-07-049613-7*) McGraw.

*****Plant Design Economy Chemical Engineer.** 5th ed. Peters. 2001. text 68.00 (*0-07-239266-5*) McGraw.

Plant Design for Safety: A User-Friendly Approach. Trevor A. Kletz. 120p. 1990. 49.95 (*1-56032-068-0*) Hemisp Pub.

Plant Design for Safety: A User Friendly Approach. 2nd ed. Trevor Kletz. LC 98-16864. 209p. 1998. boxed set 49.95 (*1-56032-619-0*, Pub. by Tay Francis Ltd) Taylor & Francis.

Plant Development: The Cellular Basis. Robert Lyndon. (Topics in Plant Physiology Ser.: No. 3). (Illus.). 220p. (C). 1990. text 75.00 (*0-04-581032-X*) Routledge.

Plant Development: The Cellular Basis. Robert Lyndon. (Topics in Plant Physiology Ser.: No. 3). (Illus.). 220p. (C). 1990. pap. 49.95 (*0-04-581033-8*) Thomson Learn.

Plant Disease Clinic & Field Diagnosis of Abiotic Diseases. Malcolm C. Shurtleff & Charles W. Averre, III. LC 96-85526. 256p. (C). 1997. text 89.00 (*0-89054-217-1*) Am Phytopathol Soc.

Plant Disease Control: Principles & Practice. 2nd ed. Otis C. Maloy. 360p. 1993. 110.00 (*0-471-57317-5*) Wiley.

Plant Disease Control: Resistance & Susceptibility. Ed. by Richard C. Staples & Gary H. Toenniessen. LC 80-22923. (Environmental Science & Technology Ser.). (Illus.). 359p. reprint ed. pap. 111.30 (*0-8357-6265-3*, 203433300089) Bks Demand.

Plant Disease Management: Principles & Practice. Ed. by H. S. Chaube. 304p. 1991. lib. bdg. 228.00 (*0-8493-5758-6*, SB562) CRC Pr.

Plant Diseases. F. T. Brooks. (C). 1981. text 210.00 (*0-89771-569-1*, Pub. by Intl Bk Distr) St Mut.

Plant Diseases. G. Swarup et al. 402p. 1989. 200.00 (*81-7041-209-9*, Pub. by Scientific Pubs) St Mut.

Plant Diseases. F. T. Brooks. 386p. 1981. reprint ed. 150.00 (*0-7855-3069-X*, Pub. by Intl Bk Distr) St Mut.

Plant Diseases. 6th ed. R. S. Singh. (C). 1989. 22.00 (*81-204-0128-X*) S Asia.

Plant Diseases: Their Biology & Social Impact. Gail L. Schumann. LC 91-70960. (Illus.). 407p. (C). 1991. text 52.00 (*0-89054-116-7*) Am Phytopathol Soc.

Plant Diseases Caused by Fastidious Prokaryotes: Third Regional Workshop on Plant Mycoplasma. Ed. by S. P. Raychaudhuri & Anupam Varma. viii, 139p. 1989. 59.00 (*1-55528-179-6*) Scholarly Pubns.

Plant Diseases Recorded in NZ, 3 vols., Set. S. R. Pennycook. 1990. 66.00 (*0-477-02547-1*, Pub. by Manaaki Whenua) Balogh.

Plant Diversity. (C). 1992. write for info. (*0-8087-7931-1*) Pearson Custom.

Plant Diversity in Forests of Western Uganda & Eastern Zaire Preliminary Results. Axel D. Poulsen. (AAU Report Ser.: No. 36). (Illus.). 76p. 1997. pap. 13.00 (*87-87600-64-1*, Pub. by Aarhus Univ Pr) David Brown.

Plant Diversity in Malesia III Pt. III: Proceedings of the Third International Floras Malesiana Symposium, 1995. J. Dransfield et al. (Illus.). 449p. 1997. pap. 66.00 (*1-900347-42-3*, Pub. by Royal Botnic Grdns) Balogh.

Plant Diversity of Malesia: Proceedings of the Flora Malesiana Symposium Commemorating Prof. Dr. C. G. G. J. van Steenis. Ed. by P. Baas et al. (C). 1990. text 129.50 (*0-7923-0883-2*) Kluwer Academic.

Plant DNA Infectious Agents. Ed. by T. Hohn & Jeff Schell. (Plant Gene Research Ser.). (Illus.). 360p. 1987. 158.95 (*0-387-81995-9*) Spr-Verlag.

Plant Dormancy: Physiology, Biochemistry & Molecular Biology. Ed. by G. A. Lang. LC 97-142321. (CAB International Publication). 408p. 1997. text 105.00 (*0-85198-978-0*) OUP.

Plant Dreaming Deep. May Sarton. 1984. 23.50 (*0-8446-6094-9*) Peter Smith.

Plant Dreaming Deep. May Sarton. 192p. 1996. reprint ed. pap. 11.00 (*0-393-31551-7*) Norton.

Plant Drug Analysis: A Thin Layer Chromatography Atlas, Vol. XII. 2nd ed. Hildebert H. Wagner & Sabine Bladt. (Illus.). 350p. 1996. 198.00 (*3-540-58676-8*) Spr-Verlag.

Plant Drug Analysis: A Thin Layer Chromatography Photo-Atlas. H. Wagner et al. Tr. by T. A. Scott. (GER., Illus.). 350p. 1992. 200.00 (*0-387-13195-7*) Spr-Verlag.

Plant-Eaters. (Funpax Ser.). (J). 1997. pap. text 2.95 (*0-7894-2115-1*) DK Pub Inc.

Plant Ecological Bibliography & Thesaurus for Southern Africa up to 1975. A. P. Backer et al. (Memoirs of the Botanical Survey of South Africa Ser.: No. 52). (Illus.). 216p. 1986. 15.00 (*0-621-08871-4*, Pub. by Natl Botanical Inst) Balogh.

Plant Ecology. 2nd ed. Ed. by M. J. Crawley. LC 96-23347. 500p. 1997. pap. 54.95 (*0-632-03639-7*) Blackwell Sci.

Plant Ecology in West Africa: Systems & Processes. Ed. by George W. Lawson. LC 84-17347. (Illus.). 376p. 1986. reprint ed. pap. 116.60 (*0-608-05276-0*, 206581400001) Bks Demand.

Plant Ecology of the Hazelwood Botanical Preserve. John G. Segelken. (Bulletin Ser.: No. 21). 1929. pap. text 2.00 (*0-86727-020-9*) Ohio Bio Survey.

Plant Ecology of the Isipingo Beach Area, Natal, South Africa. C. J. Ward. (Memoirs of the Botanical Survey of South Africa Ser.: No. 45). (Illus.). 147p. 1980. 15.00 (*0-621-05307-4*, Pub. by Natl Botanical Inst) Balogh.

*****Plant Ecology Principles & Conservation.** Bethany Keddy. 2000. pap. text. write for info. (*0-7167-4053-2*) W H Freeman.

Plant Ecophysiology. Ed. by Mular N. Prasad. LC 96-19477. 552p. 1996. 125.00 (*0-471-13157-1*) Wiley.

*****Plant Electron Microscopy & Cytochemistry.** Ed. by William V. Dashek. 300p. 2000. spiral bd. 79.50 (*0-89603-809-2*) Humana.

Plant Embryology: Embryogeny of the Spermatophytes. D. A. Johansen. (Illus.). 305p. 1990. reprint ed. text 59.50 (*81-211-0043-7*, Pub. by Mahendra Pal Singh) Lubrecht & Cramer.

Plant Energetics. Octavian S. Ksenzhek & Alexander G. Volkov. LC 97-80794. (Illus.). 389p. 1998. text 79.95 (*0-12-427350-5*) Morgan Kaufmann.

Plant Engineering Management. Donald A. Bartlett. LC 74-144106. (Manufacturing Management Ser.: Vol. 5). 233p. reprint ed. pap. 72.30 (*0-608-16167-5*, 205573700034) Bks Demand.

Plant Engineers & Managers Guide to Energy Conservation. 5th ed. Albert Thumann. (Illus.). 333p. 1991. 68.00 (*0-88173-131-5*, 0271) Fairmont Pr.

Plant Engineers & Managers Guide to Energy Conservation. 6th ed. Albert Thumann. LC 95-32306. 389p. 1995. 79.00 (*0-88173-230-3*) Fairmont Pr.

Plant Engineers & Managers Guide to Energy Conservation. 7th ed. Albert Thumann. LC 98-35001. 410p. 1998. 88.00 (*0-88173-304-0*) Fairmont Pr.

Plant Engineers & Managers to Energy Conservation. 7th ed. Albert Thumann. LC 98-35001. 411p. 1998. 88.00 (*0-13-020738-1*) P-H.

*****Plant Engineers Handbook.** Keith Mobley. (Illus.). 2000p. 2000. 125.00 (*0-7506-7328-1*) Buttrwrth-Heinemann.

Plant Engineer's Reference Book. Dennis A. Snow. 864p. 1991. 265.00 (*0-7506-1015-8*) Buttrwrth-Heinemann.

Plant-Environment Interactions. Ed. by Robert E. Wilkinson. (Books in Soils, Plants & the Environment: Vol. 35). (Illus.). 616p. 1994. text 180.00 (*0-8247-8940-7*) Dekker.

*****Plant-Environment Interactions.** 2nd ed. R. E. Wilkinson. LC 00-31592. (Books in Soils, Plants & the Environment). 2000. write for info. (*0-8247-0377-4*) Dekker.

*****Plant Evolution under Domestication.** Gideon Ladizinsky. 262p. 1999. 140.00 (*0-412-82210-5*) Kluwer Academic.

Plant Experiments. Vera Webster. LC 82-9448. (New True Books Ser.). (Illus.). 48p. (J). (gr. k-4). 1982. lib. bdg. 21.00 (*0-516-01638-5*) Childrens.

Plant Exploration & Introduction: A Source Guide. 1991. lib. bdg. 76.00 (*0-8490-4824-9*) Gordon Pr.

Plant Explorer's Guide to New England. Raymond Wiggers. (Illus.). 599p. 1999. reprint ed. pap. text 18.00 (*0-7881-6351-5*) DIANE Pub.

Plant Facilities Administrator. Jack Rudman. (Career Examination Ser.: C-2758). 1994. pap. 39.95 (*0-8373-2758-X*) Nat Learn.

Plant Families. 2nd ed. William G. Jaques. (Pictured Key Nature Ser.). 184p. (C). 1948. text. write for info. (*0-697-04840-3*, WCB McGr Hill) McGrw-H Hghr Educ.

Plant-Feeding Gall Midges of North America. Raymond J. Gagne. LC 88-47921. (Illus.). 340p. 1989. text 57.50 (*0-8014-1918-2*) Cornell U Pr.

Plant Fibers. Ed. by H. F. Linskens & J. F. Jackson. (Modern Methods of Plant Analysis Ser.: Vol. 10). (Illus.). 420p. 1989. 284.95 (*0-387-18822-3*) Spr-Verlag.

Plant Fibers for Papermaking. Lilian A. Bell. (Illus.). 132p. 1995. pap. 21.00 (*0-9625076-5-2*) Liliaceae Pr.

Plant Fibre Processing: A Handbook. Cyril Jarman. 64p. 1998. pap. 13.95 (*1-85339-385-1*, Pub. by Intermed Tech) Stylus Pub VA.

Plant Form: An Illustrated Guide to Flowering Plant Morphology. Adrian D. Bell. (Illus.). 356p. 1991. pap. text 49.95 (*0-19-854219-4*) OUP.

Plant Form & Vegetation Structure: Adaptation, Plasticity & Relation to Herbivory. Ed. by Jarinus J. Werger et al. (Illus.). xii, 356p. 1988. pap. 80.00 (*90-5103-019-3*, Pub. by SPB Acad Pub) Balogh.

Plant Fossils: The History of Land Vegetation. Christopher J. Cleal & Barry A. Thomas. LC 99-19437. (Fossils Illustrated Ser.). (Illus.). 288p. 1999. 110.00 (*0-85115-684-3*, Boydell Pr) Boydell & Brewer.

Plant Fruit & Seeds, Vol. 3039. David M. Schwartz. (Look Once, Look Again! Ser.: Vol. 12). (Illus.). 16p. (J). (gr. 1-3). 1998. pap. 2.99 (*1-57471-330-2*, 3039) Creat Teach Pr.

Plant Fruits & Seeds see Look Once, Look Again

Plant Fun: Crafts & Games for All Ages. Kathleen C. Ruppert. (Illus.). 60p. (Orig.). 1996. pap. text 7.00 (*0-916287-20-3*, SP207) Univ Fla Food.

Plant Functional Types: Their Relevance to Ecosystem Properties & Global Change. Ed. by F. I. Woodward et al. (International Geosphere-Biosphere Programme Bks.: No. 1). (Illus.). 383p. (C). 1997. text 135.00 (*0-521-48231-3*); pap. text 47.95 (*0-521-56643-6*) Cambridge U Pr.

Plant Fundamentals Instructor's Guides: A Performance-Based Training Series for the Process Industries, 12 Vols., Set. Multimedia Development Services Staff. (Plant Fundamentals Ser.). (Illus.). (Orig.). 1995. teacher ed. 975.00 (*1-57431-040-2*) Tech Trng Systs.

Plant Galls & Gall Inducers. Jean Meyer. Tr. by Suellen Cheskin. (Handbuch der Pflanzenanatomie Encyclopedia of Plant Anatomy - Traite d' Anatomie Vegetale Ser.). (Illus.). viii, 291p. 1987. 88.00 (*3-443-01023-7*, Pub. by Gebruder Borntraeger) Balogh.

*****Plant Galls of India.** 2nd ed. M. S. Mani. (Illus.). 400p. 2000. text 112.00 (*1-57808-131-9*) Science Pubs.

Plant Gene Transfer & Expression Protocols. Ed. by Heddwyn Jones. LC 95-23429. (Methods in Molecular Biology Ser.: Vol. 49). (Illus.). 482p. 1995. 79.50 (*0-89603-321-X*) Humana.

Plant Genetic Conservation: The In Situ Approach. Ed. by Nigel Maxted et al. LC 96-86665. 472p. 1997. pap. 54.95 (*0-412-63730-8*) Kluwer Academic.

Plant Genetic Conservation: The In Situ Approach. Ed. by Nigel Maxted et al. LC 96-86665. (Illus.). 472p. (C). 1997. write for info. (*0-412-63400-7*) Kluwer Academic.

Plant Genetic Engineering. Ed. by John H. Dodds. 320p. 1985. text 69.95 (*0-521-25966-5*) Cambridge U Pr.

Plant Genetic Engineering. D. Grierson. (Plant Biotechnology Ser.). (Illus.). 267p. (C). 1990. text 115.15 (*0-216-92914-8*, Pub. by B Acad & Prof) Routldge.

Plant Genetic Engineering. Ed. by Donald Grierson. (Plant Biotechonology Ser.). 320p. 1990. mass mkt. 115.15 (*0-412-02521-3*, A4217) Chapman & Hall.

*****Plant Genetic Engineering: Toward the Third Millenium: Proceedings of the International Symposium on Plant Genetic Engineering, 6-10 December, 1999, Havana, Cuba.** International Symposium on Plant Genetic Engineering Staff. Ed. by Ariel D. Arenibia. LC 99-88767. (Developments in Plant Genetics & Breeding Ser.). 2000. write for info. (*0-444-50430-3*) Elsevier.

Plant Genetic Resources of Ethiopia. Ed. by J. M. Engels & J. G. Hawkes. (Illus.). 399p. (C). 1991. text 105.00 (*0-521-38456-7*) Cambridge U Pr.

*****Plant Genetics.** James A. Birchler & Kathleen J. Newton. (Illus.). 2000. pap. 50.00 (*0-86542-244-3*) Blackwell Sci.

Plant Genome Analysis. Peter M. Gresshoff. 256p. 1994. boxed set 83.95 (*0-8493-8264-5*) CRC Pr.

Plant Genome Bibliography: Breeding for Cold Tolerance in Plants. 49p. (Orig.). (C). 1993. pap. text 25.00 (*1-56806-927-8*) DIANE Pub.

Plant Genomes. Beckmann. 1992. pap. text. write for info. (*0-7923-1631-2*) Kluwer Academic.

Plant Genomes Methods for Genetic & Physical Mapping. Ed. by Jacques S. Beckmann & Thomas C. Osborn. (C). 1992. text 189.00 (*0-7923-1630-4*) Kluwer Academic.

Plant Geography of Korea with an Emphasis on the Alpine Zones. Woo-Seok Kong & David Watts. LC 93-16490. (Geobotany Ser.: Vol. 19). 240p. 1993. text 236.00 (*0-7923-2068-9*) Kluwer Academic.

Plant Geography upon a Physiological Basis. A. F. Schimper. Tr. by W. R. Fisher. (Illus.). 1960. reprint ed. 160.00 (*3-7682-0901-6*) Lubrecht & Cramer.

Plant Groups. H. Mukherjee. (C). 1989. 100.00 (*0-89771-410-5*, Pub. by Current Dist) St Mut.

Plant Growth & Development. Abramoff. Date not set. 1.50 (*0-7167-9118-8*) W H Freeman.

Plant Growth & Development. 2nd ed. Fosket. 600p. 1998. write for info. (*0-12-262432-7*) Acad Pr.

Plant Growth & Development: A Molecular Approach. Donald E. Fosket. (Illus.). 580p. 1994. text 53.00 (*0-12-262430-0*) Acad Pr.

Plant Growth & Development: Complete Unit. National Science Resources Center Staff. (Science & Technology for Children Ser.). (Illus.). (Orig.). (J). (gr. 3). 1991. pap. text. write for info. (*0-89278-632-9*) Carolina Biological.

Plant Growth & Development Student Activity Book. National Science Resources Center Staff. (Science & Technology for Children Ser.). (Illus.). 50p. (J). (gr. 3). 1991. pap. text, student ed. write for info. (*0-89278-634-5*) Carolina Biological.

Plant Growth & Development Teacher's Guide. National Science Resources Center Staff. (Science & Technology for Children Ser.). (Illus.). 142p. (J). (gr. 3). 1991. pap. text, teacher ed. write for info. (*0-89278-633-7*) Carolina Biological.

Plant Growth & Leaf-Applied Chemicals. Ed. by Peter M. Neumann. 192p. 1988. lib. bdg. 183.00 (*0-8493-5414-5*, SB128) CRC Pr.

An Asterisk (*) at the beginning of an entry indicates that the title is appearing for the first time.

Plant Growth & Response. Frank Schaffer Publications, Inc. Staff. (Science Notes Ser.). (Illus.). 8p. 1996. 2.49 (0-86734-898-4, FS-62035) Schaffer Pubns.

Plant Growth Modeling for Resources Management, 2 vols. Ed. by Karin Wisiol & John D. Hesketh. 1987. 279.90 (0-8493-6489-2, QK731) CRC Pr.

Plant Growth Modeling for Resources Management, 2 vols., Vol. 1. Ed. by Karin Wisiol & John D. Hesketh. 176p. 1987. write for info. (0-318-62588-1) CRC Pr.

Plant Growth Modeling for Resources Management: Current Models & Methods. Karin Wisiol & J. E. Hesketh. LC 87-849. 184p. 1987. reprint ed. 106.00 (0-8493-6490-6, CRC Reprint) Franklin.

Plant Growth Modeling for Resources Management: Quantifying Plant Processes, 2 vols., Vol. 2. Ed. by Karin Wisiol & John D. Hesketh. 192p. 1987. 111.00 (0-8493-6491-4, CRC Reprint) Franklin.

Plant Growth Regulating Chemicals, 2 Vols., Vol. 1. Ed. by Louis G. Nickell. LC 82-22832. 288p. 1983. 165.00 (0-8493-5002-6, QK745, CRC Reprint) Franklin.

Plant Growth Regulating Chemicals, 2 Vols., Vol. 2. Ed. by Louis G. Nickell. LC 82-22832. 264p. 1983. 152.00 (0-8493-5003-4, QK745, CRC Reprint) Franklin.

Plant Growth Regulators. Ed. by Charles A. Stutte. LC 77-7934. (Advances in Chemistry Ser.: No. 159). 1977. 27.95 (0-8412-0344-X) Am Chemical.

Plant Growth Regulators: Agricultural Uses. Louis G. Nickell. (Illus.). 173p. 1981. 70.00 (0-387-10973-0) Spr-Verlag.

Plant Growth Regulators: Chemical Activity, Plant Responses, & Economic Potential. Ed. by Charles A. Stutte. LC 77-7934. (Advances in Chemistry Ser.: Vol. 159). 102p. 1977. reprint ed. pap. 31.70 (0-608-03863-6, 206431000008) Bks Demand.

***Plant Growth Regulators in Agriculture & Horticulture: Their Role & Commercial Uses.** Ed. by Amarjit S. Basra. LC 00-39357. (Illus.). 272p. (C). 2000. pap. text 39.95 (1-56022-896-2, Food Products); lib. bdg. 94.95 (1-56022-891-1, Food Products) Haworth Pr.

Plant Growth Substances. Ed. by N. Bhushan Mandava. LC 79-18933. (ACS Symposium Ser.: No. 111). 1979. 43.95 (0-8412-0518-3) Am Chemical.

Plant Growth Substances. Ed. by P. F. Wareing. 1983. text 157.00 (0-12-735380-1) Acad Pr.

Plant Growth Substances. Ed. by N. Bhushan Mandava. LC 79-18933. (ACS Symposium Ser.: Vol. 111). 320p. 1979. reprint ed. pap. 99.20 (0-608-03051-1, 206350400007) Bks Demand.

Plant Growth Substances, 1979: Proceedings. Ed. by F. Skoog. (Proceedings in Life Sciences Ser.). (Illus.). 527p. 1980. 94.95 (0-387-10182-9) Spr-Verlag.

Plant-Growth Substances to Potassium Compounds see Encyclopedia of Chemical Technology

Plant Guide: Successful Plants for Every Garden. David Joyce. (Illus.). 160p. 1996. 27.50 (1-85029-670-7, Pub. by Conran Octopus) Trafalgar.

Plant Guidelines for Technical Management of Chemical Process Safety. Compiled by Center for Chemical Process Safety Staff. 393p. 1992. 120.00 (0-8169-0499-5, G-10) Am Inst Chem Eng.

Plant Hairs. J. C. Uphof. (Handbuch der Pflanzenanatomie Encyclopedia of Plant Anatomy - Traite d' Anatomie Vegetale Ser.: Vol. 4, Pt. 5). (Illus.). xii, 292p. 1962. 71.00 (3-443-39005-6, Pub. by Gebruder Borntraeger) Balogh.

Plant Health Care for Woody Ornamentals: A Professional's Guide to Preventing & Managing Environmental Stresses & Pests. John Lloyd et al. (Illus.). 256p. (Orig.). 1997. pap. 45.00 (1-883097-17-7) U Ill Ofc Agricult.

Plant Hormone Ethylene. Autar K. Mattoo & Jeffrey C. Suttle. (Illus.). 352p. 1991. boxed set 249.00 (0-8493-4566-9, QK898) CRC Pr.

Plant Hormone Protocols. Ed. by Jeremy A. Roberts & Gregory A. Tucker. LC 99-58889. (Methods in Molecular Biology Ser.: Vol. 141). (Illus.). 216p. 2000. 69.50 (0-89603-577-8) Humana.

Plant Hormone Receptors. Ed. by D. Klambt. (NATO ASI Series H: Vol. 10). xii, 319p. 1987. 135.95 (0-387-17981-X) Spr-Verlag.

Plant Hormones: Physiology, Biochemistry & Molecular Biology. 836p. (C). 1995. pap. text 102.50 (0-7923-2985-6) Kluwer Academic.

Plant Hormones: Physiology, Biochemistry & Molecular Biology. rev. ed. Ed. by Peter J. Davies. LC 94-45154. Orig. Title: Plant Hormones & Their Role in Plant Growth & Development. 836p. (C). 1995. lib. bdg. 330.00 (0-7923-2984-8) Kluwer Academic.

Plant Hormones & Their Role in Plant Growth & Development see Plant Hormones: Physiology, Biochemistry & Molecular Biology

Plant Hormones & Their Role in Plant Growth & Development. Ed. by Peter J. Davies. (C). 1987. pap. text 105.00 (90-247-3498-3); lib. bdg. 323.50 (90-247-3497-5) Kluwer Academic.

Plant Hormones Signal Perception & Transduction: Proceedings of the International Symposium, Moscow, Russia, September 4-18, 1994. Ed. by M. A. Hall. LC 95-40384. 230p. (C). 1996. text 110.50 (0-7923-3768-9) Kluwer Academic.

Plant Hunters. Tyler Whittle. LC 97-15137. (Horticulture Garden Classics Ser.). (Illus.). 288p. 1997. reprint ed. pap. 16.95 (1-55821-592-1, 15921) Lyons Pr.

***Plant Hunters: Two Hundred Years of Adventure & Discovery Around the World.** Toby Musgrave. 2000. pap. 21.95 (1-84188-001-9) Seven Dials.

Plant Hunters: Two Hundred Years of Adventure & Discovery Around the World. Toby Musgrave et al. LC 99-178847. 224p. 29.95 (0-7063-7753-2, Pub. by WrLock) Sterling.

Plant Hunting in Nepal. Ray Lancaster. (C). 1988. 74.00 (0-685-25851-3) St Mut.

Plant Hunting on the Edge of the World. Frank K. Ward. (Illus.). 1976. reprint ed. 12.50 (0-913728-21-7) Theophrastus.

Plant Identification Characteristics for Deciduous Trees & Shrubs - Lesson Plans. Kathy J. Burkholder. Ed. by Muriel N. King. (Illus.). 112p. (C). 1995. pap. text, teacher ed. 24.95 (1-56502-006-5, 2214G) Ohio Agri Educ.

Plant Identification Terminology: An Illustrated Glossary. James G. Harris & Melinda W. Harris. LC 94-65026. (Illus.). 198p. 1994. pap. text 17.95 (0-9640221-5-X) Spring Lake.

Plant-Induced Soil Changes: Processes & Feedbacks. N. Breemen. LC 98-38828. (Developments in Biogeochemistry Ser.). 1998. 108.00 (0-7923-5216-5) Kluwer Academic.

Plant Infectious Agents: Viruses, Viroids, Virusoids & Satellites. Ed. by Hugh D. Robertson et al. (Current Communications in Molecular Biology Ser.). 230p. 1983. pap. text 28.00 (0-87969-159-X) Cold Spring Harbor.

Plant Integrity Assessment by Acoustic Methods. 2nd ed. Ed. by Stuart Hewerdine. 128p. 1993. pap. 30.00 (0-85295-316-X, 9CH93) Gulf Pub.

Plant Intoxicants: A Classic Text on the Use of Mind-Altering Plants. Ernst Von Bibra. LC 94-19230. (Illus.). 286p. 1995. pap. 16.95 (0-89281-498-5, Heal Arts VT) Inner Tradit.

Plant Invasions: General Aspects & Special Problems. Ed. by P. Pysek et al. (Illus.). xi, 263p. 1995. pap. 59.95 (90-5103-097-5, Pub. by SPB Acad Pub) Balogh.

Plant Invasions: Studies from North America & Europe. Ed. by J. H. Brock et al. (Illus.). 224p. 1997. pap. 53.00 (90-73348-23-4, Pub. by Backhuys Pubs) Balogh.

Plant Invasions - Ecological Mechanisms & Human Responses. Ed. by U. Starfinger et al. (Illus.). 372p. 1998. pap. 97.00 (90-5782-005-6, Pub. by Backhuys Pubs) Balogh.

Plant Kingdom. Ed. by Anne Finney Batiza. 1984. 4.95 (1-55708-197-2, MCR761) McDonald Pub Co.

Plant Kingdom. 5th ed. Harold C. Bold & John La Claire. (Illus.). 320p. (C). 1986. pap. text 39.80 (0-13-680398-9) P-H.

***Plant Kingdom: A Guide to Plant Classification & Biodiversity.** Theresa Greenaway. LC 99-31013. (Classification Ser.). 1999. 25.69 (0-8172-5886-8) Raintree Steck-V.

Plant Kingdom: 5 Kingdoms & Symbiosis. William A. Hutchinson. (Illus.). 189p. 1990. pap. 18.00 (0-9615427-1-3) W A Hutchinson.

Plant Kingdoms: The Photographs of Charles Jones. Sean Sexton. (Illus.). 128p. 1998. text 24.95 (1-55670-924-2) Stewart Tabori & Chang.

Plant Layout: A Guide to the Layout of Process Plant & Sites. J. C. Mecklenburgh. LC 74-181804. 160p. reprint ed. pap. 49.60 (0-608-13147-4, 202523400043) Bks Demand.

Plant Layout & Flow Improvement. Jay Cedarleaf. LC 94-4207. (Illus.). 240p. 1997. reprint ed. pap. 29.00 (0-9658416-1-8) Bluecreek Publ.

Plant Layout & Materials Handling. James M. Apple. LC 90-48718. 496p. (C). 1991. reprint ed. lib. bdg. 59.50 (0-89464-545-5) Krieger.

Plant Leaf Optical Properties in Visible & Near-Infrared Light. Harold W. Gausman. (Graduate Studies: No. 29). (Illus.). 78p. 1985. 25.00 (0-89672-132-9); pap. 10.00 (0-89672-131-0) Tex Tech Univ Pr.

Plant Leaves see Look Once, Look Again

Plant Lectins. Arpad Pusztai. (Chemistry & Pharmacology of Natural Products Ser.). 271p. (C). 1992. text 80.00 (0-521-32824-1) Cambridge U Pr.

Plant License Renewal Topical Meeting, Orlando, FL, June 2-6, 1991. 156p. 1991. 45.00 (0-89448-160-6, 700154) Am Nuclear Soc.

Plant Life see Understanding Science & Nature Series

Plant Life. LC 92-34975. (Understanding Science & Nature Ser.). (J). 1993. lib. bdg. write for info. (0-8094-9713-1) Time-Life.

Plant Life. Barbara Cork. (Mysteries & Marvels Ser.). (Illus.). 32p. (YA). (gr. 3-7). 1984. pap. 5.95 (0-86020-755-2); lib. bdg. 14.95 (0-88110-169-9) EDC.

***Plant Life.** Roland Ennos & Elizabeth Sheffield. LC 00-23721. (Illus.). 232p. 2000. pap. 45.00 (0-86542-737-2) Blackwell Sci.

***Plant Life.** Theresa Greenaway. LC 00-20919. (Cycles In Nature Ser.). (Illus.). (J). 2000. 25.69 (0-7398-2729-4) Raintree Steck-V.

***Plant Life.** Peter D. Riley. LC 98-34725. (Straightforward Science Ser.). 32p. 1999. lib. bdg. 6.95 (0-531-15373-8) Watts.

Plant Life. Peter D. Riley. LC 98-34725. (Straightforward Science Ser.). (J). 1999. 19.00 (0-531-14507-7) Watts.

***Plant Life.** 3rd ed. (C). 2000. 45.00 (0-536-61104-1) Pearson Custom.

Plant Life Histories: Ecological Correlates & Phylogenetic Constraints. Ed. by Jonathan Silvertown et al. LC 96-51104. (Illus.). 334p. (C). 1997. pap. text 30.95 (0-521-57495-1) Cambridge U Pr.

Plant Life in the Devonian. Patricia G. Gensel & Henry N. Andrews. (Illus.). 396p. 1984. 38.95 (0-275-91165-9, C1165, Praeger Pubs) Greenwood.

Plant Life in the World's Mediterranean Climates: California, Chile, South Africa, Australia, & the Mediterranean Basin. Peter R. Dallman. LC 97-52208. 255p. 1998. pap. 29.95 (0-520-20809-9, Pub. by U CA Pr) Cal Prin Full Svc.

Plant Life of Alabama. C. Mohr. (Illus.). 1969. reprint ed. 64.00 (3-7682-0622-X) Lubrecht & Cramer.

Plant Life of Maryland. Forrest Shreve et al. 1969. reprint ed. pap. 64.00 (3-7682-0626-2) Lubrecht & Cramer.

***Plant Life of Quarternary Cold Stages: Evidence from the British Isles.** Richard West. (Illus.). 329p. (C). 2000. text 105.00 (0-521-59397-2) Cambridge U Pr.

Plant Life of Western Australia. John S. Beard. (Illus.). 319p. 1990. 37.50 (0-86417-279-6, Pub. by Kangaroo Pr) Seven Hills Bk.

Plant Life under Oxygen Deprivation: Ecology, Physiology & Biochemistry. Ed. by M. B. Jackson et al. (Illus.). xii, 336p. 1990. 90.00 (90-5103-051-7, Pub. by SPB Acad Pub) Balogh.

Plant Lipid Biochemistry, Structure & Utilization. Ed. by P. J. Quinn & J. Harwood. 483p. (C). 1991. text 80.75 (1-85578-003-8, Pub. by Portland Pr Ltd) Ashgate Pub Co.

Plant Lipid Biosynthesis: Fundamentals & Agricultural Applications. Ed. by John L. Harwood. LC 98-21343. (Society for Experimental Biology Seminar Ser.: No. 67). (Illus.). 400p. (C). 1998. 100.00 (0-521-62074-0) Cambridge U Pr.

Plant Location Decisions of Foreign Manufacturing Investors. Hsin-Min Tong. Ed. by Gunter Dufey. LC 79-22203. (Research for Business Decisions Ser.: No. 17). 162p. 1979. reprint ed. pap. 50.30 (0-8357-1056-4, 207015200064) Bks Demand.

Plant Location in Theory & in Practice: The Economics of Space. Melvin L. Greenhut. LC 81-20230. 338p. 1982. reprint ed. lib. bdg. 75.00 (0-313-23338-1, GRPL, Greenwood Pr) Greenwood.

Plant Location Selection Techniques. Edwin M. McPherson. LC 95-22727. (Illus.). 260p. 1996. 129.00 (0-8155-1378-X) Noyes.

Plant-Lore & Garden-Craft of Shakespeare. 2nd ed. Henry N. Ellacombe. LC 76-166018. 1878. reprint ed. 45.00 (0-404-02277-4) AMS Pr.

Plant Lover's Guide to Wildcrafting: How to Protect Wild Places & Harvest Medicinal Herbs. 3rd ed. Krista Thie. LC 89-92395. (Illus.). 63p. 1995. pap. 6.00 (0-9624868-0-9) Longevity Herb Pr.

Plant Macrofossils in Quaternary Lake Sediments. Hilary H. Birks. (Advances in Limnology Ser.: Vol. 15). (GER., Illus.). 60p. 1980. 20.00 (3-510-47013-3, Pub. by E Schweizerbartsche) Balogh.

Plant Maintenance Engineer. Jack Rudman. (Career Examination Ser.: C-2480). 1994. pap. 34.95 (0-8373-2480-7) Nat Learn.

Plant Maintenance Mechanic. Jack Rudman. (Career Examination Ser.: C-1393). 1994. pap. 27.95 (0-8373-1393-7) Nat Learn.

Plant Maintenance Program. (Manual of Practice, Operations & Maintenance Ser.: No. 3). 112p. (Orig.). (C). 1982. pap. text 24.00 (0-943244-38-2, MOM3) Water Environ.

Plant Maintenance Supervisor. Jack Rudman. (Career Examination Ser.: C-1559). 1994. pap. 27.95 (0-8373-1559-X) Nat Learn.

Plant Manager's Daily Planner, 1988. Donald W. Moffat. 448p. 1988. text 32.50 (0-13-680257-5, Busn) P-H.

Plant Manager's Handbook. Charles H. Becker. 304p. 1974. 42.00 (0-685-03897-1) P-H.

Plant Manager's Handbook. Water Pollution Control Federation Staff. (Manual of Practice, Systems Management Ser.). (Illus.). 168p. 1986. pap. 37.00 (0-943244-66-8, MSM4) Water Environ.

Plant Manager's Practical Guide to Accounting & Finance. Donald W. Moffat & Greg A. Poage. LC 93-8923. (C). 1993. text 59.95 (0-13-676966-7) Prntice Hall Bks.

Plant Membrane Biology. Ed. by Ian M. Miller & Peter Brodelius. (Proceedings of the Phytochemical Society of Europe Ser.: Vol. 38). (Illus.). 310p. (C). 1996. text 135.00 (0-19-857776-1, Clarendon Pr) OUP.

Plant Membranes: A Biophysical Approach. Ya'acov Y. Leshem. 280p. (C). 1992. text 218.00 (0-7923-1353-4) Kluwer Academic.

Plant Membranes: Endo & Plasma Membranes. David G. Robinson. LC 84-7539. (Cell Biology: A Series of Monographs: Vol. 3). 352p. 1985. text 83.95 (0-471-86210-X) Krieger.

Plant Membranes: Structure, Assembly & Function. Ed. by J. L. Harwood & T. J. Watson. (Illus.). 256p. (C). 1988. text 76.50 (0-904498-23-9, Pub. by Portland Pr Ltd) Ashgate Pub Co.

Plant Metabolism. 2nd ed. David Dennis. (C). 1996. pap. text 59.06 (0-582-25906-1, Pub. by Addison-Wesley) Longman.

Plant Metabolism. 2nd ed. H. E. Street & W. Cockburn. LC 76-174629. 332p. 1972. 153.00 (0-08-016752-7, Pub. by Pergamon Repr) Franklin.

Plant-Microbe Interactions & Biological Control. Ed. by Boyland & Kuykendall. (Illus.). 464p. 1998. text 165.00 (0-8247-0043-0) Dekker.

Plant-Microbe Interactions 2, Vol. 2. Ed. by Gary Stacey & Noel T. Keen. (Plant-Microbe Interactions Ser.). 336p. (C). (gr. 13). 1997. 83.95 (0-412-08881-9) Kluwer Academic.

Plant-Microbe Interactions 3, Vol. 3. Gary Stacey & Noel T. Keen. (Illus.). 240p. 1997. write for info. (0-412-11241-8) Kluwer Academic.

Plant Microtechnique & Microscopy. Steven E. Ruzin. LC 98-40910. (Illus.). 336p. (C). 1999. pap. text 45.00 (0-19-508956-1) OUP.

***Plant Microtubules: Potential for Biotechnology.** Peter Nickel. LC 00-24394. 2000. write for info. (3-540-67105-6) Spr-Verlag.

Plant Migration: The Dynamics of Geographic Patterning in Seed Plant Species. Jonathan D. Sauer. (Illus.). 298p. 1991. reprint ed. pap. 17.95 (0-520-06871-8, Pub. by U CA Pr) Cal Prin Full Svc.

Plant Mitochondria: From Gene to Function. Ed. by I. M. Moller et al. (Illus.). 618p. 1998. 174.50 (90-5782-009-9) Backhuys Pubs.

Plant Mitochondria: With Emphasis on RNA Editing & Cytoplasmic Male Sterility. Ed. by A. Brennicke & U. Kuck. (Illus.). 432p. 1993. 150.00 (3-527-30033-3, Wiley-VCH) Wiley.

***Plant Molecular Biochemistry.** P. Jones. (Illus.). 2000. pap. 45.95 (0-387-91574-5) Spr-Verlag.

Plant Molecular Biology. Ed. by Sidney P. Colowick et al. (Methods in Enzymology Ser.: Vol. 118). 856p. 1986. text 188.00 (0-12-182018-1) Acad Pr.

Plant Molecular Biology. Ed. by D. Von Wettstein & N. H. Chua. LC 87-24389. (NATO ASI Series A, Life Sciences: Vol. 140). 710p. 1987. 145.00 (0-306-42696-X, Plenum Trade) Perseus Pubng.

Plant Molecular Biology. 2nd ed. Donald Grierson & S. N. Covey. (Tertiary Level Biology Ser.). 200p. 1988. mass mkt. 39.95 (0-412-01691-5, Chap & Hall NY) Chapman & Hall.

Plant Molecular Biology, Vol. 2. Ed. by R. G. Herrmann & B. A. Larkins. (NATO ASI Ser.: Vol. 212). (Illus.). 784p. (C). 1992. text 222.00 (0-306-44024-5, Kluwer Plenum) Kluwer Academic.

Plant Molecular Biology: A Practical Approach, No. 41. C. H. Shaw. (Practical Approach Ser.). (Illus.). 330p. 1988. pap. text 45.00 (1-85221-056-7) OUP.

Plant Molecular Biology: Essential Techniques. P. Jones & J. M. Sutton. LC 97-16266. (Essential Techniques Ser.). 232p. 1997. pap. 49.95 (0-471-97268-1) Wiley.

Plant Molecular Biology: Molecular Genetic Analysis of Plant Development & Metabolism. Ed. by Gloria Coruzzi & Pedro Puigdomenech. LC 94-9638. (NATO ASI Ser.: Vol. 81). 1994. write for info. (3-540-57733-5) Spr-Verlag.

Plant Molecular Biology: Molecular Genetic Analysis of Plant Development & Metabolism. Ed. by Gloria Coruzzi & Pedro Puigdomenech. LC 94-9638. (NATO ASI Ser.: Vol. 81). 1994. write for info. (0-387-57733-5) Spr-Verlag.

Plant Molecular Biology: Springer Lab Manual. M. Clark. 520p. 1997. pap. text 89.50 (3-540-58405-6) Spr-Verlag.

Plant Molecular Biology Labfax. Ed. by R. R. Croy. (Labfax Ser.). (Illus.). 382p. 1994. text 63.00 (0-12-198370-6) Acad Pr.

Plant Molecular Biology Manual. 2nd ed. Stanton B. Gelvin. 778p. (C). 1994. ring bd. 206.00 (0-7923-2731-4) Kluwer Academic.

Plant Molecular Biology Manual. 2nd ed. Ed. by Stanton B. Gelvin. 112p. (C). 1996. spiral bd. 112.00 (0-7923-4205-4) Kluwer Academic.

Plant Molecular Biology Manual: Supplement I. 2nd ed. Stanton B. Gelvin. (C). ring bd. 64.00 (0-7923-2858-2) Kluwer Academic.

Plant Molecular Systematics: Macromolecular Approaches. Daniel J. Crawford. LC 89-16702. 400p. 1990. 110.00 (0-471-80760-5) Wiley.

Plant Mutation Breeding for Crop Improvement, Vol. 1. IAEA Staff. 1000p. 1991. pap. 210.00 (92-0-010091-0, STI/PUB/842, Pub. by IAEA) Bernan Associates.

Plant Mutation Breeding for Crop Improvement, Vol. 2. IAEA Staff. 1000p. 1991. pap. 190.00 (92-0-010191-7, STI/PUB/842/2, Pub. by IAEA) Bernan Associates.

Plant Needles & Leaves, Vol. 3037. David M. Schwartz. (Look Once, Look Again! Ser.: Vol. 10). (Illus.). 16p. (J). (gr. 1-3). 1998. pap. 2.99 (1-57471-328-0, 3037) Creat Teach Pr.

Plant Nematode Problems & Their Control in the Near East Region. M. A. Maqbool & Brian Kerry. (Plant Production & Protection Papers: No. 09005672). 328p. 1998. 25.00 (92-5-103798-1, F37981, Pub. by FAO) Bernan Associates.

Plant Nematods. A. G. Whitehead. LC 97-22222. (A CAB International Publication). (Illus.). 400p. 1998. text 120.00 (0-85199-188-2) OUP.

Plant Nutrient Disorders, Vol. 5. Weir. 200p. 1998. pap. text 52.95 (0-909605-93-9) Buttrwrth-Heinemann.

Plant Nutrient Disorders Vol. 1: Temp & Sub. 2000. pap. text 46.95 (0-909605-89-0) Buttrwrth-Heinemann.

Plant Nutrient Facts for Hydroponics: How to Make Your Own Fully Formulated Plant Nutrient. Jim McAskill. Ed. by Dennis Germann. (Plant Nutrient Facts for Hydroponics Ser.). (Illus.). 69p. 1998. pap. 24.95 (0-9669557-0-6) Foothill.

Plant Nutrients in Desert Environments. Arden D. Day & Kenneth L. Ludeke. LC 92-32705. (Adaptations of Desert Organisms Ser.). 1993. 118.00 (3-540-55695-8); 104.95 (0-387-55695-8) Spr-Verlag.

Plant Nutrition: Introduction to Current Concepts. Anthony D. Glass. (C). 1989. 46.25 (0-86720-080-4) Jones & Bartlett.

Plant Nutrition: Molecular Biology & Genetics G. Gissel-Nielsen & Arne Jensen. LC 99-24926. 1999. write for info. (0-7923-5716-7) Kluwer Academic.

Plant Nutrition - Physiology & Applications. M. L. Van Beusichem. (Developments in Plant & Soil Sciences Ser.). (C). 1990. text 594.00 (0-7923-0740-2) Kluwer Academic.

Plant Nutrition Basics. Ed. by J. Benton Jones. (Plant Nutrition Ser.). (C). 1994. lib. bdg. 99.50 incl. VHS (1-884015-27-1) St Lucie Pr.

Plant Nutrition for Sustainable Food Production & Environment. Ed. by Tadao Ando et al. LC 98-122134. 982p. 1998. text 468.00 (0-7923-4796-X) Kluwer Academic.

Plant Nutrition, From Genetic Engineering to Field Practice: Proceedings of the Twelfth International Plant Nutrition Colloquium, 21-26 September 1993, Perth, Western Australia. N. J. Barrow. LC 93-32992. (Developments in Plant & Soil Sciences Ser.). 830p. (C). 1994. text 509.50 (0-7923-2540-0) Kluwer Academic.

Plant Nutrition Manual. J. B. Jones. LC 97-46560. (Illus.). 200p. 1997. lib. bdg. 49.95 (1-884015-31-X) St Lucie Pr.

Plant of Renown. Leonard Sheldrake. 158p. 1996. reprint ed. pap. 7.95 (1-882701-16-X) Uplook Min.

P

An Asterisk (*) at the beginning of an entry indicates that the title is appearing for the first time.

Plant Oils As Fuels: Present State of Science & Future Developments: Proceedings of the Symposium Held in Potsdam, Germany, February 16-18, 1997. N. Martini & Josef S. Schell. LC 98-27941. 1998. pap. write for info. (*3-540-64754-6*) Spr-Verlag.

Plant Operations & Optimization. Ed. by Gail Nalven. LC 96-24176. (Practical Engineering Perspectives Ser.). 372p. 1996. 85.00 (*0-8169-0710-2*, Q-2) Am Inst Chem Eng.

Plant Operations Handbook: A Tactical Guide to Everyday Management. Gerhard J. Plenert. 528p. 1992. 75.00 (*1-55623-707-3*, Irwn Prfssnl) McGraw-Hill Prof.

Plant Operators. Ed. by D. N. Halbe et al. LC 91-66740. 263p. 1991. reprint ed. pap. 81.60 (*0-608-02420-1*, 206306300004) Bks Demand.

Plant Operators' Forum, Vol. I. D. N. Halbe. LC 98-48544. (Illus.). 256p. 1999. pap. 54.00 (*0-87335-156-8*, 156-8) SMM&E Inc.

Plant Organelles: Compartmentation of Metabolism in Photosynthetic Tissue. Ed. by Alyson K. Tobin. (Society for Experimental Biology Seminar Ser.: No. 50). (Illus.). 350p. (C). 1992. text 100.00 (*0-521-40171-2*) Cambridge U Pr.

Plant-Parasitic Nematodes: A Pictorial Key to Genera. 5th ed. Howard H. Lyon et al. (Comstock Bk.). (Illus.). 288p. 1996. text 49.95 (*0-8014-3116-6*) Cornell U Pr.

Plant Parasitic Nematodes - A Check List, 1981-1985. R. L. Rajak et al. (International Bioscience Monographs: Vol. XVIII). (Illus.). 135p. 1987. 17.00 (*1-55528-143-5*) Scholarly Pubns.

Plant Parasitic Nematodes in Subtropical & Tropical Agriculture. Ed. by M. Luc et al. (Illus.). 648p. 1990. text 160.00 (*0-85198-630-7*) OUP.

Plant Parasitic Nematodes in Temperate Agriculture. Ed. by K. Evans et al. (Illus.). 666p. 1993. text 170.00 (*0-85198-808-3*) OUP.

Plant Parasitic Nematodes of India. K. Sitaramaiah. (International Bioscience Monographs: No. XV). xxii, 292p. 1984. 25.00 (*1-55528-042-0*) Scholarly Pubns.

Plant Partners. Reader's Digest Editors. LC 94-13509. (Successful Gardening Ser.). (Illus.). 176p. 1994. 18.98 (*0-89577-614-6*) RD Assn.

Plant Partners. Reader's Digest Editors. (Successful Gardening Ser.). (Illus.). 176p. 1998. pap. text 19.95 (*0-89577-961-7*, Pub. by RD Assn) Penguin Putnam.

Plant Pathogen Detection & Disease Diagnosis. P. Narayanasamy. LC 97-23414. (Books in Soils, Plants & the Environment: Vol. 59). (Illus.). 344p. 1997. text 145.00 (*0-8247-0040-6*) Dekker.

Plant Pathogenesis & Disease Resistance. Hachiro Oku. 208p. 1993. lib. bdg. 99.95 (*0-87371-727-9*, L727) Lewis Pubs.

Plant Pathogenic Bacteria. Ed. by E. L. Civerolo, Jr. et al. (Current Plant Science & Biotechnology in Agriculture Ser.). 1987. text 445.50 (*90-247-3476-2*) Kluwer Academic.

Plant Pathogenic Bacteria: Proceedings of the 7th International Conference on Plant Pathogenic Bacteria, Budapest, Hungary, June 11-16, 1989, 2 vols., Set. Z. Klement. 1061p. (C). 1990. 300.00 (*963-05-5871-8*, Pub. by Akade Kiado) St Mut.

Plant Pathogenic Fungi. J. A. Von Arx. (Nova Hedwigia, Beihefte/Supplementary Issues Ser.: Beih 87). (Illus.). 288p. 1987. pap. text 83.00 (*3-443-51009-4*, Pub. by Gebruder Borntraeger) Balogh.

Plant Pathogens: The Nematodes. R. S. Singh & K. Sitaramaiah. 320p. 1992. text 35.00 (*1-881570-34-7*) Science Pubs.

Plant Pathogens - The Prokaryotes. R. S. Singh. (C). 1989. 22.00 (*81-204-0440-8*) S Asia.

Plant Pathogens & the Worldwide Movement of Seeds. Ed. by Denis C. McGee. LC 97-75237. (Illus.). 109p. 1997. pap. 39.00 (*0-89054-185-X*) Am Phytopathol Soc.

Plant Pathogens & Their Control in Horticulture. G. R. Dixon. (Science in Horticulture Ser.). (Illus.). 265p. (Orig.). (C). 1984. pap. text 30.00 (*0-333-35912-7*) Scholium Intl.

Plant Pathologists Pocket Book. 2nd ed. Ed. by A. Johnston & C. Booth. (Illus.). 439p. 1983. text 40.00 (*0-85198-460-6*); pap. text 26.00 (*0-85198-517-3*) OUP.

***Plant Pathologists' Pocketbook.** 3rd ed. Ed. by J. M. Waller & J. M. Lenn'e. (Illus.). 450p. 2000. text 85.00 (*0-85199-458-X*); pap. text 40.00 (*0-85199-459-8*) OUP.

Plant Pathology. 4th ed. George N. Agrios. LC 96-29221. (Illus.). xvi, 635p. 1997. text 59.95 (*0-12-044564-6*) Morgan Kaufmann.

Plant Pathology: Principles & Practice. D. Gareth Jones. (Illus.). 208p. (C). 1987. text 31.00 (*0-13-680760-7*) P-H.

***Plant Pathology & Plant Pathogens.** 3rd ed. John A. Lucas & C. H. Dickinson. LC 97-48463. (Illus.). 274p. 1998. pap. 49.95 (*0-632-03046-1*) Blackwell Sci.

Plant Pheno. Morphological Studies in Mediterranean Type Ecosystems. Ed. by G. Orshan. (Geobotany Ser.). (C). 1988. text 354.00 (*90-6193-656-X*) Kluwer Academic.

Plant Physiognomies. Elisee Reclus. 1973. 69.95 (*0-8490-0840-9*) Gordon Pr.

Plant Physiology. Hans Mohr. Orig. Title: Lehrbuch der Pflanzenphysiologie. 1995. 64.95 (*3-540-58016-6*) Spr-Verlag.

Plant Physiology. Hans Mohr & Peter Schopfer. Tr. by Gudron Lawlor & David W. Lawlor from GER. LC 94-21765. Orig. Title: Lehrbuch der Pflanzenphysiologie. (Illus.). 640p. 1995. 59.95 (*0-387-58016-6*) Spr-Verlag.

Plant Physiology. Newman. 144p. (C). 1997. write for info. (*0-02-386720-5*, Macmillan Coll) P-H.

Plant Physiology. J. Sebanek. (Developments in Crop Science Ser.: Vol. 21). 454p. 1992. 243.25 (*0-444-98699-5*) Elsevier.

Plant Physiology. Lincoln Taiz & Eduardo Zeiger. (C). 1991. text 63.95 (*0-8053-0245-X*) Benjamin-Cummings.

Plant Physiology. Irwin P. Ting. LC 80-16448. (Illus.). 635p. (C). 1982. text. write for info. (*0-201-07406-0*) Addison-Wesley.

Plant Physiology. 2nd ed. Salisbury. (Biology Ser.). 1978. pap. 30.25 (*0-534-00562-4*) Wadsworth Pub.

Plant Physiology. 2nd ed. Lincoln Taiz & Eduardo Zeiger. LC 98-34409. (Illus.). (C). 1998. text 86.95 (*0-87893-831-1*) Sinauer Assocs.

Plant Physiology. 3rd ed. Frank B. Salisbury & Cleon W. Ross. 540p. (C). 1985. mass mkt. 44.00 (*0-534-04482-4*) Wadsworth Pub.

Plant Physiology. 4th ed. Frank B. Salisbury & Cleon W. Ross. 682p. (C). 1991. 69.75 (*0-534-15162-0*) Wadsworth Pub.

Plant Physiology: Biology: Form & Function. Irene Ridge. (Illus.). 372p. 1991. pap. 52.50 (*0-340-53186-X*, Pub. by Hodder & Stought Ltd) Lubrecht & Cramer.

Plant Physiology Ecology. H. Lambers et al. LC 97-33273. (Illus.). 456p. 1998. text 44.95 (*0-387-98326-0*) Spr-Verlag.

Plant Pigments. T. W. Goodwin. 325p. 1988. text 104.00 (*0-12-289847-8*) Acad Pr.

Plant Plasma Membrane. Ed. by C. Larsson & I. M. Moller. (Illus.). 432p. 1990. 227.95 (*0-387-50836-8*) Spr-Verlag.

Plant Poisoning in Animals No. 2, No. 2. Compiled by M. R. Hails. 96p. (C). 1986. pap. 39.95 (*0-85198-578-5*) OUP.

Plant Poisoning in Animals, 1983-1992, No. 3. M. R. Hails & T. D. Crane. 297p. 1994. pap. 92.00 (*0-85198-916-0*) OUP.

Plant Poisonings & Mycotoxicoses of Livestock in Southern Africa. T. S. Kellerman et al. (Illus.). 256p. 1989. 135.00 (*0-19-570488-6*) OUP.

Plant Polymeric Carbohydrates. Ed. by F. Meuser et al. 295p. 1993. 105.00 (*0-85186-645-X*) CRC Pr.

Plant Polyphenols: Synthesis, Properties & Significance. R. W. Hemingway & P. E. Laks. LC 92-22273. (Basic Life Sciences Ser.: Vol. 59). (Illus.). 1066p. (C). 1992. text 215.00 (*0-306-44252-3*, Kluwer Plenum) Kluwer Academic.

***Plant Polyphenols 2.** George G. Gross et al. LC 99-46706. (Basic Life Sciences Ser.). 1999. write for info. (*0-306-46218-4*, Kluwer Plenum) Kluwer Academic.

Plant Portraits from the Flora Danica, 1761-1769. William T. Stearn. (Illus.). 1988. 130.00 (*0-900751-20-7*, Pub. by Trade & Travel) St Mut.

***Plant Power: The Humorous Herbalist's Guide to Finding, Growing, Gathering & Using 30 Great Medicinal Herbs.** Laurel Dewey. 422p. 1999. 19.95 (*1-884820-37-9*) SAFE GOODS.

Plant Printing. Ida Geary. (Illus.). 1978. pap. 3.50 (*0-912908-03-3*) Tamal Land.

Plant-Process Model for Forecasting Iowa Corn Yields, Vol. 89-M2. David R. Krog. (Illus.). xviii, 204p. (Orig.). 1989. pap. text 15.00 (*0-936911-01-8*) Ctr Agri & Rural Dev.

Plant Processing of Natural Gas. Curtis F. Kruse & Hank Haas. (Illus.). 114p. (Orig.). (C). 1974. pap. text 15.00 (*0-88698-115-8*, 3.11010) PETEX.

Plant Production: Multilingual Illustrated Dictionary in 6 Languages: English, German, French, Spanish, Italian & Dutch. H. Steinmetz. (Illus.). 682p. 1992. pap. 33.00 (*3-8236-1126-7*, Pub. by Backhuys Pubs) Balogh.

Plant Production in Closed Ecosystems: The International Symposium on Plant Production in Closed Ecosystems Held in Narita, Japan, August 26-29, 1996. Ed. by E. Goto et al. LC 96-51037. 360p. (C). 1997. text 147.00 (*0-7923-4417-0*) Kluwer Academic.

Plant Production in Containers. rev. ed. Carl E. Whitcomb. (Illus.). 640p. 1988. 35.00 (*0-9613109-1-X*) Lacebark.

Plant Production on the Threshold of a New Century: Proceedings of the International Conference at the Occasion of the 75th Anniversary of the Wageningen Agricultural University, Wageningen, The Netherlands, June 28-July 1, 1993. Ed. by P. C. Struik. (Developments in Plant & Soil Sciences Ser.). 516p. (C). 1994. text 255.50 (*0-7923-2903-1*) Kluwer Academic.

Plant Products & the New Technology. Ed. by John R. Gallon & Keith Fuller. (Annual Proceedings of the Phytochemical Society of Europe: Vol. 26). (Illus.). 330p. 1986. text 69.00 (*0-19-854180-5*) OUP.

***Plant Projects for Young Scientists** Salvatore Tocci. LC 99-15454. 2000. 25.00 (*0-531-11704-9*) Watts.

Plant Promoters & Transcription Factors. Lutz Nover. LC 93-29266. (Results & Problems in Cell Differentiation Ser.: Vol. 20). 1994. 198.00 (*0-387-57288-0*) Spr-Verlag.

Plant Propagation. M. K. Sadhu. (C). 1989. pap. 18.50 (*0-85226-739-8*) S Asia.

Plant Propagation: Insight, Fundamentals & Techniques. Ed. by Oliver N. Menhinick. 72p. 1990. pap. 25.00 (*0-948251-74-3*, Pub. by Picton) St Mut.

Plant Propagation: Seeds, Cuttings, Division, Layering, Grafting. Peter Klock. Tr. by Elaine Richards & First Edition Translations Ltd. Staff. LC 97-176796. (Illus.). 104p. 1997. pap. text 12.95 (*0-7063-7584-X*) Ward Lock Ltd UK.

Plant Propagation: The Fully Illustrated Plant-by-Plant Manual of Practical Techniques. Ed. by Alan R. Toogood. LC 98-38933. (Illus.). 18p. 1999. 34.95 (*0-7894-4116-0*) DK Pub Inc.

Plant Propagation Practices. James E. Wells. 362p. 1985. pap. 14.95 (*1-887632-55-7*) Amer Nurseryman Pub.

Plant Propogation. 6th ed. Hudson T. Hartmann et al. LC 96-28045. 770p. (C). 1996. 105.00 (*0-13-206103-1*) P-H.

Plant Protection: An Integrated Interdisciplinary Approach. Webster H. Sill. LC 81-12323. (Illus.). 311p. 1982. reprint ed. pap. 96.50 (*0-608-00124-4*, 206088900006) Bks Demand.

Plant Protection & Quarantine: Principles, Concepts, & Problems, Vol. I-III. Robert P. Kahn. 224p. 1989. 130.00 (*0-8493-6652-6*, SB980, CRC Reprint) Franklin.

Plant Protection & Quarantine: Principles, Concepts, & Problems, Vols. I-III. Robert P. Kahn. 256p. 1988. 136.00 (*0-8493-6650-X*, SB980, CRC Reprint) Franklin.

Plant Protection & Quarantine: Principles, Concepts, & Problems, Vols. I-III. Robert P. Kahn. 280p. 1989. 157.00 (*0-8493-6651-8*, SB980, CRC Reprint) Franklin.

Plant Protein Engineering. Ed. by Peter R. Shewry & S. Gutteridge. (Plant & Microbial Biotechnology Research Ser.). 362p. (C). 1992. text 105.00 (*0-521-41761-9*) Cambridge U Pr.

Plant Proteins: Applications, Biological Effects, & Chemistry. Ed. by Robert L. Ory. LC 86-10848. (ACS Symposium Ser.: No. 312). (Illus.). 296p. 1986. text 75.00 (*0-8412-0976-6*, Pub. by Am Chemical) OUP.

Plant Proteins from European Crops: Food & Non-Food Applications. Ed. by J. Gueguen & Yves Popineau. LC 98-12110. (Illus.). 340p. 1998. 99.00 (*3-540-63291-3*) Spr-Verlag.

Plant Proteolytic Enzymes, 2 vols. Ed. by Michael J. Dalling. 1986. 239.90 (*0-8493-5684-9*, QK898) CRC Pr.

Plant Proteolytic Enzymes, Vol. 1. M. Dalling. LC 85-24319. 1986. 100.00 (*0-8493-5682-2*, CRC Reprint) Franklin.

Plant Proteolytic Enzymes, Vol. 2. M. Dalling. LC 85-24319. 176p. 1986. 103.00 (*0-8493-5683-0*, CRC Reprint) Franklin.

Plant Protoplast & Genetic Engineering, Vol. 34, Pt. VI. Contrib. by Y. P. S. Bajaj. 1995. 303.95 (*3-540-58931-7*) Spr-Verlag.

Plant Protoplasts. Ed. by Larry C. Fowke & Fred Constabel. LC 84-23179. 256p. 1985. 146.00 (*0-8493-6473-6*, QK725, CRC Reprint) Franklin.

Plant Protoplasts & Genetic Engineering. Ed. by Y. P. S. Bajaj. (Biotechnology in Agriculture & Forestry Ser.: Vol. 8, No. 1). (Illus.). 465p. 1989. 318.95 (*0-387-19194-1*) Spr-Verlag.

Plant Protoplasts & Genetic Engineering, Vol. VII. Ed. by Y. P. S. Bajaj. (Biotechnology in Agriculture & Forestry Ser.). (Illus.). xxiii, 350p. 1996. 259.00 (*3-540-60876-1*) Spr-Verlag.

Plant Protoplasts & Genetic Engineering II. Ed. by Y. P. S. Bajaj. (Biotechnology in Agriculture & Forestry Ser.: Vol. 9). (Illus.). 510p. 1989. 165.95 (*0-387-50789-2*) Spr-Verlag.

Plant Protoplasts & Genetic Engineering III. Ed. by Y. P. S. Bajaj. (Biotechnology in Agriculture & Forestry Ser.: Vol. 22). (Illus.). 320p. 1993. 242.95 (*0-387-56313-X*) Spr-Verlag.

Plant Protoplasts & Genetic Engineering IV. Ed. by Y. P. S. Bajaj. (Biotechnology in Agriculture & Forestry Ser.: Vol. 23). (Illus.). 387p. 1994. 317.95 (*0-387-56384-9*) Spr-Verlag.

Plant Protoplasts & Genetic Engineering V, 29. Ed. by Y. P. S. Bajaj. (Biotechnology in Agriculture & Forestry Ser.: Vol. 29). 426p. 1994. 334.95 (*0-387-57447-6*) Spr-Verlag.

Plant Quarantine: A Primer to Development Workers. Rhonda M. Black & A. Sweetmore. 1995. pap. 45.00 (*0-85954-397-8*, Pub. by Nat Res Inst) St Mut.

Plant Relationships, Pt. A. Ed. by G. C. Carroll & P. Tudzynski. (Mycota: Vol. 5). (Illus.). 250p. 1997. 169.00 (*3-540-58006-9*) Spr-Verlag.

Plant Relationships, Pt. B. Ed. by G. C. Carroll & P. Tudzynski. (Mycota: Vol. 5). (Illus.). 300p. 1997. 179.00 (*3-540-62018-4*) Spr-Verlag.

Plant Reproduction: From Floral Induction to Pollination. E. Lord & G. Bernicer. (C). 1991. text 165.00 (*81-7233-006-5*, Pub. by Scientific Pubs) St Mut.

Plant Reproduction: From Floral Induction to Pollination. Ed. by Elizabeth M. Lord & Georges Bernier. LC 89-80454. 250p. 1989. pap. text 25.00 (*0-943088-14-3*) Am Soc of Plan.

Plant Reproductive Ecology. Mary F. Willson. LC 82-24826. 291p. reprint ed. pap. 90.30 (*0-7837-2801-8*, 205767200006) Bks Demand.

Plant Reproductive Ecology: Patterns & Strategies. Ed. by Jon Lovett-Doust & Lesley Lovett-Doust. (Illus.). 360p. (C). 1990. pap. text 33.95 (*0-19-506394-5*) OUP.

Plant Resistance to Herbivores & Pathogens: Ecology, Evolution, & Genetics. Ed. by Robert S. Fritz & Ellen L. Simms. LC 91-5060. (Illus.). 600p. 1992. pap. text 34.50 (*0-226-26554-4*); lib. bdg. 86.50 (*0-226-26553-6*) U Ch Pr.

Plant Resistance to Insects. Ed. by Paul A. Hedin. LC 82-22622. (ACS Symposium Ser.: No. 208). 375p. 1983. lib. bdg. 54.95 (*0-8412-0756-9*) Am Chemical.

Plant Resistance to Insects. Ed. by Paul A. Hedin. LC 82-22622. (ACS Symposium Ser.: No. 208). (Illus.). 384p. 1983. reprint ed. pap. 119.10 (*0-608-03222-0*, 206374100007) Bks Demand.

Plant Resistance to Insects: A Fundamental Approach. C. Michael Smith. LC 89-30629. 294p. 1989. 110.00 (*0-471-84938-3*) Wiley.

***Plant Resistance to Parasitic Nematodes.** Ed. by J. L. Starr et al. (Illus.). 256p. 2001. text. write for info. (*0-85199-466-0*) OUP.

Plant Resistance to Viruses: Symposium No. 133. CIBA Foundation Staff. (CIBA Foundation Symposium Ser.). 226p. 1987. 152.00 (*0-471-91263-8*) Wiley.

Plant Resource Allocation. Ed. by Fakhri A. Bazzaz & John Grace. LC 97-12027. (Physiological Ecology Ser.). (Illus.). 303p. 1997. text 84.95 (*0-12-083490-1*) Morgan Kaufmann.

Plant Resources of South-East Asia: Vegetables. J. S. Siemonsma & K. Piluek. (World Biodiversity Database Ser.). 1997. 109.00 incl. cd-rom (*3-540-14626-1*) Spr-Verlag.

Plant Resources of South-East Asia Vol. 5, No. 3: Timber Trees: Lesser-known Timbers. Ed. by M. S. Sosef et al. (Illus.). 859p. 1998. 236.00 (*90-73348-88-9*, Pub. by Backhuys Pubs) Balogh.

Plant Response, 2 vols. J. C. Bose. 1991. 400.00 (*81-7158-248-6*, Pub. by Scientific Pubs) St Mut.

Plant Response to Air Pollution. Ed. by Muhammad Iqbal & Mohammad Yunus. LC 95-42780. 558p. 1996. 190.00 (*0-471-96061-6*) Wiley.

Plant Response to Stress. Ed. by J. D. Tenhunen et al. (NATO ASI Series G: Vol. 15). 680p. 1987. 313.95 (*0-387-16082-5*) Spr-Verlag.

Plant Responses to Elevated CO2: Evidence from Natural Springs. Ed. by A. Raschi et al. LC 97-8030. (Illus.). 280p. (C). 1997. text 69.95 (*0-521-58203-2*) Cambridge U Pr.

Plant Responses to Environmental Stresses: From Phytohormones to Genome Reorganization. H. R. Lerner. LC 99-30941. (Books in Soils, Plants & the Environment). (Illus.). 752p. 1999. text 195.00 (*0-8247-0044-9*) Dekker.

Plant Responses to the Environment. Peter M. Gresshoff. 208p. 1993. boxed set 99.95 (*0-8493-8263-7*, QK901) CRC Pr.

Plant Root & Its Environment: Proceedings. Virginia Polytechnic Institute on the Plant Root &. Ed. by E. W. Carson. LC 72-92877. 705p. reprint ed. pap. 200.00 (*0-8357-3279-7*, 203950200013) Bks Demand.

Plant Roots: From Cells to Systems. Ed. by H. M. Anderson et al. LC 97-29302. (Developments in Plant & Soil Sciences Ser.: No. 73). 160p. 1997. text 120.50 (*0-7923-4369-7*) Kluwer Academic.

Plant Roots: The Hidden Half. 2nd expanded rev. ed. Ed. by Yoav Waisel et al. LC 95-51805. (Books in Soils, Plants & the Environment: Vol. 47). (Illus.). 1024p. 1996. text 215.00 (*0-8247-9685-3*) Dekker.

Plant Safety. Gail Nalven. LC 96-24177. (Practical Engineering Perspectives Ser.;). 272p. 1996. 85.00 (*0-8169-0709-9*, Q-1) Am Inst Chem Eng.

Plant Science. Boy Scouts of America. (Illus.). 48p. (YA). (gr. 6-12). 1983. pap. 2.90 (*0-8395-3396-9*, 33396) BSA.

Plant Science. Anita Ganeri. LC 92-36738. (Science Questions & Answers Ser.). (Illus.). 48p. (J). (gr. 5 up). 1993. lib. bdg. 13.95 (*0-87518-580-0*, Dillon Silver Burdett) Silver Burdett Pr.

Plant Science. R. Gordon Halfacre & John A. Barden. 592p. (C). 1987. 86.88 (*0-07-003669-1*) McGraw.

***Plant Science.** 2nd ed. 440p. (C). 1998. text, student ed. 45.00 (*0-536-00752-7*) Pearson Custom.

Plant Science: Growth, Development & Utilization of Cultivated Plants. 2nd ed. William J. Flocker et al. (Illus.). 752p. (C). 1988. 100.00 (*0-13-680307-5*) P-H.

Plant Science: Growth, Development & Utilization of Cultivated Plants. 3rd ed. Hartmann. 752p. 1999. 66.75 incl. cd-rom (*0-13-955477-7*) P-H.

***Plant Science: Learning about Plant Life.** Edward Shevick. Ed. by Judy Mitchell. (Illus.). 64p. (J). 2000. pap. 8.95 (*1-57310-208-3*) Teachng & Lrning Co.

Plant Science Research in India: Present Status & Future Challenges, Pt. 1. Ed. by M. L. Trivedi et al. (Aspects of Plant Sciences Ser.: Vol. XI). xxxviii, 526p. 1989. 69.00 (*1-55528-186-9*) Scholarly Pubns.

Plant Science Research in India: Present Status & Future Challenges, Pt. 2. Ed. by M. L. Trivedi et al. (Aspects of Plant Sciences Ser.: Vol. XII). vi, 500p. 1989. 69.00 (*1-55528-188-5*) Scholarly Pubns.

***Plant Sciences for Students** 2001. 78.00 (*0-02-865430-7*); 310.00 (*0-02-865434-X*) Macmillan.

***Plant Sciences for Students, vol. 4.** 2001. 78.00 (*0-02-865433-1*) Macmillan.

***Plant Sciences for Students , vol.2.** 2001. 78.00 (*0-02-865431-5*) Macmillan.

***Plant Sciences for Students , vol.3.** 2001. 78.00 (*0-02-865432-3*) Macmillan.

***Plant Secondary Metabolism.** David S. Seigler. 704p. 1999. 460.00 (*0-412-01981-7*) Kluwer Academic.

***Plant Selector.** Susan Berry & Steve Bradley. 160p. 2000. pap. 14.95 (*1-84215-080-4*) Anness Pub.

Plant Selector: Over 1500 Garden Plants to Help You Pick Winning Combinations. Brian Davis. LC 98-120900. (Illus.). 240p. 1998. 27.95 (*0-7063-7567-X*, Pub. by WrLock) Sterling.

Plant Senescence: Its Biochemistry & Physiology. Ed. by W. W. Thomson et al. LC 87-70735. 269p. (Orig.). 1987. pap. 20.00 (*0-943088-10-0*) Am Soc of Plan.

Plant Services & Operations Handbook. Anthony L. Kohan. LC 94-48612. 544p. 1995. 62.50 (*0-07-035940-7*) McGraw.

Plant Sitter. Gene Zion. LC 59-5325. (Trophy Picture Bk.). (Illus.). 32p. (J). (ps-3). 1976. pap. 1.95 (*0-06-443012-X*, HarpTrophy) HarpC Child Bks.

Plant Sociology: The Study of Plant Communities. J. Braun-Blanquet. Ed. & Tr. by George D. Fuller & Henry S. Conrad. (Illus.). xviii, 439p. 1983. reprint ed. 75.00 (*3-87429-208-8*, 002243, Pub. by Koeltz Sci Bks) Lubrecht & Cramer.

Plant Sociology of Alpine Tundra, Trail Ridge, Rocky Mountain National Park, Colorado. Beatrice L. Willard. Ed. by Jon W. Raese. LC 79-26590. (Colorado School of Mines Quarterly Ser.: Vol. 74, No. 4). (Illus.). 119p. 1980. pap. 6.00 (*0-686-63162-5*) Colo Sch Mines.

Plant-Soil Interactions at Low pH, Principles & Management: Proceedings of the 3rd International Symposium on Plant-Soil Interactions at Low pH Held 1993, Brisbane, Queensland, Australia. Ed. by R. A. Date et al. LC 95-34329. (Developments in Plant & Soil Sciences Ser.: Vol. 64). 822p. 1995. text 481.00 (*0-7923-3198-2*) Kluwer Academic.

An Asterisk (*) at the beginning of an entry indicates that the title is appearing for the first time.

Plant Specialists Index: Index to Specialists of Plants & Fungi Based on Data from index Herbariorum. Ed. by Patricia Holmgren & Noel H. Holmgren. (Regnum Vegetabile Ser.: Vol. 124). 394p. 1992. 120.00 (*3-87429-331-9*, Pub. by Koeltz Sci Bks) Lubrecht & Cramer.

Plant Species Reportedly Possessing Pest-Control Properties: An EWC-UH Database. Michael Grainge et al. (East-West Resource Systems Institute RM Ser.: No. 84-1). vi, 249p. 1985. 25.00 (*0-86638-064-7*) EW Ctr HI.

Plant Sperm Cells As Tools for Bio-Technology. H. J. Wilms. (C). 1991. text 350.00 (*0-89771-679-5*, Pub. by Intl Bk Distr) St Mut.

Plant Sperm Cells As Tools for Biotechnology. H. J. Wilms. 187p. 1995. pap. 163.00 (*81-7089-202-3*, Pub. by Intl Bk Distr) St Mut.

Plant Spirit Medicine: Healing with the Power of Plants. Eliot Cowan. 154p. 1991. pap. 13.95 (*1-893183-11-4*, Pub. by Granite Pub) ACCESS Pubs Network.

Plant Spirit Medicine: The Healing Power of Plants. Eliot Cowan. 175p. 1995. pap. 13.95 (*0-926524-09-7*) Granite WI.

Plant Stems: Physiology & Functional Morphology. Ed. by Barbara L. Gartner. (Physiological Ecology Ser.). (Illus.). 440p. 1995. text 95.00 (*0-12-276460-9*) Acad Pr.

Plant Stems & Roots see Look Once, Look Again

Plant Stems & Roots, Vol. 3036. David M. Schwartz. (Look Once, Look Again! Ser.: Vol. 9). (Illus.). 16p. (J). (gr. 1-3). 1998. pap. 2.99 (*1-57471-327-2*, 3036) Creat Teach Pr.

Plant Strategies & the Dynamics & Structure of Plant Communities. David Tilman. Ed. by Robert M. May. (Monographs in Population Biology: No. 26). (Illus.). 376p. 1988. pap. text 29.95 (*0-691-08489-0*, Pub. by Princeton U Pr) Cal Prin Full Svc.

Plant Strategies & Vegetation Processes. John Philip Grime. LC 78-18523. (Illus.). 258p. reprint ed. pap. 80.00 (*0-8357-3736-5*, 203646200003) Bks Demand.

Plant Stress: Insect Interactions. Ed. by E. A. Heinrichs. LC 88-255. (Environmental Science & Technology Ser.). (Illus.). 492p. 1988. 150.00 (*0-471-82648-0*) Wiley.

Plant Stress from Air Pollution. Michael Treshow & Franklin K. Anderson. LC 89-9070. 296p. 1989. text 190.00 (*0-471-92374-5*) Wiley.

Plant Structure: Function & Development - A Treatise on Anatomy & Vegetative Development, With Special Reference to Woody Plants. J. A. Romberger. LC 93-20242. 1993. 219.00 (*0-387-56305-9*) Spr-Verlag.

Plant Structure & Function. 6th ed. Starr. (Biology Ser.). 1993. pap. 8.25 (*0-534-30477-X*) Wadsworth Pub.

Plant Structure & Function. 7th ed. Starr. (Biology Ser.). 1995. pap. 11.00 (*0-534-21067-8*) Wadsworth Pub.

Plant Structure & Function. 8th ed. Starr. (Biology Ser.). 1997. 17.95 (*0-534-53009-5*) Wadsworth Pub.

Plant Superintendent. Jack Rudman. (Career Examination Ser.: C-1935). 1994. reprint ed. pap. 34.95 (*0-8373-1935-8*) Nat Learn.

Plant Superintendent A. Jack Rudman. (Career Examination Ser.: C-2046). 1994. pap. 34.95 (*0-8373-2046-1*) Nat Learn.

Plant Superintendent B. Jack Rudman. (Career Examination Ser.: C-2047). 1994. pap. 34.95 (*0-8373-2047-X*) Nat Learn.

Plant Superintendent C. Jack Rudman. (Career Examination Ser.: C-2048). 1994. pap. 34.95 (*0-8373-2048-8*) Nat Learn.

Plant Survival: Adapting to a Hostile World. Brian Capon. LC 93-43342. (Illus.). 144p. (J). 1994. 24.95 (*0-88192-283-8*); pap. 15.95 (*0-88192-287-0*) Timber.

***Plant Systematics.** Gurcharan Singh. LC 99-48015. (Illus.). 348p. 1999. text 65.00 (*1-57808-081-9*); pap. text 39.50 (*1-57808-077-0*) Science Pubs.

Plant Systematics. 2nd ed. Samuel B. Jones & Arlene E. Luchsinger. 448p. (C). 1986. 84.38 (*0-07-032796-3*) McGraw.

***Plant Systematics: A Phylogenetic Approach.** Walter Judd et al. LC 99-19845. 14p. (C). 1999. text 69.95 incl. audio compact disk (*0-87893-404-9*) Sinauer Assocs.

Plant Systematics in the Age of Molecular Biology. P. Y. Ladiges & L. W. Martinelli. (Illus.). 172p. 1990. pap. 50.00 (*0-643-05098-1*, Pub. by CSIRO) Accents Pubns.

Plant Systems-Components Aging Management. Ed. by I. T. Kisisel. 155p. 1996. pap. text 80.00 (*0-7918-1779-2*, TS283) ASME Pr.

Plant Systems-Components Aging Management, 1993. Ed. by I. T. Kisisel. (PVP Ser.: Vol. 252). 212p. 1993. 50.00 (*0-7918-0979-X*, H00811) ASME.

Plant Systems-Components Aging Management, 1994: Proceedings of the Pressure Vessels & Piping Conference, Minneapolis, MN, 1994. Ed. by I. T. Kisisel. LC 93-71816. (PVP Ser.: Vol. 283). 117p. 1994. pap. 45.00 (*0-7918-1356-8*) ASME.

Plant Systems-Components Aging Management, 1995. Ed. by I. T. Kisisel et al. LC 93-71816. (Proceedings of the 1995 ASME/JSME Pressure Vessels & Piping Conference Ser.: PVP-Vol. 316). 200p. 1995. 100.00 (*0-7918-1347-9*, H00979) ASME.

Plant Systems/Components Aging Management, 1997: Proceedings ASME Pressure Vessels & Piping Conference (1997, Orlando, FL) Ed. by I. T. Kisisel & J. Sinnappan. LC 97-73336. (PVP Ser.: Vol. 349). 155p. 1997. pap. 80.00 (*0-7918-1566-8*) ASME.

Plant Taxonomic Database Standards: Plant Names in Botanical Databases, No. 3. Frank A. Bisby. 30p. 1994. pap. 8.00 (*0-913196-62-2*) Hunt Inst Botanical.

Plant Taxonomic Database Standards No. 2: World Geographic Scheme for Recording Plant Distributions, No. 2. S. Hollis & R. K. Brummitt. (Illus.). 104p. (Orig.). 1992. pap. 18.00 (*0-913196-56-8*, Pub. by Royal Botnic Grdns) Balogh.

Plant Taxonomic Literature Microfiche Collection: Bibliographic Guide. Compiled by James A. Mears. 177p. 1989. write for info. (*0-85964-217-8*) Chadwyck-Healey.

Plant Taxonomy: The Systematic Evaluation of Comparative Data. Tod F. Stuessy. 512p. 1990. text 77.00 (*0-231-06784-4*) Col U Pr.

Plant Taxonomy & Biosystematics. 2nd ed. Clive A. Stace. (Illus.). 272p. 1992. pap. text 34.95 (*0-521-42785-1*) Cambridge U Pr.

Plant Taxonomy & Biosystematics. 2nd ed. Clive A. Stace. LC 90-102463. 1989. pap. 29.95 (*0-7131-2955-7*) St Martin.

Plant Taxonomy Phytogeography & Related Subjects: The Davis & Hedge Festschrift. Ed. by Kit Tan et al. (Illus.). 310p. 1989. 85.00 (*0-85224-638-2*, Pub. by Edinburgh U Pr) Col U Pr.

Plant Technology of First Peoples in British Columbia: Including Neighbouring Groups in Washington, Alberta, & Alaska. rev. ed. Nancy J. Turner. LC 99-193038. (Illus.). 288p. 1999. pap. 24.95 (*0-7748-0687-7*) U BC Pr.

Plant That Ate Dirty Socks. Nancy McArthur. (Plant That Ate Dirty Socks Ser.: Bk. 1). 52p. (J). (gr. 2-5). Date not set. pap. 5.60 (*0-87129-240-8*, P94) Dramatic Pub.

Plant That Ate Dirty Socks. Nancy McArthur. (Plant That Ate Dirty Socks Ser.: Bk. 1). 119p. (J). (gr. 2-5). pap. 4.50 (*0-8072-1494-9*) Listening Lib.

Plant That Ate Dirty Socks, Bk. 1. Nancy McArthur. (Plant That Ate Dirty Socks Ser.: Bk. 1). 144p. (J). (gr. 2-5). 1988. mass mkt. 4.50 (*0-380-75493-2*, Avon Bks) Morrow Avon.

Plant That Ate Dirty Socks, Set. unabridged ed. Ed. by Nancy McArthur. (Plant That Ate Dirty Socks Ser.: Bk. 1). (J). (gr. 2-5). 1997. audio. write for info. (*0-8072-7751-7*, YA909SP) Listening Lib.

Plant That Ate Dirty Socks: Teacher's Guide. HarBrace Staff. (J). 1995. pap. text 13.10 (*0-15-305589-8*) Harcourt.

Plant That Ate Dirty Socks Gets a Girlfriend. Nancy McArthur. (Plant That Ate Dirty Socks Ser.: No. 8). (J). (gr. 2-5). 1997. pap. 3.99 (*0-614-28632-8*, Avon Bks) Morrow Avon.

Plant That Ate Dirty Socks Gets a Girlfriend. Nancy McArthur. (Plant That Ate Dirty Socks Ser.: Bk. 8). (J). (gr. 2-5). 1997. 9.09 (*0-606-11756-3*, Pub. by Turtleback) Demco.

Plant That Ate Dirty Socks Gets a Girlfriend, Bk. 8. Nancy McArthur. (Plant That Ate Dirty Socks Ser.: Bk. 8). 144p. (J). (gr. 2-5). 1997. mass mkt. 3.99 (*0-380-78319-3*, Avon Bks) Morrow Avon.

***Plant That Ate Dirty Socks Goes Hollywood, Vol. 9.** Nancy McArthur. (Plant That Ate Dirty Socks Ser.: Bk. 9). 144p. (J). (gr. 2-5). 1999. mass mkt. 3.99 (*0-380-79935-9*, Avon Bks) Morrow Avon.

Plant that Ate Dirty Socks Goes Up in Space. Nancy McArthur. (Plant That Ate Dirty Socks Ser.: No. 6). (J). (gr. 2-5). 1988. 9.60 (*0-606-03890-6*, Pub. by Turtleback) Demco.

Plant that Ate Dirty Socks Goes Up in Space. Nancy McArthur. (Plant That Ate Dirty Socks Ser.: Bk. 6). (J). (gr. 2-5). 1995. 9.85 (*0-606-08022-8*) Turtleback.

Plant that Ate Dirty Socks Goes Up in Space, Bk. 6. Nancy McArthur. (Plant That Ate Dirty Socks Ser.: Bk. 6). 144p. (J). (gr. 2-5). 1995. mass mkt. 4.50 (*0-380-77664-2*, Avon Bks) Morrow Avon.

Plant That Kept on Growing. Barbara Brenner. LC 95-18798. (Bank Street Ready-to-Read Ser.). (Illus.). (J). (ps-3). 1996. pap. 3.99 (*0-553-09746-6*) Bantam.

Plant that Kept on Growing. Barbara Brenner. (Bank Street Ready-to-Read Ser.). (Illus.). 32p. (J). (ps-1). 1996. pap. 4.50 (*0-553-37578-4*) BDD Bks Young Read.

***Plant This! Best Bets for Year - Round Gorgeous Gardens.** Ketzel Levine. (Illus.). 224p. 2000. pap. 19.95 (*1-57061-245-5*) Sasquatch Bks.

Plant Tissue & Cell Culture: Proceedings of the 6th International Congress on Plant Tissue & Cell Culture, Held at the University of Minnesota, August 3-8, 1986. International Congress on Plant Tissue & Cell Cult. Ed. by C. E. Green. LC 86-27527. (Plant Biology Ser.: No. 3). 523p. reprint ed. pap. 162.20 (*0-7837-2826-3*, 205764600006) Bks Demand.

Plant Tissue Culture. Ed. by A. S. Islam. 242p. 1996. lib. bdg. 80.00 (*1-886106-64-9*) Science Pubs.

Plant Tissue Culture: A Classified Bibliography. S. S. Bhojwani et al. (Developments in Crop Science Ser.: No. 9). xvi,790p. 1987. 420.00 (*0-444-42663-9*) Elsevier.

Plant Tissue Culture: An Alternative for Production of Useful Metabolites. Masanaru Misawa. (Agricultural Services Bulletin Ser.: 108). 93p. 1994. pap. 11.00 (*92-5-103391-9*, F33919, Pub. by FAO) Bernan Associates.

Plant Tissue Culture: Applications & Limitations. Ed. by S. S. Bhojwani. (Developments in Crop Science Ser.: No. 19). 462p. 1990. 158.25 (*0-444-88883-7*) Elsevier.

Plant Tissue Culture: Methods & Application in Agriculture. Ed. by Trevor A. Thorpe. 1981. text 62.00 (*0-12-690680-7*) Acad Pr.

Plant Tissue Culture: Techniques & Experiments. Roberta H. Smith. (Illus.). 171p. 1992. pap. 41.00 (*0-12-650340-0*) Acad Pr.

***Plant Tissue Culture: Techniques & Experiments.** 2nd ed. Roberta Smith. 2000. 49.95 (*0-12-650342-7*) Acad Pr.

Plant Tissue Culture: Theory & Practice. S. S. Bhojwani & M. N. Razdan. (Developments in Crop Science Ser.: Vol. 5). vii,502p. 1986. pap. 116.00 (*0-444-42526-8*) Elsevier.

Plant Tissue Culture: Theory & Practice. rev. ed. S. S. Bhojwani & M. N. Razdan. LC 96-42141. (Studies in Plant Science). 776p. 1996. 284.50 (*0-444-81623-2*) Elsevier.

Plant Tissue Culture Concepts & Laboratory Exercises. Ed. by Robert N. Trigiano & Dennis J. Gray. LC 95-47400. 400p. 1996. spiral bd. 84.95 (*0-8493-9409-0*, 9409) CRC Pr.

***Plant Tissue Culture Concepts & Laboratory Exercises.** 2nd ed. R. N. Trigiano & Dennis J. Gray. LC 99-34987. 472p. 1999. spiral bd. 79.95 (*0-8493-2029-1*) CRC Pr.

Plant Tissue Culture Manual, Suppl. 5. Ed. by K. Lindsey. 164p. (Orig.). 1995. ring bd., suppl. ed. 86.00 (*0-7923-3319-5*) Kluwer Academic.

Plant Tissue Culture Manual, Supplement 2. Ed. by K. Lindsey. (Looseleaf Product Code: LS Ser.). 75p. (Orig.). (C). 1992. ring bd. 32.00 (*0-7923-1516-2*) Kluwer Academic.

Plant Tissue Culture Manual B - W. Ed. by K. Lindsey. 585p. (C). 1991. lib. bdg. 143.00 (*0-7923-1115-9*) Kluwer Academic.

Plant Tissue Culture Studies. Robert A. Smith. (Illus.). 168p. (YA). (gr. 9-12). 1997. pap. 22.00 (*0-941212-24-6*) Natl Assn Bio Tchrs.

Plant Toxin Analysis. Ed. by H. F. Linskens & J. F. Jackson. (Modern Methods of Plant Analysis Ser.: Vol. 13). (Illus.). 368p. 1992. 251.95 (*0-387-52328-6*) Spr-Verlag.

Plant Transposable Elements: Alaskan Aviation History. Ed. by O. Nelson. LC 88-21917. (Basic Life Sciences Ser.: Vol. 47). (Illus.). 416p. 1990. 105.00 (*0-306-43001-0*, Plenum Trade) Perseus Pubng.

***Plant Trichomes Vol. 31.** Ed. by J. A. Callow. (Advances in Botanical Research Ser.). 900p. 2000. 99.95 (*0-12-005931-2*) Acad Pr.

Plant Tropisms & Other Growth Movements. James W. Hart. 388p. 1990. text 55.00 (*0-04-445370-1*) Routledge.

Plant Tumor Research. Ed. by A. C. Braun. (Progress in Experimental Tumor Research Ser.: Vol. 15). 1972. 54.00 (*3-8055-1262-7*) S Karger.

Plant Tumors. Arun Misra et al. (Illus.). xxl, 222p. (C). 1985. lib. bdg. 25.00 (*1-55528-000-5*) Scholarly Pubns.

Plant Tumors. Arun Misra et al. (Illus.). xviii, 222p. 1985. 25.00 (*1-55528-045-5*, Pub. by Today Tomorrow) Scholarly Pubns.

Plant Tutor. Steven Scheckler et al. (Life Science Ser.). Date not set. wbk. ed. 50.00 incl. cd-rom (*0-7637-0348-6*) Jones & Bartlett.

Plant Tutor Workbook. Steven Scheckler et al. (Life Science Ser.). Date not set. pap. 25.00 (*0-7637-0442-3*) Jones & Bartlett.

Plant Utilities Engineer. (Career Examination Ser.). 1997. pap. 39.95 (*0-8373-3795-X*, C3795) Nat Learn.

Plant Utilities Engineer Apprentice. (Career Examination Ser.). 1997. pap. 29.95 (*0-8373-3786-0*, C3786) Nat Learn.

***Plant Vacuole.** Leigh. (C). 1999. pap. text 59.95 (*0-12-441870-8*) Acad Pr.

Plant Vacuoles: Their Importance in Solute Compartmentation in Cells & Their Applications in Plant Biotechnology. Ed. by B. P. Marin. LC 87-14121. (NATO ASI Series A, Life Sciences: Vol. 134). (Illus.). 578p. 1987. 135.00 (*0-306-42613-7*, Plenum Trade) Perseus Pubng.

Plant Variation & Evolution. 3rd ed. D. Briggs & S. M. Walters. LC 96-39293. (Illus.). 536p. (C). 1997. text 80.00 (*0-521-45295-3*); pap. text 37.95 (*0-521-45918-4*) Cambridge U Pr.

Plant Variety Protection Act Amendments of 1993. United States Government Printing Office Staff. LC 94-135529. (S. Hrg. Ser.). iii, 117 p. 1993. write for info. (*0-16-043316-9*) USGPO.

Plant Variety Protection Act & Regulations & Rules of Practice. rev. ed. Ed. by Marsha A. Stanton. 44p. (C). 1999. reprint ed. pap. text 25.00 (*0-7881-8098-3*) DIANE Pub.

***Plant Variety Protection Act & Regulations & Rules of Practice.** rev. ed. Ed. by Marsha A. Stanton. 44p. 1999. pap. text 15.00 (*0-7881-3191-5*) DIANE Pub.

Plant Virology. 3rd ed. R. E. Matthews. (Illus.). 835p. (C). 1991. text 53.00 (*0-12-480553-1*) Acad Pr.

Plant Virology Protocols: From Virus Isolation to Transgenic Resistance. Ed. by Gary D. Foster & Sally Taylor. LC 97-32185. (Methods in Molecular Biology Ser.: Vol. 81). (Illus.). 592p. 1998. 89.50 (*0-89603-385-6*) Humana.

Plant Virus Disease Control. Ed. by A. Hadidi et al. (Illus.). 704p. 1998. 109.00 (*0-89054-191-4*) Am Phytopathol Soc.

Plant Virus Epidemics: Monitoring, Modeling & Predicting Outbreaks. Ed. by George McLean et al. 1986. text 146.00 (*0-12-485060-X*) Acad Pr.

Plant Viruses: Structure & Replication. Ed. by C. L. Mandahar. (Illus.). 368p. 1989. lib. bdg. 289.00 (*0-8493-6947-9*, QR351) CRC Pr.

Plant Viruses Vol. 1: Polyhedral Virions with Tripartite Genomes. R. I. Francki. LC 85-3528. (Viruses Ser.). (Illus.). 324p. (C). 1985. text 110.00 (*0-306-41958-0*, Kluwer Plenum) Kluwer Academic.

Plant Viruses Vol. 2: Pathology. Ed. by C. L. Mandahar. (Illus.). 368p. 1990. lib. bdg. 289.00 (*0-8493-6948-7*, QR351) CRC Pr.

Plant Viruses Vol. 2: The Rod-Shaped Plant Viruses. M. H. Van Regenmortel & H. Fraenkel-Conrat. (Illus.). 422p. 1986. 110.00 (*0-306-42258-1*, Kluwer Plenum) Kluwer Academic.

Plant Viruses Vol. 3: Polyhedral Virions with Monopartite RNA Genomes. R. Koenig. LC 87-32809. (Viruses Ser.). (Illus.). 308p. 1987. 110.00 (*0-306-42705-2*, Kluwer Plenum) Kluwer Academic.

Plant Viruses Vol. 4: The Filamentous Plant Viruses. R. G. Milne. LC 88-15221. (Viruses Ser.). (Illus.). 440p. (C). 1988. text 110.00 (*0-306-42845-8*, Kluwer Plenum) Kluwer Academic.

Plant Viruses & Virus Diseases. Frederick C. Bawden. LC 64-11825. 368p. reprint ed. pap. 114.10 (*0-7837-3427-1*, 205774800008) Bks Demand.

***Plant Viruses, Unique & Intriguing Pathogens: A Textbook of Plant Virology.** L. Bos. (Illus.). 358p. 1999. 85.00 (*90-5782-012-9*, Pub. by Backhuys Pubs) Balogh.

Plant Vitamins: Agronomic, Physiological & Nutritional Aspects. A. Mozafar. 432p. 1993. boxed set 249.00 (*0-8493-4734-3*) CRC Pr.

Plant Voices. Gary Fincke. LC 90-25920. (Illus.). 64p. (Orig.). 1991. pap. 7.95 (*0-9620251-4-3*) Yardbird Bks.

Plant Volatile Analysis. Ed. by H. F. Linskens & J. F. Jackson. (Modern Methods of Plant Analysis: Vol. 19). 200p. 1997. 157.00 (*3-540-61589-X*) Spr-Verlag.

Plant Watermelons on My Grave. Bob Bowman. 1991. 16.95 (*1-878096-20-6*) Best E TX Pubs.

Plant-Wide Process Control. Kelvin T. Erickson & John L. Hedrick. LC 98-38903. 560p. 1999. 89.95 (*0-471-17835-7*) Wiley.

Plant, Wildlife & Man: A Conservation Scenario of Bay Islands & the Himalayas. A. B. Chaudhuri. (C). 1992. 42.00 (*81-7024-464-1*, Pub. by Ashish Pub Hse) S Asia.

Plant Your Dreams, My Child. Nancy Bestmann. (Illus.). 18p. (J). 1997. 12.99 (*0-89900-665-5*) College Pr Pub.

Plant Your Feet Firmly in Mid-Air: Guidance Through Turbulent Change. Janet E. Lapp. LC 95-71616. 235p. 1996. 22.95 (*1-885365-00-4*) Demeter Pr.

Plantado: Una Cronica Desnuda y Terrible de la Experiencia de las Carceles Castristas. Hilda Perera. (SPA.). 183p. (Orig.). 1981. pap. 7.95 (*84-320-3612-9*) Ediciones.

Plantae Asiaticae Rorrieres, 3 vols. N. Wallich. (C). 1988. text 1000.00 (*0-7855-3148-3*, Pub. by Scientific) St Mut.

Plantae Cubenses Novae Vel Rariores a E. L. Ekman Rectae, 4 pts. in 1. Ignatius Urban. 1964. reprint ed. 75.00 (*90-6123-176-0*) Lubrecht & Cramer.

Plantae Davidiane Ex Sinarum Imperio, 2 pts. in 1 vol. A. R. Franchet. (Illus.). 1970. reprint ed. 240.00 (*3-7682-0670-X*) Lubrecht & Cramer.

Plantae Elmerianae Borneenses. Elmer D. Merrill. LC 29-219. (University of California Publications in Social Welfare: Vol. 15). 320p. reprint ed. pap. 99.20 (*0-608-18022-X*, 201475100096) Bks Demand.

Plantae Hartwegianae: Plantas Hartwegianas Imprimis Mexicanas Adjectis Nonullis Grahamianis Enumerat Novasque Describit. G. Bentham. 1971. reprint ed. 96.00 (*3-7682-0673-4*) Lubrecht & Cramer.

Plantae Wilsonianae: An Enumeration of the Woody Plants Collected in Western China, 3 vols. E. H. Wilson. Ed. by Charles S. Sargent. LC 88-6946. 1964p. 1988. reprint ed. 110.00 (*0-931146-01-1*, Dioscorides) Timber.

Plantagenet Ancestry: Being Tables Showing over 7,000 of the Ancestors of Elizabeth (Daughter of Edward IV & Wife of Henry VII) the Heiress of the Plantagenets. W. H. Turton. LC 68-54254. 274p. 1993. reprint ed. 50.00 (*0-8063-0330-1*) Genealog Pub.

***Plantagenet Connection, 1993-1997.** 2nd ed. Kenneth H. Finton. LC 99-90154. (Illus.). 100p. 1999. reprint ed. pap. 59.95 (*1-892977-04-4*, 04-4) H T Commun.

Plantagenet Descent: 31 Generations from William the Conqueror to Today. Thomas R. Moore. (Illus.). xviii, 242p. 1995. 49.50 (*0-9644929-0-3*) T R Moore.

Plantagenet Prelude. Jean Plaidy, pseud. 24.95 (*0-8488-0607-7*) Amereon Ltd.

Plantagenet Roll of the Blood Royal: The Anne of Exeter Volume, Containing the Descendants of Anne (Plantagenet), Duchess of Exeter. Marquis of Ruvigny & Raineval. (Illus.). 842p. 1994. 50.00 (*0-8063-1433-8*) Genealog Pub.

Plantagenet Roll of the Blood Royal: The Clarence Volume, Containing the Descendants of George, Duke of Clarence. Marquis of Ruvigny & Raineval. (Illus.). 730p. 1994. 50.00 (*0-8063-1432-X*) Genealog Pub.

Plantagenet Roll of the Blood Royal: The Isabel of Essex Volume, Containing the Descendants of Isabel (Plantagenet), Countess of Essex & Eu. Marquis of Ruvigny & Raineval. (Illus.). 698p. 1994. 45.00 (*0-8063-1434-6*) Genealog Pub.

Plantagenet Roll of the Blood Royal: The Mortimer-Percy Volume, Containing the Descendants of Lady Elizabeth Percy, Nee Mortimer. Marquis of Ruvigny & Raineval. (Illus.). 650p. 1994. 45.00 (*0-8063-1435-4*) Genealog Pub.

Plantaginaceae to Compositae (& Rubiaceae) see Flora Europaea

Plantago: A Multidisciplinary Study. Ed. by Hermann Remmert et al. (Ecological Studies: Vol. 89). (Illus.). 400p. 1992. 199.95 (*0-387-53632-9*) Spr-Verlag.

Plantaire: In Honor of the Blessed Virgin Mary Taken from a French Manuscript of the Fourteenth Century. M. Alberta Savoie. LC 73-94205. (Catholic University of America. Studies in Romance Languages & Literatures: No. 9). reprint ed. 37.50 (*0-404-50309-8*) AMS Pr.

Plantando Iglesias para una Mayor Cosecha. P. Wagner.Tr. of Church Planting for a Great Harvest. (SPA.). 100. pap. 7.99 (*0-7899-0038-6*, 497653) Editorial Unilit.

Plantar Iglesias Autoctonas: Un Viaje Practico. Charles Brock. Tr. by Norma C. Armengol.Tr. of Indigenous Church Planting: A Practical Journey. (SPA.). 262p. 1996. pap. 10.00 (*1-885504-35-7*) Church Gwth.

Plantas - Plants. Ed. by Maria J. Gomez-Navarro et al. Tr. by Maria Del Carmen Blazquez. (Diccionarios Visuales Altea Ser. - Visual Dictionary Ser.). (SPA., Illus.). 64p. (YA). (gr. 5-12). 1993. write for info. (*84-372-4529-X*) Santillana.

P

An Asterisk (*) at the beginning of an entry indicates that the title is appearing for the first time.

Plantas Curativas Mexicanas. Rivas Garcia. 1997. pap. text 9.98 (968-38-0293-1) Panorama Edit.

Plantas de los Bosques. Chelsea House Publishing Staff & B. Mavis. (SPA., Illus.). 32p. (YA). (gr. 3 up). 1996. lib. bdg. 15.95 (0-7910-4020-8) Chelsea Hse.

Plantas del Desierto see Plants of the Desert

Plantas del Desierto. Chelsea House Publishing Staff. (SPA., Illus.). 32p. (YA). (gr. 3 up). 1996. lib. bdg. 15.95 (0-7910-4018-6) Chelsea Hse.

Plantas del Mar see Plants under the Sea

***Plantas do Nordeste (Plants of the Northeast) Anais do 1 Workshop Geral (Proceedings of the First General Workshop)** Ed. by Fernando Dantas de Araujo et al. (POR.). 150p. 1999. pap. 30.00 (1-900347-79-2, Pub. by Royal Botnic Grdns) Balogh.

Plantas Medicinales. Arias Carbajal.Tr. of Healing Plants. 215p. (Orig.). 1997. pap. text 6.98 (968-15-0735-5) Ed Mex.

Plantas Medicinales de Puerto Rico: Folklore y Fundamentos Cientificos. 2nd abr. rev. ed. Esteban Nunez-Melendez. LC 82-17321. (SPA., Illus.). xii, 498p. 1989. pap. 22.95 (0-8477-2328-3) U of PR Pr.

Plantas Medicinales En el Sur Andino del Peru. Carolus M. Roersch. (ENG & SPA., Illus.). xii, 1188p. 1994. pap. 178.50 (3-87429-369-6, 057586, Pub. by Koeltz Sci Bks) Lubrecht & Cramer.

Plantas Ornamentais no Brasil: Arbustivas, Herbaceas e Trepadeiras. Harri Lorenzi. (POR., Illus.). 730p. 1997. 129.95 (85-86714-01-1, Pub. by Inst Plantarum) Balogh.

Plantas Ornamentais no Brasil: Arbustivas, Herbaceas e Trepadeiras. 2nd rev. ed. Harri Lorenzi. (POR., Illus.). 730p. 1999. 110.00 (85-86714-08-9, Pub. by Inst Plantarum) Balogh.

Plantas para Ti y para Mi. Arthur Morton. Tr. by Patricia Rodriguez-Kalson. (SPA.). (J). (gr. k-3). 1993. 12.50 (1-57842-070-9) Delmas Creat.

Plantas (Plant Life) see Enciclopedia Ilustrada de Ciencia Naturaleza (Understanding Science & Nature)

Plantas Venenosas de Puerto Rico. Esteban N. Melendez. (SPA.). 290p. 1990. pap. 12.75 (0-8477-2341-0) U of PR Pr.

Plantation. Fern Smith-Brown. LC 98-73652. 219p. 1999. 21.95 (0-9666721-3-5) GoldenIsle Pubs.

Plantation Agriculture & Social Control in Northern Peru, 1875-1933. Michael J. Gonzales. (Institute of Latin American Studies Monographs: No. 62). 251p. 1985. text 25.00 (0-292-76491-X) U of Tex Pr.

Plantation & Agri-Horticultural Resources of Kerala. P. K. Nair. (Aspects of Plant Sciences Ser.: Vol. 7). 120p. 1984. 19.00 (1-55528-165-6, Pub. by Today Tomorrow) Scholarly Pubns.

Plantation Bamboos. P. Shanmughavel. 1997. pap. 125.00 (81-7089-245-7, Pub. by Intl Bk Distr) St Mut.

Plantation Bird Legends. Martha Young. LC 70-152933. (Black Heritage Library Collection). 1977. 20.95 (0-8369-8778-0) Ayer.

Plantation Boy. Milton Murayama. LC 97-33350. 180p. 1998. 24.95 (0-8248-1965-9); pap. 14.95 (0-8248-2007-X) UH Pr.

Plantation Child & Other Stories. Eve B. Kiehm. LC 94-33410. (Illus.). 80p. (J). (gr. 3-6). 1995. 9.95 (0-8248-1596-3, Kolowalu Bk) UH Pr.

Plantation Christmas. Julia Peterkin. LC 72-4563. (Black Heritage Library Collection). (Illus.). (YA). (gr. 7 up). 1977. reprint ed. 13.95 (0-8369-9119-2) Ayer.

Plantation Christmas. Julia Peterkin. LC 78-22014. (Illus.). (J). (gr. 6 up). 1978. reprint ed. pap. 2.95 (0-89783-007-5) Cherokee.

Plantation Cookbook. Junior League of New Orleans Staff. (Illus.). 223p. 1992. reprint ed. 22.95 (0-9631925-0-7) B E Trice.

Plantation County. Morton Rubin. (Orig.). 1951. pap. 12.95 (0-8084-0247-1) NCUP.

Plantation Economy in India. Somu Giriappa. 151p. 1995. pap. 113.00 (81-85880-84-0, Pub. by Print Hse) St Mut.

Plantation Forestry in India. R. K. Luna. 509p. (C). 1989. 595.00 (0-7855-6881-6, Pub. by Intl Bk Distr); text 595.00 (0-7855-6587-6, Pub. by Intl Bk Distr) St Mut.

Plantation Forestry in India. R. K. Luna. 519p. 1989. pap. 500.00 (81-7089-141-8, Pub. by Intl Bk Distr) St Mut.

Plantation Forestry in the Amazon: The Jari Experience. Clayton E. Posey & Harold K. Steen. LC 97-36526. 1997. pap. 12.95 (0-89030-054-2) Forest Hist Soc.

Plantation Forestry in the Tropics: Tree Planting for Industrial, Social, Environmental & Agroforestry Purposes. 2nd ed. Julian Evans. (Illus.). 418p. 1992. pap. text 65.00 (0-19-854257-7) OUP.

Plantation Homes of Louisiana & the Natchez Area. David K. Gleason. LC 82-7723. (Illus.). 134p. 1982. 49.95 (0-8071-1058-2) La State U Pr.

Plantation Homes of the James River. Bruce Roberts. LC 89-39204. (Illus.). xii, 116p. (C). 1990. pap. 19.95 (0-8078-4278-8) U of NC Pr.

Plantation Homes of the Teche Country. Paul Stahls, Jr. LC 78-24283. (Illus.). 96p. 1979. pap. 17.95 (1-56554-556-7) Pelican.

Plantation Houses & Mansions of the Old South. J. Frazer Smith. LC 93-25640. Orig. Title: White Pillars. (Illus.). 256p. 1993. reprint ed. pap. text 12.95 (0-486-27848-4) Dover.

Plantation Labour, Unions, Capital, & the State in Peninsular Malaysia. P. Ramasamy. LC 93-26972. (South-East Asian Social Science Monographs). (Illus.). 220p. 1994. 55.00 (967-65-3031-X) OUP.

Plantation Landscape: Slaves & Freedom at Seabrook Plantation, Hilton Head Island, South Carolina. Rachel Campo et al. LC 98-39805. (Research Ser.: No. 34). (Illus.). 197p. 1998. pap. 30.00 (1-58317-003-0) Chicora Found.

Plantation Lays, & Other Poems. Belton O. Townsend. LC 78-173619. (Black Heritage Library Collection). 1977. reprint ed. 17.95 (0-8369-8912-0) Ayer.

Plantation Letters: Plantation Letters. Roger Elwood. LC 97-26525. (Plantation Letters Ser.: Vol. 1). 256p. 1997. pap. 12.99 (0-8499-3390-0) Word Pub.

Plantation Life: The Narratives of Mrs. Henry Rowe Schoolcraft. Mary H. Schoolcraft. LC 68-55926. 569p. 1969. reprint ed. lib. bdg. 49.50 (0-8371-2084-5, SCP&, Greenwood Pr) Greenwood.

Plantation Life in Texas. Elizabeth Silverthorne. LC 86-5810. (Clayton Wheat Williams Texas Life Ser.: Vol. 1). (Illus.). 256p. 1986. 24.95 (0-89096-288-X) Tex A&M Univ Pr.

Plantation Life in the Florida Parishes of Louisiana, 1836-1846, As Reflected in the Diary of Bennet H. Barrow. Bennet H. Barrow. Ed. by Edwin A. Davis. LC 74-163680. reprint ed. 34.50 (0-404-01989-7) AMS Pr.

Plantation Management on a Sharecropper's Budget. David A. Avant, III. LC 91-84670. (Illus.). 120p. pap. 15.00 (0-914570-12-9) LAvant Studios.

Plantation Mistress: Woman's World in the Old South. Catherine Clinton. 1984. pap. 13.00 (0-394-72253-1) Pantheon.

Plantation Mistress on the Eve of the Civil War: The Diary of Keziah Goodwyn Hopkins Brevard, 1860-1861. Ed. by John H. Moore. LC 92-23308. (Illus.). 148p. 1996. pap. 12.95 (1-57003-125-8) U of SC Pr.

Plantation Pageants. Joel Chandler Harris. LC 76-113667. (Short Story Index Reprint Ser.). 1977. 25.95 (0-8369-3396-6) Ayer.

Plantation Politics. Caroline Sargent & Stephen Bass. 1991. 26.00 (1-85383-113-1, Pub. by Escan Pubns) Island Pr.

Plantation Production & Political Power: Plantation Development in South-West India in a Long-Term Historical Perspective, 1743-1963. Paul E. Baak. LC 97-900358. (Illus.). 392p. (C). 1998. 29.95 (0-19-564103-5) OUP.

Plantation Row Slave Cabin Cooking: The Roots of Soul Food. Patricia B. Mitchell. LC 98-161648. 1998. pap. 4.00 (0-925117-89-7) Mitchells.

***Plantation Secrets.** James W. Ridout, IV. 376p. 2000. 23.95 (0-9678838-0-6) Pilot.

Plantation Silviculture. Kenneth R. Shepherd. (Forestry Sciences Ser.). 1986. text 199.50 (90-247-3379-0) Kluwer Academic.

Plantation Silviculture in Europe. Peter Savill et al. LC 97-15621. (Illus.). 308p. 1997. text 95.00 (0-19-854909-1) OUP.

Plantation Silviculture in Europe. Peter Savill et al. LC 97-15621. (Illus.). 308p. 1998. pap. text 45.00 (0-19-854908-3) OUP.

Plantation Silviculture in Temperate Regions: With Special Reference to the British Isles. Peter S. Savill & Julian Evans. (Illus.). 250p. 1986. 49.95 (0-19-854138-4) OUP.

Plantation Slavery in Barbados: An Archaeological & Historical Investigation. Jerome S. Handler & Frederick W. Lange. LC 77-22312. 384p. 1978. 37.50 (0-674-67275-5) HUP.

Plantation Slavery on the East Coast of Africa. Frederick Cooper. LC 97-5082. 314p. 1997. pap. 27.50 (0-435-07419-9) Heinemann.

Plantation Slaves of Trinidad, 1783-1816: A Mathematical & Demographic Enquiry. A. Meredith John. (Illus.). 282p. (C). 1989. text 80.00 (0-521-36166-4) Cambridge U Pr.

Plantation Societies in the Era of European Expansion. Judy Bieber. LC 96-40468. (Expanding World Ser.: No. 18). 372p. 1997. text 124.95 (0-86078-506-8, Pub. by Variorum) Ashgate Pub Co.

Plantation Societies, Race Relations, & the South: The Regimentation of Populations: Selected Papers of Edgar T. Thompson. Edgar T. Thompson. LC 75-728. (Illus.). 423p. reprint ed. pap. 131.20 (0-608-18756-9, 205223900068) Bks Demand.

Plantation Society & Race Relations: The Origins of Inequality. Ed. by Thomas J. Durant, Jr. & J. David Knottnerus. LC 98-35372. 280p. 1999. 59.95 (0-275-95808-6, Praeger Pubs) Greenwood.

Plantation Songs. Eli Shepperd & Pia-Seija Seagrave. LC 97-9670. 1997. pap. 19.95 (1-887901-11-6) Sergeant Kirk.

Plantation South. William C. Holley et al. LC 78-166955. (Research Monographs: Vol. 22). 1971. reprint ed. lib. bdg. 19.50 (0-306-70354-8) Da Capo.

Plantation South: Atlanta to Savannah & Charleston. Louis De Vorsey, Jr. & Marion Rice. LC 92-10413. (Touring North America Ser.). (Illus.). 220p. 1992. 25.00 (0-8135-1872-5); pap. 9.95 (0-8135-1873-3) Rutgers U Pr.

Plantation South, 1934-37. William C. Holley et al. LC 74-160977. (Select Bibliographies Reprint Ser.). 1977. reprint ed. 19.95 (0-8369-5844-6) Ayer.

Plantation Tales. Nancy Rhyne. LC 88-37029. (YA). (gr. 7 up). 1989. pap. 12.95 (0-87844-093-3) Sandlapper Pub Co.

Plantation, Town, & County: Essays on the Local History of American Slave Society. Ed. by Elinor Miller & Eugene D. Genovese. LC 73-20359. 463p. reprint ed. pap. 143.60 (0-608-10894-4, 202277800029) Bks Demand.

Plantation Trees. R. K. Luna. LC 96-900510. 974p. 1996. pap. 1250.00 (81-7089-235-X, Pub. by Intl Bk Distr) St Mut.

Plantations. Lynn M. Stone. LC 93-771. (Old America Ser.). 32p. (J). (gr. 3-6). 1993. lib. bdg. 21.27 (0-86625-446-3) Rourke Pubns.

Plantations & Outdoor Museums in America's Historic South. Gerald L. Gutek & Patricia A. Gutek. LC 95-38981. (Illus.). 420p. 1996. pap. 19.95 (1-57003-071-5) U of SC Pr.

Plantations & Plantation Workers. Jean-Paul Sajhau & Jurgen Von Muralt. xii, 207p. (Orig.). 1987. pap. 24.75 (92-2-105652-X) Intl Labour Office.

Plantations in the Tropics: Environmental Concerns. Jacqueline Sawyer. (IUCN Forest Conservation Programme Ser.). 83p. (C). 1993. pap. text 20.00 (2-8317-0139-2, Pub. by IUCN) Island Pr.

Plantations of the Carolina Low Country. Samuel G. Stoney. 256p. 1990. pap. 16.95 (0-486-26089-5) Dover.

Plantations of the Low Country: South Carolina, 1697-1865. William P. Baldwin, Jr. & Agnes Baldwin. LC 84-82499. (Illus.). 144p. 1986. pap. 19.95 (0-933101-03-1) Legacy Pubns.

Plantations of the Low Country: South Carolina, 1697-1865. William P. Bladwin, Jr. & Agnes Baldwin. LC 84-82499. (Illus.). 144p. 1986. 29.95 (0-933101-08-2) Legacy Pubns.

Plantations on the Mississippi River: From Natchez to New Orleans. A. Persac. 1931. 26.00 (0-911116-26-5) Pelican.

Plantations, Peasants, & State: A Study of the Mode of Sugar Production in Guyana. Clive Y. Thomas. (Afro-American Culture & Society Monographs: Vol. 5). 214p. 1984. pap. 12.95 (0-934934-19-3) CAAS Pubns.

Plantations, Proletarians, & Peasants in Colonial Asia. Ed. by Daniel Valentine et al. LC 92-30826. 299p. 1993. text 49.50 (0-7146-3467-0, Pub. by F Cass Pubs) Intl Spec Bk.

Planted. A. Sturgeon. text 40.00 (0-340-71712-2, Pub. by Hodder & Stought Ltd) Trafalgar.

Planted. Andy Sturgeon. LC 98-33714. (Illus.). 208p. 1998. pap. 22.00 (1-57959-029-2, SOMA) BB&T Inc.

Planted by the Water: 70 Days Toward a Flourishing Faith. Arnold Fleagle. LC 93-74748. 154p. 1994. pap. 9.99 (0-87509-557-7) Chr Pubns.

Planted Forests: Contributions to the Quest for Sustainable Societies. James R. Boyle. LC 98-31689. (Forestry Sciences Ser.). 1999. write for info. (0-7923-5468-0) Kluwer Academic.

Planted in Good Soil: A History of the Issei in United States Agriculture I. Masakazu Iwata. (American University Studies: History: Series IX, Vol. 57 & 58). (Illus.). XXXII, 960p. 1992. pap. 89.95 (0-8204-1307-0) P Lang Pubng.

Planted in Love: The Enneagram-Reasoning & Conversion. Elizabeth W. McNulty. 142p. 1996. pap. 39.95 (0-85439-502-4, Pub. by St Paul Pubns) St Mut.

Planted Seed. Juanita Bynum. LC 98-193799. 1997. pap. 6.99 (1-56229-122-X) Pneuma Life Pub.

Plantegenet - "Rich & Beautiful . . ." A History of the Shire of Plantagenet, Western Australia. Rhoda Glover et al. 429p. 29.95 (0-85564-175-4, Pub. by Univ of West Aust Pr) Intl Spec Bk.

Planter & Patriot, 1759-75 see George Washington: A Biography

Planter: or 13 Years in the South. LC 75-83958. (Black Heritage Library Collection). 1977. 22.95 (0-8369-8642-3) Ayer.

Planter: or 13 Years in the South. David Brown. LC 75-104423. 276p. reprint ed. pap. text 6.95 (0-89197-888-7); reprint ed. lib. bdg. 14.25 (0-8398-0174-2) Irvington.

Planter Wire: A Patent History & Collector's Catalog. Jim Guedert & Larry Greer. (Illus.). 376p. 1998. pap. write for info. (1-885591-88-8, PO2409) Morris Pubng.

Planters & Plain Folk: Agriculture in Antebellum Texas. Richard G. Lowe & Randolph B. Campbell. LC 85-27844. 240p. 1987. 22.50 (0-87074-212-4) SMU Press.

Planters & the Making of a New South: Class, Politics & Development in North Carolina, 1865-1900. Dwight B. Billings. LC 78-25952. 298p. reprint ed. pap. 92.40 (0-7837-0299-X, 204062000018) Bks Demand.

Planter's Northern Bride, 2 vols. Caroline L. Hentz. (Notable American Authors Ser.). 1992. reprint ed. lib. bdg. 75.00 (0-7812-3088-8) Rprt Serv.

Planters of Colonial Virginia. Thomas J. Wertenbaker. 260p. 1997. reprint ed. 24.50 (0-8063-4672-8) Clearfield Co.

Planters of the Commonwealth in Massachusetts: A Study of the Emigrants & Emigration in Colonial Times. Charles E. Banks. LC 67-30794. (Illus.). xiii, 231p. 1997. reprint ed. 20.00 (0-8063-0018-3) Genealog Pub.

Planters of the Landscape Garden: Botany, Trees, & the Georgics. Douglas Chambers. LC 92-35695. (Paul Mellon Centre for Studies in British Art). (Illus.). 224p. (C). 1993. 60.00 (0-300-05464-5) Yale U Pr.

Planters Peanut Collectibles, 1906-1961: A Handbook & Price Guide. Jan Lindenberger & Joyce Spontak. LC 95-10515. (Illus.). 160p. (Orig.). 1995. pap. 19.95 (0-88740-792-7) Schiffer.

Planters Peanut Collectibles, 1906-1961: A Handbook & Price Guide. 2nd rev. ed. Jan Lindenberger. (Illus.). 160p. (Orig.). 1999. pap. 19.95 (0-7643-0853-X) Schiffer.

Planters Peanut Collectibles since 1961: A Handbook & Price Guide. Jan Lindenberger & Joyce Spontak. LC 95-31083. 160p. (gr. 10). 1996. pap. 19.95 (0-88740-793-5) Schiffer.

Planters Plea. John White. LC 68-54669. (English Experience Ser.: No. 60). 84p. 1968. reprint ed. 52.00 (90-221-0060-X) Walter J Johnson.

Planter's Republic: The Search for Economic Independence in Revolutionary Virginia. Bruce A. Ragsdale. LC 95-18435. (Illus.). 320p. (C). 1996. text 34.95 (0-945612-40-0) Madison Hse.

Plantes Potageres. Jacques Barrau. (FRE., Illus.). 96p. 1996. pap. 19.95 (2-909808-27-0, Pub. by Art Bks Intl) Partners Pubs Grp.

***Plantfinder's Guide to Early Bulbs.** Rod Leeds. LC 99-41603. (Illus.). 192p. 2000. 34.95 (0-88192-443-1) Timber.

***Plantfinder's Guide to Garden Ferns.** Martin Rickard. LC 00-26329. (Illus.). 192p. 2000. 34.95 (0-88192-476-8) Timber.

Plantfinder's Guide to Ornamental Grasses. Roger Grounds. LC 98-22939. (Illus.). 192p. 1998. 34.95 (0-88192-451-2) Timber.

Plantfinder's Guide to Tender Perennials. Ian Cooke. LC 98-22940. (Illus.). 192p. 1998. 34.95 (0-88192-450-4) Timber.

Plantimal Safari. (J). (ps-6). 1986. 3.00 (0-9605656-3-9) Desert Botanical.

Planting. 3rd ed. Ed. by Deere & Company Staff. (Fundamentals of Machine Operation Ser.). (Illus.). 96p. 1992. pap. text, teacher ed. 33.95 incl. trans. (0-86691-173-1, FMO12503T) Deere & Co.

Planting. 3rd rev. ed. Ed. by Deere & Company Staff. (Fundamentals of Machine Operation Ser.). (Illus.). 224p. 1992. pap. text 29.95 (0-86691-148-0, FMO12103B); pap. text, student ed. 16.95 (0-86691-174-X, FMO12603W) Deere & Co.

Planting: A Book of Seasons. Janelle M. Burk. (Illus.). 96p. 1988. 9.95 (0-9615736-1-9) Milestone Pr.

Planting a Bible Garden. F. Nigel Hepper. LC 97-39355. (Good Book Practical Guide Ser.). (Illus.). 96p. 1998. 19.99 (0-8007-1756-2) Revell.

Planting a Rainbow. Lois Ehlert. LC 87-8528. (Illus.). 32p. (J). (ps-3). 1988. 16.00 (0-15-262609-3) Harcourt.

Planting a Rainbow. Lois Ehlert. LC 87-8528. (Illus.). 32p. (J). (ps-3). 1992. pap. 6.00 (0-15-262610-7) Harcourt.

Planting a Rainbow. large type ed. Lois Ehlert. LC 87-8528. (Illus.). 32p. (J). (ps-3). 1992. pap. 19.95 (0-15-262611-5) Harcourt.

Planting a Water Garden. Joseph L. Thimes. (Illus.). 64p. 1998. 12.95 (0-7938-0331-4, WW090) TFH Pubns.

Planting an Inheritance: Life on a Pennsylvania Farm. Edwin A. Peeples. 224p. 1994. 19.95 (0-8117-1206-0) Stackpole.

***Planting & Building: Raising a Jewish Child.** Shelomoh Volbeh. LC 00-23842. 2000. write for info. (1-58330-402-9) Feldheim.

Planting & Growing in Alabama. Lynn Edge. 138p. 1993. pap. 9.00 (1-878561-17-0) Seacoast AL.

Planting & Growing Urban Churches: From Dream to Reality. Ed. by Harvie M. Conn. LC 97-3223. (Illus.). 272p. (Orig.). (gr. 12 up). 1997. pap. 19.99 (0-8010-2109-X) Baker Bks.

Planting & Reaping Albright: Politics, Ideology, & Interpreting the Bible. Burke O. Long. LC 95-42065. 1996. 32.50 (0-271-01576-4) Pa St U Pr.

Planting by the Moon: On Life in a Mountain Hamlet. Peter Stillman. LC 94-34646. 105p. 1995. pap. 10.95 (0-86709-347-1, 0347, Pub. by Boynton Cook Pubs) Heinemann.

Planting Church-Culture at New Calabar: Some Neglected Aspects of Missionary Enterprise in the Eastern Niger Delta, 1865-1918. Waibinte Elekima Wariboko. LC 98-24863. 278p. 1998. 74.95 (1-57309-315-7, U Pr W Africa) Intl Scholars.

***Planting Churches Cross-Culturally: A Biblical Guide.** 2nd rev. ed. David J. Hesselgrave. LC 99-54928. (Illus.). 352p. (gr. 13). 2000. pap. 24.99 (0-8010-2222-3) Baker Bks.

Planting Churches in Muslim Cities: A Team Approach. Greg Livingstone. LC 93-6623. 272p. (C). 1993. pap. 17.99 (0-8010-5682-9) Baker Bks.

Planting Companions. Jill Billington. LC 96-49089. (Illus.). 160p. 1997. 32.50 (1-55670-543-3) Stewart Tabori & Chang.

Planting Corn Belt Culture: The Impress of the Upland Southerner & Yankee in the Old Northwest. Richard L. Power. LC 83-8491. (Indiana Historical Society Publications Ser.). 196p. 1983. reprint ed. lib. bdg. 55.00 (0-313-24060-4, POPC) Greenwood.

Planting Design. Robinson. 312p. 1994. pap., student ed. 43.95 (0-566-07545-8) Ashgate Pub Co.

Planting Design. 2nd ed. Theodore D. Walker. 208p. 1991. pap. 44.95 (0-471-29022-X, VNR) Wiley.

Planting Design: A Manual of Theory & Practice. William R. Nelson. (Illus.). 1985. text 25.80 (0-87563-268-8) Stipes.

Planting Design Handbook. Koepke. text 64.95 (0-471-29182-X) Wiley.

Planting Design Handbook. Nick Robinson. 1992. 87.95 (0-566-09008-2, Pub. by Gower) Ashgate Pub Co.

Planting Dreams: A Swedish Immigrant's Journey to America. Linda K. Hubalek. LC 97-92245. (Illus.). 128p. (Orig.). 1997. pap. 9.95 (1-886652-11-2) Butterfld Bks.

Planting for Privacy: A Guide to Growing Hedges & Screens. Judy Horton. (Illus.). 96p. 1993. 14.95 (0-86417-472-1, Pub. by Kangaroo Pr) Seven Hills Bk.

Planting for the Future: Forestry for Human Needs. Erik P. Eckholm. 1979. pap. write for info. (0-318-70407-2) Worldwatch Inst.

Planting Growing Churches for the Twenty-First Century: Comprehensive Guide for New Churches & Those Desiring Renewal. 2nd rev. ed. Aubrey Malphurs. LC 98-24675. 432p. 1998. pap. 22.99 (0-8010-9053-9) Baker Bks.

***Planting Light.** Anne Born. 77p. 2000. pap. 11.95 (1-902096-58-4, Pub. by Headland Pubns) Intl Spec Bk.

***Planting Missions Across Cultures.** Kenneth W. Behnken. 220p. 2000. teacher ed., ring bd. 39.95 (0-570-05251-3, 12-4061) Concordia.

Planting Noah's Garden: Further Adventures in Backyard Ecology. Sara Stein. (Illus.). 288p. 1997. 35.00 (0-395-70960-1) HM.

Planting of Civilization in Western Pennsylvania. Solon J. Buck. 1993. reprint ed. lib. bdg. 89.00 (0-7812-5439-6) Rprt Serv.

An Asterisk (*) at the beginning of an entry indicates that the title is appearing for the first time.

Planting of Civilization in Western Pennsylvania. Solon J. Buck & Elizabeth H. Buck. LC 39-25307. (Illus.). 616p. 1969. reprint ed. pap. 24.95 (*0-8229-5202-5*) U of Pittsburgh Pr.

Planting of the Presbyterian Church in Northern Virginia. James R. Graham. 190p. 1998. reprint ed. pap. 20.00 (*1-888265-30-2*) Willow Bend.

Planting of the Presbyterian Church in Northern Virginia Prior to the Organization of Winchester Presbytery, December Fourth, Seventeen Ninety-Four. James R. Graham. LC 26-22114. 168p. 1904. 10.00 (*0-685-65067-7*) VA Bk.

Planting of the Swedish Church in America: Graduation Dissertation of Tobias Eric Biorck. Ed. & Tr. by Ira O. Nothstein. LC 43-18182. (Augustana College Library Publications: No. 19). 39p. 1943. pap. 4.00 (*0-910182-14-0*) Augustana Coll.

Planting Seeds of Hope: How to Reach a New Generation of African Americans with the Gospel. abr. ed. Institute for the Black Family Staff. Ed. by Eugene Seals & Matthew Parker. 180p. 1998. 11.99 (*0-8024-5427-5*) Moody.

Planting Spiritual Seeds: 75 Nature Activities to Help Children & Youth Learn about God. Judy G. Smith. LC 93-32019. 96p. (Orig.). 1994. pap. 113.95 (*0-687-10501-3*) Abingdon.

Planting Tail Feathers: Tribal Survival & Public Law 280. Carole Goldberg-Ambrose. Tr. by Timothy C. Seward. LC 96-60473. 246p. (Orig.). (C). 1997. pap. 15.00 (*0-935626-44-1*) U Cal AISC.

Planting the Children. Lola Haskins. LC 82-1958. (University of Central Florida Contemporary Poetry Ser.). 72p. 1983. 14.95 (*0-8130-0727-5*) U Press Fla.

Planting the Country Way: A Hands-On Approach. John Brookes. LC 97-74411. (Illus.). 192p. 1997. 32.95 (*0-563-36799-7*, BBC-Parkwest) Parkwest Pubns.

Planting the Faith: A History of St. John's Episcopal Church-Memphis, Tennessee. Betty B. Larkey. (Illus.). 200p. 1996. write for info. (*0-9654666-0-4*) St Johns Episcopal.

Planting the Future: Developing an Agriculture That Sustains Land & Community. Ed. by Elizabeth A. Bird et al. LC 94-41959. (Illus.). 300p. 1995. pap. text 17.95 (*0-8138-2072-3*) Iowa St U Pr.

***Planting the Future: Saving Our Medicinal Herbs.** Ed. by Rosemary Gladstar & Pamela Hirsch. (Illus.). 320p. 2000. pap. 22.95 (*0-89281-894-8*) Inner Tradit.

Planting the Grassroots: Structuring Citizen Participation. Steven H. Haeberle. LC 89-3679. 164p. 1989. 52.95 (*0-275-93219-2*, C3219, Praeger Pubs) Greenwood.

Planting the Landscape: A Professional Approach to Garden Design. Nancy A. Leszczynski. LC 97-17966. (Illus.). 224p. 1998. 42.95 (*0-442-02429-0*, VNR) Wiley.

Planting the Landscape: A Professional Approach to Garden Design. Nancy A. Leszczynski. (Illus.). 224p. 1998. 59.95 (*0-471-29215-X*) Wiley.

Planting the Voice: Poems from Poems. Lynn Butler. (University of Central Florida Contemporary Poetry Ser.). 104p. 1989. 17.95 (*0-8130-0921-9*); pap. 10.95 (*0-8130-0937-5*) U Press Fla.

Planting the Voice: Poems from Poems. Lynn Butler. LC 88-32407. (Contemporary Poetry Ser.). 103p. 1989. reprint ed. pap. 32.00 (*0-608-04480-6*, 206522500001) Bks Demand.

Planting Trees: Special Public Works Programmes Booklet No. 7. iii, 278p. 1993. pap. 18.00 (*92-2-108518-X*) Intl Labour Office.

Planting Trees in the Developing World: A Sociology of International Organizations. Steven R. Brechin. LC 96-27636. (Illus.). 280p. 1997. text 48.50 (*0-8018-5439-3*) Johns Hopkins.

Planting Trouble: The Barzon Debtors' Movement in Mexico. Heather L. Williams. 53p. 1996. pap. 7.50 (*1-878367-35-8*) UCSD Ctr US-Mex.

Planting Wetlands & Dams: A Practical Guide to Wetland Design, Construction & Propagation. Nick Romanowski. LC 99-165249. (Illus.). 80p. 1998. pap. 22.95 (*0-86840-608-2*, Pub. by New South Wales Univ Pr) Intl Spec Bk.

Plantings. Glenn Russell. (Illus.). 47p. (Orig.). 1989. pap. 3.00 (*0-926935-34-8*) Runaway Spoon.

Plantons "Parmenides" Franz Von Kutschera. (GER.). xi, 171p. (C). 1995. pap. text 36.70 (*3-11-014557-X*); lib. bdg. 67.70 (*3-11-014910-9*) De Gruyter.

Plantos Debajo del Mar. Chelsea House Publishing Staff. (SPA., Illus.). 32p. (YA). (gr. 3 up). 1996. lib. bdg. 15.95 (*0-7910-4022-4*) Chelsea Hse.

Plants. (Make it Work Ser.). 42p. (J). (gr. 4-8). pap. write for info. (*1-882210-41-7*) Action Pub.

Plants. (Jump Ser.). (Illus.). 32p. (J). (gr. 2-7). pap. write for info. (*1-882210-31-X*) Action Pub.

Plants. 1997. 4.95 (*1-55708-491-2*, MCR749) McDonald Pub Co.

Plants. Wendy Baker & Andrew Haslam. (Make It Work! Ser.). (Illus.). (J). 15.95 (*0-590-74523-9*); pap. 9.99 (*0-590-24331-4*) Scholastic Inc.

Plants. Patricia Ball. (Hands-On Minds-On Science Ser.). (Illus.). 96p. 1994. pap., teacher ed. 11.95 (*1-55734-629-1*) Tchr Create Mat.

Plants. Melvin Berger. Ed. by Susan Evento. (Macmillan Early Science Big Bks.). (Illus.). (J). (ps-2). 1995. pap. write for info. (*1-56784-164-3*) Newbridge Educ.

Plants. David Black & Anthony Huxley. (World of Science Ser.). (Illus.). 64p. 1985. 15.95 (*0-8160-1065-X*) Facts on File.

Plants. Sue Boulais. 1995. 3.95 (*1-55708-475-0*, MCT1006) McDonald Pub Co.

Plants. Lorraine Conway. 64p. (J). (gr. 5 up). 1980. 8.99 (*0-916456-69-2*, GA 176) Good Apple.

Plants. Ed. by Christine J. Dillon. (My First Report Ser.). (Illus.). 52p. (J). (gr. 1-3). 1997. ring bd. 5.95 (*1-57896-043-6*, 2344) Hewitt Res Fnd.

Plants. Gillian Dorfman & Sheila Galbraith. (World Wildlife Ser.: No. S864-3). (Illus.). (J). (gr. k-3). 1989. pap. 3.95 (*0-7214-5214-0*, Ladybrd) Penguin Putnam.

Plants. Catherine H. Howell & National Geographic Society (U. S.) Staff. LC 97-28649. (National Geographic Nature Library). (J). 1997. write for info. (*0-7922-7045-2*) Natl Geog.

Plants. Ladybird Books Staff. (Ladybird Learners Ser.: No. 8911-9). (J). 1991. pap. 3.95 (*0-7214-5327-9*, Ladybrd) Penguin Putnam.

Plants. Adrienne Mason & Deborah Hodge. (Starting with Science Ser.). (Illus.). 32p. (J). (gr. k-4). 1998. 14.95 (*1-55074-193-4*, Pub. by Kids Can Pr) Genl Dist Srvs.

Plants. Moore & Evans. (Illus.). 16p. (J). (gr. 1-3). 1986. pap., teacher ed. 5.95 (*1-55799-091-3*, 801) Evan-Moor Edu Pubs.

***Plants.** Alexandra Parsons. (Make It Work! Science Ser.). (Illus.). (J). (gr. 4-7). 2000. pap. 6.95 (*1-58728-359-X*) Two Can Pub.

Plants. Alexandra Parsons & Jon Barnes. (Make It Work! Ser.). (Illus.). 48p. (J). pap. 7.95 (*0-590-24403-5*) Scholastic Inc.

Plants. Ed. by Penguin Books Staff. (Learners Ser.). 48p. (J). text 3.50 (*0-7214-1709-4*, Ladybrd) Penguin Putnam.

Plants. Steve Pollock. (Find Out about Ser.). (Illus.). 24p. (J). 1996. 9.95 (*0-563-37335-0*, Pub. by BBC) Parkwest Pubns.

Plants. Ed. by Scholastic, Inc. Staff. (Discovery Box Ser.). (Illus.). 32p. (J). (gr. 1-5). 1997. 11.95 (*0-590-92673-X*) Scholastic Inc.

Plants. Linda Schwartz. (Science Mini Units Ser.). (Illus.). 48p. (J). (gr. 2-5). 1990. pap. 6.95 (*0-88160-189-6*, LW 148) Learning Wks.

Plants. Alvin Silverstein et al. (Kingdoms of Life Ser.). (Illus.). 64p. (J). (gr. 5-8). 1995. lib. bdg. 21.40 (*0-8050-3519-2*) TFC Bks NY.

Plants. Lyndall Thomas. LC 98-4237. (Interfact Ser.). (Illus.). 48p. (J). (gr. 2-8). 1999. spiral bd. write for info. incl. cd-rom (*0-7166-7239-1*) World Bk.

***Plants.** Two Can Publishing Ltd. Staff. (Make It Work! Science Ser.). (Illus.). (J). 2000. 12.95 (*1-58728-367-0*) Two Can Pub.

Plants. Richard Walker. LC 93-19075. (Picturepedia Ser.). (J). 1993. 12.95 (*1-56458-383-X*) DK Pub Inc.

***Plants.** unabridged ed. Ontario Science Centre Staff. (Starting with Science Ser.). 32p. (J). (gr. k-4). 2000. pap. 6.95 (*1-55074-395-3*, Pub. by Kids Can Pr) Genl Dist Srvs.

***Plants, Vol. 2443.** Juli Snyder & Kimberlee Graves. Ed. by Wendy Blocher. (Primary Theme Ser.). (Illus.). 32p. 1999. pap. 6.98 (*1-57471-627-1*, 2443) Creat Teach Pr.

Plants, Vol. 2822. Judy Hechtman & Sandra F. Grove. Ed. by Karen P. Hall. (Explore & Discover Ser.). (Illus.). 32p. (J). (gr. 1-3). 1996. pap., teacher ed. 5.98 (*1-57471-164-4*, 2822) Creat Teach Pr.

Plants: A BBC Fact Finder Book. Andrew Charman. (Illus.). 48p. 1996. pap. text 8.95 (*0-563-35538-7*, BBC-Parkwest) Parkwest Pubns.

Plants: A Creative Hands-On Approach to Science. Wendy Baker & Andrew Haslam. LC 92-24559. (Make It Work! Ser.). (Illus.). 48p. (J). (gr. 2-5). 1993. 12.95 (*0-689-71664-8*) Aladdin.

***Plants: A Novel.** Fred Bigjim. 240p. 1999. pap. 12.95 (*0-7392-0496-3*, PO3857) Morris Pubng.

Plants: An Integrated Unit. Kathy Rogers. (Primary Thematic Units Ser.). (Illus.). 96p. (Orig.). 1994. pap. 12.95 (*0-944459-83-8*) ECS Lrn Systs.

Plants: Evolution & Diversity. 3rd ed. Barbara Crandall-Stotler & Raymond E. Stotler. 212p. 1995. spiral bd. 28.95 (*0-7872-1965-7*) Kendall-Hunt.

Plants: Grades 1-3. Jo Ellen Moor. Ed. by Marilyn Evans. (Science Picture Cards Ser.: Vol. 2). (Illus.). 24p. 1998. pap., teacher ed. 12.95 (*1-55799-693-8*, 864) Evan-Moor Edu Pubs.

Plants: Grades 1-3. Jo Ellen Moor. Ed. by Marilyn Evans. (Science Works for Kids Ser.: Vol. 6). (Illus.). 80p. 1998. pap., teacher ed. 9.95 (*1-55799-687-3*, 858) Evan-Moor Edu Pubs.

Plants: Hands-on Minds-on Science. 1997. text 11.95 (*1-55734-625-9*) Tchr Create Mat.

Plants: Life Cycles. Gail Saunders-Smith. (J). 1998. 53.00 (*0-516-29779-1*) Childrens.

Plants: Origin & Evolution. Alessandro Garassino. LC 94-3838. (Beginnings Origins & Evolution Ser.). (Illus.). 40p. (J). (gr. 3-10). 1994. lib. bdg. 24.26 (*0-8114-3332-3*) Raintree Steck-V.

Plants: Thematic Unit. Sterling. (Illus.). 80p. (J). (ps-1). 1995. pap. text, wbk. ed. 9.95 (*1-55734-244-X*) Tchr Create Mat.

Plants: 2,400 Copyright-Free Illustrations of Flowers, Trees, Fruits & Vegetables. Ed. by Jim Harter. LC 98-24685. (Illus.). 374p. 1998. pap. 19.95 (*0-486-40264-9*) Dover.

Plants Activity Book. Charlene Stout. Ed. by Kathy Rogers. (Hands-On Science Ser.). (Illus.). 48p. 1998. pap., wbk. ed. 6.95 (*1-56472-117-5*) Edupress Inc.

Plants, Agriculture & Human Society. Norman Richardson & Thomas Stubbs. LC 77-72644. 1978. pap. text 26.95 (*0-8053-8215-1*) Benjamin-Cummings.

Plants & Animals see Macmillan Encyclopedia of Science

Plants & Animals in Nature, Set. Lorraine Conway. (Superific Science Ser.). (Illus.). 64p. (J). (gr. 5 up). 1986. student ed. 7.99 (*0-86653-356-7*, GA 797) Good Apple.

Plants & Animals in the Life of the Kuna. Jorge Ventocilla et al. Tr. by Elisabeth King from SPA. (Translations from Latin America Ser.). (Illus.). 160p. (Orig.). (C). 1995. pap. 25.00 (*0-292-78725-1*); pap. 12.95 (*0-292-78726-X*) U of Tex Pr.

Plants & Animals of Hawaii. Susan Scott. LC 91-70851. (Illus.). 176p. 1991. 19.95 (*0-935848-92-4*) Bess Pr.

Plants & Animals of the Pacific Northwest: An Illustrated Guide to the Natural History of Western Oregon, Washington, & British Columbia. Eugene N. Kozloff. LC 75-40875. (Illus.). 280p. 1976. pap. 29.95 (*0-295-95597-X*) U of Wash Pr.

Plants & Animals Rare in South Dakota: A Field Guide. Michael M. Melius. LC 87-50402. (Illus.). 120p. (Orig.). 1987. pap. 3.00 (*0-937603-05-8*) Melius Pub.

Plants & Animals Source Book. (Pathways Through Science Ser.). 1993. pap. text. write for info. (*0-582-09421-6*, Pub. by Addison-Wesley) Longman.

Plants & Civilization. 2nd ed. Baker. (Biology Ser.). 1970. pap. 5.50 (*0-534-02026-7*) Wadsworth Pub.

Plants & Flowers. Sally Hewitt. LC 98-16704. (It's Science Ser.). (J). 1998. student ed. 20.00 (*0-516-21176-5*) Childrens.

Plants & Flowers. Sally Hewitt. (It's Science! Ser.). (Illus.). 32p. (J). (gr. k-3). 1999. pap. text 6.95 (*0-516-26341-2*) Childrens.

Plants & Flowers. Joyce Pope. LC 91-45378. (Nature Club Ser.). (Illus.). 32p. (J). (gr. 3-6). 1993. lib. bdg. 17.25 (*0-8167-2779-1*) Troll Communs.

Plants & Flowers. Joyce Pope. LC 91-45378. (Nature Club Ser.). (Illus.). 32p. (J). (gr. 3-6). 1996. pap. 4.95 (*0-8167-2780-5*) Troll Communs.

Plants & Flowers of Desert. (Butterly Bks.). (ARA., Illus.). 31p. 8.95 (*0-86685-402-9*, LDL252, Pub. by Librairie du Liban) Intl Bk Ctr.

Plants & Flowers of Hawaii. Seymour H. Sohmer. LC 86-19231. (Illus.). 144p. 1987. 18.95 (*0-8248-1096-1*) UH Pr.

Plants & Flowers of the Desert. Illus. by Fiona Almeleh. (Butterfly Bks.). 32p. (J). (gr. 3-5). 1985. 8.95 (*0-86685-446-0*) Intl Bk Ctr.

Plants & Flowers, 1786 Illustrations for Artists & Designers. Bassette & Chapman. (Illus.). 288p. (Orig.). pap. 14.95 (*0-486-26957-4*) Dover.

Plants & Harappan Subsistence. Steven Weber. (C). 1992. 19.00 (*81-204-0579-X*, Pub. by Oxford IBH) S Asia.

Plants & Man. Frederick O. Bower. (C). 1980. text 235.00 (*0-89771-565-9*, Pub. by Intl Bk Distr) St Mut.

Plants & Man. Frederick O. Bower. 365p. 1980. reprint ed. 500.00 (*0-7855-3073-8*, Pub. by Intl Bk Distr) St Mut.

Plants & Man on the Seychelles Coast: A Study in Historical Biogeography. Jonathan D. Sauer. LC 67-13556. (Illus.). 148p. reprint ed. pap. 45.90 (*0-8357-4753-0*, 203767500009) Bks Demand.

Plants & Nitrogen. O. A. Lewis. (Studies in Biology: No. 166). 112p. (C). 1992. pap. text 15.95 (*0-521-42776-2*) Cambridge U Pr.

Plants & People: A Walk Through a World of Plants at the Enid A. Haupt Conservatory. Allan Appel & New York Botanical Garden Staff. LC 96-54479. 1997. pap. 10.00 (*0-89327-425-9*) NY Botanical.

Plants & People: Economic Botany in Northern Europe 800-1800 A.D. Ed. by J. H. Dickson & R. R. Mill. 198p. 1995. pap. 17.50 (*0-7486-0526-6*, Pub. by Edinburgh U Pr) Col U Pr.

Plants & People: Vegetation Change in North America. Thomas R. Vale. Ed. by C. Gregory Knight. LC 82-8865. (Resource Publications in Geography). (Illus.). (Orig.). 1982. pap. 15.00 (*0-89291-151-4*) Assn Am Geographers.

Plants & People of the Golden Triangle: Ethnobotany of the Hill Tribes of Northern Thailand. Edward F. Anderson. LC 92-25857. (Illus.). 272p. 1993. 69.95 (*0-931146-25-9*, Dioscorides) Timber.

Plants & People of the Sonoran Desert. 1988. 0.75 (*0-9605656-5-5*) Desert Botanical.

***Plants & Plant Eaters.** Michael Chinery. (Secrets of the Rainforest Ser.). (Illus.). 32p. (J). (gr. k-8). 2000. pap. 7.95 (*0-7787-0228-6*); lib. bdg. 19.96 (*0-7787-0218-9*) Crabtree Pub Co.

***Plants & Plant Lore in Ancient Greece.** John Raven. (Illus.). 144p. 2000. 36.95 (*0-904920-40-2*, Pub. by Leopards Head Pr) David Brown.

***Plants & Politics.** G. Meester. 255p. 1999. pap. 67.00 (*90-74134-72-6*) Wageningen Pers.

Plants & Processes in Wetlands. Ed. by P. I. Boon & M. Brock. (Illus.). 180p. 1995. 50.00 (*0-643-05698-X*, Pub. by CSIRO) Accents Pubns.

Plants & Protected Areas: A Guide to the In-Situ Management. J. Tuxill & G. P. Nobhan. 264p. 1998. pap. 75.00 (*0-7487-3990-4*) St Mut.

Plants & Seeds: Easy Readers Science. Cindy Barden. (Easy Readers Ser.). 16p. (J). (ps-1). 1997. pap. 2.49 (*1-57690-281-1*) Tchr Create Mat.

Plants & Society. Ed. by S. L. Kochhar. (Illus.). 649p. (C). 1990. text 70.00 (*0-333-45141-4*); pap. text 30.00 (*0-333-44867-7*) Scholium Intl.

Plants & Society. Estelle Levetin & Karen McMahon. 416p. (C). 1995. text. write for info. (*0-697-14064-4*, WCB McGr Hill) McGrw-H Hghr Educ.

Plants & Society. Levitin & McMahon. 1995. teacher ed. 15.31 (*0-697-24323-0*, WCB McGr Hill) McGrw-H Hghr Educ.

Plants & Society. 2nd ed. Levetin. LC 98-18213. 496p. 1998. pap. 57.50 (*0-697-34552-1*) McGraw.

Plants & Society. 3rd ed. Estelle Levetin. 2002. 53.25 (*0-07-290949-8*) McGraw.

Plants & the Chemical Elements: Biochemistry, Uptake, Tolerance & Toxicity. Ed. by Margaret E. Farago. 292p. 1994. 205.00 (*3-527-28269-6*, Wiley-VCH) Wiley.

Plants & the Daylight Spectrum. Ed. by Harold Smith. LC 81-66697. 1982. text 184.00 (*0-12-650980-8*) Acad Pr.

Plants & the Skin. C. R. Lovell. (Illus.). 280p. 1993. 99.95 (*0-632-02562-X*) Blackwell Sci.

Plants & Trees, 4 vols. J. M. Parramon. (Illus.). 32p. (J). (ps-3). 1991. pap., boxed set 23.95 (*0-8120-7771-7*) Barron.

Plants & Us. Angela Royston. LC 98-42810. (Plants Ser.). 32p. (J). 1999. lib. bdg. write for info. (*1-57572-825-7*) Heinemann Lib.

Plants & UV-B: Responses to Environmental Change. Ed. by Peter Lumsden. (Society for Experimental Biology Seminar Ser.: Vol. 64). (Illus.). 375p. (C). 1997. text 110.00 (*0-521-57222-3*) Cambridge U Pr.

Plants, Animals & Humid Beans: Fun Tales from NEA Members. Leona Hiraoka & National Education Association of the United State. LC 97-33434. 90 p. 1997. pap. 7.95 (*0-8106-1880-X*) NEA.

Plants Are Alive. Philp & Horn. (Illus.). (Orig.). 1989. pap. text 16.95 (*1-877991-14-7*, AP4286) Flinn Scientific.

Plants Are Special Friends. Alex N. Holland. (Illus.). 14p. (J). (gr. k-4). 1997. pap. 12.88 (*1-56606-047-8*) Bradley Mann.

Plants Are Still Like People. Jerry Baker. (Orig.). 1999. pap. 18.95 (*0-452-28105-9*) NAL.

Plants Are Waters' Factories: The Book about Drought! Michael A. Weinberg. LC 75-4850. 110p. 1976. pap. 2.95 (*0-9601014-1-1*) Weinberg.

Plants Around Us. Malcolm Dixon & Karen Smith. LC 98-6975. (Young Scientists Ser.). (Illus.). 32p. (J). 1998. lib. bdg. 21.30 (*1-887068-71-6*) Smart Apple.

Plants as Biomonitors: Indicators for Heavy Metals in the Terrestrial Environment. Ed. by Bernd Markert. LC 92-34620. 645p. 1993. 236.00 (*3-527-30001-5*, Wiley-VCH) Wiley.

Plants As Indicators of Ground Water. Oscar E. Meinzer. (Illus.). 100p. 1997. reprint ed. pap. 49.95 (*0-9641628-7-3*) Karo Hollow.

Plants As Solar Collectors: Optimizing Productivity for Energy. J. Coombs et al. 1983. text 106.00 (*90-277-1625-0*) Kluwer Academic.

***Plants Bite Back!** Richard Platt. LC 99-20403. (Eyewitness Readers). 48p. (J). (gr. 2-3). 1999. 12.95 (*0-7894-4755-X*); pap. text 3.95 (*0-7894-4754-1*) DK Pub Inc.

Plants Collected by the Vernay Nyasaland Expedition of 1946: Angiospermae & General Index: Conclusion. J. P. M. Brenan et al. (Memoirs Ser.: Vol. 9 (1)). 132p. 1954. pap. 10.00 (*0-89327-028-8*) NY Botanical.

Plants Collected by the Vernay Nyasaland Expedition of 1946: Angiospermae: Continuation. J. P. M. Brenan et al. (Memoirs Ser.: Vol. 8 (5)). 102p. 1954. pap. 10.00 (*0-89327-033-4*) NY Botanical.

Plants et Leurs Noms: Essai de Phytonomie Structurale. Bruno De Foucault. (Dissertationes Botanicae Ser.: Band 201). (Illus.). iv, 64p. 1993. 30.00 (*3-443-64113-X*, Pub. by Gebruder Borntraeger) Balogh.

Plants Fed to Village Ruminants in Indonesia: Notes on 136 Species, Their Composition & Significance in Village Farming Systems. Ed. by J. Lowry et al. 60p. 1992. pap. 45.00 (*1-86320-071-1*, Pub. by ACIAR) St Mut.

Plants Feed on Sunlight: And Other Facts about Things That Grow. Helen Taylor. LC 97-51778. (You'd Never Believe It, but... Ser.). (Illus.). 32p. (J). (gr. k-2). 1998. lib. bdg. 19.90 (*0-7613-0814-8*, Copper Beech Bks) Millbrook Pr.

***Plants for a Future: Edible & Useful Plants for a Healthier World.** Ken Fern. (Illus.). 320p. 2000. pap. 30.00 (*1-85623-011-2*, Pub. by Hyden House) Chelsea Green Pub.

Plants for All Season: Creating a Garden with Year-Round Beauty. Andrew Lawson. LC 98-139483. 168p. 1998. pap. 19.95 (*0-14-027057-4*) Viking Penguin.

Plants for All Seasons: Beautiful & Versatile Plants That Change Through the Year. Ursula Buchan. 1999. 29.95 (*1-84000-051-1*, Pub. by Mitchell Beazley) Trafalgar.

Plants for American Landscapes. Neil G. Odenwald et al. LC 96-22844. (Illus.). 368p. 1996. 49.95 (*0-8071-2093-6*) La State U Pr.

Plants for Arid Lands. Ed. by Gerald E. Wickens et al. 500p. (C). 1989. pap. 54.95 (*0-04-445330-2*) Thomson Learn.

Plants for Balconies, Verandas & Window Boxes. Denise Greig. (Illus.). 72p. (Orig.). 1993. 12.95 (*0-86417-370-9*, Pub. by Kangaroo Pr) Seven Hills Bk.

***Plants for Dry Climates.** Mary Rose Duffield & Warren Jones. (Illus.). 192p. 2000. pap. 19.95 (*1-55561-270-9*) Fisher Bks.

Plants for Dry Climates: How to Select, Grow & Enjoy. Mary R. Duffield. LC 98-36073. 1998. pap. 17.95 (*1-55561-176-1*) Fisher Bks.

Plants for Dry Gardens. James Taylor. 1998. pap. 52.00 (*0-7112-0772-0*, Pub. by F Lincoln) St Mut.

***Plants for Dry Gardens: Beating the Drought.** James Taylor. (Illus.). 192p. 2000. pap. text 19.95 (*0-7112-1222-8*) F Lincoln.

Plants for Environmental Studies. Wun-Cheng Wang et al. LC 96-47075. 576p. 1997. boxed set 84.95 (*1-56670-028-0*) CRC Pr.

Plants for Food & Medicine: Proceedings of the Joint Conference of the Society for Economic Botany & the International Society for Ethnopharmacology, London, 1-6 July 1996. Ed. by H. D. Prendergast et al. (Illus.). 438p. 1998. pap. 48.00 (*1-900347-55-5*, Pub. by Royal Botnic Grdns) Balogh.

Plants for Human Consumption: An Annotated Checklist of the Edible Phanerogams & Ferns. Guenther Kunkel. xiv, 393p. 1984. reprint ed. 92.00 (*3-87429-216-9*, 006015, Pub. by Koeltz Sci Bks) Lubrecht & Cramer.

Plants for Malaria, Plants for Fever: Medicinal Species in Latin America - Bibliographic Study. W. Milliken. 150p. 1997. 50.00 (*1-900347-29-6*, Pub. by Royal Botnic Grdns) Balogh.

Plants for Natural Gardens: Southwestern Native & Adaptive Trees, Shrubs, Wildflowers & Grasses. Judith Phillips. (Illus.). 160p. 1995. pap. 27.50 (*0-89013-281-X*) Museum NM Pr.

P

Plants for People: The Psychological & Physiological Effects of Plants. Bibliography. Judith Keane. 54p. (Orig.). (C). 1994. pap. text 20.00 (*0-7881-0347-4*) DIANE Pub.

Plants for Play: A Plant Selection Guide for Children's Outdoor Environments. Robin C. Moore. LC 92-62234. 1993. pap. 16.95 (*0-944661-18-1*) MIG Comns.

***Plants for Pots & Patios.** Roger Phillips. (Book of... Garden Plants Ser.). 2000. pap. 8.99 (*0-375-75443-1*) Random.

Plants for Pots & Patios & How to Grow Them. Roger Phillips & Martyn Rix. (Pan Garden Plants Ser.). (Illus.). 96p. 1998. pap. 12.95 (*0-330-35547-3*, Pub. by Pan) Trans-Atl Phila.

Plants for Problem Places. Linda Yang. 1998. 24.25 (*0-8446-6961-X*) Peter Smith.

***Plants for Profit.** Francis X. Jozwik. Ed. by John Gist. (Illus.). 304p. 2000. 29.95 (*0-916781-21-6*) Andmar Pr.

Plants for Sale. Melanie Harrison. 1996. pap. text 10.95 (*0-86417-695-3*, Pub. by Kangaroo Pr) Seven Hills Bk.

***Plants for Shade.** Roger Phillips. (Book of... Garden Plants Ser.). (Illus.). 2000. pap. 8.99 (*0-375-75444-X*) Random.

Plants for Shade: A Complete Guide to What to Grow in Shade & Woodland. Allen Paterson. (Illus.). 160p. 1994. pap. 17.95 (*0-460-86096-8*, Pub. by J M Dent & Sons) Trafalgar.

Plants for Shade & How to Grow Them. Roger Phillips & Martyn Rix. (Pan Garden Plants Ser.). (Illus.). 96p. 1998. pap. 12.95 (*0-330-35548-1*, Pub. by Pan) Trans-Atl Phila.

Plants for Small Spaces. Stephanie Donaldson & Susan Berry. LC 97-81350. (Illus.). 144p. 1998. 29.95 (*1-57076-117-5*, Trafalgar Sq Pub) Trafalgar.

Plants for the Dry Garden. Peter Thurman. (Illus.). 64p. 1994. 8.95 (*1-85793-112-2*, Pub. by Pavilion Bks Ltd) Trafalgar.

Plants for the Future: A Gardener's Wishbook. Jerome Malitz. (Illus.). 270p. 1996. 34.95 (*0-88192-349-4*) Timber.

Plants for the Home, Vol. 1. John J. Bagnasco. 1975. 15.00 (*0-918134-01-3*) Nature Life.

Plants for Toxicity Assessment. Ed. by Wuncheng Weng et al. LC 90-40925. (Special Technical Publication (STP) Ser.: STP 1091). (Illus.). 360p. 1990. text 87.00 (*0-8031-1397-8*, STP1091) ASTM.

Plants for Toxicity Assessment, STP 1115, Vol. 2. Kenneth R. St. John. Ed. by Joseph W. Gorsuch et al. (Special Technical Publication Ser.). 400p. 1991. text 95.00 (*0-8031-1422-2*, STP1115) ASTM.

***Plants for Tropical Landscapes: A Gardener's Guide.** Fred D. Rauch & Paul R. Weissich. LC 99-26677. 2000. 39.95 (*0-8248-2034-7*) UH Pr.

***Plants for Water Gardens: The Complete Guide to Aquatic Plants.** Helen Nash & Steve Stroupe. (Illus.). 224p. 1999. pap. 19.95 (*0-8069-9980-2*) Sterling.

Plants for Winter Beauty. Rita Buchanan. LC 97-10466. (Taylor's Weekend Gardening Guides Ser.). (Illus.). 128p. 1997. pap. 12.95 (*0-395-82750-7*) HM.

Plants for You & Me. Arthur Morton. (Illus.). (J). (gr. k-3). 1992. 12.50 (*1-57842-069-5*) Delmas Creat.

Plants for You & Me. Arthur Morton. Tr. by Suon Thach. (CAM.). (J). (gr. k-3). 1995. 12.50 (*1-57842-072-5*) Delmas Creat.

Plants from Test Tubes: An Introduction to Micropropagation. 3rd rev. ed. Lydiane Kyte & John Kleyn. LC 96-33972. (Illus.). 250p. 1996. 29.95 (*0-88192-361-3*) Timber.

Plants from the Past. James Sutherland. 1988. 24.95 (*0-670-80852-0*) Grossman.

Plants Galore - The General Clerk Simulation. Lovern. (KM - Office Procedures Ser.). 1984. pap. 15.95 (*0-538-25510-2*) S-W Pub.

Plants, Genes, & Agriculture. Maarten J. Chrispeels & David E. Sadava. LC 93-45677. (Life Science Ser.). 512p. (C). 1994. 61.25 (*0-86720-871-6*) Jones & Bartlett.

***Plants in Action.** Brian Atwell. (Illus.). (YA). 1999. 74.95 (*0-7329-4439-2*) Macmill Educ.

Plants in Agriculture. James C. Forbes & Drennan Watson. (Illus.). 371p. (C). 1992. text 85.00 (*0-521-41755-4*); pap. text 34.95 (*0-521-42791-6*) Cambridge U Pr.

Plants in Agriculture. James C. Forbes & R. Drennan Watson. (Illus.). 352p. 1991. pap. 27.50 (*0-7131-2891-7*, A3024, Pub. by E A) Routldge.

Plants in Cardiology. Arthur Hollman. 49p. 1992. pap. text 4.00 (*0-7279-0744-1*, Pub. by BMJ Pub) Login Brothers Bk Co.

Plants in Changing Environments: Linking Physiological, Population, & Community Ecology. F. A. Bazzaz. (Illus.). 329p. (C). 1996. text 74.95 (*0-521-39190-3*); pap. text 30.95 (*0-521-39843-6*) Cambridge U Pr.

***Plants in Garden History: An Illustrated History of Plants & Their Influences on Garden Styles-from Ancient Egypt to the Present Day.** Penelope Hobhouse. (Illus.). 336p. 2000. reprint ed. pap. 29.95 (*1-85793-273-0*, Pub. by Pavilion Bks Ltd) Trafalgar.

Plants in Hawaiian Culture. Beatrice H. Krauss. (Illus.). 272p. (Orig.). 1993. pap. 29.95 (*0-8248-1225-5*, Kolowalu Bk) UH Pr.

Plants in Hawaiian Medicine. Beatrice Krauss. (Illus.). 144p. 2000. pap. 11.95 (*1-57306-034-8*) Bess Pr.

Plants in Human Nutrition. A. P. Simopoulos. (World Review of Nutrition & Dietetics Ser.: Vol. 77). (Illus.). xiv, 160p. 1995. 172.25 (*3-8055-6101-6*) S Karger.

***Plants in Indian Medicine, No. 4.** Anthony R. Torkelson. (Cross Name Index to Medicinal Plants Ser.). 560p. 1999. boxed set 350.00 (*0-8493-1085-7*) CRC Pr.

Plants in Indian Temple Art. Shakti M. Gupta. (C). 1996. 110.00 (*81-7018-883-0*, Pub. by BR Pub) S Asia.

Plants in the Indian Puranas: An Ethnobotanical Investigation. P. Sensarma. (C). 1989. 17.50 (*81-85109-76-1*, Pub. by Naya Prokash) S Asia.

Plants in the Landscape: Environmental Design 335. Jack Ahern. 229p. (C). 1993. student ed. 22.46 (*1-56870-046-6*) RonJon Pub.

Plants in the Landscapes. 2nd ed. Philip L. Carpenter & Theodore D. Walker. (Illus.). 401p. (C). 1998. reprint ed. text 45.95 (*1-57766-018-8*) Waveland Pr.

Plants in the Light of Healing. Lilli Botchis. (Illus.). 30p. (Orig.). 1995. pap. text 3.95 (*0-9643535-1-2*) Time Portal.

***Plants Invade the Land: Evolutionary & Environmental Perspectives.** Ed. by Patricia G. Gensel & Dianne Edwards. 512p. 2001. text 65.00 (*0-231-11160-6*); pap. text 32.00 (*0-231-11161-4*) Col U Pr.

Plants Man & Ecosystem. 2nd ed. Billings. (Biology Ser.). 1970. pap. 5.50 (*0-534-02027-5*) Wadsworth Pub.

Plants, Man & Life. Edgar Anderson. LC 52-5870. (Illus.). 265p. reprint ed. pap. 82.20 (*0-608-18284-2*, 203153100075) Bks Demand.

Plants, Man & Life. Edgar Anderson. (Illus.). 272p. 1997. reprint ed. 16.95 (*0-915279-44-4*, PLANTSMAN) Miss Botan.

Plants, Myths, & Traditions in India. Shakti & Gupta. (C). 1991. 25.00 (*0-685-50026-8*, Pub. by M Manoharial) S Asia.

Plants of Central Asia: Introduction, Ferns, Bibliography. Ed. by V. I. Grubov. LC 99-36729. (Illus.). 188p. 1999. text 69.00 (*1-57808-060-6*) Science Pubs.

Plants of Chota Nagpur Including Jaspur & Sirguja. Ed. by F. F. Wood. (C). 1979. text 150.00 (*0-89771-680-9*, Pub. by Intl Bk Distr) St Mut.

Plants of Chota Nagpur Including Jaspur & Sirguja. F. F. Wood. 97p. (C). 1979. reprint ed. 100.00 (*0-7855-3105-X*, Pub. by Intl Bk Distr) St Mut.

Plants of Coastal British Columbia Including Washington, Oregon & Alaska. Jim Pojar. (Illus.). 528p. 1994. pap. 19.95 (*1-55105-042-0*) Lone Pine.

Plants of Colonial Days. unabridged ed. Raymond L. Taylor. (Illus.). 110p. 1996. reprint ed. pap. text 3.95 (*0-486-29404-8*) Dover.

Plants of Colonial Williamsburg: How to Identify 200 of Colonial America's Flowers, Herbs, & Trees. Joan P. Dutton. LC 76-50633. (Illus.). 193p. 1979. pap. 12.95 (*0-87935-042-3*) Colonial Williamsburg.

Plants of Deep Canyon: The Central Coachella Valley of California. LC 79-63644. 1979. 14.95 (*0-942290-03-8*) Boyd Deep Canyon.

Plants of Desert Dunes. Avinoam Danin. LC 95-37101. (Adaptations of Desert Organisms Ser.). (Illus.). 192p. 1996. 99.00 (*3-540-59260-1*) Spr-Verlag.

Plants of Extremes, Contrasts, & Superlatives (Orchideen - Orchids. Pflanzen der Extreme, Gegensaetze und Superlative) Karlheinz Senghas. (ENG & GER., Illus.). 182p. 1993. 92.00 (*3-8263-2642-3*, Pub. by Blckwell Wissenschafts) Balogh.

Plants of Hawaii: How to Grow Them. rev. ed. Fortunato Teho. (Illus.). 83p. 1992. pap. 7.95 (*0-912180-48-X*) Petroglyph.

Plants of India. Cecil J. Saldhana & J. Dhawan. (C). 1987. 28.50 (*0-8364-2116-7*, Pub. by Oxford IBH) S Asia.

Plants of Life, Plants of Death. Frederick J. Simoons. LC 98-9689. 592p. 1998. 65.00 (*0-299-15900-0*); pap. 34.95 (*0-299-15904-3*) U of Wis Pr.

Plants of Love: Aphrodisiacs in Myth, History, & the Present. Christian Ratsch. LC 97-7265. (Illus.). 208p. (Orig.). 1997. pap. 19.95 (*0-89815-928-8*) Ten Speed Pr.

***Plants of Mount Cameroon: A Conservation Checklist.** S. Cable & M. Cheek. 198p. 1998. pap. 60.00 (*1-900347-57-1*, Pub. by Royal Botnic Grdns) Balogh.

Plants of Mount Kinabalu Vol. 1: Ferns. B. S. Parris et al. viii, 165p. 1992. pap. 30.00 (*0-947643-38-9*, Pub. by Royal Botnic Grdns) Balogh.

Plants of Mount Kinabalu Vol. 2: Orchids. J. J. Wood et al. (Illus.). xii, 411p. 1993. pap. 60.00 (*0-947643-46-X*, Pub. by Royal Botnic Grdns) Balogh.

***Plants of Mt. Kinabalu, Vol. 3.** John H. Beaman & Reed S. Beaman. (Illus.). 243p. 1998. 60.00 (*983-812-026-X*, Pub. by Royal Botnic Grdns) Balogh.

Plants of Mystery & Magic: A Photographic Guide. Michael Jordan. LC 97-172222. (Illus.). 128p. 1997. 27.95 (*0-7137-2645-8*, Pub. by Blandford Pr) Sterling.

Plants of 1917. Ed. by Wolfgang Hageney. (ENG, FRE, GER, ITA & SPA., Illus.). 192p. 1986. 54.95 (*88-7070-017-8*) Belvedere USA.

Plants of 1917, Vol. I-Spring 1. Ed. by Wolfgang Hageney. (Illus.). 55p. 1986. pap. 16.95 (*88-7070-087-9*) Belvedere USA.

Plants of 1917, Vol. 2-Spring 2. Ed. by Wolfgang Hageney. (Illus.). 55p. 1986. pap. 16.95 (*88-7070-088-7*) Belvedere USA.

Plants of 1917, Vol. 3-Summer 1. Ed. by Wolfgang Hageney. (Illus.). 55p. 1986. pap. 16.95 (*88-7070-089-5*) Belvedere USA.

Plants of 1917, Vol. 4-Summer 2. Ed. by Wolfgang Hageney. (Illus.). 55p. 1986. pap. 16.95 (*88-7070-090-9*) Belvedere USA.

Plants of 1917, Vol. 5-Autumn-Winter. Ed. by Wolfgang Hageney. (Illus.). 55p. 1986. pap. 16.95 (*88-7070-091-7*) Belvedere USA.

Plants of Northern British Columbia Revised. 2nd rev. ed. Andy MacKinnon et al. 1999. pap. 19.95 (*1-55105-108-7*) Lone Pine.

Plants of Old Hawaii. Lois Lucas. LC 82-72199. (Illus.). 112p. (Orig.). 1982. pap. 7.95 (*0-935848-11-8*) Bess Pr.

Plants of Pehr Forsskal's Flora Aegyptiaco-Arabica. F. N. Hepper & I. Friis. (Illus.). xii, 400p. 1994. pap. 30.00 (*0-947643-62-1*, Pub. by Royal Botnic Grdns) Balogh.

***Plants of Pennsylvania: An Illustrated Manual.** Ann F. Rhoads & Timothy A. Block. LC 99-89946. (Illus.). 1040p. 2000. 65.00 (*0-8122-3535-5*) U of Pa Pr.

Plants of Pictured Rocks National Lakeshore: A Complete, Illustrated Guide to the Plants of America's First National Lakeshore. Steve W. Chadde. (Pocketflora Guide Ser.: Vol. 2). (Illus.). 104p. (Orig.). 1996. pap. 8.95 (*0-9651385-1-8*) PocketFlora.

Plants of Prey see Nature Close-Ups

Plants of Quetico & the Ontario Shield. Shan Walshe. (Illus.). 216p. 1980. text 14.95 (*0-8020-3370-9*) U of Toronto Pr.

***Plants of Rocky Mountain National Park.** Richard G. Beidleman. (Illus.). 2000. pap. 29.95 (*1-56044-910-1*) Falcon Pub Inc.

Plants of Saratoga & Eastern New York: An Identification Manual. H. H. Howard. write for info. (*0-912756-30-6*) Union Coll.

Plants of Saratoga & Eastern New York: An Identification Manual. H. H. Howard. (FRE.). 320p. 1995. pap. 15.95 (*0-614-03742-5*) Union Coll.

Plants of South Florida. Jean Seavey. (Illus.). 1994. pap. write for info. (*1-892772-00-0*) Seavey.

Plants of Southern Interior British Columbia see Plants of Southern Interior British Columbia & the Inland Northwest

Plants of Southern Interior British Columbia. Ray Coupe & Roberta Parish. Ed. by Dennis Lloyd. LC 97-193096. (Illus.). 464p. 1996. pap. 19.95 (*1-55105-057-9*) Lone Pine.

***Plants of Southern Interior British Columbia & the Inland Northwest.** Roberta Parish et al. Orig. Title: Plants of Southern Interior British Columbia. (Illus.). 454p. 1999. pap. 19.95 (*1-55105-219-9*) Lone Pine.

Plants of Southernmost Texas. Alfred Richardson. 298p. (Orig.). 1990. pap. text 13.00 (*0-9627293-0-2*) Gorgas Sci Fndtn.

Plants of the Adelaide Plains & Hills. Gilbert Dashorst. (Illus.). 224p. 1990. 32.50 (*0-86417-323-7*, Pub. by Kangaroo Pr) Seven Hills Bk.

Plants of the Bible. Harold N. Moldenke & Alma L. Moldenke. 384p. 1986. reprint ed. pap. 11.95 (*0-486-25069-5*) Dover.

Plants of the Bible: And How to Grow Them. Allan A. Swenson. LC 93-43773. (Illus.). (Orig.). 1994. 18.95 (*1-55972-216-9*, Birch Ln Pr) Carol Pub Group.

Plants of the Bible: And How to Grow Them. Allan A. Swenson. (Illus.). 240p. (Orig.). 1995. pap. 9.95 (*0-8065-1615-1*, Citadel Pr) Carol Pub Group.

***Plants of the Black Hills & Bear Lodge Mountains. Gary E. Larson & James R. Johnson. 608p. 1999. pap. 37.95 (*0-913062-05-7*) SD Agriculture.**

Plants of the Black Hills & Bear Lodge Mountains is a color-illustrated guide with 758 photographs covering about 600 vascular plant species residing in the Black Hills of South Dakota & Wyoming. Plants are categorized into four groups, including ferns & horsetails, flowering forbs, grasses & grasslike plants & woody plants. Within these four groups, subjects are arranged alphabetically by scientific names of the family & the species. Each entry includes a description of the plant, its habitat, an account of regional & worldwide distribution & information about plant values to wildlife & human cultures, past & present. A geomorphologic map & overview of vegetation types encountered in the Black Hills is given an introductory section. Keywords: plants, Black Hills, Bear Lodge Mountains, South Dakota, Wyoming vegetation, wildflowers, grasses, trees, shrubs, ferns, plant identification, pictorial works. To order call 1-800-301-9293, or e-mail sdsu_bulletinroom@sdstate.edu or contact the Bulletin Room, South Dakota State University, Brookings, SD 57007 & ask for the book by title.

Publisher Paid Annotation.

Plants of the Chicago Region. 4th rev. ed. Floyd Swink & Gerould Wilhelm. (IAS Special Publications). 932p. (C). 1994. reprint ed. 40.00 (*1-883362-01-6*) IN Acad Sci.

Plants of the Coast of Coromandel, 3 vols. William Roxburgh. (C). 1988. text 2000.00 (*0-7855-6002-5*, Pub. by Scientific) St Mut.

Plants of the Coast of Coromandel: Selected from Drawings & Descriptions Presented to the Hon. Court of Directors of the East India Company, under the Order of Sir Joseph Banks, 3 vols. William Roxburgh. (Illus.). 20p. 1982. reprint ed. lib. bdg. 1200.00 (*0-685-44091-5*) Lubrecht & Cramer.

Plants of the Coast Redwood Region. Kathleen Lyons & Mary B. Cooney-Lazaneo. (Illus.). (Orig.). (C). 1988. pap. text 15.00 (*0-9626961-0-2*) Looking Pr.

Plants of the Copper Country: An Illustrated Guide to the Vascular Plants of Houghton & Keweenaw Counties, Michigan & Isle Royale National Park. Steve W. Chadde. (Pocketflora Guide Ser.: Vol. 1). (Illus.). 112p. (Orig.). 1996. pap. 8.95 (*0-9651385-0-X*) PocketFlora.

Plants of the Desert. Illus. by Luis Rizo. LC 95-10768. (Amazing World of Plants Ser.).Tr. of Plantas del Desierto. 32p. (J). (gr. 3-12). 1996. lib. bdg. 15.95 (*0-7910-3466-1*) Chelsea Hse.

Plants of the East Bay Parks. Glenn Keator. LC 94-66099. (Illus.). 332p. 1994. pap. 19.95 (*1-879373-42-4*) Roberts Rinehart.

Plants of the East Mojave. Adrienne Knute. LC 91-27773. (Illus.). 208p. (Orig.). 1991. pap. 12.95 (*0-938109-08-1*) Wide Horiz Pr.

Plants of the Forest. Andreu Llamas. (Incredible World of Plants Ser.). (Illus.). 32p. (J). (gr. 3-12). 1995. lib. bdg. 15.95 (*0-7910-3467-4*) Chelsea Hse.

Plants of the Gods: Their Sacred Healing, & Hallucinogenic Powers. Richard E. Schultes & Albert Hofmann. LC 92-16621. (Illus.). 192p. (Orig.). 1992. pap. 22.95 (*0-89281-406-3*, Heal Arts VT) Inner Tradit.

Plants of the Kimberley Region of Western Australia. R. J. Petheram & B. Kok. (Illus.). 556p. (Orig.). pap. 34.95 (*0-85564-215-7*, Pub. by Univ of West Aust Pr) Intl Spec Bk.

Plants of the Manua Islands. T. G. Yuncker. (BMB Ser.: No. 184). 1974. reprint ed. 25.00 (*0-527-02292-6*) Periodicals Srv.

Plants of the Metroplex. rev. ed. J. Howard Garrett. LC 97-34540. (Illus.). 90p. 1998. pap. 18.95 (*0-292-72815-8*, GARPLP) U of Tex Pr.

Plants of the Northern Provinces of South Africa: Keys & Diagnostic Characters. E. Retief et al. (Strelitzia Ser.: Vol. VI). (Illus.). 1977. 15.00 (*1-874907-30-7*, Pub. by Natl Botanical Inst) Balogh.

Plants of the Oregon Coastal Dunes. La Rea J. Dennis et al. LC 98-49879. (Illus.). 128p. (Orig.). 1999. pap. 12.95 (*0-87071-457-0*) Oreg St U Pr.

Plants of the Pacific Northwest Coast: Washington, Oregon, British Columbia, & Alaska. Jim Pojar & Andy MacKinnon. (Illus.). 528p. 1994. pap. 19.95 (*1-55105-040-4*) Lone Pine.

***Plants of the Peloponnese (Southern Part of Greece)** Walter Strasser. (Illus.). 350p. 1999. pap. 35.00 (*3-904144-11-1*, Pub. by Gantner) Lubrecht & Cramer.

Plants of the Perth Coast & Islands. Elizabeth Rippey & Barbara Rowland. LC 96-151372. (Illus.). 292p. 1995. 49.95 (*1-875560-46-7*, Pub. by Univ of West Aust Pr) Intl Spec Bk.

Plants of the Punjab. C. J. Bamber. (C). 1976. text 350.00 (*0-89771-546-2*, Pub. by Intl Bk Distr) St Mut.

Plants of the Punjab. Ed. by C. J. Bamber. 676p. 1976. reprint ed. 225.00 (*0-7855-6642-2*, Pub. by Intl Bk Distr) St Mut.

Plants of the Rain Forest. Lynn M. Stone. LC 94-20908. (Rain Forests Discovery Library). 24p. (J). (gr. k-4). 1994. lib. bdg. 10.95 (*0-86593-393-6*) Rourke Corp.

Plants of the Rain Forest. Mae Woods. LC 97-53101. (Rain Forest Ser.). (Illus.). 24p. (J). (gr. 2-4). 1999. lib. bdg. 18.60 (*1-57765-018-2*, Checkerboard Library) ABDO Pub Co.

Plants of the Rio Grande Delta. Alfred Richardson. (Gorgas Science Foundation, Inc., Treasures of Nature Ser.). (Illus.). 440p. (Orig.). 1995. pap. 24.95 (*0-292-77070-7*); text 45.00 (*0-292-77068-5*) U of Tex Pr.

Plants of the Rocky Mountains. Linda Kershaw et al. (Illus.). 384p. (Orig.). 1997. pap. 19.95 (*1-55105-088-9*) Lone Pine.

Plants of the San Francisco Bay Region: Mendocino to Monterey. Eugene N. Kozloff & Linda H. Beidleman. LC 94-68921. 448p. 1994. pap. 29.95 (*0-9643756-0-5*) Sagen Pr.

***Plants of the Tahoe Basin: Flowering Plants, Trees, & Ferns.** Michael Graf. LC 99-13267. 300p. 1999. 40.00 (*0-520-21583-4*, Pub. by U CA Pr) Cal Prin Full Svc.

***Plants of the Tahoe Basin: Flowering Plants, Trees & Ferns.** Michael Graf. LC 99-13267. (Illus.). 300p. 1999. pap. 19.95 (*0-520-21541-9*, Pub. by U CA Pr) Cal Prin Full Svc.

Plants of the Texas Shore: A Beachcomber's Guide. Mary M. Cannatella & Rita E. Arnold. LC 84-40553. (Illus.). 78p. 1985. pap. 5.95 (*0-89096-214-6*) Tex A&M Univ Pr.

Plants of the Tropics. Joyce Pope. (Plant Life Ser.). 64p. (YA). 1990. 15.95 (*0-8160-2423-5*) Facts on File.

Plants of the Western Boreal Forest & Aspen Parkland: Including Alberta, Saskatchewan, Manitoba. Derek Johnson et al. 392p. 1996. pap. 19.95 (*1-55105-058-7*) Lone Pine.

Plants of Tonga. T. G. Yuncker. (BMB Ser.: No. 220). 1974. reprint ed. 40.00 (*0-527-02328-0*) Periodicals Srv.

Plants of Waterton-Glacier National Parks & the Northern Rockies. Richard J. Shaw & Danny On. LC 79-9912. (Illus.). 160p. 1987. reprint ed. pap. 12.00 (*0-87842-114-9*) Mountain Pr.

Plants of Yellowstone & Grand Teton National Parks. (Nature & Scenic Bks.). 1981. pap. 10.95 (*0-937512-02-8*) Wheelwright UT.

Plants on Stamps, Vol. I. 167p. 1979. 10.00 (*0-318-13307-5*) Am Topical Assn.

Plants on Stamps, Vol. II. Ed. by Jeane Gould & Alice Sents. 200p. 1988. 12.00 (*0-935991-05-0*) Am Topical Assn.

Plants, People & Culture: The Science of Ethnobotany, a Scientific American Library Book. Michael J. Balick & Paul A. Cox. (Illus.). 256p. 1996. pap. text 32.95 (*0-7167-5061-9*) W H Freeman.

Plants, People, & Environmental Quality: Syllabus. 1977. pap. text 8.25 (*0-89420-021-6*, 140014); audio 70.90 (*0-89420-173-5*, 140000) Natl Book.

Plants, People & Paleoecology: Biotic Communities & Aboriginal Plant Usage in Illinois. Frances B. King. (Scientific Papers: Vol. XX). (Illus.). 224p. (Orig.). 1984. pap. 10.00 (*0-89792-100-3*) Ill St Museum.

Plants Photo Fun Activities. Mary Ellen Sterling. Ed. by Kathy Rogers. (Science Photo Fun Activities Ser.). (Illus.). 8p. 1997. 6.95 (*1-56472-081-0*) Edupress Inc.

Plants, Plants & More. Thomas-Cochran. (What a Wonderful World 2 Ser.). 1992. pap. text. write for info. (*0-582-90964-3*, Pub. by Addison-Wesley) Longman.

Plants Poisonous to People in Florida. Julia F. Morton. LC 81-71614. 1995. pap. 19.95 (*0-87024-336-5*) U of Miami Pr.

P

An Asterisk (*) at the beginning of an entry indicates that the title is appearing for the first time.

Plants Poisonous to People in Florida & Other Warm Areas. 2nd rev. ed. Julia F. Morton. LC 81-71614. (Illus.). 170p. 1982. pap. 19.75 (*0-9610184-0-2*) ECHO Inc.

***Plants Series, 10 bks.** 32p. 1999. 199.20 (*1-57572-831-1*) Heinemann Lib.

Plants Series: Life Cycles, 4 bks. Gail Saunders-Smith. Incl. Apple Trees. LC 97-23593. 24p. (J). 1997. lib. bdg. 13.25 (*1-56065-490-2*, Pebble Bks); Beans. LC 97-23585. 24p. (J). 1997. lib. bdg. 13.25 (*1-56065-487-2*, Pebble Bks); Carrots. LC 97-23586. 24p. (J). 1997. lib. bdg. 13.25 (*1-56065-488-0*, Pebble Bks); Sunflowers. LC 97-23580. 24p. (J). 1997. lib. bdg. 13.25 (*1-56065-489-9*, Pebble Bks); 53.00 (*1-56065-675-1*, Pebble Bks) Capstone Pr.

Plants Set. Melvin Berger. Ed. by Susan Evento. (Macmillan Early Science Big Bks.). (Illus.). (J). (ps-2). 1995. pap. write for info. (*1-56784-163-5*) Newbridge Educ.

Plants That Hyperaccummulate Heavy Metals. Ed. by Robert R. Brooks. LC 97-43257. (A CAB International Publication). (Illus.). 392p. 1998. text 100.00 (*0-85199-236-6*) OUP.

Plants That Merit Attention Vol. 1: Trees. Garden Club of America, Horticultural Committee St. Ed. by Janet M. Poor. LC 94-7957. (Illus.). 349p. 1984. 59.95 (*0-917304-75-6*) Timber.

Plants That Merit Attention Vol. 2: Shrubs. Ed. by Janet M. Poor & Nancy P. Brewster. LC 94-7957. (Illus.). 364p. 1996. 59.95 (*0-88192-347-8*) Timber.

Plants That Never Ever Bloom. Ruth Heller. (Illus.). 48p. (J). (ps-3). 1984. 14.95 (*0-448-18964-X*, G & D) Peng Put Young Read.

Plants That Never Ever Bloom. Ruth Heller. (Sandcastle Ser.). (Illus.). 48p. (J). (ps-3). 1992. pap. 7.95 (*0-448-41092-3*, Philomel) Peng Put Young Read.

Plants That Never Ever Bloom. Ruth Heller. (Ruth Heller's World of Nature Ser.). (Illus.). 48p. (gr. k-3). 1999. pap. 6.99 (*0-698-11558-9*, PapStar) Peng Put Young Read.

Plants That Never Ever Bloom. Ruth Heller. 1992. 13.15 (*0-606-05549-5*, Pub. by Turtleback) Demco.

Plants to Ecosystems. M. T. Michalewiz. (Advances in Computational Life Sciences Ser.). (Illus.). 133p. 1997. 64.95 (*0-643-05942-3*, Pub. by CSIRO) Accents Pubns.

Plants to Transform Your Garden. Noel Kingsbury. 1999. 29.95 (*0-7063-7711-7*) WrLock.

***Plants-2400 Copyright-Free Illustrations of Flowers, Trees, Fruits & Vegetables.** Jim Harter. (Illus.). 1999. 31.25 (*0-8446-6985-7*) Peter Smith.

Plants under Stress. Ed. by Hamlyn G. Jones et al. (Society for Experimental Biology Seminar Ser.: No. 39). (Illus.). 272p. (C). 1989. text 85.00 (*0-521-34423-9*) Cambridge U Pr.

Plants under the Sea. Illus. by Luis Rizo. LC 95-18261. (Incredible World of Plants Ser.).Tr. of Plantas del Mar. (ENG & SPA.). 32p. (J). (gr. 3 up). 1996. lib. bdg. 15.95 (*0-7910-3468-2*) Chelsea Hse.

Plants Used As Curatives by Certain Southeastern Tribes. Lyda A. Taylor. LC 76-43866. (Botanical Museum of Harvard University Ser.). reprint ed. 29.50 (*0-404-15725-4*) AMS Pr.

Plants Used in Basketry by the California Indians. fac. ed. Ruth E. Merrill. (University of California Publications in American Archaeology & Ethnology: Vol. 20: 13). 30p. (C). 1923. reprint ed. pap. text 3.44 (*1-55567-249-3*) Coyote Press.

Plants Used in Basketry by the California Indians. Ruth E. Merrill. (Illus.). 1980. reprint ed. pap. 6.95 (*0-686-77544-9*) Acoma Bks.

Plants We Need to Eat. Jeanette Ewin. 1997. 10.00 (*0-7225-3278-4*) Thorsons PA.

Plants Yielding Non-Seed Carbohydrates. Ed. by M. Flach & F. Rumawas. (Plant Resources of South-East Asia Ser.: No. 9). (Illus.). 237p. 1996. 83.00 (*90-73348-51-X*, Pub. by Backhuys Pubs) Balogh.

Plantsman in Nepal. Roy Lancaster. (Illus.). 240p. 1995. 69.50 (*1-85149-179-1*) Antique Collect.

Plantwatching: How Plants Remember, Tell Time, Form Partnerships, & More. fac. ed. Malcolm B. Wilkins. LC 88-45167. (Illus.). 207p. 1988. reprint ed. pap. 64.20 (*0-7837-8098-2*, 204785300008) Bks Demand.

Plantwide Process Control. William L. Luyben et al. LC 98-16167. 395p. 1998. 79.95 (*0-07-006779-1*) McGraw.

Plantworks. Karen Shanberg. 288p. 1991. pap. 12.95 (*0-934860-70-X*) Adventure Pubns.

Planty's Encyclopedia of Cacheted F. D. C.'s, 10 vols. Michael A. Mellone & Earl Planty. (Illus.). 1979. pap. 99.98 (*0-89794-008-3*) FDC Pub.

Planty's Encyclopedia of Cacheted F. D. C.'s, Vol. 3. Michael A. Mellone & Earl Planty. (Illus.). 1978. pap. 8.95 (*0-89794-011-3*) FDC Pub.

Planty's Encyclopedia of Cacheted F. D. C.'s, Vol. 4. Michael A. Mellone & Earl Planty. (Illus.). 1978. pap. 9.95 (*0-89794-012-1*) FDC Pub.

Planty's Encyclopedia of Cacheted F. D. C.'s, Vol. 5. Michael A. Mellone & Earl Planty. (Illus.). 1978. pap. 9.95 (*0-89794-013-X*) FDC Pub.

Planty's Encyclopedia of Cacheted F. D. C.'s, Vol. 6. Michael Mellone & Earl Planty. (Illus.). 1978. pap. 9.95 (*0-89794-014-8*) FDC Pub.

Planty's Encyclopedia of Cacheted F. D. C.'s, Vol. 7. Michael A. Mellone & Earl Planty. (Illus.). 1979. pap. 9.95 (*0-89794-015-6*) FDC Pub.

Planty's Encyclopedia of Cacheted F. D. C.'s, Vol. 8. Michael A. Mellone & Earl Planty. (Illus.). 1979. pap. 9.95 (*0-89794-016-4*) FDC Pub.

Planty's Encyclopedia of Cacheted F. D. C.'s, Vol. 9. Michael A. Mellone & Earl Planty. (Illus.). 1978. pap. 9.95 (*0-317-16573-9*) FDC Pub.

Planty's Encyclopedia of Cacheted F. D. C.'s, Vol. 10. Michael A. Meellone & Earl Planty. (Illus.). 1978. pap. 9.95 (*0-317-16574-7*) FDC Pub.

Planty's Encyclopedia of Cacheted F. D. C.'s, 1923-1928, Vol. 1. Michael A. Mellone & Earl Planty. (Illus.). 1977. pap. 9.95 (*0-89794-009-1*) FDC Pub.

Planty's Encyclopedia of Cacheted F. D. C.'s, 1928-1929, Vol. 2. Michael A. Mellone & Earl Planty. (Illus.). 1977. pap. 9.95 (*0-89794-010-5*) FDC Pub.

***Plantzilla.** Nolen. 2002. write for info. (*0-15-202412-3*) Harcourt.

Planung & Verwirklichung Von Freizeitangeboten. Moeglichkeiten & Formen der Partizipation. S. Agricola & B. Von Schmettow. Ed. by R. Schmitz-Scherzer. (Psychologische Praxis Ser.: Band 50). 1976. 21.75 (*3-8055-2361-0*) S Karger.

Planungshoheit Und Grundeigentum: Die Verfassungsrechtlichen Schranken der Stadtebaulichen Entwicklungsmassnahme. Jochen Seitz. 292p. 1998. 51.95 (*3-631-33145-2*) P Lang Pubng.

Planungshoheit Und Grundeigentum: Die Verfassungsrechtlichen Schranken der Stadtebaulichen Entwicklungsmassnahme. Jochen Seitz. 292p. 1999. 51.95 (*0-8204-3575-9*) P Lang Pubng.

Planus. Blaise Cendrars. 208p. 1989. reprint ed. pap. 17.95 (*0-7206-0740-X*, Pub. by P Owen Ltd) Dufour.

Plaque & Calculus Removal: Considerations for the Professional. David L. Cochran et al. LC 94-17876. (Illus.). 109p. 1994. pap. text 32.00 (*0-86715-285-0*) Quint Pub Co.

Plasir de Rompre see Oeuvres

Plasma Acceleration. Ed. by Sidney W. Kash. LC 60-13869. 125p. reprint ed. pap. 38.80 (*0-608-10332-2*, 200031200025) Bks Demand.

Plasma & Laser Processing of Materials. Ed. by Kamleshwar Upadhya. LC 90-64065. 389p. 1991. reprint ed. pap. 120.60 (*0-608-03831-8*, 206279300004) Bks Demand.

Plasma & the Universe: Dedicated to Hannes Alfven. Ed. by Carl-Gunne Falthammar et al. (C). 1988. text 271.50 (*90-277-2764-3*) Kluwer Academic.

***Plasma Astrophysics.** Ed. by B. Coppi et al. (International School of Physics Enrico Fermi Ser.: Vol. 142). 500p. 2000. 126.00 (*1-58603-073-6*) IOS Press.

Plasma Astrophysics. J. G. Kirk et al. (Astrophysics, Solar Physics, Plasma Physics Ser.). 352p. 1995. 74.95 (*0-387-58327-0*) Spr-Verlag.

Plasma Astrophysics, 10 vols., Set. Ed. by R. Kulsrud. LC 96-77142. (Research Trends in Physics Ser.). (Illus.). 450p. (C). 1996. 85.00 (*1-889545-01-5*) Stefan Univ Pr.

Plasma Astrophysics: Kinetic Processes in Solar & Stellar Coronae. Arnold O. Benz. LC 93-24191. (Astrophysics & Space Science Library). 320p. (C). 1993. lib. bdg. 137.00 (*0-7923-2429-3*) Kluwer Academic.

Plasma Astrophysics: Lectures Held at the Astrophysics School VII, Organized by the European Astrophysics Doctoral Network (EADN) in San Miniato, Italy, 3-14 October 1994. Ed. by Claudio Chiuderi & Giorgio Einaudi. LC 96-2418. (Lecture Notes in Physics Ser.: Vol. 468). 326p. 1996. 78.00 (*3-540-61014-6*) Spr-Verlag.

Plasma Astrophysics: Nonthermal Processes in Diffuse Magnetized Plasm: Astrophysical Applications, 2 vols., Vol. 2. D. B. Melrose. 714p. 1980. text 600.00 (*0-677-03490-3*) Gordon & Breach.

Plasma Astrophysics Vol. 1: Nonthermal Processes in Diffuse Magnetized Plasmas: The Emission, Absorption & Transfer of Waves in Plasmas. D. B. Melrose. x, 270p. 1980. text 335.00 (*0-677-02340-5*) Gordon & Breach.

Plasma Astrophysics & Cosmology: Proceedings of the 2nd IEEE International Workshop, Princeton, New Jersey, May 10-12, 1993. Ed. by Anthony L. Peratt. 297p. 1995. reprint ed. text 250.00 (*0-7923-3784-0*) Kluwer Academic.

***Plasma Astrophysics & Space Physics.** J. Buchner. LC 99-50108. 1999. write for info. (*0-7923-6002-8*) Kluwer Academic.

***Plasma Boundary of Magnetic Fusion Devices.** P. C. Stangeby. (Plasma Physics Ser.). 744p. 2000. 195.00 (*0-7503-0559-2*) IOP Pub.

Plasma Cell Dyscrasias. A. I. Pick. (Journal: Acta Haematologica: Vol. 68, No. 3). (Illus.). vi, 96p. 1982. pap. 51.50 (*3-8055-3549-X*) S Karger.

***Plasma Charging Damage.** Kin P. Cheung. LC 99-34071. 1999. write for info. (*1-85233-144-5*, Pub. by Spr-Verlag) Spr-Verlag.

Plasma Chemistry. Ed. by L. S. Polak & Yu A. Lebedev. 320p. 1995. boxed set 120.00 (*1-898326-22-3*, Pub. by CISP) Balogh.

Plasma Chemistry, Vol. IV. Ed. by S. Veprek & M. Venugopalan. (Topics in Current Chemistry Ser.: Vol. 107). (Illus.). 186p. 1982. 61.95 (*0-387-11828-4*) Spr-Verlag.

Plasma Chemistry of Polymers. Ed. by Mitchel C. Shen. LC 76-29324. 291p. reprint ed. pap. 90.30 (*0-608-16979-X*, 202710700054) Bks Demand.

Plasma Chromatography. Ed. by Timothy W. Carr. (Illus.). 274p. (C). 1984. text 102.00 (*0-306-41432-5*, Kluwer Plenum) Kluwer Academic.

Plasma Deposited Thin Films. J. Mort & F. Jansen. LC 86-23264. 256p. 1986. reprint ed. 146.00 (*0-8493-5119-7*, CRC Reprint) Franklin.

Plasma Deposition & Treatment of Polymers Vol. 544: Materials Research Society Symposium Proceedings. Ed. by W. W. Lee et al. LC 99-40522. 300p. 1999. text 94.00 (*1-55899-450-5*) Materials Res.

Plasma Deposition of Amorphous Silicon-Based Materials. Ed. by Giovanni Bruno et al. (Plasma-Materials Interactions Ser.). (Illus.). 368p. 1995. text 90.00 (*0-12-137940-X*) Acad Pr.

Plasma Deposition, Treatment & Etching of Polymers, Plasma-Materials Interactions. Ed. by Riccardo D'Agostino. 528p. 1990. text 136.00 (*0-12-200430-2*) Acad Pr.

Plasma Diagnostics. W. Lochte-Holtgreven. (AVS Classics Ser.). (Illus.). 945p. (C). 1995. text 64.95 (*1-56396-388-4*) Spr-Verlag.

Plasma Diagnostics, Vol. 2. Ed. by Orlando Auciello & Daniel L. Flamm. (Plasma Materials Interactions Ser.). 337p. 1989. text 146.00 (*0-12-067636-2*) Acad Pr.

Plasma Dynamics. R. O. Dendy. (Illus.). 172p. 1990. text 65.00 (*0-19-851991-5*); pap. text 29.95 (*0-19-852041-7*) OUP.

Plasma Electrodynamics Vol. 2: Non Linear Theory & Fluctuations. A. I. Akhiezer & I. Akhiezer. LC 74-332. (International Series of Monographs in Natural Philosophy: Vol. 80: 2). 1975. 147.00 (*0-08-018016-7*, Pub. by Pergamon Repr) Franklin.

Plasma en Todas Partes. Silvia Bravo. (Ciencia para Todos Ser.). (SPA.). pap. 6.99 (*968-16-4366-6*, Pub. by Fondo) Continental Bk.

Plasma Environments of Non-Magnetic Planets: Proceedings of the 4th COSPAR Colloquium Held in Ann Arbor, Michigan, U. S. A., 24-27 August, 1992. Ed. by Tamas I. Gombosi. (COSPAR Colloquia Ser.: Vol. 4). 344p. 1993. 155.00 (*0-08-042333-7*, Pergamon Pr) Elsevier.

***Plasma Etch.** (Illus.). 249p. (C). 1998. 59.95 (*1-58257-027-2*) TX Eng Extsn Servs.

Plasma Etch '98: Processes & Equipment for the New Millennium. 1998. pap. write for info. (*1-892568-10-1*) Smicndctr Equip.

Plasma Etching: An Introduction. Ed. by Dennis M. Manos & Daniel L. Flamm. (Plasma Materials Interactions Ser.). 476p. 1989. text 100.00 (*0-12-469370-9*) Acad Pr.

Plasma Etching: Fundamentals & Applications. M. Sugawara. (Series on Semiconductor Science & Technology: No. 7). (Illus.). 356p. 1998. text 140.00 (*0-19-856287-X*) OUP.

Plasma Etching for Integrated Silicon Sensor Applications. Yuan Xiong Li. (Illus.). xi, 221p. (Orig.). 1995. pap. 59.50 (*90-407-1177-1*, Pub. by Delft U Pr) Coronet Bks.

Plasma Exhaust Aftertreatment. 190p. 1998. pap. 49.00 (*0-7680-0309-1*, SP-1395) Soc Auto Engineers.

Plasma Fibronectin: Structure & Functions. J. McDonagh. (Hematology Ser.: Vol. 5). (Illus.). 288p. 1985. text 150.00 (*0-8247-7384-5*) Dekker.

Plasma Fractionation & Blood Transfusion. Ed. by C. T. Sibinga et al. (Developments in Hematology & Immunology Ser.). 1985. text 75.00 (*0-89838-761-2*) Kluwer Academic.

Plasma Homovanillic Acid in Schizophrenia: Implications for Presynaptic Dopamine Dysfunction. Ed. by Arnold J. Friedhoff & Farooq Amin. LC 96-30139. (Progress in Psychiatry Ser.: Vol. 52). 216p. 1997. text 34.00 (*0-88048-489-6*, 8489) Am Psychiatric.

Plasma in a Magnetic Field: A Symposium on Magnetohydrodynamics, 2nd, 1957, Palo Alto. Lockheed Symposium on Magnetohydrodynamics Staff. LC 58-11698. 139p. reprint ed. pap. 43.10 (*0-608-30253-8*, 200031700025) Bks Demand.

Plasma Instabilities in Astrophysics. Ed. by Donat A. Wentzel & Derek A. Tidman. (Illus.). xii, 418p. 1969. text 500.00 (*0-677-13520-3*) Gordon & Breach.

Plasma Isoenzymes: The Current Status. Ed. by Victor H. Blaton & A. Van Steirteghem. (Advances in Clinical Enzymology Ser.: Vol. 3). (Illus.). viii, 208p. 1986. 155.75 (*3-8055-4321-2*) S Karger.

Plasma Jets in the Development of New Materials Technology. Ed. by O. P. Solonenko & A. I. Fedorchenko. (Illus.). 730p. 1991. 265.00 (*90-6764-131-6*, Pub. by VSP) Coronet Bks.

***Plasma Kinetics in Atmospheric Gases.** M. Capitelli. LC 00-41961. (Series on Atomic, Optical & Plasma Physics). 2000. write for info. (*3-540-67416-0*) Spr-Verlag.

***Plasma Lipids & Their Role in Disease.** Ed. by Philip J. Barter & Kerry-Anne Rye. (Advances in Vascular Biology Ser.: Vol. 5). 368p. 1999. text 120.00 (*90-5702-466-7*, Harwood Acad Pubs) Gordon & Breach.

Plasma Lipoproteins, Pt. A. Ed. by Sidney P. Colowick et al. (Methods in Enzymology Ser.: Vol. 128). 992p. 1986. text 178.00 (*0-12-182028-9*) Acad Pr.

Plasma Lipoproteins, Pt. B. Ed. by Sidney P. Colowick & Nathan O. Kaplan. (Methods in Enzymology Ser.: Vol. 129). 960p. 1986. text 178.00 (*0-12-182029-7*) Acad Pr.

Plasma Lipoproteins Pt. C: Quantitation. Ed. by William A. Bradley et al. (Methods in Enzymology Ser.: Vol. 263). (Illus.). 373p. 1995. text 80.00 (*0-12-182164-1*) Acad Pr.

Plasma Loops in the Solar Corona. R. J. Bray et al. (Cambridge Astrophysics Ser.: No. 18). (Illus.). 522p. (C). 1991. text 120.00 (*0-521-35107-3*) Cambridge U Pr.

Plasma Materials. 2nd ed. Manos. 500p. 1997. write for info. (*0-12-469365-2*) Acad Pr.

Plasma Membrane ATPase of Plants & Fungi. Ramo Serrano. 184p. 1985. 109.00 (*0-8493-6134-6*, QK725, CRC Reprint) Franklin.

Plasma Membrane Oxidoreductases in Control of Animal & Plant Growth. Ed. by F. L. Crane et al. (NATO ASI Series A, Life Sciences: Vol. 157). (Illus.). 460p. 1988. 125.00 (*0-306-43092-4*, Plenum Trade) Perseus Pubng.

***Plasma Membrane Redox Systems & Their Role in Biological Stress & Disease.** Ed. by Han Asard. LC 98-31686. 332p. 1998. 180.00 (*0-7923-5467-2*) Kluwer Academic.

Plasma Physics. Richard D. Hazeltine. 1998. write for info. (*0-201-69578-2*) Addison-Wesley.

Plasma Physics. N. L. Tsintsadze. 584p. 1991. text 118.00 (*981-02-0425-6*) World Scientific Pub.

Plasma Physics. S. Chandrasekhar. LC 60-7234. (Midway Reprint Ser.). (Illus.). x, 218p. 1978. reprint ed. pap. text 15.00 (*0-226-10085-5*) U Ch Pr.

Plasma Physics: An Introduction to the Theory of Astrophysical, Geophysical, & Laboratory Plasmas. Peter A. Sturrock. (Illus.). 347p. (C). 1994. pap. text 37.95 (*0-521-44810-7*) Cambridge U Pr.

Plasma Physics: Basic Theory with Fusion Applications. 2nd rev. ed. K. Nishikawa & M. Wakatani. LC 93-36463. 340p. 1994. 59.00 (*0-387-56854-9*) Spr-Verlag.

***Plasma Physics: Basic Theory with Fusion Applications.** 3rd ed. Kyoji Nishikawa & M. Wakatani. LC 99-39641. (Series in Atoms, Molecular, Optical & Plasma Physics: Vol. 8). (Illus.). 335p. 2000. 89.95 (*3-540-65285-X*) Spr-Verlag.

Plasma Physics: Proceedings of the EUR-CNEN Association Meeting, 1969. Ed. by J. F. Linhart. 1975. pap. 16.25 (*0-08-020450-3*, Pergamon Pr) Elsevier.

Plasma Physics: Proceedings of the 1987 International Conference on Plasma Physics, 2 vols., Vols. 1 - 2. Ed. by A. G. Sitenko. 1412p. (C). 1987. text 290.00 (*9971-5-0387-5*) World Scientific Pub.

Plasma Physics: Proceedings of the 1997 Latin American Workshop on Plasma Physics Held in Caracas, Venezuela, January 20-31, 1997. Latin American Workshop on Plasma Physics Staff et al. LC 98-32183. 14p. 1999. write for info. (*0-7923-5527-X*) Kluwer Academic.

Plasma Physics Vol. 345: AIP Conference Proceedings. Ed. by Paulo H. Sakanaka & Michael Tendler. LC 95-78438. (AIP Conference Ser.: No. 345). (Illus.). 508p. 1995. 175.00 (*1-56396-496-1*) Am Inst Physics.

Plasma Physics - Basic Theory with Fusion Applications. K. Nishikawa. Ed. by G. Ecker et al. (Atoms & Plasmas Ser.: Vol. 8). (Illus.). 320p. 1990. 69.00 (*0-387-52481-9*) Spr-Verlag.

Plasma Physics & Controlled Nuclear Fusion Research see Fusion Energy, Vol. 2, 1996

Plasma Physics & Controlled Nuclear Fusion Research see Fusion Energy 1996

Plasma Physics & Controlled Nuclear Fusion Research: 14th Session 1992 (Conference Summaries), Vol. 4. IAEA Staff. 1000p. 1993. pap. 30.00 (*92-0-101393-0*, STI/PUB/906/4, Pub. by IAEA) Bernan Associates.

Plasma Physics & Controlled Nuclear Fusion Research, 1990, Vol. 1. IAEA Staff. 629p. 1991. pap. 255.00 (*92-0-130091-3*, STI/PUB/844, Pub. by IAEA) Bernan Associates.

Plasma Physics & Controlled Nuclear Fusion Research, 1992, Vol. 2. IAEA Staff. 700p. 1993. pap. 195.00 (*92-0-101193-8*, STI/PUB/906/2, Pub. by IAEA) Bernan Associates.

Plasma Physics & Controlled Nuclear Fusion Research, 1992, Vol. 3. IAEA Staff. 1993. pap. 155.00 (*92-0-101293-4*, STI/PUB/906/3, Pub. by IAEA) Bernan Associates.

Plasma Physics & Controlled Nuclear Fusion Research, 1992, 14th Session, Vol. 1. IAEA Staff. 700p. 1993. pap. 240.00 (*92-0-101093-1*, STI/PUB/906, Pub. by IAEA) Bernan Associates.

Plasma Physics & Controlled Nuclear Fusion Research, 1994, Vol. 2. 1996. pap. 260.00 (*92-0-103695-7*, STI/PUB/948/2, Pub. by IAEA) Bernan Associates.

Plasma Physics & Controlled Nuclear Fusion Research, 1994, Vol. 3. 731p. 1996. pap. 240.00 (*92-0-103795-3*, STI/PUB/948/3, Pub. by IAEA) Bernan Associates.

Plasma Physics & Controlled Thermonuclear Fusion: Proceedings, 2nd Latin-American Workshop. R. Krikorian. (CIF Ser.: Vol. 12). 400p. 1989. text 109.00 (*9971-5-0893-1*) World Scientific Pub.

Plasma Physics & Plasma Electronics. Ed. by L. M. Kovrizhnykh. (Illus.). 270p. 1988. text 175.00 (*0-941743-47-0*) Nova Sci Pubs.

Plasma Physics for Nuclear Fusion. rev. ed. Kenro Miyamoto. 640p. 1989. pap. text 35.00 (*0-262-63117-2*) MIT Pr.

Plasma Physics for Thermonuclear Fusion Reactors, Vol. 1. G. Casini. (Ispra Courses on Nuclear Engineering & Technology Ser.). vi, 492p. (C). 1981. text 349.00 (*3-7186-0091-9*) Gordon & Breach.

Plasma Physics Theory. V. Malnev & A. G. Sitenko. LC 94-71831. (Applied Mathematics & Mathematical Computation Ser.: No. 10). 403p. 1994. lib. bdg. 99.95 (*0-412-56790-3*) ASME Pr.

Plasma Physics Via Computer Simulation. C. K. Birdsall & A. B. Langdon. (Plasma Physics Ser.). (Illus.). 504p. 1991. 90.00 incl. disk (*0-7503-0117-1*) IOP Pub.

Plasma Polymerization. Ed. by Alexis T. Bell & Mitchel C. Shen. LC 79-15252. (ACS Symposium Ser.: No. 108). 1979. 43.95 (*0-8412-0510-8*) Am Chemical.

Plasma Polymerization. Ed. by Alexis T. Bell & Mitchel C. Shen. LC 79-15252. (ACS Symposium Ser.: Vol. 108). 352p. 1979. reprint ed. pap. 109.20 (*0-608-03086-4*, 206353900007) Bks Demand.

Plasma Polymerization Processes. H. Biederman & Y. Osada. (Plasma Technology Ser.: Vol. 3). x, 210p. 1992. 140.00 (*0-444-88724-5*) Elsevier.

Plasma Processes for Semiconductor Fabrication. W. N. Hitchon. LC 98-11717. (Studies in Semiconductor Physics & Microelectronic Engineering: No. 8). (Illus.). 240p. (C). 1999. text 64.95 (*0-521-59175-9*) Cambridge U Pr.

Plasma Processing: Proceedings of the 4th Symposium, Held in San Francisco, CA, 1983. Symposium on Plasma Processing Staff. Ed. by G. S. Mathad et al. LC 83-82041. (Electrochemical Society Proceedings Ser.: Vol. 83-10). 659p. 1983. reprint ed. pap. 200.00 (*0-608-04659-0*, 205257600004) Bks Demand.

Plasma Processing: Proceedings of the 5th Symposium Held 1984, New Orleans, LA. Symposium on Plasma Processing Staff. Ed. by G. S. Mathad et al. LC 85-70593. (Electrochemical Society Ser.: No. 85-1). (Illus.). 629p. 1985. reprint ed. pap. 195.00 (*0-608-05752-5*, 205264400008) Bks Demand.

P

An Asterisk (*) at the beginning of an entry indicates that the title is appearing for the first time.

Plasma Processing: Symposium on Plasma Etchins & Deposition, Proceedings. Ed. by R. G. Frieser & C. J. Mogab. LC 81-65237. (Electrochemical Society Proceedings Ser.: Vol. 81-1). (Illus.). 348p. reprint ed. pap. 107.90 (0-608-30678-9, 205174900006) Bks Demand.

Plasma Processing: 11th International Symposium. Ed. by G. S. Mathad & M. Meyyappan. (Proceedings Ser.: Vol. 96-12). (Illus.). 720p. 1996. 92.00 (1-56677-164-1) Electrochem Soc.

Plasma Processing & Synthesis of Materials II. Ed. by Diran Apelian & Julian Szekely. (Materials Research Society Symposium Proceedings Ser.: Vol. 98). 1987. text 17.50 (0-931837-65-0) Materials Res.

Plasma Processing & Synthesis of Materials III Vol. 190: Symposium Proceedings Ser. Ed. by Diran Apelian & J. Szekely. 355p. 1991. text 17.50 (1-55899-079-8) Materials Res.

Plasma Processing of Materials: Scientific Opportunities & Technological Challenges. fac. ed. National Research Council (US) Panel of Plasma Pro. LC 91-66812. (Illus.). 87p. 1991. pap. 30.00 (0-7837-7559-8, 204731200007) Bks Demand.

Plasma Processing of Polymers: Proceedings of the NATO Advanced Study Institute on Plasma Treatments & Deposition of Polymers, Acquafredda di Maratea, Italy, May 19-June 2, 1996. Ed. by Riccardo D'Agostino et al. LC 97-45510. (NATO Advanced Science Institutes Ser.: No. 346). 544p. 1997. text 307.50 (0-7923-4859-1) Kluwer Academic.

Plasma Processing of Semiconductors: Proceedings of the NATO Advanced Study Institute on Plasma Processing of Semiconductors, Chateau de Bonas, France, 1996. Ed. by P. F. Williams. LC 97-16609. 613p. 1997. text 331.50 (0-7923-4567-3) Kluwer Academic.

Plasma Processing XII. Ed. by G. S. Mathad et al. (Proceedings Ser.: Vol. 98-4). (Illus.). 292p. 1998. 58.00 (1-56677-198-6) Electrochem Soc.

Plasma Products & European Self-Sufficiency: Collection, Preparation & Use. Council of Europe Staff. 1992. 12.00 (92-871-1925-2, Pub. by Council of Europe) Manhattan Pub Co.

Plasma Properties, Deposition & Etching. Ed. by J. J. Pouch & S. A. Alterovitz. (Materials Science Forum Ser.: Vol. 140-142). (Illus.). 749p. (C). 1993. text 266.00 (0-87849-670-X, Pub. by Trans T Pub) Enfield Pubs NH.

Plasma Proteins. Ed. by Birger Blomback & Lars A. Hanson. Tr. by Desmond Hogg from SWE. LC 78-10126. (Illus.). 419p. reprint ed. pap. 129.90 (0-8357-8619-6, 203504200091) Bks Demand.

Plasma Proteins: An Introduction. M. W. Turner & B. Hulme. (Illus.). 1971. pap. 22.95 (0-8464-0725-6) Beekman Pubs.

Plasma Science: From Fundamental Research to Technological Applications. National Research Council, Panel on Opportunities. (Physics in a New Era Ser.). 224p. (Orig.). (C). 1995. pap. text 35.00 (0-309-05231-9) Natl Acad Pr.

Plasma Science & Technology. Herman V. Boenig. LC 81-15200. (Illus.). 304p. 1982. text 57.50 (0-8014-1356-7) Cornell U Pr.

Plasma Science & the Environment. Wallace Manheimer et al. LC 96-27719. 1996. 75.00 (1-56396-377-9) Spr-Verlag.

Plasma Separation & Plasma Fractionation. Ed. by H. J. Gurland & M. J. Lysaght. (Illus.). viii, 332p. 1983. 116.75 (3-8055-3822-7) S Karger.

***Plasma Source Mass Spectrometry: New Developments & Applications Ser.** Ed. by J. G. Holland & S. D. Tanner. (Special Publication Ser.: Vol. 241). 310p. 1999. 140.00 (0-85404-749-2, Pub. by Royal Soc Chem) Spr-Verlag.

Plasma Source Mass Spectrometry, No. 85. K. E. Jarvis et al. 1990. 105.00 (0-85186-567-4) CRC Pr.

Plasma Source Mass Spectrometry: Development & Applications. International Conference on Plasma Source Mass Spe. Ed. by Grenville Holland & Scott D. Tanner. 329p. 1997. text 136.00 (0-85404-727-1, QD96) Am Chemical.

Plasma Source Mass Spectroscopy. Van Loon. 1994. 99.95 (0-8493-6807-3) CRC Pr.

Plasma Space Sciences Symposium: Proceedings. Ed. by D. D. Chang & S. S. Huang. 386p. 1966. pap. 88.00 (0-677-00645-4) Gordon & Breach.

Plasma Spectrochemistry: Proceedings of the Winter Conference, Orlando , Florida, January 4-9, 1982. Ed. by R. M. Barnes. 436p. 1983. pap. 55.00 (0-08-028745-X, Pergamon Pr) Elsevier.

Plasma Spectrochemistry: Proceedings of the 1985 European Winter Conference on Plasma Spectrochemistry, 7-11 January 1985, Leysin, Switzerland. Ed. by P. W. Boumans. 1986. pap. 64.00 (0-08-033925-5, Pub. by PPL) Elsevier.

Plasma Spectroscopy: The Influence of Microwave & Laser Fields. Eugene A. Oks. LC 94-35448. (Series on Atoms & Plasmas: Vol. 9). 1995. 83.95 (0-387-54100-4) Spr-Verlag.

Plasma Spectroscopy for the Analysis of Hazardous Materials: Design & Application of Enclosed Plasma Sources. Ed. by Martin C. Edelson & J. Leland Daniel. (Special Technical Publication Ser.: No. 951). (Illus.). 160p. 1987. text 34.00 (0-8031-0951-2, STP951) ASTM.

Plasma-Spray Coating: Principles & Applications. Robert B. Heimann. (Illus.). 341p. 1996. 255.00 (3-527-29430-9, Wiley-VCH) Wiley.

Plasma Spraying: Theory & Applications. R. Suryanarayan. 308p. 1993. text 78.00 (981-02-1363-8) World Scientific Pub.

Plasma Spraying of Metallic & Ceramic Materials. D. Matejka & B. Benko. LC 89-16459. 280p. 1990. 650.00 (0-471-91876-8) Wiley.

Plasma Studies at Cornell University. Ed. by Gladys McConkey. 64p. 1988. write for info. (0-918531-01-2) Cornell Coll Eng.

Plasma Surface Engineering: Proceedings of the 1st International Conference, 1988, 2 vols. Ed. by E. Broszeit et al. (Illus.). 1310p. 1989. lib. bdg. 178.00 (0-685-44884-3, Pub. by DGM Metallurgy Info) IR Pubns.

Plasma Surface Engineering: Proceedings of the 1st International Conference, 1988, 2 vols., Vol. 1. Ed. by E. Broszeit et al. (Illus.). 1310p. 1989. write for info. (3-88355-150-3, Pub. by DGM Metallurgy Info) IR Pubns.

Plasma Surface Engineering: Proceedings of the 1st International Conference, 1988, 2 vols., Vol. 2. Ed. by E. Broszeit et al. (Illus.). 1310p. 1989. write for info. (3-88355-151-1, Pub. by DGM Metallurgy Info) IR Pubns.

Plasma-Surface Interactions & Processing of Materials. Ed. by Orlando Auciello et al. (Proceedings of the NATO Advanced Study Institute on Carbon Fibers & Filamets Held in Alvor, Portugal, May 15-27, 1989 Ser.). (C). 1990. text 285.00 (0-7923-0584-1) Kluwer Academic.

Plasma Surface Modification & Plasma Polymerization. Norihiro Inagaki. LC 95-61774. 270p. 1995. text 116.95 (1-56676-337-1) Technomic.

Plasma Surface Modification of Polymers: Relevance to Adhesion. Ed. by M. Strobel et al. (Illus.). 290p. 1994. 105.00 (90-6764-164-2, Pub. by VSP) Coronet Bks.

Plasma Synthesis & Etching of Electronic Materials, Vol. 38. Ed. by R. P. H. Chang & B. Abeles. LC 85-3085. 1985. text 17.50 (0-931837-03-0) Materials Res.

Plasma Technology: Fundamentals & Applications. M. Capitelli & C. Gorse. (Illus.). 232p. (C). 1992. text 75.00 (0-306-44207-8, Kluwer Plenum) Kluwer Academic.

Plasma Technology in Metallurgical Processing. Ed. by Jerome Feinman et al. LC 86-81742. 214p. reprint ed. pap. 66.40 (0-7837-4492-7, 204426900001) Bks Demand.

Plasma Theory & Nonlinear & Turbulent Processes in Physics: Proceedings of the 3rd International Workshop on Nonlinear & Turbulent Processes in Physics, 2 vols., I. Ed. by V. G. Baryakhtar et al. 1000p. (C). 1988. text 239.00 (9971-5-0546-0) World Scientific Pub.

Plasma Universe: Beyond the Big Bang. Anthony L. Peratt. 1999. text. write for info. (0-312-09362-4) St Martin.

Plasma Volume Expansion. Jean-Francois Baron. (Illus.). 240p. 1992. 115.00 (2-7184-0584-8) Blackwell Sci.

Plasma Waves & Instabilities at Comets & in Magnetospheres. Ed. by B. T. Tsurutani & H. Oya. (Geophysical Monograph Ser.: Vol. 53). 264p. 1989. 32.00 (0-87590-073-9) Am Geophysical.

Plasma Waves in the Magnetosphere. A. D. Walker. LC 93-20240. (Physics & Chemistry in Space Ser.: Vol. 24). 1993. 219.95 (0-387-56046-7) Spr-Verlag.

Plasmador. Luis M. Villar. (SPA.). 96p. (Orig.). 1984. pap. 6.00 (0-9606758-6-8) SLUSA.

Plasmapheresis: Therapeutic Applications & New Techniques. fac. ed. Ed. by Yukihiko Nose et al. LC 82-42896. (Illus.). 462p. pap. 143.30 (0-7837-7187-8, 204711200005) Bks Demand.

Plasmapheresis in Immunology & Oncology: Beitraege zur Onkologie. Contributions to Oncology, Vol. 10. Ed. by G. A. Nagel et al. (Illus.). viii, 266p. 1982. pap. 50.50 (3-8055-3467-1) S Karger.

Plasmas & Fluids. National Research Council Staff. (Physics Through the 1990's Ser.). 336p. 1986. pap. text 31.50 (0-309-03548-1) Natl Acad Pr.

Plasmas & Laser Light. fac. ed. Thomas P. Hughes. LC 77-357183. (Illus.). 540p. 1975. reprint ed. pap. 167.40 (0-7837-8010-9, 204776600008) Bks Demand.

Plasmas at High Temperature & Density: Applications & Implications of Laser-Plasma Interaction. Heinrich Hora. Ed. by W. Beiglbock et al. (Lecture Notes in Physics Ser.: Vol. M1). xii, 442p. 1991. 68.95 (0-387-54312-0) Spr-Verlag.

Plasmid Inheritance. Thomas. 1991. write for info. (0-8493-6175-3, CRC Reprint) Franklin.

Plasmids. Ed. by Peter Bennett. (C). 1997. text. write for info. (0-582-10125-5, Pub. by Addison-Wesley) Longman.

Plasmids. Novick. Date not set. 1.20 (0-7167-9273-7) W H Freeman.

Plasmids, No. 138. 2nd ed. Ed. by Kimber G. Hardy. (Practical Approach Ser.: Vol. 138). (Illus.). 280p. 1994. pap. text 50.00 (0-19-963444-0) OUP.

Plasminogen-Related Growth Factors, Vol. 212. Gregory Bock et al. LC 97-34811. (Ciba Foundation Symposium Ser.). 268p. 1998. 128.00 (0-471-97456-0) Wiley.

Plasmodesmata: Structure, Function, Role in Cell Communication. Ed. by Art J. Van Bel & W. J. van Kesteren. LC 99-20520. (Illus.). 350p. 1999. 219.00 (3-540-65169-1) Spr-Verlag.

Plasmodiophora Brassicae: The Cause of Cabbage Herhita. M. Woronin. (Phytopathological Classics Ser.). 32p. 1934. 22.00 (0-89054-005-5) Am Phytopathol Soc.

Plassey, 1757. Peter Harrington. (Campaign Ser.). 96p. 1994. pap. 14.95 (1-85532-352-4, 9534, Pub. by Ospry) Stackpole.

Plaste und Elaste: Ein Deutsch-Deutsches Woertebuch. 8th ed. Jule Hammer. (GER.). 98p. 1990. 19.95 (0-7859-8468-2, 3775903151) Fr & Eur.

Plaster Art: Step-by-Step. Dorothy S. Allen. Ed. by Tom Cole. LC 80-70317. (Illus.). 172p. (Orig.). 1981. pap. 12.95 (0-9605204-0-6) Dots Pubns.

Plaster of Paris Techniques from Scratch. Reid Harvey. (Illus.). 28p. 1996. pap. 9.95 (0-9650786-9-8) Gentle Br.

Plasterer. Jack Rudman. (Career Examination Ser.: C-589). 1994. pap. 23.95 (0-8373-0589-6) Nat Learn.

Plastering. 5th ed. J. B. Taylor. (Illus.). 264p. 1990. text 49.50 (0-582-05634-9, Pub. by Addison-Wesley) Trans-Atl Phila.

Plastering: Testbook, Pt. 1. California Department of Education Staff. (Apprenticeship Instructional Materials Ser.). 80p. 1972. pap. 3.50 (0-8011-0596-X) Calif Education.

Plastering: Testbook, Pt. 2. California Department of Education Staff. (Apprenticeship Instructional Materials Ser.). 68p. 1974. pap. 6.25 (0-8011-0599-4) Calif Education.

Plastering: Workbook, Pt. 1. California Department of Education Staff. (Apprenticeship Instructional Materials Ser.). (Illus.). 144p. 1972. pap. 4.00 (0-8011-0595-1) Calif Education.

Plastering: Workbook, Pt. 2. California Department of Education Staff. (Apprenticeship Instructional Materials Ser.). (Illus.). 148p. 1974. pap. 4.00 (0-8011-0598-6) Calif Education.

Plastering Skills. F. Van Den Branden & Thomas L. Hartsell. (Illus.). 543p. (Orig.). 1984. pap. 35.96 (0-8269-0657-5) Am Technical.

***Plasterwork: One Hundred Period Details.** Jeremy Musson & Michael Hall. (Illus.). 108p. 2000. pap. 24.95 (1-85410-685-6, Pub. by Aurum Pr) London Brdge.

Plasterworks. John Plowman. (Illus.). 128p. 1996. 18.99 (0-89134-707-0, North Lght Bks) F & W Pubns Inc.

***Plasterworks: A Beginner's Guide to Molding & Decorating Plaster Projects from Stars & Cherubs to Shells & Sunflowers.** John Plowman. (Illus.). 128p. 2000. reprint ed. text 19.00 (0-7881-9276-0) DIANE Pub.

Plastic: The Making of a Synthetic Century. Stephen Fenichell. 1997. pap. 13.00 (0-88730-862-7, HarpBusn) HarpInfo.

Plastic Age: A Novel. Percy Marks. LC 80-17959. (Lost American Fiction Ser.). 352p. 1980. reprint ed. 16.95 (0-8093-0984-X) S Ill U Pr.

Plastic Age: Modernity to Post-Modernity. Sparke. 1996. pap. text 39.95 (1-85177-066-6, Pub. by V&A Ent) Antique Collect.

Plastic Analysis of Concrete Frames. M. Tichy & J. Rakosnik. Tr. by Dagmar et al from CZE. (Illus.). 320p. 1977. text 50.00 (0-569-08199-8) Scholium Intl.

Plastic Analysis of Reinforced Concrete Beams. Bruno Thurlimann. (IBA Ser.: No. 86). 20p. 1980. 14.50 (0-8176-1064-2) Birkhauser.

Plastic Analysis of Reinforced Concrete Shear Walls. Peter Marti. (IBA Ser.: No. 87). 19p. 1980. 12.50 (0-8176-1065-0) Birkhauser.

Plastic & Other Limit State Methods for Design Evaluation: Proceedings of a Session Sponsored by the Committee on Analysis & Design of Structures of the Structural Division. Ed. by V. B. Watwood, Jr. 94p. 1984. 5.00 (0-87262-423-4) Am Soc Civil Eng.

Plastic & Reconstructive Breast Surgery. G. Lemperle & J. Nievergelt. (Illus.). x, 192p. 1991. 262.00 (0-387-52868-7) Spr-Verlag.

***Plastic & Reconstructive Breast Surgery.** 2nd ed. John Bostwick, 3rd. LC 99-46503. (Illus.). 1606p. 1999. text 420.00 (1-57626-104-2) Quality Med Pub.

Plastic & Reconstructive Surgery. Nancymarie Fortunato & Susan M. McCullough. LC 98-155078. (Perioperative Nursing Ser.). (Illus.). 208p. (C). (gr. 13). 1998. text 54.95 (0-8151-3305-7, 27472) Mosby Inc.

Plastic & Reconstructive Surgery of the Breast: A Surgical Atlas. Heinz Bohmert. LC 96-33255. (Illus.). 2388p. 1996. text 199.00 (0-86577-628-8) Thieme Med Pubs.

Plastic & Reconstructive Surgery of the Face & Neck, 2 vols. Ed. by John Conley & John T. Dickinson. Incl. Vol. 1. Aesthetic Surgery. 264p. 1972. 58.25 (0-8089-0750-6, W B Saunders Co); (Illus.). 1972. write for info. (0-318-52859-2, Grune & Strat) Harcrt Hlth Sci Grp.

Plastic & Reconstructive Surgery of the Head & Neck. Fred Stucker. 1990. 169.00 (1-55664-211-3) Mosby Inc.

Plastic & Reconstructive Surgery of the Nose. Nabil I. Elsahy. (Illus.). 655p. 1998. text. write for info. (0-7216-7722-3, W B Saunders Co) Harcrt Hlth Sci Grp.

Plastic & Reconstructive Surgery of the Orbitopalpebral Region. Denys Montandon et al. (Illus.). 360p. 1990. text 98.00 (0-443-04486-4) Church.

***Plastic Bag.** (C). 1999. 0.00 (0-201-61687-4) HEPC Inc.

Plastic Bending: Theory & Applications. T. X. Yu & C. Zhang. 350p. 1996. text 85.00 (981-02-2267-X) World Scientific Pub.

Plastic Bottles. Nikki Connor. LC 96-45580. (Creative Crafts from Ser.). (Illus.). 24p. (J). (ps-2). 1997. lib. bdg. 19.90 (0-7613-0553-X, Copper Beech Bks) Millbrook Pr.

Plastic Canvas All-Occasion Gifts. Ed. by Laura Scott. LC 98-73375. (Illus.). 176p. 1998. 19.95 (1-882138-41-4) Hse White Birches.

Plastic Canvas Celebration Gifts. LC 93-86079. 160p. 1994. 19.96 (0-9638031-2-3) Needlecrft Shop.

Plastic Canvas Seasonal Sensations. LC 93-85500. 160p. 1993. 19.96 (0-9638031-0-7) Needlecrft Shop.

***Plastic Canvaswork: Project for Your Home.** Meg Evans. 128p. 1999. 27.95 (0-7153-0837-8) Strlng Pub CA.

Plastic Canvaswork: 21 Quick & Easy Projects for the Home. Meg Evans. (Illus.). 80p. 1996. 19.95 (1-85470-222-X, Pub. by Collins & Br) Trafalgar.

Plastic Component Design. Paul Campbell. 1996. 40.95 (0-8311-3065-2) Indus Pr.

Plastic Components, Processes & Technology. (Special Publications). 270p. 1999. pap. 109.00 (0-7680-0342-3, SP-1410) Soc Auto Engineers.

Plastic Containers for Pharmaceuticals: Testing & Control. J. Cooper. (Offset Publications: No. 4). 1974. pap. text 28.80 (92-4-170004-1, 1120004) World Health.

Plastic Cup Collectibles. Bryan Meccariello. LC 97-80679. 128p. 1998. pap. 14.95 (0-7643-0473-9) Schiffer.

Plastic Cups. Nikki Conner. LC 96-12632. (Use Your Junk Ser.). (Illus.). 24p. (J). (ps-2). 1996. lib. bdg. 19.90 (0-7613-0539-4, Copper Beech Bks) Millbrook Pr.

Plastic Deformation of Ceramics: Proceedings of an International Engineering Conference Held in Snowbird, Utah, August 7-12, 1994. R. C. Bradt et al. (Illus.). 684p. (C). 1995. text 155.00 (0-306-45120-4, Kluwer Plenum) Kluwer Academic.

Plastic Design & Second-Order Analysis of Steel Frames. Wai-Fah Chen & I. Sohal. LC 94-11614. 1994. 109.95 (0-387-94314-5) Spr-Verlag.

Plastic Design in Steel: A Guide & Commentary. 2nd ed. (Manual & Report of Engineering Practice Ser.: No. 41). 348p. 1971. pap. 28.00 (0-87262-217-7) Am Soc Civil Eng.

Plastic Design of Braced Multistory Steel Frames. 124p. 1968. 20.00 (1-56424-005-3, M004) Am Inst Steel Construct.

Plastic Design of Complex Shape Structures. Wojciech Szczepinski & Jan Szlagowski. 1989. text 97.00 (0-470-21163-6) P-H.

Plastic Design of Low-Rise Frames. M. R. Horne & L. J. Morris. (Structural Mechanics Ser.). (Illus.). 256p. 1982. 60.00 (0-262-08123-7) MIT Pr.

Plastic Design of Steel. Mrazik et al. LC 85-5623. 420p. 1987. text 116.00 (0-470-20132-0) P-H.

Plastic Drinking Glasses & Church Fathers: Semantic Extension from the Ethnoscience Tradition. David Kronenfeld. (Illus.). 288p. 1996. pap. 29.95 (0-19-509408-5) OUP.

Plastic-Encapsulated Microelectronics: Materials, Processes, Quality, Reliability & Applications. Luu T. Nguyen. Ed. by Michael G. Pecht et al. 512p. 1995. 200.00 (0-471-30625-8) Wiley.

Plastic Enclosures in Portable Electronics, No. YP-150. Howard Kibbel. (Illus.). 138p. 1994. 2650.00 (1-56965-252-X, P-150) BCC.

***Plastic Fiber Optics: Principles, Components, Installation.** 5th ed. Andreas Weinert. 148p. 2000. 55.00 (3-89578-135-5) Wiley.

Plastic Film Technology: Extrusion of Plastic Film & Sheeting, Vol. 2. Ed. by Kier M. Finlayson. LC 89-51355. 350p. 1993. pap. text 84.95 (1-56676-018-6) Technomic.

Plastic Film Technology Vol. 1: High Barrier Plastic Films for Packaging. Ed. by Kier M. Finlayson. LC 89-51355. 276p. 1989. pap. 74.95 (0-87762-711-8) Technomic.

Plastic Films. 3rd ed. Briston. 1996. (0-582-01490-5) Addison-Wesley.

Plastic Films: Technology & Packaging Applications. Wilmer A. Jenkins & Kenton R. Osborn. LC 91-66456. 258p. 1991. 49.95 (0-87762-843-2) Technomic.

Plastic Foams, Pt. 2. Ed. by Kurt C. Frisch & James H. Saunders. LC 71-157837. (Monographs on Plastics: No. 1). (Illus.). 589p. reprint ed. pap. 182.60 (0-7837-3378-X, 204333600002) Bks Demand.

Plastic Foams, Pt.1. Ed. by Kurt C. Frisch & J. H. Saunders. LC 71-157837. (Monographs on Plastics). 464p. reprint ed. 143.90 (0-8357-9092-4, 205505900001) Bks Demand.

Plastic Foams: Proceedings of a Special Conference, Los Angeles. (Illus.). 188p. 1990. reprint ed. pap. 42.00 (0-938648-03-9) T-C Pr CA.

***Plastic Food Packaging Materials: Barrier Function, Mass Transport, Quality Assurance, Legislation.** Otto G. Piringer. 606p. 2000. 245.00 (3-527-28868-6) Wiley.

Plastic Glasses & Church Fathers: Semantic Extension from the Ethnoscience Tradition. David Kronenfeld. (Illus.). 288p. 1996. text 65.00 (0-19-509407-7) OUP.

Plastic Handbags: Sculpture to Wear. Kate E. Dooner. LC 92-85176. (Illus.). 112p. (Orig.). 1993. pap. 24.95 (0-88740-466-9) Schiffer.

Plastic Hinge Based Methods for Advanced Analysis & Design of Steel Frames: An Assessment of the State-of-the-Art. Ed. by Wai Fah Chen. 309p. (Orig.). 1993. pap. 40.00 (1-879749-53-X) Structural Stability.

Plastic Hinge Based Methods for Advanced Analysis & Design of Steel Frames: An Assessment of the State-of-the-Art. Ed. by Donald W. White & Wai-Fah Chen. 310p. (Orig.). 1994. 40.00 (0-685-75147-3, SSRC1) Am Soc Civil Eng.

Plastic Injection Molding: Manufacturing Process Fundamentals. Douglas M. Bryce. LC 96-67394. (Illus.). 277p. 1996. 76.00 (0-87263-472-8, 2457) SME.

***Plastic Injection Molding: Manufacturing Startup & Management.** Douglas M. Bryce. LC 98-61657. 208p. 1999. 76.00 (0-87263-503-1) SME.

Plastic Injection Molding: Material Selection & Product Design Fundamentals. Douglas M. Bryce. LC 97-68807. (Illus.). 380p. 1997. 76.00 (0-87263-488-4, 2599) SME.

Plastic Injection Molding: Mold Design & Construction Fundamentals. Douglas M. Bryce. LC 98-60567. (Illus.). 193p. 1998. 76.00 (0-87263-495-7, 2673) SME.

Plastic Injection Molding Made Easy. unabridged ed. R. L. Nyborg. (Illus.). 95p. 1991. pap. 22.00 (1-57002-074-4) Univ Publng Hse.

Plastic Jewelry. rev. ed. Lyngerda Kelley & Nancy Schiffer. 159p. 1996. pap. 14.95 (0-7643-0124-1) Schiffer.

Plastic Laminates, 1992: Short Course, Westin Peachtree Plaza Hotel, Atlanta, GA, August 17-20. Technical Association of the Pulp & Paper Industry. LC TS1109.T4. (TAPPI Notes Ser.). (Illus.). 226p. reprint ed. pap. 70.10 (0-7837-3401-8, 204336000008) Bks Demand.

Plastic Laminates Symposium, 1994: Hyatt Regency, Atlanta, GA, August 22-25. Technical Association of the Pulp & Paper Industry. LC TP1183.L3P53. (TAPPI Proceedings Ser.). (Illus.). 216p. 1994. pap. 67.00 (0-608-05368-6, 208241700010) Bks Demand.

P

An Asterisk (*) at the beginning of an entry indicates that the title is appearing for the first time.

Plastic Limit Analysis of Plates, Shells & Disks. M. A. Save et al. LC 97-34690. (North-Holland Series in Applied Mathematics & Mechanics). 1997. 244.00 (0-444-89479-9) Elsevier.

*Plastic Little: Captain's Log. Satoshi Urushihara. Tr. by Laura Jackson & Yoko Kobayashi from JPN. (Illus.). 160p. 1998. pap. 15.95 (1-56219-910-2, CMX 0609) Central Pk Media.

Plastic Machinery, Materials & Resins in Chile: A Strategic Entry Report, 1998. Compiled by Icon Group International Staff. (Country Industry Report). (Illus.). 120p. 1999. ring bd. 1200.00 incl. audio compact disk (0-7418-0529-4) Icon Grp.

Plastic Man Archives. Jack Cole. (Illus.). 224p. 1998. 49.95 (1-56389-468-8, Pub. by DC Comics) Time Warner.

*Plastic Mater Data Handbook. Martin. 2002. pap. 125.00 (0-07-135921-4) McGraw.

Plastic Materials & Resins in China: A Strategic Entry Report, 1997. Compiled by Icon Group International Staff. (Country Industry Report). (Illus.). 179p. 1999. ring bd. 1790.00 incl. audio compact disk (0-7418-0296-1) Icon Grp.

Plastic Materials & Resins in Egypt: A Strategic Entry Report, 1998. Compiled by Icon Group International Staff. (Country Industry Report). (Illus.). 166p. 1999. ring bd. 1660.00 incl. audio compact disk (0-7418-0297-X) Icon Grp.

Plastic Materials & Resins in Hong Kong: A Strategic Entry Report, 1998. Compiled by Icon Group International Staff. (Country Industry Report). (Illus.). 126p. 1999. ring bd. 1260.00 incl. audio compact disk (0-7418-0531-6) Icon Grp.

Plastic Materials & Resins in Pakistan: A Strategic Entry Report, 1998. Compiled by Icon Group International Staff. (Country Industry Report). (Illus.). 177p. 1999. ring bd. 1770.00 incl. audio compact disk (0-7418-0532-4) Icon Grp.

Plastic Materials & Their Properties - Student's Manual: Molding Materials & Process Troubleshooting, Module Four, Lesson 1. (Illus.). 1997. pap., student ed. write for info. (1-58677-034-9) Polymer Train.

*Plastic Materials, Resins - Polyethylenes in Colombia: A Strategic Entry Report, 1996. Compiled by Icon Group International Staff. (Illus.). 188p. 1999. ring bd. 1880.00 incl. audio compact disk (0-7418-1369-6) Icon Grp.

Plastic Model Kits. Jack C. Harris. LC 91-25201. (Hobby Guides Ser.). (Illus.). 48p. (J). (gr. 5-6). 1993. lib. bdg. 12.95 (0-89686-623-8, Crstwood Hse) Silver Burdett Pr.

*Plastic Molding Equipment in Canada: A Strategic Entry Report, 1995. Compiled by Icon Group International Staff. (Illus.). 131p. 1999. ring bd. 1310.00 incl. audio compact disk (0-7418-1629-6) Icon Grp.

Plastic Mortars, Sealants, & Caulking Compounds. Ed. by Raymond B. Seymour. LC 79-19752. (ACS Symposium Ser.: No. 113). 1979. 32.95 (0-8412-0523-X) Am Chemical.

Plastic Mortars, Sealants, & Caulking Compounds. Ed. by Raymond B. Seymour. LC 79-19752. (ACS Symposium Ser.: Vol. 113). 192p. 1979. reprint ed. pap. 59.60 (0-608-03053-8, 206350600007) Bks Demand.

Plastic Optical Fiber Data Book. 1997. 120.00 (0-614-26577-0) Info Gatekeepers.

Plastic Optical Fiber Data Communication Primer. 1997. 29.95 (0-614-26578-9) Info Gatekeepers.

Plastic Optical Fiber Design Manual - Handbook & Buyer's Guide. 208p. 1993. 49.95 (0-614-26576-2, POFHO1) Info Gatekeepers.

Plastic Optical Fiber Design Manual - Handbook & Buyers Guide. 200p. 1993. pap. 49.95 (1-56851-011-X) Info Gatekeepers.

Plastic Optical Fiber Market & Technology Assessment. 320p. 1992. pap. 1995.00 (1-56851-001-2, IGIC-76) Info Gatekeepers.

Plastic Optical Fiber Market & Technology Assessment. 320p. 1996. 1995.00 (0-614-26567-3, IGIC-57) Info Gatekeepers.

Plastic Optical Fiber, '95: Boston, MA. 1995. 125.00 (0-614-26565-7, P95PRC) Info Gatekeepers.

Plastic Optical Fiber, '94: Yokehama, Japan. 1994. 125.00 (0-614-26556-8, P94PRC) Info Gatekeepers.

Plastic Optical Fiber, '91: San Diego, CA. 1991. 125.00 (0-614-26525-8, P91PRC) Info Gatekeepers.

Plastic Optical Fiber-91 Conference Proceedings. 1991. 100.00 (0-614-26568-1, P91PRC) Info Gatekeepers.

Plastic Optical Fiber, '96: Paris, France. 1996. 125.00 (0-614-26566-5, POF96) Info Gatekeepers.

Plastic Optical Fiber Sign & Illumination Directory. 1997. 75.00 (0-614-26575-4, POFSID) Info Gatekeepers.

Plastic Optical Fibers & Applications. rev. ed. IGIC, Inc. Staff. (Fiber Optics Reprint Ser.: Vol. 25). (Illus.). 222p. 1994. pap. 75.00 (1-56851-074-8) Info Gatekeepers.

Plastic Optical Fibers for Data Communications. 1996. pap. 2995.00 (1-56851-143-4, IGIC19) Info Gatekeepers.

Plastic Optical Fibers, '90: Boston, MA. 1997. 125.00 (0-614-26520-7, P90PRC) Info Gatekeepers.

Plastic Optical Fibres: Practical Applications. LC 95-49523. 168p. 1997. 105.00 (0-471-95639-2) Wiley.

Plastic Part Design for Injection Molding: An Introduction. Robert A. Malloy. 450p. (C). 1994. 79.50 (1-56990-129-5) Hanser-Gardner.

Plastic Part Technology. Edward A. Muccio. (Illus.). 304p. 1991. 94.00 (0-87170-432-3, 6901) ASM.

*Plastic People of the Universe. Ed. by Jaroslav Riedel. 185p. 1999. 17.00 (80-86013-58-8, Pub. by Mata) SPD-Small Pr Dist.

Plastic Pipe for Subsurface Drainage of Transportation Facilities. (National Cooperative Highway Research Program Report Ser.: No. 225). 153p. 1980. 9.60 (0-309-03030-7, NR225) Transport Res Bd.

*Plastic Piping Handbook. David A. Willoughby. (Handbooks Ser.). (Illus.). 750p. 2000. 99.95 (0-07-135956-7) McGraw.

Plastic Piping Systems. 2nd ed. David A. Chasis. (Illus.). 172p. 1988. 32.95 (0-8311-1181-X) Indus Pr.

Plastic Piping Systems Development for Natural Gas Applications. Battelle Memorial Institute Staff et al. 50p. 1970. pap. 4.00 (0-318-12668-0, X10180) Am Gas Assn.

*Plastic Processes, Components, & Technology. (Special Publications). 98p. 2000. 99.00 (0-7680-0584-1, SP-1534) Soc Auto Engineers.

Plastic Processing Behavior - Student's Manual: Molding Materials & Process Troubleshooting, Module Four, Lesson 3. (Illus.). 1997. pap., student ed. write for info. (1-58677-035-7) Polymer Train.

Plastic Production Equipment in Mexico: A Strategic Entry Report, 1997. Compiled by Icon Group International Staff. (Illus.). 144p. 1999. ring bd. 1440.00 incl. audio compact disk (0-7418-1067-0) Icon Grp.

Plastic Products Design Handbook: Processes & Design for Processes, Pt. B. Ed. by Edward Miller. (Mechanical Engineering Ser.: Vol. 8). (Illus.). 392p. 1983. text 175.00 (0-8247-1886-0) Dekker.

Plastic, Reconstructive & Aesthetic Surgery. Ed. by Kiyonori Harii et al. (Illus.). 726p. 1995. text 343.00 (90-6299-118-1, Pub. by Kugler) Kugler Pubns.

Plastic Redirections in 20th Century Painting: The Meaning of Unintelligibility in Modern Art. James J. Sweeney & Edward F. Rothschild. 15.00 (0-685-11368-X, 11380) Ayer.

*Plastic Resins in Primary Forms in Hong Kong: A Strategic Entry Report, 1995. Compiled by Icon Group International Staff. (Illus.). 126p. 1999. ring bd. 1260.00 incl. audio compact disk (0-7418-1631-8) Icon Grp.

Plastic Sheeting: Its Use for Emergency Housing & Other Purposes. Jim Howard & Ron Spice. (Illus.). 40p. (C). 1988. 5.95 (0-85598-140-7, Pub. by Oxfam Pub) Stylus Pub VA.

Plastic Soup: Dream Poems. Charles Ghigna. LC 99-36168. 1998. 16.95 (1-57966-004-5, Black Belt) Black Belt Communs.

Plastic Surgery. 3rd ed. Ed. by William X. Grabb & James W. Smith. 1980. 69.50 (0-316-32269-5, Little Brwn Med Div) Lppncott W & W.

Plastic Surgery, 8 vols., Set. 3rd ed. McCarthy. (Illus.). 6448p. 1989. text 995.00 (0-7216-1514-7, W B Saunders Co) Harcrt Hlth Sci Grp.

Plastic Surgery, Vol. 1. 3rd ed. McCarthy. 1989. text 165.00 (0-7216-2542-8, W B Saunders Co) Harcrt Hlth Sci Grp.

Plastic Surgery, Vol. 2. 3rd ed. McCarthy. 1989. text 165.00 (0-7216-2543-6, W B Saunders Co) Harcrt Hlth Sci Grp.

Plastic Surgery, Vol. 3. 3rd ed. McCarthy. 1989. text 165.00 (0-7216-2544-4, W B Saunders Co) Harcrt Hlth Sci Grp.

Plastic Surgery, Vol. 4. 3rd ed. McCarthy. 1989. text 165.00 (0-7216-2545-2, W B Saunders Co) Harcrt Hlth Sci Grp.

Plastic Surgery, Vol. 5. 3rd ed. McCarthy. 1989. text 165.00 (0-7216-2546-0, W B Saunders Co) Harcrt Hlth Sci Grp.

Plastic Surgery, Vol. 6. 3rd ed. McCarthy. 1989. text 165.00 (0-7216-2547-9, W B Saunders Co) Harcrt Hlth Sci Grp.

Plastic Surgery, Vol. 7. 3rd ed. McCarthy. 1989. text 165.00 (0-7216-2548-7, W B Saunders Co) Harcrt Hlth Sci Grp.

Plastic Surgery, Vol. 8. 3rd ed. McCarthy. 1989. text 165.00 (0-7216-2549-5, W B Saunders Co) Harcrt Hlth Sci Grp.

Plastic Surgery: Past & Present. J. Gabka & E. Vaubel. (Illus.). viii, 180p. 1983. 256.75 (3-8055-3651-8) S Karger.

Plastic Surgery: What You Need to Know Before, During, & After. Richard Marfuggi. LC 97-15709. 272p. 1998. pap. 15.00 (0-399-52374-X, Perigee Bks) Berkley Pub.

Plastic Surgery Hopscotch: A Resource Guide for Those Considering Cosmetic Surgery. John McCabe. Ed. by Miriam Ingersoll. LC 93-74927. 384p. 1995. pap. 19.95 (1-884702-32-5) Carmania Bks.

Plastic Surgery in Pedeatrics. Ian Muir. 1988. 116.00 (0-316-58944-6, Little Brwn Med Div) Lppncott W & W.

Plastic Surgery Malpractice & Damages, 1. Jeffrey D. Robertson & William T. Keavy. (Medico-Legal Library Ser.). 512p. 1993. boxed set 145.00 (0-471-60831-9) Wiley.

Plastic Surgery, Nerve Repair, Burns. Ed. by Gunther O. Schlag. LC 94-41582. (Fibrin Sealing in Surgical & Nonsurgical Fields Ser.: Vol. 3). 1995. 59.95 (3-540-58550-8) Spr-Verlag.

Plastic Surgery of the Breast. Maxwell. (Illus.). 900p. 1993. text 250.00 (0-8016-5821-7) Mosby Inc.

Plastic Surgery of the Facial Skeleton. S. Anthony Wolfe. 500p. 1989. 345.00 (0-316-95105-6, Little Brwn Med Div) Lppncott W & W.

Plastic Surgery of the Head & Neck, 2 vols. Ed. by Richard B. Stark. (Illus.). 1580p. 1986. text 320.00 (0-443-08249-9) Church.

Plastic Surgery of the Orbit & Eyelids. Caludia Tessier. (gr. 13). 1981. 82.50 (0-89352-041-1) Mosby Inc.

Plastic Surgery Secrets. Jeffrey Weinzweig. LC 98-33916. (Secrets Ser.). (Illus.). 650p. 1998. pap. text 49.00 (1-56053-219-X) Hanley & Belfus.

Plastic Surgery Sourcebook. Kimberly Henry & Penny Heckaman. LC 96-49696. (Illus.). 240p. 1996. 30.00 (1-56565-464-1) Lowell Hse.

Plastic Surgery Sourcebook. 2nd ed. Kimberly Henry & Penny Heckaman. (Illus.). 240p. 1997. reprint ed. pap. 16.00 (1-56565-820-5, Anodyne) Lowell Hse.

Plastic Surgery Sourcebook. 2nd rev. ed. Kimberly A. Henry & Penny S. Heckaman. LC 99-24231. (Illus.). 272p. 1999. pap. 18.95 (0-7373-0087-6, 00876W) NTC Contemp Pub Co.

Plastic Surgery Sourcebook: Basic Consumer Health Information on Cosmetic & Reconstructive Plastic Surgery. Ed. by M. Lisa Weatherford. (Health Reference Ser.). 400p. 2000. lib. bdg. 48.00 (0-7808-0214-4) Omnigraphics Inc.

Plastic Techniques in Neurosurgery. Kalmon D. Post & James T. Goodrich. (Illus.). 168p. 1991. text 155.00 (0-86577-352-1) Thieme Med Pubs.

Plastic Templates for Traditional Patchwork Quilt Patterns: Instructions for 27 Easy-to-Make Designs. 81st ed. Rita Weiss. 32p. (Orig.). 1985. pap. 4.95 (0-486-24984-0) Dover.

Plastic Theory of Structures: In SI-Metric Units. 2nd ed. M. R. Horne. 1979. 90.00 (0-08-022737-6, Pub. by Pergamon Repr) Franklin.

Plastic Toys: Dimestore Dreams of the '50s & '60s. Bill Harlan. LC 93-85217. (Illus.). 288p. 1993. 69.95 (0-88740-460-X) Schiffer.

Plastic Twilite: A Novelette. Louis A. Marcialis. LC 97-90081. 83p. 1998. 12.95 (0-533-12283-X) Vantage.

Plastic Waste Management: Recycling & Alternatives: A Regional Technical Conference, September 24-25, 1991, Galt House Hotel, Louisville, KY. Society of Plastics Engineers Staff. LC TD0798.S62. (Illus.). 185p. reprint ed. pap. 57.40 (0-7837-1787-3, 204198600001) Bks Demand.

Plastic Waste Primer: A Handbook for Citizens. League of Women Voters Education Fund Staff. (Illus.). 152p. 1993. 10.95 (1-55821-229-9, 954) Lyons Pr.

Plastic Words: The Tyranny of a Modular Language. Uwe Poerksen. Tr. by Jutta Mason & David Cayley. LC 94-44589. (Illus.). 134p. 1995. 24.50 (0-271-01476-8) Pa St U Pr.

Plastically Crystalline State: (Orientationally-Disordered Crystals) Ed. by John N. Sherwood. LC 78-16086. 409p. reprint ed. pap. 126.80 (0-608-17669-9, 203038600069) Bks Demand.

Plasticisers: Principles & Practice. Alan S. Wilson. 316p. 1996. 90.00 (0-901716-76-6, Pub. by Inst Materials) Ashgate Pub Co.

Plasticity. Akhtar S. Khan & Sujian Huang. 440p. 1995. 110.00 (0-471-31043-3) Wiley.

Plasticity: Mathematical Theory & Numerical Analysis. Weimin Ham & B. D. Reddy. Ed. by J. E. Marsden et al. LC 98-51755. (Interdisciplinary Applied Mathematics Ser.: Vol. 9). (Illus.). 390p. 1999. 69.95 (0-387-98704-5) Spr-Verlag.

Plasticity: Theory & Application. Alexander Mendelson. LC 68-12718. (Macmillan Series in Applied Mechanics). 367p. reprint ed. pap. 113.80 (0-608-11610-6, 200354000034) Bks Demand.

Plasticity: Theory & Application. Alexander Mendelson. LC 82-21231. 368p. (C). 1983. reprint ed. lib. bdg. 43.50 (0-89874-582-9) Krieger.

Plasticity & Creep: Theory, Examples & Problems. Jacek J. Skrzypek. Ed. by Richard B. Hetnarski. LC 92-46871. 560p. 1993. boxed set 131.95 (0-8493-9936-X, BB9936) CRC Pr.

Plasticity & Failure Behaviour of Solids: Memorial Volume Dedicated to the Late Professor Yuriy Nickolaevich Rabotnov. Ed. by G. C. Sih et al. (C). 1990. text 201.00 (0-7923-0336-9) Kluwer Academic.

Plasticity & Morphology of the Central Nervous System. Ed. by C. L. Cazzulio et al. (C). 1989. text 152.50 (0-7462-0094-3) Kluwer Academic.

Plasticity & Regeneration of the Nervous System. Ed. by Paola S. Timiras et al. (Advances in Experimental Medicine & Biology Ser.: Vol. 296). (Illus.). 382p. (C). 1991. text 144.00 (0-306-43933-6, Kluwer Plenum) Kluwer Academic.

Plasticity for Engineers. C. R. Calladine. LC 85-14057. 318p. 1985. pap. text 31.95 (0-470-20235-1) P-H.

Plasticity in Epilepsy: Dynamic Aspects of Brain Function, Vol. 81. Hermann Stefan et al. 464p. text 142.00 (0-7817-1446-X) Lppncott W & W.

Plasticity in Nerve Cell Function. P. G. Kostyuk. (Illus.). 152p. 1999. text 115.00 (0-19-852418-8) OUP.

Plasticity in Structural Engineering, Fundamentals & Applications. C. C. Massonnet et al. (CISM International Centre for Mechanical Sciences Ser.: Vol. 241). (Illus.). 302p. 1980. 46.95 (0-387-81350-0) Spr-Verlag.

Plasticity in the Central Nervous System: Learning & Memory. Ed. by James L. McGaugh et al. 272p. 1995. text 39.95 (0-8058-1573-2) L Erlbaum Assocs.

Plasticity in the Nervous System. 2nd ed. B. I. Kotlyar. LC 92-1418. (Monographs in Neuroscience: Vol. 3). ix, 305p. 1992. text 141.00 (2-88124-525-0, QP376) Gordon & Breach.

Plasticity in the Somatosensory System of Developing & Mature Mammals. P. Wilson & P. J. Snow. Ed. by H. Autrum et al. (Progress in Sensory Physiology Ser.). (Illus.). 464p. 1991. 143.95 (0-387-52573-4) Spr-Verlag.

Plasticity of Development. Ed. by Steven Brauth et al. 184p. 1991. 38.50 (0-262-02326-1, Bradford Bks) MIT Pr.

Plasticity of Metals & Alloys: ISPMA-6. P. Lukac. (Key Engineering Materials Ser.: Vols. 97-98). (Illus.). 526p. (C). 1995. text 207.00 (0-87849-687-4, Pub. by Trans T Pub) Enfield Pubs NH.

Plasticity of Muscle. Ed. by D. Pette. (C). 1979. 146.15 (3-11-007961-5) De Gruyter.

Plasticity of the Central Nervous System. Ed. by Susumu Ishii & Keiji Sano. (Acta Neurochirugica - Supplementum Ser.: Supplementum 41). (Illus.). 140p. 1987. 131.00 (0-387-82027-2) Spr-Verlag.

Plasticity of the Neuromuscular System. LC 88-20780. (CIBA Foundation Symposium Ser.: No. 138). 284p. 1988. 128.00 (0-471-91902-0) Wiley.

Plasticity Theory. Jacob Lubliner. 500p. (C). 1990. text 75.00 (0-02-372161-8, Macmillan Coll) P-H.

Plasticity, Theory & Engineering Applications. S. Kaliszky. (Studies in Applied Mechanics: No. 21). 506p. 1989. 277.25 (0-444-98891-2) Elsevier.

Plasticity Today: New Solutions & Trends in Plasticity: Special Memorial Issue in Honor of Prof. Waclaw Olszak. Proceedings of the Plasticity Today Symposium, Udine, Italy, 27-30 June 1983. Antoni Sawczuk. (Illus.). 466p. 1985. pap. 61.00 (0-08-031657-3, Pub. by PPL) Elsevier.

Plasticization & Plasticizer Processes: A Symposium Sponsored by the Division of Industrial & Engineering Chemistry at the 147th Meeting of the American Chemical Society, Philadelphia, PA, April 6-7, 1964. American Chemical Society Staff. LC 65-23931. (Advances in Chemistry Ser.: Vol. 48). (Illus.). 210p. 1965. reprint ed. pap. 65.10 (0-608-06920-5, 206712800009) Bks Demand.

Plasticizers, Stabilizers & Thickeners. Ed. by Michael Ash & Irene Ash. (What Every Chemical Technologist Wants to Know About...Ser.: Vol. III). 422p. 1989. 80.00 (0-8206-0329-5) Chem Pub.

Plastics. Mark Lambert. (Spotlight on Resources Ser.). (Illus.). 48p. (J). (gr. 5 up). 1985. 12.95 (0-685-58326-0) Rourke Corp.

Plastics. Questech Staff. (Illus.). 120p. 1997. text 99.95 (1-58100-021-9) Beckley Cardy.

Plastics. 2nd ed. pap. text. write for info. (0-340-56043-6, Pub. by E A) Routldge.

*Plastics: A Laymans Guide. Maxwell. 160p. 1999. pap. 30.00 (1-86125-085-1) Institute of Management Consultants.

Plastics: America's Packaging Dilemma. Environmental Action Coalition Staff et al. LC 90-43801. 128p. 1990. pap. 15.95 (1-55963-062-0) Island Pr.

*Plastics: Collecting & Conserving. Kate Charlesworth. Ed. by Anita Quye & Colin Williamson. (Illus.). 128p. 1999. pap. 19.95 (1-901663-12-4, Pub. by Natl Mus Scotland) A Schwartz & Co.

Plastics: Components, Processes & Technology. LC 97-81304. 223p. 1998. 99.00 (0-7680-0160-9) Soc Auto Engineers.

Plastics: How Structure Determines Properties. Geza Gruenwald. 371p. 1993. 85.00 (1-56990-032-9) Hanser-Gardner.

*Plastics: Materials & Manufacturing Processes. 2nd ed. A. Brent Strong. LC 99-38587. (Illus.). 811p. 1999. 76.00 (0-13-021626-7) P-H.

Plastics: Microstructure Properties & Applications. 2nd ed. N. J. Mills. LC 93-15986. 377p. 1994. pap. text 64.95 (0-470-22132-1) Halsted Pr.

Plastics: Surface & Finish. 2nd ed. Ed. by W. Gordon Simpson. 327p. 1993. 105.00 (0-85186-209-8) CRC Pr.

Plastics ABC's: Polymer Alloys, Blends & Composites; National Technical Conference, Sheraton Bal Harbour, Bal Harbour, Florida, October 25-27, 1982. Society of Plastics Engineers Staff. LC TP1105.. 332p. reprint ed. pap. 103.00 (0-608-14339-1, 201965400013) Bks Demand.

Plastics Additives: An Industrial Guide. 2nd ed. Ernest W. Flick. LC 92-25241. 1089p. 1993. 125.00 (0-8155-1313-5) Noyes.

Plastics Additives & Modifiers Handbook. Ed. by Jesse Edenbaum. (Illus.). 1300p. 1992. mass mkt. 149.95 (0-442-23450-3) Chapman & Hall.

Plastics Additives Handbook. 4th ed. R. Gachter & H. Muller. 1001p. 1993. 99.50 (1-56990-153-8) Hanser-Gardner.

Plastics Age: From Bakelite to Beanbags & Beyond. Ed. by Penny Sparke. LC 92-35039. (Illus.). 1993. 35.00 (0-87951-471-X, Pub. by Overlook Pr) Penguin Putnam.

Plastics Age: From Bakelite to Beanbags & Beyond. Ed. by Penny Sparke. (Illus.). 160p. 1994. pap. 25.00 (0-87951-488-4, Pub. by Overlook Pr) Penguin Putnam.

Plastics & Additives in Plastics in Europe. Anthony Redverse-Mutton. LC 98-120918. (Report Ser.: No. P-163). 163p. 1997. 3350.00 (1-56965-274-0, P-163) BCC.

*Plastics & Coatings: Durability, Stabilization, Testing. Rose A. Ryntz. LC 00-39564. 2000. write for info. (1-56990-290-9) Hanser-Gardner.

Plastics & Design. Arnoldsche Art Publications Staff. (Illus.). 162p. 1997. 75.00 (3-925369-72-4, Pub. by Arnoldsche Art Pubs) Antique Collect.

Plastics & Polymers. Robert C. Mebane & Thomas R. Rybolt. (Everyday Material Science Experiments Ser.). (Illus.). 64p. (J). (gr. 5-8). 1995. lib. bdg. 18.90 (0-8050-2843-9) TFC Bks NY.

Plastics & Resin Compositions. Ed. by W. Gordon Simpson. 419p. 1995. 159.95 (0-85404-501-5, TP1130) CRC Pr.

Plastics & Technology. Ray Jaques. LC 93-31718. (Australian Technology Studies). 1994. pap. 13.95 (0-521-43886-1) Cambridge U Pr.

Plastics Are Fluid Again. I. S. Roverso. 1971. pap. 3.50 (0-913054-05-4) Poet Gal Pr.

Plastics Blow Molding Today & Tomorrow: Pushing the Process Limits: 4th Annual High Performance Blow Molding Technical Conference, October 16-17, 1989, Cherry Hill Hyatt, Cherry Hill, NJ. Society of Plastics Engineers Staff. LC TP1150.H53. (Illus.). 267p. reprint ed. pap. 82.80 (0-8357-3624-5, 203632500003) Bks Demand.

*Plastics Calculation Handbook. Margolis. 2000. 125.00 (0-07-135172-8) McGraw.

Plastics Careers. Harold Haugan. 1988. 12.50 (0-8187-0109-9) Harlo Press.

Plastics Composites for the 21st Century Construction: Proceedings of a Session. Ed. by Richard E. Chambers. LC 93-32978. 80p. 1993. 17.00 (0-87262-989-9) Am Soc Civil Eng.

An Asterisk (*) at the beginning of an entry indicates that the title is appearing for the first time.

Plastics Compounding: Equipment & Processing. David B. Todd. LC 97-33095. (Polymer Processing Institute Books from Hanser Publishers Ser.). 288p. 1998. 128.00 (*1-56990-236-4*) Hanser-Gardner.

Plastics Create a World of Difference: ANTEC 89, 47th Annual Technical Conference & Exhibits, May 1-4, 1989, New York. Society of Plastics Engineers Staff. LC TP1105.. (Conference Proceedings Ser.). 1936p. reprint ed. pap. 200.00 (*0-8357-8574-2*, 203494000091) Bks Demand.

Plastics Decorating from Start to Finish: Technical Papers Regional Technical Conference, March 3-4, 1992, Hyatt Regency, Indianapolis, IN. Society of Plastics Engineers Staff. LC TP1170.. 111p. reprint ed. pap. 34.50 (*0-7837-2153-6*, 204243900004) Bks Demand.

Plastics Disposal & Recycling: Technical Papers Regional Technical Conference, Airport Ramada Inn, Essington, PA March 9-10, 1988. Society of Plastics Engineers Staff. LC TP1105.. (Illus.). 138p. reprint ed. pap. 42.80 (*0-608-16040-7*, 203314200084) Bks Demand.

Plastics Engineering. R. J. Crawford. (Illus.). 360p. 1981. text 91.00 (*0-08-026262-7*, Pergamon Pr) Elsevier.

Plastics Engineering. R. J. Crawford. (Illus.). 360p. 1981. pap. text 32.00 (*0-08-026263-5*, Pergamon Pr) Elsevier.

Plastics Engineering. 3rd ed. R. J. Crawford. LC 97-36604. 352p. 1998. pap. text 49.95 (*0-7506-3764-1*) Buttrwrth-Heinemann.

Plastics Engineering Dictionary. Welling. 1981. 20.00 (*0-07-069220-3*) McGraw.

Plastics Engineering Dictionary. 2nd ed. Gisbert Kaliske. 648p. 1992. 210.00 (*0-7859-8914-5*) Fr & Eur.

Plastics Engineering Dictionary in English, French, German & Russian. 2nd ed. Gisbert Kaliske. (ENG, FRE, GER & RUS.). 648p. 1992. 195.00 (*0-7859-9343-6*) Fr & Eur.

Plastics-Engineering Today for Tomorrow's World: ANTEC 83, 41st Annual Technical Conference Proceedings, Hyatt Regency, Chicago, May 2-5, 1983. Society of Plastics Engineers Staff. LC TP1185.. 965p. reprint ed. pap. 200.00 (*0-608-13712-X*, 202044700018) Bks Demand.

Plastics Extrusion Equipment in Taiwan: A Strategic Entry Report, 1997. Compiled by Icon Group International Staff. (Illus.). 115p. 1999. ring bd. 1150.00 incl. audio compact disk (*0-7418-0885-4*) Icon Grp.

Plastics Extrusion Technology. 2nd ed. Friedhelm Hensen & U. Berghaus. LC 97-14385. 1997. 198.00 (*1-56990-225-9*) Hanser-Gardner.

Plastics Extrusion Technology Handbook. 2nd ed. Sidney Levy et al. (Illus.). 398p. 1989. 44.95 (*0-8311-1185-2*) Indus Pr.

Plastics Failure Guide: Cause & Prevention. Myer Ezrin. LC 96-32920. 464p. 1996. 130.00 (*1-56990-184-8*) Hanser-Gardner.

Plastics Finishing: Responding to Tomorrow's Global Requirements: RETEC Technical Papers, March 21 & 22, 1995. fac. ed. Society of Plastics Engineers Staff. LC TP1170.. 178p. 1995. reprint ed. pap. 55.20 (*0-608-00980-6*, 206183400012) Bks Demand.

Plastics for Barrier Packaging. Contrib. by J. Charles Forman. 269p. 1996. 2850.00 (*1-56965-265-1*, P-137R) BCC.

Plastics for Engineers: Materials, Properties, Applications. Hans Dominninghaus.Tr. of Die Kunststoffe und Ihre Bigenschaften. 798p. (C). 1993. 98.00 (*1-56990-011-6*) Hanser-Gardner.

Plastics for Medical Devices: What's Ahead? LC 97-120162. (Report Ser.: No. P-121R). 171p. 1996. 2950.00 (*1-56965-268-6*) BCC.

Plastics for Modellers. Alex Weiss. (Illus.). 160p. (Orig.). 1998. pap. 23.50 (*1-85486-170-0*) Nexus Special Interests.

Plastics for Portable Electronics: Proceedings, January 5-6, 1995, Las Vegas, Nevada. Society of Plastics Engineers Staff. LC TP1185.E4. (Illus.). 185p. 1995. reprint ed. pap. 57.40 (*0-7837-9717-6*, 206044800005) Bks Demand.

Plastics for Tomorrow's Medical Needs: Technical Papers; Regional Technical Conference, September 23-24, 1986, Hyatt Cherry Hill, Cherry Hill, NJ. Society of Plastics Engineers Staff. LC TP1185.M4. (Illus.). 298p. pap. 92.40 (*0-608-15530-6*, 202971100064) Bks Demand.

Plastics from Microbes: Microbial Synthesis of Polymers & Polymer Precursors. David P. Mobley. 280p. (C). 1994. 98.00 (*1-56990-128-7*) Hanser-Gardner.

Plastics Gearing: Selection & Application. Clifford E. Adams. (Mechanical Engineering Ser.: Vol. 49). (Illus.). 400p. 1986. text 175.00 (*0-8247-7498-1*) Dekker.

Plastics in a World Economy, ANTEC 1984: 42nd Technical Conference. Society of Plastics Engineers Staff. LC TP1105. 1123p. reprint ed. pap. 200.00 (*0-608-14778-8*, 202300800032) Bks Demand.

Plastics in Aircraft Interiors P-117. Business Communications Co., Inc. Staff. 218p. 1990. 2950.00 (*0-89336-765-6*) BCC.

Plastics in & for the Automotive Industry: Regional Technical Conference, Chicago, October 27, 28 & 29, 1992. Society of Plastics Engineers Staff. LC TP1185.. (Illus.). 222p. reprint ed. pap. 68.90 (*0-7837-4499-4*, 204427600001) Bks Demand.

Plastics in Architecture: A Guide to Acrylic & Polycarbonate. Ralph Montella. LC 85-1645. (Plastics Engineering Ser.: No. 10). (Illus.). 231p. reprint ed. pap. 71.70 (*0-7837-0868-8*, 204117600019) Bks Demand.

Plastics in Automobile Instrument Panels, Trim & Seating. 144p. 1990. 19.00 (*1-56091-031-3*, SP822) Soc Auto Engineers.

Plastics in Business Machines: Update. 215p. 1992. 2750.00 (*0-89336-923-3*, P-064U) BCC.

Plastics in ESD Applications. Business Communications Co., Inc. Staff. 198p. 1992. 2450.00 (*0-89336-575-0*, P-099R) BCC.

Plastics in Food Packaging: Properties, Design & Fabrication. Ed. by William E. Brown. (Packaging & Converting Technology Ser.: Vol. 5). (Illus.). 544p. 1992. text 199.00 (*0-8247-8685-8*) Dekker.

***Plastics in Germany: A Strategic Entry Report, 1996.** Compiled by Icon Group International Staff. (Illus.). 107p. 1999. ring bd. 1070.00 incl. audio compact disk (*0-7418-1370-X*) Icon Grp.

Plastics in Medical - Pharmaceutical Disposables: Driving Forces Creating New Opportunities. 1993. 2650.00 (*0-89336-958-6*, P-212) BCC.

Plastics in Medical Tubing. 108p. 1991. 1550.00 (*0-89336-861-X*, P-129) BCC.

Plastics in Medicine, Science & Law: Subject Survey Analysis with Research Bibliography. Roy R. Zimmerman. LC 85-478711. 150p. 1987. 47.50 (*0-88164-414-5*); pap. 44.50 (*0-88164-415-3*) ABBE Pubs Assn.

Plastics in Non-Packaging Medical Applications. BCC Staff. 224p. 1990. 2350.00 (*0-89336-725-7*, P121) BCC.

Plastics in the Automobile Industry. James Maxwell. (Authored (Royalty) Ser.). 200p. 1994. 69.00 (*1-56091-527-7*, R-147) Soc Auto Engineers.

Plastics in the Electrical Industry: Technical Papers, Regional Technical Conference, Milwaukee, Wisconsin, March 3-4, 1980. Society of Plastics Engineers Staff. LC TK0454.4.P55. (Illus.). 229p. reprint ed. pap. 71.00 (*0-608-10024-2*, 201201800081) Bks Demand.

Plastics Laboratory Procedures. Harry L. Hess. LC 78-26948. 1980. pap. write for info. (*0-672-97138-0*); pap., teacher ed. write for info. (*0-672-97268-9*) Macmillan.

***Plastics Machinery in Brazil: A Strategic Entry Report, 1999.** Compiled by Icon Group International. (Illus.). 162p. 1999. ring bd. 1620.00 incl. audio compact disk (*0-7418-1719-5*) Icon Grp.

Plastics Materials. 6th ed. J. A. Brydson. LC 94-44833. (Illus.). 896p. 1995. text 175.00 (*0-7506-1864-7*) Buttrwrth-Heinemann.

***Plastics Materials.** 7th ed. J. A. Brydson. LC 99-30623. 920p. 1999. text 175.00 (*0-7506-4132-0*) Buttrwrth-Heinemann.

Plastics Materials: Properties & Applications. 2nd ed. Arthur W. Birley et al. 208p. (C). (gr. 13). 1988. mass mkt. 47.50 (*0-412-01781-4*, Chap & Hall NY) Chapman & Hall.

Plastics Mold Design Engineering Handbook. 4th ed. J. Harry DuBois & Wayne I. Pribble. (Illus.). 704p. 1987. text 89.95 (*0-442-21897-4*) Chapman & Hall.

Plastics Molding, 4 vols., Vols. 1 - 4. A. Whelan. (gr. 13). 1991. text 139.95 (*0-442-30813-2*) Chapman & Hall.

Plastics Molding: Equipment, Processes, & Materials. Ed. by J. S. Robinson. LC 81-90745. x, 299p. 1981. pap. 42.00 (*0-942378-00-8*) Polymers & Plastics Tech Pub Hse.

Plastics Packaging Materials in India: A Strategic Entry Report, 1998. Compiled by Icon Group International Staff. (Country Industry Report). (Illus.). 190p. 1999. ring bd. 1900.00 incl. audio compact disk (*0-7418-0291-0*) Icon Grp.

Plastics-Pioneering the 21st Century: ANTEC 87: Conference Proceedings 45th Annual Technical Conference & Exhibit, Los Angeles, May 4-7, 1987. Society of Plastics Engineers Staff. LC TP1105.A562. (Society of Plastics Engineers, Technical Papers: Vol. 33). 1598p. reprint ed. pap. 200.00 (*0-608-17479-3*, 202997300067) Bks Demand.

Plastics Planning Conference: Proceedings, 1990. 1990. 225.00 (*0-685-38983-9*, DPP90) BCC.

Plastics Polymer Science & Technology. Ed. by Mahendra D. Baijal. LC 81-13066. (SPE Monographs). 959p. reprint ed. pap. 200.00 (*0-7837-2383-0*, 204006900006) Bks Demand.

Plastics Process Engineering. James L. Throne. LC 78-9883. (Illus.). 944p. reprint ed. pap. 200.00 (*0-608-18267-2*, 203298900082) Bks Demand.

Plastics Processing: An Introduction. Walter Michaeli. 211p. 1995. pap. 49.95 (*1-56990-144-9*) Hanser-Gardner.

Plastics Processing Data Handbook. Donald V. Rosato. (Illus.). 392p. 1989. mass mkt. 67.95 (*0-412-73920-8*, Chap & Hall NY) Chapman & Hall.

Plastics Processing Machinery in Argentina: A Strategic Entry Report, 1997. Compiled by Icon Group International Staff. (Country Industry Report). (Illus.). 142p. 1999. ring bd. 1420.00 incl. audio compact disk (*0-7418-0292-9*) Icon Grp.

Plastics Processing Technology. Edward A. Muccio. 323p. 1994. 87.00 (*0-87170-494-3*, 6614) ASM.

Plastics Product Design. R. Shastri. (Mechanical Engineering Ser.). Date not set. write for info. (*0-8247-9557-1*) Dekker.

Plastics Product Design & Process Engineering. Harold Belofsky. LC 94-48205. 552p. 1995. 139.00 (*1-56990-142-2*); pap. 69.00 (*1-56990-179-1*) Hanser-Gardner.

Plastics Production & Plastics Processing Machinery in Germany: A Strategic Entry Report, 1998. Compiled by Icon Group International Staff. (Country Industry Report). (Illus.). 108p. 1999. ring bd. 1080.00 incl. audio compact disk (*0-7418-0293-7*) Icon Grp.

***Plastics Production Equipment in Mexico: A Strategic Entry Report, 1999.** Compiled by Icon Group International. (Illus.). 145p. 1999. ring bd. 1450.00 incl. audio compact disk (*0-7418-1858-2*) Icon Grp.

Plastics Production Machinery & Parts in Indonesia: A Strategic Entry Report, 1998. Compiled by Icon Group International Staff. (Country Industry Report). (Illus.). 163p. 1999. ring bd. 1630.00 incl. audio compact disk (*0-7418-0530-8*) Icon Grp.

Plastics Production Machinery in Brazil: A Strategic Entry Report, 1997. Compiled by Icon Group International Staff. (Country Industry Report). (Illus.). 154p. 1999. ring bd. 1540.00 incl. audio compact disk (*0-7418-0294-5*) Icon Grp.

***Plastics Production Machinery in China: A Strategic Entry Report, 1999.** Compiled by Icon Group International. (Illus.). 174p. 1999. ring bd. 1740.00 incl. audio compact disk (*0-7418-1710-1*) Icon Grp.

***Plastics Production Machinery in Guatemala: A Strategic Entry Report, 1996.** Compiled by Icon Group International Staff. (Illus.). 111p. 1999. ring bd. 1110.00 incl. audio compact disk (*0-7418-1366-1*) Icon Grp.

***Plastics Production Machinery in Singapore: A Strategic Entry Report, 1995.** Compiled by Icon Group International Staff. (Illus.). 114p. 1999. ring bd. 1140.00 incl. audio compact disk (*0-7418-1630-X*) Icon Grp.

***Plastics Production Machinery in Thailand: A Strategic Entry Report, 1996.** Compiled by Icon Group International Staff. (Illus.). 140p. 1999. ring bd. 1400.00 incl. audio compact disk (*0-7418-1367-X*) Icon Grp.

Plastics Products Design: Technical Papers, Regional Technical Conference, 1984. Society of Plastics Engineers Staff. LC TA0455.. 177p. reprint ed. pap. 54.90 (*0-608-12961-5*, 202472700038) Bks Demand.

Plastics Products Design Handbook: Materials & Components, Pt. A. Ed. by Edward Miller. LC 81-9730. (Mechanical Engineering Ser.: No. 10). (Illus.). 615p. reprint ed. pap. 190.70 (*0-7837-4083-2*, 205248000001) Bks Demand.

Plastics, Properties & Testing to Polyvinyl Compounds see Ullmann's Encyclopedia of Industrial Chemistry

Plastics Recognized Component Directory, 1997. (C). 1997. pap. text 46.00 (*0-7629-0099-7*) Underwrtrs Labs.

Plastics Recognized Components Directory, 1996. (C). 1996. pap. text 42.00 (*1-55989-957-3*) Underwrtrs Labs.

Plastics Recycling. (Report Ser.: No. P-216R). 382p. 1996. 2950.00 (*1-56965-267-8*) BCC.

Plastics Recycling: Blueprint for Success: A Regional Technical Conference, The Benson Hotel, Portland, Oregon, September 24 & 25, 1992. Society of Plastics Engineers Staff. LC TP1122.. (Illus.). 140p. reprint ed. pap. 43.40 (*0-7837-4495-1*, 204427200001) Bks Demand.

Plastics Recycling: Products & Processes. Raymond J. Ehrig. 303p. 1992. 64.50 (*1-56990-015-9*) Hanser-Gardner.

Plastics Recycling: Technology Charts the Course: Technical Conference, November 3-4, 1994. Society of Plastics Engineers Staff. LC TP1122.. (Illus.). 318p. 1994. reprint ed. pap. 98.60 (*0-7837-9718-4*, 206044900005) Bks Demand.

Plastics Recycling Equipment in Argentina: A Strategic Entry Report, 1997. Compiled by Icon Group International Staff. (Country Industry Report). (Illus.). 139p. 1999. ring bd. 1390.00 incl. audio compact disk (*0-7418-0308-9*) Icon Grp.

Plastics Repair. rev. ed. Ed. by Deere & Company Staff. (Fundamentals of Service Ser.). (Illus.). 48p. 1994. pap. text 11.95 (*0-86691-223-1*, FOS6501NC) Deere & Co.

Plastics, Rubber, & Paper Recycling: A Pragmatic Approach. Ed. by Charles P. Rader. LC 95-37097. (Symposium Ser.: Vol. 609). 1995. 119.95 (*0-614-09700-2*) Am Chemical.

Plastics, Rubber, & Paper Recycling: A Pragmatic Approach. Charles P. Rader et al. (ACS Symposium Ser.: No. 609). (Illus.). 544p. 1995. text 130.00 (*0-8412-3325-X*, Pub. by Am Chemical) OUP.

Plastics South: The SPI-SPE Connection . . . Filling a Real Need: Conference Proceedings, Georgia World Congress Center, Atlanta, GA, October 8-10, 1986. Society of Plastics Engineers Staff. LC TP1150.. (Illus.). 379p. pap. 117.50 (*0-608-15529-2*, 202971000064) Bks Demand.

Plastics Technical Dictionary: English-German, German-English. Annemarie Wittfoht. (ENG & GER.). 1992. 195.00 (*0-7859-6935-7*) Fr & Eur.

Plastics Technical Dictionary: English-German/German-English. Annemarie Wittfoht. 1620p. 1992. 97.50 (*1-56990-110-4*) Hanser-Gardner.

Plastics Technical Dictionary: German-Spanish, Spanish-German. Annemarie Wittfoht. (GER & SPA.). 469p. 1981. 150.00 (*0-7859-6934-9*) Fr & Eur.

Plastics Technology Handbook. 3rd ed. Chanda & Roy. LC 98-9729. (Illus.). 1214p. 1998. text 250.00 (*0-8247-0066-X*) Dekker.

Plastics vs. Paper & Paperboard. Business Communications Co., Inc. Staff. 302p. 1994. 2650.00 (*0-89336-757-5*, P027U) BCC.

Plastics Waste: Recovery of Economic Value. Jacob Leidner. LC 81-2752. (Plastics Engineering Ser.: No. 1). 327p. reprint ed. pap. 101.40 (*0-7837-5885-5*, 204560500006) Bks Demand.

Plastics Waste Management: Disposal, Recycling, & Reuse. Mustafa. (Environmental Science & Pollution Ser.: Vol. 5). (Illus.). 432p. 1993. text 180.00 (*0-8247-8920-2*) Dekker.

Plastics Wastes: Management, Control, Recycling, & Disposal. U. S. EPA Staff et al. LC 90-23207. (Pollution Technology Review Ser.: No. 201). (Illus.). 479p. 1991. 98.00 (*0-8155-1265-1*) Noyes.

Plastics/Elastomers Under-the-Hood: A Robust Market. Melvin Schlechter. 138p. 1995. 2750.00 (*1-56965-317-8*, P-123R) BCC.

Plasticville: Poems. David Trinidad. LC 99-71392. 101p. 2000. pap. 14.99 (*1-885983-46-8*, Pub. by Turtle Point Pr) Dist Art Pubs.

Plastidaere Mosaikgene: Struktur und Funktion Des Chloroplasten-Gens Fuer die tRNALys Aus Sinapis Alba L. 1988. Heike Neuhaus. (Dissertationes Botanicae Ser.: Band 115). (GER., Illus.). v, 100p. 1988. pap. 36.00 (*3-443-64027-3*, Pub. by Gebruder Borntraeger) Balogh.

Plastination: A Tool for Teaching & Research: The 8th International Conference on Plastination, Brisbane, July 1996. Ed. by Andreas H. Weiglein. (Acta Anatomica Ser.: Vol. 158, No. 1, 1997). (Illus.). 82p. 1997. pap. 75.00 (*3-8055-6572-0*) S Karger.

Plastique, Nos. 1[00ad]5. Ed. by Hans Arp et al. LC 74-91379. (Contemporary Art Ser.). 1970. reprint ed. 15.95 (*0-405-00725-6*) Ayer.

***Plat Book of Minnesota.** 116p. 1999. pap. 15.00 (*0-915709-72-4*) Pk Geneal Bk.

Plate Bending Analysis with Boundary Elements. Ed. by M. H. Aliabadi. LC 97-67408. (Advances in Boundary Elements Ser.: Vol. 2). 368p. 1998. 148.00 (*1-85312-531-8*, 5318) Computational Mech MA.

Plate Bending & Finite Element Analysis of Spur & Helical Gear Tooth Deflection. H. R. Busby & Donald R. Houser. (1985 Fall Technical Meeting Ser.: Vol. 85FTM4). 10p. 1985. pap. text 30.00 (*1-55589-097-0*) AGMA.

Plate Reconstruction from Paleozoic Paleomagnetism. Ed. by R. Van der Voo et al. (Geodynamics Ser.: Vol. 12). 136p. 1984. 20.00 (*0-87590-512-9*) Am Geophysical.

Plate Stability by Boundary Element Method. Ed. by A. Elzein et al. (Lecture Notes in Engineering Ser.: Vol. 64). (Illus.). v, 205p. 1991. 45.95 (*0-387-53710-4*) Spr-Verlag.

Plate Techtonics. Arthur N. Strahler. LC 98-75540. (Illus.). 554p. (C). 1998. text 75.00 (*0-9668594-4-8*) Geo Bks Pubg.

Plate Tectonic Cycle - Earth's Moving Force. 1992. 18.95 (*1-56638-086-3*) Math Sci Nucleus.

Plate Tectonics. Dickinson. 384p. (C). 1999. write for info. (*0-02-329640-2*, Macmillan Coll) P-H.

Plate Tectonics. Alvin Silverstein et al. LC 98-24934. (Science Concepts Ser.). (Illus.). 64p. (J). (gr. 5-8). 1998. lib. bdg. 23.40 (*0-7613-3225-1*) TFC Bks NY.

Plate Tectonics: Assessments & Reassessments. Ed. by Charles F. Kahle. LC 74-28810. (American Association of Petroleum Geologists. Memoir Ser.: No. 23). (Illus.). 520p. reprint ed. pap. 161.20 (*0-608-18023-8*, 202796100057) Bks Demand.

Plate Tectonics: How It Works. Allan Cox & Brian R. Hart. LC 86-6138. (Illus.). 400p. 1986. pap. text 52.95 (*0-86542-313-X*) Blackwell Sci.

***Plate Tectonics: Unraveling the Mysteries of the Earth.** Jonathon S. Erickson. (Illus.). 210p. 1999. 31.95 (*0-7351-0200-7*) Replica Bks.

Plate Tectonics & Crustal Evolution. Ed. by Kent C. Condie. (Illus.). 350p. 1982. pap. text 49.50 (*0-08-028075-7*) Elsevier.

Plate Tectonics & Crustal Evolution. 2nd ed. Ed. by Kent C. Condie. (Illus.). 350p. 1982. text 110.00 (*0-08-028076-5*) Elsevier.

Plate Tectonics & Crustal Evolution. 4th ed. Kent C. Condie. LC 97-4026. 288p. 1997. pap. text 49.95 (*0-7506-3386-7*) Buttrwrth-Heinemann.

Plate Tectonics & Hydrocarbon Accumulation. William R. Dickinson & Hunter Yarborough. LC TN0871.E38. (Education Course Note Ser.: Vol. 1). (Illus.). 218p. reprint ed. pap. 67.60 (*0-608-08722-X*, 206936100004) Bks Demand.

Plateau. Ed. by Deward E. Walker. (Handbook North American Indians Ser.: No. 12). (Illus.). 816p. 1998. 61.00 (*0-87474-192-0*) Smithsonian.

***Plateau Indians.** Mir Tamim Ansary. LC 99-34897. (Illus.). 32p. 2000. lib. bdg. write for info. (*1-57572-928-8*) Heinemann Lib.

***Plateau Journal: Dwellings.** Ed. by Carol Haralson & L. Greer Price. (Illus.). 64p. 1999. pap. 9.95 (*0-938216-69-4*) GCA.

***Plateau Journal Vol. 2, No. 2: Journal.** Ed. by Carol Haralson & L. Greer Price. (Illus.). 64p. 1998. pap. 9.95 (*0-938216-67-8*) GCA.

***Plateau Journal Vol. 3, No. 2: Elements.** Ed. by Carol Haralson & L. Greer Price. (Illus.). 64p. 1999. pap. 9.95 (*0-938216-71-6*) GCA.

***Plateau Journal Vol. 4, No. 1: Law & Order.** Ed. by Carol Haralson & L. Greer Price. (Illus.). 64p. 2000. pap. 9.95 (*0-938216-73-2*) GCA.

Plateau Light. David Muench. LC 98-26898. (Illus.). 1998. 39.95 (*1-55868-416-6*) Gr Arts Ctr Pub.

Plateau Problem: The Historical Survey & The Present State of the Theory, 2 vols., Vol. 2. A. T. Fomenko. 472p. 1990. text 453.00 (*2-88124-702-4*) Gordon & Breach.

Plateau Problem Pt. I: Historical Survey, Vol. 1. A. T. Fomenko. xii, 220p. 1990. text 323.00 (*2-88124-700-8*) Gordon & Breach.

Plateau Problem Pt. II: The Present State of the Theory, Vol. 2. A. T. Fomenko. xii, 252p. 1990. text 323.00 (*2-88124-701-6*) Gordon & Breach.

***Plateaus of Destiny.** Mike Gould. Ed. by Gary Hubbell. (Illus.). 207p. 1998. pap. 19.00 (*1-893740-00-5*) Clinetop.

Plateaux, Gateaux, Chateaux. Mary D. Parnell. LC 98-140836. 214p. 1998. 25.95 (*1-85411-207-4*, Pub. by Seren Bks) Dufour.

Platee, ou Junon Jalouse see Chefs-d'Oeuvre Classiques de l'Opera Francais

Plateglass Universities. Michael Beloff. LC 70-88559. 208p. 1975. 18.50 (*0-8386-7550-6*) Fairleigh Dickinson.

Platelet-Activating Factor & Cell Immunology. Ed. by P. Braquet. (New Trends in Lipid Mediators Research Ser.: Vol. 1). viii, 180p. 1988. 146.25 (*3-8055-4684-X*) S Karger.

P

An Asterisk (*) at the beginning of an entry indicates that the title is appearing for the first time.

Platelet Activating Factor & Human Disease. Ed. by P. Barnes et al. (Frontiers in Pharmacology & Therapeutics Ser.). (Illus.). 350p. 1989. 125.00 (*0-632-02684-7*) Blackwell Sci.

Platelet-Activating Factor & Related Lipid Mediators, Vol. 1. F. Snyder. LC 87-14198. (Illus.). 492p. (C). 1987. text 125.00 (*0-306-42516-5*, Kluwer Plenum) Kluwer Academic.

Platelet-Activating Factor & Related Lipid Mediators No. 2: Roles in Health & Disease. Ed. by Santosh Nigam et al. LC 97-3871. (Advances in Experimental Medicine & Biology Ser.: No. 416). (Illus.). 414p. (C). 1997. text 144.00 (*0-306-45506-4*, Kluwer Plenum) Kluwer Academic.

Platelet-Activating Factor & Structurally Related Alkyl Ether Lipids. Ed. by Wolfgang J. Baumann. 524p. (C). 1991. 60.00 (*0-935315-40-3*) Am Oil Chemists.

Platelet-Activating Factor Antagonists: New Developments for Clinical Application. Ed. by Joseph T. O'Flaherty & Peter W. Ramwell. (Advances in Applied Biotechnology Ser.: Vol. 9). (Illus.). 256p. (C). 1990. 55.00 (*0-943255-13-9*) Portfolio Pub.

Platelet Activating Factor Receptor: Signal Mechanisms & Molecular Biology. Ed. by Shivendra D. Shukla. (Pharmacology & Toxicology Ser.). 208p. 1992. lib. bdg. 129.00 (*0-8493-7299-2*, QP752) CRC Pr.

Platelet Amine Storage Granule. Johnston. Ed. by Charles D. Barnes. 224p. 1992. lib. bdg. 110.00 (*0-8493-8838-4*, QP97) CRC Pr.

Platelet-Dependent Vascular Occlusion. Ed. by Garret A. FitzGerald et al. LC 94-7321. (Annals of the New York Academy of Sciences Ser.: Vol. 714). 328p. 1994. pap. 90.00 (*0-89766-845-6*); pap. 90.00 (*0-89766-846-4*) NY Acad Sci.

Platelet Glycoprotein IIb/IIIa Inhibitors in Cardiovascular Disease. Ed. by A. Michael Lincoff & Eric J. Topol. LC 99-30220. (Contemporary Cardiology Ser.). (Illus.). 384p. 1999. 125.00 (*0-89603-727-4*) Humana.

Platelet Heterogeneity. Ed. by J. Martin & T. Trowbridge. (Illus.). 286p. 1990. 182.00 (*0-387-19602-1*) Spr-Verlag.

Platelet Immunology. Ed. by C. Kaplan et al. (Current Studies in Hematology & Blood Transfusion: No. 55). (Illus.). viii, 188p. 1988. 143.50 (*3-8055-4693-9*) S Karger.

Platelet Kinetics & Imaging. Ed. by Phillip N. Badenhorst et al. Incl. Vol. I. Techniques & Normal Platelet Kinetics. 184p. 1985. 134.00 (*0-8493-5441-2*, RC670); Vol. II. Clinical Applications. Ed. by Philip N. Badenhorst. 128p. 1985. 79.00 (*0-8493-5442-0*, CRC Reprint); 1985. 134.00 (*0-318-60653-4*) CRC Pr.

Platelet Membrane Glycoproteins. Ed. by James N. George et al. LC 85-3498. 438p. 1985. 105.00 (*0-306-41857-6*, Plenum Trade) Perseus Pubng.

Platelet Membrane in Transfusion Medicine. Ed. by Gail A. Rock & F. Decary. (Current Studies in Hematology & Blood Transfusion: No. 54). (Illus.). viii, 156p. 1988. 126.25 (*3-8055-4657-2*) S Karger.

Platelet Protocols. Jennings. LC 98-83126. 128p. (C). 1999. 39.95 (*0-12-384260-3*) Acad Pr.

Platelet Responses & Metabolism, 3 Vols., Vols. 1 - 3. Holm Holmsen. 728p. 1987. 207.00 (*0-8493-5896-5*, QP97) CRC Pr.

Platelet Responses & Metabolism: Response-Metabolism Relationships, Vol. 3. Holm Holmsen. LC 86-135430. 336p. 1987. 185.00 (*0-8493-5899-X*, QP97) Franklin.

Platelet Responses & Metabolism Vol. 1: Responses. Holm Holmsen. LC 86-13543. 360p. 1986. 197.00 (*0-8493-5897-3*, CRC Reprint) Franklin.

Platelet Responses & Metabolism Vol. 2: Receptors & Metabolism. Holm Holmsen. LC 86-13543. 360p. 1986. 201.00 (*0-8493-5898-1*, CRC Reprint) Franklin.

Platelet Serology. Ed. by Francine Decary & Gail A. Rock. (Current Studies in Hematology & Blood Transfusion: No. 52). (Illus.). vii, 124p. 1986. 85.25 (*3-8055-4208-9*) S Karger.

Platelet-Vessel Wall Interaction. R. M. Pittilo & S. J. Machin. (Bloomsbury Series in Clinical Science). (Illus.). 195p. 1988. 103.00 (*0-387-17488-5*) Spr-Verlag.

Platelets: A Multidisciplinary Approach. fac. ed. International Symposium on Platelets Staff. Ed. by Giovanni de Gaetano & Silvio Garattini. LC 78-66352. (Monographs of the Mario Negri Institute for Pharmacological Research). (Illus.). 501p. pap. 155.40 (*0-7837-7260-2*, 204704500005) Bks Demand.

Platelets: A Practical Approach. Ed. by Stephen Watson & Kalwant Authi. (Practical Approach Ser.: Vol. 167). (Illus.). 396p. (C). 1996. text 100.00 (*0-19-963538-2*); pap. text 49.95 (*0-19-963537-4*) OUP.

Platelets Pt. B: Receptors, Adhesion, Secretion. Ed. by John N. Abelson et al. (Methods in Enzymology Ser.: Vol. 215). (Illus.). 526p. 1992. text 104.00 (*0-12-182116-1*) Acad Pr.

Platelets - Receptors, Adhesion, Secretion, Pt. A. Ed. by Jacek J. Hawiger et al. (Methods in Enzymology Ser.: Vol. 169). 512p. 1989. text 136.00 (*0-12-182070-X*) Acad Pr.

Platelets, Analgesics & Asthma. Michael Schmitz-Schumann et al. (Agents & Actions Supplements Ser.: No. 21). 206p. 1987. 70.00 (*0-8176-1806-6*) Birkhauser.

Platelets & Atherosclerosis. Ed. by C. Kessler. (Illus.). 128p. 1990. 62.95 (*0-387-53006-1*) Spr-Verlag.

Platelets & Their Factors. Kalwant S. Authi et al. LC 96-39635. (Handbook of Experimental Pharmacology Ser.). 1997. write for info. (*3-540-61997-6*) Spr-Verlag.

Platelets, Cellular Response Mechanisms & Their Biological Significance: Proceedings of the Embo Workshops on Platelets, Cellular Response Mechanisms & Their Biological Significance, 1980. Weizman Institute of Science Staff. Ed. by A. Rotman & F. A. Meyer. LC 80-41257. (Wiley-Interscience Publications). 349p. reprint ed. pap. 108.20 (*0-608-13120-2*, 205209500033) Bks Demand.

Platelets, Drugs & Thrombosis: Proceedings of the Symposium, Hamilton, Ont., Oct. 1972. Symposium, Hamilton, Ont. Staff et al. Ed. by Edward Schonbaum et al. 320p. 1974. 85.25 (*3-8055-1745-9*) S Karger.

Platelets, Prostaglandins & the Cardiovascular System. Ed. by Gian G. Serneri et al. LC 84-29840. (Advances in Prostaglandin, Thromboxane, & Leukotriene Research Ser.: No. 13). (Illus.). 421p. 1985. reprint ed. pap. 130.60 (*0-7837-9637-4*, 206039000005) Bks Demand.

***Platelets, Thrombosis & the Vessel Wall.** Michael C. Berndt. (Advances in Vascular Biology Ser.: Vol. 6). 356p. 1999. text 90.00 (*90-5702-369-5*, Harwood Acad Pubs) Gordon & Breach.

Platen-Bibliographie. Fritz Redenbacher. viii, 186p. 1972. reprint ed. write for info. (*3-487-04095-6*) G Olms Pubs.

Platero & I. Juan Ramon Jimenez. 179p. 1994. pap. 9.95 (*1-56924-944-X*) Marlowe & Co.

Platero & I. Juan Ramon Jimenez. Tr. by Eloise Roach from SPA. (Illus.). 228p. (C). 1957. pap. 14.95 (*0-292-76479-0*) U of Tex Pr.

Platero y Yo. Juan Ramon Jimenez. Ed. by Richard A. Cardwell. (Nueva Austral Ser.: Vol. 58). (SPA.). 1991. pap. text 24.95 (*84-239-1858-0*) Elliots Bks.

Platero y Yo. Tr. by Myra C. Livingston & Joseph F. Dominguez. LC 92-11634. (ENG & SPA., Illus.). 64p. (YA). (gr. 3-7). 1994. 14.95 (*0-395-62365-0*, Clarion Bks) HM.

Platero y Yo. large type ed. Juan Ramon Jimenez. (SPA.). reprint ed. 10.00 (*0-318-65684-1*) NAVH.

Platero y Yo Platero & I. Juan Ramon Jimenez. Tr. by Myra C. Livingston & Joseph F. Dominquez. (ENG & SPA., Illus.). (J). (gr. 3-7). 1994. 14.95 (*0-685-71523-X*, Clarion Bks) HM.

***Plates, 1 vol.** Mary Engelbreit. LC 99-35411. 1999. 12.95 (*0-7407-0201-7*) Andrews & McMeel.

Plates & Buckles of the American Military, 1795-1874. Sydney C. Kerksis. LC 74-76858. (Illus.). 567p. 1974. 39.95 (*0-614-29614-5*) North South Trader.

Plates & Junctions in Elastic Multi-Structures: An Asymptotic Analysis. P. G. Ciarlet. Ed. by J. L. Lions. (Recherches en Mathematiques Appliquees Ser.: Vol. 14). vii, 215p. 1990. 44.95 (*0-387-52917-9*) Spr-Verlag.

Plates & Shells. Michel Fortin. LC 99-22844. (CRM Proceedings & Lecture Notes Ser.). 1999. write for info. (*0-8218-0950-4*) Am Math.

Plates Illustrative of the Vocabulary for the Deaf & Dumb. Harvey Darton. 1972. 69.95 (*0-8490-0841-7*) Gordon Pr.

Plates in Illustration of a Handbook to the Flora of Ceylon. H. Trimen. (C). 1974. text 400.00 (*0-89771-669-8*, Pub. by Intl Bk Distr) St Mut.

Plates in Illustration of a Handbook to the Flora of Ceylon. H. Trimen. (C). 1974. reprint ed. 350.00 (*0-7855-3081-9*, Pub. by Intl Bk Distr) St Mut.

Plates, Laminates & Shells Asymptotic Analysis & Homogenization. T. Lewinski & J. J. Telega. LC 99-40193. 450p. 1999. text 58.00 (*981-02-3206-3*) World Scientific Pub.

Plates; Rolled Floor Plates: Carbon, High Strength Low Alloy & Alloy Steel. LC 90-86190. 100p. 1991. 27.00 (*0-932897-60-6*) Iron & Steel.

Platespinner: Playing with Time. Victor Margolis. 300p. (Orig.). 1995. pap. 14.95 (*0-9642973-8-8*) Marik Pubg.

Platform Abandonment & Decommissioning: History & Techniques, Vol. 1. Oilfield Publications Limited Staff. (Illus.). 200p. 1995. pap. 295.00 (*1-870945-74-3*) Oilfield Publns.

Platform for Change. Stafford Beer. LC 73-10741. (Stafford Beer Classic Library). 468p. 1995. pap. 89.95 (*0-471-94840-3*) Wiley.

Platform for Change: The Foundations of the Northern Black Community, 1775-1865. Harry Reed. LC 93-37526. 1994. 29.95 (*0-87013-341-1*) Mich St U Pr.

Platform Margin & Deep Water Carbonates No. 12: Lecture Notes for Short Course. Harry E. Cook et al. LC QE0471.15.C3. (SEPM Short Course Ser.: No. 12). (Illus.). 581p. reprint ed. pap. 180.20 (*0-8357-6266-1*, 203417800089) Bks Demand.

Platform of the Joint Opposition. Leon Trotsky. (Illus.). 117p. 1973. pap. 11.95 (*0-929087-97-6*) Mehring Bks.

Platform Officer's Guide to the Direct Deposit of Social Security Payments. Robert Strand. (Illus.). 200p. (C). 1975. 6.00 (*0-89982-068-9*) Am Bankers.

Platform Party. Alan Richardson. LC 98-55493. 1999. pap. 5.00 (*0-88734-829-7*) Players Pr.

Platform Shoes: A Big Step in Fashion. Ray Ellsworth. LC 97-80254. (Illus.). 112p. 1998. pap. 19.95 (*0-7643-0459-3*) Schiffer.

Platform Souls: The Trainspotter As 20th-Century Hero. Nicholas Whittaker. 256p. 1997. pap. 15.95 (*0-575-40011-0*, Pub. by V Gollancz) Trafalgar.

***Platform Sutra of the Sixth Partiarch, No. 2.** Ed. by Mayeda Sengaku & Kenneth K. Inada. Tr. by John R. McRae from CHI. LC 99-75770. (BDK English Tripitaka Ser.: Vol. 73). 170p. 2000. 35.00 (*1-886439-13-3*) Numata Ctr.

Platform Sutra of the 6th Patriarch. 6th ed. Tr. by Philip B. Yampolsky. LC 67-11847. (Records of Civilization: Sources & Studies: No. 76). 1978. pap. text 20.50 (*0-231-08361-0*) Col U Pr.

Platforms. John R. Maxim. Date not set. mass mkt. write for info. (*0-380-73005-7*) Morrow Avon.

***Plath: Poems.** Sylvia Plath. LC 98-23336. 1998. 12.50 (*0-375-40464-3*) Everymns Lib.

Platica de Autoestima - Conversations about Self-Esteem: Guia para el Lider y Novelas - Guide for the Leader & Short Stories. Jean I. Clarke et al. 268p. 1993. write for info. (*1-882556-00-3*); write for info. (*1-882556-01-1*); write for info. (*1-882556-02-X*); write for info. (*1-882556-03-8*); write for info. (*1-882556-04-6*); write for info. (*1-882556-05-4*); write for info. (*1-882556-06-2*); write for info. (*1-882556-07-0*) U WA Early Chldhood.

***Platicas: Conversations with Hispano Writers of New Mexico.** Nasario Garcbia. LC 99-47064. 2000. 27.95 (*0-89672-428-X*) Tex Tech Univ Pr.

Platicas Adicionales Sobre la Vida de la Iglesia. Watchman Nee.Tr. of Further Talks on the Church Life. (SPA.). 189p. per. 6.50 (*0-87083-090-2*, 08010002) Living Stream Ministry.

Platicas Adicionales Sobre la Vida de la Iglesia (Further Talks on the Church Life) Watchman Nee. (SPA.). 189p. 1982. per. 8.50 (*0-87083-236-0*, 08-010-002) Living Stream Ministry.

Platicas de Mi Barrio. Carlos Ponce. (SPA.). 120p. 1998. pap. 11.00 (*0-927534-82-7*) Biling Rev-Pr.

Platies, Keeping & Breeding Them in Captivity: Keeping & Breeding Them in Captivity. Donald Mix. (Illus.). 64p. 1996. pap. 6.95 (*0-7938-0362-4*, RE613) TFH Pubns.

Platina: On Right Pleasure & Good Health (A Critical Edition & Translation of De Honesta Voluptate et Valetudine) Ed. by Mary E. Milham. LC 97-30151. (Medieval & Renaissance Texts & Studies: No. 168). 528p. 1998. 35.00 (*0-86698-208-6*, MR168) MRTS.

Plating Aluminum on Video. R. L. Nyborg. (Illus.). 75p. 1995. pap. 45.00 incl. VHS (*1-57002-063-9*) Univ Publng Hse.

Plating Plastic on Video. R. L. Nyborg. (Illus.). 75p. 1995. pap. 26.95 incl. VHS (*1-57002-065-5*) Univ Publng Hse.

Platinum. (Environmental Health Criteria Ser.: No. 125). (ENG, FRE & SPA.). 167p. 1991. pap. text 29.00 (*92-4-157125-X*, 1160125) World Health.

Platinum & Other Metal Coordination Compounds in Cancer Chemotherapy. S. B. Howell. (Illus.). 558p. (C). 1992. text 174.00 (*0-306-44027-X*, Kluwer Plenum) Kluwer Academic.

Platinum & Other Metal Coordination Compounds in Cancer Chemotherapy. Ed. by Marino Nicolini. (Developments in Oncology Ser.). (C). 1988. text 330.00 (*0-89838-358-7*) Kluwer Academic.

Platinum & Other Metal Coornation Compounds in Cancer Chemotherapy 2: Proceeding of the 7th International Symposium Held in Amsterdam, The Netherlands, March 1-4, 1995, Vol. 2. Ed. by H. M. Pinedo & J. H. Schornagel. (Illus.). 368p. 1996. 102.00 (*0-306-45287-1*, Kluwer Plenum) Kluwer Academic.

Platinum & Palladium Buyer's Guide. Margaret Olsen. Ed. by Alison Matthews. LC 97-60830. (Illus.). 272p. (Orig.). 1998. pap. 24.95 (*0-9630498-2-8*, 97-60830) Westminster CO.

Platinum & Palladium Printing. Dick Arentz. LC 99-28233. 184p. 1999. pap. text 29.95 (*0-240-80377-9*, Focal) Buttrwrth-Heinemann.

***Platinum-Based Drugs in Cancer Therapy.** Lloyd R. Kelland & Nicholas P. Farrell. LC 99-32239. (Cancer Drug Discovery & Development Ser.: Vol. 7). 360p. 2000. 145.00 (*0-89603-599-9*) Humana.

Platinum Blues. William Deverell. 261p. 1996. mass mkt. 5.95 (*0-7710-2662-5*) McCland & Stewart.

Platinum by Cartier: Triumphs of the Jewelers' Art. Franco Cologni & Eric Nussbaum. (Illus.). 280p. 1996. 85.00 (*0-8109-3738-7*, Pub. by Abrams) Time Warner.

Platinum Edition Using HTML 3.2, Java 1.1, & GCI: 8 Contemporary Photographers. Eric Ladd & Jim O'Donnell. LC 96-71191. 1520p. 1996. 70.00 (*0-7897-0932-5*) Que.

Platinum Girl: The Life & Legends of Jean Harlow. Eve Golden. (Illus.). 248p. 1993. 35.00 (*1-55859-214-8*) Abbeville Pr.

Platinum, Gold, & Other Metal Chemotherapeutic Agents. Ed. by Stephen J. Lippard. LC 82-24333. (Symposium Ser.: No. 209). 453p. 1983. lib. bdg. 65.95 (*0-8412-0758-5*) Am Chemical.

Platinum, Gold, & Other Metal Chemotherapeutic Agents: Chemistry & Biochemistry. Ed. by Stephen J. Lippard. LC 82-24333. (ACS Symposium Ser.: No. 209). (Illus.). 464p. 1983. reprint ed. pap. 143.90 (*0-608-03221-2*, 206374000007) Bks Demand.

Platinum-Group Metals. (Metals & Minerals Ser.). 1993. lib. bdg. 250.95 (*0-8490-8961-1*) Gordon Pr.

Platinum Group Metals Industry. William Black. 192p. 2000. ring bd. 710.00 (*1-85573-346-3*, Pub. by Woodhead Pubng) Am Educ Systs.

***Platinum Keys.** Sonja Smith. LC 99-91136. 192p. 2000. pap. 12.95 (*1-56167-571-7*, Five Star Spec Ed) Am Literary Pr.

Platinum Leadership: Above & Beyond Empowerment. Al Marino. 1997. 19.95 (*1-890295-01-9*) Ldrship Resources.

Platinum, '93: Piano/Vocal/Chords. 240p. (Orig.). 1993. pap. 18.95 (*0-7692-1044-9*, VF1946) Wrner Bros.

Platinum Rule: Discover the Four Basic Business Personalities - & How They Can Lead You to Success. Tony Alessandra & Michael J. O'Connor. 304p. 1998. mass mkt. 12.99 (*0-446-67343-9*, Pub. by Warner Bks) Little.

Platinum Scenes: Photographs by Irving Herman. Ed. by Harvey Hess. (Illus.). 96p. (Orig.). 1996. pap. 29.95 (*0-9656482-1-4*) J&M Hearst.

Platitudes. Trey Ellis. LC 87-40109. (Vintage Contemporaries Ser.). 160p. (Orig.). 1988. pap. 9.00 (*0-394-75439-5*) Vin Bks.

Platitudes Undone. G. K. Chesterton. LC 96-78010. 92p. 1997. 14.95 (*0-89870-628-9*) Ignatius Pr.

Platium Group Metals & Compounds: A Symposium Sponsored by the Division of Inorganic Chemistry at the 158th Meeting of the American Chemical Society, New York, NY, September 8-9, 1969. American Chemical Society Staff. LC 76-152755. (Advances in Chemistry Ser.: No. 98). (Illus.). 173p. 1971. reprint ed. pap. 53.70 (*0-608-06758-X*, 206695500009) Bks Demand.

Plato. Ed. by Gail Fine. LC 99-13232. 700p. 2000. text 110.00 (*0-19-875207-5*) OUP.

Plato. Richard M. Hare. (Past Masters Ser.). 96p. 1983. pap. text 9.95 (*0-19-287585-X*) OUP.

Plato. Harold F. Rahmlow et al. Ed. by Danny G. Langdon. LC 79-26395. (Instructional Design Library). 112p. 1980. 27.95 (*0-87778-150-8*) Educ Tech Pubns.

***Plato.** Eric Voegelin. 288p. 2000. pap. 12.95 (*0-8262-1298-0*) U of Mo Pr.

Plato. Alfred E. Taylor. LC 71-160995. (Select Bibliographies Reprint Ser.). 1977. reprint ed. 18.95 (*0-8369-5863-2*) Ayer.

Plato, Vol. 1. Paul Friedlander. Tr. by Hans Meyerhoff from GER. LC 57-11126. (Illus.). 467p. 1973. pap. 144.80 (*0-7837-8587-9*, 204940200011) Bks Demand.

Plato: Apology. rev. ed. Plato. (ENG & GRE.). viii, 127p. 1997. pap. text 15.00 (*0-86516-348-0*) Bolchazy-Carducci.

Plato: Apology of Socrates. Plato. Ed. & Tr. by M. C. Stokes. (Classical Texts Ser.). 1997. 59.99 (*0-85668-371-X*, Pub. by Aris & Phillips); pap. 28.00 (*0-85668-372-8*, Pub. by Aris & Phillips) David Brown.

Plato: Atlantis Story: Timaeus 17-27 & Critias. Ed. by Christopher Gill. (Bristol Greek Texts Ser.). (GRE.). 122p. 1980. 18.95 (*0-906515-59-9*, Pub. by Brist Class Pr) Focus Pub-R Pullins.

Plato: Cratylus, Phaedo, Parmenides, Timaeus & Critias. Thomas Taylor. LC 73-84046. (Secret Doctrine Reference Ser.). 460p. 1975. lib. bdg. 27.00 (*0-913510-21-1*) Wizards.

Plato: Crito. Ed. by J. Adam. (Bristol Greek Texts Ser.). (GRE.). 128p. 1991. pap. 18.95 (*1-85399-032-9*, Pub. by Brist Class Pr) Focus Pub-R Pullins.

Plato: Crito. 2nd ed. Gilbert P. Rose. 1983. pap. text 6.00 (*0-929524-24-1*) Bryn Mawr Commentaries.

Plato: Das Platonbild. Konrad Gaiser. 36.00 (*0-318-70802-7*) G Olms Pubs.

Plato: Dramatist of the Life of Reason. John Randall. LC 71-106565. 288p. reprint ed. pap. 89.30 (*0-608-14583-1*, 202482600038) Bks Demand.

Plato: Euthyphro. Ed. by C. Emlyn-Jones. (Bristol Greek Texts Ser.). (GRE.). 124p. 1991. pap. 22.95 (*1-85399-132-5*, Pub. by Brist Class Pr) Focus Pub-R Pullins.

Plato: Euthyphro. 2nd ed. John E. Hare. 1985. pap. text 6.00 (*0-929524-25-X*) Bryn Mawr Commentaries.

Plato: Euthyphro, Apology, Crito. F. J. Church & Robert D. Cummings. 88p. (C). 1956. pap. text 8.00 (*0-02-322410-X*, Macmillan Coll) P-H.

***Plato: Great Philosophers.** Bernard Arthur Owen Williams. LC 99-22643. (The Great Philosophers Ser.). 64p. 1999. pap. 6.00 (*0-415-92395-6*) Routledge.

Plato: Hippias Maior. David Sider. 1986. pap. text 6.00 (*0-929524-26-8*) Bryn Mawr Commentaries.

Plato: Ion. 2nd ed. Andrew M. Miller. 1984. pap. text 6.00 (*0-929524-27-6*) Bryn Mawr Commentaries.

Plato: Laches. Penelope Rainey. 1985. pap. text 6.00 (*0-929524-28-4*) Bryn Mawr Commentaries.

Plato: Meno. Benjamin E. Jowett. 64p. (C). 1949. pap. text 4.33 (*0-02-360770-X*, Macmillan Coll) P-H.

Plato: Meno. Plato. Ed. by R. W. Sharples. (Classical Texts Ser.). 1985. 59.99 (*0-85668-248-9*, Pub. by Aris & Phillips); pap. 28.00 (*0-85668-249-7*, Pub. by Aris & Phillips) David Brown.

Plato: New Subtitle. Kraut. 224p. write for info. (*0-8133-2086-0*, Pub. by Westview) HarpC.

Plato: Phaedrus. W. C. Helmbold. Ed. by Perry G. Miller. 96p. (C). 1956. pap. text 9.20 (*0-02-352960-1*, Macmillan Coll) P-H.

Plato: Phaedrus. Plato. Ed. by C. J. Rowe. (Classical Texts Ser.). 1986. 59.99 (*0-85668-313-2*, Pub. by Aris & Phillips); pap. 28.00 (*0-85668-314-0*, Pub. by Aris & Phillips) David Brown.

Plato: Republic I. Ed. by D. J. Allan. (Bristol Greek Texts Ser.). (GRE.). 136p. 1993. pap. 20.95 (*1-85399-254-2*, Pub. by Brist Class Pr) Focus Pub-R Pullins.

Plato: Statesman. Plato. Ed. & Tr. by C. J. Rowe from GRE. (Classical Texts Ser.). 256p. 1995. 59.99 (*0-85668-612-3*, Pub. by Aris & Phillips); pap. 28.00 (*0-85668-613-1*, Pub. by Aris & Phillips) David Brown.

Plato: Symposium. C. J. Rowe. (Classical Texts Ser.). 228p. 1998. 59.95 (*0-85668-614-X*) David Brown.

***Plato: Syposium.** Ed. & Tr. by C. J. Rowe. (Classical Texts Ser.). 228p. 1998. pap. 28.00 (*0-85668-615-8*) David Brown.

***Plato: The Crito.** rev. ed. (GRE.). 200p. 1999. pap. text 27.95 (*1-85399-469-3*, Pub. by Brist Class Pr) Focus Pub-R Pullins.

Plato: The Man & His Work. 7th ed. Alfred E. Taylor. 1960. pap. 16.95 (*0-416-67590-5*, NO. 6444) Routledge.

Plato: The Martyrdom of Socrates. Plato. Ed. by F. Doherty. (Bristol Greek Texts Ser.). (GRE.). 112p. 1981. reprint ed. 16.95 (*0-906515-96-3*, Pub. by Brist Class Pr) Focus Pub-R Pullins.

Plato: The Midwife's Apprentice. I. M. Crombie. LC 81-6812. 195p. 1981. reprint ed. lib. bdg. 49.75 (*0-313-23243-1*, CRPL, Greenwood Pr) Greenwood.

Plato: The Statesman. 1987. 38.50 (*0-8453-4519-2*) Assoc Univ Prs.

Plato: 1902 Edition. David G. Ritchie. (Key Texts Ser.). 240p. 1996. reprint ed. pap. 19.95 (*1-85506-215-1*) Bks Intl VA.

Plato, No. 1 see Aquinas

Plato Pt. III: Concordantiae in Platonis Opera Omnia, Pt. III. Contrib. by Mauro Sivero. (Alpha-Omega Ser.: Reihe A., Bd. CX). (GER.). 188p. 1997. write for info. (*3-487-10483-0*) G Olms Pubs.

Plato Pt. IV: Concordantiae in Platonis Opera Omnia, 2 vols., Pt. IV. Contrib. by Mauro Sivero. (Alpha-Omega Ser.: Reihe A., Bd. CX). (GER.). xiv, 694p. 1997. write for info. (*3-487-10484-9*) G Olms Pubs.

Plato V: Republic. Plato. Ed. by Halliwell. 1992. pap. 28.00 (*0-85668-536-4*, Pub. by Aris & Phillips) David Brown.

Plato X: Republic. Plato. Ed. by S. Halliwell. (Classical Texts Ser.). 1986. 59.99 (*0-85668-405-8*, Pub. by Aris & Phillips) David Brown.

Plato X: Republic. Plato. Ed. by F. S. Halliwell. (Classical Texts Ser.). 1986. pap. 28.00 (*0-85668-406-6*, Pub. by Aris & Phillips) David Brown.

Plato - Concordantiae in Platonis Opera Omnia: Apologia. Hildesheim, Pars II. Curavit M. Siviero. (GER.). x, 304p. 1996. write for info. (*3-487-10225-0*) G Olms Pubs.

Plato - Concordantiae in Platonis Opera Omnia: Cratylus, Pars v. Curavit M. Siviero. (GER.). 570p. 1996. write for info. (*3-487-10574-8*) G Olms Pubs.

Plato - Concordantiae in Platonis Opera Omnia: Politicus, Pars VIII. Curavit M. Siviero. (GER.). 570p. 1996. write for info. (*3-487-10583-7*) G Olms Pubs.

Plato - Concordantiae in Platonis Opera Omnia: Sophista, Pars VII. Curavit M. Siviero. (GER.). 520p. 1996. write for info. (*3-487-10580-2*) G Olms Pubs.

Plato - Concorrdantiae in Platonis Opera Omnia: Theaetetur, Pars VI. Curavit M. Siviero. (GER.). 700p. 1996. write for info. (*3-487-10577-2*) G Olms Pubs.

Plato - The Man & His Dialogues - Earlier Period see History of Greek Philosophy

Plato & Aristotle. Eric Voegelin. Ed. & Intro. by Dante Germino. LC 99-53537. (Collected Works of Eric Voegelin: Vol. 16, Pt. III). 448p. 2000. 39.95 (*0-8262-1250-6*) U of Mo Pr.

Plato & Aristotle on Constitutionalism: An Exposition & Reference Source. Raymond Polin. LC 98-71971. (Avebury Series in Philosophy). 346p. 1998. text 72.95 (*1-84014-301-0*, Pub. by Ashgate Pub) Ashgate Pub Co.

Plato & Aristotle on Poetry. Gerald F. Else. Ed. by Peter Burian. LC 86-1475. 243p. 1986. pap. 75.40 (*0-608-05201-9*, 206573800001) Bks Demand.

Plato & Augustine: Taken from Vol. 1 of the Great Philosophers, Vol. 1. Karl Jaspers. Tr. by Karl Mannheim. LC 67-38117. Orig. Title: Great Philosophers, Vol. 1 (Pt. 2). 144p. 1966. pap. 8.00 (*0-15-672035-3*, Harvest Bks) Harcourt.

Plato & Greek Painting. E. C. Keuls. 1978. 23.00 (*90-04-05395-6*, CSCT, 5) Brill Academic Pubs.

Plato & His Contemporaries. Guy C. Field. LC 74-30008. (Studies in Philosophy: No. 40). 1974. lib. bdg. 75.00 (*0-8383-1992-0*) M S G Haskell Hse.

***Plato & His Predecessors: The Dramatisation of Reason.** Mary Margaret McCabe. 296p. 2000. write for info. (*0-521-65306-1*) Cambridge U Pr.

Plato & Platonism. Ed. by Johannes M. Van Ophuijsen. (Studies in Philosophy & the History of Philosophy: Vol. 33). 368p. (C). 1999. text 69.95 (*0-8132-0910-2*) Cath U Pr.

Plato & Platonism: A Series of Lectures. Walter Pater. LC 69-14031. 282p. 1970. reprint ed. lib. bdg. 79.50 (*0-8371-1151-X*, PAPP, Greenwood Pr) Greenwood.

Plato & Postmodernism. Shankman et al. Ed. by Steven Shankman. LC 94-4375. 192p. (Orig.). 1994. pap. 18.95 (*0-9620529-6-5*) Aldine Pr Ltd.

***Plato & Protagoras: Truth & Relativism in Ancient Greek Philosophy.** Oded Balaban. LC 99-37747. 368p. 1999. 75.00 (*0-7391-0075-0*) Lxngtn Bks.

Plato & the Epinomis. A. E. Taylor. (Studies in Philosophy: No. 40). (C). 1977. lib. bdg. 49.95 (*0-8383-0119-3*) M S G Haskell Hse.

Plato & the Foundations of Metaphysics: A Work on the Theory of the Principles & the Unwritten Doctrines of Plato with a Collection of the Fundamental Documents. Hans J. Kramer. Ed. & Tr. by John R. Catan from GER. LC 89-77689. (ITA.). 311p. 1990. text 21.50 (*0-7914-0433-1*) State U NY Pr.

***Plato & the Hero: Courage, Manliness & the Impersonal Good.** Angela Hobbs. 281p. 2000. write for info. (*0-521-41733-3*) Cambridge U Pr.

Plato & the Human Paradox. Robert O'Connell. LC 96-52170. xviii, 162p. (C). 1997. pap. 15.00 (*0-8232-1758-2*) Fordham.

Plato & the Human Paradox. 2nd rev. ed. Robert O'Connell. LC 96-52170. xviii, 162p. (C). 1997. 30.00 (*0-8232-1757-4*) Fordham.

Plato & the Other Companions of Sokrates: 1865 Edition, 3 vols., Set. George Grote. 1888p. 1996. reprint ed. 240.00 (*1-85506-177-5*) Bks Intl VA.

Plato & the Republic. Nickolas Pappas. LC 94-33894. (Philosophy Guidebooks Ser.). 256p. (C). (gr. 13). 1995. pap. 12.99 (*0-415-09532-8*, C0410) Routledge.

Plato & the Republic. Nickolas Pappas. LC 94-33894. (Philosophy Guidebooks Ser.). 256p. (C). (gr. 13). 1995. 60.00 (*0-415-09531-X*, C0409) Routledge.

Plato & the Socratic Dialogue: The Philosophical Use of a Literary Form. Charles H. Kahn. 454p. (C). 1998. pap. text 24.95 (*0-521-64830-0*) Cambridge U Pr.

Plato Apology. Gilbert P. Rose. (Greek Commentaries Ser.). 104p. (Orig.). (C). 1989. pap. text 7.00 (*0-929524-56-X*) Bryn Mawr Commentaries.

Plato, Aristotle, & Thomas Aquinas: An Introduction to Moral Philosophy. Ed. by Jean W. Rioux. 118p. (Orig.). (C). 1995. pap. text 12.95 (*0-943025-77-X*) Cummngs & Hath.

Plato As God As Nous. Stephen Menn. LC 94-15845. 112p. (C). 1995. pap. 26.95 (*0-8093-1970-5*) S Ill U Pr.

Plato Baptized: Towards the Interpretation of Spenser's Mimetic Fictions. Elizabeth Bieman. 335p. 1988. text 45.00 (*0-8020-5767-5*) U of Toronto Pr.

***Plato, Clitophon.** Plato. Ed. by S. R. Slings. LC 98-52085. (Cambridge Classical Texts & Commentaries Ser.: No. 37). 364p. (C). 1999. 69.95 (*0-521-62368-5*) Cambridge U Pr.

Plato Critical Assessments, 4 vols. Ed. by Nicholas D. Smith. (Critical Assessments Ser.). 1432p. (C). 1998. 655.00 (*0-415-12605-3*) Routledge.

Plato, Derrida, & Writing. Jasper P. Neel. LC 87-28439. 268p. (C). 1988. text 31.95 (*0-8093-1440-1*) S Ill U Pr.

Plato, Etc. The Problems of Philosophy & Their Resolution. Roy Bhaskar. 256p. (C). 1994. pap. 20.00 (*0-86091-649-9*, B4649, Pub. by Verso) Norton.

Plato for Beginners. Robert Cavaliere. (for Beginners Ser.). (Illus.). 176p. (Orig.). 1996. pap. 11.95 (*0-86316-039-5*) Writers & Readers.

Plato for the Modern Age. Robert S. Brumbaugh. (Illus.). 256p. (C). 1991. reprint ed. pap. text 24.50 (*0-8191-8356-3*) U Pr of Amer.

Plato in 90 Minutes. Paul Strathern. (Philosophers in 90 Minutes Ser.). 96p. 1996. pap. 6.95 (*1-56663-127-0*, Pub. by I R Dee); lib. bdg. 14.95 (*1-56663-126-2*, Pub. by I R Dee) Natl Bk Netwk.

Plato in Renaissance England. Sears Jayne. LC 94-29929. (International Archives of the History of Ideas Ser.: Vol. 141). 208p. (C). 1995. lib. bdg. 140.00 (*0-7923-3060-9*, Pub. by Kluwer Academic) Kluwer Academic.

Plato in the Italian Renaissance. James Hankins. LC 89-70823. (Columbia Studies in the Classical Tradition: Vol. 1). xxxi, 368p. 1991. pap. 46.00 (*90-04-09552-7*) Brill Academic Pubs.

Plato in the Italian Renaissance, 2 vols. 2nd rev. ed. James Hankins. LC 89-70823. (Columbia Studies in the Classical Tradition: Vol. 17). xxxii, 849p. 1994. lib. bdg. 187.50 (*90-04-10095-4*) Brill Academic Pubs.

***Plato, Not Prozac! Applying Eternal Wisdom to Everyday Problems.** Lou Marinoff. 320p. 2000. pap. 13.00 (*0-06-093136-1*, Perennial) HarperTrade.

Plato on Justice & Power: Reading Book I of Plato's Republic. Kimon Lycos. LC 86-19166. (SUNY Series in Philosophy). 201p. (C). 1987. text 21.50 (*0-88706-415-9*) State U NY Pr.

Plato on Knowledge & Reality. Nicholas P. White. LC 76-10993. 272p. (C). 1976. 37.95 (*0-915144-21-2*); pap. 16.95 (*0-915144-22-0*) Hackett Pub.

Plato on Poetry. Plato. Ed. by Penelope Murray. (Greek & Latin Classics Ser.). 260p. (C). 1996. text 64.95 (*0-521-34182-5*) Cambridge U Pr.

Plato on Poetry: Ion; Republic 376e-398b9; Republic 595-608b10. Ed. by Penelope Murray. (Greek & Latin Classics Ser.). 260p. (C). 1996. pap. text 22.95 (*0-521-34981-8*) Cambridge U Pr.

Plato on Rhetoric & Language: Four Key Dialogues. Plato. LC 98-46510. 300p. 1998. pap. write for info. (*1-880393-33-6*) L Erlbaum Assocs.

Plato on the Self-Predication of Forms: Early & Middle Dialogues. John Malcolm. 238p. 1991. text 70.00 (*0-19-823906-8*) OUP.

Plato 1: Metaphysics & Epistemology. Ed. by Gail Fine. LC 99-13233. 512p. 2000. pap. text 19.95 (*0-19-875206-7*) OUP.

***Plato Papers: A Prophecy.** Peter Ackroyd. LC 99-16573. 160p. 2000. 21.95 (*0-385-49768-7*, N A Talese) Doubleday.

***Plato Papers: A Prophecy.** Peter Ackroyd. 2001. reprint ed. pap. 12.00 (*0-385-49769-5*, Anchor NY) Doubleday.

Plato Prehistorian: 10,000 to 5,000 B. C. Myth, Religion, Archaeology. Mary Settegast. (Illus.). 334p. 1990. pap. 18.95 (*0-940262-34-7*, Lindisfarne) Anthroposophic.

Plato Prehistorian: 10000 to 5000 B.C. in Myth, Religion & Archaeology. Mary Settegast. LC 86-61988. (Illus.). 334p. (C). 1990. 36.00 (*0-9617333-1-4*, Lindisfarne) Anthroposophic.

Plato, Protagoras & Meno. W. K. Guthrie. 157p. Date not set. 18.95 (*0-8488-2288-9*) Amereon Ltd.

Plato Reader. Plato. Ed. & Tr. by Tim Chappell. 320p. 1996. pap. 24.50 (*0-7486-0788-9*, Pub. by Edinburgh U Pr) Col U Pr.

Plato Reader, 001. Plato. Ed. by Ronald B. Levinson. (YA). (gr. 9 up). 1967. pap. 13.96 (*0-395-05197-5*, RivEd) HM.

Plato Rediscovered: Human Value & Social Order. T. K. Seung. LC 95-30781. (Studies in Social, Political, & Legal Philosophy). 394p. (C). 1995. pap. 29.95 (*0-8476-8112-2*) Rowman.

Plato Rediscovered: Human Value & Social Order. T. K. Seung. LC 95-30781. (Studies in Social, Political, & Legal Philosophy). 394p. (C). 1995. 71.00 (*0-8476-8111-4*) Rowman.

Plato the Apology. abr. ed. Plato. Tr. by Benjamin E. Jowett. LC 78-752121. 1972. audio 22.00 (*0-694-50405-X*, SWC 2050, Caedmon) HarperAudio.

Plato the Myth Maker. Luc Brisson. 1997. pap. text 12.95 (*0-226-07519-2*) U Ch Pr.

Plato the Myth Maker. Luc Brisson. LC 98-8641. 176p. 1999. 27.50 (*0-226-07518-4*) U Ch Pr.

Plato, Time, & Education: Essays in Honor of Robert S. Brumbaugh. Ed. by Brian P. Hendley. LC 87-21161. 326p. (C). 1988. text 21.50 (*0-88706-733-6*) State U NY Pr.

Plato to Machiavelli, 3 vols. Michael B. Foster. (Essay Index Reprint Ser.: Vol. 1). 1977. reprint ed. 20.95 (*0-518-10154-1*) Ayer.

Plato Two: Ethics, Politics, & Philosophy of Art & Religion; a Collection of Critical Essays. Ed. by Gregory Vlastos. LC 77-19103. (Modern Studies in Philosophy). 1978. reprint ed. pap. text 14.95 (*0-268-01531-7*) U of Notre Dame Pr.

Plato 2: Ethics, Politics, Religion & the Soul. Ed. by Gail Fine. LC 99-13233. 480p. 2000. pap. text 19.95 (*0-19-875204-0*) OUP.

Platocrit Assessments, Vol. 1. 296p. (C). Date not set. write for info. (*0-415-12601-0*) Routledge.

Platocrit Assessments, Vol. 2. 328p. (C). Date not set. write for info. (*0-415-12602-9*) Routledge.

Platocrit Assessments, Vol. 3. 336p. (C). Date not set. write for info. (*0-415-12603-7*) Routledge.

Platocrit Assessments, Vol. 4. 360p. (C). Date not set. write for info. (*0-415-12604-5*) Routledge.

Platon, 3 vols. Paul Friedlaender. Incl. Vol. 1. Seinswahrheit und Lebenswirklichkeit. 3rd enl. rev. ed. (Illus.). x, 438p. 1964. 75.40 (*3-11-000137-3*); Vol. 2. Platonischen Schriften: Erste Periode. 3rd rev. ed. vi, 358p. 1964. 75.40 (*3-11-000138-1*); Vol. 3. Platonischen Schriften: Tweite & Periode. 1975. 101.55 (*3-11-004049-2*); (GER.). (C). write for info. (*0-318-51637-3*) De Gruyter.

Platon: Sein Leben, Seine Schriften, Seine Lehre, 2 vols., Vol. 1. Constantin Ritter. LC 75-13291. (History of Ideas in Ancient Greece Ser.). (GER.). 1976. reprint ed. 51.95 (*0-405-07334-8*) Ayer.

Platon: Sein Leben, Seine Schriften, Seine Lehre, 2 vols., Vol. 2. Constantin Ritter. LC 75-13291. (History of Ideas in Ancient Greece Ser.). (GER.). 1976. reprint ed. 51.95 (*0-405-07335-6*) Ayer.

Platon: Sein Leben, Seine Schriften, Seine Lehre, 2 vols., Vols. 1 [00ad] 2. Constantin Ritter. LC 75-13291. (History of Ideas in Ancient Greece Ser.). (GER.). 1976. reprint ed. 101.95 (*0-405-07333-X*) Ayer.

Platon Band 1: Sein Leben und Seine Werke. Ulrich Von Wilamowitz-Moellendorff. (GER.). xvi, 615p. 1959. write for info. (*3-296-16301-8*) G Olms Pubs.

Platon Band 2: Beilagen und Textritik. Ulrich Von Wilamowitz-Moellendorff. (GER.). ii, 460p. 1992. reprint ed. write for info. (*3-296-16302-6*) G Olms Pubs.

Platon - Concordantiae in Platonis Opera Omnia. Mauro Siviero. (Alpha-Omega, Reihe A Ser.: Bd. CX). xlii, 217p. 1978. reprint ed. write for info. (*3-487-06667-X*) G Olms Pubs.

Platon - Concordantiae in Platonis Opera Omnia Pars I: Euthyphro. Ed. by Mauro Siviero. 180p. write for info. (*0-318-70674-1*) G Olms Pubs.

Platon und die Schriftlichkeit der Philosophie: Interpretationen zu den Fruehen und Mittleren Dialogen. Thomas A. Szlezak. (GER.). x, 446p. 1985. 192.35 (*3-11-010272-2*) De Gruyter.

Platonic Bearings in Rabindranath. Bhaktivenode Chakraborty. 1986. 9.00 (*0-8364-1580-9*, Pub. by KP Bagchi) S Asia.

Platonic Blow & My Epitaph. W. H. Auden. LC 85-339. 8p. 1985. pap. 5.00 (*0-914061-04-6*) Orchises Pr.

Platonic Discourse on Love. Pico Della Mirandola. 1994. pap. 7.95 (*1-55818-279-9*) Holmes Pub.

Platonic Doctrines of Albinus. Tr. by Jeremiah Reedy from GRE. LC 91-25598. 81p. (Orig.). 1991. pap. 12.00 (*0-933999-15-1*) Phanes Pr.

Platonic Epistles. Plato. Tr. by J. Harward. LC 75-13287. (History of Ideas in Ancient Greece Ser.). 1979. reprint ed. 26.95 (*0-405-07330-5*) Ayer.

Platonic Errors: Plato, a Kind of Poet, 69. Gene Fendt & David Rozema. LC 98-23547. (Contributions in Philosophy Ser.: Vol. 69). 192p. 1998. 55.00 (*0-313-30765-2*, Greenwood Pr) Greenwood.

Platonic Ethics, Old & New. Julia Annas. LC 98-30418. (Studies in Classical Philology - Townsend Lectures). viii, 196p. 1998. pap. write for info. (*0-8014-8517-7*) Cornell U Pr.

Platonic Ethics, Old & New. Julia Annas. LC 98-30418. 256p. 1999. 35.00 (*0-8014-3518-8*) Cornell U Pr.

Platonic Love. Michael J. Bugeja. LC 90-19734. 80p. (Orig.). 1991. pap. 10.00 (*0-914061-21-6*) Orchises Pr.

Platonic Love. Thomas Gould. LC 81-6881. 216p. 1981. reprint ed. lib. bdg. 42.50 (*0-313-22520-6*, GOPT, Greenwood Pr) Greenwood.

***Platonic Political Art: A Study of Critical Reason & Democracy.** John R. Wallach. LC 00-31376. 2001. pap. write for info. (*0-271-02076-8*) Pa St U Pr.

Platonic Quest. Edward J. Urwick. xxxiv, 264p. (Orig.). (C). 1983. reprint ed. pap. 21.75 (*0-88695-001-5*) Concord Grove.

***Platonic Questions: Dialogues with the Silent Philosopher.** Diskin Clay. LC 99-56918. 2000. write for info. (*0-271-02044-X*) Pa St U Pr.

Platonic Rape: A Novel about Unfilial People. Unfilial. 124p. (Orig.). 1993. pap. 10.00 (*0-9639653-0-1*) Unfilial Pr.

Platonic Renaissance in England. Ernst Cassirer. LC 71-128186. 207p. (C). 1970. reprint ed. 50.00 (*0-87752-128-X*) Gordian.

Platonic Studies. 2nd ed. Gregory Vlastos. LC 80-8732. 520p. (C). 1981. reprint ed. pap. text 24.95 (*0-691-10021-7*, Pub. by Princeton U Pr) Cal Prin Full Svc.

Platonic Studies of Greek Philosophy: Form, Arts, Gadgets, & Hemlock. Robert S. Brumbaugh. LC 88-8578. (SUNY Series in Philosophy). 296p. (C). 1989. text 24.50 (*0-88706-897-9*) State U NY Pr.

Platonic Transformations: With & after Hegel, Heider & Levinas. Adriaan T. Peperzak. LC 96-46160. 280p. 1997. 71.00 (*0-8476-8428-8*); pap. 26.95 (*0-8476-8429-6*) Rowman.

Platonic Writings - Platonic Readings. Ed. by Charles L. Griswold, Jr. 320p. 1988. text 47.50 (*0-415-00186-2*) Routledge.

Platonick Song of the Soul. Henry More. Ed. & Intro. by Alexander Jacob. LC 97-47288. 688p. 1998. 65.00 (*0-8387-5366-3*) Bucknell U Pr.

Platonics: 1894 Edition. Ethel Arnold. Ed. by Marie M. Roberts. (Her Write His Name Ser.). 160p. 1996. reprint ed. pap. 24.95 (*1-85506-389-1*) Bks Intl VA.

Platoniker Tauros in der Darstellung des Aulus Gellius. M. L. Lakmann. (GER.). xi, 294p. 1994. 105.50 (*90-04-10096-2*, PHA, 63) Brill Academic Pubs.

Platonis. Ed. by Moore-Blunt. (GRE.). 1985. 27.95 (*3-322-00423-6*, T1588, Pub. by B G Teubner) U of Mich Pr.

Platonis Opera. 2nd ed. Plato. Ed. by E. A. Duke et al. (Classical Texts Ser.). 604p. 1995. text 36.00 (*0-19-814569-1*) OUP.

Platonische Aufsatze. Otto Apelt. LC 75-13251. (History of Ideas in Ancient Greece Ser.). (GER.). 1976. reprint ed. 21.95 (*0-405-07288-0*) Ayer.

Platonische Philosophie des Guten Lebens und Moderne Orientierungslosigkeit. Pirkko Pitkanen. Ed. by Hartmut Schroder. (Scandinavian University Studies in the Humanities & Social Sciences: Bd. 11). (GER.). 140p. 1996. 32.95 (*3-631-31051-X*) P Lang Pubng.

Platonische Staat. August A. Krohn. LC 75-13277. (History of Ideas in Ancient Greece Ser.). (GER.). 1976. reprint ed. 26.95 (*0-405-07317-8*) Ayer.

Platonische Studien. Hermann Bonitz. (GER.). xii, 323p. 1968. reprint ed. 90.00 (*0-318-70452-8*) G Olms Pubs.

Platonische Studien. Eduard Zeller. LC 75-13301. (History of Ideas in Ancient Greece Ser.). (GER.). 1976. reprint ed. 21.95 (*0-405-07344-5*) Ayer.

Platonischen Schriften: Erste Periode see Platon

Platonischen Schriften: Tweite & Periode see Platon

Platonism, 5. John Burnet. LC 83-1503. (Sather Classical Lecture: Vol. 5). 130p. (C). 1983. reprint ed. lib. bdg. 42.50 (*0-313-23699-2*, BUPL, Greenwood Pr) Greenwood.

Platonism & Anti-Platonism in Mathematics. Mark Balaguer. 240p. 1998. text 45.00 (*0-19-512230-5*) OUP.

Platonism & Its Christian Heritage. Rist. 94.95 (*0-86078-169-0*) Ashgate Pub Co.

Platonism & Positivism in Psychology. Mortimer J. Adler. LC 94-27446. 266p. 1994. pap. 24.95 (*1-56000-772-9*) Transaction Pubs.

Platonism & the English Imagination. Ed. by Anna Baldwin & Sarah Hutton. LC 93-9341. 373p. (C). 1994. text 74.95 (*0-521-40308-1*) Cambridge U Pr.

Platonism in English Poetry of the 16th & 17th Centuries. John S. Harrison. LC 80-11587. (Columbia University Studies in Comparative Literature). 235p. 1980. reprint ed. lib. bdg. 59.50 (*0-313-22374-2*, HAPL, Greenwood Pr) Greenwood.

Platonism in English Poetry of the 16th & 17th Centuries. John S. Harrison. (BCL1-PR English Literature Ser.). 235p. 1992. reprint ed. lib. bdg. 79.00 (*0-7812-7079-0*) Rprt Serv.

Platonism in Late Antiquity. Ed. by Stephen Gersh & Charles Kannengiesser. LC 91-43920. (Christianity & Judaism in Antiquity Ser.: Vol. 8). (C). 1992. text 34.50 (*0-268-01513-9*) U of Notre Dame Pr.

Platonismus und Hellenistische Philosophie. Hans J. Kraemer. 368p. (C). 1971. 130.80 (*3-11-003643-6*) De Gruyter.

Plato, Not Prozac! Applying Philosophy to Everyday Problems. Lou Marinoff. LC 99-22650. 320p. 1999. 23.95 (*0-06-019328-X*) HarpC.

Platonov: A Play in 4 Acts. Anton Chekhov. Tr. by David Magarshack from RUS. 195p. 1964. 17.95 (*0-910278-93-8*) Boulevard.

Platonov: The River Potudan (Reka Potudan) Ed. by M. Minto. (Bristol Russian Texts Ser.). (RUS.). 1995. pap. 18.95 (*1-85399-377-8*, Pub. by Brist Class Pr) Focus Pub-R Pullins.

Platons Dialektik: Die Fruhen & Mittleren Dialoge. Peter Stemmer. (Quellen und Studien zur Philosophie: No. 31). (GER.). vii, 307p. (C). 1992. lib. bdg. 121.55 (*3-11-012770-9*) De Gruyter.

Platons Ideenlehre. Gottfried Martin. LC 72-81562. (C). 1973. 89.25 (*3-11-004135-9*) De Gruyter.

Platons, Parmenides' Probleme de Interpretation. Rudolf Haegler. (LAT.). 220p. 1983. 113.10 (*3-11-009599-8*) De Gruyter.

Platons' Philosophische Entwicklung. Hans Raeder. LC 75-13288. (History of Ideas in Ancient Greece Ser.). (GER.). 1976. reprint ed. 29.95 (*0-405-07331-3*) Ayer.

Platonstudien. Hermann Gundert. (Studien zur antiken Philosophie). viii, 194p. 1977. (*90-6032-074-3*) B R Gruner.

Platoon: Bravo Company. Robert Hemphill. LC 98-36820. 1998. 24.95 (*1-887901-25-6*) Sergeant Kirk.

***Platoon: Bravo Company.** Robert Hemphill. 2001. mass mkt. write for info. (*0-312-97657-7*) St Martin.

Platoon Leader. James R. McDonough. LC 84-24839. (Illus.). 208p. 1996. pap. 14.00 (*0-89141-606-4*) Presidio Pr.

Platoon Operations Order. Matthew R. Redel. (Illus.). 33p. 1998. pap. 8.95 (*1-884778-51-8*) Old Mountain.

Platoon Sergeant. Bobby Owens. LC 93-90792. (Illus.). 224p. 1994. 25.00 (*1-884308-03-1*); pap. text 14.95 (*1-884308-04-X*) Enlisted Ldrship.

Platoro: From Mining Camp to Resort Town. Leland Feitz. (Illus.). 1969. 3.95 (*0-936564-09-1*) Little London.

Platoro Area Wildflowers: Food, Medicinal, & Craft Uses of 125 Montane, Subalpine, & Alpine Wildflowers of Southeastern Colorado. Lynn Copley. (Illus.). 112p. 1998. pap. 15.95 (*1-882849-06-X*) Platoro Pr.

Plato's Analytic Method. Kenneth M. Sayre. LC 69-15496. 261p. reprint ed. pap. 81.00 (*0-608-18240-0*, 205665400078) Bks Demand.

Platos Analytical Method. Sayre. 1994. 56.95 (*0-7512-0316-5*) Ashgate Pub Co.

Plato's Apology of Socrates: A Literary & Philosophical Study with a Running Commentary. Plato & Emile de Strycker. LC 94-20723. (Mnemosyne, Bibliotheca Classica Batava, Supplementum: Vol. 137). xvii, 405p. 1994. 135.50 (*90-04-10103-9*) Brill Academic Pubs.

Plato's Apology of Socrates: An Interpretation, with a New Translation. Plato. LC 78-11532. 240p. 1979. text 37.50 (*0-8014-1127-0*) Cornell U Pr.

Plato's Breath: Poems by Randall R. Freisinger. Randall R. Freisinger. LC 97-47427. (May Swenson Poetry Award Ser.: Vol. 1). 80p. 1997. pap. 9.95 (*0-87421-236-7*) Utah St U Pr.

An Asterisk (*) at the beginning of an entry indicates that the title is appearing for the first time.

Plato's Cave: Desire, Power, & the Specular Functions of the Media. John O'Neil. 224p. 1991. pap. 39.50 (*1-56750-080-3*) Ablx Pub.

Plato's Cave: Desire, Power, & the Specular Functions of the the Media. John O'Neil. 224p. 1991. text 73.25 (*0-89391-722-2*) Ablx Pub.

Plato's Cave Vol. 1: Interviews with the Wise. Ed. by Mount San Antonio College Philosophy Group Staff. 60p. (Orig.). 1992. pap. 9.95 (*1-56543-012-3*) Mt SA Coll Philos.

Plato's Charmides & the Socratic Ideal of Ratioality. W. Thomas Schmid. LC 97-27154. (SUNY Series in Ancient Greek Philosophy). 192p. (C). 1998. text 59.50 (*0-7914-3763-9*); pap. text 19.95 (*0-7914-3764-7*) State U NY Pr.

Plato's Conception of Philosophy. H. Gauss. LC 73-21610. (Studies in Philosophy: No. 40). 1974. lib. bdg. 75.00 (*0-8383-1759-6*) M S G Haskell Hse.

Plato's Cosmology. Francis M. Cornford. LC 97-74231. 390p. (C). 1997. reprint ed. lib. bdg. 39.95 (*0-87220-387-5*) Hackett Pub.

Plato's Cosmology. 2nd ed. Francis M. Cornford. LC 97-74231. 390p. (C). 1997. reprint ed. pap. 16.95 (*0-87220-386-7*) Hackett Pub.

Plato's Craft of Justice. Richard D. Parry. LC 95-3471. (SUNY Series in Ancient Greek Philosophy). 268p. (C). 1995. text 57.50 (*0-7914-2731-5*); pap. text 18.95 (*0-7914-2732-3*) State U NY Pr.

Plato's Cretan City: A Historical Interpretation of the Laws. Glenn R. Morrow. 646p. 1993. pap. text 29.95 (*0-691-02484-7*, Pub. by Princeton U Pr) Cal Prin Full Svc.

Plato's Defence of Poetry. Julius A. Elias. LC 83-9137. 261p. (C). 1984. text 59.50 (*0-87395-806-3*); pap. text 19.95 (*0-87395-807-1*) State U NY Pr.

***Plato's Democratic Entanglements: Athenian Politics & the Practice of Philosophy.** S. Sara Monoson. LC 99-54924. 256p. 2000. 39.50 (*0-691-04366-3*, Pub. by Princeton U Pr) Cal Prin Full Svc.

Plato's Dialectical Ethics: Phenomenological Interpretations Relating to the "Philebus" Hans-Georg Gadamer. Tr. by Robert M. Wallace from GER. LC 91-7212. 272p. (C). 1991. 37.00 (*0-300-04807-6*) Yale U Pr.

***Plato's Dialogue Form & the Care of the Soul.** Mark Moes. LC 98-50412. (New Perspectives in Philosophical Scholarship Ser.: Vol. 13). 240p. 2000. text 50.95 (*0-8204-4459-6*) P Lang Pubng.

Plato's Dialogue of the Immortality of the Soul. Plato. LC 73-161797. (Augustan Translators Ser.). reprint ed. 49.50 (*0-404-54134-8*) AMS Pr.

Plato's Dialogue on Friendship: An Interpretation of the "Lysis", with a New Translation. David Bolotin. LC 88-43323. (Agora Paperback Editions Ser.). 232p. 1989. pap. text 13.95 (*0-8014-9561-X*) Cornell U Pr.

Plato's Dialogues: New Studies & Interpretations. Ed. by Gerald A. Press. 288p. (Orig.). (C). 1993. pap. text 24.95 (*0-8476-7836-9*) Rowman.

Plato's Dialogues: The Dialogical Approach. Ed. by Richard E. Hart & Victorino Tejera. LC 97-12614. (Studies in History of Philosophy: No. 46). 280p. 1997. text 89.95 (*0-7734-8628-3*) E Mellen.

***Plato's Dialogues & Ethics.** Howard Alexander Slaatte. LC 99-41509. 152p. 1999. 39.50 (*0-7618-1500-7*) U Pr of Amer.

Plato's Dialogues One by One. V. Tejera. LC 97-45719. 1997. write for info. (*0-7618-0993-7*) U Pr of Amer.

Plato's Dialogues 1-by-1: A Structural Interpretation. Victorino Tejera. LC 83-22573. 424p. 1984. text 49.50 (*0-8290-1515-9*); pap. text 24.95 (*0-8290-1541-8*) Irvington.

Plato's Dream of Sophistry. Richard Marback. Ed. by Thomas W. Benson. LC 97-45431. (Studies in Rhetoric/Communication). 160p. 1999. lib. bdg. 24.95 (*1-57003-240-8*) U of SC Pr.

Plato's Epistemology: How Hard It Is to Know. Elizabeth A. Laidlaw-Johnson. (American University Studies V: Vol. 173). X, 137p. (C). 1997. text 33.95 (*0-8204-2721-7*) P Lang Pubng.

Plato's Ethics. Terrence H. Irwin. 464p. 1995. pap. text 28.00 (*0-19-508645-7*) OUP.

Plato's Ethics see Classical Philosophy: Collected Papers

Plato's Euthydemus: Analysis of What Is & Is Not Philosophy. Thomas H. Chance. (C). 1992. 55.00 (*0-520-07754-7*, Pub. by U CA Pr) Cal Prin Full Svc.

Plato's Euthyphro. Plato. LC 75-13272. (History of Ideas in Ancient Greece Ser.). (ENG & GRE.). 1978. reprint ed. 16.95 (*0-405-07313-5*) Ayer.

Plato's Euthyphro, Apology & Crito, Set. unabridged ed. Plato. (Theater of the Mind Ser.). 69p. 1995. pap. 12.50 incl. audio (*1-887250-05-0*) Agora Pubns.

Plato's Euthyphro, Apology, & Crito: Arranged for Dramatic Presentation from the Jowett Translation with Choruses. S. W. Emery. 90p. (C). 1995. lib. bdg. 22.50 (*0-7618-0170-7*) U Pr of Amer.

Plato's Euthyphro, Apology, Crito & Phaedo Notes. Charles H. Patterson. (Cliffs Notes Ser.). 64p. (Orig.). 1975. pap. text 4.95 (*0-8220-1044-5*, Cliff) IDG Bks.

Plato's Euthyphro, Apology of Socrates & Crito. Plato. Ed. by John Burnet. LC 76-29434. reprint ed. 45.00 (*0-404-15322-4*) AMS Pr.

***Plato's First Interpreters.** Harold Tarrant. 2000. write for info. (*0-8014-3792-X*) Cornell U Pr.

Plato's Garage. Ron Campbell. 272p. 2000. text 23.95 (*0-312-20569-4*) St Martin.

Plato's Gorgias. unabridged ed. Plato. (Theater of the Mind Ser.). 114p. (C). 1994. pap. 12.50 incl. audio (*1-887250-01-8*) Agora Pubns.

Plato's Heirs: Classic Essays. Compiled by James D. Lester. LC 95-8290. (Library of Classic Essays). 304p. 1995. pap. text, student ed. 14.95 (*0-8442-5878-4*) NTC Contemp Pub Co.

Plato's Heirs: Classic Essays. James D. Lester. (Library of Classic Essays). 1998. pap., teacher ed. 23.99 (*0-8442-5879-2*) NTC Contemp Pub Co.

Plato's Individuals. Mary M. McCabe. LC 93-42370. 360p. 1994. text 47.50 (*0-691-07351-1*, Pub. by Princeton U Pr) Cal Prin Full Svc.

***Plato's Individuals.** Mary Margaret McCabe. 360p. (C). 1999. pap. text 18.95 (*0-691-02939-3*, Pub. by Princeton U Pr) Cal Prin Full Svc.

***Plato's Introduction to the Question of Justice.** Devin Stauffer. (C). 2000. pap. text 16.95 (*0-7914-4746-4*) State U NY Pr.

***Plato's Introduction to the Question of Justice.** Devin Stauffer. (C). 2000. text 49.50 (*0-7914-4745-6*) State U NY Pr.

Plato's Ion & Meno. unabridged ed. Plato. Tr. by Benjamin Jowett. (Theater of the Mind Ser.). (Illus.). 77p. (gr. 7 up). 1998. pap. 12.50 incl. audio (*1-887250-10-7*) Agora Pubns.

Plato's Journey. Linda Talley. LC 97-13842. (Key Concepts in Personal Development Ser.). (Illus.). 32p. (J). (gr. k-4). 1998. 16.95 (*1-55942-100-2*, 7664) Marsh Media.

Platos Jugenddialoge & die Entstehungszeit des Phaidros. Hans F. Von Arnim. LC 75-13255. (History of Ideas in Ancient Greece Ser.). (GER.). 1976. reprint ed. 18.95 (*0-405-07293-7*) Ayer.

Plato's Late Ontology: A Riddle Resolved. Kenneth M. Sayre. LC 82-61382. 339p. 1983. reprint ed. pap. 105.10 (*0-608-04579-9*, 206534800003) Bks Demand.

Plato's Law of Slavery in Its Relation to Greek Law. Glenn R. Morrow. LC 75-13283. (History of Ideas in Ancient Greece Ser.). 1976. reprint ed. 15.95 (*0-405-07325-9*) Ayer.

Plato's Literary Garden: How to Read a Platonic Dialogue. Kenneth M. Sayre. LC 95-16521. (C). 1996. text 34.95 (*0-268-03808-2*) U of Notre Dame Pr.

Plato's Lysis. William H. Race. (Greek Commentaries Ser.). 59p. (Orig.). (C). 1983. pap. text 6.00 (*0-929524-29-2*) Bryn Mawr Commentaries.

Plato's Meno. Richard D. McKirahan, Jr. (Greek Commentaries Ser.). 109p. (Orig.). (C). 1986. pap. text 7.00 (*0-929524-30-6*) Bryn Mawr Commentaries.

Plato's Meno. 2nd ed. Plato. Tr. by G. M. Grube from GRE. LC 76-40412. (HPC Classics Ser.). 48p. (C). 1980. pap. 3.95 (*0-915144-24-7*) Hackett Pub.

Plato's Metaphysics & Epistemology see Classical Philosophy: Collected Papers

Plato's Metaphysics of Education. Samuel Scolnicov. (Philosophy of Education Research Library). 192p. 1988. text 27.50 (*0-415-01864-1*) Routledge.

Plato's Method of Dialectic. Julius Stenzel. Ed. & Tr. by D. J. Allan. LC 72-9305. (Philosophy of Plato & Aristotle Ser.). 1979. reprint ed. 27.95 (*0-405-04862-9*) Ayer.

***Plato's Parmenides.** Plato & Samuel Scolnicov. LC 00-21808. 2001. write for info. (*0-520-22403-5*) U CA Pr.

Plato's Parmenides. Albert K. Whitaker. (Philosophical Library). 96p. (Orig.). 1996. pap. text 6.95 (*0-941051-96-X*) Focus Pub-R Pullins.

Plato's Parmenides. rev. ed. Tr. & Comment by R. E. Allen. (Dialogues of Plato Ser.: Vol. 4). 384p. 1997. pap. 18.00 (*0-300-07729-7*) Yale U Pr.

Plato's Parmenides. rev. ed. Plato. Tr. & Comment by R. E. Allen. LC 97-128617. (Dialogues of Plato Ser.: Vol. 4). 384p. 1997. 45.00 (*0-300-06616-3*) Yale U Pr.

Plato's Parmenides: The Conversion of the Soul. Mitchell H. Miller, Jr. 314p. 1991. pap. 16.95 (*0-271-00803-2*) Pa St U Pr.

Plato's Parmenides: The Conversion of the Soul. Mitchell H. Miller. LC 85-43301. 314p. 1986. reprint ed. pap. 97.40 (*0-608-06477-7*, 206677400009) Bks Demand.

Plato's Penal Code: Tradition, Controversy, & Reform in Greek Penology. Trevor J. Saunders. 432p. 1994. reprint ed. pap. text 35.00 (*0-19-814960-3*) OUP.

Plato's Phaedo. David Bostock. 236p. (C). 1986. pap. text 32.00 (*0-19-824918-7*) OUP.

Plato's Phaedo. Eva Brann et al. (Philosophical Library). (GEC.). 140p. (C). 1998. pap. text 7.95 (*0-941051-69-2*) Focus Pub-R Pullins.

Plato's Phaedo. Plato. Tr. by G. M. Grube. LC 76-49565. (HPC Classics Ser.). 72p. (C). 1980. pap. 4.25 (*0-915144-18-2*) Hackett Pub.

Plato's Phaedo: An Interpretation. Kenneth Dorter. LC 82-217526. 245p. reprint ed. pap. 76.00 (*0-8357-6378-1*, 203573200096) Bks Demand.

Plato's Phaedrus: The Philosophy of Love. Graeme Nicholson. LC 97-46404. (In the History of Philosophy Ser.). 1998. 49.95 (*1-55753-118-8*); pap. 24.95 (*1-55753-119-6*) Purdue U Pr.

Plato's Philosophy of Mathematics. Anders Wedberg. LC 76-50071. 154p. 1977. reprint ed. lib. bdg. 38.50 (*0-8371-9405-9*, WEPP, Greenwood Pr) Greenwood.

Plato's Plant. F. Schieving. 360p. 1998. 99.00 (*90-5782-003-X*) Balogh.

Plato's Poetics: The Authority of Beauty. Morriss H. Partee. LC 81-3332. 238p. reprint ed. pap. 73.80 (*0-8357-6846-5*, 203554100095) Bks Demand.

Plato's Political Philosophy: Prudence in the Republic & the Laws. Zdravko Planinc. 328p. (C). 1991. text 37.50 (*0-8262-0798-7*) U of Mo Pr.

Plato's Portrait of Sokrates. Stephen G. Daitz. (Living Voice of Greek & Latin Ser.). (GRE.). 68p. 1988. pap. text 39.95 incl. audio (*0-88432-254-8*, S23695) Audio-Forum.

Plato's Progress. Gilbert Ryle. LC 66-15278. 319p. reprint ed. pap. 91.00 (*0-608-10014-5*, 2013248) Bks Demand.

Plato's Progress: 1966 Edition. Gilbert Ryle. (Key Texts Ser.). 320p. 1996. reprint ed. pap. 29.95 (*1-85506-321-2*) Bks Intl VA.

Plato's Protagoras: A Socratic Commentary. Plato. Ed. by B. A. Hubbard. LC 83-18122. xvi, 172p. 1993. pap. text 11.95 (*0-226-67036-8*) U Ch Pr.

Plato's Psychology. T. M. Robinson. LC 76-465044. 215p. reprint ed. pap. 66.70 (*0-608-31002-6*, 20512160093) Bks Demand.

Plato's Psychology. 2nd rev. ed. T. M. Robinson. (Phoenix Supplementary Volumes Ser.). 264p. 1995. text 60.00 (*0-8020-0635-3*); pap. text 22.95 (*0-8020-7590-8*) U of Toronto Pr.

Plato's Reception of Parmenides. John A. Palmer. LC 98-46615. 312p. 1999. text 65.00 (*0-19-823800-2*) OUP.

Plato's Republic, Bk. 1. Gilbert P. Rose. (Greek Commentaries Ser.). 91p. (Orig.). (C). 1983. pap. text 6.00 (*0-929524-31-4*) Bryn Mawr Commentaries.

Plato's Republic, Bks. 1 & 2. unabridged ed. Plato. (Theater of the Mind Ser.). 102p. (YA). (gr. 7 up). 1997. pap. 12.50 incl. audio (*1-887250-07-7*) Agora Pubns.

***Plato's Republic: An Introduction.** Sean Sayers. 192p. 2000. pap. text 18.00 (*0-7486-1188-6*) Col U Pr.

Plato's "Republic" Critical Essays. Ed. by Richard Kraut. LC 97-15773. (Critical Essays on the Classics Ser.). 240p. 1997. 36.00 (*0-8476-8492-X*); pap. 15.95 (*0-8476-8493-8*) Rowman.

***Plato's Republic: The Good Society & the Deformation of Desire.** Martha Nussbaum. LC 97-4414. (Bradley Lecture Ser.). 30p. 1998. pap. 5.00 (*0-8444-0951-0*) Lib Congress.

Plato's Republic Vol. 2: The Greek Text, Volume II; Essays. Plato. Ed. by Benjamin E. Jowett & Lewis Campbell. LC 72-9295. (Philosophy of Plato & Aristotle Ser.). (GRE.). 1974. reprint ed. 37.95 (*0-405-04846-7*) Ayer.

Plato's Republic & the Space of Discourse. Adi Ophir. 300p. (C). 1990. text 64.00 (*0-389-20930-9*) Rowman.

Plato's Republic for Readers: A Constitution. Plato. Tr. by George A. Blair. LC 98-10666. 440p. (C). 1998. pap. 36.50 (*0-7618-1044-7*) U Pr of Amer.

***Plato's Self-Corrective Development of the Concepts of Soul, Forms & Immortality in Three Arguments of the Phaedo.** Martha C. Beck. LC 99-27736. (Studies in the History of Philosophy: Vol. 52). 276p. 1999. text 89.95 (*0-7734-7950-3*) E Mellen.

Plato's Seventh Letter. L. Edelstein. 1966. pap. 37.00 (*90-04-01726-7*, PHA, 14) Brill Academic Pubs.

Plato's Socrates. Thomas C. Brickhouse & Nicholas D. Smith. 256p. 1996. reprint ed. pap. 18.95 (*0-19-510111-1*) OUP.

***Plato's Socrates as Educator.** Gary Alan Scott. (C). 2000. pap. text 20.95 (*0-7914-4724-3*) State U NY Pr.

***Plato's Socrates as Educator.** Gary Alan Scott. (C). 2000. text 62.50 (*0-7914-4723-5*) State U NY Pr.

Plato's Socratic Conversations: Drama & Dialectic in Three Dialogues. Michael C. Stokes. LC 85-24074. 534p. reprint ed. pap. 165.60 (*0-608-06109-3*, 206644100008) Bks Demand.

Plato's Sophist. Martin Heidegger. Tr. by Richard Rojcewicz & Andre Schuwer. LC 96-32709. (Studies in Continental Thought). 1997. 39.95 (*0-253-33222-2*) Ind U Pr.

Plato's Sophist. Plato. Tr. by William S. Cobb. 144p. (C). 1990. pap. text 14.95 (*0-8476-7653-6*) Rowman.

Plato's Sophist. Plato. Tr. & Intro. by William S. Cobb. 144p. (C). 1990. text 55.00 (*0-8476-7652-8*) Rowman.

Plato's Sophist: A Philosophical Commentary. L. M. de Rijk. (Verhandelingen der Koninklijke Nederlandse Akademie van Wetenschappen, Afd. Letterkunde, Nieuwe Reeks Ser.: No. 133). 396p. 1986. pap. text 115.75 (*0-444-85627-7*) Elsevier.

Plato's Sophist: The Being of the Beautiful, Pt. II. Seth Benardete. LC 85-28861. xx, 200p. 1986. pap. text 18.00 (*0-226-67032-5*) U Ch Pr.

Plato's Sophist: The Drama of Original & Image. Stanley Rosen. LC 99-13195. 352p. 1999. pap. 29.00 (*1-890318-63-9*) St Augustines Pr.

Plato's Sophist: The Professor of Wisdom. Eva Brann et al. (Philosophical Library). (Illus.). 98p. (C). 1996. pap. text 6.95 (*0-941051-51-X*) Focus Pub-R Pullins.

Plato's Statesman. Plato. Tr. by J. B. Skemp. LC 92-26568. 136p. (C). 1992. reprint ed. 29.95 (*0-87220-139-2*); reprint ed. pap. 7.95 (*0-87220-138-4*) Hackett Pub.

Plato's Statesman: The Being of the Beautiful, Pt. III. Seth Benardete. LC 85-28827. xx, 176p. 1986. pap. text 13.95 (*0-226-67033-3*) U Ch Pr.

Plato's Statesman: The Web of Politics. Stanley Rosen. LC 94-44016. 197p. 1995. 30.00 (*0-300-06264-8*) Yale U Pr.

Plato's Statesman: The Web of Politics. Stanley Rosen. 208p. 1997. pap. text 16.00 (*0-300-07281-3*) Yale U Pr.

***Plato's Symposium.** Plato et al. LC 00-32593. 2000. pap. write for info. (*0-226-04275-8*) U Ch Pr.

Plato's Symposium. Avi Sharon. (Focus Philosophical Library). 140p. (Orig.). 1998. pap. 6.95 (*0-941051-56-0*) Focus Pub-R Pullins.

Plato's Symposium. 2nd ed. Gilbert P. Rose. (Greek Commentaries Ser.). 158p. (C). 1985. pap. text 8.00 (*0-929524-32-2*) Bryn Mawr Commentaries.

Plato's Symposium. 2nd ed. Stanley Rosen. LC 99-21495. 428p. 1999. reprint ed. pap. 32.00 (*1-890318-64-7*) St Augustines Pr.

Plato's the Republic Notes. C. H. Patterson. (Cliffs Notes Ser.). 80p. 1963. pap. 4.95 (*0-8220-1129-8*, Cliff) IDG Bks.

Plato's Theatetus, Pt. I. Seth Benardete. LC 85-28863. xx, 214p. 1986. pap. text 15.50 (*0-226-67031-7*) U Ch Pr.

Plato's Theory of Explanation: A Study of the Cosmological Account in the Timaeus. Anne F. Ashbaugh. LC 87-10256. (SUNY Series in Philosophy). 195p. 1988. text 24.50 (*0-88706-607-0*) State U NY Pr.

Plato's Theory of Fine Art: "He Who Knows Not the Truth, but Pursues Opinions, will, It Seems, Attain an Art Which Is Ridiculous, & Not an Art at All" - Plato's Phaedrus, 262C. Constantine Cavarnos. 107p. 1998. 15.00 (*1-884729-34-7*) Inst Byzantine.

Plato's Theory of Fine Art: "He Who Knows Not the Truth, but Pursues Opinions, Will, It Seems, Attain an Art Which Is Ridiculous, & Not an Art at All" - Plato's Phaedrus, 262C. 2nd ed. Constantine Cavarnos. LC 98-70395. 107p. 1998. pap. 7.00 (*1-884729-35-5*) Inst Byzantine.

Plato's Theory of Ideas. William D. Ross. LC 75-36510. 250p. 1976. reprint ed. lib. bdg. 69.50 (*0-8371-8635-8*, ROPTI, Greenwood Pr) Greenwood.

Plato's Theory of Knowledge. Norman Gulley. LC 86-4622. 211p. 1986. reprint ed. lib. bdg. 41.50 (*0-313-25209-2*, GUPL, Greenwood Pr) Greenwood.

Plato's Theory of Particulars. F. C. White. Ed. by W. R. Connor. LC 80-2672. (Monographs in Classical Studies). 1981. lib. bdg. 64.95 (*0-405-14055-X*) Ayer.

Plato's Theory of Understanding. Jon Moline. LC 81-50826. 272p. 1981. reprint ed. pap. 84.40 (*0-7837-9790-7*, 206051900005) Bks Demand.

Plato's 3rd Eye: Studies in Marsilio Metaphysics & Its Sources. M. J. Allen. (Collected Studies: Vol. CS483). 350p. 1995. 113.95 (*0-86078-472-X*, Pub. by Variorum) Ashgate Pub Co.

Plato's Thought. G. M. Grube. LC 80-14588. 368p. (C). 1980. reprint ed. 34.95 (*0-915144-79-4*); reprint ed. pap. text 10.95 (*0-915144-80-8*) Hackett Pub.

Plato's Thought in the Making: A Study of the Development of His Metaphysics. John E. Raven. LC 85-10074. 256p. 1985. reprint ed. lib. bdg. 65.00 (*0-313-24958-X*, RAPT, Greenwood Pr) Greenwood.

Plato's Timaeus. Francis M. Cornford. Ed. by Oskar Piest. 144p. (C). 1959. pap. text 6.00 (*0-02-325190-5*, Macmillan Coll) P-H.

Plato's Trilogy: Theaetetus, the Sophist & the Statesman. Jacob Klein. LC 76-25642. 1977. lib. bdg. 16.00 (*0-226-43951-8*) U Ch Pr.

Plato's View of Man: Two Bowen Prize Essays Dealing with the Problem of the Destiny of Man & the Individual Life, Together with Selected Passages from Plato's Dialogues on Man & the Human Soul. Constantine Cavarnos. LC 74-27242. 95p. 1982. pap. 5.00 (*0-914744-26-7*) Inst Byzantine.

Plato's World. Joseph Cropsey. LC 94-34538. 238p. 1995. 29.95 (*0-226-12121-6*) U Ch Pr.

Plato's World. Joseph Cropsey. 1997. pap. text 12.95 (*0-226-12122-4*) U Ch Pr.

Plats du Jour: or Foreign Food. Patience Gray & Primrose Boyd. (Illus.). 299p. 1990. 33.00 (*0-907325-45-9*, Pub. by Prospect) Food Words.

Platt Brothers & Company: Small Business in American Manufacturing. Matthew W. Roth. LC 93-11001. (Illus.). 272p. reprint ed. pap. 84.40 (*0-608-09094-8*, 206972800005) Bks Demand.

Platt Genealogy in America, from the Arrival of Richard Platt in New Haven, Conn., in 1638. Charles Platt, Jr. (Illus.). 453p. 1993. reprint ed. pap. 71.00 (*0-8328-3573-0*); reprint ed. lib. bdg. 81.00 (*0-8328-3572-2*) Higginson Bk Co.

Platt Lineage: A Genealogical Research & Record. G. L. Platt. (Illus.). 398p. 1989. reprint ed. pap. 60.00 (*0-8328-0973-X*); reprint ed. lib. bdg. 68.00 (*0-8328-0972-1*) Higginson Bk Co.

Platte: Channels in Time. Paul A. Johnsgard. LC 83-10453. (Illus.). 170p. 1984. pap. 52.70 (*0-608-05114-4*, 206567300005) Bks Demand.

Platte River. Rick Bass. 160p. 1995. pap. 10.00 (*0-345-39249-3*) Ballantine Pub Grp.

Platte River Road Narratives: A Descriptive Bibliography of Travel over the Great Central Overland Route to Oregon, California, Utah, Colorado, Montana, & Other Western States & Territories, 1812-1866. Merrill J. Mattes. LC 87-1668. (Illus.). 648p. 1988. text 95.00 (*0-252-01342-5*) U of Ill Pr.

Platte River Vengeance. Jonnie Stinson. Ed. by Roy A. Gregory. LC 93-74035. 250p. (Orig.). 1993. pap. 5.95 (*0-9639047-0-1*) Blue Bonnet.

Plattentektonik in den Ostalpen. Volker J. Dietrich. (Geotektonische Forschungen Ser.: Vol. 50). (GER.). ii, 109p. 1976. 43.00 (*3-510-50016-4*, Pub. by E Schweizerbartsche) Balogh.

Plattentektonische Probleme in der Weiteren Umgebung Arabiens Sowie der Danakil Afar-Senke. Peter J. Burek. (Geotektonische Forschungen Ser.: Vol. 47). (GER.). ii, 100p. 1974. 33.00 (*3-510-50013-X*, Pub. by E Schweizerbartsche) Balogh.

Platters Anthology. (Easy Play Ser.: Vol. 137). 64p. 1991. pap. 7.95 (*0-7935-0578-X*, 00001580) H Leonard.

Platters Anthology, No. 236. 64p. 1991. pap. 6.95 (*0-7935-0529-1*, 00243002) H Leonard.

Platters Anthology: Piano, Vocal & Guitar. (Illus.). 80p. 1990. per. 12.95 (*0-88188-841-9*, 00490213) H Leonard.

Platt's Starport Guide. (Star Wars Ser.). 25.00 (*0-87431-224-8*, 40107) West End Games.

Plattsburgh (N.Y.) Traction Co. Roger Borrup. (Illus.). 51p. 1971. 7.50 (*0-910506-14-0*) De Vito.

Platus, Asinaria: Index Verborum, Lexiques Inverses, Releves Lexicaux et Grammaticaux. Laurence Denooz. Ed. by Albert Maniet. (Alpha-Omega, Reihe A: Vol. XXVI). (GER.). ix, 211p. 1992. write for info. (*3-487-09465-7*) G Olms Pubs.

Platus, Ausgewahlte Komodien Band 2: Mostellaria, Vol. 2. Contrib. by August F. Lorenz. 239p. 1981. write for info. (*3-296-15001-3*) G Olms Pubs.

Platus, Ausgewahlte Komodien Band 3: Miles Gloriosus, Vol. 3. Contrib. by August F. Lorenz. (GER.). viii, 294p. 1981. write for info. (*3-296-15002-1*) G Olms Pubs.

Platus, Ausgewahlte Komodien Band 4: Pseudolus, Vol. 4. Contrib. by August F. Lorenz. viii, 289p. 1981. write for info. (*3-296-15003-X*) G Olms Pubs.

P

An Asterisk (*) at the beginning of an entry indicates that the title is appearing for the first time.

Platus, Epidicus: Index Verborum, Lexiques Inverses, Releves Lexicaux et Grammaticaux. Laurence Denooz. (Alpha-Omega, Reihe A Ser.: Vol. CLXXXVIII). vi, 222p. 1997. write for info. (3-487-10313-3) G Olms Pubs.

Platy: The Child in Us. Grady B. Brittain. LC 81-6503. (Illus.). 53p. (Orig.). (J). (ps-8). 1981. pap. 5.00 (0-86663-761-3) Ide Hse.

Platypus. Ann G. Gaines. LC 98-20896. (Let's Investigate Ser.). (Illus.). 32p. (J). (gr. 2 up). 1999. lib. bdg. 19.95 (0-88682-612-8, Creat Educ) Creative Co.

Platypus. Pauline Reilly. (Picture Roo Bks.). (Illus.). 32p. (Orig.). (J). (ps-3). 1994. pap. 6.95 (0-86417-391-1, Pub. by Kangaroo Pr) Seven Hills Bk.

Platypus. Joan Short et al. LC 96-15299. (Illus.). (J). (gr. 2-7). 1996. pap. 4.95 (1-57255-195-X) Mondo Pubng.

Platypus. Tom Grant. (Illus.). 76p. 1984. reprint ed. 22.95 (0-86840-143-9, Pub. by New South Wales Univ Pr) Intl Spec Bk.

Platypus & the Mermaid: And Other Figments of the Classifying Imagination. Harriet Ritvo. LC 97-405. (Illus.). 304p. 1997. 31.00 (0-674-67357-3) HUP.

Platypus & the Mermaid: And Other Figments of the Classifying Imagination. Harriet Ritvo. (Illus.). 304p. 1998. pap. 15.95 (0-674-67358-1) HUP.

Platypus of Doom (And Other Nihilists) Arthur B. Cover. Ed. by A. J. Krever. 1999. pap. write for info. (1-893475-03-4) Alexander Pubg.

Platzangst: Ein Uebungsprogramm Fuer Betroffene und Angehoerige. Andrew Mathews et al. (Unveraenderte Auflage Ser.: Vol. 3, 1997). viii, 132p. 1997. pap. 28.00 (3-8055-6522-4) S Karger.

Plausible Argument in Everyday Conversation. Douglas N. Walton. LC 91-35193. (SUNY Series in Speech Communication). (Illus.). 320p. (C). 1992. text 21.50 (0-7914-1157-5) State U NY Pr.

Plausible Denial: Was the CIA Involved in the Assassination of JFK? Mark Lane. LC 98-182700. (Illus.). 416p. 1992. pap. 13.95 (1-56025-048-8, Thunders Mouth) Avalon NY.

Plausible Ghosts. Joshua P. Warren. LC 97-120362. (Illus.). 160p. (Orig.). 1995. pap. 9.95 (0-9649370-1-8, Hydra Books) Shadowbox.

Plaute, Amphitryon. Index Verborum, Lexiques Inverses, Releves Lexicaux et Grammaticaux. Plautus. Ed. by Albert Maniet & Annette Paquot. vii, 217p. 1970. write for info. (0-318-71200-8) G Olms Pubs.

Plaute, Lexique Inverse: Listes Grammaticales. Releves Divers. Plautus. Ed. by Albert Maniet. viii, 201p. 1969. write for info. (0-318-71201-6) G Olms Pubs.

Plauti Mercator, 2 vols. Titus Maccius Plautus. Ed. by W. R. Connor. LC 78-67131. (Latin Texts & Commentaries Ser.). (ENG & LAT.). 1979. reprint ed. lib. bdg. 25.95 (0-405-11601-2) Ayer.

Plauti Truculentus, 2 vols. Plautus. Ed. by W. R. Connor. LC 78-67132. (Latin Texts & Commentaries Ser.). (LAT.). 1979. reprint ed. lib. bdg. 28.95 (0-405-11602-0) Ayer.

Plautinische Akzentstudien, 2 vols. in 1. Hans Drexler. (GER.). xvi, 694p. 1967. reprint ed. write for info. (0-318-70572-9); reprint ed. write for info. (0-318-71112-5) G Olms Pubs.

Plautinische Prosodie. Carl F. Wilhelm Muller. (GER.). xvi, 159p. 1971. reprint ed. write for info. (3-487-04085-9) G Olms Pubs.

Plautinische Studien. Peter Langen. vi, 400p. 1970. reprint ed. write for info. (0-318-71159-1) G Olms Pubs.

Plautus. Miles Gloriosus. LC 97-136138. 224p. 1997. pap. text 14.00 (0-674-57437-0) HUP.

Plautus. Karl Von Reinhardstoettner. xvi, 793p. 1980. reprint ed. write for info. (3-487-06726-9) G Olms Pubs.

Plautus: Amphitruo. Ed. by W. B. Sedgwick. (Bristol Latin Texts Ser.). (LAT.). 144p. 1993. pap. 18.95 (1-85399-349-2, Pub. by Brist Class Pr) Focus Pub-R Pullins.

Plautus: Bacchides. Plautus. Ed. by J. Barsby. (Classical Texts Ser.). 1986. pap. 28.00 (0-85668-227-6, Pub. by Aris & Phillips) David Brown.

Plautus: Bacchides. J. A. Plautus. Ed. by J. Barsby. (Classical Texts Ser.). 1986. 59.99 (0-85668-226-8, Pub. by Aris & Phillips) David Brown.

Plautus: Captivi. Gail Smith. (Latin Commentaries Ser.). 137p. (Orig.). (C). 1985. pap. text 7.00 (0-929524-50-0) Bryn Mawr Commentaries.

Plautus: Captivi. Ed. by Wallace M. Lindsay. (Bristol Latin Texts Ser.). (LAT.). 120p. 1981. reprint ed. pap. 16.95 (0-906515-95-5, Pub. by Brist Class Pr) Focus Pub-R Pullins.

Plautus: Plaute, Lexique Inverse, Listes Grammaticales, Releves Divers. Ed. by Albert Maniet. viii, 201p. 1969. write for info. (0-318-71975-4) G Olms Pubs.

Plautus: Pseudolus. Ed. by Malcolm M. Willcock. (Bristol Latin Texts Ser.). (LAT.). 1987. pap. 22.95 (0-86292-089-2, Pub. by Brist Class Pr) Focus Pub-R Pullins.

Plautus: Rudens. Ed. by H. Fay. (Bristol Latin Texts Ser.). (LAT.). 1989. pap. 20.95 (0-86292-063-9, Pub. by Brist Class Pr) Focus Pub-R Pullins.

Plautus: The Comedies, Vol. 1. Ed. by David R. Slavitt & Palmer Bovie. LC 94-45317. (Complete Roman Drama in Translation Ser.: Vol. 1). 352p. 1995. pap. 15.95 (0-8018-5071-1); text 45.00 (0-8018-5070-3) Johns Hopkins.

Plautus: The Comedies, Vol. 2. Ed. by Palmer Bovie & David R. Slavitt. (Complete Roman Drama in Translation Ser.). 384p. 1995. pap. 15.95 (0-8018-5057-6) Johns Hopkins.

Plautus: The Comedies, Vol. 2. Ed. by David R. Slavitt & Palmer Bovie. (Complete Roman Drama in Translation Ser.). 384p. 1995. text 45.00 (0-8018-5056-8) Johns Hopkins.

Plautus: The Comedies, Vol. 3. Ed. by Palmer Bovie & David R. Slavitt. (Complete Roman Drama in Translation Ser.). 392p. 1995. pap. 15.95 (0-8018-5068-1) Johns Hopkins.

Plautus: The Comedies, Vol. 3. Ed. by David R. Slavitt & Palmer Bovie. (Complete Roman Drama in Translation Ser.). 392p. 1995. text 45.00 (0-8018-5067-3) Johns Hopkins.

Plautus: The Comedies, Vol. 4. Ed. by Palmer Bovie & David R. Slavitt. (Complete Roman Drama in Translation Ser.). 360p. 1995. pap. 15.95 (0-8018-5073-8) Johns Hopkins.

Plautus: The Comedies, Vol. 4. Ed. by David R. Slavitt & Palmer Bovie. (Complete Roman Drama in Translation Ser.). 360p. 1995. text 45.00 (0-8018-5072-X) Johns Hopkins.

Plautus: 3 Comedies. Robert Wind. LC 94-41092. 238p. (Orig.). (C). 1995. 26.50 (0-8191-9815-3) U Pr of Amer.

Plautus - Plaute, Amphitryon: Index Verborum, Lexiques Inverses, Releves Lexicaux et Grammaticaux. Ed. by Albert Maniet & Annette Paquot. vii, 217p. 1970. write for info. (0-318-71976-2) G Olms Pubs.

Plautus - Plaute, Amphitryon: Index Verborum, Lexiques Inverses, Releves Lexicaux et Grammaticaux. Ed. by Albert Maniet & Annette Paquot. vii, 217p. 1970. write for info. (0-318-70661-X) G Olms Pubs.

Plautus - Plaute, Asinaria: Index Verborum, Lexiques Inverses, Releves Lexicaux et Grammaticaux. Ed. by Albert Maniet. write for info. (0-318-71978-9) G Olms Pubs.

Plautus - Plaute, Lexique Inverse: Listes Grammaticales. Releves Divers. Ed. by Albert Maniet. viii, 201p. 1969. write for info. (0-318-70660-1) G Olms Pubs.

Plautus' Aulularia: The Pot of Gold; An Adaptation for Production by High School Latin Students. Ed. by Gilbert Lawall. (LAT.). 35p. 1992. spiral bd. 3.25 (0-939507-30-7, B724) Amer Classical.

Plautus' Curculio. Intro. & Notes by John Wright. LC 93-13385. (Series in Classical Culture: Vol. 17). 1993. 11.95 (0-8061-2507-1) U of Okla Pr.

***Plautus in Performance: The Theatre of the Mind.** Niall W. Slater. (Greek & Roman Theatre Archive Ser.). 244p. 1999. pap. text 35.00 (90-5755-038-5, Harwood Acad Pubs) Gordon & Breach.

***Plautus in Performance: The Theatre of the Mind.** Niall W. Slater. (Greek & Roman Theatre Archive Ser.). 228p. 2000. text 40.00 (90-5755-037-7, Harwood Acad Pubs) Gordon & Breach.

Plautus in the Convent. Conrad F. Meyer. Tr. by William G. Howard. LC 62-17089. xiv, 133p. 1964. pap. 3.95 (0-8044-6503-7) Continuum.

Plautus' Menaechmi. Ed. by Gilbert Lawall & Betty N. Quinn. (Textbook Ser.). (Illus.). 200p. (Orig.). 1981. pap. 15.00 (0-86516-007-4) Bolchazy-Carducci.

Plaxis: Finite Element Code for Soil & Rock Plasticity. P. A. Vermeer. 400p. 1998. 4250.00 (90-5410-449-X, Pub. by A A Balkema) Ashgate Pub Co.

***Play.** Ann Morris. LC 97-15728. (J). 1998. lib. bdg. 14.93 (0-688-14553-1) Lothrop.

Play. Ann Morris. LC 97-15728. (Illus.). 32p. (J). 1998. 15.00 (0-688-14552-3) Lothrop.

Play. Jan Pienkowski. 8p. (J). (ps-k). 1995. 4.50 (0-689-80431-8) Atheneum Yung Read.

Play. 2nd enl. ed. Catherine Garvey. LC 90-36281. (Developing Child Ser.). (Illus.). 176p. 1990. 26.95 (0-674-67364-6); pap. text 7.95 (0-674-67365-4) HUP.

Play see Learn-To-Read Series

Play: A Necessity for All Children. Joan Isenberg & Nancy L. Quisenberry. 1988. pap. 1.50 (0-87173-116-9) ACEI.

Play! A Reading Program. Jeffrey E. Stewart. (Illus.). 116p. (Orig.). 1989. pap. 32.50 (1-877866-04-0) J E Stewart.

Play: Around the World. Patricia Lakin. Ed. by Bruce Glassman. LC 94-38497. (We All Share Ser.). (Illus.). 32p. (J). (gr. 3-5). 1995. lib. bdg. 16.95 (1-56711-141-6) Blackbirch.

Play: Engineer & Social Scientist. Michael Z. Brooke. LC 98-11406. 224p. 1998. pap. text 22.95 (0-7658-0425-5) Transaction Pubs.

Play: Working Partner of Growth. Ed. by Judy S. McKee. LC 86-22245. 88p. 1986. pap. 11.00 (0-87173-112-6) ACEI.

Play - Commodus. Lewis Wallace. (Notable American Authors Ser.). 1999. reprint ed. lib. bdg. 125.00 (0-7812-9870-9) Rprt Serv.

Play - Play Therapy - Play Research: International Symposium, Amsterdam (The Netherlands), September 1985. R. J. Van der Kooij & J. Hellendoorn. (PAOS Ser.: Vol. 6). vi, 304p. 1987. pap. 45.25 (90-265-0754-2) Swets.

Play - The Intentional Avoidance of Work. Louis C. Androes. LC 90-70837. (Illus.). 80p. (Orig.). 1990. pap. 7.95 (0-9626575-2-2) Whoopee Hollow.

Play a Swiss Teams of 4 with Mike Lawrence. Mike Lawrence. LC 84-223798. 99p. 1982. pap. 7.95 (0-939460-19-X) Devyn Pr.

Play All Day. Julie Paschkis. LC 96-14234. (Illus.). 32p. (J). (gr. k-4). 1998. 14.95 (0-316-69043-0) Little.

Play-Along Rhymes. Disney Press Staff. 14p. 1999. 7.99 (0-7364-0187-3, Pub. by Mouse Works) Time Warner.

Play along with Brimhall Bk. 1: Piano. 47p. (Orig.). 1995. pap. 16.95 (0-7692-1014-7, AF9564CD) Wrner Bros.

Play along with Brimhall Bk. 2: Piano. 55p. (Orig.). 1996. pap. 16.95 (0-7692-1015-5, AF9609CD) Wrner Bros.

Play along with Brimhall Bk. 3: Piano. 63p. (Orig.). 1996. pap. 16.95 (1-57623-482-7, AF9665CD) Wrner Bros.

Play an Intergenerational Experience: Proceedings of the IPA - USA, 1995 National Conference. Ed. by Marcy Guddemi et al. (Illus.). 96p. 1996. pap. 4.00 (0-942388-23-2) So Early Chldhood Assn.

Play & Care - Out of School. Pat Petrie. 252p. 1994. pap. 45.00 (0-11-701844-9, HM18449, Pub. by Statnry Office) Bernan Associates.

***Play & Child Development.** Frost. 2001. pap. text. write for info. (0-13-685603-9) P-H.

***Play & Culture Studies, Vol. 2.** Stuart Reifel. 1999. 73.25 (1-56750-422-1); pap. 39.50 (1-56750-423-X) Ablx Pub.

Play & Discover. Sterling Publishing Staff. 1995. pap. text 20.95 (0-8069-4390-4) Sterling.

Play & Discover: Colors. Sterling Staff. 32p. (J). 1995. pap. 3.95 (0-8069-3822-6) Sterling.

Play & Discover: Letters. Sterling Staff. 32p. (J). 1995. pap. 3.95 (0-8069-3835-8) Sterling.

Play & Discover: Numbers. Sterling Staff. 32p. (J). 1995. pap. 3.95 (0-8069-3823-4) Sterling.

Play & Discover: Shapes. Sterling Staff. 32p. (J). 1995. pap. 3.95 (0-8069-3821-8) Sterling.

***Play & Early Childhood Development.** 2nd ed. 1999. teacher ed. write for info. (0-321-03776-6) Addison-Wesley.

***Play & Early Childhood Development.** 2nd ed. Ed. by Johnson. 288p. (C). 1999. pap. 50.00 (0-321-01166-X) Addson-Wesley Educ.

Play & Early Childhood Development. 2nd ed. James E. Johnson et al. LC 98-8742. 1998. 36.55 (0-673-99738-3) Addison-Wesley.

Play & Evolution: Second Thoughts on the Behaviour of Animals. Koenraad Kortmulder. LC 98-204429. (Illus.). 160p. 1998. pap. 24.95 (90-5727-013-7, Pub. by Intl Bks) Paul & Co Pubs.

Play & Exploration in Children & Animals. Thomas G. Power. LC 99-30955. 512p. 1999. 99.95 (0-8058-2241-0); pap. write for info. (0-8058-2242-9) L Erlbaum Assocs.

Play & Grow Rich: How to Break Free from the 9-to-5 World & Profit from What You Enjoy Most. 2nd ed. Jan L. Gault. (Illus.). 250p. (Orig.). 1992. pap. 19.95 (0-923699-00-7) Ocean Manor Pub.

Play & Imagination in Children with Autism. Pamela Wolfberg. LC 98-48404. 20. 208p. 1999. 48.00 (0-8077-3815-8) Tchrs Coll.

Play & Imagination in Children with Autism. Pamela J. Wolfberg. LC 98-48404. (Special Education Ser.). 1999. 22.95 (0-8077-3814-X) Tchrs Coll.

Play & Inter-Ethnic Communication: A Practical Ethnography of the Mescalero Apache. Claire R. Farrer. LC 90-24495. (Evolution of North American Indians Ser.). 205p. 1991. reprint ed. text 10.00 (0-8240-2502-4) Garland.

Play & Intervention. Ed. by Joop Hellendoorn et al. LC 93-28930. (SUNY Series, Children's Play in Society). 369p. (C). 1994. text 59.50 (0-7914-1933-9); pap. text 19.95 (0-7914-1934-7) State U NY Pr.

Play & Learn. Parents Magazine Staff. 1999. pap. write for info. (0-312-24559-9) St Martin.

Play & Learn. Lara Tankle. (Illus.). (J). (ps-1). 1997. pap. 4.95 (0-614-28711-1) DK Pub Inc.

***Play & Learn: A Motor-Based Preschool Curriculum for Children of All Abilities.** Mary Sullivan Coleman & Laura Krueger. Ed. by Theresa I. Curran. (Illus.). 314p. 1999. pap. 59.00 (0-9666667-2-0) AbleNet Inc.

Play & Learn: Puzzles & Fun. Chickadee Magazine Editors. (Illus.). 64p. (J). (gr. k-4). 1999. pap. 8.95 (1-895688-92-2, Pub. by Owl Bks) Firefly Bks Ltd.

Play & Learn Bk. 2: Blues & More (Bass) Willie Thomas. Ed. by Larry Clark. (Jazz Anyone...? Ser.). 76p. 1996. pap. text, wbk. ed. 19.95 (1-57623-507-6, EL9691CD) Wrner Bros.

Play & Learn Bk. 2: Blues & More (Bass Clef Edition) Willie Thomas. Ed. by Larry Clark. (Jazz Anyone...? Ser.). 56p. 1996. pap. text, wbk. ed. 14.95 (1-57623-506-8, EL9690CD) Wrner Bros.

Play & Learn Bk. 2: Blues & More (Bb Edition) Willie Thomas. Ed. by Larry Clark. (Jazz Anyone...? Ser.). 56p. 1996. pap. text, wbk. ed. 14.95 (1-57623-503-3, EL9687CD) Wrner Bros.

Play & Learn Bk. 2: Blues & More (C Edition) Willie Thomas. Ed. by Larry Clark. (Jazz Anyone...? Ser.). 56p. (Orig.). 1996. pap. text, wbk. ed. 14.95 (1-57623-502-5, EL9686CD) Wrner Bros.

Play & Learn Bk. 2: Blues & More (Drums) Willie Thomas. Ed. by Larry Clark. (Jazz Anyone...? Ser.). 72p. 1996. pap. text, wbk. ed. 19.95 (1-57623-510-6, EL9694CD) Wrner Bros.

Play & Learn Bk. 2: Blues & More (Eb Edition) Wilie Thomas. Ed. by Larry Clark. (Jazz Anyone...? Ser.). 56p. 1996. pap. text, wbk. ed. 14.95 (1-57623-504-1, EL9688CD) Wrner Bros.

Play & Learn Bk. 2: Blues & More (Guitar) Willie Thomas. Ed. by Larry Clark. (Jazz Anyone...? Ser.). 76p. 1996. pap. text, wbk. ed. 19.95 (1-57623-509-2, EL9693CD) Wrner Bros.

Play & Learn Bk. 2: Blues & More (Piano) Willie Thomas. Ed. by Larry Clark. (Jazz Anyone...? Ser.). 76p. 1996. pap. text, wbk. ed. 19.95 (1-57623-508-4, EL9692CD) Wrner Bros.

Play & Learn Bk. 2: Blues & More (Tenor Sax Edition) Willie Thomas. Ed. by Larry Clark. (Jazz Anyone...? Ser.). 56p. 1996. pap. text, wbk. ed. 14.95 (1-57623-505-X, EL9689CD) Wrner Bros.

Play & Learn Colors. DK Editors. LC 97-38164. (Play & Learn Ser.). (Illus.). 24p. (J). (ps-1). 1998. pap. 3.95 (0-7894-2912-8) DK Pub Inc.

Play & Learn Numbers. DK Editors. LC 97-38163. (Play & Learn Ser.). (Illus.). 24p. (J). (ps-1). 1998. pap. 3.95 (0-7894-2914-4) DK Pub Inc.

Play & Learn Shapes. DK Editors. LC 97-38162. (Play & Learn Ser.). (Illus.). 24p. (J). (ps-1). 1998. pap. 3.95 (0-7894-2913-6) DK Pub Inc.

Play & Learn Sizes. DK Editors. LC 97-38157. (Play & Learn Ser.). (Illus.). 24p. (J). (ps-1). 1998. pap. 3.95 (0-7894-2915-2) DK Pub Inc.

***Play & Learn with Cereal O's: Simple, Effective Activities to Help You Educate Your Preschool Child.** Talita Paolini & Kenneth Paolini. LC 00-102400. (Illus.). 108p. 2000. pap. 9.95 (0-9666213-2-8) Paolini Intl.

***Play & Learn with Your Five Year Old.** Jill Norris. Ed. by Marilyn Evans. (Play & Learn Ser.: Vol. 5). (Illus.). 80p. (J). (ps-k). 1999. pap. 9.95 (1-55799-721-7, 4504) Evan-Moor Edu Pubs.

***Play & Learn with Your Four Year Old.** Jill Norris. Ed. by Marilyn Evans. (Play & Learn Ser.: Vol. 4). (Illus.). 80p. (J). (ps). 1999. pap. 9.95 (1-55799-720-9, 4503) Evan-Moor Edu Pubs.

***Play & Learn with Your One Year Old.** Jill Norris. Ed. by Marilyn Evans. (Play & Learn Ser.: Vol. 1). (Illus.). 80p. (J). (ps). 1999. pap. 9.95 (1-55799-717-9, 4500) Evan-Moor Edu Pubs.

***Play & Learn with Your Six Year Old.** Jill Norris. Ed. by Marilyn Evans. (Play & Learn Ser.: Vol. 6). (Illus.). 80p. (J). (gr. k-1). 1999. pap. 9.95 (1-55799-722-5, 4505) Evan-Moor Edu Pubs.

***Play & Learn with Your Three Year Old.** Jill Norris. Ed. by Marilyn Evans. (Play & Learn Ser.: Vol. 3). (Illus.). 80p. (J). (ps). 1999. pap. 9.95 (1-55799-719-5, 4502) Evan-Moor Edu Pubs.

***Play & Learn with Your Two Year Old.** Jill Norris. Ed. by Marilyn Evans. (Play & Learn Ser.: Vol. 2). (Illus.). 80p. (J). (ps). 1999. pap. 9.95 (1-55799-718-7, 4501) Evan-Moor Edu Pubs.

Play & Literacy in Early Childhood: Research from Multiple Perspectives. Ed. by Kathleen Roskos & James F. Christie. 300p. 2000. write for info. (0-8058-2964-4) L Erlbaum Assocs.

***Play & Literacy in Early Childhood: Research from Multiple Perspectives.** Ed. by Kathleen Roskos & James F. Christie. LC 99-47474. 300p. 2000. pap. write for info. (0-8058-2965-2) L Erlbaum Assocs.

Play & Mental Health. John E. Davis. 1982. 21.95 (0-8434-0427-2, Pub. by McGrath NH) Ayer.

Play & Other Stories. Stephen Dixon. LC 88-30153. 224p. (Orig.). 1988. pap. 9.95 (0-918273-45-5) Coffee Hse.

Play & Place of Criticism. Murray Krieger. LC 66-24405. 271p. reprint ed. pap. 84.10 (0-8357-6620-9, 203526500094) Bks Demand.

Play & Playscapes. Joel Frost. (C). 1991. mass mkt. 30.50 (0-8273-4699-9) Delmar.

Play & Playscapes Instructors Guide. Joe L. Frost. 1992. pap., teacher ed. 10.50 (0-8273-4700-6) Delmar.

Play & Playthings: A Reference Guide. Bernard Mergen. LC 82-6139. (American Popular Culture Ser.). (Illus.). 281p. 1982. lib. bdg. 65.00 (0-313-22136-7, MGT/, Greenwood Pr) Greenwood.

Play & Playwork. Palmer & Cheesman. 1993. pap. text. write for info. (0-582-09370-8, Pub. by Addison-Wesley) Longman.

Play & Practice! Graded Games for English Language Teaching. Anthony Chamberlin & Kurt Stenburg. 128p. 1979. pap. 14.06 (0-8442-5213-1) NTC Contemp Pub Co.

Play & Practice! Blackline Masters. 48p. 1995. pap., teacher ed. 15.47 (0-8442-0707-1) NTC Contemp Pub Co.

Play & Recreation for Individuals with Disabilities: Practical Pointers. Ed. by Susan J. Grosse & Donna Thompson. 152p. (Orig.). 1993. pap. 28.00 (0-88314-554-5) AAHPERD.

Play & the Social Context of Development in Early Care & Education. Ed. by Barbara Scales et al. (Early Childhood Education Ser.: Vol. 31). 288p. (C). 1991. text 43.00 (0-8077-3067-X); pap. text 19.95 (0-8077-3066-1) Tchrs Coll.

Play Anti-Indian Systems. Egon Varnusz. (PECH Pergamon Chess Ser.). 170p. 1991. write for info. (0-08-032078-3, 6201, Pub. by CHES); pap. 13.95 (0-685-33073-7, 6201, Pub. by CHES) Macmillan.

Play as a Medium for Learning & Development. Doris Bergen. LC 98-17376. 144p. 1998. reprint ed. pap. text 18.00 (0-87173-142-8) ACEI.

Play as Exploratory Learning: Studies of Curiosity Behavior. Ed. by Mary Reilly. LC 72-98044. 317p. 1974. reprint ed. pap. 98.30 (0-608-01448-6, 205949200001) Bks Demand.

Play at the Center of the Curriculum. 2nd ed. Judith L. Van Hoorn. LC 98-11345. 337p. 1998. pap. text 39.67 (0-13-611997-2, Merrill Coll) P-H.

Play at the End of the World. Eric Felderman. LC 92-21133. (Illus.). 1993. 49.95 (0-945942-25-7); pap. 36.95 (0-945942-26-5) Portmanteau Editions.

Play at Your House. Regina Brown. (Illus.). (J). (gr. 3-7). 1962. 8.95 (0-8392-3027-3) Astor-Honor.

Play Baby Play. Ingrid Van Deer Leeden. (Illus.). 12p. (J). (ps up). 1997. 3.99 (0-689-81447-X) Atheneum Yung Read.

Play, Baby, Play: Daily Affirmations for Toddlers. Becky Daniel. (Illus.). 388p. pap. 10.00 (1-885412-01-0) R A Daniel.

Play Ball! see Juega con la Pelota!

Play Ball. Barbour Publishing, Inc. Editors. 1999. pap. 0.99 (1-57748-429-0) Barbour Pub.

Play Ball. Derenne. 1993. mass mkt. 23.25 (0-314-02575-8) West Pub.

Play Ball! Gail S. Fleagle. (Books for Young Learners). (Illus.). 8p. (J). (gr. k-2). 1998. pap. text 5.00 (1-57274-138-4, A2183) R Owen Pubs.

Play Ball! Mark Freeman. (Rookies Ser.). (J). 1989. 9.60 (0-606-04301-2, Pub. by Turtleback) Demco.

Play Ball. Margaret Hillert. (Illus.). (J). (ps-2). 1978. pap. 5.10 (0-8136-5534-X); lib. bdg. 7.95 (0-8136-5034-8) Modern Curr.

Play Ball. Dean Hughes. LC 98-14084. (Scrappers Ser.: No. 1). 128p. (J). (gr. 3-7). 1999. 14.00 (0-689-81924-2); per. 3.99 (0-689-81933-1) S&S Childrens.

An Asterisk (*) at the beginning of an entry indicates that the title is appearing for the first time.

***Play Ball!** Apple Jordan. (Naptime Tales Ser.). 14p. 2000. 4.99 (*0-307-13472-5*) Gldn Bks Pub Co.

Play Ball. Francis H. Wise & Joyce M. Wise. (Dr. Wise Learn to Read Ser.: No. 10). (Illus.). (J). (ps-1). 1975. pap. text 2.00 (*0-915766-31-0*) Wise Pub.

Play Ball: All I Ever Learned I Forgot by the Third Inning. Jeff McNelly. 1999. pap. text 9.95 (*1-57243-328-0*) Triumph Bks.

***Play Ball: Baseball Haiku.** Cor Van Den Heuvel. 24p. 1999. pap. 6.95 (*1-893959-06-6*) Red Moon Pr.

Play Ball! Great Moments & Dubious Achievements in Baseball History. John Snyder. 208p. (Orig.). 1991. pap. 6.95 (*0-8118-0038-5*) Chronicle Bks.

Play Ball: Home Runs for Life. Robert W. Lowe. LC 96-44095. 1996. write for info. (*0-87197-451-7*) Favorite Recipes.

Play Ball: Quotes on America's Favorite Pastime. Ariel Books Staff. (Illus.). 374p. 1995. pap. 4.95 (*0-8362-0721-1*, Arie Bks) Andrews & McMeel.

Play Ball: Sports Math see I Love Math Series

Play Ball: Sports Math. Time-Life Books Editors. Ed. by Sara Mark et al. (I Love Math Ser.). (Illus.). 64p. (J). (gr. k-4). 1993. lib. bdg. write for info. (*0-8094-9971-1*) Time-Life.

Play Ball: The Miracle of Children. Ron Smothermon. 100p. 1983. pap. 15.00 (*0-932654-06-1*) Context Pubns.

Play Ball! The Official Little League Fitness Guide. Frank W. Jobe et al. LC 86-17402. (Illus.). 98p. (Orig.). 1986. pap. 7.95 (*0-936691-01-8*) Champ Pr Inglewood.

***Play Ball! Level 3.** Cal Ripken, Jr. et al. Ed. by Dena Wallenstein & Cindy Kane. LC 98-26366. (Illus.). 48p. (J). (gr. k-3). 1999. 13.99 (*0-8037-2415-2*, Dial Yng Read) Peng Put Young Read.

***Play Ball, Amelia Bedelia.** Peggy Parish. (I Can Read Bks.). (J). (gr. 1-3). 1999. write for info. (*0-88103-913-6*) Econo-Clad Bks.

Play Ball, Amelia Bedelia. Peggy Parish. LC PZ7.P219Pl 1996. (I Can Read Bks.). (Illus.). 64p. (J). (gr. 1-3). 1972. 14.95 (*0-06-024655-3*); lib. bdg. 14.89 (*0-06-024656-1*) HarpC Child Bks.

Play Ball, Amelia Bedelia. Peggy Parish. (I Can Read Bks.). (Illus.). 64p. (J). (gr. 1-3). 1986. pap. 2.50 (*0-590-06203-4*) Scholastic Inc.

Play Ball, Amelia Bedelia. Peggy Parish. (I Can Read Bks.). (J). (gr. 1-3). 1978. 8.70 (*0-606-01549-3*, Pub. by Turtleback) Demco.

Play Ball, Amelia Bedelia. rev. ed. Peggy Parish. (I Can Read Bks.). (Illus.). 64p. (J). (gr. 1-3). 1995. pap. 3.95 (*0-06-444205-5*, HarpTrophy) HarpC Child Bks.

Play Ball, Amelia Bedelia. rev. ed. Peggy Parish. (I Can Read Bks.). (Illus.). 64p. (J). (gr. 1-3). 1996. lib. bdg. 15.89 (*0-06-026701-1*) HarpC Child Bks.

Play Ball, Amelia Bedelia. rev. ed. Peggy Parish. LC 94-27141. (I Can Read Bks.). (Illus.). 64p. (J). (ps-3). 1996. 15.95 (*0-06-026700-3*) HarpC Child Bks.

Play Ball, Amelia Bedelia. unabridged ed. Peggy Parish. LC 71-85028. (I Can Read Bks.). (Illus.). 64p. (J). (ps-3). 1990. pap. 8.95 incl. audio (*1-55994-241-X*) HarperAudio.

"Play-Ball" Exercise Program: A Stabilization Program for Back Pain & Dysfunction. Barbara J. Headley. (Illus.). 80p. 1990. ring bd. 450.00 incl. VHS (*0-685-54228-9*) Innovat Systems.

Play Ball, Sherman. Betty Erickson. (Illus.). 12p. (Orig.). (J). (gr. k-1). 1996. pap. 3.75 (*1-880612-53-4*) Seedling Pubns.

Play Ball, Zachary! Muriel Blaustein. LC 87-45274. (Illus.). 32p. (J). (ps-2). 1988. 11.95 (*0-06-020543-1*) HarpC Child Bks.

Play-Based Learning: A Module for Training Early Intervention Special Education Personnel. Infant Hearing Resource Staff. (Early Intervention Series II). 38p. (Orig.). (C). 1994. pap. text 89.00 incl. VHS (*1-883204-03-8*) Hearing & Speech.

Play-Based Learning: A Module for Training Personnel Serving Families of Deaf & Hard of Hearing Infants & Young Children. Ed. by Valerie Schuyler. (Early Intervention Ser.). 37p. (C). 1993. teacher ed. 89.00 incl. VHS (*0-9618297-5-3*) Hearing & Speech.

Play Behavior. Pref. by Joseph Levy. LC 83-6102. 250p. (C). 1983. reprint ed. text 29.50 (*0-89874-627-2*) Krieger.

Play Behavior & Choice of Play Materials of Pre-School Children. Dorothy Van Alstyne. LC 75-35083. (Studies in Play & Games). (Illus.). 1976. reprint ed. 15.95 (*0-405-07931-1*) Ayer.

Play Behind the Play: Hamlet & Quarto One. Maxwell E. Foster. Ed. by Anne Shiras. LC 97-44621. 1998. 24.95 (*0-325-00006-9*) Heinemann.

Play Better Baseball. 2nd ed. Bob Cluck. (Illus.). 248p. 1998. pap. 16.95 (*0-8092-2921-8*, 292180, Contemporary Bks) NTC Contemp Pub Co.

Play Better Basketball. Jim Pruitt. (Illus.). 160p. (Orig.). 1982. pap. 12.95 (*0-8092-5799-8*) NTC Contemp Pub Co.

Play Better Golf, No. 1. Jack Nicklaus. 1989. mass mkt. 5.50 (*0-671-68492-2*) PB.

Play Better Golf: Lessons from the Academy of Golf at PGA National. Mike Adams & T. J. Tomasi. 176p. 1996. 24.95 (*1-885203-35-7*) Jrny Editions.

Play Better Golf: Problems & Answers, Vol. 3. Jack Nicklaus & Ken Bowden. (Orig.). 1990. mass mkt. 4.99 (*0-671-72765-6*) PB.

Play Better Golf: The Short Game & Scoring, Vol. II. Jack Nicklaus. 1986. mass mkt. 5.50 (*0-671-63257-4*) PB.

Play Better Golf for Seniors. Mike Adams et al. LC 98-5945. (Illus.). 160p. 1999. 29.95 (*0-8050-5920-2*) H Holt & Co.

Play Better Golf for Women. Mike Adams. LC 97-72664. 1997. 27.95 (*0-8050-5694-7*) H Holt & Co.

Play Blues Harp in 60 Minutes. Pat Conway. (Illus.). 19p. 1998. pap. text 5.95 (*0-7119-5640-5*, AM 936188) Music Sales.

Play Book: A Complete Guide to Quality Productions for Christian Schools & Churches. unabridged ed. Dwight Swanson & Travis Tyre. LC 98-107777. (Illus.). 204p. (Orig.). 1996. pap. text 18.50 (*1-887710-41-8*, ArtCan Drama) Promise Prodns.

Play-Boy a Seduire. Anne McAllister. (Azur Ser.: No. 775). (FRE.). 1999. mass mkt. 3.99 (*0-373-34775-8*, 1-34775-6) Harlequin Bks.

Play Bridge! Mary A. McVey. 1983. pap. 6.50 (*0-910475-22-9*) KET.

Play Bridge with Mike Lawrence. Lawrence. 11.95 (*0-910791-09-0*, 0635) Devyn Pr.

Play by Play. Isaac Goldemberg. Tr. by Hardie St Martin. (SPA.). 180p. 1985. 13.95 (*0-89255-092-9*) Persea Bks.

Play-by-Play: 25 Years of Royals on the Radio. Denny Matthews et al. LC 99-19435. (Illus.). 240p. 1999. pap. 14.95 (*1-886110-78-6*, Pub. by Addax Pubng) Midpt Trade.

***Play-by-Play Baseball.** Don Geng & Andy King. LC 00-8879. (Illus.). (YA). 2001. pap. write for info. (*0-8225-9880-9*, LernerSports) Lerner Pub.

***Play-by-Play Mountain Biking.** rev. ed. Andy King. LC 00-8852. (Illus.). (YA). 2001. pap. write for info. (*0-8225-9879-5*, LernerSports) Lerner Pub.

Play-by-Play Sportscast Training. Alan Epstein & Lou E. Riggs. 244p. 1993. spiral bd. 51.95 (*0-8403-8871-3*, 40887101) Kendall-Hunt.

Play by the Rules: Creative Practice in Direction-Following. Greta Rasmussen. LC 89-51969. (Illus.). 112p. 1990. pap. 11.95 (*0-936110-09-0*) Tin Man Pr.

Play Called Corpus Christi. V. A. Kolve. LC 66-15301. viii, 337p. 1966. pap. 16.95 (*0-8047-0278-0*) Stanford U Pr.

Play Called Noah's Flood. Suzan L. Zeder. (J). (gr. 4 up). 1984. pap. 6.50 (*0-87602-247-6*) Anchorage.

Play Cleaning. Ed. by Scholastic, Inc. Staff. (Illus.). 8p. (J). 19.99 (*0-590-24957-6*) Scholastic Inc.

***Play Cribbage to Win.** Dan Barlow. 2000. pap. 7.95 (*0-8069-4313-0*) Sterling.

***Play Day: The Sound of Long A.** Alice K. Flanagan. LC 99-31939. (Wonder Books Ser.). (Illus.). 23p. (J). (ps-2). 1999. lib. bdg. 14.99 (*1-56766-730-9*) Childs World.

Play Day Songs Illus. by Gary Yealdhall. LC 98-234894. 1997. write for info. (*0-7853-2638-3*) Pubns Intl Ltd.

***Play Dead.** Leo Atkins. (P. I. Mysteries Ser.). 2000. mass mkt. 5.99 (*0-425-17362-3*, Prime Crime) Berkley Pub.

Play Dead. Leslie O'Kane. LC 98-96043. 261p. 1998. mass mkt. 5.99 (*0-449-00159-8*, GM) Fawcett.

***Play Dead.** large type ed. Leslie O'Kane. LC 99-56053. 377p. 2000. 27.95 (*0-7862-2329-4*) Thorndike Pr.

***Play Diagnosis & Assessment.** 2nd ed. Ed. by Karen Gitlin-Weiner et al. LC 99-24905. 792p. 2000. 75.00 (*0-471-25457-6*) Wiley.

***Play Directing: Analysis, Communication & Style.** 5th ed. Francis Hodge. LC 99-29772. 396p. 1999. 64.00 (*0-205-29561-4*) Allyn.

Play Directing in the School: A Drama Director's Survival Guide. David Grote. Ed. by Arthur L. Zapel. LC 97-31802. (Illus.). 248p. (YA). (gr. 9-12). 1997. pap. 17.95 (*1-56608-036-3*, B214) Meriwether Pub.

Play Director's Survival Kit. James W. Rodgers & Wanda C. Rodgers. 286p. 1997. pap. 29.50 (*0-87628-565-5*) Ctr Appl Res.

Play Director's Survival Kit: A Complete Step-by-Step Guide to Producing Theater in Any School or Community Setting. James W. Rodgers & Wanda C. Rodgers. LC 94-43944. (Illus.). 286p. 1995. pap. text 29.95 (*0-87628-862-X*) Ctr Appl Res.

Play Durrenmatt. Ed. by Moshe Lazar. (Interplay Ser.: Vol. 3). 219p. (C). 1983. pap. text 21.00 (*0-89003-129-0*, 82-50986) Undena Pubns.

Play Electric Bass from Chord Symbols. Roger Filiberto. 40p. 1978. pap. 6.95 (*0-87166-666-9*, 93458) Mel Bay.

Play Electric Guitar. Burrowes. 1999. text 22.95 (*0-312-24417-7*) St Martin.

Play Equipment for Kids: Great Projects You Can Build. Mike Lawrence. Ed. by Gwen Steege. LC 95-24038. (Illus.). 96p. (Orig.). 1996. pap. 18.95 (*0-88266-916-8*, 916-8, Storey Pub) Storey Bks.

Play Essential Guitar Scales in 60 Minutes. Pat Conway. 19p. 1998. pap. text 5.95 (*0-7119-5637-5*, AM 936155) Music Sales.

Play Essential Rock Chords in 60 Minutes. Pat Conway. 19p. 1998. pap. text 5.95 (*0-7119-5635-9*, AM 936133) Music Sales.

Play, Exploration & Learning: A Natural History of the Pre-School. John Hutt et al. 224p. (C). 1989. lib. bdg. 45.00 (*0-415-01286-4*) Routledge.

Play Famous Blues Guitar Rhythms in 60 Minutes. Pat Conway. (Illus.). 19p. 1998. pap. text 5.95 (*0-7119-5630-8*, AM 936089) Music Sales.

Play 50 Irish Ballads, Vol. 1. 40p. 6.95 (*0-946005-61-3*, OS 00080, Pub. by Ossian) Music Sales.

Play 50 Irish Ballads, Vol. 2. 40p. 6.95 (*0-946005-62-1*, OS 00081, Pub. by Ossian) Music Sales.

Play 50 Irish Ballads, Vol. 3. 40p. 6.95 (*0-946005-63-X*, OS 00082, Pub. by Ossian) Music Sales.

Play Football the NFL Way. 6th ed. Tom Bass. 1991. pap. 16.95 (*0-312-05947-7*) St Martin.

Play for a Kingdom: A Novel. Thomas Dyja. LC 96-53875. 384p. (C). 1997. 25.00 (*0-15-100267-3*) Harcourt.

Play for a Kingdom: A Novel. Thomas Dyja. (Illus.). 428p. (C). 1998. pap. 14.00 (*0-15-600629-4*, Harvest Bks) Harcourt.

Play for All Guidelines: Planning, Design & Management of Outdoor Play Settings for All Children. Ed. by Robin C. Moore et al. LC 87-73243. (Illus.). 266p. (Orig.). 1987. pap. text 24.00 (*0-944661-00-9*, L009) AAHPERD.

Play for All Guidelines: Planning, Design & Management of Outdoor Play Settings for All Children. 2nd ed. Ed. by Robin C. Moore et al. LC 92-64424. (Illus.). 300p. (Orig.). 1992. pap. 39.95 (*0-944661-17-3*) MIG Comns.

Play for Power: Creating Leaders Through Sport. Ed. by Fay Biles et al. 265p. (Orig.). 1996. pap. text 26.00 (*0-88314-801-3*, A801-3) AAHPERD.

Play 411, 1998. Illus. by Conrad Haberland. 100p. 1998. spiral bd. 19.00 (*1-879930-07-2*) LA Four-Eleven.

***Play 411/2000: A Guide to Entertainment Resources & Activities for the Los Angeles Area.** Ed. by Amy Haberland. 202p. 2000. pap. 10.00 (*1-879930-14-5*, Pub. by Media Pub Intl) SCB Distributors.

Play from Birth to 12 & Beyond: Contexts, Perspectives, & Meanings. Ed. by Doris P. Fromberg & Doris Bergen. LC 97-45203. (Illus.). 578p. 1998. text 100.00 (*0-8153-1745-X*, SS970) Garland.

Play Fundamentals. Hanson. 6.95 (*0-910791-46-5*, 0530) Devyn Pr.

Play, Games, & Sports in Cultural Contexts. Ed. by Janet C. Harris & Roberta J. Park. LC 82-83148. 533p. reprint ed. pap. 165.30 (*0-608-15854-2*, 203146800074) Bks Demand.

Play Gin to Win: Strategies for Internet, Tournaments, Recreation. large type ed. Charley Killebrew. Ed. by Pete Billac. LC 99-62671. (Illus.). 96p. (Orig.). 1999. pap. 9.95 (*0-943629-40-3*, Pub. by Swan Pub) Hervey's Bklink.

Play Goes On: A Memoir. Neil Simon. LC 99-36449. (Illus.). 480p. 1999. 26.50 (*0-684-84691-8*) S&S Trade.

Play Golf Effectively. Couey. (Adaptable Courseware-Softside). 1993. mass mkt. 16.75 (*0-314-02912-5*) West Pub.

***Play Golf for Juniors: The Academy of Golf at PGA National.** Mike Adams & T. J. Tomasi. LC GV966.3.A33 2000. (Illus.). 144p. (YA). (gr. 5-12). 2000. pap. 19.95 (*1-55209-446-4*) Firefly Bks Ltd.

Play Golf the Wright Way. Mickey Wright. LC 92-37340. (Illus.). 104p. 1993. reprint ed. 17.95 (*0-87833-812-8*); reprint ed. pap. 9.95 (*0-87833-813-6*) Taylor Pub.

Play Great Chord Riffs in 60 Minutes. Music Sales Corporation Staff. (Illus.). 19p. 1998. pap. text 5.95 (*0-7119-5636-7*) Music Sales.

Play Great Golf. Arnold Palmer. (Illus.). 1996. 14.99 (*0-88365-942-5*) Galahad Bks.

Play Great Golf: Mastering the Fundabmentals of Your Game. Arnold Palmer. 1998. pap. text 14.95 (*0-88486-191-0*, Bristol Park Bks) Arrowood Pr.

Play Guide 1: Building Adventures. Dawn Panttaja. (Illus.). 1989. teacher ed. 10.00 (*1-879616-00-9*, 34891) Brio Scanditoy.

Play Guide 2: Travel Through Time & Space. Janet McAlpine. (Illus.). 1990. teacher ed. 10.00 (*1-879616-01-7*, 34892) Brio Scanditoy.

Play Guitar in 60 Minutes. Pat Conway. 19p. 1998. pap. text 5.95 (*0-7119-5632-4*, AM 936100) Music Sales.

Play Guitar Overnight Basics Book. 56p. 1990. pap. 3.95 (*0-7935-2785-6*, 00660198) H Leonard.

***Play Guitar Today.** Doug Downing. 48p. 1999. pap. 9.95 incl. audio compact disk (*0-634-00410-7*) H Leonard.

Play Guitar Today! Peter Pickow. pap. 16.95 incl. audio compact disk (*0-8256-1427-9*, AM92242) Omnibus NY.

***Play Guitar With: Black Sabbath.** Compiled by Chrish Welch. 48p. 2000. pap. text 21.95 (*0-7119-7762-3*, AM955911) Music Sales.

Play Guitar With Oasis. Oasis. (Guitar Jammin Ser.). Date not set. pap. text 19.95 incl. audio compact disk (*0-7935-6873-0*) H Leonard.

Play Hard, Eat Right! A Parent's Guide to Sports Nutrition for Their Children. Ada. 160p. 1995. pap. 10.95 (*0-471-34695-0*) Wiley.

Play Hard, Eat Right! A Parent's Guide to Sports Nutrition for Their Children. Debbi S. Jennings & Suzanne N. Steen. 160p. 1995. pap. 10.95 (*1-56561-063-6*) Wiley.

***Play Hard, Score Big.** Illus. by John Patrick. 552p. 1999. pap. 14.95 (*1-877978-97-3*, STARbks Pr) FL Lit Foundation.

Play Harmonica. Hal Leighton. 6.50 (*0-87505-262-2*) Borden.

Play Healthy, Stay Healthy: Your Guide to Managing & Treating 40 Common Sports Injuries. Gary N. Guten. LC 90-28365. (Illus.). 240p. (Orig.). 1991. pap. 15.95 (*0-88011-439-8*, PGUT0439) Human Kinetics.

***Play in a Changing Society.** Marcy Guddemi et al. (Illus.). 82p. (C). 2000. 8.00 (*0-942388-26-7*) So Early Childhood Assn.

Play in Childhood. Margaret Lowenfeld. (Classics in Developmental Medicine Ser.: No. 6). (Illus.). 242p. (C). 1991. text 19.95 (*0-521-41331-1*, Pub. by Mc Keith Pr) Cambridge U Pr.

Play in Education. Joseph Lee. LC 74-143062. Date not set. 35.95 (*0-8434-0426-4*, Pub. by McGrath NH) Ayer.

Play in Family Therapy. Eliana Gil. LC 93-44074. 226p. 1994. pap. text 21.00 (*0-89862-757-5*); lib. bdg. 42.00 (*0-89862-756-7*) Guilford Pubns.

Play in Pediatric Occupational Therapy. Ed. by L. Diane Parham. (Illus.). 288p. (C). (gr. 13). 1996. text 47.00 (*0-8016-7838-2*, 07838) Mosby Inc.

Play in Practice: A Systems Approach to Making Good Play Happen. Paul Niemiec et al. (Source Books on Education). 175p. Date not set. text 30.00 (*0-8153-0217-7*) Garland.

Play in the Lives of Children. Cosby S. Rogers & Janet K. Sawyers. LC 87-62314. 135p. 1988. pap. 6.00 (*0-935989-09-9*, NAEYC #301) Natl Assn Child Ed.

Play in the Mirror: Lacanian Perspectives on Spanish Baroque Theater. Matthew D. Stroud. LC 95-40323. 1996. write for info. (*0-614-08638-8*) Bucknell U Pr.

Play in the Mirror: Lacanian Perspectives on Spanish Baroque Theater. Matthew D. Stroud. LC 95-40323. (Illus.). 248p. 1996. 39.50 (*0-8387-5315-9*) Bucknell U Pr.

Play Interactions. Ed. by Catherine C. Brown. (Pediatric Round Table Ser.: No. 11). 209p. (Orig.). (C). 1985. pap. text 10.00 (*0-931562-13-9*) J & J Consumer Prods.

Play Interviews for 4 Year Old Hospitalized Children. Florence H. Erickson. (SRCD M Ser.: Vol. 23, No. 3). 1958. pap. 25.00 (*0-527-01575-X*) Periodicals Srv.

Play Is Work. William Page. 40p. (Orig.). 1992. pap. text 6.00 (*0-935493-94-8*) Modern Learn Pr.

Play It! see Juegos para Cada Ocasion

Play It: Great Games for Groups. Wayne Rice & Mike Yaconelli. 285p. 1986. pap. 12.99 (*0-310-35191-X*, 10799P) Zondervan.

Play It Again. Stephen H. Bogart. 1996. pap. 6.99 (*0-614-98052-6*); pap. 6.99 (*0-614-98053-4*) Forge NYC.

Play It Again. Steven H. Bogart. LC 94-44452. 256p. 1996. mass mkt. 5.99 (*0-8125-5162-1*, Pub. by Tor Bks) St Martin.

Play It Again! More Great Games for Groups. Ed. by Wayne Rice & Mike Yaconelli. 240p. 1993. pap. 12.99 (*0-310-37291-7*) Zondervan.

Play It Again! More 1-Act Plays for Acting Students. Norman A. Bert & Deb Bert. Ed. by Theodore O. Zapel. LC 93-312. 288p. (Orig.). (YA). (gr. 9-12). 1993. pap. 14.95 (*0-916260-97-6*, B130) Meriwether Pub.

Play It Again: Suggestions for Drama. Sue Porter. 64p. (C). 1990. pap. 8.50 (*0-7131-0698-0*, 00641) Heinemann.

Play It Again, Sam. Victoria Alexander. 400p. (Orig.). 1998. mass mkt. 5.99 (*0-505-52247-0*, Love Spell) Dorchester Pub Co.

Play It Again, Sam. Reese & Hoffman. 7.95 (*0-910791-21-X*, 0690) Devyn Pr.

Play It Again Sam: Recurrence Equations & Recursion in Mathematics & Computer Science. Rochelle W. Meyer & Walter J. Meyer. Ed. by Joseph Malkevitch. (Explorations in Mathematics Ser.). (Illus.). 114p. (Orig.). 1990. pap. text 12.95 (*0-912843-17-9*) COMAP Inc.

Play It Again, Sam: Retakes on Remakes. Andrew Horton & Stuart Y. McDugal. LC 97-175. 340p. 1998. 50.00 (*0-520-20592-8*, Pub. by U CA Pr) Cal Prin Full Svc.

Play It Again, Sam: Retakes on Remakes. Ed. by Andrew Horton & Stuart Y. McDugal. LC 97-175. 340p. 1998. pap. 19.95 (*0-520-20593-6*, Pub. by U CA Pr) Cal Prin Full Svc.

Play It Again Spam. Tamar Myers. 262p. 1999. mass mkt. 5.99 (*0-451-19754-2*, Sig) NAL.

Play It As It Lays. Joan Didion. 214p. 1990. pap. 11.00 (*0-374-52171-9*) FS&G.

Play It As It Lies: Golf & the Spiritual Life. Mike Linder. LC 98-50849. 144p. 1999. pap. 15.00 (*0-664-25822-0*) Westminster John Knox.

Play It by Ear! Edgar L. Lowell & Marguerite Stoner. 1963. reprint ed. spiral bd. 9.00 (*0-9606312-0-8*) John Tracy Clinic.

Play It by Ear (The Festival) Manuscript Edition. Bella Spewack. 1955. pap. 13.00 (*0-8222-0897-0*) Dramatists Play.

Play It by Sign: Games in Sign Language. Suzie L. Kirchner. 39.00 (*0-917002-03-2*) Joyce Media.

Play It from the Heart. Neal Morgan. vii, 345p. 1999. pap. 14.95 (*0-9671801-0-4*, 1) Sea Rim Bks.

Play It My Way - Learning Through Play with Your Visually Impaired Child. 125p. 1995. pap. 25.00 (*0-11-701676-4*, HM16764, Pub. by Statnry Office) Bernan Associates.

Play It Safe. JoAnne Nelson. LC 93-12173. (Primarily Health Ser.). (Illus.). (J). (ps-2). 1995. 6.00 (*0-7802-3255-0*) Wright Group.

Play It Safe: Safety Tips for Boys & Girls. David Fields. (Illus.). 60p. (J). 1995. lib. bdg. 8.95 (*0-9644363-0-2*) Play It Safe.

Play It Safe: Safety Tips for Boys & Girls. David Fields. (Illus.). 23p. (J). (gr. k-4). 1996. pap. 8.95 (*0-614-14523-6*) Play It Safe.

Play It Safe in the Sun. Perry Robins. (Illus.). 40p. (J). 1994. pap. 9.95 (*0-9627688-1-2*) Skin Cancer Fndtn.

***Play It Smart Workbooks: Human Body.** Random House Staff. (J). 2001. pap. 2.99 (*0-375-80461-7*) Random Bks Yng Read.

Play Jam Tracks for Guitar in 60 Minutes. Pat Conway. 19p. 1998. pap. text 5.95 (*0-7119-5629-4*, AM 936078) Music Sales.

Play Keyboard Scales. Darryl Winston. (Step One Ser.). pap. 7.95 incl. audio compact disk (*0-8256-1612-3*) Omnibus NY.

Play Kitchen. Ed. by Scholastic, Inc. Staff. (Illus.). 8p. (J). 19.99 (*0-590-24958-4*) Scholastic Inc.

Play Lady - La Senora Juguentona. Eric Hoffman. LC 99-13778. (Anti-Bias Books for Kids). (ENG & SPA., Illus.). 32p. (J). (ps-3). 1999. pap. 10.95 (*1-884834-61-2*) Redleaf Pr.

Play, Language & Socialization. Ed. by Sue Burroughs & Roy Evans. (Special Aspects of Education Ser.: Vol. 8). vi, 264p. 1986. text 137.00 (*0-677-21510-X*); pap. text 36.00 (*0-677-21500-2*) Gordon & Breach.

Play Language & Spectacle: A Structural Reading of Selected Texts by Gabrielle Roy. Ellen R. Babby. 140p. (C). 1985. text 25.00 (*0-920763-02-2*, Pub. by ECW); pap. text 15.00 (*0-920802-97-4*, Pub. by ECW) Genl Dist Srvs.

Play, Language, & Stories: The Development of Children's Literate Behavior. Ed. by Lee Galda & Anthony D. Pellegrini. LC 08-13396. 208p. (C). 1985. text 73.25 (*0-89391-292-1*) Ablx Pub.

Play, Learn & Grow: An Annotated Guide to the Best Books & Materials for Very Young Children. James L. Thomas. 439p. 1992. 30.00 (*0-8352-3019-8*) Bowker.

Play, Learning & the Early Childhood Curriculum. Elizabeth Wood & Jane Attfield. LC 96-223611. (One-Off Ser.). (Illus.). 192p. 1996. pap. (*1-85396-252-X*) Corwin Pr.

P

Play Lightly on the Earth: Nature Activities for Children 3 to 9 Years Old. Jacqueline Horsfall. LC 98-127233. (Illus.). 176p. (J). (ps-4). 1997. pap. 12.95 (*1-883220-68-8*) Dawn CA.

Play Like a Girl: A Celebration of Women in Sports. Sue Macy & Jane Gottesman. LC 98-47754. 32p. (J). (gr. 4). 1999. 15.95 (*0-8050-6071-5*) H Holt & Co.

***Play Like a Man, Win Like a Woman: What Men Know about Success That Women Need to Learn.** Gail Evans. LC 99-462238. 256p. 2000. 23.95 (*0-7679-0462-1*) Broadway BDD.

Play Like a Pro. Stuart Isacoff & Becca Pulliam. pap. 19.95 (*0-943748-62-3*) Ekay Music.

***Play Like Elvis! How British Musicians Bought the American Dream.** Mo Foster. 2000. pap. 19.95 (*1-86074-285-8*) Sanctuary Pr.

Play-Likes for Preschoolers: Around the World Costume Patterns. Nancy Mock. Ed. by Karen Gross. (Illus.). 08p. (Orig.). (J). (ps-k). 1991. pap. text 5.95 (*1-56309-009-0*, N918101, New Hope) Womans Mission Union.

Play, Literature, Religion: Essays in Cultural Intertextuality. Ed. by Virgil Nemoianu & Robert Royal. LC 91-4056. 221p. (C). 1992. pap. text 18.95 (*0-7914-0936-8*) State U NY Pr.

Play Little Victims. Kenneth Cook. LC 79-303356. 1978. 8.00 (*0-08-023123-3*, Pergamon Pr) Elsevier.

Play Mas. David Gershator. 92p. (Orig.). 1981. pap. 3.00 (*0-917402-14-6*) Downtown Poets.

***Play Mas'! A Carnival ABC.** Dirk McLean. (Illus.). 32p. (YA). (ps-3). 2000. 18.99 (*0-88776-486-X*) Tundra Bks.

Play Mask Book: Little Red Riding Hood. Peter Stevenson. 12p. (J). (ps-3). 1991. pap. 5.95 (*0-8167-2370-2*) Troll Communs.

Play Mask Book - Cinderella. Peter Stevenson. 12p. (J). (ps-3). 1991. pap. 5.95 (*0-8167-2371-0*) Troll Communs.

Play Me a Story: 9 Tales about Musical Instruments. Naomi Adler. LC 97-25708. (Barefoot Book of Musical Tales). (Illus.). 80p. (J). (gr. 3-5). 1997. 23.40 (*0-7613-0401-0*) Millbrook Pr.

Play Memory. Joanna M. Glass. 96p. (Orig.). 1998. pap. 13.95 (*0-88754-575-0*, Pub. by Theatre Comm) Consort Bk Sales.

Play More Bridge. Mary A. McVey & Linda R. Lehtcmaa. (Bridge Ser.). 228p. 1985. pap. text 7.00 (*0-910475-32-6*) KET.

Play Movement. Claren E. Rainwater. LC 76-143068. 1982. 30.95 (*0-8434-0430-2*, Pub. by McGrath NH) Ayer.

Play Movement & Its Significance. Henry Curtis. 1982. 26.95 (*0-8434-0431-0*) McGrath NH.

Play Murder. Sky Gilbert. LC 96-157916. 64p. 1995. pap. 10.95 (*0-921368-49-6*) Blizzard Publ.

Play Next Play. June Mumme. 1998. pap. 19.95 (*1-57640-023-9*) Host Comns Inc.

Play Now! Fagan. Date not set. pap. text. write for info. (*0-582-03060-9*, Pub. by Addison-Wesley) Longman.

Play Now Library Bk. 17: Remembering the Big Bands. Ed. by Tony Esposito. 36p. (YA). 1995. pap. text 7.95 (*0-89724-668-3*, AF9504) Wrner Bros.

Play of a Fiddle: Traditional Music, Dance & Folklore in West Virginia. Gerald Milnes. LC 98-40733. 264p. 1999. 35.00 (*0-8131-2080-2*) U Pr of Ky.

Play of Allegory in the Autos Sacramentales of Pedro Calderon de la Barca. Barbara E. Kurtz. LC 90-36829. (Contexts & Literature Ser.: Vol. 2). 250p. 1991. text 34.95 (*0-8132-0733-9*) Cath U Pr.

Play of Animals. Karl Groos. LC 75-35072. (Studies in Play & Games). 1976. reprint ed. 31.95 (*0-405-07922-2*) Ayer.

***Play of Consciousness: A Spiritual Autobiography.** 3rd ed. Swami Muktananda. Tr. & Intro. by Gurumayi Chidvilasananda. LC 99-42868.Tr. of Chitshakti Vilas. (Illus.). 368p. 2000. pap. 15.95 (*0-911307-81-8*, 205570, Pub. by SYDA Found) Words Distrib.

Play of Consciousness in the Web of the Universe. Edward L. Gardner. LC 86-30006. (Illus.). 224p. 1987. reprint ed. pap. 7.25 (*0-8356-0236-2*, Quest) Theos Pub Hse.

Play of Daniel: Critical Essays. Dunbar H. Odgen & A. Marcel Zijlstra. LC 96-27276. 1997. pap. 15.00 (*1-879288-77-X*) Medieval Inst.

Play of Daniel: Critical Essays. Dunbar H. Ogden & A. Marcel Zijlstra. LC 96-27276. 1997. 30.00 (*1-879288-76-1*) Medieval Inst.

Play of Daniel, a 13th-Century Musical Drama. Ed. by Noah Greenberg & W. H. Auden. (Illus.). 1959. pap. 5.95 (*0-19-385195-4*) OUP.

Play of Double Senses. A. Bartlett Giamatti. 1990. pap. 7.95 (*0-393-30631-3*) Norton.

Play of Fictions Bk. 2: Studies in Ovid's Metamorphoses. A. M. Keith. (Monographs in Classical Antiquity). 176p. (C). 1992. text 39.50 (*0-472-10274-5*, 10274) U of Mich Pr.

Play of God: Visions of the Life of Krishna. 2nd ed. Devi Vanamal. LC 95-35071. 407p. (Orig.). 1996. pap. 19.95 (*1-884997-07-4*) Blue Dove Pr.

Play of Herod: A Twelfth-Century Musical Drama. Ed. by Noah Greenberg & W. L. Smoldon. (Illus.). 1965. pap. 12.00 (*0-19-385196-2*) OUP.

Play of Light: The Glass Lamps of Frederick Carder. Intro. by Thomas P. Dimitroff. (Illus.). 20p. (Orig.). 1991. pap. 3.00 (*0-9622038-3-1*) Rockwell NY.

Play of Love. John Heywood. LC 73-133676. (Tudor Facsimile Texts. Old English Plays Ser.: No. 16). reprint ed. 59.50 (*0-404-53316-7*) AMS Pr.

Play of Madness: A Translation of "Jeu de la Feuillee" Adam De La Halle. Tr. by Guy R. Mermier from FRE. LC 96-37492. (Studies in Humanities: Vol. 22). XXIX, 127p. (C). 1997. text 38.95 (*0-8204-2860-4*) P Lang Pubng.

Play of Man. Karl Groos. Tr. by Elizabeth L. Baldwin. LC 75-35073. (Studies in Play & Games). 1976. reprint ed. 31.95 (*0-405-07923-0*) Ayer.

Play of Masks. Frithjof Schuon. LC 91-18219. (Library of Traditional Wisdom). 96p. (Orig.). (C). 1992. pap. 9.00 (*0-941532-14-3*) Wrld Wisdom Bks.

Play of Mirrors: The Representation of Self Mirrored in the Other. Sylvia C. Novaes. Tr. by Izabel M. Burbridge from SPA. LC 97-13918. (Translations from Latin America Ser.). (Illus.). 192p. 1997. pap. 14.95 (*0-292-71196-4*) U of Tex Pr.

Play of Mirrors: 8 Major Poets of Modern Japan. Ed. by Thomas Fitzsimmons & Ooka Makoto. LC 86-21130. (Asian Poetry in Translation Ser.: No. 7). (Illus.). 312p. 1987. pap. 30.00 (*0-942668-08-1*) Katydid Bks.

Play of Musement. Thomas A. Sebeok. LC 80-8846. (Advances in Semiotics Ser.). (Illus.). 320p. (C). 1982. 14.95 (*0-253-39994-7*) Ind U Pr.

Play of Musement. Thomas A. Sebeok. LC 80-8846. (Advances in Semiotics Ser.). (Illus.). 320p. Date not set. reprint ed. pap. 99.20 (*0-608-20570-2*, 205448400002) Bks Demand.

Play of Paradox: The Play of Paradox in Early Modern England: Stage & Sermon in Renaissance England. Bryan Crockett. 240p. 1995. text 32.95 (*0-8122-3316-6*) U of Pa Pr.

Play of Power. James Eisenstein. 1995. pap. text 2.25 (*0-312-13750-8*) St Martin.

Play of Power: An Introduction to American Government. James Eisenstein. 1996. pap. text, student ed. 21.95 (*0-312-13777-X*) St Martin.

Play of Power: An Introduction to American Government. James Eisenstein. 1996. pap. text, teacher ed. 17.98 (*0-312-13778-8*) St Martin.

Play of Power: An Introduction to American Government. James Eisenstein et al. LC 94-74765. 864p. 1995. pap. 64.95 (*0-312-08655-5*); pap. 59.95 (*0-312-14212-9*) St Martin.

Play of Power: An Introduction to American Politics. abr. ed. James Eisenstein. 752p. 1995. pap. text 53.95 (*0-312-13662-5*) St Martin.

Play of Power: Mythological Court Dramas of Calderon de la Barca. Margaret R. Greer. (Illus.). 310p. 1991. text 45.00 (*0-691-06857-7*, Pub. by Princeton U Pr) Cal Prin Full Svc.

Play of Power: Nader. Eisenstein. 2000. pap. text 35.60 (*0-312-13869-5*); pap. text 51.00 (*0-312-13871-7*) St Martin.

Play of Reason: From the Modern to the Postmodern. Linda Nicholson. LC 98-39167. 240p. 1998. 39.95 (*0-8014-3517-X*); pap. 17.95 (*0-8014-8516-9*) Cornell U Pr.

Play of Terror in France. John T. Booker & Allan H. Pasco. LC 96-12771. (Illus.). 280p. 1996. 34.50 (*0-87413-589-3*) U Delaware Pr.

Play of the Cards: Self Quizzes at Bridge. Fred L. Karpin. 216p. 1996. reprint ed. pap. 13.95 (*0-89412-258-4*, B-2) Aegean Park Pr.

Play of the Double in Postmodern American Fiction. Gordon E. Slethaug. LC 92-19853. 272p. (C). 1993. 36.95 (*0-8093-1841-5*) S Ill U Pr.

Play of the Gods: Locality, Ideology, Structure & Time in the Festivals of a Bengali Town. Akos Ostor. LC 79-25661. 264p. 1993. 27.00 (*0-226-63954-1*) U Ch Pr.

Play of the Hand: Student Text for Contract Bridge. Shirley Silverman. 64p. (Orig.). 1980. pap. text 4.95 (*0-87643-030-2*) Barclay Bridge.

Play of the Platonic Dialogues. Bernard Freydberg. LC 96-6888. (Literature & the Sciences of Man Ser.: No. 12). XII, 224p. (C). 1997. text 46.95 (*0-8204-3313-6*) P Lang Pubng.

Play of the Self. Ed. by Ronald Bogue & Mihai I. Spariosu. LC 93-43552. (SUNY Series, The Margins of Literature). 268p. (C). 1994. text 59.50 (*0-7914-2079-5*); pap. text 19.95 (*0-7914-2080-9*) State U NY Pr.

Play of the Text: Max Jacob's "Le Cornet a Des" Sydney Levy. Tr. by Judith M. Schneider. LC 80-52298. 173p. 1981. reprint ed. pap. 53.70 (*0-608-01969-0*, 206262400003) Bks Demand.

Play of the Unmentionable: An Installation by Joseph Kosuth at the Brooklyn Museum. Joseph Kosuth. 168p. 1992. 40.00 (*1-56584-004-6*, Pub. by New Press NY) Norton.

Play of the Weather. John Heywood. LC 72-143209. (Tudor Facsimile Texts. Old English Plays Ser.: No. 14). reprint ed. 59.50 (*0-404-53314-0*) AMS Pr.

Play of the Weather. John Heywood. LC 70-133678. (Tudor Facsimile Texts. Old English Plays Ser.: No. 15). reprint ed. 59.50 (*0-404-53315-9*) AMS Pr.

Play of the Week: Selected from Highlights for Children. LC 92-73626. (Illus.). 96p. (J). (gr. 2-5). 1993. pap. 3.95 (*1-56397-193-3*) Boyds Mills Pr.

Play of Time: Kodi Perspectives on Calendars, History, & Exchange. Janet Hoskins. LC 92-31669. 1994. 55.00 (*0-520-08003-3*, Pub. by U CA Pr) Cal Prin Full Svc.

Play of Time: Kodi Perspectives on Calendars, History, & Exchange. Janet Hoskins. LC 92-31669. (Illus.). 1997. pap. 18.95 (*0-520-20892-7*, Pub. by U CA Pr) Cal Prin Full Svc.

Play of Truth & State: Historical Drama from Shakespeare to Brecht. Matthew H. Wikander. LC 85-23128. 300p. 1986. reprint ed. pap. 93.00 (*0-608-03666-8*, 206449200009) Bks Demand.

Play of Wisdom: Its Texts & Contexts. Milla C. Riggio. LC 86-47840. (Studies in the Middle Ages: No. 14). 32.50 (*0-404-61444-2*) AMS Pr.

Play of Wit & Science. John Redford. (Tudor Facsimile Texts. Old English Plays Ser.: No. 18). reprint ed. 59.50 (*0-404-53318-3*) AMS Pr.

Play of Words. Richard Lederer. Ed. by Elaine Pfefferblit. 288p. 1991. reprint ed. pap. 12.00 (*0-671-68909-6*) PB.

Play On! Memoirs of a Jesuit Teacher. C. J. McNaspy. LC 95-37834. 360p. (Orig.). (C). 1996. pap. 18.95 (*0-8294-0867-3*, Jesuit Way) Loyola Pr.

Play 101. Janie Currey. 108p. (Orig.). 1996. pap. 5.95 (*0-9652587-0-X*) Vegas Publng.

Play Out of Context: Transferring Plays from Culture to Culture. Ed. by Hanna Scolnicov & Peter R. Holland. (Illus.). 240p. (C). 1989. text 69.95 (*0-521-34433-6*) Cambridge U Pr.

Play Party Book: Singing Games for Children. Ed. by Ed Durlacher. (Illus.). 38p. (J). (ps-5). 1945. 9.50 (*0-8159-6505-2*) Devin.

Play-Party in Indiana. Leah J. Wolford. Ed. by W. Edson Richmond. LC 75-35086. (Studies in Play & Games). (Illus.). 1976. reprint ed. 21.95 (*0-405-07933-8*) Ayer.

Play Pennywhistle. Date not set. pap. 5.95 (*0-8256-1644-1*, AM 945593) Music Sales.

Play Pennywhistle Now! The Fun & Easy Way to Play Pennywhistle. Peter Pickow. (Illus.). 52p. 1989. pap. 16.95 (*0-8256-1779-0*, Amsco Music) Music Sales.

Play Pipes for Water Supply Testing in Fire Protection Service, UL 385. 9th ed. (C). 1994. pap. text 135.00 (*1-55989-700-7*) Underwrtrs Labs.

Play Poker, Quit Work & Sleep till Noon. rev. ed. John Fox. 1988. 17.95 (*0-940416-01-8*) Bacchus Pr.

Play, Policy & Practice. Ed. by Edgar Klugman. LC 95-26056. 219p. 1995. pap. 18.95 (*1-884834-11-6*, 1503) Redleaf Pr.

Play Power: Games & Activities for Young Children. Sharron W. Krull & Norma Don. LC 94-92243. (Illus.). 142p. 1994. pap. text 16.95 (*1-885650-00-0*) Play Power.

Play Production Today. 1996. teacher ed., ring bd. 85.31 (*0-8442-5777-X*) NTC Contemp Pub Co.

Play Production Today! 4th ed. Roy A. Beck. 336p. 1989. 26.60 (*0-8442-5085-6*) NTC Contemp Pub Co.

Play Production Today! 5th ed. LC 95-67114. 368p. 1996. student ed. 42.66 (*0-8442-5775-3*) NTC Contemp Pub Co.

Play Resumed: A Journal. D. J. Enright. LC 98-35295. 220p. 1999. 29.95 (*0-19-288108-6*) OUP.

Play Rhymes. Marc Tolon Brown. (J). 1993. 9.94 (*0-606-05977-6*, Pub. by Turtleback) Demco.

***Play Rock Drums.** Joel Rothman. (Step One Ser.). (Illus.). 44p. 1999. pap. 5.95 (*0-8256-1669-7*, AM947529, Amsco Music) Music Sales.

Play Rock Guitar. Mike Clifford. (Illus.). 128p. 1987. pap. 17.95 (*0-8256-1165-2*, AM66762) Music Sales.

Play Rock Keyboards. Dewi Evans & Mike Lindup. (Illus.). 128p. 1987. pap. 14.95 (*0-8256-1166-0*, AM66754) Music Sales.

Play Rock 'n Roll Drums. Joel Rothman. (Illus.). 32p. 1980. pap. 5.95 (*0-86001-738-9*, AM26329) Music Sales.

***Play, School & Society, Ser. 11.** George Herbert Mead. Ed. by Mary Jo Deegan. LC 97-20825. (American University Studies: Vol. 71). (Illus.). CXII, 157p. 1999. text 50.00 (*0-8204-3823-5*) P Lang Pubng.

Play School Fun: Point & Say. Lorenz. 1999. 9.98 (*1-84038-213-9*, Pub. by Hermes Hse) Random.

Play Shapes. Illus. by Claire Henley. LC 98-141062. 14p. (J). (ps up). 1997. bds. 5.95 (*0-448-41628-X*, G & D) Peng Put Young Read.

Play Smart: A Science-by-Mail Challenge about Sports. Science-by-Mail Staff. 40p. pap. text 54.00 (*0-7872-6240-4*, 41624004) Kendall-Hunt.

Play Spaces for Children: A New Beginning, Vol. II. Ed. by Lawrence D. Bruya. (Illus.). 243p. (Orig.). 1988. pap. text 9.50 (*0-88314-391-7*, A3917) AAHPERD.

Play, Symbolism & Ritual: A Study of Tamil Brahmin Women's Rites of Passage. Vasumathi K. Duvvury. LC 89-14564. (American University Studies: Anthropology & Science: Ser. XI, Vol. 41). (Illus.). X, 251p. (C). 1991. text 46.95 (*0-8204-1108-6*) P Lang Pubng.

Play Tabla: A Manual for the Benares Style of Tabla Playing. Frances Shepherd & Sharda Sahai. (Illus.). 68p. 1992. pap. 15.00 (*0-948080-27-2*, Trentham Bks) Stylus Pub VA.

Play Techniques in Interviewing Children. Virginia B. Eaddy & Ethel S. Amacher. 111p. 1985. 8.50 (*0-89695-012-3*) U Tenn CSW.

Play Tennis in the Airzone: Air Target Training System & Drill Book. Joe Dinoffer. (Illus.). 80p. 1995. student ed. write for info. (*0-9642150-2-0*) Oncourt Offcourt.

Play Tennis in the Ropezone: Target System & Drill Book. Joe Dinoffer. (Illus.). 64p. 1994. student ed. write for info. (*0-9642150-0-4*) Oncourt Offcourt.

Play-Texts in Old Spelling: Papers from the Glendon Conference. Ed. by Raymond C. Shady & G. B. Shand. LC 81-69123. (Studies in the Renaissance: No. 6). 1984. 34.50 (*0-404-62276-3*) AMS Pr.

Play the Anti-Indian Systems. Egon Varnusz. 170p. 1991. pap. 13.95 (*0-08-032077-5*, Pub. by CHES) Macmillan.

Play the Benko Gambit. Vaidyanathan M. Ravikumar. (Chess Library). (Illus.). 120p. 1991. write for info. (*0-08-029767-6*, Pub. by CHES); pap. 19.95 (*0-08-029766-8*, Pub. by CHES) Macmillan.

Play the Bogo-Indian. Shaun Taulbut. LC 84-10995. (Chess Ser.). (Illus.). 144p. 1985. 27.90 (*0-08-029729-3*, Pergamon Pr); pap. 17.90 (*0-08-029728-5*, Pergamon Pr) Elsevier.

Play the Brazilian Way: The Secret Behind the Success of the World's Greatest Soccer Team. Simon Clifford. (Illus.). 96p. 1999. pap. 24.00 (*0-7522-1347-4*) Trans-Atl Phila.

Play the Caro-Kann. Egon Varnusz. Ed. by M. Chandler. (Chess Openings Ser.). (Illus.). 175p. 1983. 17.95 (*0-08-024130-1*, Pergamon Pr) Elsevier.

Play the Caro-Kann. 2nd rev. ed. Egon Varnusz. (Chess Library). (Illus.). 180p. 1991. pap. 19.95 (*0-08-037789-0*, Pub. by CHES) Macmillan.

Play the Catalan: Closed Variation & Catalan Opening after 1 d4 d5 2 c4. J. Neishtadt. LC 87-2262. (Illus.). 190p. 1988. pap. 19.90 (*0-08-032062-7*, Pergamon Pr) Elsevier.

Play the Catalan: Open Variation, Vol. 1. J. Neishtadt. Tr. by Kenneth P. Neat. LC 87-2262. (Chess Ser.). (Illus.). 258p. 1987. pap. 23.90 (*0-08-029740-4*, Pergamon Pr) Elsevier.

Play the Evans Gambit. Tim Harding & Bernard Cafferty. 1997. pap. 21.95 (*1-85744-119-2*, Pub. by Cadgn Bks) Macmillan.

Play the French. J. L. Watson. LC 84-10990. (Chess Ser.). (Illus.). 160p. 1984. 27.90 (*0-08-029716-1*, Pergamon Pr); pap. 17.90 (*0-08-026929-X*, Pergamon Pr) Elsevier.

Play the French. John Watson. 212p. 1996. pap. 19.95 (*1-85744-101-X*) Macmillan.

Play the Game: Golf. Ian Morrison. 1998. pap. 10.95 (*0-7063-7686-2*, Pub. by WrLock) Sterling.

***Play the Game: How to Get Accepted & Succeed in Graduate School.** LC 99-91975. 2000. 25.00 (*0-7388-1460-1*); pap. 18.00 (*0-7388-1461-X*) Xlibris Corp.

Play the Game: Karate. Karl Oldgate. (Illus.). 80p. 1998. pap. 10.95 (*0-7063-7714-1*, Pub. by WrLock) Sterling.

Play the Game: Tennis. Simon Lee. (Illus.). 80p. 1998. pap. 10.95 (*0-7063-7715-X*, Pub. by WrLock) Sterling.

Play the Game: Volleyball. George Bulman. (Illus.). 80p. 1998. pap. 10.95 (*0-7063-7683-8*, Pub. by WrLock) Sterling.

Play the Harmonica Well. Douglas Tate. (Illus.). 46p. 1998. pap. 9.95 (*1-57424-061-7*) Centerstream Pub.

Play the King's Gambit. Yakov B. Estrin & I. B. Glaskov. LC 81-23469. (Russian Chess Ser.: No. 13). 1982. 39.95 (*0-08-026877-3*, Pergamon Pr); pap. 24.95 (*0-08-026876-5*, Pergamon Pr) Elsevier.

Play the King's Gambit: King's Gambit Accepted, Vol. 1. Yakov B. Estrin & I. B. Glaskov. Tr. by Kenneth P. Neat. (Illus.). 174p. 1982. 22.95 (*0-08-026873-0*, Pergamon Pr); pap. 13.95 (*0-08-026872-2*, Pergamon Pr) Elsevier.

Play the King's Gambit: King's Gambit Declined, Vol. 2. Yakov B. Estrin & I. B. Glaskov. Tr. by Kenneth P. Neat. (Chess Openings Ser.). (Illus.). 130p. 1982. 23.95 (*0-08-026875-7*, Pergamon Pr); pap. 11.95 (*0-08-026874-9*, Pergamon Pr) Elsevier.

Play the King's Indian Defense. D. Marovic. (Chess Ser.). (Illus.). 242p. 1983. 29.95 (*0-08-029727-7*, Pergamon Pr) Elsevier.

Play the Nimzo-Indian Defense. Svetozar Gligoric. (Chess Ser.). (Illus.). 175p. 1985. 27.90 (*0-08-026928-1*, Pergamon Pr); pap. 17.90 (*0-08-026927-3*, Pergamon Pr) Elsevier.

***Play the Open Games As Black.** John Emms. (Illus.). 224p. 2000. pap. 23.95 (*1-901983-27-7*, Pub. by Gambit) BHB Intl.

Play the Piano Drunk Like a Percussion Instrument until the Fingers Begin to Bleed a Bit. Charles Bukowski. LC 79-20429. 128p. 1998. reprint ed. 25.00 (*0-87685-438-2*); reprint ed. pap. 14.00 (*0-87685-437-4*) Black Sparrow.

Play the Queen's Gambit. D. Marovic. (PECH Pergamon Chess Ser.). 200p. 1991. write for info. (*0-08-029765-X*, 6201, Pub. by CHES); pap. 29.95 (*0-08-029764-1*, 6201, Pub. by CHES) Macmillan.

Play the Roman Fool & Die. large type ed. Richard Grayson. (Linford Mystery Library). 352p. 1997. pap. 16.99 (*0-7089-5162-7*) Ulverscroft.

Play the Ruy Lopez. Egon Varnusz. 200p. 1990. pap. write for info. (*0-08-037152-3*, Pub. by CHES) Macmillan.

Play the Ruy Lopez. Egon Varnusz. 1992. 14.00 (*1-85744-012-9*, Maxwell Macmillan) Macmillan.

Play the St. George. Michael Basman. (Illus.). 132p. 1982. 19.95 (*0-08-029718-8*, Pergamon Pr); pap. 13.90 (*0-08-029717-X*, Pergamon Pr) Elsevier.

Play the Tarrasch. Leonid Shamkovich & Eric Schiller. (Chess Ser.). (Illus.). 150p. 1984. 25.90 (*0-08-029748-X*, Pergamon Pr); pap. 15.90 (*0-08-029747-1*, Pergamon Pr) Elsevier.

Play the Viol: The Complete Guide to Playing the Treble, Tenor, & Bass Viol. Alison Crum & Sonia Jackson. (Early Music Ser.: No. 10). (Illus.). 200p. 1992. pap. text 29.95 (*0-19-816311-8*) OUP.

Play Theory of Mass Communication. William Stephenson. 210p. 1987. pap. 24.95 (*0-88738-705-5*) Transaction Pubs.

Play Therapy. Michael Joseph. LC 90-85709. (Illus.). 72p. (Orig.). 1991. pap. 4.95 (*0-87029-233-1*) Abbey.

Play Therapy. rev. ed. Virginia M. Axline. (Illus.). 374p. (C). 1981. mass mkt. 6.99 (*0-345-30335-0*) Ballantine Pub Grp.

Play Therapy: A Comprehensive Guide. O'Dessie O. James. LC 96-45165. 328p. 1997. 60.00 (*0-7657-0052-2*) Aronson.

Play Therapy: A Non-Directive Approach for Children & Adolescents. Kate Wilson et al. (Illus.). 245p. 1992. pap. text 26.00 (*0-7020-1487-7*, Pub. by W B Saunders) Saunders.

Play Therapy: A Strategic Approach. Stanley Kissel. 108p. 1990. pap. 19.95 (*0-398-06205-6*) C C Thomas.

Play Therapy: A Strategic Approach. Stanley Kissel. 108p. (C). 1990. text 31.95 (*0-398-05708-7*) C C Thomas.

Play Therapy: Dynamics of the Process of Counseling with Children. Garry L. Landreth. 380p. 1982. pap. 46.95 (*0-398-06221-8*) C C Thomas.

Play Therapy: Dynamics of the Process of Counseling with Children. Garry L. Landreth. 380p. (C). 1982. text 58.95 (*0-398-04716-2*) C C Thomas.

Play Therapy: From the Sky to the Underworld. Ann Cattanach. LC 93-44030. 1994. 75.00 (*1-85302-250-0*); pap. 25.00 (*1-85302-211-X*) Taylor & Francis.

Play Therapy in Action: A Casebook for Practitioners. Ed. by Terry A. Kottman & Charles E. Schaefer. LC 93-15666. 640p. 1993. 70.00 (*1-56821-058-2*) Aronson.

P

An Asterisk (*) at the beginning of an entry indicates that the title is appearing for the first time.

Play Therapy Primer: In Integration of Theories & Techniques. Kevin J. O'Connor. LC 90-19419. (Series on Personality Processes). 384p. 1991. 74.50 (*0-471-52543-X*) Wiley.

***Play Therapy Primer: In Integration of Theories & Techniques.** 2nd ed. Kevin J. O'Connor. LC 99-53399. 384p. 2000. 49.95 (*0-471-24873-8*) Wiley.

Play Therapy Theory & Practice: A Comparative Presentation. Ed. by Kevin O'Connor & Lisa M. Braverman. LC 96-21257. 432p. 1996. 64.50 (*0-471-10638-0*) Wiley.

Play Therapy Treatment Planning & Interventions: The Ecosystemic Model & Workbook. Ed. by Kevin J. O'Connor & Sue Ammen. LC 97-25959. (Illus.). 234p. 1997. pap. text 54.95 (*0-12-524135-6*) Morgan Kaufmann.

Play Therapy with Abused Children. Ann Cattanach. (Illus.). 160p. 1993. write for info. (*1-85302-193-8*, Pub. by Jessica Kingsley) Taylor & Francis.

Play Therapy with Children in Crisis: A Casebook for Practitioners. Ed. by Nancy B. Webb. LC 91-19756. 460p. 1991. lib. bdg. 38.95 (*0-89862-760-5*) Guilford Pubns.

***Play Therapy with Children in Crisis: Individual, Group & Family Treatment.** 2nd ed. Ed. by Nancy Boyd Webb. LC 99-35764. 506p. 1999. lib. bdg. 46.00 (*1-57230-485-5*, CO485) Guilford Pubns.

Play Therapy with Sexually Abused Children: A Synergistic Clinical-Developmental Approach. Robert A. Ciottone & John M. Madonna. LC 95-42102. 240p. 1996. 50.00 (*1-56821-571-1*) Aronson.

Play! Think! Grow! 234 Activities for Christian Growth. Doris Willis. 264p. (Orig.). (J). (ps-1). 1992. pap. 19.95 (*0-687-13498-6*) Abingdon.

Play Time. Roger Pare. (Illus.). 24p. (J). (ps-8). 1988. text 12.95 (*1-55037-087-1*, Pub. by Annick) Firefly Bks Ltd.

Play Time. Roger Pare. (Illus.). 24p. (J). (ps-8). 1988. pap. 4.95 (*1-55037-086-3*, Pub. by Annick) Firefly Bks Ltd.

Play Time. Murray Schisgal. 1997. pap. 5.25 (*0-8222-1586-1*) Dramatists Play.

Play Time, Bk. 6. Fagan. Date not set. pap. text. write for info. (*0-582-18332-4*, Pub. by Addison-Wesley) Longman.

Play Time: 100 Good Tunes. M. Fagan. Date not set. pap. text. write for info. (*0-582-18331-6*, Pub. by Addison-Wesley) Longman.

Play to Live. Alan Watts. Ed. by Mark Watts. LC 82-72606. 100p. (Orig.). 1982. pap. text 10.95 (*0-89708-098-X*) And Bks.

Play to Nature: Experimentation As Performance. Robert P. Crease. LC 93-2735. (Indiana Series in the Philosophy of Technology). 228p. 1993. 12.95 (*0-253-31474-7*) Ind U Pr.

Play to Win! Choosing Growth over Fear in Work & Life. Larry Wilson & Hersch Wilson. LC 98-15291. 288p. 1998. 24.95 (*1-885167-31-8*) Bard Press.

***Play Today in the Primary School Playground: Life, Learning & Creativity.** Julia C. Bishop & Mavis Curtis. LC 00-44120. 2001. pap. write for info. (*0-335-20715-4*, Pub. by OpUniv Pr) Taylor & Francis.

Play Today the Bubar Way. David N. Bubar. 130p. 1996. 29.95 incl. VHS (*1-885273-00-2*) First Century.

Play Today the Bubar Way, Vol. 1, Church ed. David N. Bubar. 130p. 1996. 29.95 incl. VHS (*1-885273-01-0*) First Century.

Play Together, Grow Together: A Cooperative Curriculum for Teachers of Young Children. rev. ed. Marilyn Segal & Don Adcock. (Illus.). 150p. (J). 1993. pap. 12.95 (*1-879744-03-1*) Nova U Fam Ctr.

***Play Together, Learn Together.** Melanie Rice. (Illus.). 160p. (YA). 2000. pap. 12.95 (*0-7534-5294-4*, Kingfisher) LKC.

***Play Together, Share Together, Fun Activities for Parents.** Cynthia Holtzschuler. 160p. 2000. pap. 14.95 (*1-57690-504-7*) Tchr Create Mat.

Play Tunes: A Supplement to "Singing & Playing" Polly Gibbs. 1971. 2.00 (*0-19-385156-3*) OUP.

***Play Winning Checkers.** Ed. by Sterling Publishing Staff. (Illus.). 2000. pap. 14.95 (*0-8069-4463-3*) Sterling.

Play Winning Checkers Official American Mensa Game Book. Robert W. Pike. LC 98-48172. 1999. pap. text 7.95 (*0-8069-3794-7*) Sterling.

Play Winning Cribbage. 2nd ed. DeLynn C. Colvert. LC 80-67576. (Illus.). 154p. 1979. write for info. (*0-9612548-1-5*) Starr Studios.

Play Winning Cribbage. 3rd ed. DeLynn C. Colvert. 1997. pap. 10.95 (*0-614-29365-0*) ISBN Agency.

Play Winning Cribbage. 3rd ed. DeLynn C. Colvert. LC 80-67576. (Illus.). 154p. 1997. pap. 10.95 (*0-9612548-0-7*) Starr Studios.

Play with A & T. Jane Belk Moncure. LC 89-774. (Sound Box Library). (Illus.). 32p. (J). (ps-2). 1989. lib. bdg. 21.36 (*0-89565-505-5*) Childs World.

Play with a Purpose for under Sevens. Elizabeth Matterson. pap. 15.95 (*0-14-010493-3*, Pub. by Pnguin Bks Ltd) Trafalgar.

Play with Big Boxes. Liz Wilmes & Dick Wilmes. (Illus.). (Orig.). 1996. pap. 12.95 (*0-943452-23-6*) Building Blocks.

Play with Computers. Jim Drake. LC 98-48088. 32p. (J). 1999. lib. bdg. 21.36 (*1-57572-786-2*) Heinemann Lib.

Play with E & D. Jane Belk Moncure. LC 73-4743. (Sound Box Library). (Illus.). 32p. (J). (ps-2). 1989. lib. bdg. 21.36 (*0-89565-508-X*) Childs World.

Play with Fire: A Kate Shugak Mystery. Dana Stabenow. (Kate Shugak Mystery Ser.). 288p. 1995. pap. 19.95 (*0-425-14717-7*, Prime Crime) Berkley Pub.

Play with Fire: A Kate Shugak Mystery. Dana Stabenow. 1996. mass mkt. 5.99 (*0-425-15254-5*) Berkley Pub.

Play with I & G. Jane Belk Moncure. LC 73-4739. (Sound Box Library). (Illus.). 32p. (J). (ps-1). 1989. lib. bdg. 21.36 (*0-89565-507-1*) Childs World.

Play with Me. (Young Dragon Readers 1 Ser.). (J). 1995. pap. text. write for info. (*962-359-528-X*) Addison-Wesley.

Play with Me. Marie H. Ets. LC 55-14845. (Picture Puffin Ser.). (J). (ps-3). 1976. pap. 5.99 (*0-14-050178-9*, PuffinBks) Peng Put Young Read.

Play with Me. Marie H. Ets. LC 55-14845. (Picture Puffin Ser.). (Illus.). (J). 1976. 10.19 (*0-606-04330-6*, Pub. by Turtleback) Demco.

Play with Me. Marie H. Ets. 1976. pap. 15.95 (*0-670-55985-7*) Viking Penguin.

Play with Me, Set. unabridged ed. Marie H. Ets. (J). (gr. k-3). 1975. pap., teacher ed. 33.95 incl. audio (*0-670-55979-2*) Live Oak Media.

Play with Me: Crafts for Preschoolers. Barbara Miles. (Illus.). (Orig.). (ps). 1990. pap. 13.98 (*0-88290-367-5*) Horizon Utah.

Play with Models. Ivan Bulloch. LC 94-14248. (Play with Crafts Ser.). 24p. (J). (ps-2). 1995. lib. bdg. 19.95 (*0-87614-866-6*, Carolrhoda) Lerner Pub.

Play with Numbers. T. Satyanarayana Raju. (Illus.). v, 190p. (Orig.). (YA). (gr. 7-12). 1996. pap. 29.95 (*0-9650901-2-4*) Inst of Vedic.

Play with O & G. Jane Belk Moncure. LC 73-4742. (Sound Box Library). (Illus.). 32p. (J). (ps-2). 1989. lib. bdg. 21.36 (*0-89565-506-3*) Childs World.

Play with Paint. Sara Lynn & Diane James. (Play with Crafts Ser.). (Illus.). 24p. (J). (ps-2). 1992. lib. bdg. 19.95 (*0-87614-755-4*, Carolrhoda) Lerner Pub.

Play with Paper. Sara Lynn & Diane James. (J). (ps-2). 1992. lib. bdg. 19.95 (*0-87614-754-6*, Carolrhoda) Lerner Pub.

***Play with Paper.** rev. ed. Ivan Bulloch. (Let's Ser.). (Illus.). (J). 2000. 9.95 (*1-58728-027-2*); pap. 4.95 (*1-58728-031-0*) Two Can Pub.

Play with Papier-Mache. Susan Moxley. LC 94-14247. (Play with Crafts Ser.). 24p. (J). (ps-2). 1995. lib. bdg. 19.95 (*0-87614-865-8*, Carolrhoda) Lerner Pub.

Play with Shakespeare: A Guide to Producing Shakespeare with Young People. Linda Burson. (Illus.). 218p. (Orig.). 1992. pap. 19.95 (*0-932720-51-X*) New Plays Inc.

Play with Small Boxes. Liz Wilmes & Dick Wilmes. (Illus.). (Orig.). 1996. pap. 12.95 (*0-943452-24-4*) Building Blocks.

Play with Them - Theraplay Groups in the Classroom: A Technique for Professionals Who Work with Children. Phyllis B. Rubin & Jeanine L. Tregay. (Illus.). 206p. 1989. pap. 33.95 (*0-398-06715-5*) C C Thomas.

Play with Them - Theraplay Groups in the Classroom: A Technique for Professionals Who Work with Children. Phyllis B. Rubin & Jeanine L. Tregay. (Illus.). 206p. (C). 1989. text 41.95 (*0-398-05579-3*) C C Thomas.

***Play with Triangles: Patchwork Designs & Projects.** Bonnie K. Browning & Phyllis D. Miller. Ed. by Cherry Pyron. 32p. 2000. pap. 15.95 (*1-57432-753-4*, Am Quilters Soc) Collector Bks.

Play with U & G. Jane Belk Moncure. LC 73-4741. (Sound Box Library). (Illus.). 32p. (J). (ps-2). 1989. lib. bdg. 21.36 (*0-89565-509-8*) Childs World.

Play with Us. (Key Words Readers Ser.: A Series, No. 641-1a). (Illus.). (J). (ps-5). pap. 3.50 (*0-7214-0001-9*, Ladybrd) Penguin Putnam.

Play with Your Food. Joost Elffers. LC 97-16557. (Illus.). 112p. 1997. 19.95 (*1-55670-630-8*) Stewart Tabori & Chang.

Play with Your Food: Postcards, 30 vols. Joost Elffers & Saxton Freymann. (Illus.). 1998. pap. 10.95 (*1-55670-849-1*) Stewart Tabori & Chang.

Play with Your Pumpkins. Joost Elffers & Saxton Freymann. LC 98-17155. (Illus.). 79p. (YA). (gr. 2 up). 1998. 10.95 (*1-55670-848-3*) Stewart Tabori & Chang.

Play Within a Play. R. J. Nelson. LC 72-87356. (Theatre, Film & the Performing Arts Ser.). 182p. 1971. reprint ed. lib. bdg. 29.50 (*0-306-71580-5*) Da Capo.

Play, Working Partner of Growth. Ed. by Judy S. McKee. LC 86-22245. (Illus.). 88p. 1986. reprint ed. pap. 30.00 (*0-608-03185-2*, 206363800007) Bks Demand.

***Play World: The Emergence of the New Ludenic Age.** James E. Combs. LC 00-22344. 208p. 2000. 53.00 (*0-275-96838-3*, C6838, Praeger Pubs) Greenwood.

Play Writing: A Study in Choices & Challenges. Paul McCusker. LC 97-171168. 1995. pap. 14.99 (*0-8341-9353-1*, MP-760) Nazarene.

Play Years: 2 to 6. rev. ed. Judith K. Schneider et al. (Competent Caregiver Ser.). (Illus.). 58p. (C). 1986. pap., student ed. 10.95 (*0-944454-17-8*); pap. text 10.95 (*0-944454-05-4*) CAPE Center.

Play Your Best. Ron Duffy. 83p. 1992. pap. write for info. (*0-9632496-0-6*) R Duffy.

Play Your Best Pool: Secrets to Winning 8 Ball & 9 Ball for All Players. Philip B. Capelle. (Illus.). 464p. 1995. pap. 29.95 (*0-9649204-0-9*) Billiards Pr.

Play Your Cards! Ed. by Stauart R. Kaplan. LC 95-81776. (Illus.). 96p. 1995. pap. 20.00 (*0-88079-959-5*, BK145) US Games Syst.

Play Your First Blues Riffs in 60 Minutes. Pat Conway. (Illus.). 19p. 1998. pap. text 5.95 (*0-7119-5639-1*, Am 936177) Music Sales.

Play Your First Rock Riffs in 60 Minutes. Pat Conway. (Illus.). 19p. 1998. pap. text 5.95 (*0-7119-5638-3*, AM 936166) Music Sales.

Playa Giron: La Verdadera Historia. 3rd ed. Enrique Ros. LC 94-71749. (Coleccion Cuba y sus Jueces). (SPA., Illus.). 314p. (Orig.). 1998. pap. 25.00 (*0-89729-738-5*) Ediciones.

Playa Vista Archaeological & Historical Project Vol. 1: Research Design. Jeffrey H. Altschul et al. (Statistical Research Technical Ser.: No. 29). (Illus.). 219p. 1991. spiral bd. 25.00 (*1-879442-27-2*) Stats Res.

Playas: Jewels of the South Plains. Jim Steiert. LC 94-12270. (Illus.). 144p. 1995. text 37.50 (*0-89672-335-6*) Tex Tech Univ Pr.

Playback. Raymond Chandler. LC 87-45920. (Crime Ser.). 240p. 1988. pap. 10.00 (*0-394-75766-1*) Vin Bks.

Playback. Richard "Cactus" Pryor. LC 95-10561. (Illus.). 176p. 1995. 19.95 (*0-292-76567-3*) U of Tex Pr.

Playback & Studies of Animal Communication. P. K. McGregor. (NATO ASI Ser.: Vol. 228). (Illus.). 248p. (C). 1992. text 95.00 (*0-306-44205-1*, Kluwer Plenum) Kluwer Academic.

Playback Equalizer Settings for 78 rpm Recordings. James R. Powell, Jr. & Randall G. Stehle. (Illus.). v, 89p. (Orig.). 1993. pap. 50.00 (*0-9634921-3-6*, 1003) Gramphne Advent.

***Playback War.** Lisa Smedman. 304p. 2000. mass mkt. 6.50 (*0-446-60489-5*, Pub. by Warner Bks) Little.

Playbill 1. Alan Durband. 152p. (C). 1989. pap. 11.95 (*0-7487-0180-X*) Dufour.

Playbills from the Harvard Theatre Collection: A Guide to the Microfilm Collection. LC 82-5313. 380p. 1982. 300.00 (*0-89235-037-7*) Primary Srce Media.

Playboar. Thomas Hagey. (Illus.). reprint ed. pap. 9.95 (*0-9628198-2-4*) W Kent.

***Playboating.** Eric Jackson. LC 99-32587. (Kayaking with Eric Jackson Ser.). 2000. pap. 16.95 (*0-8117-2894-3*) Stackpole.

Playboating the Nantahala River: An Entry-Level Guide. Kelly Fischer. LC 98-10272. (Illus.). 96p. 1998. pap. 9.95 (*1-889596-05-1*) Milestone NC.

Playbook. (Big Comfy Couch Digest Ser.). (Illus.). 64p. (J). (ps-1). 1997. pap. write for info. (*0-7666-0013-0*, Honey Bear Bks) Modern Pub NYC.

Playbook. unabridged ed. Dayna Fenker & Nancy Baker. (Illus.). 86p. (Orig.). (C). 1990. pap. text 5.95 (*0-940352-03-6*) Mesa Hse.

Playbook: A Resource for Games & Other Group Related Activities. Roger Maness et al. (Illus.). 144p. 1995. spiral bd. 17.95 (*0-9658328-0-5*) Playbook Pubs.

Playbook: 7 Plays about Women & Work, Culture, & Revolution. Maxine Klein et al. LC 86-6754. 500p. (Orig.). 1986. 35.00 (*0-89608-309-8*) South End Pr.

Playbook for Kids about Sex. Joani Blank. (Illus.). 56p. (J). (gr. 2-6). 1980. pap. 5.00 (*0-9602324-6-X*, Yes Pr) Down There Pr.

Playbook for Men about Sex. rev. ed. Joani Blank. (Illus.). 32p. 1981. pap. 4.50 (*0-9602324-8-6*) Down There Pr.

Playbook for Women about Sex. rev. ed. Joani Blank. (Illus.). 32p. 1989. pap. 4.50 (*0-940208-04-0*) Down There Pr.

Playboy. Mark Dunster. (Rin Ser.: Pt. 43). 1974. 4.00 (*0-89642-030-2*) Linden Pubs.

Playboy. William Oxley. 109p. pap. write for info. (*3-7052-0223-5*, Pub. by Poetry Salzburg) Intl Spec Bk.

Playboy & the Mommy: Tall, Dark & Irresistible. Mindy Neff. (American Romance Ser.: No. 800). 1999. per. 3.99 (*0-373-16800-4*, 1-16800-4) Harlequin Bks.

Playboy & the Nanny. Anne Mcallister. 1998. per. 3.75 (*0-373-12005-2*, 1-12005-4, Mira Bks) Harlequin Bks.

Playboy & the Nanny. large type ed. 1999. 21.95 (*0-263-15926-4*) Chivers N Amer.

Playboy & the Widow. Debbie Macomber. (Mira Bks.). 256p. 1996. per. 5.50 (*1-55166-080-6*, 1-66080-2, Mira Bks) Harlequin Bks.

***Playboy & the Widow.** Debbie Macomber. LC 00-37799. 2000. pap. write for info. (*0-7862-2607-2*) Thorndike Pr.

Playboy & the Yellow Lady. James Carney. 240p. 1986. pap. 10.95 (*0-905169-82-4*, Pub. by Poolbeg Pr) Dufour.

Playboy Assignment. Leigh Michaels. (Romance Ser.). 1998. per. 3.50 (*0-373-03500-4*, 1-03500-5) Harlequin Bks.

Playboy Assignment. large type ed. Michaels. (Finding Mr. Right Ser.). 1998. per. 3.50 (*0-373-15746-0*, Harlequin) Harlequin Bks.

***Playboy Assignment.** large type ed. Leigh Michaels. 1999. 25.99 (*0-263-15935-3*, Pub. by Mills & Boon) Ulverscroft.

Playboy Book of Science Fiction. Ed. by Alice K. Turner. 480p. 1999. pap. 16.00 (*0-06-107342-3*, HarperPrism) HarpC.

Playboy Guide to Jazz. Neil Tesser. LC 98-14753. 288p. 1998. pap. 13.95 (*0-452-27648-9*, Plume) Dutton Plume.

Playboy Interview: The Best of 3 Decades, 1962-1992. Playboy Enterprises, Inc. Staff. (Illus.). (Orig.). 24.95 (*0-87223-909-8*); pap. 9.95 (*0-87223-908-X*) Playboy Ent.

Playboy King: Carol II of Romania, 52. Paul D. Quinlan. LC 94-46945. (Contributions to the Study of World History Ser.: No. 52). 288p. 1995. 59.95 (*0-313-29519-0*, Greenwood Pr) Greenwood.

***Playboy King's Wife: Kings of the Outback.** Emma Darcy. (Harlequin Presents Ser.). 2000. mass mkt. 3.99 (*0-373-12116-4*, 1121169) Harlequin Bks.

Playboy Lover. Lindsay Armstrong. (Australians Ser.: Vol. 5). 1998. per. 4.50 (*0-373-82575-7*) Harlequin Bks.

Playboy Magazines: Price & Identification Guide. 5th rev. ed. Denis C. Jackson. 56p. 2000. pap. 5.95 (*1-888687-10-X*) Illust Collectors.

Playboy McCoy. Glenda Sanders. LC 97-10525. 216p. 1994. per. 2.99 (*0-373-25610-8*, 125610-6) Harlequin Bks.

Playboy of the West Indies. Mustapha Matura. 1988. pap. 6.95 (*0-88145-060-X*) Broadway Play.

Playboy of the Western World. John Millington Synge. 74p. 1990. pap. 6.95 (*0-85342-406-3*) Dufour.

Playboy of the Western World. John Millington Synge. 120p. (C). 1988. pap., student ed. write for info. (*0-413-51940-6*, A0215, Methuen Drama) Methn.

Playboy of the Western World. John Millington Synge. Ed. & Pref. by William-Alan Landes. 55p. 1996. pap. 7.00 (*0-88734-700-2*) Players Pr.

Playboy of the Western World. John Millington Synge. (Nick Hern Bks.). 128p. 1997. pap. 6.95 (*1-85459-210-6*) Theatre Comm.

Playboy of the Western World. 2nd ed. Ed. by Malcolm Kelsall. 1996. pap. 8.00 (*0-393-90081-9*) Norton.

Playboy of the Western World: And Two Other Irish Plays. John Millington Synge et al. LC 97-152828. 1997. pap. 9.95 (*0-14-018878-9*, Penguin Bks) Viking Penguin.

Playboy of the Western World & Other Plays. John Millington Synge. LC 96-70405. 1997. mass mkt. 5.95 (*0-451-52651-1*, Sig Classics) NAL.

Playboy of the Western World & Other Plays: Riders to the Sea; The Shadow of the Glen; The Tinker's Wedding; The Well of the Saints; The Playboy of the Western World; Deirdre of the Sorrows. John Millington Synge. Ed. & Intro. by Ann Saddlemyer. (Oxford World's Classics Ser.). 240p. 1995. text 49.95 (*0-19-812155-5*) OUP.

Playboy of the Western World & Other Plays: Riders to the Sea; The Shadow of the Glen; The Tinker's Wedding; The Well of the Saints; The Playboy of the Western World; Deirdre of the Sorrows. John Millington Synge. Ed. by Ann Saddlemyer. (Oxford World's Classics Ser.). 240p. 1998. pap. 9.95 (*0-19-283448-7*) OUP.

Playboy of the Western World & Other Plays: Riders to the Sea; The Shadow of the Glen; The Tinker's Wedding; The Well of the Saints; The Playboy of the Western World; Deirdre of the Sorrows. John Millington Synge & Ann Saddlemyer. (Oxford Drama Library). 240p. 1995. pap. 9.95 (*0-19-282611-5*) OUP.

Playboy of the Western World & Riders to the Sea. John Millington Synge. Ed. by William E. Hart. (Crofts Classics). 128p. 1966. pap. text 4.95 (*0-88295-097-5*) Harlan Davidson.

Playboy of the Western World & Riders to the Sea. John Millington Synge. (Unwin Paperbacks Ser.). 1962. pap. text 9.95 (*0-04-822041-8*) Routledge.

Playboy of the Western World & Riders to the Sea. John Millington Synge. LC 93-10455. (Thrift Editions Ser.). 64p. 1993. reprint ed. pap. 1.50 (*0-486-27562-0*) Dover.

Playboy of the Western World/Riders to the Sea: Curriculum Unit. Center for Learning Network Staff & John Millington Synge. (Drama Ser.). 75p. (YA). (gr. 11 up). 1994. spiral bd. 18.95 (*1-56077-302-2*) Ctr Learning.

Playboy of West World. abr. ed. John Millington Synge. LC 73-751026. 1988. audio 22.00 (*0-694-50920-5*, SWC 348, Caedmon) HarperAudio.

Playboy Presents: Dian Parkinson. Playboy Enterprises, Inc. Staff. (Illus.). 96p. (Orig.). 1993. pap. 5.95 (*0-87223-913-6*) Playboy Ent.

Playboy Presents International Playmates. Playboy Enterprises, Inc. Staff. (Playboy Presents Ser.). (Illus.). 112p. (Orig.). 1992. pap. 5.95 (*0-87223-900-4*, Playboy Pr) Playboy Ent.

Playboy Presents Playboy's Playmate Review. Playboy Enterprises, Inc. Staff. (Playboy Presents Ser.). (Illus.). 112p. (Orig.). 1992. pap. 5.95 (*0-87223-903-9*, Playboy Pr) Playboy Ent.

Playboy Prince. Nora Roberts. (NR Flowers Ser.: No. 39). 1994. per. 3.59 (*0-373-51039-X*, 1-51039-5) Silhouette.

Playboy Stories: The Best of 40 Years of Short Fiction. Ed. by Alice K. Turner. 1995. pap. 13.95 (*0-522-71177-4*, Plume) Dutton Plume.

Playboy's Baby: Expecting! Mary Lyons. (Presents Ser.: No. 2028). 1999. per. 3.75 (*0-373-12028-1*, 1-12028-6) Harlequin Bks.

Playboy's Bathing Beauties. Playboy Enterprises, Inc. Staff. (Illus.). 112p. (Orig.). 1992. pap. 5.95 (*0-87223-902-0*, Playboy Pr) Playboy Ent.

Playboy's Career Girls. Playboy Enterprises, Inc. Staff. (Illus.). 112p. (Orig.). 1992. pap. 5.95 (*0-87223-905-5*, Playboy Pr) Playboy Ent.

Playboy's Girls of Summer, '92. Playboy Enterprises, Inc. Staff. (Illus.). 112p. (Orig.). 1992. pap. 5.95 (*0-87223-904-7*, Playboy Pr) Playboy Ent.

Playboy's Girls of the World. Playboy Enterprises, Inc. Staff. (Illus.). 112p. (Orig.). 1992. pap. 5.95 (*0-87223-906-3*, Playboy Pr) Playboy Ent.

Playboy's Nudes. Playboy Enterprises, Inc. Staff. (Illus.). 112p. (Orig.). 1992. pap. 5.95 (*0-87223-907-1*, Playboy Pr) Playboy Ent.

***Playboy's Own Miss Prim: Bachelors of Shotgun Ridge, Vol. 834.** Windy Neff. (American Romance Ser.). 2000. mass mkt. 4.25 (*0-373-16834-9*, 1-16834-3) Harlequin Bks.

***Playboy's Proposition.** Miranda Lee. (Presents Ser.: Vol. 2128). 2000. mass mkt. 3.99 (*0-373-12128-8*, 1-12128-4) Harlequin Bks.

Playboy's Sisters. Playboy Enterprises, Inc. Staff. (Illus.). 112p. (Orig.). 1992. pap. 5.95 (*0-87223-901-2*, Playboy Pr) Playboy Ent.

***Playboy's Virgin.** Miranda Lee. (Presents Ser.: Bk. 2134). 2000. mass mkt. 3.99 (*0-373-12134-2*, 1-12134-2) Harlequin Bks.

Playbuilding. Errol Bray. LC 94-229338. 142p. 1994. pap. 13.95 (*0-435-08635-9*, 08635) Heinemann.

Playbuilding Shakespeare. Wendy Michaels. LC 96-15738. (Illus.). 175p. (C). 1997. pap. 19.95 (*0-521-57025-5*) Cambridge U Pr.

Playdays Colours & Shapes. Alison Boyle. (Illus.). 32p. (J). (ps-2). 1992. pap. 3.95 (*0-563-20887-2*, BBC-Parkwest) Parkwest Pubns.

Playdays Letters & Words. Alison Boyle. (Illus.). 32p. (J). (ps-2). 1992. pap. 3.95 (*0-563-20890-2*, BBC-Parkwest) Parkwest Pubns.

Playdays Numbers. Alison Boyle. (Illus.). 32p. (J). (ps-2). 1992. pap. 3.95 (*0-563-20889-9*, BBC-Parkwest) Parkwest Pubns.

P

An Asterisk (*) at the beginning of an entry indicates that the title is appearing for the first time.

Playdays Out & About. Alison Boyle. (Illus.). 32p. (J). (ps-2). 1992. pap. 3.95 (*0-563-20888-0*, BBC-Parkwest) Parkwest Pubns.

Played in Peoria. Jerry Klein. 176p. 1979. 11.95 (*0-933180-14-4*) Spoon Riv Poetry.

Player. Michael Tolkin. 208p. 1997. pap. 12.00 (*0-8021-3513-7*, Grove) Grove-Atltic.

Player. Michael Tolkin. 1992. pap. 10.00 (*0-394-23924-5*) Vin Bks.

Player Character Record Sheets. 2nd ed. TSR Hobbies, Inc. Staff. 1989. 9.95 (*0-88038-752-1*, Pub. by TSR Inc) Random.

***Player Character Record Sheets: A D&D Accessory.** (Dungeons & Dragons Ser.). (Illus.). 32p. (YA). 2000. pap. 9.95 (*0-7869-1642-7*) TSR Inc.

Player for a Moment: Notes from Fenway Park. John Hough, Jr. 350p. 1988. 17.95 (*0-15-172033-9*) Harcourt.

Player King: A Theme of Shakespeare's Histories. James Winny. LC 68-141502. 219 p. 1968. write for info. (*0-7011-1316-2*) Chatto & Windus.

Player of Games, The TP. Iain M. Banks. LC 96-35028. 288p. 1997. pap. 13.00 (*0-06-105356-2*, HarperPrism) HarpC.

Player Piano. Conrad Hilberry. LC 99-28003. 72p. 1999. pap. 12.95 (*0-8071-2380-3*); text 19.95 (*0-8071-2379-X*) La State U Pr.

Player Piano. Kurt Vonnegut, Jr. 352p. 1999. pap. 11.95 (*0-385-33378-1*) Dell.

Player-Piano Music of Conlon Nancarrow: An Analysis of Selected Studies. Philip Carlsen. LC 87-832360. (I.S.A.M. Monographs: No. 26). 86p. (Orig.). 1988. pap. 12.00 (*0-914678-29-9*) Inst Am Music.

Player Piano Servicing & Rebuilding. Arthur A. Reblitz. LC 85-3140. (Illus.). 224p. 1985. pap. 24.95 (*0-911572-40-6*, Vestal Pr) Madison Bks UPA.

Player Picker Software. Mark G. Catlin. 1993. pap. 24.95 (*0-9626834-3-4*) Soccer Bks.

***Player Profiles 2000.** 8th ed. STATS Inc. Staff. 600p. 1999. pap. 19.95 (*1-884064-73-6*) STATS.

Player Queen see Eleven Plays of William Butler Yeats

Player, the Rapture, the New Age: 3 Screenplays. Michael Tolkin. 240p. 1995. pap. 13.00 (*0-8021-3392-4*, Grove) Grove-Atltic.

Player under Three Reigns. Johnston Forbes-Robertson. LC 79-88537. (Illus.). 1972. 20.95 (*0-405-08525-7*) Ayer.

Players. Don DeLillo. (Vintage Contemporaries Ser.). 1989. pap. 12.00 (*0-679-72293-9*) Random.

***Players.** Terrance Dicks. 1999. mass mkt. 9.99 (*0-563-55573-4*) BBC Worldwide.

Players. Clay Reynolds. LC 97-4265. 432p. 1997. 24.00 (*0-7867-0407-1*) Carroll & Graf.

Players. Clay Reynolds. 448p. 1998. mass mkt. 5.99 (*0-7860-0598-X*, Pinncle Kensgtn) Kensgtn Pub Corp.

Players. Barbara Sherrod. 256p. 1989. mass mkt. 3.95 (*0-446-35870-3*, Pub. by Warner Bks) Little.

Players. Robbi Sommers. 192p. 1990. pap. 9.95 (*0-941483-73-8*) Naiad Pr.

***Players.** Joyce Sweeney. 225p. (YA). (gr. 7 up). 2000. 16.95 (*1-890817-54-6*, Pub. by Winslow Pr) Publishers Group.

Players: A Novel of the Young Shakespeare. Stephanie Cowell. LC 96-34987. 352p. (C). 1997. 24.00 (*0-393-04060-7*) Norton.

***Players: All the Universe a Stage & All the Men & Women Merely Players.** Joseph Fullan. 168p. 1999. per. 12.00 (*0-9672287-0-0*) Sevenlong.

Players: The Men Who Made Las Vegas. Ed. by Jack Sheehan. LC 97-24443. (Illus.). 240p. 1997. pap. 18.95 (*0-87417-306-X*) U of Nev Pr.

Players All: Performances in Contemporary Sport. Robert E. Rinehart. LC 98-19008. (Drama & Performance Studies). 240p. 1998. 35.00 (*0-253-33426-8*); pap. 15.95 (*0-253-21223-5*) Ind U Pr.

Player's & Fan's Guide to Pitching: It's Not Rocket Science. John Stuper. Ed. by Rob Rains & Sally T. Rains. (Illus.). 128p. 2001. pap. 17.95 (*0-911921-37-0*) Palmerston & Reed.

Players & Issues in International Aid. Paula Hoy. LC 97-35131. (Books on International Development). (Illus.). 190p. 1998. 45.00 (*1-56549-072-X*); pap. 21.95 (*1-56549-073-8*) Kumarian Pr.

P

Players & Their Personalities: Understanding People Who Get Involved in Addictive Relationships. Terence T. Gorski. 1989. pap. 8.00 (*0-8309-0553-7*, 17-0180-0) Herald Pub Hse.

Players & Vagabonds. Viola Roseboro. LC 70-101291. (Short Story Index Reprint Ser.). 1977. 21.95 (*0-8369-3228-5*) Ayer.

Players at Work. Morton Eustis. LC 79-84511. (Illus.). 120p. 1972. 20.95 (*0-405-08491-9*, Pub. by Blom Pubns) Ayer.

Players at Work: Acting According to the Actors. Morton Eustis. LC 67-23216. (Essay Index Reprint Ser.). 1977. 20.95 (*0-8369-0432-X*) Ayer.

Players Championship. Don Wade. 1998. 50.00 (*1-888531-03-7*) Amer Golfer.

Players Choice. Eugene V. McCaffrey & Roger A. McCaffrey. LC 86-19705. (Illus.). 240p. reprint ed. pap. 74.40 (*0-7837-1567-6*, 204185900024) Bks Demand.

Players' Choice! 17 Favorite Duets. Ed. by Carole Flatau. (Grand Duets for Piano Ser.). 112p. (Orig.). (YA). 1997. pap. text 12.95 (*0-7692-0107-5*) Wrner Bros.

Players Come Again. Amanda Cross. 240p. 1991. mass mkt. 5.99 (*0-345-36998-X*) Ballantine Pub Grp.

Players Come Again. large type ed. Amanda Cross. 1991. 27.99 (*0-7089-8615-3*, Charnwood) Ulverscroft.

Player's Guide to Greyhawk. Anne Brown. 1998. 13.95 (*0-7869-1248-0*, Pub. by TSR Inc) Random.

Player's Guide to Guitar Maintenance. Dave Burrluck. (Illus.). 84p. 1998. pap. 24.95 (*0-87930-549-5*) Miller Freeman.

Player's Guide to Tapani. Ed. by Fred E. Jandt. (Star Wars). 49p. 1997. 12.00 (*0-87431-507-7*) West End Games.

Player's Guide to the Sabbat. Steven C. Brown. (Vampire Ser.). (Illus.). 1994. per. 15.00 (*1-56504-042-2*, 2055) White Wolf.

Players in a Game. Dale Wasserman. 1989. pap. 5.25 (*0-8222-0898-9*) Dramatists Play.

Players in the Game: Destiny of Doom. Gyeorgos C. Hatonn. (Phoenix Journals). 215p. 1993. pap. 6.00 (*1-56935-022-1*) Phoenix Source.

Player's Manual for the Debtor Creditor Game. Lynn M. LoPucki. (Legal Exercise Ser.). 123p. (C). 1984. pap. text 17.50 (*0-314-89510-8*) West Pub.

Players of a Century: A Record of the Albany Stage. Henry P. Phelps. LC 78-91562. 1972. 30.95 (*0-405-08855-8*, Pub. by Blom Pubns) Ayer.

Players of a Century: A Record of the Albany Stage. Henry P. Phelps. 424p. 1993. reprint ed. lib. bdg. 99.00 (*0-7812-5284-9*) Rprt Serv.

Players of Cooperstown: Baseball's Hall of Fame. Consumer Guide Editors. LC 99-230474. 432p. 1998. mass mkt. 6.99 (*0-451-19525-6*, Sig) NAL.

Players of Cooperstown: Baseball's Hall of Fame. Publications International, Ltd. Editorial Staff. 1992. 29.95 (*1-56173-230-3*) Pubns Intl Ltd.

Players of Cooperstown: Baseball's Hall of Fame. Publications International, Ltd. Editorial Staff et al. (Illus.). 256p. 1992. 29.95 (*0-7853-0336-7*) Pubns Intl Ltd.

Players of God. David J. Knowles. LC 96-220311. 125p. 1995. pap. 9.95 (*0-9648480-0-7*) Stndpt Pubng.

Players of Shakespeare: Essays in Shakespearean Performance by Twelve Players with the Royal Shakespeare Company, No. 1. Ed. by Philip Brockbank. (Illus.). 192p. 1988. pap. text 20.95 (*0-521-36817-0*) Cambridge U Pr.

Players of Shakespeare: Further Essays in Shakespearean Performance by Players with the Royal Shakespeare Company, No. 2. Ed. by Russell Jackson & Robert Smallwood. 216p. (C). 1989. pap. text 23.95 (*0-521-38903-8*) Cambridge U Pr.

Players of Shakespeare: Further Essays in Shakespearean Performance by Players with the Royal Shakespeare Company, No. 3. Ed. by Russell Jackson & Robert Smallwood. LC 92-36175. (Illus.). 236p. (C). 1994. pap. text 20.95 (*0-521-47734-4*) Cambridge U Pr.

***Players of Shakespeare Vol. 4: Further Essays in Shakespearean Performance by Players with the Royal Shakespeare Company.** Ed. by Robert Smallwood. (Illus.). 222p. 2000. pap. write for info. (*0-521-79416-1*) Cambridge U Pr.

Players of Shakespeare 4: Further Essays in Shakespearian Performance by Players with the Royal Shakespeare Company. Ed. by Robert Smallwood. LC 98-16621. (Illus.). 222p. (C). 1999. text 44.95 (*0-521-55420-9*) Cambridge U Pr.

Players of the Present, 3 vols., 1 bk. John B. Clapp & Edwin F. Edgett. LC 72-91897. (Illus.). 432p. 1972. 32.95 (*0-405-08360-2*, Pub. by Blom Pubns) Ayer.

***Players, Opening & Tactics.** Nikolay Minev. 200p. 2000. pap. 19.95 (*1-879479-84-2*) ICE WA.

Player's Option. Rich Baker. 1996. 22.00 (*0-7869-0394-5*, Pub. by TSR Inc) Random.

Player's Option: Combat & Tactics; Advanced Dungeons & Dragons Rulebook. 2nd ed. L. Richard Baker. 1995. 20.00 (*0-7869-0096-2*, Pub. by TSR Inc) Random.

Player's Passion: Studies in the Science of Acting. Joseph R. Roach. LC 84-40059. (Illus.). 256p. 1986. 38.50 (*0-87413-265-7*) U Delaware Pr.

Player's Passion: Studies in the Science of Acting. Joseph R. Roach. (Theater & Dramatic Studies). 256p. (C). 1993. reprint ed. pap. text 17.95 (*0-472-08244-2*, 08244) U of Mich Pr.

Player's Primer. Joe Williams & Kathleen Williams. (Legendary Lives Ser.). (Illus.). 90p. (Orig.). 1989. pap. 11.95 (*0-685-30415-9*) Marquee Pr.

Players Rules: Time-Tested Secrets for Capturing Ms. Right Without Marrying Her! J Anthony Brown. 1999. pap. text 7.95 (*1-890194-08-5*) Pines One.

Players' Scepters: Fictions of Authority in the Restoration. Susan Staves. LC 78-24346. 379p. 1979. reprint ed. pap. 117.50 (*0-608-02137-7*, 206280600003) Bks Demand.

Players' Survival Guide: The OTE Players' Rulebook. John Sullivan et al. (Over the Edge Ser.). 80p. 1993. pap. 10.00 (*1-887801-02-2*, Atlas Games) Trident MN.

Player's Vendetta, 1 vol. John Lantigua. 272p. 1999. mass mkt. 5.99 (*0-451-19846-8*) NAL.

Player's Wench. large type ed. Marina Oliver. (Dales Large Print Ser.). 1994. pap. 18.99 (*1-85389-511-3*, Pub. by Mgna Lrg Print) Ulverscroft.

Playford Ball: 103 Early English Country Dances. Kate Van Winkle Keller & Genevieve Shimer. LC 90-81710. (Illus.). 136p. 1990. pap. 19.00 (*1-55652-091-3*) Pendragon NY.

Playford Ball: 103 Early English Country Dances As Interpreted by Cecil Sharp & His Followers. 2nd rev. ed. Kate Van Winkle Keller & Genevieve Shimer. LC 94-71847. (Illus.). 120p. 1994. pap. 19.00 (*0-917024-07-9*) Country Dance and Song.

Playful Activities for Powerful Presentations. Bruce Williamson. LC 93-60577. 198p. 1993. pap. 24.95 (*0-938586-77-7*) Whole Person.

***Playful & Awesome Timeless Stories, Vol. 2, set.** unabridged ed. Kumuda Reddy et al. (Timeless Wisdom Stories Ser.: Vol. 2). (J). (gr. 1-6). 1999. 18.95 incl. audio (*1-929297-13-0*) Samhita Prodns.

Playful Approaches to Serious Problems: Narrative Therapy with Children & Their Families. Jennifer Freeman et al. LC 96-52874. 288p. 1997. 35.00 (*0-393-70229-4*) Norton.

Playful Dolphins see Books for Young Explorers

***Playful Eye: An Album of Visual Delight.** Julian Rothenstein & Mel Gooding. LC 99-35698. (Illus.). 112p. 2000. pap. 19.95 (*0-8118-2696-1*) Chronicle Bks.

Playful Jungle Friends. Christopher Carrie. (Crayola Coloring Storybks.). (Illus.). 32p. (Orig.). (J). (ps). 1990. 1.99 (*0-86696-238-7*) Binney & Smith.

Playful Lady Penelope. Kasey Michaels. 192p. 1988. pap. 2.95 (*0-380-75297-2*, Avon Bks) Morrow Avon.

***Playful Learning Playful Teaching.** 1999. teacher ed. write for info. (*0-205-31868-1*) Allyn.

***Playful Learning, Playful Teaching.** Kieff. LC 98-53533. 249p. (C). 1999. pap. text 40.00 (*0-205-28547-3*, Macmillan Coll) P-H.

***Playful Origami.** Reiko Asou. (Illus.). 98p. 1998. 17.00 (*0-87040-827-5*) Japan Pubns USA.

Playful Pandas. Ed. by Jane H. Buxton. (Pop-Up Bks.: No. 6). (Illus.). (J). (ps-3). 1998. 16.00 (*0-87044-840-4*) Natl Geog.

Playful Parenting: Turning the Dilemma of Discipline into Fun & Games. Mark S. Weston & Denise C. Weston. LC 92-44229. (Illus.). 288p. 1993. pap. 15.95 (*0-87477-734-8*, Tarcher Putnam) Putnam Pub Group.

Playful Patchwork: Great Gift Ideas for Children. Ondori Publishing Company Staff. (Illus.). 84p. 1993. pap. 18.00 (*0-87040-913-1*) Kodansha.

***Playful Patchwork Projects.** Karinn Pearson & K. P. Kids & Co. Staff. LC 99-39262. 1999. 27.95 (*0-8069-2039-4*) Sterling.

Playful Penguins Independent Reader 5-Pack, EV Unit 3. (Networks Ser.). (J). (gr. 1). 1991. pap. 15.00 (*0-88106-723-7*, N136) Charlesbridge Pub.

Playful Perception: Choosing How to Experience Your World. Herbert L. Leff. LC 83-19876. (Illus.). 172p. (Orig.). 1984. 15.95 (*0-914525-01-8*); pap. 9.95 (*0-914525-00-X*) Waterfront Bks.

Playful Pete. Janet Tomita. (Illus.). 24p. 1998. boxed set 9.99 (*1-885101-92-9*) Writers Pr ID.

***Playful Pets.** Ana M. Larranaga. (Ana's Animals Bks.). (Illus.). (J). 2000. 3.95 (*1-58646-001-3*) Polka Dot.

Playful Piggy: Handpuppet & Story Book. (Read-Along Pals Ser.). (Illus.). 10p. (J). (gr. 2 up). 1998. bds. 9.95 (*1-888443-62-6*, Piggy Toes Pr) Intervisual Bks.

***Playful Puppy: Including Toy.** Jane Brett. (Animal Homes Ser.). (Illus.). (J). (ps-k). 1999. 5.98 (*0-7651-1698-7*) Smithmark.

Playful Revolution: Theatre & Liberation in Asia. Eugene Van Erven. LC 91-23369. (Drama & Performance Studies). (Illus.). 304p. 1992. text 41.95 (*0-253-36204-0*); pap. text 19.95 (*0-253-20729-0*, MB-729) Ind U Pr.

Playful Self-Discovery: A Findhorn Foundation Approach to Building Trust in Groups. David E. Platts. (Guidebooks for Growth Together). 128p. (Orig.). 1996. pap. 10.95 (*1-899171-06-1*, Pub. by Findhorn Pr) Words Distrib.

***Playful World: Interactive Toys & the Future of Imagination.** Mark Pesce. 256p. 2000. 24.00 (*0-345-43943-0*) Ballantine Pub Grp.

Playfulness in Japanese Art. Nobuo Tsuji. (Franklin D. Murphy Lectures: No. 7). (Illus.). 104p. 1986. 12.00 (*0-913689-23-8*) Spencer Muse Art.

Playgoing: An Essay. James Agate. LC 72-83870. 1972. reprint ed. 18.95 (*0-405-08191-X*, Pub. by Blom Pubns) Ayer.

Playgoing in Shakespeare's London. 2nd ed. Andrew Gurr. (Illus.). 325p. (C). 1996. pap. text 23.95 (*0-521-57449-8*) Cambridge U Pr.

Playground. rev. ed. Diane Wilmer. (Quality Time Easy Readers Ser.). (Illus.). 32p. (J). (gr. k-2). 1990. reprint ed. lib. bdg. 12.95 (*1-878363-10-7*) Forest Hse.

Playground, No. 12. Debbie Bailey. (Talk about Book Ser.: Vol. 12). (Illus.). 14p. (J). (ps). 1998. bds. 5.95 (*1-55037-511-3*, Pub. by Annick) Firefly Bks Ltd.

Playground Director. Jack Rudman. (Career Examination Ser.: C-590). 1994. pap. 34.95 (*0-8373-0590-X*) Nat Learn.

Playground Equipment: Do-It-Yourself, Indestructible, Practically Free. Lloyd Marston. LC 83-25565. (Illus.). 160p. 1984. pap. 29.95 (*0-89950-104-4*) McFarland & Co.

Playground Fun. Margie Burton et al. Ed. by Susan Evento. (Early Connections Ser.). 16p. (J). (gr. k-2). 1998. pap. text 4.25 (*1-892393-62-X*) Benchmark Educ.

Playground Fun. Sharon Gordon. LC 86-30854. (Illus.). 32p. (J). (gr. k-2). 1997. pap. 2.95 (*0-8167-0991-2*) Troll Communs.

Playground of Psychoanalytic Therapy. Jean Sanville. 312p. 1991. 45.00 (*0-88163-091-8*) Analytic Pr.

Playground of the Gods. Cathy Cash Spellman. 82p. 1996. 21.95 (*0-446-51701-1*) Warner Bks.

Playground Physics. Bob De Weese. (Science Mini Unit Intermediate Ser.). (Illus.). 16p. (J). (gr. 3-6). 1994. pap. text 5.95 (*1-55799-301-7*, EMC 841) Evan-Moor Edu Pubs.

Playground Politics: Understanding the Emotional Life of Your School-Age Child. Stanley L. Greenspan. (Illus.). 336p. 1994. pap. 14.00 (*0-201-40830-9*) Addison-Wesley.

Playground Popcorn Explosion, Vol. 17. (J). 1993. 12.99 incl. VHS (*0-310-58919-3*) Zondervan.

Playground Problem Solvers, Vol. 4413. Sandi Hill. Ed. by Joel Kupperstein. (Learn to Read Social Studies). (Illus.). 16p. (J). (ps-2). 1998. pap. 2.75 (*1-57471-336-1*, 4413) Creat Teach Pr.

Playground Propaganda: Poetry Anthology California State University Fullerton. Ken Kesey et al. Ed. & Intro. by Tatyana Melnikoff. (Illus.). 92p. (Orig.). (J). (gr. 2-7). 1992. pap. 10.00 (*0-9631219-0-1*) T Melnikoff.

Playground Push-Around: Bully & Victim Activity Book. Jim Boulden & Joan Boulden. Ed. by Evelyn M. Ward. (Illus.). 16p. (Orig.). (J). (gr. k-2). 1994. pap. 5.95 (*1-878076-36-1*) Boulden Pub.

Playground Safety: Proceedings of the 1995 International Conference. Ed. by Monty L. Christiansen. 211p. 1995. pap. 35.00 (*0-9650342-0-8*) PSU Ctr Hospitality.

Playground Sports: A Book of Ball Games. rev. ed. Marilyn Gould. (Illus.). 64p. (J). (gr. 2 up). 1999. pap. 10.95 (*0-9632305-2-2*) Allied Crafts.

***Playground Supervisor.** Raintree Steck-Vaughn Publishing Staff. LC 99-57362. (Workers You Know Ser.). (Illus.). 32p. 2000. lib. bdg. 22.83 (*0-8172-5593-1*) Raintree Steck-V.

Playground Technique & Playcraft. Arthur Leland & Lorna Leland. 1982. 23.95 (*0-8434-0432-9*, Pub. by McGrath NH) Ayer.

Playgrounds. Gail Gibbons. LC 84-19285. (Illus.). 32p. (J). (gr. k-3). 1985. lib. bdg. 16.95 (*0-8234-0553-2*) Holiday.

Playgrounds for Young Children: National Survey & Perspectives. Ed. by Sue C. Wortham & Joe L. Frost. (Illus.). 250p. (Orig.). 1990. pap. text 12.00 (*0-88314-488-3*, A4883) AAHPERD.

Playgrounds (Health Education), Men. Jack Rudman. (Teachers License Examination Ser.: T-47a). 1994. pap. 27.95 (*0-8373-8047-2*) Nat Learn.

Playgrounds (Health Education), Women. Jack Rudman. (Teachers License Examination Ser.: T-47b). 1994. pap. 27.95 (*0-685-49791-7*) Nat Learn.

Playgrounds (Kindergarten) Jack Rudman. (Teachers License Examination Ser.: T-48). 1994. pap. 27.95 (*0-8373-8048-0*) Nat Learn.

Playgrounds of Our Minds. John Barell. LC 79-27084. 207p. 1980. pap. 64.20 (*0-7837-7447-8*, 204903900010) Bks Demand.

Playgrounds of the Mind. Larry Niven. 704p. 1992. mass mkt. 5.99 (*0-8125-1695-8*, Pub. by Tor Bks) St Martin.

Playgrounds (Swimming) Jack Rudman. (Teachers License Examination Ser.: T-49). 1994. pap. 27.95 (*0-8373-8049-9*) Nat Learn.

Playgroup: Motherhood in 3 Variations. Nina Barrett. 1994. 21.00 (*0-671-74710-X*) S&S Trade.

Playgroup Handbook. 3rd ed. Laura P. Broad. 1991. pap. 12.95 (*0-312-05494-7*) St Martin.

Playhouse. Diane Alexander. LC 84-70527. (Illus.). 237p. 1984. 19.95 (*0-916329-00-3*) Dorleac-MacLeish.

Playhouse. Ada Mae Zimmerman. (Illus.). 32p. (J). 1980. pap. 2.90 (*0-7399-0072-2*, 2345) Rod & Staff.

Playhouse: Six Fantasy Plays for Children. Ed. by Joyce Doolittle. (Illus.). 206p. (J). (gr. 1-9). 1991. pap. 12.95 (*0-88995-028-8*, Pub. by Red Deer) Empire Pub Srvs.

Playhouse & Cosmos: Shakespearean Theater As Metaphor. Kent Van Den Berg. LC 82-49308. (Illus.). 256p. 1985. 32.50 (*0-87413-244-4*) U Delaware Pr.

Playhouses, Gazebos & Sheds. Percy W. Blandford. 160p. 1992. pap. 9.95 (*0-8306-3604-8*) McGraw-Hill Prof.

Playhouses You Can Build: Indoor & Backyard Designs. David Stiles & Jeanie Stiles. (Illus.). 128p. 1999. pap. 14.95 (*1-55209-315-8*) Firefly Bks Ltd.

***Playiing God: Rebellion & Grace in 1 & 2 Kings.** Dave Rogalsky. (Good Ground Ser.: No. 2, Pt. 6). 46p. 2000. pap. 5.95 (*0-87303-365-5*) Faith & Life.

Playin' Around: The Lives & Careers of Famous Session Musicians. Jennifer E. Pierce. LC 97-45588. 368p. 1998. 49.50 (*0-8108-3434-0*) Scarecrow.

Playin' Jazz on Broadway. (Jazz Ser.). 48p. 1989. pap. 6.95 (*0-7935-3409-7*, 00365135) H Leonard.

Playing. Shirley Hughes. LC 96-72499. (Illus.). 14p. (J). (ps). 1997. bds. 3.99 (*0-7636-0400-3*) Candlewick Pr.

***Playing.** Atsuko Morozumi. (Baby Bunny Board Bks.). (Illus.). 6p. (J). 2000. 4.99 (*0-375-80592-3*, Pub. by Knopf Bks Yng Read) Random.

Playing. Helen Oxenbury. (Oxenbury Board Bks.). (Illus.). 14p. (J). (ps up). 1981. bds. 4.95 (*0-671-42109-3*) Litle Simon.

Playing: A Kid's Curriculum. Sandra J. Stone. (Illus.). 240p. (Orig.). (J). (ps-1). 1992. pap. 12.95 (*0-673-36041-5*, GoodYrBooks) Addson-Wesley Educ.

***Playing a Virginia Moon.** Peter J. Neumann. 248p. (YA). (gr. 11-12). 1999. reprint ed. text 15.00 (*0-7881-6636-0*) DIANE Pub.

Playing Along: 37 Learning Activities Borrowed from Improvisational Theater. Izzy Gesell. LC 96-51245. 1997. 21.95 (*1-57025-141-X*) Whole Person.

Playing & Coaching Wheelchair Basketball. Ed Owen. LC 81-10456. (Illus.). 320p. 1982. pap. text 18.95 (*0-252-00867-7*) U of Ill Pr.

Playing & Exploring: Education Through the Discovery of Order. R. A. Hodgkin. 180p. 1985. pap. text 13.95 (*0-416-40300-X*, 9629) Routledge.

Playing & Learning Together. Eleanor Eley. (You & Your Baby Ser.). 35p. 1994. 2.65 (*0-9642374-0-7*) Corner Hlth.

Playing & Praying with God: Guided Meditations for Children. Rita A. Brink. LC 96-28991. 112p. (Orig.). (J). 1997. pap. 12.95 (*0-8091-3679-1*) Paulist Pr.

Playing & Reality. Clare Winnicott. 192p. 1982. pap. 18.99 (*0-415-03689-5*, Pub. by Tavistock) Routldge.

Playing & Reality. Donald Woods Winnicott. 1982. pap. 10.95 (*0-422-78310-2*, NO. 3741, Pub. by Tavistock) Routldge.

Playing & Teaching the Strings. Vincent Oddo. 189p. (C). 1979. pap. 20.25 (*0-534-00614-0*) Wadsworth Pub.

Playing & Teaching the Strings. 2nd ed. Vincent Oddo. LC 94-35620. 189p. 1994. 42.95 (*0-534-22971-9*) Wadsworth Pub.

Playing & Working Together: The Best Therapy Is Fun - A New Approach to Family Living. Malka Golden-Wolfe. 83p. 1991. student ed., ring bd. 50.00 (*0-9629782-0-5*) Sedona Child & Eld.

Playing Around: Scripts of One & Two Act Plays, Vol. I. B. B. Higgins. 70p. (Orig.). 1990. pap. text. write for info. (*0-937787-07-8*) Sun Star Pubns.

Playing As One. Thomas N. O'Neil & Alex Saltonstall. 103p. (Orig.). 1999. mass mkt. 4.99 (*1-55197-013-9*, Commonwealth) S Asia.

Playing at Home. John Light. (ITA.). (J). 1991. pap. 3.99 (*0-85953-600-9*) Childs Play.

Playing at Home. John Light. LC 90-34356. (Light Reading Ser.). 24p. (J). (gr. 4 up). 1991. pap. 1.99 (*0-85953-336-0*) Childs Play.

Playing at Love. Jennifer Taylor. (Romance Ser.: No. 418). 1999. mass mkt. 3.50 (*0-373-17418-7*, 1-17418-4) Harlequin Bks.

Playing at Sight for Violinists & Others in an Orchestra. Sydney Twinn. 52p. 1991. reprint ed. 59.00 (*0-7812-9305-7*) Rprt Serv.

Playing Away. Jenni Linden. 144p. (J). 1997. pap. 6.95 (*0-09-926322-X*, Pub. by Random) Trafalgar.

***Playing Away.** Adele Parks. 336p. 2000. 23.95 (*0-671-77543-X*, PB Hardcover) PB.

Playing Ball on Running Water: Living Morita Psychotherapy - The Japanese Way to Building a Better Life. David K. Reynolds. LC 84-8399. 160p. 1984. pap. 8.95 (*0-688-03913-8*, Quil) HarperTrade.

Playing Bar Chords. Ron Centola. Ed. by Aaron Stang. 68p. (Orig.). (C). 1985. pap. text 10.00 (*0-7692-1278-6*, EL02803) Wrner Bros.

Playing Bare. Dominic Champagne. Tr. by Shelley Tepperman. 112p. 1993. pap. 11.95 (*0-88922-335-1*, Pub. by Talonbks) Genl Dist Srvs.

Playing Basketball with the Viet Cong. Kevin Bowen. LC 94-30715. 63p. (Orig.). 1983. pap. 10.95 (*1-880684-20-9*) Curbstone.

Playing Better Baseball. Rick Wolff. LC 96-48349. (Illus.). 208p. (Orig.). 1997. pap. 15.95 (*0-87322-936-3*, PWOL0936) Human Kinetics.

Playing Bit Parts in Shakespeare. LC 97-43666. 296p. (C). (gr. 13). 1998. pap. 22.99 (*0-415-18242-5*) Routledge.

Playing Blackjack As a Business. Lawrence Revere. (Illus.). 192p. 1995. pap. 15.95 (*0-8184-0064-1*, Citadel Pr) Carol Pub Group.

Playing Blackjack As a Business. Lawrence Revere. 192p. 1999. reprint ed. 27.95 (*0-7351-0090-X*) Replica Bks.

Playing Blackjack As a Business. rev. ed. 1977. pap. 14.95 (*0-8184-0063-3*) Paul Mann.

Playing Boal: Theatre, Therapy, Activism. Jan Cohen-Cruz. Ed. by Mady Schutzman. LC 93-12884. 256p. (C). (gr. 13). 1993. pap. 24.99 (*0-415-08608-6*) Routledge.

***Playing Botticelli.** Liza Nelson. LC 99-47292. 288p. 2000. 23.95 (*0-399-14601-6*, Marion Wood) Putnam Pub Group.

Playing by the Rules. large type ed. Kathryn Ross. 1996. 11.50 (*0-7505-0855-8*, Pub. by Mgna Lrg Print) Ulverscroft.

Playing by the Rules: A Philosophical Examination of Rule-Based Decision Making in Law & in Life. Frederick F. Schauer. (Clarendon Law Ser.). 272p. 1993. reprint ed. pap. text 24.95 (*0-19-825831-3*) OUP.

Playing by the Rules: American Trade Power & Diplomacy in the Pacific. Michael P. Ryan. LC 94-32278. 320p. 1995. 42.50 (*0-87840-579-8*) Georgetown U Pr.

Playing by the Rules: Sport, Society, & the State. John Wilson. LC 93-19671. 430p. 1994. text 39.95 (*0-8143-2107-0*) Wayne St U Pr.

Playing by the Rules: The Mitterrand Government & the International Economy. Elizabeth Doherty. (Political Economy of Global Interdependence Ser.). (C). 2000. pap. 49.95 (*0-8133-2992-2*) Westview.

Playing Card Price Guide. Shami Maxwell & Kathryn Maxwell. (Illus.). 128p. 1992. lib. bdg. 12.95 (*0-940649-11-X*) Parnell Pub.

Playing Cards: Fournier Museum. Felix A. Fournier. (Illus.). 344p. 1982. 80.00 (*0-88079-026-1*, BK49) US Games Syst.

Playing Cards: Predicting Your Future. Hali Morag. (Astrology Complete Guide Ser.). (Illus.). 112p. 1998. pap. 6.95 (*965-494-040-X*, Pub. by Astrolog Pub) Assoc Pubs Grp.

Playing Cards & Tarots. George Beal. 1989. pap. 25.00 (*0-85263-924-4*, Pub. by Shire Pubns) St Mut.

Playing Cards Around the World see Card Games Around the World

Playing-Cards of Spain: A Guide for Historians & Collectors. Trevor Denning. LC 96-42278. (Illus.). 180p. 1996. 49.50 (*0-8386-3747-7*) Fairleigh Dickinson.

Playing Cards II: Fournier Museum. Felix A. Fournier. (Illus.). 112p. 1992. 50.00 (*0-88079-039-3*, BK82) US Games Syst.

Playing Catch with My Mother: A Memoir of Coming to Manhood When all the Rules Have Changed. Greg Lichtenberg. LC 98-42355. 272p. 1999. 23.95 (*0-553-09982-5*) Bantam.

***Playing Catch with My Mother: Coming to Manhood When All the Rules Have Changed.** Greg Lichtenberg. 256p. 2000. pap. 14.95 (*0-553-37802-3*) Bantam.

Playing Catholic. Veronica Brady. 60p. (C). 1991. pap. 11.95 (*0-86819-256-2*, Pub. by Currency Pr) Accents Pubns.

Playing Chess. S. Caldwell. (Usborne Guides Ser.). (Illus.). 64p. (J). (gr. 5-9). 1987. pap. 7.95 (*0-7460-0135-5*) EDC.

Playing Chess. S. Caldwell. (Usborne Guides Ser.). (Illus.). 64p. (J). (gr. 5 up). 1999. lib. bdg. 15.95 (*0-88110-288-1*) EDC.

Playing Chess with the Heart: Beatrice Wood at 100. Marlene Wallace. LC 93-25852. (Illus.). 72p. 1994. 14.95 (*0-8118-0607-3*) Chronicle Bks.

Playing Chord Progressions. J. Jones. 48p. 1993. pap. 5.95 (*0-7935-2750-3*, 00696518) H Leonard.

Playing Computer Chess. Al Lawrence. LC 98-130578. (Illus.). 144p. 1998. 12.95 (*0-8069-0717-7*) Sterling.

Playing Contemporary Scenes: 31 Famous Scenes & How to Play Them. Ed. by Gerald L. Ratliff & Theodore O. Zapel. LC 96-36394. (Illus.). 368p. (YA). (gr. 9 up). 1996. pap. 16.95 (*1-56608-025-8*, B100) Meriwether Pub.

Playing Corners, Counting Points, Understanding Shape & Other Amateur Go Topics. Stephen F. Likins. (Illus.). 80p. Date not set. pap. 24.95 (*0-9671321-0-X*) Stevel Enterp.

Playing Cowboys: Low Culture & High Art in the Western. Robert M. Davis. LC 91-34453. 192p. 1994. pap. 11.95 (*0-8061-2627-2*) U of Okla Pr.

Playing Cure: Individualized Play Therapy for Specific Childhood Problems. Ed. by Heidi G. Kaduson et al. 1997. 55.00 (*0-7657-0021-2*) Aronson.

Playing Daddy. Lorraine Carroll. LC 96-7298. 251p. 1996. per. 3.99 (*0-373-24020-1*, 1-24020-9) Silhouette.

Playing Darts with a Rembrandt: Public & Private Rights in Cultural Treasures. Joseph L. Sax. LC 99-26356. (Illus.). 272p. 1999. 32.50 (*0-472-11044-6*, 11044) U of Mich Pr.

Playing Dead. R. G. Belsky. 345p. 1999. mass mkt. 6.50 (*0-380-79069-6*, Avon Bks) Morrow Avon.

Playing Dead: A Hollywood Mystery. Lindsay Maracotta. LC 98-27438. 288p. 1999. 24.00 (*0-688-15867-6*, Wm Morrow) Morrow Avon.

Playing Director: A Handbook for the Beginning Director. Rick DesRochers. LC 95-4974. 144p. 1995. pap. 13.95 (*0-435-08668-5*, 08668) Heinemann.

Playing Doctor: Who Will Control Medical Practice in the Year 2000? Emily Friedman. (Papers: No. 9). 36p. 1989. 5.00 (*0-934459-57-6*) United Hosp Fund.

Playing Dolly: Technocultural Formations, Fantasies, & Fictions of Assisted Reproduction. Ed. by E. Ann Kaplan & Susan M. Squier. LC 98-48454. 256p. (C). 1999. text 50.00 (*0-8135-2648-5*); pap. text 22.00 (*0-8135-2649-3*) Rutgers U Pr.

Playing Fair. Shelly Nielsen. Ed. by Rosemary Wallner. LC 92-73043. (Values Matter Ser.). (J). 1992. lib. bdg. 14.98 (*1-56239-065-1*) ABDO Pub Co.

Playing Favorites, Bk. 2. Steven Kroll. (Hit & Run Gang Ser.: 4). 80p. (J). (gr. 4-7). 1992. pap. 3.50 (*0-380-76409-1*) Morrow Avon.

Playing Favorites: Gifted Education & the Disruption of Community. Mara Sapon-Shevin. LC 93-23451. 275p. (C). 1994. pap. text 19.95 (*0-7914-1980-0*) State U NY Pr.

Playing Fields & Sports Turf. V. I. Stewart & R. B. Gooch. (Illus.). 320p. (gr. 13). 1993. text 72.95 (*0-419-14950-3*, A9476) Chapman & Hall.

Playing for Dollars: Labor Relations & the Sports Business. Paul D. Staudohar. LC 95-49456. (ILR Press Book). (Illus.). 232p. 1996. pap. text 16.95 (*0-8014-8342-5*) Cornell U Pr.

Playing for England. David Scott. LC 89-82481. (Illus.). 64p. (Orig.). 1990. pap. 13.95 (*1-85224-071-7*, Pub. by Bloodaxe Bks) Dufour.

Playing for High Stakes: The Men, Money & Power of Corporate Wives. Elaine Denholtz. LC 86-2020. 210p. 1985. 16.95 (*0-88191-030-9*) Freundlich.

***Playing for Keeps.** Nina Alexander. (Love Stories Ser.). 192p. (YA). (gr. 7-12). 1999. mass mkt. 4.50 (*0-553-49292-6*) Bantam.

***Playing for Keeps.** C. J. Anders. (Dawson's Creek Ser.: No. 10). 192p. (YA). (gr. 8 up). 2000. mass mkt. 5.99 (*0-671-77536-7*, Pocket Pulse) PB.

Playing for Keeps. Allison Estes. (J). 1997. per. 3.99 (*0-671-00434-4*, Minstrel Bks) PB.

Playing for Keeps. Deborah Gordon. 1980. pap. 1.50 (*0-373-58050-9*, Harlequin) Harlequin Bks.

Playing for Keeps. Donald Junkins. LC 91-8498. 84p. 1991. 16.00 (*0-89924-074-7*); pap. 8.00 (*0-89924-073-9*) Lynx Hse.

Playing for Keeps. Jack Kendall. 224p. (Orig.). 1989. pap. 3.95 (*0-380-75756-7*, Avon Bks) Morrow Avon.

Playing for Keeps. Stevie Rios. 256p. 1995. pap. 10.99 (*1-883061-07-5*) Rising AZ.

Playing for Keeps. Stephanie Salinas. 1999. pap. text 8.95 (*1-885478-91-7*, Pub. by Genesis Press) BookWorld.

Playing for Keeps: A History of Early Baseball. Warren Goldstein. LC 89-42876. (Illus.). 200p. 1991. reprint ed. pap. text 14.95 (*0-8014-9924-0*) Cornell U Pr.

***Playing for Keeps: A Novel.** Peter Fowler. 300p. 1999. 22.95 (*0-929712-06-4*) Huntington Pr.

Playing for Keeps: Biblical Keys to Preservation & Increase. Tim Gilligan. LC 96-68106. 200p. 1996. pap. text 9.99 (*1-57502-164-1*, P0768) Morris Pubng.

Playing for Keeps: How the World's Most Aggressive & Admired Companies Use Core Values to Manage, Energize & Organize Their People & Promote, Advance & Achieve Their Corporate Missions. Frederick G. Harmon. LC 95-45410. 288p. 1996. 27.95 (*0-471-59847-X*) Wiley.

Playing for Keeps: Michael Jordan & the World He Made. David Halberstam. LC 99-41931. 448p. 2000. pap. 14.00 (*0-7679-0444-3*) Broadway BDD.

Playing for Keeps: Michael Jordan & the World He Made. David Halberstam. LC 98-49964. (Illus.). 352p. 1999. 24.95 (*0-679-41562-9*) Random.

Playing for Keeps Vol. 2: Supporting Children's Play. Ed. by Amy L. Phillips. LC 96-35870. (Topics in Early Childhood Education Ser.). 192p. (Orig.). (C). 1996. pap. 14.95 (*1-884834-29-9*) Redleaf Pr.

Playing for Knight: My Six Seasons with Coach Knight. Steve Alford & John Garrity. 304p. 1990. pap. 9.95 (*0-671-72441-X*, Fireside) S&S Trade Pap.

Playing for Love. Jilly Johnson. 288p. 2000. 22.50 (*0-684-86827-X*) S&S Trade.

Playing for Profit: How Digital Entertainment Is Making Big Business Out of Child's Play. Alice LaPlante & Rich Seidner. LC 98-33166. (Upside Magazine Ser.). 287p. 1999. 29.95 (*0-471-29614-7*) Wiley.

Playing for Profit: How Digital Entertainment Is Making Big Business Out of Child's Play. Peter Walker. LC 98-155526. v, 93 p. 1997. write for info. (*1-86106-528-0*, Pub. by Minerva Pr) Unity Dist.

Playing for Real: Exploring the World of Child Therapy & the Inner Worlds of Children. Richard Bromfield. LC 97-13376. 256p. 1997. reprint ed. pap. 35.00 (*0-7657-0129-4*, RA1) Aronson.

Playing for Scotland: A History of the Scottish Stage, 1715-1965. Donald Campbell. LC 96-172387. 168p. 1996. pap. 40.00 (*1-873644-57-4*, Pub. by Mercat Pr Bks) St Mut.

Playing for Stakes: German-Language Drama in Social Context. Ed. by Anna K. Kuhn & Barbara D. Wright. LC 93-4300. 256p. 1994. 49.50 (*0-85496-949-7*) Berg Pubs.

Playing for the Ashes. Elizabeth George. LC 93-50153. 675p. 1995. mass mkt. 7.50 (*0-553-57251-2*, Crimeline) Bantam.

Playing for Their Lives: Helping Troubled Children Through Play Therapy. Dorothy Singer. 240p. 1993. 27.95 (*0-02-928903-3*) Free Pr.

Playing for Thrills: A Mystery. Wang Shuo. Tr. by Howard Goldblatt from CHI. LC 96-32148. 256p. 1997. 23.00 (*0-688-13046-1*, Wm Morrow) Morrow Avon.

Playing for Thrills: A Mystery. Wang Shuo. Tr. by Howard Goldblatt. LC 96-32148. 325p. 1998. pap. 12.95 (*0-14-026971-1*) Viking Penguin.

Playing for Time. Barbara Bretton. (Men at Work Ser.: Vol. 46). 1998. mass mkt. 4.50 (*0-373-81058-X*, 1-81058-9) Harlequin Bks.

Playing for Time. Fania Fenelon & Marcelle Routier. Tr. by Judith Landry et al. LC 97-22168. ix, 262p. 1997. pap. 17.95 (*0-8156-0494-7*) Syracuse U Pr.

Playing for Time. Arthur Miller. 1985. 5.95 (*0-87129-267-X*, P59) Dramatic Pub.

***Playing from Memory.** David Milofsky. LC 99-11759. 270p. 1999. reprint ed. pap. 14.95 (*0-87081-526-1*) Univ Pr Colo.

Playing from the Heart. Roger Crawford & Michael Bowker. 200p. 1994. 17.95 (*1-55958-018-6*) Prima Pub.

***Playing from the Heart: A Portrait in Courage.** rev. ed. Roger Crawford. LC 97-26575. (Illus.). 224p. 1998. pap., per. 14.00 (*0-7615-0440-0*) Prima Pub.

***Playing from the Rough: Women of the LPGA Hall of Fame.** Jackie Williams. (Illus.). 268p. 1999. pap. 24.95 (*1-884724-15-9*) Women Diversity.

Playing Games. Jana Ellis. LC 88-12389. (Merivale Mall Ser.). 160p. (YA). (gr. 7 up). 1988. pap. text 2.50 (*0-8167-1358-8*) Troll Communs.

***Playing Games.** Donna Jo Napoli. LC 99-87418. (Angelwings Ser.: No. 8). (Illus.). 80p. (J). (gr. 2-5). 2000. pap. 3.99 (*0-689-83208-7*) Aladdin.

Playing Games: Zoa, the Greek Fertility Goddess, Shoots for the Gold. Jay Critchley. (Illus.). 40p. (Orig.). 1995. pap. 7.95 (*0-9644145-2-X*) Parfait de Cocoa.

Playing God. Maralene Wesner & Miles E. Wesner. 82p. 1997. pap. 6.95 (*0-936715-33-2*, 123) Diversity Okla.

Playing God. Sarah Zettel. LC 98-19556. 417p. 1998. 22.00 (*0-446-52322-4*, Pub. by Warner Bks) Little.

Playing God. Sarah Zettel. 464p. 1999. mass mkt. 6.99 (*0-446-60758-4*, Pub. by Warner Bks) Little.

Playing God? Dissecting Biomedical Ethics & Manipulating the Body. Ed. by R. C. Sproul, Jr. LC 96-35213. 96p. (gr. 11). 1997. pap. 8.99 (*0-8010-5725-6*) Baker Bks.

Playing God? Genetic Determinism & Human Freedom. Ted Peters. 218p. (C). 1996. pap. 19.99 (*0-415-91522-8*) Routledge.

Playing God? Genetic Determinism & Human Freedom. Ted Peters. 218p. (C). 1996. 70.00 (*0-415-91521-X*) Routledge.

Playing God: Medieval Mysteries on the Modern Stage. John R. Elliott, Jr. (Studies in Early English Drama). 186p. 1989. text 45.00 (*0-8020-5606-7*) U of Toronto Pr.

Playing God: Seven Fateful Moments When Great Men Met to Change the World. Charles L. Mee, Jr. 269p. 1999. reprint ed. text 23.00 (*0-7881-6343-4*) DIANE Pub.

Playing God . . . & Other Games. Roy Gilligan. LC 92-74052. (Pat Riordan Mystery Ser.). 180p. (Orig.). 1993. pap. 8.95 (*0-9626136-4-9*) Brendan Bks.

Playing God in Yellowstone: The Destruction of America's First National Park. Alston Chase. (Illus.). 480p. 1987. pap. 16.00 (*0-15-672036-1*, Harvest Bks) Harcourt.

Playing God's Melodies: The Psalms in Our Lives. Jane M. Milward. 160p. 1996. pap. 39.95 (*0-85439-465-6*, Pub. by St Paul Pubns) St Mut.

***Playing Grandma's Games.** Karen Arnold. LC 00-190332. (Illus.). 160p. 2000. pap. 11.95 (*1-890437-47-6*) Western Reflections.

Playing Great Songs. pap. 14.95 incl. audio compact disk (*0-7935-4389-4*, 00290025) H Leonard.

Playing Great Songs: Elementary Piano Solos. 16p. 1991. pap. 4.95 (*0-7935-0593-3*, 00290269) H Leonard.

***Playing Guitar.** Terry Burrows. LC 00-8783. (Keep It Simple Ser.). (Illus.). 352p. 2000. pap. write for info. (*0-7894-5979-5*, Pub. by DK Pub Inc) Pub Resources Inc.

Playing Guitar in a Jazz Big Band for the Beginning Jazz Guitarist. 52p. 1995. pap. 14.95 (*0-7935-4958-2*, 00030025) H Leonard.

Playing Happy Families. Julian Symons. 288p. 1995. mass mkt. 5.50 (*0-446-40412-8*, Pub. by Warner Bks) Little.

Playing Hardball: The Dynamics of Baseball Folk Speech. Lawrence Frank. LC 83-48834. 145p. (Orig.). (C). 1984. text 9.60 (*0-8204-0061-0*) P Lang Pubng.

Playing Haydn for the Angel of Death. Bill Holm. (Winter Book Ser.: Vol. 9). (Illus.). 25p. 1997. 195.00 (*1-879832-14-3*) MN Ctr Book Arts.

Playing Hide & Seek: A Non-Churchgoer's Path to Finding God. Michael Elliott. LC 96-14321. 112p. 1996. pap. 10.00 (*1-57312-057-X*) Smyth & Helwys.

Playing in the Asphalt Garden: An Anthology. Philip Arima et al. LC 95-189170. 128p. pap. 14.99 (*1-895837-20-0*) Insomniac.

Playing in the Band: An Oral & Visual Portrait of the Grateful Dead. David Gans & Peter Simon. LC 84-52537. (Illus.). 192p. 1985. pap. 16.95 (*0-312-61630-9*) St Martin.

Playing in the Band: An Oral & Visual Portrait of the Grateful Dead. David Gans & Peter Simon. (Illus.). 224p. 1996. pap. 18.95 (*0-312-14391-5*) St Martin.

Playing in the Band: My First Activity Book. (My First Activity Ser.). (J). 1997. 1.09 (*0-307-09339-5*, 09339, Goldn Books) Gldn Bks Pub Co.

Playing in the Dark. Kent Thompson. 144p. 1990. pap. 12.95 (*0-919627-83-8*, Pub. by Quarry Pr) LPC InBook.

Playing in the Dark: Whiteness & the Literary Imagination. Toni Morrison. LC 91-39671 . (Massey Lectures). xiii, 91p. 1992. 14.95 (*0-674-67377-8*) HUP.

Playing in the Dark: Whiteness & the Literary Imagination. Toni Morrison. LC 92-50581. xiii, 91 p. 1993. pap. 10.00 (*0-679-74542-4*) Vin Bks.

Playing in the Digital Funhouse. Michael Cuthbertson. LC 94-37487. 250p. 1994. pap. 21.95 (*1-55828-368-4*, MIS Pr) IDG Bks.

Playing in the Zone. Andrew Cooper. LC 98-5799. 1998. pap. 13.00 (*1-57062-151-9*, Pub. by Shambhala Pubns) Random.

***Playing Indian.** Philip J. Deloria. LC 97-30936. (Yale Historical Publications). (Illus.). 264p. 1998. 30.00 (*0-300-07111-6*) Yale U Pr.

Playing Indian. Philip Joseph Deloria. (Illus.). 264p. 1999. pap. 13.95 (*0-300-08067-0*) Yale U Pr.

Playing Inside & Out: How to Promote Social Growth & Learning in Young Children Including the Developmentally Delayed Child. Thomas D. Yawkey et al. LC 85-51121. 189p. 1985. 24.95 (*0-87762-419-4*) Scarecrow.

Playing Is Learning see Curriculum Written for Partners in Parenting Education

Playing Is the Thing: Learning to Act Through Games & Exercises. 2nd rev. ed. Anita Jesse. LC 96-61374. 208p. 1996. pap. 16.95 (*0-9639655-1-4*) Wolf Creek CA.

Playing It by Ear: Literary Essays & Reviews. William H. Pritchard. LC 94-12255. 288p. (C). 1994. pap. 18.95 (*0-87023-948-1*); lib. bdg. 45.00 (*0-87023-947-3*) U of Mass Pr.

***Playing It by Heart: Taking Care of Yourself No Matter What.** Melody Beattie. LC 99-58620. 250p. 1999. pap. text 15.00 (*1-56838-338-X*) Hazelden.

Playing It Safe. Margie Burton et al. Ed. by Susan Evento. (Early Connections Ser.). 16p. (J). (gr. k-2). 1998. pap. 4.25 (*1-892393-72-7*) Benchmark Educ.

Playing It Safe: Milady's Guide to Decontamination, Sterilization, & Personal Protection. Sheldon R. Chesky et al. LC 93-36024. (Career Development Ser.). 1993. pap. 15.75 (*1-56253-179-4*) Thomson Learn.

Playing It Safe with Mr. See-More Safety: Let's Learn about Bicycle Safety, Vol. 2. Janis Rafael. (Illus.). 24p. (Orig.). (J). (ps-8). Date not set. write for info. (*0-9655604-1-4*) Safewrld Pub.

Playing It Safe with Mr. See-More Safety: Let's Rap & Rhyme. large type ed. Janis Rafael. LC 96-71670. (Illus.). 84p. (Orig.). (J). (gr. k-6). 1997. pap. 14.95 (*0-9655604-0-6*) Safewrld Pub.

Playing It Straight: Personal Conversations on Recovery, Transformation & Success. David Dodd. 300p. 1996. pap. 12.95 (*1-55874-388-X*) Health Comm.

Playing Joan: Actresses on the Challenge of Shaw's Saint Joan. Holly Hill. LC 87-10051. (Illus.). 272p. (Orig.). 1987. pap. 10.95 (*0-930452-64-X*) Theatre Comm.

***Playing Juliet/Casting Othello.** Caleen S. Jennings. 95p. 1999. pap. 5.60 (*0-87129-924-0*, P86) Dramatic Pub.

Playing Keyboard Bass Lines. John Valerio. 96p. 1998. otabind 14.95 incl. audio compact disk (*0-7935-6927-3*) H Leonard.

***Playing, Learning, Praying: Parish Tools for Gathering Families.** Kathleen R. O'Connell. LC 99-64812. 64p. 2000. 9.95 (*0-7648-0551-7*) Liguori Pubns.

***Playing Life.** Sebastian Kusenberg. (Illus.). 96p. 1999. 35.00 (*3-931321-56-8*, Pub. by Jovis Verlags) Dist Art Pubs.

Playing Me with Your Tongue: And Other Poetry of Passion, Pleasure & Pain. Gwendolyn L. Evans & Norma I. Fortinberry. Ed. by Imani Kenyatta. LC 96-72120. 112p. (Orig.). 1997. pap. 13.95 (*1-886580-56-1*) Pinnacle-Syatt.

***Playing Music on Your PC.** DK Publishing Staff. 72p. 2000. pap. 6.95 (*0-7894-6372-5*) DK Pub Inc.

Playing My Part. Frida Leider. Tr. by Charles Osborne. LC 77-26171. (Music Reprint Ser.: 1978). (Illus.). 1978. reprint ed. lib. bdg. 32.50 (*0-306-77535-2*) Da Capo.

Playing Nice: Politics & Apologies in Women's Sports. Mary J. Festle. LC 96-4739. (Illus.). 400p. 1996. 31.50 (*0-231-10162-7*) Col U Pr.

Playing Off the Rail. David McCumber. LC 95-6955. 384p. 1997. pap. 12.50 (*0-380-72923-7*, Avon Bks) Morrow Avon.

Playing on the Keys, Prep Bk. C. large type ed. Lynne Cimorelli. (Illus.). 88p. (Orig.). (J). (gr. 1-5). 1997. pap. text 10.95 (*0-9657845-2-5*) Alex Pub.

Playing on the Keys, Prep Bk. A. large type ed. Lynne Cimorelli. (Illus.). 102p. (Orig.). (J). (gr. 1-5). 1997. pap. text 10.95 (*0-9657845-0-9*) Alex Pub.

Playing on the Keys, Prep Bk. B. large type ed. Lynne Cimorelli. (Illus.). 94p. (Orig.). (J). (gr. 1-5). 1997. pap. text 10.95 (*0-9657845-1-7*) Alex Pub.

Playing on the Mother-Ground: Cultural Routines for Children's Development. David F. Lancy. (Culture & Human Development Ser.). 240p. 1996. pap. text 21.00 (*1-57230-215-1*, 0215); lib. bdg. 39.95 (*1-57230-142-2*) Guilford Pubns.

Playing Out of the Deep Woods: Stories. G. W. Hawkes. LC 94-36965. 152p. (C). 1995. pap. 17.95 (*0-8262-0988-2*) U of Mo Pr.

P

An Asterisk (*) at the beginning of an entry indicates that the title is appearing for the first time.

Playing Out the Empire: Ben-Hur & Other Toga Plays & Films, 1883-1908. A Critical Anthology. David Mayer. (Illus.). 336p. (C). 1994. text 65.00 (*0-19-811990-9*) OUP.

Playing Place. Muyrna Combellack. (C). 1989. 50.00 (*1-85022-041-7*, Pub. by Dyllansow Truran) St Mut.

Playing Politics: The Nightmare Continues. Michael Laver. LC 97-7910. (Illus.). 182p. 1997. pap. 11.95 (*0-19-285321-X*) OUP.

***Playing Poohsticks: Die cut Board Book.** abr. ed. A. A. Milne, pseud. (Illus.). 12p. (J). (ps-1). 1999. bds. 6.99 (*0-525-46198-1*, Dutton Child) Peng Put Young Read.

Playing Possum: Riddles about Kangaroos, Koalas & Other Marsupials. (Illus.). (J). (ps-3). 1995. pap. text 3.95 (*0-8225-9674-1*, Lerner Publctns) Lerner Pub.

Playing Possum: Riddles about Kangaroos, Koalas, & Other Marsupials. John Jansen. LC 94-19553. (You Must Be Joking! Ser.). (Illus.). 32p. (J). (gr. 1-4). 1995. lib. bdg. 14.60 (*0-8225-2346-9*, Lerner Publctns) Lerner Pub.

***Playing Prodigals Home.** Quin Sherrer & Ruthanne Garlock. 2000. pap. 11.99 (*0-8307-2563-6*, Regal Bks) Gospel Lght.

Playing Recorder Sonatas: Technique & Interpretation. Anthony Rowland-Jones. (Illus.). 240p. (C). 1992. 59.95 (*0-19-879002-3*); pap. text 29.95 (*0-19-879001-5*) OUP.

***Playing Right Field.** Willy Welch. (Illus.). 32p. (J). (ps-2). 2000. pap. 5.99 (*0-439-13994-5*) Scholastic Inc.

Playing Robin Hood: The Legend As Performance in Five Centuries. Ed. by Lois Potter. LC 97-43695. (Illus.). 256p. 1998. 42.50 (*0-87413-663-6*) U Delaware Pr.

Playing Roulette As a Business: A Professional's Guide to Beating the Wheel. R. J. Smart. LC 96-25072. (Illus.). 120p. 1996. pap. 12.95 (*0-8184-0585-6*) Carol Pub Group.

***Playing Safe: Science & the Environment.** Jonathon Porritt. LC 99-66984. (Prospects for Tomorrow Ser.). 112p. 2000. pap. 12.95 (*0-500-28073-8*, Pub. by Thames Hudson) Norton.

Playing Scenes: A Sourcebook for Performers. Gerald L. Ratliff. Ed. by Theodore O. Zapel. LC 93-11356. (Illus.). 440p. (Orig.). (YA). (gr. 9 up). 1993. pap. 14.95 (*0-916260-89-5*, B109) Meriwether Pub.

Playing Scenes from Classic Literature: Short Dramatizations of the World's Most Famous Literature. Ed. by Joellen Bland. LC 96-36386. (YA). (gr. 9 up). 1996. pap. 14.95 (*1-56608-024-X*, B201) Meriwether Pub.

Playing Self: Person & Meaning in the Planetary Society. Alberto Melucci. (Cultural Social Studies). 184p. (C). 1996. text 54.95 (*0-521-56401-8*); pap. text 16.95 (*0-521-56482-4*) Cambridge U Pr.

Playing Shakespeare. John Barton. 211p. (C). 1988. pap. 13.95 (*0-413-54790-6*, A0216, Methuen Drama) Methn.

Playing Skipping & Elastic Games. Lynette Silver. (Illus.). 40p. (J). 1996. pap. 6.95 (*1-86351-185-7*, Pub. by Sally Milner) Sterling.

Playing Smart: A Parent's Guide to Enriching, Offbeat Learning Activities for Ages 4-14. Susan K. Perry. Ed. by Pamela Espeland. LC 90-40224. (Illus.). 224p. (Orig.). 1990. pap. 14.95 (*0-915793-22-9*) Free Spirit Pub.

Playing Smart: A Practical Guide to Slot Machine Play. Al D'Angelo, Jr. Ed. & Intro. by Barbara D'Angelo. LC 95-83364. (Illus.). 73p. (Orig.). 1995. pap. 8.95 (*0-9644746-0-3*) A-Fortune.

Playing Soccer. Ken Laitin & Steve Laitin. LC 79-63980. (Illus.). (J). (gr. 2-7). 1979. pap. 9.95 (*0-916802-22-1*) Soccer for Am.

Playing Soldiers in the Dark. Stephen Dueweke. 294p. (Orig.). 1992. pap. 12.95 (*0-9624627-1-3*) Bagman Pr.

***Playing Solitaire.** Nancy Antle. LC 99-30704. (Illus.). 112p. (YA). 2000. 16.99 (*0-8037-2406-3*, Dial Yng Read) Peng Put Young Read.

Playing Synthesizers. Helen Casabona & David Frederick. Ed. by Brent Hurtig. (G. P. I. Ser.). 48p. 1988. pap. 8.95 (*0-88284-362-1*, 4110) Alfred Pub.

Playing Tall: The 10 Shortest Players in NBA History. Bill Heller. (Illus.). 190p. 1995. pap. 14.95 (*1-56625-045-5*) Bonus Books.

Playing Techniques & Performance Studies 1: Trumpet Method. A. Sandoval. 56p. 1994. pap. 17.95 (*0-7935-3029-6*, 00696535); pap. 19.95 (*0-7935-3030-X*, 00696536) H Leonard.

Playing Techniques & Performance Studies 2: Trumpet Method. A. Sandoval. 60p. 1995. pap. 17.95 (*0-7935-3031-8*, 06696537); pap. 19.95 (*0-7935-3032-6*, 00696538) H Leonard.

Playing Techniques & Performance Studies 3: Trumpet Method. A. Sandoval. 64p. 1995. pap. 17.95 (*0-7935-3033-4*, 00696539) H Leonard.

Playing Techniques & Performance Studies 3: Trumpet Method. A. Sandoval. 64p. 1995. pap. 19.95 (*0-7935-3034-2*, 00696540) H Leonard.

Playing the Bass Guitar. Verdine White & Louis Satterfield. Ed. by Norman Schwartz. (Illus.). 100p. (Orig.). 1978. pap. 6.95 (*0-89705-011-8*) Almo Pubns.

Playing the Bones. Louise Redd. 1997. pap. 11.95 (*0-614-27265-3*, Plume) Dutton Plume.

Playing the Cards: Developing Competence at the Bridge Table. Norma Sands. 1984. pap. 6.95 (*0-9605648-7-X*) Rocky Mtn Bks.

Playing the Cards That Are Dealt: Mead Dixon, the Law, & Casino Gaming. Louis M. Dixon et al. (Illus.). 276p. 1992. 19.95 (*1-56475-365-4*) U NV Oral Hist.

Playing the Changes: From Afro-Modernism to the Jazz Impulse. Craig H. Werner. 368p. pap. text 17.95 (*0-252-06641-3*) U of Ill Pr.

Playing the Changes: From Afro-Modernism to the Jazz Impulse. Craig H. Werner. LC 94-711. 384p. 1994. text 39.95 (*0-252-02112-6*) U of Ill Pr.

Playing the Chord Organ & Learning to Read Music. Albert K. De Vito. (Illus.). 1974. pap. 5.95 (*0-934286-08-6*) Kenyon.

Playing the "Communal Card" Communal Violence & Human Rights. 176p. (Orig.). 1995. pap. 15.00 (*1-56432-152-5*) Hum Rts Watch.

Playing the Electric Bass. D. Bennett. 40p. 1986. pap. 4.50 (*0-7935-5532-9*, 50394220) H Leonard.

***Playing the Field: Irish Writers on Sport.** Ed. by George O'Brien. 2000. pap. 16.95 (*1-874597-81-2*, Pub. by New Island Books) Dufour.

Playing the Field: Why Sports Teams Move & Cities Fight to Keep Them. Charles C. Euchner. LC 92-43276. 224p. 1993. 37.00 (*0-8018-4572-6*) Johns Hopkins.

Playing the Field: Why Sports Teams Move & Cities Fight to Keep Them. Charles C. Euchner. 232p. 1994. reprint ed. pap. 15.95 (*0-8018-4973-X*) Johns Hopkins.

Playing the Future: How Kid's Culture Can Teach Us to Thrive in an Age of Chaos. Douglas Rushkoff. LC 99-28145. 1999. pap. text 14.00 (*1-57322-764-1*, Riverhead Books) Putnam Pub Group.

Playing the Game. Allyn. 1996. text 49.50 (*0-205-26868-4*) Allyn.

Playing the Game. Alan Lelchuk. 361p. 1995. 23.00 (*1-880909-32-4*) Baskerville.

Playing the Game. Kate Petty. (Playground Ser.). (Illus.). 24p. (J). (ps-2). 1991. pap. 4.95 (*0-8120-4659-5*) Barron.

Playing the Game. Christine Poulter. LC 90-53168. (Illus.). 150p. (Orig.). 1991. pap. 16.00 (*0-88734-611-1*) Players Pr.

Playing the Game: Inspirations for Life & Golf. Jim Sheard & Wally Armstrong. (Illus.). 144p. 1998. 12.99 (*0-8499-5433-9*) Word Pub.

Playing the Game: Sport & British Society, 1914-1945. Derek Birley. (International Studies in the History of Sport). 256p. 1996. text 29.95 (*0-7190-4497-9*, Pub. by Manchester Univ Pr) St Martin.

Playing the Game: Sport & the Physical Emancipation of English Women, 1870-1914. Kathleen E. McCrone. LC 87-32038. (Illus.). 336p. 1988. 37.50 (*0-8131-1641-4*) U Pr of Ky.

Playing the Game: The Presidential Rhetoric of Ronald Reagan. Mary E. Stuckey. LC 89-16208. 141p. 1990. 47.95 (*0-275-93413-6*, C3413, Praeger Pubs) Greenwood.

Playing the Globe: Genre & Geography in English Renaissance Drama. Ed. by John Gillies & Virginia M. Vaughan. LC 97-34945. (Illus.). 296p. 1998. 45.00 (*0-8386-3739-6*) Fairleigh Dickinson.

Playing the Guitar. 3rd ed. Frederick Noad. (Illus.). 196p. 1997. pap. 16.95 (*0-8256-1308-6*, FN 10040) Music Sales.

Playing the Hammered Dulcimer in the Irish Tradition. Karen Ashbrook. (Illus.). 90p. 1987. pap. 17.95 (*0-8256-0310-2*, OK64915, Oak) Music Sales.

Playing the Hand Life Dealt & Winning the Jackpot! Auto-Immune Illness. Barbara Mascio & Richard Mascio. LC 96-230357. (Illus.). 100p. (Orig.). 1996. pap. 10.95 (*0-9653612-4-1*, AIBM-1) Harmony Publng.

***Playing the Hand That's Dealt to You: A Guide for Parents of Children with Special Needs.** Janet Morel. LC 00-31190. 2000. write for info. (*1-887774-07-6*) Canmore Pr.

***Playing the King: Lope de Vega & the Limits of Conformity.** Melveena McKendrick. LC 99-41910. (Monografias A Ser.). 256p. 2000. 75.00 (*1-85566-069-5*) Boydell & Brewer.

Playing the Language Game. Valerie Shepherd. LC 92-18668. (English, Language & Education Ser.). 1993. 33.95 (*0-335-09939-4*) OpUniv Pr.

Playing the Love Market: Dating, Romance & the Real World. Samuel Cameron & Ian Collins. 280p. 2000. 30.00 (*1-85343-494-9*, Pub. by Free Assoc Bks) Intl Spec Bk.

***Playing the Market.** rev. ed. Karen Isaacson. (Illus.). 1999. pap. 10.95 (*0-7690-0106-8*) Seymour Pubns.

Playing the Market: Students Learn Important Math Concepts While Engaged in a Stock Market Simulation. Karen Isaacson. 54p. 1995. teacher ed. 10.95 (*0-9648289-0-1*) Real Day Educ Pubns.

Playing the Market: The Market Theatre, Johannesburg, 1976-1986, Vol. 1. Anne Fuchs. (Contemporary Theatre Studies). vii, 183p. 1990. text 64.00 (*3-7186-5044-4*, Harwood Acad Pubs); pap. text 16.00 (*3-7186-5082-7*, Harwood Acad Pubs) Gordon & Breach.

Playing the Mischief see Collected Works of John W. De Forest

Playing the Mischief. John W. De Forest. (Collected Works of John W. De Forest). 1988. reprint ed. lib. bdg. 59.00 (*0-7812-1161-1*) Rprt Serv.

Playing the Numbers. Myron Turner. 55p. (Orig.). 1986. pap. 5.00 (*0-940237-00-8*) ND Qtr Pr.

Playing the Odds. Nora Roberts. (NR Flowers Ser.: No. 12). 1992. mass mkt. 3.59 (*0-373-51012-8*) Harlequin Bks.

Playing the Other: Essays on Gender & Society in Classical Greek Literature. Froma I. Zeitlin. LC 95-2906. (Women in Culture & Society Ser.). 484p. 1995. pap. text 19.95 (*0-226-97922-9*); lib. bdg. 60.00 (*0-226-97921-0*) U Ch Pr.

Playing the Palace - Musical. June W. Rogers. 77p. 1989. pap. 5.95 (*0-87129-680-2*, P63) Dramatic Pub.

Playing the Personals: Dating in the '90s. Claudia Beakman & Karla Dougherty. LC 97-122164. 1996. mass mkt. 5.99 (*0-671-88826-9*, Pocket Books) PB.

Playing the Piano for Pleasure. Charles Cooke. LC 70-110824. (Illus.). 247p. 1971. reprint ed. lib. bdg. 43.75 (*0-8371-3224-X*, COPP, Greenwood Pr) Greenwood.

Playing the Post: Basketball Skills & Drills. Burrall Paye. LC 96-21956. (Illus.). 256p. (Orig.). 1996. pap. 15.95 (*0-87322-979-7*, PPAY0979) Human Kinetics.

***Playing the Reader: The Homoerotics of Self-Reflexive Fiction.** Michael Hardin. LC 98-46255. (Sexuality & Literature Ser.: Vol. 8). 157p. (C). 2000. text. write for info. (*0-8204-4408-1*) P Lang Pubng.

Playing the Recorder: Alto. 48p. 1984. pap. 4.95 (*0-7935-5002-5*) H Leonard.

Playing the Recorder: Soprano. Bergma White. 48p. 1984. pap. 4.95 (*0-7935-2012-6*, 6062) H Leonard.

Playing the Selective College Admissions Game. 2nd ed. Richard W. Moll. 256p. (Orig.). 1994. pap. 11.95 (*0-14-051303-5*, Penguin Bks) Viking Penguin.

Playing the Stock Market. Joan Nally Galleghe r. (Internet Investigations Ser.). (Illus.). 24p. 1999. pap. text, teacher ed. 8.95 (*1-58108-031-X*) Pencil Point.

Playing the String Game: Strategies for Teaching Cello & Strings. 6th ed. Phyllis Young. (Illus.). 102p. 1997. reprint ed. pap. text 12.50 (*0-9621416-2-3*, H44) Shar Prods.

Playing the Tuba at Midnight: The Joys & Challenges of Singleness. Roberta Rand. LC 95-20348. 180p. (Orig.). 1995. pap. 9.99 (*0-8308-1690-9*, 1690) InterVarsity.

Playing the Viola: Conversations with William Primrose. David Dalton. (Illus.). 256p. 1990. pap. text 32.00 (*0-19-816195-6*) OUP.

Playing the Wild Card. large type ed. Philip Evans. 1989. 11.50 (*0-7089-2183-3*) Ulverscroft.

Playing the Works of Cesar Franck, No. 1. Rolland Smith. LC 96-43042. (Works of Cesar Franck). 1996. 42.00 (*0-945193-79-3*) Pendragon NY.

Playing Their Game Our Way: Using the Political Process to Meet Community Needs. Greg L. Speeter. LC 79-106542. (Illus.). (Orig.). (C). 1978. pap. 7.00 (*0-934210-06-3*) Devlp Commy.

Playing Their Part: Language & Learning in the Classroom. Nancy King. LC 95-12799. 281p. 1995. pap. text 23.50 (*0-435-08672-3*, 08672) Heinemann.

Playing Their Parts: Parents & Teachers Talk about Parent Involvement in Public School. Steve Forkas et al. 51p. 1999. pap. 10.00 (*1-889483-59-1*) Public Agenda.

Playing Through: Straight Talk on Hard Work, Big Dreams & Adventures with Tiger Woods. Earl Woods. Date not set. 12.00 (*0-06-273649-3*) HarpC.

Playing Through: Straight Talk on Hard Work, Big Dreams & Adventures with Tiger Woods. Earl Woods. LC 98-5607. (Illus.). 288p. 1998. 24.00 (*0-06-270222-X*) HarpC.

Playing to the Camera: Film Actors Discuss Their Craft. Ed. by Bert Cardullo et al. LC 97-1644. (Illus.). 384p. 1997. pap. 16.95 (*0-300-07051-9*) Yale U Pr.

Playing to the Camera: Film Actors Discuss Their Craft. Ed. by Bert Cardullo et al. LC 97-1644. (Illus.). 384p. 1998. 35.00 (*0-300-06983-9*) Yale U Pr.

Playing to Win. Laurel Ames. LC 96-498. (Historical Ser.). 296p. 1995. per. 4.50 (*0-373-28880-8*, 1-28880-2) Harlequin Bks.

Playing to Win. Margo Sorenson. (Girl Sports Girl Stories Ser.). 144p. (J). (gr. 3-7). 2000. pap. 4.95 (*1-56145-202-5*) Peachtree Pubs.

Playing to Win: Sports & the American Military, 1898-1945. Wanda E. Wakefield. LC 96-19224. (SUNY Series on Sport, Culture, & Social Relations). 216p. (C). 1997. text 59.50 (*0-7914-3313-7*); pap. text 19.95 (*0-7914-3314-5*) State U NY Pr.

***Playing to Win at Bridge.** Ron Klinger. (Illus.). 216p. 2000. pap. 14.95 (*0-575-06736-5*, Pub. by V Gollancz) Trafalgar.

Playing to Win in Atlantic City. Sam Grafstein. Ed. by Brian Kleger. (Illus.). (Orig.). 1989. pap. 4.95 (*0-9622645-0-4*) Atlantic City News Pub.

Playing Together, Learning Together. Joan Barrett & Linda Thompson. 128p. (Orig.). 1995. pap., teacher ed. 8.95 (*0-673-36160-8*, GoodYrBooks) Addson-Wesley Educ.

Playing Tree & Other Stories. Mary Bird. 1995. pap. text 12.95 (*1-887650-00-8*) Factor Pr.

Playing Urban Games: The Systems Approach to Planning. Martin Kuenzlen. LC 75-189032. 1978. pap. text 12.00 (*0-262-61028-0*) MIT Pr.

Playing Wargames on the Internet. Rawn Shah & Jim Romine. LC 95-37037. 308p. 1995. pap. 19.95 (*0-471-11634-3*) Wiley.

***Playing Winning Chess.** Yasser Seirawan. 1999. pap. text 19.99 (*0-7356-0919-5*) Microsoft.

***Playing with Books.** Peggy Kaye. 2000. text (*0-374-23455-8*) FS&G.

Playing with Cobras. large type ed. Craig Thomas. LC 93-24234. 595p. 1993. 21.95 (*0-7862-0013-8*) Thorndike Pr.

Playing with Desire: Christopher Marlowe & the Art of Tantalization. Fred B. Tromly. LC 99-193027. 312p. 1998. text 50.00 (*0-8020-4355-0*) U of Toronto Pr.

Playing with Fire see Jugando Con Fuego

Playing with Fire. Kate Chester. (Hear No Evil Ser.). (J). (gr. 6-10). 1997. pap. 3.99 (*0-614-29021-X*) Scholastic Inc.

Playing with Fire. Cho Chong-Rae. Tr. by Chun Kyung-Ja from KOR. (Cornell East Asia Ser.: Vol. 85). 188p. (C). 1997. 18.70 (*1-885445-65-2*, CEAS 85); pap. 11.90 (*1-885445-85-7*, CEAS 85) Cornell East Asia Pgm.

Playing with Fire. Lucinda Edmonds. 400p. 2000. 23.00 (*0-684-86836-9*) S&S Trade.

Playing with Fire. Mary Maxwell. (Desire Ser.). 1993. per. 2.99 (*0-373-05825-X*, 5-05825-0) Silhouette.

***Playing with Fire.** Dianne Mayhew. (Arabesque Ser.). 2000. mass mkt. 5.99 (*1-58314-161-8*) BET Bks.

Playing with Fire. Dianne Mayhew. 304p. 1997. mass mkt. 4.99 (*0-7860-0457-6*, Pinncle Kensgtn) Kensgtn Pub Corp.

Playing with Fire. Created by Francine Pascal. (Sweet Valley High Ser.: No. 3). 160p. (YA). (gr. 7 up). 1984. mass mkt. 3.99 (*0-553-27669-7*) Bantam.

Playing with Fire. Dani Shapiro. 320p. 1990. 17.95 (*0-385-26722-3*) Doubleday.

Playing with Fire. Dani Shapiro. 320p. 1992. mass mkt. 5.99 (*0-446-36187-9*, Pub. by Warner Bks) Little.

Playing with Fire. Mary-Ann T. Smith. 1994. write for info. (*0-318-71661-5*) Warner Bks.

Playing with Fire. Victoria Thompson. 1990. pap. 3.95 (*0-380-75961-6*, Avon Bks) Morrow Avon.

Playing with Fire. Kate William. (Sweet Valley High Ser.: No. 3). (YA). (gr. 7 up). 1983. 9.09 (*0-606-01268-0*, Pub. by Turtleback) Demco.

Playing with Fire, 6. Kate Chester. (Hear No Evil Ser.). 1997. 9.09 (*0-606-11449-1*, Pub. by Turtleback) Demco.

Playing with Fire, Vol. 6. Kate Chester. (Hear No Evil Ser.). 1997. mass mkt. 3.99 (*0-590-87992-8*, Point) Scholastic Inc.

Playing with Fire: A Search for the Hidden Heart of Rock & Roll. Steve Ball & Scott Dunham. LC 97-5420. 304p. (Orig.). 1997. pap. 16.95 (*0-934252-72-6*, Pub. by Hohm Pr) SCB Distributors.

Playing with Fire: A Story of Genius, Madness & Music. Jonathan Eig. 288p. 2002. write for info. (*0-7868-6567-9*, Pub. by Hyperion) Little.

Playing with Fire: Creative Conflict Resolution for Young Adults. Fiona Macbeth & Nic Fine. (Illus.). 192p. 1995. pap. 19.95 (*0-86571-306-5*) New Soc Pubs.

***Playing with Fire: How the Bible Ignites Change in Your Soul.** Walter Russell. LC 00-25318. 2000. pap. 14.00 (*1-57683-142-6*) NavPress.

Playing with Fire: Queer Politics, Queer Theories. Ed. by Shane Phelan. LC 95-51728. 384p. (C). 1997. 70.00 (*0-415-91416-7*); pap. 18.99 (*0-415-91417-5*) Routledge.

Playing with Fire (after Frankenstein) (Shelley) Barbara Field. 1989. pap. 5.25 (*0-8222-0899-7*) Dramatists Play.

Playing with Form: Children Draw in Six Countries. Alexander Alland, Jr. LC 82-25269. (Illus.). 224p. 1983. pap. text 23.50 (*0-231-05609-5*) Col U Pr.

Playing with God. Jean M. Unsworth. (Illus.). 128p. (Orig.). 1992. spiral bd. 19.95 (*0-87946-064-4*, 127) ACTA Pubns.

Playing with Ideas. Susan Pfisterer & Carolyn Pickett. (Orig.). pap. 29.95 (*0-86819-565-0*, Pub. by Currency Pr) Accents Pubns.

Playing with Infinity: Mathematical Explorations & Excursions. Rozsa Peter. LC 75-26467. (Illus.). 268p. 1976. reprint ed. pap. text 7.95 (*0-486-23265-4*) Dover.

***Playing with Light.** Beatriz Rivera. 240p. 2000. pap. 12.95 (*1-55885-310-3*) Arte Publico.

Playing with Logic. Mark Schoenfield & Jeanette Rosenblatt. (J). (gr. 3-5). 1985. pap. 8.99 (*0-8224-5310-X*) Fearon Teacher Aids.

Playing with Magnets. Gary Gibson. (Science for Fun Ser.). 1995. 10.15 (*0-606-09829-1*, Pub. by Turtleback) Demco.

Playing with Magnets: With Easy-to-Make Scientific Projects. Gary Gibson. (Science for Fun Ser.). (Illus.). 32p. (J). (gr. 2-4). 1995. pap. 4.95 (*1-56294-633-1*, Copper Beech Bks) Millbrook Pr.

Playing with Paint. Diane James. (Illus.). 24p. (J). (ps-1). 1992. pap. 3.95 (*0-590-45739-X*, Cartwheel) Scholastic Inc.

Playing with Penguins & Other Adventures in Antarctica. Ann McGovern. LC 92-4646. 48p. (J). (gr. 4-7). 1995. pap. 4.95 (*0-590-44175-2*) Scholastic Inc.

Playing with Penguins & Other Adventures in Antarctica. Ann McGovern. (J). 1994. 10.15 (*0-606-08023-6*, Pub. by Turtleback) Demco.

Playing with Power in Movies, Television, & Video Games: From Muppet Babies to Teenage Mutant Ninja Turtles. Marsha Kinder. LC 91-11252. (Illus.). 277p. 1991. pap. 15.95 (*0-520-07776-8*, Pub. by U CA Pr) Cal Prin Full Svc.

Playing with Print. Carol A. Bloom. LC 97-198274. 1997. pap. text 14.95 (*0-673-36326-0*) Addson-Wesley Educ.

Playing with Shadows: Stories. Gloria Whelan. LC 87-35690. (Illinois Short Fiction Ser.). 160p. 1988. 14.95 (*0-252-01524-X*) U of Ill Pr.

Playing with Signs. V. K. Agawu. 168p. 1991. text 42.50 (*0-691-09138-2*, Pub. by Princeton U Pr) Cal Prin Full Svc.

***Playing with the Dead.** Dennis Havens. 2000. pap. 18.00 (*0-7388-2149-7*) Xlibris Corp.

Playing with the Edge: The Photographic Achievement of Robert Mapplethorpe. Arthur Danto. LC 94-38950. (Illus.). 208p. 1995. 29.95 (*0-520-20051-9*, Pub. by U CA Pr) Cal Prin Full Svc.

Playing with the Elements of Music: A Guide to Music Theory. Jean Nandi. LC 88-92717. (Illus.). 153p. (Orig.). (C). 1989. pap. 22.95 (*0-9622023-1-2*) Bon Gout Pub.

***Playing with the Numbers: How So-Called Experts Mislead Us about the Economy.** Richard A. Stimson. LC 99-93764. 284p. 1999. pap. 12.00 (*0-9671232-6-7*) Westchester Pr.

Playing with the Wind: The Whirligig Collection of the Canadian Museum of Civilization. Pierre Crepeau. (Illus.). 55p. 1991. pap. 9.95 (*0-660-12923-X*, Pub. by CN Mus Civilization) U of Wash Pr.

Playing with Time: Art & Performance in Central Mali. Mary Jo Arnoldi. LC 94-38744. (Traditional Arts of Africa Ser.). (Illus.). 256p. 1995. text 29.95 (*0-253-30900-X*) Ind U Pr.

Playing with Time: Mothers & the Meaning of Literacy. Jane Mace. LC 99-159373. 1998. 85.00 (*1-85728-890-4*) Taylor & Francis.

Playing with Time: Mothers & the Meaning of Literacy. Jane Mace. LC 99-159373. 185p. 1998. 24.95 (*1-85728-891-2*) UCL Pr Ltd.

Playing with Time: Ovid & the "Fasti" Carole E. Newlands. LC 95-2919. (Studies in Classical Philology: Vol. 55). 256p. 1995. text 45.00 (*0-8014-3080-1*) Cornell U Pr.

An Asterisk (*) at the beginning of an entry indicates that the title is appearing for the first time.

Playing with Trains. Stephen Poliakoff. (Methuen Modern Plays Ser.). 106p. (Orig.). (C). 1989. pap. 9.95 (0-413-62510-9, A0433, Methuen Drama) Methn.

Playing with Trumps. Sally Brock. LC 97-39105. (How to Play Bridge Ser.). (Illus.). 96p. 1998. pap. 8.95 (0-8442-2565-7) NTC Contemp Pub Co.

Playing with Water: Passion & Solitude on a Philippine Island. James Hamilton-Paterson. 288p. (C). 1990. reprint ed. pap. 14.95 (0-941533-82-4, NAB) I R Dee.

Playing with Words. James Howe. LC 93-48166. (Meet the Author Ser.). (Illus.). 32p. (J). (gr. 2-5). 1994. 14.95 (1-878450-40-9, 707) R Owen Pubs.

Playing with Words. Hazel Moses. (Illus.). 28p. (J). (gr. 1-4). 1996. spiral bd. 4.50 (0-9653867-0-8) Wrking Print.

***Playing without the Ball.** Rich Wallace. 160p. (ps up). 2000. lib. bdg. 25.00 (0-679-98672-3) Knopf.

***Playing Without the Ball.** Rich Wallace. 160p. (J). (ps up). 2000. 15.95 (0-679-88672-9) Knopf Bks Yng Read.

Playing Woodwind Instruments: A Guide for Teachers, Performers, & Composers. Phillip Rehfeldt. (Illus.). 211p. (C). 1998. pap. text 27.95 (1-57766-028-5) Waveland Pr.

Playing Write Field: Selected Works by Scott Pitoniak. Scott Pitoniak. 150p. (Orig.). 1997. pap. 10.95 (0-9659348-0-2) S Pitoniak.

***Playing YMCA Baseball & Softball: Bronze Edition.** YMCA of the U. S. A. Staff. (Illus.). 32p. 2000. pap. write for info. (0-7360-3040-9) Human Kinetics.

***Playing YMCA Baseball & Softball: Gold Edition.** YMCA of the U. S. A. Staff. (Illus.). 32p. 2000. pap. write for info. (0-7360-3042-5) Human Kinetics.

***Playing YMCA Baseball & Softball: Silver Edition.** YMCA of the U. S. A. Staff. (Illus.). 32p. 2000. pap. write for info. (0-7360-3041-7) Human Kinetics.

***Playing YMCA Basketball: Bronze Edition.** YMCA of the U. S. A. Staff. (Illus.). 32p. 2000. pap. write for info. (0-7360-3043-3) Human Kinetics.

***Playing YMCA Basketball: Gold Edition.** YMCA of the U. S. A. Staff. (Illus.). 32p. 2000. pap. write for info. (0-7360-3045-X) Human Kinetics.

***Playing YMCA Basketball: Silver Edition.** YMCA of the U. S. A. Staff. (Illus.). 32p. 2000. pap. write for info. (0-7360-3044-1) Human Kinetics.

***Playing YMCA Soccer.** YMCA of The U.S.A. Staff. (Illus.). 32p. 2000. pap. write for info. (0-7360-3046-8) Human Kinetics.

***Playing YMCA Soccer: Gold Edition.** YMCA of the U. S. A. Staff. (Illus.). 32p. 2000. pap. write for info. (0-7360-3048-4) Human Kinetics.

***Playing YMCA Soccer: Silver Edition.** YMCA of the U. S. A. Staff. (Illus.). 32p. 2000. pap. write for info. (0-7360-3047-6) Human Kinetics.

***Playing YMCA Volleyball: Bronze Edition.** YMCA of the U. S. A. Staff. (Illus.). 32p. 2000. pap. write for info. (0-7360-3049-2) Human Kinetics.

***Playing YMCA Volleyball: Gold Edition.** YMCA of the U. S. A. Staff. (Illus.). 32p. 2000. pap. write for info. (0-7360-3051-4) Human Kinetics.

***Playing YMCA Volleyball: Silver Edition.** YMCA of the U. S. A. Staff. (Illus.). 32p. 2000. pap. write for info. (0-7360-3050-6) Human Kinetics.

***Playing Your Position: Investing Yourself in Others.** Compiled by Larry Thomas. (We Build People Ser.). 160p. 2000. pap. 4.95 (0-88243-410-1, 02/4101) Gospel Pub.

Playland & a Place with the Pigs. Athol Fugard. 112p. 1993. 21.95 (1-55936-070-4); pap. 10.95 (1-55936-071-2) Theatre Comm.

Playland Bunnies Book. Playland Staff. (J). 13.95 (0-698-12069-8) Putnam Pub Group.

Playland Kids, Featuring Marcus Toussaint, the Recycler. Michael E. Toussaint. (Coloring Book Ser.). (Illus.). 24p. (Orig.). (J). (gr. k-6). 1992. pap. 2.95 (0-9630905-0-X) Michael T Enter.

Playland Night Before Xmas Book. Playland Staff. (J). 13.95 (0-698-13034-0) Putnam Pub Group.

Playland Three Pigs Book. Playland Staff. (J). 13.95 (0-698-12073-6) Putnam Pub Group.

***Playlistening.** Patty Wipfler. 1999. pap. 2.00 (1-58429-035-8) Rational Isl.

Playlunch: 5 Short New Zealand Plays. Ed. by Christine Prentice & Lisa Warrington. 112p. 1996. pap. 19.95 (1-877133-01-9, Pub. by Univ Otago Pr) Intl Spec Bk.

***Playmaker.** Janie Cheaney. 256p. (ps up). 2000. lib. bdg. 17.99 (0-375-90577-4) Knopf.

***Playmaker.** Janie Cheaney. 256p. (J). (ps up). 2000. 15.95 (0-375-80577-X, Pub. by Knopf Bks Yng Read) Random.

Playmaker: A New Concept of Leadership in the Post-Newtonian Age. Katherine Kline. (Illus.). 110p. 1997. pap. 19.95 (0-9668727-0-3) K Kline.

***Playmakers.** Arthur Cantor & Stuart W. Little. 352p. 2000. pap. 20.95 (1-58348-382-9, Authors Guild Backinprint) iUniversecom.

Playmaking: Children Writing & Performing Their Own Plays. Daniel J. Sklar. 184p. 1990. 24.95 (0-915924-34-X); pap. 14.95 (0-915924-35-8) Tchrs & Writers Coll.

Playmaking in the Classroom . . . And Elsewhere. Vern Adix. (Theatre Book Ser.). 87p. 1991. pap. text 7.95 (1-57514-013-6, 5002) Encore Perform Pub.

Playmasters. Eldon L. Ham. LC 99-37967. 256p. 1999. pap. 14.95 (0-8092-2602-2, 260220, Contemporary Bks) NTC Contemp Pub Co.

***Playmate & the Carpetbaggers.** Bestow R. Rudolph. LC 99-96751. 2000. 18.95 (0-533-13336-X) Vantage.

Playmate Big Book: Black & White Nellie Edge I Can Read & Sing Big Book. Illus. by Tani Draper. (J). (ps-2). 1994. pap. text 20.00 (0-922053-31-6) N Edge Res.

Playmate Lingerie Calendar, 1995. (Illus.). 12p. 1994. 12.95 (0-87223-914-4) Playboy Ent.

Playmates. Pam Adams. (Baby Carriage Ser.). (Illus.). 8p. (J). (gr. 3 up). 1991. 6.99 (0-85953-449-9) Childs Play.

Playmates. Ed. by Ginny Ballor & Carrie Newmann. 40p. (Orig.). 1997. pap. 3.00 (1-882294-23-8) Green Gate.

Playmates. Barbara J. Crane. (Crane Reading System-English Ser.). (Illus.). (gr. k-2). 1977. pap. text 4.85 (0-89075-096-3) Bilingual Ed Serv.

Playmates. Abigail McDaniels. 256p. 1993. mass mkt. 4.50 (0-8217-4296-5, Zebra Kensgtn) Kensgtn Pub Corp.

Playmates. Robert B. Parker. 1990. mass mkt. 6.99 (0-425-12001-5) Berkley Pub.

Playmates. large type ed. Robert B. Parker. LC 89-20218. 268p. 1990. lib. bdg. 11.95 (0-89621-947-X) Thorndike Pr.

Playoff Champion. Felix Von Moschzisker. (Choose Your Own Adventure Ser.: No. 135). (J). (gr. 4-8). 1993. 8.60 (0-606-05550-9, Pub. by Turtleback) Demco.

Playoff Dreams. Fred Bowen. LC 97-10447. (AllStar Sport Story Ser.). (Illus.). 112p. (Orig.). (J). (gr. 3-7). 1997. pap. 4.95 (1-56145-155-X) Peachtree Pubs.

Playoff Pressure. Renardo Barden. LC 92-9143. (Basketball Heroes Ser.). 48p. (J). (gr. 3-8). 1992. lib. bdg. 15.95 (0-86593-162-3) Rourke Corp.

Playpen to Podium: Giving Your Child the Communication Advantage in Every Area of Life. Jeff Myers. 230p. (Orig.). 1997. pap. 12.95 (1-56857-068-6, 1799) Noble Pub Assocs.

Playreaders Play Packs, 2 sets, Mixed Set 1. 1987. 18.00 (0-8123-7058-9) McDougal-Littell.

Playreaders Play Packs, 2 sets, Mixed Set 2. 1987. 18.00 (0-8123-7065-1) McDougal-Littell.

Playreadings. Louise Frankenstein. 132p. 1933. 5.00 (0-573-60074-0) French.

Playroom. Frances Hegerty. Ed. by Jane Chelius. 336p. 1992. reprint ed. mass mkt. 4.99 (0-671-73583-7) PB.

Plays. Incl. Bear. Cherry Orchard. Anton Chekhov. Ivanov. Jubilee. Anton Chekhov. Tr. by Elisaveta Fen. 1959. pap. Marriage Proposal. Anton Chekhov. Tr. by Elisaveta Fen. 1959. pap. Seagull. Three Sisters. (Classics Ser.). 464p. 1959. Set pap. 8.95 (0-14-044096-8, Penguin Classics) Viking Penguin.

***Plays.** Kelly Burkholder. LC 00-36927. (Artistic Adventures Ser.). 2000. pap. write for info. (1-57103-357-2) Rourke Bk Co.

***Plays.** Caryl Churchill. LC 85-186277. 2000. pap. 14.95 (0-413-56670-6, Methuen Drama) Methn.

Plays. Susan Glaspell. Ed. by Christopher W. Bigsby. (British & American Playwrights Ser.). (Illus.). 174p. 1987. pap. text 21.95 (0-521-31204-3) Cambridge U Pr.

Plays, 3 vols. Hudson River Editions Staff. 1991. 75.00 (0-685-74362-4) Macmillan.

Plays. D. H. Lawrence. Ed. by Hans-Wilhelm Schwarze & John Worthen. LC 98-8068. (Edition of the Works of D. H. Lawrence). (Illus.). 900p. (C). 1999. 150.00 (0-521-24277-0) Cambridge U Pr.

Plays. Friedrich Schiller. Ed. by Walter Hinderer. LC 76-17466. (German Library: Vol. 15). 346p. 1983. pap. 19.95 (0-8264-0275-5) Continuum.

Plays. Friedrich Schiller. Ed. by Walter Hinderer. LC 74-76129. (German Library: Vol. 15). 346p. (C). 1983. 39.50 (0-8264-0274-7) Continuum.

Plays. Heinrich Von Kleist. Ed. by Walter Hinderer. LC 78-178169. (German Library: Vol. 25). 340p. 1982. pap. 19.95 (0-8264-0263-1) Continuum.

Plays. Alexander Ostrovsky. Ed. by George R. Noyes. LC 70-98632. reprint ed. 41.50 (0-404-04837-4) AMS Pr.

Plays. William Shakespeare. Ed. by John P. Collier. LC 72-175850. reprint ed. 32.50 (0-404-01615-4) AMS Pr.

Plays, 8 vols. William Shakespeare. Ed. by Samuel Johnson. LC 68-59595. reprint ed. 810.00 (0-404-05810-8) AMS Pr.

Plays. Paul Valery. Tr. by David Paul & Robert Fitzgerald. LC 56-9337. (Collected Works of Paul Valery: Vol. 3). 403p. 1960. reprint ed. pap. 125.00 (0-608-02898-3, 206396200008) Bks Demand.

Plays, No. 1. Sebastian Barry. LC 97-223096. (Contemporary Dramatists Ser.). 1997. pap. 14.95 (0-413-71120-X) Methn.

Plays, No. 1. Christina Reid. LC 97-223101. (Contemporary Dramatists Ser.). 1997. pap. 14.95 (0-413-71220-6) Methn.

Plays, No. 1. Philip Ridley. LC 97-223095. (Contemporary Dramatists Ser.). 1997. pap. 14.95 (0-413-71100-5) Methn.

Plays, No. 2. Anthony Minghella. LC 98-130607. (Contemporary Dramatists Ser.). 1997. pap. 14.95 (0-413-71520-5) Methn.

Plays, 3 vols., Vol. 1. Hudson River Editions Staff & Edward Albee. (Hudson River Editions Ser.). 680p. 1991. 75.00 (0-02-501761-6) Free Pr.

Plays, Vol. 1. Saunders & Lewis. Date not set. pap. 17.95 (0-8464-4889-0) Beekman Pubs.

Plays, Vol. 1. Oscar Wilde. (Classics Library). 1998. pap. 3.95 (1-85326-184-X, 184XWW, Pub. by Wrdsworth Edits) NTC Contemp Pub Co.

Plays, Vol. 2. Saunders & Lewis. Date not set. pap. 17.95 (0-8464-4865-3) Beekman Pubs.

Plays, Vol. 2. Oscar Wilde. (Classics Library). 160p. 1998. pap. 3.95 (1-85326-185-8, 1858WW, Pub. by Wrdsworth Edits) NTC Contemp Pub Co.

Plays, Vol. 3. Edward Albee. Incl. All Over. 1982. Counting the Ways & Listening. 1982. Seascape. 1982. 1982. Set pap. 9.95 (0-689-70615-4) Atheneum Yung Read.

Plays, 3 vols., Vol. 3. Hudson River Editions Staff & Edward Albee. 464p. 1991. 75.00 (0-02-501763-2) Free Pr.

Plays, Vol. 4. Saunders & Lewis. Date not set. pap. 17.95 (0-8464-4891-2) Beekman Pubs.

Plays: A Study Guide. Mary Medland. Ed. by J. Friedland & R. Kessler. (Novel-Ties Ser.). 1990. pap. text, student ed. 15.95 (0-88122-863-X) Lrn Links.

Plays: Before Daybreak, the Weavers, the Beaver Coat. Gerhart Hauptmann. Ed. by Reinhold Grimm. LC 55-8437. (German Library). 324p. (C). 1993. 39.50 (0-8264-0726-9); pap. 19.95 (0-8264-0727-7) Continuum.

Plays: Egmont, Iphigenia in Tauris, Torquato Tasso. Johann Wolfgang Von Goethe. LC 82-40260. (German Library: Vol. 20). 324p. (C). 1993. 39.50 (0-8264-0716-1); pap. 19.95 (0-8264-0717-X) Continuum.

Plays: Man & Superman, Candida, Arms & the Man & Mrs. Warren's Profession. George Bernard Shaw. 448p. 1960. mass mkt. 5.95 (0-451-52434-9, CE1786, Sig Classics) NAL.

Plays: The Threepenny Opera, The Measures Taken, Galileo, Mother Courage & Her Children, Baal. Bertolt Brecht. LC 56-12398. 324p. 1995. pap. 24.95 (0-8264-0737-4) Continuum.

Plays: The Threepenny Opera, The Measures Taken, Galileo, Mother Courage & Her Children, Baal. Bertolt Brecht. Ed. by Reinhold Grimm & Caroline Molina y Vedia. LC 76-20409. (German Library: Vol. 75). 324p. (C). 1999. 39.95 (0-8264-0736-6) Continuum.

Plays - Brutus: or The Fall Tarquin. John H. Payne. (Notable American Authors Ser.). 1999. reprint ed. lib. bdg. 125.00 (0-7812-8709-X) Rprt Serv.

***Plays - The Contrast.** Royall Tyler. (Notable American Authors Ser.). 1999. reprint ed. lib. bdg. 125.00 (0-7812-9858-X) Rprt Serv.

Plays about Presidents. Tim Nolan. 128p. (J). 1997. pap. 16.95 (0-590-48195-9) Scholastic Inc.

Plays about the Theatre in England, 1737-1800, or the Self-Conscious Stage from Foote to Sheridan. Dane F. Smith & M. L. Lawhon. LC 77-74409. 288p. 1979. 38.50 (0-8387-2074-9) Bucknell U Pr.

Plays & Essays. Friedrich Durrenmatt. Ed. by Volkmar Sander. LC 56-12398. (German Library: Vol. 89). 316p. 1982. 39.50 (0-8264-0257-7); pap. 19.95 (0-8264-0267-4) Continuum.

Plays & Fragments, 2 vols. Sophocles. (ENG & GER.). lxix, 1150p. 1968. reprint ed. write for info. (0-318-70532-X); reprint ed. write for info. (0-318-71030-7); reprint ed. write for info. (0-318-70533-8); reprint ed. write for info. (0-318-70534-6); reprint ed. write for info. (0-318-71031-5); reprint ed. write for info. (0-318-71032-3) G Olms Pubs.

Plays & Fragments: Menander. Menander. Tr. & Intro. by Norma Miller. 272p. 1988. pap. 12.95 (0-14-044501-3, Penguin Classics) Viking Penguin.

Plays & Masques at Court During the Reigns of Elizabeth, James & Charles. Mary S. Steele. (BCL1-PR English Literature Ser.). 300p. 1992. reprint ed. lib. bdg. 79.00 (0-7812-7106-1) Rprt Serv.

Plays & Novels of Peter Handke. June Schlueter. LC 81-50242. (Critical Essays in Modern Literature Ser.). 225p. reprint ed. pap. 69.80 (0-7837-2144-7, 204243000004) Bks Demand.

Plays & Other Dramatic Writings by W. H. Auden, 1928-1938, Vol. I. W. H. Auden & Christopher Isherwood. Ed. by Edward Mendelson. 544p. 1989. text 69.50 (0-691-06740-6, Pub. by Princeton U Pr) Cal Prin Full Svc.

Plays & Other Writings of Arpad Goncz. Tr. by Katharina M. Wilson & Christopher C. Wilson from HUN. LC 90-3872. (Library of World Literature in Translation: Vol. 8). 266p. 1990. text 20.00 (0-8240-2994-1) Garland.

Plays & Pageants from the Life of the Negro. Willis Richardson. 1990. 25.00 (0-87498-028-3) Assoc Pubs DC.

Plays & Pageants from the Life of the Negro. abr. ed. Willis Richardson. LC 93-27075. (Illus.). 400p. 1993. text 40.00 (0-87805-657-2) U Pr of Miss.

Plays & Pageants from the Life of the Negro. Willis Richardson. LC 93-27075. (Illus.). 400p. 1993. reprint ed. pap. 17.95 (0-87805-658-0) U Pr of Miss.

Plays & Petersburg Tales: Petersburg Tales; Marriage; The Government Inspector. Nikolai Vasilevich Gogol. Ed. & Tr. by Christopher English. (Oxford World's Classics Ser.). (Illus.). 400p. 1999. pap. 8.95 (0-19-283552-1) OUP.

Plays & Players. Laurence Hutton. (Notable American Authors Ser.). 1992. reprint ed. lib. bdg. 75.00 (0-7812-3304-6) Rprt Serv.

Plays & Playhouses in Imperial Decadence. Ed. by Anthony N. Zahareas. (Towards a Social History of Hispanic & Luso-Brazilian Literature Ser.). 118p. (Orig.). 1987. pap. text 6.95 (0-910235-15-5) Prisma Bks.

***Plays & Playwright for the New Millenium.** Kirk Wood Bromley et al. Ed. by Martin Denton. 366p. 2000. pap. 14.00 (0-9670234-1-6) NY Theatre Exp.

Plays & Poems. George Chapman. 416p. pap. 19.95 (0-14-043636-7, Pub. by Pnguin Bks Ltd) Trafalgar.

Plays & Poems. Oskar Kokoschka. Tr. by Michael Mitchell from GER. LC 99-36779. (Studies in Austrian Literature, Culture, & Thought. Translation Ser.). 2000. 29.95 (1-57241-041-8) Ariadne CA.

Plays & Poems, 2 vols. George H. Boker. reprint ed. 84.50 (0-404-00930-1) AMS Pr.

Plays & Poems, 2 vols. George H. Boker. (Anglistica & Americana Ser.: No. 40). 1969. reprint ed. 200.00 (0-685-66434-1, 05102518) G Olms Pubs.

Plays & Poems, 2 vols. Robert Greene. Ed. by John C. Collins. LC 79-130985. reprint ed. 105.00 (0-404-01634-0) AMS Pr.

Plays & Poems, 21 vols. William Shakespeare. Ed. by James Boswell. LC 68-59049. reprint ed. 1470.00 (0-404-05870-1) AMS Pr.

Plays & Poems, 10 vols. William Shakespeare. Ed. by Edmond Malone. LC 68-59049. reprint ed. 1375.00 (0-404-05850-7) AMS Pr.

Plays & Poems see Complete Works of Henry Fielding

Plays & Poems, 1948-58. Elder Olson. LC 58-11951. (Midway Reprint Ser.). 179p. reprint ed. pap. 55.50 (0-608-09029-8, 206966400005) Bks Demand.

Plays & Poems, 1948-58. Elder Olson. LC 58-11951. (Midway Reprint Ser.). x, 170p. 1993. reprint ed. pap. text 5.95 (0-226-62896-5) U Ch Pr.

Plays & Poems of Cyril Tourneur, 2 vols. Cyril Tourneur. LC 77-38370. (Select Bibliographies Reprint Ser.). 1977. reprint ed. 37.95 (0-8369-6787-9) Ayer.

Plays & Poems of Mercy Otis Warren. Mercy Otis Warren. LC 80-16625. 392p. 1980. 60.00 (0-8201-1344-1) Schol Facsimiles.

Plays & Poems of Robert Greene, 2 Vols. Robert Greene. Ed. by J. Churton Collins. LC 79-119957. (Select Bibliographies Reprint Ser.). 1977. 39.95 (0-8369-5400-9) Ayer.

Plays & Poems of Robert Greene, 2 vols. Robert Greene. (BCL1-PR English Literature Ser.). 1992. reprint ed. lib. bdg. 150.00 (0-7812-7241-6) Rprt Serv.

***Plays & Prose of Oscar Wilde: Wilde Style.** Neil Sammells. 192p. 2000. pap. 19.00 (0-582-35759-4) Longman.

Plays & Puppets &cetera. 7th ed. Courtaney Brooks. LC 81-68933. (Illus.). 100p. (Orig.). (J). (gr. k up). 1981. pap. text 14.95 (0-941274-00-4) Belnice Bks.

Plays & Stories. Arthur Schnitzler. Ed. by Egon Schwartz. LC 82-18263. (German Library: Vol. 55). 320p. 1983. 39.50 (0-8264-0270-4) Continuum.

Plays & Stories. Arthur Schnitzler. Ed. by Egon Schwartz. LC 70-190350. (German Library: Vol. 55). 320p. (C). 1983. pap. 19.95 (0-8264-0271-2) Continuum.

Plays Around the Year: More Than 20 Thematic Plays for the Classroom. Liza Schafer. LC 95-114082. (Illus.). 200p. 1994. pap. 18.95 (0-590-49475-9) Scholastic Inc.

Plays at Home & Abroad. Norman Beim. LC 96-21006. 524p. 1996. pap. 19.95 (0-931231-07-8) Newconcept Pr.

Plays by A. P. Chekhov: Russian Reader with Explanatory Notes. Anton Chekhov. 238p. 1989. pap. text 7.95 (0-8285-4904-4) Firebird NY.

Plays by Allan Havis. Allan Havis. 1989. pap. 11.95 (0-88145-071-5) Broadway Play.

Plays by American Women, 1900-1930. rev. ed. Ed. by Judith E. Barlow. LC 84-24606. 304p. 1985. reprint ed. 24.95 (1-55783-007-X); reprint ed. pap. 10.95 (1-55783-008-8) Applause Theatre Bk Pubs.

Plays by American Women, 1930-1960. Clare Boothe Luce et al. Ed. by Judith E. Barlow. LC 94-7760. 416p. 1994. pap. 16.95 (1-55783-164-5) Applause Theatre Bk Pubs.

Plays by & about Woman: An Anthology. Ed. by Victoria Sullivan & James Hatch. 1974. pap. 11.00 (0-394-71896-8) Vin Bks.

Plays by Donald Freed. Donald Freed. 1990. pap. 11.95 (0-88145-088-X) Broadway Play.

Plays by Early American Women, 1775-1850. Ed. & Compiled by Amelia H. Kritzer. LC 94-45115. 448p. 1995. pap. text 17.95 (0-472-06598-X, 06598) U of Mich Pr.

Plays by French & Francophone Women: A Critical Anthology. Ed. by Christiane P. Makward & Judith G. Miller. (Illus.). 320p. (C). 1994. pap. text 19.95 (0-472-08258-2, 08258) U of Mich Pr.

Plays by French & Francophone Women: A Critical Anthology. Ed. by Christiane P. Makward & Judith G. Miller. LC 95-20373. (Illus.). 320p. (C). 1995. text 49.50 (0-472-10263-X, 10263) U of Mich Pr.

***Plays by Jeremy Dobrish.** Jeremy Dobrish. 148p. 1999. pap. 11.95 (0-88145-157-6) Broadway Play.

***Plays by Len Jenkin.** Len Jenkin. 153p. 1999. pap. 11.95 (0-88145-158-4) Broadway Play.

Plays by Mediterranean Women. Ed. by Marion Baraitser. 296p. 1999. pap. 16.00 (0-9515877-3-0) Theatre Comm.

***Plays by Michael McGuire.** Michael McGuire. 198p. 1999. pap. 11.95 (0-88145-160-6) Broadway Play.

Plays by Tony Kushner. Tony Kushner. 1992. pap. 11.95 (0-88145-102-9) Broadway Play.

Plays by Webster & Ford. John Webster. LC 75-41291. reprint ed. 32.50 (0-404-14628-7) AMS Pr.

Plays by Women, Vol. 4. Michelene Wandor. (Methuen New Theatrescripts Ser.). 159p. (C). 1988. pap. write for info. (0-413-56740-0, A0220, Methuen Drama) Methn.

Plays by Women, Vol. 5. Ed. by Mary Remnant. (Methuen New Theatrescripts Ser.). 181p. (C). 1988. pap. write for info. (0-413-41570-8, A0221, Methuen Drama) Methn.

Plays by Women, Vol. 6. Intro. & Selected by Mary Remnant. (Methuen New Theatrescripts Ser.). 126p. (C). 1988. pap. write for info. (0-413-14080-6, A0222, Methuen Drama) Methn.

Plays by Women, Vol. 10. Annie Castledine. 256p. (Orig.). 1993. pap. 17.95 (0-413-68000-2, A0690, Methuen Drama) Methn.

Plays by Women Bk. 2: An International Anthology Includes: The Orphanage, Game of Patience, The Widow Dylemma, The Tropical Breeze Hotel, Beware the Heart. Abla Farhoud et al. Ed. by Francoise Kourilsky. Tr. by Jill MacDougall et al. LC 89-142722. 267p. 1994. pap. 15.95 (0-913745-42-1) Ubu Repertory.

Plays by Women Vol. 3: An International Anthology, Vol. III. Denise Bonal et al. Ed. by Francoise Kourilsky. Tr. by Jill MacDougall et al. 440p. (Orig.). 1996. pap. 19.95 (0-913745-46-4) Ubu Repertory.

***Plays by Women from Africa & the Caribbean.** Francoise Kourilsky. 1999. pap. 19.95 (0-913745-50-2, Pub. by Theatre Comm) Consort Bk Sales.

Plays Children Love, Vol. 2. Coleman A. Jennings & Aurand Harris. 512p. (J). 1988. text 19.95 (0-312-01490-2) St Martin.

Edward Bond Plays: Five, Vol. 5. Edward Bond. 1996. pap. 15.95 (0-413-70390-8, Methuen Drama) Methn.

An Asterisk (*) at the beginning of an entry indicates that the title is appearing for the first time.

Plays for a New Theatre: Long Night of Medea, Methusalem or the Eternal Bourgeois, Assault upon Charles Sumner, Wax Museum, Knackery for All. Corrado Alvaro et al. LC 66-17821. 288p. 1966. 7.50 (*0-8112-0245-3*, Pub. by New Directions) Norton.

Plays for Children & Young Adults, 1989-1994, Suppl. 1. 2nd ed. Rashelle S. Karp et al. Ed. by Tonya Shockowitz. LC 90-44195. 384p. (J). 1996. text 83.00 (*0-8153-1493-0*, SS926) Garland.

Plays for Grades 2 Through 4. Michael H. Burton. (Illus.). vi, 51p. 1995. spiral bd. 12.95 (*0-945803-22-2*, 00185) R Steiner Col.

Plays for Pagans. Colin C. Clements. LC 77-94337. (One-Act Plays in Reprint Ser.). 1978. reprint ed. 20.00 (*0-8486-2035-6*) Roth Pub Inc.

Plays for Pairs: The 52nd Street Project Plays. Ed. by Willie Reale. 1995. spiral bd. 15.00 (*0-8222-1444-X*) Dramatists Play.

Plays for Players. Alun Richards. 367p. (C). 1975. text 75.00 (*0-85088-290-7*, Pub. by Gomer Pr) St Mut.

Plays for Poet-Mimes. Alfred Kreymborg. LC 76-40388. (One-Act Plays in Reprint Ser.). 1976. reprint ed. 20.00 (*0-8486-2004-6*) Roth Pub Inc.

Plays for Radio, 1964-1991. Tom Stoppard. 304p. 1994. 22.95 (*0-571-17208-3*) Faber & Faber.

Plays for the Actress. E. Lave & N. Sheilgold. LC 96-53573. 1997. pap. 18.00 (*0-679-77281-2*) McKay.

Plays for the End of the Century. Ed. by Bonnie Marrance. LC 96-21936. (PAJ Bks.). 288p. 1996. text 45.00 (*0-8018-5107-6*); pap. text 16.95 (*0-8018-5108-4*) Johns Hopkins.

Plays for the Soul. Sarah L. McNeely. 50p. (J). (ps-12). 1997. pap. 10.00 (*1-890300-03-9*) NIA Pages.

Plays for the Theatre. 6th ed. Oscar Gross Brockett. (C). 1996. pap. text 43.50 (*0-15-504462-1*) Harcourt Coll Pubs.

Plays for the Theatre. 7th ed. Brockett. LC 98-75702. 640p. (C). 1999. text 51.00 (*0-15-507230-7*, Pub. by Harcourt Coll Pubs) Harcourt.

Plays for Today. (Knockout Ser.). Date not set. pap. text. write for info. (*0-582-24392-0*, Pub. by Addison-Wesley) Longman.

Plays for Young Audiences by Max Bush: An Anthology of Selected Plays for Young Audiences. Max Bush. Ed. by Roger Ellis. LC 95-2382. 392p. (Orig.). (J). (gr. 4-12). 1995. pap. 16.95 (*1-56608-011-8*, B131) Meriwether Pub.

Plays for Young Puppeteers. Lewis Mahlmann & David C. Jones. LC 92-38529. 328p. (Orig.). (J). (gr. 1-6). 1993. pap. text 14.95 (*0-8238-0298-1*) Kalmbach.

Plays from African Folktales. unabridged ed. Carol Korty. Ed. by William-Alan Landes. LC 97-35354. (Illus.). 98p. (J). (gr. 3-12). 1998. pap. 17.00 (*0-88734-659-6*) Players Pr.

Plays from African Tales. Barbara Winther. LC 92-3965. (Orig.). (J). (gr. 1-6). 1992. pap. 13.95 (*0-8238-0296-5*) Kalmbach.

Plays from Black Australia. Jack Davis et al. (Currency Plays Ser.). (Illus.). xi, 233p. 1989. reprint ed. pap. 24.95 (*0-86819-226-0*, Pub. by Currency Pr) Accents Pubns.

Plays from Circle Rep. L. Wilson et al. 410p. (Orig.). 1986. pap. 14.95 (*0-88145-037-5*) Broadway Play.

Plays from Contemporary American Theatre. Ed. by Brooks McNamara. 1988. mass mkt. 7.99 (*0-451-62753-9*) NAL.

Plays from Famous Stories & Fairy Tales. Adele Thane. (J). (gr. 4-7). 1989. pap. 15.00 (*0-8238-0262-0*) Kalmbach.

Plays from Famous Stories & Fairy Tales: Royalty-Free Dramatizations of Favorite Children's Stories. Adele Thane. (J). 1967. 20.10 (*0-606-04404-3*, Pub. by Turtleback) Demco.

Plays from Hispanic Tales. Barbara Winther. LC 97-51973. 150p. (J). (gr. 4-8). 1998. pap. 13.95 (*0-8238-0307-4*) Kalmbach.

Plays from Playwrights Horizons. T. Cone et al. 336p. (Orig.). 1987. pap. 14.95 (*0-88145-047-2*) Broadway Play.

Plays from South Coast Rep. 1993. pap. 14.95 (*0-88145-111-8*) Broadway Play.

Plays from the Cynical Life. August Strindberg. Tr. by Walter Johnson from SWE. LC 82-13581. (Illus.). 144p. 1983. 25.00 (*0-295-95980-0*) U of Wash Pr.

Plays from the New York Shakespeare Festival. M. Cohen et al. 400p. (Orig.). 1986. pap. 14.95 (*0-88145-036-7*) Broadway Play.

Plays from the Philadelphia Young Playwrights Festival. Sally Oswald et al. 96p. 1998. pap. 5.00 (*0-87440-057-0*) Bakers Plays.

***Plays from Woolly Mammoth.** Robert Alexander et al. 1999. pap. 14.95 (*0-88145-159-2*) Broadway Play.

Plays In. 2nd ed. Ed. by Daniel Halpern. 512p. 1999. reprint ed. pap. 18.00 (*0-88001-490-3*) HarpC.

Plays in One Act. Ed. by Daniel Halpern. 1991. pap. 16.95 (*0-88001-305-2*) HarpC.

Plays in One Act. Ed. by Daniel Halpern. 502p. 1997. reprint ed. 9.98 (*1-56731-164-4*, MJF Bks) Fine Comms.

Plays in Ten. David S. Raine. 1995. 5.50 (*0-87129-588-1*, P95) Dramatic Pub.

Plays Modelled on the Noh (1916) Ezra Pound. Ed. by Donald C. Gallup. LC 87-124514. (Illus.). 38p. 1987. pap. 17.00 (*0-918160-02-2*) Friends Univ Toledo.

Plays, Movies, & Critics. Ed. by Jody McAuliffe. LC 93-17308. (Illus.). 304p. 1993. text 49.95 (*0-8223-1404-5*); pap. text 17.95 (*0-8223-1418-5*) Duke.

Plays of America from American Folklore for Children, K-6. L. E. McCullough. LC 96-6172. (Young Actors Ser.). 176p. (Orig.). (J). (gr. k-6). 1996. pap. 14.95 (*1-57525-038-1*) Smith & Kraus.

Plays of America from American Folklore for Young Actors, 7-12. L. E. McCullough. 176p. (Orig.). (YA). (gr. 7-12). 1996. pap. 14.95 (*1-57525-040-3*) Smith & Kraus.

***Plays of Ancient Israel.** L. E. McCullough. 192p. (J). (gr. k-2). 2000. pap. 15.95 (*1-57525-252-X*) Smith & Kraus.

Plays of Anton Chekhov. Anton Chekhov. 24.95 (*0-89190-432-8*) Amereon Ltd.

Plays of Anton Chekhov. Anton Chekhov. Tr. by Paul Schmidt. 400p. 1998. pap. 14.00 (*0-06-092875-1*) HarpC.

***Plays of Anton Chekhov.** Anton Chekhov. 1999. 25.25 (*0-8446-6987-3*) Peter Smith.

Plays of Anton Chekhov. Anton Chekhov. Tr. by Paul Schmidt. LC 96-42456. 400p. 1997. 30.00 (*0-06-018705-0*) HarpC.

Plays of Beaumont & Fletcher. Ernest H. Oliphant. LC 73-126657. reprint ed. 37.50 (*0-404-04814-5*) AMS Pr.

Plays of Beaumont & Fletcher: An Attempt to Determine Their Respective Shares & the Shares of Others. Ernest H. Oliphant. (BCL1-PR English Literature Ser.). 553p. 1992. reprint ed. lib. bdg. 99.00 (*0-7812-7236-X*) Rprt Serv.

Plays of Beaumont & Fletcher: An Attempt to Determine Their Respective Shares & the Shares of Others. Ernest H. Oliphant. 1971. reprint ed. 10.00 (*0-403-01138-8*) Scholarly.

Plays of Belonging: Three Plays. Rex Deverell. (Playwrights Canada Ser.). 1998. text 12.95 (*0-88754-531-9*) Theatre Comm.

Plays of Benn Levy: Between Conrad & Shaw. Susan Rusinko. LC 94-10592. (Illus.). 224p. 1994. 36.50 (*0-8386-3556-3*) Fairleigh Dickinson.

Plays of Black Americans. rev. ed. Ed. by Sylvia E. Kamerman. LC 94-9314. 160p. (Orig.). (J). (gr. 4-9). 1994. pap. 13.95 (*0-8238-0301-5*) Kalmbach.

Plays of Codco. Ed. by Helen Peters. LC 92-3833. (Illus.). XL, 446p. (Orig.). (C). 1993. pap. text 26.95 (*0-8204-1861-7*) P Lang Pubng.

Plays of Colley Cibber. Colley Cibber. LC 99-54768. 2000. write for info. (*0-8386-3624-1*) Fairleigh Dickinson.

Plays of Confession & Therapy: To Damascus I, to Damascus II & to Damascus III. August Strindberg. LC 78-20962. (Illus.). 260p. 1979. pap. 25.00 (*0-295-95567-8*) U of Wash Pr.

Plays of David Garrick Vol. 1: Garrick's Own Plays, 1740-1766. Ed. by Harry W. Pedicord & Fredrick L. Bergmann. LC 79-28443. (Plays of David Garrick). (Illus.). 480p. 1980. 49.95 (*0-8093-0862-2*) S Ill U Pr.

Plays of David Garrick Vol. 2: Garrick's Own Plays, 1767-1775. Ed. by Harry W. Pedicord & Fredrick L. Bergmann. LC 79-28443. (Illus.). 444p. 1980. 49.95 (*0-8093-0863-0*) S Ill U Pr.

Plays of David Garrick Vol. 3: Garrick's Adaptations of Shakespeare, 1744-1756. Ed. by Harry W. Pedicord & Fredrick L. Bergmann. LC 80-28443. (Illus.). 496p. 1981. 49.95 (*0-8093-0968-8*) S Ill U Pr.

Plays of David Garrick Vol. 4: Garrick's Adaptations of Shakespeare, 1759-1773. Ed. by Harry W. Pedicord & Fredrick L. Bergmann. LC 80-28443. (Illus.). 490p. 1981. 49.95 (*0-8093-0969-6*) S Ill U Pr.

Plays of David Garrick Vol. 5: Garrick's Alterations of Others, 1742-1750. Ed. by Harry W. Pedicord & Fredrick L. Bergmann. LC 80-28443. 485p. 1982. 51.95 (*0-8093-0993-9*) S Ill U Pr.

Plays of David Garrick Vol. 6: Garrick's Alterations of Others, 1751-1756. Ed. by Harry W. Pedicord & Fredrick L. Bergmann. LC 80-28443. 453p. 1982. 51.95 (*0-8093-0994-7*) S Ill U Pr.

Plays of David Garrick Vol. 7: Garrick's Alterations of Others, 1757-1773. Ed. by Harry W. Pedicord & Fredrick L. Bergmann. LC 80-28443. 399p. 1982. 50.00 (*0-8093-1051-1*) S Ill U Pr.

Plays of David Hare. Carol Homden. LC 93-42187. 274p. (C). 1995. pap. text 19.95 (*0-521-42718-5*) Cambridge U Pr.

Plays of David Storey: A Thematic Study. William Hutchings. LC 87-35985. 220p. (C). 1988. text 26.95 (*0-8093-1461-4*) S Ill U Pr.

Plays of Edward Bond. Richard G. Scharine. 302p. 1972. 38.50 (*0-8387-1538-9*) Bucknell U Pr.

Plays of Ernst Toller: A Revelation. Cecil Davies. (Contemporary Theatre Studies: Vol. 10). 685p. 1996. text 55.00 (*3-7186-5614-0*, ECU70, Harwood Acad Pubs); pap. text 25.00 (*3-7186-5615-9*, ECU32, Harwood Acad Pubs) Gordon & Breach.

Plays of Eugene O'Neill: A Study in Myths & Symbols. Avadhesh K. Singh. 1993. 25.00 (*81-85231-11-7*, Pub. by Creative Pubs) Advent Bks Div.

Plays of Eva Gore-Booth. Eva Gore-Booth. Ed. by Frederick S. Lapisardi. LC 91-23060. 244p. 1991. pap. 29.95 (*0-7734-9912-1*) E Mellen.

Plays of Exploration & Discovery. L. E. McCullough. LC 99-30020. 128p. (J). (gr. 4-6). 1999. pap. 14.95 (*1-57525-113-2*) Smith & Kraus.

Plays of Fairy Tales for Grades K-3. L. E. McCullough. LC 97-32881. (Plays for Young Actors Ser.). 224p. (Orig.). (J). (gr. k-3). 1998. pap. 14.95 (*1-57525-109-4*) Smith & Kraus.

Plays of Frances Sheridan. Ed. by Robert T. Hogan & Jerry C. Beasley. LC 82-49304. (Illus.). 216p. 1985. 35.00 (*0-87413-243-6*) U Delaware Pr.

Plays of George Chapman: The Tragedies with Sir Gyles Goosecappe, A Critical Edition. Ed. by Alan Holaday. 1987. 130.00 (*0-85991-243-4*) Boydell & Brewer.

Plays of George Fitzmaurice: Folkplays, Vol. 2. George Fitzmaurice. 153p. 1970. 15.95 (*0-85105-013-1*) Dufour.

Plays of George Fitzmaurice: Realistic Plays, Vol. 3. George Fitzmaurice. Ed. by Howard K. Slaughter. 166p. 1970. 15.95 (*0-85105-174-X*) Dufour.

***Plays of Girish Karnad: Critical Perspectives** Jaydipsinh Dodiya. LC 99-932707. 304p. 1999. write for info. (*81-7551-061-7*, Pub. by Prestige) Advent Bks Div.

Plays of Great Achievers. Ed. by Sylvia E. Kamerman. LC 92-13505. 366p. (Orig.). (J). (gr. 4-9). 1992. pap. 16.95 (*0-8238-0297-3*) Kalmbach.

Plays of Heinrich von Kleist: Ideals & Illusions. Sean Allan. (Studies in German). (Illus.). 333p. (C). 1996. text 64.95 (*0-521-49511-3*) Cambridge U Pr.

Plays of Henry Fielding: A Critical Study of His Dramatic Career. Albert J. Rivero. LC 88-35304. 170p. 1989. text 30.00 (*0-8139-1228-8*) U Pr of Va.

Plays of Henry Medwall. Henry Medwall. Ed. by Alan H. Nelson. (Tudor Interludes Ser.: No. II). 245p. 1980. 75.00 (*0-85991-054-7*) Boydell & Brewer.

Plays of Hrotswitha of Gandersheim. Tr. by Larissa Bonfante & Alexandra Bonfante-Warren from LAT. LC 79-90053. 1986. reprint ed. pap. 18.00 (*0-86516-178-X*) Bolchazy-Carducci.

Plays of Ibsen, Vols. III, IV. Tr. by Michael Meyer. 1986. pap. 4.95 (*0-317-43114-5*) PB.

Plays of Impasse: Contemporary Drama Set in Confining Institutions. Carol Rosen. LC 82-61381. 357p. 1983. reprint ed. pap. 110.70 (*0-608-02887-8*, 206395100007) Bks Demand.

***Plays of Israel Reborn.** L. E. McCullough. 192p. (J). (gr. k-3). 2000. 15.95 (*1-57525-253-8*) Smith & Kraus.

Plays of James Reaney. James S. Reaney. 110p. 1977. pap. 7.00 (*0-920763-30-8*, Pub. by ECW) LPC InBook.

Plays of Jewish Interest on the American Stage. Edward D. Coleman. 1972. 59.95 (*0-8490-0842-5*) Gordon Pr.

Plays of John Heywood. Ed. by Richard Axton & Peter Happe. (Tudor Interludes Ser.: No. VI). 368p. (C). 1991. 90.00 (*0-85991-319-8*) Boydell & Brewer.

Plays of John Lyly. Ed. by Carter A. Daniel. LC 87-47849. 384p. 1988. 45.00 (*0-8387-5119-9*) Bucknell U Pr.

Plays of John Lyly: Eros & Eliza. Michael Pincombe. LC 95-47235. 224p. 1997. text 79.95 (*0-7190-3858-8*) Manchester Univ Pr.

Plays of John Marston, 3 vols. John Marston. 1988. reprint ed. lib. bdg. 290.00 (*0-7812-0324-4*) Rprt Serv.

Plays of John Marston, 3 vols. John Marston. reprint ed. 225.00 (*0-403-04206-2*) Somerset Pub.

***Plays of Kalidasa: Theater of Memory.** Barbara Stoler Miller. Ed. by Edwin Gerow. 387p. 1999. pap. 125.00 (*81-208-1681-1*, Pub. by Motilal Bnarsidass) St Mut.

Plays of Lord Byron. Ed. by Robert F. Gleckner & Bernard Beatty. (Liverpool English Texts & Studies: No. 29). 320p. 1997. pap. 21.95 (*0-85323-891-X*, Pub. by Liverpool Univ Pr); boxed set 44.95 (*0-85323-881-2*, Pub. by Liverpool Univ Pr) Intl Spec Bk.

***Plays of Mahasweta Devi.** E. Satyanarayana. 2000. 29.50 (*81-7551-081-1*, Pub. by Prestige) S Asia.

Plays of Michael Vinaver: Political Theatre in France. Kevin Elstob. LC 91-37696. (American University Studies: Romance Languages & Literature: Ser. II, Vol. 178). 215p. (C). 1992. text 40.95 (*0-8204-1646-0*) P Lang Pubng.

Plays of Mythology. L. E. McCullough. LC 97-32882. 224p. (YA). (gr. 4-6). 1997. pap. 14.95 (*1-57525-110-8*) Smith & Kraus.

Plays of Negro Life: A Sourcebook of Native American Drama. Alain L. Locke. LC 77-132077. 430p. 1971. reprint ed. lib. bdg. 35.00 (*0-8371-5037-X*, IPN&, Greenwood Pr) Greenwood.

Plays of Old Japan. Ed. by Leo Duran. LC 77-94339. (One-Act Plays in Reprint Ser.). 1978. reprint ed. 20.00 (*0-8486-2037-2*) Roth Pub Inc.

Plays of Oscar Wilde. Oscar Wilde. LC 87-40358. 440p. 1988. pap. 13.00 (*0-394-75788-2*) Vin Bks.

Plays of Oscar Wilde. Oscar Wilde. 238p. Date not set. 21.95 (*0-8488-2545-4*) Amereon Ltd.

Plays of Our Forefathers & Some of the Traditions upon Which They Were Founded. Charles M. Gayley. LC 68-25810. (Illus.). 1968. reprint ed. 30.00 (*0-8196-0209-4*) Biblo.

Plays of People at Work. L. E. McCullough. 128p. (J). (gr. k-3). 1998. pap. 14.95 (*1-57525-140-X*) Smith & Kraus.

Plays of Philip Massinger, 4 vols., Set. 2nd ed. Philip Massinger. Ed. by William Gifford. LC 12-36722. reprint ed. write for info. (*0-404-04280-5*) AMS Pr.

Plays of Protest. Upton Sinclair. LC 75-115275. 1970. reprint ed. 39.00 (*0-403-00293-1*) Scholarly.

Plays of Richard Steele. Richard Steele. Ed. by Shirley S. Kenny. (C). 1971. 79.00 (*0-19-812414-7*) OUP.

Plays of Robert Munford. Robert Munford. 105p. 1992. pap. 7.95 (*0-929408-06-3*) Amer Eagle Pubns Inc.

Plays of Roswitha. Roswitha. Tr. by Christopher St. John. LC 65-20048. 1972. reprint ed. 22.95 (*0-405-08900-7*) Ayer.

Plays of Roswitha. Roswitha. Tr. by Christopher St. John. LC 65-20048. 1989. reprint ed. pap. 18.95 (*0-88143-106-0*) Ayer.

Plays of Saki. Saki, pseud. 16.95 (*0-8488-0842-8*) Amereon Ltd.

Plays of Samuel Beckett. Eugene Webb. LC 73-174798. 160 p. 1972. write for info. (*0-7206-0352-8*) P Owen Ltd.

Plays of Saunders Lewis, Vol. 3. Saunders & Lewis. 1985. pap. 17.95 (*0-8464-4890-4*) Beekman Pubs.

***Plays of Shakespeare: A Thematic Guide.** Victor L. Cahn. LC 00-22337. 296p. 2000. 50.00 (*0-313-30981-7*, GR0981, Greenwood Pr) Greenwood.

Plays of Susan Glaspell: A Contextual Study. Gainor. (Illus.). (C). text. write for info. (*0-472-10650-3*) U of Mich Pr.

Plays of the Cretan Renaissance. Georgios Chortatsis. Ed. by Rosemary Bancroft-Marcus. 1150p. 2001. 125.00 (*0-19-815808-4*) OUP.

Plays of the 47 Workshop: 1st Series. Forty-Seven Workshop Staff. (BCL1-PS American Literature Ser.). 113p. 1992. reprint ed. lib. bdg. 69.00 (*0-7812-6648-3*) Rprt Serv.

Plays of the 47 Workshop: 2nd Series. Forty-Seven Workshop Staff. (BCL1-PS American Literature Ser.). 139p. 1992. reprint ed. lib. bdg. 69.00 (*0-7812-6649-1*) Rprt Serv.

Plays of the 47 Workshop: 3rd Series. Forty-Seven Workshop Staff. (BCL1-PS American Literature Ser.). 92p. 1992. reprint ed. lib. bdg. 69.00 (*0-7812-6650-5*) Rprt Serv.

Plays of the Greek Dramatists: Selections from Aeschylus, Sophocles, Euripides & Aristophanes. Ed. by Arthur Zieger. 20.00 (*0-8196-2794-1*) Biblo.

Plays of the Holocaust: An International Anthology. Ed. by Elinor Fuchs. LC 87-9997. 340p. (Orig.). 1987. pap. 16.75 (*0-930452-63-1*) Theatre Comm.

Plays of the Irish Renaissance, 1880-1930. Ed. by Curtis Canfield. LC 73-4881. (Play Anthology Reprint Ser.). 1980. reprint ed. 34.95 (*0-8369-8248-7*) Ayer.

Plays of the Italian Theatre. Giovanni Verga et al. Tr. by Isaac Goldberg. LC 76-40394. (One-Act Plays in Reprint Ser.). 1976. reprint ed. 25.00 (*0-8486-2009-7*) Roth Pub Inc.

Plays of the Marquis de Sade: Count Oxtiern, The Bedroom, The Madness of Misfortune, The Haunted Tower, The Shyster, Vol. 1. Marquis De Sade, pseud. Tr. by John Franceschina & Ben Ohmart from FRE. LC 92-17131. 250p. (C). 1993. text 35.00 (*0-89341-708-4*); pap. text 18.50 (*0-89341-709-2*) Hollowbrook.

Plays of the Marquis de Sade: Tancrede, Fanny, The Antique Dealers, Love Makes the Misanthrope, Festival of Friendship, Vol. 3. Marquis De Sade, pseud. Tr. by John Franceschina & Ben Ohmart from FRE. LC 92-17131. 225p. 1995. text 35.00 (*0-89341-745-9*); pap. text 18.50 (*0-89341-746-7*) Hollowbrook.

Plays of the Marquis de Sade: The Self-Proclaimed Philosopher, Jeanne Laine, The Twins, Truth & Treason, Henriette & St. Clair, Vol. 2. Marquis De Sade, pseud. Tr. by John Franceschina from FRE. LC 92-17131. 250p. (C). 1993. text 35.00 (*0-89341-710-6*); pap. text 18.50 (*0-89341-711-4*) Hollowbrook.

Plays of the Marquis de Sade: The Wedding of the Century, The Marriage of the Arts, The Freak, Prefaces & Theatrical Essays, Vol. 4. Marquis De Sade, pseud. Tr. by John Franceschina & Ben Ohmart from FRE. LC 92-17131. 325p. 1995. text 35.00 (*0-89341-747-5*); pap. text 18.50 (*0-89341-748-3*) Hollowbrook.

Plays of the Natural & the Supernatural. Theodore Dreiser. LC 73-97893. 1969. reprint ed. 32.50 (*0-404-02179-4*) AMS Pr.

***Plays of the Natural & the Supernatural.** Theodore Dreiser. (Collected Works of Theodore Dreiser). 288p. 1998. reprint ed. lib. bdg. 88.00 (*1-58201-624-0*) Classic Bks.

Plays of the Natural & the Supernatural. Theodore Dreiser. LC 74-131690. reprint ed. 69.00 (*0-403-00577-9*) Scholarly.

Plays of the New Democratic Spain (1975-1990) Patricia W. O'Connor. 500p. (Orig.). (C). 1992. pap. text 44.00 (*0-8191-8442-X*); lib. bdg. 72.50 (*0-8191-8441-1*) U Pr of Amer.

Plays of the Passion. Linn Creighton. LC 98-15539. 124p. 1998. 13.95 (*1-57895-053-8*) Bridge Resources.

Plays of the Pioneers: A Book of Historical Pageant Plays. Constance D. Mackay. LC 76-40389. (One-Act Plays in Reprint Ser.). 1976. reprint ed. 20.00 (*0-8486-2005-4*) Roth Pub Inc.

Plays of the Present. John B. Clapp & Edwin F. Edgett. LC 73-83498. (Illus.). 331p. 1972. 24.95 (*0-405-08361-0*, Pub. by Blom Pubns) Ayer.

***Plays of the 70's, Vol. 1.** Ed. by Katharine Brisbane. LC 99-196480. (Orig.). 1998. pap. 24.95 (*0-86819-548-0*, Pub. by Currency Pr) Accents Pubns.

Plays of the Seventies: An Anthology. Intro. & Selected by Bill Findlay. 400p. 1994. pap. 30.00 (*1-84017-028-X*) St Mut.

Plays of the 60's, Vol. 3. Ed. by Katharine Brisbane. (Orig.). pap. 24.95 (*0-86819-562-6*, Pub. by Currency Pr) Accents Pubns.

Plays of the Songs of Christmas. L. E. McCullough. LC 96-22834. (Young Actors Ser.). 128p. 1996. pap. 19.95 (*1-57525-062-4*) Smith & Kraus.

Plays of the Southern Americas. Stanford University Dramatists' Alliance Staff. LC 74-173626. (Play Anthology Reprint Ser.). 1977. reprint ed. 22.95 (*0-8369-8231-2*) Ayer.

Plays of the Wild West: Grades K-3. L. E. McCullough. LC 97-14729. (Plays for Young Actors Ser.: No. 1). 160p. (J). (gr. 1-5). 1997. pap. 14.95 (*1-57525-104-3*) Smith & Kraus.

Plays of the Wild West: Grades 4-6, Vol. II. L. E. McCullough. (Plays for Young Actors Ser.). (Illus.). 160p. (Orig.). (J). (gr. 4-6). 1997. pap. 14.95 (*1-57525-105-1*) Smith & Kraus.

Plays of the Year, Vol. 35. Ed. by J. C. Trewin. 416p. 1969. 16.95 (*0-910278-78-4*) Boulevard.

An Asterisk (*) at the beginning of an entry indicates that the title is appearing for the first time.

Plays of the Year, Vol. 36. Ed. by J. C. Trewin. 488p. 1969. 16.95 (*0-910278-79-2*) Boulevard.

Plays of the Year, Vol. 37. Ed. by J. C. Trewin. 416p. 1970. 16.95 (*0-910278-80-6*) Boulevard.

Plays of the Year, Vol. 38. Ed. by J. C. Trewin. 502p. 1970. 16.95 (*0-910278-81-4*) Boulevard.

Plays of Three Decades: Thunder Rock, Jeb, Shadow of Heroes. Robert Ardrey. LC 67-19963. 255p. 1968. 18.95 (*0-910278-89-X*) Boulevard.

Plays of Today, Vol. 1. Elizabeth Baker et al. LC 76-132137. (Play Anthology Reprint Ser.). 1977. 19.95 (*0-8369-8214-2*) Ayer.

Plays of Today, Vol. 2. Laurence Housman et al. LC 76-132137. (Play Anthology Reprint Ser.). 1925. 17.25 (*0-8369-8215-0*) Ayer.

Plays of Today, Vol. 3. Ashley Dukes et al. LC 76-132137. (Play Anthology Reprint Ser.). 1977. 21.95 (*0-8369-8216-9*) Ayer.

Plays of W. B. Yeats: Yeats & the Dancer. Sylvia C. Ellis. 256p. 1999. pap. 19.95 (*0-312-21069-8*) St Martin.

Plays of William Mountfort. William Mountfort. LC 77-21660. 280p. 1977. 50.00 (*0-8201-1292-5*) Schol Facsimiles.

Plays Old & New. Ed. by Stella B. Finney. 20.00 (*0-8196-2812-3*) Biblo.

Plays Old & New: Children's Edition. Stella B. Finney. student ed. 25.00 (*0-8196-1386-X*) Biblo.

Plays on Classic Themes. Franz Grillparzer. Tr. by Samuel Solomon from GER. LC 72-85607. 554p. 1969. 39.95 (*0-910278-25-3*) Boulevard.

Plays on Women: Anon, Arden of Faversham; Middleton & Dekker, The Roaring Girl; Middleton, A C. Kathleen McLuskie. 1999. 69.95 (*0-7190-1564-2*, Pub. by Manchester Univ Pr) St Martin.

Willy Russell: Plays One, Vol. 1. Willy Russell. LC 97-153162. 1996. pap. 15.95 (*0-413-70220-0*, Methuen Drama) Methn.

Sue Townsend: Plays One, Vol. 1. Sue Townsend. 1996. pap. 15.95 (*0-413-70250-2*, Methuen Drama) Methn.

Play's Place in Public Education for Young Children. Victoria J. Dimidjian. 96p. 1992. pap. 15.95 (*0-8106-0364-0*) NEA.

Plays, Players & Playing: How to Start Your Own Children's Theatre Company. Judith A. Hackbarth. LC 94-18425. (Illus.). 208p. 1994. pap. 25.00 (*0-941599-29-9*, Pub. by Piccadilly Bks) Empire Pub Srvs.

Plays, Prefaces & Postscripts of Tawfiq al-Hakim Vol. 1: Theater of the Mind. Tawfiq Al-Hakim. Tr. & Intro. by William M. Hutchins. LC 80-80887. 301p. 1981. 15.00 (*0-89410-148-X*, Three Contnts); pap. 8.95 (*0-89410-134-X*, Three Contnts) L Rienner.

Plays, Prefaces & Postscripts of Tawfiq al-Hakim Vol. 2: Theater of Society. Tawfiq Al-Hakim. Tr. & Intro. by William M. Hutchins. LC 80-80887. 350p. 1984. 15.00 (*0-89410-280-X*, Three Contnts) L Rienner.

Plays, Prose Writings & Poems. Oscar Wilde. 430p. 1996. pap. 9.95 (*0-460-87655-4*, Everyman's Classic Lib) Tuttle Pubng.

***Plays Slaves in Algiers.** Susanna Haswell Rowson. (Notable American Authors Ser.). 1999. reprint ed. lib. bdg. 125.00 (*0-7812-8843-6*) Rprt Serv.

Plays That Teach: Plays, Activities, & Songs with a Message. Judy T. Mecca. Ed. by Jan Keeling. (Illus.). 96p. (Orig.). (J). (gr. 3-6). 1992. pap. text 10.95 (*0-86530-153-0*, 195-2) Incentive Pubns.

Play's the Thing. J. K. Forte. (C). 1988. 135.00 (*1-85077-950-3*, Pub. by Darf Pubs Ltd) St Mut.

Play's the Thing. Marina Jenkins. 256p. (C). 1996. pap. 25.99 (*0-415-11498-5*) Routledge.

Play's the Thing. Marina Jenkins. 256p. (C). 1997. 85.00 (*0-415-11497-7*) Routledge.

***Play's the Thing.** Valerie Whiteson. 208p. 1999. 16.99 incl. audio (*0-521-65789-X*) Cambridge U Pr.

Play's the Thing. Valerie Whiteson & Nava Horovitz. 208p. (C). 1998. pap. text 17.95 (*0-521-65791-1*) Cambridge U Pr.

Play's the Thing: A Story about William Shakespeare. Ruth Turk. LC 97-10849. (Carolrhoda Creative Minds Book Ser.). (Illus.). 64p. (J). (gr. 3-5). 1997. 19.93 (*1-57505-212-1*, Carolrhoda) Lerner Pub.

Play's the Thing: An Introduction to Drama. Nedra P. Roberts. 417p. (Orig.). (gr. 9-12). 1981. pap. text 10.50 (*0-88334-141-7*) Longman.

Play's the Thing: Instructor's Manual. Valerie Whiteson & Nava Horovitz. 30p. (C). 1998. pap. text, teacher ed. 6.00 (*0-521-65790-3*) Cambridge U Pr.

Play's the Thing: Teachers' Roles in Children's Plays. Elizabeth Jones & Gretchen Reynolds. (Early Childhood Education Ser.). 160p. (C). 1992. pap. 17.95 (*0-8077-3171-4*) Tchrs Coll.

Peter Barnes Plays, Vol. 3. Peter Barnes. (Methuen Contemporary Dramatists). 1996. pap. 17.95 (*0-413-69980-3*, Methuen Drama) Heinemann.

Plays to Play with in Class. Sally-Anne Milgrim. LC 85-60244. (Illus.). 208p. 1991. pap. 10.95 (*0-89390-060-5*, Pub. by Resource Pubns) Empire Pub Srvs.

Plays Unpleasant. George Bernard Shaw. 288p. 1989. pap. 10.95 (*0-14-045021-1*) Viking Penguin.

Plays Well with Others. Allan Gurganus. 368p. 1999. pap. 14.00 (*0-375-70203-2*) Vin Bks.

Plays with Songs. Adrian Mitchell. (Oberon Bks.). 264p. 1997. pap. 18.95 (*1-870259-40-8*) Theatre Comm.

Plays without Theatres. Pamela Dellar. (C). 1989. text 35.00 (*0-948929-27-8*) St Mut.

Playsmen. Jeri Westerson. 320p. 1998. 21.00 (*1-891488-00-7*) Russn Hill Pr.

Playspaces: Architecture for Children. Julia Brown-Turrell. LC 89-50429. (Illus.). 59p. (Orig.). 1989. pap., spiral bd. 25.00 (*0-9614615-7-8*) Edmundson.

PlayStation, Vol. 3. PCS Staff. 1996. pap., per. 12.99 (*0-7615-0527-X*) Prima Pub.

PlayStation: The Unauthorized Edition, Vol. 2. Vince Matthews. 128p. 1996. pap. text 12.99 (*0-7615-0515-6*) Prima Pub.

PlayStation Bundle Bks. 1 & 2: Official Playstation Games. Bradygames Staff. 1996. pap. text 19.98 (*1-56686-587-5*) Brady Pub.

PlayStation Game Secrets, Vol. 4. Ed. by Judie Svabik. 144p. 1997. per. 12.99 (*0-7615-1154-7*) Prima Pub.

PlayStation Game Secrets: The Unauthorized Edition, Vol. 1. Vince Matthews. 128p. 1996. pap. text 12.99 (*0-7615-0200-9*) Prima Pub.

PlayStation Game Secrets Vol. 7: Prima's Unauthorized Strategy Guide, Vol. 7. Ed. by Steve Faragher et al. (Illus.). 143p. 1999. pap. 14.99 (*0-7615-2102-X*) Prima Pub.

PlayStation Game Secrets Unauthorized, Vol. 5. Prima Publishing Staff. 144p. 1998. per. 12.99 (*0-7615-1463-5*) Prima Pub.

PlayStation Game Secrets Unauthorized, Vol. 6. Prima Creative Services Staff & Vince Matthews. 96p. 1998. per. 12.99 (*0-7615-1643-3*) Prima Pub.

PlayStation Games Book, Vol. 4. 4th ed. Brady Publishing Staff & Christine Cain. 112p. 1997. 11.99 (*1-56686-704-5*) Brady Pub.

PlayStation Games Secrets. Proteus Group Staff. (Illus.). 153p. (Orig.). 1995. 9.99 (*1-56686-408-9*) Brady Pub.

PlayStation Player's Guide. Zach Meston & John Ricciardi. (Gaming Mastery Ser.). (Illus.). 320p. (Orig.). 1996. pap. 14.95 (*1-884364-22-5*) Sandwich Islands.

PlayStation Player's Guide, Vol. 2. Zach Meston & J. Douglas Arnold. (Gaming Mastery Ser.). 288p. (Orig.). (YA). (gr. 7 up). 1997. pap. 14.95 (*1-884364-49-7*) Sandwich Islands.

PlayStation Pocket Power Guide, Vol. 3. Prima Publishing Staff. LC 96-70918. Vol. 3. 96p. 1998. per. 7.99 (*0-7615-1466-X*) Prima Pub.

PlayStation Pocket Power Guide: Unauthorized. Prima Publishing Staff. LC 96-70918. 96p. 1996. pap. 7.99 (*0-7615-0973-9*) Prima Pub.

PlayStation Pocket Power Guide Vol. 2: Unauthorized. Prima Publishing Staff. LC 96-70918. (Secrets of the Game Ser.). 96p. 1997. per. 7.99 (*0-7615-1120-2*) Prima Pub.

PlayStation Power Pocket Guide Vol. 4: Prima's Unauthorized Game Secrets. Prima Publishing Staff. LC 96-70918. (Games Ser.). 96p. 1998. per. 7.99 (*0-7615-1818-5*) Prima Pub.

PlayStation RPG Secrets. Chris Jensen. LC 97-69923. 224p. 1997. per. 14.99 (*0-7615-1331-0*) Prima Pub.

***PlayStation Secret Codes, 4.** Bradygames Staff. LC 99-72444. 1999. pap. text 7.99 (*1-56686-893-9*) Brady Pub.

***PlayStation Ultimate Strategy Guide.** 4th ed. Bart Farkas. (PlayStation Ultimate Strategy Guides Ser.). 1999. pap. 14.99 (*0-7821-2687-1*) Sybex.

Playtexts: Ludics in Contemporary Literature. Warren F. Motte. LC 94-19827. (Stages Ser.). ix, 233p. 1995. text 40.00 (*0-8032-3181-4*) U of Nebr Pr.

Playtherapy with Children. Sue Jennings. (Illus.). 224p. 1993. pap. 36.95 (*0-632-02442-9*) Blackwell Sci.

***Plaything.** Penny Birch. 2000. mass mkt. 6.95 (*0-352-33493-2*) Nexus.

Playthings & Pastimes in Japanese Prints. Lea Baten. LC 94-43737. (Illus.). 160p. 1995. 39.95 (*0-8348-0344-5*) Weatherhill.

Playthings, Selected Toys from the Collection of the Westmoreland Museum of Art. Paul A. Chew. (Illus.). 36p. (Orig.). 1994. pap. text 9.95 (*0-931241-26-X*) Westmoreland.

Playtime see Critter Sitters Cloth Books

Playtime. Dorothea Ackroyd. 1999. 3.95 (*1-58185-202-9*) Quadrillion Media.

Playtime. Deni Bown. (Treasure Hunt Board Bks.). 10p. (J). 1996. 4.95 (*0-7894-0627-6*) DK Pub Inc.

Playtime. D K Publishing Staff. (Bath Bks.). 1999. pap. text 4.95 (*0-7894-4324-4*) DK Pub Inc.

Playtime. Murphy. (Razzle Dazzle Bks.). (Illus.). 12p. (J). (ps-1). 1998. 4.99 (*0-689-82056-9*) S&S Childrens.

Playtime. Linda G. Richman. (Illus.). 252p. 1995. spiral bd. 29.00 (*1-884135-18-8*) Mayer-Johnson.

Playtime. Denyse Worland. LC 92-31077. (Voyages Ser.). (Illus.). (J). 1993. 4.25 (*0-383-03590-2*) SRA McGraw.

Playtime. Ronald Heuninck. (Illus.). 14p. (J). (ps). 1991. reprint ed. bds. 5.50 (*0-86315-124-8*, Pub. by Floris Bks) Gryphon Hse.

Playtime: Activity Book. Ed. by Sara Strange. (Illus.). 96p. 1991. pap. 12.95 (*0-563-34351-6*, BBC-Parkwest) Parkwest Pubns.

Playtime: Bright Ideas for Pre-School Play. Delphine Evans. (Illus.). 128p. 1992. 11.95 (*0-09-174163-7*, Pub. by Hutchnson) Trafalgar.

Playtime: First Words, Rhymes & Actions. LC 98-83014. (Illus.). 16p. (J). 1999. bds. 7.99 (*0-7636-0933-1*) Candlewick Pr.

Playtime: Supplementary Music, Pt. A. 5th ed. Ed. by Frances Clark & Louise Goss. (Frances Clark Library for Piano Students). 16p. (J). (gr. 1-3). 1976. reprint ed. pap. 5.95 (*0-87487-137-9*, 0137) Summy-Birchard.

Playtime Activity Books. Dover Staff. 1991. text 8.00 (*0-486-26972-8*) Dover.

***Playtime Art for Preschoolers.** Delphine Boswell. LC 98-34859. 96p. 1998. pap. 14.99 (*0-7644-2111-5*) Group Pub.

***Playtime at Barney's House!** Guy Davis. LC 00-105008. (Illus.). (J). (ps). 2000. 9.95 (*1-58668-051-X*) Lyrick Studios.

Playtime Baby: Baby Books. Illus. by Alison Ross. 8p. (J). (ps). 1992. text 3.50 (*0-7214-1514-8*, S9212-2, Ladybrd) Penguin Putnam.

Playtime Boutique: 50 Fun, Fun & Easy-to-Make Projects. Ann Poe & Kandy Schneider. LC 99-23628. 128p. Date not set. pap. 19.95 (*0-8442-0092-1*, 00921, Contemporary Bks) NTC Contemp Pub Co.

Playtime Crafts & Activities: Fun Things to Make & Do. Liz Dwyer. LC 93-73232. (Illus.). 32p. (J). (gr. 2-7). 1994. pap. 4.95 (*1-56397-348-0*) Boyds Mills Pr.

***Playtime for Piglet.** Frances Coe. (Play-Along Puppet Bks.). (Illus.). 4p. (J). (ps-k). 2000. bds. 4.99 (*0-448-42098-8*, G & D) Peng Put Young Read.

Playtime for Recorder: Animal Songs. (Illus.). 32p. 1993. pap. 7.95 (*0-7119-3464-9*, AM91221) Music Sales.

Playtime for Recorder: Hymn Tunes. (Illus.). 32p. 1993. pap. 7.95 (*0-7119-3461-4*, AM91218) Music Sales.

Playtime for Recorder: Traditional Folk Tunes. (Illus.). 32p. 1993. pap. 7.95 (*0-7119-3462-2*, AM91219) Music Sales.

Playtime for Rosie Rabbit. Patrick Yee. LC 96-142242. (Illus.). 14p. (J). (ps-3). 1996. 6.99 (*0-689-80717-1*) Litle Simon.

Playtime for Zoo Animals. Caroline Arnold. LC 98-24380. (Zoo Animals Ser.). (Illus.). 32p. (J). (gr. k-2). 1999. 21.27 (*1-57505-287-3*, Carolrhoda) Lerner Pub.

***Playtime for Zoo Animals.** Caroline Arnold. LC 98-24380. (Zoo Animals Ser.). 32p. (J). (gr. k-2). 1999. 9.95 (*1-57505-391-8*, Carolrhoda) Lerner Pub.

Playtime Friends: Victorian Pop-Up. Stephen L. Nelson. 1994. 4.99 (*0-8407-6957-1*) Nelson.

Playtime Is Science: An Equity-Based Parent/Child Science Program. Barbara Sprung et al. LC 96-39701. 1997. 69.95 (*0-931629-11-X*) Educ Equity Con.

Playtime Learning Games for Young Children. Alice S. Honig. LC 82-16794. (Illus.). 128p. 1982. pap. 12.95 (*0-8156-0178-6*) Syracuse U Pr.

PlayTime Piano Christmas Level 1: 5 Finger Melodies. Nancy Faber & Randall Faber. Ed. by Edwin McLean. (Faber & Faber Piano Library). (Illus.). 24p. (J). (gr. 1-3). 1988. pap. 4.95 (*0-929666-02-X*) FJH Music Co Inc.

PlayTime Piano Hymns Level 1: 5 Finger Melodies. Nancy Faber & Randall Faber. Ed. by Edwin McLean. (Faber & Faber Piano Library). (Illus.). 24p. (J). (gr. 1-3). 1988. pap. 4.95 (*0-929666-00-3*) FJH Music Co Inc.

PlayTime Piano Popular Level 1: 5 Finger Melodies. Nancy Faber & Randall Faber. Ed. by Edwin McLean. (Faber & Faber Piano Library). (Illus.). 24p. (J). (gr. 1-3). 1988. pap. 4.95 (*0-929666-01-1*) FJH Music Co Inc.

Playtime Poems. Illus. by Nick Sharratt. 32p. (J). Date not set. write for info. (*0-19-276128-5*) OUP.

Playtime Pottery & Porcelain: From Europe & Asia. Lorraine Punchard. LC 95-52684. (Illus.). 192p. (YA). (gr. 10-13). 1996. pap. write for info. (*0-88740-974-1*) Schiffer.

Playtime Pottery & Porcelain: From the United Kingdom & the United States. Lorraine Punchard. LC 95-44164. (Illus.). 160p. (YA). (gr. 10-13). 1996. pap. 29.95 (*0-88740-958-X*) Schiffer.

Playtime Props for Toddlers. Carol Gnojewski. LC 97-62227. (Time for Toddlers Ser.). (Illus.). 160p. (J). (ps). 1998. pap. 14.95 (*1-57029-204-3*, 4701) Totline Pubns.

Playtime Rhymes. (Happytime Ser.: No. S871-8). (Illus.). (J). (ps). pap. 1.25 (*0-7214-9552-4*, Ladybrd) Penguin Putnam.

***Playtime Rhymes.** Kindersley Dorling. LC 99-54784. (Read & Listen Ser.). (Illus.). 32p. (J). (ps-3). 2000. pap. text 7.95 (*0-7894-5465-3*, D K Ink) DK Pub Inc.

Playtime Rhymes: And Songs for the Very Young. Priscilla Lamont. LC 97-36187. (Illus.). 29p. (J). (ps-4). 1998. 12.95 (*0-7894-2861-X*) DK Pub Inc.

Playtime Surprises: An Antique Moving Picture Book. Ernest Nister. LC 84-16579. (Illus.). 12p. (J). (gr. k up). 1985. 13.95 (*0-399-21214-0*, Philomel) Peng Put Young Read.

***Playtime Treasury.** (Illus.). 96p. (YA). 2000. pap. 10.95 (*0-7534-5296-0*, Kingfisher) LKC.

Playtime with Big Bird. Random House Staff. (Board Bks.). (J). 1997. 2.50 (*0-679-88881-0*, Pub. by Random Bks Yng Read) Random.

Playtime with Captain Kangaroo & Friends. (Captain Kangaroo Coloring Bks.: Vol. 4). (Illus.). 24p. (J). 1998. pap. write for info. (*0-7666-0222-2*, Honey Bear Bks) Modern Pub NYC.

Playtime with Simba & Nala. Golden Books Family Entertainment Staff. (Illus.). (J). 1998. pap. text 3.99 (*0-307-09206-2*, 09206, Goldn Books) Gldn Bks Pub Co.

Playtraining Your Dog. Patricia G. Burnham. (Illus.). 256p. 1985. pap. 11.95 (*0-312-61691-0*) St Martin.

Playwise: 365 Fun-Filled Activities for Building Character, Conscience & Emotional Intelligence in Children. Denise C. Weston & Mark S. Weston. LC 96-3858. (Illus.). 304p. (Orig.). 1996. pap. 17.95 (*0-87477-808-5*, Tarcher Putnam) Putnam Pub Group.

***Playwork: A Guide to Good Practice.** 2nd ed. Paul Bonel & Jennie Liindon. (Illus.). 268p. 2000. pap. 39.50 (*0-7487-5496-2*, Pub. by S Thornes Pubs) Trans-Atl Phila.

Playworld of Sanskrit Drama. Robert E. Goodwin. LC 98-915809. 217 p. 1998. 175.00 (*81-208-1589-0*, Pub. by Motilal Bnarsidass) St Mut.

Playwright & Historical Change: Dramatic Strategies in Brecht, Hauptmann, Kaiser & Wedekind. Leroy R. Shaw. LC 75-106042. 195p. 1970. reprint ed. pap. 60.50 (*0-608-01978-X*, 206263300003) Bks Demand.

Playwright As Magician: Shakespeare's Image of the Poet in the English Public Theater. Alvin B. Kernan. LC 79-10829. 164p. 1979. 27.00 (*0-300-02379-0*) Yale U Pr.

Playwright Plays Vol. 9: Complete Plays 9: Tatters, Still Still. Manuel P. Garcia. 110p. 1998. 4.95 (*1-885901-59-3*, Liberts) Presbyters Peartree.

Playwright Power: A Concise How-to-Book for the Dramatist. Robert Friedman. LC 96-17741. 164p. 1996. pap. text 24.50 (*0-7618-0362-9*) U Pr of Amer.

Playwright vs. Director: Authorial Intentions & Performance Interpretations, 54. Ed. by Jeane Luere & Sidney Berger. LC 93-44134. (Contributions in Drama & Theatre Studies: No. 54). 200p. 1994. 59.95 (*0-313-28679-5*, Greenwood Pr) Greenwood.

Playwrighting: A Course. Robert Spira. (Illus.). 83p. (C). 1991. pap. text 20.00 (*0-911455-04-3*) Quartz Pr.

Playwrights & Acting: Acting Methodologies of Brecht, Ionesco, Pinter & Shepard, 59. James H. McTeague. LC 94-17979. (Contributions in Drama & Theatre Studies). 216p. 1994. 55.00 (*0-313-28975-1*, Greenwood Pr) Greenwood.

Playwrights & Plagiarists in Early Modern England: Gender, Authorship, Literary Property. Laura J. Rosenthal. LC 96-22233. 256p. 1996. text 39.95 (*0-8014-3252-9*) Cornell U Pr.

Playwright's Art: Conversations with Contemporary American Dramatists. Ed. by Jackson R. Bryer. LC 94-14070. (Illus.). 359p. (C). 1995. pap. 18.00 (*0-8135-2129-7*) Rutgers U Pr.

Playwright's Art: Stage, Radio, Television, Motion Pictures. Roger M. Busfield. LC 78-139125. 260p. (C). 1971. reprint ed. lib. bdg. 65.00 (*0-8371-5741-2*, BUPA, Greenwood Pr) Greenwood.

***Playwrights at Work.** Paris Review Staff. LC 99-44064. (Illus.). 320p. 2000. pap. 15.95 (*0-679-64021-5*) Modern Lib NY.

Playwright's Companion, 1998: A Practical Guide to Script Opportunities in the U. S. A. 14th rev. ed. Ed. by Mollie A. Meserve. 416p. 1998. pap. 20.95 (*0-937657-35-2*) Feedbk Theabks & Prospero.

Playwrights for Tomorrow, Vol. 13. Ed. by Arthur H. Ballet. LC 66-19124. 314p. pap. 97.40 (*0-8357-6527-X*, 203589600013) Bks Demand.

Playwrights for Tomorrow: A Collection of Plays, 5. Ed. by Arthur H. Ballet. LC 66-19124. 166p. 1969. reprint ed. pap. 51.50 (*0-608-08307-0*, 205583800005) Bks Demand.

Playwrights for Tomorrow: A Collection of Plays, 6. Ed. by Arthur H. Ballet. LC 66-19124. 148p. 1969. reprint ed. pap. 45.90 (*0-608-08308-9*, 205583800006) Bks Demand.

Playwrights for Tomorrow: A Collection of Plays, Vol. 1. Ed. by Arthur H. Ballet. LC 66-19124. 280p. 1966. reprint ed. pap. 86.80 (*0-8357-6528-8*, 203589600001) Bks Demand.

Playwrights for Tomorrow: A Collection of Plays, Vol. 3. Ed. by Arthur H. Ballet. LC 66-19124. 352p. reprint ed. pap. 109.20 (*0-8357-6529-6*, 203589600003) Bks Demand.

Playwrights for Tomorrow: A Collection of Plays, Vol. 4. Ed. by Arthur H. Ballet. LC 66-19124. 349p. reprint ed. pap. 108.20 (*0-8357-6530-X*, 203589600004) Bks Demand.

Playwrights for Tomorrow: A Collection of Plays, Vol. 7. Ed. by Arthur H. Ballet. LC 66-19124. 221p. reprint ed. pap. 68.60 (*0-8357-6531-8*, 203589600007) Bks Demand.

Playwrights for Tomorrow: A Collection of Plays, Vol. 8. Ed. by Arthur H. Ballet. LC 66-19124. 220p. reprint ed. pap. 68.20 (*0-8357-6532-6*, 203589600008) Bks Demand.

Playwrights for Tomorrow: A Collection of Plays, Vol. 9. Ed. by Arthur H. Ballet. LC 66-19124. 216p. reprint ed. pap. 67.00 (*0-8357-6533-4*, 203589600009) Bks Demand.

Playwrights for Tomorrow: A Collection of Plays, Vol. 10. Ed. by Arthur H. Ballet. LC 66-19124. 201p. reprint ed. pap. 62.40 (*0-8357-6534-2*, 203589600010) Bks Demand.

Playwrights for Tomorrow: A Collection of Plays, Vol. 11. Ed. by Arthur H. Ballet. LC 66-19124. 237p. reprint ed. pap. 73.50 (*0-8357-6525-3*, 203589600011) Bks Demand.

Playwrights for Tomorrow: A Collection of Plays, Vol. 12. Ed. by Arthur H. Ballet. LC 66-19124. 274p. reprint ed. pap. 85.00 (*0-8357-6526-1*, 203589600012) Bks Demand.

Playwright's Handbook. rev. ed. Frank Pike & Thomas G. Dunn. LC 85-318. 272p. 1996. pap. 13.95 (*0-452-27588-1*, Plume) Dutton Plume.

Playwrights in Rehearsal. Susan L. Cole. (Illus.). 256p. (C). (gr. 13). 1999. 65.00 (*0-415-91969-X*, Thtre Arts Bks) Routledge.

Playwrights of Color. Ed. by Meg Swanson. LC 99-14126. 714p. 1999. pap. text 59.95 (*1-877864-35-8*) Intercult Pr.

Playwrights of Exile: An International Anthology. Eduardo Manet et al. Ed. by Francoise Kourilsky. Tr. by Stephen J. Vogel et al from FRE. 456p. 1997. pap. 19.95 (*0-913745-48-0*) Ubu Repertory.

Playwrights of the New American Theater. Thomas H. Dickinson. LC 67-26731. (Essay Index Reprint Ser.). 1977. 23.95 (*0-8369-0373-0*) Ayer.

Playwrights of the New American Theater. Thomas H. Dickinson. (BCL1-PS American Literature Ser.). 331p. 1992. reprint ed. lib. bdg. 89.00 (*0-7812-6634-3*) Rprt Serv.

Playwrights on Playmaking: Other Studies of the Stage. Brander Matthews. LC 67-26765. (Essay Index Reprint Ser.). 1977. 23.95 (*0-8369-0698-5*) Ayer.

Playwright's Process: Learning the Craft from Today's Leading Dramatists. Buzz Mclaughlin. LC 97-7977. 288p. 1997. pap. text 18.95 (*0-8230-8833-2*, Back Stage Bks) Watsn-Guptill.

***Playwright's Survival Guide: Keeping the Drama in Your Work & Out of Your Life.** Gary Garrison. LC 99-27323. 144p. 1999. pap. text 14.95 (*0-325-00165-0*) Heinemann.

P

An Asterisk (*) at the beginning of an entry indicates that the title is appearing for the first time.

Playwright's Workbook. Jean-Claude Van Itallie. LC 97-28471. 160p. 1998. pap. 16.95 (*1-55783-302-8*) Applause Theatre Bk Pubs.

Playwriting. Downs. LC 97-72178. (C). 1997. pap. text 22.50 (*0-15-503861-3*, Pub. by Harcourt Coll Pubs) Harcourt.

Playwriting: A Complete Guide to Creating Theater. Shelly Frome. LC 89-42715. 191p. 1990. pap. 28.50 (*0-89950-425-6*) McFarland & Co.

Playwriting: A Manual for Beginners. Debra A. Peterson. 51p. (gr. 10 up). 1999. pap. 9.95 (*0-87129-822-8*, P85) Dramatic Pub.

Playwriting: The 1st Workplace. Kathleen E. George. 202p. 1994. pap. text 28.95 (*0-240-80190-3*, Focal) Buttrwrth-Heinemann.

Playwriting: Writing, Producing & Selling Your Play. Louis E. Catron. Orig. Title: Writing, Producing & Selling Your Play. 272p. (C). 1990. reprint ed. pap. text 16.95 (*0-88133-564-9*) Waveland Pr.

Playwriting for the Puppet Theatre. Jean M. Mattson. LC 97-8165. 235p. 1997. pap. 24.95 (*0-8108-3324-7*) Scarecrow.

Playwriting for Theater, Film, & Television. Laura A. Shamas. LC 91-19479. 176p. (Orig.). 1998. reprint ed. pap. 20.00 (*1-55870-213-X*, Betrwy Bks) F & W Pubns Inc.

Playwriting-in-Process: Thinking & Working Theatrically. Michael Wright. LC 97-1815. 208p. 1997. pap. 17.95 (*0-435-07034-7*) Heinemann.

***Playwriting Master Class: The Personality of Process & the Art of Rewriting.** Michael Wright. 224p. 2000. pap. 18.95 (*0-325-00169-3*) Heinemann.

Playwriting Self of Bernard Shaw. John A. Bertolini. LC 89-49568. 208p. (C). 1991. 26.95 (*0-8093-1650-1*) S Ill U Pr.

Playwriting Step by Step. Marsh Cassady. LC 92-3406. 114p. 1990. pap. 11.95 (*0-89390-056-7*, Pub. by Resource Pubns) Empire Pub Srvs.

Playwriting Women: 7 Plays from the Women's Project. Ed. by Julia Miles. 325p. (C). 1993. pap. 17.95 (*0-435-08617-0*, 08617) Heinemann.

Plaza Chica. Maria I. Fornes. (SPA.). 67p. 1994. pap. text 4.95 (*1-885901-12-7*) Presbyters Peartree.

Plaza First & Always. William Worley & Michael McKenzie. LC 97-18963. (Illus.). 192p. 1997. 36.00 (*1-886110-19-0*) Addax Pubng.

***Plazas.** Hershberger. (C). 2000. pap., teacher ed. 25.00 (*0-8384-1179-7*) Heinle & Heinle.

***Plazas.** L. Pellettieri. (C). 2000. pap., wbk. ed., lab manual ed. 3.50 (*0-8384-1182-7*) Heinle & Heinle.

***Plazas.** L. Pellettieri. (C). 2000. pap., wbk. ed., lab manual ed. 25.00 (*0-8384-1129-0*) Heinle & Heinle.

***Plazas.** annot. ed. Hershberger. (C). 2000. pap., teacher ed. 45.00 (*0-8384-1180-0*) Heinle & Heinle.

***Plazas-Activities File.** Curry. (C). 2000. pap. 15.00 (*0-8384-1187-8*) Heinle & Heinle.

Plazas Mayores de Espana, I. L. Cervera Vera. (SPA., Illus.). 408p. 1993. 295.00 (*84-239-5285-1*) Elliots Bks.

PLC Selected Applications, Vol. 1. 2nd ed. Luis A. Bryan & Eric A. Bryan. Ed. by Stephanie Phillipo & Lisa Dupree. (Selected Application Ser.). (Illus.). 435p. (Orig.). 1997. pap. text 45.95 (*0-944107-25-7*, 106) Indust Text.

PLC Workbook & Study Guide. 2nd ed. Luis A. Bryan & Eric A. Bryan. Ed. by Stephanie Phillipo. (Illus.). 327p. 1997. pap. text, student ed., wbk. ed. 25.00 incl. VHS (*0-944107-33-8*, 224) Indust Text.

Plea Against Extremism. Tallach. 1994. pap. 3.99 (*1-871676-11-8*, Pub. by Christian Focus) Spring Arbor Dist.

Plea Bargaining: The Experiences of Prosecutors, Judges, & Defense Attorneys. Milton Heumann. LC 77-9970. (Illus.). 1978. lib. bdg. 18.00 (*0-226-33187-3*) U Ch Pr.

Plea Bargaining: The Experiences of Prosecutors, Judges & Defense Attorneys. Milton Huemann. LC 77-9970. (Illus.). 232p. 1981. pap. text 18.00 (*0-226-33188-1*) U Ch Pr.

Plea Bargaining: 1997 Edition, 1998 Supplement. G. N. Herman. LC 97-68450. 1997. text, suppl. ed. 85.00 (*1-55834-568-X*, 65718-10, MICHIE) LEXIS Pub.

Plea Bargaining, 1999 Cumulative Supplement. G. Nicholas Herman. 75p. 1999. 35.00 (*0-327-01158-0*, 6571911) LEXIS Pub.

P

Plea Book 1, Halifax County, Virginia, 1752-1755. Marian D. Chiarito. 146p. (Orig.). 1988. per. 25.00 (*0-945503-14-8*) Clarkton Pr.

Plea for a Measure of Abnormality. Joyce McDougall. LC 92-29739. 493p. 1992. reprint ed. pap. text 39.95 (*0-87630-701-2*) Brunner-Mazel.

Plea for a New Look at Lepidoptera: Special Reference to the Scent Distributing Organs of Male Moths. G. C. Varley. 1962. write for info. (*0-7855-2552-1*) St Mut.

Plea for Liberty. Ed. by Thomas Mackay. LC 81-80950. 565p. 1982. reprint ed. 20.00 (*0-913966-95-9*); reprint ed. pap. 7.00 (*0-913966-96-7*) Liberty Fund.

Plea for Old Cap Collier. Irvin S. Cobb. (Collected Works of Irvin S. Cobb). 56p. 1998. reprint ed. lib. bdg. 88.00 (*1-58201-606-2*) Classic Bks.

Plea for Peasant Proprietors: With the Outlines of a Plan for Their Establishment in Ireland. William T. Thornton. LC 68-58028. (Reprints of Economic Classics Ser.). xii, 256p. 1969. reprint ed. 39.50 (*0-678-00569-9*) Kelley.

Plea for Purity: Sex, Marriage & God. 2nd rev. expanded ed. Johann C. Arnold. LC 98-33914. 224p. 1998. pap. 12.00 (*0-87486-960-9*) Plough.

Plea for the Abolition of Tests in the University of Oxford. 2nd ed. Goldwin A. Smith. Ed. by Walter P. Metzger. (Academic Profession Ser.). 1977. reprint ed. lib. bdg. 17.95 (*0-405-10026-4*) Ayer.

***Plea for the Indians.** John Beeson. (Illus.). 149p. 1998. pap. 11.95 (*0-87770-676-X*) Ye Galleon.

Plea for the Poor. John Woolman. (Notable American Authors Ser.). 1999. reprint ed. lib. bdg. 125.00 (*0-7812-7785-X*) Rprt Serv.

Plea for the West. Lyman Beecher. Ed. by Gerald N. Grob. LC 76-46067. 1977. lib. bdg. 19.95 (*0-405-09941-X*) Ayer.

Plea for the West. Lyman Beecher. (Works of Lyman Beecher). 190p. 1985. reprint ed. lib. bdg. 49.00 (*0-932051-00-6*) Rprt Serv.

Plea for Woman. Marion Reid. LC 88-61923. 98p. 1988. reprint ed. pap. 12.95 (*0-948275-56-1*) Dufour.

Plea from the Angels: Messages from Michael the Archangel. 2nd ed. Denise Cooney. (Orig.). 1996. pap. 12.95 (*0-944256-74-0*) ACCESS Pubs Network.

Plea from the Angels: Messages from Michael, the Archangel. 2nd ed. Denise R. Cooney. 160p. 1996. pap. 12.95 (*0-9673784-0-0*, Pub. by Angel Work Pr) ACCESS Pubs Network.

Plea of Insanity in Criminal Cases. Forbes Winslow. (Historical Foundations of Forensic Psychiatry & Psychology Ser.). viii, 78p. 1983. reprint ed. lib. bdg. 17.50 (*0-306-76180-7*) Da Capo.

Plea of Pan (1901) Henry W. Nevisnon. 212p. 1998. reprint ed. pap. 17.95 (*0-7661-0552-5*) Kessinger Pub.

Plea of Puerto Rico. Luis A. Ferre. (Studies in Puerto Rican History, Literature & Culture). 1980. lib. bdg. 59.95 (*0-8490-3087-0*) Gordon Pr.

Plea of the Negro Soldier & 100 Other Poems. Charles F. White. LC 78-133164. (Black Heritage Library Collection). 1977. 24.95 (*0-8369-8720-9*) Ayer.

Plead Your Case. Kenneth E. Hagin. 1979. pap. 1.00 (*0-89276-058-3*) Faith Lib Pubns.

Pleaders & Protesters: The Future of Citizens' Organizations in Israel. Eliezer D. Jaffe. LC 80-68431. 40p. 1980. pap. 2.50 (*0-87495-028-7*) Am Jewish Comm.

Pleading & Procedure - State & Federal: 1996 Supplement to Cases & Materials On. 7th ed. Geoffrey C. Hayard, Jr. et al. (University Casebook Ser.). 92p. 1996. pap. text. write for info. (*1-56662-382-0*) Foundation Pr.

Pleading & Procedure - State & Federal: 1997 Supplement to Cases & Materials. 7th ed. Geoffrey C. Hazard, Jr. et al. (University Casebook Ser.). 122p. (C). 1997. pap. text. write for info. (*1-56662-496-7*) Foundation Pr.

Pleading & Procedure Casebooks: 1995 Civil Procedure Supplement for Use with All. Jack Friedenthal. (American Casebook Ser.). 440p. (C). 1995. pap. text 17.50 (*0-314-06861-9*) West Pub.

Pleading & Procedure, State & Federal: Cases & Materials. 7th ed. Geoffrey C. Hazard, Jr. Ed. by Colin C. Tait & William A. Fletcher. (University Casebook Ser.). 321p. 1994. pap. text, teacher ed. write for info. (*1-56662-247-6*) Foundation Pr.

Pleading & Procedure, State & Federal: Cases & Materials. 7th ed. Geoffrey C. Hazard, Jr. & Colin C. Tait. Ed. by William A. Fletcher. (University Casebook Ser.). 1417p. 1994. text 49.00 (*1-56662-157-7*) Foundation Pr.

Pleading Guilty. Scott Turow. 386p. 1993. 24.00 (*0-374-23457-4*) FS&G.

Pleading Guilty. abr. ed. Scott Turow. 1993. audio 24.00 (*0-671-87043-2*) S&S Audio.

Pleading Guilty. large type ed. Scott Turow. LC 93-4746. 495p. 1993. lib. bdg. 25.95 (*0-8161-5746-4*, G K Hall Lrg Type) Mac Lib Ref.

Pleading Guilty. Scott Turow. 480p. 1994. reprint ed. mass mkt. 7.99 (*0-446-36550-5*, Pub. by Warner Bks) Little.

Pleading Precedents. 5th ed. Malcolm M. Britts. LC 95-103131. 359p. 1994. pap. 69.00 (*0-455-21267-8*, Pub. by LawBk Co) Gaunt.

Pleading Without Tears: A Guide to Legal Drafting. 2nd ed. William M. Rose. 316p. (C). 1992. pap. 32.00 (*1-85431-216-2*, Pub. by Blackstone Pr) Gaunt.

Pleadings & Pretrial Practice: A Deskbook for Connecticut Litigators. Jeanne M. Dumont. LC 95-104164. iii, 157 p. 1994. write for info. (*0-910051-33-X*) CT Law Trib.

Pleadings Game: An Artificial Intelligence Model of Procedural Justice. Thomas F. Gordon. (Diverse Ser.). 260p. (C). 1995. lib. bdg. 110.50 (*0-7923-3607-0*, Pub. by Kluwer Academic) Kluwer Academic.

Pleadings Without Tears: A Guide to Legal Drafting. 4th ed. William M. Rose. 353p. 1997. pap. 34.00 (*1-85431-639-7*, Pub. by Blackstone Pr) Gaunt.

***Pleadings Without Tears: A Guide to Legal Drafting under the Civil Procedure Rules.** 5th ed. William R. Rose. 1999. pap. 31.00 (*1-85431-890-X*, Pub. by Blackstone Pr) Gaunt.

Pleadings Without Tears in Australia. Peter Young & Hugh Selby. 256p. 1997. pap. 49.00 (*1-86287-234-1*, Pub. by Federation Pr) Gaunt.

***Pleasant Activities: COPE Program for Depression.** John H. Greist et al. 56p. 1999. pap. write for info. (*0-9702974-3-2*) Healthcare Sys.

***Pleasant Bay: Stories of a Cape Cod Place.** (Illus.). 200p. 1999. pap. 25.00 (*0-9676220-0-X*) Bog House.

Pleasant Beth. Robert L. Merriam. (Illus.). 24p. (Orig.). 1975. pap. 2.00 (*0-686-32490-0*) R L Merriam.

Pleasant Conceited Historie, Called the Taming of a Shrew. Ed. by Graham Holderness & Bryan Loughrey. 144p. (C). 1992. text 57.50 (*0-389-20998-8*) B&N Imports.

Pleasant Disport of Divers Noble Personages Entitled Philocopo. Giovanni Boccaccio. LC 71-25579. (English Experience Ser.: No. 277). 116p. 1970. reprint ed. 35.00 (*90-221-0277-7*) Walter J Johnson.

***Pleasant Dreams: Nighttime Meditations for Peace of Mind.** Amy E. Dean. LC 99-57405. 128p. 2000. 9.95 (*1-56170-693-0*, L460) Hay House.

Pleasant Grove Families: Saline County, Arkansas, Recollections of a Church, a Cemetery, a Community of the Past. 2nd ed. Carolyn E. Billingsley. (Illus.). 216p. 1997. pap. 28.00 (*1-56546-108-8*) Arkansas Res.

Pleasant Grove Families (Saline County, Arkansas) Recollections of a Church, a Cemetery, a Community of the Past. Carolyn E. Billingsley. (Illus.). 202p. 1988. pap. 23.50 (*0-9618123-5-4*) C E Billingsley.

***Pleasant Hill - Shaker Canaan in Kentucky: An Architectural & Social Study.** Clay Lancaster. LC 98-90411. (Illus.). 134p. 2000. 35.00 (*1-892106-14-0*) Warwick Pubns.

***Pleasant Places: The Rustic Landscape from Bruegel to Ruisdael** Walter S. Gibson. LC 99-29336. 290p. 2000. 55.00 (*0-520-21698-9*) U CA Pr.

Pleasant Quippes for Upstart Newfangled Gentlewomen. limited ed. Stephen Gosson. Ed. by Edwin J. Howard. 1942. 30.00 (*0-686-17402-X*) R S Barnes.

Pleasant Refuge: "Experiences" Lewis E. Forrest. ii, 51p. 1997. pap. 10.00 (*0-9666519-1-X*) LEMLS.

Pleasant Suite, for Tenor Viol, Alto Recorder, & Bass Viol. David Goldstein. (Contemporary Consort Ser.: No. 28). i, 13p. 1994. pap. text 10.00 (*1-56571-081-9*, CC028) PRB Prods.

Pleasant the Scholar's Life: Irish Intellectuals & the Construction of the Nation State. Maurice Goldring. 192p. 1998. pap. 17.50 (*1-897959-06-0*, Pub. by Serif) IPG Chicago.

Pleasant Valley. Louis Bromfield. LC 97-18639. (Illus.). 320p. 1997. pap. 14.00 (*1-888683-56-2*) Wooster Bk.

Pleasant Valley. Louis Bromfield. 1976. reprint ed. lib. bdg. 25.95 (*0-88411-504-6*) Amereon Ltd.

Pleasant Vices. Judy Astley. 288p. 1998. mass mkt. write for info. (*0-552-99565-7*, Pub. by Corgi Bks Ltd) Doubleday.

Pleasant Ways of the Jewish Daughter. S. Wagschal. 1995. 13.95 (*1-58330-161-5*); pap. 8.95 (*1-58330-113-5*) Feldheim.

Pleasant Weather Ratings: Enjoy Travel More & Save Money by Planning for the Weather. Thomas Whitmore. LC 96-83608. 116p. (Orig.). 1996. pap. 10.95 (*0-9645785-7-3*) Consumer Travel.

***Pleasantness of a Religious Life.** Christian Focus U. K. Staff. 1998. 6.99 (*1-85792-391-X*, Pub. by Christian Focus) Spring Arbor Dist.

Pleasantness of a Religious Life. Matthew Henry. 192p. 1996. reprint ed. 18.95 (*1-57358-044-9*) Soli Deo Gloria.

Pleasantries. C. Pleasants York. Ed. by Sam McKay. (Illus.). 60p. (Orig.). 1996. pap. write for info. (*0-614-14903-7*) Green Jade.

Pleasantries of Old Quong, Vol. 1. Thomas Burke. LC 72-5861. (Short Story Index Reprint Ser.). 1977. reprint ed. 23.95 (*0-8369-4195-0*) Ayer.

Pleasantries of the Incredible Mulla Nasrudin. Ed. by Idries Shah. 169p. 1983. reprint ed. 25.00 (*0-86304-023-3*, Pub. by Octagon Pr) ISHK.

Pleasantries of the Incredible Mullah Nasrudin. Mullah Nasrudin. 224p. 1993. pap. 12.95 (*0-14-019357-X*, Penguin Bks) Viking Penguin.

Pleasantville, 1893: A Charming Piece of Americana That Never Existed. 60p. 1992. 7.50 (*0-9632035-0-9*) Flambro Imports.

Pleasantville, 1893: A Charming Piece of Americana That Never Existed. deluxe limited ed. 60p. 1992. write for info. (*0-9632035-1-7*) Flambro Imports.

Please. Chariot Books Staff. LC 50-6526. (Talking with God Ser.). 22p. (J). (ps). 1993. bds. 3.29 (*0-7814-0107-0*, Chariot Bks) Chariot Victor.

***Please.** Ruth S. Odor. LC 99-25377. (Illus.). 32p. (J). 1999. lib. bdg. 18.50 (*1-56766-672-8*) Childs World.

Please Adjust Your Set: 59 Graphical Adventures. fac. ed. Ed Weston. (Illus.). 59p. 1995. 8.50 (*0-9646772-0-2*) Eirenicon Design.

Please Adjust Your Set: 59 Graphical Adventures. Ed Weston. (Illus.). 59p. 1995. reprint ed. 14.95 (*0-9646772-1-0*) Eirenicon Design.

***Please & Thank-You.** Lise Caldwell. 2000. pap. text. write for info. (*0-7847-1109-7*) Standard Pub.

***Please & Thank You.** Keith Faulkner. (Illus.). 4p. (J). 1998. bds. 7.99 (*1-58048-037-3*) Sandvik Pub.

Please Ask. Cecelia Kroll. LC 85-90128. 241p. (Orig.). 1985. pap. 9.00 (*0-9614913-0-2*) C Kroll.

***Please, Baby, Please.** Spike Lee & Tonya Lewis Lee. LC 99-462286. (Illus.). (J). 2001. write for info. (*0-689-83233-8*) S&S Childrens.

Please Be Ad-Vised: The Legal Reference for the Advertising Executive. Doug Wood. 420p. 1995. pap. text 59.95 (*1-56318-021-9*) Assn Natl Advertisers.

***Please Be Quiet!** Mary Murphy. LC 98-47802. (Illus.). 32p. (J). 1999. 9.95 (*0-395-97113-6*) HM.

***Please Call Back!** Steck-Vaughn Company Staff. (Illus.). (J). 2000. pap. 2.95 (*0-8114-9306-7*) Raintree Steck-V.

Please Call the Tower! A Pilot's Guide to FAA Enforcement Program. Keith Bumsted & Kelly Reeser. (Illus.). 235p. 1994. pap. 14.95 (*0-9670342-0-5*) Paragon Commns Inc.

Please Carry Me Lord. Rose Cornelsen. 1989. pap. 7.95 (*0-919797-91-1*) Kindred Prods.

Please Come for Dinner: 12 Easy & Elegant Menus for Busy Cooks. Pat Ross. LC 97-42911. (Illus.). 84p. (YA). (gr. 11). 1999. 14.95 (*0-7835-5308-0*) Time-Life.

Please Communicate. Mary Oldfield. 1956. pap. 5.25 (*0-8222-0900-4*) Dramatists Play.

Please Die I Want a Promotion: How to Maximize Employee Contribution & Flexibility. Richard Allison. 216p. (Orig.). 1996. pap. 17.95 (*1-57502-139-0*) Morris Pubng.

Please Do Not Touch: A Collection of Stories. Judith Gorog. 144p. (J). (gr. 7-9). 1995. mass mkt. 3.50 (*0-590-46683-6*) Scholastic Inc.

Please Do Not Touch, a Collection of Stories. Judith Gorog. 1993. 8.60 (*0-606-08024-4*, Pub. by Turtleback) Demco.

Please Dr., I'd Rather Do It Myself with Herbs. LaDean Griffin. 1979. pap. 4.95 (*0-89036-058-8*) Liahona Pub Trust.

Please Don't Ask Me to Sing in the Choir. Thomas L. Are. 120p. (Orig.). 1985. pap. 8.95 (*0-916642-28-3*, 905) Hope Pub.

Please Don't Be Mine, Julie Valentine. Todd Strasser. 128p. (J). (gr. 4-6). 1995. pap. 3.99 (*0-590-48153-3*) Scholastic Inc.

Please Don't Bug the Dog. C. Uhrig. (Illus.). 24p. (ps-3). 1998. pap. text 5.25 (*0-9681925-3-X*) Hushion Hse.

Please Don't Call It Soviet Georgia. Mary Russell. (Illus.). 268p. (Orig.). 1992. pap. 16.99 (*1-85242-216-5*) Serpents Tail.

Please Don't Call Me Collect on Mother's Day. Mary McBride & Veronica McBride. Ed. by Helen Duffy. (Illus.). 105p. (Orig.). 1995. pap. 5.95 (*0-9627601-6-1*) Bros Grinn.

Please Don't Call Me Human. Wang Shuo. Tr. by Howard Goldblatt from CHI. LC 99-53596. 320p. 2000. 23.95 (*0-7868-6419-2*, Pub. by Hyperion) Time Warner.

Please Don't Call My Dog a Dog. Shirley F. Marks. LC 92-73384. (Illus.). 96p. 1993. pap. 9.95 (*0-942963-29-6*) Distinctive Pub.

***Please Don't Call My Mother: An Administrative Philosophy & Parental Intervention Plan That Works.** John Lazares. 1999. pap. text 12.95 (*1-886021-33-3*) J W Wood.

***Please Don't Come Out While We're Eating: Coming Out Cartoons.** Julian Lake. LC 99-98253. (Illus.). 100p. 2000. pap. 8.95 (*0-9663454-3-6*, Pub. by Rubicon Media) Bookazine Co Inc.

Please Don't Die. Lurlene McDaniel. 192p. (YA). (gr. 10 up). 1993. mass mkt. 4.50 (*0-553-56262-2*) Bantam.

Please Don't Die. Lurlene McDaniel. 1993. 9.60 (*0-606-07972-6*, Pub. by Turtleback) Demco.

Please Don't Eat the Daisies. Jean Kerr. 1976. 18.95 (*0-8488-0552-6*) Amereon Ltd.

Please Don't Eat the Daisies. Jean Kerr. 1994. reprint ed. lib. bdg. 28.95 (*1-56849-298-7*) Buccaneer Bks.

Please Don't Eat the Teacher! Scott Ciencin. (Dinoverse Ser.: No. 4). (Illus.). 192p. (YA). (gr. 4-7). 2000. pap. 4.99 (*0-679-88846-2*, Pub. by Random Bks Yng Read) Random.

Please Don't Feed the Anxiety Monster. Judy M. Stamper. (Illus.). 16p. 1995. 6.95 (*0-9667751-0-4*) Just in Time.

Please Don't Feed the Bears. Allan Fowler. LC 91-3130. (Rookie Read-About Science Ser.). (Illus.). 32p. (J). (ps-2). 1991. pap. 4.95 (*0-516-44916-8*) Childrens.

Please Don't Feed the Children! Tales of Tarry-a-While. Barbara L. Jenni. 106p. 1994. 7.00 (*0-9643271-0-4*) Appenzeller.

Please Don't Feed the Egos: And Other Tips for Corporate Survival. Scott Adams. LC 97-228609. (Illus.). 40p. 1997. 6.95 (*0-8362-3224-0*) Andrews & McMeel.

Please Don't Feed the Lions. Michael A. Vander Klipp. LC 94-46166. (J). 1995. pap. 7.95 (*1-56212-062-X*) CRC Pubns.

Please Don't Feed the Vampire! R. L. Stine, pseud. (Give Yourself Goosebumps Ser.: No. 15). 1997. pap. 3.99 (*0-590-93477-5*, Apple Paperbacks) Scholastic Inc.

Please Don't Feed the Vampire! R. L. Stine, pseud. (Give Yourself Goosebumps Ser.: No. 15). 1997. 9.09 (*0-606-11391-6*, Pub. by Turtleback) Demco.

Please Don't Go. MaryJo Valley. LC 97-195102. (Illus.). 93p. (Orig.). (J). (gr. 5-7). 1996. pap. 9.99 (*0-88092-097-1*) Royal Fireworks.

Please Don't Go Back Where You Came From. John O'Brien. 1994. 5.50 (*0-87129-434-6*, P75) Dramatic Pub.

Please Don't Hit It to Me. Adoff Jaime Levi. 1924. write for info. (*0-688-17532-5*); lib. bdg. write for info. (*0-688-17533-3*) Lothrop.

Please Don't Hurt Me, Doc! Humourous Experiences from 40 Years of Practice. Daniel L. Thomas, Jr. LC 97-35779. (Illus.). 79p. (Orig.). 1997. pap. 10.00 (*1-888683-57-0*) Wooster Bk.

***Please Don't Kill the Umpire! Reminiscences of an Obscure Man in Blue.** John Massaro. 229p. 1999. pap. 14.00 (*0-9670092-1-9*) Springbok.

Please Don't Kiss Me at the Bus Stop: Over 600 Things Parents. Merry B. Jones. LC 97-1219. (Illus.). 224p. (Orig.). 1997. pap. 7.95 (*0-8362-3589-4*) Andrews & McMeel.

Please Don't Mind My Bubbles. Christopher A. Fitts. (Illus.). 42p. 1992. text 20.00 (*0-9635689-1-4*) Storm Grove.

Please Don't Quote Me, Vol. 1. Caralee Aschenbrenner. (Illus.). 344p. 1994. 32.00 (*0-9647651-0-1*) Straddle Creek.

Please Don't Say Good-Bye. Adalu Justus. Ed. & Des. by Michel Justus. LC 97-42818. vii, 430p. 1998. 23.95 (*0-937109-06-1*, 1); pap., per. 19.95 (*0-937109-08-8*, 1) J Ike Bks.

Please Don't Say Hello: Living with Childhood Autism. Phyllis Gold. LC 74-13185. (Illus.). 48p. 1975. pap. 10.95 (*0-89885-199-8*, Kluwer Acad Hman Sci) Kluwer Academic.

Please Don't Say You Need Me: Biblical Answers for Co-Dependency. Jan Silvious. 176p. 1989. pap. 10.99 (*0-310-34391-7*) Zondervan.

***Please Don't Shoot the Messenger! How to Talk to Demanding Bosses, Clueless Colleagues, Tough Customers & Difficult Clients Without Losing Your Cool (Or Your Job)** Gary S. Goodman. LC 99-38814. 224p. 2000. pap. 14.95 (*0-8092-2520-4*, 252040, Contemporary Bks) NTC Contemp Pub Co.

***Please Don't Sit Next to Me!** Matthew Ellis. (Illus.). 130p. 2000. pap. 9.95 (*1-930669-00-3*) A & S.

An Asterisk (*) at the beginning of an entry indicates that the title is appearing for the first time.

Please Don't Sit on the Kids: Alternatives to Punitive Discipline. Clare Cherry. LC 82-81981. (J). (ps-3). 1982. pap. 13.99 (*0-8224-5474-2*) Fearon Teacher Aids.

Please Don't Squeeze Your Boa Noah. Marilyn Singer. 88p. (J). 1995. 15.95 (*0-8050-3277-0*) H Holt & Co.

Please Don't Step on Me. Elly-Kree George. (Illus.). 20p. (J). (gr. 1-3). 1981. 4.00 (*0-935741-07-0*) Cherokee Pubns.

Please Don't Stop. Art Freifeld. (Illus.). 1987. teacher ed. 12.95 (*0-916177-02-5*); student ed. 9.95 (*0-916177-13-0*); 5.95 (*0-916177-14-9*); 10.95 (*0-916177-15-7*) Am Eng Pubns.

Please Don't Stop, Set. Art Freifeld. (Illus.). 1987. 35.95 (*0-916177-16-5*) Am Eng Pubns.

Please Don't Tailgate the Real Estate. William C. Anderson. 224p. 1997. 16.95 (*0-934798-51-6*) TL Enterprises.

Please Don't Tell My Parents. Dawson McAllister. 176p. (YA). 1992. pap. 8.99 (*0-8499-3311-0*) Word Pub.

Please Don't Wish Me a Merry Christmas: A Critical History of the Separation of Church & State. Stephen M. Feldman. LC 96-35601. 400p. (C). 1996. 55.00 (*0-8147-2637-2*) NYU Pr.

Please Don't Wish Me a Merry Christmas: A Critical History of the Separation of Church & State. Stephen M. Feldman. (Critical America Ser.). 396p. 1998. pap. text 20.00 (*0-8147-2684-4*) NYU Pr.

Please Explain! Pauline Hanson's Electoral Appeal. Murray Goot. 128p. 1999. pap. 16.95 (*0-86840-481-0*, Pub. by New South Wales Univ Pr) Intl Spec Bk.

Please Follow Me see Suite Venitienne (Please Follow Me)

Please Forgive Me. Created by Francine Pascal. (Sweet Valley High Ser.: No. 140). 208p. (YA). (gr. 7 up). 1998. mass mkt. 3.99 (*0-553-49230-6*, Sweet Valley) BDD Bks Young Read.

Please Give Me Another Chance, Lord. Lorraine Peterson. 16p. (YA). 1995. pap. 7.99 (*1-55661-583-3*) Bethany Hse.

Please, God see Por Favor, Dios

Please, God. Anne Riley. (My First Prayers Bks.). (Illus.). (J). 1997. 2.50 (*1-85608-026-9*) Hunt GBR.

Please Hang Up. Arthur S. Rosenblatt. 18p. 1984. pap. 3.50 (*0-87129-107-X*, P58) Dramatic Pub.

Please Help Me Hold On. Charles Dickson. Ed. by Becky Nelson. 22p. (Orig.). (YA). (gr. 7-12). 1992. pap. text 1.95 (*1-56309-037-6*, C926106, Wrld Changers Res) Womans Mission Union.

Please Help Me! I Hurt! A Guide for Self-Therapy. Maralene Wesner & Miles Wesner. 160p. (Orig.). 1990. pap. 9.95 (*0-936715-34-0*) Diversity Okla.

Please Help Me with This Family: Using Consultants As Resources in Family Therapy. Ed. by Maurizio Andolfi & Russell Haber. LC 94-25864. 294p. 1995. text 35.95 (*0-87630-748-9*) Brunner-Mazel.

Please Help, Miss Nightingale! Stewart Ross. (Coming Alive Ser.). (Illus.). 62p. (J). (ps-4). 1998. write for info. (*0-237-51749-3*) EVN1 UK.

Please Help Yourself! Self-Starting Ideas & Step-by-Step Recipes for Cocktail Parties & Elegant Buffet Meals. Robert Ackart. 132p. 1995. pap. 12.95 (*1-887678-07-7*) Finley-Greene Pubns.

Please Hold: 102 Things to Do While You Wait on the Phone. Wallace Wilkins. LC 95-81421. 102p. 1996. pap. 6.95 (*1-883697-46-8*) Hara Pub.

Please Hold My Hand. Geneva R. Newcomb. (Illus.). 78p. (Orig.). 1989. 9.95 (*0-9622762-1-9*); pap. 4.95 (*0-9622762-0-0*) Non-Fictitious.

Please Kill Me: The Uncensored Oral History of Punk. Ed. by Legs McNeil & Gillian McCain. LC 98-139308. (Illus.). 512p. 1997. pap. 14.95 (*0-14-026690-9*) Viking Penguin.

Please Leave Quietly: People, Power & Purpose at Work. Ed. by Graham Guest. 128p. (C). 1988. pap. text 50.00 (*0-7152-0610-9*) St Mut.

Please Leave Your Shoes at the Door. Barbara Hibschman. (Junior Jaffray Collection: Bk. 5). (Illus.). 30p. (J). (ps-2). 1992. pap. 3.99 (*0-87509-486-4*) Chr Pubns.

Please Leave Your Shoes at the Door. Corrine Sahlberg. LC 91-77848. (Jaffray Collection of Missionary Portraits: Bk. 5). 191p. 1992. pap. 9.99 (*0-87509-481-3*) Chr Pubns.

Please Let Me Be Who I Am. Beverly J. Williams. 24p. (Orig.). 1998. pap. 1.25 (*1-889552-01-1*) B J Williams.

Please Listen . . . Ed. by Helen Olson. LC 94-69790. 153p. 1994. pap. text 5.95 (*1-882972-52-X*, 3155) Queenship Pub.

Please Listen to Me: Your Guide to Understanding Teenagers & Suicide. 2nd ed. Marion Crook. 112p. 1992. pap. 9.95 (*0-88908-544-7*) Self-Counsel Pr.

Please, Lord, Make Me a Famous Poet: Or Everything You Always Wanted to Know about Poetry but Were Afraid If You Asked Someone Would Start Talking about Whatchamajigger Pentameter. Dean Blehert. LC 98-96522. (Illus.). 416p. 1999. pap. 19.95 (*1-892261-03-0*) Wrds & Pictres.

Please Make Me Cry! see Senor, Hazme Llorar

Please Miss. A. C. Griffiths. 1987. 21.00 (*0-7223-2176-7*, Pub. by A H S Ltd) St Mut.

***Please, Mr. Crocodile! Poems about Animals.** Illus. by Rosslyn Moran. 40p. (J). (gr. 1-5). 1999. 16.95 (*1-902283-62-7*) Barefoot Bks NY.

Please Mrs. Butler. Allan Ahlberg. 1984. pap. 7.95 (*0-14-031494-6*, Pub. by Pnguin Bks Ltd) Trafalgar.

Please, No Police: A Novella. Aras Oren. Tr. by Teoman Sipahigil from TUR. LC 92-75236. (Modern Middle Eastern Literature in Translation Ser.). 174p. 1992. pap. 8.95 (*0-292-76038-8*, Pub. by Ctr Mid East Stud) U of Tex Pr.

Please Pass the Roses. Colleen K. Kanieski. Ed. by J. Allen Kirsch. 222p. (Orig.). 1995. pap. 12.95 (*1-878569-26-0*) Badger Bks Inc.

Please Pass up the Salt. Lucy M. Williams. 48p. (J). (gr. k-4). 1995. 14.95 (*0-945080-18-2*) Sandridge Pub.

Please Pass up the Salt. Lucy M. Williams. (Illus.). (J). (gr. k-4). 1995. cd-rom 19.95 (*0-945080-12-3*) Sandridge Pub.

Please Please Please. Renee Swindle. LC 96-37895. 320p. 1999. 23.95 (*0-385-31863-4*, Dial Pr) Dell.

***Please Please Please.** Renee Swindle. 400p. 2000. mass mkt. 6.50 (*0-440-22376-8*) Dell.

Please Please Please. Renee Swindle. Date not set. write for info. (*0-614-18293-X*) Dial Pub.

Please, Please, Please: CJ. Rachel Vail. (The Friendship Ring Ser.). 240p. (J). (gr. 5-8). 1998. pap. 4.99 (*0-590-37452-4*) Scholastic Inc.

Please, Please, Please: CJ. Rachel Vail. LC 97-32547. (The Friendship Ring Ser.). 240p. (J). (gr. 4-8). 1998. 14.95 (*0-590-00327-5*) Scholastic Inc.

***Please, Please, Please: CJ.** Rachel Vail. (The Friendship Ring Ser.:). 240p. (J). (gr. 4-8). 1999. pap. 3.99 (*0-439-08762-7*, Pub. by Scholastic Inc) Penguin Putnam.

***Please Pray for Us: Praying for Persecuted Christians in 52 Nations.** Johan Companjen. 192p. 2000. pap. 9.99 (*0-7642-2416-6*) Bethany Hse.

Please Pray with Me: Prayers for People at Worship. Earle W. Fike. LC 90-41490. 125p. 1990. reprint ed. pap. 38.80 (*0-608-04171-8*, 206490500011) Bks Demand.

Please Put Me: Simple Spatial Concepts. Marilyn M. Toomey. (Illus.). 48p. 1989. 17.95 (*0-923573-12-7*) Circuit Pubns.

Please Remind Me How Far I've Come: Meditations for Codependents. Jan Silvious & Carolyn Capp. 304p. 1990. pap. 8.99 (*0-310-34341-0*) Zondervan.

Please Remind Me I Am the Presence of Love: Awakening to the Awareness of Love. Brother Bob. LC 94-69510. (Illus.). 159p. (Orig.). 1995. pap. 12.95 (*0-9644021-5-7*) Peaceful Express.

Please Remove Your Elbow from My Ear. Martyn N. Godfrey. 128p. (Orig.). (YA). 1993. mass mkt. 3.99 (*0-380-76580-2*, Avon Bks) Morrow Avon.

Please Say "I Do" Karen T. Whittenburg. 1997. per. 3.75 (*0-373-16698-2*, 1-16698-2) Harlequin Bks.

Please Set My Table, Psalm 23:5a. Ricki King. 116p. 1995. pap. 9.95 (*0-9649718-0-1*) Break N Bread.

Please, Somebody Love Me! Surviving Abuse & Becoming Whole. Jillian Ryan & Joseph A. Ryan. 160p. (YA). (gr. 10). 1996. mass mkt. 5.99 (*0-8007-8640-8*, Spire) Revell.

Please Stand By. Michael Ritchie. 1995. 22.95 (*0-8050-1973-1*) H Holt & Co.

Please Stand By: The Prehistory of Television. Michael Ritchie. (Illus.). 247p. 1994. 23.95 (*0-87951-546-5*, Pub. by Overlook Pr) Penguin Putnam.

Please Stand By: The Prehistory of Television. Michael Ritchie. 280p. 1995. pap. 15.95 (*0-87951-615-1*, Pub. by Overlook Pr) Penguin Putnam.

Please Stand by-Your Mother's Missing. Shirley B. Tallman & Nancy P. Gilsenan. LC 78-61590. 1980. 15.00 (*0-87212-097-X*) Libra.

Please Take Care of Willie. Tracy Sinclair. (Cupid's Little Helpers Ser.). 1997. per. 3.99 (*0-373-24101-1*, 1-24101-7) Silhouette.

Please Take Your Dead Bird Home Today: Portrait of an Alternative School. Rita K. Mitchell. LC 77-79578. 1978. 15.00 (*0-87212-094-5*) Libra.

Please Talk with Me: A Guide to Teen-Adult Dialogue. Ronald J. Gaetano et al. 96p. 1994. spiral bd. 11.95 (*0-8403-6488-1*) Kendall-Hunt.

Please! Teach ALL of Me: Multisensory Activities for Preschoolers. Jackie Crawford et al. (Illus.). 182p. 1994. pap. text, teacher ed. 19.50 (*1-57035-001-9*, 52ALL) Sopris.

Please Tease Me. R. Ambrose. mass mkt. 6.95 (*0-7472-5472-9*, Pub. by Headline Bk Pub) Trafalgar.

Please Tell! see Por Favor, Di!: Un Cuento Para Ninos Sobre el Abuso Sexual

Please Tell: A Child's Story about Sexual Abuse. Jessie. (Illus.). 32p. (J). (ps-7). pap. 8.00 (*0-89486-776-8*, 5169A) Hazelden.

Please Tell Me: Questions People Ask about Free Masonry - & the Answers. Tom McKenney. LC 94-75443. 224p. 1994. pap. 10.99 (*1-56384-013-8*) Huntington Hse.

Please Tell Me How to Be Saved. Rena K. Goss. (Little Library Ser.). 1999. pap. 0.99 (*1-57748-438-X*) Barbour Pub.

Please Tell Me What the Rebbe Said: Torah Insights Adapted from the Works of the Lubavitcher Rebbe, No. 1. Malka Touger. LC 96-117694. 150p. (J). 1993. 12.95 (*1-881400-04-2*) S I E.

Please Tell Me What the Rebbe Said: Torah Insights Adapted from the Works of the Lubavitcher Rebbe, No. 2. Malka Touger. LC 96-117694. 148p. (J). 1995. 12.95 (*1-881400-14-X*) S I E.

Please to the Table: The Russian Cookbook. Anya Von Bremzen & John Welchman. LC 90-50360. (Illus.). 704p. 1990. pap. 18.95 (*0-89480-753-6*, 1753) Workman Pub.

Please Touch: Sensory Tours for People with Disabilities, a Workbook. Taft Museum Staff. 16p. 1995. pap. 5.00 (*0-915577-26-7*) Taft Museum.

Please Touch Cookbook. Please Touch Museum Staff. Ed. by Bonnie Brook. (Illus.). 64p. (J). (ps-2). 1990. lib. bdg. 7.95 (*0-671-70558-X*) S&S Bks Yung.

Please Touch Museum Move It! A Play-&-Learn Kit. The Please Touch Museum Staff & Ann Keech. (Please Touch Museum Ser.). (Illus.). 32p. (J). 1998. 14.95 (*0-7624-0012-9*) Running Pr.

Please Tough Museum Bugs: A Play & Learn Kit. Ann Keech. LC 97-196817. (Please Touch Museum Ser.). (Illus.). 32p. (J). 1999. pap. 14.95 (*0-7624-0011-0*) Running Pr.

Please Try to Remember the 1st of October. Theo LeSieg, pseud. LC 77-4504. (Illus.). 48p. (J). (gr. k-3). 1977. lib. bdg. 11.99 (*0-394-93563-2*) Beginner.

Please Try to Remember the 1st of October. Theo LeSleg & Art Cumings. LC 77-4504. (Illus.). 48p. (J). (gr. k-3). 1977. 7.99 (*0-394-83563-8*, 565683) Beginner.

Please Understand Me: Character & Temperament Types. David West Keirsey & Marilyn Bates. 207p. 1978. pap. 11.95 (*0-9606954-0-0*) Prometheus Nemesis.

Please Understand Me II: Temperament, Character, & Intelligence. rev. ed. David West Keirsey. Ed. by Stephen Montgomery. LC 98-218142. 346p. (C). 1998. pap. 15.95 (*1-885705-02-6*) Prometheus Nemesis.

Please Understand Us! Is the World As I See It?; My Little World Book; Open Minded Kids!; Fence Me In...with Understanding, 33 vols., Set. Judy Mohr-Stephens. Ed. by Evelyn Riegert. (Illus.). 500p. (J). (gr. k-8). 1990. 139.95 (*0-935323-00-7*) Barrington Hse.

Please, Wind? Carol Greene. LC 82-4548. (Rookie Readers Ser.). (Illus.). 32p. (J). (ps-3). 1982. lib. bdg. 17.00 (*0-516-02033-1*) Childrens.

Please Wonderful Mommy. Anne De Graff. (Tiny Triumphs Ser.). (Illus.). 22p. (J). 1997. pap. text 2.95 (*0-687-07099-6*) Abingdon.

Please Write: A Beginning Composition Text for Students of ESL. Patricia Ackert. (Illus.). 192p. (C). 1995. pap. text 28.60 (*0-13-683418-3*) P-H.

***Pleasing for Our Use: David Tannenberg & the Organs of the Moravians.** Carol A. Traupman-Carr. LC 99-40651. (Illus.). 168p. 2000. 35.00 (*0-934223-60-2*) Lehigh Univ Pr.

Pleasing God. Jack Kuhatschek. (Life Guide Bible Studies Ser.). 60p. 1999. pap. 4.99 (*0-8308-3086-3*, 3086) InterVarsity.

Pleasing God. R. C. Sproul. 234p. 1994. pap. 10.99 (*0-8423-5024-1*) Tyndale Hse.

Pleasing God: A Self-Directed Bible Study for Living the Christian Life. Peggy Musgrove. 80p. 1991. pap. text 3.95 (*0-88243-651-1*, 02-0651) Gospel Pub.

Pleasing God in Our Worship. Robert Godfrey. (Today's Issues Ser.). 48p. 1999. pap. 4.99 (*1-58134-079-6*) Crossway Bks.

***Pleasing God Outside the Comfort Zone.** Greg Sealy. Ed. by Harriet Whipkey. 255p. 1999. pap. 11.99 (*0-9673872-0-5*) G Sealy Outreach.

Pleasing God, Pleasing You: Twenty Church Leaders Share Biblical Principles for Successful Christian Living. Hal Donaldson & Kenneth M. Dobson. 200p. 1992. 14.95 (*1-880689-01-4*) Onward Bks.

***Pleasing Hour.** Lily King. LC 99-25528. 237p. (YA). 1999. 24.00 (*0-87113-754-2*, Atlntc Mnthly) Grove-Atltic.

***Pleasing Hour: A Novel.** Lily King. LC 00-35761. 2000. pap. 12.00 (*0-7432-0164-7*, Scribner Pap Fic) S&S Trade Pap.

***Pleasing Hours: The Travels of James Caulfeild, 1st Earl of Charlemont, Ireland, 1728-1799.** Cynthia O'Connor. LC 99-196839. (Illus.). 288p. 1999. 35.95 (*1-898256-66-7*, Pub. by Collins Press) Irish Bks Media.

Pleasing Novelty: Bunkio Matsuki & the Japan Craze in Victorian Salem. Frederic A. Sharf et al. (Illus.). 112p. (Orig.). 1993. pap. 15.00 (*0-88389-098-4*, PEMP198) Peabody Essex Mus.

Pleasing Polish Recipes. Jacek Nowakowski. 160p. 1989. spiral bd. 6.95 (*0-941016-63-3*) Penfield.

Pleasing the Father: Minibook. Gloria Copeland. (Illus.). 25p. (Orig.). 1996. pap. 1.00 (*1-57562-121-5*, 30-0543) K Copeland Pubns.

Pleasing the Ghost. Sharon Creech. LC 95-52280. (Illus.). 96p. (J). (gr. 4-7). 1996. 14.95 (*0-06-026985-5*); lib. bdg. 14.89 (*0-06-026986-3*) HarpC Child Bks.

Pleasing the Ghost. Sharon Creech. (J). 1997. 9.70 (*0-606-11757-1*, Pub. by Turtleback) Demco.

Pleasing the Ghost. Sharon Creech. LC 95-52280. (Trophy Bk.). (Illus.). 96p. (J). (gr. 2-5). 1997. reprint ed. mass mkt. 4.95 (*0-06-440686-5*, HarpTrophy) HarpC Child Bks.

Pleasing the Lord: Know God's Will & Receive His Rewards. Norvel Hayes. LC 97-220837. 128p. 1997. pap. 7.99 (*1-57794-033-4*, HH2-033) Harrison Hse.

Pleasing the Spirits, 1. Douglas C. Ewing. 1998. 60.00 (*1-55821-793-2*) Lyons Pr.

Pleasing Your Partner: An Intimate Guide to Love & Sex. Gilbert Tordjman. 1997. 17.99 (*1-85833-711-9*, Pub. by CLib Bks) Whitecap Bks.

Pleasurable Husband/Wife Childbirth: The Real Consummation of Married Love. Marilyn A. Moran. (Illus.). 228p. (Orig.). 1997. pap. 22.95 (*0-940128-05-5*) Terra Publng.

Pleasure & Beauty. Kahlil Gibran. 1999. 4.95 (*0-375-40459-7*) Knopf.

Pleasure & Business in Western Pennsylvania: The Journal of Joshua Gilpin, 1809. Ed. by Joseph E. Walker. LC 75-623536. (Illus.). 156p. 1975. 9.00 (*0-911124-78-0*) Pa Hist & Mus.

Pleasure & Dancer. Vance. 1986. 11.95 (*0-7102-0248-2*, Routledge Thoemms) Routledge.

Pleasure & Danger: Exploring Female Sexuality. Carole S. Vance. 1990. pap. 11.95 (*0-7100-0248-3*, Routledge Thoemms) Routledge.

Pleasure & Danger: Exploring Female Sexuality. Ed. by Carole S. Vance. (Illus.). 512p. 1993. reprint ed. pap. text 20.00 (*0-04-440867-6*) NYU Pr.

Pleasure & Frustration: A Resynthesis of Clinical & Theoretical Psychoanalysis. Leon Wallace. LC 84-3787. xiv, 193p. (C). 1984. 30.00 (*0-8236-4161-9*) Intl Univs Pr.

Pleasure & Guilt Grand Tour. Chard. 1999. pap. 24.95 (*0-7190-4805-2*) St Martin.

***Pleasure & Guilt Grand Tour.** Chard. LC 99-52388. 1999. text 79.95 (*0-7190-4804-4*) St Martin.

Pleasure & Pain: Reminiscences of Georgia in the 1840's. Emily Burke. 100p. 1991. 15.00 (*0-88322-006-7*) Beehive GA.

Pleasure & Perils of Mexico. Ed. by Vanetta E. VanScoyk. (Illus.). 148p. 1998. pap. 12.95 (*0-9670282-0-5*) V VanScoyk.

Pleasure & Quality of Life. David M. Warburton & Neil Sherwood. LC 96-10653. 326p. 1997. 150.00 (*0-471-96511-1*) Wiley.

***Pleasure & the Good Life: Plato, Aristotle & the Neoplatonists.** Gerd Van Riel. (Philosophia Antiqua, 85 Ser.). 176p. 2000. text 84.00 (*90-04-11797-0*) Brill Academic Pubs.

Pleasure Beach. Syl Labrot. 1976. 100.00 (*0-614-18204-2*) Visual Studies.

Pleasure Beyond the Pleasure Principle: An Integration. Robert A. Glick & Stanley Bone. 352p. (C). 1991. 45.00 (*0-300-04793-2*) Yale U Pr.

***Pleasure Boats & Accessories in Japan: A Strategic Entry Report, 1996.** Compiled by Icon Group International Staff. (Illus.). 159p. 1999. ring bd. 1590.00 incl. audio compact disk (*0-7418-1363-7*) Icon Grp.

Pleasure Boats & Accessories in Netherlands: A Strategic Entry Report, 1997. Compiled by Icon Group International Staff. (Illus.). 122p. 1999. ring bd. 1220.00 incl. audio compact disk (*0-7418-0882-X*) Icon Grp.

***Pleasure Boats & Marine Sports Accessories in Singapore: A Strategic Entry Report, 1996.** Compiled by Icon Group International Staff. (Illus.). 113p. 1999. ring bd. 1130.00 incl. audio compact disk (*0-7418-1364-5*) Icon Grp.

Pleasure Boats in Denmark: A Strategic Entry Report, 1998. Compiled by Icon Group International Staff. (Country Industry Report). (Illus.). 100p. 1999. ring bd. 1000.00 incl. audio compact disk (*0-7418-0290-2*) Icon Grp.

Pleasure Boats in France: A Strategic Entry Report, 1997. Compiled by Icon Group International Staff. (Illus.). 121p. 1999. ring bd. 1210.00 incl. audio compact disk (*0-7418-0883-8*) Icon Grp.

***Pleasure Boats in France: A Strategic Entry Report, 1999.** Compiled by Icon Group International. (Illus.). 122p. 1999. ring bd. 1220.00 incl. audio compact disk (*0-7418-1857-4*) Icon Grp.

Pleasure Boats in Germany: A Strategic Entry Report, 1997. Compiled by Icon Group International Staff. (Illus.). 106p. 1999. ring bd. 1060.00 incl. audio compact disk (*0-7418-0884-6*) Icon Grp.

***Pleasure Bound.** 256p. 1999. mass mkt. 7.95 (*1-56201-139-1*, Pub. by Blue Moon Bks) Publishers Group.

Pleasure Bound. 1999. mass mkt. 7.95 (*0-7867-0645-7*) Carroll & Graf.

Pleasure Business. Patrick Anderson. 291p. 1989. 17.95 (*0-15-172047-9*) Harcourt.

Pleasure by the Busload. Emily Kimbrough. 286p. Date not set. 23.95 (*0-8488-2345-1*) Amereon Ltd.

***Pleasure Chateau.** Jeremy Reed. 242p. (Orig.). 2000. pap. 14.95 (*1-84068-046-6*, Pub. by Creation Bks) Subterranean Co.

Pleasure Chateau. Jeremy Reed. (Velvet Ser.: Vol. 3). 192p. (Orig.). 1996. pap. 12.95 (*1-871592-52-6*) Creation Books.

Pleasure Connection: How Endorphins Affect Our Health & Happiness. Deva Beck & James Beck. LC 87-60379. 235p. (Orig.). 1987. pap. 12.95 (*0-9617972-0-7*) Synthesis Pr.

***Pleasure Cruise Nurse.** Jane Converse. LC 00-23528. 2000. write for info. (*0-7862-2508-4*) Five Star.

Pleasure Dome: On Reading Modern Poetry. Lloyd Frankenberg. LC 68-57701. 384p. (C). 1968. reprint ed. 50.00 (*0-87752-038-0*) Gordian.

Pleasure-Dome of Kubla Khan. C. Griffes. 20p. 1993. pap. 7.95 (*0-7935-2536-5*) H Leonard.

Pleasure Dome of Kubla Khan: For Orchestra Full Score. C. Griffes. 52p. 1994. pap. 12.50 (*0-7935-3527-1*, 50482198) H Leonard.

Pleasure Garden: An Illustrated History of British Gardening. large type ed. Anne Scott-James & Osbert Lancaster. (Illus.). 158p. 1992. 20.95 (*1-85089-322-5*, Pub. by ISIS Lrg Prnt) Transaction Pubs.

Pleasure Gardens of the Mind. Stephen Market. (Jane Greenough Green Collection of Indian Paintings). (Illus.). 168p. 1997. 50.00 (*0-944142-93-1*) Grantha.

Pleasure Gardens of the Mind: Indian Paintings from the Jane Greenough Green Collection. Pratapaditya Pal et al. (Illus.). 160p. 1993. 50.00 (*81-85822-15-8*, Pub. by Mapin Pubng) Antique Collect.

Pleasure Grounds: Andrew Jackson Downing & Montgomery Place. Alexander J. Davis. (Illus.). 96p. 1988. 19.95 (*0-912882-65-4*) Sleepy Hollow.

Pleasure Horse. Bonnie Bryant. (Saddle Club Ser.: No. 51). (J). (gr. 4-6). 1996. 9.09 (*0-606-09805-4*, Pub. by Turtleback) Demco.

Pleasure in the Eighteenth Century. Ed. by Roy Porter & Marie M. Roberts. LC 96-12952. 273p. (C). 1996. text 37.50 (*0-8147-6644-7*) NYU Pr.

Pleasure in the Word: Erotic Writing by Latin American Women. Ed. by Lizabeth P. Gebert & Margarite Fernandez-Olmos. 240p. 1993. 19.95 (*1-877727-31-8*) White Pine.

Pleasure Island: Tourism & Temptation in Cuba. Rosalie Schwartz. LC 96-40476. (Illus.). xxiv, 247p. 1997. text 50.00 (*0-8032-4257-3*) U of Nebr Pr.

Pleasure Island: Tourism & Temptation in Cuba. Contrib. by Rosalie Schwartz. (Illus.). 247p. 1999. pap. 15.00 (*0-8032-9265-1*, Bison Books) U of Nebr Pr.

P

An Asterisk (*) at the beginning of an entry indicates that the title is appearing for the first time.

***Pleasure King's Bride.** Emma Darcy. (Presents Ser.). 2000. mass mkt. 3.99 (0-373-12122-9, 1-12122-7) Harlequin Bks.

Pleasure, Knowledge, & Being: An Analysis of Plato's Philebus. Cynthia Hampton. LC 89-11603. (SUNY Series in Ancient Greek Philosophy). 144p. (C). 1990. text 64.50 (0-7914-0259-2); pap. text 21.95 (0-7914-0260-6) State U NY Pr.

Pleasure of Angling with Rod & Reel. George Dawson. 264p. 45.00 (1-56416-120-X) Derrydale Pr.

Pleasure of Being Oneself. Cyril E. Joad. LC 74-111841. (Essay Index Reprint Ser.). 1977. 20.95 (0-8369-1665-4) Ayer.

Pleasure of Believing. Anastasia Hobbet. LC 96-37223. 336p. 1997. 24.00 (1-56947-085-5) Soho Press.

Pleasure of Believing. Anastasia Hobbet. 325p. 1998. pap. 12.00 (1-56947-115-0) Soho Press.

***Pleasure of Children Literature.** 3rd ed. 2000. teacher ed. write for info. (0-8013-3085-8) Longman.

***Pleasure of Discernment.** Carol Thyself. (Oxford Studies in Historical Theology). 208p. 2000. text 45.00 (0-19-513845-7) OUP.

***Pleasure of Finding Things Out.** Richard P. Feynman. 288p. 2000. pap. text 14.00 (0-7382-0349-1, Pub. by Perseus Pubng) HarpC.

***Pleasure of Finding Things Out: The Best Short Works of Richard Feynman.** Richard Phillips Feynman. LC 99-64775. (Illus.). 288p. 1999. text 24.00 (0-7382-0108-1, Pub. by Perseus Pubng) HarpC.

Pleasure of Gardens: A Literary Companion. Joyce Lindsay & Maurice Lindsay. (Aberdeen University Press Bks.). (Illus.). 224p. 1991. pap. text 16.95 (0-08-041209-2, Pub. by Aberdeen U Pr) Macmillan.

Pleasure of Herbs: A Month-by-Month Guide to Growing, Using, & Enjoying Herbs. Phyllis V. Shaudys. LC 86-14856. (Illus.). 288p. (Orig.). 1986. pap. 17.95 (0-88266-423-9, Garden Way Pub) Storey Bks.

Pleasure of Herbs: A Month-by-Month Guide to Growing, Using, & Enjoying Herbs. Phyllis V. Shaudys. LC 86-14856. (Illus.). 288p. (Orig.). 1986. 22.50 (0-88266-430-1, Garden Way Pub) Storey Bks.

Pleasure of His Company. Samuel Taylor. 1961. pap. 5.25 (0-8222-0901-2) Dramatists Play.

Pleasure of His Company. Lee Venden. LC 94-141260. 112p. 1995. pap. 8.99 (0-8280-0825-6) Review & Herald.

Pleasure of Miss Pym. Charles Burkhart. LC 87-5829. reprint ed. pap. 43.40 (0-608-20099-9, 2071371) Bks Demand.

Pleasure of Reading in an Ideological Age. Robert Alter. 256p. 1996. pap. 13.00 (0-393-31499-5) Norton.

Pleasure of the Crown: Anthropology, Law & First Nations. Dara Culhane. LC 98-150773. 416p. 1998. pap. 21.95 (0-88922-315-7, Pub. by Talonbks) Genl Dist Srvs.

Pleasure of the Play. Bert O. States. (Illus.). 240p. 1994. text 39.95 (0-8014-3036-4); pap. text 14.95 (0-8014-8217-8) Cornell U Pr.

Pleasure of Their Company. Bonnie M. Doane. LC 97-46150. 224p. 1998. pap. 27.95 (0-87605-594-3) Howell Bks.

Pleasure of Their Company. Bonnie M. Doane. 1998. 27.95 (0-87605-614-1) Macmillan.

***Pleasure of Their Company.** Doris Grumbach. 128p. 2000. 22.00 (0-8070-7222-2) Beacon Pr.

Pleasure of Their Company: A Reminiscence. Howard Taubman. LC 94-21716. (Illus.). 352p. 1994. 24.95 (0-931340-78-0, Amadeus Pr) Timber.

Pleasure of Whole Grain Breads. Beth Hensperger. LC 98-51735. 176p. 2000. pap. 24.95 (0-8118-1455-6) Chronicle Bks.

***Pleasure of Writing: Critical Essays on Dacia Maraini.** Rodica Blumenfeld & Ada Testaferri. LC 99-89306. (Studies in Romance Literatures: Vol. 20). 2000. 43.95 (1-55753-197-8) Purdue U Pr.

Pleasure of Your Company. Molly O'Neill. 1996. 26.95 (0-614-19404-0) Viking Penguin.

Pleasure of Your Company: A Socio-Psychological Analysis of Modern Sociability. Emile J. Pin & Jamie Turndorf. 288p. 1985. 59.95 (0-275-91755-X, C1755, Praeger Pubs) Greenwood.

***Pleasure of Your Company: Simple Ideas for Enjoyable Entertaining.** Ann Platz & Susan Wales. LC 99-18437. (Illus.). 112p. 1999. 14.99 (0-7369-0111-6) Harvest Hse.

Pleasure Paradises. John P. Radulski & William Weathersby. LC 96-5730. (Illus.). 184p. 1997. text 42.50 (0-86636-496-X) St Martin.

Pleasure Paradises: International Clubs & Resorts. John P. Radulski. LC 96-5730. 1999. pap. text 34.95 (0-86636-536-2) PBC Intl Inc.

Pleasure Park. (Kake Ser.: No. 20). 1997. pap. 10.00 (1-879055-07-4) Tom Finland.

Pleasure Pavilions & Follies: In the Gardens of the Ancien Regime. Bernd H. Dams & Andrew Zega. LC 97-177521. (Illus.). 192p. 1995. 50.00 (2-08-013561-9, Pub. by Flammarion) Abbeville Pr.

Pleasure, Power & Technology: Some Tales of Gender, Engineering, & the Cooperative Workplace. Sally L. Hacker. 240p. 1989. 39.95 (0-04-445096-6); pap. 12.95 (0-318-41853-3) Routledge.

Pleasure Prescription: To Love, to Work, to Play-Life in the Balance. Paul Pearsall. 288p. 1996. pap. 13.95 (0-89793-207-2) Hunter Hse.

Pleasure Prescription: To Love, to Work, to Play-Life in the Balance. Paul Pearsall. 288p. 1997. 23.95 (0-89793-208-0) Hunter Hse.

Pleasure Principle. Michael Bronski. LC 97-7983. 304p. 1998. text 24.95 (0-312-15625-1) St Martin.

***Pleasure Principle.** Maria Del Rey. 2000. mass mkt. 6.95 (0-352-33482-7) Nexus.

Pleasure Principle. Chris Steele-Perkins. 1990. 37.95 (0-89381-436-9) Aperture.

Pleasure Principle: Discovering a New Way to Health. Paul Pearsall. 1995. 16.00 incl. audio (0-671-52116-0) S&S Trade.

***Pleasure Principle: Sex, Backlash, & the Struggle for Gay Freedom.** Michael Bronski. 304p. 2000. pap. 13.95 (0-312-25287-0) St Martin.

Pleasure Principle Diet: How to Lose Weight Permanently, Eating the Foods That Made You Fat. Robert E. Willner. LC 84-29121. 225p. 1985. 18.95 (0-685-09453-7); pap. 7.95 (0-685-09454-5) P-H.

Pleasure Principles: Politics, Sexuality & Ethics. Ed. by Victoria Harwood et al. 256p. (C). 1993. pap. 19.95 (0-85315-791-X, Pub. by Lawrence & Wishart) NYU Pr.

Pleasure, Profit, Proselytism: British Culture & Sport at Home & Abroad, 1700-1914. Ed. by James A. Mangan. 250p. 1986. 45.00 (0-7146-3289-9, Pub. by F Cass Pubs); pap. 22.50 (0-7146-4050-6, Pub. by F Cass Pubs) Intl Spec Bk.

Pleasure Program: The Lifestyle & Weight Management Guide for Busy People. Jeanette Robinson. 250p. 1996. pap. text, per. 19.95 (0-7872-2457-X) Kendall-Hunt.

***Pleasure, Recreational Boats in Chile: A Strategic Entry Report, 1996.** Compiled by Icon Group International Staff. (Illus.). 108p. 1999. ring bd. 1080.00 incl. audio compact disk (0-7418-1365-3) Icon Grp.

Pleasure Ring. K. Gerrard. 1997. mass mkt. 6.95 (0-7472-5580-6, Pub. by Headline Bk Pub) Trafalgar.

Pleasure Seekers. Roberta Latow. 320p. 1997. pap. 11.95 (0-7472-5305-6, Pub. by Headline Bk Pub) Trafalgar.

Pleasure Seeker's Guide. Judith Leet. (New Poetry Ser.). 1976. 6.95 (0-395-24313-0) HM.

Pleasure, the Politics & the Reality. Ed. by David M. Warburton & Maureen Kéw. 180p. 1994. 175.95 (0-471-94229-4) Wiley.

Pleasure Time Stories for Girls & Boys. Cecile Dahlstrom. (Illus.). 64p. (Orig.). pap. 9.95 (1-886094-03-9) Chicago Spectrum.

Pleasure Tree. Robley Wilson. LC 89-39345. (Poetry Ser.). 72p. 1990. pap. 10.95 (0-8229-5427-3) U of Pittsburgh Pr.

Pleasure Trove. Edward V. Lucas. LC 68-57329. (Essay Index Reprint Ser.). 1977. 19.95 (0-8369-0631-4) Ayer.

Pleasure Vessels: The Winners of the 1995 Ian St. James Awards. Angela Royal Publishing Staff. 1997. pap. text 12.95 (1-899860-60-6, Pub. by A Royal Pub) Red Sea Pr.

Pleasure Wars: The Bourgeois Experience: Victoria to Freud. Peter Gay. (Illus.). 352p. 1999. pap. 16.00 (0-393-31827-3, Norton Paperbks) Norton.

Pleasure Wars: The Bourgeois Experience: Victoria to Freud, Vol. 5. Peter Gay. 400p. 1998. 29.95 (0-393-04570-6) Norton.

Pleasure Zone: Why We Resist Good Feelings & How to Let Go & Be Happy. Stella Resnick. LC 97-15651. 320p. 1997. 21.95 (1-57324-071-0) Conari Press.

Pleasure Zone: Why We Resist Good Feelings & How to Let Go & be Happy. Stella Resnick. 320p. 1998. pap. text 14.95 (1-57324-150-4) Conari Press.

Pleasures. Robbi Sommers. 224p. 1989. pap. 11.95 (0-941483-49-5) Naiad Pr.

Pleasures: Women Write Erotica. Lonnie G. Barbach. LC 85-42550. 368p. 1985. reprint ed. pap. 13.50 (0-06-097002-2, PL 7002, Perennial) HarperTrade.

Pleasures & Days: And Other Writings. Marcel Proust. Tr. by Louise Varese et al from FRE. LC 78-2432. 1978. reprint ed. 35.00 (0-86527-293-X) Fertig.

Pleasures & Pains: Opium & the Orient in Nineteenth-Century British Culture. Barry Milligan. 192p. (C). 1995. text 29.50 (0-8139-1571-6) U Pr of Va.

Pleasures & Palaces. Frances L. Warner & Gertrude Chandler Warner. LC 68-58817. (Essay Index Reprint Ser.). 1977. 18.95 (0-8369-0132-0) Ayer.

Pleasures & Pastimes. Elisabeth R. Fairman. LC 89-52081. (Illus.). 40p. (Orig.). 1990. pap. 4.95 (0-930606-62-0) Yale Ctr Brit Art.

Pleasures & Pastimes in Medieval England. Compton Reeves. (Illus.). 248p. 1998. pap. 16.95 (0-19-521423-4) OUP.

***Pleasures & Pastimes in Medieval England.** Compton Reeves. (Illus.). 228p. 1999. reprint ed. text 30.00 (0-7881-6670-0) DIANE Pub.

Pleasures & Pastimes in Tudor England. Alison Sim. 1998. 39.95 (0-7509-1833-0, Pub. by Sutton Pub Ltd) Intl Pubs Mktg.

Pleasures & Pastimes of Victorian England. Pamela Horn. 1999. 34.95 (0-7509-1666-4) A Sutton.

Pleasures & Perils of Genius: Mostly Mozart. Ed. by Peter F. Ostwald & Leonard S. Zegans. LC 93-24461. (Mental Health Library: Monograph 2). 228p. (C). 1993. 35.00 (0-8236-4162-7) Intl Univs Pr.

Pleasures & Regrets. Marcel Proust. 236p. 1986. reprint ed. 33.00 (0-7206-0655-1) Dufour.

Pleasures & Regrets. Marcel Proust. Tr. by Louise Varese from FRE. LC 84-6120. (Neglected Books of the 20th Century Ser.). 221p. 1984. reprint ed. pap. 7.50 (0-88001-063-0) HarpC.

Pleasures & Speculations. Walter J. De La Mare. LC 76-90630. (Essay Index Reprint Ser.). 1977. 23.95 (0-8369-1255-1) Ayer.

Pleasures Childrens Literature. 2nd ed. Perry Nodelman. LC 95-23477. 336p. (C). 1996. pap. text 38.44 (0-8013-1576-X) Longman.

Pleasure's Daughter. Sedalia Johnson. 1998. mass mkt. 5.95 (0-352-33237-9, Pub. by BLA4) London Brdge.

***Pleasures Evermore: The Life-Changing Power of Enjoying God.** Sam Storms. 317p. 2000. pap. 15.00 (1-57683-188-4) NavPress.

Pleasures of Academe: A Celebration & Defense of Higher Education. James Axtell. LC 97-51865. xix, 293p. 1998. text 40.00 (0-8032-1049-3) U of Nebr Pr.

Pleasures of Academe: A Celebration & Defense of Higher Education. James Axtell. 1999. pap. 15.00 (0-8032-5938-7) U of Nebr Pr.

Pleasures of Aesthetics: Philosophical Essays. Jerrold Levinson. (Illus.). 320p. 1996. text 52.50 (0-8014-3059-3); pap. text 18.95 (0-8014-8226-7) Cornell U Pr.

Pleasures of an Absentee Landlord: And Other Essays. Samuel M. Crothers. LC 72-1326. (Essay Index Reprint Ser.). 1977. reprint ed. 20.95 (0-8369-2844-X) Ayer.

Pleasures of Children's Literature: Pleasures. Perry Nodelman. 260p. (C). 1991. pap. text 31.33 (0-8013-0219-6, 75877) Longman.

Pleasures of Cocaine: If You Enjoy the Pleasures of Cocaine This Book May Say Your Life. Adam Gottlieb. (Illus.). 1996. pap. 12.95 (0-914171-81-X) Ronin Pub.

Pleasures of Cooking, 10 bks. in 1. deluxe ed. (Illus.). 608p. 1993. 29.95 (1-56173-900-6, 2020200) Pubns Intl Ltd.

Pleasures of Cooking Fruits & Vegetables. Ed. by Carl Sontheimer. LC 97-18009. (Illus.). 304p. 1998. 25.00 (0-88001-525-X) HarpC.

Pleasures of Counting. T. W. Korner. LC 97-108334. (Illus.). 544p. (C). 1996. text 85.00 (0-521-56087-X); pap. text 36.00 (0-521-56823-4) Cambridge U Pr.

***Pleasures of Cruelty.** 144p. 2000. mass mkt. 7.95 (1-56201-176-6, Pub. by Blue Moon Bks) Publishers Group.

Pleasures of Entomology: Portraits of Insects & the People Who Study Them. Howard E. Evans. LC 84-600318. (Illus.). 238p. 1985. pap. 16.95 (0-87474-421-0, EVPEP) Smithsonian.

Pleasures of Exile. George Lamming. (Ann Arbor Paperbacks Ser.). 300p. (C). 1991. reprint ed. pap. 17.95 (0-472-06466-5, 06466); reprint ed. text 49.50 (0-472-09466-1, 09466) U of Mich Pr.

***Pleasures of God: Meditation on God's Delight in Being God.** John Piper. 400p. 2000. pap. 14.99 (1-57673-665-2, Pub. by Multnomah Pubs) GL Services.

Pleasures of Helen. Lawrence Sanders. 304p. 1986. mass mkt. 6.99 (0-425-10168-1) Berkley Pub.

Pleasures of Ikebana. Koji Hinata. (Illus.). 160p. 1996. 39.95 (4-07-976250-X, Pub. by Shufunotomo) Weatherhill.

Pleasures of Irish Nature Poetry. Ed. by Malachi McCormick. 32p. 1984. 10.00 (0-943984-18-1) Stone St Pr.

Pleasures of Japanese Literature. Donald Keene. Ed. by William T. De Bary. (Companions to Asian Studies). (Illus.). 133p. (C). 1993. pap. 16.50 (0-231-06737-2); text 29.50 (0-231-06736-4) Col U Pr.

Pleasures of JessicaLynn: An Erotic Novel. Joan Elizabeth Lloyd. 208p. 1996. pap. 8.95 (0-7867-0327-X) Carroll & Graf.

Pleasures of Love: The Ultimate Guide to Sexual Fulfillment for You & Your Partner. Pierre Habert & Marie Habert. (Illus.). 304p. (Orig.). 1996. pap. 24.50 (0-572-02212-3, Pub. by W Foulsham) Trans-Atl Phila.

Pleasures of Loving God, Vol. 1. Mike Bickle. 2000. pap. 12.99 (0-88419-662-3) Creation House.

Pleasures of Music: An Anthology of Writings about Music & Musicians from Cellini to Bernard Shaw. abr. ed. Ed. by Jacques Barzun. 382p. 1977. pap. text 13.50 (0-226-03854-8, P727) U Ch Pr.

Pleasures of Painting Outdoors: A Diary of the 13 Part PBS WorldScape Series. John Stobart. 127p. 1993. 29.95 (0-9635775-0-6); pap. 19.95 (0-685-63477-9) Wrldscape Prods.

Pleasures of Paris: From Daumier to Picasso. Barbara S. Shapiro. LC 91-72212. (Illus.). 192p. 1991. 50.00 (0-87923-919-0) Godine.

Pleasures of Porch. Daria P. Bowman & Maureen Lamarca. LC 96-70340. 144p. 1997. 35.00 (0-8478-2005-X, Pub. by Rizzoli Intl) St Martin.

Pleasures of Probability. Richard Isaac. LC 94-39140. (Undergraduate Texts in Mathematics Ser.). (Illus.). 241p. 1995. 29.50 (0-387-94415-X) Spr-Verlag.

***Pleasures of Recluses.** Sheila Grimaldi-Craig. 236p. 2000. pap. 19.50 (0-88214-384-0, Pub. by Spring Pubns) Continuum.

Pleasures of Staying. Jennifer Williams. LC 97-46705. (Illus.). 192p. 1998. 22.00 (0-688-15440-9, Hearst) Hearst Commns.

Pleasures of Tea. Victoria Magazine Editors. LC 98-32092. 1999. 20.00 (0-688-16751-9, Hearst) Hearst Commns.

Pleasures of the Belle Epoque: Entertainment & Festivity in Turn-of-the-Century France. Charles Rearick. LC 85-40468. 263p. 1985. pap. 81.60 (0-7837-8653-0, 208236600009) Bks Demand.

Pleasures of the Belle Epoque: Entertainment & Festivity in Turn-of-the-Century France. Charles Rearick. LC 85-40468. 240p. (C). 1988. reprint ed. pap. 25.00 (0-300-04381-3) Yale U Pr.

Pleasures of the Canary Islands: Wine, Food, Beauty, & Mystery. Ann Walker & Larry Walker. (Illus.). 144p. pap. 12.95 (0-932664-75-X, 6640) Wine Appreciation.

Pleasures of the Cottage Garden. 27.50 (0-676-57339-8) Random.

Pleasures of the Cottage Garden. Rand B. Lee. LC 98-43511. (Illus.). 144p. 1998. 27.50 (1-56799-695-7, Friedman-Fairfax) M Friedman Pub Grp Inc.

***Pleasures of the Flesh.** John Patrick. 1999. pap. 14.95 (1-891855-03-4) FL Lit Foundation.

Pleasures of the Imagination: English Culture in the Eighteenth Century. John Brewer. LC 97-60984. (Illus.). 688p. 1997. 40.00 (0-374-23458-2) FS&G.

Pleasures of the Palate. Harris Golden. Ed. by Candice Miles. LC 88-81018. (Illus.). 246p. 1989. 40.00 (0-9620669-0-7) Goldens Kitchen.

Pleasures of the Palettes. Kirsten Ross. 1997. pap. 24.95 (1-885590-22-9) Golden West Pub.

Pleasures of the Palettes II. Kirsten Ross. (Illus.). 144p. 1998. pap. 24.95 (1-885590-34-2) Golden West Pub.

Pleasures of the Past: Reflections in Modern British History. David Cannadine. 1991. pap. 10.95 (0-393-30749-2) Norton.

Pleasures of the Table. G. H. Ellwanger. 1972. 59.95 (0-8490-0843-3) Gordon Pr.

Pleasures of the Table. Florence Fabricant. 1989. 12.98 (0-88365-748-1) Galahad Bks.

Pleasures of the Text. Roland Barthes. 80p. 1975. pap. 9.00 (0-374-52160-3) FS&G.

Pleasures of Virtue: Political Thought in the Novels of Jane Austin. Anne C. Ruderman. LC 95-32349. 214p. (C). 1995. pap. text 25.95 (0-8476-8101-7); lib. bdg. 65.00 (0-8476-8100-9) Rowman.

Pleasures of Women. James Jennings. 1996. mass mkt. 6.99 (0-515-12052-9, Jove) Berkley Pub.

Pleasures of Your Food Processor. Norene Gilletz. 368p. 1985. mass mkt. 12.95 (0-446-38373-2, Pub. by Warner Bks) Little.

Pleasures of Your Food Processor, 1. Norene Gilletz. 1994. ring bd. 33.95 (0-9697972-0-6) GOUR.

Pleasures Taken: Performances of Sexuality & Loss in Victorian Photographs. Carol Mavor. LC 94-41559. (Illus.). 208p. 1995. text 49.95 (0-8223-1603-X); pap. text 17.95 (0-8223-1619-6) Duke.

Pleasuring Painting: Matisse's Feminine Representations. John Elderfield. LC 95-61353. (Walter Neurath Memorial Lectures). (Illus.). 64p. 1996. 14.95 (0-500-55028-X, Pub. by Thames Hudson) Norton.

Plebs & Princeps. Zvi Yavetz. 192p. 1987. 44.95 (0-88738-154-5) Transaction Pubs.

Plectrum Banjo Melody Chord Playing System. Mel Bay Staff. 112p. 1979. spiral bd. 11.95 (1-56222-332-1, 93628) Mel Bay.

Plectrum Picking. Howard Roberts. (Illus.). 1998. 9.98 (0-89915-025-X) Playback Mus Pub.

Pledge. Rob Kean. LC 99-19765. 496p. 1999. 24.95 (0-446-52497-2, Pub. by Warner Bks) Little.

***Pledge.** Rob Kean. 2000. mass mkt. 7.50 (0-446-60848-3) Warner Bks.

Pledge. large type ed. Jane Peart. LC 98-4362. 1998. 22.95 (0-7862-1469-4) Thorndike Pr.

Pledge: Calling Adolescents to Maturity, Purity, & Ministry. Chris Brown & Dave Earley. Ed. by Cindy G. Spear. 127p. 1997. ring bd. 99.95 incl. audio (1-57052-081-X) Chrch Grwth VA.

Pledge Class, Vol. 2. Stephanie Prince. (Sorority Sisters Ser.: No. 2). 224p. (J). 1997. mass mkt. 4.50 (0-06-106508-0) HarpC Child Bks.

Pledge of Allegiance. Stuart A. Kallen. LC 94-12217. (Famous Illustrated Speeches). 1994. lib. bdg. 14.96 (1-56239-316-2) ABDO Pub Co.

Pledge of Allegiance. Douglas M. Rife. Ed. by Judy Mitchell. (Illus.). 32p. (J). (gr. 4-8). 1998. pap., teacher ed. 5.95 (1-57310-128-1) Teachng & Lrning Co.

Pledge of Allegiance. large type ed. Mark Lapin. LC 91-18381. 396p. 1991. reprint ed. 19.95 (1-56054-195-4) Thorndike Pr.

Pledge of the Twin Knights. Margaret Sutton. Date not set. lib. bdg. 19.95 (0-8488-2129-7) Amereon Ltd.

Pledger Family History. Florence M. Pledger. 176p. 1991. 29.95 (0-942407-13-X) Father & Son.

Pledging Allegiance: American Identity & the Bond Drive of World War II. Lawrence R. Samuel. (Illus.). 336p. 1997. 29.95 (1-56098-707-3) Smithsonian.

Plehve: Repression & Reform in Imperial Russia, 1902 to 1904. Edward H. Judge. 312p. 1983. text 45.00 (0-8156-2295-3) Syracuse U Pr.

Pleiades Stones. Raven Hail. LC 87-61690. 200p. 1987. pap. 12.95 (0-9617696-4-5) Raven Hail.

Pleiadian Agenda: A New Cosmology for the Age of Light. Barbara H. Clow. (Illus.). 334p. 1995. pap. 15.00 (1-879181-30-4) Bear & Co.

Pleiadian Mission: A Time of Awareness. Randolph Winters. Ed. by Ann Tremaine. (Illus.). 275p. (Orig.). 1994. pap. 20.00 (1-885757-07-7) Pleiades Proj.

Pleiadian Perspectives on Human Evolution. Amorah Quan-Yin. 304p. (Orig.). 1996. pap. 15.00 (1-879181-33-9) Bear & Co.

Pleiadian Workbook: Awakening Your Divine KA. Amorah Quan-Yin. Ed. by Gail Vivino. (Illus.). 352p. (Orig.). 1996. pap. 16.00 (1-879181-31-2) Bear & Co.

Pleidian Tantric Workbook: Awakening Your Divine BA, Vol. II. Amorah Quan Yin. LC 97-28684. (Illus.). 320p. (Orig.). 1997. pap. 16.00 (1-879181-45-2) Bear & Co.

Pleier's Arthurian Romances: Garel of the Blooming Valley Tandareis & Flordibel Meleranz. Ed. & Tr. by J. W. Thomas. LC 92-11337. (Library of Medieval Literature: Vol. 91B). 536p. 1992. text 20.00 (0-8153-0919-8) Garland.

PL8-QIZ (Plate Quiz) A Game of License Plates & What They Say 2 U. Earl Heintzelman. Ed. by Donna Heintzelman. (Illus.). 64p. (Orig.). 1993. per. 8.95 (0-9636058-0-1) Faro Green Pr.

Plein Air Painters of California: The North. Ruth Westphal. LC 86-50631. (Illus.). 216p. 1986. 65.00 (0-9610520-1-5) Westphal Pub.

Plein Air Painters of California: The Southland. Ruth L. Westphal. LC 82-90314. (Illus.). 228p. 1982. 65.00 (0-9610520-0-7) Westphal Pub.

***Plein la Vue.** Alex Thiltges & Richard Bourmaut. 28p. 1999. pap. 8.00 (1-888662-14-X) Vinegar Hill.

Pleiocene Fossils of South Carolina No. 12: Special Publication. Michael Tuomey & Francis S. Holmes. (Illus.). 152p. 1974. reprint ed. 12.00 (0-87710-365-8) Paleo Res.

Pleistocene. Tage A. Nilsson. 1983. text 376.50 (90-277-1466-5) Kluwer Academic.

P

An Asterisk (*) at the beginning of an entry indicates that the title is appearing for the first time.

Pleistocene Amphibians & Reptiles in Britain & Europe. J. Alan Holman. (Oxford Monographs on Geology & Geophysics: No. 38). (Illus.). 264p. 1998. text 65.00 (*0-19-511232-6*) OUP.

Pleistocene Amphibians & Reptiles of North America. J. Alan Holman. (Monographs on Geology & Geophysics: No. 32). (Illus.). 256p. 1995. text 90.00 (*0-19-508610-4*) OUP.

Pleistocene & Holocene Carbonate Environments on San Salvador Island, Bahamas, No. T175. Ed. by Curran. (IGC Field Trip Guidebooks Ser.). 56p. 1989. 21.00 (*0-87590-610-9*) Am Geophysical.

Pleistocene & Recent Faunas from the Brynjulfson Caves, Missouri. Paul W. Parmalee & Ronald D. Oesch. (Reports of Investigations: No. 25). (Illus.). 52p. 1972. pap. 2.00 (*0-89792-049-X*) Ill St Museum.

Pleistocene & Recent Vertebrate Faunas from Crankshaft Cave, Missouri. Paul W. Parmalee et al. (Reports of Investigations: No.14). (Illus.). 37p. 1969. pap. 1.00 (*0-89792-036-8*) Ill St Museum.

Pleistocene Birds of the Palearctic: A Catalogue. Tommy Tyrberg. (Publications of the Nuttall Ornithological Club: Vol. 27). (Illus.). 720p. 1998. 50.00 (*1-877973-39-4*) Nuttall Ornith.

Pleistocene Boundary & the Beginning of the Quaternary. Ed. by John A. Van Couvering. (World & Regional Geology Ser.: No. 9). (Illus.). 317p. (C). 1996. text 130.00 (*0-521-34115-9*) Cambridge U Pr.

Pleistocene Extinctions Vol. 6: The Search for a Cause: Proceedings of the VII Congress of the International Association for Quaternary Research. International Association for Quaternary Research. Ed. by P. S. Martin & H. E. Wright, Jr. LC 67-24502. 463p. reprint ed. pap. 143.60 (*0-8357-8269-7*, 203381300087) Bks Demand.

Pleistocene Fauna & Holocene Humans: A Gazetteer of Paleontological & Early Archaeological Sites on Cyprus. Steve O. Held. (Studies in Mediterranean Archaeology: Vol. XCV). (Illus.). 197p. (Orig.). 1992. pap. 67.50 (*91-7081-025-7*, Pub. by P Astroms) Coronet Bks.

Pleistocene History of the Lower Thames Valley. Philip L. Gibbard. LC 93-31544. (Illus.). 239p. (C). 1994. text 110.00 (*0-521-40209-3*) Cambridge U Pr.

Pleistocene Mammals of Florida. Ed. by Sawney D. Webb. LC 74-3115. 280p. reprint ed. pap. 86.80 (*0-608-17501-3*, 203001100067) Bks Demand.

Pleistocene Mammals of North America. Bjorn Kurten & Elaine Anderson. LC 79-26679. 1980. text 105.50 (*0-231-03733-3*) Col U Pr.

Pleistocene of the Middle Region of North America & Its Vertebrated Animals. Oliver P. Hay. LC 24-24625. (Carnegie Institution of Washington Publication Ser.: Vol. 322A). 393p. reprint ed. pap. 121.90 (*0-608-06205-7*, 206625000008) Bks Demand.

Pleistocene Old World: Regional Perspectives. O. Soffer. LC 87-12329. (Interdisciplinary Contributions to Archaeology Ser.). (Illus.). 402p. (C). 1987. 57.50 (*0-306-42438-X*, Plenum Trade) Perseus Pubng.

Pleistocene Palaeoecology of Central Norfolk. Richard West. (Illus.). 120p. (C). 1991. text 85.00 (*0-521-40368-5*) Cambridge U Pr.

Pleistocene Redemption. Dan Gallagher. LC 97-66273. (Illus.). 344p. 1997. 14.95 (*0-9666929-0-X*) AncientProphecies.com.

Pleistocene Redemption: Prehistoric Terror in the 21st Century. rev. ed. Dan Gallagher. Ed. by Ed Stacker. LC 98-93588. (Illus.). 320p. (J). 1998. 9.95 (*0-9666929-2-6*) AncientProphecies.com.

Pleistocene Shoreline & Shelf Deposits at Fort Funston & Their Relation to Sea-Level Changes: Latest Cretaceous & Early Tertiary Depositional Systems of the Northern Diablo Range, California: Depositional Facies of Sedimentary Serpentinite: Selected Examples from the Coast Ranges, California. Ralph E. Hunter et al. (Guidebook Ser.: No. 3). 125p. 1984. pap. 21.00 (*0-918985-45-5*) SEPM.

Pleistocene Vertebrates in the British Isles. A. J. Stuart. LC 81-8389. (Illus.). 222p. reprint ed. pap. 68.90 (*0-8357-6267-X*, 203448300090) Bks Demand.

Plekhanov in Russian History & Soviet Historiography. Samuel H. Baron. (Pitt Series in Russian & East European). 274p. (C). 1994. text 59.95 (*0-8229-3788-3*) U of Pittsburgh Pr.

Ple'ma Spot? Eric Hill. (C). 1989. 45.00 (*1-85022-004-2*, Pub. by Dyllansow Truran) St Mut.

Plemons - Plemmons & Kin A-Z. Janet Webb. LC 98-100427. viii, 797p. 1997. pap. 39.50 (*0-7884-0741-4*, W100) Heritage Bk.

Plenary Lectures/Movement of Copper & Industry Outlook: Copper Applications & Fabrication, 1. G. A. Eltringham et al. (Illus.). write for info. (*0-87339-435-6*) Minerals Metals.

Plenary Papers: World Congress of Rehabilitation International, 14th, Winnipeg, Canada, 1980. 55p. 10.00 (*0-686-94883-1*) Rehab Intl.

Plenary Review: A Macro-Policy Approach to Improve Public Policy. David G. Williams. 1992. 24.95 (*1-879727-02-1*) Think About Pr.

***Plenary Volume.** Ed. by Han-Fu Chen et al. 268p. 1999. pap. 126.00 (*0-08-042756-1*, Pergamon Pr) Elsevier.

Pleneurethic: A New Approach to Life & Health. R. B. Collier. Ed. by Iris Myers. (Illus.). 1974. text 4.50 (*0-533-01143-4*) Pleneurethic Intl.

Pleneurethic & the Brain. R. B. Collier. LC 65-81608. 2.50 (*0-686-17437-2*) Pleneurethic Intl.

Pleneurethics: A New Concept of Healing, Vol. 1. 2nd ed. Richard B. Collier. Ed. by John N. Terrey. xlvii, 292p. (C). 1992. 17.95 (*1-882152-08-5*); pap. 11.95 (*1-882152-09-3*) R B Collier Pleneurethics.

Pleneurethics: A New Concept of Healing, Vol. 2. 2nd ed. Richard B. Collier. xxvi, 288p. 1993. 17.95 (*1-882152-10-7*); pap. 11.95 (*1-882152-11-5*) R B Collier Pleneurethics.

Pleneurethics: A Philosophical System Uniting Body, Brain & Mind. 2nd ed. Richard B. Collier. Ed. by John N. Terrey. xxiv, 436p. (C). 17.95 (*1-882152-06-9*); pap. 11.95 (*1-882152-07-7*) R B Collier Pleneurethics.

Plenishment in the Earth: An Ethic of Inclusion. Stephen D. Ross. LC 94-9881. 430p. (C). 1995. text 74.50 (*0-7914-2309-3*); pap. text 24.95 (*0-7914-2310-7*) State U NY Pr.

Plenitud de Vida - Hunger for Reality. George Verwer. (SPA.). 1990. write for info. (*0-614-24394-7*) Editorial Unilit.

Plenitude Restored of Trompe l'Oeil: The Problematic of Fragmentation & Integration in the Prose Works of Pierre Jean Jouve & Michael Tournier, Vol. 11. Jane K. Stribling. LC 95-30238. (Francophone Cultures & Literatures Ser.). XIII, 339p. (C). 1998. text 57.95 (*0-8204-2868-X*) P Lang Pubng.

Pleno Perdon. Richard Coss. Tr. by John Cosby from ENG. (Friendship Ser.). (SPA., Illus.). 48p. 1992. pap. 0.70 (*1-882536-29-0*, A110-0014) Bible League.

Plentiful Water Through Market Forces. Stephen F. Williams. (Issue Papers: No. 13-87). 19p. 1987. pap. text 8.00 (*1-57655-016-8*) Independ Inst.

***Plenty: A Collection of Sarah McLachlan's Favorite Recipes.** Jaime Laurita & Sarah McLachlan. 1999. pap. text 24.95 (*1-894160-01-0*) MP Ltd.

Plenty Coups. Michael P. Doss. (Raintree-Rivilo American Indian Stories Ser.). (J). 1996. 10.15 (*0-606-12480-2*, Pub. by Turtleback) Demco.

Plenty-Coups: Chief of the Crows. Frank B. Linderman. LC 30-11369. (Illus.). ix, 327p. 1962. pap. 14.95 (*0-8032-5121-1*, Bison Books) U of Nebr Pr.

Plenty Coups: Great Crow Chief. Flora Hatheway. (Indian Culture Ser.). 36p. 1995. 6.95 (*0-89992-135-3*) Coun India Ed.

Plenty for Everyone. Corrie Ten Boom. 1993. pap. 5.99 (*0-87508-023-5*) Chr Lit.

Plenty Good Room. Teresa McClain-Watson. LC 97-23995. (Discoveries Ser.: No. 1). 272p. 1997. pap. 14.00 (*0-940242-74-5*) Fjord Pr.

Plenty Good Room: The Spirit & Truth of American Catholic Worship. Liturgy Training Publications. LC 92-125332. 1998. pap. 9.95 (*1-55586-385-X*) US Catholic.

Plenty of Nothing: The Downsizing of the American Dream & the Case for Structural Keynesianism. Thomas I. Palley. LC 97-34907. 227p. 1998. 27.95 (*0-691-04847-9*, Pub. by Princeton U Pr) Cal Prin Full Svc.

***Plenty of Nothing: The Downsizing of the American Dream & the Case for Structural Keynesianism.** Thomas I. Palley. (Illus.). 240p. 2000. pap. 16.95 (*0-691-05031-7*) Princeton U Pr.

Plenty of Penguins. Sonia W. Black. LC 99-26237. (Hello Reader! Science Ser.). (Illus.). 32p. (J). (ps-k). 1999. 3.99 (*0-439-09832-7*) Scholastic Inc.

***Plenty of Pockets.** Ann Braybrooks. LC 98-53784. (Illus.). 34p. (J). (gr. 1-4). 2000. 16.00 (*0-15-202173-6*, Harcourt Child Bks) Harcourt.

Plenty of Puppets to Make. Robyn Supraner & Lauren Supraner. LC 80-23785. (Illus.). 48p. (J). (gr. 1-5). 1981. lib. bdg. 16.65 (*0-89375-432-3*) Troll Communs.

Plenty of Puppets to Make. Robyn Supraner & Lauren Supraner. LC 80-23785. (Illus.). 48p. (J). (gr. 1-5). 1997. pap. 3.95 (*0-89375-433-1*) Troll Communs.

Plenty of Room & Air. Dan Cushman. LC 75-20626. 1975. 16.95 (*0-911436-04-9*) Stay Away.

***Plenty of Room Between the Trees.** Charles Fowler. (Illus.). 36p. (J). (gr. k-6). 1999. pap. 15.00 (*0-9675506-9-6*) Mirth.

Plenty to Do at MSU. Dianne K. Holman. (Illus.). 32p. (Orig.). (J). 1989. pap. 5.95 (*0-9626188-0-2*) Cupery Pr.

Plenty to Eat: The Story of Joseph & His Brothers. Patricia L. Nederveld. LC 97-37036. (God Loves Me Ser.). (Illus.). 24p. (J). (ps). 1998. pap. 2.45 (*1-56212-279-7*, 1105-0110) CRC Pubns.

Plenty to Say. Ramsey. Date not set. pap. text. write for info. (*0-582-00299-0*, Pub. by Addison-Wesley) Longman.

***Plenum.** Ben Norwood. Ed. by James M. Robbins. LC 99-72886. 80p. 1999. pap. 10.00 (*0-9657687-5-9*) Sulphur River.

Pleroma: An Essay on the Origin of Christianity. Paul Carus. 163p. 1997. pap. 12.00 (*0-89540-258-0*, SB-258) Sun Pub.

Pleroma: Reading in Hegel. Werner Hamacher. 400p. 1997. 49.50 (*0-8047-2183-1*); pap. 19.95 (*0-8047-2185-8*) Stanford U Pr.

***Plerygium Surgery.** Lucio Buratto et al. 200p. (C). 2000. pap. text 59.00 (*1-55642-492-2*) SLACK Inc.

Plesiosaurus. Stuart A. Kallen. Ed. by Julie Berg. LC 94-6356. (If the Dinosaurs Could Talk Ser.). (J). 1994. 14.98 (*1-56239-287-5*) ABDO Pub Co.

Plesiosaurus: The Swimming Reptile. Elizabeth Sandell. Ed. by Marjorie Oelerich & Howard Schroeder. LC 88-962. (Dinosaur Discovery Era Ser.). (Illus.). 32p. (J). (gr. k-5). 1988. pap. 5.95 (*0-944280-10-2*); lib. bdg. 12.95 (*0-944280-04-8*) Bancroft-Sage.

Plesiosaurus (Jurassic Period) see New Dinosaur Collection

Plesiosaurus-Minibeast. David Hawcock. (J). 1995. 5.95 (*0-8050-3196-0*) H Holt & Co.

Plessy Case: A Legal-Historical Interpretation. Charles A. Lofgren. 288p. 1988. reprint ed. pap. text 19.95 (*0-19-505684-1*) OUP.

Plessy vs. Ferguson. Thomas. LC 96-84942. 205p. 1996. pap. text 11.95 (*0-312-13743-5*) St Martin.

Plessy vs. Ferguson. Brook Thomas. LC 96-84942. 192p. 1996. text 39.95 (*0-312-16284-7*) St Martin.

Plessy vs. Ferguson: Separate but Equal? Harvey Fireside. LC 96-53651. (Landmark Supreme Court Cases Ser.). (Illus.). 128p. (YA). (gr. 6 up). 1997. lib. bdg. 20.95 (*0-89490-860-X*) Enslow Pubs.

Plessy vs. Ferguson Separate but Equal. (My Ancestors--My Heroes Ser.: Vol. 21). (J). (gr. 3-4). 2000. write for info. (*1-893091-20-1*) F R Parker.

Pleterni Ukras Od Najstarijih Vremena Do Danas: Njegov Likovni Oblik I Nutarnje Znacenje - Supplement: The Principal Conclusions of This Research: The Twist or Guilloche As Ornament from Ancient Times to Present: Its Exterior Form & Inner Meaning. Vinko D. Lasic. Ed. by Ziral Staff. Tr. by Dusko Condic from CRO. (CRO., Illus.). 920p. 1995. 100.00 (*1-880829-02-9*) Z I R A L.

Plethonis, Georgii Gemisti: Contra Scholarii Pro Aristotele Obiectiones. Ed. by Maltese. (GRE.). 1988. 22.95 (*3-322-00460-0*, T1589, Pub. by B G Teubner) U of Mich Pr.

Plethonis, Georgii Gemisti: Opuscula de Historia Graeca. Ed. by Maltese. (GRE.). 1989. 22.95 (*3-322-00674-3*, T1590, Pub. by B G Teubner) U of Mich Pr.

Plethora. unabridged ed. John Repar. 150p. 1995. pap. 5.00 (*0-9661910-0-5*) J Repar.

Plethora of Puzzles. Stanley Newman. 1995. 75.45 (*0-394-27306-0*) Random.

Plethysmography: Safety, Effectiveness, & Clinical Utility in Diagnosing Vascular Disease. Thomas V. Holohan. 46p. (C). 1998. reprint ed. pap. text 20.00 (*0-7881-4191-0*) DIANE Pub.

Pletzl of Paris: Jewish Immigrant Workers in the Belle Epoque. Nancy L Green. LC 84-27937. 278p. 1985. 45.00 (*0-8419-0995-4*) Holmes & Meier.

Pleura in Health & Disease. Chretien et al. (Lung Biology in Health & Disease Ser.: Vol. 30). (Illus.). 906p. 1985. text 295.00 (*0-8247-7380-2*) Dekker.

Pleural Diseases. 3rd ed. Richard W. Light. LC 94-44122. (Illus.). 408p. 1995. 79.00 (*0-683-05017-6*) Lppncott W & W.

Pleurocarpous Mosses of the West Indies. William R. Buck. LC 97-48734. (Memoirs of the New York Botanical Garden Ser.: Vol. 82). (Illus.). 400p. 1998. text 49.00 (*0-89327-418-6*, MEM 82) NY Botanical.

Pleurot, Hohenbuehelia, Hypsizygus, Calocybe, Lepista, Armillar, Amanita, Pluteus, Phaeolepiota, Crepidotus, Lactar. Aurel Dermek. (Fungorum Rariorum Icones Coloratae Ser.: Pars XVII). (FRE., Illus.). 23p. 1987. pap. 27.00 (*3-443-69003-3*, Pub. by Gebruder Borntraeger) Balogh.

Pleurotus Unter Stress: Oekophysiologische Untersuchungen Zu Wasserhaushalt und Sporulation. Angelika Achhammer. (Bibliotheca Mycologica: Vol. 141). (GER., Illus.). xii, 206p. 1992. 77.00 (*3-443-59042-X*, Pub. by Gebruder Borntraeger) Balogh.

Pleut De Coups Durs II. Chester B. Himes. (FRE.). 224p. 1988. pap. 10.95 (*0-7859-2652-6*, 207037923X) Fr & Eur.

Plexers. 1997. pap. text 8.95 (*0-86651-110-5*) Seymour Pubns.

Plexus see Rosy Crucifixion

Plexus. Henry Miller. 1987. pap. 9.95 (*0-394-62370-3*) Random.

Plexus: The Rosy Crucifixion II, Vol. II. Henry Miller. LC 86-33722. 640p. 1987. pap. 14.95 (*0-8021-5179-5*, Grove) Grove-Atltic.

Plexus Anesthesia: Perivascular Techniques of Brachial Plexus Block, Vol. 1. rev. ed. Alon P. Winnie. (Illus.). 272p. 1984. text 142.00 (*0-7216-1172-9*, W B Saunders Co) Harcrt Hlth Sci Grp.

Pleyel Violin Duets. Burton Isaac. 56p. 1997. pap. 9.95 (*0-7866-3126-0*, 93651) Mel Bay.

Pleyn Delit: Medieval Cookery for Modern Cooks. rev. ed. Constance B. Hieatt & Sharon Butler. LC 76-29734. (Illus.). 1979. pap. 16.95 (*0-8020-6366-7*) U of Toronto Pr.

Pleyto y Querella de los Guajolotes: Un Estudio. Gerardo Saenz. LC 87-81915. (Coleccion Cuba y sus Jueces). (SPA.). 122p. (Orig.). 1988. pap. 16.00 (*0-89729-454-8*) Ediciones.

PLFP's Changing Role in the Middle East. Harold M. Cubert. LC 96-42486. 256p. 1997. 52.50 (*0-7146-4772-1*, Pub. by F Cass Pubs); pap. 24.50 (*0-7146-4329-7*, Pub. by F Cass Pubs) Intl Spec Bk.

PLI Continuing Legal Assistant Training: More Litigation Techniques for Legal Assistants: Beyond the Basics - A Satellite Program. (Litigation & Administrative Practice Course Handbook, 1983-84 Ser.: Vol. 447). 445p. 1992. 70.00 (*0-685-65525-3*, H4-5141) PLI.

PLI Continuing Legal Assistant Training - Workshop for Legal Assistants, 1992: Bankruptcy. (Commercial Law & Practice Course Handbook Ser.). 333p. 1992. pap. 70.00 (*0-685-69473-9*) PLI.

PLI Continuing Legal Assistant Training - Workshop for Legal Assistants, 1992: Litigation; Legal Research & Writing; Environmental Law & Toxic Tort Litigation. (Litigation & Administrative Practice Course Handbook, 1983-84 Ser.). 536p. 1992. pap. 17.50 (*0-685-69474-7*) PLI.

PLI Continuing Legal Training: Workshops for Legal Assistants 1993: Basic Litigation: Legal Research & Writing. (Litigation & Administrative Practice Course Handbook, 1983-84 Ser.: Vol. 461). 732p. 1993. 70.00 (*0-685-69734-7*, H4-5155) PLI.

Plic . . . Plic . . . Tombe la Pluie. European Language Institute Staff. (Raconte et Chante Ser.). (FRE., Illus.). 27p. (Orig.). (J). (gr. k-2). 1992. pap. 19.95 (*88-85148-66-2*, Pub. by Europ Lang Inst) Midwest European Pubns.

Plicul Negru see Black Envelope

Pliers. David Armentrout & Patricia Armentrout. LC 94-46473. (Learning about Tools Discovery Library). 24p. (J). (gr. k-4). 1995. lib. bdg. 15.93 (*1-55916-120-5*) Rourke Bk Co.

Plight & Promise of Arid Land Agriculture. C. Wiley Hinman & Jack W. Hinman. 253p. 1992. text 39.00 (*0-231-06612-0*) Col U Pr.

Plight in Common: Hawthorne & Percy. Elzbieta Oleksy. LC 92-4487. (American University Studies: American Literature: Ser. XXIV, Vol. 34). VI, 244p. (C). 1993. text 35.95 (*0-8204-1848-X*) P Lang Pubng.

Plight of a Flight Attendant. Roy Orason. Ed. by Sierra Publishing Staff. LC 94-68493. (Illus.). 315p. (Orig.). 1994. pap. 6.95 (*0-9642392-2-1*) Orason.

Plight of Emulation: Ernest Meissonier & French Salon Painting. Marc J. Gotlieb. LC 95-12058. 264p. 1996. text 45.00 (*0-691-04374-4*, Pub. by Princeton U Pr) Cal Prin Full Svc.

Plight of Feeling. Julia A. Stern. LC 97-14419. 312p. 1997. pap. text 18.95 (*0-226-77311-6*); lib. bdg. 48.00 (*0-226-77310-8*) U Ch Pr.

***Plight of the Children.** LC 00-91800. (Tim MacCulfsky Mystery Ser.). 288p. 2000. pap. 19.95 (*0-9700458-0-8*) Koenisha Pubns.

Plight of the Church Traditionalist: A Last Apology. Donald D. Hook. 166p. (Orig.). 1991. pap. 9.95 (*1-879793-00-8*) Prayer Book.

Plight of the Kamaiyas: A Report of the Kamaiya Conference. Ratna Pustak Bhandar. 1997. pap. 22.00 (*0-7855-7477-8*, Pub. by Ratna Pustak Bhandar) St Mut.

Plight of the Lesser Sawyer's Cricket. Curtis Zahn. 199p. 1989. 20.00 (*0-88496-262-8*); pap. 11.00 (*0-88496-264-4*) Players Pr.

Plight of the Lesser's Sawyers Cricket: Playscript. Curtis Zahn. LC 90-53083. (Orig.). 1990. pap. 6.00 (*0-88734-223-X*) Players Pr.

***Plight of the Minorities: Problems & Grievances in Their Education.** R. N. Thakur. LC 99-931874. 1999. 27.50 (*81-212-0624-3*, Pub. by Gyan Publishing Hse) S Asia.

Plight of the Montagnards: Hearing before the Committee on Foreign Relations, United States Senate, One Hundred Fifth Congress, Second Session, March 10, 1998. United States Staff. LC 98-182904. (S. Hrg. Ser.). iii, 53p. 1998. write for info. (*0-16-056574-X*) USGPO.

Plight of the Thrift Institutions. Andrew S. Carron. LC 81-71434. (Studies in the Regulation of Economic Activity). 96p. 1982. 18.95 (*0-8157-1300-2*); pap. 8.95 (*0-8157-1299-5*) Brookings.

Plight of This Grey Wolf. Jeff Winters. 1997. pap. 6.95 (*0-9660702-1-6*) Babylon Pub.

Plight Through 7 Houses. Ernestine Tanner. 128p. 1997. 16.00 (*0-8059-4005-7*) Dorrance.

PLILP/ALP'98: Proceedings of the 10th International Symposium, PLILP '98: Held Jointly with the 6th International Conference, ALP '98, Pisa, Italy, September, 1998. Ed. by C. Palamidessi et al. LC 98-41640. (Lecture Notes in Computer Science Ser.: Vol. 1490). xi, 497p. 1998. pap. 75.00 (*3-540-65012-1*) Spr-Verlag.

Plimoth Plantation Day Packet. Ed. by Elizabeth L. Youmans. (Illus.). 107p. (Orig.). 1995. pap. 12.00 (*0-912498-16-1*, PPDP) F A C E.

Plimoth Plantation New England Cookery Book. Malabar Hornblower & Plimoth Plantation Staff. LC 90-5269. 224p. 1990. pap. 12.95 (*1-55832-027-X*) Harvard Common Pr.

Plini, Vol. I. Ed. by Jan & Mayhoff. (LAT.). 1996. reprint ed. 69.50 (*3-519-11650-2*, T1650, Pub. by B G Teubner) U of Mich Pr.

Plini, Vol. II. Ed. by Jan & Mayhoff. (LAT.). 1986. reprint ed. 72.50 (*3-519-01651-6*, T1651, Pub. by B G Teubner) U of Mich Pr.

Plini, Vol. III. Ed. by Jan & Mayhoff. (LAT.). 1987. reprint ed. 59.50 (*3-519-01652-4*, T1652, Pub. by B G Teubner) U of Mich Pr.

Plini, Vol. IV. Ed. by Jan & Mayhoff. (LAT.). 1967. reprint ed. 59.50 (*3-519-01653-2*, T1653, Pub. by B G Teubner) U of Mich Pr.

Plini, Vol. V. Ed. by Jan & Mayhoff. (LAT.). 1986. reprint ed. 59.50 (*3-519-01654-0*, T1654, Pub. by B G Teubner) U of Mich Pr.

Plini Vol. VI: Indices. Ed. by Jan. (LAT.). 1987. reprint ed. 69.50 (*3-519-01655-9*, T1655, Pub. by B G Teubner) U of Mich Pr.

Plini Secundi. Ed. by Schuster & Hanslik. (LAT.). 1992. reprint ed. pap. 29.95 (*3-8154-1657-4*, T1657, Pub. by B G Teubner) U of Mich Pr.

Plinius: Concordantiae in C. Plinii Caecilii Secundi Opera, 4 vols., Set. Plinius Minor. Ed. by Friedrich Heberlein & Wolfgang Slaby. (Alpha-Omega, Reihe A Ser.: Bd. CXIV-2). (GER.). 3128p. 1991. write for info. (*3-487-09403-7*) G Olms Pubs.

Plinius: Konkordanz Zur Naturalis Historia des C. Plinius Secundus, 3 vols. Ed. by Peter Rosumek & Dietmar Najock. write for info. (*0-318-71980-0*) G Olms Pubs.

Plinius Maior: Concordantia in C. Plinii Secundi Naturalem Historiam. Peter Rosumek & Dietmar Najock. (GER.). iv, 934p. 1995. write for info. (*3-487-10016-9*) G Olms Pubs.

Plinius Maior: Concordantia in C. Plinii Securdi Naturalem Historiam. Peter Rosumek & Dietmar Najock. (GER.). 5036p. 1995. write for info. (*3-487-09949-7*) G Olms Pubs.

Plinius Minor - Concordantiae in C. Plinii Caecilii Secundi Opera. Pars Prior: Epistulae, 4 vols., Set. Ed. by Friedrich Heberlein & Wolfgang Slaby. (Alpha-Omega, Reihe A Ser.: Bd. CXIV/1). (GER.). xviii, 3128p. 1991. write for info. (*3-487-09467-3*) G Olms Pubs.

P

An Asterisk (*) at the beginning of an entry indicates that the title is appearing for the first time.

Plinius Minor Pars Altera: Panegyricus. (GER.). 500p. write for info. (0-318-70607-5) G Olms Pubs.

Plins Pouvoirs. Jean Giraudoux. pap. 9.95 (0-685-33923-8) Fr & Eur.

Pliny Epistle X: Correspondence. Ed. by Williams. (Classical Texts Ser.). 1990. 59.99 (0-85668-407-4, Pub. by Aris & Phillips); pap. 22.00 (0-85668-408-2, Pub. by Aris & Phillips) David Brown.

Pliny Moore: North Country Pioneer. Allan S. Everest. (Illus.). 136p. 1990. pap. 12.95 (1-890402-17-6) Clinton Cnty Hist.

Pliny the Elder on Science & Technology. John F. Healy. LC 99-24316. (Illus.). 484p. 2000. text 110.00 (0-19-814687-6) OUP.

Pliny the Elder's Chapters on the History of Art. Ed. by J. B. Sellers. 252p. 1974. 35.00 (0-89005-055-4) Ares.

Pliny the Younger's Character As Revealed Through His Letters: An Intermediate Reader-Grammar Review. 2nd ed. 92p. (C). 1995. 17.95 (0-9628450-5-1) P L Chambers.

Pliny the Younger's Character As Revealed Through His Letters: Teacher Key. 2nd ed. 43p. (C). 1995. pap., teacher ed. 7.95 (0-9628450-6-X) P L Chambers.

Pliny's Images Through Prose. Esmond Blair. (C). 1991. pap. 8.98 (0-913412-53-8) Brandon Hse.

Plio-Pleistocene Genetic Sequences of the Southwestern Louisiana Continental Shelf & Slope RIO 210: Geologic Framework, Sedimentary Facies, & Hydrocarbon Distribution. R. A. Morton & W. B. Ayers, Jr. (Illus.). 74p. 1992. pap. 7.00 (0-317-05177-6, RI 210) Bur Econ Geology.

Pliocene Carbonates & Related Facies Flanking the Gulf of California, Baja California, Mexico. Ed. by M. E. Johnson & J. L. Vazquez. LC 97-16527. (Special Papers: No. 318). 1997. pap. 57.00 (0-8137-2318-3) Geol Soc.

***Plip, Plop.** Concordia Publishing House Staff. (Hear Me Read Ser.). (SPA., Illus.). 24p. (J). (ps-3). 2000. 2.95 (0-570-09910-2) Concordia.

PLI's Annual Institutes on Securities Regulation Transcripts. 1975. write for info. (0-318-72261-5) PLI.

Pliska Alphabet, the Cyrillic & the Glacolitic Alphabets. V. Yontchev. (Illus.). 184p. 1997. 94.95 (954-90178-1-8) Intl Scholars.

PLO & Israel: From Armed Conflict to Political Solutions, 1964-1994. Avraham Sela & Moshe Maoz. LC 97-10190. 292p. 1997. text 45.00 (0-312-12906-8) St Martin.

PLO-The Palestine Liberation Organization: Its Function & Structure. Sami Mussalam. 70p. (Orig.). (C). 1988. pap. 6.95 (0-915597-72-1) Amana Bks.

PLO under Arafat: Between Gun & Olive Branch. Shaul Mishal. LC 86-9140. 206p. reprint ed. pap. 63.90 (0-7837-4541-9, 208031000005) Bks Demand.

Plodding Princes of the Palouse. Nona Hengen. (Illus.). xi, 184p. (Orig.). 1984. 14.95 (0-931474-29-9) TBW Bks.

Ploesti: The Great Ground-Air Battle of 1 August 1943. Stewart Dugan et al. LC 97-31258. (Illus.). 318p. 1998. pap. 19.95 (1-57488-144-2) Brasseys.

Plomb-Rennaissance see Grande Encyclopedie

Plombier. Allen Morgan. (FRE.). 24p. 1999. pap. write for info. (2-89021-362-5, Pub. by La Courte Ech) Firefly Bks Ltd.

Plongee dans Mon Essentiel. Claude Peloquin.Tr. of Dive into My Essence. (FRE.). 119p. 1985. pap. 10.00 (2-89135-011-1) Guernica Editions.

Plop! Martin Baxendale. (Illus.). 64p. 1998. pap. 6.95 (1-889647-36-5) Boston Am.

PlopLop, No. 1. Ed. by John Clark & Scott Franke. (Adventures of PlopLop Ser.). 16p. 1991. pap. 5.00 (1-885710-00-3) Geekspeak Unique.

PlopLop, No. 2. Ed. by John Clark. (Adventures of PlopLop Ser.). 16p. 1992. pap. 5.00 (1-885710-01-1) Geekspeak Unique.

PlopLop No. 3: An "Antholozine" of Poetry, Prose & Artwork. Kitrell Andis et al. 32p. 1993. pap. 5.00 (1-885710-02-X) Geekspeak Unique.

PlopLop No. 4: An "Antholozine" of Poetry, Prose & Artwork. Kitrell Andis et al. 48p. 1993. pap. 6.00 (1-885710-03-8) Geekspeak Unique.

PlopLop No. 5: An "Antholozine" of Poetry, Prose & Artwork. Kitrell Andis et al. Ed. & Illus. by John Clark. Illus. by Bart Quinet. 50p. 1994. pap. 5.00 (1-885710-05-4) Geekspeak Unique.

PlopLop No. 6: An "Antholozine" of Poetry, Prose & Artwork. Kitrell Andis et al. 50p. 1995. pap. 5.00 (1-885710-11-9) Geekspeak Unique.

PlopLop No. 7: An "Antholozine" of Poetry, Prose & Artwork. Kitrell Andis et al. Ed. by John Clark. (Illus.). 50p. 1995. pap. 5.00 (1-885710-14-3) Geekspeak Unique.

PlopLop No. 8: An "Antholozine" of Poetry, Prose & Artwork. Fielding Dawson et al. Ed. by Kitrell Andis. (Illus.). 35p. 1996. pap. 5.00 (1-885710-15-1) Geekspeak Unique.

PlopLop No. 9: An "Antholozine" of Poetry, Prose & Artwork. B. Z. Niditch et al. Ed. & Illus. by John Clark. 50p. (Orig.). 1997. pap. 5.00 (1-885710-20-8) Geekspeak Unique.

Ploplop No. 10: An "Antholozine" of Poetry, Prose, & Artwork. Kitrell Andis et al. Ed. & Illus. by John Clark. 50p. 1998. pap. 5.00 (1-885710-23-2) Geekspeak Unique.

***Plot.** H. C. Bailey. 252p. 2000. pap. 9.95 (0-594-00162-5) Eightn Hundrd.

Plot. Ansen Dibell. (Elements of Fiction Writing Ser.). 176p. 1988. 15.99 (0-89879-303-3, Wrtrs Digest Bks) F & W Pubns Inc.

Plot. Ansen Dibell. (Elements of Fiction Writing Ser.). 176p. 1999. pap. 12.00 (0-89879-946-5, 10644, Wrtrs Digest Bks) F & W Pubns Inc.

Plot Vol. 1: The Big Picture Resolves Ten Doctrinal Debates. Bob Enyart. (Illus.). 311p. 1997. pap. 49.95 (1-891451-02-2) B Enyart.

Plot - Dealing with Feelings: Victims, Villains & Heroines. Loy Young. LC 98-96448. (Illus.). 272p. 1998. 24.95 (1-882888-49-9); pap. 17.95 (1-882888-50-2) Aquarius Hse.

***Plot Against Christianity.** Elizabeth Dilling. 310p. 1998. pap. 15.00 (0-944379-10-9) CPA Bk Pub.

Plot Against Christianity. unabridged ed. Elizabeth Dilling. 310p. 1970. reprint ed. pap. 20.00 (0-945001-71-1) GSG & Assocs.

Plot Against the Catholic Church: Communism, Free Masonry & the Jewish Fifth Column in the Clergy. Maurice Pinay. 1979. lib. bdg. 69.95 (0-8490-2984-8) Gordon Pr.

Plot & Point of View in the Iliad. Robert J. Rabel. LC 96-51313. 264p. 1997. text 44.50 (0-472-10768-2, 10768) U of Mich Pr.

Plot in Rabbitville. Earl J. Scheel. (J). 1999. pap. 6.95 (0-533-12904-4) Vantage.

Plot-It-Yourself Adventure: Goonies Cavern of Horror. William Rotsler. Ed. by Diane Arico. 128p. (Orig.). (J). (gr. 3-7). 1985. pap. 3.95 (0-671-60135-0) S&S Trade.

***Plot of a Strangemaker.** Francis H. Raven. (Poetry Chapbks.). 2000. pap. 8.00 (1-930259-11-5) Anabasis.

Plot of Aeschylus' "Oresteia" A Literary Commentary. Harou Konishi. (Classical & Byzantine Monographs: Vol. 19). vii, 284p. 1990. pap. 72.00 (90-256-0994-5, Pub. by AM Hakkert) BookLink Distributors.

Plot of Her Own: The Female Protagonist in Russian Literature. Ed. by Sona S. Hoisington. LC 95-1989. (Studies in Russian Literature & Theory). 1995. 49.95 (0-8101-1224-8); pap. 16.95 (0-8101-1298-1) Northwestern U Pr.

Plot of the Future: Utopia & Dystopia in Modern Drama. Dragan Klaic. (Theater: Theory - Text - Performance Ser.). 272p. (C). 1992. text 47.50 (0-472-10217-6, 10217) U of Mich Pr.

Plot Outlines of One Hundred Famous Plays. Ed. by Van H. Cartmell. 1979. 16.50 (0-8446-0539-5) Peter Smith.

Plot Pak: Precalculus Tutorials with Computer Graphics. John Mowbray. (Software Ser.). 191p. (C). 1987. pap. text 53.95 incl. disk (0-534-07542-8) PWS Pubs.

Plot Snakes & the Dynamics of Narrative Experience. Allen Tilley. (Illus.). 176p. 1992. 49.95 (0-8130-1151-5); pap. 17.95 (0-8130-1166-3) U Press Fla.

Plot, Story, & the Novel: From Dickens & Poe to the Modern Period. Robert L. Caserio. LC 79-4321. 326p. 1979. reprint ed. pap. 101.10 (0-608-02538-0, 206318200004) Bks Demand.

Plot, the Cause, the Solution. 3rd ed. Malik H. Jabbar. 35p. reprint ed. pap. 4.95 (1-57154-001-6) Rare Bks Dist.

Plot Thickens. Ed. by Mary Higgins Clark. 1997. per. 5.99 (0-671-01557-5) PB.

Plot to Destroy the Armed Forces of Ibero-America. Dennis Small & Gretchen Small. LC 94-71140. (Illus.). 500p. 1994. pap. text 15.00 (0-943235-11-1) Exec Intel Review.

***Plot to Get Bill Gates: An Irreverent Investigation of the World's Richest Man.** Gary Rivlin. 2000. pap. 14.00 (0-8129-9073-0, Times Bks) Crown Pub Group.

Plot to Get Bill Gates: An Irreverent Investigation of the World's Richest Man ... & the People Who Hate Him. Gary Rivlin. LC 99-18228. 360p. 1999. 25.00 (0-8129-3006-1) Times Pub TX.

***Plot to Kill Jesus: A Contextual Study of John 11.47-53.** Camillus Umoh. (European University Studies: Vol. 696). xx,309p. 2000. pap. text 47.95 (3-631-36203-X) P Lang Pubng.

Plot to Win the White House: And How It Succeeded. Jack Catran. 200p. (Orig.). 1994. pap. 14.95 (0-937399-22-1) Jade Pubns.

***Plot Twist.** Jane Rubino. 304p. 2000. 24.95 (1-885173-80-6, Pub. by Write Way) Midpt Trade.

Plotbusters Case of the Toxic Trous. C. Gifford. 1996. mass mkt. 10.95 (0-340-65596-8, Pub. by Hodder & Stought Ltd) Trafalgar.

Plotin & L'Occident: Firmicus Maternus, Marius Victorinus, Saint Augustin, et Macrobe. P. Henry. (Classical Studies). (FRE.). reprint ed. lib. bdg. 42.50 (0-697-00039-7) Irvington.

Plotinian & Christian Studies. A. Hilary Armstrong. (Collected Studies: No. CS102). 384p. (C). 1979. reprint ed. lib. bdg. 112.95 (0-86078-047-3, Pub. by Variorum) Ashgate Pub Co.

Plotinus. Lloyd P. Gerson. LC 93-49382. (Arguments of the Philosophers Ser.). 328p. (C). (gr. 13). 1994. 90.00 (0-415-05662-4, B4274) Routledge.

Plotinus. Lloyd P. Gerson. LC 97-50000. (Arguments of the Philosophers Ser.). 356p. (C). 1998. pap. 27.99 (0-415-17409-0) Routledge.

Plotinus. G. R. Mead. 1983. reprint ed. pap. 8.95 (0-916411-01-X) Holmes Pub.

Plotinus. Ralph Shirley. 1993. reprint ed. pap. 6.95 (1-55818-241-1) Holmes Pub.

Plotinus: An Introduction to the Enneads. Dominic J. O'Meara. (Illus.). 154p. 1995. pap. text 17.95 (0-19-875147-8) OUP.

Plotinus: Essay on the Beautiful. Plotinus. Tr. by Thomas Taylor. 1984. pap. 8.95 (0-916411-86-9) Holmes Pub.

Plotinus: On the Descent of the Soul. Tr. by Thomas Taylor from GRE. 1990. pap. text 5.95 (1-55818-159-8) Holmes Pub.

Plotinus: The Theosophy of the Greeks. B. A. Mead. 48p. 1996. reprint ed. spiral bd. 9.00 (0-7873-0601-0) Hlth Research.

Plotinus: The Theosophy of the Greeks (1895) G. R. Mead. 51p. 1996. reprint ed. pap. 7.95 (1-56459-743-1) Kessinger Pub.

Plotinus & Freedom: A Study of Enneads 6.8. Laura Westra. LC 88-38807. (Studies in the History of Philosophy). 264p. 1990. lib. bdg. 89.95 (0-88946-312-3) E Mellen.

***Plotinus on Body & Beauty: Society, Philosophy & Religion in 3rd Century Rome.** Margaret R. Miles. LC 99-32105. 224p. 1999. 64.95 (0-631-21274-4); pap. text 26.95 (0-631-21275-2) Blackwell Pubs.

Plotinus on the Beautiful (1908) Stephen MacKenna. 50p. 1998. reprint ed. pap. 9.95 (0-7661-0345-5) Kessinger Pub.

Plotinus on the Good or the 1 (Enneads) Vol. 9: An Analytical Commentary. P. A. Meijer. (Amsterdam Classical Monographs (ACM): Vol. I). 397p. 1992. pap. 80.00 (90-5063-082-0, Pub. by Gieben) J Benjamins Pubng Co.

Plotinus: or The Simplicity of Vision. Pierre Hadot. Tr. by Michael Chase. (Illus.). 144p. 1999. 24.95 (0-226-31193-7) U Ch Pr.

Plotinus Psychology: His Doctrines of the Embodied Soul. H. J. Blumenthal. 170p. 1971. text 65.00 (90-247-5037-7) Kluwer Academic.

Plotinus Simplicity Vision. Pierre Hadot. Tr. by Michael Chase. 152p. 1998. pap. text 13.00 (0-226-31194-5) U Ch Pr.

Plotinus' Theory of Matter-Evil. E. Peters. 1998. 90.95 (90-6831-752-0, Pub. by Peeters Pub) Bks Intl VA.

***Plotinus (204/5-270 A.D.) The Triumph of Spirit.** Eugene T. Woolf. (The/Great Minds Revisited Ser.: Vol. 1). 87p. 1999. 12.00 (0-910153-14-0) E T Woolf.

Plotius, Tolma, & the Descent of Being: An Exposition & Analysis. N. Joseph Torchia. LC 91-35593. (American University Studies: Philosophy: Ser. V, Vol. 135). 170p. (C). 1993. text 43.95 (0-8204-1768-8) P Lang Pubng.

Plots: A Funereal Comedy in One-Act. Jerome McDonough. 24p. 1981. pap. 3.25 (0-88680-154-0) I E Clark.

Plots Against Presidents. 2nd ed. John M. Potter. 1969. 14.95 (0-8392-1178-3) Astor-Honor.

Plots & Characters. Millard Kaufman. LC 98-89055. 262p. 1999. 24.95 (1-893329-03-8) Really Great Bks.

Plots & Conspiracies. Andrew Shirley. LC 75-27686. (Illus.). 142p. 1975. reprint ed. lib. bdg. 59.50 (0-8371-8459-2, SHPC, Greenwood Pr) Greenwood.

Plots & Counterplots see Marble Woman: Unknown Thrillers of Louisa May Alcott

Plots & Errors. Jill McGown. LC 99-14226. 1999. 22.95 (0-345-43313-0) Ballantine Pub Grp.

***Plots & Errors.** Jill McGown. 384p. 2000. mass mkt. 6.99 (0-449-00253-5) Fawcett.

Plots & Paranoia: A History of Political Espionage in Britain, 1790-1988. Bernard Porter. 304p. 1989. 34.95 (0-04-445258-6) Routledge.

Plots & Players. Pamela Melnikoff. LC 96-3777. (Illus.). (J). (gr. 3 up). 1996. pap. 9.95 (0-8276-0576-5) JPS Phila.

Plots & Proposals: American Women's Fiction, 1850-90. Karen Tracey. LC 99-6380. 2000. 16.95 (0-252-06839-4) U of Ill Pr.

***Plots of Enlightenment: Education & The Novel in Eighteenth-century England.** Richard A Barney. LC 99-21524. 1999. 49.50 (0-8047-2978-6) Stanford U Pr.

Plots of Time: An Inquiry into History, Myth, & Meaning. Allen Tilley. LC 94-48704. (Illus.). 144p. 1995. 39.95 (0-8130-1357-7) U Press Fla.

Plots, Quarks & Strange Particles: Proc of the Dalitz Conference, 1990. Ian J. Aitchison et al. 220p. 1991. pap. 28.00 (981-02-0471-X); text 84.00 (981-02-0470-1) World Scientific Pub.

Plots, Transformations & Regression: An Introduction to Graphical Methods of Diagnostic Regression Analysis. A. C. Atkinson. (Oxford Statistical Science Ser.). (Illus.). 296p. 1987. pap. text 45.00 (0-19-853371-3) OUP.

Plots Unlimited: A Creative Source for Generating a Virtually Limitless Number & Variety of Story Plots & Outlines. Tom Sawyer & Arthur D. Weingarten. LC 90-83939. 296p. (Orig.). 1995. pap. 25.00 (0-9627476-0-2) Ashleywilde.

Plotted, Shot & Painted: Cultural Representation of Biblical Women. J. Cheryl Exum. LC 97-100777. (JSOT Supplement Ser.: No. 215). 260p. 1996. 75.00 (1-85075-592-2, Pub. by Sheffield Acad) CUP Services.

Plotted, Shot & Painted: Cultural Representations of Biblical Women. J. Cheryl Exum. LC 97-100777. (JSOT Supplement Ser.: No. 215). 260p. 1996. pap. 19.50 (1-85075-778-X, Pub. by Sheffield Acad) CUP Services.

Plotters & Patterns of American Land Surveying. Ed. by Roy Minnick. 232p. 1986. pap. 30.00 (0-910845-28-X, 974) Landmark Ent.

Plotting America's Past: Fenimore Cooper & the Leatherstocking Tales. William P. Kelly. LC 83-4779. 208p. 1984. 26.95 (0-8093-1144-5) S Ill U Pr.

Plotting & Writing Suspense Fiction. Patricia Highsmith. 160p. 1990. pap. 12.95 (0-312-04867-X) St Martin.

Plotting Change: Contemporary Women's Fiction. Ed. by Linda Anderson. (Stratford-upon-Avon Ser.). 160p. 1990. pap. 13.95 (0-7131-6603-7, A4124, Pub. by E A) Routldge.

Plotting Course Act. Ryan. 1997. mass mkt., wbk. ed. 20.50 (0-314-06792-2) West Pub.

Plotting Directions: An Activist's Guide. Chris Robinson. LC 82-80105. (Illus.). 68p. 1982. pap. 5.00 (0-916894-02-9) Recon Pubns.

Plotting Hitler's Death: The German Resistance to Hitler, 1933-1945. Joachim C. Fest. Tr. by Bruce Little. LC 96-7306. (Illus.). 448p. 1995. 30.00 (0-8050-4213-X) H Holt & Co.

Plotting Hitler's Death: The German Resistance, 1933-1945. Joachim C. Fest. Tr. by Bruce Little from GER. LC 96-7306.Tr. of Staatsstreich. 1996. write for info. (0-08-050421-3) H Holt & Co.

Plotting Hitler's Death: The Story of the German Resistance. Joachim Fest. 448p. 1997. pap. text 16.95 (0-8050-5648-3) H Holt & Co.

Plotting Pictures: Coordinate Graphing & Number Skills. Paula Rozell. Ed. by Joan Gideon. (Illus.). 64p. (J). (gr. 5-8). 1994. student ed. 10.95 (0-86651-854-1) Seymour Pubns.

Plotting Points & Position. Andrew King. LC 98-18034. (Math for Fun Ser.). 32p. (J). (gr. 2-4). 1998. pap. 5.95 (0-7613-0746-X, Copper Beech Bks) Millbrook Pr.

Plotting Points & Position. Andrew King. LC 98-18034. (Math for Fun Ser.). (Illus.). 32p. (J). (gr. 2-4). 1998. 20.90 (0-7613-0852-0, Copper Beech Bks) Millbrook Pr.

Plotting Sheets & Sight Forms for Yachtsmen. Des. by Rod McCallum. (C). 1989. 35.00 (0-7855-5957-4, Pub. by Laurie Norie & Wilson Ltd) St Mut.

Plotting the Past: Metamorphoses of Historical Narrative in Modern Italian Fiction. Cristina Della Coletta. LC 96-31663. (Studies in Romance Literatures: Vol. 12). 232p. 1996. pap. 38.95 (1-55753-091-2) Purdue U Pr.

Plotting to Kill. Armine K. Mortimer. LC 90-19208. (Writing about Women Ser.: Vol. 1). XIV, 222p. (C). 1991. text 41.95 (0-8204-1435-2) P Lang Pubng.

Plotting Women: Gender & Narration in the Eighteenth- & Nineteenth-Century British Novel. Alison A. Case. LC 99-28818. 1999. 37.50 (0-8139-1895-2) U Pr of Va.

Plotting Women: Gender & Representation in Mexico. Jean Franco. (Gender & Culture Ser.). 256p. 1991. pap. text 19.00 (0-231-06423-3) Col U Pr.

Plough & the Pen: Paul S. Gross & the Establishment of the Spokane Hutterian Brethren. Vance J. Youmans. LC 94-21473. (Illus.). xii, 150p. (Orig.). (C). 1994. pap. 25.00 (0-9635752-5-2) Pkway Pubs.

Plough & the Swastika: The NSDAP & Agriculture in Germany, 1928-45. John E. Farquharson. LC 74-31570. (Sage Studies in 20th Century History: Vol. 5). 320p. reprint ed. pap. 99.20 (0-608-14233-6, 202189700026) Bks Demand.

Plough in Field Arable: Western Agribusiness in Third World Agriculture. Sarah P. Voll. LC 80-50490. 224p. reprint ed. pap. 69.50 (0-8357-5548-7, 203516700093) Bks Demand.

Plough, Sword & Book: The Structure of Human History. Ernest Gellner. 288p. 1990. pap. 17.95 (0-226-28702-5) U Ch Pr.

Plough, Sword & Book: The Structure of Human History. Ernest Gellner. LC 88-32452. 288p. 1995. 29.95 (0-226-28701-7) U Ch Pr.

Plough Woman. Rachel Katznelson-Shazar. 1975. 7.95 (0-685-82599-X); pap. 3.95 (0-685-82600-7) Herzl Pr.

***Ploughing Sand: British Rule in Palestine, 1917-1948.** Naomi Shephard. LC 99-42669. (Illus.). 290p. (C). 2000. 28.00 (0-8135-2765-1) Rutgers U Pr.

Ploughing the Clouds: The Soma Ceremony in Ancient Ireland. Peter L. Wilson. LC 97-118. 184p. (Orig.). 1998. per. 14.95 (0-87286-326-3) City Lights.

Ploughman's Progress. Alfred Hall. (Illus.). 164p. 1992. text 33.95 (0-85236-209-9, Pub. by Farming Pr) Diamond Farm Bk.

Ploughman's Punch. Thelwell. (Illus.). 128p. pap. 12.95 (0-85236-296-X, Pub. by Farming Pr) Diamond Farm Bk.

Ploughmen of the Glacier. George Ryga. 80p. 1977. pap. 9.95 (0-88922-118-9, Pub. by Talonbks) Genl Dist Srvs.

Ploughs & Ploughing. Roy Brigden. (Album Ser.: No. 125). (Illus.). 32p. 1998. pap. 6.25 (0-85263-695-4, Pub. by Shire Pubns) Parkwest Pubns.

Ploughs & Politicks: Charles Read of New Jersey & His Notes on Agriculture, 1715-1744. Carl R. Woodward. LC 73-16351. (Perspectives in American History Ser.: No. 24). (Illus.). xxvi, 468p. 1974. reprint ed. lib. bdg. 49.50 (0-87991-338-X) Porcupine Pr.

***Ploughshare of War: The Origins of the Anglo-Zulu War of 1879.** Richard Cope. LC 99-456901. (Illus.). 282p. 1999. pap. 12.75 (0-86980-944-X, Pub. by Univ Natal Pr) Intl Spec Bk.

Ploughshare Village Pasis: Culture & Context in Taiwan. S. Harrell. LC 82-8333. (Publications on Asia of the School of International Studies: No. 35). (Illus.). 248p. 1982. pap. 25.00 (0-295-95946-0) U of Wash Pr.

Ploughshares Fall, 1998: Fiction Issue Edited by Lorrie Moore, Vol. 24, Nos. 2 & 3. Ed. by Lorrie Moore. 247p. 1998. pap. 9.95 (0-933277-23-7) Ploughshares.

Ploughshares Fall, 1995: Living Rooms. Ed. by Ann Beattie. 254p. (Orig.). 1995. pap. 8.95 (0-933277-14-8) Ploughshares.

Ploughshares Fall, 1994: Intimate Exile. Ed. by Rosellen Brown. (Ploughshares Ser.). 251p. (Orig.). (C). 1994. pap. 8.95 (0-933277-11-3) Ploughshares.

***Ploughshares, Fall 1999 Vol. 25: Fiction Issue.** Ed. by Charles Baxter. 233p. 1999. pap. 9.95 (0-933277-26-1) Ploughshares.

Ploughshares Fall, 1997. Ed. by Mary Gordon. 242p. 1997. pap. 9.95 (0-933277-20-2) Ploughshares.

Ploughshares Fall, 1996. Ed. by Richard Ford. 252p. (Orig.). 1996. pap. 8.95 (0-933277-17-2) Ploughshares.

Ploughshares Fall, 1992: Stories. Ed. by Tobias Wolff. 226p. (Orig.). (C). 1992. pap. 8.95 (0-933277-05-9) Ploughshares.

Ploughshares into Swords? Israelis & Jews in the Shadow of the Intifada. Colin Shindler. 1991. text 49.50 (1-85043-324-0, Pub. by I B T) St Martin.

Ploughshares into Swords: Josiah Gorgas & Confederate Ordnance. Frank E. Vandiver. LC 94-15117. (Military History Ser.: No. 36). (Illus.). 368p. 1994. reprint ed. 35.00 (0-89096-630-3) Tex A&M Univ Pr.

Ploughshares into Swords: Josiah Gorgas & Confederate Ordnance. Frank E. Vandiver. LC 94-15117. (Military History Ser.: No. 36). (Illus.). 368p. 1994. reprint ed. pap. 16.95 (0-89096-632-X) Tex A&M Univ Pr.

An Asterisk (*) at the beginning of an entry indicates that the title is appearing for the first time.

Ploughshares into Swords: Race, Rebellion, & Identity in Gabriel's Virginia, 1730-1810. James Sidbury. (Illus.). 302p. (C). 1997. text 54.95 (*0-521-58454-X*); pap. text 18.95 (*0-521-59860-5*) Cambridge U Pr.
Ploughshares Poetry Reader. Ed. & Intro. by Joyce Peseroff. LC 86-6319. 336p. 1987. 25.00 (*0-933277-02-4*) Ploughshares.
Ploughshares Spring, 1998: Stories & Poems Edited by Stuart Dabek & Jane Hirshfield, Vol. 24, No. 1. Ed. by Stuart Dybek & Jane Hirshfield. 225p. 1998. pap. 9.95 (*0-933277-22-9*) Ploughshares.
Ploughshares Spring, 1995: Everyday Seductions. Ed. by Gary Soto. (Ploughshares Ser.). 211p. (Orig.). 1995. pap. 8.95 (*0-933277-13-X*) Ploughshares.
Ploughshares Spring, 1994: Tribes. Ed. by James Welch. (Ploughshares Ser.). 210p. (Orig.). (C). 1994. pap. 8.95 (*0-933277-10-5*) Ploughshares.
***Ploughshares Spring 1999 Vol. 25, No. 1: Poems & Stories Edited by Mark Doty.** Ed. by Mark Doty. 207p. 1999. pap. 9.95 (*0-933277-25-3*) Ploughshares.
Ploughshares Spring, 1997. Ed. by Yusef Komunyakaa. 227p. (Orig.). 1997. pap. 9.95 (*0-933277-19-9*) Ploughshares.
Ploughshares Spring, 1996. Ed. by Marilyn Hacker. 217p. (Orig.). 1996. pap. 8.95 (*0-933277-16-4*) Ploughshares.
Ploughshares Spring, 1993: Believers. Ed. by Al Young. 234p. (Orig.). (C). 1993. pap. 8.95 (*0-933277-07-5*) Ploughshares.
***Ploughshares Spring 2000 Vol. 26: Poems & Stories Edited by Paul Muldoon.** Ed. by Paul Muldoon. 226p. 2000. pap. 9.95 (*0-933277-28-8*) Ploughshares.
Ploughshares Winter, 1995-96. Ed. by Tim O'Brien & Mark Strand. 225p. (Orig.). 1995. pap. 8.95 (*0-933277-15-6*) Ploughshares.
Ploughshares Winter, 1994-95: Regrets Only. Ed. by Don Lee & David Daniel. (Ploughshares Ser.). 230p. (Orig.). (C). 1994. pap. text 8.95 (*0-933277-12-1*) Ploughshares.
***Ploughshares, Winter 1999-00 Vol. 25: Stories & Poems.** Ed. by Madison Smartt Bell & Elizabeth Spires. 238p. 1999. pap. write for info. (*0-933277-27-X*) Ploughshares.
Ploughshares Winter, 1997-98. Ed. by Howard Norman & Jane Shore. 234p. 1997. pap. 9.95 (*0-933277-21-0*) Ploughshares.
Ploughshares Winter, 1996-97. Ed. by Robert Boswell & Ellen B. Voigt. 247p. (Orig.). 1996. pap. 8.95 (*0-933277-18-0*) Ploughshares.
Ploughshares Winter, 1993-94: Borderlands. Ed. by Russell Banks & Chase Twichell. 231p. (Orig.). (C). 1993. pap. 8.95 (*0-933277-09-1*) Ploughshares.
Ploughshares Winter, 1992-93: Voices from the Other Room. Ed. by Marie Howe & Christopher Tilghman. 254p. (Orig.). (C). 1993. pap. 8.95 (*0-933277-06-7*) Ploughshares.
***Ploughshares Winter, 1998-99: Poems & Stories Edited by Thomas Lux.** Ed. by Thomas Lux. 243p. 1998. pap. 9.95 (*0-933277-24-5*) Ploughshares.
Plovers. Richard Vaughan. (Illus.). 160p. (C). 1988. 90.00 (*0-900963-36-0*, Pub. by T Dalton) St Mut.
Plovers, Sandpipers, & Snipes of the World. Paul A. Johnsgard. LC 80-22712. 575p. 1981. reprint ed. pap. 178.30 (*0-608-03483-5*, 206419600008) Bks Demand.
Plow Naked: Selected Writings on Poetry. Fred Chappell. LC 93-23791. (Poets on Poetry Ser.). 160p. (C). 1993. pap. 13.95 (*0-472-06542-4*, 06542) U of Mich Pr.
Plow Reader: Selections from an Appalachian Alternative Newsmagazine of the Late 1970's. Ed. by Ann F. Richman. (Illus.). xxiv, 328p. (Orig.). 1996. reprint ed. pap. 15.00 (*1-885912-09-9*) Sows Ear Pr.
Plow That Broke the Plains Brass Quintet. V. Thomson. 1994. pap. 36.00 (*0-7935-2988-3*) H Leonard.
Plow, the Hammer, & the Knout: An Economic History of Eighteenth-Century Russia. Arcadius Kahan. Ed. by Richard Hellie. LC 84-16338. (Illus.). xii, 412p. 1985. lib. bdg. 78.00 (*0-226-42253-4*) U Ch Pr.
Plow to Pulpit. H. L. Inabnit. 130p. (Orig.). 1989. pap. text 12.50 (*0-9620902-1-2*) Vernon Print & Pub.
Plowboys, Cowboys & Slanted Pigs: A Collection. Jerry Flemmons. LC 84-2421. (Illus.). 230p. 1984. 15.95 (*0-912646-90-X*); pap. 8.95 (*0-912646-95-0*) Tex Christian.
***Plowing in Hope: Toward a Biblical Theology of Culture.** David B. Hegeman. 128p. 1999. pap. 10.00 (*1-885767-63-3*) Canon Pr ID.
Plowing My Own Furrow. Howard W. Moore. LC 93-7918. (Studies on Peace & Conflict Resolution). 224p. 1993. reprint ed. pap. 19.95 (*0-8156-0276-6*) Syracuse U Pr.
***Plowing the Dark.** Richard Powers. LC 99-45084. 400p. 2000. 25.00 (*0-374-23461-2*) FS&G.
Plowing the Sea: Nurturing the Hidden Sources of Growth in the Developing World. Michael Fairbanks & Stace Lindsay. LC 96-35391. 320p. 1997. 29.95 (*0-87584-761-7*) Harvard Busn.
Plowing the Steppes: And Other Gulag Stories. A. Meyer Galler. LC 97-79551. (Illus.). ix, 179p. (Orig.). 1997. pap. 10.95 (*0-943376-65-3*) Magnes Mus.
Plowman: A Register of Plowmans in America & Extr. from English & American Records. B. H. Plowman. 90p. 1991. reprint ed. pap. 17.50 (*0-8328-1828-3*) Higginson Bk Co.
Plowman's Folly & a Second Look. Edward H. Faulkner & Paul B. Sears. LC 87-82036. (Conservation Classics Ser.). 193p. (C). 1988. reprint ed. text 38.00 (*0-933280-51-3*) Island Pr.
Plowman's Tale: The c. 1532 & 1606 Editions of a Spurious Canterbury Tale. rev. ed. Mary R. McCarl. LC 96-37836. (Renaissance Imagination Ser.). 320p. 1997. text 72.00 (*0-8153-1711-5*) Garland.
***Plows.** Hal Rogers. LC 99-89469. 2000. lib. bdg. write for info. (*1-56766-755-4*) Childs World.
Plows & Planting Implements. April Halberstadt. LC 97-16143. (Farm Tractor Color History Ser.). (Illus.). 128p. 1997. pap. 21.95 (*0-7603-0099-2*) MBI Pubg.
Plows, Peacocks & Stars. Dan McLary. Date not set. write for info. (*0-9659632-6-8*) Verda Publ.
Plows, Prosperity, & Cooperation at Agbassa: The Change from Hoes to Plows on a Government-Sponsored Land Settlement Project in Northern Togo. Dana A. Farnham. LC 96-21396. 264p. 1996. 42.50 (*0-945636-98-9*) Susquehanna U Pr.
Plowshare in Heaven. 2nd ed. Jesse H. Stuart. Ed. by Jerry A. Herndon et al. LC 90-62718. (Illus.). 268p. (YA). (gr. 7 up). 1991. reprint ed. 22.00 (*0-945084-21-8*) J Stuart Found.
Plowshares: Poems for Nuclear Disarmament & a Play. Jocelyn Hollis. LC 87-31912. 80p. 1988. 19.95 (*0-930933-07-9*); pap. 9.95 (*0-930933-08-7*); lib. bdg. 19.95 (*0-930933-06-0*) Am Poetry & Lit.
Plowshares into Swords. Grant T. Hammond. (WVSS in International Relations Ser.). (C). 1996. text 35.00 (*0-8133-7561-4*) Westview.
Plowshares to Printouts. Hiram R. Drache. (Illus.). 263p. 1985. 20.95 (*0-8134-2459-3*, 2459) Interstate.
Plowzone Archeology: Contributions to Theory & Technique. Ed. by Michael J. O'Brien & Dennis E. Lewarch. (Vanderbilt University Publications in Anthropology: No. 27). 214p. 1981. pap. 12.15 (*0-935462-18-X*) VUPA.
Ploy of Cooking. Charles C. Wehrenberg. 224p. 1995. pap. 11.00 (*1-886163-03-0*) SoloZone.
PLS Educator Learning Styles Inventory: Directions & Application. Bill Haggart. (Illus.). 84p. 1997. pap. 19.95 (*0-9621766-7-2*) Perf Lrn Systs.
PLS Educator Learning Styles Inventory: Directions & Applications see Kaleidoscope Profile: Guide for Educators
PLS Student Learning Styles Inventory: Directions & Applications. Bill Haggart. (Illus.). 50p. 1995. pap. 15.00 (*0-9621766-1-3*) Perf Lrn Systs.
PLS Student Learning Styles Inventory: Directions & Applications see Kaleidoscope Profile: Guide for Students
PLTMG: A Software Package for Solving Elliptic Partial Differential Equations Users' Guide 8.0. 3rd rev. ed. Randy Bank. LC 98-11767. (Software, Environments & Tools Ser.: Vol. 5). (Illus.). xi, 110p. 1998. pap. 32.50 (*0-89871-409-5*, SE05) Soc Indus-Appl Math.
Pluck & Luck. Robert Benchley. 296p. reprint ed. lib. bdg. 23.95 (*0-88411-308-6*) Amereon Ltd.
Plucked Chickens. James Magorian. LC 80-68263. (Illus.). 32p. (J). (gr. 4-6). 1981. 5.00 (*0-930674-04-9*) Black Oak.
Pluckin' Corn on the Sabbath. Steven C. Collins. (Illus.). 72p. 1997. pap. 9.00 (*1-877603-47-3*) Pecan Grove.
***Plucking from the Tree of the Smarandache Functions & Sequences.** Charles Ashbacher. LC 99-200248. (Smarandache Notions Ser.). 85 p. (C). 1999. pap. text. write for info. (*1-879585-61-8*) Erhus Univ Pr.
Plucking the Apple. Elizabeth Palmer. (Mira Bks.). 378p. 1999. mass mkt. 5.99 (*1-55166-493-3*, 1-66493-7, Mira Bks) Harlequin Bks.
Plucking the Apple. large type ed. Elizabeth Palmer. LC 99-14582. 396p. 1999. 26.95 (*0-7838-8624-1*) Mac Lib Ref.
Plug & Play Book. Bigelow. 1999. 29.99 (*0-07-134775-5*) McGraw.
***Plug & Play Book.** Steven J. Bigelow. LC 99-14542. (Illus.). 243p. 1999. pap. 29.99 incl. cd-rom (*0-07-134774-7*) McGraw.
Plug & Play Linux. 96p. 1994. pap. 34.95 (*1-883601-09-6*) Yggdrasil Comput.
Plug & Play Programming an Object-Oriented Construction Kit. William G. Wong. 1995. 39.95 incl. disk (*1-55851-302-7*, M&T Bks) IDG Bks.
Plug & Play Software for Agile Manufacturing, Vol. 2913. Ed. by Barbara L. Goldstein. LC 96-69765. 354p. 1997. 56.00 (*0-8194-2315-7*) SPIE.
Plug & Play System Architecture. Tom Shanley. LC 95-30802. (PC System Architecture Ser.). 352p. (C). 1995. pap. text 34.95 (*0-201-41013-3*) Addison-Wesley.
Plug & Transplant Production: A Grower's Guide. Roger C. Styer & David S. Koranski. LC 96-37957. (Illus.). 400p. 1997. 84.95 (*1-883052-14-9*, B031) Ball Pub.
Plug Fishing for Steelhead. Mike Laverty. 64p. 1994. pap. 8.95 (*1-878175-92-0*) F Amato Pubns.
Plug Fuses: 198 F. 5th ed. 1995. write for info. (*1-55989-814-3*, UL 198F) Underwrtrs Labs.
Plug-In Drug: Television, Children & the Family. Marie Winn. (Nonfiction Ser.). 288p. 1985. pap. 12.95 (*0-14-007698-0*, Penguin Bks) Viking Penguin.
Plug-In, Locking Type Photocontrols for Use with Area Lighting, UL 773. 4th ed. (C). 1995. pap. text 95.00 (*1-55989-748-1*) Underwrtrs Labs.
Plug-in Power: Energize Your Graphics Software with Add-in Utilities. Stephen Beale. LC 96-194091. (Illus.). 240p. 1995. pap. 27.95 (*0-941845-15-X*) Micro Pub Pr.
Plug-In Smart: How to Choose & Use Photoshop Plug-Ins. Joe Farace. (Smart Design Ser.). (Illus.). 160p. 1998. pap. 35.00 incl. cd-rom (*1-56496-431-0*) Rockport Pubs.
Plug in the Sun. Lori J. Bennett. (J). (gr. 1-8). 1992. pap. 12.95 (*1-878347-20-9*) NL Assocs.
Plug-In to Life: Strategies & Resources for Catholic Youth Ministry from Life Teen. Dale Fushek et al. LC 98-147696. 112p. 1998. spiral bd. 14.95 (*0-87793-644-7*) Ave Maria.
Plug into Electronics Reuse. Brenda Platt & Jennifer Hyde. LC 97-97. 1997. pap. 15.00 (*0-917582-92-6*) Inst Local Self Re.
Plug into the Power: Helping Younger Youth Make Faithful Choices. Tom Everson. (Journey of Faith Ser.). 48p. 1998. pap. 8.95 (*0-687-05675-6*) Abingdon.
Plug-n-Play JavaScript. Kevin Ready & Paul Vachier. 450p. 1996. 34.99 (*1-56205-674-3*) New Riders Pub.
Plugged Arteries & a Clogged Immune System. Milton G. Crane. LC 98-88032. (Illus.). 110p. 1998. per. 18.95 (*1-57258-145-X*) Teach Servs.
Plugged In. Ted Gurley. 1996. 29.95 incl. cd-rom (*0-614-14497-3*) P-H.
Plugged In: Electric Riddles. Scott K. Peterson. (Illus.). 32p. (J). (gr. 1-4). 1995. pap. 1.98 (*0-8225-9700-4*) Lerner Pub.
Plugged in & Turned On: Planning, Coordinating, & Managing Computer-Supported Instruction. Charles H. McCain. 216p. 1996. pap. 24.95 (*0-8039-6432-3*); text 55.95 (*0-8039-6431-5*) Corwin Pr.
Plugged-In Parent: What You Should Know about Kids, Computers, & Technology. Steve Bennett. LC 98-9514. 1998. pap. 15.00 (*0-8129-6378-4*) Random.
Plugged Nickel. Ed. by Robert Campbell & Jane Chelius. 1988. mass mkt. 4.99 (*0-671-64363-0*) PB.
Plugger: Wade Fishing the Gulf Coast. Rudy Grigar. Ed. by W. R. McAfee. LC 97-4128. (Illus.). 192p. 1996. 24.95 (*0-89672-377-1*) Tex Tech Univ Pr.
Plugging into Canada: Prospects for U. S. - Canadian Electricity Trade. Dina W. Kruger. 74p. (Orig.). 1988. pap. 15.00 (*0-931035-26-0*) IRRC Inc DC.
Plugging into Utilities: A Safe & Sound Way to Superior Returns in the Stock Market. Donald L. Cassidy. 250p. 1993. text 24.95 (*1-55738-498-3*, Irwn Prfssnl) McGraw-Hill Prof.
Plugs & Plug Circles: A Basic Form of Patterned Ground, Cornwallis Island, Arctic Canada - Origin & Implications. Ed. by A. L. Washburn. LC 97-12288. (Memoir Ser.: No. 190). 1997. 45.00 (*0-8137-1190-8*) Geol Soc.
Plugs, Receptacles, & Cable Connectors, of the Pin & Sleeve Type, UL 1682. (C). 1993. pap. text 135.00 (*1-55989-546-2*) Underwrtrs Labs.
Plugs, Receptacles, & Connectors of the Pin & Sleeve Type for Hazardous Locations. 1988. 34.00 (*0-318-18028-6*, PB 2.2-1984) Natl Elec Mfrs.
Pluie et le Beau Temps. Jacques Prevert. (FRE.). 1972. pap. 10.95 (*0-7859-2264-4*, 2070360903) Fr & Eur.
Pluie et le Beau Temps. Jacques Prevert. (Folio Ser.: No. 90). (FRE.). 256p. 1955. 8.95 (*2-07-036090-3*) Schoenhof.
Pluie et Vent sur Telumee. Andre Schwarz-Bart. (FRE.). 1980. pap. 14.95 (*0-7859-2681-X*, 2020055473) Fr & Eur.
Plum. Alan M. Hofmeister et al. (Reading for All Learners Ser.). (Illus.). (J). pap. write for info. (*1-56861-220-6*) Swift Lrn Res.
***Plum & Jaggers.** Susan Richards Shreve. LC 99-47619. 208p. 2000. 20.00 (*0-374-23462-0*) FS&G.
Plum Beach Light: The Birth, Life, & Death of a Lighthouse. Lawrence H. Bradner. (Illus.). 196p. (Orig.). 1989. pap. 19.95 (*0-9624248-0-3*) L H Bradner.
Plum Blossom: A Poetic Novelette. 137p. 1987. 9.95 (*0-930061-17-9*) Interspace Bks.
Plum Book: U. S. Government Policy & Supporting Positions for 9,000 Federal Civil Service Positions. 265p. (Orig.). 1996. pap. text 35.00 (*0-7881-3570-8*) DIANE Pub.
Plum Book: U. S. Government Policy & Supporting Positions: Salaries for 9,000 Federal Civil Service Positions. (Illus.). 211p. (Orig.). (C). 1993. pap. text 35.00 (*0-7881-0233-8*) DIANE Pub.
Plum Book, 1996-2000: U. S. Government Policy & Supporting Positions: Salaries for 9000+ Federal Civil Service Positions, 2 vols. 274p. (Orig.). 1996. pap. 42.00 (*0-9656560-3-9*) DIANE Pub.
Plum Bun: A Novel Without a Moral. Jessie R. Fauset. LC 90-52590. (Black Women Writers Ser.). 408p. 1999. pap. 14.00 (*0-8070-0919-9*) Beacon Pr.
Plum Crazy, a Book about Beach Plums. Elizabeth P. Mirel. (Illus.). 160p. 1986. reprint ed. pap. 6.95 (*0-940160-34-X*) Parnassus Imprints.
Plum Crazzzy! Vol. 1: I Will Survive Giving God the Glory. Monique J. Anderson. 300p. (Orig.). 1996. pap. 12.95 (*0-9653696-0-9*) Spirit Filled Creat.
Plum Creek Bride. Lynna Banning. 1999. per. 4.99 (*0-373-29074-8*, 1-29074-1) Harlequin Bks.
Plum Creek Timber Company, L. P. A Report on the Company's Environmental Policies & Practices. (Illus.). 43p. (C). 1994. reprint ed. pap. text 40.00 (*0-7881-0965-0*, Coun on Econ) DIANE Pub.
Plum Dead. G. L. Sundance. Ed. by Gloria D. Ladd & James E. Gilliland. 159p. 1997. 16.95 (*1-890668-03-6*) Electronic Books.
Plum Full of Prunes see Ciruela Lleno de Ciruelas Pasas
Plum Full of Prunes. large type ed. Phillip E. Hauck. Ed. by Casper Wilhem & Robert A. Folchi. (Illus.). 32p. (J). (gr. 3-4). 1999. 12.95 (*0-9662228-5-7*, Pub. by Dab Pub Co) Amer West Books.
Plum in the Golden Vase: Chin P'ing Mei The Gathering, Vol. 1. Tr. by David T. Roy. LC 92-45054. (Library of Asian Translations). (Illus.). 544p. 1993. text 65.00 (*0-691-06932-8*, Pub. by Princeton U Pr) Cal Prin Full Svc.
Plum Island. Nelson DeMille. 1998. mass mkt. 287.64 (*0-446-16544-1*) Warner Bks.
Plum Island. large type ed. Nelson DeMille. LC 97-11760. 1997. 28.95 (*0-7862-0979-8*) Thorndike Pr.
Plum Island. large type ed. Nelson DeMille. LC 97-11760. 821p. 1999. pap. 26.95 (*0-7862-0980-1*) Thorndike Pr.
Plum Island. Nelson DeMille. 592p. 1998. reprint ed. mass mkt. 7.99 (*0-446-60540-9*, Pub. by Warner Bks) Little.
Plum Island: The Way It Was. Nancy V. Weare. (Illus.). 112p. (Orig.). 1993. pap. write for info. (*1-882266-02-1*) Newburyport.
Plum Island: The Way It Was. 2nd ed. Nancy V. Weare. (Illus.). 120p. (Orig.). 1996. pap. 17.95 (*1-882266-05-6*) Newburyport.
Plum Island Recollections. Vincent L. Wood. (Illus.). 96p. (Orig.). 1995. pap. 16.95 (*1-882266-04-8*) Newburyport.
Plum Lake: Visits to the North Woods. David Nyweide. Ed. by J. Allen Kirsch. 96p. (YA). 1999. pap. 9.95 (*1-878569-59-7*) Badger Bks Inc.
***Plum Local IV: A Primer on Economics.** Bob Komives. Orig. Title: For Love of Wealth & Biosphere. 201p. 1998. spiral bd. 14.00 (*0-9629281-1-9*) RPK Pr.
Plum Plum Pickers. 2nd ed. Raymond Barrio. LC 84-70568. 232p. 1984. pap. 16.00 (*0-916950-51-4*) Biling Rev-Pr.
Plum Poems. Svein Myreng. LC 99-24382. (Illus.). 80p. (Orig.). 1998. pap. 10.00 (*1-888375-06-X*) Parallax Pr.
Plum Pudding. Christopher Morley. 256p. 22.95 (*0-8488-2491-1*) Amereon Ltd.
***Plum Purdy.** Renee Mullins. (Illus.). 52p. 2000. pap. 10.95 (*1-57377-102-3*, 0-19884-02342) Easl Pubns.
Plum Thicket. Janice H. Giles. LC 95-7889. 284p. 1996. 30.00 (*0-8131-1947-2*); pap. 17.00 (*0-8131-0859-4*) U Pr of Ky.
Plum Tree. David C. Phillips. (Collected Works of David G. Phillips). 1988. reprint ed. lib. bdg. 59.00 (*0-7812-1328-2*) Rprt Serv.
Plum Tree. David G. Phillips. LC 68-57547. (Muckrakers Ser.). (Illus.). 389p. reprint ed. lib. bdg. 20.50 (*0-8398-1566-2*) Irvington.
Plum Tree. David G. Phillips. (Muckrakers Ser.). (Illus.). 389p. (C). 1986. reprint ed. pap. text 9.95 (*0-8290-1884-0*) Irvington.
Plum Tree. David G. Phillips. (American Author Ser.). 1981. reprint ed. lib. bdg. 49.00 (*0-686-71938-7*) Scholarly.
Plum Tree Lane. Lodwick Hartley. LC 78-53759. (Illus.). 204p. 1978. 1.00 (*0-87844-042-9*) Sandlapper Pub Co.
Plum Tree War. Bonnie Pryor. LC 88-32426. (Illus.). 128p. (J). (gr. 4-7). 1989. 14.00 (*0-688-08142-8*, Wm Morrow) Morrow Avon.
Plum Village Chanting & Recitation Book. rev. ed. Thich Nhat Hanh. LC 98-19539. 350p. 2000. 17.50 (*0-938077-91-0*, Pub. by Parallax Pr) SCB Distributors.
Pluma e il Cucciolo di Husky. Hans De Beer.Tr. of Little Polar Bear & the Husky Pup. (ITA., Illus.). (J). (ps-3). pap. 15.95 (*88-8203-183-7*, Pub. by North-South Bks NYC) Chronicle Bks.
Pluma Magica. Ilan Stavans. (College Spanish Ser.). (FRE.). (C). 1994. mass mkt. 23.95 (*0-8384-5876-9*) Heinle & Heinle.
***Pluma y la Represion: Escritoras Argentinas Contemporaneas.** Maria del Mar Lopez Cabrales. (Wor(l)ds of Change: Vol. 44). (SPA.). 200p. (C). 2000. text 46.95 (*0-8204-4286-0*) P Lang Pubng.
***Plumage.** Nancy Springer. 240p. 2000. 23.00 (*0-380-80120-5*, Wm Morrow) Morrow Avon.
Plumage of the Sun. Margaret K. Biggs. LC 85-62534. (Illus.). 92p. 1986. 12.00 (*0-942544-10-2*) Negative Capability Pr.
Plumas Estelares de Puerto Rico Bk. 2: Siglo XX. Cesareo R. Nieves. 518p. (C). 1971. 5.00 (*0-8477-3148-0*) U of PR Pr.
Plumas National Forest Fly Fishing Guide. Andrew Harris. (Illus.). 124p. 1999. pap. 15.95 (*1-57188-175-1*) F Amato Pubns.
Plumas para Almorzar. Lois Ehlert. Tr. by Alma F. Ada & F. Isabel Campoy. LC 89-29459. (SPA.). 40p. (J). (ps-3). 1996. pap. 6.00 (*0-15-201021-1*, Voyager Bks) Harcourt.
Plumas para Almorzar. Lois Ehlert. LC 95-22798. 1996. 11.45 (*0-606-09755-4*) Turtleback.
Plumbate: A Mesoamerican Trade Ware. Anna O. Shepard. LC 77-11522. (Carnegie Institution of Washington. Publications: No. 573). reprint ed. 42.50 (*0-404-16289-4*) AMS Pr.
Plumbate, a Mesoamerican Trade Ware. Anna O. Shepard. LC 48-10528. (Carnegie Institution of Washington Publication Ser.: No. 573). 190p. reprint ed. pap. 58.90 (*0-7837-2024-6*, 204229900002) Bks Demand.
Plumber. Frank Endersby. 12p. (J). (gr. 4 up). 1981. 2.99 (*0-85953-272-0*) Childs Play.
Plumber. Frank Endersby. (GRE.). (J). 1981. 3.99 (*0-85953-867-2*); 3.99 (*0-85953-630-0*) Childs Play.
Plumber. Jack Rudman. (Career Examination Ser.: C-591). 1994. pap. 27.95 (*0-8373-0591-8*) Nat Learn.
Plumber & a Man. Joe Corrie. LC 96-8659. 55p. (Orig.). 1996. pap. 6.00 (*0-88734-380-5*) Players Pr.
Plumbers. Tracey Boraas. LC 98-16855. (Community Helpers Ser.). (J). 1998. 14.00 (*0-7368-0073-5*, Bridgestone Bks) Capstone Pr.
Plumbers. Dee Ready. (Community Helpers Ser.). (J). 1998. 14.00 (*0-516-21347-4*) Childrens.
Plumbers. Robert Stewart. LC 88-6249. 64p. 1988. 8.50 (*0-933532-68-7*) BkMk.
Plumber's & Pipe Fitter's Calculations Manual. R. Dodge Woodson. LC 98-35387. (Illus.). 352p. 1998. 49.95 (*0-07-071857-1*) McGraw-Hill Prof.
Plumber's Exam Preparation Guide. Howard C. Massey. LC 85-19050. 320p. (Orig.). 1985. pap. 29.00 (*0-934041-04-0*) Craftsman.
Plumber's Field Manual. R. Dodge Woodson. (Illus.). 448p. 1996. pap. 47.95 (*0-07-071779-6*) McGraw.
Plumber's Handbook. 3rd rev. ed. Howard C. Massey. LC 98-18088. (Illus.). 352p. 1998. pap. 32.00 (*1-57218-056-0*) Craftsman.
Plumbers' Handbook. 6th ed. Joseph P. Almond, Sr. LC 82-1342. 1982. write for info. (*0-672-23370-3*) Macmillan.
Plumber's Handbook. 8th ed. Joseph P. Almond. 368p. 1991. pap. 15.95 (*0-02-501570-2*) Macmillan.
Plumber's Helper. Jack Rudman. (Career Examination Ser.: C-592). 1994. pap. 23.95 (*0-8373-0592-6*) Nat Learn.
Plumbers Maintenance/Troubleshooting Pocket Manual. 9th ed. Joseph P. Almond. 352p. 1997. 16.95 (*0-02-861501-8*, Aude IN) IDG Bks.
***Plumbers Pricing Manual.** Ed. by Mert Kennedy. (Illus.). 190p. 2000. pap. 35.00 (*0-915955-18-0*) Trade Srv Corp.

P

Plumber's Quick-Reference Manual: Tables, Charts & Calculations. R. Dodge Woodson. (Illus.). 320p. 1995. pap. 47.50 (*0-07-071799-0*) McGraw.

Plumber's Standard Handbook. Woodson. (Illus.). 700p. 1999. 89.95 (*0-07-134244-3*) McGraw.

***Plumber's Standard Handbook.** R. Dodge Woodson. LC 98-47578. 1999. 89.95 (*0-07-134386-5*) McGraw-Hill Sch.

Plumber's Toolbox Manual. Louis J. Mahiau. (On-the-Job Reference Ser.). 352p. 1992. pap. text 10.00 (*0-13-683806-5*) P-H.

Plumber's Troubleshooting Guide. Dodge Woodson. LC 94-4065. 385p. 1994. pap. 44.95 (*0-07-071777-X*) McGraw.

Plumbing. Jeff Beneke. Ed. by David W. Toht. (Easy-Step Ser.). (Illus.). 64p. (Orig.). 1997. pap. 6.95 (*0-89721-335-1*, 05958, Ortho Bks) Meredith Bks.

Plumbing. Contrib. by Jeff Beneke. LC 99-182114. (Easy-Step Ser.). (Illus.). 64p. (Orig.). 1998. pap. 4.95 (*0-8069-7051-0*) Sterling.

Plumbing. Boy Scouts of America. (Illus.). 48p. (YA). (gr. 6-12). 1989. pap. 2.90 (*0-8395-3386-1*, 33386) BSA.

Plumbing. Leslie V. Ripka. LC 94-23444. (Illus.). 384p. 1994. 36.96 (*0-8269-0612-5*) Am Technical.

Plumbing. Jack Rudman. (Occupational Competency Examination (OCE) Ser.: Vol. 29). 47.95 (*0-8373-5779-9*) Nat Learn.

Plumbing. Jack Rudman. (Occupational Competency Examination Ser.: OCE-29). 1994. pap. 27.95 (*0-8373-5729-2*) Nat Learn.

Plumbing. Time-Life Books Editors. LC 94-48025. (Home Repair & Improvement Ser.). (Illus.). 128p. (gr. 11). 1999. 14.95 (*0-7835-3866-9*) Time-Life.

Plumbing. R. D. Treloar. 416p. 1994. pap. 29.95 (*0-632-03761-X*) Blackwell Sci.

Plumbing. rev. ed. Time-Life Books Editors. (Home Repair & Improvement Ser.). (Illus.). 127p. 1989. 14.60 (*0-8094-7370-4*); pap. write for info. (*0-8094-7373-9*) Time-Life.

Plumbing, Level 1. (C). 1996. pap. text 50.00 (*0-13-245994-9*) P-H.

Plumbing, Level 2. National Center for Construction Education & Reseach Staff. (Wheels of Learning Ser.). (C). 1996. teacher ed., ring bd. 80.00 (*0-13-265521-7*) P-H.

Plumbing, Level 2. National Center for Construction Education & Reseach Staff. (Wheels of Learning Ser.). (C). 1996. student ed., ring bd. 80.00 (*0-13-265919-0*) P-H.

Plumbing, Level 3. National Center for Construction Education & Reseach Staff. (Trainee Ser.). 1996. student ed., ring bd. 80.00 (*0-13-265927-1*) P-H.

Plumbing, Level 3. National Center for Construction Education & Reseach Staff. (Wheels of Learning Ser.). (C). 1996. teacher ed., ring bd. 80.00 (*0-13-265539-X*) P-H.

Plumbing, Level 4. National Center for Construction Education & Reseach Staff. (Wheels of Learning Ser.). (C). 1996. teacher ed., ring bd. 80.00 (*0-13-265547-0*); student ed., ring bd. 80.00 (*0-13-265935-2*) P-H.

***Plumbing: A Field Guide to the Plumbing Codes.** Redwood Kardon. (Code Check Ser.). (Illus.). 32p. 2000. pap. text 16.95 (*1-56158-409-6*) Taunton.

Plumbing: Basic & Advanced Projects. rev. ed. Mort Schultz. Ed. by Timothy O. Bakke. LC 97-75259. (Illus.). 176p. 1998. pap. 14.95 (*1-58011-008-8*) Creative Homeowner.

***Plumbing: Heating & Gas Installations.** 2nd ed. Roy Treloar. LC 99-88766. 2000. pap. write for info. (*0-632-05332-1*) Blackwell Sci.

Plumbing: Installation & Design. Thomas Philbin. 227p. (C). 1988. teacher ed. write for info. (*0-15-570676-4*); text 53.00 (*0-15-570675-6*, Pub. by SCP) Harcourt.

Plumbing: Instructor's Guide, Level 1. (C). 1996. teacher ed., per. 50.00 (*0-13-246000-9*) P-H.

Plumbing: Instructor's Guide, Level 1. National Center for Construction Education & Reseach Staff. (Wheels of Learning Ser.). (C). 1996. teacher ed., ring bd. 50.00 (*0-13-265513-6*) P-H.

Plumbing: Instructor's Guide, Level 3. (C). 1996. teacher ed., per. 80.00 (*0-13-246042-4*) P-H.

Plumbing: Instructors Guide, Level 3. (C). 1996. per. 80.00 (*0-13-246034-3*) P-H.

Plumbing: Instructor's Guide, Level 4. (C). 1996. teacher ed., per. 80.00 (*0-13-246067-X*) P-H.

Plumbing: Instructors Guide to Plumbing, Trainee Guide Wheels Learning Service, Level 2. (C). 1996. teacher ed., per. 80.00 (*0-13-246026-2*) P-H.

Plumbing: Sounding Modern Architecture. Ed. by Daniel S. Friedman & Nadir Lahiji. LC 97-10075. (Illus.). 288p. (Orig.). 1997. pap. 19.95 (*1-56898-107-4*) Princeton Arch.

Plumbing: Trainee Guide, Level 1. National Center for Construction Education & Reseach Staff. (Wheels of Learning Ser.). (C). 1996. pap. text, student ed. 50.00 (*0-13-266453-4*) P-H.

Plumbing: Trainee Guide, Level 2. (C). 1996. per. 80.00 (*0-13-246018-1*) P-H.

Plumbing: Trainee Guide, Level 4. National Center for Construction Education & Reseach Staff. (Wheels of Learning Ser.). (C). 1996. per. 80.00 (*0-13-246059-9*) P-H.

Plumbing a House. Peter Hemp. LC 94-33843. (Illus.). 205p. 1994. pap. 29.95 (*0-942391-40-3*, 070102) Taunton.

Plumbing & Domestic Heating, 1955. 7th ed. Ed. by Tweeds, Chartered Quantity Staff. (Spon's Contractors' Handbooks). 384p. (Orig.). (C). 1994. pap. 49.99 (*0-419-18580-1*, E & FN Spon) Routledge.

Plumbing & HVAC Manhour Estimates: A Guide to Competitive Bidding. Ray E. Prescher. LC 97-6514. (Illus.). 224p. (Orig.). 1997. pap. 28.25 (*1-57218-041-2*) Craftsman.

Plumbing & Mechanical Services, Pt. 1. A. H. Masterman & R. M. Boyce. (Illus.). 246p. (C). 1984. pap. 40.00 (*0-7487-0368-3*, Pub. by S Thornes Pubs) Trans-Atl Phila.

Plumbing & Mechanical Services, Pt. 2. 2nd ed. A. H. Masterman & R. M. Boyce. (Illus.). 224p. (C). 1990. pap. 36.50 (*0-7487-0232-6*, Pub. by S Thornes Pubs) Trans-Atl Phila.

Plumbing & Mechanical Services, Pt. 3. 3rd ed. A. H. Masterman & R. M. Boyce. 232p. (C). 1990. pap. 36.50 (*0-7487-0233-4*, Pub. by S Thornes Pubs) Trans-Atl Phila.

Plumbing & Pipefitting. 1991. lib. bdg. 76.00 (*0-8490-4120-1*) Gordon Pr.

Plumbing & Pipefitting. Patrick J. Galvin. (Opportunities In . . . Ser.). (Illus.). 160p. pap. 11.95 (*0-8442-4414-7*, 44147, VGM Career) NTC Contemp Pub Co.

Plumbing & Pipefitting. Patrick J. Galvin. (Opportunities in...Ser.). (Illus.). 160p. 1994. 14.95 (*0-8442-4413-9*, 44139, VGM Career) NTC Contemp Pub Co.

Plumbing Apprentice Handbook. R. Dodge Woodson. LC 93-15862. 366p. 1994. pap. 54.95 (*0-07-071772-9*) McGraw.

***Plumbing Basics.** Rick Peters. LC 99-86644. (Illus.). 128p. 2000. pap. 14.95 (*0-8069-3669-X*) Sterling.

Plumbing Contractor: Start & Run a Money Making Business. R. Dodge Woodson. 1993. pap. 17.95 (*0-8306-4323-0*) McGraw-Hill Prof.

***Plumbing Cost Data: 2000 Edition.** 23rd ed. R. S. Means Company Staff. (Illus.). 540p. 1999. pap. text 89.95 (*0-87629-546-4*) R S Means.

Plumbing Design & Installation Details. Jerome F. Mueller. 1987. text 55.00 (*0-07-043963-X*) McGraw.

Plumbing Encyclopedia. 2nd rev. ed. R. D. Treloar. LC 95-47346. 576p. 1996. pap. text 34.95 (*0-632-04056-4*) Blackwell Sci.

Plumbing Engineer. Jack Rudman. (Career Examination Ser.: C-2713). 1994. pap. 34.95 (*0-8373-2713-X*) Nat Learn.

Plumbing Equipment & Supplies in Japan: A Strategic Entry Report, 1997. Compiled by Icon Group International Staff. (Illus.). 166p. 1999. ring bd. 1660.00 incl. audio compact disk (*0-7418-0777-7*) Icon Grp.

Plumbing Essentials. Cowles Creative Publishing Staff. (Black & Decker Quick Steps Ser.). (Illus.). 80p. (Orig.). 1996. pap. 9.95 (*0-86573-651-0*) Creat Pub Intl.

***Plumbing Estimating Methods.** 2nd rev. ed. Joseph J. Galeno & Sheldon Greene. (Illus.). 1999. pap. 59.95 (*0-87629-536-7*, 67283A) R S Means.

Plumbing for Dummies. Gene Hamilton & Katie Hamilton. LC 99-63191. (Illus.). 264p. 1999. pap. 16.99 (*0-7645-5174-4*, Dummies Trade Pr) IDG Bks.

Plumbing for Dummies: A Guide to the Maintenance & Repair of Everything Including the Kitchen Sink. Don Fredriksson. LC 82-17790. (Illus.). 256p. 1983. pap. 10.95 (*0-672-52738-3*) Macmillan.

Plumbing for the Kitchen & Bathroom: Installation Techniques. National Kitchen & Bath Association Staff. (Illus.). 166p. 1998. pap. text 50.00 (*1-887127-36-4*, 5205) Natl Kit Bath.

Plumbing Fundamentals. James L. Thiesse. (Contemporary Construction Ser.). (Illus.). 192p. (gr. 10-12). 1981. text 29.96 (*0-07-064191-9*) McGraw.

Plumbing Inspector. Jack Rudman. (Career Examination Ser.: C-593). 1994. pap. 29.95 (*0-8373-0593-4*) Nat Learn.

Plumbing Level 1: Trainee Guide, Level 1. (C). 1996. student ed., ring bd. 80.00 (*0-13-264896-2*, Prentice Hall) P-H.

***Plumbing Products in United Arab Emirates: A Strategic Entry Report, 1999.** Compiled by Icon Group International. (Illus.). 95p. 1999. ring bd. 950.00 incl. audio compact disk (*0-7418-1774-8*) Icon Grp.

Plumbing Supervisor. Jack Rudman. (Career Examination Ser.: C-2583). 1994. pap. 34.95 (*0-8373-2583-8*) Nat Learn.

Plumbing Systems. Tim Wentz. LC 96-20096. 216p. (C). 1996. 64.00 (*0-13-235284-2*) P-H.

Plumbing Tech: Design & Installation. 3rd ed. Lee Smith. LC 99-57896. (Construction/Building Trades). (C). 2000. pap. 57.95 (*0-7668-1084-4*) Delmar.

Plumbing Technology. Justin Duncan. Ed. by Joanna Turpin. LC 93-11615. (Illus.). 384p. 1994. text 29.95 (*0-912524-76-6*) Busn News.

Plumbing Technology. 2nd ed. Hall. 1987. pap. text. write for info. (*0-582-41397-4*, Pub. by Addison-Wesley) Longman.

Plumbing Technology: Design & Installation. 2nd ed. Lee Smith. 83p. 1994. teacher ed. 16.95 (*0-8273-5524-6*); text 38.00 (*0-8273-5523-8*) Delmar.

Plumbing Technology: Design & Installation. 2nd ed. Lee Smith & Harry Slater. (Construction & Building Trades Ser.). 1988. pap., teacher ed. 13.50 (*0-8273-2445-6*) Delmar.

Plumbing Workbook. Jack Rudman. (Workbook (W) Ser.: Vol. 3160). 43.95 (*0-8373-7930-X*) Nat Learn.

Plumbing Workbook. Jack Rudman. (Workbook Ser.: W-3160). 1994. pap. 23.95 (*0-8373-7905-9*) Nat Learn.

Plume: Lointain Interieur. Henri Michaux. (FRE.). 1985. pap. 14.95 (*0-7859-3379-4*) Fr & Eur.

Plume & Le Zinc: Writers in the Cafes of Paris. Jeanne Hilary. (Illus.). 120p. 1998. pap. text 22.95 (*2-85025-650-1*) Hazan.

Plume au Pays des Tigres. Hans De Beer.Tr. of Little Polar Bear, Take Me Home!. (FRE., Illus.). (J). 15.95 (*3-314-21007-8*, Pub. by North-South Bks NYC) Chronicle Bks.

Plume dans L'Alambic. Ed. by J. Buzelin. 88p. 1993. text 23.00 (*2-906077-40-2*) Elsevier.

Plume en Bateau. Hans De Beer. (FRE., Illus.). 32p. (J). (gr. k-3). 1992. 13.95 (*3-314-20647-X*, Pub. by North-South Bks NYC) Chronicle Bks.

Plume et la Station Polaire. Tr. of Little Polar Bear & the Brave Little Hare. (FRE., Illus.). 32p. (J). (gr. k-3). 1996. 12.95 (*3-314-20760-3*, Pub. by North-South Bks NYC) Chronicle Bks.

Plume et la Station Polaire. Hans De Beer.Tr. of Little Polar Bear & the Brave Little Hare. (FRE., Illus.). (J). (gr. 1-3). pap. 15.95 (*3-314-21162-7*, Pub. by North-South Bks NYC) Chronicle Bks.

Plume et le Chien de Traineau. Hans De Beer.Tr. of Little Polar Bear & the Husky Pup. (FRE., Illus.). (J). (ps-3). pap. 15.95 (*3-314-21211-9*, Pub. by North-South Bks NYC) Chronicle Bks.

Plume Rise. G. A. Briggs. LC 77-603261. (AEC Critical Review Ser.). 81p. 1969. pap. 10.00 (*0-87079-304-7*, TID-25075); fiche 9.00 (*0-87079-305-5*, TID-25075) DOE.

Plume S'Echappe. Tr. of Little Polar Bear Finds a Friend. (FRE., Illus.). 32p. (J). (gr. k-3). 1996. 13.95 (*3-314-20719-0*, Pub. by North-South Bks NYC) Chronicle Bks.

Plumed Serpent. D. H. Lawrence. 480p. 1992. pap. 16.00 (*0-679-73493-7*) McKay.

Plumer's Principles & Practice of Intravenous Therapy. 4th ed. Ada L. Plumer & Cosentino. (Illus.). 567p. (C). 1987. text 31.50 (*0-673-39403-4*) Lppncott W & W.

Plumer's Principles & Practice of Intravenous Therapy. 6th ed. Sharon Weinstein. LC 96-20620. 592p. 1996. pap. text 34.95 (*0-397-55311-0*) Lppncott W & W.

Plumer's Principles & Practice of Intravenous Therapy. 7th ed. Sharon M. Weinstein. 688p. pap. text 34.95 (*0-7817-1988-7*) Lppncott W & W.

Plumes: Poems from Hollywood. Mark Dunster. 11p. 1999. pap. 5.00 (*0-89642-654-8*) Linden Pubs.

Plumes & Visibility. Ed. by Warren White. (Illus.). 230p. 1981. pap. 73.00 (*0-08-028733-6*, Pergamon Pr) Elsevier.

Plumes & Visibility. Ed. by Warren White. (Illus.). 230p. 1982. pap., suppl. ed. 36.00 (*0-08-028741-7*, Pergamon Pr) Elsevier.

Plumes 'n' Blooms. Terra Parma. (Illus.). 52p. 1997. pap. 12.95 (*0-936459-37-9*) Stained Glass.

Plumes of Paradise: Trade Cycles in Outer Southeast Asia & Their Impact on New Guinea & Nearby Islands until 1920. Pamela Swadling. LC 96-147932. (Illus.). 352p. 1997. text 60.00 (*9980-85-103-1*, Pub. by Papua New Guinea) UH Pr.

Plumming in America: The Game: Poor Little Unfortunate Me. Milton A. Rubin. (Illus.). 90p. 1989. pap. write for info. (*0-9624702-0-1*) Behav Psychol Servs.

***Plump: Survival of the Fattest.** Linda F. Carlson. Ed. by Laurie Boucke. LC 99-43574. (Illus.). 1999. pap. 12.50 (*1-888580-12-7*) White-Boucke.

***Plump Pups & Fat Cats.** Steve Duno. LC 99-34014. (Illus.). 208p. (ps-3). 1999. pap. 14.95 (*0-312-24436-3*) St Martin.

Plump Woman: A Treasury of Stories. Anil Chandra. 1998. 20.00 (*81-241-0368-2*) Har-Anand Pubns.

***Plumply, Dumply Pumpkin.** Mary Serfozo. LC 00-32421. (Illus.). 2001. write for info. (*0-689-83834-4*) McElderry Bks.

Plumpton Correspondence. Ed. by Thomas Stapleton. 160p. (C). 1991. text 86.50 (*0-86299-656-2*, Pub. by Sutton Pub Ltd) Intl Pubs Mktg.

Plumpton Correspondence. Edward Plumpton. Ed. by Thomas Stapleton. (Camden Society, London. Publications, First Ser.: No. 4). reprint ed. 95.00 (*0-404-50104-4*) AMS Pr.

Plumpton Letters & Papers. Ed. by Joan Kirby. (Camden Fifth Ser.: No. 8). 370p. 1997. text 59.95 (*0-521-57394-7*) Cambridge U Pr.

Plums & Ashes. David N. Moolten. LC 94-29229. (Samuel French Morse Poetry Prize Ser.). 64p. 1994. pap. text 11.95 (*1-55553-208-X*) NE U Pr.

Plums from a Tree. Andrea F. Litkei. (Illus.). 102p. 1978. 9.95 (*1-880165-03-1*) Hanlit Pubns.

Plums in a Wicker Basket. Ann Gasser. 33p. (Orig.). 1996. pap. 4.00 (*1-884257-14-3*) AGEE Keyboard.

Plums of New York. U. P. Hedrick. 615p. 1993. reprint ed. lib. bdg. 109.00 (*0-7812-5237-7*) Rprt Serv.

Plum's Peaches. P. G. Wodehouse. 336p. 1995. pap. 12.95 (*1-55882-129-5*) Intl Polygonics.

Plums, Stones, Kisses & Hooks: Poems. Ronald Wallace. LC 80-15907. 80p. (Orig.). 1982. pap. 12.95 (*0-8262-0400-7*) U of Mo Pr.

Plunder: A Play. Fredy Perlman. 1962. pap. 1.50 (*0-934868-18-2*) Black & Red.

Plunder: Poems from Hollywood. Mark Dunster. 20p. 1998. 5.00 (*0-89642-424-3*) Linden Pubs.

Plunder & Preservation: Cultural Property Law & Practice in the People's Republic of China. J. David Murphy. (Illus.). 222p. 1995. text 65.00 (*0-19-586874-9*) OUP.

Plunder Canyon. large type ed. Todhunter Ballard. (Sagebrush Large Print Westerns Ser.). 1996. lib. bdg. 17.95 (*1-57490-048-X*, Sagebrush LP West) T T Beeler.

Plunder of Art. H. Bhisham Pal. (C). 1992. 72.00 (*81-7017-285-3*, Pub. by Abhinav) S Asia.

***Plunder of Jewish Property During the Holocaust.** Avi Beker. LC 00-55041. 2000. write for info. (*0-8147-9867-5*) NYU Pr.

Plunder, Profit & Paroles: A Social History of the War of 1812 in Upper Canada. George Sheppard. (Illus.). 344p. 1994. 55.00 (*0-7735-1137-7*, Pub. by McG-Queens Univ Pr) CUP Services.

Plunder Valley. Lee Morgan. (McMasters Ser.: No. 3). 192p. (Orig.). 1995. mass mkt. 4.50 (*0-515-11731-5*, Jove) Berkley Pub.

Plundered Kitchens, Empty Wombs: Threatened Reproduction & Identity in the Cameroon Grassfields. Pamela Feldman-Savelsberg. LC 98-51223. (Illus.). 280p. 1999. text 49.50 (*0-472-10989-8*, 10989) U of Mich Pr.

Plundered Loyalties: World War II & the Greek Civil War. Giannes Koliopoulos. LC 98-8396. 288p. 1999. text 45.00 (*0-8147-4730-2*) NYU Pr.

Plundered Seas. Michael Berrill. LC 97-6192. 1997. 22.50 (*0-87156-945-0*, Pub. by Sierra) Random.

Plunderers Llewellyn P. Holmes. LC 77-14142. 349p. (J). 1978. write for info. (*0-89340-119-6*) Chivers N Amer.

Plunderers. Edwin Lefevre. LC 83-80981. (Illus.). 334p. 1983. reprint ed. pap. 19.00 (*0-87034-067-0*) Fraser Pub Co.

Plunderers: A Novel. Edwin Lefevre. LC 75-152945. (Short Story Index Reprint Ser.). 1977. reprint ed. 23.95 (*0-8369-3804-6*) Ayer.

Plundering Africa's Past. Ed. by Peter R. Schmidt & Roderick J. McIntosh. (Illus.). 320p. 1996. 39.95 (*0-253-33040-8*) Ind U Pr.

Plundering of Agriculture in Developing Countries. Maurice Schiff & Alberto Valdes. LC 92-26620. 42p. 1992. pap. 22.00 (*0-8213-2184-6*, 12184) World Bank.

Plundering Paradise: The Struggle for the Environment in the Philippines. Robin Broad. 1994. pap. 16.95 (*0-520-08921-9*, Pub. by U CA Pr) Cal Prin Full Svc.

***Plundering Pirates: A Where's Waldo? Fun Fact Book.** Rachel Wright & Martin Handford. LC 00-23144. (Illus.). 2000. pap. write for info. (*0-7636-1300-2*) Candlewick Press.

Plunderphonics, 'Pataphysics & Pop Mechanics: An Introduction to "Musique Actuelle" Andrew Jones. 1999. pap. 18.95 (*0-946719-15-2*) Interlink Pub.

Plunge. Christopher Kyle. 1998. pap. 5.25 (*0-8222-1670-1*) Dramatists Play.

Plunger: A Tale of the Wheat Pit. Edward J. Dies. Ed. by Dan C. McCurry & Richard E. Rubenstein. LC 74-30627. (American Farmers & the Rise of Agribusiness Ser.). (Illus.). 1975. reprint ed. 25.95 (*0-405-06789-5*) Ayer.

Plunging Through the Clouds: Constructive Living Currents. Ed. by David K. Reynolds. LC 91-45686. 199p. (C). 1993. text 19.50 (*0-7914-1313-6*) State U NY Pr.

***Plunkett's Biotech & Genetics Industry Almanac: The Only Complete Reference to the Biotech Business.** Jack W. Plunkett. 650p. 2001. pap. 199.99 incl. cd-rom (*1-891775-18-9*) Plunkett Res.

Plunkett's Companion to the Almanac of American Employers: Mid-Size Firms. Jack W. Plunkett. LC 98-212699. 640p. 1999. pap. 149.99 incl. disk (*1-891775-02-2*) Plunkett Res.

***Plunkett's Companion to the Almanac of American Employers, 2000-2001: Mid Size Firms.** Jack W. Plunkett. 693p. 2000. pap. 149.99 incl. cd-rom (*1-891775-13-8*) Plunkett Res.

Plunkett's E-Commerce & Internet Business Almanac: The Only Complete Guide to the Business Side of the Internet. Jack W. Plunkett. 500p. 2000. pap. 199.99 incl. cd-rom (*1-891775-11-1*) Plunkett Res.

Plunkett's Employers' Internet Sites with Careers Information: The Only Complete Guide to Careers Websites Operated by Major Employers. Jack W. Plunkett. 701p. 1999. pap. 149.99 incl. disk (*1-891775-01-4*) Plunkett Res.

Plunkett's Energy Industry Almanac: The Only Complete Guide to the Energy & Utilities Industry. Jack W. Plunkett. 610p. 1999. pap. 149.99 incl. disk (*0-9638268-8-3*) Plunkett Res.

Plunkett's Engineering & Research Industry Almanac: The Only Complete Guide to the Hottest Research & Engineering Firms. Jack W. Plunkett. 680p. 2000. pap. 179.99 incl. cd-rom (*1-891775-10-3*) Plunkett Res.

Plunkett's Entertainment & Media Industry Almanac: The Complete Guide to America's Publishing, Broadcasting & Entertainment Business. Jack W. Plunkett. 626p. 1998. pap. 149.99 incl. disk (*0-9638268-6-7*) Plunkett Res.

***Plunkett's Entertainment & Media Industry Almanac, 2000-2001: The Complete Guide to America's Publishing, Broadcasting & Entertainment Business.** Jack W. Plunkett. 642p. 2000. pap. 179.99 incl. cd-rom (*1-891775-14-6*) Plunkett Res.

Plunkett's Financial Services Industry Almanac, 2000-2001. Jack W. Plunkett. 754p. 1999. pap. 179.99 incl. cd-rom (*1-891775-03-0*) Plunkett Res.

Plunkett's Health Care Industry Almanac, 1999-2000: The Only Complete Guide to America's Health Care Industry. Jack W. Plunkett. 740p. 1999. pap. 179.99 incl. cd-rom (*1-891775-04-9*) Plunkett Res.

Plunkett's InfoTech Industry Almanac, 1999-2000: The Only Complete Guide to the Technologies & Companies Changing the Way the World Thinks, Works, & Shares Information. 2nd rev. ed. Jack W. Plunkett. 695p. 1998. pap. 149.99 incl. disk (*1-891775-00-6*) Plunkett Res.

Plunkett's On-Line Trading, Finance & Investment Web Sites Almanac: The Only Complete Guide to Investment, Finance, Accounting, Economics, Banking & Financial Services Web Sites. Jack W. Plunkett. 547p. 2000. pap. 149.99 incl. disk (*1-891775-08-1*) Plunkett Res.

Plunkett's Retail Industry Almanac, 1999-2000: The Only Complete Guide to the Hottest Retail Companies & Hottest Retail Trends. Jack W. Plunkett. 648p. 1999. pap. 179.99 incl. cd-rom (*1-891775-05-7*) Plunkett Res.

Plunkett's Telecommunications Industry Almanac: The Only Complete Guide to the Firms Changing the Way the World Communicates Via Wired & Wireless Systems. Jack W. Plunkett. 680p. 2000. pap. 179.99 incl. cd-rom (*1-891775-06-5*) Plunkett Res.

Plunkitt of Tammany Hall. William L. Riordan. 101p. reprint ed. lib. bdg. 17.95 (*0-88411-977-7*) Amereon Ltd.

Plunkitt of Tammany Hall. William L. Riordan. 1993. reprint ed. lib. bdg. 14.95 (*1-56849-215-4*) Buccaneer Bks.

Plunkitt of Tammany Hall: A Series of Very Plain Talks on Very Practical Politics. William L. Riordan. (C). 1995. mass mkt. 5.95 (*0-451-52620-1*) NAL.

Plunkitt of Tammany Hall: A Series of Very Plain Talks On Very Practical Politics. William L. Riordan. Ed. by Terrence J. McDonald. LC 92-72221. (Books in American History). 160p. (C). 1993. text 35.00 (*0-312-09666-6*) St Martin.

Plunkitt of Tammany Hall: A Series of Very Plain Talks On Very Practical Politics. William L. Riordan. Ed. by Terrence J. McDonald. LC 92-72221. (Books in American History). 148p. (C). 1993. pap. text 11.95 (*0-312-08444-7*) St Martin.

Plupart du Temps, Vol. 1. Pierre Reverdy. (FRE.). 1970. pap. 10.95 (*0-8288-3870-4*, F121000) Fr & Eur.

Plupart du Temps, Vol. 2. Pierre Reverdy. (FRE.). 1989. pap. 10.95 (*0-8288-3871-2*, F121001) Fr & Eur.

Plupart du Temps, 1915-1922. Pierre Reverdy. (Poesie Ser.). pap. 18.95 (*2-07-032532-6*) Schoenhof.

Plural & Conflicting Values. Michael Stocker. 372p. 1990. text 70.00 (*0-19-824447-9*) OUP.

Plural & Conflicting Values. Michael Stocker. 368p. 1992. reprint ed. pap. text 26.00 (*0-19-824055-4*) OUP.

Plural Desires: Writing Bisexual Women's Realities. Bisexual Anthology Collective Staff. LC 95-231609. 320p. Date not set. pap. 19.95 (*0-920813-19-4*) Sister Vis Pr.

Plural Event: Descartes, Hegel, Heidegger. Andrew Benjamin. LC 93-16570. 224p. (C). 1993. pap. 27.99 (*0-415-09529-8*, B2461) Routledge.

Plural Event: Descartes, Hegel, Heidegger. Andrew Benjamin. LC 93-16570. 240p. (C). (gr. 13). 1993. 75.00 (*0-415-09528-X*, B2457) Routledge.

Plural I - & After. William E. Coles, Jr. 298p. (Orig.). (C). 1988. pap. text 23.00 (*0-86709-217-3*, 0217, Pub. by Boynton Cook Pubs) Heinemann.

Plural Marriage for Our Times: A Reinvented Option? Philip L. Kilbride. LC 94-4753. 160p. 1994. 59.95 (*0-89789-314-X*, Bergin & Garvey); pap. 17.95 (*0-89789-315-8*, Bergin & Garvey) Greenwood.

Plural Medical Systems in North-East Africa: The Legacy of "Sheikh" Hippocrates. Leendert J. Slikkerveer. (Monographs from the African Studies Centre, Leiden). 200p. 1989. 69.50 (*0-7103-0203-7*) Routledge.

Plural of Bus Is Buses Isn't It? A Guide to Word Usage. rev. ed. Michael Paul. LC 87-91305. (Illus.). 85p. 1988. pap. 5.00 (*0-9616367-2-6*) Michael Paul.

Plural Psyche: Personality, Morality & the Father. Andrew Samuels. 272p. 1989. 25.00 (*0-415-01759-9*, 9841) Routledge.

Plural Psyche: Personality, Morality & the Father. Andrew Samuels. 272p. (C). 1990. pap. 25.99 (*0-415-01760-2*, A9854) Routledge.

Plural Rationality & Interactive Decision Processes. Ed. by M. Grauer et al. (Lecture Notes in Economics & Mathematical Systems Ser.: Vol. 248). (Illus.). vi, 354p. 1985. 47.50 (*0-387-15675-5*) Spr-Verlag.

Plural Self: Multiplicity in Everyday Life John Rowan. LC 98-61585. 278 p. 1999. write for info. (*0-7619-6076-7*) Sage.

Pluralism. Greg McLennan. Ed. by Frank Parkin. (Concepts in the Social Sciences Ser.). 128p. 1995. 74.00 (*0-335-19155-X*); pap. 18.95 (*0-335-19154-1*) OpUniv Pr.

Pluralism. Gregory McLennan. (Concepts in Social Thought Ser.). 1995. pap. 14.95 (*0-8166-2815-7*); text 37.95 (*0-8166-2814-9*) U of Minn Pr.

Pluralism: A New Paradigm for Theology. Chester Gillis. (Louvain Theological & Pastoral Monographs). 1993. pap. text 25.00 (*0-8028-0572-8*) Eerdmans.

Pluralism: Against the Demand for Consensus. Nicholas Rescher. (Clarendon Library of Logic & Philosophy). (Illus.). 216p. 1995. reprint ed. pap. text 19.95 (*0-19-823601-8*) OUP.

Pluralism: Cultural Maintenance & Evolution. Brian M. Bullivant. 126p. 1984. 69.00 (*0-905028-27-9*, Pub. by Multilingual Matters); pap. 24.95 (*0-905028-26-0*, Pub. by Multilingual Matters) Taylor & Francis.

Pluralism: Unravelling a Riddle of Our Time. Kevin McNamara. 1989. 15.00 (*0-86217-265-9*, Pub. by Veritas Pubns) St Mut.

Pluralism & Consensus: Conceptions of the Good in the American Polity. Christopher Beem. LC 97-68132. (Studies in Religion, Society & Personality). ix, 153p. 1998. text 29.95 (*0-913348-29-5*) Ctr Sci Study.

Pluralism & Education: Current World Trends in Policy, Law, & Administration. Ed. by Peter M. Roeder et al. LC 95-42849. 345p. (Orig.). 1995. pap. 21.95 (*0-87772-366-4*) UCB IGS.

Pluralism & Identity: Studies in Ritual Behavior. Ed. by Jan Platvoet & Karel Van der Toorn. LC 95-16624. (Studies in the History of Religions: Vol. 67). vi, 376p. 1995. 119.00 (*90-04-10373-2*) Brill Academic Pubs.

Pluralism & Inequality in Quebec. Leslie S. Laczko. 288p. 1995. text 55.00 (*0-312-10064-7*) St Martin.

Pluralism & Inequality in Quebec. Leslie S. Laczko. 252p. 1996. text 55.00 (*0-8020-0892-5*) St Martin.

Pluralism & Liberal Neutrality. Richard Bellamy & Martin Hollis. LC 98-20005. 128p. 1999. 49.50 (*0-7146-4916-3*); pap. 24.50 (*0-7146-4470-6*) F Cass Pubs.

Pluralism & Oppression: Theology in World Perspective - R. Panikkar, T. Berry, J. Sobrino, E. Dussel & Others. Ed. by Paul F. Knitter. (College Theology Society Publications, 1988: Vol. 34). 290p. (C). 1990. lib. bdg. 50.00 (*0-8191-7904-3*) U Pr of Amer.

Pluralism & Particularity in Religious Belief. Brad Stetson. LC 94-13738. 168p. 1994. 49.95 (*0-275-94739-4*, Praeger Pubs) Greenwood.

Pluralism & Personality: William James & Some Contemporary Cultures of Psychology. Don S. Browning. LC 78-75196. 280p. 1970. 38.50 (*0-8387-2265-2*) Bucknell U Pr.

Pluralism & Progressives: Hull House & the New Immigrants, 1890-1919. Rivka S. Lissak. (Illus.). 264p. 1989. 42.00 (*0-226-48502-1*) U Ch Pr.

Pluralism & Social Conflict: A Social Analysis of the Communist World. Silviu Brucan. LC 89-48745. 216p. 1990. 55.00 (*0-275-93475-6*, C3475, Greenwood Pr) Greenwood.

Pluralism & the Personality of the State. David Runciman. (Ideas in Context Ser.: Vol. 47). 297p. (C). 1997. text 59.95 (*0-521-55191-9*) Cambridge U Pr.

Pluralism & the Politics of Difference: State, Culture & Ethnicity in Comparative Perspective. Ralph Grillo. LC 98-2538. 288p. 1999. text 35.00 (*0-19-829426-3*) OUP.

Pluralism & the Religions: The Theological & Political Dimensions. John May. LC 98-187158. 99p. 1998. pap. text 17.95 (*0-304-70259-5*) Continuum.

Pluralism & Truth in Religion. John F. Kane. LC 80-20659. (American Academy of Religion, Dissertation Ser.). 193p. 1981. pap. 15.95 (*0-89130-414-2*, 01-01-33) OUP.

Pluralism by Design: Environmental Policy & the American Regulatory State. George Hoberg. LC 91-22259. 256p. 1992. 55.00 (*0-275-94126-4*, C4126, Praeger Pubs) Greenwood.

Pluralism by the Rules: Conflict & Cooperation in Environmental Regulation. Edward P. Weber. LC 97-37976. (American Governance & Public Policy Ser.). 336p. 1998. 55.00 (*0-87840-671-9*); pap. 23.95 (*0-87840-672-7*) Georgetown U Pr.

***Pluralism Comes of Age: American Religious Culture in the Twentieth Century.** Charles H. Lippy. LC 99-88431. 264p. 2000. text 34.95 (*0-7656-0150-8*) M E Sharpe.

Pluralism, Corporatism, & Confucianism: Political Association & Conflict Regulation in the United States, Europe, & Taiwan. Harmon Zeigler. LC 87-20161. 272p. (C). 1988. 39.95 (*0-87722-529-X*) Temple U Pr.

Pluralism in a Democratic Society. Ed. by Melvin M. Tumin & Walter Plotch. LC 76-12877. 248p. 1977. 42.95 (*0-275-90275-7*, C0275, Praeger Pubs) Greenwood.

Pluralism in Economics: New Perspectives in History & Methodology. Ed. by Andrea Salanti & Ernesto Screpanti. LC 96-15996. 328p. 1997. 90.00 (*1-85898-140-9*) E Elgar.

Pluralism in Education in Europe: Report of the International Conference, Alden Biesen, 18-20 May, 1995. D. De Neve & Raad van het Pluralistisch Onderwijs Staff. LC 98-230055. 216p. 1997. pap. write for info. (*90-5487-182-2*) VUB Univ Pr.

***Pluralism in Philosophy: Changing the Subject.** John Kekes. LC 00-9351. (C). 2000. write for info. (*0-8014-3805-5*) Cornell U Pr.

***Pluralism in Self Psychology Vol. 15: Progress in Self Psychology.** Ed. by Arnold Goldberg. 380p. 1999. 47.50 (*0-88163-312-7*) Analytic Pr.

***Pluralism in Theory & Practice: Richard McKeon & American Philosophy.** Ed. by Eugene Garver & Richard Buchanan. (Library of American Philosophy). 320p. 2000. 39.95 (*0-8265-1340-9*, Pub. by Vanderbilt U Pr) U of Okla Pr.

Pluralism, Justice, & Equality. Ed. by David Miller & Michael Walzer. (Illus.). 318p. 1995. pap. text 21.00 (*0-19-828008-4*) OUP.

Pluralism, Politics & Ideology in the Creole Caribbean. M. G. Smith. (Vera Rubin Caribbean Ser.: No. 1). 1991. pap. text 7.50 (*0-9633741-0-9*) RI Study of Man.

Pluralism, Socialism, & Political Legitimacy: Reflections on Opening up Communism. F. M. Barnard. 203p. (C). 1991. text 52.95 (*0-521-40252-2*) Cambridge U Pr.

Pluralist Game: Pluralism, Liberalism & the Moral Conscience. Francis Canavan. LC 95-4609. 192p. (C). 1995. pap. text 22.95 (*0-8476-8094-0*); lib. bdg. 56.50 (*0-8476-8093-2*) Rowman.

***Pluralist Thinking & the State in Britain & France, 1900-25** Cecile Laborde. LC 99-42554. (St. Antony's Ser.). 2000. text 65.00 (*0-312-22934-8*) St Martin.

Pluralistic Approaches to Art Criticism. Ed. by Doug E. Blandy & Kristin G. Congdon. LC 91-78362. 200p. (C). 1992. 29.95 (*0-87972-543-5*) Bowling Green Univ Popular Press.

Pluralistic Philosophy of Stephen Crane. Patrick K. Dooley. (Illus.). 224p. (C). 1993. pap. text 17.95 (*0-252-06390-2*) U of Ill Pr.

Pluralistic Universe. William James. LC 76-45464. (Works of William James). 517p. 1977. 50.00 (*0-674-67391-3*) HUP.

Pluralistic Universe. William James. LC 96-28484. xx, 405p. 1996. pap. 15.00 (*0-8032-7591-9*, Bison Books) U of Nebr Pr.

Pluralistic Universe. William James. (Notable American Authors Ser.). 1992. reprint ed. lib. bdg. 75.00 (*0-7812-3478-6*) Rprt Serv.

Pluralistic Vision: Presbyterians & Mainstream Protestant Education & Leadership. Ed. by Milton J. Coalter et al. (Presbyterian Presence Ser.). 320p. (Orig.). 1992. pap. 24.95 (*0-664-25243-5*) Westminster John Knox.

Pluralite Culturelle et Education en Suisse: Etre Migrant II. Ed. by Eho Poglia et al. 472p. 1995. 47.95 (*3-906753-56-5*, Pub. by P Lang) P Lang Pubng.

Pluralities. Roger Schwarzschild. (Studies in Linguistics & Philosophy: Vol. 61). 1996. text 100.50 (*0-7923-4007-8*) Kluwer Academic.

Plurality & Ambiguity: Hermeneutics, Religion, Hope. David Tracy. LC 93-50894. 160p. 1994. reprint ed. pap. text 12.95 (*0-226-81126-3*) U Ch Pr.

Plurality & Christian Ethics. Ian S. Markham. (New Studies in Christian Ethics: No. 4). 239p. (C). 1994. text 59.95 (*0-521-45328-3*) Cambridge U Pr.

Plurality & Christian Ethics. rev. ed. Ian S. Markham. 208p. (C). 1998. pap. text 19.95 (*1-889119-06-7*) Seven Bridges.

Plurality & Continuity. David A. Seargent. 164p. 1985. lib. bdg. 98.50 (*90-247-3185-2*, Pub. by M Nijhoff) Kluwer Academic.

Plurality & Quantification Vol. 69: Studies in Linguistics & Philosophy. Ed. by Fritz Hamm & Erhard Hinrichs. LC 97-35078. (Studies in Linguistics & Philosophy Ser.). 392p. 1998. text 117.50 (*0-7923-4841-9*) Kluwer Academic.

Plurality, Conjunction & Events. Peter Lasersohn. LC 94-38629. (Studies in Linguistics & Philosophy: Vol. 55). 316p. 1994. lib. bdg. 117.50 (*0-7923-3238-5*, Pub. by Kluwer Academic) Kluwer Academic.

Plurality of Truth: A Critique of Research on the State & European Integration. Hanna Ojanen. LC 98-24497. 377p. 1998. text 72.95 (*1-84014-402-5*, JA86.O46, Pub. by Ashgate Pub) Ashgate Pub Co.

Plurality of Worlds of Lewis. Jacques Roubaud. Tr. by Rosmarie Waldrop from FRE. LC 94-7327. 109p. (Orig.). 1995. pap. 9.95 (*1-56478-069-4*) Dalkey Arch.

Pluralizing Journalism Education: A Multicultural Handbook. Ed. by Carolyn A. Martindale. LC 92-35923. 264p. 1993. lib. bdg. 65.00 (*0-313-28592-6*, MZG/) Greenwood.

Pluralizing World in Formation. Ed. by Harold D. Lasswell. LC 79-21108. (Propaganda & Communication in World History Ser.: Vol. 3). 576p. reprint ed. pap. 178.60 (*0-608-09994-5*, 202958800003) Bks Demand.

Plurals & Events. Barry Schein. LC 92-47494. (Current Studies in Linguistics: Vol. 23). 400p. 1994. 46.50 (*0-262-19334-5*) MIT Pr.

Plurals & Possessives Through Pictures. Harris Winitz. (Language Through Pictures Ser.). (Illus.). 28p. (YA). (gr. 2-12). 1982. pap. 5.00 (*0-939990-37-7*) Intl Linguistics.

Pluricentric Languages: Differing Norms in Different Nations. Ed. by Michael Clyne. LC 91-35828. (Contributions to the Sociology of Language Ser.: No. 62). vi, 481p. (C). 1991. lib. bdg. 152.35 (*3-11-012855-1*) Mouton.

***Pluricentric Languages in an Immigrant Context: Spanish, Arabic & Chinese.** Michael Clyne & Sandra Kipp. LC 99-29118. (Contributions to the Sociology of Language Ser.: No. 82). 360p. 1999. 155.00 (*3-11-016577-5*) De Gruyter.

***Plurigenera of Surface Singularities: Tomohiro Okuma.** 187p. 2000. lib. bdg. 79.00 (*1-56072-802-7*) Nova Sci Pubs.

Pluripotential Theory, Vol. 6. Maciej Klimek. (London Mathematical Society Monographs: New Series 6). 288p. 1992. 65.00 (*0-19-853568-6*) OUP.

Plurisubharmonic Functions & Positive Differential Forms. P. Lelong. (Notes on Mathematics & Its Applications Ser.). x, 78p. 1969. text 142.00 (*0-677-30220-7*) Gordon & Breach.

Pluriverse: An Essay in the Philosophy of Pluralism. Benjamin P. Blood. LC 75-3057. reprint ed. 20.50 (*0-404-59055-1*) AMS Pr.

Pluriverse: An Essay in the Philosophy of Pluralism. Benjamin P. Blood. LC 75-36829. (Occult Ser.). 1976. reprint ed. 25.95 (*0-405-07941-9*) Ayer.

Plurry: A Scheme for a Musical Instrument. Guy Ottewell. (Illus.). 36p. 1992. 6.00 (*0-934546-45-2*) Univ Wrkshop.

Plus Anciens Monuments de la Langue Francaise. (Societe Des Anciens Textes Francais Ser.). 67.50 (*0-685-34016-3*) Fr & Eur.

Plus Anciens Monuments de la Musique Francaise see Melanges de Musicologie Critique

***Plus Beau Noel de Jackie.** Day Leclaire. (Horizon Ser.: No. 537). (FRE.). 2000. mass mkt. 3.99 (*0-373-39537-X*, 1-39537-5, Harlequin French) Harlequin Bks.

***Plus Belle des Surprises.** Marie Ferrarella. (Horizon Ser.: No. 525). (FRE.). 1999. mass mkt. 3.99 (*0-373-39525-6*, 1-39525-0) Harlequin Bks.

Plus Belle Histoire du Monde. Rudyard Kipling. (FRE.). 320p. 1974. pap. 10.95 (*0-7859-2348-9*, 2070366170) Fr & Eur.

Plus Belle Historie du Monde see Origins: Cosmos, Earth & Mankind

Plus Belles Chamsons, 1900-40. Date not set. pap. 34.95 (*0-7692-1045-7*, 01020601) Wrner Bros.

Plus Belles Melodies de Schubert: For Guitar. Ed. by Michael Lefferts. (FRE.). 12p. (Orig.). (C). 1997. pap. text 11.95 (*0-7692-1310-3*, 01020302) Wrner Bros.

Plus Ca Change... For the Love of France. William D. Romey. LC 96-85369. (Illus.). 352p. (Orig.). 1996. pap. 19.95 (*0-915492-04-0*) Ash Lad Pr.

Plus Ca Change: La France Entre Hier et Demain. Edward C. Knox & Huguette-Laure Knox. (FRE., Illus.). 157p. (C). 1994. pap. text 22.95 (*2-278-04015-4*, U0978) Hatier Pub.

Plus Essential Sociolgy. 3rd ed. Henslin. 1999. pap. 21.00 (*0-205-29986-5*, Longwood Div) Allyn.

Plus 15: Fifteen Days to Lower Blood Pressure & Cholesterol. rev. ed. Samuel L. DeShay & Bernice A. DeShay. (YA). (gr. 10). 1992. 14.95 (*0-945460-16-3*) Upward Way.

Plus Fort Que la Peur. Debra Cowan. (Amours d'Aujourd'Hui Ser.: Vol. 322). (FRE.). 1999. mass mkt. 4.99 (*0-373-38322-3*, 1-38322-3) Harlequin Bks.

Plus Fort Que la Vengeance. Kay Thorpe. (Azur Ser.: Bk. 737). 1999. mass mkt. 3.50 (*0-373-34737-5*, 1-34737-6) Harlequin Bks.

Plus Fou Des Paris. Leigh Michaels. (Horizon Ser.: No. 487). (FRE.). 1998. mass mkt. 3.50 (*0-373-39487-X*, 1-39487-3) Harlequin Bks.

Plus Haute des Solitudes, Misere Affective et Sexuelle d'Emigres Nord-Amerique. Tahar B. Jelloun. (FRE.). 1979. pap. 14.95 (*0-7859-2676-3*) Fr & Eur.

Plus Long Circuit see Longest Home Run

Plus Long Circuit. Roch Carrier. LC 92-62362. (FRE., Illus.). 24p. (J). (gr. 2 up). 1993. 15.95 (*0-88776-301-4*) Tundra Bks.

Plus 1090 Game: 52 High Impact Leverage Points for Enhancing Sales, Customer Loyalty & Teamwork. Mark Rosenberger. (Illus.). 160p. 1997. 19.95 (*0-9656567-0-5*) WOW Pubng.

Plus Proche Voisin. Helene Vachon. (Best-Sellers Ser.).Tr. of Nearest Neighbor. (FRE.). (J). (ps-2). 2000. pap. 9.95 incl. audio (*2-921997-36-3*) Coffragants.

Plus Shipping. Bob Hicok. LC 98-712193. (American Poets Continuum Ser.: No. 50). 96p. 1998. pap. 12.50 (*1-880238-67-5*) BOA Edns.

Plus Sign on the Roof. Paul K. Van Thomson. 200p. 1991. pap. 9.95 (*0-932506-86-0*) St Bedes Pubns.

Plus Style: The Plus-Size Guide to Looking Great. Suzan Nanfeldt. (Illus.). 384p. (Orig.). 1996. pap. 19.95 (*0-452-27596-2*, Plume) Dutton Plume.

Plus Text. Cranbrook Academy of Art, Architecture Studio Staf. 63p. 1991. pap. 6.00 (*1-880337-02-9*) Cranbrook Acad.

Plus Ultra. Joseph Glanvill. LC 58-9452. 208p. 1978. reprint ed. 50.00 (*0-8201-1243-7*) Schol Facsimiles.

Plus Ultra: or The Progress & Advancement of Knowledge since the Days of Aristotle. Joseph Glanvill. Ed. by Bernhard Fabian. (Collected Works: Vol. IV). 154p. 1979. reprint ed. 45.37 (*3-487-02690-2*) G Olms Pubs.

Plush Toy-Scaredy Kittens. Childs Play Staff. 1995. 24.99 (*0-85953-410-3*) Childs Play.

Plutarach, Moralia Vol. XIII, PT. 2: Stoic Essays: Loeb No. 470. Tr. by Harold Cherniss. 21.25 (*0-674-99517-1*) HUP.

Plutarch. rev. ed. Brian P. Hillyard. Ed. by W. R. Connor. LC 80-2653. (Monographs in Classical Studies). 1981. lib. bdg. 35.95 (*0-405-14040-1*) Ayer.

Plutarch: Life of Cicero. Plutarch. Ed. by J. L. Moles. (Classical Texts Ser.). 1989. 59.99 (*0-85668-360-4*, Pub. by Aris & Phillips); pap. 28.00 (*0-85668-361-2*, Pub. by Aris & Phillips) David Brown.

Plutarch: Life of Themistocles. Ed. & Tr. by John L. Marr from GRE. (Classical Texts Ser.). 172p. (C). 1998. 59.95 (*0-85668-676-X*, Pub. by Aris & Phillips); pap. 22.00 (*0-85668-677-8*, Pub. by Aris & Phillips) David Brown.

Plutarch: Lives of Aristedes & Cato. Plutarch. Ed. by David Sansone. (Classical Texts Ser.). 1989. 59.99 (*0-85668-421-X*, Pub. by Aris & Phillips) David Brown.

Plutarch: Lives of Aristedes & Catro. Plutarch. Ed. by David Sansone. (Classical Texts Ser.). 1989. pap. 28.00 (*0-85668-422-8*, Pub. by Aris & Phillips) David Brown.

Plutarch: The Malice of Herodotus. Plutarch. 1992. 59.99 (*0-85668-568-2*, Pub. by Aris & Phillips); pap. 22.00 (*0-85668-569-0*, Pub. by Aris & Phillips) David Brown.

Plutarch & His Intellectual World: Essays on Plutarch. Ed. by Judith Mossman. 250p. 1997. 49.50 (*0-7156-2778-3*, Pub. by Classical Pr) David Brown.

Plutarch & His Times. Reginald H. Barrow. LC 76-6599. (BCL Ser. II). 1979. reprint ed. 39.50 (*0-404-15276-7*) AMS Pr.

Plutarch, Moralia Vol. XIII, Pt. 1: Platonic Essays. Tr. by Harold Cherniss. 392p. 1957. text 18.95 (*0-674-99470-1*) HUP.

Plutarch, the Parallel Lives: Agesilaus & Pompey, Pelopidas & Marcellus. Plutarch. 19.95 (*0-674-99097-8*) HUP.

Plutarch, the Parallel Lives Vol. IV: Alcibiades & Coriolanus, Lysander & Sulla. Tr. by Beradotte Perrin. 1989. text 18.95 (*0-674-99089-7*) HUP.

Plutarch Themistocles. David J. Ladouceur. (Bryn Mawr Greek Commentaries Ser.). 80p. (Orig.). (C). 1989. pap. text 6.00 (*0-929524-60-8*) Bryn Mawr Commentaries.

Plutarch Uber Isis und Osiris, 2 vols. in 1. Theodor Hopfner. (Monographien des Archiv Orientalni, Prag: Band IX). (GER.). x, 319p. 1991. reprint ed. write for info. (*3-487-05051-X*) G Olms Pubs.

Plutarchi: De Heroditi Malignitate. Ed. by Petrus A. Hansen. (GRE & LAT.). xviii, 77p. 1979. pap. 38.00 (*90-256-0695-4*, Pub. by AM Hakkert) BookLink Distributors.

Plutarchi Vol. I: De Liberis Educandis. Ed. by Paton et al. (GRE.). 1993. reprint ed. 100.00 (*3-8154-1678-7*, T1678, Pub. by B G Teubner) U of Mich Pr.

Plutarchi Vol. I, Fascicule 1: Theseus et Romulus - Solon et Publicola - Themistocles et Camillus - Aristides et Cato Maior - Cimon et Lucullus. Ed. by Ziegler & Gartner. (GRE.). 1997. reprint ed. 100.00 (*3-322-00249-7*, T1672, Pub. by B G Teubner) U of Mich Pr.

Plutarchi Vol. I, Fascicule 2: Pericles et Fabius Maximus - Nicias et Crassus - Alcibiades et Coriolanus - Demosthenes et Cicero. rev. ed. Ed. by Ziegler & Gartner. (GRE.). 1994. 85.00 (*3-8154-1671-X*, T1671, Pub. by B G Teubner) U of Mich Pr.

Plutarchi Vol. II: Regum et Imperatorum Apophthegmata. Ed. by Paton et al. (GRE.). 1972. reprint ed. 53.50 (*3-322-00200-4*, T1679, Pub. by B G Teubner) U of Mich Pr.

P

Plutarchi Vol. II, Fascicule 1: Phocion et Cato Minor - Dion et Brutus - Aemilius Paulus et Timoleon - Sertorius et Eumenes. rev. ed. Ed. by Ziegler & Gartner. (GRE.). 1993. 75.00 (*3-8154-1673-6*, T1673, Pub. by B G Teubner) U of Mich Pr.

Plutarchi Vol. II, Fascicule 2: Philopoemen et Titus Flamininus - Pelopidas et Marcellus - Alexander et Caesar. rev. ed. Ed. by Ziegler & Gartner. (GRE.). 1994. 79.50 (*3-8154-1674-4*, T1674, Pub. by B G Teubner) U of Mich Pr.

Plutarchi Vol. III, Fascicule 1: Demetrius et Antonius - Phrrhus et Marius - Aratus et Artaxerxes - Agis et Cleomenes et Ti. rev. ed. Ed. by Ziegler & Gartner. (GRE.). 1996. 110.00 (*3-8154-1675-2*, T1675, Pub. by B G Teubner) U of Mich Pr.

Plutarchi Vol. III, Fascicule 2: Lycurgus et Numa - Lysander et Sulla - Agesilaus et Pompeius - Galba et Otho. Ed. by Ziegler & Gartner. (GRE.). 1973. 49.50 (*3-322-00251-9*, T1676, Pub. by B G Teubner) U of Mich Pr.

Plutarchi Vol. IV: Indices. Ed. by Ziegler & Gartner. (GRE.). 1997. 62.50 (*3-8154-1677-9*, T1677, Pub. by B G Teubner) U of Mich Pr.

Plutarchi Vol. VI, Fascicule 3: De Musica. Ed. by Pohlenz & Ziegler. (GRE.). 1966. 19.95 (*3-322-00248-9*, T1688, Pub. by B G Teubner) U of Mich Pr.

Plutarchi Phythici Dialogi: De E Apud Delphos - De Pythiae Oraculis - De Defectu Oraculorum. Ed. by Sieveking & Gartner. (GRE.). 1997. reprint ed. pap. 26.95 (*3-8154-1695-7*, T1695, Pub. by B G Teubner) U of Mich Pr.

Plutarch's Advice to the Bride & Groom & A Consolation to His Wife: English Translations, Commentary, Interpretive Essays & Bibliography. Plutarch. LC 98-27968. (Illus.). 240p. 1999. text 55.00 (*0-19-512023-X*) OUP.

Plutarch's Essay on the Life & Poetry of Homer. Ed. by John J. Keaney & Robert Lamberton. LC 96-13850. (American Philological Association, American Classical Studies: No. 40). 321p. (C). 1996. pap. 21.95 (*0-7885-0260-3*, 400440) OUP.

Plutarch's Historical Methods: An Analysis of the Mulierum Virtutes. Philip A. Stadter. LC 65-13850. 171p. reprint ed. pap. 53.10 (*0-8357-8270-0*, 203394000087) Bks Demand.

Plutarch's Life of Pericles. H. Holden. 303p. 1984. reprint ed. 20.00 (*0-86516-026-0*) Bolchazy-Carducci.

Plutarch's Lives. Ed. by Leonard S. Davidow. 30.00 (*0-8196-2860-3*) Biblo.

Plutarch's Lives. Plutarch. Ed. by John S. White. LC 66-28487. (Illus.). 468p. (YA). (gr. 7 up). 1995. 25.00 (*0-8196-0174-8*) Biblo.

Plutarch's Lives: Exploring Virtue & Vice. Tim Duffy. LC 98-40794. 448p. 2000. text 95.00 (*0-19-815058-X*) OUP.

Plutarch's Lives of the Noble Grecians & Romans, 6 vols. Plutarch. Ed. by Thomas North. LC 70-158307. (Tudor Translations, First Ser.: Nos. 7-12). reprint ed. 345.00 (*0-404-51870-2*) AMS Pr.

Plutarch's Political Thought. G. J. D. Aalders. (Verhandelingen der Koninklijke Nederlandse Akademie van Wetenschappen, Afd. Letterkunde, Nieuwe Reeks Ser.: No. 116). 68p. 1982. pap. text 25.00 (*0-444-85554-8*) Elsevier.

Plutarch's Rules of Health. Plutarch. (Longevity Ser.). 1991. lib. bdg. 75.00 (*0-8490-4183-X*) Gordon Pr.

Plutarch's Schrift Non Posse Suaviter Vivi Secundum Epicurum. Hella Adam. LC 72-96778. (Studien zur antiken Philosophie). (GER.). vi, 95p. (C). 1974. 38.00 (*90-6032-015-8*, Pub. by B R Gruner) Humanities.

Plutarch's Sertorius: A Historical Commentary. C. F. Konrad. LC 93-36131. lvi, 260p. (C). 1994. 65.00 (*0-8078-2139-X*) U of NC Pr.

Plutarch's Themistocles. F. J. Frost. LC 99-192407. xiii, 237p. 1997. 25.00 (*0-89005-556-4*) Ares.

Plutarco Elias Calles: Reformar Desde. Enrique Krauze. (Political Biographies of the Mexican Revolution Ser.). (SPA., Illus.). 156p. 1987. pap. 9.99 (*968-16-2292-8*, Pub. by Fondo) Continental Bk.

Plutinische Forschungen Zur Kritik und Geschichte der Komodie. Friedrich Leo. (GER.). vii, 375p. 1973. write for info. (*3-296-14210-X*) G Olms Pubs.

***Pluto.** Carmen Bredeson. LC 00-35179. (Library). 2001. write for info. (*0-531-11784-7*) Watts.

Pluto. Larry Dane Brimmer. (True Bks.). 1999. lib. bdg. 6.95 (*0-516-26499-0*) Childrens.

Pluto. Larry D. Brimner. LC 98-26740. (Space Ser.). 47p. (J). 1999. 21.50 (*0-516-21155-2*) Childrens.

Pluto. Robert Daily. LC 94-58. (First Bks.). 64p. (J). (gr. 4-6). 1994. lib. bdg. 22.00 (*0-531-20166-X*) Watts.

Pluto. Caleb Owens. LC 97-31356. Date not set. write for info. (*1-56766-512-8*) Childs World.

***Pluto.** Luke Thompson. LC 00-24766. (Library of the Planets). (Illus.). (J). 2000. write for info. (*0-8239-5650-4*, PowerKids) Rosen Group.

***Pluto.** Gregory L. Vogt. LC 99-51640. (Galaxy Ser.). (Illus.). 24p. (J). (ps-3). 2000. lib. bdg. 15.93 (*0-7368-0514-1*, Bridgestone Bks) Capstone Pr.

Pluto. Gregory L. Vogt. LC 93-11224. (Gateway Solar System Ser.). (Illus.). 32p. (J). (gr. 2-4). 1994. lib. bdg. 19.90 (*1-56294-393-6*) Millbrook Pr.

Pluto. Gregory L. Vogt. (Gateway Solar System Ser.). (Illus.). 32p. (J). (gr. 2-4). 1996. 6.95 (*0-7613-0158-5*) Millbrook Pr.

Pluto. Robert Daily. (First Bks.). (Illus.). 64p. (J). (gr. 4-6). 1996. reprint ed. pap. 6.95 (*0-531-15770-9*) Watts.

Pluto: The Evolutionary Journey of the Soul. Jeff Green. LC 85-45290. (Modern Astrology Library). (Illus.). 384p. (Orig.). 1999. pap. 15.00 (*0-87542-296-9*) Llewellyn Pubns.

***Pluto: The Key to the Expansion of Consciousness.** 136p. 1999. 14.95 (*0-86690-498-0*) Am Fed Astrologers.

Pluto: Transforming the New You. Karen Lustrup. LC 96-181131. 1995. pap. 13.00 (*0-86690-448-4*) Am Fed Astrologers.

Pluto & Charon. Stern et al. LC 97-27746. 756p. (C). 1997. 90.00 (*0-8165-1840-8*) U of Ariz Pr.

Pluto & Charon: Ice Worlds on the Ragged Edge of the Solar System. Alan Stern & Jacqueline Mitton. LC 97-9502. 232p. 1997. 34.95 (*0-471-15297-8*) Wiley.

***Pluto & Charon: Ice Worlds on the Ragged Edge of the Solar System.** Alan Stern & Jacqueline Mitton. 232p. 1999. pap. 19.95 (*0-471-35384-1*) Wiley.

Pluto Ephemeris, 1900-2000. Lynne Palmer. LC 74-181511. 316p. 1974. 15.00 (*0-86690-200-7*, P1680-004) Am Fed Astrologers.

Pluto in Libra. Manly P. Hall. pap. 4.95 (*0-89314-342-1*) Philos Res.

Pluto, Planet of Magic & Power. Ginger Chalford. LC 83-73607. 200p. 1984. 18.50 (*0-86690-270-8*, C2524-014) Am Fed Astrologers.

***Pluto Rising: A Katy Klein Mystery.** Karen Irving. 336p. 2000. pap. 8.95 (*1-896095-95-X*) Polstar Bk.

Pluto II: The Evolutionary Journey of the Soul Through Relationships. Jeffrey W. Green. (Illus.). 432p. (Orig.). 1999. pap. 12.95 (*1-56718-333-6*) Llewellyn Pubns.

Plutocracy & Politics in New York City. Gabriel Abraham Almond. LC 97-27164. (Urban Policy Challenges Ser.). 288p. (C). 1997. pap. 28.00 (*0-8133-9983-1*, Pub. by Westview) HarpC.

Pluton von Loch Doon in Suedschottland: Theoretisches Zu Bewegungen in Festen Korpern Bei der Deformation. Gerhard Oertel. (Geotektonische Forschungen Ser.: Vol. 11). (GER.). ii, 107p. 1955. pap. 18.00 (*3-510-50902-1*, Pub. by E Schweizerbartsche) Balogh.

Plutonian Ode & Other Poems, 1977-1980. Allen Ginsberg. LC 81-7657. (Pocket Poets Ser.: No. 40). 80p. 1981. pap. 8.95 (*0-87286-125-2*) City Lights.

Plutonian Phoenix. Dale Richardson. 168p. 1974. 12.00 (*0-86690-145-0*, R1398-014) Am Fed Astrologers.

Plutonism from Antarctica to Alaska. Ed. by S. M. Kay & C. W. Rapela. (Special Papers: No. 241). (Illus.). 236p. 1990. pap. 20.00 (*0-8137-2241-1*) Geol Soc.

Plutonium - Deadly Gold of the Nuclear Age: The Health & Environmental Problems of Plutonium Production & Disposal. International Physicians for the Prevention of Nuc & Institute for Energy & Environmental Research Staf. 256p. 1992. pap. 15.00 (*0-9634455-0-2*) Intl Phys PONW.

Plutonium & Highly Enriched Uranium, 1996: World Inventories, Capabilities, & Policies. David Albright et al. (SIPRI Publication). (Illus.). 534p. 1997. text 79.00 (*0-19-828009-2*) OUP.

Plutonium & the Rio Grande: Environmental Change & Contamination in the Nuclear Age. William L. Graf. LC 93-40028. (Illus.). 356p. 1994. text 65.00 (*0-19-508933-2*) OUP.

Plutonium Chemistry. Ed. by William T. Carnall & Gregory R. Choppin. LC 83-6057. (Symposium Ser.: No. 216). 484p. 1983. lib. bdg. 60.95 (*0-8412-0772-0*) Am Chemical.

Plutonium Chemistry. Ed. by William T. Carnall & Gregory R. Choppin. LC 83-6057. (ACS Symposium Ser.: No. 216). (Illus.). 496p. 1983. reprint ed. pap. 153.80 (*0-608-03200-X*, 206371900007) Bks Demand.

***Plutonium Files.** Eileen Welsome. 592p. 2000. pap. 16.95 (*0-385-31954-1*, Dial Pr) Dell.

***Plutonium Files: America's Secret Medical Experiments in the Cold War.** Eileen Welsome. LC 99-10991. 576p. 1999. 26.95 (*0-385-31402-7*) Delacorte.

Plutonium for Japan's Nuclear Reactors: Paying Both the Proliferation & Dollar Price to Assure Long-Term Fuel Supply. Kenneth A. Solomon. LC 93-10298. 1993. pap. 13.00 (*0-8330-1367-X*, MR-186-CC) Rand Corp.

***Plutonium Futures - The Science: Topical Conference on Plutonium & Actinides.** Ed. by K. K. S. Pillay & K. C. Kim. LC 00-104645. (AIP Conference Proceedings Ser.: Vol. 532). (Illus.). xviii, 439p. 2000. 115.00 (*1-56396-948-3*) Am Inst Physics.

Plutonium Handbook, Set. rev. ed. O. J. Wick. LC 80-7679. 992p. 1980. 173.00 (*0-89448-023-5*, 250005) Am Nuclear Soc.

***Plutonium Metallurgy at Los Alamos, 1943-1945.** Edward F. Hammel. LC 98-45594. (Illus.). 8p. 1999. pap. 20.00 (*0-941232-20-4*) Los Alamos Hist Soc.

Plutonium Murders. Robert Davis. 392p. 1997. pap. 24.95 (*1-890248-00-2*) Horizon Pr MI.

Plutonium Nineteen-Seventy & Other Actinides: Proceedings of the 4th International Conference on Plutonium & Other Actinides, Santa Fe, New Mexico, October 5-9, 1970, Pt. I. Ed. by William N. Miner. LC QD0181.P9. (Nuclear Metallurgy Ser.: Vol. 17). 550p. 1970. reprint ed. pap. 170.50 (*0-608-08310-0*, 200117000066) Bks Demand.

Plutonium Nineteen-Seventy & Other Actinides: Proceedings of the 4th International Conference on Plutonium & Other Actinides, Santa Fe, New Mexico, October 5-9, 1970, Pt. II. Ed. by William N. Miner. LC QD0181.P9. (Nuclear Metallurgy Ser.: Vol. 17). 532p. 1970. reprint ed. pap. 165.00 (*0-608-08309-7*, 200117000065) Bks Demand.

Plutonium Recycle: Reports of 3 Contract Studies, 3 pts. Incl. Part II. Cost Impact Analysis of Delay in Plutonium Recycle. W. V. Macnabb. 1975. Pt.i. Legal Aspects of Nuclear Regulatory Commission's Provisional Policy Statement on GESMO. Gerald Charnoff & J. E. Silberg. 1975. Part III. 1975. (Technical & Economic Reports: Nuclear Fuelcycle). 120p. 1975. 20.00 (*0-318-13587-6*) US Coun Energy Awareness.

Plutonium Recycling Scenario in Light Water Reactors: Assessment of Environmental Impact in the European Community, Vol. 5. Ed. by Commission of European Communities. viii, 240p. 1982. text 156.00 (*3-7186-0118-4*) Gordon & Breach.

Plutonium Story: The Journals of Professor Glenn T. Seaborg, 1939-1946. Ed. by Ronald L. Kathren et al. LC 94-9113. (Illus.). 920p. 1994. 49.95 (*0-935470-75-1*) Battelle.

***Pluto's Words of Wisdom.** Disney Staff. (Illus.). 48p. (J). (ps-3). 2000. pap. 4.95 (*0-7407-0080-4*) Andrews & McMeel.

Plutot Deux Fois Qu'une. Pascal Laine. (Folio Ser.: No. 2063). (FRE.). pap. 9.95 (*2-07-038150-1*) Schoenhof.

Ply. limited ed. P. Inman. 60p. (C). 1997. 26.00 (*0-937013-71-4*) Potes Poets.

Plymouth. Lani B. Johnson. LC 97-119385. (Images of America Ser.). 1998. pap. 16.99 (*0-7524-0517-9*) Arcadia Publng.

Plymouth. Plymouth Historical Society Staff. LC 98-86584. (Images of America Ser.). 1997. pap. 16.99 (*0-7524-0518-7*) Arcadia Publng.

Plymouth Cloak. large type ed. Kate Sedley. 317p. 1994. 27.99 (*0-7505-0614-8*, Pub. by Mgna Lrg Print) Ulverscroft.

***Plymouth Colony.** Andrew Santella. (We the People Ser.). (Illus.). 48p. (J). 2000. write for info. (*0-7565-0046-X*) Compass Point.

Plymouth Colony: Its History & People, 1620-1691. Eugene A. Stratton. LC 86-72003. (Illus.). 481p. 1986. pap. 19.95 (*0-916489-18-3*) Ancestry.

Plymouth Colony Probate Guide: Where to Find Wills & Related Data for 800 People of Plymouth Colony, 1620-1691. Ruth W. Sherman & Robert S. Wakefield. LC 83-2362. (Plymouth Colony Research Group Ser.: No.2). xxi, 167p. 1983. 12.50 (*0-910233-01-2*) Plymouth Col.

Plymouth Colony Records Vol. 1: Wills & Inventories, 1633-1666. Charles H. Simmons. 640p. 1995. 59.50 (*0-89725-245-4*, 1608) Picton Pr.

Plymouth Commercial Vehicles Photo Archive. Jim Benjaminson. (Photo Archive Ser.). (Illus.). 128p. 1999. pap. 29.95 (*1-58388-004-6*, Pub. by Iconografix) Motorbooks Intl.

Plymouth County Heritage. Plymouth County Heritage Book Committee. LC 97-76566. 216 p. 1998. write for info. (*1-890105-03-1*) Taylor Publishing.

Plymouth County, 1685. Cynthia H. Krusell. (Illus.). 64p. (Orig.). 1986. pap. 9.95 (*0-940628-43-0*) Pilgrim Soc.

Plymouth Court Records, 1686-1859, 16 vols., Set. Ed. by David T. Konig. LC 78-62076. 1978. 1200.00 (*0-89453-096-8*) Scholarly Res Inc.

Plymouth Harbours & Rivers. Imray, Laurie, Norie & Wilson Ltd. Staff. (Illus.). (C). 1987. text 60.00 (*0-7855-5799-7*, Pub. by Laurie Norie & Wilson Ltd) St Mut.

Plymouth Heritage Cookbook. Lennie Bowser. LC 97-67590. (Illus.). 104p. (Orig.). 1997. spiral bd. 19.95 (*1-882792-45-9*) Proctor Pubns.

Plymouth in the Nineteenth Century. Laurence R. Pizer. (Pilgrim Society Notes Ser.: No. 31). 1983. 2.00 (*0-940628-48-1*) Pilgrim Soc.

Plymouth, 1968-1976. LC 76-9517. 280p. 1976. 16.95 (*0-8019-6552-7*) Nichols Pub.

***Plymouth Pioneers.** Colleen L. Reece. (American Adventure Ser.: No. 2). (J). (gr. 3-6). 1998. pap. 3.97 (*1-57748-060-0*) Barbour Pub.

Plymouth Pioneers. Colleen L. Reece. LC 98-7225. (American Adventure Ser.: No. 2). (Illus.). 142p. (J). (gr. 4-7). 1998. lib. bdg. 15.95 (*0-7910-5042-4*) Chelsea Hse.

Plymouth Plantation. Terry J. Dunnahoo. LC 93-39625. (Places in American History Ser.). (Illus.). 72p. (J). (gr. 4 up). 1995. lib. bdg. 14.95 (*0-382-24968-2*) Silver Burdett Pr.

Plymouth Rock: History & Significance. Rose T. Briggs. 1968. 5.95 (*0-940628-03-1*) Pilgrim Soc.

***Plymouth Rock & the Pilgrims: And Other Speeches.** Mark Twain, pseud. Ed. by Charles Neider. 2000. reprint ed. pap. 17.95 (*0-8154-1104-9*, Pub. by Cooper Sq) Natl Bk Netwk.

Plymouth Settlement: Of Plimoth Plantation. William Bradford. (Illus.). 354p. 1998. reprint ed. 18.00 (*1-889128-48-1*) Mantle Ministries.

***Plymouth State College.** Bruce D. Heald. (Images of America Ser.). 128p. 1999. pap. 18.99 (*0-7385-0184-0*) Arcadia Publng.

Plyometric Exercises with the Medicine Ball. Donald A. Chu. LC 89-60633. (Illus.). 136p. (Orig.). 1989. pap. 12.95 (*0-931255-05-8*) Bittersweet Pub.

Plyometric Exercises with the Medicine Ball. 2nd rev. ed. Donald A. Chu. (Illus.). (Orig.). 1999. pap. 14.95 (*0-931255-09-0*, Pub. by Bittersweet Pub) Rivers & Mnts.

Plyometric Power: The Martial Artist's New Training Method for Explosive Power. 2nd ed. Tom Skotidas. LC 95-94126. (Illus.). 104p. 1995. pap. 19.95 (*1-885083-01-7*) ATS Pubs Inc.

Plyometrics. Will Freeman & Evelyn Freeman. 54p. (Orig.). 1984. pap. 8.95 (*0-89279-068-7*) Championship Bks & Vid Prodns.

Plywood & Adhesive Technology. Terry Sellers. (Illus.). 680p. 1985. text 250.00 (*0-8247-7407-8*) Dekker.

Plywood & Veneer-Based Products: Manufacturing Practices. Richard F. Baldwin. (Illus.). 388p. 1995. 59.00 (*0-87930-371-9*, 417) Miller Freeman.

Plywood Headers for Residential Construction, Vol. 5. NAHB Research Foundation Staff. (Research Report Ser.). 48p. 1983. pap. 8.00 (*0-86718-200-8*) Home Builder.

PM. Danny Lekas. LC 84-91446. 1985. pap. 2.00 (*0-930759-05-2*) D Lekas.

PM: A New Deal in Journalism. Paul Milkman. LC 97-5675. (Illus.). 240p. 1997. text 45.00 (*0-8135-2434-2*) Rutgers U Pr.

PM & the Art of Not Taking Out the Garbage. I. Will Lader. 1991. pap. write for info. (*1-878515-41-1*) W S Dawson.

P/M Applications. (Special Publications). 220p. 1999. pap. 95.00 (*0-7680-0379-2*, SP-1447) Soc Auto Engineers.

P/M in Aerospace & Defense Technologies, 1991: Proceedings of the P/M in Aerospace & Defense Technologies Symposium, Sponsored by the Metal Powder Industries Federation, Held in Tampa, FL, March 4-6, 1991. P/M in Aerospace & Defense Technologies Symposium. LC 91-19049. 424p. 1991. reprint ed. pap. 131.50 (*0-608-01820-1*, 206246900003) Bks Demand.

P/M in Aerospace, Defense, & Demanding Applications, 1993: Proceedings of the Third International Conference on Powder Metallurgy in Aerospace, Defense, & Demanding Applications. International Conference on Powder Metallurgy in A. Ed. by F. H. Froes. LC 93-7184. 402p. 1993. reprint ed. pap. 124.70 (*0-608-01819-8*, 206246800003) Bks Demand.

P/M in Aerospace, Defense, & Demanding Applications, 1995: Proceedings of the 4th International Conference on P/m in Aerospace, Defense & Demanding Applications. Ed. by F. H. Froes. LC 96-216398. (Illus.). 375p. (Orig.). (C). 1995. pap. 150.00 (*1-878954-57-1*) Metal Powder.

PM-My First Book: Prayer Boy-Baptist. Catholic Edition. 1996. 12.95 (*0-88271-323-X*) Regina Pr.

PM Ninety World Conference of Powder Metallurgy, Vol. 1. 576p. 1990. 90.00 (*0-901462-94-2*, Pub. by Inst Materials) Ashgate Pub Co.

PM Ninety World Conference of Powder Metallurgy, Vol. 2. 460p. 1990. pap. text 70.00 (*0-901462-97-7*, Pub. by Inst Materials) Ashgate Pub Co.

PM Ninety World Conference of Powder Metallurgy, Vol. 3. 292p. 1990. 50.00 (*0-901462-98-5*, Pub. by Inst Materials) Ashgate Pub Co.

PM Ninety World Conference of Powder Metallurgy, Vol. 4. 57p. 1990. pap. text 20.00 (*0-901462-99-3*, Pub. by Inst Materials) Ashgate Pub Co.

***PM 101: According to the Olde Curmudgeon: An Introduction to the Basic Concepts of Modern Project Management.** Francis M. Webster & Project Management Institute Staff. LC 99-41261. 1999. pap. write for info. (*1-880410-55-9*) Proj Mgmt Inst.

Pm/Am: New & Selected Poems. Linda Pastan. 128p. 1982. pap. 9.95 (*0-393-30055-2*) Norton.

PMBOK Q & A: A Pocket Guide of Questions & Answers to Learn More About the Project Management Body of Knowledge. 176p. 1997. pap. 24.95 (*1-880410-21-4*) Proj Mgmt Inst.

PMI Book of Project Management Forms. Ed. by Project Management Institute Staff. LC 97-27953. 416p. 1997. ring bd. 49.95 (*1-880410-31-1*) Proj Mgmt Inst.

PMP Challenge! 2nd ed. J. Leroy Ward & Ginger Levin. Ed. by Dixie Richards. LC 99-206696. 560p. 1998. spiral bd. 44.95 (*1-890367-14-1*) ESI Int.

PMP Challenge! 480 Mind-Bending, Thought-Provoking Questions for PMP Exam Preparation. J. LeRoy Ward & Ginger Levin. Ed. by Dixie Richards. (Illus.). 489p. 1996. spiral bd. 44.95 (*0-9626190-7-8*) ESI Int.

PMP Exam: Practice Test & Study Guide. Ed. by LeRoy Ward. 218p. (Orig.). 1997. pap. 29.95 (*0-9626190-8-6*) ESI Int.

PMP Exam Practice Test & Study Guide: Practice Test & Study Guide. 2nd ed. Ed. by J. Leroy Ward. 224p. 1998. student ed., spiral bd. 29.95 (*1-890367-11-7*) ESI Int.

***PMP Exam Prep.** 2nd rev. ed. Rita Mulcahy. (Illus.). 336p. 1999. pap. 89.00 (*1-890676-42-X*, Pub. by Beavers Pond) Bookman Bks.

***PMS: A Woman Doctor's Guide: Essential Facts & Up-to-the-Minute Information on Premenstrual Syndrome.** Andrea J. Rapkin. 2000. mass mkt. 6.99 (*1-57566-602-2*, Knsington) Kensgtn Pub Corp.

PMS: Everything You Need to Know about. Helen Batchelder. LC 98-49608. (Natural Pharmacist Ser.). (Illus.). 177p. 2000. pap. 6.99 (*0-7615-1615-8*) Prima Pub.

PMS: Pre-Menstrual Syndrome. Ronald V. Norris & Colleen Sullivan. 50p. 1987. mass mkt. 4.95 (*0-425-10332-3*) Berkley Pub.

PMS: Self Help Book. Susan M. Lark. LC 89-25292. 240p. 1995. pap. 16.95 (*0-89087-587-1*) Celestial Arts.

PMS: Women Tell Women How to Control Premenstrual Syndrome. 2nd rev. ed. Stephanie D. Bender & Kathleen Kelleher. LC 96-67940. Orig. Title: PMS: A Positive Program to Gain Control. (Illus.). 256p. 1996. pap. 13.95 (*1-57224-052-0*) New Harbinger.

PMS: A Positive Program to Gain Control see PMS: Women Tell Women How to Control Premenstrual Syndrome

PMS & Alcoholism. Therese Casey. 20p. (Orig.). (C). 1984. pap. 2.00 (*0-89486-247-2*, 1377B) Hazelden.

PMS & Perimenopause Sourcebook: A Guide to the Emotional, Mental, & Physical Patterns of a Woman's Life. Lori A. Futterman & John E. Jones. 272p. 1998. pap. 16.00 (*1-56565-859-0*, 08590W, Pub. by Lowell Hse) NTC Contemp Pub Co.

PMS & You. Elizabeth K. White et al. (Illus.). 40p. 1994. pap. 3.60 (*0-910304-20-3*) Budlong.

PMS Crazed: Touch Me & I'll Kill You. Jan B. King. Ed. by Cliff Carle. 64p. 1994. pap. 5.95 (*0-918259-70-3*) CCC Pubns.

PMS Diet Cookbook: With an Overview of Premenstrual Syndrome Plus Self-Help Recommendations for Every Woman. Sharon A. Heinz. 69p. (Orig.). 1987. pap. 10.00 (*0-9619495-0-3*) Heinz Pr.

An Asterisk (*) at the beginning of an entry indicates that the title is appearing for the first time.

PMS Handbook for Men. rev. ed. Ted Manuel & Doreen Ramirez. (Illus.). 56p. (Orig.). 1994. write for info. (0-9628011-1-9) Desert Palm Pub.

*__PMS Outlaws.__ Sharyn McCrumb. Vol. 9. 304p. 2000. 24.00 (0-345-38231-5, Ballantine) Ballantine Pub Grp.

*__PMS, Perimenopause & You: A Guide to the Physical, Mental & Emotional Patterns of a Woman'__ 2nd ed. Lori A. Futterman. 2000. pap. 16.95 (0-7373-0511-8) Lowell Hse.

PMS-Prudent Mans Survival Cookbook. Ted Manuel. Ed. by Doreen Ramirez. 100p. (Orig.). 1995. write for info. (0-9628011-4-3) Desert Palm Pub.

PMS Puzzle. Holli Kenley. 156p. 1993. pap. 10.00 (0-939513-76-5) Joy Pub SJC.

PMS Relief: Natural Approaches to Treating Symptoms. Judy E. Marshel. 1998. mass mkt. 5.99 (0-425-16395-4) Berkley Pub.

PMS Solution: A Nutritional Approach to Premenstrual Syndrome. Ann Nazzaro et al. 156p. (Orig.). 1985. 7.95 (0-86683-793-0, AY8554) Harper SF.

PMS Solving the Puzzle: Sixteen Causes of Premenstrual Syndrome & What to Do about It. Linaya Hahn. (Illus.). 176p. (Orig.). 1995. pap. 16.95 (1-886094-15-2) Chicago Spectrum.

PMS Zone. Rose M. Brown. (Illus.). 80p. (Orig.). (YA). 1988. pap. 7.95 (0-9622109-0-0) Skeetoonies.

*__PMSE Preprints: Polymeric Materials Science & Engineering.__ J. Weber & A. Mesli. (European Materials Research Society Symposia Proceedings Ser.: Vol. 81). (Illus.). 623p. 1999. pap. 66.00 (0-8412-3683-6) Am Chemical.

PN Junction Diode. Gerold W. Neudeck. LC 81-14979. (Modular Series on Solid State Devices: No. 2). (Illus.). 120p. 1983. pap. 7.00 (0-201-05321-7) Addison-Wesley.

PN Junction Diode. 2nd ed. Gerold W. Neudeck. (Modular Series on Solid State Devices). (Illus.). 176p. (C). 1988. pap. text 23.40 (0-201-12296-0) Addison-Wesley.

PN-VN NCLEX Review Cards. (C). 1999. boxed set 32.95 (1-56930-093-3) Skidmore Roth Pub.

PNA: A Centennial History of the Polish National Alliance of the U. S. A. Donald E. Pienkos. 485p. 1984. text 72.00 (0-88033-060-0, Pub. by East Eur Monographs) Col U Pr.

*__Pndr, Psychologists' Neuropsychotropic Drug Reference.__ Louis A. Pagliaro. LC 98-32463. 1999. 54.95 (0-87630-956-2) Brunner-Mazel.

Pneuma Hagion. Hans Leisegang. vi, 150p. 1970. reprint ed. write for info. (0-318-70959-7) G Olms Pubs.

Pneumatic: Machines & Postal Markings. Reg Morris & Robert J. Payne. 176p. (C). 1992. pap. 15.00 (1-880065-00-2) Machine Cancel Soc.

Pneumatic & Hydraulic Components & Instruments in Automatic Control: Proceedings of the IFAC Symposium, Warsaw, Poland, May, 1980. IFAC Symposium Staff. Ed. by H. J. Leskiewicz & M. Zaremba. LC 80-41658. (IFAC Proceedings Ser.). (Illus.). 308p. 1981. 126.00 (0-08-027317-3, Pub. by Pergamon Repr) Franklin.

Pneumatic & Hydraulic Control Systems. M. Aizerman & P. Linnik. LC 66-19864. (Seminar Pneumohydraulic Automation 1st Session Ser.: Vol. 1). 1968. 184.00 (0-08-009977-7, Pub. by Pergamon Repr) Franklin.

Pneumatic & Hydraulic Control Systems: 2nd & 3rd Sessions, 2 vols. M. Aizerman & R. Matthews. LC 66-19864. (Seminar Pneumohydraulic Automation Ser.: Vol, 2). 1968. 111.00 (0-08-011147-5, Pub. by Pergamon Repr) Franklin.

Pneumatic & Hydraulic Conveying of Solids. O. A. Williams. (Chemical Industries Ser.: Vol. 13). (Illus.). 336p. 1983. text 175.00 (0-8247-1855-0) Dekker.

Pneumatic & Hydraulic Systems. W. Bolton. LC 97-222388. 248p. 1997. pap. text 34.95 (0-7506-3836-2) Buttrwrth-Heinemann.

Pneumatic Controls for Industrial Application: A Practical & Comprehensive Presentation of Pneumatic Control System Fundamentals, Control Devices, Associated Facilities, & Application Circuitry for Manual, Semiautomatic, & Automatic Industrial Operations. American Society of Tool & Manufacturing Engineers. Ed. by Frank W. Wilson. LC 65-13379. (Manufacturing Data Ser.). 174p. reprint ed. pap. 54.00 (0-608-13149-0, 202417800035) Bks Demand.

Pneumatic Conveying Design. David Mills. 607p. 1990. text 205.00 (0-408-04707-0) Buttrwrth-Heinemann.

Pneumatic Conveying of Solids. R. D. Marcus et al. 528p. (gr. 13). 1990. text 102.95 (0-412-21490-3, 6647) Chapman & Hall.

Pneumatic Data, Vol. 2. Institute for Power System Staff. 130p. 1979. 75.00 (0-7855-7242-2) St Mut.

Pneumatic Data, Vol. 3. Institute for Power System Staff. 100p. 1979. 75.00 (0-7855-7243-0) St Mut.

Pneumatic Engineering Calculations. Institute for Power System Staff. 120p. 1979. 65.00 (0-7855-7244-9) St Mut.

Pneumatic Handbook. 5th ed. Institute for Power System Staff. 700p. 1979. 275.00 (0-7855-2853-9) St Mut.

Pneumatic Handbook. 8th ed. Ed. by Barber. LC 97-33006. 650p. 1997. text 230.00 (1-85617-249-X) Elsevier.

Pneumatic Instrumentation. 3rd ed. Dale R. Patrick & Steven R. Patrick. LC 92-31773. 434p. 1993. mass mkt. 42.50 (0-8273-5482-7) Delmar.

Pneumatic Measurement & Control Applications, 3 vol. set. E. M. Eacho et al. (Illus.). (C). 1981. teacher ed., ring bd. 595.00 (0-87683-014-9) GP Courseware.

Pneumatic Measurement & Control Applications, 3 vol. set, Set. E. M. Eacho et al. (Illus.). (C). 1981. lib. bdg. 195.00 (0-87683-010-6) GP Courseware.

Pneumatic Measurement & Control Applications, 3 vol. set, Vol. 1. E. M. Eacho et al. (Illus.). 400p. (C). 1981. ring bd. 95.00 (0-87683-011-4) GP Courseware.

Pneumatic Measurement & Control Applications, 3 vol. set, Vol. 2. E. M. Eacho et al. (Illus.). 160p. (C). 1981. ring bd. 79.50 (0-87683-013-0) GP Courseware.

Pneumatic Measurement & Control Applications, 3 vol. set, Vol. 3. E. M. Eacho et al. (Illus.). 160p. (C). 1981. student ed., ring bd. 79.50 (0-685-09257-7) GP Courseware.

Pneumatic Power Glossary. Institute for Power System Staff. 80p. 1979. 60.00 (0-7855-7245-7) St Mut.

Pneumatic Steelmaking, Vol. 2. Iron & Steel Society Staff. Ed. by Steward K. Mehlman. LC 88-82120. 171p. 1988. pap. 53.10 (0-608-01268-8, 206201800002) Bks Demand.

Pneumatic Steelmaking: Refractories, Vol. III. M. A. Rigaud & R. A. Landy. 180p. 1996. 75.00 (1-886362-08-4) Iron & Steel.

Pneumatic Steelmaking: Tuyere Design, Vol. 1. N. L. Kotraba. LC 88-82120. 200p. 1988. 70.00 (0-932897-38-X) Iron & Steel.

Pneumatic Systems: Principles & Maintenance. S. R. Majumdar. 282p. 1995. 65.00 (0-07-460231-4) McGraw.

Pneumatic Systems Optimized. Fleischer. 1998. pap. 49.50 (0-07-134530-2) McGraw.

Pneumatics. Questech Staff. (Illus.). 120p. 1997. text 99.95 (1-58100-012-X) Beckley Cardy.

Pneumatics Explained. Leo Rizzo. LC 84-730253. 1984. student ed. 7.00 (0-8064-0038-2, 530) Bergwall.

Pneumocystic Carinii: Index of New Information. Jennifer G. Rescar. 1998. 47.50 (0-7883-1814-4); pap. 47.50 (0-7883-1815-2) ABBE Pubs Assn.

Pneumocystis Carinii. Julian Hopkin. (Illus.). 152p. 1991. 45.00 (0-19-261654-4, 10903) OUP.

Pneumocystis Carinii, Vol. I. Walter T. Hughes, Jr. 144p. 1987. 86.00 (0-8493-4665-7, CRC Reprint) Franklin.

Pneumocystis Carinii, Vol. II. Hughes, Jr. 152p. 1987. 88.00 (0-8493-4666-5, CRC Reprint) Franklin.

Pneumocystis Carinii Pneumonia. 2nd ed. Ed. by Peter D. Walzer. LC 93-11338. (Lung Biology in Health & Disease Ser.: Vol. 69). (Illus.). 744p. 1993. text 255.00 (0-8247-8854-0) Dekker.

*__Pneumological Aspects of Gastroesophageal Reflux.__ L. Allegra & R. Dal Negro. LC 99-24353. 190p. 1999. 89.00 (88-470-0049-1, Pub. by Spr-Verlag) Spr-Verlag.

Pneumonia, Set. Benjamin White. Incl. Biology of the Pneumococcus. LC 78-10579. 818p. 1979. text LC 78-10579. (Commonwealth Fund Publications). (Illus.). 1105p. 1990. 135.00 (0-674-67444-8) HUP.

Pneumonias. Monroe Karetzky et al. LC 92-49615. (Illus.). 328p. 1993. 110.00 (0-387-97945-X) Spr-Verlag.

Pneumonias. Monroe Karetzky et al. xv, 328p. 1993. write for info. (3-540-97945-X) Spr-Verlag.

Pneumonias. Hobart A. Reimann. LC 78-166458. (Illus.). 224p. 1971. 12.50 (0-87527-119-7) Green.

Pneumonias: Clinical Approaches to Infectious Diseases of the Lower Respiratory Tract. Ed. by Matthew E. Levison. LC 83-10473. 592p. reprint ed. pap. 183.60 (0-8357-7864-9, 203628100002) Bks Demand.

Pneumorhythm: Relief from Stress Through Breathing. Oscar Ichazo. (Illus.). 32p. 1979. pap. 20.00 (0-916554-09-0) Arica Inst Pr.

PNF in Practice: An Illustrated Guide. Susan S. Adler et al. LC 93-5234. (Illus.). 240p. 1995. 49.95 (0-387-52649-8) Spr-Verlag.

*__PNF in Practice: An Illustrated Guide.__ 2nd rev. ed. Susan S. Adler et al. (Illus.). xiii, 401p. 2000. pap. text 52.00 (3-540-66395-9) Spr-Verlag.

PNG: A Fact Book on Modern Papua New Guinea. 2nd ed. Jackson Rannells. (Illus.). 224p. 1995. pap. 49.95 (0-19-553679-7) OUP.

PNG: The Definitive Guide. Greg Roelofs. Ed. by Richard Koman. (Illus.). 321p. 1999. reprint ed. pap. 34.95 (1-56592-542-4) OReilly & Assocs.

PNGV Battery Test Manual, Rev. O. Idaho National Engineering & Environmental Laborat. (Electric Vehicle Information Ser.: Vol. 28). (Illus.). 50p. 1997. pap. 85.00 (0-89934-323-6, BT080); lib. bdg. 115.00 (0-89934-324-4, BT980) Bus Tech Bks.

*__PNH & the GPI Linked Proteins.__ Neal S. Young. LC 99-65876. (Illus.). 304p. 2000. 109.95 (0-12-772940-2) Acad Pr.

PNI: The New Mind - Body Healing Program. Elliott S. Dacher. 224p. 1994. pap. 12.95 (1-56924-928-8) Marlowe & Co.

PNI Healing Stories for Children, Vol. I. Carl Brahe. Ed. by Victoria Hall. 84p. (J). (ps-6). 1999. pap. 11.95 (1-893351-05-X) Asclepian Pr.

Pnin. Vladimir Nabokov. Tr. by G. Barabtarlo from ENG. (RUS.). 175p. 1983. 25.00 (0-88233-737-8); pap. 12.50 (0-88233-738-6) Ardis Pubs.

Pnin. Vladimir Nabokov. (International Ser.). 1989. pap. 11.00 (0-679-72341-2) Vin Bks.

Pnin. Vladimir Nabokov. LC 82-1208. 192p. 1982. reprint ed. 16.00 (0-8376-0465-6) Bentley Pubs.

Pniniad: Vladimir Nabokov & Marc Szeftel. Galya Diment. LC 97-10871. (McLellan Book Ser.). (Illus.). 256p. 1997. 35.00 (0-295-97634-9) U of Wash Pr.

PNL-18 Sing & 10 Children Favorites: Piano. 40p. (Orig.). (J). 1995. pap. 8.95 (0-7692-1016-3, AF9553) Wrner Bros.

PNL-11 Crazy for You Bk. II: Piano. (Play Now Library). 41p. (Orig.). 1994. pap. 8.95 (0-89724-326-9, PF0921) Wrner Bros.

PNL-16 Tradition Music/Israel: Piano. 24p. (Orig.). 1995. pap. 7.95 (0-89724-592-X, AF9507) Wrner Bros.

PNL 10 - The Secret Garden Bk. 10: Piano. (Play Now Library). 64p. (Orig.). 1994. pap. 9.95 (0-89724-313-7, PF0920) Wrner Bros.

PNL-13 Songs of the 20's Bk. 13: Piano, Book 13. (Play Now Library). 48p. (Orig.). 1994. pap. 8.95 (0-89724-329-3, PF0924) Wrner Bros.

PNL-12 George & Ira Gershwin: Piano. 40p. (Orig.). 1994. pap. 8.95 (0-89724-327-7, PF0922) Wrner Bros.

PNL 2 Vintage Broadway: Piano. (Play Now Library). 52p. (Orig.). 1994. pap. 8.95 (0-89724-206-8, PF0894) Wrner Bros.

PN's Advanced DOS Guide, SE. 29.95 (1-56686-138-1) Brady Pub.

PN's DOS Guide, SE. 24.95 (1-56686-139-X) Brady Pub.

Po Beyond Yes & No. Edward De Bono. 1990. pap. 30.00 (0-14-013782-3) Intl Ctr Creat Think.

*__Po Chhu-i: Selected Poems.__ Chhu-i Pai & Burton Watson. LC 99-24284. (Translations from the Asian Classics Ser.). 2000. 14.50 (0-231-11839-2) Col U Pr.

Po Follows a Path. (Teletubbies Coloring Activity Book Ser.: Vol. 4). (Illus.). 32p. (J). 1998. pap. write for info. (0-7666-0258-3, Honey Bear Bks) Modern Pub NYC.

Po Man's Child: A Novel. Marci Blackman. LC 99-6198. 240p. 1999. pap. 12.95 (0-916397-59-9, Pub. by Manic D Pr) SPD-Small Pr Dist.

Po Obe Storony Steny. Victor Nekrasov. LC 84-81387. (Povesti i Rasskazy Ser.). (RUS.). 216p. 1985. 12.50 (0-911971-12-2) Effect Pub.

Po Obye Storoni Orgasma. Mikhail Armalinskii, pseud. LC 88-90891. (RUS.). 150p. 1988. pap. 10.00 (0-916201-04-X) M I P Co.

Po-on. Jose F. Sionil. LC 97-39435. 256p. 1998. pap. 12.95 (0-375-75144-0) Modern Lib NY.

Po Pai Mo: The Search for White Buffalo Woman. Robert Boissiere. LC 83-4668. (Illus.). 96p. (Orig.). 1983. pap. 8.95 (0-86534-024-2) Sunstone Pr.

Po, Pb, Ra, Pu, Cur, U, Th, Am, CF, Mo, & Tc Radionuclides in Teeth & Bones. Florence T. Cua. 363p. 1994. 50.00 (0-9645418-2-3) F T Cua.

Po Pravuiu Ruku Sana: The 2nd Book of Poems. Nina Kossman. (RUS., Illus.). 60p. (Orig.). 1996. pap. 10.00 (0-9654454-0-2) Coast.

*__Po Tu Storonu Vospitanita.__ Diana Vinkovetsky. LC 99-35224. (RUS., Illus.). 160p. 1999. pap. 9.00 (1-55779-118-X) Hermitage Pubs.

Po Tu Styoronu Sambationa: Etiudy o Russko-Everiskikh Kul'turnykh, Iasykovykh i Literaturnykh Kontaktakh V V-XVI Vekakh. Andrey Arkhipov. (Monuments of Early Russian Literation Ser.: Vol. 9). (RUS.). 296p. (Orig.). 1995. pap. 20.00 (1-57201-011-8) Berkeley Slavic.

Po' White Trash & Other 1-Act Dramas. Evelyn G. Sutherland. LC 77-70363. (One-Act Plays in Reprint Ser.). 1977. reprint ed. 20.00 (0-8486-2023-2) Roth Pub Inc.

*__Poaceae (Gramineae)__ Ed. by L. I. Kashina et al. (Flora of Siberia Ser.: Vol. 2). (Illus.). 2000. write for info. (1-57808-101-7) Science Pubs.

Poach of Ouch. (Illus.). 28p. (J). 1997. pap. 5.95 (0-9644574-0-7) Shoeless Pub.

Poachers: Stories. Tom Franklin. LC 98-51982. 208p. 1999. 22.00 (0-688-16740-3, Wm Morrow) Morrow Avon.

*__Poachers: Stories.__ Tom Franklin. (Illus.). 208p. 2000. pap. 12.00 (0-688-17771-9) Morrow Avon.

Poacher's Daughter. Mary Nichols. 384p. 1995. 26.00 (1-85797-696-7, Pub. by Orion Pubng Grp) Trafalgar.

Poacher's Payback. Curant Road Elementary & Middle School Students. LC 95-83048, (Illus.). 27p. (J). (gr. k-6). 1995. write for info. (0-9649125-0-3) Durant Rd Elem.

Poacher's Way. John Bailey. (Illus.). 160p. 1996. 34.95 (1-85223-859-3, Pub. by Cro1wood) Trafalgar.

Poaching & the Illegal Trade in Wildlife & Wildlife Parts in Canada. L. J. Gregorich & Canadian Wildlife Federation Staff. LC 92-243495. ix, 117 p. 1992. write for info. (1-55029-052-5) CWFI.

Poaching Rights. Bernard O'Donoghue. 32p. 1987. pap. 11.95 (1-85235-014-8) Dufour.

Poakalani Hawaiian Quilt Cushion Patterns & Design. 2nd ed. Poakalani Serrao & John Serrao. (Illus.). 56p. pap. 5.95 (1-56647-265-2) Mutual Pub HI.

Pobblebonk the Frog Picture Roo. Pauline Reilly. (Picture Roo Bks.). (Illus.). 32p. (Orig.). (J). (gr. 2-7). 1997. pap. 6.95 (0-86417-802-6, Pub. by Kangaroo Pr) Seven Hills Bk.

*__Pobby & Dingan.__ Ben Rice. (Illus.). 80p. 2000. 16.00 (0-375-41127-5) Knopf.

Pobedonostsev: His Life & Thought. Robert F. Byrnes. LC 68-14598. 509p. reprint ed. 157.80 (0-8357-9231-5, 201302200083) Bks Demand.

Poberezny: The Story Begins . . . Paul H. Poberezny et al. LC 96-92890. (Illus.). 350p. 1997. 24.95 (0-9655654-0-8) Red One Pub.

Poberezny: The Story Begins . . . limited ed. Paul H. Poberezny et al. LC 96-92890. (Illus.). 350p. 1997. lthr. 46.95 (0-9655654-1-6) Red One Pub.

Poblacion. Rafael M. Salas. 1981. write for info. (0-08-026099-3, Pergamon Pr); pap. write for info. (0-08-026098-5, Pergamon Pr) Elsevier.

Pobladores Prehispanicos de Acapulco: Proyecto Arqueologico Renacimiento. Martha E. Cabrera. 245p. 1990. pap. 9.00 (968-6487-44-1, IN014) UPLAAP.

Pobre Ana. Blaine Ray. (TPRS First-Year Spanish Novels Ser.). (SPA.). ii, 39p. (gr. 7-12). 1999. pap. 3.95 (0-929724-47-X) Command Performance.

Pobre Raza! Arturo Rosales. LC 98-58049. 304p. 1999. 45.00 (0-292-77094-4); pap. 19.95 (0-292-77095-2) U of Tex Pr.

Pobreza, Desigualdad y Formacion del Capital Humano en America Latina, 1950-2025. Juan L. Londono. (World Bank Latin American & Caribbean Studies).Tr. of Poverty, Inequality, & Human Capital Development in Latin America, 1950-2025. (SPA.). 48p. 1996. pap. 22.00 (0-8213-3692-4, 13692) World Bank.

Pocachicha. 4th ed. Fernando Almena. (Punto Juvenil Ser.). (SPA.). (J). 1988. 10.05 (0-606-05551-7, Pub. by Turtleback) Demco.

Pocahontas. LC 96-215753. (Classics Ser.). (Illus.). 96p. (J). (ps-4). 1995. 7.98 (1-57082-114-3, Pub. by Mouse Works) Time Warner.

Pocahontas. LC 97-163230. (Little Library). (Illus.). 40p. (J). (ps up). 1995. 5.98 (1-57082-115-1, Pub. by Mouse Works) Little.

Pocahontas. (Disney Read-Alongs Ser.). (J). 7.99 incl. audio (1-55723-739-5) W Disney Records.

Pocahontas. Stuart E. Brown, Jr. 34p. 1989. pap. 9.95 (0-685-56616-1) VA Bk.

Pocahontas. Susan Donnell. 416p. 1993. mass mkt. 6.50 (0-425-13620-5) Berkley Pub.

Pocahontas. Jan Gleiter. 32p. (J). (gr. 1-6). 1995. pap. text 5.95 (0-8114-9350-4) Raintree Steck-V.

Pocahontas. Jan Gleiter & Kathleen Thompson. LC 94-24005. (Illus.). 32p. (J). 1995. lib. bdg. 21.40 (0-8114-8450-5) Raintree Steck-V.

Pocahontas. Leslie Gourse. LC 96-1522. (Childhood of Famous Americans Ser.). (Illus.). 176p. (J). (ps-3). 1996. mass mkt. 4.99 (0-689-80808-9) Aladdin.

Pocahontas. Leslie Gourse. LC 96-1522. (Childhood of Famous Americans Ser.). 1996. 10.09 (0-606-10285-X, Pub. by Turtleback) Demco.

Pocahontas. Aurand Harris. (J). 1961. 6.00 (0-87602-177-1) Anchorage.

Pocahontas. Cynthia Holzschuher. (Literature Unit Ser.). (Illus.). 48p. 1995. pap., teacher ed. 7.95 (1-55734-769-7) Tchr Create Mat.

Pocahontas. Margaret Hudson. LC 97-51457. (Lives & Times Ser.). (J). 1998. (1-57572-670-X) Heinemann.

Pocahontas. Gina Ingoglia. (Wonderful World of Disney Ser.). (Illus.). 80p. (J). (gr. 3-7). 1997. pap. 3.25 (0-7868-4216-4, Pub. by Disney Pr) Time Warner.

*__Pocahontas.__ Tim Vicary. (Illus.). 48p. 1999. pap. 5.95 (0-19-422877-0) OUP.

Pocahontas. Ingri Parim D'Aulaire & Edgar Parim D'Aulaire. LC 97-78469. (Illus.). 45p. (J). (gr. k-6). 1998. reprint ed. pap. 11.95 (0-9643803-6-6) Beautiful Feet.

Pocahontas. Grace S. Woodward. LC 68-15687. (Civilization of the American Indian Ser.: No. 93). (Illus.). 238p. 1980. reprint ed. pap. 14.95 (0-8061-1642-0) U of Okla Pr.

Pocahontas: Alias Matoaka, & Her Descendants Through Her Marriage at Jamestown, Virginia, with John Rolfe, Gentleman. W. Robertson. 84p. 1993. reprint ed. pap. 10.00 (0-8328-3385-1); reprint ed. lib. bdg. 20.00 (0-8328-3384-3) Higginson Bk Co.

*__Pocahontas: An American Princess.__ Joyce Milton. (All Aboard Reading Ser.). (Illus.). 48p. (J). (gr. 2-3). 2000. 13.89 (0-448-42298-0, Planet Dexter); pap. 3.99 (0-448-42181-X, Planet Dexter) Peng Put Young Read.

Pocahontas: An Animated Flip Book. Walt Disney's Feature Animation Department Staff. (Illus.). 96p. (J). 1995. pap. 3.95 (0-7868-8061-9, Pub. by Hyperion) Time Warner.

Pocahontas: An Historical Drama. Robert D. Owen. (Notable American Authors Ser.). 1999. reprint ed. lib. bdg. 125.00 (0-7812-4681-4) Rprt Serv.

Pocahontas: An Unlikely Pair. Disney Enterprises, Inc. Staff. (Disney's "Storytime Treasures" Library: Vol. 10). (Illus.). 44p. (J). (gr. 1-6). 1997. 3.49 (1-57973-006-X) Advance Pubs.

Pocahontas: Daughter of a Chief. Carol Greene. LC 88-11978. (Rookie Biographies Ser.). (Illus.). 48p. (J). (gr. k-3). 1988. pap. 4.95 (0-516-44203-1) Childrens.

Pocahontas: Full-Color Sturdy Book. Pat Ronson Stewart. (Little Activity Bks.). (Illus.). 16p. (Orig.). (J). 1995. pap. text 1.00 (0-486-28697-5) Dover.

Pocahontas: Looking for Meeko. Illus. by Isidre Mones. LC 95-83655. (Follow the Tracks Bk.). 16p. (J). (ps-k). 1996. 12.95 (0-7868-3094-8, Pub. by Disney Pr) Little.

Pocahontas: Painting with the Wind: A Book about Colors. Teddy Slater. LC 94-71797. (Illus.). 24p. (J). (ps-k). 1995. 12.95 (0-7868-3041-7, Pub. by Disney Pr); lib. bdg. 13.49 (0-7868-5031-0, Pub. by Disney Pr) Little.

Pocahontas: Powhatan Peacemaker see North American Indians of Achievement

Pocahontas: Princess of the River Tribes. Raphael Bolognese et al. 32p. (J). (ps-3). 1995. pap. 4.95 (0-590-44372-0) Scholastic Inc.

Pocahontas: The Evolution of an American Narrative. Robert S. Tilton. (Cambridge Studies in American Literature & Culture: No. 83). (Illus.). 272p. (C). 1994. pap. text 19.95 (0-521-46959-7) Cambridge U Pr.

Pocahontas: The Life & the Legend. Frances Mossiker. LC 95-43815. (Illus.). 424p. 1996. reprint ed. pap. 15.95 (0-306-80699-1) Da Capo.

Pocahontas: The True Story of an American Hero & Her Faith. Andy Holmes. LC 95-79435. 1995. 6.99 (0-345-40361-4, Moorings) Ballantine Pub Grp.

Pocahontas: The True Story of the Powhatan Princess see Junior World Biographies

Pocahontas: True Princess. Mari Hanes. 1995. pap. Price not set. (0-88070-873-5) Zondervan.

Pocahontas: True Princess. Mari D. Hanes. (Illus.). 151p. 1995. pap. 7.99 (0-88070-856-5, Gold n Honey) Zondervan.

Pocahontas: Who's Making that Sound? (My First Read-Alongs Ser.). (Illus.). (J). 7.99 incl. audio (1-55723-961-4) W Disney Records.

Pocahontas - Powhatan Peacemaker see North American Indians of Achievement

Pocahontas & the Strangers. Clyde R. Bulla. LC 77-139094. (Illus.). 176p. (J). (ps-3). 1987. pap. 3.50 (0-590-43481-0) Scholastic Inc.

Pocahontas & the Strangers. Clyde Robert Bulla. (J). 1971. 9.09 (0-606-03892-2, Pub. by Turtleback) Demco.

Pocahontas Bead Book & Kit. Illus. by Brainwaves Studio Staff. LC 95-67717. 32p. (J). (gr. 3-7). 1995. pap. 12.95 (0-7868-4035-8, Pub. by Disney Pr) Little.

Pocahontas Coloring Book. Brian Doherty. (Illus.). (J). (gr. k-3). 1994. pap. 2.95 (0-486-28040-3) Dover.

P

Pocahontas' Descendants with Corrections & Additions. Stuart E. Brown, Jr. et al. (Illus.). 715p. 1994. 50.00 (*0-317-40516-0*) VA Bk.

Pocahontas Discovers America. Miriam Sagan. 20p. (Orig.). 1993. pap. 9.50 (*0-938566-57-1*) Adastra Pr.

Pocahontas en Espanol. (Spanish Classics Ser.). (SPA., Illus.). 96p. (J). (ps-4). 1995. 7.98 (*1-57082-116-X*, Pub. by Mouse Works) Time Warner.

Pocahontas (1585-1750) Sally Isaacs. LC 98-25164. (J). 1998. 24.22 (*1-57572-745-5*) Heinemann Lib.

*__Pocahontas, 1590-1754.__ Sally Senzell Isaacs. (America in the Time of...Ser.). 48p. 1999. 7.95 (*1-57572-978-4*) Heinemann Lib.

Pocahontas' Forest Friends. (J). 1995. write for info. (*0-7853-1337-0*) Pubns Intl Ltd.

Pocahontas, Girl of Jamestown. Kate Jassem. LC 78-18045. (Illus.). 48p. (J). (gr. 4-6). 1979. pap. 3.50 (*0-89375-142-1*) Troll Communs.

Pocahontas, Girl of Jamestown. Kate Jassem. (J). 1979. 8.70 (*0-606-01708-9*, Pub. by Turtleback) Demco.

Pocahontas Illustrated Classic. Gina Ingoglia. LC 94-71795. (Illustrated Classics Ser.). (Illus.). 96p. (J). 1995. lib. bdg. 14.89 (*0-7868-5023-X*, Pub. by Disney Pr) Little.

Pocahontas (In the Words of Her Contemporaries) Stuart E. Brown, Jr. (Illus.). 36p. 1998. pap. 9.95 (*0-8063-4605-1*) Clearfield Co.

Pocahontas Junior Novelization. Gina Ingoglia. LC 94-71796. (Junior Novelization Ser.). (Illus.). 80p. (J). (gr. 2-6). 1995. pap. 3.50 (*0-7868-4036-6*, Pub. by Disney Pr) Little.

Pocahontas Junior Novelization. Tr. by Gina Ingoglia. LC 94-69681. (Junior Novelization Ser.). (SPA., Illus.). 80p. (J). (gr. 2-6). 1995. pap. 3.50 (*0-7868-4046-3*, Pub. by Disney Pr) Time Warner.

Pocahontas Nature Guide: Woods & Wildlife. Gina Ingoglia. LC 95-70030. (Illus.). 64p. (J). (gr. 1-4). 1995. pap. 5.95 (*0-7868-4055-2*, Pub. by Disney Pr) Little.

Pocahontas Piano/Vocal/Guitar. 72p. 1995. per. 16.95 (*0-7935-4507-2*) H Leonard.

Pocahontas Play-Along. 1995. 22.78 incl. audio (*1-55723-744-1*) W Disney Records.

Pocahontas, Powhatan Peacemaker. Anne Holler. (North American Indians of Achievement Ser.). (J). 1993. 14.15 (*0-606-08025-2*) Turtleback.

Pocahontas, Powhatan Princess. Diane Shaughnessy. LC 96-30024. (Famous Native Americans Ser.). (J). (gr. k-4). 1997. lib. bdg. 15.93 (*0-8239-5106-5*, PowerKids) Rosen Group.

Pocahontas, Princess of the River Tribes. Elaine Raphael & Don Bolognese. LC 92-41990. 32p. (J). (gr. 1-3). 1993. 12.95 (*0-590-44371-2*) Scholastic Inc.

Pocahontas's People: The Powhatan Indians of Virginia Through Four Centuries. Helen C. Rountree. LC 90-33598. (Civilization of the American Indian Ser.: Vol. 196). (Illus.). 416p. 1996. pap. 14.95 (*0-8061-2849-6*) U of Okla Pr.

Poccamandas: Adapted from My Mother's Adaptation of a Storyteller's Adaptation of a Southern Folktale. Papa Joe. (Step into a Story Book Ser.). 12p. 1996. pap. 3.50 (*1-889238-09-0*) Papa Joes.

Pochacco & Friends: Silly Time Races. Scholastic, Inc. Staff. (Sanrio Ser.). (Illus.). 48p. (J). (gr. 2-5). 1998. pap. text 6.99 (*0-590-55825-0*, Cartwheel) Scholastic Inc.

Pocho. Jose A. Villarreal. LC 71-11196. 192p. 1970. reprint ed. pap. 10.95 (*0-385-06118-8*, Anchor NY) Doubleday.

Pocion Secreta de Mi Abuelito see Homeplay: La Alegria de Aprender Entre Ninos y Adultos, Series I

Pocitajme Hravo (Arithmetics by Playing) E. Dinerova. (SLO.). 80p. 1997. pap. write for info. (*80-08-02587-5*, Pub. by Slov Pegagog Naklad) IBD Ltd.

Pocket: Rereading America. 3rd ed. Diana Hacker. 2000. pap. text 27.45 (*0-312-13801-6*) St Martin.

Pocket Acapulco. 3rd ed. Fodor's Staff. 1998. pap. 9.00 (*0-679-00050-X*) Fodors Travel.

Pocket Ad Writer: For Real Estate Professionals. unabridged ed. Ernie Blood. 241p. 1986. reprint ed. pap. 29.95 (*1-893572-00-5*) Carmel Pubg.

Pocket Addresses: Lily Pad. Photos by Anne Geddes. (Illus.). 1996. 9.95 (*1-55912-240-4*) CEDCO Pub.

Pocket Almanac. Godin, Seth, Productions Staff. (Cader Flip Ser.). 1997. pap. text 3.95 (*0-8362-2548-1*, Cader Bks) Andrews & McMeel.

Pocket America, Vol. 2. Henretta. 1997. pap. text 30.40 (*0-312-19003-4*) St Martin.

Pocket Amsterdam. 1988. 5.95 (*0-671-84846-1*) S&S Trade.

Pocket Amsterdam. Fodor Staff. 1999. pap. 9.00 (*0-679-00243-X*) Fodors Travel.

Pocket Aquinas. Ed. by Vernon Bourke. 372p. 1991. per. 5.99 (*0-671-73991-3*, WSP) PB.

Pocket Architecture: A Walking Tour Guide to the Architecture of Downtown Minneapolis & St. Paul. 2nd rev. ed. Bernard Jacob & Carol Morphew. (Illus.). 140p. 1987. pap. 7.95 (*0-945056-00-1*) AIA MN.

Pocket Aristotle. Aristotle. Ed. by Justin E. Kaplan. 400p. 1983. mass mkt. 5.99 (*0-671-46377-2*, WSP) PB.

Pocket Assistant's Guide: For Real Estate Professionals. unabridged ed. Ernie Blood. 191p. 1997. reprint ed. pap. 29.95 (*1-893572-05-6*) Carmel Pubg.

Pocket Athletic Director. Dick King. 96p. 1999. pap. 9.95 (*1-58151-037-3*) BookPartners.

*__Pocket Atlas of Acupuncture.__ Hans-Ulrich Hecker & Angelika Steveling. (Illus.). 274p. 2000. pap. 29.00 (*0-86577-938-4*) Thieme Med Pubs.

Pocket Atlas of Anatomy. 3rd ed. Victor Pauchet & S. Dupret. (Illus.). 1976. pap. 14.95 (*0-19-263131-4*) OUP.

Pocket Atlas of Cardiac & Thoracic MRI. Jeffrey J. Brown & Charles B. Higgins. (Illus.). 72p. 1989. pap. text 16.95 (*0-88167-488-5*, 1961) Lppncott W & W.

Pocket Atlas of Cranial Magnetic Resonance Imaging. Victor M. Haughton & David L. Daniels. (Illus.). 64p. 1986. pap. text 16.95 (*0-88167-171-1*) Lppncott W & W.

Pocket Atlas of Cross-Sectional Anatomy: Computer Tomography & Magnetic Resonance Imaging, Head, Neck, Spine & Joints, Vol. 1. Emil Reif et al. Tr. by Clifford Bergman. LC 93-43883. 1993. pap. 28.50 (*0-86577-510-9*) Thieme Med Pubs.

Pocket Atlas of Cross-Sectional Anatomy: Computer Tomography & Magnetic Resonance Imaging Thorax, Abdomen & Pelvis, Vol. 2. Torsten B. Moeller & Emil Reif. LC 93-43883. 246p. 1994. pap. 28.50 (*0-86577-511-7*) Thieme Med Pubs.

Pocket Atlas of Cross-Sectional Anatomy Vol. 1: Head, Neck, Spine & Joints. 2nd ed. Moeller. 1998. pap. 28.50 (*0-86577-813-2*) Thieme Med Pubs.

Pocket Atlas of Cytology & Microscopic Anatomy. Wolfgang Kuhnel. 1981. 21.00 (*0-8151-5208-6*) Mosby Inc.

Pocket Atlas of Cytology, Histology & Microscopic Anatomy. 3rd rev. ed. Wolfgang Kuhnel. Tr. & Intro. by H. M. Beier. (Flexibook Ser.). (Illus.). 410p. 1992. pap. text 29.90 (*0-86577-388-2*) Thieme Med Pubs.

Pocket Atlas of Dermatology. 2nd rev. ed. G. K. Steigleder & Howard I. Maibach. (Flexibook Ser.). (Illus.). 304p. 1993. pap. text 28.50 (*0-86577-491-9*) Thieme Med Pubs.

*__Pocket Atlas of Emergency Medicine.__ Kevin Knoop et al. (Illus.). 334p. 1999. pap. 49.95 (*0-07-135807-2*) McGraw.

Pocket Atlas of Head & Neck MRI Anatomy. Robert B. Lufkin & William N. Hanafee. (Illus.). 83p. 1989. pap. text 16.95 (*0-88167-498-2*) Lppncott W & W.

Pocket Atlas of Hematology. Theml. pap. 29.90 (*0-86577-210-X*) Thieme Med Pubs.

Pocket Atlas of Human Anatomy. 3rd ed. Heinz Feneis & Worfgang Dauber. (Illus.). 480p. 1994. text 29.50 (*0-86577-479-X*) Thieme Med Pubs.

*__Pocket Atlas of Human Anatomy: Based on the International Nomenclature.__ 4th ed. H. Feneis & W. Dauber. (Illus.). 480p. 2000. pap. 32.00 (*0-86577-928-7*) Thieme Med Pubs.

Pocket Atlas of MRI Body Anatomy. 2nd ed. Thomas H. Bequist. LC 95-17885. (Illus.). 104p. 1995. pap. text 16.95 (*0-7817-0336-0*) Lppncott W & W.

Pocket Atlas of MRI Musculoskeletal Anatomy. Thomas H. Berquist. LC 95-16479. (Illus.). 96p. 1995. pap. text 16.95 (*0-7817-0337-9*) Lppncott W & W.

Pocket Atlas of MRI of the Pelvis. Zella Campos et al. LC 92-49417. (Illus.). 128p. 1993. pap. text 16.95 (*0-88167-987-9*) Lppncott W & W.

Pocket Atlas of Normal CT Anatomy. James B. Weinstein et al. (Illus.). 88p. 1985. pap. text 16.95 (*0-88167-070-7*) Lppncott W & W.

Pocket Atlas of Normal CT Anatomy of the Head & Brain. Anton N. Hasso & Miyuki Shakudo. 96p. 1990. pap. text 16.95 (*0-88167-663-2*) Lppncott W & W.

Pocket Atlas of Normal Ultrasound Anatomy. Matthew D. Rifkin & Larry Waldroup. (Illus.). 72p. 1985. pap. text 16.95 (*0-88167-163-0*) Lppncott W & W.

Pocket Atlas of Obstetric Ultrasound. John C. Hobbins et al. LC 95-45314. (Illus.). 89p. 1996. pap. text 16.95 (*0-397-51623-1*) Lppncott W & W.

Pocket Atlas of Ophthalmology. 2nd ed. Fritz Hollwich. Tr. by Frederick C. Blodi. (Flexibook Ser.). (Illus.). 192p. 1981. pap. 29.90 (*0-86577-244-4*) Thieme Med Pubs.

Pocket Atlas of Oral Diseases. G. Laskaris. (Illus.). 444p. 1997. pap. text 22.00 (*0-86577-635-0*) Thieme Med Pubs.

Pocket Atlas of Pediatric Emergency Procedures. Fred M. Henretig & Christopher King. 450p. pap. text 34.95 (*0-683-30666-9*) Lppncott W & W.

Pocket Atlas of Pediatric Ultrasound. Carol M. Rumack et al. 120p. 1990. pap. text 16.95 (*0-88167-620-9*) Lppncott W & W.

Pocket Atlas of Pharmacology. Heinz Luellmann et al. LC 92-48531. (Flexibook Ser.).Tr. of Tashenatlas der Pharmakologie. (ENG & GER., Illus.). 374p. 1993. pap. text 29.90 (*0-86577-455-2*) Thieme Med Pubs.

Pocket Atlas of Radiographic Anatomy. Torsten B. Moeller et al. Ed. by Emil Reif. Tr. by Michael Robertson. LC 92-49310. 356p. 1993. pap. 28.50 (*0-86577-459-5*) Thieme Med Pubs.

*__Pocket Atlas of Radiographic Anatomy.__ 2nd ed. Emil Reif & Toreten B. Moeller. LC 99-40802. (Illus.). 391p. 1999. pap. 34.00 (*0-86577-874-4*) Thieme Med Pubs.

Pocket Atlas of Radiographic Positioning. Emil Reif & Therald B. Moeller. LC 97-110619. (Illus.). 290p. 1996. pap. text 19.90 (*0-86577-640-7*) Thieme Med Pubs.

Pocket Atlas of Rheumatology. Dieter Wessinghage. Tr. by Gottfried Stiasny. (Flexibook Ser.). (Illus.). 256p. 1986. pap. 29.90 (*0-86577-221-5*) Thieme Med Pubs.

*__Pocket Atlas of Sectional Anatomy Vol. 2: Computed Tomography & Magnetic Resonance Imaging.__ 2nd ed. Torsten B. Moeller & Emil Reif. (Illus.). 264p. 2000. pap. 32.00 (*0-86577-872-8*) Thieme Med Pubs.

Pocket Atlas of Spinal MRI. Leo F. Czervionke & Victor M. Haughton. 90p. 1989. pap. text 16.95 (*0-88167-546-6*) Lppncott W & W.

*__Pocket Atlas of the Moving Body: For All Students of Human Biology, Medicine, Sports & Physical Therapy.__ Mel Cash. (Illus.). 68p. 2000. spiral bd. 15.95 (*0-09-186512-3*, Pub. by Ebury Pr) Trafalgar.

*__Pocket Atlas of the World.__ (Illus.). 304p. 1999. pap. 9.95 (*0-7641-1130-2*) Barron.

Pocket Austria & Switzerland. Ed. by Pocket Books Staff. 1988. mass mkt. 5.95 (*0-671-88280-5*) PB.

Pocket Babies. Katherine M. Marko. (First Bks.). (Illus.). 64p. (J). (gr. 4-6). 1995. lib. bdg. 22.00 (*0-531-20211-9*) Watts.

Pocket Battleship: The Admiral Graf Spee. Siegfried Breyer. LC 89-84177. (Illus.). 48p. 1989. pap. 9.95 (*0-88740-183-X*) Schiffer.

*__Pocket Battleships of the Deutschland Class.__ Gerhard Koop & Klaus-Peter Schmolke. Tr. by Geoffrey Brooks. (Illus.). 224p. 2000. 45.00 (*1-55750-426-1*) Naval Inst Pr.

Pocket Bhagavad Gita. Winthrop Sargeant. 199p. (C). 1994. pap. text 9.95 (*0-7914-2030-2*) State U NY Pr.

Pocket Bi Story-David, 1. Luis Gonzalez Palma. 1994. pap. text 5.90 (*0-7814-1528-4*) Chariot Victor.

Pocket Bi Story-Noahs AR. Luis Gonzalez Palma. 1994. pap. text 5.90 (*0-7814-1526-8*) Chariot Victor.

Pocket Bi Stry-Daniel. Luis Gonzalez Palma. 1994. pap. text 5.90 (*0-7814-1529-2*) Chariot Victor.

Pocket Bi Stry-Good Neig. Luis Gonzalez Palma. 1994. pap. text 5.90 (*0-7814-1535-7*) Chariot Victor.

Pocket Bible see Biblias de Bolsillo

Pocket Bible see Biblia de Bolsillo

Pocket Bible. 1997. 35.99 (*1-55819-720-6*) Broadman.

*__Pocket Bible.__ 1999. 21.95 (*5-550-00740-1*); 21.95 (*5-550-00741-X*); 25.95 (*5-550-00743-6*); 25.95 (*5-550-00744-4*); 23.95 (*5-550-00745-2*); 23.95 (*5-550-00746-0*); 27.95 (*5-550-00747-9*); 27.95 (*5-550-00748-7*) Nairi.

Pocket Bible. 1988. 32.99 (*0-529-06059-0*) World Publng.

*__Pocket Bible.__ 1998. 26.99 (*0-529-10859-3*) World Publng.

*__Pocket Bible.__ Broadman & Holman Publishing Staff. (SPA.). 1999. 31.99 (*1-55819-997-7*); 31.99 (*1-55819-998-5*); 31.99 (*1-55819-999-3*) Broadman.

*__Pocket Bible.__ Pckt Staff. 1998. write for info. (*1-55819-723-0*) Broadman.

Pocket Bible Commentary. William Neil. 1997. 10.98 (*0-7858-0813-2*) Bk Sales Inc.

Pocket Bible Guide. 1981. pap. 0.95 (*0-89942-056-7*, 56/00) Catholic Bk Pub.

Pocket Bible Handbook see Manual Biblico de Bolsillo

Pocket Bible-Jesus Heals. Luis Gonzalez Palma. (Illus.). 12p. (J). (ps-k). 1995. pap. text 4.90 (*0-7814-0222-0*) Chariot Victor.

Pocket Bible Ready Reference for Personal Workers. 31st ed. Ernest A. Clevenger, Jr. (Parchment Ready Reference Ser.). 24p. (Orig.). 1994. pap. 2.00 (*0-88428-011-X*) Parchment Pr.

Pocket Billiard Guidebook for Pool Players, Tournament Directors & Spectators. Ed. by James R. Lawson. 192p. (Orig.). 1994. pap. 39.95 (*0-945071-55-8*) Lawco.

Pocket Billiards: Fundamentals of Technique & Play. Bogdan Pejcic & Rolf Meyer. LC 93-8557. (Illus.). 80p. 1993. pap. 9.95 (*0-8069-0458-5*) Sterling.

Pocket Billiards Tips & Trick Shots. Steve Mizerak & Michael E. Panozzo. (Illus.). 176p. 1982. pap. 12.95 (*0-8092-5779-3*, 577930, Contemporary Bks) NTC Contemp Pub Co.

Pocket Book: A Child's Activity Book. Sas Colby & Lorraine Shirkus. (Illus.). 10p. (J). (ps). 1988. 39.95 (*0-922656-00-2*) Design Matters Inc.

Pocket Book Infectious Disease Therapy, 1997. 8th ed. John G. Bartlett. 379p. 1997. pap. 14.95 (*0-683-30357-0*) Lppncott W & W.

Pocket Book of Catholic Devotions. Lawrence Lovasik. (Pocket Book Ser.). (Illus.). 96p. 1997. pap. 3.95 (*0-89942-034-6*, 34/04) Catholic Bk Pub.

Pocket Book of Catholic Novenas. Lawrence G. Lovasik. (Pocket Book Ser.). (Illus.). 96p. 1997. pap. 3.95 (*0-89942-037-0*, 36/04) Catholic Bk Pub.

Pocket Book of Catholic Prayers see Libro de Bolsillo de Oraciones Catolicas

Pocket Book of Catholic Prayers. Lawrence G. Lovasik. (Pocket Book Ser.). (Illus.). 96p. 1997. pap. 3.95 (*0-89942-032-X*, 32/04) Catholic Bk Pub.

Pocket Book of Catholic Prayers & Devotions. Victor Hoagland. 1999. pap. text 125.00 (*0-88271-621-2*) Regina Pr.

Pocket Book of Cats. Joan Palmer. (Illus.). 137p. 1998. text 17.00 (*0-7881-5384-6*) DIANE Pub.

Pocket Book of Critical Care Pharmacotherapy. Ed. by Bart Chernow & Lisa D. Sparks. LC 94-37822. (Illus.). 430p. 1995. pap. text 19.00 (*0-683-01535-4*) Lppncott W & W.

Pocket Book of Electrical Engineering Formulas. Ronald J. Tallarida & Richard C. Dorf. LC 93-9634. 224p. 1993. per. 26.95 (*0-8493-4473-5*, TK153) CRC Pr.

Pocket Book of Emergency & Disability Scores. Jonathan Handler. 40p. (C). 1999. pap. 6.00 (*1-883205-46-8*) Intl Med Pub.

Pocket Book of Favorite Catholic Prayers. Victor Hoagland. 1999. pap. text 125.00 (*0-88271-622-0*) Regina Pr.

Pocket Book of Foreplay: The Art of Sexual Excitement Explained. Richard Craze. (Illus.). 96p. 1999. pap. 10.95 (*0-89793-252-8*) Hunter Hse.

Pocket Book of Golf Rules. Steve Newell. 1999. pap. text 7.99 (*1-84100-144-9*) Quadrillion Media.

Pocket Book of Healing. Ed. by David Maclennan. (C). 1990. pap. 35.00 (*0-85305-220-4*, Pub. by Arthur James) St Mut.

Pocket Book of Integrals & Mathematical Formulas. Ed. by Ronald J. Tallarida. (Illus.). 224p. 1989. pap. 19.95 (*0-8493-0161-0*, QA, CRC Reprint) Franklin.

Pocket Book of Integrals & Mathematical Formulas. 3rd ed. Ronald J. Tallarida. LC 99-31157. 304p. (C). 1999. per. 19.95 (*0-8493-0263-3*) CRC Pr.

Pocket Book of Manners for Young People. Elizabeth Hammond. LC 90-90325. (Illus.). 96p. (Orig.). (J). (gr. 4-8). 1990. pap. 5.95 (*0-9627061-0-8*) Trotwood Press.

Pocket Book of O. Henry Short Stories. Harry Hansen. 256p. 1989. mass mkt. 5.50 (*0-671-68861-8*, WSP) PB.

Pocket Book of Ogden Nash. Ogden Nash. 1976. 19.95 (*0-8488-1439-8*) Amereon Ltd.

Pocket Book of Ogden Nash. Ogden Nash. 197p. 1990. mass mkt. 5.50 (*0-671-72789-3*) PB.

Pocket Book of Ogden Nash. Ogden Nash. 200p. 1991. reprint ed. lib. bdg. 18.95 (*0-89966-867-4*) Buccaneer Bks.

Pocket Book of Pediatric Antimicrobial Therapy, 1995. 11th ed. John D. Nelson. LC 88-26186. (Illus.). 106p. 1995. pap. 13.95 (*0-683-06406-1*) Lppncott W & W.

Pocket Book of Pediatric Antimicrobial Therapy, 1996-1997. 12th ed. John D. Nelson. 108p. 1997. pap. 14.95 (*0-683-18053-3*) Lppncott W & W.

Pocket Book of Puzzles. Nancy Hite. 200p. (J). (ps up). 1979. 8.99 (*0-916456-47-1*, GA98) Good Apple.

Pocket Book of Romantic Love Songs & Short Stories. James P. Herrmann. (Illus.). 80p. (C). 1991. reprint ed. 9.95 (*0-9635777-0-0*) Pocket Bk Romant.

*__Pocket Book of Scottish Quotations.__ David Ross. 256p. 1999. pap. (*1-84158-011-2*, Pub. by Birlinn Ltd) Dufour.

*__Pocket Book of Sexual Fantasy: The Art of Sexual Excitement Explained.__ Richard Craze. 2000. pap. 10.95 (*0-89793-294-3*) Hunter Hse.

Pocket Book of Short Sermon Starters: A Help for All Ministers: Young & Experienced. Morris A. Curry, Sr. 92p. (Orig.). 1995. pap. text 5.00 (*1-882581-09-1*) Campbell Rd Pr.

Pocket Book of Short Stories. Ed. by Edmund M. Speare. 336p. (Orig.). (gr. 9 up). 1989. pap. 5.50 (*0-671-68955-X*, WSP) PB.

Pocket Book of Social & Community Paediatrics. 2nd ed. Tinker. pap. text 19.95 (*0-340-51764-6*, Pub. by E A) Routldge.

Pocket Book of Statistical Tables. Robert E. Odeh. LC 76-28106. (Statistics, Textbooks & Monographs: Vol. 22). 178p. reprint ed. pap. 55.20 (*0-608-08970-2*, 206960500005) Bks Demand.

*__Pocket Book of Technical Writing for Engineers & Scientists.__ Leo Finkelstein. LC 99-44806. 336p. 1999. pap. 19.38 (*0-07-237080-7*) McGraw.

*__"Pocket Brain" on ETT (Exercise Treadmill Testing)__ (Illus.). iv, 60p. 1999. pap. text 10.00 (*0-9663389-8-7*) KG-EKG.

Pocket Britain. 1988. 5.95 (*0-671-84843-7*) S&S Trade.

Pocket Budapest. 2nd ed. Fodors Staff. 1999. pap. 9.00 (*0-679-00052-6*) Fodors Travel.

Pocket Bunny. Illus. by Pam Adams. (Pocket Pals Ser.). (J). 1995. bds. 2.99 (*0-85953-907-5*) Childs Play.

*__Pocket Bushtucker.__ Peter Latz. (Illus.). 240p. 1999. pap. 22.95 (*1-86465-023-0*, Pub. by IAD Pr) Intl Spec Bk.

Pocket Business Dictionary, Polish/English-English/Polish. (ENG & POL.). Date not set. pap. 59.95 (*0-7859-9579-X*) Fr & Eur.

Pocket California Goldenwest. Ed. by Pocket Books Staff. 1988. mass mkt. 5.95 (*0-671-84894-1*) PB.

Pocket Call Conversation Guide: For Real Estate Professionals. unabridged ed. Ernie Blood. 130p. 1989. reprint ed. pap. 29.95 (*1-893572-01-3*) Carmel Pubg.

Pocket Canons: Books of the Bible. Grove Press Staff. 1999. 24.95 (*0-8021-3609-5*, Grove) Grove-Atltic.

Pocket Canons: Corinthians. Grove Press Staff. LC 99-45007. 64p. 1999. pap. 2.95 (*0-8021-3620-6*, Grove) Grove-Atltic.

Pocket Canons: Ecclesiastes. Grove Press Staff. LC 99-45020. 64p. 1999. pap. 2.95 (*0-8021-3614-1*) Grove-Atltic.

Pocket Canons: Exodus. Grove Press Staff. LC 99-45021. 128p. 1999. pap. 2.95 (*0-8021-3611-7*) Grove-Atltic.

*__Pocket Canons: Genesis.__ Grove Press Staff. LC 99-45008. 144p. 1999. pap. 2.95 (*0-8021-3610-9*) Grove-Atltic.

Pocket Canons: Job. Grove Press Staff. LC 99-482759. 96p. 1999. pap. 2.95 (*0-8021-3612-5*) Grove-Atltic.

Pocket Canons: John. Grove Press Staff. LC 99-45018. 80p. 1999. pap. 2.95 (*0-8021-3619-2*) Grove-Atltic.

Pocket Canons: Luke. Grove Press Staff. LC 99-45005. 96p. 1999. pap. 2.95 (*0-8021-3618-4*) Grove-Atltic.

Pocket Canons: Mark. Grove Press Staff. LC 99-45004. 64p. 1999. pap. 2.95 (*0-8021-3617-6*) Grove-Atltic.

Pocket Canons: Matthew. Grove Press Staff. LC 99-45022. 96p. 1999. pap. 2.95 (*0-8021-3616-8*) Grove-Atltic.

Pocket Canons: Proverbs. Grove Press Staff. LC 99-45019. 112p. 1999. pap. 2.95 (*0-8021-3613-3*) Grove-Atltic.

Pocket Canons: Revelation. Grove Press Staff. LC 99-45017. 64p. 1999. pap. 2.95 (*0-8021-3621-4*) Grove-Atltic.

Pocket Canons: Song of Solomon. Intro. by A. S. Byatt. (Pocket Canons Ser.). 48p. 1999. pap. 2.50 (*0-8021-3615-X*) Grove-Atltic.

Pocket Card with Segregation Table. International Maritime Organization Staff. 1992. text 45.00 (*0-89771-873-9*, Pub. by Intl Maritime Org) St Mut.

Pocket Cathedrals: Pre-Raphaelite Book Illustration. Susan P. Casteras. LC 91-65082. (Illus.). 112p. 1991. pap. 18.95 (*0-930606-65-5*) Yale Ctr Brit Art.

Pocket Catholic Catechism. John J. Hardon. 336p. 1989. pap. 10.95 (*0-385-24293-X*) Doubleday.

Pocket Catholic Dictionary. John A. Hardon. LC 85-5790. 528p. 1985. pap. 10.95 (*0-385-23238-1*, Image Bks) Doubleday.

Pocket Chameleon. Pam Adams. (J). 1996. bds. 2.99 (*0-85953-918-0*) Childs Play.

Pocket Change. Dawn L. Watkins. Ed. by Mark Sidwell. (Illus.). 40p. (J). (ps). 1992. pap. 5.49 (*0-89084-645-6*, 062893) Bob Jones Univ.

*__Pocket Change: The Towpath Anthology 2000.__ Ed. by Ellen Compton et al. 48p. 2000. 5.00 (*1-893959-12-0*) Red Moon Pr.

Pocket Chart Book: Build Literacy with More Than 35 Fun, Interactive, Cross-Curricular Charts. Valier Schiffer-Danoff. 1996. pap. text 12.95 (*0-590-59927-5*) Scholastic Inc.

P

Pocket Chart Math Activities, Vol. 4036. Mary Kurth. Ed. by Joel Kupperstein. (Illus.). 96p. 1996. pap. text, teacher ed. 9.98 (*1-57471-161-X*, 4036) Creat Teach Pr.

Pocket Charts for Emergent Readers: 30 Fun, Interactive Cross-Curricular Charts That Build Literacy. Valerie Schifferdanoff. 112p. 1998. 12.95 (*0-590-31470-X*) Scholastic Inc.

***Pocket Charts for Math.** Valerie Schifferdanoff. (Illus.). 80p. (YA). 1999. pap. 11.95 (*0-590-98336-9*) Scholastic Inc.

***Pocket Chinese Dictionary.** (CHI & ENG.). 2000. 13.95 (*1-58573-057-2*, Insight Guides) Langenscheidt.

***Pocket Chinese-Russian-English Dictionary: Arranged by the Rosenberg Graphical System.** John S. Barlow. (CHI, RUS & ENG.). 406p. 2000. pap. text 25.00 (*0-8248-2294-3*) UH Pr.

Pocket Church History for Orthodox Christians. Aidan Keller. 72p. (Orig.). 1994. pap. 5.00 (*0-923864-08-3*) St Hilarion Pr.

***Pocket City Atlas.** Ed. by Rand McNally Staff. (Illus.). 64p. 1999. pap. 2.95 (*0-528-84135-1*) Rand McNally.

Pocket Classic Series. R. W. Schambach. 1995. pap. 7.00 incl. VHS (*1-888361-09-3*) Power Publns.

Pocket Clinical & Drug Guide. 3rd ed. Paul Debello. 672p. (Orig.). (C). 1992. pap. text 25.00 (*0-9627160-2-2*) Tortoise NV.

Pocket Clinical & Drug Guide. 4th ed. Paul Debello. 672p. (Orig.). (C). pap. text 25.00 (*0-9627160-3-0*) Tortoise NV.

Pocket Coach to Parenthood: Good Sports Make Winning Parents. Asa Odback. LC 97-71097. 192p. 1997. pap. 13.95 (*0-9657760-8-5*) Light Beams.

Pocket Companion: A Rule of Life. Ferdinand Valentine. 192p. 1994. pap. 5.00 (*0-87343-056-5*) Magi Bks.

Pocket Companion for Cancer Nursing. Ed. by Ruth McCorkle & Marcia Grant. LC 94-6847. (Illus.). 537p. 1994. pap. text 38.95 (*0-7216-5410-X*, W B Saunders Co) Harcrt Hlth Sci Grp.

Pocket Companion for Critical Care Nursing. Sheila Melander & Linda Bucher. Ed. by Robin Carter. LC 98-43361. 475p. 1999. pap. text 23.95 (*0-7216-6919-0*, W B Saunders Co) Harcrt Hlth Sci Grp.

Pocket Companion for Home Health Nurses. Springhouse Publishing Company Staff. Ed. by June Norris. LC 96-17975. (Illus.). 512p. (Orig.). 1996. 26.95 (*0-87434-853-6*) Springhouse Corp.

Pocket Companion for Medical-Surgical Nursing. 2nd ed. Donna D. Ignatavicius & Kathy A. Hausman. (Illus.). 775p. 1994. pap. text 22.00 (*0-7216-4867-3*, W B Saunders Co) Harcrt Hlth Sci Grp.

Pocket Companion for Medical-Surgical Nursing: Foundations for Clinical Practice. 2nd ed. Monahan. 1997. pap. 17.95 (*0-7216-7334-1*, W B Saunders Co) Harcrt Hlth Sci Grp.

Pocket Companion for Pharmacology: A Nursing Process Approach. 2nd ed. Evelyn R. Hayes & Joyce L. Kee. LC 96-43504. 1996. pap. text 20.95 (*0-7216-5957-8*, W B Saunders Co) Harcrt Hlth Sci Grp.

Pocket Companion for Physical Examination & Health Assessment. 2nd ed. Carolyn Jarvis. LC 95-24471. (Illus.). 329p. 1996. pap. text 24.00 (*0-7216-5899-7*, W B Saunders Co) Harcrt Hlth Sci Grp.

Pocket Companion for the Textbook of Physical Diagnosis. 2nd ed. Mark H. Swartz. Ed. by William Schmitt. LC 97-23179. (Illus.). 288p. 1997. pap. text 22.95 (*0-7216-7517-4*, W B Saunders Co) Harcrt Hlth Sci Grp.

Pocket Companion of Critical Care: Immediate Concerns. Robert R. Kirby et al. (Illus.). 760p. 1990. text 44.95 (*0-397-51030-6*) Lppncott W & W.

Pocket Companion of Inspiration Thought. Compiled by James H. Fedor. 102p. 1986. pap. 3.95 (*0-929896-01-7*) MindArt Pub.

***Pocket Companion to Cecil Textbook of Medicine.** 21st ed. Lee Goldman & J. Claude Bennett. (Illus.). 765p. 2001. write for info. (*0-7216-8972-8*, W B Saunders Co) Harcrt Hlth Sci Grp.

Pocket Companion to Equine Medicine & Surgery. Colahan et al. LC 98-35658. (Illus.). 800p. (C). (gr. 13). 1999. pap. text 39.95 (*0-8151-1741-8*, 28581) Mosby Inc.

***Pocket Companion to Home Health Nursing.** Karen E. Monks. LC 99-44468. 475p. 2000. pap. text. write for info. (*0-7216-8558-7*, W B Saunders Co) Harcrt Hlth Sci Grp.

Pocket Companion to Neurology in Clinical Practice. 3rd ed. Walter G. Bradley et al. LC 96-28924. 758p. 2000. pap. text 25.00 (*0-7506-9787-3*) Buttrwrth-Heinemann.

***Pocket Companion to Neurology in Clinical Practice.** 3rd ed. Walter G. Bradley et al. (Illus.). 768p. 2000. pap. 45.00 (*0-7506-7264-1*) Buttrwrth-Heinemann.

Pocket Companion to Obstetrics: Normal & Problem Pregnancies. J. Gabbe et al. LC 98-41893. (Illus.). 400p. (C). 1998. pap. text. write for info. (*0-443-07982-X*) Church.

Pocket Companion To Opera: Including More Than 150 Works. John Allison. 1999. pap. 9.95 (*1-85732-253-3*) Mitchell Beazley.

Pocket Companion to Pathologic Basis of Disease. 5th ed. Stanley L. Robbins et al. (Illus.). 630p. 1995. pap. text 26.95 (*0-7216-5742-7*, W B Saunders Co) Harcrt Hlth Sci Grp.

Pocket Companion to Physical Exam & Health Assessment. 3rd ed. Jarvis. 1999. pap. text Price not set. (*0-7216-8434-3*, W B Saunders Co) Harcrt Hlth Sci Grp.

Pocket Companion to Principles & Practice of Medical Intensive Care. James A. Kruse et al. (Illus.). 608p. 1995. pap. text 44.00 (*0-7216-5633-1*, W B Saunders Co) Harcrt Hlth Sci Grp.

***Pocket Companion to Shakespeare's Plays: The Newly Revised Reference to All 38 Plays.** J C Trewin. 1999. 9.95 (*1-85732-340-8*) Mitchell Beazley.

Pocket Companion to Textbook of Critical Care. 3rd ed. William C. Shoemaker et al. 608p. 1996. pap. text 43.00 (*0-7216-5833-4*, W B Saunders Co) Harcrt Hlth Sci Grp.

Pocket Companion to Textbook of Medical Physiology. 10th ed. Arthur C. Guyton & John E. Hall. (Illus.). 605p. Date not set. text. write for info. (*0-7216-8729-6*, W B Saunders Co) Harcrt Hlth Sci Grp.

Pocket Companion to Textbook of Physiology. Arthur C. Guyton & John E. Hall. Ed. by William Schmitt. LC 97-7746. (Illus.). 640p. 1997. pap. text 19.95 (*0-7216-7118-7*, W B Saunders Co) Harcrt Hlth Sci Grp.

Pocket Companion to Textbook of Small Animal Surgery. 2nd ed. Douglas H. Slatter. LC 94-13110. 864p. 1995. pap. text 52.50 (*0-7216-5544-0*, W B Saunders Co) Harcrt Hlth Sci Grp.

Pocket Companion to Textbook of Veterinary Internal Medicine. 2nd ed. Stephen J. Ettinger. (Illus.). 900p. 1995. pap. text 43.00 (*0-7216-5766-4*, W B Saunders Co) Harcrt Hlth Sci Grp.

Pocket Computer Primer. Hank Librach. LC 82-80270. 96p. (Orig.). 1982. pap. 9.95 (*0-942412-00-1*); audio 8.95 (*0-686-87024-7*) Micro Text Pubns.

Pocket Computer Programming Made Easy. Jim Cole. (Illus.). 128p. (Orig.). 1982. pap. 8.95 (*0-86668-009-8*) ARCsoft.

Pocket Computer Programs for Astronomers. Fred Klein. 100p. (Orig.). 1983. pap. 12.95 (*0-913051-01-2*) F Klein Pubns.

Pocket Concise Chinese-English Dictionary. Commercial Press Staff. (CHI & ENG.). 620p. 1978. pap. 14.95 (*0-8288-5262-6*, M9182) Fr & Eur.

Pocket Concordance to the New Testament. rev. ed. Charles J. Hazelton. 640p. 1992. lib. bdg. 7.95 (*0-9634753-1-2*) NTPC.

***Pocket Condition of Education.** Jeanne H. Nathanson. 28p. 1999. pap. 2.00 (*0-16-050214-4*) USGPO.

Pocket Consultant for Small Business. Chandler H. Everett. LC 96-75843. 128p. 1996. pap. 6.75 (*1-886966-04-4*) In Print.

Pocket Consultant in Gastroenterology. S. P. Travis et al. (Pocket Consultant Ser.). (Illus.). 432p. 1991. pap. 36.95 (*0-632-01098-3*) Blackwell Sci.

Pocket Course in Creative Thinking. (Illus.). 80p. 1993. write for info. (*0-945100-35-3*) Parlay Intl.

Pocket Course in Goal Setting. (Illus.). 80p. 1993. write for info. (*0-945100-33-7*) Parlay Intl.

Pocket Course in Innovation. (Illus.). 80p. 1993. write for info. (*0-945100-31-0*) Parlay Intl.

Pocket Course in Leadership. (Illus.). 80p. 1993. write for info. (*0-945100-32-9*) Parlay Intl.

Pocket Course in Teamwork. (Illus.). 80p. 1993. write for info. (*0-945100-34-5*) Parlay Intl.

Pocket Crossword Puzzle Dictionary. Langenscheidt Staff. (Insight Guides). 1998. pap. 11.95 (*0-88729-215-1*) Langenscheidt.

Pocket Cruisers & Tabloid Yachts, Vol. 1. rev. ed. Jay R. Benford. LC 99-234170. (Illus.). 96p. 1996. pap. 17.95 (*1-888671-04-1*) Tiller.

Pocket Dictionary. large type ed. Vianna F. DeMello. 392p. (YA). (gr. 10 up). 1985. reprint ed. 102.89 (*0-317-01921-X*, 4-21900-00) Am Printing Hse.

***Pocket Dictionary.** 4th ed. Ed. by Websters New World Staff. 384p. 2000. pap. 4.95 (*0-7645-6147-2*) IDG Bks.

Pocket Dictionary: Dutch - Indonesian. Thomas G. Oey. (Illus.). 1994. pap. write for info. (*0-945971-94-X*) Periplus.

Pocket Dictionary: English-Indonesian - Indonesian-English. Thomas G. Oey. (IND & ENG.). 72p. (Orig.). 1992. pap. 3.95 (*0-945971-66-4*) Periplus.

Pocket Dictionary-Flag Blue, Blue. Resource Staff. 326p. 1994. pap. text 7.95 (*0-15-900257-5*) Harcourt Legal.

Pocket Dictionary-Hunter Green, Green. Resource Staff. 326p. 1994. pap. text 7.95 (*0-15-900258-3*) Harcourt Legal.

Pocket Dictionary-Maroon, Burgundy. Resource Staff. 326p. 1994. pap. text 7.95 (*0-15-900256-7*) Harcourt Legal.

Pocket Dictionary Michaelis: English-Portuguese/ Portuguese-English. Michaelis. 1999. pap. 8.95 (*85-06-01486-7*) Midwest European Pubns.

Pocket Dictionary of Astrological Terms. Gayle Bachicha. LC 94-11441. 64p. (Orig.). 1994. pap. 6.95 (*1-885084-11-0*) Tickerwick.

Pocket Dictionary of Automotive Technology. Hans-Dieter Junge. (ENG & GER.). 232p. 1987. pap. 28.00 (*3-433-02815-X*, Wiley-VCH) Wiley.

Pocket Dictionary of Banjo Chords. Neil Lambard. 1966. pap. 2.95 (*0-934286-19-1*) Kenyon.

Pocket Dictionary of Baritone Ukulele Chords. Charles Allen. 1971. pap. 2.95 (*0-934286-21-3*) Kenyon.

Pocket Dictionary of Botany: English-German, German-English. Theodor Cole. (ENG & GER.). 156p. 1994. 59.95 (*0-7859-9975-2*) Fr & Eur.

Pocket Dictionary of Cantonese. 3rd ed. Toy T. Cowles. 448p. 1986. pap. 29.50 (*962-209-122-9*, Pub. by HK Univ Pr) Coronet Bks.

Pocket Dictionary of Chinese English & Pekingese Syllabary. Chauncey Goodrich. 342p. 1982. reprint ed. pap. 33.00 (*962-209-069-9*, Pub. by HK Univ Pr) Coronet Bks.

Pocket Dictionary of Data Communication. (ENG, FRE & GER.). 286p. 1982. pap. 95.00 (*0-8288-0266-1*, M 14376) Fr & Eur.

Pocket Dictionary of Fire Prevention: Brandschutz Taschenwoerterbuch. Klaus P. Hecker. (ENG & GER.). 252p. 1982. 45.00 (*0-8288-0569-5*, M15390) Fr & Eur.

Pocket Dictionary of Guitar Chords. Howard Ries. 1965. pap. 2.95 (*0-934286-22-1*) Kenyon.

Pocket Dictionary of Horseman's Terms in English, German, French & Spanish. Hanns Muller. (FRE.). 1971. 9.95 (*0-685-00343-4*) Transatl Arts.

Pocket Dictionary of Laboratory Equipment: English-German. Hans-Dieter Junge. 201p. 1987. pap. 45.00 (*0-89573-596-2*, Wiley-VCH) Wiley.

Pocket Dictionary of Mandolin Chords. Charles Allen. 1971. pap. 2.95 (*0-934286-23-X*) Kenyon.

Pocket Dictionary of Music Terms. Albert De Vito. 48p. 1986. pap. 4.25 (*0-7935-5533-7*, 50395370) H Leonard.

Pocket Dictionary of Philosophy: Diccionario de Filosofia de Bolsillo, 2 vols. Jose Ferrater Mora. (SPA.). 785p. 1983. pap. 27.95 (*0-8288-2282-4*, S39820) Fr & Eur.

Pocket Dictionary of Saints. John J. Delaney. LC 82-45479. 528p. 1983. pap. 10.95 (*0-385-18274-0*, Image Bks) Doubleday.

Pocket Dictionary of Signing. Rod R. Butterworth. 1992. 12.05 (*0-606-02844-7*, Pub. by Turtleback) Demco.

Pocket Dictionary of Signing. rev. ed. Rod R. Butterworth & Mickey Flodin. LC 91-30462. (Illus.). 224p. (YA). 1992. pap. 6.95 (*0-399-51743-X*, Perigee Bks) Berkley Pub.

Pocket Dictionary of Technology & Science: German-English, English-German. 6th ed. Karl Breuer. (ENG & GER.). 405p. 1971. 75.00 (*0-7859-7117-3*) Fr & Eur.

Pocket Dictionary of Tenor Banjo Chords. Charles Allen. 1971. pap. 2.95 (*0-934286-20-5*) Kenyon.

Pocket Dictionary of the German & English Languages. K. Wichmann. (ENG & GER.). 1976. 15.00 (*0-7100-2290-5*, Routledge Thoemms) Routledge.

Pocket Dictionary of the Spoken Arabic of Cairo: English-Arabic. Virginia Stevens & Maurice Salib. 226p. 1987. pap. 13.00 (*977-424-157-6*, Pub. by Am Univ Cairo Pr) Col U Pr.

Pocket Dictionary of Theological Terms. Stanley J. Grenz et al. LC 99-18214. 122p. 1999. pap. 6.99 (*0-8308-1449-3*, 1449) InterVarsity.

Pocket Dictionary of Verb Conjugation. Antoine El-Dahdah. (ARA.). 243p. 1997. pap. 12.00 (*0-86685-588-2*) Intl Bk Ctr.

Pocket Dictionary of Zoology: English-German, German-English. Theodor Cole. (ENG & GER.). 200p. 1995. 69.95 (*0-7859-9974-4*) Fr & Eur.

Pocket Dictionary/Nursing Assistant & Health Care. Hampton. (Home Care Aide Ser.). 1995. 12.95 (*0-8273-6475-X*) Delmar.

Pocket Diesel & Electric Guide: A Quick Reference Handbook to Locomotives in Service. LC 74-80803. (Illus.). 1974. pap. 4.00 (*0-913556-12-2*); spiral bd. 5.00 (*0-913556-11-4*) Spec Pr NJ.

Pocket Dietitian. J. H. Tilden. 109p. 1993. reprint ed. spiral bd. 12.50 (*0-7873-0877-3*) Hlth Research.

Pocket Dietitian (1918) J. H. Tilden. 112p. 1996. reprint ed. pap. 10.95 (*1-56459-871-3*) Kessinger Pub.

Pocket Digest of OSHA Construction Standards. William Finch, III. 96p. 1998. pap. 5.95 (*0-9662979-1-1*) Occup Safe Consult.

Pocket Digest of OSHA Standards. abr. ed. Ed. by William H. Finch, 3rd. 116p. 1998. pap. 5.95 (*0-9662979-0-3*) Occup Safe Consult.

Pocket Directory of the California Legislative, 1988: Photo Edition. 80p. 1988. pap. 11.95 (*0-917982-35-5*) Capitol Enquiry.

Pocket Directory of the California Legislature, 1986. Compiled by Capitol Enquiry Staff. 64p. (Orig.). 1986. pap. 5.95 (*0-917982-32-0*) Capitol Enquiry.

Pocket Directory of the California Legislature, 1987. 56p. 1987. pap. 6.95 (*0-917872-33-9*) Capitol Enquiry.

Pocket Directory of the California Legislature, 1988. 64p. 1988. pap. 6.95 (*0-917982-34-7*) Capitol Enquiry.

Pocket Directory of the California Legislature, 1989. 80p. 1989. pap. 10.95 (*0-917982-36-3*) Capitol Enquiry.

Pocket Directory of the California Legislature, 1990. (Illus.). 1990. pap. 11.95 (*0-917982-38-X*) Capitol Enquiry.

Pocket Directory of the California Legislature, 1991. (Illus.). 1991. pap. 11.95 (*0-917982-40-1*) Capitol Enquiry.

Pocket Directory of the California Legislature, 1992. (Illus.). 1992. pap. 11.95 (*0-917982-41-X*) Capitol Enquiry.

Pocket Directory of the California Legislature, 1993. (Illus.). 88p. (Orig.). 1993. pap. 11.95 (*0-917982-45-2*) Capitol Enquiry.

Pocket Directory of the California Legislature, 1994. (Illus.). (Orig.). 1994. pap. 11.95 (*0-917982-47-9*) Capitol Enquiry.

Pocket Directory of the California Legislature, 1995. annuals (Illus.). 96p. (Orig.). (C). 1995. pap. text 11.95 (*0-917982-51-7*) Capitol Enquiry.

Pocket Directory of the California Legislature, 1997. 24th rev. ed. (Illus.). 104p. 1997. pap. 11.95 (*0-917982-58-4*, D7) Capitol Enquiry.

Pocket Directory of the California Legislature, 1998. (Illus.). 120p. 1998. pap. 11.95 (*0-917982-63-0*) Capitol Enquiry.

Pocket Doctor: A Passport to Healthy Travel. 3rd ed. Stephen Bezruchka. LC 98-52801. 96p. 1999. pap. 6.95 (*0-89886-614-6*) Mountaineers.

Pocket Doctor: Your Ticket to Good Health While Traveling. 2nd ed. Stephen Bezruchka. LC 92-19995. (Illus.). 96p. 1992. pap. 4.95 (*0-89886-345-7*) Mountaineers.

Pocket Doctor: 500 Medical Tips You Need to Stay Healthy & Calm Your Fears. Michael A. LaCombe. LC 96-7960. 374p. (Orig.). 1996. pap. 5.95 (*0-8362-2166-4*) Andrews & McMeel.

Pocket Doctor 1999. Michael S. Sherman & Edward S. Schulman. 176p. 1999. pap. 12.95 (*0-9672263-0-9*) Ed Commns NY.

***Pocket Doctor 2000-2001.** Michael S. Sherman & Edward S. Schulman. 176p. 2000. pap. 13.95 (*0-9672263-1-7*, Pub. by Ed Commns NY) Login Brothers Bk Co.

Pocket Dolphin. Michael Twinn & Pam Adams. (Pocket Pals Ser.). (Illus.). (J). 1997. bds. 2.99 (*0-85953-981-4*) Childs Play.

Pocket Drawing Book: On to the Basics. R. R. Dvorak. (Illus.). 162p. (Orig.). 1987. reprint ed. pap. 9.95 (*0-945625-00-6*) Inkwell Pr.

Pocket Drawing Book & the Pocket Drawing Pad. 2nd ed. R. R. Dvorak. (Illus.). 160p. 1993. reprint ed. pap. 12.95 (*0-945625-02-2*) Inkwell Pr.

Pocket Drug Guide. Constantine J. Gean et al. 257p. 1989. pap. text 25.00 (*0-683-03440-5*) Lppncott W & W.

Pocket Drug Guide. 3rd ed. Frederick H. Meyers & Constantine J. Gean. LC 98-13760. 265p. 1998. pap. 24.95 (*0-683-30597-2*) Lppncott W & W.

Pocket Earwig. Pam Adams. (J). 1996. bds. 2.99 (*0-85953-916-4*) Childs Play.

Pocket Economist. Rupert Pennant-Rea & William Emmott. LC 83-15054. (Illus.). 194p. 1984. text 31.95 (*0-521-26070-1*) Cambridge U Pr.

Pocket Edition Jackson's Hallmarks of England, Scotland & Ireland. Ian Pickford. 172p. 1991. 25.00 (*1-85149-128-7*) Antique Collect.

Pocket Edition Jackson's Hallmarks of England, Scotland & Ireland. Ed. by Ian Pickford. (Illus.). 172p. 1993. 14.50 (*1-85149-169-4*) Antique Collect.

Pocket Encyclopedia of American Wine, East of the Rockies. William I. Kaufman. 144p. 1986. pap. 8.95 (*0-932664-41-5*) Wine Appreciation.

Pocket Encyclopedia of California Wine & Other Western States. William I. Kaufman. 336p. 1985. pap. 5.95 (*0-932664-40-7*) Wine Appreciation.

Pocket Encyclopedia of California Wine & Other Western States. 11th ed. William I. Kaufman. 448p. 1998. pap. 12.95 (*0-932664-42-3*, 641) Wine Appreciation.

Pocket Encyclopedia of Dogs. Ivan Swedrup. 1981. 8.95 (*0-02-615610-5*) Macmillan.

***Pocket Encyclopedia of Mind, Body, Spirit & Earth.** Joanna Crosse. (Illus.). 160p. (YA). (gr. 4 up). 1999. pap. 8.95 (*1-902618-10-6*, Pub. by Element Childrns) Penguin Putnam.

Pocket English-Chinese Dictionary. Commercial Press Staff. (CHI & ENG.). 451p. 1980. 9.95 (*0-8288-1600-X*, M9580) Fr & Eur.

Pocket English-Chinese (Pinyin) Dictionary. 1991. 19.95 (*0-8288-2482-7*) Fr & Eur.

Pocket Enneagram: Understanding the 9 Types of people. Helen Palmer. LC 95-14044. (Illus.). 96p. 1995. pap. 9.00 (*0-06-251327-3*, Pub. by Harper SF) HarpC.

Pocket Essentials of Clinical Medicine. 2nd ed. Anne Ballinger & Stephen Patchett. LC 99-23407. (Illus.). 600p. 1998. pap. write for info. (*0-7020-2289-6*) W B Saunders.

Pocket Essentials of Clinical Surgery. Ed. by S. Walker & C. Holcombe. (Illus.). 530p. 1997. write for info. (*0-7020-2064-8*, W B Saunders Co) Harcrt Hlth Sci Grp.

Pocket Essentials of Pathology. N. Woolfe & A. C. Wotherspoon. (Illus.). 510p. 2002. pap. text. write for info. (*0-7020-2394-9*) W B Saunders.

Pocket Evangelism Kit. James G. McCarthy. 1996. pap. 2.99 (*1-884833-05-5*) Lumen Prodns.

Pocket Examiner in Obstetrics & Gynaecology. 2nd ed. Peter Bowen-Simpkins & David Pugh. 260p. 1993. pap. text 19.95 (*0-443-03929-1*) Church.

Pocket Examiner in Pathology. 2nd ed. P. N. Cowen & F. G. Smiddy. LC 95-33681. 148p. 1996. pap. text 22.00 (*0-443-05418-5*) Church.

Pocket Examiner in Regional & Clinical Anatomy see Problem Solving for Tutorials in Anatomy

Pocket Examiner in Surgery. 2nd ed. Tom Treasure et al. LC 96-26055. 1999. pap. text 29.95 (*0-443-04894-0*, Pub. by C Lvngstone UK) HarBrace.

Pocket Examiner Paediatrics. Lissauer. 1985. pap. text 22.00 (*0-443-03815-5*, W B Saunders Co) Harcrt Hlth Sci Grp.

Pocket Fat Counter. Annette B. Natow & Jo-Ann Heslin. 1996. pap. 2.99 (*0-671-53260-X*, PB Trade Paper) PB.

Pocket Fat Counter. 2nd ed. Annette Natow. 1998. per. 2.99 (*0-671-00450-6*, Pocket Books) PB.

Pocket Fisherman's Catch. Dorling Kindersley Staff. 1995. pap. write for info. (*0-7894-0195-9*) HM.

Pocket Florida. 1988. 5.95 (*0-671-84873-9*) S&S Trade.

Pocket Fly Fishing. Charles Jardine. LC 96-13243. 128p. 1996. pap. 18.95 (*0-7894-1098-2*) DK Pub Inc.

Pocket Flyers Paper Airplane Book. Ken Blackburn & Jeff Lammers. LC 98-36689. (Illus.). 160p. 1998. pap. 7.95 (*0-7611-1362-2*) Workman Pub.

Pocket Food & Exercise Diary. 3rd rev. ed. Allan Borushek. (Illus.). 96p. 1996. pap. 3.95 (*0-9587991-3-X*) A Borushek.

Pocket for Corduroy. Don Freeman. LC 77-16123. (Corduroy Ser.). (Illus.). 32p. (J). (gr. k-1). 1978. 14.99 (*0-670-56172-X*, Viking Child) Peng Put Young Read.

Pocket for Corduroy. Don Freeman. LC 79-92744. (Corduroy Ser.). (Illus.). (J). (ps-3). 1980. pap. 5.99 (*0-14-050352-8*, PuffinBks) Peng Put Young Read.

Pocket for Corduroy. Don Freeman. (Corduroy Ser.). (Illus.). (J). (ps-3). 1993. audio 8.99 (*0-14-095124-5*, PuffinBks) Peng Put Young Read.

Pocket for Corduroy. Don Freeman. (Corduroy Ser.). (Illus.). (J). (gr. k-1). 1980. 10.19 (*0-606-01785-2*, Pub. by Turtleback) Demco.

Pocket for Corduroy. unabridged ed. Don Freeman. (Corduroy Ser.). (Illus.). (J). (gr. k-1). 1982. 24.95 incl. audio (*0-941078-17-5*); pap. 15.95 incl. audio (*0-941078-15-9*) Live Oak Media.

Pocket for Corduroy, 4 cass., Set. unabridged ed. Don Freeman. (Corduroy Ser.). (Illus.). (J). (gr. k-1). 1982. pap., student ed. 33.95 incl. audio (*0-941078-16-7*) Live Oak Media.

Pocket Fox. Pam Adams. (J). 1996. bds. 2.99 (*0-85953-912-1*) Childs Play.

P

Pocket France. 1988. 5.95 (*0-671-84875-5*) S&S Trade.

Pocket Frog. Illus. by Pam Adams. (Pocket Pals Ser.). (J). 1995. bds. 2.99 (*0-85953-908-3*) Childs Play.

Pocket Full of . . . Parables. Helen Haidle & Elizabeth Haidle. (Pocket Full Ser.). 25p. (J). 1995. bds. 5.99 (*0-88070-796-8*, Gold n Honey) Zondervan.

Pocket Full of . . . Prayer. Helen Haidle & Elizabeth Haidle. (Pocket Full Ser.). 25p. (J). 1995. bds. 5.99 (*0-88070-795-X*, Gold n Honey) Zondervan.

Pocket Full of . . . Psalms. Helen Haidle & Elizabeth Haidle. LC 96-115139. 25p. (J). 1995. bds. 5.99 (*0-88070-794-1*, Gold n Honey) Zondervan.

Pocket Full of Birthday Memories. Theresa M. Dean & Rhonda Lucadamo. (Illus.). 24p. (J). 1997. spiral bd. 19.95 (*1-57102-204-X*, Ideals Child) Hambleton-Hill.

Pocket Full of Christmas Memories. Theresa M. Dean. (Illus.). 20p. (J). 1993. pap. 19.95 (*1-881511-01-4*) Pockets Pr.

Pocket Full of Christmas Memories. Theresa M. Dean et al. (Illus.). 20p. (J). 1995. reprint ed. spiral bd. 19.95 (*1-57102-202-3*, Ideals Child) Hambleton-Hill.

Pocket Full of Kryptonite: With Notes & Tablature. 96p. 1993. otabind 19.95 (*0-7935-2432-6*, 00694885) H Leonard.

Pocket Full of Memories Journal. Theresa M. Dean. (Illus.). 24p. (J). (gr. 4-7). 1994. pap. 9.95 (*1-881511-03-0*) Pockets Pr.

Pocket Full of Miracles. Don Black. 1991. pap. 8.95 (*1-57734-649-1*) Covenant Comms.

Pocket Full of Pennies. Rick Amato. LC 94-68469. 1994. pap. 8.99 (*0-8407-3430-1*) Nelson.

Pocket Full of Posies. Provo Craft Designers Staff. (Illus.). 24p. 1998. 7.99 (*1-58050-060-9*, 40-6178) Provo Craft.

Pocket Full of Praises. Helen Haidle & Elizabeth Haidle. (Pocket Full Ser.). 25p. (J). 1994. bds. 5.99 (*0-88070-712-7*, Gold n Honey) Zondervan.

Pocket Full of Promises. Helen Haidle & Elizabeth Haidle. (Pocket Full Ser.). 25p. (J). 1994. bds. 5.99 (*0-88070-713-5*, Gold n Honey) Zondervan.

Pocket Full of Proverbs. Helen Haidle & Elizabeth Haidle. (Pocket Full Ser.). 25p. (J). 1994. bds. 5.99 (*0-88070-714-3*, Gold n Honey) Zondervan.

Pocket Full of Pye: A Miss Marple Mystery. Agatha Christie. 192p. 1991. mass mkt. 5.99 (*0-425-13028-2*) Berkley Pub.

***Pocket Full of Pythons, Vol. 2.** John Cleese. (Illus.). 64p. 2000. pap. 9.99 (*0-413-74160-5*) Methn.

***Pocket Full of Rye.** Agatha Christie. 2000. mass mkt. 5.99 (*0-451-19986-3*, Sig) NAL.

Pocket Full of School Memories. Theresa Dean & Rhonda Lucadamo. (Illus.). 26p. (J). (ps-8). 1992. 18.95 (*1-881511-00-6*) Pockets Pr.

Pocket Full of School Memories. Theresa M. Dean et al. (Illus.). 26p. (J). 1995. reprint ed. spiral bd. 19.95 (*1-57102-200-7*, Ideals Child) Hambleton-Hill.

Pocket Full of Seeds. Marilyn Sachs. LC 93-36243. (Illus.). 144p. (J). (gr. 5-9). 1994. pap. 4.99 (*0-14-036593-1*, PuffinBks) Peng Put Young Read.

Pocket Full of Seeds. Marilyn Sachs. 1995. 19.00 (*0-8446-6796-X*) Peter Smith.

Pocket Full of Seeds. Marilyn Sachs. 1994. 9.09 (*0-606-05978-4*, Pub. by Turtleback) Demco.

Pocket Full of Sports Memories. Illus. & Created by Theresa M. Dean. 20p. 1994. pap. 19.95 (*1-881511-02-2*) Pockets Pr.

Pocket Full of Sports Memories. Theresa M. Dean et al. (Illus.). 20p. (J). 1995. reprint ed. spiral bd. 13.95 (*1-57102-201-5*, Ideals Child) Hambleton-Hill.

Pocket Full of Wry. Sally Lutyens. Ed. by Jane Weinberger. LC 94-61887. (Illus.). 84p. (Orig.). 1995. pap. 6.00 (*1-883650-14-3*) Windswept Hse.

Pocket Fund. 5th ed. Halliday. LC 96-233488. 1996. pap. text 11.00 (*0-471-09675-X*) Wiley.

Pocket Garden Herbs. Lesley Bremness. LC 96-30981. 96p. 1997. pap. 9.95 (*0-7894-1466-X*) DK Pub Inc.

Pocket Garden Herbs. Storey Publishing Staff. 1997. 9.95 (*0-676-57028-3*) Random.

***Pocket Gardens: Big Ideas for Small Spaces.** James Grayson Trulove. LC 99-43601. (Illus.). 208p. 2000. 30.00 (*0-688-16830-2*, Hearst) Hearst Commns.

Pocket Gastronomical Dictionary: France. Ed. by Elisabeth Consigny et al. 225p. 1999. pap. 12.95 (*0-9666899-1-7*, Pub. by Mariposa Pr NM) Consort Bk Sales.

***Pocket Gatronomical Dictionary.** Laurie Blum. 2001. pap. 12.95 (*0-9666899-3-3*) Mariposa Pr NM.

Pocket German. rev. ed. Langenscheidt Editorial Staff. (Pocket Dictionaries Ser.). 1999. vinyl bd. 12.95 (*0-88729-121-X*) Langenscheidt.

Pocket Germany. 1988. 5.95 (*0-671-84876-3*) S&S Trade.

Pocket Gillie: Fly Fishing Essentials. Scott Richmond. 224p. 1992. pap. 14.95 (*0-9633067-0-7*) Four Rivers Pr.

Pocket Girdles: And Other Confessions of a Northwest Farmgirl. Marianne Love. Ed. by Noelle Sullivan. LC 94-76285. (Illus.). 213p. (Orig.). 1994. pap. 9.95 (*1-56044-293-X*) Falcon Pub Inc.

Pocket Glossary of Pneumatic Conveying Terms No. 805: CEMA 805. 14p. 1992. pap. 5.00 (*1-891171-16-X*) Conveyor Equip Mfrs.

Pocket Golf Etiquette. 128p. 1996. pap. 16.95 (*0-7894-1099-0*) DK Pub Inc.

Pocket Good Sex Guide. David Devlin. (Illus.). 96p. 1999. 10.95 (*0-7867-0616-3*) Carroll & Graf.

Pocket Gopher & Other Poems from the Gopher State. Garry De Young. (Illus.). 31p. pap. 7.50 (*0-936128-00-3*) De Young Pr.

Pocket Gophers (Genus Thomomys) of Utah. Stephen D. Durrant. (Museum Ser.: Vol. 1, No. 1). 82p. 1946. pap. 4.25 (*0-686-80277-2*) U KS Nat Hist Mus.

Pocket Gourmet Instant Menu Translator: France, Italy, Germany, Spain. Foulsham Editors. 222p. (Orig.). 1995. pap. 6.95 (*0-572-01164-4*, Pub. by Foulsham UK) Assoc Pubs Grp.

***Pocket Guide.** Janet Davies. 160p. 1999. pap. (*0-7083-1516-X*, Pub. by Univ Wales Pr) Paul & Co Pubs.

***Pocket Guide: The History of Wales.** J. Graham Jones. (Illus.). 210p. 1999. pap. 9.95 (*0-7083-1491-0*, Pub. by Univ Wales Pr) Paul & Co Pubs.

Pocket Guide: WordStar. Anthony Bove & Cheryl Rhodes. (Micro Computer Ser.). 1983. pap. 7.25 (*0-201-07754-X*) Addison-Wesley.

Pocket Guide: 45-70 Springfield: Changes & Modifications by Serial Number, Models & Specifications. 1994. pap. 6.95 (*1-882391-04-7*) N Cape Pubns.

***Pocket Guide Athens.** 4th ed. (Illus.). 2000. pap. 12.95 (*0-88729-405-7*, Insight Guides) Langenscheidt.

***Pocket Guide Brisbane.** (Illus.). 2000. pap. 12.95 (*0-88729-366-2*, Insight Guides) Langenscheidt.

Pocket Guide-Cigar Aficionado. Marvin R. Shanken. (Illus.). 48p. 1997. 5.95 (*1-881659-45-3*, Wine Spectator) M Shanken Comm.

Pocket Guide for Asthma Management & Prevention: A Pocket Guide for Physicians & Nurses. (Illus.). 28p. 1996. reprint ed. pap. text 15.00 (*0-7881-3543-0*) DIANE Pub.

Pocket Guide for Chemistry. 3rd ed. Mary L. Kotz. (C). 1995. pap. text 12.50 (*0-03-017562-3*) Harcourt Coll Pubs.

Pocket Guide for Chiropractic Skeletal Radiography. Rhonda J. Boone. (Illus.). 320p. (C). 1999. pap. 34.95 (*0-8385-8130-7*) McGraw.

Pocket Guide for Documentation: EMT-B Skills. Ron Milewski & Rick Lang. LC 98-38471. 1998. 13.00 (*0-7637-0879-8*) Jones & Bartlett.

Pocket Guide for Electrophysiology. John H. Hummel et al. Ed. by Robin Carter. LC 99-23883. (Illus.). 175p. 1999. pap. text. write for info. (*0-7216-7369-4*, W B Saunders Co) Harcrt Hlth Sci Grp.

Pocket Guide for HVAC&R - IP. Ed. by Mildred Geshwiler. (Illus.). 219p. 1997. text 24.00 (*1-883413-48-6*) Am Heat Ref & Air Eng.

Pocket Guide for HVAC&R - SI. Ed. by Mildred Geshwiler. (Illus.). 219p. 1997. text 24.00 (*1-883413-49-4*) Am Heat Ref & Air Eng.

Pocket Guide for Maternal & Child Health Nursing. Adele Pillitteri. 816p. 1995. pap. text 19.95 (*0-397-55114-2*) Lppncott W & W.

Pocket Guide for Medical-Surgical Nursing. Carol Neel & Mark Wallerstein. (Illus.). 448p. (C). 1985. pap. text 27.95 (*0-89303-772-9*, D7729-9) Appleton & Lange.

Pocket Guide for the Church Choir Member. Kenneth W. Osbeck. 48p. 1969. pap. 2.50 (*0-8254-3408-4*) Kregel.

Pocket Guide for the Home Care Aide. Barbara S. Gingerich & Deborah A. Ondeck. LC 98-26061. 350p. (gr. 6). 1998. pap. 29.00 (*0-8342-1161-0*, 11610) Aspen Pub.

Pocket Guide for the Textbook of Pharmacotherapy for Child & Adolescent Psychiatric Disorders. David Rosenberg et al. LC 97-33193. 192p. 1997. pap. 24.95 (*0-87630-871-X*) Brunner-Mazel.

***Pocket Guide French Riviera.** 4th ed. Insight Guides Staff. (Illus.). 2000. pap. 12.95 (*0-88729-500-2*, Insight Guides) Langenscheidt.

Pocket Guide General Chemistry. 5th ed. Whitten. (C). 1995. pap. text 9.50 (*0-03-018043-0*) Harcourt.

Pocket Guide Geo-Metrics: Dimensioning & Tolerating the Metric Version. 3rd ed. Lowell Foster. 36p. (C). 1995. ring bd. 34.95 (*0-201-63476-7*) Addison-Wesley.

***Pocket Guide Ireland.** 4th ed. (Illus.). 2000. pap. 12.95 (*0-88729-406-5*, Insight Guides) Langenscheidt.

***Pocket Guide London.** 5th ed. (Illus.). 2000. pap. 12.95 (*0-88729-421-9*, Insight Guides) Langenscheidt.

***Pocket Guide Melbourne.** Insight Guides Staff. (Illus.). 2000. pap. 12.95 (*0-88729-118-X*, Insight Guides) Langenscheidt.

***Pocket Guide Paris.** 5th ed. (Illus.). 2000. pap. 12.95 (*0-88729-422-7*, Insight Guides) Langenscheidt.

***Pocket Guide Sri Lanka.** 3rd ed. (Illus.). 2000. pap. 12.95 (*0-88729-414-6*, Insight Guides) Langenscheidt.

***Pocket Guide Sydney.** 4th ed. (Illus.). 2000. pap. 12.95 (*0-88729-450-2*, Insight Guides) Langenscheidt.

Pocket Guide Thesaurus. Arthur H. Bell. LC 92-9427. (Barron's Pocket Guides Ser.). 1992. vinyl bd. 7.95 (*0-8120-4845-8*) Barron.

***Pocket Guide to Acne.** Amrit Darvay & Anthony Chu. LC 00-22607. (Illus.). 56p. 2000. pap. 29.95 (*0-632-05437-9*) Blackwell Sci.

Pocket Guide to Acupressure Points for Women. Cathryn Bauer. LC 97-11570. (Crossing Press Pocket Ser.). (Illus.). 102p. (Orig.). 1997. pap. 6.95 (*0-89594-879-6*) Crossing Pr.

Pocket Guide to All the Tea in China. rev. ed. Kit Chow & Ione Kramer. 175p. 1998. pap. 6.95 (*0-8351-2629-3*) China Bks.

Pocket Guide to Animal Tracks. Ron Cordes et al. (Illus.). 28p. 1995. spiral bd. 12.95 (*1-886127-03-4*) Greycliff Pub.

Pocket Guide to Aromatherapy. Kathi Keville. (Crossing Press Pocket Ser.). (Illus.). 112p. (Orig.). 1996. pap. 6.95 (*0-89594-815-X*) Crossing Pr.

Pocket Guide to Astrology. Alan Oken. (Crossing Press Pocket Ser.). (Illus.). 128p. 1996. pap. 6.95 (*0-89594-820-6*) Crossing Pr.

Pocket Guide to Auto Maintenance & Emergency Car Repair. Wally Stewart et al. (Illus.). 28p. 1995. spiral bd. 12.95 (*1-886127-05-0*) Greycliff Pub.

Pocket Guide to Ayurvedic Healing. Candis C. Packard. (Crossing Press Pocket Ser.). (Illus.). 144p. (Orig.). 1996. pap. text 6.95 (*0-89594-764-1*) Crossing Pr.

Pocket Guide to Babysitting. (Illus.). 64p. (Orig.). (C). 1995. pap. text 14.95 (*0-7881-2273-8*) DIANE Pub.

Pocket Guide to Bach Flower Essences. Rachelle Hasnas. LC 97-11517. (Crossing Press Pocket Ser.). 128p. 1997. pap. 6.95 (*0-89594-865-6*) Crossing Pr.

Pocket Guide to Basic Canoeing. Bruce Newell et al. (Illus.). 28p. 1994. spiral bd. 12.95 (*1-886127-00-X*) Greycliff Pub.

Pocket Guide to Basic Dysrhythmias: Interpretation & Management. 2nd ed. Robert J. Huszar. (Illus.). 126p. 1995. write for info. (*0-8151-4743-0*, 25903) Mosby Inc.

Pocket Guide to Basic Dysrhythmias Interpretation & Management. Robert J. Huszar. (Illus.). 128p. 1995. pap. text 9.95 (*0-8151-4746-5*) Mosby Inc.

Pocket Guide to Basic Fly Tying Techniques. Ron Cordes & Gary LaFontaine. (Illus.). 28p. 1995. spiral bd. 12.95 (*1-886127-11-5*) Greycliff Pub.

Pocket Guide to Basic Skills & Procedures, Vol. 4. 4th ed. Anne G. Perry. LC 99-187163. (Illus.). 576p. (C). (gr. 13). 1998. text 22.95 (*0-8151-2714-6*, 31635) Mosby Inc.

Pocket Guide to Being Long Term Care. 3rd ed. Judith B. Eighmy & Will. (C). 1991. pap. 11.20 (*0-89303-130-5*, Medical Exam) Appleton & Lange.

Pocket Guide to Biking on Mt. Desert Island. Audrey S. Minutolo. LC 96-83694. (Illus.). 64p. (Orig.). 1996. pap. 7.95 (*0-89272-367-X*) Down East.

Pocket Guide to Biotherapy. Paula Rieger. (Nursing Ser.). 200p. Date not set. pap. 31.25 (*0-7637-0543-8*) Jones & Bartlett.

Pocket Guide to Bowhunting Whitetail Deer. 1989. pap. 2.95 (*1-879206-10-2*) Outdoor World Pr.

Pocket Guide to Brain Injury, Cognitive' & Neurobehavioral Rehabilitation. Thomas J. Guilmette. LC 97-22897. (Illus.). 324p. (Orig.). 1997. pap. 45.00 (*1-56593-833-X*, 1628) Thomson Learn.

Pocket Guide to Breast Cancer. Karen H. Dow. (Nursing Ser.). 320p. Date not set. pap. 31.25 (*0-7637-0683-3*) Jones & Bartlett.

***Pocket Guide to Breast Cancer.** Karen Hassey-Dow. (Illus.). (C). 1998. pap. text 31.25 (*0-7637-0988-3*) JB Pubns.

Pocket Guide to Breastfeeding & Human Lactation. Kathleen G. Auerbach & nice Riordan. LC 96-25990. 1996. pap. 18.75 (*0-7637-0258-7*) Jones & Bartlett.

Pocket Guide to Business Writing. Nancy A. Pipes. (Illus.). 150p. (Orig.). 1990. pap. write for info. (*0-923768-03-3*) Tekne Pr.

Pocket Guide to Cardiovascular Care, No. 2. 2nd ed. Susan B. Stillwell & Edith M. Randall. LC 93-35578. (Illus.). 368p. (C). (gr. 13). 1993. text 22.95 (*0-8016-7725-4*, 07725) Mosby Inc.

***Pocket Guide to Cardiovascular Disease.** Edward K. Chung & Dennis A. Tighe. LC 98-45297. (Illus.). 1998. pap. 35.95 (*0-86542-508-6*) Blackwell Sci.

Pocket Guide to Cases of Medicine & Public Health Collaboration. Roz D. Lasker et al. LC 98-22071. 1998. write for info. (*0-924143-08-8*) NY Acad Med.

Pocket Guide to Celtic Spirituality. Sirona Knight. LC 98-5023. (Crossing Press Pocket Ser.). 112p. 1998. pap. 6.95 (*0-89594-907-5*) Crossing Pr.

***Pocket Guide to Chemical Engineering.** Carl Branan. LC 99-45424. (Illus.). 160p. 1999. 30.00 (*0-88415-311-8*) Gulf Pub.

Pocket Guide to Chicago Architecture. Judith P. McBrien. LC 96-38750. (Illus.). 120p. 1997. pap. 15.95 (*0-393-73013-1*) Norton.

Pocket Guide to Chinese Patent Medicines. Bill Schoenbart. LC 98-47925. (Crossing Press Pocket Ser.). 112p. 1999. pap. 6.95 (*0-89594-978-4*) Crossing Pr.

Pocket Guide to Choosing Woody Ornamentals. Gerd Krussman. Ed. & Tr. by Michael E. Epp from GER. LC 82-13690. Orig. Title: Taschenbuch Der Geholzverwendung. (Illus.). 140p. 1982. pap. 12.95 (*0-917304-24-1*) Timber.

Pocket Guide to Cleveland Update. Lynn A. Howell. Ed. by Denise J. Knecht. (Illus.). (Orig.). 1993. pap. 4.95 (*0-9632245-3-0*) Pocket Guide.

Pocket Guide to Cliches. Arthur H. Bell. LC 98-21311. 160p. 1999. pap. 6.95 (*0-7641-0672-4*) Barron.

Pocket Guide to Clinical Examination. Nicholas J. Talley. 1998. pap. 24.95 (*0-632-05152-3*) Blackwell Sci.

Pocket Guide to Clinical Immunology. 2nd rev. ed. James D. Folds & David E. Normansell. LC 99-25642. 300p. 1999. pap. 29.95 (*1-55581-134-5*) ASM Pr.

Pocket Guide to Clinical Laboratory Instrumentation. Terence C. Karselis. LC 94-6969. (Illus.). 524p. 1994. 25.95 (*0-8036-5223-2*) Davis Co.

Pocket Guide to Clinical Microbiology. 2nd rev. ed. Patrick R. Murray. LC 98-21385. 350p. 1998. pap. 29.95 (*1-55581-137-X*) ASM Pr.

Pocket Guide to Cold Water Survival. IMO Staff. (C). 1992. 30.00 (*0-7855-0019-7*, IMO 946E, Pub. by Intl Maritime Org); 30.00 (*0-318-69904-4*, IMO 947F, Pub. by Intl Maritime Org) St Mut.

Pocket Guide to Collecting Police Badges & Patches. William B. Hedges. LC 92-90501. (Illus.). 60p. (Orig.). 1992. pap. text 9.95 (*0-9620487-2-0*) Baird-Hedges Pub.

***Pocket Guide to Colleges 2001.** Ed. by Princeton Review Publishing Staff. (Illus.). 2000. pap. 9.95 (*0-375-75631-0*, Pub. by PRP NY) Random.

Pocket Guide to Colleges, 2000 Edition. Lishing L.L.C. Pr Pub. 1999. pap. 9.95 (*0-375-75416-4*) Random.

Pocket Guide to Color Reproduction. Miles F. Southworth. LC 79-53546. (Illus.). 109p. (Orig.). 1979. pap. 7.95 (*0-933600-01-1*) Tech & Ed Ctr Graph Arts RIT.

Pocket Guide to Color Reproduction. 3rd ed. Miles F. Southworth & Donna Southworth. (Orig.). 1994. 16.95 (*0-933600-09-7*) Graph Arts Pub.

Pocket Guide to Color with Digital Applications: Reproduction & Printing with Digital Applications. Thomas Schildgen et al. LC 97-18609. (Graphic Communications Ser.). (Illus.). 352p. 1997. mass mkt. 17.95 (*0-8273-7298-1*) Delmar.

Pocket Guide to Colorado. 2nd ed. Ed. by Karl Kocivar. (Illus.). 176p. 1985. pap. 6.95 (*0-939396-01-7*) Colorado Expr.

Pocket Guide to Columbus. Brenda Custodio. (Illus.). 120p. (Orig.). 1992. pap. 6.95 (*0-9632245-0-6*) Pocket Guide.

Pocket Guide to Columbus: 1992 Update. rev. ed. Brenda Custodio. (Illus.). 1992. pap. 2.95 (*0-9632245-1-4*) Pocket Guide.

Pocket Guide to Common Drugs. Springhouse Publishing Company Staff. 336p. 1998. pap. text 18.95 (*0-87434-948-6*) Springhouse Corp.

Pocket Guide to Commonly Prescribed Drugs. 2nd ed. Glenn N. Levine. (C). 1996. pap. text 18.95 (*0-8385-8099-8*, A8099-2) Appleton & Lange.

Pocket Guide to Commonly Prescribed Drugs. 3rd ed. Glenn N. Levine. 480p. 1999. pap. 19.95 (*0-8385-8146-3*, Apple Lange Med) McGraw.

Pocket Guide to Cooking in the Great Outdoors. Earl Shelsby. 1993. pap. 4.95 (*0-917131-04-5*) FIM Pub.

Pocket Guide to Correct English. 3rd ed. Michael Temple. LC 97-633. 128p. 1997. pap. 6.95 (*0-8120-9816-1*) Barron.

Pocket Guide to Correct Grammar. 3rd ed. Vincent F. Hopper et al. LC 96-54635. 180p. 1997. pap. 6.95 (*0-8120-9815-3*) Barron.

Pocket Guide to Correct Punctuation. 3rd ed. Robert E. Brittain & Benjamin W. Griffith. LC 97-634. 128p. 1997. pap. 6.95 (*0-8120-9814-5*) Barron.

Pocket Guide to Correct Spelling. 3rd ed. Francis J. Griffith & Barron's Educational Editors. LC 96-52693. (Barron's Pocket Guides Ser.). 220p. 1997. pap. 6.95 (*0-8120-9813-7*) Barron.

Pocket Guide to CPR for Infants & Children. Ed. by Gloria Blatti. LC 99-207577. 128p. 1998. per. 3.99 (*0-671-00975-3*) PB.

Pocket Guide to Critical Appraisal. Ed. by I. K. Crombie. 66p. 1996. pap. text 18.00 (*0-7279-1099-X*, Pub. by BMJ Pub) Login Brothers Bk Co.

Pocket Guide to Critical Care Assessment. 3rd ed. Laura A. Talbot. LC 96-44664. (Illus.). 400p. (C). (gr. 13). 1997. text 22.95 (*0-8151-5608-1*, 29562) Mosby Inc.

Pocket Guide to Critical Care Monitoring. 2nd ed. Anna Owen. (Illus.). 288p. (C). (gr. 13). 1996. text 22.95 (*0-8151-7374-1*, 28101) Mosby Inc.

***Pocket Guide to Critical Thinking.** Epstein. (Philosophy Ser.). 1999. 12.95 (*0-534-55844-5*) Wadsworth Pub.

Pocket Guide to Cross Country Skiing. Greg Vivian et al. (Illus.). 28p. 1994. spiral bd. 12.95 (*1-886127-02-6*) Greycliff Pub.

Pocket Guide to Crystals & Gemstones. Sirona Knight. LC 98-26906. (Pocket Ser.). 96p. 1998. pap. 6.95 (*0-89594-947-4*) Crossing Pr.

Pocket Guide to Cultural Assessment. 2nd ed. Elaine Marie Geissler. LC 98-25821. (Illus.). 320p. (C). (gr. 13). 1998. spiral bd. 22.95 (*0-8151-3633-1*, 31285) Mosby Inc.

Pocket Guide to Cutaneous Medicine & Surgery. Philip E. LeBoit et al. (Illus.). 416p. 1995. pap. text 39.00 (*0-7216-5409-6*, W B Saunders Co) Harcrt Hlth Sci Grp.

Pocket Guide to Depression Glass & More: 1920s-1960s Identification & Values. 11th ed. Gene Florence. 192p. 1998. pap. 9.95 (*1-57432-081-5*) Collector Bks.

***Pocket Guide to Depression Glass & More, 1920s-1960s: Identification & Values.** 12th ed. Gene Florence. (Illus.). 192p. 2000. pap. 9.95 (*1-57432-202-8*) Collector Bks.

Pocket Guide to Diagnostic Tests. 2nd rev. ed. Diana Nicoll et al. 457p. (C). 1998. pap. 24.95 (*0-8385-8100-5*, A8100-8, Apple Lange Med) McGraw.

Pocket Guide to Diagnostic Tests. 3rd ed. Nicoll. (Illus.). 500p. (C). 1999. pap. text 19.95 (*0-8385-8135-8*) Appleton & Lange.

Pocket Guide to Digital Design. Ronald A. Labuz. (Graphic Communications Ser.). 352p. 1996. pap. 12.95 (*0-8273-7591-3*) Delmar.

Pocket Guide to Digital Imaging. Klein. (Graphic Communications Ser.). 1997. pap. 12.95 (*0-8273-7299-X*) Delmar.

Pocket Guide to Digital Imaging. Henry Lim. (Graphic Communications Ser.). 1996. pap. 11.95 (*0-8273-7506-9*) Delmar.

Pocket Guide to Digital Prepress. Frank Romano. LC 95-20087. 352p. (C). 1995. pap. 17.95 (*0-8273-7198-5*) Delmar.

Pocket Guide to Digital Printing. Frank Cost. (Graphic Communications Ser.). (Illus.). 228p. 1996. mass mkt. 17.95 (*0-8273-7592-1*) Delmar.

Pocket Guide to Dry Fly Fishing. Ron Cordes & Gary LaFontaine. (Illus.). 28p. 1994. spiral bd. 12.95 (*0-9633024-3-4*) Greycliff Pub.

Pocket Guide to ECG Diagnosis. Edward K. Chung. LC 96-3795. (Illus.). 495p. 1996. pap. text 34.95 (*0-86542-499-3*) Blackwell Sci.

***Pocket Guide to ECG Diagnosis.** 2nd ed. Edward K. Chung. (Illus.). 512p. 2000. pap. 36.95 (*0-86542-589-2*) Blackwell Sci.

Pocket Guide to Economics for the Global Investor. John Calverley. 1996. 19.95 (*1-55738-924-1*, Irwn Prfssnl) McGraw-Hill Prof.

Pocket Guide to Economics Today Printed & Electronic Supplements (the 1999-2000 Edition) 10th ed. Leroy Miller & Roger Miller. 112p. 1998. pap. text 145.00 (*0-321-03364-7*) Addison-Wesley.

***Pocket Guide to Electrical Equipment.** R. R. Lee. LC 99-39142. (Illus.). 1999. 30.00 (*0-88415-305-3*) Gulf Pub.

P

An Asterisk (*) at the beginning of an entry indicates that the title is appearing for the first time.

Pocket Guide to Electrical Equipment & Instrumentation. 2nd ed. R. R. Lee. (Illus.). 340p. (Orig.). 1991. pap. 30.00 (*0-87201-234-4*, 1234) Gulf Pub.

Pocket Guide to Electrocardiography. 4th ed. Mary Boudreau Conover. LC 97-39597. (Illus.). 288p. (C). (gr. 13). 1997. text 22.95 (*0-8151-3695-1*, 31037) Mosby Inc.

***Pocket Guide to Emergency Bicycle Repair.** Eric Grove & Gary LaFontaine. (Illus.). 28p. 1999. spiral bd. 12.95 (*1-886127-18-2*) Greycliff Pub.

Pocket Guide to Emergency First Aid. Betty Cordes et al. (Illus.). 28p. 1993. spiral bd. 12.95 (*0-9633024-2-6*) Greycliff Pub.

Pocket Guide to Emergency Medical. Howell. 1998. pap. 44.00 (*0-7216-5823-7*, W B Saunders Co) Harcrt Hlth Sci Grp.

Pocket Guide to EMS Run Reports. Armando S. Bevelacqua. 16.00 (*0-685-50512-X*) P-H.

Pocket Guide to EMT Prehospital Care. Alice T. Dalton et al. LC 93-23587. (Illus.). 256p. 1994. pap. text 17.95 (*0-7216-3781-7*, W B Saunders Co) Harcrt Hlth Sci Grp.

Pocket Guide to Environmental Bad Guys: And a Few Ideas on How to Stop Them. James Ridgeway. LC 98-34022. (Illus.). 178p. 1998. pap. text 10.95 (*1-56025-153-0*, Thunders Mouth) Avalon NY.

Pocket Guide to Eponyms & Subtle Signs of Disease. Scott M. Tenner & Thomas M. Masterson. 78p. (Orig.). (C). 1993. pap. text 7.50 (*0-9634063-6-1*) Intl Med Pub.

Pocket Guide to Essential of Diagnosis & Treatment. Lawrence M. Tierney. (C). 1997. pap. text 22.95 (*0-8385-3605-0*, Apple Lange Med) McGraw.

Pocket Guide to Evaluations of Drug Interactions. 3rd rev. ed. Ed. by Frederic J. Zucchero et al. 450p. 1999. pap. 35.00 (*0-917330-93-5*, T59-3) Am Pharm Assn.

Pocket Guide to Examination of the Musculoskeletal System. Richard J. Hawkins & Kiefer. LC 94-28871. (Illus.). 304p. (C). (gr. 13). 1994. pap. text 27.00 (*0-8151-4162-9*, 20943) Mosby Inc.

Pocket Guide to Fetal Monitoring & Assessment. 3rd ed. Ed. by Susan M. Tucker. LC 95-48296. (Illus.). 304p. (C). (gr. 13). 1996. text, pap. text, spiral bd. 22.95 (*0-8151-8883-8*, 26418) Mosby Inc.

***Pocket Guide to Fetal Monitoring & Assessment.** 4th ed. Susan M. Tucker. (Illus.). 315p. 2000. pap. text 24.95 (*0-323-00884-4*) Mosby Inc.

***Pocket Guide to Field Dressing Big Game.** Steve Gilbert. (Illus.). 28p. 2000. spiral bd. 12.95 (*1-886127-19-0*) Greycliff Pub.

Pocket Guide to Field Dressing, Butchering & Cooking Deer. 1986. pap. 2.95 (*1-879206-08-0*) Outdoor World Pr.

Pocket Guide to Finance. David J. Leahigh. 176p. (C). 1995. pap. text 23.00 (*0-03-015718-8*) Dryden Pr.

Pocket Guide to Financial Products & Services. 2nd ed. Dwight S. Ritter. 240p. 1996. per. 12.95 (*0-7863-1110-X*, Irwn Prfssnl) McGraw-Hill Prof.

Pocket Guide to Financial Products & Services: Product Information/Customer Profile/Cross Selling Checklist. 2nd rev. ed. Dwight S. Ritter. 48p. 1996. 50.00 (*0-7863-1109-6*, Irwn Prfssnl) McGraw-Hill Prof.

Pocket Guide to First Aid for Scuba Diving. Dan Orr & Bill Clendenen. (Illus.). 28p. 1998. pap. text 12.95 (*1-886127-17-4*) Troutbeck Pub.

***Pocket Guide to Fishing Knots.** Peter Owen. LC 98-21947. (Illus.). 80p. 1998. 9.95 (*1-58080-064-5*) Burford Bks.

Pocket Guide to Fishing Lakes & Reservoirs. W. Cary DeRussy. (Pocket Guide to Fishing Ser.). (Illus.). 96p. (Orig.). 1989. pap. 4.95 (*0-917131-01-0*) FIM Pub.

Pocket Guide to Fishing Rivers & Streams. W. Cary DeRussy. (Pocket Guide to Fishing Ser.). (Illus.). 96p. (Orig.). 1989. pap. 4.95 (*0-917131-02-9*) FIM Pub.

Pocket Guide to Flanges, Fittings, & Piping Data. Robert R. Lee. LC 84-669. 151p. 1984. reprint ed. pap. 46.90 (*0-608-00831-1*, 206162100010) Bks Demand.

Pocket Guide to Flanges, Fittings, & Piping Data. 2nd ed. R. R. Lee. (Illus.). 176p. (Orig.). 1992. pap. 30.00 (*0-88415-023-2*, 5023) Gulf Pub.

***Pocket Guide to Flanges, Fittings & Piping Data.** 3rd ed. R. R. Lee. LC 99-38352. 1999. 30.00 (*0-88415-310-X*) Gulf Pub.

Pocket Guide to Flow Blue: With Prices. Jeffrey B. Snyder. LC 95-22124. (Illus.). 160p. (Orig.). 1995. pap. 19.95 (*0-88740-856-7*) Schiffer.

Pocket Guide to Fluids & Electrolytes. 3rd ed. Mima M. Horne et al. LC 96-10272. (Illus.). 320p. (C). (gr. 13). 1996. text 22.95 (*0-8151-4663-9*, 27461) Mosby Inc.

Pocket Guide to Fly Casting. Michael C. Maloney et al. (Illus.). 28p. 1995. spiral bd. 12.95 (*1-886127-10-7*) Greycliff Pub.

Pocket Guide to Fly Fishing. Ron Cordes & Gary LaFontaine. (Illus.). 26p. 1992. spiral bd. 12.95 (*1-886127-16-6*) Greycliff Pub.

Pocket Guide to Fly Fishing for Largemouth Bass. Ron Cordes & Gary LaFontaine. (Illus.). 28p. 1999. spiral bd. 12.95 (*1-886127-12-3*) Greycliff Pub.

Pocket Guide to Fly Fishing for Steelhead. Jay Rowland et al. (Illus.). 28p. 1994. spiral bd. 12.95 (*0-9633024-9-3*) Greycliff Pub.

Pocket Guide to Fly Fishing for Trout. Jim Gilford. LC 97-187924. (Pocket Guide to Fishing Ser.). (Illus.). 96p. 1996. pap. text 4.95 (*0-917131-06-1*) FIM Pub.

Pocket Guide to Fly Fishing Knots. Stan Bradshaw et al. (Illus.). 28p. 1997. 12.95 (*1-886127-14-X*) Greycliff Pub.

Pocket Guide to Fly Fishing the Lakes. Ron Cordes & Gary LaFontaine. (Illus.). 28p. 1993. spiral bd. 12.95 (*0-9633024-4-2*) Greycliff Pub.

Pocket Guide to Food Additives. Donald S. Saulson & Elisabeth M. Saulson. LC 91-90996. 64p. (Orig.). 1991. pap. 1.95 (*0-9629606-0-8*) VPS Pub.

***Pocket Guide to Fortified & Sweet Wines.** John Radford & Stephen Brook. 204p. 2000. 14.95 (*1-84000-248-4*, Pub. by Mitchell Beazley) Antique Collect.

Pocket Guide to Fortunetelling. Scott Cunningham. LC 97-26024. (Crossing Press Pocket Ser.). (Illus.). 140p. (Orig.). 1997. pap. 6.95 (*0-89594-875-3*) Crossing Pr.

***Pocket Guide to Fungal Infection.** Malcolm Richardson & Elizabeth Johnson. (Illus.). 120p. 2000. pap. 29.95 (*0-632-05325-9*) Blackwell Sci.

Pocket Guide to Gene Level Diagnostics in Clinical Practice. Victor A. Bernstam. 560p. 1992. lib. bdg. 69.95 (*0-8493-4485-9*, RB155) CRC Pr.

Pocket Guide to Gerontologic Assessment. 3rd ed. Annette Lueckenotte. LC 97-34218. (Illus.). 432p. (C). (gr. 13). 1997. text 22.95 (*0-8151-2799-5*, 31133) Mosby Inc.

Pocket Guide to Gerontologic Assessment, No. 2. Annette Lueckenotte. 310p. 1994. write for info. (*0-08-151778-5*) Mosby Inc.

Pocket Guide to Golf. Michael Brady et al. (Illus.). 28p. 1995. spiral bd. 12.95 (*1-886127-13-1*) Greycliff Pub.

Pocket Guide to Good Food: A Shopper's Resource. Margaret M. Wittenberg. LC 95-50885. (Crossing Press Pocket Ser.).Tr. of C'est Pas Juste!. (Illus.). 160p. 1996. pap. text 6.95 (*0-89594-747-1*) Crossing Pr.

***Pocket Guide to Good Tuning.** Gregory K. McMillan. LC 00-36958. 2000. write for info. (*1-55617-726-7*) ISA.

Pocket Guide to Grant Applications. Ed. by Iain K. Crombie & Charles D. Florey. 68p. 1998. pap. text 29.00 (*0-7279-1219-4*, Pub. by BMJ Pub) Login Brothers Bk Co.

Pocket Guide to Great Relationships. James J. McCarthy. LC 94-74379. 91p. 1995. pap. 6.95 (*1-883697-37-9*) Hara Pub.

Pocket Guide to Harp Composing. 2nd rev. ed. Darhon Rees-Rohrbacher. (Illus.). 80p. 1995. pap. text 9.00 (*1-882712-14-5*) Dragonflower.

Pocket Guide to Hatha Yoga. Michele Picozzi. LC 98-5022. (Crossing Press Pocket Ser.). (Illus.). 112p. 1998. pap. 6.95 (*0-89594-911-3*) Crossing Pr.

Pocket Guide to Hawaii's Birds. H. Douglas Pratt. (Illus.). 112p. 1996. pap. 8.95 (*1-56647-145-1*) Mutual Pub HI.

Pocket Guide to Hawaii's Flowers. Leland Miyano. (Illus.). 112p. 1997. pap. 8.95 (*1-56647-149-4*) Mutual Pub HI.

Pocket Guide to Hawaii's Trees & Shrubs. H. Douglas Pratt. (Pocket Guides Ser.). (Illus.). 136p. 1999. pap. 8.95 (*1-56647-219-9*) Mutual Pub HI.

Pocket Guide to Hawaii's Underwater Paradise. John P. Hoover. (Illus.). 96p. 1997. pap. 8.95 (*1-56647-151-6*) Mutual Pub HI.

***Pocket Guide to Healing Headaches.** Pat Thomas. LC 00-30712. 2000. pap. 6.95 (*1-58091-083-1*) Crossing Pr.

Pocket Guide to Health Assessment. 4th ed. Potter. LC 97-47169. (Illus.). 416p. (C). (gr. 13). 1998. text 22.95 (*0-8151-8396-8*, 31696) Mosby Inc.

Pocket Guide to Herbal First Aid. Nancy Evelyn. LC 98-26032. (Pocket Ser.). 96p. 1998. pap. 6.95 (*0-89594-967-9*) Crossing Pr.

Pocket Guide to Hiking - Backpacking. Ron Cordes & Gary LaFontaine. (Illus.). 28p. 1993. spiral bd. 12.95 (*0-9633024-7-7*) Greycliff Pub.

Pocket Guide to Hiking on Mt. Desert Island. Earl Brechlin. LC 95-71936. (Illus.). 72p. (Orig.). 1996. pap. 7.95 (*0-89272-356-4*) Down East.

***Pocket Guide to How to Hula.** Ed. by Patricia Murray. (Illus.). 88p. 1999. pap. 8.95 (*1-56647-163-X*) Mutual Pub HI.

***Pocket Guide to I. V. Drugs.** Dawn N. Philp & Deborah L. Walz. LC 99-52578. 2000. otabind. write for info. (*1-58255-044-1*) Springhouse Corp.

***Pocket Guide to ICD - 10 Classification of Mental & Behavioural Disorders with Glossary & Diagnostic Criteria for Research DCR - 10.** World Health Organization Staff. Ed. by J. E. Cooper. 419p. 1998. pap. write for info. (*0-443-04909-2*) Church.

Pocket Guide to Infection Prevention & Safe Practice. Susan D. Schaffer et al. LC 95-32784. (Illus.). 384p. (C). (gr. 13). 1995. 22.95 (*0-8151-7593-0*, 23641) Mosby Inc.

Pocket Guide to Infectious Disease. Gorbach. 1999. pap. text. write for info. (*0-7216-5525-4*) Harcourt.

Pocket Guide to Injectable Chemotherapeutic Agents: Drug Information & Dosages. 2nd rev. ed. Byron G. Peters et al. xiii, 152p. 1998. pap. 24.95 (*0-9663138-0-1*) Oncology Educ.

***Pocket Guide to Injectable Chemotherapeutic Agents: Drug Information & Dosages.** 3rd rev. ed. Byron G. Peters et al. xvi, 168p. 2000. pap. 24.95 (*0-615-11127-0*) Midwest Bk.

Pocket Guide to Injectable Drugs: Companion to Handbook on Injectable Drugs. 8th rev. ed. Lawrence A. Trissel. 296p. 1994. pap. text 31.00 (*1-879907-50-X*) Am Soc Hlth-Syst.

Pocket Guide to Injectable Drugs: Companion to Handbook on Injectable Drugs. 9th ed. Lawrence A. Trissel. LC 97-116598. 300p. 1996. pap. text 31.00 (*1-879907-67-4*) Am Soc Hlth-Syst.

Pocket Guide to Injectable Drugs: Companion to Handbook on Injectable Drugs. 10th ed. Lawrence A. Trissel. 352p. 1998. pap. text 38.00 (*1-879907-89-5*) Am Soc Hlth-Syst.

***Pocket Guide to Instrumentation.** R. R. Lee. LC 99-41792. 1999. 30.00 (*0-88415-308-8*) Gulf Pub.

Pocket Guide to Intravenous Therapy. 3rd ed. Joanne C. LaRocca & Shirley E. Otto. LC 96-14139. (Illus.). 464p. (C). (gr. 13). 1996. text 22.95 (*0-8151-5298-1*, 28205) Mosby Inc.

Pocket Guide to Irish Genealogy. Brian Mitchell. (Illus.). 63p. 1999. pap. 10.95 (*0-8063-1300-5*, 9240) Clearfield Co.

Pocket Guide to Irish Genealogy. Brian S. Mitchell. 103p. 1988. pap. text 7.95 (*1-55856-000-9*, 137) Closson Pr.

Pocket Guide to IV Therapy. 4th ed. Joanne C. Larocca. (Illus.). 213p. (C). (gr. 13). 1993. spiral bd. 28.95 (*0-8016-6910-3*, 06910) Mosby Inc.

Pocket Guide to John Wesley's Message Today. Lovett H. Weems. 1991. pap. 5.95 (*0-687-31681-2*) Abingdon.

***Pocket Guide to Kids Are Worth It! Giving Your Child the Gift of Inner Discipline.** Barbara Coloroso. 216p. 1998. write for info. (*1-894042-08-5*) Somerville Hse.

Pocket Guide to Louisiana Native Trees. Friends of Hilltop, a Native Trees Committee. 80p. (Orig.). 1997. pap. 6.00 (*0-614-29819-9*) Frnds Hilltop.

Pocket Guide to Lure Fishing for Trout in a Stream. Harley W. Reno et al. (Illus.). 28p. 1995. spiral bd. 12.95 (*1-886127-06-9*) Greycliff Pub.

***Pocket Guide to Lymphoma Classification.** D. Mason. (Illus.). 1998. pap. 26.95 (*0-632-05096-9*) Blackwell Sci.

Pocket Guide to Macrobiotics. Carl Ferre. LC 97-24472. (Crossing Press Pocket Ser.). (Illus.). 140p. (Orig.). 1997. pap. 6.95 (*0-89594-848-6*) Crossing Pr.

***Pocket Guide to Making Successful Small Talk: How to Talk to Anyone Anytime Anywhere about Anything.** unabridged ed. Bernardo J. Carducci. 90p. 1999. pap. 9.95 (*0-9677517-0-5*, PGP001) Pocket Guide IN.

***Pocket Guide to Malignant Melanoma.** John Buchan & Dafydd Lloyd Roberts. LC 99-53650. (Illus.). 72p. 2000. pap. 29.95 (*0-632-05421-2*) Blackwell Sci.

***Pocket Guide to Managing Contraception: 2000-2001 Edition.** Robert A. Hatcher & Anita Nelson. (Illus.). 168p. 2000. text 24.95 (*0-8290-5216-X*); pap. text 15.95 (*0-8290-5217-8*) Ardent Media.

Pocket Guide to Manwatching. Desmond Morris. pap. 9.95 (*0-586-05628-9*) HarpC.

Pocket Guide to Maryland's Chesapeake Bay. Howard A. Chatterton. (Illus.). 48p. (Orig.). 1984. pap. 5.95 (*0-933852-46-0*) Nautical & Aviation.

Pocket Guide to Maternal & Neonatal Nursing. Kathryn A. May & Laura R. Mahlmeister. LC 93-30921. 1993. write for info. (*0-397-55125-8*) Lppncott W & W.

Pocket Guide to Medications Used in Dermatology. 4th ed. Andrew J. Scheman & David L. Severson. LC 94-21217. 1994. 16.00 (*0-683-07593-4*) Lppncott W & W.

Pocket Guide to Medications Used in Dermatology. 5th ed. Andrew J. Scheman & David L. Severson. LC 96-36534. 228p. 1997. pap. 19.00 (*0-683-30106-3*) Lppncott W & W.

***Pocket Guide to Medications Used in Dermatology.** 6th ed. Andrew J. Scheman & David L. Severson. LC 99-10896. 1999. write for info. (*0-7817-2100-8*) Lppncott W & W.

Pocket Guide to Meditation. Alan L. Pritz. LC 97-26037. (Crossing Press Pocket Ser.). (Illus.). 112p. (Orig.). 1997. pap. 6.95 (*0-89594-886-9*) Crossing Pr.

Pocket Guide to Meditation Fundamentals. unabridged ed. John J. Kelly & N. Tracy Childers. (Illus.). 82p. 1997. pap. 4.95 (*1-890639-00-1*) Synergy Systs.

Pocket Guide to Menopause. Ruth Appleby. LC 99-37388. Orig. Title: Menopause - The Common Sense Approach. 96p. 2000. pap. 6.95 (*1-58091-012-2*) Crossing Pr.

Pocket Guide to Midwifery Care. Aviva J. Romm. LC 98-10584. (Crossing Press Pocket Ser.). (Illus.). 112p. 1998. pap. 6.95 (*0-89594-855-9*) Crossing Pr.

Pocket Guide to MR Procedures & Metallic Objects: Update 1997. Frank G. Shellock. LC 97-187631. 136p. 1997. pap. text 18.00 (*0-7817-1452-4*) Lppncott W & W.

Pocket Guide to MR Procedures & Metallic Objects: Update 1998. Frank G. Shellock. 1998. pap. text 18.95 (*0-7817-1784-1*) Lppncott W & W.

Pocket Guide to MR Procedures & Metallic Objects: Update 1999. Frank G. Shellock. 200p. pap. text 19.95 (*0-7817-2345-0*) Lppncott W & W.

Pocket Guide to MR Procedures & Metallic Objects: Update 2000. Frank G. Shellock. 244p. pap. text 19.95 (*0-7817-2868-1*) Lppncott W & W.

Pocket Guide to Multimedia. abr. rev. ed. David D. Peck. (Graphic Communications Ser.). (Illus.). 224p. (C). 1998. text 16.95 (*0-8273-7383-X*) Delmar.

Pocket Guide to Musculoskeletal Assessment. Richard Baxter. Ed. by Margaret Biblis. LC 97-18626. (Illus.). 208p. 1998. pap. text 24.95 (*0-7216-3337-4*, W B Saunders Co) Harcrt Hlth Sci Grp.

Pocket Guide to National Parks. H. M. Gousha. 1995. 2.95 (*0-671-50062-7*) S&S Trade.

Pocket Guide to Naturopathic Medicine. Judith Boice. (Crossing Press Pocket Ser.). (Illus.). 128p. (Orig.). 1996. pap. 6.95 (*0-89594-821-4*) Crossing Pr.

Pocket Guide to Neonatal EKG Interpretation. Jobeth Pilcher. LC 97-26769. (Illus.). 53p. 1998. spiral bd. 17.95 (*1-887571-02-7*) NICU Ink.

Pocket Guide to Neuroanatomy & the Neurologic Exam. Ralph F. Jozefowicz & David L. Felten. 200p. 1998. pap. text 19.95 (*0-7817-1653-5*) Lppncott W & W.

Pocket Guide to Numerology. Alan Oken. (Crossing Press Pocket Ser.). 96p. (Orig.). 1996. pap. 6.95 (*0-89594-826-5*) Crossing Pr.

Pocket Guide to Nursing Diagnosis. 7th ed. MiJa Kim et al. 528p. (C). (gr. 13). 1997. text 24.00 (*0-8151-4989-1*, 28270) Mosby Inc.

Pocket Guide to Nutrition & Diet Therapy. 3rd ed. Mary C. Moore. LC 96-15024. (Illus.). 496p. (C). (gr. 13). 1996. text 22.95 (*0-8151-7370-9*, 28269) Mosby Inc.

Pocket Guide to Nymph Fishing. Ron Cordes & Gary LaFontaine. (Illus.). 28p. 1994. spiral bd. 12.95 (*0-9633024-6-9*) Greycliff Pub.

Pocket Guide to Obstetrics & Gynecology. Frank Ling & Patrick Duff. (C). 2000. 30.00 (*0-8385-8134-X*) Appleton & Lange.

Pocket Guide to Occupied Japan. Monica L. Clements & Patricia R. Clements. LC 98-88135. (Illus.). 160p. (Orig.). 1999. pap. 16.95 (*0-7643-0728-2*) Schiffer.

Pocket Guide to Old Time Catfish Techniques. 1989. pap. 2.95 (*1-879206-11-0*) Outdoor World Pr.

Pocket Guide to Oncology Nursing. Shirley E. Otto. (Illus.). 640p. (C). (gr. 13). 1995. text 22.95 (*0-8151-6547-1*, 23768) Mosby Inc.

***Pocket Guide to Ophthalmology Review.** Willie Y. W. Chen. 144p. (C). 2000. pap. text 29.00 (*1-55642-478-7*) SLACK Inc.

Pocket Guide to Oregon Birds. Alan Contreras. 65p. 1996. 5.00 (*1-877693-23-5*) Oregon Field.

Pocket Guide to Organic Chemistry. Rosenfeld. (C). 1999. pap. text 13.50 (*0-15-601654-0*) Harcourt Coll Pubs.

Pocket Guide to Outdoor Photography. Mary Mather. (Illus.). 28p. 1993. spiral bd. 12.95 (*0-9633024-5-0*) Greycliff Pub.

Pocket Guide to Outdoor Survival. Stan Bradshaw et al. (Illus.). 28p. 1994. spiral bd. 12.95 (*1-886127-04-2*) Greycliff Pub.

Pocket Guide to Paddling the Waters of Mt. Desert Island. Earl Brechlin. LC 96-83695. (Illus.). 64p. (Orig.). 1996. pap. 7.95 (*0-89272-357-2*) Down East.

Pocket Guide to Pediatric Assessment. 3rd ed. Joyce K. Engel. (Illus.). 384p. (C). (gr. 13). 1996. pap. text 22.95 (*0-8151-3157-7*, 27512) Mosby Inc.

Pocket Guide to Physical Agents. Alain Yvan Belanger. 352p. spiral bd. write for info. (*0-7817-2108-3*) Lppncott W & W.

Pocket Guide to Physical Diagnosis. Janice L. Willms & Henry Schneiderman. (Illus.). 400p. 1996. pap. 22.95 (*0-683-09116-6*) Lppncott W & W.

Pocket Guide to Physical Examination & Nutritional Assessment. Jane E. McDonald. (Illus.). 156p. 1994. pap. text 29.00 (*0-920513-21-2*, Pub. by Saulnders) Saunders.

***Pocket Guide to Pink Depression Era Glass.** Patricia Clements & Monica L. Clements. (Illus.). 160p. 1999. pap. 16.95 (*0-7643-1008-9*) Schiffer.

Pocket Guide to Prayer. Gary Egeberg. LC 99-34648. 160p. 1999. mass mkt. 6.99 (*0-8066-3958-X*, Augsburg) Augsburg Fortress.

***Pocket Guide to Preventing Process Plant Materials Mix-Ups.** Bert Moriz. LC 00-25085. 180p. 2000. pap. 30.00 (*0-88415-344-4*) Gulf Pub.

***Pocket Guide to Psoriasis.** Simon Davison et al. LC 99-53651. (Illus.). 72p. 2000. pap. 29.95 (*0-632-05208-2*) Blackwell Sci.

Pocket Guide to Psychiatry. Allan Tasman. 1997. pap. text 36.95 (*0-7216-5241-7*, W B Saunders Co) Harcrt Hlth Sci Grp.

Pocket Guide to Punctuation & Style. Langenscheidt Staff. (Insight Guides Ser.). 1998. pap. 10.95 (*0-88729-218-6*) Langenscheidt.

Pocket Guide to Radiography. 3rd ed. Philip W. Ballinger. LC 95-6295. (Illus.). 400p. (C). (gr. 13). 1995. spiral bd. 22.95 (*0-8151-0401-4*, 24273) Mosby Inc.

Pocket Guide to Radiography. 4th ed. (Illus.). 400p. 1999. spiral bd. 23.95 (*0-8151-2649-2*, 31647) Mosby Inc.

Pocket Guide to Reading Katakana. Carl Shaad. (Illus.). 102p. 1988. 9.95 (*0-8348-0219-8*) Weatherhill.

***Pocket Guide to Recognising & Treating Pig Diseases.** 301p. 1999. pap. 94.00 (*0-9530150-1-7*, Pub. by FiveM Enterprises) St Mut.

Pocket Guide to Recommended World Restaurants. A. G. Small. LC 83-91446. (Orig.). 1984. pap. 6.95 (*0-915457-00-8*) A G Small Pubns.

Pocket Guide to Respiratory Disease. Robert L. Wilkins et al. 180p. 14.95 (*0-8036-0566-8*) Davis Co.

Pocket Guide to Rudolph's Pediatrics. (C). 2001. 30.00 (*0-8385-8287-7*) Appleton & Lange.

Pocket Guide to Safe Babysitting. Betty Cordes et al. (Illus.). 28p. 1995. spiral bd. 12.95 (*1-886127-09-3*) Greycliff Pub.

Pocket Guide to Saltwater Fly Fishing. Ron Cordes & Gary LaFontaine. (Illus.). 28p. 1994. spiral bd. 12.95 (*0-9633024-8-5*) Greycliff Pub.

Pocket Guide to Scotch Whisky. Charles MacLean. 224p. 1998. pap. 14.95 (*1-84000-022-8*, Pub. by Mitchell Beazley) Antique Collect.

Pocket Guide to Seasonal Largemouth Bass Patterns. 1990. pap. 2.95 (*1-879206-12-9*) Outdoor World Pr.

Pocket Guide to Seasonal Walleye Tactics. 1990. pap. 2.95 (*1-879206-13-7*) Outdoor World Pr.

Pocket Guide to Seattle: And Surrounding Areas. 5th ed. Duse McLean. LC 96-60636. 1996. pap. text 10.95 (*0-9621935-6-9*) Thistle Pr.

Pocket Guide to Seattle: And Surrounding Areas. 6th rev. ed. Duse F. McLean. LC 98-60791. (Illus.). 1998. pap. 10.95 (*0-9621935-8-5*) Thistle Pr.

Pocket Guide to Seattle, 1989: A Complete Guide to Seattle & Surrounding Areas. Duse F. McLean. Ed. by Elisha Hampton. (Illus.). 160p. 1996. pap. 10.95 (*0-9621935-0-X*) Thistle Pr.

Pocket Guide to Sectional Anatomy. Kelley & Petersen. (Illus.). 256p. (gr. 13). 1997. spiral bd. 21.95 (*0-8151-8666-5*, 28945) Mosby Inc.

Pocket Guide to Self-Hypnosis. Adam Burke. LC 97-12914. (Crossing Press Pocket Ser.). (Illus.). 112p. 1997. pap. 6.95 (*0-89594-824-9*) Crossing Pr.

Pocket Guide to Selling Services & Products. Malcolm H. McDonald & Peter Morris. 96p. 1995. pap. text 15.95 (*0-7506-2641-0*) Buttrwrth-Heinemann.

Pocket Guide to Shakespeare's Plays. Kenneth McLeish & Stephen F. Unwin. 288p. (Orig.). 1999. pap. 14.00 (*0-571-19183-5*) Faber & Faber.

Pocket Guide to Shamanism. Tom Cowan. LC 97-9449. (Crossing Press Pocket Ser.). (Illus.). 128p. 1997. pap. 6.95 (*0-89594-845-1*) Crossing Pr.

***Pocket-Guide to Southern African Birds.** Burger Cillie & Ulrich Oberprieler. 2000. pap. 14.95 (*0-627-01979-X*, Pub. by J L Van Schaik) BHB Intl.

Pocket Guide to Southern African Mammals. Burger Cillie. (Illus.). 124p. 1999. pap. 14.95 (*0-627-01686-3*, Pub. by J L Van Schaik) BHB Intl.

P

Pocket Guide to Spring & Fall Turkey Hunting. 1989. pap. 2.95 (*1-879206-09-9*) Outdoor World Pr.

Pocket Guide to Stress Reduction. Brenda O'Hanlon. LC 99-36916. (Crossing Press Pocket Ser.). Orig. Title: Stress - The Common Sense Approach. 112p. 1999. pap. 6.95 (*1-58091-011-4*) Crossing Pr.

Pocket Guide to Stress Testing. Edward K. Chung & Dennis A. Tighe. LC 96-40175. (Illus.). 1997. pap. 36.95 (*0-86542-509-4*) Blackwell Sci.

Pocket Guide to Study Tips. 3rd ed. William H. Armstrong et al. LC 96-19015. 290p. 1997. pap. 6.95 (*0-8120-9812-9*) Barron.

***Pocket Guide to Successful Consulting.** Leslie Powell. Ed. by Harvey Imeson. 50p. 2000. pap. 7.95 (*0-9625738-6-8*) Gala Pub.

Pocket Guide to Surgical Critical Care Medicine. (C). 2001. 39.00 (*0-8385-8163-3*, Medical Exam) Appleton & Lange.

Pocket Guide to Syndrome Identification for Audiologists. Shprinzens. 2001. pap. 35.25 (*0-7693-0020-0*) Singular Publishing.

***Pocket Guide to Syndromes.** Robert J. Shprintzen. LC 99-40684. 508p. 1999. pap. 65.00 (*0-7693-0019-7*) Singular Publishing.

Pocket Guide to Synonyms. Arthur H. Bell. (Barron's Pocket Guides Ser.). 1992. vinyl bd. 7.95 (*0-8120-4843-1*) Barron.

Pocket Guide to Synonyms & Antonyms. Langenscheidt Staff. (Insight Guides Ser.). 1998. pap. 10.95 (*0-88729-220-8*) Langenscheidt.

Pocket Guide to Target - Field Archery. Harley W. Reno et al. (Illus.). 28p. 1994. spiral bd. 12.95 (*1-886127-01-8*) Greycliff Pub.

Pocket Guide to Tarot. Alan Oken. (Crossing Press Pocket Ser.). (Illus.). 176p. (Orig.). 1996. pap. 6.95 (*0-89594-822-2*) Crossing Pr.

Pocket Guide to Teaching for Medical Instructors. Ed. by Kevin Mackway-Jones & Mike Walker. 91p. 1998. pap. text 18.95 (*0-7279-1380-8*) Login Brothers Bk Co.

Pocket Guide to Technical Writing. William S. Pfeiffer. LC 97-1404. 170p. 1997. pap. text 14.00 (*0-13-242157-7*) P-H.

***Pocket Guide to Technical Writing.** 2nd ed. William S. Pfeiffer. LC 00-27689. (Illus.). 240p. 2000. pap. 13.33 (*0-13-026102-5*) P-H.

***Pocket Guide to Telecommunications, Electronic Comm. & Information Technology.** Ajayi. LC 98-43746. 208p. 1999. 32.95 (*0-7668-0170-5*) Delmar.

Pocket Guide to the ADA: Americans with Disabilities Act Accessibility Guidelines for Buildings & Facilities. 2nd rev. ed. Evan Terry Associates Staff. LC 97-1549. (Illus.). 144p. 1997. pap. 29.95 (*0-471-18137-4*) Wiley.

Pocket Guide to the Baldrige Award Criteria. Mark G. Brown. 66p. (Orig.). 1994. pap. text 4.50 (*0-527-76315-2*, 762466) Productivity Inc.

Pocket Guide to the Baldrige Award Criteria. 4th rev. ed. Mark G. Brown. 66p. (Orig.). 1997. pap. 4.50 (*0-527-76331-4*, 763314) Productivity Inc.

Pocket Guide to the Baldrige Award Criteria. 5th ed. Mark G. Brown. 64p. (Orig.). 1998. pap. 4.50 (*0-527-76347-0*, 763470) Productivity Inc.

***Pocket Guide to the Baldrige Award Criteria.** 7th ed. Mark Graham Brown. 2000. pap. 5.25 (*1-56327-233-4*) Productivity Inc.

***Pocket Guide to the Best of Los Angeles.** deluxe ed. Gary McBroom. Ed. by Charlotte McBroom. LC 99-66044. 224p. 2000. pap. 12.95 (*0-9674258-0-8*) GPS Advent.

Pocket Guide to the Birds of Britain & North-West Europe. Chris Kightley & Steve Madge. LC 97-80503. (Illus.). 300p. 1998. pap. 20.00 (*0-300-07455-7*) Yale U Pr.

Pocket Guide to the Carriage Roads of Acadia National Park. 2nd expanded rev. ed. Diana F. Abrell. 40p. 1995. pap. 4.95 (*0-89272-349-1*) Down East.

Pocket Guide to the Chakras. Joy Gardner-Gordon. LC 98-24642. (Pocket Ser.). 112p. 1998. pap. 6.95 (*0-89594-949-0*) Crossing Pr.

Pocket Guide to the Common Birds of Ireland. Eric Dempsey & Michael O'Clery. (Illus.). 249p. (Orig.). 1995. pap. 17.95 (*0-7171-2296-4*, Pub. by Gill & MacMill) Irish Bks Media.

***Pocket Guide to the Hawaiian Lei: A Tradition of Aloha.** Ronn Ronck. (Illus.). 80p. 1999. pap. 8.95 (*1-56647-181-8*) Mutual Pub HI.

Pocket Guide to the Identification of First Editions. 5th ed. Ed. by William M. McBride. 100p. 1995. pap. 9.95 (*0-930313-03-8*) McBride Pub.

Pocket Guide to the Internet. Ed. by Dave Stern. 1996. 5.99 (*0-614-14482-5*) PB.

Pocket Guide to the Internet: The No Sweat Guide to the Information Superhighway. Gary Gach. LC 96-154952. 1996. mass mkt. 5.99 (*0-671-56850-7*) PB.

Pocket Guide to the Location of Art in the United States. Ed. by Emma L. Fundaburk & Mary D. Foreman. 314p. 1977. 7.00 (*0-910642-04-4*) Am Bicent Mus.

Pocket Guide to the Maine Outdoors. 2nd ed. Eben Thomas. LC 89-32517. (Illus.). 242p. (Orig.). 1989. pap. 11.95 (*0-945980-13-2*) Nrth Country Pr.

Pocket Guide to the National Electrical Code. Marvin J. Fischer. 288p. (C). 1984. 9.95 (*0-13-683995-9*) P-H.

Pocket Guide to the National Electrical Code. 1987th ed. Marvin J. Fischer. 288p. 1987. 11.50 (*0-13-684606-8*) P-H.

Pocket Guide to the National Electrical Code 1999 Edition. Marvin J. Fischer. 448p. 1998. pap. text 24.95 (*0-13-020724-1*) P-H.

Pocket Guide to the Oesophagus. David Evans. 1998. pap. text 29.95 (*0-632-05085-3*) Blackwell Sci.

Pocket Guide to the Operating Room. 2nd ed. Maxine A. Goldman. (Illus.). 655p. (C). 1995. pap. text 34.95 (*0-8036-0033-X*) Davis Co.

Pocket Guide to the Place-Names of Wales. Hywel W. Owen. LC 98-217939. (Pocket Guides Ser.). 120p. 1998. pap. 9.95 (*0-7083-1458-9*, Pub. by Univ Wales Pr) Paul & Co Pubs.

Pocket Guide to the Southeast Aegean. Rod Heikell & Mike Harper. 105p. (C). 1985. 75.00 (*0-85288-101-0*, Pub. by Laurie Norie & Wilson Ltd) St Mut.

Pocket Guide to the 12 Steps. Kathleen S. LC 97-11609. (Crossing Press Pocket Ser.). (Illus.). 128p. 1997. pap. 6.95 (*0-89594-864-8*) Crossing Pr.

***Pocket Guide to the 2000 Olympics.** Bob Knotts. Ed. by Margaret Sieck. 96p. (J). (gr. 2-8). 2000. pap. 3.99 (*1-886749-94-9*) SI For Kids.

***Pocket Guide to the Wines of Australia.** James Halliday. 208p. 2000. 14.95 (*1-84000-249-2*, Pub. by Mitchell Beazley) Antique Collect.

Pocket Guide to TQM. Oakland & Morris. 96p. 1998. pap. text 16.95 (*0-7506-3986-5*) Buttrwrth-Heinemann.

Pocket Guide to Treasure Signs. Thomas P. Terry. (Illus.). 24p. (Orig.). 1977. pap. 1.95 (*0-939850-08-7*) Spec Pub.

Pocket Guide to Treatment in Occupational Therapy. Stein. LC 99-36125. 381p. 1999. pap. 40.00 (*0-7693-0025-1*) Thomson Learn.

Pocket Guide to Treatment in Speech-Language Pathology. M. N. Hegde. (Illus.). 320p. (Orig.). (C). 1995. pap. text 45.00 (*1-56593-274-9*, 0596) Thomson Learn.

Pocket Guide to Trees. Keith D. Rushforth. 1981. 7.95 (*0-686-73804-7*) S&S Trade.

Pocket Guide to 12 Lead ECG Interpretation. Gerry C. Mulholland. LC 97-42698. 1998. 19.95 (*0-683-40235-8*) Lppncott W & W.

Pocket Guide to U. S. Electric Utilities. 4th rev. ed. Ed. by John Crass. 400p. 1996. pap. 110.00 (*1-56760-039-5*) Utility Data Inst.

Pocket Guide to Vaccination & Prophylaxis. Hal B. Jenson. Ed. by Lisette Bralow. LC 98-38330. (Illus.). 270p. (C). 1998. pap. text 19.95 (*0-7216-7993-5*, W B Saunders Co) Harcrt Hlth Sci Grp.

Pocket Guide to Valuable Old Lace & Lacy Linens. Elizabeth M. Kurella. 96p. (Orig.). 1997. pap. text 18.00 (*0-9642871-1-0*) Lace Merchant.

Pocket Guide to Visualization. Helen Graham. LC 97-25970. (Crossing Press Pocket Ser.). (Illus.). 144p. (Orig.). 1997. pap. 6.95 (*0-89594-885-0*) Crossing Pr.

Pocket Guide to Vitamins. Susan K. Podell. LC 93-2344. 56p. 1994. pap. 2.99 (*0-385-46823-7*) Doubleday.

Pocket Guide to Vocabulary. 3rd ed. Samuel C. Brownstein et al. LC 97-117. 256p. 1997. pap. 6.95 (*0-8120-9818-8*) Barron.

Pocket Guide to Walleye Fishing in Lakes. Lester Cordes, II et al. (Illus.). 28p. 1995. spiral bd. 12.95 (*1-886127-08-5*) Greycliff Pub.

Pocket Guide to Westmoreland's Paneled Grape Pattern in Milk Glass. Lorraine Kovar. LC 97-218165. (Illus.). 32p. 1997. pap. 9.95 (*0-9659807-0-7*) L Kovar.

Pocket Guide to Wicca. Paul Tuitean & Estelle Daniels. LC 98-5017. (Crossing Press Pocket Ser.). (Illus.). 112p. 1998. pap. 6.95 (*0-89594-904-0*) Crossing Pr.

Pocket Guide to Wild Edible & Medicinal Plants. Kathryn Cox. (Illus.). 80p. (Orig.). 1996. spiral bd. 12.95 (*0-9651749-0-5*) Motherlove Herbal.

Pocket Guide to Wood Finishes. Nigel Lofthouse. (Illus.). 64p. 1993. spiral bd. 16.95 (*1-55870-272-5*, Betrwy Bks) F & W Pubns Inc.

***Pocket Guide to Writing History.** Mary Lynn Rampolla. LC 97-74969. 85p. 1998. pap. text 8.95 (*0-312-18006-3*) St Martin.

***Pocket Guide to Writing History.** 3rd ed. Mary Lynn Rampolla. 2000. pap. text, student ed. write for info. (*0-312-24766-4*) St Martin.

***Pocket Guide Tokyo.** (Illus.). 2000. pap. 12.95 (*0-88729-402-2*, Insight Guides) Langenscheidt.

***Pocket Guide Wales in Quotations.** Meic Stephens. 152p. 2000. 12.95 (*0-7083-1560-7*, Pub. by U Wales Pr) Paul & Co Pubs.

Pocket Guidebook on Environmental Auditing. 2nd ed. M. A. Ruiz & Paul N. Cheremisinoff. (Illus.). 109p. 1989. 24.95 (*0-925760-31-5*) SciTech Pubs.

Pocket Guides to the Internet, 6 vols., Vol. 1. Mark D. Veljkov & George Hartnell. LC 93-40260. 1993. 9.95 (*0-88736-943-X*) Mecklermedia.

Pocket Guides to the Internet, 6 vols., Vol. 2. Mark D. Veljkov & George Hartnell. LC 93-40260. 1993. 9.95 (*0-88736-944-8*) Mecklermedia.

Pocket Guides to the Internet, 6 vols., Vol. 3. Mark D. Veljkov & George Hartnell. LC 93-40260. 1993. 9.95 (*0-88736-945-6*) Mecklermedia.

Pocket Guides to the Internet, 6 vols., Vol. 4. Mark D. Veljkov & George Hartnell. LC 93-40260. 1993. 9.95 (*0-88736-946-4*) Mecklermedia.

Pocket Guides to the Internet, 6 vols., Vol. 5. Mark D. Veljkov & George Hartnell. LC 93-40260. 1993. 9.95 (*0-88736-947-2*) Mecklermedia.

Pocket Guides to the Internet, 6 vols., Vol. 6. Mark D. Veljkov & George Hartnell. LC 93-40260. 1993. 9.95 (*0-88736-948-0*) Mecklermedia.

Pocket Handbook: Radiographic Positioning & Techniques. 2nd ed. Kenneth L. Bontrager. (Illus.). 294p. 1995. pap. text 27.75 (*0-9641723-1-3*) Bontrager Pub.

Pocket Handbook for Living the Christian Life: A Simple Guide to Christian Living. Charles F. Gilmore. 1990. reprint ed. pap. 1.95 (*0-9627630-1-2*) Light & Living.

Pocket Handbook for Solid-Liquid Separations. Nicholas P. Cheremisinoff. LC 84-8970. (Illus.). 160p. 1984. reprint ed. pap. 49.60 (*0-608-07939-1*, 206791200012) Bks Demand.

Pocket Handbook of Clinical Psychiatry. Harold I. Kaplan & Benjamin J. Sadock. 352p. 1990. 33.00 (*0-683-04523-7*) Lppncott W & W.

Pocket Handbook of Clinical Psychiatry. 2nd ed. Harold I. Kaplan & Benjamin J. Sadock. (Illus.). 352p. 1996. pap. 35.00 (*0-683-04583-0*) Lppncott W & W.

Pocket Handbook of Electroanalytical Instrumental Techniques for Analytical Chemistry. Osteryoung. (C). 2001. 14.95 (*0-13-738907-8*, Macmillan Coll) P-H.

Pocket Handbook of Emergency Psychiatric Medicine. Harold I. Kaplan & Benjamin J. Sadock. LC 93-18379. 376p. 1993. 33.00 (*0-683-04539-3*) Lppncott W & W.

Pocket Handbook of Image Processing Algorithms in C. Harley R. Myler. 303p. (C). 1993. 30.00 (*0-13-642240-3*) P-H.

Pocket Handbook of Juice Power. Carlson Wade. 88p. 1992. pap. 3.95 (*0-87983-591-5*, 35915K, Keats Publng) NTC Contemp Pub Co.

Pocket Handbook of Primary Care Psychiatry. Harold I. Kaplan & Benjamin J. Sadock. LC 96-32243. (Illus.). 486p. 1996. pap. 37.00 (*0-683-30017-2*) Lppncott W & W.

Pocket Handbook of Psychiatric Drug Treatment. Harold I. Kaplan & Benjamin J. Sadock. LC 92-22846. (Illus.). 288p. 1992. pap. 33.00 (*0-683-04538-5*) Lppncott W & W.

Pocket Handbook of Psychiatric Drug Treatment. 2nd ed. Harold I. Kaplan & Benjamin J. Sadock. 328p. 1996. 35.00 (*0-683-18006-1*) Lppncott W & W.

Pocket Handbook, Radiographic Positioning & Techniques: Student Edition. Kenneth L. Bontrager. (Illus.). 290p. (Orig.). (C). 1994. pap. text 24.00 (*0-9641723-0-5*) Bontrager Pub.

Pocket Harmonica Songbook. David Harp. 64p. 1993. pap. 4.95 (*0-918321-97-2*) Musical I Pr.

Pocket Harmonica Songbook, Incl. Harmonica. David Harp. 64p. 1992. pap. 11.95 (*0-918321-96-4*) Musical I Pr.

Pocket Herbal Reference. Rita Elkins. 1997. pap. text 5.95 (*1-885670-37-0*) Woodland UT.

Pocket Herbal Reference Guide. Debra Nuzzi. (Crossing Press Pocket Ser.). (Illus.). 144p. (Orig.). 1992. pap. 6.95 (*0-89594-568-1*) Crossing Pr.

Pocket Highway Atlas. rev. ed. 64p. 1984. 1.25 (*0-88098-057-5*, H M Gousha) Prntice Hall Bks.

***Pocket History of Gaelic Culture.** Alan Titley. 112p. 2000. pap. 7.95 (*0-86278-569-3*, Pub. by OBrien Pr) IPG Chicago.

Pocket History of Ireland. Breandan O. Heithir. LC 89-82005. 112p. 1997. pap. 7.95 (*0-86278-188-4*, Pub. by OBrien Pr) Irish Amer Bk.

***Pocket History of Ireland.** 2nd ed. Breandan O'Heithir. 112p. 2000. pap. 7.95 (*0-86278-633-9*, Pub. by OBrien Pr) IPG Chicago.

Pocket History of Irish Literature. A. Norman Jeffares. (Illus.). 160p. 1997. pap. 7.95 (*0-86278-502-2*, Pub. by OBrien Pr) Irish Amer Bk.

***Pocket History of Irish Rebels.** Morgan Llywelyn. 112p. 2000. pap. 7.95 (*0-86278-580-4*, Pub. by OBrien Pr) IPG Chicago.

Pocket History of Irish Traditional Music. Gearoid O'Hallmurain. (Pocket History Ser.). 144p. 1998. pap. 7.95 (*0-86278-555-3*, Pub. by OBrien Pr) Irish Amer Bk.

Pocket History of the Banshee. Patricia Lysaght. 144p. 1997. pap. 7.95 (*0-86278-501-4*, Pub. by OBrien Pr) Irish Amer Bk.

Pocket History of the IRA. Brendan O'Brien. (Illus.). 144p. 1997. pap. 7.95 (*0-86278-511-1*, Pub. by OBrien Pr) Irish Amer Bk.

***Pocket History of the IRA.** Brendan O'Brien. 112p. 2000. pap. 7.95 (*0-86278-642-8*, Pub. by OBrien Pr) IPG Chicago.

Pocket History of the U. S. Allan Nevins. Ed. by Maryanne Sacco. 736p. 1992. mass mkt. 7.99 (*0-671-79023-4*) PB.

Pocket History of the U. S. Allan Nevins & Henry S. Commager. (YA). (gr. 10 up). 1991. mass mkt. 4.95 (*0-671-62992-1*) PB.

Pocket History of the World. Mary Winters. Ed. by Roy Zarucchi. (Chapbook Ser.). (Illus.). 56p. (Orig.). 1996. pap. 9.95 (*1-879205-66-1*) Nightshade Pr.

Pocket History of Ulster. Brian Barton. (Illus.). 224p. 1997. pap. 8.95 (*0-86278-428-X*, Pub. by OBrien Pr) Irish Amer Bk.

Pocket Holland, Belguim, Luxembourg. Ed. by Pocket Books Staff. 1988. mass mkt. 5.95 (*0-671-84842-9*) PB.

Pocket Honolulu & Waikiki. Fodors Staff. 1998. pap. 8.50 (*0-679-00238-3*) Fodors Travel.

Pocket I-Ching. Gary G. Melyan. 1999. 5.99 (*0-7858-1122-2*) Bk Sales Inc.

Pocket I-Ching. Gary Melyan. LC 88-50327. (Illus.). 182p. 1988. reprint ed. pap. 8.95 (*0-8048-1566-6*) Tuttle Pubng.

Pocket Idiot Guide to Your Portable Office. 192p. 1998. 15.95 (*0-02-862927-2*) Macmillan Gen Ref.

Pocket Idiot's Guide to America's Golf Courses. (Pocket Idiot's Guides Ser.). 192p. 1998. pap. 9.95 (*0-02-862944-2*) Macmillan Gen Ref.

***Pocket Idiot's Guide to Baby Names.** Sonia Weiss. (Pocket Idiot's Guide Ser.). (Illus.). 192p. 1999. pap. 7.95 (*0-02-863182-X*, Pub. by Macmillan) S&S Trade.

Pocket Idiot's Guide to Bartending. Palyers Club Staff. (Pocket Idiot's Guides Ser.). 1998. pap. 9.95 (*0-02-862700-8*) Macmillan Gen Ref.

Pocket Idiot's Guide to Beanie Babies. Holly Stowe. LC 98-88317. (Illus.). 196p. 1998. pap. 9.95 (*0-02-863078-5*, Pub. by Macmillan Gen Ref) S&S Trade.

***Pocket Idiot's Guide to Being a Groom.** Jennifer Lata & Mark Rung. (Pocket Idiot's Guide Ser.). 200p. 1999. pap. 7.95 (*0-02-863649-X*) Macmillan.

Pocket Idiot's Guide to Betting on Horses. Sharon Smith. (Pocket Idiot's Guides Ser.). (Illus.). 216p. 1999. pap. 7.95 (*1-58245-109-5*) Macmillan Gen Ref.

Pocket Idiot's Guide to Car Repair. Dan Ramsey. (Pocket Idiot's Guides Ser.). (Illus.). 192p. 1997. pap. 9.95 (*0-02-862014-3*) Macmillan Gen Ref.

Pocket Idiot's Guide to Choosing & Training a Dog. Sarah Hodgson. LC 97-20855. (Pocket Idiot's Guides Ser.). (Illus.). 192p. 1997. pap. 9.95 (*0-87605-281-2*) Macmillan Gen Ref.

***Pocket Idiot's Guide to Choosing Cigars.** Tad Gage. LC 98-88159. (Pocket Idiot's Guides Ser.). 192p. 1998. pap. 9.95 (*0-02-862701-6*) Macmillan Gen Ref.

Pocket Idiot's Guide to Choosing Wine. Philip Seldon. LC 97-73177. (Pocket Idiot's Guides Ser.). (Illus.). 208p. 1997. pap. 9.95 (*0-02-862016-X*) Macmillan Gen Ref.

Pocket Idiot's Guide to Dog Tricks. Sarah Hodgson. LC 99-20878. (Pocket Idiot's Guides Ser.). (Illus.). 184p. 1999. pap. 7.95 (*1-58245-105-2*) Macmillan Gen Ref.

Pocket Idiot's Guide to First Aid. Stephen J. Rosenberg & Karla Dougherty. LC 97-73179. (Pocket Idiot's Guides Ser.). (Illus.). 192p. 1997. pap. 9.95 (*0-02-862015-1*) Macmillan Gen Ref.

Pocket Idiot's Guide to French. Gail Stein. (Pocket Idiot's Guides Ser.). 1999. pap. 9.95 (*0-02-863146-3*) Macmillan Gen Ref.

Pocket Idiot's Guide to Freshwater Aquariums. Michael Wickland. (Pocket Idiot's Guides Ser.). (Illus.). 218p. 1999. pap. 7.95 (*1-58245-110-9*) Macmillan Gen Ref.

Pocket Idiot's Guide to German. Alice Mueller & Stephen Mueller. (Pocket Idiot's Guides Ser.). 184p. 1999. pap. 9.95 (*0-02-863177-3*) Macmillan Gen Ref.

Pocket Idiot's Guide to Getting a Good Night's Sleep. Martin C. Moore-Ede & Suzanne LeVert. (Pocket Idiot's Guides Ser.). (Illus.). 215p. 1999. pap. 9.95 (*0-02-863380-6*, Pub. by Macmillan Gen Ref) S&S Trade.

***Pocket Idiot's Guide to Golf Accessories.** Rich Mintzer. (Pocket Idiot's Guides Ser.). 192p. 1999. pap. 9.95 (*0-02-863376-8*, Pub. by Macmillan Gen Ref) S&S Trade.

Pocket Idiot's Guide to Golf Courses. 180p. 1998. 9.95 (*0-02-862704-0*, Pub. by Macmillan) S&S Trade.

Pocket Idiot's Guide to Home Repair. David J. Tenenbaum. LC 97-80973. (Pocket Idiot's Guides Ser.). 208p. 1997. pap. 9.95 (*0-02-862118-2*) Macmillan Gen Ref.

Pocket Idiot's Guide to Horoscopes. Madeline Gerwick-Brodeur. (Pocket Idiot's Guides Ser.). 1998. pap. 9.95 (*0-02-862702-4*) Macmillan Gen Ref.

***Pocket Idiot's Guide to Italian.** Gabrielle Euvino. LC 97-80973. (Pocket Idiot's Guides Ser.). 1999. pap. 9.95 (*0-02-863147-1*) Macmillan Gen Ref.

***Pocket Idiot's Guide to Living on a Budget.** Jennifer Basye Sander & Peter J. Sander. (Pocket Idiot's Guides Ser.). (Illus.). 192p. 1999. pap. 9.95 (*0-02-863389-X*, Pub. by Macmillan Gen Ref) S&S Trade.

Pocket Idiot's Guide to Living with a Cat. Carol Janik & Ruth Rejnis. LC 98-49276. (Pocket Idiot's Guides Ser.). (Illus.). 186p. 1999. pap. 7.95 (*1-58245-111-7*) Macmillan Gen Ref.

***Pocket Idiot's Guide to One-Minute Managing.** Arthur R. Pell. LC 99-64050. (Pocket Idiot's Guides Ser.). (Illus.). 202p. 1999. pap. 9.95 (*0-02-863343-1*, Pub. by Macmillan Gen Ref) S&S Trade.

Pocket Idiot's Guide to Photography. Roger Woodson. LC 97-80974. (Pocket Idiot's Guides Ser.). (Illus.). 192p. 1997. pap. 9.95 (*0-02-862129-8*) Macmillan Gen Ref.

Pocket Idiot's Guide to Portable Office. 180p. 1998. 9.95 (*0-02-862705-9*, Pub. by Macmillan) S&S Trade.

***Pocket Idiot's Guide to Reading Stocks.** 192p. 1999. 7.95 (*0-02-863851-4*) Macmillan.

Pocket Idiot's Guide to Spanish Phrases. Alpha Development Group Staff. LC 99-60218. (Pocket Idiot's Guides Ser.). (Illus.). 242p. 1998. pap. 9.95 (*0-02-862703-2*) Macmillan Gen Ref.

***Pocket Idiot's Guide to Vitamins.** Alan H. Pressman & Sheila Buff. (Pocket Idiot's Guides Ser.). 192p. 1999. pap. 9.95 (*0-02-863397-0*, Pub. by Macmillan Gen Ref) S&S Trade.

***Pocket Immuno Facts.** John D. Grabenstein. (Illus.). 1999. pap. 34.95 (*1-57439-061-9*) Facts & Comparisons.

Pocket Impressionists. (Illus.). 432p. 1999. pap. 9.95 (*1-86205-108-9*, Pub. by Pavilion Bks Ltd) Trafalgar.

Pocket International Encyclopedia of Business Management. Ed. by Malcolm Warner. LC 97-12149. 320p. 1997. pap. 15.99 (*1-86152-113-8*) Thomson Learn.

Pocket Internet Directory Dictionary. Bryan Pfaffenberger. 400p. 1997. 5.95 (*0-02-861889-0*) Macmillan.

Pocket Internet Guide: For Real Estate Professionals. unabridged ed. Ernie Blood. 130p. 1996. reprint ed. pap. 29.95 (*1-893572-06-4*) Carmel Pubg.

Pocket Interpreter: Chinese. Lydia Chen & Ying Bian. (Illus.). 216p. 1988. pap. 7.95 (*0-8351-2320-0*) China Bks.

***Pocket Investor.** Ed. by Philip Ryland. LC 98-40637. (Economist Ser.). 215p. 1998. pap. 14.95 (*0-471-29597-3*) Wiley.

Pocket Irish Dictionary. Seosamh Watson. (Pocket Guide Ser.). 72p. 1985. pap. 7.95 (*0-86281-150-3*, Pub. by Appletree Pr) Irish Bks Media.

Pocket Israel Holy. 1988. 5.95 (*0-671-84874-7*) S&S Trade.

Pocket Istanbul. Fodors Staff. 1999. pap. 9.00 (*0-679-00291-X*) Fodors Travel.

***Pocket Italian Dictionary.** (ITA & ENG.). 672p. 2000. 12.95 (*1-58573-039-4*, Insight Guides) Langenscheidt.

Pocket Jamaica. 4th ed. Fodor's Staff. 1998. pap. 8.50 (*0-679-00054-2*) Fodors Travel.

Pocket Japanese. Langenscheidt Staff. (Insight Guides Ser.). 1998. pap. 12.95 (*0-88729-171-6*) Langenscheidt.

***Pocket Japanese Dictionary.** (JPN & ENG.). 2000. pap. 13.95 (*1-58573-038-6*, Insight Guides) Langenscheidt.

Pocket Journal - Blue. (Masquerade Ser.). 128p. 1995. 4.95 (*0-8069-3954-0*) Sterling.

P

***Pocket Journal for Creative Ideas, Thoughts, Notes, Drawings & Inspirations.** Tom Rauscher. 62p. 2000. pap. 8.95 (*0-9672613-1-7*) Inventors Place.

Pocket Kitten. Illus. by Pam Adams. (Pocket Pals Ser.). (J). 1995. bds. 2.99 (*0-85953-905-9*) Childs Play.

Pocket Knife Price Guide Winchester & Marble, Bk. 3. Larry Ehrhardt & Jack Ferrell. 128p. 1974. spiral bd. 25.00 (*0-913902-08-X*) Heart Am Pr.

Pocket Koala. Pam Adams. (J). 1996. bds. 2.99 (*0-85953-917-2*) Childs Play.

***Pocket Korean Dictionary.** (KOR & ENG.). 2000. 13.95 (*1-58573-056-4*, Insight Guides) Langenscheidt.

Pocket Lawyer: Solve Your Own Legal Disputes. Marilyn D. Sullivan. Ed. by Jean B. Howard. LC 96-49952. 320p. (Orig.). 1997. pap. 24.95 (*0-9629239-2-3*) Venture Two.

Pocket Lexicon & Concordance to the Temple Shakespeare. Marian Edwardes. LC 74-164759. reprint ed. 47.50 (*0-404-02261-8*) AMS Pr.

Pocket Library of Letters: For Real Estate Professionals. unabridged ed. Ernie Blood. 283p. 1989. reprint ed. pap. 29.95 (*1-893572-02-1*) Carmel Pubg.

Pocket Library of Letters II: For Real Estate Professionals. unabridged ed. Ernie Blood. 1999. reprint ed. pap. 29.95 (*1-893572-08-0*) Carmel Pubg.

Pocket London. 1988. 5.95 (*0-671-84293-5*) S&S Trade.

***Pocket London 2000.** (Guides Ser.). (Illus.). 1999. 9.00 (*0-679-00349-5*, Compass Amrcn) Fodors Travel.

Pocket Louvre: A Vistor's Guide to 500 Works. Claude Mignot. LC 99-18384. (Illus.). 540p. (J). 2000. 19.95 (*0-7892-0578-5*, Abbeville Kids) Abbeville Pr.

Pocket Machzor Set: Ashkenaz, 5 vols. 150.00 (*0-89906-022-6*) Mesorah Pubns.

Pocket Mad. (Mad Ser.). (Illus.). 1980. mass mkt. 1.75 (*0-446-94594-3*, Pub. by Warner Bks) Little.

Pocket Magic: Graphic Games for the Pocket Computer. Bill L. Behrendt. LC 82-80271. (Illus.). 96p. (Orig.). (YA). 1982. 17.95 (*0-685-05521-3*); pap. 9.95 (*0-942412-01-X*); audio 8.95 (*0-686-87025-5*) Micro Text Pubns.

Pocket Manual for Radiographic Anatomy & Positioning. Madigan. 320p. (C). 1997. pap. 23.95 (*0-8385-8237-0*, A-8237-8, Apple Lange Med) McGraw.

Pocket Manual of Basic Surgical Skills. Charles W. Van Way & Buerk. (Illus.). 240p. (C). (gr. 13). 1986. spiral bd. 29.00 (*0-8016-5231-6*, 05231) Mosby Inc.

Pocket Manual of Differential Diagnosis. 3rd ed. Stephen N. Adler et al. LC 93-33819. 392p. 1994. pap. text 24.95 (*0-316-01109-6*) Lppncott W & W.

***Pocket Manual of Differential Diagnosis.** 4th ed. Stephen N. Adler et al. LC 99-42878. 352p. 1999. pap. text 24.95 (*0-7817-1943-7*) Lppncott W & W.

Pocket Massage for Stress Relief. Clare Maxwell-Hudson. 96p. 1996. 9.95 (*0-7894-0438-9*) DK Pub Inc.

Pocket Matchsafes: Reflections of Life & Art, 1840-1920. W. Eugene Sanders, Jr. & Christine C. Sanders. LC 97-28363. (Schiffer Book for Collectors Ser.). (Illus.). 176p. 1997. pap. 34.95 (*0-7643-0324-4*) Schiffer.

Pocket Medical French. Russell Dollinger. (FRE & ENG.). 262p. 1995. spiral bd. 11.95 (*0-945585-03-9*) Booksmythe.

Pocket Medical Russian. Russell Dollinger. (FRE & ENG.). 1995. spiral bd. 11.95 (*0-945585-04-7*) Booksmythe.

Pocket Medical Spanish. Russell Dollinger. (Medical Interpreting Aid Ser.). (ENG & SPA.). 262p. 1991. spiral bd. 11.95 (*0-945585-02-0*) Booksmythe.

Pocket Medicinal Herbs. Penelope Ody. LC 96-30991. 96p. 1997. pap. 9.95 (*0-7894-1616-6*) DK Pub Inc.

Pocket Medicinal Herbs. Storey Publishing Staff. 1997. 9.95 (*0-676-57029-1*) Random.

Pocket Medicine. Marc S. Sabatine. 192p. 24.95 (*0-7817-1649-7*) Lppncott W & W.

***Pocket Mentor: A Handbook for Teachers.** Chris Niebrand & Horn. LC 98-54370. 268p. 1999. 27.50 (*0-205-29693-9*) Allyn.

Pocket Mentor: A Handbook for Teachers. Chris Niebrand et al. LC 93-145416. xviii, 248 p. 1992. write for info. (*0-8251-2123-X*) J W Walch.

Pocket Mentor: How to Get Every Promotion You Want from Now On! Susan J. Powers. 390p. 1995. 29.95 (*1-886573-02-6*); pap. 19.95 (*1-886573-01-8*) Change Pubns.

***Pocket Menu Reader China.** 2000. pap. 7.95 (*1-58573-040-8*, Insight Guides) Langenscheidt.

***Pocket Menu Reader France.** (Illus.). 2000. pap. 7.95 (*0-88729-305-0*) Langenscheidt.

***Pocket Menu Reader Germany.** 2000. pap. 7.95 (*0-88729-310-7*) Langenscheidt.

***Pocket Menu Reader Greece.** 2000. pap. 7.95 (*0-88729-311-5*) Langenscheidt.

***Pocket Menu Reader Italy.** 2000. pap. 7.95 (*0-88729-313-1*) Langenscheidt.

***Pocket Menu Reader Mexico.** 175p. 2000. pap. 7.95 (*1-58573-041-6*, Insight Guides) Langenscheidt.

***Pocket Menu Reader Russia.** 189p. 2000. pap. 7.95 (*1-58573-042-4*, Insight Guides) Langenscheidt.

***Pocket Menu Reader Spain.** 2000. pap. 7.95 (*0-88729-315-8*) Langenscheidt.

Pocket Mexico. 1988. 5.95 (*0-671-84847-X*) S&S Trade.

Pocket Mexico City. Fodor's Staff. 1998. pap. 9.00 (*0-679-00244-8*) Fodors Travel.

Pocket Mirror. Janet Frame. LC 67-18210. 121p. 1991. pap. 6.95 (*0-8076-1272-3*) Braziller.

Pocket Mnemonics for Practitioners. abr. ed. Robert Bloomfield & Ted Chandler. 1983. pap. 4.95 (*0-9612242-2-3*) Harbinger Med Pr NC.

***Pocket Modern Welsh Dictionary: A Guide to the Living Language.** Ed. by Gareth King. 576p. 2000. pap. 16.95 (*0-19-864531-7*) OUP.

Pocket Monologues for Men. Ed. by Roger Karshner. LC 98-22435. 128p. 1998. pap. 9.95 (*0-940669-41-2*, D-46) Dramaline Pubns.

Pocket Monologues for Women. Susan Pomerance. LC 97-24251. 96p. 1997. pap. 9.95 (*0-940669-36-6*, D-42) Dramaline Pubns.

Pocket Mouse. Pam Adams. (J). 1996. bds. 2.99 (*0-85953-911-3*) Childs Play.

Pocket Munich. 2nd ed. Fodor's Staff. 1998. pap. 9.00 (*0-679-00051-8*) Fodors Travel.

***Pocket New Testament.** 2000. pap. text 3.25 (*5-550-02384-9*) Nairi.

Pocket New York City. 1988. 5.95 (*0-671-84406-7*) S&S Trade.

***Pocket OB/GYN.** C. Scott Naylor. LC 99-44469. 1999. write for info. (*0-7817-1770-1*, Lippnctt) Lppncott W & W.

Pocket Obstetrics & Gynecology. 11th ed. Ed. by Stanley G. Clayton & John R. Newton. (Illus.). 392p. 1988. pap. text 25.00 (*0-443-03777-9*) Church.

Pocket Oxford Book of Prayer. George Appleton. 128p. 1989. pap. 14.00 (*0-19-122441-3*) OUP.

Pocket Oxford Dictionary & Thesaurus. Ed. by Frank R. Abate. 992p. 1999. pap. 12.95 (*0-19-513097-9*) OUP.

Pocket Oxford Dictionary of Current English. 8th rev. ed. Ed. by Della Thompson. 1,088p. 1996. 16.95 (*0-19-860045-3*) OUP.

Pocket Oxford-Duden German Dictionary. 2nd rev. ed. Ed. by M. Clark & O. Thyen. LC 99-174797. 856p. 1998. pap. 11.95 (*0-19-860131-X*) OUP.

Pocket Oxford German Dictionary, 2 vols. Incl. Pt. 1. German-English. 3rd ed. (ENG & GER.). 1975. Pt. 2. English-German. Compiled by C. T. Carr. (ENG & GER.). 1975. (GER.). 712p. 1981. Set pap. 8.95 (*0-19-864138-9*) OUP.

***Pocket Oxford Greek Dictionary.** Ed. by J. T. Pring. 592p. 2000. pap. 15.95 (*0-19-860327-4*) OUP.

Pocket Oxford-Hachette French Dictionary. Ed. by Marie-Helene Correard. 800p. 1997. pap. 11.95 (*0-19-864534-1*) OUP.

Pocket Oxford Italian Dictionary. Ed. by Deborah Mazza et al. LC 97-228867. 704p. 1997. pap. 11.95 (*0-19-860007-0*) OUP.

***Pocket Oxford Latin Dictionary.** Ed. by James Morwood. 368p. 2000. pap. 11.95 (*0-19-860283-9*) OUP.

Pocket Oxford Latin Dictionary. James Morwood. (Illus.). 368p. 1995. reprint ed. pap. 11.95 (*0-19-864228-8*) OUP.

Pocket Oxford Latin Dictionary. 2nd ed. Ed. by S. E. Woodhouse & James Morwood. LC 94-11749. (LAT.). 366p. 1994. 17.95 (*0-19-864227-X*) OUP.

***Pocket Oxford Russian Dictionary.** Ed. by Jessie Coulson et al. 636p. 2000. pap. 11.95 (*0-19-860150-6*) OUP.

Pocket Oxford Russian Dictionary. 2nd ed. Ed. by Jessie Coulson et al. LC 99-176653. 636p. 1995. pap. 11.95 (*0-19-864526-0*) OUP.

Pocket Oxford Russian-English/English-Russian Dictionary. 2nd rev. ed. Ed. by Della Thompson et al. 638p. (YA). (gr. 9-12). 1994. 25.00 (*0-19-864500-7*) OUP.

Pocket Oxford Spanish Dictionary. Ed. by Carol S. Carvajal & Jane Horwood. LC 97-3814. 992p. 1997. pap. 9.95 (*0-19-521346-7*) OUP.

Pocket Pal. 16th ed. International Paper Staff. 233p. 11.00 (*0-614-25523-6*, 00DC4423) Print Indus Am.

Pocket Pal. 16th ed. International Paper Staff. 233p. 11.00 (*0-614-25541-4*, 00DC4423) Print Indus Am.

Pocket Pal Spanish Edition: Manual de Artes Graficas. 15th rev. ed. Ed. by Michael H. Bruno. (SPA., Illus.). 264p. 1993. pap. text 20.00 (*0-88362-255-6*, OODC44482) GATFPress.

Pocket Pals: To Knit by Hand or Machine. Val Love. (Illus.). 32p. 1995. pap. 10.00 (*1-886828-00-8*) Dovetail Desgn.

Pocket Panda. Pam Adams. (J). 1996. bds. 2.99 (*0-85953-915-6*) Childs Play.

***Pocket Paper Engineer Vol. I: How to Make Pop-Ups.** Carol Barton. (Illus.). 50p. 2000. pap. 40.00 (*0-9627752-0-7*) Pop Kinetics.

***Pocket Partner.** 2nd ed. Dennis H. Evers et al. LC 00-131473. 576p. 2000. pap. 9.95 (*1-885071-26-4*) Sequoia Pub Inc.

Pocket Parts Pal: A Catalog of HO Scale Car Parts. John K. Timothy. 52p. 1992. pap. text 3.50 (*1-883796-00-8*) What It Is.

Pocket Parts Pal: Ho Scale Parts Guide. 3rd rev. ed. Kevin Timothy. Ed. by Joanne Collison. (Illus.). 72p. (Orig.). 1994. pap. text 4.95 (*1-883796-05-9*) What It Is.

Pocket Parts Pal: The Complete Guide to Ho Scale Car Parts. 3rd ed. Kevin Timothy. Ed. by Joanne Collison. (Illus.). 72p. (Orig.). pap. text 4.95 (*88-379-6059-X*) What It Is.

Pocket Patch, Vol. 4. Sara Massey. (Illus.). 72p. (C). 1998. pap. 10.50 (*1-56770-446-8*) S Scheewe Pubns.

***Pocket Patch, Vol. 5.** Sara Massey. (Illus.). 72p. 2000. pap. 10.50 (*1-56770-486-7*) S Scheewe Pubns.

Pocket Pathology. Ivan Damjanov & Emanuel Rubin. 550p. 1998. pap. text 23.95 (*0-397-58407-5*) Lppncott W & W.

Pocket Pathology. 7th ed. Ivan Damjanov & Emanuel Rubin. LC 98-21735. 20p. 1999. text. write for info. (*0-7817-1636-5*) Lppncott W & W.

Pocket Patriot. 2nd ed. Robert Woods & Marco Fiorini. (Illus.). 86p. 1997. reprint ed. per. 6.95 (*0-9670373-0-1*, 001) Unity Intl Pubg.

***Pocket Patriot: An Introduction to the Principles of Freedom.** rev. ed. George Grant. LC 99-88254. 256p. 2000. pap. 9.95 (*1-58182-092-5*, Cumberland Hearthside) Cumberland Hse.

Pocket PC Clear & Simple. Craig Peacock. Date not set. pap. 12.95 (*0-7506-7354-0*, Digital DEC) Buttrwrth-Heinemann.

***Pocket PCRef.** 9th ed. Thomas J. Glover & Millie M. Young. LC 91-90581. 608p. 1999. pap. 14.95 (*1-885071-19-1*) Sequoia Pub Inc.

***Pocket PCRef.** 10th ed. Thomas J. Glover & Millie M. Young. 576p. 2000. pap. 14.95 (*1-885071-27-2*) Sequoia Pub Inc.

Pocket PCs Made Simple. Peacock. 160p. pap. text. write for info. (*0-7506-4900-3*) Buttrwrth-Heinemann.

Pocket PDR. 1997. 129.95 (*1-56712-353-8*, F0987) Franklin Elect.

Pocket Pediatrician. David Zigelman. 1996. pap. 17.95 (*0-385-42735-2*) Doubleday.

Pocket Pediatrician: An A-Z Guide to Your Child's Health. David Zigelman. LC 94-11969. 448p. 1994. pap. 13.95 (*0-385-47088-6*) Doubleday.

Pocket Pediatrician: The BC Children's Hospital Manual. Ed. by M. Seear. (Illus.). 626p. (C). 1996. pap. text 32.95 (*0-521-56881-1*) Cambridge U Pr.

Pocket Pediatrics. Mary Lieh-Lai. 200p. 24.95 (*0-7817-2567-4*) Lppncott W & W.

Pocket Pediatrics. Terence Stephenson & Chris O'Callaghan. (Illus.). 394p. (Orig.). 1992. pap. text 30.00 (*0-443-04360-4*) Church.

Pocket Penguin. Michael Twinn. (Pocket Pals Ser.). (Illus.). (J). 1997. bds. 2.99 (*0-85953-980-6*) Childs Play.

Pocket Pep Talk. Jill Spiegel. (Illus.). 72p. (Orig.). 1997. pap. 6.99 (*0-9643325-1-5*) Goal Gtrs MN.

Pocket Performance Specs for Thermoplastics. 670p. (Orig.). 1996. pap. 49.95 (*0-9642570-2-5*) Abby Communs.

Pocket Persian-English Dictionary. Aryanpur. (ENG & PER.). 1049p. 1986. 24.95 (*0-8288-1121-0*, F98990) Fr & Eur.

***Pocket Personal Coach: A Collection of 356 Tips to Energize Your Body, Mind & Spirit.** Eric Harr. 176p. 1999. pap. 12.95 (*1-928595-02-2*) Citron Bay.

Pocket Personal Trainer: A Total Nutrition & Fitness Planner for Busy People. Gay Riley. Ed. by Patricia Rodriguez. 290p. 1994. pap. text 9.95 (*0-9642204-0-7*) Lipo-Visuals.

Pocket Personality Quiz. Lagoon Books Staff. 1999. 6.95 (*1-899712-90-9*) Lagoon Bks.

Pocket Pests: Beetle. Tucker Slingsby Ltd., Staff. (Illus.). 16p. (J). (gr. k-3). 1997. 5.99 (*0-689-81129-2*) S&S Childrens.

Pocket Pests: Cockroach. Tucker Slingsby Ltd., Staff. (Illus.). 16p. (J). (gr. k-3). 1997. 5.99 (*0-689-81130-6*) S&S Childrens.

Pocket Pests: Spider. Tucker Slingsby Ltd., Staff. (Illus.). 16p. (J). (gr. k-3). 1997. 5.99 (*0-689-81131-4*) S&S Childrens.

Pocket Pests: Worm. Tucker Slingsby Ltd., Staff. (Illus.). 16p. (J). (gr. k-3). 1997. 5.99 (*0-689-81132-2*) S&S Childrens.

Pocket Pets. Alvin Silverstein. LC 98-47616. (What a Pet! Ser.). 48p. (J). (gr. 5-8). 1999. 21.40 (*0-7613-1370-2*) TFC Bks NY.

Pocket Picture Guide to Cardiology. 3rd ed. Adam D. Timmis. 1995. text 20.95 (*0-7234-2443-8*, Pub. by Martin Dunitz) Mosby Inc.

Pocket Pilot Handbook: Flight Calculations, Weather Decoder, Aviation Acronyms, Charts & Checklists Pilot Memory Aids. Art Parma. LC 99-209328. (Illus.). 53p. 1998. pap. 6.95 (*0-9631973-8-X*) Flight Time.

Pocket Place Names of Hawaii. Mary K. Pukui et al. LC 88-27747. (Illus.). 96p. (Orig.). 1989. pap. 3.95 (*0-8248-1187-9*) UH Pr.

Pocket Poetry Parenting Guide. Ed. by Jennifer Bosveld. 1999. pap. 12.95 (*0-944754-59-7*) Pudding Hse Pubns.

Pocket Poets Series, 4 vols., Set. LC 73-12817. (Illus.). 1964p. 1973. reprint ed. 200.00 (*0-527-71600-6*) Periodicals Srv.

Pocket Pointers: A Quick Reminder on Any Shot. Pocket Pointers, Inc. Staff. Ed. by Golf Magazine Editors. 1988. pap. 3.00 (*1-878728-18-0*) Golf Gifts.

Pocket Polar Bear. Michael Twinn. (Pocket Pals Ser.). (Illus.). (J). 1997. bds. 2.99 (*0-85953-982-2*) Childs Play.

Pocket Pony. Pam Adams. (J). 1996. bds. 2.99 (*0-85953-913-X*) Childs Play.

Pocket Portfolio Jokes. Braude. 16p. (C). 1989. pap. text 9.95 (*0-13-683871-5*) P-H.

Pocket Power No. 1: Medical. Joseph M. Leonard. 48p. (Orig.). 1988. pap. 2.95 (*0-945893-00-0*) Pocket Power.

Pocket Power No. 2: Taxes. Lois L. Leonard. Ed. by Joseph M. Leonard. 48p. (Orig.). 1988. pap. text 2.95 (*0-945893-01-9*) Pocket Power.

Pocket Power No. 3: Legal. Douglas A. Stoodt. Ed. by Joseph M. Leonard. 48p. (Orig.). 1988. pap. 2.95 (*0-945893-02-7*) Pocket Power.

Pocket Power No. 4: Dental. Wayne A. Brannon & Joseph M. Leonard. 48p. (Orig.). 1988. pap. 2.95 (*0-945893-03-5*) Pocket Power.

Pocket Power No. 5: Veterinary. John L. Augustine & Joseph M. Leonard. 48p. (Orig.). 1988. pap. 2.95 (*0-945893-04-3*) Pocket Power.

Pocket Power No. 6: Travel. Allyson C. Burnette. Ed. by Joseph M. Leonard. 48p. (Orig.). 1988. pap. 2.95 (*0-945893-05-1*) Pocket Power.

Pocket Power Book of Integrity. Byrd Baggett. LC 99-17237. 1999. 4.95 (*1-55853-739-2*) Rutledge Hill Pr.

Pocket Power Book of Leadership. Byrd Baggett. LC 97-191698. 96p. 1997. 4.95 (*1-55853-461-X*) Rutledge Hill Pr.

Pocket Power Book of Motivation. Byrd Baggett. LC 99-17238. 96p. 1999. 4.95 (*1-55853-740-6*) Rutledge Hill Pr.

Pocket Power Book of Performance. Byrd Baggett. LC 97-191705. 96p. 1997. 4.95 (*1-55853-462-8*) Rutledge Hill Pr.

Pocket Powter: Questions & Answers to Help You Change the Way You Look & Feel Forever. Susan Powter. 224p. 1994. pap. 6.99 (*0-671-89456-0*, Fireside) S&S Trade Pap.

Pocket Prague. 3rd ed. Fodors Staff. 1999. pap. 9.00 (*0-679-00053-4*) Fodors Travel.

Pocket Prayer Book. pap. 7.40 (*0-687-60896-1*) Abingdon.

Pocket Prayer Book, White. 1983. pap. text 4.95 (*0-687-60895-3*) Abingdon.

Pocket Prayer Book: St. Joseph Edition. 1997. pap. 0.75 (*0-89942-030-3*, 30/04) Catholic Bk Pub.

Pocket Prayerbook. Date not set. 0.99 (*0-88271-059-1*, 1590) Regina Pr.

Pocket Prayerbook. (SPA.). Date not set. 0.99 (*0-88271-267-5*, 1591); 0.99 (*0-88271-268-3*, 1592) Regina Pr.

Pocket Prayers. Gertrud M. Nelson. 176p. 1995. pap. 6.00 (*0-385-47847-X*) Doubleday.

Pocket Prayers for Lent. Simeon Thole. 29p. (Orig.). 1982. pap. 0.95 (*0-8146-1270-9*) Liturgical Pr.

Pocket Pre-Hospital Spanish. Russell Dollinger. (SPA.). Date not set. spiral bd. write for info. (*0-945585-07-1*) Booksmythe.

Pocket Pressures: Who Benefits from Economic Growth? Public Agenda Foundation Staff. 48p. (C). 1995. pap. 12.19 (*0-07-052213-8*) McGraw.

Pocket Price Guide to British Painting, 1830-1980. Ed. by ACC Research Project Editors. 160p. 1990. 25.00 (*1-85149-124-4*) Antique Collect.

Pocket Print Production Guide. Pira Staff. Date not set. 15.00 (*1-85713-005-7*, Pub. by Pira Pub) Bks Intl VA.

Pocket Printer Series, 6 vols. Michael P. Shanley & Nita G. Coldiron. Incl. Flat Printing for Textile Printers. (Illus.). 64p. (Orig.). 1996. pap. 14.95 (*1-889920-06-1*, PP4); Introduction to T-Shirt Printing. (Illus.). 64p. (Orig.). 1996. pap. 14.95 (*1-889920-03-7*, PP1); Making the Automatic Decision. (Illus.). 64p. (Orig.). 1996. pap. 14.95 (*1-889920-05-3*, PP3); Printing on Specialty Items. (Illus.). 64p. (Orig.). 1996. pap. 14.95 (*1-889920-07-X*, PP5); Troubleshooting Screens & Stencil Systems. (Illus.). 64p. (Orig.). 1996. pap. 14.95 (*1-889920-04-5*, PP2); Upgrading Textile Printing Equipment. (Illus.). 64p. (Orig.). 1996. pap. 14.95 (*1-889920-08-8*, PP6); 1996. Set pap. 75.00 (*1-889920-02-9*) S & C Enterprises.

Pocket Professor Philosophy: Everything You Need to Know about Philosophy. Steven Sherman & Gregg Stebben. Ed. by Denis Boyles. LC 99-31305. 256p. 1999. per. 12.00 (*0-671-53488-2*) PB.

Pocket Professor Religion: Everything You Need to Know about Religion. Gregg Stebben. Ed. by Denis Boyles. LC 99-30402. 256p. 1999. per. 12.00 (*0-671-53489-0*) PB.

Pocket Programmable Calculators in Biochemistry. John E. Barnes & Alan J. Waring. LC 79-2547. 385p. reprint ed. pap. 119.40 (*0-608-16761-4*, 202680900052) Bks Demand.

Pocket Promises for Kids: Verses to Learn from A to Z. Ed. by Susan Jahns. LC 94-219129. (Pocketpacs Ser.). (Illus.). 64p. (J). 1994. pap. text 2.99 (*0-87788-657-1*, H Shaw Pubs) Waterbrook Pr.

Pocket Proof of Facts: Proof of Facts & How to Deal with the Difficult Judge. Ronald Carlson. 1993. 29.95 (*0-614-06017-6*, 4324); audio 95.00 (*0-614-06018-4*) Natl Prac Inst.

Pocket Property Management Guide: For Real Estate Professionals. unabridged ed. Ernie Blood. 1999. reprint ed. pap. 29.95 (*1-893572-09-9*) Carmel Pubg.

Pocket Prophecy. Catherine J. Duane & Orla Duane. (Illus.). 64p. 1997. 7.95 (*1-86204-133-4*, Pub. by Element MA) Penguin Putnam.

Pocket Prophecy. Patricia Farrell. (Pocket Prophecy Ser.). (Illus.). 64p. 1997. 7.95 (*1-86204-132-6*, Pub. by Element MA) Penguin Putnam.

Pocket Prophecy. Romayne Magellan. (Illus.). 64p. 1997. 7.95 (*1-86204-131-8*, Pub. by Element MA) Penguin Putnam.

Pocket Prophecy: Dreams. Evelyn M. Young. 64p. 1998. 7.95 (*1-86204-254-3*, Pub. by Element MA) Penguin Putnam.

Pocket Prophecy: I Ching. Mary Clark. LC 98-22601. (Illus.). 64p. 1998. 7.95 (*1-86204-265-9*, Pub. by Element MA) Penguin Putnam.

Pocket Prophecy: Tarot. Suzy Johns. LC 97-32783. (Illus.). 64p. 1997. 7.95 (*1-86204-130-X*, Pub. by Element MA) Penguin Putnam.

Pocket Proposal Style Manual. 2nd ed. Ross Pipes & Associates Inc., Staff. 68p. (Orig.). 1989. pap. 12.95 (*0-923768-02-5*) Tekne Pr.

Pocket Proposal Style Manual. 2nd deluxe ed. Ross Pipes & Associates Inc., Staff. 68p. (Orig.). 1989. 49.95 (*0-923768-01-7*) Tekne Pr.

Pocket Prospecting Guide: For Real Estate Professionals. unabridged ed. Ernie Blood. 219p. 1988. reprint ed. pap. 29.95 (*1-893572-03-X*) Carmel Pubg.

Pocket Protein Counter. Natow Annette B. & Jo-Ann Heslin. 96p. 1997. per. 2.99 (*0-671-00380-1*) PB.

***Pocket Protocols: Notifying Survivors about Sudden, Unexpected Deaths.** Kenneth V. Iserson. 65p. 1999. pap. 6.95 (*1-883620-05-8*) Galen AZ.

Pocket Protocols for Ultrasound Scanning. Betty B. Tempkin. Ed. by Andrew Allen. (Illus.). 670p. (C). 1998. pap. text 50.00 (*0-7216-6881-X*, W B Saunders Co) Harcrt Hlth Sci Grp.

Pocket Psychiatry. Bhui. (C). 1996. pap. text 51.00 (*0-7020-2151-2*) Harcourt.

Pocket Psychic: (Tells Your Future Instantly) Dezra-Lehr Guthrie. 100p. 1999. pap. 6.95 (*1-881542-43-2*) Blue Star Prodns.

Pocket Puerto Rico. 5th ed. Fodors Staff. 1998. pap. 8.50 (*0-679-00064-X*) Fodors Travel.

P

Pocket Puppy. Illus. by Pam Adams. (Pocket Pals Ser.). (J). 1995. bds. 2.99 (*0-85953-906-7*) Childs Play.

Pocket Python. Pam Adams. (J). 1996. bds. 2.99 (*0-85953-910-5*) Childs Play.

Pocket R. I. Dictionary. Mark Patinkin. (Illus.). 64p. 2000. 4.95 (*1-58066-003-7*, Covered Brdge Pr) Douglas Charles Ltd.

Pocket Rad Tech. Mary J. Hagler. (Illus.). 608p. 1992. pap. text 30.00 (*0-7216-3981-X*, W B Saunders Co) Harcrt Hlth Sci Grp.

Pocket Ref. 2nd ed. Thomas J. Glover. (Illus.). 544p. 1999. pap. 9.95 (*0-02-645744-X*) Glencoe.

Pocket Reference: A Guide to the World of Measures. Group Diagram Staff. (Illus.). 320p. 1994. pap. 10.00 (*0-00-470322-7*) Collins.

Pocket Reference Bible Trivia. TNP Staff. 640p. 2000. pap. 4.99 (*0-7852-4269-4*) Nelson.

***Pocket Reference Book for Missionaries, Parents & Instructors: Doctrine & Information, Inspiration.** Adrian Parker Call. 1999. pap. text. write for info. (*1-890558-57-5*) Granite UT.

Pocket Reference for EMT - B, 1. Elling. 144p. 1998. spiral bd. 21.80 (*0-8359-5191-X*) Globe Fearon.

Pocket Reference for Long Term Care Nursing Assistant. Barbara R. Hegner & Joan F. Needham. 1992. pap. 14.95 (*0-8273-4840-1*) Delmar.

***Pocket Reference for Pediatric ECG's.** 3rd rev. ed. Susan Duszynski. (Illus.). 76p. 2000. pap. 13.00 (*1-930605-00-5*, 104001) Maxishare.

***Pocket Reference for Pediatric Primary Care.** Catherine E. Burns. LC 00-37159. 2001. write for info. (*0-7216-8466-1*, W B Saunders Co) Harcrt Hlth Sci Grp.

Pocket Reference for Psychiatrists. Susan C. Jenkins et al. LC 90-276. 255p. 1990. reprint ed. pap. 79.10 (*0-608-02028-1*, 206268400003) Bks Demand.

Pocket Reference for Psychiatrists. 2nd ed. Susan C. Jenkins & Mark R. Hansen. LC 95-2541. 240p. 1995. pap. text 24.50 (*0-88048-721-6*, 8721) Am Psychiatric.

***Pocket Reference for Psychiatrists.** 3rd ed. Susan C. Jenkins et al. 2000. pap. 24.50 (*1-58562-008-4*) Am Psychiatric.

Pocket Reference of Diagnosis & Management for the Speech-Language Pathologist. Patricia F. White. LC 96-39070. 454p. 1996. pap. text 40.00 (*0-7506-9818-7*) Buttrwrth-Heinemann.

***Pocket Reference of Diagnosis & Management for the Speech-Language Pathologist.** Patricia F. White. 484p. 2000. pap. 40.00 (*0-7506-7248-X*) Buttrwrth-Heinemann.

Pocket Reference to American English Grammar, Punctuation & Usage. 2nd rev. ed. Linda A. Sikorski. Tr. by Babetta S. Frazier. 54p. 1990. pap. 10.95 (*1-883574-06-4*, 3605) LDS & Asocs.

Pocket Reference to Radiographic Exposure Techniques. Kathleen Kath. (Illus.). 97p. (C). (gr. 13). 1993. spiral bd. 19.95 (*0-8016-6907-3*, 06907) Mosby Inc.

***Pocket Retreat for Catholics: Thirty Simple Steps to Holiness - In Just Ten Minute a Day!** F. Maucourant. Orig. Title: The Life of Union with OUr Divine Lord. 224p. 2000. reprint ed. pap. 10.95 (*1-928832-12-1*) Sophia Inst Pr.

Pocket Review of Surgery. Sergio Huerta & Theodore X. O'Connell. 2000. pap. 34.00 (*1-888308-06-0*) J & S Pub VA.

***Pocket Review of Surgery.** Huerta Sergio. (Illus.). 200p. 2000. pap. 36.00 (*0-8036-0759-8*) Davis Co.

Pocket Road Atlas. Rand McNally Staff. 1998. pap. 2.95 (*0-528-84042-8*) Rand McNally.

***Pocket Road Atlas.** Rand McNally Staff. (Illus.). 64p. 1999. pap. 2.95 (*0-528-84134-3*) Rand McNally.

Pocket Road Atlas, 1997. Rand McNally Staff. 64p. 1996. pap. text 2.95 (*0-528-81562-8*) Rand McNally.

Pocket Rome. 1988. 5.95 (*0-671-84295-1*) Macmillan.

Pocket Rome. 3rd ed. Fodor's Staff. 1998. pap. 9.00 (*0-679-00055-0*) Fodors Travel.

Pocket Russian. rev. ed. Langenscheidt Editorial Staff. (Pocket Dictionaries Ser.). 1999. vinyl bd. 12.95 (*0-88729-120-1*) Langenscheidt.

***Pocket Sack: A Story of the Brightness of Love & the Darkness of Hate.** (Illus.). x, 481p. 2000. per. 14.95 (*0-9679384-0-6*) Cottage Rose Pubng.

Pocket Salesman. Dimond. 1993. pap. 4.95 (*0-9640173-0-X*) Stadot Pubns.

Pocket Sampling Guide for Operators of Small Water Systems: Phases 2 & 5. Government Printing Office Staff. 119p. 1994. pap. 6.50 (*0-16-045682-7*) USGPO.

Pocket Santa Fe. Fodors Staff. 1999. pap. 9.00 (*0-679-00306-1*) Fodors Travel.

Pocket Scandinavia. 1988. 5.95 (*0-671-84864-X*) S&S Trade.

Pocket School Dictionary. (Pocket Guides Ser.). (Illus.). (YA). (gr. 4 up). 1998. pap. 6.95 (*0-7894-2808-3*) DK Pub Inc.

Pocket Science Encyclopedia. Deni Bown. LC 97-80368. (Pocket Guides Ser.). (Illus.). 512p. (YA). (gr. 5 up). 1998. pap. 9.95 (*0-7894-2871-7*) DK Pub Inc.

Pocket Scots Dictionary. Iseabail Macleod et al. 320p. 1988. pap. 9.95 (*0-08-036581-7*, Pub. by Aberdeen U Pr) Macmillan.

Pocket Scripture Reference. Arline H. Heaton. 14p. 1983. pap. text 1.15 (*0-9644423-0-2*) A H Heaton.

Pocket Seahorse. Michael Twinn. (Pocket Pals Ser.). (Illus.). (J). 1997. bds. 2.99 (*0-85953-983-0*) Childs Play.

Pocket Self Promotion, Marketing, & Advertising Guide: For Real Estate Professionals. unabridged ed. Ernie Blood. 233p. 1994. reprint ed. pap. 29.95 (*1-893572-07-2*) Carmel Pubg.

Pocket Selling & Closing Guide: For Real Estate Professionals. unabridged ed. Ernie Blood. 231p. 1992. reprint ed. pap. 29.95 (*1-893572-04-8*) Carmel Pubg.

Pocket Singing in Latin. Harold Copeman. (C). 1988. spiral bd. 30.00 (*0-9515798-1-9*, Pub. by H Copeman) St Mut.

Pocket Size Carpenter's Helper. Robert F. Bailey. (Illus.). 123p. (Orig.). (C). 1996. pap. 12.95 (*0-937635-00-6*) R S Wood.

***Pocket-Size Classic Bible.** Broadman & Holman Publishers Staff. 1999. 35.99 (*1-55819-840-7*) Broadman.

Pocket Size Law Dictionary - Black, Black. Gilbert Law Summaries Staff. 326p. 1997. pap. text 7.95 (*0-15-900316-4*) Harcourt Legal.

Pocket-Size Machzor: Shavuos. 18.99 (*0-89906-627-5*, MPVH); pap. 15.99 (*0-89906-628-3*, MPVP) Mesorah Pubns.

Pocket Spanish - French, French - Spanish see Diccionario de Bolsillo Frances-Espanol, Espanol-Francais: Pocket Spanish - French, French - Spanish Dictionary

Pocket Spanish Dictionary. Payne. (SPA., Illus.). 32p. (J). (ps-3). 1999. 17.00 (*0-395-97910-2*) HM.

Pocket Spanish-English Dictionary. rev. ed. Langenscheidt Editorial Staff. (Pocket Dictionaries Ser.). 1999. vinyl bd. 12.95 (*0-88729-123-6*) Langenscheidt.

Pocket Specs for Injection Molding. 4th ed. Ides Inc. Abby Commons Staff. 630p. 1999. pap. 39.95 (*1-893677-00-1*) Abby Communs.

Pocket Star Finder: Guide to the Northern Sky. Larry Deckman. (C). 1992. pap. 5.99 (*0-945200-00-5*) Star Finders.

Pocket Statistician: A Practical Guide to Quality Improvement. Shirley Coleman et al. (An Arnold Publication). 260p. 1996. pap. text 29.95 (*0-340-67721-X*, Pub. by E A) OUP.

Pocket Student Dictionaries: Arabic-English. Wagdi Rizk Ghali. 400p. 1996. pap. 7.95 (*0-86685-696-X*) Intl Bk Ctr.

Pocket Student Dictionaries: English-Arabic. Wagdi Rizk Ghali. 400p. 1996. pap. 7.95 (*0-86685-695-1*) Intl Bk Ctr.

Pocket Student Dictionaries: English-Arabic & Arabic-English. Wagdi Rizk Ghali. 400p. 1996. pap. 14.95 (*0-86685-694-3*) Intl Bk Ctr.

***Pocket Style Manual.** 2nd ed. Diane T. Hacker. 1999. pap. text 13.95 (*0-312-24752-4*) St Martin.

***Pocket Style Manual.** 3rd ed. Hacker. 2000. pap. text 13.95 (*0-312-20488-4*) St Martin.

Pocket Supermarket Guide: Food Choices for You & Your Family. Mary Abbott Hess. 128p. 1997. pap. 6.95 (*0-471-34707-8*) Wiley.

Pocket Tao Reader. Eva Wong. LC 98-33138. 208p. 1999. pap. 6.95 (*1-57062-460-7*, Pub. by Shambhala Pubns) Random.

Pocket Telephone & Addresses: Teddy Bears. Anne Geddes. (Illus.). 1997. 9.95 (*0-7683-2015-1*) CEDCO Pub.

Pocket Therapist Guide for Problem Drinkers: Self-Help in Your Pocket. Robert Heller. 12p. 1994. pap. 5.95 (*0-9666918-0-6*) Robert F Heller.

Pocket Thesaurus. DK Editors. LC 97-80388. (Pocket Guides Ser.). (Illus.). 512p. (YA). (gr. 5 up). 1998. pap. 6.95 (*0-7894-2809-1*) DK Pub Inc.

Pocket Thesaurus. Langenscheidt Staff. (Insight Guides Ser.). 1998. pap. 10.95 (*0-88729-219-4*) Langenscheidt.

***Pocket Thesaurus.** 2nd ed. Charlton Laird. 320p. 2000. pap. 4.95 (*0-7645-6148-0*) IDG Bks.

Pocket Thin New Testament: With Psalms & Proverbs. 1999. pap. text 4.99 (*0-310-90213-4*); im. lthr. 7.99 (*0-310-90214-2*) Zondervan.

Pocket-Thin New Testament with Psalms & Proverbs. 528p. 1986. bond lthr. 18.99 (*0-310-90570-2*) Zondervan.

Pocket Thinline New Testament Psalms & Proverbs. 1997. pap. text 5.99 (*0-8423-3314-2*) Tyndale Hse.

Pocket Thinline New Testament Psalms & Proverbs. 1998. 9.99 (*0-8423-3383-5*) Tyndale Hse.

***Pocket Thinline NT Psalms & Proverbs.** 1998. bond lthr. 17.99 (*0-8423-3384-3*) Tyndale Hse.

Pocket Tin Whistle Tutor. Francis McPeake. (Appletree Pocket Guides Ser.). 72p. 1983. pap. 7.95 (*0-86281-112-0*, Pub. by Appletree Pr) Irish Bks Media.

***Pocket Trainer: Strength Training Guide.** Jack Holleman & Ginny Porter. LC 99-91029. (Illus.). 72p. 1999. 19.95 (*1-929376-01-4*) Flexor Pr.

Pocket Traveler. Frank Hill. (Pocket Pac Ser.). 1990. 4.00 (*0-88699-057-2*) Travel Sci.

***Pocket Treasury of Bible Promises Gift Book.** Compiled by Garborg's Inc. Staff. (Pocket Treasury Ser.). 352p. 1999. pap. 3.99 (*1-58375-476-8*) Garborgs.

***Pocket Treasury of Inspirational Verse Gift Book.** Compiled by Garborg's Inc. Staff. 352p. 1999. pap. 3.99 (*1-58375-477-6*) Garborgs.

Pocket Treasury of Irish Verse. Michael Diggin. 1998. pap. 7.99 (*1-85833-861-1*) Quadrillion Pubng.

***Pocket Vietnamese Dictionary.** (VIE & ENG.). 2000. 13.95 (*1-58573-059-9*, Insight Guides) Langenscheidt.

Pocket Watch Price Indicator. Roy Ehrhardt. (Illus.). 1980. spiral bd. 25.00 (*0-913902-32-2*) Heart Am Pr.

Pocket Watch Price Indicator, 1979. Roy Ehrhardt. (Illus.). 1979. spiral bd. 25.00 (*0-913902-29-2*) Heart Am Pr.

Pocket Watch Price Indicator, 1977. Roy Ehrhardt. (Illus.). 1976. ring bd. 25.00 (*0-913902-21-7*) Heart Am Pr.

Pocket Watch Price Indicator, 1978. Roy Ehrhardt. (Illus.). 1978. ring bd. 25.00 (*0-913902-26-8*) Heart Am Pr.

Pocket Watch Price Indicator, 1976. Roy Ehrhardt. (Illus.). 1975. reprint ed. ring bd. 25.00 (*0-913902-15-2*) Heart Am Pr.

Pocket Watches. Reinhard Meis. LC 86-63367. (Illus.). 316p. 1987. 79.95 (*0-88740-084-1*) Schiffer.

Pocket Watches: L'Orologio da Tasca. Leonardo Leonardi & Gabriele Ribolini. LC 93-48527. (Bella Cosa Ser.). (ITA & ENG., Illus.). 144p. 1994. pap. 12.95 (*0-8118-0753-3*) Chronicle Bks.

Pocket Watches (American) Price Guide, Bk. 1. Roy Ehrhardt. (Illus.). 150p. 1972. spiral bd. 25.00 (*0-913902-01-2*) Heart Am Pr.

Pocket Watches of the 19th & 20th Century: 19th & 20th Century. Alan Shenton & Rita Shenton. LC 96-147098. (Illus.). 480p. 1995. 79.50 (*1-85149-211-9*) Antique Collect.

Pocket Webster School & Office Dictionary. Ed. by Thomas A. Layman. 888p. 1990. per. 4.99 (*0-671-70016-2*) PB.

Pocket Welsh Dictionary. 1998. pap. 17.95 (*0-8464-4905-6*) Beekman Pubs.

Pocket Whiskey Book: A Guide to Malt, Grain, Liquor & Leading Blended Whiskies. Charles MacLean. LC 96-139074. 192p. 1993. 12.95 (*1-85732-171-5*, Pub. by Reed Illust Books) Antique Collect.

Pocket Wine Guide 2000. Clarke. 1999. write for info. (*0-15-601074-7*) Harcourt.

Pocket with a Hole. large type ed. Brenda Bullock. 1997. 24.95 (*0-7531-5034-4*, Pub. by ISIS Lrg Prnt) Transaction Pubs.

Pocket Word Finder Thesaurus. Microlytics, Inc. Staff. 1990. mass mkt. 4.99 (*0-671-68613-5*) PB.

Pocket World Atlas. Rand McNally Staff. 1992. pap. 2.50 (*0-528-83517-3*) Rand McNally.

***Pocket World Atlas.** 3rd ed. Oxford University Press Staff. (Illus.). 224p. 2000. 15.95 (*0-19-521588-5*) OUP.

Pocket Zen Reader. Thomas Cleary. LC 98-39908. 160p. 1999. pap. text 6.95 (*1-57062-447-X*, Pub. by Shambhala Pubns) Random.

Pocketax, 1997. 80p. 1996. pap. 7.00 (*0-614-26806-0*, 13496BLS03) CCH INC.

Pocketbook in Vascular Surgery. 1997. pap. write for info. (*0-7020-2062-1*, Pub. by W B Saunders) Saunders.

Pocketbook of Daily Prayers. F. B. Meyer. 1997. pap. text 2.99 (*0-87788-620-2*, H Shaw Pubs) Waterbrook Pr.

***Pocketbook of Drug Eruptions & Interactions.** J. Z. Litt. 2001. write for info. (*1-84214-031-0*) Prthnon Pub.

Pocketbook of Drug Eruptions & Interactions: Millennium Edition. J. Z. Litt. 328p. 1999. pap. 32.00 (*1-85070-077-X*) Prthnon Pub.

Pocketbook of Hair & Scalp Disorders: An Illustrated Guide. John Gray & R. P. Dawber. LC 98-26852. (Illus.). 1998. pap. 31.95 (*0-632-05189-2*) Blackwell Sci.

Pocketbook of Infectious Disease Therapy, 1994. John G. Bartlett. (Illus.). 272p. 1994. 13.95 (*0-683-00444-1*) Lppncott W & W.

Pocketbook of Obstetrics & Gynecology. N. O. Sjoberg & B. Astedt. 204p. 1989. 28.00 (*1-85070-207-1*) Prthnon Pub.

Pocketbook of Palliative Care. Robin Hull. (Illus.). 118p. 1995. 26.00 (*0-07-470138-X*) McGraw-Hill HPD.

Pocketbook of Porcelain & Pottery Marks. Peter Darty. 1974. 15.00 (*0-685-53252-6*) Ars Ceramica.

Pocketbook Pressures: Who Benefits from Economic Growth? Keith Melville. LC 96-154973. (National Issues Forums Ser.). 28p. 1995. write for info. (*0-7872-1637-2*) Kendall-Hunt.

Pocketbook Shaliach: Aliyah Advice for the Pragmatic Idealist. Ephraim Bluth. LC 96-36973. 78p. 1996. pap. 12.95 (*965-229-168-4*, Pub. by Gefen Pub Hse) Gefen Bks.

Pocketful of Blessings. LC 97-42930. 64p. 1998. pap. 4.95 (*1-57587-065-7*) Crane Hill AL.

Pocketful of Cricket. Rebecca Caudill. LC 64-12617. (Illus.). 48p. (J). (gr. k-2). 1995. pap. 5.95 (*0-8050-1275-3*, Bks Young Read) H Holt & Co.

Pocketful of Dream. Denise Linn. LC 97-93661. 1997. pap. 12.00 (*0-345-40003-8*) Ballantine Pub Grp.

Pocketful of Dreams. Mary A. VanderWeele. (Illus.). 256p. 1987. 13.95 (*0-943273-01-3*); pap. 9.49 (*0-943273-00-5*) Bolton FL.

Pocketful of Goobers: A Story about George Washington Carver. Barbara Mitchell. (Creative Minds Ser.). (Illus.). 64p. (J). (gr. 3-6). 1986. lib. bdg. 19.95 (*0-87614-292-7*, Carolrhoda) Lerner Pub.

Pocketful of Goobers: A Story about George Washington Carver. Barbara Mitchell. (Creative Minds Bks.). (Illus.). 56p. (J). (gr. 3-6). 1987. reprint ed. pap. 5.95 (*0-87614-474-1*, Lerner Publctns) Lerner Pub.

Pocketful of Hymns. 64p. 1998. pap. 4.95 (*1-57587-067-3*) Crane Hill AL.

Pocketful of Laughs: Stories, Poems, Jokes & Riddles. Joanna Cole. (J). 1995. 9.95 (*0-385-32154-6*) Doubleday.

Pocketful of Miracles. Joan Borysenko. 432p. (Orig.). 1994. mass mkt. 12.95 (*0-446-39536-6*, Pub. by Warner Bks) Little.

Pocketful of Miracles Holiday: Filefolder Games, Patterns & Directions. Connie Eisenhart & Ruth Bell. 1985. pap. 7.95 (*0-933212-24-0*) Partner Pr.

Pocketful of Paradise. Kathleen Kane. 1997. mass mkt. 5.99 (*0-312-96090-5*) St Martin.

Pocketful of Pets. Jane Belk Moncure. LC 87-11748. (Magic Castle Readers Ser.). (Illus.). 32p. (J). (ps-2). 1988. lib. bdg. 21.36 (*0-89565-370-2*) Childs World.

Pocketful of Plays: Sample Edition. David Madden. (C). 1995. pap. text 8.00 (*0-15-503630-0*) Harcourt Coll Pubs.

Pocketful of Plays: Vintage. David Madden. (C). 1995. pap. text 12.00 (*0-15-502543-0*, Pub. by Harcourt Coll Pubs) Harcourt.

Pocketful of Plums: Jim River Days. Jack Botts. (Illus.). 1995. pap. 9.95 (*0-911007-42-3*) Twin Pines Pub.

***Pocketful of Poems.** Nikki Grimes & Javaka Steptoe. LC 00-24232. 2000. pap. write for info. (*0-395-93868-6*, Clarion Bks) HM.

Pocketful of Poems. Babe Hart et al. LC 85-73259. 68p. (Orig.). 1985. pap. 4.95 (*0-9615829-0-1*) Baja Bks.

Pocketful of Poems: Sample Edition. David Madden. (C). 1995. pap. text 8.00 (*0-15-503628-9*) Harcourt Coll Pubs.

Pocketful of Poetry: Vintage. David Madden. LC 95-79366. (C). 1995. pap. text 12.00 (*0-15-502544-9*, Pub. by Harcourt Coll Pubs) Harcourt.

Pocketful of Poohisms. Walt Disney Staff. LC 98-140795. (J). 1997. 2.98 (*1-57082-761-3*, Pub. by Mouse Works) Time Warner.

Pocketful of Praise. Compiled by Ken Bible. 62p. (J). (gr. 3-7). 1987. 4.99 (*0-8341-9283-7*, MB-574) Lillenas.

Pocketful of Prevention: Preventive Care Guidelines. Ed. by Thomas Masterson. 40p. (C). 1998. pap. 7.50 (*1-883205-44-1*) Intl Med Pub.

Pocketful of Promises. 96p. (J). 1997. write for info. (*1-55513-012-7*, Chariot Bks) Chariot Victor.

Pocketful of Prose: Contemporary Short Fiction. David Madden. 236p. (C). 1991. pap. text. write for info. (*0-318-69117-5*) Harcourt Coll Pubs.

Pocketful of Prose: Contemporary Short Fiction. David Madden. 230p. (C). 1992. pap. text 12.00 (*0-03-054934-5*, Pub. by Harcourt Coll Pubs); 13.50 (*0-03-014289-X*) Harcourt Coll Pubs.

Pocketful of Prose: Vintage. David Madden. (C). 1995. pap. text 12.00 (*0-15-502545-7*, Pub. by Harcourt Coll Pubs) Harcourt.

Pocketful of Prose: Vintage Short Fiction. David Madden. 288p. (C). 1992. pap. text 11.50 (*0-03-054937-X*, Pub. by Harcourt Coll Pubs); disk. write for info. (*0-318-69139-6*) Harcourt Coll Pubs.

Pocketful of Prose Poems & Plays. Madden. (C). 1995. 34.00 (*0-15-503786-2*) Harcourt.

Pocketful of Puppets: Activities for the Special Child. Debbie Sullivan & Nancy Renfro. (Puppetry in Education Ser.). (Illus.). 48p. (Orig.). 1982. spiral bd. 10.95 (*0-931044-07-3*) Renfro Studios.

Pocketful of Puppets: Mother Goose Rhymes. Nancy Refro & Tamara Hunt. Ed. by Ann W. Schwalb. (Puppetry in Education Ser.). (Illus.). 80p. (Orig.). (J). (ps-2). 1982. spiral bd. 12.95 (*0-931044-06-5*) Renfro Studios.

Pocketful of Puppets: Poems for Church School. Lynn Irving. Ed. by Merily H. Keller. (Puppetry in Education Ser.). (Illus.). 48p. (Orig.). (J). (ps-3). 1982. pap. 10.95 (*0-931044-05-7*) Renfro Studios.

Pocketful of Puppets: Three Plump Fish & Other Short Stories. Yvonne Winer. Ed. by Merily H. Keller. (Puppetry in Education Ser.). (Illus.). 48p. (Orig.). (J). (ps-4). 1982. pap. 10.95 (*0-931044-08-1*) Renfro Studios.

***Pocketful of Python, Vol. 1.** Jones Terry. (Illus.). 64p. 2000. pap. 9.99 (*0-413-73290-8*) Methn.

Pocketful of Rainbows. Clarice Burrell. 1967. 5.00 (*0-87511-014-2*); pap. 3.95 (*0-87511-013-4*) Claitors.

Pocketful of Rye. A. J. Cronin. 1976. 22.95 (*0-88411-526-7*) Amereon Ltd.

Pocketful of Saints. LC 97-42931. 64p. 1998. pap. 4.95 (*1-57587-066-5*) Crane Hill AL.

Pocketful of Smiles. Earl W. Engleman. (Illus.). 1979. pap. 4.50 (*0-933992-03-3*) Coffee Break.

Pocketful of Stars: Poems about the Night. Illus. by Emma Shaw-Smith. 40p. (J). (gr. 1-5). 1999. 16.95 (*1-902283-84-8*) Barefoot Bks NY.

Pocketful of Stars: Rhymes, Chants & Lap Games. Felicity Williams. (Illus.). 56p. (Orig.). (J). (ps). 1997. pap. 12.95 (*1-55037-386-2*, Pub. by Annick) Firefly Bks Ltd.

Pocketful of Whimsy: Wee Patchwork Gifts. Kathleen R. Brooks. Ed. by Debra Feece. LC 99-32787. (Illus.). 32p. 1999. pap. 12.95 (*1-885588-27-5*) Chitra Pubns.

Pocketful of Wisdom. Michael Lynberg. 160p. 1996. pap. 6.95 (*0-312-14392-3*) St Martin.

PocketGuide for Family Planning Service Providers. 2nd ed. Paul D. Blumenthal & Noel McIntosh. Ed. by Elizabeth Oliveras. (Illus.). (Orig.). 1996. pap. text 15.00 (*0-929817-45-1*) JHPIEGO.

PocketGuide for Family Planning Service Providers. 2nd rev. ed. Noel McIntosh & Paul Blumenthal. Ed. by Elizabeth Oliveras. (POR., Illus.). 200p. (Orig.). 1998. pap. 15.00 (*0-929817-53-2*) JHPIEGO.

PocketGuide for Family Planning Service Providers. 2nd rev. ed. Ed. by Noel McIntosh & Elizabeth Oliveras. (RUS., Illus.). (Orig.). 1996. pap. text 15.00 (*0-929817-48-6*) JHPIEGO.

Pocketguide to Assessment in Speech-Language Pathology. M. N. Hegde. LC 96-44665. 420p. (Orig.). 1996. pap. 45.00 (*1-56593-273-0*, 0595) Thomson Learn.

Pocketguide to The Art Institute of Chicago. 4th ed. Ed. by Robert V. Sharp. (Illus.). 64p. 1997. reprint ed. pap. text 3.95 (*0-86559-054-0*) Art Inst Chi.

PocketRef. 2nd rev. ed. Thomas J. Glover. (Illus.). 544p. 1994. pap. 9.95 (*1-885071-00-0*) Sequoia Pub Inc.

Pockets. Jennifer Armstrong. LC 97-10962. (Illus.). (J). (gr. 1-6). 1998. lib. bdg. 18.99 (*0-517-70927-9*, Pub. by Crown Bks Yng Read) Random.

Pockets. Jennifer Armstrong. LC 97-10962. (J). (gr. 1-6). 1998. 17.00 (*0-517-70926-0*) Random.

Pockets. Claudette C. Mitchell et al. (Illus.). 8p. (Orig.). (J). (gr. k-1). 1996. pap. text 3.00 (*1-57518-055-3*) Arborlake.

Pockets. large type ed. Joseph Lynch. (Illus.). (J). pap. 16.98 (*0-932970-83-4*) Prinit Pr.

Pockets & Pouches. Moore et al. (Illus.). 48p. (J). (ps-1). 1995. pap., teacher ed. 9.95 (*1-55799-391-2*, 543) Evan-Moor Edu Pubs.

Pockets of Craziness: Examining Suspected Incest. Kathryn Hagans. 112p. 1991. 17.95 (*0-669-24483-X*) Lxngtn Bks.

Pockets of Love. Russell Marano. 58p. 1984. 5.00 (*0-318-03893-5*) Back Fork Bks.

Pockets of Pride. Miller. 1994. 17.95 (*0-02-921690-7*) S&S Trade.

An Asterisk (*) at the beginning of an entry indicates that the title is appearing for the first time.

Pockets of Resistance. Will Sundown. 224p. 1990. mass mkt. 4.95 (*0-445-21024-9*, Mysterious Paperbk) Warner Bks.

Pockets of Time. Anita L. Hamm. 1982. 6.95 (*0-935513-04-3*) Samara Pubns.

Pockets of Wheat. Geoffrey Young. (Illus.). 44p. (Orig.). (C). 1996. pap. 8.00 (*0-935724-85-0*) Figures.

Pockets Spelling Dictionary. DK Publishing Staff. LC 97-80395. (DK Pockets Ser.). 432p. (J). 1998. pap. 6.95 (*0-7894-3073-8*) DK Pub Inc.

Pockets Zippers Colors: Clothing Designs for Kids. Sallie J. Russell. (Illus.). 44p. (Orig.). 1992. pap. 8.95 (*1-883777-00-3*) SJR Sew.

***Pocketsize Central Boston & Rapid Transit.** Michael E. Brown. (Illus.). 1998. 2.95 (*0-935039-98-8*) Stwise Maps.

***Pocketsize Downtown Chicago & Transit.** Michael E. Brown. (Illus.). 1998. 2.95 (*0-935039-97-X*) Stwise Maps.

***Pocketsize Downtown Washington D. C. & Metrorail.** Michael E. Brown. (Illus.). 1998. 2.95 (*1-886705-00-3*) Stwise Maps.

***Pocketsize Manhattan Bus/Subway.** Michael E. Brown. (Illus.). 1998. 2.95 (*1-886705-01-1*) Stwise Maps.

Pocketwatch. Mille Kirn. (Account Ability Ser.). 140p. 1992. student ed. 18.00 (*0-9632915-1-3*) Ellim & Ange.

Poco a Poco. 2nd ed. Hendrickson. (College Spanish Ser.). (C). 1990. pap., teacher ed. 17.25 (*0-8384-1860-0*); pap., student ed. 28.95 (*0-8384-1859-7*) Heinle & Heinle.

Poco a Poco. 2nd ed. Hendrickson. (College Spanish Ser.). (C). 1990. pap., wbk. ed. 15.25 (*0-8384-1840-6*); 30.95 (*0-8384-1858-9*) Heinle & Heinle.

Poco a Poco. 2nd annot. ed. Hendrickson. (C). 1990. pap., teacher ed. 48.95 (*0-8384-1851-1*); pap., teacher ed. 48.95 (*0-8384-1852-X*) Heinle & Heinle.

Poco a Poco. 3rd ed. James M. Hendrickson. (C). 1993. text 57.95 (*0-8384-4753-8*) Heinle & Heinle.

Poco a Poco. 3rd ed. James M. Hendrickson. (College Spanish Ser.). (C). 1993. text, teacher ed. 57.95 (*0-8384-4754-6*) Heinle & Heinle.

Poco a Poco. 3rd ed. James M. Hendrickson. (C). 1994. pap. 36.95 (*0-8384-4755-4*); text, teacher ed. 21.95 (*0-8384-4756-2*) Heinle & Heinle.

Poco a Poco. 3rd ed. James M. Hendrickson. (College Spanish Ser.). (C). 1994. 109.95 (*0-8384-4764-3*) Heinle & Heinle.

Poco a Poco. 3rd ed. James M. Hendrickson. (College Spanish Ser.). (SPA.). (C). 1994. text, suppl. ed. 21.95 (*0-8384-4759-7*) Heinle & Heinle.

Poco a Poco. 3rd ed. James M. Hendrickson. (College Spanish Ser.). (SPA.). (C). 1994. text, suppl. ed. 36.95 (*0-8384-4757-0*) Heinle & Heinle.

Poco a Poco. 4th ed. Hendrickson. (College Spanish Ser.). (C). 1997. pap., teacher ed. 57.95 (*0-8384-7852-2*) Heinle & Heinle.

Poco a Poco. 4th ed. Hendrickson. (C). 1998. pap., wbk. ed., lab manual ed. 31.00 (*0-8384-3868-7*) Heinle & Heinle.

Poco A Poco. 4th ed. Hendrickson. (College Spanish). (C). 1997. pap., wbk. ed. 1.00 (*0-8384-8142-6*) Heinle & Heinle.

Poco a Poco. 4th ed. James M. Hendrickson. LC 97-31617. (College Spanish Ser.). (C). 1997. text, student ed. 73.95 (*0-8384-7843-3*) Heinle & Heinle.

Poco a Poco: Spanish for Proficiency. James M. Hendrickson. 492p. (C). 1986. mass mkt. 38.95 (*0-8384-1350-1*) Heinle & Heinle.

Poco A Poco Testing Program. Hendrickson. (College Spanish Ser.). (C). 1998. pap. 25.00 (*0-8384-8169-8*) Heinle & Heinle.

Pocono Ghosts Bk. 2: Legends & Lore. Charles J. Adams, III & David J. Seibold. 1995. pap. 8.95 (*1-880683-08-3*) Exeter Hse.

Pocono Ghosts, Legends & Lore. David J. Seibold & Charles J. Adams, III. (Illus.). 114p. (Orig.). 1991. pap. 8.95 (*1-880683-00-8*) Exeter Hse.

Pocono Mountain Beauty. 2000. 15.95 (*0-9654700-9-1*) F R Parker.

Pocono Weather. Ben Gelber. LC 92-85403. (Illus.). 304p. (Orig.). 1993. pap. 17.95 (*0-9624020-9-5*) Uriel Pub PA.

Pocono Weather: A Weather History of Eastern Pennsylvania, the Poconos, Western New Jersey. 2nd rev. ed. Ben Gelber. LC 97-62355. (Illus.). 370p. 1998. pap. 24.95 (*0-9624020-8-7*) Uriel Pub PA.

Poconos: An Illustrated Natural History Guide. Carl S. Oplinger & J. Robert Halma. (Illus.). 280p. (C). 1988. pap. 14.95 (*0-8135-1294-8*) Rutgers U Pr.

Pocumtuck Housewife: A Guide to Domestic Cookery. Deerfield Parish Guild Staff. 55p. 1985. reprint ed. pap. 4.95 (*0-9612876-4-0*) Pocumtuck Valley Mem.

Pod of Gray Whales: An Affectionate Portrait. Francois Gohier. LC 94-31824. (Close Up Ser.). (Illus.). 40p. (YA). (gr. 5 up). 1994. pap. 7.95 (*0-382-24884-8*); lib. bdg. 14.95 (*0-382-24882-1*) Silver Burdett Pr.

***Pod of Gray Whales: An Affectionate Portrait.** Francois Gohier. Ed. by Vicki Leon. (Illus.). 40p. 1999. reprint ed. pap. 7.95 (*0-945092-45-8*, Pub. by EZ Nature) Cntrl Coast Pr.

Pod of Killer Whales: The Mysterious & Beautiful Life of the Orca. Vicki Leon. LC 94-30906. (Close Up Ser.). (Illus.). 40p. (YA). (gr. 5 up). 1994. pap. 7.95 (*0-382-24901-1*); lib. bdg. 14.95 (*0-382-24900-3*) Silver Burdett Pr.

***Pod of Killer Whales: The Mysterious & Beautiful Life of the Orca.** Ed. by Vicki Leon. (Illus.). 40p. 2000. reprint ed. pap. 7.95 (*0-945092-46-6*, Pub. by EZ Nature) Cntrl Coast Pr.

Pod Run. 2nd ed. Ada Chambers & Anna Chambers. 228p. 1989. reprint ed. pap. 10.95 (*0-9621954-0-5*) A Cataldo.

Pod Sztandarem Z Gwiazd. Halina Bonikowska. LC 85-61376. (POL.). 112p. (Orig.). 1985. pap. text 8.00 (*0-930401-01-8*) Artex Pub.

PODC, 95: 14th Annual ACM Symposium on Principles of Distributed Computing. 284p. 1995. pap. text 40.00 (*0-89791-710-3*, 536950) Assn Compu Machinery.

PODC, 94: 13th Annual ACM Symposium on Principles os Distributed Computing. 416p. 1994. pap. text 60.00 (*0-89791-654-9*, 536940) Assn Compu Machinery.

PODC 97: 16th Annual ACM Symposium on Principles of Distributed Computing. 1997. pap. 42.00 (*0-89791-952-1*, 536970) Assn Compu Machinery.

PODC, 96: 15th Annual ACM Symposium on Principles of Distributed Computing. 1996. text 50.00 (*0-89791-800-2*, 536960) Assn Compu Machinery.

PODC, 93: 12th Annual ACM Symposium on Principles of Distributed Computing. 280p. 1993. pap. text 39.00 (*0-89791-613-1*, 536930) Assn Compu Machinery.

PODC 98: PODC: 17th Annual ACM Symposium on Principles of Distributed Computing. 1998. 42.00 (*0-89791-977-7*, 536980) Assn Compu Machinery.

Podemos. Bob Reese. Tr. by Gloria Schaffer-Melendez. (Libro de Diaz Palabras Ser.). (SPA., Illus.). (J). (gr. k-3). 1994. pap. 3.95 (*0-89868-256-8*, Read Res); lib. bdg. 9.95 (*0-89868-255-X*, Read Res) ARO Pub.

Podemos Confiar en Dios. Jerry Bridges. (Serie Realidades - Realities Ser.).Tr. of You Can Trust God. (SPA.). 90p. 1994. 1.99 (*1-56063-927-X*, 498131) Editorial Unilit.

Podemos Construir see Homeplay: La Alegria de Aprender Entre Ninos y Adultos, Series I

Poder Creador de Dios. Charles Capps. (Mini-Bks.).Tr. of God's Creative Power Will Work for You. (SPA.). 32p. 1980. pap. 0.99 (*0-89274-335-2*, HH-335) Harrison Hse.

Poder Creador de Dios para Sanar. Charles Capps.Tr. of God's Creative Power for Healing. (SPA.). 64p. (Orig.). 1995. mass mkt. 1.00 (*0-89274-825-7*, HH-825) Harrison Hse.

***Poder Creativo de Dios: Obrara para Usted.** Charles Capp. (SPA.). 32p. 1999. pap. write for info. (*1-58633-005-5*) Libros Intern.

***Poder Creativo de Dios para Sanar.** Charles Capp. (SPA.). 64p. 1999. pap. write for info. (*1-58633-004-7*) Libros Intern.

***Poder Creativo del Sonido.** Elizabeth Clare Prophet. (SPA.). 2000. pap. 4.95 (*968-19-0581-4*) Aguilar.

Poder Cuartivo del Ajo. Paul Bergner. (SPA.). 1997. pap. text 7.98 (*970-643-033-4*) Selector.

Poder Curativo de la Biblia. Gibson. (SPA.). 1997. pap. text 7.98 (*968-403-420-2*) Selector.

***Poder Curativo de la Mente (The Healing Power of the Mind) Practical Techniques for Health & Empowerment.** Rolf Alexander. (SPA.). 128p. 2000. pap. 10.95 (*0-89281-590-6*, Inner Trad Espanol) Inner Tradit.

Poder Curativo de la Oracion. Ciro Sepulveda. (SPA.). 96p. (Orig.). 1995. pap. 6.95 (*1-888867-04-3*) Biblos Pr.

Poder Curativo de las Semillas. Murry Prisant Guillermo. (SPA.). 173p. 1997. pap. text 8.98 (*970-643-127-6*) Selector.

Poder Curativo de los Jugos. Murray Prisant Guillermo. (SPA.). 1997. pap. text 8.98 (*970-643-036-9*) Selector.

Poder Curativo de Soya. Sarubbi. (SPA.). 1997. pap. text 7.98 (*970-643-081-4*) Selector.

Poder de la Alabanza. Merlin R. Carothers. (SPA.). 224p. 1996. pap. 6.99 (*0-8297-0444-2*) Vida Pubs.

Poder de la Confesion Positiva. Don Gossett. (SPA.). 170p. 1990. pap. 4.95 (*0-938127-12-8*) Publ Senda de Vida.

Poder De la Espada. Lectorum Staff. 1998. 24.95 (*84-01-49624-1*) Lectorum Pubns.

***Poder de la Espada.** Wilbur Smith. (SPA.). 1999. 24.95 (*84-01-32301-0*) Plaza.

Poder de la Esperanza. Charles R. Swindoll.Tr. of Hope Again. (SPA.). 1997. 10.99 (*0-88113-437-6*, B008-4376) Caribe Betania.

Poder de la Iglesia Para Ayudar O Danar: The Church, the Power to Help & to Hurt. Daniel G. Bagby. Tr. by Mabel G. De Gherman. (SPA.). 112p. 1990. pap. 6.99 (*0-311-17034-X*) Casa Bautista.

***Poder de la Integridad.** John F. MacArthur, Jr. (SPA.). 192p. 1999. pap. 8.99 (*0-8254-1468-7*, Edit Portavoz) Kregel.

Poder de la Lengua. Kenneth Copeland. Tr. by Copeland, Kenneth, Publications Staff. (SPA.). 32p. (Orig.). 1985. pap. 0.75 (*0-88114-307-3*) K Copeland Pubns.

Poder de la Lengua (The Power of the Tongue) Kenneth Copeland. (SPA.). 62p. 1996. 1.00 (*0-88114-997-7*, S30-0014) K Copeland Pubns.

Poder de las Afirmaciones. Jerry Fankhauser. (Orig.). 1981. pap. 6.00 (*0-9617006-6-1*) J Fankhauser.

Poder de los Debiles. C. De Vinck.Tr. of Power of the Powerless. (SPA.). 1996. pap. 7.99 (*0-8297-0591-0*) Vida Pubs.

Poder de Su Presenciq. Alberto Mottesi.Tr. of Power of His Presence. (SPA.). 240p. 1997. pap. 9.99 (*0-88113-464-3*) Caribe Betania.

Poder de una Pormesa Cumplida. Gregg Lewis.Tr. of Power of a Promise Kept. (SPA.). 240p. 1995. 8.99 (*0-7899-0147-1*, 497272) Editorial Unilit.

Poder del Espiritu Santo. Charles H. Spurgeon. Tr. by Gisela Sawin. LC 98-20657.Tr. of Holy Spirit Power. (SPA.). 144p. 1998. pap. 9.99 (*0-88368-538-8*) Whitaker Hse.

Poder del Telefono en las Ventas. Teri K. Gamble & Mike Gamble.Tr. of Phone Power. (SPA.). 154p. 1996. pap. text 16.95 (*0-7931-1953-7*, 1913-4001) Dearborn.

Poder Detras de Sus Ojos. Robert-Michael Kaplan.Tr. of Power Behind Your Eyes. (SPA., Illus.). 208p. 1996. pap. 16.95 (*0-89281-576-0*) Inner Tradit.

Poder Empresarial en Mision Integral. H. R. Suter.Tr. of Businessman's Power in Important Missions. (SPA.). 5.99 (*0-7899-0443-8*, 498659) Editorial Unilit.

Poder en Tu Boca. Victor Ricardo. 26p. 1992. pap. 1.15 (*1-885630-02-6*) HLM Producciones.

Poder en Tus Manos: God Doing Extraordinary Miracles Through Ordinary People. rev. ed. Wallace H. Heflin, Jr.Tr. of Power in Your Hand. (SPA.). 154p. 1997. pap. 6.99 (*1-884369-04-9*) McDougal Pubng.

Poder Esta Dentro de Ti. Louise L. Hay. (SPA.). 1997. pap. 19.98 (*968-13-2304-1*) Edit Diana.

Poder Esta Dentro de Ti - The Power Is Within You. Hay House Staff. 1993. pap. 12.95 (*1-56170-131-9*) Hay House.

Poder Judicial en Cuba. Vicente Vinuela. LC 91-73597. (Coleccion Cuba y sus Jueces). (SPA.). 396p. (Orig.). 1991. pap. 25.00 (*0-89729-617-6*) Ediciones.

Poder Liberador de la Gracia. David Seamands.Tr. of Healing Grace. (SPA.). 240p. 1991. mass mkt. 1.50 (*0-8297-0832-4*) Vida Pubs.

Poder Magico de los Santos (The Magical Power of the Saints) Ray T. Malbrough. (SPA., Illus.). 240p. 1999. pap. 7.95 (*1-56718-453-7*) Llewellyn Pubns.

Poder Milagroso. Jamie Buckingham.Tr. of Miracle Power. (ENG & SPA.). 100. pap. 8.99 (*1-56063-649-1*, 550108) Editorial Unilit.

***Poder Preservador de Dios.** Living Stream Ministry Staff. 1999. pap. 10.00 (*0-7363-0333-2*) Living Stream Ministry.

Poder Secreto de las Piramides. Ed Pettit. (SPA.). 1997. pap. 17.98 (*968-13-1697-5*, Pub. by Edit Diana) Libros Fronteras.

Poder Sin Limites La Nueva Ciencia Del Desarrollo Personal. Anthony Robbins. 1997. pap. text 17.98 (*970-05-0202-3*) Grijalbo Edit.

Poder Sutil de Abuso Espiritual. Johnstone.Tr. of Subtle Power of Spiritual Abuse. (SPA.). 333p. 1995. 10.99 (*1-56063-510-X*, 498527) Editorial Unilit.

Poder y Derecho: Estrategias de las Mujeres del Tercer Mundo. Ed. by Margaret Schuler. Tr. by Guillermo Delgado from ENG. LC 87-62631.Tr. of Empowerment & the Law: Strategies of Third World Women. (SPA.). 472p. (Orig.). 1986. pap. 16.00 (*0-912917-17-2*) UNIFEM.

Poder y Desarrolo Organizacional. (SPA.). 216p. (C). 1990. text 9.66 (*0-201-62913-5*) Addison-Wesley.

Poder y la Bendicion. Jack W. Hayford.Tr. of Power & the Blessing. (SPA.). 280p. 1995. 9.99 (*1-56063-718-8*, 497720) Editorial Unilit.

Poder y transgresion: Peru, Metafora e Historia. Marta Bermudez-Gallegos. (SPA.). 196p. (Orig.). 1996. pap. text 26.00 (*0-9640795-5-0*) Latinoam Edit.

***Podere Fiume.** Leavitt. 2000. 24.00 (*1-58243-061-6*, Pub. by Counterpt DC) HarpC.

***Poderes Terrenales: Tecnicas Para la Magia Natural.** Scott Cunningham. 2000. pap. text 8.95 (*1-56718-187-2*) Llewellyn Pubns.

Poderoso Principe De la Oracion see Daniel Nash: Prevailing Prince of Prayer

Podhale: A Companion Guide to the Polish Highlands. Jan G. Mostowy. Tr. by Maria De Gorgey from POL. (Illus.). 276p. 1997. 19.95 (*0-7818-0522-8*, 652) Hippocrene Bks.

Podiatric Medical Assisting. 2nd ed. Ed. by Leonard A. Levy & Anne K. Thompson. (Illus.). 295p. 1992. pap. text 56.00 (*0-443-08760-1*) Church.

***Podiatric Radiology.** Mandraachi. 2001. text. write for info. (*0-7216-9123-4*) Harcrt Hlth Sci Grp.

Podiatry: Index of Modern Information. Victor A. Chandra. LC 88-48010. 150p. 1989. 47.50 (*1-55914-054-2*); pap. 44.50 (*1-55914-055-0*) ABBE Pubs Assn.

Podiatry Office Manual. Robert D. Sowell & William F. Munsey. (Office Manual Ser.). 201p. 1994. 89.00 (*1-890018-03-1*) Anadem Pubng.

***Podiatry Sourcebook: Basic Consumer Health Information about Foot Conditions, Diseases & Injuries.** Ed. by M. Lisa Weatherford. (Health Reference Ser.). 600p. 2000. lib. bdg. 78.00 (*0-7808-0215-2*) Omnigraphics Inc.

Podium Humor Ri. James C. Humes. LC 85-42572. 320p. 1993. pap. 13.00 (*0-06-273234-X*, Harper Ref) HarpC.

Podium Pointers. James P. King. 1986. pap. text 7.50 (*0-936895-02-0*) Brown House.

Podkayne of Mars. Robert A. Heinlein. 256p. 1995. mass mkt. 5.99 (*0-671-87671-6*) Baen Bks.

Podkayne of Mars. Robert A. Heinlein. 1999. lib. bdg. 20.95 (*1-56723-164-0*) Yestermorrow.

Podkayne of Mars. Robert A. Heinlein. 256p. 1993. reprint ed. pap. 10.00 (*0-671-72179-8*) Baen Bks.

Podos: External Diseases. Chandler. 1993. 99.00 (*1-56375-101-1*) Gower-Mosby.

***Podracer!** Lisa Findlay. (Star Wars: Episode 1). (Illus.). 80p. (J). (ps-3). 2000. pap. 2.99 (*0-375-80510-9*, Pub. by Random Bks Yng Read) Random.

***Podracer Punch-Out Book.** Ed. by Lucas Books Staff. (Illus.). (J). 2000. pap. 3.99 (*0-375-80566-4*) Random.

***Podracing Book Plus Magnets.** Kerry Milliron. 2000. 8.99 (*0-375-80522-2*, Pub. by Random Bks Yng Read) Random.

Podreczny Slownik Polsko-Niemiecki (Manual Dictionary Polish-German) A. Bzdega et al. (GER & POL.). 1018p. 1977. 49.95 (*0-8288-5510-2*, M9129) Fr & Eur.

Podria Haber Sido Peor. A. H. Benjamin. Tr. by Teresa Mlawer.Tr. of It Could Have Been Worse. (SPA., Illus.). 32p. (J). (gr. 1-3). 1998. 14.95 (*1-880507-40-4*) Lectorum Pubns.

PODS 98: PODS: Principles of Data Base Systems. 1998. 40.00 (*0-89791-996-3*, 475980) Assn Compu Machinery.

PODS, 97: 16th Annual Symposium Principles of Database Systems. 1997. pap. 37.00 (*0-89791-910-6*, 475970) Assn Compu Machinery.

PODS, 96: 15th ACM Symposium on the Principles of Database System. 260p. 1996. pap. text 37.00 (*0-89791-781-2*, 475960) Assn Compu Machinery.

PODS, 93: 12th Annual ACM Symposium on the Principles of Database Systems. 320p. 1993. pap. text 44.00 (*0-89791-593-3*, 475930) Assn Compu Machinery.

Podstawowe Wiadomosci o Sprzedawaniu: Podrecznik dla Osob Pragnacych Rozwinac Umiejetnosc Sprzedawania. Ellwood Chapman. Ed. by Czeslaw J. Grycz & Andrzej Salski. Tr. by Agata Filipczak from ENG. (POL., Illus.). iv, 74p. (Orig.). (C). 1991. pap. 7.95 (*1-56513-001-4*) W Poniecki Charit.

Poe. Nancy Loewen. (Illus.). 64p. (YA). (gr. 6-12). 1993. 22.60 (*1-56846-084-8*, Creat Educ) Creative Co.

***Poe, Vol. 1.** Jason Asala. (Illus.). 128p. 1998. pap. 14.95 (*1-57989-018-0*) Sirius Ent.

Poe: A Critical Study. Edward H. Davidson. LC 57-12965. 310p. reprint ed. pap. 96.10 (*0-7837-3834-X*, 204365500010) Bks Demand.

Poe: Selected Stories & Poems. Edgar Allan Poe. (Airmont Classics Ser.). (J). (gr. 9 up). 1962. mass mkt. 3.95 (*0-8049-0008-6*, CL-8) Airmont.

Poe - Master of Macabre. P. H. Bellas. (Illus.). 24p. 1996. pap. 7.95 (*0-9670556-0-1*) Xavier Pubg.

Poe Abroad: Influence, Reputation & Affinities. Ed. by Lois D. Vines. LC 99-36989. 284p. 1999. text 39.95 (*0-87745-697-6*) U of Iowa Pr.

Poe & His Poetry. Lewis N. Chase. LC 72-120973. (Poetry & Life Ser.). reprint ed. 16.00 (*0-404-52506-7*) AMS Pr.

Poe & His Poetry. Lewis N. Chase. LC 75-38649. (Studies in Poe: No. 23). 1976. reprint ed. lib. bdg. 75.00 (*0-8383-2112-7*) M S G Haskell Hse.

Poe & Pog. Norma M. Bracy. (Illus.). 22p. (J). (ps-12). 1986. pap. text 2.50 (*0-915783-02-9*) Book Binder.

***Poe & the Printed Word.** Kevin J. Hayes. (Studies in American Literature & Culture: Vol. 124). 163p. (C). 2000. text 49.95 (*0-521-66276-1*) Cambridge U Pr.

Poe & the Southern Literary Messenger. D. K. Jackson. LC 71-95432. (Studies in Poe: No. 23). 1970. reprint ed. lib. bdg. 75.00 (*0-8383-0983-6*) M S G Haskell Hse.

Poe Cinema: A Critical Filmography of Theatrical Releases Based on the Works of Edgar Allan Poe. Don G. Smith. LC 98-3271. (Illus.). 315p. 1998. boxed set 55.00 (*0-7864-0453-1*) McFarland & Co.

Poe, Death, & the Life of Writing. J. Gerald Kennedy. LC 86-15981. 256p. 1987. text 32.50 (*0-300-03773-2*) Yale U Pr.

Poe Encyclopedia. Frederick S. Frank & Anthony S. Magistrale. LC 96-22005. 480p. 1997. lib. bdg. 89.50 (*0-313-27768-0*, Greenwood Pr) Greenwood.

Poe in the Media: Screen, Songs, & Spoken Word Recordings. Ronald L. Smith. LC 89-27483. 236p. 1990. text 15.00 (*0-8240-5614-0*, H1272) Garland.

Poe Log: A Documentary Life of Edgar Allan Poe. Dwight Thomas & David K. Jackson. (Reference Bks.). (Illus.). 880p. 1987. 90.00 (*0-8161-8734-7*, Hall Reference) Macmillan.

Poe Log: A Documentary Life of Edgar Allan Poe 1809-1849. Dwight Thomas & David Jackson. 1995. 29.95 (*0-7838-1401-1*) Macmillan.

Poe! Poe! Poe! A Play Based on the Life & Writings of Edgar Allan Poe. Kathryn S. Miller. (Illus.). 24p. (J). (gr. 4-12). 1984. pap. 3.25 (*0-88680-224-5*) I E Clark.

Poe Poe Poe Poe Poe Poe Poe. Daniel Hoffman. LC 98-24405. 352p. 1998. pap. 16.95 (*0-8071-2321-8*) La State U Pr.

Poe-Pourri: A North Carolina Cavalcade. Clarence Poe & Charles A. Poe. LC 87-90549. (Illus.). 157p. 1987. 11.95 (*0-9618716-0-1*) Charles Poe.

Poem. Francis Neilson. 1971. 59.95 (*0-87700-066-2*) Revisionist Pr.

Poem. 3rd ed. Stanley B. Greenfield et al. 605p. (C). 1989. pap. text 28.20 (*0-13-684143-0*) P-H.

Poem a Day. Ed. by Nicholas Albery & Karen McCosker. LC 96-32784. 485p. 1996. pap. 18.00 (*1-883642-38-8*) Steerforth Pr.

Poem a Day: More Than 200 Cross-Curricular Poems That Teach & Delight. Professional Books Staff. LC 97-198073. 1997. pap. text 14.95 (*0-590-29433-4*) Scholastic Inc.

Poem a Day - Keeps Depression Away: One Woman's Philosophy in Verse. Maralene Wesner. 100p. (Orig.). 1991. pap. 7.95 (*0-936715-35-9*) Diversity Okla.

Poem about Music. Anthony Barnett. (Burning Deck Poetry Ser.). 1974. 15.00 (*0-930900-00-6*); pap. 4.00 (*0-930900-01-4*) Burning Deck.

Poem & Music in the German Lied from Gluck to Hugo Wolf. Jack M. Stein. LC 70-152772. 250p. reprint ed. pap. 77.50 (*0-7837-4193-6*, 205904300012) Bks Demand.

Poem & Revolution Before Breakfast: The Life of Edward Abbey. Jack Loeffler. 1993. 25.00 (*0-517-58632-0*, Crown) Crown Pub Group.

Poem & Symbol: A Brief History of French Symbolism. Wallace Fowlie. LC 89-16120. 160p. 1990. pap. text 15.95 (*0-271-00696-X*); lib. bdg. 25.00 (*0-271-00683-8*) Pa St U Pr.

Poem & the Book: Interpreting Collections of Romantic Poetry. Neil Fraistat. LC 84-10381. 255p. reprint ed. pap. 79.10 (*0-7837-5233-4*, 204496700005) Bks Demand.

Poem & the Insect: Aspects of Twentieth Century Hispanic Culture. David Spooner. 212p. 1998. 74.95 (*1-57309-324-6*) Intl Scholars.

Poem & the World: An International Anthology of Poetry, Bk. III. International Poets Staff. Ed. by Poem & the World Editorial Committee. 95p. (Orig.). 1995. pap. 10.00 (*0-9636124-2-5*) Poem & The Wrld.

Poem & the World: An International Anthology of Poetry, Bk. IV. Ed. by Poem & the World Editorial Committee. (Orig.). 1996. pap. 10.00 (*0-9636124-4-1*) Poem & The Wrld.

P

Poem & the World: The Literary Center's Sister City Poetry Anthology, Bk. 1. International Poets Staff & Poem & the World Editorial Committee. 72p. 1993. pap. 10.00 (*0-9636124-0-9*) Poem & The Wrld.

Poem & the World: The Literary Centers Sister City Poetry Anthology, Bk. 2. International Poets Staff & Poem & the World Editorial Committee. 96p. 1994. pap. 10.00 (*0-9636124-1-7*) Poem & The Wrld.

Poem as a Plant: A Biological View of Goethe's Faust. Salm Peter. LC 71-141461. 169p. reprint ed. pap. 52.40 (*0-608-30811-0*, 200325900021) Bks Demand.

Poem As Green Girdle: Commercium in Sir Gawain & the Green Knight. R. A. Shoaf. LC 84-2285. (University of Florida Humanities Monographs: No. 55). 116p. 1984. pap. 19.95 (*0-8130-0766-6*) U Press Fla.

Poem As Initiation. Charles Tomlinson. LC 68-56436. 1968. 8.00 (*0-912568-03-8*) Colgate U Pr.

Poem As Relic. John Logan. (Poetry/Rare Books Collection). 1989. pap. 6.00 (*0-922668-03-5*) SUNYB Poetry Rare Bks.

***Poem as Sacrament: The Theological Aesthetic of Gerard Manley Hopkins.** Phillip A. Ballinger. 272p. 2000. pap. text 30.00 (*0-8028-4737-4*) Eerdmans.

Poem at the Right Moment: Remembered Verses from Premodern South India. LC 96-29616. (Voices from Asia Ser.). 195p. 1997. 45.00 (*0-520-20847-1*, Pub. by U CA Pr) Cal Prin Full Svc.

Poem at the Right Moment: Remembered Verses from Premodern South India. Vlcheru N. Rao. Tr. by David Shulman. LC 96-29616. (Voices from Asia Ser.). 195p. 1997. pap. 16.95 (*0-520-20849-8*, Pub. by U CA Pr) Cal Prin Full Svc.

Poem Beyond My Reach. Selma Stefanile. (Vagrom Chap Bk.: No. 19). (Illus.). 56p. (Orig.). 1982. pap. 4.00 (*0-935552-03-0*) Sparrow Pr.

***Poem Called Lost.** Margaret Peacock. 222p. 1999. pap. 7.95 (*0-88028-210-X*, 1497) Forward Movement.

Poem Concerning the Death of the Prophet Muhammad - Utendi Wa Kutawafu Nabii. Ed. by J. W. Allen et al. LC 91-32526. (Studies in African Literature: Vol. 6). (Illus.). 172p. 1991. lib. bdg. 79.95 (*0-7734-9705-6*) E Mellen.

Poem Containing History: Textual Studies in "The Cantos" Ed. by Lawrence S. Rainey. LC 96-41212. 288p. (C). 1997. text 57.50 (*0-472-10232-X*, 10232) U of Mich Pr.

Poem for Every Student: Creating Community in a Public School Classroom. Sheryl Laim. (Illus.). 116p. 1998. pap. 11.00 (*1-883920-13-2*) Nat Writing Proj.

Poem for Flute & Orchestra & Piano. C. Griffes. 16p. 1986. pap. 4.95 (*0-7935-0584-4*, 50275980) H Leonard.

Poem for Guatemala. Judith Kazantzis. (C). 1990. 40.00 (*0-906887-28-3*, Pub. by Greville Pr) St Mut.

Poem for Lottie see Cake for Herbie

Poem for My Children: The Fate of Nation & Family. Orig. Title: Bai Tho Cho Con. 157p. pap. 25.00 (*0-9629578-7-9*) Intl Long WA.

Poem for You. Poet Project Staff. 48p. 1998. pap. 6.00 (*0-9655816-8-3*) Wings of Dawn.

Poem from a Single Pallet. Fanny Howe. 32p. 1980. 4.50 (*0-932716-10-5*) Kelsey St Pr.

Poem in Time: Reading George Herbert's Revisions of The Church. Janis Lull. LC 88-40586. (Illus.). 168p. 1990. 32.50 (*0-87413-357-2*) U Delaware Pr.

Poem Is Where the Heart Is: A Chronicle of Verse. Ed. by Mary J. Rillera. 226p. (Orig.). 1991. pap. 15.95 (*0-910143-03-X*) Pure CA.

Poem Itself. Ed. by Stanley Burnshaw et al. LC 94-22928. (ENG, FRE, GER, ITA & POR.). 1995. pap. 24.00 (*1-55728-328-1*) U of Ark Pr.

Poem-Making: Ways to Begin Writing Poetry. Myra C. Livingston. LC 90-5012. (Charlotte Zolotow Bk.). 176p. (J). (gr. 4-8). 1991. 16.95 (*0-06-024019-9*) HarpC Child Bks.

Poem of Ecstasy & "Prometheus Poem of Fire" in Full Score. Alexander Scriabin. 192p. 1995. pap. 13.95 (*0-486-28461-1*) Dover.

Poem of Empedocles: A Text & Translation with a Commentary. Ed. by Brad Inwood. (Phoenix Supplementary Volumes Ser.: No. XXIX: Pre-Socratics III). 420p. 1992. text 45.00 (*0-8020-5971-6*) U of Toronto Pr.

Poem of Job: A Literary Study with a New Translation. W. B. Stevenson. (British Academy, London, Schweich Lectures on Biblical Archaeology Series, 1930). 1974. reprint ed. pap. 35.00 (*0-8115-1285-1*) Periodicals Srv.

Poem of My Cid. Ed. by Peter Such. (Hispanic Classics Ser.). 1987. pap. 25.00 (*0-85668-322-1*, Pub. by Aris & Phillips) David Brown.

Poem of My Cid. Ed. by Peter Such. (Hispanic Classics Ser.). 1987. 59.95 (*0-85668-321-3*, Pub. by Aris & Phillips) David Brown.

Poem of Queen Esther. Joao Pinto Delgado. Tr. by David R. Slavitt from SPA. LC 98-19437. 112p. 1999. 19.95 (*0-19-512374-3*) OUP.

Poem of the Cid. Ed. by George Economou. Tr. by Paul Blackburn. LC 97-43704. 192p. 1998. pap. 12.95 (*0-8061-3022-9*) U of Okla Pr.

Poem of the Cid. Rita Hamilton. (Classics Ser.). 256p. 1985. pap. 10.95 (*0-14-044446-7*, Penguin Classics) Viking Penguin.

Poem of the Cid. W. S. Merwin. 1975. pap. 11.95 (*0-452-01060-8*, Mer) NAL.

Poem of the Cid. Tr. by Lesley B. Simpson. 1957. pap. 12.95 (*0-520-01176-7*, Pub. by U CA Pr) Cal Prin Full Svc.

Poem of the Deep Song. Federico Garcia Lorca. Tr. by Carlos Bauer from SPA. (Orig.). 1987. pap. 12.95 (*0-87286-205-4*) City Lights.

Poem of the End: Selected Lyrical & Narrative Poetry. Marina I. Tsvetaeva. Tr. by Nina Kossman from RUS. LC 94-7868. 190p. 1997. 25.00 (*0-87501-112-8*) Ardis Pubs.

Poem of the New River. Patricia G. Johnson. LC 90-91348. (Illus.). 30p. (Orig.). 1993. pap. 10.00 (*1-878188-00-3*) Walpa Pub.

***Poem of the Week: 50 Irresistible Poems with Activities That Teach Key Reading & Writing Skills.** Maria Fleming. (Illus.). 128p. (J). 2000. pap. 14.95 (*0-439-07751-6*) Scholastic Inc.

Poem Paintings. Gladys C. Strong. (Illus.). 66p. 1997. 16.95 (*0-945199-07-4*); pap. 9.95 (*0-945199-12-0*) Double SS Pr.

Poem Patterns: Integrate Poems & Pattern Projects with Thematic Activities Across the Curriculum - Grades PS-2. Linda Milliken. (Illus.). 40p. 1995. pap., wbk. ed. 5.95 (*1-56472-059-4*) Edupress Inc.

Poem Portraits. James J. Metcalfe. 270p. 1992. reprint ed. lib. bdg. 29.95 (*0-89966-893-3*) Buccaneer Bks.

Poem Rising out of the Earth & Standing up in Someone. James Grabill. LC 94-10672. 1994. 19.95 (*0-89924-087-9*); pap. 9.95 (*0-89924-086-0*) Lynx Hse.

Poem Sacred to the Memory of the Honorable Josiah Willard. Peter Oliver. (Notable American Authors Ser.). 1999. reprint ed. lib. bdg. 125.00 (*0-7812-4668-7*) Rprt Serv.

Poem Stew. Ed. by William Cole. (Illus.). (J). (gr. 3-6). 1981. 7.66 (*0-397-31963-0*, 229850) Lppncott W & W.

Poem Stew. William Cole. (J). 1983. 10.15 (*0-606-02564-2*, Pub. by Turtleback) Demco.

Poem Stew. Illus. by Karen A. Weinhaus. LC 81-47106. (Trophy Bk.). 96p. (J). (ps-3). 1983. pap. 4.95 (*0-06-440136-7*, HarpTrophy) HarpC Child Bks.

Poem to Poets. deluxe ed. Richard Eberhart. (Illus.). 40p. 1975. 50.00 (*0-915778-04-1*) Penmaen Pr.

Poem to the Memory of Mr. Urian Oakes. Cotton Mather. (Notable American Authors Ser.). 1999. reprint ed. lib. bdg. 125.00 (*0-7812-3950-8*) Rprt Serv.

Poem with No Point see Poema Bez Predmeta

Poem Without a Hero & Selected Poems. Anna Andreevena Akhmatova. Tr. by Lenore Mayhew & William McNaughton from RUS. LC 89-60154. No. 14. 193p. 1989. 17.95 (*0-932440-51-7*); pap. 9.95 (*0-932440-50-9*) Oberlin Coll Pr.

Poem You Asked For. Marianne Wolfe. (Outstanding Author Ser.: No. 2). (Illus.). 1977. 3.00 (*0-930370-01-5*) Spirit That Moves.

Poema Bez Predmeta. Valeriy Pereleshin. Ed. by Roman Levin. LC 89-92891.Tr. of Poem with No Point. (RUS., Illus.). 422p. 1989. pap. text 25.00 (*0-914265-28-8*) New Eng Pub MA.

Poema de Fernan Gonzalez. Ed. by John Lihani. (Medieval Texts & Studies: No. 4). 188p. 1991. text 26.95 (*0-937191-21-3*) Mich St U Pr.

Poema de Fernan Gonzalez. Ed. by H. Salvador Martinez. (Nueva Austral Ser.: No. 195). (SPA.). 1991. pap. text 24.95 (*84-239-1995-1*) Elliots Bks.

Poema de Jose: A Transcription & Comparison of the Extant Manuscripts. William W. Johnson. LC 73-93265. (Romance Monographs: No. 6). 1974. 22.00 (*84-399-1996-4*) Romance.

Poema de Mio Cid. (Clasicos Ser.). (SPA.). 270p. 1996. pap. write for info. (*0-929441-38-9*) Pubns Puertorriquenas.

Poema de Mio Cid. Anonimo. (SPA.). pap. 12.95 (*84-206-9981-0*, Pub. by Alianza Editorial) Continental Bk.

Poema del Cante Jondo. Federico Garcia Lorca. Ed. by Luis Garcia Montero. (Nueva Austral Ser.: Vol. 161). (SPA.). 1991. pap. text 24.95 (*84-239-1961-7*) Elliots Bks.

Poema del Cante Jondo: Romancero Gitano. 12th ed. Federico Garcia Lorca. (SPA.). 320p. 1989. pap. 12.95 (*0-7859-4980-1*) Fr & Eur.

Poema del Cante Jondo Romancero Gitano. Federico Garcia Lorca. Ed. by Allen Josephs & Juan Caballero. (SPA.). pap. 11.95 (*84-376-0114-2*, Pub. by Ediciones Catedra) Continental Bk.

Poema del Cid. Anonimo. (SPA.). 249p. 1963. 9.95 (*0-8288-7093-4*, S7515) Fr & Eur.

Poema del Cid & the Poema de Fernan Gonzalez: The Transformation of an Epic Tradition. Matthew Bailey. (Spanish Ser.: No. 78). vi, 144p. 1993. 20.00 (*0-940639-88-2*) Hispanic Seminary.

***Poema del Esposo.** Patricia Guzman. (Poesia Ser.: Vol. 1). (SPA.). 24p. 1999. pap. 4.00 (*0-9673260-0-1*) Pen Pr.

Poema en Veinte Surcos. Julia De Burgos. LC 83-82116. (Illus.). 64p. (Orig.). 1982. pap. 6.75 (*0-940238-23-3*) Ediciones Huracan.

Poema Fernan Gonzalez. Anonimo. (SPA.). 139p. 1973. 9.95 (*0-8288-7076-4*) Fr & Eur.

Poema Mio, 1920-1944. Eugenio Florit. (SPA.). 503p. 4.50 (*0-318-14300-3*) Hispanic Inst.

Poemario. Angel Gaztelu. LC 94-70245. (Coleccion Arte). (Illus.). 52p. 1994. pap. 29.00 (*0-89729-726-1*) Ediciones.

Poemario de Fray Luis de Leon. Julio Baena. (American University Studies: Romance Languages & Literature: Ser. II, Vol. 107). X, 232p. (C). 1989. text 35.95 (*0-8204-1015-2*) P Lang Pubng.

***Poemas.** Alma Flor Ada. (SPA., Illus.). 1999. pap. text 5.95 (*1-58105-408-4*) Santillana.

Poemas. Fernando Perez. LC 88-81563. (Coleccion Espejo de Paciencia). (SPA.). 89p. (Orig.). 1989. pap. 9.95 (*0-89729-496-3*) Ediciones.

Poemas. Jennicel Velez. LC 83-3526. (UPREX, Literatura Infantil Ser.: No. 63). (SPA.). xvii, 51p. (J). (gr. 3-7). 1983. pap. 2.50 (*0-8477-0063-1*) U of PR Pr.

Poemas. 7th ed. Amado N. Ordaz. 1983. pap. 9.95 (*0-7859-5191-1*) Fr & Eur.

Poemas: Edicion Facsimil del Manuscrito (Siglo XIV) Gonzalo De Berceo. (Real Academia Ediciones Ser.). (SPA.). 1993. 750.00 (*84-600-3319-8*) Elliots Bks.

Poemas Amorosos. Vicente Aleixandre. (SPA.). 120p. 1960. 6.95 (*0-8288-7024-1*, BC283) Fr & Eur.

Poemas Arabigoandaluces. E. Garcia Gomez. (SPA.). 147p. 1971. 9.95 (*0-8288-7129-9*, S6091) Fr & Eur.

Poemas Breves Medievales. Antonio G. Solalinde. Ed. by Ivy A. Corfis. xiv, 99p. 1987. 12.50 (*0-940639-01-7*) Hispanic Seminary.

Poemas Clasicos Para Jovenes. Jose Hernandez. (SPA.). 1997. pap. text 7.98 (*968-403-854-2*) Selector.

Poemas de Amor, 1. Antonio Gala. LC 97-183951. 1998. 19.95 (*84-08-01995-3*) Planeta.

***Poemas de Amor.** Antonio Gala. 1998. pap. text 9.95 (*84-08-02784-0*) Planeta.

Poemas de Amor. Mexicanos Editores Staff. (SPA.). 1997. pap. text 4.98 (*968-15-0446-1*) Ed Mex.

Poemas de Israel. Israel Rodriguez. LC 80-51403. (SPA.). 91p. 1980. pap. 12.00 (*0-89295-016-1*) Society Sp & Sp-Am.

***Poemas de la Isla.** Josefina de la Torre. Tr. by Carlos Reyes. (SPA.). 122p. 2000. 24.00 (*0-910055-59-9*, Pub. by East Wash Univ) U of Wash Pr.

***Poemas de la Isla (The Island Poems)** Josephina de la Torre. Tr. by Carlos Reyes. (SPA & ENG.). 90p. 2000. pap. 15.95 (*0-910055-58-0*, Pub. by East Wash Univ) U of Wash Pr.

Poemas de la Nieve Negra. Juan M. Rivera. LC 84-62597. (Serie de Poesia Guampara: No. 3). (SPA.). 96p. (Orig.). 1985. pap. text 5.95 (*0-910235-09-0*) Prisma Bks.

Poemas de las Madres (The Mothers' Poems) Gabriela Mistral, pseud. Tr. by Christiane J. Kyle. (Illus.). 39p. 1996. pap. 25.00 (*0-910055-29-7*) East Wash Univ.

Poemas del Hombre y las Desolaciones. Odon Betanzos-Palacios. 1986. pap. 3.00 (*0-86515-014-1*) Edit Mensaje.

Poemas en Prosa. Carmela V. De Rodriguez. 1978. 2.50 (*84-399-8110-4*) Edit Mensaje.

***Poemas Escogidos.** Ruben Dario. 1999. 13.00 (*84-481-0978-3*, McGrw-H College) McGrw-H Hghr Educ.

Poemas Escogidos. Pedro Salinas. Ed. by Francisco J. Diez De Revenga. (Nueva Austral Ser.: Vol. 226). (SPA.). 1991. pap. text 24.95 (*84-239-7226-7*) Elliots Bks.

Poemas Majicos y Dolientes. Juan Ramon Jimenez. (SPA.). 121p. 1965. 4.50 (*0-8288-7133-7*, S20022) Fr & Eur.

***Poemas Mayas.** Calixta Gabriel. (SPA.). 100p. 2000. pap. 10.95 (*1-886502-35-8*) Yax Te Found.

Poemas para Combatir la Calvicie (Poetry Against Hairloss) Nicanor Parra. (SPA.). 382p. 1993. pap. 25.99 (*968-16-3931-6*, Pub. by Fondo) Continental Bk.

Poemas para Todas Ocasiones. Alfredo D. Noble. Tr. by William Ortiz. (SPA.). 46p. 1998. pap. 7.95 (*1-887653-02-3*) Papito.

Poemas Sem Poesia; Imigramar; Vinte e Cinco Anos de Poesia see Poems Without Poetry: Twenty Five Years of Poetry

Poemas Tradicionales. Leslie C. Stockham. (SPA., Illus.). 52p. (Orig.). (J). (ps-2). 1991. pap. 5.98 (*0-9624096-0-X*) Bilingual Lang Mat.

Poemata Arcana. C. Moreschini. Tr. by D. A. Sykes. (Theological Monographs). 310p. 1997. text 95.00 (*0-19-826732-0*) OUP.

***Poematics of the Hyperbloody Real: Poems 1980-2001.** Harrison Fisher. LC 00-190995. 2000. 25.00 (*0-7388-2177-2*); pap. 18.00 (*0-7388-2178-0*) Xlibris Corp.

Poemcrazy: Freeing Your Life with Words. Susan Wooldridge. 1997. pap. 13.00 (*0-609-80098-1*) Random Hse Value.

Poeme de Versailles. Andre Maurois. pap. 9.50 (*0-685-36952-8*) Fr & Eur.

Poeme Heroique sur le Bataille de Qadech (1288 Av. J. C.) Gregoire Loukianoff. (FRE.). 24p. (Orig.). (C). 1988. reprint ed. pap. 10.00 (*0-933175-18-3*) Van Siclen Bks.

Poemes. Alfred De Vigny. Ed. by Jean Chuzeville. 276p. 1953. 12.95 (*0-8288-9668-2*, M2667) Fr & Eur.

Poemes. Jean Genet. pap. 19.95 (*0-685-33953-X*) Fr & Eur.

Poemes. Leopold S. Senghor. (FRE.). 412p. 1984. pap. 59.95 (*0-685-67479-7*, 2020067579) Fr & Eur.

Poemes see Oeuvres Choisies

Poemes: De Mouvement et de l'Immobilitie de Douve, Hier Regnant Desert, Pierre Ecrit, Dans le Leurre du Seuil. Yves Bonnefoy. (FRE.). 1982. pap. 10.95 (*0-8288-3814-3*, F88690) Fr & Eur.

Poemes: Du Mouvement et de l'Immobilite de Douve; Hier Regnant Desert; Pierre Ecrite, etc. Yves Bonnefoy. (Poesie Ser.). (FRE.). pap. 13.95 (*2-07-032221-1*) Schoenhof.

Poemes a Lou. II y A. Guillaume Apollinaire. (FRE.). 266p. 1969. pap. 11.95 (*0-7859-2755-7*, F82220) Fr & Eur.

Poemes a Lou. II y A. Guillaume Apollinaire. Ed. by Decaudin. (Poesie Ser.). pap. 9.95 (*2-07-030009-9*) Schoenhof.

Poemes Antiques et Modernes: Les Destinees. Alfred De Vigny. (FRE.). 1973. pap. 14.95 (*0-7859-2773-5*) Fr & Eur.

Poemes Antiques et Modernes & les Destinees. Alfred De Vigny. (Poesie Ser.). (FRE.). 320p. 1973. pap. 11.95 (*2-07-032049-9*) Schoenhof.

Poemes Barbares. Charles-Rene-Marie Leconte De Lisle. (Poesie Ser.). (FRE.). pap. 16.95 (*2-07-032326-9*) Schoenhof.

Poemes (Chants d'Ombre, Hosties Noires, Nocturnes, Ethopiques, Ballade Toucoulore de Samba-Foul, Ballade Khassonkaise du Dioudi. Leopold S. Senghor. 19.95 (*0-685-35641-8*) Fr & Eur.

Poemes d'Amour de Baudelaire: Avec des Documents Nouveaux. Charles Baudelaire. LC 77-10249. (Illus.). reprint ed. 20.50 (*0-404-16305-X*) AMS Pr.

Poemes de l'Infortune et Autres Poemes (Medieval & Modern French) Rutebeuf. (Poesie Ser.). (FRE.). 308p. 1986. pap. 13.95 (*2-07-032378-1*) Schoenhof.

Poemes de Morven le Gaelique. M. Jacob. (FRE.). 1991. pap. 10.95 (*0-7859-2823-5*) Fr & Eur.

Poemes de Renee Vivien, 2 vols. Renee Vivien. LC 75-12354. (Homosexuality Ser.). (FRE.). 1975. reprint ed. 41.95 (*0-405-07397-6*) Ayer.

Poemes d'Edgar Allan Poe. Edgar Allan Poe. Tr. by Stephane Mallarme. LC 77-11473. (FRE., Illus.). reprint ed. 57.50 (*0-404-16335-1*) AMS Pr.

Poemes et Paroles Durant la Guerre de Trente Ans. Paul Claudel. (FRE.). 216p. 1945. 10.95 (*0-7859-1120-0*, 2070215105) Fr & Eur.

Poemes et Petits Poemes Abstraits. Paul Valery. Ed. by Judith Robinson-Valery. (FRE.). 1992. pap. 24.95 (*0-7859-2832-4*) Fr & Eur.

Poemes et Poesies, 1914-1973. Philippe Soupault. (FRE.). 1987. pap. 19.95 (*0-7859-3048-5*) Fr & Eur.

Poemes et Prose Choisis. Rene Char. 320p. 1957. 7.95 (*0-8288-9090-0*) Fr & Eur.

Poemes I, 1945-1967: Les Testaments. Alain Bosquet. (FRE.). 1985. pap. 16.95 (*0-7859-2796-4*) Fr & Eur.

Poemes Lyriques. Emile Zola. 6.95 (*0-686-55797-2*) Fr & Eur.

Poemes, Pieces, Prose: Introduction a l'Analyse de Textes Litteraires Francais. Ed. by Peter Schofer et al. (FRE., Illus.). 742p. (C). 1973. text 41.95 (*0-19-501643-2*) OUP.

Poemes pour le Cours Avance, 1985-1986. rev. ed. Andre O. Hurtgen. 148p. (YA). (gr. 9-12). 1981. pap. text 13.95 (*0-8013-0239-0*) Longman.

Poemes Saturniens. unabridged ed. Paul M. Verlaine. (FRE.). pap. 5.95 (*2-87714-191-8*, Pub. by Bookking Intl) Distribks Inc.

Poemes Saturniens: Avec: Confessions. Paul M. Verlaine & Jean Gaudon. (FRE.). 375p. 1977. pap. 10.95 (*0-7859-1433-1*, 2080702890) Fr & Eur.

Poemes Saturniens Fetes Galantes. Paul Verlaine. (FRE.). 1961. pap. 10.95 (*0-7859-3071-X*, 2253006254) Fr & Eur.

Poeming Elusions. Robley E. Whitson. LC 92-72897. 104p. (C). 1992. pap. text 12.00 (*1-55605-213-8*) Wyndham Hall.

Poems. Anna Andreevena Akhmatova. Tr. by Lyn Coffin from RUS. 1983. pap. 10.95 (*0-393-30014-5*) Norton.

Poems. Maya Angelou. 224p. 1986. mass mkt. 5.50 (*0-553-85173-X*) Bantam.

Poems. Arden. 1985. pap. 8.95 (*0-416-27870-1*) Routledge.

Poems, 2 vols. Ausonius. No. 96, 115. write for info. (*0-318-53140-2*) HUP.

Poems. William Blake. LC 91-52990. Vol. 34. 496p. 1991. 20.00 (*0-679-40552-6*) Everymns Lib.

Poems. Bray. (Australian National University Press Ser.). 1979. text 17.50 (*0-08-032934-9*, Pergamon Pr) Elsevier.

Poems. Rosalia de Castro. Ed. & Tr. by Barbara N. Gantt from GAE. Tr. by Anna-Marie Aldaz et al from GAE. LC 90-9895. (SUNY Series, Women Writers in Translation). 216p. (C). 1991. pap. text 19.95 (*0-7914-0583-4*) State U NY Pr.

Poems, 2 vols. Claudian. No. 135, 136. 19.95 (*0-318-53141-0*) HUP.

Poems. Samuel Taylor Coleridge. 400p. 1991. 17.00 (*0-679-40669-7*) Everymns Lib.

Poems. Samuel Taylor Coleridge. Ed. by John B. Beer. 412p. 1993. pap. 7.95 (*0-460-87316-4*, Everyman's Classic Lib) Tuttle Pubng.

Poems. John Davies. Ed. by Robert Krueger. (Oxford English Texts Ser.). (Illus.). 522p. 1975. text 85.00 (*0-19-812716-2*) OUP.

Poems. Richard Dehmel. 1972. 59.95 (*0-8490-0846-8*) Gordon Pr.

Poems. Emily Dickinson. LC 94-45647. (Pocket Classics Ser.). 208p. 1995. pap. 6.00 (*1-57062-099-7*, Pub. by Shambhala Pubns) Random.

Poems. John Donne. 576p. 1991. 20.00 (*0-679-40558-5*) Everymns Lib.

Poems. John Donne. LC 95-15330. (Everyman's Library of Pocket Poets). 256p. 1994. 12.50 (*0-679-44467-X*) Knopf.

Poems. Mihail Eminescu. 1976. 250.00 (*0-87968-466-6*) Gordon Pr.

Poems. Carl A. Faber. LC 59-4760. 1974. 4.95 (*0-918026-01-6*) Perseus Pr.

Poems. Alvin Feinman. 78p. (Orig.). 1990. text 17.95 (*0-691-06819-4*, Pub. by Princeton U Pr) Cal Prin Full Svc.

Poems. John Fowles. LC 72-96853. 100p. 1985. pap. 7.50 (*0-912946-03-2*, Ecco Press) HarperTrade.

Poems. Robert Frost. 256p. 1997. 12.50 (*0-679-45514-0*) Everymns Lib.

***Poems.** Allen Ginsberg. 1998. write for info. (*0-375-40465-1*) Everymns Lib.

Poems. Fulke Greville. (C). 1990. 60.00 (*0-906887-06-2*, Pub. by Greville Pr) St Mut.

Poems. Gerard Manley Hopkins. LC 95-15331. (Everyman's Library of Pocket Poets). 256p. 1995. 12.50 (*0-679-44469-6*) Knopf.

***Poems.** Gerard Manley Hopkins. LC 99-222471. 1999. pap. 5.95 (*0-460-87714-3*, Everyman's Classic Lib) Tuttle Pubng.

Poems. Langston Hughes. LC 98-55136. 256p. 1999. 12.50 (*0-375-40551-8*) Everymns Lib.

Poems. Samuel Johnson. Ed. by E. L. McAdam, Jr. & George Milne. (Works of Samuel Johnson Ser.: Vol. 6). (Illus.). 1965. 65.00 (*0-300-00734-5*) Yale U Pr.

Poems. Ben Jonson. Ed. by Ian Donaldson. (Oxford Standard Authors Ser.). 448p. 1976. 35.00 (*0-19-254166-8*) OUP.

Poems. Tr. by Guy Lee. LC 96-164134. (World's Classics WC Ser.). 230p. (Orig.). (C). 1996. pap. 8.95 (*0-19-283198-4*) OUP.

Poems. C. S. Lewis. Ed. by Walter Hooper. LC 77-4733. 168p. 1977. pap. 10.00 (*0-15-672248-8*, Harvest Bks) Harcourt.

An Asterisk (*) at the beginning of an entry indicates that the title is appearing for the first time.

Poems. Dierdre Lichtenberg. (Illus.). 60p. (Orig.). pap. 5.00 (*0-9617811-0-6*) Chandrabala Pr.

Poems. Francis Neilson. 1971. 250.00 (*0-87700-006-9*) Revisionist Pr.

Poems. James Oppenheimer. 1972. 69.95 (*0-8490-0847-6*) Gordon Pr.

Poems. Oppian. (Loeb Classical Library: No. 219). 15.50 (*0-674-99241-5*) HUP.

Poems. Nick Piombino. 88p. (Orig.). 1988. pap. 8.95 (*1-55713-011-6*) Sun & Moon CA.

Poems. J. H. Prynne. (Agneau 2 Paperbook Ser.: 1). 320p. 1982. pap. 18.00 (*0-907954-01-4*, Pub. by Allardyce Barnett) SPD-Small Pr Dist.

Poems. J. H. Prynne. 440p. 1998. 59.95 (*1-85224-491-7*, Pub. by Bloodaxe Bks); pap. 29.95 (*1-85224-492-5*, Pub. by Bloodaxe Bks) Dufour.

***Poems.** Sean Rafferty. 173p. 1999. pap. 13.50 (*1-901538-15-X*, Pub. by etruscan bks) SPD-Small Pr Dist.

Poems. Rainer Maria Rilke. Tr. by J. B. Leishman & Stephen Spender. 1996. 12.50 (*0-679-45098-X*) McKay.

Poems. Arthur Rimbaud. LC 94-2496. 288p. 1994. 12.50 (*0-679-43321-X*) Random.

Poems. W. R. Rodgers & Michael Longley. 108p. 1993. pap. 16.95 (*1-85235-106-3*) Dufour.

Poems. Bruce Ruddick. LC 93-46450. 60p. (Orig.). 1994. pap. 10.95 (*1-878818-26-0*, Pub. by Sheep Meadow) U Pr of New Eng.

Poems. Sappho. Tr. by Willis Barstone. (Green Integer Bks.: No. 26). 152p. 1999. pap. text 10.95 (*1-892295-13-X*, Pub. by Green Integer) Consort Bk Sales.

Poems. Aram Saroyan. 47p. (Orig.). 1986. pap. 4.00 (*0-9606772-5-9*) Blackberry Bks.

Poems. William Shakespeare. (Illus.). 1994. 12.50 (*0-679-43320-1*) Random.

Poems. William Shakespeare. Ed. by David Bevington et al. LC 87-19540. (Classics Ser.). 368p. 1988. mass mkt. 4.95 (*0-553-21309-1*, Bantam Classics) Bantam.

Poems. William Shakespeare. 1995. pap. 11.95 (*0-17-443628-9*) Thomson Learn.

Poems. William Shakespeare. (English Ser.). (C). 2001. mass mkt. 9.95 (*0-17-443532-0*) Wadsworth Pub.

Poems. Virginia Sheahen. LC 87-81640. (Illus.). 72p. (Orig.). 1990. pap. 7.95 (*0-910725-04-7*) Gain Pubns.

Poems. Arseny Tarkovsky. (C). 1990. 40.00 (*0-906887-53-4*, Pub. by Greville Pr) St Mut.

Poems, 2 vols. Theocritus. Tr. by A. S. Gow. 990p. 1952. text 200.00 (*0-521-06616-6*) Cambridge U Pr.

Poems. Ioanna Tsatsos. Tr. by Jean Demos from GRE. 200p. 1984. 20.00 (*0-935476-15-6*) Nostos Bks.

Poems. Victor Urin. 1986. 4.00 (*0-685-22664-6*) RWCPH.

Poems. large type ed. Maya Angelou. 224p. 1997. pap. 12.00 (*0-553-37985-2*) Bantam.

Poems see Works of Oscar Wilde

Poems see Writings of George Eliot

Poems see Works of George Meredith

Poems see Complete Works of John Ruskin

Poems. Aimeric De Peguilhan. LC 70-128941. reprint ed. 34.50 (*0-404-50724-7*) AMS Pr.

Poems. William Allingham. LC 78-148741. reprint ed. 20.00 (*0-404-00345-1*) AMS Pr.

Poems. George Bancroft. (Works of George Bancroft). 1989. reprint ed. lib. bdg. 79.00 (*0-685-27844-1*) Rprt Serv.

Poems. George Bannatyne. LC 78-144411. (Bannatyne Club, Edinburgh. Publications: No. 4a). reprint ed. 35.00 (*0-404-52705-1*) AMS Pr.

Poems. Eloise Bibb. LC 71-173601. (Black Heritage Library Collection). 1977. reprint ed. 20.95 (*0-8369-8897-3*) Ayer.

Poems, 2 vols. William Browne. 1988. reprint ed. lib. bdg. 99.00 (*0-317-90892-8*) Rprt Serv.

Poems. William C. Bryant. (Works of William Cullen Bryant). 1989. reprint ed. lib. bdg. 79.00 (*0-685-27995-2*) Rprt Serv.

Poems. Henry Carey. (BCL1-PR English Literature Ser.). 261p. 1992. reprint ed. lib. bdg. 79.00 (*0-7812-7329-3*) Rprt Serv.

Poems. William E. Channing. LC 72-4955. (Romantic Tradition in American Literature Ser.). 162p. 1972. reprint ed. 23.95 (*0-405-04627-8*) Ayer.

Poems. William E. Channing, II. (Works of William Ellery Channing II). 1990. reprint ed. lib. bdg. 79.00 (*0-7812-2261-3*) Rprt Serv.

Poems. Tristan Corbiere. Tr. by Walter McElroy from FRE. LC 77-10257. 80p. reprint ed. 27.50 (*0-404-16312-2*) AMS Pr.

Poems. Emily Dickinson. (Notable American Authors Ser.). 1992. reprint ed. lib. bdg. 75.00 (*0-7812-2628-7*) Rprt Serv.

Poems. William Drummond. Ed. by Thomas Maitland. LC 77-144419. (Maitland Club, Glasgow. Publications: No. 18). reprint ed. 67.50 (*0-404-52956-9*) AMS Pr.

Poems. William Drummond. LC 76-6156. (English Experience Ser.: No. 83). 128p. 1969. reprint ed. 20.00 (*90-221-0083-9*) Walter J Johnson.

Poems. Mary M. Eddy. (Notable American Authors Ser.). 1992. reprint ed. lib. bdg. 75.00 (*0-7812-2756-9*) Rprt Serv.

Poems. Ralph Waldo Emerson. (Notable American Authors Ser.). 1992. reprint ed. lib. bdg. 75.00 (*0-7812-2808-5*) Rprt Serv.

Poems. James T. Fields. (Notable American Authors Ser.). 1992. reprint ed. lib. bdg. 75.00 (*0-7812-2832-8*) Rprt Serv.

Poems. Bob Grumman. 34p. 1997. reprint ed. pap. 3.00 (*1-57141-036-8*) Runaway Spoon.

Poems. Henry Harbaugh. (Notable American Authors Ser.). 1992. reprint ed. lib. bdg. 75.00 (*0-7812-3012-8*) Rprt Serv.

Poems. Frances Ellen Watkins Harper. LC 73-18576. reprint ed. 27.50 (*0-404-11387-7*) AMS Pr.

Poems. John M. Hay. (Notable American Authors Ser.). 1992. reprint ed. lib. bdg. 75.00 (*0-7812-3054-3*) Rprt Serv.

Poems. Paul H. Hayne. LC 74-101918. (Illus.). reprint ed. 49.50 (*0-404-03167-6*) AMS Pr.

Poems. Paul H. Hayne. (BCL1-PS American Literature Ser.). 386p. 1992. reprint ed. lib. bdg. 89.00 (*0-7812-6735-8*) Rprt Serv.

Poems. Charles F. Hoffman. (BCL1-PS American Literature Ser.). 238p. 1992. reprint ed. lib. bdg. 79.00 (*0-7812-6738-2*) Rprt Serv.

Poems. Charles F. Hoffman. Ed. by E. F. Hoffman. (Notable American Authors Ser.). 1992. reprint ed. lib. bdg. 75.00 (*0-7812-3138-8*) Rprt Serv.

Poems. Oliver W. Holmes. (Notable American Authors Ser.). 1992. reprint ed. lib. bdg. 75.00 (*0-7812-3161-2*) Rprt Serv.

Poems. William Dean Howells. (Notable American Authors Ser.). 1992. reprint ed. lib. bdg. 75.00 (*0-7812-3269-4*) Rprt Serv.

Poems. Helen Maria Hunt Jackson. LC 72-4966. (Romantic Tradition in American Literature Ser.). (Illus.). 326p. 1980. reprint ed. 34.95 (*0-405-04637-5*) Ayer.

Poems. Francis S. Key. LC 79-104503. reprint ed. lib. bdg. 37.50 (*0-8398-1053-9*) Irvington.

Poems. Anne Killigrew. LC 67-10177. 112p. 1967. reprint ed. 50.00 (*0-8201-1030-2*) Schol Facsimiles.

Poems. Charles Kingsley. (BCL1-PR English Literature Ser.). 236p. 1992. reprint ed. lib. bdg. 79.00 (*0-7812-7705-1*) Rprt Serv.

Poems. A. M. Klein. LC 74-27993. (Modern Jewish Experience Ser.). 1975. reprint ed. 16.95 (*0-405-06720-8*) Ayer.

Poems. Jan Kochanowski. Tr. by Dorothea P. Radin et al from POL. LC 76-29471. (ENG.). reprint ed. 20.00 (*0-404-15313-5*) AMS Pr.

Poems. Sidney Lanier. (Notable American Authors Ser.). 1999. reprint ed. lib. bdg. 125.00 (*0-7812-3715-7*); reprint ed. lib. bdg. 125.00 (*0-7812-3723-8*) Rprt Serv.

Poems. Lucy Larcom. (Notable American Authors Ser.). 1999. reprint ed. lib. bdg. 125.00 (*0-7812-3746-7*) Rprt Serv.

Poems. Emma Lazarus. (Notable American Authors Ser.). 1999. reprint ed. lib. bdg. 125.00 (*0-7812-3773-4*) Rprt Serv.

Poems. Henry Wadsworth Longfellow. (Notable American Authors Ser.). 1999. reprint ed. lib. bdg. 125.00 (*0-7812-3827-7*) Rprt Serv.

Poems. James Russell Lowell. (Notable American Authors Ser.). 1999. reprint ed. lib. bdg. 125.00 (*0-7812-3875-7*); reprint ed. lib. bdg. 125.00 (*0-7812-3876-5*); reprint ed. lib. bdg. 125.00 (*0-7812-3882-X*); reprint ed. lib. bdg. 125.00 (*0-7812-3883-8*) Rprt Serv.

Poems. Robert T. Lowell. (Notable American Authors Ser.). 1999. reprint ed. lib. bdg. 125.00 (*0-7812-3905-2*) Rprt Serv.

Poems. Stephane Mallarme. Tr. by Roger Fry from ENG. LC 77-10279. 320p. reprint ed. 32.00 (*0-404-16330-0*) AMS Pr.

Poems. David Murray. LC 70-144428. (Bannatyne Club, Edinburgh. Publications: No. 2). reprint ed. 27.50 (*0-404-52702-7*) AMS Pr.

Poems. Arthur O'Shaughnessy. (BCL1-PR English Literature Ser.). 104p. 1992. reprint ed. lib. bdg. 69.00 (*0-7812-7611-X*) Rprt Serv.

Poems. Edward C. Pinkney. LC 72-4970. (Romantic Tradition in American Literature Ser.). 76p. 1972. reprint ed. 21.95 (*0-405-04640-5*) Ayer.

Poems. Edgar Allan Poe. (BCL1-PS American Literature Ser.). 332p. 1992. reprint ed. lib. bdg. 89.00 (*0-7812-6831-1*) Rprt Serv.

Poems. William B. Scott. LC 77-140034. (Illus.). reprint ed. 45.00 (*0-404-05647-4*) AMS Pr.

Poems. Robert Southey. (BCL1-PR English Literature Ser.). 768p. 1992. reprint ed. lib. bdg. 109.00 (*0-7812-7659-4*) Rprt Serv.

Poems. Edmund C. Stedman. (BCL1-PS American Literature Ser.). 475p. 1992. reprint ed. lib. bdg. 99.00 (*0-7812-6864-8*) Rprt Serv.

Poems. Robert Louis Stevenson. (BCL1-PR English Literature Ser.). 259p. 1992. reprint ed. lib. bdg. 79.00 (*0-7812-7665-9*) Rprt Serv.

Poems. Charles W. Stoddard. Ed. by Ina Coolbrith. LC 79-144690. reprint ed. 31.50 (*0-404-06279-2*) AMS Pr.

Poems. Charles W. Stoddard. (BCL1-PS American Literature Ser.). 144p. 1992. reprint ed. lib. bdg. 69.00 (*0-7812-6866-4*) Rprt Serv.

Poems. Charles W. Stoddard. (Notable American Authors Ser.). 1999. reprint ed. lib. bdg. 125.00 (*0-7812-8939-4*) Rprt Serv.

Poems. Alfred Lord Tennyson. (BCL1-PR English Literature Ser.). 752p. 1992. reprint ed. lib. bdg. 109.00 (*0-7812-7690-X*) Rprt Serv.

Poems. Henry Timrod. (BCL1-PS American Literature Ser.). 130p. 1992. reprint ed. lib. bdg. 69.00 (*0-7812-6887-7*) Rprt Serv.

Poems. Henry T. Tuckerman. (Notable American Authors Ser.). 1999. reprint ed. lib. bdg. 125.00 (*0-7812-9851-2*) Rprt Serv.

Poems. Paul M. Verlaine. Tr. by Jacques Leclercq. LC 77-13574. (Illus.). 61p. 1977. reprint ed. lib. bdg. 45.00 (*0-8371-9859-3*, VEPO, Greenwood Pr) Greenwood.

Poems. Edmund Waller. Ed. by G. Thorn Drury. LC 69-14135. 352p. 1969. reprint ed. lib. bdg. 65.00 (*0-8371-0735-0*, WAEW, Greenwood Pr) Greenwood.

Poems. Edmund Waller. (BCL1-PR English Literature Ser.). 352p. 1992. reprint ed. lib. bdg. 89.00 (*0-7812-7417-6*) Rprt Serv.

Poems. Frances E. Watkins Harper. LC 98-67628. (Illus.). 96p. 1998. reprint ed. pap. 12.95 (*1-892616-01-7*) Post Oak Pubns.

Poems. Henrik A. Wergeland. Tr. by Geoffrey M. Gathorne-Hardy et al. LC 74-98798. 203p. 1970. reprint ed. lib. bdg. 59.50 (*0-8371-3159-6*, WEPO, Greenwood Pr) Greenwood.

Poems. Sarah H. Whiteman. (Notable American Authors Ser.). 1999. reprint ed. lib. bdg. 125.00 (*0-7812-9942-X*) Rprt Serv.

Poems. Nathaniel P. Willis. LC 72-144703. reprint ed. 34.00 (*0-404-06989-4*) AMS Pr.

Poems. Nathaniel P. Willis. (BCL1-PS American Literature Ser.). 304p. 1992. reprint ed. lib. bdg. 89.00 (*0-7812-6904-0*) Rprt Serv.

Poems. William Winter. (Notable American Authors Ser.). 1999. reprint ed. lib. bdg. 125.00 (*0-7812-7765-5*); reprint ed. lib. bdg. 125.00 (*0-7812-7767-1*); reprint ed. lib. bdg. 125.00 (*0-7812-7761-2*) Rprt Serv.

Poems. 3rd ed. William Shakespeare. (English Ser.). (C). 2001. mass mkt. 45.00 (*0-17-443565-7*) Wadsworth Pub.

Poems. 3rd ed. William Shakespeare. Ed. by F. T. Prince. (Arden Shakespeare Ser.). 1960. reprint ed. 9.95 (*0-415-02752-7*, NO. 2489) Routledge.

Poems. 3rd ed. William Shakespeare. Ed. by F. T. Prince. (Arden Shakespeare Ser.). 1960. reprint ed. pap. 45.00 (*0-416-47610-4*, NO. 2488) Thomson Learn.

Poems, 2 Vols, 1. Ausonius. (Loeb Classical Library: No. 96, 115). 442p. 1919. 19.95 (*0-674-99107-9*) HUP.

Poems, 2 vols., 1. Tr. by Maurice Platnauer. (Loeb Classical Library: No. 135, 136). 420p. 1922. 18.95 (*0-674-99150-8*) HUP.

Poems, 2 Vols, 2. Ausonius. (Loeb Classical Library: No. 96, 115). 374p. 1921. 19.95 (*0-674-99127-3*) HUP.

Poems, 2 vols., 2. Tr. by Maurice Platnauer. (Loeb Classical Library: No. 135, 136). 420p. 1922. 18.95 (*0-674-99151-6*) HUP.

Poems, 3rd Series. Emily Dickinson. (Notable American Authors Ser.). 1992. reprint ed. lib. bdg. 75.00 (*0-7812-2631-7*) Rprt Serv.

***Poems, Bk. 1.** Esther Trussell. 1999. pap. write for info. (*1-58235-172-4*) Watermrk Pr.

Poems, 2 vols., Set. William T. Browne. 1971. reprint ed. 69.00 (*0-403-00846-8*) Scholarly.

Poems, 3 vols., Set. William Dunbar. Ed. by John Small. (Anglistica & Americana Ser.: No. 136). (Illus.). 1973. reprint ed. 161.20 (*3-487-04650-4*) G Olms Pubs.

Poems, 2 vols., Set. Richard Lovelace. Ed. by C. H. Wilkinson. (BCL1-PR English Literature Ser.). 1992. reprint ed. lib. bdg. 150.00 (*0-7812-7369-2*) Rprt Serv.

Poems, Vol. 1. Prudentius. Tr. by M. Clement Eagan. LC 63-5499. (Fathers of the Church Ser.: Vol. 43). 280p. 1962. 31.95 (*0-8132-0043-1*) Cath U Pr.

Poems, Vol. 1. Alexander Brome. Ed. by Roman R. Dubinski. LC 83-107902. 407p. reprint ed. pap. 126.20 (*0-7837-1231-6*, 204136800001) Bks Demand.

Poems, Vol. 2. Prudentius. Tr. by M. Clement Eagan. LC 63-5499. (Fathers of the Church Ser.: Vol. 52). 230p. 1965. 31.95 (*0-8132-0052-0*) Cath U Pr.

Poems, Vol. 2. Alexander Brome. Ed. by Roman R. Dubinski. LC 83-107902. 156p. reprint ed. pap. 48.40 (*0-7837-1232-4*, 204136800002) Bks Demand.

Poems, 3 vols., Vols. 1 - 3. George Crabbe. Ed. by Adolphus W. Ward. LC 75-41067. (BCL Ser. II). reprint ed. 210.00 (*0-404-14860-3*) AMS Pr.

Poems: A Selection. John Cowper Powys. Ed. by Kenneth Hopkins. 224p. 1964. text 29.95 (*0-912568-00-3*) Colgate U Pr.

Poems: About People & Rivers of Appalachia. Silas E. Coomer. (Illus.). 46p. 1993. pap. text 8.95 (*1-883045-00-2*) Trning Materials.

Poems: Auden. W. H. Auden. 1995. 12.50 (*0-679-44367-3*) Knopf.

Poems: Baudelaire. Charles Baudelaire. LC 93-14363. (Pocket Poets Ser.). (ENG & FRE.). 256p. 1993. 12.50 (*0-679-42910-7*) Everymns Lib.

***Poems: By Julie Marie.** Julie Marie. 2000. pap. 6.95 (*0-533-13504-4*) Vantage.

Poems: Collected & Selected. Hildegarde Flanner. LC 86-32817. 112p. (Orig.). 1988. pap. 10.00 (*0-936784-27-X*) J Daniel.

Poems: Descriptive, Dramatic, Legendary & Contemplative. William Gilmore Simms. LC 72-4973. (Romantic Tradition in American Literature Ser.). 712p. 1972. reprint ed. 51.95 (*0-405-04643-X*) Ayer.

Poems: Dickinson. Emily Dickinson. LC 93-14360. (Pocket Poets Ser.). 256p. 1993. 12.50 (*0-679-42907-7*) Everymns Lib.

Poems: Emily Bronte. Emily Jane Bronte. LC 96-140866. 254p. 1996. 12.50 (*0-679-44725-3*) Random.

Poems: Friendship. Everymans Library Staff & Carolyn B. Mitchell. 1995. 12.50 (*0-679-44370-3*) Everymns Lib.

Poems: Glenings from Spare Hours of a Business Life. James Lawson. (Notable American Authors Ser.). 1999. reprint ed. lib. bdg. 125.00 (*0-7812-3764-5*) Rprt Serv.

Poems: Hardy. Thomas Hardy. 1995. 10.95 (*0-679-44368-1*) Everymns Lib.

Poems: Insomnia in the Afternoon. Michael Foley. 108p. 1994. pap. 11.95 (*0-85640-515-9*, Pub. by Blackstaff Pr) Dufour.

Poems: Just Give Me a Cool Drink of Water 'Fore I Die/Oh Pray My Wings Are Gonna Fit Me Well & Still I Rise/ Shaker, Why Don't You Sin. large type ed. Maya Angelou. 224p. 1996. mass mkt. 5.99 (*0-553-25576-2*) Bantam.

Poems: Keats. John Keats. LC 94-2495. (Everyman's Library Pocket Poets Ser.). 253p. 1994. 10.95 (*0-679-43319-8*) Random.

Poems: Lord Byron. George Gordon Byron. 256p. 1994. 12.50 (*0-679-43630-8*) Everymns Lib.

Poems: Medley & Palestina. John W. DeForest. 1902. 100.00 (*0-685-89770-2*) Elliots Bks.

Poems: Medley & Palestina see Collected Works of John W. De Forest

Poems: Medley & Palestina. John W. De Forest. (Collected Works of John W. De Forest). 1988. reprint ed. lib. bdg. 59.00 (*0-7812-1168-9*) Rprt Serv.

Poems: New & Selected. Grace Cavalieri. Ed. by Cindy Comitz & Robert Sargent. 100p. (Orig.). 1994. pap. 10.00 (*0-938572-06-7*) Bunny Crocodile.

Poems: New & Selected. Frederick Morgan. LC 86-30844. 280p. 1987. 12.95 (*0-252-01434-0*); text 24.95 (*0-252-01433-2*) U of Ill Pr.

Poems: New & Selected. Thomas F. Parkinson. 140p. 1988. pap. 14.95 (*0-915032-96-1*) Natl Poet Foun.

Poems: On Writing Poetry. John Travers Moore. LC 79-181366. 1971. 5.00 (*0-87212-025-2*) Libra.

Poems: Partly Medical. Benjamin F. Miller. (Countway Library Associates Historical Publication: No. 4). 85p. 1978. 9.95 (*0-686-23786-2*) F A Countway.

Poems: Reinvestigations & Descent from the Cross. Kostas Kindinis. Tr. by Kimon Friar from GRE. (Modern Greek History & Culture Ser.). 1980. 10.00 (*0-935476-05-9*) Nostos Bks.

Poems: Rossetti. Christina Georgina Rossetti. LC 93-14362. (Pocket Poets Ser.). 256p. 1993. 0.12 (*0-679-42908-5*) Everymns Lib.

Poems: Second Series. Emily Dickinson. (Notable American Authors Ser.). 1992. reprint ed. lib. bdg. 75.00 (*0-7812-2629-5*) Rprt Serv.

Poems: Selected & New. Tony Curtis. LC 86-60368. (Poetry Ser.). 86p. (Orig.). 1986. 15.00 (*0-934257-07-8*); pap. 8.00 (*0-934257-06-X*) Story Line.

Poems: Selected & New, 1967-1991. Robert Peters. LC 92-71208. 190p. (Orig.). 1992. 20.00 (*1-878580-30-2*); pap. 11.95 (*1-878580-31-0*) Asylum Arts.

Poems: Shelley. Percy Bysshe Shelley. LC 93-78335. (Pocket Poets Ser.). 250p. 1993. 10.95 (*0-679-42909-3*) Everymns Lib.

Poems: Stevens. Wallace Stevens. 1993. 10.95 (*0-685-66616-6*) Everymns Lib.

Poems: The Collected Works of William Butler Yeats, Vol. 1. 2nd ed. William Butler Yeats. Ed. by Richard J. Finneran. LC 97-23065. (The Collected Works of W. B. Yeats Ser.). (Illus.). 784p. 1997. 40.00 (*0-684-83935-0*) S&S Trade.

Poems: The Poetry of Arlie Petree. Arlie Petree. 80p. (Orig.). Date not set. pap. 5.00 (*0-9646344-1-4*) M Padgett.

Poems: The Weight of Oranges, Miner's Pond, Skin Divers. Anne Michaels. LC 99-47105. 192p. 2000. 25.00 (*0-375-40140-7*) Knopf.

Poems: The 1645 Edition. John Milton. LC 68-24444. 369p. 1968. reprint ed. 75.00 (*0-87752-075-5*) Gordian.

Poems: Translated with Explanatory Notes. Propertius. Tr. by Guy Lee. LC 93-42190. 230p. (C). 1994. text 55.00 (*0-19-814497-0*, Clarendon Pr) OUP.

Poems: Venus & Adonis, The Rape of Lucrece, The Phoenix & the Turtle, The Passionate Pilgrim, A Lover's Complaint. William Shakespeare. Ed. by John Roe. (New Cambridge Shakespeare Ser.). (Illus.). 315p. (C). 1992. text 44.95 (*0-521-22231-1*); pap. text 11.95 (*0-521-29411-8*) Cambridge U Pr.

Poems: Wallace. Wallace Stevens. LC 93-14361. (Pocket Poets Ser.). 256p. 1993. 12.50 (*0-679-42911-5*) Everymns Lib.

Poems: Walt Whitman. Walt Whitman. LC 95-105153. 256p. 1994. 12.50 (*0-679-43632-4*) Everymns Lib.

Poems: William Blake. William Blake. LC 95-105107. 256p. 1994. 12.50 (*0-679-43633-2*) Random.

Poems: With Elegies on the Author's Death. John Donne. (Anglistica & Americana Ser.: No. 94). 406p. 1974. reprint ed. 83.20 (*3-487-05441-8*) G Olms Pubs.

Poems: With Elegies on the Author's Death. John Donne. LC 72-191. (English Experience Ser.: No. 240). 408p. 1970. reprint ed. 50.00 (*90-221-0240-8*) Walter J Johnson.

Poems: Wordsworth. William Wordsworth. 1995. 12.50 (*0-679-44369-X*) Everymns Lib.

Poems: Written on the Journey from Sense to Soul. 4th ed. Augusta E. Stetson. LC 92-82753. (Illus.). 132p. 1992. reprint ed. 15.00 (*1-879135-10-8*) Emma Pub Soc.

Poems: 2D Series. James Russell Lowell. (Notable American Authors Ser.). 1999. reprint ed. lib. bdg. 125.00 (*0-7812-3878-1*) Rprt Serv.

Poems - The Wooling of Malkatoon. Lewis Wallace. (Notable American Authors Ser.). 1999. reprint ed. lib. bdg. 125.00 (*0-7812-9869-5*) Rprt Serv.

Poems, a Life Primer. Edwin Alonig. 150p. 10.00 (*0-685-53107-4*) Soft Teach Inc.

***Poems about Family & Nations.** Bernard Mikofsky. 1999. pap. write for info. (*1-58235-307-7*) Watermrk Pr.

***Poems about Life.** Wilbur R. FitzGerno. (Illus.). iv, 168p. 1999. pap. 12.95 (*0-9670614-0-7*) TLC ETC.

Poems about Life. David Thompson. 64p. 1984. 5.95 (*0-89697-182-1*) Intl Univ Pr.

Poems about Little Angels: A Precious Child I Am. Marjorie R. Craig. 1998. pap. 6.95 (*0-533-12699-1*) Vantage.

Poems about War. Robert Graves. 92p. (Orig.). 1992. pap. 12.95 (*1-55921-030-3*) Moyer Bell.

Poems Across the Pavement. Luis J. Rodriguez. LC 90-119897. (Illus.). 48p. (Orig.). (C). 1989. pap. 7.95 (*0-9624287-0-1*) Tia Chucha Pr.

Poems Against Death. Karl Krolow. Tr. by Herman Salinger. LC 71-82716. 1980. 7.50 (*0-910350-07-8*) Charioteer.

Poems Alone. Harry Solomon. LC 94-70152. 80p. 1994. pap. 15.00 (*0-9630376-3-3*) Figure Eight.

Poems along the Path: Ad Adventure in Poetry. Judith Rafaela. 48p. 1994. pap. 7.50 (*0-9644196-0-2*) Sherman Asher Pub.

***Poems Along the Way.** Kenneth Hlavinka. 2000. pap. write for info. (*1-58235-388-3*) Watermrk Pr.

Poems & a Play in Irish. Brendan Behan. 76p. 1989. pap. 12.95 (*0-904011-15-1*) Dufour.

Poems & Adolphe, 1920. John Rodker. LC 96-182524. 280p. 1996. pap. 27.95 (*1-85754-060-3*, Pub. by Carcanet Pr) Paul & Co Pubs.

Poems & Annotations. Brooks et al. 31p. (Orig.). 1994. pap. 18.00 (*1-887648-05-4*) A-A Bks Pub.

Poems & Annotations. limited ed. Meade Brooks et al. 31p. (C). pap. 15.00 (*0-9632718-5-7*) A-A Bks Pub.

Poems & Balads of Heinrich Heine. Emma Lazarus. (Notable American Authors Ser.). 1999. reprint ed. lib. bdg. 125.00 (*0-7812-3770-X*) Rprt Serv.

Poems & Carols. Selwin Image et al. LC 93-41350. (Decadents, Symbolists, Anti-Decadents Ser.). 1994. 43.00 (*1-85477-148-5*) Continuum.

Poems & Carols. Selwyn Image. 1987. reprint ed. pap. 7.50 (*0-89979-051-8*) British Am Bks.

Poems & Contradictions. 2nd rev. ed. Rex Warner. LC 83-45483. 1945. 29.50 (*0-404-20281-0*, PR6045) AMS Pr.

Poems & Days. Michael Hannon. (Orig.). 1986. pap. 7.95 (*0-931037-03-4*) Isis Pr CA.

Poems & Dramas of Fulke Greville First Lord Brooke, 2 vols. Fulke G. Brooke. reprint ed. 95.00 (*0-403-04210-0*) Somerset Pub.

Poems & Epigrams. Richard O'Connell. 1929. pap. 25.00 (*0-87556-227-2*) Saifer.

Poems & Essays: With a Biographical Sketch by James Freeman Clarke. Jones Very. LC 72-4980. (Romantic Tradition in American Literature Ser.). 558p. 1978. reprint ed. 46.95 (*0-405-04649-9*) Ayer.

Poems & Essays of a Texas Expatriate. Wilburn L. Kirkpatrick. 56p. 1999. pap. 8.00 (*0-8059-4725-6*) Dorrance.

Poems & Essays of Herbert Krause. Arthur R. Huseboe. LC 90-2009. (Illus.). 300p. 1990. pap. 9.95 (*0-931170-49-4*); text 24.95 (*0-931170-48-6*) Ctr Western Studies.

Poems & Essays on Poetry. Edgar Allan Poe. Ed. & Intro. by C. H. Sisson. xvi, 150p. 1995. pap. 17.95 (*1-85754-120-0*, Pub. by Carcanet Pr) Paul & Co Pubs.

Poems & Fables. Robert Henryson. Ed. by Harvey H. Wood. 304p. (C). 1989. pap. 24.00 (*0-901824-53-4*, Pub. by Mercat Pr Bks) St Mut.

Poems & Fancies. Edward E. Hale. (Notable American Authors Ser.). 1992. reprint ed. lib. bdg. 75.00 (*0-7812-2981-2*) Rprt Serv.

Poems & Fragments. Friedrich Holderlin & Michael Hamburger. 750p. 1994. pap. 39.95 (*0-85646-245-4*, Pub. by Anvil Press) Dufour.

Poems & Fragments. Bacchylides. Tr. & Intro. by Richard Claverhouse. xviii, 524p. 1967. reprint ed. 130.00 (*3-487-09858-X*) G Olms Pubs.

Poems & Glyphs No. 17: Io Journal. Charles Stein. (Illus.). 100p. 1973. pap. 7.50 (*0-913028-18-5*) North Atlantic.

Poems & Growth: From Me to Me. Dee Frances. Ed. by Harry Koster. 70p. (Orig.). 1993. pap. 8.95 (*0-9635341-1-4*) DDDD Pubns.

Poems & Hums of Winnie-the-Pooh. A. A. Milne, pseud. (Illus.). 10p. (J). (gr. 4-7). 1994. 5.99 (*0-525-45205-2*, Dutton Child) Peng Put Young Read.

Poems & Hymn Tunes As Songs: Metrical Partners. Joseph Jones. 84p. 1983. pap. 24.50 incl. audio (*0-88432-588-1*, S1560); pap. 8.95 (*0-88432-119-3*, B21193) Audio-Forum.

Poems & Letters, 2 vols. Sidonius. Nos. 296, 420. write for info. (*0-318-53144-5*) HUP.

Poems & Letters. Sidney Lanier. (American Autobiography Ser.). 227p. 1995. reprint ed. lib. bdg. 79.00 (*0-7812-8574-7*) Rprt Serv.

Poems & Letters, 2 vols., 1. Tr. by W. B. Anderson. (Loeb Classical Library: Nos. 296, 420). 560p. 1936. 18.95 (*0-674-99327-6*) HUP.

Poems & Letters, 2 vols., 2. Tr. by W. B. Anderson. (Loeb Classical Library: Nos. 296, 420). 668p. 1965. 18.95 (*0-674-99462-0*) HUP.

Poems & Letters of C. H. Spurgeon. Eric W. Hayden. 1997. pap. 6.00 (*1-56186-204-5*) Pilgrim Pubns.

Poems & Masques of Aurelian Townshend: With Music by Henry Lawes & William Webb. Ed. by Cedric C. Brown. 126p. 1983. 37.00 (*0-7049-0108-0*, WK1) Pegasus Pr.

Poems & Melodrama. Donald Davie. LC 97-143398. 128p. pap. 14.95 (*1-85754-290-8*, Pub. by Carcanet Pr) Paul & Co Pubs.

Poems & Other Pieces. Henry Headley. LC 92-24826. (Augustan Reprints Ser.: No. 121). 1966. reprint ed. 14.50 (*0-404-70121-3*, PR4779) AMS Pr.

Poems & Other Ramblings about "Zis" & "Zat" Norman M. Trieff. LC 94-75655. 110p. (Orig.). 1994. pap. 9.95 (*0-9627775-4-4*) Ledero Pr.

Poems & Other Writings. Jeffrey G. Reese. (Illus.). (Orig.). 1994. pap. 20.00 (*0-9641717-0-8*) Am Vision Gallery.

Poems & Other Writings: Herbert. George Herbert. 1995. 20.00 (*0-679-44359-2*) Knopf.

***Poems & Parables: A Collection of Short Stories, Prose & Dramatic Readings.** Hannah Shively. (Illus.). 240p. 1999. pap. 14.95 (*0-9660304-1-9*) Illus Word.

Poems & Plays. Oliver Goldsmith. Ed. by Tom Davis. 328p. 1993. pap. 8.95 (*0-460-87390-3*, Everyman's Classic Lib) Tuttle Pubng.

Poems & Plays, 2 vols. William Vaughn Moody. LC 70-80719. reprint ed. 97.50 (*0-404-04388-7*) AMS Pr.

Poems & Plays, 2 vols., Set. William Vaughn Moody. (BCL1-PS American Literature Ser.). 1992. reprint ed. lib. bdg. 150.00 (*0-7812-6801-X*) Rprt Serv.

Poems & Plays of Thomas Wade. Ed. by John L. McLean. LC 95-61177. xiv, 699p. 1997. 65.00 (*0-87875-463-6*) Whitston Pub.

Poems & Poem Outlines see Centennial Edition of the Works of Sidney Lanier

Poems & Poems. Gerard Manley Hopkins. Ed. by W. H. Gardner. (Poets Ser.). 266p. 1953. pap. 14.95 (*0-14-042015-0*, Penguin Classics) Viking Penguin.

Poems & Poetical Fragments. Nicander. Ed. by W. R. Connor. LC 78-18579. (Greek Texts & Commentaries Ser.). (Illus.). 1979. reprint ed. lib. bdg. 23.95 (*0-405-11422-2*) Ayer.

Poems & Poets. Geoffrey Grigson. LC 68-55232. 1969. 24.95 (*0-8023-1195-4*) Dufour.

Poems & Points. Gomer Press Staff. (C). 1983. pap. 23.00 (*0-85088-526-4*, Pub. by Gomer Pr) St Mut.

Poems & Political Letters of F. I. Tyutchev. Fedor I. Tiutchev. Tr. & Intro. by Jesse Zeldin. LC 73-4397. 248p. reprint ed. pap. 76.90 (*0-7837-3022-5*, 204291800006) Bks Demand.

Poems & Prayers. Walter Lee. (Illus.). 54p. 1995. pap. 6.95 (*1-887409-06-8*) Faun Pub Co.

Poems & Prayers. Walter Lee. (Illus.). 54p. 1996. 11.95 (*1-887409-07-6*) Faun Pub Co.

Poems & Prayers for the Very Young see Santa's Take-Along Library: Five Favorite Read-to-Me Books

Poems & Prayers for the Very Young. Martha Alexander. (Illus.). (J). (ps-1). 1974. pap. 3.25 (*0-394-82705-8*, Pub. by Random Bks Yng Read) Random.

Poems & Prayers of Medjugorje. Margaret Gunnell. 21p. (Orig.). 1991. pap. 4.95 (*1-879877-03-1*) Moccasins Pr.

Poems & Profundities: Bits & Verses of Wit & Wisdom. Wilfred C. Gleason. LC 96-94041. 78p. (Orig.). 1996. pap. 11.95 (*0-9650810-0-1*) W C Gleason.

Poems & Prose. Edgar Allan Poe. LC 95-15329. (Everyman's Library of Pocket Poets). 256p. 1995. 12.50 (*0-679-44505-6*) Knopf.

Poems & Prose. Christina Georgina Rossetti. Ed. by Jan Marsh. 288p. 1995. lib. bdg. 7.95 (*0-460-87536-1*, Everyman's Classic Lib) Tuttle Pubng.

Poems & Prose. rev. ed. Percy Bysshe Shelley. Ed. by Timothy Webb. LC 92-29780. 320p. 1995. pap. 7.95 (*0-460-87449-7*, Everyman's Classic Lib) Tuttle Pubng.

Poems & Prose: Complete Writings, 10 vols., Set. Walt Whitman. LC 02-25501. 1902. reprint ed. 695.00 (*0-403-00114-5*) Scholarly.

Poems & Prose: Glimpses of Visions. Barbara A. Haugh. 40p. (Orig.). 1991. pap. 2.00 (*0-9617236-2-9*) B A H Publishing.

Poems & Prose from the Eastern Kentucky Hills. Lawrence Helton. LC 97-90904. 40p. 1998. 12.95 (*0-533-12510-3*) Vantage.

Poems & Prose from the Old English. Ed. by Alexandra Hennessey Olsen. Tr. by Burton Raffel from ANG. LC 97-22556. 273p. 1998. 32.50 (*0-300-06994-4*) Yale U Pr.

Poems & Prose from the Old English. Burton Raffel & Alexandra Hennessey Olsen. LC 97-22556. 273p. 1998. pap. 15.00 (*0-300-06995-2*) Yale U Pr.

***Poems & Prose of Mihai Eminescu.** Ed. by Kurt W. Treptow. 240p. 2000. 39.95 (*973-9432-10-7*, Pub. by Ctr Romanian Studies) Intl Spec Bk.

Poems & Prose Remains of Arthur Hugh Clough, 2 vols., Set. Arthur H. Clough. (BCL1-PR English Literature Ser.). 1992. reprint ed. lib. bdg. 150.00 (*0-7812-7499-0*) Rprt Serv.

Poems & Prose Writings. Richard Henry Dana. (Notable American Authors Ser.). 1992. reprint ed. lib. bdg. 75.00 (*0-7812-2611-2*) Rprt Serv.

Poems & Psalms of the Hebrew Bible. S. E. Gillingham. (Bible Ser.). (Illus.). 324p. 1994. pap. text 22.00 (*0-19-213243-1*) OUP.

Poems & Rhymes & Things to Do Now That I'm a Toddler, Too. Connie Smrke. (Illus.). 96p. (Orig.). (J). (ps). 1992. pap. text 10.95 (*0-86530-107-7*, 197-1) Incentive Pubns.

Poems & Selected Letters. Veronica Franco. LC 98-25551. 224p. 1998. pap. text 17.00 (*0-226-25987-0*); lib. bdg. 45.00 (*0-226-25986-2*) U Ch Pr.

Poems & Short Stories for Study. Thomas Barthel. 245p. (C). 1999. pap. text 25.00 (*1-891877-02-X*) Sheron Ent.

Poems & Some Letters of James Thomson. James Thomson. LC PR5655.A2. (Centaur Classics Ser.). 328p. reprint ed. pap. 101.70 (*0-8357-6670-5*, 205231500094) Bks Demand.

Poems & Songs. Robert Burns. (Thrift Editions Ser.). 96p. 1991. pap. 1.00 (*0-486-26863-2*) Dover.

Poems & Songs. 2nd ed. Robert Burns. Ed. by James Kinsley. (Oxford Standard Authors Ser.). 802p. 1971. pap. text 21.00 (*0-19-281114-2*) OUP.

Poems & Songs of the Civil War. Lois Hill. 256p. 1990. 6.99 (*0-517-69918-4*) Random Hse Value.

Poems & Sonnets of William Shakespeare. William Shakespeare. (Poetry Library). 256p. pap. 7.95 (*1-85326-416-4*, 4164WW, Pub. by Wrdsworth Edits) NTC Contemp Pub Co.

Poems & Stories. Richard Blessing. LC 82-22177. 75p. 1983. 14.00 (*0-937872-12-1*); pap. 6.00 (*0-937872-13-X*) Dragon Gate.

Poems & Stories. J. R. R. Tolkien. LC 81-455744. 342 p. 1980. write for info. (*0-04-823174-6*) Routledge.

Poems & Stories of a Salt Grass Cowboy. Bob Kahla. (Illus.). 52p. (Orig.). Date not set. pap. 12.00 (*1-882820-01-0*) Cracked Egg.

Poems & Stories of Fitz-James O'Brien. Fitz-James O'Brien. 1972. reprint ed. text 27.95 (*0-8422-8102-9*) Irvington.

***Poems & Stories of Reality: Always Believe in Yourself.** Tyrone Barnes. 24p. 1999. pap. 6.00 (*0-8059-4466-4*) Dorrance.

Poems & Tales of Edgar Allan Poe at Fordham. 2nd ed. Edgar Allan Poe. Ed. by Elizabeth Beirne. (Illus.). 42p. 1999. pap. 15.00 (*0-941980-06-5*) Bronx County.

Poems & Texts: An Anthology of French Poems. Serge Gavronsky. 1969. 10.00 (*0-8079-0150-4*) October.

Poems & Things, Vol. 1. George F. Johnson. 98p. (Orig.). (YA). (gr. 9-12). 1989. write for info. (*0-318-65121-1*) G F Johnson.

Poems & Things for Pondering. Anita Carlson-Mineau. 20p. 1995. pap. 5.00 (*0-9662539-3-0*) Bks By Anita.

Poems & Thoughts for Everyone. Ed. by L. Jack Stevenson. (Illus.). 112p. 1999. 14.95 (*1-58244-042-5*) Rutledge Bks.

Poems & Thoughts in Rhyme. Alfred G. Huber. 1997. pap. write for info. (*1-57553-553-X*) Watermrk Pr.

Poems & Translations. Robin Flower. LC 94-204628. 176p. 1994. pap. 14.95 (*1-874675-32-5*) Dufour.

Poems & Translations. Emma Lazarus. (Notable American Authors Ser.). 1999. reprint ed. lib. bdg. 125.00 (*0-7812-3766-1*) Rprt Serv.

Poems & Translations. John Millington Synge. (BCL1-PR English Literature Ser.). 44p. 1992. reprint ed. lib. bdg. 59.00 (*0-7812-7685-3*) Rprt Serv.

Poems & Translations, 1850-1870, Together with the Prose Story "Hand & Soul" Dante Gabriel Rossetti. (BCL1-PR English Literature Ser.). 492p. 1992. reprint ed. lib. bdg. 99.00 (*0-7812-7627-6*) Rprt Serv.

Poems & Translations of Hi-Lo. John Peck. LC 93-38629. 181p. (Orig.). 1993. pap. 14.95 (*1-878818-28-7*, Pub. by Sheep Meadow) U Pr of New Eng.

Poems & Translations of Robert Fletcher. Daniel H. Woodward. LC 73-79525. (Illus.). 316p. reprint ed. pap. 98.00 (*0-8357-6727-2*, 203536800095) Bks Demand.

Poems & Translations of Sir Richard Fanshawe, Vol. I. Richard Fanshaw. Ed. by Peter Davidson. LC 96-31088. (Oxford English Texts Ser.). 428p. 1998. text 125.00 (*0-19-811737-X*) OUP.

Poems & Translations of Sir Richard Fanshawe, Vol. 2. Richard Fanshawe. Ed. by Peter Davidson. (Oxford English Texts Ser.). (Illus.). 704p. 1999. text 200.00 (*0-19-818299-6*) OUP.

Poems & Verses. Augusta T. Reid. 50p. (Orig.). 1997. pap. 20.00 (*0-9634518-2-0*) Longinus Pr.

Poems Are for Children: Welcome to My World. Vernelle B. Allen. 78p. (J). 1994. pap. write for info. (*1-885984-10-3*) Wings of Healing.

Poems Are Hard to Read. William Meredith. 258p. 1990. pap. 13.95 (*0-472-06427-4*, 06427, Ann Arbor Bks) U of Mich Pr.

Poems Before & After: Collected English Translations. Miroslav Holub. Tr. by Ian Milner et al from CZE. 274p. 1990. 40.00 (*1-85224-121-7*, Pub. by Bloodaxe Bks) Dufour.

Poems Before & After: Collected English Translations. Miroslav Holub. Tr. by Ian Milner et al from CZE. 274p. 1995. pap. 19.95 (*1-85224-122-5*, Pub. by Bloodaxe Bks) Dufour.

Poems Between Women: Four Centuries of Love, Romantic Friendship, & Desire. Emma Donoghue. LC 96-49693. 272p. (C). 1997. 26.50 (*0-231-10924-5*) Col U Pr.

Poems Between Women: Four Centuries of Love, Romantic Friendship, & Desire. Ed. by Emma Donoghue. 1999. pap. 17.50 (*0-231-10925-3*) Col U Pr.

Poems Browning V2 1841 46, Vol. II, 1841-1846. Ed. by John Woolford & Daniel Karlin. (Annotated English Poets Ser.). (Illus.). 544p. (C). 1990. text 103.95 (*0-582-06399-X*, 78810) Longman.

Poems Browning V1 1826, Vol. I, 1826-1840. Ed. by John Woolford & Daniel Karlin. (Annotated English Poets Ser.). (Illus.). 856p. (C). 1990. text 103.95 (*0-582-48100-7*, 78653) Longman.

Poems by a Painter. Joseph N. Paton. LC 73-112941. reprint ed. 32.00 (*0-404-04905-2*) AMS Pr.

Poems by Andrea Zanzotto. Andrea Zanzotto. Tr. & Illus. by Anthony Barnett. (ITA.). 44p. (Orig.). 1993. pap. write for info. (*0-907954-19-7*, Pub. by Allardyce Barnett) SPD-Small Pr Dist.

Poems by Andrea Zanzotto, Little Stars & Straw Breasts & The Poetry of Anthony Barnett, 3 bks., Set. 1993. pap. 30.00 (*0-907954-22-7*, Pub. by Allardyce Barnett) SPD-Small Pr Dist.

Poems by Beulah, Vol. 3. 416p. (Orig.). 1983. 8.00 (*0-911870-04-0*) Beulah.

Poems by Beulah, Vol. 4. 300p. (Orig.). 1996. pap. 8.00 (*0-614-13836-1*) Beulah.

Poems by Bill: Also Poems to Live By. William Boyer. 130p. 1997. pap. write for info. (*1-57502-610-4*, PO1752) Morris Pubng.

Poems by Bonnie Paques, the Poet Pooch. Jeanette Comer. LC 91-78093. (Illus.). 1993. 8.95 (*0-8158-0482-2*) Chris Mass.

Poems by Contemporary Women. Ed. by Theodore Roscoe & Mary W. Were. LC 79-51967. (Granger Poetry Library). 1980. reprint ed. 20.00 (*0-89609-195-3*) Roth Pub Inc.

Poems by Ephelia (c. 1679) The Premier Facsimile Edition of the Collected Manuscript & Published Poems. With a Critical Essay & Apparatus. Ephelia. Ed. by Maureen Mulvihill. LC 92-15119. (Scholars' Facsimiles & Reprints Ser.: Vol. 463). (Illus.). 278p. 1992. reprint ed. 50.00 (*0-8201-1463-4*) Schol Facsimiles.

Poems by Father & Son. Trinidad V. Sanchez & Trinidad Sanchez, Jr. (Illus.). 127p. 1996. pap. 12.00 (*1-877603-41-4*) Pecan Grove.

Poems by Gloria Champagne. 3rd rev. ed. Gloria F. Champagne. (Illus.). 26p. (Orig.). 1996. pap. 12.00 (*0-9655506-0-5*) Champagne Falcon Pub.

Poems by Grades: Grammar, Vol. 2. Charles B. Gilbert & Ada V. Harris. LC 78-149103. (Granger Index Reprint Ser.). 1977. 25.95 (*0-8369-6228-1*) Ayer.

Poems by Grades: Primary, Vol. 1. Charles B. Gilbert & Ada V. Harris. LC 74-149102. (Granger Index Reprint Ser.). 1977. 23.95 (*0-8369-6227-3*) Ayer.

Poems by Joan Murray, 1917-1942. Joan Murray. Ed. by Grant Code. LC 71-144751. (Yale Series of Younger Poets: No. 45). reprint ed. 18.00 (*0-404-53845-2*) AMS Pr.

Poems by Lee Sangak. unabridged ed. Kim Unsong. 100p. (Orig.). 1997. pap. 15.00 (*0-942049-08-X*) One Mind Pr.

Poems by Mae, 10 vols., Bk. 1. Annie Teegardin. 50p. (Orig.). Date not set. pap. 10.95 (*0-9647790-2-1*) Exerbian Pr.

Poems by Marjorie Kinnan Rawlings: Songs of a Housewife. Marjorie Kinnan Rawlings. Ed. by Rodger L. Tarr. LC 96-50245. 288p. 1997. 24.95 (*0-8130-1491-3*) U Press Fla.

***Poems by Moses Grady Farmer.** Moses Grady Farmer. 64p. 1999. pap. 8.00 (*1-56411-229-2*) Untd Bros & Sis.

Poems by Naomi. Naomi Harvey. 25p. 1991. pap. 4.00 (*0-9628208-3-0*) Canal Side Pubs.

Poems by Nicholas Breton. Nicholas Breton. LC 72-161960. 229p. 1952. 39.00 (*0-403-01335-6*) Scholarly.

Poems by Nicholas Breton. Nicholas Breton. 1988. reprint ed. lib. bdg. 59.00 (*0-7812-0343-0*) Rprt Serv.

Poems by Ray Ford. Raymond W. Ford. Ed. by Virginia Parry. (Illus.). 80p. 1997. pap. 10.00 (*0-9652145-1-6*) Eshleday Specday.

Poems by Richard C. Richard C. Craven. 1987. pap. 4.00 (*0-932526-15-2*) Nexus Pr.

Poems by Robert Frost: A Boy's Will & North of Boston. Robert Frost. LC 89-12182. 160p. (YA). 1990. mass mkt. 4.95 (*0-451-52413-6*, Ment) NAL.

Poems by Robert Frost: A Boy's Will & North of Boston. Robert Frost. (J). 1989. 10.05 (*0-606-02249-X*, Pub. by Turtleback) Demco.

Poems by Roberto Sosa. Ed. & Tr. by Edward V. Coughlin from SPA. LC 83-72296. 119p. 1984. 14.00 (*0-938972-06-5*) Spanish Lit Pubns.

Poems by Sir John Salusbury & Robert Chester. John Salusbury. Ed. by K. Paul. (ETS ES: No. 113). 1974. reprint ed. 35.00 (*0-527-00315-8*) Periodicals Srv.

***Poems by the Dozen.** John Cawthron. (Illus.). 57p. (J). (gr. 2-4). 1999. 12.95 (*1-888565-06-3*) Trinity Rivrs.

***Poems by the Dozen.** John Cawthron. LC 99-62973. (Illus.). 57p. (J). (gr. 2-4). 1999. pap. 9.95 (*1-888565-07-1*) Trinity Rivrs.

Poems by the Dozen. Wayne Walden. (Illus.). 20p. (Orig.). 1991. pap. 2.00 (*1-879200-02-3*) Livingworks.

Poems by the End of the Oregon Trail. J. Verne Laswell. Ed. & Intro. by E. Stiltner. 76p. (Orig.). 1990. 7.75 (*1-878457-54-3*); pap. 7.75 (*0-685-30411-6*) Skunk Creek Computing Servs.

Poems by the Most Deservedly Admired Mrs. Katherine Phillips: The Matchless Orinda. Katherine Philips. LC 92-1093. (Scholars' Facsimiles & Reprints Ser.). 200p. 1992. reprint ed. 50.00 (*0-8201-1462-6*) Schol Facsimiles.

Poems by the Way: 1911 Edition. Ed. by Peter Faulkner. (William Morris Library). 282p. 1996. reprint ed. pap. 24.75 (*1-85506-255-0*) Bks Intl VA.

Poems by Three Friends. (Thomas Raffles, Baldwin Brown, & J. H. Wiffen), Repr. of 1813 Ed. Jeremiah H. Wiffen. Ed. by Donald H. Reiman. LC 75-31272. (Romantic Context: Poetry 1789-1830 Ser.). 1978. lib. bdg. 57.00 (*0-8240-2218-1*) Garland.

***Poems, Cartoons, Revelations, by Codger.** William McGowan. 1999. pap. write for info. (*1-58235-168-6*) Watermrk Pr.

Poems, Chiefly in the Scottish Dialect. Robert Burns. LC 72-153518. reprint ed. 41.50 (*0-404-08977-1*) AMS Pr.

Poems Chiefly in the Scottish Dialect. Robert Burns. LC 91-7154. 252p. 1991. reprint ed. 55.00 (*1-85477-060-8*) Continuum.

Poems, Chiefly Lyrical, 1830. Alfred Lord Tennyson. LC 91-32477. (Revolution & Romanticism Ser.). 170p. 1991. reprint ed. 48.00 (*1-85477-081-0*) Continuum.

Poems, Chiefly Lyrical, from Romances & Prose-Tracts of the Elizabethan Age: With Chosen Poems of Nicholas Breton see Collections of Lyrics & Poems: Sixteenth & Seventeenth Centuries

Poems Children Love. Penrhyn Coussens. LC 72-98078. (Granger Index Reprint Ser.). 1977. 20.95 (*0-8369-6073-4*) Ayer.

Poems Descriptive of Rural Life & Scenery. Ed. by John Clare. 176p. 1986. 45.00 (*0-948697-01-6*, Pub. by Lark Pubns) St Mut.

Poems Downeast. Mary R. Palmer. Ed. by Kate Whitaker. LC 93-61629. (Illus.). 96p. 1994. pap. 8.95 (*1-883650-10-0*) Windswept Hse.

Poems-Drawings. Louis Simpson & Nicolo D'Alessandro. Tr. by Nat Scammacca. (Illus.). 63p. 1989. 30.00 (*0-89304-585-3*); pap. 15.00 (*0-89304-586-1*) Cross-Cultrl NY.

Poems (1880) Edwin Arnold. 246p. 1998. reprint ed. pap. 19.95 (*0-7661-0239-4*) Kessinger Pub.

Poems, 1890-1896, 3 Vols. in 1. Emily Dickinson. LC 67-25640. 624p. 1967. 75.00 (*0-8201-1014-0*) Schol Facsimiles.

Poem's 1890. fac. ed. Emily Dickinson. (Library of American Poets). 1994. reprint ed. 50.00 (*1-56515-002-3*) Collect Reprints.

Poems, 1895. William E. Henley. LC 93-50736. (Decadents, Symbolists, Anti-Decadents Ser.). 1994. 55.00 (*1-85477-146-9*) Continuum.

Poems, 1895. Lionel Johnson. LC 93-30369. (Decadents, Symbolists, Anti-Decadents Ser.). 1994. 48.00 (*1-85477-149-3*) Continuum.

Poems, 1895. William Butler Yeats. LC 93-46500. (Decadents, Symbolists, Anti-Decadents Ser.). xi,285p. 1994. 49.50 (*1-85477-161-2*) Continuum.

Poems, 1894. Francis Thompson. LC 93-25722. (Decadents, Symbolists, Anti-Decadents Ser.). 120p. 1993. 43.00 (*1-85477-157-4*) Continuum.

Poems, 1892. Oscar Wilde. LC 95-24125. (Decadents, Symbolists, Anti-Decadents Ser.). 1995. 55.00 (*1-85477-158-2*) Continuum.

Poems 1807-1824 & Beppo: A Facsimile of the Original Manuscripts in the British Library & in the Pforzheimer Library at the New York Public Library. George Gordon Byron. Ed. & Intro. by

P

Andrew Nicholson. LC 36-3645. (Manuscripts of the Younger Romantics Ser.: Vol. 12). 324p. 1998. text 225.00 (*0-8153-1149-4*) Garland.

Poems, 1817: A Facsimile of Richard Woodhouse's Annotated Copy in the Huntington Library. John Keats. Ed. by Jack Stillinger. LC 87-109527. (Manuscripts of the Younger Romantics & the Bodleian Shelley Manuscripts: Vol. 1). (Illus.). xvi, 255p. 1985. text 40.00 (*0-8240-6254-X*) Garland.

Poems, 1816. George Gordon Byron. LC 90-14257. (Revolution & Romanticism Ser.). 48p. 1990. reprint ed. 35.00 (*1-85477-039-X*) Continuum.

***Poems (1860)** Gerald Massey. 456p. 1999. reprint ed. pap. 29.95 (*0-7661-0743-4*) Kessinger Pub.

Poems, 1833. Samuel Taylor Coleridge. LC 90-12670. (Revolution & Romanticism Ser.). 176p. 1990. reprint ed. 48.00 (*1-85477-043-8*) Continuum.

Poems, English & Latin. Edward H. Herbert. (BCL1-PR English Literature Ser.). 169p. 1992. reprint ed. lib. bdg. 69.00 (*0-7812-7211-4*) Rprt Serv.

Poems, English & Latin, of Edward Lord Herbert of Cherbury. Edward H. Herbert. Ed. by G. C. Smith. LC 76-29466. reprint ed. 44.50 (*0-404-15306-2*) AMS Pr.

Poems Especially for You. Jim O'Neal. 24p. 1993. pap. 9.95 (*1-883457-32-7*) J ONeal Publng.

Poems, Essays & Comments for Everyone. Ian Mayo-Smith. LC 94-39164. 92p. (Orig.). 1994. pap. 9.95 (*1-56549-043-6*) Kumarian Pr.

***Poems, Essays, & Short Stories for Sharing: Portraits of a Writer's Soul!** Denise Michelle Phillips. 163p. 2000. pap. text 16.00 (*1-55605-300-2*) Wyndham Hall.

***Poems, Followed by an Humble Supplication to Her Majesty.** Robert Southwell. Ed. by Charles S. Kraszewski. 1999. pap. 10.50 (*1-930205-02-3*) Libella.

***Poems for a Friend.** Ed. by Elizabeth Kea. 2000. 9.95 (*0-8249-4194-2*) Ideals.

***Poems for a Friend: Kind Thoughts.** Thorunn McCoy. LC 00-35019. 2000. write for info. (*0-8249-4176-4*) Ideals.

Poems for a Small Planet: Contemporary American Nature Poetry. Ed. by Robert Pack & Jay Parini. LC 92-56909. (Bread Loaf Anthology Ser.). 320p. 1993. pap. 19.95 (*0-87451-621-8*) U Pr of New Eng.

Poems for Adults & Other Children. Dean Blehert. Ed. by Jeff Bates. (Illus.). 55p. 1988. 5.95 (*0-938823-01-9*) Wrds & Pictres.

Poems for Adults & Other Children. M. Dean Blehert. (Poetry Ser.: No. 1). (Illus.). 64p. 1988. pap. 5.95 (*0-685-23290-5*) Pogment Pr.

Poems for All Occasions. Alfredo D. Noble. 42p. (Orig.). 1991. pap. 5.70 (*0-9622849-3-9*) Papito.

Poems for All Occasions. rev. ed. Alfredo D. Noble. Ed. by Jean Noble et al. 72p. (Orig.). (YA). 1998. reprint ed. pap. 8.95 (*1-887653-06-6*) Papito.

Poems for All Purposes: Selected Poems of G. K. Chesterton. Ed. by Stephen Medcalf. (Illus.). 208p. 1994. 19.95 (*0-7126-5881-5*, Pub. by Pimlico) Trafalgar.

Poems for All Seasons. Alan Rothman. 1998. pap. write for info. (*1-58235-028-0*) Watermrk Pr.

Poems for Bessie Smith. Anthony S. Koeninger. 198p. (Orig.). 1992. pap. 15.95 (*0-9625767-4-3*) Chumash Pr.

Poems for Billie Holiday. Kainoa A. Koeninger. 92p. (Orig.). 1993. pap. text 10.95 (*0-9625767-5-1*) Chumash Pr.

Poems for Boys & Girls with Hopes to Build a Better World. Janice McCarthy. (Illus.). 43p. (YA). (gr. k-12). 1996. pap. 8.95 (*0-9665720-0-9*) Jan McCarthy.

Poems for Children Nowhere. Carl Sandburg. LC 98-39551. (Illus.). 48p. (J). (gr. 5-9). 1999. lib. bdg. 16.99 (*0-679-98990-0*, Pub. by Random Bks Yng Read) Random.

Poems for Children Nowhere Near Old Enough to Vote. Carl Sandburg. LC 98-39551. (Illus.). 48p. (J). 1999. 15.00 (*0-679-88990-6*, Pub. by Knopf Bks Yng Read) Random.

***Poems for Christmas: Joyous Thoughts.** Thorunn McCoy. Ed. by Elizabeth Kea. LC 00-27772. 2000. 9.95 (*0-8249-4193-4*) Ideals.

Poems for Chromosomes. 1998. pap. write for info. (*1-58235-051-5*) Watermrk Pr.

***Poems for Easter.** Ideals Publications. 88p. 2000. 9.95 (*0-8249-4174-8*) Ideals.

Poems for Ecumencity. Edward M. Robbins. 59p. 1985. 7.95 (*0-89697-236-4*) Intl Univ Pr.

Poems for Eternity. Ellwood F. Saxton. 1998. pap. write for info. (*1-58235-032-9*) Watermrk Pr.

Poems for Everyday People. Kim F. Layman. 57p. (Orig.). 1993. pap. 9.95 (*0-9639836-0-1*) K F Layman.

Poems for Family & Friends: Flowers That Bloom with Much Care see Always Come Rejoicing

Poems for Free Spirits: Candid Views of Sacred Cows. M. Scott Myers. (Illus.). 168p. 1996. pap. 10.00 (*0-9639930-3-8*) Choctaw Pubng.

Poems for Ghosts. Peter Finch. (Illus.). 96p. 1991. pap. 15.95 (*1-85411-057-8*, Pub. by Seren Bks) Dufour.

Poems for Jewish Holidays. Illus. by Lloyd Bloom. LC 85-27179. 32p. (J). (gr. k-3). 1986. lib. bdg. 15.95 (*0-8234-0606-7*) Holiday.

Poems for Life. Nightingale Bamford School Staff. LC 96-28793. 1997. per. 10.00 (*0-684-82695-X*) S&S Trade.

Poems for Life: Famous People Select Their Favorite Poem & Say Why It Inspires Them. Ed. by Nightingale-Bamford School Staff. LC 94-39896. (Illus.). 128p. 1995. 16.45 (*1-55970-286-9*, Pub. by Arcade Pub Inc) Time Warner.

Poems for Little Cataraqui. Eric Folsom. 1994. pap. 8.25 (*0-921411-28-6*) Genl Dist Srvs.

Poems for Living. Kathryn Renata. 39p. 1998. pap. 5.00 (*1-892019-01-9*) G D Frummox.

Poems for Lost & Un-Lost Boys. Michael Lassell. LC 85-73772. (Amelia Chapbooks Ser.). (Illus.). 92p. (Orig.). 1985. pap. 10.95 (*0-936545-00-3*) Amelia.

***Poems for Love Letters: A Hawaiian Mystery.** Tom S. Adair. LC 99-91864. 2000. 25.00 (*0-7388-1344-3*); pap. 18.00 (*0-7388-1345-1*) Xlibris Corp.

Poems for Lovers. Dutch Keen. (Illus.). 78p. 1998. pap. 12.95 (*0-89896-192-0*) Larksdale.

***Poems for Lovers.** H. D. Reiss. LC 99-93893. 1999. pap. 7.95 (*0-533-13178-2*) Vantage.

Poems for Memorization. Illus. by Lester Miller. 199p. (J). (gr. 1-10). 1988. pap. 6.75 (*0-7399-0166-4*, 2354) Rod & Staff.

Poems for Men. Damon Runyon. 22.95 (*0-8488-1145-3*) Amereon Ltd.

Poems for Men Who Dream of Lolita. Kim Morrissey. 80p. 1992. text 19.95 (*1-55050-030-9*, Pub. by Coteau) Genl Dist Srvs.

Poems for Men Who Dream of Lolita. Kim Morrissey. 72p. 1992. pap. 8.95 (*1-55050-029-5*, Pub. by Coteau) Genl Dist Srvs.

***Poems for Mothers.** Ideals Publications. LC 99-58055. 96p. 2000. 9.95 (*0-8249-4175-6*) Ideals.

Poems for My Family. Philip Overly. 116p. (Orig.). 1996. pap. write for info. (*1-57502-216-8*, P0869) Morris Pubng.

Poems for My Grandchildren, 1996: Collected from the Family. Rose M. Denney. 32p. (Orig.). (J). (gr. k-6). 1996. pap. 4.95 (*0-9654698-5-9*) Denney Literary.

Poems for Nine Year Olds & Under. Kit Wright. 1192p. (J). (ps-4). 1985. pap. 9.95 (*0-14-031490-3*, Pub. by Pnguin Bks Ltd) Trafalgar.

Poems for Old Geezers & Young Whippersnappers. Jefferson D. Bates. (Poetry Ser.: No. 4). (Illus.). 96p. (Orig.). 1990. pap. 6.95 (*0-938823-04-3*) Pogment Pr.

Poems for Our Time. Jack D. Simco. (Orig.). 1997. pap. write for info. (*1-57553-441-X*) Watermrk Pr.

Poems for Paula. Frederick Morgan. 72p. (Orig.). 1995. 14.00 (*1-885266-14-6*); pap. 8.00 (*1-885266-18-9*) Story Line.

***Poems for Peace & Last Poems.** Jocelyn Hollis. LC 00-33145. 2000. pap. 9.95 (*0-930933-30-3*) Am Poetry & Lit.

Poems for Peaceful People: A Collection of Feeling Love. Elmer A. Spiezio. 60p. (Orig.). 1996. pap. 9.95 (*1-57502-323-7*, P01088) Morris Pubng.

Poems for Peter. rev. ed. Lysbeth B. Borie. Ed. by I. Murphy Lewis. LC 96-67927. (Illus.). 112p. (J). (ps-5). 1996. 14.95 (*1-888959-25-8*) Shank Painter Pub.

Poems for Pianists & Other Musical People. Morton Stimler. 80p. 1995. pap. 8.95 (*0-9643392-0-X*) M Stimler.

Poems for Piano: Poems (with Descriptive Music) Karla Carey. (Reflections in Thought, from Dawn to Dusk Ser.). 50p. 1988. pap. 10.00 (*1-55768-518-5*); audio 8.00 (*1-55768-538-X*) LC Pub.

Poems for Pleasure, Book 2. Ed. by A. F. Scott. 275p. reprint ed. pap. 78.40 (*0-608-12085-5*, 2024584) Bks Demand.

Poems for Praise & Power. Pauline Ressler. (Illus.). 157p. 1978. pap. 5.90 (*0-7399-0167-2*, 2350) Rod & Staff.

Poems for Seniors, No. 2. Carl F. Becker. 100p. (Orig.). 1991. pap. 8.00 (*0-9633350-0-6*) C F Becker.

Poems for Seven Year Olds. Helen Nicoll. (J). 1984. pap. 9.95 (*0-14-031489-X*, Pub. by Pnguin Bks Ltd) Trafalgar.

Poems for Shakespeare. Selected by Anthony Astbury. (C). 1990. 35.00 (*0-906887-48-8*, Pub. by Greville Pr) St Mut.

Poems for Special Days & Occasions. Thomas C. Clark. 168p. 1977. 24.95 (*0-8369-6128-2*) Ayer.

Poems for Terry. Brendan Tripp. 28p. 1981. pap. 5.00 (*1-57353-004-2*) Eschaton Prods.

Poems for the Asking. Joan Albarella. (Illus.). 24p. 1975. pap. 2.00 (*0-914620-02-9*) Alpha Pr.

Poems for the Beekeeper: An Anthology of Modern Poetry. Ed. by Robert Gent. 156p. (Orig.). 1996. pap. 14.95 (*0-907123-82-1*, Pub. by Five Leaves) AK Pr Dist.

Poems for the City & the Country Too. Mary L. Burkhalter. 30p. 1998. pap. 20.00 (*0-934284-11-3*) Jolean Pub Co.

Poems for the Common People. Pauline Waugh. 38p. 1998. 3.99 (*0-7541-0145-2*) Communs Plus.

Poems for the Dead. Hart D. Fisher. (Illus.). 156p. (Orig.). (C). 1995. pap. 10.95 (*0-9646027-0-9*) Boneyard Pr.

Poems for the Dead. Ed. by Greg Kuzma. 104p. (Orig.). 1984. pap. write for info. (*0-916891-00-3*) Pebble Cellar.

Poems for the Glancing Eye. Roberto Valenza. (Illus.). 44p. 1993. pap. 7.00 (*1-878888-13-7*) Nine Muses Books.

Poems for the Great Days. Compiled by Thomas C. Clark & Robert E. Clark. LC 72-11861. (Granger Index Reprint Ser.). 1977. reprint ed. 24.95 (*0-8369-6401-2*) Ayer.

Poems for the Holidays. Dina Mapelli. 50p. 1998. pap. 9.95 (*1-892896-38-9*) Buy Books.

Poems for the Insomniac. Samuel Davidowitz. 1998. pap. write for info. (*1-57553-666-8*) Watermrk Pr.

Poems for the Ladies. Sheryl Nadler. (Illus.). 40p. 1998. pap. 6.00 (*0-9662606-1-9*) S Nadler.

Poems for the Man Who Weighs Light. Mary O'Dell. LC 98-48975. 72p. 1999. pap. 14.95 (*0-7734-3118-7*, Mellen Poetry Pr) E Mellen.

Poems for the Manly-Man: A State of Mind. rev. ed. J. Buddy Rodgers & Chuck LeFever. (Illus.). 64p. 1997. reprint ed. pap. 9.95 (*0-9657732-0-5*) Protocol Grp.

Poems for the Millennium Vol. 1: The University of California Book of Modern & Postmodern Poetry: From Fin-de-Siecle to Negritude. Ed. by Jerome Rothenberg & Pierre Joris. LC 93-49839. (Illus.). 839p. 1995. 70.00 (*0-520-07225-1*, Pub. by U CA Pr); pap. 24.95 (*0-520-07227-8*, Pub. by U CA Pr) Cal Prin Full Svc.

Poems for the Millennium Vol. 2: From Postwar to Millennium. Jerome Rothenberg. 912p. 1998. 70.00 (*0-520-20863-3*, Pub. by U CA Pr) Cal Prin Full Svc.

Poems for the Millennium Vol. 2: From Postwar to Millennium. Ed. by Jerome Rothenberg & Pierre Joris. 912p. 1998. pap. 24.95 (*0-520-20864-1*, Pub. by U CA Pr) Cal Prin Full Svc.

***Poems for the Nation: A Collection of Contemporary Political Poems.** Allen Ginsberg et al. LC 99-41330. (Open Media Pamphlet Ser.: No. 15). 64p. 1999. pap. text 5.95 (*1-58322-012-7*) Seven Stories.

***Poems for the Occasion: Three Essays on Neo-Latin Poetry from Seventeenth-Century Sweden.** Claes Gejrot & Annika Strom. (Studia Latina Stockholmiensia XLIV). (Illus.). 200p. 1999. pap. 43.50 (*91-22-01852-2*, Pub. by Almqvist) Coronet Bks.

Poems for the People. Carl Sandburg. Ed. by George Hendrick & Willene Hendrick. LC 98-44501. 192p. 1999. 22.50 (*1-56663-236-6*, Pub. by I R Dee) Natl Bk Netwk.

***Poems for the Pocket & the Soul.** J. Richard Freeman & Criswell Freeman. 128p. 2000. pap. 4.95 (*1-58334-078-5*, Pub. by Walnut Gr Pr) Midpt Trade.

Poems for the Purpose. Golda L. Morrison. Ed. by Aleen M. Pacitti. (Illus.). 136p. 1996. pap. text 4.95 (*0-9643424-2-1*) A J Morrison.

Poems for the Soul. Barbara S. Woodley. LC 97-904907. 1998. pap. 9.95 (*0-533-12384-4*) Vantage.

Poems for the Very Young. Ed. by Michael Rosen. LC 92-45574. (Illus.). 80p. (J). (ps-3). 1993. 17.95 (*1-85697-908-3*, Kingfisher) LKC.

Poems for the Whole Family. Daniel Krakauer. 1994. pap. 7.00 (*0-935992-00-6*) United Art Bks.

Poems for the Wild Earth. Ed. by Gary Lawless. 96p. (Orig.). 1995. pap. 8.95 (*0-942396-72-3*) Blackberry ME.

***Poems for the Wretched Child & Pets for the Wretched Child.** Paul Richard. 2000. pap. write for info. (*1-58235-433-2*) Watermrk Pr.

Poems for Young Children. Mimi Roes. (Illus.). (J). (ps-6). 1979. pap. 1.95 (*0-89780-003-6*) NAR Pubns.

Poems for Youth. Emily Dickinson. LC 95-33497. (Illus.). 128p. (J). (gr. k-3). 1996. 15.95 (*0-316-18435-7*) Little.

***Poems Forged in a Forest of Words.** Herschel Silverman. Ed. by Joyce Metzger. 56p. 1999. pap. 5.95 (*1-878116-89-4*) JVC Bks.

Poems from a Broken Soul. Cheryl L. Ferry. (Orig.). 1997. pap. write for info. (*1-57553-480-0*) Watermrk Pr.

Poems from a Brother. Tariq A. Shabazz. 32p. 1998. pap. 5.00 (*0-9669536-1-4*) T&M.

Poems from a Dog's Point of View: A Collection of Some Down-to-Earth (And Some Not-So-down-to-Earth) Canine Poetry By Summerset's Toby. Jeanne Hess. LC 91-91009. (Illus.). 72p. 1991. pap. 5.00 (*0-9629745-0-1*) Summerset Ent.

Poems from a Mountain Ghetto. Russell Marano. (Illus.). 76p. (Orig.). 1979. pap. 5.00 (*0-686-37048-1*) Back Fork Bks.

Poems from a Multiple Heart. unabridged ed. Suzanne J. Hardy-Winters. (Illus.). 100p. 1998. pap. 10.95 (*1-892896-02-8*) Buy Books.

Poems from a Purple Heart: Expressions of Joy, Sorrow, Love & Inspiration. LC 97-65058. (Illus.). 100p. (Orig.). 1997. pap. 10.00 (*0-9656658-0-1*) RYBA Pub.

Poems from a Spiritual Journey. G. G. Hall. LC 94-75762. 147p. (Orig.). 1994. pap. 12.00 (*1-883709-71-7*) Gold Crest Pubns.

Poems from Arab Andalusia. Ed. & Tr. by Cola Franzen. 96p. (Orig.). 1989. pap. 8.95 (*0-87286-242-9*) City Lights.

Poems from Captured Documents: A Bilingual Edition. Tr. by Thanh T. Nguyen & Bruce Weigl from VIE. LC 93-46189. 80p. 1994. pap. 10.95 (*0-87023-922-8*) U of Mass Pr.

Poems "From Deep Within" Maxine Mountcastle. LC 94-96059. 56p. 1994. lib. bdg. 5.00 (*0-9639403-0-9*) Maish & Mountcastle.

Poems from East Anglia. Kevin Crossley-Holland. LC 98-143977. 92p. 1998. pap. 18.95 (*1-900564-60-2*, Pub. by Enitha Pr) Dufour.

Poems from Farmers Valley: A Celebration of Rural Life. Ed. by Dorothy Prell. LC 99-203974. (Illus.). 256p. (Orig.). 1999. pap. 16.95 (*1-889406-00-7*) Prell Pub.

***Poems from 42nd Street.** 2nd ed. Rufus Goodwin. Ed. by Doug Holper. (Illus.). 98p. 1999. pap. 6.00 (*0-9678131-0-7*) Ibbetson St Pr.

Poems from 4 Corners. John Brandi. 5.00 (*0-686-15301-4*) Great Raven Pr.

***Poems from Holland & Belgium.** Tr. by C. J. Stevens. 104p. 1999. pap. 12.00 (*1-882425-13-8*) J Wade.

Poems from Italy. Ed. by William J. Smith. LC 77-158700. (Poems of the World Ser.). (Illus.). (J). (gr. 3 up). 1972. 11.74 (*0-690-63915-5*) HarpC Child Bks.

Poems from Jobe. Hannah J. Brackett. LC 95-92190. 24p. (J). (gr. 1-3). 1995. pap. write for info. (*0-9646501-0-X*) Paw Pub.

Poems from Life. James P. Massey. Ed. by David B. Reyner & Carole J. Massey-Reyner. LC 96-94327. (Collective Works of James P. Massey Ser.: Vol. III). 80p. (Orig.). 1996. pap. 14.95 (*0-9650514-2-0*) Massey-Reyner.

Poems from Little Sister. Ed. by Ana Takseena. 23p. (Orig.). 1988. pap. text 4.00 (*0-944667-02-3*) Little Sister Pubns.

Poems from Mandelstam. Tr. by R. H. Morrison. LC 88-46184. 120p. 1990. 26.50 (*0-8386-3382-X*) Fairleigh Dickinson.

Poems from Me to You. Kecia R. Libron. Ed. by Gerald Shultz. 1997. pap. 5.00 (*0-9659049-0-3*) K R Libron.

Poems from Other Centuries. Tissier. 1994. pap. text. write for info. (*0-582-22585-X*, Pub. by Addison-Wesley) Longman.

Poems from Pawleys. George F. Brown, Sr. et al. (Illus.). 32p. (Orig.). 1996. pap. text 12.00 (*0-9645242-3-6*) OceanFront IA.

Poems from Prison. Johnny Baranski. (Sunburst Originals Ser.: No. 7). 16p. (Orig.). 1979. pap. 2.00 (*0-934648-02-6*) Sunburst Pr.

Poems from Prison. Etheridge Knight. LC 68-22139. (YA). (gr. 12 up). 1968. pap. 4.00 (*0-910296-15-4*) Broadside Pr.

Poems from Providence. Brett Rutherford. (Illus.). 180p. 1991. pap. 10.00 (*0-922558-06-X*) Poets Pr.

Poems from Santa. large type ed. John M. Guthrie & Kari H. Guthrie. (Illus.). 69p. (J). (gr. 2 up). 1996. pap. 16.95 (*1-887492-00-3*) Hi I Que Pub.

Poems from Seventy Seven Barrow Street. Emilie Glen. 42p. 1984. write for info. (*0-318-64128-3*) Poets Pr.

Poems from Swedenborg. Ed. by Leon C. Le Van. LC 87-60469. 178p. (Orig.). 1987. pap. 5.95 (*0-87785-134-4*, Pub. by Swedenborg) Words Distrib.

Poems from the Alamo Saloon. Paul T. Lillard. LC 98-90154. 1998. pap. 10.95 (*0-533-12728-9*) Vantage.

***Poems from the Archive of the Pearl Roth Institute.** Billy Wisse. 1999. pap. 10.00 (*0-9675229-0-0*) P Roth Inst.

Poems from the Blue Horizon. Rob McLennan. 1995. pap. text 3.00 (*0-921411-34-0*) Genl Dist Srvs.

Poems from the Body Bag. Michael H. Brownstein. (Offset Offshoot Ser.: No. 11). 21p. 1989. pap. 4.00 (*0-941240-14-2*) Ommation Pr.

Poems from the Book of Hours. Rainer Maria Rilke. Tr. & Intro. by Babette Deutsch. LC 42-21208. 64p. 1975. pap. 6.95 (*0-8112-0595-9*, NDP408, Pub. by New Directions) Norton.

Poems from the Book of Taliesin. Taliesin The Bard. Ed. by J. G. Evans. LC 78-72673. (Series of Old Welsh Texts: Vol. 9B). reprint ed. 37.50 (*0-404-60592-3*) AMS Pr.

Poems from the Burnt Woods. Boyd Chubbs. 72p. 1995. pap. 9.95 (*1-895387-50-7*) Creative Bk Pub.

Poems from the Desert. Eighth Army Staff. LC 76-110519. (Granger Index Reprint Ser.). 1977. 16.95 (*0-8369-6132-3*) Ayer.

Poems from the Dindshenchas. Dinnseanchus. Ed. & Tr. by Edward Gwynn. LC 78-72686. (Royal Irish Academy. Todd Lecture Ser.: Vol. 7). reprint ed. 16.50 (*0-404-60567-2*) AMS Pr.

Poems from the Edge. 104p. (Orig.). 1996. pap. text. write for info. (*0-9639999-7-4*) Jay St Pubs.

Poems from the Floating World, Vol. 1-5. reprint ed. 38.50 (*0-404-19541-5*) AMS Pr.

Poems from the German of Ferdinand Freiligrath. Ferdinand Freiligrath. 1972. 59.95 (*0-8490-0848-4*) Gordon Pr.

Poems from the Greek Anthology. expanded ed. Kenneth Rexroth. LC 99-32302. (Ann Arbor Paperbacks Ser.). 152p. 1999. pap. text 15.95 (*0-472-08608-1*, 08608) U of Mich Pr.

Poems from the Greek Anthology, in English Paraphrase. Anthologia Graeca Selections. Tr. by Dudley Fitts. LC 78-13574. 141p. 1978. reprint ed. lib. bdg. 49.50 (*0-313-21017-9*, AGPG, Greenwood Pr) Greenwood.

***Poems From the Heart.** Christine Gleseke. 1999. pap. write for info. (*1-58235-415-4*) Watermrk Pr.

Poems from the Heart. Marvin Hager. 60p. (Orig.). 1996. pap. 9.95 (*1-57502-271-0*, P0962) Morris Pubng.

***Poems from the Heart.** David Macy. 36p. 1999. pap. 3.95 (*0-9668443-5-1*) Macy Intl.

***Poems from the Heart.** Margaret McDowell. 1999. pap. write for info. (*1-58235-078-7*) Watermrk Pr.

Poems from the Heart. Timothy Scott. 200p. 1992. text 20.00 (*0-685-59548-X*) T Scott Pub.

Poems from the Heart. L. B. Strawn. 1998. pap. write for info. (*1-57553-867-9*) Watermrk Pr.

***Poems from the Heart.** Ron Yablon. 2000. 16.95 (*0-533-13461-7*) Vantage.

Poems from the Heart. expanded rev. ed. Marvin D. Hager. 126p. 1997. pap. write for info. (*1-57502-550-7*, P00962A) Morris Pubng.

Poems from the Heart. unabridged ed. Thompson Lennox. 66p. (Orig.). 1996. pap. 12.00 (*1-890283-06-1*, 9601) L Thompson NY.

***Poems from the Heart: A Writer's Dreams Flow Like a River.** Charlotte G. Dillon. Ed. by Kendrick Taylor & Helen W. Searle. (Illus.). 52p. 1999. pap. 12.00 (*0-9664709-2-3*) Mountain Empire.

Poems from the Heart: Intimate Thoughts of Life & My Faith. Cletus S. Cottrell. (Illus.). 32p. 1999. pap. 8.00 (*0-8059-4601-2*) Dorrance.

***Poems from the Heart...& the Funny Bone.** Sandi Cohen. 1999. pap. write for info. (*1-58235-316-6*) Watermrk Pr.

Poems from the Hearth. Helen M. Price. 133p. 1992. pap. 14.95 (*0-9635029-0-5*) W Price & Assocs.

Poems from the Heartland. Ed. by Charles E. Cravey. 1993. pap. 9.95 (*0-938645-87-0*) In His Steps.

***Poems from the Heartland.** Steve McGurk. 2000. pap. 10.95 (*0-533-13283-5*) Vantage.

***Poems from the Heron Clan.** Xve Di et al. 144p. 1999. pap. 11.95 (*0-9673855-0-4*) K James Bks.

***Poems from the Hobbit.** J. R. R. Tolkien. LC 99-31805. 48p. 1999. 5.95 (*0-618-00934-5*) HM.

Poems from the Madhouse - Now Millennium. Jeffs & Deborah Staines. 144p. 1993. pap. 12.95 (*1-875559-20-5*, Pub. by SpiniFex Pr) LPC InBook.

Poems from the Oregon Sea Coast. large type ed. Marilyn R. Riddle. (Illus.). 24p. 1979. pap. 10.00 (*0-9603748-0-9*) Sandpiper OR.

***Poems from the Quill of Duane & Shane.** Duane K. Schell. 40p. 1999. 19.50 (*1-57529-076-6*) Kabel Pubs.

Poems from the Rooms Below. Renee Ruderman. LC 95-34861. (Illus.). 72p. (Orig.). 1995. pap. 11.95 (*0-938075-58-6*) Ocean View Bks.

Poems from the Sangamon. John Knoepfle. LC 85-1133. 128p. 1985. pap. 9.95 (*0-252-01243-7*) U of Ill Pr.

P

***Poems from the Schoolhouse.** Sterling Phillips. iii, 37p. 2000. pap. 9.95 (0-9700467-1-5) Pollyanna Pr.

***Poems from the Southend of the Rink.** Richard E. Parham. LC 99-94707. viii, 103p. 1999. 9.95 (0-9670748-0-0) Black Duck.

Poems from the Virginia Quarterly Review, 1925-1967. Ed. by Charlotte Kohler. LC 69-18860. 274p. reprint ed. 85.00 (0-8357-9812-7, 2010032000071) Bks Demand.

Poems from 3 Decades. Richard Lattimore. LC 80-39709. xiv, 288p. 1999. pap. text 17.00 (0-226-46946-8) U Ch Pr.

***Poems Galore/Inspirational Writings.** Irene Armstrong. 70p. 2000. pap. 8.95 (0-9661337-2-2) Son-Kin.

Poems Go Clang! Debi Gliori. LC 96-30750. (Illus.). 32p. (J). (gr. k-4). 1997. 13.99 (0-7636-0148-9) Candlewick Pr.

Poems Have Roots. Lillian Moore. (Illus.). 48p. (J). (gr. 3-8). 1997. 15.00 (0-689-80029-0) Atheneum Yung Read.

Poem's Heartbeat: A Manual of Prosody. Alfred Dewitt Corn. LC 97-5766. (Story Line Writers Guide Ser.). 224p. (Orig.). 1997. pap. 12.00 (1-885266-40-5) Story Line.

Poems Here at Home. James Whitcomb Riley. (Notable American Authors Ser.). 1999. reprint ed. lib. bdg. 125.00 (0-7812-8787-1) Rprt Serv.

Poems Hitherto Uncollected. Francis L. Hawks. (Notable American Authors Ser.). 1992. reprint ed. lib. bdg. 75.00 (0-7812-3035-7) Rprt Serv.

Poems Humorous & Inconsequential. Picton Publishing (Chippenham) Ltd. Staff. (C). 1987. 35.00 (0-948251-30-1, Pub. by Picton) St Mut.

Poems I Wish I'd Written: Translations from the Irish. Tr. by Gabriel Fitzmaurice from IRI. LC 97-164299. 132p. pap. 11.95 (1-900693-14-3, Pub. by Clo Iar-Chonnachta) Dufour.

Poems in Black & White with Shades of Color, No. 1000. Edward D. Anderson. (Illus.). 52p. (Orig.). 1996. pap. 6.95 (0-9655341-0-3) Small Caps.

Poems in Contempt of Progress by Jerome Tichenor. Ed. by Joel W. Hedgpeth. 1974. pap. 2.95 (0-910286-36-1) Boxwood.

Poems in English, 2 vols., Set. John Milton. LC 27-273. (Illus.). 1968. reprint ed. 79.00 (0-403-00349-0) Scholarly.

Poems in English, with Illustrations by William Blake, 2 vols., Set. John Milton. (BCL1-PR English Literature Ser.). (Illus.). 1992. reprint ed. lib. bdg. 150.00 (0-7812-7375-7) Rprt Serv.

Poems in Many Voices. Mary Hampden-Jackson. 70p. 1984. 22.00 (0-7212-0557-7, Pub. by Regency Pr GBR) St Mut.

Poems in My Earphone. Agard. 1995. pap. text. write for info. (0-582-22587-6, Pub. by Addison-Wesley) Longman.

Poems in Our Absence. Claes Andersson. Tr. by Lennart Bruce & Sonja Bruce from FIN. LC 94-1387. 128p. (Orig.). 1994. pap. 12.95 (0-9638398-5-3) Bonne Chance.

Poems in Persons: An Introduction to the Psychoanalysis of Literature. Norman N. Holland. (Morningside Bk.). 192p. 1989. pap. text 18.00 (0-231-06983-9) Col U Pr.

Poems in Persons: An Introduction to the Psychoanalysis of Literature. Norman N. Holland. LC 73-4691. xi, 183p. 1973. write for info. (0-393-01099-6) Norton.

Poems in Prose see Works of Oscar Wilde

Poems in Prose: In Russian & English. Ivan Sergeevich Turgenev & S. M. Konovalov. Tr. by Constance Garnett & Roger Rees from RUS. 219p. 1951. pap. 32.50 (0-8236-4140-6) Intl Univs Pr.

Poems in Prose & la Fanfarlo. Charles Baudelaire. 270p. 1989. pap. 16.95 (0-85646-170-9, Pub. by Anvil Press) Dufour.

Poems in Scots & English. rev. ed. Robert Burns. Ed. by Donald Law. (Everyman Paperback Classics Ser.). 256p. (C). 1996. pap. 8.95 (0-460-87786-0, Everyman's Classic Lib) Tuttle Pubng.

***Poems in the Afternoon.** Hedda Rogers. 56p. 2000. pap. write for info. (0-7541-0952-6, Pub. by Minerva Pr) Unity Dist.

Poems in the Autograph of Lord Byron: Once in the Possession of Teresa Guicciolo, Don Juan, Cantos I-V: A Facsimile of the Original Draft Manuscripts in the Pierpont Morgan Library, Vol. II. George Gordon Byron. Ed. by Jerome J. McGann & Alice Levine. LC 88-2416. (Manuscripts of the Younger Romantics & the Bodleian Shelley Manuscripts). 376p. 1985. text 50.00 (0-8240-6251-5) Garland.

Poems in the Key of Life. Charles A. Davis. (Illus.). 64p. 1994. pap. 6.95 (0-9636197-1-3) Davis & Assocs.

Poems in the Season. Colin Zarhett. 1998. pap. write for info. (1-57553-928-4) Watermrk Pr.

Poems in the Tree of Life. Cleo B. Ross. LC 96-92482. (Illus.). 80p. 1996. spiral bd. 32.95 (0-9653709-0-9) Ginga Pr.

Poems in the Tree of Life, Act II. Cleo B. Ross. 43p. 1997. spiral bd. 21.95 (0-9653709-1-7) Ginga Pr.

Poems in Their Place: Intertextuality & Order of Poetic Collections. Ed. by Neil Fraistat. LC 85-28926. vii, 344p. (C). 1987. 55.00 (0-8078-1695-7) U of NC Pr.

Poems, in 2 Volumes & Other Poems, 1800-1807. William Wordsworth. Ed. by Jared Curtis. LC 81-3124. (Cornell Wordsworth Ser.). 760p. 1982. text 115.00 (0-8014-1445-8) Cornell U Pr.

Poems Inspired by God. Jennie V. Harris. 52p. 1997. pap. write for info. (1-57502-645-7, PO1826) Morris Pubng.

Poems Just for Us! 50 Read-Aloud Poems with Cross-Curricular Activities for Young Learners. Bobbi Katz. 1996. pap. text 10.95 (0-590-53544-7) Scholastic Inc.

Poems, Knots, & Conundra. Jean H. Thoresen. 1997. pap. 56.95 (1-57553-506-8) Watermrk Pr.

***Poems, Litanies & Meditations.** Nancy Bright. (Illus.). 80p. 1999. lib. bdg. 22.00 (0-9650485-2-7) Phoenix Intl AR.

Poems Lyrical & Idyllic. Edmund C. Stedman. (Notable American Authors Ser.). 1999. reprint ed. lib. bdg. 125.00 (0-7812-8905-X) Rprt Serv.

Poems Made & Remade. Howard Meroney. 1966. pap. 10.00 (0-685-62615-6) Atlantis Edns.

Poems, New & Collected, 1957-1997. Wislawa Szymborska. Tr. by Stanisaw Baranczak & Clare Cavanagh from POL. LC 97-32277. 288p. (C). 1998. 27.00 (0-15-100353-X) Harcourt.

Poems, New & Old. John Freeman. 319p. 1920. reprint ed. 59.00 (0-403-01761-0) Scholarly.

Poems New & Selected. Frederick Candelaria. 84p. 1984. pap. 6.95 (0-86492-029-6, Pub. by Goose Ln Edits) Genl Dist Srvs.

Poems New & Selected. Patrick Lane. 1980. pap. 5.95 (0-19-540296-0) OUP.

Poems New & Selected. James Laughlin. LC 97-52320. 294p. 1998. pap. 12.95 (0-8112-1375-7, NDP857, Pub. by New Directions) Norton.

Poems New & Selected, 1962-1992. H. Lloyd Van Brunt. LC 93-83655. (Illus.). 256p. 1993. pap. 14.95 (1-882986-00-8) Smith.

Poems, 1918-1975: The Complete Poems of Charles Reznikoff. Charles Reznikoff. LC 89-17816. 450p. (C). 1995. reprint ed. pap. 17.50 (0-87685-790-X) Black Sparrow.

Poems, 1980. Brendan Tripp. 45p. 1983. pap. 5.00 (1-57353-007-7) Eschaton Prods.

Poems, 1988. Brendan Tripp. 252p. 1989. pap. 25.00 (1-57353-017-4) Eschaton Prods.

Poems, 1985-1986. Brendan Tripp. 161p. 1987. pap. 15.00 (1-57353-013-1) Eschaton Prods.

Poems, 1984. Brendan Tripp. 252p. 1986. pap. 25.00 (1-57353-012-3) Eschaton Prods.

Poems, 1984: Orwellian Themes. Valerie Hannah. 25p. (Orig.). 1984. pap. 2.95 (0-9610912-2-3) V H Pub.

Poems, 1989. Brendan Tripp. 252p. 1990. pap. 25.00 (1-57353-018-2) Eschaton Prods.

Poems, 1981. Brendan Tripp. 102p. 1983. pap. 10.00 (1-57353-008-5) Eschaton Prods.

Poems, 1987. Brendan Tripp. 252p. 1988. pap. 25.00 (1-57353-015-8) Eschaton Prods.

Poems, 1983. Brendan Tripp. 202p. 1984. pap. 20.00 (1-57353-011-5) Eschaton Prods.

Poems, 1980-1994. John Kinsella. LC 97-158288. 1997. pap. 19.95 (1-86368-177-9, Pub. by Fremantle Arts) Intl Spec Bk.

Poems, 1980-1994: The Hunt. John Kinsella. 352p. 1998. pap. 22.95 (1-85224-453-4, Pub. by Bloodaxe Bks) Dufour.

Poems, 1982. Brendan Tripp. 162p. 1983. pap. 15.00 (1-57353-009-3) Eschaton Prods.

Poems, 1911 to 1940. F. Scott Fitzgerald. 1981. 20.00 (0-89723-026-4) Bruccoli.

Poems, 1911-1931. Herbert E. Read. LC 78-64052. (Des Imagistes; Literature of the Imagist Movement Ser.). reprint ed. 37.50 (0-404-17092-7) AMS Pr.

Poems, 1959-1979. Frederick Seidel. 1989. pap. 11.95 (0-685-28297-X) Knopf.

Poems, 1956-1986. James Simmons. 202p. 1986. 32.00 (1-85224-019-9, Pub. by Bloodaxe Bks); pap. 17.95 (1-85224-020-2, Pub. by Bloodaxe Bks) Dufour.

Poems, 1956-1986. James Simmons. 184p. 1986. pap. 14.95 (1-85235-002-4) Dufour.

Poems, 1942-1992. I. Lesley Briggs. LC 92-73124. 1994. 10.95 (0-8158-0489-X) Chris Mass.

Poems, 1990. Brendan Tripp. 252p. 1991. pap. 25.00 (1-57353-020-4) Eschaton Prods.

Poems, 1991. Brendan Tripp. 252p. 1992. pap. 25.00 (1-57353-021-2) Eschaton Prods.

Poems, 1993. Brendan Tripp. 252p. 1994. pap. 25.00 (1-57353-024-7) Eschaton Prods.

Poems, 1992. Brendan Tripp. 252p. 1993. pap. 25.00 (1-57353-023-9) Eschaton Prods.

***Poems, 1975-1995: Hail! Madam Jazz & a Fragile City.** Michael O'Siadhail. 238p. 2000. pap. 22.95 (1-85224-495-X, Pub. by Bloodaxe Bks) Dufour.

Poems, 1976-1979. Brendan Tripp. 100p. 1983. pap. 10.00 (1-57353-010-7) Eschaton Prods.

Poems, 1970-1992. Fay Zwicky. LC 93-226772. 241p. 1993. pap. 19.95 (0-7022-2466-9, Pub. by Univ Queensland Pr) Intl Spec Bk.

Poems, 1968-1972: Including Relearning the Alphabet, To Stay Alive & Footprints. Denise Levertov. LC 86-5389. 288p. 1987. pap. 12.95 (0-8112-1005-7, NDP629, Pub. by New Directions) Norton.

Poems, 1963-1983. C. K. Williams. 244p. 1988. 19.95 (0-374-23516-3) FS&G.

Poems, 1963-1983. C. K. Williams. 1989. pap. 14.00 (0-374-52204-9) FS&G.

Poems, 1960-1967: Including The Jacob's Ladder, O Taste & See, & The Sorrow Dance. Denise Levertov. LC 82-2263. 256p. 1983. pap. 11.95 (0-8112-0859-1, NDP549, Pub. by New Directions) Norton.

Poems, 1937-1947. Gottfried Benn. Tr. by Simona Draghici from GER. LC 91-282. 108p. (C). 1991. pap. text 4.95 (0-943045-06-1) Plutarch Pr OR.

Poems, 1923-1941. Carl Rakosi. Ed. by Andrew Crozier. (Sun & Moon Classics Ser.: No. 64). 180p. (Orig.). 1995. pap. 12.95 (1-55713-185-6) Sun & Moon CA.

Poems, Non-Poems & Nonsense. Doris Goldberg. Ed. by Carol Spelius. (Illus.). 277p. (Orig.). 1989. pap. 10.95 (0-941363-06-6) Lake Shore Pub.

Poems Now First Collected. Edmund C. Stedman. (Notable American Authors Ser.). 1999. reprint ed. lib. bdg. 125.00 (0-7812-8910-6) Rprt Serv.

Poems of a Civil War Veteran. Matthew Cowlin. LC 91-73855. (Illus.). 35p. (Orig.). 1991. pap. 5.00 (0-9633524-2-3) JB Press.

Poems of a Cowboy I. unabridged ed. Bill Halbert. (Illus.). 50p. 1995. spiral bd. 6.00 (1-929326-30-0) Hal Bar Pubg.

Poems of a Cowboy II. unabridged ed. Bill Halbert. (Illus.). 20p. 1996. spiral bd. 6.00 (1-929326-31-9) Hal Bar Pubg.

Poems of A. E. Housman. Alfred E. Housman. Ed. by Archie Burnett. LC 97-16259. (Oxford English Texts Ser.). 640p. 1998. text 150.00 (0-19-812322-1) OUP.

***Poems of a Lifetime.** Salvatore Gianquinto. 2000. pap. write for info. (1-58235-393-X) Watermrk Pr.

Poems of a Lifetime. David E. Morton. 1999. pap. write for info. (1-58235-075-2) Watermrk Pr.

Poems of a Manic Depressive. Judith C. Maiman. (Illus.). 96p. (Orig.). 1992. pap. 10.95 (0-9627860-4-7) Lone Oak MN.

Poems of a Mountain Home. Saigyo. Tr. by Burton Watson from JPN. 256p. 1991. 29.50 (0-231-07492-1) Col U Pr.

Poems of a Mountain Home. Burton Watson. 256p. 1992. pap. 18.00 (0-231-07493-X) Col U Pr.

Poems of a Son, Prayers of a Father. Matthew L. Watley & William D. Watley. LC 92-11599. 96p. 1992. pap. 11.00 (0-8170-1183-8) Judson.

Poems of a Wanderer. So Chong-Ju & Kevin D. O'Rourke. 136p. 1995. pap. 15.95 (1-873790-73-2) Dufour.

***Poems of a Woman.** Marilyn Peretti. (Illus.). 32p. 1999. pap. 5.00 (0-9673333-2-6) Splendid Pr.

Poems of a Yosemite Packer. William D. Fouts. LC 87-91031. (Illus.). 89p. (Orig.). 1987. pap. text 6.95 (0-944798-00-4) Spurs Pub.

Poems of Abraham Lincoln. Abraham Lincoln. 28p. 1991. 8.95 (1-55709-133-1) Applewood.

Poems of Aemelia Lanyer: Salve Deus Rex Judaeorum. Aemelia Lanyer. Ed. by Susanne Woods. (Women Writers in English Ser.). (Illus.). 192p. 1993. pap. text 16.95 (0-19-508361-X) OUP.

Poems of Akhmatova. Anna Andreevena Akhmatova. Tr. by Stanley Kunitz & Max Hayward. LC 97-19949. (RUS & ENG.). 192p. 1997. pap. 13.00 (0-395-86003-2) HM.

Poems of Al-Mutanabbi: A Selection with Introduction, Translations & Notes. Al-Mutanabbi & Abu al-Tayyib Ahmad ibn al-Husan. Tr. by Arthur J. Arberry. LC 66-17060. 161p. reprint ed. pap. 45.90 (0-608-10870-7, 2051447) Bks Demand.

Poems of Alan Dugan. Alan Dugan. LC 79-144761. (Yale Series of Younger Poets: No. 57). reprint ed. 18.00 (0-404-53857-6) AMS Pr.

Poems of Alan Seeger. Alan Seeger. LC 72-1678. reprint ed. 21.00 (0-404-08498-2) AMS Pr.

Poems of Alcimus Ecdicius Avitus: Translation & Introduction. Avitus & George W. Shea. LC 96-52898. (Medieval & Renaissance Texts & Studies: No. 172). 168p. 1997. 24.00 (0-86698-214-0, MR172) MRTS.

Poems of Alexander Pope: A 1 Volume Edition of the Twickenham Text with Selected Annatations. Alexander Pope. Ed. by John Butt. (Illus.). 1966. pap. 19.00 (0-300-00030-8, Y163) Yale U Pr.

Poems of Alexander Pope: Index. (Twickenhaus Edition of the Poems of Alexander Pope Ser.: Vol. XI). 175p. 1969. 59.50 (0-416-44380-X) Elliots Bks.

Poems of Alexander Scott. Alexander Scott. Ed. by A. K. Donald. (ETS ES: No. 85). 1974. reprint ed. 35.00 (0-527-00288-7) Periodicals Srv.

Poems of Algernon Charles Swinburne. Algernon Charles Swinburne. 252p. Date not set. 22.95 (0-8488-2495-4) Amereon Ltd.

Poems of Algernon Charles Swinburne, 6 vols. Algernon Charles Swinburne. LC 77-148312. reprint ed. 445.00 (0-404-08930-5) AMS Pr.

Poems of Allan Ramsay, 2 vols. Allan Ramsay. LC 71-144498. reprint ed. 110.00 (0-404-08584-9) AMS Pr.

Poems of Ambrose Bierce. Ambrose Bierce. Ed. & Intro. by M. E. Grenander. LC 94-13761. xliv, 202p. 1995. pap. 12.00 (0-8032-6133-0, Bison Books) U of Nebr Pr.

Poems of American History. Ed. by Burton E. Stevenson. LC 72-116416. (Granger Index Reprint Ser.). 1977. 38.95 (0-8369-6159-5) Ayer.

Poems of American Patriotism. Ed. by Frederic L. Knowles. LC 76-109142. (Granger Index Reprint Ser.). 1977. 19.95 (0-8369-6126-9) Ayer.

Poems of American Patriotism. Ed. by Brander Matthews. LC 70-133072. (Granger Index Reprint Ser.). 1977. 19.95 (0-8369-6202-8) Ayer.

Poems of Andre Breton: A Bilingual Anthology. Andre Breton. Tr. by Jean-Pierre Cauvin & Mary A. Caws. 298p. 1982. text 35.00 (0-292-76476-6) U of Tex Pr.

Poems of Anna Letitia Barbauld. Ed. by William McCarthy & Elizabeth Kraft. LC 92-39712. (Illus.). 448p. 1994. 65.00 (0-8203-1528-1) U of Ga Pr.

Poems of Anne, Countess of Winchelsea. Anne K. Finch. Ed. & Intro. by Myra Reynolds. reprint ed. 49.50 (0-404-56856-4) AMS Pr.

Poems of Aphra Behn: A Selection. Ed. by Janet Todd. LC 94-31330. (C). 1995. text 50.00 (0-8147-8216-7) NYU Pr.

Poems of Arouet. Joseph B. Ladd. (Notable American Authors Ser.). 1999. reprint ed. lib. bdg. 125.00 (0-7812-3679-7) Rprt Serv.

Poems of Arthur Henry Hallam. Arthur H. Hallam. Ed. by Richard Le Gallienne. LC 75-148794. reprint ed. 34.00 (0-404-08825-2) AMS Pr.

Poems of Arthur Hugh Clough. Arthur H. Clough. Ed. by A. L. Norrington. 340p. 1986. pap. 18.95 (0-19-812343-4) OUP.

Poems of Arthur Hugh Clough. 2nd ed. Arthur H. Clough. Ed. by Frederick L. Mulhauser. (Oxford English Texts Ser.). 852p. (C). 1974. text 89.00 (0-19-811898-8) OUP.

Poems of Arthur O'Shaughnessy. Arthur E. O'Shaughnessy. Ed. by William A. Percy. LC 78-13947. 104p. 1979. reprint ed. lib. bdg. 49.50 (0-313-21101-9, OSPO, Greenwood Pr) Greenwood.

Poems of Augie Prime: New Poems. George Wallace. Ed. by David B. Axelrod. pap. 12.00 (0-925062-19-7) Writers Ink Pr.

Poems of B. R. Whiting. B. R. Whiting. LC 91-11885. 105p. 1991. pap. text 12.95 (1-878818-08-2, Pub. by Sheep Meadow) U Pr of New Eng.

***Poems of Boston & Beyond: From the Back Bay to the Back Ward.** Douglas S. Holder. 28p. 1998. pap. 4.00 (0-9678131-2-3) Ibbetson St Pr.

Poems of Byron Vazakas see Nostalgias for a House of Cards: Poems

Poems of Cabin & Field. Paul Laurence Dunbar. LC 72-83917. (Black Heritage Library Collection). (Illus.). 1977. 35.95 (0-8369-8564-8) Ayer.

Poems of Cabin & Field. Paul Laurence Dunbar. LC 74-164803. (Illus.). reprint ed. 19.50 (0-404-00041-X) AMS Pr.

Poems of Cabin & Field. Paul Laurence Dunbar. (Illus.). 1991. reprint ed. pap. 22.95 (0-88143-132-X) Ayer.

***Poems of Callimachus.** Callimachus. 300p. 2000. pap. text 24.95 (0-19-815224-8) OUP.

***Poems of Callimachus.** Callimachus. Tr. by Frank Nisetich. 300p. 2000. text 70.00 (0-19-814760-0) OUP.

Poems of Catullus. Gaius Valerius Catullus. Tr. by Charles Martin from LAT. LC 89-45486. 208p. 1989. pap. 13.95 (0-8018-3926-2); text 35.00 (0-8018-3925-4) Johns Hopkins.

Poems of Catullus. Gaius Valerius Catullus. 224p. 1998. pap. 10.95 (0-19-283587-4) OUP.

Poems of Catullus. Gaius Valerius Catullus. Tr. by Peter Whigham from LAT. (Classics Ser.). 254p. 1966. pap. 16.99 (0-14-044180-8, Penguin Classics) Viking Penguin.

Poems of Catullus. Gaius Valerius Catullus. Tr. by James Michie. 240p. 1989. pap. 18.95 (1-85399-129-5, Pub. by Brist Class Pr) Focus Pub-R Pullins.

Poems of Celia Thaxter. Celia L. Thaxter. (Illus.). 360p. 1996. reprint ed. pap. 20.00 (0-914339-57-5, Pub. by P E Randall Pub) U Pr of New Eng.

Poems of Charles Baudelaire. Charles Baudelaire. Tr. by F. P. Sturm. LC 77-10250. 192p. reprint ed. 49.50 (0-404-16306-8) AMS Pr.

Poems of Charles Fenno Hoffman. Charles F. Hoffman. Ed. by Edward F. Hoffman. LC 72-80627. reprint ed. 37.50 (0-404-03299-0) AMS Pr.

Poems of Charles Kingsley. Charles Kingsley. reprint ed. lib. bdg. 79.00 (0-7812-0307-4) Rprt Serv.

Poems of Charles Kingsley. Charles Kingsley. LC 78-131762. 1970. reprint ed. 39.00 (0-403-00649-X) Scholarly.

Poems of Charles Warren Stoddard. Charles W. Stoddard. (Notable American Authors Ser.). 1999. reprint ed. lib. bdg. 125.00 (0-7812-8950-5) Rprt Serv.

Poems of Charlotte Smith. Charlotte Smith. Ed. by Stuart Curran. (Women Writers in English Ser.). 368p. 1993. pap. text 19.95 (0-19-508358-X) OUP.

Poems of Childhood. Joan W. Anglund. LC 95-30937. (Illus.). 32p. 1996. 13.00 (0-15-262961-0) Harcourt.

Poems of Childhood. Eugene Field. (Airmont Classics Ser.). (Illus.). (J). (gr. 4 up). 1969. mass mkt. 2.95 (0-8049-0211-9, CL-211) Airmont.

Poems of Childhood. Eugene Field. LC 95-25851. (Scribner Illustrated Classics Ser.). (Illus.). 216p. (YA). (gr. 7 up). 1996. per. 25.00 (0-689-80757-0) Atheneum Yung Read.

Poems of Cicero. Marcus Tullius Cicero. Ed. by W. Eubank. (LAT.). 280p. 1997. pap. text 29.95 (1-85399-529-0, Pub. by Brist Class Pr) Focus Pub-R Pullins.

Poems of Cicero. Marcus Tullius Cicero. ix, 267p. write for info. (0-318-71097-8) G Olms Pubs.

Poems of Cloister & Jungle, a Buddhist Anthology. Rhys Davids. 1972. 59.95 (0-8490-0849-2) Gordon Pr.

Poems of Color: Knitting in the Bohus Tradition. Wendy Keele. (Illus.). 144p. 1995. pap. 19.95 (1-883010-12-8) Interweave.

Poems of Comfort for the Sick & the Bereaved: Flowers That Bloom a Message of Cheer see Always Come Rejoicing

Poems of Cupid, God of Love. Ed. by Thelma S. Fenster & Mary C. Erler. vii, 237p. 1990. 73.50 (90-04-09218-8) Brill Academic Pubs.

Poems of Cuthbert Shaw & Thomas Russell. Ed. by Eric Partridge. LC 74-117908. (Select Bibliographies Reprint Ser.). 1977. 19.95 (0-8369-5360-6) Ayer.

Poems of Doctor Zhivago. Boris Pasternak. Ed. & Tr. by Donald Davie. LC 76-1980. 204p. 1977. reprint ed. lib. bdg. 38.50 (0-8371-8294-8, PAPDZ, Greenwood Pr) Greenwood.

Poems of Dylan Thomas. rev. ed. Dylan Thomas. Ed. by Daniel Jones. LC 79-145935. 1971. 23.95 (0-8112-0398-0, Pub. by New Directions) Norton.

Poems of Early Buddhist Nuns: Therigatha. Tr. by C. A. Davids & K. R. Norman from PLI. (C). 1989. pap. 14.00 (0-86013-289-7, Pub. by Pali Text) Elsevier.

Poems of Edgar Allan Poe. Edgar Allan Poe. Ed. by Floyd Stovall. LC 65-23455. 400p. reprint ed. pap. 124.00 (0-7837-1246-4, 204138300020) Bks Demand.

Poems of Edgar Allan Poe. Edgar Allan Poe. Ed. by Thomas O. Mabbott. LC 79-28853. 511p. reprint ed. pap. 158.50 (0-7837-4168-5, 205901700012) Bks Demand.

Poems of Edgar Allan Poe: Illustrated & Decorated by W. Heath Robinson. Edgar Allan Poe. LC 71-536276. xxi, 225 p. 1970. write for info. (0-7135-1603-8) CE10.

Poems of Edward Taylor. Edward Taylor. Ed. by Donald E. Sanford. LC 60-6432. (Yale Paperbound Ser.: No. Y-308). 607p. reprint ed. pap. 188.20 (0-8357-8271-9, 203389500087) Bks Demand.

An Asterisk (*) at the beginning of an entry indicates that the title is appearing for the first time.

Poems of Edward Taylor. Edward Taylor. Ed. by Donald E. Stanford. LC 88-40555. xlii, 370p. (C). 1989. reprint ed. pap. 24.95 (*0-8078-4248-6*) U of NC Pr.

Poems of Egan O'Rahilly: To Which Are Added Miscellaneous Pieces Illustrating Their Subjects & Language. Egan O'Rahilly. Ed. by Patrick S. Dinneen. LC 75-28837. reprint ed. 30.00 (*0-404-13826-8*) AMS Pr.

Poems of Emerson: Selected Criticism from the Coming Age & the Arena, 1899-1905. Charles Malloy. LC 80-2539. 1981. 55.00 (*0-404-19265-3*) AMS Pr.

Poems of Emily Bronte. Emily Jane Bronte. Ed. by Barbara Lloyd-Evans. 224p. (C). 1992. text 54.50 (*0-389-20977-5*) B&N Imports.

Poems of Emily Bronte. Emily Jane Bronte. Ed. by Derek Roper & Edward Chitham. (English Texts Ser.). 326p. 1996. text 74.00 (*0-19-812641-7*) OUP.

Poems of Emily Dickinson, 3 vols. Emily Dickenson. 1998. 156.00 (*0-674-67601-7*) HUP.

Poems of Emily Dickinson. Emily Dickinson. Ed. by Helen Plotz. LC 64-12111. (Harper Poets Ser.). (Illus.). (J). (gr. 4 up). 1964. 12.95 (*0-690-63365-3*) HarpC Child Bks.

***Poems of Emily Dickinson.** Emily Dickinson. Ed. by R. W. Franklin. LC 99-11821. 704p. 1999. 29.95 (*0-674-67624-6*) HUP.

Poems of Emily Dickinson, 3 vols. variorum ed. Emily Dickinson. Ed. by R. W. Franklin. LC 98-20854. 1680p. 1998. 125.00 (*0-674-67622-X*) HUP.

Poems of Emily Dickinson: An Annotated Guide to the Commentary in English, 1978-1989. Joseph Duchac. (G. K. Hall Reference Ser.). 525p. 1993. 70.00 (*0-8161-7352-4*, G K Hall & Co) Mac Lib Ref.

Poems of Endre Ady. Tr. & Intro. by Anton N. Nyerges. (Illus.). 500p. 1987. reprint ed. lib. bdg. 58.50 (*0-8191-6568-9*) U Pr of Amer.

Poems of Eugene Field. Eugene Field. (BCL1-PS American Literature Ser.). 553p. 1992. reprint ed. lib. bdg. 99.00 (*0-7812-6711-0*) Rprt Serv.

***Poems of Fact & Fantasy.** Virgina Snyder. 1999. pap. text 11.95 (*0-9674935-0-1*) NY Knott.

Poems of Faith. Helen Steiner Rice. 1984. 14.95 (*0-89952-086-3*) Littlebrook.

Poems of Faith & Hope: Flowers That Bloom to Clear the Way see Always Come Rejoicing

Poems of Faith & Inspiration. E. M. Johnson. Ed. by Elizabeth Coon. (Illus.). 128p. 1997. pap. 11.95 (*1-886028-21-4*) Savage Pr.

Poems of Faiz Ahmad Faiz: A Poet of the Third World. Tr. by Mohammed Zakir & M. N. Menai.Tr. of No. 1. 83p. 1995. pap. 60.00 (*0-7855-2727-3*, Pub. by Print Hse) St Mut.

Poems of Faiz Ahmad Faiz: A Poet of the Third World. Tr. by Mohammed Zakir & M. N. Menai. LC 95-902328. (Oriental Literature in Translation Ser.: Vol. 1).Tr. of No. 1. 83p. 1998. pap. 55.00 (*81-85880-67-0*, Pub. by Print Hse) St Mut.

Poems of Fear & Delight. David Bernatchez. 36p. 1994. pap. 5.00 (*0-9626735-9-5*) Rabeth Pub Co.

Poems of Fernando Pessoa. Fernando Pessoa. (Modern European Poets Ser.). 215p. 1988. pap. 10.50 (*0-88001-123-8*) HarpC.

Poems of Fernando Pessoa. Fernando Pessoa. Ed. by Edwin Honig & Susan M. Brown. LC 98-11043. 236p. 1998. reprint ed. pap. 15.95 (*0-87286-342-5*) City Lights.

Poems of Flowers. (Illus.). 20p. 1986. 4.00 (*0-930061-11-X*) Interspace Bks.

Poems of Frances E. W. Harper. Frances Ellen Watkins Harper. LC 74-133155. (Black Heritage Library Collection). 1977. 11.95 (*0-8369-8710-1*) Ayer.

Poems of Francis Thompson. rev. ed. Francis Thompson. Ed. by Terence L. Connolly. LC 78-10371. 587p. 1979. reprint ed. lib. bdg. 45.50 (*0-313-21003-9*, THFT, Greenwood Pr) Greenwood.

Poems of Francois Villon. Francois Villon. Tr. & Intro. by Galway Kinnell. LC 81-71907. (FRE & ENG.). 270p. 1982. reprint ed. pap. 17.95 (*0-87451-236-0*) U Pr of New Eng.

Poems of General George S. Patton, Jr. Lines of Fire. George S. Patton, Jr. Ed. by Carmine A. Prioli. LC 90-30990. (Studies in American Literature: Vol. 8). 232p. 1991. 89.95 (*0-88946-162-7*) E Mellen.

Poems of George Crabbe: A Literary & Historical Study. John H. Evans. 1977. 22.95 (*0-8369-7108-6*, 7942) Ayer.

Poems of George Herbert. George Herbert. LC 75-41132. (Illus.). reprint ed. 55.00 (*0-404-14553-1*) AMS Pr.

Poems of George Marion M'Clellan. George M. McClellan. LC 79-133159. (Black Heritage Library Collection). 1977. 12.00 (*0-8369-8714-4*) Ayer.

Poems of George Meredith. George Meredith. Ed. by Phyllis B. Bartlett. LC 73-77142. 1978. 175.00 (*0-300-01283-7*) Yale U Pr.

Poems of Gerard Manley Hopkins. 4th ed. Gerard Manley Hopkins. Ed. by W. H. Gardner & Norman H. MacKenzie. (Illus.). 428p. 1976. pap. 19.95 (*0-19-281094-4*) OUP.

Poems of Goethe. Johann Wolfgang Von Goethe. 1974. 300.00 (*0-87968-151-9*) Gordon Pr.

Poems of Goethe. Johann Wolfgang Von Goethe. Ed. by Edwin H. Zeydel. LC 72-168176. (North Carolina. University. Studies in the Germanic Languages & Literatures: No. 20). reprint ed. 27.00 (*0-404-50920-7*) AMS Pr.

Poems of Governor Thomas Burke of North Carolina. Ed. by Richard Walser. vii, 69p. 1961. 6.00 (*0-86526-070-2*) NC Archives.

Poems of Grzegorz Musial: Berliner Tagebuch & Taste of Ash. Grzegorz Musia et al. LC 98-24573. 168p. 1998. 32.50 (*0-8386-3783-3*) Fairleigh Dickinson.

Poems of Hafez. Reza Saberi. 404p. (C). Date not set. lib. bdg. 44.50 (*0-7618-0075-1*) U Pr of Amer.

Poems of Heaven & Hell from Ancient Mesopotamia. Thomas Wyatt. Tr. & Intro. by N. K. Sandars. 192p. 1989. pap. 11.95 (*0-14-044249-9*, Penguin Classics) Viking Penguin.

Poems of Heinrich Heine. Heinrich Heine. 1974. 300.00 (*0-8490-0850-6*) Gordon Pr.

Poems of Henry Howard, Earl of Surrey. Henry H. Surrey. Ed. by M. Frederick. LC 68-682. 1970. reprint ed. lib. bdg. 75.00 (*0-8383-0606-3*) M S G Haskell Hse.

Poems of Henry Timrod: With a Sketch of the Poet's Life. Henry Timrod. Ed. by Paul H. Hayne. LC 72-4976. (Romantic Tradition in American Literature Ser.). 236p. 1978. reprint ed. 23.95 (*0-405-04646-4*) Ayer.

Poems of Henry Van Dyke. Henry Van Dyke. (BCL1-PS American Literature Ser.). 467p. 1992. reprint ed. pap. text 79.00 (*0-685-51470-6*); reprint ed. lib. bdg. 99.00 (*0-7812-6889-3*) Rprt Serv.

***Poems of Herman Melville.** rev. ed. Herman Melville & Douglas Robillard. LC PS2382.R63 2000. 2000. pap. 29.00 (*0-87338-660-4*) Kent St U Pr.

Poems of Hesiod. Hesiod. LC 82-40451. (Illus.). 160p. 1983. pap. 10.95 (*0-8061-1846-6*) U of Okla Pr.

Poems of Hesiod. Hesiod. Tr. & Intro. by R. M. Frazer. LC 82-40451. (Illus.). 160p. 1983. 21.95 (*0-8061-1837-7*) U of Okla Pr.

Poems of Home & Travel. Bayard Taylor. (Notable American Authors). 1999. reprint ed. lib. bdg. 125.00 (*0-7812-8985-8*) Rprt Serv.

Poems of Horace. Horace. Tr. by Richard Brome. LC 71-161791. (Augustan Translator Ser.). reprint ed. 63.00 (*0-404-54119-4*) AMS Pr.

Poems of Illumination. Richard Angilly. (Illus.). (Orig.). 1980. pap. 11.95 (*0-931290-27-9*) Blue Dragon.

Poems of Inspiration. Marion J. Gilbert. 52p. 1998. pap. 5.00 (*1-57502-791-7*, PO2185) Morris Pubng.

Poems of Inspiration. Randal R. Rossow. 1998. pap. write for info. (*1-57553-855-5*) Watermrk Pr.

Poems of Inspiration & Guidance. Marion Lewellyn. 1998. pap. write for info. (*1-57553-972-1*) Watermrk Pr.

Poems of Interest, Vol. 1. Louis R. Stagnaro. (C). 1995. 9.95 (*0-9654817-1-9*) L R Stagnaro.

Poems of J. V. Cunningham. J. V. Cunningham. Ed. by Timothy Steele. LC 97-355. 253p. 1997. pap. 16.95 (*0-8040-0998-8*); text 28.95 (*0-8040-0997-X*) Swallow.

Poems of Jacobus Bellamy. Ed. by P. J. Buijnsters. (Illus.). 64p. (C). 1994. pap. text 12.95 (*90-5356-107-2*, Pub. by Amsterdam U Pr) U of Mich Pr.

Poems of Jane Turell & Martha Brewster. LC 78-9933. 136p. 1979. reprint ed. 50.00 (*0-8201-1327-1*) Schol Facsimiles.

Poems of Jerusalem & Love Poems. Yehuda Amichai. LC 92-31558. (ENG & HEB.). 277p. 1992. pap. 13.95 (*1-878818-19-8*, Pub. by Sheep Meadow) U Pr of New Eng.

Poems of John Audelay. Ed. by Ella K. Whiting. (EETS, OS Ser.: No. 184). 1974. reprint ed. 63.00 (*0-685-02859-3*) Periodicals Srv.

Poems of John Collop. John Collop. Ed. by Conrad Hilberry. LC 61-5905. 239p. 1962. reprint ed. pap. 74.10 (*0-608-01981-X*, 206263600003) Bks Demand.

Poems of John Dewey. John Dewey. Ed. by Jo Ann Boydston. LC 77-4718. 220p. 1977. 16.95 (*0-8093-0800-2*) S Ill U Pr.

Poems of John Dryden. John Dryden. Ed. by Paul Hammond. LC 94-14270. (Longman Annotated English Poets Ser.). (C). 1995. text 251.25 (*0-8013-1430-5*, Pub. by Addison-Wesley) Longman.

Poems of John Gray. Ian Fletcher. LC 87-2528. (British Authors, 1880-1920 Ser.). 360p. (C). 1988. lib. bdg. 30.00 (*0-944318-00-2*) ELT Pr.

Poems of John Keats. John Keats. Ed. by Stanley Kunitz. LC 64-22174. (Harper Poets Ser.). (Illus.). (J). (gr. 6 up). 1964. 11.74 (*0-690-63933-3*) HarpC Child Bks.

Poems of John Keats. John Keats. Ed. by Gerald Bullett. LC 91-53231. (Everyman's Library: No. 53). xxxv, 396p. 1992. 20.00 (*0-679-40553-4*) McKay.

Poems of Jonathan Swift. write for info. (*0-87413-207-X*) U Delaware Pr.

Poems of Jose Bergamin (1896-1983) Echoes of a Distant Sea. Jose Bergamin. Tr. by David Garrison from SPA. LC 91-4715. (Hispanic Literature Ser.: Vol. 12). (ENG & SPA., Illus.). 114p. 1991. lib. bdg. 59.95 (*0-7734-9778-1*) E Mellen.

Poems of Joseph Fletcher. Joseph Fletcher. LC 73-21063. (Fuller Worthies' Library). 272p. 1983. reprint ed. 76.50 (*0-404-11482-2*) AMS Pr.

Poems of Joseph Mary Plunkett. Joseph M. Plunkett. LC 75-28839. reprint ed. 29.50 (*0-404-13828-4*) AMS Pr.

Poems of Joseph Sheridan Le Fanu. Joseph Sheridan Le Fanu. Ed. by Alfred P. Graves. LC 78-148812. reprint ed. 32.50 (*0-404-08878-3*) AMS Pr.

Poems of Joseph Sheridan Le Fanu. Joseph Sheridan Le Fanu. Ed. by Alfred P. Graves. LC 76-5273. (Collected Works). 1977. reprint ed. 23.95 (*0-405-09224-5*) Ayer.

Poems of Joy & Hope: A Little Treasury of Gold. Kay A. Carson. 1993. 7.98 (*0-88486-072-8*) Arrowood Pr.

Poems of Jules Laforgue. Jules Laforgue & Peter Dale. 456p. 1986. pap. 19.95 (*0-85646-146-6*, Pub. by Anvil Press) Dufour.

Poems of Jules Laforgue. Jules LaForgue. Tr. by Patricia Terry. LC 86-4617. 217p. 1986. reprint ed. lib. bdg. 59.50 (*0-313-25210-6*, LFPO, Greenwood Pr) Greenwood.

Poems of Lady Mary Wroth. Ed. by Josephine A. Roberts. LC 82-20843. (Illus.). 304p. (C). 1992. pap. text 17.95 (*0-8071-1799-4*) La State U Pr.

Poems of Lake George: Proses & Posey. Thomas R. Lord. 198p. 1995. pap. 21.75 (*0-9640267-2-4*) Pinelands Pr.

Poems of Laughter & Violence: Selected Poems, 1981-1986. Billy Childish. 204p. (Orig.). 1992. pap. 18.95 (*1-871894-76-X*, Pub. by Hangman Bks) AK Pr Dist.

Poems of Laura Riding. Laura Riding. 420p. (C). 1985. reprint ed. pap. 14.95 (*0-89255-087-2*) Persea Bks.

***Poems of Laura Riding: A Newly Revised Edition of the 1938/1980 Collection.** rev. ed. Laura Riding Jackson. 2001. 17.95 (*0-89255-258-1*, Pub. by Persea Bks) Norton.

Poems of Laurence Minot, 1333-1352. Ed. by Richard H. Osberg. LC 96-6482. (Middle English Texts Ser.). (Illus.). 1996. pap. 12.00 (*1-879288-67-2*) Medieval Inst.

***Poems of Lauris Edmond.** Read by Lauris Edmond & Frances Edmonds. 2000. 24.95 incl. audio compact disk (*1-86940-234-0*, Pub. by Auckland Univ) Paul & Co Pubs.

Poems of Lawrence Minot. Ed. by James & Simons. 116p. 1989. pap. text 15.95 (*0-85989-234-4*, Pub. by Univ Exeter Pr) Northwestern U Pr.

Poems of Lee Bassett, 1973-2000. Lee Bassett. (Illus.). 190p. 1999. 40.00 (*0-911287-37-X*, Pub. by Blue Begonia); pap. 15.00 (*0-911287-34-5*, Pub. by Blue Begonia) Partners Pubs Grp.

Poems of Lewis Carroll. Lewis Carroll, pseud. Ed. by Myra C. Livingston. LC 73-7914. (Harper Poets Ser.). (Illus.). 128p. (YA). (gr. 7 up). 1986. lib. bdg. 11.89 (*0-690-04540-9*) HarpC Child Bks.

Poems of Li Ho, 791-817. Li Ho. Tr. by J. D. Frodsham. (Oxford Library of East Asian Literature Ser.). 1970. 26.00 (*0-19-815436-4*) OUP.

Poems of Life. Ed. by Delores W. Brooks. (Illus.). 60p. (Orig.). 1987. pap. 9.95 (*0-932471-10-2*) Falsoft.

***Poems of Life.** George Murphy. 1999. pap. write for info. (*1-58235-202-X*) Watermrk Pr.

***Poems of Life: Pet Tales Spun with Gold.** Shirley D. Cleveland. 1999. pap. 5.95 (*0-9671225-1-1*) Lyons Media.

***Poems of Life: Silver Memories Spun with Gold-"Yesterdays" on the Farm.** Shirley D. Cleveland. (Illus.). 2000. per. 9.98 (*0-9671225-2-X*) Lyons Media.

***Poems of Life: Silver Thoughts Spun with Gold-Love-Hope-Faith.** Shirley D. Cleveland. 1999. per. 12.95 (*0-9671225-0-3*) Lyons Media.

Poems of Life & Nature. George Ray. 1995. pap. 4.95 (*1-57087-048-9*) Prof Pr NC.

Poems of Light. Ed. by Carl Japikse. 160p. 1991. pap. 12.95 (*0-89804-156-2*, Enthea Pr) Ariel GA.

Poems of Longfellow. Henry Wadsworth Longfellow. 23.95 (*0-8488-2652-3*) Amereon Ltd.

***Poems of Louisa May Alcott. Louisa May Alcott. LC 99-51490. (American Classics Ser.). 147p. 2000. pap. 15.95 (0-9655309-5-7) Ironweed Pr.**
The Poems of Louisa May Alcott is the first comprehensive volume of her poems, many of which are collected here for the first time. This book will delight & surprise those who know Louisa May Alcott principally through her fiction. All Ironweed American Classics books are printed on acid-free paper. Available to trade via Baker & Taylor, Brodart, & Ingram. ***Publisher Paid Annotation.***

Poems of Love. Selected by Margaret Browning. 64p. 1992. text 8.95 (*0-312-07065-9*) St Martin.

***Poems of Love.** Jonathan Orion. 35p. 1999. (*1-891232-09-6*, Closet Bks) R Crane Pub.

***Poems of Love & Faith.** Linda L. LaMar. 54p. 1999. pap. 6.00 (*1-929302-00-2*, 001) FnQualPoets Pubg Servs.

***Poems of Love & Faith.** deluxe rev. ed. Linda L. LaMar. 78p. 2000. pap. 12.95 (*1-929302-07-X*) FnQualPoets Pubg Servs.

Poems of Love & Marriage. John Ciardi. LC 88-17229. 48p. (Orig.). 1989. 16.00 (*1-55728-053-3*) U of Ark Pr.

Poems of Love & Strife, Death & Life by Francisco de Quevedo. Ed. & Tr. by Carl W. Cobb from SPA. LC 89-64207. 290p. 1991. 37.50 (*0-938972-16-2*) Spanish Lit Pubns.

Poems of Love & War: From the 8 Anthologies & the 10 Songs of Classical Tamil. A. K. Ramanujan. LC 84-12182. 320p. 1985. pap. text 23.50 (*0-231-05107-7*) Col U Pr.

***Poems of Love, Inspiration & Other Things.** Jim Comstock. 120p. 2000. pap. write for info. (*0-7541-1035-4*, Pub. by Minerva Pr) Unity Dist.

Poems of Madness & Angel. Ray Bremser. LC 86-50905. (Illus.). 90p. 1986. pap. 8.95 (*0-934953-11-2*) Water Row Pr.

Poems of Mao Tsetung. Kim Unsong. LC 93-87737. (Illus.). 200p. (Orig.). 1994. 20.00 (*0-942049-05-5*) One Mind Pr.

Poems of Maria Lowell, with Unpublished Letters & a Biography. Hope J. Vernon. LC 37-13958. (Brown University Studies: Vol. 2). 198p. reprint ed. 61.40 (*0-608-16570-0*, 202751500055) Bks Demand.

Poems of Meleager. Peter Whigham. Date not set. 18.95 (*0-85646-000-1*, Pub. by Anvil Press) Dufour.

Poems of Memory Trips. Michael Mbabuike. LC 98-60016. (Poetry Ser.). (Illus.). 96p. 1998. 19.95 (*1-889218-08-1*); pap. 6.95 (*1-889218-09-X*) Sungai Bks.

Poems of Michael Wigglesworth. Ed. by Ronald A. Bosco. LC 88-34214. 374p. (C). 1989. lib. bdg. 48.00 (*0-8191-7345-2*) U Pr of Amer.

***Poems of Misery & Love.** Anthony Mazzini. 1999. pap. write for info. (*1-58235-310-7*) Watermrk Pr.

Poems of Modern Sijo. Kim Unsong. LC 95-68802. 200p. (Orig.). (C). 1995. 20.00 (*0-942049-06-3*) One Mind Pr.

Poems of Modern Thought & Spiritual Truths. E. W. Sprague. 76p. 1998. reprint ed. pap. 14.95 (*0-7661-0343-9*) Kessinger Pub.

Poems of Mourning. Ed. by Peter Washington. LC 98-27662. (Pocket Poets Ser.). 256p. 1999. 12.50 (*0-375-40456-2*) Everymns Lib.

Poems of Mrs. Anne Bradstreet (1612-1672) Anne D. Bradstreet. 1976. reprint ed. 69.00 (*0-685-71977-4*, Regency) Scholarly.

Poems of N. M. Rashed: A Poet of the Third World (Oriental Literature in Translation 2) Tr. by Mohammed Zakir. LC 95-902329. (Oriental Literature in Translation Ser.: Vol. 2).Tr. of No. 2. 165p. 1998. pap. 75.00 (*81-85880-68-9*, Pub. by Print Hse) St Mut.

***Poems of Nation, Anthems of Empire: English Verse in the Long Eighteenth Century.** Suvir Kaul. LC 00-27526. 416p. 2000. 55.00 (*0-8139-1967-3*); pap. 19.50 (*0-8139-1968-1*) U Pr of Va.

Poems of Nature & Wildlife. Verla Tollefson. LC 96-94979. (Illus.). 250p. (Orig.). 1996. pap. 8.00 (*0-9654570-0-1*) V Tollefson.

Poems of Nazim Hikmet. Nazim Hikmet. Tr. by Randy Blasing & Mutlu Konuk from TUR. 256p. (Orig.). 1993. pap. 12.95 (*0-89255-198-4*) Persea Bks.

Poems of Nepali Women. S. K. Singh. 1994. pap. 30.00 (*0-7855-2758-3*, Pub. by Ratna Pustak Bhandar) St Mut.

Poems of Nia, Bk. I. Runett N. Ebo. (Illus.). 26p. (Orig.). 1990. pap. 6.00 (*1-883753-00-7*) Jwand Ent.

Poems of Nia, Bk. II. Runett N. Ebo. (Illus.). 61p. (Orig.). 1994. pap. 10.00 (*1-883753-04-X*) Jwand Ent.

Poems of O. V. de L. Milosz (1877-1939) David Gascoyne. 24p. 1993. pap. 7.95 (*1-870612-73-6*, Pub. by Enitha Pr) Dufour.

Poems of Ossian, 2 vols. James Macpherson. LC 76-144459. reprint ed. 195.00 (*0-404-08697-7*) AMS Pr.

Poems of Ossian. James MacPherson. (BCL1-PR English Literature Ser.). 298p. 1992. reprint ed. lib. bdg. 79.00 (*0-7812-7370-6*) Rprt Serv.

Poems of Ossian. Ossian. 492p. reprint ed. lib. bdg. 79.00 (*0-7812-0259-0*) Rprt Serv.

Poems of Ossian. Ossian. Ed. by James Macpherson. LC 76-107180. 1970. reprint ed. 49.00 (*0-403-00036-X*) Scholarly.

Poems of Ossian & Related Works. James Macpherson. Ed. by Howard Gaskill et al. 480p. 1996. pap. 28.00 (*0-7486-0707-2*, Pub. by Edinburgh U Pr) Col U Pr.

Poems of Ossian in the Original Gaelic, 3 vols. James Macpherson. Ed. by John M'Arthur. LC 70-144460. reprint ed. 185.00 (*0-404-08730-2*) AMS Pr.

Poems of Our Time. Nellie Wheatley. 1986. 9.00 (*0-7223-2026-4*, Pub. by A H S Ltd) St Mut.

Poems of Park Benjamin. Park Benjamin. LC 70-160914. (Biography Index Reprint Ser.). 1977. reprint ed. 23.95 (*0-8369-8077-8*) Ayer.

Poems of Passion. Rommiet Gilbert. 1998. pap. 8.95 (*0-533-12636-3*) Vantage.

Poems of Passion (1911) Ella W. Wilcox. 160p. 1998. reprint ed. pap. 17.95 (*0-7661-0291-2*) Kessinger Pub.

Poems of Patrick Branwell Bronte: A New Text & Commentary. Victor A. Neufeldt. LC 90-38464. 590p. 1990. text 25.00 (*0-8240-4590-4*, H1050) Garland.

Poems of Paul Celan. Paul Celan. Tr. & Intro. by Michael Hamburger. (ENG & GER.). 350p. 1989. 24.95 (*0-89255-140-2*) Persea Bks.

Poems of Paul Celan. Paul Celan. Tr. by Michael Hamburger from GER. LC 88-22567. 350p. 1990. reprint ed. pap. 16.95 (*0-89255-134-8*) Persea Bks.

Poems of Pearls & Praise. Connie V. Barrow. 1998. pap. write for info. (*1-57553-692-7*) Watermrk Pr.

Poems of Peter Davison. Peter Davison. 336p. 1997. pap. 17.50 (*0-679-76589-1*) Knopf.

Poems of Peter Davison, 1957-1995. Peter Davison. 1995. 25.00 (*0-679-44180-8*) Knopf.

Poems of Petronius. E. Courtney. 86p. 1991. pap. 13.95 (*1-55540-588-6*, 40 04 25) OUP.

Poems of Phillis Wheatley. Phillis Wheatley. LC 94-40958. 160p. 1995. pap. 9.95 (*1-55709-233-8*) Applewood.

Poems of Phillis Wheatley. rev. ed. Phillis Wheatley. Ed. by Julian D. Mason, Jr. LC 88-23280. (Illus.). xviii, 236p. 1989. pap. 18.95 (*0-8078-4245-1*) U of NC Pr.

Poems of Pleasure. Ella W. Wilcox. 158p. 1999. reprint ed. pap. 16.95 (*0-7661-0752-3*) Kessinger Pub.

Poems of Power & Praise. Daniel H. Carson. Ed. by Mildred Carson. (Orig.). 1990. pap. 8.95 (*0-9627561-0-5*) Wordsmith NV.

Poems of Praise: A Metaphysician's Psalter. Friend Stuart. 112p. 1982. pap. 12.95 (*0-912132-13-2*) Dominion Pr.

Poems of Praise & Thanksgiving: Flowers That Bloom with Heads Toward the Sky see Always Come Rejoicing

Poems of Protest. Ed. by Robin Wright. (Pocket Poet Ser.). 1966. pap. 3.95 (*0-8023-9052-8*) Dufour.

Poems of Protest & Enjoyment. Zebade Why. v, 58p. 1997. pap. 8.50 (*0-9662354-0-1*) C Keeler.

Poems of Pure Imagination: Robert Penn Warren & the Romantic Tradition. Lesa C. Corrigan. LC 99-32047. (Southern Literary Studies). 160p. 1999. text 35.00 (*0-8071-2408-7*); pap. text 19.95 (*0-8071-2506-7*) La State U Pr.

Poems of Queen Elizabeth I. Leicester Bradner. LC 64-17778. (Brown University Bicentennial Publications). 111p. reprint ed. 34.50 (*0-608-16491-7*, 202750300055) Bks Demand.

Poems of R. S. Thomas. R. S. Thomas. LC 85-1152. 216p. 1985. 22.00 (*0-938626-46-9*) U of Ark Pr.

***Poems of Reflection: Being Within Incadescence & Luminescence.** Charlotte Ann Frick. (Love Poem Trilogy Ser.: Bk. 2). 134p. 1999. pap. write for info. (*0-9676746-2-X*) J Grey Pr.

Poems of Robert Browning, 001. Robert Browning. Ed. by Donald Smalley. LC 56-3004. (YA). (gr. 9 up). 1956. pap. 13.96 (*0-395-05103-7*, RivEd) HM.

Poems of Robert Frost: An Explication. Mordecai Marcus. 288p. (C). 1991. 40.00 (*0-8161-7267-6*, Hall Reference) Macmillan.

P

An Asterisk (*) at the beginning of an entry indicates that the title is appearing for the first time.

Poems of Robert Henryson. Robert Henryson. Ed. by Denton Fox. (Oxford English Texts Ser.). 1981. 135.00 (*0-19-812703-0*) OUP.

Poems of Robert Henryson. Robert Henryson. Ed. by Denton Fox. (Oxford English Texts Ser.). 280p. 1987. pap. 29.95 (*0-19-812324-8*) OUP.

Poems of Robert Sidney, Edited from the Poet's Autograph Notebook with Introduction & Commentary. Robert Sidney. Ed. by P. J. Croft. (Illus.). 372p. 1984. text 79.00 (*0-19-812726-X*) OUP.

***Poems of St. John of the Cross.** Roy Campbell. 96p. 2000. pap. 13.00 (*1-86046-589-7*) Harvill Press.

Poems of St. John of the Cross. Tr. by Kenneth Krabbenhoft. LC 98-35251. 96p. (C). 1999. 20.00 (*0-15-100327-0*) Harcourt.

Poems of Saisseval. Pierre Garnier. Tr. by Alex Fischler. (ENG & FRE., Illus.). 64p. 1995. pap. 12.95 (*0-9614462-9-3*) Black Hat Pr.

Poems of Samuel Taylor Coleridge. Samuel Taylor Coleridge. LC 98-125159. 256p. 1997. 12.50 (*0-375-40072-9*) Everymns Lib.

***Poems of Shelley, Vol. 2.** Kelvin Everest & Geoffrey Matthews. 920p. 2000. 124.95 (*0-582-03082-X*) Longman.

***Poems of Shelley, Vol. 3.** K. Everest. 648p. 2000. 99.95 (*0-582-03083-8*) Longman.

Poems of Shelly, Vol. 1. Percy Bysshe Shelley. Ed. by Geoffrey Matthews & Kelvin Everest. (Annotated English Poets Ser.). 648p. (C). 1989. text 59.66 (*0-582-48448-0*, 78288) Longman.

Poems of Sidney Lanier. Ed. by Mary D. Lanier. 320p. 1999. reprint ed. pap. 17.95 (*0-8203-2155-9*) U of Ga Pr.

Poems of Sidney Lanier. Sidney Lanier. 262p. 1998. reprint ed. lib. bdg. 89.00 (*0-7812-4776-4*) Rprt Serv.

Poems of Sir Richard Maitland, Knight of Lethingtoun. Richard Maitland. Ed. by Joseph Bain. LC 77-144427. reprint ed. 41.50 (*0-404-52927-5*) AMS Pr.

Poems of Sir Samuel Ferguson. Samuel Ferguson. LC 75-28814. reprint ed. 62.50 (*0-404-13807-1*) AMS Pr.

***Poems of Sir Walter Ralegh: A Historical Edition.** Walter Raleigh & Michael Rudick. LC 99-54887. (Renaissance English Text Society Ser.: Vol. 209). 1999. write for info. (*0-86698-251-5*) MRTS.

Poems of 65 Years. William E. Channing, II. Ed. by F. B. Sanborn. LC 72-4956. (Romantic Tradition in American Literature Ser.). 232p. 1979. reprint ed. 28.95 (*0-405-04628-6*) Ayer.

Poems of 65 Years. William E. Channing, II. (Works of William Ellery Channing II). 1990. reprint ed. lib. bdg. 79.00 (*0-7812-2268-0*) Rprt Serv.

Poems of Social Revolt. Myles Greene. LC 85-70604. 52p. 1985. pap. text 2.50 (*0-9606994-4-9*) Greenview Pubns.

Poems of Sophia. (Aviarium Poetarum Variorum Ser.: Vol. 2). 42p. 1996. pap. 4.00 (*1-929829-05-1*) Variable Pr.

Poems of St. John of the Cross. Tr. & Intro. by Kathleen Jones. 96p. 1994. pap. 40.00 (*0-86012-210-7*, Pub. by Srch Pr) St Mut.

Poems of St. John of the Cross. St. John of the Cross. Tr. by Willis Barnstone. LC 68-14597. (ENG & SPA.). 144p. 1972. reprint ed. pap. 9.95 (*0-8112-0449-9*, NDP341, Pub. by New Directions) Norton.

Poems of St. John of the Cross. 3rd ed. Tr. by John F. Nims. LC 79-12943. 160p. 1979. pap. 12.00 (*0-226-40110-3*, P845) U Ch Pr.

Poems of St. John of the Cross. 3rd ed. St. John of the Cross. Tr. by John F. Nims. LC 79-12943. (Midway Reprint Ser.). viii, 152p. 1995. reprint ed. pap. text 12.95 (*0-226-40111-1*) U Ch Pr.

Poems of St. Paulinus of Nola. Ed. by J. Quasten et al. Tr. by P. G. Walsh. (Ancient Christian Writers Ser.: No. 40). 1975. 29.95 (*0-8091-0197-1*) Paulist Pr.

Poems of Stephen Crane: A Critical Edition. Joseph Katz. LC 65-17181. 1966. 59.00 (*0-8154-0125-6*) Cooper Sq.

***Poems of Suradasa.** Krishna Bahadur. LC 99-931369. 364p. 1999. 32.00 (*81-7017-369-8*, Pub. by Abhinav Pubns) S Asia.

Poems of T. S. Eliot. T. S. Eliot. 256p. 1998. 12.50 (*0-375-40185-7*) Everymns Lib.

Poems of T. Sturge Moore, 4 vols., Set. T. Sturge Moore. 1982. reprint ed. lib. bdg. 125.00 (*0-403-01114-0*) Scholarly.

Poems of Tai Chi Chuan: Selected Readings from the Masters. Ed. by James C. O'Leary. Tr. by Yang Jwing-Ming. LC 98-61694. (Tai Chi Treasures Ser.). 128p. 1999. pap. 12.95 (*1-886969-71-X*, B035\71X) YMAA Pubn.

Poems of Tennyson, 3 vols., Vol. Set. 2nd ed. Alfred Lord Tennyson. Ed. by Christopher Ricks. 1987. 425.00 (*0-520-06012-1*, Pub. by U CA Pr) Cal Prin Full Svc.

Poems of the Aztec Peoples. Tr. by Edward Kissam & Michael Schmidt. LC 83-70274. 144p. 1983. pap. 15.00 (*0-916950-35-2*) Biling Rev-Pr.

Poems of the Big Sur. Joel Rothberg. (Illus.). 114p. (Orig.). 1989. pap. 12.95 (*0-9610386-0-8*) Dragons Tail Pr.

Poems of the Divided Self. Gary W. Crawford. (Blue Meadow Poets Ser.: No. 3). (Illus.). 12p. (Orig.). 1992. pap. 3.00 (*0-910151-04-0*) Nashville Hse.

Poems of the Elder Edda. rev. ed. Tr. by Patricia Terry. LC 89-70689. (Middle Ages Ser.). 300p. (C). 1990. text 39.95 (*0-8122-8235-3*); pap. text 18.95 (*0-8122-8220-5*) U of Pa Pr.

Poems of the English Race. Ed. by Raymond M. Alden. LC 77-149099. (Granger Index Reprint Ser.). 1977. 27.95 (*0-8369-6224-9*) Ayer.

Poems of the Fantastic. Glenn R. Sweatman. LC 89-82518. (Modern Poets Ser.). 88p. (YA). 1993. pap. 9.95 (*0-938991-07-8*) Colonial Pr AL.

Poems of the 5 Mountains: An Introduction to the Literature of the Zen Monasteries. 2nd rev. ed. Marian Ury. LC 91-32839. (Michigan Monographs in Japanese Studies: No. 10). xx, 105p. 1992. 15.95 (*0-939512-53-X*) U MI Japan.

Poems of the 4 Seas. Joshua H. Jones. LC 76-178478. (Black Heritage Library Collection). 1977. reprint ed. 13.95 (*0-8369-8927-9*) Ayer.

Poems of the Great War. Ed. by John W. Cunliffe. LC 72-160904. (Granger Index Reprint Ser.). 1977. reprint ed. 21.95 (*0-8369-6267-2*) Ayer.

Poems of the Heart. Danny L. Doss. 16p. (Orig.). 1995. pap. write for info. (*1-885206-27-5*, Iliad Pr) Cader Pubng.

Poems of the Heart. Patricia A. Frazier Rivers. 1998. pap. write for info. (*1-57553-921-7*) Watermrk Pr.

Poems of the Hidden Way. Catherine De Vinck. LC 91-76162. 142p. (Orig.). 1991. pap. 9.75 (*0-911726-53-5*, PHW) Alleluia Pr.

Poems of the Holocaust. Jacob E. Melek. (Illus.). 276p. (Orig.). 1996. pap. 24.00 (*0-614-95918-7*) J Melek.

Poems of the Kingdom. Mel L. Piper. 16p. (Orig.). (YA). (gr. 7 up). 1996. pap. 2.95 (*1-881477-51-7*) Piper Hse.

Poems of the Known World. William Kistler. LC 94-43024. 96p. 1995. 14.45 (*1-55970-301-6*, Pub. by Arcade Pub Inc) Time Warner.

Poems of the Late Francis Scott Key. Francis S. Key. (Notable American Authors Ser.). 1999. reprint ed. lib. bdg. 125.00 (*0-7812-3676-2*) Rprt Serv.

Poems of the Later Years. Irving Wilner. 64p. 1981. pap. 8.95 (*0-931848-31-8*) Dryad Pr.

Poems of the Life Beyond & Within (1880) Giles B. Stebbins. 262p. 1998. reprint ed. pap. 18.95 (*0-7661-0654-3*) Kessinger Pub.

Poems of the Middle Period, 1822-1837, Vol. I. John Clare. Ed. by David Powell et al. (Oxford English Texts Ser.). 406p. 1996. text 110.00 (*0-19-812340-X*) OUP.

Poems of the Middle Period, 1822-1837, Vol. II. John Clare. Ed. by Eric Robinson et al. (English Texts Ser.). 416p. 1996. text 105.00 (*0-19-812387-6*) OUP.

Poems of the Morning & Poems of the Storm. Wyatt. 1973. 6.00 (*0-685-36817-3*); pap. 2.50 (*0-685-36818-1*) Oyez.

Poems of the Nazareth & the Cross. William Allen. (Works of William Allen). 1989. reprint ed. lib. bdg. 79.00 (*0-7812-1774-1*) Rprt Serv.

Poems of the Old West. Ed. by Levette J. Davidson. LC 68-58824. (Granger Index Reprint Ser.). 1977. 27.95 (*0-8369-6012-2*) Ayer.

Poems of the Orient. Bayard Taylor. (Notable American Authors). 1999. reprint ed. lib. bdg. 125.00 (*0-7812-8984-X*) Rprt Serv.

Poems of the Passing. Ruhiyyih Rabbani. 136p. (Orig.). 1996. pap. 29.95 (*0-85398-410-7*) G Ronald Pub.

Poems of the Pearl Manuscript. 3rd ed. Ed. by Malcolm Andrew & Ronald Waldron. (Exeter Medieval English Texts & Studies Ser.). 382p. 1997. pap. 19.95 (*0-85989-514-9*, Pub. by Univ Exeter Pr) Northwestern U Pr.

Poems of the Pearl Manuscript: Pearl, Cleanness, Patience & Sir Gawain & the Green Knight. Ed. by Malcom Andrew & Ronald Waldron. 384p. 1995. pap. text 17.95 (*0-85989-273-5*, Pub. by Univ Exeter Pr) Northwestern U Pr.

Poems of the Persian Gulf War. Jocelyn Hollis & J. Topham. LC 97-52121. 1998. write for info. (*0-930933-27-3*); pap. write for info. (*0-930933-28-1*) American Poets Cooperative Pubns.

Poems of the River Spirit. Maurice K. Guevara. (Pitt Poetry Ser.). 65p. (C). 1996. pap. 10.95 (*0-8229-5591-1*); text 24.95 (*0-8229-3934-7*) U of Pittsburgh Pr.

Poems of the Scottish Minor Poets. Ed. by George B. Douglas. LC 73-144505. reprint ed. 44.50 (*0-404-08634-9*) AMS Pr.

Poems of the Sixt Sense. Mariah Taracatac & Earl Sixt. (Illus.). 85p. 1988. 9.50 (*0-9674569-0-8*, 14911) R Sixt.

Poems of the 6th Decade. Marilyn Zuckerman. 76p. 1993. pap. 10.00 (*1-882329-01-5*) Garden St Pr.

Poems of the Spirit, Vols. 1-5. 95p. 1999. pap. 12.95 (*0-9632204-5-4*) J Alfieri.

Poems of the Tarot. Malcolm K. Smith. 84p. 1984. 8.95 (*0-89697-218-6*) Intl Univ Pr.

Poems of the Troubadour Raimbaut de Vaqueiras. Raimbaut de Vaqueiras. Ed. by Joseph Linskill. LC 80-2190. reprint ed. 45.00 (*0-404-19014-6*) AMS Pr.

Poems of the 2 Worlds. Frederick Morgan. LC 76-51907. 132p. 1977. 14.95 (*0-252-00604-6*) U of Ill Pr.

Poems of the Vietnam War. rev. ed. Jocelyn Hollis. LC 86-28776. 51p. 1987. 19.95 (*0-933486-67-7*); pap. 9.95 (*0-933486-69-3*); lib. bdg. 19.95 (*0-933486-68-5*) Am Poetry & Lit.

Poems of the Vikings: The Elder Edda. Ed. by Patricia Terry. LC 69-16528. (Library of Liberal Arts). (C). 1969. pap. write for info. (*0-672-60332-2*, LLA128) Macmillan.

Poems of the War. George H. Boker. LC 72-4949. (Romantic Tradition in American Literature Ser.). 204p. 1980. reprint ed. 28.95 (*0-405-04623-5*) Ayer.

Poems of the Way. Seyyed Hossein Nasr. 94p. (C). 2000. pap. 14.95 (*0-9629984-6-X*, Pub. by Foun Trad Studies) Kazi Pubns.

Poems of the West & East: Bi-Lingual Edition of the Complete Poems. Johann Wolfgang Von Goethe. Tr. by John Whaley. (Germanic Studies in America: No. 68). (ENG & GER.). 490p. 1998. text 70.95 (*0-8204-4220-8*) P Lang Pubng.

Poems of Theocritus. Anna Risk. LC 77-20042. 264p. reprint ed. pap. 81.90 (*0-8357-3887-6*, 203661900004) Bks Demand.

Poems of Thomas Carew. Thomas Carew. Ed. by Arthur Vincent. LC 76-38343. (Select Bibliographies Reprint Ser.). 1977. 19.95 (*0-8369-6760-7*) Ayer.

Poems of Thomas Gordon Hake. Thomas G. Hake. LC 75-131504. reprint ed. 32.00 (*0-404-03026-2*) AMS Pr.

Poems of Thomas Sheridan. Ed. by Robert Hogan. LC 94-8797. 1994. 49.50 (*0-87413-495-1*) U Delaware Pr.

Poems of Thomas Washbourne. Thomas Washbourne. LC 73-21068. (Fuller Worthies' Library). 240p. 1983. reprint ed. 76.50 (*0-404-11498-9*) AMS Pr.

Poems of Tibullus. Albius Tibullus. Tr. by Constance Carrier. LC 68-14614. (Greek & Latin Classics Series Midland Bks.: No. 116). 128p. reprint ed. 39.70 (*0-8357-9232-3*, 201301400083) Bks Demand.

***Poems of Time.** Brian Garrett. 2000. pap. write for info. (*1-58235-394-8*) Watermrk Pr.

Poems of Tristan Corbiere. Tr. by C. E. MacIntyre from FRE. (Illus.). 105p. 1989. 185.00 (*0-933861-03-6*) H Berliner.

Poems of Trumbull Stickney. Trumbull Stickney. LC 72-4975. (Romantic Tradition in American Literature Ser.). 336p. 1972. reprint ed. 31.95 (*0-405-04645-6*) Ayer.

Poems of Truth: A Guide Within Spiritual Development. Sharon A. Tyng. (Illus.). 64p. 1993. 7.95 (*0-9634388-0-8*) Creat Within.

Poems of Truth & Meditations (1924) Ida Mingle. 160p. 1998. reprint ed. pap. 17.95 (*0-7661-0341-2*) Kessinger Pub.

Poems of Tukarama. Ed. by J. Nelson Fraser & K. B. Marathe. 1981. reprint ed. 15.00 (*0-8364-0747-4*, Pub. by Motilal Bnarsidass) S Asia.

Poems of Two Friends (with J. J. Piatt) William Dean Howells. (Notable American Authors Ser.). 1992. reprint ed. lib. bdg. 75.00 (*0-7812-3266-X*) Rprt Serv.

Poems of Walter of Wimborne. Walter of Wimborne. Ed. by A. George Rigg. (ENG & LAT.). xii, 349p. pap. text 47.43 (*0-88844-042-1*) Brill Academic Pubs.

Poems of Wilfrid Owen. Ed. by Jon Stallworthy. 200p. 1986. pap. 12.95 (*0-393-30385-3*) Norton.

Poems of William B. Greene. William B. Greene. 1977. lib. bdg. 59.95 (*0-8490-2447-1*) Gordon Pr.

Poems of William Cowper, 1782-1785 Vol. 2, Vol. 2. William Cowper. Ed. by John D. Baird & Charles Ryskamp. (Oxford English Texts Ser.). (Illus.). 484p. (C). 1996. text 120.00 (*0-19-812339-6*) OUP.

Poems of William Cowper, 1785-1800 Vol. 3, Vol. 3. William Cowper. Ed. by John D. Baird & Charles Ryskamp. (Oxford English Texts Ser.). (Illus.). 466p. 1996. text 98.00 (*0-19-818296-1*) OUP.

Poems of William Cowper, 1748-1782 Vol. I, Vol. 1. William Cowper. Ed. by John D. Baird & Charles Ryskamp. (Oxford English Texts Ser.). (Illus.). 642p. 1980. text 115.00 (*0-19-811875-9*) OUP.

Poems of William Dunbar. Ed. by Kinsley. 188p. 1989. pap. text 15.95 (*0-85989-329-4*, Pub. by Univ Exeter Pr) Northwestern U Pr.

Poems of William Dunbar. W. Mackay Mackenzie. 272p. 1989. pap. 21.00 (*0-901824-94-1*, Pub. by Mercat Pr Bks) St Mut.

Poems of William Dunbar. William Dunbar. LC 70-161970. reprint ed. 29.00 (*0-403-01321-6*) Scholarly.

Poems of William of Shoreham. William Shoreham. Ed. by M. Konrath. (EETS, ES Ser.: No. 86). 1974. reprint ed. 45.00 (*0-527-00289-5*) Periodicals Srv.

Poems of William T. Costello, SJ. 2nd ed. William T. Costello. 128p. 1993. pap. 7.95 (*0-9629578-3-6*) Intl Long WA.

Poems of Yesteryear. Hazel Dover. (Illus.). 2p. 1998. pap. write for info. (*1-887804-12-9*) Cent Mont Pubng.

Poems of Z. Paul Hyland. 1982. pap. 10.95 (*0-906427-44-4*, Pub. by Bloodaxe Bks) Dufour.

Poems Old & New, 1918-1978. Janet Lewis. LC 80-26209. xvi, 112p. 1981. pap. 10.95 (*0-8040-0372-6*) Swallow.

Poems on a White Page. Frank Cady. (Flowering Quince Poetry Ser.: No. 4). (Illus.). 24p. (Orig.). 1982. pap. 7.50 (*0-940592-13-4*) Heyeck Pr.

Poems on Affairs of State: Augustan Satirical Verse, 1660-1714, Vol. 1, 1669-1678. Ed. by George D. Lord. Vol. 1. (Illus.). 1963. 70.00 (*0-300-00726-4*) Yale U Pr.

Poems on Affairs of State: Augustan Satirical Verse, 1660-1714, Vol. 2. Ed. by Elias F. Mengel, Jr. 575p. 1965. 150.00 (*0-300-00766-3*) Elliots Bks.

Poems on Affairs of State: Augustan Satirical Verse, 1660-1714, Vol. 7. Ed. by Frank H. Ellis. 732p. 1975. 150.00 (*0-300-01772-3*) Elliots Bks.

Poems on Affairs of State: Augustan Satirical Verse, 1660-1714, Vol. 7, 1704-1714. George D. Lord. Ed. by Frank H. Ellis. LC 63-7938. 830p. reprint ed. pap. 200.00 (*0-7837-2363-6*, 202202000023) Bks Demand.

Poems on Affairs of State Vol. 4: Augustan Satirical Verse, 1660-1714. Ed. by Galbraith M. Crump. LC 63-7938. (Illus.). 1968. 67.50 (*0-300-00389-7*) Yale U Pr.

Poems on Affairs of State Vol. 5: Augustan Satirical Verse, 1660-1774. Ed. by William J. Cameron. LC 63-7983. (Illus.). 1972. 80.00 (*0-300-01190-3*) Yale U Pr.

Poems on Events of the Day, 1582-1607. John Ross. LC 91-20371. 244p. 1991. 50.00 (*0-8201-1456-1*) Schol Facsimiles.

Poems on Land & on Water. Carmelita McGrath. 80p. 1992. pap. 7.15 (*1-895387-11-6*) Creative Bk Pub.

Poems on Love & Life. Frederick D. Harper. LC 84-73550. 125p. 1985. 19.95 (*0-935392-06-8*) Douglass Pubs.

Poems on Man in His Various Aspects under the American Republic. Cornelius Mathews. (Notable American Authors Ser.). 1999. reprint ed. lib. bdg. 125.00 (*0-7812-3987-7*) Rprt Serv.

Poems on Several Occasions. Sarah F. Egerton. LC 86-31375. 260p. 1987. 50.00 (*0-8201-1423-5*) Schol Facsimiles.

Poems on Several Occasions Written in the Eighteenth Century. Kathleen Campbell. (BCL1-PR English Literature Ser.). 212p. 1992. reprint ed. lib. bdg. 79.00 (*0-7812-7139-8*) Rprt Serv.

Poems on Slavery. Henry Wadsworth Longfellow. (Notable American Authors Ser.). 1999. reprint ed. lib. bdg. 125.00 (*0-7812-3825-0*) Rprt Serv.

Poems on the Abolition of the Slave Trade. James Montgomery et al. LC 79-149871. (Black Heritage Library Collection). 1977. 24.95 (*0-8369-8751-9*) Ayer.

Poems on the Reign of William the Third. Intro. & Selected by Earl Miner. LC 92-22021. (Augustan Reprints Ser.: No. 166). 1974. reprint ed. 14.50 (*0-404-70166-3*, PR565) AMS Pr.

Poems on the Rising Glory of America see Millennium in America: From the Puritan Migration to the Civil War

Poems on Various Subjects, Religious & Moral. Phillis Wheatley. LC 75-177828. reprint ed. 18.00 (*0-404-00126-2*) AMS Pr.

Poems on Various Subjects, 1787. Ann Yearsley. LC 94-22014. (Revolution & Romanticism, 1789-1834 Ser.). 1994. 95.00 (*1-85477-196-5*) Continuum.

Poems Only a Dog Could Love. John B. Lee. 1979. pap. 3.95 (*0-919910-06-8*) Genl Dist Srvs.

Poems, Original & Translated. Charles T. Brooks. Ed. by W. P. Andrews. LC 72-4952. (Romantic Tradition in American Literature Ser.). 256p. 1972. reprint ed. 21.95 (*0-405-04624-3*) Ayer.

Poems Out of Harlan County. Vivian Shipley. (Ithaca House Poetry Ser.). 60p. (Orig.). 1989. pap. 9.95 (*0-87886-132-7*) Greenfld Rev Lit.

Poems Pensive & Peculiar. Picton Publishing (Chippenham) Ltd. Staff. (C). 1987. 40.00 (*0-7855-5326-6*, Pub. by Picton) St Mut.

Poems, People, Places: Travels on My Own. David Wilde. (Sun Also Sets Ser.). (Illus.). 120p. 1994. pap. 12.95 (*0-9625472-2-0*) Wilde Pub.

Poems, Performance Pieces, Proses (sic), Plays, Poetics. Kurt Schwitters. Ed. & Tr. by Jerome Rothenberg & Pierre Joris from GER. LC 92-17365. (Border Lines Ser.).Tr. of Das Litterarische Werk. (Illus.). 320p. (C). 1993. 54.95 (*0-87722-894-9*) Temple U Pr.

Poems, Performance Pieces, Proses (sic), Plays, Poetics. Kurt Schwitters. Ed. & Tr. by Jerome Rothenberg & Pierre Joris. LC 92-17365. (Border Lines Ser.).Tr. of Das Litterarische Werk. (Illus.). 320p. 1994. pap. 29.95 (*1-56639-264-0*) Temple U Pr.

Poems Plain & Fancy. Dick Higgins. 136p. (Orig.). 1998. pap. 7.95 (*1-886449-71-6*, P9716, Pub. by Barrytown Ltd) Consort Bk Sales.

Poems, Plays & Other Remains of Sir John Suckling, 2 Vols. John Suckling. Ed. by William C. Hazlitt. LC 71-103669. (Select Bibliographies Reprint Ser.). 1977. 44.95 (*0-8369-5169-7*) Ayer.

Poems, Plays, & The Briton. Tobias George Smollett. Ed. by Byron Gassman. LC 91-36319. (Illus.). 592p. 1993. 50.00 (*0-8203-1428-5*) U of Ga Pr.

Poems Poets & Story, Vol. 1. 4th ed. Vendler. 1997. pap. text 47.25 (*0-312-18446-8*) St Martin.

Poems, Prayers & Exhortations. Cynthia Winton-Henry. 43p. 1994. pap. 9.95 (*0-9636755-3-2*) Wing It Pr.

Poems, Prayers & Logics. Delbert L. Tibbs. LC 84-80264. (Illus.). 80p. (Orig.). 1984. pap. 6.00 (*0-915867-02-8*) ENAAQ Pubns.

***Poems, Prayers & Promises...** Prophet Andromeda. Ed. by Sherry Knecht. 56p. (Orig.). 1999. pap. 9.95 (*1-929589-10-7*) Branching Leaf.

Poems, Prayers & Promises. Charles E. Cravey. (Illus.). 120p. (Orig.). 1988. pap. 9.95 (*0-938645-02-1*) In His Steps.

***Poems, Prayers & Promises...** 2nd rev. ed. Andromeda Knecht. (Illus.). 62p. 1999. pap. 9.95 (*1-929589-18-2*) Branching Leaf.

Poems, Prose & Poetry, Vol. 1. Marjorie V. Weber. (Illus.). 68p. 1978. lib. bdg. 10.00 (*1-891150-55-3*) M V Weber.

Poems, Prose & Poetry, Vol. 2. Marjorie V. Weber. (Illus.). 64p. 1979. lib. bdg. 10.00 (*1-891150-56-1*) M V Weber.

Poems, Protest & a Dream. Sor J. De La Cruz. Tr. by Margaret Sayers Peden. LC 96-30638. 304p. 1997. pap. 12.95 (*0-14-044703-2*, Penguin Classics) Viking Penguin.

Poems, Quotes, Mini Stories & True Life Experiences in God Power. Edna McNeil. Ed. by Denise Moore. (Orig.). 1989. pap. text 24.94 (*0-9613082-3-0*, TX369163) Bootstrap.

Poems Retrieved. 2nd rev. ed. Frank O'Hara. Ed. by Donald Allen. LC 77-554. 272p. 1996. pap. 13.95 (*0-912516-19-4*) Grey Fox.

Poems, Sacred, Passionate, & Humorous, of Nathaniel Parker Willis. Nathaniel P. Willis. LC 72-4983. (Romantic Tradition in American Literature Ser.). 388p. 1972. reprint ed. 33.95 (*0-405-04652-9*) Ayer.

Poems-2nd Series. William E. Channing, II. (Works of William Ellery Channing II). 1990. reprint ed. lib. bdg. 79.00 (*0-7812-2262-1*) Rprt Serv.

Poems Selected & New. Joan McBreen. 1998. pap. 13.95 (*1-897648-86-3*, Pub. by Salmon Poetry) Dufour.

***Poems Selected & New.** Heather Spears. LC 99-458651. 1998. write for info. (*0-919897-61-4*) Wolsak & Wynn.

Poems, 1786. Helen M. Williams. LC 93-46508. (Revolution & Romanticism, 1789-1834 Ser.). 1994. 65.00 (*1-85477-173-6*) Continuum.

Poems, 1799, Robert Southey. LC 96-35547. (Revolution & Romanticism Ser.). 1997. 65.00 (*1-85477-203-1*) Continuum.

Poems, 1791. Mary Robinson. LC 94-29215. (Revolution & Romanticism Ser.). 262p. 1994. 55.00 (*1-85477-191-4*) Continuum.

Poems, 1797. Samuel Taylor Coleridge et al. LC 96-35546. (Revolution & Romanticism Ser.). 1997. 75.00 (*1-85477-197-3*) Continuum.

Poems, 1792. Anna L. Barbauld. LC 93-17413. (Revolution & Romanticism Ser.). 168p. 1993. reprint ed. 48.00 (*1-85477-127-2*) Continuum.

Poems 6. Alan Dugan. 1989. 17.95 (*0-88001-199-8*) HarpC.

Poems (Stikhi) Stikhotvorenia. Nikolai Shatrov. Ed. by Ian Probstein & Feliks Goneonsky. LC 95-77393. (RUS.). 216p. (Orig.). 1995. pap. 12.00 (*1-882725-06-9*) Arch-Arcada.

Poems That Clang Inside My Head. Rosemary J. Schmidt. Ed. by Gabriel Blue. 40p. (Orig.). 1993. pap. 3.00 (*1-882294-03-3*) Green Gate.

Poems That Every Child Should Know: A Selection of the Best Poems of All Times for Young People. Ed. by Mary E. Burt. LC 71-168776. (Granger Index Reprint Ser.). 1977. reprint ed. 49.92 (*0-8369-6296-6*) Ayer.

***Poems That Have Helped Me.** Ed. by S. E. Kiser. (Illus.). 64p. 2000. reprint ed. pap. 5.95 (*1-883211-26-3*) Laughing Elephant.

Poems That Lift the Soul: A Treasury of Faith & Inspiration. Jack M. Lyon. LC 97-43382. 1998. pap. 19.95 (*1-57345-364-1*, Shadow Mount) Deseret Bk.

Poems That Live Forever: America's Favorite Poems of Love & Friendship, Humor & Whimsy, Faith & Inspiration. Ed. by Hazel Felleman. LC 65-13987. 480p. 1965. 18.95 (*0-385-00358-7*) Doubleday.

Poems That Preach. 1982. pap. text 1.95 (*0-87398-652-0*) Sword of Lord.

Poems That Sing to You. Ed. by Michael Strickland. LC 92-81078. (Illus.). 64p. (YA). (gr. 5 up). 1993. 14.95 (*1-56397-178-X*, Wordsong) Boyds Mills Pr.

Poems That Tell Me Who I Am. Margaret L. McWhorter. LC 80-51481. (Illus.). 57p. 1978. reprint ed. pap. 5.95 (*0-9604342-0-8*) Ransom Hill.

Poems That Touch the Heart. Mary L. Harris. LC 90-62239. (Illus.). 84p. 1990. pap. 7.95 (*0-9620115-1-7*) Post Oak Pubns.

Poems That Touch the Heart. enl. rev. ed. Compiled by A. L. Alexander. LC 56-11498. 425p. 1984. 19.95 (*0-385-04401-1*) Doubleday.

Poems That Touch Your Soul. Joyce Kelley. LC 97-91046. 105p. 2000. pap. 9.95 (*0-533-12550-2*) Vantage.

Poems That Warm Your Heart. Ottis L. Cotton. 256p. 1998. write for info. (*0-933380-44-5*) Olive Pr Pubns.

***Poems Throughout the Year 2nd Beyond.** Linda Taylor. LC 99-97582. (J). (gr. 1-3). 2000. pap. 15.00 (*0-533-13437-4*) Vantage.

Poems to Be Read Aloud: A Victorian Drawing Room Entertainment. Tom Atkinson. (Illus.). 113p. 1999. pap. 9.95 (*0-946487-00-6*, Pub. by Luath Pr Ltd) Midpt Trade.

Poems to Break the Harts of Impossible Princesses. Billy Childish. (Illus.). 69p. (Orig.). 1994. pap. 13.95 (*1-871894-86-7*, Pub. by Hangman Bks) AK Pr Dist.

Poems to Count On: 30 Terrific Poems & Activities to Help Teach Math Concepts. Sandra Liatsos. (Illus.). 1995. pap. 9.95 (*0-590-60340-X*) Scholastic Inc.

Poems to Ease the Spirit. Sharon E. Borges. 195p. pap. 15.00 (*0-9648658-0-7*) S Borges.

Poems to Keep. Phillip Corwin. 42p. 1985. 4.95 (*0-9615475-0-2*) Catnip Pr.

Poems to Lisi. De Quevdo. (Exeter Hispanic Text Ser.: No. 45). (SPA.). 136p. Date not set. pap. text 17.95 (*0-85989-274-3*, Pub. by Univ Exeter Pr) Northwestern U Pr.

Poems to Love & the Body. Dave Malone. LC 98-93926. 56p. 1999. pap. 7.95 (*0-9667744-0-X*) Bliss Sta.

Poems to Our Therapists. Many Voices Readers Staff. Ed. by Lynn W. (Illus.). 120p. (Orig.). 1996. pap. 10.00 (*0-9637277-1-0*) Many Voices Pr.

Poems to Ponder from the Pen of C. Gordon K. Clifford G. Kershner. 1999. pap. 5.95 (*0-9656015-5-2*) C G Kershner.

Poems to Read to the Very Young. Ed. by Josette Frank. LC 87-23234. (Pictureback Ser.). (Illus.). 32p. (J). (ps-1). 1988. pap. 3.25 (*0-394-89768-4*, Pub. by Random Bks Yng Read) Random.

Poems to Read to the Very Young. Frank & Wilson. 1p. 1998. pap. text 53.33 (*0-205-30294-7*) Allyn.

***Poems to Read to Very Young Children.** (J). 2001. bds. 7.99 (*0-375-80475-7*) Random Bks Yng Read.

***Poems to Relate To.** Katherine Zimbrick. 1999. pap. write for info. (*1-58235-226-7*) Watermrk Pr.

Poems to Remember. Pollee Freier. (J). 1996. pap. 15.95 (*1-57502-247-8*, P0927) Morris Pubng.

Poems to Share. Ed. by Kathleen Paton. (Real Mother Goose Library). (Illus.). 24p. (J). (ps-3). 1990. 4.95 (*1-56288-050-0*) Checkerboard.

Poems to Share. Nell Wommack. LC 92-74620. (Illus.). 170p. (Orig.). 1992. pap. 10.00 (*1-878149-18-0*) Counterpoint Pub.

Poems to Shiva. Narasimhan. 19.00 (*0-06-066080-5*) HarpC.

Poems to Treasure. Clara Baugus. 1997. pap. write for info. (*1-57553-550-5*) Watermrk Pr.

Poems to Vishnu the Lord. Narasimhan. 20.00 (*0-06-066079-1*) HarpC.

Poems to Younger Women. Michael Hartnett. 34p. 1988. pap. 11.95 (*1-85235-022-9*) Dufour.

Poems, Transcripts, Letters: Facsimiles of Richard Woodhouse's Scrapbook Materials in the Pierpont Morgan Library. John Keats. Ed. & Intro. by Jack Stillinger. LC 83-49279. (Manuscripts of the Younger Romantics & the Bodleian Shelley Manuscripts: Vol. 4). xix, 322p. 1985. text 45.00 (*0-8240-6257-4*) Garland.

Poem's Two Bodies: The Poetics of the 1590 Faerie Queene. David L. Miller. LC PR2358.M48. 311p. 1991. reprint ed. pap. 96.50 (*0-608-02541-0*, 206318500004) Bks Demand.

Poems West from Ballina. Gerald J. Shea. 50p. (Orig.). 1987. pap. 3.00 (*0-9618637-0-6*) Oak St Bks.

Poems with a Message. Carla S. Bell. (Orig.). 1997. pap. write for info. (*1-57553-453-3*) Watermrk Pr.

***Poems Without Poetry: Twenty Five Years of Poetry.** abr. ed. Jose Brites. Ed. by Peregrinacao Publications Staff. (Poetry/ Poesia Ser.: No. 7). Orig. Title: Poemas Sem Poesia; Imigramar; Vinte e Cinco Anos de Poesia. (ENG & POR.). 192p. 2001. reprint ed. boxed set 18.00 (*1-889358-13-4*, 26) Peregrinacao.

Poems Written & Published During the American Revolutionary War. Philip M. Freneau. LC 76-11754. 616p. 1976. reprint ed. lib. bdg. 90.00 (*0-8201-1173-2*) Schol Facsimiles.

Poems Written Between the Years 1768 & 1794. Philip Freneau. 1972. 59.95 (*0-8490-0852-2*) Gordon Pr.

Poems Written Between the Years 1768 & 1794. Philip M. Freneau & Lewis Leary. LC 76-11752. 480p. 1976. reprint ed. lib. bdg. 75.00 (*0-8201-1172-4*) Schol Facsimiles.

Poems Written for Sbek's Mummies, Marie Menken & Other Important Persons, Places & Things. Ed. by Anne Paolucci. 1977. pap. 6.95 (*0-918680-03-4*) Griffon House.

Poems You Ought to Know. Elia W. Peattie. LC 75-98084. (Granger Index Reprint Ser.). 1977. 20.95 (*0-8369-6085-8*) Ayer.

Poems 1819-1822, Poems in the Autograph of Lord Byron: Facsimile of Manuscripts in Pierpont Morgan Library, Vol. III. George Gordon Byron. Ed. by Jerome J. McGann & Alice Levine. LC 88-2416. (Manuscripts of the Younger Romantics & the Bodleian Shelley Manuscripts). 468p. 1988. text 90.00 (*0-8240-6252-3*) Garland.

Poems 1974-1996. Jeffrey Carson. LC 98-108716. 1997. pap. 24.95 (*3-7052-0085-2*, Pub. by Poetry Salzburg) Intl Spec Bk.

***Poems/Poems: Poems by Gerardo Deniz.** Gerardo Deniz. 2000. 12.00 (*0-918786-51-7*) Lost Roads.

Poemthought Equation(s) Mark Sonnenfeld. 36p. 1995. pap. 3.00 (*1-887379-01-0*) M Sonnenfeld.

***Poe's Children: Connections Between Tales of Terror & Detection.** Tony Magistrale & Sidney Poger. LC 98-53779. 148p. (C). 1999. pap. text 25.95 (*0-8204-4070-1*) P Lang Pubng.

Poe's Helen. C. Ticknor. LC 72-6294. (Studies in Poe: No. 23). (Illus.). 1972. reprint ed. lib. bdg. 75.00 (*0-8383-1632-8*) M S G Haskell Hse.

Poe's Helen Remembers. Ed. by John C. Miller. LC 79-742. (Illus.). 528p. 1980. text 40.00 (*0-8139-0771-3*) U Pr of Va.

Poe's Major Crisis: His Libel Suit & New York's Literary World. Sidney P. Moss. LC 74-100089. 256p. reprint ed. pap. 79.40 (*0-608-11984-9*, 202342400033) Bks Demand.

Poe's Mother: Selected Drawings of Djuna Barnes. Djuna Barnes. LC 95-42960. (Illus.). 240p. (Orig.). 1993. 29.95 (*1-55713-143-0*) Sun & Moon CA.

Poe's "Pym" Critical Explorations. Ed. by Richard Kopley. LC 92-2775. 367p. 1992. text 49.95 (*0-8223-1235-2*); pap. text 19.95 (*0-8223-1246-8*) Duke.

Poe's Rhymes. Helen Ensley. 1981. pap. 2.50 (*0-910556-17-2*) Enoch Pratt.

Poe's Short Stories: Notes. J. M. Lybyer. (Cliffs Notes Ser.). 72p. (Orig.). (C). 1981. pap. text 4.95 (*0-8220-1046-1*, Cliff) IDG Bks.

Poe's Tell-Tale Clocks. Dennis Eddings. 1994. pap. 3.95 (*0-910556-30-X*) Enoch Pratt.

Poeseys Forever. Wendell Metzger. Ed. by Joyce Carbone. 94p. 1997. pap. 6.95 (*1-878116-73-8*) JVC Bks.

Poeseys Only. Wendell Metzger. Ed. by Joyce Carbone. (Illus.). 52p. (Orig.). 1997. pap. 5.95 (*1-878116-66-5*) JVC Bks.

Poeseys Then but Mostly Now II. Wendell Metzger. Ed. by Joyce Carbone. 56p. 1997. pap. 5.95 (*1-878116-80-0*) JVC Bks.

Poesia. 224p. 1982. pap. 12.95 (*0-7859-5148-2*) Fr & Eur.

Poesia. Ramon De Campoamor Y Campoosorio. (SPA.). 192p. 1983. pap. 10.95 (*0-7859-5140-7*) Fr & Eur.

Poesia. Miguel De Cervantes Saavedra. (SPA.). 125p. 1972. 8.95 (*0-8288-7169-8*, S7742) Fr & Eur.

Poesia. Garcilaso De La Vega. (SPA.). 132p. 1977. 4.95 (*0-8288-7127-2*) Fr & Eur.

Poesia. Luis De Leon. (SPA.). 129p. 1977. 11.95 (*0-8288-7120-5*, S7942) Fr & Eur.

Poesia. Salvador De Madariaga. (Nueva Austral Ser.: Vol. 89). (SPA.). 1991. pap. text 24.95 (*84-239-1889-0*) Elliots Bks.

Poesia. Gongora. (SPA.). 126p. 1979. 4.95 (*0-8288-7124-8*, S7977) Fr & Eur.

Poesia. Juan Ramon Jimenez. (SPA.). 129p. 1946. 4.50 (*0-8288-7134-5*, S5643) Fr & Eur.

Poesia. Antonio Machado. (SPA.). pap. 10.95 (*84-206-1602-8*, Pub. by Alianza Editorial) Continental Bk.

Poesia. unabridged ed. Leon. (SPA.). pap. 5.95 (*84-410-0049-2*, Pub. by Bookking Intl) Distribks Inc.

Poesia. unabridged ed. Angel Manrique. (SPA.). pap. 5.95 (*84-410-0011-5*, Pub. by Bookking Intl) Distribks Inc.

Poesia. 8th ed. Ruben Dario. 144p. 1991. pap. 9.95 (*0-7859-5206-3*) Fr & Eur.

Poesia - Novo (Poetry - Novo) 2nd ed. Salvador Novo. (SPA.). 180p. 1993. 13.99 (*968-16-4449-2*, Pub. by Fondo) Continental Bk.

Poesia Afroantillana. Leslie N. Wilson. LC 79-54892. (Coleccion Ebano y Canela). (SPA.). 182p. (Orig.). 1981. pap. 10.00 (*0-89729-237-5*) Ediciones.

Poesia Afroantillana y Negrista: Puerto Rico, Republica Dominica, Cuba. Jorge L. Morales. LC 80-25893. 456p. 1981. pap. 10.00 (*0-8477-3230-4*) U of PR Pr.

Poesia, Casi Siempre: Ensayos. Eugenio Florit. (SPA.). 1978. pap. 10.00 (*84-399-8746-3*) Edit Mensaje.

Poesia Castellana Completa. unabridged ed. Garcilaso De La Vega. (SPA.). pap. 5.95 (*84-410-0010-7*, Pub. by Bookking Intl) Distribks Inc.

Poesia Completa. Garcilaso De la Vega. Ed. by Juan F. Alcina. (Nueva Austral Ser.: No. 96). (SPA.). 1991. pap. text 24.95 (*84-239-1896-3*) Elliots Bks.

Poesia Completa (Complete Poetry) Efrain Huerta. (SPA.). 623p. 1992. reprint ed. 27.99 (*968-16-3002-5*, Pub. by Fondo) Continental Bk.

Poesia de Jose Gautier Benitez. Miriam Curet De Anda. LC 80-17629. (Coleccion Mente y Palabra). (Illus.). 158p. 1980. 5.00 (*0-8477-0570-6*); pap. 4.00 (*0-8477-0571-4*) U of PR Pr.

Poesia De Luis Pales Matos. 2nd ed. Miguel Enguidanos. LC 76-8010. (UPREX, Estudios Literarios Ser.: No. 47). (SPA.). 111p. 1976. pap. 1.50 (*0-8477-0047-X*) U of PR Pr.

Poesia de Nicolas Guillen: Cuatro Elementos Sustancialez. Jorge M. Ruscalleda. LC 76-1828. 310p. (C). 1975. 5.00 (*0-8477-0518-8*); pap. 4.00 (*0-8477-0519-6*) U of PR Pr.

Poesia de Pales Matos. Luis Pales Matos & Mercedes Lopez-Baralt. (SPA.). 800p. 1995. 34.95 (*0-8477-0193-X*) U of PR Pr.

Poesia de Valle-Inclan: Del Simbolismo Al Expresionism. Lopez E. Gonzalez. 197p. (C). 1973. 5.00 (*0-8477-0506-4*); pap. 4.00 (*0-8477-0507-2*) U of PR Pr.

Poesia en Exodo: Antologia de Poesias Cubanas del Exilio 1959-1969. Ana R. Nunez. (SPA.). 1970. pap. 12.00 (*0-89729-006-2*) Ediciones.

Poesia en Jose Marti, Juan Ramon Jimenez, Alfonso Reyes, Federico Garcia Lorca y Pablo Neruda. Eugenio Florit. LC 78-55266. 1978. pap. 10.95 (*0-89729-194-8*) Ediciones.

Poesia Espanola y Otros Estudios, Vol. 9. Damaso Alonso. (SPA.). 706p. 1993. pap. 150.00 (*84-249-1408-2*) Elliots Bks.

Poesia Femenina Actual de Sudamerica. Franklin Proano. 59.50 (*1-882528-04-2*) Scripta.

Poesia in Voz Alta in the Theater of Mexico. Roni J. Unger. LC 80-25889. 184p. 1981. text 27.50 (*0-8262-0333-7*) U of Mo Pr.

Poesia Juglaresca & Juglares. Origenes de las Literaturas Romanicas. Ramon Menendez Pidal. (Nueva Austral Ser.: No. 159). (SPA.). 1991. pap. text 39.95 (*84-239-1959-5*) Elliots Bks.

Poesia Lirica. Espronceda. (SPA.). 126p. 1976. 4.50 (*0-8288-7125-6*, S20231) Fr & Eur.

Poesia Lirica. 8th ed. Lope de Vega. 154p. 1984. pap. 7.95 (*0-7859-5188-1*) Fr & Eur.

***Poesia Medieval.** Spain. (SPA.). 1999. 13.00 (*84-481-0668-7*, McGraw-H College) McGrw-H Hghr Educ.

Poesia Moral (Polimnia), No. 42. Francisco De Quevedo. Ed. by Alfonso Rey. (Textos B Ser.). 360p. 1999. 72.00 (*1-85566-058-X*, Pub. by Tamesis Bks Ltd) Boydell & Brewer.

Poesia, 1915-1956. 5th rev. ed. Luis Pales Matos. (SPA.). 304p. 1974. 5.00 (*0-88473-212-6*) U of PR Pr.

Poesia No Eres Tu (Poetry . . . It's Not You!) 2nd ed. Rosario Castellanos. (SPA.). 336p. 1975. pap. 16.99 (*968-16-1004-0*, Pub. by Fondo) Continental Bk.

Poesia Paisajistica Espanola, 1940-1970: Estudio Y Antologia. Diego Marin. (Monagrafias A Ser.: Vol. LVII). (SPA.). 296p. (C). 1976. 45.00 (*0-7293-0026-9*, Pub. by Tamesis Bks Ltd) Boydell & Brewer.

Poesia Popular Contempranea: Poesia General. Julia Aguilar. (SPA.). 52p. 1992. pap. 4.99 (*1-882263-00-6*) J A Pubns.

Poesia Popular Quechua see Quechua Peoples Poetry

***Poesia Renacentista.** Garcilaso De La Vega. (SPA.). 1999. 13.00 (*84-481-0619-9*, McGraw-H College) McGrw-H Hghr Educ.

Poesia, Sociedad y Cultura: Dialogos y Retratos Del Peru Colonial. Marta Bermudez-Gallegos. 189p. 49.50 (*0-916379-99-X*) Scripta.

Poesia y Poetas. Luis Mario. LC 83-81718. (SPA.). 126p. (Orig.). 1984. pap. 8.95 (*0-89729-337-1*) Ediciones.

Poesia y Poetica de Vicente Huidobro. Mireya Camurati. (SPA.). 210p. 1980. pap. 12.50 (*0-685-13896-8*, 3024) Ediciones Norte.

Poesia y Politica in Pablo Neruda: Analisis del "Canto General" Maria M. Sola. (Coleccion Mente y Palabra). (SPA.). 294p. 1980. 10.00 (*0-8477-0560-9*); pap. 9.00 (*0-8477-0561-7*) U of PR Pr.

Poesia y Profecia del Antiquo Testamento. C. H. Benson. Tr. by Fernando P. Villalobos from ENG. (Curso para Maestros Cristianos Ser.: No. 2).Tr. of Broadening Your Biblical Horizon. (SPA.). 122p. 1972. pap. 7.99 (*0-89922-010-X*) Caribe Betania.

Poesia y Prosa Literaria Vol. X: Obras Completas. Damaso Alonso. (SPA.). 1994. pap. 150.00 (*0-614-00241-9*) Elliots Bks.

Poesia y Sociedad. Hugo Achugar. (SPA.). 229p. 1988. pap. 12.00 (*0-318-39832-X*) Ediciones Norte.

Poesias. Luis De Leon. (SPA.). 200p. 1953. 6.95 (*0-8288-7135-3*) Fr & Eur.

Poesias. Juan Melendez Valdes. Ed. by Cesar Real Ramos. (Nueva Austral Ser.: Vol. 217). (SPA.). 1991. pap. text 24.95 (*84-239-7217-8*) Elliots Bks.

Poesias. Francisco De Sa De Miranda. cxxxvi, 965p. reprint ed. write for info. (*0-318-71629-1*) G Olms Pubs.

Poesias. 3rd ed. Miguel Hernandez. 304p. 1979. pap. 13.95 (*0-7859-5196-2*) Fr & Eur.

Poesias Completas. Luis Cartana. (SPA.). Date not set. pap. write for info. (*0-89729-541-2*) Ediciones.

***Poesias Completas.** Federico Garcia Lorca. (SPA.). 1999. pap. 9.98 (*968-15-0472-0*) Ed Mex.

Poesias Completas. Antonio Machado. Ed. by Manuel Alvar. (Nueva Austral Ser.: Vol. 33). (SPA.). 1991. pap. text 29.95 (*84-239-1833-5*) Elliots Bks.

Poesias Completas. Jorge Manrique. Ed. by Miguel A. Perez Priego. (Nueva Austral Ser.: Vol. 152). (SPA.). 1991. pap. text 24.95 (*84-239-1952-8*) Elliots Bks.

Poesias Completas. Escuela Salmantina. Fray L. De Leon. (Nueva Austral Ser.: Vol. 41). (SPA.). 1991. pap. text 24.95 (*84-239-1841-6*) Elliots Bks.

Poesias Completas y Otras Paginas. San Juan De La Cruz. (SPA.). 125p. 1976. 12.95 (*0-8288-7167-1*, S39827) Fr & Eur.

Poesias Completas y Pequenos Poemas en Prosa en Orden Cronologico. Julian De Casal. Ed. by Esperanza Figueroa. LC 93-71467. (Coleccion Clasicos Cubanos). (SPA., Illus.). 400p. (Orig.). 1993. pap. 39.00 (*0-89729-688-5*) Ediciones.

Poesias de Antonio Garcia Gutierrez. Antonio Garcia Gutierrez. Ed. by Joaquin de Entrambasabuas. (SPA.). 421p. 1968. pap. 100.00 (*0-614-00224-9*) Elliots Bks.

Poesias de Lucila E. Azcuy: Poesias de Ayer y de Hoy. Para Siempre... Lucila E. Azcuy. LC 81-69540. (Coleccion Espejo de Paciencia). (SPA., Illus.). 67p. (Orig.). 1982. pap. 5.95 (*0-89729-267-7*) Ediciones.

Poesias Escogidas. Miguel de Unamuno. (SPA.). 185p. 1972. 7.95 (*0-8288-7096-9*) Fr & Eur.

Poesias Ineditas de Cristobal Mosquera. Cristobal Mosquera. Ed. by Guillermo Diaz Plaja. (SPA.). 239p. 1968. pap. 100.00 (*0-614-00213-3*) Elliots Bks.

Poesias Ineditas de Juan Melendez Valdes. Juan Melendez Valdes. Ed. by Antonio Rodriguez Monino. (SPA.). 259p. 1968. 100.00 (*0-614-00218-4*) Elliots Bks.

Poesias Ineditas U Olvidadas. Emilia P. Bazan. Ed. by Maurice Hemingway. (Exeter Hispanic Text Ser.: No. 51). (SPA.). 200p. 1996. pap. text 17.95 (*0-85989-339-1*, Pub. by Univ Exeter Pr) Northwestern U Pr.

Poesias Inmortales para Toda Ocasion. Rene De la Puente. (SPA.). 1997. pap. 16.98 (*968-13-2529-X*) Edit Diana.

Poesias Liricas. Tirso De Molina. (SPA.). 228p. 1980. 10.25 (*0-8288-7026-8*) Fr & Eur.

Poesias Liricas, el Estudiante de Salamanca. Jose de Espronceda. (SPA.). pap. 10.95 (*84-239-0917-4*, Pub. by Espasa Calpe) Continental Bk.

Poesias Para la Infancia. Maria U. Alicia. (SPA.). (ps-k). 1997. pap. text 9.98 (*968-409-940-1*) Edamex.

Poesias para Recordar un Pasado. Hector M. Cotto-Falcon. (SPA.). 16p. (Orig.). 1996. pap. 4.95 (*0-9652064-0-8*) Edit Naboria.

Poesias, Prosas y Pensamientos: La Familia, 3 vols., Set. Ed. by Gloria Sepulveda. (SPA., Illus.). 234p. (Orig.). 1996. pap. 14.95 (*1-888867-07-8*) Biblos Pr.

Poesie. Saint-John Perse, pseud. (FRE.). 16p. 1961. pap. 10.95 (*0-7859-1315-7*, 2070256790) Fr & Eur.

Poesie Allemande de Roumanie: Entre Heteronomie et Dissidence (1944-1990) Claire De Oliveira. (Contacts Ser.: Series III, Vol. 32). (FRE.). 400p. 1995. 54.95 (*3-906754-17-0*, Pub. by P Lang) P Lang Pubng.

Poesie Bis ca. 1430 H. Fuat Sezgin. (Geschichte des Arabischen Schrifttums Ser.: Vol. 2). (GER.). xii, 808p. 1996. 235.50 (*90-04-04376-4*) Brill Academic Pubs.

Poesie de Langue Francaise: Anthologie Thematique. Ed. by Anne De Ravel et al. (Illus.). 196p. 1985. pap. 14.00 (*0-86980-471-5*, Pub. by Univ Natal Pr) Intl Spec Bk.

Poesie Depuis Baudelaire. Henri Lemaitre. 368p. 1965. 39.95 (*0-8288-7422-0*) Fr & Eur.

Poesie der Niedersachsen, 6 vols. Ed. by Christian F. Weichmann. 1990. reprint ed. 430.00 (*3-262-01216-5*) Periodicals Srv.

Poesie der Teilnahme Kritiken, 1980-1994. Peter Schjeldahl. (GER.). 320p. 1996. text 19.50 (*3-364-00356-4*) Gordon & Breach.

Poesie der Troubadours. Friedrich C. Diez. xxii, 314p. 1966. reprint ed. write for info. (*0-318-71454-X*) G Olms Pubs.

Poesie des Dilettantismus: Zur Rezeption und Wirkung Leopold von Sacher-Masochs. Svetlana Milojevic. (German Studies in Canada: Vol. 11). (GER.). 282p. 1998. 48.95 (*3-631-33230-0*) P Lang Pubng.

Poesie Di Peire Raimon De Tolosa. Peire Raimon. Ed. by Alfredo Cavaliere. LC 80-2181. reprint ed. 29.50 (*0-404-19010-3*) AMS Pr.

Poesie du Journalisme. Jean Cocteau. (FRE.). 260p. 1973. 19.95 (*0-8288-9131-1*, M3309) Fr & Eur.

Poesie Erotique de Germain Nouveau: Une Lecture des Valentines. Alexandre L. Amprimoz. (Stanford French & Italian Studies: Vol. 28). 76p. 1983. pap. 56.50 (*0-915838-09-5*) Anma Libri.

Poesie Est Impossible en 1981. Geoffrey Strickland. (C). 1989. 30.00 (*0-907839-16-9*, Pub. by Brynmill Pr Ltd) St Mut.

Poesie et Profondeur. J. P. Richard. (FRE.). 1976. pap. 14.95 (*0-7859-2673-9*) Fr & Eur.

Poesie Francaise: Premiers Excercises d'Analyse. Jean-Paul Carton. XII, 291p. (C). 1998. pap. text 29.95 (*0-8204-4054-X*) P Lang Pubng.

Poesie Galloise des XII-XIIIe Siecles. Joseph Vendryes. LC 78-72652. (Celtic Language & Literature Ser.: Goidelic & Brythonic). reprint ed. 39.50 (*0-404-17605-4*) AMS Pr.

Poesie Ininterrompue. Paul Eluard. (Poesie Ser.). (FRE.). 160p. 1969. pap. 7.95 (*2-07-030097-8*) Schoenhof.

Poesie Ininterrompue et la Poetique de Paul Eluard. Vernier. (De Proprietatibus Litterarum Ser.: Practica XXVII). 18.95 (*0-685-34115-1*) Fr & Eur.

Poesie Interrompue. Paul Eluard. (FRE.). 1969. pap. 10.95 (*0-8288-3857-7*, F100040) Fr & Eur.

Poesie Lyrique des Troubadors, 2 vols. in 1. Alfred Jeanroy. LC 72-1608. reprint ed. 52.50 (*0-404-08350-1*) AMS Pr.

Poesie, 1913-1926. Paul Eluard. (FRE.). 1970. pap. 10.95 (*0-8288-3858-5*, F100030) Fr & Eur.

Poesie per I Romeni: Italian Poetry. Angelo Pendola.Tr. of Poetry for the Romanians. (ITA.). 99p. 1990. 20.00 (*0-89304-539-X*); pap. 10.00 (*0-89304-538-1*) Cross-Cultrl NY.

Poesie Scherzevoli: Italian Poetry. Giuseppe M. Calvino. 251p. 1990. pap. 10.00 (*0-89304-665-5*) Cross-Cultrl NY.

Poesie Symboliste. P. M. Roinard et al. LC 77-11482. reprint ed. 40.00 (*0-404-16343-2*) AMS Pr.

P

Poesie und Kunst der Araber in Spanien und Sicilien, 2 vols. in 1. Adolf F. Schack. xii, 733p. 1979. reprint ed. write for info. (*3-487-06731-5*) G Olms Pubs.
Poesie Volgari, 2 vols. Lorenzo De Medici. LC 71-172718. (Renaissance Library: No. 2). reprint ed. 34.50 (*0-404-07872-9*) AMS Pr.
Poesies see Oeuvres Completes
Poesies. Paul Claudel. (FRE.). 1970. pap. 10.95 (*0-8288-3852-6*, F105180) Fr & Eur.
Poesies. Paul Claudel. (Poesie Ser.). (FRE.). pap. 7.95 (*2-07-030375-6*) Schoenhof.
Poesies. Marceline Desbordes-Valmore. (Poesie Ser.). (FRE.). pap. 13.95 (*2-07-032243-2*) Schoenhof.
Poesies. Kenneth Gaburo. 1976. 7.00 (*0-939044-07-2*) Lingua Pr.
Poesies. Arthur Rimbaud. (FRE.). pap. 5.95 (*2-87714-132-2*, Pub. by Bookking Intl) Distribks Inc.
Poesies. Arthur Rimbaud. (FRE.). 1984. pap. 10.95 (*0-7859-3122-8*) Fr & Eur.
Poesies. Paul Valery. (Coll. Soleil Ser.). 14.50 (*0-685-36606-5*); pap. 9.95 (*2-07-030282-2*) Schoenhof.
Poesies. François Villon. Ed. by Roger Dufournet. (FRE.). 1973. pap. 12.95 (*0-7859-2774-3*) Fr & Eur.
Poesies. Francois Villon. (Poesie Ser.). (FRE.). pap. 9.95 (*2-07-032069-3*) Schoenhof.
Poesies. unabridged ed. Stephane Mallarme. (FRE.). pap. 5.95 (*2-87714-162-4*, Pub. by Bookking Intl) Distribks Inc.
Poesies: Album de Vers. Paul Valery. (FRE.). 1966. pap. 11.95 (*0-7859-2767-0*) Fr & Eur.
Poesies: Avec: Une Saison en Enfer, Illuminations. Arthur Rimbaud. Ed. by Louis Forestier. (FRE.). 157p. 1992. pap. 8.95 (*0-7859-1493-5*, 2277231533) Fr & Eur.
Poesies: Edition Critique. Arthur Rimbaud. (FRE.). 232p. 1966. pap. 24.95 (*0-7859-5381-7*) Fr & Eur.
Poesies: Poesies Choix de Vers de Circonstance. Stephane Mallarme. (FRE.). 1966. pap. 10.95 (*0-8288-3865-8*, F67270) Fr & Eur.
Poesies: (Poesies Choix de vers de Circonstance; Poemes d'Enfance et de Jeunesse) Stephane Mallarme. (Poesie Ser.). (FRE.). pap. 11.95 (*2-07-032716-7*) Schoenhof.
Poesies - Ecrits Politiques, Vol. I. Louis-Claude De Saint-Martin. Ed. by Robert Amadou. viii, 314p. reprint ed. write for info. (*0-318-71409-4*) G Olms Pubs.
Poesies Choisies. Alfred De Vigny. (FRE., Illus.). 96p. 1967. 6.95 (*0-8288-9671-2*, F75785) Fr & Eur.
Poesies Choisies. Pierre De Ronsard. Ed. by Francois Joukovsky. (FRE., Illus.). 539p. 1989. 45.00 (*0-7859-1271-1*, 2040173234) Fr & Eur.
Poesies Completes. La Peruse. Ed. by Coleman. (Exeter French Texts Ser.: Vol. 81). (FRE.). 125p. Date not set. pap. text 19.95 (*0-85989-363-4*, Pub. by Univ Exeter Pr) Northwestern U Pr.
Poesies Completes. Arthur Rimbaud. (FRE.). (C). 1984. pap. 7.95 (*0-8442-1957-6*, VF1957-6) NTC Contemp Pub Co.
Poesies Completes. Francois Villon. (FRE.). 1972. pap. 10.95 (*0-7859-3095-7*) Fr & Eur.
Poesies Completes. Francois Villon. (FRE.). 383p. 1991. pap. 16.95 (*0-7859-1471-4*, 2253057029) Fr & Eur.
Poesies Completes, 3 vols., Set. rev. ed. Theophile Gautier. (FRE.). 842p. 1970. 38.95 (*0-7859-0071-3*, M2350) Fr & Eur.
Poesies Completes see Oeuvres Completes
Poesies Completes Tome 1: Les Complaintes. Premiers Poemes. Jules Laforgue. (Poesie Ser.). (FRE.). 1979. pap. 15.95 (*2-07-032181-9*) Schoenhof.
Poesies Completes Tome 2: L'Imitation de Notre Dame la Lune. Le Concile Feerique. Etc... Jules LaForgue. (Poesie Ser.). (FRE.). 1979. pap. 11.95 (*2-07-032182-7*) Schoenhof.
Poesies de A. O. Barnabooth: Poesies Divers. V. Larbaud. (FRE.). 1987. pap. 10.95 (*0-8288-3863-1*, F109090) Fr & Eur.
Poesies de P. de Ronsard et Autres Poetes see Maitres Musiciens de la Renaissance Francaise
Poesies de Theodore De Banville, "Les Cariatides" Theodore De Banville. LC 75-41015. 1976. reprint ed. 39.50 (*0-404-14504-3*) AMS Pr.
Poesies de Theodore De Banville, "Odes Funambulesques" Theodore De Banville. LC 75-41016. (BCL Ser. II). reprint ed. 45.00 (*0-404-14505-1*) AMS Pr.
Poesies du Roi Francois 1er, de Louise de Savoie, Duchesse D'Angouleme, de Marguerite, Reine de Navarre. Marguerite D'Angouleme. (FRE.). 243p. 1970. reprint ed. 75.00 (*0-7859-5529-1*) Fr & Eur.
Poesies Du Troubadour Albertet. Albertet de Sestero. Ed. by Jean Boutiere. LC 80-2173. reprint ed. 24.50 (*0-404-19001-4*) AMS Pr.
Poesies et Souvenirs. Gerard De Nerval. Ed. by Maurice Richier. (FRE.). 1974. pap. 18.95 (*0-7859-2775-1*) Fr & Eur.
Poesies et Souvenirs. Gerard De Nerval. (Poesie Ser.). (FRE.). 1974. pap. 14.95 (*2-07-032127-4*) Schoenhof.
Poesies, Melanges, Variete see Oeuvres
Poesies, 1960-1961. Roland Morisseau. (FRE.). 170p. 1993. pap. write for info. (*2-89135-042-1*) Guernica Editions.
Poesies, 1913-1926. Paul Eluard. (Poesie Ser.). (FRE.). 224p. 1970. pap. 9.95 (*2-07-031808-7*) Schoenhof.
Poesies, 1934-1943: La Pluie sur les Boulevards, Des Tonnes de Semences, Toujours. Jacques Audiberti. (FRE.). 266p. 1976. pap. 26.95 (*0-7859-1144-8*, 2070294765) Fr & Eur.
Poesies, Une Saison en Enfer, Illuminations. Arthur Rimbaud. (Poesie Ser.). (FRE.). 318p. 1981. pap. 9.95 (*2-07-031955-5*) Schoenhof.
Poet. Michael Connelly. 1996. 22.95 (*0-614-15483-9*) Little.
Poet. large type ed. Michael Connelly. LC 96-16366. 1996. 25.95 (*1-56895-330-5*, Compass) Wheeler Pub.
Poet. Michael Connelly. 512p. 1997. reprint ed. mass mkt. 7.99 (*0-446-60261-2*, Pub. by Warner Bks) Little.
Poet? Criminal? Madman? Poems. Ewa Lipska. Tr. by B. Plebanek & T. Howard from POL. LC 91-72165. 96p. (Orig.). 1991. pap. 16.95 (*1-85610-011-1*, Pub. by Forest Bks) Dufour.
Poet & a Filthy Play-Maker: New Essays on Christopher Marlowe. Ed. by Kenneth Friedenreich et al. LC 85-47999. (Studies in the Renaissance: No. 14). 1988. 52.50 (*0-404-62284-4*) AMS Pr.
Poet & Audience in the Argonautica of Apollonius. Robert V. Albis. 168p. 1996. 52.50 (*0-8476-8315-X*); pap. 21.95 (*0-8476-8316-8*) Rowman.
Poet & Hero in the Persian Book of Kings. Olga M. Davidson. (Myth & Poetics Ser.). 208p. 1994. text 42.50 (*0-8014-2780-0*) Cornell U Pr.
Poet & Killer Chronicles. Kei Kunihiro. LC 95-77864. (Illus.). 128p. (Orig.). 1995. pap. 15.00 (*1-55618-154-X*) Brunswick Pub.
Poet & Other Poems. Raymond G. Dandridge. LC 73-18573. reprint ed. 21.50 (*0-404-11384-2*) AMS Pr.
Poet & Painter. Andrew Causey. 280p. (C). 1989. 85.00 (*1-872971-15-6*, Pub. by Redcliffe Pr Ltd) St Mut.
Poet & Painter: Allan Ramsay, Father & Son, 1684-1784. Iain Gordon Brown & National Library of Scotland. LC 85-117162. 51 p. 1984. 0.00 (*0-902220-63-2*) Nat Lib Scot.
Poet & Peasant: Through Peasant Eyes. Kenneth E. Bailey. 1983. pap. 25.00 (*0-8028-1947-8*) Eerdmans.
Poet & Pilot: Antoine de Saint-Exupery. John Phillips. (Illus.). 1994. 40.00 (*1-881616-23-1*, Pub. by Scalo Pubs) Dist Art Pubs.
Poet & Politician of Puerto Rico: Don Luis Munoz Marin. Carmen T. Bernier-Grand. LC 94-21985. (Illus.). 128p. (J). (gr. 4 up). 1995. 15.95 (*0-531-06887-0*); lib. bdg. 16.99 (*0-531-08737-9*) Orchard Bks Watts.
Poet & Printer in Colonial & Federal America: Some Bibliographical Perspectives. Roger E. Stoddard. (Illus.). 97p. 1983. pap. 10.00 (*0-912296-59-3*) Am Antiquarian.
***Poet & the Countess: Hugo Von Hofmannsthal's Correspondence with Countess Ottonie Degenfeld.** Ed. by Marie-Therese Miller-Degenfeld. (Studies in German Literature, Linguistics & Culture). 384p. 2000. 65.00 (*1-57113-030-6*, Pub. by Camden Hse) Boydell & Brewer.
Poet & the Donkey. May Sarton. 128p. 1996. pap. 11.00 (*0-393-31553-3*) Norton.
Poet & the Donkey. May Sarton. (Illus.). 128p. 1984. reprint ed. pap. 3.95 (*0-393-30159-1*) Norton.
Poet & the Dream Girl: The Love Letters of Lilian Steichen & Carl Sandburg. Ed. by Margaret Sandburg. LC 86-25001. (Illus.). 292p. 1987. 16.95 (*0-252-01386-7*) U of Ill Pr.
Poet & the Dream Girl: The Love Letters of Lilian Steichen & Carl Sandburg. Margaret Sandburg. 292p. 1999. pap. text 22.95 (*0-252-06849-1*) U of Ill Pr.
Poet & the Flea: On Beat, Image & Milieu of Poetry. G. W. Sherman. (Orig.). 1971. pap. 4.00 (*0-685-00354-X*) Cobra Pr.
Poet & the Historian: Essays in Literary & Historical Biblical Criticism. Ed. by Richard E. Friedman. LC 83-9035. (Harvard Semitic Studies: Vol. 26). 171p. 1983. reprint ed. pap. 53.10 (*0-608-02836-3*, 206390300007) Bks Demand.
Poet & the Machine. Paul Ginestier. Tr. by Martin B. Friedman. 1961. pap. 14.95 (*0-8084-0248-X*) NCUP.
Poet & the Natural World in the Age of Gongora. M. J. Woods. (Oxford Modern Languages & Literature Monographs). 1978. 34.95 (*0-19-815533-6*) OUP.
Poet & the Paragon. Rita Boucher. 224p. 1999. mass mkt. 4.99 (*0-451-19578-7*, Sig) NAL.
Poet & the Prince: Ovid & Augustan Discourse. Alessandro Barchiesi. LC 96-49230. 285p. 1997. 48.00 (*0-520-20223-6*, Pub. by U CA Pr) Cal Prin Full Svc.
Poet & the Thief. S. J. Revich. (Tales from the East Ser.). (Illus.). 158p. (J). (gr. 5-7). 1989. 13.95 (*0-935063-71-4*); pap. 10.95 (*0-935063-72-2*) CIS Comm.
Poet Apart: A Literary Biography of the Bengali Poet. Clinton B. Seely. LC 88-40262. (Jibanananda Das (1899-1954) Ser.). 344p. 1991. 55.00 (*0-87413-356-4*) U Delaware Pr.
Poet As a Citizen, & Other Papers. Arthur T. Quiller-Couch. LC 75-41219. reprint ed. 27.50 (*0-404-14585-X*) AMS Pr.
Poet As Critic. Ed. by Frederick P. McDowell. LC 67-12675. 127p. reprint ed. 39.40 (*0-8357-9466-0*, 201476700093) Bks Demand.
Poet As Mythmaker: A Study of Edwin Muir. Ed. by Don Y. Lee. 121p. (C). 1990. 34.50 (*0-939758-21-0*) Eastern Pr.
Poet As Mythmaker: A Study of Symbolic Meaning in Taras Sevcenko. George G. Grabowicz. LC 82-81227. (Harvard Ukrainian Research Institute Monograph). 186p. 1990. text 20.00 (*0-674-67852-4*) Harvard Ukrainian.
Poet As Performer. Don Cusic. 136p. (Orig.). (C). 1991. pap. text 18.00 (*0-8191-8397-0*); lib. bdg. 44.00 (*0-8191-8396-2*) U Pr of Amer.
Poet As Philosopher. Charles E. Trinkaus. 1979. 37.00 (*0-300-02327-8*) Yale U Pr.
***Poet As Provocateur: Heinrich Heine & His Critics.** George F. Peters. LC 99-49775. (Literary Criticism in Perspective Ser.). (Illus.). 256p. 2000. 55.00 (*1-57113-161-2*) Camden Hse.
Poet As Thinker: Holderlin in France. Geert Lernout. (COMLIT Ser.). xii, 138p. 1994. 60.00 (*1-879751-98-4*) Camden Hse.
Poet As Warrior. Chuck Taylor. 40p. (Orig.). (C). 1989. pap. 4.00 (*0-941720-73-X*) Slough Pr TX.
Poet Assassinated. Guillaume Apollinaire. Tr. by Matthew Josephson. (Illus.). 158p. 1999. reprint ed. pap. 13.95 (*1-878972-29-4*, Pub. by Exact Change) SPD-Small Pr Dist.
Poet at Its Desk. Brita Bergland. 1987. pap. 8.00 (*0-942433-12-2*) Awede Pr.
Poet at the Breakfast-Table. Oliver W. Holmes. 1986. reprint ed. lib. bdg. 24.95 (*0-89966-546-2*) Buccaneer Bks.
Poet at the Breakfast Table. Oliver W. Holmes. (Notable American Authors Ser.). 1992. reprint ed. lib. bdg. 75.00 (*0-7812-3158-2*) Rprt Serv.
Poet at the Breakfast Table: He Talks with His Fellow Boarders & the Reader. Oliver W. Holmes. 360p. 1968. reprint ed. 18.00 (*0-403-00069-6*) Scholarly.
Poet Auden: A Personal Memoir. A. L. Rowse. LC 87-149279. 138p. 1987. write for info. (*0-413-40390-4*) Heinemann.
Poet Be Like God: Jack Spicer & the San Francisco Renaissance. Lewis Ellingham & Kevin Killian. LC 97-32883. (Illus.). 459p. 1998. 35.00 (*0-8195-5308-5*, Wesleyan Univ Pr) U Pr of New Eng.
Poet-Chief: The Native American Poetics of Walt Whitman & Pablo Neruda. James Nolan. LC 93-2379. 270p. 1994. 16.95 (*0-8263-1484-8*) U of NM Pr.
Poet Could Not but Be Gay: Some Legends of My Lost Youth. James Kirkup. 240p. 1991. 34.00 (*0-7206-0823-6*, Pub. by P Owen Ltd) Dufour.
Poet Dying: Heinrich Heine's Last Years in Paris. Ernst Pawel. LC 94-40744. 209p. 1995. 23.00 (*0-374-23538-4*) FS&G.
Poet from Prison. Jude Benton. 32p. (Orig.). 1994. pap. 6.00 (*1-878149-27-X*) Counterpoint Pub.
Poet from the City of the Angels: Poems & Photographs: 1969-1989. Michael Andrews. (Illus.). 234p. (Orig.). 1990. pap. 19.95 (*0-941017-16-8*) Bombshelter Pr.
***Poet Game: A Novel.** Salar Abdoh. LC 99-55845. 240p. 2000. text 23.00 (*0-312-20954-1*, Picador USA) St Martin.
Poet in America: Winfield Townley Scott. Scott Donaldson. LC 75-38568. 414p. reprint ed. pap. 128.40 (*0-8357-7736-7*, 203609300002) Bks Demand.
Poet in Despair: A Diary of the Great Depression. Royal Murdoch. LC 73-89987. 1974. write for info. (*0-914290-00-2*) Royal Murdoch.
Poet in Motion: Through Poetry. Dee Frances. Date not set. pap. 8.95 (*1-885519-02-8*) DDDD Pubns.
Poet in New York. rev. ed. Federico Garcia Lorca. Ed. by Christopher Maurer. Tr. by Greg Simon & Steven F. White. LC 97-49953. (Illus.). 320p. 1998. pap. text 16.00 (*0-374-52540-4*, Noonday) FS&G.
Poet in Pomfret, Poems by Maxim Konecky. Maxim Konecky. Ed. by John E. Westburg. (Illus.). 68p. 1968. pap. 7.00 (*0-87423-004-7*) Westburg.
Poet in the Desert. Charles E. Wood. 1973. 250.00 (*0-8490-0854-9*) Gordon Pr.
Poet in the Poem. George T. Wright. LC 74-2404. 167p. (C). 1974. reprint ed. 25.00 (*0-87752-169-7*) Gordian.
Poet in the Theatre. Ronald Peacock. LC 86-22749. 211p. 1986. reprint ed. lib. bdg. 59.50 (*0-313-25220-3*, PPOE, Greenwood Pr) Greenwood.
***Poet in Waiting.** Kaizer Ukinstoff. 56p. 2000. pap. 9.99 (*1-892668-16-5*) Prospect Pr.
Poet Is a Little God: Creationist Verse by Vicente Huidobro. 2nd rev. ed. Vicente Huidobro. Tr. by Jorge Garcia-Gomez. LC 89-24984. (Xenos Dual-Language Book Ser.). (SPA.). xxxii, 182p. (C). 1996. pap. 13.00 (*0-89370-945-X*) Xenos Riverside.
Poet L'a Dit. Charles Peguy. pap. 5.95 (*0-685-37045-3*) Fr & Eur.
Poet Lucan. M. Morford. (Bristol Classical Paperbacks Ser.). 104p. 1996. pap. text 25.95 (*1-85399-488-X*, Pub. by Brist Class Pr) Focus Pub-R Pullins.
Poet Moropanta's Kekavali: A Series of the Peacock's Screams. Tr. by P. V. Bobde. LC 94-900471. (C). 1994. 18.00 (*81-208-1115-1*, Pub. by Motilal Bnarsidass) S Asia.
Poet, Mystic, Modern Hero: Fernando Rielo Pardal. Zelda I. Brooks. 200p. 1991. 49.50 (*0-916379-85-X*) Scripta.
Poet, 1981. Ed. by Doris I. Nemeth et al. (Autumn Ser.). (Illus.). 400p. 1981. pap. 11.00 (*0-932192-03-3*) Fine Arts Soc.
Poet, 1983. Ed. by Doris I. Nemeth et al. (Autumn Ser.: 1983). (Illus.). 400p. 1983. pap. 11.50 (*0-932192-05-X*) Fine Arts Soc.
***Poet of a Morning: Herman Melville & the "Redburn Poem"** Jeanne Howes. 2000. 37.95 (*0-932274-57-9*) Cadmus Eds.
Poet of Civic Courage: The Films of Francesco Rosi. Ed. by Carlo Testa. LC 96-28759. 208p. 1996. pap. 20.95 (*0-275-95800-0*, Praeger Pubs) Greenwood.
Poet of Civic Courage: The Films of Francesco Rosi, 59. Ed. by Carlo Testa. LC 96-28759. (Contributions to the Study of Popular Culture Ser.). 208p. 1996. 65.00 (*0-313-30278-2*, Greenwood Pr) Greenwood.
Poet of Expressionist Berlin: The Life & Work of Georg Heym. Patrick Bridgwater. (Illus.). 320p. 1992. text 59.95 (*1-870352-75-0*, Pub. by Libris) Paul & Co Pubs.
Poet of the Dunes: Songs of the Dunes & the Outer Shore; with Others in Varying Modes & Moods. Harry Kemp. LC 88-70770. (Provincetown Classics in History, Literature, & Art Ser.: No. 1). 104p. 1988. reprint ed. pap. 6.00 (*0-945135-00-9*) Cape Cod Pilgrim.
Poet of the Ghetto: Morris Rosenfeld. Edgar J. Goldenthal. LC 97-40778. (YID.). 412p. 1998. 39.50 (*0-88125-613-7*) Ktav.
Poet of Wall Street. Nelson J. Kjos. 80p. (C). 1992. 11.95 (*0-9620917-1-5*) James Pub Ltd.
Poet of Wall Street. 2nd ed. Nelson J. Kjos. 88p. 1995. 12.95 (*0-9620917-2-3*) James Pub Ltd.
Poet on Demand: The Life, Letters, & Works of Celia Thaxter. 2nd ed. Jane E. Vallier. LC 94-13822. (Illus.). 309p. 1994. reprint ed. pap. 14.95 (*0-914339-47-8*, Pub. by P E Randall Pub) U Pr of New Eng.
***Poet on Watch.** Angela Williamston. Ed. by Esther Abercrombie. (Illus.). 96p. 1999. pap. 14.95 (*0-9674984-9-X*, ISBN713) Freeverse Pubng.
Poet or Nothing at All: The Tubingen & Basel Years of Hermann Hesse. Richard C. Helt. LC 96-11390. (Illus.). 272p. 1996. pap. 59.95 (*1-57181-049-8*); pap. 19.95 (*1-57181-075-7*) Berghahn Bks.
Poet-Painter: Paintings by Rabindranath Tagore. Mulk-Raj Anand. (Illus.). 86p. 1992. 18.00 (*1-85127-039-6*, Pub. by Tricolour Bks) Asia Pub Hse.
Poet Philosophers. Goldie L. Morales. (Illus.). 48p. (Orig.). 1983. pap. 3.00 (*0-910083-16-9*) Heritage Trails.
Poet-Physician: Keats & Medical Science. Donald C. Goellnicht. LC 83-47618. 303p. 1984. reprint ed. pap. 94.00 (*0-608-00905-9*, 206169900010) Bks Demand.
Poet President of Texas: The Life of Mirabeau B. Lamar, President of the Republic of Texas. Stanley Siegel. 176p. 1977. 15.00 (*0-8363-0153-6*, PA7-39-7226) Jenkins.
Poet, Public, & Performance in Ancient Greece. Ed. by Lowell Edmunds & Robert W. Wallace. LC 97-676. 200p. 1997. text 37.50 (*0-8018-5575-6*) Johns Hopkins.
Poet Reclining. Ken A. Smith. 1982. pap. 18.95 (*0-906427-51-7*, Pub. by Bloodaxe Bks) Dufour.
Poet Reclining. Ken A. Smith. 1989. 29.95 (*0-906427-50-9*, Pub. by Bloodaxe Bks) Dufour.
Poet Robert Browning & His Kinsfolk by His Cousin Cyrus Mason. Ed. by W. Craig Turner. LC 81-86286. (Illus.). 268p. 1983. 24.00 (*0-918954-38-X*) Baylor Univ Pr.
Poet Sa'di: A Persian Humanist. John D. Yohannan. (Persian Studies: No. 11). 162p. (Orig.). 1987. pap. text 19.50 (*0-8191-5740-6*) U Pr of Amer.
Poet Saints of India. M. Sivaramkrishna & Sumita Roy. 1996. write for info. (*81-207-1864-X*) Sterling Pubs.
Poet Shen Yueh, (441-513) The Reticent Marquis. Richard B. Mather. LC 87-1138. 272p. 1988. reprint ed. pap. 84.40 (*0-608-06469-6*, 206670200009) Bks Demand.
Poet, the People, the Spirit. Dorn. (NFS Canada Ser.). 1993. pap. 8.95 (*0-88922-101-4*) Genl Dist Srvs.
Poet to His Beloved: The Early Love Poems of William Butler Yeats. 9th ed. William Butler Yeats. 64p. 1985. text 9.95 (*0-312-61986-3*) St Martin.
Poet Toilers in Many Fields. Robert A. Watson. LC 72-8528. (Essay Index Reprint Ser.). 1977. reprint ed. 23.95 (*0-8369-7336-4*) Ayer.
Poet Tree. Jeanine Jensen. 168p. (Orig.). 1996. pap. write for info. (*1-57502-167-6*, PO775) Morris Pubng.
Poet Tree. Sharron L. Mcelmeel. LC 93-20268. (Illus.). xvi, 186p. 1993. pap. text 23.50 (*1-56308-102-4*) Teacher Ideas Pr.
Poet Tree Proof! Pat'rick N. Pugh. 1995. 18.00 (*1-883184-15-0*); pap. 9.95 (*1-883184-11-8*) PNP.
Poet under Black Banners: The Case of Ornulf Tigerstedt & Extreme Right-Wing Swedish Literature in Finland 1918-1944. Goran Walta. 347p. (Orig.). 1993. pap. 55.00 (*91-88300-28-5*) Coronet Bks.
Poet Within. Ed. by Diane Tait. LC 97-24555. 104p. (Orig.). 1997. pap. 9.95 (*0-9646450-6-8*) DeeMar Commun.
Poet Without a Name: Gray's "Elegy" & the Problem of History. Henry Weinfield. LC 90-9892. 304p. (C). 1991. 36.95 (*0-8093-1652-8*) S Ill U Pr.
Poet Wordsworth. Helen Darbishire. LC 79-14336. 182p. 1980. reprint ed. lib. bdg. 35.00 (*0-313-21483-2*, DAWO, Greenwood Pr) Greenwood.
Poeta Creator: Studien Zu Einer Figur der Antiken Dichtung. Godo Lieberg. (GER.). 189p. (C). 1982. pap. 40.00 (*90-70265-53-2*, Pub. by Gieben) J Benjamins Pubng Co.
Poeta de Tristibus: or The Poet's Complaint: A Poem in Four Canto's. Intro. by Harold Love. LC 92-24287. (Augustan Reprints Ser.: No. 149). 1971. reprint ed. 14.50 (*0-404-70149-3*, PR3291) AMS Pr.
Poeta en Nueva York. Federico Garcia Lorca. Ed. by Piero Menarini. (Nueva Austral Ser.: Vol. 146). (SPA.). 1991. pap. text 12.95 (*84-239-1946-3*) Elliots Bks.
Poeta en Nueva York. 8th ed. Federico Garcia Lorca. (SPA.). 184p. 1990. pap. 15.95 (*0-7859-4981-X*) Fr & Eur.
Poeta Nino (The Child Poet) Homero Aridjis. (SPA.). 175p. 1984. pap. 6.99 (*968-16-1655-3*, Pub. by Fondo) Continental Bk.
Poeta y la Escultura: La Espana Que Huntington Conocio. Jose Garcia-Mazas. (Illus.). 1962. 10.00 (*0-87535-097-6*) Hispanic Soc.
Poeta y Su Obra. Claudio Rodriguez. 146p. 1994. 10.00 (*84-599-3368-7*) Hispanic Inst.
Poetae Comici Graeci. Ed. by Rudolfo Kassel & C. Austin. (LAT.). xxxiii, 582p. (C). 1991. lib. bdg. 344.45 (*3-11-012840-3*, 239-91) De Gruyter.
Poetae Comici Graeci, Vol. IV. Ed. by Rudolfo Kassel & C. Austin. (GER.). 367p. 1983. 203.70 (*3-11-002405-5*) De Gruyter.
Poetae Comici Graeci: Damoxenus - Magnes, Band V. Ed. by Rudolfo Kassel & C. Austin. xxxii, 640p. 1987. lib. bdg. 332.15 (*3-11-010922-0*) De Gruyter.
Poetae Comici Graeci Band 7: Menecrates-Xenophon. Ed. by Rudolfo Kassel & C. Austin. xxxiii, 813p. (C). 1989. lib. bdg. 433.35 (*3-11-012035-6*) De Gruyter.
Poetae Comici Graeci Vol. VIII: Adespota. Ed. by Rudolfo Kassel & C. Austin. (LAT.). xxx, 525p. (C). 1995. lib. bdg. 300.00 (*3-11-014534-0*) De Gruyter.
Poetae Comici Graeci (PCG), Vol. VI. Ed. by R. Kassel & C. Austin. 448p. 1998. 225.00 (*3-11-015825-6*) De Gruyter.
Poetarum Comicorum Graecorum Fragmenta. August Meineke. x, 807p. 1989. reprint ed. write for info. (*3-487-09213-1*) G Olms Pubs.

An Asterisk (*) at the beginning of an entry indicates that the title is appearing for the first time.

Poetarum Epicorum Graecorum, Pt. I. rev. ed. Ed. by Bernabe. (GRE.). 1996. 69.50 (*3-8154-1706-6*, T1706, Pub. by B G Teubner) U of Mich Pr.

Poetarum Melicorum Graecorum Fragmenta, Vol. I: Alcman, Stesichorus, Ibycus. Ed. by Malcolm Davies. (GRE & LAT.). 350p. 1991. text 100.00 (*0-19-814046-0*) OUP.

Poetas Cubanos: Los Vidaurretta Antolgia. Ed. by Antolin Gonzalez-del-Valle & Luis Gonzalez-del-Valle. LC 88-61943. (SPA.). 183p. 1989. pap. 10.00 (*0-89295-056-0*) Society Sp & Sp-Am.

***Poetas de Hispanoamerica.** Spain. 1999. 13.00 (*84-481-1058-7*, McGrw-H College) McGrw-H Hghr Educ.

Poetas y Novelistas Ante la Musica. Federico Sopena. (Nueva Austral Ser.: Vol. 112). (SPA.). 1991. pap. text 24.95 (*84-239-1912-9*) Elliots Bks.

Poetaster. Ben Jonson. (Illus.). 304p. 1996. text 24.95 (*0-7190-1637-1*, Pub. by Manchester Univ Pr) St Martin.

Poete . . . Vos Papiers! Leo Ferre. (FRE.). 181p. 1977. pap. 10.95 (*0-7859-2389-6*, 2070369269) Fr & Eur.

Poete Assassine. Guillaume Apollinaire. 12.50 (*0-685-37175-1*) Fr & Eur.

Poete Assassine. Guillaume Apollinaire. (Poesie Ser.). (FRE.). pap. 15.95 (*2-07-032179-7*) Schoenhof.

Poete et le Shamisen: Avec: Le Poete et le Vase d'Encens, Jules ou l'Homme-aux-deux-cravates. Paul Claudel. 368p. 1970. 30.00 (*0-686-54419-6*) Fr & Eur.

Poete Noir et Autres Textes. Antonin Artaud. (ENG & FRE.). 64p. 1966. pap. 9.95 (*0-7859-5319-1*) Fr & Eur.

Poete Regarde la Croix. Paul Claudel. (FRE.). 290p. 1938. 10.95 (*0-7859-1114-6*, 2070215016) Fr & Eur.

Poetes. Louis Aragon. (FRE.). 256p. 1976. pap. 14.95 (*0-7859-3463-4*, 2070321614) Fr & Eur.

Poetes du XVI Siecle: Marot, Sceve, Louise Labe, J. du Bellay, Belleau, J. de Sponde, etc. 1120p. 9.95 (*0-686-56552-5*) Fr & Eur.

Poetes et Romanciers du Moyer Age: Poetes et Romanciers. deluxe ed. (Pleiade Ser.). (FRE.). 1312p. 68.95 (*0-686-56545-2*) Schoenhof.

Poetes Maudits. Paul M. Verlaine. LC 77-11495. (Symbolists Ser.). (FRE., Illus.). reprint ed. 34.50 (*0-404-16354-8*) AMS Pr.

Poetess. Helen Ruggieri. LC 79-18883. 1980. 8.00 (*0-931588-09-X*); pap. 3.50 (*0-931588-10-3*) Allegany Mtn Pr.

Poetheralogist: A Reference. A. Doyle. 50p. 1998. pap., wbk. ed. 21.95 (*1-890928-41-0*) Frieda Carrol.

Poethics: And Other Strategies of Law & Literature. Richard H. Weisberg. 384p. 1992. 44.00 (*0-231-07454-9*) Col U Pr.

Poeti Prieteni: Traduceri Din Franceza Si Engleza. Ed. by Xiquan Publishing House Staff. Tr. by Florentin Smarandache from ENG. (RUM.). 54p. (Orig.). (C). 1992. pap. 4.99 (*1-879585-22-7*) Erhus Univ Pr.

Poetic Abstract. Sue Hu. LC 90-90198. (Illus.). 116p. (Orig.). 1991. pap. 24.95 (*0-9623736-1-3*) WE Enterprises.

Poetic Abstract. limited ed. Sue Hu. LC 90-90198. (Illus.). 116p. (Orig.). 1991. 250.00 (*0-9623736-4-8*) WE Enterprises.

***Poetic Achievement of Ezra Pound.** Michael Alexander. 256p. 1998. pap. 22.50 (*0-7486-0981-4*, Pub. by Edinburgh U Pr) Col U Pr.

***Poetic Adventures of a Romantic Rogue.** Alipio A. DeVeyrz. 68p. 1999. pap. write for info. (*0-7392-0267-7*, PO3348) Morris Pubng.

Poetic Allusion & Poetic Embrace in Ovid & Virgil. R. A. Smith. LC 97-21532. 240p. (C). 1997. text 42.50 (*0-472-10706-2*, 10706) U of Mich Pr.

***Poetic & Didactic Literatures of Indian Buddhism.** M. Hahn. 2000. 202.00 (*90-04-10510-7*) Brill Academic Pubs.

Poetic & Musical Reflections: About Life, People, Living & Events. Benjamin B. Weybrew. LC 98-72952. (Illus.). 132p. 1998. lib. bdg. 25.95 (*0-923687-47-5*) Celo Valley Bks.

Poetic & Pictorial Elements in Works by 5 Writers in English - Milton, Pope, Wordsworth, Ruskin, Pound. Peter F. Morgan. LC 92-9968. (Illus.). 268p. 1992. lib. bdg. 89.95 (*0-7734-9503-7*) E Mellen.

Poetic & Verse-Criticism in the Reign of Elizabeth. Felix E. Schelling. (English Literature Ser.: No. 33). (C). 1970. reprint ed. pap. 29.95 (*0-8383-0068-5*) M S G Haskell Hse.

Poetic Anthlogy see Amado Nervo, Antologia Poetica

Poetic Argument: Studies in Modern Poetry. Jonathan Kertzer. 216p. (C). 1989. text 60.00 (*0-7735-0679-9*, Pub. by McG-Queens Univ Pr) CUP Services.

Poetic Art, Vol. 1. John Sasser. 1997. write for info. (*1-57074-362-2*) Greyden Pr.

Poetic Art of A. E. Housman: Theory & Practice. Bobby J. Leggett. LC 77-15792. 173p. reprint ed. pap. 53.70 (*0-7837-6032-9*, 204584500008) Bks Demand.

Poetic Art of A. K. Ramanujan. A. N. Dwivedi. LC 94-907323. (C). 1995. 16.00 (*81-7018-832-6*, Pub. by BR Pub) S Asia.

Poetic Art of Aldhelm. Andy Orchard. (Cambridge Studies in Anglo-Saxon England: No. 8). (Illus.). 328p. (C). 1994. text 85.00 (*0-521-45090-X*) Cambridge U Pr.

Poetic Artifice: A Theory of Twentieth-Century Poetry Veronica Forrest-Thomson. LC 79-303820. 168 p. 1978. 9.95 (*0-7190-0714-3*) St Martin.

Poetic Asides 1. Peter Russell. 121p. pap. write for info. (*3-7052-0205-7*, Pub. by Poetry Salzburg) Intl Spec Bk.

Poetic Asylum: Poems Written in Canada, 1968-1990. Jesus Lopez-Pacheco. 80p. 1991. pap. 9.95 (*0-919626-54-8*, Pub. by Brick Bks) Genl Dist Srvs.

Poetic Authority: Spenser, Milton, & Literary History. John Guillory. 224p. 1983. text 57.50 (*0-231-05540-4*); pap. text 20.00 (*0-231-05541-2*) Col U Pr.

Poetic Avant-Garde: The Groups of Borges, Auden, & Breton. Beret E. Strong. LC 97-18785. (Avant-Garde & Modernism Studies). 1997. 79.95 (*0-8101-1508-5*); pap. 24.95 (*0-8101-1509-3*) Northwestern U Pr.

Poetic Avant-Garde in Poland, 1918-1939. Bogdana Carpenter. LC 83-1126. (Publications on Russia & Eastern Europe of the School of International Studies: No. 11). (Illus.). 254p. 1983. 25.00 (*0-295-95996-7*) U of Wash Pr.

Poetic Bouquet Journal. Bramley. 1999. 9.95 (*1-84100-109-0*) Quadrillion Media.

Poetic Calm after the Desert Storm. Ed. by Ron R. Hansen. 192p. (Orig.). 1991. pap. 10.95 (*0-9630108-1-6*) Monterey Poetry.

Poetic Canvas. Theresa B. Meyerowitz. LC 87-46429. (Illus.). 128p. 1989. 30.00 (*0-8453-4817-5*, Cornwall Bks) Assoc Univ Prs.

Poetic Classics of 1997. Ed. by Kevin Piantanida. LC 97-65159. 300p. (Orig.). 1997. pap. 32.00 (*0-9656699-0-4*) Delta Pubns NJ.

Poetic Closure: A Study of How Poems End. Barbara H. Smith. LC 68-15034. 1996. pap. text 16.00 (*0-226-76343-9*, P381) U Ch Pr.

Poetic College. Davydd A. Saille. LC 95-36106. 115p. (Orig.). (C). 1996. pap. 9.95 (*1-887786-07-4*) Sky & Sage Bks.

***Poetic Concoctions: Grades 2-4.** Patricia Buob & Sally Eyre. (Illus.). 64p. 1999. pap., teacher ed. 6.95 (*1-889369-38-1*, TI0800) Teaching Ink.

Poetic Configurations: Essays in Literary History & Criticism. Lowry Nelson, Jr. 352p. 1992. text 45.00 (*0-271-00800-8*) Pa St U Pr.

Poetic Craft in the Early Greek Elegists. Arthur W. Adkins. LC 84-16203. 262p. 1985. lib. bdg. 42.00 (*0-226-00725-1*) U Ch Pr.

Poetic Craft in the Early Greek Elegists. Arthur W. Adkins. LC 84-16203. 262p. Date not set. reprint ed. 81.30 (*0-608-20976-7*, 205450400003) Bks Demand.

Poetic Craft of Bella Akhmadulina. Sonia I. Ketchian. LC 92-30850. (Illus.). 208p. 1993. 37.50 (*0-271-00916-0*) Pa St U Pr.

Poetic Creation: Inspiration or Craft. Carl Fehrman. LC 79-17901. 239p. 1980. reprint ed. pap. 74.10 (*0-7837-2965-0*, 205748900006) Bks Demand.

Poetic Creativity. Charlotte Dunn. 52p. (Orig.). 1993. pap. 4.95 (*0-9622849-6-3*) Papito.

Poetic Culture: Contemporary American Poetry Between Community & Institution. Christopher Beach. LC 99-27504. (Avant-Garde & Modernism Studies). 248p. 1999. pap. 17.95 (*0-8101-1678-2*) Northwestern U Pr.

Poetic Culture: Contemporary American Poetry Between Community & Institution. Christopher Beach. LC 99-27504. 248p. 1999. 59.95 (*0-8101-1677-4*) Northwestern U Pr.

Poetic Debussy: A Collection of His Song Texts & Selected Letters. Ed. by Margaret G. Cobb. Tr. by Richard Miller. LC 93-21462. (Eastman Studies in Music: Vol. 1). (Illus.). 350p. (C). 1994. reprint ed. 39.95 (*1-878822-33-0*) Univ Rochester Pr.

Poetic Delight. 2nd rev. ed. Lillian Thorp. LC 97-68326. 136p. 1997. reprint ed. 7.50 (*1-890869-13-9*) Chelsey Publ.

Poetic Designs: An Introduction to Meters, Verse Forms, & Figures of Speech. Stephen Adams. 240p. (C). 1997. pap. 16.95 (*1-55111-129-2*) Broadview Pr.

Poetic Dewdrops for Children. Mabel G. Haldeman. (Illus.). 304p. 1986. 12.95 (*0-9617506-0-X*) Inc Trustees Gospel Worker Soc.

Poetic Dialect of Sappho & Alcaeus. Anus M. Bowie. 1981. 24.95 (*0-88143-020-X*) Ayer.

Poetic Dialect of Sappho & Alcaeus. rev. ed. Angus M. Bowie. Ed. by W. R. Connor. LC 80-2641. (Monographs in Classical Studies). 1981. lib. bdg. 22.00 (*0-405-14029-0*) Ayer.

Poetic Diction: A Study in Meaning. 2nd ed. Owen Barfield. LC 87-22985. 238p. 1984. pap. 17.95 (*0-8195-6026-X*, Wesleyan Univ Pr) U Pr of New Eng.

Poetic Diction: A Study of Eighteenth Century Verse. Thomas Quayle. (BCL1-PR English Literature Ser.). 212p. 1992. reprint ed. lib. bdg. 79.00 (*0-685-54571-7*) Rprt Serv.

Poetic Diction in the Old English Meters of Boethius. Allan A. Metcalf. LC 72-94487. (De Proprietatibus Litterarum, Ser. Practica: No. 50). 164p. 1973. pap. text 32.35 (*90-279-2537-2*) Mouton.

Poetic Digs. Mabel D. Gilmore. 1997. pap. 10.00 (*0-87012-586-9*) McClain.

Poetic Drama of Paul Claudel. Joseph Chiari. LC 71-90365. (C). 1969. reprint ed. 50.00 (*0-87752-018-6*) Gordian.

Poetic Edda. Tr. by Carolyne Larrington. LC 96-5465. 367p. 1999. pap. 12.95 (*0-19-283946-2*) OUP.

Poetic Edda. Tr. by Henry A. Bellows from ICE. LC 91-39918. 472p. 1991. reprint ed. lib. bdg. 109.95 (*0-88946-783-8*) E Mellen.

Poetic Edda. rev. ed. Tr. by Lee M. Hollander. 375p. (C). 1986. reprint ed. pap. 16.95 (*0-292-76499-5*) U of Tex Pr.

Poetic Edda: Mythological Poems, Vol. II. Ed. & Comment by Ursula Dronke. (Illus.). 458p. 1997. text 120.00 (*0-19-811181-9*) OUP.

Poetic Edda in the Light of Archaeology. Birger Nerman. LC 76-43954. (Viking Society for Northern Research: Extra Ser.: Vol. 4). (Illus.). reprint ed. 39.50 (*0-404-60024-7*) AMS Pr.

***Poetic Effects: A Relevance Theory Perspective.** Adrian Pilkington. LC 99-88714. (Pragmatics & Beyond New Ser.: Vol. 75). xii, 209p. 2000. 65.00 (*1-55619-922-8*); pap. 34.95 (*1-55619-923-6*) J Benjamins Pubng Co.

Poetic Epistemologies: Gender & Knowing in Women's Language-Oriented Writing. Megan Simpson. LC 99-37947. (C). 2000. pap. text 18.95 (*0-7914-4446-5*) State U NY Pr.

Poetic Epistemologies: Gender & Knowing in Women's Language-Oriented Writing. Megan Simpson. LC 99-37947. 264p. (C). 2000. text 57.50 (*0-7914-4445-7*) State U NY Pr.

Poetic Equation: Conversations Between Nikki Giovanni & Margaret Walker. 1983. pap. 12.95 (*0-88258-088-4*) Howard U Pr.

***Poetic Expressions.** Viola E. Iverson. 52p. 1999. pap. 6.95 (*0-9644483-1-9*) Viola Iverson.

Poetic Expressions. Lovel G. Waiters. 1998. pap. write for info. (*1-888139-28-5*) Y Morris Carib.

Poetic Expressions in Nursing... Sharing the Caring. Susan J. Farese. Ed. by Mary A. Liotta. LC 93-61138. 128p. 1993. pap. 9.95 (*1-880254-10-7*) Vista.

Poetic Expressions of God's Love. Vaughn A. Foster. 90p. 1999. pap. write for info. (*0-7392-0086-0*, P02957) Morris Pubng.

Poetic Fantastic: Studies in an Evolving Genre, 40. Ed. by Patrick D. Murphy & Vernon Hyles. LC 89-11930. (Contributions to the Study of Science Fiction & Fantasy Ser.: No. 40). 226p. 1989. 59.95 (*0-313-26160-1*, MYT/, Greenwood Pr) Greenwood.

Poetic Feelings. Mary Ann Madgett. LC 95-94235. (Illus.). 60p. (Orig.). 1995. pap. 7.95 (*0-9645227-9-9*) Madgett Pub.

Poetic Feelings, Vol. I. Hoai Van Tu. LC 94-43310. 64p. 1995. pap. 12.95 (*0-7734-2744-9*) E Mellen.

Poetic Feelings, Vol. II. Hoai Van Tu. LC 94-43310. 64p. 1995. pap. 12.95 (*0-7734-2745-7*) E Mellen.

Poetic Fiction of Jose Lezama Lima. Raymond D. Souza. LC 83-1056. 160p. 1983. text 24.95 (*0-8262-0406-6*) U of Mo Pr.

Poetic Flights: Poems on Assorted Subjects. Harry A. Poole. 70p. 1995. 15.00 (*1-887189-06-8*); pap. 7.50 (*1-887189-15-7*) Symi Pub.

Poetic for Sociology: Toward a Logic of Discovery for the Human Sciences. Richard H. Brown. xvi, 320p. 1989. pap. text 17.95 (*0-226-07619-9*) U Ch Pr.

Poetic Form & British Romanticism. Stuart Curran. 288p. 1990. pap. text 22.00 (*0-19-506072-5*) OUP.

Poetic Friends: A Study of Literary Relations During the English Romantic Period. Warren Stevenson. LC 89-13048. (American University Studies: English Language & Literature: Ser. IV, Vol. 97). 209p. (C). 1989. text 35.95 (*0-8204-1043-8*) P Lang Pubng.

Poetic Garlands: Hellenistic Epigrams in Context. Kathryn J. Gutzwiller. LC 97-5676. (Hellenistic Culture & Society Ser.). 420p. 1997. 45.00 (*0-520-20857-9*, Pub. by U CA Pr) Cal Prin Full Svc.

Poetic Identity in Guillaume de Machaut. Kevin Brownlee. LC 83-14498. 279p. 1984. reprint ed. pap. 86.50 (*0-608-07460-8*, 206768700009) Bks Demand.

Poetic Image. Cecil Day Lewis. LC 83-45427. reprint ed. 29.50 (*0-404-20075-3*) AMS Pr.

***Poetic Imagination: An Anglican Spiritual Tradition.** William L. Countryman. LC 99-49300. (Traditions of Christian Spirituality Ser.). 214p. 2000. pap. 16.00 (*1-57075-307-5*) Orbis Bks.

Poetic Imagination in Black Africa: Essays on African Poetry. Tanure Ojaide. LC 96-16122. 168p. (Orig.). 1996. pap. 20.00 (*0-89089-855-3*) Carolina Acad Pr.

Poetic Injustice: A Rhyme Crime. George Statham. 120p. (Orig.). 1996. pap. 11.95 (*1-57502-165-X*, PO769) Morris Pubng.

Poetic Interaction: Language, Freedom, Reason. John McCumber. LC 88-19831. 504p. 1989. lib. bdg. 72.00 (*0-226-55703-0*) U Ch Pr.

Poetic Interaction: Language, Freedom, Reason. John McCumber. LC 88-19831. 504p. 1997. pap. text 30.00 (*0-226-55704-9*) U Ch Pr.

***Poetic Interlude.** Millie Crouch. 107p. 1999. pap. 5.95 (*1-888796-18-9*) ABWE Pubng.

Poetic Investigations: Singing the Holes in History. Paul Naylor. LC 99-29032. (Avant-Garde & Modernism Studies). 222p. 1999. pap. 19.95 (*0-8101-1668-5*) Northwestern U Pr.

Poetic Investigations: Singing the Holes in History. Paul Naylor. LC 99-29032. 208p. 1999. 59.95 (*0-8101-1667-7*) Northwestern U Pr.

Poetic Journeys of the Heart. Ed. by Charles E. Cravey. 1990. pap. 9.95 (*0-938645-44-7*) In His Steps.

Poetic Justice. S. G. Carrier. 104p. 1999. pap. 11.00 (*0-8059-4637-3*) Dorrance.

Poetic Justice. Amanda Cross. 176p. 1979. mass mkt. 4.99 (*0-380-44222-1*, Avon Bks) Morrow Avon.

Poetic Justice. Alicia Ralsey. 320p. 1994. mass mkt. 3.99 (*0-8217-4599-9*, Zebra Kensgtn) Kensgtn Pub Corp.

Poetic Justice. Fraser Sampson. (Illus.). 80p. (C). 1990. pap. 30.00 (*1-85352-903-6*, Pub. by HLT Pubns) St Mut.

Poetic Justice. L. A. Taylor. 1988. 16.95 (*0-8027-5701-4*) Walker & Co.

Poetic Justice. Nigel Tranter. 320p. 1997. text 27.00 (*0-340-62581-3*, Pub. by Hodder & Stought Ltd) Trafalgar.

Poetic Justice. Nigel Tranter. 320p. 1997. pap. 11.95 (*0-340-62582-1*, Pub. by Hodder & Stought Ltd) Trafalgar.

Poetic Justice: A DCI Jim Ashworth Investigation. Brian Battison. mass mkt. 9.95 (*0-7490-0419-3*) Allison & Busby.

Poetic Justice: A Memoir of My Father Roy Campbell. Anna C. Lyle. 156p. 1986. 100.00 (*0-930126-17-3*) Typographeum.

Poetic Justice: The Funniest, Meanest Things Ever Said About Lawyers. Jonathan Roth & Andrew Roth. LC 87-63575. 128p. (Orig.). 1994. pap. 9.95 (*0-87337-072-4*) Nolo com.

Poetic Justice: The Literary Imagination & Public Life. Martha C. Nussbaum. 128p. 1997. pap. 14.00 (*0-8070-4109-2*) Beacon Pr.

Poetic Knowledge: The Recovery of Education. James S. Taylor. LC 97-26325. 211p. (C). 1997. text 59.50 (*0-7914-3585-7*); pap. text 19.95 (*0-7914-3586-5*) State U NY Pr.

Poetic Land, Political Territory: Contemporary Art from Ireland. David Brett. (Illus.). 164p. 1995. pap. 25.00 (*0-9525020-0-3*, Pub. by Lund Humphries) Antique Collect.

***Poetic Landscape: A Contemporary Visual & Psychological Exploration.** Elizabeth Mowry. (Illus.). 160p. 2000. pap. 24.95 (*0-8230-4067-4*) Watsn-Guptill.

Poetic Landscape: The Art & Experience of Sandford R. Gifford. Ila Weiss. LC 84-40805. (American Art Ser.). (Illus.). 384p. 1988. 85.00 (*0-87413-199-5*) U Delaware Pr.

***Poetic Landscapes of Samuel Colman (1832-1920)** Maribeth Flynn. (Illus.). 12p. 1999. mass mkt. write for info. (*0-87920-009-X*) Kennedy Gall.

Poetic License: Essays on Modernist & Postmodernist Lyric. Marjorie Perloff. (Illus.). 352p. 1990. 49.95 (*0-8101-0843-7*); pap. 18.95 (*0-8101-0844-5*) Northwestern U Pr.

Poetic Madness & the Romantic Imagination. Frederick Burwick. (Illus.). 376p. 1996. 55.00 (*0-271-01488-1*) Pa St U Pr.

Poetic Medicines: The Healing Art of Poem-Making. John Fox. LC 97-8832. (Inner Work Bks.). 304p. 1997. pap. 16.95 (*0-87477-882-4*, Tarcher Putnam) Putnam Pub Group.

Poetic Memoirs of Lady Daibu. Tr. by Phillip T. Harries from JPN. LC 79-65519. 336p. 1980. 37.50 (*0-8047-1077-5*) Stanford U Pr.

Poetic Memories. Alan Rothman. 1998. pap. write for info. (*1-58235-106-6*) Watermrk Pr.

Poetic Messages from Mesa. unabridged ed. Monte Anderson. 20p. 1997. spiral bd. 5.00 (*1-929326-39-4*) Hal Bar Pubg.

Poetic Messages to My Students & Other Poems. Juan Pinaula. 1998. pap. write for info. (*1-57553-865-2*) Watermrk Pr.

Poetic Meter & Poetic Form. rev. ed. Paul Fussell, Jr. 190p. (C). 1979. pap. 25.63 (*0-07-553606-4*) McGraw.

Poetic Mind. Frederick C. Prescott. LC 83-1547. 308p. 1983. reprint ed. lib. bdg. 69.50 (*0-313-23925-8*, PRPO, Greenwood Pr) Greenwood.

***Poetic Negotiation of Identity in the Works of Brathwaite, Harris, Senior & Dabydeen: Tropical Paradise Lost & Regained.** Emily Allen Williams. LC 99-41710. (Caribbean Studies: Vol. 5). 172p. 1999. text 79.95 (*0-7734-7931-7*) E Mellen.

Poetic New-World. Ed. by Lucy H. Humphrey. LC 75-149105. (Granger Index Reprint Ser.). 1977. 31.95 (*0-8369-6230-3*) Ayer.

Poetic Notions. Elizabeth Ragsdale. 16p. 1993. pap. text 6.00 (*0-9641217-0-0*) Sea-Lark Print.

***Poetic Occasion From Milton to Wordsworth.** John Dolan. LC 98-54305. 242p. 2000. text 59.95 (*0-312-22094-4*) St Martin.

Poetic Odyssey. Don Petrucelle. 64p. (Orig.). 1996. pap. 9.95 (*0-9654297-0-9*) D Petrucelle.

Poetic Odysseys. Francine Swann. 52p. 1994. pap. 5.00 (*0-9645451-0-1*) F Swann Pubns.

Poetic Path. Eva O. Scott. 1998. pap. write for info. (*1-57553-996-9*) Watermrk Pr.

Poetic Patterns in Rutebeuf: A Study in Noncourtly Poetic Modes of the Thirteenth Century. Nancy F. Regalado. LC 70-104620. (Yale Romanitc Series, Second Ser.: No. 21). 384p. reprint ed. pap. 119.10 (*0-608-14258-1*, 202203300024) Bks Demand.

Poetic Penguins. William L. Boyd. LC 91-66936. 108p. 1992. 14.95 (*0-933598-36-X*) NC Wesleyan Pr.

Poetic Penguins. deluxe limited ed. William L. Boyd. LC 91-66936. 108p. 1992. 30.00 (*0-933598-37-8*) NC Wesleyan Pr.

Poetic Perception. Cherron M. Payne. 127p. 1997. pap. write for info. (*0-9662550-0-3*) C M Payne.

Poetic Perspectives Vol. 1: Preview Collection of Poems. 30p. 1996. 7.00 (*0-614-30276-5*) Costa Pubng.

Poetic Potentials in Information of Astronomy. Polish Academy of Science Staff. 1976. pap. 1.95 (*0-934982-05-8*) Primary Pr.

Poetic Potpourri. Jimmie Ahmed. (Illus.). 53p. 1997. pap. 12.00 (*0-9656152-0-0*) Jimmie Ahmed.

Poetic Power of Place: Comparative Perspectives on Austronesian Ideas of Locality. James J. Fox & Australian National University Staff. LC 98-205136. vi, 204p. 1997. 35.00 (*0-7315-2841-7*, Pub. by Aust Nat Univ) UH Pr.

Poetic Praise, Vol. I. Arica L. Coleman. 50p. (Orig.). 1993. pap. 10.00 (*1-883435-01-3*) Insight Pubns.

Poetic Presence & Illusion: Essays in Critical History & Theory. Murray Krieger. LC 79-14598. (Illus.). 351p. 1979. reprint ed. pap. 108.90 (*0-608-04034-7*, 206477000011) Bks Demand.

Poetic Process. W. G. Kudszus. LC 94-33678. (Texts & Contexts Ser.: Vol. 15). vii, 145p. 1995. text 35.00 (*0-8032-2727-2*) U of Nebr Pr.

Poetic Process. George Whalley. LC 73-5274. 256p. 1973. reprint ed. lib. bdg. 65.00 (*0-8371-6878-3*, WHPP, Greenwood Pr) Greenwood.

Poetic Prophecy: Life Cycles Within the Circle of Life. S. L. Williams. 103p. (Orig.). 1997. pap., per. 9.95 (*0-9657842-2-3*) S Williams.

Poetic Prophecy in Western Literature. Jan Wojcik & Raymond-Jean Frontain. LC 83-49339. 224p. 1984. 35.00 (*0-8386-3191-6*) Fairleigh Dickinson.

Poetic Realism in Scandinavia & Central Europe, 1820-1895. Clifford A. Bernd. (GERM Ser.). xvi, 243p. 1995. 65.00 (*1-57113-010-1*) Camden Hse.

Poetic Reflections. Gamalial H. Gooding. LC 99-98259. (Illus.). xi, 108p. (Orig.). pap. 12.00 (*0-9679367-0-5*, 04055) Divine Life.

P

An Asterisk (*) at the beginning of an entry indicates that the title is appearing for the first time.

Poetic Reflections. D. A. Pattie. LC 87-72042. 58p. (Orig.). 1987. pap. 1.95 (*0-911789-02-2*) Pattie Prop Inc.

Poetic Remaking: The Art of Browning, Yeats, & Pound. George Bornstein. LC 87-25789. 176p. 1988. lib. bdg. 35.00 (*0-271-00620-X*) Pa St U Pr.

Poetic Resemblance. Barbara Broughel. (Illus.). 24p. 1986. pap. 5.00 (*0-936739-00-2*) Hallwalls Inc.

Poetic Rhythm: An Introduction. Derek Attridge. 294p. (C). 1995. text 59.95 (*0-521-41302-8*) Cambridge U Pr.

Poetic Rhythm: An Introduction. Derek Attridge. 294p. (C). 1996. pap. text 18.95 (*0-521-42369-4*) Cambridge U Pr.

Poetic Rhythm: Structure & Performance: An Empirical Study in Cognitive Poetics. Reuven Tsur. (Illus.). 378p. 1998. write for info. (*3-906760-00-6*) P Lang.

Poetic Rhythm: Structure & Performance: An Empirical Study in Cognitive Poetics. Reuven Tsur. (Illus.). 378p. 1998. pap. text 50.95 (*0-8204-3444-2*) P Lang Pubng.

Poetic Shapes. Trina Gerson. (Illus.). 52p. (J). (ps-7). 1981. pap. text 2.95 (*0-9605878-0-2*) Anirt Pr.

Poetic Spirit. Ed. by Jef Sturm. 300p. 1998. 59.95 (*1-888680-31-8*) Poetry Guild.

Poetic Statement & Critical Dogma. Gerald Graff. LC 80-14318. 208p. 1994. pap. text 7.00 (*0-226-30601-1*) U Ch Pr.

Poetic Statement & Critical Dogma. Gerald Graff. LC 80-14318. 205p. reprint ed. pap. 63.60 (*0-608-08735-1*, 206937400004) Bks Demand.

Poetic Structure of the World: Copernicus & Kepler. Fernand Hallyn. Tr. by Donald Leslie from FRE. LC 89-35295. (Illus.). 367p. 1990. 28.95 (*0-942299-60-4*) Zone Bks.

Poetic Structure of the World: Copernicus & Kepler. Fernand Hallyn. Tr. by Donald Leslie from FRE. 1993. pap. 18.00 (*0-942299-61-2*) Zone Bks.

Poetic Style of Corneille's Tragedies: An Aesthetic Interpretation. Sharon Harwood-Gordon. (Studies in French Literature: Vol. 6). 224p. 1990. write for info. (*0-88946-569-X*) E Mellen.

Poetic Style of Erich Kaestner. John Winkleman. LC 57-63699. (Nebraska University Ser.: No. 13). 57p. reprint ed. pap. 30.00 (*0-608-30814-5*, 200288600015) Bks Demand.

***Poetic Sunrise.** Natasha Eisenman. 150p. 1999. pap. write for info. (*0-7392-0349-5*, PO3531) Morris Pubng.

***Poetic Tales.** Alfred H. Knight. 1999. pap. write for info. (*1-58235-238-0*) Watermrk Pr.

***Poetic Tales of the Longhorn Trail.** unabridged ed. Marybelle Land. (Illus.). 20p. 1998. spiral bd. 7.00 (*1-929326-37-8*) Hal Bar Pubg.

Poetic Theology of Love: Cupid in Medieval & Renaissance Literature. Thomas Hyde. LC 84-40368. (Illus.). 216p. 1986. 36.50 (*0-87413-273-8*) U Delaware Pr.

Poetic Theory, Poetic Practice: Papers of the Midwest Modern Language Association Presented at the Annual Meeting for 1968, October 17, 18 & 19, in Cincinnati, Ohio. fac. ed. Ed. by Robert E. Scholes. LC PN1031.S2. (Papers of the Midwest Modern Language Association: No. 1). 174p. 1969. reprint ed. pap. 54.00 (*0-7837-8034-6*, 204779000008) Bks Demand.

Poetic Thinking: An Approach to Heidegger. David Halliburton. LC 81-7542. (C). 1993. 22.50 (*0-226-31372-7*) U Ch Pr.

Poetic Thinking: An Approach to Heidegger. David Halliburton. LC 81-7542. 247p. reprint ed. pap. 76.60 (*0-608-09325-4*, 205419900004) Bks Demand.

***Poetic Thoughts.** Lydia Castillo. 2000. write for info. (*1-58235-572-X*) Watermrk Pr.

Poetic Thoughts. Eva O. Scott. 20p. (Orig.). 1995. pap. write for info. (*1-885206-19-4*, Iliad Pr) Cader Pubng.

Poetic Time Scroll's: A Journey into Sentimental Time! Frank Armanno, Sr. (Illus.). 48p. 1999. pap. 7.95 (*0-9671820-1-8*) Prog Time Corp.

Poetic Traditions of the English Renaissance. Ed. by Maynard Mack & George D. Lord. LC 82-1941. 336p. 1982. 40.00 (*0-300-02785-0*) Yale U Pr.

Poetic Tranquility. Gregory A. Dente. 1998. pap. 8.95 (*0-533-12679-7*) Vantage.

Poetic Truth. Robin Skelton. LC 78-57849. 131p. 1978. text 41.00 (*0-06-496253-9*, N6679) B&N Imports.

***Poetic Truth about Illict Drugs.** Kenneth E. Wimberly. LC 98-73640. (Illus.). 1998. mass mkt. 14.95 (*0-9666547-0-6*, 9809801) Anti-Drug Prods.

Poetic Truth & Transvaluation in Nietzsche's Zarathustra: A Hermeneutic Study. Ernest Joos. (American University Studies: Philosophy: Ser. V, Vol. 31). XIX, 180p. 1992. text 17.95 (*0-8204-0432-2*) P Lang Pubng.

Poetic Truths. Mia Sillanpaa. LC 94-90834. (Illus.). 46p. (Orig.). 1994. pap. 16.95 (*0-9643761-0-5*) M Sillanpaa.

Poetic Unreason & Other Studies. Robert Graves. LC 68-59244. 1968. reprint ed. 30.00 (*0-8196-0227-2*) Biblo.

Poetic Variables & Other Thoughts. Moritz E. Pape. (Illus.). 50p. (Orig.). 1990. text 4.50 (*0-9630599-1-2*, TXU432-733) Ltd Ex Pr.

Poetic Variety Show: Featuring Life, Love & Laughter. Harry S. Hunting. LC 91-90657. 133p. (Orig.). 1991. pap. 8.95 (*0-9631370-0-X*) H S Hunting.

Poetic Ventures Vol. 1: Introspection of a Poet. L. Louis Robinson. LC 90-92023. 138p. (Orig.). 1991. pap. text 12.95 (*0-9628034-0-5*) L L Robinson.

Poetic Vibrations of a Matured Butterfly. 2nd rev. ed. Arthur L. Conway. LC 92-73855. (Illus.). 120p. (Orig.). 1992. pap. 10.95 (*0-9633352-1-9*) A L Conway.

Poetic Vibrations of a Matured Butterfly, Poems & Parables. Arthur L. Conway. LC 92-90290. (Illus.). 117p. (Orig.). 1992. pap. 10.95 (*0-9633352-0-0*) A L Conway.

Poetic Vision: The Photographs of Anne Brigman. Susan Ehrens. 1995. write for info. (*0-89951-091-4*) Santa Barb Mus Art.

Poetic Vision of Robert Penn Warren. Victor H. Strandberg. LC 76-9503. 304p. 1977. 34.95 (*0-8131-1347-4*) U Pr of Ky.

Poetic Visions. Rochelle White. (Orig.). 1995. pap. write for info. (*1-57553-080-5*) Watermrk Pr.

Poetic Voice of America, Spring, 1997. Patricia Hamilton. LC 90-660082. (Illus.). 300p. 1997. lib. bdg. 44.95 (*0-923242-51-1*) Sparrowgrass Poetry.

Poetic Voice of Charles Cros: A Centennial Study of His Songs. Robert L. Mitchell. LC 76-24891. (Romance Monographs: No. 21). 1976. 26.00 (*84-399-5835-8*) Romance.

Poetic Voices: Discourse Linguistics & the Poetic Text. Timothy R. Austin. LC 93-41329. 240p. (Orig.). 1994. pap. text 24.95 (*0-8173-0726-5*) U of Ala Pr.

Poetic Voices of America, Fall 1996. Ed. by Patricia Hamilton. LC 90-660082. (Illus.). 395p. 1996. lib. bdg. 44.95 (*0-923242-49-X*) Sparrowgrass Poetry.

Poetic Voices of America, Fall 1997. Ed. by Patricia Hamilton. LC 90-640795. (Illus.). 360p. 1997. lib. bdg. 44.95 (*0-923242-55-4*) Sparrowgrass Poetry.

Poetic Voices of America, Fall 1998. Ed. by Patricia Hamilton. LC 90-660082. (Illus.). 333p. 1998. lib. bdg. 64.95 (*0-923242-62-7*) Sparrowgrass Poetry.

Poetic Voices of America, Fall 1990. Ed. by William H. Trent. LC 90-60975. 400p. 1990. lib. bdg. 44.95 (*0-923242-08-2*) Sparrowgrass Poetry.

Poetic Voices of America, Fall 1991. Ed. by William H. Trent. LC 91-60962. (Illus.). 340p. 1991. lib. bdg. 44.95 (*0-923242-14-7*) Sparrowgrass Poetry.

Poetic Voices of America, Fall 1992. Ed. by Patricia Hamilton. LC 90-660082. (Illus.). 460p. 1992. lib. bdg. 44.95 (*0-923242-20-1*) Sparrowgrass Poetry.

Poetic Voices of America, Fall 1994. Ed. by Patricia Hamilton. LC 90-660082. (Illus.). 448p. 1994. lib. bdg. 44.95 (*0-923242-34-1*) Sparrowgrass Poetry.

Poetic Voices of America, Fall 1995. Ed. by Patricia Hamilton. LC 90-660082. (Illus.). 454p. 1995. lib. bdg. 44.95 (*0-923242-43-0*) Sparrowgrass Poetry.

Poetic Voices of America, Spring 1998. Patricia Hamilton. LC 90-660082. (Illus.). 472p. 1998. lib. bdg. 59.95 (*0-923242-57-0*) Sparrowgrass Poetry.

Poetic Voices of America, Spring 1991. Ed. by William H. Trent. LC 90-62147. (Illus.). 296p. 1991. lib. bdg. 44.95 (*0-923242-10-4*) Sparrowgrass Poetry.

Poetic Voices of America, Spring 1992. Ed. by Patricia Hamilton. LC 91-62378. (Illus.). 376p. 1992. lib. bdg. 44.95 (*0-923242-16-3*) Sparrowgrass Poetry.

Poetic Voices of America, Spring 1993. Ed. by Patricia Hamilton. LC 90-660082. (Illus.). 336p. 1993. lib. bdg. 44.95 (*0-923242-22-8*) Sparrowgrass Poetry.

Poetic Voices of America, Spring 1994. Ed. by Patricia Hamilton. LC 90-660082. (Illus.). 408p. 1994. lib. bdg. 44.95 (*0-923242-30-9*) Sparrowgrass Poetry.

Poetic Voices of America, Spring 1995. Ed. by Patricia Hamilton. LC 90-660082. (Illus.). 404p. 1995. lib. bdg. 44.95 (*0-923242-36-8*) Sparrowgrass Poetry.

Poetic Voices of America, Spring 1996. Ed. by Patricia Hamilton. LC 90-660082. (Illus.). 360p. 1996. lib. bdg. 59.95 (*0-923242-45-7*) Sparrowgrass Poetry.

Poetic Voices of America, Summer 1995. Ed. by Patricia Hamilton. LC 90-660082. (Illus.). 364p. 1995. lib. bdg. 44.95 (*0-923242-40-6*) Sparrowgrass Poetry.

Poetic Voices of America, Summer 1997. Patricia Hamilton. LC 90-660082. (Illus.). 776p. 1997. lib. bdg. 44.95 (*0-923242-53-8*) Sparrowgrass Poetry.

Poetic Voices of America, Summer 1996. Ed. by Patricia Hamilton. LC 90-660082. (Illus.). 336p. 1996. lib. bdg. 39.95 (*0-923242-47-3*) Sparrowgrass Poetry.

Poetic Voices of America, Summer 1998. Ed. by Patricia Hamilton. LC 90-660082. (Illus.). 319p. 1998. lib. bdg. 64.95 (*0-923242-59-7*) Sparrowgrass Poetry.

Poetic Voices of America, Summer 1990. Ed. by William H. Trent. LC 90-660082. (Illus.). 335p. 1990. lib. bdg. 44.95 (*0-923242-06-6*) Sparrowgrass Poetry.

Poetic Voices of America, Summer 1991. Ed. by William H. Trent. LC 91-60035. (Illus.). 256p. 1991. lib. bdg. 44.95 (*0-923242-12-0*) Sparrowgrass Poetry.

Poetic Voices of America, Summer 1992. Ed. by Patricia Hamilton. LC 90-660082. (Illus.). 336p. 1992. lib. bdg. 44.95 (*0-923242-18-X*) Sparrowgrass Poetry.

Poetic Voices of America, Summer 1994. Ed. by Patricia Hamilton. LC 90-660082. (Illus.). 432p. 1994. lib. bdg. 44.95 (*0-923242-32-5*) Sparrowgrass Poetry.

***Poetic Wanderings.** Steve Baba. LC 99-61939. 140p. 1999. 25.00 (*0-7388-0374-X*); pap. 18.00 (*0-7388-0375-8*) Xlibris Corp.

Poetic Will: Shakespeare & the Play of Language. David Willbern. LC 96-37484. xix, 237p. 1997. text 37.50 (*0-8122-3389-1*) U of Pa Pr.

Poetic Wisdom: Poetic Wisdom: Revealing & Healing. Susan R. Makin. LC 98-16987. 246p. 1998. text 50.95 (*0-398-06878-X*); pap. text 37.95 (*0-398-06879-8*) C C Thomas.

Poetic Works of Flavien Ranaivo: L'Ombre et le Vent, Mes Chansons de Tourjours, Le Retour au Bercail. Flavien Ranaivo. (B. E. Ser.: No. 29). 1962. 25.00 (*0-8115-2980-0*) Periodicals Srv.

Poetic Works of Maurice de Guerin. Tr. by James Vest & Nancy F. Vest from FRE. LC 92-81519. 384p. 1992. lib. bdg. 43.95 (*0-87786-87-4*) Summa Pubns.

Poetic Works of Pilar E. Barrios: Piel Negra, Mis Cantos, Campo Afuera. Pilar E. Barrios. (B. E. Ser.: No. 25). 1959. 50.00 (*0-8115-2976-2*) Periodicals Srv.

Poetic Writings of Thomas Cradock, 1718-1770. Ed. by David C. Skaggs. LC 81-72059. (Illus.). 312p. 1983. 42.50 (*0-87413-206-1*) U Delaware Pr.

Poetica de Escritoras Hispanoamericanas al Alba del Proximo Milenio. Rojas-Trempe & Catharina Vallejo. LC 97-80049. (Coleccion Polymita). (SPA.). 248p. 1998. pap. 16.00 (*0-89729-850-0*, 850-0) Ediciones.

Poetica de la Frialdad: La Narrativa de Virgilio Pinera. Ed. by Fernando Valerio-Holguin. 128p. 1996. 34.50 (*0-7618-0549-4*) U Pr of Amer.

Poetica de la Oscuridad: La Recepcion Critica de las Soledades en el Siglo XVII. Joaquin R. Lozano. (Monagrafias A Ser.: No. 155). (SPA.). 234p. (C). 1994. 72.00 (*1-85566-026-1*, Pub. by Tamesis Bks Ltd) Boydell & Brewer.

Poetica de la Poblacion Marginal: Sensibilidades Determinantes. Ed. by James V. Romano. (Literature & Human Rights Ser.: No. 2). (SPA.). 488p. (Orig.). 1988. pap. 14.95 (*0-910235-20-1*) Prisma Bks.

Poetica de Transgresion en la Novelistica de Luisa Valenuela. Junamaria Cordones-Cook. LC 91-27570. (American University Studies: Romance Languages & Literature: Ser. II, Vol. 173). (SPA.). 118p. (C). 1992. text 35.95 (*0-8204-1584-7*) P Lang Pubng.

Poetica Erotica. Ronne R. Gleason. Ed. by Bob Lewanski. (Illus.). 167p. (Orig.). 1985. 3.50 (*0-9608030-1-7*) Taoist Pubs.

Poetical Alphabet. Benjamin P. Blood. (Surrealist Research & Development Monographs). 24p. 1972. pap. 10.00 (*0-941194-04-3*) Black Swan Pr.

Poetical & Dramatic Works, 2 vols. Charles Sedley. Ed. by Vivian De Sola Pinto. LC 70-85905. 1969. reprint ed. 87.50 (*0-404-05692-X*) AMS Pr.

Poetical & Dramatic Works, 2 vols. Charles Sedley. (BCL1-PR English Literature Ser.). 1992. reprint ed. lib. bdg. 150.00 (*0-7812-7399-4*) Rprt Serv.

Poetical & Dramatic Works of Thomas Randolph, 2 vols. Thomas Randolph. Ed. by William C. Hazlitt. LC 68-57192. 1972. reprint ed. 48.95 (*0-405-08874-4*) Ayer.

Poetical Books see Oxford Illustrated Old Testament: With Drawings by Contemporary Artists

Poetical Books: A Sheffield Reader. Ed. by David J. Clines. (Biblical Seminar Ser.: No. 41). 370p. 1997. pap. 19.95 (*1-85075-787-9*, Pub. by Sheffield Acad) CUP Services.

Poetical Career of Alexander Pope. Robert K. Root. 1990. 16.50 (*0-8446-1392-4*) Peter Smith.

Poetical Cat. rev. ed. Felicity Bast. 1996. 15.00 (*0-374-23540-6*) FS&G.

Poetical Cook-Book. Maria J. Moss. 144p. 1972. 3.95 (*0-405-02213-1*) Arno Press.

Poetical, Dramatic, & Miscellaneous Works, 6 vols. John Gay. LC 73-137415. reprint ed. 345.00 (*0-404-02790-3*) AMS Pr.

Poetical Effusions, 1814. Isabella Lickbarrow. LC 93-46504. (Revolution & Romanticism Ser.). 1994. 48.00 (*1-85477-167-1*) Continuum.

Poetical Eurythmics of an African Griot. limited unabridged ed. David Abdulai. Ed. by Henry Kyambalesa. 1997. pap. 9.95 (*0-9647012-7-8*, Dawn of a New Day) Konkori Intl.

Poetical Favorites: Yours & Mine. Compiled by Warren Snyder. LC 79-167482. (Granger Index Reprint Ser.). 1977. reprint ed. 26.95 (*0-8369-6287-7*) Ayer.

Poetical Histories, Repr. of 1671 Ed. Pierre Gautruche. Tr. by Marius D'Assigny. LC 75-27877. (Renaissance & the Gods Ser.: Vol. 32). (Illus.). 1976. lib. bdg. 34.00 (*0-8240-2081-2*) Garland.

Poetical Jest - My Gestful World. Robert G. English. 1997. pap. write for info. (*1-57553-602-1*) Watermrk Pr.

Poetical Manuscripts of Mark Akenside. Mark Akenside. (Illus.). 32p. (Orig.). 1988. pap. 15.00 (*0-943184-02-9*) Amherst Coll Pr.

Poetical Meditations - Meditations Poetiques. Alphonse De Lamartine. Tr. by Gervase Hittle from FRE. LC 92-43538. (Studies in French Literature: Vol. 14). 248p. 1993. text 89.95 (*0-7734-9221-6*) E Mellen.

Poetical Pathway of Life. Alvie C. Hutton. LC 97-91259. 1998. 13.95 (*0-533-12611-8*) Vantage.

Poetical Quotations from Chaucer to Tennyson. Samuel A. Allibone. 1972. 59.95 (*0-8490-0855-7*) Gordon Pr.

Poetical Quotations from Chaucer to Tennyson. Samuel A. Allibone. (Principle Works of Samuel Austin Allibone). 1989. reprint ed. lib. bdg. 79.00 (*0-7812-1787-3*) Rprt Serv.

***Poetical Reflections.** Tudor Whitticombe. 1999. pap. write for info. (*1-58235-311-5*) Watermrk Pr.

Poetical Review of the Literary & Moral Character of the Late Samuel Johnson. 3rd rev. ed. John Courtenay. LC 92-22689. (Augustan Reprints Ser.: No. 133). 1969. reprint ed. 14.50 (*0-404-70133-7*, PR4508) AMS Pr.

Poetical Tributes to the Memory of Abraham Lincoln. Ed. by J. N. Plotts. 1972. reprint ed. lib. bdg. 20.00 (*0-8422-8105-3*) Irvington.

Poetical Vagaries, Repr. of 1812 Ed. George Colman. LC 75-31182. (Romantic Context: Poetry 1789-1830 Ser.: Vol. 34). 1976. lib. bdg. 52.00 (*0-8240-2133-9*) Garland.

Poetical Vagaries of a Knight of the Folding Stick of Paste-Castle. deluxe limited ed. 62p. 1994. boxed set 235.00 (*1-886015-05-8*) Sandlins Bks.

Poetical Whims of Wilson: Come Walk with Me. Archie W. Wilson. Ed. by Melissa Cox. 120p. (Orig.). 1997. pap. 6.00 (*0-9658785-0-3*) A W Wilson.

***Poetical Works.** Samuel Taylor Coleridge & J. C. Mays. LC 00-21206. (Bollinger Ser.). 2001. write for info. (*0-691-09883-2*) Princeton U Pr.

Poetical Works. Alexander Pope. Ed. by Herbert Davis. (Oxford Paperbacks Ser.). (Illus.). 776p. 1978. pap. text 19.95 (*0-19-281246-7*) OUP.

Poetical Works. Edmund Spenser. Ed. by J. C. Smith & Ernest De Selincourt. (Oxford Standard Authors Ser.). 808p. 1961. pap. text 22.00 (*0-19-281070-7*) OUP.

Poetical Works, 5 vols. William Wordsworth. Ed. by Ernest De Selincourt & Helen Darbishire. Incl. Vol. 5. 508p. 1948. 105.00 (*0-19-811831-7*); (Oxford English Texts Ser.). write for info. (*0-318-54883-6*) OUP.

Poetical Works. deluxe ed. Percy Bysshe Shelley. Ed. by Thomas Hutchinson. (Oxford Standard Authors Ser.). 1971. 125.00 (*0-685-03767-3*) OUP.

Poetical Works. Mark Akenside. (BCL1-PR English Literature Ser.). 353p. 1992. reprint ed. lib. bdg. 89.00 (*0-7812-7317-X*) Rprt Serv.

Poetical Works. James Beattie. LC 72-25. (Select Bibliographies Reprint Ser.). 1977. reprint ed. 19.95 (*0-8369-9953-3*) Ayer.

Poetical Works. James M. Bell. Ed. by Bishop Arnett. LC 70-39423. reprint ed. 31.50 (*0-404-00005-3*) AMS Pr.

Poetical Works. William Blake. Ed. by William M. Rosetti. LC 79-13496. reprint ed. 47.50 (*0-404-07259-3*) AMS Pr.

Poetical Works. William Blake. (BCL1-PR English Literature Ser.). 453p. 1992. reprint ed. lib. bdg. 99.00 (*0-7812-7441-9*) Rprt Serv.

Poetical Works. William C. Bryant. (BCL1-PS American Literature Ser.). 130p. 1992. reprint ed. lib. bdg. 69.00 (*0-7812-6681-5*) Rprt Serv.

Poetical Works. Thomas M. Campbell. Ed. by Alfred Hill. LC 73-39665. (Select Bibliographies Reprint Ser.). 1977. reprint ed. 22.95 (*0-8369-9932-0*) Ayer.

Poetical Works. John Denham. (BCL1-PR English Literature Ser.). 362p. 1992. reprint ed. lib. bdg. 89.00 (*0-7812-7344-7*) Rprt Serv.

Poetical Works. Austin Dobson. 1988. reprint ed. lib. bdg. 75.00 (*0-7812-0033-4*) Rprt Serv.

Poetical Works. Ernest C. Dowson. 1988. reprint ed. lib. bdg. 49.00 (*0-317-90186-9*) Rprt Serv.

Poetical Works. Ernest C. Dowson. 1980. reprint ed. 49.00 (*0-403-00948-0*) Scholarly.

Poetical Works, 2 vols. in 1. Ebenezer Elliott. Ed. by Edwin Elliott. (Anglistica & Americana Ser.: No. 151). xviii, 834p. 1975. reprint ed. 122.20 (*3-487-05326-8*) G Olms Pubs.

Poetical Works, 2 vols. Giles Fletcher & Phineas Fletcher. 1981. reprint ed. lib. bdg. 59.00 (*0-403-00091-2*) Scholarly.

Poetical Works. John Gay. (BCL1-PR English Literature Ser.). 700p. 1992. reprint ed. lib. bdg. 109.00 (*0-7812-7353-6*) Rprt Serv.

Poetical Works. Charles G. Halpine. Ed. by R. B. Roosevelt. (Notable American Authors Ser.). 1992. reprint ed. lib. bdg. 75.00 (*0-7812-2998-7*) Rprt Serv.

Poetical Works. Joaquin Miller. (BCL1-PS American Literature Ser.). 587p. 1992. reprint ed. lib. bdg. 99.00 (*0-7812-6798-6*) Rprt Serv.

Poetical Works. Thomas Parnell. LC 70-39664. (Select Bibliographies Reprint Ser.). 1977. reprint ed. 19.95 (*0-8369-9942-8*) Ayer.

Poetical Works. Thomas Parnell. Ed. by John Mitford. (Anglistica & Americana Ser.: No. 158). xxxii, 185p. 1976. reprint ed. 37.70 (*3-487-05844-8*) G Olms Pubs.

Poetical Works. Christina Georgina Rossetti. (BCL1-PR English Literature Ser.). 507p. 1992. reprint ed. lib. bdg. 99.00 (*0-7812-7623-3*) Rprt Serv.

Poetical Works. William Shenstone. (BCL1-PR English Literature Ser.). 284p. 1992. reprint ed. lib. bdg. 79.00 (*0-7812-7400-1*) Rprt Serv.

Poetical Works. William Shenstone. 1854. reprint ed. 15.00 (*0-403-00124-2*) Scholarly.

Poetical Works, 10 vols. in 5. Robert Southey. (Anglistica & Americana Ser.: No. 79). (Illus.). 1977. reprint ed. 507.00 (*3-487-06244-5*) G Olms Pubs.

Poetical Works. Edmund C. Stedman. (Notable American Authors Ser.). 1999. reprint ed. lib. bdg. 125.00 (*0-7812-8908-4*) Rprt Serv.

Poetical Works. Bayard Taylor. (BCL1-PS American Literature Ser.). 361p. 1992. reprint ed. lib. bdg. 89.00 (*0-7812-6877-X*) Rprt Serv.

Poetical Works, 2 vols. James Thomson. (BCL1-PR English Literature Ser.). 1992. reprint ed. lib. bdg. 150.00 (*0-7812-7516-4*) Rprt Serv.

Poetical Works. John T. Trowbridge. (Notable American Authors). 1999. reprint ed. lib. bdg. 125.00 (*0-7812-9818-0*) Rprt Serv.

Poetical Works. John Trumbull. 1988. reprint ed. lib. bdg. 59.00 (*0-317-90280-6*) Rprt Serv.

Poetical Works, 2 vols. John Trumbull. (BCL1-PS American Literature Ser.). 1992. reprint ed. lib. bdg. 150.00 (*0-7812-6663-7*) Rprt Serv.

Poetical Works, 2 vols. John Trumbull. LC 30-20909. 1968. reprint ed. 59.00 (*0-403-00049-1*) Scholarly.

Poetical Works, 2 vols. Edward Young. (BCL1-PR English Literature Ser.). 1992. reprint ed. lib. bdg. 150.00 (*0-7812-7420-6*) Rprt Serv.

Poetical Works. 2nd ed. Percy Bysshe Shelley. Ed. by Thomas Hutchinson. (Oxford Standard Authors Ser.). 960p. 1970. pap. text 11.50 (*0-19-281069-3*) OUP.

Poetical Works. 3rd rev. ed. George Gordon Byron. Ed. by Frederick Page & John D. Jump. (Oxford Standard Authors Ser.). (Illus.). 934p. 1961. pap. text 21.00 (*0-19-281068-5*) OUP.

***Poetical Works, Pt. I.** Mary Christina Pegg. 48p. 1999. pap. 4.95 (*1-885206-79-8*) Cader Pubng.

Poetical Works see Complete Works of Algernon Charles Swinburne

Poetical Works: Definitive Edition, 2 vols. John Payne. LC 73-128418. 1973. reprint ed. 110.00 (*0-404-04946-X*) AMS Pr.

Poetical Works Vol. 1: Paradise Lost, Vol. 1. John Milton. Ed. by Helen Darbishire. 364p. 1953. text 75.00 (*0-19-811819-8*) OUP.

Poetical Works, 1842. Susanna Blamire. LC 93-47133. (Revolution & Romanticism, 1789-1834 Ser.). 1994. 55.00 (*1-85477-165-5*) Continuum.

Poetical Works of Ann Radcliffe, 2 vols. Ann Radcliffe. LC 70-37714. reprint ed. 85.00 (*0-404-56805-X*) AMS Pr.

An Asterisk (*) at the beginning of an entry indicates that the title is appearing for the first time.

Poetical Works of Anna Seward: With Extracts from Her Literary Correspondence, 3 vols. Anna Seward. Ed. by Sir Walter Scott. LC 70-37722. (Women of Letters Ser.). reprint ed. 230.00 (*0-404-56850-5*) AMS Pr.

Poetical Works of Beattie, Blair, & Falconer. James Beattie. Ed. by George Gilfillian. LC 73-144580. reprint ed. 34.50 (*0-404-08552-0*) AMS Pr.

Poetical Works of Charles Mackay. Charles Mackay. LC 70-144452. reprint ed. 37.50 (*0-404-08564-4*) AMS Pr.

Poetical Works of Christopher Smart Vol. I: Jubilate Agno, Vol. 1. Christopher Smart. Ed. by Karina Williamson. (Oxford English Texts Ser.). (Illus.). 176p. 1980. text 65.00 (*0-19-811869-4*) OUP.

Poetical Works of Christopher Smart Vol. III: A Translation of the Psalms of David, Vol. 3. Christopher Smart. Ed. by Marcus Walsh. (Oxford English Texts Ser.). 488p. (C). 1988. text 145.00 (*0-19-812771-5*) OUP.

Poetical Works of Christopher Smart Vol. IV: Miscellaneous Poems, English & Latin. Christopher Smart. Ed. by Karina Williamson. (Illus.). 548p. (J). (gr. 5 up). 1987. text 130.00 (*0-19-812768-5*) OUP.

Poetical Works of Christopher Smart Vol. V: Translations of the Works of Horace. Christopher Smart. Ed. by Karina Williamson. (Oxford English Texts Ser.). 512p. (C). 1996. text 105.00 (*0-19-812772-3*) OUP.

Poetical Works of Christopher Smart Vol. VI: A Poetical Translation of the Fables of Phaedrus. Christopher Smart. Ed. by Karina Williamson. (Oxford English Texts Ser.). (Illus.). 176p. 1996. text 55.00 (*0-19-818360-7*) OUP.

Poetical works [of] Coleridge, including poems & versions of poems herein. Samuel Taylor Coleridge. Ed. by E. H. Coleridge. (Oxford Standard Authors Ser.). 638p. 1961. pap. 21.00 (*0-19-281051-0*) OUP.

Poetical Works of David Garrick, 2 vols. David Garrick. LC 68-21214. 1972. reprint ed. 47.95 (*0-405-08553-2*) Ayer.

Poetical Works of David Garrick, 2 vols., Vol. 1. David Garrick. LC 68-21214. 1972. reprint ed. 24.95 (*0-405-08554-0*) Ayer.

Poetical Works of David Garrick, 2 vols., Vol. 2. David Garrick. LC 68-21214. 1972. reprint ed. 24.95 (*0-405-08555-9*) Ayer.

Poetical Works of Edward Rowland Sill. Edward R. Sill. LC 72-4972. (Romantic Tradition in American Literature Ser.). 462p. 1972. reprint ed. 39.95 (*0-405-04642-1*) Ayer.

Poetical Works of Edward Taylor. Edward Taylor. Ed. by Thomas H. Johnson. LC 45-4662. 231p. 1971. reprint ed. pap. 71.70 (*0-7837-9286-7*, 206002500004) Bks Demand.

Poetical Works of Elizabeth Margaret Chandler. Elizabeth M. Chandler. LC 71-83930. (Black Heritage Library Collection). 1977. 27.95 (*0-8369-8534-6*) Ayer.

Poetical Works of Fitz-Greene Halleck. J. G. Wilson. 1972. 59.95 (*0-8490-0856-5*) Gordon Pr.

Poetical Works of Fitz-Greene Halleck. Fitz-Greene Halleck. (Notable American Authors Ser.). 1992. reprint ed. lib. bdg. 75.00 (*0-7812-2991-X*) Rprt Serv.

Poetical Works of Gavin Douglas, Bishop of Dunkeld, 4 vols. Gavin Douglas. Ed. by John Small. (Anglistica & Americana Ser.: No. 80). (Illus.). 1970. reprint ed. 193.70 (*0-685-66460-0*, 05103095) G Olms Pubs.

Poetical Works of Geoffrey Chaucer, 6 vols. Geoffrey Chaucer. Ed. by Harris Nicolas & Richard Morris. LC 72-971. reprint ed. 495.00 (*0-404-01560-3*) AMS Pr.

Poetical Works of George Crabbe. George Crabbe. Ed. by A. J. Carlyle. reprint ed. lib. bdg. 79.00 (*0-7812-0304-X*) Rprt Serv.

Poetical Works of George MacDonald, Vol. I. George MacDonald. (George MacDonald Original Works Ser.: Series VIII). 448p. 1997. reprint ed. 22.00 (*1-881084-50-7*) Johannesen.

Poetical Works of George MacDonald, Vol. II. George MacDonald. (George MacDonald Original Works Ser.: Series VIII). 424p. 1997. reprint ed. 22.00 (*1-881084-51-5*) Johannesen.

Poetical Works of Gerard Manley Hopkins. Gerard Manley Hopkins. Ed. by Norman H. MacKenzie. (Oxford English Texts Ser.). (Illus.). 624p. (C). 1990. 200.00 (*0-19-811883-X*) OUP.

Poetical Works of Hector Macneill, 2 vols. Hector Macneill. LC 74-144453. reprint ed. 13.50 (*0-404-08565-2*) AMS Pr.

Poetical Works of James Madison Bell. James M. Bell. LC 78-133148. (Black Heritage Library Collection). 1977. 21.95 (*0-8369-8704-7*) Ayer.

Poetical Works of James Thomson. John Thomson. LC 73-145328. 1971. reprint ed. 49.00 (*0-403-01239-2*) Scholarly.

Poetical Works of John Keats. John Keats. Ed. by Heathcote W. Garrod. (Oxford Standard Authors Ser.). 508p. 1961. pap. text 21.00 (*0-19-281067-7*) OUP.

Poetical Works of John Milton, 6 vols. John Milton. Ed. by Egerton Brydges. LC 75-172735. (Illus.). reprint ed. 435.00 (*0-404-04380-1*) AMS Pr.

Poetical Works of John Milton - With Notes of Various Authors, 7 vols. John Milton. (BCL1-PR English Literature Ser.). 1992. reprint ed. lib. bdg. 525.00 (*0-7812-7376-5*) Rprt Serv.

Poetical Works of John Skelton, 2 vols. John Skelton. Ed. by Alexander Dyce. LC 75-133856. reprint ed. 155.00 (*0-404-06105-2*) AMS Pr.

Poetical Works of John Townsend Trowbridge. John T. Trowbridge. LC 72-4978. (Romantic Tradition in American Literature Ser.). 372p. 1972. reprint ed. 31.95 (*0-405-04647-2*) Ayer.

Poetical Works of John Trumbull. John Trumbull. (Notable American Authors). 1999. reprint ed. lib. bdg. 125.00 (*0-7812-9828-8*) Rprt Serv.

Poetical Works of Leigh Hunt. Leigh Hunt. Ed. by H. S. Milford. LC 75-41147. reprint ed. 124.50 (*0-404-14556-6*) AMS Pr.

Poetical Works of Letitia Elizabeth Landon "L. E. L." Letitia E. Landon. LC 90-8789. 676p. 1990. 75.00 (*0-8201-1443-X*) Schol Facsimiles.

Poetical Works of Lionel Johnson. Lionel P. Johnson. LC 75-28820. reprint ed. 45.00 (*0-404-13812-8*) AMS Pr.

Poetical Works of Marcus Garvey. Ed. by Tony Martin. LC 83-61114. (New Marcus Garvey Library: No. 2). (Illus.). viii, 123p. (C). 1983. 17.95 (*0-912469-02-1*); pap. 9.95 (*0-912469-03-X*) Majority Pr.

Poetical Works of Mark Akenside. Ed. by Robin Dix. LC 95-25560. (Illus.). 600p. 1996. 69.50 (*0-8386-3535-0*) Fairleigh Dickinson.

Poetical Works of Mark Akenside. Mark Akenside. Ed. by Alexander Dyce. LC 71-94924. reprint ed. 54.00 (*0-404-00299-4*) AMS Pr.

Poetical Works of Patrick Hannay. Patrick Hannay. LC 68-21217. 245p. 1972. reprint ed. 23.95 (*0-405-08596-6*, Pub. by Blom Pubns) Ayer.

Poetical Works of Robert Bridges, Excluding the 8 Dramas. 2nd ed. Robert S. Bridges. LC 75-41036. (BCL Ser. II). reprint ed. 72.50 (*0-404-14511-6*) AMS Pr.

Poetical Works of Robert Browning Books I-IV: The Ring & the Book, Vol. VII. Robert Browning. Ed. by Stefan Hawlin & T. A. J. Burnett. (Oxford English Texts Ser.). 398p. 1998. text 120.00 (*0-19-812356-6*) OUP.

Poetical Works of Robert Browning Vol. 1: Pauline & Paracelsus, Vol. 1. Robert Browning. Ed. by Ian Jack & Margaret Smith. (Oxford English Texts Ser.). 570p. (C). 1983. text 125.00 (*0-19-811893-7*) OUP.

Poetical Works of Robert Browning Vol. 2: Strafford, Sordello, Vol. 2. Robert Browning. Ed. by Jack Ian & Margaret Smith. (Oxford English Texts Ser.). 536p. 1984. text 115.00 (*0-19-812317-5*) OUP.

Poetical Works of Robert Browning Vol. 3: Bells & Pomegranates I-VI (Including Pippa Passes & Dramatic Lyrics) Robert Browning. Ed. by Ian Jack & Rowena Fowler. (Oxford English Texts Ser.). 560p. 1988. text 140.00 (*0-19-812762-6*) OUP.

Poetical Works of Robert Browning Vol. 4: Bells & Pomegranates VII. Robert Browning. Ed. by Ian Jack et al. (Oxford English Texts Ser.). (Illus.). 478p. (C). 1991. text 150.00 (*0-19-812789-8*) OUP.

Poetical Works of Robert Browning Vol. 5: Men & Women, Vol. 5. Robert Browning. Ed. by Ian Jack & Robert Inglesfield. (Oxford English Texts Ser.). (Illus.). 556p. (C). 1996. text 130.00 (*0-19-812790-1*) OUP.

Poetical Works of Robert Southey, 10 vols. in 5. Robert Southey. LC 76-7328. reprint ed. 225.00 (*0-404-15180-9*) AMS Pr.

Poetical Works of Rupert Brooke. Rupert Brooke. 20.95 (*0-8488-0351-5*) Amereon Ltd.

Poetical Works of Rupert Brooke. Rupert Brooke. Ed. by Geoffrey Keynes. 216p. 1970. pap. 14.95 (*0-571-04704-1*) Faber & Faber.

Poetical Works of Sir Thomas Wyatt. Thomas Wyatt. LC 76-119967. (Select Bibliographies Reprint Ser.). 1977. 23.95 (*0-8369-5410-6*) Ayer.

Poetical Works of Taras Shevchenko. Taras Shevchenko. Tr. by C. H. Andrusyshen & Watson Kirkconnell. LC 66-2188. (Illus.). 1964. text 32.50 (*0-8020-3114-5*) U of Toronto Pr.

Poetical Works of Thomas Chatterton, 2 vols. Thomas Chatterton. Ed. by Walter W. Skeat. LC 68-59008. (BCL Ser.: No. I). reprint ed. 125.00 (*0-404-01484-4*) AMS Pr.

Poetical Works of Thomas Chatterton, 2 vols. Thomas Chatterton. (BCL1-PR English Literature Ser.). 1992. reprint ed. lib. bdg. 150.00 (*0-7812-7330-7*) Rprt Serv.

Poetical Works of Thomas Little. Thomas Moore. LC 90-31439. (Revolution & Romanticism Ser.). 204p. 1990. reprint ed. 48.00 (*1-85477-050-0*) Continuum.

Poetical Works of Thomas MacDonagh. Thomas MacDonagh. LC 75-28822. reprint ed. 24.00 (*0-404-13814-4*) AMS Pr.

Poetical Works of Thomas Moore. Thomas Moore. Ed. by A. D. Godley. LC 75-41197. reprint ed. 42.50 (*0-404-14688-0*) AMS Pr.

Poetical Works of Thomas Moore. Thomas Moore. (BCL1-PR English Literature Ser.). 751p. 1992. reprint ed. lib. bdg. 109.00 (*0-7812-7604-7*) Rprt Serv.

Poetical Works of Wilfrid Scawen Blunt, 2 vols. Wilfrid S. Blunt. (BCL1-PR English Literature Ser.). 1992. reprint ed. lib. bdg. 150.00 (*0-7812-7448-6*) Rprt Serv.

Poetical Works of Wilfrid Scawen Blunt, 2 vols. Wilfrid S. Blunt. LC 14-22324. 1968. reprint ed. 59.00 (*0-403-00110-2*) Scholarly.

Poetical Works of William Cowper. 4th ed. William Cowper. Ed. by H. S. Milford. LC 75-41066. (BCL Ser. II). reprint ed. 49.50 (*0-404-14525-6*) AMS Pr.

Poetical Works of William Cullen Bryant. William C. Bryant. Date not set. lib. bdg. 26.95 (*0-8488-1895-4*) Amereon Ltd.

Poetical Works of William Cullen Bryant. William C. Bryant. LC 79-85192. 1969. reprint ed. 42.50 (*0-404-01143-8*) AMS Pr.

Poetical Works of William Drummond of Hawthornden, 2 Vols. W. Drummond. Ed. by L. E. Kastner. LC 68-24906. (Studies in Poetry: No. 38). 1969. reprint ed. lib. bdg. 150.00 (*0-8383-0157-6*) M S G Haskell Hse.

Poetical Works of William Drummond of Hawthornden, with "A Cypresse Grove" William Drummond. (BCL1-PR English Literature Ser.: 2 vols.). 1992. reprint ed. lib. bdg. 150.00 (*0-7812-7206-8*) Rprt Serv.

Poetical Works of Wordsworth with Introduction & Notes. rev. ed. William Wordsworth. Ed. by Thomas Hutchinson & Ernest De Selincourt. (Oxford Standard Authors Ser.). 810p. 1961. reprint ed. pap. text 22.00 (*0-19-281052-9*) OUP.

Poetical Writings of Fitz-Greene Halleck: With Extracts from Those of Joseph Rodman Drake. Fitz-Greene Halleck. Ed. by James G. Wilson. LC 70-80010. reprint ed. 52.50 (*0-404-03047-5*) AMS Pr.

Poetical Writings of Fitz-Greene Halleck: With Extracts from Those of Joseph Rodman Drake. Fitz-Greene Halleck. (BCL1-PS American Literature Ser.). 389p. 1992. reprint ed. lib. bdg. 89.00 (*0-7812-6717-X*) Rprt Serv.

Poetically, Just Us. Valada S. Flewellyn. 128p. (J). (gr. 5-12). 1992. text 24.95 (*1-880997-01-0*) Parker Init Pubns.

Poetically Speaking. Norma Wise. Ed. by Ginny L. Ballor & Carrie Neumann. 40p. (Orig.). (C). 1996. pap. 3.00 (*1-882294-21-1*) Green Gate.

***Poetically Yours.** Janet Parker & Mary Gribble. LC 99-61337. 76p. 1999. pap. 6.00 (*1-886467-49-8*) WJM Press.

Poeticas del Ensayo Venezoland del Siglo XX: La Forma de lo Diverso. Miguel Gomes. (SPA.). 260p. 1996. pap. 25.00 (*1-888135-01-8*) Ediciones Inti.

Poeticized Language: Studies in Contemporary French Poetry. Jean-Jacques Thomas & Steven Winspur. LC 98-17597. 1999. 55.00 (*0-271-01812-7*); pap. 23.00 (*0-271-01813-5*) Pa St U Pr.

Poetic'ly Speaking: Views & Blues (Urban Whirl) Oscar Washington. (Illus.). 134p. 1998. pap. 10.95 (*1-883069-02-5*) NESB Pubs.

Poetics see Classical Literary Criticism

Poetics see Poetique d'Aristote

Poetics. Aristotle. LC 94-5113. 342p. 1981. pap. text 26.00 (*0-19-814024-X*) OUP.

Poetics. Aristotle. Tr. by Kenneth MacLeish from GRE. LC 99-18986. (Dramatic Contexts Ser.). 64p. 1999. pap. 9.95 (*1-55936-170-0*, Pub. by Theatre Comm) Consort Bk Sales.

Poetics. Aristotle. Tr. by Gerald F. Else. LC 94-5113. 136p. 1967. pap. text 11.95 (*0-472-06166-6*, 06166) U of Mich Pr.

Poetics. Aristotle. Tr. & Notes by Richard Janko. LC 94-5113. (Classics Ser.). 261p. (Orig.). (C). 1987. pap. 9.95 (*0-87220-033-7*); lib. bdg. 34.95 (*0-87220-034-5*) Hackett Pub.

Poetics. Aristotle. Tr. by S. H. Butcher from GRE. (Mermaid Dramabook Ser.). 118p. (Orig.). 1961. pap. 6.00 (*0-8090-0527-1*) Hill & Wang.

Poetics. Aristotle. Tr. & Intro. by James Hutton. (Illus.). 120p. (Orig.). (C). 1982. pap. 11.25 (*0-393-95216-9*) Norton.

Poetics. Aristotle. Tr. by Theodore Buckley. LC 92-33258. (Great Books in Philosophy). 77p. (Orig.). 1992. pap. 5.95 (*0-87975-776-0*) Prometheus Bks.

Poetics. Aristotle. Tr. & Intro. by Malcolm Heath. LC 97-138026. 144p. (Orig.). 1997. pap. 10.95 (*0-14-044636-2*) Viking Penguin.

Poetics. Aristotle. Ed. by W. Hamiltin Fyfe et al. Tr. by Stephen Halliwell et al. LC 94-5113. (Loeb Classical Library: No. 199). 500p. 1995. text 18.95 (*0-674-99563-5*, L199) HUP.

Poetics. Aristotle. Ed. by John Baxter & J. P. Atherton. Tr. & Comment by George Whalley. 224p. 1997. 55.00 (*0-7735-1611-5*, Pub. by McG-Queens Univ Pr); pap. 19.95 (*0-7735-1612-3*, Pub. by McG-Queens Univ Pr) CUP Services.

Poetics. Aristotle. Ed. by Stephen Halliwell. LC 86-4299. 381p. 1986. pap. 118.20 (*0-608-05227-2*, 206576400001) Bks Demand.

Poetics. Aristotle. Ed. & Intro. by Stephen Halliwell. LC 98-36373. 384p. 1999. pap. text 22.00 (*0-226-31394-8*) U Ch Pr.

Poetics. Aristotle et al. LC 89-64029. (Apostle Translations of Aristotle's Works: Vol. 8). 167p. 1990. pap. 12.00 (*0-911589-09-0*) Peripatetic.

Poetics. Charles Bernstein. 240p. (C). 1992. 44.50 (*0-674-67854-0*); pap. 17.95 (*0-674-67857-5*) HUP.

***Poetics.** Ed. by Joel Kuszai. 192p. 1999. pap. 18.95 (*0-937804-79-7*, Roof Bks) Segue NYC.

Poetics. Julian Mall. 74p. pap. write for info. (*3-7052-0939-6*, Pub. by Poetry Salzburg) Intl Spec Bk.

Poetics. Tr. by W. Rhys Roberts & W. Hamilton Fyfe. (Loeb Classical Library: No. 199). 15.50 (*0-674-99219-9*) HUP.

Poetics. Aristotle. Ed. by S. H. Butcher. LC 96-47116. (Thrift Editions Ser.). (Illus.). 64p. (Orig.). 1997. reprint ed. pap. 1.00 (*0-486-29577-X*) Dover.

Poetics: Sighs of Relief, of Joy, for Thanks & Love: Lyricalfeelthoughtoder: A Written Transcendent Walk. abr. ed. Eric Fortmeyer. (Illus.). 132p. 1997. 50.00 (*1-928620-02-7*, EFX-799107R0398, Poms Healing) AGI Prods.

Poetics - Poetica. Eduardo Cortils. (Artists' Books Ser.). (Illus.). 96p. 1995. 20.00 (*0-89822-115-3*) Visual Studies.

Poetics & Interpretation of Biblical Narrative. Adele Berlin. LC 94-4841. 180p. 1994. pap. 15.95 (*1-57506-002-7*) Eisenbrauns.

Poetics & Literature of the Sicilian Diaspora: Studies in Oral History & Story-Telling. Justin Vitiello. 528p. 1993. 119.95 (*0-7734-2226-9*) E Mellen.

Poetics & Politics: The Revolutions of Wordsworth. Yu Liu. LC 98-26877. (Studies in Nineteenth-Century British Literature: Vol. 12). IX, 138p. (C). 1999. text 39.95 (*0-8204-4168-6*) P Lang Pubng.

Poetics & Politics in the Art of Rudolf Baranik. David Craven. LC 96-18347. (Illus.). 224p. (C). 1996. text 49.95 (*0-391-03988-1*) Humanities.

Poetics & Politics of Tuareg Aging: Life Course & Personal Destiny in Niger. Susan J. Rasmussen. LC 96-43794. 208p. 1997. lib. bdg. 32.00 (*0-87580-220-6*) N Ill U Pr.

Poetics & Praxis, Understanding & Imagination: The Collected Essays of O. B. Hardison, Jr. Ed. by Arthur F. Kinney. LC 95-39534. 1997. 75.00 (*0-8203-1819-1*) U of Ga Pr.

Poetics Architecture Design: Theory of Design. Anthony C. Antoniades. 320p. 1992. pap. 39.95 (*0-471-28530-7*, VNR) Wiley.

Poetics@ Poets on the Internet. Ed. by Joel Kuszai. 1997. pap. 18.95 (*0-614-29447-9*, Roof Bks) Segue NYC.

***Poetics for Screenwriters.** Lance Lee. LC 00-36415. 160p. 2001. 30.00 (*0-292-74718-7*); pap. 15.95 (*0-292-74719-5*) U of Tex Pr.

Poetics in the Poem: Critical Essays on American Self-Reflexive Poetry. Ed. by Dorothy Baker. (American University Studies: Vol. 184, No. 4). X, 322p. (C). 1998. text 51.95 (*0-8204-3329-2*) P Lang Pubng.

Poetics of Alfarabi & Avicenna. Salim Kemal. LC 90-27148. (Islamic Philosophy, Theology & Science, Studies & Texts Ser.: No. 9). vii, 285p. 1991. 116.00 (*90-04-09371-0*) Brill Academic Pubs.

Poetics of Anarchy: David Edelshtat's Revolutionary Poetry. Ori Kritz. (European University Studies Comparative LIterature: Series 18, Vol. 88). 210p. 1997. 42.95 (*3-631-32559-2*) P Lang Pubng.

Poetics of Appalachian Space. Ed. by Parks Lanier, Jr. LC 90-45244. (Illus.). 232p. 1991. text 26.00 (*0-87049-692-1*) U of Tenn Pr.

Poetics of Appropriation: The Literary Theory & Practice of Huang Tingjian. David Palumbo-Liu. LC 92-22990. 280p. 1993. 39.50 (*0-8047-2126-2*) Stanford U Pr.

Poetics of Architecture. Anthony C. Antoniades. 1992. pap. 32.95 (*0-442-01330-2*, VNR) Wiley.

Poetics of Aristotle. Tr. by Preston H. Epps. xii, 70p. (C). 1967. reprint ed. pap. 10.95 (*0-8078-4017-3*) U of NC Pr.

Poetics of Aristotle: Translation & Commentary. Stephen Halliwell. 206p. (C). 1987. pap. 12.95 (*0-8078-4203-6*) U of NC Pr.

Poetics of Aristotle & the Tractatus Coislinianus: A Bibliography from about 900 till 1996. Omert J. Schrier. LC 98-6542. (Mnemosyne, Bibliotheca Classica Batava Ser.). 1998. 121.00 (*90-04-11132-8*) Brill Academic Pubs.

Poetics of Art Criticism: The Case of Baudelaire. Timothy B. Raser. LC 88-27319. (North Carolina Studies in the Romance Languages & Literatures: Vol. 234). 202p. 1989. reprint ed. pap. 62.70 (*0-608-02060-5*, 206271300003) Bks Demand.

Poetics of Ascent: Theories of Language in a Rabbinic Ascent Text. Naomi Janowitz. LC 87-9993. (SUNY Series in Judaica: Hermeneutics, Mysticism, & Religion). 176p. (C). 1988. pap. text 21.95 (*0-88706-637-2*) State U NY Pr.

***Poetics of Authorship in the Later Middle Ages: The Emergence of the Modern Literary Persona.** 2nd ed. Burt Kimmelman. (Studies in the Humanities: Vol. 21). 288p. 1999. pap. text 34.95 (*0-8204-4567-3*, 45673) P Lang Pubng.

Poetics of Biblical Narrative. Robert W. Funk. 336p. (C). 1988. pap. 19.95 (*0-944344-04-6*) Polebridge Pr.

Poetics of Biblical Narrative: Ideological Literature & the Drama of Reading. Meir Sternberg. LC 85-42752. (Indiana Studies in Biblical Literature). (Illus.). 596p. 1985. 59.95 (*0-253-34521-9*) Ind U Pr.

Poetics of Biblical Narrative: Ideological Literature & the Drama of Reading. Meir Sternberg. LC 85-42752. (Indiana Studies in Biblical Literature). (Illus.). 596p. 1987. pap. 22.95 (*0-253-20453-4*, MB-453) Ind U Pr.

Poetics of Cavafy: Textuality, Eroticism, History. Gregory Jusdanis. LC 87-3390. 215p. 1987. reprint ed. pap. 66.70 (*0-608-07644-9*, 205996100010) Bks Demand.

Poetics of Change: The New Spanish-American Narrative. Julio Ortega. Tr. by Galen D. Greaser. (Texas Pan American Ser.). 200p. (C). 1984. reprint ed. pap. 10.95 (*0-292-76508-8*); reprint ed. text 20.00 (*0-292-76488-X*) U of Tex Pr.

Poetics of Cinema. Raoul Ruiz. 128p. 1995. pap. 19.50 (*2-906571-38-5*, Pub. by Editions Dis Voir) Dist Art Pubs.

Poetics of Cities: Designing Neighborhoods That Work. Mike Greenberg. LC 94-26658. (Urban Life & Urban Landscape Ser.). (Illus.). 288p. 1995. text 60.00 (*0-8142-0656-5*) Ohio St U Pr.

Poetics of Cities: Designing Neighborhoods That Work. Mike Greenberg. LC 94-26658. (Urban Life & Urban Landscape Ser.). (Illus.). 288p. 1995. pap. 21.95 (*0-8142-0657-3*) Ohio St U Pr.

Poetics of Colonization: From City to Text in Archaic Greece. Carol Dougherty. LC 92-41090. (Illus.). 224p. 1993. text 55.00 (*0-19-508399-7*) OUP.

Poetics of Death: The Short Prose of Kleist & Balzac. Beatrice M. Guenther. LC 95-52864. (SUNY Series, The Margins of Literature). 216p. (C). 1996. text 71.50 (*0-7914-3023-5*); pap. text 24.95 (*0-7914-3024-3*) State U NY Pr.

Poetics of Decadence: Chinese Poetry of the Southern Dynasties & Late Tang Periods. Fusheng Wu. LC 97-37507. (SUNY Series in Chinese Philosophy & Culture). 288p. (C). 1998. text 71.50 (*0-7914-3751-5*); pap. text 23.95 (*0-7914-3752-3*) State U NY Pr.

Poetics of Derek Walcott: Intercultural Perspectives, Vol. 96, No. 2. Ed. by Gregson Davis. 250p. 1997. pap. 12.00 (*0-8223-6444-1*) Duke.

Poetics of Desire: Essay on Dorothy Livesay. Nadine McInnis. 114p. 1997. pap. 10.95 (*0-88801-181-4*, Pub. by Turnstone Pr) Genl Dist Srvs.

***Poetics of Disappointment: Wordsworth to Ashbery.** Laura Quinney. LC 98-55128. 1999. 30.00 (*0-8139-1858-8*) U Pr of Va.

P

Poetics of Disguise: The Autobiography of the Work in Homer, Dante, & Shakespeare. Franco Ferrucci. Tr. by Ann Dunnigan from ITA. LC 80-11242. 178p. 1980. text 37.50 (0-8014-1262-5) Cornell U Pr.

Poetics of Ecstasy. Willis Barnstone. LC 82-9283. 331p. (C). 1983. pap. 18.95 (0-8419-0849-4) Holmes & Meier.

***Poetics of Empire: A Study of James Grainger's the Sugar Cane.** John Gilmore & James Grainger. LC 99-54614. 2000. write for info. (0-485-12148-4, Pub. by Athlone Pr) Transaction Pubs.

***Poetics of Empire in the Indies: Prophecy & Imitation in La Araucana & Os Lusbiadas.** James Nicolopulos. LC 99-42052. (Series in Romance Literature). 2000. 55.00 (0-271-01990-5) Pa St U Pr.

Poetics of English Nationhood, 1590-1612. Claire McEachern. (Cambridge Studies in Renaissance Literature & Culture: No. 13). (Illus.). 250p. (C). 1996. text 59.95 (0-521-57031-X) Cambridge U Pr.

Poetics of Eros in Ancient Greece. Claude Calame & Janet Lloyd. LC 98-37129. 1999. 35.00 (0-691-04341-8, Pub. by Princeton U Pr) Cal Prin Full Svc.

Poetics of Experiment: A Study of the Work of George Perec. Warren F. Jr. Motte. LC 83-81599. (French Forum Monographs: No. 51). 163p. (Orig.). 1984. pap. 12.95 (0-917058-51-8) French Forum.

Poetics of Expressiveness: A Theory & Application. Yuri Shcheglov & Alexander Zholkovsky. LC 86-3572. (Linguistic & Literary Studies in Eastern Europe: Vol. 18). x, 362p. 1987. 118.00 (90-272-1522-7) J Benjamins Pubng Co.

Poetics of Fascism: Ezra Pound, T. S. Eliot, Paul de Man. Paul Morrison. 192p. 1996. text 45.00 (0-19-508085-8) OUP.

Poetics of French Verse: Studies in Reading. Clive Scott. LC 97-44994. 304p. 1998. text 75.00 (0-19-815944-7) OUP.

Poetics of Gardens. Charles W. Moore et al. (Illus.). 288p. 1988. 50.00 (0-262-13231-1) MIT Pr.

Poetics of Gardens. Charles W. Moore et al. (Illus.). 272p. 1993. pap. text 26.95 (0-262-63153-9) MIT Pr.

Poetics of Gender. Ed. & Intro. by Nancy K. Miller. LC 85-29904. (Gender & Culture Ser.). 272p. 1987. pap. text 21.00 (0-231-06311-3) Col U Pr.

Poetics of Historical Perspectivism: Breitinger's Critische Dichtkunst & the Neoclassic Tradition. Jill A. Kowalik. LC 91-23614. (Germanic Languages & Literatures Ser.: No. 114). xvi, 150p. (C). 1992. lib. bdg. 39.95 (0-8078-8114-7) U of NC Pr.

Poetics of Imagining: Modern & Post Modern. Richard Kearney. LC 98-8607. (Perspectives in Continental Philosophy Ser.: No. 6). 260p. 1998. 35.00 (0-8232-1871-6); pap. 19.95 (0-8232-1872-4) Fordham.

Poetics of Imitation: Anacreon & the Anacreontic Tradition. Patricia A. Rosenmeyer. (Illus.). 297p. (C). 1992. text 69.95 (0-521-41044-4) Cambridge U Pr.

Poetics of Imperialism: Translation & Colonization from the Tempest to Tarzan. Eric Cheyfitz. LC 96-45596. (Illus.). 272p. 1997. pap. 17.50 (0-8122-1609-1) U of Pa Pr.

Poetics of Impersonality: T. S. Eliot & Ezra Pound. Maud Ellmann. LC 87-7422. 224p. 1988. 37.95 (0-674-67858-3) HUP.

Poetics of Inconstancy: Etienne Durand & the End of Renaissance Verse. Hoyt Rogers. LC 98-4924. (North Carolina Studies in the Romance Languages & Literatures: Vol. 256). 1998. pap. 29.95 (0-8078-9260-2) U of NC Pr.

Poetics of Indeterminacy: Rimbaud to Cage. Marjorie Perloff. LC 99-46824. 368p. 1999. pap. 18.95 (0-8101-1764-9) Northwestern U Pr.

Poetics of Indeterminacy: Rimbaud to Cage. Marjorie Perloff. 346p. 1981. reprint ed. pap. 18.95 (0-8101-0661-2) Northwestern U Pr.

Poetics of Influence: New & Selected Criticism of Harold Bloom. Harold Bloom. Ed. & Intro. by John Hollander. 500p. 1988. 49.95 (0-939681-00-5); pap. 24.95 (0-939681-01-3) H R Schwab.

Poetics of Jacobean Drama. Coburn Freer. LC 81-47599. 288p. 1982. text 41.00 (0-8018-2545-8) Johns Hopkins.

***Poetics of Japanese Verse: Imagery, Structure & Meter.** Koju Kawamoto. Tr. by Stephen Collington et al. 320p. 1999. 42.00 (0-86008-526-0, Pub. by U of Tokyo) Col U Pr.

Poetics of Jonah: Art in the Service of Ideology. Kenneth M. Craig, Jr. LC 99-19934. 208p. 1999. pap. 19.95 (0-86554-614-2) Mercer Univ Pr.

Poetics of Korolenko's Fiction. Radha Balasubramanian. LC 96-2775. (Middlebury Studies in Russian Language & Literature: No. 12). 146p. (C). 1997. text 39.95 (0-8204-3305-5) P Lang Pubng.

Poetics of Manhood: Contest & Identity in Cretan Mountain Village. Michael Herzfeld. LC 84-26530. (Illus.). 330p. 1985. pap. text 19.95 (0-691-10244-9, Pub. by Princeton U Pr) Cal Prin Full Svc.

Poetics of Military Occupation: Mzeina Allegories of Bedouin Identity under Israeli & Egyptian Rule. Smadar Lavie. 1990. 45.00 (0-520-06880-7, Pub. by U CA Pr) Cal Prin Full Svc.

Poetics of Mind: Figurative Thought, Language, & Understanding. Raymond W. Gibbs, Jr. 437p. (C). 1994. text 59.95 (0-521-41965-4); pap. text 19.95 (0-521-42992-7) Cambridge U Pr.

Poetics of Modernity: Toward a Hermeneutic Imagination. Richard Kearney. LC 94-18237. (Philosophy & Literary Theory Ser.). 336p. (C). 1995. reprint ed. text 55.00 (0-391-03798-6) Humanities.

Poetics of Modernity: Toward a Hermeneutic Imagination. Richard Kearney. (Philosophy & Literary Theory Ser.). 272p. 1998. reprint ed. pap. 19.95 (0-391-04080-4) Humanities.

Poetics of Music in the Form of Six Lessons. Igor Stravinsky. LC 79-99520. (Charles Eliot Norton Lectures). (ENG & FRE.). 199p. 1970. pap. text 12.50 (0-674-67856-7) HUP.

Poetics of Myth. Eleazar M. Meletinsky. Ed. by Robert A. Segal. Tr. by Guy Lanoue & Alexandre Sadetsky. LC 97-24453. (Theorists of Myth Ser.: Vol. 9). 520p. 1998. text 85.00 (0-8153-2134-1) Garland.

Poetics of Natural History: From John Bartram to William James. Christoph Irmscher. LC 98-40434. (Illus.). 320p. (C). 1999. text 42.00 (0-8135-2615-9) Rutgers U Pr.

Poetics of Old Age in Greek Epic, Lyric & Tragedy. Thomas M. Falkner. LC 95-17116. (Oklahoma Classical Culture Ser.: Vol. 19). 368p. 1995. 42.50 (0-8061-2775-9) U of Okla Pr.

Poetics of Old Age in Greek Epic, Lyric & Tragedy. Thomas M. Falkner. LC 95-17116. (Oklahoma Classical Culture Ser.: Vol. 19). 368p. 1996. pap. 16.95 (0-8061-2798-8) U of Okla Pr.

Poetics of Painting in the Works of Proust & Matisse see Poetique des Tableaux Chez Proust et Matisse

Poetics of Personification. James J. Paxson. (Literature, Culture, Theory Ser.: No. 6). 222p. (C). 1994. text 54.95 (0-521-44539-6) Cambridge U Pr.

Poetics of Perspective. James Elkins. LC 94-16310. (Illus.). 1995. text 42.50 (0-8014-2796-7) Cornell U Pr.

Poetics of Perspective. James Elkins. (Illus.). 344p. 1996. pap. text 16.95 (0-8014-8379-4) Cornell U Pr.

Poetics of Place. Paul M. Edwards. 1994. pap. text 5.00 (0-8309-0658-4) Herald Pub Hse.

Poetics of Place. Photos by Lynn Geesaman. (Illus.). 80p. 1999. 45.00 (0-89381-865-8) Aperture.

***Poetics of Place.** Photos by Lynn Geesaman. LC 99-227420. (Illus.). 80p. 1998. 45.00 (1-884167-01-2, Pub. by Umbrage Edits) Aperture.

Poetics of Place: The Poetry of Ralph Gustafson. Dermot McCarthy. 352p. (C). 1990. text 55.00 (0-7735-0815-5, Pub. by McG-Queens Univ Pr) CUP Services.

Poetics of Plot: The Case of English Renaissance Drama. Thomas G. Pavel. LC 84-15663. (Theory & History of Literature Ser.: Vol. 18). 192p. 1985. pap. 14.95 (0-8166-1375-3) U of Minn Pr.

Poetics of Political Economy in Egypt. Kristin Koptiuch. LC 99-17927. 1999. pap. text 17.95 (0-8166-2539-5) U of Minn Pr.

***Poetics of Portraiture in the Italian Renaissance.** Jodi Cranston. LC 99-59861. (Illus.). 304p. 2000. write for info. (0-521-65324-X) Cambridge U Pr.

Poetics of Postmodernism: History, Theory & Fiction. Linda Hutcheon. 300p. (C). 1988. pap. 22.99 (0-415-00706-2) Routledge.

Poetics of Postmodernism: History, Theory & Fiction. Linda Hutcheon. 300p. 1988. text 49.95 (0-415-00705-4) Routledge.

Poetics of Primitive Accumulation: English Renaissance Culture & the Genealogy of Capital. Richard Halpern. LC 90-55757. (Illus.). 400p. 1991. text 49.95 (0-8014-2539-5); pap. text 19.95 (0-8014-9772-8) Cornell U Pr.

Poetics of Prose. Tzvetan Todorov. Tr. by Richard Howard. LC 76-28124. 272p. 1977. text 42.50 (0-8014-0857-1); pap. text 15.95 (0-8014-9165-7) Cornell U Pr.

Poetics of Protest: Literary Form & Political Implication in the Victim-of-Society Novel. George Goodin. LC 83-27179. 232p. 1985. text 26.95 (0-8093-1173-9) S Ill U Pr.

Poetics of Quotation in the European Novel. Herman Meyer. LC 65-17152. 288p. reprint ed. pap. 89.30 (0-8357-3701-2, 203642500003) Bks Demand.

Poetics of Rasalia De Castro's Sombra Negra. Joanna Courteau. LC 94-36502. (Hispanic Literature Ser.: No. 23). 136p. 1995. text 69.95 (0-7734-9055-8) E Mellen.

Poetics of Reading: Approaches to the Novel. Inge C. Wimmers. LC 88-17898. 201p. 1988. reprint ed. pap. 62.40 (0-608-07525-6, 206774100009) Bks Demand.

Poetics of Reading Vol. 2: Textuality & Subjectivity. Eitel Timm. Ed. by Kenneth Mendoza. LC 92-29486. (GERM Ser.). x, 130p. 1993. 50.00 (1-879751-31-3) Camden Hse.

Poetics of Relation. Edouard Glissant. Tr. by Betsy Wing. LC 97-6997. 252p. (C). 1997. pap. text 15.95 (0-472-06629-3, 06629) U of Mich Pr.

Poetics of Resistance: Heidegger's Line. Michael Roth. LC 96-378. (Studies in Phenomenology & Existential Philosophy). (Illus.). 420p. 1996. 75.00 (0-8101-1317-1); pap. 29.95 (0-8101-1318-X) Northwestern U Pr.

Poetics of Resistance: Narrative & the Writings of Pier Paolo Pasolini. David Ward. LC 95-6297. 216p. 1995. 35.00 (0-8386-3585-7) Fairleigh Dickinson.

Poetics of Resistance: Women Writing in El Salvador, South Africa, & the United States. Mary K. DeShazer. LC 94-6207. 368p. (C). 1994. pap. text 18.95 (0-472-06563-7, 06563) U of Mich Pr.

Poetics of Revelation: Recognition in the Narrative Tradition. Diana Culbertson. LC 88-37662. 120p. (C). 1988. 24.95 (0-86554-310-0, MUP/H251); pap. 16.95 (0-86554-351-8, MUP/P081) Mercer Univ Pr.

Poetics of Reverie: Childhood, Language & the Cosmos. Gaston Bachelard. 1971. reprint ed. pap. 16.50 (0-8070-6413-0) Beacon Pr.

Poetics of Revitalization: Adam Mickiewicz Between Forefathers' Eve, Part 3 & Pan Tadeusz. Roman Koropeckyj. 360p. 1999. 48.50 (0-88033-434-7, 536, Pub. by East Eur Monographs) Col U Pr.

Poetics of Roman Ingarden. Eugene H. Falk. LC 79-29655. 235p. reprint ed. pap. 72.90 (0-7837-3763-7, 204358000010) Bks Demand.

Poetics of Scepticism: Gottfried Keller & Die Leute von Seldwyla. Erika Swales. LC 93-33396. (Berg Monographs in German Literature). 216p. 1994. 49.50 (0-85496-903-9) Berg Pubs.

***Poetics of Science Fiction.** Peter Stockwell. LC 00-30958. 2000. write for info. (0-582-36993-2) Addison-Wesley.

Poetics of Self-Consciousness: Twentieth-Century Spanish Poetry. Jonathan Mayhew. LC 92-56608. 1994. 29.50 (0-8387-5256-X) Bucknell U Pr.

Poetics of Sensibility: A Revolution in Literary Style. Jerome J. McGann. 232p. (C). 1996. text 39.95 (0-19-818370-4) OUP.

Poetics of Sensibility: A Revolution in Literary Style. Jerome McGann. 228p. 1998. reprint ed. pap. text 19.95 (0-19-818478-6) OUP.

Poetics of Sexual Myth: Gender & Ideology in the Verse of Swift & Pope. Ellen Pollak. LC 84-28125. (Women in Culture & Society Ser.). 1994. 18.95 (0-226-67345-6) U Ch Pr.

***Poetics of Simple Mathematics in Music.** (Illus.). 120p. 1999. pap. 25.00 (0-9634500-5-0) Pubn Contact Intl.

Poetics of Space. Gaston Bachelard. LC 93-27874. 288p. 1994. reprint ed. pap. 15.00 (0-8070-6473-4) Beacon Pr.

***Poetics of Spice: Romantic Consumerism & the Exotic.** Timothy Morton. LC 99-87472. (Illus.). 328p. 2000. write for info. (0-521-77146-3) Cambridge U Pr.

Poetics of Supplication: Homer's "Iliad" & "Odyssey" Kevin Crotty. (Myth & Poetics Ser.). 256p. 1994. text 37.50 (0-8014-2998-6) Cornell U Pr.

Poetics of the Americas: Race, Founding, & Textuality. Ed. by Bainard Cowan & Jefferson Humphries. LC 96-52687. (Horizons in Theory & American Culture Ser.). (Illus.). 240p. 1997. text 35.00 (0-8071-2142-8); pap. text 12.95 (0-8071-2181-9) La State U Pr.

Poetics of the Antarctic: A Study in Nineteenth-Century American Cultural Perceptions. William E. Lenz. LC 94-27300. (Studies in Nineteenth-Century American Literature: Vol. 5). (Illus.). 248p. 1995. text 46.00 (0-8153-1473-6, H1785) Garland.

Poetics of the Common Knowledge. Don Byrd. LC 92-42637. (SUNY Series, The Margins of Literature). 404p. (C). 1993. pap. text 18.95 (0-7914-1686-0) State U NY Pr.

Poetics of the Common Knowledge. Don Byrd. LC 92-42637. (SUNY Series, The Margins of Literature). 404p. (C). 1993. text 57.50 (0-7914-1685-2) State U NY Pr.

Poetics of the Elements in the Human Condition: The Sea. Ed. by Anna-Teresa Tymieniecka. 532p. 1985. text 248.50 (90-277-1906-3, D Reidel) Kluwer Academic.

Poetics of the Elements in the Human Condition Pt. 2: The Airy Elements in Poetic Imagination: Breath, Breeze, Wind, Tempest, Thunder, Snow, Flame, Fire, Volcano... Anna-Teresa Tymieniecka. 448p. (C). 1988. lib. bdg. 215.00 (90-277-2569-1, Pub. by Kluwer Academic) Kluwer Academic.

Poetics of the Elements in the Human Condition Pt. 3: The Elemental Passions of the Soul. Anna-Teresa Tymieniecka. 668p. (C). 1990. lib. bdg. 336.00 (0-7923-0180-3, Pub. by Kluwer Academic) Kluwer Academic.

Poetics of the Feminine: Authority & Literary Tradition in William Carlos Williams, Mina Loy, Denise Levertov, & Kathleen Fraser. Linda A. Kinnahan. (Cambridge Studies in American Literature & Culture: No. 74). 302p. (C). 1994. text 69.95 (0-521-45127-2) Cambridge U Pr.

Poetics of the Holy: A Reading of "Paradise Lost" Michael Lieb. LC 80-29159. (Illus.). 464p. 1981. reprint ed. pap. 143.90 (0-7837-7073-1, 204688500004) Bks Demand.

Poetics of the Literary Self-Portrait. Michel Beaujour. (Studies in French Culture & Civilization). 419p. (C). 1992. pap. text 20.00 (0-8147-1192-8) NYU Pr.

Poetics of the Mind's Eye: Literature & the Psychology of Imagination. Christopher Collins. LC 91-20561. (Illus.). 224p. (Orig.). (C). 1991. text 35.00 (0-8122-3133-3); pap. text 15.95 (0-8122-1360-2) U of Pa Pr.

Poetics of the New History: French Historical Discourse from Braudel to Chartier. Philippe Carrard. LC 91-20585. (Parallax: Re-Visions of Culture & Society Ser.). 272p. 1991. text 42.50 (0-8018-4254-9) Johns Hopkins.

Poetics of the New History: French Historical Discourse from Braudel to Chartier. Philippe Carrard. (Parallax). 220p. 1995. reprint ed. pap. text 17.95 (0-8018-5233-1) Johns Hopkins.

Poetics of the New Poetries. Ed. by Richard Kostelanetz & Benjamin Hrushovski. 256p. 1983. pap. 8.00 (0-932360-45-9) Archae Edns.

Poetics of the Occasion: Mallarme & the Poetry of Circumstance. Marian Z. Sugano. LC 91-20228. (Illus.). 288p. 1992. 39.50 (0-8047-1946-2) Stanford U Pr.

Poetics of the Pretext: Reading Lautreamont. Roland-Francois Lack. 250p. 1998. 60.00 (0-85989-498-3, Pub. by Univ Exeter Pr) Northwestern U Pr.

Poetics of the Ramakian. Theodora H. Bofman. (Special Reports: No. 21). 258p. (C). 1984. pap. 16.95 (1-877979-71-6) SE Asia.

Poetics of Transformation: Prudentius & Classical Mythology. Martha A. Malamud. LC 88-43290. (Cornell Studies in Classical Philology). 224p. 1989. 35.00 (0-8014-2249-3) Cornell U Pr.

Poetics of Transformation: Prudentius & Classical Mythology. Martha A. Malamud. LC 88-43290. (Cornell Studies in Classical Philology: Vol. 49). 208p. reprint ed. pap. 64.50 (0-608-20920-1, 207201900003) Bks Demand.

***Poetics of Transition: Emerson, Pragmatism, & American Literary Modernism.** Jonathan Levin. LC 98-8840. (New Americanists Ser.). 1999. write for info. (0-8223-2277-3) Duke.

Poetics of Transition: Emerson, Pragmatism & American Literary Modernism. Jonathan Levin. LC 98-8840. (New Americanists Ser.). 1999. pap. 17.95 (0-8223-2296-X) Duke.

Poetics of Translatio Studii & Conjointure: Chretien de Troyes's Cliges. Michelle A. Freeman. LC 78-54262. (Edward C. Armstrong Monographs on Medieval Literature: No. 12). 199p. (Orig.). 1979. pap. 12.95 (0-917058-11-9) French Forum.

Poetics of Translation: History, Theory, Practice. Willis Barnstone. 1995. pap. 20.00 (0-300-06300-8) Yale U Pr.

Poetics of Valentin Kataev's Prose of the 1960's & 1970's. Ireneusz Szarycz. (American University Studies: Slavic Languages & Literature: Ser. XII, Vol. 5). 205p. (C). 1989. text 35.95 (0-8204-1081-0) P Lang Pubng.

Poetics of Vision: Photographs from the Collection of Harry M. Drake. Christian A. Peterson & Minneapolis Institute of Arts. LC 97-73720. (Illus.). 1997. write for info. (0-912964-62-6) Minneapolis Inst Arts.

Poetics of Women's Autobiography: Marginality & the Fictions of Self-Representation. Sidonie Smith. LC 86-45990. 223p. 1987. reprint ed. pap. 69.20 (0-608-01077-4, 205938500001) Bks Demand.

Poetics of Yury Olesha. Victor Peppard. (University of Florida Humanities Monographs: No. 63). 176p. 1989. 49.95 (0-8130-0950-2) U Press Fla.

Poetics of Yves Bonnefoy. John T. Naughton. LC 87-5097. (Illus.). x, 224p. 1984. 24.00 (0-226-56947-0) U Ch Pr.

Poetics on Indeterminacy: Rimbaud to Cage. Marjorie Perloff. LC 80-8569. (Illus.). 363p. 1981. reprint ed. pap. 112.60 (0-608-02540-2, 206318400004) Bks Demand.

Poetics Religious Experience. Keshavjee. 1998. text 9.95 (1-86064-240-3, Pub. by I B T) St Martin.

Poetics, Speculation, & Judgment: The Shadow of the Work of Art from Kant to Phenomenology. Jacques Taminiaux. Ed. & Tr. by Michael Gendre. LC 92-35025. (SUNY Series in Contemporary Continental Philosophy). 191p. (C). 1993. text 59.50 (0-7914-1547-3); pap. text 19.95 (0-7914-1548-1) State U NY Pr.

Poetics, the Imitation of Action: Essays in Interpretation. E. San Juan, Jr. LC 78-4345. 134p. 1979. 26.50 (0-8386-2273-9) Fairleigh Dickinson.

Poetics/Politics. Kumar. LC 99-22576. 280p. 1999. text 55.00 (0-312-21865-6) St Martin.

Poetics/Politics: Radical Aesthetics for the Classroom. Amitava Kumar. LC 99-22576. 288p. 1999. pap. 18.95 (0-312-21866-4) St Martin.

Poetika Kino. Boris M. Eikhenbaum et al. (RUS.). 191p. 1984. pap. 7.50 (0-933884-40-0) Berkeley Slavic.

Poetique d'Aristote. Aristotle. Tr. & Comment by Andre Dacier.Tr. of Poetics. xxxii, 527p. 1976. reprint ed. 130.00 (3-487-05591-0) G Olms Pubs.

Poetique de la Prose: Nouvelles Recherches sur le Recit. Tzvetan Todorov. (FRE.). 1980. pap. 14.95 (0-7859-2682-8) Fr & Eur.

Poetique de la Reverie. 3rd ed. Gaston Bachelard. (FRE.). 192p. 1990. pap. 19.95 (0-7859-3012-4) Fr & Eur.

Poetique de L'Espace. 5th ed. Gaston Bachelard. (FRE.). 214p. 1992. pap. 19.95 (0-7859-3019-1) Fr & Eur.

Poetique des Tableaux Chez Proust et Matisse. Martine Blanche. LC 96-68095.Tr. of Poetics of Painting in the Works of Proust & Matisse. (Illus.). 206p. 1996. 39.95 (1-883479-10-X) Summa Pubns.

Poetiques: Theorie et Critique Litteraires. Ed. by Floyd Gray. LC 81-50963. (Michigan Romance Studies: Vol. 1). 207p. 1980. pap. 15.00 (0-939730-00-6) Mich Romance.

Poetische Werke. Ed. by James R. Hightower. Tr. by Erwin Von Zach. LC 52-5409. (Harvard-Yenching Institute Studies: No. 7). 404p. 1952. 21.00 (0-674-67860-5) HUP.

***Poetisches Pathos: Eine Idee Bei Friedrich Nietzsche und im Deutschen Expressionismus.** Peter Stucheli. (Europaische Hochschulschriften Ser.). 235p. 1999. 37.95 (3-906763-94-3, Pub. by P Lang) P Lang Pubng.

Poetivities - Intermediate. James Wainwright. 64p. (J). (gr. 4-6). 1989. 8.99 (0-86653-488-1, GA1090) Good Apple.

Poetivities - Primary. James Wainwright. 64p. (J). (gr. 1-3). 1989. 8.99 (0-86653-484-9, GA1089) Good Apple.

Poetography: Images of the Soul. Nancy E. Holderfield. (Illus.). 35p. 1998. spiral bd. 15.00 (0-9668585-0-6) Eternal Images.

Poetria Nova & Its Sources in Early Rhetorical Doctrine. Ernest A. Gallo. (De Proprietatibus Litterarum, Ser. Major: No. 10). 1971. text 50.80 (90-279-1794-9) Mouton.

Poetries: Their Media & Ends. I. A. Richards. LC 73-93947. (De Proprietatibus Litterarum, Ser. Major: No. 30). 256p. 1974. pap. text 56.95 (90-279-3482-7) Mouton.

Poetries & Sciences. I. A. Richards. LC 68-22862. (C). 1972. pap. 3.00 (0-393-00652-2) Norton.

Poetries of America: Essays on the Relation of Character to Style. Irvin Ehrenpreis. Ed. by Daniel Albright. LC 88-10699. 292p. 1989. reprint ed. pap. 90.60 (0-7837-8571-2, 204938600011) Bks Demand.

Poetry. (C). 1990. (0-8013-0572-1) Longman.

Poetry. Jill P. Bamgaertner & Linda A. Dover. 703p. (C). 1989. pap. text 41.50 (0-15-570680-2) Harcourt Coll Pubs.

Poetry. Jill P. Bamgaertner & Linda A. Dover. 703p. (C). 1990. pap. text 34.00 (0-15-570681-0) Harcourt Coll Pubs.

***Poetry.** Kelly Burkholder. LC 00-25371. (Artistic Adventures Ser.). (Illus.). (J). 2000. write for info. (1-57103-354-8) Rourke Bk Co.

P

An Asterisk (*) at the beginning of an entry indicates that the title is appearing for the first time.

Poetry. James Halon. LC 91-76664. 80p. 1992. 12.95 (*0-923687-14-9*) Celo Valley Bks.

Poetry. Peggy Hapke Lewis. 1994. 6.95 (*1-55708-421-1*, MCC922) McDonald Pub Co.

Poetry. Jeffrey D. Hoeper. 480p. (C). 1990. pap. text 25.80 (*0-02-395465-5*, Macmillan Coll) P-H.

Poetry. Ann Leschen. 1981. 4.95 (*1-55708-233-2*, MCR243) McDonald Pub Co.

Poetry. Bernadette Mayer. 1976. 7.00 (*0-686-16289-7*); pap. 3.50 (*0-686-16290-0*) Kulchur Foun.

Poetry. Ed. by Stephany Mendelsohn. 1979. 4.95 (*1-55708-175-1*, MCR263) McDonald Pub Co.

Poetry. Meyer. (Bedford Introduction to Literature Ser.). 2000. pap. text 52.20 (*0-312-13896-2*) St Martin.

Poetry. MQ Publications Staff. (Infatuations Ser.). (Illus.). 256p. 1998. 12.95 (*1-897954-65-4*, Pub. by Mus Quilts Pub) Sterling.

***Poetry.** Lyle Paulsen. Ed. by Ann Kozachik. 106p. 2000. pap. 10.00 (*0-9619354-2-1*) Victoria Productions.

Poetry. O. Tlyiha. 120p. 1985. 18.00 (*0-935090-16-9*) Almanac Pr.

Poetry, 2 vols. George Wither. (BCL1-PR English Literature Ser.). (J). 1992. reprint ed. lib. bdg. 150.00 (*0-7812-7231-9*) Rprt Serv.

***Poetry.** 3rd ed. (C). 1999. 18.40 (*0-8087-2295-6*) Pearson Custom.

Poetry, Vol. 1. Richard Oldham. 32p. 1997. pap. 6.30 (*0-9655710-7-6*) With Heart Bks.

Poetry, Vol. 2. unabridged ed. Richard Oldham. 30p. 1997. pap. 6.30 (*0-9655710-8-4*) With Heart Bks.

Poetry: A Blueprint for Key Stage 3. James Sale. 112p. 1998. pap. 120.00 (*0-7487-3134-2*, Pub. by S Thornes Pubs) Trans-Atl Phila.

Poetry: A Collection of Poems Written by Medical Students 1983-1985. Ed. by Susan Jamison et al. 48p. (Orig.). 1986. pap. 5.00 (*0-614-08002-9*) NE Ohio Univs.

Poetry: A Collection of Poems Written by Medical Students 1983-1991, 3 vols. Ed. by Martin F. Kohn & Delese Wear. 122p. (Orig.). 1992. pap. 16.50 (*0-925664-02-2*) NE Ohio Univs.

Poetry: A Collection of Poems Written by Medical Students 1989-1991. Ed. by Martin F. Kohn & Delese Wear. 38p. (Orig.). 1992. pap. 7.95 (*0-925664-01-4*) NE Ohio Univs.

Poetry: A Collection of Poems Written by Medical Students 1992-1996. Ed. by Nancy A. McDonald. 79p. (Orig.). 1996. pap. text 8.95 (*0-925664-03-0*) NE Ohio Univs.

Poetry: A Harper Collins Pocket Anthology. 2nd ed. Ed. by R. S. Gwynn. LC 97-16030. 350p. (C). 1997. pap. 19.13 (*0-321-01113-9*) Addson-Wesley Educ.

Poetry: A Magazine of Verse, 1912-81, 138 vols. write for info. (*0-404-19577-6*) AMS Pr.

Poetry: A Study Guide. Alice Sheff. Ed. by J. Friedland & R. Kessler. (Novel-Ties Ser.). 1989. pap. text, student ed. 15.95 (*0-88122-864-8*) Lrn Links.

Poetry: An Introduction. Meyer. 1994. pap. text, teacher ed. 10.00 (*0-312-11712-4*) St Martin.

***Poetry: An Introduction.** John Strachan & Richard Terry. LC 00-41896. 2001. write for info. (*0-8147-9797-0*) NYU Pr.

Poetry: Lyrical, Narrative, & Satirical of the Civil War. Ed. by Richard G. White. LC 72-4981. (Romantic Tradition in American Literature Ser.). 360p. 1972. reprint ed. 30.95 (*0-405-04650-2*) Ayer.

Poetry: Nature. Rosemary R. Wilkinson. 75p. (Orig.). 1996. pap. text 10.00 (*0-9642261-0-3*) EJ Co.

Poetry: Reading, Reacting. Laurie G. Kirszner. (C). 1994. pap. text, teacher ed. 33.75 (*0-15-501213-4*) Harcourt Coll Pubs.

Poetry: Ryms & Odes, Heart & Mind: Poem Feelings Expressing Life--A Sojourner's Steps. abr. ed. Eric Fortmeyer. (Illus.). 112p. 1996. 70.00 (*1-928620-00-0*, EFX-699106M0399, Poms Healing); pap. 30.00 (*1-928620-01-9*, EFX-699106M0399, Poms Healing) AGI Prods.

Poetry: Starting from Scratch, a Two Week Lesson Plan for Teaching Poetry Writing. Michael Carey. LC 88-82550. 120p. 1989. pap. 5.95 (*0-934988-17-X*) Foun Bks.

Poetry: Telling It Like It Is. B. J. Moore. 80p. 1996. 10.00 (*0-533-11375-X*) Vantage.

***Poetry: Telling It Like It Is - II.** B. J. Moore. 87p. 2000. 11.95 (*0-533-12771-8*) Vantage.

Poetry: Treasures of the Heart. Walterrean Salley. LC 89-85680. 50p. (Orig.). 1989. pap. 6.00 (*0-9622600-1-0*) Christ Assn.

***Poetry No. 3: Collection.** 2000. 14.00 (*0-9657552-6-6*) P L Mackenzie.

Poetry - A Legacy of Love: Featuring an Era of Poetry Then & Now. Shirley B. Paoli. 55p. (Orig.). 1989. pap. 5.95 (*0-685-44869-X*) S B Paoli.

Poetry - An Elegy on the Death of Mr. Buckingham St. John. John Trumbull. (Notable American Authors). 1999. reprint ed. lib. bdg. 125.00 (*0-7812-9821-0*) Rprt Serv.

Poetry - Close Reading for Cooperative Learning Groups. 2nd rev. ed. James Scott. 55p. (YA). (gr. 7-12). 1997. pap., wbk. ed. 3.00 (*1-58049-108-1*, CO02A) Prestwick Hse.

Poetry - Mind - Body. Helen Jaskoski. 88p. (Orig.). (C). 1991. lib. bdg. 11.00 (*0-8191-8312-1*) U Pr of Amer.

Poetry - Ontwa: The Son of the Forest. James Lawson. (Notable American Authors Ser.). 1999. reprint ed. lib. bdg. 125.00 (*0-7812-3763-7*) Rprt Serv.

Poetry - Poems. Richard H. Stoddard. (Notable American Authors Ser.). 1999. reprint ed. lib. bdg. 125.00 (*0-7812-8951-3*) Rprt Serv.

Poetry - The Book of Gold & Other Poems. John T. Trowbridge. (Notable American Authors). 1999. reprint ed. lib. bdg. 125.00 (*0-7812-9815-6*) Rprt Serv.

Poetry - The Convent & Other Poems. William Winter. (Notable American Authors Ser.). 1999. reprint ed. lib. bdg. 125.00 (*0-7812-7760-4*) Rprt Serv.

Poetry - Windows & Mirrors: The Sketchbook Approach to Writing & Reading Poetry. Priscilla Adams. LC 93-74573. (Illus.). 188p. (J). (gr. 6-10). 1995. pap. text 14.95 (*0-89089-571-6*) Carolina Acad Pr.

Poetry--Plain & Simple. Ingeborg Z. Seymour. 64p. 1999. pap. 14.95 (*1-892668-10-6*) Prospect Pr.

Poetry across the Curriculum: An Action Guide for Elementary Teachers. Aaren Y. Perry. LC 96-42531. 192p. 1996. pap. text 30.00 (*0-205-19807-4*) Allyn.

Poetry after Lunch: Poems to Read Aloud. Ed. by Joyce A. Carroll & Edward E. Wilson. 164p. (Orig.). 1997. pap. 17.95 (*1-888842-03-2*, 1040) Absey & Co.

Poetry after Modernism. Ed. by Robert McDowell. (New Criticism Ser.). 378p. 1991. 24.95 (*0-934257-36-1*) Story Line.

Poetry after Modernism. 2nd rev. ed. Ed. by Robert McDowell. LC 97-2209. 288p. 1998. pap. 17.95 (*1-885266-34-0*) Story Line.

Poetry Alaska Women: Top of the World. Illus. by Jennifer Dominick. 64p. (Orig.). 1993. pap. 10.00 (*0-9637003-0-8*) ArtsVenture.

Poetry among Friends. Dorothy Lloyd Gilbert Thorne. LC 63-18398. 1963. pap. 4.00 (*0-87574-130-4*) Pendle Hill.

Poetry & Ambition: Essays, Nineteen Eighty-Two to Eighty-Eight. Donald Hall. (Poets on Poetry Ser.). 216p. 1988. pap. 13.95 (*0-472-06387-1*, 06387) U of Mich Pr.

Poetry & Anarchism. Herbert E. Read. 1972. 59.95 (*0-8490-0857-3*) Gordon Pr.

Poetry & Anarchism. Herbert E. Read. LC 72-290. (Essay Index Reprint Ser.). 1977. reprint ed. 13.95 (*0-8369-2819-9*) Ayer.

Poetry & Antipoetry: A Study of Selected Aspects of Max Jacob's Poetic Style Annette Thau. LC 74-32437. (Studies in the Romance Languages & Literatures). 128p. 1976. write for info. (*0-88438-005-X*) U NC Studies Rom.

Poetry & Career of Li Po. Arthur Waley. (Ethical & Religious Classics of East & West Ser.). 1951. 19.95 (*0-04-895012-2*) Routledge.

Poetry & Civil War in Lucan's "Bellum Civile" Jamie Masters. (Cambridge Classical Studies). (Illus.). 285p. (C). 1992. text 59.95 (*0-521-41460-1*) Cambridge U Pr.

Poetry & Colortypes of the 1915 Exposition. Max G. Harrington. (Illus.). 36p. 1998. pap. 17.99 (*1-892571-01-3*) TDC Pr.

Poetry & Consciousness. Daisy Aldan. 1985p. 1985. pap. 3.50 (*0-913152-16-1*) Folder Edns.

Poetry & Consciousness. C. K. Williams. LC 98-5418. (Poets on Poetry Ser.). 144p. (C). 1998. pap. 13.95 (*0-472-06672-2*, 06672); text 39.50 (*0-472-09672-9*, 09672) U of Mich Pr.

Poetry & Doubt in the Work of Jose Angel Valente & Guillermo Carnero. C. R. Christie. LC 95-19530. 290p. 1996. text 89.95 (*0-7734-8901-0*) E Mellen.

Poetry & Film: 2 Symposiums. Arthur Miller et al. 1973. pap. 5.50 (*0-910664-24-2*) Gotham.

Poetry & Gender: Statements & Essays on Australian Women Poets. Ed. by David Brooks & Brenda Walker. 1989. pap. 14.95 (*0-7022-2240-2*, Pub. by Univ Queensland Pr) Intl Spec Bk.

Poetry & Humanism. Molly M. Mahood. (C). 1970. reprint ed. pap. 3.00 (*0-393-00533-X*) Norton.

Poetry & Ireland since 1800: A Source Book. Ed. by Mark Storey. 256p. 1988. pap. 14.95 (*0-415-00332-6*); lib. bdg. 57.50 (*0-415-00331-8*) Routledge.

Poetry & Its Public in Ancient Greece: From Homer to the Fifth Century. Bruno Gentili. Tr. by A. Thomas Cole from ITA. LC 87-26852. 408p. 1990. pap. text 18.95 (*0-8018-4019-8*) Johns Hopkins.

Poetry & Jacobite Politics in Eighteenth-Century Britain & Ireland. Murray G. Pittock. LC 93-42500. (Studies in Eighteenth-Century English Literature & Thought: No. 23). 270p. (C). 1995. text 69.95 (*0-521-41092-4*) Cambridge U Pr.

Poetry & Knowing: Speculative Essays & Interviews. Ed. by Tim Lilburn. 192p. 1995. pap. 19.95 (*1-55082-116-4*, Pub. by Quarry Pr) LPC InBook.

Poetry & Life. Ed. by Clyde S. Kilby. LC 72-12510. (Granger Index Reprint Ser.). 1977. reprint ed. 32.95 (*0-8369-6405-5*) Ayer.

***Poetry & Life of Allen Ginsberg: A Narrative Poem.** Ed. by Edward Sanders. LC 00-26619. 240p. 2000. 27.95 (*1-58567-037-5*, Pub. by Overlook Pr) Penguin Putnam.

Poetry & Life Series, 34 vols. Ed. by William Henry Hudson. reprint ed. 544.00 (*0-404-52500-8*) AMS Pr.

Poetry & Mathematics. Scott Buchanan. (Midway Reprint Ser.). 156p. 1975. reprint ed. pap. text 9.95 (*0-226-07821-3*) U Ch Pr.

Poetry & Moral Dialectic: Baudelaire's "Secret Architecture" James R. Lawler. LC 97-19940. 224p. 1997. 36.00 (*0-8386-3758-2*) Fairleigh Dickinson.

Poetry & Music from Under the Watchful Eye. James Deahl. audio 8.95 (*0-921411-32-4*) Genl Dist Srvs.

Poetry & Music in Seventeenth-Century England. Diane K. McColley. LC 97-7581. (Illus.). 330p. (C). 1998. text 59.95 (*0-521-59363-8*) Cambridge U Pr.

Poetry & Mysticism. Colin Wilson. LC 70-88225. pap. 12.95 (*0-87286-182-1*) City Lights.

Poetry & Mysticism in Islam: The Heritage of Rumi. Ed. by Amin Banani et al. (Levi Della Vida Symposia Ser.: No. 11). 214p. (C). 1994. text 69.95 (*0-521-45476-X*) Cambridge U Pr.

Poetry & Mysticism in Islam: The Heritage of Rumi. Amin Banani & Georges Sabagh. 214p. 1996. 59.95 (*0-614-21327-4*, 1439) Kazi Pubns.

Poetry & Opinion. Archibald Macleish. LC 74-2189. (Studies in Poetry: No. 38). (C). 1974. lib. bdg. 75.00 (*0-8383-2043-0*) M S G Haskell Hse.

***Poetry & Painting in Song China: The Subtle Art of Dissent.** Alfreda Murck. LC 99-44492. Vol. 50. (Illus.). 400p. 2000. 60.00 (*0-674-00243-1*) HUP.

Poetry & Paintings of the 1st Bible of Charles the Bald. Paul E. Dutton & Herbert L. Kessler. LC 97-4833. (Recentiores Ser.). 198p. (C). 1998. text 69.50 (*0-472-10815-8*, 10815) U of Mich Pr.

Poetry & Personality: Reading, Exegesis, & Hermeneutics in Traditional China. Steven Van Zoeren. LC 90-38044. 352p. 1991. 45.00 (*0-8047-1854-7*) Stanford U Pr.

Poetry & Philosophy of Browning. Edward H. Griggs. 1972. 59.95 (*0-8490-0858-1*) Gordon Pr.

Poetry & Philosophy of George Meredith. George M. Trevelyan. (BCL1-PR English Literature Ser.). 234p. 1992. reprint ed. lib. bdg. 79.00 (*0-7812-7598-9*) Rprt Serv.

***Poetry & Poetics in a New Millennium: Interviews with Major Contemporary Poets.** Ed. by E. H. Foster. 2000. 39.95 (*1-58498-015-X*); pap. 18.95 (*1-58498-014-1*) Talisman Hse.

Poetry & Poetics of Amiri Baraka: The Jazz Aesthetic. William J. Harris. LC 85-1000. 184p. 1985. text 27.50 (*0-8262-0483-X*) U of Mo Pr.

Poetry & Poetics of Ancient Japan. Makoto Ooka. Tr. by Thomas Fitzsimmons from JPN. LC 97-19908. (Reflections Ser.: No. 6). (Illus.). 144p. 1997. 30.00 (*0-942668-51-0*); pap. text 19.95 (*0-942668-52-9*) Katydid Bks.

Poetry & Poetics of Cesar Vallejo: The Fourth Angle of the Circle. Ed. by Adam Sharman. LC 97-45854. 200p. 1997. text 749.95 (*0-7734-8461-2*) E Mellen.

Poetry & Poetics of Constantine P. Cavafy: Aesthetic Visions of Sensual Reality. John P. Anton. LC 95-233198. (Greek Poetry Archives Ser.: Vol. 1). 387p. 1995. text 74.00 (*3-7186-5551-9*, Harwood Acad Pubs); pap. text 27.00 (*3-7186-5552-7*, Harwood Acad Pubs) Gordon & Breach.

Poetry & Poetics of Nishiwaki Junzaburo: Modernism in Translation. Hosea Hirata. LC 92-42404. (Studies of the East Asian Institute, Columbia University). 272p. (C). 1993. text 42.50 (*0-691-06981-6*, Pub. by Princeton U Pr) Cal Prin Full Svc.

Poetry & Poets. Amy Lowell. LC 77-162298. 1971. reprint ed. 30.00 (*0-8196-0274-4*) Biblo.

Poetry & Politics. Ed. by Kate Flint. LC 97-200101. (English Association: No. 49). 176p. 1996. 55.00 (*0-85991-504-2*) Boydell & Brewer.

Poetry & Politics in the Cockney School: Keats, Shelley, Hunt & Their Circle. Jeffrey N. Cox. LC 98-12838. (Studies in Romanticism: No. 31). (Illus.). 250p. (C). 1999. text 59.95 (*0-521-63100-9*) Cambridge U Pr.

Poetry & Politics in the English Renaissance. David Norbrook. 280p. 1984. 32.50 (*0-7100-9778-6*, Routledge Thoemms) Routledge.

Poetry & Popcorn. Linda J. Hubbard. (Illus.). 112p. (J). (gr. 2-4). 1996. pap. 11.00 (*0-8059-3997-0*) Dorrance.

Poetry & Possibility. Michael Edwards. 224p. 1987. 53.00 (*0-389-20770-5*, N8329) B&N Imports.

Poetry & Pragmatism. Richard Poirer. 240p. 1992. pap. 16.00 (*0-674-67991-1*) HUP.

Poetry & Pragmatism. Richard Poirier. 208p. (C). 1992. 30.00 (*0-674-67990-3*) HUP.

Poetry & Prophecy: The Anthropology of Inspiration. John H. Leavitt. LC 97-25223. 224p. (C). 1997. text 44.50 (*0-472-10688-0*, 10688) U of Mich Pr.

Poetry & Prophecy: The Beginnings of a Literary Tradition. Ed. by James L. Kugel. LC 90-55128. (Myth & Poetics Ser.). 256p. 1991. 42.50 (*0-8014-2310-4*); pap. text 17.95 (*0-8014-9568-7*) Cornell U Pr.

Poetry & Prose. John Donne. Ed. by Frank J. Warnke. (Modern Library College Editions). 437p. (C). 1967. pap. 8.44 (*0-07-553663-3*, T89) McGraw.

Poetry & Prose. Heinrich Heine. Ed. by Jost Hermand & Robert C. Holub. LC 73-77054. (German Library: Vol. 32). 288p. 1982. 39.50 (*0-8264-0255-0*) Continuum.

Poetry & Prose. Heinrich Heine. Ed. by Jost Hermand & Robert C. Holub. LC 74-16788. (German Library: Vol. 32). 288p. 1982. pap. 19.95 (*0-8264-0265-8*) Continuum.

Poetry & Prose. Ed. by Evelyn G. Klapp. 1991. pap. 12.00 (*0-685-60196-X*) Aegis Pub Co.

Poetry & Prose. Walt Whitman. Ed. by Justin Kaplan. 1380p. 1982. 35.00 (*0-940450-02-X*, 81-20768, Pub. by Library of America) Penguin Putnam.

Poetry & Prose. Walt Whitman. LC 95-52466. (Library of America College Editions). 1407p. (C). 1996. pap. text 16.95 (*1-883011-35-3*, Pub. by Library of America) Penguin Putnam.

Poetry & Prose. Walter Savage Landor. LC 76-29435. reprint ed. 24.50 (*0-404-15314-3*) AMS Pr.

Poetry & Prose, Vol. de-1001. Barbara D. DeVault. 55p. 1997. pap. 4.99 (*1-891536-03-6*, BD8197A) DeVault Ents.

Poetry & Prose in the Sixteenth Century. C. S. Lewis. (Oxford History of English Literature Ser.: Vol. IV). 704p. (C). 1990. text 75.00 (*0-19-812231-4*) OUP.

Poetry & Prose of Alexander Pope, 001. Alexander Pope. Ed. by Aubrey Williams. LC 76-4880. (C). 1969. pap. 13.96 (*0-395-05156-8*, RivEd) HM.

Poetry & Prose of the Han, Wei & Six Dynasties. 228p. 1986. 6.95 (*0-8351-1606-9*) China Bks.

Poetry & Prose of the Tang & Song. Wang Wei et al. Tr. by Yan Xianyi & Gladys Yang from CHI. 310p. 1984. pap. 7.95 (*0-8351-1164-4*) China Bks.

Poetry & Prose with a Purpose. Ruth Newman. 1998. pap. write for info. (*1-57553-756-7*) Watermrk Pr.

Poetry & Prose, with Izaac Walton's Life, Appreciations by Ben Jonson, Dryden, Coleridge & Others. John Donne. LC 75-41077. reprint ed. 20.00 (*0-404-14769-0*) AMS Pr.

Poetry & Prose, with Thomas Sprat's Life, & Observations by Dryden, Addison, Johnson & Others. Abraham Cowley. 1988. reprint ed. lib. bdg. 49.00 (*0-7812-0276-0*) Rprt Serv.

Poetry & Revolution: An Anthology of British & Irish Verse, 1625-1660. Ed. by David Davidson. LC 97-44267. 716p. 1998. text 135.00 (*0-19-818441-7*) OUP.

Poetry & Revolution: Boris Pasternak's "My Sister Life" Ed. by Lazar Fleishman. (Stanford Slavic Studies: Vol. 21). (ENG & RUS.). 244p. (C). 1999. pap. text 25.00 (*1-57201-054-1*) Berkeley Slavic.

Poetry & Revolution in Russia, 1905-1930: An Exhibition of Books & Manuscripts. Lazar Fleishman. LC 89-188526. (Illus.). 63p. (Orig.). 1989. pap. 18.00 (*0-911221-10-7*) Stanford U Libraries.

Poetry & Selected Prose of Camillo Sbarbaro. Vittorio Felaco. Tr. by Franco Fido. 1985. 25.00 (*0-916379-19-1*) Scripta.

Poetry & Short Stories of Dorothy Parker. Dorothy R. Parker. (Illus.). 504p. 1994. 16.50 (*0-679-60132-5*) Modern Lib NY.

Poetry & Society: The Role of Poetry in Ancient Greece. Bruno Snell. LC 73-165808. (Select Bibliographies Reprint Ser.). 1977. reprint ed. 17.95 (*0-8369-5965-5*) Ayer.

Poetry & Song of Old Ireland. Compiled by John B. O'Reilly. (Illus.). 852p. 1985. 35.00 (*0-940134-43-8*) Irish Genealog.

***Poetry & Style.** Sheryle DeNonno. 1999. pap. write for info. (*1-57553-860-1*) Watermrk Pr.

Poetry & Tales. Edgar Allan Poe. Ed. by Patrick F. Quinn. 1408p. 1984. 37.50 (*0-940450-18-6*, Pub. by Library of America) Penguin Putnam.

Poetry & the Age. Randall Jarrell. LC 52-12173. 271p. 1979. reprint ed. pap. 8.50 (*0-912946-70-9*, Ecco Press) HarperTrade.

Poetry & the Body. John Vernon. LC 78-11552. 176p. 1979. text 19.95 (*0-252-00699-2*) U of Ill Pr.

Poetry & the Common Life. Macha L. Rosenthal. 148p. 1987. reprint ed. pap. 8.95 (*0-89255-118-6*) Persea Bks.

Poetry & the Criticism of Life. Heathcote W. Garrod. LC 76-58446. (Charles Eliot Norton Lectures Ser.: 1929-1930). 168p. 1978. reprint ed. lib. bdg. 55.00 (*0-8371-9445-8*, GAPO, Greenwood Pr) Greenwood.

Poetry & the Cult of the Martyrs: The Liber Peristephanon on Prudentius. Michael Roberts. (Recentiores: Later Latin Texts & Contexts Ser.). 232p. 1993. text 52.50 (*0-472-10449-7*, 10449) U of Mich Pr.

Poetry & the Practical. William Gilmore Simms. LC 96-12926. (Simms Ser.). (C). 1996. text 24.00 (*1-55728-435-0*) U of Ark Pr.

Poetry & the Practical. William Gilmore Simms. Ed. & Intro. by James E. Kibler, Jr. 1998. pap. 16.00 (*1-55728-540-3*) U of Ark Pr.

Poetry & the Realm of Politics: Shakespeare to Dryden. Howard Erskine-Hill. (Illus.). 298p. 1996. text 60.00 (*0-19-811731-0*) OUP.

Poetry & the Stars. Hyacinthe Hill. LC 86-61691. 88p. (Orig.). 1986. 10.95 (*0-9616986-0-8*); pap. 5.95 (*0-9616986-1-6*) Scop & Gleeman.

Poetry & the System. Brian Lee. (C). 1989. 30.00 (*0-907839-05-3*, Pub. by Brynmill Pr Ltd) St Mut.

Poetry And The World. 11th ed. Robert Pinsky. LC 88-4411. 1992. pap. 10.95 (*0-88001-217-X*) HarpC.

Poetry & Truth. Dennis Rasmussen. LC 74-75364. (De Proprietatibus Litterarum, Ser. Minor: No. 20). 123p. 1974. pap. text 20.80 (*90-279-3462-2*) Mouton.

Poetry & Truth in the Spanish Works of Fray Luis de Leon. David J. Hildner. (Monagrafias A Ser.: No. 151). 185p. (C). 1992. 72.00 (*1-85566-017-2*, Pub. by Tamesis Bks Ltd) Boydell & Brewer.

***Poetry & Violence on Mexico's Costa Chica.** John H. McDowell. LC 99-51010. (Music in American Life Ser.). (Illus.). 248p. 2000. text 39.95 (*0-252-02588-1*) U of Ill Pr.

Poetry & War: An Introductory Reader. Simon Featherstone. LC 94-16861. (Critical Readers in Theory & Practice Ser.). 256p. (C). 1995. pap. 22.99 (*0-415-09570-0*, B4271) Routledge.

Poetry & Wisdom. Peter Enns. LC 97-33543. (IBR Bibliographies Ser.). 176p. 1998. pap. 12.99 (*0-8010-2161-8*) Baker Bks.

Poetry Anthology. Robert Creeley. LC 92-74507. (Illus.). 118p. 1992. pap. 14.00 (*1-879003-07-4*) Edmundson.

Poetry Anthology. Eloise Greenfield. 32p. (ps-3). 15.95 (*0-06-028993-7*); pap. 5.95 (*0-06-443692-6*); lib. bdg. 15.89 (*0-06-028994-5*) HarpC.

Poetry Anthology. Charles H. Rowell. 1997. pap. 65.00 (*0-8133-3014-9*) Westview.

Poetry Anthology. Charles H. Rowell. 2000. pap. 22.50 (*0-8133-3015-7*) Westview.

Poetry Anthology, 1912-1977: 65 Years of America's Most Distinguished Verse Magazine. Ed. by Daryl Hine & Joseph Parisi. 1978. pap. 10.95 (*0-395-26547-9*, 86, SenEd) HM.

Poetry Appreciation Toolkit: A Guide to Reading & Understanding Poetry. Marc Polonsky. LC 97-347. 1997. write for info. (*0-8442-5989-6*) NTC Contemp Pub Co.

Poetry As a Means of Grace. Charles G. Osgood. LC 68-25106. 131p. 1965. reprint ed. 50.00 (*0-87752-081-X*) Gordian.

Poetry As a Performance Art on & off the Page. 1976. pap. 1.95 (*0-934982-06-6*) Primary Pr.

Poetry as Communication. David A. Williams. LC 92-7440. xiv, 148p. (C). 1992. pap. text 22.50 (*0-8191-8665-1*) U Pr of Amer.

Poetry As Discourse: New Accents. Anthony Easthope. LC 82-18856. 200p. 1983. pap. 13.95 (*0-416-32730-3*, NO. 2975) Routledge.

Poetry As Epitaph: Representation & Poetic Language. Karen Mills-Courts. LC 89-13533. 352p. 1990. text 50.00 (*0-8071-1568-1*); pap. text 19.95 (*0-8071-1657-2*) La State U Pr.

Poetry As Experience. Philippe Lacoue-Labarthe. Tr. by Andrea Tarnowski. LC 98-33880. (Meridian Ser.). 180p. 1998. 39.50 (*0-8047-3426-7*) Stanford U Pr.

Poetry As Experience. Philippe Lacoue-Labarthe. Tr. by Andrea Tarnowski. LC 98-33880. (Meridian Ser.). 180p. 1999. pap. 14.95 (*0-8047-3427-5*) Stanford U Pr.

Poetry As Labor & Privilege: The Writings of W. S. Merwin. Edward J. Brunner. (Illus.). 352p. 1991. text 44.95 (*0-252-01775-7*) U of Ill Pr.

Poetry As Performance: Homer & Beyond. Gregory Nagy. 264p. (C). 1996. pap. text 19.95 (*0-521-55848-4*) Cambridge U Pr.

***Poetry As Persuasion.** Carl Dennis. LC 00-44728. 2001. pap. write for info. (*0-8203-2248-2*) U of Ga Pr.

Poetry As Play: "Gongorismo" & the "Comedia" Maria C. Quintero. LC 91-40886. (Purdue University Monographs in Romance Languages: No. 38). xviii, 260p. 1991. 80.00 (*1-55619-304-1*); pap. 27.95 (*1-55619-305-X*) J Benjamins Pubng Co.

Poetry as Prayer: The Hound of Heaven. Robert Waldron. LC 99-12708. (Illus.). 161p. 1999. pap. 8.95 (*0-8198-5914-1*) Pauline Bks.

***Poetry As Prayer: Thomas Merton.** Robert Waldron. LC 99-55540. (Illus.). 2000. pap. 8.95 (*0-8198-5919-2*) Pauline Bks.

***Poetry as Prayer Vol. 3: Jessica Powers.** Robert F. Morneau. (Illus.). 145p. 2000. pap. 8.95 (*0-8198-5921-4*) Pauline Bks.

Poetry As Text in Twentieth Century Vocal Music: From Stravinsky to Reich. Joseph Coroniti. LC 91-43310. (Studies in the History & Interpretation of Music: Vol. 35). 112p. 1992. lib. bdg. 59.95 (*0-7734-9774-9*) E Mellen.

Poetry As Therapy. Morris R. Morrison. LC 86-15281. 229p. 1987. 35.95 (*0-89885-312-5*, Kluwer Acad Hman Sci) Kluwer Academic.

Poetry at Court in Trastamaran Spain: From the Cancionero de Baena to the Cancionero General. Ed. by E. Michael Gerli & Julian Weiss. LC 98-8302. (Medieval & Renaissance Texts & Studies: Vol. 181). 1998. 30.00 (*0-86698-223-X*, MR181) MRTS.

Poetry at Midnight. Ted Thomas. (Illus.). 197p. 1999. 18.95 (*0-9668452-2-6*) Brown Bks TX.

***Poetry at One Remove: Essays.** John Koethe. LC 99-6806. (Poets on Poetry Ser.). 128p. 2000. pap. 14.95 (*0-472-06709-5*, 06709); text 39.50 (*0-472-09709-1*, 09709) U of Mich Pr.

Poetry at Present. Charles W. Williams. LC 69-17595. (Essay Index Reprint Ser.). 1977. 19.95 (*0-8369-0098-7*) Ayer.

Poetry at Present. Charles Williams. (BCL1-PR English Literature Ser.). 216p. 1992. reprint ed. lib. bdg. 79.00 (*0-7812-7074-X*) Rprt Serv.

Poetry at Stake: Lyric Aesthetics & the Challenge of Technology. Carrie Noland. 280p. 55.00 (*0-691-00416-1*, Pub. by Princeton U Pr) Cal Prin Full Svc.

Poetry at Stake: Lyric Aesthetics & the Challenge of Technology. Carrie Noland. LC 99-25333. (Illus.). 280p. 1999. 19.95 (*0-691-00417-X*, Pub. by Princeton U Pr) Cal Prin Full Svc.

Poetry at the End of the Mind: Poems, 1984-1990 & Postmodern Poems. Louis Hammer. LC 92-19380. 191p. 1992. pap. 11.95 (*0-937584-16-9*) Sachem Pr.

Poetry Australia. John Millet. 128p. (C). 1990. 80.00 (*0-909185-38-7*, Pub. by Pascoe Pub) St Mut.

Poetry Beat: Reviewing the 80's. Tom Clark. 244p. 1990. pap. 13.95 (*0-472-06428-2*, 06428) U of Mich Pr.

Poetry Book, Vol. 4. Ed. by Miriam B. Huber et al. LC 79-51968. (Granger Poetry Library). (Illus.). (J). (gr. 4). 1980. reprint ed. 20.00 (*0-89609-183-X*) Roth Pub Inc.

Poetry Bookshop, 1912-1935: A Bibliography. J. Howard Woolmer. LC 87-51103. (Illus.). 218p. 1988. 75.00 (*0-913506-19-2*, 50295, Pub. by Woolmer-Brotherson) Oak Knoll.

Poetry Bouquet. Mary H. Kegel. (Orig.). 1995. pap. write for info. (*1-57553-045-7*) Watermrk Pr.

Poetry Break: An Annotated Anthology with Ideas for Introducing Children to Poetry. Caroline Feller Bauer. LC 93-42069. 372p. 1994. 45.00 (*0-8242-0852-8*) Wilson.

Poetry Bum: Lyrics of Loss, Love, & Wonder. Mark Selden. 80p. (Orig.). 1995. pap. 12.00 (*0-9645971-1-X*) BloomingFlds.

Poetry by American Women, 1900-1975: A Bibliography. Joan Reardon & Kristine A. Thorsen. LC 78-11944. 631p. 1979. 39.50 (*0-8108-1173-1*) Scarecrow.

Poetry by American Women, 1975-1989: A Bibliography. Joan Reardon. LC 90-21020. 242p. 1990. 32.50 (*0-8108-2366-7*) Scarecrow.

Poetry by Doing. Patricia Osborn. 240p. 1991. pap. 22.59 (*0-8442-5662-5*) NTC Contemp Pub Co.

Poetry by Geraldo Bessa Victor: Debaixo de Ceu, Mucanda, Cubata Abandonada. Geraldo Bessa Victor. (B. E. Ser.: No. 33). 1966. 35.00 (*0-8115-2984-3*) Periodicals Srv.

Poetry by Medieval Welsh Bards. Ed. by John G. Evans. LC 78-72677. (Series of Old Welsh Texts: Vol. 11B). reprint ed. 64.50 (*0-404-60595-8*) AMS Pr.

Poetry by the Kids: Our Times Together. Ed. by Mia Sillanpaa. LC 95-94099. 60p. 1995. pap. 12.95 (*0-9643761-9-9*) M Sillanpaa.

Poetry by Women to 1900: A Bibliography of American & British Writers. Ed. by Beverly A. Joyce. (Bibliographies of Women Writers to 1900 Ser.). 400p. 1991. text 100.00 (*0-8020-5966-X*) U of Toronto Pr.

Poetry Can Be Fun: A Child's Guide to Poetry Writing. Elizabeth Bowers. (Illus.). 60p. (Orig.). (J). (gr. 3-6). 1997. pap. write for info. (*0-9644473-1-2*) Adept Pubng.

***Poetry Church.** John Waddington-Feather. 224p. 1999. 40.00 (*0-85305-429-0*, Pub. by Arthur James) St Mut.

Poetry Class Poem. James Russell Lowell. (Notable American Authors Ser.). 1999. reprint ed. lib. bdg. 125.00 (*0-7812-3873-0*) Rprt Serv.

Poetry Collection. Ed. by Stephen Mitchell. 96p. 1998. pap. 12.00 (*0-06-095049-8*) HarpC.

Poetry Collection: A Compilation of Original Verse. Doris Parker. LC 96-92399. 70p. (Orig.). 1996. pap. 3.00 (*1-57502-243-5*) Morris Pubng.

***Poetry Comes up Where It Can: Poems from "The Amicus Journal," 1990-2000.** Ed. by Brian Swann. LC 99-51678. (Illus.). 168p. 2000. 12.95 (*0-87480-644-5*) U of Utah Pr.

Poetry Corner: Grades 4-6. Arnold B. Cheyney. (Illus.). 128p. (Orig.). 1982. pap. 12.95 (*0-673-16461-6*, GoodYrBooks) Addson-Wesley Educ.

Poetry, Creativity & Aesthetic Experience: Sanskrit Poetics & Literary Criticism. Natavarlal Joshi. xvi, 251p. (C). 1994. 20.00 (*81-85133-94-8*, Pub. by Eastern Bk Linkers) Nataraj Bks.

***Poetry Criticism, 24.** Gale Research Staff. 500p. 1999. text 105.00 (*0-7876-2015-7*) Gale.

Poetry Criticism, Vol. 1. Ed. by Robyn V. Young. 560p. 1990. text 105.00 (*0-8103-5450-0*, 100782-M94801) Gale.

Poetry Criticism, Vol. II. Jane Kosek. 500p. 1995. text 105.00 (*0-8103-5615-5*) Gale.

Poetry Criticism, Vol. 2. Robyn V. Young. 500p. 1991. text 105.00 (*0-8103-5539-6*) Gale.

Poetry Criticism, Vol. 3. Robyn V. Young. 560p. 1991. text 105.00 (*0-8103-5540-X*, 100985-M99348) Gale.

Poetry Criticism, Vol. 4. Young. 500p. 1992. text 105.00 (*0-8103-5541-8*) Gale.

Poetry Criticism, Vol. 5. Young. 500p. 1992. text 105.00 (*0-8103-8333-0*) Gale.

Poetry Criticism, Vol. 6. Young. 500p. 1993. text 105.00 (*0-8103-8334-9*) Gale.

Poetry Criticism, Vol. 7. Young. 500p. 1993. text 105.00 (*0-8103-8335-7*) Gale.

Poetry Criticism, Vol. 8. Young. 500p. 1994. text 105.00 (*0-8103-8460-4*, 101342) Gale.

Poetry Criticism, Vol. 9. Young. 500p. 1994. text 105.00 (*0-8103-8461-2*, 101343) Gale.

Poetry Criticism, Vol. 10. Jane Kosek. 557p. 1994. text 105.00 (*0-8103-5614-7*) Gale.

Poetry Criticism, Vol. 12. Jane Kosek. 500p. 1995. text 105.00 (*0-8103-9273-9*) Gale.

Poetry Criticism, Vol. 13. Jane Kosek. 500p. 1995. text 105.00 (*0-8103-9274-7*) Gale.

Poetry Criticism, Vol. 14. Jane Kosek. 500p. 1996. text 105.00 (*0-7876-0473-9*) Gale.

Poetry Criticism, Vol. 15. Jane Kosek. 500p. 1996. text 105.00 (*0-7876-0474-7*) Gale.

Poetry Criticism, Vol. 16. 500p. 1996. text 105.00 (*0-7876-0475-5*, 00152722) Gale.

Poetry Criticism, Vol. 17. 500p. 1997. text 105.00 (*0-7876-0957-9*, 00155994) Gale.

Poetry Criticism, Vol. 18. 500p. 1997. text 105.00 (*0-7876-0958-7*, 00155995) Gale.

Poetry Criticism, Vol. 19. 500p. 1997. text 105.00 (*0-7876-1546-3*, 00156821) Gale.

***Poetry Criticism, Vol. 20.** 500p. 1998. text 105.00 (*0-7876-1591-9*, 00156894) Gale.

***Poetry Criticism, Vol. 21.** 500p. 1998. text 105.00 (*0-7876-2012-2*, 00157529) Gale.

***Poetry Criticism, Vol. 22.** 500p. 1998. text 105.00 (*0-7876-2013-0*) Gale.

***Poetry Criticism, Vol. 23.** 500p. 1999. text 105.00 (*0-7876-2014-9*) Gale.

***Poetry Criticism, Vol. 25.** Gale Research Staff. 500p. 1999. text 102.00 (*0-7876-3073-X*) Gale.

***Poetry Criticism, Vol. 26.** Gale Group Staff. 500p. 1999. text 105.00 (*0-7876-3074-8*) Gale.

***Poetry Criticism, Vol. 27.** 500p. 2000. text 102.00 (*0-7876-3075-6*) Gale.

***Poetry Criticism, Vol. 28.** 500p. 2000. text 102.00 (*0-7876-3076-4*) Gale.

***Poetry Criticism, Vol. 29.** 500p. 2000. text 102.00 (*0-7876-3077-2*) Gale.

Poetry Dictionary. John Drury. 352p. 1995. 18.99 (*1-884910-04-1*, Story Press) F & W Pubns Inc.

Poetry, 1870-1914. Bergonzi. 1983. pap. text. write for info. (*0-582-35147-2*, Pub. by Addison-Wesley) Longman.

Poetry Essays: From Context Journal. Stan Proper. 32p. (Orig.). (C). 1995. pap. 2.00 (*0-9619992-4-1*) Walden Sudbury.

Poetry Everywhere: Teaching Poetry Writing in School & in the Community. Jack Collom & Sheryl Noethe. LC 93-32351. 280p. 1994. pap. 17.95 (*0-915924-98-6*) Tchrs & Writers Coll.

Poetry Express, 1988: A Collection of Poetry by the Children of California. Elementary School Children of California. Ed. by Lillian E. Gillman. 192p. (J). (ps-6). 1988. 8.95 (*0-317-93373-6*) Other Eye.

Poetry for a Child - By a Child. large type ed. Brittney Grimes. LC 98-60989. (Illus.). 40p. (J). 1998. pap. write for info. (*1-889732-12-5*, Key-A-Teese Prod) Word-For-Word.

Poetry for a Lifetime: All-Time Favorite Poems to Delight & Inspire All Ages. Ed. by Samuel Norfleet Etheredge. (Illus.). 488p. 1999. 21.95 (*0-9665804-0-0*, Pub. by MiraVista) IPG Chicago.

Poetry for a Midsummer's Night: In the Spirit of William Shakespeare's A Midsummer Night's Dream. Marvin Bell. LC 97-62533. (Illus.). 4p. 1998. 19.50 (*0-9655702-1-5*) Seventy Fourth St.

***Poetry for All Occasions: A Collection of Conscious Poems.** Frank Wallace. 95p. 1998. pap. 10.95 (*1-881524-32-9*, Prof Busn) Milligan Bks.

Poetry for All Those Breathing. Amy Marschak. 50p. (Orig.). 1996. pap. 10.00 (*0-9653298-0-1*) Human Theatre.

***Poetry for Bouncers, Straphangers, Teenagers & Lovers.** Alice A. Robinson. LC 98-91119. 1999. pap. 10.95 (*0-533-13055-7*) Vantage.

Poetry for Cats: The Definitive Anthology of Distinguished Feline Verse. Ed. by Henry Beard. LC 94-15358. (Illus.). 1994. write for info. (*0-679-43502-6*) Villard Books.

Poetry for Cats: The Definitive Anthology of Distinguished Feline Verse. Henry Beard. (Illus.). 96p. 1994. 12.95 (*0-679-43582-4*) Villard Books.

Poetry for Children. Ed. by Samuel Eliot. LC 76-160905. (Granger Index Reprint Ser.). 1977. reprint ed. 23.95 (*0-8369-6268-0*) Ayer.

Poetry for Children. Samuel Eliot. (Notable American Authors Ser.). 1992. reprint ed. lib. bdg. 75.00 (*0-7812-2790-9*) Rprt Serv.

Poetry for Enjoyment. Geraldyne I. Garrett. pap. write for info. (*1-57553-578-5*) Watermrk Pr.

Poetry for Home & School. Anna C. Brackett & Ida M. Eliot. LC 79-38593. (Granger Index Reprint Ser.). 1977. reprint ed. 21.95 (*0-8369-6325-3*) Ayer.

Poetry for Life: A Practical Guide to Teaching Poetry in the Primary School. Linda Hall. 160p. 1989. text 100.00 (*0-304-31770-5*) Continuum.

Poetry for Men to Speak Chorally. Marion Robinson & Rozetta L. Thurston. 148p. 3.00 (*0-686-15465-7*) Expression.

***Poetry for Patrons: Literary Communication in the Age of Domitian.** Ruurd R. Nauta. 375p. 2000. 98.00 (*90-04-10885-8*) Brill Academic Pubs.

Poetry for People, Vol. I. Clifton A. Wiles. LC 85-60785. (Illus.). 64p. (Orig.). 1985. pap. 5.95 (*0-9614593-0-1*) hell box.

Poetry for People, Vol. II. Clifton A. Wiles. LC 85-60785. 55p. (Orig.). 1986. pap. 5.95 (*0-9614593-2-8*) hell box.

Poetry for People, Vol. III. Clifton A. Wiles. LC 85-60785. 53p. (Orig.). 1988. pap. 5.95 (*0-9614593-3-6*) hell box.

Poetry for People (Who Don't Like Poetry) Lucille M. Wall. 110p. (Orig.). 1994. pap. 8.95 (*0-9628837-0-0*); text 15.95 (*0-9628837-1-9*) Bradford Enterprise.

Poetry for Sailors & Sea Lovers. Howard Prescott. Ed. by Judy Knop et al. LC 98-91575. 93p. 1998. pap. 9.95 (*1-892109-00-X*) Founders Hill.

Poetry for School Reading. Ed. by Marcus White. LC 72-160912. (Granger Index Reprint Ser.). 1977. reprint ed. 19.95 (*0-8369-6277-X*) Ayer.

***Poetry for Students.** 8th ed. 350p. 2000. text 60.00 (*0-7876-3569-3*) Gale.

Poetry for Students, Vol. 1. 350p. (YA). 1997. text 60.00 (*0-7876-1688-5*, 111089) Gale.

Poetry for Students, Vol. 2. 350p. (YA). 1997. text 60.00 (*0-7876-1689-3*, 111090) Gale.

***Poetry for Students, Vol. 3.** Contrib. by Ruby Hill. 350p. (YA). 1998. text 60.00 (*0-7876-2724-0*, GML00198-112251) Gale.

***Poetry for Students, Vol. 4.** Marowski. 350p. 1998. text 60.00 (*0-7876-2725-9*, GML00298-112252) Gale.

***Poetry for Students, Vol. 5.** Ed. by Mary K. Ruby. 350p. 1999. text 60.00 (*0-7876-3566-9*, GML00299-113189, Gale Res Intl) Gale.

***Poetry for Students, Vol. 6.** Gale Group Publishing Staff. 350p. 1999. text 60.00 (*0-7876-3567-7*) Gale.

***Poetry for Students, Vol. 7.** Gale Group Publishing Staff. 350p. 1999. text 60.00 (*0-7876-3568-5*) Gale.

***Poetry for Students, Vol. 9.** 350p. 2000. text 60.00 (*0-7876-3570-7*, UXL) Gale.

Poetry for the Common Man. Raul Maldonado. 96p. 1998. pap. 10.00 (*0-8059-4377-3*) Dorrance.

Poetry for the Earth. Ed. by Sara Dunn & Alan Scholefield. 288p. 1992. pap. 10.00 (*0-449-90599-3*, Columbine) Fawcett.

Poetry for the Healing. Deborah Stoechel. 1998. pap. write for info. (*1-57553-941-1*) Watermrk Pr.

***Poetry for the Heart.** Fred Gregg, III. 16p. 2000. pap. 11.00 (*1-58374-018-X*) Chicago Spectrum.

Poetry for the Hungry. Gordon Elston. 1997. pap. write for info. (*1-57553-561-0*) Watermrk Pr.

Poetry for the Peace Movement. A. C. Doyle. 17p. 1984. pap. text 7.00 (*0-913597-56-2*) Prosperity & Profits.

Poetry for the Reflective Soul. Robert Wickboldt. LC 96-90150. (Illus.). 150p. (Orig.). 1996. pap. 10.95 (*0-533-11918-9*) Vantage.

Poetry for the Romanians see Poesie per I Romeni: Italian Poetry

Poetry for the Soul: A Poetic Review of 12 Best Sellers. Nick Ortz. 208p. 1998. pap. 14.95 (*1-892896-09-5*) Buy Books.

***Poetry for the Soul: Divinely Inspired Poetic Writings.** Arlette Thomas-Fletcher. 2000. 14.95 (*1-878647-74-1*) APU Pub Grp.

Poetry for the Soul: 700 Best Loved Christian Poems. large type ed. Mary Batchelor. 1996. 20.00 (*0-7838-1683-9*, G K Hall Lrg Type) Mac Lib Ref.

***Poetry for the Spirit: Poem Meditations.** Toyin Olakanpo. 60p. 1999. pap. 10.00 (*0-9673126-6-3*) T K D Bks.

Poetry for Wee Folks. Charlotte M. Hill. Ed. by Fred D. Hill. LC 88-70281. (Illus.). 28p. (J). (gr. k-3). 1988. 11.95 (*0-9620182-0-1*); pap. 6.95 (*0-9620182-2-8*) Charill Pubs.

***Poetry 4 Ya Mind: A Collection of Poetry & Artwork from Getting Ready.** Ed. by Lee White. (Illus.). 128p. (J). (gr. 7-12). 1999. pap. 9.95 (*1-892194-22-8*) NW Media.

Poetry from A to Z: A Guide for Young Writers. Illus. by Cathy Bobak. LC 94-10528. 176p. (J). (gr. 4-8). 1994. mass mkt. 16.00 (*0-02-747672-3*, Mac Bks Young Read) S&S Childrens.

Poetry from Angola: Ao Som das Marimbas, Poemes Africians. Geraldo Bessa Victor. (B. E. Ser.: No. 110). 1967. 25.00 (*0-8115-3041-8*) Periodicals Srv.

Poetry from Bengal. Ron Banerjee. LC 89-82066. 160p. (Orig.). 1990. pap. 19.95 (*0-948259-79-5*, Pub. by Forest Bks) Dufour.

Poetry from Heaven. Brian E. Miller. Ed. by Rene Trezise. (Illus.). 50p. 1998. pap. 15.00 (*0-9664602-0-0*) Vic Crown Pub.

***Poetry from Interface 2000.** Ann S. Gagliardi & Sharon Harmon. 21p. 2000. pap. 3.00 (*1-884540-56-2*) Haleys.

Poetry from Literature for Our Time. Ed. by Harlow O. Waite & Benjamin P. Atkinson. LC 72-108589. (Granger Index Reprint Ser.). 1977. 18.95 (*0-8369-6117-X*) Ayer.

Poetry from Pakistan: An Anthology. Intro. by Maya Jamil. LC 98-135946. (Jubilee Ser.). 132p. (C). 1998. 21.00 (*0-19-577814-6*) OUP.

***Poetry From the Heart.** Evan Thompson. 2000. write for info. (*1-58235-448-0*) Watermrk Pr.

Poetry from the Valley of Virginia: 1996 Edition. Ed. by Ann A. Hunter. (Illus.). 128p. 1996. 19.95 (*0-9630797-2-7*) Loft Pr.

Poetry from the Valley of Virginia: 1998 Edition. Ed. by Ann A. Hunter. (Illus.). 112p. 1997. 20.00 (*0-9630797-5-1*) Loft Pr.

Poetry Fun Book. Claire Ottenstein. (Illus.). 40p. (Orig.). (J). 1992. pap. 7.95 (*1-878149-20-2*) Counterpoint Pub.

Poetry Fun by the Ton with Jack Prelutsky. Cheryl Potts. LC 95-36069. (Illus.). 64p. (J). 1995. pap. 13.95 (*0-917846-55-9*, 34003, Alleyside) Highsmith Pr.

Poetry Galore & More with Shel Silverstein. Cheryl Potts. 64p. 1993. pap. 13.95 (*0-913853-35-6*, 32554, Alleyside) Highsmith Pr.

Poetry Gazzette, 2. unabridged ed. Michael Lizza. (Illus.). 38p. 1996. pap. 7.50 (*1-929326-58-0*) Hal Bar Pubg.

***Poetry Grand Slam Finale.** Alan Scott Macdougall. Ed. by Barbara G. Dan. LC 99-97407. (Illus.). 164p. 2000. pap. 19.95 (*1-884898-09-2*) Eden Pubng OR.

Poetry Handbook. Kim Addonizio. LC 96-40451. 224p. 1997. 23.00 (*0-393-04081-X*) Norton.

Poetry Handbook. Mary Oliver. LC 93-49676. 132p. 1994. pap. 12.00 (*0-15-672400-6*, Harvest Bks) Harcourt.

Poetry Handbook: A Dictionary of Terms. 4th ed. Babette Deutsch. 224p. 1982. reprint ed. pap. 14.00 (*0-06-463548-1*, EH 548) HarpC.

Poetry Handbook: A Guide to Reading Poetry in English for Pleasure & Practical Criticism. John Lennard. 238p. 1996. pap. text 14.95 (*0-19-871149-2*) OUP.

Poetry Handbook: A Guide to Reading Poetry in English for Pleasure & Practical Criticism. John Lennard. 238p. 1997. text 60.00 (*0-19-871154-9*) OUP.

Poetry Highway. Cheryl A. Dennin. 1999. pap. 6.95 (*0-533-12923-0*) Vantage.

***Poetry H2O.** Charles Peters & Kenneth Dillon. Ed. by Patricia Demings. LC 99-90525. (Illus.). 109p. 1999. pap. 12.95 (*1-891601-17-2*) Ladies Caliber.

Poetry Hunter, No. 1. Ed. by Richard A. Spiegel & Barbara Fisher. (Illus.). 92p. (Orig.). (J). (gr. k-6). 1981. pap. 2.00 (*0-934830-21-5*) Ten Penny.

Poetry I Write! Mary A. Bandemer. 48p. (Orig.). 1994. pap. 4.00 (*1-884257-05-4*) AGEE Keyboard.

Poetry in a Divided World: The Clark Lectures, 1985. Henry Gifford. 128p. 1986. text 59.95 (*0-521-30944-1*) Cambridge U Pr.

Poetry in America: Expression & Its Values in the Times of Bryant, Whitman, & Pound. Bernard I. Duffey. LC 77-81281. 372p. reprint ed. pap. 115.40 (*0-608-18755-0*, 205223600068) Bks Demand.

Poetry in Blue: Reflections in the Eye of a Cop. James P. McMann. LC 95-41606. 128p. (Orig.). 1995. pap. 12.95 (*0-9639290-3-8*) Good Times.

Poetry in Context: I Was Wandering Through Green Fields. Joseph A. Uphoff, Jr. LC 96-45248. 140p. 1996. pap. text 7.00 (*0-943123-31-3*) Arjuna Lib Pr.

Poetry in East Germany: Adjustments, Visions & Provocations 1945-1970. John Flores. LC 77-115368. (Yale Germanic Studies: No. 5). 368p. reprint ed. 114.10 (*0-8357-9442-3*, 201677700005) Bks Demand.

Poetry in English: An Anthology. Ed. by Macha L. Rosenthal. (Illus.). 1234p. 1987. pap. text 41.95 (*0-19-520539-1*) OUP.

Poetry in France: Metamorphosis of a Muse. Ed. by Ketih Aspley & Peter France. 288p. 1992. 76.50 (*0-7486-0335-2*, Pub. by Edinburgh U Pr) Col U Pr.

Poetry in Hell. Greg Gerding. LC 94-74875. (Illus.). 58p. (Orig.). 1995. pap. 8.95 (*0-9637704-1-1*) Red Dragon VA.

Poetry in Motion. (Illus.). 24p. 1996. pap. 7.95 (*1-55670-494-1*) Stewart Tabori & Chang.

Poetry in Motion. Ed. by Jef Sturm. 300p. 1998. 59.95 (*1-888680-35-0*) Poetry Guild.

Poetry in Motion: Postcard Book. Poetry Society of America et al. 1996. pap. 7.95 (*1-56924-805-2*) Marlowe & Co.

Poetry in Motion: 100 Poems from the Subways & Buses. Neil Neches et al. (Illus.). 128p. 1996. pap. 13.00 (*0-393-31458-8*, Norton Paperbks) Norton.

Poetry in Motion: 100 Poems from the Subways & Buses. Ed. by Elise Paschen et al. 128p. 1996. 18.95 (*0-393-03977-3*) Norton.

Poetry in Motion/Words from the Heart. (Illus.). 141p. (Orig.). 1997. pap. 12.95 (*0-9657419-0-7*) Glo Pub TX.

Poetry in Our Time. Babette Deutsch. LC 73-191121. 457p. 1975. reprint ed. lib. bdg. 35.00 (*0-8371-7309-4*, DEPT, Greenwood Pr) Greenwood.

Poetry in Prose. T. S. Eliot et al. LC 78-64019. (Des Imagistes: Literature of the Imagist Movement Ser.). reprint ed. 27.50 (*0-404-17090-0*) AMS Pr.

P

An Asterisk (*) at the beginning of an entry indicates that the title is appearing for the first time.

Poetry in Song Literature. Donna Harrison. LC 89-15753. (Illus.). 250p. (Orig.). (C). 1989. pap. 22.95 (*0-940473-07-0*) Wm Caxton.

Poetry in Speech: Orality & Homeric Discourse. Egbert J. Bakker. LC 96-3197. (Myth & Poetics Ser.). 256p. 1996. text 49.95 (*0-8014-3295-2*) Cornell U Pr.

Poetry in the Age of Democracy: The Literary Criticism of Matthew Arnold. Mary W. Schneider. LC 88-29096. xii, 228p. 1989. 25.00 (*0-7006-0380-8*) U Pr of KS.

Poetry in the British Isles: Non-Metropolitan Perspectives. Lother Ludwig & Hans-Werner Fietz. 288p. pap. 27.95 (*0-7083-1266-7*, Pub. by Univ Wales Pr) Paul & Co Pubs.

Poetry in the Dark Ages. H. Waddell. (Studies in Poetry: No. 38). 1948. pap. 39.95 (*0-8383-0079-0*) M S G Haskell Hse.

Poetry in the Garden. Ed. by Jacqueline M. Bachar. LC 96-75021. (Illus.). 128p. 1996. 19.95 (*1-886934-07-X*) Intl Forum.

***Poetry in the Hebrew Bible, Selected Studies from Vetus Testamentum.** D. E. Orton. (Readers in Biblical Studies). 2000. 35.00 (*90-04-11161-1*) Brill Academic Pubs.

Poetry in the Latin Class. Mary D. Lyons. 9p. 1991. spiral bd. 1.60 (*0-939507-15-3*, B16) Amer Classical.

Poetry in the Making: An Anthology. Ed. by Ted Hughes. 124p. 1967. pap. 13.95 (*0-571-09076-1*) Faber & Faber.

Poetry in the Red Book of Hergest. Ed. by John G. Evans. LC 78-72676. (Series of Old Welsh Texts: Vol. 11A). reprint ed. 32.50 (*0-404-60594-X*) AMS Pr.

Poetry in the Sixt Dimension. Earl Sixt. Ed. by Ruby Sixt. 144p. 1994. 12.00 (*0-9674569-1-6*, 27212) R Sixt.

Poetry in the Therapeutic Experience. Arthur Lerner. (Illus.). 144p. (Orig.). (C). 1994. pap. 14.95 (*0-918812-79-8*) MMB Music.

Poetry in the Wars. Edna Longley. LC 86-25069. 264p. 1987. 38.50 (*0-87413-322-X*) U Delaware Pr.

Poetry in Watercolor. Thomas C. Wilczewski. (Illus.). 39p. 1997. pap. 4.95 (*0-9657853-0-0*) Wilczewski.

Poetry in Waters. Edna Longley. 270p. 1996. pap. 22.95 (*0-906427-99-1*, Pub. by Bloodaxe Bks) Dufour.

Poetry Index Annual, 1988. Ed. by Roth Publishing, Inc. Staff. 320p. 1989. 54.99 (*0-89609-283-6*, Poetry Index Pr) Roth Pub Inc.

Poetry Index Annual, 1985. Granger Book Company, Editorial Board Staff. 680p. 1985. 54.99 (*0-89609-259-3*) Roth Pub Inc.

Poetry Index Annual, 1984. Granger Book Company, Editorial Board Staff. 1984. 54.99 (*0-89609-240-2*) Roth Pub Inc.

Poetry Index Annual, 1989. Ed. by Roth Publishing, Inc. Staff. 305p. 1990. 54.99 (*0-89609-296-8*) Roth Pub Inc.

Poetry Index Annual, 1987. Ed. by Roth Publishing, Inc. Staff. 328p. 1988. 54.99 (*0-89609-269-0*) Roth Pub Inc.

Poetry Index Annual, 1986. Roth Publishing, Inc. Staff. 470p. 1987. 54.99 (*0-89609-264-X*) Roth Pub Inc.

Poetry Index Annual, 1983. Ed. by Granger Book Company, Editorial Board Staff. LC 83-641946. 337p. 1983. 54.99 (*0-89609-237-2*) Roth Pub Inc.

Poetry Index Annual, 1982. Granger Book Company, Editorial Board Staff. 372p. 1982. 54.99 (*0-89609-223-2*) Roth Pub Inc.

Poetry Index Annual, 1990. Ed. by Roth Publishing, Inc. Staff. 270p. 1991. 54.99 (*0-89609-311-5*) Roth Pub Inc.

Poetry Index Annual, 1991. Roth Publishing, Inc. Staff. 1992. 54.99 (*0-89609-321-2*) Roth Pub Inc.

Poetry Index Annual, 1993. Roth Publishing, Inc. Staff. 1994. 54.99 (*0-89609-329-8*) Roth Pub Inc.

Poetry Index Annual, 1992. Roth Publishing, Inc. Staff. 1993. 54.99 (*0-89609-324-7*) Roth Pub Inc.

Poetry Index, 1912-1997. Compiled & Intro. by Jayne Marek. LC 98-158147. 86p. 1998. lib. bdg. 98.00 (*1-881505-09-X*, Poetry Pr) Modern Poetry.

Poetry into Song: Performance & Analysis of Lieder. Deborah Stein & Robert Spillman. (Illus.). 432p. 1996. 45.00 (*0-19-509328-3*) OUP.

Poetry Introduction. 2nd ed. Meyer. LC 97-72374. 1997. pap. text 39.95 (*0-312-14835-6*) St Martin.

Poetry Is Dangerous: The Poet Is an Outlaw. Tony Moffeit. (Illus.). 104p. (Orig.). 1995. 10.00 (*0-912449-44-6*) Floating Island.

***Poetry Is to Be Consumed.** Philip R. Pearson, Jr. LC 99-93872. 1999. pap. 8.95 (*0-533-13170-7*) Vantage.

Poetry, Language, Thought. Martin Heidegger. Tr. by Albert Hofstadter from GER. 256p. 1975. pap. 13.00 (*0-06-090430-5*, CN430, Perennial) HarperTrade.

***Poetry-Leaves of Grass.** Walt Whitman. (Notable American Authors Ser.). 1999. reprint ed. lib. bdg. 125.00 (*0-7812-9944-6*) Rprt Serv.

***Poetry Like Bread.** 25th anniversary ed. Martin Espada. 2000. pap. text 15.95 (*1-880684-74-8*) Curbstone.

Poetry Like Bread: Poets of the Political Imagination from Curbstone Press. Ed. by Martin Espada. LC 94-2135. 282p. 1994. pap. 12.95 (*1-880684-15-2*) Curbstone.

Poetry London: February 1939 to Winter 1951, 5 vols. Ed. by Tambimuttu. (Illus.). 1328p. 1970. reprint ed. 285.00 (*0-7146-2112-9*, Pub. by F Cass Pubs) Intl Spec Bk.

Poetry London - Apple Magazine, Vol. 2. Ed. by Tambimuttu. (Illus.). 96p. 1982. pap. 7.95 (*0-9502506-4-3*) Synerg CA.

Poetry Manuscripts, 16th Century see Diccionario de Pliegos Sueltos Poeticos

Poetry Markets for Canadians. 6th ed. Ed. by James Deahl. 240p. pap. 15.95 (*1-55128-030-2*, Pub. by Mercury Bk) LPC InBook.

Poetry Miscellany, 1992. Ed. by Boyd White & Richard Jackson. 100p. 1992. pap. 5.00 (*1-881489-03-5*) Poetry Miscellany.

Poetry My Arse: A Riotous Epic Poem. Brendan Kennelly. 352p. 1996. 55.00 (*1-85224-322-8*, Pub. by Bloodaxe Bks); pap. 22.95 (*1-85224-323-6*, Pub. by Bloodaxe Bks) Dufour.

Poetry 'n Motion: Rhymes for All Times. Tom Catalano. 96p. (Orig.). 1996. pap. 9.95 (*1-882646-03-7*) Wordsmith Bks.

Poetry Nation: The North American Anthology of Fusion Poetry. Regie Cabico & Todd Swift. LC 99-191799. 288p. 1999. pap. 17.95 (*1-55065-112-9*) Vehicule Pr.

Poetry, 1900-1975. George MacBeth. 1980. pap. text. write for info. (*0-582-35149-9*, Pub. by Addison-Wesley) Longman.

Poetry Notebooks of Ralph Waldo Emerson. Ralph Waldo Emerson. Ed. by Ralph H. Orth et al. LC 84-2184. 1024p. 1986. text 70.00 (*0-8262-0444-9*) U of Mo Pr.

***Poetry of a Rich Project Girl.** Tyronica Johnson-Seaton. Ed. by Alexandria N. Hooks. 2000. lib. bdg. write for info. (*0-9701437-1-0*) Writing for Soul.

***Poetry of a Rich Project Girl.** Tyronica Johnson-Seaton. Ed. by Alexandria N. Hooks. (YA). 2000. pap. 12.95 (*0-9701437-0-2*) Writing for Soul.

Poetry of Abraham Cowley. David Trotter. LC 78-31613. 162p. 1979. 36.00 (*0-8476-6157-1*) Rowman.

Poetry of ad-Dindan: A Bedouin Bard in Southern Najd. Ed. by Marcel Kurpershoek. (Studies in Arabic Literature: No. 17). 436p. 1994. 124.00 (*90-04-09894-1*, NLG185) Brill Academic Pubs.

Poetry of African-American Invention Vol. I: When One Doors Closes, Another Opens, 4 vols., Vol. 1. Wina Marchi. 114p. (Orig.). (J). (gr. 3 up). 1996. pap. 17.95 (*0-9655039-0-9*) Reklaw Prodns.

Poetry of Alex Pope. abr. ed. Alexander Pope. LC 66-1794. 1970. audio 14.00 (*0-694-50127-1*, SWC 1171, Caedmon) HarperAudio.

Poetry of Allusion: Virgil & Ovid in Dante's 'Commedia' Ed. by Rachel Jacoff & Jeffrey T. Schnapp. LC 90-40182. 352p. 1991. 42.50 (*0-8047-1860-1*) Stanford U Pr.

Poetry of American Wit & Humor. Frederic L. Knowles. LC 78-98082. (Granger Index Reprint Ser.). 1977. 23.95 (*0-8369-6079-3*) Ayer.

***Poetry of Ancient Egypt.** Kenneth A. Kitchen. (Documenta Mundi-Aegyptiaca Ser.). (Illus.). 504p. 1999. 92.50 (*91-7081-150-4*, Pub. by P Astroms) Coronet Bks.

Poetry of Anne Finch: An Essay in Interpretation. Charles J. Hinnant. LC 92-50829. 1994. 42.50 (*0-87413-469-2*) U Delaware Pr.

Poetry of Anthony Barnett. Paul Auster et al. Tr. by Anthony Barnett. (FRE, ITA & RUS.). 192p. (Orig.). 1993. pap. write for info. (*0-907954-21-9*, Pub. by Allardyce Barnett) SPD-Small Pr Dist.

***Poetry of Arab Women: A Contemporary Anthology.** Ed. by Nathalie Handal. 2000. pap. 20.00 (*1-56656-374-7*) Interlink Pub.

Poetry of Architecture. John Ruskin. LC 74-148294. reprint ed. 29.50 (*0-404-05463-3*) AMS Pr.

Poetry of Architecture. John Ruskin. LC 78-115265. (Illus.). 274p. 1972. reprint ed. 69.00 (*0-403-00305-9*) Scholarly.

Poetry of Architecture. John Ruskin. 300p. 1998. reprint ed. lib. bdg. 79.00 (*0-7812-7707-8*) Rprt Serv.

***Poetry of Architecture: Cottage, Villa Etc. to Which Is Added Suggestions on Works of Art.** John Ruskin. LC 99-68874. (Illus.). 246p. 1999. reprint ed. pap. 24.95 (*1-930423-00-4*) Brohan Pr.

Poetry of Architecture or the Architecture of the Nations of Europe. John Ruskin. 1972. 59.95 (*0-8490-0859-X*) Gordon Pr.

Poetry of Basil Bunting. Victoria Forde. 300p. 1991. 55.00 (*1-85224-047-4*, Pub. by Bloodaxe Bks) Dufour.

Poetry of Being. Yosef Ben Shlomo. 122p. 1990. pap. 12.00 (*965-05-0525-3*, Pub. by Israel Ministry Def) Gefen Bks.

Poetry of Ben Jonson. J. G. Nichols. LC 75-7260. x, 177p. 1969. write for info. (*0-389-01010-3*) B&N Imports.

Poetry of Black America: Anthology of the Twentieth Century. Ed. by Arnold Adoff. LC 72-76518. 584p. (YA). (gr. 7 up). 1973. 25.95 (*0-06-020089-8*) HarpC Child Bks.

Poetry of Boethius. Gerard O'Daly. LC 90-2528. xii, 252p. (C). 1991. 59.95 (*0-8078-1989-1*) U of NC Pr.

Poetry of Brecht: Seven Studies. Philip Thomson. LC 88-14834. (Germanic Languages & Literatures Ser.: No. 107). xii, 212p. (C). 1989. lib. bdg. 37.50 (*0-8078-8107-4*) U of NC Pr.

Poetry of Business Life: An Anthology. Ed. by Ralph Windle. LC 94-38199. (Illus.). 200p. 1994. pap. 16.95 (*1-881052-59-1*) Berrett-Koehler.

Poetry of Byron: Power,&Tyrone. abr. ed. Byron. 1996. audio 12.00 (*0-694-51707-0*, CPN 1042) HarperAudio.

Poetry of Charles Olson: A Primer. Thomas F. Merrill. LC 81-40341. 224p. 1982. 32.50 (*0-87413-196-0*) U Delaware Pr.

Poetry of Charles Potts. Hugh Fox. (American Dust Ser.: No. 12). 1979. pap. 2.95 (*0-913218-44-8*) Dustbooks.

Poetry of Chaucer. John Gardner. LC 76-22713. 445p. 1978. pap. 19.95 (*0-8093-0871-1*) S Ill U Pr.

Poetry of Chaucer: A Guide to Its Study & Appreciation. rev. ed. Robert K. Root. 1990. 16.50 (*0-8446-1391-6*) Peter Smith.

Poetry of Chess. Andrew Waterman. 160p. 1981. pap. 17.95 (*0-85646-067-2*, Pub. by Anvil Press) Dufour.

Poetry of Christian Hofmann von Hofmannswaldau: A New Reading. Fritz G. Cohen. LC 85-72042. (GERM Ser.: Vol. 22). (Illus.). 195p. 1986. 35.00 (*0-938100-38-6*) Camden Hse.

Poetry of Cino da Pistoia. Ed. by Christopher Kleinhenz. LC 83-48059. (Publications in Medieval Studies). 420p. lib. bdg. 43.00 (*0-8240-9411-5*) Garland.

Poetry of Civil Virtue: Eliot, Malraux, Auden. Nathan A Scott. LC 76-7871. 176p. reprint ed. pap. 54.60 (*0-608-16396-1*, 202689600053) Bks Demand.

Poetry of Civilization: Mythopoeic Displacement in the Verse of Milton, Dryden, Pope, & Johnson. Sanford Budick. LC 73-86887. 195p. reprint ed. pap. 60.50 (*0-608-14189-5*, 202198400024) Bks Demand.

Poetry of Cold: A Collection of Writings about Winter, Wolves & Love. LC 97-77675. 1997. pap. 14.95 (*1-891609-00-9*) Home Brew Pr.

Poetry of Conrad Ferdinand Meyer. Heinrich Henel. LC 54-8534. 347p. reprint ed. pap. 107.60 (*0-608-30797-1*, 200547600054) Bks Demand.

Poetry of D. H. Lawrence: Texts & Contexts. Ross C. Murfin. LC 82-10940. 281p. reprint ed. pap. 87.20 (*0-7837-4661-X*, 204438600002) Bks Demand.

Poetry of Dante G. Rossetti: A Critical Reading & Source Study. Florence S. Boos. (Studies in English Literature: No. 104). 1976. text 61.55 (*90-279-3471-1*) Mouton.

Poetry of Dante (1922) Benedetto Croce. 319p. reprint ed. 15.00 (*0-911858-12-1*) Appel.

Poetry of David Shapiro. Thomas Fink. LC 91-58946. 128p. 1993. 28.50 (*0-8386-3495-8*) Fairleigh Dickinson.

Poetry of Dino Frescobaldi: Romance Language & Literature. Joseph Alessia. LC 83-5482. (American University Studies: Romance Languages & Literature: Ser. II, Vol. 2). 157p. (Orig.). (C). 1983. pap. text 15.80 (*0-8204-0008-4*) P Lang Pubng.

Poetry of Discovery: The Spanish Generation of 1956-1971. Andrew P. Debicki. LC 82-40171. 248p. 1982. 29.95 (*0-8131-1461-6*) U Pr of Ky.

***Poetry of Dr. Ashraf Siddiqui.** Ahmad Nawaz. LC 00-133578. 56p. 2000. pap. 10.00 (*1-58225-383-8*) Ananta Prakashani.

Poetry of Dylan Thomas. Elder Olson. LC 54-9580. 1993. pap. 1.75 (*0-226-62917-1*, P72) U Ch Pr.

Poetry of E. A. Robinson. Edwin Arlington Robinson. LC 98-31800. 256p. 1999. 19.95 (*0-679-60262-3*) Modern Lib NY.

Poetry of Edwin Arlington Robinson. Lloyd Morris. LC 70-99664. (Select Bibliographies Reprint Ser.). 1977. 20.95 (*0-8369-5093-3*) Ayer.

Poetry of Edwin Arlington Robinson. L. Morris. LC 73-92976. (Studies in Poetry: No. 38). (C). 1969. reprint ed. lib. bdg. 75.00 (*0-8383-0996-8*) M S G Haskell Hse.

Poetry of Edwin Arlington Robinson: An Essay in Appreciation. Lloyd Morris & W. Van Whitall. LC 70-99664. (Select Bibliographies Reprint Ser.). 116p. reprint ed. 16.50 (*0-8290-0486-6*) Irvington.

Poetry of Elizabeth Singer Rowe (1674-1737) Madeleine F. Marshall. LC 87-24399. (Studies in Women & Religion: Vol. 25). (Illus.). 380p. 1987. lib. bdg. 99.95 (*0-88946-524-X*) E Mellen.

Poetry of Emily Dickinson. Charlotte A. Alexander. 1965. 4.25 (*0-671-00780-7*, Arco) Macmillan Gen Ref.

Poetry of Enlightenment: Poems of Ancient Ch'an Masters. Tr. & Intro. by Sheng-Yen Chang. LC 90-84326. 103p. (Orig.). 1989. pap. 12.00 (*0-9609854-1-7*) Dharma Drum Pubs.

Poetry of Ernest Dowson. Ed. by Desmond Flower. LC 75-88560. 165p. 1975. 38.50 (*0-8386-7551-4*, 8386-7551-4) Fairleigh Dickinson.

Poetry of Everyday Life. John Hollander. LC 98-39034. (Poets on Poetry Ser.). 184p. 1998. pap. 14.95 (*0-472-06684-5*, 06684) U of Mich Pr.

Poetry of Everyday Life. John Hollander. LC 98-39034. (Poets on Poetry Ser.). 184p. 1998. text 39.50 (*0-472-09684-2*, 09684) U of Mich Pr.

Poetry of Experience: The Dramatic Monologue in Modern Literary Tradition. Robert Langbaum. LC 85-14861. 256p. 1996. reprint ed. pap. text 12.00 (*0-226-46872-0*) U Ch Pr.

Poetry of Eyvind Earle. Eyvind Earle. Ed. by Kristin E. Thompson. 156p. 1997. 20.00 (*0-9650587-1-9*) E Earle.

Poetry of Flight. Ed. by Selden Rodman. LC 75-76939. (Granger Index Reprint Ser.). 1977. 19.95 (*0-8369-6041-6*) Ayer.

Poetry of Flowers: A Bouquet of Romantic Verse & Paper Flowers. Illus. by Patricia Whittaker. 14p. 1992. 17.95 (*0-8109-3718-2*, Pub. by Abrams) Time Warner.

Poetry of Force & Darkness: The Fiction of John Hawkes. Eliot Berry. LC 79-282. (Milford Ser.: Popular Writers of Today: Vol. 22). 64p. 1979. pap. 13.00 (*0-89370-232-3*) Millefleurs.

Poetry of Form: Richard Tuttle Drawings from The Vogel Collection. Susan Harris et al. (Illus.). 92p. 1994. pap. 24.95 (*90-800968-2-2*) Ind U Pr.

Poetry of Francisco Brines: The Deconstructive Effects of Language. Judith Nantell. LC 93-30378. 1995. 29.50 (*0-8387-5277-2*) Bucknell U Pr.

Poetry of Freemasonry. Rob Morris. 416p. 1997. reprint ed. pap. 35.00 (*0-7661-0032-4*) Kessinger Pub.

Poetry of Gabriel Celaya. Zelda I. Brooks. 26.00 (*0-916379-27-2*) Scripta.

Poetry of Gabriel Celaya. Tr. by Betty J. Craige. LC 83-45367. 160p. 1984. 29.50 (*0-8387-5062-1*) Bucknell U Pr.

Poetry of Geoffrey Hill. Henry Hart. LC 85-2122. 320p. (C). 1986. 26.95 (*0-8093-1236-0*) S Ill U Pr.

Poetry of Geology. Robert M. Hazen. 96p. 1982. 15.95 (*0-04-808032-2*) Routledge.

Poetry of George Gissing. Ed. by Bouwe Postmus. LC 94-5679. 204p. 1994. 69.95 (*0-7734-9148-1*) E Mellen.

Poetry of George Herbert. Helen H. Vendler. LC 74-16803. 320p. 1975. 37.95 (*0-674-67959-8*) HUP.

Poetry of George Wither, 2 vols. George Wither. Ed. by Frank Sidgwick. 1970. reprint ed. 19.00 (*0-403-00236-2*) Scholarly.

Poetry of George Wither, 2 vols., Set. George Wither. Ed. by Frank Sidgwick. LC 68-59006. reprint ed. 62.75 (*0-404-07006-X*) AMS Pr.

Poetry of Giacomo Da Lentino: Sicilian Poet of the Thirteenth Century. Ernest Langley. 1977. lib. bdg. 59.95 (*0-8490-2448-X*) Gordon Pr.

Poetry of Golf. Michael D. Ebeling. 64p. 1998. 29.95 (*0-9663042-0-9*) Unsoma Inc.

Poetry of Grammar & Grammar of Poetry see Selected Writings

***Poetry of Gwendolyn MacEwen Vol. 1: The Early Years,** 2nd ed. Gwendolyn MacEwen. (Picas Ser.: No. 18). 176p. 1999. reprint ed. pap. 7.00 (*1-55096-543-3*, Pub. by Exile Edns) Paul & Co Pubs.

***Poetry of Gwendolyn Macewen Vol. 2: The Later Years,** 2nd ed. Gwendolyn MacEwen. (Picas Ser.: No. 19). 148p. 1999. reprint ed. pap. 7.00 (*1-55096-547-6*, Pub. by Exile Edns) Paul & Co Pubs.

Poetry of H: Lost Poet of Lincoln's Illinois. Ed. by John E. Hallwas. 240p. 1982. 22.95 (*0-933180-38-1*) Ellis Pr.

Poetry of Han-Shan: A Complete, Annotated Translation of Cold Mountain. Robert G. Henricks. LC 89-4452. (SUNY Series in Buddhist Studies). 486p. (C). 1990. text 24.50 (*0-88706-977-0*) State U NY Pr.

Poetry of Healing: A Doctor's Education in Empathy, Identity, & Desire. Rafael Campo. LC 96-23121. 192p. 1997. 23.00 (*0-393-04009-7*) Norton.

Poetry of Heinrich Heine. Ed. by Frederic Ewen. 320p. (C). 1983. reprint ed. pap. 5.95 (*0-8065-0076-X*, Citadel Pr) Carol Pub Group.

Poetry of Henry Newbolt: Patriotism Is Not Enough. Vanessa F. Jackson. LC 93-71682. (British Authors, 1880-1920 Ser.: No. 9). 250p. (C). 1994. lib. bdg. 30.00 (*0-944318-08-8*) ELT Pr.

Poetry of History: The Contribution of Literature & Literary Scholarship to the Writing of History Since Voltaire. Emery E. Neff. LC 47-30933. 258p. (C). 1961. pap. text 23.00 (*0-231-08525-7*) Col U Pr.

Poetry of Home. Ed. by Charlotte Moss. (Illus.). 152p. 1998. 29.95 (*0-9669503-0-5*, Boxwood Press) CM Retail.

Poetry of Horses. Olwen Way. (Illus.). 330p. 1995. 60.00 (*0-85131-611-5*, Pub. by J A Allen); pap. 35.00 (*0-85131-642-5*, Pub. by J A Allen) Trafalgar.

***Poetry of Hugo Von Hofmannsthal & French Symbolism.** 240p. 2000. 74.00 (*0-19-816003-8*) OUP.

Poetry of Ibn Khafajah: A Literary Analysis. Magda M. Al-Nowaihi. LC 92-21985. (Studies in Arabic Literature: Vol. 16). 176p. 1993. 83.00 (*90-04-09660-4*) Brill Academic Pubs.

Poetry of Industry: Two Literary Reactions to the Industrial Revolution 1755-1757. Ed. by Arno Press Staff & Leonard Silk. LC 70-38474. (Evolution of Capitalism Ser.). 1972. reprint ed. 21.95 (*0-405-04131-4*) Ayer.

Poetry of Inspiration for All Occasions & Situations: Something Special for Someone Special. Louella Kingston. Ed. by Sonya Kingston et al. 84p. (Orig.). 1995. pap. 18.95 (*0-9649631-0-8*) LL&L Pr.

Poetry of Irving Feldman: 9 Essays. Ed. by Harold Schweizer. LC 90-56169. (Illus.). 192p. 1992. 32.50 (*0-8387-5209-8*) Bucknell U Pr.

Poetry of James Wright. Andrew Elkins. LC 90-10879. 288p. 1991. text 34.95 (*0-8173-0496-7*) U of Ala Pr.

Poetry of Jane Austen & the Austen Family. Jane Austen. Ed. by David Selwyn. LC 96-61382. 124p. (Orig.). 1997. pap. 12.95 (*0-87745-580-5*) U of Iowa Pr.

Poetry of Janie Luelling Byrnes. Illus. by John Finger. LC 89-81879. 128p. 1990. 20.00 (*0-9625195-0-2*) Byrnes Finger.

Poetry of Jaroslav Seifert. Jaroslav Seifert. Ed. & Tr. by George Gibian from CZE. Tr. by Ewald Osers from CZE. LC 97-40802. 255p. 1998. pap. 14.95 (*0-945774-39-7*) Catbird Pr.

Poetry of John Donne: A Study in Explication. Doniphan Louthan. LC 75-40927. 193p. 1976. reprint ed. lib. bdg. 49.75 (*0-8371-8693-5*, LOPJ, Greenwood Pr) Greenwood.

Poetry of John Dryden. Mark Van Doren. LC 79-95450. (Studies in Dryden: No. 10). 1969. reprint ed. lib. bdg. 75.00 (*0-8383-1207-1*) M S G Haskell Hse.

Poetry of John Dryden. Mark Van Doren. (BCL1-PR English Literature Ser.). 361p. 1992. reprint ed. lib. bdg. 89.00 (*0-7812-7347-1*) Rprt Serv.

***Poetry of John Greenleaf Whittier: A Reader's Edition.** Ed. by William Jolliff. 275p. (C). 2000. pap. text 18.00 (*0-944350-48-8*) Friends United.

Poetry of Jonathan Swift: Allusion & the Development of a Poetic Style. Peter J. Schakel. LC 78-53292. 229p. 1978. reprint ed. pap. 71.00 (*0-7837-9794-X*, 206052300005) Bks Demand.

Poetry of Julia Uceda. Julia Uceda. Tr. by Noel Valis from SPA. LC 93-38925. (Nuestra Voz Ser.: Vol. 2). XII, 216p. (C). 1995. 42.95 (*0-8204-2409-9*) P Lang Pubng.

Poetry of Julian Del Casal: A Critical Edition, 2 vols., Vol. 1. Julian Del Casal. Ed. by Robert J. Glickman. LC 76-22800. (SPA., Illus.). 304p. 1976. reprint ed. pap. 94.30 (*0-7837-4878-7*, 204478800001) Bks Demand.

Poetry of Julian Del Casal: A Critical Edition, 2 vols., Vol. 2. Julian Del Casal. Ed. by Robert J. Glickman. LC 76-22800. (SPA & ENG., Illus.). 486p. 1978. reprint ed. pap. 150.70 (*0-7837-4879-5*, 204478800002) Bks Demand.

Poetry of Julian Del Casal: A Critical Edition, Vol. 3. Julian Del Casal. Ed. by Robert J. Glickman. LC 76-22800. (SPA., Illus.). 509p. reprint ed. pap. 157.80 (*0-608-04453-9*, 204478800003) Bks Demand.

Poetry of Keats: Richardson,&Sir Ralph. abr. ed. John Keats. 1996. audio 12.00 (*0-694-51706-2*, CPN 1087) HarperAudio.

Poetry of Laetitia Pilkington (1712-1750) & Constantia Grierson (1706-1733) Ed. by Bernard Tucker. LC 95-38166. (Studies in British Literature: Vol. 20). 200p. 1996. text 79.95 (*0-7734-8866-9*) E Mellen.

Poetry of Life. Leelia Cornell. 1998. pap. 10.49 (*0-9648730-9-5*) Shoe Hse.

Poetry of Life. Rose M. Gerlach. LC 98-84411. (Illus.). 68p. 1998. pap. 5.00 (*1-886467-31-5*) WJM Press.

P

Poetry of Life: And the Life of Poetry. David Mason. LC 99-14959. 248p. 2000. pap. 15.95 (*1-885266-80-4*, Pub. by Story Line) Consort Bk Sales.

Poetry of Life: Shelley & Literary Form. Ronald Tetreault. 290p. 1987. text 40.00 (*0-8020-5696-2*) U of Toronto Pr.

***Poetry of Life in Literature.** Anna-Teresa Tymieniecka. LC 00-33088. (Analecta Husserliana Ser.). 2000. write for info. (*0-7923-6408-2*) Kluwer Academic.

Poetry of Living Japan. Ed. by Takamichi Ninomiya & D. J. Enright. LC 78-11863. 104p. 1979. reprint ed. lib. bdg. 49.50 (*0-313-21210-4*, NIPL, Greenwood Pr) Greenwood.

Poetry of Love: Baby Boomers. Belva Carey. (Poetry...Mostly Faith Ser.). (Illus.). 72p. (Orig.). (J). (gr. 6 up). 1987. pap. 5.95 (*0-9617859-0-X*) Careys Pub Co.

Poetry of Love & Pets. Marie D. Spivack. 1998. pap. write for info. (*1-57553-948-9*) Watermrk Pr.

Poetry of Lucy Maud Montgomery. L. M. Montgomery. 1999. pap. text 9.95 (*1-55041-402-X*) Fitzhenry & W Ltd.

***Poetry of Luis Cernuda: Order in a World of Chaos.** Neil C. McKinlay. LC 99-18395. 192p. 1999. 54.00 (*1-85566-063-6*, Pub. by Tamesis Bks Ltd) Boydell & Brewer.

Poetry of Marjorie V. Weber. Marjorie V. Weber. (Illus.). 246p. 1992. pap., per. 10.00 (*1-891150-54-5*) M V Weber.

Poetry of Mary Barber (1690-1757) Ed. by Bernard Tucker. LC 91-48162. 252p. 1992. lib. bdg. 89.95 (*0-7734-9465-0*) E Mellen.

Poetry of Meditation: A Study in English Religious Literature of the Seventeenth Century. rev. ed. Louis L. Martz. LC 54-9520. 405p. reprint ed. pap. 125.60 (*0-8357-8272-7*, 203381400087) Bks Demand.

Poetry of Meng Chiao & Han Yu. Stephen Owen. LC 74-29732. 304p. reprint ed. pap. 94.30 (*0-8357-8273-5*, 203385000087) Bks Demand.

Poetry of Meredith. Meredith. 55p. 1995. pap. 2.99 (*1-886820-01-5*) Meredith WA.

Poetry of Michelangelo. Christopher Ryan. LC 97-50387. 352p. 1998. 47.50 (*0-8386-3802-3*) Fairleigh Dickinson.

Poetry of Michelangelo: An Annotated Translation. James M. Saslow. LC 90-48480. (Illus.). 576p. (C). 1993. reprint ed. pap. 22.00 (*0-300-05509-9*) Yale U Pr.

Poetry of Modern Quebec: An Anthology. Ed. by Fred Cogswell. LC 77-362075. (French Writers of Canada Ser.). 206p. reprint ed. pap. 63.90 (*0-608-13918-1*, 202375000033) Bks Demand.

Poetry of Modernity: Anglo-American Encodings. Dennis Brown. LC 93-48922. 1994. text 55.00 (*0-312-12093-1*) St Martin.

Poetry of Mourning: The Modern Elegy from Hardy to Heaney. Jahan Ramazani. LC 93-31581. 436p. 1994. pap. text 16.95 (*0-226-70340-1*) U Ch Pr.

Poetry of Mourning: The Modern Elegy from Hardy to Heaney. Jahan Ramazani. LC 93-31581. 419p. 1995. lib. bdg. 42.00 (*0-226-70339-8*) U Ch Pr.

Poetry of Nature: Rural Perspectives in Poetry from Wordsworth to the Present. W. J. Keith. 1980. text 35.00 (*0-8020-5494-3*) U of Toronto Pr.

Poetry of Neil Munro. Pref. by John Buchan. 88p. 1989. 12.95 (*0-907590-24-1*, Pub. by SPA Bks Ltd) Seven Hills Bk.

Poetry of Nino Martoglio: Selections from Centona. Tr. by Gaetano Cipolla from ITA. LC 93-28682. (Poets of Arba Sicula Ser.). (ENG & ITA.). 304p. (Orig.). (C). 1993. pap. 10.00 (*1-881901-03-3*) LEGAS.

***Poetry of Nizami Ganjavi.** Kamran Talattof. LC 99-56710. 2000. text 49.95 (*0-312-22810-4*) St Martin.

Poetry of Opposition & Revolution: Dryden to Wordsworth. Howard Erskine-Hill. (Illus.). 284p. 1997. text 68.00 (*0-19-812177-6*) OUP.

Poetry of Our Times. Ed. by Sharon Brown. LC 79-51956. (Granger Poetry Library). 1980. reprint ed. 40.00 (*0-89609-179-1*) Roth Pub Inc.

Poetry of Our World. Ed J. Paine. 320p. 2000. pap. 17.00 (*0-06-095193-1*, Perennial) HarperTrade.

Poetry of Our World: An International Anthology of Contemporary Poetry. Ed. by Jeffrey Paine. LC 99-34921. 528p. 2000. 35.00 (*0-06-055369-3*) HarpC.

Poetry of Pablo Neruda. Rene De Costa. LC 78-18008. (Illus.). 225p. 1979. 24.00 (*0-674-67980-6*) HUP.

Poetry of Pablo Neruda. Rene De Costa. (Illus.). 225p. 1979. pap. 14.95 (*0-674-67981-4*) HUP.

Poetry of Pain: Poems of Truth, Acceptance & Hope for Those Who Suffer Chronic Pain. Linda Martinson. LC 95-92651. 60p. (Orig.). 1996. pap. 9.95 (*0-9648978-2-2*) Simply Books.

Poetry of Paul Celan: Papers from the Conference at the State University of New York at Binghamton, October 28-29, 1988. Ed. by Haskell M. Block. LC 91-31335. (American University Studies: Comparative Literature: Ser. III, Vol. 42). 69p. (C). 1992. text 23.95 (*0-8204-1615-0*) P Lang Pubng.

Poetry of Philosophy: On Aristotle's Poetics. Michael Davis. LC 99-21188. 203p. 1999. reprint ed. pap. 19.00 (*1-890318-62-0*) St Augustines Pr.

Poetry of Pierre Le Moyne (1602-1671) Richard G. Maber. 311p. 1982. pap. 45.00 (*3-261-04945-6*) P Lang Pubng.

Poetry of Pope's Dunciad. John E. Sitter. LC 71-167298. 144p. reprint ed. pap. 44.70 (*0-608-14148-8*, 205591700039) Bks Demand.

Poetry of Postwar Japan. Ed. by Kijima Hajime. LC 75-17718. (Iowa Translations Ser.). 319p. reprint ed. pap. 98.90 (*0-608-15069-X*, 202593500047) Bks Demand.

Poetry of Presence: The Writing of William Carlos Williams. Bernard Duffey. LC 85-40760. (Wisconsin Project on American Writers Ser.). 352p. 1986. text 24.95 (*0-299-10470-2*) U of Wis Pr.

Poetry of Probably Rare Beauty. Max L. Christensen. LC 98-73079. 85p. 1998. pap. 9.95 (*0-9648562-1-2*) Aspermont.

Poetry of Protest. Fuller. 1992. pap. text. write for info. (*0-582-08550-0*, Pub. by Addison-Wesley) Longman.

Poetry of Protest under Franco. Eleanor Wright. (Monagrafias A Ser.: Vol. LXXXIX). (ENG & SPA.). 195p. 1986. 58.00 (*0-7293-0210-5*, Pub. by Tamesis Bks Ltd) Boydell & Brewer.

Poetry of Puerto Rico. Ed. by Raoul Gordon. 1976. lib. bdg. 59.95 (*0-8490-0862-X*) Gordon Pr.

Poetry of Rafael Alberti: A Visual Approach. Robert C. Manteiga. (Monagrafias A Ser.: Vol. LXXV). 130p. (C). 1978. 51.00 (*0-7293-0069-2*, Pub. by Tamesis Bks Ltd) Boydell & Brewer.

Poetry of Reality: Composing with Recorded Sound. Ed. by Katharine Norman. (Contemporary Music Review Ser.). 179p. 1997. pap. text 30.00 incl. audio compact disk (*3-7186-5932-8*, Harwood Acad Pubs) Gordon & Breach.

Poetry of Relationship: The Wordsworths & Coleridge, 1797-1800. Richard Matlak. LC 96-48921. 244p. 1997. text 39.95 (*0-312-10166-X*) St Martin.

Poetry of Resistance: Seamus Heaney & the Pastoral Tradition. Sidney Burris. LC 89-25502. 182p. (C). 1990. text 32.95 (*0-8214-0951-4*) Ohio U Pr.

Poetry of Richard Aldington. Norman T. Gates. 1975. text 40.00 (*0-271-01119-X*) Pa St U Pr.

***Poetry of Rimbaud.** Robert Greer Cohn. 460p. 1999. pap. 29.95 (*1-57003-332-3*) U of SC Pr.

Poetry of Robert Browning. Stopford A. Brooke. LC 02-24748. reprint ed. 29.50 (*0-404-01114-4*) AMS Pr.

Poetry of Robert Burns, 4 vols., Set. Robert Burns. Ed. by William E. Henley & Thomas F. Henderson. LC 78-113567. reprint ed. 120.00 (*0-404-01250-7*) AMS Pr.

Poetry of Robert Frost. Ed. by Edward C. Lathem. LC 68-24759. 632p. 1995. 27.50 (*0-8050-0502-1*) H Holt & Co.

Poetry of Robert Frost: The Collected Poems, Complete & Unabridged. unabridged ed. Robert Frost. Ed. by Edward Connery Lathem. LC 68-24759. 607p. 1979. pap. 15.95 (*0-8050-0501-3*, Owl) H Holt & Co.

Poetry of Robert Tofte, 1597-1620: A Critical Old-Spelling Edition. Ed. by Jeffrey N. Nelson. LC 94-9802. (Renaissance Imagination Ser.). 360p. 1994. text 35.00 (*0-8153-1091-9*) Garland.

Poetry of Rock: The Golden Years. David R. Pichaske. 192p. (Orig.). 1981. pap. 5.95 (*0-933180-17-9*) Ellis Pr.

Poetry of Roses. Photos by Carolyn Parker. LC 94-42121. (Illus.). 64p. 1995. 19.95 (*0-8109-3736-0*, Pub. by Abrams) Time Warner.

Poetry of Rudyard Kipling: Rousing the Nation. Ann Parry. 160p. 1992. 113.00 (*0-335-09495-3*); pap. 36.95 (*0-335-09494-5*) OpUniv Pr.

Poetry of Ryuichi Tamura, No. 1. Tr. by Samuel Grolmes & Yumiko Tsumura from JPN. LC 97-95369. (Illus.). 160p. 1998. pap. 25.00 (*0-9662832-0-1*) CCC Bks.

***Poetry of Seamus Heaney.** Elmer Andrews. LC 99-41368. (Critical Guides Ser.). 2000. pap. 14.50 (*0-231-11927-5*) Col U Pr.

Poetry of Shelley: Price, & Vincent. abr. ed. Percy Bysshe Shelley. 1996. audio 12.00 (*0-694-51708-9*, CPN 1059) HarperAudio.

Poetry of Sight. Avis Berman. 2000. write for info. (*0-517-70567-2*) Random.

Poetry of Sir Thomas Wyatt: A Selection & a Study by E. M. W. Tillyard. Thomas Wyatt. (BCL1-PR English Literature Ser.). 179p. 1992. reprint ed. lib. bdg. 69.00 (*0-7812-7232-7*) Rprt Serv.

Poetry of Sir Thomas Wyatt: A Selection & a Study by E. M. W. Tillyard. Thomas Wyatt. reprint ed. 29.00 (*0-403-08614-0*) Somerset Pub.

Poetry of Solitude: A Tribute to Edward Hopper. Gail Levin. (Illus.). 80p. 1995. 19.95 (*0-7893-0017-6*, Pub. by Universe) St Martin.

Poetry of St. Therese of Lisieux. Tr. by Donald Kinney from FRE. LC 95-295. 352p. (Orig.). 1996. pap. 12.95 (*0-935216-56-1*) ICS Pubns.

Poetry of Stephen Crane. Daniel G. Hoffman. LC 57-11017. 1971. pap. text 23.00 (*0-231-08662-8*) Col U Pr.

Poetry of Stevie Smith: "Little Girl Lost" Arthur C. Rankin. LC 84-16896. (Illus.). 120p. 1985. 43.00 (*0-389-20508-7*, BNB-08066) B&N Imports.

Poetry of T. S. Eliot. Hugh Ross-Williamson. LC 71-156296. (Studies in T. S. Eliot: No. 11). 1971. reprint ed. lib. bdg. 75.00 (*0-8383-1291-8*) M S G Haskell Hse.

Poetry of T. S. Eliot. Hugh R. Williamson. 1972. reprint ed. lib. bdg. 250.00 (*0-8490-0863-8*) Gordon Pr.

Poetry of Teaching. Hermon R. Card. 65p. 1998. pap. 10.00 (*0-9664103-2-7*) Thornetree Hill.

Poetry of Tennyson. Alastair W. Thomson. 288p. 1986. 55.00 (*0-7102-0716-6*, 07166, Routledge Thoemms) Routledge.

Poetry of Tennyson. Henry Van Dyke. LC 72-3195. (Studies in Tennyson: No. 27). 1972. reprint ed. lib. bdg. 75.00 (*0-8383-1517-8*) M S G Haskell Hse.

Poetry of the Aeneid. Michael C. Putnam. LC 88-47774. 256p. 1988. pap. text 14.95 (*0-8014-9518-0*) Cornell U Pr.

Poetry of the Age of Fable. Thomas Bulfinch. 1972. 250.00 (*0-8490-0864-6*) Gordon Pr.

Poetry of the Age of Fable. Thomas Bulfinch. (Works of Thomas Bulfinch). 1989. reprint ed. lib. bdg. 79.00 (*0-7812-2166-8*) Rprt Serv.

Poetry of the Age of Wordsworth. Ed. by John D. Wilson. LC 72-104291. 275p. 1970. reprint ed. lib. bdg. 65.00 (*0-8371-4083-8*, WIPW, Greenwood Pr) Greenwood.

Poetry of the Age of Wordsworth. John D. Wilson. (BCL1-PR English Literature Ser.). 1992. reprint ed. lib. bdg. 75.00 (*0-7812-7142-8*) Rprt Serv.

Poetry of the American Civil War. 2nd ed. Ed. by Lee Steinmetz. LC 59-15220. 264p. (C). 1991. reprint ed. pap. 14.95 (*0-87013-310-1*) Mich St U Pr.

Poetry of the American Renaissance: A Diverse Anthology from the Romantic Period. Ed. & Intro. by Paul Kane. LC 95-17681. 384p. 1995. pap. 14.95 (*0-8076-1398-3*, Pub. by Braziller) Norton.

Poetry of the American West. Ed. by Alison H. Deming. (Illus.). 392p. 1996. 28.50 (*0-231-10386-7*) Col U Pr.

Poetry of the American West. Alison H. Deming. 328p. 1999. pap. text 18.95 (*0-231-10387-5*) Col U Pr.

***Poetry of the Angels: Inspiration For Us All.** 2nd ed. Eric Brodsky. 53p. 2000. pap. 8.00 (*0-9676406-0-1*) Universal One.

Poetry of the Anti-Jacobin. George Canning & John H. Frere. LC 91-3943. 260p. 1991. reprint ed. 48.00 (*1-85477-067-5*) Continuum.

Poetry of the Canadian People, 1720 to 1920, Vol. 1. Ed. by Brian Davis. (Illus.). 288p. (Orig.). 1995. pap. 10.95 (*0-919600-50-6*, Pub. by NC Ltd) U of Toronto Pr.

Poetry of the Canadian People 1900-1950, Vol. 2. Ed. by Brian Davis. (Illus.). 224p. 1978. pap. 12.95 (*0-919600-97-2*, Pub. by NC Ltd) U of Toronto Pr.

Poetry of the Carolingian Renaissance. Ed. by Peter Godman. LC 84-40699. (Illus.). 384p. 1985. 55.00 (*0-8061-1939-X*) U of Okla Pr.

Poetry of the Chartist Movement: A Literary & Historical Study. Ulrike Schwab. (Studies in Social History). 260p. (C). 1993. lib. bdg. 188.00 (*0-7923-2110-3*) Kluwer Academic.

Poetry of the Deformed. Kenn Mitchell. 64p. (Orig.). 1996. pap. 10.00 (*0-944550-42-8*) Pygmy Forest Pr.

Poetry of the First World War. (Poetry Library). 240p. pap. 7.95 (*1-85326-444-X*, 444XWW, Pub. by Wrdsworth Edits) NTC Contemp Pub Co.

Poetry of the Gogynfeirdd from the Myvyrian Archaeology of Wales. Owen Jones. LC 78-72633. (Celtic Language & Literature Ser.: Goidelic & Brythonic). reprint ed. 30.00 (*0-404-17558-9*) AMS Pr.

Poetry of the Heavens. Jerome J. Knuiit. (Illus.). 153p. (Orig.). 1989. pap. 19.95 (*0-9625168-0-5*) Mira Pubns.

Poetry of the Literary Revolution in Haiti. Jean de La Fontaine et al. (B. E. Ser.: No. 77). 1958. 60.00 (*0-8115-3028-0*) Periodicals Srv.

Poetry of the Minor Connecticut Wits, 1791-1818. Ed. by Benjamin Franklin. LC 68-17015. 1970. 90.00 (*0-8201-1066-3*) Schol Facsimiles.

Poetry of the '90's. Ed. by C. E. Andrews & M. O. Percival. LC 78-116392. (Granger Index Reprint Ser.). 1977. 20.95 (*0-8369-6133-1*) Ayer.

Poetry of the Orient. A. W. Rounseville. 1973. 59.95 (*0-8490-0865-4*) Gordon Pr.

Poetry of the Passion: Studies in 12 Centuries of English Verse. Jack A. Bennett. 250p. 1984. pap. text 22.50 (*0-19-812832-0*) OUP.

***Poetry of the Past & Present.** Ginevar Curenton. 2000. 8.95 (*0-533-11835-2*) Vantage.

Poetry of the People: Poems to the President, 1929-1945. Donald W. Whisenhunt. LC 96-20028. (Illus.). 235p. 1996. 45.95 (*0-87972-703-9*); pap. 19.95 (*0-87972-704-7*) Bowling Green Univ Popular Press.

Poetry of the Reincarnation of a King: A Black Man's View. Ajamu Bandele. 360p. 1997. pap. 16.00 (*1-57502-428-4*, PO1309) Morris Pubng.

Poetry of the Scots. Duncan Glen. 160p. 1991. text 60.00 (*0-7486-0297-6*, Pub. by Edinburgh U Pr) Col U Pr.

Poetry of the Seasons. Compiled by Mary I. Lovejoy. LC 71-98083. (Granger Index Reprint Ser.). 1977. 23.95 (*0-8369-6082-3*) Ayer.

Poetry of the Silver Age: The Various Voices of Russian Modernism. Victor Terras. Tr. by Alexander Landman. 480p. 1998. 55.00 (*3-931828-71-9*, Pub. by Dresden Univ Pr) Paul & Co Pubs.

Poetry of the Spirit. Ed. by Gerard E. Goggins. LC 96-79064. 164p. 1996. pap. 9.95 (*0-9646439-7-9*) Ambasdr Bks.

Poetry of the Stewart Court. Hughes & Ramson. (Australian National University Press Ser.). 1983. text 86.00 (*0-08-033020-7*, Pergamon Pr) Elsevier.

Poetry of the Transition, 1850-1914. Ed. by Thomas M. Parrott & Willard Thorp. LC 72-5594. (Granger Index Reprint Ser.). 1977. reprint ed. 44.95 (*0-8369-6384-9*) Ayer.

Poetry of the Universe: The Mathematical Imagination & the Nature of the Cosmos. Robert Osserman. (Illus.). 224p. 1996. pap. 11.95 (*0-385-47429-6*, Anchor NY) Doubleday.

Poetry of the Victorian Period. 3rd ed. Jerome H. Buckley & George B. Woods. 1097p. (C). 1997. 77.00 (*0-673-05630-9*) Addson-Wesley Educ.

Poetry of the Web Vol. I: 1999. Ed. by Laura Lammers. LC 99-90294. 150p. (YA). (gr. 9 up). 1999. pap. 19.99 (*1-893231-02-X*) Poet Born.

Poetry of the World. Robert Pinsky. 256p. (C). 2000. pap. 10.95 (*0-88001-216-1*) HarpC.

Poetry of the World Wars. Ed. by Michael Foss. (Illus.). 224p. 1990. 18.95 (*0-87226-336-3*, P Bedrick Books) NTC Contemp Pub Co.

Poetry of Thomas Hardy: A Handbook & Commentary. James O. Bailey. LC 77-97015. 740p. reprint ed. pap. 200.00 (*0-7837-2076-9*, 204235000004) Bks Demand.

Poetry of Tony Harrison. Sandie Byrne. LC 97-47407. 240p. 2000. 74.95 (*0-7190-5294-7*, Pub. by Manchester Univ Pr); pap. 19.95 (*0-7190-5295-5*, Pub. by Manchester Univ Pr) St Martin.

Poetry of Travelling in the United States. Caroline Gilman. LC 71-104465. 430p. 1977. reprint ed. lib. bdg. 32.00 (*0-8398-0660-4*) Irvington.

Poetry of Travelling in the United States. Caroline Gilman. 430p. (C). 1986. reprint ed. pap. text 8.95 (*0-8290-1885-9*) Irvington.

***Poetry of Two Minds.** Sherod Santos. (Life of Poetry Ser.). 2000. 40.00 (*0-8203-2244-X*) U of Ga Pr.

***Poetry of Two Minds.** Sherod Santos. LC 99-57977. 2000. pap. 17.95 (*0-8203-2204-0*) U of Ga Pr.

Poetry of Vachel Lindsay, Vol. 1. Vachel Lindsay. Ed. by Dennis Camp. (Illus.). 408p. 1984. 39.95 (*0-933180-45-4*) Spoon Riv Poetry.

Poetry of Vachel Lindsay, Vol. 2. Vachel Lindsay. Ed. by Dennis Camp. (Illus.). 408p. 1984. 39.95 (*0-933180-67-5*) Spoon Riv Poetry.

Poetry of Vachel Lindsay, Vol. 3. Ed. by Dennis Camp. 190p. 1986. 14.95 (*0-933180-77-2*) Spoon Riv Poetry.

Poetry of Vasko Popa. Anita Lekic. LC 92-7285. (Balkan Studies: Vol. 2). XIV, 178p. (C). 1993. text 44.95 (*0-8204-1777-7*) P Lang Pubng.

Poetry of Villon & Baudelaire: Two Worlds, One Human Condition. Robert R. Daniel. LC 96-24067. (Currents in Comparative Romance Languages & Literatures Ser.: Vol. 52). VI, 196p. (C). 1997. text 44.95 (*0-8204-3472-8*) P Lang Pubng.

Poetry of Vision: Five Eighteenth-Century Poets. Patricia A. Spacks. LC 67-10942. 247p. reprint ed. pap. 76.60 (*0-7837-4438-2*, 205796700012) Bks Demand.

***Poetry of W. B. Yeats.** Contrib. by Nicholas Drake. (Penguin Critical Studies). 136p. 2000. pap. 9.95 (*0-14-077132-8*, Pub. by Pnguin Bks Ltd) Trafalgar.

Poetry of W. D. Snodgrass: Everything Human. Stephen H. Haven. (Under Discussion Ser.). 328p. 1993. text 49.50 (*0-472-10252-4*, 10252) U of Mich Pr.

Poetry of W. S. Graham. Tony Lopez. 240p. 1989. 45.00 (*0-85224-587-4*, Pub. by Edinburgh U Pr) Col U Pr.

Poetry of W. S. Graham. Tony Lopez. 176p. 1990. pap. text 25.00 (*0-85224-588-2*, Pub. by Edinburgh U Pr) Col U Pr.

Poetry of Wang Wei: New Translations & Commentary. Wang Wei. LC 79-3623. (Chinese Literature in Translation Ser.). 288p. reprint ed. pap. 89.30 (*0-608-18848-4*, 205672800081) Bks Demand.

Poetry of War Book B. B. C. Fuller. Date not set. pap. text. write for info. (*0-582-05811-2*, Pub. by Addison-Wesley) Longman.

Poetry of Wickedness & Other Poems. Lyn Coffin. LC 81-20085. 65p. (Orig.). 1981. pap. 4.00 (*0-87886-116-5*, Greenfld Rev Pr) Greenfld Rev Lit.

Poetry of Yevgeny Yevtushenko. enl. rev. ed. Yevgeny Yevtushenko. 1964. 10.00 (*0-8079-0105-9*) October.

Poetry of Yunus Emre, a Turkish Sufi Poet. Grace M. Smith. LC 93-12561. (Publications in Modern Philology: Vol. 127). 1993. pap. 17.95 (*0-520-09781-5*, Pub. by U CA Pr) Cal Prin Full Svc.

Poetry on a Journey of Remembrance: A Collection. Nancy Keats. 101p. 1992. pap. 11.00 (*0-9633740-0-1*) Purple Finch.

Poetry on & off the Page: Essays for Emergent Occasions. Marjorie Perloff. LC 97-50432. (Avant-Garde & Modernism Studies). 320p. 1998. 79.95 (*0-8101-1560-3*); pap. 19.95 (*0-8101-1561-1*) Northwestern U Pr.

Poetry Out Loud. Ed. by Robert A. Rubin. 240p. 1995. pap. 9.95 (*1-56512-122-8*, 72122) Algonquin Bks.

Poetry Pad. Sue Thomas. 1994. pap. 14.99 (*0-88092-079-3*) Royal Fireworks.

Poetry Parade. Pamela A. Klawitter. (Learning Works Creative Writing Ser.). (Illus.). (J). (gr. 4-6). 1987. pap. 6.95 (*0-88160-156-X*, LW 274) Learning Wks.

Poetry Party. Linda Spellman. (Learning Works Creative Writing Ser.). (Illus.). 48p. (J). (gr. 4-6). 1981. pap. 6.95 (*0-88160-038-5*, LW 223) Learning Wks.

Poetry Pathology. Donald Ryburn & Robin Gould. 87p. (Orig.). 1996. pap. text 7.95 (*1-888406-00-3*) Phoenix Access.

***Poetry Patterns.** Eleanor Orndorf & Jo Ellen Moore. Ed. by Marilyn Evans. (Illus.). 96p. 1999. pap., teacher ed. 10.95 (*1-55799-733-0*, 733) Evan-Moor Edu Pubs.

Poetry Patterns. Karen A. Schuler. LC 98-71187. (Illus.). 32p. (J). (gr. 3-7). 1998. pap. 9.95 (*1-889590-01-0*) Cherubic Pr.

Poetry Patterns. 2nd expanded ed. Charla Jones. (Illus.). 48p. 1992. pap. 8.95 (*1-880505-58-4*) Pieces of Lrning.

Poetry Peddlers: Two from Music City Country. Craig Deitschmann & Tom C. Armstrong. 127p. (Orig.). 1984. pap. 7.95 (*0-939298-46-5*, 465) AD HOC Bks.

Poetry Place Anthology. Scholastic, Inc. Staff. 192p. (J). (gr. k-7). 1993. pap. 18.95 (*0-590-49017-6*) Scholastic Inc.

Poetry Play Any Day with Jane Yolen. Cheryl Potts. LC 99-29784. 64p. (J). (gr. 2-5). 1999. pap. 13.95 (*1-57950-038-2*, Alleyside) Highsmith Pr.

Poetry Please! Compiled by Charles Causley. (Everyman's Poetry Ser.). 116p. 1997. pap. 1.95 (*0-460-87824-7*, Everyman's Classic Lib) Tuttle Pubng.

Poetry Plus. Sidney Taylor. LC 96-90371. 1998. 10.95 (*0-533-12017-9*) Vantage.

Poetry Plus! Grades K-6. Troll Books Staff. 96p. 1999. pap. text 12.95 (*0-8167-2594-2*) Troll Communs.

Poetry Pointers. Martha Rohrer. 48p. (YA). (gr. 7). 1989. pap. 2.15 (*0-7399-0243-1*, 2435) Rod & Staff.

Poetry Power. 72p. 9.95 (*0-932269-36-2*) Interspace Bks.

Poetry, Prayer, & Praise. Wilma Goolsby-Gibbs. LC 89-91294. 106p. (C). 1989. text 20.00 (*0-9623487-0-8*) W Goolsby-Gibbs.

***Poetry, Prayers, & Haiku.** William Sutherland. 1999. pap. write for info. (*1-58235-198-8*) Watermrk Pr.

Poetry Project, Vol. 4. Ed. by Joel Rudinger. (Poetry Projects Ser.). 104p. (Orig.). 1985. pap. 7.00 (*0-918342-22-8*) Cambric.

Poetry Project: American Anthology, Vol. 1. 1981. pap. 5.50 (*0-932436-02-1*) Cykx.

Poetry Project: Poets of the World, Vol. 2. 1981. pap. 5.50 (*0-932436-05-6*) Cykx.

Poetry Project CPP, Vol. 3. Ed. by Joel Rudinger. 128p. (Orig.). (C). 1983. pap. 7.95 (*0-918342-16-3*) Cambric.

P

An Asterisk (*) at the beginning of an entry indicates that the title is appearing for the first time.

Poetry, Prose, & Listry. Pierce S. Ketchum. 1997. pap. write for info. (*1-57553-517-3*) Watermrk Pr.

***Poetry, Prose & Other Voyages to the Edge.** Violet Ampersand. LC 99-90883. 1999. 25.00 (*0-7388-0554-8*); pap. 18.00 (*0-7388-0555-6*) Xlibris Corp.

Poetry, Prose, & Popular Culture in Hausa. Graham Furniss. 368p. (Orig.). 1996. pap. text 34.95 (*1-56098-695-6*) Smithsonian.

Poetry, Prose & Prayers for Joyous Christian Living. large type rev. ed. John S. Girard. LC 97-74918. (Illus.). 127p. 1998. pap. 19.95 (*0-9651099-1-7*) Angels Wings.

Poetry, Prose & Prayers for Joyous Christian Living, Vol. 1. John S. Girard. (Illus.). 108p. 1996. pap. 9.95 (*0-9651099-0-9*, 00001) Angels Wings.

Poetry Put the Po' in Poor Boy: A Collection of Humerous Poems. Richard Jones. Ed. by Gaynelle Hughes. 78p. (Orig.). 1996. pap. 12.50 (*0-9652459-1-8*) TSFP.

***Poetry Quartets, Vol. 1.** Simon Armitage et al. 1999. (*1-85224-468-2*, Pub. by Bloodaxe Bks) Dufour.

***Poetry Quartets, Vol. 2.** Fleur Adcock et al. 1999. 24.95 (*1-85224-469-0*, Pub. by Bloodaxe Bks) Dufour.

***Poetry Quartets, Vol. 3.** James Fenton et al. 1999. (*1-85224-470-4*, Pub. by Bloodaxe Bks) Dufour.

***Poetry Quartets 5: Women Poets.** Helen Dunmore. 2000. 26.95 incl. audio (*1-85224-499-2*, Pub. by Bloodaxe Bks) Dufour.

***Poetry Quartets 4: Irish Poets.** Paul Durcan. 2000. 26.95 incl. audio (*1-85224-498-4*, Pub. by Bloodaxe Bks) Dufour.

Poetry Quintet. Georgina Hammick et al. (Gollancz Poets Ser.). 1977. pap. 7.50 (*0-575-02156-X*) Transatl Arts.

Poetry Read, React & Writing. Kirszne. (C). 1994. pap. text 37.00 (*0-15-501015-8*, Pub. by Harcourt Coll Pubs) Harcourt.

Poetry Reader's Toolkit: A Guide to Reading & Understanding Poetry. Marc Polonsky. LC 97-347. (Illus.). 176p. 1997. pap. 22.45 (*0-8442-5988-8*, 59888) NTC Contemp Pub Co.

Poetry Reading at Panama Hotel. Denella Kimura. 64p. 1991. pap. 6.95 (*0-939513-44-7*) Joy Pub SJC.

Poetry Reading, 1982: An Anthology. limited ed. 24p. 1983. 3.00 (*0-943018-06-4*) Backstreet.

Poetry Realized in Nature: Samuel Taylor Coleridge & Early Nineteenth-Century Science. Trevor H. Levere. LC 81-1930. 296p. 1981. text 69.95 (*0-521-23920-6*) Cambridge U Pr.

Poetry References in the Junior High School. Lucy Kangley. LC 75-176927. (Columbia University. Teachers College. Contributions to Education Ser.: No. 758). reprint ed. 37.50 (*0-404-55758-9*) AMS Pr.

Poetry Ritual for Grammar Schools. Robert McGovern. 42p. 1974. pap. 2.50 (*0-912592-23-0*) Ashland Poetry.

Poetry Room. Lewis MacAdams, Jr. LC 73-123978. 65p. 1970. 12.50 (*0-89366-104-X*) Ultramarine Pub.

Poetry Self-Taught. 2nd rev. ed. Barbara Morris Fischer. 60p. 1998. 34.95 (*0-912658-63-0*); pap. text 24.95 (*0-912658-65-7*) J Mark Pr.

Poetry since 1939. Stephen Spender. LC 74-7038. (Studies in Poetry: No. 38). (C). 1974. lib. bdg. 75.00 (*0-8383-1930-0*) M S G Haskell Hse.

Poetry since the Liberation. (Yale French Studies: No. 21). 1974. reprint ed. 25.00 (*0-527-01727-2*) Periodicals Srv.

Poetry Slam. M. Lewis Peterson. (Illus.). 150p. 1997. pap. 29.95 (*1-885721-03-X*) L P Prods.

***Poetry Slam: The Competitive Art of Performance Poetry.** Ed. by Gary Glazner. 240p. 2000. pap. 15.00 (*0-916397-66-1*) Manic D Pr.

Poetry Society of America Anthology. Ed. by Amy Bonner et al. LC 76-75709. (Granger Index Reprint Ser.). 1977. 23.95 (*0-8369-6003-3*) Ayer.

Poetry, Space, Landscape: Toward a New Theory. Chris Fitter. (Literature, Culture, Theory Ser.: No. 13). (Illus.). 336p. (C). 1995. text 64.95 (*0-521-46301-7*) Cambridge U Pr.

Poetry Street 1. Orme & Sale. 1991. pap. text. write for info. (*0-582-03924-X*, Pub. by Addison-Wesley) Longman.

Poetry Street 2. Orme & Sale. 1992. pap. text. write for info. (*0-582-03925-8*, Pub. by Addison-Wesley) Longman.

Poetry Street 3. Orme & Sale. 1992. pap. text. write for info. (*0-582-03926-6*, Pub. by Addison-Wesley) Longman.

Poetry, Tales & Selected Essays. Edgar Allan Poe. LC 96-8922. (Library of America College Editions). 1506p. (C). 1996. pap. text 16.95 (*1-883011-38-8*, Pub. by Library of America) Penguin Putnam.

***Poetry That Ministers.** Mary Kramer. 1999. pap. write for info. (*1-58235-189-9*) Watermrk Pr.

Poetry That Stirs the Soul. Compiled by M. L. Smith. LC 92-75904. 120p. 1993. pap. text 6.00 (*1-882581-00-8*) Campbell Rd Pr.

Poetry, the Healer. Jack J. Leedy. 1973. 12.75i (*0-397-59057-1*, Lippnctt) Lppncott W & W.

Poetry, the Magic Language: Children Learn to Read & Write It. Maureen W. Armour. xvii, 215p. 1994. pap. text 17.50 (*1-56308-033-8*) Teacher Ideas Pr.

Poetry, Themes, & Activities: Exploring the Fun & Fantasy of Language. Les Parsons. 112p. (C). 1992. pap. text 16.50 (*0-435-08730-4*, 08730) Heinemann.

***Poetry Therapy: Interface of the Arts & Psychology.** Nicholas Mazza. LC 99-29951. (Innovations in Psychology Ser.). 232p. 1999. boxed set 39.95 (*0-8493-0350-8*) CRC Pr.

***Poetry Therapy: Interface of the Arts & Psychology.** Nicholas Mazza. LC 99-29951. (Innovations in Psychology Ser.). 1999. 39.95 (*1-57444-183-3*) CRC Pr.

Poetry Therapy - Notebook of Stories & Poetry to Duplicate & Use. A. Doyle. 70p. (Orig.). 1996. ring bd. 34.95 (*1-56820-164-8*) Story Time.

Poetry Time with Dr. Seuss Rhyme. Cheryl Potts & Dr. Seuss. LC 97-31434. (Illus.). 64p. (J). 1998. pap. text 13.95 (*0-917846-99-0*, Alleyside) Highsmith Pr.

Poetry to Devour. David Bowden. (Illus.). 47p. (Orig.). (YA). (gr. 6-12). 1995. pap. text 7.95 (*1-887172-08-4*) G Bowden.

Poetry to Heal Your Inner Self. Carolyn T. Laskey. Ed. by Patty Hutchings. LC 94-62011. 136p. 1994. pap. 9.95 (*1-880254-29-8*) Vista.

***Poetry to Live by.** Eugene Kitt. 1999. pap. write for info. (*1-58235-112-0*) Watermrk Pr.

Poetry to Make You Smile. Muriel R. Kulwin. 83p. 1996. pap. 20.00 (*1-889080-06-3*) Doublem Bks.

Poetry to My Lovers. Karen M. Miller. 34p. (Orig.). 1996. pap. 9.43 (*0-9654907-0-X*) kilo mike bks.

Poetry to the Rescue. Steven Herrick. LC 99-210729. 1998. pap. 10.95 (*0-7022-3006-5*, Pub. by Univ Queensland Pr) Intl Spec Bk.

Poetry Today. 2nd ed. Anthony Thwaite. LC 95-21683. 192p. (C). 1996. pap. 26.73 (*0-582-21511-0*) Addison-Wesley.

Poetry Tribune Primer. Eugene Field. (Notable American Authors Ser.). 1992. reprint ed. lib. bdg. 75.00 (*0-7812-2640-6*) Rprt Serv.

Poetry Trifold: Choices in Relationships. 6th ed. Knox & Schacht. (Sociology-Upper Level Ser.). 1999. pap. text 1.50 (*0-534-57374-6*) Wadsworth Pub.

***Poetry under Oath: From the Testimony of William Jefferson Clinton & Monica S. Lewinsky.** Tom Simon. 1998. pap. 71.40 (*0-7611-1621-4*) Workman Pub.

Poetry under Oath: From the Testimony of William Jefferson Clinton & Monica S. Lewinsky. Ed. by Tom Simon. LC 99-185372. 115p. 1998. mass mkt. 5.95 (*0-7611-1620-6*) Workman Pub.

Poetry Unfolding. Incl. Guide to Poetry Unfolding Film-Strip. 1983. (*0-915291-17-7*); 1983. write for info. (*0-318-57617-1*) Know Unltd.

Poetry Ventured, Four Years of PV's Best Poems: A Poetry Anthology. Ed. by Marjorie M. Schuck & George Garrott. 172p. 1972. pap. 10.00 (*0-912760-00-1*) Valkyrie Pub Hse.

Poetry Wales: 25 Years. Ed. by Cary Archard. 280p. (Orig.). (YA). (gr. 10-12). 1990. pap. 17.95 (*1-85411-031-4*, Pub. by Seren Bks) Dufour.

Poetry with a Porpoise. Rick Peoples. (J). (gr. 1-6). 1998. 12.95 (*0-9668328-0-9*) Appenzell Pr.

Poetry with a Porpoise. Rick Peoples. (Illus.). 128p. (J). (ps-6). 1998. reprint ed. 21.95 incl. cd-rom (*0-9668328-3-3*) Appenzell Pr.

Poetry with a Purpose. Barbara Malley & Frances Allen. (Illus.). 128p. (J). (gr. 4-7). 1987. pap. 12.99 (*0-86653-415-6*, GA 1018) Good Apple.

Poetry with an Edge. Ed. by Neil Astley. LC 88-51307. 320p. 1993. pap. 22.95 (*1-85224-061-X*, Pub. by Bloodaxe Bks) Dufour.

***Poetry with Some Flowers, Birds & Teddy Bears: Inspirational, Romance & Life.** Robert J. Lessig. LC 00-104494. (Illus.). 104p. 2000. pap. 17.95 (*0-9667763-0-5*) Biblical Rsrch.

Poetry with Wanda Marie. Wanda M. Gallagher. (J). 1998. pap. 7.95 (*0-533-12646-0*) Vantage.

Poetry, Word-Play, & Word-War in Wallace Stevens. Eleanor Cook. LC 88-4817. 339p. 1988. reprint ed. pap. 105.10 (*0-608-04582-9*, 206535200003) Bks Demand.

Poetry Workbook: A Poet's Workbook. 3rd ed. Ed. by S. Diane Bogus. 25p. (YA). (gr. 11-12). 1995. reprint ed. pap. 10.00 (*0-934172-20-X*) WIM Pubns.

***Poetry Works.** Pamela Amick Klawitter. Ed. by Kimberley Clark & Clark Editorial & Design Staff. (Illus.). 56p. (J). (gr. 3-7). 2000. pap. 8.95 (*0-88160-302-3*, LW371) Learning Wks.

Poetry World 1. Daniel Weissbort. 160p. 1986. pap. 17.95 (*0-85646-174-1*, Pub. by Anvil Press) Dufour.

Poetry World 2. Daniel Weissbort. 160p. 1988. pap. 17.95 (*0-85646-184-9*, Pub. by Anvil Press) Dufour.

Poetry Writing. Peggy Hapke Lewis. 1993. 5.95 (*1-55708-410-6*, MCS953) McDonald Pub Co.

Poetry Writing: Theme & Variations David Starkey. LC 99-21611. 1999. write for info. (*0-8442-0343-2*) NTC Contemp Pub Co.

Poetry Writing Handbook: Definitions, Examples, Lessons. Greta B. Lipson. Ed. by Judy Mitchell. (Illus.). 112p. (J). (gr. 4-6). 1998. pap., teacher ed. 10.95 (*1-57310-108-7*) Teachng & Lrning Co.

Poetry Writing Self-Taught. Pauline Durrett Robertson. (Illus.). 204p. 2000. pap. 17.95 (*0-942376-10-2*) Paramount TX.

***Poetry's Appeal: 19th-Century French Lyric & the Political Space.** E S Burt. LC 99-39452. (Meridian Ser.). 1999. pap. text 19.95 (*0-8047-3873-4*) Stanford U Pr.

Poetry's Catbird Seat: The Consultantship in Poetry in the English Language at the Library of Congress, 1937-1987. William McGuire. LC 87-33876. 512p. 1988. 21.00 (*0-685-48152-2*, 030-000-00204-1) Lib Congress.

Poetry's Old Air. Marianne Boruch. LC 94-44312. (Poets on Poetry Ser.). 160p. 1995. pap. 13.95 (*0-472-06584-X*, 06584); text 39.50 (*0-472-09584-6*, 09584) U of Mich Pr.

Poetry's Self-Portrait: The Visual Arts As Mirror & Muse in Rene Char & John Ashbery. Mary E. Eichbauer. LC 91-43606. (New Connections: Studies in Interdisciplinarity: Vol. 7). XV, 160p. (C). 1993. 44.95 (*0-8204-1817-X*) P Lang Pubng.

***Poetry's Whatever.** Jeremiah Schultz. 32p. 2000. pap. 7.00 (*0-923242-99-6*) Sparrowgrass Poetry.

Poets. Greville Pr. Staff. (C). 1990. 45.00 (*0-906887-04-6*, Pub. by Greville Pr) St Mut.

Poets see Great Writers of the English Language

Poets: American & British, Vol. 1. Scribner. LC 98-36811. 1998. 70.00 (*0-684-80606-1*) S&S Trade.

***Poets: American & British, Vol. 2.** Scribner. 1998. 70.00 (*0-684-80607-X*) S&S Trade.

***Poets: American & British, Vol. 3.** Scribner. 1998. 70.00 (*0-684-80608-8*) S&S Trade.

Poet's Africa: Africanness in the Poetry of Nicolas Guillen & Aime Cesaire, 138. Josaphat B. Kubayanda. LC 90-3161. (Contributions in Afro-American & African Studies: No. 138). 192p. 1990. 52.95 (*0-313-26298-5*, KUP, Greenwood Pr) Greenwood.

***Poet's Alibi.** Nikia Taylor. 50p. 1999. pap. 10.00 (*0-9677743-0-6*) Kazuri Pub Co.

***Poets & Critics Read Virgil.** Sarah Spence. LC 00-33445. 2001. write for info. (*0-300-08376-9*) Yale U Pr.

Poets & Critics, Their Means & Meanings: Including Essays on Browning, Ruskin, Stevens, Heaney, & Others. Ashby B. Crowder. LC 93-9540. (Illus.). 228p. 1993. 89.95 (*0-7734-9268-2*) E Mellen.

Poets & Dreamers: Studies & Translations from the Irish. Lady Gregory. LC 73-17133. (Studies in Irish Literature: No. 16). 1974. lib. bdg. 75.00 (*0-8383-1725-1*) M S G Haskell Hse.

Poets & Emperors: Frankish Politics & Carolingian Poetry. Peter Godman. 250p. 1987. 59.00 (*0-19-812820-7*) OUP.

Poets & Gay Poets. Edward Lau. 150p. 1996. pap. text 10.00 (*1-888065-09-5*) New Wrld Poetry.

Poets & Murder: A Judge Dee Mystery. Robert H. Van Gulik. (Illus.). vi, 176p. 1996. pap. 7.95 (*0-226-84876-0*) U Ch Pr.

Poets & Music. Edward W. Naylor. LC 80-16489. (Music Reprint Ser.). 1980. reprint ed. 29.50 (*0-306-76038-X*) Da Capo.

Poets & Mystics. Edward I. Watkin. LC 68-55862. (Essay Index Reprint Ser.). 1977. 21.95 (*0-8369-0979-8*) Ayer.

Poets & Painters. David Shapiro. LC 79-55555. (Illus.). 80p. (Orig.). 1979. pap. 6.00 (*0-914738-17-8*) Denver Art Mus.

***Poets & Pals of Picardy: A Weekend on the Somme'.** Mary Ellen Freedman. (Illus.). 2000. pap. 16.95 (*0-85052-703-1*, Pub. by Leo Cooper) Combined Pub.

Poets & Players: Last Interview - Exchange Simone de Beauvoir - Jean-Paul Sartre. Ed. & Tr. by Ann B. Krooth. 1976. pap. 6.00 (*0-939074-01-X*) Harvest Pubns.

Poets & Poetry: Being Articles Reprinted from the Literary Supplement of 'The Times' John C. Bailey. LC 67-30196. (Essay Index Reprint Ser.). 1977. 18.95 (*0-8369-0170-3*) Ayer.

Poets & Poetry of Europe. Henry Wadsworth Longfellow. (Notable American Authors Ser.). 1999. reprint ed. lib. bdg. 125.00 (*0-7812-3829-3*) Rprt Serv.

Poets & Poetry of Munster. Tr. & Compiled by James Clarence Mangan. LC 96-23326. (Hibernia Ser.). 1996. 75.00 (*1-85477-217-1*) Continuum.

Poets & Poetry of Munster: A Selection of Irish Songs by the Poets of the Last Century. 5th ed. Tr. by James C. Mangan. LC 75-28824. reprint ed. 34.50 (*0-404-13816-0*) AMS Pr.

Poets & Poetry of the West: With Biographical & Critical Notices. William T. Coggeshall. LC 75-92. (Mid-American Frontier Ser.). 1975. reprint ed. 57.95 (*0-405-06859-X*) Ayer.

***Poets & Politics: Continuity & Reaction in Irish Poetry, 1558-1625.** Marc Caball. LC 98-42848. (Critical Conditions Ser.: 8). 280p. 1999. pap. 30.00 (*0-268-03856-2*, Pub. by U of Notre Dame Pr) Chicago Distribution Ctr.

Poets & Presidents: Selected Essays, 1977-1992. E. L. Doctorow. 206p. (Orig.). 1994. pap. 26.50 (*0-333-61606-5*, Pub. by Papermac) Trans-Atl Phila.

Poets & Princepleasers: Literature & the English Court in the Late Middle Ages. Richard F. Green. 1980. text 35.00 (*0-8020-5409-9*) U of Toronto Pr.

Poets & Prophets: Essays on Medieval Studies by G. T. Shepherd. G. T. Shepherd. Ed. by J. D. Pickles. 238p. (C). 1990. 75.00 (*0-85991-289-2*) Boydell & Brewer.

Poets & the Poetics of Sin. George Kane. (Morton W. Bloomfield Lectures on Medieval English Literature Ser.: No. I). 25p. 1989. pap. 3.95 (*0-674-68045-6*) HUP.

Poets & the Poetry of the Nineteenth Century, 12 vols. rev. ed. Ed. by Alfred H. Miles. LC 16-2291. reprint ed. 780.00 (*0-404-05120-0*) AMS Pr.

Poets & Their Art. Harriet Monroe. 322p. 1977. 18.95 (*0-8369-0714-0*) Ayer.

Poets & Their Art. Harriet Monroe. (BCL1-PS American Literature Ser.). 300p. 1992. reprint ed. lib. bdg. 79.00 (*0-7812-6630-0*) Rprt Serv.

Poet's Anthology: The Range of Japanese Poetry. Tr. by Janine Beichman from JPN. (Reflections Ser.: No. 3). (ENG.). 224p. (C). 1994. pap. text 19.95 (*0-942668-38-3*) Katydid Bks.

Poet's Anthology: The Range of Japanese Poetry. Ed. by Thomas Fitzsimmons. Tr. by Janine Beichman from JPN. (Reflections Ser.: No. 3). (ENG.). 224p. (C). 1994. 30.00 (*0-942668-37-5*) Katydid Bks.

Poets Are People. Maurine Fergueson. (Orig.). 1997. pap. write for info. (*1-57553-510-6*) Watermrk Pr.

Poet's Art. Macha L. Rosenthal. 1989. pap. 7.95 (*0-393-30584-8*) Norton.

Poets As Players: Theme & Variation in Late Medieval French Poetry. Leonard W. Johnson. LC 90-33954. 376p. 1991. 42.50 (*0-8047-1828-8*) Stanford U Pr.

Poets at Large: 25 Poets in 25 Homes. Ed. by H. L. Hix. LC 97-3587. 1997. 12.95 (*1-884235-19-0*) Helicon Nine Eds.

Poets at Play. J. L. Malone. 1990. pap. text. write for info. (*0-582-86818-1*, Pub. by Addison-Wesley) Longman.

Poets at Play: Irony & Parody in the Harley Lyrics. Daniel J. Ransom. LC 85-544. 160p. (C). 1985. 29.95 (*0-937664-67-7*) Pilgrim Bks OK.

Poets at Prayer. Mary J. Power. LC 68-29239. (Essay Index Reprint Ser.). 1977. 20.95 (*0-8369-0797-3*) Ayer.

Poets at Work: Contemporary Poets-Lives, Poems, Process. Ed. by Betty Cohen. 309p. (Orig.). (YA). (gr. 7-12). 1995. pap. 15.00 (*0-9647047-0-6*) Just Buffalo.

Poets at Work: 32 Poems & a Story by Children in Phillipston. Ed. by Christine Tarantino. (Illus.). 56p. (J). (gr. 2-8). 1996. spiral bd. 3.95 (*1-887480-24-2*) Wrds Lght Intl.

Poet's Bazaar: A Journey to Greece, Turkey & up the Danube. Hans Christian Andersen. Tr. by Grace Thornton from DAN. LC 87-30993.Tr. of Digters bazar. (Illus.). 208p. 1990. pap. 15.95 (*0-935576-34-7*) Kesend Pub Ltd.

Poets Behind Barbed Wire. Keiho Soga et al. Ed. & Tr. by Jiro Nakano & Kay Nakano from JPN. LC 83-71474. 73p. 1983. pap. 8.00 (*0-910043-05-1*) Bamboo Ridge Pr.

Poets Between the Wars. New Canadian Library Staff. 198p. 1996. pap. text 7.95 (*0-7710-9475-2*) McCland & Stewart.

Poets' Book of Psalms: The Complete Psalter As Rendered by Twenty-Five Poets from the Sixteenth to the Twentieth Centuries. Ed. by Laurence Wieder. LC 98-55749. 336p. 1999. pap. 15.95 (*0-19-513058-8*) OUP.

Poet's Calling in the English Ode. Paul H. Fry. LC 79-20554. 1980. 50.00 (*0-300-02400-2*) Yale U Pr.

Poet's Car: Poems. James Ralston. LC 91-62670. 60p. (Orig.). 1992. pap. 7.00 (*0-945073-15-1*) Nightsun MD.

Poet's Cat. Ed. by Mona Gooden. LC 74-75711. (Granger Index Reprint Ser.). 1977. 11.95 (*0-8369-6017-3*) Ayer.

Poets' Cat. Frances May. 69p. 1990. pap. 7.00 (*1-878660-09-8*) Fireweed WI.

Poets Choice. Robert Hass. LC 97-23792. 224p. 1998. 23.00 (*0-88001-566-7*) HarpC.

Poet's Choice. Elizabeth Jennings. LC 97-164311. 180p. 1997. pap. 16.95 (*1-85754-262-2*, Pub. by Carcanet Pr) Paul & Co Pubs.

Poet's Choice, Vol 1, No. 1. Ed. by Charles E. Cravey. 1993. pap. 12.95 (*0-938645-98-6*) In His Steps.

Poet's Choice: Poems for Everyday Life. Ed. by Robert Hass. 224p. 1999. reprint ed. pap. 15.00 (*0-88001-613-2*) HarpC.

Poet's Choice: 100 American Poets' Favorite Poems. Ed. by George E. Murphy, Jr. 176p. 1980. 12.95 (*0-937504-01-7*); pap. 5.95 (*0-937504-00-9*) Tendril.

Poet's Companion: A Guide to the Pleasures of Writing Poetry. Kim Addonizio & Dorianne Laux. LC 96-40451. 224p. 1997. pap. 13.00 (*0-393-31654-8*, Norton Paperbks) Norton.

Poet's Concord. Ed. by Avon Fields. (Illus.). 24p. 1997. pap. 6.95 (*1-879629-99-2*) Galaxy Pub CO.

Poet's Corner. Roderic Vickers. 44p. 1995. pap. 5.95 (*1-886956-00-6*) Star Concepts.

Poet's Craft. Ed. by Helen F. Daringer & Anne T. Eaton. LC 72-8284. (Granger Index Reprint Ser.). (Illus.). 1977. reprint ed. 23.95 (*0-8369-6385-7*) Ayer.

***Poets' Dante: Essays on Dante by Twentieth-Century Poets.** Ed. by Peter Hawkins & Rachel Jacoff. 256p. 2001. 25.00 (*0-374-23536-8*) FS&G.

Poet's Dictionary: A Handbook of Prosody & Poetic Devices. William Packard. LC 88-45899. 240p. 1994. reprint ed. pap. 15.00 (*0-06-272045-7*, Harper Ref) HarpC.

Poets' Digest. Ed. by Ronald D. Hardcastle. LC 98-72997. (Illus.). xxx, 325p. 1998. 47.50 (*0-9665781-3-9*) Inst Contemp Amer Poetry.

Poet's Domain: We Wear the Mask. Ed. by Patricia Adler. 120p. (Orig.). 1999. pap. 10.95 (*0-9672885-0-9*) Live Wire Pr.

Poet's Dreams & Visualization of Reality. Abraham J. Heller. 1998. pap. write for info. (*1-58235-068-X*) Watermrk Pr.

Poets '88: The New Generation. Ed. by Ken Norris & Bob Hilderley. 160p. 1988. pap. 12.95 (*0-919627-88-9*, Pub. by Quarry Pr) LPC InBook.

Poets' Encyclopedia. John M. Cage & Allen Ginsberg. Ed. by Michael Andre & Erika Rothenberg. (Illus.). 1979. 35.00 (*0-934450-02-1*) Unmuzzled Ox.

Poets' Encyclopedia. John M. Cage et al. (Illus.). 1980. pap. 17.00 (*0-934450-03-X*) Unmuzzled Ox.

***Poet's Feelings, Thoughts & Fantasies.** Abraham Heler. 1999. pap. write for info. (*1-58235-306-9*) Watermrk Pr.

Poets for Life: 76 Poets Respond to AIDS. Ed. by Michael Klein. LC 88-35219. 256p. 1992. reprint ed. pap. 12.95 (*0-89255-170-4*) Persea Bks.

Poets Fortnightly, 1973-74: A Newsletter for Poets. Ed. by Barbara A. Holland & Brett Rutherford. write for info. (*0-318-64129-1*) Poets Pr.

Poets from the North of Ireland. Frank Ormsby. 312p. 1990. pap. 22.00 (*0-85640-444-6*, Pub. by Blackstaff Pr) Dufour.

Poet's Gift: Toward the Renewal of Pastoral Care. Donald Capps. 176p. (Orig.). 1993. pap. 19.95 (*0-664-25403-9*) Westminster John Knox.

Poet's Grandmother. John Ash. (Illus.). (C). text. write for info. (*0-472-09644-3*); pap. text. write for info. (*0-472-06644-7*) U of Mich Pr.

Poet's Guide: How to Publish & Perform Your Work. Michael J. Bugeja. (SLP Writer's Guides Ser.). 152p. (Orig.). 1995. pap. 12.95 (*1-885266-00-6*) Story Line.

Poet's Guide to Freelance Selling. Kathleen Gilbert. (Illus.). 27p. 1983. pap. 4.50 (*0-915913-00-3*) Violetta Bks.

Poet's Guide to Poetry. Mary Kinzie. LC 98-10248. 508p. 1999. pap. 18.00 (*0-226-43739-6*); lib. bdg. 47.00 (*0-226-43738-8*) U Ch Pr.

Poet's Handbook. Judson Jerome. 224p. 1986. pap. 14.99 (*0-89879-219-3*, Wrtrs Digest Bks) F & W Pubns Inc.

Poet's Harvest Home. William B. Scott. LC 79-148298. reprint ed. 40.00 (*0-404-05648-2*) AMS Pr.

Poets Historical: Dynastic Epic in the Renaissance. Andrew Fichter. LC 81-19795. 237p. 1982. 40.00 (*0-300-02721-4*) Yale U Pr.

P

An Asterisk (*) at the beginning of an entry indicates that the title is appearing for the first time.

Poet's Homecoming. George MacDonald & Michael R. Phillips. 192p. 1990. pap. 7.99 (*1-55661-135-8*) Bethany Hse.

Poets' Homes: Pen & Pencil Sketches of American Poets & Their Homes, 2 Vols. Richard H. Stoddard et al. LC 72-3491. (Essay Index Reprint Ser.). 1977. reprint ed. 48.95 (*0-8369-2926-8*) Ayer.

Poet's "I" in Archaic Greek Lyric. Ed. by S. R. Slings. 79p. 1991. pap. text 22.95 (*90-6256-940-4*, Pub. by VU Univ Pr) Paul & Co Pubs.

Poets in a Changing World. K. P. Sasidharan. xiv, 206p. 1991. 27.50 (*81-220-0236-6*) Advent Bks Div.

***Poets in a Frieze & a Valentine.** James Liddy. (Poetry New York Pamphlet Ser.: No. 26). 1999. pap. 5.00 (*0-923389-36-9*) Meet Eyes Bind.

Poets in Motion. Louis R. Rivera et al. (Illus.). (Orig.). 1976. pap. text 3.00 (*0-917886-00-3*) Shamal Bks.

Poets in Person: A Listener's Guide. 2nd ed. Joseph Parisi. LC 99-208341. (Illus.). 1997. pap. 11.95 (*1-881505-08-1*) Modern Poetry.

Poets in Their Time: Essays on English Poetry from Donne to Larkin. Barbara Everett. 272p. 1992. pap. text 24.95 (*0-19-811281-5*) OUP.

Poet's Ink. Tom Collins. 85p. (Orig.). 1995. pap. 6.95 (*0-9649165-0-9*) Marion Prods.

***Poets' Jesus: Representations at the End of the Millennium.** Peggy Rosenthal. LC 99-23029. 184p. 2000. 29.95 (*0-19-513114-2*) OUP.

Poet's Journal. Bayard Taylor. (Notable American Authors). 1999. reprint ed. lib. bdg. 125.00 (*0-7812-8986-6*) Rprt Serv.

Poet's Journal: Days of 1945-1951. George Seferis. Tr. by Athan Angnostopoulos from GRE. LC 73-92634. 208p. 1974. pap. 10.50 (*0-674-68041-3*) Belknap Pr.

Poet's Kiss. Valerie King. 288p. 1997. mass mkt. 4.99 (*0-8217-5789-X*, Zebra Kensgtn) Kensgtn Pub Corp.

Poet's Life. Tzvetan Todorov. (Bennington Chapbooks in Literature Ser.). 32p. (Orig.). 1994. pap. text 5.00 (*1-878603-06-X*) Bennington Coll.

Poet's Life. Harriet Monroe. LC 71-93777. reprint ed. 22.50 (*0-404-04349-6*) AMS Pr.

Poet's Life. unabridged ed. Tzvetan Todorov. (Ben Belitt Lectureship Ser.: Vol. 16). (Illus.). 28p. (Orig.). 1994. pap. 5.00 (*0-614-10188-3*) Bennington Coll.

Poet's Life: 70 Years in a Changing World. Harriet Monroe. (American Biography Ser.). 488p. 1991. reprint ed. lib. bdg. 89.00 (*0-7812-8288-8*) Rprt Serv.

Poet's Life: 70 Years in a Changing World. Harriet Monroe. (BCL1-PS American Literature Ser.). 488p. 1993. reprint ed. lib. bdg. 99.00 (*0-7812-6995-4*) Rprt Serv.

Poets' Life of Christ. Norman Ault. LC 72-2513. (Select Bibliographies Reprint Ser.). 1977. reprint ed. 24.95 (*0-8369-6847-6*) Ayer.

***Poet's Market: 1,800 Places to Publish Your Poetry.** Ed. by Chantelle Bentley. 608p. 2000. pap. 23.99 (*0-89879-981-3*) F & W Pubns Inc.

Poet's Mind: L6. James A. Emanuel. Ed. by Jean A. McConochie. (Regents Readers Ser.). 1987. pap. text. write for info. (*0-13-683962-2*, 20975) Prentice ESL.

Poet's Myth of Fernan Gonzalez. Jean P. Keller. LC 90-22462. (Scripta Humanistica Ser.: No. 81). 1991. 47.50 (*0-916379-87-6*) Scripta.

Poets Never Kill. Roy Gilligan. LC 90-92285. (Pat Riordan Mystery Ser.). 200p. 1991. pap. 8.95 (*0-9626136-1-4*) Brendan Bks.

Poet's Notebook. Edith Sitwell. LC 71-152605. 276p. 1972. reprint ed. lib. bdg. 35.00 (*0-8371-6040-5*, SIPN, Greenwood Pr) Greenwood.

Poet's Notebook: Excerpts from the Notebooks of 26 American Poets. Ed. by Stephen Kuusisto et al. 320p. (C). 1997. pap. 13.00 (*0-393-31655-6*, Norton Paperbks) Norton.

Poet's Odyssey: Joachim du Bellay & the Antiquitez de Rome. George H. Tucker. 318p. 1991. text 90.00 (*0-19-815865-3*) OUP.

Poets of Action. G. Wilson Knight. LC 81-43479. 320p. 1982. reprint ed. pap. text 27.00 (*0-8191-2074-X*) U Pr of Amer.

Poets of America. Edmund C. Stedman. LC 18-13421. 13.00 (*0-403-00058-0*) Scholarly.

Poets of America. Edmund C. Stedman. 1988. reprint ed. lib. bdg. 49.00 (*0-7812-0535-2*) Rprt Serv.

Poets of Bulgaria. Ed. by William Meredith. Tr. by Denise Levertov et al from BUL. 150p. 1985. 25.00 (*0-87775-189-7*); pap. 15.00 (*0-87775-190-0*) Unicorn Pr.

Poets of Bulgaria. Ed. & Tr. by William Meredith. 92p. 1988. reprint ed. pap. 16.95 (*0-948259-39-6*, Pub. by Forest Bks) Dufour.

Poets of Chile: A Bilingual Anthology, 1965-1985. Ed. by Steven F. White. LC 85-16479. (Illus.). 283p. (Orig.). 1986. 29.95 (*0-87775-179-X*); pap. 19.95 (*0-87775-180-3*) Unicorn Pr.

Poets of Contemporary Canada. New Canadian Library Staff. 144p. 1996. pap. text 7.95 (*0-7710-9506-6*) McCland & Stewart.

***Poets of Contemporary Latin America: History & the Inner Life.** William Rowe. (Illus.). 288p. 2000. 65.00 (*0-19-815892-0*) OUP.

Poets of Ellicott Street. Ed. by Marijane G. Ricketts & Gonny Van den Broek. (Illus.). 48p. (Orig.). 1989. pap. 5.00 (*0-9618223-1-7*) M G Ricketts.

Poets of Great Britain & Ireland, 1945-1960. Ed. by Vincent B. Sherry, Jr. (Dictionary of Literary Biography Ser.: Vol. 27). 416p. 1984. text 155.00 (*0-8103-1705-2*) Gale.

Poets of Great Britain & Ireland since 1960, 2 vols. Ed. by Vincent B. Sherry, Jr. (Dictionary of Literary Biography Ser.: Vol. 40). 702p. 1985. text 296.00 (*0-8103-1718-4*, 006440-M99348) Gale.

Poets of Greece. Edwin Arnold. LC 70-39680. (Essay Index Reprint Ser.). 1977. reprint ed. 23.95 (*0-8369-2738-9*) Ayer.

Poets of Ireland. David J. O'Donoghue. 1972. 59.95 (*0-8490-0867-0*) Gordon Pr.

Poets of Modern France. Ludwig Lewisohn. (Collected Works of Ludwig Lewisohn). 199p. 1998. reprint ed. lib. bdg. 88.00 (*1-58201-684-4*) Classic Bks.

Poets of Modern Ireland: Text, Context, Intertext. Ed. by Neil Corcoran. LC 99-30718. 200p. 1988. pap. 21.95 (*0-8093-2290-0*) S Ill U Pr.

Poets of Munster. Ed. by Sean Dunne. Date not set. pap. 18.95 (*0-85646-122-9*, Pub. by Anvil Press) Dufour.

Poets of Munster. Ed. by Sean Dunne. 224p. 1985. 29.95 (*0-85646-121-0*, Pub. by Anvil Press) Dufour.

Poets of Nicaragua: A Bilingual Anthology, 1918-1979. Ed. by Steven F. White. 1982. 29.95 (*0-87775-132-3*); pap. 19.95 (*0-87775-133-1*) Unicorn Pr.

Poets of Ohio. Emerson Venable. 1993. reprint ed. lib. bdg. 89.00 (*0-7812-5410-8*) Rprt Serv.

Poets of Our Time: An Anthology. Compiled by Finn. 160p. 1976. pap. 7.95 (*0-7195-3243-4*) Transatl Arts.

Poets of the Church: A Series of Biographical Sketches of Hymn-Writers, with Notes on Their Hymns. Edwin F. Hatfield. 1999. reprint ed. 110.00 (*1-55888-208-1*) Omnigraphics Inc.

Poets of the English Language Vol. 4: Romantic Poets. Ed. by W. H. Auden & Norman H. Pearson. (Portable Library: No. 52). 576p. 1977. pap. 15.95 (*0-14-015052-8*, P52, Penguin Bks) Viking Penguin.

***Poets of the Great War.** Ed. by Tonie & Valmai Holt. (Illus.). 2000. pap. 23.95 (*0-85052-706-6*, Pub. by Leo Cooper) Combined Pub.

Poets of the Insurrection. LC 75-28840. reprint ed. 29.50 (*0-404-13832-2*) AMS Pr.

Poets of the New York School. John Ashbery et al. (Illus.). 1969. 10.00 (*0-910664-14-5*) Gotham.

Poets of the Pacific. Ed. by Yvor Winters. LC 68-57068. (Second Ser.). 1977. 15.95 (*0-8369-6049-1*) Ayer.

Poets of the Pacific. Ed. by Yvor Winters. LC 49-9205. (Second Ser.). 136p. 1949. reprint ed. pap. 30.00 (*0-608-08292-9*, 205195700016) Bks Demand.

Poets of the South. Franklin V. Painter. LC 68-57064. (Granger Index Reprint Ser.). 1977. 17.95 (*0-8369-6037-8*) Ayer.

Poets of the Younger Generation. William Archer. LC 76-120572. (BCL Ser. I). reprint ed. 76.50 (*0-404-00367-2*) AMS Pr.

Poets of the Younger Generation. William Archer. (BCL1-PR English Literature Ser.). 564p. 1992. reprint ed. lib. bdg. 99.00 (*0-7812-7092-8*) Rprt Serv.

Poets of the Younger Generation. William Archer. LC 72-8574. 564p. reprint ed. 12.00 (*0-403-00240-0*) Scholarly.

Poets of Tin Pan Alley: A History of America's Great Lyricists. Philip Furia. 336p. 1992. pap. 13.95 (*0-19-507473-4*) OUP.

Poets of Transcendentalism: An Anthology. George W. Cooke. 1972. 59.95 (*0-8490-0868-9*) Gordon Pr.

***Poets of WWI.** Harold Bloom. (Major Poets Ser.). 2000. 19.95 (*0-7910-5932-4*) Chelsea Hse.

Poets on Painters: Essays on the Art of Painting by Twentieth-Century Poets. Ed. by J. D. McClatchy. (Illus.). 228p. 1988. pap. 17.95 (*0-520-06971-4*, Pub. by U CA Pr) Cal Prin Full Svc.

Poets on Poets: An Anthology. Ed. by N. Rennison & M. Schmidt. LC 98-146544. 420p. 1998. pap. 18.95 (*1-85754-339-4*, Pub. by Carcanet Pr) Paul & Co Pubs.

Poets on the Classics: An Anthology. Ed. by Stuart Gillespie. 256p. 1988. text 39.50 (*0-415-00328-8*) Routledge.

Poets on the Horizon: A Collection of Poetry. 1988. pap. 12.00 (*0-89073-080-6*, 317) Boston Public Lib.

Poet's Other Voice: Conversations on Literary Translation. Edwin Honig. LC 84-28066. (Illus.). 232p. 1985. lib. bdg. 30.00 (*0-87023-476-5*) U of Mass Pr.

Poets, Painters, Paupers, Fools: Indiana's Stein Family. Robert C. Kriebel. LC 90-30697. (Illus.). 194p. 1990. pap. 21.95 (*1-55753-006-8*) Purdue U Pr.

***Poet's Palette: Selected Works by Hobson Pittman.** Meade B. Horne. Ed. by Daphne Hamm O'Brien. (Illus.). xi, 63p. 1999. 50.00 (*0-9674327-0-7*) Blount-Bridgers.

Poet's Parents: The Courtship Letters of Emily Norcross & Edward Dickinson. Emily N. Dickinson. Ed. by Vivian R. Pollak. LC 87-35868. (Illus.). 274p. reprint ed. pap. 85.00 (*0-608-06013-5*, 206634100008) Bks Demand.

Poets, Patrons, & Printers: Crisis of Authority in Late Medieval France. Cynthia J. Brown. (Illus.). 320p. 1995. text 42.50 (*0-8014-3071-2*) Cornell U Pr.

Poet's Pen, Vol. 4, No. 3. Charles E. Cravey. 1992. 10.00 (*0-938645-64-1*) In His Steps.

Poet's Pen, Vol. 4, No. 4. Ed. by Charles E. Cravey. 1992. 10.00 (*0-938645-70-6*) In His Steps.

Poet's Pen, Vol. 5, No. 1. Ed. by Charles E. Cravey. 1992. 10.00 (*0-938645-76-5*) In His Steps.

Poet's Pen, Vol. 5, No. 2. Ed. by Charles E. Cravey. 1992. 10.00 (*0-938645-81-1*) In His Steps.

Poet's Pen, Vol. 5, No. 3. Ed. by Charles E. Cravey. 1993. 10.00 (*0-938645-86-2*) In His Steps.

Poet's Pen, Vol. 5, No. 4. Ed. by Charles E. Cravey. 1993. 10.00 (*0-938645-88-9*) In His Steps.

Poet's Pen, Vol. 6, No. 1. Ed. by Charles E. Cravey. 1993. 10.00 (*0-938645-92-7*) In His Steps.

Poet's Pen, Vol. 6, No. 2. Ed. by Charles E. Cravey. 1993. 10.00 (*0-938645-97-8*) In His Steps.

Poets' Perspectives: Reading, Writing & Teaching Poetry. Ed. by Charles R. Duke & Sally A. Jacobsen. LC 92-8499. 256p. (J). 1992. pap. text 18.50 (*0-86709-304-8*, 0304, Pub. by Boynton Cook Pubs) Heinemann.

Poets, Poems, Movements. Ed. by A. Walton Litz. LC 86-30910. (Studies in Modern Literature: No. 64). 340p. reprint ed. pap. 105.40 (*0-8357-1783-6*, 207074800004) Bks Demand.

Poets, Poetics, & Politics: America's Literary Community Viewed from the Letters of Rolfe Humphries, 1910-1969. Ed. by Richard Gillman & Michael P. Novak. LC 91-29496. (Illus.). xx, 300p. 1992. 35.00 (*0-7006-0508-8*) U Pr of KS.

Poets, Poetics, & Politics: America's Literary Community Viewed from the Letters of Rolfe Humphries, 1910-1969. Ed. by Richard Gillman & Michael P. Novak. LC 91-29496. (Illus.). xx, 300p. 1992. pap. 14.95 (*0-7006-0589-4*) U Pr of KS.

Poets, Politics & the People. Victor G. Kiernan. 320p. (C). 1989. pap. 19.00 (*0-86091-957-9*, A3345, Pub. by Verso) Norton.

Poets, Princes, & Private Citizens: Literary Alternatives to Postmodern Politics. Ed. by Joseph M. Knippenberg & Peter A. Lawler. LC 96-10739. 334p. 1996. pap. text 25.95 (*0-8476-8200-5*); lib. bdg. 66.00 (*0-8476-8199-8*) Rowman.

Poets, Prophets, & Sages: Essays in Biblical Interpretation. Robert Gordis. LC 79-98984. 446p. reprint ed. pap. 138.30 (*0-608-14594-7*, 205549800023) Bks Demand.

Poet's Prose: The Crisis in American Verse. 2nd ed. Stephen Fredman. (Cambridge Studies in American Literature & Culture: No. 44). 210p. (C). 1990. text 64.95 (*0-521-39098-2*); pap. text 18.95 (*0-521-39994-7*) Cambridge U Pr.

Poets Reading: The Field Symposia. Ed. by David Walker. LC 99-60376. 615p. 1999. pap. 25.00 (*0-932440-84-3*) Oberlin Coll Pr.

Poets Revolution see Koltok Forradalma: Antologia, 1953-1956

Poet's Sketch of His Biography. Dean Nichols. 96p. 1979. 12.50 (*0-682-49420-8*) Binford Mort.

Poets Talking: Poet of the Month Interviews from BBC Radio 3. Clive Wilmer. 160p. 1995. pap. 24.95 (*1-85754-075-1*, Pub. by Carcanet Pr) Paul & Co Pubs.

Poets Teaching Poets: Self & the World. Ed. by Gregory Orr & Ellen B. Voight. LC 96-4234. 288p. (C). 1996. text 47.50 (*0-472-09621-4*, 09621) U of Mich Pr.

Poets Teaching Poets: Self & the World. Ed. by Gregory Orr & Ellen B. Voigt. LC 96-4234. 288p. 1996. pap. 17.95 (*0-472-06621-8*, 06621) U of Mich Pr.

Poet's Testament: Poems & 2 Plays. George Santayana. LC 75-3339. reprint ed. 22.00 (*0-404-59424-7*) AMS Pr.

Poets Tongue. W. H. Auden & Garrett Auden. 1988. reprint ed. lib. bdg. 49.00 (*0-7812-0243-4*) Rprt Serv.

Poet's Tongue. Ed. by W. H. Auden & John Garrett. LC 75-161942. 222p. 1935. reprint ed. 49.00 (*0-403-01326-7*) Scholarly.

Poet's Touch. Valerie King. (Zebra Regency Romance Ser.). 224p. 1998. mass mkt. 4.99 (*0-8217-5901-9*, Zebra Kensgtn) Kensgtn Pub Corp.

Poet's Truth: A Study of the Poet in Virgil's Georgics. Christine Perkell. 1989. 45.00 (*0-520-06323-6*, Pub. by U CA Pr) Cal Prin Full Svc.

Poet's Universe. Joseph A. Uphoff, Jr. 130p. 1992. pap. text 7.00 (*0-943123-20-8*) Arjuna Lib Pr.

Poet's Vignette of Human Emotions & Behaviour. Abraham J. Heller. 1998. pap. write for info. (*1-57553-949-7*) Watermrk Pr.

Poet's Vision & Magic of Words: Muhammad Iqbal. I. Hussaini & Muhammad Iqbal. 145p. (Orig.). 1985. 14.50 (*1-56744-355-9*) Kazi Pubns.

Poet's Voice. Ed. by Fred Beake et al. 1997. pap. 8.95 (*3-7052-0084-4*, Pub. by Poetry Salzburg) Intl Spec Bk.

Poet's Voice: Poets Reading Aloud & Commenting upon Their Works. Ed. by Stratis Haviaras. (Harvard Audio Visual Materials Ser.). 1978. pap. 70.00 (*0-674-67853-2*) HUP.

Poet's Voice & Craft. Ed. by C. B. McCully. 200p. 1995. pap. 25.00 (*1-85754-020-4*, Pub. by Carcanet Pr) Paul & Co Pubs.

Poets Walk In. Anna P. Broomell. LC 54-8405. (C). 1954. pap. 4.00 (*0-87574-077-4*) Pendle Hill.

Poet's Way with Music: Humanism in Jorge de Sena's Poetry. Francisco C. Fagundes. LC 88-72191. 375p. (Orig.). 1988. pap. 12.50 (*0-943722-15-2*) Gavea-Brown.

Poets West: An Anthology of Contemporary Poems from the Eleven Western States. Ed. by Lawrence P. Spingarn. LC 73-79233. 182p. 1976. pap. 11.95 (*0-912288-05-1*) Perivale Pr.

Poet's Work. Sam Hamill. LC 97-76756. (Poets in Prose Ser.). 229p. 1998. pap. 19.95 (*0-88748-225-2*) Carnegie-Mellon.

Poets Work: An Introduction to Czeslaw Milosz. Leonard Nathan. 1991. pap. 15.00 (*0-674-68970-4*) HUP.

Poet's Work: An Introduction to Czeslaw Milosz. Leonard Nathan & Arthur Quinn. (C). 1991. pap. 9.95 (*0-685-48477-7*) HUP.

Poet's Work: 29 Poets on the Origins & Practice of Their Art. Ed. by Reginald Gibbons. LC 88-27772. xiv, 320p. 1989. pap. 16.95 (*0-226-29054-9*) U Ch Pr.

Poet's World. Rita Dove. LC 95-5323. 107p. 1995. pap. 9.50 (*0-8444-0874-3*) Lib Congress.

Poetspeak: In Their Work, about Their Work: A Special Kind of Poetry Anthology. Paul B. Janeczko. LC 91-15532. 256p. (YA). (gr. 7 up). 1991. reprint ed. mass mkt. 9.95 (*0-02-043850-8*, Collier Bks Young) S&S Childrens.

***Poetwoman - Dreamscapes.** C. A. Willett. LC 99-58516. 92p. 2000. pap. text 19.95 (*0-7734-1248-4*) E Mellen.

POF Data Book. 120.00 (*0-614-18420-7*) Info Gatekeepers.

Poff Der Kater, Oder Wenn Wir Lieben see Poff the Cat or When We Care

Poff the Cat or When We Care. Hartmut Von Hentig. Tr. by Joel Agee from GER. LC 83-82754.Tr. of Poff Der Kater, Oder Wenn Wir Lieben. 56p. 1993. 7.95 (*0-940242-09-5*) Fjord Pr.

Poganuc People. Harriet Beecher Stowe. (Notable American Authors Ser.). 1999. reprint ed. lib. bdg. 125.00 (*0-7812-8964-5*) Rprt Serv.

Poganuc People: Their Loves & Lives. Harriet Beecher Stowe. LC 76-56587. (Illus.). 375p. (C). 1996. reprint ed. pap. 17.00 (*0-917482-06-9*) Rutgers U Pr.

Poggius Florentinus: Leben und Werke. Ernst Walser. (Beitrage Zur Kulturgeschichte des Mittelalters und der Renaissance, Heft Ser.: No. 14). (Illus.). viii, 567p. 1974. reprint ed. write for info. (*3-487-05250-4*) G Olms Pubs.

Pogo, Vol. 5. Walt Kelly. 80p. 1996. pap. 9.95 (*1-56097-252-1*) Fantagraph Bks.

Pogo, Vol. 6. Walt Kelly. 88p. 1997. pap. 9.95 (*1-56097-262-9*) Fantagraph Bks.

Pogo, Vol. 7. Walt Kelly. pap. 9.95 (*1-56097-268-8*, Pub. by Fantagraph Bks) Seven Hills Bk.

Pogo, Vol. 8. Walt Kelly. 1998. pap. text 9.95 (*1-56097-285-8*) Fantagraph Bks.

***Pogo, Vol. 9.** Walt Kelly. (Illus.). 80p. 1999. pap. 9.95 (*1-56097-342-0*, Pub. by Fantagraph Bks) Seven Hills Bk.

Pogo, Vol. 10. Walt Kelly. (Pogo Ser.). 80p. 1999. pap. text 9.95 (*1-56097-324-2*, Pub. by Fantagraph Bks) Seven Hills Bk.

Pogo, Vol. 11. Walt Kelly. 80p. 1999. pap. 9.95 (*1-56097-339-0*) Fantagraph Bks.

Pogo: We Have Met the Enemy & He Is Us. Walt Kelly. (Pogo Collector's Edition Ser.). 127p. 1995. 19.95 (*1-886460-09-4*) Sunday Comics.

Pogo Files for Pogophiles: A Retrospective on 50 Years of Walt Kelly's Classic Comic Strip. Selby D. Kelly & Steve A. Thompson. LC 92-18008. (Illus.). 256p. (Orig.). 1992. 35.00 (*0-945185-04-9*); pap. 19.95 (*0-945185-03-0*) Spring Hollow Bks.

Pogo Puce Stamp Catalog. Walt Kelly. (Pogo Collector's Edition Ser.). 96p. 1995. 19.95 (*1-886460-01-9*) Sunday Comics.

Pogo Sunday Book. Walt Kelly. (Pogo Collector's Edition Ser.). 132p. 1995. 19.95 (*1-886460-05-1*) Sunday Comics.

Pogo User's Manual, General Aids to Graphic Programming. J. E. Rieber & V. R. Lamb. LC 70-131898. 191p. 1970. 25.00 (*0-403-04531-2*) Scholarly.

Pogo's Sunday Punch. Walt Kelly. (Pogo Collector's Edition Ser.). 140p. 1995. 19.95 (*1-886460-06-X*) Sunday Comics.

Pogreshnosti Izmerenii see Measurement Errors: Theory & Practice

Pogrom: A Novel of Armenian History. Aleksandr Shaginyan. Tr. by David Floyd from RUS. LC 93-43509. 165p. 1994. 21.95 (*1-883695-00-7*) Edition Q.

Pogroms: Anti-Jewish Violence in Modern Russian History. Ed. by John D. Klier & Shlomo Lambroza. (Illus.). 413p. (C). 1992. text 80.00 (*0-521-40532-7*) Cambridge U Pr.

Pogue-Pollock-Polk Genealogy As Mirrored in History: From Scotland to Northern Ireland-Ulster, Ohio & Westward. Lloyd W. Pogue. Ed. by John M. Pogue. LC 84-73111. (Illus.). 720p. 1990. 35.00 (*0-9622395-0-X*) Gateway Balto.

Pohaku: Hawaiian Stones. June Gutmanis. (Pacific Polynesia Ser.: No. 5). (Illus.). 36p. (C). 1986. 3.50 (*0-939154-44-7*) Inst Polynesian.

Pohnpei & Tourism: Managing the Balance Between Development & Conservation. 31p. 1990. pap. 35.00 (*1-882866-51-7*) Pac Asia Trvl.

Poi Dogs & Popoki. Hawaiian Humane Society Staff. LC 97-74269. (Illus.). viii, 136p. 1997. 24.95 (*0-9631154-6-4*) Watermark.

Poids du Ciel. Jean Giono. (FRE.). 1971. pap. 10.95 (*0-7859-2841-3*) Fr & Eur.

Poiesis: The Language of Psychology & the Speech of the Soul. Stephen K. Levine. LC 97-200969. 141p. 1997. pap. 24.95 (*1-85302-488-0*, Pub. by Jessica Kingsley) Taylor & Francis.

Poiesis of History: Experimenting with Genre in Postwar Italy. Keala Jewell. LC 92-52762. (Illus.). 288p. 1992. 39.95 (*0-8014-2645-6*) Cornell U Pr.

Poiesis of History: Experimenting with Genre in Postwar Italy. Keala J. Jewell. LC 92-52762. 277p. reprint ed. pap. 85.90 (*0-608-20906-6*, 207200500003) Bks Demand.

Poiesis Poetry Guide for Colorado: Poetry Resources, Venues, Bookstores, Events, Readings, & Workshops. Catherine O'Neill Thorn. 80p. 1997. pap. 11.95 (*0-938075-73-X*, ONeill Pub) Ocean View Bks.

Poignant Relations: Three Modern French Women James S. Allen. LC 99-28341. 2000. write for info. (*0-8018-6204-3*) Johns Hopkins.

Poil de Carotte see Oeuvres

Poil de Carotte. Jules Renard. (FRE.). 1957. pap. 6.95 (*0-8288-6913-8*) Fr & Eur.

Poil de Carotte. Jules Renard. 90p. 1965. 6.95 (*0-685-61098-5*) Fr & Eur.

Poil de Carotte. unabridged ed. Jules Renard. (FRE.). pap. 5.95 (*2-87714-171-3*, Pub. by Bookking Intl) Distribks Inc.

Poil de Carotte: Level A. Jules Renard. text 7.95 (*0-8219-1450-2*) EMC-Paradigm.

Poil de Carotte la Bigote. Jules Renard. (Folio Ser.: No. 1090). (FRE.). pap. 9.95 (*2-07-037090-9*) Schoenhof.

Poil de Carotte Suivi de la Bigote. Jules Renard. (FRE.). 1979. pap. 11.95 (0-7859-4114-2) Fr & Eur.

Poils, Poils et Repoils - Hairs on Bears. Geraldine Ryan-Lush. (FRE., Illus.). 32p. (J). 1996. pap. 5.95 (1-55037-980-1, Pub. by Annick); lib. bdg. 14.95 (1-55037-981-X, Pub. by Annick) Firefly Bks Ltd.

Poimandres As Myth: Scholarly Theory & Gnostic Meaning. Robert A. Segal. (Religion & Reason Ser.: No. 33). 216p. 1986. lib. bdg. 89.25 (0-89925-146-3) Mouton.

Poincare & the Three Body Problem. June Barrow-Green. LC 96-11112. (History of Mathematics Ser.: Vol. 11). 272p. 1996. 49.00 (0-8218-0367-0, HMATH/11) Am Math.

Poincare Half-Plane. Saul Stahl. (Math Ser.). 312p. (C). 1993. 53.75 (0-86720-298-X) Jones & Bartlett.

***Poincare Maps for Orbits near Lagrangian Points.** Gerard Gomez. (Illus.). 2000. 68.00 (981-02-4210-7) World Scientific Pub.

Poinconnement. 1980. 33.50 (0-8176-1370-6) Birkhauser.

Poincons d'Argent du Monde Entier. 6th ed. J. Divis. (FRE.). 246p. 1991. 49.95 (0-8288-7300-3, 2859170820) Fr & Eur.

Poindexter of Washington: A Study in Progressive Politics. Howard W. Allen. LC 80-20123. 352p. 1981. 36.95 (0-8093-0952-1) S Ill U Pr.

Poinsett County Arkansas Census, 1850. Courtney York & Gerlene York. 54p. (Orig.). pap. 12.00 (0-916660-05-2) Hse of York.

Poinsettia & Firefighters. Felicia Bond. (J). 1984. 12.95 (0-690-04400-3) HarpC Child Bks.

Poinsettia & Her Family. Michael Bond. (J). 1981. 12.95 (0-690-04144-6) HarpC Child Bks.

Poinsettia & Her Family. Felicia Bond. LC 81-43035. (Trophy Picture Bk.). (Illus.). 32p. (J). (ps-3). 1985. reprint ed. pap. 4.95 (0-06-443076-6, HarpTrophy) HarpC Child Bks.

Poinsettia & the Firefighters. Felicia Bond. LC 83-46169. (Illus.). 32p. (J). (ps-3). 1984. lib. bdg. 16.89 (0-690-04401-1) HarpC Child Bks.

Poinsettia Manual. Paul Ecke, Jr. et al. (Illus.). 300p. (C). 1989. write for info. (0-9623551-1-9) P Ecke Ranch Pr.

***Poinsettia Tradition.** Christine Anderson. LC 99-94939. 1999. 9.95 (0-9656224-7-9) Wtrs Edge.

Poinsettias: Myth & Legend - History & Botanical Fact. Christine Anderson. LC 96-60667. (Illus.). 64p. 1997. 21.95 (0-9656224-9-5) Wtrs Edge.

Poinsot: Tractatus de Signis (Macintosh) John Poinsot. Ed. & Tr. by John Deely. (Past Masters Ser.). (C). write for info. (1-57085-032-1) Intelex.

Poinsot: Tractatus de Signis (Windows) John Poinsot. Ed. by John Deely. (Past Masters Ser.). (C). write for info. (1-57085-120-4) Intelex.

Point. Charles D'Ambrosio. 256p. 1996. pap. 11.95 (0-316-17125-5) Little.

***Point.** Charles D'Ambrosio. 1998. pap. 11.95 (0-316-19095-0, Back Bay) Little.

***Point!** J. Horace Lytle. (Illus.). 208p. 2000. 24.95 (1-58667-031-X, Pub. by Derrydale Pr) Natl Bk Netwk.

Point! A Book about Bird Dogs. 2nd ed. Horace Lytle. (Fifty Greatest Bks.). (Illus.). 200p. 1992. reprint ed. 50.00 (1-56416-036-X) Derrydale Pr.

Point: Instant of Time. John A. Ebe. Vol. 1. 60p. lib. bdg. write for info. (0-318-51802-3) Ebe.

Point! Training the All-Seasons Birddog. James B. Spencer. LC 94-48548. (Illus.). 288p. 1995. 29.95 (0-87605-780-6) Howell Bks.

Point: Where Teaching & Writing Intersect. Ed. by Nancy Larson Shapiro & Ron Padgett. 145p. 1983. pap. 10.95 (0-915924-33-1) Tchrs & Writers Coll.

Point . . . Click . . . & Learn!!! Camilla K. Hileman. 169p. 1997. pap. 19.95 (1-885477-43-0) Fut Horizons.

Point - Counterpoint. Mcgrath. (C). 1998. pap. text 40.50 (0-15-503983-0) Harcourt.

Point After: Advice from God's Athletes. Elliot Johnson. 128p. 1987. pap. 5.95 (0-310-26171-6, 12416P) Zondervan.

Point & Extended Defects in Semiconductors. Ed. by G. Benedek et al. (NATO ASI Series B, Physics: Vol. 202). (Illus.). 300p. 1989. 89.50 (0-306-43336-2, Plenum Trade) Perseus Pubng.

Point & Figure Charting: The Complete Guide. rev. ed. Carroll D. Aby, Jr. LC 97-172657. 296p. 1996. 35.00 (0-934380-30-9, 538-A) Traders Pr.

Point & Figure Charting: The Essential Application for Forecasting & Tracking Market Prices. Thomas J. Dorsey. LC 95-3091. (Finance Editions Ser.). 256p. 1995. 59.95 (0-471-11961-X) Wiley.

Point & Figure Commodity & Stock Trading Techniques. Kermit Zieg. (Illus.). 220p. 1997. pap. 35.00 (0-934380-38-4, 1162) Traders Pr.

Point & Figure Method of Anticipating Stock Price. Victor DeVilliers. 82p. 1995. pap. 19.95 (1-883272-16-5) Traders Lib.

Point & Figure Method of Anticipating Stock Price Movements. Victor De Villiers. 1973. pap. 15.00 (0-685-42039-6) Windsor.

Point & Figure Method of Anticipating Stock Prices. Victor De Villiers. 64p. 1998. pap. 15.00 (0-930233-64-6, Pub. by Windsor) Natl Bk Netwk.

***Point & Line.** Thalia Field. LC 99-89048. 160p. 2000. pap. 14.95 (0-8112-1442-7, NDP899, Pub. by New Directions) Norton.

Point & Line to Plane. Wassily Kandinsky. LC 79-50616. (Illus.). 192p. 1979. reprint ed. pap. text 6.95 (0-486-23808-3) Dover.

***Point & Say: All About Nature.** Anness Publishing Staff. 2001. 10.00 (1-85967-982-X) Anness Pub.

***Point & Say: Playschool Fun.** Anness Publications Staff. (J). 2001. 10.00 (1-85967-974-9) Time Warner.

***Point & Shoot.** Henry Bond. 2000. pap. 39.95 (3-7757-0894-4) Gerd Hatje.

Point au Fer on Lake Champlain. Allan S. Everest. (Illus.). 53p. 1992. pap. 10.95 (1-890402-19-2) Clinton Cnty Hist.

Point Blank: Guns & Violence in America. Gary Kleck. (Social Institutions & Social Change Ser.). 527p. 1991. lib. bdg. 59.95 (0-202-30419-1) Aldine de Gruyter.

Point Click & Drag. 4th ed. Ed. by Peterson. (C). 1996. text 31.88 (0-673-67646-3) Addison-Wesley.

Point, Click & Learn Visual Basic 4. Marco Mason. 528p. 1996. pap. 34.99 (1-56884-317-8) IDG Bks.

Point, Click, & Wow!! A Quick Guide to Brilliant Laptop Presentations. Claudyne Wilder & David Fine. (Illus.). 128p. 1996. pap. 29.95 (0-88390-484-5) Jossey-Bass.

Point Conception. Gretel Ehrlich. 1998. write for info. (0-679-44201-4) Pantheon.

Point Conception to Mexico: A Common Man Kayak Adventure. David D. Powdrell. (Illus.). 110p. 1998. pap. 14.95 (0-9663634-0-X) Cuatro Casas.

Point Count Bidding. 2nd rev. ed. Charles Goren. 1996. pap. 11.00 (0-684-81398-X) Free Pr.

Point Counter Point. Aldous Huxley. 1976. 23.95 (0-8488-1379-0) Amereon Ltd.

Point Counter Point. Aldous Huxley. 300p. 1991. reprint ed. lib. bdg. 22.95 (0-89966-849-6) Buccaneer Bks.

Point Counter Point. Aldous Huxley. LC 96-7376. 448p. 1996. reprint ed. pap. 13.95 (1-56478-131-3) Dalkey Arch.

Point Counterpoint. 5th ed. Levine. 1994. pap. text, teacher ed. 5.00 (0-312-11143-6) St Martin.

Point Counterpoint. 6th ed. Levine. LC 97-65190. 400p. 1997. pap. text 24.95 (0-312-14987-5) St Martin.

Point Counterpoint: Universal Grammar in the Second Language. Ed. by Lynn Eubank. LC 91-16723. (Language Acquisition & Language Disorders (LALD) Ser.: Vol. 3). x, 439p. 1991. 83.00 (1-55619-236-3); pap. 29.95 (1-55619-239-8) J Benjamins Pubng Co.

Point Counterpoint: 8 Cases for Composition. 2nd ed. Thayle Anderson & Kent Forrester. LC 92-73716. 512p. (C). 1993. pap. text 37.00 (0-15-500169-8) Harcourt Coll Pubs.

Point-Counterpoint Vol. 1: False Prophets. Duane Magnani. 1986. pap. 8.95 (1-883858-16-X) Witness CA.

***Point Crime: Bored to Death.** Margaret Bingley. 1999. 16.95 (0-7540-6071-3) Chivers N Amer.

Point de Croix. Marie C. Allegre-Papadacci. (FRE., Illus.). 192p. 1998. 34.00 (2-84229-045-3, DE19, Pub. by C Armand) Lacis Pubns.

Point Defect in Metal's II: Dynamical Properties & Diffusion Controlled Reactions. P. H. Dederichs et al. (Tracts in Modern Physics Ser.: Vol. 87). 1980. 49.00 (0-387-09623-X) Spr-Verlag.

Point Defects in Crystals. R. K. Watts. LC 76-43013. 326p. reprint ed. 101.10 (0-8357-9956-5, 201352200086) Bks Demand.

Point Defects in Materials. F. Agullo-Lopez & C. R. Catlow. 445p. 1988. text 128.00 (0-12-044510-7) Acad Pr.

Point Defects in Semiconductors I. M. Lannoo & J. Bourgoin. (Solid-State Sciences Ser.: Vol. 22). (Illus.). 260p. 1981. 53.00 (0-387-10518-2) Spr-Verlag.

Point Defects in Semiconductors II: Experimental Aspects. J. Bourgoin & M. Lannoo. (Solid-State Sciences Ser.: Vol. 35). (Illus.). 295p. 1983. 60.95 (0-387-11515-3) Spr-Verlag.

Point du Jour. Andre Breton. (FRE.). 192p. 1992. pap. 10.95 (0-7859-1680-6, 2070326489) Fr & Eur.

Point du Jour. Andre Breton. (Idees Ser.). (FRE.). pap. 8.95 (2-07-035213-7) Schoenhof.

Point Elliott Treaty, 1855. Lynn Kickingbird & Curtis Berkey. (Treaty Manuscripts Ser.: No. 9). 28p. 9.00 (0-944253-31-8) Inst Dev Indian Law.

Point Engraving on Glass. Laurence Whistler. (Decorative Arts Library). (Illus.). 93p. 1997. 19.95 (0-7445-1894-6) Antique Collect.

Point 4, Near East & Africa: A Selected Bibliography of Studies on Economically Underdeveloped Countries. U. S. Department of State, Division of Library & R. LC 68-55124. (Illus.). 136p. 1969. reprint ed. lib. bdg. 57.50 (0-8371-1732-1, ROFO) Greenwood.

Point Ground Patterns from Australia. 2nd ed. Elwyn Kenn. (Illus.). 37p. 1997. reprint ed. pap. 12.95 (1-56659-049-3) Robin & Russ.

Point Group Symmetry Applications: Methods & Tables. Philip H. Butler. LC 80-17947. 578p. 1981. 125.00 (0-306-40523-7, Plenum Trade) Perseus Pubng.

Point-Group Theory Tables. Simon L. Altmann & Peter Herzig. (Illus.). 716p. 1994. text 145.00 (0-19-855226-2) OUP.

***Point Groups, Space Groups, Crystals & Molecules.** R. Mirman. 1999. 68.00 (981-02-3732-4) World Scientific Pub.

Point Hope, an Eskimo Village in Transition. James W. Vanstone. LC 84-45530. (American Ethnological Society Monographs: No. 35). 1988. reprint ed. 31.50 (0-404-62934-2) AMS Pr.

***Point Horror Unleashed: Transformer.** Philip Gross. 1999. 16.95 (0-7540-6057-8) Chivers N Amer.

Point in Time. Linda O. Johnston. 368p. (Orig.). 1998. mass mkt. 5.50 (0-505-52244-6, Love Spell) Dorchester Pub Co.

***Point Is That Which Has No Part.** Liz Waldner. LC 99-56175. (Iowa Poetry Prize Ser.). 84p. 2000. pap. 10.95 (0-87745-702-6) U of Iowa Pr.

Point Lace & Diamonds. George A. Baker, Jr. LC 74-103080. (Granger Index Reprint Ser.). 1977. 17.95 (0-8369-6095-5) Ayer.

Point Last Seen: A Woman Tracker's Story of Domestic Violence & Personal Triumph. Hannah Nyala. LC 96-18397. 176p. 1998. pap. 11.95 (0-14-027463-4) Viking Penguin.

Point-Ligne-Plan. Wassily Kandinsky. (Ed. Ser.). (FRE.). 249p. 1991. pap. 17.95 (0-7859-2625-9, 207032639X) Fr & Eur.

Point Loma Community in California, 1897-1942: A Theosophical Experiment. Emmett A. Greenwalt. LC 76-42802. reprint ed. 42.50 (0-404-60068-9) AMS Pr.

Point Loma Theosophical Society: A List of Publications, 1898 - 1942. Loren R. Brown. LC 81-187499. (Illus.). 136p. (C). 1977. pap. 10.00 (0-913510-46-7) Wizards.

Point Man see Hombre Guia: Como ser li der de su Familia

Point Man. James Watson, Jr. 360p. 1995. mass mkt. 6.99 (0-380-71986-X, Avon Bks) Morrow Avon.

Point Man: How a Man Can Lead a Family. rev. ed. Steve Farrar. 336p. 1992. pap. 12.99 (0-88070-643-0, Multnomah Bks) Multnomah Pubs.

Point Man: Taking New Ground. Steve Farrar. 222p. 1996. pap. 9.99 (0-88070-825-5, Multnomah Bks) Multnomah Pubs.

Point Me in the Right Direction. Kaitlyn Gallagher. 39p. (Orig.). 1995. pap. 5.00 (1-887289-04-6) Rodent Pr.

Point No Point: Selected Poems. Sujata Bhatt. LC 97-221814. 144p. 1997. pap. 14.95 (1-85754-306-8, Pub. by Carcanet Pr) Paul & Co Pubs.

Point-No-Point Treaty, 1855. Lynn Kickingbird & Curtis Berkey. (Treaty Maunuscrips Ser.: No. 10). 29p. 9.00 (0-944253-32-6) Inst Dev Indian Law.

Point of Americas II: Poems. Louis D. Brodsky. LC 98-21767. 1998. spiral bd. 9.95 (1-56809-049-8) Time Being Bks.

Point of Arrival. Graham-Yoo. (C). 49.95 (0-7453-0671-3, Pub. by Pluto GBR); pap. 18.95 (0-7453-0672-1, Pub. by Pluto GBR) Stylus Pub VA.

Point-of-Care IVD Testing: Proposed Guideline. Contrib. by Barbara M. Goldsmith. 1995. 150.00 (0-614-20206-X, AST2-P) NCCLS.

Point-of-Care IVD Testing: Proposed Guideline (1995) 552nd ed. 1995. 75.00 (1-56238-266-7, AST2-P) NCCLS.

***Point-of-Care Testimg.** Ed. by Jocelyn M. Hicks & Christopher P. Price. 1999. 79.00 (1-890883-23-9, 341) Am Assn Clinical Chem.

Point-of-Care Testing. (Specialty Collections). ring bd. 200.00 (1-56238-294-2, SC17-L) NCCLS.

Point of Care Testing. Greg Nunemacher. (Market Research Reports: No. 430). (Illus.). 91p. 1994. 795.00 (0-614-09925-0) Theta Corp.

Point of Care Testing: Principles, Management, & Clinical Practice. Gerald J. Kost. (Illus.). 288p. 1999. write for info. (0-07-038306-5) McGraw-Hill HPD.

Point of Christology. Schubert M. Ogden. LC 91-52783. 206p. 1992. reprint ed. pap. text 12.95 (0-87074-331-7) SMU Press.

Point of Departure: The Autobiography of Jean Devanny. Jean Devanny. Ed. by Carole Ferrier. LC 86-7068. (Illus.). 332p. 1987. text 44.95 (0-7022-1979-7, Pub. by Univ Queensland Pr) Intl Spec Bk.

Point of Departure: Women of Glory, That Special Woman. Lindsay McKenna. (Special Edition Ser.). 1993. per. 3.50 (0-373-09853-7, 5-09853-8) Silhouette.

Point of Departure: 19 Stories of Youth & Discovery. Ed. by Robert S. Gold. 192p. (Orig.). (YA). (gr. 7 up). 1967. mass mkt. 4.99 (0-440-96983-2, LLL BDD) BDD Bks Young Read.

Point of Entry: A Study of Client Reception in the Social Services. Anthony S. Hall. 1974. 30.00 (0-317-05811-8, Pub. by Natl Inst Soc Work) St Mut.

Point of Existence: Transformations of Narcissism in Self-Realization. A. H. Almaas. LC 96-84403. 602p. 1996. pap. 21.50 (0-936713-09-7) Diamond Bks CA.

Point of Fracture: Voices of Heinous Crime Survivors. Ed. by Karen Nystedt. (Illus.). 164p. 1998. per. 29.95 (0-9662909-0-9) A Zuckerman.

***Point of Grace.** CCM Staff. (Lifelines Ser.). 128p. 2001. pap. 8.99 (0-7369-0443-3) Harvest Hse.

Point of Honor. Dorothy J. Heydt. 320p. 1998. mass mkt. 5.99 (0-88677-791-7, Pub. by DAW Bks) Penguin Putnam.

Point of Honor. Maurice Medland. 304p. 1997. 21.95 (1-57566-193-4, Knsington) Kensgtn Pub Corp.

Point of Honor. Maurice Medland. 384p. 1998. pap. 5.99 (0-7860-0489-4, Pinncle Kensgtn) Kensgtn Pub Corp.

***Point of Honor.** Robins. 1999. write for info. (0-8125-7647-0) Tor Bks.

Point of Hopes. Melissa Scott. 1997. mass mkt. 6.99 (0-8125-5099-4, Pub. by Tor Bks) St Martin.

Point of Hopes. Melissa Scott & Lisa A. Barnett. 384p. 1995. 23.95 (0-312-85844-2) Tor Bks.

Point of Impact. Stephen Hunter. 592p. 1985. mass mkt. 7.50 (0-553-56351-3) Bantam.

***Point of Impact.** Don Pendelton. (Executioner Ser.: Vol. 256). 2000. per. 4.50 (0-373-64256-3) Harlequin Bks.

***Point of Impact.** Clair M. Poulson. 1999. pap. 12.95 (1-55517-403-5) CFI Dist.

Point of Light & Naked Truth. unabridged ed. Sharon Flynn. (Illus.). 20p. (Orig.). 1997. pap. 5.00 (1-929326-61-0) Hal Bar Pubg.

Point of Murder. Margaret Yorke. LC 99-19633. 1999. 19.95 (0-7838-8575-X, G K Hall & Co) Mac Lib Ref.

Point of No Return. Martha Gelhorn. Orig. Title: The Wine of Astonishment. 1989. pap. 8.95 (0-317-02808-1) NAL.

Point of No Return. Martha Gellhorn. LC 94-43697. iv, 333p. 1995. pap. 12.00 (0-8032-7051-8) U of Nebr Pr.

Point of No Return. Rachel Lee. 1994. per. 3.50 (0-373-07566-9) Silhouette.

Point of No Return. John P. Marquand. 559p. 1985. pap. 12.00 (0-89733-174-5) Academy Chi Pubs.

Point of No Return. Paul McCusker. LC 95-19068. (Adventures in Odyssey Ser.: No. 8). (J). (gr. 3-7). 1995. pap. 5.99 (1-56179-401-5) Focus Family.

Point of No Return: An Aviator's Story. Ralph E. Piper. LC 89-27919. (Illus.). 222p. 1990. 34.95 (0-8138-0158-3) Iowa St U Pr.

Point of No Return: Tackling Your Next New Assignment with Courage & Common Sense. Rick Renner. 176p. 1996. pap. 9.99 (1-880089-20-3, Pub. by Albury Pub) Appalach Bk Dist.

Point of No Return: The Deadly Struggle for Middle East Peace. Geoffrey Kemp & Jeremy Pressman. LC 97-29939. 265p. 1997. 44.95 (0-87003-020-5); pap. 18.95 (0-87003-021-3) Carnegie Endow.

Point of Order: The Ready Reference for Simple Rules of Order & Parliamentary Procedure. Marjorie M. Cann. 80p. (Orig.). 1993. pap. 7.95 (0-399-51815-0, Perigee Bks) Berkley Pub.

***Point of Origin.** Patricia Cornwell. LC 98-10479. 368p. 1999. 25.95 (0-399-14394-7, G P Putnam) Peng Put Young Read.

Point of Origin. large type ed. Patricia Cornwell. LC 98-23618. 542p. 1998. write for info. (0-7540-2149-1) Chivers N Amer.

Point of Origin. large type ed. Patricia Cornwell. LC 98-23618. 543p. 1998. pap. 20.00 (0-7862-1478-3) Thorndike Pr.

Point of Origin. large type ed. Patricia Cornwell. LC 98-23618. 582p. 1998. 20.00 (0-7862-1477-5) Thorndike Pr.

***Point of Origin.** limited ed. Patricia Cornwell. 350p. 1998. 150.00 (0-399-14412-9, G P Putnam) Peng Put Young Read.

Point of Origin. Patricia Cornwell. 397p. 1999. reprint ed. mass mkt. 7.99 (0-425-16986-3) Berkley Pub.

Point of Pines, Arizona: A History of the University of Arizona Archaeological Field School. Emil W. Haury. LC 88-29523. (Anthropological Papers). 140p. 1989. pap. 23.00 (0-8165-1096-2) U of Ariz Pr.

Point of Power. Kay Snow-Davis. 1995. pap. 10.95 (1-85230-633-5, Pub. by Element MA) Penguin Putnam.

Point of Production: Work Environment in Advanced Industrial Societies. John Wooding & Charles Levenstein. LC 99-18040. (Democracy & Ecology Ser.). 166p. 1999. lib. bdg. 16.95 (1-57230-447-2) Guilford Pubns.

Point of Purchase. 6th ed. Retail Reporting Staff. 1999. 39.95 (0-688-16475-7, Wm Morrow) Morrow Avon.

Point of Purchase: Design Annual, Bk. 7. 4th ed. Point of Purchase Institute Staff. 1998. 49.95 (0-934590-40-0) Watsn-Guptill.

Point of Purchase Design Annual. (Illus.). 240p. 1994. 49.99 (1-56496-063-3, 30558) Rockport Pubs.

Point of Purchase Design Annual, No. 5. Point of Purchase Advertising Institute Staff. (Illus.). 176p. 1997. 59.95 (0-934590-96-6) Visual Refer.

***Point of Purchase Design Annual, No. 7.** Ed. by Point of Purchase Advertising Institute Staff. 176p. 2000. 59.95 (1-58471-010-1) Visual Refer.

Point of Purchase Design Annual: The 40th Merchandising Awards. Ed. by Point-of-Purchase Advertising Inst. Staff. (Illus.). 176p. 1998. text 59.95 (0-934590-74-5) Visual Refer.

Point of Purchase Design Annual No. 2: The 36th Merchandising Awards. 2nd ed. Point of Purchase Advertising Institute Staff. (Illus.). 240p. 1994. 49.95 (0-934590-64-8) Visual Refer.

Point of Purchase Design Annual No. 3: The 37th Merchandising Awards. (Illus.). 224p. 1995. 59.95 (0-934590-76-1) Visual Refer.

Point of Purchase Design Annual No. 4: The 38th Merchandising Awards. annuals Ed. by Point of Purchase Advertising Institute Staff. (Illus.). 208p. 1996. 59.95 (0-934590-88-5) Visual Refer.

Point-of-Purchase Design Annual No. 6: The 41st Annual Merchandising Awards. Ed. by Point-of-Purchase Advertising Inst. Staff. (Illus.). 176p. 1999. 59.95 (0-934590-63-X) Visual Refer.

Point-of-Sale Retail Automation in the 1990's: New Technologies & Applications. 1992. 2450.00 (0-89336-876-8, G-135) BCC.

Point of Sale Terminals in Saudi Arabia: A Strategic Entry Report, 1997. Compiled by Icon Group International Staff. (Illus.). 131p. 1999. ring bd. 1310.00 incl. audio compact disk (0-7418-0795-5) Icon Grp.

Point of the Graver. Wesley W. Bates. 160p. 1994. pap. write for info. (0-88984-182-9) Porcup Quill.

Point of Theory: Practices of Cultural Analysis. Meike Bal & Inge Boer. (Illus.). 326p. 1994. 34.95 (0-8264-0657-2) Continuum.

Point-of-Use - Point-of-Entry. Benjamin W. Lykins, Jr. et al. 368p. 1991. lib. bdg. 89.95 (0-87371-354-0, L354) Lewis Pubs.

Point of Use Water Devices, No. GB-140. Business Communications Co., Inc. Staff. 1992. 1950.00 (0-89336-810-5) BCC.

Point of View. David Campton. 1967. pap. 3.50 (0-87129-147-9, P43) Dramatic Pub.

Point of View. Martine Glowinski. (Orig.). 1996. mass mkt. 5.95 (1-56333-433-X) Masquerade.

Point of View. Soren Kierkegaard. Tr. by Howard V. Hong & Edna H. Hong from DAN. LC 97-34909. (Kierkegaard's Writings). 376p. 1998. text 55.00 (0-691-05855-5, Pub. by Princeton U Pr) Cal Prin Full Svc.

Point of View. Photos by Henrik Saxgher. LC 97-75182. (Illus.). 112p. 1998. pap. 68.00 (0-89381-771-6) Aperture.

Point of View see Works of Henry James Jr.: Collected Works

Point of View: A Personal Response to Life, Literature & Politics. Nayantara Sahgal. LC 97-901517. 202p. 1997. pap. 150.00 (81-7551-017-X, Pub. by Print Hse) St Mut.

Point of View: Landscapes from the Addison Collection. Susan C. Faxon. LC 92-73513. (Illus.). 148p. (Orig.). 1992. pap. 30.00 (1-879886-33-2) Addison Gallery.

P

An Asterisk (*) at the beginning of an entry indicates that the title is appearing for the first time.

Point of View: The Art of Architectural Photography. Emanuel E. Abraben. 202p. 1993. 62.95 (0-442-00984-4, VNR) Wiley.

Point of View: The Art of Architectural Photography. Emanuel M. Abraben. (Illus.). 202p. 1993. 62.95 (0-471-28463-7, VNR) Wiley.

Point of View: Twentieth-Century Art from a Long Island Collection. Anna C. Noll. LC 90-84052. (Illus.). 48p. (Orig.). 1990. pap. text 9.95 (1-879195-05-4) Heckscher Mus.

Point of View: Where Horsemanship Begins. Ethel Gardner. 416p. mass mkt. 17.95 (1-55197-155-0) Picasso Publ.

Point of View in the Cinema: A Theory of Narration & Subjectivity in Classical Film. Edward Branigan. (Approaches to Semiotics Ser.: No. 66). xvi, 246p. 1984. 49.95 (90-279-3079-1) Mouton.

Point of Words: Children's Understanding of Metaphor & Irony. Ellen Winner. LC 87-21092. 226p. 1988. 29.95 (0-674-68125-8) HUP.

Point of Words: Children's Understanding of Metaphor & Irony. Ellen Winner. 224p. 1997. pap. text 18.50 (0-674-68126-6) HUP.

.1 (Point One) deluxe limited ed. John Lowther. 32p. 1997. 20.00 (0-937013-72-2) Potes Poets.

Point Park College: The First 25 Years; An Oral History. Albert F. McLean. 1985. write for info. (0-318-60297-0) Point Park.

Point Pattern Analysis. B. N. Boots & Arthur Getis. LC 88-60304. (Scientific Geography Ser.: No. 8). 93p. 1988. reprint ed. pap. 30.00 (0-608-01449-4, 205949300001) Bks Demand.

Point Pleasant. Jerry A. Woolley. (Images of America Ser.). (Illus.). (Orig.). 1995. pap. 16.99 (0-7524-0096-7) Arcadia Publng.

Point Pleasant, Vol. II. Jerry A. Woolley. (Images of America Ser.). (Illus.). (Orig.). 1997. pap. 16.99 (0-7524-0457-1) Arcadia Publng.

***Point Pleasant, Vol. III.** Jerry A. Woolley. (Images of America Ser.). (Illus.). (Orig.). 1999. pap. 18.99 (0-7385-0026-7) Arcadia Publng.

Point Process Models: With Applications to Safety & Reliability. W. A. Thompson. 250p. 1988. text 39.95 (0-412-01481-5, Chap & Hall NY) Chapman & Hall.

Point Processes. D. R. Cox & V. Isham. (Monographs on Statistics & Applied Probability). 200p. 1980. boxed set 19.95 (0-412-21910-7, NO. 2962) Chapman & Hall.

Point Processes & Queues: Martingale Dynamics. P. Bremaud. (Series in Statistics). (Illus.). 352p. 1981. 87.95 (0-387-90536-7) Spr-Verlag.

Point Processes & Their Statistical Inference. 2nd ed. Alan F. Karr. (Probability Ser.: Vol. 7). (Illus.). 512p. 1991. text 175.00 (0-8247-8532-0) Dekker.

Point Purchase: Merchandizing. Retail Reporting Staff. 1998. 39.95 (0-688-16473-0, Wm Morrow) Morrow Avon.

Point Reyes. 3rd rev. ed. Dorothy L. Whitnah. LC 97-7535. (Illus.). 114p. 1997. pap. 12.95 (0-89997-173-3) Wilderness Pr.

Point Reyes: A Children's Guide. Judy Beach-Balthis. Ed. by Frank S. Balthis. (Children's Guides on the National Parks Ser.). (Illus.). 24p. (Orig.). (J). (gr. k-8). 1993. pap. 3.95 (0-918355-03-6) Firehole Pr.

Point Reyes: Secret Places & Magic Moments. 3rd rev. ed. Phil Arnot. LC 88-50274. (Illus.). 224p. 1992. pap. 9.95 (0-933174-84-5) Wide World-Tetra.

Point Reyes National Seashore: A Hiking & Nature Guide. 2nd rev. ed. Don Martin & Key Martin. (Illus.). 136p. 1997. pap. 9.95 (0-9617044-6-2) Martin Press.

Point Reyes Poems. Robert Bly. (Orig.). 1989. pap. 6.00 (0-912449-32-2) Floating Island.

Point Reyes Poems. Robert Bly. (Orig.). 1989. 10.00 (0-941220-15-X) Jungle Garden.

Point Reyes Poems. rev. ed. Robert Bly. 32p. (Orig.). 1993. pap. 6.00 (0-912449-46-2) Floating Island.

***Point Reyes Visions: Photographs & Essays, Point Reyes National Seashore & West Marin.** unabridged ed. Kathleen P. Goodwin. (Illus.). 198p. 1999. 45.00 (0-9671527-4-7) Color & Light.

Point Set Theory. Morgan. (Pure & Applied Mathematics Ser.: Vol. 131). (Illus.). 296p. 1989. text 155.00 (0-8247-8178-3) Dekker.

Point System. Joyce W. Tea. LC 98-30106. (Illus.). (J). 1998. pap. write for info. (1-56763-399-4) Ozark Pub.

Point System. Joyce W. Teal. LC 98-30106. (Illus.). (J). 1998. lib. bdg. write for info. (1-56763-398-6) Ozark Pub.

Point to Point. Elizabeth Graham & Angela Munro. 48p. (J). (gr. 1-4). pap. 9.95 (1-871098-05-X, Pub. by Claire Pubns) Parkwest Pubns.

Point to the Future: A Principal's Technology Planning Guide. Jim Brennan. LC 98-194955. 70p. 1997. pap. 12.00 (1-55833-197-2) Natl Cath Educ.

Point Twill with Color & Weave. Margaret B. Windeknecht. LC 89-90330. 76p. (Orig.). 1990. pap. 13.95 (0-9618797-1-8) T G Windeknecht.

Point Well Taken: The Guide to Success with Needles & Threads. Debbie Garbers & Janet F. O'Brien. (Illus.). vi, 60p. (Orig.). 1996. pap. 12.95 (0-9653079-0-5) In Cahoots.

Point Where All Things Meet: Essays on Charles Wright. Ed. & Pref. by Tom Andrews. LC 95-67732. 300p. (Orig.). 1995. pap. 19.95 (0-932440-72-X) Oberlin Coll Pr.

Point Within a Circle: A System of Masonry Veiled in Allegory & Illustrated by Symbols. Albert Pike. (Illus.). 1994. pap. 3.95 (1-55818-305-1, Sure Fire) Holmes Pub.

Point Zero Bliss: A Prisoner's Quest for Freedom. Sean Legacy. 292p. 1997. pap. 14.95 (0-9645561-1-1) Greathse Co.

***La Pointe: Village Outpost on Madeline Island.** Ross Nelson Hamilton et al. LC 00-38799. (Illus.). 2000. pap. write for info. (0-87020-321-5) State Hist Soc Wis.

Pointe Book: Shoes, Training & Technique. rev. ed. Janice Barringer & Sarah Schlesinger. LC 96-43844. 208p. 1998. pap. 18.95 (0-87127-204-0) Princeton Bk Co.

Pointed Brush Writing Manual. 2nd rev. ed. Fran Strom. (Illus.). 50p. 1991. pap. 15.00 (1-880133-00-8) AHA Calligraphy.

Pointer: Hunter, Showman, Companion. Karen Ashe. Ed. by Mark Anderson. (Pure Breds Ser.). (Illus.). 320p. Date not set. 28.50 (0-944875-60-2) Doral Pub.

Pointer Champions, 1889-1980. Jan L. Pata. (Illus.). 108p. 1981. pap. 36.95 (0-940808-00-5) Camino E E & Bk.

Pointer Champions, 1981-1986. Camino E. E. & Bk. Co. Staff. (Illus.). 145p. 1987. pap. 28.95 (0-940808-43-9) Camino E E & Bk.

Pointer Champions, 1987-1992. Camino E. E. & Bk. Co. Staff. (Illus.). 150p. 1993. pap. 32.95 (1-55893-031-0) Camino E E & Bk.

Pointer Junior. 48p. 1970. pap. 4.95 (0-7935-3860-2, 00050108) H Leonard.

Pointer System for Guitar Bk. 1: Instruction Book 1. Z. Van Auken. 48p. 1970. pap. 3.95 (0-7935-5123-4) H Leonard.

Pointer System for the Piano, Bk. 1. 36p. 1970. pap., teacher ed. 4.95 (0-7935-2455-5, 00082001) H Leonard.

Pointer System for the Piano, Bk. 2. 32p. 1970. pap. 4.95 (0-7935-2075-4, 00082002) H Leonard.

Pointer System for the Piano, Bk. 3. 28p. 1970. pap. 4.95 (0-7935-2167-X, 00082003) H Leonard.

Pointer System for the Piano, Bk. 4. 32p. 1970. pap., teacher ed. 4.95 (0-7935-2203-X, 00082004) H Leonard.

Pointers. E. H. Hart. (Illus.). 192p. 1990. 9.95 (0-86622-752-0, KW-184) TFH Pubns.

Pointers. Ernest H. Hart. (Illus.). 192p. Date not set. 9.95 (0-7938-1478-2, KW-184) TFH Pubns.

Pointers & Setters. Derry Argue. (Illus.). 192p. 1993. 40.00 (1-85310-239-3, Pub. by Swan Hill Pr) Voyageur Pr.

Pointers for Self Publishers: Putting a Price on Your Dream. Robert S. Giovannucci. Ed. by Toni Valdez. (Illus.). 16p. 1997. pap. 6.95 (1-891164-00-7) RSG Indust.

Pointers for Sunday School Teachers. Lester Showalter. 84p. 1991. pap. 3.65 (0-7399-0325-X, 2358) Rod & Staff.

Pointers from Nisargadatta Maharaj. Ramesh s. Balsekar. LC 82-71505. xiv, 223p. 1998. reprint ed. pap. 14.95 (0-89386-033-6) Acorn NC.

Pointers in C. Kenneth Reek. LC 97-10744. 636p. (C). 1997. pap. text 51.00 (0-673-99986-6) Addison-Wesley.

Pointers on Parliamentary Procedure. 50p. (Orig.). 1993. pap. 10.00 (1-884048-01-3) Natl Assn Parliamentarians.

Pointers to Cancer Prognosis. Ed. by Basil A. Stoll. (Developments in Oncology Ser.). 1987. pap. text 101.50 (0-89838-876-7); lib. bdg. 222.00 (0-89838-841-4) Kluwer Academic.

Pointing at the Direction of Sound. Brad O'Sullivan. 44p. (Orig.). 1996. pap. 5.00 (1-887289-12-7) Rodent Pr.

Pointing Dogs Made Easy: How to Train, Nurture, & Appreciate Your Bird Dog. limited ed. Steven J. Mulak. Ed. by Doug Traux & Art DeLaurier, Jr. LC 95-31114. (Illus.). 184p. 1995. 25.00 (0-924357-54-1) Countrysport Pr.

Pointing Hands. Maggie Kate. 1998. pap. 1.00 (0-486-27836-0) Dover.

Pointing Out the Sky. Roy Scheele. LC 85-50680. (Plains Poetry Ser.: Vol. 3). (Illus.). 64p. (Orig.). 1985. 13.00 (0-911015-10-8); pap. 6.95 (0-911015-11-6) Sandhills Pr.

Pointing the Way. Martin Buber. LC 77-134063. (Essay Index Reprint Ser.). 1977. 18.95 (0-8369-2149-6) Ayer.

Pointing the Way. James Hoffman. LC 95-68380. (Bumble Bear Ser.). (J). 1995. pap. 4.99 (0-88743-580-7, 06402) Sch Zone Pub Co.

Pointing the Way. Sutton E. Griggs. LC 75-144622. reprint ed. 29.50 (0-404-00167-X) AMS Pr.

Pointing the Way: Collected Essays. 2nd ed. Martin Buber. LC 90-32310. 264p. (C). 1990. pap. 15.95 (0-391-03655-6) Humanities.

Pointing the Way: Spiritual Insights from Sfas Emes Rabbi Yehudah Aryeh Leib Alter. Tr. by Moshe Braun. LC 96-27842. 216p. 1997. pap. 30.00 (1-56821-996-2) Aronson.

***Pointing Toward Home & Song of Yasuka: Poems.** Carrie Allison & Stacey Starr. 71p. 1999. pap. 10.00 (0-910479-07-0) Mid-America Pr.

PointMaker Devotions for Youth Ministry. Ed. by Amy Simpson. LC 97-13441. 128p. (Orig.). 1997. pap. 15.99 (0-7644-2003-8) Group Pub.

***PointMaker Object Lessons for Youth Ministry.** Katrina Arbuckle & Group Publishing Staff. LC 99-58642. (Illus.). 109p. 2000. pap. 14.99 (0-7644-2196-4) Group Pub.

Points: Interviews. Jacques Derrida. Ed. by Elisabeth Weber. Tr. by Peggy Kamuf from FRE. LC 94-26823. (Meridian: Crossing Aesthetics Ser.). Orig. Title: Points de Suspension. (ENG.). xiv, 502p. 1995. 57.50 (0-8047-2395-8); pap. 18.95 (0-8047-2488-1) Stanford U Pr.

Points: The Most Practical Program Ever to Improve Your Self-Image. David A. Gustafson. LC 92-5016. 192p. (Orig.). 1992. pap. 12.95 (0-931892-74-0) B Dolphin Pub.

Points & Lines. Seicho Matsumoto. Tr. by Makiko Yamamoto & Paul C. Blum. 160p. pap. 9.00 (4-7700-0937-2) FS&G.

Points & Lines. Seicho Matsumoto. Ed. by Shaw. Tr. by Makiko Tamamoto & Paul C. Blum from JPN. LC 72-117385. 160p. 1986. pap. 11.95 (0-87011-456-5) Kodansha.

Points & Lines: Charat Ram: A Biography. M. V. Kamath. LC 93-911128. (C). 1994. 28.50 (81-86112-15-4, Pub. by UBS Pubs Dist) S Asia.

Points & Manners of Articulation As They Relate to the Teaching & Learning of Language in a Sociolinguistic Context. Ed. by D. W. Graham. 22p. (Orig.). (C). 1996. spiral bd. 10.00 (1-889868-00-0, Educatnl Insights) Shiloh Press.

Points at Issue: A Bookseller Looks at Bibliography. Anthony Rota. LC 84-600230. 22p. 1984. 3.95 (0-8444-0471-3) Lib Congress.

Points at Issue, & Some Other Points. Henry A. Beers. LC 67-22055. (Essay Index Reprint Ser.). 1977. 19.95 (0-8369-0183-5) Ayer.

Points Created Pro Basketball Book, 1992-93. Bob Bellotti. 275p. (Orig.). 1992. pap. 15.95 (0-9621147-3-1) Night Work Pub.

Points Created Pro Basketball Book, 1991-92. Robert S. Bellotti. 350p. (Orig.). 1991. pap. 14.95 (0-9621147-2-3) Night Work Pub.

Points Created Pro Basketball Book, 1993-94. Bob Bellotti. 360p. (Orig.). 1993. pap. 15.95 (0-9621147-4-X) Night Work Pub.

Points de Nash des Ensembles Sous-Analytiques. W. Pawlucki. LC 89-18471. (Memoirs Ser.: No. 425). 76p. 1990. pap. 18.00 (0-8218-2430-9, MEMO/84/425) Am Math.

Points de Suspension see Points: Interviews

Points Discount Disclosure Tables. Financial Publishing Co. Staff. 256p. 1999. pap. 20.00 (0-87600-654-3) Finan Pub.

Points for Emphasis 1999-2000. Trent C. Butler. (Points for Emphasis Ser.). 224p. 1999. pap. 6.99 (0-8054-1269-7); pap. 5.99 (0-8054-1270-0) Broadman.

Points for Parents Perplexed about Drugs. David C. Hancock. 16p. (Orig.). 1975. pap. 1.15 (0-89486-031-3, 1405B) Hazelden.

Points in Time. Paul Bowles. LC 83-16571. 96p. (C). 1999. pap. 9.95 (0-88001-117-3) HarpC.

Points in Time. Louis D. Brodsky. LC 95-35333. 106p. 1995. spiral bd. 9.95 (1-56809-026-9) Time Being Bks.

Points in Time: Building a Life in Western Pennsylvania. Paul Roberts et al. LC 80-80284. (Illus.). 124p. (Orig.). 1998. pap. 30.95 (0-936340-00-2) Hist Soc West PA.

Points in Time: Structure & Event in a Late Northern Plains Hunting Society. P. G. Duke. LC 91-12002. (Illus.). 239p. 1991. reprint ed. pap. 74.10 (0-608-08861-7, 206950000004) Bks Demand.

Points, Lines & Walls: In Liquid Crystals, Magnetic Systems & Various Ordered Media. Maurice Kleman. LC 81-21976. (Wiley-Interscience Publications). (Illus.). 352p. reprint ed. pap. 109.20 (0-8357-8641-2, 203506500092) Bks Demand.

Points of Action Lists: To-Do Lists. (Believer's Life System Women's Edition Ser.). 1998. ring bd. 3.50 (0-8024-6979-5) Moody.

Points of Contact: A Study of the Interplay & Intersection of Traditional & Non-Traditional Literatures, Cultures, & Mentalities. Norman Simms. 238p. (C). 1991. lib. bdg. 52.50 (0-944473-04-0) Pace Univ Pr.

Points of Contact: Disability, Art & Culture. Ed. by Susan Crutchfield & Marcy Epstein. LC 99-86129. 312p. 2000. pap. 17.95 (0-472-06711-7, 06711); text 47.50 (0-472-09711-3, 09711) U of Mich Pr.

Points of Contention. O'Riorden. 1996. pap. 22.19 (0-07-048192-X) McGraw.

Points of Controversy. Tr. by S. Z. Aung & Mrs. C. A. Davids from PLI. (C). 1915. 37.00 (0-86013-002-9, Pub. by Pali Text) Elsevier.

Points of Cosmic Energy. Blanche Merz. (Illus.). 184p. (Orig.). pap. 20.95 (0-8464-4271-X) Beekman Pubs.

Points of Cosmic Energy. Blanche Merz. 188p. (Orig.). 1988. pap. 15.95 (0-85207-194-9, Pub. by C W Daniel) Natl Bk Netwk.

Points of Departure: Essays & Stories for College English. Ed. by Arthur J. Carr & William R. Steinhoff. LC 74-167324. (Essay Index Reprint Ser.). (C). 1977. reprint ed. 39.95 (0-8369-2449-5) Ayer.

Points of Departure: International Writers on Writing & Politics. 248p. (C). 1992. pap. text 15.95 (0-472-06471-1, 06471) U of Mich Pr.

Points of Departure: Origins in Video. Jacqueline Kain & William D. Judson. (Illus.). 32p. 1990. 8.00 (0-916365-31-X) Ind Curators.

Points of Departure: Poems. Miller Williams. LC 94-26824. 88p. 1995. 18.95 (0-252-02142-8); 15.95 (0-252-06451-8) U of Ill Pr.

Points of Departure: Zen Buddhism with a Rinzai View. Eido T. Shimano. 195p. 1991. 17.00 (0-9629246-1-X) Zen Studies Society Pr.

Points of Departure: Zen Buddhism with a Rinzai View. Eido T. Shimano. 196p. 1992. pap. 12.95 (0-9629246-0-1) Zen Studies Society Pr.

Points of Entry: Reframing America. large type ed. Terence Pitts & Andrei Codrescu. (Illus.). 144p. (Orig.). (C). 1995. pap. write for info. (0-933286-70-8) Frnds Photography.

Points of Entry: Three Rivers Arts Festival. Contrib. by Mary Jane Jacob & David Levi Strauss. (Illus.). 72p. 1997. 25.00 (0-9658529-0-3, Pub. by Three Rivers) RAM Publications.

Points of Friction. Agnes Repplier. LC 77-121505. (Essay Index Reprint Ser.). 1977. 23.95 (0-8369-2027-9) Ayer.

***Points of Grace.** Thomasina Miller. 1999. pap. write for info. (1-58235-334-4) Watermrk Pr.

Points of Honor. Thomas A. Boyd. LC 72-5859. (Short Story Index Reprint Ser.). 1977. reprint ed. 24.95 (0-8369-4192-6) Ayer.

Points of Influence: A Guide to Using Personality Theory at Work. Morley Segal. 1996. 41.95 (0-7879-0260-8) Jossey-Bass.

Points of Issue: A Compendium of Points of Issue of Books by 20th Century Authors. 3rd ed. Ed. by William M. McBride & Amy A. Arledge. 104p. 1996. pap. 12.95 (0-930313-04-6) McBride Pub.

Points of Light. Linda G. Sexton. 288p. 1988. 16.95 (0-316-78200-9) Little.

Points of Light. Linda G. Sexton. 384p. 1989. mass mkt. 4.50 (0-380-70684-9, Avon Bks) Morrow Avon.

Points of Light: New Approaches to Ending Welfare Dependency. Ed. by Tamar A. Mehuron. 154p. (C). 1991. pap. 12.95 (0-89633-152-0); lib. bdg. 38.50 (0-89633-151-2) Ethics & Public Policy.

Points of Light Foundation Youth Management Books. 1996. write for info. (1-58534-012-X) Points of Light.

Points of Resistance: Women, Power, & Politics in the New York Avant-Garde Cinema, 1943-71. Lauren Rabinovitz. (Illus.). 264p. 1991. text 34.95 (0-252-01744-7); pap. text 14.95 (0-252-06139-X) U of Ill Pr.

Points of the Compass: Stories by Sahar Tawfiq. Sahar Tawfiq. Tr. & Intro. by Marilyn Booth. LC 95-17242. 96p. 1995. pap. 12.00 (1-55728-384-2); text 20.00 (1-55728-385-0) U of Ark Pr.

Points of View. LC 78-76910. (Essay Index Reprint Ser.). 1977. 18.95 (0-8369-0026-X) Ayer.

Points of View, 2 Vols. Frederick E. Birkenhead. LC 77-111815. (Essay Index Reprint Ser.). 1977. 40.95 (0-8369-1594-1) Ayer.

Points of View. A. W. Moore. LC 97-200685. (Illus.). 328p. (C). 1997. text 35.00 (0-19-823692-1) OUP.

***Points of View.** A. W. Moore. 2000. pap. 19.95 (0-19-825062-2) OUP.

Points of View. Stuart P. Sherman. (BCL1-PS American Literature Ser.). 363p. 1992. reprint ed. lib. bdg. 89.00 (0-7812-6614-9) Rprt Serv.

Points of View. rev. ed. Ed. by James Moffett & Kenneth R. McElheny. 608p. 1995. mass mkt. 7.99 (0-451-62872-1, Sig) NAL.

Points of View. 8th ed. Diclerico. 2000. 25.00 (0-07-232268-3) McGraw.

Points of View, Vol. 1. Frederick E. Smith. (Essay Index Reprint Ser.). 255p. 1982. reprint ed. lib. bdg. 19.00 (0-8290-0807-1) Irvington.

Points of View, Vol. 2. Frederick E. Smith. (Essay Index Reprint Ser.). 250p. 1982. reprint ed. lib. bdg. 19.00 (0-8290-0779-2) Irvington.

Points of View: An Anthology of Short Stories. James Moffett. 1995. 11.09 (0-606-00840-3, Pub. by Turtleback) Demco.

Points of View: Five Essays. W. Somerset Maugham. LC 75-25374. (Works of W. Somerset Maugham). 1977. reprint ed. 23.95 (0-405-07827-7) Ayer.

Points of View: Readings in American Government & Politics. 4th ed. Robert E. DiClerico & Allan S. Hammock. (Illus.). 352p. (C). 1989. pap. text. write for info. (0-318-62941-0) McGraw.

Points of View: Readings in American Government & Politics. 5th ed. Robert E. DiClerico & Allan S. Hammock. (C). 1991. text 25.25 (0-07-016849-0) McGraw.

Points of View: Readings in American Government & Politics. 6th ed. Ed. by Robert E. DiClerico & Allan S. Hammock. LC 94-33042. 1994. pap. text 26.00 (0-07-016866-0) McGraw.

Points of View: Readings in American Government & Politics. 7th ed. Robert E. DiClerico & Allan S. Hammock. LC 97-30864. 312p. 1997. pap. 34.06 (0-07-016870-9) McGraw.

Points of View: Readings of Kierkegaard. Louis H. Mackey. LC 85-22713. (Kierkegaard & Postmodernism Ser.). 240p. (Orig.). 1986. pap. 24.95 (0-8130-0824-7) U Press Fla.

***Points of View: Stories of Psychopathology.** James E. Mitchell. 2000. pap. 29.95 (1-58391-005-0) Brunner-Mazel.

Points of View on American Higher Education: A Selection of Important Contributions Appearing in "The Chronicle of Higher Education", Vol. 1. Ed. by Stephen H. Barnes. LC 89-38747. (Studies in Education: Vols. 4-6). 296p. 1990. lib. bdg. 89.95 (0-88946-939-3) E Mellen.

Points of View on American Higher Education: A Selection of Important Contributions Appearing in "The Chronicle of Higher Education", Vol. 2. Ed. by Stephen H. Barnes. LC 89-38747. (Studies in Education: Vols. 4-6). 296p. 1990. lib. bdg. 89.95 (0-88946-940-7) E Mellen.

Points of View on American Higher Education: A Selection of Important Contributions Appearing in "The Chronicle of Higher Education", Vol. 3. Ed. by Stephen H. Barnes. LC 89-38747. (Studies in Education: Vols. 4-6). 296p. 1990. lib. bdg. 89.95 (0-88946-941-5) E Mellen.

Points of Viewing Children's Thinking: A Digital Ethnographer's Journey. Ricki Goldman-Segall. LC 97-17260. 224p. 1997. pap. write for info. (0-8058-2432-4) L Erlbaum Assocs.

Points of Viewing Children's Thinking: A Digital Ethnographer's Journey. Ricki Goldman-Segall. LC 97-17260. 224p. 1997. 59.95 (0-8058-2431-6) L Erlbaum Assocs.

***Points on a Hazard Map.** John Vieira. 32p. 1999. pap. 5.00 (1-57141-046-5) Runaway Spoon.

***Points, Pit Houses & Pioneers: Tracing Durango's Archaeological Past.** Philip Duke & Gary Matlock. 136p. 1999. 45.00 (0-87081-519-9) Univ Pr Colo.

***Points, Pithouses & Pioneers: Tracing Durango's Archaeological Past.** Philip Duke & Gary Matlock. 136p. 1999. pap. 24.95 (0-87081-556-3) Univ Pr Colo.

Points, Plugs & a Roadmap see Career Drive: How to Arrive at the Job You Really Want

P

An Asterisk (*) at the beginning of an entry indicates that the title is appearing for the first time.

Points + Lines: Diagrams & Projects for the City. Stan Allen. LC 98-38817. (Illus.). 144p. 1999. pap. 35.00 (*1-56898-155-4*) Princeton Arch.

Points Schmoints: Bergen's Winning Bridge Secrets. Marty Bergen. 224p. 1995. 19.95 (*0-9637533-2-0*) Bergen Bks.

Points Schmoints: Bergen's Winning Bridge Secrets. Marty Bergen. Tr. by Kassie Ohtaka. (ENG & JPN.). 215p. 1997. 26.50 (*0-9658055-0-6*) Knockout Bks.

Points to Ponder (Commentary on Acts) Marlin E. Hotle. 1989. pap. 13.99 (*0-88019-256-9*) Schmul Pub Co.

***Points to Ponder from Hebrews.** Marlin R. Hotle. 112p. 1999. pap. 5.99 (*0-88019-389-1*) Schmul Pub Co.

***Points Unknown: A Century of Great Exploration.** Ed. by David Roberts. 500p. 2000. 29.95 (*0-393-05000-9*) Norton.

***Points Unknown: A Photographic Guide to Big Bear Lake & the San Bernardino...** Illus. by Rick Keppler & John Bratton. 64p. 2000. pap. 19.95 (*0-9677967-0-9*) Fifty-Three.

Pointy-Hatted Princesses. Nick Sharratt. LC 94-14580. (Illus.). (J). (ps up). 1996. pap. 2.99 (*1-56402-477-6*) Candlewick Pr.

Poiret Francois Baudot. LC 98-160735. (Fashion Memoir Ser.). 79 p. 1997. write for info. (*0-500-01814-6*) Thames Hudson.

Poiret Fashion Design Paper Dolls in Full Color. 81st ed. Tom Tierney. (J). 1985. pap. 3.95 (*0-486-24952-2*) Dover.

***Poirot Investigates.** Agatha Christie. (Hercule Poirot Mysteries Ser.). 256p. 2000. mass mkt. 5.99 (*0-425-17472-7*) Berkley Pub.

Poirot Investigates. Agatha Christie. pap. 14.95 (*0-8161-4590-3*, G K Hall & Co) Mac Lib Ref.

Poirot Investigates. large type ed. Agatha Christie. (General Ser.). 330p. 1992. lib. bdg. 19.95 (*0-8161-4589-X*, G K Hall Lrg Type) Mac Lib Ref.

Poirot Investigates: A Hercule Poirot Mystery. Agatha Christie. 256p. 1992. mass mkt. 5.99 (*0-06-100287-9*, Harp PBks) HarpC.

Poirot Loses a Client. large type ed. Agatha Christie. (Agatha Christie Ser.). 420p. 1992. 14.95 (*0-8161-4592-X*, G K Hall Lrg Type) Mac Lib Ref.

***Poised for Plenty: Moving Your Business to the Web.** Martin Brauns. 2000. 24.95 (*1-886939-43-8*) OakHill Pr VA.

Poised for Success. John Rosemond. Ed. by Mary Cox & Pam Fettig. (Illus.). 24p. 1997. mass mkt., wbk. ed. 24.95 incl. audio (*0-9663173-0-0*) MC Mktging.

Poised Power: A Guide for Everyone Who Wishes to Communicate with Greater Ease. Sheryll Hirschberger. (Illus.). 105p. (Orig.). 1994. pap. 10.00 (*0-9643714-0-5*) IZIA Hse.

Poisen-Damsels & Other Essays in Folklore & Anthropology. Norman M. Penzer. Ed. by Richard M. Dorson. LC 80-669. (Folklore of the World Ser.). 1981. reprint ed. lib. bdg. 34.95 (*0-405-13336-7*) Ayer.

Poiski Lugvi. Andrei Klenov. (Illus.). 560p. 1989. write for info. (*0-318-64829-6*) Parus.

Poison. Ed. by Jeannette DeLisa & Aaron Stang. (Guitar Anthology Ser.). 116p. (Orig.). (YA). 1995. pap. text 19.95 (*0-89898-913-2*, P1054GTX) Wrner Bros.

Poison. Alane Ferguson. LC 94-10560. 256p. (J). (gr. 7 up). 1994. mass mkt. 16.95 (*0-02-734528-9*, Mac Bks Young Read) S&S Childrens.

Poison. Kathryn Harrison. 336p. 1996. pap. 12.00 (*0-380-72741-2*, Avon Bks) Morrow Avon.

Poison. Diane Hoh. (Med Center Ser.). 1997. 9.09 (*0-606-11611-7*, Pub. by Turtleback) Demco.

Poison. Ed McBain, pseud. 256p. 1988. mass mkt. 4.99 (*0-380-70030-1*, Avon Bks) Morrow Avon.

Poison. Jane Yolen. (Med Center Ser.: No. 6). 176p. (J). (gr. 6-10). 1997. mass mkt. 3.99 (*0-590-89755-1*) Scholastic Inc.

Poison & Vision: Poems & Prose of Baudelaire, Mallarme & Rimbaud. Charles Baudelaire & Stephane Mallarme. 350p. 1996. pap. 24.95 (*3-7052-0640-0*, Pub. by Poetry Salzburg) Intl Spec Bk.

Poison Animals. LC 97-43025. (Inside-Out Guides Ser.). (Illus.). 48p. (J). (gr. 5-10). 1998. 12.95 (*0-7894-2828-8*) DK Pub Inc.

***Poison Apples.** Nancy Wright. 336p. 2000. 24.95 (*0-312-26220-5*, Minotaur) St Martin.

Poison-Arrow Frogs: Their Natural History & Care in Captivity. rev. ed. Ralph Heselhaus. (Illus.). 128p. 1996. pap. 15.95 (*0-88359-031-X*, Pub. by R Curtis Pubng) Chelsea Green Pub.

Poison Belt. Arthur Conan Doyle. 1976. 22.95 (*0-8488-0991-2*) Amereon Ltd.

Poison Belt. Arthur Conan Doyle. (BCL1-PR English Literature Ser.). 252p. 1992. reprint ed. lib. bdg. 79.00 (*0-7812-7521-0*) Rprt Serv.

Poison! Beware! Be an Expert Poison Spotter. Steve Skidmore. (Lighter Look Bk.). (Illus.). 40p. (J). (gr. 2-6). 1991. pap. 3.80 (*1-878841-41-6*) Millbrook Pr.

Poison Conspiracy. Karl Grossman. 281p. 1983. 22.00 (*0-932966-26-8*) Permanent Pr.

Poison Dart Frogs. Jennifer Owings Dewey. LC 97-74194. (Illus.). 32p. (J). (gr. 2-4). 1998. 15.95 (*1-56397-655-2*) Boyds Mills Pr.

***Poison Dart Frogs.** William Samples. (Illus.). 1999. 12.95 (*0-7938-3013-3*) TFH Pubns.

Poison Detection in Human Organs. 4th ed. Alan S. Curry. (Illus.). 358p. 1988. 78.95 (*0-398-05425-8*); pap. 51.95 (*0-398-06082-7*) C C Thomas.

Poison Drops in the Federal Senate. Ed. by Zach Montgomery. LC 72-172221. (Right Wing Individualist Tradition in America Ser.). iv, 138 p. 1972. reprint ed. 19.95 (*0-405-00430-3*) Ayer.

Poison Drops in the Federal Senate: The School Question from a Parental & Non-Sectarian Standpoint. Zach Montgomery. 138p. 1983. reprint ed. pap. 4.95 (*0-685-04742-3*) St Thomas.

***Poison du Doute.** Lois F. Dyer. (Amours d'Aujourd'Hui Ser.: No. 338). (FRE.). 1999. mass mkt. 5.50 (*0-373-38338-X*, 1-38338-9) Harlequin Bks.

Poison Elves Vol. 1: Requiem for a Elf. Drew Hayes. (Illus.). 144p. 1996. pap. 14.95 (*1-57989-001-6*) Sirius Ent.

Poison Elves Vol. 2: Traumatic Dogs. Drew Hayes. (Illus.). 144p. 1996. pap. 14.95 (*1-57989-002-4*) Sirius Ent.

Poison Elves Vol. 3: Desert of the Third Sin. Drew Hayes. (Illus.). 144p. 1997. pap. 14.95 (*1-57989-003-2*) Sirius Ent.

***Poison Elves Vol. 4: Patrons.** Drew Hayes. (Illus.). 48p. 1998. pap. 4.95 (*1-57989-017-2*) Sirius Ent.

***Poison Elves Vol. 5: Sanctuary.** Drew Hayes. (Illus.). 288p. 1998. pap. 14.95 (*1-57989-022-9*) Sirius Ent.

Poison Fangs. Lynn M. Stone. LC 96-8998. (Animal Weapons Ser.). 1996. lib. bdg. 14.60 (*1-57103-164-2*) Rourke Pr.

Poison Flesh & Blood Tab: Guitar Personality Book. 1p. (Orig.). 1994. pap. 18.95 (*0-7935-0315-9*, HL00660188) Wrner Bros.

Poison Flowers. large type ed. Natasha Cooper. (Mystery Ser.). 544p. 1992. 25.99 (*0-7089-2726-2*) Ulverscroft.

Poison for the Prince. Elizabeth Eyre. LC 94-7333. 1994. 19.95 (*0-15-172540-3*) Harcourt.

Poison Frog Mystery. Created by Gertrude Chandler Warner. LC 99-43097. (Boxcar Children Ser.: No. 74). (Illus.). 128p. (J). (gr. 2-5). 2000. lib. bdg. 13.95 (*0-8075-6586-5*); mass mkt. 3.95 (*0-8075-6587-3*) A Whitman.

***Poison Frog Mystery.** Gertrude Chandler Warner. (Boxcar Children Ser.: Vol. 74). (J). 2000. 9.30 (*0-606-18767-7*) Turtleback.

Poison Frogs. J. Walls. (Illus.). 64p. 1995. pap. text 9.95 (*0-7938-0252-0*, RE108) TFH Pubns.

Poison Frogs, Jewels of Rainforest. Jerry G. Walls. (Illus.). 288p. 1994. 89.95 (*0-7938-0299-7*, TS223) TFH Pubns.

Poison Gas: The Myths Versus Reality, 178. James W. Hammond. LC 98-50234. (Contributions in Military Studies Ser.: Vol. 178). 184p. 1999. 55.00 (*0-313-31038-6*) Greenwood.

Poison Heart: Surviving the Ramones. Dee Dee Ramone. (Illus.). 192p. 1998. pap. 16.95 (*0-946719-19-5*, Pub. by Helter Skelter) Interlink Pub.

Poison Heart: Surviving the Ramones see Lobotomy: Surviving the Ramones

Poison in Paradise! Diana G. Gallagher. (Secret World of Alex Mack Ser.: No. 9). (J). (gr. 3-6). 1996. pap. 3.99 (*0-671-00083-7*) PB.

Poison in the Blood. Fay N. Zachary. 336p. (Orig.). 1994. mass mkt. 5.50 (*0-515-11472-3*, Jove) Berkley Pub.

Poison in the Gift: Ritual, Prestation, & the Dominant Caste in North Indian Village. Gloria G. Raheja. (Illus.). xiv, 300p. 1988. lib. bdg. 51.00 (*0-226-70728-8*) U Ch Pr.

Poison in the Pen: A Miss Silver Mystery. Patricia Wentworth. 1976. reprint ed. lib. bdg. 23.95 (*0-88411-739-1*) Amereon Ltd.

Poison in the Pot: The Legacy of Lead. Curtus. LC 84-2296. 287p. 1984. 31.95 (*0-8093-1156-9*) S Ill U Pr.

***Poison in the Pot: The Legacy of Lead.** Richard P. Wedeen. (Illus.). 274p. 2000. reprint ed. text 30.00 (*0-7881-9172-1*) DIANE Pub.

Poison Ivy & Eyebrow Wigs. Bonnie Pryor. LC 92-38881. (Illus.). 176p. (J). (gr. 3 up). 1993. 15.00 (*0-688-11200-5*, Wm Morrow) Morrow Avon.

Poison Ivy & Eyebrow Wigs. Bonnie Pryor. (J). 1995. 10.30 (*0-606-08026-0*) Turtleback.

Poison Ivy & Eyebrow Wigs. Bonnie Pryor. LC 92-38881. (Illus.). 176p. (J). (gr. 3 up). 1995. reprint ed. pap. 4.95 (*0-688-13562-5*, Wm Morrow) Morrow Avon.

Poison Ivy, Oak & Sumac Book: A Short Natural History & Cautionary Account. Thomas E. Anderson. LC 95-75276. (Illus.). 152p. (Orig.). 1995. pap. 14.95 (*0-9639371-8-9*) Acton Circle.

Poison Ivy, Poison Oak, Poison Sumac & their Relatives. Edward Frankel. 1991. 9.95 (*0-940168-18-9*) Boxwood.

Poison Maiden & the Great Bitch: Female Stereotypes in Marvel Superhero Comics. Susan Wood. LC 86-2268. (Essays on Fantastic Literature Ser.: No. 5). 28p. 1989. lib. bdg. 23.00 (*0-89370-537-3*) Millefleurs.

Poison Mind. Jeffrey Good. 1996. mass mkt. 6.50 (*0-312-96016-6*) St Martin.

Poison Mind: A True Story of Evil Genius & an Undercover Cop. Jeffrey Good & Susan Goreck. LC 94-44132. 1995. write for info. (*0-614-32190-5*, Wm Morrow) Morrow Avon.

***Poison Oak.** Paul J. Willis. 48p. 1999. pap. 6.00 (*1-890887-08-0*) Mille Grazie.

Poison Oak - Ivy: A New & Effective Coping Strategy. Bill Sturgeon. 20p. 1995. pap. 10.00 (*0-9633979-8-2*) Green Fir Pub.

***Poison on a Plate: The Dangers in the Food We Eat & How to Avoid Them.** Richard Lacey. (Illus.). 288p. 1999. pap. 19.95 (*1-900512-45-9*, Pub. by Metro Bks) Trafalgar.

Poison Palace. Mary E. Lyons. LC 96-53678. (Illus.). 160p. (J). (gr. 7 up). 1997. 16.00 (*0-689-81146-2*) S&S Childrens.

Poison Pen. George Carpozi. 368p. 1997. 20.00 (*1-56980-112-6*) Barricade Bks.

Poison Pen. Mary Towne. (J). 1997. pap. 3.95 (*0-8167-4287-1*) Troll Communs.

Poison Pen Letters: Using the Mail for Revenge. Keith Wade. LC 84-81633. 104p. (Orig.). 1984. pap. 12.95 (*0-915179-15-6*) Loompanics.

Poison Pen Mystery. Dandi Daley Mackall. LC 98-147736. (Puzzle Club Mystery Ser.). (gr. 1-5). 1998. pap. text 4.99 (*0-570-05052-9*, 56-1876) Concordia.

Poison Pill Anti-Takeover Defense: The Price of Strategic Deterrence. Robert F. Bruner. (Orig.). 1991. pap. text 20.00 (*0-943205-11-5*) RFICFA.

Poison Place. Mary Lyons. (J). 1997. 16.00 (*0-614-29300-6*) Atheneum Yung Read.

Poison Place. Mary E. Lyons. LC 96-53678. 160p. (J). (gr. 5 up). 1999. per. 4.50 (*0-689-82678-8*, 076714004993) Aladdin.

Poison Politics: Are Negative Campaigns Destroying Democracy? Victor Kamber. LC 97-30034. (Illus.). 340p. (C). 1997. 27.95 (*0-306-45628-1*, Plen Insight) Perseus Pubng.

Poison Pool. Patricia Hall. (WWL Mystery Ser.). 1996. per. 4.99 (*0-373-26198-5*, 1-26198-1, Wrldwide Lib) Harlequin Bks.

***Poison Prevention Week: Teacher's Manual.** Edmund F. Benson & Susan Benson. (Illus.). 1999. pap. text, teacher ed. 25.00 (*1-58614-009-4*) Arise Found.

Poison River: An Unbelievable True Story of Betrayal & Redemption. Steve Raymond & Mal Karman. (Illus.). 354p. (Orig.). (C). 1994. 19.95 (*0-9642533-9-9*); pap. 12.95 (*0-9642533-8-0*) New Amstrdm Pr.

Poison Runoff: A Guide to State & Local Control of Non-Point Source Water Pollution. Paul Thompson et al. 484p. (Orig.). (C). 1989. pap. write for info. (*0-9609358-6-X*) Natl Resources Defense Coun.

***Poison Sky.** John Shannon. (Jack Liffey Mystery Ser.). 241p. 2000. mass mkt. 5.99 (*0-425-17424-7*, Prime Crime) Berkley Pub.

Poison Sky: Myth & Apocalypse in Ruskin. Raymond E. Fitch. LC 70-122097. 732p. 1986. 40.00 (*0-8214-0090-8*); pap. text 20.00 (*0-8214-0642-6*) Ohio U Pr.

Poison Stronger Than Love: The Destruction of an Ojibwa Community. Anastasia M. Shkilnyk. LC 84-40202. (Illus.). 276p. 1985. pap. 18.00 (*0-300-03325-7*) Yale U Pr.

Poison Traders. large type ed. James Pattinson. LC 95-20451. 250p. 1995. pap. 18.95 (*0-7838-1439-9*, G K Hall Lrg Type) Mac Lib Ref.

Poison Tree. Tony Strong. 400p. 1998. mass mkt. 6.50 (*0-440-22498-5*) Dell.

Poison Tree: A Children's Fairy Tale. Linda J. Moll. (Illus.). 40p. (J). (gr. 1). 1994. 12.95 (*0-9641641-1-6*) Punking Pr.

Poison Tree: A True Story of Family Violence & Revenge. Alan Prendergast. 336p. 1987. mass mkt. 4.95 (*0-380-70346-7*, Avon Bks) Morrow Avon.

Poison Tree: Selected Writings of Rumphius on the Natural History of the Indies. Rumphius. Tr. by E. M. Beekman from DUT. LC 81-7605. (Library of the Indies). (Illus.). 272p. 1981. lib. bdg. 32.50 (*0-87023-329-7*) U of Mass Pr.

Poison Widow: A True Story of Witchcraft, Arsenic, & Murder. George Cooper. LC 98-43796. 288p. 1999. text 24.95 (*0-312-19947-3*) St Martin.

***Poison Wood.** F. King. 1999. 168.00 (*0-06-095625-9*) HarpC.

Poisoned Blood. Philip E. Ginsburg. 480p. 1989. mass mkt. 5.99 (*0-446-35312-4*, Pub. by Warner Bks) Little.

Poisoned by a Lie. Oscar J. Underwood, Jr. (Illus.). 32p. (Orig.). 1996. mass mkt. 5.95 (*0-9656062-0-1*) OJU Pubns.

Poisoned Chalice: Being the Second Journal of Sir Roger Shallot Concerning Wicked Conspiracies & Horrible Murders Perpetrated in the Reign of King Henry VIII. Michael Clynes. LC 93-48844. 288p. 1994. reprint ed. 20.00 (*1-883402-48-4*) S&S Trade.

Poisoned Ivy. M. D. Lake. 256p. 1992. mass mkt. 5.50 (*0-380-76573-X*, Avon Bks) Morrow Avon.

Poisoned Ivy: Lesbian & Gay Academics Confronting Homophobia. Toni A. McNaron. LC 96-35334. 256p. (C). 1996. 54.95 (*1-56639-487-2*); pap. 19.95 (*1-56639-488-0*) Temple U Pr.

Poisoned Needle. Elanor McBean. 230p. 1993. reprint ed. pap. 18.50 (*0-7873-0594-4*) Hlth Research.

Poisoned Patient: The Role of the Laboratory. CIBA Foundation Staff. LC 75-317672. (CIBA Foundation Symposium: New Ser.: No. 26). 333p. reprint ed. pap. 103.30 (*0-608-13983-1*, 202215500024) Bks Demand.

Poisoned Pen. Arthur B. Reeve. LC 70-150561. (Short Story Index Reprint Ser.). (Illus.). 1977. reprint ed. 23.95 (*0-8369-3858-5*) Ayer.

Poisoned Places: Seeking Environmental Justice in a Contaminated World. Michael R. Edelstein. 225p. 2000. text 25.00 (*0-8133-8741-8*) Westview.

Poisoned Places: Seeking Environmental Justice in A Contaminated World. Michael R. Edelstein. (C). 1998. 19.95 (*0-8133-8742-6*) Westview.

Poisoned Power: The Case Against Nuclear Power Before & After Three Mile Island. John W. Gofman & Arthur R. Tamplin. LC 79-16781. 353p. 1979. pap. 9.95 (*0-87857-288-0*) Comm Nuclear Respon.

Poisoned Prosperity: Development, Modernization, & the Environment in South Korea. Norman R. Eder. LC 95-34229. (Illus.). 224p. (C). (gr. 13). 1995. 75.95 (*1-56324-686-4*, East Gate Bk); pap. 34.95 (*1-56324-687-2*, East Gate Bk) M E Sharpe.

***Poisoned Serpent.** Joan Wolf. LC 99-51770. 304p. 2000. 23.00 (*0-06-019239-9*) HarpC.

Poisoned Stream: Gay Influence in Human History. Scott Lively. (Germany 1900-1945 Ser.: Vol. 1). 136p. 1997. pap. 9.95 (*0-9647609-2-4*) Fndrs Pubng.

Poisoned Vows. Clifford L. Linedecker. 1995. mass mkt. 5.50 (*0-312-95513-8*, Pub. by Tor Bks) St Martin.

Poisoned Well. Sierra Club Legal Defense Fund Staff. LC 89-1940. (Illus.). 420p. (C). 1989. text 40.00 (*0-933280-56-4*); pap. text 24.95 (*0-933280-55-6*) Island Pr.

***Poisoners & Pretenders.** Michael Chinery. (Secrets of the Rainforest Ser.). (Illus.). 32p. (J). (gr. k-8). 2000. pap. 7.95 (*0-7787-0229-4*); lib. bdg. 19.96 (*0-7787-0219-7*) Crabtree Pub Co.

Poisoning & Drug Overdose. 2nd ed. Kent R. Olson. (Illus.). 592p. (C). 1994. pap. text 32.95 (*0-8385-1108-2*, A1108-8) Appleton & Lange.

Poisoning & Drug Overdose: A Lange Clinical Manual. 4th ed. Kent R. Olson. 1998. pap. text 36.95 (*0-8385-8172-2*) Appleton & Lange.

Poisoning & Drug Overdose: Clinical Manual. 3rd ed. Kent R. Olson. (Illus.). 569p. 1999. spiral bd. 36.95 (*0-8385-0260-1*, Apple Lange Med) McGraw.

Poisoning & Promotion in Catalysis Based on Surface Science Concepts & Experiments. M. P. Kiskinova. (Studies in Surface Science & Catalysis: Vol. 70). 346p. 1991. 228.50 (*0-444-86947-6*) Elsevier.

Poisoning & Toxicology Compendium. Leikin. 1997. 74.75 (*0-916589-61-7*) Lexi-Comp.

Poisoning Arms Control: The Soviet Union & Chemical-Biological Weapons. Mark C. Storella. LC 84-10832. (Special Reports). 99p. 1984. 11.95 (*0-89549-063-3*) Inst Foreign Policy Anal.

Poisoning of Eros: Sexual Values in Conflict. Raymond J. Lawrence, Jr. LC 89-92038. 281p. (C). 1989. 19.95 (*0-9623310-0-7*) Augustine Moore.

Poisoning of Louisiana. Ed. by Maxine Alexander et al. (Southern Exposure Ser.). (Illus.). 72p. (Orig.). (C). 1984. pap. 4.00 (*0-943810-28-0*) Inst Southern Studies.

Poisoning Our Children: Surviving in a Toxic World. Nancy S. Green. LC 90-63429. 270p. (Orig.). 1991. pap. 12.95 (*0-9622683-7-2*) Noble Pr.

Poisoning the Ivy: The 7 Deadly Sins & Other Vices of Higher Education in America. Michael Lewis. LC 96-40284. 230p. (C). (gr. 13). 1997. 33.95 (*0-7656-0071-4*) M E Sharpe.

Poisoning the Minds of the Lower Orders. Don Herzog. LC 98-5126. 472p. 1998. text 29.95 (*0-691-04831-2*, Pub. by Princeton U Pr) Cal Prin Full Svc.

***Poisoning the Minds of the Lower Orders.** Don Herzog. 472p. 2000. pap. 19.95 (*0-691-05741-9*) Princeton U Pr.

Poisonous & Hazardous Marine Life: Animals That Bite, Sting, Cut, or Are Poisonous or Dangerous to Eat. Sandra Romashko. (Illus.). 64p. 1998. pap. 4.95 (*0-89317-045-3*) Windward Pub.

Poisonous & Useful Fungi of Africa South of the Sahara. R. Walleyn & J. Rammeloo. (Scripta Botanica Belgica Ser.: Vol. 10). 56p. 1994. 21.00 (*90-72619-22-6*, Pub. by Natl Botanic Grdn Belgium) Balogh.

Poisonous & Venomous Animals. Matthew Landau. 84p. 1996. pap. text, per. 29.95 (*0-7872-0731-4*) Kendall-Hunt.

Poisonous & Venomous Marine Animals of the World. 2nd rev. ed. Bruce W. Halstead. LC 84-70414. (Illus.). 1500p. 1988. 250.00 (*0-87850-050-2*) Darwin Pr.

Poisonous Animals: Facts & Fun Books. Peter M. Spizzirri. Ed. by Linda Spizzirri. (Illus.). 32p. (J). (ps-2). 1997. pap. 1.25 (*0-86545-285-7*) Spizzirri.

Poisonous Cocktail? Aum Shinrikyo's Path to Violence. Ian Reader. 116p. 1998. pap. 19.95 (*87-87062-55-0*, Pub. by NIAS) Paul & Co Pubs.

Poisonous Dwellers of the Desert. Trevor Hare. Ed. by Sandra Scott. LC 94-69816. (Illus.). 32p. 1995. pap. 5.95 (*1-877856-53-3*) SW Pks Mnmts.

Poisonous Lizards: Gila Monsters & Mexican Beaded Lizards see Animals & the Environment

Poisonous Plant Contamination of Edible Plants. Abdel-Fattah M. Rizk. (Illus.). 192p. 1990. lib. bdg. 149.00 (*0-8493-6369-1*, RA1250) CRC Pr.

Poisonous Plants. Betty J. Arnold. LC 77-9240. 141p. 1978. pap. 10.00 (*0-9670441-0-3*) Terra.

Poisonous Plants. Suzanne M. Coil. (First Bks.). (Illus.). 64p. (J). (gr. 5-8). 1992. pap. 6.95 (*0-531-15647-8*) Watts.

Poisonous Plants. Richard A. Howard & Gordon P. DeWolf. (Illus.). 48p. reprint ed. pap. text 3.95 (*1-878297-01-5*) Arnold Arboretum.

Poisonous Plants: A Magna Colour Guide. Frantisek Stary. (Illus.). 224p. 1998. pap. text 25.00 (*0-7881-5721-3*) DIANE Pub.

Poisonous Plants: A Source Guide. 1991. lib. bdg. 75.00 (*0-8490-4825-7*) Gordon Pr.

Poisonous Plants & Animals of Florida & the Caribbean. David W. Nellis. LC 96-21971. (Illus.). 416p. 1997. 29.95 (*1-56164-111-1*); pap. 21.95 (*1-56164-113-8*) Pineapple Pr.

Poisonous Plants & Fungi: An Illustrated Guide. Marian R. Cooper & Anthony W. Johnson. (Illus.). 134p. 1998. pap. 115.00 (*0-11-242981-5*, Pub. by Statnry Office) Bernan Associates.

Poisonous Plants & Fungi: An Illustrated Guide. 4th ed. Marion R. Cooper & Anthony R. Johnson. (Illus.). 134p. 1996. pap. 21.95 (*0-11-242718-9*, Pub. by Statnry Office) Bernan Associates.

Poisonous Plants & Venomous Animals of Alabama & Adjoining States. Whit Gibbons et al. LC 88-34003. (Illus.). 368p. 1990. pap. 24.95 (*0-8173-0442-8*) U of Ala Pr.

Poisonous Plants in Britain & Ireland: An Identification System on CD-ROM. Guy's & St. Thomas Hospital Staff & Royal Botanic Gardens Kew Staff. 1995. pap. 86.00 incl. cd-rom (*0-11-526474-4*, HM64744) Balogh.

Poisonous Plants of All Countries, 1923. Ed. by B. Bernardr. (C). 1923. 170.00 (*0-7855-2284-0*, Pub. by Scientific) St Mut.

Poisonous Plants of California. Thomas C. Fuller & Elizabeth McClintock. (California Natural History Guides Ser.: No. 53). (Illus.). 384p. (C). 1987. pap. 13.95 (*0-520-05569-1*, Pub. by U CA Pr) Cal Prin Full Svc.

P

An Asterisk (*) at the beginning of an entry indicates that the title is appearing for the first time.

Poisonous Plants of India. R. N. Chopra et al. 762p. (C). 1984. 750.00 (0-7855-1984-X, Pub. by Scientific); 210.00 (0-7855-2270-0, Pub. by Scientific) St Mut.

***Poisonous Plants of Paradise: First Aid & Medical Treatment of Injuries from Hawai'i's Plants.** Susan Scott & Craig Thomas. LC 99-50088. (Illus.). 184p. 2000. pap. 19.95 (0-8248-2251-X) UH Pr.

Poisonous Plants of Pennsylvania. Robert J. Hill. (Illus.). 175p. 1986. pap. 6.35 (0-8182-0078-2) Commonweal PA.

Poisonous Plants of Southern California. Ed. by James Bauml. LC 98-201697. (Illus.). 36p. 1998. pap. 4.00 (0-9660222-2-X) Arboretum LA Cty.

Poisonous Plants of the Central United States. H. A. Stephens. LC 79-28161. (Illus.). xiv, 166p. 1980. pap. 15.95 (0-7006-0204-6) U Pr of KS.

Poisonous Power: Childhood Roots of Tyranny. June Stephenson. LC 98-209926. 700p. 1998. pap. 19.95 (0-941138-15-1) Diemer-Smith.

Poisonous Snakes. Tony Phelps. LC 81-670067. 1981. 27.50 (0-7137-0877-8) Blandford Pr.

Poisonous Snakes. Seymour Simon. (YA). 1981. 11.95 (0-590-07513-6) Scholastic Inc.

Poisonous Snakes: Educational Coloring Book. Spizzirri Publishing Co. Staff. Ed. by Linda Spizzirri. (Illus.). 32p. (J). (gr. 1-8). 1984. pap. 1.99 (0-86545-054-4) Spizzirri.

Poisonous Snakes of Alabama. Christine A. Wimberly. (Illus.). 46p. (Orig.). (J). (gr. 4-12). 1970. pap. 3.35 (0-9605938-0-2) Explorer Bks.

Poisonous Snakes of India. Joseph Ewart. 64p. (C). 1988. 250.00 (0-7855-6735-6, Pub. by Himalayan Bks) St Mut.

Poisonous Snakes of India. Joseph Ewart. (Illus.). 64p. 1987. reprint ed. 39.50 (0-88359-019-0) R Curtis Pubng.

Poisonous Snakes of the World. 1997. lib. bdg. 250.95 (0-8490-6222-5) Gordon Pr.

Poisonous Snakes of the World. U. S. Department of the Navy Staff. 1991. pap. 15.95 (0-486-26629-X) Dover.

Poisonous Snakes of the World: Manual for Use by the United States Amphibious Forces. Granville M. Moore. (Illus.). 220p. 1979. reprint ed. boxed set 31.00 (0-16-002014-X, S/N 008-045-00009-7) USGPO.

Poisonous, Venomous, & Electric Marine Organisms of the Atlantic Coast, Gulf of Mexico, & the Caribbean. Matthew Landau. (Illus.). 218p. 1997. 29.95 (0-937548-36-7); pap. 19.95 (0-937548-33-2) Plexus Pub.

Poisons & Antidotes Sourcebook. Carol Turkington. LC 98-55190. 1999. 16.95 (0-8160-3960-7) Facts on File.

***Poisons & Antidotes Sourcebook.** 2nd ed. Carol Turkington. LC 98-55190. (Facts for Life Ser.). 408p. 1999. 35.00 (0-8160-3959-3) Facts on File.

Poisons & Toxins. Marc Kusinitz. (Encyclopedia of Health Ser.). (Illus.). 116p. (YA). (gr. 7 up). 1992. lib. bdg. 19.95 (0-7910-0074-5) Chelsea Hse.

Poisons Around Us: Toxic Metals in Food, Air, & Water. Henry A. Schroeder. LC 73-15283. 156p. reprint ed. pap. 48.40 (0-608-13220-9, 205605600044) Bks Demand.

Poisons in Our Path: Plants That Harm & Heal. Anne O. Dowden. LC 92-9518. (Illus.). 64p. (J). 1994. lib. bdg. 17.89 (0-06-020862-7) HarpC Child Bks.

Poisons of the Past: Molds, Epidemics, & History. Mary K. Matossian. (Illus.). 208p. (C). 1991. reprint ed. pap. 14.00 (0-300-05121-2) Yale U Pr.

Poisons That Heal. Eileen Nauman. 270p. 1995. pap. 14.95 (0-929385-62-4) Light Tech Pubng.

Poisonwood Bible. Barbara Kingsolver. LC 98-19901. 546p. 1998. 26.00 (0-06-017540-0, HarperFlamingo) HarpC.

Poisonwood Bible. Barbara Kingsolver. LC 98-19901. 560p. 1999. pap. 14.00 (0-06-093053-5) HarpC.

Poisonwood Bible. large type ed. Barbara Kingsolver. LC 98-48529. (Large Print Bks.). 712p. 1950. pap. 27.95 (0-7838-8468-0, G K Hall Lrg Type) Mac Lib Ref.

Poisson Approximation. A. D. Barbour et al. (Studies in Probability: No. 2). 288p. 1992. text 55.00 (0-19-852235-5) OUP.

Poisson D'Avril. Steven Kroll & Jeni Bassett. (FRE.). (J). mass mkt. 6.99 (0-590-73953-0) Scholastic Inc.

Poisson Processes. J. F. Kingman. LC 92-25532. (Studies in Probability: Vol. 3). (Illus.). 112p. 1993. text 50.00 (0-19-853693-3, Clarendon Pr) OUP.

Poissons de Mer de l'Ouest Africain Tropical (The Sea Fish of Tropical West Africa) 3rd rev. ed. B. Seret & P. Opic. (Initiations Documentations Techniques Ser.: No. 49).Tr. of Sea Fish of Tropical West Africa. (FRE., Illus.). 450p. 1990. pap. 34.00 (2-7099-1016-0, Pub. by LInstitut Francais) Balogh.

Poisson's Exponential Binomial Limit. E. C. Molina. 56p. 1973. reprint ed. pap. 10.50 (0-88275-107-7) Krieger.

Poissons Rouges see Nouvelles Pieces Grincantes

Poissons Rouges. Jean Anouilh. (FRE.). 1972. pap. 10.95 (0-7859-1684-9, 2070360067) Fr & Eur.

Poissons Rouges. Jean Anouilh. (Folio Ser.: No. 6). (FRE.). pap. 10.95 (2-07-036006-7) Schoenhof.

Poitiers City Plan. (Grafocarte Maps Ser.). 1994. 8.95 (2-7416-0067-8, 80067) Michelin.

Poitou-Vendee-Charentes Green Guide. 3rd ed. Michelin Staff. (FRE.). 1995. pap. 19.95 (0-7859-9155-7) Fr & Eur.

Poitou/Charentes Map. 1996. 8.95 (2-06-700233-3, 233) Michelin.

***Pojo's Unofficial Big Book of Pokeman: The Ultimate Player & Collector's Guide.** Ed. by Nancy Davis. (Pokemon Ser.). 2000. pap. 19.95 (1-57243-361-2) Triumph Bks.

Poka-Yoke: Improving Product Quality by Preventing Defects. Ed. by NKS-Factory Magazine Staff. LC 88-62593. (Illus.). 295p. 1989. 65.00 (0-915299-31-3) Productivity Inc.

Poka-Yoke: Mejorando la Calidad Del Producto Evitando los Defectos. Ed. by Nikkan K. Shimbun. (SPA., Illus.). 316p. (Orig.). 1991. pap. 60.00 (84-87022-73-1) Productivity Inc.

Pokagon Township Reflections. Barbara W. Cook & Grafton H. Cook, II. (Illus.). v, 252p. 1998. pap. 20.00 (0-9601340-1-8) The Cooks.

Pokagons, Sixteen Eighty-Three to Nineteen Eighty-Three: Catholic Potawatomi Indians of the St. Joseph River Valley. James A. Clifton. (Illus.). 182p. (Orig.). 1985. pap. text 23.00 (0-8191-4283-2) U Pr of Amer.

Poke in the Public Eye: Media Manipulation for Aspiring Politicians & Other Undesirables. David J. Climenhaga. (Illus.). 128p. (Orig.). 1995. pap. write for info. (1-55059-110-X) Detselig Ents.

***Pokemon: Electric Pikachu Boogaloo.** Toshihiro Ono. (Illus.). 168p. 2000. pap. 12.95 (1-56931-436-5, Pub. by Viz Commns Inc) Publishers Group.

***Pokemon: Gotta Catch 'em All!** Golden Books Staff. (Pokemon Tattoo Ser.). 16p. (J). 1999. pap. text 3.99 (0-307-10401-X, Goldn Books) Gldn Bks Pub Co.

***Pokemon: Gotta Catch 'em All!** Emilie Kong. 48p. (J). 1999. pap. 3.99 (0-307-10311-0, Goldn Books); pap. text 3.99 (0-307-10310-2, Goldn Books) Gldn Bks Pub Co.

***Pokemon: Gotta Catch 'em All!** Leif Peng. 48p. (J). 1999. pap. 3.99 (0-307-10313-7, Goldn Books) Gldn Bks Pub Co.

***Pokemon: Gotta Catch 'em All!** Michael Teitelbaum. (Illus.). 44p. (gr. 3-7). 1999. pap. 3.95 (0-8167-6527-8) Troll Communs.

***Pokemon: Gym Challenge.** Wizards of the Coast Staff. (Illus.). 160p. 2000. pap. 12.95 (0-7869-1786-5) TSR Inc.

***Pokemon: Gym Heroes.** Wizards of the Coast Staff. (Illus.). 160p. 2000. pap. 12.95 (0-7869-1787-3) TSR Inc.

***Pokemon: Night/Haunted Tower, Vol. 4.** Scholastic, Inc. Staff. (Illus.). 70p. (gr. 2-5). 1999. pap. text 4.50 (0-439-13742-X) Scholastic Bk Fairs.

***Pokemon: Pikachu Shocks Back.** Toshihiro Ono. (Illus.). 160p. 1999. pap. 12.95 (1-56931-411-X, Viz Comics) Viz Commns Inc.

Pokemon: Prima's Official Strategy Guide. Elizabeth Hollinger. LC 98-67343. (Games Ser.). 1998. per. 12.99 (0-7615-1812-6, Prima Games) Prima Pub.

Pokemon: The Electric Tale of Pikachu! Toshihiro Ono. (Illus.). 160p. (J). (gr. 4-7). 1999. pap. 12.95 (1-56931-378-4, Pub. by Viz Commns Inc) Publishers Group.

***Pokemon: The First Movie Animation Comics: Mewtwo Strikes Back.** Takeshi Shudo. (Illus.). (J). 2000. pap. 15.95 (1-56931-505-1, Viz Comics) Viz Commns Inc.

***Pokemon Adventures Vol. 1: Desperado Pikachu.** Hidenori Kusaka. (Illus.). (YA). 2000. pap. 13.95 (1-56931-507-8, Viz Comics) Viz Commns Inc.

***Pokemon Adventures Vol. 2: Legendary Pokemon.** Hidenori Kusaka. (Illus.). (YA). 2000. pap. 13.95 (1-56931-508-6, Viz Comics) Viz Commns Inc.

Pokemon (Blue) Official Strategy Guide. Prima Development Staff. 96p. 1999. pap. 12.99 (0-7615-2282-4, Prima Games) Prima Pub.

***Pokemon Card Collector's Guide.** Consumer Guide Editors. (Illus.). 2000. pap. 7.99 (0-7853-4045-9) Pubns Intl Ltd.

***Pokemon Collectible Magnet Book, Vol. 1.** Golden Books Publishing Company Staff. (Illus.). (J). 2000. pap. 4.99 (0-307-10237-8) Gldn Bks Pub Co.

***Pokemon Collectible Magnet Book, Vol. 2.** Golden Books Publishing Company Staff. (Illus.). (J). 2000. pap. 4.99 (0-307-10238-6) Gldn Bks Pub Co.

***Pokemon Collectible Magnet Book, Vol. 3.** Golden Books Publishing Company Staff. Vol. 3. (Illus.). 56p. (J). (ps-3). 2000. pap. 4.99 (0-307-10239-4) Gldn Bks Pub Co.

***Pokemon Collector's Value Guide.** 2nd ed. CheckerBee Publishing Staff. 270p. 2000. pap. text 12.95 (1-888914-88-2) CheckerBee.

***Pokemon Counting Book.** Golden Books Staff. 32p. 1999. pap. 5.99 (0-307-10464-8) Gldn Bks Pub Co.

***Pokemon Edition of Swap: Create Your Own Trading Cards.** Alexander Gekko & Gille Myotis. 60p. (J). 1999. pap. 13.95 (1-883573-33-5) Pride & Imprints.

***Pokemon Fever: The Unauthorized Guide.** Hank Schlesinger. 256p. 1999. mass mkt. 5.99 (0-312-97530-9, St Martins Paperbacks) St Martin.

***Pokemon Future: The Unauthorized Guide.** Hank Schlesinger. 256p. 2000. pap. 5.99 (0-312-97758-1, St Martins Paperbacks) St Martin.

***Pokemon Gold & Silver Japanese Translation Guide.** J. Douglas Arnold. (Illus.). (J). 2000. pap. 12.95 (1-884364-51-9) Sandwich Islands.

***Pokemon Holiday.** Yumi Tsukirino. (Magical Pokemon Journey Ser.: Vol. 3). (Illus.). 40p. (ps-3). 2000. pap. 4.95 (1-56931-457-8, Pub. by Viz Commns Inc) Publishers Group.

***Pokemon Made Simple!** Ed. by Wizards of the Coast Staff. (Pokemon Ser.). (Illus.). 160p. (J). 2000. mass mkt. 4.99 (0-7869-1766-0) TSR Inc.

***Pokemon Master Collection, 1 vol., Vol. 1.** Golden Books Staff. 1999. pap. text 5.99 (0-307-10430-3, Goldn Books) Gldn Bks Pub Co.

***Pokemon Master Collector's Book.** Golden Books Publishing Company Staff. (Pokemon Ser.). (Illus.). (J). 2000. 19.99 (0-307-10129-0) Gldn Bks Pub Co.

***Pokemon Master Game Book & Magic Cube.** Golden Books Publishing Company Staff. (Pokemon Ser.). (Illus.). (J). 2000. pap. 12.99 (0-307-10141-X) Gldn Bks Pub Co.

***Pokemon Math Challenge.** Ed. by Golden Book Staff. (Illus.). (J). 2000. pap. 5.99 (0-307-30615-1, Goldn Books) Gldn Bks Pub Co.

***Pokemon Math Challenge.** Ed. by Golden Book Staff. (Illus.). (J). (gr. 4-5). 2000. pap. 5.99 (0-307-30614-3, Goldn Books) Gldn Bks Pub Co.

***Pokemon Math Challenge.** Ed. by Golden Books Staff. (Illus.). (J). (gr. 3-4). 2000. pap. 5.99 (0-307-30613-5, Goldn Books) Gldn Bks Pub Co.

***Pokemon Math Challenge: Grade 2.** Golden Books Staff. (Pokemon Math Challenge Ser.). 2000. pap. 5.99 (0-307-30610-0, Goldn Books) Gldn Bks Pub Co.

Pokemon Origami. Ryoko Nishida. (Illus.). 80p. (J). (gr. 4-7). 1999. pap. 8.95 (1-56931-391-1, Pub. by Viz Commns Inc) Publishers Group.

***Pokemon Origami, Vol.2.** Ryoko Nishida. (Illus.). 80p. (ps-3). 2000. pap. 8.95 (1-56931-415-2, Pub. by Viz Commns Inc) Publishers Group.

Pokemon: Pathways to Adventure. Jason Rich. LC 98-89150. (Illus.). 102p. (J). (gr. 3-7). 1998. pap. 9.99 (0-7821-2503-4) Sybex.

***Pokemon Piano Fun!** Hal Leonard Publishing Company Staff. 1999. pap. 19.95 (1-57560-308-X, Pub. by Cherry Lane) H Leonard.

***Pokemon Pop Quiz!** Scholastic, Inc. Staff. (Illus.). 80p. (J). (gr. 2-7). 2000. pap. 4.99 (0-439-15406-5) Scholastic Inc.

***Pokemon Postcard Book, Vol. 1, Vol. 1.** Golden Books Staff. 6p. 1999. pap. 5.99 (0-307-10463-X) Gldn Bks Pub Co.

***Pokemon Punch-Out Playset, Vol. 1, Vol. 1.** Golden Books Staff. 8p. 1999. pap. 5.99 (0-307-10500-8) Gldn Bks Pub Co.

***Pokemon Recorder Fun.** Ed. by Cherry Lane Music Staff. (Illus.). (J). 2000. pap. 9.95 (1-57560-324-1, Pub. by Cherry Lane) H Leonard.

***Pokemon Snap.** Prima Development Staff. 1999. pap. 12.99 (0-7615-2275-1) Prima Pub.

***Pokemon Snap.** 3rd ed. Sybex, Inc. Staff. (Illus.). 112p. (J). 1999. pap. 9.99 (0-7821-2666-9) Sybex.

***Pokemon Stadium: Prima's Official Strategy Guide.** Prima Development Staff et al. LC 99-63696. (Illus.). 111p. 2000. pap. 12.99 (0-7615-2278-6) Prima Pub.

***Pokemon Stadium Official Strategy Guide.** Jeffery Nelson. (Strategy Guides Ser.). (Illus.). 128p. (J). 2000. pap. 12.99 (1-56686-974-9, BradyGAMES) Brady Pub.

***Pokemon Stick'n Play Book.** Viz Comics Staff. (Illus.). 10p. (J). (ps up). 2000. 11.95 (1-56931-417-9, Viz Comics) Viz Commns Inc.

***Pokemon Tales Box Set 1.** Viz Comics Staff. (Illus.). (J). 2000. 19.95 (1-56931-525-6, Viz Comics) Viz Commns Inc.

***Pokemon Tales Box Set 2.** Viz Comics Staff. 2000. 19.95 (1-56931-526-4, Viz Comics) Viz Commns Inc.

***Pokemon Tattoo, 1.** Golden Books Staff. 1999. pap. text 3.99 (0-307-10400-1) Gldn Bks Pub Co.

***Pokemon Team Rocket Strategy Guide.** Ed. by Wizards of the Coast Staff. (Pokemon Ser.). (Illus.). 128p. (J). 2000. pap. 12.95 (0-7869-1762-8) TSR Inc.

***Pokemon Theme.** (Easy Piano Ser.). 4p. 1999. pap. 3.95 (1-57560-267-9, Pub. by Cherry Lane) H Leonard.

***Pokemon Trading Card Game: Gameboy Color.** Elizabeth M. Hollinger. LC 00-10174. (Official Strategy Guides Ser.). (Illus.). 144p. (YA). 2000. pap. 14.99 (0-7615-2798-2) Prima Pub.

***Pokemon Trading Card Game: Official Strategy Guide.** IMGS Inc. Staff et al. LC 99-63280. (Illus.). 143p. 1999. pap. 14.99 (0-7615-2238-7, Prima Games) Prima Pub.

***Pokemon Trading Card Game - Fossil Expansion - Player's Guide Vol. 2: Fossil Expansion & Japanese Card.** Brian Brokaw & J. Douglas Arnold. (Illus.). 144p. 2000. pap. 12.95 (1-884364-39-X, Pub. by Sandwich Islands) Login Pubs Consort.

***Pokemon Trading Card Game Player's Guide.** J Douglas Arnold & Brian Brokaw. (Illus.). 144p. (YA). 1999. pap. 12.95 (1-884364-50-0, Pub. by Sandwich Islands) Login Pubs Consort.

***Pokemon Trading Card Game Player's Guide.** Brian Brokaw. (Illus.). (YA). 2000. pap. 12.95 (1-884364-53-5) Sandwich Islands.

Pokemon Trainers Survival Guide. Mark MacDonald. 1999. pap. 11.95 (1-884364-33-0) Sandwich Islands.

Pokemon Trainer's Survival Guide. rev. ed. Mark MacDonald et al. 144p. 1999. pap. 12.95 (1-884364-25-X) Sandwich Islands.

***Pokemon 2 B. A. Master: E-Z Play Songbook.** Cherry Lane Music Company Staff. (Pokemon Ser.). (Illus.). 64p. (J). 2000. otabind 12.95 (1-57560-289-X, Pub. by Cherry Lane) H Leonard.

***Pokemon 2000 Collector's Value Guide.** CheckerBee Publishing Staff. (Illus.). 250p. 1999. pap. 9.95 (1-888914-68-8) CheckerBee.

***Pokemon 2000 Collector's Value Guide.** CheckerBee Publishing Staff. (Illus.). 256p. 1999. pap. 9.95 (1-888914-67-X) CheckerBee.

***Pokemon Write Your Own Adventures!, Vol. 2.** Golden Books Publishing Company Staff. (Illus.). (J). 2000. pap. 4.99 (0-307-10466-4) Gldn Bks Pub Co.

***Pokemon Yellow.** Elizabeth Hollinger. 1999. pap. 12.99 (0-7615-2277-8) Prima Pub.

***Pokemon #12 Scyther, Heart of a Champion Display.** Sheila Sweeny. (Illus.). 2000. pap. text 54.00 (0-439-21190-5) Scholastic Inc.

Poker. 2000. mass mkt. 8.95 (0-446-73698-8, Pub. by Warner Bks) Little.

Poker: A Winner's Guide. Andy Nelson. 288p. 1996. pap. 11.00 (0-399-52212-3, Perigee Bks) Berkley Pub.

Poker: How to Win at the Great American Game. David A. Daniel. LC 96-21024. 384p. 1997. 20.00 (1-56980-093-6) Barricade Bks.

***Poker Club.** Ed Gorman. 400p. 2000. mass mkt. 5.99 (0-8439-4683-0, Leisure Bks) Dorchester Pub Co.

***Poker Club.** Ed Gorman. 352p. 1999. 40.00 (1-881475-68-9) Cemetery Dance.

Poker Essays. 2nd ed. Mason Malmuth. Ed. by Lynne Loomis. 262p. 1996. pap. text 24.95 (1-880685-09-4) Two Plus NV.

Poker Essays, Vol. II. Mason Malmuth. Ed. by Paula Cizmar. (Illus.). 286p. 1996. pap. 24.95 (1-880685-15-9) Two Plus NV.

Poker Expertise Through Probability. Robert T. Riley. (Illus.). 186p. 1996. spiral bd. write for info. (0-9701586-0-2) R T Riley.

Poker Farce & Poker Truth: The Actual & Real World Of Poker. Ray Michael B. LC 99-229011. (Illus.). 246p. 1999. pap. 19.95 (1-880685-20-5) Two Plus NV.

***Poker for Dummies.** Richard Harroch & Lou Krieger. 256p. 2000. pap. 14.99 (0-7645-5232-5) IDG Bks.

Poker for Fun & Profit. Irwin Steig. (Illus.). 1959. 10.95 (0-8392-1085-X) Astor-Honor.

Poker for Profit. Carroll Volm. 67p. 1987. pap. 12.95 (0-9622525-0-6) Evon Pub.

Poker for the Family. Joseph P. Wergin & Beatrice S. Smith. LC 94-75669. (Illus.). 84p. (J). (gr. 3-8). 1994. pap. 9.95 (1-885114-00-1, Huron Prss) Wergin Bks.

Poker, Gaming, & Life: Fighting Fuzzy Thinking In. David Sklansky. LC 97-185768. (Illus.). 207p. (Orig.). 1997. reprint ed. pap. text 24.95 (1-880685-17-5) Two Plus NV.

Poker Humor. Gary Oliver. 100p. 1993. pap. 5.95 (0-9635909-0-1) Poker Tips Pr.

Poker, 7-Card Stud & Hold'em. Tony Korfman. (Playing to Win Ser.). 47p. (Orig.). 1985. pap. text 3.50 (0-934047-06-5) Gaming Bks Intl.

***Poker Strategy: Proven Principles for Winning Play.** A. D. Livingston. 240p. 2000. pap. 14.95 (1-58574-064-0) Lyons Pr.

Poker Talk: A Complete Guide to the Vocabulary of Poker. Michael Wiesenberg. 186p. (Orig.). 1995. pap. 14.95 (1-884466-14-1) Poker Plus.

Poker Tournament Strategies. Sylvester Suzuki & Paula Cizmar. LC 99-163511. (Illus.). 187p. 1998. pap. 19.95 (1-880685-19-1) Two Plus NV.

Poker Tournament Tactics for Winners Vol. I: How to Play Like a Fox & Outwit the Maniacs, Rocks & Desperadoes. D. R. Sherer. LC 98-67031. 176p. 1998. pap. 24.95 (1-884466-33-8) Poker Plus.

Poketales. Schandra K. Thompkinsel Alston. LC 98-91595. (Illus.). 280p. 1998. 29.99 (0-9664695-5-0) Mason & Mellonstein.

Pokeweed & Mrs. Gasp: And Other One-Acts with a Point of View. Anita Higman. 77p. 1994. pap. 8.99 (0-8341-9052-4, MP-696) Lillenas.

Pokey: The Good Fight. Pokey Allen. LC 97-71515. (Illus.). 200p. 1997. pap. 14.95 (0-9658911-0-0) Bootleg Bks.

Pokey & Horse Latitudes: Manuscript Edition. Stephen Black. 1976. pap. 13.00 (0-8222-0903-9) Dramatists Play.

Pokey Opossum. Dave Sargent & Pat L. Sargent. (Animal Pride Ser.: No. 18). (Illus.). 39p. (J). (gr. 2-8). 1996. pap. 2.95 (1-56763-043-X); lib. bdg. 12.95 (1-56763-042-1) Ozark Pub.

Pokhara. 64p. 1988. pap. 35.00 (1-882866-57-6) Pac Asia Trvl.

Pokhara: A Valley in the Himalayas. Prakash A. Raj. (C). 1993. 30.00 (0-7855-0203-3, Pub. by Ratna Pustak Bhandar) St Mut.

Poking Holes in the Darkness. Jaki Parlier. 192p. 1994. pap. 8.95 (0-939497-34-4) Promise Pub.

Poklosie: Gleanning. Leokadia Rowinska. (Illus.). 200p. (Orig.). 1987. pap. 10.95 (0-930401-07-7) Artex Pub.

Pokot. Ciarunji C. Swinimer. LC 94-5071. (Heritage Library of African Peoples: Set 1). (Illus.). 64p. (YA). (gr. 7-12). 1994. lib. bdg. 16.95 (0-8239-1756-8) Rosen Group.

***Poky: Tails of Friendship.** Talkington. (Illus.). 20p. (J). 1999. write for info. (0-307-16077-7) Gldn Bks Pub Co.

***Poky & Friends Travel Case, 5 bks.** Golden Books Publishing Company Staff. (Illus.). (J). 2000. boxed set 9.99 (0-307-15893-4, 15893, Goldn Books) Gldn Bks Pub Co.

***Poky Little Puppy.** Golden Books Publishing Company Staff. (Illus.). 16p. (J). 2001. bds. 9.99 (0-307-17306-2, 17306, Goldn Books) Gldn Bks Pub Co.

***Poky Little Puppy.** Golden Books Staff. 1999. 12.99 (0-307-33726-X) Gldn Bks Pub Co.

Poky Little Puppy. Naomi Kleinberg. LC 98-88682. 24p. 1999. 3.99 (0-307-16263-X) Gldn Bks Pub Co.

Poky Little Puppy. Janette S. Lowrey. (Little Golden Bks.). (Illus.). 24p. (J). (ps-2). 1992. bds. 2.29 (0-307-02134-3, 98100, Goldn Books) Gldn Bks Pub Co.

Poky Little Puppy. Jeanette S. Lowrey. (Little Golden Storybks.). (J). 1998. 3.99 (0-307-16026-2, 16026, Goldn Books) Gldn Bks Pub Co.

Poky Little Puppy. deluxe ed. Janette Sebring Lowrey. (Illus.). 23p. (J). (ps-2). Date not set. reprint ed. write for info. (1-929566-56-5) Cronies.

Poky Little Puppy: Classic Edition. Janette Sebring Lowrey. (Illus.). 23p. (J). (ps-1). Date not set. reprint ed. write for info. (1-929566-50-6) Cronies.

Poky Little Puppy's Book of Colors. Golden Staff. LC 94-77231. (Shaped Little Nugget Bks.). (Illus.). 14p. (J). (ps). 1995. bds. 3.99 (0-307-12725-7, 12725, Goldn Books) Gldn Bks Pub Co.

Poky Little Puppy's Busy Counting Book. Rita Balducci. (Super Shape Bks.). (Illus.). 24p. (J). (ps-3). 1994. pap. 3.29 (0-307-10015-4, 10015) Gldn Bks Pub Co.

Poky Little Puppy's First Christmas. (Golden Book 'n' Tapes Ser.). (Illus.). 24p. (J). (ps-3). 1995. bds. 6.99 incl. audio (0-307-14460-7, 14460) Gldn Bks Pub Co.

Poky Little Puppy's First Christmas. Julie Korman. (Little Golden Storybks.). (J). 1997. 3.99 (0-307-16169-2, 16169, Goldn Books) Gldn Bks Pub Co.

***Poky's Bathtime Adventure.** Eva Nagorski. (Illus.). (J). 2000. 7.99 (0-307-12199-2) Gldn Bks Pub Co.

***Pol Mexico.** (C). 1998. pap. 0.00 (0-321-01351-4) HEPC Inc.

P

An Asterisk (*) at the beginning of an entry indicates that the title is appearing for the first time.

Pol Pot. Rebecca Stefoff. (World Leaders Past & Present Ser.). (Illus.). 120p. (YA). (gr. 5 up). 1990. lib. bdg. 19.95 (*1-55546-848-9*) Chelsea Hse.

Pol Pot Plans the Future: Confidential Leadership Documents from Democratic Kampuchea, 1976-1977. Ed. & Tr. by David P. Chandler et al. Tr. by Ben Kiernan et al. (Monographs: No. 33). xviii, 346p. 1989. pap. 20.00 (*0-938692-35-6*) Yale U SE Asia.

Pol Pot Regime: Race, Power, & Genocide in Cambodia under the Khmer Rouge, 1975-79. Ben Kiernan. LC 95-18669. (Illus.). 512p. 1996. 45.00 (*0-300-06113-7*) Yale U Pr.

Pol Pot Regime: Race, Power, & Genocide in Cambodia under the Khmer Rouge, 1975-79. Ben Kiernan. (Illus.). 512p. 1998. pap. 18.00 (*0-300-07052-7*) Yale U Pr.

***Pol Roger.** Cynthia Parzych & John Turner. (Illus.). 168p. 2000. 45.00 (*0-9702611-0-1*) C Parzych.

Poland see Festivals of the World

Poland see Fiesta 2!

Poland. Denise Allard. LC 95-53804. (Postcards From Ser.). (J). 1996. lib. bdg. 21.40 (*0-8172-4025-X*) Raintree Steck-V.

Poland. Clifford R. Barnett et al. LC 58-11469. (Area & Country Surveys Ser.). 479p. 1958. 15.00 (*0-87536-901-4*) HRAFP.

***Poland.** Laurel Corona. LC 99-50797. (Modern Nations of the World Ser.). (Illus.). 144p. (YA). (gr. 4-12). 2000. 18.96 (*1-56006-600-8*) Lucent Bks.

Poland. Insight Guides Staff. (Euro-Atlas Ser.). 1998. pap. 19.95 (*0-8416-0541-6*) Am Map.

Poland. Insight Guides Staff. (Insight Guides). 1998. pap. text 22.95 (*0-88729-741-2*); pap. text 7.95 (*0-88729-555-X*) Langenscheidt.

Poland. Sean Mccollum. LC 98-8831. (Globe-Trotters Club Ser.). 48p. (J). (gr. 3-5). 1999. lib. bdg. 22.60 (*1-57505-106-0*, Carolrhoda) Lerner Pub.

Poland. Sean McCollum. LC 98-49042. (Ticket to . . . Ser.). (Illus.). 48p. (J). (gr. 1-3). 1999. lib. bdg. 16.95 (*1-57505-131-1*) Lerner Pub.

***Poland.** Gordon McLachlan. (Illus.). 2000. pap. 19.95 (*1-84162-009-2*) Bradt Pubns.

Poland. James A. Michener. 768p. 1984. mass mkt. 6.99 (*0-449-20587-8*, Crest) Fawcett.

Poland. Nelles Verlag Staff. (Nelles Guides Ser.). (Illus.). 256p. 1999. pap. 15.95 (*3-88618-088-3*) Hunter NJ.

Poland. Steven Otfinoski. LC 95-17252. (Nations in Transition Ser.). (Illus.). 144p. (YA). (gr. 7-12). 1995. 19.95 (*0-8160-3063-4*) Facts on File.

***Poland** Patrick Ryan. LC 99-37426. 2000. write for info. (*1-56766-716-3*) Childs World.

Poland. Dominique Sein. (Countries of the World Ser.: No. 27). (Illus.). 83p. (J). lib. bdg. 14.95 (*0-8288-3938-7*) Fr & Eur.

Poland. U. S. Government Staff. (Country Studies). 1994. 21.00 (*0-614-30812-7*, UPOLAN) Claitors.

Poland. William R. Morfill. LC 75-39494. (Select Bibliographies Reprint Ser.). 1977. reprint ed. 23.95 (*0-8369-9919-3*) Ayer.

Poland. rev. ed. Alexander Jordan. (Insider's Guides Ser.). (Illus.). 233p. 1990. pap. 9.95 (*0-87052-880-7*) Hippocrene Bks.

Poland see Cultures of the World - Group 8

Poland. 2nd ed. Ed. by Sebastian Wormell. (Illus.). 691p. 1998. pap. text 27.95 (*1-873429-22-3*, Pub. by Pallas Athene) Cimino Pub Grp.

Poland. 2nd rev. ed. George Sanford. LC 93-190996. (World Bibliographical Ser.). 276p. 1993. lib. bdg. 84.00 (*1-85109-180-7*) ABC-CLIO.

Poland. 4th ed. Rough Guides Staff. 704p. 1999. pap. 18.95 (*1-85828-423-6*, Pub. by Rough Guides) Penguin Putnam.

Poland, Vol. III. Paul H. Gleye & Waldemar R. Szczerba. (Historic Preservation in Other Countries Ser.). (Illus.). 74p. (Orig.). 1990. pap. text 15.00 (*0-911697-05-5*) US ICOMOS.

Poland: A Country Study. Glenn E. Curtis. 405p. 1994. boxed set 30.00 (*0-16-061164-4*) USGPO.

***Poland: A Country Study.** Global Investment & Business Center, Inc. Staff. (World Country Study Guides Library: Vol. 137). (Illus.). 350p. 2000. pap. 59.00 (*0-7397-2435-5*) Intl Business Pubns.

Poland: A Troubled Past, a New Start see Exploring Cultures of the World - Group 2

***Poland: An Illustrated History.** Iwo C. Pogonowski. (Illustrated History Ser.). (Illus.). 150p. 2000. 14.95 (*0-7818-0757-3*) Hippocrene Bks.

Poland: Behind the Crisis. Sam Marcy. 168p. 1982. pap. 3.95 (*0-89567-076-3*) World View Forum.

***Poland: Complying with EU Environmental Legislation.** Julia Bucknall. LC 99-47657. (Technical Paper Ser.: No. 454). 1999. 22.00 (*0-8213-4595-8*, 14595) World Bank.

Poland: Country Commercial Guide, 1998. Ed. by Barry Leonard. (Illus.). 88p. (C). 1999. pap. text 25.00 (*0-7881-7564-5*) DIANE Pub.

Poland: Decentralization & Reform of the State. World Bank Staff. LC 92-23415. (Country Study Ser.). 120p. 1992. pap. 22.00 (*0-8213-2213-3*, 12213) World Bank.

Poland: Directory of Affordable Accomodations. Ray Kulvicki. (Illus.). 192p. 1996. pap. 14.95 (*0-9652982-0-5*) Polskie B&B Inns.

Poland: Economic Restructuring & Donor Assistance. Ed. by Louis H. Zanardi et al. (Illus.). 83p. 1997. reprint ed. pap. text 30.00 (*0-7881-4112-0*) DIANE Pub.

Poland: Edged Weapons, Sixteenth Century Thru Twentieth Century - A Collectors Guide. J. Skoviera & Martin M. Kozlowski. (Illus.). 54p. (Orig.). (C). 1994. pap. 10.00 (*0-929757-47-5*, Pub. by Militaria Hse) Trafalgar.

Poland: Income Support & the Social Safety Net During the Transition. LC 92-45645. (Country Study Ser.). 164p. 1993. 10.95 (*0-8213-2370-9*, 12370) World Bank.

Poland: Land of Freedom Fighters. Christine Pfeiffer. LC 90-26093. (Discovering Our Heritage Ser.). (Illus.). 144p. (YA). (gr. 5 up). 1991. lib. bdg. 14.95 (*0-87518-464-2*, Dillon Silver Burdett) Silver Burdett Pr.

Poland: Major World Nations. Julian Popescu. LC 99-13405. (Major World Nations Ser.). (Illus.). 144p. 1999. 19.95 (*0-7910-5394-6*) Chelsea Hse.

Poland: Policies for Growth with Equity. LC 94-48162. (Country Study Ser.). 148p. 1995. pap. 22.00 (*0-8213-3158-2*, 13158) World Bank.

Poland: Politics, Economics & Society. G. Kolankiewicz. 220p. 1988. text 17.50 (*0-86187-437-4*, Pub. by P P Pubs) Cassell & Continuum.

Poland: Politics, Economics & Society. G. Kolankiewicz. (Marxist Regimes Ser.). 220p. 1988. text 49.00 (*0-86187-436-6*) St Martin.

Poland: Prison Conditions in Poland, June, 1988. Helsinki Watch Staff. (Orig.). 1988. pap. 7.00 (*0-938579-62-2*) Hum Rts Watch.

Poland: The Conquest of History. George Sanford. 113p. 1999. pap. text 19.95 (*90-5702-347-4*) Gordon & Breach.

***Poland: The Conquest of History.** George Sanford. 113p. 1999. text 33.00 (*90-5702-346-6*, Harwood Acad Pubs) Gordon & Breach.

Poland: The Economy in the 1980's. Ed. by Roger A. Clarke. (Perspectives on Eastern Europe Ser.). 149p. 1989. lib. bdg. 25.00 (*1-55862-045-1*) St James Pr.

Poland: The Path to a Market Economy. Liam Ebrill et al. LC 94-22746. (Occasional Papers: Vol. 113). 1994. 15.00 (*1-55775-411-X*) Intl Monetary.

Poland: The Politics of Crisis. Jack Bielasiak. (WVSS on the Soviet Union & Eastern Europe Ser.). 1996. text 26.50 (*0-86531-441-1*) Westview.

Poland: The Protracted Crisis. Adam Bromke. 280p. 1994. pap. 14.95 (*0-88962-194-2*) Mosaic.

Poland: The Role of the Press in Political Change, 102. Madeleine K. Albright. LC 83-16144. (Washington Papers). 168p. 1983. pap. 13.95 (*0-275-91559-X*, B1559, Praeger Pubs) Greenwood.

Poland - A Country Study Guide: Basic Information for Research & Pleasure. Global Investment Center, USA Staff. (World Country Study Guide Library: Vol. 137). (Illus.). 350p. 1999. pap. 59.00 (*0-7397-1534-8*) Intl Business Pubns.

Poland - Military Medals & Decorations: The Peoples Republic of Poland - 1943 to 1975. Marian Furlan & Martin M. Kozlowski. (Illus.). 60p. (Orig.). 1990. pap. 10.00 (*0-929757-40-8*, Pub. by Militaria Hse) Trafalgar.

Poland - Military Medals & Decorations, 1939-45. Marian Furlan & martin M. Kozlowski. (Illus.). 84p. 1988. pap. 10.00 (*0-929757-13-0*, Pub. by Militaria Hse) Trafalgar.

Poland after Solidarity: Social Movements versus the State. Ed. by Bronislaw Misztal. 1985. 34.95 (*0-88738-049-2*) Transaction Pubs.

Poland & Hungary: Economic Transition & U. S. Assistance. (Illus.). 61p. (Orig.). (C). 1993. pap. text 20.00 (*1-56806-652-X*) DIANE Pub.

***Poland & the European Union.** Karl Cordell & Andrzej Antoszewski. LC 00-20055. (Studies of Societies in Transition). 2000. write for info. (*0-415-23885-4*) Routledge.

Poland & the European Union: Between Association & Membership. Peter C. Mhuller-Graff et al. LC 97-178367. (ECSA Ser.). 320p. 1997. write for info. (*3-7890-4652-3*) Nomos Verlags.

Poland & the Minority Races. Arthur L. Goodhart. LC 71-135809. (Eastern Europe Collection). 1971. reprint ed. 17.95 (*0-405-02751-6*) Ayer.

Poland & Ukraine: Past & Present. Ed. by Peter J. Potichnyj. LC 80-91019. xiv, 365p. pap. 9.95 (*0-920862-07-1*) Ukrainian Acad.

Poland Between East & West: Soviet & German Diplomacy Toward Poland, 1919-1933. Josef Korbel. LC 63-9993. 335p. 1963. reprint ed. pap. 103.90 (*0-608-00007-8*, 206010500004) Bks Demand.

Poland Between East & West: The Controversies over Self-Definition & Modernization in Partitioned Poland (The August Zaleski Lectures, Harvard University, 18-22 April 1994) Andrzej Walicki. (Harvard Papers in Ukrainian Studies). (Illus.). 63p. 1994. pap. text 5.00 (*0-916458-71-7*) Harvard Ukrainian.

Poland Between the Wars, 1918-1939. Peter D. Stachura. LC 98-7134. 168p. 1998. text 59.95 (*0-312-21680-7*) St Martin.

Poland Business & Investment Opportunities Yearbook-98: Business, Investment, Export-Import. Contrib. by Russian Information & Business Center, Inc. Staff. (Business & Investment Opportunity Library-98). (Illus.). 350p. 1998. pap. 99.00 (*1-57751-938-8*) Intl Business Pubns.

***Poland Business Intelligence Report, 190 vols.** Global Investment & Business Center, Inc. Staff. (World Business Intelligence Library: Vol. 137). (Illus.). 350p. 2000. pap. 99.95 (*0-7397-2635-8*) Intl Business Pubns.

***Poland Business Law Handbook.** Global Investment & Business Center, Inc. Staff. (Global Business Law Handbooks Library: Vol. 137). (Illus.). 2000. pap. 99.95 (*0-7397-2035-X*) Intl Business Pubns.

Poland Business Law Handbook-98. Russian Information & Business Center, Inc. Staff. (World Business Law Library-98). (Illus.). 350p. 1998. pap. 99.00 (*1-57751-808-X*) Intl Business Pubns.

***Poland Business Opportunity Yearbook.** Global Investment & Business Center, Inc. Staff. (Global Business Opportunity Yearbooks Library: Vol. 137). (Illus.). 2000. pap. 99.95 (*0-7397-2235-2*) Intl Business Pubns.

***Poland Business Opportunity Yearbook: Export-Import, Investment & Business Opportunities.** International Business Publications, U. S. A. Staff & Global Investment Center, U. S. A. Staff. (Global Business Opportunity Yearbooks Library: Vol. 137). (Illus.), 350p. 1999. pap. 99.95 (*0-7397-1335-3*) Intl Business Pubns.

Poland Challenges a Divided World. John Rensenbrink. LC 88-1393. 256p. 1988. text 35.00 (*0-8071-1446-4*) La State U Pr.

Poland Country Assistance Review: Partnership in a Transition Economy. Luis Landau. LC 97-17871. (Operations & Evaluation Study Ser.). 152p. 1997. pap. 22.00 (*0-8213-3980-X*, 13980) World Bank.

***Poland Country Review 2000.** Robert C. Kelly et al. (Illus.). 60p. 1999. pap. 39.95 (*1-58310-561-1*) CountryWatch.

Poland Country Studies: Area Handbook. 3rd ed. Ed. by Glenn E. Curtis. LC 93-46235. (Area Handbook Ser.). 1994. 21.00 (*0-8444-0827-1*) Lib Congress.

Poland Economic & Business Guide: Strategic & Business Information for Corporate Executives. Russian Information & Business Center, Inc. Staff. (Eastern European Business Library). (Illus.). 200p. 1997. pap. 69.00 (*1-57751-285-5*) Intl Business Pubns.

***Poland Foreign Policy & Government Guide.** Contrib. by Global Investment & Business Center, Inc. Staff. (World Foreign Policy & Government Library: Vol. 131). (Illus.). 350p. 1999. pap. 99.00 (*0-7397-3629-9*) Intl Business Pubns.

***Poland Foreign Policy & Government Guide.** Global Investment & Business Center, Inc. Staff. (World Foreign Policy & Government Library: Vol. 131). (Illus.). 350p. 2000. 99.95 (*0-7397-3835-6*) Intl Business Pubns.

***Poland Government & Business Contacts Handbook: Strategic Government & Business Contacts for Conducting Succesful Business, Export-Import & Investment Activity.** International Business Publications, USA Staff & Global Investment Center, USA Staff. (World Export-Import & Business Library: 110). (Illus.). 250p. 2000. pap. 99.95 (*0-7397-6099-8*) Intl Business Pubns.

Poland in a World in Change: Constitutions, Presidents & Politics. Ed. by Kenneth W. Thompson. (Miller Center Series on a World of Change: Vol. 4). 258p. (Orig.). (C). 1992. pap. text 29.00 (*0-8191-8518-3*); lib. bdg. 58.00 (*0-8191-8517-5*) U Pr of Amer.

Poland in Pictures. LC 93-10769. (J). 1994. lib. bdg. 19.95 (*0-8225-1885-6*, Lerner Publctns) Lerner Pub.

Poland in the British Parliament: Documentary Material Relating to the Cause of Poland During World War Two, 3 vols., 2. Pilsudski Institute of America Staff. Ed. by Waclaw Jedrzejewicz. 1834p. write for info. (*0-940962-26-8*) Polish Inst Art & Sci.

Poland in the British Parliament: Documentary Material Relating to the Cause of Poland During World War Two, 3 vols., 3. Pilsudski Institute of America Staff. Ed. by Waclaw Jedrzejewicz. 1834p. write for info. (*0-940962-27-6*) Polish Inst Art & Sci.

Poland in the Twentieth Century. Stachura. LC 98-49490. 180p. 1999. text 45.00 (*0-312-22027-8*) St Martin.

Poland in Transition, 1989-1991. David R. Pichaske. (Illus.). 256p. (Orig.). 1994. pap. 11.95 (*0-944024-27-0*) Ellis Pr.

Poland in World War II: An Illustrated Military History. Andrew Hempel. (Illus.). 150p. 2000. 11.95 (*0-7818-0758-1*) Hippocrene Bks.

***Poland Investment & Business Guide.** Global Investment & Business Center, Inc. Staff. (Global Investment & Business Guide Library: Vol. 137). (Illus.). 2000. pap. 99.95 (*0-7397-1835-5*) Intl Business Pubns.

Poland Investment & Business Guide: Economy, Export-Import, Business & Investment Climate, Business Contacts. Contrib. by Russian Information & Business Center, Inc. Staff. (Russia, NIS & Emerging Markets Investment & Business Library-98). (Illus.). 350p. 1998. pap. 99.00 (*1-57751-858-6*) Intl Business Pubns.

***Poland Investment & Business Guide: Export-Import, Investment & Business Opportunities.** International Business Publications, USA Staff & Global Investment Center, USA Staff. (World Investment & Business Guide Library-99: Vol. 137). (Illus.). 350p. 1999. pap. 99.95 (*0-7397-0332-3*) Intl Business Pubns.

Poland, Military Medals & Decorations, 1638-1940. Martin M. Kozlowski. (Illus.). 88p. 1989. pap. 10.00 (*0-929757-22-X*, Pub. by Militaria Hse) Trafalgar.

Poland, 1980 to 1982. Henri Simon. 1985. pap. 3.00 (*0-934868-26-3*) Black & Red.

Poland, 1944 to 1962: The Sovietization of a Captive People. Richard F. Staar. LC 75-1297. (Illus.). 300p. 1975. reprint ed. lib. bdg. 41.50 (*0-8371-8008-2*, STPO, Greenwood Pr) Greenwood.

Poland, 1946: The Photographs & Letters of John Vachon. Ed. by Ann Vachon. LC 95-17074. (Illus.). 188p. 1995. 45.00 (*1-56098-540-2*) Smithsonian.

Poland, 1992. (Country Profile Ser.). 142p. 1994. pap. 16.00 (*92-826-7026-0*, CA-80-93-105ENC, Pub. by Comm Europ Commun) Bernan Associates.

Poland, 1935 to 1947. John Coutouvidis & Jaime Reynolds. Ed. by Geoffrey Warner & David M. Ellwood. LC 86-14814. (Politics of Liberation Ser.). (Illus.). 393p. 1986. 65.00 (*0-8419-1093-6*) Holmes & Meier.

Poland, Nineteen Thirty-One. Jerome Rothenberg. LC 74-8646. (Illus.). 160p. 1974. pap. 3.25 (*0-8112-0542-8*, NDP379, Pub. by New Directions) Norton.

Poland Past & Present: Select Bibliography of Works in English. Norman Davies. (Illus.). 175p. 1976. lib. bdg. 26.00 (*0-89250-010-7*) Orient Res Partners.

Poland-Silesian Uprising, 1919-1921: Badges & Decorations - A Collectors Guide. J. Skoviera & Martin M. Kozlowski. (Illus.). 52p. (Orig.). (C). 1994. pap. 10.00 (*0-929757-46-7*, Pub. by Militaria Hse) Trafalgar.

Poland since 1956: Readings & Essays on Polish Government & Politics. Ed. by Tadeusz N. Cieplak. LC 79-125262. 482p. 1972. text 42.50 (*0-8290-0193-X*); pap. text 19.50 (*0-8290-0374-6*) Irvington.

Poland Spring to Summer. J. Cordoza. (Images of America Ser.). Date not set. pap. 16.99 (*0-7524-0442-3*) Arcadia Publng.

Poland, the Captive Satellite: A Study in National Psychology. Joseph W. Zurawski. (Illus.). 1962. 4.75 (*0-685-09286-0*) Endurance.

Poland to 2005. 1996. 695.00 (*0-614-25463-9*, P815) Econ Intel.

Poland to 2005. 1997. 515.00 (*0-85058-991-6*) Economist Intell.

Poland Today: The State of the Republic. Experience & the Future Discussion Group Staff. Tr. by Andrew Swidlicki. LC 81-8782. 255p. 1981. reprint ed. pap. 79.10 (*0-7837-9938-1*, 206066500006) Bks Demand.

Poland under Black Light. Janusz Anderman. Tr. by Andrew Short & Nina Taylor from POL. (Readers International Ser.). 131p. (Orig.). 1988. 12.50 (*0-930523-13-X*); pap. 6.95 (*0-930523-14-8*) Readers Intl.

Poland, What Have I to Do with Thee? Essays Without Prejudice. Raphael F. Scharf. LC 98-30088. 220p. 1998. pap. 25.00 (*0-85303-350-1*, Pub. by M Vallentine & Co) Intl Spec Bk.

Poland's Caribbean Tragedy: A Study of Polish Legions in the Haitian War of Independence 1802-1803. Jan Pachonski & Reuel K. Wilson. (East European Monographs: No. 199). (Illus.). 386p. 1986. text 63.00 (*0-88033-093-7*, Pub. by East Eur Monographs) Col U Pr.

Poland's Commitment to Its Past: A Report on 2 Study Tours. Krystyna Puc. LC 85-21716. (Illus.). 48p. (Orig.). 1985. pap. 7.00 (*0-941182-16-9*) Partners Livable.

Poland's Financial Services. Paczyriski. (Euromoney Country Guide Ser.). 183p. 1997. 170.00 (*1-85564-569-6*, Pub. by Euromoney) Am Educ Systs.

Poland's First Post-Communist Generation. K. Roberts & B. Jung. 240p. 1995. pap. 72.95 (*1-85628-897-8*, Pub. by Avebry) Ashgate Pub Co.

Poland's Ghettos at War. Alfred Katz. LC 78-120535. 1978. reprint ed. 37.50 (*0-8290-0194-8*); reprint ed. pap. text 12.95 (*0-8290-0195-6*) Irvington.

Poland's Gourmet Cuisine. Bernard Lussiana & Mary Pininska. (Illus.). 143p. 1999. 35.00 (*0-7818-0790-5*) Hippocrene Bks.

Poland's Holocaust: Ethnic Strife, Collaboration with Occupying Forces & Genocide in the Second Republic, 1918-1947. Tadeusz Piotrowski. LC 97-26233. (Illus.). 451p. 1997. boxed set 55.00 (*0-7864-0371-3*) McFarland & Co.

Poland's International Affairs, 1919-1960. Stephan M. Horak. LC 64-63009. (Indiana University Russian & East European Ser.: Vol. 31). 268p. reprint ed. 83.10 (*0-8357-9233-1*, 201545500094) Bks Demand.

Poland's Journalists: Professionalism & Politics. Jane L. Curry. (Cambridge Russian, Soviet & Post-Soviet Studies: No. 66). 312p. (C). 1990. text 69.95 (*0-521-36201-6*) Cambridge U Pr.

Poland's Jump to the Market Economy. Jeffrey D. Sachs. (Lionel Robbins Lectures). (Illus.). 144p. 1993. 24.00 (*0-262-19312-4*) MIT Pr.

Poland's Jump to the Market Economy. Jeffrey D. Sachs. (Lionel Robbins Lectures). 144p. 1994. pap. text 12.00 (*0-262-69174-4*) MIT Pr.

Poland's Last King & English Culture: Stanislaw August Poniatowski, 1732-1792. Richard Butterwick. (Oxford Historical Monographs). (Illus.). 400p. 1998. text 95.00 (*0-19-820701-8*) OUP.

Poland's Millenium of Christianity. Canadian Polish Millenium Fund Staff. (ENG & FRE.). 50p. 1966. 1.00 (*0-940962-29-2*) Polish Inst Art & Sci.

Poland's Navy, 1918-1945. Michael A. Peszke. (Illus.). 250p. 1999. reprint ed. 29.95 (*0-7818-0672-0*) Hippocrene Bks.

Poland's Permanent Revolution: People vs. Elites, 1956-1990. Ed. by Jane L. Curry & Luba Fajfer. 300p. (C). 1995. pap. text 30.50 (*1-879383-46-2*); lib. bdg. 71.50 (*1-879383-45-4*) Am Univ Pr.

Poland's Place in Europe: General Sikorski & the Origin of the Oder-Neisse Line, 1939-1943. Sarah M. Terry. LC 82-47617. 411p. 1983. reprint ed. pap. 127.50 (*0-7837-9459-2*, 206020100004) Bks Demand.

Poland's Politics: Idealism vs. Realism. Adam Bromke. LC 66-21331. (Harvard University, Russian Research Center Studies: Vol. 51). 330p. reprint ed. pap. 102.30 (*0-608-10068-4*, 201775400007) Bks Demand.

Poland's Protracted Transition: Institutional Change & Economic Growth, 1971-1993. Kazimierz Z. Poznanski. LC 97-160980. (Cambridge Russian, Soviet & Post-Soviet Studies: No. 98). 360p. (C). 1997. text 74.95 (*0-521-55396-2*); pap. text 29.95 (*0-521-55639-2*) Cambridge U Pr.

Poland's Self-Limiting Revolution. Jadwiga Staniszkis. Ed. by Jan T. Gross. LC 82-61387. 365p. 1984. reprint ed. pap. 113.20 (*0-7837-9452-5*, 206019400004) Bks Demand.

Polanski. John Parker. (Illus.). 288p. 1995. 29.95 (*0-575-05615-0*, Pub. by V Gollancz) Trafalgar.

Polar & Alpine Tundra. Ed. by F. E. Wielgolaski. LC 97-19344. (Ecosystems of the World Ser.: Vol. 3). 930p. 1997. text 497.00 (*0-444-88265-0*) Elsevier.

P

An Asterisk (*) at the beginning of an entry indicates that the title is appearing for the first time.

Polar & Arctic Lows. Ed. by Paul Twitchell et al. LC 89-23495. (Illus.). 421p. 1989. 81.00 (*0-937194-19-0*) A Deepak Pub.

Polar Animals. D. Harper. (Information Ser.). 32p. (J). text 3.50 (*0-7214-1747-7*, Ladybrd) Penguin Putnam.

Polar Animals. Paul Hess. (Illus.). 24p. (J). 1999. bds. 5.95 (*1-84089-167-X*) LKC.

Polar Animals. Preluts. LC 98-60344. (Animal Worlds Ser.). (Illus.). (J). (ps). 1998. 6.95 (*1-84089-009-6*, 868229) Zero to Ten.

Polar Attack: From Canada to the North Pole & Back. Richard Weber & Mikhail Malakhov. LC 97-122983. (Illus.). 232p. 1997. 24.95 (*0-7710-8902-3*) McCland & Stewart.

Polar Attack: From Canada to the North Pole, & Back. Richard Weber & Mikhail Malakhov. (Illus.). 232p. 1997. pap. 19.99 (*0-7710-8903-1*) McClelland & Stewart.

Polar Babies. Susan Ring. LC 98-49207. (Early Step into Reading Ser.). (Illus.). (J). 2000. lib. bdg. 11.99 (*0-679-99387-8*) Random.

Polar Bear see Osito Polar

***Polar Bear.** Sarah Jane Brian. (All-Star Readers Ser.). (Illus.). 48p. (J). (gr. 2-3). 2000. pap. 3.99 (*1-57584-660-8*, Pub. by Rdrs Digest) S&S Trade.

Polar Bear. Christine Economos. (American Museum of Natural History Book & Diorama Ser.). (Illus.). 64p. (J). (gr. 1-4). 1996. pap. 10.95 (*0-7611-0170-5*, 10170) Workman Pub.

Polar Bear. Photos & Pref. by Dan E. Guravich. (Illus.). 112p. 1993. pap. 18.95 (*0-8118-0204-3*) Chronicle Bks.

Polar Bear. Annie Hemstock. LC 98-3482. (Wildlife of North America Ser.). (Illus.). 48p. (J). 1998. 19.00 (*0-7368-0031-X*) Capstone Pr.

***Polar Bear.** Malcolm Perry. (Natural World Ser.). (J). 2000. pap. 7.95 (*0-7398-1816-3*) Raintree Steck-V.

***Polar Bear.** Jason Stoneking & Jody H. Stone. LC 00-8123. (Wild Bears! Ser.). (Illus.). 24p. (J). (ps-3). 2000. 16.95 (*1-56711-344-3*) Blackbirch.

Polar Bear, 10. Annie Hemstock. (Wildlife of North America Ser.). (J). 1998. 19.00 (*0-516-21483-7*) Childrens.

***Polar Bear: A Book of Postcards.** Photos by Norbert Rosing. (Illus.). 24p. 1998. pap. 9.95 (*1-55209-306-9*) Firefly Bks Ltd.

***Polar Bear: Habitats, Life Cycles, Food Chains, Threats.** Malcolm Penny. LC 99-32666. (Natural World Ser.). (Illus.). 48p. (J). (gr. 4-7). 2000. lib. bdg. 25.69 (*0-7398-1060-X*) Raintree Steck-V.

Polar Bear & Grizzly Bear. Rod Theodorou & Carole Telford. LC 96-7244. (Discover the Difference Ser.). (Illus.). (J). 1998. (*1-57572-105-8*) Heinemann Lib.

Polar Bear & His New Friend see Osito Polar y Su Nueva Amiga

***Polar Bear Biologist at Work.** Dorothy Hinshaw Patent. LC 00-38151. (Illus.). 2001. write for info. (*0-531-11850-9*) Watts.

Polar Bear Can Swim. Harriet Ziefert. LC 97-27542. (Lodestar Science Easy-to-Read Bk.). (Illus.). (J). 1998. write for info. (*0-525-67557-4*) NAL.

Polar Bear Can Swim. Harriet Ziefert. (Puffin Easy-to-Read Program Ser.). 32p. (J). (gr. k-3). 1998. pap. 3.99 (*0-14-038692-0*, PuffinBks) Peng Put Young Read.

Polar Bear Can Swim: What Animals Can & Cannot Do. Harriet Ziefert. LC 97-27542. (Illus.). (J). (gr. k-2). 1998. 13.89 (*0-670-88056-6*) Viking Penguin.

Polar Bear Family Book. Thor Larsen. (Illus.). 64p. (J). (gr. 1-5). 1996. pap. 8.95 (*1-55858-613-X*, Pub. by North-South Bks NYC) Chronicle Bks.

Polar Bear Journey. Debbie S. Miller. LC 96-42284. (Illus.). 32p. (J). (gr. k-3). 1997. 15.95 (*0-316-57244-6*) Little.

Polar Bear, Master of the Ice. Valerie Tracqui. LC 93-30167. (Animal Close-Ups Ser.). (Illus.). 28p. (J). (ps-3). 1994. pap. 6.95 (*0-88106-432-7*) Charlesbridge Pub.

Polar Bear, Master of the Ice. Valerie Tracqui. LC 93-30167. (Animal Close-Ups Ser.). (J). 1994. 12.15 (*0-606-06674-8*, Pub. by Turtleback) Demco.

Polar Bear, Polar Bear, What Do You Hear? Bill Martin, Jr. (Illus.). 32p. (J). (ps). 1995. 15.95 (*0-8050-1759-3*, Bks Young Read) H Holt & Co.

Polar Bear, Polar Bear, What Do You Hear? Bill Martin, Jr. (Illus.). 32p. (J). (ps-2). 1995. pap. 16.95 (*0-8050-2815-3*, Bks Young Read) H Holt & Co.

Polar Bear, Polar Bear, What Do You Hear? Bill Martin, Jr. (Illus.). (J). 1997. bds. 6.95 (*0-8050-5388-3*) H Holt & Co.

Polar Bear, Polar Bear, What Do You Hear? Big Book. Bill Martin, Jr. LC 91-13322. (Illus.). 32p. (J). (ps-2). 1995. pap. 19.95 (*0-8050-2346-1*, Bks Young Read) H Holt & Co.

Polar Bear Reflections. Ken Jenkins. LC 96-51620. (Reflections of the Wilderness Ser.). (Illus.). 64p. (Orig.). 1999. pap. 11.95 (*1-57034-068-4*) Globe Pequot.

Polar Bear Son: An Inuit Tale. Lydia Dabcovich. (FRE., Illus.). 32p. (J). (ps-2). 1999. pap. 5.95 (*0-395-97567-0*) HM.

***Polar Bear Son: An Inuit Tale.** Lydia Dabcovich. LC 96-4780. (Illus.). 32p. (J). (ps-2). 1999. 16.00 (*0-395-72766-9*, Clarion Bks) HM.

Polar Bear Strategy: Reflections on Risk in Modern Life. John F. Ross. LC HM1101.R67 1999. 288p. 1999. 23.00 (*0-7382-0117-0*, Pub. by Perseus Pubng) HarpC.

Polar Bear Who Hated Snow. Linda Garber. (Illus.). 55p. (J). (gr. 2-5). 1998. pap. 9.95 (*1-892218-00-3*) Murlin Pubns.

Polar Bears see Zoobooks

Polar Bears see Osos Polares

Polar Bears. Susan Canizares et al. LC 97-34209. (Science Emergent Readers Ser.). (J). 1998. pap. 3.50 (*0-590-76153-6*) Scholastic Inc.

Polar Bears. Lesley A. Dutemple. LC 97-4131. (Early Bird Nature Bks.). (Illus.). (J). (ps-4). 1997. lib. bdg. 19.95 (*0-8225-3025-2*, Lerner Publctns) Lerner Pub.

Polar Bears. Freeman. LC 98-19943. (J). 1998. 14.00 (*0-7368-0099-9*, Pebble Bks) Capstone Pr.

Polar Bears. Marcia S. Freeman. (J). 1998. 13.25 (*0-516-21487-X*) Childrens.

Polar Bears. Diana S. Helmer. LC 96-47207. (Bears of the World Ser.). (J). 1997. lib. bdg. 17.27 (*0-8239-5130-8*, PowerKids) Rosen Group.

Polar Bears. Stuart A. Kallen. LC 95-52341. (Bears Ser.). (J). 1997. lib. bdg. 13.98 (*1-56239-593-9*) ABDO Pub Co.

Polar Bears. Emilie U. Lepthien. LC 91-8892. (New True Books Ser.). (Illus.). 48p. (J). (ps-3). 1991. pap. 5.50 (*0-516-41127-6*); lib. bdg. 21.00 (*0-516-01127-8*) Childrens.

Polar Bears. Nikita Ovsyanikov. LC 98-3431. (Worldlife Library). 72p. (YA). 1998. pap. 16.95 (*0-89658-358-9*) Voyageur Pr.

Polar Bears. Sarah Palmer. (Sea Mammal Discovery Library). (Illus.). 24p. (J). (gr. k-4). 1989. lib. bdg. 14.60 (*0-86592-360-4*) Rourke Enter.

***Polar Bears.** Dorothy Hinshaw Patent. LC 99-29601. (Nature Watch Ser.). (Illus.). 48p. (J). (gr. 2-7). 2000. 22.60 (*1-57505-020-X*, Carolrhoda) Lerner Pub.

Polar Bears. Wendy Pfeffer. LC 95-25790. (Creatures in White Ser.). (Illus.). 32p. (J). 1996. pap. 5.95 (*0-382-39326-0*); lib. bdg. 14.95 (*0-382-39327-9*) Silver Burdett Pr.

***Polar Bears.** Ian Stirling. LC 88-14244. (Illus.). 232p. 1998. pap. 27.95 (*0-472-08108-X*, 08108) U of Mich Pr.

Polar Bears. Wildlife Education, Ltd. Staff. (Illus.). 20p. (J). (gr. k-12). 1997. pap. 2.75 (*0-937934-36-4*) Wildlife Educ.

Polar Bears. Wildlife Education, Ltd. Staff & Timothy Levibiel. (Zoobooks Ser.). (Illus.). 24p. (J). 1993. 13.95 (*0-937934-85-2*) Wildlife Educ.

Polar Bears: Living with the White Bear. Nikita Ovsyanikov. LC 96-33764. (Illus.). 144p. 1996. 29.95 (*0-89658-323-6*) Voyageur Pr.

Polar Bears: Living with the White Bear. Nikita Ovsyanikov. LC 96-33764. (Illus.). 144p. 1999. pap. 19.95 (*0-89658-426-7*) Voyageur Pr.

Polar Bears: Monty's Left Flank: From Normandy to the Relief of Holland with the 49th Division. Patrick Delaforce. LC 96-212600. (British Army Divisional History Ser.). (Illus.). 240p. 1996. pap. 19.95 (*0-7509-1062-3*, Pub. by Sutton Pub Ltd) Intl Pubs Mktg.

Polar Bears: Proceedings of the 10th Working Meeting of the IUCN-SSC Polar Bear Specialist Group. Ed. by Oystein Wiig. (Occasional Papers of the IUCN Species Survival Commission). (Illus.). 107p. (Orig.). 1991. pap. 22.00 (*2-8317-0039-6*, Pub. by IUCN) Island Pr.

Polar Bears Past Bedtime. Mary Pope Osborne. LC 97-15624. (Magic Tree House Ser.: No. 12). (Illus.). (J). (gr. k-3). 1998. pap. 3.99 (*0-679-88341-X*, Pub. by Random Bks Yng Read); lib. bdg. 11.99 (*0-679-98341-4*, Pub. by Random Bks Yng Read) Random.

***Polar Bears Past Bedtime, 12.** Mary Pope Osborne. (Magic Tree House Ser.: No. 12). (Illus.). (J). (gr. k-3). 1998. 9.09 (*0-606-13018-7*, Pub. by Turtleback) Demco.

***Polar Bolero: A Bedtime Dance.** Debi Gliori. LC 00-9183. (Illus.). (J). 2000. write for info. (*0-15-202436-0*, Harcourt Child Bks) Harcourt.

Polar Cap Boundary Phenomena: Proceedings of the NATO Advanced Study Institute on Polar Cap Boundary Phenomena, Longyearbyen, 4-13 June 1997. Advanced Study Institute on Polar Cap Boundary Phe et al. LC 98-9255. (NATO ASI Ser.). 1998. 184.00 (*0-7923-4976-8*) Kluwer Academic.

Polar Cusp. Ed. by Jan Anstein Holtet & Alv Egeland. (NATO Advanced Study Institutes Series C, Mathematical & Physical Sciences). 1985. text 195.50 (*90-277-1923-3*) Kluwer Academic.

Polar Dance: Born of the North Wind. Photos by Thomas D. Mangelsen. LC 97-71666. (Illus.). 264p. 1997. 65.00 (*1-890310-03-4*) Thomas D Mangelsen Inc Images.

Polar Dance: Born of the North Wind. deluxe ed. Thomas D. Mangelsen & Fred Bruemmer. (Illus.). 264p. 1997. 65.00 (*0-9633080-8-4*) Thomas D Mangelsen Inc Images.

Polar Exploration: Journeys to the Arctic & Antarctic. LC 98-4221. (J). 1998. 14.95 (*0-7894-3421-0*) DK Pub Inc.

***Polar Exploration Adventures.** Barbara Saffer. (Dangerous Adventures Ser.). 48p. (YA). (gr. 5 up). 2000. lib. bdg. 21.26 (*0-7368-0572-9*, Capstone Bks) Capstone Pr.

***Polar Express.** (J). 1999. 9.95 (*1-56137-196-3*) Novel Units.

Polar Express. Susan Kilpatrick. (Literature Unit Ser.). 48p. 1996. pap., teacher ed. 7.95 (*1-55734-543-0*) Tchr Create Mat.

Polar Express, 001. Chris Van Allsburg. LC 85-10907. (Illus.). 32p. (J). (gr. 2 up). 1985. 18.95 (*0-395-38949-6*) HM.

***Polar Express.** 15th anniversary ed. Allsburg C. Van. 2000. 29.95 (*0-618-07736-7*) HM.

Polar Express: Gift Set. Chris Van Allsburg & William Hurt. (Illus.). 32p. (J). (gr. 2 up). 1989. 24.95 incl. audio (*0-395-48880-X*) HM.

Polar Journeys: The Role of Food & Nutrition in Early Exploration. Robert E. Feeney. LC 97-49810. (Illus.). xxx, 279p. 1998. pap. 27.95 (*0-912006-97-8*, 6978) U of Alaska Pr.

***Polar Journeys: The Role of Food & Nutrition in Early Explorations.** Robert E. Feeney. LC 97-49810. (An American Chemical Society & University of Alaska Press Co-Publication). 258p. 1998. text 41.95 (*0-8412-3349-7*, Pub. by Am Chemical) OUP.

Polar Knight: The Mystery of Sir John Franklin. B. J. Rule. LC 98-22705. 1998. pap. 14.95 (*1-877633-40-2*) Luthers.

Polar Lands. Rodney Aldis. LC 91-34170. (Ecology Watch Ser.). (Illus.). 48p. (J). (gr. 5 up). 1992. lib. bdg. 13.95 (*0-87518-494-4*, Dillon Silver Burdett) Silver Burdett Pr.

Polar Lands. World Book Staff & Monica Byles. LC 98-3593. (Interfact Ser.). (Illus.). 48p. (J). (gr. 2-8). 1998. spiral bd. write for info. incl. cd-rom (*0-7166-7227-8*) World Bk.

Polar Mammals. (True Bk.). (Illus.). 48p. (J). (gr. 2-4). 1996. lib. bdg. 21.00 (*0-516-20042-9*) Childrens.

Polar Mammals. Larry D. Brimner. LC 96-34192. (True Bks.). 48p. (J). 1997. pap. 6.95 (*0-516-26112-6*) Childrens.

Polar Marine Diatoms. L. Medlin & J. Priddle. (Illus.). 214p. 1990. 45.00 (*0-85665-140-0*, Pub. by Brit Antarctic Surv) Balogh.

Polar Oceanography, 2 vols. Smith. 1990. 219.00 (*0-12-653030-0*) Acad Pr.

Polar Oceanography Pt. A: Physical Science. Ed. by Walker O. Smith, Jr. 406p. 1990. text 110.00 (*0-12-653031-9*) Acad Pr.

Polar Oceanography Pt. B: Chemistry, Biology, Geology. Ed. by Walker O. Smith, Jr. 353p. 1990. text 110.00 (*0-12-653032-7*) Acad Pr.

Polar Oceans & Their Role in Shaping the Global Environment: The Nansen Centennial Volume. Ed. by O. M. Johannessen et al. LC 94-35047. (Geophysical Monographs: Vol. 85). 540p. 1994. 70.00 (*0-87590-042-9*) Am Geophysical.

Polar Orbiter Satellite Imagery Interpretation. National Environmental Satellite, Data & Informati & Satellite Applications Lab Staff. (NWA Publication: No. 2-88). 42p. (C). 1988. pap. text 84.00 incl. sl. (*1-883563-06-2*) Natl Weather.

Polar Passage. Jeff MacInnis & Wade Rowland. 224p. 1990. mass mkt. 4.95 (*0-8041-0650-9*) Ivy Books.

Polar Peoples: Native Inhabitants of the Far North. Ian Creery et al. LC 94-204813. (Orig.). pap. 24.95 (*1-873194-51-X*, Pub. by Minority Rts Pubns) Paul & Co Pubs.

Polar Peoples: Native Inhabitants of the Far North. Ian Creery et al. (Illus.). 250p. (Orig.). 1994. text 49.95 (*1-873194-55-2*, Pub. by Minority Rts Pubns); pap. text 19.95 (*1-873194-50-1*, Pub. by Minority Rts Pubns) Paul & Co Pubs.

Polar Pioneers: John Ross & James Clark Ross. M. J. Ross. (Illus.). 464p. 1994. 32.95 (*0-7735-1234-9*, Pub. by McG-Queens Univ Pr) CUP Services.

Polar Politics: Creating International Environmental Regimes. Ed. by Oran R. Young & Gail Osherenko. LC 92-54972. (Cornell Studies in Political Economy). (Illus.). 304p. 1993. text 45.00 (*0-8014-2793-2*); pap. text 18.95 (*0-8014-8069-8*) Cornell U Pr.

Polar Rearrangements. L. M. Harwood. (Oxford Chemistry Primers Ser.: No. 5). (Illus.). 100p. (C). 1992. pap. text 12.95 (*0-19-855670-5*) OUP.

***Polar Regions.** (Exploration Into... Ser.). (Illus.). (J). 2000. 17.95 (*0-7910-6026-8*) Chelsea Hse.

Polar Regions. Gilda Berger. (Smart Science Ser.). (Illus.). 16p. (J). (gr. 2-5). Date not set. pap. 5.95 (*1-58273-509-3*) Newbridge Educ.

Polar Regions. Nigel Bonner. (Habitats Ser.). (Illus.). 48p. (J). (gr. 4-6). 1995. lib. bdg. 24.26 (*1-56847-386-9*) Raintree Steck-V.

Polar Regions. Mel Higginson. (This Earth of Ours Discovery Library). 24p. (J). (gr. k-4). 1994. lib. bdg. 10.95 (*0-86593-378-2*) Rourke Corp.

Polar Regions. David Lambert. (Our World Ser.). (Illus.). 48p. (J). (gr. 5-8). 1987. lib. bdg. 12.95 (*0-382-09502-2*) Silver Burdett Pr.

***Polar Regions,** Quadrillion Media Staff. (Start Me Up Ser.: Vol. 13). (Illus.). 2000. 12.95 (*1-58185-017-4*) Quadrillion Media.

Polar Regions. Claire Watts. (Launch Pad Library). (Illus.). 32p. (J). (gr. k-4). 1998. 11.95 (*1-58087-004-X*) C D Stampley Ent.

Polar Regions. John Richardson. LC 74-5869. reprint ed. 39.50 (*0-404-11676-0*) AMS Pr.

Polar Regions: A Political Geography. Sanjay Chaturvedi. LC 95-44829. (Polar Research Ser.). 330p. 1996. 145.00 (*0-471-94898-5*) Wiley.

Polar Regions: Geographical & Historical Data for Consideration in a Study of Claims to Sovereignty in the Arctic & Antarctic Regions. Samuel W. Boggs. LC 89-85449. (Illus.). 138p. 1990. reprint ed. lib. bdg. 37.50 (*0-89941-726-4*, 306380) W S Hein.

Polar Regions Activity Book: Explore the Arctic & Antarctic Through Arts & Crafts - Grades 3-6. Mary J. Keller. Ed. by Kathy Rogers. (Illus.). 48p. 1995. pap., wbk. ed. 6.95 (*1-56472-066-7*) Edupress Inc.

Polar Regions & the Development of International Law. Donald R. Rothwell. (Cambridge Studies in International & Comparative Law). 530p. (C). 1996. text 95.00 (*0-521-56182-5*) Cambridge U Pr.

Polar Regions Photo Fun Activities. Mary Jo Keller. Ed. by Kathy Rogers. (Social Studies Photo Fun Activities Ser.). (Illus.). 8p. 1995. 6.95 (*1-56472-067-5*) Edupress Inc.

Polar Seas. Malcolm Penny. LC 96-27732. (Seas & Oceans Ser.). 48p. (J). 1997. lib. bdg. 24.26 (*0-8172-4513-8*) Raintree Steck-V.

Polar Seas Encyclopedia Coloring Book. Julia Pinkham. (NaturEncyclopedia Ser.). (Illus.). 48p. (Orig.). 1996. pap. 6.95 (*0-88045-120-3*) Stemmer Hse.

***Polar Star.** Sally Grindley. (Illus.). 32p. (J). (ps-3). 1999. (*1-84121-149-4*) Orchard Bks.

Polar Star. Sally Grindley. LC 97-52593. (Illus.). 32p. (J). (ps-3). 1998. 15.95 (*1-56145-181-9*) Peachtree Pubs.

Polar Star. Martin Cruz Smith. 384p. 1990. mass mkt. 5.99 (*0-345-36765-0*) Ballantine Pub Grp.

***Polar Star.** Martin Cruz Smith. 2000. mass mkt. 6.99 (*0-345-91706-5*) Ballantine Pub Grp.

Polar Star. large type ed. Martin Cruz Smith. LC 90-10735. 571p. 1990. pap. 14.95 (*0-89621-981-X*) Thorndike Pr.

Polar Structures in the Book of Qohelet. Jamer A. Loader. (Beiheft zur Zeitschrift fuer die Alttestamentliche Wissenschaft Ser.). 150p. (C). 1979. text 65.40 (*3-11-007636-5*) De Gruyter.

Polar Sun. Sandi Piccione. LC 79-4685. 1979. pap. 4.00 (*0-918366-12-7*) Slow Loris.

Polar the Titanic Bear. Daisy C. S. Spedden. LC 94-75240. (Illus.). 64p. (J). (gr. 3-7). 1994. 17.95 (*0-316-80625-0*) Little.

Polar the Titanic Bear. Daisy C. S. Spedden. 1998. 17.95 (*0-316-80924-1*) Little.

Polar Tourism: Tourism in the Arctic & Antarctic Regions. Ed. by Colin M. Hall & Margaret E. Johnston. LC 94-32093. 346p. 1995. 135.00 (*0-471-94921-3*) Wiley.

Polar Twins: Scottish History & Scottish Literature. E. W. Cowan. 230p. 1998. pap. 45.00 (*0-85976-494-X*, Pub. by J Donald) St Mut.

Polar Wandering & Continental Drift. Ed. by Arthur C. Munyan. LC 64-6318. (Society of Economic Paleontologists & Mineralogists, Special Publication Ser.: No. 10). 175p. reprint ed. pap. 54.30 (*0-608-12957-7*, 202473600038) Bks Demand.

Polar Wildlife. Jinny Johnson. (Up-Close Ser.). (Illus.). 24p. (J). (gr. 4-7). 1993. 9.95 (*0-89577-538-7*) RD Assn.

Polar Wildlife. Kamini Khanduri. (World Wildlife Ser.). (Illus.). 32p. (J). (gr. 3-7). 1993. pap. 6.95 (*0-7460-0938-0*); lib. bdg. 14.95 (*0-88110-601-1*) EDC.

Polaria: The Gift of the White Stone. W. H. Muller. (Illus.). 210p. (Orig.). 1996. pap. 14.95 (*0-914732-34-X*) Bro Life Inc.

***Polarimetric Doppler Weather Radar: Principles & Applications.** V. N. Bringi & V. Chandrasekar. (Illus.). 500p. 2000. write for info. (*0-521-62384-7*) Cambridge U Pr.

Polarimetry & Ellipsometry, Vol. 3094. Ed. by Maksymilian Pluta & Tomasz R. Wolinski. LC 97-200960. 392p. 1997. 80.00 (*0-8194-2509-5*) SPIE.

Polarimetry of the Interstellar Medium, Vol. 97. Ed. by W. G. Roberge & D. C. Whillet. (ASP Conference Series Proceedings). 632p. 1996. 34.00 (*1-886733-18-X*) Astron Soc Pacific.

Polaris ATV Shop Manual, 1985-1995. LC 96-75544. (Illus.). 424p. 1996. pap. 28.95 (*0-89287-668-9*, M496) Intertec Pub.

Polaris, 1984-1989. (Illus.). 488p. Date not set. reprint ed. pap. 34.95 (*0-89287-537-2*, S832) Intertec Pub.

Polaris, 1990-1995. LC 94-79862. (Illus.). 608p. Date not set. reprint ed. pap. 34.95 (*0-89287-649-2*, S833) Intertec Pub.

Polaris Personal Watercraft, 1992-97, Vol. 4. Seloc Publications Staff. LC 98-158124. (Marine Tune-Up & Repair Manuals). (C). 1998. pap. text 34.95 (*0-89330-045-4*, Pub. by Seloc) Natl Bk Netwk.

Polaris System Development: Bureaucratic & Programmatic Success in Government. Harvey M. Sapolsky. LC 72-79311. (Illus.). 281p. 1972. 36.50 (*0-674-68225-4*) HUP.

Polaris, the Robot King. Lane Riosley. (Lucky Hightops & the Cosmic Cat Patrol Ser.: No. 3). (Illus.). (J). (gr. 2-8). pap. 3.00 (*1-57514-269-4*, 1028) Encore Perform Pub.

Polaris Water Vehicles, 1992-1995. LC 96-77869. (Illus.). 296p. 1996. pap. 36.95 (*0-89287-672-7*, W819) Intertec Pub.

Polaris Writings. Shannon D. Russell & Toni N. Russell. 187p. (Orig.). 1997. pap. 12.95 (*0-9657274-0-8*) Nrth Star Pub.

***Polarisation de la Lumiere et L'observation Astronomique.** Jean-Louis Leroy. 212p. 1998. text 70.00 (*90-5699-110-8*, Harwood Acad Pubs); pap. text 30.00 (*90-5699-111-6*, Harwood Acad Pubs) Gordon & Breach.

Polarisation of Elizabethan Politics: The Political Career of Robert Devereux, 2nd Earl of Essex, 1585-1597. Paul E. Hammer. LC 98-35139. (Cambridge Studies in Early Modern British History). (Illus.). 398p. (C). 1999. text 69.95 (*0-521-43485-8*) Cambridge U Pr.

Polarities. David R. Pichaske. (Illus.). 28p. (Orig.). 1997. pap. 9.95 (*0-944024-34-3*) Spoon Riv Poetry.

Polarities in the Evolution of Mankind: West & East, Materialism & Mysticism, Knowledge & Belief. Rudolf Steiner. 183p. 1987. 20.00 (*0-88010-214-4*, 1175) Anthroposophic.

Polarities in the Evolution of Mankind: West & East, Materialism & Mysticism, Knowledge & Belief. Rudolf Steiner. 183p. 1990. pap. 12.95 (*0-88010-556-9*, 1175) Anthroposophic.

Polarities of Human Existence in Biblical Perspective. rev. ed. Frank Stagg. 208p. 1994. reprint ed. pap. 17.00 (*1-880837-49-8*) Smyth & Helwys.

Polariton - Mediated Light Scattering & Electronic Structure of Noble Metals. Bernard Bendow & B. Langeler. (Tracts in Modern Physics Ser.: Vol. 82). (Illus.). 1978. 36.95 (*0-387-08814-8*) Spr-Verlag.

Polarity & Analogy. 1987. 50.00 (*0-8453-4517-6*) Assoc Univ Prs.

Polarity & Analogy: Two Types of Argumentation in Early Greek Thought. G. E. Lloyd. LC 92-17832. 512p. (C). 1992. reprint ed. pap. text 16.95 (*0-87220-140-6*) Hackett Pub.

Polarity Control for Synthesis. Tse-Lok Ho. LC 90-23148. 403p. 1991. 125.00 (*0-471-53850-7*) Wiley.

Polarity, Dialectic, & Organicity. Archie J. Bahm. LC 77-81834. 293p. 1976. reprint ed. pap. 10.00 (*0-911714-18-9*) World Bks.

Polarity Management: Identifying & Managing Unsolvable Problems. Barry Johnson. 250p. 1992. pap. 24.95 (*0-87425-176-1*) HRD Press.

P

An Asterisk (*) at the beginning of an entry indicates that the title is appearing for the first time.

Polarity of Mexican Thought. Michael A. Weinstein. LC 76-23159. 1977. 28.50 (*0-271-01232-3*) Pa St U Pr.

Polarity Process. Franklyn Sills. 1993. pap. 15.95 (*1-85230-052-3*, Pub. by Element MA) Penguin Putnam.

Polarity Sensitivity As (Non) Veridical Dependency. Anastasia Giannakidou. LC 98-39786. (Linguistik Aktuell/Linguistics Today Ser.: Vol. 23). xvi, 282p. 1998. 60.00 (*1-55619-907-4*) J Benjamins Pubng Co.

Polarity Therapy, Vol. 1. Randolph Stone. 1999. pap. text 35.00 (*1-57067-079-X*) Book Pub Co.

Polarity Therapy, Vol. 2. Randolph Stone. 240p. 1999. pap. text 35.00 (*1-57067-080-3*) Book Pub Co.

Polarity Therapy: The Complete Collected Works, Vol. 1. Randolph Stone. LC 84-71548. (Illus.). 330p. 1986. pap. 35.00 (*0-916360-48-2*) CRCS Pubns CA.

Polarity Therapy: The Complete Collected Works, Vol. 2. Randolph Stone. LC 84-71548. (Illus.). 240p. 1987. pap. 35.00 (*0-916360-25-3*) CRCS Pubns CA.

Polarity Therapy Workbook. John Beaulou. 225p. 1994. write for info. (*0-9640604-0-X*) Bio Sonic Ent.

Polarization: Measurement, Analysis & Remote Sensing. Ed. by Dennis H. Goldstein & Russell A. Chipman. 74p. 1997. pap. 116.00 (*0-8194-2543-5*) SPIE.

***Polarization, Alignment & Orientation in Atomic Collisions.** Nils Anderson. (Illus.). 2000. write for info. (*0-387-98989-7*) Spr-Verlag.

***Polarization & Color Techniques in Industrial Inspection.** Ed. by Elsbieta A. Marszalec & Emanuele Trucco. 324p. 1999. pap. text 72.00 (*0-8194-3312-8*) SPIE.

Polarization & Intensity of Light in the Atmosphere. Kinsell L. Coulson. LC 88-25698. 596p. 1988. 105.00 (*0-937194-12-3*) A Deepak Pub.

Polarization Bremsstrahlung. V. N. Tstovich & I. M. Oiringel. (Physics of Atoms & Molecules Ser.). (Illus.). 396p. (C). 1992. text 110.00 (*0-306-44217-5*, Kluwer Plenum) Kluwer Academic.

Polarization Dynamics in Nuclear & Particle Physics. Asim O. Barut et al. 450p. 1993. text 121.00 (*981-02-1423-5*) World Scientific Pub.

Polarization in Antennas & Radar. Harold Mott. LC 86-1349. 320p. 1986. 162.50 (*0-471-01167-3*) Wiley.

Polarization Interferometers: Applications in Microscopy & Macroscopy. Maurice Francon & S. Mallick. LC 75-147194. (Wiley Series in Pure & Applied Optics). 172p. reprint ed. pap. 53.40 (*0-608-14055-4*, 202402100035) Bks Demand.

Polarization Method of Seismic Studies. E. I. Galperin. 1983. text 206.50 (*90-277-1555-6*) Kluwer Academic.

Polarization of Light. Serge Huard. LC 96-9365. 348p. 1997. 185.00 (*0-471-96536-7*) Wiley.

Polarization of Light in Nonlinear Optics. Yu P. Svirko & N. I. Zheludev. LC 98-8795. 240p. 1998. 140.00 (*0-471-97640-7*) Wiley.

Polarization of the Vacuum & a Quantum Relativistic Gas in an Extreme Field. A. Y. Shabad. (Proceedings of the Lebedev Physics Institute Ser.: Vol. 191). (Illus.). 231p. (C). 1991. pap. text 175.00 (*1-56072-044-1*) Nova Sci Pubs.

Polarization Phenomena in Nuclear Physics: 8th International Symposium, Vol. CP 339. Edward J. Stephenson & Steven E. Vigdor. (AIP Conference Proceedings Ser.). (Illus.). 816p. 1995. 145.00 (*1-56396-482-1*) Am Inst Physics.

Polarization Phenomena in Nuclear Physics, 1980: 5th International Symposium, Santa Fe. Ed. by G. G. Ohlsen et al. (AIP Conference Proceedings Ser.: No. 69). 1536p. 1981. lib. bdg. 84.00 (*0-88318-168-1*) Am Inst Physics.

Polarization Phenomena in Nuclear Reactions: Proceedings. International Symposium on Polarization Phenomena. Ed. by Henry H. Barschall & W. Haeberli. LC 71-143762. (Illus.). 960p. 1971. reprint ed. pap. 200.00 (*0-7837-6662-9*, 204627400011) Bks Demand.

Polarization Properties of Liquid Crystals, Vol. 11. S. A. Pikin et al. (Soviet Scientific Reviews Ser.: Vol. 11, Pt. 3). ii, 100p. 1989. pap. text 107.00 (*3-7186-4904-7*) Gordon & Breach.

Polarization Spectroscopy of Ionized Gases. S. A. Kazantsev & J. C. Henoux. LC 95-12384. (Astrophysics & Space Science Library: Vol. 200). 1995. text 118.00 (*0-7923-3474-4*) Kluwer Academic.

Polarized Beams & Polarized Gas Targets: Proceedings of the International Workshop. 476p. 1996. 59.00 (*981-02-2592-X*) World Scientific Pub.

Polarized Beams at SCC & Polarized Antiprotons. Ed. by Alan D. Krisch et al. LC 86-71343. (AIP Conference Proceedings Ser.: No.145). 270p. 1986. lib. bdg. 60.00 (*0-88318-344-7*) Am Inst Physics.

Polarized Collider Workshop. Ed. by John Collins et al. LC 91-71303. (AIP Conference Proceedings Ser.: No. 223, 42). (Illus.). 400p. 1991. lib. bdg. 95.00 (*0-88318-826-0*) Am Inst Physics.

Polarized Development & Regional Policies. Ed. by Antoni Kuklinski. 518p. 1981. 107.70 (*90-279-3099-6*) Mouton.

Polarized Electron/Polarized Photon Physics: Proceedings of Two United Kingdom Engineering & Physical Science Research Committee Workshops Held in York, England, September 22-23, 1993 & April 15-16, 1994. H. Kleinpoppen & W. R. Newell. LC 95-37115. (Physics of Atoms & Molecules Ser.). (Illus.). 364p. (C). 1995. text 114.00 (*0-306-45131-X*, Kluwer Plenum) Kluwer Academic.

Polarized Electrons. 2nd ed. J. Kessler. (Atoms & Plasmas Ser.: Vol. 1). (Illus.). 310p. 1985. 86.95 (*0-387-15736-0*) Spr-Verlag.

Polarized Electrons in Surface Physics. Ed. by R. Feder. (Advanced Series in Surface Science: Vol. 1). 632p. 1986. pap. 47.00 (*9971-978-50-4*); text 127.00 (*9971-978-49-0*) World Scientific Pub.

Polarized Gas Targets & Polarized Beams: Seventh International Workshop. Ed. by Roy J. Holt & Michael A. Miller. LC 97-78196. (AIP Conference Proceedings Ser.: Vol. 421). (Illus.). xv, 549p. 1998. 145.00 (*1-56396-700-6*) Am Inst Physics.

Polarized Ion Sources & Polarized Gas Targets. Ed. by L. W. Anderson. (AIP Conference Proceedings Ser.: No. 293). 320p. 1994. text 288.00 (*1-56396-220-9*) Am Inst Physics.

Polarized Law (With an English Translation of the Hague Conventions on Private International Law) Three Lectures on Conflicts of Law, Delivered at the University of London. T. Baty. (Legal Reprint Ser.). xv, 210p. 1986. reprint ed. 35.00 (*0-421-35520-4*) W S Hein.

Polarized Light: Production & Use. William A. Shurcliff. LC 62-11405. 218p. reprint ed. pap. 67.60 (*0-608-30595-2*, 205198000023) Bks Demand.

Polarized Light & Optical Measurements. D. Clarke & J. F. Grainger. 1971. 94.00 (*0-08-016320-3*, Pub. by Pergamon Repr) Franklin.

Polarized Light in Optics & Spectroscopy. David S. Kliger et al. 304p. 1990. text 71.00 (*0-12-414975-8*) Acad Pr.

Polarized Light Microscopy. 8th ed. Walter C. McCrone et al. LC 78-61047. (Illus.). 1979. 39.50 (*0-250-40262-9*) Microscope Pubns.

Polarized Neutron Reflectometry on Thin Magnetic Films. Anja Van Der Graaf. (Illus.). 142p. 1997. pap. 45.00 (*90-407-1526-2*, Pub. by Delft U Pr) Coronet Bks.

Polarized Neutrons. W. Gavin Williams. (Oxford Series on Neutron Scattering in Condensed Matter: No. 1). (Illus.). 360p. 1988. 85.00 (*0-19-851005-5*) OUP.

***Polarized Politics: Congress & the President in a Partisan Era.** Jon R. Bond & Richard Fleisher. LC 99-59253. 2000. 24.95 (*1-56802-493-2*) Congr Quarterly.

Polarized Proton Ion Sources: Ann Arbor, 1981. Ed. by Alan D. Krisch & A. M. Lin. LC 82-71025. (AIP Conference Proceedings Ser.: No. 80). 214p. 1982. lib. bdg. 30.00 (*0-88318-179-7*) Am Inst Physics.

Polarized Proton Ion Sources: Conference Proceedings, TRIUMF, Vancouver, 1983. Ed. by G. Roy & P. Schmor. LC 84-71235. (AIP Conference Proceedings Ser.: No. 117). 209p. 1984. lib. bdg. 37.00 (*0-88318-316-1*) Am Inst Physics.

Polarized Radiation of Circumstellar Origin. Ed. by George V. Coyne et al. 795p. 1989. pap. 48.00 (*0-8165-1120-9*) U of Ariz Pr.

Polarized Spectroscopy of Ordered Systems. Ed. by B. Samori & Erik W. Thulstrup. (C). 1988. text 282.00 (*90-277-2784-8*) Kluwer Academic.

***Polarizing Mexico: The Impact of Liberalization Strategy.** Enrique Dussel Peters. (Critical Perspectives on Latin America's Economy & Society Ser.). 210p. 2000. lib. bdg. 49.95 (*1-55587-861-X*) L Rienner.

Polarografia. (Serie de Quimica: No. 13). (SPA.). 1974. pap. 3.50 (*0-8270-6385-7*) OAS.

Polarographic Oxygen Sensor: Its Theory of Operation & Its Application in Biology, Medicine & Technology. Irving Fatt. LC 82-6581. 290p. (Orig.). 1982. reprint ed. 59.95 (*0-89874-511-X*) Krieger.

Polarographic Techniques. 2nd ed. Louis Meites. LC 65-19735. (Illus.). 770p. reprint ed. pap. 200.00 (*0-608-18196-X*, 205659800078) Bks Demand.

Polaroid: And Other Poems of View. Betsy G. Hearne. LC 90-45577. (Illus.). 80p. (YA). (gr. 7-12). 1991. 13.95 (*0-689-50530-2*) McElderry Bks.

Polaroid Education Program: Lesson Plan - Activity Book. Ed. by John Schaefer. 1989. pap. text 7.00 (*0-9629348-0-1*) Polaroid Ed.

Polaroid Man. Michael Cormany. 1991. 15.95 (*1-55972-069-7*, Birch Ln Pr) Carol Pub Group.

Polaroid Man. Michael Cormany. 240p. 1993. reprint ed. mass mkt. 3.99 (*0-8439-3542-1*) Dorchester Pub Co.

***Polaroid Stories.** Naomi Iizuka. 88p. 1999. pap. 5.95 (*0-87129-939-9*, P91) Dramatic Pub.

Polaroid Transfers: A Complete Visual Guide to Creating Image & Emulsion Transfers. Kathleen T. Carr. LC 97-1132. (Illus.). 144p. 1997. pap. text 35.00 (*0-8174-5554-X*, Amphoto) Watsn-Guptill.

Polaroids. Andy Warhol. 1992. pap. 24.95 (*1-879532-03-4*) Pace-MacGill.

Polaroids from the Dead. Douglas Coupland. (Illus.). 208p. 1997. pap. 15.00 (*0-06-098721-9*, ReganBks) HarperTrade.

Polarons & Applications. Ed. by Victor D. Lakhno. (Proceedings in Nonlinear Science Ser.). 528p. 1995. text 250.00 (*0-471-95514-0*) Wiley.

Polarons & Bipolarons. A. S. Alexandrov & Sir Nevill Francis Mott. LC 96-146435. 300p. 1996. text 52.00 (*981-02-2298-X*) World Scientific Pub.

Polarons & Bipolarons in High-T*c Superconductors & Related Materials. Ed. by E. K. Salje et al. (Illus.). 474p. (C). 1996. text 105.00 (*0-521-48175-9*) Cambridge U Pr.

Poldark's Cornwall N-E. Winston Graham. (Illus.). 224p. 1998. pap. 24.95 (*0-7538-0131-0*, Pub. by Orion Pubng Grp) Trafalgar.

Polden' I Polnoch' Aleksandr Glezer. LC 83-63004. (Russica Poetry Ser.: No. 7). (RUS.). 120p. 1986. pap. 7.95 (*0-89830-076-2*) Russica Pubs.

***Poldi Pezzoli Museum in Milan.** Alessandra M. Molfino. 1999. pap. text 30.00 (*88-422-0827-2*) Allemandi.

***Pole Assignment for Uncertain Systems.** Mehmet Turan Soylemez. LC 99-17678. 275p. 1999. 97.00 (*0-86380-246-X*) Research Studies Pr Ltd.

Pole Cats: A North Coast Short Story. unabridged ed. Marilyn S. Wagner. (Illus.). 30p. 1997. pap. 7.95 (*0-9664234-0-2*) M S Wagner.

Pole Line Hardware, 1995. 128p. 80.00 (*1-55937-444-6*, SH94216) IEEE Standards.

Pole Position William F1: Behind the Scenes of Williams - Renault F1. Jon Nicholson & Maurice Hamilton. LC 97-116801. (Illus.). 216p. 1996. 14.98 (*0-7603-0256-1*) MBI Pubg.

Pole Shift: A Scientific-Psychic Forecast of the Ultimate Disaster. 3rd ed. John White. (Illus.). 413p. 1985. reprint ed. pap. 9.95 (*0-87604-162-4*, 8014) ARE Pr.

Pole to Pole. (Natural World Ser.). (Illus.). 32p. (gr. 5 up). 1999. pap. 5.95 (*0-7641-0639-2*) Barron.

Pole to Pole: North to South by Camel, River Raft, & Balloon. Michael Palin. LC 95-6608. (Illus.). 326p. 1995. pap. 18.95 (*0-912333-41-3*) BB&T Inc.

Pole to Pole: With Michael Palin. Michael Palin. (Illus.). 320p. 1993. 29.95 (*0-563-36283-9*, BBC-Parkwest) Parkwest Pubns.

Pole 2 Locker: Devotional. Barry St. Clair et al. (Illus.). (Orig.). 1996. pap. 4.99 (*0-9634354-3-4*) Reach Out Minist.

Pole 2 Locker: Interactive Sessions. Barry St. Clair et al. (Illus.). (Orig.). (YA). 1996. pap. 11.99 (*0-9634354-2-6*) Reach Out Minist.

Pole 2 Locker: Leader's Guide. Barry St. Clair et al. (Illus.). (Orig.). 1996. pap., teacher ed. 9.99 (*0-9634354-1-8*) Reach Out Minist.

Poleas. Capstone Press Staff. Price not set. (*1-56065-794-4*) Capstone Pr.

Poleas. Capstone Press Staff. (J). 1998. 14.00 (*0-516-21383-0*) Childrens.

Polec: Dictionary of Politics & Economics. 2nd enl. rev. ed. Ed. by Harry Back et al. (ENG, FRE & GER.). (C). 1967. 76.15 (*3-11-000892-0*) De Gruyter.

Polec Dictionary of Politics & Economics German-English-French. 2nd ed. Harry Back. (ENG, FRE & GER.). 1037p. 1967. 150.00 (*0-7859-6857-1*, 3110008920) Fr & Eur.

Poled Polymers & Their Applications to SHG & EO Devices. Ed. by S. Miyata & H. Sasabe. (Advances in Nonlinear Optics Ser.: Vol. 4). 292p. 1997. text 98.00 (*90-5699-025-X*) Gordon & Breach.

Polemic on the General Line of the International Communist Movement: Hung Ch'i. LC 71-38078. (China Classic & Contemporary Works in Reprint Ser.). reprint ed. 45.00 (*0-404-56942-0*) AMS Pr.

Polemical Papers. Jenny Teichman. LC 97-73457. (Avebury Series in Philosophy). 184p. 1997. text 64.95 (*1-85972-670-4*, Pub. by Ashgate Pub) Ashgate Pub Co.

Polemical Pulps: The Martin Beck Novels of Maj Sjowall & Per Wahloo. J. Kenneth Van Dover. LC 87-716. (Brownstone Mystery Guides Ser.: Vol. 11). 96p. 1993. pap. 15.00 (*0-89370-284-6*) Millefleurs.

***Polemicization.** Benjamin Arditi. LC 99-41201. 157p. 1999. pap. text 18.50 (*0-8147-0689-4*) NYU Pr.

***Polemicization.** Benjamin Arditi & Jeremy Valentine. LC 99-41201. (Taking on the Political Ser.). 192p. 1999. text 55.00 (*0-8147-0688-6*) NYU Pr.

Polemics. Anselm Hollo et al. 208p. 1998. pap. 8.00 (*1-57027-070-8*) Autonomedia.

Polemics & Poems of Rachel Speght. Rachel Speght. Ed. by Barbara K. Lewalski. (Women Writers in English 1350-1850 Ser.). 144p. (C). 1996. pap. 18.95 (*0-19-508615-5*); text 55.00 (*0-19-508614-7*) OUP.

Polemics & Prophecies, Vol. 1. I. F. Stone. 1989. pap. 9.95 (*0-316-81747-3*) Little.

Polemics in Marxist Philosophy. George Novack. LC 77-70457. 344p. 1978. pap. 19.95 (*0-87348-820-2*) Pathfinder NY.

Polemics in Marxist Philosophy. George Novack. LC 77-70457. 344p. 1978. reprint ed. lib. bdg. 55.00 (*0-913460-63-X*) Pathfinder NY.

Polemics of Poetry: The Harlem Renaissance & Sixties in Retrospect. Margaret A. Reid. LC 94-11768. (Studies in African & African-American Culture: Vol. 8). 1994. write for info. (*0-8204-2482-X*) P Lang Pubng.

Polemische und Apologetische Literatur in Arabischer Sprache. Moritz Steinschneider. x, 456p. 1966. reprint ed. write for info. (*0-318-71568-6*); reprint ed. write for info. (*0-318-71868-5*) G Olms Pubs.

Polenta. Brigit L. Binns. (Illus.). 120p. 1996. pap. 14.95 (*0-8118-1185-9*) Chronicle Bks.

Polenta: 100 Innovative Recipes - From Appetizers to Desserts. Michele A. Jordan. LC 96-31712. 160p. 1996. pap. 16.95 (*0-553-06732-X*) Broadway BDD.

Poles & Gridwork No. 26: Threshold Picture Guide. Jane Wallace. (Illus.). 24p. (YA). 1993. pap. 12.00 (*1-872082-44-0*, Pub. by Kenilworth Pr) Half Halt Pr.

Poles & Jews: A Failed Brotherhood. Magdalena Opalski & Israel Bartal. LC 92-53865. (Tauber Institute Ser.: Vol. 13). 205p. 1992. pap. 17.95 (*0-87451-602-1*) U Pr of New Eng.

Poles & Residues of Eisenstein Series for Symplectic & Unitary Groups. P. Feit. LC 86-3386. (Memoirs of the AMS Ser.: No. 61/346). 89p. 1986. pap. 18.00 (*0-8218-2347-7*, MEMO/61/346) Am Math.

Poles & Saxons of the Napoleonic Wars. George F. Nafziger et al. (Illus.). 266p. 1991. 35.00 (*0-9626655-3-3*, Pub. by Emperors Pr) Combined Pub.

Poles Apart. Thomas. (Clipper Fiction Ser.). 1994. pap. text. write for info. (*0-582-80267-9*, Pub. by Addison-Wesley) Longman.

Poles Apart: Parallel Visions of the Arctic & Antarctic. Galen Rowell. LC 94-42048. (Illus.). 184p. 1995. 45.00 (*0-520-20174-4*, Pub. by U CA Pr) Cal Prin Full Svc.

Poles Apart: Parallel Visions of the Arctic & Antarctic. Galen Rowell. LC 94-42048. (Illus.). 1997. pap. 24.95 (*0-520-20902-8*, Pub. by U CA Pr) Cal Prin Full Svc.

Poles Apart: Solidarity & the New Poland. Jacqueline Hayden. LC 94-184554. (Illus.). 224p. 1994. 37.50 (*0-7165-2532-1*, Pub. by Irish Acad Pr); pap. 19.50 (*0-7165-2533-X*, Pub. by Irish Acad Pr) Intl Spec Bk.

Poles Apart: The First Polish Airborne at Arnhem. George F. Cholewczynski. (Illus.). 352p. 1993. 21.95 (*0-9627613-5-4*) Sarpedon.

Poles Apart: The Gospel in Creative Tension. Ed. by D. S. Russell. 160p. (Orig.). (C). 1991. pap. text 59.00 (*86-15-30646-X*, Pub. by St Andrew) St Mut.

Poles Apart: The Gospel in Creative Tension. D. S. Russell. 160p. (Orig.). 1993. text 25.00 (*0-7152-0646-X*, Pub. by St Andrew) St Mut.

Poles in America. Paul Fox. LC 70-129397. (American Immigration Collectio. Series 2). (Illus.). 1973. reprint ed. 15.95 (*0-405-00551-2*) Ayer.

Poles in American History & Traditions. Joseph A. Wytrwal. 1969. 7.50 (*0-685-09287-9*) Endurance.

***Poles in Defence of Britain: A Day-by-Day Chronology of Polish Day & Night Fighter Pilot Operations, July1940-June 1941.** Robert Gretzyngier. 2000. 45.00 (*1-902304-54-3*, Pub. by Grub St) Seven Hills Bk.

***Poles in the Central & Western States, Vol. IV.** James S. Pula. 2001. 59.95 (*0-8132-0923-4*) Cath U Pr.

Poles in the 19th Century Southwest. Francis C. Kajencki. LC 90-61764. (Illus.). 288p. (C). 1991. 25.00 (*0-9627190-1-3*) SW Polonia Pr.

Poles in the 19th Century Southwest. Francis C. Kajencki. LC 90-61764. 288p. 1990. reprint ed. pap. 89.30 (*0-608-00693-9*, 206146400009) Bks Demand.

Polestar of the Ancients: Aristotelian Tradition in Classical & English Literary Criticism. John O. Hayden. LC 77-74411. 237p. 1979. 34.50 (*0-87413-125-1*) U Delaware Pr.

Poletje Molka see Summer of Silence

Poletown: Community Betrayed. Jeanie Wylie. (Illus.). 288p. 1989. pap. text 14.95 (*0-252-06153-5*) U of Ill Pr.

Poletown, Detroit: A Case Study in Public Use & Reindustrialization. Armond Cohen. LC KF9922.C6. (Lincoln Institute Monograph: No. 82-5). 53p. reprint ed. pap. 30.00 (*0-7837-2161-7*, 204246600004) Bks Demand.

Poleward Flows along Eastern Ocean Boundaries. Ed. by Steve Neshyba et al. (Coastal & Estuarine Studies: Vol. 34). ix, 374p. 1989. 65.00 (*0-387-97175-0*) Spr-Verlag.

Polgar Sisters, Training or Genius? Cathy Forbes. 176p. 1995. pap. 16.95 (*0-8050-2426-3*, Pub. by Batsford Chess) H Holt & Co.

Polgara the Sorceress. David Eddings & Leigh Eddings. LC 97-14785. 656p. 1997. 25.95 (*0-345-41662-7*, Del Rey) Ballantine Pub Grp.

Polgara the Sorceress. David Eddings & Leigh Eddings. 1998. mass mkt. 6.99 (*0-345-42474-3*) Ballantine Pub Grp.

Polgara the Sorceress. David Eddings & Leigh Eddings. 754p. 1999. mass mkt. 6.99 (*0-345-42255-4*, Del Rey) Ballantine Pub Grp.

Poli - A Mexican Boy in Early Texas. Jay Neugeboren. LC 88-64094. (Multicultural Texas Ser.). (Illus.). 120p. (YA). (gr. 7 up). 1992. pap. 7.95 (*0-931722-74-8*) Corona Pub.

Poli Formal Ontology. Nip. LC 96-185793. 1996. text 161.50 (*0-7923-4104-X*) Kluwer Academic.

Poliakoff: Plays One. Stephen Poliakoff. (Methuen World Dramatists Ser.). 461p. (Orig.). (C). 1989. pap. 13.95 (*0-413-62460-9*, A0414, Methuen Drama) Methn.

Poliakoff: Plays Two. Date not set. pap. write for info. (*0-614-96392-3*, A0711) Heinemann.

Poliatrics: The Art of Conspiracy. Cole Silvers, pseud. 99p. (Orig.). (C). 1991. pap. text 10.95 (*0-9630732-7-3*) C E Silvestri.

Police, No. 23. 48p. 1984. pap. 6.95 (*0-7935-2701-5*, 00243620) H Leonard.

Police: An Introduction. Lyman. LC 98-20842. 502p. 1998. 73.00 (*0-13-260365-9*) P-H.

Police: Autonomy & Consent. Michael Brogden. (Law, State & Society Ser.). 1983. text 109.00 (*0-12-135180-7*) Acad Pr.

Police: Greatest Hits. (Piano-Vocal-Guitar Ser.). (Illus.). 84p. 1990. per. 14.95 (*0-7935-0626-3*, 00490533) H Leonard.

Police: Practices, Perspectives, Problems. Cox. LC 95-684. 300p. 1995. 72.00 (*0-205-16198-7*) Allyn.

Police: Practices, Perspectives, Problems. Steven M. Cox. (C). 1995. teacher ed. write for info. (*0-205-18480-4*, H8480-9) Allyn.

Police: Streetcorner Politicians. William K. Muir, Jr. LC 76-8085. (Illus.). 318p. 1979. pap. text 14.95 (*0-226-54633-0*, P825) U Ch Pr.

Police: The Constitution & the Community. Ed. by John Baxter & Lawrence Koffman. 274p. 1985. 25.00 (*0-7855-1462-7*, Pub. by NCCL) St Mut.

Police - Health, Risks, Shift Work, Attitudes, & Brutality Force. Walter E. Schultz. LC 95-17303. 1995. pap. write for info. (*0-7883-0697-9*) ABBE Pubs Assn.

Police - Health, Risks, Shift Work, Attitudes, & Brutality Force: Index od New Information for Reference & Research. Walter E. Schultz. LC 95-17303. 1995. write for info. (*0-7883-0696-0*) ABBE Pubs Assn.

Police Abuse & Killings of Street Children in India. Human Rights Watch Helsinki Staff. LC 96-77861. 200p. 1996. pap. 15.00 (*1-56432-205-X*) Hum Rts Watch.

Police Academy: A Preparation Guide. Phillip M. Satterfield. 96p. (Orig.). 1985. pap. 12.95 (*0-9616014-0-X*) P M Satterfield.

***Police Accountability: The Role of Citizen Oversight.** Walker. 2000. pap. 25.00 (*0-534-58158-7*) Wadsworth Pub.

Police Actions: A Practical Guide. Richard Clayton & Hugh Tomlinson. 200p. 1997. pap. 36.00 (*1-84113-077-X*, Pub. by Hart Pub) Intl Spec Bk.

Police Administration. Larry K. Gaines et al. 512p. (C). 1991. 66.25 (*0-07-557127-7*) McGraw.

Police Administration. Southerland. 1990. text, teacher ed. 21.56 (*0-07-022736-5*) McGraw.

***Police Administration.** 2nd ed. Gaines. 2000. write for info. (*0-07-022809-4*) McGraw.

P

Police Administration. 3rd ed. Robert Sheehan & Gary W. Cordner. LC 94-70963. 504p. (C). 1994. pap. text 39.95 (*0-87084-788-0*) Anderson Pub Co.

Police Administration. 4th ed. Gary W. Cordner & Robert Sheehan. LC 98-51021. 1998. pap. 45.95 (*0-87084-794-5*) Anderson Pub Co.

Police Administration. 5th ed. Jack R. Greene et al. LC 96-75689. 646p. (C). 1996. 64.06 (*0-07-022566-4*) McGraw.

Police Administration: A Critical Study of Police Organizations in the United States & Abroad. Leonhard Felix Fuld. LC 70-152105. (Criminology, Law Enforcement, & Social Problems Ser.: No. 141). (Illus.). 583p. 1971. reprint ed. 28.00 (*0-87585-141-X*) Patterson Smith.

Police Administration: An Introduction. 2nd ed. Alfred R. Stone & Stuart M. DeLuca. LC 93-14128. 498p. 1994. 88.00 (*0-13-681602-9*) P-H.

Police Administration & Management. Sam S. Souryal. (Criminal Justice Ser.). 462p. 1977. pap. text, teacher ed. write for info. (*0-314-35440-9*) West Pub.

Police Administration & Progressive Reform: Theodore Roosevelt as Police Commissioner of New York, 19. Jay S. Berman. LC 87-8651. (Contributions in Criminology & Penology Ser.: No. 19). 167p. 1987. 49.95 (*0-313-25554-7*, BMO/, Greenwood Pr) Greenwood.

Police Administration & Supervision. Jack Rudman. (General Aptitude & Abilities Ser.: No. CS-32). pap. 39.95 (*0-8373-6732-8*, CS-32) Nat Learn.

Police Administration in Ancient India. K. K. Mira. (C). 1987. 20.00 (*81-7099-005-X*, Pub. by Mittal Pubs Dist) S Asia.

Police Administration in Boston: Survey of Crime & Criminal Justice in Boston Conducted by the Harvard Law School, Vol. 3. Leonard V. Harrison. LC 70-154584. (Police in America Ser.). 1971. reprint ed. 18.95 (*0-405-03371-0*) Ayer.

Police Administration: Structures, Processes & Behaviors Study Guide: Based on the Text by Swanson, Territo & Taylor. 2nd ed. Davis Publishing Company Staff. Ed. by Robert Dahl. 108p. (C). 1991. 28.95 (*1-56325-000-4*, DS097) Davis Pub Law.

Police Administration: Structures, Processes & Behaviors Study Guide: Based on the Text by Swanson, Territo & Taylor. 3rd ed. Davis Publishing Company Staff. Ed. by Robert Dahl. 108p. (C). 1995. 28.95 (*1-56325-057-8*, DS097) Davis Pub Law.

Police Administration Study Guide. 4th ed. Ralph E. Hendel. 293p. 1979. student ed. 28.95 (*1-56325-020-9*, DS170) Davis Pub Law.

Police Administrative Aide. Jack Rudman. (Career Examination Ser.: C-640). 1994. pap. 23.95 (*0-8373-0640-X*) Nat Learn.

Police Administrator Looks at Police Corruption. William McCarthy. (Criminal Justice Center Monographs). 1978. pap. text 3.50 (*0-318-37488-9*) John Jay Pr.

Police Administrators: Reminiscences. S. K. Ghosh. (C). 1989. 26.50 (*81-7024-220-7*, Pub. by Ashish Pub Hse) S Asia.

Police Aid & Political Will: U. S. Policy in El Salvador & Honduras, 1962-1987. Washington Office on Latin America Staff. 82p. (Orig.). 1987. pap. 6.00 (*0-929513-02-9*) WOLA.

***Police Analysis & Planning for Chemical, Biological & Radiological Attacks.** John W. Ellis. LC 99-28266. 1999. 31.95 (*0-398-06982-4*) C C Thomas.

***Police Analysis & Planning for Chemical, Biological & Radiological Attacks: Prevention, Defense, Response.** John W. Ellis. LC 99-28266. (Illus.). 238p. 1999. text 43.95 (*0-398-06981-6*) C C Thomas.

Police Analysis & Planning for Vehicular Bombings: Prevention, Defense & Response. John W. Ellis. LC HV8079.B62E55 1999. (Illus.). 1999. text 77.95 (*0-398-06938-7*); pap. text 57.95 (*0-398-06939-5*) C C Thomas.

Police & Community Conflicts: Role Play Peacegames. David W. Felder. LC 95-90516. 126p. 1996. 24.95 (*0-910959-20-X*, B&G 20H); teacher ed. 44.95 (*0-910959-40-4*, B&G 20T) Wellington Pr.

Police & Community Relations: Critical Issues. Steven M. Cox & Jack D. Fitzgerald. 208p. (C). 1983. pap. write for info. (*0-697-08219-9*) Brown & Benchmark.

***Police & Criminal Evidence Act 1984 Explained.** John Beggs. 2000. 50.00 (*0-11-702396-5*, Pub. by Statnry Office) Balogh.

Police & Criminal Evidence Act, 1984: A Guide for Duty Solicitors. Anna Turnbull-Walker. 30p. 1986. 45.00 (*1-85190-019-5*, Pub. by Fourmat Pub) St Mut.

***Police & Criminal Evidence Act 1984: Code of Practice on Stop & Search, Effective 1 March 1999.** LC 99-201573. 15p. 1999. write for info. (*0-11-341230-4*, Pub. by Statnry Office) Bernan Associates.

Police & Drug Control: A Home Field Advantage. John E. Eck. LC 89-62596. 22p. (Orig.). 1989. pap. 3.00 (*1-878734-12-1*) Police Exec Res.

Police & Fire Communications Handbook. Communications Research Council Staff. 376p. 1995. pap. 19.95 (*0-917963-16-4*) Artsci Inc.

Police & Fire Station. Yes! Entertainment Corporation Staff. (Pop-Up Sound-Up Bks.). 2p. (J). (ps-2). 1993. write for info. (*1-883366-05-4*) YES Ent.

Police & Government: Histories of Policing in Australia. Mark Finnane. (Illus.). 248p. 1994. pap. text 32.00 (*0-19-553474-3*) OUP.

***Police & Human Rights.** Ralph Crawshaw. LC 99-29580. 1999. 72.00 (*90-411-1209-X*) Kluwer Law Intl.

Police & Law Enforcement. 2nd ed. R. Deb. (C). 1989. 125.00 (*0-7855-4795-9*) St Mut.

Police & Law Enforcement, 1973-1993, 6 vols. Ed. by James T. Curran et al. LC 73-7210. 1973. lib. bdg. write for info. (*0-404-19542-3*) AMS Pr.

Police & Legal Dictionary: Polish to English-French-German-Russian. G. Sostek. 315p. 1996. pap. 58.00 (*83-85703-30-6*, Pub. by Wyzsa Szk Pol) IBD Ltd.

Police & Legal Dictionary, Polish to English/French/German/Russian. G. Sostek. (ENG, FRE, GER, POL & RUS.). 1996. 58.00 (*0-7859-9690-7*) Fr & Eur.

Police & Modern Society. August Vollmer. LC 72-129309. (Criminology, Law Enforcement, & Social Problems Ser.: No. 131). 273p. (C). 1971. reprint ed. lib. bdg. 24.00 (*0-87585-131-2*) Patterson Smith.

Police & Other Law Enforcement Examinations. 4th ed. Harry W. Koch. 1984. 8.00 (*0-910553-00-9*) Ken-Bks.

Police & Policing: Contemporary Issues. 2nd ed. Ed. by Dennis Jay Kenney & Robert P. McNamara. LC 98-33609. 320p. 1999. 69.50 (*0-275-95498-6*, Praeger Pubs); pap. 24.95 (*0-275-95499-4*, Praeger Pubs) Greenwood.

Police & Policing in India: A Select Bibliography. Ed. by Nehal Ashraf. (C). 1992. 27.50 (*0-8364-2799-8*, Commonwealth) S Asia.

Police & Politics in 20th Century Punjab: A Saga of the Punjab. B. S. Danewalia. LC 99-931640. (C). 1997. 42.00 (*81-202-0453-0*, Pub. by Aditya Prakashan) S Asia.

Police & Social Change in India. Rashmi Mishra & Samarendra Mohanty. xiv, 229p. 1992. 22.95 (*1-881338-32-0*) Nataraj Bks.

Police & Social Conflict: Rhetoric & Reality. Nigel G. Fielding. LC 90-41705. (Conflict & Change in Britain - A New Audit Ser.: Vol. 2). 240p. (C). 1991. pap. 19.95 (*0-485-80102-7*, Pub. by Athlone Pr); text 50.00 (*0-485-80002-0*, Pub. by Athlone Pr) Humanities.

Police & Social Workers. 2nd ed. Terry Thomas. 208p. 1994. pap. 31.95 (*1-85742-157-4*, Pub. by Arena) Ashgate Pub Co.

Police & Society. Roy R. Roberg & Jack Kuykendall. LC 92-35788. 484p. 1993. 43.25 (*0-534-19872-4*) Wadsworth Pub.

Police & Society. 2nd rev. ed. Roy R. Roberg et al. LC 99-35450. (Illus.). 490p. (C). 2000. pap. text. write for info. (*1-891487-17-5*) Roxbury Pub Co.

***Police & Society: Instructor's Manual.** 2nd ed. Cary Heck & Gary T. Banet. 2000. pap., teacher ed. write for info. (*1-891487-63-9*) Roxbury Pub Co.

Police & Society: Touchstone Readings. 2nd ed. Ed. by Victor E. Kappeler. LC 99-234238. (Illus.). 512p. (C). 1999. pap. text 23.95 (*1-57766-045-5*) Waveland Pr.

Police & Sting. Chris Welch. (Illus.). 112p. (Orig.). 1996. pap. 8.95 (*0-7119-5302-3*, OP47800) Omnibus NY.

Police & the Blacks: U. S. Civil Rights Commission Hearings. 1973. 23.95 (*0-405-03381-8*) Ayer.

Police & the Community. 6th ed. David L. Carter & Louis A. Radelet. LC 98-14531. 585p. 1998. 71.00 (*0-13-619677-2*) P-H.

Police & the Crime Problem. American Academy of Political & Social Science. Ed. by Thorsten D. Sellin. reprint ed. 42.50 (*0-404-09145-8*) AMS Pr.

Police & the Crime Problem. Ed. by Thorsten D. Sellin. LC 78-154589. (Police in America Ser.). 1975. reprint ed. 23.95 (*0-405-03385-0*) Ayer.

Police & the Elderly. Arnold P. Goldstein & William J. Hoyer. (C). 1979. 42.95 (*0-205-14352-0*, H4352) Allyn.

Police & the Elderly. Aronald P. Goldstein. (C). 1979. pap. 21.95 (*0-205-14351-2*, H4351) Allyn.

Police & the Homeless: Creating a Partnership Between Law Enforcement & Social Service Agencies in the Development of Effective Policies & Programs. Martin L. Forst. LC 96-43226. (Illus.). 248p. 1997. text 57.95 (*0-398-06689-2*); pap. text 42.95 (*0-398-06690-6*) C C Thomas.

Police & the Social Order in German Cities: The Dusseldorf Administrative District, 1848-1914. Elaine G. Spencer. LC 92-1279. 260p. 1992. lib. bdg. 34.00 (*0-87580-170-6*) N Ill U Pr.

Police & the Use of Force: The Savannah Study. Vance McLaughlin. LC 92-10154. 176p. 1992. 49.95 (*0-275-94344-5*, C4344, Praeger Pubs) Greenwood.

Police & Their Many Publics. Donald W. McEvoy. LC 76-6851. 154p. reprint ed. pap. 47.80 (*0-608-15229-3*, 202749400055) Bks Demand.

Police & Thieves: A Novel. Peter Plate. LC 98-55232. 192p. 1999. text 20.00 (*1-888363-95-9*, Pub. by Seven Stories) Publishers Group.

Police & Young People in Australia. Ed. by Rob White & Christine Alder. LC 93-23286. (Illus.). 288p. (C). 1994. pap. write for info. (*0-521-43574-9*); text 64.95 (*0-521-43426-2*) Cambridge U Pr.

Police Antidrug Tactics: New Approaches & Applications. Deborah Weisel et al. LC 96-67353. 196p. (Orig.). (C). 1996. pap. 18.50 (*1-878734-43-1*) Police Exec Res.

Police As Problem Solvers. H. Toch & J. D. Grant. (Illus.). 296p. (C). 1991. 49.50 (*0-306-43845-3*, Plenum Trade) Perseus Pubng.

Police Assessment Center. Harry W. More & Peter C. Unsinger. (Illus.). 232p. 1987. 54.95 (*0-398-05331-6*); pap. 38.95 (*0-398-06299-4*) C C Thomas.

Police Assessment Center Examination. (Career Examination Ser.: C-3595). 1994. pap. 29.95 (*0-8373-3595-7*) Nat Learn.

Police Assessment Testing: An Assessment Center Handbook for Law Enforcement Personnel. 2nd ed. John L. Coleman. (Illus.). 182p. 1992. pap. 26.95 (*0-398-06065-7*) C C Thomas.

Police Assessment Testing: An Assessment Center Handbook for Law Enforcement Personnel. 2nd ed. John L. Coleman. (Illus.). 182p. (C). 1992. text 41.95 (*0-398-05809-1*) C C Thomas.

Police at the Funeral. Margery Allingham. 232p. 1994. mass mkt. 3.95 (*0-7867-0169-2*) Carroll & Graf.

Police at the Funeral. Margery Allingham. 1998. lib. bdg. 21.95 (*1-56723-017-2*) Yestermorrow.

Police at Work: Policy Issues & Analysis. Ed. by Richard R. Bennett. LC 82-23126. (Perspectives in Criminal Justice Ser.: No. 5). 168p. reprint ed. pap. 52.10 (*0-8357-8469-X*, 203473700091) Bks Demand.

Police Attendant. Jack Rudman. (Career Examination Ser.: C-982). 1994. pap. 23.95 (*0-8373-0982-4*) Nat Learn.

Police Auditing: Theories & Practice. Allan Y. Jiao. LC 99-28166. (Illus.). 200p. 1999. pap. text 31.95 (*0-398-06980-8*) C C Thomas.

***Police Auditing: Theories & Practice.** Allan Y. Jiao. LC 99-28166. (Illus.). 200p. 1999. text 44.95 (*0-398-06979-4*) C C Thomas.

Police Authorities During the Miners' Strike. Sarah Spencer. (C). 1988. 21.00 (*0-900137-25-8*, Pub. by NCCL) St Mut.

Police Bibliography. Jack E. Whitehouse. LC 77-15909. (Studies in Criminal Justice: No. 3). 1980. 95.00 (*0-404-16040-9*) AMS Pr.

Police Brutality. 20p. (Orig.). 1995. pap. 3.95 (*1-884855-25-3*) Secretarius.

Police Brutality. Kelly C. Anderson. LC 94-9707. (Overview Ser.). (Illus.). (YA). (gr. 5-8). 1995. 22.45 (*1-56006-164-2*) Lucent Bks.

Police Brutality. Ed. by Tamara L. Roleff. LC 98-26633. (Current Controversies Ser.). 226p. (YA). (gr. 9-12). 1998. lib. bdg. 27.45 (*0-7377-0013-0*) Greenhaven.

***Police Brutality.** Ed. by Tamara L. Roleff. LC 98-26633. (Current Controversies Ser.). 170p. (YA). (gr. 9-12). 1998. pap. 17.45 (*0-7377-0012-2*) Greenhaven.

***Police Brutality: An Anthology.** Ed. by Jill Nelson. 320p. 2000. 24.95 (*0-393-04883-7*) Norton.

***Police Brutality: Opposing Viewpoints.** Helen Cothran. LC 00-32996. (Opposing Viewpoints Ser.). 2001. lib. bdg. write for info. (*0-7377-0515-9*) Greenhaven.

Police Cadet. Jack Rudman. (Career Examination Ser.: C-594). 1994. pap. 23.95 (*0-8373-0594-2*) Nat Learn.

Police Captain. Jack Rudman. (Career Examination Ser.: C-2803). 1994. pap. 39.95 (*0-8373-2803-9*) Nat Learn.

Police Card Discord. Maxwell T. Cohen. LC 93-4173. (Studies in Jazz: No. 15). (Illus.). 194p. 1993. 26.50 (*0-8108-2638-0*) Scarecrow.

Police Cars. Freeman. LC 98-7056. (Community Vehicles Ser.). (J). 1998. 13.25 (*0-7368-0103-0*, Pebble Bks) Capstone Pr.

Police Cars. Marcia S. Freeman. (Community Vehicles Ser.). (J). 1998. 13.25 (*0-516-21491-8*) Childrens.

Police Cars. Ian Kerr. 1998. 14.99 (*0-7858-0948-1*) Bk Sales Inc.

Police Cars: A Graphic History. Bruce W. Cameron. LC 96-71797. (Illus.). 216p. 1997. write for info. (*0-7853-2196-9*) Pubns Intl Ltd.

Police Cars: A Photographic History. Monty McCord. LC 91-61303. (Illus.). 304p. 1991. pap. 14.95 (*0-87341-171-4*, PC01) Krause Pubns.

Police Cars in Action. Robert Genat. LC 99-13090. (Enthusiast Color Ser.). (Illus.). 96p. 1999. pap. text 13.95 (*0-7603-0521-8*, Pub. by MBI Pubg) Motorbooks Intl.

Police Chief. Jack Rudman. (Career Examination Ser.: C-2754). 1994. pap. 44.95 (*0-8373-2754-7*) Nat Learn.

Police Chief's Guide to Using Microcomputers. Ernie Hernandez, Jr. (Illus.). 160p. 1984. 16.95 (*0-910657-05-X*) Frontline.

Police Civil Liability, 2 vols. Isidore Silver. LC 86-70621. 1986. ring bd. 255.00 (*0-8205-1543-4*) Bender.

Police Clerk. Jack Rudman. (Career Examination Ser.: C-639). 1994. pap. 23.95 (*0-8373-0639-6*) Nat Learn.

Police Collectibles Pictorial Guide. 2nd ed. George Virgines. (Illus.). 111p. 1989. reprint ed. pap. 12.95 (*0-9623724-3-9*) Baird Pub.

***Police Combating Violence Against Women: Documentation of the Conference Experts.** Ed. by Albin P. Dearing & Elisabeth Forg. 271p. 1999. pap. 48.00 (*90-5095-085-X*, 18662, Pub. by Intersentia Uitgevers) Gaunt.

Police Communications & Teletype Operator. Jack Rudman. (Career Examination Ser.: C-1847). 1994. pap. 23.95 (*0-8373-1847-5*) Nat Learn.

Police Communications & Teletype Operator Supervisor. Jack Rudman. (Career Examination Ser.: C-1437). 1994. pap. 29.95 (*0-8373-1437-2*) Nat Learn.

Police Communications in Traffic Stops. Angela V. Woodhull. LC 92-42397. 364p. (C). 1993. text 29.95 (*0-87047-062-0*); pap. text 18.95 (*0-87047-063-9*) Schenkman Bks Inc.

Police Communications Technician. Jack Rudman. (Career Examination Ser.: C-3526). 1994. pap. 23.95 (*0-8373-3526-4*) Nat Learn.

Police Community: Theory & Practice Alternatives, Preliminary Edition. Jim Chambers. 164p. (C). 1994. per. 22.95 (*0-8403-9284-2*) Kendall-Hunt.

Police-Community Relations: Crisis in Our Time. 3rd ed. Howard H. Earle. (Illus.). 304p. 1980. 49.95 (*0-398-03900-3*); pap. 37.95 (*0-398-06103-3*) C C Thomas.

Police Community Relations & the Administration of Justice. 5th ed. (C). 2000. text. write for info. (*0-13-026002-9*) P-H.

***Police Community Relations & the Administration of Justice.** 5th ed. Pamela D. Mayhall. LC 99-36908. (Illus.). 402p. 1999. 78.67 (*0-13-020997-X*) P-H.

Police Complete. 224p. 1982. per. 22.95 (*0-88188-361-1*, 00307900) H Leonard.

Police, Courts & Correction. Robert Winslow. 256p. (C). 1999. per. 35.00 (*0-7872-5715-X*, 41571501) Kendall-Hunt.

Police, Crimes & Offenses & Motor Vehicle Laws of Virginia, 2 vols. Michie Company Editorial Staff. 1992. 80.00 (*0-685-62339-4*, MICHIE); 80.00 (*0-685-62355-6*, MICHIE) LEXIS Pub.

***Police, Crimes & Offenses & Motor Vehicle Laws of Virginia with CD-ROM Vol. 1 & 2: 1999 Edition, 2 vols., Set.** 1878p. 1999. pap. 92.00 (*0-327-09451-6*, 3545315) LEXIS Pub.

Police, Crimes & Offenses & Motor Vehicle Laws of Virginia, 1994 Edition. write for info. (*0-614-05946-1*, MICHIE) LEXIS Pub.

Police, Crimes & Offenses & Motor Vehicle Laws of Virginia, 1998 Edition, 2 vols. LC 98-202645. 1872p. 1998. write for info. (*0-327-05486-7*, 35453-14) LEXIS Pub.

Police Crisis Intervention. 1991. lib. bdg. 79.00 (*0-8490-4478-2*) Gordon Pr.

Police Crowd Control: Risk-Reduction Strategies for Law Enforcement. Charles Beene. (Illus.). 128p. 1992. pap. 16.00 (*0-87364-674-6*) Paladin Pr.

***Police Detective.** Tracey Boraas. (Career Explorations Ser.). 48p. (YA). (gr. 5 up). 2000. lib. bdg. 21.26 (*0-7368-0597-4*) Capstone Pr.

Police Detention: A Practical Guide to Advising the Suspect. Christopher J. Lethem. (Waterlow Procedure Notes Ser.). (Illus.). 208p. 1991. pap. 33.90 (*0-685-48858-6*) Macmillan.

Police Deviance. 3rd ed. Thomas Barker & David L. Carter. LC 90-82315. 442p. (C). 1994. pap. 35.95 (*0-87084-714-7*) Anderson Pub Co.

Police Dictionary: English-Arabic Dictionary. Shafiq Ismat. (ARA & ENG.). 1980. 25.00 (*0-86685-068-6*) Intl Bk Ctr.

Police Dictionary & Encyclopedia. John J. Fay. 378p. 1988. pap. text 49.95 (*0-398-06965-4*) C C Thomas.

Police Dictionary & Encyclopedia. John J. Fay. 378p. (C). 1988. text 64.95 (*0-398-05494-0*) C C Thomas.

Police Dispatcher. Jack Rudman. (Career Examination Ser.: C-2256). 1994. reprint ed. pap. 23.95 (*0-8373-2256-1*) Nat Learn.

Police Dog Tactics. Bryson. (C). 1995. pap. text 47.50 (*0-07-008649-4*) McGraw.

***Police Dogs.** Charles George & Linda George. LC 97-31740. (Dogs at Work Ser.). (Illus.). 48p. (J). (gr. 4-7). 1998. lib. bdg. 19.93 (*1-56065-752-9*) Capstone Pr.

Police Dogs. Linda George & Charles George. (Dogs at Work Ser.). 48p. (J). 1998. lib. bdg. 19.00 (*0-531-11556-9*) Watts.

Police Dogs: Helping to Fight Crime. Alice B. McGinty. LC 97-52013. (Dogs Helping People Ser.). 24p. (J). (gr. k-4). 1999. 15.93 (*0-8239-5218-5*, PowerKids) Rosen Group.

Police Dogs in North America. Samuel G. Chapman. 254p. 1990. pap. 35.95 (*0-398-06053-3*) C C Thomas.

Police Dogs in North America. Samuel G. Chapman. 254p. (C). 1990. text 51.95 (*0-398-05693-5*) C C Thomas.

Police Drug Testing. (Illus.). 105p. (Orig.). (C). 1993. pap. text 25.00 (*1-56806-826-3*) DIANE Pub.

Police, Drugs & Community. Mike Collison. 275p. (C). 1995. 55.00 (*1-85343-318-7*, Pub. by Free Assoc Bks) NYU Pr.

Police, Drugs & Community. Mike Collison. (C). 1995. pap. 25.00 (*1-85343-319-5*, Pub. by Free Assoc Bks) NYU Pr.

Police Education & Minority Recruitment: The Impact of a College Requirement. David L. Carter & Allen D. Sapp. LC 90-62532. 27p. (Orig.). 1991. pap. 4.00 (*1-878734-23-7*) Police Exec Res.

Police Entrance Examinations Handbook. rev. ed. Davis Publishing Company Staff. (Illus.). 219p. 1991. reprint ed. pap. 28.95 (*1-56325-004-7*, T46) Davis Pub Law.

Police Equipment. Ian Kerr. LC 99-42732. (Illus.). 144p. 1998. 17.98 (*1-57145-157-9*, Thunder Bay) Advantage Pubs.

Police Ethics. Patricia Haggard. LC 93-41922. 94p. 1994. text 49.95 (*0-7734-9409-X*) E Mellen.

Police Ethics. David A. Hansen. 96p. 1973. pap. 23.95 (*0-398-02648-3*) C C Thomas.

Police Ethics. Seumas Miller et al. LC 97-200044. 256p. 1998. pap. 29.95 (*1-86448-308-3*, Pub. by Allen & Unwin Pty) Paul & Co Pubs.

Police Ethics: Crisis in Law Enforcement. Tom Barker. LC 96-3551. 94p. 1996. 36.95 (*0-398-06613-2*); pap. 20.95 (*0-398-06614-0*) C C Thomas.

***Police Ethics: The Corruption of Noble Cause.** John P. Crank & Michael A. Caldero. LC 99-38850. 275p. 1999. pap. 32.95 (*1-58360-504-5*) Anderson Pub Co.

Police Executive Leadership. Donald G. Hanna. 127p. 1990. pap. 14.80 (*0-87563-355-2*) Stipes.

Police Field Operations. 4th ed. National Center for Construction Education & Reseach Staff. LC 96-48358. 452p. 1997. 84.00 (*0-13-266362-7*) P-H.

Police Field Operations Study Guide. 3rd ed. Davis Publishing Company Staff. 156p. (C). 1997. pap., student ed. 28.95 (*1-56325-012-8*, DS444) Davis Pub Law.

Police Files: The Spokane Experience, 1853-1995 : Personal & Historical Accounts by a Career Staffer. M. Kienholz. (Illus.). 1999. write for info. (*0-87062-286-2*, Millwood Pub) A H Clark.

Police, Fire, EMS see Community Service for Teens

Police, Firefighter & Paramedic Stress: An Annotated Bibliography, 6. Compiled by John J. Miletich. LC 89-28649. (Bibliographies & Indexes in Psychology Ser.: No. 6). 239p. 1990. lib. bdg. 65.00 (*0-313-26682-4*, MOF/, Greenwood Pr) Greenwood.

Police for the Future. David H. Bayley. (Studies in Crime & Public Policy). 208p. 1996. pap. text 17.95 (*0-19-510458-7*) OUP.

Police Forces in History. Ed. by George L. Mosse. LC 74-84258. 344p. reprint ed. pap. 106.70 (*0-608-14199-2*, 202193500026) Bks Demand.

Police Function. 5th ed. Frank W. Miller et al. 640p. 1991. pap. text 23.95 (*0-88277-881-1*) Foundation Pr.

An Asterisk (*) at the beginning of an entry indicates that the title is appearing for the first time.

Police Function & the Investigation of Crime. J. Brian Morgan. (Illus.). 201p. 1990. text 72.95 (*0-566-07127-4*) Ashgate Pub Co.

Police Governance in England & Wales. Arthur Brown. LC 98-196562. xxvi, 193p. 1998. pap. 36.00 (*1-85941-395-1*, Pub. by Cavendish Pubng) Gaunt.

Police Guide to the Young Offender's Act. Platt. 224p. 1991. pap. 27.00 (*0-409-89340-4*, MICHIE) LEXIS Pub.

Police Handbook for Applying the Systems Approach & Computer Technology. Ernie Hernandez, Jr. LC 82-17662. (Illus.). 231p. 1982. 26.95 (*0-910657-00-9*); pap. 19.95 (*0-910657-01-7*) Frontline.

Police Handbook for Applying the Systems Approach & Computer Technology. 2nd rev. ed. Ernie Hernandez, Jr. (Illus.). 279p. (C). 1992. pap. 25.00 (*0-910657-06-8*) Frontline.

Police Health: A Physician's Guide for the Assessment of Police Officers. Alain Trottier. 182p. (Orig.). 1994. pap. text 64.95 (*0-660-15391-2*, Pub. by Canadian Govt Pub) Accents Pubns.

Police Higher Education & Training in the United Kingdom. Ian Watt. 1988. pap. 5.95 (*0-942511-17-4*) OICJ.

Police Horses. Judith Campbell. 1975. pap. 2.00 (*0-87980-199-9*) Wilshire.

***Police in a Multicultural Society: An American Story.** David E. Barlow & Melissa Hickman Barlow. 313p. (C). 2000. 21.95 (*1-57766-129-X*) Waveland Pr.

Police in America, 35 bks. Ed. by Robert M. Fogleson. 1971. reprint ed. 660.00 (*0-405-03360-5*) Ayer.

Police in America: An Introduction. 2nd ed. Samuel Walker. (C). 1991. text 39.75 (*0-07-067869-3*) McGraw.

Police in America: An Introduction. 3rd ed. Samuel Walker. LC 98-19785. 432p. 1998. pap. 45.94 (*0-07-067911-8*) McGraw.

Police in Community Relations: Critical Issues. 3rd ed. Steven M. Cox & Jack D. Fitzgerald. LC 94-73759. 240p. (C). 1995. text. write for info. (*0-697-25119-5*) Brown & Benchmark.

Police in Community Relations: Critical Issues. 3rd ed. Steven M. Cox & Jack D. Fitzgerald. 240p. (C). 1997. student ed., per. write for info. (*0-07-114136-7*) Brown & Benchmark.

Police in Community Relations: Critical Issues. 4th ed. Steven M. Cox & Jack D. Fitzgerald. 1999. pap. text 25.00 (*0-697-35610-8*) McGraw.

Police in Contradiction: The Evolution of the Police Function in Society, 44. Cyril D. Robinson & Richard Scaglion. LC 93-25071. (Contributions in Criminology & Penology Ser.: No. 44). 216p. 1993. 62.95 (*0-313-28891-7*, GM8891, Greenwood Pr) Greenwood.

Police in Ferment. S. K. Ghosh. 140p. 1981. 17.95 (*0-317-12335-1*, Pub. by Light & Life Pubs) Asia Bk Corp.

Police in Free India: Its Facets & Drawbacks. B. P. Saha. 189p. 1989. text 22.50 (*81-220-0121-1*, Pub. by Konark Pubs Pvt Ltd) Advent Bks Div.

Police in Great Britain, 6 vols. Ed. by Robert M. Fogelson. 1971. reprint ed. 281.00 (*0-405-03405-9*) Ayer.

Police in Los Angeles: Reform & Professionalization. Gerald Woods. LC 92-34899. (Modern American History Ser.). 368p. 1993. text 35.00 (*0-8153-1096-X*) Garland.

Police in New York City: An Investigation. Board of Aldermen Staff. LC 79-154565. (Police in America Ser.). 1971. reprint ed. 29.95 (*0-405-03382-6*) Ayer.

Police in Occupation Japan: Control Corruption & Resistance to Reform. Christopher Aldous. (Routledge Studies in the Modern History of Asia: 1). 328p. (C). 1997. 90.00 (*0-415-14526-0*) Routledge.

***Police in Society.** Terence J. Fitzgerald. LC 00-36642. (Reference Shelf Ser.). (Illus.). 2000. pap. write for info. (*0-8242-0983-4*) Wilson.

Police in the Community. 3rd ed. Cox & Fitzgerald. 1995. teacher ed. 7.81 (*0-697-27548-5*, WCB McGr Hill) McGrw-H Hghr Educ.

Police in the Community. 3rd ed. Hess Miller. (Criminal Justice Ser.). 2001. pap. text 55.75 (*0-534-53946-7*) Brooks-Cole.

Police in the Community: Strategies in the 21st Century. 2nd ed. Linda S. Miller & Karen M. Hess. LC 97-37745. (C). 1997. 77.95 (*0-534-53789-8*) Wadsworth Pub.

Police Informant Management. Jack Morris. LC 83-63214. (Illus.). 95p. 1983. pap. 15.00 (*0-912479-02-7*) Palmer Pr.

Police Informers: Negotiation & Power. Rod Settle. LC 95-189894. 288p. 1995. pap. 39.00 (*1-86287-148-5*, Pub. by Federation Pr) Gaunt.

Police Innovation & Control of the Police: Problems of Law, Order, & Community. Ed. by David Weisburd & Craig Uchida. LC 92-45633. 1993. 102.00 (*0-387-94013-8*) Spr-Verlag.

Police Inspector. Jack Rudman. (Career Examination Ser.: C-1383). 1994. pap. 39.95 (*0-8373-1383-X*) Nat Learn.

Police Integrity: Public Service with Honor. 104p. 1997. pap. text 40.00 (*1-57979-232-4*) DIANE Pub.

Police Integrity: Public Service with Honor. Ed. by Sheldon F. Greenberg. 96p. (C). 1999. pap. text 25.00 (*0-7881-7565-3*) DIANE Pub.

Police Integrity: The Role of Psychological Screening of Applicants. Allen E. Shealy. (Criminal Justice Center Monographs). 1978. pap. text 3.00 (*0-318-37490-0*) John Jay Pr.

Police Intelligence: The Operations of an Investigative Unit. Anthony V. Bouza. LC 75-8667. (Studies in Criminal Justice: No. 2). 1976. 32.50 (*0-404-13138-7*) AMS Pr.

Police Intelligence Reports. Charles C. Frost & Jack Morris. LC 83-62701. (Illus.). 135p. 1983. pap. 15.00 (*0-912479-03-5*) Palmer Pr.

Police Intelligence System. John B. Wolf. (Criminal Justice Center Monographs). 1978. pap. text 5.00 (*0-89444-048-9*) John Jay Pr.

Police Interrogation & Confessions: A Rebuttal to Misconceived Objections. Joseph D. Grano. Ed. by Graham Hughes. (Occasional Papers: Vol. I). 21p. (Orig.). (C). 1987. pap. 5.00 (*1-878429-50-7*) NYU Ctr for Rsch in Crime Justice.

Police Intervention in Marital Violence. Alan Bourlet. 160p. 1990. 113.00 (*0-335-09293-4*); pap. 36.95 (*0-335-09292-6*) OpUniv Pr.

Police Investigation & Prosecution. K. Krishnamurthi. 900p. 1986. 45.95 (*0-318-37218-5*) Asia Bk Corp.

Police Investigation Handbook. Barton I. Ingraham & Thomas Mauriello. 1990. 140.00 (*0-8205-1673-2*, 673) Bender.

Police Know Everything: And Other Maine Stories. Sanford Phippen. Ed. by Constance Hunting. 149p. (Orig.). 1982. pap. 8.95 (*0-913006-27-0*) Puckerbrush.

Police Lab: Using Science to Solve Crimes see Science Lab Series

***Police Ladies.** Yolanda Celbridge. 2000. mass mkt. 6.95 (*0-352-33489-4*) Nexus.

Police, Law & Internal Security. Krishna M. Mathur. (C). 1994. 32.00 (*81-212-0455-0*, Pub. by Gian Publng Hse) S Asia.

Police Law Primer. 4th ed. Kenneth Sloan. 384p. 1992. pap. 30.00 (*0-406-00879-5*, UK, MICHIE) LEXIS Pub.

Police Law Problems & Solutions. 249p. (Orig.). (C). 1993. pap. text 50.00 (*1-56806-880-8*) DIANE Pub.

Police Law Problems & Solutions. Stanley Cohen. 249p. 1995. text 24.95 (*0-685-29114-6*) PA PCLB.

Police Leadership in America: Crisis & Opportunity. William A. Geller. LC 85-6284. 544p. 1985. 55.00 (*0-275-90205-6*, C0205, Praeger Pubs); pap. 29.95 (*0-275-91672-3*, B1672, Praeger Pubs) Greenwood.

Police Leadership in Australia. Ed. by Barbara Etter & Mick Palmer. LC 95-232110. 336p. 1995. pap. 50.00 (*1-86287-183-3*, Pub. by Federation Pr) Gaunt.

Police Lieutenant. Jack Rudman. (Career Examination Ser.: C-2802). 1994. pap. 34.95 (*0-8373-2802-0*) Nat Learn.

Police Lieutenants & Captains Handbook, Vol. I. J. Robert Lansberry & Ralph E. Hendel. (Illus.). 225p. (Orig.). 1971. pap. 28.95 (*1-56325-023-3*, DH007) Davis Pub Law.

Police Lieutenants & Captains Handbook, Vol. II. J. Robert Lansberry. 88p. (Orig.). 1971. pap. 28.95 (*0-685-46276-5*, DH008) Davis Pub Law.

Police Lieutenants & Captains Handbook, Vol. III. Ralph E. Hendel. 233p. (Orig.). 1976. pap. 28.95 (*1-56325-022-5*, DH009) Davis Pub Law.

Police Make House Calls. Armand Hernandez. LC 90-25121. 80p. 1991. pap. 9.00 (*0-927534-09-6*) Biling Rev-Pr.

Police Management. 2nd ed. A. J. Butler. 300p. (Orig.). 1992. pap. text 43.95 (*1-85521-215-3*, Pub. by Dartmth Pub) Ashgate Pub Co.

Police Management. 2nd ed. Roy R. Roberg & Jack Kuykendall. LC 96-46541. (Illus.). 440p. (C). 1997. text. write for info. (*0-935732-85-3*) Roxbury Pub Co.

Police Management: Issues & Perspectives. Ed. by Larry T. Hoover. LC 92-64236. 380p. (Orig.). 1992. pap. 20.00 (*1-878734-28-8*) Police Exec Res.

Police Management & Organizational Behavior: A Contingency Approach. Roy R. Roberg. (Criminal Justice Ser.). (Illus.). 348p. 1979. pap. text, teacher ed. write for info. (*0-314-44225-1*) West Pub.

Police Management Examinations Preparation Guide. Larry F. Jetmore. LC 96-195988. (Cliffs Test Preparation Ser.). (Illus.). 101p. (Orig.). 1996. pap. text 17.95 (*0-8220-2049-1*, Cliff) IDG Bks.

Police Management for the 1990's: A Practitioner's Road Map. John W. Bizzack. 170p. 1989. 41.95 (*0-398-05583-1*); pap. 29.95 (*0-398-06020-7*) C C Thomas.

Police Management in South Africa. W. Fox et al. LC 99-163451. 206p. 1999. pap. 25.00 (*0-7021-4676-5*, Pub. by Juta & Co) Intl Spec Bk.

Police Manager. 3rd ed. Ronald C. Lynch. 352p. (C). 1986. 61.88 (*0-07-554818-6*) McGraw.

Police Manager. 5th rev. ed. Ronald G. Lynch. LC 98-24145. 273p. (C). 1998. pap. 33.95 (*0-87084-710-4*) Anderson Pub Co.

Police Manager: Professional Leadership Skills. 3rd ed. Davis Publishing Company Staff. 96p. (C). 1989. pap. 28.95 (*1-56325-014-4*, DS036) Davis Pub Law.

Police Markets of North America & The European Union. Charles LeMesurier & Marc Arnold. (Law Enforcement - Related Special Report Ser.). 1997. 695.00 (*0-7106-1511-6*) Janes Info Group.

Police, Military, & Ethnicity. Cynthia Enloe. LC 79-64569. 179p. 1980. text 39.95 (*0-87855-302-9*) Transaction Pubs.

Police-Minority Community Relations: The Control & Structuring of Police Discretion. Spring Hill Center Staff. Ed. by Donna Hoel & John Ziegenhagen. 1978. pap. text 2.50 (*0-932676-04-9*) Spring Hill.

Police Misconduct: Law & Litigation. 2nd ed. Michael Avery & David Rudovsky. LC 80-23165. (Civil Rights Ser.). 1980. ring bd. 135.00 (*0-87632-112-0*) West Group.

Police Misconduct: Law & Litigation. 3rd ed. Michael Avery et al. LC 96-37113. 1996. write for info. (*0-8366-1099-7*) West Group.

Police Misconduct: Scope of the Problems & Remedies. William A. Geller. LC HV7924.. (American Bar Foundation Research Reporter Ser.: No.23). 10p. reprint ed. pap. 30.00 (*0-608-14590-4*, 202481900038) Bks Demand.

Police Mystique: An Insider's Look at Cops, Crime & the Criminal Justice System. Anthony V. Bouza. LC 89-29450. (Illus.). 312p. (C). 1990. 23.50 (*0-306-43464-4*, Plenum Trade) Perseus Pubng.

Police of France. Phillip J. Stead. 1983. 19.95 (*0-02-930820-8*) Free Pr.

Police of Sri Lanka: Police-Public Relations. Nandasena Ratnapala. (Illus.). 100p. (C). 1988. reprint ed. pap. text 4.95 (*0-942511-13-1*) OICJ.

Police Officer. Jack Rudman. (Career Examination Ser.: C-1939). 1994. reprint ed. pap. 23.95 (*0-8373-1939-0*) Nat Learn.

Police Officer. 12th ed. Hugh O'Neill. (Illus.). 480p. 1994. pap. 14.00 (*0-671-89231-2*) P-H.

Police Officer. 13th ed. Hugh O'Neill & Hy Hammer. 1996. 13.95 (*0-02-861188-8*) Macmillan.

Police Officer. 13th ed. Hugh O'Neill et al. 480p. 1996. pap. 13.95 (*0-02-861518-2*, Arco) Macmillan Gen Ref.

Police Officer. 14th ed. 480p. 1999. 13.95 (*0-02-862808-X*, Arc) IDG Bks.

***Police Officer.** 15th ed. Fred Rafilson. 480p. 2000. pap. text 13.95 (*0-02-863741-0*) Macmillan Gen Ref.

***Police Officer Exam: The Complete Preparation Guide.** Learning Express Staff. LC 98-44289. 384p. 1999. pap. 14.95 (*1-57685-207-5*) LrningExprss.

Police Officer Exam, California. Learning Express Staff. LC 95-51010. (Law Enforcement Library). 352p. 1996. pap. 35.00 (*1-57685-002-1*) LrningExprss.

Police Officer Exam, Chicago. Ed. by Jim Gish. (Law Enforcement Library). 256p. 1997. pap. 25.00 (*1-57685-073-0*) LrningExprss.

Police Officer Exam, Massachusetts. LC 96-18056. (Law Enforcement Library). 288p. 1996. pap. 30.00 (*1-57685-044-7*) LrningExprss.

Police Officer Exam, New Jersey. LC 96-11283. (Law Enforcement Library). 208p. 1996. pap. 35.00 (*1-57685-021-8*) LrningExprss.

Police Officer Exam New York City & Nassau County. 2nd ed. Learning Express Staff. LC 98-9243. 322p. 1998. pap. 25.00 (*1-57685-159-1*) LrningExprss.

Police Officer Exam the South. Learning Express Staff. Ed. by Jim Gish. LC 97-22391. (Law Enforcement Library). 304p. (Orig.). 1997. pap. 25.00 (*1-57685-033-1*) LrningExprss.

Police Officer Examination Preparation Guide. Larry F. Jetmore. (Cliffs Test Preparation Ser.). 101p. 1994. pap. text 17.95 (*0-8220-2075-0*, Cliff) IDG Bks.

Police Officer, Florida. LC 96-4717. (Law Enforcement Library). 352p. 1996. pap. 35.00 (*1-57685-013-7*) LrningExprss.

Police Officer Friendly Safety Tips Activity & Coloring Book see Police Officer Safety Tips Activity & Coloring Book

Police Officer Jones. Harry Bornstein & Lillian B. Hamilton. (Signed English Ser.). (Illus.). 16p. (J). (ps). 1976. pap. 3.50 (*0-913580-53-8*, Pub. by K Green Pubns) Gallaudet Univ Pr.

Police Officer, Los Angeles Police Department. Jack Rudman. (Career Examination Ser.: C-2441). 1994. pap. 23.95 (*0-8373-2441-6*) Nat Learn.

Police Officer, Nassau County Police Department. Jack Rudman. (Career Examination Ser.: C-1755). 1994. pap. 23.95 (*0-8373-1755-X*) Nat Learn.

Police Officer, New York Police Department. Jack Rudman. (Career Examination Ser.: C-1739). 1994. reprint ed. pap. 23.95 (*0-8373-1739-8*) Nat Learn.

Police Officer Safety Tips Activity & Coloring Book. 2nd rev. ed. Veronica Mora et al. (Children's Safety: Vol. V). Orig. Title: Police Officer Friendly Safety Tips Activity & Coloring Book. (Illus.). 32p. (J). (gr. k-4). 1997. pap. 2.79 (*1-884888-00-3*, 537-T) Student Lifeline.

Police Officer Selection: A Handbook for Law Enforcement Administrators. Anthony R. Moriarty & Mark W. Field. LC 94-17514. (Illus.). 372p. (C). 1994. 80.95 (*0-398-05922-5*); pap. 47.95 (*0-398-05970-5*) C C Thomas.

Police Officer, Suffolk County Police Department. Jack Rudman. (Career Examination Ser.: C-1741). 1994. reprint ed. pap. 23.95 (*0-8373-1741-X*) Nat Learn.

Police Officer Survival & Weapons Use: Seminar Textbook. Wayne N. Hill, Sr. (Illus.). 45p. (C). 1995. pap. text 25.00 (*0-7881-1867-6*) DIANE Pub.

Police Officer, Texas. LC 96-343. (Law Enforcement Library). 352p. 1996. pap. 35.00 (*1-57685-003-X*) LrningExprss.

***Police Officer That's What I'll Be!** Ronald Pinkston. (Illus.). 26p. (J). (gr. k-2). 1999. 12.99 (*0-9671708-0-X*) Pinkston Pubg.

Police Officers see Community Helpers Series

***Police Officers.** Paulette Bourgeois. (Illus.). (J). 2000. 11.40 (*0-606-18226-8*) Turtleback.

***Police Officers.** Alice K. Flanagan. (Community Workers Ser.). (Illus.). 32p. (J). (gr. 1-2). 2000. write for info. (*0-7565-0011-7*) Compass Point.

Police Officers. Dee Ready. (Community Helpers Ser.). (Illus.). (J). 1997. lib. bdg. 14.00 (*0-516-20505-6*) Childrens.

***Police Officers.** unabridged ed. Paulette Bourgeois. (In My Neighborhood Ser.). (Illus.). 32p. (J). (gr. k-3). 2000. pap. 5.95 (*1-55074-787-8*, Pub. by Kids Can Pr) Genl Dist Srvs.

Police Officers. unabridged ed. Peter Bourgeois & Kim LaFave. LC 98-93196. (In My Neighborhood Ser.). (Illus.). 32p. (J). (ps-2). 1998. 14.95 (*1-55074-502-6*, Pub. by Kids Can Pr) Genl Dist Srvs.

Police Officers: A to Z. Jean Johnson. (Walker's Community Helpers Ser.). (Illus.). 48p. (J). (gr. k-3). 1986. 11.95 (*0-8027-6614-5*); lib. bdg. 12.85 (*0-8027-6615-3*) Walker & Co.

Police Officer's Guide. 2nd rev. ed. Bill Clede. LC 88-24987. (Illus.). 384p. (Orig.). 1995. pap. 21.95 (*0-9630016-2-0*) Lakeland Pub.

Police Officer's Guide to Civil Liability. Carl J. Franklin. LC 93-49335. (Illus.). 298p. 1993. pap. 40.95 (*0-398-06130-0*) C C Thomas.

Police Officer's Guide to Civil Liability. Carl J. Franklin. LC 93-49335. (Illus.). 298p. (C). 1993. text 60.95 (*0-398-05881-4*) C C Thomas.

Police Officers Guide to Community Based Policing. C. E. Pratt. (Illus.). iv, 119p. 1995. pap. text 12.95 (*0-9658709-0-1*) Police Mgmt.

Police Officer's Guide to Survival, Health & Fitness. John F. Reintzell. 152p. 1990. pap. 24.95 (*0-398-06344-3*) C C Thomas.

Police Officer's Guide to Survival, Health & Fitness. John F. Reintzell. 152p. 1990. 36.95 (*0-398-05711-7*) C C Thomas.

Police Officer's Handbook. 2nd ed. Ed. by Mahendra Singh. (C). 1991. 110.00 (*0-7855-5450-5*) St Mut.

Police Officers Protect People. Carol Greene. LC 96-13839. (Community Helpers Ser.). (Illus.). 32p. (J). (gr. k-3). 1996. lib. bdg. 21.36 (*1-56766-311-7*) Childs World.

Police Officer's Response Guide to Crimes: Incidents in Progress Field Manual. Nate Tanguay. 1998. 31.95 (*0-930137-81-7*) Looseleaf Law.

Police on Patrol: The Other Side of the Story. Linda Kleinschmidt. Ed. by Deena A. Quilty. (Illus.). 154p. (Orig.). 1996. pap., per. 14.95 (*0-9652255-0-X*) A J Pubng.

Police on Skid-Row: A Study of Peace Keeping. Egon Bittner. (Reprint Series in Social Sciences). (C). 1993. reprint ed. pap. text 5.00 (*0-8290-3743-8*, S-551) Irvington.

Police Operations. Karen M. Hess & Henry M. Wrobleski. Ed. by Jucha. LC 92-10983. 400p. (C). 1993. pap. text 56.00 (*0-314-00926-4*) West Pub.

Police Operations. Sutor. Date not set. pap. text, teacher ed. write for info. (*0-314-35441-7*) West Pub.

Police Operations. 2nd ed. Karen M. Hess & Henry M. Wrobleski. LC 96-38397. 550p. 1996. 92.95 (*0-314-20225-0*) West Pub.

Police Operations: Analysis & Evaluation. Gary W. Cordner et al. LC 96-84653. 538p. (C). 1996. pap. 36.95 (*0-87084-118-1*) Anderson Pub Co.

Police Operations - Tactical Approaches to Crimes in Progress. Andrew P. Sutor. LC 76-16911. (Criminal Justice Ser.). 1976. 19.95 (*0-685-05354-7*); teacher ed. write for info. (*0-8299-0611-8*); pap. text. write for info. (*0-8299-0609-6*) West Pub.

Police Operations Aide. Jack Rudman. (Career Examination Ser.: C-3402). 1994. pap. 23.95 (*0-8373-3402-0*) Nat Learn.

Police Organisation & Legitimacy: Case Studies in England, Wales, & Turkey. Ahmet H. Aydin. 216p. 1997. text 64.95 (*1-85972-644-5*, Pub. by Avebry) Ashgate Pub Co.

Police Organization & Management. 8th ed. V. A. Leonard & Harry W. More. (Police Science Ser.). 650p. (C). 1993. text 34.95 (*1-56662-049-X*) Foundation Pr.

Police Organization & Management: Behavior, Theory & Processes. 2nd ed. Roy R. Roberg. 480p. 1996. 37.95 (*0-534-51418-9*) Wadsworth Pub.

Police Organization & Management: Yesterday, Today & Tomorrow. Mark L. Dantzker. LC 98-18426. 298p. 1998. pap. 49.95 (*0-7506-7101-7*) Buttrwrth-Heinemann.

Police Organization & Management, Instructor's Guide To. 8th ed. Harry W. More. (Police Science Ser.). 93p. 1993. pap. text. write for info. (*1-56662-086-4*) Foundation Pr.

Police Passages. John G. Stratton. (Illus.). 350p. (C). 1984. text 24.95 (*0-317-11361-5*) Glennon Pub.

Police Patrol. Katherine K. Winkleman. LC 96-10761. (Illus.). (J). 1996. 15.95 (*0-8027-8453-4*); lib. bdg. 16.85 (*0-8027-8454-2*) Walker & Co.

Police Patrol: Operations & Management. Charles D. Hale. LC 80-36814. 328p. (C). 1981. text 42.50 (*0-471-03291-3*); pap. text, teacher ed. 10.50 (*0-471-08901-X*) P-H.

Police Patrol: Operations & Management. 2nd ed. Charles D. Hale. LC 93-29722. 397p. 1994. 97.00 (*0-13-814484-2*) P-H.

Police Patrol: Tactics & Techniques. Thomas F. Adams. LC 71-138484. (Essentials of Law Enforcement Ser.). 1971. 24.95 (*0-685-03898-X*) P-H.

Police Patrol Operations. Mark Miller. LC 95-67382. (Illus.). 503p. (C). 1995. pap. 31.95 (*0-942728-59-9*) Copperhouse.

Police Patrolman. Jack Rudman. (Career Examination Ser.: C-595). 1994. pap. 23.95 (*0-8373-0595-0*) Nat Learn.

Police Personnel Selection Process. Leonard Territo et al. LC 76-30889. (Illus.). 1977. pap. text 10.95 (*0-672-61403-0*, Bobbs) Macmillan.

Police Photography. 4th ed. Larry S. Miller & Sam J. Sansone. LC 98-18745. 270p. 1998. pap. 35.95 (*0-87084-816-X*) Anderson Pub Co.

Police Pictures: The Photograph As Evidence. Sandra S. Phillips. LC 97-14539. (Illus.). 144p. 1997. 24.95 (*0-8118-1984-1*) Chronicle Bks.

Police, Pleaders, & Prisoners Too Few for Too Many. William B. Sinclair. (Confusion Beyond Imagination Ser.: Bk. 6). (Illus.). 211p. 1989. 24.50 (*0-937577-10-3*) J F Whitley.

P

some approaches to lessening the corruptive influence of politics; thus positioning his book as a "primer" in the study of law enforcement in all jurisdictions. The book may be ordered from Polis Publishing, 4107 Park St., Camp Hill, PA 17011. Single copy price = $14.00 plus $3.00 shipping & handling, plus 6% Sales Tax, Total=$18.02 Checks or Money Orders accepted.
Publisher Paid Annotation.

Police Politics & Prejudices. Delbert F. Gray. 175p. 1992. text 19.95 (*0-9632288-0-3*) Sweetwater Lit.

Police Power: Public Policy & Constitutional Rights. Ernst Freund. LC 75-17223. (Social Problems & Social Policy Ser.). 1976. reprint ed. 74.95 (*0-405-07493-X*) Ayer.

Police Power: Public Policy & Constitutional Rights. Ed. by Ernst Freund et al. LC 80-84868. (Historical Writings in Law & Jurisprudence Ser.: No. 22, Bk. 32). xcii, 918p. 1981. reprint ed. lib. bdg. 75.00 (*0-89941-084-7*, 302180) W S Hein.

Police Power & Colonial Rule, Madras, 1859-1947. David Arnold. LC 86-900007. 277p. 1987. 29.95 (*0-19-561893-9*) OUP.

Police Powers & Duties: A Practical Guide to the Pace Act, 1984. John Marston & Robin E. Nottridge. 168p. (C). 1985. 100.00 (*0-906840-82-1*, Pub. by Fourmat Pub) St Mut.

Police Powers Arising under the Law of Overruling Necessity. W. P. Prentice. xli, 516p. 1993. reprint ed. 52.50 (*0-8377-2523-2*, Rothman) W S Hein.

Police Powers in Canada: The Evolution & Practice of Authority. Ed. by R. C. MacLeod & David Schneiderman. 370p. 1994. text 50.00 (*0-8020-2863-2*); pap. text 24.95 (*0-8020-7362-X*) U of Toronto Pr.

Police Practice in the '90s: Key Management Issues. Ed. by James J. Fyfe. (Practical Management Ser.). (Illus.). 174p. 1990. 23.95 (*0-87326-058-9*) Intl City-Cnty Mgt.

Police Practices: An International Review. Ed. by Dilip K. Das. LC 94-18256. 475p. 1994. 58.00 (*0-8108-2908-8*) Scarecrow.

Police Principles & the Problem of War. Charles Reith. 1992. lib. bdg. 88.75 (*0-8490-5299-8*) Gordon Pr.

Police, Probation & Protecting the Public. Mike Nash. LC 99-205096. 228p. 1999. pap. 34.00 (*1-85431-735-0*, Pub. by Blackstone Pr) Gaunt.

Police Procedural. George N. Dove. LC 81-84214. 1982. 21.95 (*0-87972-188-X*) Bowling Green Univ Popular Press.

Police Procedural: A Writer's Guide to the Police & How They Work. Russell Bintliff. (Howdunit Ser.). 272p. 1993. pap. 16.99 (*0-89879-596-6*, Wrtrs Digest Bks) F & W Pubns Inc.

Police Procedurals. Martin Harry Greenberg & Bill Pronzini. LC 85-18557. Vol. 2. 232p. 1985. pap. 8.00 (*0-89733-158-3*) Academy Chi Pubs.

Police Procedure & Search & Seizure. James A. Girard & Ronald P. Leavell. 400p. (C). 1993. text. write for info. (*0-9637609-1-2*); pap. text. write for info. (*0-9637609-0-4*) Prof Police.

Police Professionalism in New York City: The Zuccotti Committee in Historical Context. Joseph P. Viteritti. Ed. by Graham Hughes. (Occasional Papers: Vol. III). 26p. (Orig.). (C). 1987. pap. 5.00 (*1-878429-52-3*) NYU Ctr for Rsch in Crime Justice.

Police Program Evaluation. Ed. by Larry Hoover. LC 97-69292. 240p. 1997. pap. 21.00 (*1-878734-54-7*) Police Exec Res.

Police Promotion Course. Jack Rudman. (General Aptitude & Abilities Ser.: No. CS-18). pap. 39.95 (*0-8373-6718-2*, CS-18) Nat Learn.

Police Promotion Manual. 1994. 16.95 (*0-930137-23-X*) Looseleaf Law.

Police Psychology: Collected Papers. Martin Reiser. LC 81-82247. 1982. 24.95 (*0-934486-01-8*) Martin Reiser.

Police Psychology into the 21st Century. Ed. by Martin I. Kurke & Ellen M. Scrivner. (Applied Psychology Ser.). 544p. 1995. text 39.95 (*0-8058-1344-6*) L Erlbaum Assocs.

Police, Public Order & Civil Liberties: Legacies of Miners' Strike. Ed. by Sarah McCabe et al. 256p. (C). 1988. lib. bdg. 45.00 (*0-415-00724-0*) Routledge.

Police, Public Order & Civil Liberties: Legacies of the Miners' Strike. Sarah McCabe et al. LC 88-190050. 221p. reprint ed. pap. 68.60 (*0-608-20398-X*, 207165100002) Bks Demand.

Police Pursuit Driving: Controlling Responses to Emergency Situations, 27. Geoffrey P. Alpert & Roger G. Dunham. LC 89-23247. (Contributions in Criminology & Penology Ser.: No. 27). 200p. 1990. 52.95 (*0-313-27261-1*, ALC/, Greenwood Pr) Greenwood.

Police Pursuit Driving Handbook. Donald O. Schultz. LC 79-50244. (Illus.). 96p. (Orig.). reprint ed. pap. 30.00 (*0-608-18155-2*, 203284600081) Bks Demand.

Police Reading Comprehension. Jack Rudman. (General Aptitude & Abilities Ser.: No. CS-23). pap. 23.95 (*0-8373-6723-9*, CS-23) Nat Learn.

Police Records & Recollections or Boston by Daylight & Gaslight for Two Hundred & Forty Years. Edward H. Savage. LC 74-154048. (Criminology, Law Enforcement, & Social Problems Ser.: No. 123). (Illus.). 1970. reprint ed. 24.00 (*0-87585-123-1*) Patterson Smith.

Police Referral to Drug Treatment. 1986. lib. bdg. 79.95 (*0-8490-3516-3*) Gordon Pr.

Police Research: Some Future Prospects. Mollie Weatheritt. 200p. 1989. text 63.95 (*0-566-07030-8*, Pub. by Avebry) Ashgate Pub Co.

Police Research in the Federal Republic of Germany: 15 Years Research Within the "Bundeskriminalamt" Ed. by E. Kube et al. (Illus.). 304p. 1991. 135.00 (*0-387-50395-1*) Spr-Verlag.

Police Response to People with Mental Illnesses: Trainer's Guide. LC 97-75599. 140p. 1997. pap. 5.50 (*1-878734-55-5*) Police Exec Res.

Police Response to the Homeless: A Status Report. Martha R. Plotkin & Tony Narr. LC 93-86619. 312p. (Orig.). 1993. pap. 26.00 (*1-878734-31-8*) Police Exec Res.

Police Retirement: The Impact of Change. John M. Violanti. (Illus.). 200p. 1992. pap. 26.95 (*0-398-06474-1*) C C Thomas.

Police Retirement: The Impact of Change. John M. Violanti. (Illus.). 200p. (C). 1992. text 39.95 (*0-398-05786-9*) C C Thomas.

Police Rifles: Selecting the Right Rifle for Street Patrol & Special Tactical Situations. Richard Fairburn. (Illus.). 248p. 1994. pap. 30.00 (*0-87364-799-8*) Paladin Pr.

Police Science Fundamentals. 1973rd ed. Henry J. Mulhearn. 220p. pap. 14.95 (*0-87526-160-4*) Gould.

Police Selection: A Case Study. Ed. by Suzanne O. Hazlett. (Center for Responsive Psychology Monograph). 14p. (Orig.). 1985. pap. 4.00 (*0-318-19260-8*) Ctr Respon Psych.

Police Selection & Evaluation: Issues & Techniques. Charles D. Spielberger. LC 78-9958. (Praeger Special Studies). 313p. 1979. 65.00 (*0-275-90428-8*, C0428, Praeger Pubs) Greenwood.

Police Selection & Training. Ed. by John C. Yuille. 1986. lib. bdg. 234.00 (*90-247-3369-3*) Kluwer Academic.

Police Sergeant * Lieutenant * Captain. Francis M. Connolly & George J. Mullins. 336p. 1993. per. 19.95 (*0-671-84686-8*, Arc) IDG Bks.

Police Sergeant Examination Preparation Guide. Larry F. Jetmore. (Cliffs Test Preparation Ser.). 312p. (Orig.). 1989. pap. text 9.95 (*0-8220-2044-0*, Cliff) IDG Bks.

Police Sergeants Handbook, Vol. I. Robert A. Davis, Sr. 195p. (Orig.). 1968. pap. 28.95 (*1-56325-024-1*, DH011) Davis Pub Law.

Police Sergeants Handbook, Vol. II. J. Robert Lansberry. 279p. (Orig.). 1972. pap. 28.95 (*1-56325-050-0*, DH012) Davis Pub Law.

Police Sergeants Handbook, Vol. III. Ralph E. Hendel. 250p. (Orig.). 1976. pap. 28.95 (*1-56325-051-9*, DH013) Davis Pub Law.

Police Service: Public Needs & Community Policing in America. David Kessler. (Illus.). 260p. 1998. pap. 54.95 (*1-57292-068-8*) Austin & Winfield.

Police Service: Public Needs & Community Policing in America. David Kessler. (Illus.). 260p. 1998. 74.95 (*1-57292-069-6*) Intl Scholars.

Police Services: The Private Challenge. Erwin A. Blackstone & Simon Hakim. (Independent Policy Reports). 44p. (Orig.). 1996. pap. 6.95 (*0-945999-49-6*) Independent Inst.

Police Shootings & the Prosecutor in Los Angeles County: An Evaluation of Operation Rollout. Craig D. Uchida et al. LC 81-85315. (Illus.). 1981. pap. 15.00 (*0-318-57302-4*) Police Found.

Police Shotgun Manual: How to Survive Against All Odds. Bill Clede. LC 86-948. 128p. 1986. reprint ed. pap. 39.70 (*0-608-00473-1*, 206129200007) Bks Demand.

Police Sniper. Craig Roberts. Ed. by Eric Tobias. 320p. (Orig.). 1993. mass mkt. 5.99 (*0-671-79459-0*) PB.

Police Staff College: Bramshill. Ian Watt. LC 94-20677. (Studies in International Criminal Justice Ser.). 1994. 4.95 (*0-942511-64-6*) OICJ.

***Police Station.** Steven James Petruccio. (Little Activity Bks.). (Illus.). (J). 1999. pap. 1.00 (*0-486-40748-9*) Dover.

***Police Station.** Lola M. Schaefer. LC 99-40768. (Who Works Here? Ser.). (Illus.). (J). 2000. lib. bdg. write for info. (*1-57572-520-7*) Heinemann Lib.

Police Station Connected Burglar Alarm Units & Systems, UL 365. 4th ed. (C). 1997. pap. text 95.00 (*1-55989-409-1*) Underwrtrs Labs.

Police Stations see Estaciones de Policia

Police Stations. Jason Cooper. LC 92-12575. (J). 1992. 9.50 (*0-685-59406-8*) Rourke Corp.

Police Stations. Jason Cooper. LC 92-12575. (Great Places to Visit Ser.). 24p. (J). (gr. k-4). 1992. lib. bdg. 10.95 (*0-86593-213-1*) Rourke Corp.

Police Stress at Work. David A. Alexander et al. (Aberdeen University Press Bks.). 176p. 1991. pap. text 19.90 (*0-08-041199-1*, Pub. by Aberdeen U Pr) Macmillan.

Police Suicide: Epidemic in Blue. John M. Violanti. LC 96-8389. (American Series in Behavioral Science & Law). (Illus.). 132p. 1996. 35.95 (*0-398-06665-5*); pap. 26.95 (*0-398-06666-3*) C C Thomas.

Police Supervision. Ronald W. Glensor et al. LC 98-8620. 408p. 1998. 57.19 (*0-07-303342-1*) McGraw.

Police Supervision: Theory & Practice. 2nd ed. Paul M. Whisenand. (Illus.). 576p. 1976. text 46.80 (*0-13-686311-6*) P-H.

Police Supervision Study Guide. Robert Fischer & Ronald Moser. 64p. 1995. pap., student ed., per. 13.95 (*0-7872-1660-7*) Kendall-Hunt.

Police Supervisor's Guide to Discipline & Commendation. Barbara J. Birkland et al. Ed. by Ed Mund. (Police Supervision Ser.). (Illus.). 48p. 1997. pap. 7.95 (*0-937935-09-3*) Justice Syst Pr.

Police Supervisor's Test Manual Database. Cliff Mariani. 290p. 1996. ring bd. 24.95 (*0-930137-84-1*) Looseleaf Law.

Police Surgeon. Jack Rudman. (Career Examination Ser.: C-596). 1994. pap. 49.95 (*0-8373-0596-9*) Nat Learn.

***Police Surgeon.** large type ed. Abigail Gordon. 288p. 2000. 25.99 (*0-263-16270-2*, Pub. by Mills & Boon) Ulverscroft.

Police Systems & Practices: An Introduction. Thomas Barker et al. LC 93-39495. 354p. 1994. 63.80 (*0-13-682865-5*) P-H.

Police, the Court & Injustice. James Vadackumchery. LC 97-901012. (Illus.). xiii, 188p. 1997. 28.00 (*81-7024-806-X*, Pub. by APH Pubng) Nataraj Bks.

Police, the People & Criminal Justice. James Vadackumchery. LC 97-905308. xiv, 210p. 1997. 30.00 (*81-7024-862-0*, Pub. by APH Pubng) Nataraj Bks.

Police Traffic Control Function. 5th ed. Paul B. Weston. LC 95-25888. (Illus.). 228p. 1996. 41.95 (*0-398-06567-5*); pap. 28.95 (*0-398-06568-3*) C C Thomas.

Police Trainee. Jack Rudman. (Career Examination Ser.: C-597). 1994. pap. 23.95 (*0-8373-0597-7*) Nat Learn.

Police Training Concerning Migrants & Ethnic Relations. 1994. 18.00 (*92-871-2459-0*, Pub. by Council of Europe) Manhattan Pub Co.

Police Training in Community Relations: Perspectives on the United States & India. R. P. Joshi. (C). 1993. 20.00 (*81-7033-190-0*, Pub. by Rawat Pubns) S Asia.

Police Transportation Management. G. Ray Wynne. (Illus.). 1965. pap. 15.00 (*0-910390-03-7*) Coda Publications.

Police Trauma: Psychological Aftermath of Civilian Combat. John M. Violanti & Douglas Paton. LC 99-17948. (Illus.). 276p. 1999. pap. text 49.95 (*0-398-06955-7*) C C Thomas.

***Police Trauma: Psychological Aftermath of Civilian Combat.** Ed. by John M. Violanti & Douglas Paton. LC 99-17948. (Illus.). 352p. 1999. text 64.95 (*0-398-06954-9*) C C Thomas.

***Police under Fire.** Ted Gottfried. LC 98-55074. (Issue & Debate Ser.). (Illus.). 128p. (YA). (gr. 6-9). 1999. lib. bdg. 22.90 (*0-7613-1313-3*) TFC Bks NY.

Police under Pressure: Resolving Disputes, 40. Robert Coulson. LC 92-35551. (Criminology & Crime Control Policy Ser.: No. 40). 176p. 1993. 47.95 (*0-313-28791-0*, GM8791, Greenwood Pr) Greenwood.

Police Uniform & Equipment. A. A. Clarke. 1989. pap. 6.25 (*0-7478-0126-6*, Pub. by Shire Pubns) St Mut.

***Police Uniform Patches of Central Arizona.** Stanley G. Benjamin. (Illus.). 25p. 2000. pap. write for info. (*1-930012-01-2*) Benjamin & Co.

***Police Uniform Patches of Northern Arizona.** Stanley G. Benjamin. 25p. 2000. pap. write for info. (*1-930012-02-0*) Benjamin & Co.

Police Unions. International Association of Chiefs of Police Staf. LC 79-154573. (Police in America Ser.). 1975. reprint ed. 16.95 (*0-405-03400-8*) Ayer.

Police Use of Force. Donald O. Schultz & J. Gregory Service. (Illus.). 136p. 1981. 33.95 (*0-398-04563-1*) C C Thomas.

Police Use of Force: A Statistical Analysis of the Metro-Dade Police Department. Geoffrey P. Alpert & Roger Dunham. LC 95-71262. (Police Research & Evaluation Ser.: Vol. 1). 44p. (Orig.). 1995. pap. text 6.50 (*1-878734-38-5*) Police Exec Res.

Police Use of Force: Official Reports, Citizen Complaints, & Legal Consequences, 2 vols., Set only. Antony M. Pate et al. LC 93-86909. (Illus.). 173p. (Orig.). 1993. pap. text. write for info. (*1-884614-01-9*); pap. text. write for info. (*1-884614-02-7*) Police Found.

Police Use of Force: Official Reports, Citizen Complaints, & Legal Consequences, 2 vols., Vols. 1 - 2. Antony M. Pate et al. LC 93-86909. (Illus.). 383p. (Orig.). 1993. pap. text 60.00 (*1-884614-00-0*) Police Found.

Police Use of Force Vol. 1: A Line Officer's Guide. Thomas T. Gillespie et al. LC 98-60230. 120p. (Orig.). 1998. pap. 29.95 (*1-888644-82-6*) Varro Pr.

Police Vehicles & Firearms: Instruments of Deadly Force. Geoffrey P. Alpert & Lorie Fridell. 167p. (C). 1992. pap. text 13.95 (*0-88133-613-0*) Waveland Pr.

Police Violence: Understanding & Controlling Police Abuse of Force. Ed. by William A. Geller & Hans Toch. LC 96-33939. 384p. 1996. reprint ed. 40.00 (*0-300-06429-2*) Yale U Pr.

Police Violence in Argentina: Torture & Police Killings in Buenos Aires. Ed. by Human Rights Watch Staff. 56p. (Orig.). 1991. pap. 7.00 (*1-56432-051-0*) Hum Rts Watch.

Police Witness: Effectiveness in the Courtroom. Michael W. Whitaker. 124p. 1985. 30.95 (*0-398-05119-4*); pap. 18.95 (*0-398-06495-4*) C C Thomas.

Police Work: On Patrol in the Inner City. LC 96-95241. (Illus.). 224p. 1997. pap. write for info. (*0-9655590-0-9*) M D Mello.

Police Work: The Social Organization of Policing. 2nd rev. ed. Peter K. Manning. LC 98-115517. (Illus.). 372p. (C). 1997. pap. text 22.95 (*0-88133-953-9*) Waveland Pr.

Police Work with Juveniles & the Administration of Juvenile Justice. 8th ed. John P. Kenney et al. LC 94-33970. 334p. (C). 1994. text 45.95 (*0-398-05938-1*) C C Thomas.

Police/Law Enforcement. 6th ed. 1991. pap. 12.00 (*0-910553-29-7*) Ken-Bks.

Policeman. Cornelius F. Cahalane. LC 75-112529. (Rise of Urban America Ser.). 1974. reprint ed. 25.95 (*0-405-02440-1*) Ayer.

Policeman & Public. Arthur Woods. 1978. 18.95 (*0-405-03391-5*, 16957) Ayer.

Policeman & Public: With Introduction & Index Added. Arthur Woods. LC 71-172604. (Criminology, Law Enforcement, & Social Problems Ser.: No. 194). (Illus.). 1975. reprint ed. 20.00 (*0-87585-194-0*) Patterson Smith.

Policeman Bluejay. L. Frank Baum. LC 81-9044. 152p. (J). (gr. 1-6). 1981. reprint ed. 50.00 (*0-8201-1367-0*) Schol Facsimiles.

***Policeman Small.** Lois Lenski. (J). 2001. mass mkt. 11.95 (*0-375-81072-2*) Random.

***Policeman Small.** Lois Lenski. (J). 2001. mass mkt. 13.99 (*0-375-91072-7*, Pub. by Random Bks Yng Read) Random.

Policeman's Art: As Taught in the New York State School for Police. George F. Chandler et al. LC 70-156009. reprint ed. 32.50 (*0-404-09172-5*) AMS Pr.

Policeman's Guide to Crime & Criminal Investigation. S. S. Mangat. (C). 1979. 160.00 (*0-7855-5451-3*) St Mut.

***Policeman's Ireland: Recollections of Samuel Waters, R. I. C.** Ed. by Stephen Ball. LC 99-197984. 96p. 1999. pap. 12.95 (*1-85918-189-9*, Pub. by Cork Univ) Intl Spec Bk.

Policeman's Position Today & Tomorrow: An Examination of the Victoria Police Force. Paul R. Wilson & John S. Western. LC 72-192932. xi, 128p. 1972. write for info. (*0-7022-0754-3*) Intl Spec Bk.

Policewoman. Jack Rudman. (Career Examination Ser.: C-598). 1994. pap. 23.95 (*0-8373-0598-5*) Nat Learn.

Policewoman: Her Service & Ideals. Mary E. Hamilton. LC 74-154596. (Police in America Ser.). 1980. reprint ed. 21.95 (*0-405-03370-2*) Ayer.

Policework: The Need for a Noble Character. Rickey D. Lashley. LC 94-32921. 144p. 1995. 55.00 (*0-275-95013-1*, Praeger Pubs) Greenwood.

Policia de la Biblioteca. Stephen King.Tr. of Library Policeman. (SPA.). 1999. mass mkt. 4.99 (*0-451-18660-5*, Sig) NAL.

Policias. Capstone Press Staff. (J). 1998. 14.00 (*0-516-21370-9*) Childrens.

Policias. Dee Ready. 15.93 (*1-56065-802-9*, Bridgestone Bks) Capstone Pr.

Policies Affecting Fertility & Contraceptive Use: An Assessment of Twelve Sub-Saharan Countries. Susan Scribner. LC 94-29410. (Discussion Paper, Africa Technical Department Ser.: 259). 98p. 1995. pap. 22.00 (*0-8213-2994-4*, 12994) World Bank.

Policies & Organizations for Urban Water Management. Victor A. Koelzer & Alexander B. Bigler. LC 74-28617. 1975. pap. 20.00 (*0-918334-06-3*) WRP.

Policies & Perceptions of Insurance: An Introduction to Insurance Law. Malcolm Clarke. 354p. 1997. pap. text (*0-19-876341-7*) OUP.

Policies & Perceptions of Insurance: An Introduction to Insurance Law. Malcolm Clarke. (Clarendon Law Ser.). 354p. 1998. text 80.00 (*0-19-876340-9*) OUP.

Policies & Persons: A Casebook in Business Ethics. 3rd ed. Kenneth E. Goodpaster et al. LC 97-25773. 552p. 1997. pap. 50.31 (*0-07-024509-6*) McGraw.

Policies & Persons: A Casebook in Ethics. 2nd ed. John B. Matthews et al. 512p. (C). 1991. teacher ed. write for info. (*0-318-72116-3*); text 49.00 (*0-07-040999-4*) McGraw.

Policies & Practice: A Focus on Higher Education Retention. American Association of State Colleges & Universit. LC 97-35812. 1997. write for info. (*0-88044-136-4*) AASCU Press.

Policies & Practices in Preventive Child Care. Pauline Hardiker et al. 195p. 1991. text 66.95 (*1-85628-108-6*, Pub. by Avebry) Ashgate Pub Co.

Policies & Practices of Transnational Corporations Regarding Their Activities in South Africa & Namibia. 55p. (Orig.). 1984. pap. 7.00 (*92-1-104147-3*, E.84.11.A.5) UN.

Policies & Procedures in Association Management, 1996. American Society of Association Executives Staff. 210p. 1996. pap. 125.00 (*0-88034-108-4*) Am Soc Assn Execs.

Policies & Procedures. Robert A. Pearson. 1984. reprint ed. pap. write for info. (*0-9608378-1-7*) B Pearson.

Policies & Procedures: Adult Correctional Institutions. 396p. 1991. 60.00 (*0-929310-62-4*, 318) Am Correctional.

Policies & Procedures: Adult Local Detention Facilities. American Correctional Association Staff. 428p. 1992. pap. 60.00 (*0-929310-71-3*, 325) Am Correctional.

Policies & Procedures: Juvenile Community Residential Facilities. American Correctional Association Staff. 145p. (Orig.). 1990. 28.00 (*0-929310-30-6*) Am Correctional.

Policies & Procedures: Juvenile Detention Facilities. American Correctional Association Staff. 206p. (Orig.). 1992. pap. text 27.00 (*0-929310-61-6*, 458) Am Correctional.

Policies & Procedures for Long-Term Care Dietetic Services. Ann P. Hunter. 320p. 1990. 149.00 (*0-8342-0128-3*, 20128) Aspen Pub.

***Policies & Procedures for the Electroneurodiagnostic Laboratory.** ASET Committee. 150p. 1999. spiral bd. 80.00 (*1-57797-039-X*) ASET.

Policies & Procedures Guidebook for Assisted Living Centers. Joan Bachman. 194p. 77.00 (*0-929442-56-3*) Prof Prnting & Pub.

Policies & Procedures Handbook for Induction & Foundation Training. Compiled by George Mahon. 1991. pap. 21.00 (*0-7855-2689-7*, Pub. by Natl Inst Soc Work) St Mut.

***Policies & Procedures Manual Accouting & Financial Control.** 2000. 89.95 (*0-13-088001-9*) P-H.

Policies & Procedures Manual for Accounting & Financial Control. DOUGLAS W. KURZ. 1992. 89.95 (*0-13-020879-5*) P-H.

Policies & Procedures of Orchestra Administration: A Survey & Study by the American Symphony Orchestra League. 116p. 1992. pap. 30.00 (*0-614-04618-1*) Am Symphony Orch.

Policies & Procedures of Orchestra Governing Boards, 3. 2nd ed. 1995. pap. 30.00 (*0-614-04621-1*) Am Symphony Orch.

Policies & Programs for Social & Human Development: Experiences from Developing Countries. Antonio Sancho. LC 96-12886. 106p. 1996. pap. 19.95 (*1-55815-487-6*) ICS Pr.

Policies & Strategies to Combat Drugs in Europe: The Treaty on European Union: Framework for a New European Strategy to Combat Drugs. Ed. by Georges Estievenart. LC 94-46675. 448p. (C). 1995. lib. bdg. 136.00 (*0-7923-3336-5*, Pub. by M Nijhoff) Kluwer Academic.

P

An Asterisk (*) at the beginning of an entry indicates that the title is appearing for the first time.

Policies & Systems of Environmental Impact Assessment. (Environmental Ser.: No. 4). 44p. 1990. 19.00 (*92-1-116492-3*, 90.II.E.36) UN.

Policies for African Development: From the 1890s to the 1990s. Ed. by I. G. Patel. LC 92-15526. 293p. 1992. pap. 24.00 (*1-55775-232-X*) Intl Monetary.

Policies for America's Public Schools: Teacher, Equity, & Indicators. Ed. by Ron Haskins et al. LC 87-27057. (Child & Family Policy Ser.: Vol. 6). 320p. 1988. text 73.25 (*0-89391-444-4*) Ablx Pub.

Policies for Competition & Competitiveness: Case Study of Industry in Turkey. LC 96-122918. (UNIDO General Studies). 300p. 45.00 (*92-1-106298-5*) UN.

***Policies for Competitiveness: Comparing Business-Government Relationships in the 'Golden Age of Capitalism'** Ed. by Hideaki Miyajima et al. LC 99-21238. (Fuji Conference Ser.). (Illus.). 356p. 1999. text 85.00 (*0-19-829323-2*) OUP.

Policies for Coping with Oil Supply Disruptions. Ed. by George Horwich & Edward J. Mitchell. LC 82-1630. (AEI Symposia Ser.: No. 82A). 200p. reprint ed. pap. 62.00 (*0-8357-4523-6*, 203738400008) Bks Demand.

Policies for Developing Forward Foreign Exchange Markets. Peter J. Quirk et al. (Occasional Papers: No. 60). 51p. 1988. pap. 7.50 (*1-55775-017-3*) Intl Monetary.

Policies for Growth: The Latin American Experience: Proceedings of a Conference Held in Mangaratiba, Rio de Janeiro, Brazil, March 16-19, 1994. Contrib. by Andre L. Resende. 1995. 24.00 (*1-55775-517-5*) Intl Monetary.

Policies for Improving Schools in South Dakota: The Financial & Knowledge Resources for Teacher Education. Robert L. Emans. 1984. 1.00 (*1-55614-079-7*) U of SD Gov Res Bur.

Policies for Promoting the Use of Environmentally Sound Technologies. LC 98-108480. pap. 19.00 (*92-1-112397-6*) UN.

Policies for Prosperity: Essays in a Keynesian Mode. James Tobin. Ed. by Peter M. Jackson. 528p. 1989. pap. text 25.00 (*0-262-70036-0*) MIT Pr.

Policies for Public Service Transformation. Fanie Cloete & Job Mokgoro. LC 95-206520. 1995. pap. 32.00 (*0-7021-3319-1*, Pub. by Juta & Co) Intl Spec Bk.

Policies for Seismic Safety: Elements of a State Governmental Program. Stanley Scott. LC 79-19189. 112p. (Orig.). reprint ed. pap. 34.80 (*0-608-20135-9*, 207140700011) Bks Demand.

Policies, Institutions & the Dark Side of Economics. Vito Tanzi. LC 97-44605. 296p. 2000. 95.00 (*1-85898-729-6*) E Elgar.

Policies into Practice. Lewis & Walla. 1984. text 72.95 (*0-435-83488-6*); text 35.95 (*0-435-83489-4*) Ashgate Pub Co.

Policies, Law & Regulations on Transfer, Application & Development of Technology, 1990. 32p. 1992. 15.00 (*92-1-112318-6*, E.92.II.D.2) UN.

Policies of Chaos: The Organizational Causes of Violence in China's Cultural Revolution. Lynn T. White. LC 88-15235. 378p. 1989. reprint ed. pap. 117.20 (*0-608-02573-9*, 206321800004) Bks Demand.

Policies of Deceit: In Our Public Schools & Colleges. Jim Martin. Ed. by Gregor McGavin & Evelyn Martin. 310p. (Orig.). 1998. pap. 16.00 (*0-9663249-0-0*) Mustang Publ.

Policies of Genocide: Jews & Soviet Prisoners of War in Nazi Germany. Ed. by Gerhard Hirschfeld. (Illus.). 176p. 1986. text 24.95 (*0-04-943045-9*); pap. text 14.95 (*0-04-943046-7*) Routledge.

Policies of Publishers: A Handbook for Order Librarians. David U. Kim & Craig A. Wilson. LC 95-6262. 303p. 1995. 39.50 (*0-8108-3017-5*) Scarecrow.

Policies of Publishers: A Handbook for Order Librarians, 1989. David U. Kim & Craig A Wilson. LC 89-6406. 285p. 1989. 31.00 (*0-8108-2233-4*) Scarecrow.

Policies on Health & Safety in 13 Countries of the European Union Vol. II: The European Situation. Francoise Piotet. 102p. 1996. pap. 18.00 (*92-827-6642-X*, SY94-96-938-ENC, Pub. by Comm Europ Commun) Bernan Associates.

Policies on Imports from Economies in Transition: Two Case Studies. Peter D. Ehrenhaft et al. LC 97-10334. (Studies of Economies in Transformation: No. 22). 56p. 1997. pap. 22.00 (*0-8213-3916-8*, 13916) World Bank.

Policies on Labour Relations & Social Dialogue in European Countries: The Portuguese & German Cases. Rainer Pitschas. LC 98-177126. 176 p. 1997. write for info. (*3-7890-4982-4*) Nomos Verlags.

Policies, Plans & People: Culture & Health Development in Nepal. Judith Justice. 1986. pap. 15.95 (*0-520-06788-6*, Pub. by U CA Pr) Cal Prin Full Svc.

Policies, Plans, & People: Foreign Aid & Health Development. Judith Justice. 1989. pap. 120.00 (*0-7855-7475-1*, Pub. by Ratna Pustak Bhandar) St Mut.

***Policies, Policies & the Future of Lifelong Learning.** Ann Hodgson. 192p. 2000. pap. 35.00 (*0-7494-3202-0*, Pub. by Kogan Page Ltd) Stylus Pub VA.

Policies, Strategies & Plans for Computing in Higher Education: Proceedings. 200p. 12.00 (*0-318-14030-6*) EDUCOM.

Policies That Work for Personal Trainers. Susan Cantwell. LC 97-76871. (Business Ser.: Vol. 1). 114p. 1997. per. 24.95 (*1-887781-02-1*, C899002) IDEA Pr.

Policies to Combat Depression. Universities-National Bureau Staff. (Conference Ser.: No. 7). 427p. 1956. reprint ed. 111.10 (*0-87014-198-8*) Natl Bur Econ Res.

Policies to Combat Depression: Proceedings. Conference of the Universities. LC 75-19701. (National Bureau of Economic Research Ser.). (Illus.). 1975. reprint ed. 35.95 (*0-405-07581-2*) Ayer.

Policies to Improve Linkages with the Global Economy: Policies to Improve Linkages with the Global Economy. Economic Commission for Latin America & the Caribb. LC 96-198318. (Libros de la CEPAL: No. 40). 308p. 25.00 (*92-1-121200-6*) UN.

Policies to Prevent Crime: Neighborhood, Family & Employment Strategies, Vol. 494. Ed. by Lynn A. Curtis. 1987. 26.00 (*0-8039-3008-9*); pap. 17.00 (*0-8039-3009-7*) Sage.

***Policies Towards Full Employment.** OECD Staff. (Proceedings Ser.). 224p. 2000. pap. 45.00 (*92-64-17661-6*, 03 2000 03 1 P, Pub. by Org for Econ) OECD.

Policing. Dempsey. Date not set. pap. text, teacher ed. write for info. (*0-314-03337-8*) West Pub.

Policing. Light. (Criminal Justice Ser.). 2001. text 43.00 (*0-534-54230-1*) Wadsworth Pub.

Policing, 2 vols., Vols. I & II. Robert Reiner. (International Library of Criminology, Criminal Justice & Penology). (Illus.). 1000p. 1996. text 349.95 (*1-85521-390-7*, Pub. by Dartmth Pub) Ashgate Pub Co.

Policing: An Introduction to Law Enforcement. John S. Dempsey. Ed. by Baxter. LC 93-21287. 400p. (C). 1994. pap. 36.25 (*0-314-02774-2*) West Pub.

Policing: Concepts, Strategies, & Current Issues in American Police Forces. Michael J. Palmiotto. LC 97-13942. 386p. (C). 1997. pap. 28.00 (*0-89089-867-7*) Carolina Acad Pr.

Policing a Class Society: The Experience of American Cities, 1865 to 1915. Sidney L. Harring. (Crime, Law & Deviance Ser.). 310p. 1983. text 45.00 (*0-8135-1000-7*) Rutgers U Pr.

Policing a Multicultural Community. Henry T. DeGeneste & John P. Sullivan. LC 97-69036. 28p. 1997. pap. 6.50 (*1-878734-53-9*) Police Exec Res.

Policing a Socialist Society: The German Democratic Republic, 34. Nancy T. Wolfe. LC 91-27274. (Contributions in Criminology & Penology Ser.: No. 34). 264p. 1992. 65.00 (*0-313-26530-5*, WCJ/, Greenwood Pr) Greenwood.

Policing Accounting Knowledge: The Market for Excuses Affair. Tony Tinker & Anthony Puxty. (Critical Accounting Research Ser.). 320p. (C). 1995. text 39.95 (*1-55876-085-7*) Wiener Pubs Inc.

Policing Across National Boundaries. Malcolm Anderson & Monica Den Boer. LC 93-42935. 256p. 1994. text 55.00 (*1-85567-195-6*) St Martin.

Policing Across the World: Issues for the Twenty-First Century. R. I. Mawby. LC 99-175617. 1999. 72.00 (*1-85728-488-7*); pap. text 23.95 (*1-85728-489-5*) UCL Pr Ltd.

***Policing Africa: Internal Security & the Limits of Liberalization.** Alice Hills. LC 99-37488. 214p. 2000. 53.00 (*1-55587-715-X*) L Rienner.

Policing America: Methods, Issues, Challenges. 3rd ed. Kenneth J. Peak. LC 99-19289. (Illus.). 394p. 1999. 81.00 (*0-13-021884-7*) P-H.

Policing American Society. 2nd ed. Randy L. LaGrange. LC 97-3889. (Illus.). 572p. (C). 1997. text 63.95 (*0-8304-1471-1*) Thomson Learn.

Policing & Crime Control see Crime & Justice in American History

Policing & Democracy in the Netherlands. Trevor Jones. 192p. (C). 1995. pap. 19.95 (*0-85374-581-1*, Pub. by Pol Studies Inst) Brookings.

Policing & Human Rights. 2nd ed. Ed. by Francisca Nel & Jan Bezuidenhout. LC 97-198501. 472p. 1997. pap. 52.50 (*0-7021-3905-X*, Pub. by Juta & Co) Gaunt.

Policing & Prosecution in Britain, 1750-1850. Ed. by Francis G. Snyder & Douglas Hay. (Illus.). 488p. 1989. 95.00 (*0-19-822999-2*) OUP.

Policing & Punishing the Drinking Driver. R. Homel. (Research in Criminology Ser.). (Illus.). 370p. 1988. 118.00 (*0-387-96715-X*) Spr-Verlag.

Policing & Punishment in China: From Patriarchy to "the People" Michael R. Dutton. (Illus.). 401p. (C). 1992. text 80.00 (*0-521-40097-X*) Cambridge U Pr.

Policing as Social Discipline. Satnam Choongh. (Clarendon Studies in Criminology). 274p. 1998. text 69.00 (*0-19-826478-X*) OUP.

Policing As Though People Matter. Dorothy Guyot. 448p. 1991. 39.95 (*0-87722-755-1*); pap. 24.95 (*0-87722-766-7*) Temple U Pr.

Policing Athens: Social Control in the Attic Lawsuits, 420-320 B. C. Virginia J. Hunter. LC 93-23879. (Illus.). 296p. 1993. text 39.50 (*0-691-03268-8*, Pub. by Princeton U Pr) Cal Prin Full Svc.

Policing Change, Changing Police: International Perspectives. Otwin Marenin. LC 95-37407. (Reference Library of Social Science: Vol. 1025). 1995. write for info. (*0-614-08568-3*) Garland.

Policing Change, Changing Police: International Perspectives. Ed. by Otwin Marenin. LC 95-37407. (Current Issues in Criminal Justice Ser.: Vol. 14). (Illus.). 368p. 1996. text 65.00 (*0-8153-1995-9*, SS1025) Garland.

***Policing Citizens: Authority & Rights.** P. A. J. Waddington. 1998. pap. text 24.95 (*1-85728-693-6*) Taylor & Francis.

Policing Communities: Understanding Crime & Solving Problems (An Anthology) Ronald W. Glensor et al. LC 98-19442. 320p. (C). 1999. pap. text. write for info. (*1-891487-07-8*) Roxbury Pub Co.

Policing Desire: Pornography, Aids & the Media. 3rd ed. Simon Watney. LC 96-38959. xvi, 172 p. 1997. pap. 16.95 (*0-8166-3025-9*); text 39.95 (*0-8166-3024-0*) U of Minn Pr.

Policing 'Domestic' Violence: Women, the Law, & the State. Susan S. Edwards. 256p. (C). 1989. text 45.00 (*0-8039-8032-9*); pap. text 18.95 (*0-8039-8033-7*) Sage.

Policing Drugs. Karim Murji. LC 98-73752. 202p. 1998. text 59.95 (*1-84014-383-5*) Ashgate Pub Co.

Policing Europe: Co-Operation, Conflict & Control. Bill Hebenton & Terry Thomas. LC 94-27003. 1997. text 49.95 (*0-312-12423-6*) St Martin.

Policing for a New South Africa. Michael Brogden & Clifford D. Shearing. LC 92-47078. 256p. (C). (gr. 13). 1997. 85.00 (*0-415-08321-4*) Routledge.

Policing for Prevention: Reducing Crime, Public Intoxication & Injury. Ed. by Ross Home. (Crime Prevention Studies: Vol. 7). (Illus.). 240p. 1997. text 47.50 (*1-881798-10-0*, Criminal Justice) Willow Tree NY.

Policing for Profit: The Private Security Sector & the New Division of Policing Labour. Nigel South. (Contemporary Criminology Ser.). 192p. (C). 1989. pap. 16.95 (*0-8039-8175-9*); text 69.95 (*0-8039-8174-0*) Sage.

Policing Futures: The Police, Law Enforcement & the Twenty-First Century. Ed. by Peter Francis. LC 97-13024. 248p. 1997. text 65.00 (*0-312-17597-3*) St Martin.

Policing Haiti: Preliminary Assessment of the Civilian Police Force. Rachel Nield. Ed. by Washington Office on Latin America Staff. 56p. (Orig.). 1995. pap. text 7.00 (*0-929513-30-4*) WOLA.

Policing in a Divided Society: A Study of Part-Time Policing in Northern Ireland. Richard Mapstone. 139p. 1994. 61.95 (*1-85628-598-7*, Pub. by Avebry) Ashgate Pub Co.

Policing in America. 2nd ed. Larry K. Gaines et al. LC 96-83688. (Illus.). 438p. (C). 1996. pap. text 43.95 (*0-87084-705-8*) Anderson Pub Co.

Policing in America. 3rd ed. Larry K. Gaines et al. LC 99-18636. 7p. 1999. pap. 48.95 (*0-87084-708-2*) Anderson Pub Co.

Policing in America: A Balance of Forces. 2nd ed. Robert H. Langworthy. LC 98-25251. 460p. 1998. 80.00 (*0-13-646217-0*) P-H.

Policing in Emerging Democracies: Workshop Papers & Highlights. Ed. by Jeremy Travis. 108p. (C). 1999. text 25.00 (*0-7881-7913-6*) DIANE Pub.

Policing in Europe: Diversity in Uniform. Bill Tupman. LC 99-179696. 96p. 1998. pap. 17.95 (*1-871516-90-0*) Intl Spec Bk.

Policing in Indian Country. Michael L. Barker. LC 97-52328. 150p. (C). 1998. pap. text 22.50 (*0-911577-44-0*, Criminal Justice) Willow Tree NY.

***Policing in Modern Society.** Bruce L. Berg. LC 98-48869. 480p. 1999. pap. 44.95 (*0-7506-9867-5*) Buttrwrth-Heinemann.

Policing in the Community. Dean J. Champion & George E. Rush. LC 96-28494. 483p. 1996. 90.00 (*0-13-681248-1*) P-H.

Policing Industrial Disputes, Eighteen Ninety-Three to Nineteen Eighty-Five. Roger Geary. LC 85-9632. 179p. reprint ed. pap. 51.10 (*0-608-15725-2*, 2031657) Bks Demand.

Policing Islam: The British Occupation of Egypt & the Anglo-Egyptian Struggle over Control of the Police, 1882-1914, 38. Harold Tollefson. LC 98-44254. (Contributions in Comparative Colonial Studies: Vol. 38). 216p. 1999. 59.95 (*0-313-30714-8*) Greenwood.

Policing Liberal Society. Steve Uglow. (Illus.). 176p. 1988. 35.00 (*0-19-219222-1*) OUP.

Policing Mass Transit: A Comprehensive Approach to Designing a Safe, Secure, & Desirable Transit Policing & Management System. Kurt R. Nelson. LC 98-44029. 224p. 1999. text 46.95 (*0-398-06919-0*); pap. text 33.95 (*0-398-06920-4*) C C Thomas.

Policing Morals: The Metropolitan Police & the Home Office 1870-1914. Stefan Petrow. (Illus.). 360p. 1994. 65.00 (*0-19-820165-6*) OUP.

Policing Multi-Ethnic Neighborhoods: The Miami Study & Findings for Law Enforcement in the United States, 20. Geoffrey P. Alpert & Roger G. Dunham. LC 88-3112. (Contributions in Criminology & Penology Ser.: No. 20). 176p. 1988. 42.95 (*0-313-26290-X*, ATP/) Greenwood.

***Policing Northern Ireland: Proposals for a New Start.** John McGarry & Brendan O'Leary. LC 99-196638. (Orig.). 1999. pap. 22.95 (*0-85640-648-1*, Pub. by Blackstaff Pr) Dufour.

Policing of Families. Jacques Donzelot. Tr. by Robert Hurley. LC 97-1666. 242p. 1997. reprint ed. pap. text 15.95 (*0-8018-5649-3*) Johns Hopkins.

Policing of Politics in the 20th Century: Historical Perspectives. Ed. by Mark Mazower. LC 95-37154. 288p. 1997. 59.95 (*1-57181-873-1*) Berghahn Bks.

Policing Ontario: The OPP Today. Michael Barnes. (Illus.). 208p. 29.95 (*1-55046-015-3*, Pub. by Boston Mills) Genl Dist Srvs.

Policing Perspectives: An Anthology. Ed. by Larry K. Gaines & Gary W. Cordner. LC 97-39253. (Illus.). 450p. (C). 1998. pap. text. write for info. (*1-891487-04-3*) Roxbury Pub Co.

Policing Places with Drug Problems. Lorraine A. Green. (Drugs, Health, & Social Policy Ser.: Vol. 2). 144p. 1995. 42.00 (*0-8039-7018-8*); pap. 17.95 (*0-8039-7019-6*) Sage.

Policing Police Violence. Uildrik. 1991. lib. bdg. 42.50 (*90-6544-589-7*) Kluwer Academic.

Policing Police Violence. Niels Uildriks & Hans Van Mastrigt. 246p. 1991. pap. 25.40 (*1-85752-000-9*, Pub. by Aberdeen U Pr) Macmillan.

Policing Policy in France. Christine Horton. LC 96-229461. 177p. (C). 1995. pap. 19.95 (*0-85374-580-3*, Pub. by Pol Studies Inst) Brookings.

Policing Politics: Security Intelligence & the Liberal Democratic State. Peter Gill. LC 93-31498. (Studies in Intelligence). 365p. 1994. 54.50 (*0-7146-3490-5*, Pub. by F Cass Pubs); pap. 29.50 (*0-7146-4097-2*, Pub. by F Cass Pubs) Intl Spec Bk.

Policing Prostitution in Nineteenth-Century Paris. Jill Harsin. LC 84-42887. 442p. 1985. reprint ed. pap. 137.10 (*0-608-07643-0*, 205996000010) Bks Demand.

Policing Protest: The Control of Mass Demonstrations in Western Democracies. Donatella Della Porta & Herbert Reiter. LC 97-48500. (Social Movements, Protest, & Contention Ser.). 1998. pap. 22.95 (*0-8166-3064-X*) U of Minn Pr.

Policing Protest: The Control of Mass Demonstrations in Western Democracies. Donatella Della Porta & Herbert Reiter. LC 97-48500. (Social Movements, Protest & Contention Ser.). 1998. 57.95 (*0-8166-3063-1*) U of Minn Pr.

Policing Provincial England, 1829-1856: The Politics of Reform. David Philips & Robert D. Storch. LC 98-26883. 1999. 75.00 (*0-7185-0112-8*) Bks Intl VA.

Policing Public Housing Projects. Jack H. Glymph. 86p. 1998. 74.95 (*1-57292-107-2*); pap. 54.95 (*1-57292-106-4*) Austin & Winfield.

Policing Public Order: Theoretical & Practical Ideas. David Waddington & Chas Critcher. 280p. 1996. text 77.95 (*1-85972-299-7*, Pub. by Avebry) Ashgate Pub Co.

Policing Public Sex: Queer Politics & the Future of AIDS Activism. Ed. by Ephen G. Colter et al. LC 96-12714. (Illus.). 416p. 1996. 40.00 (*0-89608-550-3*); pap. 20.00 (*0-89608-549-X*) South End Pr.

Policing Rio de Janeiro: Repression & Resistance in a 19th-Century City. Thomas H. Holloway. LC 92-45685. 392p. (C). 1993. 47.50 (*0-8047-2056-8*) Stanford U Pr.

Policing Sexual Assault. Jeanne Gregory & Sue Lees. LC 98-8111. (Illus.). 240p. (C). 1999. 85.00 (*0-415-16387-0*); pap. 25.99 (*0-415-16388-9*) Routledge.

Policing Shanghai, 1927-1937. Frederic Wakeman, Jr. (Philip E. Lilienthal Bk.). (Illus.). 478p. (C). 1996. pap. 19.95 (*0-520-20761-0*, Pub. by U CA Pr) Cal Prin Full Svc.

Policing South Africa: The SAP & the Transition from Apartheid. Gavin Cawthra. LC 93-37608. 240p. (C). 1993. text 59.95 (*1-85649-065-3*, Pub. by Zed Books); text 22.50 (*1-85649-066-1*, Pub. by Zed Books) St Martin.

Policing Soviet Society. Louise I. Shelley. LC 95-34020. 296p. (C). 1996. 75.00 (*0-415-10469-6*); pap. 29.99 (*0-415-10470-X*) Routledge.

Policing Space: Territoriality & the Los Angeles Police Department. Steve Herbert. 160p. (C). 1996. pap. 17.95 (*0-8166-2865-3*); text 44.95 (*0-8166-2864-5*) U of Minn Pr.

Policing Technology: Asia Pacific Police Technology Conference. Ed. by J. Vernon & D. Berwick. (Australian Institute Conference Proceedings Ser.: Vol. 18). 1993. pap. 35.00 (*0-642-19060-7*, Pub. by Aust Inst Criminology) Advent Bks Div.

Policing the Conflict in South Africa. Ed. by Mary Mathews et al. LC 93-7218. 240p. 1993. 49.95 (*0-8130-1224-4*) U Press Fla.

Policing the Elephant: Crime, Punishment, & Social Behavior on the Overland Trail. John P. Reid. LC 96-30677. (Illus.). (Orig.). 1996. pap. 15.00 (*0-87328-159-4*) Huntington Lib.

Policing the European Union. Malcolm Anderson & Monica Den Boer. (Clarendon Studies in Criminology). 346p. 1996. text 85.00 (*0-19-825965-4*) OUP.

Policing the Future. Ed. by A. B. Hoogenboom et al. LC 97-14346. 1997. 100.00 (*90-411-0416-X*) Kluwer Law Intl.

***Policing the Media: Street Cops & Public Perceptions of Law Enforcement.** David D. Perlmutter. LC 99-50428. 160p. 2000. 69.95 (*0-7619-1104-9*) Sage.

Policing the Miners Strike. Robert Millar. Ed. by Ben Fine. (C). 1985. pap. 19.50 (*0-85315-633-6*, Pub. by Lawrence & Wishart); text 52.50 (*0-85315-632-8*, Pub. by Lawrence & Wishart) NYU Pr.

***Policing the New World Disorder: Peace Operations & Public Security.** Ed. by Robert B. Oakley et al. 573p. 1999. pap. text 45.00 (*0-7881-8114-9*) DIANE Pub.

***Policing the New World Disorder: Peace Operations & Public Security.** Robert B. Oakley. 587p. 1998. per. 27.00 (*0-16-061216-0*) USGPO.

Policing the New World Disorder: Peace Operations & Public Security. Robert B. Oakley et al. LC 97-43986. 587p. 1998. pap., per. 27.00 (*1-57906-006-4*) Natl Defense.

Policing the Poor in 18th-Century France. Robert M. Schwartz. LC 87-6039. (Illus.). xxi, 321p. (C). 1987. text 70.00 (*0-8078-1735-X*) U of NC Pr.

Policing the Risk Society. Richard V. Ericson & Kevin D. Haggerty. LC 97-160534. 487p. 1997. text 65.00 (*0-8020-4121-3*, HV7921) U of Toronto Pr.

Policing the Southern City: New Orleans, 1805-1889. Dennis C. Rousey. LC 95-50128. (Illus.). 288p. (C). 1997. text 35.00 (*0-8071-2046-4*) La State U Pr.

Policing the World: Interpol & the Politics of International Police Co-Operation. Malcolm Anderson. (Illus.). 222p. 1989. text 49.95 (*0-19-827597-8*) OUP.

Policing Transportation Facilities. Henry I. DeGeneste & John P. Sullivan. LC 94-26575. (Illus.). 172p. (C). 1994. text 41.95 (*0-398-05929-2*) C C Thomas.

Policing Transportation Facilities. Henry I. DeGeneste & John P. Sullivan. LC 94-26575. (Illus.). 172p. (C). 1994. pap. text 28.95 (*0-398-05946-2*) C C Thomas.

Policing under Fire: Ethnic Conflict & Police-Community Relations in Northern Ireland. Ronald Weitzer. LC 94-816. (SUNY Series in New Directions in Crime & Justice Studies). 350p. (C). 1994. text 59.50 (*0-7914-2247-X*); pap. text 19.95 (*0-7914-2248-8*) State U NY Pr.

Policing Urban America. 3rd rev. ed. Geoffrey P. Alpert & Roger G. Dunham. LC 97-205587. (Illus.). 312p. (C). 1996. pap. text 17.95 (*0-88133-917-2*) Waveland Pr.

P

***Policing Urban Poverty.** Christy Crowther & Jo Campling. LC 99-40401. 2000. text 65.00 (*0-312-22846-5*) St Martin.

Policing Victorian London: Political Policing, Public Order & the London Metropolitan Police, 7. Phillip T. Smith. LC 84-6666. (Contributions in Criminology & Penology Ser.: No. 7). 229p. 1985. 62.95 (*0-313-24437-5*, SPV/, Greenwood Pr) Greenwood.

Policing Western Europe: Politics, Professionalism, & Public Order, 1850-1940, 33. Ed. by Clive Emsley & Barbara Weinberger. LC 91-8944. (Contributions in Criminology & Penology Ser.: No. 33). 272p. 1991. 69.50 (*0-313-28219-6*, EYW, Greenwood Pr) Greenwood.

Policing Women: The Sexual Politics of Law Enforcement & the LAPD. Janis Appier. LC 97-9965. (Critical Perspectives on the Past Ser.). 256p. 1998. 59.95 (*1-56639-559-3*); pap. 19.95 (*1-56639-560-7*) Temple U Pr.

Policraticus: Of the Frivolities of Courtiers & the Footprints of Philosophers. John of Salisbury. Ed. by Cary J. Nederman. (Cambridge Texts in the History of Political Thought Ser.). 270p. (C). 1990. text 59.95 (*0-521-36399-3*); pap. text 19.95 (*0-521-36701-8*) Cambridge U Pr.

Policy. H. K. Colebatch. LC 97-36034. (Concepts in Social Thought Ser.). 1998. 37.95 (*0-8166-3137-9*); pap. 14.95 (*0-8166-3138-7*) U of Minn Pr.

Policy. Elaine A. Kille et al. (School Board Library Ser.: Vol. 2). (Illus.). 48p. 1998. 29.90 (*0-912337-08-7*) NJ Schl Bds.

***Policy.** Patrick Lynch. 1999. reprint ed. mass mkt. 6.99 (*0-451-19326-1*, Sig) NAL.

Policy: An International Perspective. Ed. by Carlye Honig. (Collected Papers Ser.). 152p. 1995. pap. 55.00 (*0-7123-0822-9*, Pub. by SRIS) L Erlbaum Assocs.

Policy Alternatives for a New International Economic Order. William Cline. LC 79-87553. 392p. 1979. 65.00 (*0-275-90342-7*, C0342, Praeger Pubs) Greenwood.

***Policy Analysis.** Munger. LC 99-47240. 1999. pap. 22.50 (*0-393-97399-9*) Norton.

Policy Analysis. David L. Weimer & Aidan Vining. 480p. (C). 1988. boxed set. write for info. (*0-318-63666-2*) P-H.

Policy Analysis: Concepts & Practices. 3rd ed. David L. Weimer & Aidan Vining. LC 98-27838. 486p. 1998. pap. text 49.33 (*0-13-109083-6*) P-H.

Policy Analysis Vol. 6: Perspectives, Concepts, & Methods. Ed. by William Dunn & Stuart S. Nagel. LC 85-23152. (Public Policy Ser.). 396p. 1986. 73.25 (*0-89232-371-X*) Jai Pr.

Policy Analysis & Deductive Reasoning. Ed. by Gordon Tullock & Richard E. Wagner. (Organization Ser.). 213p. 1978. 15.00 (*0-317-35631-3*) Pol Studies.

Policy Analysis & Deductive Reasoning. Ed. by Gordon Tullock & Ricard E. Wagner. 220p. 1985. reprint ed. lib. bdg. 42.00 (*0-8191-5143-2*) U Pr of Amer.

Policy Analysis & Economics: Developments, Tensions, Prospects. Ed. by David L. Weimer. (Recent Economic Thought Ser.). 240p. 1991. lib. bdg. 98.00 (*0-7923-9154-3*) Kluwer Academic.

Policy Analysis & Policy Innovation: Patterns, Problems & Potentials. Ed. by Peter R. Baehr & Bjorn Wittrock. LC 80-41079. (Sage Modern Politics Ser.: No. 5). 244p. reprint ed. pap. 75.70 (*0-8357-4721-2*, 203763500009) Bks Demand.

Policy Analysis & Problem-Solving for Social Systems: Toward Understanding, Monitoring, & Managing Complex Real World Problems. P. N. Rastogi. (Illus.). 150p. (C). 1992. 27.50 (*0-8039-9425-7*) Sage.

Policy Analysis & Public Choice: Selected Papers by William A. Niskanen. William A. Niskanen, Jr. LC 97-29956. (John Locke Ser.). 448p. 1998. 100.00 (*1-85898-702-4*) E Elgar.

Policy Analysis & Research Technology: Political & Ethical Considerations. Thomas M. Meenaghan & Keith Kilty. LC 93-30524. 248p. 1994. pap. text 28.95 (*0-925065-46-3*) Lyceum IL.

Policy Analysis & the Federal Income Tax: Text & Readings. William A. Klein. (University Casebook Ser.). 614p. 1991. reprint ed. text 26.50 (*0-88277-419-0*) Foundation Pr.

Policy Analysis by Design. Davis B. Bobrow & John S. Dryzek. LC 87-5974. (Political Science Ser.). (Illus.). 256p. 1987. pap. 16.95 (*0-8229-5392-7*) U of Pittsburgh Pr.

Policy Analysis for Food & Agricultural Development. FAO Staff. (Basic Data Series & Their Uses). 150p. 1994. 16.00 (*92-5-103567-9*, F99913, Pub. by FAO) Bernan Associates.

Policy Analysis for Public Decisions. Duncan MacRae, Jr. & James A. Wilde. 344p. 1985. reprint ed. pap. text 25.50 (*0-8191-4835-0*) U Pr of Amer.

Policy Analysis in Education. Lorne W. Downey. 107p. (Orig.). (C). 1988. pap. text 14.95 (*0-920490-83-2*) Temeron Bks.

Policy Analysis Matrix for Agricultural Development. Eric Monke & Scott R. Pearson. LC 88-47938. 312p. 1989. text 47.50 (*0-8014-1953-0*); pap. text 18.95 (*0-8014-9551-2*) Cornell U Pr.

***Policy Analysis Methods.** Ed. by Stuart Nagel. 267p. 1999. 49.00 (*1-56072-657-1*) Nova Sci Pubs.

Policy-Analysis Methods & Super-Optimum Solutions. Stuart S. Nagel. 227p. 1994. lib. bdg. 95.00 (*1-56072-135-9*) Nova Sci Pubs.

Policy Analysis of Alternative Military Retirement Systems. Beth J. Asch & John T. Warner. LC 94-28238. 1994. pap. 15.00 (*0-8330-1565-6*, MR-465-OSD) Rand Corp.

***Policy Analysis of Child Labor.** Grootaert. LC 99-17086. 168p. 1999. text 45.00 (*0-312-22122-3*) St Martin.

Policy Analysis of Professional Development & Personnel Preparation for Serving Special Populations. N. Alan Sheppard. 37p. 1984. 4.25 (*0-318-22168-3*, IN279) Ctr Educ Trng Employ.

Policy Analysis Through Macro-Models: Issues, Techniques & Applications in Selected Developing Asian Countries. (Development Papers: No. 14). 344p. 35.00 (*92-1-119613-2*, E.93.II.F.10) UN.

Policy & Applied Research, Vol. 2. Ed. by Stuart S. Nagel & John P. Crecine. (Research in Public Policy Analysis & Management Ser.). 382p. 1981. 78.50 (*0-89232-210-1*) Jai Pr.

Policy & Change in Thatcher's Britain: Policy & Planning & Critical Theory. Ed. by Paul J. Cloke. (Policy, Planning & Critical Theory Ser.). 350p. 1992. text 59.95 (*0-08-040647-5*, Prgamon Press) Buttrwrth-Heinemann.

Policy & Debate. O. Mosley. 1972. 59.95 (*0-8490-0869-7*) Gordon Pr.

Policy & Development of Energy Resources. Ed. by T. L. Shaw et al. LC 83-10197. (World Energy Options Ser.). (Illus.). 261p. reprint ed. pap. 81.00 (*0-8357-3085-9*, 203934200012) Bks Demand.

Policy & Ethics in Business. Carl F. Taeusch. LC 73-2535. (Big Business; Economic Power in a Free Society Ser.). 1973. reprint ed. 38.95 (*0-405-05113-1*) Ayer.

Policy & Government in Northern Ireland: Lessons of Devolution. Derek Birrell & Alan Murie. LC 79-53790. 353p. 1980. 50.00 (*0-389-20019-0*, 06348) B&N Imports.

Policy & Health: Implications for Development in Asia. John W. Peabody et al. LC 99-24255. (Rand Studies in Policy Analysis). (Illus.). 464p. (C). 1999. 44.95 (*0-521-66164-1*) Cambridge U Pr.

Policy & Impact Assessment. Ed. by Robert Bartlett. (Orig.). 1988. pap. 15.00 (*0-944285-06-6*) Pol Studies.

Policy & Institutional Reform in Central European Agriculture. Ed. by Johan F. Swinnen. (LICOS Studies on the Transitions in Central & Eastern Europe). 258p. 1994. 77.95 (*1-85628-896-X*, Pub. by Avebry) Ashgate Pub Co.

Policy & Law Enforcement, 1987-1993, 5 vols. Ed. by Robert J. Homant & Daniel B. Kennedy. LC 73-7210. (Illus.). 1987. write for info. (*0-404-11199-8*) AMS Pr.

***Policy & Law in Heritage Conservation.** Robert Pickard. LC 00-44057. (Conservation of the European Built Heritage Ser.). 2000. pap. write for info. (*0-419-23280-X*, E & FN Spon) Routledge.

Policy & Methods in German & American Antitrust Law: A Comparative Study. James R. Maxeiner. LC 86-8108. 188p. 1986. 57.95 (*0-275-92113-1*, C2113, Praeger Pubs) Greenwood.

Policy & Operations in the Mediterranean, 1912 to 1914. Ed. by E. W. Lumby. 1986. 80.00 (*0-7855-1151-2*) St Mut.

Policy & Opinion in the Gulf War. John Mueller. LC 93-21226. 398p. 1994. pap. text 19.95 (*0-226-54565-2*) U Ch Pr.

Policy & Opinion in the Gulf War. John Mueller. LC 93-21226. 398p. 1994. lib. bdg. 55.00 (*0-226-54564-4*) U Ch Pr.

***Policy & Planning As Public Choice.** David Lewis & Fred Williams. LC 99-72332. 304p. 1999. 78.95 (*0-7546-1067-5*) Ashgate Pub Co.

Policy & Planning for Economic Upgradation. Ed. by Virendra P. Singh. (Caste Culture & Society Ser.: No. 4). (C). 1992. text 44.00 (*81-7169-241-9*, Commonwealth) S Asia.

Policy & Politics: Essays in Honour of Norman Chester. Daniel Norman Chester et al. LC 78-318575. 214 p. 1978. write for info. (*0-333-23561-4*) Macmillan.

Policy & Politics in American Governments. Marsh. (C). 1975. pap. text, teacher ed. 16.87 (*0-07-056429-9*) McGraw.

Policy & Politics in Britain: The Limits of Consensus. Douglas E. Ashford. LC 80-19771. (Policy & Politics in Industrial States Ser.). 330p. 1980. pap. text 19.95 (*0-87722-195-2*) Temple U Pr.

Policy & Politics in Canada: Institutionalized Ambivalence. Carolyn J. Tuohy. (Policy & Politics in Industrial States Ser.). (C). 1992. pap. 22.95 (*0-87722-871-X*) Temple U Pr.

Policy & Politics in Canada: Institutionalized Ambivalence. Carolyn J. Tuohy. (Policy & Politics in Industrial States Ser.). (C). 1992. 54.95 (*0-87722-870-1*) Temple U Pr.

Policy & Politics in France: Living with Uncertainty. Douglas E. Ashford. LC 82-5771. (Policy & Politics in Industrial States Ser.). 365p. 1982. pap. text 22.95 (*0-87722-262-2*) Temple U Pr.

Policy & Politics in Japan: Creative Conservatism. T. J. Pempel. LC 81-14464. (Policy & Politics in Industrial States Ser.). 330p. 1982. pap. 22.95 (*0-87722-250-9*) Temple U Pr.

Policy & Politics in Nursing & Health Care. 3rd ed. Diana J. Mason & Judith K. Leavitt. LC 98-21520. (Illus.). 784p. (C). 1998. pap. text 42.00 (*0-7216-7038-5*, W B Saunders Co) Harcrt Hlth Sci Grp.

Policy & Politics in Sweden: Principled Pragmatism. Hugh Heclo & Henrik Madsen. LC 85-27803. (Policy & Politics in Industrial States Ser.). 352p. 1987. pap. 22.95 (*0-87722-266-5*) Temple U Pr.

Policy & Politics in the United States: The Limits of Localism. E. W. Kelley. LC 87-5042. (Policy & Politics in Industrial States Ser.). 416p. (C). 1987. pap. 19.95 (*0-87722-268-1*) Temple U Pr.

Policy & Practice: Certified Home Health Care in New York City. Kimberley S. Fox. (Papers: No. 11). 48p. 1990. 5.00 (*0-934459-59-2*) United Hosp Fund.

Policy & Practice: Essays in Memory of Sir John Crawford. Ed. by L. T. Evans & J. D. Miller. (Illus.). 226p. 1987. text 30.00 (*0-08-034390-2*, Pergamon Pr) Elsevier.

Policy & Practice for the Protection of Groundwater. 2nd ed. Environment Agency Staff. 59p. 1998. pap. 60.00 (*0-11-310145-7*, Pub. by Statnry Office) Balogh.

Policy & Practice in Bibliographic Control of Nonbook Media. Ed. by Sheila S. Intner & Richard P. Smiraglia. LC 87-1849. 208p. 1987. pap. text 10.00 (*0-8389-0468-8*) ALA.

Policy & Practice in European Human Resource Management. Ed. by Chris Brewster & Ariane Hegewisch. LC 93-43235. 432p. (C). 1994. pap. 36.95 (*0-415-06530-5*) Thomson Learn.

Policy & Practice in Further Education: Managing the Process of Change. Geoffrey Elliott. LC 96-213805. (Higher Education Policy Ser.: No. 36). 250p. 1996. pap. text 34.95 (*1-85302-393-0*, Pub. by Jessica Kingsley) Taylor & Francis.

Policy & Practice in the Education of Culturally & Linguistically Diverse Students: Views from Language Educators. Ed. by G. Richard Tucker. LC 97-61489. 22p. 1993. pap. 12.95 (*0-939791-50-1*) Tchrs Eng Spkrs.

Policy & Practice in the Justice System. C. Aaron McNeece & Albert R. Roberts. LC 96-11325. (Social Work). (Illus.). 1997. pap. text 48.95 (*0-8304-1417-7*) Thomson Learn.

Policy & Practice in the Management of Tropical Watersheds. H. C. Pereira. 237p. 1989. pap. 180.00 (*81-7089-123-X*, Pub. by Intl Bk Distr) St Mut.

Policy & Practices in Bilingual Education: A Reader Extending the Foundations. Ed. by Ofelia Garcia & Colin Baker. (Bilingual Education & Bilingualism Ser.: No. 2). 298p. 1995. 89.00 (*1-85359-267-6*, Pub. by Multilingual Matters); pap. 28.95 (*1-85359-266-8*, Pub. by Multilingual Matters) Taylor & Francis.

Policy & Procedure Manual for Church & Synagogue Libraries: A Do-It-Yourself Guide. Martin Ruoss. LC 79-28676. (Guide Ser.: No. 9). 14p. 1998. pap. 9.00 (*0-915324-17-2*) CSLA.

Policy & Procedure Manual for Church & Synagogue Libraries Guide No. 9: A Do-It-Yourself Guide. 2nd rev. ed. 22p. 1998. pap. text 9.00 (*0-915324-41-5*) CSLA.

Policy & Procedures for Supervisors. (Training in a Box Ser.). 54p. 1997. ring bd. 49.00 (*1-57927-028-X*) APCO Inst.

Policy & Procedures Manual for Commercial Loan Asset Administrators. 240p. 1999. spiral bd. 95.00 (*0-945359-47-0*) Mortgage Bankers.

Policy & Procedures Manual for Purchasing & Materials Control. 2nd ed. R. Jerry Baker et al. LC 92-20166. 480p. (C). 1992. pap. 79.95 (*0-13-689969-2*) P-H.

Policy & Provision for the Single Homeless: Research Paper. Madeline Drake & Tony Biebuych. 1977. 30.00 (*0-7855-0567-9*, Pub. by Natl Inst Soc Work) St Mut.

Policy & Rationality: The Regulation of Canadian Trucking. Harold Kaplan. 221p. 1989. text 37.50 (*0-8020-5725-X*) U of Toronto Pr.

Policy & Regulation. (VDT-2000 Ser.: Vol. 5). 1995. 2995.00 (*0-614-18342-1*, IGIC-96) Info Gatekeepers.

Policy & Research in Adult Education. Ed. by J. Daines et al. 150p. (C). 1982. text 65.00 (*0-7855-3193-9*, Pub. by Univ Nottingham) St Mut.

Policy & Research in Adult Education: The 1st Nottingham International Colloquium 1981. Harvey et al. (C). 1981. 29.00 (*0-902031-60-0*, Pub. by Univ Nottingham) St Mut.

Policy & Theory in Criminal Justice. Don Gottfresdon & Ronald Clarke. 214p. 1990. text 74.95 (*1-85628-021-7*, Pub. by Avebry) Ashgate Pub Co.

Policy Anveshan: Police Investigation in Hindi. B. L. Babel. (C). 1984. 50.00 (*0-89771-790-2*, Pub. by Eastern Book) St Mut.

Policy Approach to Political Representation: Lessons from the Four Corners States. Helen M. Ingram et al. LC 79-3644. xviii, 270 p. 1980. write for info. (*0-8018-2369-2*) Johns Hopkins.

Policy Arguments in Judical Decisions. John S. Bell. LC 83-4207. 1985. pap. 19.95 (*0-19-825522-5*) OUP.

***Policy as Practice: Toward a Comparative Sociocultural Analysis of Educational Policy.** Ed. by Margaret A. Sutton & Bradley Levinson. Vol. V.1. 2000. write for info. (*1-56750-517-1*); pap. write for info. (*1-56750-516-3*) Greenwood.

Policy-Based Finance: The Experience of Postwar Japan & the Japan Economic Research Institute. Kozo Kato. LC 93-31025. (Discussion Papers: No. 221). 268p. 1994. pap. 22.00 (*0-8213-2716-X*, 12716) World Bank.

Policy Based Finance & Market Alternatives: East Asian Lessons for Latin America & the Caribbean. Kim B. Staking. 195p. 1997. pap. text 18.50 (*1-886938-23-7*) IADB.

Policy-Based Networking: Architecture & Algorithms. 500p. 1900. 55.00 (*1-57870-226-7*) Macmillan Tech.

Policy Based Profession: An Introduction to Social Welfare Policy for Social Workers. Philip R. Popple & Leslie Leighninger. LC 97-2260. 368p. 1997. 61.00 (*0-205-18606-8*) P-H.

***Policy-Based Profession: An Introduction to Social Welfare Policy for Social Workers.** 2nd ed. Philip R. Popple & Leslie Leighninger. LC 00-41630. 2001. boxed set. write for info. (*0-205-31739-1*) Allyn.

Policy Calculated to Benefit China: The United States & the China Arms Embargo, 1919 to 1929, 25. Stephen J. Valone. LC 90-20734. (Contributions to the Study of World History Ser.: No. 25). 176p. 1991. 49.95 (*0-313-27621-8*, VUD/, Greenwood Pr) Greenwood.

Policy Capturing in Target Selection: U. S. & Swedish Army Aviators & Social Judgment Theory. Anders Carlstrom. LC 97-170685. (Studia Psychologica Upsaliensia: No. 15). (Illus.). 74p. (Orig.). 1996. pap. 33.50 (*91-554-3810-5*, Pub. by Uppsala Univ Acta Univ Uppsaliensis) Coronet Bks.

Policy Challenge of Ethnic Diversity: Immigrant Politics in France & Switzerland. Patrick R. Ireland. LC 93-28583. 336p. (C). 1994. text 57.00 (*0-674-68375-7*) HUP.

Policy Choice & Economic Structure. John B. Taylor. (Occasional Paper Ser.: No. 9). 23p. 1982. pap. 7.00 (*1-56708-008-1*) Grp of Thirty.

Policy Choices: Creating Michigan's Future. Phyllis T. Grummon. Ed. by Brendan Mullan. 1995. pap. 17.95 (*0-87013-382-9*) Mich St U Pr.

Policy Choices: Framing the Debate for Michigan's Future. Ed. by Timothy S. Bynum & Phyllis T. Grummon. LC 93-31939. 211p. 1993. 19.95 (*0-87013-344-6*) Mich St U Pr.

Policy Choices: NAFTA & Michigan's Future. Ed. by Karen Roberts & Mark Wilson. LC 96-26073. (Policy Choices Ser.: Vol. 3). (Illus.). 230p. 1996. pap. 21.95 (*0-87013-415-9*) Mich St U Pr.

Policy Choices & Practical Problems in Health Economics: Cases from Latin America & the Caribbean. Ed. by Catherine A. Overholt & Margaret K. Saunders. LC 94-29559. (EDI Learning Resources Ser.: Vol. 3). 242p. 1997. pap. 22.00 (*0-8213-3012-8*, 13012) World Bank.

Policy Choices in Vocational Education. Gregory Schmid. 68p. 1979. 7.50 (*0-318-14417-4*, R48A) Inst Future.

Policy Coherence in Development Co-operation. Ed. by Olav Stokke & Jacques Forster. LC 99-14823. (EADI Book Ser.: No. 22). 512p. 1999. 64.50 (*0-7146-4914-7*, Pub. by F Cass Pubs); pap. 28.50 (*0-7146-4464-1*, Pub. by F Cass Pubs) Intl Spec Bk.

Policy Compendium on Reproductive Health Issues Affecting Adolescents. Janet E. Gans Epner & American Medical Association. LC 98-147775. 80 p. 1996. write for info. (*0-89970-768-4*) AMA.

Policy Competition & Foreign Direct Investment in Europe. Ed. by Philip Raines & Ross Brown. LC 98-74932. 7p. 1999. 61.95 (*1-84014-768-7*, Pub. by Ashgate Pub) Ashgate Pub Co.

Policy Conflicts in Post-Mao China: A Documentary Survey with Analysis. Ed. by John P. Burns & Stanley Rosen. LC 86-907. 384p. (gr. 13). 1986. pap. text 36.95 (*0-87332-338-6*, East Gate Bk) M E Sharpe.

Policy Conflicts in Post-Mao China: A Documentary Survey with Analysis. Ed. by John P. Burns & Stanley Rosen. LC 86-907. (Illus.). 384p. 1986. reprint ed. pap. 119.10 (*0-7837-9991-8*, 206071800006) Bks Demand.

Policy Consequences of John Maynard Keynes. Ed. by Harold L. Wattel. LC 84-23542. 176p. (gr. 13). 1986. pap. text 40.95 (*0-87332-317-3*) M E Sharpe.

Policy Consequences of John Maynard Keynes. Ed. by Harold L. Wattel. LC 84-23542. 171p. 1985. reprint ed. pap. 53.10 (*0-7837-9976-4*, 206070300006) Bks Demand.

Policy Controversies in Higher Education, 19. Ed. by Samuel K. Gove & Thomas M. Stauffer. LC 86-4646. (Contributions to the Study of Education Ser.: No. 19). 285p. 1986. 49.95 (*0-313-25381-1*, GPC/, Greenwood Pr) Greenwood.

Policy Controversy in Biotechnology: An Insider's View. Henry I. Miller. 1997. text 69.95 (*0-12-496725-6*) Acad Pr.

Policy Controversy in Biotechnology: An Insider's View. Henry I. Miller. LC 96-35982. (Biotechnology Intelligence Unit Ser.). 1996. write for info. (*1-57059-408-2*) Chapman & Hall.

Policy Coordination in the European Monetary System. Manuel Guitian et al. (Occasional Papers: No. 61). vii, 82p. 1988. pap. 7.50 (*1-55775-028-9*) Intl Monetary.

Policy Cycle. Ed. by Judith V. May & Aaron B. Wildavsky. LC 78-15351. (Sage Yearbooks in Politics & Public Policy Ser.: No. 5). (Illus.). 332p. reprint ed. pap. 103.00 (*0-8357-4775-1*, 203771200009) Bks Demand.

Policy Deployment: Setting the Direction for Change. Chuni Li. Ed. by Mari-Lynn Hankinson. (AT&T Quality Library). (Illus.). 97p. (Orig.). 1992. pap. 24.95 (*0-932764-31-2*, 500-453) AT&T Customer Info.

Policy Design & the Politics of Implementation: The Case of Child Health Care in the American States. Malcolm L. Goggin. LC 86-11333. (Illus.). 312p. 1987. reprint ed. pap. 96.80 (*0-608-07786-0*, 206787400010) Bks Demand.

Policy Design for Democracy. Anne L. Schneider & Helen Ingram. LC 97-20360. (Studies in Government & Public Policy). 256p. 1997. 35.00 (*0-7006-0843-5*); pap. 15.95 (*0-7006-0844-3*) U Pr of KS.

Policy Development & Big Science: Proceedings of the Colloquium, 18-19 September 1989. Ed. by E. E. Hicks & W. van Rossum. (Verhandelingen der Koninklijke Nederlandse Akademie van Wetenschappen, Afd. Letterkunde, Nieuwe Reeks Ser.: No. 147). vii, 64p. 1991. pap. text 22.00 (*0-444-85740-0*) Elsevier.

Policy Development for Cellular Telephone Service in the United States & the United Kingdom. Christopher W. Mines. (Illus.). 58p. 1993. pap. text. write for info. (*1-879716-01-1*, P-93-3) Ctr Info Policy.

Policy Development in Sport Management. Harold J. Vanderzwaag. LC 98-4973. 248p. 1998. text 45.00 (*0-275-96089-7*, Praeger Pubs) Greenwood.

Policy Education & Inequalities in Communist China since 1949. Xiaodong Niu. 122p. (C). 1992. lib. bdg. 35.00 (*0-8191-8335-0*) U Pr of Amer.

Policy Employee Health. B. Swanton & J. Walker. 97p. 1989. pap. 15.00 (*0-642-14890-2*, Pub. by Aust Inst Criminology) Advent Bks Div.

An Asterisk (*) at the beginning of an entry indicates that the title is appearing for the first time.

***Policy Entrepreneurs & School Choice.** Michael Mintrom. LC 99-36842. (American Governance & Public Policy Ser.). 336p. 2000. pap. text 24.95 (*0-87840-771-5*) Georgetown U Pr.

***Policy Entrepreneurs & School Choice.** Michael Mintrom. LC 99-36842. (American Governance & Public Policy Ser.). (Illus.). 336p. 2000. text 65.00 (*0-87840-770-7*) Georgetown U Pr.

Policy Evaluation: Linking Theory to Practice. Ed. by Ray C. Rist. LC 94-32281. (Reference Collection: International Library of Comparative Public Policy: Vol. 3). 608p. 1995. 230.00 (*1-85278-946-8*) E Elgar.

Policy Evaluation: Making Optimum Decisions. Stuart S. Nagel. LC 81-12123. 329p. 1982. 49.95 (*0-275-90866-6*, C0866, Praeger Pubs) Greenwood.

Policy Evaluation for Local Government. Ed. by Terry Busson & Philip Coulter. (Orig.). 1983. pap. 15.00 (*0-918592-69-0*) Pol Studies.

Policy Evaluation in Innovation & Technology: Towards Best Practices. OECD Staff. LC 98-121817. (Proceedings Ser.). 468p. 1998. pap. 27.00 (*92-64-15697-6*, 92-97-10-1, Pub. by Org for Econ) OECD.

Policy Evaluation in the Public Sector: Approaches & Methods. Colin Palfrey et al. 182p. 1992. 72.95 (*1-85628-393-3*, Pub. by Avebry) Ashgate Pub Co.

Policy Evalution for Local Government, 182. Ed. by Terry Busson & Phillip Coulter. LC 87-7532. (Contributions in Political Science Ser.: No. 182). 286p. 1987. 65.00 (*0-313-25953-4*, BEV/, Greenwood Pr) Greenwood.

Policy Evolution. Decker & Berolzheimer. 388p. (C). 1997. 62.00 (*0-13-673716-1*) P-H.

Policy Evolution: Energy Conservation to Energy Efficiency: A Series of Speeches from the Energy Efficiency Forums. Douglas A. Decker & Alan R. Berolzheimer. LC 97-12267. 365p. 1997. 62.00 (*0-88173-274-5*) Fairmont Pr.

Policy Experiences & Issues in the Baltic Countries, Russia & Other FSU Countries. Ed. by Daniel A. Citrin & Ashok K. Lahiri. LC 96-118846. (Occasional Papers: No. 133). 1995. pap. 15.00 (*1-55775-518-3*) Intl Monetary.

Policy Expert: A Supplement for Courses in Business Policy & Strategic Management. 3rd ed. Kirk P. Arnett et al. (C). 1992. text 29.56 incl. 5.25 hd (*0-395-63003-7*) HM.

Policy Expert: A Supplement for Courses in Business Policy & Strategic Management. 3rd ed. Kirk P. Arnett et al. (C). 1992. text 29.56 incl. 3.5 hd (*0-395-63004-5*) HM.

Policy Factor: Agricultural Performance in Kenya & Tanzania. Michael F. Lofchie. LC 88-18396. (Food in Africa Ser.). 236p. 1988. lib. bdg. 35.00 (*1-55587-136-4*) L Rienner.

Policy for American Agriculture: Choices & Consequences. M. C. Hallberg. LC 91-36670. (Illus.). 386p. (C). 1992. text 54.95 (*0-8138-1368-9*) Iowa St U Pr.

Policy for Educational Renewal. Calvin Frazier. (Agenda for Education in a Democracy Ser.). 1999. pap. text 28.95 (*0-7879-4559-5*) Jossey-Bass.

Policy for Land: Law & Ethics. Kristin S. Shrader-Frechette & Lynton K. Caldwell. LC 92-28586. 340p. (Orig.). (C). 1993. pap. text 27.95 (*0-8476-7779-6*); lib. bdg. 75.00 (*0-8476-7778-8*) Rowman.

Policy for School Boards. Linda Leopardi. (School Board Library Ser.). 68p. (Orig.). 1983. pap. 9.95 (*0-912337-03-6*) NJ Schl Bds.

Policy Formation & Resource Allocation. Brian Caldwell & Jim Spinks. 121p. (C). 1986. 48.00 (*0-7300-0378-7*, Pub. by Deakin Univ) St Mut.

Policy Game: How Special Interests & Ideologues Are Stealing America. Peter Navarro. 360p. (C). 1986. 18.95 (*0-669-14112-7*) Free Pr.

***Policy Governance Fieldbook: Practical Lessons, Tips & Tools from the Experiences of Real-World.** Caroline Oliver. LC 99-6258. 256p. 1999. pap. text 29.95 (*0-7879-4366-5*) Jossey-Bass.

Policy Grants Directory. Ed. by Stuart S. Nagel & Marian Neef. 1977. pap. 15.00 (*0-918592-25-9*) Pol Studies.

Policy Handbook for Flood Control. T. V. Hromadka, II et al. (Illus.). 94p. 1990. 19.50 (*0-914055-08-9*) Lighthouse Pubns.

Policy Hits the Ground: Environment, Equity, & Participation in Policy Making. Aaron Zazueta. 60p. 1995. pap. 20.00 (*1-56973-002-4*) World Resources Inst.

Policy Implementation: Penalties or Incentives? Ed. by John Brigham & Don W. Brown. LC 80-16765. (Sage Focus Editions Ser.: Vol. 25). 271p. 1980. reprint ed. pap. 84.10 (*0-608-03378-2*, 205964200008) Bks Demand.

Policy Implementation & Social Welfare in the 1980s: Israel & the United States. Frederick A. Lazin. 145p. (Orig.). 1986. 34.95 (*0-88738-084-0*) Transaction Pubs.

Policy Implementation in Federal & Unitary Systems: Questions of Analysis & Design. Ed. by Kenneth Hanf & A. J. Toonen. 1985. lib. bdg. 184.00 (*90-247-3137-2*) Kluwer Academic.

Policy Implications of Anti-Dumping Measures. Ed. by P. K. Tharakan. (Advanced Series in Management: No. 14). 314p. 1995. 101.25 (*0-444-88713-X*, North Holland) Elsevier.

Policy Implications of Greenhouse Warming. Ed. by Synthesis Panel Staff, National Academy of Science. 144p. 1991. pap. 14.95 (*0-309-04440-5*) Natl Acad Pr.

Policy Implications of Greenhouse Warming: Mitigation, Adaptation, & the Science Base. National Academy of Science Staff et al. 944p. (C). 1992. text 89.95 (*0-309-04386-7*) Natl Acad Pr.

Policy Implications of U. S. Involvement in Bosnia: Hearings Before the Committee on Armed Services, House of Representatives, 103rd Congress, 1st Session, Hearings Held May 25 & 26, 1993. USGPO Staff. LC 94-176127. iii, 72 p. 1994. pap. write for info. (*0-16-043646-X*) USGPO.

Policy Implications on Environment: The Case of Villagization in Tanzania. Idris Kikula. LC 98-138746. 1997. pap. text 26.95 (*91-7106-405-2*) Transaction Pubs.

Policy in Love: Lyric & Public in Ovid, Petrarch & Shakespeare. Christopher Martin. LC 94-30961. (Duquesne Studies: Language & Literature Ser.: Vol. 17). 240p. (C). 1995. text 44.95 (*0-8207-0260-9*) Duquesne.

Policy Indicators: Links Between Social Science & Public Debate. Duncan MacRae, Jr. LC 84-17294. (Urban & Regional Policy & Development Studies). xvi, 414p. 1985. 59.95 (*0-8078-1628-0*) U of NC Pr.

Policy Innovation in State Government. David C. Nice. LC 93-24017. 182p. (C). 1993. text 54.95 (*0-8138-0658-5*) Iowa St U Pr.

Policy Insurance. rev. ed. Compiled by A. P. Braga. LC 93-90021. (Illus.). 146p. 1993. 14.95 (*0-939205-52-1*) S Station Bks.

Policy Issues & Community Life in Texas: State Tax Issues, Child Care, Crime & Justice, & Hazardous Materials. Laura Lein & Robert C. Rickards. (Special Project Reports). 80p. 1989. pap. 7.00 (*0-89940-868-0*) LBJ Sch Pub Aff.

***Policy Issues & Strategies Affecting Public Libraries in the National Networked Environment: Moving Beyond Connectivity.** John Carlo Bertot. 32p. 1998. pap. 2.75 (*0-16-061878-9*) USGPO.

Policy Issues for Interdependent Economics. Ed. by Anthony Courakis & Mark P. Taylor. (Illus.). 456p. 1991. pap. text 32.50 (*0-19-828325-3*) OUP.

Policy Issues for the 1990s. Ed. by Ray C. Rist. (Policy Studies Review Annual: Vol. 9). 800p. 1988. 89.95 (*0-88738-265-7*) Transaction Pubs.

Policy Issues in Aerospace Offsets: Report of a Workshop. National Research Council Staff. Ed. by Charles W. Wessner & Alan W. Wolff. LC 97-220794. 44p. (C). 1997. pap. text 10.00 (*0-309-05840-6*) Natl Acad Pr.

Policy Issues in Bangladesh. Habib Zafarullah. (C). 1994. text 27.50 (*81-7003-165-6*, Pub. by S Asia Pubs) S Asia.

Policy Issues in Employment Testing. Ed. by Linda C. Wing & Bernard R. Gifford. LC 93-10783. 1993. lib. bdg. 134.00 (*0-7923-9363-5*) Kluwer Academic.

Policy Issues in Modern Cartography. D. R. Taylor. LC 98-25805. 1998. 155.00 (*0-08-043111-9*, Pergamon Pr) Elsevier.

Policy Issues in National Assessment. Ed. by Patricia Broadfoot et al. LC 92-38545. (BERA Dialogues Ser.: No. 7). 1992. 69.00 (*1-85359-171-8*, Pub. by Multilingual Matters); pap. 24.95 (*1-85359-170-X*, Pub. by Multilingual Matters) Taylor & Francis.

Policy Issues in Nursing. Ed. by Jane Robinson et al. 192p. 1991. pap. 37.95 (*0-335-09466-X*) OpUniv Pr.

Policy Issues in Residential Care: Discussion Paper. 1978. 60.00 (*0-7855-0566-0*, Pub. by Natl Inst Soc Work) St Mut.

Policy Issues in the European Union: A Reader in the Political Economy of European Integration. Ed. by Mehmet Ugur. 388p. (C). 1996. pap. text 39.00 (*1-874529-38-8*) NYU Pr.

Policy Issues in the Evolving International Monetary System. Morris Goldstein et al. (Occasional Papers: No. 96). 74p. 1992. 15.00 (*1-55775-234-6*) Intl Monetary.

Policy Issues in the Operation of Currency Unions. Ed. by Paul R. Masson & Mark P. Taylor. LC 92-20210. (Illus.). 324p. (C). 1993. text 59.95 (*0-521-43455-6*) Cambridge U Pr.

Policy Issues in Work & Retirement. Herbert S. Parnes. LC 83-4950. 288p. 1983. pap. text 14.00 (*0-88099-010-4*) W E Upjohn.

Policy Kit: A Collection of Sample Insurance Forms, 1995-1996. Alliance of American Insurers Staff. 546p. 1995. pap. text 22.95 (*1-887271-19-8*) Alliance Am Insurers.

Policy Kit: A Collection of Sample Insurance Forms, 1997-1998. rev. ed. 568p. 1997. pap. 22.95 (*1-887271-32-5*) Alliance Am Insurers.

Policy Kit, 1996-1997: A Collection of Sample Insurance Forms. rev. ed. 560p. 1996. pap. 22.95 (*1-887271-25-2*) Alliance Am Insurers.

Policy Lessons of the Development Experience. Helen Hughes. (Occasional Paper Ser.: No. 16). 27p. 1985. pap. 7.00 (*1-56708-015-4*) Grp of Thirty.

Policy Makers & Critics: Conflicting Theories of American Foreign Policy. rev. ed. Cecil V. Crabb, Jr. LC 86-16901. 311p. 1986. pap. 18.95 (*0-275-92210-3*, B2210, Praeger Pubs) Greenwood.

Policy Makers & Critics: Conflicting Theories of American Foreign Policy. rev. ed. Cecil V. Crabb, Jr. LC 86-16901. 311p. 1986. 69.50 (*0-275-92209-X*, C2209, Praeger Pubs) Greenwood.

Policy-Making & Diversity in Europe: Escape from Deadlock. Adrienne Heritier. (Theories of Institutional Design Ser.). 150p. (C). 1999. 49.95 (*0-521-65296-0*); pap. 18.95 (*0-521-65384-3*) Cambridge U Pr.

Policy Making & Effective Leadership. J. Victor Baldridge et al. LC 77-82909. (Jossey-Bass Series in Higher Education). 318p. reprint ed. pap. 98.60 (*0-8357-4932-0*, 203786200009) Bks Demand.

Policy Making in a Disorderly World Economy. Gunnar Eliasson et al. 418p. (Orig.). 1983. pap. 52.00 (*91-7204-166-8*) Coronet Bks.

Policy Making in a Three-Party System Committees, Coalitions & Parliament. Ian A. Marsh. 256p. 1986. text 57.50 (*0-416-92090-X*, 1021) Routledge.

Policy Making in an Era of Global Environmental Change. Ed. by R. E. Munn. (Environment & Policy Ser.). 256p. (C). 1996. text 59.00 (*0-7923-3872-3*) Kluwer Academic.

Policy Making in an Era of Global Environmental Change. R. E. Munn et al. LC 96-1781. (Environment & Policy Ser.). 1996. write for info. (*0-7923-4072-8*) Kluwer Academic.

Policy Making in Britain. Maurice Mullard & Paul Spicker. LC 97-53073. 240p. (C). 1998. 80.00 (*0-415-16540-7*) Routledge.

Policy Making in Britain: An Introduction. Maurice Mullard. 240p. (C). 1995. pap. 24.99 (*0-415-10850-0*, C0052) Routledge.

Policy Making in Britain: An Introduction. Maurice Mullard. LC 94-48178. 240p. (C). (gr. 13). 1995. 85.00 (*0-415-10849-7*, C0051) Routledge.

Policy Making in Education. Ed. by Ann Lieberman & Milbrey W. McLaughlin. LC 81-85130. (National Society for the Study of Education Publication Ser.: 81st; Pt. 1). 304p. (C). 1982. lib. bdg. 15.00 (*0-226-60132-3*) U Ch Pr.

Policy Making in Israel: Routines for Simple Problems & Coping with the Complex. Ira Sharkansky. LC 97-4756. (Series in Policy & Institutional Studies). 220p. 1997. pap. 19.95 (*0-8229-5633-0*); text 45.00 (*0-8229-3984-3*) U of Pittsburgh Pr.

Policy-Making in the European Community. 2nd fac. ed. Ed. by Helen S. Wallace. LC 83-1118. 467p. 1983. reprint ed. pap. 144.80 (*0-7837-8266-7*, 204904700009) Bks Demand.

Policy-Making in the European Union. 3rd ed. Ed. by Helen Wallace. LC 96-228127. (Illus.). 538p. (C). 1996. pap. text 22.00 (*0-19-878129-6*) OUP.

Policy-Making in the European Union. 3rd ed. Ed. by Helen Wallace & William Wallace. LC 96-228127. (Illus.). 544p. (C). 1996. text 78.00 (*0-19-878128-8*) OUP.

***Policy-Making in the European Union.** 4th ed. Helen Wallace. (New European Union Ser.). 645p. 2000. pap. 24.95 (*0-19-878242-X*) OUP.

Policy Making in the European Union: Conceptual Lenses & the Integration Process. Laura Cram. LC 98-108264. (European Public Policy Ser.). 200p. (C). 1997. pap. 27.99 (*0-415-14626-7*) Routledge.

Policy Making in the European Union: Conceptual Lenses & the Integration Process. 2nd ed. Laura Cram. LC 98-108264. (European Public Policy Ser.). 200p. (C). 1997. 90.00 (*0-415-14625-9*) Routledge.

Policy-Making in the Federal Executive Branch. Ed. by Randall B. Ripley & Grace A. Franklin. LC 74-33093. (Illus.). 1975. 27.95 (*0-02-926490-1*) Free Pr.

Policy Making Process: Foundations of Modern Political Science Ser. 3rd ed. Charles E. Lindblom & Edward J. Woodhouse. LC 92-28729. 176p. (C). 1992. pap. text 32.80 (*0-13-682360-2*) P-H.

Policy-Making Russian Industry. Fortescue. LC 96-46424. 196p. 1997. text 65.00 (*0-312-17270-2*) St Martin.

Policy Manual Bloodborne Pathogens. Victoria Wetle. 480p. 1994. pap. text 99.95 (*0-86720-778-7*) Jones & Bartlett.

***Policy Measures for Low-Wage Employment in Europe.** Wiemer Salverda et al. LC 00-39397. 2000. write for info. (*1-84064-410-9*) E Elgar.

Policy Mental Health Partnership: A Community-Based Response to Urban Violence. Steven Marans et al. LC 95-18519. 1995. 22.50 (*0-300-06420-9*) Yale U Pr.

Policy Modeling in the Small Island Economies of the South Pacific: The Case of Vanuatu. Mark Sturton. (Research Reports: No. 11). (Illus.). 141p. 1989. pap. text 8.00 (*0-86638-110-4*) EW Ctr HI.

Policy Networks & European Structural Funds: A Comparison Between European Union Member States. Ed. by Hubert Heinelt & Randall Smith. (Perspectives on Europe Ser.). 330p. 1997. text 77.95 (*1-85972-238-5*, Pub. by Avebry) Ashgate Pub Co.

Policy Networks in British Government. Ed. by David Marsh & R. A. Rhodes. (Illus.). 320p. 1992. 75.00 (*0-19-827852-7*) OUP.

Policy Networks under Pressure: Pollution Control, Policy Reform & the Power of Farmers. Carsten Daugbjerg. (Illus.). 232p. 1998. text 59.95 (*1-84014-140-9*, Pub. by Ashgate Pub) Ashgate Pub Co.

Policy of the United States As Regards Intervention. Charles E. Martin. LC 21-3655. (Columbia University. Studies in the Social Sciences: No. 211). reprint ed. 21.50 (*0-404-51211-9*) AMS Pr.

Policy of the United States Toward the Neutrals, 1917-1918. Thomas A. Bailey. 1979. 44.95 (*0-405-10578-9*) Ayer.

Policy of the United States Towards Its Territories with Special Reference to Puerto Rico. Jose Lopez-Baralt. LC 98-5820. 1998. write for info. (*0-8477-0341-X*) U of PR Pr.

Policy, Office or Votes? How Political Parties in Western Europe Make Hard Decisions. Ed. by Kaare Strom et al. LC 98-49530. (Cambridge Studies in Comparative Politics). (Illus.). 336p. (C). 1999. write for info. (*0-521-63135-1*) Cambridge U Pr.

Policy, Office or Votes? How Political Parties in Western Europe Make Hard Decisions. Ed. by Kaare Strom & Wolfgang C. Muller. LC 98-49530. (Cambridge Studies in Comparative Politics). (Illus.). 336p. (C). 1999. pap. 21.95 (*0-521-63723-6*) Cambridge U Pr.

Policy Officer Exam, Midwest. Learning Express Staff. Ed. by Jim Gish. LC 97-8772. (Law Enforcement Library). 320p. (Orig.). 1997. pap. 30.00 (*1-57685-097-8*) LrningExprss.

Policy Officer, Long Island Railroad. (Career Examination Ser.: C-3685). pap. 23.95 (*0-8373-3685-6*) Nat Learn.

Policy on Drug & Alcohol Abuse Prevention: An Employer's Development & Implementation Guide. Mark A. De Bernardo. (Employer Guide Ser.: Vol. 1). 16p. (Orig.). 1994. pap. 4.50 (*1-889437-10-7*) Inst Drug-Free Wrkpl.

Policy on Geometric Design of Highways & Streets. (Design Ser.). 1052p. (C). 1994. 62.50 (*1-56051-068-4*, GDHS-3) AASHTO.

Policy on Geometric Design of Highways & Streets. AASHTO Staff. (Design & Traffic Ser.). (Illus.). i, 136p. (C). 1990. pap. text 37.00 (*1-56051-001-3*, GDHS-2) AASHTO.

Policy on Health & Well-Being (In Canada) Marc-Yvan Cote. 170p. 1999. reprint ed. pap. text 35.00 (*0-7881-8018-5*) DIANE Pub.

Policy on Land Use & Source Control Aspects of Traffic Noise Attenuation. 1980. 2.75 (*0-686-29469-6*, TNA-1) AASHTO.

Policy Options for Army Involvement in Youth Development. Elizabeth H. Ondaatje. LC 93-21331. 1993. pap. 15.00 (*0-8330-1460-9*, MR-352-A) Rand Corp.

Policy Options for Intermodal Freight Transportation National Research Council (U.S.). LC 98-16533. (Special Report Ser.). viii, 315p. 1998. write for info. (*0-309-06451-1*) Natl Acad Pr.

Policy Options for Intermodal Freight Transportation, Vol. 252. National Research Council Staff (U.S.). LC 98-16533. (Special Reports). 1998. write for info. (*0-309-06220-9*) Natl Acad Pr.

Policy Options for Reform of Chinese State-Owned Enterprises. Harry G. Broadman. (World Bank Discussion Papers: No. 335). 248p. 1996. pap. 22.00 (*0-8213-3686-X*, 13686) World Bank.

Policy Options for Stabilizing Global Climate. Daniel Lashof & Dennis A. Tirpak. 825p. 1990. 160.00 (*1-56032-072-9*) Hemisp Pub.

Policy Options in Long-Term Care. Ed. by Judith Meltzer et al. LC 81-10445. (C). 1995. lib. bdg. 34.00 (*0-226-51973-2*) U Ch Pr.

Policy Options in Long-Term Care. Ed. by Judith Meltzer et al. LC 81-10445. (C). 1995. pap. text 15.00 (*0-226-51974-0*) U Ch Pr.

Policy Options in Long-Term Care. Ed. by Judith Meltzer et al. LC 81-10445. (Illus.). 254p. reprint ed. pap. 78.80 (*0-608-09021-2*, 206965600005) Bks Demand.

Policy Paradox. 2nd ed. Deborah Stone. (C). pap. text. write for info. (*0-393-97625-4*) Norton.

Policy Paradox: The Art of Political Decision Making. Deborah A. Stone. LC 96-52119. (C). 1996. pap. 23.50 (*0-393-96857-X*) Norton.

Policy, Pedagogy & Social Inequality: Community College Student Realities in Post-Industrial America. Penelope E. Herideen. LC 98-18505. (Critical Studies in Education & Culture). 160p. 1998. 49.95 (*0-89789-593-2*, Bergin & Garvey) Greenwood.

Policy Perspectives. Henry M. Wriston. LC 64-17776. (Brown University Bicentennial Publications). 188p. reprint ed. pap. 58.30 (*0-608-14776-1*, 202322900032) Bks Demand.

Policy Perspectives in Indian Economic Development: Essays in Honour of Professor G. S. Bhana. Ed. by G. K. Chadha. (C). 1994. 27.50 (*81-241-0142-6*, Pub. by Har-Anand Pubns) S Asia.

Policy Perspectives on Educational Testing. Ed. by Bernard R. Gifford. LC 92-5610. (Evaluation in Education & Human Services Ser.). 416p. (C). 1992. lib. bdg. 137.00 (*0-7923-9238-8*) Kluwer Academic.

Policy, Politics & Gender: Women Gaining Ground. Kathleen Staudt. LC 98-5309. 252p. 1998. 55.00 (*1-56549-080-0*); pap. 24.95 (*1-56549-079-7*) Kumarian Pr.

Policy Positions, 1988-89. National Governors' Association Staff. (Policy Positions Ser.). 280p. (Orig.). 1988. pap. text 15.00 (*1-55877-023-2*) Natl Governor.

Policy Positions, 1989-90. National Governors' Association Staff. Ed. by Mark Miller. 316p. (Orig.). 1989. pap. text 15.00 (*1-55877-064-X*) Natl Governor.

Policy Positions, 1991-92. Ed. by Mark Miller. 350p. (Orig.). 1991. pap. text 15.00 (*1-55877-131-X*) Natl Governor.

Policy Positions, 1990-91. Ed. by Mark Miller. 350p. (Orig.). 1990. pap. text 15.00 (*1-55877-123-9*) Natl Governor.

Policy, Practice, & Provision for Children with Specific Learning Difficulties. Jill Duffield et al. LC 95-77822. 256p. 1995. 72.95 (*1-85628-928-1*, LC4706, Pub. by Avebry) Ashgate Pub Co.

Policy Process. Stuart S. Nagel. LC 99-26784. 1999. 49.00 (*1-56072-650-4*) Nova Sci Pubs.

Policy Process: A Reader. 2nd ed. Ed. by Michael J. Hill. LC 97-10252. 1997. pap. 41.95 (*0-13-616947-3*) P-H.

Policy Process & Super-Optimum Solutions. Stuart S. Nagel. 274p. 1994. lib. bdg. 95.00 (*1-56072-134-0*) Nova Sci Pubs.

***Policy Process in a Petro-State.** Cesar E. Baena. (Political Economy of Latin America Ser.). 274p. 1999. text 69.95 (*0-7546-1070-5*, Pub. by Ashgate Pub) Ashgate Pub Co.

Policy Process in the Modern State. Michael Hill & Christopher Ham. 264p. 1997. pap. 27.00 (*0-13-269226-0*) P-H.

Policy, Program Evaluation & Research in Disability: Community Support for All. Julie Ann Racino. LC 99-17248. 473p. 1999. 69.95 (*0-7890-0597-2*) Haworth Pr.

***Policy, Program Evaluation & Research in Disability: Community Support for All.** Julie Ann Racino. LC 99-17248. 473p. 1999. pap. 39.95 (*0-7890-0598-0*) Haworth Pr.

Policy Programme Options for Urban Poverty Reduction: A Framework for Action at the Municipal Level. Franz Vanderschueren et al. LC 96-30834. (Urban Management Program Ser.: No. 20). 72p. 1996. pap. 22.00 (*0-8213-3716-5*, 13716) World Bank.

P

An Asterisk (*) at the beginning of an entry indicates that the title is appearing for the first time.

Policy Puzzle: Finding Solutions in the Diverse American Systems. Donald T. Wells & Chris R. Hamilton. LC 95-25290. 331p. 1995. 49.00 (*0-13-300088-5*) P-H.

Policy Reference Guide of the American Academy of Pediatrics: A Comprehensive Guide to AAP Statements Issued Through December 1997. 11th ed. American Academy of Pediatrics Staff. 1998. pap. 79.95 (*0-910761-98-1*) Am Acad Pediat.

Policy Reform & Poverty in Malawi: A Survey of a Decade of Experience. David E. Sahn et al. (Monographs). (Illus.). 254p. (C). 1990. pap. text 12.00 (*1-56401-007-4*) Cornell Food.

Policy Reform for Sustainable Development in the Caribbean. Ed. by M. Garrity & L. A. Picard. LC 96-7643. (International Institute of Administrative Sciences Monographs: Vol. 2). 140p. (YA). (gr. 12). 1996. 50.00 (*90-5199-271-8*, 271-8) IOS Press.

***Policy Reform in American Agriculture: Analysis & Prognosis.** David Orden et al. LC 98-55710. (Illus.). 248p. 1999. 38.00 (*0-226-63264-4*) U Ch Pr.

Policy Reform in India. Isher Judge Ahluwalia et al. 168p. (Orig.). 1996. pap. 30.00 (*92-64-15308-X*, 41-96-10-1) OECD.

Policy Reform in India. Isher Judge Ahluwalia et al. LC 97-914056. (Development Centre Seminars Ser.). 166p. (Orig.). 1997. pap. write for info. (*81-204-1188-9*) Oxford & IBH Pubng.

***Policy Regimes & Industrial Competitiveness: A Comparative Study of East Asia & India.** Pradeep Agrawal et al. LC 00-27831. (International Political Economy Ser.). 2000. write for info. (*0-312-23452-X*) St Martin.

Policy, Regulation, & Legislation, 1995. (Telecom Power-2000 Ser.: Vol. 5). 1995. 2495.00 (*0-614-18336-7*, IGIC-91) Info Gatekeepers.

Policy Report of the Physician Consortium on Substance Abuse Education. (Illus.). 24p. (Orig.). (C). 1993. pap. text 20.00 (*1-56806-433-0*) DIANE Pub.

Policy Representation in Western Democracies. Warren Miller et al. LC 99-25727. 192p. 2000. text 65.00 (*0-19-829570-7*) OUP.

Policy Research Centers Directory. Ed. by Stuart S. Nagel & Marian Neef. 1978. pap. 15.00 (*0-918592-30-5*) Pol Studies.

***Policy Research in Educational Settings: Contested Terrain.** Jennifer Ozga. LC 99-24211. (Doing Qualitative Research in Educational Settings Ser.). 1999. pap. 25.95 (*0-335-20295-0*) Taylor & Francis.

Policy Research in Telecommunications: Proceedings from the 11th Annual Telecommunications Policy Research Conference. Ed. by Vincent Mosco & Melvin J. Voigt. LC 83-12340. (Communication & Information Science Ser.). 472p. 1984. text 82.50 (*0-89391-260-3*) Ablx Pub.

Policy Responses Globalization: U. S. Foreign Policy & American Commercial Banks. Peter Dombrowski. (Policy & Institutional Studies). (Illus.). 247p. (C). 1996. text 34.95 (*0-8229-3901-0*) U of Pittsburgh Pr.

Policy Responses to Resource Depletion: The Case of Mercury. Nigel Roxburgh. Ed. by Edward I. Altman & Ingo I. Walter. LC 77-24395. (Contemporary Studies in Economic & Financial Analysis: Vol. 21). 219p. 1980. 78.50 (*0-89232-093-1*) Jai Pr.

***Policy Responses to Social Exclusion.** Janie Percy-Smith. LC 99-88206. 2000. write for info. (*0-335-20474-0*) Taylor & Francis.

***Policy Responses to Social Exclusion Towards Inclusion?** Janie Percy-Smith. LC 99-88206. 2000. pap. text 28.95 (*0-335-20473-2*) OpUniv Pr.

Policy Sciences State of the Art. Ed. by Gideon Doron & Alex Mintz. (Orig.). 1992. pap. 15.00 (*0-944285-30-9*) Pol Studies.

Policy Series. Alan C. Walter. Ed. by Beverly Miles. 70p. (Orig.). 1995. pap. text 17.97 (*1-57569-026-8*) Wisdom Pubng.

Policy Simulations in the European Union. Amedeo Fossati & John J. Hutton. LC 97-28275. 336p. (C). 1998. 110.00 (*0-415-15335-2*) Routledge.

Policy Simulations with an Econometric Model. Gary Fromm & Paul Taubman. LC 67-30593. 195p. reprint ed. pap. 60.50 (*0-608-12197-5*, 202537800043) Bks Demand.

Policy Stability & Democratic Change: Energy in Spain's Transition. Thomas D. Lancaster. LC 87-43185. (Illus.). 256p. 1990. lib. bdg. 30.00 (*0-271-00634-X*) Pa St U Pr.

Policy Statement Manual. James M. Mataya. 135p. (Orig.). 1994. pap. 95.00 (*1-882097-51-3*) Amers Comm Bank.

Policy Studies: Integration & Evaluation. Stuart S. Nagel. LC 88-4148. 320p. 1989. pap. 22.95 (*0-275-93007-6*, B3007, Praeger Pubs) Greenwood.

Policy Studies: Integration & Evaluation, 216. Stuart S. Nagel. LC 88-3122. (Contributions in Political Science Ser.: No. 216). 320p. 1988. 65.00 (*0-313-26256-X*, NSP/, Greenwood Pr) Greenwood.

Policy Studies & Developing Nations Vol. 6: The Policy Implementation in Developing Nations, No. 6. Stuart Nagel & Fred Lazin. (Policy Studies & Developing Nations: Vol. 6). 1999. 78.50 (*0-7623-0221-6*) Jai Pr.

Policy Studies & the Social Sciences. Ed. by Stuart S. Nagel. (Organization Ser.). 329p. 1975. pap. 15.00 (*0-317-35632-1*) Pol Studies.

Policy Studies & the Social Sciences. Ed. by Stuart S. Nagel. LC 77-82859. 315p. 1979. reprint ed. pap. text 21.95 (*0-87855-641-9*) Transaction Pubs.

Policy Studies Around the World. Ed. by Stuart S. Nagel. 1973. pap. 15.00 (*0-918592-02-X*) Pol Studies.

Policy Studies Directory. Stuart S. Nagel & Marian Neef. 1976. pap. 15.00 (*0-918592-18-6*) Pol Studies.

Policy Studies for Educational Leaders. Fowler. LC 99-21265. (Illus.). 382p. 1999. 63.00 (*0-13-267832-2*) P-H.

Policy Studies in America & Elsewhere. Ed. by Stuart S. Nagel. (Organization Ser.). 229p. 1975. 15.00 (*0-317-35633-X*) Pol Studies.

Policy Studies in Canada: The State of the Art. Ed. by Laurent Dobuzinskis et al. 360p. 1996. text 55.00 (*0-8020-0528-4*); pap. text 24.95 (*0-8020-6966-5*) U of Toronto Pr.

Policy Studies in Developing Nations, Vol. 2: Political Reform & Developing Nations. Ed. by Stuart S. Nagel. 363p. 1995. 78.50 (*1-55938-106-X*) Jai Pr.

Policy Studies in Developing Nations Vol. 3: Public Budgeting & Financial Administration in Developing Nations. Ed. by Stuart S. Nagel. 1996. 78.50 (*1-55938-190-6*) Jai Pr.

Policy Studies Personnel Directory. Ed. by Stuart S. Nagel & Nancy Munshaw. 1979. pap. 15.00 (*0-918592-33-X*) Pol Studies.

Policy Studies Review Annual, Vol. 1. Ed. by Stuart S. Nagel. 704p. 1977. text 69.95 (*0-8039-0848-2*) Transaction Pubs.

Policy Studies Review Annual, Vol. 2. Ed. by Howard E. Freeman. 752p. 1978. text 69.95 (*0-8039-1100-9*) Transaction Pubs.

Policy Studies Review Annual, Vol. 3. Ed. by Robert H. Haveman & B. Bruce Zellner. 800p. 1979. text 69.95 (*0-8039-1183-1*) Transaction Pubs.

Policy Studies Review Annual, Vol. 4. Ed. by Bertram H. Raven. 768p. 1980. text 69.95 (*0-8039-1119-X*) Transaction Pubs.

Policy Studies Review Annual, Vol. 5. Ed. by Irving L. Horowitz. 768p. 1981. text 69.95 (*0-8039-1315-X*) Transaction Pubs.

Policy Studies Review Annual, Vol. 6. Ed. by Ray C. Rist. 776p. 1982. text 69.95 (*0-8039-1875-5*) Transaction Pubs.

Policy Studies Review Annual, Vol. 7. Ed. by Ray C. Rist. 700p. (C). 1985. text 69.95 (*0-88738-008-5*) Transaction Pubs.

Policy Studies Review Annual, Vol. 8. Ed. by Ray C. Rist. 726p. 1987. pap. 34.95 (*0-88738-673-3*); text 79.95 (*0-88738-116-2*) Transaction Pubs.

Policy Styles in Western Europe. Ed. by Jeremy J. Richardson. 224p. (C). 1982. text 49.95 (*0-04-350062-5*) Routledge.

Policy Systems in An Australian Metropolitan Region: Political & Economic Determinants of Change in Victoria, Vols. 22 & 23. N. P. Low & J. M. Power. (Illus.). 70p. 1984. pap. 22.00 (*0-08-032329-4*, Pergamon Pr) Elsevier.

Policy Theory & Evaluation Concepts, Knowledge, Causes & Norms, 258. Ed. by Stuart S. Nagel & William N. Dunn. LC 89-25784. (Contributions in Political Science Ser.: No. 258). 256p. 1990. 75.00 (*0-313-27356-1*, NPT/, Greenwood Pr) Greenwood.

Policy Through Impact Assessment: Institutionalized Analysis As a Policy Strategy, 235. Ed. by Robert V. Bartlett. LC 89-2122. (Contributions in Political Science Ser.: No. 235). 212p. 1989. 62.95 (*0-313-26775-8*, BPZ, Greenwood Pr) Greenwood.

Policy Toward Public-Private Relations: A Symposium. Ed. by Dennis Thompson. (C). 1983. pap. 15.00 (*0-918592-63-1*) Pol Studies.

***Policy Transfer & British Social Policy: Learning from the U. S. A.?** David P. Dolowitz. LC 99-29252. (Public Policy & Management Ser.). 1999. pap. 32.95 (*0-335-19991-7*) OpUniv Pr.

Policy vs. Paper Clips: Selling the Corporate Model to Your Nonprofit Board. rev. ed. Eugene H. Fram & Vicki Brown. 176p. 1995. pap. 17.95 (*0-87304-279-4*) Manticore Pubs.

Policy vs. the Law: The Reinterpretation of the ABM Treaty. Raymond L. Garthoff. LC 87-72297. 117p. 1987. pap. 10.95 (*0-8157-3049-7*) Brookings.

Policy Within & Across Developing Nations. Stuart S. Nagel. LC 97-27228. (Policy Studies Organization). (Illus.). 200p. 1997. text 72.95 (*1-84014-019-4*, Pub. by Ashgate Pub) Ashgate Pub Co.

Policyholder's Guide to the Law of Insurance Coverage. Peter J. Kalis. LC 97-7867. 600p. 1997. ring bd. 164.00 (*1-56706-341-1*) Panel Pubs.

Policymaker's Guide to Accrual Funding of Military Retirement. William M. Hix & William W. Taylor. LC 96-48479. 1997. pap. 15.00 (*0-8330-2464-7*, MR-760-A) Rand Corp.

Policymakers' Views of Student Assessment. Lorraine M. McDonnell. LC 94-12141. ix, 48p. 1994. pap. 7.50 (*0-8330-1542-7*, MR-348) Rand Corp.

***Policymaking: From the Top Down.** Thomas R. Dye. (Illus.). 208p. (C). 2000. pap. text 21.95 (*1-889119-33-4*, Chatham House Pub) Seven Bridges.

Policymaking & Politics in the Federal District Courts. Robert A. Carp & C. K. Rowland. LC 82-13462. 220p. 1983. text 30.00 (*0-87049-369-8*) U of Tenn Pr.

Policymaking, Communication, & Social Learning. Geoffrey Vickers. Ed. by Guy B. Adams et al. 246p. 1986. 39.95 (*0-88738-115-4*) Transaction Pubs.

Policymaking for Conservation in Latin America: National Parks, Reserves, & the Environment. Jack W. Hopkins. LC 95-19741. 232p. 1995. 59.95 (*0-275-95349-1*, Praeger Pubs) Greenwood.

Policymaking for School Library Media Programs. Marian E. Karpisek. 176p. 1989. pap. 10.00 (*0-8389-0520-X*) ALA.

Policymaking for Social Security. Martha Derthick. LC 78-24811. 446p. 1979. 36.95 (*0-8157-1816-0*); pap. 16.95 (*0-8157-1815-2*) Brookings.

Policymaking in a Newly Industrialized Nation: Foreign & Domestic Policy Issues in Brazil. Robert Wilson & Lawrence Graham. (Policy Research Project Report Ser.: No. 83). 201p. 1988. pap. 12.00 (*0-89940-689-0*) LBJ Sch Pub Aff.

Policymaking in a Redemocratized Brazil, Vols. 1 & 2. Vilmar E. Faria et al. 1996. pap. 32.00 (*0-89940-729-3*) LBJ Sch Pub Aff.

Policymaking in a Redemocratized Brazil Vol. 1: Decentralization & Social Policy. Vilmar E. Faria et al. (Policy Research Project Report Ser.: Vol. 119). 484p. 1997. pap. 22.00 (*0-89940-727-7*) LBJ Sch Pub Aff.

Policymaking in a Redemocratized Brazil Vol. 2: Public Policy & Social Exclusion. Robert S. Graham. LC 96-77963. (Policy Research Project Report Ser.: Vol. 119). 146p. 1997. pap. 12.00 (*0-89940-728-5*) LBJ Sch Pub Aff.

Policymaking in American Public Education: A Framework for Analysis. John T. Thompson. LC 75-5841. (Illus.). 304p. 1975. 25.95 (*0-685-03899-8*) P-H.

Policymaking in Mexico: From Boom to Crisis. Judith A. Teichman. (Thematic Studies in Latin America). 192p. 1988. text 44.95 (*0-04-445033-8*); pap. text 14.95 (*0-04-445049-4*) Routledge.

Policymaking in the Open Economy: Concepts & Case Studies in Economic Performance. Ed. by Rudiger Dornbusch. LC 92-33405. (World Bank Publications). (Illus.). 272p. 1993. text 18.95 (*0-19-520884-6*, 60884) OUP.

Policymaking on the Front Lines: Memoirs of a Korean Practitioner, 1945-79. Chong-Yum Kim. LC 94-22730. (EDI Retrospectives in Policymaking Ser.). 136p. 1994. pap. 22.00 (*0-8213-3014-4*) World Bank.

Policymaking, Politics, & Urban Governance in Chihuahua: The Experience of Recent Panista Governments. Peter Ward & Victoria E. Rodriguez. (U. S. - Mexican Policy Reports: No. 3). 152p. 1992. pap. 15.00 (*0-89940-317-4*) LBJ Sch Pub Aff.

Policymaking under Adversity. Yehezkel Dror. 450p. 1987. pap. 29.95 (*0-88738-721-7*) Transaction Pubs.

Policymaking with Macroeconomic Models. Andrew Britton. 282p. 1989. text 82.95 (*0-566-05748-4*, Pub. by Dartmth Pub) Ashgate Pub Co.

Poliester #27 Death. D. A. P. Plubishing Staff. 1999. pap. text 10.00 (*1-56466-066-4*) Archer Fields.

Poliester #28 Design. D. A. P. Plubishing Staff. 1999. pap. text 10.00 (*1-56466-071-0*) ACOA.

Polignac's Texas Brigade: With a New Preface. Alwyn Barr. LC 97-51441. (Military History Ser.). (Illus.). 104p. 1998. pap. 12.95 (*0-89096-814-4*) Tex A&M Univ Pr.

Polihale & Other Kaua'i Legends. Frederick B. Wichman. LC 91-24204. (Bamboo Ridge Ser.: Nos. 53-54). (Illus.). 184p. 1991. pap. 12.00 (*0-910043-24-8*) Bamboo Ridge Pr.

Polikanpov Fighters in Action, Pt. 2. Hans-Heiri Stapfer. (Aircraft in Action Ser.). (Illus.). 50p. 1996. pap. 9.95 (*0-89747-355-8*, 1162) Squad Sig Pubns.

Polikarpov Fighters in Action, Pt. 1. Hans-Heiri Stapfer. (Aircraft in Action Ser.). (Illus.). 50p. 1995. pap. 9.95 (*0-89747-343-4*) Squad Sig Pubns.

Polin, Vol. 3. Ed. by Antony Polonsky. (Illus.). 458p. 1989. 55.00 (*0-631-16694-7*) Intl Spec Bk.

Polin, Vol. 4. Ed. by Antony Polonsky. (Illus.). 502p. 1990. 55.00 (*0-631-17303-X*) Intl Spec Bk.

Polin, Vol. 5. Ed. by Antony Polonsky. (Illus.). 512p. 1991. 55.00 (*0-631-17886-4*) Intl Spec Bk.

Polin, Vol. 6. Ed. by Antony Polonsky. 512p. 1991. 55.00 (*0-631-18167-9*) Intl Spec Bk.

Polin: Focusing on Galicia: Jews, Poles & Ukrainians, 1772-1918. Ed. by Israel Bartal & Antony Polonsky. (Studies in Polish Jewry: Vol. 12). (Illus.). 416p. 1999. 55.00 (*1-874774-59-5*, Pub. by Littman Lib); pap. 29.50 (*1-874774-40-4*, Pub. by Littman Lib) Intl Spec Bk.

Polin: Focusing on Religion: Aspects & Experiences. Ed. by Antony Polonsky. (Polin: Vol. 11). (Illus.). 480p. 1998. text 55.00 (*1-874774-05-6*, Pub. by Littman Lib); pap. text 29.50 (*1-874774-34-X*, Pub. by Littman Lib) Intl Spec Bk.

Polin: Studies in Polish Jewry, Vol. 2. Ed. by Antony Polonsky. 496p. 1987. 55.00 (*1-874774-24-2*) Intl Spec Bk.

Polin: Studies in Polish Jewry, Vol. 7. Ed. by Antony Polonsky. 350p. 1987. 55.00 (*0-631-18932-7*) Intl Spec Bk.

Polinka Saks & the Story of Aleksei Dmitrich. Aleksandr Druzhinin. Tr. & Intro. by Michael R. Katz. (Studies in Russian Literature & Theory). 225p. (Orig.). 1992. 49.95 (*0-8101-1052-0*); pap. 16.95 (*0-8101-1077-6*) Northwestern U Pr.

Polio. Ed. by Thomas M. Daniel & Frederick C. Robbins. LC 97-18522. (Illus.). 216p. 1997. 29.95 (*1-878822-90-X*) Univ Rochester Pr.

***Polio.** Ed. by Thomas M. Daniel & Frederick C. Robbins. (Illus.). 216p. 1999. pap. 19.95 (*1-58046-066-6*) Univ Rochester Pr.

***Polio.** Allison Stark Draper. LC 00-9371. (Epidemics! Ser.). (Illus.). (J). 2000. write for info. (*0-8239-3348-2*, PowerKids) Rosen Group.

Polio, a Special Ride? One Nurse's Real Life Story of Her Experiences with Polio. Diane Zemke Hawksford. (Illus.). 68p. (Orig.). 1997. pap. 11.95 (*1-891421-00-X*) Diagnostic Ctr.

***Polio Epidemic: Crippling Virus Outbreak.** Victoria Sherrow. LC 00-9472. (Illus.). (J). 2001. write for info. (*0-7660-1555-6*) Enslow Pubs.

Polioakoff Plays 2, No. 2. Stephen Poliakoff. 1995. pap. 15.95 (*0-413-68660-4*, Methuen Drama) Methn.

Polio's Legacy: An Oral History. Edmund J. Sass et al. 296p. (C). 1996. pap. text 28.50 (*0-7618-0144-8*); lib. bdg. 57.00 (*0-7618-0143-X*) U Pr of Amer.

Poliovirus Attenuation: Molecular Mechanisms & Practical Aspects. Ed. by F. Brown & B. P. Lewis. (Developments in Biological Standardization Ser.: Vol. 78). (Illus.). viii, 192p. 1993. pap. 156.75 (*3-8055-5744-2*) S Karger.

Poliquin Principles: Successful Methods for Strength & Mass Development. Charles Poliquin. (Illus.). 160p. 1997. pap. 39.95 (*0-9662752-0-9*) Dayton Pubns.

POLIS, 2 vols. 1991. 50.00 (*0-317-05656-5*, P91013PRO) Assn Bay Area.

POLIS: The Land Use Information & Transportation System for the San Francisco Bay Area. 58p. 1984. 35.00 (*0-318-22681-2*); 35.00 (*0-317-05655-7*, P84002PRO) Assn Bay Area.

Polis & Polemos: Essays on Politics, War, & History in Ancient Greece in Honor of Donald Kagan. Ed. by Charles D. Hamilton & Peter Krentz. LC 97-3189. 368p. 1997. text 39.50 (*0-941690-76-8*); pap. text 19.50 (*0-941690-75-X*) Regina Bks.

Polis & Politics: Essays in Greek Moral & Political Philosophy. Andros Loizou & Harry Lesser. (Avebury Series in Philosophy). 166p. 1990. text 72.95 (*1-85628-052-7*, Pub. by Avebry) Ashgate Pub Co.

Polis & Praxis: Exercises in Contemporary Political Theory. Fred R. Dallmayr. 312p. 1987. pap. text 14.50 (*0-262-54048-7*) MIT Pr.

Polis & the Divine Order: The Oresteia, Sophocles, & the Defense of Democracy. William F. Zak. LC 95-8247. 320p. 1996. 45.00 (*0-8387-5275-6*) Bucknell U Pr.

Poliscide: Big Government, Big Science, Lilliputian Politics. Theodore J. Lowi & Benjamin Ginsberg. LC 89-25001. 330p. (C). 1990. reprint ed. pap. text 24.50 (*0-8191-7654-0*) U Pr of Amer.

Polish: An Essential Grammar. Dana Bielec. LC 97-44254. (POL & ENG.). 296p. (C). 1998. 75.00 (*0-415-16405-2*); pap. 22.99 (*0-415-16406-0*) Routledge.

Polish: LANGUAGE/30. rev. ed. Educational Services Corporation Staff. (POL.). 1995. pap. 16.95 incl. audio (*0-910542-83-X*) Educ Svcs DC.

Polish: Textbook of the Polish Language for English-Speaking People. Joseph Wira. LC 87-91220. (Illus.). 672p. (C). 1987. 32.50 (*0-9618215-0-7*) Belweder Pr.

Polish Aces of World War 2. Robert Fretzyngier. (Illus.). 96p. 1998. pap. 16.95 (*1-85532-726-0*, Pub. by Ospry) Motorbooks Intl.

Polish Air Force at War: The Official History, 1939-1943. Jerzy B. Cynk. 336p. 1998. 59.95 (*0-7643-0559-X*) Schiffer.

Polish Air Force at War The Official History: The Official History, 1943-1945. Jerzy B. Cynk. 336p. 1998. 59.95 (*0-7643-0560-3*) Schiffer.

Polish Alternative, Old Myths, Hard Facts & New Strategies in the Successful Transformation of the Polish Economy. 66p. 8.00 (*952-9520-50-6*) UN.

Polish-American Answer Book. Ed. by Reed Ueda & Sandra Stotsky. (Ethnic Answer Bks.). (Illus.). 136p. (YA). (gr. 5 up). 1999. pap. 8.95 (*0-7910-4802-0*); lib. bdg. 8.95 (*0-7910-4801-2*) Chelsea Hse.

Polish American Archives at Orchard Lake Yearbook. Roman Nir. 1996. write for info. (*0-9649869-3-0*) Orchrd Lake Sch.

Polish American Eff Pol, No. 311. Donald E. Pienkos. 400p. 1992. text 75.50 (*0-88033-208-5*, Pub. by East Eur Monographs) Col U Pr.

***Polish-American Folklore.** Deborah Anders Silverman. LC 99-6985. (Folklore & Society Ser.). 272p. 2000. text 29.95 (*0-252-02569-5*) U of Ill Pr.

Polish-American Politics in Chicago, 1888-1940. Edward Kantowicz. Ed. by Arthur Mann. LC 74-16682. (Illus.). xii, 278p. 1975. lib. bdg. 19.50 (*0-226-42380-8*) U Ch Pr.

Polish-American Politics in Chicago, 1888-1940. Edward Kantowicz. Ed. by Arthur Mann. LC 74-16682. (Illus.). 1995. reprint ed. pap. text 7.00 (*0-226-42381-6*) U Ch Pr.

Polish Americans. Sean Dolan. LC 95-30995. (Immigrant Experience Ser.). 120p. (YA). (gr. 5 up). 1996. lib. bdg. 19.95 (*0-7910-3364-3*) Chelsea Hse.

Polish Americans. Sean Dolan. LC 95-30995. (Immigrant Experience Ser.). (Illus.). 120p. (YA). (gr. 7 up). 1996. pap. 9.95 (*0-7910-3386-4*) Chelsea Hse.

Polish Americans. Helena Z. Lopata & Mary Erdmans. LC 92-41516. 376p. (C). 1993. text 39.95 (*1-56000-100-3*) Transaction Pubs.

Polish Americans. James S Pula. LC 94-20514. (Twayne's Immigrant Heritage of America Ser.). 1995. 33.00 (*0-8057-8427-6*, Twyne); pap. 20.00 (*0-8057-8438-1*, Twyne) Mac Lib Ref.

Polish Americans & Their History: Community, Culture & Politics. John J. Bukowczyk. LC 96-10071. 278p. 1996. text 49.95 (*0-8229-3953-3*) U of Pittsburgh Pr.

Polish & Other Ethnic Jokes. E. C. Stangland. (Mitzi's Office Jokes Ser.). (Illus.). 1980. pap. 2.50 (*0-9602692-1-5*) Norse Pr.

Polish & Publish. Clothilde Belk. Ed. by Kathie Nee. (Illus.). 70p. (Orig.). 1995. pap. text 6.95 (*0-9620258-7-9*) Babe Pub.

Polish Arabian Horse in North America. Neil L. Wood. 500p. 1992. 97.50 (*0-9634613-0-3*) Myerswood.

Polish Armies, 1569-1696, Vol. 2. Richard Brzezinski. (Men-at-Arms Ser.: No. 188). (Illus.). 48p. pap. 11.95 (*0-85045-744-0*, 9121, Pub. by Ospry) Stackpole.

Polish Armour, 1939-45. Krzysztof Barbarski. (Vanguard Ser.: No. 30). (Illus.). 48p. pap. 10.95 (*0-85045-467-0*, 9319, Pub. by Ospry) Stackpole.

Polish Army, 1569-1696, Vol. 1. Richard Brzezinski. (Men-at-Arms Ser.: No. 184). (Illus.). 48p. pap. 11.95 (*0-85045-736-X*, 9116, Pub. by Ospry) Stackpole.

Polish Army, 1939-45. Steven J. Zaloga. (Men-at-Arms Ser.: No. 117). (Illus.). 48p. pap. 11.95 (*0-85045-417-4*, 9050, Pub. by Ospry) Stackpole.

Polish Arrivals at the Port of Baltimore, 1880-1884. Ed. by Jeanne Davis-White. 168p. 1994. pap. 5.95 (*1-887124-09-8*, PG 109) Historyk Pr.

P

An Asterisk (*) at the beginning of an entry indicates that the title is appearing for the first time.

Polish August: Documents from the Beginnings of the Polish Workers' Rebellion. Ed. by Oliver MacDonald. (Illus.). 177p. 1982. pap. 2.00 (*0-939306-02-6*) Left Bank.

Polish Avant Garde Architecture, Rassegna 65. Milobedzki. (Illus.). 110p. 1996. pap. 35.00 (*88-85322-23-9*, Pub. by Birkhauser) Princeton Arch.

Polish Baroque & Enlightenment Literature: An Anthology. Michael J. Mikos. (Illus.). 382p. 1996. 29.95 (*0-89357-266-7*) Slavica.

Polish Biographical Dictionary. Stanley S. Sokol & Sharon F. Kissane. (Illus.). 478p. 1991. 35.00 (*0-86516-245-X*) Bolchazy-Carducci.

Polish-Black Encounters: A History of Polish & Black Relations in America Since 1619. Joseph A. Wytrwal. 5572p. 1982. text 15.00 (*0-317-02855-3*) Endurance.

Polish Catholics in Chicago, 1850-1920: A Religious History. Joseph J. Parot. LC 81-11297. 298p. 1982. 18.00 (*0-87580-081-5*) N Ill U Pr.

Polish Cemetery Inscriptions: Connecticut. Jonathan D. Shea & Constance M. Ochnio. LC 91-60068. (Illus.). 500p. (Orig.). 1991. pap. text. write for info. (*0-945440-05-7*) Pol Geneal CT.

Polish Cemetery Inscriptions: New Hampshire. Jonathan D. Shea et al. LC 88-64169. (Illus.). 100p. 1991. pap. 10.00 (*0-945440-01-4*) Pol Geneal CT.

Polish Cemetery Inscriptions: Vermont. Jonathan D. Shea. LC 88-61600. (Illus.). 88p. 1988. pap. 10.00 (*0-945440-00-6*) Pol Geneal CT.

Polish Champions, Sketches in Human Dignity. Zbigniew Tyburski. LC 99-475862. (Illus.). 208p. 1998. pap. write for info. (*1-55805-999-7*) Franc Pubs WI.

Polish Cities: Travels in Cracow & the South, Gdansk, Malbork, & Warsaw. Philip Ward. LC 89-8426. (International Guide Ser.). (Illus.). 216p. 1989. reprint ed. pap. 17.95 (*0-88289-739-X*) Pelican.

Polish Civilization - Essays & Studies. Ed. by Mieczyslaw Giergielewicz. 304p. 1979. 16.00 (*0-940962-39-X*) Polish Inst Art & Sci.

Polish Coal & European Energy Market Integration. Marian Radetski. 137p. 1995. 56.95 (*1-85972-140-0*, Pub. by Avebry) Ashgate Pub Co.

Polish Coal Miners' Union. John J. Kulczycki. LC 96-45039. 1997. 65.00 (*1-85973-158-9*, Pub. by Berg Pubs) NYU Pr.

Polish Coin see Moneta Polska

Polish Complex. Tadeusz Konwicki. Tr. & Intro. by Richard Lourie. LC 98-23365. 224p. 1998. reprint ed. pap. 12.95 (*1-56478-201-8*) Dalkey Arch.

Polish Contributions to Latin American Culture. Edmund Urbanski. LC 96-83399. 1996. 22.50 (*0-930401-97-2*) Am Inst Polish.

Polish Contributions to the Science. Bohdan Walentynowicz. 1983. lib. bdg. 206.50 (*90-277-1233-6*) Kluwer Academic.

Polish, Conversational: A Beginner's Guide. Maria Swiecicka-Ziemianek. 327p. pap. text 185.00 incl. audio (*0-88432-099-5*, AFP500) Audio-Forum.

Polish Cookbook. Jan Kaluza. Ed. by Polish Book Fair, Inc. Staff. 120p. 1995. 19.00 (*1-885889-60-7*) Home Tutor.

Polish Cookery. Marja Ochorowicz-Monatowa. Ed. & Tr. by Jean Karsavina. (International Cookbook Ser.). 1968. 15.00 (*0-517-50526-6*, Crown) Crown Pub Group.

Polish Crisis: American Policy Options. Jerry F. Hough. LC 82-72742. 80p. 1982. pap. 8.95 (*0-8157-3743-2*) Brookings.

Polish Cuisine: Traditional Recipes in Polish & English. Ed. by Maria De Gorgey. (Hippocrene Bilingual Cookbks.). (ENG & POL.). 146p. 1999. 11.95 (*0-7818-0738-7*) Hippocrene Bks.

Polish Customs, Traditions & Folklore. 2nd ed. Sophie H. Knab. (Illus.). 340p. 1996. 22.50 (*0-7818-0515-5*) Hippocrene Bks.

Polish Debt Crises. Karin Lassakers. (Pew Case Studies in International Affairs). 50p. (C). 1994. pap. text 3.50 (*1-56927-209-3*, GU Schl Foreign) Geo U Inst Dplmcy.

Polish Defense. Thomas Kapitaniak. (Orig.). 1988. pap. 6.50 (*0-931462-80-0*) Chess Ent.

Polish Democratic Thought from the Renaissance to the Great Emigration: Essays & Documents. Ed. by James S. Pula & M. B. Biskupski. (East European Monographs: No. 289). 224p. 1990. 44.50 (*0-88033-186-0*) East Eur Monographs.

Polish Detroit & the Kolasinski Affair. Lawrence D. Orton. LC 80-25290. 230p. reprint ed. pap. 71.30 (*0-608-10595-3*, 207121600009) Bks Demand.

Polish Dictionary: English-Polish--Polish English Pocket Dictionary. K. Stanislawski. (ENG & POL.). 712p. 1992. pap. 29.00 (*0-7859-8915-3*) Fr & Eur.

Polish Directory for the City of Chicago, 1908. Thomas L. Hollowak. 39p. 4.75 (*0-317-57779-4*) Polish Genealog.

Polish Dissident Publications. J. Preibisz. LC 82-7677. 382p. 1982. 65.00 (*0-275-90878-X*, C0878, Praeger Pubs) Greenwood.

Polish Economy: Crisis, Reform, & Transition. Ben Slay. LC 93-44823. 248p. 1994. text 45.00 (*0-691-03616-0*, Pub. by Princeton U Pr) Cal Prin Full Svc.

Polish Economy: Legacies from the Past, Prospects for the Future. Raphael Shen. LC 91-16683. 256p. 1992. 59.95 (*0-275-93886-7*, C3886, Praeger Pubs) Greenwood.

Polish Encyclopaedia, 3 vols. Narodowy P. Wydzia. LC 72-135828. 1972. reprint ed. 52.95 (*0-405-02770-2*) Ayer.

Polish-English see Kosciuszko Foundation Dictionary

Polish-English - English-Polish. Davidovic Mladen. (ENG & POL.). 240p. (Orig.). 1996. pap. 8.95 (*0-7818-0496-5*) Hippocrene Bks.

Polish-English - English-Polish Concise Dictionary: With Complete Phonetics. 4th rev. ed. Iwo C. Pogonowski. 408p. 1993. pap. 9.95 (*0-7818-0133-8*) Hippocrene Bks.

Polish-English - English-Polish Dictionary. (ENG & POL.). 39.50 (*0-87557-131-X*) Saphrograph.

Polish-English - English-Polish Dictionary: Large Edition. large type ed. W. Kierst. (ENG & POL.). 1984. 49.50 (*0-87557-060-7*) Saphrograph.

Polish-English - English-Polish Practical Dictionary. 15th ed. Iwo C. Pogonowski. (Practical Language Dictionaries Ser.). 703p. 1993. pap. 11.95 (*0-7818-0085-4*) Hippocrene Bks.

Polish-English - English-Polish Standard Dictionary: With Business Terms. rev. ed. Iwo C. Pogonowski. (Standard Dictionaries Ser.). 780p. 1994. pap. 19.95 (*0-7818-0282-2*) Hippocrene Bks.

Polish-English & English-Polish Culinary Terms. Marta Sieron. 200p. 1990. pap. text 12.00 (*0-930401-32-8*) Artex Pub.

Polish-English Dictionary of Science & Technology. Sergiusz Czerni & Maria Skrzynska. 846p. 1983. 49.75 (*83-204-1380-X*) IBD Ltd.

Polish-English Dictionary of Science & Technology. 8th ed. Sergiusz Czerni & Maria Skrzynska. (ENG & POL.). 881p. 1994. 150.00 (*0-8288-0650-0*, M15313) Fr & Eur.

Polish-English Dictionary of Slang & Colloquialism. Maelej Widawski. LC 97-38303. (ENG & POL.). 361p. (Orig.). 1997. pap. 19.95 (*0-7818-0570-8*) Hippocrene Bks.

Polish-English, English-Polish Dictionaries. A. Reskiewicz. (ENG & POL.). 1992. write for info. (*0-8288-7279-1*) Fr & Eur.

Polish-English, English-Polish Technical Dictionary. Maria Skrzynska. (ENG & POL.). 498p. 1991. 49.95 (*0-8288-7241-4*, 8320413850) Fr & Eur.

Polish-English, English-Polish Technical Dictionary: Maly Slownik Techniczny Angielsko-Polski - Polsko-Angielski. Maria Skrzynska et al. (ENG & POL.). 498p. 1991. 55.75 (*83-204-1385-0*, Pub. by WNT Warzawa) IBD Ltd.

Polish-English Medical Dictionary. 2nd ed. Przemyslaw Slomski. (ENG & POL.). 802p. 1991. 150.00 (*0-7859-9335-5*) Fr & Eur.

Polish-English Medical Dictionary: Slownik Lekarski Polsko-Angielski. Przemyslaw Stomski. (ENG & POL.). 899p. 1986. 75.00 (*0-8288-0576-8*, F 105610) Fr & Eur.

Polish-English-Russian Data Processing Dictionary. Z. Pezinska & A. Topulos. (ENG, POL & RUS.). 119p. 1981. pap. 24.95 (*0-8288-0274-2*, M 9489) Fr & Eur.

Polish-English Unabridged Dictionary, 3 vols., Set. Iwo C. Pogonowski. LC 97-14300. (ENG & POL.). 3800p. 1997. 200.00 (*0-7818-0441-8*) Hippocrene Bks.

Polish Entrepreneurs & American Entrepreneurs: A Comparative Study of Role Motivations. rev. ed. John O'Del. LC 96-30014. (Studies in Entrepreneurship). (Illus.). 104p. 1997. text 37.00 (*0-8153-2850-8*) Garland.

Polish Essays in the Methodology of the Social Sciences. Ed. by Jerzy J. Wiatr. (Boston Studies in the Philosophy of Science: No. 29). 273p. 1979. pap. text 70.50 (*90-277-0956-4*, D Reidel); lib. bdg. 80.00 (*90-277-0723-5*, D Reidel) Kluwer Academic.

Polish Essays in the Philosophy of the Natural Sciences. Wladislaw Krajewski. 515p. 1982. pap. text 95.00 (*90-277-1287-5*, D Reidel); lib. bdg. 187.00 (*90-277-1286-7*, D Reidel) Kluwer Academic.

Polish Fables: Bilingual Edition. Ignacy Krasicki. Tr. by Gerard Kapolka. (POL., Illus.). 250p. 1997. reprint ed. 19.95 (*0-7818-0548-1*) Hippocrene Bks.

Polish Family Research. rev. ed. J. Konrad. 63p. 1987. pap. 10.00 (*0-685-20960-1*, Heritge House) Ye Olde Genealogie Shoppe.

Polish Family Research. rev. ed. J. Konrad. (Illus.). 72p. 1992. pap. 10.00 (*1-878311-13-1*, Heritge House) Ye Olde Genealogie Shoppe.

***Polish First Names.** Sophie H. Hodorowicz Knab. 128p. 1999. 11.95 (*0-7818-0749-2*) Hippocrene Bks.

Polish Folk Embroidery. Jadwiga Turska. (Illus.). 336p. 1998. 75.00 (*0-7818-0719-0*) Hippocrene Bks.

Polish Folk Legends. Illus. by Daniel Haskin. 72p. (Orig.). 1992. pap. text 11.95 (*0-9634152-0-4*) Polish-Amer Jrnl.

Polish Folk Music: Slavonic Heritage - Polish Tradition - Contemporary Trends. Anna Czekanowska. (Cambridge Studies in Ethnomusicology). (Illus.). 240p. (C). 1991. text 74.95 (*0-521-30090-8*) Cambridge U Pr.

Polish Folkdances & Songs: A Step by Step Guide. Ada Dziewanowska. LC 97-26137. (ENG & POL., Illus.). 800p. 1997. 39.50 (*0-7818-0420-5*) Hippocrene Bks.

Polish Folkways in America: Community & Family. Eugene Obidinski & Helen S. Zand. (Polish Studies: Vol. I). 162p. (Orig.). 1987. pap. text 23.00 (*0-8191-5882-8*); lib. bdg. 44.50 (*0-8191-5881-X*) U Pr of Amer.

Polish Foreign Policy Reconsidered: Challenges of Independence. Ed. by Ilya Prizel & Andrew A. Michta. LC 94-35327. 224p. 1995. text 45.00 (*0-312-12293-4*) St Martin.

Polish-French Medical Dictionary: Dictionnaire Medical Polonais-Francais. 2nd ed. Brunon Neuman. 1984. 50.00 (*0-8288-1854-1*, M15407) Fr & Eur.

Polish-German Boderlands: An Annotated Bibliography, 35. Barbara D. Paul. LC 94-13054. (Bibliographies & Indexes in World History Ser.: Vol. 35). 224p. 1994. lib. bdg. 75.00 (*0-313-29162-4*, Greenwood Pr) Greenwood.

Polish-German Medical Dictionary: Polnisch-Deutsches Medizinisches Woerterbuch. 2nd ed. B. Zlotnicki. 762p. 1985. 95.00 (*0-8288-1855-X*) Fr & Eur.

Polish-German Scientific & Technical Dictionary: Polnisch-Deutsches Wissenschaftlich - Technisches Woerterbuch. 5th ed. Z. J. Koch. (GER & POL.). 598p. 1984. 125.00 (*0-8288-2125-9*, M9217) Fr & Eur.

Polish Handy Extra Dictionary. Krystyna M. Olszer & Ryszard Olszer. (POL.). 125p. (Orig.). 1996. pap. 11.95 (*0-7818-0504-X*) Hippocrene Bks.

Polish Herbs, Flowers & Folk Medicine. Sophie H. Knab. (Illus.). 207p. 1995. 19.95 (*0-7818-0319-5*) Hippocrene Bks.

Polish Herbs, Flowers & Folk Medicine. rev. ed. Sophie Knab. LC 99-39042. (Illus.). 216p. 1999. 22.50 (*0-7818-0786-7*) Hippocrene Bks.

Polish Heritage Cookery. Robert Strybel & Maria Strybel. (Illus.). 895p. 1992. 35.00 (*0-7818-0069-2*) Hippocrene Bks.

Polish Heritage Cookery. Robert Strybel & Maria Strybel. (Illus.). 915p. 1997. 39.95 (*0-7818-0558-9*, 658) Hippocrene Bks.

Polish Heritage of Joseph Conrad. Gustav Morf. LC 65-26452. (Studies in Conrad: No. 8). 1969. reprint ed. lib. bdg. 75.00 (*0-8383-0597-0*) M S G Haskell Hse.

Polish Heritage Songbook. Marek Sart. 166p. 1995. pap. 14.95 (*0-7818-0425-6*) Hippocrene Bks.

Polish-Hungarian Pocket Dictionary. Ed. by I. Varsanyi. 784p. (C). 1988. 35.00 (*963-205-233-1*, Pub. by Akade Kiado) St Mut.

Polish Immigrants & Industrial Chicago: Workers on the South Side, 1880-1922. Dominic A. Pacyga. LC 90-25391. (Urban Life & Urban Landscape Ser.). 298p. 1991. text 21.50 (*0-8142-0541-0*) Ohio St U Pr.

Polish in Three Months. Danusia Stok. LC 98-48010. (Hugo Ser.). 256p. 1999. pap. text 14.95 (*0-7894-4217-5*) DK Pub Inc.

Polish Independent Publications, 1976-1990: Guide to the Collection in the Hoover Institution Archives. Compiled by Christopher Lazarski & Maciej Siekierski. LC 98-44721. (Bibliography Ser.: Vol. 77). 510p. 1998. pap. 25.95 (*0-8179-2772-7*) Hoover Inst Pr.

Polish Institute of Arts & Sciences in America: Origin & Development. Stanislaw Strzetelski. 54p. 1960. 4.00 (*0-940962-32-2*) Polish Inst Art & Sci.

Polish Institutions of Higher Learning. Jan Wepsiec. 110p. 1959. 2.00 (*0-940962-33-0*) Polish Inst Art & Sci.

Polish Intellegentsia in Nazi Concentration Camps & American Exile: A Study of Values in Crisis Situations. Alicja Iwanska. LC 98-17569. 200p. 1998. text 79.95 (*0-7734-8388-8*) E Mellen.

Polish-Jewish Relations During the Second World War. Emmanuel Ringelblum. Tr. by Dafna Allon et al. LC 76-1394. 330p. 1976. 35.00 (*0-86527-155-0*) Fertig.

Polish-Jewish Relations During the Second World War. annot. ed. Emmanuel Ringelblum. Ed. by Shmuel Krakowski. Tr. by Dafna Allon et al from YID. 671p. 1992. reprint ed. pap. 19.95 (*0-8101-0963-8*) Northwestern U Pr.

Polish Jews, 1914-1939. Ed. by Nachman Tamir. LC 85-47709. (Illus.). 216p. 1986. 19.95 (*0-8453-4791-8*, Cornwall Bks) Assoc Univ Prs.

Polish Law Collection. Ed. by Danuta Kierzkowska. 1000p. (C). 1996. ring bd. 450.00 (*83-85430-27-X*, Pub. by Tepis Pubng Hse) Intl Info Srvcs Inc.

Polish Letters, 2 vols. Jean-Paul Marat. 1972. 200.00 (*0-8490-0871-9*) Gordon Pr.

Polish Localities in the Russian Partition & Their Parish Affiliations: Bialystok, Drohiczyn, Lomza, Plock Dioceses. Jonathan D. Shea & William F. Hoffman. (Illus.). 168p. (Orig.). 1994. pap. 15.00 (*0-9631579-1-4*) Lang & Lineage.

Polish Love Story. Ron Manske. LC 79-84322. (Illus.). 144p. 1979. pap. 2.50 (*0-89221-060-5*) New Leaf.

Polish Masters from the Kosciuszko Foundation Collection. Wladyslawa Jaworska. Ed. by Elizabeth K. Skrabonja. (Illus.). 88p. 1995. 40.00 (*0-917004-23-X*); pap. 20.00 (*0-917004-24-8*) Kosciuszko.

Polish Memoirs of William John Rose. William J. Rose. Ed. by Daniel Stone. LC 74-79986. 274p. 1975. reprint ed. pap. 85.00 (*0-608-08211-2*, 202367300033) Bks Demand.

Polish Music & Chopin, Its Laureate. Ethel Rayson. 64p. 1991. reprint ed. lib. bdg. 59.00 (*0-7812-9344-8*) Rprt Serv.

Polish Music Literature, (1515-1990) A Selected Annotated Bibliography. Ed. by Gillian Olechno-Huszcza et al. (Polish Music History Ser.: No. 4). 244p. 1991. 25.00 (*0-916545-04-0*, ML 120 P6 1991) Friends of Pol Mus.

Polish National Catholic Church, Independent Movements, & Old Catholic Church: Annotated Bibliography. Bernard Wielewinski. (East European Monographs). 768p. 1989. text 138.50 (*0-88033-176-3*, Pub. by East Eur Monographs) Col U Pr.

Polish National Liberation Struggles & the Genesis of the Modern Nation. Emanuel Halicz. (Odense Studies in History & Social Sciences: No. 73). 197p. (Orig.). 1982. pap. 37.50 (*87-7492-374-9*, Pub. by Odense Universitets Forlag) Coronet Bks.

Polish Paradox. Anatole C. Bogacki. 1991. text 50.00 (*0-88033-200-X*, Pub. by East Eur Monographs) Col U Pr.

Polish Paradox: Communism & National Renewal. William E. Schaufele. LC 81-70157. (Headline Ser.: No. 256). (Illus.). 72p. (gr. 11-12). 1981. pap. 5.95 (*0-87124-071-8*) Foreign Policy.

Polish Peasant in Europe & America. William I. Thomas & Florian Znaniecki. Ed. by Eli Zaretsky. LC 95-838. 152p. 1995. pap. text 13.95 (*0-252-06484-4*) U of Ill Pr.

Polish People's Republic. James F. Morrison. LC 68-18209. (Integration & Community Building in Eastern Europe Ser.: No. 2). 184p. reprint ed. pap. 57.10 (*0-608-10161-3*, 200228000012) Bks Demand.

***Polish Pharse Book.** (Phrase Book & Dictionary Ser.). (Illus.). 192p. 1999. pap. 8.95 (*2-8315-7197-9*) Berlitz.

Polish Phrase Book. DK Publishing Staff. LC 99-21840. (Eyewitness Travel Guide Phrase Bks.). 128p. 1999. pap. 6.95 (*0-7894-4869-6*) DK Pub Inc.

Polish Phrase Book & Dictionary. 2nd rev. ed. Iwo C. Pogonowski. 252p. 1993. pap. 11.95 (*0-7818-0134-6*) Hippocrene Bks.

Polish Phrasebook: For Business & Pleasure. Jan Kaluza. Ed. by Polish Book Fair, HTP Staff. (POL.). 350p. 1998. pap. 9.95 (*1-885889-55-0*) Home Tutor.

Polish Piano Music: Works by Paderewski, Scharwenka, Moszkowski. Ignance Jan Paderewski. Date not set. pap. text 12.95 (*0-486-40624-5*) Dover.

Polish Plays in English Translations: A Bibliography. Boleslaw Taborski. 74p. 1968. pap. 3.50 (*0-940962-34-9*) Polish Inst Art & Sci.

Polish Poetry of the Last Two Decades of Communist Rule: Spoiling Cannibals' Fun. Ed. by Stanislaw Baranczak & Clare Cavanagh. 204p. (Orig.). 1991. 29.95 (*0-8101-0968-9*); pap. 12.95 (*0-8101-0982-4*) Northwestern U Pr.

Polish Politics: Edge of the Abyss. Ed. by Jack Bielasiak. LC 83-24759. 366p. 1984. 65.00 (*0-275-91128-4*, C1128, Praeger Pubs) Greenwood.

Polish Politics & National Reform, 1775-1788. Daniel Stone. (East European Monographs: No. 22). 122p. 1976. text 60.00 (*0-914710-15-X*, Pub. by East Eur Monographs) Col U Pr.

***Polish Politics & Society.** F. Millard. LC 99-12745. 1999. write for info. (*0-415-15903-2*) Routledge.

Polish Politics in Transition: The Camp of National Unity & the Struggle for Power, 1935-1939. Edward D. Wynot. LC 73-85024. 312p. reprint ed. pap. 96.80 (*0-608-15801-1*, 203106400073) Bks Demand.

Polish Portrait. Michael Tarnowski. 192p. 1972. 25.00 (*0-89388-044-2*) Okpaku Communications.

Polish Presence in America. Illus. by Julian Zebrowski. 178p. 1990. pap. 35.00 (*1-881284-12-3*) Am Inst Polish.

Polish Problem at the Paris Peace Conference: A Study of the Great Powers & the Poles, 1918-1919. Kay Lundgreen-Nielsen. (Odense Studies in History & Social Sciences: No. 59). 603p. (Orig.). 1979. pap. 42.50 (*87-7492-261-0*, Pub. by Odense Universitets Forlag) Coronet Bks.

Polish Proverbs. Compiled by Joanne Asala. 1995. pap. 10.95 (*1-57216-011-X*) Penfield.

Polish Question During World War II. John Harper & Andrew Parlin. (Pew Case Studies in International Affairs). 50p. (C). 1995. pap. text 3.50 (*1-56927-419-3*) Geo U Inst Dplmcy.

Polish Question in the Russian State Duma. Edward Chmielewski. LC 77-100411. 196p. reprint ed. pap. 60.80 (*0-608-14260-3*, 202221300025) Bks Demand.

Polish Radio Broadcasting in the United States. Joseph Migala. 309p. 1987. text 55.50 (*0-88033-112-7*, 216, Pub. by East Eur Monographs) Col U Pr.

Polish Reference Grammar. Maria Z. Brooks. LC 74-78500. (Slavistic Printings & Reprintings Ser.: No. 2). 580p. 1976. text 123.10 (*90-279-3313-8*) Mouton.

Polish Renaissance. Bernard Jacobson. LC 96-196301. (Twentieth Century Composers Ser.). (Illus.). 240p. (Orig.). (C). 1996. pap. 19.95 (*0-7148-3251-0*, Pub. by Phaidon Press) Phaidon Pr.

Polish Renaissance in Its European Context. Ed. by Samuel Fiszman. LC 88-1717. (Illus.). 506p. 1988. pap. 156.90 (*0-608-05018-0*, 205967900004) Bks Demand.

Polish Renaissance Literature: An Anthology. Michael J. Mikos. (Illus.). 275p. 1995. 24.95 (*0-89357-257-8*) Slavica.

Polish Review. write for info. (*0-318-60008-0*); write for info. (*0-318-60009-9*) Polish Inst Art & Sci.

Polish Review: Index: 1956-1966. Ed. by Irene Sokol & Ludwik Krzyzanowski. 66p. 1967. 2.00 (*0-940962-06-3*) Polish Inst Art & Sci.

Polish Review: Index: 1969-1970. Ed. by Irene Sokel. 39p. 1971. 1.00 (*0-940962-07-1*) Polish Inst Art & Sci.

Polish Revolutionary Populism: A Study in Agrarian Socialist Thought from the 1830s to the 1850s. Peter Brock. LC 77-2840. 134p. reprint ed. pap. 41.60 (*0-608-18024-6*, 202648400049) Bks Demand.

Polish Road from Socialism: The Economics, Sociology & Politics of Transition. Ed. by Walter Connor et al. LC 91-27626. 320p. (C). (gr. 13). 1992. text 87.95 (*0-87332-886-8*) M E Sharpe.

Polish Romantic Drama: Three Plays in English Translation. Ed. by Harold B. Segel. (Polish Theatre Archive Ser.). 304p. 1997. text 47.00 (*90-5702-087-4*, Harwood Acad Pubs); pap. text 23.00 (*90-5702-088-2*, Harwood Acad Pubs) Gordon & Breach.

Polish Romantic Literature. Julian Krzyzanowski. LC 68-22922. (Essay Index Reprint Ser.). 1977. 20.95 (*0-8369-0602-0*) Ayer.

Polish Roots (Korzenie Polskie) Rosemary A. Chorzempa. (Illus.). 262p. 2000. pap. 17.95 (*0-8063-1378-1*, 983) Genealog Pub.

Polish-Russian Dictionary of Economics. deluxe ed. M. N. Osmowej. (POL & RUS.). 494p. 1977. 35.00 (*0-8288-5511-0*, M9121) Fr & Eur.

Polish-Russian, Russian-Polish Dictionary. deluxe ed. I. Mitronowa. (POL & RUS.). 575p. 1980. 14.95 (*0-8288-4712-6*, M9102) Fr & Eur.

Polish Sacred Philology in the Reformation & the Counter-Reformation: Chapters in the History of the Controversies (1551-1632) David A. Frick. LC 88-27853. (University of California Publications in Modern Philology: No. 123). 302p. reprint ed. pap. 93.70 (*0-7837-7481-8*, 204920300010) Bks Demand.

Polish School of Philosophy of Medicine: From Tytus Chalubinski (1820-1889) to Ludwick Fleck (1896-1961) Iklana Lowey & Inserm. (Philosophy & Medicine Ser.). 296p. 1990. lib. bdg. 135.00 (*0-7923-0958-8*, Pub. by Kluwer Academic) Kluwer Academic.

Polish 2nd Corps & the Italian Campaign. Ed. by W. Victor Madeja. LC 84-81892. (Illus.). 186p. 1984. 14.00 (*0-941052-51-6*) Valor Pub.

Polish 2nd Corps & the Italian Campaign. Ed. by W. Victor Madeja. LC 84-81892. (Illus.). 186p. 1985. pap. 14.00 (*0-941052-34-6*) Valor Pub.

Polish Short Story in English: A Guide & Critical Bibliography. Jerzy J. Maciuszko. LC 68-12253. 474p. reprint ed. pap. 147.00 (*0-7837-3617-7*, 204348300009) Bks Demand.

Polish Society. Adam Podgorecki. LC 93-25056. 208p. 1993. 62.95 (*0-275-94728-9*, C4728, Praeger Pubs) Greenwood.

Polish Solidarity Movement: Revolution, Democracy & Natural Rights. Arista M. Cirtautas. LC 97-5239. (Routledge Studies of Societies in Transition). 336p. (C). 1997. 90.00 (*0-415-16940-2*) Routledge.

Polish Speaking in Poland. Oscar E. Swan. 140p. 1993. pap. text 49.95 incl. audio (*0-88432-693-4*, AFP650) Audio-Forum.

Polish Surnames: Origins & Meanings. William F. Hoffman. viii, 296p. (Orig.). 1993. pap. text 16.50 (*0-924207-00-0*) Polish Genealog.

Polish Syllables: The Role of Prosody in Phonology & Morphology. Christina Y. Bethin. (Illus.). 278p. (Orig.). 1992. pap. 22.95 (*0-89357-234-9*) Slavica.

Polish Taxation. Paiz. 1993. pap. text 53.50 (*90-6544-737-7*) Kluwer Academic.

Polish Texans. T. Lindsay Baker. (Illus.). 120p. 1982. pap. 7.95 (*0-933164-99-8*) U of Tex Inst Tex Culture.

Polish Touches: Recipes & Traditions. Ed. by Jacek Nowakowski. 1996. pap. 12.95 (*1-57216-016-0*) Penfield.

Polish Traditional Folklore: The Magic of Time. Anna Brzozowska-Krajka. 224p. 1998. 31.00 (*0-88033-395-2*, 498, Pub. by East Eur Monographs) Col U Pr.

***Polish Transition Ten Years on: Processes & Perspectives.** Ed. by Sue Faulkner & Jim McLoughlin. LC 99-73323. 222p. 1999. text 65.95 (*1-84014-944-2*, Pub. by Ashgate Pub) Ashgate Pub Co.

Polish Trivia Book. John M. Vraniak. LC 87-71341. 169p. 1990. 7.95 (*0-910977-03-8*) Avenue Pub.

Polish U. S. Industrial Cooperation in the 1980's: Findings of a Joint Research Project. Ed. by Paul Marer & Eugeniusz Tabaczynski. LC 81-47884. (Studies in East European & Soviet Planning, Development, & Trade: No. 30). 438p. 1981. reprint ed. pap. 135.80 (*0-7837-9660-9*, 205929300005) Bks Demand.

Polish Underground State. Stefan Korbonski. 288p. 1981. pap. 9.95 (*0-88254-517-5*) Hippocrene Bks.

***Polish up Your Punctuation & Grammar: Master the Basics of the English Language & Write with Greater Confidence.** Marion Field. (General Reference Ser.). (Illus.). 144p. 2000. pap. 19.95 (*1-85703-585-2*, Pub. by How To Bks) Midpt Trade.

Polish Viewpoint: Poland's Entry into the Second World War. S. X. Delaska. 1991. lib. bdg. 67.95 (*0-8490-4417-0*) Gordon Pr.

Polish Way: A Thousand Year History of the Poles & Their Culture. Adam Zamoyski. (Illus.). 422p. 1993. pap. 19.95 (*0-7818-0200-8*) Hippocrene Bks.

Polish Weddings: Customs & Traditions. Sophie H. Knab. LC 97-26010. 250p. 1997. 19.95 (*0-7818-0530-9*) Hippocrene Bks.

Polish Wycinanki Designs. Frances Drwal. (International Design Library). (Illus.). 48p. (Orig.). 1984. pap. 5.95 (*0-88045-058-4*) Stemmer Hse.

Polish Your Furniture with Panty Hose: And Hundreds of Offbeat Uses for Brand-Name Products. Joey Green. LC 95-16399. (Illus.). 160p. (J). 1995. pap. 8.70 (*0-7868-8108-9*, Pub. by Hyperion) Time Warner.

Polish Your Soul & Spruce up Your Heart: How to Like What You See in the Mirror. 160p. 1996. text 10.00 (*0-9641725-3-4*) Canticle Press.

Polished Ebony. Octavus R. Cohen. LC 74-128725. (Short Story Index Reprint Ser.). (Illus.). 1977. 18.95 (*0-8369-3616-7*) Ayer.

Polished Politician: The Political Candidate's Personal Handbook. Lillian Brown. 87p. 1995. pap. 9.95 (*0-9641061-0-8*) LB-LTD Pr.

Polished Stone Articles Used by the New York Aborigines Before & During European Occupation. William M. Beauchamp. LC 74-7930. reprint ed. 34.50 (*0-404-11816-X*) AMS Pr.

Polish/English, Level 1. Penton Overseas Inc. Staff. (VocabuLearn Ser.). (ENG & POL.). 1990. pap. 15.95 incl. audio (*0-939001-04-7*) Penton Overseas.

Polish/English, Level 2. unabridged ed. Penton Overseas Inc. Staff. (VocabuLearn Ser.). (ENG & POL.). 1990. pap. 15.95 incl. audio (*0-939001-05-5*) Penton Overseas.

Polish/English-English/Polish Dictionary. Tadeusz Piotrowski. (ENG & POL.). 790p. 1997. 49.95 (*0-7859-9645-1*) Fr & Eur.

Polish/English-English/Polish Medical Dictionary. Przemyslaw Slomski. (ENG & POL.). 1996. 83.00 (*0-7859-9703-2*) Fr & Eur.

Polishing Apples. Christie Woods. 244p. (C). 1996. pap. text, per. 25.95 (*0-7872-2506-1*, 41250601) Kendall-Hunt.

Polishing Apples Vol. II: Of Bicycles & Blimps. Christie Woods. 232p. (C). 1996. pap. text, per. 23.95 (*0-7872-2510-X*, 41251001) Kendall-Hunt.

Polishing Cloth. 5th ed. DeKalb College Staff. 272p. (C). 1996. pap. text, per. 15.95 (*0-7872-2462-6*) Kendall-Hunt.

Polishing Cloth. 6th ed. DeKalb College Staff. 200p. (C). 1997. per. 11.00 (*0-7872-4402-3*) Kendall-Hunt.

Polishing Cloth. 7th ed. DeKalb College Staff. 202p. (C). 1998. per. 11.95 (*0-7872-5115-1*, 41511501) Kendall-Hunt.

***Polishing Cloth.** 8th ed. Georgia Perimeter. 212p. (C). 1999. per. 12.95 (*0-7872-6103-3*, 41610301) Kendall-Hunt.

***Polishing Cloth.** 9th ed. Georgia Perimeter College Staff. 210p. (C). 2000. per. 12.95 (*0-7872-7204-3*) Kendall-Hunt.

Polishing the Bayonet. Elisabeth A. Belile. LC 97-130533. 150p. (Orig.). 1994. pap. 12.00 (*1-884615-05-8*) Incommcdo San Diego.

Polishing the Diamond, Enlightening the Mind: Reflections of a Korean Buddhist Master. Jae Woong Kim. LC 98-43093. 320p. 1999. pap. 18.95 (*0-86171-145-9*, Pub. by Wisdom MA) Natl Bk Netwk.

***Polishing the Jewel: An Administrative History of Grand Canyon National Park.** Michael F. Anderson. LC 00-9110. (Monograph/Grand Canyon Association Ser.). (Illus.). 2000. pap. write for info. (*0-938216-72-4*) GCA.

Polishing the Petoskey Stone. Luci Shaw. (Wheaton Literary Ser.). 288p. 1990. 14.99 (*0-87788-658-X*, H Shaw Pubs) Waterbrook Pr.

Polishing Wear. A. Milburn et al. (Nineteen Ninety Fall Technical Meeting Ser.: Vol. 90FTM5). (Illus.). 13p. 1990. pap. text 30.00 (*1-55589-557-3*) AGMA.

Polishing Your Professional Image. Bobbi Linkemer. LC 86-47814. (Successful Office Skills Ser.). 64p. 1987. pap. 4.00 (*0-8144-7670-8*) AMACOM.

***Polisi vs. Clark & Parker & Gould: Sexual Harassment.** Anthony J. Bocchino & David A. Sonenshein. 188p. 1998. pap. 22.95 (*1-55681-629-4*) Natl Inst Trial Ad.

Politcs in America: Texas Edition. 3rd ed. G. Gibson. 948p. 1998. 78.00 (*0-13-095511-6*) P-H.

Polite Americans: A Wide-Angle View of Our More or Less Good Manners over 300 Years. Gerald Carson. LC 80-11824. (Illus.). 346p. 1980. reprint ed. lib. bdg. 59.75 (*0-313-22417-X*, CAPO, Greenwood Pr) Greenwood.

***Polite & Commercial People: England, 1727-1783.** Paul Langford. (Illus.). 820p. 1998. 55.00 (*0-19-820733-6*) OUP.

Polite & Commercial People: England, 1727-1783. Paul Langford. (New Oxford History of England Ser.). (Illus.). 820p. 1994. reprint ed. pap. text 22.00 (*0-19-285253-1*) OUP.

Polite & Profane Russian Business Terms: Words & Expressions. T. J. Straub. 42p. 1995. pap. 21.95 (*0-9651660-2-3*) Profit Mgnt.

Polite Essays. Ezra Pound. LC 67-22111. (Essay Index Reprint Ser.). 1977. 23.95 (*0-8369-0796-5*) Ayer.

Polite Farces for the Drawing Room. Arnold Bennett. Date not set. 20.95 (*0-518-19147-8*) NY Times Lib.

Polite Farces for the Drawing Room. (Collected Works of Arnold Bennett: Vol. 66). 1976. reprint ed. 15.75 (*0-685-72140-X*, 19147) Ayer.

Polite Landscapes: Gardens & Society in Eighteenth-Century England. Tom Williamson. 1999. pap. text 22.95 (*0-7509-2023-8*) A Sutton.

Polite Landscapes: Gardens & Society in 18th-Century England. Tom Williamson. (Illus.). viii, 182p. 1995. text 39.95 (*0-8018-5205-6*) Johns Hopkins.

Polite Lies: On Being a Woman Caught Between Cultures. Kyoko Mori. 258p. 1999. pap. 11.95 (*0-449-00428-7*) Fawcett.

Polite Lies: On Being a Woman Caught Between Cultures. Kyoko Mori. LC 97-10445. 256p. 1998. text 22.50 (*0-8050-4079-X*) St Martin.

Polite Marriage. Joyce M. Tompkins. LC 77-80403. (Essay Index Reprint Ser.). 1977. 18.95 (*0-8369-1053-2*) Ayer.

Polite or Commercial Concerts? Concert Management & Orchestral Repertoire in Edinburgh, Bath, Oxford, Manchester & Newcastle, 1730-1799. Jenny Burchell. LC 96-1839. (Outstanding Dissertations in Music from British Universities Ser.). (Illus.). 432p. 1996. text 105.00 (*0-8153-2462-6*) Garland.

Polite Politics in Hong-kong. Ho. 67.95 (*1-84014-333-9*) Ashgate Pub Co.

Polite Protesters: The American Peace Movement of the 1980s. John Lofland. (Studies on Peace & Conflict Resolution). 320p. (C). 1993. text 49.95 (*0-8156-2604-5*); pap. text 19.95 (*0-8156-2605-3*) Syracuse U Pr.

Polite Satires. Clifford Bax. LC 76-40385. (One-Act Plays in Reprint Ser.). 1976. reprint ed. 20.00 (*0-8486-2001-1*) Roth Pub Inc.

Polite Sex. James Wilcox. 1999. pap. write for info. (*0-316-94010-0*) Little.

Polite Sex: A Novel. James Wilcox. 288p. 1999. pap. 13.00 (*0-316-94134-4*, Back Bay) Little.

Polite Society. Arthur Devis. (Illus.). 122p. 1983. pap. 8.95 (*0-9591141-2-2*) Antique Collect.

***Polite Tourist.** Adrian Tinniswood. LC 98-234585. (Illus.). 224p. 1999. 39.95 (*0-8109-6372-8*, Pub. by Abrams) Time Warner.

Polite Wisdom: Heathen Rhetoric in Milton's Areopagitica. Paul M. Dowling. 146p. (C). 1995. pap. text 24.95 (*0-8476-8053-3*); lib. bdg. 58.50 (*0-8476-8052-5*) Rowman.

Politeness: Some Universals in Language Usage. Penelope Brown & Stephen C. Levinson. (Illus.). 352p. 1987. pap. text 22.95 (*0-521-31355-4*) Cambridge U Pr.

***Politeness & Face in Chinese Culture.** Song Mei Lee-Wong. 2000. 48.95 (*3-631-32022-1*) P Lang Pubng.

***Politeness & Face in Chinese Culture.** Song Mei Lee-Wong. LC 99-89976. (Cross Cultural Communication Ser.: Vol. 6). 344p. 2000. pap. text 48.95 (*0-8204-3295-4*) P Lang Pubng.

Politeness & Its Discontents: Problems in French Classical Culture. Peter France. (Cambridge Studies in French: No. 35). 257p. (C). 1992. text 69.95 (*0-521-37070-1*) Cambridge U Pr.

Politeness & Poetry in the Age of Pope. Thomas Woodman. LC 88-45806. 168p. 1989. 32.50 (*0-8386-3348-X*) Fairleigh Dickinson.

Politeness in Language: Studies in Its History, Theory & Practice. Ed. by Richard J. Watts et al. LC 91-45519. (Trends in Linguistics, Studies & Monographs: No. 59). (Illus.). x, 381p. (C). 1992. lib. bdg. 116.95 (*3-11-013184-6*, 47-92) Mouton.

Politeness Phenomena in England & Greece: A Cross-Cultural Perspective. Maria Sifianou. LC 92-11078. (Illus.). 272p. (C). 1993. text 59.00 (*0-19-823972-6*, Clarendon Pr) OUP.

Politian: An Unfinished Tragedy. Edgar Allan Poe. (BCL1-PS American Literature Ser.). 89p. 1992. reprint ed. lib. bdg. 59.00 (*0-7812-6832-X*) Rprt Serv.

Politica. Johannes Althusius. Tr. & Abr. by Frederick S. Carney. LC 94-30586. (Liberty Classics Ser.). Orig. Title: Politica Methodice Digesta. lxii, 240p. 1995. 19.50 (*0-86597-114-5*); pap. 7.50 (*0-86597-115-3*) Liberty Fund.

Politica. Ed. by W. David Ross. (Oxford Classical Texts Ser.). 292p. 1957. text 26.00 (*0-19-814515-2*) OUP.

Politica - Sexualidad: Nudo en la Escritura de Mujeres Latino Americanas. Liliana Trevizan. 194p. 1997. text 37.50 (*0-7618-0664-4*) U Pr of Amer.

Politica Cambiaria, Desarrollo Exportador y Estabilizacion en Chile, 1990-92, Vol. 12. Andres Bianchi. (SPA.). 54p. 1994. pap. text 8.00 (*0-940602-87-3*) IADB.

Politica de las Drogas: Quin Sufre, Quien Trafica, Quien Se Lucra. David Perez. 26p. 1989. pap. 0.50 (*0-89567-098-4*) World View Forum.

Politica de los Empresarios Puertorriquenos. Emilio G. Diaz. (SPA.). 124p. 1991. pap. 6.50 (*0-929157-13-3*) Ediciones Huracan.

Politica delle Idee: Giovan Pietro Vieusseux e Giuseppe Montanelli Nella Toscana Preunitaria. Paolo Bagnoli. (ITA.). 269p. 1996. pap. 30.00 (*0-913298-04-2*) S F Vanni.

Politica e il Tempo: Idee e Problemi Della Transizione Italiana. Paolo Bagnoli. (ITA.). 114p. 1998. pap. 18.00 (*0-913298-16-6*) S F Vanni.

Politica Espanola en Puerto Rico Durante el Siglo XIX. Maria A. Garcia Ochoa. LC 78-14035. 697p. 1982. 12.50 (*0-8477-0854-3*); pap. 10.50 (*0-8477-0855-1*) U of PR Pr.

Politica Methodice Digesta see Politica

Politica Methodice Digesta of Johannes Althusius. Johannes Althusius. Ed. by J. P. Mayer. LC 78-67326. (European Political Thought Ser.). 1979. reprint ed. lib. bdg. 42.95 (*0-405-11673-X*) Ayer.

Politica Militar y Dominacion. Jorge Rodriguez. LC 88-80499. 270p. 1988. pap. 9.50 (*0-940238-59-4*) Ediciones Huracan.

Politica Monetaria: En Busca de Asidero. Gerald K. Bouey. LC HG0655.B68. (Conferencia Per Jacobsson de 1982 Ser.). (SPA.). 37p. reprint ed. pap. 30.00 (*0-608-08759-9*, 206939800004) Bks Demand.

Politica, Pressures & Tariff. Elmer E. Schattscheider. 1974. 23.95 (*0-405-05898-5*) Ayer.

Politica Puertorriquena y el Nuevo Trato. Thomas Mathews. Tr. by Antonio J. Colorado. 349p. (C). 1975. 4.00 (*0-8477-0831-4*); pap. 3.00 (*0-8477-0832-2*) U of PR Pr.

Politica Sacra et Civilis. George Lawson. Ed. by Conal Condren. (Cambridge Texts in the History of Political Thought Ser.). 336p. (C). 1993. text 23.95 (*0-521-39248-9*) Cambridge U Pr.

Politica Sexual en Puerto Rico. Margarita Ostolaza. LC 88-83952. 204p. 1989. pap. 12.50 (*0-929157-00-1*) Ediciones Huracan.

Politica Social Ante los Nuevos Desafios: Cuba y Puerto Rico. Dagmar Guardiola et al. (SPA.). 186p. 1995. pap. write for info. (*0-929441-77-X*) Pubns Puertorriquenas.

Politica y la Ilustracion. Isabel Guiterrez Del Arroyo. (SPA.). 336p. 1995. pap. 14.95 (*0-8477-0206-5*) U of PR Pr.

Political - The Policy of Emanicipation. Robert D. Owen. (Notable American Authors Ser.). 1999. reprint ed. lib. bdg. 125.00 (*0-7812-4678-4*) Rprt Serv.

Political Abolitionism in Wisconsin, 1840-1861: Michael J. McManus. Michael J. McManus. LC 98-12683. 288p. 1998. text 39.00 (*0-87338-601-9*) Kent St U Pr.

Political Action: Mass Participation in 5 Western Democracies. Samuel H. Barnes et al. LC 78-19649. 607p. 1979. reprint ed. pap. 188.20 (*0-608-01450-8*, 205949400001) Bks Demand.

Political Action: The Key to Understanding Politics. George Beam & Dick Simpson. LC 84-5976. xiii, 253p. 1984. 24.95 (*0-8040-0834-5*); pap. 12.95 (*0-8040-0835-3*) Ohio U Pr.

Political Action - Themes of Geography: Sing & Learn. John Carratello. 1994. pap. 9.95 incl. audio (*0-7604-0021-0*, JPC003) Wrner Bros.

Political Action Handbook for Nurses. Diana J. Mason & Susan W. Talbott. 640p. (C). 1985. pap. text 29.75 (*0-201-16368-3*, Health Sci) Addison-Wesley.

Political Action, Public Policy & Catholic Schools. John E. Coons & Frank J. Monahan. (National Congress Catholic Schools for the 21st Century Ser.). 37p. 1991. pap. 2.00 (*1-55833-070-4*) Natl Cath Educ.

Political Activists: Ndp In Convention. Keith Archer & Alan Whitehorn. 320p. 1998. pap. text 29.95 (*0-19-541145-5*) OUP.

Political Activists from Hesse, Germany, 1832-1834: Among Whom Many Immigrants to America. Clifford N. Smith. (German-American Genealogical Research Monographs: No. 29). i, 25p. (Orig.). 1993. pap. 20.00 (*0-915162-73-3*) Westland Pubns.

Political Activists in America: The Identity Construction Model of Political Participation. Nathan Teske. 190p. 1997. text 39.95 (*0-521-58114-1*) Cambridge U Pr.

Political Activities of Philip Freneau. Samuel E. Forman. LC 77-125693. (American Journalists Ser.). 1975. reprint ed. 17.95 (*0-405-01670-0*) Ayer.

Political Activities of the Johnson White House, 1963-1969. Paul Kesaris et al. LC 88-17182. (Research Collections in American Politics Ser.). 1987. write for info. (*0-89093-926-8*) U Pubns Amer.

***Political Activity & the Federal Employee.** 13p. 1999. per. 1.25 (*0-16-049909-7*) USGPO.

***Political Activity & the State & Local Employee.** 11p. 1999. pap. 1.25 (*0-16-063563-2*) USGPO.

Political Activity of Nonprofit Organizations. Mathew D. Staver. LC 98-86448. (Faith & Freedom Ser.). (Illus.). vi, 35p. 1998. pap. write for info. (*0-9662079-2-0*) Liberty Counsel.

Political Advancement in the South Pacific: A Comparative Study of Colonial Practice in Fiji, Tahiti & American Samoa. Francis J. West. LC 84-6745. 188p. 1984. reprint ed. lib. bdg. 55.00 (*0-313-24533-9*, WPSP, Greenwood Pr) Greenwood.

Political Advertising in Western Democracies: Parties & Candidates on Television. Ed. by Lynda L. Kaid & Christina Holtz-Bacha. 331p. 1994. 46.00 (*0-8039-5351-8*); pap. 21.50 (*0-8039-5352-6*) Sage.

Political Advocacy & Cultural Communication: Organizing the Nation's Public Diplomacy. Gifford D. Malone. (Exxon Education Foundation Series on Rhetoric & Political Discourse: Vol. 11). 178p. (Orig.). (C). 1988. pap. text 20.00 (*0-8191-6620-0*) U Pr of Amer.

Political Advocacy & Cultural Communication: Organizing the Nation's Public Diplomacy. Gifford D. Malone. (Exxon Education Foundation Series on Rhetoric & Political Discourse: Vol. 11). 178p. (Orig.). (C). 1988. lib. bdg. 41.00 (*0-8191-6619-7*, Pub. by White Miller Center) U Pr of Amer.

Political Advocacy Handbook. Jaclyn A. Bootel & Cynthia L. Warger. 193p. 1997. pap. 85.70 (*0-86586-291-5*) Coun Exc Child.

Political Aesthetic of Yeats, Eliot & Pound. Michael North. 249p. (C). 1992. text 64.95 (*0-521-41432-6*) Cambridge U Pr.

Political Affiliations of American Economic Elites: Wayne County, Michigan, 1844-1860 As a Test Case. Alexandra McCoy. (Nineteenth Century American Political & Social History Ser.). 291p. 1989. reprint ed. 20.00 (*0-8240-4069-4*) Garland.

Political Agendas for Education: From the Christian Coalition to the Green Party. Joel H. Spring. LC 97-8976. (Sociocultural, Political, & Historical Studies in Education). 1997. 32.50 (*0-8058-2766-8*); pap. 17.50 (*0-8058-2767-6*) L Erlbaum Assocs.

Political Alienation & Voting Turnout in the United States, 1960-1988. Kevin Chen. LC 92-20375. 272p. 1992. text 89.95 (*0-7734-9833-8*) E Mellen.

Political Alignment in the French National Assembly, 1789-1791. Harriet B. Applewhite. LC 92-32493. 304p. (C). 1993. text 45.00 (*0-8071-1751-X*) La State U Pr.

Political Alignments in Colonial Virginia Politics, 1698-1750. D. Alan Williams. (Outstanding Studies in Early American History). 392p. 1990. reprint ed. 25.00 (*0-8240-6296-5*) Garland.

Political Allegory in Late-Medieval England. Ann W. Astell. LC 98-42272. 1999. 35.00 (*0-8014-3560-9*) Cornell U Pr.

Political Ambition. Linda Fowler. 1990. pap. 18.00 (*0-300-04901-3*) Yale U Pr.

Political Ambition: Who Decides to Run for Congress. Linda L. Fowler & Robert D. McClure. LC 88-22713. 264p. (C). 1989. 37.50 (*0-300-04405-4*) Yale U Pr.

Political Analysis. Joseph Linzmeier. 120p. 1997. pap., teacher ed. 6.95 (*1-57087-299-6*) Prof Pr NC.

Political Analysis. 4th ed. White. (C). 1998. pap. text 51.50 (*0-15-505522-4*, Pub. by Harcourt Coll Pubs) Harcourt.

Political Analysis, Vol. 5. Ed. by John R. Freeman. 250p. 1996. text 49.50 (*0-472-10635-X*, 10635) U of Mich Pr.

Political Analysis: The Methodology Section of the American Political Science, Vol. 7. annuals Walter R. Mebane. (Political Analysis Ser.). 218p. 1999. text 49.50 (*0-472-11074-8*, 11074) U of Mich Pr.

Political Analysis Vol. 3: An Annual Publication of the Methodology Section of the American Political Science Association, 1992. Ed. by James A. Stimson. 184p. (C). 1992. text 49.50 (*0-472-10335-0*, 10335) U of Mich Pr.

Political Analysis Vol. 4: An Annual Publication of the Methodology Section of the American Political Science Association. Ed. by John R. Freeman. 272p. 1994. text 49.50 (*0-472-10435-7*, 10435) U of Mich Pr.

Political Analysis Vol. 6: An Annual Volume of the Methodology Section of the American Political Science Association. Ed. by John R. Freeman. 264p. (C). 1997. text 49.50 (*0-472-10743-7*, 10743) U of Mich Pr.

Political Analysis, 1990: An Annual Publication of the Methodology Section of the American Political Science Association, Vol. I. Ed. by James A. Stimson. 290p. 1990. text 49.50 (*0-472-10137-4*, 10137) U of Mich Pr.

Political Analysis, 1990 Vol. 2: An Annual Publication of the Methodology Section of the American Political Science Association. Ed. by James A. Stimson. 216p. (C). 1991. text 49.50 (*0-472-10226-5*, 10226) U of Mich Pr.

Political Analysis of Deviance. Ed. by Pat Lauderdale. LC 79-27057. 257p. 1980. reprint ed. pap. 79.70 (*0-608-00791-9*, 205934000010) Bks Demand.

Political Analysis of Postcommunism: Understanding Postcommunist Ukraine. Volodymyr Polokhalo. LC 97-41505. (Eastern European Studies: No. 6). 368p. 1997. pap. 21.95 (*0-89096-783-0*) Tex A&M Univ Pr.

Political Analysis Through the Prince System. William D. Coplin & Michael K. O'Leary. (Learning Packages in the Policy Sciences Ser.: No. 23). (Illus.). 100p. (Orig.). 1983. pap. text 10.75 (*0-936826-18-5*) PS Assocs Croton.

Political & Administrative Set-Up of Union Territories in India. Sudhir Kumar. (C). 1991. text 29.50 (*81-7099-304-0*, Pub. by Mittal Pubs Dist) S Asia.

Political & Civil History of the United States of America from the Year 1763 to the Close of the Administration of President Washington in March,

P

An Asterisk (*) at the beginning of an entry indicates that the title is appearing for the first time.

1797, 2 vols. Timothy Pitkin. LC 79-109613. (Era of the American Revolution Ser.). 1970. reprint ed. lib. bdg. 135.00 (0-306-71908-8) Da Capo.

Political & Constitutional Ideas of the Court Whigs. Reed Browning. LC 81-19372. 295p. 1982. pap. 91.50 (0-7837-8529-1, 204933800011) Bks Demand.

***Political & Constitutional Ideas of the Philippine Revolution.** Cesar Adib Majul. (Illus.). 252p. 1999. pap. text 23.00 (971-542-115-6, Pub. by U of Philippines Pr) UH Pr.

Political & Constitutional Law of the United States of America. William O. Bateman. xiv, 386p. 1993. reprint ed. 47.50 (0-8377-1919-4, Rothman) W S Hein.

Political & Demographic Aspects of Migration Flows to Europe. (Population Studies: No. 25). 1993. 18.00 (92-871-2360-8, Pub. by Council of Europe) Manhattan Pub Co.

Political & Diplomatic Documents of the State of Israel, December, 1947-May, 1948, 2 vols. Ed. by Gedalia Yogev. (Documents on the Foreign Policy of Israel Ser.). 1980. 79.95 (0-87855-396-7) Transaction Pubs.

Political & Ecclesiastical Allegory of the First Book of the Fairie Queen. Frederick M. Padelford. LC 70-111785. reprint ed. 20.00 (0-404-04856-0) AMS Pr.

Political & Economic Development of Pakistan. Omar Noman. 260p. 1988. lib. bdg. 55.00 (0-7103-0211-8) Routledge.

***Political & Economic Developments in the Third World.** Ed. by Harold Isaacs. (Journal of Third World Studies: Vol. XVII, No. 2). 360p. 2000. pap. 23.00 (0-931971-32-2) Assn Third Wld.

***Political & Economic Dictionary of Eastern Europe.** 500p. 1999. 115.00 (1-85743-063-8, Pub. by EurP) Gale.

Political & Economic Encyclopedia of the Pacific. Ed. by Gerald Siegal. 1990. 85.00 (1-55862-033-8) St James Pr.

Political & Economic Encyclopedia of the Soviet Union & Eastern Europe. Ed. by Stephen White. 380p. 1990. 85.00 (1-55862-070-2) St James Pr.

Political & Economic Encyclopedia of Western Europe. Ed. by Frances Nicholson. 380p. 1990. 85.00 (1-55862-072-9) St James Pr.

Political & Economic Liberalization: Dynamics & Linkages in Comparative Perspective. Ed. by Gerd Nonneman. 332p. 1996. lib. bdg. 59.95 (1-55587-639-0, 87-639-0) L Rienner.

***Political & Economic Transition in East Asia: Strong Market, Weakening State.** Ed. by Xiaoming Huang. 296p. 2000. text 55.00 (0-87840-818-5) Georgetown U Pr.

Political & Economic Trends in Central Asia. Ed. by Shirin Akiner. 350p. 1994. text 69.50 (1-85043-516-2, Pub. by I B T) St Martin.

Political & Economic Writings. Alfred R. Orage. 1973. 250.00 (0-8490-0872-7) Gordon Pr.

Political & Economic Writings from the New English Weekly, 1932-1934. Alfred R. Orage. LC 67-28762. (Essay Index Reprint Ser.). 1977. 19.95 (0-8369-0753-1) Ayer.

***Political & Economic Writings of Daniel Defoe, 8 vols.** W. R. Owens & P. N. Furbank. (Pickering Masters Ser.). 3200p. 2000. 880.00 (1-85196-465-7, Pub. by Pickering & Chatto) Ashgate Pub Co.

Political & Electoral Confrontation in Revolutionary Nicaragua. Alexander H. McIntire, Jr. 65p. (C). 1985. pap. text 18.95 (1-56000-660-9, LA204) Transaction Pubs.

Political & Idealogical Confrontations in 20th Century Europe: Essays in Honor of Milorad M. Drachkovitch. Ed. by Robert Conquest & Dusan Djordjevich. 300p. 1996. text 55.00 (0-312-12373-6) St Martin.

Political & Institutional Issues of the New International Economic Order. Ed. by Ervin Laszlo & Joel Kurtzman. (Policy Studies on the New International Economic Order). 208p. 1981. 52.00 (0-08-025122-6, Pergamon Pr) Elsevier.

Political & Legal Framework of Trade Relations Between the European Community & Eastern Europe. Ed. by Marc Maresceau. (C). 1989. lib. bdg. 139.00 (0-7923-0046-7) Kluwer Academic.

Political & Legal Philosophy of James Wilson, 1742-1798. Mark D. Hall. LC 97-1473. 248p. 1997. spiral bd. 37.50 (0-8262-1103-8) U of Mo Pr.

Political & Legal Remedies for War. Sheldon Amos. 254p. 1982. reprint ed. 35.00 (0-8377-0213-5, Rothman) W S Hein.

Political & Literary Essays: 1st Series. Evelyn B. Cromer. LC 68-8453. (Essay Index Reprint Ser.). 1977. 26.95 (0-8369-1058-3) Ayer.

Political & Literary Essays: 2nd Series. Evelyn B. Cromer. LC 73-108636. (Essay Index Reprint Ser.). 1977. 23.95 (0-8369-1564-X) Ayer.

Political & Literary Essays: 3rd Series. Evelyn B. Cromer. LC 74-107690. (Essay Index Reprint Ser.). 1977. 23.95 (0-8369-1494-5) Ayer.

Political & Military Episodes in the Latter Half of the Eighteenth Century Derived from the Life & Correspondence of the Right Hon. John Burgoyne. Edward B. DeFonblanque. LC 72-8667. (American Revolutionary Ser.). (Illus.). 516p. reprint ed. lib. bdg. 66.00 (0-8398-0378-8) Irvington.

***Political & Military Transformation Of England, 1490-1690 - Rise Of England' The Rise of England's Maritime Empire.** David Loades. 224p. 2000. 69.95 (0-582-35629-6) Longman.

Political & Philosophical Writings of William Godwin, 7 vols. Ed. by Mark Philp et al. LC 99-58650. (Pickering Masters Ser.). 1993. 635.00 (1-85196-026-0, Pub. by Pickering & Chatto) Ashgate Pub Co.

***Political & Religious Ideas in the Works of Arnold Schoenberg.** Ed. by Charlotte M. Cross & A. Berman Russell. LC 99-31282. (Border Crossings Ser.: Vol. 5). 400p. 1999. 75.00 (0-8153-2831-1) Garland.

Political & Social Action in Homophile Organizations. Roxanna T. Sweet. LC 75-13729. (Homosexuality Ser.). 1975. 19.95 (0-405-07372-0) Ayer.

Political & Social Change in China since 1978: Contributions in Political Science, 250. Charles Burton. LC 89-17208. 225p. 1990. 59.95 (0-313-26834-7, BSQ/, Greenwood Pr) Greenwood.

Political & Social Doctrine of Fascism. Benito Mussolini. 1976. 250.00 (0-87968-434-8) Gordon Pr.

Political & Social Economy: Its Practical Applications. John H. Burton. LC 68-55499. (Reprints of Economic Classics Ser.). xii, 345p. 1970. reprint ed. 49.50 (0-678-00621-0) Kelley.

Political & Social Economy of Commodity Control. Christopher P. Brown. LC 79-88568. 394p. 1980. 75.00 (0-275-90458-X, C0458, Praeger Pubs) Greenwood.

Political & Social History of Khurasan under Abbasid Rule 747-820. Elton L. Daniel. LC 79-53302. 1979. 28.00 (0-88297-025-9) Bibliotheca.

Political & Social Ideas of St. Augustine. Herbert A. Deane. LC 63-9809. 356p. (C). 1966. pap. text 25.50 (0-231-08569-9) Col U Pr.

Political & Social Issues in Poland, As Reflected in the Polish Novel. Anna R. Dadlez. 289p. 1989. text 55.50 (0-88033-166-6, Pub. by East Eur Monographs) Col U Pr.

Political & Social Movements. Diane K. Moser & Raymond Spangenburg. LC 97-28096. (American Historic Places Ser.). (Illus.). 130p. (YA). (gr. 7-12). 1998. 19.95 (0-8160-3404-4) Facts on File.

Political & Social Philosophy of Ze'ev Jabotinsky: Selected Writings. Mordechai Sarig & Vladimir Jabotinsky. LC 98-46521. 192p. 1999. 45.00 (0-85303-360-9); pap. 22.50 (0-85303-359-5) Intl Spec Bk.

Political & Social Theory of Max Weber: Collected Essays. Wolfgang J. Mommsen. LC 88-36950. 240p. 1989. 47.95 (0-226-53398-0) U Ch Pr.

Political & Social Theory of Max Weber: Collected Essays. Wolfgang J. Mommsen. LC 88-36950. xiv, 240p. 1992. pap. text 15.50 (0-226-53400-6) U Ch Pr.

Political & Social Thought in the Contemporary Middle East. rev. ed. Ed. by Kemal H. Karpat. LC 81-11877. 557p. 1982. 49.95 (0-275-90834-8, C0834, Praeger Pubs); pap. 25.95 (0-275-91541-7, B1541, Praeger Pubs) Greenwood.

Political & Social Writings Vol. 1: From the Critique of Bureaucracy to the Positive Content of Socialism. Cornelius Castoriadis. 347p. 1988. pap. 19.95 (0-8166-1617-5) U of Minn Pr.

Political & Social Writings Vol. 2: From the Worker's Struggle Against Bureaucracy to Revolution in the Age of Modern Capitalism. Cornelius Castoriadis. LC 87-10893. 384p. 1988. pap. 19.95 (0-8166-1619-1) U of Minn Pr.

Political & Social Writings Vol. 3: Recommencing the Revolution: From Socialism to the Autonomous Society, 1961-1979. Cornelius Castoriadis. Tr. by David A. Curtis from FRE. (C). 1992. pap. 19.95 (0-8166-2168-3); text 49.95 (0-8166-2069-5) U of Minn Pr.

Political & Social Writings Vol. 3: Recommencing the Revolution: From Socialism to the Autonomous Society, 1961-1979, 3 vols., Set. Cornelius Castoriadis. Tr. by David A. Curtis from FRE. 1318p. (C). 1992. pap. 45.00 (0-8166-2264-7) U of Minn Pr.

Political & Socioeconomic Transformation of Turkey. Ed. by Birol A. Yesilada et al. LC 92-46638. 256p. 1993. 62.95 (0-275-93204-4, C3204, Praeger Pubs) Greenwood.

Political & Strategic Issues in the Gulf. Hassan A. Sayed. 327p. 1984. 125.00 (0-946706-07-7, Pub. by Royston Ltd) St Mut.

Political Animal: Biology, Ethics, & Politics. Stephen R. Clark. LC 98-35441. 1999. pap. 24.99 (0-415-18911-X) Routledge.

Political Animal: Biology, Ethics & Politics. Stephen R. Clark. LC 98-35441. 1999. 75.00 (0-415-18910-1) Routledge.

Political Animal: The Conquest of Speciesism. Richard D. Ryder. LC 98-19445. (Illus.). 157p. 1998. lib. bdg. 32.00 (0-7864-0530-9) McFarland & Co.

Political Animals. Garner. LC 97-38262. 286p. 1998. text 65.00 (0-312-21208-9) St Martin.

***Political Anthropology.** Kurtz. 2000. 45.00 (0-8133-3803-4, Pub. by Westview); pap. 20.00 (0-8133-3804-2, Pub. by Westview) HarpC.

Political Anthropology: An Introduction. 2nd ed. Ted C. Lewellen. LC 91-44660. 248p. 1992. 57.95 (0-89789-289-5, H289, Bergin & Garvey); pap. 24.95 (0-89789-290-9, G290, Bergin & Garvey) Greenwood.

Political Anthropology: The State of the Art. Ed. by S. Lee Seaton & Henry J. Claessen. (World Anthropology Ser.). iv, 412p. 1979. text 61.55 (90-279-7770-4) Mouton.

Political Anti-Semitism in England, 1918-1939. Gisela C. Lebzelter. LC 78-16795. 222p. 1979. 49.50 (0-8419-0426-X) Holmes & Meier.

***Political Apocalypse: A Study of Dostoevsky's Grand Inquisitor.** Ellis Sandoz. 2000. 24.95 (1-882926-51-X) ISI Books.

Political Apocalypse: A Study of Dostoevsky's Grand Inquisitor. fac. ed. Ellis Sandoz. LC 77-152707. 281p. 1971. reprint ed. pap. 87.20 (0-7837-7771-X, 204752700007) Bks Demand.

Political Appointees: Turnover Rates in Executive Schedule Positions Requiring Senate Confirmation. (Illus.). 40p. (Orig.). (C). 1995. pap. text 20.00 (0-7881-1332-1) DIANE Pub.

Political Approach to Pacifism, Bk. 1. Will Morrisey. LC 95-12482. (Studies in World Peace: Vol. 6a). 472p. 1996. 109.95 (0-7734-8910-X) E Mellen.

Political Approach to Pacifism, Bk. 2. Will Morrisey. LC 95-12482. (Studies in World Peace: Vol. 6b). 460p. 1996. 109.95 (0-7734-8912-6) E Mellen.

Political Approaches to Injury Control at the State Level. Ed. by Abraham B. Bergman. LC 91-40227. 128p. 1992. pap. text 9.95 (0-295-97176-2) U of Wash Pr.

Political Argument: A Reissue with a New Introduction. Brian Barry. (California Series on Social Choice & Political Economy: No. 20). 335p. 1990. pap. 18.95 (0-520-07051-8, Pub. by U CA Pr) Cal Prin Full Svc.

Political Arithmetic: Containing Observations on the Present State of Great Britain. Arthur Young. LC 67-29462. (Reprints of Economic Classics Ser.). xii, 366p. 1967. reprint ed. 57.50 (0-678-00338-6) Kelley.

Political Arm. Joseph D. Ketner & Chris Scoates. LC 90-72071. 42p. 1991. pap. 20.00 (0-936316-13-6) Wash U Gallery.

Political Arrangements: Power & the City. Ed. by Henri Lustiger-Thaler. LC 92-72628. 224p. 1993. 48.99 (1-895431-55-7, Pub. by Black Rose); pap. 19.99 (1-895431-54-9, Pub. by Black Rose) Consort Bk Sales.

Political Art of Greek Tragedy. Christian Meier. 250p. (C). 1993. text 37.50 (0-8018-4727-3) Johns Hopkins.

Political Ascent: Contemporary Islamic Movements in North Africa. Emad Shahin. (Series on State, Culture, & Society in Arab North Africa). 288p. (C). 1998. pap. text 27.00 (0-8133-3617-1, Pub. by Westview) HarpC.

Political Aspects of the Panama Canal: The Problem of Location. James L. Busey. LC 73-84606. (Arizona University, Institute of Government Research, Comparative Government Studies: No. 5). 55p. reprint ed. pap. 30.00 (0-608-13643-3, 205524900011) Bks Demand.

Political Assassinations by Jews: A Rhetorical Device for Justice. Nachman Ben-Yehuda. LC 91-36690. (SUNY Series in Deviance & Social Control). 527p. (C). 1992. pap. text 24.95 (0-7914-1166-4) State U NY Pr.

Political Atlas of Illinois. Paul Kleppner et al. LC 87-24765. (Illus.). 112p. (Orig.). 1988. pap. 15.00 (0-87580-136-6) N Ill U Pr.

Political Attitudes & Preferences of South Dakotans in the 1968 Presidential Election. Alan L. Clem. 1972. 1.00 (0-685-05041-6); write for info. (1-55614-080-0) U of SD Gov Res Bur.

Political Attitudes in Venezuela: Societal Cleavages & Political Opinion. Enrique A. Baloyra & John D. Martz. LC 78-14241. (Texas Pan-American Ser.). 320p. reprint ed. pap. 99.20 (0-8357-7723-5, 203608000002) Bks Demand.

Political Attitudes over the Life Span: The Bennington Women after 50 Years. Duane F. Alwin et al. LC 91-50319. (Life Course Studies). (Illus.). 352p. 1992. pap. 22.95 (0-299-13014-2) U of Wis Pr.

Political Authority: A Comparative Study. Satinder N. Mahajan. 113p. 1986. 12.00 (1-881338-72-X) Nataraj Bks.

Political Authority & Bureaucratic Power: A Comparative Analysis. Edward Page & James B. Van Treese. LC 84-21895. 202p. 1985. pap. 62.70 (0-608-05190-X, 206572700001) Bks Demand.

Political Authority & Moral Judgement. Glenn R. Negley. LC 65-13654. 173p. reprint ed. pap. 53.70 (0-608-11981-4, 202342700033) Bks Demand.

Political Authority & Party Secretaries in Poland, 1975-1986. Paul G. Lewis. (Illus.). 368p. (C). 1989. text 69.95 (0-521-36369-1) Cambridge U Pr.

Political Awakening in Kashmir. Ravinderjit Kaur. (Illus.). xvi, 226p. (C). 1996. 29.00 (81-7024-709-8, Pub. by Ashish Pub Hse) Nataraj Bks.

Political Awakening in Kashmir. Narinder Singh. 202p. 1992. 22.00 (81-7249-012-7, Pub. by H K Pubs & Dist) Nataraj Bks.

Political Awakening in Nepal: The Search for a New Identity. Ed. by Prem R. Uprety. (C). 1992. 58.00 (0-7855-0210-6, Pub. by Ratna Pustak Bhandar) St Mut.

Political Awakening in Nepal: The Search for a New Identity. Prem R. Uprety. (C). 1992. text 23.00 (81-7169-190-0, Commonwealth) S Asia.

Political Awakening in the Belgian Congo. Rene Lemarchand et al. LC 82-2986. (Illus.). 357p. 1982. reprint ed. lib. bdg. 75.00 (0-313-23415-9, LEPOL, Greenwood Pr) Greenwood.

Political Babylon. 32p. (Orig.). 1982. pap. 0.95 (0-937408-16-6) GMI Pubns Inc.

Political Behavior. Abdul K. Bangura et al. 176p. (C). 1996. pap. text 29.00 (0-7618-0223-1); lib. bdg. 39.00 (0-7618-0222-3) U Pr of Amer.

Political Behavior: Patterns in Everyday Life. Ed. by Steven A. Peterson. (Library of Social Research: Vol. 177). 296p. (C). 1990. text 59.95 (0-8039-3729-6); pap. text 26.00 (0-8039-3730-X) Sage.

Political Behavior: Patterns in Everyday Life. Steven A. Peterson. LC 89-27838. (Sage Library of Social Research: Vol. 177). (Illus.). 296p. 1990. reprint ed. pap. 91.80 (0-608-01725-6, 206238200003) Bks Demand.

Political Behavior: Studies in Election Statistics. Herbert Tingsten. LC 74-25791. (European Sociology Ser.). 236p. 1975. reprint ed. 24.95 (0-405-06543-4) Ayer.

Political Behavior & Public Issues in Ohio. Ed. by John J. Gargan & James G. Coke. LC 72-78408. 398p. reprint ed. pap. 123.40 (0-608-17126-3, 202730200055) Bks Demand.

Political Behavior & Social Interaction among Caribbean & African American Residents in New York. Ed. by J. A. Irish & E. W. Rivere. 161p. (Orig.). 1990. pap. text 15.00 (1-878433-04-0) Caribbean Diaspora Pr.

Political Behavior & the Local Context. John W. Books & Charles L. Prysby. LC 91-429. 184p. 1991. 52.95 (0-275-93629-5, C3629, Praeger Pubs) Greenwood.

Political Behavior in the American States. Gimpel. 1999. pap. text 33.33 (0-205-30295-5) Allyn.

Political Behavior of Adolescents in China: The Cultural Revolution in Kwangchow. David M. Raddock. LC 76-19640. (Monographs: No. 32). vii, 242p. 1977. 22.00 (0-8165-0607-8) Assn Asian Studies.

Political Behavior of American Jews. Lawrence H. Fuchs. LC 79-28711. (Illus.). 220p. 1980. reprint ed. lib. bdg. 59.50 (0-313-22282-7, FUPB, Greenwood Pr) Greenwood.

Political Behavior of Chicago's Ethnic Groups, 1918-1932. John M. Allswang. LC 80-837. (American Ethnic Groups Ser.). 1981. lib. bdg. 35.95 (0-405-13401-0) Ayer.

Political Behavior of Older Americans. Steven A. Peterson & Albert Somit. LC 94-4762. (Issues in Aging Ser.: Vol. 4). 200p. 1994. text 39.00 (0-8153-1321-7, SS972) Garland.

Political Behavior of the American Electorate. 8th ed. William H. Flanigan & Nancy H. Zingale. LC 94-2163. 220p. (YA). (gr. 11). 1994. pap. text 22.95 (0-87187-797-X) Congr Quarterly.

***Political Behavior of the American Electorate.** 9th ed. William H. Flanigan. 1999. pap. 29.50 (1-56802-533-5) CQ Pr.

Political Behavior of the American Electorate. 9th ed. William H. Flanigan & Nancy H. Zingale. LC 97-47675. 208p. (C). 1998. pap. text 23.95 (1-56802-332-4) Congr Quarterly.

Political Bias, Censorship & the Dissolution of the "Official" Press in Eighteenth-Century France. Christopher Todd. LC 91-21823. (Studies in French Civilization: Vol. 8). 444p. 1991. lib. bdg. 109.95 (0-7734-9719-6) E Mellen.

Political Bibliography of Afro-Asian Nations. 1985. 150.00 (0-7855-1823-1, Pub. by Archives Pubs) St Mut.

Political Bibliography of Politically Advanced Nations. 1985. 120.00 (0-7855-1825-8, Pub. by Archives Pubs) St Mut.

Political Biography of David Lawrence Gregg: American Diplomat & Hawaiian Official. Pauline K. Joerger. 1981. 35.95 (0-405-14093-2) Ayer.

Political Biography of Walter Reuther. 2nd ed. Beatrice Hansen & Farrell Dobbs. 27p. 1987. pap. 2.50 (0-87348-492-4) Pathfinder NY.

Political Blacklist in the Broadcasting Industry. K. Sue Foley. Ed. by Christopher H. Sterling. LC 78-21718. (Dissertations in Broadcasting Ser.). 1980. lib. bdg. 40.95 (0-405-11757-4) Ayer.

Political Bossism in Mid-America: Tom Dennison's Omaha, 1900-1933. Orville D. Menard. LC 88-33697. (Illus.). 360p. (C). 1989. lib. bdg. 50.00 (0-8191-7342-8) U Pr of Amer.

Political Bribery in Japan. Richard H. Mitchell. 224p. 1996. pap. text 25.00 (0-8248-1819-9) UH Pr.

Political Broadcast Catechism. 103p. 1996. pap. write for info. (0-89324-243-8, 3831) Natl Assn Broadcasters.

Political Brokers: People, Organizations, Money & Power. Ed. by Judith G. Smith. (Illus.). 320p. 1972. pap. 3.45 (0-87140-261-0, Pub. by Liveright) Norton.

Political Business Cycles. Ed. by Bruno S. Frey. LC 96-52256. (International Library of Critical Writings in Economics Ser.: No. 79). 528p. 1997. 165.00 (1-85898-399-1) E Elgar.

Political Business Cycles: The Political Economy of Money, Inflation, & Unemployment. Ed. by Thomas D. Willett. LC 88-7148. (Duke Press Policy Studies). xxii, 521p. (C). 1988. text 69.95 (0-8223-0824-X); pap. text 29.95 (0-8223-0842-8) Duke.

Political Buttons, 1920-1976, Bk. 2. Theodore L. Hake. LC 73-93793. (Illus.). 1977. 40.00 (0-918708-00-1) Hake.

Political Buttons, 1920-1976, Bk. II. 2nd ed. Theodore L. Hake. LC 73-93793. (Illus.). 256p. 1977. reprint ed. pap. 30.00 (0-918708-01-X) Hake.

Political Buttons Seventeen Eighty-Nine to Nineteen Sixteen, Bk. III: 1789-1916. 2nd ed. Theodore L. Hake. LC 73-93793. (Illus.). 256p. 1977. reprint ed. 40.00 (0-918708-02-8); reprint ed. pap. 30.00 (0-918708-03-6) Hake.

Political Calculus: Essays on Machiavelli's Philosophy. Ed. by Anthony J. Parel. LC 77-185729. 232p. reprint ed. pap. 72.00 (0-608-30272-4, 201433000093) Bks Demand.

Political Calypso: True Opposition in Trinidad & Tabago, 1962-1987. Louis Regis. LC 97-37804. 320p. 1998. 49.95 (0-8130-1580-4) U Press Fla.

Political Campaign Communication: A Bibliography & Guide to the Literature 1973-1982. Lynda L. Kaid & Anne J. Wadsworth. LC 84-23508. 223p. 1985. 24.00 (0-8108-1764-0) Scarecrow.

Political Campaign Communication: Principles & Practices. 4th ed. Judith S. Trent & Robert V. Friedenberg. LC 99-14854. (Praeger Series in Political Communication). 408p. 2000. pap. 27.95 (0-275-96405-1) Greenwood.

Political Campaign Communication: Principles & Practices. 4th ed. Judith S. Trent & Robert V. Viendenburg. LC 99-14854. 408p. 2000. 75.00 (0-275-96404-3, Praeger Pubs) Greenwood.

Political Campaign Craftsmanship: A Professional's Guide to Campaigning for Public Office. 3rd ed. Edward Schwartzman. 356p. 1994. pap. 24.95 (0-88738-742-X) Transaction Pubs.

Political Campaign Stamps. Mark Warda. LC 98-84100. (Illus.). 224p. 1998. pap. 19.95 (0-87341-616-3, PCS) Krause Pubns.

Political Capacity & Economic Behavior. Ed. by Marina Arbetman & Jacek Kugler. LC 98-157765. (Political Economy of Global Interdependence Ser.). 352p. (C). 1997. pap. 29.00 (0-8133-3364-4, Pub. by Westview) HarpC.

P

An Asterisk (*) at the beginning of an entry indicates that the title is appearing for the first time.

Political Capital: The Motives, Tactics & Goals of Politicized Businesses in South Africa. Kris W. Kobach. LC 89-5510. (Illus.). 184p. (Orig.). (C). 1990. pap. text 23.00 (*0-8191-7405-X*); lib. bdg. 45.00 (*0-8191-7404-1*) U Pr of Amer.

Political Career of Floyd B. Olson. George H. Mayer. LC 86-33332. xxii, 329p. 1987. reprint ed. pap. 10.95 (*0-87351-206-5*, Borealis Book) Minn Hist.

Political Career of Oliver St. John, 1637-1649. William Palmer. LC 91-51138. 160p. (C). 1992. 32.50 (*0-87413-453-6*) U Delaware Pr.

Political Career of Sir Adolphe Chapleau, Premier of Quebec, 1879-1882. Kenneth J. Munro. LC 92-4338. 244p. 1992. lib. bdg. 89.95 (*0-7734-9494-4*) E Mellen.

Political Careers: Recruitment Through the Legislature. Leonard I. Ruchelman. LC 70-99325. 216p. 1975. 25.00 (*0-8386-7613-8*) Fairleigh Dickinson.

Political Cartoons in the Middle East: Cultural Representation in the Middle East. Ed. by Fatma M. Gocek. LC 97-34020. (Illus.). 160p. (C). 1997. text 39.95 (*1-55876-156-X*); pap. text 16.95 (*1-55876-157-8*) Wiener Pubs Inc.

Political Cartoons in the 1988 Presidential Campaign: Image, Metaphor, & Narrative. Janis L. Edwards. LC 97-10605. (Studies in American Popular History & Culture). (Illus.). 184p. 1997. text 48.00 (*0-8153-2858-3*) Garland.

Political Catholicism & the Czechoslovak People's Party, 1918-1939. Milos Trapl. 280p. 1995. 41.00 (*0-88033-306-5*, 409, Pub. by East Eur Monographs) Col U Pr.

Political Catholicism in Europe, 1918-1965. Ed. by Tom Buchanan & Martin Conway. LC 95-25450. (Illus.). 322p. (C). 1996. text 85.00 (*0-19-820319-5*, Clarendon Pr) OUP.

Political Centers & Cultural Regions in Early Bengal. Barrie M. Morrison. LC 76-92469. (Monographs: No. 25). xii, 189p. 1969. 17.00 (*0-8165-0154-8*) Assn Asian Studies.

Political Centralization & Decentralization in Europe & North America. Ed. by John Agnew. (Orig.). 1990. pap. 15.00 (*0-944285-14-7*) Pol Studies.

Political Change. David E. Apter. 245p. 1973. 32.50 (*0-7146-2941-3*, BHA-02941, Pub. by F Cass Pubs); pap. 19.50 (*0-7146-4012-3*, BHA-00097, Pub. by F Cass Pubs) Intl Spec Bk.

Political Change & Industrial Development in Japan: Government Enterprise, 1868-1880. Thomas C. Smith. viii, 126p. 1955. 22.50 (*0-8047-0469-4*) Stanford U Pr.

Political Change & Industrial Development in Japan: Government Enterprise, 1868-1880. Thomas C. Smith. LC 55-6687. 136p. 1955. reprint ed. pap. 30.00 (*0-7837-5127-3*, 204485500004) Bks Demand.

Political Change & the Economic Future of East Asia. Ed. by Robert B. Hewett. (Illus.). 189p. (C). 1981. pap. text 10.00 (*0-317-91348-4*) Pac Forum.

Political Change & Underdevelopment: A Critical Introduction to Third World Politics. Vicky Randall & Robin Theobald. LC 85-10176. ix, 215p. 1985. text 49.95 (*0-8223-0564-X*); pap. text 18.95 (*0-8223-0662-X*) Duke.

Political Change & Underdevelopment: A Critical Introduction to Third World Politics. 2nd ed. Vicky Randall & Robin Theobald. LC 97-52380. 1998. write for info. (*0-8223-2079-7*) Duke.

Political Change & Underdevelopment: A Critical Introduction To Third World Politics. 2nd ed. Vicky Randall & Robin Theobald. LC 97-52380. 1998. pap. 18.95 (*0-8223-2093-2*) Duke.

Political Change in an Indian State, Mysore, 1917-1955. James Manor. 1978. 12.50 (*0-8364-0069-0*) S Asia.

Political Change in Baja California: Democracy in the Making? Victoria E. Rodriguez & Peter M. Ward. (Monographs). 140p. (C). 1994. pap. 13.95 (*1-878367-25-0*, MN-40) UCSD Ctr US-Mex.

Political Change in Britain, 1963-1970, 2 vols. David Butler & Donald E. Stokes. 1972. write for info. (*0-89138-055-8*) ICPSR.

Political Change in Britain, 1963-1970, 2 vols., 1. David Butler & Donald E. Stokes. 1972. write for info. (*0-89138-056-6*) ICPSR.

Political Change in Britain, 1963-1970, 2 vols., 2. David Butler & Donald E. Stokes. 1972. write for info. (*0-89138-057-4*) ICPSR.

Political Change in California: Critical Elections & Social Movements, 1890-1966, 5. Michael P. Rogin & John L. Shover. LC 72-95506. (Contributions in American History Ser.: No. 5). 231p. 1970. 55.00 (*0-8371-2346-1*, ROP/, Greenwood Pr) Greenwood.

Political Change in Eastern Europe Since 1989: Prospects for Liberal Democracy & Market Economies. Robert Zuzowski. LC 97-32998. 176p. 1998. 57.95 (*0-275-96145-1*, Praeger Pubs) Greenwood.

Political Change in France under Richelieu & Mazarin, 1624-1661. Richard Bonney. (Illus.). 1978. text 69.00 (*0-19-822537-7*) OUP.

Political Change in New York City: Politics & Policy since 1960. Charles Brecher et al. 1993. write for info. (*0-318-69291-0*) OUP.

Political Change in South Korea. Ed. by Ilpyong J. Kim & Young W. Kihl. LC 88-11069. 263p. 1988. text 24.95 (*0-943852-59-5*); pap. text 17.95 (*0-943852-60-9*) Prof World Peace.

Political Change in Southeast Asia, Vol. 61, No. 5. Ed. by Donald Altschiller. (Reference Shelf Ser.). 220p. (C). 1989. pap. 25.00 (*0-8242-0784-X*) Wilson.

Political Change in Southeast Asia: Trimming the Banyan Tree. Michael R. Vatikiotis. (Politics in Asia Ser.). 248p. (C). 1996. pap. 25.99 (*0-415-13484-6*) Routledge.

Political Change in Thailand: Democracy & Participation. Kevin Hewison. LC 97-5094. (Politics in Asia Ser.). 320p. (C). 1997. pap. 29.99 (*0-415-17971-8*) Routledge.

Political Change in the Metropolis. 5th ed. John J. Harrigan. LC 92-26301. (C). 1993. pap. text 47.81 (*0-673-52245-8*) Addson-Wesley Educ.

Political Change in the Metropolis. 6th ed. Ed. by Harrigan. LC 99-26210. 512p. (C). 1999. pap. text 52.00 (*0-321-01105-8*) Addson-Wesley Educ.

Political Change in the Third World. Charles F. Andrain. 1988. 44.95 (*0-04-497029-3*); pap. 17.95 (*0-04-497030-7*) Routledge.

Political Change on Taiwan: A Study of Ruling Party Adaptability. Peter R. Moody, Jr. LC 91-15311. 224p. 1991. 62.95 (*0-275-94035-7*, C4035, Praeger Pubs) Greenwood.

Political Character of Adolescence: The Influence of Families & Schools. M. Kent Jennings & Richard G. Niemi. LC 73-16779. 375p. reprint ed. pap. 116.30 (*0-8357-2782-3*, 203990800014) Bks Demand.

Political Choice & Social Structure: An Analysis of Actors, Interests & Rationality. Barry Hindess. (Illus.). 224p. 1989. text 95.00 (*1-85278-093-2*) E Elgar.

Political Choice in Canada. H. Clarke et al. 1979. text 24.95 (*0-07-082783-4*) McGraw.

***Political Choice in Global Markets.** Evelyne Huber. 2000. pap. text 18.00 (*0-226-35647-7*); lib. bdg. 54.00 (*0-226-35646-9*) U Ch Pr.

Political Choices & Electoral Consequences: A Study of Organized Labour & the New Democratic Party. Keith Archer. 128p. (C). 1990. text 60.00 (*0-7735-0744-2*, Pub. by McG-Queens Univ Pr) CUP Services.

Political Class Economy. Murray Milgate. pap. 0.00 (*0-691-00390-4*) Princeton U Pr.

Political Classics: A Guide to the Essential Texts from Plato to Rousseau. Ed. by Murray Forsyth & Maurice Keens-Soper. LC 92-6370. 210p. 1993. pap. 19.95 (*0-19-285282-5*) OUP.

Political Classics: Green to Dworkin. Ed. by Murray Forsyth & Maurice Keens-Soper. (Illus.). 300p. 1996. text 65.00 (*0-19-878094-X*); pap. text 21.00 (*0-19-878095-8*) OUP.

Political Classics: Hamilton to Mill. Ed. by Murray Forsyth et al. LC 92-41448. 256p. 1993. text 49.95 (*0-19-878025-7*); pap. text 18.95 (*0-19-878026-5*) OUP.

***Political Cleavages: Issues, Parties & the Consolidation of Democracy.** Alejandro Moreno. LC 99-30615. 224p. 1999. text 65.00 (*0-8133-3550-7*) Westview.

Political Clientelism, Patronage & Development. Samuel N. Eisenstadt. Ed. by Rene Lemarchand. LC 80-41955. (Sage Studies in Contemporary Political Sociology: No. 3). 338p. reprint ed. pap. 104.80 (*0-8357-4784-0*, 203772100009) Bks Demand.

Political Code of the State of New York, 1860 see New York Field Codes, 1850-1865

Political Cognition: The 19th Annual Carnegie Mellon Symposium on Cognition. Ed. by Richard R. Lau & David O. Sears. (Carnegie Symposium on Cognition Ser., 19th Annual). 424p. (C). 1986. text 79.95 (*0-89859-652-1*) L Erlbaum Assocs.

Political Commentators in the United States: A Bio-Critical Sourcebook, 1930 to the Present. Dan Nimmo & Chevelle Newsome. LC 96-28069. 448p. 1997. lib. bdg. 99.50 (*0-313-29585-9*) Greenwood.

Political Communication. Graig A. Smith. 263p. (C). 1989. pap. text 32.50 (*0-15-570709-4*, Pub. by Harcourt Coll Pubs) Harcourt.

Political Communication: Engineering Visions of Order in the Socialist World. Ed. by Sarah S. King & Donald P. Cushman. LC 91-45329. (SUNY Series, Human Communication Processes). 212p. (C). 1993. text 59.50 (*0-7914-1201-6*); pap. text 19.95 (*0-7914-1202-4*) State U NY Pr.

Political Communication: Issues & Strategies for Research. Ed. by Steven H. Chaffee. LC 75-14629. (Sage Annual Reviews of Communication Research Ser.: No. 4). 319p. reprint ed. pap. 98.90 (*0-7837-1122-0*, 204165200022) Bks Demand.

Political Communication: Issues, Ideas, Impact. Richard Perloff. LC 97-21794. (Communication Ser.). 375p. 1997. write for info. (*0-8058-1794-8*) L Erlbaum Assocs.

Political Communication: Politics, Press, & Public in America. Richard Perloff. LC 97-21794. (Communication Ser.). 1997. pap. 45.00 (*0-8058-1795-6*) L Erlbaum Assocs.

Political Communication: Rhetoric, Government, & Citizens. Dan F. Hahn. LC 97-34149. 304p. (C). 1998. pap. text 29.95 (*0-9634489-3-5*) Strata Pub Co.

Political Communication Across Cultures. Ed. by Alberto Gonzalez & Dolores V. Tanno. (International & Intercultural Communication Annual (IICA) Ser.: Vol. 20). 353p. (C). 1997. 59.95 (*0-7619-0741-6*, 07416); pap. 26.00 (*0-7619-0742-4*, 07424) Sage.

***Political Communication Ethics: An Oxymoron?** Robert E. Denton, Jr. LC 99-55872. (Praeger Series in Political Communication). 288p. 2000. 69.50 (*0-275-96482-5*, Praeger Pubs) Greenwood.

***Political Communication Ethics: An Oxymoron?** Ed. by Robert E. Denton, Jr. LC 99-55872. 288p. 2000. pap. 19.95 (*0-275-96483-3*, Praeger Pubs) Greenwood.

Political Communication in Action: States, Institutions, Movements, Audiences. Ed. & Tr. by David L. Paletz. LC 95-36519. (Communication Series). 352p. (C). 1995. text 72.50 (*1-57273-000-5*); pap. text 26.50 (*1-57273-001-3*) Hampton Pr NJ.

Political Communication in America. 3rd ed. Robert E. Denton, Jr. & Gary C. Woodward. LC 98-24557. 328p. 1998. 65.00 (*0-275-95782-9*, Praeger Pubs); pap. 22.95 (*0-275-95783-7*, Praeger Pubs) Greenwood.

Political Communication in the Information Society: The Findings of a German-American Workshop. Ingrid Hamm. 1998. 9.95 (*3-89204-334-5*) Bertelsmann Stiftung.

Political Communication Research Vol. I: Approaches, Studies, Assessments. Ed. by Melvin J. Voigt. LC 86-17475. (Communication & Information Science Ser.). 288p. (C). 1987. text 73.25 (*0-89391-329-4*) Ablx Pub.

Political Communication Research Vol. II: Approaches, Studies, Assessments. Hans M. Kepplinger et al. Ed. by David L. Paletz. (Illus.). 293p. 1997. pap. 39.50 (*1-56750-164-8*); text 73.25 (*1-56750-163-X*) Ablx Pub.

Political Communication Yearbook, 1984. Ed. by Keith R. Sanders et al. 304p. 1985. text 36.95 (*0-8093-1183-6*) S Ill U Pr.

Political Communications: The General Election Campaign of 1992. Ed. by Ivor Crewe & Brian Gosschalk. LC 93-47235. (Illus.). 292p. (C). 1995. text 64.95 (*0-521-45396-8*); pap. text 24.95 (*0-521-46964-3*) Cambridge U Pr.

Political Communications: Why Labour Won the General Election of 1997. Ed. by Ivor Crewe et al. 288p. 1998. 49.50 (*0-7146-4923-6*, Pub. by F Cass Pubs) Intl Spec Bk.

Political Communications: Why Labour Won the General Election of 1997. Ed. by Ivor Crewe et al. LC 98-38304. 288p. 2000. pap. 22.50 (*0-7146-4482-X*, Pub. by F Cass Pubs) Intl Spec Bk.

***Political Communities & Calculus: Sociological Analysis in the Italian Scientific Tradition 1924 -1943.** Mino B. Garzia. (European University Studies: Series 22, Vol. 322). xi, 324p. 1998. 48.95 (*3-906760-53-7*, Pub. by P Lang) P Lang Pubng.

Political Communities & Calculus: Sociological Analysis in the Italian Scientific Tradition (1924-1943), Vol. 322. Mino B. Garzia. LC 98-44040. (European University Studies: No. 22). XI, 324p. 1998. pap. text 48.95 (*0-8204-4200-3*) P Lang Pubng.

Political Communities & Gendered Ideologies in Contemporary Ukraine: The Petryshyn Memorial Lecture, Harvard University, 26 April 1994. Martha Bohachevsky-Chomiak. (Harvard Papers in Ukrainian Studies). (Illus.). 27p. 1994. pap. text 5.00 (*0-916458-72-5*) Harvard Ukrainian.

Political Community & the North Atlantic Area: International Organization in the Light of Historical Experience. Karl W. Deutsch et al. LC 69-13882. 228p. 1969. reprint ed. lib. bdg. 38.50 (*0-8371-1054-8*, DEPO, Greenwood Pr) Greenwood.

Political Companion to American Film. Ed. by Gary Crowdus. 1996. lib. bdg. 95.00 (*1-884964-53-2*) Fitzroy Dearborn.

Political Companion to American Film. Ed. by Gary Crowdus. LC 93-41593. (Illus.). 512p. 1994. 60.00 (*0-941702-37-5*) Lake View Pr.

Political Companion to American Film. Ed. by Gary Crowdus. (Illus.). 512p. 1996. pap. 29.95 (*0-941702-42-1*, 42-1) Lake View Pr.

Political Competition, Innovation & Growth: A Historical Analysis. Ed. by P. Bernholz et al. LC 98-27595. viii, 308p. 1998. 92.00 (*3-540-64680-9*) Spr-Verlag.

***Political Complexity: Nonlinear Models of Politics.** Diana Richardson. 352p. (C). 2000. text 59.50 (*0-472-10964-2*, 10964) U of Mich Pr.

Political Concepts: A Reconstruction. Felix E. Oppenheim. LC 80-23846. 240p. 1996. pap. text 7.00 (*0-226-63185-0*) U Ch Pr.

Political Concepts: An Introduction. David A. Freeman. LC 95-107780. 224p. (C). 1993. per. 39.95 (*0-8403-9062-9*) Kendall-Hunt.

Political Concepts: An Introduction. 2nd ed. David Freeman. LC 97-72281. 232p. (C). 1997. per. 52.95 (*0-7872-3750-7*, 41375001) Kendall-Hunt.

***Political Concepts: An Introduction.** 3rd ed. David Freeman. 140p. (C). 2000. per. 52.95 (*0-7872-7186-1*) Kendall-Hunt.

Political Concepts, a Reconstruction. Felix E. Oppenheim. LC 80-23846. 237p. reprint ed. pap. 73.50 (*0-608-09490-0*, 205429100005) Bks Demand.

Political Concepts & Political Theories. Gaus. LC 00-27305. 224p. 2000. pap. 20.00 (*0-8133-3331-8*) HarpC.

Political Conditionality. Ed. by Georg Srensen. LC 93-24139. 1993. 25.00 (*0-7146-4101-4*, Pub. by F Cass Pubs) Intl Spec Bk.

Political Conditions & Physical States. Tom Savage. 70p. (Orig.). 1993. pap. 7.00 (*0-935992-18-9*) United Art Bks.

Political Conflict & Constitutional Change in Puerto Rico, 1898-1952. Alfredo Montalvo-Barbot. LC 97-33539. 176p. (C). 1997. 37.00 (*0-7618-0901-5*) U Pr of Amer.

Political Conflict & Economic Change in Nigeria. Henry S. Bienen. 192p. 1985. 35.00 (*0-7146-3266-X*, Pub. by F Cass Pubs) Intl Spec Bk.

Political Conflict in Southern Europe: Regulation, Regression & Morphogenesis. Eduard A. Ziegenhagen & Kleomenis S. Koutsoukis. LC 91-18923. 176p. 1992. 55.00 (*0-275-94019-5*, C4019, Praeger Pubs) Greenwood.

Political Conflict on the Horn of Africa. Robert F. Gorman. LC 81-5183. 243p. 1981. 45.00 (*0-275-90636-1*, C0636, Praeger Pubs) Greenwood.

Political Conflict, Political Development, & Public Policy. Ed. by Eduard A. Ziegenhagen. LC 93-15350. 224p. 1993. 62.95 (*0-275-94174-4*, C4174, Praeger Pubs) Greenwood.

Political Confrontation Arts. Werckmeister. 1992. lib. bdg. 34.95 (*0-226-89363-4*) U Ch Pr.

Political Consciousness & American Democracy. James F. Lea. LC 81-13133. 218p. 1982. pap. text 16.95 (*0-87805-151-1*) U Pr of Miss.

Political Consequence of Social Networks, Vol. 4. Ed. by Gwen Moore & J. Allen Whitt. (Research in Politics & Society Ser.). 360p. 1993. 73.25 (*0-89232-994-7*) Jai Pr.

Political Consequences of Being a Woman: How Stereotypes Influence the Conduct & Consequences of Political Campaigns. Kim Kahn. LC 96-10979. (Power, Conflict, & Democracy Ser.). (Illus.). 224p. 1996. pap. 17.50 (*0-231-10303-4*) Col U Pr.

Political Consequences of Modernization. John H. Kautsky. LC 80-16087. 286p. 1989. reprint ed. text 27.50 (*0-89464-366-5*) Krieger.

Political Consequences of the Addis Ababa Agreement. Abu B. El Obeld. 167p. 1980. write for info. (*91-38-05528-7*, Pub. by Nordic Africa) Transaction Pubs.

Political Consequences of Thinking: Gender & Judaism in the Work of Hannah Arendt. Jennifer Ring. LC 96-47278. (SUNY Series in Political Theory). 358p. (C). 1997. text 54.50 (*0-7914-3483-4*) State U NY Pr.

Political Consequences of Thinking: Gender & Judaism in the Work of Hannah Arendt. Jennifer Ring. LC 96-47278. (SUNY Series in Political Theory). (C). 1998. pap. text 22.95 (*0-7914-3484-2*) State U NY Pr.

Political Constraints on Brazil's Economic Development: (North-South Center, University of Miami, in Cooperation with the Getulio Vargas Foundation & University of Sao Paulo) Ed. by Siegfried Marks. LC 92-43075. 202p. (C). 1993. pap. 18.95 (*1-56000-683-8*, Pub. by U Miami N-S Ctr) L Rienner.

Political Construction of Education: The State, School Expansion, & Economic Change. Ed. by Bruce Fuller & Richard Rubinson. LC 91-33893. 280p. 1992. 49.95 (*0-275-93831-X*, C3831, Praeger Pubs) Greenwood.

Political Constructions: Defoe, Richardson, & Sterne in Relation to Hobbes, Hume, & Burke. Carol Kay. LC 88-3741. 288p. 1988. text 39.95 (*0-8014-2043-1*) Cornell U Pr.

Political Consultants & Negative Campaigning: The Secrets of the Pros. Kerwin C. Swint. LC 97-46437. 192p. (C). 1998. text 49.00 (*0-7618-1008-0*); pap. text 26.50 (*0-7618-1009-9*) U Pr of Amer.

Political Context of Collective Action: Power Argumentation & Democracy. Ed. by Ricca Edmondson. LC 98-117259. (European Political Science Ser.). 256p. (C). 1997. 85.00 (*0-415-16941-0*) Routledge.

Political Context of Law. Ed. by Richard Eales & David Sullivan. 184p. 1987. 60.00 (*0-907628-84-2*) Hambledon Press.

Political Control, Human Rights & the U. N. Mission in Cambodia. Ed. by Human Rights Watch Staff. 78p. (Orig.). 1992. pap. 7.00 (*1-56432-085-5*) Hum Rts Watch.

Political Control of Czechoslovakia. Ivan Gadourek. LC 74-2841. 285p. 1974. reprint ed. lib. bdg. 75.00 (*0-8371-7437-6*, GACZ, Greenwood Pr) Greenwood.

Political Control of the Economy. Edward R. Tufte. LC 77-85570. 192p. 1978. pap. text 14.95 (*0-691-02180-5*, Pub. by Princeton U Pr) Cal Prin Full Svc.

Political Controversy: A Study in 18th-Century Propaganda, 34. Robert D. Spector. LC 91-34158. (Contributions to the Study of Mass Media & Communications Ser.: No. 34). 200p. 1992. 55.00 (*0-313-28206-4*, SOT/, Greenwood Pr) Greenwood.

Political Conundrum. Clive Betts. Ed. by Meic Stephens. (Changing Wales Ser.). 65p. 1993. pap. 11.95 (*0-8464-4713-4*) Beekman Pubs.

Political Correctness: A Critique. Peter Duignan & L. H. Gann. LC 95-36921. (Hoover Essays Ser.: No. 11). 43p. 1995. pap. 5.00 (*0-8179-3742-0*) Hoover Inst Pr.

Political Correctness: A Response from the Cultural Left. Richard Feldstein. LC 96-31332. 232p. (C). 1997. pap. 18.95 (*0-8166-2476-3*); text 47.95 (*0-8166-2475-5*) U of Minn Pr.

"Political Correctness" For & Against. Marilyn Friedman & Jan Narveson. 160p. (C). 1994. pap. text 21.95 (*0-8476-7986-1*); lib. bdg. 62.50 (*0-8476-7985-3*) Rowman.

***Political Correctness & Public Finance.** Dennis O'Keeffe. 114p. 1999. 22.50 (*0-255-36478-4*, Pub. by Inst Economic Affairs) Coronet Bks.

Political Correctness, Censorship & Liberal-Jewish Strongarm Tactics in High-IQ/Low-Morals Mensa: A Case Study. John Bryant. 60p. (Orig.). 1997. pap. 4.95 (*1-886739-37-4*) Socratic Pr.

Political Correctness Exposed: A Piranha in Your Bathtub. Marvin Sprouse. LC 94-66615. 208p. 1995. pap. 9.95 (*0-914984-62-4*) Starburst.

Political Correctness Invades the Classroom: The Public Speaks Out! Ed. by Steve Baldwin & Karen Holgate. LC 98-56505. 304p. 1999. pap. 15.00 (*0-938453-07-6*) Small Helm Pr.

Political Corruption: A Handbook. 2nd rev. ed. Ed. by Arnold J. Heidenheimer et al. 1017p. 1988. 39.95 (*0-88738-163-4*) Transaction Pubs.

Political Corruption: Readings in Comparative Analysis. Arnold J. Heidenheimer. LC 77-10874. 582p. 1978. reprint ed. pap. text 24.95 (*0-87855-636-2*) Transaction Pubs.

Political Corruption & Political Geography. Peter J. Perry. LC 97-1226. (Illus.). 176p. 1997. text 72.95 (*1-85521-901-8*, Pub. by Ashgate Pub) Ashgate Pub Co.

Political Corruption in Africa. Williams. 1987. 77.95 (*1-85521-214-5*) Ashgate Pub Co.

Political Crime. A. M. Gibson. LC 69-16851. (Select Bibliographies Reprint Ser.). 1977. 23.95 (*0-8369-5007-0*) Ayer.

Political Crime. Louis Proal. LC 70-172565. (Criminology, Law Enforcement, & Social Problems Ser.: No. 146). 1973. reprint ed. 24.00 (*0-87585-146-0*) Patterson Smith.

Political Crime: Ideology & Criminality. Frank E. Hagan. 214p. 1996. pap. text 41.00 (*0-02-348993-6*, Macmillan Coll) P-H.

An Asterisk (*) at the beginning of an entry indicates that the title is appearing for the first time.

Political Crime in Contemporary America: A Critical Approach. Ed. by Kenneth D. Tunnell. LC 92-45728. (Current Issues in Criminal Justice Ser.: Vol. 863). 264p. 1994. text 48.00 (*0-8153-0928-7*, 92-45728) Garland.

Political Criminality: The Defiance & Defense of Authority. Austin T. Turk. LC 81-18531. (Sage Library of Social Research: No. 136). 232p. reprint ed. pap. 72.00 (*0-7837-6715-3*, 204634200011) Bks Demand.

Political Crisis - Fiscal Crisis: The Collapse & Revival of New York City. Martin Shefter. 336p. 1992. pap. text 19.00 (*0-231-07943-5*) Col U Pr.

Political Crisis & Debt Negotiations: The Case of the Philippines, 1983-1986. Penlope Walker. (Pew Case Studies in International Affairs). 50p. (C). 1992. pap. text 3.50 (*1-56927-133-X*) Geo U Inst Dplmcy.

Political Crisis of the 1850's. Michael F. Holt. 352p. (C). 1983. pap. text 14.00 (*0-393-95370-X*) Norton.

Political Criticism. Ian Shapiro. 1990. 50.00 (*0-520-06672-3*, Pub. by U CA Pr) Cal Prin Full Svc.

Political Criticism. Ian Shapiro. (C). 1990. pap. 17.95 (*0-520-08032-7*, Pub. by U CA Pr) Cal Prin Full Svc.

Political Crossroads: The 1989 Queensland Election. Ed. by Rosemary Whip & Colin A. Hughes. 1991. pap. 32.95 (*0-7022-2362-X*, Pub. by Univ Queensland Pr) Intl Spec Bk.

Political Culture & Behavior of Latin America. Louis K. Harris & Victor Alba. LC 74-79151. 231p. reprint ed. pap. 71.70 (*0-7837-0283-3*, 204060400018) Bks Demand.

Political Culture & Constitutionalism: A Comparative Approach. Ed. by Daniel P. Franklin & Michael J. Baun. LC 94-29697. (Comparative Politics Ser.). (Illus.). 254p. (gr. 13). 1994. text 76.95 (*1-56324-415-2*); pap. text 36.95 (*1-56324-416-0*) M E Sharpe.

Political Culture & Cultural Politics in Early Modern England: Essays Presented to David Underdown. Ed. by Susan D. Amussen & Mark A. Kishlansky. LC 95-3505. 1995. text 69.95 (*0-7190-4695-5*, Pub. by Manchester Univ Pr) St Martin.

Political Culture & Democracy in Developing Countries: Textbook Edition. Ed. by Larry Diamond. LC 94-2568. 266p. (C). 1994. pap. text 19.95 (*1-55587-515-7*) L Rienner.

Political Culture & Foreign Policy in Latin America: Case Studies from the Circum-Caribbean. Roland H. Ebel et al. LC 90-9951. (SUNY Series in the Making of Foreign Policy). 238p. (C). 1991. pap. text 24.95 (*0-7914-0605-9*) State U NY Pr.

Political Culture & Foreign Policy in Latin America: Case Studies from the Circum-Caribbean. Roland H. Ebel et al. LC 90-9951. (SUNY Series in the Making of Foreign Policy). 238p. (C). 1991. text 67.50 (*0-7914-0604-0*) State U NY Pr.

Political Culture & Leadership in India. Bharati Mukherjee. (C). 1991. 36.00 (*81-7099-320-2*, Pub. by Mittal Pubs Dist) S Asia.

Political Culture & Leadership in Soviet Russia: From Lenin to Gorbachev. Robert C. Tucker. (C). 1988. pap. text 14.00 (*0-393-95798-5*) Norton.

Political Culture & Political Change in Communist States. 2nd rev. ed. Ed. by Archie Brown & Jack Gray. LC 76-41832. 375p. (C). 1979. reprint ed. 35.00 (*0-8419-0508-8*) Holmes & Meier.

***Political Culture & Public Policy in Canada & the United States: Only a Border Apart?** John C. Pierce et al. LC 99-47699. (Canadian Studies: Vol. 22). 428p. 2000. text 109.95 (*0-7734-7897-3*) E Mellen.

Political Culture, Foreign Policy & Conflict: The Palestine Area Conflict System, 63. Basheer Meibar. LC 81-427. (Contributions in Political Science Ser.: No. 63). (Illus.). 312p. 1982. 59.95 (*0-313-22941-4*, MEP/, Greenwood Pr) Greenwood.

Political Culture in East Central Europe. Ed. by Fritz Plasser & Andreas Pribersky. 242p. 1996. 69.95 (*1-85972-259-8*, Pub. by Avebry) Ashgate Pub Co.

Political Culture in France & West Germany: A Comparative Perspective. Ed. by John Gaffney & Eva Kolinsky. 272p. 1991. 55.00 (*0-415-02321-1*, A4571) Routledge.

Political Culture in Germany. Ed. by Dirk Berg-Schlosser & Ralf Rytlewski. LC 92-12880. 1993. text 49.95 (*0-312-08530-3*) St Martin.

Political Culture in Israel: Cleavage & Integration among Israeli Jews. Eva Etzioni-Halevy & Rina Shapira. LC 76-24350. (Special Studies). 249p. 1977. 59.95 (*0-275-90263-3*, C0263, Praeger Pubs) Greenwood.

***Political Culture in Libya.** Amal Obeidi. 320p. 2000. 80.00 (*0-7007-1229-1*, Pub. by Curzon Pr Ltd) Paul & Co Pubs.

Political Culture in Modern Britain. Malcolm Bean. 1987. text 57.50 (*0-231-06678-3*) Col U Pr.

***Political Culture in Post-communist Russia: Formlessness & Recreation.** James Alexander. LC 00-21164. 240p. 2000. text 65.00 (*0-312-23194-6*) St Martin.

Political Culture in the 19th-Century South: Mississippi, 1830-1900. Bradley G. Bond. LC 95-11134. 392p. 1995. text 40.00 (*0-8071-1976-8*) La State U Pr.

Political Culture in the Reign of Elizabeth I: Queen & Commonwealth, 1558-1585. Anne McLaren. LC 99-22403. (Ideas in Context Ser.: No. 56). 286p. 2000. text 54.95 (*0-521-65144-1*) Cambridge U Pr.

Political Culture of China's University Students: A Comparative Study of University Students in Mainland China, Hong Kong, Macau, & Taiwan. Herbert S. Yee. LC 98-44559. 1998. 49.00 (*1-56072-626-1*) Nova Sci Pubs.

Political Culture of Contemporary Britain: People & Politicians, Principles & Practice. William L. Miller et al. (Illus.). 540p. 1996. text 95.00 (*0-19-827984-1*) OUP.

Political Culture of Language: Swahili, Society, & the State. Ali A. Mazrui & Alamin M. Mazrui. (Studies on Global Africa). 320p. (C). 1996. reprint ed. pap. 17.00 (*1-883058-06-6*, Studies Global) Global Pubns.

***Political Culture of Secession Mississippi, 1830-1860.** Christopher J. Olsen. LC 99-49213. (Illus.). 320p. 2000. text. write for info. (*0-19-513147-9*) OUP.

Political Culture of Tanzania. Michael Okema. LC 95-30882. 172p. 1996. 79.95 (*0-7734-8921-5*) E Mellen.

Political Culture of the American Whigs. Daniel W. Howe. LC 79-12576. 2000. lib. bdg. 25.00 (*0-226-35478-4*) U Ch Pr.

Political Culture of the American Whigs. Daniel W. Howe. LC 79-12576. x, 414p. (C). 1984. reprint ed. pap. text 19.00 (*0-226-35479-2*) U Ch Pr.

***Political Culture of the Russian 'Democrats'** Alexander Lukin. LC 99-57191. 352p. 2000. write for info. (*0-19-829558-8*) OUP.

Political Cycles & the Macroeconomy. Alberto Alesina & Nouriel Roubini. LC 97-14051. (Illus.). 300p. 1997. 45.00 (*0-262-01161-1*) MIT Pr.

Political Cycles & the Macroeconomy. Alberto Alesina & Nouriel Roubini. 300p. 1997. pap. text 22.50 (*0-262-51094-4*) MIT Pr.

Political Cycles in International Relations: The Cold War & Africa. L. F. Marte. 496p. 1994. 57.00 (*90-5383-280-7*, Pub. by VU Univ Pr) Paul & Co Pubs.

Political Data Handbook: OECD Countries. 2nd ed. Jan-Erik Lane et al. LC 97-164375. (Comparative Politics Ser.). (Illus.). 366p. 1997. text 95.00 (*0-19-828053-X*) OUP.

Political Death: A Jemima Shore Mystery. Antonia Fraser. 240p. 1997. mass mkt. 5.99 (*0-553-57203-2*, Crimeline) Bantam.

Political Deliverance: The Mormon Quest for Utah Statehood. Edward L. Lyman. LC 85-1204. (Illus.). 352p. 1986. text 22.95 (*0-252-01239-9*) U of Ill Pr.

Political Development: Dilemmas & Challenges. Monte Palmer. LC 96-70031. Orig. Title: Dilemmas of Political Development. (Illus.). 400p. (C). 1997. pap. text 35.00 (*0-87581-406-9*, PD) F E Peacock Pubs.

Political Development & Ethnic Identity in Africa: A Study of Angola since 1960. Susama Mohanty. vii, 246p. (C). 1992. text 27.95 (*0-685-55354-X*, Pub. by Radiant Pubs) S Asia.

Political Development & Political Decay. Samuel P. Huntington. (Reprint Series in Political Science). (C). 1993. reprint ed. pap. text 3.90 (*0-8290-3653-9*, PS-482) Irvington.

Political Development & Social Change. 2nd ed. Jason L. Finkle & Richard W. Gable. LC 72-149769. 703p. reprint ed. pap. 200.00 (*0-608-11862-1*, 202321500032) Bks Demand.

Political Development & the New Realism in Sub-Saharan Africa. David E. Apter & Carl G. Rosberg. LC 93-2428. 1994. pap. text 19.50 (*0-8139-1480-9*) U Pr of Va.

Political Development in Macau. Lo S. Hing. LC 97-178513. 260p. (Orig.). (C). 1997. pap. text 28.95 (*962-201-658-8*, Pub. by Chinese Univ) U of Mich Pr.

Political Development in Modern Japan. Ed. by Robert E. Ward. LC 66-14309. (Studies in the Modernization of Japan: No. 4). 649p. reprint ed. pap. 200.00 (*0-8357-4675-5*, 203762200008) Bks Demand.

Political Development in Nepal. Ed. by B. R. Bajracharya. (C). 1993. 22.00 (*81-7041-844-5*, Pub. by Anmol) S Asia.

Political Development in Pacific Asia. David M. Jones. LC 97-39514. (Illus.). 256p. (C). 1997. 57.95 (*0-7456-1504-X*, Pub. by Polity Pr); pap. 26.95 (*0-7456-1505-8*, Pub. by Polity Pr) Blackwell Pubs.

Political Development of Bangladesh. V. P. Puchkov. (C). 1989. 32.00 (*81-7050-084-2*) S Asia.

Political Development of the British Isles, 1100-1400. Robin Frame. (Illus.). 278p. 1995. pap. text 28.00 (*0-19-820604-6*) OUP.

Political Developments & Prospects for Peace in Mozambique & Review of the Electorial Process in Angola: Hearing Before the Subcommittee on Africa of the Committee on Foreign Affairs, House of Representatives, One Hundred Second Congress, Second Session, October 8, 1992. USGPO Staff. LC 93-233872. iii, 148 p. 1993. write for info. (*0-16-041141-6*) USGPO.

Political Dialogue in Northern Ireland: The Brooke Initiative, 1989-92. David Bloomfield. LC 97-22915. 1998. text 59.95 (*0-312-17726-7*) St Martin.

Political Diaries of the Arab World, 1882-1965, 80 vols. Ed. by R. L. Jarman. 20000p. 1998. reprint ed. lib. bdg. 14755.00 (*1-85207-725-5*, Pub. by Archive Editions) N Ross.

Political Diaries of the Persian Gulf, 1904-1965, 20 vols. Archives Research Ltd. Staff. (C). 1987. text 11000.00 (*0-318-68197-8*, Pub. by Archive Res Ltd) St Mut.

Political Diaries of the Persian Gulf, 1904-1965, 24 vols., Set. Archives Research Ltd. Staff. 13000p. (C). 1990. reprint ed. lib. bdg. 3995.00 (*1-85207-250-4*, Pub. by Archive Editions) N Ross.

Political Dictionaries of the Arab World & State of Israel, 2 vols. Susan H. Rolef & Shim. 1988. 90.00 (*0-02-916423-0*) S&S Trade.

***Political Dictionary of Israel.** Bernard Reich & David H. Goldberg. (Illus.). 528p. 2000. 75.00 (*0-8108-3778-1*) Scarecrow.

Political Dictionary of Modern Middle East. Agnes C. Korbani. LC 94-16764. 262p. (Orig.). 1995. reprint ed. pap. text 37.50 (*0-8191-9580-4*); reprint ed. lib. bdg. 56.50 (*0-8191-9579-0*) U Pr of Amer.

Political Dimension in Teacher Education: Comparative Perspectives on Policy Formation, Socialization & Society. Ed. by Mark B. Ginsburg & Beverly Lindsay. LC 94-36884. 210p. 1995. 95.00 (*0-7507-0392-X*, Falmer Pr); pap. 27.95 (*0-7507-0393-8*, Falmer Pr) Taylor & Francis.

Political Dimension of Economic Growth: Proceedings of the IEA Conference, held in San Jose, Costa Rica. Silvio Borner et al. LC 97-22800. (IEA Conference Ser.). 352p. 1998. text 79.95 (*0-312-21008-6*) St Martin.

Political Dimensions of Aristotle's Ethics. Richard Bodeus. Tr. by Jan Garrett. LC 92-34024. (SUNY Series in Ancient Greek Philosophy). 250p. (C). 1993. pap. text 19.95 (*0-7914-1610-0*) State U NY Pr.

Political Dimensions of Aristotle's Ethics. Richard Bodeus. Tr. by Jan Garrett. LC 92-34024. (SUNY Series in Ancient Greek Philosophy). 250p. (C). 1993. text 59.50 (*0-7914-1609-7*) State U NY Pr.

Political Dimensions of Arthur Schnitzler's Late Fiction. Felix W. Tweraser. LC 97-36199. (GERM Ser.). 163p. 1998. 55.00 (*1-57113-106-X*) Camden Hse.

Political Dimensions of Development. Iqbal Narain. (C). 1994. 18.50 (*81-7033-253-2*, Pub. by Rawat Pubns) S Asia.

Political Dimensions of India - U. S. S. R. Relations. S. P. Singh. 302p. 1987. 37.95 (*0-318-37253-3*) Asia Bk Corp.

Political Dimensions of Land Reforms in India. P. Eashvaraish. 1985. 18.00 (*0-8364-1382-2*, Pub. by Ashish Pub Hse) S Asia.

Political Dimensions of Religion. Ed. by Said A. Arjomand. LC 92-28757. (SUNY Series in Near Eastern Studies). 293p. (C). 1993. text 64.50 (*0-7914-1557-0*); pap. text 21.95 (*0-7914-1558-9*) State U NY Pr.

Political Dimensions of South Asian Cooperation. V. Kanesalingam. (C). 1991. 47.00 (*0-7855-0206-8*, Pub. by Ratna Pustak Bhandar) St Mut.

Political Discourse in Early Modern Britain. Ed. by Nicholas Phillipson & Quentin Skinner. (Ideas in Context Ser.: No. 24). 460p. (C). 1993. text 69.95 (*0-521-39242-X*) Cambridge U Pr.

Political Discourse in Exile: Karl Marx & the Jewish Question. Dennis Fischman. LC 90-24603. 160p. (C). 1991. lib. bdg. 22.50 (*0-87023-746-2*) U of Mass Pr.

Political Discourse in Transition in Europe 1989-1991. Ed. by Paul A. Chilton et al. LC 97-44191. (Pragmatics & Beyond Ser.: No. 36). xi, 272p. 1998. lib. bdg. 69.00 (*1-55619-329-7*) J Benjamins Pubng Co.

Political Discourse of Anarchy: A Disciplinary History of International Relations. Brian C. Schmidt. LC 97-1724. (SUNY Series in Global Politics). 309p. (C). 1997. pap. text 19.95 (*0-7914-3578-4*) State U NY Pr.

Political Discourse of Anarchy: A Disciplinary History of International Relations. Brian C. Schmidt. LC 97-1724. (SUNY Series in Global Politics). 309p. (C). 1997. text 59.50 (*0-7914-3577-6*) State U NY Pr.

Political Discourses in African Thought: 1860 to the Present. Pieter Boele van Hensbroek. LC 98-44539. 248p. 1999. 59.95 (*0-275-96494-9*, Praeger Pubs) Greenwood.

Political Dissent & Opposition in Poland: The Workers' Defense Committee "KOR" Robert Zuzowski. LC 92-2685. 320p. 1992. 75.00 (*0-275-94138-8*, C4138, Praeger Pubs) Greenwood.

Political Dissent in Democratic Athens: Intellectual Critics of Popular Rule. Josiah Ober. LC 98-7110. (Martin Classical Lectures). 388p. 1998. text 35.00 (*0-691-00122-7*, Pub. by Princeton U Pr) Cal Prin Full Svc.

Political Dissidence under Nero. Vasily Rudich. LC 92-7604. 388p. (C). (gr. 13). 1993. 80.00 (*0-415-06951-3*, A7048) Routledge.

Political Doctrine of Al-Baqillani. Yusuf Ibish. 1966. 19.95 (*0-8156-6029-4*, Pub. by Am U Beirut) Syracuse U Pr.

Political Doctrine of the Isma'ilis. Abu A. Ya'qub. Tr. by Sami N. Makarim. LC 77-16600. 156p. 1990. pap. 15.00 (*0-88206-507-6*) Caravan Bks.

Political Doctrines of Sun Yat-Sen, No. 24--24. Paul M. Linebarger. LC 73-3926. 278p. 1973. lib. bdg. 38.50 (*0-8371-6855-4*, LISY, Greenwood Pr) Greenwood.

Political Doctrines of Sun Yat-Sen: An Exposition of the San Min Chu I. Paul M. Linebarger. LC 78-64293. (Johns Hopkins University. Studies in the Social Sciences. Thirtieth Ser. 1912: 24). reprint ed. 27.50 (*0-404-61393-4*) AMS Pr.

Political Dramaturgy of Nicodemus Frischlin: Essays on Humanist Drama in Germany. David Price. LC 89-16733. (Germanic Languages & Literatures Ser.: No. 111). xii, 156p. (C). 1990. 37.50 (*0-8078-8111-2*) U of NC Pr.

Political Dynamics & Security in the Arabian Peninsula Through the 1990s. Joseph A. Kechichian. LC 93-3480. 1993. pap. 15.00 (*0-8330-1353-X*, MR-167-AF/A) Rand Corp.

Political Dynamics in Contemporary Japan. Ed. by Gary D. Allinson & Yasunori Sone. LC 92-56777. (Illus.). 336p. 1993. text 49.95 (*0-8014-2852-1*); pap. text 17.95 (*0-8014-8096-5*) Cornell U Pr.

Political Dynamics in the Middle East. Ed. by Paul Y. Hammond & Sidney S. Alexander. LC 71-161688. (Middle East Ser.). 704p. reprint ed. pap. 200.00 (*0-608-30669-X*, 200764000065) Bks Demand.

Political Dynamics of American Education. rev. ed. Frederick M. Wirt & Michael W. Kirst. LC 97-70792. 356p. 1997. 40.00 (*0-8211-2273-8*) McCutchan.

Political Dynamics of Constitutional Law. Neal Devins & Louis Fisher. 333p. (C). 1992. pap. text 21.00 (*0-314-00657-5*) West Pub.

Political Dynamics of Constitutional Law. 2nd ed. Louis Fisher & Neal Devins. (Misacellaneous Ser.). 316p. (C). 1996. pap. text 22.00 (*0-314-09012-6*) West Pub.

Political Dynamics of Direct Foreign Investment. Veenaskay & Sahar Muakasa. 150p. 1985. 30.00 (*0-944025-02-1*) Advance Research.

Political Dynamics of European Economic Integration. Leon N. Lindberg. LC 63-14129. 381p. 1963. reprint ed. pap. 30.00 (*0-608-08293-7*, 203097600073) Bks Demand.

***Political Dynamics of Hong Kong under the Chinese Sovereignty.** Jermain T. M. Lam. LC 00-28422. 251p. 2000. lib. bdg. 59.00 (*1-56072-806-X*) Nova Sci Pubs.

Political Dynamics of Japan. Jun-Ichi Kyogoku. Tr. by Nobutaka Ike. 250p. 1993. pap. 24.50 (*0-86008-500-7*, Pub. by U of Tokyo) Col U Pr.

Political Dynamics of Japan. Jun-Ichi Kyogoku. Tr. by Nobutaka Ike from JPN.Tr. of Nihon no Seiji. 240p. 1987. 32.50 (*0-86008-409-4*, Pub. by U of Tokyo) Col U Pr.

Political Ecologist. David Wells & Tony Lynch. LC 99-76343. 148p. 61.95 (*0-7546-1119-1*) Ashgate Pub Co.

Political Ecology: Beyond Environmentalism. Dimitrios I. Roussopoulos. LC 93-72749. 180p. 1994. 44.99 (*1-895431-81-6*, Pub. by Black Rose); pap. 15.99 (*1-895431-80-8*, Pub. by Black Rose) Consort Bk Sales.

Political Ecology: Global & Local. LC 98-13484. 408p. (C). (gr. 13). 1998. 110.00 (*0-415-18380-4*) Routledge.

Political Ecology: Global & Local. Ed. by David Bell & Roger Keil. LC 98-13484. 400p. (C). 1998. pap. 32.99 (*0-415-18381-2*) Routledge.

Political Ecology of Bananas: Contract Farming, Peasants & Agrarian Change in the Eastern Caribbean. Lawrence S. Grossman. LC 97-40002. 1998. pap. 19.95 (*0-8078-4718-6*); lib. bdg. 49.95 (*0-8078-2410-0*) U of NC Pr.

Political Ecology of Forestry in Burma, 1824-1994. Raymond L. Bryant. LC 96-30877. 1997. text 39.00 (*0-8248-1909-8*) UH Pr.

Political Ecology of the Modern Peasant: Calculation & Community. Leslie E. Anderson. LC 93-5388. 1994. text 49.95 (*0-8018-4708-7*) Johns Hopkins.

Political Ecology of the Water Crisis in Israel. Susan H. Lees. 208p. (C). 1997. 36.00 (*0-7618-0969-4*) U Pr of Amer.

Political Economic Analysis of U. S. Dairy Policies & European Community Dairy Policy Comparisons. Mary A. Marchant. LC 92-40968. (Government & the Economy Ser.). 280p. 1993. text 10.00 (*0-8153-1231-8*) Garland.

Political, Economic, & Cultural Developments in the Third World. Ed. by Harold Isaacs. (Journal of Third World Studies: Vol. VIII, No. 1). 432p. 1991. pap. 11.25 (*0-931971-13-6*) Assn Third Wld.

Political, Economic, & Labor Climate in Argentina. David R. Decker. LC 83-81084. (Multinational Industrial Relations Ser.: No. 4). (Illus.). 148p. 1983. reprint ed. pap. 45.90 (*0-608-04367-2*, 206514800001) Bks Demand.

Political, Economic, & Labor Climate in Colombia. David R. Decker & Ignacio Duran. LC 82-82996. (Multinational Industrial Relations Ser.: No. 4). (Illus.). 146p. 1982. reprint ed. pap. 45.30 (*0-608-04366-4*, 206514700001) Bks Demand.

Political, Economic, & Labor Climate in India. Viswanathan Venkatachalam. LC 82-80931. (Multinational Industrial Relations Ser.: No. 8). (Illus.). 164p. 1982. reprint ed. pap. 50.90 (*0-608-04365-6*, 206514600001) Bks Demand.

Political, Economic, & Labor Climate in Spain. Mario Gobbo. LC 81-52617. (Multinational Industrial Realtions Ser.: No. 10). (Illus.). 148p. 1981. reprint ed. pap. 45.90 (*0-608-04362-1*, 206514300001) Bks Demand.

Political, Economic, & Labor Climate in the Philippines. Jaime T. Infante. LC 80-53988. (Multinational Industrial Relations Ser.: No. 8). (Illus.). 162p. 1980. reprint ed. pap. 50.30 (*0-608-04363-X*, 206514400001) Bks Demand.

Political, Economic, & Labor Climate in Turkey. Anwar M. Shabon. LC 84-62547. (Multinational Industrial Relations Ser.: No. 10). (Illus.). 296p. 1985. reprint ed. pap. 91.80 (*0-608-04364-8*, 206514500001) Bks Demand.

Political, Economic, & Social Issues in the Third World, Vol. XV, No. 2. Ed. by Harold Isaacs. (Journal of Third World Studies). 272p. 1998. pap. 23.00 (*0-931971-28-4*) Assn Third Wld.

Political, Economic, & Social Problems of the Latin-American Nations of Southern South America, 6--6. Texas University Institute of Latin-American Studi. LC 69-19006. 107p. 1969. reprint ed. lib. bdg. 57.50 (*0-8371-1031-9*, TLPE, Greenwood Pr) Greenwood.

Political Economic Development. Pranab Bardhan. (C). 35.00 (*0-691-04280-2*, Pub. by Princeton U Pr) Cal Prin Full Svc.

Political Economic Development. Pranab Bardhan. (C). 1992. pap. text 10.95 (*0-691-00389-0*, Pub. by Princeton U Pr) Cal Prin Full Svc.

Political-Economic Issues in Tanzania: The Nyerere Years, 1965-1985. Meta K. Townsend. LC 97-50275. 336p. 1998. text 99.95 (*0-7734-4233-2*) E Mellen.

Political Economic Management of India, by India, for India: Creation of Wealth from Public Investment. Ajit N. Haksar. 473p. 1988. text 40.00 (*0-7069-3859-3*, Pub. by Vikas) S Asia.

Political Economics. Biel. (C). 1998. pap. 30.00 (*0-06-500864-2*) HarpC.

***Political Economics: Explaining Economic Policy.** Torsten Persson & Guido Enrico Tabellini. LC 00-28245. (Zeuthen Lecture Ser.). (Illus.). 544p. 2000. 55.00 (*0-262-16195-8*) MIT Pr.

Political Economics & International Money. John Williamson. (C). 1989. pap. text 18.50 (*0-8147-5447-3*) NYU Pr.

P

An Asterisk (*) at the beginning of an entry indicates that the title is appearing for the first time.

Political Economics in Retrospect: Essays in Memory of Adolph Lowe. Ed. by Harald Hagemann & Heinz D. Kurz. LC 97-22600. 352p. (C). 1998. 95.00 (*1-85898-057-7*) E Elgar.

Political Economics of International Bank Lending. David Gisselquist. LC 81-8636. 251p. 1981. 55.00 (*0-275-90632-9*, C0632, Praeger Pubs) Greenwood.

Political Economics of North American Free Trade. Ed. by Ricardo S. Grinspun & Maxwell A. Cameron. LC 93-14764. 400p. 1993. text 19.95 (*0-312-07599-5*) St Martin.

Political Economy. Francisco L. Rivera-Batiz. pap. 0.00 (*0-691-00385-8*) Princeton U Pr.

Political Economy. Ed. by Larry L. Wade. 1983. lib. bdg. 85.50 (*0-89838-083-9*) Kluwer Academic.

Political Economy: A Comparative Approach. 2nd ed. Barry Clark. LC 98-15657. 376p. 1998. 69.50 (*0-275-95869-8*, Praeger Pubs); pap. 24.95 (*0-275-96370-5*, Praeger Pubs) Greenwood.

Political Economy: A Condensed Course. L. Leontyev. (Rus. Ser.). (Illus.). 248p. 1974. pap. 19.95 (*0-8464-1268-3*) Beekman Pubs.

Political Economy: A Marxist Textbook. rev. ed. John Eaton. 253p. (C). 1966. pap. text 4.25 (*0-7178-0157-8*) Intl Pubs Co.

Political Economy: An Inquiry into the Natural Grounds of Right to Vendible Property. Samuel Read. LC 68-56570. (Reprints of Economic Classics Ser.). xxxiv, 398p. 1976. reprint ed. 57.50 (*0-678-00959-7*) Kelley.

Political Economy: An Introductory Text. Edmund S. Phelps. (C). 1985. text 48.75 (*0-393-95312-2*) Norton.

Political Economy: Institutions, Competition & Representation: Proceedings of the 7th International Symposium. Ed. by William A. Barnett et al. LC 92-43595. (International Symposia in Economic Theory & Econometrics Ser.: No. 7). (Illus.). 536p. (C). 1993. text 89.95 (*0-521-41781-3*); pap. text 37.95 (*0-521-42831-9*) Cambridge U Pr.

Political Economy: Public Policies in the United States & Britain. Ed. by Jerold L. Waltman & Donley T. Studlar. LC 87-10425. 285p. 1987. text 32.50 (*0-87805-313-1*); pap. text 15.95 (*0-87805-314-X*) U Pr of Miss.

Political Economy: Readings in the Politics & Economics of American Public Policy. Thomas Ferguson & Joel Rogers. LC 84-3111. 380p. (C). (gr. 13). 1984. text 81.95 (*0-87332-276-2*); pap. text 43.95 (*0-87332-272-X*) M E Sharpe.

***Political Economy Adult Education & Development.** Frank Youngman. LC 99-52390. 256p. 2000. pap. 25.00 (*1-85649-676-7*) Zed Books.

Political Economy & American Capitalism. Rodney D. Peterson. 240p. (C). 1991. lib. bdg. 80.50 (*0-7923-9142-X*) Kluwer Academic.

Political Economy & Capitalism: Some Essays in Economic Tradition. Maurice H. Dobb. LC 76-108389. 357p. (C). 1972. reprint ed. lib. bdg. 38.50 (*0-8371-3812-4*, DOPE, Greenwood Pr) Greenwood.

***Political Economy & Contemporary Capitalism: Radical Perspectives on Economic Theory & Policy.** Ron P. Baiman et al. LC 99-47226. (Illus.). 368p. 2000. text 69.95 (*0-7656-0529-5*) M E Sharpe.

***Political Economy & Fiction in the Early Works of Harriet Martineau.** Claudia Orazem. (Anglo-American Studies). 212p. 1999. pap. 35.95 (*3-631-35458-4*) P Lang Pubng.

***Political Economy & Fiction in the Early Works of Harriet Martineau.** Claudia Orazem. LC 99-57824. (Anglo-American Studies: Vol. 16). 212p. (C). 1999. pap. text 35.95 (*0-8204-4398-0*) P Lang Pubng.

Political Economy & Freedom: A Collection of Essays. G. Warren Nutter. Ed. by Jane C. Nutter. LC 82-48106. (Illus.). 328p. 1983. 14.00 (*0-86597-024-6*); pap. 5.50 (*0-86597-025-4*) Liberty Fund.

Political Economy & Ideology in the Managerial - Technological Society. Daniel Pound. 144p. 1990. per. 31.95 (*0-8403-5697-8*) Kendall-Hunt.

Political Economy & International Economics. Jagdish N. Bhagwati. (Illus.). 490p. 1991. 49.95 (*0-262-02322-9*) MIT Pr.

Political Economy & International Economics. Jagdish N. Bhagwati. (Illus.). 576p. 1996. pap. text 29.00 (*0-262-52218-7*) MIT Pr.

Political Economy & Laissez-Faire Economics & Ideology in the Ricardian Age. Rajani K. Kanth. LC 85-30345. 208p. (C). 1986. 58.00 (*0-8476-7488-6*) Rowman.

Political Economy & Modern Capitalism: Mapping Convergence & Diversity. Colin Crouch & Wolfgang Streeck. LC 97-68597. 240p. 1997. 79.95 (*0-7619-5652-2*); pap. 26.95 (*0-7619-5653-0*) Sage.

***Political Economy & New Capitalism: Essays in Honour of Sam Aaronovitch.** Sam Aaronovitch & Jan Toporowski. LC 99-22500. (Frontiers of Political Economy Ser.). 1999. text. write for info. (*0-415-20221-3*) Routledge.

Political Economy & Politics: Collected Writings, Vol. IX. Thomas De Quincey. Ed. by David Masson. LC 66-21670. (Reprints of Economic Classics Ser.). vii, 444p. 1970. reprint ed. 49.50 (*0-678-00680-6*) Kelley.

Political Economy & Public Policy. Deepak Lal. 36p. 1990. pap. 9.95 (*1-55815-101-X*) ICS Pr.

***Political Economy & Public Policy Vol. 12.** 1999. 73.25 (*0-7623-0545-2*) Jai Pr.

Political Economy & Soviet Socialism. Alec Nove. pap. text 14.95 (*0-04-335037-2*) Routledge.

Political Economy & Statesmanship: Smith, Hamilton, & the Foundation of the Commerical Republic. Peter McNamara. LC 97-12499. 256p. 1997. lib. bdg. 35.00 (*0-87580-228-1*) N Ill U Pr.

Political Economy & the Changing Global Order. Ed. by Richard Stubbs & Geoffrey R. Underhill. 780p. 1994. pap. 22.95 (*0-312-12197-0*) St Martin.

***Political Economy & the Changing Global Order.** 2nd ed. Ed. by Richard Stubbs & Geoffrey R. D. Underhill. LC 99-461929. (Illus.). 432p. (C). 1999. pap. text 27.95 (*0-19-541464-0*) OUP.

Political Economy & the Philosophy of Government: A Series of Essays Selected from the Works of M. de Sismondi. Jean C. Simonde De Sismondi. LC 65-19654. (Reprints of Economic Classics Ser.). iii, 455p. 1966. reprint ed. 49.50 (*0-678-00119-7*) Kelley.

Political Economy & the Rise of Capitalism: A Reinterpretation. David McNally. 345p. 1989. pap. 16.95 (*0-520-07192-1*, Pub. by U CA Pr) Cal Prin Full Svc.

Political Economy (1815) Jean C. Simonde De Sismondi. LC 87-17084. (Reprints of Economic Classics Ser.). 128p. 1991. reprint ed. lib. bdg. 35.00 (*0-678-01458-2*) Kelley.

Political Economy Financial Integrity: The Battle of the Systems. Story. LC 97-5363. (European Policy Research Unit Ser.). 1997. pap. write for info. (*0-7190-4313-1*) Manchester Univ Pr.

Political Economy for Beginners, 1870 Edition. (Works of Henry & Millicent Garrett Fawcett). 218p. 1996. reprint ed. 68.00 (*1-85506-372-7*) Bks Intl VA.

Political Economy for the People. George Tucker. LC 68-23040. (Reprints of Economic Classics Ser.). xix, 238p. 1970. reprint ed. 39.50 (*0-678-00589-3*) Kelley.

Political Economy for the People. George Tucker. (Notable American Authors). 1999. reprint ed. lib. bdg. 125.00 (*0-7812-9838-5*) Rprt Serv.

Political Economy for the 21st Century: Contemporary Views on the Trend of Economics. Ed. by Charles J. Whalen. LC 95-22497. 304p. (C). 1995. text 79.95 (*1-56324-648-1*) M E Sharpe.

Political Economy for the 21st Century: Contemporary Views on the Trend of Economics. Ed. by Charles J. Whalen. LC 95-22497. 304p. (C). (gr. 13). 1995. pap. text 38.95 (*1-56324-649-X*) M E Sharpe.

Political Economy, Growth, & Business Cycles. Ed. by Alex Cukierman et al. (Illus.). 400p. 1992. 55.00 (*0-262-03194-9*) MIT Pr.

Political Economy, Ideology, & the Impact of Economics on the Third World. Derrick K. Gondwe. LC 91-37624. 208p. 1992. 49.95 (*0-275-94025-X*, C4025, Praeger Pubs) Greenwood.

Political Economy in Haiti: The Drama of Survival. Simon M. Fass. 416p. (C). 1990. 39.95 (*0-88738-158-8*); pap. 24.95 (*0-88738-855-8*) Transaction Pubs.

Political Economy in the 20th Century. Ed. by Maxine Berg. 192p. 1989. lib. bdg. 45.00 (*0-389-20896-5*, N8452) B&N Imports.

Political Economy in Vietnam. Kathleen Gough. (Sunderlal Series in Humanistic Social Sciences: No. 2). 400p. (C). 1989. 40.00 (*0-9623432-0-X*) Folklore Inst.

Political Economy in Western Democracies. Ed. by Norman J. Vig & Steven E. Schier. LC 84-25320. 328p. 1985. 39.50 (*0-8419-0989-X*); pap. 19.75 (*0-8419-0990-3*) Holmes & Meier.

Political Economy of a Dual Labor Market in Africa: The Copper Industry & Dependency in Zambia, 1929-1969. Buy C. Mhone. LC 80-70184. (Illus.). 256p. 1982. 34.50 (*0-8386-3063-4*) Fairleigh Dickinson.

***Political Economy of a Frontier: Southwest China, 1250-1850.** James Z. Lee. (Harvard East Asian Monographs: Vol. 190). 2000. text 49.50 (*0-674-00241-5*) HUP.

Political Economy of a Social Europe. Kluth. LC 98-17439. x, 179 p. 1998. text 65.00 (*0-312-21557-6*) St Martin.

***Political Economy of Adult Education & Development.** Frank Youngman. LC 99-52390. 256p. 2000. text 69.50 (*1-85649-675-9*) Zed Books.

Political Economy of Africa: Selected Readings. Ed. by Dennis L. Cohen & John Daniel. LC 82-101006. 295p. reprint ed. pap. 91.50 (*0-8357-6269-6*, 203449800090) Bks Demand.

Political Economy of African Famine, Vol. 9. Ed. by R. E. Downs. (Food & Nutrition in History & Anthro Ser.). 389p. 1991. text 130.00 (*2-88124-476-9*); pap. text 49.00 (*2-88124-477-7*) Gordon & Breach.

Political Economy of Agrarian Change: Nanchilnadu, 1880-1939. M. S. Pandian. (Illus.). 196p. (C). 1990. 25.00 (*0-8039-9642-X*) Sage.

Political Economy of Agrarian Reform in Central & Eastern Europe. Ed. by Johan F. Swinnen. LC 97-71710. (LICOS Studies on the Transitions in Central & Eastern Europe). (Illus.). 432p. 1997. text 91.95 (*1-85972-560-0*, Pub. by Ashgate Pub) Ashgate Pub Co.

Political Economy of Agricultural Markets in South Asia: Masters of the Countryside. Barbara Harriss-White. LC 95-51259. 404p. 1996. 39.95 (*0-8039-9299-8*) Sage.

Political Economy of Agricultural Price Intervention in Latin America. Anne O. Krueger et al. LC 91-43697. 40p. 1992. pap. 14.95 (*1-55815-180-X*) ICS Pr.

Political Economy of Agricultural Pricing Policy Vol. 1: Latin America. Ed. by Anne O. Krueger et al. 288p. 1991. 32.95 (*0-8018-4029-5*, 44029) Johns Hopkins.

Political Economy of Agricultural Pricing Policy Vol. 2: Asia. Ed. by Anne O. Krueger et al. 312p. 1991. 32.95 (*0-8018-4030-9*, 44030) Johns Hopkins.

Political Economy of Agricultural Pricing Policy Vol. 3: Africa & the Mediterranean. Ed. by Anne O. Krueger et al. 360p. 1991. text 32.95 (*0-8018-4031-7*, 44031) Johns Hopkins.

Political Economy of Agricultural Pricing Policy Vol. 4: A Synthesis of the Economics in Developing Countries. Ed. by Maurice Schiff & Alberto Valdes. 256p. 1992. text 32.95 (*0-8018-4531-9*, 44531) Johns Hopkins.

Political Economy of Agricultural Pricing Policy Vol. 5: A Synthesis of the Political Economy in Developing Countries. Anne O. Krueger. 176p. 1992. 32.95 (*0-8018-4294-8*, 44294) Johns Hopkins.

Political Economy of AIDS. Ed. by Merrill Singer. LC 97-6399. (Critical Approaches in the Health Social Sciences Ser.). 236p. 1998. text 44.00 (*0-89503-177-9*) Baywood Pub.

***Political Economy of American Industrialization, 1877 - 1900.** Richard Franklin Bensel. (Illus.). 512p. 2001. write for info. (*0-521-77233-8*); pap. write for info. (*0-521-77604-X*) Cambridge U Pr.

Political Economy of American Monetary Policy. Ed. by Thomas Mayer. (Illus.). 324p. (C). 1993. pap. text 21.95 (*0-521-44651-1*) Cambridge U Pr.

Political Economy of American Trade Policy. Ed. by Anne O. Krueger. LC 95-21949. 470p. 1995. 70.00 (*0-226-45489-4*) U Ch Pr.

Political Economy of Australian Urbanization, Vol. 22. M. Berry. (Illus.). 84p. 1984. pap. 22.00 (*0-08-031741-3*, Pergamon Pr) Elsevier.

Political Economy of Austria. Ed. by Sven W. Arndt. LC 82-11661. (AEI Symposia Ser.: No. 82D). (Illus.). 240p. reprint ed. pap. 74.40 (*0-8357-4524-4*, 203738500008) Bks Demand.

Political Economy of Basic Human Needs. Bruce E. Moon. LC 91-14912. 336p. 1991. 49.95 (*0-8014-2448-8*); pap. text 17.95 (*0-8014-9982-8*) Cornell U Pr.

Political Economy of Brazilian Oil. Laura Randall. LC 92-15781. 328p. 1993. 69.50 (*0-275-94091-8*, C4091, Praeger Pubs) Greenwood.

Political Economy of Burma. David I. Steinberg. 1996. pap. text 19.95 (*0-8133-0897-6*) Westview.

Political Economy of Cameroon: SAIS Study on Africa. Ed. by Michael G. Schatzberg & I. William Zartman. LC 85-20492. 284p. 1985. 45.00 (*0-275-90223-4*, C0223, Praeger Pubs) Greenwood.

Political Economy of Canada: An Introduction. 2nd ed. Michael Howlett et al. (Illus.). 392p. 1999. pap. text 29.95 (*0-19-541348-2*) OUP.

Political Economy of Capital Controls. Gunther G. Schulze. (Illus.). 304p. (C). 2000. 64.95 (*0-521-58222-9*) Cambridge U Pr.

Political Economy of Central-Bank Independence. Sylvester C. Eijffinger & Jakob De Haan. LC 96-14334. (Special Papers in International Economics: Vol. 19). 1996. pap. 13.50 (*0-88165-308-X*) Princeton U Int Finan Econ.

Political Economy of Central Banking. Ed. by Philip Arestis & Malcolm C. Sawyer. LC 98-12817. 256p. 1998. 85.00 (*1-85898-742-3*) E Elgar.

Political Economy of Change. Warren F. Ilchman & Norman T. Uphoff. LC 97-13293. 330p. 1997. pap. text 24.95 (*1-56000-961-6*) Transaction Pubs.

***Political Economy Of China's Provinces Comparative & Competitive Advantage.** Hans J. Hendrischke. 1999. write for info. (*0-415-20775-4*) Routledge.

Political Economy of China's Provinces: Competitive & Comparative Advantage. Hans J. Hendrischke. LC 98-31541. 1999. pap. text 32.99 (*0-415-20776-2*) Routledge.

Political Economy of China's Special Economic Zones. George T. Crane. LC 89-10759. (Studies on Contemporary China). 206p. (C). (gr. 13). 1990. text 70.95 (*0-87332-514-1*, East Gate Bk) M E Sharpe.

Political Economy of Chinese Development. Mark Selden. LC 92-22899. (Socialism & Social Movements Ser.). 288p. (C). (gr. 13). 1992. text 75.95 (*0-87332-763-2*, East Gate Bk); pap. text 28.95 (*1-56324-092-0*, East Gate Bk) M E Sharpe.

Political Economy of Chinese Socialism. Mark Selden. LC 88-4666. (Socialism & Social Movements Ser.). 252p. (gr. 13). 1988. pap. text 31.95 (*0-87332-504-4*, East Gate Bk) M E Sharpe.

Political Economy of Civil Society & Human Rights. Gary B. Madison. LC 97-8645. 320p. (C). 1998. 85.00 (*0-415-16677-2*) Routledge.

Political Economy of Colonialism: The State & Industrialization in Puerto Rico. Sherrie L. Baver. LC 92-46553. 176p. 1993. 55.00 (*0-275-94503-0*, C4503, Praeger Pubs) Greenwood.

Political Economy of Colonialism in Ghana. Ed. by Geoffrey Kay & Stephen Mymer. (Modern Revivals in African Studies). 460p. 1992. 72.95 (*0-7512-0079-4*, Pub. by Gregg Revivals) Ashgate Pub Co.

Political Economy of Communication: Rethinking & Renewal. Vincent Mosco. LC 98-2647. (Media, Culture & Society Ser.). (Illus.). 336p. 1996. 75.00 (*0-8039-8560-6*); pap. 26.95 (*0-8039-8561-4*) Sage.

Political Economy of Communications: A Special Issue of Media Economics. Ed. by Gerald Sussman. 80p. 1999. pap. 20.00 (*0-8058-9798-4*) L Erlbaum Assocs.

Political Economy of Comparative Development into the 21st Century Vol. 1: Essays in Memory of John C. H. Fei, Vol. 1. Ed. by Gustav Ranis et al. LC 98-29702. 416p. 1999. 100.00 (*1-85898-878-0*) E Elgar.

***Political Economy of Competitiveness: Essays on Employment, Public Policy & Corporate Performance.** Jonathan Michie & Michael Kitson. LC 99-57353. 1999. write for info. (*0-415-20495-X*) Routledge.

***Political Economy of Competitiveness: Essays on Employment, Public Policy & Corporate Performance.** Jonathan Michie & Michael Kitson. LC 99-57353. (Contemporary Political Economy Ser.). 1999. pap. write for info. (*0-415-20496-8*) Routledge.

Political Economy of Conflict & Appropriation. Ed. by Michelle R. Garfinkel & Stergios Skaperdas. (Illus.). 224p. (C). 1996. text 54.95 (*0-521-56063-2*) Cambridge U Pr.

Political Economy of Contemporary Africa. 2nd ed. Ed. by Peter C. Gutkind & Immanuel Wallerstein. LC 84-27647. (Sage Series on African Modernization & Development: No. 1). 344p. 1985. reprint ed. pap. 106.70 (*0-608-01451-6*, 205949500001) Bks Demand.

Political Economy of Contemporary Egypt. Ed. by Ibrahim M. Oweiss. 330p. (Orig.). 1990. text 34.95 (*0-932568-20-3*); pap. text 16.95 (*0-932568-21-1*) GU Ctr CAS.

Political Economy of Corruption in China. Julia Kwong. LC 97-13320. (Studies on Contemporary China Ser.). 192p. (C). (gr. 13). 1997. text 72.95 (*0-7656-0086-2*, East Gate Bk); pap. text 30.95 (*0-7656-0087-0*, East Gate Bk) M E Sharpe.

Political Economy of Customs & Culture: Informal Solutions to the Common Problem. Terry L. Anderson & Randy Simmons. (Political Economy Forum Ser.). 260p. (C). 1993. text 54.00 (*0-8476-7786-9*) Rowman.

Political Economy of Defense: Issues & Perspectives, 112. Ed. by Andrew L. Ross. LC 90-25280. (Contributions in Military Studies Ser.: No. 112). 240p. 1991. 62.95 (*0-313-26462-7*, RPD/, Greenwood Pr) Greenwood.

***Political Economy of Defense Spending Around the World.** Uk Heo. LC 99-21898. (Studies in World PEace: Vol. 42). 164p. 1999. text 79.95 (*0-7734-8017-X*) E Mellen.

Political Economy of Democratic Decentralization. James Manor. LC 99-11245. (Directions in Development Ser.). 144p. 1999. pap. 22.00 (*0-8213-4470-6*) World Bank.

***Political Economy of Democratic Institutions.** Peter Moser. LC 99-88523. (Locke Institute Ser.). 208p. 2000. 85.00 (*1-85898-966-3*) E Elgar.

Political Economy of Democratic Transitions. Stephen Haggard & Robert R. Kaufman. LC 94-49595. 360p. 1995. pap. text 19.95 (*0-691-02775-7*, Pub. by Princeton U Pr) Cal Prin Full Svc.

Political Economy of Development: Theoretical & Empirical Contributions. Ed. by Norman T. Uphoff & Warren F. Ilchman. LC 77-161999. 518p. reprint ed. pap. 160.60 (*0-608-18430-6*, 203228100080) Bks Demand.

Political Economy of Development & Underdevelopment. 6th ed. Ed. by Kenneth P. Jameson & Charles K. Wilber. LC 95-8588. 672p. (C). 1995. pap. 39.38 (*0-07-070189-X*) McGraw.

Political Economy of Development & Underdevelopment: Appraisal of Radical Theories. B. N. Ghosh. (C). 1996. 32.00 (*81-7100-821-6*, Pub. by Deep & Deep Pubns) S Asia.

Political Economy of Development in India: Expanded Edition with an Epilogue on the Political Economy of Reform in India. Pranab Bardhan. LC 99-220256. 162p. 1999. pap. text 9.95 (*0-19-564770-X*) OUP.

Political Economy of Dictatorship. Ronald Wintrobe. LC 97-24262. (Illus.). 400p. (C). 1998. text 59.95 (*0-521-58329-2*) Cambridge U Pr.

***Political Economy of Dictatorship.** Ronald Wintrobe. 400p. 2000. pap. write for info. (*0-521-79449-8*) Cambridge U Pr.

Political Economy of Diet & Health. Ben Fine. LC 99-163026. 192p. (C). 1998. 75.00 (*0-415-16366-8*) Routledge.

Political Economy of Discontinuous Development: Regional Disparities & Inter-Regional Conflict. Milica Z. Bookman. LC 91-10659. 288p. 1991. 59.95 (*0-275-93777-1*, C3777, Praeger Pubs) Greenwood.

Political Economy of Diversity: Evolutionary Perspectives on Economic Order & Disorder. Ed. by Robert Delorme & Kurt Dopfer. LC 94-6264. (European Association for Evolutionary Political Economy Ser.). 328p. 1994. 95.00 (*1-85278-874-7*) E Elgar.

Political Economy of Dowry: Institutionalization & Expansion in North India. Ranjana Sheel. LC 99-932394. 229 p. 1999. 30.00 (*81-7304-264-0*, Pub. by Manohar) S Asia.

***Political Economy of Drugs in the Caribbean.** Ivelaw L. Griffith. LC 99-87197. 272p. 2000. text 65.00 (*0-312-23258-6*) St Martin.

Political Economy of Dual Transformations: Market Reforms & Democratization in Hungary. David L. Bartlett. LC 96-36553. 320p. (C). 1997. text 54.50 (*0-472-10794-1*, 10794) U of Mich Pr.

Political Economy of East Asia, 6 vols. Ed. by John Ravenhill. Incl. Vol. 2. China, Korea & Taiwan., **2 bks. set** LC 95-7192. 1995. 400.00 (*1-85898-253-7*); Vol. 3. Singapore, Indonesia, Malaysia, the Philippines & Thailand., **2 bks. set** LC 95-7193. 1120p. 1995. 400.00 (*1-85898-254-5*); 3444p. 1995. 1150.00 (*1-85898-031-3*) E Elgar.

Political Economy of East German Privatization. Phyllis Dininio. LC 98-47764. 152p. 1999. 55.00 (*0-275-96484-1*, Praeger Pubs) Greenwood.

Political Economy of Economic Decline & Reform in Africa: The Role of the State, Markets, & Civil Institutions. CFNPP Staff et al. (Working Papers). (C). 1992. pap. 7.00 (*1-56401-125-9*) Cornell Food.

Political Economy of Economic Freedom. Alan Peacock. LC 96-48251. 352p. 1997. 100.00 (*1-85898-535-8*) E Elgar.

Political Economy of Economic Policy: The Quest for Human Betterment. Wilfred L. David. LC 88-9961. 283p. 1988. 65.00 (*0-275-93015-7*, C3015, Praeger Pubs) Greenwood.

Political Economy of Edmund Burke: The Role of Property in His Thought. Francis Canavan. xi, 185p. (C). 1994. text 30.00 (*0-8232-1590-3*); pap. text 17.95 (*0-8232-1591-1*) Fordham.

Political Economy of Education in Ghana, 1920-1979: A Study of Education & National Development in Ghana. Kwaku Osei-Hwedie & Yaw Agyeman-Badu. LC 84-61224. 189p. (Orig.). 1985. pap. 10.95 (*0-943324-13-0*) Omenana.

Political Economy of Education in India. J. B. Tilak. (Special Studies in Comparative Education: No. 24). 63p. (Orig.). 1990. pap. text 10.00 (*0-937033-14-6*) Grad Schl of Educ.

An Asterisk (*) at the beginning of an entry indicates that the title is appearing for the first time.

Political Economy of Energy. Stephen C. Stamos. (C). 1996. pap. text 24.00 (*0-8133-0270-6*) Westview.

Political Economy of Environmental Policy: A Public Choice Approach to Market Instruments. Bouwe R. Dijkstra. LC 98-53752. 400p. 1999. 100.00 (*1-85898-964-7*) E Elgar.

Political Economy of Environmental Protection. Horst Siebert et al. Ed. by Edward I. Altman. LC 78-13843. (Contemporary Studies in Economic & Financial Analysis: Vol. 24). 202p. 1979. 78.50 (*0-89232-116-4*) Jai Pr.

Political Economy of Environmental Protection: Analysis & Evidence. Ed. by Roger D. Congleton. LC 96-25. 304p. (C). 1996. text 57.50 (*0-472-10602-3*, 10602) U of Mich Pr.

***Political Economy of Environmental Protectionism.** Achim Korber. LC 99-49368. (New Horizons in Environmental Economics Ser.). 168p. 2000. 75.00 (*1-84064-242-4*) E Elgar.

***Political Economy of Environmental Taxes.** Nicholas Wallart. LC 99-15585. (New Horizons in Environmental Economics Ser.). 224p. 1999. write for info. (*1-84064-185-1*) E Elgar.

Political Economy of Ethiopia. Ed. by Marina Ottaway. LC 89-77108. (SAIS Studies of Africa). 264p. 1990. 59.95 (*0-275-93472-1*, C3472, Greenwood Pr) Greenwood.

Political Economy of Ethnic Discrimination & Affirmative Action: A Comparative Perspective. Ed. by Michael L. Wyzan. LC 90-31364. 288p. 1990. 59.95 (*0-275-93334-2*, C3334, Praeger Pubs) Greenwood.

Political Economy of European Integration. Ed. by Finn Laursen. LC 95-527. 1995. lib. bdg. 118.00 (*90-411-0086-5*) Kluwer Academic.

Political Economy of European Integration: Markets & Institutions. Ed. by Paolo Guerrieri & Pier C. Padoan. 284p. (C). 1989. lib. bdg. 51.00 (*0-389-20891-4*, N 8448) B&N Imports.

Political Economy of European Integration: The Challenges Ahead. Ed. by Jeffry Frieden & Barry Eichengreen. LC 97-36700. 352p. (C). 1998. text 57.50 (*0-472-10840-9*, 10840) U of Mich Pr.

***Political Economy of European Monet.** Barry Eichengreen. 2000. 35.00 (*0-8133-9761-8*, Pub. by Westview) HarpC.

Political Economy of Fairness. Edward E. Zajac. (Illus.). 320p. 1995. 32.50 (*0-262-24038-6*) MIT Pr.

Political Economy of Fairness. Edward E. Zajac. (Illus.). 344p. 1996. pap. text 20.00 (*0-262-74019-2*) MIT Pr.

Political Economy of Federal Government Growth. James T. Bennett & Manuel H. Johnson. 148p. 1980. 12.95 (*0-86599-001-8*); pap. 4.95 (*0-86599-002-6*) PERC.

Political Economy of Financial Integration in Europe: The Battle of the Systems. Jonathan Story & Ingo Walter. LC 97-72739. (Illus.). 351p. 1997. 50.00 (*0-262-19396-5*); pap. text 25.00 (*0-262-69203-1*) MIT Pr.

Political Economy of Fiscal Decisions: The Strategic Role of Public Debt. J. De Wolff. (Contributions to Economics Ser.). (Illus.). xvi, 150p. 1998. pap. 56.00 (*3-7908-1130-0*) Spr-Verlag.

Political Economy of Fiscal Policy. 350p. 30.00 (*92-808-0696-3*) UN.

Political Economy of Food & Nutrition Policies. Ed. by Per Pinstrup-Andersen. LC 92-25287. (International Food Policy Research Institute Ser.). 352p. 1993. text 38.50 (*0-8018-4480-0*) Johns Hopkins.

Political Economy of Food in Nigeria: A Discussion on Peasants, State & World Economy. Hans-Otto Sano. (Research Report Ser.: No. 65). 108p. 1983. write for info. (*91-7106-210-6*, Pub. by Nordic Africa) Transaction Pubs.

Political Economy of Foreign Aid in the Third World. M. Dharamdasani. 1984. pap. 32.00 (*0-7855-7476-X*, Pub. by Ratna Pustak Bhandar) St Mut.

Political Economy of Foreign Investment in Mexico: Nationalism, Liberalism, & Constraints on Choice. Van R. Whiting, Jr. LC 91-17669. 384p. 1992. text 55.00 (*0-8018-4227-1*) Johns Hopkins.

Political Economy of Foreign Policy Behavior. Ed. by Charles W. Kegley, Jr. & Pat McGowan. LC 80-25248. (Sage International Yearbook of Foreign Policy Studies: No. 6). 295p. reprint ed. pap. 91.50 (*0-8357-8436-3*, 203470000091) Bks Demand.

Political Economy of Foreign Policy in ECOWAS. Ed. by Julius E. Okolo & Timothy M. Shaw. LC 93-29482. (International Political Economy Ser.). 1994. text 65.00 (*0-312-10646-7*) St Martin.

Political Economy of Forest Resource Use: Case Studies of Social Forestry in Bangladesh. Niaz A. Khan. LC 98-71400. (Studies in Green Research). 368p. 1998. text 72.95 (*1-84014-573-0*, Pub. by Ashgate Pub) Ashgate Pub Co.

Political Economy of Forest Use & Management. M. V. Nadkarni et al. 184p. (C). 1989. text 22.50 (*0-8039-9591-1*) Sage.

Political Economy of Freedom: Essays in Honor of F. A. Hayek. W. W. Bartley, III et al. Ed. by Kurt R. Leube & Albert H. Zlabinger. (International Carl Menger Library). 320p. 1985. 52.00 (*3-88405-057-5*) Philosophia Pr.

Political Economy of Full Employment: Conservationism, Corporatism & Institutional Change. Ed. by Philip Arestis & Mike Marshall. 296p. 1995. 95.00 (*1-85278-880-1*) E Elgar.

Political Economy of German Unification. Ed. by Thomas Lange & J. R. Shackleton. LC 97-28863. 192p. 1997. 45.00 (*1-57181-880-4*) Berghahn Bks.

Political Economy of Germany in the 20th Century. Karl Hardach. LC 78-64754. 240p. 1980. pap. 15.95 (*0-520-04023-6*, Pub. by U CA Pr) Cal Prin Full Svc.

Political Economy of Global Energy. R. K. Pachauri. LC 84-21825. (Illus.). 207p. reprint ed. pap. 64.20 (*0-608-06112-3*, 206644500008) Bks Demand.

Political Economy of Global Restructuring Vol. 1: Economic Organization & Production. Ed. by Ingrid H. Rima. LC 93-12027. 256p. 1993. 85.00 (*1-85278-638-8*) E Elgar.

Political Economy of Globalization. Ed. by Satya D. Gupta. LC 97-5090. (Illus.). 344p. 1997. lib. bdg. 121.00 (*0-7923-9903-X*) Kluwer Academic.

***Political Economy of Globalization.** Ngaire Woods. LC 99-86149. 2000. text 65.00 (*0-312-23319-1*) St Martin.

Political Economy of Government Debt. Ed. by Frans A. Van Winden & Harrie A. Verbon. LC 93-14167. (Contributions to Economic Analysis Ser.: Vol. 219). 340p. 1993. 98.50 (*0-444-89052-1*, North Holland) Elsevier.

Political Economy of Growth. Paul A. Baran. LC 57-7953. 352p. 1968. pap. 15.00 (*0-85345-076-5*, Pub. by Monthly Rev) NYU Pr.

Political Economy of Growth. Ed. by Dennis C. Mueller. LC 81-15955. (Illus.). 292p. reprint ed. pap. 90.60 (*0-7837-5197-4*, 205768100006) Bks Demand.

Political Economy of Gunnar Myrdal: An Institutional Basis for the Transformation Problem. James Angresano. LC 97-12121. 224p. 1997. 85.00 (*1-85898-530-7*) E Elgar.

Political Economy of Health. Lesley Doyal & Pennell. (C). pap. 19.95 (*0-86104-074-0*, Pub. by Pluto GBR) Stylus Pub VA.

Political Economy of Health Care Development & Reforms in Hong Kong. Victor C. Wong. LC 98-74643. (Social & Political Studies from Hong Kong). 21p. 1999. text 74.95 (*1-84014-868-3*, Pub. by Ashgate Pub) Ashgate Pub Co.

Political Economy of Health in Africa. Ed. by Toyin Falola & Dennis Ityavyar. LC 91-39117. (Monographs in International Studies, Africa: No. 60A). 258p. (Orig.). (C). 1991. pap. text 20.00 (*0-89680-168-3*) Ohio U Pr.

Political Economy of Hope & Fear: Capitalism & the Black Condition in America. Marcellus Andrews. LC 98-58107. 1999. 29.95 (*0-8147-0679-7*) NYU Pr.

***Political Economy of Housing & Urban Development in Africa: Ghana's Experience from Colonial Times to 1998.** Kwadwo Konadu-Agyemang. LC 00-29846. 272p. 2000. 62.00 (*0-275-97003-5*, Praeger Pubs) Greenwood.

Political Economy of Human Rights Vol. 1: The Washington Connection & Third World Fascism, Vol. 1. Noam Chomsky & Edward S. Herman. 441p. write for info. (*0-919618-89-8*); pap. write for info. (*0-919618-88-X*) Black Rose.

Political Economy of Human Rights Vol. 2: After the Cataclysm: Postwar Indochina & the Reconstruction of Imperial Ideology, Vol. 2. Noam Chomsky & Edward S. Herman. 392p. write for info. (*0-919618-91-X*); pap. write for info. (*0-919618-90-1*) Black Rose.

Political Economy of Human Service Programs. David M. Austin. Ed. by Judith A. Levy. LC 88-9043. (Contemporary Studies in Applied Behavioral Science: Vol. 5). 257p. 1988. 73.25 (*0-89232-958-0*) Jai Pr.

Political Economy of Hunger. Jean Dreze & Amartya K. Sen. (WIDER Studies in Development Economics). (Illus.). 642p. 1995. pap. text 24.00 (*0-19-828883-2*) OUP.

Political Economy of Hunger: The Silent Holocaust. George Kent. LC 84-18281. 176p. 1984. 52.95 (*0-275-91206-X*, Praeger Pubs) Greenwood.

Political Economy of Hunger Vol. 1: Entitlement & Well-Being. Ed. by Jean Dreze & Amartya K. Sen. (WIDER Studies in Development Economics). (Illus.). 512p. 1991. text 79.00 (*0-19-828635-X*) OUP.

Political Economy of Hunger Vol. 2: Famine Prevention. Ed. by Jean Dreze & Amartya K. Sen. (WIDER Studies in Development Economics). (Illus.). 420p. 1991. text 69.00 (*0-19-828636-8*) OUP.

Political Economy of Hunger Vol. 3: Endemic Hunger. Ed. by Jean Dreze & Amartya K. Sen. (WIDER Studies in Development Economics). (Illus.). 408p. 1991. text 75.00 (*0-19-828637-6*, 12216) OUP.

Political Economy of Imperialism: Critical Appraisals. Ronald H. Chilcote. LC 99-12023. (Recent Economic Thought Ser.). 1999. write for info. (*0-7923-8470-9*) Kluwer Academic.

Political Economy of Income Distribution in Egypt. Ed. by Robert L. Tignor & Goudal Abdel-Khalek. LC 80-26932. (Political Economy of Income Distribution in Developing Countries Ser.: Vol. I). 525p. (C). 1982. 85.00 (*0-8419-0633-5*) Holmes & Meier.

Political Economy of Income Distribution in Mexico. Ed. by Henry S. Bienen et al. (Political Economy of Income Distribution in Developing Countries Ser.: Vol. IV). 562p. 1984. 85.00 (*0-8419-0907-5*) Holmes & Meier.

Political Economy of Income Distribution in Nigeria. Ed. by Henry S. Bienen & V. P. Diejomaoh. LC 80-16860. (Political Economy of Income Distribution in Developing Countries Ser.). 520p. 1981. 85.00 (*0-8419-0618-1*) Holmes & Meier.

Political Economy of Income Distribution in Turkey. Ed. by Ergun Ozbudun & Aydin Ulusan. LC 79-2781. (Political Economy of Income Distribution in Developing Countries Ser.: Vol. III). 1980. 85.00 (*0-8419-0563-0*) Holmes & Meier.

***Political Economy of Independent Ukraine.** Hans van Zon. LC 00-36911. 2000. write for info. (*0-312-23593-3*) St Martin.

Political Economy of Indian Agriculture. Ashok Rudra. (C). 1992. 28.50 (*0-685-61702-5*, Pub. by KP Bagchi) S Asia.

Political Economy of Indian Sugar: State Intervention & Structural Change. Sanjaya Baru. 240p. 1990. 21.00 (*0-19-562423-8*) OUP.

Political Economy of India's Public Sector: Policy & Performance. Baldev R. Nayar. 1990. 48.50 (*0-86132-264-9*, Pub. by Popular Prakashan) S Asia.

Political Economy of Industrial Democracies. Douglas A. Hibbs. LC 86-9799. 339p. 1987. reprint ed. pap. 105.10 (*0-7837-6072-8*, 205911800007) Bks Demand.

Political Economy of Industrial Policy. Wyn Grant. LC 82-145987. xii, 160p. 1982. write for info. (*0-408-10765-0*) Buttrwrth-Heinemann.

Political Economy of Industrial Policy in East Asia: The Semiconductor Industry in Taiwan & South Korea. Sung G. Hong. LC 97-24224. 208p. 1997. 75.00 (*1-85898-520-X*) E Elgar.

Political Economy of Industrial Promotion: Indian, Brazilian, & Korean Electronics in Comparative Perspective 1969-1994. Eswaran Sridharan. LC 95-43766. 256p. 1996. 67.95 (*0-275-95418-8*, Praeger Pubs) Greenwood.

Political Economy of Industrialisation: From Self-Reliance to Globalisation. Dalip S. Swamy. LC 93-34796. (Illus.). 320p. (C). 1993. text 36.00 (*0-8039-9473-7*) Sage.

***Political Economy of Inequality.** Frank Ackerman. LC 99-48264. (Frontier Issues in Economic Thought Ser.). 2000. pap. write for info. (*1-55963-786-2*) Island Pr.

***Political Economy of Inequality.** Ed. by Kevin Gallagher et al. (Frontier Issues in Economic Thought Ser.). 448p. 2000. 60.00 (*1-55963-797-8*); pap. 35.00 (*1-55963-798-6*) Island Pr.

Political Economy of Inflation in the United States. Paul Peretz. LC 82-24738. 264p. 1993. lib. bdg. 30.00 (*0-226-65671-3*) U Ch Pr.

Political Economy of Inflation in the United States. Paul Peretz. LC 82-24738. 280p. 1996. pap. text 17.00 (*0-226-65672-1*) U Ch Pr.

Political Economy of Information. Ed. by Vincent Mosco & Janet Wasko. LC 87-40369. (Studies in Communication & Society). 368p. (C). 1988. pap. text 12.95 (*0-299-11574-7*) U of Wis Pr.

***Political Economy of Integration in the European Union.** 3rd ed. Jeffrey Harrop. LC 99-49222. 360p. 2000. 100.00 (*1-84064-099-5*); pap. 30.00 (*1-84064-114-2*) E Elgar.

Political Economy of International & Domestic Monetary Relations. Ed. by Raymond E. Lombra & Willard E. Witte. LC 82-15320. (Illus.). 374p. 1982. reprint ed. pap. 116.00 (*0-608-00166-X*, 206094800006) Bks Demand.

Political Economy of International Co-Operation. Ed. by Paolo Guerrieri & Pier C. Padoan. 272p. 1988. lib. bdg. 57.50 (*0-318-35458-6*, Pub. by C Helm) Routldge.

Political Economy of International Communications: International & European Dimensions. Ed. by Kenneth H. Dyson & Peter Humphreys. 320p. (C). (gr. 13). 1990. text 85.00 (*0-415-03794-8*, A5552) Routledge.

Political Economy of International Debt: What, Who, How Much, & Why? Michael H. Bouchet. LC 87-2474. 238p. 1987. 67.95 (*0-89930-185-1*, BTP/, Quorum Bks) Greenwood.

Political Economy of International Environmental Cooperation. Changhua Sun Rich et al. Ed. by Alan Richards. (Policy Papers Ser.: Vol. 29). 99p. (Orig.). (C). 1997. pap. 3.50 (*0-934637-45-8*) U of CA Inst Global.

Political Economy of International Financial Instability. Pier C. Padoan. 240p. 1986. 45.00 (*0-7099-4003-3*, Pub. by C Helm) Routldge.

Political Economy of International Labour Migration. Hassan N. Gardezi. 210p. 1995. 48.99 (*1-55164-017-1*, Pub. by Black Rose); pap. 19.99 (*1-55164-016-3*, Pub. by Black Rose) Consort Bk Sales.

Political Economy of International Oil. George Philip. (Commodities in the International Economy Ser.). 256p. 1994. 60.00 (*0-7486-0490-1*, Pub. by Edinburgh U Pr) Col U Pr.

***Political Economy of International Reform & Reconstruction, Vol. 3.** Ludwig Von Mises & Richard M. Ebeling. LC 99-16126. 2000. 19.00 (*0-86597-270-2*); pap. 12.00 (*0-86597-271-0*) Liberty Fund.

Political Economy of International Relations. Robert Gilpin. 432p. 1987. pap. text 17.95 (*0-691-02262-3*, Pub. by Princeton U Pr) Cal Prin Full Svc.

Political Economy of International Shipping in Developing Countries. Okechukwu C. Iheduru. LC 95-22392. 304p. 1996. 46.50 (*0-87413-552-4*) U Delaware Pr.

Political Economy of International Technology Transfer. Ed. by John R. McIntyre & Daniel S. Papp. LC 85-28128. (Illus.). 280p. 1986. 72.95 (*0-89930-128-2*, MYP/, Quorum Bks) Greenwood.

Political Economy of Iran under the Shah. M. M. Malek. 288p. 1987. 42.00 (*0-7099-3519-6*, Pub. by C Helm) Routldge.

Political Economy of Israel. Ira Sharkansky. 224p. 1986. 39.95 (*0-88738-117-0*) Transaction Pubs.

Political Economy of Israel: From Ideology to Stagnation. Yakir Plessner. LC 93-203. (SUNY Series in Israeli Studies). 328p. (C). 1993. text 64.50 (*0-7914-1741-7*); pap. text 21.95 (*0-7914-1742-5*) State U NY Pr.

Political Economy of James Buchanan. Ed. by David Reisman. LC 89-4435. (Economics Ser.: No. 10). 216p. 1990. 39.50 (*0-89096-430-0*) Tex A&M Univ Pr.

***Political Economy of Japan.** Gordon Cheung. 1999. write for info. (*981-210-109-8*, Pub. by Times Academic) Intl Spec Bk.

Political Economy of Japan: Cultural & Social Dynamics, Vol. 3. Ed. by Shumpei Kumon & Henry Rosovsky. 540p. (C). 1992. 57.50 (*0-8047-1991-8*); pap. 19.95 (*0-8047-1992-6*) Stanford U Pr.

Political Economy of Japan Vol. 1: The Domestic Transformation. Ed. by Kozo Yamamura & Yasukichi Yasuba. LC 86-30037. 696p. 1987. 59.50 (*0-8047-1380-4*); pap. 19.95 (*0-8047-1381-2*) Stanford U Pr.

Political Economy of Japan Vol. 2: The Changing International Context. Ed. by Takashi Inoguchi & Daniel I. Okimoto. LC 86-30037. 592p. 1988. pap. 19.95 (*0-8047-1481-9*) Stanford U Pr.

Political Economy of Japanese & Asian Development. S. Ichimura. (Illus.). xvi, 292p. 1998. 79.95 (*4-431-70220-2*) Spr-Verlag.

Political Economy of Japanese Foreign Direct Investment in the U. K. & the U. S. Multinationals, Subnational Regions & the Investment Location Decision. Carl Aaron. LC 97-44367. (St. Antony's Ser.). 256p. 1998. text 69.95 (*0-312-21314-X*) St Martin.

Political Economy of Japanese Monetary Policy. Thomas F. Cargill et al. LC 97-3717. 248p. 1997. 35.50 (*0-262-03247-3*) MIT Pr.

Political Economy of Japanese Money. Shigeo Nakao. 215p. 1995. 48.00 (*0-86008-507-4*, Pub. by U of Tokyo) Col U Pr.

Political Economy of Japanese Society: Internationalization & Domestic Issues, Vol. 2. Ed. by Junji Banno. (The Political Economy of Japanese Society Ser.). (Illus.). 382p. 1998. text 85.00 (*0-19-828034-3*) OUP.

Political Economy of Japanese Society: The State or the Market?, Vol. 1. Ed. by Junji Banno. LC 97-23116. (The Political Economy of Japanese Society Ser.). (Illus.). 376p. 1998. text 90.00 (*0-19-828033-5*) OUP.

Political Economy of Kenya. Ed. by Michael G. Schatzberg. LC 87-22889. 253p. 1987. 65.00 (*0-275-92672-9*, C2672, Praeger Pubs) Greenwood.

***Political Economy of Labour Market Institutions.** Gilles Saint-Paul. (Illus.). 272p. 2000. text 60.00 (*0-19-829332-1*) OUP.

Political Economy of Large Natural Disasters: With Special Reference to Developing Countries. J. M. Albala-Bertrand. LC 92-28248. (Illus.). 272p. 1993. text 65.00 (*0-19-828765-8*, Clarendon Pr) OUP.

Political Economy of Latin American Development: 7 Exercises in Retrospection. Albert O. Hirschman. (Co-Publications: No. 3). 57p. (Orig.). (C). 1986. ring bd. 7.50 (*0-935391-64-9*, CE-03) UCSD Ctr US-Mex.

Political Economy of Latin American in the Postwar Period. Ed. by Laura Randall. LC 97-34275. (Critical Reflections on Latin America Ser.). (Illus.). 288p. 1997. 30.00 (*0-292-77086-3*); pap. 15.95 (*0-292-77083-9*) U of Tex Pr.

***Political Economy of Legal Information: The New Landscape.** Ed. by Samuel E. Trosow. LC 99-31546. (Legal Reference Services Quarterly Ser.: Vol. 17, Nos. 1/2). 200p. (C). 1999. 39.95 (*0-7890-0764-9*) Haworth Pr.

Political Economy of Market Reform in Jordan. Timothy J. Piro. LC 98-24370. 152p. 1998. 54.00 (*0-8476-8881-X*); pap. 19.95 (*0-8476-8882-8*) Rowman.

Political Economy of Medicine: Great Britain & the United States. Joseph R. Hollingsworth. LC 86-2720. 333p. 1986. reprint ed. pap. 103.30 (*0-608-03703-6*, 206452800009) Bks Demand.

Political Economy of Merchant Empires: State Power & World Trade, 1350-1750. Ed. by James D. Tracy. (Illus.). 512p. (C). 1991. text 80.00 (*0-521-41046-0*) Cambridge U Pr.

Political Economy of Merchant Empires: State Power & World Trade, 1350-1750. Ed. by James D. Tracy. (Studies in Comparative Early Modern History). (Illus.). 512p. 1997. pap. text 20.95 (*0-521-57464-1*) Cambridge U Pr.

Political Economy of Mexican Oil. Laura Randall. LC 89-16099. 238p. 1989. 59.95 (*0-275-93372-5*, C3372, Praeger Pubs) Greenwood.

Political Economy of Mexico, Two Studies. William P. Glade & Charles W. Anderson. LC 63-10531. 254p. reprint ed. pap. 78.80 (*0-8357-6771-X*, 203544600095) Bks Demand.

Political Economy of Mexico under de la Madrid: The Crisis Deepens, 1985-1986. Wayne A. Cornelius. (Research Reports: No. 43). 50p. (Orig.). (C). 1986. pap. 5.00 (*0-935391-65-7*, RR-43) UCSD Ctr US-Mex.

Political Economy of Middle East Peace: The Impact of Competing Arab & Israeli Trade. Ed. by J. W. Wright, Jr. (Frontiers of Political Economy Ser.: No. 19). 256p. (C). (gr. 13). 1999. 85.00 (*0-415-18395-2*, D5997) Routledge.

Political Economy of Modern Britain. Andrew Cox et al. LC 96-48952. 288p. 1997. 90.00 (*1-85278-411-3*) E Elgar.

Political Economy of Modern Britain. Andrew Cox et al. LC 96-48952. 288p. 1998. pap. text 30.00 (*1-85898-616-8*) E Elgar.

Political Economy of Modern Spain: Policy-Making in an Authoritarian System. Charles W. Anderson. LC 72-106036. 296p. reprint ed. pap. 91.80 (*0-7837-7019-7*, 204683500004) Bks Demand.

***Political Economy of Monetary Union.** Malcolm Levitt & Christopher Lord. LC 99-88066. 2000. write for info. (*0-312-23189-X*) St Martin.

Political Economy of Monetary Union: Towards the Euro. Francesco Giordano & Sharda Persaud. LC 97-29026. 256p. (C). 1998. 85.00 (*0-415-17442-2*) Routledge.

Political Economy of Money: Emerging Fiat Monetary Regime. George Macesich. LC 99-17922. 152p. 1999. 49.95 (*0-275-96572-4*) Greenwood.

Political Economy of Monopoly: Business, Labor, & Government Policies. Fritz Machlup. LC 53-6338. 560p. reprint ed. pap. 173.60 (*0-8357-8274-3*, 203412100088) Bks Demand.

Political Economy of Morocco: A SAIS Study on Africa. Ed. by I. William Zartman. LC 87-6955. 278p. 1987. 65.00 (*0-275-92593-5*, C2593, Praeger Pubs) Greenwood.

Political Economy of Mountain Java: An Interpretive History. Robert W. Hefner. LC 89-49222. (Illus.). 352p. 1990. 45.00 (*0-520-06933-1*, Pub. by U CA Pr); pap. 17.95 (*0-520-08269-9*, Pub. by U CA Pr) Cal Prin Full Svc.

Political Economy of Namibia: An Annotated Critical Bibliography. 2nd ed. Tore L. Eriksen & Richard Moorsom. (Scandinavian Institute of African Studies). 370p. 1989. 53.50 (*91-7106-297-1*) Coronet Bks.

Political Economy of National Security. Ethan B. Kapstein. 288p. (C). 1991. 32.81 (*0-07-034256-3*) McGraw.

Political Economy of Nationalisation in Britain, 1920-50. Ed. by Robert E. Millward & John Singleton. (Illus.). 339p. (C). 1995. text 64.95 (*0-521-45096-9*) Cambridge U Pr.

Political Economy of NATO: Past, Present, & into the 21st Century. Todd Sandler. LC 98-39564. (Illus.). 292p. (C). 1999. pap. 22.95 (*0-521-63880-1*) Cambridge U Pr.

Political Economy of NATO: Past, Present, & into the 21st Century. Todd Sandler & Keith Hartley. LC 98-39564. (Illus.). 250p. (C). 1999. text 69.95 (*0-521-63093-2*) Cambridge U Pr.

Political Economy of Neotribal Capitalism. Elizabeth Rata. LC 99-28297. 288p. 2000. 65.00 (*0-7391-0068-8*) Lxngtn Bks.

Political Economy Of New Labou. Hay. 1999. text 72.95 (*0-7190-5481-8*) St Martin.

***Political Economy of New Labour: Labouring under False Pretences?** Colin Hay. 1999. pap. text 24.95 (*0-7190-5482-6*, Pub. by Manchester Univ Pr) St Martin.

Political Economy of New Zealand. 2nd ed. Ed. by Chris Rudd & Brian Roper. LC 97-200086. (Illus.). 324p. 1997. pap. text 45.00 (*0-19-558331-0*) OUP.

Political Economy of Nicaragua. Rose J. Spalding. (Thematic Studies in Latin America). 256p. (C). 1986. text 44.95 (*0-04-497014-5*); pap. text 15.95 (*0-04-497015-3*) Routledge.

Political Economy of Nonalignment: Indonesia & Malaysia. Kalyani Bandyopadhyaya. (C). 1990. 24.00 (*81-7003-113-3*, Pub. by S Asia Pubs) S Asia.

Political Economy of North American Indians. John H. Moore. LC 92-50719. 320p. 1993. 29.95 (*0-8061-2505-5*) U of Okla Pr.

Political Economy of North-South Relations. Toivo Miljan. 712p. 1987. pap. 29.95 (*0-921149-11-5*) Broadview Pr.

Political Economy of Pan African Nationalism: Historical Origins & Contemporary Forms. Linus A. Hoskins. (International Affairs Ser.). 57p. (Orig.). 1987. pap. 4.95 (*0-939841-00-2*) Pyramid MD.

Political Economy of Participation in Local Development Programs: Short-Term Impasse & Long-Term Change in South Asia & the United States from the 1950s to the 1970s. Harry W. Blair. (Monograph). 180p. (Orig.). 1981. pap. text 10.65 (*0-86731-055-3*) Cornell CIS RDC.

Political Economy of Participatory Socialism. Michael Albert & Robin Hahnel. 176p. 1990. text 55.00 (*0-691-04274-8*, Pub. by Princeton U Pr) Cal Prin Full Svc.

***Political Economy of Pension Reform in Central-Eastern Europe.** Katharina Muller. LC 99-44830. (Studies in Comparative Economic Systems). 240p. 2000. 80.00 (*1-84064-238-6*) E Elgar.

Political Economy of Peru, Nineteen Fifty-Six to Nineteen Seventy-Eight: Economic Development & the Restructuring of Capital. Edmund Fitzgerald. LC 78-72086. 372p. reprint ed. pap. 106.10 (*0-608-15721-X*, 2031649) Bks Demand.

Political Economy of Policy Coordination: International Adjustment since 1945. Michael C. Webb. (Studies in Political Economy). 256p. 1995. text 39.95 (*0-8014-2929-3*) Cornell U Pr.

Political Economy of Policy-Making: Essays in Honor of Will E. Mason. Ed. by Michael P. Dooley et al. LC 78-25960. (Comparative Political Economy & Public Policy Ser.: Vol. 4). (Illus.). 248p. reprint ed. pap. 76.90 (*0-608-10733-6*, 202188900026) Bks Demand.

Political Economy of Policy Reform. Ed. by John Williamson. 601p. 1994. pap. text 25.00 (*0-88132-195-8*) Inst Intl Eco.

Political Economy of Policy Reform in Developing Countries. Anne O. Krueger. LC 92-41790. (Ohlin Lectures). (Illus.). 183p. 1993. 27.50 (*0-262-11178-0*) MIT Pr.

Political Economy of Population Ageing. William A. Jackson. LC 97-39375. 256p. 1998. 85.00 (*1-85278-692-2*) E Elgar.

Political Economy of Post-Cold War Africa. Aloy Chife. LC 97-2366. (Studies in African Economic & Social Development: Vol. 9). 264p. 1997. pap. 89.95 (*0-7734-8683-6*) E Mellen.

***Political Economy of Post-Soviet Russia.** V. I. Tikhomirov. LC 99-53112. 2000. text 65.00 (*0-312-23086-9*) St Martin.

Political Economy of Postwar Reconstruction. Peter Burnham. LC 91-164362. xiv, 228 p. 1990. write for info. (*0-333-48289-1*) Macmillan.

Political Economy of Poverty, Equity, & Growth: A Comparative Study. Deepak Lal & H. Myint. (Illus.). 476p. 1999. reprint ed. pap. text 24.95 (*0-19-829432-8*) OUP.

Political Economy of Poverty, Equity, & Growth: Costa Rica & Uruguay. Ed. by Simon Rottenberg. (Comparative Study Ser.). (Illus.). 440p. 1993. text 49.95 (*0-19-520883-8*, 60883) OUP.

Political Economy of Poverty, Equity, & Growth: Egypt & Turkey. Bent Hansen. (World Bank Publications). (Illus.). 592p. 1992. text 55.00 (*0-19-520825-0*, 60825) OUP.

Political Economy of Poverty, Equity & Growth: Five Small Open Economies. Ronald Findlay & Stanislaw Wellisz. (World Bank Comparative Study Ser.). (Illus.). 352p. (C). 1993. text 55.00 (*0-19-520880-3*, 60880) OUP.

***Political Economy of Poverty, Equity & Growth: Nigeria & Indonesia.** David Bevan et al. (A World Bank Publication). 432p. 1999. 60.00 (*0-19-520986-9*) OUP.

Political Economy of Power: Hegemony & Economic Liberalism. Anthony T. Gadzey. LC 93-34314. (International Political Economy Ser.). 1994. text 49.95 (*0-312-12019-2*) St Martin.

Political Economy of Power: Hegemony & Economic Liberalism. Anthony Tuo-Kofi Gadzey. (International Political Economy Ser.). 216p. 1996. pap. 19.95 (*0-312-16416-5*) St Martin.

Political Economy of Privatization & Deregulation. Ed. by Elizabeth E. Bailey & Janet R. Peck. (International Library of Critical Writings in Economics: Vol. 44). 672p. 1995. 270.00 (*1-85278-831-3*) E Elgar.

Political Economy of Progressive Taxation. Ed. by Dieter Bos & Bernhard Felderer. (Illus.). ix, 220p. 1989. 74.95 (*0-387-51554-2*) Spr-Verlag.

Political Economy of Property Rights. Ed. by David L. Weimer. LC 96-36258. (Political Economy of Institutions & Decisions Ser.). 380p. 1997. text 64.95 (*0-521-58101-X*) Cambridge U Pr.

Political Economy of Prosperity. Arthur M. Okun. LC 76-108835. 122p. 1970. 19.95 (*0-8157-6478-2*) Brookings.

Political Economy of Protection, Vol. 32. A. L. Hillman. viii, 172p. 1989. pap. text 75.00 (*3-7186-4873-3*) Gordon & Breach.

Political Economy of Protest & Patience: East European & Latin American Transformations Compared. Bela Greskovits. LC 98-34528. (Illus.). 320p. (C). 1998. 49.95 (*963-9116-14-9*); pap. 21.95 (*963-9116-13-0*) Ctrl Europ Univ.

Political Economy of Public Administration: Institutional Choice in the Public Sector. Murray J. Horn. (Political Economy of Institutions & Decisions Ser.). 275p. (C). 1995. text 64.95 (*0-521-48201-1*); pap. text 22.95 (*0-521-48436-7*) Cambridge U Pr.

Political Economy of Public Distribution of Food in India. Kamal N. Kalra. 1990. 37.00 (*81-202-0273-2*, Pub. by Ajanta) S Asia.

Political Economy of Race & Class in South Africa. Bernard M. Magubane. LC 78-13917. 364p. 1980. pap. 18.00 (*0-85345-506-6*, Pub. by Monthly Rev) NYU Pr.

Political Economy of Racism: A History. Leiman. LC 92-8518. 421p. (C). 63.00 (*0-7453-0488-5*, Pub. by Pluto GBR); pap. 18.95 (*0-7453-0487-7*, Pub. by Pluto GBR) Stylus Pub VA.

Political Economy of Reform. Ed. by Federico Sturzenegger & Mariano Tommasi. LC 97-46390. (Illus.). 389p. 1998. 47.50 (*0-262-19400-7*) MIT Pr.

Political Economy of Reform & Change: A Case of Eastern Europe. Jan Winiecki. LC 97-30123. 237p. (C). 1997. lib. bdg. 75.00 (*1-56072-449-8*) Nova Sci Pubs.

Political Economy of Reform in Post-Mao China. Ed. by Christine P. Wong. (Harvard Contemporary China Ser.: No. 2). 352p. 1985. pap. 18.00 (*0-674-68590-3*) HUP.

Political Economy of Regional Co-Operation: Comparative Case Studies. Ed. by Andrew Axline. 256p. 1994. 90.00 (*1-85567-190-5*) Bks Intl VA.

Political Economy of Regional Cooperation in the Middle East. Carko Glu Ali et al. LC 98-17666. 272p. (C). 1998. 100.00 (*0-415-19445-8*) Routledge.

Political Economy of Regional Corporation: Comparative Case Studies. W. Andrew Axline. LC 94-20226. 256p. 1994. 39.50 (*0-8386-3608-X*) Fairleigh Dickinson.

Political Economy of Regionalism. Ed. by Michael Keating & John Loughlin. LC 96-20554. (Regional & Federal Studies). 504p. (C). 1997. 57.50 (*0-7146-4658-X*, Pub. by F Cass Pubs); pap. 27.50 (*0-7146-4187-1*, Pub. by F Cass Pubs) Intl Spec Bk.

Political Economy of Regionalism. Edward D. Mansfield & Helen V. Milner. LC 96-54832. (New Directions in World Politics Ser.). 1997. 47.50 (*0-231-10662-9*); pap. 19.50 (*0-231-10663-7*) Col U Pr.

Political Economy of Regionalism in Africa: The Case of the Economic Community of West African States. S. K. Asante. LC 85-16740. 286p. 1985. 69.50 (*0-275-90194-7*, C0194, Praeger Pubs) Greenwood.

Political Economy of Regulation: The Case of Insurance. Kenneth J. Meier. LC 87-33769. (SUNY Series in Public Administration). (Illus.). 230p. (C). 1988. pap. text 24.95 (*0-88706-732-8*) State U NY Pr.

Political Economy of Regulation: The Case of Insurance. Kenneth J. Meier. LC 87-33769. (SUNY Series in Public Administration). (Illus.). 230p. (C). 1988. text 74.50 (*0-88706-731-X*) State U NY Pr.

Political Economy of Rent Seeking. Ed. by Charles K. Rowley et al. 1988. lib. bdg. 192.50 (*0-89838-241-6*) Kluwer Academic.

Political Economy of Risk & Choice in Senegal. Ed. by Mark Gersovitz & John Waterbury. 370p. 1986. 54.50 (*0-7146-3297-X*, Pub. by F Cass Pubs) Intl Spec Bk.

Political Economy of Romanian Socialism. William E. Crowther. LC 87-29244. 212p. 1988. 65.00 (*0-275-92840-3*, C2840, Praeger Pubs) Greenwood.

Political Economy of Rural Development in China, 1978-1999. Weixing Chen. LC 99-15397. 192p. 1999. 55.00 (*0-275-96687-9*) Greenwood.

***Political Economy of Russian Oil.** David Lane. LC 99-15556. 240p. 1999. text 69.00 (*0-8476-9508-5*) Rowman.

***Political Economy of Russian Oil.** David S. Lane. LC 99-15556. 240p. 1999. pap. text 29.95 (*0-8476-9509-3*) Rowman.

Political Economy of Sanctions Against Apartheid. Haider Ali Khan. LC 89-34521. 120p. 1989. lib. bdg. 26.50 (*1-55587-145-3*) L Rienner.

Political Economy of Schooling. John Freeland. 129p. (C). 1986. 65.00 (*0-7300-0432-5*, Pub. by Deakin Univ) St Mut.

Political Economy of Science, Technology & Innovation. Ed. by Ben R. Martin & Paul Nightingale. LC 99-53193. 736p. 2000. 265.00 (*1-85898-961-2*) E Elgar.

Political Economy of Senegal under Structural Adjustment. Ed. by Christopher L. Delgado & Sidi Jammeh. LC 90-40946. 232p. 1991. 59.95 (*0-275-93525-6*, C3525, Praeger Pubs) Greenwood.

Political Economy of Shopkeeping in Milan, 1886-1922. Jonathan Morris. (Past & Present Publications). (Illus.). 328p. (C). 1993. text 69.95 (*0-521-39119-9*) Cambridge U Pr.

Political Economy of Sino-American Relations: A Greater Chinese Perspective. Ed. by Y. Y. Kueh. LC 98-156604. 368p. (Orig.). 1997. pap. 45.00 (*962-209-440-6*, Pub. by HK Univ Pr) Coronet Bks.

Political Economy of Slavery: Studies in Economy & Society of the Slave South. Eugene D. Genovese. 1967. pap. 7.16 (*0-394-70400-2*, V400) Vin Bks.

Political Economy of Slavery: Studies in the Economy & Society of the Slave South. 2nd rev. ed. Eugene D. Genovese. LC 89-5607. 368p. 1989. pap. text 19.95 (*0-8195-6208-4*, Wesleyan Univ Pr) U Pr of New Eng.

Political Economy of Small States. Anand Aditya. 1997. pap. 30.00 (*0-7855-7482-4*, Pub. by Ratna Pustak Bhandar) St Mut.

Political Economy of Small Tropical Islands: The Importance of Being Small. Ed. by Helen Hintjens & Newitt. 269p. 1992. text 62.00 (*0-85989-372-3*, Pub. by Univ Exeter Pr) Northwestern U Pr.

Political Economy of Smog in Southern California. Jeffry Fawcett. LC 90-45456. (Environment: Problems & Solutions Ser.). 239p. 1990. text 20.00 (*0-8240-2525-3*) Garland.

Political Economy of Social Control in Singapore. Christopher Tremewan. 260p. 1996. pap. 21.95 (*0-312-15865-3*) St Martin.

Political Economy of Social Credit & Guild Socialism. Frances Hutchinson & Brian Burkitt. LC 97-6276. (Illus.). 208p. (C). 1997. 80.00 (*0-415-14709-3*) Routledge.

Political Economy of Social Policy. A. J. Culyer. (Modern Revivals in Economics Ser.). 352p. 1992. 65.95 (*0-7512-0025-5*, Pub. by Gregg Revivals) Ashgate Pub Co.

Political Economy of Socialism: A Marxist Social Theory. Branko Horvat. LC 81-9430. (Illus.). 691p. 1982. reprint ed. pap. 200.00 (*0-7837-9946-2*, 206067300006) Bks Demand.

Political Economy of Soil Erosion in Developing Countries. Balaikie Piers. 1985. pap. text 30.95 (*0-582-30089-4*) Addison-Wesley.

Political Economy of South Africa. Ed. by Albert Venter. 164p. 1991. pap. text 10.95 (*0-943852-84-6*) Prof World Peace.

Political Economy of South Africa's Transition. Michie. (ITBP Reference Ser.). 1998. pap. 18.99 (*1-86152-455-2*) Thomson Learn.

Political Economy of South Korea. John Lie. LC 97-34019. 1998. 49.50 (*0-8047-3055-5*) Stanford U Pr.

Political Economy of Southeast-Asia: An Introduction. Ed. by Garry Rodan et al. LC HC441.P647 1997. (Illus.). 314p. 1998. pap. text 19.95 (*0-19-553736-X*) OUP.

Political Economy of Soviet Socialism: The Formative Years, 1918-1928. Peter J. Boettke. (C). 1990. lib. bdg. 118.50 (*0-7923-9100-4*) Kluwer Academic.

Political Economy of Special-Purpose Government. Kathryn A. Foster. LC 96-46603. (American Governance & Public Policy Ser.). 288p. 1999. reprint ed. pap. 22.95 (*0-87840-753-7*) Georgetown U Pr.

Political Economy of Special-Purpose Government. Kathryn A. Foster. Ed. by Barry Rabe & John Tierney. LC 96-46603. (American Governance & Public Policy Ser.). 288p. 1999. reprint ed. 55.00 (*0-87840-638-7*) Georgetown U Pr.

Political Economy of State Economic Development Programs. Robert Wilson. (Working Paper Ser.: No. 52). 38p. 1989. pap. 5.00 (*0-89940-533-9*) LBJ Sch Pub Aff.

Political Economy of Suppressed Markets: Controls, Rent Seeking & Interest-Group Behaviour in the Indian Sugar & Cement Industries. Shyam J. Kamath. (Illus.). 264p. 1993. text 32.00 (*0-19-562637-0*) OUP.

Political Economy of Syria under ASAD. Volker Perthes. 272p. 1995. text 65.00 (*1-85043-910-9*, Pub. by I B T) St Martin.

Political Economy of Syria under ASAD. Volker Perthes. 272p. 1997. text 19.95 (*1-86064-192-X*, Pub. by I B T) St Martin.

Political Economy of Taiwan's Development into the 21st Century Vol. 2: Essays in Memory of John C. H. Fei, Vol. 2. Ed. by Gustav Ranis et al. LC 98-49231. 360p. 1999. 95.00 (*1-85898-879-9*) E Elgar.

Political Economy of Tax Reform. Ed. by Takatoshi Ito & Anne O. Krueger. LC 92-9001. (National Bureau of Economic Research East Asia Seminar on Economics Ser.). (Illus.). x, 358p. 1992. 69.00 (*0-226-38667-8*) U Ch Pr.

Political Economy of Telecommunications Reform in Developing Countries: Privatization & Liberalization in Comparative Perspective. Ben A. Petrazzini. LC 95-7552. 248p. 1995. 65.00 (*0-275-95294-0*, Praeger Pubs) Greenwood.

***Political Economy of Telecommunications Reforms in Thailand.** Sakkarin Niyomsilpa Staff. LC 99-23340. 1999. 99.95 (*1-85567-541-2*) P P Pubs.

Political Economy of Texas. Bernard Weinstein & Harold T. Gross. 1992. write for info. (*1-56000-041-4*) Transaction Pubs.

Political Economy of the American Revolution. 2nd ed. Ed. by Nancy B. Spannaus & Christopher White. (Illus.). 450p. (C). 1996. pap. 15.00 (*0-943235-14-6*) Exec Intel Review.

Political Economy of the American West. Ed. by Terry L. Anderson & Peter J. Hill. 194p. (C). 1994. lib. bdg. 47.00 (*0-8476-7911-X*) Rowman.

***Political Economy of the Asian Financial Crisis.** Stephen Haggard. 165p. 2000. pap. 17.95 (*0-88132-283-0*) Inst Intl Eco.

The Asian crisis has sparked a thoroughgoing reappraisal of current international financial norms, the policy prescriptions of the International Monetary Fund & the adequacy of the existing financial architecture. To draw proper policy conclusions from the crisis, however, it is necessary to understand its domestic politics. In this study, political scientist Stephan Haggard focuses on the most seriously affected countries - Indonesia, Korea, Malaysia & Thailand - while also drawing lessons from those economies, such as Taiwan, that escaped the most severe distress. Haggard focuses on the political economy of the crisis, emphasizing the longer-run problems of moral hazard & corruption, the politics of crisis management & the political consequences if severe economic downturn. Looking forward, he focuses on two critical policy issues: changes in social safety nets in the crisis countries & efforts at corporate & financial restructuring.

Publisher Paid Annotation.

Political Economy of the Brazilian State, 1889-1930. Steven Topik. LC 87-5835. (Latin American Monographs: No. 71). (Illus.). 255p. reprint ed. pap. 79.10 (*0-8357-6736-1*, 203539200095) Bks Demand.

Political Economy of the Cotton South. Ed. by Gavin Wright. 205p. (C). 1978. pap. text 12.50 (*0-393-09038-8*) Norton.

Political Economy of the Educational Process. Richard B. McKenzie. (Studies in Public Choice: Vol. 2). 1979. lib. bdg. 97.50 (*0-89838-012-X*) Kluwer Academic.

Political Economy of the Environment. Ken Walker. LC 95-166285. 260p. 1994. pap. 32.95 (*0-86840-070-X*, Pub. by New South Wales Univ Pr) Intl Spec Bk.

Political Economy of the Family Farm: The Agrarian Roots of American Capitalism. Sue Headlee. LC 91-19354. (Praeger Series in Political Economy). 224p. 1991. 57.95 (*0-275-93806-9*, C3806, Praeger Pubs) Greenwood.

Political Economy of the Gulf States. Pradeep Bhargava. (C). 1988. 17.50 (*81-7003-098-6*, Pub. by S Asia Pubs) S Asia.

Political Economy of the Ivory Coast: An SAIS Study on Africa. Ed. by I. William Zartman & Christopher L. Delgado. LC 84-1998. 268p. 1984. 59.95 (*0-275-91295-7*, C1295, Praeger Pubs) Greenwood.

Political Economy of the Media, 2 vols. Ed. by Peter Golding & Graham Murdock. LC 96-35918. (International Library of Studies in Media & Culture: No. 2). 1424p. 1997. 480.00 (*1-85278-777-5*) E Elgar.

Political Economy of the Middle East. 2nd ed. Alan Richards & John Waterbury. LC 96-24374. 464p. (C). 1996. pap. text 35.00 (*0-8133-2411-4*, Pub. by Westview) HarpC.

***Political Economy of the Middle East, 6 Vol., Set.** Incl. Vol. I. Economic Development. 384p. 1999. 135.00 (*1-85898-935-3*); Vol. II. International Economic Relations. 320p. 1999. 110.00 (*1-85898-936-1*); Vol. III. Islamic Economics. 528p. 1999. 185.00 (*1-85898-937-X*); Vol. IV. Economic & Political Liberalisation. 384p. 1999. 135.00 (*1-85898-938-8*); Vol. V. Role of the State. 448p. 1999. 160.00 (*1-85898-939-6*); Vol. VI. Oil. 392p. 1999. 145.00 (*1-85898-940-X*); LC 99-34289. (Mini Ser.). 2432p. 1999. 870.00 (*1-85898-443-2*) E Elgar.

Political Economy of the Minimal State. Ed. by Charles K. Rowley. LC 95-40192. (Shaftesbury Papers). 348p. 1996. 95.00 (*1-85898-199-9*) E Elgar.

Political Economy of the New Asian Industrialism. Ed. by Frederic C. Deyo. LC 86-29103. (Cornell Studies in Political Economy). (Illus.). 254p. (C). 1987. pap. text 16.95 (*0-8014-9449-4*) Cornell U Pr.

Political Economy of the New Deal. Jim F. Couch & William F. Shughart, II. LC 98-27149. (Locke Institute Ser.). 264p. 1998. 85.00 (*1-85898-899-3*) E Elgar.

Political Economy of the New Right. Grahame Thompson. (Twayne's Themes in Right-Wing Politics & Ideology Ser.: No. 4). 250p. 1990. pap. 16.95 (*0-8057-9557-X*, Twyne); text 30.95 (*0-8057-9556-1*, Twyne) Mac Lib Ref.

Political Economy of the Peace Process in a Changing Middle East. LC 97-194193. (World Development Studies: No. 8). 82p. pap. 12.00 (*952-9520-34-4*) UN.

Political Economy of the Punjab: An Insider's Account. Pritam Singh. LC 99-931516. 332p. 1997. pap. 287.50 (*81-7533-031-7*, Pub. by Print Hse) St Mut.

Political Economy of the Sherman Act: The First 100 Years. Ed. by E. Thomas Sullivan. 344p. 1991. text 60.00 (*0-19-506642-1*) OUP.

P

An Asterisk (*) at the beginning of an entry indicates that the title is appearing for the first time.

Political Economy of the Social Sciences. Ed. by Frederick Gareau. LC 91-4357. (Library of Sociology: Vol. 19). 376p. 1991. text 25.00 (*0-8240-7267-7*, 699) Garland.

Political Economy of the Space Program. Mary A. Holman. LC 79-180902. (Science & Technology Management Ser.: No. 1). (Illus.). xviii, 398p. 1974. 34.95 (*0-87015-199-1*) Pacific Bks.

Political Economy of the State. Ed. by Dimitrios I. Roussopoulos. 196p. 1973. 35.99 (*0-919618-02-2*, Pub. by Black Rose); pap. 6.99 (*0-919618-01-4*, Pub. by Black Rose) Consort Bk Sales.

Political Economy of the Swiss National Bank. B. Jeitziner. LC 99-30480. (Contributions to Economics Ser.). (Illus.). xiv, 270p. 1999. pap. 67.00 (*3-7908-1209-9*) Spr-Verlag.

Political Economy of the Third World Countries. Ed. by Devendra Thakur. 212p. 1987. 34.95 (*81-7100-007-X*) Asia Bk Corp.

Political Economy of the Transition Process in Eastern Europe. Ed. by Laszlo Somogyi. 400p. 1993. 95.00 (*1-85278-857-7*) E Elgar.

Political Economy of the United States. Ed. by Mucciaroni. (C). 1998. text. write for info. (*0-321-01157-0*) Addson-Wesley Educ.

Political Economy of the Urban Ghetto. Daniel R. Fusfeld & Timothy Bates. LC 83-20424. (Political & Social Economy Ser.). 304p. 1984. pap. text 21.95 (*0-8093-1158-5*) S Ill U Pr.

Political Economy of the Welfare State. James Buchanan. 32p. (Orig.). 1988. pap. 17.50 (*91-7204-296-6*, Pub. by Industriens) Coronet Bks.

Political Economy of the World Trading System: From GATT to WTO. 2nd ed. Bernard Hoekman & Michel Kostecki. 416p. 1999. text 76.00 (*0-19-829434-4*) OUP.

Political Economy of the World Trading System: From GATT to WTO. 2nd ed. Bernard Hoekman & Michel Kostecki. 350p. 2000. pap. text 29.00 (*0-19-829431-X*) OUP.

Political Economy of Third World Intervention: Mines, Money, & U. S. Policy in the Congo Crisis. David N. Gibbs. LC 91-9798. (American Politics & Political Economy Ser.). (Illus.). 332p. 1991. 34.95 (*0-226-29071-9*) U Ch Pr.

Political Economy of Tourism in Africa. Ed. by Peter U. Dieke. (Tourism Dynamics Ser.). (C). 2000. 62.00 (*1-882345-26-6*); pap. text. write for info. (*1-882345-25-8*) Cognizant Comm.

Political Economy of Trade: Case Studies in U. S. Policy. Mark R. Eaker & Faith J. Rubenstein. LC 97-31791. 1997. 44.95 (*0-538-87517-8*) S-W Pub.

Political Economy of Trade & Growth: An Analytical Interpretation of Sir James Steuart's Inquiry. Hong-Seok Yang. 336p. 1994. 95.00 (*1-85898-093-3*) E Elgar.

Political Economy of Trade Conflicts: The Management of Trade Relations in the U.S.-EU-Japan Triad. Ed. by Franz Waldenberger. LC 94-31036. (Europe-Asia-Pacific Studies in Economy & Technology). 1994. 62.95 (*3-540-58395-5*) Spr-Verlag.

Political Economy of Trade Integration. O. Fratzscher. 181p. 1996. pap. 59.00 (*3-7908-0945-4*) Spr-Verlag.

Political Economy of Trade Policy: Papers in Honor of Jagdish Bhagwati. Ed. by Robert C. Feenstra et al. (Illus.). 320p. (C). 1996. 44.00 (*0-262-06186-4*) MIT Pr.

Political Economy of Trade Protection. Ed. by Anne O. Krueger. LC 95-4789. (National Bureau of Economic Research Project Report Ser.). 112p. 1995. 24.95 (*0-226-45491-6*) U Ch Pr.

Political Economy of Transformation. Ed. by H. J. Wagener. (Studies in Contemporary Economics). (Illus.). viii, 241p. 1994. 61.95 (*0-387-91475-7*) Spr-Verlag.

Political Economy of Transition: Coming to Grips with History & Methodology. Jozef M. Van Brabant. LC 97-31300. 416p. (C). 1998. 125.00 (*0-415-16946-1*) Routledge.

Political Economy of Transition in Central & Eastern Europe: The Light(s) at the End of the Tunnel. Ed. by Jens Bastian. LC 98-73760. 5p. 1998. text 59.95 (*1-85972-661-5*) Ashgate Pub Co.

Political Economy of Turkey in the Post-Soviet Era: Going West & Looking East? Ed. by Libby Rittenberg. LC 97-26174. 240p. 1998. 59.95 (*0-275-95596-6*, Praeger Pubs) Greenwood.

Political Economy of U. S. Agriculture: Challenges for the 1990s. Ed. by Carol S. Kramer. LC 89-13023. 285p. 1989. pap. 30.00 (*0-915707-49-7*) Resources Future.

Political Economy of U. S.-Taiwan Trade. Robert E. Baldwin et al. LC 95-13471. (Studies in International Trade Policy). 232p. 1995. text 75.00 (*0-472-10551-5*, 10551) U of Mich Pr.

Political Economy of U. S. Trade Policy. Keith Alger. LC 90-3611. (Foreign Economic Policy of the United States Ser.). 272p. 1990. reprint ed. text 10.00 (*0-8240-7467-X*) Garland.

Political Economy of under Development. T. Szentes. 432p. (C). 1988. pap. 72.00 (*963-05-4943-3*, Pub. by Akade Kiado) St Mut.

Political Economy of Underdevelopment. B. S. Butola. (C). 1992. text 27.50 (*0-7069-6024-6*, Pub. by Vikas) S Asia.

Political Economy of Underdevelopment: Dependence in Senegal. Ed. by Rita C. O'Brien. LC 78-27183. (Sage Series on African Modernization & Development: No. 3). 277p. reprint ed. pap. 85.90 (*0-8357-8502-5*, 203477900091) Bks Demand.

Political Economy of Uneven Development: The Case of China. Wang Shaoguang & Hu Angang. LC 99-11412. (Asia & the Pacific Ser.). (Illus.). 280p. 1999. text 69.95 (*0-7656-0203-2*, East Gate Bk) M E Sharpe.

***Political Economy of Uneven Development: The Case of China.** Wang Shaoguang & Hu Angang. (Asia & the Pacific Ser.). (Illus.). 280p. 2000. pap. text 24.95 (*0-7656-0204-0*, East Gate Bk) M E Sharpe.

Political Economy of Unorganised Industry: A Study of the Labour Process. Manjit Singh. 236p. (C). 1990. text 27.50 (*0-8039-9647-0*) Sage.

Political Economy of Urban Schools. Martin C. Katzman. LC 70-139723. (Joint Center for Urban Studies). (Illus.). 249p. 1971. 35.95 (*0-674-68576-8*) HUP.

Political Economy of War & Peace. Murray Wolfson. LC 98-30948. (Recent Economic Thought Ser.). 1998. 130.00 (*0-7923-8310-9*) Kluwer Academic.

***Political Economy of Water Pricing Reforms.** Ed. by Ariel Dinar. LC 99-59024. (World Bank Publications). 412p. 2000. 50.00 (*0-19-521594-X*, 61594) OUP.

Political Economy of West Germany: Modell Deutschland. Ed. by Andrei S. Markovits. LC 81-20996. 240p. 1982. 55.00 (*0-275-90854-2*, C0854, Praeger Pubs) Greenwood.

Political Economy of Western Europe. O'Cleireacain. 1999. text. write for info. (*0-312-04776-2*) St Martin.

Political Economy of World Energy: A Twentieth-Century Perspective. John G. Clark. LC 90-37657. 417p. 1990. reprint ed. pap. 129.30 (*0-608-08015-2*, 206798000001) Bks Demand.

Political Economy of World Energy: A 20th-Century Perspective. John G. Clark. LC 90-37657. xx, 397p. (C). 1991. pap. 19.95 (*0-8078-4306-7*) U of NC Pr.

Political Economy of Zimbabwe. Ed. by Michael G. Schatzberg. LC 84-8252. 276p. (C). 1984. 31.95 (*0-275-91261-2*, C1261, Praeger Pubs) Greenwood.

Political Economy, Oligopoly & Experimental Games Vol. 1: The Selected Essays of Martin Shubik. Martin Shubik. LC 99-16257. (Economists of the Twentieth Century Ser.). 592p. 1999. 120.00 (*1-85898-241-3*) E Elgar.

***Political Economy, Power & the Body.** Gillian Youngs. LC 99-15310. (International Political Economy Ser.). 2000. text 65.00 (*0-312-22588-1*) St Martin.

Political Editorial, 1916-1988: From War-Related Conflicts to Metropolitan Disputes. Ed. by Heinz-Dietrich Fischer & Erika J. Fischer. (Pulitzer Prize Archive: Vol. 4). 376p. 1990. lib. bdg. 95.00 (*3-598-30174-X*) K G Saur Verlag.

Political Education: A Washington Memoir. Harry McPherson. LC 94-32805. (Illus.). 520p. 1995. pap. 19.95 (*0-292-75181-8*) U of Tex Pr.

Political Education & Stability: Elite Responses to Political Conflict. Edward Tapper. LC 75-30817. 277p. reprint ed. pap. 85.90 (*0-608-14087-2*, 202428600035) Bks Demand.

Political Education in European Democracies. Susanne M. Shafer. Ed. by Edward R. Beauchamp. (Reference Books in International Education). 300p. 1997. text 45.00 (*0-8153-0613-X*) Garland.

Political Education in the Southern Farmers Alliance, 1887-1900. Theodore R. Mitchell. LC 87-40141. 256p. 1987. reprint ed. pap. 79.40 (*0-608-01980-1*, 206263500003) Bks Demand.

Political Education of Henry Adams. Brooks D. Simpson. LC 95-4371. 1996. text 24.95 (*1-57003-053-7*) U of SC Pr.

Political Element in the Development of Economic Theory. Gunnar Myrdal. 311p. (C). 1990. pap. 24.95 (*0-88738-827-2*) Transaction Pubs.

Political Element in the Port Geography of Trieste. Duesan Mihelic. LC 69-18024. (University of Chicago, Department of Geography, Research Paper Ser.: No. 120). (Illus.). 117p. reprint ed. pap. 36.30 (*0-7837-0397-X*, 204071800018) Bks Demand.

Political Elite: A Sociological Study of Legislators in Rajasthan. R. C. Swarankar. (C). 1988. 32.00 (*81-7033-046-7*, Pub. by Rawat Pubns) S Asia.

Political Elite in Tribal Society. P. K. Panigrahi. LC 98-901418. 1998. 30.00 (*81-7169-496-9*, Pub. by Commonwealth) S Asia.

Political Elite of Iran. Marvin Zonis. LC 74-90966. (Princeton Studies on the Near East). 305p. 1971. reprint ed. pap. 94.60 (*0-608-02588-7*, 206324500004) Bks Demand.

Political Elites. Geraint Parry. (Studies in Political Science). 1969. pap. text 15.95 (*0-04-320059-1*) Routledge.

Political Elites & Social Change: Studies of Elite Roles & Attitudes. Ed. by Moshe M. Czudnowski. LC 83-2461. (International Yearbook for Studies of Leaders & Leadership Ser.). 255p. 1983. 32.00 (*0-87580-093-9*); pap. 18.00 (*0-87580-530-2*) N Ill U Pr.

Political Elites in Anglo-American Democracies. Ed. by Harold D. Clarke & Moshe M. Czudnowski. LC 86-21822. (International Yearbook for Studies of Leaders & Leadership Ser.). 1987. 32.00 (*0-87580-126-9*) N Ill U Pr.

Political Elites in Bangladesh. Rangalal Sen. 355p. (C). 1987. 28.50 (*0-8364-2170-1*, Pub. by KP Bagchi) S Asia.

Political Elites in Modern Societies: Empirical Research & Democratic Theory. Samuel J. Eldersveld. 96p. 1989. text 24.95 (*0-472-08094-6*, 08094) U of Mich Pr.

Political Elites in the Middle East. Ed. by George Lenczowski. LC 75-10898. (Foreign Affairs Study Ser.: No. 19). 235p. reprint ed. pap. 72.90 (*0-8357-4522-8*, 203738300008) Bks Demand.

Political Elites in the U. S. S. R. Central Leaders & Local Cadres from Lenin to Gorbachev. Thomas H. Rigby. 308p. 1990. text 95.00 (*1-85278-303-6*) E Elgar.

Political Empiricism: Communication Strategies in State & Regional Elections. Rita K. Whillock. LC 91-19412. (Praeger Series in Political Communication). 272p. 1991. 55.00 (*0-275-93554-X*, C3554, Praeger Pubs) Greenwood.

Political Encyclopedia of the Middle East. Ed. by Avraham Sela. LC 97-51280. (Illus.). 800p. 1998. 125.00 (*0-8264-1053-7*) Continuum.

Political Environment of Public Management. Peter Kobrak. 450p. (C). 1997. pap. text 49.00 (*0-673-46945-X*) Addson-Wesley Educ.

Political Equality in a Democratic Society: Women in the United States, 45. Mary Lou Kendrigan. LC 83-12569. (Contributions in Women's Studies: No. 45). 149p. 1984. 52.95 (*0-313-23775-1*, KPE/, Greenwood Pr) Greenwood.

Political Equilibrium. Peter C. Ordeshook & Kenneth A. Shepsle. (Studies in Public Choice). 1982. lib. bdg. 111.00 (*0-89838-073-1*) Kluwer Academic.

Political Essay on the Kingdom of New Spain, 4 vols. Alexander Von Humboldt. Tr. by John Black. LC 01-20796. reprint ed. 345.00 (*0-404-03450-0*) AMS Pr.

Political Essays. David Hume. Ed. by Knud Haakonssen. LC 93-36183. (Cambridge Texts in the History of Political Thought Ser.). 414p. (C). 1994. pap. text 19.95 (*0-521-46639-3*) Cambridge U Pr.

Political Essays. David Hume. Ed. by Charles W. Hendel. LC 54-6. 1953. pap. 5.10 (*0-672-60198-2*, Bobbs) Macmillan.

Political Essays. Richard Kostelanetz. 289p. 1999. pap. 14.00 (*1-57027-090-2*, Pub. by Autonomedia) SPD-Small Pr Dist.

Political Essays. John Locke. Ed. by Mark Goldie. (Cambridge Texts in the History of Political Thought Ser.). 456p. (C). 1997. text 59.95 (*0-521-47269-5*); pap. text 19.95 (*0-521-47861-8*) Cambridge U Pr.

Political Essays. Roy A. Medvedev. (European Socialist Thought Ser.: No. 8). 151p. 1976. 33.50 (*0-85124-151-4*, Pub. by Spkesman) Coronet Bks.

Political Essays. John E. Cairnes. LC 66-22615. viii, 350p. 1967. reprint ed. 45.00 (*0-678-00206-1*) Kelley.

Political Essays. James Russell Lowell. (Notable American Authors Ser.). 1999. reprint ed. lib. bdg. 125.00 (*0-7812-3897-8*) Rprt Serv.

Political Ethics: An Alternative to Democratic Tyranny. John D. Garcia. (Illus.). 252p. 1997. write for info. (*0-614-14319-5*) Noetic Pr.

Political Ethics & Public Office. Dennis F. Thompson. 272p. 1990. pap. 18.50 (*0-674-68606-3*) HUP.

Political Ethics of International Relations. Stanley Hoffmann. (Seventh Morgenthau Memorial Lectures). 36p. 1988. pap. 4.00 (*0-87641-229-0*) Carnegie Ethics & Intl Affairs.

Political Events Project, 1948 to 1965. Ivo Feierabend et al. 1976. write for info. (*0-89138-017-5*) ICPSR.

***Political Evolution & Democratic Practice in Uganda, 1952-1996.** Jim Ocitti. LC 99-53203. (African Studies: Vol. 51). 468p. 2000. 109.95 (*0-7734-7860-4*) E Mellen.

Political Evolution of the Hungarian Nation. C. M. Knatchbull-Hugessen. LC 79-135843. (Eastern Europe Collection). 1971. reprint ed. 44.95 (*0-405-02785-0*) Ayer.

Political Executive: Politicians & Management in European Local Government. Ed. by Richard Batley & Adrian Campbell. 85p. 1992. text 25.00 (*0-7146-3480-8*, Pub. by F Cass Pubs) Intl Spec Bk.

Political Expression & Ethnicity: Statecraft & Mobilization in the Maori World. Kayleen M. Hazelhurst. LC 92-35349. 248p. 1993. 62.95 (*0-275-94458-1*, C4458, Praeger Pubs) Greenwood.

Political Facts of the United States since 1789. Erik W. Austin & Jerome M. Clubb. LC 86-2605. 450p. 1986. text 104.00 (*0-231-06094-7*) Col U Pr.

Political Failure of Employment Policy, 1945-1982. Gary Mucciaroni. LC 90-31987. (Political Science Ser.). 328p. 1991. pap. 19.95 (*0-8229-5474-5*) U of Pittsburgh Pr.

Political Feasibility of Adjustment in Developing Countries. S. Haggard et al. LC 95-220564. 134p. (Orig.). 1995. pap. 27.00 (*92-64-14395-5*, Pub. by Org for Econ) OECD.

Political Feasibility of Reform in School Financing: The Case of California. Arnold J. Meltsner et al. LC 72-92461. (Special Studies in U. S. Economic, Social & Political Issues). 1973. 39.50 (*0-685-70526-9*) Irvington.

Political Fiction & the American Self. John Whalen-Bridge. LC 97-33737. 224p. 1998. text 39.95 (*0-252-02388-9*); text 17.95 (*0-252-06688-X*) U of Ill Pr.

Political Fiction, the Spirit of the Age, & Allen Drury. Tom Kemme. LC 87-71029. 250p. 1987. 32.95 (*0-87972-373-4*); pap. 16.95 (*0-87972-374-2*) Bowling Green Univ Popular Press.

Political Film. 2nd ed. Genovese. 146p. (C). 1998. pap. text 19.50 (*0-536-01250-4*) Pearson Custom.

Political Films of Andrzej Wajda: Dialogism in Man of Marble, Man of Iron & Danton. Janina Falkowska. LC 95-16394. (Illus.). 208p. (C). 1996. 55.00 (*1-57181-005-6*) Berghahn Bks.

Political Finance. Ed. by Herbert E. Alexander. LC 78-24439. (Sage Electoral Studies Yearbook: Vol. 5). (Illus.). 272p. reprint ed. pap. 84.40 (*0-608-10080-3*, 202186700026) Bks Demand.

Political Finance: Reform & Reality. Ed. by Herbert E. Alexander & Richard D. Lambert. LC 75-45503. (Annals Ser.: No. 425). 250p. 1976. pap. 18.00 (*0-87761-201-3*) Am Acad Pol Soc Sci.

Political Forces in Argentina. 3rd ed. Peter G. Snow & Luigi Manzetti. LC 92-19595. 224p. 1992. 57.95 (*0-275-93384-9*, C3384, Praeger Pubs); pap. 19.95 (*0-275-93810-7*, B3810, Praeger Pubs) Greenwood.

Political Forgiveness in Old Athens: The Amnesty of 403 B.C. Alfred P. Dorjahn. (Northwestern University. Humanities Ser.: No. 13). reprint ed. 27.50 (*0-404-50713-1*) AMS Pr.

Political Forms of Modern Society Bureaucracy: Democracy, Totalitarianism. Claude Lefort. Ed. by John B. Thompson. 352p. (Orig.). 1986. pap. text 18.50 (*0-262-62054-5*) MIT Pr.

Political Foundation of Law & the Need for Theory with Practical Value: The Theories of Ronald Dworkin & Roberto Unger. John J. Burke. 319p. (Orig.). 1992. 64.95 (*1-880921-46-4*); pap. text 44.95 (*1-880921-05-7*) Austin & Winfield.

Political Foundations of Development Policies. Oskar Kurer. LC 96-46349. 252p. 1997. 42.50 (*0-7618-0617-2*) U Pr of Amer.

***Political Freedom.** Howard G. Davis. 256p. 2001. 90.95 (*0-8264-5030-X*) Continuum.

Political Frontiers & Boundaries. J. R. Prescott. 320p. 1987. text 49.95 (*0-04-341030-8*) Routledge.

Political Future of Northern Ireland. Paul Bew et al. LC 93-150256. 160p. (C). 1997. pap. 18.50 (*0-85315-771-5*, Pub. by Lawrence & Wishart) NYU Pr.

Political Gain & Civilian Pain: Humanitarian Impacts of Economic Sanctions. Ed. by Thomas G. Weiss et al. LC 97-25040. (Illus.). 256p. 1997. 62.00 (*0-8476-8702-3*); pap. 24.95 (*0-8476-8703-1*) Rowman.

***Political Genealogy after Foucault: Savage Identities.** Michael Clifford. LC 00-44632. 2001. pap. write for info. (*0-415-92916-4*) Routledge.

Political Geography. Ed. by John Agnew. (Arnold Publications). (Illus.). 384p. 1996. text 75.00 (*0-340-67742-2*) OUP.

Political Geography. 2nd ed. Martin I. Glassner. LC 95-32362. 736p. 1995. text 78.95 (*0-471-11496-0*) Wiley.

Political Geography. 3rd ed. Peter J. Taylor. (C). 1993. pap. text 45.94 (*0-582-09862-9*) Addison-Wesley.

Political Geography: A Comprehensive Systematic Bibliography. B. L. Sukhwal & Lilawati Sukhwal. LC 91-57956. (International Studies: No. 1). 1992. 159.50 (*0-404-63151-7*) AMS Pr.

Political Geography: A New Introduction. Richard Muir. LC 97-5293. 352p. 1997. pap. text 39.95 (*0-470-23744-9*) Halsted Pr.

Political Geography: A Reader. Ed. by John Agnew. (Arnold Publications). (Illus.). 384p. 1996. pap. text 35.00 (*0-340-67743-0*) OUP.

Political Geography: Recent Advances & Future Directions. Ed. by Peter Taylor & John House. LC 84-6493. (Illus.). 250p. (C). 1984. 50.00 (*0-389-20493-5*, N8055) B&N Imports.

***Political Geography: World Economy, Nation-State & Locality.** 4th ed. Peter J. Taylor & Colin Flint. 412p. (C). 1999. pap. 54.00 (*0-582-35733-0*) Longman.

Political Geography of California. T. Anthony Quinn. 132p. 1981. pap. text 23.75 (*1-883638-18-6*) Rose Inst.

Political Geography of Countries & Concepts. 6th ed. 40p. (C). 1997. write for info. (*0-13-789371-X*, Macmillan Coll) P-H.

Political Geography of Latin America. Jonathan R. Barton. LC 96-47376. (Illus.). 264p. (C). 1997. 85.00 (*0-415-12189-2*); pap. 25.99 (*0-415-12190-6*) Routledge.

Political Geography of the New World Order. Colin H. Williams. LC 93-10054. 224p. 1993. 110.00 (*0-471-94792-X*) Wiley.

Political Geography of the United States. Fred M. Shelley & J. Clark Archer. LC 96-10814. 364p. 1996. lib. bdg. 47.95 (*1-57230-047-7*) Guilford Pubns.

Political Geography of the United States. Fred M. Shelley et al. LC 96-10814. 364p. 1996. pap. text 30.00 (*1-57230-048-5*, 0048) Guilford Pubns.

Political Gerrymandering & the Courts. Ed. by Bernard N. Grofman. LC 89-29830. (Representation Ser.: Vol. 3). 360p. 1990. 42.00 (*0-87586-092-3*) Agathon.

Political Groups in Chile: The Dialogue Between Order & Change. Ben G. Burnett. LC 70-135759. (Latin American Monographs: No. 21). 333p. reprint ed. pap. 103.30 (*0-8357-7730-8*, 203608700002) Bks Demand.

Political Guide to Latin America. 1992. lib. bdg. 79.95 (*0-8490-8762-7*) Gordon Pr.

Political Gumbo: A Collection of Editorial Cartoons. Walt Handelsman. LC 94-6025. (Editorial Cartoonists Ser.). (Illus.). 160p. 1994. pap. 8.95 (*1-56554-054-9*) Pelican.

Political Hand: Policy Implementation & Youth Employment Programs. Martin A. Levin & Barbara Ferman. (Government & Politics Ser.). 160p. 1985. text 37.50 (*0-08-031604-2*, Pergamon Pr); pap. text 18.95 (*0-08-031603-4*, Pergamon Pr) Elsevier.

Political Handbook for Student Government Operations: A Guide to Candidacy, Campaigning, Leadership & Management & Advisory Functions. Henry C. Landa & Douglas C. Landa. 158p. (Orig.). 1998. pap. 18.00 (*0-931974-17-8*) FICOA.

Political Handbook of the World, 1986. Ed. by Arthur S. Banks et al. LC 81-643916. (Illus.). 803p. 1986. 79.95 (*0-933199-01-5*) CSA Pubn.

Political Handbook of the World, 1987. Ed. by Arthur S. Banks et al. LC 81-643916. (Illus.). 850p. 1987. 84.95 (*0-933199-03-1*) CSA Pubn.

Political Handbook of the World, 1990. Ed. by Arthur S. Banks et al. LC 81-643916. (Illus.). 956p. 1990. 89.95 (*0-933199-06-6*) CSA Pubn.

Political Handbook of the World, 1991. Ed. by Arthur S. Banks et al. LC 81-643916. (Illus.). 1016p. 1991. 89.95 (*0-933199-07-4*) CSA Pubn.

Political Handbook of the World, 1984-1985. Arthur S. Banks et al. LC 81-643916. (Illus.). 768p. 1985. 79.95 (*0-933199-00-7*) CSA Pubn.

Political Handbook of the World, 1993. Arthur S. Banks et al. LC 81-643916. (Illus.). 1224p. 1993. 104.50 (*0-933199-09-0*) CSA Pubn.

Political Handbook of the World, 1994-1995. 60th ed. Ed. by Arthur S. Banks. LC 81-643916. (Political Handbook of the World Ser.). 1226p. (C). 1995. 104.95 (*0-933199-10-4*) CSA Pubn.

Political Handbook of the World, 1995-1996. 61st ed. Ed. by Arthur S. Banks et al. LC 81-643916. (Political Handbook of the World Ser.). 1322p. (C). 1996. 109.95 (*0-933199-11-2*) CSA Pubn.

P

An Asterisk (*) at the beginning of an entry indicates that the title is appearing for the first time.

Political Handbook of the World, 1997. 62nd rev. ed. Ed. by Arthur S. Banks et al. LC 81-643916. 1220p. 1997. 115.00 (*0-933199-12-0*) CSA Pubn.

Political Handbook of the World, 1998. 63rd rev. ed. Ed. by Arthur S. Banks & Thomas C. Muller. LC 81-643916. (Political Handbook of the World Ser.). (Illus.). 1297p. 1998. 119.00 (*0-933199-13-9*) CSA Pubn.

***Political Handbook of the World, 1999.** 64th ed. Ed. by Arthur S. Banks & Thomas C. Muller. LC 81-643916. (Illus.). 1325p. 2000. 125.00 (*0-933199-14-7*) CSA Pubn.

Political Handbook of the World, 1988: 1988. Ed. by Arthur S. Banks. LC 81-643916. (Illus.). 877p. 1988. 89.95 (*0-933199-04-X*) CSA Pubn.

***Political Handbook of the World, 2000.** 64th ed. Arthur S. Banks & Thomas C. Muller. LC 81-643916. (Political Handbook of the World Ser.). (Illus.). 1375p. (C). 2000. 130.00 (*0-933199-15-5*) CSA Pubn.

Political Handbook of the World, 1992: 1992. Arthur S. Banks et al. LC 81-643916. (Illus.). 1120p. 1992. 94.95 (*0-933199-08-2*) CSA Pubn.

Political Hermeneutics: The Early Thinking of Hans-Georg Gadamer. Robert R. Sullivan. LC 88-43435. 176p. 1990. lib. bdg. 35.00 (*0-271-00670-6*) Pa St U Pr.

***Political High Court: How the High Courts Shapes Politics.** David Solomon. 288p. 2000. 29.95 (*1-86448-716-X*, Pub. by Allen & Unwin Pty) Paul & Co Pubs.

Political History of Ancient India. Hemchandra Raychaudhuri. LC 78-174301. reprint ed. 49.50 (*0-404-05228-2*) AMS Pr.

Political History of Ancient India: From the Accession of Parikshit to the Extinction of the Gupta Dynasty. 8th ed. Hemchandra Raychaudhuri. (Illus.). 885p. 1998. reprint ed. pap. text 14.95 (*0-19-564376-3*) OUP.

Political History of Carnatic under the Nawabs. N. S. Ramaswami. 1985. 40.00 (*0-8364-1262-1*, Pub. by Abhinav) S Asia.

Political History of Chandalas. R. K. Dixit. 1977. 16.00 (*0-8364-0446-7*) S Asia.

Political History of Eastern Europe in the Twentieth Century: The Struggle Between Democracy & Dictatorship. Sten Berglund & Frank H. Aarebrot. LC 96-41938. (Studies of Communism in Transition). 208p. 1997. 70.00 (*1-85898-478-5*) E Elgar.

Political History of Eighteenth-Century Scotland. John S. Shaw. LC 99-21982. (British History in Perspective Ser.). 151p. 1999. text 39.95 (*0-312-22430-3*) St Martin.

Political History of England, 12 vols. Ed. by William Hunt & Reginald L. Poole. reprint ed. 540.00 (*0-404-50770-0*) AMS Pr.

Political History of Imperial Guptas: From Gupta to Skand Gu. Tej R. Sharma. (C). 1989. 22.50 (*81-7022-251-6*, Pub. by Concept) S Asia.

Political History of Italy: The Postwar Years. Norman Kogan. LC 83-3963. 365p. 1983. pap. 16.95 (*0-275-91576-X*, B1576, Praeger Pubs) Greenwood.

Political History of Italy: The Postwar Years. Norman Kogan. LC 83-3963. 365p. 1983. 40.95 (*0-275-91029-6*, C1029, Praeger Pubs) Greenwood.

Political History of Italy: The Postwar Years. Norman Kogan. LC 83-3963. xviii, 365 p. 1983. write for info. (*0-03-062961-6*) Holt R&W.

Political History of Jackson County, Missouri. Marshall & Morrison. (Illus.). 276p. 1997. reprint ed. pap. 22.00 (*0-7884-0709-0*, M069) Heritage Bk.

Political History of Japan During the Meiji Era, 1867-1912. Walter W. McLaren. 379p. 1966. 35.00 (*0-7146-2018-1*, Pub. by F Cass Pubs) Intl Spec Bk.

Political History of Modern Iran: From Tribalism to Theocracy. Mehran Kamrava. LC 92-23068. 192p. 1992. 57.95 (*0-275-94445-X*, C4445, Praeger Pubs) Greenwood.

Political History of Modern Japan, 1868-1952: The Afro-Asian Nations: History & Culture. R. L. Sims. 1991. text 35.00 (*0-7069-5334-7*, Pub. by Vikas) S Asia.

Political History of New York State During the Period of the Civil War. Sidney D. Brummer. LC 11-19977. (Columbia University. Studies in the Social Sciences: No. 103). reprint ed. 37.50 (*0-404-51103-1*) AMS Pr.

Political History of Newfoundland, 1832-1864. Gertrude E. Gunn. LC 67-397. (Canadian Studies in History & Government: No. 7). 257p. reprint ed. pap. 79.70 (*0-608-16275-2*, 202652200050) Bks Demand.

Political History of Parthia. Neilson C. Debevoise. LC 68-56330. (Illus.). 303p. 1970. reprint ed. lib. bdg. 59.75 (*0-8371-0374-6*, DEPA, Greenwood Pr) Greenwood.

Political History of Public Health. D. Porter. LC 98-21836. (Wellcome Institute Series in the History of Medicine). 256p. (C). 1999. 85.00 (*0-415-12244-9*) Routledge.

Political History of Secession, to the Beginning of the American Civil War. Daniel W. Howe. LC 77-88436. 649p. 1970. reprint ed. lib. bdg. 75.00 (*0-8371-1734-8*, HOP&, Greenwood Pr) Greenwood.

Political History of Slavery in the United States. James Z. George. LC 77-92429. 1915. 15.00 (*0-403-00162-5*) Scholarly.

Political History of Slavery in the United States. James Z. George. LC 72-181080. 342p. 1970. reprint ed. lib. bdg. 59.50 (*0-8371-1991-X*, GEP&, Greenwood Pr) Greenwood.

Political History of Slavery in the United States see Political History of Slavery in the United States

Political History of Slavery in the United States, 2 bks, Set. James Z. George et al. Incl. Bk. 1. Political History of Slavery in the United States. LC 73-83944. Vol. 2. Legislative History of Reconstruction. LC 73-83944. LC 73-83944. (Black Heritage Library Collection). 1977. reprint ed. 26.95 (*0-8369-8577-X*) Ayer.

Political History of the Achaemenid Empire. M. A. Dandamaev. Tr. by W. J. Vogelsang from RUS. (Illus.). xv, 373p. 1990. 144.00 (*90-04-09172-6*) Brill Academic Pubs.

Political History of the Civil War in Angola, 1974-1990. W. Martin James. 296p. (C). 1992. text 49.95 (*0-88738-418-8*) Transaction Pubs.

Political History of the State of New York, 3 vols., Set. D. S. Alexander. 1993. reprint ed. lib. bdg. 225.00 (*0-7812-5165-6*) Rprt Serv.

Political History of the State of New York, 1865-1869. Homer A. Stebbins. LC 13-15791. (Columbia University. Studies in the Social Sciences: No. 135). reprint ed. 36.50 (*0-404-51135-X*) AMS Pr.

Political History of the Texas Republic. Stanley Siegel. LC 72-6676. (American History & Americana Ser.: No. 47). (Illus.). (C). 1972. reprint ed. lib. bdg. 75.00 (*0-8383-1648-4*) M S G Haskell Hse.

Political History of the U. S. A. During the Period of Reconstruction. Edward McPherson. Ed. by Harold Hyman & Hans Trefousse. LC 77-127288. (Studies in American History & Government). 648p. 1973. reprint ed. lib. bdg. 85.00 (*0-306-71206-7*) Da Capo.

Political History of the United States of America During the Great Rebellion. Edward McPherson. LC 73-127287. (American Constitutional & Legal History Ser). 1972. reprint ed. lib. bdg. 75.00 (*0-306-71207-5*) Da Capo.

Political History of Tripura. J. Gan Chaudhuri. 1986. 27.95 (*0-318-36961-3*) Asia Bk Corp.

Political History of Virginia During the Reconstruction. Hamilton J. Eckenrode. LC 76-164387. (Black Heritage Library Collection). 1977. reprint ed. 22.95 (*0-8369-8846-9*) Ayer.

Political History of Virginia During the Reconstruction. Hamilton J. Eckenrode. (BCL1 - United States Local History Ser.). 128p. 1991. reprint ed. lib. bdg. 69.00 (*0-7812-6295-X*) Rprt Serv.

Political History of Western Europe since 1945. 5th ed. Derek W. Urwin. LC 96-35274. (C). 1997. write for info. (*0-582-31618-9*, Pub. by Addison-Wesley) Longman.

Political History of Western Europe since 1945. 5th ed. Derek W. Urwin. LC 96-35274. 376p. (C). 1997. pap. 29.06 (*0-582-25374-8*) Longman.

Political Holiness: A Spirituality of Liberation - Espiritualidad de la Liberacion. Pedro Casaldaliga & Jose M. Vigil. Tr. by Paul Burns & Francis McDonagh from SPA. LC 94-22056. (Theology & Liberation Ser.). 275p. 1994. reprint ed. pap. 17.00 (*0-88344-979-X*) Orbis Bks.

Political Hospitality & Tourism: Cuba & Nicaragua. Paul Hollander. 32p. 1986. 3.00 (*0-317-90498-1*) Cuban Amer Natl Fndtn.

Political Humor. Charles E. Schutz. LC 74-197. 349p. 1976. 39.50 (*0-8386-1536-8*) Fairleigh Dickinson.

Political Humor in America. Stephen M. Forman. LC 97-78306. (Perspectives on History Ser.: Pt. III). (Illus.). 58p. 1998. pap. 6.95 (*1-57960-020-4*) Disc Enter Ltd.

Political Ideals. Houston S. Chamberlain. Tr. by Alexander Jacob from GER. Orig. Title: Politische Ideale. 135p. (Orig.). 1996. pap. 15.00 (*0-937944-08-4*) Natl Vanguard.

Political Ideals. Bertrand Russell. 80p. (C). 1988. pap. 14.99 (*0-415-10907-8*) Routledge.

Political Ideals. Bertrand Russell. (Unwin Paperbacks Ser.). 1980. reprint ed. pap. 9.95 (*0-04-320120-2*) Routledge.

Political Ideals in Medieval Italian Art: The Frescoes in the Palazzo dei Priori, Perugia, 1297. Jonathan B. Riess. LC 81-12950. (Studies in the Fine Arts: Iconography: No. 1). (Illus.). 201p. reprint ed. pap. 62.40 (*0-8357-1238-9*, 207025200065) Bks Demand.

Political Ideas. David Thomson. 1990. pap. 16.95 (*0-14-013543-X*, Pub. by Pnguin Bks Ltd) Trafalgar.

Political Ideas & Concepts. Andrew Heywood. 369p. 1994. pap. text 26.95 (*0-312-11220-3*) St Martin.

Political Ideas & Concepts: An Introduction. Andrew Heywood. LC 93-44097. 1994. text 49.95 (*0-312-12108-3*) St Martin.

Political Ideas & Institutions under the Mauryas. Satya N. Singh. (C). 1992. 18.00 (*81-85078-63-7*, Pub. by Manohar) S Asia.

Political Ideas & the Enlightenment in the Romanian Principalities, 1750-1831. Vladimir Georgescu. (East European Monographs: No. 1). 232p. (C). 1972. text 52.50 (*0-231-02842-3*, Pub. by East Eur Monographs) Col U Pr.

Political Ideas in Contemporary Poland. Jan Zielonka. 220p. 1989. text 82.95 (*0-566-07012-X*, Pub. by Dartmth Pub) Ashgate Pub Co.

Political Ideas in Modern Britain: In & after the 20th Century. 2nd ed. Rodney Barker. 360p. (C). 1997. 85.00 (*0-415-16166-5*); pap. 25.99 (*0-415-07121-6*) Routledge.

Political Ideas in Opera: From Monteverdi to Henze. John Bokina. LC 96-53455. 264p. 1997. 30.00 (*0-300-06935-9*) Yale U Pr.

Political Ideas in the Pancamahakavyas. Mangala Mirasdar. LC 95-910681. xix, 348p. 1995. 29.00 (*81-86339-10-8*, Pub. by Eastern Bk Linkers) Nataraj Bks.

Political Ideas of Benoy Kumar Sarkar. Bholanath Bandyopadhyay. 1985. 15.00 (*0-8364-1336-9*, Pub. by KP Bagchi) S Asia.

Political Ideas of James Wilson, 1742-1798. Jean M. Pascal. LC 91-10728. (Political Theory & Political Philosophy Ser.). 368p. 1991. text 10.00 (*0-8153-0139-1*) Garland.

Political Ideas of Justice Holmes. David H. Burton. LC 91-55095. 128p. 1992. 29.50 (*0-8386-3457-5*) Fairleigh Dickinson.

Political Ideas of M. N. Roy. Reeta Sinha. (C). 1981. 21.00 (*81-85135-62-2*, Pub. by Natl Bk Orgn) S Asia.

Political Ideas of M. N. Roy & Jaya Prakash Narayan: A Comparative Study. Bhola Singh. xii, 296p. 1985. 22.00 (*0-685-67625-0*, Pub. by Ashish Pub Hse) Nataraj Bks.

Political Ideas of M. N. Roy & Jaya Prakash Narayan: A Comparative Study. Bhola Singh. 1986. 32.00 (*81-7024-022-0*, Pub. by Ashish Pub Hse) S Asia.

Political Ideas of M. S. Golwalker. Ritu Kohli. (C). 1993. 14.00 (*81-7100-566-7*, Pub. by Deep & Deep Pubns) S Asia.

Political Ideas of Marx & Engels, Vol. 2: Classical Marxism 1850-1895. Pref. by Richard N. Hunt. LC 84-5218. 440p. 1984. text 49.95 (*0-8229-3496-5*) U of Pittsburgh Pr.

Political Ideas of St. Thomas Aquinas: Representative Selections. Aquinas, Thomas, Saint. Ed. by Dino Bigongiari. (Library of Classics: No. 15). 255p. 1997. pap. 15.95 (*0-684-83641-6*) Hafner.

Political Ideas of the Greeks. John L. Myres. 436p. 1927. 25.00 (*0-8196-1163-8*) Biblo.

Political Ideas of the Greeks. John L. Myres. LC 71-137278. reprint ed. 22.50 (*0-404-04549-9*) AMS Pr.

Political Identities of Ezra Pound & T. S. Eliot. William M. Chace. LC 73-80620. 256p. 1973. 32.50 (*0-8047-0843-6*) Stanford U Pr.

Political Identities of Ezra Pound & T. S. Eliot. William M. Chace. LC 73-80620. 256p. 1973. reprint ed. pap. 30.00 (*0-608-00552-5*, 206143500008) Bks Demand.

Political Identity of Andrew Marvell. Conal Condren & A. D. Cousins. 256p. 1990. text 78.95 (*0-85967-818-0*, Pub. by Scolar Pr) Ashgate Pub Co.

Political Ideologies. 2nd ed. Robert Eccleshall et al. LC 94-21697. 272p. (C). 1994. pap. 22.99 (*0-415-09982-X*, B3110) Routledge.

Political Ideologies. 3rd ed. Ed. by Charles Funderburk. 280p. (C). 1997. pap. text 40.00 (*0-673-67590-4*) Addison-Wesley.

Political Ideologies: A Comparative Approach. Mostafa Rejai. 216p. 1991. pap. text 34.95 (*0-87332-807-8*) M E Sharpe.

Political Ideologies: A Comparative Approach. Mostafa Rejai. LC 90-26349. 216p. (C). (gr. 13). 1991. text 69.95 (*0-87332-806-X*) M E Sharpe.

Political Ideologies: A Comparative Approach. 2nd ed. Mostafa Rejai. LC 94-29696. 260p. (YA). (gr. 13). 1994. pap. text 32.95 (*1-56324-142-0*) M E Sharpe.

Political Ideologies: An Australian Introduction. 2nd ed. Robert Leach. 260p. 1994. 64.95 (*0-7329-2002-7*, Pub. by Macmill Educ); pap. 32.95 (*0-7329-2001-9*, Pub. by Macmill Educ) Paul & Co Pubs.

Political Ideologies: An Introduction. Robert Eccleshall et al. LC 92-35536. 1992. write for info. (*0-415-09442-9*) Routledge.

Political Ideologies: An Introduction. Heywood. 1998. 18.00 (*1-57259-723-2*) Worth.

Political Ideologies: Their Origins & Impact. 7th ed. Ed. by Prentice-Hall Staff. LC 99-12299. 338p. (C). 1999. pap. text 29.40 (*0-13-020888-4*) P-H.

***Political Ideologies & the Democratic Ideal.** 3rd ed. Ball. 1999. 45.93 (*0-201-66695-2*); 46.87 (*0-201-66696-0*); 48.75 (*0-201-66697-9*); 46.87 (*0-201-66698-7*) Addison-Wesley.

Political Ideologies & the Democratic Ideal. 3rd ed. Ball. LC 98-7260. 320p. (C). 1998. pap. text 51.00 (*0-321-00541-4*) Addson-Wesley Educ.

Political Ideologies in Contemporary France. Christopher Flood & Laurence Bell. LC 96-47167. 192p. 1997. 65.00 (*1-85567-237-5*); pap. 21.95 (*1-85567-238-3*) Bks Intl VA.

Political Ideologies of Organized Labor: The New Deal Era. Ruth L. Horowitz. LC 76-58229. 260p. 1978. text 34.95 (*0-87855-208-1*) Transaction Pubs.

***Political Ideology.** 3rd ed. Ball. 1999. 48.75 (*0-201-66694-4*) Addison-Wesley.

Political Ideology & Class Formation: A Study of the Middle Class. Carolyn Howe. LC 92-15988. 216p. 1992. 49.95 (*0-275-94151-5*, C4151, Praeger Pubs) Greenwood.

Political Ideology & Educational Reform in Chile, 1964-1976. Kathleen B. Fischer. LC 79-620018. (Latin American Studies: Vol. 46). 1979. 14.95 (*0-87903-046-1*) UCLA Lat Am Ctr.

Political Ideology & Voting: An Exploratory Study. Elinor Scarbrough. (Illus.). 257p. 1985. 49.95 (*0-19-827469-6*) OUP.

***Political Ideology in Ireland, 1541-1641.** Ed. by Hiram Morgan. 256p. 2000. 55.00 (*1-85182-440-5*, Pub. by Four Cts Pr) Intl Spec Bk.

Political Ideology in Malaysia: Reality & the Beliefs of an Elite. James C. Scott. LC 68-27766. (Yale Southwest Asia Studies: No. 3). 316p. reprint ed. pap. 98.00 (*0-608-30044-6*, 201680300005) Bks Demand.

Political Ideology Today. Ian Adams. (Politics Today Ser.). 208p. (C). 1993. text 19.95 (*0-7190-3347-0*) Manchester Univ Pr.

Political Impact of Colonial Administration. Arthur J. Vidich. Ed. by Harriet Zuckerman & Robert K. Merton. LC 79-9036. (Dissertations on Sociology Ser.). 1980. lib. bdg. 36.95 (*0-405-13003-1*) Ayer.

Political India, 1832 to 1932: A Cooperative Survey of a Century. Ed. by John G. Cumming. 332p. 1968. text 20.00 (*0-685-13736-8*) Coronet Bks.

Political India, 1935-42: Anatomy of Indian Politics. Ramji Lal. 308p. 1986. 28.00 (*81-202-0160-4*, Pub. by Ajanta) S Asia.

Political Influence. Edward C. Banfield. LC 82-6245. 354p. 1982. lib. bdg. 41.50 (*0-313-22645-8*, BAPF, Greenwood Pr) Greenwood.

Political Influence of Global NGOs: Case Studies on the Climate & Biodiversity Conventions. Bas Arts. 300p. 1998. pap. 29.95 (*90-5727-012-9*, Pub. by Intl Bks) Paul & Co Pubs.

Political Influence of Ideas: Policy Communities & the Social Sciences. Ed. by Stephen Brooks & Alain-G. Gagnon. LC 93-23680. 256p. 1994. 65.00 (*0-275-94333-X*, Praeger Pubs) Greenwood.

Political Influence of the Military: A Comparative Reader. Amos Perlmutter & Valerie P. Bennett. LC 78-26154. 518p. reprint ed. pap. 160.60 (*0-8357-8275-1*, 203385500087) Bks Demand.

Political Innovation in America: The Politics of Policy Initation. Nelson W. Polsby. LC 83-14749. 200p. 1984. 37.50 (*0-300-03089-4*) Yale U Pr.

***Political Instability as a Source of Growth.** Bruce Bueno de Mesquita. LC 00-23814. (Essays in Public Policy Ser.: 99). 18p. 2000. pap. 5.00 (*0-8179-4342-0*) Hoover Inst Pr.

Political Instability, Interstate Conflict Adverse Changes in Host Government Policies & Foreign Direct Investment: A Sensitivity Analysis. Braimoh D. Oseghale. LC 92-40969. (Foreign Economic Policy of the United States Ser.). 192p. 1993. text 10.00 (*0-8153-1254-7*) Garland.

Political Institution of Private Property. Itai Sened. (Theories of Institutional Design Ser.). 218p. 1997. text 54.95 (*0-521-57247-9*) Cambridge U Pr.

Political, Institutional & Fiscal Alternatives for Nonpoint Pollution Abatement Programs: Proceedings of a Conference Held in Milwaukee, Wisconsin, December 7-9, 1987. Ed. by Vladimir Novotny. LC 88-61504. 210p. 1988. reprint ed. pap. 65.10 (*0-608-04196-3*, 206493100011) Bks Demand.

Political Institutionalization: A Political Study of Two Sardinian Communities. Francesco Kjellberg. LC 74-20693. 160p. reprint ed. pap. 49.60 (*0-608-30707-6*, 201616100098) Bks Demand.

Political Institutions & Economic Growth in Latin America: Essays in Policy, History & Political Economy. Ed. by Stephen Haber. LC 99-50375. (Publication Ser: Vol. 462). Date not set. 18.95 (*0-8179-9662-1*) Hoover Inst Pr.

Political Institutions & Military Change: Lessons from Peripheral Wars. Deborah D. Avant. (Studies in Security Affairs). 176p. 1994. text 35.00 (*0-8014-3034-8*) Cornell U Pr.

Political Institutions & Public Policy: Perspectives on European Decision Making. Bernard Steunenberg & Frans VanVught. LC 97-1389. 1997. lib. bdg. 124.00 (*0-7923-4471-5*) Kluwer Academic.

Political Institutions in Europe. Ed. by Josep Colomer. 304p. (C). 1996. pap. 25.99 (*0-415-10820-9*) Routledge.

Political Institutions in Virginia. Jon Kukla. (Outstanding Studies in Early American History). 284p. 1989. reprint ed. 20.00 (*0-8240-6188-8*) Garland.

Political Integration of Women: Roles, Socialization, & Politics. Virginia Sapiro. LC 82-2672. 216p. 1984. pap. text 10.95 (*0-252-01141-4*) U of Ill Pr.

Political Intelligence for America's Future. Ed. by Bertram M. Gross & Richard D. Lambert. LC 78-112787. (Annals of the American Academy of Political & Social Science Ser.: No. 388). (C). 1970. 28.00 (*0-685-00184-9*); pap. 18.00 (*0-87761-125-4*) Am Acad Pol Soc Sci.

Political Interests of Gender: Developing Theory & Research with a Feminist Face. Ed. by Kathleen B. Jones & Anna G. Jonasdottir. (Modern Politics Ser.: Vol. 20). 256p. (C). 1988. text 47.50 (*0-8039-8085-X*); pap. text 18.95 (*0-8039-8086-8*) Sage.

Political, International, Social & Economic Aspects see Czechoslovakia Past & Present

Political Interpretations of Educational Administration. David K. Wiles. 288p. 1977. text 32.50 (*0-8422-5267-3*); pap. text 15.95 (*0-8422-0557-8*) Irvington.

Political Intrigue in the Establishment of the Identity of Jesus & Mary. James H. Boykin. LC 86-90757. 285p. 1986. pap. 11.99 (*0-9603342-6-2*) Boykin.

Political Inversions: Homosexuality, Fascism, & the Modernist Imaginary. Andrew Hewitt. LC 96-828. 1996. 49.50 (*0-8047-2639-6*); pap. 16.95 (*0-8047-2641-8*) Stanford U Pr.

Political Investments in Food Production. Ed. by Barbara Huddleston & Jon McLin. LC 79-5025. (Illus.). 256p. reprint ed. pap. 79.40 (*0-608-17407-6*, 205642400067) Bks Demand.

Political Islam: Essay from Middle East Report. Ed. by Joel Beinin & Joe Stork. LC 95-39810. 383p. (C). 1996. 55.00 (*0-520-20447-6*, Pub. by U CA Pr) Cal Prin Full Svc.

Political Islam: Essay from Middle East Report. Ed. by Joel Beinin & Joe Stork. LC 95-39810. (Illus.). 383p. 1996. pap. 22.50 (*0-520-20448-4*, Pub. by U CA Pr) Cal Prin Full Svc.

Political Islam: Religion & Politics in the Arab World. Nazih Ayubi. 304p. (C). 1993. pap. 27.99 (*0-415-10385-1*) Routledge.

Political Islam: U. S. Policy Implications: A Conference Report. Date not set. pap. 15.00 (*0-9644523-2-4*) Jewish Inst Nat Secur.

Political Islam & the United States, 1. Pinto Maria Do Ceu. 1999. 40.00 (*0-86372-245-8*) Garnet-Ithaca.

Political "ISMS" & the Democratic Mind: A Treatise on the Origin, Nature & Outcome of the Modern Conflict over Political Sovereignty. Raymann Newton. Ed. by Gene De Roin. LC 88-92701. 160p. (Orig.). (C). 1989. pap. text 7.95 (*0-9622647-0-9*) Baron & Roth Pub.

***Political Issues.** Sink. 450p. 1999. pap. text 47.00 (*0-536-02793-5*) Pearson Custom.

Political Issues Debated: An Introduction to Politics. Herbert M. Levine. (Illus.). 352p. (C). 1982. pap. 15.95 (*0-13-685032-4*) P-H.

An Asterisk (*) at the beginning of an entry indicates that the title is appearing for the first time.

Political Issues Debated: An Introduction to Politics. 4th ed. Herbert M. Levine. 322p. 1992. pap. text 34.60 (*0-13-681644-4*) P-H.

Political Issues in America Today: The 1990's Revisited. 2nd ed. Ed. by Philip J. Davies & Fredric A. Waldstein. (Politics Today Ser.). 272p. 1996. text 69.95 (*0-7190-4225-9*); text 24.95 (*0-7190-4226-7*, Pub. by Manchester Univ Pr) St Martin.

Political Issues in Britain Today. Bill Jones. 1999. text 69.95 (*0-7190-5431-1*) St Martin.

Political Issues in Britain Today. 4th ed. Ed. by Bill Jones. (Politics Today Ser.). 300p. 1994. text 14.95 (*0-7190-3772-7*, Pub. by Manchester Univ Pr) St Martin.

Political Issues in Britain Today. 5th ed. Bill Jones. 1999. pap. 19.95 (*0-7190-5432-X*) St Martin.

Political Issues in Ireland Today. 2nd ed. Neil Collins. LC 99-41937. 210p. 1999. 69.95 (*0-7190-5403-6*, Pub. by Manchester Univ Pr) St Martin.

Political Issues in Ireland Today, 2nd Ed. 2nd ed. Neil Collins. LC 99-41937. 1999. pap. text 24.95 (*0-7190-5404-4*, Pub. by Manchester Univ Pr) St Martin.

Political Issues in Luke - Acts. Ed. by Richard J. Cassidy & Philip J. Scharper. LC 82-19060. 192p. (Orig.). reprint ed. pap. 59.60 (*0-8357-2669-X*, 204020500015) Bks Demand.

Political Judgement. Ronald S. Beiner. LC 83-50829. (C). 1984. pap. text 9.50 (*0-226-04165-4*) U Ch Pr.

Political Judgements. Dick Howard. 352p. (C). 1996. pap. text 28.95 (*0-8476-8163-7*) Rowman.

Political Judgment. Ronald S. Beiner. LC 83-50829. (C). 1984. lib. bdg. 20.00 (*0-226-04164-6*) U Ch Pr.

Political Judgment. Ronald Beiner. LC 83-50829. 215p. Date not set. reprint ed. pap. 66.70 (*0-608-21002-1*, 205453000003) Bks Demand.

Political Judgment: Structure & Process. Ed. by Milton Lodge & Kathleen M. McGraw. 320p. (C). 1995. text 47.50 (*0-472-10541-8*, 10541) U of Mich Pr.

Political Judgments. Dick Howard. 352p. (C). 1996. lib. bdg. 73.00 (*0-8476-8162-9*) Rowman.

Political Justice. William Godwin. 1972. 250.00 (*0-8490-0873-5*) Gordon Pr.

Political Justice: A Poem in a Letter to the Right Hon. the Lord. Intro. by Burton R. Pollin & John W. Wilkes. LC 92-24282. (Augustan Reprints Ser.: No. 111). 1965. reprint ed. 14.50 (*0-404-70111-6*) AMS Pr.

Political Justice: Foundations for a Critical Philosophy of Law & the State. Otfried Hoffe. Tr. by Jeffrey Cohen. 320p. 1995. 68.95 (*0-7456-0887-6*) Blackwell Pubs.

Political Justice in the Soviet Union: Dissent & Repression in Lithuania, 1969-1987. Thomas Oleszczuk. (East European Monographs: No. 247). 221p. 1988. text 59.50 (*0-88033-144-5*, Pub. by East Eur Monographs) Col U Pr.

Political Justice, 1793, 2 vols., Set. William Godwin. LC 92-36380. (Revolution & Romanticism Ser.). 978p. 1992. reprint ed. 275.00 (*1-85477-115-9*) Continuum.

Political Kingdom in Uganda: A Study in Bureaucratic Nationalism. 2nd ed. LC 67-18831. (Illus.). 528p. reprint ed. pap. 163.70 (*0-608-11807-9*, 205159900097) Bks Demand.

Political Kingdom in Uganda: A Study in Bureaucratic Nationalism. 3rd ed. David E. Apter. LC 97-13495. 498p. (C). 1997. 59.50 (*0-7146-4696-2*, Pub. by Irish Acad Pr); pap. 27.50 (*0-7146-4234-7*, Pub. by Irish Acad Pr) Intl Spec Bk.

Political Landscape: An Art History of Nature. Martin Warnke. (Essays in Art & Culture Ser.).Tr. of Politische Landschaft. (Illus.). 165p. 1995. text 42.00 (*0-674-68616-0*, WARPOL) HUP.

Political Landscape: An Art History of Nature. Martin Warnke. (Essays in Art & Culture Ser.).Tr. of Politische Landschaft. (Illus.). 168p. 1996. pap. 23.50 (*0-674-68617-9*) HUP.

Political Language of Film & the Avant-Garde. Dana B. Polan. Ed. by Diane Kirkpatrick. LC 84-24062. (Studies in Cinema: No. 30). 151p. reprint ed. pap. 46.90 (*0-8357-1604-X*, 207075100004) Bks Demand.

Political Language of Islam. Bernard Lewis. LC 87-19222. (Exxon Lectures). viii, 184p. 1991. pap. 12.00 (*0-226-47693-6*) U Ch Pr.

Political Language of Islam. Bernard Lewis. (Illus.). x, 168p. 1992. 19.95 (*0-226-47692-8*) U Ch Pr.

Political Languages of Race & the Politics of Exclusion. Andy R. Brown. LC 98-73857. (Research in Migration & Ethnic Relations Ser.). 7p. 1999. text 74.95 (*1-84014-516-1*) Ashgate Pub Co.

Political Leaders see Women in Profile Series

Political Leaders. Lindop. 1996. write for info. (*0-8050-5257-7*) H Holt & Co.

Political Leaders. Ed. by S. O'Brien & James Cockcroft. (Illus.). 112-128p. (gr. 5). 1996. 139.65 (*0-7910-3528-X*) Chelsea Hse.

Political Leaders & Military Figures of the Second World War: A Bibliography. Steven D. Chambers. LC 95-47697. (Illus.). 464p. 1996. text 101.95 (*1-85521-646-9*, Pub. by Dartmth Pub) Ashgate Pub Co.

Political Leaders in Black Africa: A Biographical Dictionary of Major Politicians since Independence. John A. Wiseman. 272p. 1991. text 120.00 (*1-85278-047-9*) E Elgar.

Political Leaders of Contemporary Africa South of the Sahara: A Biographical Dictionary. Ed. by Harvey Glickman. LC 91-39641. 392p. 1992. lib. bdg. 75.00 (*0-313-26781-2*, GPF/, Greenwood Pr) Greenwood.

Political Leaders of Contemporary Western Europe: A Biographical Dictionary. David Wilsford. LC 94-39084. 536p. 1995. lib. bdg. 135.00 (*0-313-28623-X*, Greenwood Pr) Greenwood.

Political Leaders of Provincial Pennsylvania. Isaac Sharpless. LC 75-169774. (Select Bibliographies Reprint Ser.). 1977. reprint ed. 21.95 (*0-8369-5994-9*) Ayer.

Political Leaders of the Contemporary Middle East & North Africa: A Biographical Dictionary. Ed. by Bernard Reich. LC 89-7498. 570p. 1990. lib. bdg. 99.50 (*0-313-26213-6*, RPC/, Greenwood Pr) Greenwood.

Political Leaders of Upper Canada. William Smith, Jr. LC 68-26475. (Essay Index Reprint Ser.). 1977. 23.95 (*0-8369-0886-4*) Ayer.

Political Leadership: A Source Book. Barbara Kellerman. LC 85-26436. (Series in Policy & Institutional Studies). 480p. 1986. pap. 19.95 (*0-8229-5382-X*) U of Pittsburgh Pr.

Political Leadership: Jawaharlal Nehru. Akhileshwar Singh. 1986. 27.50 (*0-8364-1906-5*, Pub. by Deep & Deep Pubns) S Asia.

Political Leadership among Swat Pathans. 5th ed. Fredrik Barth. (London School of Economics Monographs on Social Anthropology: No. 19). 144p. (C). 1959. pap. 16.50 (*0-485-19619-0*, Pub. by Athlone Pr) Humanities.

Political Leadership & Educational Failure. Seymour B. Sarason. LC 97-38547. (Education Ser.). 1998. 32.95 (*0-7879-4061-5*) Jossey-Bass.

Political Leadership & Nihilism: A Study of Weber & Nietzsche. Robert Eden. LC 83-17075. 348p. 1984. 49.95 (*0-8130-0758-5*) U Press Fla.

Political Leadership in an Age of Restraint: The Australian Experience. Colin Campbell & John Halligan. LC 92-27355. (Series in Policy & Institutional Studies). 284p. (C). 1993. text 29.95 (*0-8229-1170-1*) U of Pittsburgh Pr.

Political Leadership in Contemporary Japan. Ed. by Terry E. MacDougall. LC 82-9634. (Michigan Papers in Japanese Studies: No. 1). xiv, 146p. 1982. pap. 7.00 (*0-939512-06-8*) U MI Japan.

Political Leadership in Jefferson's Virginia. Daniel P. Jordan. LC 82-23867. 298p. reprint ed. pap. 92.40 (*0-8357-6444-3*, 203581500097) Bks Demand.

Political Leadership in Korea. Ed. by Dae-Sook Suh & Chae-Jin Lee. LC 76-5480. (Publications on Asia of the Institute for Comparative & Foreign Area Studies: No. 27). 276p. 1976. 25.00 (*0-295-95437-X*) U of Wash Pr.

Political Leadership in Liberal Democracies. Robert Elgie. LC 95-19326. (Comparative Government & Politics Ser.). 208p. 1995. text 55.00 (*0-312-12893-2*) St Martin.

Political Leadership in Sierra Leone. John R. Cartwright. LC 79-300056. 308p. reprint ed. pap. 95.50 (*0-608-12846-5*, 202360200033) Bks Demand.

***Political Learning & Redemocratization in Latin America: Do Politicians Learn from Crises?** Jennifer McCoy. LC 99-47546. 1999. pap. 21.95 (*1-57454-066-1*, Pub. by U Miami N-S Ctr) L Rienner.

Political Learning in Adulthood: A Sourcebook of Theory & Research. Ed. by Roberta S. Sigel. LC 88-20522. 500p. 1989. lib. bdg. 78.00 (*0-226-75693-9*) U Ch Pr.

Political Learning in Adulthood: A Sourcebook of Theory & Research. Ed. by Roberta S. Sigel. LC 88-20522. 500p. 1998. pap. text 24.00 (*0-226-75694-7*) U Ch Pr.

***Political Learning in the Historical Context.** Dieter Schmidt-Sinns. (International Studies in Political Socialization: Vol. 9). 137p. 2000. 35.00 (*3-931397-27-0*) Galda & Wilch.

Political Left in the American Theatre of the 1930's: A Bibliographic Sourcebook. Compiled by Susan Duffy. LC 92-10822. 218p. 1992. 32.00 (*0-8108-2577-5*) Scarecrow.

Political Legacy of Aung San. Aung San Suu Kyi. LC 73-174143. (Cornell University, Southeast Asia Program, Data Paper Ser.: No. 86). 121p. reprint ed. pap. 37.60 (*0-8357-6270-X*, 201048300068) Bks Demand.

Political Legacy of Aung San. rev. ed. Compiled by Josef Silverstein. (Southeast Asia Program Ser.: No. 11). 169p. (Orig.). 1993. reprint ed. pap. text 16.00 (*0-87727-128-3*) Cornell SE Asia.

Political Legacy of George D. Aiken: Wise Old Owl of the U. S. Senate. Ed. by Michael Sherman. (Illus.). 172p. 1995. pap. 16.00 (*0-88150-352-5*, Pub. by Countryman) Norton.

Political, Legal & Ecomonic Overview see Integration Through Law - Europe & the American Federal Experience, Vol. I: Methods , Tools, & Institutions

Political Legitimacy & Housing: Stakeholding in Singapore. Beng-Huat Chua. LC 97-14249. 208p. (C). 1997. 85.00 (*0-415-16690-X*) Routledge.

Political Legitimacy & the Administration of Education. Laurence Iannaccone. 105p. (C). 1984. 65.00 (*0-7300-0013-3*, Pub. by Deakin Univ) St Mut.

Political Legitimacy & the State. Rodney Barker. 224p. 1990. 55.00 (*0-19-827495-5*) OUP.

Political Legitimacy in Southeast Asia: The Quest for Moral Authority. Ed. by Muthiah Alagappa. LC 95-1075. (Contemporary Issues in Asia & the Pacific Ser.). 448p. 1995. 60.00 (*0-8047-2504-7*); pap. 19.95 (*0-8047-2560-8*) Stanford U Pr.

Political Legitimacy of Markets & Governments. Ed. by Thomas R. Dye et al. LC 89-71749. (Political Economy & Public Policy Ser.: Vol. 7). 215p. 1990. 78.50 (*1-55938-103-5*) Jai Pr.

***Political Libels: A Comparative Style.** Ian Loveland. 224p. 2000. 45.00 (*1-84113-115-6*, Pub. by Hart Pub) Intl Spec Bk.

Political Liberalism. John Rawls. 401p. (C). 1993. 46.50 (*0-231-05248-0*) Col U Pr.

Political Liberalism. John Rawls. 401p. 1996. pap. 18.00 (*0-231-05249-9*) Col U Pr.

Political Liberalization & Democratization in the Arab World Vol. 1: Theoretical Perspectives. Ed. by Rex Brynen et al. 350p. 1995. lib. bdg. 58.00 (*1-55587-559-9*) L Rienner.

Political Liberalization & Democratization in the Arab World Vol. 2: Comparative Experiences. Bahgat Korany et al. 300p. 1998. lib. bdg. 58.00 (*1-55587-590-4*) L Rienner.

Political Liberalization & Democratization in the Arab World Vol. 2: Experiences. Bahgat Korany et al. 300p. 1998. pap. 22.50 (*1-55587-599-8*) L Rienner.

Political Liberalization in an Authoritarian Regime: The Case of Mexico. Kevin J. Middlebrook. (Research Reports: No. 41). 36p. (Orig.). (C). 1985. pap. 5.00 (*0-935391-40-1*, RR-41) UCSD Ctr US-Mex.

Political Liberty. Alexander J. Carlyle. 220p. 1963. 26.00 (*0-7146-1551-X*, Pub. by F Cass Pubs) Intl Spec Bk.

Political Liberty: A History of the Conception in the Middle Ages & Modern Times. Alexander J. Carlyle. LC 80-18967. 220p. 1980. reprint ed. lib. bdg. 59.50 (*0-313-21482-4*, CAPL, Greenwood Pr) Greenwood.

Political Life & Letters of Cavour, 1848-1861. Arthur J. Whyte. LC 74-30983. (Illus.). 478p. 1975. reprint ed. lib. bdg. 55.00 (*0-8371-7939-4*, WHPL, Greenwood Pr) Greenwood.

Political Life in Assam During the 19th Century. B. B. Hazarika. (C). 1987. 19.50 (*81-212-0069-5*, Pub. by Gian Publng Hse) S Asia.

Political Life in Eighteenth-Century Virginia. Jack P. Greene. (Foundations of America Ser.). (Illus.). 52p. (Orig.). 1986. pap. 9.95 (*0-87935-116-0*) Colonial Williamsburg.

Political Life in Japan: Democracy in a Reversible World. Takako Kishima. (Illus.). 169p. 1992. text 32.50 (*0-691-07895-5*, Pub. by Princeton U Pr) Cal Prin Full Svc.

Political Life in Medieval England, 1300-1450. W. M. Ormrod. LC 95-8258. (British History in Perspective Ser.). 1995. text 45.00 (*0-312-12722-7*) St Martin.

Political Life in Washington: Governing the Evergreen State. Ed. by Thor Swanson et al. LC 85-13824. (Illus.). 236p. reprint ed. pap. 73.20 (*0-7837-1213-8*, 204174500023) Bks Demand.

***Political Life of Children.** Robert Coles. 352p. 2000. pap. 13.50 (*0-87113-771-2*, Atlntc Mnthly) Grove-Atltic.

Political Life of the American States: American Political Parties & Elections. Ed. by Gerald M. Pomper et al. LC 83-17756. 344p. 1984. pap. 14.95 (*0-275-91630-8*, B1630, Praeger Pubs) Greenwood.

Political Limits of Environmental Regulation: Tracking the Unicorn. Bruce Yandle. LC 89-32919. 192p. 1989. 59.95 (*0-89930-431-1*, YGM/, Quorum Bks) Greenwood.

Political Literacy: Rhetoric, Ideology, & the Possibility of Justice. Fredric G. Gale. LC 93-16871. (SUNY Series, Interruptions: Border Testimony(ies) & Critical Discourse(s)). 189p. (C). 1994. text 49.50 (*0-7914-1805-7*); pap. text 16.95 (*0-7914-1806-5*) State U NY Pr.

Political Lives. Ed. by Judith Brett. (Illus.). 216p. 1998. pap. 19.95 (*1-86448-309-1*, Pub. by Allen & Unwin Pty) Paul & Co Pubs.

***Political Lives of Dead Bodies.** Katherine Verdery. 2000. reprint ed. pap. 14.95 (*0-231-11231-9*) Col U Pr.

Political Lives of Dead Bodies: Reburial & Post-Socialist Change. Katherine Verdery. LC 98-45114. 208p. 1999. 22.50 (*0-231-11230-0*) Col U Pr.

Political Logic of Economic Reform in China. Susan L. Shirk. LC 92-12030. (California Series on Social Choice & Political Economy: No. 24). 1993. 55.00 (*0-520-07706-7*, Pub. by U CA Pr); pap. 17.95 (*0-520-07707-5*, Pub. by U CA Pr) Cal Prin Full Svc.

Political Logic of Privatization: Lessons from Great Britain & Poland. Mariusz M. Dobek. LC 93-6770. 184p. 1993. 55.00 (*0-275-94618-5*, C4618, Praeger Pubs) Greenwood.

Political Love Poems. Thomas Hastings. (Chapbook Series I: No. 5). 20p. 1980. pap. 2.00 (*1-880649-05-5*) Writ Ctr Pr.

Political Loyalty & Public Service in West Germany: The 1972 Decree Against Radicals & Its Consequences. Gerard Braunthal. LC 89-28435. 272p. (C). 1990. lib. bdg. 32.50 (*0-87023-707-1*) U of Mass Pr.

Political Macroeconomics. Keizo Nagatani. (Illus.). 288p. 1990. text 75.00 (*0-19-828642-2*) OUP.

Political Man: The Social Bases of Politics. Seymour M. Lipset. LC 80-8867. 608p. (C). 1981. reprint ed. pap. text 17.95 (*0-8018-2522-9*) Johns Hopkins.

Political Management: Redefining the Public Sphere. H. T. Wilson. LC 84-17608. (Studies in Organization: No. 2). x, 316p. 1984. 87.90 (*3-11-009902-0*) De Gruyter.

Political Management in Canada: Conversations on Statecraft. 2nd ed. Allan Blakeney & Sanford Borins. LC 99-167884. 320p. 1998. text 60.00 (*0-8020-4290-2*); pap. text 21.95 (*0-8020-8123-1*) U of Toronto Pr.

Political Market Place U. S. A. Ed. by George Thomas Kurian & Jeffrey D. Schultz. LC 98-33513. (Illus.). 352p. 1999. pap. 65.00 (*1-57356-226-2*) Oryx Pr.

***Political Marketing.** Harris. 2000. 49.95 (*0-7506-4537-7*) Buttrwrth-Heinemann.

Political Marketing: An Approach to Campaign Strategy. Gary A. Mauser. Ed. by Steven E. Permut. LC 82-25973. (Praeger Series in Public & Nonprofit Sector Marketing). 304p. 1983. 57.95 (*0-275-91721-5*, C1721, Praeger Pubs) Greenwood.

Political Marketing: An Approach to Campaign Strategy. Gary A. Mauser. LC 82-25973. 1983. 34.95 (*0-03-052591-8*) Holt R&W.

Political Marketing: Readings & Annotated Bibliography. Ed. by Bruce I. Newman & Jagdish N. Sheth. LC 85-26866. 269p. (Orig.). reprint ed. pap. 83.40 (*0-7837-2494-2*, 204265900005) Bks Demand.

Political Marketing & Commun. Lutton Staff. 1997. pap. 39.95 (*0-86196-377-6*, Pub. by J Libbey Med) Bks Intl VA.

***Political Meaning of Christianity: An Interpretation.** Glenn E. Tinder. 272p. 2000. pap. 24.00 (*1-57910-426-6*) Wipf & Stock.

Political Memoir: Essays on the Politics of Memory. Ed. by George Egerton. LC 93-30585. 370p. 1994. pap. 27.50 (*0-7146-4093-X*, Pub. by F Cass Pubs); boxed set 47.50 (*0-7146-3471-9*, Pub. by F Cass Pubs) Intl Spec Bk.

Political Memoirs by Aurel Kolnai. Aurel Kolnai. Ed. by Francesca Murphy. LC 99-13920. (Religion & Society in the New Millennium Ser.). 320p. 1999. 40.00 (*0-7391-0065-3*) Lxngtn Bks.

Political Memoirs, 1914-17. Nicholas Prince of Greece. LC 72-1274. (Select Bibliographies Reprint Ser.). 1977. reprint ed. 34.95 (*0-8369-6833-6*) Ayer.

Political Memoranda: Revision of Instructions to Political Officers on Subjects Chiefly Political & Administrative, 1913-1918. 3rd rev. ed. Frederick J. Lugard. 480p. 1970. 59.50 (*0-7146-1693-1*, Pub. by F Cass Pubs) Intl Spec Bk.

Political Mercenaries & Citizen Soldiers: A Profile of North Indian Party Activists. Yogendra Malik & Jesse Marquette. 1990. 24.50 (*81-7001-081-0*, Pub. by Chanakya) S Asia.

***Political Metaphors.** Archibald C. Coolidge, Jr. 80p. (C). 1999. pap. 7.95 (*0-944266-26-6*) Maecenas Pr.

***Political-military Relations & the Stability of Arab Regimes.** Risa Brooks. LC 99-219926. (Adelphi Papers: 324). (Illus.). 92p. 1999. pap. text 25.95 (*0-19-922420-X*) OUP.

Political Mirages: Russia at the Crossroads. Leonid M. Batkin. 1995. 115.00 (*1-56072-265-7*) Nova Sci Pubs.

Political, Miscellaneous, & Philosophical Pieces. Benjamin Franklin. (Notable American Authors Ser.). 1992. reprint ed. lib. bdg. 75.00 (*0-7812-2893-X*) Rprt Serv.

Political Mischief: Smear, Sabotage, & Reform in U. S. Elections. Bruce L. Felknor. LC 91-22105. 312p. 1992. 59.95 (*0-275-94183-3*, C4183, Praeger Pubs) Greenwood.

Political Mobilization & Industry in Libya. Maja Naur. (Illus.). 268p. (Orig.). 1986. pap. text 52.50 (*87-500-2648-8*) Coronet Bks.

Political Mobilization & Social Change. Kriesi Hanspeter. (Public Policy & Social Welfare Ser.: Vol. 12). 292p. 1993. 41.95 (*1-85628-518-9*, Pub. by Avebry) Ashgate Pub Co.

Political Mobilization of Religious Beliefs. Ted G. Jelen. LC 90-45485. 208p. 1991. 57.95 (*0-275-93439-X*, C3439, Praeger Pubs) Greenwood.

Political Mobilization of the Venezuelan Peasant. John D. Powell. LC 70-134947. (Center for International Affairs Ser.). (Illus.). 275p. 1971. 35.95 (*0-674-68626-8*) HUP.

***Political Modernisation & the Environment: The Renewal of Environmental Policy Arrangements.** Jan Van Tatenhove et al. LC 00-39115. (Environment & Policy Ser.). 2000. write for info. (*0-7923-6312-4*) Kluwer Academic.

Political Modernization in the Gulf. Shahid J. Ansari. LC 99-932606. ix, 235p. 1998. write for info. (*81-7211-088-X*, Pub. by Northern Bk Centre) Nataraj Bks.

Political Modernization in Three Guatemalan Indian Communities see Community Culture & National Change

Political Moments in the Classroom. Ed. by Margaret Himley et al. LC 96-45559. (Orig.). (C). 1997. pap. text 22.50 (*0-86709-388-9*, 0388, Pub. by Boynton Cook Pubs) Heinemann.

Political Money: A Strategy for Companion Financing in America. David W. Adamany & George E. Agree. LC 75-11351. 254p. reprint ed. pap. 78.80 (*0-608-14599-8*, 202582000046) Bks Demand.

***Political Money: Deregulating American Politics, Selected Writings on Campaign Finance Reform.** Annelise Graener Anderson. LC 00-21268. 2000. write for info. (*0-8179-9672-9*) Hoover Inst Pr.

Political Money: The New Prohibition. Annelise G. Anderson. LC 97-42649. (Essays in Public Policy Ser.: No. 83). 1997. pap. 5.00 (*0-8179-5882-7*) Hoover Inst Pr.

Political Morality of the International Monetary Fund. Ed. by Robert S. Browne. (Ethics in Foreign Policy Ser.: Vol. 3). 164p. 1987. text 39.95 (*0-88738-143-X*) Transaction Pubs.

Political Mothers. Jean B. Elshtain. 224p. 1997. 19.95 (*0-465-05952-X*, Pub. by Basic) HarpC.

Political Mothers. Jean B. Elshtain. 224p. 1998. pap. 15.00 (*0-465-05888-4*, Pub. by Basic) HarpC.

Political Murder: From Tyrannicide to Terrorism. Franklin L. Ford. (Illus.). 456p. 1985. pap. text 10.95 (*0-674-68636-5*) HUP.

Political Murder: From Tyrannicide to Terrorism. Franklin L. Ford. LC 85-5837. (Illus.). 456p. 1985. 42.50 (*0-674-68635-7*) HUP.

Political Murder & Reform in Colombia: The Violence Continues. Ed. by Human Rights Watch Staff. 128p. (Orig.). 1992. pap. 10.00 (*1-56432-064-2*) Hum Rts Watch.

Political Murder in Central America: Death Squads & U. S. Policies. Ed. by Gary E. McCuen. (Ideas in Conflict Ser.). (Illus.). 136p. (YA). (gr. 7-12). 1985. lib. bdg. 15.95 (*0-86596-050-X*) G E M.

Political Myth: A Theoretical Introduction. Christopher Flood. Ed. by Robert A. Segal. LC 95-53716. (Theorists of Myth Ser.: Vol. 8). 328p. 1996. text 61.00 (*0-8153-0096-4*, H1433) Garland.

Political Mythology & Popular Fiction, 197. Ed. by Ernest J. Yanarella & Lee Sigelman. LC 87-18702. (Contributions in Political Science Ser.: No. 197). 210p. 1988. 55.00 (*0-313-25976-3*, SYT/, Greenwood Pr) Greenwood.

Political Networks: The Structural Perspective. David Knoke. (Structural Analysis in the Social Sciences Ser.: No. 3). (Illus.). 304p. (C). 1990. text 59.95 (*0-521-37552-5*) Cambridge U Pr.

P

Political Networks: The Structural Perspective. David Knoke. (Structural Analysis in the Social Sciences Ser.: No. 4). (Illus.). 304p. (C). 1994. pap. text 18.95 (*0-521-47762-X*) Cambridge U Pr.

Political Networks & the Chinese Policy Process. John W. Lewis. (Occasional Paper of the Northeast Asia-United States Forum on International Policy, Stanford University). 32p. (Orig.). pap. 6.00 (*0-935371-15-X*) CFISAC.

Political Novel. Joseph L. Blotner. LC 78-9868. 100p. 1979. reprint ed. lib. bdg. 55.00 (*0-313-21228-7*, BLPN, Greenwood Pr) Greenwood.

Political Novel: Its Development in England & in America. Morris E. Speare. (BCL1-PR English Literature Ser.). 377p. 1992. reprint ed. lib. bdg. 89.00 (*0-7812-7122-3*) Rprt Serv.

Political Novels of Joseph Conrad: A Critical Study with a New Preface. Eloise K. Hay. LC 80-29356. (Midway Reprint Ser.). (Illus.). 364p. reprint ed. pap. 112.90 (*0-608-18230-3*, 205663800078) Bks Demand.

Political Obligation. Simmons. 256p. (C). 1998. 60.00 (*0-415-10949-3*) Routledge.

Political Obligation in a Liberal State. Steven M. DeLue. LC 88-39159. (SUNY Series in Political Theory: Contemporary Issues). 179p. (C). 1989. pap. text 21.95 (*0-7914-0093-X*) State U NY Pr.

Political Offence Exception to Extradition. Christine Van den Wijngaert. 270p. 1980. lib. bdg. 48.00 (*90-268-1185-3*) Kluwer Academic.

Political Olympics: Moscow, Afghanistan & the 1980 U. S. Boycott. Derick Hulme. LC 89-78402. 192p. 1990. 52.95 (*0-275-93466-7*, C3455, Praeger Pubs) Greenwood.

Political Ontology of Martin Heidegger. Pierre Bourdieu. Tr. by Peter Collier from FRE. LC 90-70309. 146p. 1991. 37.50 (*0-8047-1698-6*) Stanford U Pr.

Political Ontology of Martin Heidegger. Pierre Bourdieu. 1996. pap. text 12.95 (*0-8047-2960-3*) Stanford U Pr.

Political Opinion in Massachusetts During Civil War & Reconstruction. Edith E. Ware. LC 77-76697. (Columbia University. Studies in the Social Sciences: No. 175). reprint ed. 29.50 (*0-404-51175-9*) AMS Pr.

Political Opposition & Foreign Policy in Comparative Perspective. Joe D. Hagan. LC 93-15853. 275p. 1993. lib. bdg. 52.00 (*1-55587-027-9*) L Rienner.

Political Opposition & Local Politics in Japan. Ed. by Kurt Steiner et al. LC 80-7555. (Illus.). 495p. 1980. reprint ed. pap. 153.50 (*0-608-02570-4*, 206321500004) Bks Demand.

Political Opposition in Post-Confucian Society. Peter R. Moody, Jr. LC 88-11759. 296p. 1988. 59.95 (*0-275-93063-7*, C3063, Praeger Pubs) Greenwood.

Political Oppositions in Industrialising Asia. Garry Rodan. LC 96-3329. (New Rich in Asia Ser.). 360p. (C). 1996. pap. 27.99 (*0-415-14865-0*) Routledge.

Political Oppositions in Industrialising Asia. 2nd ed. Garry Rodan. LC 96-3329. (New Rich in Asia Ser.). 360p. (C). 1996. 90.00 (*0-415-14864-2*) Routledge.

Political Order. Ed. by Ian Shapiro & Russell Hardin. (Nomos Ser.: Vol. XXXVIII). 544p. 1998. pap. text 20.00 (*0-8147-8103-9*) NYU Pr.

Political Order No. XXXIX: Yearbook of the American Society for Political & Legal Philosophy. Ed. by Ian Shapiro & Russell Hardin. (Illus.). 544p. (C). 1996. text 55.00 (*0-8147-8029-6*) NYU Pr.

Political Order & Power Transition in Hong Kong. Ed. by Li Pang-Kwong. 280p. 1998. pap. text 27.50 (*962-201-783-5*, Pub. by Chinese Univ) U of Mich Pr.

Political Order in Changing Societies. Samuel P. Huntington. (Henry L. Stimson Lectures). 1969. pap. 20.00 (*0-300-01171-7*) Yale U Pr.

Political Order in Post-Communist Afghanistan. William Maley & Fazel H. Saikal. LC 92-32723. (Internaational Peace Academy Occasional Papers). 80p. 1992. pap. text 7.95 (*1-55587-361-8*) L Rienner.

Political Organization & the Interwar Crisis in Europe. Lauri Karvonen. (Social Science Monographs). 185p. 1993. 31.00 (*0-88033-967-5*, 381, Pub. by East Eur Monographs) Col U Pr.

Political Organization Approach to Transnational Terrorism, 141. Kent L. Oots. LC 85-17030. (Contributions to Political Science Ser.: No. 141). (Illus.). 188p. 1986. 49.95 (*0-313-25105-3*, OPO/, Greenwood Pr) Greenwood.

Political Organization of Attica. John S. Traill. LC 74-17324. (Hesperia Supplement Ser.: No. 14). (Illus.). xviii, 122p. 1975. pap. 15.00 (*0-87661-514-0*) Am Sch Athens.

Political Organization of the Plains Indians: With Special Reference to the Council. Maurice G. Smith. LC 76-43837. (Nebraska Univ. Studies: Vol. 24, Nos. 1 & 2). reprint ed. 32.50 (*0-404-15691-6*) AMS Pr.

Political Organization of Unyamwezi. R. G. Abrahams. LC 67-12842. (Cambridge Studies in Social Anthropology: No. 1). 228p. reprint ed. pap. 65.00 (*0-608-17017-8*, 2027274) Bks Demand.

Political Organizations in the Soviet Armed Forces: The Role of the Party & Komsomol. Sergei Zamascikov. Ed. by Barbara Dash. 100p. (Orig.). 1982. pap. text 75.00 (*1-55831-057-6*) Delphic Associates.

Political Organizing in Grassroots Politics. Daniel M. Russell. LC 89-22757. 170p. (Orig.). (C). 1990. pap. text 22.50 (*0-8191-7619-2*); lib. bdg. 39.00 (*0-8191-7618-4*) U Pr of Amer.

Political Organs, Integration Techniques & Judicial Processes see Integration Through Law - Europe & the American Federal Experience, Vol. I: Methods, Tools, & Institutions

***Political Orphan? The Prolife Cause after 25 Years of Roe vs. Wade.** Kenneth D. Whitehead. ix, 353p. 1998. pap. 14.95 (*1-892875-02-0*, 0130, Remnant Israel) New Hope Publicatns.

Political Palate: A Feminist Vegetarian Cookbook. Bloodroot Collective Staff. LC 80-53521. (Illus.). 325p. (Orig.). 1980. pap. 12.95 (*0-9605210-0-3*) Sanguinaria.

Political Paranoia: The Psychopolitics of Hatred. Robert S. Robins & Jerrold M. Post. LC 96-40336. 353p. 1997. 30.00 (*0-300-07027-6*) Yale U Pr.

Political Participation & American Democracy, 279. Ed. by William Crotty. LC 91-9175. (Contributions in Political Science Ser.: No. 279). 248p. 1991. 62.95 (*0-313-27652-8*, CPR/, Greenwood Pr) Greenwood.

***Political Participation & Ethnic Minorities: Chinese Overseas in Malaysia Indonesia & the United States.** Amy L. Freedman. LC 99-55075. 224p. (C). 2000. text. write for info. (*0-415-92445-6*) Routledge.

***Political Participation & Ethnic Minorities: Chinese Overseas in Malaysia Indonesia & United States.** Amy L. Freedman. LC 99-55075. 224p. 2000. pap. write for info. (*0-415-92446-4*) Routledge.

Political Participation Goverment. Peltzman. LC 98-14276. 1998. pap. text 22.00 (*0-226-65417-6*) U Ch Pr.

Political Participation Government. Peltzman. LC 98-14276. 1998. lib. bdg. 60.00 (*0-226-65416-8*) U Ch Pr.

Political Participation in a Non-Electoral Setting: The Urban Poor in Lima, Peru. Henry A. Dietz & Richard J. Moore. LC 79-14218. (Papers in International Studies: Latin America Ser.: No. 6). 110p. reprint ed. pap. 34.10 (*0-7837-1329-0*, 204147700021) Bks Demand.

Political Participation in America, 1967. Sidney Verba & Norman H. Nie. LC 75-43068. 1976. write for info. (*0-89138-152-X*) ICPSR.

Political Participation in Beijing. Tianjian Shi. LC 96-53018. (Illus.). 416p. 1997. 51.95 (*0-674-68640-3*); pap. 23.95 (*0-674-68641-1*) HUP.

Political Participation in Communist Systems. Donald E. Schulz. (Policy Studies). 1981. 88.00 (*0-08-024665-6*, Pergamon Pr) Elsevier.

Political Participation in Latin America Vol. 2: Politics & the Poor. Ed. by John A. Booth & Mitchell A. Seligson. 1979. 34.50 (*0-8419-0405-7*); pap. 15.95 (*0-8419-0406-5*) Holmes & Meier.

Political Participation in Modern Indonesia. Ed. by R. William Liddle et al. LC 73-89521. (Monographs: No. 19). (Illus.). 206p. 1973. 9.50 (*0-938692-11-9*) Yale U SE Asia.

Political Participation in the United States. 2nd ed. M. Margaret Conway. LC 90-47357. 204p. 1990. text 24.95 (*0-87187-539-X*) Congr Quarterly.

***Political Participation in the United States.** 3rd rev. ed. M. Margaret Conway. 200p. 2000. pap. text 24.95 (*0-87187-792-9*) Congr Quarterly.

Political Participation of Asian Americans: Voting Behavior in Southern California. rev. ed. Pei-te Lien. Ed. by Franklin Ng. LC 97-33628. (Asian Americans). (Illus.). 200p. 1997. text 53.00 (*0-8153-2984-9*) Garland.

Political Participation, Public Investment, & Support for the System: A Comparative Study of Rural Communities in Mexico. Carlos Salinas De Gortari. (Research Reports: No. 35). 45p. (Orig.). (C). 1982. pap. 5.00 (*0-935391-34-7*, RR-35) UCSD Ctr US-Mex.

Political Parties. Ed. by William E. Leuchtenburg. LC 76-54572. (Great Contemporary Issues Ser.). 1977. lib. bdg. 27.95 (*0-405-09866-9*) Ayer.

Political Parties. Lindop. 1996. write for info. (*0-8050-5264-X*) H Holt & Co.

Political Parties. Edmund Lindop. LC 96-11428. (J). 1995. lib. bdg. 15.98 (*0-8050-4618-6*) H Holt & Co.

Political Parties. Robert Michels. LC 98-27094. 379p. 2000. pap. 29.95 (*0-7658-0469-7*) Transaction Pubs.

Political Parties. John R. Petrocik. (C). 1999. pap. text 36.00 (*0-15-502963-0*, Pub. by Harcourt Coll Pubs) Harcourt.

Political Parties. Steven B. Wolinetz. LC 98-12752. (The International Library of Politics & Comparative Government). 570p. 1998. text 178.95 (*1-85521-854-2*, JF2051.W66, Pub. by Ashgate Pub) Ashgate Pub Co.

Political Parties: Development & Decay. Louis Meisel & Joseph Cooper. LC 76-46782. (Sage Electoral Studies Yearbook: Vol. 4). 344p. reprint ed. pap. 106.70 (*0-608-31006-9*, 202192700026) Bks Demand.

Political Parties & American Democracy. Sidney M. Milkis. LC 99-14370. (Interpreting American Politics Ser.). 364p. 1999. 49.50 (*0-8018-6194-2*) Johns Hopkins.

Political Parties & American Democracy: Remaking American Democracy. Sidney M. Milkis. LC 99-14370. (Interpreting American Politics Ser.). 364p. 1999. pap. 17.95 (*0-8018-6195-0*) Johns Hopkins.

Political Parties & Civic Action Groups, 4. Edward L. Schapsmeier & Frederick H. Schapsmeier. LC 80-1714. (Encyclopedia of American Institutions Ser.: No. 4). (Illus.). 554p. 1981. lib. bdg. 115.00 (*0-313-21442-5*, SPC/, Greenwood Pr) Greenwood.

Political Parties & Coalitional Behavior in Italy: An Interpretive Study. Geoffrey Pridham. 256p. 1987. lib. bdg. 57.50 (*0-415-00503-5*) Routledge.

Political Parties & Democracy: Explorations in History & Theory. Arthur Lipow. LC 95-52788. 256p. 1996. 59.95 (*0-7453-1099-0*) Pluto GBR.

Political Parties & Democracy: Explorations in History & Theory. Arthur Lipow. 256p. 1996. pap. 22.95 (*0-7453-1098-2*, Pub. by Pluto GBR) Stylus Pub VA.

Political Parties & Democracy in Turkey. Ed. by Metin Heper & Jacob M. Landau. 300p. 1990. 49.50 (*0-685-38702-X*, Pub. by I B T) St Martin.

Political Parties & Elections in Japan: The Post-1993 System. 3rd ed. Ronald J. Hrebenar. LC 99-51526. 288p. 1999. text 65.00 (*0-8133-3056-4*); pap. text 25.00 (*0-8133-3057-2*) Westview.

Political Parties & Elections in the United States. Jose Marti. Ed. by Philip S. Foner. Tr. by Elinor Randall from SPA. 208p. (C). 1989. 27.95 (*0-87722-604-0*) Temple U Pr.

Political Parties & Elections in the United States: An Encyclopedia, 2 vols., Set. Ed. by Louis S. Maisel. LC 91-6940. 1367p. 1991. text 75.00 (*0-8240-7975-2*, SS498) Garland.

Political Parties & Generations in Paraguay's Liberal Era, 1869-1940. Paul H. Lewis. LC 92-21164. xvi, 228p. 1992. 49.95 (*0-8078-2078-4*) U of NC Pr.

***Political Parties & Interest Groups: Shaping Democratic Governance.** Ed. by Clive S. Thomas. 350p. 2001. 59.95 (*1-55587-978-0*) L Rienner.

Political Parties & Linkage: A Comparative Perspective. Ed. by Kay Lawson. LC 79-26751. 416p. reprint ed. pap. 129.00 (*0-7837-4532-X*, 208021600003) Bks Demand.

Political Parties & Party Systems. Alan Ware. (Illus.). 454p. 1995. text 72.00 (*0-19-878076-1*); pap. text 19.95 (*0-19-878077-X*) OUP.

Political Parties & Political Development. Ed. by Myron Weiner & Joseph G. LaPalombara. LC 66-10558. (Studies in Political Development: No. 6). (Illus.). 495p. reprint ed. pap. 153.50 (*0-8357-6271-8*, 203464700090) Bks Demand.

Political Parties & Primaries in Kentucky. Penny M. Miller & Malcolm E. Jewell. LC 89-70690. 336p. 1990. text 39.95 (*0-8131-1753-4*) U Pr of Ky.

Political Parties & Terrorist Groups. Ed. by Leonard Weinberg. LC 92-17599. 144p. 1993. text 37.50 (*0-7146-3491-3*, Pub. by F Cass Pubs) Intl Spec Bk.

Political Parties & the Callapse of the Old Orders. Ed. by John K. White & Philip J. Davies. LC 98-6506. (SUNY Series in Political Party Development). 256p. (C). 1999. text 62.50 (*0-7914-4067-2*); pap. text 20.95 (*0-7914-4068-0*) State U NY Pr.

Political Parties & the European Union. Ed. by John Gaffney. LC 95-9649. 352p. (C). 1996. pap. 25.99 (*0-415-09060-1*) Routledge.

Political Parties & the Labour Politics, 1937-47: With Special Reference to Bengal. Nirban Basu. (C). 1992. 14.00 (*81-85195-48-X*, Pub. by Minerva) S Asia.

Political Parties & the Maintenance of Liberal Democracy. Kelly D. Patterson. (Illus.). 240p. 1996. pap. 17.50 (*0-231-10257-7*) Col U Pr.

Political Parties & the Maintenance of Liberal Democracy. Kelly D. Patterson. Ed. by Robert Y. Shapiro. (Illus.). 240p. 1996. 47.50 (*0-231-10256-9*) Col U Pr.

Political Parties & the State: The American Historical Experience. Martin Shefter. LC 93-25806. (Studies in American Politics). 320p. 1994. text 55.00 (*0-691-03284-X*, Pub. by Princeton U Pr); pap. text 16.95 (*0-691-00044-1*, Pub. by Princeton U Pr) Cal Prin Full Svc.

Political Parties & the Winning of Office. Joseph A. Schlesinger. 248p. (C). 1994. pap. text 20.95 (*0-472-08256-6*, 08256) U of Mich Pr.

Political Parties Before the Constitution. Jackson T. Main. LC 71-184228. 501p. reprint ed. pap. 155.40 (*0-7837-0291-4*, 204061200018) Bks Demand.

Political Parties Before the Constitution. Jackson T. Main. Vol. 718. (Illus.). 512p. (C). 1974. reprint ed. pap. 5.75 (*0-393-00718-9*) Norton.

***Political Parties, Campaigns & Elections.** Robert E. DiClerico. LC 99-48852. 299p. 2000. pap. 28.00 (*0-13-040030-0*) P-H.

***Political Parties, Games & Redistribution.** Rosa Mule. (Illus.). 222p. 2001. write for info. (*0-521-79008-5*); pap. write for info. (*0-521-79358-0*) Cambridge U Pr.

Political Parties, Growth & Equality: Conservative & Social Democratic Economic Strategies in the World Economy. Carles Boix. LC 97-27896. (Cambridge Studies in Comparative Politics). (Illus.). 272p. (C). 1998. pap. 19.95 (*0-521-58595-3*); text 59.95 (*0-521-58446-9*) Cambridge U Pr.

Political Parties in American Society. Samuel J. Eldersveld. 2000. text 35.00 (*0-312-22688-8*) St Martin.

***Political Parties in American Society.** 2nd ed. Samuel J. Eldersveld. 1999. pap. text 42.95 (*0-312-24164-X*) St Martin.

Political Parties in Britain. Moshe Maor. LC 96-36203. 296p. (C). 1997. 85.00 (*0-415-08284-6*); pap. 25.99 (*0-415-08285-4*) Routledge.

Political Parties in China. Jermyn C. Lynn. LC 75-42523. (Studies in Chinese Government & Law). 255p. 1975. reprint ed. lib. bdg. 62.50 (*0-313-26961-0*, U6961, Greenwood Pr) Greenwood.

Political Parties in Europe. Theo Stammen. LC 80-26948. 336p. 1981. lib. bdg. 75.00 (*0-313-28132-7*, SZT/, Greenwood Pr) Greenwood.

Political Parties in India: Their Ideology & Organization. 1990. 48.50 (*81-7099-205-2*, Pub. by Mittal Pubs Dist) S Asia.

Political Parties in Local Areas. Ed. by William Crotty. LC 86-7093. 272p. 1987. text 34.00 (*0-87049-511-9*) U of Tenn Pr.

Political Parties in Puerto Rico, 1897-1976. Ed. by Raoul Gordon. 1976. lib. bdg. 59.95 (*0-8490-0874-3*) Gordon Pr.

Political Parties in Revolutionary Massachusetts. Stephen E. Patterson. LC 72-7991. 311p. reprint ed. pap. 96.50 (*0-608-01895-3*, 206254700003) Bks Demand.

Political Parties in Russia. Ed. by Alexander Dallin. LC 93-15341. (Research Ser.: No. 88). x, 102p. 1993. pap. text 10.95 (*0-87725-188-6*) U of Cal IAS.

Political Parties in Sri Lanka since Independence: A Bibliography. H. A. Peiris. (C). 1988. 22.50 (*81-7013-027-1*, Pub. by Navarang) S Asia.

Political Parties in the American Mold. Leon D. Epstein. LC 86-40050. 448p. 1989. pap. text 16.95 (*0-299-10704-3*) U of Wis Pr.

Political Parties in the American Mold. Leon D. Epstein. LC 86-40050. 454p. reprint ed. pap. 140.80 (*0-608-20427-7*, 207168000002) Bks Demand.

***Political Parties in the Electronic Age.** White & Shea. 2000. pap. text 38.95 (*0-312-15254-X*) St Martin.

Political Parties in the European Union. Simon Hix & Christopher Lord. LC 96-40842. (The European Union Series). 272p. 1997. pap. 19.95 (*0-312-17292-3*); text 59.95 (*0-312-17291-5*) St Martin.

Political Parties in the Southern States: Party Activists in Partisan Coalitions. Ed. by Tod A. Baker et al. LC 89-26557. 264p. 1990. 55.00 (*0-275-93027-0*, C3027, Greenwood Pr) Greenwood.

Political Parties in the Third World. Ed. by Vicky Randall. 256p. (C). 1988. text 69.95 (*0-8039-8143-0*); pap. text 16.95 (*0-8039-8144-9*) Sage.

Political Parties in the 21st Century. Ed. by Crotty. (C). 1998. text. write for info. (*0-321-01354-9*) Addson-Wesley Educ.

Political Parties in the United States. Jesse Macy. (Notable American Authors Ser.). 1999. reprint ed. lib. bdg. 125.00 (*0-7812-3911-7*) Rprt Serv.

Political Parties in the United States, 1846-1861. Jesse Macy. LC 73-19160. (Politics & People Ser.). 344p. 1974. reprint ed. 26.95 (*0-405-05882-9*) Ayer.

Political Parties in Turkey: The Role of Islam. Mehmet Y. Geyikdagi. LC 83-24470. 177p. 1984. 27.95 (*0-275-91167-5*, C1167, Praeger Pubs) Greenwood.

Political Parties in Western Democracies. Leon D. Epstein. LC 79-64858. 386p. (C). 1992. pap. text 24.95 (*0-87855-716-4*) Transaction Pubs.

***Political Parties Information.** John K. White. LC 00-22270. 336p. 2000. text 35.00 (*0-312-23255-1*) St Martin.

Political Parties, Interest Groups & Political Campaigns. Ronald J. Hrebenar et al. LC 99-20304. 384p. (C). 1999. pap. 69.00 (*0-8133-8007-3*, Pub. by Westview); pap. text 25.00 (*0-8133-8008-1*, Pub. by Westview) HarpC.

Political Parties of Asia & the Pacific, 2 vols. Haruhiro Fukui. Ed. by Colin A. Hughes et al. LC 84-19252. (Historical Encyclopedia of the World's Political Parties Ser.). (Illus.). 1362p. 1985. lib. bdg. 250.00 (*0-313-21350-X*, FUA/) Greenwood.

Political Parties of Asia & the Pacific, 2 vols., Vol. 1. Haruhiro Fukui. Ed. by Colin A. Hughes et al. LC 84-19252. (Historical Encyclopedia of the World's Political Parties Ser.). (Illus.). xviii, 1328p. 1985. lib. bdg. 150.00 (*0-313-25143-6*, FUA/01) Greenwood.

Political Parties of Asia & the Pacific, 2 vols., Vol. 2. Haruhiro Fukui. Ed. by Colin A. Hughes et al. LC 84-19252. (Historical Encyclopedia of the World's Political Parties Ser.). (Illus.). xviii, 1328p. 1985. lib. bdg. 150.00 (*0-313-25144-4*, FUA/02) Greenwood.

Political Parties of Europe, 2 vols. Ed. by Vincent McHale & Sharon Skowronski. LC 82-15408. (Greenwood Encyclopedia of the World's Political Parties Ser.). (Illus.). 1400p. 1983. lib. bdg. 195.00 (*0-313-21405-0*, MPP/) Greenwood.

Political Parties of Europe, 2 vols., Vol. 1. Ed. by Vincent McHale & Sharon Skowronski. LC 82-15408. (Greenwood Encyclopedia of the World's Political Parties Ser.). (Illus.). xix, 700p. 1983. lib. bdg. 125.00 (*0-313-23804-9*, MPP/01) Greenwood.

Political Parties of Europe, 2 vols., Vol. 2. Ed. by Vincent McHale & Sharon Skowronski. LC 82-15408. (Greenwood Encyclopedia of the World's Political Parties Ser.). (Illus.). 1297p. 1983. lib. bdg. 100.00 (*0-313-23805-7*, MPP/02) Greenwood.

Political Parties of the Americas: Canada, Latin America, & the West Indies, 2 vols. Ed. by Robert J. Alexander. LC 81-6952. (Greenwood Historical Encyclopedia of the World's Political Parties Ser.). (Illus.). 1274p. 1982. lib. bdg. 195.00 (*0-313-21474-3*, APA/) Greenwood.

Political Parties of the Americas: Canada, Latin America, & the West Indies, 2 vols., Vol. 1. Ed. by Robert J. Alexander. LC 81-6952. (Greenwood Historical Encyclopedia of the World's Political Parties Ser.). (Illus.). xxviii, 1274p. 1982. lib. bdg. 100.00 (*0-313-23753-0*, APA/01) Greenwood.

Political Parties of the Americas: Canada, Latin America, & the West Indies, 2 vols., Vol. 2. Ed. by Robert J. Alexander. LC 81-6952. (Greenwood Historical Encyclopedia of the World's Political Parties Ser.). (Illus.). xxviii, 1274p. 1982. lib. bdg. 100.00 (*0-313-23754-9*, APA/02) Greenwood.

Political Parties of the Americas, 1980s to 1990s: Canada, Latin America, & the West Indies. Ed. by Charles D. Ameringer. LC 92-3032. 696p. 1992. lib. bdg. 115.00 (*0-313-27418-5*, AAP/, Greenwood Pr) Greenwood.

Political Parties of the Middle East & North Africa: The Greenwood Historical Encyclopedia of the World's Political Parties. Ed. by Frank Tachau. LC 93-25067. 744p. 1994. lib. bdg. 145.00 (*0-313-26649-2*, TPP/, Greenwood Pr) Greenwood.

Political Parties of the United States. Michael Kronenwetter. LC 95-15928. (American Government in Action Ser.). (Illus.). 128p. (YA). (gr. 6 up). 1996. lib. bdg. 20.95 (*0-89490-537-6*) Enslow Pubs.

Political Parties of the World. 3rd ed. 527p. 1988. 85.00 (*0-912289-94-5*) St James Pr.

Political Parties of To-Day: A Study in Republican & Democratic Politics. Arthur N. Holcombe. LC 73-19153. (Politics & People Ser.). 410p. 1974. reprint ed. 30.95 (*0-405-05875-6*) Ayer.

Political Partisanship in the American Middle Colonies, 1700-1776. Benjamin H. Newcomb. LC 94-39764. 328p. (C). 1995. text 45.00 (*0-8071-1875-3*) La State U Pr.

Political Partnerships: Neighborhood Residents & Their Council Members. Jeffrey L. Davidson. LC 79-13107. (City & Society Ser.: No. 5). 231p. 1979. reprint ed. pap. 71.70 (*0-608-01452-4*, 205949600001) Bks Demand.

An Asterisk (*) at the beginning of an entry indicates that the title is appearing for the first time.

Political Party As a Social Process. Viva B. Boothe. LC 73-19131. (Politics & People Ser.). (Illus.). 130p. 1974. reprint ed. 13.95 (*0-405-05856-X*) Ayer.

***Political Party Matrix: The Persistence of Organization.** J. P. Monroe. (C). 2001. pap. text 16.95 (*0-7914-4918-1*) State U NY Pr.

***Political Party Matrix: The Persistence of Organization.** J. P. Monroe. (C). 2001. text 49.50 (*0-7914-4917-3*) State U NY Pr.

Political Party Systems & Democratic Development in East & Southeast Asia Vol. I: Southeast Asia, 2 vols. Wolfgang Sachsenroder & Ulrike E. Frings. LC 98-70121. (Illus.). 768p. (C). 1998. pap. text 43.95 (*1-84014-509-9*, Pub. by Ashgate Pub) Ashgate Pub Co.

Political Party Systems & Democratic Developments in East & Southeast Asia Vol. II: East Asia. Ed. by Wolfgang Sachsenroder & Ulrike E. Frings. LC 98-70121. (Illus.). 224p. 1998. pap. 39.95 (*1-84014-510-2*, Pub. by Ashgate Pub) Ashgate Pub Co.

Political Passage: The Career of Stratton of Illinois. David Kenney. LC 89-11587. (Illus.). 256p. (C). 1990. 31.95 (*0-8093-1549-1*) S Ill U Pr.

***Political Passions: Gender the Family & Political Argument.** Rachel Weil. 2000. text 79.95 (*0-7190-5622-5*, Pub. by Manchester Univ Pr) St Martin.

Political Performers: CBS Broadcasts in the Public Interest. Michael D. Murray. LC 93-30985. 272p. 1994. 59.95 (*0-275-94490-5*, Praeger Pubs) Greenwood.

Political Persuaders: The Techniques of Modern Election Campaigns. 2nd ed. Dan D. Nimmo. LC 99-13923. 214p. 1999. write for info. (*0-7658-0613-4*) Transaction Pubs.

Political Persuasion & Attitude Change. Ed. by Diana C. Mutz et al. LC 96-10248. 304p. (C). 1996. pap. text 23.95 (*0-472-06555-6*, 06555) U of Mich Pr.

Political Persuasion in Presidential Campaigns. Ed. by L. Patrick Develin. 275p. (Orig.). 1986. 34.95 (*0-88738-078-6*) Transaction Pubs.

Political Philosophers of the Twentieth Century. Michael Lessnoff. LC 98-22987. 300p. 1998. 59.95 (*0-631-20260-9*); pap. 29.95 (*0-631-20261-7*) Blackwell Pubs.

Political Philosophy. Jean Hampton. (Dimensions of Philosophy Ser.). 288p. (C). 1996. text 69.00 (*0-8133-0857-7*, Pub. by Westview); pap. text 26.00 (*0-8133-0858-5*, Pub. by Westview) HarpC.

Political Philosophy. Ed. by Anthony Quinton. (Oxford Readings in Philosophy Ser.). 208p. (Orig.). 1978. pap. 18.95 (*0-19-875002-1*) OUP.

Political Philosophy: A History of the Search for Order. James L. Wiser. 400p. (C). 1982. text 37.60 (*0-13-684845-1*) P-H.

Political Philosophy: Essential Selections. Aeon J. Skoble & Tibor R. Machan. LC 98-5773. 559p. 1998. pap. text 57.00 (*0-13-629577-0*) P-H.

Political Philosophy: From the Rights to the Republican Idea, No. 3. Luc Ferry & Alain Renaut. Tr. by Franklin Philip. LC 91-43341. 156p. (C). 1992. 27.95 (*0-226-24473-3*) U Ch Pr.

Political Philosophy: The Search for Humanity & Order. Jene Porter. LC 98-122422. 514p. 1997. pap. text 55.00 (*0-13-063991-5*) P-H.

Political Philosophy & Ideology: A Critique of Political Essentialism. Hugh P. McDonald. LC 96-46101. 440p. 1996. 64.50 (*0-7618-0594-X*); pap. 39.50 (*0-7618-0595-8*) U Pr of Amer.

Political Philosophy & Rhetoric: A Study of the Origins of American Party Politics. John Zvesper. LC 76-11097. (Cambridge Studies in the History & Theory of Politics). 246p. reprint ed. pap. 70.20 (*0-608-10258-X*, 2022480) Bks Demand.

Political Philosophy & the Human Soul: Essays in Memory of Allan Bloom. Ed. by Michael Palmer & Thomas L. Pangle. LC 95-9024. 320p. (C). 1995. 34.95 (*0-8476-8059-2*) Rowman.

Political Philosophy & the Issues of Politics. Joseph Cropsey. LC 76-22960. 340p. 1996. pap. text 9.00 (*0-226-12124-0*) U Ch Pr.

Political Philosophy & Time: Plato & the Origins of Political Vision. John G. Gunnell. LC 86-25012. xx, 314p. 1994. reprint ed. pap. text 12.95 (*0-226-31079-5*) U Ch Pr.

Political Philosophy As Therapy: Marcuse Reconsidered, 11. Gertrude A. Steuernagel. LC 78-73790. (Contributions in Political Science Ser.: No. 11). 147p. 1979. 55.00 (*0-313-20315-6*, SPP/, Greenwood Pr) Greenwood.

Political Philosophy at the Closure of Metaphysics. Bernard Flynn. LC 91-863. (Contemporary Studies in Philosophy & the Human Sciences). 248p. (C). 1992. text 55.00 (*0-391-03739-0*) Humanities.

Political Philosophy at the Closure of Metaphysics. Bernard Flynn. LC 91-863. (Contemporary Studies in Philosophy & the Human Sciences Ser.). 248p. (C). 1996. pap. 19.95 (*0-391-03961-X*) Humanities.

Political Philosophy of Blessed Robert Bellarmine see Political Philosophy of St. Robert Bellarmine

Political Philosophy of Hannah Arendt. Maurizio P. D'Entreves. LC 93-18492. 224p. (C). (gr. 13). 1993. pap. 23.99 (*0-415-08791-0*, B2462) Routledge.

Political Philosophy of Herbert Spencer: Individualist & Organicist. Tim Gray. LC 95-83292. (Avebury Series in Philosophy). 264p. 1996. 82.95 (*1-85972-279-2*, Pub. by Avebry) Ashgate Pub Co.

Political Philosophy of Hobbes: Its Basis & Its Genesis. Leo Strauss. 172p. 1996. pap. text 12.95 (*0-226-77696-4*) U Ch Pr.

Political Philosophy of Hobbes: Its Basis & Its Genesis. Leo Strauss. Tr. by Elsa M. Sinclair. LC 52-9720. 1996. reprint ed. pap. text 13.95 (*0-226-77705-7*) U Ch Pr.

***Political Philosophy of James Madison.** Garrett Ward Sheldon. LC 00-8659. 152p. 2000. 32.00 (*0-8018-6479-8*) Johns Hopkins.

Political Philosophy of John Dewey: Towards a Constructive Renewal. Terry Hoy. LC 98-15623. 152p. 1998. 49.95 (*0-275-96341-1*, Praeger Pubs) Greenwood.

Political Philosophy of Luis de Molina, S. J. Frank B. Costello. 1974. pap. 18.00 (*88-7041-338-1*) Jesuit Hist.

Political Philosophy of Martin Luther King, Jr. Hanes Walton, Jr. LC 76-111260. (Contributions in Afro-American & African Studies: No. 10). 137p. (C). 1971. pap. 4.95 (*0-8371-8931-4*, WMK/) Negro U Pr.

Political Philosophy of Martin Luther King, Jr., 10. Hanes Walton, Jr. LC 76-111260. (Contributions in Afro-American & African Studies: No. 10). 137p. (C). 1971. 49.95 (*0-8371-4661-5*, WMKPB) Greenwood.

Political Philosophy of Merleau-ponty. Sonia Kruks. 168p. 1994. 56.95 (*0-7512-0277-0*) Ashgate Pub Co.

Political Philosophy of Michael Oakeshott. Paul Franco. LC 89-29189. 288p. (C). 1990. 40.00 (*0-300-04686-3*) Yale U Pr.

Political Philosophy of Modern Shinto: A Study of the State Religion of Japan. Daniel C. Holtom. LC 84-3072. (BCC Ser.). 338p. 1984. reprint ed. 49.50 (*0-404-15937-0*) AMS Pr.

Political Philosophy of Montaigne. David L. Schaefer. LC 90-1586. 424p. 1990. pap. text 18.95 (*0-8014-9741-8*) Cornell U Pr.

Political Philosophy of Poststructuralist Anarchism. Todd May. LC 93-30551. 1994. 32.50 (*0-271-01045-2*); pap. 15.95 (*0-271-01046-0*) Pa St U Pr.

Political Philosophy of Rousseau. Roger D. Masters. LC 67-12348. 488p. reprint ed. pap. 151.30 (*0-608-18440-3*, 203263800080) Bks Demand.

Political Philosophy of Spinoza. Robert J. McShea. LC 73-89037. 835p. reprint ed. pap. 200.00 (*0-608-08662-2*, 206918500003) Bks Demand.

Political Philosophy of St. Robert Bellarmine. 2nd unabridged ed. John C. Rager. Orig. Title: The Political Philosophy of Blessed Robert Bellarmine. 96p. 1995. reprint ed. pap. 5.95 (*1-888516-00-3*) Apostlte Our Lady.

Political Philosophy of Subash Chandra Bose. D. D. Pattnaik. 1990. text 22.50 (*81-7045-066-7*, Pub. by Assoc Pub Hse) Advent Bks Div.

Political Philosophy of the Frankfurt School. George Friedman. LC 80-66890. 315p. reprint ed. pap. 97.70 (*0-608-08091-8*, 206905000002) Bks Demand.

Political Philosophy of the New Deal. fac. ed. Hubert H. Humphrey. LC 71-122356. 152p. 1970. reprint ed. pap. 47.20 (*0-7837-7773-6*, 204752900007) Bks Demand.

Political Philosophy of the Orthodox Church. Apostolos Makrakis. Ed. by Orthodox Christian Educational Society Staff. Tr. by Denver Cummings. Orig. Title: The Orthodox Definition of Political Science. 163p. (Orig.). (C). 1965. pap. 4.95 (*0-938366-11-4*) Orthodox Chr.

Political Philosophy of Thomas Jefferson. Garrett W. Sheldon. 160p. (C). 1993. reprint ed. pap. text 13.95 (*0-8018-4714-1*) Johns Hopkins.

Political Philosophy I: Rights - The New Quarrel between the Ancients & the Moderns. Luc Ferry. Tr. by Franklin Philip. LC 89-20335. 160p. 1990. 25.50 (*0-226-24471-7*) U Ch Pr.

Political Philosophy 2: The System of Philosophies of History. Luc Ferry. Tr. by Franklin Philip. (Illus.). 210p. (C). 1992. 29.95 (*0-226-24472-5*) U Ch Pr.

Political Pilgrims see Peregrinos de la Habana

Political Pilgrims: Travels of Western Intellectuals to the Soviet Union, China, & Cuba 1928-1978. Paul Hollander. LC 89-32825. 574p. (C). 1990. reprint ed. pap. text 13.95 (*0-8191-7384-3*) U Pr of Amer.

Political Pilgrims: Western Intellectuals in Search of the Good Society. 4th ed. Paul Hollander. LC 97-7925. 600p. 1997. pap. text 27.95 (*1-56000-954-3*) Transaction Pubs.

Political Plans of Mexico. Thomas B. Davis & Amado Ricon. LC 87-10568. 704p. 1987. lib. bdg. 68.50 (*0-8191-6426-7*) U Pr of Amer.

Political Plays for Children: The Grips Theater of Berlin. G. P. Deshpande. LC 98-901897. xxiv, 154p. 1998. write for info. (*81-7046-132-4*) Seagull Bks.

***Political Plays of Langston Hughes.** Langston Hughes. Ed. by Susan Duffy. LC 99-31502. 240p. 2000. 39.95 (*0-8093-2295-1*); pap. 16.95 (*0-8093-2296-X*) S Ill U Pr.

Political Poems & Songs Relating to English History, Composed During the Period from the Accession of Edward III to That of Richard III, 2 vols. Ed. by Thomas Wright. (Rolls Ser.: No. 14). 1974. reprint ed. 140.00 (*0-8115-1019-0*) Periodicals Srv.

***Political Poetry in Periodicals & the Shaping of German National Consciousness in the Nineteenth Century.** Lorie A. Vanchena. LC 99-30006. (North American Studies in Nineteenth-Century German Literature). 304p. 2000. text 56.95 incl. cd-rom (*0-8204-4547-9*) P Lang Pubng.

Political Poison: A Paul Turner Mystery. Mark R. Zubro. 208p. 1994. pap. 11.95 (*0-312-11044-8*, Stonewall Inn) St Martin.

Political Policing: The United States & Latin America. Martha K. Huggins. LC 97-52378. 1998. 49.95 (*0-8223-2159-9*); pap. 17.95 (*0-8223-2172-6*) Duke.

Political Policing in Wales. Ed. by John Davies et al. 1984. 20.00 (*0-7855-1463-5*, Pub. by NCCL) St Mut.

Political Polytheism: The Myth of Pluralism. Gary North. LC 89-27431. 771p. 1989. 22.50 (*0-930464-32-X*) Inst Christian.

Political Portrait of Northern Ireland in Transition. Stevenson. 1996. 25.00 (*0-02-874080-7*) Free Pr.

Political Portraits. fac. ed. Charles Whibley. LC 74-105050. (First Ser.). 1977. 23.95 (*0-8369-1586-0*) Ayer.

Political Portraits. Charles Whibley. LC 76-117859. (Second Ser.). 1977. 21.95 (*0-8369-1734-0*) Ayer.

***Political Posters Central & East Europe 1945-95: Signs of the Times.** James Aulich. (Illus.). 300p. 2000. pap. 29.95 (*0-7190-5419-2*, Pub. by Manchester Univ Pr) St Martin.

***Political Posters Central East.** James Aulich. 2000. text 69.95 (*0-7190-5418-4*, Pub. by Manchester Univ Pr) St Martin.

Political Posters in Ethiopia & Mozambique: Visual Imagery in a Revolutionary Context. Berit Sahlstrom. (Acta Universitatis Upsaliensis Figura, Nova Ser.: No. 24). (Illus.). 180p. 1990. 84.00 (*91-554-2642-5*) Coronet Bks.

Political Power: U. S. A. - U. S. S. R. Zbigniew K. Brzezinski & Samuel P. Huntington. LC 82-9178. 461p. 1982. reprint ed. lib. bdg. 79.50 (*0-313-23497-3*, BRZP, Greenwood Pr) Greenwood.

Political Power & Social Theory, Vol. 1. Ed. by Diane Davis et al. 334p. 1980. 78.50 (*0-89232-115-6*) Jai Pr.

Political Power & Social Theory, Vol. 2. Maurice Zeitlin. Ed. by Diane Davis & Howard Kimeldorf. 375p. 1981. 78.50 (*0-89232-143-1*) Jai Pr.

Political Power & Social Theory, Vol. 3. Ed. by Diane Davis et al. 352p. 1982. 78.50 (*0-89232-204-7*) Jai Pr.

Political Power & Social Theory, Vol. 4. Ed. by Diane Davis et al. 302p. 1984. 78.50 (*0-89232-330-2*) Jai Pr.

Political Power & Social Theory, Vol. 5. Maurice Zeitlin. Ed. by Diane Davis & Howard Kimeldorf. 324p. 1985. 78.50 (*0-89232-523-2*) Jai Pr.

Political Power & Social Theory, Vol. 6. Ed. by Diane Davis & Howard Kimeldorf. 374p. 1987. 78.50 (*0-89232-741-3*) Jai Pr.

Political Power & Social Theory, Vol. 7. Ed. by Diane Davis & Howard Kimeldorf. 320p. 1989. 78.50 (*0-89232-895-9*) Jai Pr.

Political Power & Social Theory, Vol. 8. Ed. by Diane Davis & Howard Kimeldorf. 295p. 1994. 78.50 (*1-55938-042-X*) Jai Pr.

Political Power & Social Theory, Vol. 9. Ed. by Diane Davis & Howard Kimeldorf. 221p. 1995. 78.50 (*1-55938-111-6*) Jai Pr.

Political Power & Social Theory, Vol. 10. Ed. by Diane Davis & Howard Kimeldorf. 1996. 78.50 (*0-7623-0037-X*) Jai Pr.

Political Power & Social Theory, Vol. 11. Ed. by Diane Davis. 1997. 78.50 (*0-7623-0242-9*) Jai Pr.

Political Power & Social Theory, Vol. 12. Diane Davis. 1998. 78.50 (*0-7623-0270-4*) Jai Pr.

Political Power & the Governmental Process. Karl Lowenstein. LC 65-8901. (Chicago University Charles R. Walgreen Foundation for the Study of American Institutions, Lecture Ser.). 474p. reprint ed. pap. 147.00 (*0-608-10788-3*, 202010900016) Bks Demand.

Political Power in Alabama: The More Things Change. Anne Permaloff & Carl Grafton. LC 94-38515. 1995. 50.00 (*0-8203-1721-7*) U of Ga Pr.

Political Power in Birmingham, 1871-1921. Carl V. Harris. LC 77-1110. (Twentieth-Century America Ser.). (Illus.). 351p. reprint ed. pap. 108.90 (*0-8357-8988-8*, 203336600085) Bks Demand.

Political Power in the Soviet Union: A Study of Decision-Making in Stalingrad. Philip D. Stewart. LC 68-17706. 1968. 42.50 (*0-672-51163-0*) Irvington.

Political Power in the Soviet Union: A Study of Decision-Making in Stalingrad. Philip D. Stewart. LC 68-17706. (C). 1968. pap. write for info. (*0-672-60764-6*) Macmillan.

Political Practice of Environmental Organizations. U. Hjelmar. (Avebury Studies in Green Research). 160p. 1996. 72.95 (*1-85972-239-3*, Pub. by Avebry) Ashgate Pub Co.

Political Prairie Fire: The Nonpartisan League, 1915-1922. Robert L. Morlan. LC 74-9275. (Illus.). 408p. 1974. reprint ed. lib. bdg. 35.00 (*0-8371-7639-5*, MOPF, Greenwood Pr) Greenwood.

Political Presidency: Practice of Leadership from Kennedy Through Reagan. Barbara Kellerman. 316p. 1986. pap. text 23.95 (*0-19-504037-6*) OUP.

Political Pressure & Economic Policy: British Government 1970-1974. Martin Holmes. LC 82-170177. 164 p. 1982. 39.95 (*0-408-10830-4*) Buttrwrth-Heinemann.

Political Presuppositions & Implicatures of the Most Popular African-American Hymns. Abdul K. Bangura. (Illus.). 189p. (C). 1996. lib. bdg. 85.00 (*1-56072-351-3*) Nova Sci Pubs.

Political Principles of Mencius. Cho-Min Wei. LC 77-72187. (Studies in Chinese Government & Law). 99p. 1977. reprint ed. lib. bdg. 45.00 (*0-313-27030-9*, U7030, Greenwood Pr) Greenwood.

Political Principles of Some Notable Prime Ministers of the 19th Century. Ed. by Fossey J. Hearnshaw. LC 74-107710. (Essay Index Reprint Ser.). 1977. 23.95 (*0-8369-1512-7*) Ayer.

Political Prisms. Mike Cluff. (Illus.). 46p. (Orig.). 1994. 5.95 (*1-878116-33-9*) JVC Bks.

Political Prisoner. Cesare Pavese. Tr. by W. J. Strachan. 237p. 1969. reprint ed. 28.00 (*0-7206-6202-8*) Dufour.

Political Prisoners & Trials: A Worldwide Annotated Bibliography, 1900-1993. James R. Bennett. LC 95-6232. 375p. 1995. lib. bdg. 79.50 (*0-7864-0023-4*) McFarland & Co.

Political Prisoners in India. Ujjwal K. Singh. LC 98-903531. (School of Oriental & African Studies). 310p. 1998. text 29.95 (*0-19-564188-4*) OUP.

***Political Prisoners in India.** Ujjwal Kumar Singh. (School of Oriental & African Studies). 312p. 2000. pap. 13.95 (*0-19-565388-2*) OUP.

Political Prisoners in Tibet. Ed. by Human Rights Watch Staff. 76p. (Orig.). 1992. pap. 7.00 (*1-56432-055-3*) Hum Rts Watch.

Political Process. David Cohen. (Task Force on the Eighties Ser.). 34p. 1981. pap. 2.50 (*0-87495-040-6*) Am Jewish Comm.

Political Process & Development of Black Insurgency,1930-70. 2nd ed. Doug McAdam. LC 99-32405. 304p. 1999. pap. text 14.00 (*0-226-55553-4*) U Ch Pr.

Political Process & Economic Change. Ed. by Kristen R. Monroe. LC 83-11866. 250p. 1983. 42.00 (*0-87586-063-X*); pap. 18.00 (*0-87586-062-1*) Agathon.

Political Process & Foreign Policy: The Making of the Japanese Peace Settlement. Bernard C. Cohen. LC 80-19832. 293p. 1980. reprint ed. lib. bdg. 75.00 (*0-313-22715-2*, COPF, Greenwood Pr) Greenwood.

Political Process & Role of Courts Verinder Grover. LC 98-905090. xiv, 744 p. 1997. write for info. (*81-7100-882-8*) Deep & Deep Pubns.

Political Process & the Development of Black Insurgency, 1930 to 1970. Douglas McAdam. LC 82-2712. (Illus.). viii, 312p. (C). 1985. pap. text 12.95 (*0-226-55552-6*) U Ch Pr.

Political Process & the Development of Black Insurgency, 1930 to 1970. Douglas McAdam. LC 82-2712. (Illus.). viii, 304p. (C). 1993. 27.50 (*0-226-55551-8*) U Ch Pr.

Political Process in India, 1947-1990. C. P. Bhambhri. 1991. text 27.50 (*0-7069-5596-X*, Pub. by Vikas) S Asia.

Political Profiles. Leon Trotsky. Tr. by R. Chappell. (Illus.). 171p. 1972. pap. 16.95 (*0-929087-91-7*) Mehring Bks.

Political Profiles, Vol. 4. Ed. by Nelson Lichtenstein. LC 76-20897. 765p. reprint ed. pap. 200.00 (*0-7837-6489-8*, 204508900004) Bks Demand.

Political Profiles Vol. 3: The Kennedy Years. Ed. by Nelson Lichtenstein & Eleanora W. Schoenebaum. LC 76-20897. 647p. reprint ed. pap. 200.00 (*0-7837-5346-2*, 204508900003) Bks Demand.

Political Program Operation, Urban Poverty Reduction. (FRE.). 72p. 1996. pap. 22.00 (*0-8213-3814-5*, 13914); pap. 22.00 (*0-8213-3813-7*, 13813) World Bank.

Political Promenade. Stephan R. Hutchinson. (Icon Cowboy Ser.: Bk. 2). 300p. 1998. pap. 5.95 (*0-9663394-1-X*) Earl Wayne.

Political Promises & Performance. S. P. Sharma. (C). 1991. 21.00 (*81-7024-406-4*, Pub. by Ashish Pub Hse) S Asia.

Political Prophecy in England. Rupert Taylor. LC 11-23809. reprint ed. 32.50 (*0-404-06357-8*) AMS Pr.

Political Protest & Cultural Revolution: Nonviolent Direct Action in the 1970s & 1980s. Barbara Epstein. LC 90-44230. (Illus.). 332p. 1991. 40.00 (*0-520-07010-0*, Pub. by U CA Pr) Cal Prin Full Svc.

Political Protest & Cultural Revolution: Nonviolent Direct Action in the 1970s & 1980s. Barbara Epstein. (C). 1993. pap. 17.95 (*0-520-08433-0*, Pub. by U CA Pr) Cal Prin Full Svc.

Political Protest & Social Change: Analyzing Politics. Charles F. Andrain & David E. Apter. LC 94-30981. 387p. (C). 1995. text 50.00 (*0-8147-0630-4*) NYU Pr.

Political Protest & Social Change: Analyzing Politics. Charles F. Andrain & David E. Apter. 387p. (C). 1995. pap. text 20.00 (*0-8147-0634-7*) NYU Pr.

Political Protest & Street Art: Popular Tools for Democratization in Hispanic Countries, 40. Lyman G. Chaffee. LC 92-45084. (Contributions to the Study of Mass Media & Communications Ser.: No. 40). 208p. 1993. 62.95 (*0-313-28808-9*, GM8808, Greenwood Pr) Greenwood.

Political Psyche. Andrew Samuels. LC 92-39941. 448p. (C). 1993. pap. 27.99 (*0-415-08102-5*, A7318) Routledge.

Political Psychology. Jon Elster. LC 92-17779. 214p. (C). 1993. text 64.95 (*0-521-41110-6*); pap. text 18.95 (*0-521-42286-8*) Cambridge U Pr.

Political Psychology. Neil J. Kressel. 416p. 1994. pap. 24.95 (*1-56924-894-X*) Marlowe & Co.

Political Psychology. Rose McDermott. (Analytical Perspectives on Politics Ser.). (Illus.). (C). text. write for info. (*0-472-09701-6*); pap. text. write for info. (*0-472-06701-X*) U of Mich Pr.

Political Psychology: A Special Issue of the Journal of Applied Psychology: An International Review. Klaus Boehnke. 126p. 1998. 24.95 (*0-86377-969-7*, Pub. by Psychol Pr) Taylor & Francis.

Political Psychology: Cultural & Cross-Cultural Foundations. Stanley A. Renshon & J. H. Duckitt. LC 99-26248. 2000. pap. text 22.50 (*0-8147-7537-3*) NYU Pr.

***Political Psychology: Cultural & Cross-Cultural Foundations.** Ed. by Stanley A. Renshon & John Duckitt. LC 99-26248. 400p. 2000. text 65.00 (*0-8147-7536-5*) NYU Pr.

Political Psychology in Japan: Behind the Nails Which Sometimes Stick Out (& Get Hammered Down) Ofer Feldman. LC 98-48628. 1998. 69.00 (*1-56072-636-9*) Nova Sci Pubs.

Political Psychology of Appeasement: Finlandization & Other Unpopular Essays on World Affairs. Walter Laqueur. LC 79-6854. 283p. 1980. text 34.95 (*0-87855-336-3*) Transaction Pubs.

Political Psychology of the Gulf War: Leaders, Publics, & the Process of Conflict. Stanley A. Renshon. LC 92-34182. (Series in Policy & Institutional Studies). 408p. (C). 1993. pap. 22.95 (*0-8229-5495-8*); text 49.95 (*0-8229-3744-1*) U of Pittsburgh Pr.

Political Psychology of the White Collar Worker in Martin Walser's Novels: The Impact of Work Ideology on the Reception of Martin Walser's Novels, 1957-1978. Franz Oswald. LC 98-36233. 238p. 1998. pap. text 39.95 (*0-8204-3559-7*) P Lang Pubng.

Political Psychology of the White Collar Worker In Martin Walser's Novels: The Impact of Work Ideology on the Reception of Martin Walser's Novels 1957-1978. Franz Oswald. 238p. 1998. 39.95 (*3-631-32838-9*) P Lang Pubng.

P

Political Psychos. Gyeorgos C. Hatonn. (Phoenix Journals). 213p. 1994. pap. 6.00 (*1-56935-030-2*) Phoenix Source.

Political Pundits. Dan Nimmo & James E. Combs. LC 91-34491. (Praeger Series in Political Communication). 208p. 1992. 57.95 (*0-275-93541-8*, C3541, Praeger Pubs); pap. 16.95 (*0-275-93545-0*, B3545, Praeger Pubs) Greenwood.

Political Puppies. Stephan R. Hutchinson. (Icon Cowboy Ser.: Bk. 3). 300p. 1999. pap. write for info. (*0-9663394-2-8*) Earl Wayne.

***Political Question & Article 356.** P. Rathnaswamy. 1998. 34.00 (*81-7049-083-9*, Pub. by Manas Pubns) S Asia.

Political Questions: Political Philosophy from Plato to Rawls. 2nd ed. Larry Arnhart. 406p. (C). 1993. pap. text 21.95 (*0-88133-728-5*) Waveland Pr.

Political Questions Judicial Answers: Does the Rule of Law Apply to Foreign Affairs? Thomas M. Franck. 216p. 1992. text 35.00 (*0-691-09241-9*, Pub. by Princeton U Pr) Cal Prin Full Svc.

Political Quotations: A Collection of Notable Sayings on Politics from Antiquity Through 1988. Ed. by Daniel B. Baker. 508p. 1990. 55.00 (*0-8103-4920-5*, 030121) Gale.

Political Quotations: A Worldwide Dictionary of Thoughts & Pronouncements from Politicians, Literary Figures, Humorists & Others. Ed. by Jean F. Thomsett. LC 93-41206. 352p. 1994. lib. bdg. 45.00 (*0-89950-951-7*) McFarland & Co.

Political Racket: Deceit, Self-Interest & Corruption in American Politics. Martin L. Gross. 336p. (Orig.). 1996. pap. 12.50 (*0-345-38777-5*) Ballantine Pub Grp.

Political Radicalism in Late Imperial Vienna: Origins of the Christian Social Movement, 1848-1897. John W. Boyer. LC 80-17302. (Illus.). 1981. 40.00 (*0-226-06957-5*) U Ch Pr.

Political Radicalism in Late Imperial Vienna: Origins of the Christian Social Movement, 1848-1897. John W. Boyer. 592p. 1995. pap. text 24.95 (*0-226-06956-7*) U Ch Pr.

Political Re-Mapping of Africa: Transnational Ideology & the Redefinition of Africa in World Politics. Tukumbi Lumumba-Kasongo. LC 93-30867. 170p. (C). 1993. lib. bdg. 39.00 (*0-8191-9299-6*) U Pr of Amer.

Political Realism & the Crisis of World Politics: An American Approach to Foreign Policy. Kenneth W. Thompson. LC 82-45061. 270p. 1982. reprint ed. pap. text 24.00 (*0-8191-2352-8*) U Pr of Amer.

Political Realism in American Thought. John W. Coffey. 217p. 1978. 32.50 (*0-8387-1903-1*) Bucknell U Pr.

Political Realism in International Theory. Roger D. Spegele. (Studies in International Relations: No. 47). 203p. (C). 1996. text 59.95 (*0-521-55403-9*) Cambridge U Pr.

Political Realism in International Theory. Roger D. Spegele. (Cambridge Studies in International Relations: No. 47). 303p. (C). 1996. pap. text 19.95 (*0-521-55635-X*) Cambridge U Pr.

Political Realism of Reinhold Niebuhr: A Pragmatic Approach to the Just War. Colm McKeogh. LC 97-13670. 224p. 1997. text 65.00 (*0-312-17629-5*) St Martin.

Political Reality of Freedom of the Press in Zambia. Robert C. Moore. 158p. (C). 1992. lib. bdg. 41.00 (*0-8191-8649-X*) U Pr of Amer.

Political Reasoning. Evert Vedung. Tr. by David McCune from SWE. LC 82-5532. (Illus.). 232p. reprint ed. pap. 72.00 (*0-8357-8402-9*, 203467600091) Bks Demand.

Political Reasoning & Cognition: A Piagetian View. Shawn Rosenberg et al. LC 88-16225. 192p. (C). 1988. text 45.95 (*0-8223-0856-8*) Duke.

Political Recollections, 1840-1872. George W. Julian. LC 78-83885. (Black Heritage Library Collection). 1977. 20.95 (*0-8369-8615-6*) Ayer.

Political Reconstruction of China. Eu-Yang Kwang. LC 76-55089. (Studies in Chinese Government & Law). 190p. 1976. reprint ed. lib. bdg. 55.00 (*0-313-27017-1*, U7017, Greenwood Pr) Greenwood.

Political Recruitment Across Two Centuries: Mexico, 1884-1991. Roderic A. Camp. 304p. (Orig.). (C). 1995. pap. 17.95 (*0-292-71173-5*); text 40.00 (*0-292-71172-7*) U of Tex Pr.

Political Redistricting & Geographic Theory. Richard L. Morrill. Ed. by C. Gregory Knight. LC 81-69235. (Resource Publications in Geography). (Orig.). 1981. pap. 15.00 (*0-89291-159-X*) Assn Am Geographers.

***Political Reference Almanac.** Anthony J. Quain. Ed. by Jill E. Hershey & Edward T. Pietropaoli. (Illus.). 904p. 1999. pap. 44.95 (*0-9670286-0-4*, Polisci Bks) Keynote Pubng.

Political Reflections on the Finances & Commerce of France. Charles Dutot. LC 76-146461. (Reprints of Economic Classics Ser.). xiii, 304p. 1974. reprint ed. lib. bdg. 57.50 (*0-678-00842-6*) Kelley.

Political Reform in Francophone Africa. David Gardinier. Ed. by John Clark. LC 96-38176. 8p. (C). 1996. pap. text 32.00 (*0-8133-2786-5*, Pub. by Westview) HarpC.

Political Reform in Wisconsin: A Historical Review of the Subjects of Primary Election, Taxation & Railway Regulation. Emanuel L. Philipp. Ed. by Stanley P. Caine & Roger Wyman. LC 73-620042. (Illus.). 197p. 1973. reprint ed. 12.00 (*0-87020-123-9*) State Hist Soc Wis.

Political Reformism in Mexico: An Overview of Contemporary Mexican Politics. Stephen D. Morris. LC 95-3472. 262p. 1995. pap. text 19.95 (*1-55587-594-7*); lib. bdg. 49.95 (*1-55587-572-6*) L Rienner.

Political Regimes, Public Policy & Economic Development: Agricultural Performance & Rural Change in Two Punjabs. Holly Sims. 204p. (C). 1988. text 26.00 (*0-8039-9571-7*) Sage.

Political Register, Setting Forth the Principles of the Whig & Locofoco Parties in the United States, with the Life & Public Services of Henry Clay. William G. Brownlow. LC 73-23063. 348p. 1974. reprint ed. 27.50 (*0-87152-153-9*) Reprint.

Political Religions. Eric Voegelin. LC 85-28524. (Toronto Studies in Theology: Vol. 23). 200p. 1985. lib. bdg. 79.95 (*0-88946-767-6*) E Mellen.

Political, Religious, & Love Poems. Ed. by F. J. Furnival. (EETS, OS Ser.: Vol. 15). 1974. reprint ed. 30.00 (*0-8115-3346-8*) Periodicals Srv.

Political, Religious & Love Poems from Lambeth MS. 306 & Other Sources. Ed. by F. J. Furnivall. (EETS Original Ser.: Vol. 15). 1965. reprint ed. 30.00 (*0-19-722015-0*, Pub. by EETS) Boydell & Brewer.

Political Reorientation of Japan, 1945-1948, 2 vols. Supreme Commander for the Allied Powers - Governme. 1968. 75.00 (*0-403-00028-9*) Scholarly.

Political Representation & Legitimacy in the European Union. Ed. by Hermann Schmitt & Jacques Thomassen. (Illus.). 322p. 1999. text 70.00 (*0-19-829661-4*) OUP.

Political Representation & Recruitment: Gender, Race & Class in the British Parliament. Pippa Norris & Joni Lovenduski. (Illus.). 334p. (C). 1995. pap. text 21.95 (*0-521-46961-9*) Cambridge U Pr.

Political Representation in France. Philip E. Converse & Roy Pierce. LC 85-15789. (Illus.). 1040p. 1986. 83.00 (*0-674-68660-8*) Belknap Pr.

Political Repression in America: A History. 1991. lib. bdg. 79.95 (*0-8490-4635-1*) Gordon Pr.

Political Research & Political Theory. Avery Leiserson et al. Ed. by Oliver Garceau. LC 68-28693. (Illus.). 268p. reprint ed. pap. 83.10 (*0-7837-4470-6*, 204417800001) Bks Demand.

Political Research Experience. 2nd ed. Marcus E. Ethridge. 416p. (C). 1995. text 17.50 (*1-56134-317-X*, Dshkn McG-Hill) McGrw-H Hghr Educ.

Political Resource Directory, 1989: National Edition--Includes the Official Directory of the American Association of Political Consultants. Ed. by Carol Hess. 496p. 1988. pap. text 95.00 (*0-944320-01-5*) Politic Rescs.

Political Resource Directory, 1996: National Edition. 1996. 95.00 (*0-944320-07-4*) Politic Rescs.

Political Resource Directory, 1997: National Edition. Ed. by Carol Hess. 350p. (Orig.). 1997. pap. 95.00 (*0-944320-09-0*) Politic Rescs.

Political Resource Directory, 1994: National Edition. 7th ed. Ed. by Carol Hess. 1994. pap. text 95.00 (*0-944320-06-6*) Politic Rescs.

Political Resource Directory, 1990: National Edition, "Includes the Official Directory of the American Association of Political Consultants" Ed. by Carol Hess. 496p. 1989. pap. 95.00 (*0-944320-03-1*) Politic Rescs.

Political Responsibility of the Critic. Jim Merod. LC 86-47977. 288p. 1987. 39.95 (*0-8014-1976-X*); pap. 16.95 (*0-8014-9555-5*) Cornell U Pr.

Political Responsibility of the Critic. Jim Merod. LC 86-47977. (Cornell Paperbacks Ser.). 283p. reprint ed. pap. 87.80 (*0-608-20923-6*, 207202200003) Bks Demand.

***Political Revolution & Literary Experiment in the Spanish Romantic Period, 1830-1850.** Andrew Ginger. LC 99-16082. (Hispanic Literature Ser.: Vol. 47). 424p. 1999. text 109.95 (*0-7734-7995-3*) E Mellen.

Political Rhetoric, Power, & Renaissance Women. Ed. by Carole Levin & Patricia A. Sullivan. LC 94-32811. (SUNY Series in Speech Communication). 293p. (C). 1995. text 57.50 (*0-7914-2545-2*); pap. text 19.95 (*0-7914-2546-0*) State U NY Pr.

***Political Right in Postauthoritarian Brazil: Elites, Institutions & Democratization.** Timothy J. Power. LC 99-56473. 2000. 55.00 (*0-271-02009-1*); pap. 19.95 (*0-271-02010-5*) Pa St U Pr.

Political Rights for European Citizens. Guido V. Berghe. 256p. (Orig.). 1982. text 79.95 (*0-566-00524-7*) Ashgate Pub Co.

Political Rights of Migrant Workers in Western Europe. Ed. by Zig Layton-Henry. (Modern Politics Ser.: Vol. 25). 256p. (C). 1990. text 45.00 (*0-8039-8271-2*) Sage.

Political Risk Assessment: An Annotated Bibliography, 3. Ed. by David A. Jodice. LC 84-19784. (Bibliographies & Indexes in Law & Political Science Ser.: No. 3). 279p. 1985. lib. bdg. 59.95 (*0-313-24444-8*, JOP/, Greenwood Pr) Greenwood.

Political Risk Management: International Lending & Investing under Environmental Uncertainty. Charles R. Kennedy, Jr. LC 86-25588. 177p. 1987. 55.00 (*0-89930-157-6*, KPK/, Quorum Bks) Greenwood.

Political Risks in International Business: New Directions for Research, Management & Public Policy. Ed. by Thomas L. Brewer. LC 84-24801. 384p. 1985. 75.00 (*0-275-90066-5*, C0066, Praeger Pubs) Greenwood.

Political Role of Labor in Developing Countries. Bruce H. Millen. LC 79-29735. 148p. 1980. reprint ed. lib. bdg. 59.50 (*0-313-22286-X*, MIPO, Greenwood Pr) Greenwood.

Political Role of Mongol Buddhism. Larry W. Moses. LC 81-622859. (Uralic & Altaic Ser.: Vol. 133). x, 299p. 1977. 15.00 (*0-933070-01-2*) Res Inst Inner Asian Studies.

Political Role of the General Assembly, Vol. 7. Henry F. Haviland. LC 78-2808. (Carnegie Endowment for International Peace, United Nations Studies: No. 7). 190p. 1978. reprint ed. lib. bdg. 45.00 (*0-313-20334-2*, HAPG, Greenwood Pr) Greenwood.

Political Role of the Military: An International Handbook. Ed. by Constantine P. Danopoulos & Cynthia Watson. LC 95-46134. 536p. 1996. lib. bdg. 125.00 (*0-313-28837-2*, Greenwood Pr) Greenwood.

Political Role of the United Nations: Advancing the World Community. LC 81-13948. 217p. 1981. 55.00 (*0-275-90639-6*, C0639, Praeger Pubs) Greenwood.

Political Roles & Military Rulers. Amos Perlmutter. 314p. 1981. 42.50 (*0-7146-3122-1*, Pub. by F Cass Pubs) Intl Spec Bk.

Political Roles in a New State: Tanzania's First Decade. Raymond F. Hopkins. LC 70-140532. (Yale Studies in Political Science: No. 23). (Illus.). 308p. reprint ed. 95.50 (*0-8357-9454-7*, 201678400005) Bks Demand.

Political Romanticism. Carl Schmitt. Tr. by Guy Oakes from GER. (Studies in Contemporary German Social Thought). 220p. 1986. 25.00 (*0-262-19252-7*) MIT Pr.

Political Romanticism. Carl Schmitt. Tr. by Guy Oakes. (Studies in Contemporary German Social Thought). 216p. 1991. reprint ed. pap. text 15.00 (*0-262-69142-6*) MIT Pr.

Political Roster: National Asian Pacific American Political Roster & Resource Guide, No. 8. 8th rev. ed. Ed. by Donald T. Nakanishi & James S. Lai. 322p. 1998. pap. 15.00 (*0-934052-30-1*) UCLA Asian Am Studies Ctr.

Political Russian: An Intermediate Course in Russian Language for International Relations. 3rd ed. ACTR Staff. 568p. 1996. pap., per. 46.00 (*0-7872-1904-5*, 41190401) Kendall-Hunt.

Political Satire in English Poetry. Charles W. Previte-Orton. 244p. (C). 1966. lib. bdg. 75.00 (*0-8383-0676-4*) M S G Haskell Hse.

Political Satire in the Bible. Jeev Weisman. (Biblical Encyclopaedia Library: Vol. XIII). (HEB.). ii, 287p. 1996. pap. text 27.00 (*965-342-667-2*, Pub. by Bialik) Eisenbrauns.

Political Savvy: Systematic Approaches to Leadership Behind-the-Scenes. Joel M. DeLuca. LC 91-33528. (Illus.). 250p. 1992. 32.50 (*0-934753-60-1*) LRP Pubns.

Political Savvy: Systematic Approaches to Leadership Behind-the-Scenes. 2nd ed. Joel R. DeLuca. (Illus.). 1999. 28.50 (*0-9667636-0-2*) Evergreen Bus Grp.

***Political Scandal.** John B. Thompson. 2000. 54.95 (*0-7456-2549-5*, Pub. by Polity Pr); pap. 22.95 (*0-7456-2550-9*, Pub. by Polity Pr) Blackwell Pubs.

***Political Scandals.** William Dudley. LC 00-29408. 2000. pap. write for info. (*0-7377-0518-3*) Greenhaven.

Political Scandals - Our Democratic System Prevails. David C. King. LC 97-77860. (Perspectives on History Ser.: Pt. III). (Illus.). 60p. 1998. pap. 6.95 (*1-57960-012-3*) Disc Enter Ltd.

Political Scandals & Causes Celebres since 1945. 1991. 85.00 (*1-55862-009-5*) St James Pr.

Political Scandals in the U. S. A. Robert Williams. LC 98-149424. 160p. 1998. pap. 22.00 (*1-85331-189-8*, Pub. by Edinburgh U Pr) Col U Pr.

Political Scandals in the United States. Robert Williams. (Illus.). 140p. 1998. 35.00 (*1-57958-039-4*) Fitzroy Dearborn.

Political Science, 4 bks. Kenneth Holland & Toby Fulwiler. Ed. by Arthur W. Biddle. LC 86-82754. (Writer's Guide Ser.). 182p. (C). 1990. pap. text 24.36 (*0-669-11778-1*) HM Trade Div.

Political Science. Jack Rudman. (Graduate Record Examination (GRE) Ser.: Vol. 16). 43.95 (*0-8373-5266-5*) Nat Learn.

Political Science. Jack Rudman. (Undergraduate Program Field Tests (UPFT) Ser.: Vol. 20). 43.95 (*0-8373-6070-6*) Nat Learn.

Political Science. Jack Rudman. (Graduate Record Examination Ser.: GRE-16). 1994. pap. 23.95 (*0-8373-5216-9*) Nat Learn.

Political Science. Jack Rudman. (Undergraduate Program Field Tests (UPFT) Ser.: Vol. UPFT-20). 1994. pap. 23.95 (*0-8373-6020-X*) Nat Learn.

Political Science. Gregory M. Scott & Steve Garrison. LC 96-33648. 425p. (C). 1996. text 53.00 (*0-13-207572-5*) P-H.

Political Science: A Comparative Introduction. Rod Hague et al. LC 92-61002. (Illus.). 504p. (C). 1992. pap. text 24.95 (*0-312-08427-7*) St Martin.

Political Science: A Philosophical Analysis. Vernon Van Dyke. LC 60-11836. 235p. 1960. reprint ed. pap. 30.00 (*0-608-08294-5*, 202501900040) Bks Demand.

Political Science: An Introduction. 5th ed. Michael G. Roskin et al. LC 93-26956. 416p. (C). 1993. text 81.00 (*0-13-156423-4*) P-H.

***Political Science: An Introduction.** 7th ed. 1999. text, teacher ed. write for info. (*0-13-021521-X*) P-H.

Political Science: An Introduction. 7th ed. Michael G. Roskin. LC 99-15765. 398p. (C). 1999. pap. text 49.00 (*0-13-020872-8*) P-H.

Political Science: An Overview of the Fields. 2nd ed. Peterson et al. 304p. (C). 1997. per. 38.95 (*0-7872-4179-2*, 41417901) Kendall-Hunt.

Political Science: Discipline Analysis, Vol. 7M. Virginia Sapiro. (Women in the Curriculum Ser.). 52p. (Orig.). 1997. pap. 7.00 (*1-885303-22-X*) Towson St Univ.

Political Science: Illustrated Search Strategy & Sources. Roger C. Lowery & Sue A. Cody. (Library Research Guides Ser.: No. 12). 224p. 1993. pap. 25.00 (*0-87650-290-7*) Pierian.

Political Science: The Science of Politics. Ed. by Herbert F. Weisberg. LC 85-15082. (Illus.). 320p. 1986. 38.00 (*0-87586-066-4*); pap. 18.00 (*0-87586-075-3*) Agathon.

Political Science: The State of the Discipline. rev. ed. Ed. by Ada W. Finifter. 548p. (Orig.). 1993. pap. 36.00 (*1-878147-08-0*) Am Political.

Political Science Vol. 1: Looking to the Future: The Theory & Practice of Political Science. Intro. by William Crotty. 237p. (Orig.). 1991. pap. 17.95 (*0-8101-0923-9*) Northwestern U Pr.

Political Science Vol. 2: Looking to the Future: Comparative Politics, Policy, & International Relations. Intro. by William Crotty. 294p. (Orig.). 1991. pap. 19.95 (*0-8101-0950-6*) Northwestern U Pr.

Political Science Vol. 3: Looking to the Future: Political Behavior. Intro. by William Crotty. 240p. (Orig.). 1991. pap. 17.95 (*0-8101-0952-2*) Northwestern U Pr.

Political Science Vol. 4: Looking to the Future: American Institutions. Intro. by William Crotty. 298p. (Orig.). 1991. pap. 19.95 (*0-8101-0954-9*) Northwestern U Pr.

Political Science Abstracts: 1989 Annual Supplement. (Illus.). 1855p. (C). 714.00 (*0-306-69039-X*, Kluwer Plenum) Kluwer Academic.

Political Science Abstracts: 1996 Annual Supplement, 3 vols. Compiled by IFI-Plenum Data Company Staff. (Illus.). 2174p. (C). 1998. 695.00 (*0-306-69046-2*, Kluwer Plenum) Kluwer Academic.

Political Science Abstracts, 1987: Annual Supplement. LC 78-6367. (Illus.). 1644p. (C). 1988. 714.00 (*0-306-69037-3*, Kluwer Plenum) Kluwer Academic.

Political Science Abstracts, 1988: Annual Supplement. (Illus.). 1974p. (C). 1990. 714.00 (*0-306-69038-1*, Kluwer Plenum) Kluwer Academic.

Political Science Abstracts, 1986: Annual Supplement. Compiled by IFI-Plenum Data Company Staff. LC 73-6367. (Illus.). 2284p. (C). 1988. 714.00 (*0-306-69036-5*, Kluwer Plenum) Kluwer Academic.

Political Science Abstracts, 1990: Annual Supplement. (Illus.). 1971p. (C). 1992. 714.00 (*0-306-69040-3*, Kluwer Plenum) Kluwer Academic.

Political Science Abstracts, 1991: Annual Supplement. Ed. by R. W. Hemingway. (Illus.). 1916p. (C). 1992. 714.00 (*0-306-69041-1*, Plenum Trade) Perseus Pubng.

Political Science Abstracts, 1992: Annual Supplement. Ed. by Raif O. Onvural. (Illus.). 2086p. (C). 1993. 750.00 (*0-306-69042-X*, Plenum Trade) Perseus Pubng.

Political Science Abstracts, 1994: Annual Supplement, 3 vols., Set. Compiled by IFI/Plenum Data Company Staff. (Illus.). 2121p. (C). 1995. 774.00 (*0-306-69044-6*, Kluwer Plenum) Kluwer Academic.

Political Science Abstracts, 1993: Annual Supplement, 3 vols., Set. Compiled by IFI-Plenum Data Company Staff. (Illus.). 2018p. (C). 1994. 750.00 (*0-306-69043-8*, Plenum Trade) Perseus Pubng.

Political Science & Area Studies: Rivals or Partners? Ed. by Lucian W. Pye. LC 74-15711. 253p. reprint ed. 78.50 (*0-8357-9234-X*, 201583200097) Bks Demand.

***Political Science & Comparative Constitutional Law.** John W. Burgess. 2000. reprint ed. write for info. (*1-57588-640-5*) W S Hein.

Political Science & Educational Administration. William L. Boyd. 134p. (C). 1983. 45.00 (*0-7300-0006-0*, Pub. by Deakin Univ) St Mut.

Political Science & Political Behaviour. Dennis A. Kavanagh. (Illus.). 224p. (C). 1983. text 44.95 (*0-04-322008-8*) Routledge.

Political Science & Political Theory. Ed. by Jessica Kuper. (Social Science Lexicons Ser.). 258p. 1987. pap. text 14.95 (*0-7102-1171-6*, Routledge Thoemms) Routledge.

Political Science & Regime Change in 20th Century Germany. Rainer Eisfeld et al. (C). Date not set. lib. bdg. 85.00 (*1-56072-412-9*) Nova Sci Pubs.

Political Science & School Politics: The Princes & Pundits. Ed. by Samuel K. Gove & Frederick M. Wirt. 160p. 1976. boxed set 39.95 (*0-669-00739-0*) Transaction Pubs.

Political Science & School Politics: The Princes & Pundits. Ed. by Samuel K. Gove & Frederick M. Wirt. 160p. 1985. reprint ed. lib. bdg. 37.50 (*0-8191-5141-6*) U Pr of Amer.

Political Science Annual: An International Review, Vol. 3. annuals James A. Robinson. LC 66-29710. 1972. 17.95 (*0-672-51743-4*, Bobbs) Macmillan.

Political Science Annual: An International Review, Vol. 4. annuals Ed. by Cornelius P. Cotter. LC 66-29710. 1973. 16.25 (*0-672-51808-2*, Bobbs) Macmillan.

Political Science Annual: An International Review, Vol. 5. annuals Cornelius P. Cotter. LC 66-29710. 1974. write for info. (*0-672-61318-2*, Bobbs) Macmillan.

Political Science Annual: An International Review, Vol. 6. annuals Ed. by Cornelius P. Cotter. LC 66-29710. 352p. 1975. text 20.85 (*0-672-61319-0*, Bobbs) Macmillan.

Political Science as Puzzle Solving. Ed. by Bernard Grofman. (Illus.). 184p. (C). text 59.50 (*0-472-11176-0*, 11176); pap. text 19.95 (*0-472-08723-1*, 08723) U of Mich Pr.

Political Science Fiction. Ed. by Donald M. Hassler & Clyde Wilcox. LC 96-10073. (Illus.). 320p. 1997. text 34.95 (*1-57003-113-4*) U of SC Pr.

Political Science in History: Research Programs & Political Traditions. Ed. by James Farr et al. 379p. (C). 1995. pap. text 22.95 (*0-521-47955-X*) Cambridge U Pr.

Political Science in History: Research Programs & Political Traditions. Ed. by James Farr et al. 379p. (C). 1995. text 64.95 (*0-521-47422-1*) Cambridge U Pr.

Political Science in Theory & Practice: The 'Politics' Model. Ruth Lane. LC 96-21984. 188p. (C). (gr. 13). 1996. text 58.95 (*1-56324-939-1*) M E Sharpe.

Political Science in Theory & Practice: The 'Politics' Model. Ruth Lane. LC 96-21984. 188p. (C). (gr. 13). 1996. pap. text 27.95 (*1-56324-940-5*) M E Sharpe.

Political Science Journal Information see Getting Published in Political Science Journals: A Guide for Authors, Editors & Librarians

Political Science Majors. Mark Rowh. LC 98-7263. (Great Jobs for... Ser.). 208p. 1998. pap. 11.95 (*0-8442-4724-3*, 47243) NTC Contemp Pub Co.

Political Science of John Adams. Correa M. Walsh. LC 70-102259. (Select Bibliographies Reprint Ser.). 1977. 35.95 (*0-8369-5144-1*) Ayer.

Political Science of Poverty & Welfare. Ed. by Dorothy James. 1974. pap. 15.00 (*0-918592-06-2*) Pol Studies.

***Political Science on the Internet: 1999-2000.** Ed. by Prentice-Hall Staff. (C). 1999. text. write for info. (*0-13-022075-2*) P-H.

An Asterisk (*) at the beginning of an entry indicates that the title is appearing for the first time.

Political Science on the Internet 1997-1998. Stull. 96p. (C). 1997. write for info. (*0-13-646175-1*) P-H.

Political Science Research: A Handbook of Scope & Methods. Laurence Jones & Edward C. Olson. 328p. (C). 1997. pap. text 62.00 (*0-06-501637-8*) Addson-Wesley Educ.

Political Science Research: A Methods Handbook. M. Lal Goel. LC 87-35264. (Illus.). 310p. (C). 1988. text 44.95 (*0-8138-1439-1*) Iowa St U Pr.

Political Science Research: A Methods Workbook. M. Lal Goel. LC 87-35264. (Illus.). 202p. (C). 1988. pap. text 29.95 (*0-8138-1438-3*) Iowa St U Pr.

Political Science Research Methods. 3rd ed. Janet B. Johnson & Richard A. Joslyn. LC 94-30135. 450p. (YA). (gr. 11). 1994. pap. text 39.95 (*0-87187-807-0*) Congr Quarterly.

***Political Science Research Methods.** 4th ed. Janet B. Johnson & Richard A. Joslyn. 2000. pap. 39.95 (*1-56802-329-4*) CQ Pr.

***Political Science Research Methods: Solutions Manual.** 4th ed. Janet B. Johnson & Richard A. Joslyn. 2000. pap. write for info. (*1-56802-351-0*) CQ Pr.

Political Science Student Writer's Manual. 3rd ed. Gregory M. Scott & Stephen M. Garrison. LC 99-14484. (Illus.). 335p. 1999. pap. text 23.33 (*0-13-022558-4*, Prentice Hall) P-H.

Political Science Thesaurus. Carl Beck et al. LC 75-326011. 471p. reprint ed. pap. 146.10 (*0-608-11111-2*, 201779900008) Bks Demand.

Political Science Utilization Directory. Stuart S. Nagel & Marian Neef. 1975. pap. 15.00 (*0-918592-19-4*) Pol Studies.

Political Sermons of the American Founding Era, 1730-1805. Ed. by Ellis Sandoz. LC 90-20027. (Illus.). 1636p. (C). 1991. pap. 16.00 (*0-86597-091-2*); text 32.00 (*0-86597-090-4*) Liberty Fund.

Political Shakespeare: Essays in Cultural Materialism. 2nd ed. Ed. by Jonathan Dollimore & Alan Sinfield. LC 94-15983. 304p. 1994. 45.00 (*0-8014-3091-7*); pap. text 16.95 (*0-8014-8243-7*) Cornell U Pr.

Political Shorts. Glenn Liebman. LC 98-54960. 256p. 1999. 14.95 (*0-8092-2780-0*, 278000, Contemporary Bks) NTC Contemp Pub Co.

Political Significance of Gulliver's Travels. C. H. Firth. 1990. 7.75 (*0-8446-1181-6*) Peter Smith.

Political Situation in Egypt During the Second Intermediate Period, C. 1800-1550 B.C. K. S. B. Ryholt & Adam Bulow-Jacobsen. LC 98-198517. (CNI Publications). xiv, 463 p. 1997. write for info. (*87-7289-421-0*) Mus Tusculanum.

Political Slang, 1750 to 1850. U. N. Philipson. (Lund Studies in English: Vol. 9). 1974. reprint ed. pap. 45.00 (*0-8115-0552-9*) Periodicals Srv.

Political Social Philosophy. Sher. (C). 1998. text 51.50 (*0-15-503746-3*, Pub. by Harcourt Coll Pubs) Harcourt.

Political Socialization. Diana M. Owen. (C). 1998. pap. 34.00 (*0-205-19433-8*, Macmillan Coll) P-H.

Political Socialization & Women Voters. D. M. Shukla. 1987. 34.95 (*0-318-37067-0*) Asia Bk Corp.

Political Socialization, Citizenship Education, & Democracy. Ed. by Orit Ichilov. 384p. (C). 1989. pap. text 23.95 (*0-8077-2973-6*) Tchrs Coll.

Political Socialization in the New Nations of Africa. Penelope Roach. LC 66-24873. (Columbia University, Center for Education in Asia, Publications). 41p. reprint ed. pap. 30.00 (*0-608-14831-8*, 202605800048) Bks Demand.

Political Socialization of Soviet Youth. Albert Hughes. LC 92-1055. 232p. 1992. lib. bdg. 89.95 (*0-7734-9484-7*) E Mellen.

Political Socialization of the Mexican American People. Ralph C. Guzman. Ed. by Carlos E. Cortes. LC 76-1264. (Chicano Heritage Ser.). (Illus.). 1977. 23.95 (*0-405-09504-X*) Ayer.

Political Socialization of the Young in East & West. Ed. by Bernhard Claussen & Horst Mueller. (International Studies in Political Socialization & Political Education: Vol. 5). (Illus.). 336p. 1990. pap. 69.00 (*3-631-43116-3*) P Lang Pubng.

Political Society in Lancastrian England: The Greater Gentry in Nottinghamshire. S. J. Payling. (Oxford Historical Monographs). (Illus.). 290p. 1991. text 72.00 (*0-19-820209-1*) OUP.

Political Society in Modern Israel: Myths & Realities. 2nd ed. Adam Garfinkle. LC 99-44578. 336p. 1999. text 72.95 (*0-7656-0514-7*) M E Sharpe.

***Political Society in Modern Israel: Myths & Realities.** 2nd ed. Adam Garfinkle. LC 99-44578. 336p. 1999. pap. text 28.95 (*0-7656-0515-5*) M E Sharpe.

Political Sociology. 2nd ed. Bottomore. (C). 1996. 53.95 (*0-7453-0651-9*) Westview.

Political Sociology. 2nd ed. Robert E. Dowse & John A. Hughes. LC 88-672451. 410p. reprint ed. pap. 127.10 (*0-7837-4732-2*, 204451700004) Bks Demand.

Political Sociology: A Comparative Historical Approach. Berch Berberoglu. LC 90-80204. (Illus.). 200p. (Orig.). 1990. text 35.95 (*0-930390-09-1*); pap. text 18.95 (*0-930390-08-3*) Gen Hall.

***Political Sociology: A Critical Introduction.** Keith Faulks. LC 99-56086. 1999. pap. text 19.50 (*0-8147-2709-3*) NYU Pr.

Political Sociology: An Australian Perspective. Reynolds. Date not set. pap. text. write for info. (*0-582-66397-0*, Pub. by Addison-Wesley) Longman.

Political Sociology: Readings in Research & Theory. Geroge E. Kourvetaris & Betty A. Dobratz. 350p. 1980. pap. 29.95 (*0-87855-717-2*) Transaction Pubs.

Political Sociology: Structure & Process. George A. Kourvetaris. LC 96-15327. 293p. 1996. 67.00 (*0-205-14793-1*) Allyn.

Political Sociology: Structure & Process, Incl. Test Bank. George A. Kourvetaris. (C). 1997. teacher ed. write for info. (*0-205-19685-3*, H9685-2) Allyn.

Political Sociology of C. Wright Millas. Bipul K. Bhadra. 1989. 23.50 (*81-85195-24-2*, Pub. by Minerva) S Asia.

Political Sociology of Educational Reform: Power - Knowledge in Teaching, Teacher Education, & Research. Thomas S. Popkewitz. 304p. (C). 1991. text 49.00 (*0-8077-3091-2*); pap. text 22.95 (*0-8077-3090-4*) Tchrs Coll.

Political Sociology of the State: Essays on the Origins, Structure, & Impact of the Modern State. Ed. by Richard G. Braungart & Margaret M. Braungart. 400p. 1991. pap. 25.75 (*1-55938-315-1*) Jai Pr.

Political Songs of England: From the Reign of John to That of Edward II. Ed. by Thomas Wright. (Anglistica & Americana Ser.: No. 34). xviii, 408p. 1968. reprint ed. 63.70 (*0-685-66503-8*, 05102201) G Olms Pubs.

Political Songs of England, from the Reign of John to That of Edward II. Tr. by Thomas Wright. (Camden Society, London. Publications, First Ser.: No. 6). reprint ed. 95.00 (*0-404-50106-0*, A17-1188) AMS Pr.

Political Sources of Humanitarian Emergencies. K. J. Holsti & World Institute for Development Economics Research. LC 98-178593. (Research for Action Ser.). 40p. 1997. write for info. (*952-9520-53-0*) UN.

Political Speeches & Journalism, 1923-1929. Miguel de Unamuno. Ed. by Stephen G.H. Roberts. (Exeter Hispanic Text Ser.: No. 54). (SPA.). 103p. 1996. pap. 17.95 (*0-85989-440-1*, Pub. by Univ Exeter Pr) Northwestern U Pr.

Political Stability & Democracy in Mexico: The Perfect Dictatorship? Dan A. Cothran. LC 93-23679. 272p. 1994. 65.00 (*0-275-94345-3*, Praeger Pubs) Greenwood.

Political Stability & Development: A Comparative Analysis of Kenya, Tanzania, & Uganda. Dirk Berg-Schlosser & Rainer Siegler. LC 90-8249. 226p. 1990. lib. bdg. 40.00 (*1-55587-165-8*) L Rienner.

Political Stability & Economic Growth. Ed. by Winberg Chai & Cal Clark. 1991. write for info. (*0-318-68599-X*) Third Wrld Inst.

Political Stability in Federal Governments. Jonathan Lemco. LC 91-6777. 224p. 1991. 57.95 (*0-275-93854-9*, C3854, Praeger Pubs) Greenwood.

Political Stability in the Philippines: Framework & Analysis. Daniel Druckman & Justin Green. (Monograph Series in World Affairs: Vol. 22, Bk. 3). (Orig.). 1986. pap. 9.95 (*0-87940-082-X*) Monograph Series.

Political State of New Jersey. Ed. by Gerald M. Pomper. 240p. (C). 1986. text 40.00 (*0-8135-1150-X*); pap. text 16.00 (*0-8135-1151-8*) Rutgers U Pr.

Political Status of the Negro in the Age of FDR. Ralph J. Bunche. Ed. by Dewey W. Grantham. LC 72-96327. (Illus.). 715p. Date not set. reprint ed. pap. 200.00 (*0-608-20617-2*, 205458500003) Bks Demand.

Political Structure. 2nd ed. Grace A. Jones. LC 76-7409. (Aspects of Modern Sociology Ser.: The Social Structure of Modern Britain). 133p. reprint ed. pap. 41.30 (*0-608-13225-X*, 202526400043) Bks Demand.

Political Structure & Change in the Prehistoric Southeastern United States. Ed. by John F. Scarry. LC 95-47459. (Ripley P. Bullen Ser.). (Illus.). 304p. (C). 1996. 49.95 (*0-8130-1433-6*) U Press Fla.

Political Structure of the Chinese Community in Cambodia. W. E. Willmott. (London School of Economics Monographs on Social Anthropology: No. 42). 213p. (C). 1970. text 38.50 (*0-485-19542-9*, Pub. by Athlone Pr) Humanities.

Political Structure of the Federal Health Planning Program. Lawrence D. Brown. LC 81-70468. 47p. 1982. pap. 7.95 (*0-8157-1159-X*) Brookings.

Political Structures & Democracy in Uruguay. Luis E. Gonzalez. LC 90-70850. 224p. (C). 1991. text 33.50 (*0-268-01589-9*) U of Notre Dame Pr.

Political Structures of Early Medieval South India, 600-1300 A. D. Kesavan Veluthat. 1993. text 18.50 (*0-86311-309-5*) Sangam Bks Ltd.

Political Studies on Yemen. Ed. by Abdu Al-Sharif. (Translations of Western-Language Articles into Arabic for Use in Yemeni Universities Ser.: Vol. 1). 1996. write for info. (*1-882557-03-4*) Am Inst Yemeni.

Political Style: The Artistry of Power. Robert Hariman. 272p. 1995. pap. text 14.95 (*0-226-31630-0*) U Ch Pr.

Political Style: The Artistry of Power. Robert Hariman. LC 94-36285. (New Practices of Inquiry Ser.). 272p. 1995. lib. bdg. 42.50 (*0-226-31629-7*) U Ch Pr.

Political Succession in the U. S. S. R. Myron Rush. LC 65-14778. xv, 223p. 1965. text 64.50 (*0-231-02825-3*) Col U Pr.

Political Suicide. Robert Barnard. 224p. 1995. pap. 7.95 (*0-88150-326-6*, Foul Play) Norton.

Political Suicide in Latin America: And Other Essays. James Dunkerley. LC 91-38676. 278p. (C). 1992. pap. 19.00 (*0-86091-560-3*, A6411, Pub. by Verso) Norton.

Political Support in Canada: The Crisis Years. Allan Kornberg & Harold D. Clarke. LC 83-11567. xvi, 463p. 1983. text 59.95 (*0-8223-0546-1*) Duke.

Political Symbolism in Modern Europe: Essays in Honor of George L. Mosse. Ed. by Seymour Drescher et al. LC 80-26544. (Illus.). 310p. 1982. 49.95 (*0-87855-422-X*) Transaction Pubs.

***Political Symbols, Symbolic Politics: European Identities in Transformation.** Ed. by Ulf Hedetoft. LC 98-72853. 304p. 1998. text 67.95 (*1-84014-355-X*) Ashgate Pub Co.

Political System: An Inquiry into the State of Political Science. David Easton. LC 80-39678. 408p. reprint ed. pap. 126.50 (*0-608-09453-6*, 205425300005) Bks Demand.

Political System - A Survey of Research in Political Science, 3 vols. Indian Council of Social Science Research Staff. 1981. 18.95 (*0-318-36597-9*) Asia Bk Corp.

Political System & Constitution of India, 10 vols. Verinder Grover. 8000p. 1997. 5500.00 (*81-7100-884-4*, Pub. by Print Hse) St Mut.

Political System in India, 10 vols. Verinder Grover. (C). 1989. 5500.00 (*0-7855-4752-5*) St Mut.

Political System in Pakistan, 10 vols. Verinder Grover & Ranjana Arora. 1955. 4750.00 (*81-7100-744-9*, Pub. by Print Hse) St Mut.

Political System of Brazil. Ronald M. Schneider. LC 75-154860. 431p. 1973. reprint ed. text 81.00 (*0-231-03506-3*) Col U Pr.

Political System of European. Blacky Hix. LC 99-21956. 1999. text 55.00 (*0-312-22535-0*) St Martin.

Political System of the Anuak of the Anglo-Egyptian Sudan. Edward E. Evans-Pritchard. LC 74-15036. (London School of Economics & Political Science Monographs on Social Anthropology: No. 4). reprint ed. 37.50 (*0-404-12041-5*) AMS Pr.

Political System of the European Union Simon Hix. LC 99-21956. (European Union Ser.). 1999. pap. 22.95 (*0-312-22536-9*) St Martin.

Political Systems--Conditions, Care, Ideology, Service, Progress & Reactions: Index of New Information. Howie L. Underwood. 150p. 1994. 47.50 (*0-7883-0076-8*); pap. 44.50 (*0-7883-0077-6*) ABBE Pubs Assn.

Political Systems of Empires. Samuel N. Eisenstadt. LC 92-16335. 574p. (C). 1992. reprint ed. pap. 29.95 (*1-56000-641-2*) Transaction Pubs.

Political Systems of Highlands Burma: A Study of Kachin Social Structure. 4th ed. Edmund R. Leach. (Monographs on Social Anthropology: No.44). (Illus.). 324p. (C). 1954. pap. 25.00 (*0-485-19644-1*, Pub. by Athlone Pr) Humanities.

Political Systems of the World. 2nd ed. J. Denis Derbyshire & Ian Derbyshire. 698p. 1996. text 95.00 (*0-312-16172-7*) St Martin.

Political Tactics. Jeremy Bentham. Ed. by Catherine Pease-Watkin. 308p. 1999. text 90.00 (*0-19-820772-7*) OUP.

Political Terminology in the Quran. Muhammad T. Sayyid. Tr. by Laleh Bakhtiar from PER. 64p. (Orig.). (C). 1989. pap. text 4.50 (*1-871031-12-5*) Abjad Bk.

Political Terrain: Washington, D.C., from Tidewater Town to Global Metropolis. Carl Abbott. LC 98-41013. (Illus.). 272p. 1999. pap. 19.95 (*0-8078-4805-0*); lib. bdg. 39.95 (*0-8078-2478-X*) U of NC Pr.

Political Terror in Communist Systems. Alexander Dallin & George W. Breslauer. xvi, 176p. 1970. pap. 11.95 (*0-8047-1085-6*) Stanford U Pr.

Political Terrorism, Vol. 1. Ed. by Lester A. Sobel. LC 74-84438. 317p. 1975. reprint ed. pap. 98.30 (*0-608-09966-X*, 202721800001) Bks Demand.

Political Terrorism, Vol. 2. Ed. by Lester A. Sobel. LC 74-84438. 287p. 1978. reprint ed. pap. 89.00 (*0-608-09967-8*, 202721800002) Bks Demand.

Political Terrorism: A Research Guide to Concepts, Theories, Data Bases, & Literature. 2nd expanded rev. ed. Alex P. Schmid & A. J. Jongman. 700p. 61.25 (*0-444-85659-5*) Elsevier.

Political Terrorism: Theory, Tactics & Counter Measures. 2nd ed. Grant Wardlaw. 264p. (C). 1989. pap. text 19.95 (*0-521-36841-3*) Cambridge U Pr.

Political Terrorism & Energy: The Threat & the Response. Ed. by Yonah Alexander & Charles K. Ebinger. LC 81-15695. 258p. 1982. 55.00 (*0-275-90750-3*, C0750, Praeger Pubs) Greenwood.

Political Testament of Cardinal Richelieu: The Significant Chapters & Supporting Selections. Tr. by Henry B. Hill. (Illus.). 148p. 1964. pap. 13.95 (*0-299-02424-5*) U of Wis Pr.

Political Testament of Hermann Goering. H. W. Goering. Tr. by H. W. Blood-Ryan. LC 71-180403. reprint ed. 39.50 (*0-404-56127-6*) AMS Pr.

***Political Theatre During the Spanish Civil War.** Jim McCarthy. 200p. 1999. (*0-7083-1523-2*, Pub. by Univ Wales Pr) Paul & Co Pubs.

Political Theatre of Early Seventeenth-Century Spain, with Special Reference to Juan Ruiz de Alarcon. Cynthia L. Halpern. LC 92-20890. (Iberica Ser.: Vol. 6). X, 179p. (C). 1993. text 39.95 (*0-8204-1976-1*) P Lang Pubng.

Political Theories & Social Reconstruction: A Critical Survey of the Literature on India. Thomas Pantham. LC 94-45237. 200p. 1995. 24.00 (*0-8039-9216-5*) Sage.

Political Theories of International Relations: From Thucydides to the Present. David Boucher. LC 99-179454. 456p. 1998. pap. text 24.95 (*0-19-878054-0*) OUP.

Political Theories of International Relations: From Thucydides to the Present. DAvid Boucher. LC 99-179454. 456p. 1998. 110.00 (*0-19-878053-2*) OUP.

Political Theories of the Ancient World. Westel W. Willoughby. LC 79-95083. (Select Bibliographies Reprint Ser.). 1977. 30.95 (*0-8369-5082-8*) Ayer.

Political Theories of the Middle Age. Otto Gierke. Tr. & Intro. by Frederic W. Maitland. (Key Texts Ser.). 278p. 1996. pap. 19.95 (*1-85506-478-2*) Bks Intl VA.

Political Theory. Heywood. LC 98-43696. 1999. pap. 22.95 (*0-312-22164-9*) St Martin.

Political Theory. 2nd ed. Andrew Heywood. LC 98-43696. 1999. text 59.95 (*0-312-22163-0*) St Martin.

Political Theory, Vol. 1. Klosko. LC 92-53970. (C). 1994. pap. text 47.50 (*0-03-074016-9*, Pub. by Harcourt Coll Pubs) Harcourt.

Political Theory, Vol. 2. Klosko. (C). 1995. pap. text 44.50 (*0-03-074014-2*, Pub. by Harcourt Coll Pubs) Harcourt.

Political Theory: The Foundations of Twentieth Century Political Thought. Arnold Brecht. LC 59-5591. 607p. reprint ed. pap. 188.20 (*0-608-30088-8*, 201501100092) Bks Demand.

Political Theory: Tradition & Diversity. Ed. & Contrib. by Andrew Vincent. LC 97-19623. (Illus.). 280p. 1997. text 59.95 (*0-521-57358-0*); pap. text 22.95 (*0-521-57500-1*) Cambridge U Pr.

Political Theory: Tradition & Interpretation. John G. Gunnell. (Illus.). 192p. (C). 1987. reprint ed. pap. text 18.50 (*0-8191-5954-9*) U Pr of Amer.

Political Theory & Animal Rights. Linzey. 256p. (C). 49.95 (*0-7453-0386-2*, Pub. by Pluto GBR); pap. 18.95 (*0-7453-0391-9*, Pub. by Pluto GBR) Stylus Pub VA.

Political Theory & Christian Vision: Essays in Memory of Bernard Zylstra. Ed. by Jonathan Chaplin & Paul A. Marshall. LC 94-8990. 304p. (C). 1994. pap. text 29.00 (*0-8191-9530-8*); lib. bdg. 64.00 (*0-8191-9529-4*) U Pr of Amer.

Political Theory & Ecological Values. Tim Hayward. LC 98-11701. 1999. pap. 21.95 (*0-312-21876-1*); text 65.00 (*0-312-21874-5*) St Martin.

Political Theory & Institutions of the Khawarij. Elie A. Salem. LC 78-64226. (Johns Hopkins University. Studies in the Social Sciences. Thirtieth Ser. 1912: 2). reprint ed. 37.50 (*0-404-61328-4*) AMS Pr.

Political Theory & International Relations. Charles R. Beitz. LC 79-83976. 212p. 1979. pap. text 14.95 (*0-691-02192-9*, Pub. by Princeton U Pr) Cal Prin Full Svc.

Political Theory & International Relations, Revised Edition. Charles R. Beitz. LC 99-12992. 1999. pap. text 14.95 (*0-691-00915-5*, Pub. by Princeton U Pr) Cal Prin Full Svc.

Political Theory & Modernity. 2nd ed. Epil. by William E. Connolly. LC 93-193. 240p. 1993. pap. text 16.95 (*0-8014-8108-2*) Cornell U Pr.

Political Theory & Organization. L. S. Rathore & S. A. Haqqi. (C). 1988. 65.00 (*0-7855-3520-9*) St Mut.

Political Theory & Organization for Law Students. R. Rathore & S. A. Haqqi. (C). 1991. text 60.00 (*0-89771-505-5*) St Mut.

***Political Theory & Partisan Politics.** Ed. by Edward B. Portis et al. LC 99-44721. (C). 2000. text 59.50 (*0-7914-4591-7*) State U NY Pr.

***Political Theory & Partisan Politics.** Ed. by Edward Bryan Portis et al. LC 99-44721. (C). 2000. pap. text 19.95 (*0-7914-4592-5*) State U NY Pr.

Political Theory & Postmodernism. Stephen K. White. (Modern European Philosophy Ser.). 169p. (C). 1991. text 49.95 (*0-521-40122-4*); pap. text 15.95 (*0-521-40948-9*) Cambridge U Pr.

Political Theory & Praxis: New Perspectives. Ed. by Terence Ball. LC 77-73320. 291p. reprint ed. pap. 90.30 (*0-8357-7664-6*, 205699100097) Bks Demand.

Political Theory & Public Choice Vol. 1: The Selected Essays of Anthony Downs. Anthony Downs. LC 98-12621. 192p. 1998. 70.00 (*1-85898-733-4*) E Elgar.

Political Theory & Public Policy. Robert E. Goodin. LC 81-23120. 296p. 1983. reprint ed. pap. text 19.00 (*0-226-30297-0*) U Ch Pr.

Political Theory & Societal Ethics. Robert R. Chambers. LC 91-20513. 165p. 1992. 26.95 (*0-87975-696-9*) Prometheus Bks.

Political Theory & the Displacement of Politics. Bonnie Honig. LC 92-56772. (Contestations Ser.). 288p. 1993. pap. text 17.95 (*0-8014-8072-8*) Cornell U Pr.

Political Theory & the European Union: Legitimacy, Constitutional Choice & Citizenship. Ed. by Michael Nentwich & Albert Weale. LC 98-4174. (European Political Science Ser.). (Illus.). 232p. (C). (gr. 13). 1998. 75.00 (*0-415-17313-2*, D5999) Routledge.

Political Theory & the Modern State: Essays on State, Power, & Democracy. David Held. LC 89-61405. 273p. 1989. 39.50 (*0-8047-1748-6*); pap. 14.95 (*0-8047-1749-4*) Stanford U Pr.

***Political Theory & the Rights of Indigenous Peoples.** Ed. by Duncan Ivison et al. 320p. 2000. write for info. (*0-521-77048-3*); pap. write for info. (*0-521-77937-5*) Cambridge U Pr.

Political Theory for Mortals: Shades of Justice, Images of Death. John E. Seery. (Contestations Ser.). 248p. 1996. text 39.95 (*0-8014-3259-6*); pap. text 16.95 (*0-8014-8376-X*) Cornell U Pr.

Political Theory in Modern Germany: An Introduction. Chris Thornhill. LC 99-32964. 260p. 2000. 59.95 (*0-7456-1999-1*, Pub. by Polity Pr); pap. 26.95 (*0-7456-2000-0*, Pub. by Polity Pr) Blackwell Pubs.

Political Theory in Retrospect: From the Ancient Greeks to the 20th Century. Geraint Williams. 200p. 1991. pap. 25.00 (*1-85278-641-8*) E Elgar.

Political Theory in Retrospect: From the Ancient Greeks to the 20th Century. Geraint Williams. 200p. 1991. text 80.00 (*1-85278-168-8*) E Elgar.

Political Theory in the Welfare State. Niklas Luhmann. vi, 239p. (C). 1990. lib. bdg. 46.95 (*3-11-011932-3*) De Gruyter.

***Political Theory in Transition.** Nohel O'Sullivan. LC 99-52540. 2000. pap. write for info. (*1-85728-855-6*) Taylor & Francis.

Political Theory, Modernity & Postmodernity. N. J. Rengger. 200p. (C). 1995. pap. 24.95 (*0-631-19159-3*) Blackwell Pubs.

Political Theory, Modernity & Postmodernity. N. J. Rengger. 200p. (C). 1995. 61.95 (*0-631-19158-5*) Blackwell Pubs.

Political Theory of a Compound Republic: Designing the American Experiment. 2nd ed. Vincent Ostrom. LC 86-7063. xxx, 240p. 1987. 24.95 (*0-8032-3554-2*) ICS Pr.

Political Theory of Arthur J. Penty. Asa D. Sokolow. 1940. pap. 49.50 (*0-686-83707-X*) Elliots Bks.

P

An Asterisk (*) at the beginning of an entry indicates that the title is appearing for the first time.

Political Theory of Beatrice Webb. Barbara E. Nolan. LC 87-12592. (Studies in Social History: No. 7). 1988. 47.50 (*0-404-61607-0*) AMS Pr.

Political Theory of Eric Voegelin. Barry Cooper. LC 86-23517. (Toronto Studies in Theology: Vol. 27). 256p. 1986. lib. bdg. 89.95 (*0-88946-771-4*) E Mellen.

Political Theory of Islam. S. Abul Ala Maududi. 1994. pap. 3.00 (*1-56744-189-0*) Kazi Pubns.

Political Theory of John Taylor of Caroline. C. William Hill, Jr. LC 75-39115. 343p. 1977. 38.50 (*0-8386-1902-9*) Fairleigh Dickinson.

Political Theory of Liberal Democracy. Paul Wilkinson. 1999. write for info. (*0-631-14246-0*); pap. write for info. (*0-631-15647-X*) Blackwell Pubs.

Political Theory of Liberation Theology: Toward a Reconvergence of Social Values & Social Sciences. John R. Pottenger. LC 88-34838. 264p. (C). 1989. pap. text 21.95 (*0-7914-0119-7*) State U NY Pr.

Political Theory of Rights. Attracta Ingram. 244p. 1995. pap. text 32.00 (*0-19-827963-9*) OUP.

Political Theory of the Constitution. Ed. by Kenneth W. Thompson. (Miller Center Bicentennial Series on Constitutionalism: Vol. III). 230p. (C). 1990. pap. text 22.50 (*0-8191-7678-8*) U Pr of Amer.

Political Theory of "The Federalist" David F. Epstein. LC 83-17858. x, 234p. (C). 1986. pap. text 9.95 (*0-226-21300-5*) U Ch Pr.

Political Theory Primer. Peter C. Ordeshook. (Illus.). 272p. (C). 1992. pap. 20.99 (*0-415-90241-X*, A4116) Routledge.

Political Theory Today. Ed. by David Held. LC 91-65150. 350p. 1991. 47.50 (*0-8047-1886-5*) Stanford U Pr.

Political Thinkers of Modern India. Adi H. Doctor. vii, 141p. 1997. 22.00 (*81-7099-661-9*, Pub. by Mittal Pubs Dist) Nataraj Bks.

Political Thinkers of Modern India, 10 vols., Set. Verinder Grover. (C). 1990. 3000.00 (*0-89771-136-X*) St Mut.

Political Thinkers of the Twentieth Century. P. Lassman & S. Buckler. 240p. (C). 1999. 59.99 (*0-415-10876-4*, D4207) Routledge.

Political Thinkers of the Twentieth Century. P. Lassman & S. Buckler. 240p. (C). 1999. pap. 17.99 (*0-415-10877-2*, D4211) Routledge.

Political Thinking. 6th ed. Glenn Tinder. LC 94-18671. 264p. (C). 1997. pap. text 36.93 (*0-673-99389-2*) Addson-Wesley Educ.

Political Thinking: The Perennial Questions. 7th ed. Tinder. (C). 1999. pap. text. write for info. (*0-321-00527-9*) Addson-Wesley Educ.

Political Thinking of the Indonesian Chinese, 1900-1995: A Sourcebook. 2nd expanded ed. Ed. by Leo Suryadinata. LC 97-941512. 265p. 1997. pap. 49.50 (*9971-69-201-5*, Pub. by Sngapore Univ Pr) Coronet Bks.

Political Thinking, Political Theory, & Civil Society. Steven M. DeLue. LC 95-50511. 368p. (C). 1996. pap. text 43.00 (*0-205-16487-0*) Allyn.

Political Thought. Jacob Mayer et al. LC 72-134114. (Essay Index Reprint Ser.). 1977. 29.95 (*0-8369-1932-7*) Ayer.

***Political Thought.** Ed. by Jonathan Wolff & Michael Rosen. LC 99-21005. 464p. (C). 1999. pap. text 21.95 (*0-19-289278-9*) OUP.

Political Thought: From Plato to the Present. 2nd ed. Harmon. (C). 1994. pap. text 38.25 (*0-07-026626-3*) McGraw.

***Political Thought & German Reunification: The New German Ideology?** Howard Williams et al. LC 99-43352. 2000. text 65.00 (*0-312-22924-0*) St Martin.

Political Thought & the American Judiciary. Ed. by H. L. Pohlman. LC 92-30025. 344p. (C). 1993. pap. 19.95 (*0-87023-830-2*); lib. bdg. 45.00 (*0-87023-829-9*) U of Mass Pr.

Political Thought & Thinkers. Judith N. Shklar. LC 97-27074. 402p. 1998. pap. text 21.00 (*0-226-75346-8*) U Ch Pr.

***Political Thought & Thinkers.** Judith N. Shklar. LC 97-27074. 408p. 1998. lib. bdg. 60.00 (*0-226-75344-1*) U Ch Pr.

P

Political Thought from Plato to NATO. Ed. by Brian Redhead. 288p. (C). 1988. pap. text 32.50 (*0-534-10801-6*) Harcourt.

Political Thought in America: An Anthology. 2nd ed. Michael Levy. 596p. (C). 1992. reprint ed. pap. text 30.95 (*0-88133-688-2*) Waveland Pr.

Political Thought in America: Conversations & Debates. 2nd rev. ed. Philip Abbott. LC 99-197252. 350p. (C). 1998. pap. text 22.95 (*1-57766-027-7*) Waveland Pr.

Political Thought in Ancient India: Emergence of the State, Evolution of Kingship & Inter-State Relations Based on the Saptanga Theory of State. G. P. Singh. (Reconstructing Indian History & Culture Ser.: No. 2). 152p. (C). 1993. 14.00 (*81-246-0001-5*, Pub. by D K Printwrld) Nataraj Bks.

Political Thought in Early Meiji Japan, 1868-1889. Joseph Pittau. LC 65-22065. (Harvard East Asian Ser.: No. 24). 261p. reprint ed. pap. 81.00 (*0-608-10278-4*, 200378100033) Bks Demand.

Political Thought in England, 1848 to 1914, 104. 2nd ed. Ernest Barker. LC 80-19766. (Home University Library of Modern Knowledge: 104). 256p. 1980. reprint ed. lib. bdg. 65.00 (*0-313-22216-9*, BAPL, Greenwood Pr) Greenwood.

Political Thought in England from Bacon to Halifax. George P. Gooch. LC 75-41115. reprint ed. 34.50 (*0-404-14754-2*) AMS Pr.

Political Thought in Europe, 1250-1450 see Pensamiento Politico en Europa, 1250-1450

Political Thought in Europe, 1250-1450. Antony Black. (Cambridge Medieval Textbooks Ser.). 223p. (C). 1992. text 54.95 (*0-521-38451-6*); pap. text 18.95 (*0-521-38609-8*) Cambridge U Pr.

Political Thought in France. J. P. Mayer. LC 78-67367. (European Political Thought Ser.). 1980. reprint ed. lib. bdg. 17.95 (*0-405-11718-3*) Ayer.

Political Thought in Japanese Historical Writing: From Kojiki (712) to Tokushi Yoron (1712) John S. Brownlee. 168p. (C). 1991. text 35.00 (*0-88920-997-9*) W Laurier U Pr.

Political Thought in Medieval Islam: An Introductory Outline. Erwin I. Rosenthal. LC 85-21909. 324p. 1985. reprint ed. lib. bdg. 55.50 (*0-313-25094-4*, ROPTH, Greenwood Pr) Greenwood.

Political Thought in Medieval Times. John B. Morrall. (Medieval Academy Reprints for Teaching Ser.). 1980. reprint ed. pap. text 12.95 (*0-8020-6413-2*) U of Toronto Pr.

Political Thought in Medieval Times. 3rd ed. John B. Morrall. LC 72-187548. (History Ser.). 154p. 1971. write for info. (*0-09-107680-3*) Hutchinson.

***Political Thought in Seventeenth-Century Ireland: Kingdom or Colony.** Ed. by Jane H. Ohlmeyer. LC JA84.I76P66 2000. (Illus.). 304p. (C). 2000. text 59.95 (*0-521-65083-6*) Cambridge U Pr.

Political Thought in the United States: A Documentary History. Lyman T. Sargent. LC 97-4664. 1997. text 60.00 (*0-8147-8047-4*); pap. text 22.50 (*0-8147-8048-2*) NYU Pr.

Political Thought of American Statesmen: Selected Writings & Speeches. Ed. by Morton J. Frisch & Richard G. Stevens. LC 72-89723. 384p. reprint ed. pap. 119.10 (*0-7837-1434-3*, 204181100023) Bks Demand.

Political Thought of Andre Gorz. Adrian Little. LC 96-7013. (Studies in Social & Political Thought). 224p. (C). 1996. 80.00 (*0-415-13866-3*) Routledge.

Political Thought of Benjamin Franklin. Ed. by Ralph Ketcham. LC 65-22344. 1965. pap. 8.95 (*0-672-60100-1*, AHS64, Bobbs) Macmillan.

Political Thought of Dr. Babasaheb Ambedkar. K. R. Kamaji. (C). 1992. 21.00 (*0-8364-2818-8*, Pub. by Intellectual) S Asia.

Political Thought of Dr. Babasaheb Ambedkar. R. K. Kshirsagar. vi, 246p. 1992. 16.00 (*81-7076-464-5*, Pub. by Intellect Pub Hse) Nataraj Bks.

Political Thought of G. W. F. Hegel. Henry Paolucci. LC 78-62416. 1978. pap. 2.50 (*0-918680-06-9*) Griffon House.

Political Thought of Hannah Arendt. Michael G. Gottsegen. LC 92-47131. 311p. 1993. text 21.50 (*0-7914-1729-8*) State U NY Pr.

Political Thought of Ibn Tamiyah. Qamar-ud-Din Khan. 216p. 1992. pap. 16.50 (*1-56744-190-4*) Kazi Pubns.

Political Thought of John Locke: An Historical Account of the Argument of the 'Two Treatises of Government' John Dunn. 306p. 1983. pap. text 24.95 (*0-521-27139-8*) Cambridge U Pr.

Political Thought of Karl Popper. Jeremy Sheamur. 240p. 1999. 49.95 (*0-415-09727-4*) Routledge.

Political Thought of Karl Popper. Jeremy Shearmur. LC 96-7016. 240p. (C). 1996. 75.00 (*0-415-09726-6*) Routledge.

Political Thought of Lord Durham. Janet Ajzenstat. 160p. (C). 1988. text 65.00 (*0-7735-0637-3*, Pub. by McG-Queens Univ Pr) CUP Services.

Political Thought of Max Weber: In Quest of Statesmanship. Ilse Dronberger. LC 70-133904. (Orig.). (C). 1971. 49.00 (*0-89197-349-4*); pap. text 17.95 (*0-89197-350-8*) Irvington.

Political Thought of Thomas G. Masaryk. Roman Szporluk. (East European Monographs: No. 85). 224p. 1981. text 46.00 (*0-914710-79-6*, Pub. by East Eur Monographs) Col U Pr.

Political Thought of Woodrow Wilson, 1875-1910. Niels A. Thorsen. LC 88-2495. (Supplementary Volumes to the Papers of Woodrow Wilson). 287p. 1988. reprint ed. pap. 89.00 (*0-608-07501-9*, 206772400009) Bks Demand.

Political Thought of Yu F. Samarin, 1840-1864. Loren D. Calder. (Modern European History Ser.). 358p. 1987. text 15.00 (*0-8240-8052-1*) Garland.

Political Thought since 1945: Philosophy, Science, Ideology. Ed. by Leonard Tivey & Anthony Wright. 240p. 1992. text 100.00 (*1-85278-311-7*) E Elgar.

Political Thought Today: An Introduction. Ed. by Adam Lent. LC 98-199743. 224p. 1998. pap. 20.00 (*0-85315-859-2*, Pub. by Lawrence & Wishart) NYU Pr.

Political Thoughts & Polemics. Bernard Crick. 238p. 1990. 70.00 (*0-7486-0120-1*, Pub. by Edinburgh U Pr) Col U Pr.

Political Thoughts & Polemics. Bernard Crick. 238p. 1991. pap. text 30.00 (*0-7486-0145-7*, Pub. by Edinburgh U Pr) Col U Pr.

Political Tides in the Arab World. Augustus R. Norton & Muhammad Y. Muslih. Ed. by Nancy L. Hoepli. LC 91-78231. (Headline Ser.: No. 296). (Illus.). 72p. (Orig.). 1992. pap. 5.95 (*0-87124-142-0*, 296) Foreign Policy.

Political Timber. Chris Lynch. LC 96-5750. 176p. (J). (gr. 7 up). 1996. lib. bdg. 14.89 (*0-06-027361-5*) HarpC Child Bks.

Political Timber. Chris Lynch. LC 96-5750. (Illus.). 176p. (YA). (gr. 7 up). 1996. 14.95 (*0-06-027360-7*) HarpC Child Bks.

Political Timber. Chris Lynch. 1997. 10.05 (*0-606-11758-X*, Pub. by Turtleback) Demco.

Political Timber. Chris Lynch. LC 96-5750. (Trophy Bk.). 176p. (YA). (gr. 7 up). 1997. reprint ed. pap. 4.95 (*0-06-447141-1*, HarpTrophy) HarpC Child Bks.

Political Tolerance: Balancing Community & Diversity. Robert Weissberg. LC 98-8983. (Contemporary American Politics Ser.). 275p. 1998. 54.00 (*0-8039-7342-X*); pap. 31.25 (*0-8039-7343-8*) Sage.

Political Tolerance & American Democracy. John L. Sullivan et al. LC 81-16406. 256p. (C). 1989. pap. text 17.95 (*0-226-77991-2*) U Ch Pr.

Political Tolerance & American Democracy. John L. Sullivan et al. x, 288p. (C). 1993. pap. text 16.95 (*0-226-77992-0*) U Ch Pr.

Political Tradition of the West: A Study in the Development of Modern Liberalism. Frederick M. Watkins. LC 82-9157. 368p. 1982. reprint ed. lib. bdg. 79.50 (*0-313-23368-3*, WAPT, Greenwood Pr) Greenwood.

Political Traditions in Modern France. Sudhir Hazareesingh. 368p. 1994. text 70.00 (*0-19-878074-5*); pap. text 21.00 (*0-19-878075-3*) OUP.

Political Trajectory of J. T. Murphy. Ralph Darlington. LC 99-182477. 256p. 1998. 44.95 (*0-85323-733-6*, Pub. by Liverpool Univ Pr); pap. 19.95 (*0-85323-743-3*, Pub. by Liverpool Univ Pr) Intl Spec Bk.

Political Transformation of Spain after Franco. John F. Coverdale. LC 78-19777. (Praeger Special Studies). 150p. 1979. 45.00 (*0-275-90343-5*, C0343, Praeger Pubs) Greenwood.

Political Transformation of the Brazilian Catholic Church. Thomas C. Bruneau. LC 73-79318. (Perspective on Development Ser.: Vol. 2). 284p. (J). (gr. 4-7). reprint ed. pap. 81.00 (*0-608-13317-5*, 2025579) Bks Demand.

Political Transition & the Rule of Law in Guatemala. Washington Office on Latin America Staff. 46p. 1988. pap. 5.00 (*0-931723-05-1*) WOLA.

***Political Transition in Cambodia, 1991-1999: Power, Elitism & Democracy.** David W. Roberts. LC 00-40451. 2000. write for info. (*0-312-23855-X*) St Martin.

Political Transitions & Foreign Affairs in Britain & France: Their Relevance for the United States. Don K. Price & Robert H. Evans. Ed. & Intro. by Frederick C. Mosher. (Papers on Presidential Transitions & Foreign Policy: Vol. III). 100p. (Orig.). (C). 1986. pap. text 15.00 (*0-8191-5314-1*) U Pr of Amer.

Political Transitions & Foreign Affairs in Britain & France: Their Relevance for the United States. Don K. Price & Robert H. Evans. Ed. & Intro. by Frederick C. Mosher. (Papers on Presidential Transitions & Foreign Policy: Vol. III). 100p. (Orig.). (C). 1986. lib. bdg. 34.50 (*0-8191-5313-3*, Pub. by White Miller Center) U Pr of Amer.

Political Trashing. Victor Santoro. LC 87-81102. 160p. (Orig.). 1987. pap. 12.95 (*0-915179-64-4*) Loompanics.

***Political Treatise.** Benedictus De Spinoza et al. LC 00-33422. 2000. write for info. (*0-87220-544-4*) Hackett Pub.

Political Trends in the Arab World: The Role of Ideas & Ideals in Politics. Majid Khadduri. LC 79-112361. 312p. reprint ed. 96.80 (*0-8357-9281-1*, 201657400004) Bks Demand.

Political Trends in the Arab World: The Role of Ideas & Ideals in Politics. Majid Khadduri. LC 83-12729. 298p. 1983. reprint ed. lib. bdg. 38.50 (*0-313-24181-3*, KHP0, Greenwood Pr) Greenwood.

Political Trials. Ed. by Theodore L. Becker. LC 78-126303. (C). 1971. pap. write for info. (*0-672-60744-1*, Bobbs) Macmillan.

Political Trials: Gordian Knots in the Law. Ronald S. Christenson. 252p. (Orig.). 1989. pap. 24.95 (*0-88738-776-4*) Transaction Pubs.

Political Trials: Gordian Knots in the Law. 2nd expanded rev. ed. Ron Christenson. LC 98-27092. 327p. 1998. pap. 29.95 (*0-7658-0473-5*) Transaction Pubs.

Political Trials in History: From Antiquity to the Present. Ed. by Ronald J. Christenson. 420p. (C). 1991. 59.95 (*0-88738-406-4*) Transaction Pubs.

Political Trials in Poland: Nineteen Eighty-One to Nineteen Eighty-Six. Andrezej Swidlicki. 432p. 1988. lib. bdg. 59.00 (*0-7099-4444-6*, Pub. by C Helm) Routldge.

Political Truth: A Voter's Guide to the 1996 Presidential Candidates & Elections. Ed. by Michael D. Barnes & Frank J. Fahrenkopf, Jr. (Orig.). Date not set. 14.95 (*0-614-10307-X*) Apolitical Pr.

Political Turmoil in Serbia. Ed. by Christopher H. Smith. 64p. (C). 1999. reprint ed. text 20.00 (*0-7881-7935-7*) DIANE Pub.

Political Unconscious: Narrative As a Socially Symbolic Act. Fredric Jameson. LC 80-21459. 320p. 1982. pap. text 16.95 (*0-8014-9222-X*) Cornell U Pr.

Political Unification of Korea in the 1990s: Key to World Peace. Young Jeh Kim. LC 88-27212. (Studies in World Peace: Vol. 3). (Illus.). 216p. 1989. lib. bdg. 89.95 (*0-88946-595-9*) E Mellen.

Political Unions Popular Politics of the Great Reform Act of 1832. Lopatin. LC 98-20136. 256p. 1999. text 65.00 (*0-312-21564-9*) St Martin.

Political University: Policy, Politics, & Presidential Leadership in the American Research University. Robert M. Rosenzweig. LC 97-25109. 200p. 1998. text 31.95 (*0-8018-5721-X*) Johns Hopkins.

Political Unrest in Upper Canada, 1815-1836. Aileen Dunham. LC 74-3751. 210p. 1975. reprint ed. lib. bdg. 59.50 (*0-8371-7474-0*, DUPU, Greenwood Pr) Greenwood.

Political Unrest in Upper Canada, 1815-1836. Aileen Dunham. (BCL1 - History - Canada Ser.). 210p. 1991. reprint ed. lib. bdg. 79.00 (*0-7812-6370-0*) Rprt Serv.

Political Upsurges in Post-War India, 1945-6. Keka D. Ray. (C). 1992. 15.00 (*0-685-63242-3*, Pub. by Intellectual) S Asia.

Political Use of the Radio. Thomas Grandin. LC 73-161178. (History of Broadcasting: Radio to Television Ser.). 1975. reprint ed. 18.95 (*0-405-03584-5*) Ayer.

Political Uses of Photography in the Third French Republic, 1871-1914. Donald E. English. LC 83-24239. (Studies in Photography: No. 3). (Illus.). 278p. reprint ed. pap. 86.20 (*0-8357-1473-X*, 207054200001) Bks Demand.

Political Uses of Sea Power. Edward N. Luttwak. LC 74-8219. (Washington Center of Foreign Policy Research. Studies in International Affairs: No. 23). 90p. reprint ed. pap. 30.00 (*0-608-16366-X*, 202632400049) Bks Demand.

Political Values & Ideological Trends in Africa. Ali A. Mazrui & Omari H. Kokole. 29p. 1992. 3.00 (*0-9633277-5-5*, Studies Global) Global Pubns.

Political Values on Health Care: The German Experience. Ed. by Donald W. Light & Alexander Schuller. (Humanistic & Social Dimensions of Medicine Ser.). (Illus.). 550p. 1986. 65.00 (*0-262-12109-3*) MIT Pr.

Political Vegetables? Businessman & Bureaucrat in the Development of Egyptian Agriculture. Yahya M. Sadowski. 396p. 1991. 42.95 (*0-8157-7662-4*); pap. 18.95 (*0-8157-7661-6*) Brookings.

Political Verse & Song from Britain & Ireland. Mary Asbraf. 1976. 12.95 (*0-8464-0731-0*) Beekman Pubs.

Political Violence & Stability in the States of the Northern Persian Gulf. Daniel L. Byman & Jerrold D. Green. LC 99-25031. (Illus.). 116p. 1999. pap. 15.00 (*0-8330-2726-3*, MR-1021-OSD) Rand Corp.

***Political Violence & the Palestinian Family: Implications for Mental Health & Well-Being.** Ed. by Vivian Khamis. LC 99-462145. (Illus.). 137p. 2000. 39.95 (*0-7890-0898-X*, Maltreatment & Trauma Pr); pap. text 19.95 (*0-7890-1112-3*, Maltreatment & Trauma Pr) Haworth Pr.

Political Violence, Crisis & Revolutions: Theories & Research. Ekkart Zimmerman. 792p. 1983. pap. text 24.95 (*0-87073-894-1*) Schenkman Bks Inc.

Political Violence in Drama: Classical Models, Contemporary Variations. Mary K. Dahl. Ed. by Oscar G. Brockett. LC 86-19246. (Theater & Dramatic Studies: No. 36). 171p. reprint ed. pap. 53.10 (*0-8357-1754-2*, 207070700004) Bks Demand.

Political Violence in Ireland: Government & Resistance since 1848. Charles Townshend. (Illus.). 456p. 1985. pap. text 22.50 (*0-19-820084-6*) OUP.

Political Violence in Northern Ireland: Conflict & Conflict Resolution. Ed. by Alan O'Day. LC 96-20681. 264p. 1997. 65.00 (*0-275-95414-5*, Praeger Pubs) Greenwood.

Political Violence in Sri Lanka, 1977-1990: Riots, Insurrections, Counter-Insurgencies, Foreign Intervention. Jagath P. Seneratne. 200p. 1998. pap. 27.50 (*90-5383-524-5*, Pub. by VU Univ Pr) Paul & Co Pubs.

Political Violence under the Swastika: 581 Early Nazis. Peter H. Merkl. LC 74-12143. 751p. 1975. reprint ed. pap. 200.00 (*0-7837-8593-3*, 204940800011) Bks Demand.

Political Visions: A Christian Analysis. Stephen C. Mott. LC 92-25045. (Illus.). 352p. 1993. pap. text 35.00 (*0-19-508138-2*) OUP.

Political Voice: Citizen Demand for Urban Public Services. Philip B. Coulter. LC 86-14617. (University of Alabama, Institute for Social Science Research Ser.: No. 1). 123p. reprint ed. pap. 38.20 (*0-608-09219-3*, 205272300005) Bks Demand.

Political Vulnerability of Justice Studies Pt. I: A Case Study of the Attempt to Eliminate the School of Human Justice in the 1980s. Jim Harding. LC 98-12607. (PJR Working Paper Ser.: Vol. 2). 39p. 1998. write for info. (*0-7731-0283-3*) U Regina.

Political Warfare & Psychological Operations: Rethinking the U. S. Approach. Ed. by Carnes Lord & Frank R. Barnett. 242p. (Orig.). (C). 1996. reprint ed. pap. text 35.00 (*0-7881-3051-X*) DIANE Pub.

Political Will & Personal Belief: The Decline & Fall of Soviet Communism. Paul Hollander. LC 99-31370. 354p. 1999. 35.00 (*0-300-07620-7*) Yale U Pr.

Political Wives, Veiled Lives. Joyce Schuck. 1991. 22.95 (*0-8191-8068-8*) Madison Bks UPA.

Political Women: Current Roles in State & Local Government. Ed. by Janet A. Flammang. LC 84-6922. (Sage Yearbooks in Women's Policy Studies: No. 8). 320p. 1984. reprint ed. pap. 99.20 (*0-608-01453-2*, 205949700001) Bks Demand.

***Political Women: Florence Luscomb & the Legacy of Radical Reform.** Sharon Hartman Strom. (Critical Perspectives on the Past Ser.). (Illus.). 384p. 2001. 79.50 (*1-56639-818-5*); pap. 24.95 (*1-56639-819-3*) Temple U Pr.

Political Women, 1800-1850. Edmund Frow. Ed. by Ruth Frow. 240p. 37.95 (*0-7453-0557-1*, Pub. by Pluto GBR) Stylus Pub VA.

***Political Work of Northern Women Writers & the Civil War, 1850-1872.** Lyde C. Sizer. LC 99-87015. (Civil War America Ser.). (Illus.). 368p. 2000. 45.00 (*0-8078-2554-9*) U of NC Pr.

***Political Work of Northern Women Writers & the Civil War, 1850-1872.** Lyde Cullen Sizer. LC 99-87015. (Civil War America Ser.). 368p. 2000. pap. 18.95 (*0-8078-4885-9*) U of NC Pr.

Political Works. James Harrington. Ed. by J. G. Pocock. LC 75-41712. (Studies in the History & Theory of Politics: No. 27). 850p. 1977. text 130.00 (*0-521-21161-1*) Cambridge U Pr.

Political World. Ed. by Scott Morris. LC 92-22284. (Using & Understanding Maps Ser.). (Illus.). 48p. (YA). (gr. 5 up). 1993. lib. bdg. 17.95 (*0-7910-1802-4*) Chelsea Hse.

Political World of a Small Town: A Mirror Image of American Politics, 317. Nelson Wikstrom. LC 92-36258. (Contributions in Political Science Ser.: No. 317). 232p. 1993. 59.95 (*0-313-28786-4*, GM8786, Greenwood Pr) Greenwood.

Political World of American Zionism. LC 61-10126. 449p. reprint ed. pap. 139.20 (*0-608-30397-6*, 200133200075) Bks Demand.

Political World of the Clergy. Ted G. Jelen. LC 92-37526. 192p. 1993. 49.95 (*0-275-93904-9*, C3904, Praeger Pubs) Greenwood.

An Asterisk (*) at the beginning of an entry indicates that the title is appearing for the first time.

Political World of Thomas Wentworth, Earl of Strafford, 1621-1641. Ed. by J. F. Merritt. 307p. (C). 1996. text 64.95 (*0-521-56041-1*) Cambridge U Pr.

Political Writings. Augustine, Saint. Ed. by E. L. Fortin. Tr. by Douglas Kries & Michael W. Tkacz from LAT. 256p. (Orig.). (C). 1994. pap. text 9.95 (*0-87220-210-0*); lib. bdg. 34.95 (*0-87220-211-9*) Hackett Pub.

Political Writings. Augustine, Saint. Ed. by Henry Paolucci. LC 96-23273. 358p. (Orig.). 1996. pap. 12.95 (*0-89526-704-7*, Gateway Editions) Regnery Pub.

Political Writings. Henry Bolingbroke. Ed. by David Armitage. (Cambridge Texts in the History of Political Thought Ser.). 352p. (C). 1997. text 69.95 (*0-521-44393-8*); pap. text 25.95 (*0-521-58697-6*) Cambridge U Pr.

Political Writings. Henry S. Bolingbroke. Ed. by Isaac Kramnick. (Crofts Classics Ser.). 112p. 1970. pap. text 4.95 (*0-88295-015-0*) Harlan Davidson.

Political Writings. Benjamin Constant. Ed. by Biancamaria Fontana. (Cambridge Texts in the History of Political Thought Ser.). 368p. 1988. pap. text 19.95 (*0-521-31632-4*) Cambridge U Pr.

Political Writings. John Dewey. Ed. by Ian Shapiro. LC 93-8944. (Hackett Classics Ser.). 288p. (Orig.). (C). 1993. pap. text 9.95 (*0-87220-190-2*); lib. bdg. 32.95 (*0-87220-191-0*) Hackett Pub.

Political Writings. Denis Diderot. Ed. by Robert Wokler & John H. Mason. (Cambridge Texts in the History of Political Thought Ser.). 256p. (C). 1992. text 59.95 (*0-521-36044-7*); pap. text 19.95 (*0-521-36911-8*) Cambridge U Pr.

Political Writings. David Hume. Ed. by Stuart D. Warner & Donald W. Livingston. LC 93-50572. 304p. 1994. pap. text 12.95 (*0-87220-160-0*); lib. bdg. 37.95 (*0-87220-161-9*) Hackett Pub.

Political Writings. Thomas Jefferson. Ed. by Joyce Appleby & Terence Ball. LC 98-40304. (Cambridge Texts in the History of Political Thought Ser.). 645p. (C). 1999. 59.95 (*0-521-64051-2*) Cambridge U Pr.

***Political Writings.** Samuel Johnson & Donald J. Greene. LC 99-16127. 2000. 12.00 (*0-86597-275-3*) Liberty Fund.

Political Writings. Gottfried Wilhelm Leibniz. Ed. by Patrick Riley. (Cambridge Texts in the History of Political Thought Ser.). 264p. 1988. text 64.95 (*0-521-35380-7*) Cambridge U Pr.

Political Writings. Gottfried Wilhelm Leibniz. Ed. by Patrick Riley. (Cambridge Texts in the History of Political Thought Ser.). 264p. 1988. pap. text 21.95 (*0-521-35899-X*) Cambridge U Pr.

Political Writings. Jean-Francois Lyotard. Tr. by Bill Readings & Kevin P. Geiman. 380p. (C). 1993. pap. 19.95 (*0-8166-2045-8*) U of Minn Pr.

Political Writings. Jean-Francois Lyotard. Tr. by Bill Readings & Kevin P. Geiman. 380p. (C). 1993. text 49.95 (*0-8166-2043-1*) U of Minn Pr.

Political Writings. James Mill. Ed. by Terence Ball. (Cambridge Texts in the History of Political Thought Ser.). 356p. (C). 1992. text 59.95 (*0-521-38323-4*); pap. text 19.95 (*0-521-38748-5*) Cambridge U Pr.

Political Writings. John Milton. Ed. by Martin Dzelainis. Tr. by Claire Gruzelier. (Cambridge Texts in the History of Political Thought Ser.). 304p. (C). 1991. pap. text 19.95 (*0-521-34866-8*) Cambridge U Pr.

Political Writings. Richard Price. Ed. by D. O. Thomas. (Cambridge Texts in the History of Political Thought Ser.). 234p. (C). 1992. text 59.95 (*0-521-40162-3*); pap. text 19.95 (*0-521-40969-1*) Cambridge U Pr.

Political Writings. Joseph Priestley. Ed. by Peter Miller. LC 92-27753. (Cambridge Texts in the History of Political Thought Ser.). 189p. (C). 1993. text 49.95 (*0-521-41540-3*); pap. text 16.95 (*0-521-42561-1*) Cambridge U Pr.

Political Writings. Mary Wollstonecraft Shelley. Ed. by Janet Todd. (The World's Classics Ser.). 450p. 1994. pap. 10.95 (*0-19-282311-6*) OUP.

Political Writings. Ed. by Johann P. Sommerville. (Cambridge Texts in the History of Political Thought Ser.). 375p. (C). 1995. text 59.95 (*0-521-44209-5*); pap. text 22.95 (*0-521-44729-1*) Cambridge U Pr.

Political Writings. Herbert Spencer. Ed. by John Offer. LC 92-35996. (Cambridge Texts in the History of Political Thought Ser.). 224p. (C). 1993. text 59.95 (*0-521-43142-5*); pap. text 20.95 (*0-521-43740-7*) Cambridge U Pr.

Political Writings. Francisco Vitoria. Ed. by Anthony Pagden. Tr. & Pref. by Jeremy Lawrance. (Cambridge Texts in the History of Political Thought Ser.). 442p. (C). 1992. pap. text 23.95 (*0-521-36714-X*) Cambridge U Pr.

Political Writings. Voltaire. Ed. by David Williams. (Cambridge Texts in the History of Political Thought Ser.). 344p. (C). 1994. pap. text 19.95 (*0-521-43727-X*) Cambridge U Pr.

Political Writings. Max Weber. Ed. by Peter Lassman & Ronald Speirs. LC 93-5718. (Cambridge Texts in the History of Political Thought Ser.). 424p. (C). 1994. pap. text 16.95 (*0-521-39719-7*) Cambridge U Pr.

Political Writings. 2nd ed. Immanuel Kant. Ed. by H. S. Reiss. Tr. by H. B. Nisbet. (Cambridge Texts in the History of Political Thought Ser.). 327p. (C). 1991. text 54.95 (*0-521-39185-7*); pap. text 17.95 (*0-521-39837-1*) Cambridge U Pr.

Political Writings: Contributions to Justice & Commonweal 1883-1890. Ed. by Nicholas Salmon & Peter Faulkner. (William Morris Library: First Series). 450p. 1994. 96.00 (*1-85506-251-8*); pap. 29.75 (*1-85506-252-6*) Bks Intl VA.

Political Writings: Rights of Men, Rights of Women, French Revolution. Mary Wollstonecraft Shelley. LC 92-95496. 445p. 1993. text 65.00 (*0-8020-2995-7*); pap. text 24.95 (*0-8020-7445-6*) U of Toronto Pr.

Political Writings: The Works of Samuel Johnson, Vol. 10. Samuel Johnson. Ed. by Donald J. Greene. LC 57-11918. Vol. 10. (Illus.). 1977. 75.00 (*0-300-01593-3*) Yale U Pr.

Political Writings, Including "A Defence of Poetry" Percy Bysshe Shelley. Ed. by Roland A. Duerksen. (Crofts Classics). 256p. 1970. pap. text 1.95 (*0-88295-089-4*) Harlan Davidson.

Political Writings of Dr. Johnson: A Selection. Samuel Johnson & John P. Hardy. LC 68-77844. xxii, 152 p. 1968. write for info. (*0-7100-2937-3*) Routledge.

Political Writings of James Harrington: Representative Selections, 38. James Harrington. Ed. by Charles Blitzer. LC 80-21163. (Library of Liberal Arts: No. 38). 165p. 1980. reprint ed. lib. bdg. 55.00 (*0-313-22670-9*, HAWR, Greenwood Pr) Greenwood.

***Political Writings of John Adams.** John Adams. 2000. 35.00 (*0-89526-292-4*) Regnery Pub.

Political Writings of John Dickinson, Esq. John Dickinson. (Notable American Authors Ser.). 1992. reprint ed. lib. bdg. 75.00 (*0-7812-2638-4*) Rprt Serv.

Political Writings of John Knox: The First Blast of the Trumpet Against the Monstrous Regiment of Women & Other Selected Works. Ed. by Marvin Breslow. LC 84-47549. 160p. 1985. 29.50 (*0-918016-75-4*) Folger Bks.

Political Writings of John Locke. John Locke. 592p. (Orig.). 1993. mass mkt. 6.99 (*0-451-62861-6*, Ment) NAL.

Political Writings of Mary Wollstonecraft. 69.95 (*1-85196-019-8*) Ashgate Pub Co.

Political Writings of Samuel Pufendorf. Samuel Pufendorf. Ed. by Craig L. Carr. Tr. by Michael J. Seidler. 304p. 1994. text 65.00 (*0-19-506560-3*) OUP.

Political Writings of the 1790s: French Revolution Debate in Britain, 8 vols. Gregory Claeys. 353p. 1995. 880.00 (*1-85196-320-0*) Ashgate Pub Co.

Political Writings of Thomas Jefferson. Ed. by Merrill D. Peterson. (Monticello Monographs). 213p. (Orig.). 1993. pap. 12.95 (*1-882886-01-1*) T J Mem Fnd.

Political Writings of William Morris. Ed. & Intro. by A. L. Morton. 246p. (C). 1973. pap. 9.95 (*0-85315-257-8*, Pub. by Lawrence & Wishart) NYU Pr.

Political Writings of William Morris. rev. ed. Ed. by A. L. Morton. 259p. 1973. text 9.95 (*0-85315-586-0*, Pub. by Lawrence & Wishart) NYU Pr.

Political Year 1970. Robin Oakley & Peter Rose. LC 78-855312. v, 250 p. 1970. write for info. (*0-273-31529-3*, Pub. by F T P-H) Natl Bk Netwk.

Political Year 1971. Robin Oakley. LC 72-185984. v, 314 p. 1971. write for info. (*0-273-36124-4*, Pub. by F T P-H) Natl Bk Netwk.

Political Years, 1967-1973 see Copyright, Congress & Technology: The Public Record

Political/Cultural Identity: Nations & Citizens in a Global Era. Peter W. Preston. 208p. 1997. 69.95 (*0-7619-5025-7*); pap. 26.95 (*0-7619-5026-5*) Sage.

Politicalisation of Agricultural Workers in Kerala. Jose George. 1985. 11.50 (*0-8364-1400-4*, Pub. by KP Bagchi) S Asia.

Politically Correct: The Ultimate Storybook, 3 vols. James Finn Garner. LC 98-216300. (Illus.). 296p. 1998. 7.98 (*0-7651-0867-4*) Smithmark.

Politically Correct: The Ultimate Storybook, 3 bks., Set. James Finn Garner. (Illus.). 288p. 1996. boxed set 29.95 (*0-02-860726-0*) Macmillan.

Politically Correct American History. Edward P. Moser. 1996. 10.00 (*0-614-97105-5*) Crown Pub Group.

Politically Correct Bedtime Stories. 1995. 8.95 (*0-02-860719-8*) Macmillan.

Politically Correct Bedtime Stories: A Collection of Modern Tales of Our Life & Times. James Finn Garner. LC 93-11481. 79p. 1997. 9.95 (*0-02-542730-X*) Macmillan.

Politically Correct Bedtime Stories: Modern Tales for Our Life & Times. large type ed. James Finn Garner. LC 95-17984. 1995. 17.95 (*1-56895-237-6*) Wheeler Pub.

Politically Correct Bible Stories. David Melbourne. 1995. 12.95 (*1-888121-11-4*) ST Publ.

***Politically Correct Cigar Smoking for Social Terrorists.** unabridged ed. Jack Riepe. Ed. by John J. Reilly & Leslie Marsh. LC 99-93281. (Illus.). xi, 177p. 1999. pap. 14.95 (*0-9672987-0-9*, A-01) Croften & Stone Pubs.

Politically Correct Death: Answering the Arguments for Abortion Rights. Francis J. Beckwith. LC 92-31659. 256p. 1993. pap. 19.99 (*0-8010-1050-0*) Baker Bks.

Politically Correct Duo, Bellybanded, Politically Correct Bedtime Stories & Once upon a More... James Finn Garner. 1996. 19.96 (*0-02-861399-6*) Macmillan.

Politically Correct Environment. Alan Gottlieb & Ron Arnold. LC 95-43981. (Illus.). 180p. 1995. pap. 14.95 (*0-936783-15-X*) Merril Pr.

Politically Correct Guide to American History, 000. Edward P. Moser. LC 98-50014. 1999. pap. 10.00 (*0-609-80188-0*) Three Rivers Pr.

Politically Correct Guide to Getting Laid. X. (Illus.). 98p. (Orig.). 1993. pap. 6.00 (*1-872819-08-7*, Pub. by Tuppy Owens) AK Pr Dist.

Politically Correct Guide to the Bible, 000. Edward P. Moser. 1999. pap. 10.00 (*0-609-80187-2*) Three Rivers Pr.

Politically Correct Guns. Alan Gottlieb. Ed. by Ron Arnold. (Illus.). 180p. (Orig.). 1996. pap. 14.95 (*0-936783-16-8*) Merril Pr.

Politically Correct Holiday Stories. James F. Gardner. (Illus.). 96p. 1995. 9.95 (*0-02-860420-2*) Macmillan.

***Politically Correct Holiday Stories.** James Finn Garner. 1999. pap. 5.98 (*0-671-04425-7*) PB.

Politically Correct Holiday Stories. James Finn Garner. 1995. audio 9.95 (*0-671-53452-1*) S&S Audio.

Politically Correct Hunting. Ken Jacobson. Ed. by Ron Arnold. (Illus.). x, 160p. (Orig.). 1995. pap. 14.95 (*0-936783-14-1*) Merril Pr.

Politically Correct Murder. John H. Hagar. LC 99-60637. 335p. 2000. pap. 15.95 (*0-88739-256-3*) Creat Arts Bk.

***Politically Correct Netherlands: Since the 1960s, 76.** Herman T. Vuijsje. Tr. & Anno. by Mark T. Hooker. LC 99-462061. (Contributions to the Study of World History Ser.: Vol. 76). 244p. 2000. 62.00 (*0-313-31509-4*, GM1509, Greenwood Pr) Greenwood.

Politically Correct Old Testament Stories. Robert M. Walker. LC 96-48036. 96p. (Orig.). 1997. 9.95 (*0-8362-3198-8*) Andrews & McMeel.

Politically Correct Parables. Robert M. Walker. (Illus.). 96p. 1996. 9.95 (*0-8362-1440-4*) Andrews & McMeel.

Politically Correct 'Twas the Night Before Christmas. Jamee Ruth et al. (Illus.). 20p. (Orig.). 1995. pap. 2.95 (*0-9648745-0-4*) Stickman Prods.

Politically, Fashionably & Aerodynamically Incorrect: The First Outland Collection. Berkeley Breathed. 1992. pap. 10.95 (*0-316-10701-8*) Little.

Politically Incorrect Cheese Weasel. Jim Ridings. (Illus.). 200p. 1993. pap. 11.95 (*0-9664974-3-0*, Side Show Comics) Ink & Feathers.

Politically Incorrect Cookbook: The Facts, Fantasies & Fallacies of the Endangered Species Act. Karl W. Drexel. Ed. by Roxanne Wright. (Illus.). 176p. (Orig.). 1996. pap. 12.95 (*0-9650435-0-9*) Whitney-Hill.

Politically Incorrect Dialogues: Topics Not Discussed in Polite Circles. Howard P. Kainz. (Value Inquiry Book Ser.: Vol. 82). vii, 126p. 1999. pap. 27.50 (*90-420-0686-2*) Editions Rodopi.

Politically Incorrect Joke Book. Joey West. LC 92-80466. (Illus.). 128p. (Orig.). 1992. pap. 6.95 (*0-929957-07-5*, Push-Pull Pr) JSA Pubns.

***Politically Incorrect Jokes from the Net.** Phillip Adams & Patrice Newell. 2000. pap. 11.95 (*0-285-63445-3*, Pub. by Souvenir Pr Ltd) IPG Chicago.

***Politically Incorrect Non-Animal Rights Wacko Wild Game & Fish Cookbook.** Doc Hunter & Bunney Hunter. 196p. 1999. spiral bd. 10.95 (*0-9674743-0-2*) Heavenly Insp.

***Politically Incorrect Poetry.** Mad German. (Illus.). 48p. 1999. pap. 13.00 (*1-883821-15-0*) Mother Bird.

Politically Incorrect's Greatest Hits. Bill Maher. 1996. 12.95 (*0-614-96847-X*) Villard Books.

Politically, Socially Correct? William G. White. 102p. 1995. pap. write for info. (*1-888296-02-X*) Jen Comp.

Politically Speaking: A Worldwide Examination of Language Used in the Public Sphere. Ed. by Ofer Feldman & Christ'l De Landtsheer. LC 97-49249. 224p. 1998. 69.50 (*0-275-96122-2*, Praeger Pubs) Greenwood.

Politicans & Party Politics. John G. Geer. LC 98-10047. 385p. 1998. 45.00 (*0-8018-5845-3*); pap. 18.95 (*0-8018-5846-1*) Johns Hopkins.

Politicas de Ajuste y Pobreza: Falsos Dilemas, Verdaderos Problemas. Ed. by Jose Nunez del Arco. (SPA.). 243p. 1994. pap. text 18.50 (*0-940602-88-1*) IADB.

***Politicas Forestales en America Latina.** Ed. by Kari Keipi. (SPA.). 313p. 2000. 18.50 (*1-886938-73-3*) IADB.

Politicas y Estrategias de Comunicacion y Publicidad. J. M. Ferre Trenzano. (SPA.). 109p. 1996. pap. 14.95 (*84-7978-256-0*, Pub. by Ediciones Diaz) IBD Ltd.

Politicas y Estrategias de Distribucion. J. M. Ferre Trenzano. (SPA.). 131p. 1996. pap. 16.00 (*84-7978-247-1*, Pub. by Ediciones Diaz) IBD Ltd.

Politicas y Estrategias de Gamas de Producto y Precios. J. M. Ferre Trenzano. 150p. 1995. pap. 16.00 (*84-7978-233-1*, Pub. by Ediciones Diaz) IBD Ltd.

Politician. Piers Anthony. (Bio of a Space Tyrant Ser.: No. 3). 352p. 1985. mass mkt. 4.99 (*0-380-89685-0*, Avon Bks) Morrow Avon.

Politician. Jack Luchsinger. LC 96-69944. 499p. 1996. pap. 10.00 (*0-9648622-8-X*) Pine Grve Pr.

***Politician: Bio of a Space Tyrant, Vol. 3.** Piers Anthony. LC 99-91254. 2000. 25.00 (*0-7388-0696-X*); pap. 18.00 (*0-7388-0697-8*) Xlibris Corp.

Politician: His Habits. James H. Wallis. LC 73-19183. (Politics & People Ser.). (Illus.). 368p. 1974. reprint ed. 28.95 (*0-405-05904-3*) Ayer.

Politician Goes to War: The Civil War Letters of John White Geary. Ed. by William A. Blair. LC 94-6497. (Illus.). 286p. 1995. 29.50 (*0-271-01338-9*) Pa St U Pr.

Politician Goes to War: The Civil War Letters of John White Geary. Ed. by William A. Blair. 259p. 1997. reprint ed. pap. text 27.00 (*0-7881-5057-X*) DIANE Pub.

Politician, Party & People. Henry C. Emery. 1913. 59.50 (*0-685-89771-0*) Elliots Bks.

Politicians. Cornelius Mathews. (Notable American Authors Ser.). 1999. reprint ed. lib. bdg. 125.00 (*0-7812-3986-9*) Rprt Serv.

Politicians. rev. ed. Robert C. Long. 210p. (Orig.). 1997. pap. 18.00 (*0-9653792-1-3*) C Long.

Politicians & Ethics. Ed. by Charles P. Cozic. LC 96-11848. (Current Controversies Ser.). 208p. (J). (gr. 5-12). 1996. pap. text 16.20 (*1-56510-406-4*); lib. bdg. 26.20 (*1-56510-407-2*) Greenhaven.

Politicians & Moralists of the 19th Century. Emile Faguet. LC 75-128239. (Essay Index Reprint Ser.). 1977. 21.95 (*0-8369-1828-2*) Ayer.

Politicians & Other Scoundrels. Ferdinand Lundberg. LC 92-17314. 1992. pap. 7.95 (*0-942637-72-0*) Barricade Bks.

Politicians & Other Scoundrels. Ferdinand Lundberg. 160p. 1988. reprint ed. pap. 6.95 (*0-8184-0483-3*) Carol Pub Group.

Politicians & Poachers: The Political Economy of Wildlife Policy in Africa. Clark C. Gibson. LC 98-39627. (Political Economy of Institutions & Decisions Ser.). (Illus.). 232p. (C). 1999. text 59.95 (*0-521-62385-5*) Cambridge U Pr.

Politicians & Poachers: The Political Economy of Wildlife Policy in Africa. Clark C. Gibson. (Political Economy of Institutions & Decisions Ser.). (Illus.). 264p. (C). 1999. pap. 24.95 (*0-521-66378-4*) Cambridge U Pr.

Politicians & Soldiers in Ghana, 1966-1972. Ed. by Dennis Austin & Robin Lucuham. (Studies in Commonwealth Politics & History: No. 3). 332p. 1975. 40.00 (*0-7146-3049-7*, Pub. by F Cass Pubs); pap. 19.50 (*0-7146-4019-0*, Pub. by F Cass Pubs) Intl Spec Bk.

Politicians & Virtuosi: Essays in Early Modern History. H. G. Koenigsberger. 288p. 1986. 55.00 (*0-907628-65-6*) Hambledon Press.

Politician's Dilemma: Building State Capacity in Latin America. Barbara Geddes. LC 93-14439. (California Series on Social Choice & Political Economy: Vol. 25). 1994. 45.00 (*0-520-07250-2*, Pub. by U CA Pr) Cal Prin Full Svc.

Politician's Dilemma: Building State Capacity in Latin America. Barbara Geddes. (California Series on Social Choice & Political Economy: Vol. 25). 256p. 1996. pap. 17.95 (*0-520-20762-9*, Pub. by U CA Pr) Cal Prin Full Svc.

Politicians, Diplomacy & War in Modern British History. Keith Robbins. LC 94-2354. 336p. 1994. 60.00 (*1-85285-111-2*) Hambledon Press.

***Politicians Don't Pander.** Lawrence R. Jacobs & Robert Y. Shapiro. LC 99-86011. 368p. 1999. lib. bdg. 48.00 (*0-226-38982-0*) U Ch Pr.

***Politicians Don't Pander: Political Manipulation & the Loss of Democratic Responsiveness.** Lawrence R. Jacobs & Robert Y. Shapiro. (Studies in Communication, Media & Public Opinion). 368p. 1999. pap. 17.00 (*0-226-38983-9*) U Ch Pr.

Politician's Guide to Assisted Suicide, Cloning & Other Current Controversies. George J. Marlin. 1998. pap. 12.95 (*0-9660597-1-9*) Morley Bks.

Politicians in Red Palace. Fam Wenbing. Ed. by Weihua Ma. (CHI., Illus.). 1998. pap. 19.00 (*0-9663964-1-3*) Pacific Internat.

***Politicians in the Pulpit: Christian Radicalism in Britain from the Fall of the Bastille to the Disintegration of Chartism.** Eileen Groth Lyon. 310p. 1999. 78.95 (*0-7546-0029-7*, Pub. by Ashgate Pub) Ashgate Pub Co.

Politicians, Judges & City Schools: Reforming School Finance in New York. Joel S. Berke et al. LC 84-60265. 228p. 1985. 34.00 (*0-87154-108-4*) Russell Sage.

Politicians, Judges, & the People: A Study in Citizens' Participation, 36. Charles H. Sheldon & Frank P. Weaver. LC 79-7472. (Contributions in Political Science Ser.: No. 36). 206p. 1980. 55.00 (*0-313-21492-1*, SPJ/, Greenwood Pr) Greenwood.

Politicians, Legislation, & the Economy: An Inquiry into the Interest-Group Theory of Government. Robert E. McCormick & Robert D. Tollison. (Rochester Studies in Economics & Policy Issues). 160p. 1981. lib. bdg. 111.00 (*0-89838-058-8*) Kluwer Academic.

Politicians, Planters & Plain Folk: Courthouse & Statehouse in the Upper South, 1850-1860. Ralph A. Wooster. LC 74-32339. 220p. reprint ed. pap. 68.20 (*0-608-14033-3*, 202222400025) Bks Demand.

Politicians, Poets, & Con Men: Emotional History in Late Victorian America. Burton Raffel. LC 86-1178. xi, 220p. (C). 1986. lib. bdg. 32.00 (*0-208-02067-5*, Archon Bks) Shoe String.

Politicians, Pupils, & Priests: Argentino Education since 1743. Virginia Leonard. (American University Studies: Ser. XXII, Vol. 2). XIV, 456p. (C). 1989. text 59.95 (0-8204-0748-8) P Lang Pubng.

Politicians Say the Dumbest Things. Carol A. Roessler. (Illus.). 228p. 1999. per. 11.95 (0-9668446-0-2) Wright Strategies.

***Politicians, the Press & Propaganda: Lord Northcliffe & the Great War, 1914-1919.** J. Lee Thompson. LC 99-24205. 344p. 1999. text 39.00 (0-87338-637-X) Kent St U Pr.

Politicisation of Business in Western Europe. R. Jackson. Ed. by M. P. Van Schendelen. 208p. 1987. lib. bdg. 59.95 (0-7099-2632-4, Pub. by C Helm) Routldge.

Politicisation of Islam: A Case Study of Tunisia. Mohamed E. Hamdi. LC 97-52574. (Series on State, Culture, & Society in Arab North Africa: Vol. 168). 224p. (C). 1998. 49.00 (0-8133-3458-6, Pub. by Westview) HarpC.

Politicization of Foster Care in New York City, Vol. 1. L. Trevor Grant. LC 96-90454. (Illus.). xv, 144p. (Orig.). (C). 1996. pap. 13.95 (0-9653734-0-1) Yacos Publns.

***Politicization of Islam: Reconstructing Identity, State, Faith, & Community in the Late Ottoman State.** Kemal H. Karpat. (Studies in Middle Eastern History Ser.). 640p. 2000. text 55.00 (0-19-513618-7) OUP.

Politicization of Society. Ed. by Kenneth S. Templeton, Jr. LC 78-17491. 1979. 15.00 (0-913966-48-7) Liberty Fund.

Politicization of Society During Nigeria's Second Republic, 1979-83. Ed. by Segun Gbadegesin. LC 91-26052. (African Studies: Vol. 22). 212p. 1991. lib. bdg. 89.95 (0-7734-9676-9) E Mellen.

Politicization of the United Nations Specialized Agencies: A Case Study of UNESCO. Sagarika Dutt. LC 94-13281. 340p. 1994. 99.95 (0-7734-9106-6) E Mellen.

Politicized Economies: Monarchy, Monopoly, & Mercantilism. Robert B. Ekelund, Jr. & Robert D. Tollison. LC 96-38971. (Economics Ser.: Vol. 14). (Illus.). 320p. (C). 1997. text 39.95 (0-89096-745-8) Tex A&M Univ Pr.

Politicized Ethnicity in the Russian Federation: Dilemmas of State Formation. James W. Warhola. LC 95-18592. 164p. 1996. text 79.95 (0-7734-8893-6) E Mellen.

Politicized Medicine. Intro. by Hans F. Sennholz. (Freeman Classics Ser.). 161p. (Orig.). 1993. pap. 9.95 (0-910614-87-3) Foun Econ Ed.

Politicized Muse: Medici Festivals, 1512-1537. Anthony M. Cummings. (Essays on the Arts Ser.). (Illus.). 250p. 1992. text 49.50 (0-691-09142-0, Pub. by Princeton U Pr) Cal Prin Full Svc.

Politicizing Gender: Narrative Strategies in the Aftermath of the French Revolution. Doris Y. Kadish. (Illus.). 220p. (C). 1991. text 40.00 (0-8135-1708-7) Rutgers U Pr.

Politicizing Presidency: The White House Personnel Office, 1948-1994. Thomas J. Weko. LC 94-41099. (Studies in Government & Public Policy). 256p. 1995. 35.00 (0-7006-0695-5); pap. 17.95 (0-7006-0696-3) U Pr of KS.

***Politickles: Limericks Lampooning the Liberal Left.** F. R. Duplantier. LC 99-88628. (Illus.). 120p. 2000. pap. 14.95 (0-936783-25-7, Pub. by Merril Pr) Midpt Trade.

Politico: Buddhist Manifesto. Chris Eann. Ed. by Don Lee. LC 94-78181. 250p. (C). 1994. 33.50 (0-939758-30-X) Eastern Pr.

Politico-Economic Writings. Ed. by J. C. Nyiri. (Viennese Heritage Ser.: No. 1). (GER.). xl, 240p. 1984. reprint ed. pap. 22.95 (90-272-3881-2) J Benjamins Pubng Co.

Politico-Geographical Analysis of the Arthasastra. Rajendra Prasad. (C). 1989. 30.00 (81-210-0224-9, Pub. by Inter-India Pubns) S Asia.

Politico-Legal India, 5 vols. Shiv Lal. 1986. 1950.00 (81-7051-000-7, Pub. by Archives Pubs) St Mut.

Politico-Peasantry Conflict in India: Dynamics of Agrarian Change. Suresh Misra. (C). 1991. 15.00 (81-7099-306-7, Pub. by Mittal Pubs Dist) S Asia.

Politicos, Dumbbells & Quacks. Maksymilian B. Necker. (Illus.). 170p. (Orig.). 1993. pap. 14.50 (1-877582-15-8) Ardor Pub.

Politics. Aristotle. Tr. by Carnes Lord from GRE. LC 84-215. (Illus.). vi, 290p. (C). 1985. pap. 13.50 (0-226-02669-8) U Ch Pr.

Politics. Aristotle. Tr. by H. Rackham. (Loeb Classical Library: No. 264). 712p. 1932. 18.95 (0-674-99291-1) HUP.

Politics. Aristotle. Tr. & Intro. by C. D. C. Reeve. LC 97-46398. (Classics Ser.). 384p. (C). 1998. pap. 8.95 (0-87220-388-3); lib. bdg. 34.95 (0-87220-389-1) Hackett Pub.

Politics. Aristotle. Tr. by Ernest Barker from GEC. LC 98-215869. (Oxford World's Classics Ser.). (Illus.). 470p. 1998. pap. 10.95 (0-19-283393-6) OUP.

Politics. Aristotle. Tr. by Lloyd P. Gerson & Hippocrates G. Apostle from GEC. LC 86-60430. (Apostle Translations of Aristotle's Works: Vol. 7). 399p. 1986. pap. 17.00 (0-911589-05-8) Peripatetic.

Politics. Aristotle. Tr. by William Ellis. LC 86-70378. (Great Books in Philosophy). 259p. 1986. pap. text 7.95 (0-87975-346-3) Prometheus Bks.

***Politics.** Aristotle & Benjamin Jowett. LC 00-31841. (Thrift Editions Ser.). 2000. pap. write for info. (0-486-41424-8) Dover.

Politics. Tr. by Ernest Barker. 490p. (YA). (gr. 9 up). 1962. pap. text 19.95 (0-19-500306-3) OUP.

Politics. Edward Irving Koch. 336p. 1986. mass mkt. 4.50 (0-446-32300-4) Warner Bks.

Politics. Kenneth Minogue. (Very Short Introductions Ser.). 132p. 1995. pap. 8.95 (0-19-285309-0) OUP.

Politics, 2 vols. Heinrich G. Von Treitschke. LC 72-970. reprint ed. 115.00 (0-404-13141-7) AMS Pr.

Politics. 4th ed. Johnson. 1995. 3.25 (0-697-29108-1, WCB McGr Hill) McGrw-H Hghr Educ.

Politics, Bks. I & II. Aristotle. Tr. & Comment by Trevor J. Saunders. (Clarendon Aristotle Ser.). 210p. 1996. text 55.00 (0-19-824892-X); pap. text 18.95 (0-19-824894-6) OUP.

Politics, Bks. I[00ad]IV. rev. ed. Aristotle. LC 75-13363. (History of Ideas in Ancient Greece Ser.: Bks. 1-5). (ENG & GRE.). 1976. reprint ed. 56.95 (0-405-07291-0) Ayer.

Politics, Bks. III & IV. Aristotle. Tr. & Comment by Richard Robinson. LC 97-158552. (Clarendon Aristotle Ser.). 186p. 1996. text 46.00 (0-19-823591-7) OUP.

Politics, Bks. III & IV. Aristotle. Tr. & Intro. by Richard Robinson. LC 97-158552. (Clarendon Aristotle Ser.). 186p. 1996. pap. text 19.95 (0-19-823592-5) OUP.

Politics, Bks. VII & VIII. Aristotle. Tr. & Comment by Richard Kraut. LC 97-11500. (Clarendon Aristotle Ser.). 240p. 1998. text 58.00 (0-19-875113-3, Clarendon Pr); pap. text 24.00 (0-19-875114-1) OUP.

Politics, Vols. 5-6. Aristotle. Tr. & Comment by David Keyt. LC 98-43637. 284p. 1999. text 72.00 (0-19-823535-6) OUP.

Politics, Vols. 5-6 Aristotle. Tr. & Comment by David Keyt. LC 98-43637. (Illus.). 284p. 1999. pap. text 19.95 (0-19-823536-4) OUP.

Politics: A Handbook for Students. Robert Weissberg. 422p. (C). 1985. pap. text 31.00 (0-15-570740-X, Pub. by Harcourt Coll Pubs) Harcourt.

Politics: A Selection. Roberto Unger. LC 96-49384. 1997. pap. 22.00 (1-85984-131-7, Pub. by Verso) Norton.

Politics: A Selection. Roberto M. Unger. LC 96-49384. (C). 1997. 65.00 (1-85984-870-2) Routledge.

***Politics: A Very Short Introduction.** 144p. 2000. 8.95 (0-19-285388-0) OUP.

Politics: An American Perspective: Uneasy Democracy: The Tension of Citizenship & Ideology. Earl Klee. (Citizen of Democracy Ser.). (Illus.). 219p. (Orig.). 1989. pap. 15.00 (0-936339-16-0) Circa Pr Portland.

Politics: An Introduction. Barry Axford & Gary Browning. LC 97-180623. 512p. (C). 1997. 90.00 (0-415-11074-2) Routledge.

Politics: An Introduction. Barry Axford et al. LC 97-180623. 512p. (C). 1997. pap. 24.99 (0-415-11075-0) Routledge.

Politics: An Introduction to Democratic Government. Munroe Eagles & Larry Johnston. 492p. (C). 1999. pap. 34.95 (1-55111-192-6) Broadview Pr.

Politics: An Introduction to the Modern Democratic State. Larry Johnston. 560p. (C). 1997. pap. 34.95 (1-55111-149-7) Broadview Pr.

Politics: An Irreverent Look at the Mighty & the Misguided. (Quote-a-Page Ser.). 374p. (Orig.). 1996. pap. 4.95 (0-8362-1094-8) Andrews & McMeel.

Politics: Aristotle. rev. ed. Aristotle. Tr. & Intro. by T. A. Sinclair. (Classics Ser.). 512p. 1981. pap. 12.95 (0-14-044421-1, Penguin Classics) Viking Penguin.

***Politics: Basics.** 2nd ed. Stephen D. Tansey. LC 99-30454. 272p. 1999. pap. write for info. (0-415-19199-8) Routledge.

***Politics: Basics.** 2nd ed. Stephen D. Tansey. LC 99-30454. 272p. (C). 1999. text. write for info. (0-415-19198-X) Routledge.

Politics: Canada. 7th ed. Paul Fox & Graham White. (C). 1991. pap. text 34.25 (0-07-551101-0) McGraw.

Politics: The Basics. Stephen D. Tansey. LC 95-5719. 240p. (C). 1995. pap. 16.99 (0-415-10263-4) Routledge.

Politics: The Basics. Stephen D. Tansey. LC 95-5719. 240p. (C). (gr. 13). 1995. 60.00 (0-415-10262-6) Routledge.

Politics: The Citizen's Business. William A. White. LC 73-19186. (Politics & People Ser.). 338p. 1974. reprint ed. 25.95 (0-405-05906-X) Ayer.

Politics: Who Gets What, When & How. Harold D. Lasswell. 1990. 22.25 (0-8446-1277-4) Peter Smith.

Politics - Sense - Experience: A Pragmatic Inquiry into the Promise of Democracy. Timothy V. Kaufman-Osborn. LC 91-6325. 348p. reprint ed. pap. 107.90 (0-608-20912-0, 207201100003) Bks Demand.

Politics, Administration & Public Policy in Developing Countries: Examples from Africa, Asia, & Latin America. Ed. by H. K. Asmerom & R. B. Jain. 208p. 1993. pap. 40.00 (90-5383-187-8, Pub. by VU Univ Pr) Paul & Co Pubs.

Politics Aesthetics & Culture: A Study of Indo-Anglian Political Novel. Asha Kaushik. (C). 1988. 18.50 (81-85054-47-9, Pub. by Manohar) S Asia.

Politics after Hitler: The Western Allies & the German Party System. Daniel E. Rogers. (C). 1995. text 45.00 (0-8147-7461-X) NYU Pr.

***Politics after Television: Hindu Nationalism & the Reshaping of the Public in India.** Arvind Rajagopal. 325p. 2001. write for info. (0-521-64053-9); pap. write for info. (0-521-64839-4) Cambridge U Pr.

Politics America: The Texas Edition. 2nd ed. Thomas R. Dye et al. LC 96-38827. 963p. 1996. 74.67 (0-13-257015-7) P-H.

Politics, American Style: Political Parties in American History. Isobel V. Morin. LC 98-53523. (Illus.). 144p. (YA). (gr. 5-8). 1999. lib. bdg. 22.40 (0-7613-1267-6) TFC Bks NY.

Politics among Nations. 6th rev. ed. Hans J. Morgenthau. Ed. by Kenneth W. Thompson. 688p. (C). 1985. 76.56 (0-07-554469-5) McGraw.

Politics among Nations: The Struggle for Power & Peace. Hans J. Morgenthau & Kenneth W. Thompson. 448p. (C). 1992. pap. 34.69 (0-07-043306-2) McGraw.

Politics among the Ungoverned: International Relations in the Modern World. Robert Art. 528p. (C). 2001. pap. 30.00 (0-02-303991-4, Macmillan Coll) P-H.

Politics, an American Perspective: Uneasy Democracy, the Tensions of Citizenship & Ideology. 2nd ed. Earl Klee. LC 95-49442. (Citizen of Democracy Ser.: Vol. 1). 1995. write for info. (0-936339-18-7) Circa Pr Portland.

Politics, an Initial Inquiry. Lepak. (C). 2001. pap. 33.33 (0-205-28901-0, Longwood Div) Allyn.

Politics Ancient & Modern. Pierre Vidal-Naquet. Tr. by Janet Lloyd from FRE. (Illus.). 216p. (C). 1996. text 58.95 (0-7456-1080-3) Blackwell Pubs.

Politics & a Belly-Full. Curtiss S. Johnson. LC 73-16948. (Illus.). 209p. 1974. reprint ed. lib. bdg. 35.00 (0-8371-7246-2, JOPB, Greenwood Pr) Greenwood.

Politics & Administration: Woodrow Wilson & American Public Administration. Jack Rabin & James Bowman. (Public Administration & Public Policy Ser.: Vol. 22). (Illus.). 344p. 1984. text 95.00 (0-8247-7068-4) Dekker.

Politics & Administration at the Top: Lessons from down Under. Delmer D. Dunn. LC 97-4770. (Series in Policy & Institutional Studies). 194p. 1997. pap. 19.95 (0-8229-5650-0); text 45.00 (0-8229-4045-0) U of Pittsburgh Pr.

Politics & Administration of Privatization Vol. 24:4: Efforts among Local Governments. Ed. by Dennis Daley. 51p. 1996. pap. 15.00 (0-944285-48-1) Pol Studies.

***Politics & Aesthetics in the Arts.** Salim Kemal & Ivan Gaskell. LC 99-11073. (Cambridge Studies in Philosophy & the Arts). (Illus.). 272p. (C). 2000. 59.95 (0-521-45418-2) Cambridge U Pr.

***Politics & Aesthetics of Kateb Yacine: From Francophone Literature to Popular Theatre in Algeria & Outside.** Kamal Salhi. LC 99-50295. 448p. 1999. text 109.95 (0-7734-7871-X) E Mellen.

Politics & Aesthetics of "New Negro" Literature. Ed. & Intro. by Cary D. Wintz. LC 96-16126. (Harlem Renaissance 1920-1940 Ser.: Vol. 2). (Illus.). 400p. 1996. text 90.00 (0-8153-2213-5) Garland.

Politics & Ambiguity. William Connolly. LC 86-15819. (Rhetoric of the Human Sciences Ser.). 256p. 1987. text 27.95 (0-299-10990-9) U of Wis Pr.

Politics & Budgeting in the World Health Organization. Francis W. Hoole. LC 76-19. (Studies in Development: No. 11). 240p. reprint ed. pap. 74.40 (0-608-17080-1, 205623000056) Bks Demand.

Politics & Bureaucracy in the Modern Presidency: Careerists & Appointees in the Reagan Administration, 311. Robert Maranto. LC 92-30014. (Contributions in Political Science Ser.: No. 311). 200p. 1993. 55.00 (0-313-28332-X, MTR/, Greenwood Pr) Greenwood.

Politics & Change in Developing Countries: Studies in the Theory & Practice of Development. Ed. by Colin T. Leys. 301p. reprint ed. pap. 85.80 (0-608-30039-X, 2051389) Bks Demand.

Politics & Change in Spain. Ed. by Thomas D. Lancaster & Gary Prevost. LC 84-18107. 240p. 1985. 55.00 (0-275-90133-5, C0133, Praeger Pubs) Greenwood.

Politics & Change in the Middle East: Sources of Conflict & Accommodation. 5th ed. Roy R. Andersen & Robert F. Seibert. LC 97-2062. 396p. 1997. pap. text 49.00 (0-13-621822-9) P-H.

***Politics & Change in the Middle East: Sources of Conflict & Accommodation.** 6th ed. Roy Andersen et al. LC 00-29804. 2000. write for info. (0-13-026009-6) P-H.

Politics & Civil Rights. Angela S. Medearis. (J). 1997. lib. bdg. 16.98 (0-8050-4486-8) H Holt & Co.

Politics & Class in Zaire: Bureaucracy, Business, & Beer in Lisala. Michael C. Schatzberg. LC 79-11852. (Illus.). 228p. 1980. 39.95 (0-8419-0438-3, Africana) Holmes & Meier.

Politics & Commentary. Joe Devany. LC 96-60008. (Illus.). 212p. 1996. 19.95 (0-9650890-0-2) J A Devany.

Politics & Constitution in the History of the United States, 3 vols. William W. Crosskey & William Jeffrey, Jr. 2040p. 1980. lib. bdg. 168.00 (0-226-12134-8) U Ch Pr.

***Politics & Constitutionalism: The Louis Fisher Connection.** Ed. by Robert J. Spitzer. LC 99-49908. (C). 2000. text 57.50 (0-7914-4639-5); pap. text 18.95 (0-7914-4640-9) State U NY Pr.

Politics & Corruption in Africa: A Case Study of Sierra Leone. Sahr J. Kpundeh. 262p. (Orig.). (C). 1994. pap. text 32.50 (0-8191-9697-5); lib. bdg. 57.00 (0-8191-9696-7) U Pr of Amer.

Politics & Criminal Prosecution. Raymond Moley. LC 73-19161. (Politics & People Ser.). 256p. 1974. reprint ed. 20.95 (0-405-05883-7) Ayer.

Politics & Cultural Values. Toshio Yatsushiro. Ed. by Roger Daniels. LC 78-54848. (Asian Experience in North America Ser.). 1979. lib. bdg. 50.95 (0-405-11299-8) Ayer.

Politics & Culture: Working Hypotheses for a Post-Revolutionary Society. Michael Ryan. LC 88-31746. (Parallax). 280p. 1989. text 42.00 (0-8018-3827-4) Johns Hopkins.

***Politics & Culture in 18th Century Russia.** Madariaga. LC 98-18989. 312p. (C). 1998. pap. 29.06 (0-582-32255-3) Longman.

Politics & Culture in International History: From the Ancient Near East to the Opening of the Modern Age. 2nd ed. Adda B. Bozeman. LC 94-8483. 620p. (C). 1994. pap. 29.95 (1-56000-735-4) Transaction Pubs.

***Politics & Culture in Modern Germany: Essays from the New York Review of Books.** Gordon Alexander Craig. LC 99-45708. 400p. 2000. pap. 24.50 (0-930664-22-1) SPOSS.

Politics & Culture in Renaissance Naples. Jerry H. Bentley. LC 87-945511. 342p. reprint ed. pap. 106.10 (0-608-06392-4, 206675300008) Bks Demand.

Politics & Culture in the Age of Christina. Ed. by Marie-Louise Roden. LC 99-184327. (Suecoromana Ser.: No. IV). (Illus.). 129p. 1997. 59.50 (91-7042-156-0) Coronet Bks.

Politics & Culture in Wartime Japan. Ben-Ami Shillony. 252p. 1991. pap. text 22.00 (0-19-820260-1, 8765) OUP.

Politics & Culture in Wilhelmine Germany: The Case of Industrial Architecture. Matthew Jefferies. 284p. 1995. 47.50 (0-85496-945-4) Berg Pubs.

Politics & Culture 18TH Century Russia. Madariaga. LC 98-53064. (C). 1998. text 68.44 (0-582-32256-1) Longman.

***Politics & Development: A Critical Introduction.** Olle Thornquist. LC 98-61793. 197 p. 1999. write for info. (0-7619-5934-3) Sage.

***Politics & Development: A Critical Introduction.** Olle Tornquist. LC 98-61793. 224p. 1998. 69.00 (0-7619-5933-5) Sage.

***Politics & Development in Latin America.** Mauricio Font. 175p. 1999. pap. 15.95 (0-8133-1513-1) Westview.

Politics & Development in Nepal: Some Issues. Narayan Khadka. (Illus.). xiv, 477p. 1994. 38.00 (81-85693-21-8, Pub. by Nirala Pubns) Nataraj Bks.

Politics & Development in the Caribbean Basin: Central America & the Caribbean in the New World Order. Jean Grugel. LC 94-24352. 224p. 1995. pap. 16.95 (0-253-20954-4); text 39.95 (0-253-32683-4) Ind U Pr.

Politics & Development of the Federal Income Tax. John F. Witte. LC 84-40506. (Illus.). 464p. 1985. text 35.00 (0-299-10200-9) U of Wis Pr.

Politics & Development of the Federal Income Tax. John F. Witte. LC 84-40506. (Illus.). 464p. 1986. pap. 15.95 (0-299-10204-1) U of Wis Pr.

Politics & Diplomacy. Dutton. 248p. 1998. text 59.50 (1-86064-112-1, Pub. by I B T) St Martin.

***Politics & Diplomacy in Early Modern Italy: The Structure of Diplomatic Practice, 1450-1800.** Ed. by Daniela Frigo. (Cambridge Studies in Italian History & Culture). 270p. (C). 2000. text 59.95 (0-521-56189-2) Cambridge U Pr.

Politics & Diplomacy in Egypt: The Diaries of Sir Miles Lampson, 1935-1937. Ed. by M. E. Yapp. (Oriental & African Archives Ser.: No. 5). (Illus.). 1,060p. 1998. text 185.00 (0-19-726155-8) OUP.

Politics & Dirty Tricks: A Guide to How Screwing up the System. V. R. Farb. (Illus.). 104p. 1995. pap. 14.00 (0-87364-821-8) Paladin Pr.

Politics & Economic Growth: A Cross-Country Data Perspective. Aymo Brunetti. LC 98-121829. 160p. 1998. pap. 23.00 (92-64-16017-5, 41-98-02-1, Pub. by Org for Econ) OECD.

Politics & Economic Policy in the United States. Jeffrey E. Cohen. 384p. (C). 1997. pap. text 33.56 (0-395-74603-5) HM.

Politics & Economics in America: The Way We Came to Be. Richard E. Carmichael. LC 97-20172. 384p. 1997. 29.50 (1-57524-056-4) Krieger.

Politics & Economics in Northeast. Akaha. LC 99-25809. 398p. 1999. text 55.00 (0-312-22288-2) St Martin.

Politics & Economics in the '80s. Ed. by Alberto Alesina & Geoffrey Carliner. (Illus.). 306p. 1991. pap. text 21.00 (0-226-01281-6) U Ch Pr.

Politics & Economics in the '80s. Ed. by Alberto Alesina & Geoffrey Carliner. (Illus.). 320p. 1992. lib. bdg. 45.00 (0-226-01280-8) U Ch Pr.

Politics & Economics in the Russian Far East: Changing Ties with the Asia Pacific. Thuneo Akaha. LC 96-53636. 256p. (C). 1997. 90.00 (0-415-16029-4) Routledge.

Politics & Economics in the Russian Far East: Changing Ties with the Asia Pacific. Tsuneo Akaha. 280p. 1996. pap. 18.95 (0-415-16329-3) Routledge.

Politics & Economics in the Russian Far East: Changing Ties with the Asia Pacific. Tsuneo Akaha. LC 96-53636. 256p. (C). 1997. pap. 29.99 (0-415-16473-7) Routledge.

Politics & Economics of Columbia River Water. Ed. by Charles F. Broches & Michael S. Spranger. LC 85-11506. (Orig.). 1985. pap. 10.00 (0-934539-02-2, WSG-WO) Wash Sea Grant.

Politics & Economics of Earthquake Hazard Mitigation: Unreinforced Masonry Buildings in Southern California. Daniel J. Alesch & William J. Petak. (Program on Environment & Behavior Monograph Ser.: No. 43). 300p. (Orig.). (C). 1986. pap. 20.00 (0-685-28117-5) Natural Hazards.

Politics & Economics of Eric Kierans: A Man for All Canadas. John N. McDougall. 320p. 1993. 55.00 (0-7735-1122-9, Pub. by McG-Queens Univ Pr) CUP Services.

Politics & Economics of Global Defence Industries. Ed. by Efraim Inbar & Ben-Zion Zilberfarb. LC 97-37993. (BESA Studies in International Security: Vol. 5). 240p. (C). 1998. 52.50 (0-7146-4852-3, Pub. by F Cass Pubs); pap. 24.50 (0-7146-4410-2, Pub. by F Cass Pubs) Intl Spec Bk.

Politics & Economics of Hong Kong. Ed. by S. G. Rioni. LC 98-103974. 247p. 1997. lib. bdg. 85.00 (1-56072-497-8) Nova Sci Pubs.

Politics & Economics of Japan: An Annotated Bibliography. Ed. by W. D. Alema. 82p. (C). 1992. pap. text 95.00 (1-56072-049-2) Nova Sci Pubs.

Politics & Economics of Power. Ed. by Samuel Bowles et al. LC 98-35367. (The Siena Summer School Ser.). 320p. (C). (gr. 13). 1999. 75.00 (0-415-18542-4, D6266) Routledge.

Politics & Economics of Privatization: The Case of Wastewater Treatment. John G. Heilman & Gerald W. Johnson. LC 91-43291. 240p. (Orig.). (C). 1992. pap. text 24.95 (0-8173-0569-6) U of Ala Pr.

Politics & Economics of the European Union: An Introductory Text. Robert A. Jones. LC 96-18296. (Illus.). 352p. (C). 1996. pap. 30.00 (1-85278-898-4); text 90.00 (1-85278-896-8) E Elgar.

Politics & Economics of the Internet & Cyberspace. Mary-Lea Cox & Eric J. Kruger. 192p. 1998. 39.00 (1-883223-13-X) Pacific NY.

P

An Asterisk (*) at the beginning of an entry indicates that the title is appearing for the first time.

Politics & Economics of the Soviet Union: An Annotated Bibliography. Ed. by G. P. Manat. 82p. (C). 1992. pap. text 95.00 (*1-56072-048-4*) Nova Sci Pubs.

Politics & Economics of India's Foreign Policy. Ramesh Thakur. LC 93-44718. 1994. text 55.00 (*0-312-12105-9*) St Martin.

Politics & Education. Paulo Freire. Tr. by Pia L. Wong from POR. LC 97-40743. (Latin American Studies Ser.). 1997. pap. write for info. (*0-87903-084-4*) UCLA Lat Am Ctr.

Politics & Education in Argentina, 1946-1962. Monica Rein. Tr. by Martha Grenzeback. LC 97-29381. (Latin American Realities Ser.). (Illus.). 240p. (C). (gr. 13). 1998. text 65.95 (*0-7656-0209-1*); pap. text 29.95 (*0-7656-0210-5*) M E Sharpe.

Politics & Education in Israel: Comparisons with the United States. Shlomo Swirski. Ed. by Mark B. Ginsburg. LC 99-40928. (Studies in Education & Politics: Vol. 3). 312p. 1999. text 65.00 (*0-8153-1616-X*, SS0946) Garland.

Politics & Elections in 19th Century Liverpool. Neil Collins. (Nineteenth Century Ser.). (Illus.). 256p. 1994. 86.95 (*1-85928-076-5*, Pub. by Scolar Pr) Ashgate Pub Co.

Politics & Empire in Victorian Britain. Antoinette Burton. text. write for info. (*0-312-22997-6*) St Martin.

*__Politics & Eternity: Studies in the History of Medieval & Early Modern Political Thought.__ Francis Oakley. LC 99-29170. (Studies in the History of Christian Thought). 384p. 1999. 103.00 (*90-04-11327-4*) Brill Academic Pubs.

Politics & Ethics: Machiavelli to Niebuhr. Erwin A. Gaede. LC 83-19751. 168p. (Orig.). (C). 1984. lib. bdg. 46.00 (*0-8191-3603-4*) U Pr of Amer.

Politics & Ethics of Fieldwork. Maurice Punch. (Qualitative Research Methods Ser.: No. 3). 96p. 1985. text 24.00 (*0-8039-2562-X*); pap. text 10.50 (*0-8039-2517-4*) Sage.

Politics & Ethnicity on the Rio Yaqui: Potam Revisited. Thomas R. McGuire. LC 86-11445. (PROFMEX Ser.). 186p. 1986. 28.50 (*0-8165-0893-3*) U of Ariz Pr.

Politics & Excellence: The Political Philosophy of Alfarabi. Miriam Galston. LC 90-32877. 252p. 1990. reprint ed. pap. 78.20 (*0-608-04645-0*, 206533200003) Bks Demand.

Politics & Experience: Essays Presented to Professor Michael Oakeshott on the Occasion of His Retirement. Ed. by Preston T. King & B. C. Parekh. LC 68-24482. 434p. reprint ed. pap. 123.70 (*0-608-13042-7*, 2024509) Bks Demand.

*__Politics & Fate.__ Andrew Gamble. 2000. 56.95 (*0-7456-2167-8*, Pub. by Polity Pr); pap. 21.95 (*0-7456-2168-6*, Pub. by Polity Pr) Blackwell Pubs.

Politics & Feminism: An Introduction. Barbara Arneil. LC 98-29203. 325p. 1999. pap. 62.95 (*0-631-19812-1*); pap. 29.95 (*0-631-19813-X*) Blackwell Pubs.

Politics & Feminist Standpoint Theories. Ed. by Sally J. Kenney & Helen Kinsella. LC 97-37008. (Women & Politics Monograph Ser.: Vol. 18, No. 3). 113p. 1997. pap. 19.95 (*0-7890-0366-X*) Haworth Pr.

Politics & Feminist Standpoint Theories. Helen Kinsella. Ed. by Sally J. Kenney. LC 97-37008. (Women & Politics Monograph Ser.: Vol. 18, No. 3). 113p. 1997. 29.95 (*0-7890-0364-3*) Haworth Pr.

Politics & Finance in the 18th Century. Lucy Sutherland. 550p. (C). 1984. 70.00 (*0-907628-46-X*) Hambledon Press.

Politics & Foreign Policy in Australia: The Impact of Vietnam & Conscription. Henry S. Albinski. LC 76-101128. 240p. reprint ed. pap. 74.40 (*0-8357-9114-9*, 201787800010) Bks Demand.

Politics & Form in Postmodern Poetry: O'Hara, Bishop, Ashbery, & Merrill. Mutlu K. Blasing. (Studies in American Literature & Culture: No. 94). 235p. (C). 1995. text 59.95 (*0-521-49607-1*) Cambridge U Pr.

Politics & Freedom: Human Will & Action in the Thought of Hannah Arendt. Gabriel M. Tlaba. 224p. (Orig.). (C). 1987. lib. bdg. 44.50 (*0-8191-6468-2*) U Pr of Amer.

*__Politics & Globalisation: Knowledge, Ethics & Agency.__ Ed. by Martin Shaw. (Routledge Advances in International Relations & Politics Ser.). 208p. (C). 1999. text 85.00 (*0-415-20698-7*) Routledge.

Politics & Government. Richard Wood. (Legacies Ser.). (Illus.). 48p. (J). (gr. 4-6). 1995. lib. bdg. 24.26 (*1-56847-394-X*) Raintree Steck-V.

Politics & Government: A Brief Introduction to the Politics of the U. S., Great Britain, France, Germany, Russia, Eastern Europe, Japan, Mexico & the Third World. 3rd ed. Lawrence S. Graham et al. LC 94-6041. (Illus.). 320p. (C). 1994. pap. text 19.95 (*1-56643-008-9*, Chatham House Pub) Seven Bridges.

Politics & Government: A Collection of Essays. Ed. by Neil L. Shumsky. LC 95-38632. (American Cities Ser.: Vol. 3). (Illus.). 528p. 1995. reprint ed. text 88.00 (*0-8153-2188-0*) Garland.

Politics & Government in Algeria. Ed. by Abu B. Fattah. 1988. 30.00 (*0-946706-37-9*, Pub. by Royston Ltd) St Mut.

Politics & Government in California. 13th ed. David H. Provost & Bernard L. Hyink. 272p. (C). 1997. pap. 45.00 (*0-673-99304-3*) Addson-Wesley Educ.

Politics & Government in California. 14th ed. Bernard L. Hyink. LC 97-33573. 304p. (C). 1997. pap. text 48.00 (*0-8013-3012-2*) Addison-Wesley.

*__Politics & Government in California.__ 15th ed. 240p. (C). 2000. pap. text 46.00 (*0-321-05268-4*) Addison-Wesley.

Politics & Government in Europe Today, 2 vols. 2nd ed. Colin Campbell et al. 658p. (C). 1994. text 57.56 (*0-395-66128-5*) HM.

Politics & Government in Germany, 1944-1994: Basic Documents. rev. ed. Donald P. Kommers et al. LC 94-25228. 493p. (C). 1995. pap. 24.50 (*1-57181-855-3*) Berghahn Bks.

Politics & Government in Germany, 1944-1994: Basic Documents. rev. ed. Donald P. Kommers et al. Ed. by Carl-Christoph Schweitzer. LC 94-25228. 493p. (C). 1995. 75.00 (*1-57181-854-5*) Berghahn Bks.

Politics & Government in Japan. 3rd ed. Theodore McNelly. (Illus.). 284p. (Orig.). 1985. reprint ed. pap. text 18.50 (*0-8191-4359-6*) U Pr of Amer.

Politics & Government in the Middle East & North Africa. Tareq Y. Ismael & Jacqueline S. Ismael. 400p. 1991. pap. 24.95 (*0-8130-1062-4*) U Press Fla.

Politics & Government in the Middle East & North Africa. Tareq Y. Ismael et al. 400p. 1991. 49.95 (*0-8130-1043-8*) U Press Fla.

Politics & Government in Turkey. Clement H. Dodd. LC 78-85453. 351p. reprint ed. pap. 108.90 (*0-608-17469-6*, 202995100066) Bks Demand.

Politics & Government of N.J., 1900-1980: An Annotated Bibliography, Vol. XXIII. Benjamin R. Beede & Anne Brugh. 420p. 1989. 40.00 (*0-911020-22-5*) NJ Hist Soc.

Politics & Grass: The Administration of Grazing on the Public Domain. Philip O. Foss. LC 75-90508. (Illus.). 236p. 1970. reprint ed. lib. bdg. 65.00 (*0-8371-2136-1*, FOPG, Greenwood Pr) Greenwood.

*__Politics & Guilt: The Destructive Power of Silence.__ Gesine Schwan. Tr. by Thomas Dunlap. (European Horizons Ser.). 2001. text 50.00 (*0-8032-4280-8*) U of Nebr Pr.

Politics & Health Care Organization: HMO's As Federal Policy. Lawrence D. Brown. LC 81-70466. 540p. 1983. 44.95 (*0-8157-1158-1*); pap. 19.95 (*0-8157-1157-3*) Brookings.

Politics & History. Raymond Aron. Ed. by Miriam B. Conant. 304p. 1984. reprint ed. pap. 24.95 (*0-87855-944-2*) Transaction Pubs.

Politics & History in Band Societies. Ed. by Eleanor B. Leacock & Richard B. Lee. (Illus.). 512p. 1982. pap. text 35.95 (*0-521-28412-0*) Cambridge U Pr.

*__Politics & Human Nature: Ideological Rooting of the Left.__ S. K. Leung. 195p. 2000. 29.95 (*1-902835-08-5*, Pub. by Empiricus Bks); pap. 16.95 (*1-902835-02-6*, Pub. by Empiricus Bks) Paul & Co Pubs.

Politics & Ideas in Early Stuart England. Kevin Sharpe. 256p. 1989. pap. text 17.50 (*0-685-61125-6*) St Martin.

Politics & Ideas in Early Stuart England. Kevin Sharpe. 256p. 1989. 45.00 (*0-86187-708-X*) St Martin.

Politics & Ideology: A Philosophical Approach. Oded Balaban. 304p. 1995. 69.95 (*1-85972-020-X*, Pub. by Avebry) Ashgate Pub Co.

Politics & Ideology in Allende's Chile. Ricardo I. Z. LC 87-9370. 306p. 1989. text 39.50 (*0-87918-064-1*) ASU Lat Am St.

Politics & Ideology in Canada: Elite & Public Opinion in the Transformation of the Welfare State. H. Michael Stevenson & Michael D. Ornstein. 65.00 (*0-7735-1829-0*) McG-Queens Univ Pr.

Politics & Ideology in the Italian Workers' Movement: Union Development & the Changing Role of the Catholic & Communist Subcultures in Postwar Italy. Gino Bedani. LC 95-145333. (Illus.). 365p. 1995. 53.00 (*0-85496-827-X*) Berg Pubs.

Politics & Industrialization: Early Railroads in the United States & Prussia. Colleen A. Dunlavy. LC 93-17455. (Studies in American Politics: Historical, International, & Comparative Perspectives). 283p. (C). 1993. text 49.50 (*0-691-04769-3*, Pub. by Princeton U Pr) Cal Prin Full Svc.

Politics & Institutions in an Integrated Europe. Barry J. Eichengreen. Ed. by Jurgen Von Hagen et al. (European & Transatlantic Studies). 1995. 95.00 (*3-540-59420-5*) Spr-Verlag.

Politics & Institutions in Capetian France. Elizabeth A. Brown. (Collected Studies: No. CS 350). 336p. 1991. text 109.95 (*0-86078-298-0*, Pub. by Variorum) Ashgate Pub Co.

Politics & International Relations in the Middle East: Continuity & Change. Ed. by Jane Davis. LC 94-45149. 176p. 1995. 85.00 (*1-85898-234-0*) E Elgar.

Politics & Irish Life, 1913-1921: Provincial Experience of War & Revolution. David Fitzpatrick. (Modern Revivals in History Ser.). 1993. 72.95 (*0-7512-0133-2*, Pub. by Gregg Pub) Ashgate Pub Co.

Politics & Irish Life, 1913-1921: Provincial Experiences of War & Revolution. David Fitzpatrick. LC 98-234071. 416p. 1998. pap. 34.95 (*1-85918-174-0*, Pub. by Cork Univ) Intl Spec Bk.

Politics & Islam in Contemporary Sudan. Abdel S. Sidahmed. 248p. 1996. 65.00 (*0-7007-0409-4*, Pub. by Curzon Pr Ltd) Paul & Co Pubs.

Politics & Islam in Contemporary Sudan. Abdel S. Sidahmed. LC 96-48414. (Illus.). 240p. 1997. text 55.00 (*0-312-16144-1*) St Martin.

Politics & Judgment in Federal District Courts. C. K. Rowland & Robert A. Carp. LC 95-46680. 240p. (C). 1996. 29.95 (*0-7006-0776-5*) U Pr of KS.

Politics & Justice in Russia: Major Trials of the Post-Stalin Era. Yuri Feofanov & Donald D. Barry. LC 95-42355. 360p. (C). (gr. 13). 1996. text 77.95 (*1-56324-344-X*); pap. text 32.95 (*1-56324-345-8*) M E Sharpe.

Politics & Language: Spanish & English in the United States. Ed. by D. J. Bruckner. (Orig.). 1980. pap. 4.00 (*0-686-28732-0*) U Chi Ctr Policy.

Politics & Language in Dryden's Poetry: The Arts of Disguise. Steven N. Zwicker. LC 84-42550. (Illus.). 261p. 1984. reprint ed. pap. 81.00 (*0-608-02517-8*, 206316100004) Bks Demand.

Politics & Law in South Africa: Essays on Race Relations. Julius Lewin. LC DT0763. 116p. reprint ed. pap. 36.00 (*0-608-11630-0*, 200169500014) Bks Demand.

Politics & Law of Term Limits. Roger Pilon. LC 94-35217. 152p. 1994. 19.95 (*1-882577-12-4*); pap. 10.95 (*1-882577-13-2*) Cato Inst.

Politics & Literature: The Case of Maurice Blanchot. Deborah M. Hess. LC 97-51838. (Currents in Comparative Romance Languages & Literatures Ser.: Vol. 74). VII, 272p. (C). 1999. text 50.95 (*0-8204-4015-9*) P Lang Pubng.

Politics & Markets: The World's Political-Economic Systems. Charles E. Lindblom. LC 77-75250. 416p. 1980. pap. 20.00 (*0-465-05958-9*, Pub. by Basic) HarpC.

*__Politics & Markets in the Wake of the Asian Crisis.__ Richard Robison et al. LC 99-31669. (Asian Capitalisms Ser.). 1999. pap. write for info. (*0-415-22057-2*) Routledge.

*__Politics & Markets in Wake of the Asian Crisis.__ Ed. by Richard Robison et al. LC 99-31669. 304p. (C). 1999. text. write for info. (*0-415-22056-4*) Routledge.

Politics & Method: Contrasting Studies in Industrial Geography. Ed. by Doreen Massey & Richard Meegan. 200p. pap. 14.95 (*0-317-19448-8*, 9123) Routledge.

Politics & Military Morale: Current Affairs & Citizenship Education in the British Army 1914-1950. S. P. MacKenzie. (Oxford Historical Monographs). (Illus.). 258p. 1992. text 65.00 (*0-19-820244-X*) OUP.

Politics & Modernity. Velody. 192p. 1992. pap. 25.95 (*0-8039-8826-5*) Sage.

Politics & Morality of Deviance: Moral Panics, Drug Abuse, Deviant Science, & Reversed Stigmatization. Nachman Ben-Yehuda. LC 89-4201. (SUNY Series in Deviance & Social Control). 348p. (C). 1989. pap. text 24.95 (*0-7914-0123-5*) State U NY Pr.

Politics & Narratives of Birth: Gynocolonization from Rousseau to Zola. Carol A. Mossman. (Cambridge Studies in French: No. 41). 271p. (C). 1993. text 69.95 (*0-521-41586-1*) Cambridge U Pr.

Politics & Nation: England, 1450-1660. D. M. Loades. LC 98-51868. 512p. 1999. 62.95 (*0-631-21459-3*); pap. 28.95 (*0-631-21460-7*) Blackwell Pubs.

Politics & Nationalist Awakening in South India, 1852-1891. fac. ed. R. Suntharalingam. LC 73-93408. (Association for Asian Studies, Monographs & Papers: No. 27). (Illus.). 416p. 1974. pap. 129.00 (*0-7837-7675-6*, 204742800007) Bks Demand.

Politics & Nuclear Power: Energy Policy in Western Europe. Michael T. Hatch. LC 85-29545. 232p. 1986. 29.95 (*0-8131-1583-3*) U Pr of Ky.

Politics & Painting: Murals & Conflict in Northern Ireland. Bill Rolston. LC 89-45981. (Illus.). 1991. 60.00 (*0-8386-3386-2*) Fairleigh Dickinson.

Politics & Paradigms: Changing Theories of Change in Social Science. Andrew C. Janos. 200p. 1986. 35.00 (*0-8047-1332-4*); pap. 12.95 (*0-8047-1333-2*) Stanford U Pr.

Politics & Parentela in Paraiba: A Case Study of Family-Based Oligarchy in Brazil. Linda Lewin. LC 86-42850. 524p. 1987. reprint ed. pap. 162.50 (*0-7837-9375-8*, 206011900004) Bks Demand.

Politics & Participation under Communist Rule. Ed. by Peter J. Potichnyj et al. LC 82-15082. 282p. 1983. 59.95 (*0-275-91060-1*, C1060, Praeger Pubs) Greenwood.

Politics & Partitions: Human Boundaries & the Growth of Social Complexity. Ed. by Kathryn M. Trinkaus. LC 87-70155. (Anthropological Research Papers: No. 37). (Illus.). iv, 251p. (Orig.). (C). 1987. pap. 20.00 (*0-936249-00-5*) AZ Univ ARP.

Politics & Patronage in the Gilded Age: The Correspondence of James A. Garfield & Charles E. Henry. Ed. by James D. Norris & Arthur H. Shaffer. LC 70-629850. (Illus.). 304p. 1970. 15.00 (*0-87020-107-7*) State Hist Soc Wis.

Politics & People, 58 bks. Ed. by Leon Stein. 1974. 1483.50 (*0-405-05850-0*) Ayer.

Politics & People in Ethology: Personal Reflections on the Study of Animal Behavior. Peter H. Klopfer. LC 98-28140. (Illus.). 168p. 1999. 34.50 (*0-8387-5405-8*) Bucknell U Pr.

Politics & Performance: Theatre, Poetry & Song in Southern Africa. Ed. by Liz Gunner. (Illus.). 304p. 1995. 35.00 (*0-253-32947-7*) Ind U Pr.

Politics & Performance in Contemporary Northern Ireland. Ed. by John P. Harrington & Elizabeth J. Mitchell. LC 98-32257. 240p. 1999. 50.00 (*1-55849-196-1*); pap. 15.95 (*1-55849-197-X*) U of Mass Pr.

Politics & Personalities, with Other Essays. George W. Russell. (Essay Index Reprint Ser.). 1977. 23.95 (*0-8369-0844-9*) Ayer.

Politics & Personality. M. J. Barnes. (History Today Ser.). 1967. 14.95 (*0-8023-9074-9*) Dufour.

Politics & Personality, 1760-1827. Ed. by Michael J. Barnes. LC 68-97214. (Selections from History Today Ser.: No. 6). (Illus.). 1967. 10.95 (*0-686-85915-4*) Dufour.

Politics & Personality, 1760-1827. Ed. by Michael J. Barnes. LC 68-97214. (Selections from History Today Ser.: No. 6). (Illus.). 1967. pap. 9.95 (*0-05-001535-4*) Dufour.

Politics & Personnel Management: An Outline History, 1960-1976. Winifred Marks. 240p. (C). 1978. 50.00 (*0-85292-189-6*) St Mut.

Politics & Persuasion in Aristophanes' Ecclesiazusae. Kenneth S. Rothwell, Jr. (Mnemosyne Ser.: Supplement 111). xii, 118p. 1990. pap. 41.50 (*90-04-09185-8*) Brill Academic Pubs.

Politics & Petroleum in Ecuador. John D. Martz. 345p. 1987. 44.95 (*0-88738-132-4*) Transaction Pubs.

Politics & Philosophy in the Early Novels of Ramon J. Sender, 1930-1936. Francis Lough. LC 95-19531. (Hispanic Literature Ser.: Vol. 28). 228p. 1996. text 89.95 (*0-7734-8897-9*) E Mellen.

Politics & Philosophy of Economics: Marxians, Keynesians & Economics. T. W. Hutchinson. (Modern Revivals in Economics Ser.). 318p. 1992. 63.95 (*0-7512-0089-1*, Pub. by Gregg Pub) Ashgate Pub Co.

Politics & Philosophy of Political Correctness. Jung Min Choi & John W. Murphy. LC 92-19834. 186p. 1992. 49.95 (*0-275-94286-4*, C4286, Praeger Pubs) Greenwood.

Politics & Planners: Economic Development Policy in Central America. Gary W. Wynia. LC 72-1382. 240p. 1972. reprint ed. pap. 74.40 (*0-608-01864-3*, 206251600003) Bks Demand.

Politics & Planning: A National Study of American Planners. Michael L. Vasu. LC 78-10440. (Institute for Research in Social Science Ser.). 255p. reprint ed. pap. 79.10 (*0-8357-4419-1*, 203723900008) Bks Demand.

Politics & Planning in the NHS. Neil Small. 224p. 1989. pap. 39.95 (*0-335-09259-4*) OpUniv Pr.

Politics & Plea Bargaining: Victims' Rights in California. Candace McCoy. LC 92-46518. (Law in Social Context Ser.). 248p. (Orig.). (C). 1993. text 39.95 (*0-8122-3190-2*); pap. text 19.95 (*0-8122-1433-1*) U of Pa Pr.

Politics & Poetic Form. Andrews et al. (Roof Bks.). 250p. 1989. 21.95 (*0-937804-36-3*); pap. 12.95 (*0-937804-35-5*) Segue NYC.

Politics & Poetic Value. Ed. by Robert Von Hallberg. 342p. 1987. pap. text 19.50 (*0-226-86496-0*) U Ch Pr.

Politics & Poetic Value. Ed. by Robert Von Hallberg. 342p. 1996. lib. bdg. 36.00 (*0-226-86495-2*) U Ch Pr.

Politics & Poetics of Camp. Ed. by Moe Meyer. LC 93-18913. (Illus.). 240p. (C). 1993. pap. 25.99 (*0-415-08248-X*) Routledge.

Politics & Poetics of Journalistic Narrative: The Timely & the Timeless. Phyllis Frus. 318p. (C). 1994. text 64.95 (*0-521-44324-5*) Cambridge U Pr.

Politics & Poetics of Transgression. Peter Stallybrass & Allon White. LC 85-48241. 224p. 1986. text 42.50 (*0-8014-1893-3*); pap. text 15.95 (*0-8014-9382-X*) Cornell U Pr.

Politics & Poetry in Restoration England: The Case of Dryden's Annus Mirabilis. Michael McKeon. LC 75-4508. (Illus.). 350p. reprint ed. pap. 108.50 (*0-7837-3867-6*, 204368900010) Bks Demand.

Politics & Policy: The Eisenhower, Kennedy, & Johnson Years. James L. Sundquist. LC 68-31837. 560p. 1968. 34.95 (*0-8157-8222-5*) Brookings.

Politics & Policy: United States & Texas. Dometrius. 256p. (C). 1993. pap. text 13.95 (*0-8403-8372-X*) Kendall-Hunt.

Politics & Policy Implementation: Project Renewal in Israel. Frederick A. Lazin. LC 92-40308. (SUNY Series in Israeli Studies). 201p. (C). 1993. pap. text 21.95 (*0-7914-1692-5*) State U NY Pr.

Politics & Policy Implementation: Project Renewal in Israel. Frederick A. Lazin. LC 92-40308. (SUNY Series in Israeli Studies). 201p. (C). 1993. text 59.50 (*0-7914-1691-7*) State U NY Pr.

Politics & Policy Implementation in the Third World. Ed. by Merilee S. Grindle. LC 79-3213. 327p. reprint ed. pap. 101.40 (*0-8357-2783-1*, 203990900014) Bks Demand.

Politics & Policy in America. 2nd ed. Dresang & Gosling. LC 98-27117. 488p. 1998. 65.00 (*0-205-29118-X*) Allyn.

Politics & Policy in Britain. Leonard Freedman. 368p. (Orig.). (C). 1995. pap. text. write for info. (*0-8013-1690-1*) Addison-Wesley.

*__Politics & Policy in Democratic Spain--No Longer Different? /__ Paul Heywood. LC 98-47601. 248p. 1999. write for info. (*0-7146-4910-4*) Intl Spec Bk.

Politics & Policy in Democratic Spain--No Longer Different? Paul Heywood. LC 98-47601. 248p. 1999. pap. 24.50 (*0-7146-4467-6*) F Cass Pubs.

Politics & Policy in Public Education. Ed. by Hochschild. (C). 1999. pap. text. write for info. (*0-321-01032-9*) Addson-Wesley Educ.

*__Politics & Policy in States & Communities.__ 7th ed. (C). 2000. write for info. (*0-321-05267-6*) Addison-Wesley.

*__Politics & Policy in States & Communities.__ 7th ed. (C). 2000. 67.00 (*0-321-08236-2*); 26.00 (*0-321-08237-0*) Addison-Wesley Educ.

Politics & Policy in the European Union. 3rd ed. Stephen George. (Illus.). 322p. 1996. pap. text 22.00 (*0-19-878189-X*) OUP.

Politics & Policy in the New Korean State: From Roh Tae-Woo to Kim Young-Sam. James Cotton. 232p. 1995. text 59.95 (*0-312-12549-6*) St Martin.

Politics & Policy in Traditional Korea. James B. Palais. (East Asian Monographs: No. 159). (Illus.). 390p. (C). 1992. pap. text 16.00 (*0-674-68771-X*) HUP.

Politics & Policy in Traditional Korea, 1864-1876. James B. Palais. (East Asian Monographs). 288p. 1990. 24.50 (*0-674-19058-0*) HUP.

Politics & Policy Making in Developing Countries. Gerald M. Meier. 369p. 1991. 34.95 (*1-55815-095-1*); pap. 19.95 (*1-55815-079-X*); 6.95 (*1-55815-135-4*) ICS Pr.

Politics & Policy Making in Israel's Education System. Haim Gaziel. LC 97-126077. 200p. 1996. pap. 24.95 (*1-898723-42-7*, Pub. by Sussex Acad Pr) Intl Spec Bk.

Politics & Politicians in American Film. Phillip L. Gianos. LC 97-33245. (Praeger Series in Political Communication). 232p. 1998. 59.95 (*0-275-96071-4*, Praeger Pubs) Greenwood.

Politics & Politicians in American Film. Phillip L. Gianos. 232p. 1999. pap. 21.95 (*0-275-96766-2*) Greenwood.

Politics & Popular Culture. John Street. LC 97-28845. 224p. 1997. 59.95 (*1-56639-602-6*); pap. 19.95 (*1-56639-603-4*) Temple U Pr.

P

***Politics & Popular Opinion in East Germany, 1945-1968.** Mark Allinson. LC 99-43348. 1999. 74.95 (0-7190-5554-7) Manchester Univ Pr.

Politics & Poverty: Modernization & Response in Five Poor Neighborhoods. Stanley B. Greenberg. LC 73-10273. (Wiley Series in Urban Research). 301p. reprint ed. pap. 93.40 (0-608-10321-7, 205132900095) Bks Demand.

Politics & Power in a Slave Society: Alabama, 1800-1860. J. Mills Thornton, III. LC 77-4296. (Illus.). xxiv, 492p. 1978. pap. 24.95 (0-8071-0891-X) La State U Pr.

Politics & Practice of Situational Crime Prevention. Ed. by Ross Homel. (Crime Prevention Studies: Vol. 5). 230p. (C). 1996. text 47.50 (1-881798-06-2, Criminal Justice) Willow Tree NY.

Politics & Practice of Situational Crime Prevention. Ed. by Ross Homel. (Crime Prevention Studies: No. 5). (Illus.). 192p. 1998. reprint ed. pap. 37.50 (1-881798-17-8) Willow Tree NY.

Politics & Practices of Intergovernmental Evaluation. Ed. by Jacques Toulemonde & Olaf Rieper. LC 96-3078. 182p. 1996. text 29.95 (1-56000-256-5) Transaction Pubs.

Politics & Preservation 1882-1996: Policy History of the Built Heritage. John Delafons. 192p. (C). (gr. 13). 1997. 85.00 (0-419-22390-8) Routledge.

Politics & Primary Medical Care: Dehumanization & Overutilization. Zeev Ben-Sira. 232p. 1988. text 72.95 (0-566-05566-X, Pub. by Avebry) Ashgate Pub Co.

Politics & Processes of Scholarship, 66. Ed. by Joseph M. Moxley & Lagretta T. Lenker. LC 95-16147. (Contributions to the Study of Education Ser.: No. 66). 280p. 1995. 57.95 (0-313-29572-7, Greenwood Pr) Greenwood.

Politics & Production in the Early Nineteenth Century. Clive Behagg. LC 89-34005. 283p. reprint ed. pap. 87.80 (0-608-20315-7, 207156800002) Bks Demand.

Politics & Productivity: How Japan's Development Strategy Works. Ed. by Chalmers A. Johnson et al. LC 88-31238. 348p. 1989. text 34.95 (0-88730-350-1, HarpBusn) HarpInfo.

Politics & Progress: The Rise of Urban Progressivism in Baltimore, 1895 to 1911. James B. Crooks. LC 68-21805. 281p. reprint ed. pap. 87.20 (0-608-14445-2, 205187700013) Bks Demand.

Politics & Property Rights: The Closing of the Open Range in the Postbellum South. Kantor. LC 97-25887. (Illus.). 208p. 1998. lib. bdg. 45.00 (0-226-42375-1) U Ch Pr.

Politics & Property Rights: The Closing of the Open Range in the Postbellum South. Shawn E. Kantor. LC 97-25887. (Illus.). 208p. 1998. pap. text 18.00 (0-226-42377-8) U Ch Pr.

Politics & Protestant Theology: An Interpretation of Tillich, Barth, Bonhoeffer, & Brunner. fac. ed. Rene D. Williamson. LC 76-20817. 190p. 1976. reprint ed. pap. 58.90 (0-7837-7761-2, 204751700007) Bks Demand.

Politics & Psychology: Contemporary Psychodynamic Perspectives. J. Offerman-Zuckerberg. (Illus.). 336p. (C). 1991. 59.50 (0-306-43864-X, Plenum Trade) Perseus Pubng.

***Politics & Public Culture of American Jews.** Arthur A. Goren. LC 98-52677. (Modern Jewish Experience Ser.). (Illus.). 274p. 1999. pap. 17.95 (0-253-21318-5); text 39.95 (0-253-33535-3) Ind U Pr.

Politics & Public Health in Revolutionary Russia, 1890-1918. John F. Hutchinson. LC 89-39102. (Henry E. Sigerist Series in the History of Medicine). (Illus.). 280p. 1990. reprint ed. pap. 86.80 (0-608-06720-2, 206691700009) Bks Demand.

Politics & Public Morality: The Great Welfare Reform Debate. Gary Bryner. LC 97-33693. (Illus.). 300p. (C). 1998. pap. 16.75 (0-393-97173-2) Norton.

Politics & Public Policies in California. John H. Culver. 1995. pap. text. write for info. (0-07-015095-8) McGraw.

Politics & Public Policies in California. John H. Culver. LC 96-18017. 304p. (C). 1996. pap. 34.06 (0-07-015094-X) McGraw.

***Politics & Public Policy: A Christian Response; Crucial Considerations for Governing Life.** Timothy J. Demy. 2000. 19.99 (0-8254-2362-7) Kregel.

Politics & Public Policy in Arizona. 2nd ed. Ed. by Zachary A. Smith. LC 96-2206. 288p. 1996. text 39.95 (0-275-95274-6, Praeger Pubs) Greenwood.

Politics & Public Policy in Hawaii. Ed. by Zachary A. Smith & Richard Pratt. LC 91-13267. 273p. 1992. text 16.50 (0-7914-0949-X) State U NY Pr.

Politics & Purges in China: Rectification & the Decline of Party Norms, 1950-1965. Frederick C. Teiwes. LC 79-51182. 744p. reprint ed. 200.00 (0-608-17091-7, 202762500055) Bks Demand.

Politics & Purges in China: Rectification & the Decline of Party Norms, 1950-1965. 2nd ed. Frederick C. Teiwes. LC 93-1545. (Studies on Contemporary China). 664p. (C). (gr. 13). 1993. text 103.95 (1-56324-226-5, East Gate Bk) M E Sharpe.

Politics & Purges in China: Rectification & the Decline of Party Norms, 1950-1965. 2nd ed. Frederick C. Teiwes. LC 93-1545. (Studies on Contemporary China). 664p. (C). (gr. 13). 1993. pap. text 47.95 (1-56324-227-3, East Gate Bk) M E Sharpe.

Politics & Rationality: Rational Choice in Application. Ed. by William J. Booth et al. (Illus.). 319p. (C). 1994. text 59.95 (0-521-43409-2); pap. text 20.95 (0-521-43568-4) Cambridge U Pr.

Politics & Regimes. Ed. by Paul Gottfried. (Religion & Public Life Ser.: No. 30). 107p. (Orig.). 1997. pap. text 19.95 (1-56000-908-X) Transaction Pubs.

Politics & Religion. Ed. by Edgard Pisani. (Contemporary European Affairs Ser.: No. 2). 204p. 1990. pap. 12.50 (0-08-040794-3, Pergamon Pr) Elsevier.

Politics & Religion in Ancient & Medieval Europe & China. Ed. by Frederick H. Cheung & Ming-Chiu Lai. (Illus.). 210p. (C). pap. text 30.00 (962-201-850-5, Pub. by Chinese Univ) U of Mich Pr.

Politics & Religion in Central & Eastern Europe: Traditions & Transitions. Ed. by William H. Swatos. LC 94-13737. 248p. 1994. 65.00 (0-275-94753-X, Praeger Pubs) Greenwood.

Politics & Religion in the U. S. Ed. by Corbett. (C). 1998. text. write for info. (0-321-01151-1) Addson-Wesley Educ.

Politics & Religion in the United States. Michael Corbett & Julia M. Corbett. LC 98-19364. (Garland Reference Library of Social Science). 488p. 1998. 60.00 (0-8153-3141-X); pap. 24.95 (0-8153-3143-6) Garland.

Politics & Religious Authority: American Catholics since the Second Vatican Council, 36. Richard J. Gelm. LC 93-1650. 168p. 1993. 55.00 (0-313-28903-4, Greenwood Pr) Greenwood.

Politics & Religious Consciousness in America. George A. Kelly. LC 83-9284. 312p. 1983. 39.95 (0-87855-484-X) Transaction Pubs.

Politics & Remembrance: Republican Themes in Machiavelli, Burke & Tocqueville. Bruce J. Smith. LC 84-15946. (Studies in Moral, Political, & Legal Philosophy). 300p. 1985. reprint ed. pap. 93.00 (0-608-02521-6, 206316500004) Bks Demand.

Politics & Responsibility of the North American Breadbasket. Lester R. Brown. 1975. pap. write for info. (0-318-70405-6) Worldwatch Inst.

Politics & Revelation: Mawardi & After. Hanna Mikhail. (Islamic Surveys Ser.). 128p. 1995. 50.00 (0-7486-0519-3, Pub. by Edinburgh U Pr) Col U Pr.

Politics & Reviewers: The Edinburgh & the Quarterly in the Early Victorian Age. Joanne Shattock. 220p. 1989. text 49.00 (0-7185-1269-3) St Martin.

Politics & Rhetoric in the Corinthian Epistles. Laurence L. Welborn. LC 97-41427. (C). 1997. text 29.95 (0-86554-463-8, MUP/H437) Mercer Univ Pr.

Politics & Rhetoric of Scientific Method. Ed. by John A. Schuster & Richard R. Yeo. 346p. 1986. lib. bdg. 176.50 (90-277-2152-1, D Reidel) Kluwer Academic.

Politics & Scholarship: Feminist Academic Journals & the Production of Knowledge. Patrice McDermott. LC 93-31206. 208p. (C). 1994. text 36.95 (0-252-02078-2); pap. text 14.95 (0-252-06369-4) U of Ill Pr.

Politics & Science in the U. S. S. R. & Russia: Biographical Memoir. N. N. Moiseev. LC 99-15145. (Russian Documents, Bibliography, & Memoirs Ser.: Vol. 1). (RUS.). 540p. 1999. 119.95 (0-7734-3244-2) E Mellen.

Politics & Security in the Southern Region of the Atlantic Alliance. Ed. by Douglas T. Stuart. LC 86-21081. (Illus.). 219p. reprint ed. pap. 67.90 (0-608-06158-1, 206649100008) Bks Demand.

Politics & Sinology: The Case of Naito Konan, 1866-1934. Joshua A. Fogel. (East Asian Monographs: No. 114). 1984. 30.00 (0-674-68790-6) HUP.

Politics & Social Equality: A Comparative Analysis. Robert W. Jackman. LC 74-24725. (Comparative Studies in Behavioral Science). (Illus.). 239p. reprint ed. pap. 74.10 (0-7837-3449-2, 205777500008) Bks Demand.

Politics & Social Structure in Latin America. James F. Petras. LC 73-122737. 382p. 1970. reprint ed. pap. 118.50 (0-7837-9613-7, 206037000005) Bks Demand.

Politics & Social Welfare Policy in the United States. Robert X. Browning. LC 85-17837. 220p. (C). 1986. pap. text 20.00 (0-87049-714-6) U of Tenn Pr.

Politics & Society in Contemporary Africa. 3rd ed. Naomi Chazan et al. LC 99-24154. 1999. pap. 23.50 (1-55587-679-X) L Rienner.

***Politics & Society in Contemporary Africa.** 3rd ed. Naomi Chazan et al. LC 99-24154. 1999. 59.95 (1-55587-668-4) L Rienner.

Politics & Society in Contemporary France. Ed. by Ezra N. Suleiman. 186p. (Orig.). 1977. pap. text 21.95 (0-87855-679-6) Transaction Pubs.

***Politics & Society in Developing World.** 2nd ed. Mehran Kamrava. LC 99-34151. 248p. (C). 1999. text. write for info. (0-415-21233-2) Routledge.

Politics & Society in Early Modern Iraq. Tom Nieuwenhuis. 1982. lib. bdg. 106.00 (90-247-2576-3) Kluwer Academic.

Politics & Society in Great Yarmouth, 1660-1722. Perry Gauci. LC 95-30137. (Historical Monographs). (Illus.). 312p. (C). 1996. text 72.00 (0-19-820605-4, Clarendon Pr) OUP.

Politics & Society in Israel. Ed. by Ernest Krausz. (Studies of Israeli Society: Vol. III). 400p. (C). 1984. text 44.95 (0-88738-012-3); pap. text 24.95 (0-87855-969-8) Transaction Pubs.

Politics & Society in Modern Israel: Myths & Realities. Adam Garfinkle. LC 96-35070. 336p. (C). (gr. 13). 1997. text 70.95 (0-7656-0005-6); pap. text 30.95 (0-7656-0006-4) M E Sharpe.

Politics & Society in Ottoman Palestine: The Arab Struggle for Survival & Power. Donna R. Divine. LC 93-40820. 230p. 1994. lib. bdg. 45.00 (1-55587-473-8) L Rienner.

***Politics & Society in Post-communist.** Carey. 2000. 70.00 (0-8133-3743-7, Pub. by Westview) HarpC.

Politics & Society in Post-War Naples. P. A. Allum. LC 75-174259. 426p. reprint ed. pap. 121.50 (0-608-12327-7, 2024408) Bks Demand.

Politics & Society in Provincial Russia: Saratov, 1590-1917. Ed. by Rex A. Wade & Scott J. Seregny. LC 89-36185. (Illus.). 480p. reprint ed. pap. 148.80 (0-608-09892-2, 206985800006) Bks Demand.

Politics & Society in Scotland. Ed. by Alice Brown et al. 272p. 1996. text 59.95 (0-312-16040-2) St Martin.

***Politics & Society in the Developing World.** 2nd ed. Mehran Kamrava. LC 99-34151. 248p. 1999. pap. 29.99 (0-415-21234-0) Routledge.

Politics & Society in the South. Earl Black & Merle Black. LC 86-18421. (Illus.). 384p. 1987. 41.50 (0-674-68958-5) HUP.

Politics & Society in the South. Earl Black & Merle Black. 384p. 1989. reprint ed. pap. 20.50 (0-674-68959-3) HUP.

Politics & Society in the Third World. Mehran Kamrava. LC 92-32057. (Illus.). 256p. (C). 1993. pap. 25.99 (0-415-09048-2, B0571) Routledge.

Politics & Society in the Third World. Jean Y. Calvez. Tr. by M. J. O'Connell. LC 72-85792.Tr. of Aspects Politiques et Sociaux des Pays en Voie de Developpment. 333p. (Orig.). reprint ed. pap. 103.30 (0-8357-8990-X, 203352500086) Bks Demand.

Politics & Society in the Third World: An Introduction. Susan Calvert & Peter Calvert. LC 95-37428. 256p. (C). 1996. pap. text 31.50 (0-13-355231-4) P-H.

***Politics & Society in Ukraine.** Paul D'Anieri et al. LC 99-30503. 352p. 1999. 60.00 (0-8133-3537-X); pap. 24.00 (0-8133-3538-8) Westview.

Politics & Society in Western Europe. rev. ed. Jan-Erik Lane & Svante O. Ersson. (Illus.). 320p. (C). 1991. pap. text 19.95 (0-8039-8407-3) Sage.

Politics & Society in Western Europe. 2nd rev. ed. Jan-Erik Lane & Svante O. Ersson. (Illus.). 320p. (C). 1991. text 55.00 (0-8039-8406-5) Sage.

Politics & Society in Western Europe. 3rd ed. Jan-Erik Lane & Svante O. Ersson. 432p. 1994. 69.95 (0-8039-7795-6); pap. 28.00 (0-8039-7796-4) Sage.

***Politics & Society in Western Europe.** 4th ed. Ed. by Jan-Erik Lane & Svante O. Ersson. LC 98-61733. 432p. 1998. 84.00 (0-7619-5861-4) Sage.

Politics & Society on Colonial America. 2nd ed. Michael G. Kammen. LC 78-13376. 160p. 1978. reprint ed. pap. text 10.50 (0-88275-747-4) Krieger.

***Politics & Society under the Bolsheviks: Selected Papers from the 5th World Congress of Central & East European Studies, Warsaw, 1995.** Ed. by Kevin McDermott & John Morison. LC 99-23351. 302p. 1999. text 79.95 (0-312-22593-8) St Martin.

***Politics & Sociolinguistic Reflexes: Palestinian Border Villages.** Muhammad Hasan Amara. LC 99-22264. (Studies in Bilingualism: Vol. 19). xx, 261p. 1999. 79.00 (1-55619-950-3) J Benjamins Pubng Co.

Politics & Space: Image Making by NASA. Mark E. Byrnes. LC 94-13727. 224p. 1994. 59.95 (0-275-94950-8, Praeger Pubs) Greenwood.

Politics & Steel in Britain, 1967-1988: The Life & Times of the British Steel Corporation. G. F. Dudley & J. J. Richardson. 314p. 1990. text 82.95 (1-85521-072-X, Pub. by Dartmth Pub) Ashgate Pub Co.

Politics & Strategy in the Second World War: Germany, Great Britain, Japan, the Soviet Union & the United States. Ed. by International Committee for the History of the Sec. 113p. 1976. pap. text 12.95 (0-89126-024-2) MA-AH Pub.

Politics & Strategy of Nuclear Weapons in the Middle East: Opacity, Theory, & Reality, 1960-1991 - An Israeli Perspective. Shlomo Aronson. LC 91-46244. (SUNY Series in Israeli Studies). 398p. (C). 1992. pap. text 24.95 (0-7914-1208-3) State U NY Pr.

Politics & Structure: Essentials of American National Government. 6th ed. Thomas G. Ingersoll et al. 224p. (C). 1993. pap. text 37.00 (0-534-18840-0) Harcourt.

Politics & Sustainable Development: Guinea-Bissau & Hazardous Waste Imports. Mark A. Montgomery. (Pew Case Studies in International Affairs). 50p. (C). 1996. pap. text 3.50 (1-56927-214-X, GU Schl Foreign) Geo U Inst Dplmcy.

Politics & Sustainable Growth in the Arctic. Jyrki Kakonen. 128p. 1993. 72.95 (1-85521-333-8, Pub. by Dartmth Pub) Ashgate Pub Co.

Politics & Symbols: The Italian Communish Party & the Fall of Communism. David I. Kertzer. 224p. 1996. pap. 15.00 (0-300-07724-6) Yale U Pr.

Politics & Symbols: The Italian Communist Party & the Fall of Communism. David I. Kertzer. LC 95-47703. 224p. (C). 1996. 32.50 (0-300-06612-0) Yale U Pr.

Politics & Technology. John Street. LC 92-3440. (Conduct of Science Ser.). 216p. 1992. pap. text 17.95 (0-89862-019-8) Guilford Pubns.

Politics & Technology of Nuclear Proliferation. Robert F. Mozley. LC 98-12070. 1998. write for info. (0-295-97725-6) U of Wash Pr.

Politics & Technology of Nuclear Proliferation. Robert F. Mozley. LC 98-12070. (Illus.). 384p. 1998. pap. 25.00 (0-295-97726-4) U of Wash Pr.

Politics & Television Reviewed. Gladys E. Lang & Kurt Lang. LC 84-11637. 223p. 1984. reprint ed. pap. 69.20 (0-608-01454-0, 205949800001) Bks Demand.

Politics & the Academy: Arnold Toynbee & the Koraes Chair. Richard Clogg. 128p. 1986. 30.00 (0-7146-3290-2, Pub. by F Cass Pubs) Intl Spec Bk.

Politics & the African Development Bank. Karen A. Mingst. LC 90-30935. 216p. 1990. text 29.95 (0-8131-1754-2) U Pr of Ky.

Politics & the American Economy. James J. Gosling. LC 99-46530. 175p. (C). 1999. pap. text 34.00 (0-321-07044-5) Addison-Wesley.

Politics & the American Future. 3rd ed. John A. Harrigan & Larry A. Elowitz. 1992. text. write for info. (0-07-026781-2) McGraw.

Politics & the American Future: Dilemmas of Democracy. 4th ed. John J. Harrigan. LC 95-25249. (C). 1995. pap. text 41.50 (0-07-912084-9) McGraw.

Politics & the American Public Library: Creating Political Support for Library Goals. Edwin Beckerman. LC 95-50135. 224p. 1996. 37.50 (0-8108-3115-5) Scarecrow.

Politics & the Arts: Letter to M. D'Alembert on the Theatre. Jean-Jacques Rousseau. Tr. by Allan Bloom. 196p. 1968. reprint ed. pap. text 11.95 (0-8014-9071-5) Cornell U Pr.

Politics & the Bureaucracy. 4th ed. Meier. (C). 1999. text 28.00 (0-15-505523-2, Pub. by Harcourt Coll Pubs) Harcourt.

Politics & the Catholic Church in Nicaragua. John M. Kirk. (Illus.). 272p. 1992. 49.95 (0-8130-1138-8) U Press Fla.

Politics & the Churches in Great Britain, 1869-1921. G. I. Machin. LC 87-1620. 386p. 1987. text 72.00 (0-19-820106-0) OUP.

Politics & the Class Divide: Working People & the Middle Class Left. David Croteau. (Labor & Social Change Ser.). 320p. (Orig.). (C). 1994. text 69.95 (1-56639-254-3); pap. text 22.95 (1-56639-255-1) Temple U Pr.

Politics & the Constitution: Essays on British Government. Ed. by Vernon Bogdanor. LC 95-44460. 304p. 1996. text 79.95 (1-85521-760-0, Pub. by Dartmth Pub) Ashgate Pub Co.

Politics & the Constitution in the History of the United States Vol. 3: The Political Background of the Federal Convention. William W. Crosskey & William Jeffrey, Jr. LC 53-7433. 608p. 2000. 42.00 (0-226-12138-0) U Ch Pr.

Politics & the Constitution of Athens. 2nd rev. ed. Aristotle. Ed. by Stephen Everson. LC 96-28275. (Cambridge Texts in the History of Political Thought Ser.). 325p. (C). 1996. pap., student ed. 10.95 (0-521-48400-6); pap., student ed. 29.95 (0-521-48243-7) Cambridge U Pr.

Politics & the Courts: Toward a General Theory of Public Law. Barbara M. Yarnold. LC 91-33886. 168p. 1992. 52.95 (0-275-94166-3, C4166, Praeger Pubs) Greenwood.

Politics & the Crisis of 1860. William E. Baringer et al. LC 61-14350. 170p. reprint ed. pap. 52.70 (0-608-13738-3, 202024300016) Bks Demand.

Politics & the Emergence of an Activist International Court of Justice. Thomas J. Bodie. LC 94-37739. 128p. 1995. 49.95 (0-275-95014-X, Praeger Pubs) Greenwood.

Politics & the End of History: Essays in Post-Modernist Thought. Fabio B. Dasilva & Mathew J. Kanjirathinkal. LC 92-32632. (Major Concepts in Politics & Political Theory Ser.). VII, 292p. (C). 1993. 49.95 (0-8204-2033-6) P Lang Pubng.

Politics & the Ends of Identity. Kathryn Dean. (Avebury Series in Philosophy). 312p. 1997. text 83.95 (1-85972-372-1, Pub. by Ashgate Pub) Ashgate Pub Co.

Politics & the Environment. James Connelly & Graham Smith. LC 98-28002. 1999. write for info. (0-415-15067-1); pap. 25.99 (0-415-15068-X) Routledge.

Politics & the Environment. Elim Papadakis. 240p. (Orig.). 1993. pap. text 22.95 (1-86373-363-9, Pub. by Allen & Unwin Pty) Paul & Co Pubs.

Politics & the Ethiopian Famine. Jason W. Clay & Bonnie K. Holcomb. (Cultural Survival Reports: No. 20). 237p. 1986. 29.95 (0-939521-34-2); pap. 9.95 (0-939521-25-3) Cultural Survival.

Politics & the Ethiopian Famine, 1984-1985. Jason W. Clay & Bonnie K. Holcomb. 224p. 1987. pap. 21.95 (0-685-14275-2) Transaction Pubs.

Politics & the Ethiopian Famine, 1984-1985. Jason W. Clay & Bonnie K. Holcomb. 224p. 1987. pap. text 21.95 (0-88738-147-2) Transaction Pubs.

Politics & the Expanding Physician Supply. Michael L. Millman. LC 78-73591. (Conservation of Human Resources Ser.: No. 11). (Illus.). 176p. 1980. text 34.50 (0-916672-84-0) Rowman.

Politics & the Human Body: Assault on Dignity. Ed. by Jean B. Elshtain & J. Timothy Cloyd. LC 94-48390. (Illus.). 340p. (Orig.). 1995. 39.95 (0-8265-1259-3) Vanderbilt U Pr.

Politics & the Human Body: Assault on Dignity. Ed. by Jean B. Elshtain & J. Timothy Cloyd. LC 94-48390. (Illus.). 340p. (Orig.). (C). 1995. pap. 18.95 (0-8265-1260-7) Vanderbilt U Pr.

Politics & the Immigrant. George E. Pozzetta. (Immigration & Ethnicity Ser.: Vol. 8). 480p. 1991. reprint ed. text 83.00 (0-8240-7408-4) Garland.

Politics & the Individual's Life. Helen Silver. 190p. Date not set. write for info. (0-9657552-0-7) P L Mackenzie.

Politics & the Mass Media. Mark C. Wheeler. LC 96-28693. 256p. (C). 1997. text 66.95 (0-631-19783-4); pap. text 25.95 (0-631-19784-2) Blackwell Pubs.

Politics & the Mass Media in Britain. Ralph M. Negrine. (Illus.). 284p. 1989. 45.00 (0-415-01529-4, A3282); pap. 17.95 (0-415-01530-8, A3286) Routledge.

Politics & the Media. Colton. (Political Science Ser.). 2000. pap. 24.00 (0-534-55827-5) Wadsworth Pub.

Politics & the Media: Harlots & Prerogatives at the Turn of the Millennium. Ed. by Jean Seaton. LC 97-36548. (Political Quarterly Special Issues Ser.). 144p. 1999. pap. 29.95 (0-631-20941-7, Pub. by Blckwll Scitfc UK) Blackwell Pubs.

Politics & the Military in Israel, 1967-1977. Amos Perlmutter. 1978. 27.50 (0-7146-3079-9, Pub. by F Cass Pubs) Intl Spec Bk.

Politics & the Muse: Studies in the Politics of Recent American Literature after WWI. Ed. by Adam Sorkin. LC 88-64054. 248p. (C). 1989. 34.95 (0-87972-447-1); pap. 17.95 (0-87972-448-X) Bowling Green Univ Popular Press.

***Politics & the Museum of the American Indian: The Heye & the Mighty.** Roland W. Force. LC 99-70260. (Illus.). 504p. 1999. 45.00 (0-9668654-0-5) Mechas.

P

An Asterisk (*) at the beginning of an entry indicates that the title is appearing for the first time.

Politics & the News Media in Japan. Ofer Feldman. 234p. (C). 1993. text 49.50 (*0-472-10451-9*, 10451) U of Mich Pr.

Politics & the Novel. Irving Howe. LC 74-117810. (Essay Index Reprint Ser.). 1977. 20.95 (*0-8369-1710-3*) Ayer.

Politics & the Novel. Irving Howe. 272p. 1992. text 46.00 (*0-231-07994-X*, Mrngside) Col U Pr.

Politics & the Other Scene. Etienne Balibar. Tr. by Daniel Hahn. 60.00 (*1-85984-725-0*) Norton.

***Politics & the Other Scene.** Etienne Balibar. Tr. by Daniel Hahn. 1999. pap. 20.00 (*1-85984-267-4*, Pub. by Verso) Norton.

Politics & the Oval Office: Towards a Presidential Governance. Ed. by Arnold J. Meltsner. 332p. 1981. 39.95 (*0-87855-428-9*); pap. 24.95 (*0-685-07094-8*) Transaction Pubs.

Politics & the "Parlement" of Paris under Louis the Fifteenth, 1754-1774. Julian Swann. 400p. (C). 1995. pap. text 29.95 (*0-521-48362-X*) Cambridge U Pr.

Politics & the People Vol. I: In Search of a Humane India. Rajni Kothari. 260p. 1989. 33.50 (*0-945257-19-8*) Apex Pr.

Politics & the People Vol. II: In Search of a Humane India. Rajni Kothari. 294p. 1989. 28.50 (*0-945257-20-1*) Apex Pr.

Politics & the People of London: The London County Council, 1889-1965. Ed. by Andrew Saint. 302p. 1989. 60.00 (*1-85285-029-9*) Hambledon Press.

Politics & the Political Imagination in Later Stuart Britain: Essays Presented to Lois Green Schwoerer. Ed. by Howard Nenner. LC 97-40133. 240p. 1998. 75.00 (*1-878822-95-0*) Univ Rochester Pr.

Politics & the Pound: The Tories, Sterling & Europe. Philip Stephens. (Illus.). 350p. 1995. 52.50 (*0-333-63296-6*, Pub. by Macmillan) Trans-Atl Phila.

Politics & the Press. Schweitzer & Black. (Journal of History & Politics (Revue d'Histoire et de Politique) Ser.: Vol. 7). (ENG & FRE.). 1990. 49.95 (*0-7734-8942-8*) E Mellen.

Politics & the Press: The News Media & Its Influences. Pippa Norris. LC 97-3827. 336p. 1997. pap. 59.95 (*1-55587-681-1*) L Rienner.

Politics & the Press: The News Media & Its Influences. Pippa Norris. LC 97-3827. 336p. 1997. 58.00 (*1-55587-670-6*) L Rienner.

Politics & the Restraint of Science. Leonard A. Cole. LC 83-2992. (Illus.). 200p. 1983. 29.50 (*0-86598-125-6*) Rowman.

Politics & the Sciences of Culture in Germany, 1840-1920. Woodruff D. Smith. 320p. 1991. text 65.00 (*0-19-506536-0*) OUP.

Politics & the State As Employer. Peter Fairbrother. LC 93-32442. 224p. 1994. 99.00 (*0-7201-2137-X*) Continuum.

Politics & the Support of Libraries. Ed. by E. J. Josey & Kenneth Shearer. 200p. 1990. pap. text 38.50 (*1-55570-073-X*) Neal-Schuman.

Politics & the Urban Poor see Arrabal y la Politica

Politics & the Warren Court. Alexander M. Bickel. LC 73-398. (American Constitutional & Legal History Ser). 314p. 1973. reprint ed. lib. bdg. 35.00 (*0-306-70573-7*) Da Capo.

***Politics & Theater: The Crisis of Legitimacy in Restoration France, 1815-1830.** Sheryl Kroen. LC 99-48330. Vol. 40. (Illus.). 424p. 2000. 55.00 (*0-520-22214-8*, Pub. by U CA Pr) Cal Prin Full Svc.

Politics & Theopolitics in the Bible & Post-Bibilical Literature. Yair Hoffman et al. (JSOTS Ser.: Vol. 171). 200p. 1994. 57.50 (*1-85075-461-6*, Pub. by Sheffield Acad) CUP Services.

Politics & Trade in the Indian Ocean World: Essays in Honour of Ashin Das Gupta. Ed. by Rudrangshu Mukherjee & Lakshmi Subramanian. LC 98-915484. (Illus.). 290p. 1999. text 24.95 (*0-19-564420-4*) OUP.

Politics & Transcendent Wisdom: The Scripture for Humane Kings in the Creation of Chinese Buddhism. Charles D. Orzech. LC 96-52407. (Hermeneutics Ser.: No. 8). 424p. 1998. 55.00 (*0-271-01715-5*) Pa St U Pr.

Politics & Truth: Political Theory & the Postmodernist Challenge. Theresa M. Lee. LC 97-3267. (SUNY Series in Political Theory). 243p. (C). 1997. pap. text 17.95 (*0-7914-3504-0*) State U NY Pr.

Politics & Truth: Political Theory & the Postmodernist Challenge. Theresa M. Ling Lee. LC 97-3267. (SUNY Series in Political Theory). 243p. (C). 1997. text 54.50 (*0-7914-3503-2*) State U NY Pr.

Politics & Tyranny: Lessons in Pursuit of Freedom. Milton Friedman et al. LC 84-61364. (Illus.). 80p. 1984. pap. 5.95 (*0-936488-00-X*) PRIPP.

Politics & Uncertainty: Theory, Models & Applications. Claudio Cioffi-Revilla. LC 97-23646. (Illus.). 364p. (C). 1998. text 64.95 (*0-521-58121-4*); pap. text 23.95 (*0-521-58915-0*) Cambridge U Pr.

Politics & Urban Growth in Buenos Aires, 1910-1942. Richard J. Walter. LC 93-2918. (Cambridge Latin American Studies: No. 74). (Illus.). 292p. (C). 1993. text 74.95 (*0-521-44165-X*) Cambridge U Pr.

Politics & Urban Policies. Brett W. Hawkins. LC 77-151612. (Policy Analysis Ser.). (C). 1971. write for info. (*0-672-51474-5*, Bobbs); pap. 4.95 (*0-672-61060-4*, Bobbs) Macmillan.

Politics & Urban Policy. Brett W. Hawkins. 144p. 1971. reprint ed. pap. text 17.95 (*0-8290-0331-2*) Irvington.

Politics & Value in English Studies: A Discipline in Crisis? Josephine M. Guy & Ian Small. LC 92-47281. 205p. (C). 1993. text 54.95 (*0-521-44253-2*) Cambridge U Pr.

Politics & Verbal Play: The Ludic Poetry of Angel Gonzalez. Martha L. Miller. LC 94-24276. 232p. 1995. 38.50 (*0-8386-3552-0*) Fairleigh Dickinson.

Politics & Vision: Royalty Only. Wolin. 1992. write for info. (*0-316-95200-1*) Little.

Politics & War: European Conflict from Philip II to Hitler. David Kaiser. LC 90-4166. 448p. 1990. text 42.50 (*0-674-68815-5*) HUP.

Politics & War: European Conflict from Philip II to Hitler. David Kaiser. 448p. 1992. pap. text 14.95 (*0-674-68816-3*) HUP.

***Politics & War: European Conflict from Philip II to Hitler.** enl. ed. David Kaiser. 2000. pap. text 17.95 (*0-674-00272-5*) HUP.

Politics & Welfare in Birmingham, 1900-1975. Edward S. LaMonte. LC 94-7186. 320p. 1995. text 34.95 (*0-8173-0754-0*) U of Ala Pr.

Politics are for People. Shirley Williams. LC 81-80916. 230p. 1981. 22.00 (*0-674-68910-0*) HUP.

Politics As a Noble Calling: The Memoirs of F. Clifton White. F. Clifton White. LC 98-128329. 269p. 1995. 21.95 (*0-915463-64-4*) Jameson Bks.

Politics As Development: The Emergence of Political Parties in Nineteenth-Century Serbia. Gale Stokes. LC 89-39903. 416p. (C). 1990. text 54.95 (*0-8223-1016-3*) Duke.

Politics as If Women Mattered: A Political Analysis of the National Action Committee on the Status of Women. Jill Vickers. LC 93-184367. 347p. 1994. pap. text 20.95 (*0-8020-6757-3*) U of Toronto Pr.

Politics As If Women Mattered: A Political Analysis of the National Action Committee on the Status of Women. Jill Vickers et al. 347p. 1993. text 50.00 (*0-8020-5850-7*) U of Toronto Pr.

Politics As Leadership. rev. ed. Robert C. Tucker. LC 95-21253. (Paul Anthony Brick Lectures). 192p. (C). 1995. pap. 15.95 (*0-8262-1023-6*) U of Mo Pr.

***Politics as Public Choice.** James M. Buchanan. LC 99-41676. (Collected Works of James M. Buchanan : Vol. 13). 2000. 20.00 (*0-86597-237-0*); pap. 12.00 (*0-86597-238-9*) Liberty Fund.

Politics As Rational Action: Essays in Public Choice & Policy Analysis. Ed. by Leif Lewin & Evert Vedung. (Theory & Decision Library: No. 23). 276p. 1980. lib. bdg. 96.00 (*90-277-1040-6*) Kluwer Academic.

Politics as Usual: The Age of Truman & Eisenhower. Gary W. Reichard. Ed. by A. S. Eisenstadt & John H. Franklin. LC 87-20726. 222p. (C). 1988. pap. text 11.95 (*0-88295-856-9*) Harlan Davidson.

***Politics as Usual: The Cyberspace Revolution.** Michael Margolis & David M. Resnick. LC 99-50650. (Contemporary American Politics Ser.). 2000. write for info. (*0-7619-1331-9*) Sage.

Politics at Mao's Court: Gao Gang & Party Factionalism in the Early 1950s. Frederick C. Teiwes. LC 90-35927. (Studies on Contemporary China Ser.). 342p. (C). (gr. 13). 1990. text 79.95 (*0-87332-590-7*, East Gate Bk) M E Sharpe.

Politics at Mao's Court: Gao Gang & Party Factionalism in the Early 1950s. Frederick C. Teiwes. LC 90-35927. (Studies on Contemporary China). 342p. (C). (gr. 13). 1990. pap. text 42.95 (*0-87332-709-8*, East Gate Bk) M E Sharpe.

***Politics at the Edge.** Chris Pierson. 330p. 2000. text 75.00 (*0-312-23137-7*) St Martin.

Politics at the Margin: Historical Studies of Public Expression Outside the Mainstream. Susan Herbst. LC 93-41566. (Illus.). 243p. (C). 1994. text 69.95 (*0-521-46184-7*); pap. text 19.95 (*0-521-47763-8*) Cambridge U Pr.

Politics at the Periphery: Third Parties in Two-Party America. J David Gillespie. LC 92-43973. (Illus.). 343p. (Orig.). (C). 1993. pap. text 14.95 (*0-87249-843-3*) U of SC Pr.

Politics at Work. Bob Lee & Peter Lawrence. 208p. 1999. pap. 67.50 (*0-7487-1113-9*, Pub. by S Thornes Pubs) Trans-Atl Phila.

Politics, Barbecue, & Balderdash. John R. Cole, Jr. (Illus.). 120p. 1995. pap. text 7.95 (*0-9648472-0-5*) Durham Herald.

Politics by Humans: Research on American Leadership. James D. Barber. LC 87-36593. xii, 517p. 1988. text 64.95 (*0-8223-0837-1*); pap. text 25.95 (*0-8223-0848-7*) Duke.

Politics by Other Means: Higher Education & Group Thinking. David Bromwich. 296p. (C). 1992. pap. 14.00 (*0-300-05920-5*) Yale U Pr.

Politics by Other Means: Law & the Struggle Against Apartheid. Richard Abel. (After the Law Ser.). 600p. (C). 1995. pap. 23.99 (*0-415-90817-5*, B0758) Routledge.

Politics by Other Means: Law in the Struggle Against Apartheid, 1980-1994. Richard Abel. (After the Law Ser.). 664p. (C). 1995. 90.00 (*0-415-90816-7*, B0754) Routledge.

Politics by Other Means: Politicians, Prosecutors, & the Press from Watergate to Whitewater. Benjamin Ginsberg & Martin Shefter. LC 98-37671. 224p. 1999. pap. 15.00 (*0-393-31877-X*) Norton.

Politics by Other Means: The ANC's War on South Africa. Morgan Norval. Ed. by Robert Krederas. 350p. 1993. 25.00 (*0-944273-11-4*) Selous Found Pr.

Politics by Other Means: The Declining Importance of Elections in America. Benjamin Ginsberg & Martin Shefter. LC 89-43090. xii, 226 p. 1990. 19.95 (*0-465-01973-0*) Basic.

Politics by Principle, Not Interest: Towards Nondiscriminatory Democracy. James M. Buchanan & Roger D. Congleton. LC 97-40983. (Illus.). 186p. (C). 1998. text 44.95 (*0-521-62187-9*) Cambridge U Pr.

Politics Caspian Oil. Gokay. 1999. text 65.00 (*0-312-21507-X*) St Martin.

Politics, Censorship & the English Reformation. Ed. by David M. Loades. 227p. 1992. text 65.00 (*0-86187-861-2*, Pub. by P P Pubs) Cassell & Continuum.

Politics, Character, & Culture: Perspectives from Hans Gerth, 41. Ed. by Joseph Bensman et al. LC 81-13426. (Contributions in Sociology Ser.: No. 41). 290p. 1982. 65.00 (*0-313-22863-9*, VSP/, Greenwood Pr) Greenwood.

Politics, Civil Rights & Law in Black Atlanta. Herman S. Mason, Jr. (Black America Ser.). (Illus.). 128p. 2000. pap. 18.99 (*0-7524-0985-9*) Arcadia Publng.

Politics, Crime & the International Scene: An Inter-American Focus. Ed. by Freda Adler & G. O. Mueller. x, 403p. 1972. reprint ed. pap. 12.00 (*0-8377-0203-8*, Rothman) W S Hein.

Politics, Crime Control & Culture. Ed. by Stuart A. Scheingold. LC 97-18965. (International Library of Criminology, Criminal Justice & Penology). 7p. 1997. text 189.95 (*1-85521-963-8*, Pub. by Dartmth Pub) Ashgate Pub Co.

Politics, Culture & Class in the French Revolution. Lynn A. Hunt. LC 83-27528. (Studies on the History of Society & Culture: No. 1). 270p. 1984. pap. 16.95 (*0-520-05740-6*, Pub. by U CA Pr) Cal Prin Full Svc.

Politics, Culture & Class in the French Revolution. Lynn A. Hunt. LC 83-27528. (Studies on the History of Society & Culture: No. 1). (Illus.). 267p. reprint ed. pap. 82.80 (*0-7837-4832-9*, 204447900003) Bks Demand.

Politics, Cultures & Communications: European Vs. American Approaches to Communications Policy Making. Roland S. Homet. LC 79-9817. (Praeger Special Studies). 124p. 1979. 45.00 (*0-275-90362-1*, C0362, Praeger Pubs) Greenwood.

Politics, Death, & the Devil: Self & Power in Max Weber & Thomas Mann. Harvey Goldman. 350p. (C). 1992. 48.00 (*0-520-07750-4*, Pub. by U CA Pr) Cal Prin Full Svc.

Politics, Democracy & the Supreme Court: Essays on the Frontier of Constitutional Theory, 83. Arthur S. Miller. LC 85-5604. (Contributions in American Studies: No. 83). 368p. 1985. 65.00 (*0-313-24831-1*, MLP/, Greenwood Pr) Greenwood.

Politics, Diplomacy, & Intrigue in the Early Republic: The Cabinet Career of Robert Smith, 1801-1811. Thom Armstrong. 240p. (C). 1991. pap. text, per. 32.95 (*0-8403-7055-5*) Kendall-Hunt.

Politics, Diplomacy & the Media: Gorbachev's Legacy in the West. Anthony R. Deluca. LC 98-4931. 176p. 1998. 55.00 (*0-275-95968-6*, Praeger Pubs) Greenwood.

Politics Dispossession. Edward W. Said. 1995. pap. 18.00 (*0-679-76145-4*) Knopf.

Politics East & West: A Comparison of Japanese & British Political Culture. Curtis H. Martin & Bruce Stronach. LC 92-26273. 352p. (C). (gr. 13). 1992. pap. text 32.95 (*1-56324-108-0*) M E Sharpe.

Politics East & West: A Comparison of Japanese & British Political Culture. Curtis H. Martin & Bruce Stronach. LC 92-26273. 352p. (C). (gr. 13). 1992. text 75.95 (*0-87332-895-7*) M E Sharpe.

Politics, Economics & Men of Modern Spain, 1808-1946. Oliveira A. Ramos. Tr. by Teener Hall. LC 72-4285. (World Affairs Ser.: National & International Viewpoints). 720p. 1972. reprint ed. 41.95 (*0-405-04578-6*) Ayer.

Politics, Economics, & Society in the Two Germanies, 1945-75: A Bibliography of English-Language Works. Compiled by Anna J. Merritt & Richard L. Merritt. LC 77-26853. 288p. 1978. text 29.95 (*0-252-00684-4*) U of Ill Pr.

Politics, Economics, & Welfare. Robert A. Dahl & Charles E. Lindblom. 612p. (C). 1991. pap. text 29.95 (*1-56000-575-0*) Transaction Pubs.

Politics Economoy of Venezuelan Oil. Laura Randall. LC 87-15848. 260p. 1987. 65.00 (*0-275-92823-3*, C2823, Praeger Pubs) Greenwood.

Politics, Economy, & Society in Contemporary China. Bill Brugger & Stephen Reglar. 376p. (C). 1994. 47.50 (*0-8047-2349-4*) Stanford U Pr.

Politics, Economy, & Society in Contemporary China. Bill Brugger & Stephen Reglar. viii, 367p. 1994. pap. 17.95 (*0-8047-2350-8*) Stanford U Pr.

***Politics, Education & Citizenship.** Ed. by Mal Leicester et al. LC 99-36830. (Education, Culture & Values Ser.: Vol. VI). 368p. 1999. 140.00 (*0-7507-1007-1*, Pub. by Falmer Pr UK) Taylor & Francis.

***Politics, Elections & the Law.** Noel Whelan. 192p. 1999. pap. 33.75 (*1-901657-69-8*, 18431, Pub. by Blackhall Pub) Gaunt.

Politics, Elections, Government, Military, Criminal Handbook for Reporters & Captioners. Monette Benoit. (Handbooks for Reporters Ser.: No. 4). 255p. 1995. pap. text 26.95 (*1-881149-08-0*) CRRB.

Politics, Fat-Cats & Honey-Money Boys: The Mem-Wars of Jerry Sadler. Told to James Neyland. LC 83-63199. 336p. 1984. 15.95 (*0-915677-01-6*) Roundtable Pub.

Politics, Feminism & the Reformation of Gender. Jennifer Chapman. LC 92-9372. 368p. (C). (gr. 13). 1992. 110.00 (*0-415-01698-3*, A7694) Routledge.

Politics for a Rational Left: Political Writing, 1977-1988. Eric J. Hobsbawm. 256p. 1989. 45.00 (*0-86091-246-9*, A3730); pap. 15.95 (*0-86091-958-7*, A3734) Routledge.

Politics for Dummies. Ann Delaney. (For Dummies Ser.). 368p. 1995. pap. 19.99 (*1-56884-381-X*) IDG Bks.

Politics for Evangelicals. Paul B. Henry. LC 74-2893. 127p. reprint ed. pap. 39.40 (*0-7837-2176-5*, 204251400004) Bks Demand.

Politics for People. David Mathews. Tr. by Afif Talhouk. 1997. text 9.00 (*1-886604-06-1*) Lebanese Ctr.

Politics for People: Finding a Responsible Public Voice. David Mathews. Tr. by Afif Talhouk. (ARA.). 235p. 1997. pap. write for info. (*1-886604-05-3*) Lebanese Ctr.

Politics for People: Finding a Responsible Public Voice. David Mathews. LC 93-5794. 240p. 1994. text 24.95 (*0-252-02088-X*) U of Ill Pr.

Politics for People: Finding a Responsible Public Voice. 2nd ed. Forrest D. Mathews. LC 98-18786. 1998. write for info. (*0-252-02456-7*) U of Ill Pr.

Politics For People: Finding a Responsible Public Voice. 2nd ed. Forrest D. Mathews. LC 98-18786. 1998. pap. 12.95 (*0-252-06763-0*) U of Ill Pr.

Politics for the People. Bruce Barron. LC 95-49665. 167p. (Orig.). 1996. pap. 9.99 (*0-8308-1984-3*, 1984) InterVarsity.

Politics for the People, Vol. 1, Nos. 1-17. LC 69-13752. 284p. 1971. reprint ed. 57.50 (*0-678-00663-6*) Kelley.

Politics, Gender, & the Arts: Women, the Arts, & Society. Ed. by Ronald Dotterer & Susan R. Bowers. LC 38-14370. (Susquehanna Studies). (Illus.). 216p. 1993. 34.50 (*0-945636-30-X*) Susquehanna U Pr.

Politics, Gender & the Islamic Past: The Legacy of 'A'isha Bint abi Bakr. D. A. Spellberg. LC 94-25025. 243p. 1994. 41.00 (*0-231-07998-2*) Col U Pr.

Politics, Gender & the Islamic Past: The Legacy of 'A'isha Bint abi Bakr. D. A. Spellberg. 243p. 1996. pap. 18.50 (*0-231-07999-0*) Col U Pr.

Politics, Gender & the Islamic Past: The Legacy of 'A'isha Bint abi Bakr. D. A. Spellberg. 242p. 1996. 35.00 (*0-614-21393-2*, 967) Kazi Pubns.

Politics, Gender, & the Mexican Novel, 1968-1988: Beyond the Pyramid. Cynthia Steele. LC 91-30491. (Texas Pan American Ser.). (Illus.). 223p. (Orig.). (C). 1992. pap. 15.95 (*0-292-77661-6*); text 30.00 (*0-292-76530-4*) U of Tex Pr.

Politics, Geography & Behavior. Richard Muir & Ronan Paddison. 1981. pap. 13.95 (*0-416-31340-X*, NO. 3460) Routledge.

Politics, Geography, & "Political Geography" A Critical Approach. Joe Painter. 1995. text. write for info. (*0-340-63215-1*, Pub. by E A) Routldge.

***Politics, Governance & Technology: A Postmodern Narrative on the Virtual State.** Paul H. A. Frissen. LC 99-38281. (New Horizons in Public Policy Ser.). 320p. 2000. 95.00 (*1-85898-877-2*) E Elgar.

Politics, Government, & Related Policy Issues, 1977-1982. Ed. by Harriet Nathan & Stanley Scott. LC 83-26374. (Emerging Issues in Public Policy: Research Reports & Essays). 45p. reprint ed. pap. 30.00 (*0-7837-2129-3*, 204241100004) Bks Demand.

Politics, Government & Society in the German Democratic Republic: Basic Documents. Ed. by James Mellis & J. K. Thomaneck. 373p. 1989. 19.50 (*0-85496-247-6*) Berg Pubs.

Politics, Housing & Race Relations: California's Rumford Act & Proposition 14. Thomas W. Casstevens. LC 67-64842. 103p. reprint ed. pap. 32.00 (*0-608-15396-6*, 202942100060) Bks Demand.

Politics, Ideology, & Literary Discourse in Modern China: Theoretical Interventions & Cultural Critique. Ed. by Liu Kang & Xiaobing Tang. LC 93-4448. (Illus.). 328p. 1994. text 49.95 (*0-8223-1403-7*) Duke.

Politics, Ideology, & Literary Discourse in Modern China: Theoretical Interventions & Cultural Critique. Ed. by Liu Kang & Xiaobing Tang. LC 93-4448. (Illus.). 328p. 1994. pap. text 19.95 (*0-8223-1416-9*) Duke.

Politics, Ideology & the Law in Early Modern Europe: Essays in Honor of J. H. M. Salmon. Ed. by Adrianna E. Bakos. LC 94-20552. (Illus.). 208p. (C). 1995. 85.00 (*1-878822-39-X*) Univ Rochester Pr.

Politics in a Changing World. Randall Fegley. (Illus.). 211p. (C). 1994. pap. text 29.95 (*0-9629113-1-3*) Cottage Comm.

Politics in a Changing World: A Comparative Introduction to Political Science. Marcus E. Ethridge & Howard Handelman. 608p. 1993. pap. 59.95 (*0-312-07410-7*) St Martin.

Politics in a Plural Society: A Study of Non-Communal Political Parties in West Malaysia. R. K. Vasil. LC 70-29366. (East Asian Historical Monographs). 350p. reprint ed. pap. 108.50 (*0-608-17891-8*, 205667500080) Bks Demand.

Politics in a Pluralist Democracy. Lucy S. Dawidowicz & Leon J. Goldstein. LC 74-9630. 100p. 1974. reprint ed. lib. bdg. 59.75 (*0-8371-7599-2*, DAPD, Greenwood Pr) Greenwood.

Politics in Africa. Edie. (C). 1999. pap. write for info. (*0-15-508460-7*) Harcourt Coll Pubs.

Politics in Africa. Shaw & Heard. 1982. pap. text. write for info. (*0-582-64378-3*, Pub. by Addison-Wesley) Longman.

Politics in America. 2nd ed. 1996. write for info. (*0-13-619743-4*) P-H.

Politics in America. 2nd ed. (Prentice Hall College Titles Ser.). 1997. write for info. (*0-13-258393-3*) P-H.

Politics in America. 2nd ed. Corey. 240p. 1997. pap. text, student ed. 20.80 (*0-13-258369-0*) P-H.

Politics in America. 2nd ed. Dye. 1996. pap. text, teacher ed. write for info. (*0-13-258310-0*) Allyn.

Politics in America. 2nd ed. Thomas R. Dye. 1996. text 65.00 (*0-13-257007-6*) P-H.

***Politics in America.** 3rd ed. 1999. write for info. (*0-13-095899-9*) P-H.

Politics in America. 3rd ed. Dye. LC 98-27686. 708p. 1998. 65.33 (*0-13-095689-9*) P-H.

Politics in America. 3rd ed. Dye. (C). 1998. pap. text, student ed. 18.67 (*0-13-095903-0*) P-H.

***Politics in America.** 4th ed. Thomas R. Dye. LC 00-29805. 2000. write for info. (*0-13-027109-8*) P-H.

***Politics in America.** 4th ed. L. Tucker Gibson & Clay Robison. LC 00-29357. 2001. write for info. (*0-13-027100-4*) P-H.

Politics in America: Texas. 3rd ed. Gibson. 312p. 1999. pap., student ed. 22.00 (*0-13-958927-9*) S&S Trade.

Politics in America 2000: The 106th Congress. Ed. by Philip D. Duncan & Brian Nutting. 1650p. 1999. 98.95 (*1-56802-470-3*); pap. 55.95 (*1-56802-471-1*) CQ Pr.

P

Politics in America 1992. CQ Inc. Staff. Ed. by Phil Duncan. 1991. 79.95 (*0-87187-599-3*); pap. 49.95 (*0-87187-641-8*) Congr Quarterly.

Politics in America 1996. Ed. by Phil Duncan et al. LC 93-11559. 1541p. 1995. pap. 54.95 (*0-87187-844-5*) Congr Quarterly.

Politics in America 1996. Ed. by Philip D. Duncan et al. LC 93-11559. 1541p. 1995. 89.95 (*0-87187-843-7*) Congr Quarterly.

Politics in America, 1998: The 105th Congress. Ed. by Christine C. Lawrence & Phil Duncan. LC 93-11559. (Illus.). 1647p. (C). (gr. 11). 1997. text 96.95 (*0-87187-909-3*) Congr Quarterly.

Politics in America, 1998: The 105th Congress. Ed. by Christine C. Lawrence & Phil Duncan. LC 93-11559. (Illus.). 1647p. (YA). (gr. 11). 1997. pap. text 55.95 (*0-87187-917-4*) Congr Quarterly.

Politics in an Antipolitical Age. G. J. Mulgan. 220p. 1994. pap. 26.95 (*0-7456-0813-2*) Blackwell Pubs.

Politics in an Arabian Oasis. Madawi A. Rasheed. (Illus.). 300p. 1997. text 19.95 (*1-86064-193-8*, Pub. by I B T) St Martin.

Politics in an Arabian Oasis: The Rashidi Tribal Dynasty. Madawi Al-Rasheed. 224p. 1991. text 70.00 (*1-85043-320-8*) I B T.

Politics in an Interdependent World: Essays Presented to Ghita Ionescu. Ed. by Geraint Parry. LC 93-42473. 208p. 1994. text 90.00 (*1-85278-737-6*) E Elgar.

Politics in Australia. 3rd ed. Ed. by Rodney Smith. LC 97-130452. 400p. 1997. pap. 32.95 (*1-86373-955-6*, Pub. by Allen & Unwin Pty) Paul & Co Pubs.

Politics in Austria: Still a Case for Consociationalism. Ed. by Kurt R. Luther & Wolfgang C. Muller. 232p. 1992. text 32.00 (*0-7146-3461-1*, Pub. by F Cass Pubs) Intl Spec Bk.

Politics in Bangladesh: A Study of Awami Leaugue, 1949-1958. M. B. Nair. 1990. 40.00 (*81-85119-79-1*, Pub. by Northern Bk Ctr) S Asia.

Politics in Black & White: Race & Power in Los Angeles. Raphael J. Sonenshein. 360p. 1993. pap. text 18.95 (*0-691-02548-7*, Pub. by Princeton U Pr) Cal Prin Full Svc.

Politics in Britain. Leys. 1983. 16.95 (*0-435-83493-2*) Ashgate Pub Co.

Politics in Britain. 2nd ed. Colin T. Leys. 400p. 1989. pap. text 19.95 (*0-8020-6751-4*) U of Toronto Pr.

Politics in Britain: An Introduction. Colin T. Leys. LC 83-213340. (Illus.). 360p. (Orig.). reprint ed. pap. 111.60 (*0-8357-3645-8*, 203637200003) Bks Demand.

Politics in Britain: From Labourism to Thatcherism. Colin T. Leys. 384p. 1989. 50.00 (*0-86091-240-X*, A3888); pap. 17.95 (*0-86091-954-4*, A3892) Routledge.

***Politics in Canada.** 44p. 1999. write for info. (*0-13-003700-1*) P-H.

***Politics in Canada.** 4th ed. R. J. Jackson. LC 98-104552. 650p. 1998. pap. 73.27 (*0-13-633165-3*, Prentice Hall) P-H.

***Politics in Canada: Culture, Institutions, Behaviour & Public Policy.** 5th ed. Robert J. Jackson & Doreen Jackson. 672p. 2000. pap. write for info. (*0-13-027315-5*) P-H.

Politics in Canada: Cultures, Institutions, Behavior & Public Policy. 3rd ed. Robert J. Jackson. 1994. 50.67 (*0-13-064007-7*) P-H.

***Politics in Canada & Public Policy: Culture, Institutions, Behaviour & Public Policy.** 5th ed. 2000. write for info. (*0-13-028045-3*) P-H.

Politics in Central America: Guatemala, El Salvador, Honduras, & Nicaragua. rev. ed. Thomas P. Anderson. LC 87-29944. 264p. 1988. 59.95 (*0-275-92805-5*, C2805, Praeger Pubs); pap. 17.95 (*0-275-92883-7*, B2883, Praeger Pubs) Greenwood.

Politics in Changing India. Iqbal Narain & P. C. Mathur. (C). 1994. text 34.00 (*81-7033-227-3*, Pub. by Rawat Pubns) S Asia.

Politics in Changing World. 2nd ed. Ethridge. 1997. pap. text 33.95 (*0-312-18402-6*) St Martin.

Politics in Changing World. 2nd ed. Marcus E. Ethridge. LC 97-65188. 543p. 1997. pap. text 55.95 (*0-312-06245-1*) St Martin.

Politics in Chile: Democracy, Authoritarianism, & the Search for Development. 2nd ed. Lois Oppenheim. LC 98-20755. 320p. 1998. text 65.00 (*0-8133-3565-5*, Pub. by Westview) HarpC.

Politics in Chile: Democracy, Authoritarianism & the Search for Development. 2nd ed. Lois H. Oppenheim. LC 98-20755. 320p. (C). 1998. pap. text 28.00 (*0-8133-3415-2*, Pub. by Westview) HarpC.

Politics in Context: Assimilation & Conflict in Urban Neighborhoods. Robert Huckfeldt. LC 85-28771. 200p. 1986. 38.00 (*0-87586-067-2*); pap. 18.00 (*0-87586-068-0*) Agathon.

Politics in Contmeporary Georgia: From Instability to Statehood. Jonathan Aves. 62p. 1996. pap. text 12.95 (*1-899658-17-3*, Pub. by Royal Inst Intl Affairs) Brookings.

Politics in Czechoslovakia, 1945-1989. J. F. Bradley. 200p. 1991. text 42.00 (*0-88033-212-3*, Pub. by East Eur Monographs) Col U Pr.

Politics in Developing Countries: Comparing Experiences with Democracy. 2nd ed. Seymour M. Lipset et al. 500p. 1995. pap. text 23.50 (*1-55587-541-6*) L Rienner.

Politics in Eastern Europe, 1945-1992. George Schopflin. LC 92-45695. 256p. 1993. pap. 32.95 (*0-631-14724-1*) Blackwell Pubs.

Politics in Eighteenth-Century Wales. Peter D. Thomas. LC 98-131561. 288p. 1998. 50.00 (*0-7083-1444-9*, Pub. by Univ Wales Pr) Paul & Co Pubs.

***Politics in England: Change & Persistance.** 6th ed. Rose. (C). 1999. pap. text Price not set. (*0-321-00523-6*) Addison-Wesley.

***Politics in England: Change & Persistence.** 6th ed. (C). 2000. write for info. (*0-321-05272-2*) Addison-Wesley.

Politics in England: Change & Persistence (Scott Foresman/Little Brown Series in Political Science) 5th ed. Richard Rose. (C). 1989. text 38.44 (*0-673-39892-7*) Addison-Wesley Educ.

Politics in English Romantic Poetry. Carl R. Woodring. LC 74-111490. (Illus.). 403p. reprint ed. pap. 125.00 (*0-7837-4467-6*, 204417500001) Bks Demand.

***Politics in Europe.** 3rd ed. M. Donald Hancock et al. (Illus.). 512p. (C). 2001. pap. text 42.95 (*1-889119-34-2*, Chatham House Pub) Seven Bridges.

Politics in Familiar Contexts: Projecting Politics Through Popular Media. Ed. by Robert L. Savage et al. LC 89-14901. (Communication: The Human Context Ser.: Vol. 2). 288p. (C). 1990. text 73.25 (*0-89391-508-4*) Ablx Pub.

Politics in Florida. Thomas R. Dye. LC 98-10060. 234p. (C). 1998. pap. text 25.80 (*0-13-690330-4*) P-H.

Politics in Gaullist France: Coping with Chaos. Charles Hauss. LC 90-37788. 208p. 1990. 57.95 (*0-275-93734-8*, C3734, Praeger Pubs) Greenwood.

Politics in Georgia. Arnold Fleischmann & Carol Pierannunzi. LC 97-8601. (Illus.). 368p. (C). 1997. pap. 25.00 (*0-8203-1911-2*) U of Ga Pr.

Politics in Georgia. Arnold Fleischmann & Carol Pierannunzi. LC 97-8601. (Illus.). 368p. (C). 1997. 50.00 (*0-8203-1910-4*) U of Ga Pr.

Politics in German Literature: Essays in Memory of Frank G. Ryder. Ed. by Beth Bjorklund & Mark Cory. LC 97-31383. (Studies in German Literature & Culture). 230p. 1998. 60.00 (*1-57113-082-9*) Camden Hse.

Politics in Hard Times: Comparative Responses to International Economic Crises. Peter Gourevitch. LC 86-47631. (Cornell Studies in Political Economy). 272p. 1986. pap. text 15.95 (*0-8014-9436-2*) Cornell U Pr.

Politics in Hungary: For a Democratic Alternative. Janos Kis. (Atlantic Studies on Society in Change, Social Science Monographs). 275p. 1989. text 44.50 (*0-88033-963-2*, Pub. by East Eur Monographs) Col U Pr.

Politics in India. Ed. by Sudipta Kaviraj. LC 98-112189. (Oxford in India Readings in Sociology & Social Anthropology Ser.). (Illus.). 414p. 1997. text 35.00 (*0-19-563133-1*) OUP.

***Politics in India.** Ed. by Sudipta Kaviraj. (Oxford in India Readings in Sociology & Social Anthropology Ser.). 416p. 1999. pap. 14.95 (*0-19-564873-0*) OUP.

Politics in India, 1992-93. C. P. Bhambhri. xi, 308p. 1993. 25.95 (*1-881338-10-X*) Nataraj Bks.

Politics in Indonesia: Democracy Islam & the Ideology of Tolerance. Douglas E. Ramage. (Politics in Asia Ser.). 296p. (C). 1997. pap. 27.99 (*0-415-16467-2*) Routledge.

Politics in Industrial Societies: A Comparative Perspective. Lawrence C. Mayer & John A. Burnett. LC 76-54694. 399p. reprint ed. pap. 123.70 (*0-608-30092-6*, 205549100022) Bks Demand.

Politics in Jamaica. Anthony J. Payne. 226p. 1995. pap. 21.95 (*0-312-12526-7*) St Martin.

Politics in Jamaica. 2nd rev. ed. Anthony J. Payne. LC 95-125043. 223p. 1995. text 59.95 (*0-312-12525-9*) St Martin.

Politics in Japan. Bradley M. Richardson & Scott C. Flanagan. (Comparative Politics Ser.). (C). 1984. pap. text 31.00 (*0-673-39472-7*) Addison-Wesley Educ.

Politics in Japan. 2nd ed. Ed. by Flanagan. (C). 1998. text. write for info. (*0-321-01106-6*) Addison-Wesley Educ.

Politics in Leadership: A Comparative Perspective. Ed. by William A. Shack & Percy S. Cohen. (Illus.). 1979. text 49.95 (*0-19-823193-8*) OUP.

Politics in Liberation: An Introductory Reader on Political Life & Government in U. S. 2nd ed. Nicky Yuen. LC 97-168721. 482p. (C). 1997. per. 63.95 (*0-7872-3665-9*, 41366501) Kendall-Hunt.

Politics in Mexico: The Decline of Authoritarianism. 3rd ed. Roderic A. Camp. LC 98-29058. (Illus.). 288p. (C). 1999. pap. 22.95 (*0-19-512412-X*) OUP.

Politics in Minnesota: The Directory, 1999-2000. 3rd ed. Sarah Janecek. pap. 19.95 (*0-9645333-2-4*) Minn Polit Pr.

Politics in Modern Greece. Keith R. Legg. LC 69-18495. xii, 367p. 1969. 47.50 (*0-8047-0705-7*) Stanford U Pr.

Politics in Nepal, 1980-1991. R. Shah. (C). 1992. 110.00 (*0-7855-0204-1*, Pub. by Ratna Pustak Bhandar) St Mut.

Politics in Nepal, 1980-1990. Rishikesh Shah. (C). 1991. text 70.00 (*0-7855-0151-7*, Pub. by Ratna Pustak Bhandar) St Mut.

Politics in Nepal, 1980-1990. Ed. by Rishikesh Shaha. (C). 1989. 150.00 (*0-89771-090-8*, Pub. by Ratna Pustak Bhandar) St Mut.

Politics in Nepal, 1980-1991: Referendum, Stalemate & Triumph of People Power. Rishikesh Shaha. 1992. 135.00 (*0-7855-0295-5*, Pub. by Ratna Pustak Bhandar) St Mut.

Politics in Nepal, 1980-1991: Referendum, Stalemate & Triumph of People Power. 3rd ed. Rishikesh Shaha. (C). 1993. reprint ed. text 32.00 (*81-7304-020-6*, Pub. by Manohar) S Asia.

Politics in New York State, 1800-1830. Alvin Kass. LC 65-11679. 233p. 1965. reprint ed. pap. 72.30 (*0-608-07613-9*, 205992800010) Bks Demand.

Politics in New Zealand. 2nd rev. ed. Richard Mulgan. 332p. 1997. pap. 24.95 (*1-86940-171-9*, Pub. by Auckland Univ) Paul & Co Pubs.

Politics in Nigeria. Ed. by Aborisade. (C). 1999. text. write for info. (*0-673-99284-5*) Addison-Wesley.

Politics in Nigeria. Oladimeji Aborisade. (Longman Series in Comparative Politics). 250p. 1998. pap. 38.00 (*0-321-02539-3*) Addison-Wesley Educ.

Politics in Northern Ireland. Ed. by Paul Mitchell & Rick Wilford. LC 98-27569. (Studies in Irish Politics). 352p. 1998. 75.00 (*0-8133-3527-2*, Pub. by Westview); pap. text 29.00 (*0-8133-3528-0*, Pub. by Westview) HarpC.

Politics in Palestine: Arab Factionalism & Social Disintegration, 1939-1948. Issa Khalaf. LC 90-10167. (SUNY Series in the Social & Economic History of the Middle East). (Illus.). 318p. (C). 1991. text 21.50 (*0-7914-0707-1*) State U NY Pr.

Politics in Performance: The Production Work of Edward Bond, 1978-1990. Ian Stuart. (Artists & Issues in the Theatre Ser.: Vol. 6). 191p. (C). 1996. text 37.95 (*0-8204-3014-5*) P Lang Pubng.

Politics in Place: Social Power Relations in an Australian Country Town. Ian Gray. (Illus.). 224p. (C). 1992. text 59.95 (*0-521-40426-6*) Cambridge U Pr.

***Politics in Post-Revolutionary Turkey, 1908-1913.** Aykut Kansu. LC 99-53922. (Social, Economic & Political Studies of the Middle East & Asia). 1999. write for info. (*90-04-11587-0*) Brill Academic Pubs.

Politics in Postwar Japanese Society. Joji Watanuki. LC 78-318773. (Illus.). 181p. reprint ed. pap. 56.20 (*0-608-18106-4*, 203224000078) Bks Demand.

***Politics in Republic of Ireland.** 3rd ed. John Coakley & Michael Gallagher. LC 99-31724. 392p. (C). 1999. text. write for info. (*0-415-22193-5*) Routledge.

Politics in Rhodesia: White Power in an African State. Larry W. Bowman. LC 73-75057. 224p. 1973. 34.95 (*0-674-68786-8*) HUP.

Politics in Russia. Ed. by Remington. (C). 1999. text. write for info. (*0-673-99358-2*) Addison-Wesley.

Politics in Russia. Thomas F. Remington. LC 98-4968. 368p. (C). 1998. pap. 41.40 (*0-321-00493-0*) Addison-Wesley Educ.

Politics in Sierra Leone, 1947-57. John R. Cartwright. LC 71-18592. (Scholarly Reprint Ser.). 306p. reprint ed. pap. 94.90 (*0-608-16264-7*, 202651400050) Bks Demand.

Politics in Southeast Asia. rev. ed. Clark D. Neher. 322p. 1987. 24.95 (*0-87047-010-8*); pap. 18.95 (*0-87047-011-6*) Schenkman Bks Inc.

Politics in States America: People, Parties, & Policy. Frank M. Bryan. (Special Studies). 320p. (Orig.). (C). 1981. text 41.50 (*0-89158-561-3*); pap. text 14.90 (*0-89158-984-8*) Westview.

***Politics in States & Communities.** 10th ed. 218p. 2000. teacher ed. write for info. (*0-13-022594-0*) P-H.

***Politics in States & Communities.** 10th ed. Thomas R. Dye. LC 99-29096. 536p. 1999. 56.00 (*0-13-020680-6*) P-H.

***Politics in States & Communities: Win Ph Custom Test.** 10th ed. 1999. write for info. (*0-13-022595-9*) P-H.

***Politics in Taiwan: Voting for Democracy.** Shelley Rigger. (Illus.). 256p. (Orig.). (C). 1999. text 90.00 (*0-415-17208-X*) Routledge.

Politics in Taiwan: Voting for Democracy. Shelley Riggers. LC 99-22354. 1999. pap. 27.99 (*0-415-17209-8*) Routledge.

Politics in Texasville: Locating the Texasville Regional Medical. Neiheisel. 1998. pap. text 15.73 (*0-205-29758-7*) Allyn.

Politics in Thailand: Power, Oppositions & Democratisation. Kevin Hewison. LC 97-5094. 320p. (C). 1997. 90.00 (*0-415-14795-6*) Routledge.

Politics in the African-American Novel: James Weldon Johnson, W. E. B. Dubois, Richard Wright, & Ralph Ellison, 143. Richard Kostelanetz. LC 90-19912. (Contributions in Afro-American & African Studies: No. 143). 200p. 1991. 49.95 (*0-313-27471-1*, KPM/, Greenwood Pr) Greenwood.

Politics in the Altiplano: The Dynamics of Change in Rural Peru. Edward Dew. LC 77-79542. (University of Texas, Institute of Latin American Studies, Latin American Monographs: No. 15). 234p. reprint ed. pap. 72.60 (*0-608-16492-5*, 202732900055) Bks Demand.

Politics in the American Democracy. Maggiotto. (C). 1999. pap. text 37.50 (*0-15-502199-0*, Pub. by Harcourt Coll Pubs) Harcourt.

Politics in the American Drama. Caspar H. Nannes. LC 60-50101. 272p. reprint ed. pap. 84.40 (*0-608-17236-7*, 202949500061) Bks Demand.

Politics in the American States: A Comparative Analysis. 7th ed. Virginia Gray et al. LC 99-11401. 565p. 1999. 45.95 (*1-56802-342-1*) Congr Quarterly.

Politics in the American States: A Comparative Approach. 6th ed. Ed. by Virginia Gray & Herbert Jacob. LC 95-33573. 604p. (C). (gr. 11). 1995. text 38.95 (*1-56802-035-X*) Congr Quarterly.

Politics in the American States & Communities: A Contemporary Reader. Jack R. Van Der Slik. LC 95-23598. 448p. (C). 1995. pap. text 44.00 (*0-205-16490-0*) Allyn.

Politics in the Ancient World. Moses I. Finley. (Canto Book Ser.). 160p. (C). 1991. pap. 10.95 (*0-521-40673-0*) Cambridge U Pr.

Politics in the Communist World. Leslie Holmes. (Illus.). 474p. 1987. pap. text 24.00 (*0-19-876147-3*) OUP.

Politics in the Dutch Community: The Economics of Institutional Interaction. Bart Snels. LC 99-72242. 8p. 1999. 61.95 (*1-84014-813-6*, Pub. by Ashgate Pub) Ashgate Pub Co.

Politics in the Gilded Age in New York State & Rockland County: A Biography of Senator Clarence Lexow. Isabelle K. Savelle. LC 84-10822. (Illus.). 241p. 1984. 15.00 (*0-911183-21-3*) Rockland County Hist.

Politics in the Impasse: Explorations in Postsecular Social Theory. Bill Martin, Jr. LC 95-13739. (SUNY Series in Radical, Socical & Political Theory). 300p. (C). 1996. text 59.50 (*0-7914-2793-5*); pap. text 19.95 (*0-7914-2794-3*) State U NY Pr.

***Politics in the Middle East.** 5th ed. Bill. LC 99-29689. 350p. (C). 1999. pap. text 48.00 (*0-321-00537-6*) Addison-Wesley.

Politics in the Netherlands: How Much Change. Ed. by Hans Daalder & Galen I. Irwin. 1989. lib. bdg. 30.00 (*0-7146-3361-5*, F3361, Pub. by F Cass Pubs) Intl Spec Bk.

Politics in the New South: Republicanism, Race, & Leadership in the Twentieth Century. 2nd ed. Richard K. Scher. LC 96-30362. 432p. (C). 1997. text 76.95 (*1-56324-847-6*) M E Sharpe.

Politics in the New South: Republicanism, Race, & Leadership in the Twentieth Century. 2nd ed. Richard K. Scher. LC 96-30362. 432p. (C). (gr. 13). 1997. pap. text 27.95 (*1-56324-848-4*) M E Sharpe.

Politics in the Poetry of Coleridge. Carl R. Woodring. LC 61-11643. 272p. reprint ed. pap. 84.40 (*0-8357-9778-3*, 201537400002) Bks Demand.

Politics in the Portuguese Empire: The State, Industry, & Cotton, 1926-1974. M. Anne Pitcher. LC 92-41457. (Illus.). 344p. (C). 1993. text 75.00 (*0-19-827373-8*, Clarendon Pr) OUP.

Politics in the Postwar American West. Ed. by Richard Lowitt. LC 94-43095. (Illus.). 400p. 1995. 49.50 (*0-8061-2711-2*) U of Okla Pr.

Politics in the Postwar American West. Ed. by Richard Lowitt. LC 94-43095. (Illus.). 416p. 1995. pap. 21.95 (*0-8061-2741-4*) U of Okla Pr.

Politics in the Purple Kingdom: The Derailment of Vatican II. George A. Schlichte. Ed. by Joan Stockbridge. LC 92-44098. 160p. (Orig.). 1993. pap. 9.95 (*1-55612-607-7*) Sheed & Ward WI.

***Politics in the Republic of Ireland.** 3rd ed. John Coakley & Michael Gallagher. LC 99-31724. 392p. 1999. pap. 22.99 (*0-415-22194-3*) Routledge.

Politics in the Street. Bob Purdie. 352p. 1990. pap. 19.95 (*0-85640-437-3*, Pub. by Blackstaff Pr) Dufour.

Politics in the Twentieth Century. Hans J. Morgenthau. LC 62-18111. 1962. 45.00 (*0-226-53824-9*) U Ch Pr.

Politics in the Twentieth Century, 3 vols. Incl. Vol. 1. Decline of Democratic Politics. LC 62-18111. 443p. 1962. pap. 137.40 (*0-608-18598-1*, 202012600001); Vol. 2. Impasse of American Foreign Policy. LC 62-18111. 320p. 1962. pap. 99.20 (*0-608-18599-X*, 202012600002); Vol. 3. Restoration of American Politics. LC 62-18111. 401p. 124.40 (*0-608-16078-4*, 202012600003); LC 62-18111. reprint ed. pap. write for info. (*0-608-18684-8*, 2020126) Bks Demand.

Politics in the Twenty-First Century. National Issues Institute Staff. 48p. 1993. 4.00 incl. disk (*0-8403-8393-2*) Kendall-Hunt.

Politics in the U. S. Julian Foster. LC 96-116518. 288p. (C). 1995. pap. text, per. write for info. (*0-7872-0573-7*) Kendall-Hunt.

***Politics in the U. S. A.** M. J. Vile. LC 98-49516. 1999. write for info. (*0-415-18729-X*); pap. 24.99 (*0-415-18730-3*) Routledge.

Politics in the United Nations: A Study of United States Influence in the General Assembly. Robert E. Riggs. LC 83-20164. 208p. 1984. reprint ed. lib. bdg. 59.50 (*0-313-24298-4*, RIP0, Greenwood Pr) Greenwood.

Politics in the United Nations System. Ed. by Lawrence S. Finkelstein. LC 87-27240. xvi, 503p. (C). 1988. text 79.95 (*0-8223-0804-5*); pap. text 29.95 (*0-8223-0820-7*) Duke.

***Politics in the Vernacular: Nationalism, Multiculturalism, & Citizenship.** Will Kymlicka. 240p. 2000. pap. 18.95 (*0-19-924098-1*); text 65.00 (*0-19-829665-7*) OUP.

Politics in Transition: Restructuring Britain. Ed. by Allan Cochrane & James Anderson. 264p. (C). 1989. text 47.00 (*0-8039-8201-1*); pap. text 17.95 (*0-8039-8202-X*) Sage.

Politics in War: The Bases of Political Community in South Vietnam. Allan E. Goodman. LC 72-96629. 328p. 1973. 34.50 (*0-674-68825-2*) HUP.

Politics in West Africa, Series X (1965) William A. Lewis. LC 81-13317. (Whidden Lectures for 1965). 90p. 1982. reprint ed. lib. bdg. 55.00 (*0-313-23202-4*, LEPW, Greenwood Pr) Greenwood.

Politics in West Germany. Russell J. Dalton. 376p. (C). 1989. pap. text 29.73 (*0-673-39887-0*) Addison-Wesley Educ.

Politics in Western Europe. 2nd ed. Ed. by Gerald A. Dorfman & Peter J. Duignan. (Publication Ser.: No. 404). 438p. 1991. pap. 18.95 (*0-8179-9122-0*) Hoover Inst Pr.

Politics in Western Europe: A Comparative Analysis. 5th ed. Gordon Smith. LC 83-22878. 350p. 1989. pap. 19.95 (*0-8419-1263-7*) Holmes & Meier.

Politics in Western Europe: A Comparative Analysis. 5th ed. Gordon Smith. LC 83-22878. 350p. 1989. 44.50 (*0-8419-1262-9*) Holmes & Meier.

Politics in Western Europe: An Introduction to the Politics of the United Kingdom, France, Germany, Italy, Sweden, & the European Union. 2nd ed. M. Donald Hancock et al. LC 96-9309. (Illus.). 640p. (C). 1998. pap. text 42.95 (*1-56643-039-9*, Chatham House Pub) Seven Bridges.

Politics in Western Europe Today: Perspectives, Policies & Problems since 1980. Derek W. Urwin. (C). 1990. text 45.25 (*0-582-05824-4*, Pub. by Addison-Wesley) Longman.

Politics in Western Europe Today: Perspectives, Policies & Problems since 1980. Ed. by Derek W. Urwin & William E. Paterson. 299p. (C). 1990. pap. text 42.00 (*0-582-00295-8*, 78499) Longman.

Politics in Wired Nations. Ithiel De Sola Pool. Ed. by Lloyd S. Etheredge. LC 97-51703. 395p. 1997. text 28.95 (*1-56000-344-8*) Transaction Pubs.

P

An Asterisk (*) at the beginning of an entry indicates that the title is appearing for the first time.

Politics in Wisconsin. Leon D. Epstein. LC 58-13445. (Illus.). 232p. reprint ed. pap. 72.00 (*0-7837-5900-2*, 204569100007) Bks Demand.

Politics, Innocence & the Limits of Goodness. Peter Johnson. 320p. 1989. 35.00 (*0-415-01046-2*) Routledge.

Politics, Innocence & the Limits of Goodness. Peter Johnson. LC 88-11376. 293p. reprint ed. pap. 90.90 (*0-608-20351-3*, 207160400002) Bks Demand.

Politics, Institutions & the Economic Performance of Nations. Clemens L. Siermann. LC 98-9826. 272p. 1998. 90.00 (*1-85898-609-5*) E Elgar.

Politics, Interdenominational Relations & Education in the Public Ministry of Bishop James Doyle of Kildare & Leighlin, 1786-1834: A Study of Politics Interdenominational Relations & Education. Thomas McGrath. LC 99-191730. 368p. 1999. boxed set 55.00 (*1-85182-372-7*, Pub. by Four Cts Pr) Intl Spec Bk.

Politics, Language, & Thought: The Somali Experience. David D Laitin. LC 76-22958. (Illus.). 280p. 1977. lib. bdg. 28.00 (*0-226-46791-0*) U Ch Pr.

Politics, Language & Time: Essays on Political Thought & History. J. G. Pocock. viii, 304p. 1989. pap. text 16.95 (*0-226-67139-9*) U Ch Pr.

***Politics, Law & Counsel in Tudor & Early Stuart England.** 330p. 2000. 105.95 (*0-86078-832-6*, Pub. by Ashgate Pub) Ashgate Pub Co.

***Politics, Law & Morality: Essays.** Vladimir S. Solovyov & Vladimir Wozniuk. LC 99-41463. (Russian Literature & Thought Ser.). (Illus.). 384p. 2000. 40.00 (*0-300-07995-8*) Yale U Pr.

Politics, Law & Order in 19th Century Ireland. Virginia Crossman. 300p. 1996. 70.00 (*0-7171-2001-5*, Pub. by Gill & MacMill) Irish Bks Media.

Politics, Law, & Social Change: Selected Essays. Otto Kircheimer. Ed. by Frederic S. Burin & Kurt L. Shell. LC 69-16955. (Records of Civilization: Sources & Studies). 483p. 1969. text 58.00 (*0-231-03191-2*) Col U Pr.

Politics, Law & the Church: An Examination of the Relationship Between Catholicism & American Law. Gregory M. Faulhaber. LC 96-42953. (Distinguished Research Ser.). 472p. 1996. 69.95 (*1-57309-103-0*); pap. 49.95 (*1-57309-102-2*) Intl Scholars.

Politics, Leadership, & Justice: An International Collection of Literature, Philosophy, & Poetry Specially Selected for Book Discussion Groups by the Great Books Foundation. Ed. & Intro. by Great Bks. Foundation Staff. LC 98-13670. (Fiftieth Anniversary Ser.). 384p. (Orig.). 1998. pap. 14.95 (*1-880323-81-8*) Great Bks Found.

***Politics, Literature & National Character.** Germaine De Stael & Morroe Berger. 321p. 2000. pap. 29.95 (*0-7658-0645-2*) Transaction Pubs.

Politics, Logic & Love: The Life of Jean van Heijenoort. 2nd ed. Anita Burdman Feferman. LC 93-9854. (Illus.). 432p. 1993. 44.00 (*1-56881-022-9*) AK Peters.

Politics Mainly Indian. W. H. Morris-Jones. 392p. 1978. 19.95 (*0-318-36605-3*) Asia Bk Corp.

Politics, Markets, & America's Schools. John E. Chubb & Terry M. Moe. 318p. 1990. 39.95 (*0-8157-1410-6*) Brookings.

Politics, Markets, & America's Schools. John E. Chubb & Terry M. Moe. 318p. 1990. pap. 18.95 (*0-8157-1409-2*) Brookings.

Politics, Markets & Congressional Policy Choices. Peter M. VanDoren. (Illus.). 216p. 1991. text 47.50 (*0-472-10238-9*, 10238) U of Mich Pr.

Politics, Markets & Grand Strategy. Lars S. Skalnes. (Illus.). 320p. (C). text 52.50 (*0-472-11031-4*, 11031) U of Mich Pr.

Politics, Markets, & Security: European Military & Civil Aircraft Collaboration, 1954-1994. Bonnie Gold. LC 94-41431. 1995. 34.50 (*0-8191-9809-9*) U Pr of Amer.

Politics, Media, & Modern Democracy: An International Study of Innovations in Electoral Campaigning & Their Consequences. Ed. by David L. Swanson & Paolo Mancini. LC 95-43773. (Praeger Series in Political Communication). 304p. 1996. 75.00 (*0-275-95182-0*, Praeger Pubs); pap. 22.95 (*0-275-95183-9*, Praeger Pubs) Greenwood.

Politics, Minerals, & Survival: Proceedings of a Symposium. Ed. by Ralph W. Marsden. LC 74-27310. 103p. reprint ed. pap. 32.00 (*0-8357-6792-2*, 203546900095) Bks Demand.

Politics, Misunderstandings, Misconceptions: The History of Colonial Universities. Shiame Okunor. LC 90-22144. (American University Studies: Education: Ser. XIV, Vol. 26). 196p. (C). 1991. text 34.95 (*0-8204-1176-0*) P Lang Pubng.

Politics, Morality, & Higher Education: Essays in Honor of Samuel DuBois Cook. Ed. by F. Thomas Trotter & Charles E. Cole. LC 97-67344. 128p. (Orig.). 1997. pap. 12.95 (*1-57736-058-3*) Providence Hse.

Politics, Movies & the Role of Government. John W. Cones. (Hollywood Ser.). 298p. 1996. pap. 23.95 (*1-890341-05-3*) Rivas Canyon.

Politics Needs Literature. Ed. by Brynmill Press Ltd. Staff. (C). 1989. 40.00 (*0-907839-13-4*, Pub. by Brynmill Pr Ltd) St Mut.

Politics of a Colonial Career: Jose Baquijano & the Audiencia of Lima. Mark A. Burkholder. LC 80-52279. 205p. reprint ed. pap. 63.60 (*0-608-15372-9*, 202932200060) Bks Demand.

Politics of a Colonial Career: Jose Baquijano & the Audiencia of Lima. 2nd ed. Mark A. Burkholder. LC 89-39564. (Latin American Silhouettes Ser.). 184p. (C). 1989. reprint ed. pap. 17.95 (*0-8420-2352-6*) Scholarly Res Inc.

Politics of a Colonial Career: Jose Baquijano & the Audiencia of Lima. 2nd ed. Mark A. Burkholder. LC 89-39564. (Latin American Silhouettes Ser.). 184p. (C). 1990. reprint ed. 45.00 (*0-8420-2353-4*) Scholarly Res Inc.

Politics of a Literary Man: William Gilmore Simms, 5. Jon L. Wakelyn. LC 72-845. (Contributions in American Studies: No. 5). 306p. 1973. 65.00 (*0-8371-6414-1*, WPL/, Greenwood Pr) Greenwood.

Politics of a Persian Dynasty: The Hecatomnids in the Fourth Century B. C. Stephen Ruzicka. LC 92-54138. (Oklahoma Series in Classical Culture: Vol. 14). 256p. 1992. 42.50 (*0-8061-2460-1*) U of Okla Pr.

Politics of a Popular Uprising: Bundelkhand in 1857. Tapti Roy. (Illus.). 302p. 1995. text 28.00 (*0-19-563612-0*) OUP.

Politics of a Prison Riot. Adolph Saenz. (Illus.). 190p. (Orig.). 1986. pap. 8.50 (*0-936455-00-4*) Rhombus Pub.

Politics of Abortion. Raymond Tatalovich et al. LC 81-11914. 248p. 1981. 55.00 (*0-275-90730-9*, C0730, Praeger Pubs) Greenwood.

Politics of Abortion & Birth Control in Historical Perspective. Ed. by Donald T. Critchlow. (Issues in Policy History Ser.: Vol. 5). 184p. 1996. pap. 16.95 (*0-271-01570-5*) Pa St U Pr.

Politics of Abortion in the United States & Canada: A Comparative Study. Raymond Tatalovich. LC 96-23923. (Comparative Politics Ser.). (Illus.). 278p. (gr. 13). 1996. pap. text 30.95 (*1-56324-418-7*) M E Sharpe.

Politics of Abortion in the United States & Canada: A Comparative Study. Raymond Tatalovich. LC 96-23923. (Comparative Politics Ser.). (Illus.). 278p. (C). (gr. 13). 1996. text 64.95 (*1-56324-417-9*) M E Sharpe.

Politics of Academic Culture: Foibles, Fables, & Facts. Heinz Eulau. LC 97-33756. 224p. 1997. pap. 24.95 (*1-56643-061-5*, Chatham House Pub) Seven Bridges.

Politics of Accommodation: Pluralism & Democracy in the Netherlands. 2nd rev. ed. Arend Lijphart. LC 68-11667. 255p. reprint ed. pap. 79.10 (*0-608-18025-4*, 202905100058) Bks Demand.

***Politics of Accommodation & Resistance in the Black Church: A Gramscian Analysis.** Rupe Simms. LC 00-38659. (Studies in Religion & Society: Vol. 46). 252p. 2000. 89.95 (*0-7734-7696-2*) E Mellen.

Politics of Accountability: Educative & International Perspectives. Reynold J. Macpherson. LC 98-154496. (Yearbook of the Politics of Education Association Ser.). 240p. 1998. pap. 24.95 (*0-8039-6687-3*) Corwin Pr.

Politics of Administration: The Malaysian Experience. Mavis Puthucheary. 1978. 32.50 (*0-19-580386-8*) OUP.

Politics of Affirmative Action: Women, Equality & Category Politics. Carol L. Bacchi. 224p. 1996. 75.00 (*0-8039-8792-7*); pap. 24.95 (*0-8039-8793-5*) Sage.

Politics of Afghanistan. Richard S. Newell. Ed. by Richard L. Park. LC 78-176487. (Illus.). 254p. 1972. text 42.50 (*0-8014-0688-9*) Cornell U Pr.

Politics of Africa: Dependence & Development. Ed. by Timothy M. Shaw & Kenneth A. Heard. LC 83-5749. (Dalhousie African Studies). 412p. 1979. reprint ed. pap. 127.80 (*0-608-03610-2*, 206443300009) Bks Demand.

Politics of Africa's Economic Recovery. Richard Sandbrook. LC 92-10888. (African Society Today Ser.). (Illus.). 180p. (C). 1993. text 54.95 (*0-521-41543-8*); pap. text 15.95 (*0-521-42563-8*) Cambridge U Pr.

Politics of Age & Gerontocracy in Africa. Ed. by Mario I. Aguilar. LC 98-27563. 250p. 1997. 79.95 (*0-86543-597-9*); pap. 21.95 (*0-86543-598-7*) Africa World.

Politics of Agrarian Change in Asia & Latin America. Ed. by Howard Handelman. LC 81-47565. (Illus.). 144p. reprint ed. pap. 44.70 (*0-608-18253-2*, 205670300081) Bks Demand.

Politics of Agricultural Cooperativization in China: Mao, Deng Zihui & the High Tide of 1955. Ed. by Frederick C. Teiwes & Warren Sun. Tr. by Hongyi Lai from CHI. LC 93-6434. 230p. (C). (gr. 13). 1993. pap. text 62.95 (*1-56324-382-2*, East Gate Bk) M E Sharpe.

Politics of Agricultural Labor: From Slavery to Freedom in a Cotton Culture, 1862-1902. rev. ed. Robert Hinton. LC 97-8412. (Studies in the History of American Labor). 193p. 1997. text 58.00 (*0-8153-2541-X*) Garland.

Politics of Agricultural Policy-Making in Canada. Grace D. Skogstad. 229p. 1987. text 35.00 (*0-8020-5728-4*) U of Toronto Pr.

Politics of Agricultural Research. Don F. Hadwiger. LC 81-24077. 240p. reprint ed. pap. 74.40 (*0-8357-3801-9*, 203652900003) Bks Demand.

Politics of Agricultural Support in Britain: The Development of the Agricultural Policy Community. Martin J. Smith. (Illus.). 264p. 1990. text 77.95 (*1-85521-001-0*, Pub. by Dartmth Pub) Ashgate Pub Co.

***Politics of Agriculture in Japan.** Aurelia George. LC 99-41427. 800p. 1999. 125.00 (*0-415-22346-6*) Routledge.

Politics of Agriculture in Tropical Africa. Ed. by Jonathan Barker. LC 84-2013. (Sage Series in African Modernization & Development: No. 9). 320p. 1984. reprint ed. pap. 99.20 (*0-608-01499-0*, 205954300001) Bks Demand.

Politics of AIDS. Virginia Van der Vliet. 160p. 1995. pap. 14.95 (*0-906097-24-X*) LPC InBook.

Politics of Airline Deregulation. Anthony E. Brown. LC 86-30888. 240p. 1987. reprint ed. pap. 74.40 (*0-608-07983-9*, 206794800012) Bks Demand.

Politics of Alcoholism: Building An Arena Around a Social Problem. Carolyn Wiener. LC 79-66450. 310p. 1981. 39.95 (*0-87855-379-7*) Transaction Pubs.

Politics of Alternative Theatre in Britain, 1968-1990: The Case of 7:84 (Scotland) Maria DiCenzo. LC 97-5359. (Studies in Modern Theatre). (Illus.). 261p. (C). 1996. text 59.95 (*0-521-55456-X*) Cambridge U Pr.

Politics of Ambiguity: Self, Culture, & Society in the Works of Jean-Jacques Rousseau. Mira Morgenstern. LC 95-44174. 1996. 45.00 (*0-271-01572-1*); pap. 18.95 (*0-271-01573-X*) Pa St U Pr.

Politics of America in Texas. 2nd ed. Dye. 1997. pap. text, student ed. 20.80 (*0-13-259276-2*) P-H.

Politics of American Cities: Private Power & Public Policy. 3rd ed. Dennis R. Judd. (C). 1988. pap. text 29.33 (*0-673-39730-0*) Addson-Wesley Educ.

Politics of American Discontent: How a New Party Can Make Democracy Work Again. Gordon S. Black & Benjamin Black. 262p. 1994. 22.95 (*0-471-59853-4*) Wiley.

Politics of American Economic Policy Making. Ed. by Paul Peretz. LC 87-12827. 464p. (C). (gr. 13). 1987. text 83.95 (*0-87332-406-4*); pap. text 32.95 (*0-87332-407-2*) M E Sharpe.

Politics of American Economic Policy Making. 2nd ed. Ed. by Paul Peretz. LC 95-41956. (Illus.). 520p. (C). (gr. 13). 1996. text 79.95 (*1-56324-566-3*); pap. text 38.95 (*1-56324-567-1*) M E Sharpe.

Politics of American Government. 2nd ed. Stephen J. Wayne et al. LC 96-69851. 864p. 1996. pap. text 63.95 (*0-312-13775-3*); pap. text 53.95 (*0-312-13915-2*) St Martin.

***Politics of American Government.** 3rd ed. Wayne. 1999. pap. text 66.95 (*0-312-19093-X*); pap. text 50.95 (*0-312-19094-8*) St Martin.

Politics of American Government: Basic Edition. Wayne et al. 2000. pap. text 37.00 (*0-312-11944-5*) St Martin.

Politics of American Government: Complete Edition. Wayne et al. 2000. pap. text 44.50 (*0-312-11946-1*) St Martin.

Politics of American Government: Instructor's Manual. 2nd ed. Herbert M. Levine. 1997. teacher ed. 13.33 (*0-312-15315-5*) St Martin.

Politics of American Government: Study Guide. 2nd ed. Herbert M. Levine. 1997. pap. text, student ed. 23.95 (*0-312-11148-7*) St Martin.

Politics of American Government: Test Item File. 2nd ed. Paul Benson & Pauletta Otis. 1997. 33.32 (*0-312-15316-3*) St Martin.

Politics of American Government - State & Local: Basic Edition. Wayne et al. 2000. text 38.00 (*0-312-11953-4*) St Martin.

Politics of American Government - State & Local: Complete Edition. Wayne et al. 2000. pap. text 44.50 (*0-312-11954-2*) St Martin.

Politics of American Government Brief Edition. Stephen Wayne et al. LC 97-80010. 464p. 1997. pap. text 42.95 (*0-312-17786-0*) St Martin.

Politics of American Individualism: Herbert Hoover in Transition, 1918-1921. Gary D. Best. LC 75-16960. 202p. 1975. 52.95 (*0-8371-8160-7*, BPA/, Greenwood Pr) Greenwood.

Politics of American Science: 1939 to the Present. rev. ed. James L. Penick et al. 250p. 1972. reprint ed. pap. text 12.50 (*0-262-66014-8*) MIT Pr.

Politics of an Emerging Profession: The American Library Association, 1876-1917, 56. Wayne A. Wiegand. LC 85-12679. (Contributions in Librarianship & Information Science Ser.: No. 56). (Illus.). 331p. 1986. 55.00 (*0-313-25022-7*, WPD/) Greenwood.

Politics of an Erasmian Lawyer: Vasco de Quiroga. Ross Dealy. (Humana Civilitas Ser.: Vol.3). 33p. (C). 1976. pap. 6.00 (*0-89003-015-4*) Undena Pubns.

Politics of Annexation: Oligarchic Power in a Southern City. John V. Moeser & Rutledge M. Dennis. 232p. 1982. 22.95 (*0-87073-501-2*); pap. 15.95 (*0-87073-502-0*) Schenkman Bks Inc.

Politics of Antagonism: Understanding Northern Ireland. Brendan Oleary. (Conflict & Change in Britain - A New Audit Ser.). (C). 1996. pap. 22.50 (*0-485-80110-8*) Humanities.

Politics of Anthropology: From Colonialism & Sexism Toward a View from Below. Ed. by Gerrit Huizer & Bruce Mannheim. (World Anthropology Ser.). xii, 520p. 1979. text 73.10 (*90-279-7750-X*) Mouton.

Politics of Anti-Japanese Sentiment in Korea: Japanese-South Korean Relations under American Occupation, 1945-1952, 24. Sung-Hwa Cheong. LC 90-47325. (Contributions to the Study of World History Ser.: No. 24). 208p. 1991. 55.00 (*0-313-27410-X*, CJK/, Greenwood Pr) Greenwood.

Politics of Antipolitics: The Military in Latin America. 3rd rev. ed. Ed. by Brian Loveman et al. LC 96-9466. (Latin American Silhouettes Ser.). 438p. (C). 1996. 55.00 (*0-8420-2609-6*); pap. 23.95 (*0-8420-2611-8*) Scholarly Res Inc.

Politics of Aristocratic Empires. John H. Kautsky. LC 96-17936. 430p. 1997. pap. text 24.95 (*1-56000-913-6*) Transaction Pubs.

Politics of Aristocratic Empires. John H. Kautsky. LC 81-12983. 432p. reprint ed. pap. 134.00 (*0-8357-3905-8*, 203663900004) Bks Demand.

Politics of Aristotle. Aristotle. Tr. & Intro. by Peter L. Phillips Simpson. LC 96-30395. 1997. 45.00 (*0-8078-2327-9*) U of NC Pr.

Politics of Aristotle. Aristotle. Tr. & Intro. by Peter L. Phillips Simpson. LC 96-30395. 336p. (C). (gr. 13). 1997. pap. 14.95 (*0-8078-4637-6*) U of NC Pr.

Politics of Aristotle, 4 vols. Aristotle. LC 72-9297. (Philosophy of Plato & Aristotle Ser.). (ENG & GRE.). 1973. reprint ed. 169.95 (*0-405-04848-3*) Ayer.

Politics of Aristotle, 4 vols., 1. Aristotle. LC 72-9297. (Philosophy of Plato & Aristotle Ser.). (ENG & GRE.). 1976. reprint ed. 42.95 (*0-405-04849-1*) Ayer.

Politics of Aristotle, 4 vols., Vol. 2. Aristotle. LC 72-9297. (Philosophy of Plato & Aristotle Ser.). (ENG & GRE.). 1976. reprint ed. 42.95 (*0-405-04850-5*) Ayer.

Politics of Aristotle, 4 vols., Vol. 3. Aristotle. LC 72-9297. (Philosophy of Plato & Aristotle Ser.). (ENG & GRE.). 1976. reprint ed. 42.95 (*0-405-04851-3*) Ayer.

Politics of Aristotle, 4 vols., Vol. 4. Aristotle. LC 72-9297. (Philosophy of Plato & Aristotle Ser.). (ENG & GRE.). 1976. reprint ed. 42.95 (*0-405-04852-1*) Ayer.

Politics of Arms Control Treaty Ratification. Ed. by Michael Krepon & Dan Caldwell. (Henry L. Stimson Center Bk.). 380p. 1992. text 45.00 (*0-312-06604-X*) St Martin.

Politics of Assimilation: Hegemony & Its Aftermath. Charles F. Doran. LC 77-148241. 237p. reprint ed. pap. 73.50 (*0-608-12098-7*, 202413700035) Bks Demand.

Politics of Association in Europe. John N. Kinnas. 122p. 1982. 17.95 (*3-593-32371-0*) Irvington.

Politics of Attachment: Towards a Secure Society. Ed. by Sebastian Kraemer & Jane Roberts. 200p. (C). 1997. 45.00 (*1-85343-343-8*); pap. 19.50 (*1-85343-344-6*) NYU Pr.

Politics of Australia. Dean Jaensch. 452p. 1994. 69.95 (*0-7329-0397-1*); pap. 36.95 (*0-7329-0396-3*) Paul & Co Pubs.

Politics of Australian Child Care: Philanthropy to Feminism & Beyond. rev. ed. Deborah Brennan. LC 97-52187. (Illus.). 272p. (C). 1998. pap. text 24.95 (*0-521-63510-1*) Cambridge U Pr.

Politics of Authenticity. Douglas Rossinow. 1999. pap. 18.50 (*0-231-11057-X*) Col U Pr.

Politics of Authenticity: Liberalism, Christianity, & the New Left in America. Douglas C. Rossinow. LC 97-42950. (Contemporary American History Ser.). 520p. 1998. 34.50 (*0-231-11056-1*) Col U Pr.

Politics of Automobile Insurance Reform: Ideas, Institutions & Public Policy in North America. Edward L. Lascher, Jr. LC 99-18215. (American Governance & Public Policy Ser.). 160p. 1999. 69.00 (*0-87840-739-1*) Georgetown U Pr.

***Politics of Bacteria, Docile Bodies, Ronde de Nuit.** Lewis Baltz. (Illus.). 60p. 1998. 26.00 (*0-914357-57-3*, Pub. by Los Angeles Mus Contemp) RAM Publications.

Politics of Bad Faith: The Radical Assault on America's Future. David Horowitz. LC 98-21614. 224p. 1998. 25.00 (*0-684-85023-0*) S&S Trade.

***Politics of Bad Faith: The Radical Assault on Americas Future.** David Horowitz. 224p. 2000. per. 13.00 (*0-684-85679-4*) S&S Trade.

Politics of Balanced Interdependence: Nepal & SAARC. Lok R. Baral. 1988. 50.00 (*0-7855-0294-7*, Pub. by Ratna Pustak Bhandar) St Mut.

Politics of Balanced Interdependence: Nepal & Saarc. Lok R. Baral. 140p. (C). 1988. 150.00 (*0-89771-089-4*, Pub. by Ratna Pustak Bhandar) St Mut.

***Politics of Ballistic Missile.** Bowen. LC 99-16201. 1999. text 65.00 (*0-312-22618-7*) St Martin.

Politics of Bargaining: The Merger Process & British Trade Union Structural Development, 1892-1987. Jeremy Waddington. LC 94-48179. 256p. 1995. 100.00 (*0-7201-2245-7*) Continuum.

Politics of "Basic Needs" Urban Aspects of Assaulting Poverty in Africa. Richard Sandbrook. 320p. 1982. text 35.00 (*0-8020-2428-9*); pap. text 15.95 (*0-8020-6439-6*) U of Toronto Pr.

Politics of Bavaria: A Guide to the Political System of Germany's Largest Federal State. Peter James. LC 95-78043. 240p. 1995. 72.95 (*1-85972-166-4*, Pub. by Avebry) Ashgate Pub Co.

Politics of Being: The Political Thought of Martin Heidegger. Richard Wolin. 221p. (C). 1992. pap. text 18.50 (*0-231-07315-1*) Col U Pr.

Politics of Being Mortal. Alfred G. Killilea. LC 88-9422. 184p. 1988. 25.00 (*0-8131-1643-0*) U Pr of Ky.

Politics of Belief in Nineteenth-Century France. Philip Spencer. LC 77-80592. 284p. 1973. reprint ed. 35.00 (*0-86527-156-9*) Fertig.

Politics of Belonging: Migrants & Minorities in Contemporary Europe. Ed. by Andrew Geddes & Adrian Favell. LC 98-47214. (Contemporary Trends in European Social Sciences Ser.). 227p. (C). 1999. text 61.95 (*1-84014-177-8*, Pub. by Ashgate Pub) Ashgate Pub Co.

Politics of Benevolence: Revival Religion & American Voting Behavior. John L. Hammond. LC 78-16050. 256p. 1979. text 73.25 (*0-89391-013-9*) Ablx Pub.

Politics of Biblical Theology: A Postmodern Reading. David Penshansky. LC 95-5759. (Studies in American Biblical Hermeneutics: Vol. 10). 1995. 18.00 (*0-86554-462-X*, MUP-P115) Mercer Univ Pr.

Politics of Black Empowerment: The Transformation of Black Activism in Urban America. James Jennings. LC 91-25944. (African American Life Ser.). 234p. 1992. 31.95 (*0-8143-2317-0*) Wayne St U Pr.

Politics of Black Nationalism: From Harlem to Soweto. Kinfe Abraham. LC 89-81532. 1991. 34.95 (*0-86543-155-8*); pap. 12.95 (*0-86543-156-6*) Africa World.

Politics of Blame: Family Planning, Abortion & the Poor. Patricia Donovan. LC 97-229030. (Illus.). 48p. 1994. pap. 20.00 (*0-939253-37-2*, PP9) Guttmacher Inst.

Politics of Breast Cancer Screening. Alison Mann. (Developments in Nursing & Health Care Ser.: Vol. 8). 176p. 1996. 63.95 (*1-85972-323-3*, Pub. by Avebry) Ashgate Pub Co.

Politics of Breastfeeding. Gabrielle Palmer. (Illus.). 309p. 1993. pap. text 15.00 (*0-04-440877-3*) NYU Pr.

Politics of Breastfeeding. Gabrielle Palmer. 1989. pap. 14.95 (*0-86358-220-6*, Pub. by Pandora) Harper SF.

Politics of Britain Defence 1979-98. Lawrence Freedman. LC 98-35648. 1999. text 65.00 (*0-312-22273-4*) St Martin.

P

Politics of Britain, 1688-1800. Jeremy Black. LC 93-10228. (New Frontiers in History Ser.). 1993. text 29.95 (*0-7190-3761-1*, Pub. by Manchester Univ Pr) St Martin.

***Politics of British Arms Sales since 1964: To Secure Our Rightful Share.** Mark Phythian. LC 00-21988. 2000. pap. write for info. (*0-7190-5907-0*, Pub. by Manchester Univ Pr) St Martin.

Politics of British Arms Sales Since 1964: To Secure Our Rights. Mark Phythian. text. write for info. (*0-7190-5196-7*, Pub. by Manchester Univ Pr) St Martin.

Politics of British Feminism, 1918-1970. Oliver Banks. 160p. 1993. 85.00 (*1-85278-108-4*) E Elgar.

Politics of Budget Control: Congress, the Presidency & Growth of the Administrative State. John A. Marini. 300p. 1992. 79.95 (*0-8448-1716-3*, Crane Russak); pap. 32.95 (*0-8448-1717-1*, Crane Russak) Taylor & Francis.

Politics of Building Your Own Home: How to Deal with Building Codes. 1991. lib. bdg. 79.95 (*0-8490-4739-0*) Gordon Pr.

Politics of Bureaucracy. 3rd ed. B. Guy Peters. 300p. (C). 1989. pap. text 26.95 (*0-8013-0066-5*, 75730) Longman.

Politics of Bureaucracy. 4th ed. Peter Guy. (C). 1995. pap. text. write for info. (*0-8013-1538-7*) Addison-Wesley.

Politics of Bureaucracy. 4th ed. Peter Guy. (C). 1995. pap. text. write for info. (*0-8013-1475-5*) Addison-Wesley.

Politics of Business Organizations: Understanding the Role of State Chambers of Commerce. William De Soto. LC 95-36957. 160p. (Orig.). (C). 1995. pap. text 26.50 (*0-7618-0098-0*); lib. bdg. 48.00 (*0-7618-0097-2*) U Pr of Amer.

Politics of Canada's Airlines: From Diefenbaker to Mulroney. Garth Stevenson. (State & Economic Life Ser.). 254p. 1984. pap. 14.95 (*0-8020-6637-2*); text 37.50 (*0-8020-5713-6*) U of Toronto Pr.

Politics of Canadian Broadcasting, 1920-1951. Frank W. Peers. LC 78-430275. 474p. reprint ed. pap. 147.00 (*0-608-15413-X*, 202934200060) Bks Demand.

Politics of Canadian Public Policy. Ed. by Michael M. Atkinson & Marsha A. Chandler. 296p. 1983. pap. text 18.95 (*0-8020-6517-1*) U of Toronto Pr.

Politics of Cancer Revisited. Samuel S. Epstein. LC 98-41094. 1998. pap. 21.95 (*0-914896-47-4*) East Ridge Pr.

Politics of Cancer Revisited. Samuel S. Epstein. LC 98-41094. 790p. 1998. 34.95 (*0-914896-46-6*) East Ridge Pr.

Politics of Capital Investment: The Case of Philadelphia. Carolyn T. Adams. LC 88-2274. (SUNY Series in Urban Public Policy). 202p. (C). 1988. text 24.50 (*0-88706-847-2*) State U NY Pr.

Politics of Catherinian Russia: The Panin Party. David L. Ransel. LC 74-29736. 337p. reprint ed. pap. 104.50 (*0-8357-8276-X*, 203386500087) Bks Demand.

Politics of Central Banks. Robert Elgie & Helen Thompson. LC 98-4866. 200p. (C). 1998. 85.00 (*0-415-14422-1*) Routledge.

Politics of Central Europe. Atilla Agh. LC 98-60274. (Politics Texts Ser.). ix, 244 p. 1998. write for info. (*0-7619-5032-X*) Sage.

Politics of Change. Karen Vogel. (C). 1996. pap. text. write for info. (*0-8013-1692-8*) Addison-Wesley.

Politics of Change. Karen Vogel. (C). 1998. pap. text. write for info. (*0-8013-0830-5*) Addison-Wesley.

***Politics of Change: A Brief History.** Robert N. Crittenden. 352p. 2000. pap. 16.95 (*0-9671290-1-X*) Hargrave Pubg.

Politics of Change: A Jamaican Testament. rev. ed. Michael Manley. 1990. pap. 15.95 (*0-88258-029-9*) Howard U Pr.

***Politics of Change: Globalization, Ideology & Critique.** Werner Bonefeld & Kosmas Psychopedis. LC 00-42063. 2000. write for info. (*0-312-23559-3*) St Martin.

Politics of Change: The Soviet Union & Its Successor States. Carol Barner-Barry & Cynthia A. Hody. 372p. 1995. pap. text 34.95 (*0-312-09079-X*) St Martin.

Politics of Change: The Transformation of the Former Soviet Union. Carol Barner-Barry & Cynthia A. Hody. 384p. 1995. text 45.00 (*0-312-12264-0*) St Martin.

Politics of Change in a Zambian Community. George C. Bond. LC 75-12228. (Illus.). 189p. Date not set. reprint ed. pap. 58.60 (*0-608-20592-3*, 205455700003) Bks Demand.

Politics of Change in Georgia: A Political Biography of Ellis Arnall. Harold P. Henderson. LC 90-48689. (Illus.). 336p. 1991. 35.00 (*0-8203-1306-8*) U of Ga Pr.

Politics of Character Development: A Marxist Reappraisal of the Moral Life, 52. Kit R. Christensen. LC 93-44512. (Contributions in Philosophy Ser.: Vol. 52). 152p. 1994. 57.95 (*0-313-29213-2*, Greenwood Pr) Greenwood.

Politics of Chemical Risk: Scenarios for a Regulatory Future. Roland Bal & Willem Halffman. LC 98-23057. 367p. 1998. 175.00 (*0-7923-4891-5*) Kluwer Academic.

Politics of Chicano Liberation. Ed. by Olga Rodriguez. 1977. pap. 15.95 (*0-87348-514-9*); lib. bdg. 40.00 (*0-87348-513-0*) Pathfinder NY.

Politics of Child Abuse in America. Lela B. Costin et al. (Child Welfare: A Series in Child Welfare Practice, Policy, & Research). (Illus.). 208p. 1997. reprint ed. pap. 17.95 (*0-19-511668-2*) OUP.

***Politics of Child Daycare in Britain.** Vicky Randall. 260p. 2000. text 65.00 (*0-19-828048-3*) OUP.

Politics of Childcare. Jennifer Marchbank. 1999. pap. text 27.95 (*1-85728-288-4*) UCL Pr Ltd.

Politics of Children's Survival. George Kent. LC 90-7578. 216p. 1990. 55.00 (*0-275-93723-2*, C3723, Praeger Pubs) Greenwood.

Politics of China: The Eras of Mao & Deng. 2nd ed. Ed. by Roderick MacFarquhar. 608p. 1997. text 69.95 (*0-521-58141-9*); pap. text 25.95 (*0-521-58863-4*) Cambridge U Pr.

Politics of Chinese Language & Culture: The Art of Reading Dragons. Bob Hodge & Kam Louie. LC 99-159360. (Culture & Communication in Asia Ser.). (Illus.). 208p. (C). (gr. 13). 1998. 75.00 (*0-415-17265-9*, D6268); pap. 25.99 (*0-415-17266-7*, D6272) Routledge.

Politics of Chinese Trotskyism. Joseph T. Miller. 200p. (C). 1990. pap. text 29.00 (*0-8133-7875-3*) Westview.

Politics of Christian Zionism, 1891-1948. Paul C. Merkley. LC 98-13351. 240p. 1998. 52.50 (*0-7146-4850-7*, Pub. by F Cass Pubs); pap. 24.50 (*0-7146-4408-0*, Pub. by F Cass Pubs) Intl Spec Bk.

Politics of City-County Merger: The Lexington-Fayette County Experience. William E. Lyons. LC 77-73706. 192p. 1977. reprint ed. pap. 59.60 (*0-608-02125-3*, 206277400004) Bks Demand.

Politics of Civil Rights in the Truman Administration. William C. Berman. LC 70-114736. 273p. 1970. reprint ed. pap. 84.70 (*0-608-04445-8*, 206497700012) Bks Demand.

Politics of Civil Service Reform. David A. Schultz & Robert Maranto. LC 96-24399. (Teaching Texts in Law & Politics Ser.: Vol. 1). 243p. (C). 1998. pap. text 29.95 (*0-8204-3379-9*) P Lang Pubng.

***Politics of Civil Society Building: European Private Aid Agencies & Democratic Transitions in Central America.** Kees Biekart. LC 99-514789. 400p. 1999. pap. 29.95 (*90-5727-025-0*, Pub. by Intl Bks) Paul & Co Pubs.

Politics of Classroom Life: Classroom Management in International Perspective. Nobuo K. Shimahara. Ed. by Edward Beauchamp. LC 97-43497. (Reference Books in International Education, Reference Library of Social Science: Vol. 40). (Illus.). 350p. 1998. text 65.00 (*0-8153-2466-9*, SS1125) Garland.

Politics of Clean Air: EPA Standards for Coal Burning Power Plants. Elizabeth H. Haskell. LC 81-13863. 206p. 1982. 55.00 (*0-275-90816-X*, C0816, Praeger Pubs) Greenwood.

Politics of Clientelism: Democracy & the State in Colombia. John D. Martz. 370p. 1996. text 44.95 (*1-56000-264-6*) Transaction Pubs.

Politics of Climate Change: A European Perspective. Ed. by Tim O'Riordan & Jill Jager. LC 95-42459. (Global Environmental Change Ser.). (Illus.). 416p. (C). 1996. 85.00 (*0-415-12573-1*); pap. 27.99 (*0-415-12574-X*) Routledge.

Politics of Codification: The Lower Canadian Civil Code of 1866. Brian Young. (Studies on the History of Society & Culture). (Illus.). 216p. 1994. 49.95 (*0-7735-1235-7*, Pub. by McG-Queens Univ Pr) CUP Services.

Politics of Coexistence: Soviet Methods & Motives. Michael P. Gehlen. LC 79-16999. 334p. 1980. reprint ed. lib. bdg. 67.50 (*0-313-21290-2*, GEPC, Greenwood Pr) Greenwood.

Politics of Collegiality: Retrenchment Strategies in Canadian Universities. Cynthia Hardy. LC 96-226486. 240p. 1996. 55.00 (*0-7735-1362-0*, LA417, Pub. by McG-Queens Univ Pr) CUP Services.

Politics of Colombia. Robert H. Dix. LC 86-21168. 265p. 1986. 59.95 (*0-275-92315-0*, C2315, Praeger Pubs) Greenwood.

Politics of Colonial Exploitation: Java, the Dutch & the Cultivation System. Cornelis Fasseur. Ed. by R. E. Elson. Tr. by R. E Elson & Ary Kraal from DUT. (Studies on Southeast Asia: No. 8). 266p. (Orig.). (C). 1992. pap. text 18.00 (*0-87727-707-9*) Cornell SE Asia.

Politics of Color in the Fiction of Jessie Fauset & Nella Larsen. Jacquelyn Y. McLendon. 160p. (C). 1995. text 29.50 (*0-8139-1553-8*) U Pr of Va.

Politics of Command: Factions & Ideas in Confederate Strategy. Thomas L. Connelly & Archer Jones. LC 99-160634. (Illus.). 256p. 1998. pap. 14.95 (*0-8071-2349-8*) La State U Pr.

Politics of Communalism. Zenab Banu. (C). 1989. 32.00 (*0-86132-183-9*, Pub. by Popular Prakashan) S Asia.

Politics of Communalism & Secularism: Keeping Indians Divided. Ed. by N. S. Gehlot. (C). 1993. 24.00 (*81-7100-497-0*, Pub. by Deep & Deep Pubns) S Asia.

Politics of Community: A Feminist Critique of the Liberal-Communitarian Debate. Elizabeth Frazer & Nicola Lacey. LC 93-94657. 278p. (C). 1994. text 50.00 (*0-8020-0430-X*); pap. text 19.95 (*0-8020-7220-8*) U of Toronto Pr.

Politics of Community: Migration & Politics in Antebellum Ohio. Kenneth J. Winkle. (Interdisciplinary Perspectives on Modern History Ser.). (Illus.). 256p. 1988. text 59.95 (*0-521-34372-0*) Cambridge U Pr.

Politics of Community Action. Jan O'Malley. 180p. (C). 1988. 60.00 (*0-85124-184-0*); pap. 45.00 (*0-85124-183-2*) St Mut.

Politics of Community Conflict: The Fluoridation Decision. Robert L. Crain et al. LC 68-31777. 1969. pap. text 6.95 (*0-672-60840-5*) Irvington.

Politics of Community Conflict: The Fluoridation Decision. Robert L. Crain et al. LC 68-31777. 1969. 7.50 (*0-672-51164-9*, Bobbs) Macmillan.

Politics of Community Policing: Rearranging the Power to Punish. William T. Lyons. LC 98-40135. (Law, Meaning & Violence Ser.). (Illus.). 256p. 1999. text 39.50 (*0-472-10953-7*, 10953) U of Mich Pr.

Politics of Community Policing: The Case of Seattle. Wilson Edward Reed. Ed. by Victor Kappeler et al. (Current Issues in Criminal Justice Ser.: Vol. 25). 168p. 1998. 44.00 (*0-8153-3029-4*, SS1179) Garland.

Politics of Compassion & Transformation. Dick Simpson. LC 88-29445. 350p. 1989. pap. 15.95 (*0-8040-0904-X*); text 29.95 (*0-8040-0903-1*) Swallow.

Politics of Compensation: Truman, the Wool Bill of 1947, & the Shaping of Postwar U. S. Trade Policy. A. Imtiaz Hussain. LC 92-34577. (Foreign Economic Policy of the United States Ser.). 336p. 1993. text 10.00 (*0-8153-1105-2*) Garland.

Politics of Comprehensive Manpower Legislation. Roger H. Davidson. LC 72-10874. (Policy Studies in Employment & Welfare: No. 15). 128p. reprint ed. pap. 39.70 (*0-608-11886-9*, 202309200032) Bks Demand.

Politics of Compromise: Coalition Government in Colombia. Ed. by R. Albert Berry et al. LC 78-64478. 504p. reprint ed. pap. 156.30 (*0-7837-2124-2*, 204240600004) Bks Demand.

Politics of Compromise: NATO & AWACS. Arnold L. Tessmer. 212p. (Orig.). (C). 1995. pap. text 40.00 (*0-7881-2154-5*) DIANE Pub.

Politics of Compromise: State & Religion in Israel. Ervin Birnbaum. LC 70-92557. 348p. 1975. 39.50 (*0-8386-7567-0*) Fairleigh Dickinson.

Politics of Conciliation: The Pursuit of Catholic Emancipation in Ireland, England & Scotland, 1660-1829. Gerard O'Brien. 240p. 1997. 45.00 (*0-7165-2535-6*, Pub. by Irish Acad Pr) Intl Spec Bk.

Politics of Confrontation. Ed. by Samuel Hendel. LC 75-148865. 1971. pap. text 15.95 (*0-89197-893-3*) Irvington.

Politics of Confrontation: The Babri Masjid Rajanmabhuoomi Controversy Run Riot. Asghar Ali Engineer. (C). 1992. 51.00 (*81-202-0360-7*, Pub. by Ajanta) S Asia.

Politics of Congress. 6th ed. David J. Vogler. 288p. (C). 1992. text. write for info. (*0-697-11136-9*) Brown & Benchmark.

Politics of Congressional Elections. 3rd ed. Gary C. Jacobson. (C). 1997. pap. text 28.00 (*0-06-500075-7*) Addison-Wesley Educ.

Politics of Congressional Elections. 4th ed. Gary C. Jacobson. LC 96-17458. 248p. (C). 1997. pap. 39.06 (*0-673-99637-9*) Addison-Wesley Educ.

***Politics of Congressional Elections.** 5th ed. Gary C. Jacobson. 272p. 2000. pap. text 35.00 (*0-321-07069-0*) Longman.

Politics of Conscience. Patricia W. Wallace. 1995. 24.95 (*0-614-15426-X*, Praeger Pubs) Greenwood.

Politics of Conscience: A Biography of Margaret Chase Smith. Patricia W. Wallace. LC 95-4288. 272p. 1995. 24.95 (*0-275-95130-8*, Praeger Pubs) Greenwood.

Politics of Conscience: T. H. Green & His Age. Melvin Richter. Ed. by Peter Johnson. (Idealism Ser.: No. 4). 415p. 1996. 72.00 (*1-85506-486-3*) Bks Intl VA.

Politics of Conscience: T. H. Green & His Age. Melvin Richter. Ed. by Peter Johnson. (Idealism Ser.: No. 4). (Illus.). 415p. 1996. pap. 25.00 (*1-85506-487-1*) Bks Intl VA.

Politics of Constructionism. Irving Velody & Robin Williams. LC 98-60207. ix, 241p. 1998. write for info. (*0-7619-5042-7*) Sage.

Politics of Continuity: British Foreign Policy & the Labour Government, 1945-6. John Saville. 280p. (C). (gr. 13). 1993. 60.00 (*0-86091-456-9*, B2492, Pub. by Verso) Norton.

Politics of Continuity: Maryland Political Parties from 1858 to 1870. Jean H. Baker. LC 72-12354. (Goucher College Ser.). (Illus.). 254p. 1973. 40.00 (*0-8018-1418-9*) Johns Hopkins.

Politics of Conversion: Missionary Protestantism & the Jews in Prussia 1728-1941. Christopher Clark. 348p. 1995. text 68.00 (*0-19-820456-6*) OUP.

Politics of Corporate Taxation in the European Union: Knowledge & International Policy Agendas. Claudio Maria Radaelli. LC 97-9647. 272p. (C). 1997. 85.00 (*0-415-14999-1*) Routledge.

Politics of Corruption: Organized Crime in an American City. John A. Gardiner. LC 79-107958. 130p. 1970. 24.95 (*0-87154-299-4*) Russell Sage.

Politics of Corruption: The Goddess That Failed. S. B. Sahai. LC 93-900338. vii, 228p. 1995. 20.00 (*81-212-0489-5*, Pub. by Gyan Publishing Hse) Nataraj Bks.

Politics of Corruption in Contemporary China: An Analysis of Policy Outcomes. Ting Gong. LC 93-24829. 216p. 1994. 59.95 (*0-275-94689-4*, C4689, Praeger Pubs) Greenwood.

Politics of Courtly Dancing in Early Modern England. Skiles Howard. LC 97-32623. (Massachusetts Studies in Early Modern Culture). (Illus.). 224p. (C). 1998. 37.50 (*1-55849-144-9*) U of Mass Pr.

Politics of Crime & Conflict: A Comparative History of Four Cities. Ted R. Gurr et al. LC 76-45429. 805p. reprint ed. pap. 200.00 (*0-608-14227-1*, 202191000026) Bks Demand.

Politics of Crime Control. Kevin Stenson & David Cowell. 224p. 1992. 55.00 (*0-8039-8341-7*); pap. 19.95 (*0-8039-8342-5*) Sage.

Politics of Crime Prevention. Brigitte C. Koch. LC 97-77390. 226p. 1998. text 59.95 (*1-84014-181-6*, Pub. by Ashgate Pub) Ashgate Pub Co.

Politics of Crisis Reporting: Learning to Be a Foreign Correspondent. John C. Pollock. LC 81-15350. (Praeger Special Studies). 240p. 1981. 55.00 (*0-275-90703-1*, C0703, Praeger Pubs) Greenwood.

Politics of Cruelty: An Essay on the Literature of Political Imprisonment. Kate Millett. 336p. 1995. pap. 13.00 (*0-393-31312-3*, Norton Paperbks) Norton.

Politics of Cultural Despair: A Study in the Rise of the Germanic Ideology. Fritz R. Stern. 1961. reprint ed. pap. 16.95 (*0-520-02626-8*, Pub. by U CA Pr) Cal Prin Full Svc.

Politics of Cultural Difference in Northern Cameroon. Philip Burnham. 272p. 1996. text 45.00 (*1-56098-694-8*) Smithsonian.

Politics of Cultural Diversity. L. Bolaria. 1993. pap. text. write for info. (*0-7730-5174-0*) Addison-Wes.

Politics of Cultural Performance. Ed. by David Parkin et al. LC 95-26832. 1995. pap. 19.95 (*1-57181-925-8*) Berghahn Bks.

Politics of Cultural Performance. David Parkin et al. LC 95-26832. 224p. 1996. 59.95 (*1-57181-898-7*) Berghahn Bks.

Politics of Cultural Pluralism. Crawford Young. LC 74-27318. (Illus.). 574p. 1976. 35.00 (*0-299-06740-8*) U of Wis Pr.

Politics of Cultural Pluralism. Crawford Young. LC 74-27318. (Illus.). 574p. 1979. pap. 19.95 (*0-299-06744-0*) U of Wis Pr.

***Politics of Cultural Practice: Thinking Through Theatre in an Age of Globalization.** Rustom Bharucha. LC 99-85991. 324p. 2000. 19.95 (*0-8195-6439-7*, Wesleyan Univ Pr); 45.00 (*0-8195-6440-0*, Wesleyan Univ Pr) U Pr of New Eng.

Politics of Culture. Ed. by Brett Williams. LC 90-9610. (Anthropological Society of Washington Ser.). (Illus.). 280p. 1991. text 35.00 (*0-87474-931-X*) Smithsonian.

***Politics of Culture: A Study of Three Kirata Communities in the Eastern Himalayas.** Subba. 1999. pap. 12.00 (*81-250-1693-7*, Pub. by Orient Longman Ltd) S Asia.

Politics of Culture: And Other Essays. unabridged ed. Roger Scruton. 245p. 1998. reprint ed. 25.00 (*1-890318-61-2*) St Augustines Pr.

Politics of Culture: Essays for a New Field. Ed. by Gigi Bradford et al. 288p. 2000. pap. 18.95 (*1-56584-572-2*) Norton.

Politics of Culture: Race, Violence, & Democracy. Jung Min Choi et al. LC 95-3333. 192p. 1995. 55.00 (*0-275-94889-7*, Praeger Pubs) Greenwood.

Politics of Culture in Nicaragua. David E. Whisnant. LC 94-41811. 1995. pap. text 24.95 (*0-8078-4523-X*); lib. bdg. 59.95 (*0-8078-2209-4*) U of NC Pr.

Politics of Culture in Soviet-Occupied Germany, 1945-1949. David W. Pike. 700p. (C). 1993. 59.50 (*0-8047-2093-2*) Stanford U Pr.

Politics of Culture in the Shadow of Capital. Ed. by David Lloyd & Lisa Lowe. LC 97-8900. (Post-Contemporary Interventions Ser.). 1997. lib. bdg. 69.95 (*0-8223-2033-9*) Duke.

Politics of Culture in the Shadow of Capital. Ed. by David Lloyd & Lisa Lowe. LC 97-8900. (Post-Contemporary Interventions Ser.). 593p. 1997. pap. text 23.95 (*0-8223-2046-0*) Duke.

Politics of Curriculum & Testing: Yearbook of the Politics of Education Association, 1990. Ed. by Susan H. Fuhrman & Betty Malen. (Education Policy Perspectives Ser.). 224p. 1991. pap. 29.95 (*1-85000-975-9*, Falmer Pr) Taylor & Francis.

Politics of Curriculum Decision-Making: Issues in Centralizing the Curriculum. Ed. by M. Frances Klein. LC 90-30939. (SUNY Series in Curriculum Issues & Inquiries). 236p. (C). 1991. text 64.50 (*0-7914-0487-0*); pap. text 21.95 (*0-7914-0488-9*) State U NY Pr.

Politics of Cyberspace: A New Political Science Reader. Ed. by Chris Toulouse & Timothy W. Luke. LC 98-23865. (New Political Science Reader Ser.). 208p. (C). 1998. pap. 20.99 (*0-415-92167-8*, D5961) Routledge.

Politics of Daylight Time. Frederick W. Zuercher. 1966. 1.00 (*1-55614-081-9*) U of SD Gov Res Bur.

Politics of Deafness. Owen Wrigley. LC 96-5266. (Illus.). 310p. 1996. text 49.95 (*1-56368-052-1*) Gallaudet Univ Pr.

Politics of Deafness. Owen Wrigley. LC 96-5266. 310p. 1997. pap. text 24.95 (*1-56368-064-5*) Gallaudet Univ Pr.

Politics of Debt in Argentina, Brazil, & Mexico: Economic Stabilization in the 1980s. Robert R. Kaufman. LC 88-32792. (Research Ser.: No. 72). (Illus.). ix, 137p. 1988. pap. text 11.50 (*0-87725-172-X*) U of Cal IAS.

Politics of Decolonization: Kenya Europeans & the Land Issue, 1960-1965. Gary Wasserman. LC 75-2735. (African Studies: No. 17). 235p. reprint ed. pap. 67.00 (*0-608-17534-X*, 2030628) Bks Demand.

Politics of Deeper Integration: National Attitudes & Politics in Japan. Akihiko Tanaka. (Integrating National Economies: Promise & Pitfalls Ser.). 1997. 34.95 (*0-8157-4058-1*); pap. 14.95 (*0-8157-4057-3*) Brookings.

***Politics of Deeply Divided Society.** Guelke. 2000. pap. 18.00 (*0-8133-3501-9*, Pub. by Westview) HarpC.

Politics of Deeply Divided Society: New Subtitle. Guelke. 192p. write for info. (*0-8133-3500-0*, Pub. by Westview) HarpC.

Politics of Defeat: Campaigning for Congress. Robert J. Huckshorn & Robert C. Spencer. LC 71-123538. 272p. 1971. 32.50 (*0-87023-082-4*) U of Mass Pr.

Politics of Defense Contracting. Kenneth R. Mayer. 240p. 1991. 37.50 (*0-300-04524-7*) Yale U Pr.

Politics of Deference: A Study of the Mid-Ninteenth Century English Political System. David C. Moore. (Modern Revivals in History Ser.). 576p. 1994. 96.95 (*0-7512-0236-3*, Pub. by Gregg Revivals) Ashgate Pub Co.

Politics of Democracy: American Parties in Action. P. Herring. (Illus.). 1990. 15.50 (*0-8446-2246-X*) Peter Smith.

Politics of Democratic Consolidation: Southern Europe in Comparative Perspective. Ed. by Richard Gunther et al. LC 95-2570. 493p. 1995. text 60.00 (*0-8018-4981-0*); pap. text 17.95 (*0-8018-4982-9*) Johns Hopkins.

Politics of Democratic Socialism: An Essay on Social Policy. Evan F. Durbin. LC 71-83799. 384p. 1969. reprint ed. 45.00 (*0-678-06513-6*) Kelley.

***Politics of Democratization in Korea: The Role of Civil Society.** Sunhyuk Kim. (Political Science Ser.). 196p. 2000. pap. 19.95 (*0-8229-5736-1*) U of Pittsburgh Pr.

Politics of Demonology: The European Witchcraze & the Mass Production of Deviance. Jon Oplinger. LC 89-43149. 312p. 1990. 44.50 (*0-945636-11-3*) Susquehanna U Pr.

P

An Asterisk (*) at the beginning of an entry indicates that the title is appearing for the first time.

Politics of Denial. Michael A. Milburn & Sheree D. Conrad. (Illus.). 304p. 1998. reprint ed. pap. text 15.00 (*0-262-63184-9*) MIT Pr.

Politics of Denial: Reactionary Rage. Michael A. Milburn & Sheree D. Conrad. LC 96-16100. (Illus.). 304p. 1996. 30.00 (*0-262-13330-X*) MIT Pr.

Politics of Dependency: Urban Reform in Istanbul, 3. Steven T. Rosenthal. LC 79-7588. (Contributions in Comparative Colonial Studies: No. 3). (Illus.). 220p. 1980. 69.50 (*0-313-20927-8*, RPO/, Greenwood Pr) Greenwood.

Politics of Depoliticization in Republic China: Guomindang Policy Towards Student Political Activism, 1927-1949. Jianli Huang. 242p. 1998. 52.95 (*3-906756-46-7*) P Lang Pubng.

Politics of Depoliticization in Republican China: Guomindang Policy Towards Student Political Activism, 1927-1949. 2nd rev. ed. Jianli Huang. LC 99-174301. 242 p. 1999. write for info. (*3-906760-66-9*, Pub. by P Lang) P Lang Pubng.

Politics of Depoliticization in Republican China: Guomindang Policy Towards Student Political Activism, 1927-1949. 2nd rev. ed. Jianli Huang. LC 99-174301. 242p. 1998. 46.95 (*0-8204-4207-0*) P Lang Pubng.

Politics of Deregulation. Martha Derthick & Paul J. Quirk. LC 85-16602. 265p. 1985. 36.95 (*0-8157-1818-7*) Brookings.

Politics of Design in French Colonial Urbanism. Gwendolyn Wright. LC 90-45063. (Illus.). 398p. 1991. lib. bdg. 75.00 (*0-226-90846-1*) U Ch Pr.

Politics of Design in French Colonial Urbanism. Gwendolyn Wright. LC 90-45063. (Illus.). 398p. 1999. pap. text 28.95 (*0-226-90848-8*) U Ch Pr.

***Politics of Desire.** Micela Wakil Janan. LC 99-55385. 293p. 2000. pap. 19.95 (*0-520-22321-7*, Pub. by U CA Pr) Cal Prin Full Svc.

***Politics of Desire: Propertius IV.** Micaela Wakil Janan. LC 99-55385. 293p. 2000. 50.00 (*0-520-22318-7*, Pub. by U CA Pr) Cal Prin Full Svc.

Politics of Despair: Power & Resistance in the Tobacco Wars. Tracy Campbell. LC 92-47277. 240p. 1993. text 29.95 (*0-8131-1821-2*) U Pr of Ky.

Politics of Developed Socialism: The Soviet Union As a Post-Industrial State, 149. Donald R. Kelley. LC 85-30562. (Contributions in Political Science Ser.: No. 149). (Illus.). 226p. 1986. 59.95 (*0-313-25243-2*, KPD/, Greenwood Pr) Greenwood.

Politics of Development see Global Issues: An Introduction

Politics of Development: Perspectives on Twentieth-Century Asia. Robert A. Scalapino. LC 89-11041. (Edwin O. Reischauer Lectures). 144p. 1989. 31.00 (*0-674-68757-4*) HUP.

Politics of Development: Perspectives on Twentieth-Century Asia. Robert A. Scalapino. (Edwin O. Reischauer Lectures). 152p. 1994. pap. text 15.00 (*0-674-68758-2*, SCAPOX) HUP.

Politics of Development: Transportation Policy in Nepal. Aran Schloss. LC 83-6807. (Monographs: No. 22). (Illus.). 198p. (Orig.). (C). 1983. pap. text 22.50 (*0-8191-3251-9*); lib. bdg. 50.50 (*0-8191-3250-0*) U Pr of Amer.

Politics of Development Co-Operation: Ngos, Gender & Partnership in Kenya. Lisa M. Aubrey. LC 97-14343. (Routledge Studies in Development & Society). (Illus.). 256p. (C). 1997. 75.00 (*0-415-15185-6*) Routledge.

Politics of Dietary Change. Mike Mills. 160p. 1992. text 77.95 (*1-85521-226-9*, Pub. by Dartmth Pub) Ashgate Pub Co.

Politics of Difference: Artists Explore Issues of Identity. Amelia Jones. (University Art Gallery, 1992 Ser.). (Illus.). 16p. (Orig.). (C). 1992. pap. text 7.50 (*0-932173-09-8*) Sweeney Art Gallery.

Politics of Differences: Ethnic Premises in a World of Power. Ed. by Patrick A. McAllister & Edwin Wilmsen. LC 95-35762. 208p. 1996. pap. text 13.95 (*0-226-90017-7*) U Ch Pr.

Politics of Differences: Ethnic Premises in a World of Power. Ed. by Edwin N. Wilmsen & Patrick A. McAllister. LC 95-35762. 208p. 1996. lib. bdg. 38.00 (*0-226-90016-9*) U Ch Pr.

Politics of Disablement. Oliver. 1997. text 21.95 (*0-333-43293-2*, Pub. by Macmillan) St Martin.

Politics of Disablement: A Sociological Approach. Michael Oliver. LC 90-8133. 168p. 1990. text 29.95 (*0-312-04658-8*) St Martin.

Politics of Discretion. Leonard Krieger. LC 65-14428. 1993. lib. bdg. 18.00 (*0-226-45359-6*) U Ch Pr.

Politics of Disenchantment: Bush, Clinton, Perot, & the Press. James B. Lemert et al. LC 95-51055. 384p. 1996. text 75.00 (*1-57273-058-7*); pap. text 28.50 (*1-57273-059-5*) Hampton Pr NJ.

Politics of Disillusionment: The Chinese Communist Party under Deng Xiaoping, 1978-1989. Hsi-sheng Ch'i. LC 90-20867. (Studies on Contemporary China). 352p. (C). (gr. 13). 1991. pap. text 35.95 (*0-87332-690-3*, East Gate Bk) M E Sharpe.

Politics of Disillusionment: The Chinese Communist Party under Deng Xiaoping, 1978-1989. Hsi-Sheng Ch'i. LC 90-20867. (Studies on Contemporary China). 352p. (C). (gr. 13). 1991. text 77.95 (*0-87332-689-X*, East Gate Bk) M E Sharpe.

Politics of Display: Museums, Science & Culture. Sharon MacDonald. LC 97-3319. (Illus.). 264p. (C). 1998. 85.00 (*0-415-15325-5*); pap. 29.99 (*0-415-15326-3*) Routledge.

Politics of Dissatisfaction: Citizens, Services & Urban Institutions. W. E. Lyons et al. LC 91-35287. (Bureaucracies, Public Administration & Public Policy Ser.). 248p. (C). (gr. 13). 1992. text 74.95 (*0-87332-898-1*) M E Sharpe.

Politics of Dissatisfaction: Citizens, Services & Urban Institutions. W. E. Lyons et al. LC 91-35287. (Bureaucracies, Public Administration & Public Policy Ser.). 248p. (C). (gr. 13). 1993. pap. text 35.95 (*1-56324-378-4*) M E Sharpe.

Politics of Dissolution: The Quest for a National Identity & the American Civil War. Ed. by Marshall L. DeRosa. LC 97-29445. 356p. 1997. text 39.95 (*1-56000-349-9*) Transaction Pubs.

Politics of Diversity: Immigration, Resistance & Change in Monterey Park, California. John Horton. LC 94-23618. 1995. pap. 22.95 (*1-56639-328-0*) Temple U Pr.

Politics of Diversity: Immigration, Resistance & Change in Monterey Park, California. John Horton. (Illus.). 296p. (C). 1995. lib. bdg. 69.95 (*1-56639-327-2*) Temple U Pr.

Politics of Diversity in the United States: Positive Dreams & Pyrrhic Victories. Paul Barton-Kriese. 88p. (Orig.). (C). 1993. pap. text 18.50 (*0-8191-9222-8*); lib. bdg. 32.00 (*0-8191-9221-X*) U Pr of Amer.

Politics of Divided Nations: China, Korea, Germany & Vietnam - Unification, Conflict Resolution & Political Development, No. 5. Ed. by Quansheng Zhao & Robert G. Sutter. 198p. 1991. 12.00 (*0-925153-17-6*, 106) Occasional Papers.

Politics of Domestic Consumption: Critical Readings. Ed. by Stevi Jackson & Shaun Moores. LC 95-6416. 320p. (C). 1995. pap. text 37.50 (*0-13-433343-8*) P-H.

Politics of Domesticity: Women, Evangelism, & Temperence in Nineteenth-Century America. Barbara L. Epstein. LC 80-16671. 198p. reprint ed. pap. 61.40 (*0-608-09079-4*, 206971300005) Bks Demand.

Politics of Downtown Development. Stephen J. McGovern. LC 97-53074. (Illus.). 342p. (C). 1998. 44.95 (*0-8131-2052-7*) U Pr of Ky.

Politics of Dreaming in the Carolingian Empire. Paul E. Dutton. LC 93-38615. (Regents Studies in Medieval Culture). (Illus.). xviii, 346p. 1994. text 50.00 (*0-8032-1653-X*) U of Nebr Pr.

Politics of Drugs: Who Suffers, Who Deals, Who Profits. David Perez et al. 26p. 1988. pap. 0.50 (*0-89567-093-3*) World View Forum.

Politics of Duplicity: Controlling Reproduction in Ceausescu's Romania. Gail Kligman. LC 97-49421. 350p. 1998. 50.00 (*0-520-21074-3*, Pub. by U CA Pr); pap. 19.95 (*0-520-21075-1*, Pub. by U CA Pr) Cal Prin Full Svc.

***Politics of Early Childhood Education.** Lourdes Diaz Soto. LC 98-38989. (Rethinking Childhood Ser.: Vol. 10). 248p. (C). 2000. pap. text 29.95 (*0-8204-4164-3*) P Lang Pubng.

Politics of Earthquake Prediction. Richard S. Olson. LC 88-22101. 199p. 1989. reprint ed. pap. 61.70 (*0-608-06481-5*, 206677800009) Bks Demand.

Politics of East-West Communication in Europe. Karl E. Birnbaum. 182p. 1979. text 82.95 (*0-566-00254-X*, Pub. by Dartmth Pub) Ashgate Pub Co.

Politics of East-West Migration. Ed. by Solon Ardittis. LC 93-48290. 1994. text 69.95 (*0-312-12140-7*) St Martin.

Politics of Eastern Cape Separatism, 1820-1854. Basil A. Le Cordeur. (Illus.). 1981. 45.00 (*0-19-570196-8*) OUP.

Politics of Economic Adjustment: Fragile Coalitions. Ed. by Joan M. Nelson et al. 224p. 1990. pap. 17.95 (*0-88738-787-X*) Transaction Pubs.

Politics of Economic Adjustment: International Constraints, Distributive Conflicts. Stephan Haggard. 376p. (C). 1992. text 65.00 (*0-691-04300-0*, Pub. by Princeton U Pr) Cal Prin Full Svc.

Politics of Economic Adjustment: International Constraints, Distributive Politics, & the State. Ed. by Stephen Haggard & Robert R. Kaufman. 352p. 1992. pap. text 19.95 (*0-691-00394-7*, Pub. by Princeton U Pr) Cal Prin Full Svc.

Politics of Economic Adjustment: Pluralism, Corporatism, & Privatization, 237. Ed. by Richard E. Foglesong & Joel D. Wolfe. LC 89-2180. (Contributions in Political Science Ser.: No. 237). 198p. 1989. 55.00 (*0-313-26627-1*, WDN, Greenwood Pr) Greenwood.

Politics of Economic & Human Resource Development. Randall B. Ripley. LC 79-173977. (Policy Analysis Ser.). (C). 1972. write for info. (*0-672-51479-6*, Bobbs) Macmillan.

Politics of Economic & Monetary Union. Ed. by Petri Minkkinen & Heikki Patomaki. LC 97-38342. 252p. 1997. 121.00 (*0-7923-8041-X*, D Reidel) Kluwer Academic.

Politics of Economic Crisis: Lessons from Western Europe. E. Damgaard et al. 1989. text 77.95 (*0-566-05517-1*, Pub. by Dartmth Pub) Ashgate Pub Co.

Politics of Economic Decline in East Germany, 1945-1989. Jeffrey Kopstein. LC 96-11614. 288p. (C). (gr. 13). 1997. text 45.00 (*0-8078-2303-1*) U of NC Pr.

Politics of Economic Despair: Shopkeepers & German Politics, 1890-1914. Robert Gellately. LC 74-81024. (Sage Studies in 20th Century History: Vol. 1). 334p. reprint ed. pap. 103.60 (*0-608-14228-X*, 202190500026) Bks Demand.

Politics of Economic Development in Indonesia: Contending Perspectives. Iain Chalmers & Vedi R. Hadiz. LC 96-25077. 304p. (C). 1997. 90.00 (*0-415-14502-3*) Routledge.

Politics of Economic Planning Alan Budd. LC 78-324079. (Political Issues of Modern Britain Ser.). 172p. 1978. write for info. (*0-7190-0708-9*) Manchester Univ Pr.

Politics of Economic Policy. Stuart Cochrane. LC 88-208248. (Topics in British Politics Ser.). 50 p. 1988. write for info. (*0-582-33196-X*) Addison-Wesley.

Politics of Economic Policy, 97. Volkmar Lauber. 128p. 1983. pap. 14.95 (*0-275-91579-4*, B1579, Praeger Pubs) Greenwood.

Politics of Economic Power in Southern Africa. Ronald T. Libby. LC 87-2406. 391p. reprint ed. pap. 121.30 (*0-608-06431-9*, 206664400008) Bks Demand.

Politics of Economic Reform in Zimbabwe: Continuity & Change in Development. Tor Skalnes. LC 94-43719. (International Political Economy Ser.). 1995. text 65.00 (*0-312-12574-7*) St Martin.

Politics of Economic Restructuring & Democracy in Africa, 207. Obioma M. Iheduru. LC 98-8234. (Contributions in Economics & Economic History: Vol. 207). 184p. 1999. 49.95 (*0-313-30833-0*, Greenwood Pr) Greenwood.

Politics of Economic Restructuring in Mexico: State-Society Relations & Regime Change in Mexico. Ed. by Kevin J. Middlebrook et al. (U. S. - Mexico Contemporary Perspectives Ser.: No. 7). 351p. 1994. pap. 21.95 (*1-878367-18-8*) UCSD Ctr US-Mex.

Politics of Economic Stagnation in the Soviet Union: The Role of Local Political Organs in Economic Management. Peter Rutland. (Cambridge Russian, Soviet & Post-Soviet Studies: No. 88). (Illus.). 320p. (C). 1992. text 69.95 (*0-521-39241-1*) Cambridge U Pr.

Politics of Economics. Dominick Harrod & British Broadcasting Corporation Staff. LC 79-302713. 80p. 1978. write for info. (*0-563-16270-8*) BBC.

Politics of Ecosystem Management. Hanna J. Cortner & Margaret A. Moote. LC 98-34883. (Illus.). 224p. 1998. pap. text 25.00 (*1-55963-672-6*, Shearwater Bks) Island Pr.

***Politics of Ecosystem Management.** Hanna J. Cortner & Margaret A. Moote. LC 98-34883. (Illus.). 224p. 1998. text 50.00 (*1-55963-671-8*, Shearwater Bks) Island Pr.

Politics of Ecstasy see Turn on, Tune in, Drop Out

Politics of Ecstasy. 6th ed. Timothy Leary. 230p. 1998. reprint ed. pap. 14.95 (*1-57951-031-0*) Ronin Pub.

Politics of Editing. Ed. by Nicholas Spadaccini & Jenaro Talens. (Hispanic Issues Ser.: Vol. 8). 208p. (C). 1992. pap. 14.95 (*0-8166-2029-6*); text 39.95 (*0-8166-2028-8*) U of Minn Pr.

Politics of Editing Medieval Texts: Papers Given at the Twenty-Seventh Annual Conference on Editorial Problems, University of Toronto, 1-2 November 1991. Ed. by Roberta Frank. LC 92-46368. 1993. 42.50 (*0-404-63677-2*) AMS Pr.

Politics of Education: Commonwealth Schools Policy, 1973-1993. Ed. by Janice Dudley & Lesley Vidovich. 1995. pap. 65.00 (*0-86431-177-X*, Pub. by Aust Council Educ Res) St Mut.

Politics of Education: Culture, Power, & Liberation. Paulo Freire. Tr. by Donaldo P. Macedo from POR. LC 84-18572. (Critical Studies in Education). 240p. 1984. 55.00 (*0-89789-042-6*, Bergin & Garvey); pap. 22.95 (*0-89789-043-4*, Bergin & Garvey) Greenwood.

Politics of Education: Essays from Radical Teacher. Ed. by Susan Gushee O'Malley et al. LC 89-27745. 357p. (C). 1990. pap. text 21.95 (*0-7914-0356-4*) State U NY Pr.

Politics of Education & the New Institutionalism: Reinventing the American School: PEA Yearbook 1995. Ed. by Robert L. Crowson et al. 208p. 1996. text 69.95 (*0-7507-0532-9*, Falmer Pr); pap. text 27.95 (*0-7507-0533-7*, Falmer Pr) Taylor & Francis.

Politics of Education in the States. Harmon Zeigler & Karl F. Johnson. LC 70-175225. 1972. 37.50 (*0-697-00221-7*) Irvington.

Politics of Education in the States. Harmon Zeigler & Karl F. Johnson. LC 70-175225. (Policy Analysis Ser.). 1972. pap. 5.00 (*0-672-61066-3*, Bobbs) Macmillan.

Politics of Educational Decision Making: Historically Black Colleges & Universities & Federal Assistance Programs. Marian M. Elbert. LC 95-52998. 1997. text. write for info. (*0-275-95301-7*, Praeger Pubs) Greenwood.

Politics of Educational Innovations in Developing Countries: An Analysis of Knowledge & Power. Ed. by Nelly P. Stromquist & Michael L. Basile. (Reference Books in International Education: No. 46). (Illus.). 280p. 1999. 60.00 (*0-8153-3155-X*, SS1190) Garland.

Politics of Educational Reform. Simon & Schuster Staff. (C). 1974. pap. 19.50 (*0-85315-350-7*, Pub. by Lawrence & Wishart) NYU Pr.

Politics of Educators' Work & Lives. Ed. by Mark B. Ginsburg. LC 94-13184. (Studies in Education & Politics: Vol. 1). 304p. (Orig.). 1995. text 51.00 (*0-8153-1435-3*) Garland.

Politics of Elections in Southeast Asia: Delusion or Necessity? Ed. by R. H. Taylor. (Woodrow Wilson Center Press Ser.). 269p. (C). 1996. pap. text 18.95 (*0-521-56443-3*) Cambridge U Pr.

Politics of Elections in Southeast Asia: Delusion or Necessity? Ed. by R. H. Taylor. (Woodrow Wilson Center Press Ser.). 269p. (C). 1996. text 59.95 (*0-521-56404-2*) Cambridge U Pr.

Politics of Electoral College Reform. 2nd ed. Lawrence D. Longley & Alan G. Braun. LC 72-75202. 238p. reprint ed. pap. 73.80 (*0-8357-8277-8*, 203380500087) Bks Demand.

***Politics of Emerging of Resurgent Infectious Diseases.** Jim Whitman. LC 99-58996. 2000. text 69.95 (*0-312-22854-6*) St Martin.

Politics of Empire: Ethiopia, Great Britain & the United States, 1941-1974. Harold G. Marcus. LC 94-48479. 1995. 49.95 (*1-56902-005-1*); pap. 16.95 (*1-56902-006-X*) Red Sea Pr.

Politics of Empowerment? Peter McLaverty. (Illus.). 208p. 1996. text 77.95 (*1-85521-803-8*, Pub. by Dartmth Pub) Ashgate Pub Co.

Politics of Empowerment. Robert Weissberg. LC 98-38285. 272p. 1999. 45.00 (*0-275-96426-4*, Praeger Pubs) Greenwood.

Politics of Ending Homelessness. Susan Yeich. LC 93-38163. 108p. (C). 1994. lib. bdg. 32.50 (*0-8191-9366-6*) U Pr of Amer.

Politics of Ending Homelessness. Susan Yeich. 108p. 1996. pap. 19.50 (*0-7618-0359-9*) U Pr of Amer.

Politics of Energy Conservation. Pietro S. Nivola. LC 85-48265. 294p. 1986. 34.95 (*0-8157-6088-4*); pap. 14.95 (*0-8157-6087-6*) Brookings.

Politics of Energy Forecasting: A Comparative Study of Energy Forecasting in Western Europe & North America. Thomas Baumgartner & Atle Midttun. LC 86-23885. 328p. 1987. 74.00 (*0-19-828547-7*) OUP.

Politics of Energy Policy Change in Sweden. Robert C. Sahr. LC 84-26961. 277p. reprint ed. pap. 85.90 (*0-7837-5654-2*, 205907900005) Bks Demand.

Politics of Energy Research & Development. Ed. by John Byren & Daniel Rich. (Energy Policy Studies: Vol. 3). 170p. 1986. pap. 24.95 (*0-88738-653-9*) Transaction Pubs.

Politics of English Jacobinism: Writings of John Thelwall. Ed. by Gregory Claeys. LC 94-20695. 608p. 1995. 85.00 (*0-271-01347-8*); pap. 25.00 (*0-271-01348-6*) Pa St U Pr.

Politics of Environment: A Profile. Vandana Asthana. (C). 1992. 20.00 (*81-7024-453-6*, Pub. by Ashish Pub Hse) S Asia.

Politics of Environmental Control in Northeastern Tanzania, 1840-1940. James L. Giblin. (Ethnohistory Ser.). (Illus.). 232p. (C). 1992. text 32.50 (*0-8122-3177-5*) U of Pa Pr.

Politics of Environmental Discourse: Ecological Modernization & the Policy Process. Maarten A. Hajer. (Illus.). 344p. 1997. reprint ed. pap. text 29.95 (*0-19-829333-X*) OUP.

Politics of Environmental Policy. Ed. by Lester W. Milbrath et al. LC 75-27013. (Sage Contemporary Social Science Issues Ser.: No. 18). 136p. reprint ed. pap. 42.20 (*0-608-10739-5*, 202193200026) Bks Demand.

Politics of Environmental Reform: Controlling Kentucky Strip Mining. Marc K. Landy. LC 76-15907. (RFF Working Paper Ser.: PD-2). (Illus.). 414p. reprint ed. pap. 128.40 (*0-608-17386-X*, 203020800067) Bks Demand.

Politics of Envy: Statism As Theology. Doug Bandow. 322p. (C). 1994. 39.95 (*1-56000-171-2*) Transaction Pubs.

***Politics of Equality: Hubert Humphrey & the African American Freedom Struggle, 1945-1978.** Timothy Thurber. LC 98-36359. (Columbia Studies in Contemporary American History). 352p. 1998. pap. 19.50 (*0-231-11047-2*); lib. bdg. 49.50 (*0-231-11046-4*) Col U Pr.

Politics of Ernest Hemingway. Stephen Cooper. LC 87-5872. (Studies in Modern Literature: No. 71). 174p. reprint ed. pap. 54.00 (*0-8357-1799-2*, 207064400012) Bks Demand.

Politics of Ethics: Methods for Acting, Learning & Sometimes Fighting with Others in Addressing Problems in Organizational Life. Richard P. Neilsen. (Ruffin Series in Business Ethics). (Illus.). 272p. 1996. pap. 35.00 (*0-19-509666-5*) OUP.

Politics of Ethnic & Racial Inequality. 2nd ed. J. Owens Smith. 368p. (C). 1995. pap. text, per. 31.50 (*0-8403-8056-9*) Kendall-Hunt.

Politics of Ethnic Conflict Regulation: Case Studies of Protracted Ethnic Conflicts. Ed. by John McGarry & Brendan O'Leary. LC 92-45848. 336p. (C). 1993. pap. 25.99 (*0-415-09931-5*, B2390) Routledge.

Politics of Ethnic Pressure: The American Jewish Committee Fight Against Immigration Restriction, 1906-1917. Judith Goldstein. LC 90-3488. (European Immigrants & American Society Ser.). 360p. 1990. reprint ed. text 25.00 (*0-8240-0244-X*) Garland.

Politics of Ethnicity. Michael Walzer et al. (Dimensions in Ethnicity Ser.). 160p. 1982. pap. 13.50 (*0-674-68753-1*) HUP.

***Politics of Ethnicity, Identity & Religion: Turkish Muslims in Britain.** Talip Kucukcan. 284p. 1999. text 69.95 (*0-7546-1134-5*, Pub. by Ashgate Pub) Ashgate Pub Co.

***Politics of Ethnicity in Central Europe.** Karl Cordell. LC 99-39505. 2000. text 65.00 (*0-312-22790-6*) St Martin.

Politics of Ethnicity in Eastern Europe. Ed. by George Klein & Milan J. Reban. (ASN Series in Issues Studies: No. 93). 279p. 1981. text 58.00 (*0-914710-87-7*, Pub. by East Eur Monographs) Col U Pr.

Politics of Ethnicity in Southern Mexico. Ronald M. Spores et al. (Vanderbilt University Publications in Anthropology: Vol. 50). 132p. (Orig.). 1996. pap. 16.50 (*0-935462-41-4*) VUPA.

Politics of Euro-Communism. Ed. by Carl Boggs & David Plotke. 479p. write for info. (*0-919618-32-4*); pap. write for info. (*0-919618-31-6*) Black Rose.

Politics of European Defense Cooperation: Bridging Theory & Practice. David Garnham. 216p. 1988. text 34.95 (*0-88730-302-1*, HarpBusn) HarpInfo.

Politics of European Integration. Ed. by Michael O'Neill. 360p. (C). 1996. pap. 24.99 (*0-415-11298-2*) Routledge.

Politics of European Integration. Ed. by Mochael O'Neill. 360p. (C). 1996. 90.00 (*0-415-11297-4*) Routledge.

Politics of European Integration in the Twentieth Century. David Arter. LC 93-18110. 316p. 1993. 72.95 (*1-85521-216-1*, Pub. by Dartmth Pub); pap. text 29.95 (*1-85521-255-2*, Pub. by Dartmth Pub) Ashgate Pub Co.

Politics of European Treaty Reform. Ed. by Geoffrey Edwards & Alfred Pijpers. LC 96-49889. 416p. (C). 1997. 95.00 (*1-85567-358-4*); pap. 24.95 (*1-85567-359-2*) Bks Intl VA.

Politics of European Union Regional Policy: Multi-Level Governance or Flexable Gatekeeping? Ian Bache. (Contemporary European Studies: Vol. 3). 172p. 1998. pap. 15.00 (*1-85075-863-8*, Pub. by Sheffield Acad) CUP Services.

P

Politics of Everyday Fear. Ed. by Brian Massumi. (Illus.). 341p. (C). 1993. pap. 19.95 (*0-8166-2163-2*); text 49.95 (*0-8166-2162-4*) U of Minn Pr.

Politics of Evolution: Morphology, Medicine, & Reform in Radical London. Adrian Desmond. (Science & Its Conceptual Foundations Ser.). (Illus.). 514p. 1990. 41.95 (*0-226-14346-5*) U Ch Pr.

Politics of Evolution: Morphology, Medicine, & Reform in Radical London. Adrian Desmond. LC 89-5137. (Science & Its Conceptual Foundations Ser.). (Illus.). 514p. 1992. pap. text 22.95 (*0-226-14374-0*) U Ch Pr.

Politics of Excellence: Nobel, Vol. 1. Friedman. 1999. pap. text. write for info. (*0-7167-3103-7*) W H Freeman.

Politics of Exemption: Tax Revenue vs. Community Benefit - Not-for-Profit Hospitals. 84p. 1999. pap. 70.00 (*0-9667828-3-6*) VHA Inc.

Politics of Exile: Ideology of Henry James, F. Scott Fitzgerald & James Baldwin. Bryan R. Washington. LC 94-27077. 1995. text 37.50 (*1-55553-209-8*) NE U Pr.

***Politics of Exile in Renaissance Italy.** Christine Shaw. (Cambridge Studies in Italian History & Culture). 272p. (C). 2000. text 64.95 (*0-521-66325-3*) Cambridge U Pr.

Politics of Experience. R. D. Laing. 1983. pap. 10.00 (*0-394-71475-X*) Pantheon.

Politics of Expertise in Congress: The Rise & Fall of the Office of Technology Assessment. Bruce Bimber. LC 96-7386. 127p. (C). 1996. text 48.50 (*0-7914-3059-6*); pap. text 15.95 (*0-7914-3060-X*) State U NY Pr.

Politics of Expertise in Latin America. Miguel A. Centeno et al. LC 97-29474. (Latin American Studies). 224p. 1998. text 65.00 (*0-312-21026-4*) St Martin.

Politics of External Influence in the Dominican Republic. Michael J. Kryzanek & Howard J. Wiarda. LC 87-38484. (Politics in Latin America Ser.). (Illus.). 199p. 1988. 55.00 (*0-275-92992-2*, C2992, Praeger Pubs) Greenwood.

Politics of Faction: Christian Democratic Rule in Italy. Alan S. Zuckerman. LC 78-23838. 269p. reprint ed. pap. 83.40 (*0-7837-4533-8*, 208022500004) Bks Demand.

***Politics of Faculty Unionization: The Experience of Three New England Universities.** Gordon B. Arnold. 2000. write for info. (*0-89789-716-1*, Bergin & Garvey) Greenwood.

Politics of Faith & the Politics of Scepticism. Michael Oakeshott. Ed. by Timothy Fuller. LC 96-3852. (Selected Writings of Michael Oakeshott Ser.). 139p. 1996. 30.00 (*0-300-06625-2*) Yale U Pr.

Politics of Fallen Man. Illus. by M. M. Goldsmith & T. A. Horne. Date not set. pap. 18.95 (*0-907845-04-5*) Philos Document.

Politics of Fantasy: C. S. Lewis & J. R. R. Tolkien. Lee D. Rossi. Ed. by Robert Scholes. LC 84-16116. (Studies in Speculative Fiction: No. 10). 153p. 1984. reprint ed. 47.50 (*0-8357-1597-3*, 207043700089) Bks Demand.

Politics of Fat: Food & Nutrition Policy in America. Laura S. Sims. LC 97-26608. 328p. 1998. text 66.95 (*0-7656-0193-1*) M E Sharpe.

Politics of Fat: Food & Nutrition Policy in America. Laura S. Sims. LC 97-26608. 328p. (gr. 13). 1998. pap. text 29.95 (*0-7656-0194-X*) M E Sharpe.

Politics of Fear: Joseph R. McCarthy & the Senate. 2nd ed. Robert Griffith. LC 87-13766. 392p. 1987. reprint ed. pap. 20.95 (*0-87023-555-9*) U of Mass Pr.

Politics of Federal Aid to Education in 1965: A Study in Political Innovation. Philip J. Meranto. LC 67-16846. (Orig.). 1967. pap. 16.95 (*0-8156-2107-8*) Syracuse U Pr.

Politics of Federal Judicial Administration. Peter G. Fish. LC 76-39785. 542p. reprint ed. pap. 168.10 (*0-8357-8989-6*, 203340100085) Bks Demand.

Politics of Federal Reorganization: Creating the U. S. Department of Education. Beryl A. Radin & W. D. Howley. LC 87-6972. (Illus.). 250p. 1988. 40.00 (*0-08-033978-6*, Pergamon Pr); pap. 18.95 (*0-08-033977-8*, Pergamon Pr) Elsevier.

Politics of Federalism: Ontario's Relations with the Federal Government 1867-1942. Christopher Armstrong. (Ontario Historical Studies). 316p. 1981. text 30.00 (*0-8020-2434-3*) U of Toronto Pr.

P

Politics of Fertility Control: Family Planning & Abortion Policies in the American States. Deborah R. McFarlane & Kenneth J. Meier. LC 99-50685. (Illus.). 308p. 2000. pap. text 24.95 (*1-889119-39-3*, Pub. by Seven Bridges) Stylus Pub VA.

Politics of Field Research: Beyond Enlightenment. Ed. by Jaber F. Gubrium. 256p. (C). 1989. text 39.95 (*0-8039-8226-7*) Sage.

***Politics of Fieldwork: Research in an American Concentration Camp.** Lane R. Hirabayashi. LC 98-25489. xii, 219 p. 1999. 35.00 (*0-8165-1864-5*) U of Ariz Pr.

Politics of Finance in Developing Countries. Ed. by Stephan Haggard et al. (Cornell Studies of Finance in Developing Countries). 352p. 1993. text 49.95 (*0-8014-2892-0*); pap. text 17.95 (*0-8014-8130-9*) Cornell U Pr.

Politics of Fiscal Stress: Organizational Management of Budget Cutbacks. Landon Curry. LC 90-42937. 110p. (Orig.). 1990. pap. 9.95 (*0-87772-326-5*) UCB IGS.

Politics of Fishing. Gray. LC 98-10620. 1998. text 69.95 (*0-312-21410-3*) St Martin.

Politics of Fishing in Britain & France. Michael Shackleton. 400p. 1986. text 82.95 (*0-566-05161-3*, Pub. by Dartmth Pub) Ashgate Pub Co.

Politics of Flexibility: Restructuring State & Industry in Britain, Germany & Scandinavia. Ed. by Bob Jessop et al. 400p. 1991. text 95.00 (*1-85278-548-9*) E Elgar.

Politics of Focus. Smith. LC 98-17825. 200p. 1998. text 74.95 (*0-7190-4260-7*, Pub. by Manchester Univ Pr) St Martin.

Politics of Focus. Smith. LC 98-17825. (Illus.). 200p. 1998. text 29.95 (*0-7190-4261-5*, Pub. by Manchester Univ Pr) St Martin.

Politics of Food in Mexico: State Power & Social Mobilization. Jonathan Fox. LC 92-25948. (Food Systems & Agrarian Change Ser.). (Illus.). 296p. 1993. 42.50 (*0-8014-2716-9*) Cornell U Pr.

Politics of Food in Mexico: State Power & Social Mobilization. Jonathan Fox. LC 92-25948. (Food Systems & Agrarian Change Ser.). 295p. reprint ed. pap. 91.50 (*0-608-20890-6*, 207198900003) Bks Demand.

***Politics of Force.** Regina G. Lawrence. LC 99-53115. (Illus.). 279p. 2000. pap. 17.95 (*0-520-22192-3*, Pub. by U CA Pr) Cal Prin Full Svc.

Politics of Force: Bargaining During International Crises. Oran R. Young. LC 68-27408. (Center of International Studies). 450p. reprint ed. 139.50 (*0-8357-9509-8*, 201602000006) Bks Demand.

***Politics of Force: Media, Policy Discourse, & the Construction of Police Brutality.** Regina G. Lawrence. LC 99-53115. (Illus.). 279p. 2000. 45.00 (*0-520-22191-5*, Pub. by U CA Pr) Cal Prin Full Svc.

Politics of Foreign Aid: U. S. Foreign Assistance & Aid to Israel. Mohamed Rabie. LC 88-3096. 200p. 1988. 55.00 (*0-275-93000-9*, C3000, Praeger Pubs) Greenwood.

Politics of Foreign Aid in the Brazilian Northeast. Riordan Roett. LC 73-166403. 214p. 1972. reprint ed. pap. 66.40 (*0-7837-9886-5*, 206061200006) Bks Demand.

Politics of Freedom: African Americans & the Political Process During Reconstruction. Intro. by Donald G. Nieman. LC 93-36875. (Illus.). 432p. 1994. text 83.00 (*0-8153-1442-6*) Garland.

***Politics of Freer Trade in Europe: Three-level Games in The Common Commercial Policy of The Eu,** Klaus-Gunter Deutsch. LC 99-12710. 1999. text 59.95 (*0-312-22347-1*) St Martin.

Politics of French Trade Unionism. Jeff Bridgford. 206p. 1992. text 59.00 (*0-7185-1350-9*, Pub. by Leicester U Pr) Cassell & Continuum.

Politics of French Trade Unionism. Jeff Bridgford. 208p. 1994. pap. 17.95 (*0-7185-1487-4*, Pub. by Leicester U Pr) Cassell & Continuum.

Politics of Friendship. Jacques Derrida. Tr. by George Collins. LC 97-11930. 1997. pap. 20.00 (*1-85984-033-7*, Pub. by Verso) Norton.

Politics of Fun: Cultural Policy & Debate in Contemporary France. David L. Looseley. 256p. 1995. 49.50 (*1-85973-013-2*); pap. 19.50 (*1-85973-153-8*, Pub. by Berg Pubs) MBIPubg.

Politics of Fun & Games. Shea. LC 98-84997. 1998. pap. text 23.95 (*0-312-17101-3*) St Martin.

Politics of Garbage: A Community Perspective on Solid Waste Policy Making. Larry S. Luton. LC 96-10050. (Pitt Series in Policy & Institutional). (Illus.). 272p. 1997. pap. 22.95 (*0-8229-5605-5*); text 49.95 (*0-8229-3946-0*) U of Pittsburgh Pr.

***Politics of Gay Rights.** Craig A. Rimmerman et al. LC 99-55589. (Series on Sexuality, History & Society). (Illus.). 376p. 1998. pap. text 19.00 (*0-226-71999-5*) U Ch Pr.

***Politics of Gender after Socialism: A Comparative-Historical Essay.** Susan Gal. 168p. 2000. 39.50 (*0-691-04893-2*, Pub. by Princeton U Pr); pap. text 15.95 (*0-691-04894-0*, Pub. by Princeton U Pr) Cal Prin Full Svc.

Politics of Gender & Domestic Service. Andall. 61.95 (*0-7546-1088-8*) Ashgate Pub Co.

***Politics of Genocide: Punjab, 1984-1998.** Inderjit Singh Jaijee. LC 99-938985. (Illus.). 1999. 30.00 (*81-202-0415-8*, Pub. by Ajanta Pubns) S Asia.

Politics of Genocide: The Holocaust in Hungary. Randolph L. Braham. LC 99-20739. 368p. 1999. 18.95 (*0-8143-2691-9*) Wayne St U Pr.

Politics of Genocide: The Holocaust in Hungary, 2 vols., Set. 2nd ed. Randolph L. Braham. (East European Monographs: No. 350). 2200p. 1992. 298.00 (*0-88033-247-6*, Pub. by East Eur Monographs) Col U Pr.

Politics of German Child Welfare from the Empire to the Federal Republic. Edward R. Dickinson. LC 95-38644. (Historical Studies). 384p. 1996. 45.00 (*0-674-68862-7*) HUP.

Politics of German Protestantism: The Rise of the Protestant Church Elite in Prussia, 1815-1848. Robert M. Bigler. LC 77-142055. 314p. reprint ed. pap. 97.40 (*0-608-18274-5*, 203150000075) Bks Demand.

Politics of German Regulation. Kenneth Dyson. 250p. 1992. 72.95 (*1-85521-273-0*, Pub. by Dartmth Pub) Ashgate Pub Co.

Politics of Glamour: Ideology & Democracy in the Screen Actors Guild. David F. Prindle. LC 88-40194. (Illus.). 240p. (C). 1988. 27.95 (*0-299-11810-X*) U of Wis Pr.

Politics of Global Economic Relations. 4th ed. David H. Blake & Robert H. Walters. 208p. (C). 1991. pap. text 45.00 (*0-13-682394-7*) P-H.

Politics of Global Governance: International Organizations in an Interdependent World. Ed. by Paul F. Diehl. 421p. (Orig.). 1996. 55.00 (*1-55587-654-4*); pap. 24.95 (*1-55587-638-2*) L Rienner.

Politics of God: Christian Theologies & Social Justice. Kathryn Tanner. LC 92-19360. 272p. (Orig.). 1992. pap. 21.00 (*0-8006-2613-3*, 1-2613, Fortress Pr) Augsburg Fortress.

Politics of God: Scriptures & Prophets Are Used to Evaluate Contemporary Conservative & Liberal Positions. Robert L. Hamson. LC 96-92494. (Illus.). 352p. 1997. 26.00 (*0-940356-02-3*) Sandpiper CA.

Politics of Grand Strategy: Britain & France Prepare for War, 1904-1914. Samuel R. Williamson, Jr. LC 89-27401. 432p. (C). 1990. pap. 19.95 (*0-948660-13-9*, Pub. by Ashfield Pr) Humanities.

Politics of Guilt & Pity. Rousas J. Rushdoony. 400p. 1995. reprint ed. text. write for info. (*1-879998-07-6*) Ross Hse Bks.

Politics of Gun Control. 2nd ed. Robert J. Spitzer. LC 98-34527. (Illus.). 224p. (C). 1998. pap. text 21.95 (*1-56643-072-0*, Chatham House Pub) Seven Bridges.

Politics of Hallowed Ground: Wounded Knee & the Struggle for Indian Sovereignty. Mario Gonzalez & Elizabeth Cook-Lynn. LC 97-4777. 360p. 1998. 21.95 (*0-252-06669-3*); text 49.95 (*0-252-02354-4*) U of Ill Pr.

Politics of Harmony: Civil Service, & Social Reform in Baden, 1800-1850. Lloyd E. Lee. LC 77-92569. 272p. 1980. 38.50 (*0-87413-143-X*) U Delaware Pr.

Politics of Harmony: Land Dispute Strategies in Swaziland. Laurel L. Rose. (African Studies: No. 69). (Illus.). 254p. (C). 1992. text 74.95 (*0-521-39296-9*) Cambridge U Pr.

Politics of Hazardous Waste Management. Ed. by James P. Lester & Ann Bowman. LC 83-16595. (Duke Press Policy Studies). x, 317p. (Orig.). 1983. pap. text 20.95 (*0-8223-0523-2*) Duke.

Politics of Health. 2nd ed. Gardner. LC 96-118212. 1995. text 41.00 (*0-443-04775-8*, W B Saunders Co) Harcrt Hlth Sci Grp.

***Politics of Health Care: Towards a Holistic Approach.** Ledwith & Walker. 224p. 2000. pap. text 36.00 (*0-7506-4310-2*) Buttrwrth-Heinemann.

Politics of Health Care Reform: Lessons from the Past, Prospects for the Future. Ed. by James A. Morone & Gary S. Belkin. LC 94-10005. 552p. 1994. text 54.95 (*0-8223-1461-4*); pap. text 21.95 (*0-8223-1489-4*) Duke.

***Politics of Health in Europe.** Richard Freeman. 2000. text 69.95 (*0-7190-4213-5*, Pub. by Manchester Univ Pr); pap. text 24.95 (*0-7190-4214-3*, Pub. by Manchester Univ Pr) St Martin.

Politics of Health Legislation: An Economic Perspective. 2nd ed. Paul J. Feldstein. LC 96-11238. 1996. pap. 48.00 (*1-56793-045-X*) Health Admin Pr.

Politics of Health Policy: The U. S. Reforms, 1980-1993. Vicente Navarro. LC 93-40683. 260p. 1994. pap. 29.95 (*1-55786-318-0*) Blackwell Pubs.

Politics of Heredity: Essays on Eugenics, Biomedicine, & the Nature-Nurture Debate. Diane B. Paul. LC 97-45212. (SUNY Series in Philosophy & Biology). 224p. (C). 1998. text 59.50 (*0-7914-3821-X*); pap. text 19.95 (*0-7914-3822-8*) State U NY Pr.

Politics of Heroin: CIA Complicity in the Global Drug Trade. Alfred W. McCoy. LC 90-47398. (Illus.). 654p. 1991. pap. 24.95 (*1-55652-125-1*, Lawrence Hill) Chicago Review.

Politics of Himalayan River Waters: An Analysis of the River Water Issues of Nepal, India & Bangladesh. B. C. Upreti. (Illus.). iv, 224p. 1993. 25.00 (*81-85693-32-3*, Pub. by Nirala Pubns) Nataraj Bks.

Politics of Himalayan River Waters: An Analysis of the River Water Issues of Nepal, India & Bangladesh. B. C. Upreti. (C). 1993. 71.00 (*0-7855-0205-X*, Pub. by Ratna Pustak Bhandar) St Mut.

Politics of Hispanic Education: Un Paso Pa'lante y Dos Pa'tras. Kenneth J. Meier & Joseph Stewart, Jr. LC 90-33101. (SUNY Series, United States Hispanic Studies). 275p. (C). 1991. text 64.50 (*0-7914-0507-9*); pap. text 21.95 (*0-7914-0508-7*) State U NY Pr.

Politics of Historical Vision: Marx, Foucalt, Habermas. Steven Best. LC 94-44894. (Critical Perspectives Ser.). 294p. 1995. lib. bdg. 37.95 (*0-89862-851-2*) Guilford Pubns.

Politics of Historical Vision: Marx, Foucault, Habermas. Steven Best. LC 94-44894. (Critical Perspectives Ser.). 294p. 1996. pap. text 17.95 (*1-57230-145-7*, 0145) Guilford Pubns.

Politics of History. 2nd ed. Howard Zinn. 408p. 1990. pap. text 14.95 (*0-252-06122-5*) U of Ill Pr.

Politics of History: Writing the History of the American Revolution, 1783-1815. Arthur H. Shaffer. LC 75-7865. 228p. 1975. 21.95 (*0-913750-09-3*) Transaction Pubs.

Politics of Home: Postcolonial Relocations & Twentieth-Century Fiction. Rosemary M. George. 274p. 1996. text 59.95 (*0-521-45334-8*) Cambridge U Pr.

Politics of Home: Postcolonial Relocations & Twentieth-century Fiction. Rosemary M. George. LC 99-20036. 274p. 1999. pap. 16.95 (*0-520-22012-9*, Pub. by U CA Pr) Cal Prin Full Svc.

Politics of Hong Kongs Reversi. Chuang Chang. LC 96-52814. 274p. 1999. pap. 24.95 (*0-312-22633-0*) St Martin.

Politics of Hope. Bernard P. Dauenhauer. (Critical Social Thought Ser.). 200p. 1986. 49.50 (*0-7102-0823-5*, 08235, Routledge Thoemms) Routledge.

Politics of Hostility: Castro's Revolution & United States Policy. Lynn-Darrell Bender. Ed. by John Zebrowski et al. LC 74-78314. (Illus.). 160p. 1974. 7.95 (*0-913480-24-X*) Inter Am U Pr.

Politics of Households in Ottoman Egypt: The Rise of the Qazaglis. Jane Hathaway. (Cambridge Studies in Islamic Civilization). 199p. 1997. text 54.95 (*0-521-57110-3*) Cambridge U Pr.

Politics of Housework. Ed. & Compiled by Ellen Malos. 256p. 1995. 45.00 (*1-873797-19-2*); pap. 19.95 (*1-873797-18-4*) Paul & Co Pubs.

Politics of Human Nature. Thomas Fleming. 276p. 1993. pap. 24.95 (*1-56000-693-5*) Transaction Pubs.

***Politics of Human Rights.** 1999. 25.00 (*1-85984-727-7*, Pub. by Verso) Norton.

Politics of Human Rights & Civil Liberties. Attar Chand. 377p. 1985. 32.95 (*0-317-39866-0*) Asia Bk Corp.

Politics of Human Rights in Argentina: Protest, Change, & Democratization. Alison Brysk. LC 93-34802. xvi, 291p. 1994. 45.00 (*0-8047-2275-7*) Stanford U Pr.

***Politics of Human Rights in East Asia.** Kenneth Christie & Denny Roy. LC 00-9420. 2001. write for info. (*0-7453-1419-8*, Pub. by Pluto GBR) Stylus Pub VA.

Politics of Human Science. Ed. by Siebren Miedema et al. 229p. 1995. pap. 19.95 (*90-5487-095-8*) Paul & Co Pubs.

Politics of Hunger: The Global Food System. John W. Warnock. LC 87-1659. 288p. 1987. pap. 15.95 (*0-458-80630-7*) Routledge.

***Politics of Hunger in India: A Study of Democracy, Governance & Kalahandi's Poverty.** Bob Currie. LC 99-53055. 2000. text 65.00 (*0-312-22954-2*) St Martin.

Politics of Ideas: Intellectual Challenges to the Party after 1992. Ed. by John K. White & John C. Green. LC 95-24132. 128p. (C). 1995. pap. text 19.95 (*0-8476-8103-3*); lib. bdg. 39.50 (*0-8476-8102-5*) Rowman.

Politics of Ideas: Political Theory & American Public Policy. Lawrence J. Herson. 358p. (C). 1990. reprint ed. pap. text 21.95 (*0-88133-512-6*) Waveland Pr.

***Politics of Ideas & the Spread of Enterprise Zones.** Karen Mossberger. LC 00-26360. (American Governance & Public Policy Ser.). 288p. 2000. text 60.00 (*0-87840-800-2*); pap. text 24.95 (*0-87840-801-0*) Georgetown U Pr.

Politics of Identity. James W. McAuley. LC 94-161479. 204p. 1993. 66.95 (*1-85628-537-5*, Pub. by Avebry) Ashgate Pub Co.

Politics of Identity: Class, Culture, Social Movements. Stanley Aronowitz. 288p. (C). 1992. pap. 19.99 (*0-415-90437-4*, A5748) Routledge.

Politics of Identity: Migrants & Minorities in Multicultural States. Robert Hudson & Fred Rbeno. LC 99-25941. 2000. text 65.00 (*0-312-22547-4*) St Martin.

Politics of Identity in Australia. Ed. by Geoffrey Stokes. 234p. (C). 1997. text 64.95 (*0-521-58356-X*) Cambridge U Pr.

Politics of Ideocracy. Jaroslaw Piekalkiewicz & Alfred W. Penn. LC 94-8841. 274p. (C). 1995. text 49.50 (*0-7914-2297-6*); pap. text 16.95 (*0-7914-2298-4*) State U NY Pr.

Politics of Illusion: A Political History of the IRA. Henry Patterson. 320p. 1998. pap. 24.95 (*1-897959-31-1*, Pub. by Serif) IPG Chicago.

Politics of Illusion: The Bay of Pigs Invasion Reexamined. James G. Blight & Peter Kornbluh. LC 97-23213. (Studies in Cuban History). 284p. 1997. 49.95 (*1-55587-783-4*) L Rienner.

***Politics of Illusion: The Bay of Pigs Invasion Reexamined.** Ed. by James G. Blight & Peter Kornbluh. (Studies in Cuban History). 284p. 1998. pap. 22.50 (*1-55587-822-9*) L Rienner.

Politics of Illusion: The Military Coups in Fiji. Deryck Scaar. 180p. 1989. write for info. (*0-8448-1589-6*); pap. write for info. (*0-8448-1590-X*) Taylor & Francis.

Politics of Illusion & Empire: German Occupation Policy in the Soviet Union, Nineteen Forty-Two to Nineteen Forty Three. Timothy P. Mulligan. LC 87-32702. 220p. 1988. 57.95 (*0-275-92837-3*, C2837, Praeger Pubs) Greenwood.

Politics of Immigrant Workers: Labor Activism & Migration in the World Economy since 1830. 2nd rev. ed. Ed. by Camille Guerin-Gonzales & Carl Strikwerda. LC 98-34975. 368p. 1998. pap. 20.00 (*0-8419-1298-X*) Holmes & Meier.

Politics of Immigrant Workers: Labor Activism & the World Economy Since 1830. Camille Guerin-Gonzales & Carl Strikwerda. LC 91-36174. 368p. 1993. 40.00 (*0-8419-1297-1*) Holmes & Meier.

***Politics of Immigration: Current Issues & Future Directions.** Ed. by A. M. Babkina. 187p. 2000. text 59.00 (*1-56072-733-0*) Nova Sci Pubs.

Politics of Immigration in Western Europe. Ed. by Martin Baldwin-Edwards & Martin A. Schain. LC 94-11485. (Illus.). 216p. (C). 1994. 49.50 (*0-7146-4593-1*, Pub. by F Cass Pubs); pap. 19.50 (*0-7146-4137-5*, Pub. by F Cass Pubs) Intl Spec Bk.

Politics of Improving Urban Air Quality. Wyn P. Grant et al. LC 98-30465. 200p. 1999. 80.00 (*1-85898-696-6*) E Elgar.

Politics of Inclusion & Exclusion: Jews & Nationalism in Hungary. Vera Ranki. LC 98-45937. 274p. 1999. pap. 18.95 (*0-8419-1402-8*); text 45.00 (*0-8419-1401-X*) Holmes & Meier.

Politics of Indecision: Origins & Implications of American Involvement with the Palestine Problem. Daniel Tschirgi. LC 82-15115. 368p. 1983. 47.95 (*0-275-91092-X*, C1092, Praeger Pubs) Greenwood.

Politics of Independence: A Study of a Scottish Town. Frank W. Bealey & John Sewel. 280p. 1981. 36.00 (*0-08-025736-4*, Pergamon Pr) Elsevier.

Politics of Independent Kenya, 1963-8. Cherry J. Gertzel. LC 73-124293. 192p. reprint ed. pap. 59.60 (*0-608-11809-5*, 201529600093) Bks Demand.

Politics of India since Independence. 2nd ed. Paul R. Brass. LC 93-30782. (New Cambridge History of India Ser.: No. IV: 1). (Illus.). 423p. (C). 1994. text 69.95 (*0-521-45362-3*); pap. text 24.95 (*0-521-45970-2*) Cambridge U Pr.

Politics of Indian Removal: Creek Government & Society in Crisis. Michael D. Green. LC 81-14670. xvi, 237p. 1982. pap. text 14.00 (*0-8032-7015-1*) U of Nebr Pr.

Politics of Indians' English: Linguistic Colonialism & the Expanding English Empire. N. Krishnaswamy & Archana S. Burde. LC 98-909292. 214p. 1998. text 22.50 (*0-19-564368-2*) OUP.

***Politics of India's Conventional Cinema: Imaging a Universe, Subverting a Multiverse.** Fareed Kazmi. LC 98-44786. 1998. write for info. (*0-7619-9310-X*); pap. write for info. (*0-7619-9311-8*) Sage.

An Asterisk (*) at the beginning of an entry indicates that the title is appearing for the first time.

Politics of Individualism: Liberalism, Liberal Feminism & Anarchism. L. Susan Brown. LC 93-72750. 212p. 1994. 48.99 (*1-895431-79-4*, Pub. by Black Rose); pap. 19.99 (*1-895431-78-6*, Pub. by Black Rose) Consort Bk Sales.

Politics of Individualism: Parties & the American Character in the Jacksonian Era. Lawrence F. Kohl. 288p. 1991. reprint ed. pap. text 19.95 (*0-19-506781-9*) OUP.

***Politics of Indonesia.** Damien Kingsbury. LC 99-200268. 296p. 1999. pap. text 19.95 (*0-19-550626-X*) OUP.

Politics of Industrial Change: Railway Policy in North America. R. Kent Weaver. LC 85-24274. 291p. 1985. 36.95 (*0-8157-9260-3*); pap. 16.95 (*0-8157-9259-X*) Brookings.

Politics of Industrial Recruitment: Japanese Automobile Investment & Economic Development in the American States, 104. Ed. by Ernest J. Yanarella & William C. Green. LC 89-25997. (Contributions in Economics & Economic History Ser.: No. 104). 248p. 1990. 62.95 (*0-313-26359-0*, YPC/) Greenwood.

Politics of Industrial Restructuring: Canadian Textiles. Rianne Mahon. (State & Economic Life Ser.: No. 7). xii, 204p. 1984. pap. 13.95 (*0-8020-6546-5*); text 30.00 (*0-8020-2538-2*) U of Toronto Pr.

Politics of Industrialization in Tsarist Russia: The Association of Southern Coal & Steel Producers, 1874-1914. Susan P. McCaffray. LC 95-37346. 320p. 1996. lib. bdg. 35.00 (*0-87580-204-4*) N Ill U Pr.

Politics of Inertia: The Election of 1876 & the End of Reconstruction. Keith I. Polakoff. LC 72-96400. 357p. reprint ed. pap. 110.70 (*0-7837-8693-X*, 204943900011) Bks Demand.

Politics of Inflation & Economic Stagnation. Ed. by Leon N. Lindberg & Charles S. Maier. LC 84-23263. 612p. 1985. 44.95 (*0-8157-5264-4*); pap. 19.95 (*0-8157-5263-6*) Brookings.

Politics of Informal Justice Vol. 2: Comparative Studies. Ed. by Richard L. Abel. LC 81-14920. (Studies on Law & Social Control). 1981. text 74.95 (*0-12-041502-X*) Acad Pr.

Politics of Information Management: Policy Guidelines. Paul A. Strassmann. (Illus.). 540p. 1994. mass mkt. 49.95 (*0-9620413-4-3*) Info Econ Pr.

Politics of Innocence: Sexual Responsibility. 101p. 1998. pap. write for info. (*0-9660456-6-1*) Glovebox Guidebks.

***Politics of Institutional Choice: The Formation of the Russian State Duma.** Steven S. Smith. 2001. 42.50 (*0-691-05736-2*); pap. 16.95 (*0-691-05737-0*) Princeton U Pr.

Politics of Integration: Is There a Desk with My Name On it Too? Ed. by Roger Slee. 256p. 1993. 89.95 (*0-7507-0174-9*, Falmer Pr); pap. 34.95 (*0-7507-0175-7*, Falmer Pr) Taylor & Francis.

Politics of Intergovernmental Relations. 2nd ed. David C. Nice & Patricia Fredericksen. LC 94-15923. 1995. pap. text 32.95 (*0-8304-1357-X*) Thomson Learn.

Politics of International Aviation. Eugene Sochor. LC 90-70524. 308p. 1991. text 39.95 (*0-87745-307-1*) U of Iowa Pr.

Politics of International Credit: Private Finance & Foreign Policy in Germany & Japan. Andrew J. Spindler. LC 84-73394. 220p. 1983. 32.95 (*0-8157-8070-2*); pap. 12.95 (*0-8157-8069-9*) Brookings.

Politics of International Crisis Escalation. P. Stuart Robinson. LC 95-62324. 224p. 1996. text 65.00 (*1-86064-064-8*, Pub. by I B T) St Martin.

Politics of International Economic Relations. Ramashray Roy. 234p. 1982. 24.95 (*0-318-37261-4*) Asia Bk Corp.

Politics of International Economic Relations. Joan E. Spero. 416p. 1996. pap. text 44.95 (*0-312-08476-5*) St Martin.

Politics of International Environmental Management. Ed. by Arild Underdal. LC 95-35309. (Environment, Science & Society Ser.: Vol. 4). 184p. 1998. text 107.00 (*0-7923-3685-2*) Kluwer Academic.

Politics of International Health: The Children's Vaccine Initiative & the Struggle to Develop Vaccines for the Third World. William Muraskin. LC 97-51725. 288p. (C). 1998. text 65.50 (*0-7914-3999-2*); pap. text 21.95 (*0-7914-4000-1*) State U NY Pr.

Politics of International Humanitarian Aid Operations. Ed. by Eric A. Belgrad & Nitza Nachmias. LC 96-44677. 240p. 1997. 62.95 (*0-275-95273-8*, Praeger Pubs) Greenwood.

Politics of International Law: U. S. Foreign Policy Reconsidered. David P. Forsythe. LC 90-32486. 184p. (C). 1990. pap. text 17.95 (*1-55587-208-5*) L Rienner.

Politics of International Sport: Games of Power. Wallace Irwin, Jr. LC 88-82097. (Headline Ser.: No. 286). (Illus.). 72p. (Orig.). 1988. pap. 5.95 (*0-87124-121-8*) Foreign Policy.

Politics of International Standards: France & the Color TV War. Rhonda J. Crane. LC 79-4231. (Communication & Information Science Ser.). 124p. 1979. text 73.25 (*0-89391-019-8*) Ablx Pub.

Politics of Interpretation. rev. ed. Ed. by W. J. Mitchell. LC 83-3581. 1993. pap. text 14.95 (*0-226-53220-8*) U Ch Pr.

Politics of Interpretation. rev. ed. Ed. by W. J. Mitchell. LC 83-3581. 1994. lib. bdg. 25.00 (*0-226-53219-4*) U Ch Pr.

Politics of Interpretation: Alterity & Ideology in Old Yiddish Studies. Jerold C. Frakes. LC 87-37479. 320p. (C). 1988. pap. text 19.95 (*0-88706-846-4*) State U NY Pr.

Politics of Interpretation: Ideology, Professionalism, & the Study of Literature. Patrick C. Hogan. 272p. 1990. text 55.00 (*0-19-506272-8*) OUP.

Politics of Intervention: The United States in Central America. Ed. by Roger Burbach & Patricia Flynn. LC 83-42526. 272p. 1984. pap. 12.00 (*0-85345-635-6*, Pub. by Monthly Rev) NYU Pr.

Politics of Interventionism in Ottoman Lebanon, 1830-1861, 2 vols. Ceasar E. Farah. (Illus.). 832p. 1999. text 85.00 (*1-86064-056-7*) St Martin.

Politics of Irish Dissent, 1650-1800. Ed. by Kevin Herlihy. 128p. 1997. pap. 20.00 (*1-85182-302-6*, Pub. by Four Cts Pr); boxed set 39.50 (*1-85182-301-8*, Pub. by Four Cts Pr) Intl Spec Bk.

Politics of Irish Drama: Plays in Context from Boucicault to Friel. Nicholas Grene. LC 99-10289. (Cambridge Studies in Modern Theatre). 320p. (C). 2000. 59.95 (*0-521-66051-3*); pap. 22.95 (*0-521-66536-1*) Cambridge U Pr.

Politics of Irish Social Policy, 1600-1990. Frederick W. Powell. LC 91-48166. 384p. 1992. lib. bdg. 99.95 (*0-7734-9463-4*) E Mellen.

Politics of Irony: Essays in Self-Betrayal. Ed. by Daniel W. Conway & John E. Seery. LC 91-44679. 288p. 1992. text 39.95 (*0-312-04801-7*) St Martin.

Politics of Islamic Revivalism: Diversity & Unity. Ed. by Shireen T. Hunter. LC 87-21380. (Indiana Series in Arab & Islamic Studies). 319p. 1988. reprint ed. pap. 98.90 (*0-7837-1755-5*, 205729100024) Bks Demand.

***Politics of Italian National Identity.** Ed. by Gino Bedani & Bruce Haddock. 224p. 2000. 75.00 (*0-7083-1622-0*, Pub. by U Wales Pr) Paul & Co Pubs.

***Politics of James Bond: From Fleming's Novels to the Big Screen.** Jeremy Black. LC 00-25127. 264p. 2000. 25.00 (*0-275-96859-6*, Praeger Trade) Greenwood.

Politics of James Connolly. Allen. 256p. (C). 44.95 (*0-7453-0394-3*, Pub. by Pluto GBR); pap. 17.95 (*0-7453-0473-7*, Pub. by Pluto GBR) Stylus Pub VA.

Politics of Jane Austen. Neill. LC 98-31055. 192p. 1999. text 59.95 (*0-312-21872-9*) St Martin.

Politics of Japanese Defense: Managing Internal & External Pressures. Joseph P. Keddell, Jr. LC 92-45246. 256p. (gr. 13). 1993. text 70.95 (*1-56324-129-3*) M E Sharpe.

Politics of Japan's Energy Strategy. Ed. by Ronald A. Morse. (Research Papers & Policy: No. 3). (Orig.). 1981. pap. 7.00 (*0-912966-45-9*) IEAS.

Politics of Jerusalem since 1967. Michael Dumper. (Institute for Palestine Studies). (Illus.). 320p. 1996. 31.00 (*0-231-10640-8*) Col U Pr.

Politics of Jesus: Vicit Agnus Noster. 2nd rev. ed. John H. Yoder. LC 93-39532. 256p. (C). 1994. pap. text 18.00 (*0-8028-0734-8*) Eerdmans.

Politics of John Dewey. Gary Bullert. LC 83-62872. 223p. 1983. 37.95 (*0-87975-208-4*) Prometheus Bks.

***Politics of Judgment: Aesthetics, Identity & Political Theory.** Kennan Ferguson. LC 98-55970. 176p. 1999. 40.00 (*0-7391-0058-0*) Lxngtn Bks.

Politics of Jurisprudence: A Critical Introduction to Legal Philosophy. R. B. Cotterell. 255p. 1989. pap. 34.00 (*0-406-50088-6*, UK, MICHIE) LEXIS Pub.

Politics of Jurisprudence: A Critical Introduction to Legal Philosophy. Roger Cotterell. LC 91-40233. 296p. (C). 1992. pap. text 18.95 (*0-8122-1393-9*) U of Pa Pr.

Politics of Justice: A. B. Fall & the Teapot Dome Scandal, a New Perspective. Herman B. Weisner. 291p. (Orig.). (C). 1992. 24.95 (*1-880047-05-5*); pap. text 12.95 (*1-880047-03-9*) Creative Des.

Politics of Justice: Lower Federal Judicial Selection & the Second Party System, 1829-1861. Kermit L. Hall. LC 79-9238. 288p. reprint ed. pap. 89.30 (*0-7837-1822-5*, 204202200001) Bks Demand.

Politics of Justice: The Attorney General & the Making of Legal Policy. Cornell W. Clayton. LC 92-30711. (American Political Institutions & Public Policy Ser.). 296p. (gr. 13). 1992. text 75.95 (*1-56324-018-1*); pap. text 38.95 (*1-56324-019-X*) M E Sharpe.

Politics of Justice & Justice Reform in Latin America: The Peruvian Case in Comparative Perspective. Linn Ann Hammergren. LC 97-38743. (C). 1997. text 79.00 (*0-8133-3418-7*, Pub. by Westview) HarpC.

Politics of Juvenile Crime. John Pitts. (Contemporary Criminology Ser.: Vol. 2). 192p. (C). 1988. text 69.95 (*0-8039-8132-5*); pap. text 16.50 (*0-8039-8133-3*) Sage.

Politics of King Lear. Edwin Muir. 1972. 200.00 (*0-87968-032-6*) Gordon Pr.

Politics of King Lear. E. Muir. LC 76-99171. (Studies in Shakespeare: No. 24). 1970. reprint ed. lib. bdg. 59.00 (*0-8383-0331-5*) M S G Haskell Hse.

Politics of Kinship: A Study in Social Manipulation Among the Lakeside Tonga of Malawi. J. Van Velsen & University of Zambia Staff. LC 72-181804. xxix, 338 p. 1971. write for info. (*0-7190-1023-3*) St Martin.

Politics of Knowledge: Activist Movements in Medicine & Planning. Lily M. Hoffman. LC 88-17447. (SUNY Series in the Sociology of Work). 290p. (C). 1989. text 67.50 (*0-88706-948-7*); pap. text 24.95 (*0-88706-949-5*) State U NY Pr.

Politics of Knowledge: The Carnegie Corporation, Philanthropy, & Public Policy. Ellen C. Lagemann. LC 89-16634. xvi, 364p. 1992. pap. text 18.95 (*0-226-46780-5*) U Ch Pr.

Politics of Knowledge: The Carnegie Corporation, Philanthropy & Public Policy. Ellen C. Lagemann. LC 89-16634. 363p. 1989. reprint ed. pap. 112.60 (*0-608-03014-7*, 206346400006) Bks Demand.

Politics of Labor. Thomas P. Thompson. LC 75-9924. (Social History of Canada Ser.: No. 28). 292p. reprint ed. pap. 90.60 (*0-8357-6369-2*, 203572300096) Bks Demand.

Politics of Labour under Late Colonialism: Workers, Unions & the State in Chota Nagpur 1928-1939. Dilip Simeon. LC 95-902573. (C). 1995. 38.00 (*81-7304-036-2*, Pub. by Manohar) S Asia.

Politics of Land Reform in Chile, 1950-1970: Public Policy, Political Institutions, & Social Change. Robert R. Kaufman. LC 72-75407. (Center for International Affairs Ser.). (Illus.). 333p. 1972. 34.50 (*0-674-68920-8*) HUP.

Politics of Land-Use Reform. Frank Popper et al. LC 80-23255. 333p. reprint ed. pap. 103.30 (*0-608-09921-X*, 206925900003) Bks Demand.

***Politics of Language: Conflict, Identity, & Cultural Pluralism in Comparative Perspective.** Carol L. Schmid. (Illus.). 240p. 2000. pap. 19.95 (*0-19-513776-0*); text 65.00 (*0-19-513775-2*) OUP.

Politics of Language: Liberalism As Word & Symbol. Ronald D. Rotunda. LC 85-24548. 148p. reprint ed. pap. 45.90 (*0-8357-3406-4*, 203966300013) Bks Demand.

Politics of Language in Australia. Uldis Ozolins. LC 92-30377. (Illus.). 303p. (C). 1993. text 74.95 (*0-521-41794-5*) Cambridge U Pr.

***Politics of Language in Ireland, 1366-1922: Sourcebook.** Tony Crowley. LC 99-32500. (Politics of Language Ser.). 2000. pap. 25.99 (*0-415-15718-8*) Routledge.

***Politics of Language in Ireland, 1366-1922: Sourcebook.** Ed. by Tony Crowley. LC 99-32500. 248p. (C). 2000. text. write for info. (*0-415-15717-X*) Routledge.

Politics of Language in Socialist Albania. Arshi Pipa. 283p. 1989. text 61.00 (*0-88033-168-2*, Pub. by East Eur Monographs) Col U Pr.

***Politics of Language in Spanish-Speaking World.** Clare Mar-Molinero. LC 99-58473. 256p. (C). 2000. pap. write for info. (*0-415-15655-6*); text. write for info. (*0-415-15654-8*) Routledge.

Politics of Language Purism. Ed. by Bjorn H. Jernudd & Michael J. Shapiro. (Contributions to the Sociology of Language Ser.: No. 54). vi, 250p. (C). 1989. pap. 95.40 (*0-89925-483-7*) Mouton.

Politics of Language, 1791-1819. Olivia Smith. 288p. 1986. pap. 22.50 (*0-19-812878-9*) OUP.

Politics of Large Numbers: A History of Statistical Reasoning. Alain Des Rosieres. Tr. by Camille Naish from FRE. LC 98-3199. 368p. 1998. 45.00 (*0-674-68932-1*) HUP.

Politics of Latin American Development. 3rd ed. Gary W. Wynia. (Illus.). 364p. (C). 1990. pap. text 22.95 (*0-521-38924-0*) Cambridge U Pr.

Politics of Latin American Development. 3rd ed. Gary W. Wynia. (Illus.). 364p. (C). 1990. text 69.95 (*0-521-38027-8*) Cambridge U Pr.

Politics of Latin Literature: Writing, Identity & Empire in Ancient Rome. Thomas N. Habinek. LC 97-40074. 248p. 1998. text 39.50 (*0-691-06827-5*, Pub. by Princeton U Pr) Cal Prin Full Svc.

Politics of Law: A Progressive Critique. 3rd ed. Ed. by David Kairys. LC 97-46000. 752p. 1998. pap. 20.00 (*0-465-05959-7*, Pub. by Basic) HarpC.

Politics of Law & the Courts in Nineteenth-Century Egypt. Byron Cannon. LC 88-14315. 345p. reprint ed. pap. 107.00 (*0-7837-6872-9*, 204670200003) Bks Demand.

***Politics of Lawmaking in Post-Mao China: Institutions, Processes & Democratic Prospects.** Murray Scott Tanner. LC 98-50034. (Illus.). 294p. 1999. text 75.00 (*0-19-829339-9*) OUP.

Politics of Letters. Richard Ohmann. LC 87-2152. (Illus.). 336p. 1987. pap. 22.95 (*0-8195-6213-0*, Wesleyan Univ Pr); text 40.00 (*0-8195-5175-9*, Wesleyan Univ Pr) U Pr of New Eng.

Politics of Liberal Education. Ed. by Darryl J. Gless & Barbara H. Smith. LC 91-29303. (Post-Contemporary Interventions Ser.). 288p. 1991. text 49.95 (*0-8223-1183-6*); pap. text 17.95 (*0-8223-1199-2*) Duke.

Politics of Liberation: Paths from Freire. Ed. by Peter McLaren & Colin Lankshear. LC 93-825. 288p. (C). 1994. pap. 24.99 (*0-415-09127-6*, B0844) Routledge.

Politics of Liberation: Paths from Freire. Ed. by Peter McLaren & Colin Lankshear. LC 93-825. 280p. (C). (gr. 13). 1994. text 62.50 (*0-415-09126-8*, B0840) Routledge.

Politics of Life: Four Plays by Asian American Women. Asian American Women. LC 92-13090. (Asian American History & Culture Ser.). 288p. (C). 1993. pap. 22.95 (*1-56639-001-X*) Temple U Pr.

Politics of Life: Four Plays by Asian American Women. Ed. & Intro. by Velina H. Houston. LC 92-13090. (Asian American History & Culture Ser.). 288p. (C). 1993. 59.95 (*1-56639-000-1*) Temple U Pr.

Politics of Life in Schools: Power, Conflict, & Cooperation. Ed. by Joseph R. Blase. LC 91-13614. 288p. 1991. pap. 26.95 (*0-8039-3893-4*) Corwin Pr.

Politics of Linguistics. Frederick J. Newmeyer. LC 86-11225. 192p. (C). 1987. 23.95 (*0-226-57720-1*) U Ch Pr.

Politics of Linguistics. Frederick J. Newmeyer. viii, 184p. 1988. pap. text 12.00 (*0-226-57722-8*) U Ch Pr.

Politics of Linking Schools & Social Services: The Yearbook of the Politics of Education Association, 1993. Ed. by Louise Adler et al. (Education Policy Perspectives Ser.). 224p. 1994. pap. 29.95 (*0-7507-0223-0*, Falmer Pr) Taylor & Francis.

Politics of Literacy. Ed. by Martin Hoyles. (Education Ser.). 216p. 1980. 14.00 (*0-904613-47-X*); pap. 5.95 (*0-904613-28-3*) Writers & Readers.

Politics of Literary Expression: A Study of Major Black Writers, 63. Donald B. Gibson. LC 80-27284. (Contributions in Afro-American & African Studies: No. 63). 225p. 1981. 42.95 (*0-313-21271-6*, GPE/, Greenwood Pr) Greenwood.

Politics of Literary Theory: An Introduction to Marxist Criticism. Philip Goldstein. 224p. 1990. 49.95 (*0-8130-0949-9*); pap. 19.95 (*0-8130-0976-6*) U Press Fla.

Politics of Local Economic Policy: The Problems & Possibilities of Local Initiative. Aram Eisenschitz & Jamie Gough. LC 94-179983. (Public Policy & Politics Ser.). xvi, 309 p. 1993. write for info. (*0-333-52175-7*) Macmillan.

Politics of Local Government Finance. Tony Travers. Ed. by P. G. Richards. LC 86-3331. (New Local Government Ser.: No. 27). 250p. 1987. text 49.95 (*0-04-352215-7*) Routledge.

Politics of Location. Andrew Kirby. (Illus.). 1982. 29.50 (*0-416-33900-X*, NO.3726); pap. 15.95 (*0-416-33910-7*, NO.3727) Routledge.

***Politics of Long Division: The Birth of the Second Party System in Ohio, 1818-1828.** Donald J. Ratcliffe. LC 99-50991. (Illus.). 344p. (C). 2000. text 65.00 (*0-8142-0849-5*) Ohio St U Pr.

Politics of Loyalty, 2. Alan D. Harper. LC 73-95509. (Contributions in American History Ser.: No. 2). (Illus.). 318p. 1970. 55.00 (*0-8371-2343-7*, HAL/, Greenwood Pr) Greenwood.

***Politics of Lying: Implications for Democracy.** Lionel Cliffe et al. LC 99-53561. 288p. 2000. text 45.00 (*0-312-23139-3*) St Martin.

Politics of Madness. Niri St.-Amand. 170p. 1988. pap. 14.95 (*0-88780-060-2*, Pub. by Formac Publ Co) Formac Dist Ltd.

Politics of Madness: A Theory of the Function of Madness in a Stratified Society. Hope Landrine. LC 91-16889. (American University Studies: Psychology: Ser. VIII, Vol. 22). XVI, 217p. 1992. 44.95 (*0-8204-1571-5*) P Lang Pubng.

Politics of Magic: Tom Murphy. Fintan O'Toole. LC 94-184679. 121994p. 1994. pap. 21.00 (*1-874597-75-8*) Dufour.

Politics of Management. Philip B. Heymann. LC 86-51340. 264p. 1987. 35.00 (*0-300-03777-5*) Yale U Pr.

Politics of Management Knowledge: A Critical Perspective. Ed. by Stewart Clegg et al. LC 96-69550. 256p. 1996. 65.00 (*0-8039-7933-9*); pap. 26.95 (*0-8039-7934-7*) Sage.

Politics of Manhood: Profeminist Men Respond to the Mythopoetic Men's Movement (& the Mythopoetic Leaders Answer) Ed. by Michael S. Kimmel. LC 95-34527. 368p. (C). 1995. pap. 22.95 (*1-56639-366-3*) Temple U Pr.

Politics of Marxism. write for info. (*0-8386-3612-8*) Fairleigh Dickinson.

Politics of Marxism: The Key Debates. Jules Townsend. 224p. 1996. 79.95 (*0-7185-1420-3*); pap. 19.95 (*0-7185-0004-0*) Bks Intl VA.

Politics of Masculinities: Men in Movements. Michael A. Messner. LC 96-35667. (Gender Lens Ser.). 128p. 1997. 35.00 (*0-8039-5576-6*); pap. 14.95 (*0-8039-5577-4*) Sage.

Politics of Mass Housing in Britain, 1945-1975: A Study of Corporate Power & Professional Influence in the Welfare State. Patrick Dunleavy. (Illus.). 1981. 55.00 (*0-19-827426-2*) OUP.

Politics of Maternity Care: Services for Childbearing Women in Twentieth Century Britain. Ed. by Jo Garcia et al. (Illus.). 356p. 1990. 75.00 (*0-19-827288-X*); pap. 19.95 (*0-19-827287-1*) OUP.

Politics of Mathematics Education. Stieg Mellin-Olsen. (Mathematics Education Library: Vol. 4). 264p. 1987. lib. bdg. 155.50 (*90-277-2350-8*, D Reidel) Kluwer Academic.

Politics of Meaning: A Dark Comedy about Today's Politics. Daniel Graham, Jr. 246p. 1995. pap. 14.50 (*0-9644495-3-6*) Preview Pr.

Politics of Meaning: Power & Explanation in the Construction of Social Reality. Peter C. Sederberg. LC 84-2739. 308p. 1984. pap. 95.50 (*0-608-05652-9*, 206610600006) Bks Demand.

Politics of Meaning: Restoring Hope & Possibility in an Age of Cynicism. Michael Lerner. LC 97-194468. 355p. 1996. pap. 13.00 (*0-201-15489-7*) Addison-Wesley.

Politics of Medical Encounters: How Patients & Doctors Deal with Social Problems. Howard B. Waitzkin. LC 90-45611. 320p. (C). 1991. 42.50 (*0-300-04949-8*) Yale U Pr.

Politics of Medical Encounters: How Patients & Doctors Deal with Social Problems. Howard B. Waitzkin. LC 90-45611. 320p. (C). 1993. reprint ed. pap. 20.00 (*0-300-05511-0*) Yale U Pr.

Politics of Medicare. 2nd ed. Theodore R. Marmor. LC 99-52364. (Social Institutions & Social Change Ser.). 228p. 2000. pap. text 16.95 (*0-202-30425-6*); lib. bdg. 35.95 (*0-202-30399-3*) Aldine de Gruyter.

***Politics of Memory.** Lfi Amadiume. LC 99-87433. 2000. text 65.00 (*1-85649-842-5*, Pub. by Zed Books) St Martin.

Politics of Memory: The Journey of a Holocaust Historian. Raul Hilberg. LC 96-11953. 208p. 1996. 22.50 (*1-56663-116-5*, Pub. by I R Dee) Natl Bk Netwk.

***Politics of Memory: Truth, Healing & Social Justice.** Ifi Amadiume. LC 99-87433. 2000. pap. 22.50 (*1-85649-843-3*) Zed Books.

Politics of Mental Handicap. Joanna Ryan & Frank Thomas. 190p. (C). 1987. pap. 14.50 (*0-946960-92-5*, Pub. by Free Assoc Bks) NYU Pr.

Politics of Mental Health Legislation. Clive Unsworth. LC 86-26813. 384p. 1987. text 75.00 (*0-19-825512-8*) OUP.

Politics of Mexican Development. Roger D. Hansen. LC 77-134300. (Illus.). 298p. 1971. pap. 15.95 (*0-8018-1651-3*) Johns Hopkins.

Politics of Michigan, 1865-1878. Harriette M. Dilla. (Columbia University. Studies in the Social Sciences: No. 118). reprint ed. 37.50 (*0-404-51118-X*) AMS Pr.

Politics of Middle East Oil: The Deliberations of the Royaumont Group. Ed. by Paul Tempest. LC 93-4576. 272p. (C). 1993. lib. bdg. 75.00 (*1-85333-922-9*, Pub. by Graham & Trotman) Kluwer Academic.

Politics of Migration. Ed. by Robin Cohen & Zig Layton-Henry. LC 97-22599. (International Library of Studies on Migration: No. 5). 360p. 1997. 135.00 (*1-85898-014-3*) E Elgar.

P

Politics of Migration Policies, Settlement & Integration: The First World into the 1990s. 2nd ed. Ed. by Daniel Kubat. LC 92-42228. 369p. 1993. 14.50 (*0-913256-34-X*) CMS.

Politics of Military Revolution in Korea. Se-Jin Kim. LC 71-123101. 256p. reprint ed. pap. 79.40 (*0-8357-3868-X*, 203660000004) Bks Demand.

***Politics of Military Rule & the Dilemmas of Democratization in Bangladesh.** Bhuian M. Kabir. LC 98-908917. viii, 275 p. 1999. write for info. (*81-7003-218-0*) S Asia.

Politics of Milton's Prose Style. Keith W. Stavely. LC 74-20086. 146p. reprint ed. pap. 45.30 (*0-608-30998-2*, 202204200024) Bks Demand.

Politics of Minority Coalitions: Race, Ethnicity & Shared Uncertainties. Ed. by Wilbur C. Rich. LC 96-10428. 288p. 1996. pap. 24.95 (*0-275-95489-7*, Praeger Pubs) Greenwood.

Politics of Minority Coaltions: Race, Ethnicity & Shared Uncertainties. Ed. by Wilbur C. Rich. LC 96-10428. 288p. 1996. 65.00 (*0-275-95488-9*, Praeger Pubs) Greenwood.

Politics of Mirth: Jonson, Herrick, Milton, Marvell, & the Defense of Old Holiday Pastimes. Leah S. Marcus. LC 86-7133. (Illus.). 330p. (C). 1989. pap. text 19.95 (*0-226-50452-2*) U Ch Pr.

Politics of Mirth: Jonson, Herrick, Milton, Marvell, & the Defense of Old Holiday Pastimes. Leah S. Marcus. LC 86-7133. (Illus.). 328p. (C). 1996. 34.95 (*0-226-50451-4*) U Ch Pr.

Politics of Miscalculation in the Middle East. Richard B. Parker. LC 92-23947. (Indiana Series in Arab & Islamic). 320p. (C). 1993. 46.95 (*0-253-34298-8*); pap. 18.95 (*0-253-20781-9*, MB-781) Ind U Pr.

Politics of Modern Criticism. Denis Donoghue. (Chapbooks in Literature Ser.). 31p. 1981. pap. text 5.00 (*0-9614940-5-0*) Bennington Coll.

Politics of Modern Europe: The State & Political Authority in the Major Democracies. 2nd ed. Michael Keating. LC 99-13613. 544p. 1999. 95.00 (*1-85898-962-0*) E Elgar.

***Politics of Modern Europe: The State & Political Authority in the Major Democracies.** 2nd ed. Michael Keating. LC 99-13613. 544p. 1999. pap. 30.00 (*1-85898-963-9*) E Elgar.

Politics of Modernism: Against the New Conformists. rev. ed. Raymond Williams. (Classics Ser.). 294p. (C). 1996. pap. 18.00 (*1-85984-161-9*, Pub. by Verso) Norton.

Politics of Modernization. David E. Apter. LC JF0051.A7. (Phoenix Bks.). (Illus.). 503p. reprint ed. pap. 156.00 (*0-608-18231-1*, 205663900078) Bks Demand.

Politics of Monetarism: Its Historical & Institutional Development. George Macesich. (Illus.). 170p. 1984. 50.00 (*0-8476-7344-8*) Rowman.

Politics of Motherhood: Activist Voices from Left to Right. Ed. by Alexis Jetter et al. LC 96-26125. (Illus.). 398p. 1997. pap. 22.95 (*0-87451-780-X*); text 45.00 (*0-87451-779-6*) U Pr of New Eng.

Politics of Motherhood: British Writing & Culture, 1680-1760. Toni Bowers. LC 96-227991. (Illus.). 278p. (C). 1996. text 59.95 (*0-521-55174-9*) Cambridge U Pr.

Politics of Mothering: Womanhood, Identity & Resistance in African Literature. Ed. by Obioma Nnaemeka. LC 96-20491. (Opening Out: Feminism for Today Ser.). (Illus.). 256p. (C). 1997. 75.00 (*0-415-13789-6*); pap. 22.99 (*0-415-13790-X*) Routledge.

***Politics of Mourning.** Jacques Derrida. 1999. 22.00 (*0-226-14316-3*) U Ch Pr.

***Politics of Multiculturalism & Bilingual Education: Students & Teachers Caught in the Cross Fire.** Carlos Ovando & Peter McLaren. 264p. (C). 1999. pap. 28.75 (*0-07-366076-0*) McGrw-H Hghr Educ.

Politics of Multiculturalism in the New Europe: Racism, Identity, & Community. Tariq Modood & Pnina Werbner. LC 97-13316. (Postcolonial Encounters Ser.). 1997. pap. 22.50 (*1-85649-422-5*) Humanities.

Politics of Multiculturalism in the New Europe: Racism, Identity, & Community. Tariq Modood & Pnina Werbner. LC 97-13316. (Postcolonial Encounters Ser.). 1997. text 62.50 (*1-85649-421-7*) Humanities.

Politics of Multinationals. M. K. Saini. 342p. 1981. 32.95 (*0-318-37254-1*) Asia Bk Corp.

Politics of Multiracial Education. Madan Sarup. (Education Bks.). 160p. (Orig.). (C). 1986. pap. text 19.95 (*0-7102-0570-8*, Routledge Thoemms) Routledge.

Politics of Music in the Third Reich. Michael Meyer. (American University Studies: History: Ser. IX, Vol. 49). (Illus.). XIV, 434p. 1993. text 69.95 (*0-8204-0805-0*) P Lang Pubng.

Politics of Muslim Cultural Reform: Jadidism in Central Asia. Adeeb Khalid. LC 98-4189. (Comparative Studies on Muslim Societies). 1999. 55.00 (*0-520-21355-6*, Pub. by U CA Pr); pap. 22.00 (*0-520-21356-4*, Pub. by U CA Pr) Cal Prin Full Svc.

Politics of My Heart. William Slaughter. LC 96-68145. 96p. (Orig.). 1996. pap. 12.95 (*0-9651413-0-6*) Pleasure Boat.

Politics of Myth: A Study of C. G. Jung, Mircea Eliade & Joseph Campbell. Robert Ellwood. LC 98-54277. (SUNY Series, Issues in the Study of Religion). 224p. (C). 1999. pap. text 17.95 (*0-7914-4306-X*, Suny Pr) State U NY Pr.

Politics of Myth: A Study of C. G. Jung, Mircea Eliade & Joseph Campbell. Robert Ellwood. LC 98-54277. (SUNY Series, Issues in the Study of Religion). 224p. (C). 1999. text 54.50 (*0-7914-4305-1*, Suny Pr) State U NY Pr.

Politics of Narration: James Joyce, William Faulkner & Virginia Woolf. Richard Pearce. LC 90-8977. 200p. (C). 1991. text 40.00 (*0-8135-1656-0*) Rutgers U Pr.

Politics of Narrative Ideology & Social Change in William Godwin's "Caleb Williams" Kenneth W. Graham. LC 89-45880. (Studies in the Eighteenth Century: No. 16). 1990. 37.50 (*0-404-63516-4*) AMS Pr.

***Politics of National Minority Participation in Post-Communist Europe: State-Building & Democracy.** Jonathan Stein. 320p. 1999. 76.95 (*0-7656-0528-7*, Sharpe Ref) M E Sharpe.

Politics of National Party Conventions. rev. ed. Paul T. David et al. 394p. 1984. reprint ed. pap. text 29.00 (*0-8191-4002-3*) U Pr of Amer.

Politics of National Security. Marcus G. Raskin. LC 78-55935. (Issues in Contemporary Civilization Ser.). 320p. 1979. 39.95 (*0-87855-239-1*) Transaction Pubs.

Politics of National Security: Congress & U. S. Defense Policy. Barry M. Blechman & W. Philip Ellis. 272p. 1992. reprint ed. pap. text 22.00 (*0-19-507705-9*) OUP.

Politics of Nationalism & Devolution. Henry M. Drucker & Gordon Brown. LC 79-41025. 144p. reprint ed. pap. 44.70 (*0-608-13104-0*, 202521900043) Bks Demand.

***Politics of Nationhood: Sovereignty, Britishness, & Conservative Politics.** Philip Lynch. LC 98-28308. 33p. 1999. text 65.00 (*0-312-21835-4*) St Martin.

Politics of Nature. Ed. by Andrew Dobson & Paul Lucardie. 256p. (C). 1995. pap. 25.99 (*0-415-12471-9*, C0556) Routledge.

Politics of Negotiation: America's Dealings with Allies, Adversaries, & Friends. Linda P. Brady. LC 91-13. xiv, 269p. (C). 1991. 49.95 (*0-8078-1971-9*); pap. 19.95 (*0-8078-4320-2*) U of NC Pr.

Politics of New Europe. Ian Budge. LC 96-47848. (C). 1997. pap. text 26.25 (*0-582-23434-4*, Pub. by Addison-Wesley) Longman.

Politics of News: The News of Politics. Ed. by Doris Graber & Denis McQuail. LC 98-2661. 200p. (C). 1998. 28.95 (*1-56802-412-6*) Congr Quarterly.

***Politics of News: The News of Politics.** Ed. by Denis McQuail & Doris Graber. LC 98-2661. 200p. (C). 1998. 39.95 (*1-56802-413-4*) Congr Quarterly.

Politics of NGO's in Southeast Asia: Participation & Protest in the Philippines. Gerard Clarke. LC 97-38363. (Politics in Asia Ser.). 272p. (C). 1998. 85.00 (*0-415-17140-7*) Routledge.

Politics of Nonformal Education in Latin America. Carlos A. Torres. LC 89-36651. 204p. 1990. 55.00 (*0-275-93419-5*, C3419, Praeger Pubs) Greenwood.

Politics of Nonviolent Action, 3 vols. Gene Sharp. Ed. by Marina Finkelstein. LC 72-95483. (Extending Horizons Ser.). (C). 1973. 24.95 (*0-87558-068-8*) Porter Sargent.

Politics of Nonviolent Action, 3 vols. Gene Sharp. Ed. by Marina Finkelstein. Incl. Politics of Nonviolent Action Vol. 1: Power & Struggle. LC 72-95483. 144p. (C). 1974. pap. 7.95 (*0-87558-070-X*); Politics of Nonviolent Action Vol. 3: The Dynamics of Nonviolent Action. LC 72-95483. 480p. (C). 1974. pap. 13.95 (*0-87558-072-6*); Politics of Nonviolent Action Part II: The Methods of Nonviolent Action. LC 72-95483. 368p. (C). 1974. pap. 10.95 (*0-87558-071-8*); LC 72-95483. (Extending Horizons Ser.). (C). 1973. reprint ed. 25.95 (*0-87558-143-9*) Porter Sargent.

Politics of Nonviolent Action, Vol. 1, Power & Struggle see Politics of Nonviolent Action

Politics of Nonviolent Action, Vol. 3, The Dynamics of Nonviolent Action see Politics of Nonviolent Action

Politics of Nonviolent Action Part II: The Methods of Nonviolent Action see Politics of Nonviolent Action

Politics of Nuclear Power: A History of the Shoreham Nuclear Power Plant. David P. McCaffrey. (Technology, Risk & Society Ser.). 276p. 1991. lib. bdg. 155.00 (*0-7923-1035-7*) Kluwer Academic.

Politics of Nuclear Proliferation. George H. Quester. LC 73-8119. 264p. reprint ed. pap. 81.90 (*0-608-11992-X*, 202300200030) Bks Demand.

Politics of Numbers. Ed. by William Alonso & Paul Starr. LC 86-10060. (Population of the United States in the 1980s: A Census Monograph Ser.). 480p. 1989. pap. 18.50 (*0-87154-016-9*) Russell Sage.

Politics of Nursing in Victorian, 1987. Fay Marles. (C). 1989. pap. 65.00 (*0-7300-0691-3*, NPR803, Pub. by Deakin Univ) St Mut.

Politics of Obedience: The Discourse of Voluntary Servitude. Etienne De la Boetie. Tr. by Harry Kurz.Tr. of De la Servitude Volontaire. (FRE.). 100p. 1975. 44.99 (*1-55164-089-9*, Pub. by Black Rose) Consort Bk Sales.

Politics of Obedience: The Discourse of Voluntary Servitude. Etienne De la Boetie. LC 96-79525.Tr. of De la Servitude Volontaire. 100p. 1996. pap. 15.99 (*1-55164-088-0*, Pub. by Black Rose) Consort Bk Sales.

Politics of Obedience: The Discourse of Voluntary Servitude. Etienne De la Boetie.Tr. of De la Servitude Volontaire. 1984. lib. bdg. 79.95 (*0-87700-648-2*) Revisionist Pr.

Politics of Obedience: The Discourse of Voluntary Servitude. Etienne De la Boetie. Tr. by Harry Kurz from FRE.Tr. of De la Servitude Volontaire. 88p. 1975. reprint ed. 19.95 (*0-919618-58-8*, Pub. by Black Rose) Consort Bk Sales.

Politics of Objectivity. Randall Albury. 79p. (C). 1995. pap. 21.00 (*0-949823-10-4*, Pub. by Deakin Univ) St Mut.

Politics of Obscenity: Group Litigation in a Time of Legal Change, 64. Joseph G. Kobylka. LC 90-46698. (Contributions in Legal Studies: No. 64). 224p. 1991. 57.95 (*0-313-26882-7*, KPH/, Greenwood Pr) Greenwood.

Politics of Official Discourse in Twentieth-Century South Africa. Adam Ashforth. (Oxford Studies in African Affairs). 312p. 1990. 69.00 (*0-19-827702-4*) OUP.

Politics of Offshore Oil. Joan Goldstein. LC 82-7697. 192p. 1982. 55.00 (*0-275-90805-4*, C0805, Praeger Pubs) Greenwood.

Politics of Oil & Revolution in Iran. Shaul B. Bakhash. LC 82-72116. 37p. 1982. pap. 6.95 (*0-8157-0781-9*) Brookings.

Politics of Oil in the Caucasus & Central Asia. Rosemarie Forsythe. LC 97-195125. (Adelphi Papers: No. 300). 67p. 1996. pap. text 26.00 (*0-19-828092-0*) OUP.

***Politics of Oil-producer Cooperation.** Dag Harald Claes. 270p. 2000. 70.00 (*0-8133-6843-X*, Pub. by Westview) HarpC.

Politics of Old Age in Europe. Alan Walker & Gerhard Naegele. LC 98-8177. (Rethinking Ageing Ser.). 1998. pap. 28.95 (*0-335-20007-9*) OpUniv Pr.

Politics of Old Age in Europe. Alan Walker & Gerhard Naegele. LC 98-8177. (Rethinking Ageing Ser.). 1998. 85.00 (*0-335-20008-7*) Taylor & Francis.

Politics of Oligarchy: Institutional Choice in Imperial Japan. J. Mark Ramseyer & Frances M. Rosenbluth. (Political Economy of Institutions & Decisions Ser.). (Illus.). 224p. (C). 1995. text 54.95 (*0-521-47397-7*) Cambridge U Pr.

Politics of Oligarchy: Institutional Choice in Imperial Japan. J. Mark Ramseyer & Frances M. Rosenbluth. (Political Economy of Institutions & Decisions Ser.). (Illus.). 224p. (C). 1998. pap. text 19.95 (*0-521-63649-3*) Cambridge U Pr.

Politics of Open Economies: Indonesia, Malaysia, the Philippines & Thailand. Alasdair Bowie & Danny Unger. LC 96-49358. (Asia-Pacific Studies: Vol. 4). (Illus.). 258p. (C). 1997. text 59.95 (*0-521-58343-8*); pap. text 19.95 (*0-521-58683-6*) Cambridge U Pr.

Politics of Opera in Turn-of-the-Century Italy: As Seen Through the Letters of Alfredo Catalani. Ed. & Tr. by Richard M. Berrong. LC 92-40031. (Studies in the History & Interpretation of Music: Vol. 38). 160p. 1993. text 69.95 (*0-7734-9230-5*) E Mellen.

Politics of Opposition in Contemporary Africa. Ed. by Adebayo O. Olukoshi. LC 98-215444. 230p. 1998. pap. 26.95 (*91-7106-419-2*) Transaction Pubs.

Politics of Organizational Change, 26. Iain L. Mangham. LC 79-23. (Contributions in Economics & Economic History Ser.: No. 26). 221p. 1979. 55.00 (*0-313-20981-2*, MPC/, Greenwood Pr) Greenwood.

Politics of Pan-Islam: Ideology & Organization. Jacob M. Landau. 448p. 1990. 110.00 (*0-19-827709-1*) OUP.

Politics of Pan-Islam: Ideology & Organization. Jacob M. Landau. 448p. 1994. reprint ed. pap. 22.00 (*0-19-827948-5*) OUP.

Politics of Parliamentary Reform. David Judge. LC 83-25378. 220p. 1984. 32.50 (*0-8386-3221-1*) Fairleigh Dickinson.

Politics of Parousia: Reading Mark Intercontextually. Tat-Siong Benny Liew. LC 99-19920. (Biblical Interpretation Ser.). 192p. 1999. 71.00 (*90-04-11360-6*) Brill Academic Pubs.

Politics of Partition: King Abdullah, the Zionists & Palestine, 1921-1951. Avi Shlaim. LC 99-188465. (Illus.). 496p. 1999. pap. text 24.95 (*0-19-829459-X*) OUP.

Politics of Passion: Norman Bethune's Writing & Art. Larry Hannant. LC 99-164031. (Illus.). 400p. 1998. text 45.00 (*0-8020-0907-7*) U of Toronto Pr.

Politics of Passion: Structure & Strategy in Sikh Society. Harry Izmirlian. 1979. 14.00 (*0-8364-0551-X*) S Asia.

Politics of Peace - Maintenance. Ed. by Jorat Chopra. LC 98-6172. 150p. 1998. pap. 14.95 (*1-55587-757-5*); lib. bdg. 28.50 (*1-55587-756-7*) L Rienner.

***Politics of Pearl: Court Poetry in the Age of Richard II.** John M. Bowers. LC 00-39842. 2001. write for info. (*0-85991-599-9*, DS Brewer) Boydell & Brewer.

Politics of Penal Reform. M Ryan. Date not set. pap. text. write for info. (*0-582-29539-4*, Pub. by Addison-Wesley) Longman.

***Politics of Pension Reform: Institutions & Policy Change in Western Europe.** Giuliano Bonoli. LC 99-87065. (Illus.). 204p. 2000. write for info. (*0-521-77232-X*); pap. write for info. (*0-521-77606-6*) Cambridge U Pr.

Politics of Pensions: A Comparative Analysis of Britain, Canada, & the United States, 1880-1940. Ann S. Orloff. LC 92-50256. (Illus.). 398p. (Orig.). (C). 1993. pap. 19.95 (*0-299-13224-2*); lib. bdg. 60.00 (*0-299-13220-X*) U of Wis Pr.

Politics of People's Action: The Communist Party in the '72 Elections. Henry Winston. 48p. 1972. pap. 0.50 (*0-87898-077-6*) New Outlook.

Politics of Performance: Radical Theatre As Cultural Intervention. Ben Kershaw. LC 91-39875. 296p. (C). 1992. pap. 25.99 (*0-415-05763-9*, A7476) Routledge.

Politics of Performance in Early Renaissance Drama. Greg Walker. LC 97-43342. (Illus.). 249p. (C). 1998. 59.95 (*0-521-56331-3*) Cambridge U Pr.

Politics of Persuasion: British Policy & French African Neutrality, 1940-1942. Desmond Dinan. LC 88-10690. 320p. (Orig.). (C). 1988. pap. text 25.50 (*0-8191-6983-8*); lib. bdg. 55.00 (*0-8191-6982-X*) U Pr of Amer.

Politics of Persuasion: Implementation of Foreign Policy by the Netherlands. Ed. by Philip Everts & Guido Walraven. 368p. 1989. text 82.95 (*0-566-05745-X*, Pub. by Dartmth Pub) Ashgate Pub Co.

Politics of Pessimism: Albert de Broglie & Conservative Politics in the Early Third Republic. Alan Grubb. LC 95-35998. (Illus.). 440p. 1996. 55.00 (*0-87413-575-3*) U Delaware Pr.

Politics of Philanthropy: Abraham Flexner & Medical Education. Steven C. Wheatley. LC 88-40199. (History of American Thought & Culture Ser.). 256p. (Orig.). 1988. pap. text 16.95 (*0-299-11754-5*) U of Wis Pr.

Politics of Philanthropy: Abraham Flexner & Medical Education. Steven C. Wheatley. LC 88-40199. (History of American Thought & Culture Ser.). (Illus.). 269p. reprint ed. pap. 83.40 (*0-608-20484-6*, 207173600002) Bks Demand.

Politics of Philo Judaeus. Erwin R. Goodenough. xii, 348p. 1967. reprint ed. write for info. (*0-318-70928-7*) G Olms Pubs.

Politics of Philo Judaeus: Practice & Theory. Erwin R. Goodenough. xii, 348p. 1967. reprint ed. 63.70 (*0-685-66472-4*, 05101723) G Olms Pubs.

Politics of Philosophy: A Commentary on Aristotle's Politics. Michael Davis. LC 95-48150. 176p. (C). 1996. pap. text 24.95 (*0-8476-8206-4*); lib. bdg. 57.50 (*0-8476-8205-6*) Rowman.

Politics of Physician Assisted Suicide. rev. ed. Nina Clark. LC 96-48392. (Studies on the Elderly in America). (Illus.). 148p. 1997. text 33.00 (*0-8153-2645-9*) Garland.

Politics of Pictures: Creation of the Public in the Age of Popular Media. John Hartley. (Illus.). 256p. (C). 1993. pap. 22.99 (*0-415-01542-1*) Routledge.

Politics of Piety: The Ottoman Ulema in the Postclassical Age (1600-1800) Madeline C. Zilfi. (Studies in Middle Eastern History: No. 8). 1988. pap. 20.00 (*0-88297-050-X*) Bibliotheca.

Politics of Plagiarism. Meltzer. 300p. (C). 1990. pap. text 14.95 (*0-226-51968-6*); lib. bdg. 34.95 (*0-226-51967-8*) U Ch Pr.

Politics of Planning. Francis Gladstone. 1977. 25.00 (*0-85117-106-0*) Transatl Arts.

Politics of Planning: The Debate on Economic Planning in Britain in the 1930's. Daniel Ritschel. LC 97-221670. (Oxford Historical Monographs). 378p. 1997. text 90.00 (*0-19-820647-X*) OUP.

Politics of Planning & Development. Anthony J. Catanese. LC 84-8334. (Sage Library of Social Research: No. 156). 231p. 1984. reprint ed. pap. 71.70 (*0-608-01500-8*, 205954400001) Bks Demand.

Politics of Plant Closings. John Portz. LC 90-32817. (Studies in Government & Public Policy). x, 214p. 1990. 29.95 (*0-7006-0472-3*); pap. 12.95 (*0-7006-0473-1*) U Pr of KS.

Politics of Planting: Israeli-Palestinian Competition for Control of Land in the Jerusalem Periphery. Shaul E. Cohen. (Geography Research Papers: Vol. 236). (Illus.). 222p. (C). 1993. lib. bdg. 19.00 (*0-226-11276-4*) U Ch Pr.

Politics of Pleasure. Ed. by Stephen Regan. LC 92-19298. (Ideas & Production Ser.). 1992. pap. 34.95 (*0-335-09759-6*) OpUniv Pr.

Politics of Plunder: Aitolians & Their Koinon in the Early Hellenistic Era, 279-217. Joseph B. Scholten. LC 96-26732. (Hellenistic Culture & Society Ser.). 338p. 2000. 65.00 (*0-520-20187-6*, Pub. by U CA Pr) Cal Prin Full Svc.

Politics of Plunder: Misgovernment in Washington. Doug Bandow. 385p. 1990. 34.95 (*0-88738-309-2*) Transaction Pubs.

Politics of Pluralism: A Comparative Study of Lebanon & Ghana. David R. Smock & Audrey C. Smock. LC 75-8278. 379p. reprint ed. pap. 117.50 (*0-608-16329-5*, 202626500049) Bks Demand.

Politics of Policy. Ed. by Uday Desai et al. (Policy Studies Journal: Vol. 26:3). 232p. 1998. pap. write for info. (*0-944285-56-2*) Pol Studies.

Politics of Policy Making in Defense & Foreign Affairs: Conceptual Models & Bureaucratic Politics. 3rd ed. Roger Hilsman. 384p. (C). 1993. pap. text 36.80 (*0-13-681651-7*) P-H.

Politics of Popular Representation: Reagan, Thatcher, AIDS, & the Movies. Kenneth MacKinnon. LC 91-58581. 256p. 1992. 38.50 (*0-8386-3474-5*) Fairleigh Dickinson.

Politics of Population. W. Petersen. 1990. 16.50 (*0-8446-0845-9*) Peter Smith.

Politics of Populism: Dissent in Colorado. James E. Wright. LC 74-75404. (Yale Western Americana Ser.: No. 25). (Illus.). 326p. reprint ed. pap. 101.10 (*0-8357-8278-6*, 203392800087) Bks Demand.

Politics of Pork: A Study of Congressional Appropriation Earmarks. Scott A. Frisch. LC 98-37454. (Financial Sector of the American Economy Ser.). 1998. 58.00 (*0-8153-3258-0*) Garland.

Politics of Postive Incentives in Arms Control. Ed. by Thomas Bernauer et al. LC 98-58082. (Studies in International Relations). 202p. 1999. 34.95 (*1-57003-301-3*) U of SC Pr.

Politics of Postmodernism. Linda Hutcheon. 192p. 1989. 45.00 (*0-415-03991-6*, A3623) Routledge.

Politics of Postmodernism. Linda Hutcheon. (New Accents Ser.). 192p. (C). 1989. pap. 18.99 (*0-415-03992-4*, A3627) Routledge.

Politics of Postmodernity. Ed. by James Good & Irving Velody. LC 97-42128. 232p. (C). 1998. pap. 19.95 (*0-521-46727-6*); text 59.95 (*0-521-46162-6*) Cambridge U Pr.

Politics of Poverty & Land Hunger in Nepal (Forest of Farm?) Krishna B. Ghimire. (C). 1992. 70.00 (*0-7855-0209-2*, Pub. by Ratna Pustak Bhandar) St Mut.

Politics of Power. 4th ed. Katznelson. (C). 1999. pap. text 37.50 (*0-15-501698-9*, Pub. by Harcourt Coll Pubs) Harcourt.

Politics of Power: A Critical Introduction to American Government. 3rd ed. Ira Katznelson & Mark Kesselman. 427p. (Orig.). (C). 1987. pap. text 43.00 (*0-15-570735-3*, Pub. by Harcourt Coll Pubs) Harcourt.

Politics of Power: Ontario Hydro & Its Government, 1906-1995. Neil B. Freeman. 300p. 1996. text 55.00 (*0-8020-0798-8*); pap. text 19.95 (*0-8020-7160-0*) U of Toronto Pr.

***Politics of Pragmatism: Women, Representation, & Constitutionalism in Canada.** Alexandra Dobrowolsky. 2000. pap. 24.95 (*0-19-541379-2*) OUP.

Politics of Prayer: Feminist Language & the Worship of God. Helen H. Hitchcock. LC 92-73724. 437p. 1992. pap. 16.95 (*0-89870-418-9*) Ignatius Pr.

An Asterisk (*) at the beginning of an entry indicates that the title is appearing for the first time.

Politics of Preference: Democratic Institutions & Affirmative Action in the United States & India. Sunita Parikh. LC 96-25176. 248p. (C). 1997. text 42.50 (0-472-10745-3, 10745) U of Mich Pr.

Politics of Pregnancy: Adolescent Sexuality & Public Policy. Annette Lawson. 1993. pap. 19.00 (0-300-06548-5) Yale U Pr.

Politics of Pregnancy: Adolescent Sexuality & Public Policy. Ed. by Annette Lawson & Deborah L. Rhode. LC 92-38539. (Illus.). 360p. 1993. reprint ed. pap. 111.60 (0-608-07830-1, 205400600010) Bks Demand.

Politics of Pregnancy: Policy Dilemmas in the Maternal-Fetal Relationship. Ed. by Janna C. Merrick & Robert H. Blank. LC 93-5723. (Women & Politics Ser.: Vol. 13, Nos. 3 & 4). (Illus.). 245p. 1994. pap. 14.95 (1-56023-047-9, Harrington Park); lib. bdg. 49.95 (1-56024-478-X) Haworth Pr.

Politics of Prejudice: The Anti-Japanese Movement in California & The Struggle for Japanese Exclusion. Roger Daniels. 1978. pap. 13.95 (0-520-03411-2) U CA Pr.

Politics of Prejudice: The Anti-Japanese Movement in California & The Struggle for Japanese Exclusion. Roger Daniels. 181p. 1999. pap. 14.95 (0-520-21950-3, Pub. by U CA Pr) Cal Prin Full Svc.

Politics of Presence. Anne Phillips. (Oxford Political Theory Ser.). 220p. 1998. pap. text 19.95 (0-19-829415-8) OUP.

Politics of Presence: Contacts Between Missionaries & Waluguru in Late Colonial Tanganyika. Peter Pels. (Studies in Anthropology & History: Vol. 22). 372p. 1998. text 58.00 (90-5702-304-0, ECU49) Gordon & Breach.

Politics of Presence: Democracy & Group Representation. Anne Phillips. (Oxford Political Theory Ser.). 220p. 1995. text 38.00 (0-19-827942-6) OUP.

Politics of Presidential Commissions: A Public Policy Perspective. David Flitner, Jr. 260p. 1986. lib. bdg. 42.50 (0-941320-42-1) Transnatl Pubs.

Politics of Presidential Selection. John S. Jackson & William J. Crotty. 250p. (C). 1997. pap. 33.53 (0-673-99627-1) Addson-Wesley Educ.

Politics of Pressure: American Arms & Israeli Policy Since the Six Day War, 79. David Pollock. LC 81-23720. (Contributions in Political Science Ser.: No. 79). 328p. 1982. 59.95 (0-313-22113-8, POP/, Greenwood Pr) Greenwood.

Politics of Primary Education. Cedric Cullingford. LC 96-52126. 1997. 108.00 (0-335-19579-2); pap. 30.95 (0-335-19578-4) OpUniv Pr.

Politics of Prison Expansion: Winning Elections by Waging War on Crime. Joseph D. Davey. LC 97-49278. 168p. 1998. 55.00 (0-275-96209-1, Praeger Pubs) Greenwood.

Politics of Privacy: Planning for Personal Data Systems As Powerful Technologies. Douglas McAdam et al. LC 80-13788. 212p. 1981. lib. bdg. 42.50 (0-444-99074-7, RPP/) Greenwood.

Politics of Privatisation in Western Europe. Ed. by John Vickers & V. Wright. 153p. 1989. text 35.00 (0-7146-3358-5, Pub. by F Cass Pubs) Intl Spec Bk.

Politics of Privilege: Governing the Affluent Suburb. Donald Greenberg. 104p. (Orig.). (C). 1993. pap. text 19.50 (0-8191-9264-3); lib. bdg. 42.50 (0-8191-9263-5) U Pr of Amer.

Politics of Privilege: Old Regime & Revolution in Lille. Gail Bossenga. 285p. (C). 1991. text 59.95 (0-521-39282-9) Cambridge U Pr.

Politics of Problem Definition: Shaping the Policy Agenda. Ed. by David A. Rochefort & Roger W. Cobb. LC 94-11031. (Studies in Government & Public Policy). 240p. 1994. 29.95 (0-7006-0646-7); pap. 14.95 (0-7006-0647-5) U Pr of KS.

Politics of Problem-Solving in Postwar Democracies: Institutionalizing Conflict & Consensus. Hans Keman. LC 96-7688. 224p. 1997. text 65.00 (0-312-15818-1) St Martin.

Politics of Procrustes: Contradictions of Enforced Equality. Antony G. Flew. 216p. 1981. text 32.95 (0-87975-150-9) Prometheus Bks.

***Politics of Professionalism.** Gary McCulloch et al. 176p. 2000. 74.95 (0-304-70296-X); pap. 24.95 (0-304-70297-8) Continuum.

***Politics of Professionalism: Teachers & the Curriculum.** Gary McCulloch et al. 2000. pap. 24.95 (0-8264-4798-8) Continuum.

Politics of Professionalism, Opportunity, Employment & Gender. Ed. by Sarah Slavin. LC 86-29491. (Women & Politics Ser.: Vol. 6, No. 3). 110p. 1987. text 39.95 (0-86656-626-0) Haworth Pr.

Politics of Program Evaluation. Ed. by Dennis J. Palumbo. 304p. (C). 1987. text 44.00 (0-8039-2736-3); pap. text 21.95 (0-8039-2737-1) Sage.

Politics of Program Evaluation. Ed. by Dennis J. Palumbo. LC 86-13899. (Sage Yearbooks in Politics & Public Policy Ser.: No. 15). 309p. 1987. reprint ed. pap. 95.80 (0-608-01501-6, 205954500001) Bks Demand.

Politics of Progress: The Origins & Development of the Commercial Republic, 1600-1835. Hiram Caton. LC 86-30886. 639p. 1988. 49.95 (0-8130-0847-6) U Press Fla.

Politics of Progressive Education: The Odenwaldschule in Nazi Germany. Dennis Shirley. (Illus.). 296p. (C). 1992. 42.50 (0-674-68759-0) HUP.

Politics of Prose: Essay on Sartre. Denis Hollier. Tr. by Jeffrey Mehlman from FRE. LC 86-11205. (Theory & History of Literature Ser.: Vol. 35). 242p. 1987. pap. 17.95 (0-8166-1510-1) U of Minn Pr.

Politics of Protection: Lord Derby & the Protectionist Party 1841-1852. Robert Stewart. (Modern Revivals in History Ser.). 248p. 1994. 61.95 (0-7512-0283-5, Pub. by Gregg Revivals) Ashgate Pub Co.

Politics of Protest: The Israeli Peace Movement & the Palestinian Intifada. Reuven Kaminer. LC 96-148017. 248p. 1995. 49.95 (1-898723-28-1, Pub. by Sussex Acad Pr); pap. 19.95 (1-898723-29-X, Pub. by Sussex Acad Pr) Intl Spec Bk.

Politics of Proverbs: From Traditional Wisdom to Proverbial Stereotypes. Wolfgang Mieder. LC 96-41944. (Illus.). 288p. 1997. 52.95 (0-299-15450-5); pap. 19.95 (0-299-15454-8) U of Wis Pr.

Politics of Provincialism: The Democratic Party in Transition, 1918-1932. David Burner. 320p. 1986. pap. 17.00 (0-674-68940-2) HUP.

Politics of Provocation: Participation & Protest in Israel. Gadi Wolfsfeld. LC 87-24623. (SUNY Series in Israeli Studies). (Illus.). 240p. (C). 1988. pap. text 21.95 (0-88706-769-7) State U NY Pr.

Politics of Prudence. Russell Kirk. LC 93-77172. 304p. 1993. 19.95 (1-882926-01-3) ISI Books.

Politics of Prudence. Russell Kirk. 304p. 1995. pap. 12.95 (1-882926-00-5) ISI Books.

Politics of Psychiatry in Revolutionary Cuba. Charles J. Brown & Armando M. Lago. LC 91-7537. 215p. (C). 1991. 39.95 (1-56000-020-1); pap. 24.95 (1-56000-585-8) Transaction Pubs.

***Politics of Psychoanalysis: An Introduction to Freudian & Post-Freudian Theory.** 2nd ed. Stephen Frosh. LC 99-20333. 272p. 1999. text 55.00 (0-8147-2699-2) NYU Pr.

Politics of Psychoanalysis: An Introduction to Freudion & Post-Freudian Theory 2nd ed. Stephen Frosh. LC 99-20333. 1999. pap. text 18.50 (0-8147-2700-X) NYU Pr.

Politics of Public Budgeting: Getting & Spending, Borrowing & Balancing. 3rd ed. Irene S. Rubin. LC 96-32924. (Illus.). 320p. (Orig.). (C). 1996. pap. text 29.95 (1-56643-033-X, Chatham House Pub) Seven Bridges.

Politics of Public Budgeting: Getting & Spending, Borrowing & Balancing. 4th ed. Irene S. Rubin. LC 99-86159. (Illus.). 320p. (Orig.). 2000. pap. text 29.95 (1-889119-42-3, Chatham House Pub) Seven Bridges.

Politics of Public Enterprise: Oil & the French State. Harvey B. Feigenbaum. LC 84-42883. 212p. 1985. reprint ed. pap. 65.80 (0-608-02575-5, 206322000004) Bks Demand.

Politics of Public Health. Meredeth Turshen. LC 88-36976. 300p. (C). 1989. text 45.00 (0-8135-1421-5); pap. text 19.00 (0-8135-1422-3) Rutgers U Pr.

Politics of Public Librarianship, 12. David Shavit. LC 86-7573. (New Directions in Information Management Ser.: No. 12). (Illus.). 170p. 1986. 47.95 (0-313-24816-8, SVP/, Greenwood Pr) Greenwood.

Politics of Public Management. Philip B. Heymann. LC 86-40577. 264p. (C). 1989. reprint ed. pap. 14.00 (0-300-04291-4) Yale U Pr.

Politics of Public Memory: Tourism, History, & Ethnicity in Monterey, California. Martha K. Norkunas. LC 92-42168. (SUNY Series in Oral & Public History). 123p. (C). 1993. text 57.50 (0-7914-1483-3); pap. text 19.95 (0-7914-1484-1) State U NY Pr.

Politics of Public Spending in Canada. Donald J. Savoie. 400p. 1990. pap. text 20.95 (0-8020-6755-7) U of Toronto Pr.

Politics of Puerto Rican University Students. Arthur Liebman. LC 78-630381. (Latin American Monographs: No. 20). 217p. reprint ed. pap. 67.30 (0-8357-7719-7, 203607600002) Bks Demand.

***Politics of Punishing in Democratic Athens.** Danielle S. Allen. LC 99-34848. 371p. 1999. 39.50 (0-691-05869-5, Pub. by Princeton U Pr) Cal Prin Full Svc.

Politics of Punishment: Prision Reform in Russia, 1863-1917. Bruce A. Adams. LC 96-10422. (Illus.). 320p. 1996. lib. bdg. 35.00 (0-87580-215-X) N Ill U Pr.

***Politics of Pure Science.** 2nd ed. Daniel Greenberg. LC 98-52458. 336p. 1999. pap. 15.00 (0-226-30632-1) U Ch Pr.

***Politics of Pure Science.** 2nd ed. Daniel Greenberg. LC 98-52458. 336p. 1999. lib. bdg. 49.00 (0-226-30631-3) U Ch Pr.

Politics of Purity: Harvey Washington Wiley & the Origins of Federal Food Regulation. Clayton Coppin & Jack High. LC 99-13530. 232p. 1999. text 49.50 (0-472-10984-7, 10984) U of Mich Pr.

Politics of Quality in the Public Sector: The Management of Change. Ed. by Ian Kirkpatrick & Miguel Martinez-Lucio. LC 94-29560. 224p. (C). 1995. pap. 19.99 (0-415-10666-4, C0032) Thomson Learn.

Politics of Quality in the Public Sector: The Management of Change. Ed. by Ian Kirkpatrick & Miguel Martinez-Lucio. LC 94-29560. 224p. (C). (gr. 13). 1995. pap. 80.95 (0-415-10665-6, C0031) Thomson Learn.

Politics of Race. Hillel Ticktin. (C). pap. 13.95 (0-7453-0493-1, Pub. by Pluto GBR) Stylus Pub VA.

Politics of Race: African Americans & the Political System. Ed. by Theodore Rueter. LC 95-5901. 416p. (gr. 13). 1995. text 77.95 (1-56324-564-7) M E Sharpe.

Politics of Race: African Americans & the Political System. Ed. by Theodore Rueter. LC 95-5901. 416p. (C). (gr. 13). 1995. pap. text 26.95 (1-56324-565-5) M E Sharpe.

Politics of Race: Discrimination in South Africa. Hillel Ticktin. 115p. (C). 39.95 (0-7453-0494-X, Pub. by Pluto GBR) Stylus Pub VA.

Politics of Race & Gender in Therapy. Ed. by Lenora Fulani. LC 88-657. (Women & Therapy Ser.: Vol. 6, No. 4). 120p. 1988. text 39.95 (0-86656-723-2) Haworth Pr.

Politics of Race & International Sport: The Case of South Africa, 1. Richard E. Lapchick. LC 74-11705. (Studies in Human Rights: No. 1). 268p. 1975. 38.50 (0-8371-7691-3, LPR/, Greenwood Pr) Greenwood.

Politics of Race & Schooling: Public Education in Georgia, 1900-1961. Thomas V. O'Brien. LC 99-10348. 256p. 1999. 45.00 (0-7391-0060-2) Lxngtn Bks.

Politics of Racial Inequality: A Systematic Comparative Macro-Analysis from the Colonial Period to 1970, 22. J. Owens Smith. LC 87-225. (Contributions in Ethnic Studies: No. 22). 217p. 1987. 65.00 (0-313-25731-0, SHQ/, Greenwood Pr) Greenwood.

Politics of Rage: George Wallace, the Origins of the New Conservatism, & the Transformation of American Politics. Dan T. Carter. LC 95-31477. (Illus.). 592p. 1996. pap. 17.95 (0-8071-2113-4) La State U Pr.

***Politics of Rage: George Wallace, the Origins of the New Conservatism & the Transformation of American Politics.** 2nd rev. ed. Dan T. Carter. LC 99-54330. (Illus.). 608p. 2000. pap. 17.95 (0-8071-2597-0) La State U Pr.

Politics of Railroad Coordination, 1933-1936. Earl Latham. LC 59-9279. 348p. 1959. 40.50 (0-674-68951-8) HUP.

Politics of Rape: The Victim's Perspective. Diana E. Russell. LC 73-90697. 312p. 1984. pap. 10.95 (0-8128-1860-1, Scrbrough Hse) Madison Bks UPA.

Politics of Rapid Urbanization: Government & Growth in Modern Turkey. Michael N. Danielson & Rusen Keles. (Illus.). 304p. 1985. 39.95 (0-8419-0951-2); pap. 19.50 (0-8419-0952-0) Holmes & Meier.

Politics of Rational Man. Robert E. Goodin. LC 82-3375. 146p. reprint ed. pap. 45.30 (0-608-08661-4, 206918400003) Bks Demand.

Politics of Reading: Power, Opportunity, & Prospects for Change in America's Public Schools. Jo M. Fraatz. 256p. (C). 1987. pap. text 19.95 (0-8077-2857-8) Tchrs Coll.

Politics of Readjustment: Vietnam Veterans since the War. Wilbur J. Scott. LC 93-13488. (Social Problems & Social Issues Ser.): 308p. 1993. pap. text 27.95 (0-202-30406-X); lib. bdg. 51.95 (0-202-30405-1) Aldine de Gruyter.

Politics of Reality: Essays in Feminist Theory. Marilyn Frye. LC 83-2082. (Illus.). 176p. 1983. pap. 12.95 (0-89594-099-X) Crossing Pr.

Politics of Reapportionment. Ed. by Malcolm E. Jewell. LC 82-18695. (Atherton Press Political Science Ser.). 334p. 1982. reprint ed. lib. bdg. 45.50 (0-313-23317-9, JERA, Greenwood Pr) Greenwood.

Politics of Reception: Critical Constructions of Mikhail Zoshenko. Gregory Carleton. LC 98-29222. (Studies in Russian Literature & Theory). 248p. 1998. text 54.95 (0-8101-1609-X) Northwestern U Pr.

***Politics of Reception: Globalizing Third World Women's Texts.** Amal Amireh & Lisa Suhair-Majaj. 300p. 2000. 55.00 (0-8153-3605-5) Garland.

Politics of Reclusion: Painting & Power in Momoyama Japan. Kendall H. Brown. LC 96-39173. (Illus.). 224p. 1997. text 52.00 (0-8248-1779-6); pap. text 34.95 (0-8248-1913-6) UH Pr.

Politics of Reconciliation: Zimbabwe's First Decade. Victor De Waal. LC 90-81935. 150p. (C). 1990. 39.95 (0-86543-186-8); pap. 12.95 (0-86543-187-6) Africa World.

Politics of Reconstruction, 1863-1867. David Herbert Donald. 128p. 1984. pap. 9.95 (0-674-68953-4) HUP.

Politics of Reconstruction, 1863-1867. David Herbert Donald. LC 82-1015. (Walter Lynwood Fleming Lectures in Southern History). 105p. 1982. reprint ed. lib. bdg. 55.00 (0-313-23481-7, DONP, Greenwood Pr) Greenwood.

Politics of Redistributing Urban Aid. Douglas J. Watson & John G. Heilman. LC 93-25054. 160p. 1994. 55.00 (0-275-94716-5, C4716, Praeger Pubs) Greenwood.

Politics of Redress. Willem De Haan. 224p. 1990. text 49.95 (0-04-445441-4) Routledge.

Politics of Reflexivity: Narrative & the Constitutive Poetics of Culture. Robert Siegle. LC 86-2700. 286p. reprint ed. pap. 88.70 (0-608-06145-X, 206647800008) Bks Demand.

Politics of Reform: Works Compensation from Woodhouse to Workcare, Vol. 1. Mark Considine. 118p. 1991. pap. 52.50 (0-7855-2673-0, PTSSSO, Pub. by Deakin Univ) St Mut.

Politics of Reform No. 1: Workers Compensation from Woodhouse to Workcare. Mark Considine. 118p. (C). 1991. 53.00 (0-7300-1472-X, Pub. by Deakin Univ) St Mut.

Politics of Reform in Ghana: 1982-1991. Jeffrey Herbst. 192p. 1993. 50.00 (0-520-07752-0, Pub. by U CA Pr); pap. 16.95 (0-520-07753-9, Pub. by U CA Pr) Cal Prin Full Svc.

Politics of Reform in Medical Education & Health Services: The Negev Project, No. 14. Basil Porter & William E. Seidelman. LC 91-4826. (Medical Education Ser.). 144p. (C). 1991. text 29.95 (0-8261-7730-1) Springer Pub.

Politics of Reform in Peru: The Aprista & Other Mass Parties of Latin America. Grant Hilliker. LC 76-128763. (Illus.). 221p. reprint ed. pap. 68.60 (0-608-14699-4, 202585000046) Bks Demand.

Politics of Reform in Thailand: Education in the Reign of King Chulalongkorn. David K. Wyatt. LC 77-81435. (Yale Southeast Asia Studies: No. 4). 446p. reprint ed. pap. 138.30 (0-608-14244-1, 202205500024) Bks Demand.

Politics of Regime Transitions. Ronald A. Francisco. 192p. (C). 1999. text 65.00 (0-8133-8851-1) Westview.

Politics of Region & Religion in India. Prabhat K. Datta. (C). 1991. 18.00 (81-85024-83-9, Pub. by Uppal Pub Hse) S Asia.

Politics of Regional Integration: The Central American Case. James D. Cochrane. LC 79-12590. (Tulane Studies in Political Science: No. 12). 235p. Date not set. reprint ed. pap. 72.90 (0-608-20654-7, 207209100003) Bks Demand.

Politics of Regional Integration: The Central American Case, Vol. 12. James D. Cochrane. LC 79-12590. 1969. 11.00 (0-930598-11-3) Tulane Stud Pol.

Politics of Regional Integration in East Africa. Z. M. Khan. 215p. 1985. 30.00 (0-944025-03-X) Advance Research.

Politics of Regional Policy in Japan: Localities Incorporated? Richard J. Samuels. LC 83-42575. (Illus.). 317p. 1983. reprint ed. pap. 98.30 (0-7837-9439-8, 206018100004) Bks Demand.

Politics of Regional Trade in Iraq, Arabia, & the Gulf, 1745-1900. Hala Fattah. LC 96-42069. (SUNY Series in the Social & Economic History of the Middle East). 254p. (C). 1997. text 57.50 (0-7914-3113-4); pap. text 18.95 (0-7914-3114-2) State U NY Pr.

Politics of Regions: The Economics & Politics of Territory. Ann R. Markusen. LC 87-4359. 320p. (C). 1987. 60.50 (0-8476-7394-4, R7394) Rowman.

Politics of Regulatory Change: A Tale of Two Agencies. 2nd ed. Richard A. Harris & Sidney M. Milkis. 432p. (C). 1996. pap. text 23.95 (0-19-508191-9) OUP.

Politics of Religion & Social Change. Ed. by Jeffrey K. Hadden & Anson Shupe. LC 85-21664. (Religion & the Political Order Ser.: Vol. I). 284p. 1986. pap. 12.95 (0-913757-53-5) Paragon Hse.

Politics of Religion & Social Change. Ed. by Anson Shupe & Jeffrey K. Hadden. LC 87-24480. (Religion & the Political Order Ser.: Vol. II). 284p. 1988. 24.95 (0-913757-76-4); pap. 12.95 (0-913757-77-2) Paragon Hse.

***Politics of Religion & the Religion of Politics: Looking at Israel.** Ira Sharkansky. 208p. 2000. 40.00 (0-7391-0109-9) Lxngtn Bks.

Politics of Religion in Russia & the New States of Eurasia. Ed. & Intro. by Michael Bourdeaux. 352p. 1995. pap. text 19.95 (0-563-24357-0) M E Sharpe.

Politics of Religious Apostasy: The Role of Apostates in the Transformation of Religious Movements. Ed. by David G. Bromley. LC 97-34747. (Religion in the Age of Transformation Ser.). 256p. 1998. 62.50 (0-275-95508-7, Praeger Pubs) Greenwood.

Politics of Religious Studies: The Continuing Conflict with Theology in the Academy. Donald Wiebe. LC 98-41099. 336p. 1998. text 49.95 (0-312-17696-1) St Martin.

Politics of Representation: Continuities in Theory & Research. Heinz Eulau & John C. Wahlke. LC 78-17128. 312p. reprint ed. pap. 96.80 (0-608-14236-0, 202189400026) Bks Demand.

Politics of Reputation: The Critical Reception of Tennessee Williams' Later Plays. Annette J. Saddik. LC 98-12432. 176p. 1999. 33.50 (0-8386-3772-8) Fairleigh Dickinson.

Politics of Rescue: The Roosevelt Administration & the Holocaust 1938-1945. Henry L. Feingold. LC 80-81713. (Illus.). 432p. (Orig.). 1970. pap. 12.95 (0-89604-019-4, Holocaust Library) US Holocaust.

Politics of Research. Ed. by E. Ann Kaplan & George Levine. (Millennial Shifts Ser.). 256p. (C). 1997. text 50.00 (0-8135-2418-0); pap. text 18.95 (0-8135-2419-9) Rutgers U Pr.

Politics of Retirement in Britain, 1878-1948. John Macnicol. LC 97-41842. 416p. (C). 1998. text 74.95 (0-521-62273-5) Cambridge U Pr.

Politics of Retrenchment: How Local Governments Manage Fiscal Stress. Charles H. Levine et al. LC 81-9241. (Sage Library of Social Research: No. 130). 224p. reprint ed. pap. 69.50 (0-8357-8490-8, 203476400091) Bks Demand.

Politics of Retribution: The 1996 Federal Election. Ed. by C. Bean et al. LC 97-183720. (Illus.). 288p. 1997. pap. 24.95 (1-86448-386-5, Pub. by Allen & Unwin Pty) Paul & Co Pubs.

***Politics of Retribution in Europe: World War II & Its Aftermath.** Ed. by Istvan Deak et al. 2000. 55.00 (0-691-00953-8, Pub. by Princeton U Pr); pap. 19.95 (0-691-00954-6, Pub. by Princeton U Pr) Cal Prin Full Svc.

Politics of Revelation & Reason: Religion & Civic Life in the New Nation. John G. West, Jr. LC 95-51171. (American Political Thought Ser.). 272p. 1996. 35.00 (0-7006-0780-3) U Pr of KS.

Politics of Revelation in the English Renaissance. Esther G. Richey. LC 98-3089. 264p. 1998. 37.50 (0-8262-1166-6) U of Mo Pr.

Politics of Revenge: Fascism & the Military in Twentieth Century Spain. Paul Preston. 240p. (C). 1995. pap. 25.99 (0-415-12000-4, C0394) Routledge.

Politics of Revenue Sharing. Paul R. Dommel. LC 74-376. (Illus.). 223p. reprint ed. 69.20 (0-8357-9235-8, 201761700007) Bks Demand.

Politics of Rhetoric: Richard M. Weaver & the Conservative Tradition, 51. Bernard K. Duffy & Martin J. Jacobi. LC 92-36514. (Contributions in Philosophy Ser.: No. 51). 244p. 1993. 62.95 (0-313-25713-2, DRC, Greenwood Pr) Greenwood.

Politics of Righteousness: Idaho Christian Patriotism. James A. Aho. LC 90-30168. (Samuel & Althea Stroum Bks.). (Illus.). 334p. (C). 1995. pap. 14.95 (0-295-97494-X) U of Wash Pr.

Politics of Rights: Lawyers, Public Policy & Political Change. Stuart A. Scheingold. LC 74-79972. 240p. 1974. pap. 15.00 (0-300-01811-8) Yale U Pr.

Politics of Risk Society. Ed. by Jane Franklin. LC 97-29584. 128p. 1997. 52.95 (0-7456-1924-X, Pub. by Polity Pr); pap. 20.95 (0-7456-1925-8, Pub. by Polity Pr) Blackwell Pubs.

Politics of Ritual & Remembrance: Laos since 1975. Grant Evans. (Illus.). 230p. 1998. pap. text 20.00 (0-8248-2054-1) UH Pr.

P

***Politics of Ritual in an Aboriginal Settlement: Kinship, Gender & the Currency of Knowledge.** Francoise Dussart. LC 00-36548. (Series in Ethnographic Inquiry). (Illus.). 2000. write for info. (*1-56098-393-0*) Smithsonian.

Politics of Ritual Kinship: Confraternities & Social Order in Early Modern Italy. Ed. by Nicholas Terpstra. LC 98-43693. (Cambridge Studies in Italian History & Culture). 359p. (C). 1999. 69.95 (*0-521-62185-2*) Cambridge U Pr.

Politics of River Trade: Tradition & Development in the Upper Plata, 1780-1870. Thomas Whigham. LC 91-3493. (Illus.). 292p. 1991. reprint ed. pap. 90.60 (*0-608-07866-2*, 205404900011) Bks Demand.

***Politics of Romantic Poetry: In Search of the Pure Commonwealth.** Richard Cronin. LC 99-36364. (Romanticism in Perspective Ser.). 1999. text 59.95 (*0-312-22749-3*) St Martin.

Politics of Rural Life: Political Mobilization in the French Countryside 1846-1852. Peter McPhee. (Illus.). 320p. 1992. text 75.00 (*0-19-820225-3*) OUP.

Politics of Rural Russia, 1905-1914. Ed. by Leopold H. Haimson. LC 78-62420. (Studies of the Russian Institute, Columbia University & Harvard Series in Ukrainian Studies). 319p. reprint ed. pap. 98.90 (*0-608-17406-8*, 205642200067) Bks Demand.

Politics of Salvation: The Hegelian Idea of the State. Paul Lakeland. LC 83-17875. (SUNY Series in Hegelian Studies). 197p. (C). 1985. pap. text 21.95 (*0-87395-847-0*) State U NY Pr.

Politics of San Antonio: Community, Progress, & Power. Ed. by David R. Johnson et al. LC 83-5766. 262p. reprint ed. pap. 81.30 (*0-7837-4652-0*, 204437600002) Bks Demand.

Politics of Scandal: Power & Process in Liberal Democracies. Ed. by Andrei S. Markovitz & Mark Silverstein. LC 88-11045. 288p. (C). 1988. 39.50 (*0-8419-1097-9*); pap. 19.95 (*0-8419-1098-7*) Holmes & Meier.

Politics of Scarcity: Public Pressure & Political Response in India. Myron Weiner. LC 62-15047. 271p. reprint ed. pap. 84.10 (*0-608-11703-X*, 202017700016) Bks Demand.

***Politics of School Choice.** Hubert Mŏrken & Jo R. Formicola. LC 99-36303. 416p. 1999. pap. 24.95 (*0-8476-9721-5*); text 70.00 (*0-8476-9720-7*) Rowman.

Politics of School-Community Relations. Frank Lutz & Carol Merz. 224p. (C). 1992. text 19.95 (*0-8077-3162-5*); pap. text 19.95 (*0-8077-3161-7*) Tchrs Coll.

Politics of School Desegregation: Comparative Case Studies of Community Structure & Policy-Making. Robert L. Crain. LC 67-27390. (Monographs in Social Research: No. 14). (Illus.). 1968. 15.00 (*0-202-30033-1*) Natl Opinion Res.

Politics of School Government. Ed. by G. Baron. LC 80-40913. (International Studies in Education & Social Change). 304p. 1981. 142.00 (*0-08-025213-3*, CRC Reprint) Franklin.

Politics of School Reform, 1870-1940. Paul E. Peterson. LC 85-1042. x, 256p. 1985. pap. text 14.50 (*0-226-66295-0*) U Ch Pr.

Politics of School Reform, 1870-1940. Paul E. Peterson. LC 85-1042. x, 242p. 1985. lib. bdg. 27.50 (*0-226-66294-2*) U Ch Pr.

Politics of Second Generation Discrimination in American Indian Education: Incidence, Explanation & Mitigating Strategies. David E. Wright, III et al. LC 97-16131. 192p. 1998. 49.95 (*0-89789-531-2*, Bergin & Garvey) Greenwood.

Politics of Secrecy. James Michael. 1979. 20.00 (*0-901108-80-4*, Pub. by NCCL) St Mut.

Politics of Security: Towards a Political Philosophy of Continental Thought. Michael Dillon. LC 96-3435. 272p. (C). 1996. 85.00 (*0-415-12960-5*); pap. 24.99 (*0-415-12961-3*) Routledge.

Politics of Security in the Nordic Area see Security & Politics in the Nordic Area

Politics of Seduction. Trudy Hayes. (C). 1989. 35.00 (*0-946211-94-9*) St Mut.

***Politics of Self-Determination.** Timothy Leary. LC 99-68418. (Self-Mastery Ser.). (Illus.). 112p. 2000. pap. 12.95 (*1-57951-015-9*) Ronin Pub.

Politics of Sensibility: Race, Gender & Commerce in the Sentimental Novel. Markman Ellis. (Studies in Romanticism: No. 18). (Illus.). 278p. (C). 1996. text 59.95 (*0-521-55221-4*) Cambridge U Pr.

Politics of Sentencing Reform. Ed. by C. M. Clarkson & Rod Morgan. (Illus.). 296p. 1995. text 62.00 (*0-19-825872-0*) OUP.

Politics of Sentiment: Churches & Foreign Investment in South Africa. Richard E. Sincere, Jr. LC 84-28642. 176p. (Orig.). 1987. pap. 17.75 (*0-89633-088-5*) Ethics & Public Policy.

Politics of Sentiment: Churches & Foreign Investment in South Africa. Richard E. Sincere, Jr. LC 84-28642. 176p. (Orig.). 1987. 41.25 (*0-89633-116-4*) Ethics & Public Policy.

Politics of Serbia in the 1990s. Robert Thomas. LC 98-17989. 1998. 47.50 (*0-231-11380-3*); pap. 18.50 (*0-231-11381-1*) Col U Pr.

Politics of Sex: Prostitution & Pornography in Australia since 1945. Barbara Sullivan. LC 97-2336. 293p. (C). 1997. text 64.95 (*0-521-55408-X*); pap. text 22.95 (*0-521-55630-9*) Cambridge U Pr.

***Politics of Sex & Other Essays: On Conservatism, Culture & Imagination.** Robert Grant. LC 99-48156. 240p. 2000. text 55.00 (*0-312-23024-9*) St Martin.

Politics of Sexual Morality in Ireland, 1922-1995. Chrystel Hug. LC 98-7078. 296p. 1999. text 65.00 (*0-312-21685-8*) St Martin.

Politics of Sexuality. Terrell Carver & V. Eronique Mottier. LC 98-21485. 224p. (C). 1998. 95.00 (*0-415-16953-4*) Routledge.

***Politics of Sexuality.** Ed. by Barry M. Dank & Roberto Refinetti. (Sexuality & Culture Ser.: Vol. 3). 221p. 2000. pap. 24.95 (*0-7658-0651-7*) Transaction Pubs.

Politics of Shakespeare. Derek Cohen. LC 93-8141. 1993. text 55.00 (*0-312-10187-2*) St Martin.

Politics of Shared Power: Congress & the Executive. Louis Fisher. LC 97-33461. (Illus.). 320p. 1998. pap. 15.95 (*0-89096-821-7*) Tex A&M Univ Pr.

Politics of Shared Power: Congress & the Executive. 3rd ed. Louis Fisher. LC 92-26319. 257p. 1992. pap. text 24.95 (*0-87187-708-2*) Congr Quarterly.

Politics of Shared Power: Congress & the Executive. 4th ed. Louis Fisher. LC 97-33461. (Joseph V. & Polly Oldfield Hughes Series in the Presidency & Leadership Studies). 320p. 1998. 25.95 (*0-89096-806-3*) Tex A&M Univ Pr.

Politics of Sikh Homeland, 1940-1990. Gopal Singh. LC 94-907522. (C). 1994. 37.00 (*81-202-0419-0*, Pub. by Ajanta) S Asia.

Politics of Sikhs. Jitender Kaur. 280p. 1986. 24.00 (*0-8364-1795-X*, Pub. by Manohar) S Asia.

Politics of Silence. Paul Monette. LC 93-33721. (National Book Week Lectures Ser.). 21p. 1994. write for info. (*0-8444-0808-5*) Lib Congress.

Politics of Sin: Drugs, Alcohol & Public Policy. Kenneth J. Meier. LC 93-14454. (Bureaucracies, Public Administration & Public Policy Ser.). (Illus.). 279p. (C). (gr. 13). 1994. pap. text 32.95 (*1-56324-299-0*) M E Sharpe.

Politics of Sin: Drugs, Alcohol & Public Policy. Kenneth J. Meier. LC 93-14454. (Bureaucracies, Public Administration & Public Policy Ser.). (Illus.). 279p. (C). (gr. 13). 1994. text 76.95 (*1-56324-298-2*) M E Sharpe.

Politics of Size: Representation in the United States, 1776-1850. Rosemarie Zagarri. LC 87-47609. (Illus.). 192p. (C). 1987. text 37.50 (*0-8014-2019-9*) Cornell U Pr.

Politics of Skepticism in the Ancients, Montaigne, Hume, & Kant. John C. Laursen. LC 92-28512. (Brill's Studies in Intellectual History: Vol. 35). vi, 253p. 1992. 99.00 (*90-04-09459-8*) Brill Academic Pubs.

***Politics of Slave Trade Suppression in Britain & France, 1814-48.** LC 00-27113. 2000. write for info. (*0-312-23472-4*) St Martin.

Politics of Small Business. Harmon Zeigler. Ed. by Stuart Bruchey & Vincent P. Carosso. LC 78-18154. (Small Business Enterprise in America Ser.). 1979. reprint ed. lib. bdg. 17.95 (*0-405-11511-3*) Ayer.

Politics of Social Change in the Middle East & North Africa. Manfred Halpern. LC 63-12670. (Princeton Paperbacks Ser.: No. 17). 457p. 1965. reprint ed. pap. 141.70 (*0-7837-8172-5*, 204787700008) Bks Demand.

Politics of Social Class in Secondary School: Views of Affluent & Impoverished Youth. Ellen A. Brantlinger. LC 93-10134. 256p. 1993. text 44.00 (*0-8077-3270-2*); pap. text 19.95 (*0-8077-3269-9*) Tchrs Coll.

Politics of Social Ecology: Libertarian Municipalism. Janet Biehl. 204p. 1997. pap. 19.99 (*1-55164-100-3*, Pub. by Black Rose) Consort Bk Sales.

Politics of Social Ecology: Libertarian Municipalism. Janet Biehl. 204p. 1997. 48.99 (*1-55164-101-1*, Pub. by Black Rose) Consort Bk Sales.

Politics of Social Knowledge. Larry D. Spence. LC 77-10543. 1978. 40.00 (*0-271-00521-1*) Pa St U Pr.

Politics of Social Order: The Peak Country, 1520-1770. Andy Wood. LC 98-48331. (Cambridge Studies in Early Modern British History). (Illus.). 368p. (C). 1999. 74.95 (*0-521-56114-0*) Cambridge U Pr.

Politics of Social Policy in Europe. Ed. by Maurice Mullard & Simon Lee. LC 96-52265. 304p. 1997. 90.00 (*1-85898-367-3*) E Elgar.

Politics of Social Policy in the United States. Ed. by Margaret Weir et al. (Studies from the Project on the Federal Social Role). (Illus.). 480p. 1988. pap. text 20.95 (*0-691-02841-9*, Pub. by Princeton U Pr) Cal Prin Full Svc.

Politics of Social Protest: Comparitive Perspectives on States & Social Movements. Ed. by J. Craig Jenkins & Bert Klandermans. LC 94-22704. (Social Movements, Protest & Contention Ser.: Vol. 3). 1995. pap. 19.95 (*0-8166-2422-4*) U of Minn Pr.

Politics of Social Research. Martyn Hammersley. 240p. 1995. text 69.95 (*0-8039-7718-2*); pap. text 22.95 (*0-8039-7719-0*) Sage.

Politics of Social Solidarity: Class Bases of the European Welfare State, 1875-1975. Peter Baldwin. 367p. (C). 1992. pap. text 24.95 (*0-521-42893-9*) Cambridge U Pr.

Politics of Social Theory: Habermas, Freud, & the Critique of Positivism. Russell Keat. LC 81-40532. 256p. 1993. pap. text 9.00 (*0-226-42876-1*) U Ch Pr.

Politics of Social Transformation in Afghanistan, Iran, & Pakistan. Ed. by Myron Weiner & Ali Banuazizi. LC 93-16345. (Contemporary Issues in the Middle East Ser.). 448p. 1993. pap. text 19.95 (*0-8156-2609-6*) Syracuse U Pr.

Politics of Social Welfare: The Collapse of the Centre & Rise of the Right. Alex Waddan. LC 96-38187. 224p. 1997. 80.00 (*1-85898-366-5*) E Elgar.

Politics of Solzhenitsyn. Stephen Carter. LC 76-28346. 161p. 1977. 22.00 (*0-8419-0244-5*) Holmes & Meier.

Politics of South India, 1920-1937. Christopher J. Baker. LC 75-2716. (Cambridge South Asian Studies: 17). 387p. reprint ed. pap. 110.30 (*0-608-17036-4*, 2027279) Bks Demand.

Politics of Soviet Agriculture, 1960-1970. Werner G. Hahn. LC 72-151. 336p. 1972. reprint ed. pap. 104.20 (*0-608-03685-4*, 206451100009) Bks Demand.

Politics of Soviet Culture: Anatolii Lunacharskii. Timothy E. O'Connor. LC 83-18231. (Studies in the Fine Arts: The Avant-Garde: No. 42). (Illus.). 211p. reprint ed. pap. 65.50 (*0-8357-1468-3*, 207056600001) Bks Demand.

Politics of Soviet Education. Ed. by George Z. Bereday & Jaan Pennar. LC 75-28662. 217p. 1976. reprint ed. lib. bdg. 75.00 (*0-8371-8477-0*, BEPS, Greenwood Pr) Greenwood.

Politics of Space: A History of U.S.-Soviet/Russian Competition & Cooperation in Space. Matthew J. Von Bencke. LC 96-32067. 272p. (C). 1996. text 75.00 (*0-8133-3192-7*, Pub. by Westview) HarpC.

Politics of Space: Architecture, Painting & Theater in Postmodern Germany, Vol. 107. Douglas Nash. LC 94-36388. (American University Studies Germanic Languages & Literature Ser.: Ser. I). X, 232p. (C). 1996. 44.95 (*0-8204-2599-0*) P Lang Pubng.

Politics of Spanish American Modernismo: By Exquisite Design. Gerard Aching. LC 97-218373. (Studies in Latin American & Iberian Literature: Vol. 11). 192p. (C). 1997. text 54.95 (*0-521-57249-5*) Cambridge U Pr.

Politics of Special Educational Needs. Len Barton. 200p. 1988. 75.00 (*1-85000-370-X*, Falmer Pr); pap. 37.95 (*1-85000-371-8*, Falmer Pr) Taylor & Francis.

Politics of Spirituality: A Study of a Renewal Process in an English Diocese. Michael P. Hornsby-Smith et al. (Illus.). 290p. 1995. text 59.00 (*0-19-827776-8*) OUP.

Politics of Staffing the United Nations Secretariat, Vol. 8. Houshang Ameri. (Major Concepts in Politics & Political Theory Ser.). XX, 604p. (C). 1996. 74.95 (*0-8204-2810-8*) P Lang Pubng.

Politics of State & City Administration. Glenn Abney & Thomas P. Lauth. LC 85-14873. (SUNY Series in Public Administration). 260p. 1986. text 21.50 (*0-88706-255-5*) State U NY Pr.

Politics of State Courts. Harry P. Stumpf & John H. Culver. 182p. (Orig.). (C). 1991. pap. text 60.00 (*0-8013-0051-7*, 75715) Longman.

Politics of Steel: Western Europe & the Steel Industry in the Crisis Years (1974-1984) Ed. by Yves Meny & Vincent Wright. (European University Institute, Series C (Political & Social Science): No. 7). x, 812p. 1986. lib. bdg. 242.35 (*3-11-010517-9*) De Gruyter.

Politics of Story in Victorian Social Fiction. Rosemarie Bodenheimer. LC 87-17313. 264p. 1988. 39.95 (*0-8014-2099-7*) Cornell U Pr.

Politics of Story in Victorian Social Fiction. Rosemarie Bodenheimer. LC 87-17313. 264p. 1990. reprint ed. pap. text 16.95 (*0-8014-9920-8*) Cornell U Pr.

Politics of Strategic Adjustment. Peter Trubowitz. Ed. by Emily Goldman & Edward Rhodes. LC 98-17371. (Illus.). 331p. 1998. 45.00 (*0-231-11074-X*) Col U Pr.

Politics of Strategic Adjustment. Peter Trubowitz. LC 98-17371. (Illus.). 368p. 1998. pap. 19.50 (*0-231-11075-8*) Col U Pr.

Politics of Strategic Aircraft Modernization. David S. Sorenson. LC 95-6947. 256p. 1995. 65.00 (*0-275-95258-4*, Praeger Pubs) Greenwood.

Politics of Street Crime: Criminal Process & Cultural Obsession. Stuart A. Scheingold. 250p. 1991. 59.95 (*0-87722-825-6*) Temple U Pr.

Politics of Street Crime: Criminal Process & Cultural Obsession. Stuart A. Scheingold. 256p. 1992. pap. 22.95 (*1-56639-024-9*) Temple U Pr.

Politics of Structural Adjustment in Nigeria. Adebayo O. Olukoshi. 144p. (C). 1993. text 50.00 (*0-435-08072-5*, 08072) Heinemann.

Politics of Style: Language as Theme in the Fiction of Berger, McGuane & McPherson. Jon Wallace. LC 91-38372. 172p. (C). 1993. text 35.00 (*0-89341-705-X*) Hollowbrook.

Politics of Subjectivity: Between Foucault & Merleau-Ponty. Nick Crossley. LC 94-9863. (Avebury Series in Philosophy). 1994. 69.95 (*1-85628-886-2*, Pub. by Avebury) Ashgate Pub Co.

Politics of Subnational Governance. 2nd ed. Deirdre A. Zimmerman & Joseph F. Zimmerman. 324p. (Orig.). (C). 1991. pap. text 28.50 (*0-8191-8388-1*); lib. bdg. 54.00 (*0-8191-8387-3*) U Pr of Amer.

Politics of Subversion: A Manifesto for the Twenty-First Century. Antonio Negri. Tr. by James Newell. 200p. 1989. text 61.95 (*0-7456-0601-6*) Blackwell Pubs.

***Politics of Subversion: A Manifesto for the Twenty-First Century.** Antonio Negri. Tr. by James Newell. 232p. 2000. reprint ed. text 25.00 (*0-7881-6969-6*) DIANE Pub.

Politics of Survival: Artisans in Twentieth-Century France. Steven M. Zdatny. (Illus.). 272p. 1990. text 70.00 (*0-19-505940-9*) OUP.

Politics of Survival: Resolving the Seven Deadly Trends. 2nd ed. Joseph A. Bagnall. (C). 1997. pap. 22.19 (*0-07-289259-5*) McGrw-H Hghr Educ.

Politics of Survivorship. Rosana Champagne. 248p. (C). 1998. pap. text 16.50 (*0-8147-1543-5*) NYU Pr.

Politics of Survivorship: Incest, Women's Literature, & Feminist Theory. Rosaria Champagne. 248p. (C). 1996. text 50.00 (*0-8147-1542-7*) NYU Pr.

Politics of Sustainable Development. Ed. by Susan Baker & Maria Kousis. LC 96-29598. 288p. (C). 1997. 85.00 (*0-415-13873-6*); pap. 25.99 (*0-415-13874-4*) Routledge.

Politics of Sustainable Development: A European Perspective. Ed. by Tim O'Riordan & Heather Voisey. 288p. 1997. write for info. (*1-85383-469-6*, Pub. by Escan Pubns) Island Pr.

Politics of Sustainable Development: Citizens, Unions & the Corporations. Laurie E. Adkin. LC 96-79518. (Illus.). 250p. 1996. 52.99 (*1-55164-081-3*, Pub. by Black Rose); pap. 28.99 (*1-55164-080-5*, Pub. by Black Rose) Consort Bk Sales.

Politics of Symbolism in the Mixtec Codices. John M. Pohl. Ed. by Ronald M. Spores. (Vanderbilt University Publications in Anthropology: No. 46). (Illus.). 157p. (Orig.). 1994. pap. 14.00 (*0-935462-37-6*) VUPA.

Politics of Taxation. Thomas J. Reese. LC 79-8413. (Illus.). 237p. 1980. 55.00 (*0-89930-003-0*, RPT/, Quorum Bks) Greenwood.

Politics of Taxation: Revenue Without Representation. Susan B. Hansen. LC 83-4043. 287p. 1983. 55.00 (*0-275-90996-4*, C0996, Praeger Pubs) Greenwood.

***Politics of Teacher Education Reform: The National Commission on Teaching & America's Future.** Ed. by Karen Symms Gallagher & Jerry D. Bailey. (Politics of Education Association Yearbook Ser.: Vol. 13). (Illus.). 189p. 2000. pap. 22.95 (*0-7619-7678-7*); lib. bdg. 51.95 (*0-7619-7677-9*) Corwin Pr.

Politics of Technology Transfer in Mexico. Van R. Whiting, Jr. (Research Reports: No. 37). 61p. (Orig.). (C). 1984. pap. 5.00 (*0-935391-36-3*, RR-37) UCSD Ctr US-Mex.

Politics of Telecommunications: National Institutions, Convergences, & Change in Britain & France. Mark Thatcher. LC 99-15994. 384p. 2000. 74.00 (*0-19-828074-2*) OUP.

***Politics of Telecommunications in Mexico: Privatization & State-Labour Relations, 1982-95.** Judith Clifton. LC 99-49938. (St. Antony's Ser.). 2000. text 69.95 (*0-312-23019-2*) St Martin.

Politics of Telecommunications Regulation: The States & the Divestiture of AT&T. Jeffrey E. Cohen. LC 92-9815. (Bureaucracies, Public Administration & Public Policy Ser.). 202p. (gr. 13). 1992. text 66.95 (*1-56324-050-5*) M E Sharpe.

Politics of Tensions: The Articles of Confederation & American Political Ideas. Robert W. Hoffert. 304p. 1992. 24.95 (*0-87081-254-8*) Univ Pr Colo.

Politics of Terror: The Macedonian Revolutionary Movements, 1893-1903. Duncan M. Perry. LC 87-33062. (Illus.). 275p. (C). 1988. text 39.95 (*0-8223-0813-4*) Duke.

Politics of Terrorism. 3rd enl. rev. ed. Ed. by Michael Stohl. (Public Administration & Public Policy Ser.: Vol. 33). (Illus.). 672p. 1988. text 65.00 (*0-8247-7814-6*) Dekker.

Politics of Terrorism in India. Sharda Jain. (C). 1995. 36.00 (*81-7100-807-0*, Pub. by Deep & Deep Pubns) S Asia.

Politics of Textiles: The Indian Cotton-Mill Industry & the Legacy of Swadeshi, 1900-1985. Simon R. Leadbeater. LC 92-17600. (Illus.). 312p. (C). 1993. text 36.00 (*0-8039-9440-0*) Sage.

Politics of the Administrative Process. 2nd ed. James W. Fesler & Donald F. Kettl. LC 95-50155. 512p. 1996. pap. text 42.95 (*1-56643-025-9*, Chatham House Pub) Seven Bridges.

***Politics of the Administrative Process.** 3rd ed. James W. Fesler & Donald F. Kettl. (Illus.). 540p. (C). 2000. pap. text. write for info. (*1-889119-44-X*, Chatham House Pub) Seven Bridges.

Politics of the American Civil Liberties Union. William A. Donohue & Aaron Wildavsky. 390p. 1985. pap. 24.95 (*0-87855-983-3*) Transaction Pubs.

Politics of the Ancient Constitution: An Introduction to English Political Thought, 1600-1642. Glenn Burgess. LC 92-17255. 256p. (C). 1993. 50.00 (*0-271-00903-9*); pap. 18.95 (*0-271-00926-8*) Pa St U Pr.

Politics of the Archaic Peloponnese. Adshead. 1986. 72.95 (*0-86127-024-X*) Ashgate Pub Co.

***Politics of the Arts in Britain.** Clive Gray. LC 00-38236. (Illus.). 2000. pap. write for info. (*0-312-23565-8*) St Martin.

***Politics of the Asian Economic Crisis.** Ed. by T. J. Pempel. LC 99-38107. 1999. 49.95 (*0-8014-3722-9*); pap. 19.95 (*0-8014-8634-3*) Cornell U Pr.

Politics of the Ayodhya Dispute. Pradeep Nayak. (C). 1993. 22.50 (*81-7169-252-4*, Commonwealth) S Asia.

Politics of the Basin: A Perspective on the Church As Community. D. Robert Kennedy. 196p. (Orig.). (C). 1994. pap. text 26.50 (*0-8191-9568-5*); lib. bdg. 49.00 (*0-8191-9567-7*) U Pr of Amer.

Politics of the British Annexation of India, 1757-1857. Ed. by Michael Fisher. (India Readings: Themes in Indian History Ser.). (Illus.). 332p. 1994. text 27.00 (*0-19-562860-8*) OUP.

Politics of the British Annexation of India, 1757-1857. Michael H. Fisher. (Oxford in India Readings). (Illus.). 330p. 1997. pap. text 14.95 (*0-19-563920-0*) OUP.

Politics of the British Army. Hew Strachan. LC 97-2241. 322p. 1997. text 55.00 (*0-19-820670-4*) OUP.

Politics of the British Constitution. Foley. 1999. pap. 24.95 (*0-7190-4552-5*); text 69.95 (*0-7190-4551-7*) St Martin.

Politics of the Caribbean Basin Sugar Trade. Ed. by Scott B. MacDonald & Georges A. Fauriol. LC 90-20868. 176p. 1991. 52.95 (*0-275-93052-1*, C3052, Praeger Pubs) Greenwood.

Politics of the Center: The Juste Milieu in Theory & Practice, France, & England, 1815-1848. Vincent E. Starzinger. 164p. (C). 1990. pap. 19.95 (*0-88738-862-0*) Transaction Pubs.

Politics of the Chinese Cultural Revolution: A Case Study. Hong Y. Lee. LC 76-19993. (Center for Chinese Studies, UC Berkeley: No. 17). 1978. pap. 17.95 (*0-520-04065-1*, Pub. by U CA Pr) Cal Prin Full Svc.

Politics of the Communications Revolution in Western Europe. Ed. by Kenneth Dyson & Peter Humphreys. 224p. 1986. 35.00 (*0-7146-3284-8*, Pub. by F Cass Pubs) Intl Spec Bk.

Politics of the Criminal Justice System: An Organizational Analysis. Ralph A. Rossum. LC 78-18519. (Political Science Ser.: No. 6). (Illus.). 303p. reprint ed. pap. 94.00 (*0-7837-0823-8*, 204113700019) Bks Demand.

P

An Asterisk (*) at the beginning of an entry indicates that the title is appearing for the first time.

Politics of the Developing Areas. Ed. by Gabriel Abraham Almond & James S. Coleman. LC 60-9763. 608p. reprint ed. pap. 188.50 (*0-8357-2929-X*, 203916700011) Bks Demand.

Politics of the Earth: Environmental Discourses. John S. Dryzek. LC 97-7366. (Illus.). 234p. (C). 1997. text 71.00 (*0-19-878160-1*); pap. text 21.95 (*0-19-878159-8*) OUP.

Politics of the Endless Frontier: Postwar Research Policy in the United States. Daniel L. Kleinman. LC 94-41440. (Illus.). 240p. 1995. text 49.95 (*0-8223-1583-1*); pap. text 16.95 (*0-8223-1598-X*) Duke.

Politics of the Environment. Ed. by Robert E. Goodin. LC 94-6262. (Schools of Thought in Politics Ser.: Vol. 5). 624p. 1994. 230.00 (*1-85278-872-0*) E Elgar.

Politics of the Environment in Southeast Asia. Ed. by Philip Hirsch & Carol Warren. LC 98-158615. 304p. (C). 1998. 85.00 (*0-415-17298-5*); pap. 27.99 (*0-415-17299-3*) Routledge.

Politics of the Essay: Feminist Perspectives. Ed. by Ruth-Ellen B. Joeres & Elizabeth Mittman. LC 92-25121. 240p. 1993. 36.95 (*0-253-33109-9*); pap. 13.95 (*0-253-20788-6*, MB-788) Ind U Pr.

Politics of the European Court of Justice. Richard Kruper. 1998. pap. text 25.00 (*0-7494-2607-1*) Kogan Page Ltd.

***Politics of the Extreme Right: From the Margins to the Mainstream.** Paul Hainsworth. LC 99-44977. 352p. 2000. pap. 28.95 (*1-85567-459-9*) P P Pubs.

Politics of the Family. Ed. by Helen Jones & Jane Millar. 240p. 1996. 72.95 (*1-85972-086-2*, Pub. by Avebury) Ashgate Pub Co.

Politics of the Family: From Homo Sapiens to Homo Economicus. C. L. Shannon. (American University Studies Anthropology & Sociology: Ser. XI, Vol. 24). 208p. (C). 1989. text 34.95 (*0-8204-0773-9*) P Lang Pubng.

***Politics of the Family & Other Essays** R. D. Laing. LC 99-194016. 133p. 1999. write for info. (*0-415-19822-4*) Routledge.

Politics of the Feminist Novel. Judi M. Roller. LC 85-12718. (Contributions in Women's Studies: No. 63). 206p. 1986. pap. 12.95 (*0-313-25445-1*, RPNPB) Greenwood.

Politics of the Feminist Novel, 63. Judi M. Roller. LC 85-12718. (Contributions in Women's Studies: No. 63). 206p. 1986. 49.95 (*0-313-24663-7*, RPN) Greenwood.

Politics of the Gender Gap: The Social Construction of Political Influence. Ed. by Carol M. Mueller. (Yearbooks in Women's Policy Studies: Vol. 12). 320p. (C). 1988. text 44.00 (*0-8039-2732-0*); pap. text 21.95 (*0-8039-2733-9*) Sage.

Politics of the Gender Gap: The Social Construction of Political Influence. Ed. by Carol M. Mueller. LC 87-22454. (Sage Yearbooks in Women's Policy Studies: No. 12). 316p. reprint ed. pap. 98.00 (*0-7837-6719-6*, 204634600011) Bks Demand.

Politics of the German Gothic Revival: August Reichensperger. Michael J. Lewis. LC 92-38723. (Architectural History Foundation Ser.). (Illus.). 318p. 1993. 55.00 (*0-262-12177-8*) MIT Pr.

Politics of the Heart: A Lesbian Parenting Anthology. Ed. by Sandra Pollack & Jeanne Vaughn. LC 87-27250. 360p. (Orig.). 1987. pap. 12.95 (*0-932379-35-4*); lib. bdg. 26.95 (*0-932379-36-2*) Firebrand Bks.

***Politics of the Jamiat-i-ulema-i-islam Pakistan; 1971-1977.** Sayyid A. S. Pirzada. 345p. 2000. text 26.00 (*0-19-579302-1*) OUP.

Politics of the Lesser Evil: Leadership, Democracy, & Jaruzelski's Poland. Anton Pelinka. LC 97-51254. 1998. 44.95 (*1-56000-367-7*) Transaction Pubs.

Politics of the Mass Media. Calvin F. Exoo. Ed. by Baxter. LC 93-34599. 300p. (C). 1994. 25.50 (*0-314-02891-9*) West Pub.

Politics of the Media. Ian Ward. LC 95-205683. 320p. 1994. 64.95 (*0-7329-2790-0*, Pub. by Macmill Educ); pap. 32.95 (*0-7329-2789-7*, Pub. by Macmill Educ) Paul & Co Pubs.

***Politics of the Minimum Wage.** Jerold L. Waltman. LC 99-6830. 2000. 24.95 (*0-252-02545-8*) U of Ill Pr.

Politics of the Miraculous in Peru: Haya de la Torre & the Spiritualist Tradition. Fredrick B. Pike. LC 85-1162. (Illus.). 409p. 1986. reprint ed. pap. 126.80 (*0-608-08000-4*, 206796500012) Bks Demand.

***Politics of the New Centre.** Bodo Hombach. 208p. 2000. pap. 24.95 (*0-7456-2461-8*, Pub. by Polity Pr) Blackwell Pubs.

Politics of the Northwest Passage. Ed. by Franklyn Griffiths. 324p. 1987. 65.00 (*0-7735-0613-6*, Pub. by McG-Queens Univ Pr) CUP Services.

Politics of the Nuclear Freeze. Adam M. Garfinkle. LC 84-6030. (Philadelphia Policy Papers). (Orig.). 1984. pap. 7.95 (*0-910191-08-5*) For Policy Res.

Politics of the Ordinary. Thomas L. Dumm. LC 98-40234. 240p. 1999. text 55.00 (*0-8147-1896-5*) NYU Pr.

***Politics of the Ordinary.** Thomas L. Dumm. LC 98-40234. 215p. 1999. pap. 18.50 (*0-8147-1897-3*) NYU Pr.

Politics of the Pacific Nations. Ed. by F. Q. Quo. (Replica Edition Ser.). 275p. (C). 1984. pap. text 10.00 (*0-86531-951-0*) Westview.

Politics of the Past. Ed. by P. Gathercole & D. Lowenthal. (One World Archaeology Ser.). (Illus.). 352p. (Orig.). (C). 1994. pap. 37.99 (*0-415-09554-9*, B4653) Routledge.

Politics of the Peace Corps & VISTA. T. Zane Reeves. LC 86-19194. (Illus.). 232p. 1988. text 34.95 (*0-8173-0323-5*) U of Ala Pr.

Politics of the People in Eighteenth-Century Britain. H. T. Dickinson. 358p. 1996. pap. 19.95 (*0-312-16033-X*) St Martin.

Politics of the Police. Robert Reiner. 280p. 2000. text 55.00 (*0-19-876544-4*) OUP.

Politics of the Police. 2nd ed. Robert Reiner. 334p. 1993. text 60.00 (*0-8020-2942-6*); pap. text 19.95 (*0-8020-7769-2*) U of Toronto Pr.

Politics of the Polish Military after Communism. Andrew A. Michta. LC 97-21999. 160p. 1997. text 49.95 (*0-312-17302-4*) St Martin.

Politics of the Possible: The Brazilian Rural Workers' Trade Union Movement, 1964-1985. Biorn Maybury-Lewis. LC 93-26985. 320p. 1994. 69.95 (*1-56639-166-0*); pap. 22.95 (*1-56639-167-9*) Temple U Pr.

Politics of the Post: Canada's Postal System from Public Service to Privatization. Robert M. Campbell. 500p. 1994. 49.95 (*1-55111-034-2*) Broadview Pr.

***Politics of the Post-Communist World.** Nelson White. 1080p. 2000. 139.95 (*1-85521-907-7*) Ashgate Pub Co.

Politics of the Presidency. 4th ed. Norman C. Thomas & Joseph A. Pika. LC 97-20161. 499p. (YA). 1997. 35.95 (*1-56802-316-2*) Congr Quarterly.

Politics of the Prussian Army, 1640-1945. Gordon A. Craig. 556p. 1964. reprint ed. pap. text 25.95 (*0-19-500257-1*) OUP.

Politics of the Prussian Nobility: The Development of a Conservative Ideology, 1770-1848. Robert M. Berdahl. LC 88-17616. 398p. reprint ed. pap. 123.40 (*0-608-06303-7*, 206666500008) Bks Demand.

Politics of the Reformation in Germany: Jacob Sturm (1489-1553) of Strasbourg. Thomas A. Brady. 336p. (C). 1996. pap. 19.95 (*0-391-04004-9*) Humanities.

Politics of the Right to Work: The Labor Federations as Special Interests, Nineteen Forty-Three to Nineteen Seventy-Nine, 24. Gilbert J. Gall. LC 87-29564. (Contributions in Labor Studies: No. 24). 257p. 1988. 59.95 (*0-313-24910-5*, GRT/) Greenwood.

Politics of the Second Front: American Military Planning & Diplomacy in Coalition Warfare, 1941-1943, 12. Mark A. Stoler. LC 76-47171. (Contributions in Military History Ser.: No 12). 244p. 1977. 59.95 (*0-8371-9438-5*, SPF/, Greenwood Pr) Greenwood.

Politics of the Self: Feminism & the Postmodern in West German Literature & Film. Richard W. McCormick. LC 90-47160. (Illus.). 274p. 1991. reprint ed. pap. 85.00 (*0-608-02571-2*, 206321600004) Bks Demand.

Politics of the Soul: Eric Voegelin on Religious Experience. Ed. by Glenn Hughes. LC 98-37875. 192p. 1999. 58.00 (*0-8476-9232-9*); pap. 22.95 (*0-8476-9233-7*) Rowman.

Politics of the South Africa Run: European Shipping & Pretoria. Geoffrey R. Berridge. LC 87-1600. (Illus.). 268p. 1987. 59.00 (*0-19-827484-X*) OUP.

Politics of the Soviet Cinema, Nineteen Seventeen to Nineteen Twenty-Nine. Richard Taylor. LC 78-67809. (International Studies). 230p. reprint ed. pap. 65.60 (*0-608-15612-4*, 2031732) Bks Demand.

Politics of the Spirit: Understanding the Holy Spirit in the Community Called Church. D. Robert Kennedy. LC 96-24531. 294p. 1996. lib. bdg. 42.50 (*0-7618-0425-0*) U Pr of Amer.

Politics of the Stuart Court Masque. Ed. by David Bevington & Peter Holbrook. LC 97-52957. (Illus.). 368p. (C). 1998. 64.95 (*0-521-59436-7*) Cambridge U Pr.

Politics of the Texas Sheriff: From Frontier to Bureaucracy. James G. Dickson. (Texas History Ser.). (Illus.). 68p. 1983. pap. text 9.95 (*0-89641-131-1*) American Pr.

Politics of the Textbook. Michael W. Apple & Linda K. Christian-Smith. 296p. (C). 1991. pap. 17.99 (*0-415-90223-1*) Routledge.

Politics of the Theological: Beyond the Piety & Power of a World Come of Age. Barry Harvey. LC 94-13600. (American University Studies, Series VII: Vol. 133). XI, 266p. (C). 1995. text 46.95 (*0-8204-1874-9*) P Lang Pubng.

Politics of the UCS Work-In: Class Alliances & the Right to Work. Charles Woolfson. Ed. by John Foster. (Illus.). 448p. (C). 1986. pap. 29.95 (*0-85315-663-8*, Pub. by Lawrence & Wishart) NYU Pr.

Politics of the Universe: Edward Beecher, Abolition, & Orthodoxy. Robert Merideth. LC 68-21869. 286p. reprint ed. pap. 88.70 (*0-608-06263-4*, 206659200008) Bks Demand.

Politics of the Unpolitical: German Writers & the Problem of Power, 1770-1871. Gordon A. Craig. 208p. 1995. text 45.00 (*0-19-509499-9*) OUP.

Politics of the Urban Crisis. A. Sills & G. Taylor. 192p. (C). 1988. pap. text 29.95 (*0-09-173129-1*) Routledge.

Politics of the Verm Worst. Paul Virilio. Ed. by Sylvere Letringer. Tr. by Michael Cavaliere from FRE. Orig. Title: Cubermonde: Politique du Pire. 128p. 1998. pap. 8.00 (*1-57027-084-8*) Autonomedia.

Politics of the Visible: Writing Women, Culture, & Fascism. Robin Pickering-Iazzi. 240p. (C). 1997. pap. 21.95 (*0-8166-2923-4*); text 54.95 (*0-8166-2922-6*) U of Minn Pr.

Politics of the World Economy: The States, the Movements & the Civilisations. Immanuel Wallerstein. LC 83-20853. (Studies in Modern Capitalism-Etudes sur le Capitalisme Moderne). 200p. 1984. pap. text 16.95 (*0-521-27760-4*) Cambridge U Pr.

Politics of This War. Ray F. Harvey et al. LC 68-58793. (Essay Index Reprint Ser.). 1977. 21.95 (*0-8369-1038-9*) Ayer.

Politics of Threat: Minuteman Vulnerability in American National Security Policy. David H. Dunn. LC 97-13669. 289p. 1997. text 65.00 (*0-312-17611-2*) St Martin.

Politics of Time: Modernity & Avant-Garde. Peter Osborne. LC 95-30097. 224p. (C). (gr. 13 up). 1995. 65.00 (*0-86091-482-8*, Pub. by Verso) Norton.

Politics of Tobacco: Policy Networks & the Cigarette Industry. Melvyn Read. LC 96-84592. 215p. 1996. 68.95 (*1-85628-661-4*, Pub. by Avebury) Ashgate Pub Co.

***Politics of Toleration: Ethics & Virtue.** Glen Newey. 224p. 1999. 65.00 (*0-7486-1244-0*, Pub. by Edinburgh U Pr) Col U Pr.

Politics of Toleration: Tolerance & Intolerance in Modern Life. Susan Mendus. LC 99-32392. 170p. 2000. 16.95 (*0-8223-2498-9*) Duke.

Politics of Torah: The Jewish Political Tradition & the Founding of Agudat Israel. Alan L. Mittleman. LC 95-49366. 200p. (C). 1996. text 59.50 (*0-7914-3077-4*); pap. text 19.95 (*0-7914-3078-2*) State U NY Pr.

Politics of Tourism. James Elliot. LC 96-52245. 296p. (C). 1997. pap. 27.99 (*0-415-07158-5*) Routledge.

Politics of Toxic Waste. Ed. by Dianne Rahm. (Policy Studies Journal: Vol. 26:4). 1998. pap. write for info. (*0-944285-57-0*) Pol Studies.

Politics of Trade: American Political Development & Foreign Economic Policy. Cynthia A. Hody. LC 95-8765. (Nelson A. Rockefeller Series in Social Science & Public Policy). 222p. 1996. 45.00 (*0-87451-729-X*) U Pr of New Eng.

Politics of Trade in Latin American Development. Steven E. Sanderson. LC 91-39863. 307p. (C). 1992. 47.50 (*0-8047-1983-7*); pap. 17.95 (*0-8047-2021-5*) Stanford U Pr.

Politics of Trade in Safavid Iran: Silk for Silver, 1600-1730. Rudolph P. Matthee. LC 99-12830. (Cambridge Studies in Islamic Civilization). (Illus.). 312p. (C). 2000. 64.95 (*0-521-64131-4*) Cambridge U Pr.

Politics of Trade Negotiations Between Africa & the European Economic Community: The Weak Confront the Strong. I. William Zartman. LC 76-120765. (Studies in Peaceful Change). 255p. 1971. reprint ed. pap. 79.10 (*0-7837-9490-8*, 206023300004) Bks Demand.

***Politics of Trade Pressure: American-Soviet Relations, 1980-88.** Mohammed Ishaq. 206p. 1999. text 65.95 (*1-84014-764-4*, Pub. by Ashgate Pub) Ashgate Pub Co.

Politics of Tradition: Continuity & Change in Northern Nigeria Nineteen Forty-Six to Nineteen Sixty-Six. C. S. Whitaker. LC 79-5234. 563p. reprint ed. pap. text 9.95 (*0-88357-098-X*) NOK Pubs.

Politics of Tradition Continuity & Change in Northern Nigeria, 1946-1966. C. S. Whitaker. LC 68-56323. 576p. 1970. reprint ed. pap. 178.60 (*0-608-02922-X*, 206398700008) Bks Demand.

Politics of Transformation: Local Activism in the Peace & Environmental Movements. Betty H. Zisk. LC 92-9099. (Praeger Series in Transformational Politics & Political Science). 280p. 1992. 59.95 (*0-275-94057-8*, C4057, Praeger Pubs) Greenwood.

Politics of Transition: Shaping a Post-Soviet Future. Stephen White et al. LC 92-42520. 287p. (C). 1993. text 64.95 (*0-521-44094-7*); pap. text 18.95 (*0-521-44634-1*) Cambridge U Pr.

***Politics of Transition: The Hidden History of South Africa's Negotiated Settlement.** Richard Spitz & Matthew Chaskalosn. 304p. 2000. 45.00 (*1-84113-178-4*, Pub. by Hart Pub) Intl Spec Bk.

Politics of Transport in Twentieth-Century France. Joseph Jones. 336p. 1984. 65.00 (*0-7735-0428-1*, Pub. by McG-Queens Univ Pr) CUP Services.

Politics of Truth. Maurice Foucault. 1997. pap. 8.00 (*1-57027-027-9*) Autonomedia.

Politics of Truth: From Marx to Foucault. Michele Barrett. LC 91-66613. 208p. (C). 1992. 39.50 (*0-8047-2004-5*); pap. 13.95 (*0-8047-2005-3*) Stanford U Pr.

Politics of Truth & Other Untimely Essays: The Crisis of Civic Consciousness. Ellis Sandoz. LC 98-45474. 256p. 1999. 39.95 (*0-8262-1213-1*) U of Mo Pr.

Politics of TV Violence: Policy Uses of Communication Research. Willard D. Rowland. LC 82-23009. (People & Communication Ser.: No. 16). 320p. 1983. reprint ed. pap. 99.20 (*0-608-01502-4*, 205954600001) Bks Demand.

Politics of Two Sudans: The South & the North, 1821-1969. Deng D. Ray. 183p. 1994. pap. 42.50 (*91-7106-344-7*) Coronet Bks.

***Politics of Tyranny: U. S. Foreign Policy & Korea, 1958-1988.** Woo Jung Ju. (Illus.). 160p. 1999. 15.00 (*0-8059-4817-1*) Dorrance.

***Politics of U. S. Foreign Policy.** 2nd ed. Rosati. LC 98-71719. (C). 1998. pap. text 49.00 (*0-03-018063-5*, Pub. by Harcourt Coll Pubs) Harcourt.

Politics of U. S. International Trade. Stephanie A. Lenway. LC 84-25395. (Business & Public Policy Ser.). 288p. 1986. text 28.00 (*0-273-02250-4*, HarpBusn) HarpInfo.

Politics of U. S. Labor: From the Great Depression to the New Deal. David Milton. LC 80-8934. 189p. reprint ed. pap. 58.60 (*0-7837-3915-X*, 204376300010) Bks Demand.

Politics of Uncertainty: Attachment in Private & Public Life. Peter Marris. 208p. (C). 1996. 75.00 (*0-415-13171-5*); pap. 22.99 (*0-415-13172-3*) Routledge.

Politics of Unease in the Plays of John Fletcher. Gordon McMullan. LC 93-28554. (Massachusetts Studies in Early Modern Culture). 352p. 1994. lib. bdg. 40.00 (*0-87023-892-2*) U of Mass Pr.

Politics of Unemployment. Hans F. Sennholz. 356p. 1987. 21.95 (*0-910884-17-X*) Libertarian Press.

Politics of Unfunded Mandates: Whither Federalism? Paul L. Posner. Ed. by Barry Rabe & John Tierney. LC 98-16020. (American Governance & Public Policy Ser.). 320p. 1998. 55.00 (*0-87840-708-1*) Georgetown U Pr.

Politics of Unfunded Mandates: Whither Federalism? Paul L. Posner. Ed. by Barry Rabe & John Tierney. LC 98-16020. (American Governance & Public Policy Ser.). (Illus.). 320p. 1998. pap. 24.95 (*0-87840-709-X*) Georgetown U Pr.

Politics of Union: Northern Politics During the Civil War. James A. Rawley. LC 80-17173. 216p. 1980. reprint ed. pap. 61.60 (*0-608-01402-8*, 2062165) Bks Demand.

Politics of United States Foreign Policy. Jeral A. Rosati. 560p. (C). 1993. pap. text 46.00 (*0-03-047024-2*) Harcourt Coll Pubs.

Politics of Unreason: Right Wing Extremism in America. 2nd ed. Seymour M. Lipset & Earl Raab. LC 77-92800. 1993. pap. text 7.95 (*0-226-48457-2*, P750) U Ch Pr.

Politics of Unreason: Right-Wing Extremism in America. 2nd ed. Seymour M. Lipset & Earl Raab. LC 77-92800. (Phoenix Book Ser.: Vol. P75). 608p. reprint ed. pap. 188.50 (*0-608-09465-X*, 205426500005) Bks Demand.

Politics of Urban America. 2nd ed. Judd & Kantor. LC 97-27884. 374p. 1997. pap. text 36.93 (*0-205-19771-X*) P-H.

Politics of Urban Development. Ed. by Clarence N. Stone & Heywood T. Sanders. LC 87-13311. (Studies in Government & Public Policy). viii, 312p. (C). 1987. 35.00 (*0-7006-0332-8*); pap. 14.95 (*0-7006-0333-6*) U Pr of KS.

Politics of Urban Development in Singapore. Robert E. Gamer. LC 78-37778. (Illus.). 288p. reprint ed. pap. 89.30 (*0-608-08093-4*, 206905200002) Bks Demand.

Politics of Urban Education in the United States: The Politics of Education Association Yearbook, 1991. Ed. by James G. Cibulka et al. 210p. 1992. pap. 29.95 (*0-7507-0090-4*, Falmer Pr) Taylor & Francis.

Politics of Urban Fiscal Policy. Ed. by Terrence J. McDonald & Sally K. Ward. LC 84-13431. (New Approaches to Social Science History Ser.: No. 5). 176p. 1984. reprint ed. pap. 54.60 (*0-608-01503-2*, 205954700001) Bks Demand.

Politics of Urban Liberation. Stephen Schecter. 203p. 1978. 38.99 (*0-919618-79-0*, Pub. by Black Rose); pap. 9.99 (*0-919618-78-2*, Pub. by Black Rose) Consort Bk Sales.

Politics of Urban Planning see Urban Planning & Politics

Politics of Urban Planning Policy. Efraim Torgovnik. 216p. (C). 1990. pap. text 29.00 (*0-8191-7796-2*) U Pr of Amer.

Politics of Urban Planning Policy. Efraim Torgovnik. 216p. (C). 1990. lib. bdg. 49.00 (*0-8191-7795-4*) U Pr of Amer.

Politics of Urban Redevelopment: A Study of Old Delhi. Mehra. 176p. 1991. 28.50 (*0-8039-9671-3*) Sage.

Politics of Urban Renewal: The Chicago Findings. Peter H. Rossi & Robert A. Dentler. LC 81-6327. (Illus.). 308p. 1981. reprint ed. lib. bdg. 69.50 (*0-313-22780-2*, ROPR, Greenwood Pr) Greenwood.

Politics of Usability: A Practical Guide to Designing Usable Systems in Industry. Ed. by Lesley Trenner & Joanna Bawa. LC 98-4708. (Practitioner Ser.). (Illus.). xxii, 194p. 1998. pap. 59.95 (*3-540-76181-0*) Spr-Verlag.

Politics of Usurpation in the Seventh Century: Rhetoric & Revolution in Byzantium. David M. Olster. vii, 209p. 1993. pap. 80.00 (*90-256-1010-2*, Pub. by AM Hakkert) BookLink Distributors.

***Politics of Verification.** Nancy W. Gallagher. LC 98-36543. 336p. 1999. 45.00 (*0-8018-6017-2*) Johns Hopkins.

Politics of Victimization. Robert Elias. 408p. 1986. pap. text 26.95 (*0-19-503981-5*) OUP.

Politics of Violence: Dawn of a Dangerous Era. S. K. Ghosh. (C). 1992. 20.00 (*81-7024-448-X*, Pub. by Ashish Pub Hse) S Asia.

Politics of Violence: Dawn of a Dangerous Era. S. K. Ghosh. vi, 174p. 1992. 15.95 (*1-881338-15-0*) Nataraj Bks.

Politics of Violence: From Ayodhya to Behrampada. John McGuire et al. LC 96-35431. (Studies on Contemporary South Asia). 1996. 44.00 (*0-8039-9351-X*) Sage.

Politics of Virtue: Hinduism, Sexuality, & Countercolonial Discourse in Fiji. John D. Kelly. 282p. 1991. pap. text 18.95 (*0-226-43031-6*) U Ch Pr.

Politics of Virtue: Hinduism, Sexuality, & Countercolonial Discourse in Fiji. John D. Kelly. 282p. 1991. lib. bdg. 46.00 (*0-226-43030-8*) U Ch Pr.

Politics of Virtue: Is Abortion Debatable? Elizabeth Mensch & Alan Freeman. LC 92-41302. 279p. 1993. text 49.95 (*0-8223-1331-6*); pap. text 17.95 (*0-8223-1349-9*) Duke.

Politics of Vision. Linda Nochlin. LC 89-45055. (Illus.). 224p. 1991. pap. 24.00 (*0-06-430187-7*, Icon Edns) HarpC.

Politics of War. Walter Karp & Mary-Ellen Ross. Date not set. pap. 16.95 (*1-879957-51-5*, Franklin Sq Pr) Harpers Mag Found.

Politics of Warfare: The Great Powers in the Twentieth Century. Stephen Cimbala. LC 96-6450. 208p. 1997. pap. 18.95 (*0-271-01598-5*) Pa St U Pr.

Politics of Warfare: The Great Powers in the Twentieth Century. Stephen J. Cimbala. LC 96-6450. 208p. 1997. 50.00 (*0-271-01597-7*) Pa St U Pr.

Politics of Wartime Aid: American Economic Assistance to France & French Northwest Africa, 1940-1946, 71. James J. Dougherty. LC 77-84770. (Contributions in American History Ser.: No. 71). 264p. 1978. 65.00 (*0-8371-9882-8*, DPW/, Greenwood Pr) Greenwood.

Politics of Water: Urban Protest, Gender, & Power in Monterrey, Mexico. Vivienne Bennett. (Latin American Ser.). (Illus.). 256p. (C). 1995. text 39.95 (*0-8229-3908-8*) U of Pittsburgh Pr.

Politics of Water: Urban Protest, Gender & Power in Monterrey, Mexico. Vivienne Bennett. (Latin American Ser.). 256p. 1995. pap. 19.95 (*0-8229-5616-0*) U of Pittsburgh Pr.

Politics of Welfare Reform. Donald F. Norris & Lyke Thompson. 215p. 1995. text 52.00 (*0-8039-5700-9*); pap. text 25.50 (*0-8039-5701-7*) Sage.

Politics of Welfare State. Oakley. LC 94-12566. 224p. 1994. 65.00 (*1-85728-205-1*, Pub. by UCL Pr Ltd); pap. 24.95 (*1-85728-206-X*, Pub. by UCL Pr Ltd) Taylor & Francis.

P

Politics of Western Science, 1640-1990. Ed. by Margaret C. Jacob. LC 93-8055. 240p. (C). 1994. pap. 15.00 (*0-391-03834-6*) Humanities.

Politics of Wilderness Preservation, 64. Craig W. Allin. LC 81-6234. (Contributions in Political Science Ser.: No. 64). 304p. 1982. 65.00 (*0-313-21458-1*, ALP/, Greenwood Pr) Greenwood.

Politics of Women's Biology. Ruth Hubbard. LC 89-10242. 229p. (Orig.). (C). 1990. text 40.00 (*0-8135-1489-4*); pap. text 17.00 (*0-8135-1490-8*) Rutgers U Pr.

Politics of Women's Bodies: Sexuality, Appearance, & Behavior. Ed. by rose Weitz. (Illus.). 304p. (C). 1998. pap. 22.95 (*0-19-510995-3*) OUP.

Politics of Women's Bodies: Sexuality, Appearance, & Behavior. Ed. by Rose Weitz. (Illus.). 304p. (C). 1998. text 50.00 (*0-19-510994-5*) OUP.

Politics of Women's Education. Conway & Bourque. 272p. (C). 1995. pap. text 18.95 (*0-472-08328-7*, 08328) U of Mich Pr.

Politics of Women's Health: Exploring Agency & Autonomy. Susan Sherwin. LC 98-16025. 320p. 1998. text 59.95 (*1-56639-632-8*) Temple U Pr.

Politics of Women's Health: Exploring Agency & Autonomy. Susan Sherwin. LC 98-16025. 320p. (C). 1998. pap. 19.95 (*1-56639-633-6*) Temple U Pr.

Politics of Women's Health Care: Medicalization As a Form of Social Control. Karen B. Levy. LC 92-39492. (Woman in History Ser.: Vol. 60). (Illus.). 133p. 1992. pap. 10.00 (*0-86663-201-8*) Ide Hse.

Politics of Womens Rights. Carter. 1988. pap. text. write for info. (*0-582-29519-X*, Pub. by Addison-Wesley) Longman.

***Politics of Women's Studies: Testimony from Thirty Founding Mothers.** unabridged ed. Ed. by Florence Howe. (Women's Studies History Ser.). (Illus.). 480p. 2000. 55.00 (*1-55861-240-8*, Pub. by Feminist Pr); pap. 24.95 (*1-55861-241-6*, Pub. by Feminist Pr) Consort Bk Sales.

Politics of Women's Work: The Paris Garment Trades, 1750-1915. Judith G. Coffin. LC 95-25915. (Illus.). 240p. 1996. text 37.50 (*0-691-03447-8*, Pub. by Princeton U Pr) Cal Prin Full Svc.

Politics of Woodrow Wilson. Woodrow Wilson. Ed. by August Heckscher. LC 74-117861. (Essay Index Reprint Ser.). 1977. 29.95 (*0-8369-1737-5*) Ayer.

Politics of Work: Gender & Labour in Victoria, 1880-1939. Raelene Frances. (Studies in Australian History). (Illus.). 279p. (C). 1994. text 64.95 (*0-521-40199-2*) Cambridge U Pr.

Politics of Work & Occupations. Ed. by Geoff Esland & Graeme Salaman. LC 81-139670. 422p. reprint ed. pap. 130.90 (*0-8357-3638-5*, 203636600003) Bks Demand.

Politics of Workplace Literacy: A Case Study. Sheryl G. Gowen. (Language & Literacy Ser.). 168p. (C). 1992. text 34.00 (*0-8077-3214-1*); pap. text 15.95 (*0-8077-3213-3*) Tchrs Coll.

Politics of World Communication. Cees J. Hamelink. (Communication & Human Values Ser.). 352p. 1995. 75.00 (*0-8039-7822-7*); pap. 28.50 (*0-8039-7823-5*) Sage.

Politics of Worship: Reforming the Language & Symbols of Liturgy. William Johnson Everett. LC 99-34493. 160p. (C). 1999. pap. 17.95 (*0-8298-1341-1*) Pilgrim OH.

Politics of Writing. Romy Clark & Roz Ivanic. LC 97-213182. 272p. (C). 1997. pap. 24.99 (*0-415-13483-8*) Routledge.

Politics of Writing. Romy Clark & Roz Ivanic. LC 97-213182. 272p. (C). 1997. 75.00 (*0-415-13482-X*) Routledge.

***Politics of Writing Centers.** Jane Nelson & Kathy Evertz. 2000. pap. write for info. (*0-86709-569-5*, Pub. by Boynton Cook Pubs) Heinemann.

***Politics of Writing in Iran: A History of Modern Persian Literature.** Kamran Talattof. LC 99-37867. 232p. 1999. 49.95 (*0-8156-2818-8*); pap. text 24.95 (*0-8156-2819-6*) Syracuse U Pr.

Politics of Writing Instruction: Postsecondary. Ed. by Richard Bullock et al. LC 90-5217. 311p. (Orig.). (C). (gr. 13). 1991. pap. text 27.50 (*0-86709-272-6*, 0272, Pub. by Boynton Cook Pubs) Heinemann.

Politics of Yiddish: Studies in Language, Literature & Society. Ed. by Dov-Ber Kerler. LC 98-15714. (Illus.). 216p. (C). 1998. 62.00 (*0-7619-9024-0*); pap. 24.95 (*0-7619-9025-9*) AltaMira Pr.

Politics of Young Americans. Charles Nordhoff. (Notable American Authors Ser.). 1999. reprint ed. lib. bdg. 125.00 (*0-7812-4643-1*) Rprt Serv.

Politics of Zionist Fundamentalism in Israel. Ehud Sprinzak. LC 85-52449. 40p. 1986. pap. 3.50 (*0-87495-076-7*) Am Jewish Comm.

Politics on Paper: Finland's South Africa Policy, 1945-1991. Timo-Erkki Heino. (Research Report Ser.: No. 90). 121p. 1992. 16.95 (*91-7106-326-9*, Pub. by Nordic Africa) Transaction Pubs.

Politics on the Fringe: The People, Policies, & Organization of the French National Front. Edward G. Declair. LC 98-25265. (Illus.). 261p. 1999. 49.95 (*0-8223-2237-4*); pap. 17.95 (*0-8223-2139-4*) Duke.

Politics on the Net: Wiring the Political Process. Wayne Rash, Jr. LC 96-46740. 256p. 1997. pap. text 22.95 (*0-7167-8324-X*) W H Freeman.

Politics on the Periphery: Factions & Parties in Georgia, 1783-1806. George R. Lamplugh. LC 85-40662. (Illus.). 224p. 1986. 38.50 (*0-87413-288-6*) U Delaware Pr.

Politics or Principle? Filibustering in the United States Senate. Sarah A. Binder & Steven S. Smith. 247p. 1997. 38.95 (*0-8157-0952-8*); pap. 16.95 (*0-8157-0951-X*) Brookings.

Politics, Parties & Elections in America. 4th ed. John F. Bibby. LC 99-12827. 1999. 35.95 (*0-8304-1547-5*) Thomson Learn.

Politics, Peoples, & Government: Themes in British Political Thought since the Nineteenth Century. Rodney Barker. LC 93-30828. 1994. text 49.95 (*0-312-10382-4*) St Martin.

Politics, Personality & Social Science in the Twentieth Century: Essays in Honor of Harold D. Lasswell. Ed. by Arnold A. Rogow. LC 76-75812. 466p. 1969. lib. bdg. 40.00 (*0-226-72399-2*) U Ch Pr.

***Politics, Philosophy & Terror.** Dana R. Villa. LC 99-21302. 269p. 1999. 65.00 (*0-691-00934-1*, Pub. by Princeton U Pr) Cal Prin Full Svc.

Politics, Philosophy, & the Production of Romantic Texts. Terence Hoagwood. LC 95-50637. (Illus.). 240p. 1996. lib. bdg. 32.00 (*0-87580-206-0*) N Ill U Pr.

Politics, Philosophy, Culture: Interviews & Other Writings, 1977-1984. Ed. by Lawrence D. Kritzman. Tr. by Alan Sheridan. 330p. (C). (gr. 13). 1990. pap. 22.99 (*0-415-90149-9*, A3426) Routledge.

***Politics, Philosophy, Terror: Essays on the Thought of Hannah Arendt.** Dana R. Villa. LC 99-21302. 269p. 1999. pap. 17.95 (*0-691-00935-X*, Pub. by Princeton U Pr) Cal Prin Full Svc.

Politics, Pitchforks & Pickle Jars: 75 Years of Organized Farm Women in Alberta. Nanci Langford. LC 97-190911. (Illus.). 176p. (Orig.). 1997. pap. write for info. (*1-55059-147-9*) Detselig Ents.

Politics, Plague & Shakespeare's Theater: The Stuart Years. J. Leeds Barroll. 264p. 1995. pap. text 15.95 (*0-8014-8275-5*) Cornell U Pr.

Politics, Poetics & Hermeneutics in Milton's Prose. Ed. by David Loewenstein & James G. Turner. (Illus.). 296p. (C). 1990. text 69.95 (*0-521-34458-1*) Cambridge U Pr.

***Politics, Poetics & the Algerian Novel.** Zahia Smail Salhi. LC 99-40378. 304p. 1999. lib. bdg. 99.95 (*0-7734-7957-0*) E Mellen.

Politics, Policy & Finance under Henry III, 1216-1245. Robert C. Stacey. 288p. 1987. text 59.00 (*0-19-820086-2*) OUP.

Politics, Policy, & Government in British Columbia. Ed. by Ken Carty. LC 96-221740. 396p. 1996. 65.00 (*0-7748-0582-X*) U of Wash Pr.

Politics, Policy, & Government in British Columbia. Ed. by Ken Carty. LC 96-221740. 396p. 1997. pap. 26.95 (*0-7748-0583-8*) U of Wash Pr.

Politics, Policy & Management in the American States. (C). 1989. teacher ed. write for info. (*0-8013-0266-8*) Longman.

Politics, Policy & Nursing. Derek Fatchett. (C). 1995. pap. text 19.00 (*0-7020-1791-4*) Harcourt.

Politics, Policy & Practice in Physical Education. M. Penney. LC 98-38800. 208p. 1998. pap. 24.95 (*0-419-21950-1*) Thomson Learn.

***Politics Policy States Communities.** 6th ed. (C). 1998. text 24.00 (*0-321-01886-9*) Addson-Wesley Educ.

Politics, Position & Power: The Dynamics of Federal Organization. 5th ed. Harold Seidman. LC 97-26624. 288p. (C). 1997. pap. text 22.95 (*0-19-509072-1*) OUP.

Politics, Power, & Bureaucracy in France: The Administrative Elite. Ezra N. Suleiman. LC 72-6524. (Illus.). 459p. reprint ed. pap. 142.30 (*0-8357-7896-7*, 203631500002) Bks Demand.

Politics, Power & Old Age. John A. Vincent. LC 99-20483. (Rethinking Ageing Ser.). 1999. 27.95 (*0-335-20165-2*) OpUniv Pr.

Politics, Power & Policy Making: The Case of Health Care Reform in the 1990s. Mark E. Rushefsky & Kant Patel. LC 97-33625. 316p. (C). (gr. 13). 1998. text 70.95 (*1-56324-955-3*) M E Sharpe.

***Politics, Power & Policy Making: The Case of Health Care Reform in the 1990s.** Mark E. Rushefsky et al. LC 97-33625. 316p. (C). (gr. 13). 1998. pap. text 30.95 (*1-56324-956-1*) M E Sharpe.

Politics, Power & the Struggle for Democracy in South-East Europe. Ed. by Karen Dawisha & Bruce Parrott. (Democratization & Authoritarianism in Post-Communist Societies Ser.: Vol. 2). 492p. (C). 1997. text 64.95 (*0-521-59244-5*) Cambridge U Pr.

***Politics, Prayer & Parliament.** David Rogers. LC 99-48976. 2000. pap. 21.95 (*0-304-70633-7*) Continuum.

Politics Presidents Make: Leadership from John Adams to Bill Clinton. Stephen Skowronek. LC 97-7818. 1997. 19.95 (*0-674-68937-2*) HUP.

Politics Presidents Make: Leadership from John Adams to George Bush. Stephen Skowronek. (Illus.). 538p. 1995. pap. text 16.95 (*0-674-68936-4*, SKOPOX) Belknap Pr.

Politics Presidents Make: Leadership from John Adams to George Bush. Stephen Skowronek. (Illus.). 544p. 1993. text 29.95 (*0-674-68935-6*) HUP.

Politics, Process & American Trade Policy. Sharyn O'Halloran. 216p. 1994. text 47.50 (*0-472-10516-7*, 10516) U of Mich Pr.

Politics, Professionalism, & Power: Modern Party Organization & the Legacy of Ray C. Bliss. Intro. by John C. Green. 312p. (Orig.). (C). 1994. pap. text 29.50 (*0-8191-9352-6*); lib. bdg. 57.50 (*0-8191-9351-8*) U Pr of Amer.

Politics, Projects, & People: Institutional Development in Haiti. Ed. by Derick W. Brinkerhoff & Jean-Claude Garcia-Zamor. LC 85-16979. 304p. 1985. 69.50 (*0-275-90035-5*, C0035, Praeger Pubs) Greenwood.

Politics, Property & Law in the Philippine Uplands. Melanie G. Wiber. 152p. (C). 1993. pap. 24.95 (*0-88920-222-2*) W Laurier U Pr.

Politics Public Policy in the Contemporary American West. C. Thomas. LC 90-15473. (University of New Mexico Public Policy Ser.). (Illus.). 589p. (C). 1991. pap. 12.95 (*0-8263-1251-9*) U of NM Pr.

Politics, Punishment, & Populism. Lord Windlesham. (Studies in Crime & Public Policy). 288p. 1998. text 35.00 (*0-19-511530-9*) OUP.

Politics Quaker Style: A History of the Quakers from 1624-1718. John H. Ferguson. LC 95-1515. (Stokvis Studies in Historical Chronology & Thought: No. 15). viii, 208p. 1995. pap. 23.00 (*0-8095-1101-0*) Millefleurs.

Politics, Race, & Schools: Racial Integration, 1954-1994. Joseph Watras & Mark B. Ginsburg. LC 96-24099. (Studies in Education & Politics: No. 2). 362p. 1997. text 54.00 (*0-8153-1766-2*, SS989) Garland.

Politics, Race, & Youth in Guyana. Madan M. Gopal. LC 91-47948. 480p. 1992. lib. bdg. 109.95 (*0-7734-9964-4*) E Mellen.

Politics, Regulation & the Modern Welfare State. Jacob Torfing. LC 97-40266. 312p. 1998. text 69.95 (*0-312-21182-1*) St Martin.

Politics, Religion & Classical Poltical Economy in Britain: John Stuart Mill & His Followers. Jeff Lipkes. LC 98-23640. (Studies in the History of Economics). 240p. 1999. text 79.95 (*0-312-21741-2*) St Martin.

Politics, Religion, & Love: The Story of H. H. Asquith, Venettia Stanley & Edward Montagu, Based on the Life & Letters of Edwin Samuel Montagu. Naomi B. Levine. (Illus.). 843p. (C). 1991. text 45.00 (*0-8147-5057-5*) NYU Pr.

Politics, Religion, & Rockets: Essays in Twentieth-Century American History. Paul A. Carter. LC 90-21111. 224p. 1991. 43.00 (*0-8165-1213-2*) U of Ariz Pr.

Politics, Religion, & Sex: All the Things You're Not Supposed to Talk: Performers' Edition. Harold Moss. (Illus.). 100p. (Orig.). 1997. pap. 7.00 (*1-890173-01-0*, Pasigram) P Shoemaker.

Politics, Religion, & Sex: All the Things You're Not Supposed to Talk: Reader's Edition. 2nd ed. Harold Moss. (Illus.). 150p. (Orig.). 1996. pap. 10.95 (*1-890173-00-2*, Pasigram) P Shoemaker.

Politics, Religion & Society, 1679-1742. Geoffrey Holmes. 1986. 60.00 (*0-907628-75-3*) Hambledon Press.

Politics, Religion & the British Revolutions: The Mind of Samuel Rutherford. John Coffey. (Cambridge Studies in Early Modern British History). 320p. (C). 1997. text 59.95 (*0-521-58172-9*) Cambridge U Pr.

***Politics, Religion & the Common Good: Advancing a Distinctly American Conversation about Religion's Role in Our Shared Life.** Martin E. Marty & Jonathan Moore. LC 99-50450. 240p. 2000. 22.50 (*0-7879-5031-9*) Jossey-Bass.

***Politics, Religion & the Common Good: Advancing a Distinctly American Conversion about Religion's Role in Our Shared Life.** Martin E. Marty & Jonathan Moore. 225p. 2000. 23.00 (*0-7879-5033-5*) Jossey-Bass.

Politics Righteousness: Idaho Christian Patriotism. James Aho. LC 90-30168. (Illus.). 320p. 1990. 24.95 (*0-295-96997-0*) U of Wash Pr.

Politics, Science, & Dread Disease: A Short History of the United States Medical Research Policy. Stephen P. Strickland. LC 72-78427. (Commonwealth Fund Publications). 345p. 1972. 43.00 (*0-674-68955-0*) HUP.

Politics, Security & Development in Small States. Ed. by Colin Clarke & Tony Payne. LC 87-1199. 238p. 1987. 55.00 (*0-04-320203-9*) Routledge.

Politics, Self, & Society: A Theme & Variations. Heinz Eulau. (Illus.). 592p. 1986. 58.50 (*0-674-68760-4*) HUP.

Politics, Social Change, & Economic Restructuring in Latin America. Ed. by William C. Smith & Roberto P. Korzeniewicz. LC 97-19640. 280p. 1998. pap. 23.95 (*1-57454-018-1*, 540181, Pub. by U Miami N-S Ctr) L Rienner.

Politics, Society & Christianity in Vichy France. W. D. Halls. Ed. by John E. Flower. (French Studies Ser.). 419p. 1995. 65.00 (*1-85973-071-X*, Pub. by Berg Pubs) NYU Pr.

Politics, Society & Christianity in Vichy France. W. D. Halls. Ed. by John E. Flower. (French Studies Ser.). 419p. 1995. pap. 22.50 (*1-85973-081-7*, Pub. by Berg Pubs) NYU Pr.

Politics, Society, & Cosmology in India's North East. N. Vijaylakshmi Brara. LC 98-902935. (Illus.). 272p. 1998. text 24.95 (*0-19-564331-3*) OUP.

Politics, Society & Democracy: Juan J. Linz - Untranslated Writings & Complete Annotated Bibliography, Vol. 2. Ed. by H. E. Chehabi. (C). 2000. pap. 44.00 (*0-8133-8547-4*) Westview.

Politics, Society & Democracy: Latin America, Vol. 3. Arturo Valenzuela. LC 97-33166. (C). 1997. pap. 75.00 (*0-8133-8548-2*, Pub. by Westview) HarpC.

Politics, Society & Stalinism in the U. S. S. R. John Channon. LC 97-40880. (Studies in Russian & East European History & Society). 208p. 1998. text 65.00 (*0-312-21126-0*) St Martin.

Politics, Society, & the Klan in Alabama, 1915-1949. Glenn Feldman. LC 99-6123. 1999. pap. 19.95 (*0-8173-0984-5*) U of Ala Pr.

Politics, Society & the Klan in Alabama, 1915-1949. Glenn Feldman. LC 99-6123. 1999. 49.95 (*0-8173-0983-7*) U of Ala Pr.

Politics, Sociology & Economics of the Municipal Area. Gordon Diem. 124p. (C). 1997. pap. text 21.35 (*1-56226-388-9*) CAT Pub.

Politics, Sociology, & Social Theory: Encounters with Classical & Contemporary Social Thought. Anthony Giddens. 300p. 1995. 45.00 (*0-8047-2622-1*); pap. 16.95 (*0-8047-2624-8*) Stanford U Pr.

Politics, Subsidies & Competition: The New Politics of State Intervention in the European Union. Kostas A. Lavdas & Maria M. Mendrinou. LC 98-53416. 200p. 1999. 80.00 (*1-85898-324-X*) E Elgar.

Politics Sunshine Politics. Thomas R. Dye. 48p. (C). 1995. pap. text 4.00 (*0-13-229600-4*) P-H.

Politics, Technology & the Environment: Technology, Assessment & Nuclear Energy. William T. Keating. Ed. by Stuart Bruchey. LC 78-22691. (Energy in the American Economy Ser.). 1979. lib. bdg. 33.95 (*0-405-11994-1*) Ayer.

Politics, Theory, & Contemporary Culture. Ed. by Mark Poster. LC 92-23573. 336p. (C). 1993. pap. 20.00 (*0-231-08057-3*); text 69.00 (*0-231-08056-5*) Col U Pr.

Politics Through a Looking-Glass: Understanding Political Cultures Through a Structuralist Interpretation of Narratives, 184. Eloise A. Buker. LC 87-8671. (Contributions in Political Science Ser.: No. 184). 264p. 1987. 59.95 (*0-313-25662-4*, BPK/) Greenwood.

Politics, Trade & Development: Soviet Economic Aid to the Non-Communist Third World 1955-89. Charles Dannehl. (Illus.). 150p. 1995. text 72.95 (*1-85521-658-2*, Pub. by Dartmth Pub) Ashgate Pub Co.

Politics, Truth & Law - Very Little Truth: Poetic Commentary by Sol the Sage. Sol Finkelman. 128p. 1995. pap. 19.95 (*0-9641973-2-4*) Genie Pubng.

Politics U. K. 3rd ed. Bill Jones. LC 97-3711. 1997. pap. write for info. (*0-13-269606-1*) P-H.

***Politics U. K.** 4th ed. Bill Jones. LC 00-22359. 624p. 2000. pap. 37.33 (*0-582-42333-3*) P-H.

Politics Under the Later Stuarts: Party Conflict in a Divided Society, 1660-1715 (Studies in Modern History) Tim Harris. LC 92-13841. (Studies in Modern History). 224p. (C). 1992. text 63.50 (*0-582-04081-7*) Longman.

Politics, Values, & Functions: International Law in the 21st Century: Essays in Honor of Professor Louis Henkin. Ed. by Jonathan I. Charney et al. LC 97-46629. 488p. 1998. 134.00 (*90-411-0514-X*) Kluwer Law Intl.

Politics, Values, & Public Policy. Frank Fischer. (Special Studies). 275p. 1981. text 47.00 (*0-89158-799-3*) Westview.

Politics vs. Economics in World Steel Trade. Kent A. Jones. (World Industry Studies). 250p. 1986. text 60.00 (*0-04-338118-9*) Routledge.

Politics, War & Empire: The Rise of Britain to a World Power, 1688-1792. Earl A. Reitan. Ed. by Keith Eubank. (European History Ser.). 200p. (C). 1994. pap. text 11.95 (*0-88295-899-2*) Harlan Davidson.

Politics Without a Past: The Absence of History in Post-Communist Nationalism. Shari J. Cohen. LC 99-28322. 304p. 1999. pap. 18.95 (*0-8223-2399-0*) Duke.

***Politics Without a Past: The Absence of History in Postcommunist Nationalism.** Shari J. Cohen. LC 99-28322. 304p. 1999. 54.95 (*0-8223-2378-8*) Duke.

***Politics Without Democracy, 1815-1914: Perception & Preoccupation in British Government.** Michael Bentley. LC 99-26095. (Classic Histories of England Ser.). (Illus.). 352p. 1999. pap. text 32.95 (*0-631-21813-0*) Blackwell Pubs.

Politics Without Democracy, 1815-1914: Perception & Preoccupation in British Government. 2nd ed. Michael Bentley. LC 99-26095. (Classic Histories of England Ser.). (Illus.). 352p. 1999. text 64.95 (*0-631-21812-2*) Blackwell Pubs.

Politics Without Parliaments, 1629-1640. Esther S. Cope. 256p. (C). 1987. text 55.00 (*0-04-941020-2*) Routledge.

Politics Without Parties. Gaetano Quagliariello. (Avebury Series in Philosophy). 272p. 1996. 69.95 (*1-85972-256-3*, Pub. by Avebry) Ashgate Pub Co.

Politics Without Process: Administering Development in the Arab World. Jamil Jreisat. LC 96-39894. 261p. 1997. lib. bdg. 52.00 (*1-55587-333-2*) L Rienner.

Politics, Work, & Daily Life in the U. S. S. R. A Survey of Former Soviet Citizens. Ed. by James R. Millar. (Illus.). 444p. 1987. pap. text 33.95 (*0-521-34890-0*) Cambridge U Pr.

Politiek-Politionelle Overzichten van Nederlandsch-Indie, Deel IV, 1935-41. Compiled by Harry A. Poeze. (Illus.). 583p. (Orig.). 1995. pap. 44.00 (*90-6718-051-3*, Pub. by KITLV Pr) Cellar.

Polities: Authority, Identities, & Change. Yale H. Ferguson & Richard W. Mansbach. LC 95-50229. (Studies in International Relations). (Illus.). 476p. 1996. text 49.95 (*1-57003-128-2*) U of SC Pr.

Polities: Authority, Identities, & Change. Yale H. Ferguson & Richard W. Mansbach. LC 95-50229. (Studies in International Relations). (Illus.). 476p. (C). 1996. pap. text 24.95 (*1-57003-077-4*) U of SC Pr.

Politik als Beruf see Profession of Politics

Politik und Kriegskunst der Assyrer. Walter Mayer. (Abhandlvorgen zur Literatur Alt-Syrien-Palastinas und Mesopatamieus Ser.: No. 9). xvi, 545p. 1995. text 122.00 (*3-927120-26-X*, Pub. by UGARIT) Eisenbrauns.

Politik und Praxis der Umwelterziehung. Norbert Reichel. 170p. 1995. 27.95 (*3-631-49925-6*) P Lang Pubng.

Politik, Wirtschaft, Offentliches Leben (In German) see International Biographical Dictionary of Central European Emigres: 1933-1945

Politika: The Official Strategy Guide. Ted Chapman. LC 97-76450. 192p. 1997. per. 19.99 (*0-7615-1349-3*) Prima Pub.

Politika, Ideologiia, Byt I Uchenye Trudy Russkoi Emigratsii, 1918-1945 Bibliografiia Iz Kataloga Biblioteki R.Z.I. Arkhiva, GG, Set. Sergei P. Postnikov. Ed. by Sergei Blinov. xix, 256p. 1993. lib. bdg. 135.00 (*0-88354-355-9*) N Ross.

Politikwissenschaft. Jurgen Hartmann. 272p. 1995. text 59.00 (*3-7186-5775-9*, Harwood Acad Pubs); pap. text 24.00 (*3-7186-5729-5*, Harwood Acad Pubs) Gordon & Breach.

Politique de Redevances et de Concessions Forestieres: Gestion des Futaies en Afrique Occidentale et Centrale. Mikael Grut et al. (Technical Papers: No. 143). (FRE.). 92p. 1993. pap. 22.00 (*0-8213-2592-2*, 12592) World Bank.

P

Politique des Grands Travaux en France, 1929-1939. Pierre Saly. Ed. by Stuart Bruchey. LC 77-77184. (Dissertations in European Economic History Ser.). (FRE.). 1978. lib. bdg. 40.95 (*0-405-10797-8*) Ayer.

Politique Edilitaire dans les Provinces de l'Empire Romain: IIeme-IVeme Siecles Apres J. C.: Actes du IIe Colloque Roumano-Suisse. Ed. by Regula Frei-Stolba & Heinz E. Herzig. (FRE., Illus.). 317p. 1995. 48.95 (*3-906755-47-9*, Pub. by P Lang) P Lang Pubng.

Politique et Societe en Sicile 12e - 15e Siecles. Henri Bresc. (Collected Studies: No. CS329). 320p. 1991. text 115.95 (*0-86078-285-9*, Pub. by Variorum) Ashgate Pub Co.

Politique Europeenne de la Suisse: L'Echec d'Une Communication. Christian Scharer. (Publications Universitaires Europeennes Ser.: Series 31, Vol. 308). (FRE.). 152p. 1996. 25.95 (*3-906754-56-1*, Pub. by P Lang) P Lang Pubng.

Politique Monetaire: A la Recherche d'un Point Dancrage. Gerald K. Bouey. LC 91-10906. (Fondation Per Jacobsson Ser.). (FRE.). 39p. reprint ed. pap. 30.00 (*0-608-08758-0*, 206939700004) Bks Demand.

Politique Naturelle, 2 vols. in 1. Paul H. D'Holbach. viii, 512p. 1971. reprint ed. 120.00 (*3-487-04191-X*) G Olms Pubs.

Politique Urbaine a Montreal. Ed. by J. H. Roy & B. Weston. (FRE.). 374p. 1990. pap. 15.00 (*2-89135-038-3*) Guernica Editions.

Politiques de l'Esriture, Bataille/Derrida: Le Sens du Sacre dans la Pensee Francaise du Surrealisme a Nos Jours. Jean-Michel Heimonet. LC 87-20435. (North Carolina Studies in the Romance Languages & Literatures: No. 229). (FRE.). 232p. reprint ed. pap. 72.00 (*0-608-20069-7*, 207134100011) Bks Demand.

Politiques de Tenure et Gestion des Ressources Naturelles en Afrique de l'Ouest Sahelienne. Steven W. Lawry. (LTC Paper Ser.: Vol. 130-F). (FRE.). v, 24p. (C). 1990. pap. 4.00 (*0-934519-46-3*, LTC130-F) U of Wis Land.

Politische Autobiographien in der Fruhen Amerikanischen Republik: Benjamin Franklin, John Adams, Thomas Jefferson und James Monroe. Britta A. Moser. (Europaische Hochschulschriften, Reihe 14: No. 329). 387p. 1997. 63.95 (*3-631-31034-X*) P Lang Pubng.

Politische Bildung in Hessen von 1945 Bis 1965. Johann Zilien. 458p. 1997. 76.95 (*3-631-31641-0*) P Lang Pubng.

Politische Denken Von David Hume. Filadelfo Linares. (Studien und Materialien Zur Geschichte der Philosophie Ser.: Vol. 24). (GER.). vi, 125p. 1984. write for info. (*3-487-07551-2*) G Olms Pubs.

Politische Geschichte see Aufstieg und Niedergang der romischen Welt: Section 1, von den Anfangen Roms bis zum Ausgang der Republik

Politische Geschichte: Provinzen und Randvoelker: Latenischer Donau-Balkanraum, Kleinasien see Aufstieg und Niedergang der Roemischen Welt: Selection 2, Principat

Politische Geschichte, Vol. 1, Allgemeines see Aufstieg und Niedergang der Roemischen Welt: Selection 2, Principat

Politische Geschichte, Vol. 2, Kaisergeschichte see Aufstieg und Niedergang der Roemischen Welt: Selection 2, Principat

Politische Geschichte, Vol. 3, Provinzen und Randvoelker: Allgemeins; Britannien, Hispanien, Gallien see Aufstieg und Niedergang der Roemischen Welt: Selection 2, Principat

Politische Geschichte, Vol. 4, Provinzen und Randvoelker; Gallien see Aufstieg und Niedergang der Roemischen Welt: Selection 2, Principat

Politische Geschichte, Vol. 5, Pt. I, Provinzen und Randvoelker: Germanien; Alpenprokuraten; Raetien, Part I see Aufstieg und Niedergang der Roemischen Welt: Selection 2, Principat

Politische Geschichte, Vol. 5, Pt. II, Provinzen und Randvoelker: Germanien; Alpenprokuraturen; Raetien, Part II see Aufstieg und Niedergang der Roemischen Welt: Selection 2, Principat

Politische Geschichte, Vol. 7, Pt. I, Provinzen und Randvoelker: Griesschischer Balkanrum, Kleinasien see Aufstieg und Niedergang der Roemischen Welt: Selection 2, Principat

Politische Geschichte, Vol. 7, Pt. II, Provinzen und Randvoelker: Griescher Balkanraum: Kleinasien see Aufstieg und Niedergang der Roemischen Welt: Selection 2, Principat

Politische Geschichte, Vol. 8, Provinzen und Randvoelker: Syrien, Palastina, Arabien see Aufstieg und Niedergang der Roemischen Welt: Selection 2, Principat

Politische Geschichte, Vol. 9, Pt. I, Provinzen und Randvoelker: Mespotamien, Armenien, Iran, Sudarabien, Rom und der Ferne Osten see Aufstieg und Niedergang der Roemischen Welt: Selection 2, Principat

Politische Geschichte, Vol. 9, Pt. II, Provinzen und Randvoelker: Rome und der Ferne Osten see Aufstieg und Niedergang der Roemischen Welt: Selection 2, Principat

Politische Geschichte, Vol. 10, Pt. II, Provinzen und Randvoelker: Africa mit Agypten, Fortezung see Aufstieg und Niedergang der Roemischen Welt: Selection 2, Principat

Politische Ideale see Political Ideals

Politische Katholizismus. Ludwig Bergstrasser. (Deutsche Staatsgedanke Ser.: Bd. III, 1,2). (GER.). 700p. 1976. reprint ed. write for info. (*3-487-05897-9*) G Olms Pubs.

Politische Landschaft see Political Landscape: An Art History of Nature

Politische Legitimitat, Theorien, Konzepte, Empirische Befunde. Bettina Westle. (GER.). 372p. 1989. 81.00 (*3-7890-1720-5*, Pub. by Nomos Verlags) Intl Bk Import.

Politische Leitvokabeln in der Adenauer-Aera. Karin Boeke et al. (Sprache, Politik, Oeffentlichkeit Ser.: Vol. 8). (GER.). xii, 496p. (C). 1996. lib. bdg. 161.50 (*3-11-014236-8*) De Gruyter.

***Politische Okonomie Des East Asian Miracle: Ursachen Fur Erfolg und Miaerfolg Einer Protektionistischen Wirtschaftspolitik Am Beispiel Taiwans und der Philippinen.** Roland Rohde. (GER., Illus.). xxi, 419p. 1999. 67.95 (*3-631-34423-6*) P Lang Pubng.

Politische Philosophie des Nihilismus: Neitzsches Neubestimmung des Verhaeltnisses von Politik & Metaphysik. Jin-Woo Lee. (Monographien und Texte zur Nietzscge-Forschung Ser.: Bd. 26). (GER.). xi, 441p. (C). 1992. lib. bdg. 166.15 (*3-11-012908-6*) De Gruyter.

Politische Schlagworter Aus der Zeit Aes Peloponnesischen Krieges. Gustav Grosmann. LC 72-7893. (Greek History Ser.). (GER.). 1973. reprint ed. 20.95 (*0-405-04789-4*) Ayer.

***Politische (Un-)Person: Politisches Denken Am Ubergang Vom Jugendlichen Zum Erwachsenen.** Thomas Link. (GER.). 184p. 1999. 37.95 (*3-631-34459-7*) P Lang Pubng.

Politische und gesellschaftliche intermediare Gewalten im sozialen Rechtsstaat, 22. Paul Trappe. 1990. 28.95 (*3-906764-19-2*, Pub. by P Lang) P Lang Pubng.

***Politische und Okonomische Landerrisiken.** A. P. Backer. (GER.). 240p. 1998. text 49.00 (*90-5708-031-1*, Harwood Acad Pubs); pap. text 23.00 (*90-5708-032-X*, Harwood Acad Pubs) Gordon & Breach.

Politische und Soziale Bedeutung der Naqsbandiyya in Mittelasien Im 15. Jahrhundert. Juergen Paul. (Studien zur Sprache, Geschichte und Kultur des Islamischen Orients: Bd. 13). (GER.). x, 275p. (C). 1991. lib. bdg. 136.95 (*3-11-012720-2*) De Gruyter.

***Politische und Soziale Implikationen des Zarathustrismus: Eine Untersuchung von Den Ursprungen Bis Zur Gegenwart.** Dariusch Rafiy. (Europaische Hochschulschriften Ser.: Vol. 31). XI, 313p. 1999. 48.95 (*3-631-35483-5*) P Lang Pubng.

Politische und Theologische Schriften, Monucleus Aureus see Saemtliche Schriften

Politische Witz in der NS-Zeit Am Beispiel Ausgesuchter SD-Berichte und Gestapo-Akten. Meike Wohlert. (Europaische Hochschulschriften Ser.: Reihe 3, Bd. 725). (GER.). 184p. 1996. 42.95 (*3-631-30779-9*) P Lang Pubng.

Politisches Konversations-Lexikon. H. Normann & Hermann Mensch. (GER.). iv, 336p. 1979. reprint ed. write for info. (*3-487-06854-0*) G Olms Pubs.

Politisches Woerterbuch. Siegfried Landshut. (GER.). 1958. pap. 75.00 (*0-8288-6852-2*, M-7589) Fr & Eur.

Politocal Economy of Botswana: A Study of Growth & Distribution. Christopher Colclough & Stephen McCarthy. (Illus.). 1980. 45.00 (*0-19-877136-3*) OUP.

Polity. Norton E. Long. (Reprint Series in Sociology). reprint ed. pap. 9.95 (*0-685-70259-6*); reprint ed. lib. bdg. 27.50 (*0-685-70258-8*) Irvington.

Polity: The Journal of the Northeastern Political Science Association. Ed. by Jerome M. Mileur. (Illus.). 200p. 1992. lib. bdg. 50.00 (*0-317-00292-9*) Polity NE Poli Sci.

Polity & Economy: An Interpretation of the Principles of Adam Smith, No. 8-- Joseph Cropsey. LC 76-56126. 101p. 1977. reprint ed. lib. bdg. 35.00 (*0-8371-9418-0*, CRPE, Greenwood Pr) Greenwood.

Polity & Economy of the Punjab: During the Late Eighteenth Century. Veena Sachdeva. (C). 1993. 20.00 (*81-7304-033-8*, Pub. by Manohar) S Asia.

Polity & Praxis: A Program for American Practical Theology. Dennis P. McCann & Charles R. Strain. 176p. 1985. 21.00 (*0-86683-986-0*, AY8571) Harper SF.

Polity & Praxis: A Program for American Practical Theology. Dennis P. McCann & Charles R. Strain. 252p. (C). 1990. reprint ed. pap. text 26.50 (*0-8191-7847-0*) U Pr of Amer.

Polity & Society: Philosophical Underpinnings of Social Science Paradigms. Michael Haas. LC 91-16669. 320p. 1991. 69.50 (*0-275-93558-2*, C3558, Praeger Pubs) Greenwood.

Polity Law Lost Art: Law Arithmetic. abr. ed. Luanna C. Blagrove. (Illus.). 237p. 1988. 29.95 (*0-939776-46-4*) Blagrove Pubns.

Polity, Political Process & Social Control in South Asia: The Tribal & Rural Perspectives. Ed. by Manis K. Raha & Iar A. Khan. (C). 1993. 32.00 (*81-212-0413-5*, Pub. by Gian Publng Hse) S Asia.

Polity, Practice, & the Mission of the United Methodist Church. Thomas E. Frank. LC 96-53515. 288p. 1997. pap. 19.95 (*0-687-33180-3*) Abingdon.

Politz Papers: Science & Truth in Marketing Research. Ed. by Hugh S. Hardy. LC 90-36688. (Illus.). 369p. 1990. reprint ed. pap. 114.40 (*0-7837-9766-4*, 206049400005) Bks Demand.

Poliuretany Chemia Technologia Zastosowanie see Polyurethanes: Chemistry, Technology, & Applications

Poliziano's Science of Tropes. Paul Colilli. (American University Studies: Romance Languages & Literature: Ser. 2, Vol. 98). XIV, 189p. 1988. 31.95 (*0-8204-0788-7*) P Lang Pubng.

***Polk: Character in Time: The U. S. Presidents.** 1999. 5.95 (*1-929403-20-8*) History Proj.

Polk: The Diary of a Presidency, 1845-1849, Covering the Mexican War, the Acquisition of Oregon, & the Conquest of California & the Southwest. James K. Polk. (American Biography Ser.). 412p. 1991. reprint ed. lib. bdg. 89.00 (*0-7812-8318-3*) Rprt Serv.

Polk & the Presidency. Charles A. McCoy. LC 72-10451. (American Biography Ser.: No. 32). 1973. reprint ed. lib. bdg. 75.00 (*0-8383-1686-7*) M S G Haskell Hse.

Polk County. Polk County Historical Society Staff. LC 98-85880. (Images of America Ser.). (Illus.). 128p. 1998. pap. 16.99 (*0-7524-0882-8*) Arcadia Publng.

Polk County Arkansas Census, 1850. Courtney York & Gerlene York. (Orig.). 1969. pap. 12.00 (*0-916660-06-0*) Hse of York.

***Polk County, Florida: Lakeland - Winter Haven - Bartow.** C. J. Janis. 265p. 1999. spiral bd. 34.95 (*1-882829-06-9*, 59478-82906) Map & Globe.

Polk Family & Kinsmen. William H. Polk et al. 279p. 1993. 34.95 (*1-56869-036-3*); pap. 23.95 (*1-56869-037-1*) Oldbuck Pr.

Polk Family & Kinsmen. W. Harrison Polk. (Illus.). 742p. 1994. reprint ed. pap. 105.00 (*0-8328-4280-X*); reprint ed. lib. bdg. 115.00 (*0-8328-4279-6*) Higginson Bk Co.

Polka. Earl Atkinson. (Ballroom Dance Ser.). 1986. lib. bdg. 250.00 (*0-8490-3637-2*) Gordon Pr.

Polka All-Timers. Ed. by John Haag. (Illus.). 96p. 1997. pap. 14.95 (*1-56922-145-6*, 07-1110) Creat Cncpts.

Polka & March Beats, Vol. 19. 48p. 1970. pap. 5.95 (*0-7935-3297-3*, 00100540) H Leonard.

Polka-bats & Octopus Slacks: 14 Stories. Calef Brown. LC 97-12011. 32p. (J). 1998. 15.00 (*0-395-85403-2*) HM.

Polka Dot Horse. Elizabeth Thiel. LC 92-10221. (Illus.). (J). 1993. pap. 14.00 (*0-671-79419-1*) S&S Bks Yung.

Polka Dot! Polka Dot! William Joyce. (J). 2000. pap. 9.99 (*0-7364-0173-3*, Pub. by Mouse Works) Time Warner.

Polka-Dot Puppy. Jane Belk Moncure. LC 87-15813. (Magic Castle Readers Ser.). (Illus.). 32p. (J). (ps-2). 1988. lib. bdg. 21.36 (*0-89565-407-5*) Childs World.

Polka Dotted Pals, Pt. 2. Sheila Jenkins. Ed. by Irene Goodwin & Rath Silvers. LC 80-84112. (Orig.). (J). (gr. k). 1996. pap. 8.95 (*0-932970-20-6*) Prinit Pr.

Polka Happiness. Charles Keil et al. (Illus.). 288p. (C). 1992. 32.95 (*0-87722-819-1*) Temple U Pr.

Polka Happiness. Charles Keil et al. (Visual Studies). (Illus.). 288p. (C). 1996. pap. 24.95 (*1-56639-462-7*) Temple U Pr.

Polka Party Dances. Valerie Plezia. (Ethnic Dance Bks.: No.280). 130p. 1982. pap. 12.00 (*0-9609368-0-7*) V Plezia.

Polka Time, No. 86. 64p. 1987. pap. 5.95 (*0-7935-1675-7*, 00243621) H Leonard.

Polkadots. Geri S. Hunter. 183p. 1998. pap. 13.00 (*0-9639147-5-8*) ReGeJe Press.

Polkas/Galoppe/Marsche see Werke fur Pianoforte

Polkinghor Quantum World. J. C. Polkinghorne. LC 83-9411. (Illus.). 112p. 1984. text 14.95 (*0-582-44682-1*) Longman.

***Polk's Folly: An American Family History.** William R. Polk. LC 99-24552. (Illus.). 544p. 2000. 29.95 (*0-385-49150-6*) Doubleday.

Polky Dot's Gift. Thomas F. Cummings. LC 97-91104. (Illus.). 28p. (J). (ps-6). 1998. pap. 5.95 (*0-9660798-0-9*, PD1) ToLo Pub CT.

Poll Books, c. 1696-1872: A Directory of Holdings in Great Britain. 3rd ed. J. S. W. Gibson & Colin D. Rogers. 56p. 1994. pap. 9.00 (*0-8063-1566-0*) Genealog Pub.

Poll Tax Rebellion. Danny Burns. (Illus.). 208p. 1992. pap. 10.00 (*1-873176-50-3*, AK Pr San Fran) AK Pr Dist.

Poll Taxes of 1377, 1379 & 1381 Pt. 1: Bedfordshire-Leicestershire. Ed. by Carolyn C. Fenwick. LC 98-209988. (Records of Social & Economic History Ser.: No. 27). (Illus.). 686p. 1998. text 125.00 (*0-19-726186-8*) OUP.

Poll with a Human Face: The National Issues Convention Experiment in Political Communication. Ed. by Amy Reynolds & Maxwell McCombs. LC 98-42667. (LEA's Communication Ser.). 272p. 1999. 49.95 (*0-8058-2974-1*) L Erlbaum Assocs.

***Pollack: A Critical Filmography.** Janet L. Meyer. LC 98-25890. (Illus.). 248p. 1998. lib. bdg. 38.50 (*0-7864-0486-8*) McFarland & Co.

Pollak on Jurisdiction. D. Pistorius. 231p. 1993. write for info. (*0-7021-2953-4*, Pub. by Juta & Co) Gaunt.

Pollard, Parpworth & Hughes: Constitutional & Administrative Law - Cases & Materials. 2nd ed. David Pollard et al. 1997. pap. write for info. (*0-406-04591-7*, PHCA2, MICHIE) LEXIS Pub.

Pollbooks: How Victorians Voted. John R. Vincent. LC 67-10160. 206p. reprint ed. pap. 58.80 (*0-608-18620-1*, 2024555) Bks Demand.

Pollen Analysis. 2nd ed. P. D. Moore et al. (Illus.). 224p. 1994. pap. 49.95 (*0-86542-895-6*) Blackwell Sci.

Pollen & Plant Macrofossil Evidence of Vegetation Change at Wallisellen-Langachermoos (Switzerland) During the Mesolithic-Neolithic Transition 8500 to 6500 Years Ago. Ken N. Haas & Jean N. Haas. (Dissertationes Botanicae Ser.: Band 267). (Illus.). viii, 67p. 1996. pap. 42.00 (*3-443-64179-2*, Pub. by Gebruder Borntraeger) Balogh.

***Pollen & Pollination.** Amots Dafni et al. LC 00-44575. 2000. write for info. (*3-211-83514-8*) Spr-Verlag.

Pollen & Spores: Patterns of Diversification. Ed. by Stephen Blackmore & S. H. Barnes. (Systematics Association Special Volume Ser.: Vol. 44). 408p. 1992. 125.00 (*0-19-857746-X*) OUP.

Pollen & Spores of Chile: Modern Types of The Pteridophyta, Gymnospermae, & Angiospermae. Calvin J. Heusser. LC 75-114322. 180p. reprint ed. pap. 55.80 (*0-608-16753-3*, 205621000055) Bks Demand.

Pollen Biology: A Laboratory Manual. K. R. Shivanna & N. S. Rangaswamy. (Illus.). 120p. 1992. 54.95 (*0-387-55170-0*) Spr-Verlag.

Pollen Biotechnology for Crop Production & Improvement. Ed. by K. R. Shivanna & V. K. Sawhney. LC 96-14026. (Illus.). 462p. (C). 1997. text 85.00 (*0-521-47180-X*) Cambridge U Pr.

Pollen-Collecting Bees of the Anthidiini of California: Hymenoptera: Megachilidae. Albert A. Grigarick & L. A. Stange. LC 68-64309. (Bulletin of the California Insect Survey Ser.: No. 9). (Illus.). 119p. reprint ed. pap. 36.90 (*0-608-18790-9*, 203030500068) Bks Demand.

Pollen Development in Copper Deficient Cereals. University of London Staff. 22p. 1983. write for info. (*0-318-60406-X*) Intl Copper.

Pollen Flora of China. 2nd ed. Wang Fu-hsiung. (CHI & LAT.). 1995. 158.00 (*0-7855-0525-3*, Pub. by Wanhai Books) St Mut.

Pollen Flora of Maharashtra State. T. S. Nayar. (International Bioscience Ser.: No. 14). (Illus.). 175p. 1990. 65.00 (*1-55528-221-0*) Scholarly Pubns.

Pollen Flora of the Gangetic Plain. A. R. Rao & Priti Shukla. (Indian Pollen Spore Flora Ser.: Vol. I). 140p. 1977. 15.00 (*0-88065-179-2*) Scholarly Pubns.

Pollen Flora of the Native Plants of South Australia & Southern Northern Territory. William E. Boyd. (SA Geographical Papers: No. 3). (Illus.). 212p. (C). 1992. 75.00 (*0-7855-0331-5*, Pub. by Royal Geograp Soc) St Mut.

Pollen Grains: Their Structure, Identification, & Significance in Science & Medicine. Roger P. Wodehouse. LC 59-15783. 590p. reprint ed. pap. 182.90 (*0-608-13973-4*, 205559600029) Bks Demand.

Pollen Grains of Canadian Honey Plants. C. W. Crompton. (Illus.). 228p. (Orig.). 1993. pap. 51.95 (*0-660-14818-8*, Pub. by Canadian Govt Pub) Accents Pubns.

Pollen Grains of New Zealand Dicotyledonous Plants. N. T. Moar. 1993. 60.00 (*0-478-04500-X*, Pub. by Manaaki Whenua) Balogh.

Pollen Morphology & Systematic Relationships of Families Sabiaceae & Connaraceae. M. S. Mondal. (Advances in Pollen Spore Research Ser.: Vol. 12). (Illus.). 152p. 1990. 65.00 (*1-55528-222-9*, Pub. by Today Tomorrow) Scholarly Pubns.

Pollen Morphology of Angiosperms: A Historical & Phylogenetic Study. Ed. by P. K. Nair. 200p. (C). 1991. text 200.00 (*0-89771-607-8*, Pub. by Intl Bk Distr) St Mut.

Pollen Morphology of Indian Compositae. P. K. Nair & R. Lawrence. (Advances in Pollen Spore Research Ser.: Vol. XIV). (Illus.). 176p. 1985. 25.00 (*1-55528-043-9*) Scholarly Pubns.

Pollen Morphology of Indian Geraniales: A Research Monograph. Durdana Yunus & P. K. Nair. (Advances in Pollen Spore Research Ser.: Vol. XV-XVI). 168p. 1989. 59.00 (*1-55528-158-3*) Scholarly Pubns.

Pollen Path: A Collection of Navajo Myths. Margaret S. Link. LC 98-66271. (Illus.). 240p. 1998. pap. 14.95 (*1-885772-09-2*) Kiva Pubng.

Pollen Path: A Collection of Navajo Myths. Retold by Margaret S. Link. LC 56-7272. (Illus.). xiv, 210p. 1956. 32.50 (*0-8047-0473-2*) Stanford U Pr.

Pollen Physiology & Biotechnology. Ed. by C. P. Malik. (Advances in Pollen-Spore Research Ser.: Vol. XIX). (Illus.). 196p. 1992. 65.00 (*1-55528-267-9*, Pub. by Today Tomorrow) Scholarly Pubns.

Pollen Rain, Vegetation & Climate in Lowland East Java, Indonesia. K. R. Buening. Ed. by G. J. Bartstra & W. A. Caspari. (Modern Quarternary Research in Southeast Asia Ser.: Vol. 14). 112p. (C). 1996. text 76.00 (*90-5410-629-8*, Pub. by A A Balkema) Ashgate Pub Co.

Pollen Records of Late-Quaternary North American Sediments. Ed. by Vaughn M. Bryant, Jr. & Richard G. Holloway. LC 85-71610. (Illus.). 440p. (C). 1985. 35.00 (*0-931871-01-8*) Am Assn Strat.

Pollen Room: A Novel. Zoe Jenny. Tr. by Elizabeth Gaffney from GER. LC 98-47401. 160p. 1999. 20.00 (*0-684-85458-9*) S&S Trade.

Pollen Room: A Novel. Zoe Jenny. 144p. 2000. per. 10.00 (*0-684-85459-7*) S&S Trade.

Pollen Wasps: Ecology & Natural History of the Masarinae. Sarah Gess. LC 95-38003. (Illus.). 352p. 1996. 54.00 (*0-674-68964-X*) HUP.

Pollenanalysen an Mooren Des Hohen Vogelsberges (Hessen) - Beitraege Zur Vegetationsgeschichte und Anthropogenen Nutzung Eines Mittelgebirges. Monika Schafer. (Dissertationes Botanicae Ser.: Band 265). (Illus.). 280p. 1996. pap. 83.00 (*3-443-64177-6*, Pub. by Gebruder Borntraeger) Balogh.

Pollenanalytische und Stratigraphische Untersuchungen im Sewensee. Ein Beitrag Zur Spaet- und Postglazealen Vegetations-Geschichte der Suedvogesen. S. Schloss. (Dissertationes Botanicae Ser.: Vol. 52). (GER., Illus.). 1980. lib. bdg. 32.00 (*3-7682-1240-8*) Lubrecht & Cramer.

Pollenanalytische Untersuchungen Zur Vegetations- und Klimageschichte Des Val Camonica (Norditalien) Regula Gehrig. (Dissertationes Botanicae Ser.: Band 276). (Illus.). iv, 152p. 1997. pap. 53.00 (*3-443-64188-1*, Pub. by Gebruder Borntraeger) Balogh.

Pollenation Wand. Harry A. Poole. 77p. (J). (gr. 6-7). 1995. 15.00 (*1-887189-04-1*); pap. 7.95 (*1-887189-05-X*) Symi Pub.

***Pollicino.** 1999. pap. text 7.95 (*88-450-5939-1*) Fabbri.

Pollinating a Flower. Paul Bennett. (Nature's Secrets Ser.). (Illus.). 32p. (J). (gr. 1-5). 1994. lib. bdg. 21.40 (*1-56847-206-4*) Raintree Steck-V.

Pollination Ecology & Evolution in Composite (Asterceae) M. S. Mani. LC 99-23855. (Illus.). 166p. 1999. text 49.50 (*1-57808-058-4*) Science Pubs.

Pollination Mechanisms, Reproduction & Plant Breeding. R. Frankel & E. Galun. (Monographs on Theoretical & Applied Genetics: Vol. 2). 1977. 64.00 (*0-387-07934-3*) Spr-Verlag.

Pollinator Protection: A Bee & Pesticide Handbook. Carl A. Johansen & Daniel F. Mayer. (Illus.). 212p. (Orig.). (C). 1990. pap. text 17.95 (*1-878075-00-4*) Wicwas Pr.

P

An Asterisk (*) at the beginning of an entry indicates that the title is appearing for the first time.

Polling & Presidential Election Coverage. Ed. by Paul J. Lavrakas & Jack K. Holley. (Focus Editions Ser.: Vol. 127). (Illus.). 264p. (C). 1990. text 59.95 (*0-8039-4073-4*); pap. text 26.00 (*0-8039-4074-2*) Sage.

Polling & Presidential Election Coverage. Ed. by Paul J. Lavrakas & Jack K. Holley. LC 90-43950. (Sage Focus Editions Ser.: Vol. 127). (Illus.). 244p. reprint ed. pap. 75.70 (*0-608-09792-6*, 206996600007) Bks Demand.

Polling & Survey Research Methods, 1935-1979: An Annotated Bibliography, 25. Graham R. Walden. LC 96-33127. (Bibliographies & Indexes in Law & Political Science: No. 25). 616p. 1996. lib. bdg. 105.00 (*0-313-27790-7*, Greenwood Pr) Greenwood.

Polling & the Public: What Every Citizen Should Know. 3rd ed. Herbert Asher. LC 95-10464. 199p. (YA). (gr. 11). 1995. pap. text 23.95 (*0-87187-755-4*) Congr Quarterly.

Polling & the Public: What Every Citizen Should Know. 4th ed. Herbert Asher. LC 98-11341. 200p. (C). 1998. pap. text 23.95 (*1-56802-400-2*) Congr Quarterly.

Polling for Democracy: Public Opinion & Political Liberalization in Mexico. Ed. by Roderic A. Camp et al. (Latin American Silhouettes Ser.). 180p. (C). 1996. 45.00 (*0-8420-2583-9*) Scholarly Res Inc.

Pollinosis. Ed. by Paolo Falagiani. 272p. 1989. lib. bdg. 191.00 (*0-8493-6482-5*, RC589) CRC Pr.

Pollita Chiquita. Zimmerman.Tr. of Henny Penny. (SPA.). 32p. (J). (ps-3). 1989. 19.95 (*0-590-73225-0*) Scholastic Inc.

Pollita Chiquita. H. Werner Zimmerman.Tr. of Henny Penny. 10.15 (*0-606-13713-0*, Pub. by Turtleback) Demco.

Pollita Chiquita: (Henny Penny) H. Werner Zimmerman. Tr. by Ann Freeman. (SPA.). 32p. (J). (gr. k-3). 1991. pap. 4.99 (*0-590-44192-2*) Scholastic Inc.

Pollita Pequenita. Steven Kellogg.Tr. of Chicken Little. (SPA.). (J). 1996. pap. 5.95 (*84-241-3328-5*) Lectorum Pubns.

Pollitiaue Plott, for the Honour of the Prince. Robert Hitchcock. LC 77-38110. (English Experience Ser.: No. 388). 54p. 1971. reprint ed. 15.00 (*90-221-0388-9*) Walter J Johnson.

Politicke Courtier: Spenser's the Faerie Queene As a Rhetoric of Justice. Michael F. Dixon. LC 97-200926. (UND.). 256p. 1996. 55.00 (*0-7735-1425-2*, PR2358, Pub. by McG-Queens Univ Pr) CUP Services.

Pollitos. Diane Snowball. Tr. by Martha Gonzalez-Prats. (SPA., Illus.). 16p. (J). (ps-3). 1998. pap. 4.95 (*1-57255-490-8*) Mondo Pubng.

Pollitos: Black & White Nellie Edge I Can Read & Sing Book. Tr. by Hector Pichardo. (Illus.). (J). (ps-2). 1996. 20.00 (*0-922053-42-1*) N Edge Res.

Pollitos Dicen. Nancy Abraham Hall & Jill Syverson-Stork.Tr. of Baby Chicks Sing. 32p. (J). (gr. k-3). 1999. pap. 5.95 (*0-316-33852-4*) Little.

Pollo de los Domingos (Chicken Sunday) Illus. by Patricia Polacco. LC 97-2237. (SPA.). (gr. 2-4). 1997. 15.95 (*1-880507-31-5*) Lectorum Pubns.

Pollock Painting. Hans Namuth. Ed. by Barbara Rose. LC 79-57621. (Illus.). 112p. 1980. 95.00 (*0-9601068-6-3*); pap. 65.00 (*0-9601068-5-5*) Agrinde Pubns.

***Pollos.** Peter Brady. Ed. by Isabel Schon. Tr. by Martin Luis Guzman Ferrer. (Animales de La Granja Ser.). (Illus.). 24p. 1999. 15.93 (*1-56065-787-1*, Bridgestone Bks) Capstone Pr.

Pollos. Peter Brady. (Animales de la Granja). (SPA.). (J). 1998. 14.00 (*0-516-21374-1*) Childrens.

Pollos. Lynn M. Stone. (Animales de Granja Ser.).Tr. of Chickens. 24p. (J). (gr. k-4). 1991. lib. bdg. 14.60 (*0-86592-949-1*) Rourke Enter.

Polls & Surveys: Understanding What They Tell Us. Norman M. Bradburn & Seymour Sudman. LC 88-42778. (Social & Behavioral Science Ser.). 269p. 1988. 35.95 (*1-55542-098-2*) Jossey-Bass.

Polls & the Awareness of Public Opinion. Leo Bogart. 250p. (C). 1985. pap. 21.95 (*0-88738-620-2*) Transaction Pubs.

Polls, Politics & Populism. John Clemens. 208p. 1983. text 82.95 (*0-566-00602-2*, Pub. by Dartmth Pub) Ashgate Pub Co.

Pollutant Industries. Fire Protection Association Staff. (C). 1990. 110.00 (*0-902167-05-7*, Pub. by Fire Protect Assn) St Mut.

Pollutant Materials in the American Environment: Index of New Information. Alan S. Kauffman. 1998. 47.50 (*0-7883-1840-3*); pap. 44.50 (*0-7883-1841-1*) ABBE Pubs Assn.

Pollutant Studies in Marine Animals. Ed. by C. S. Giam & L. E. Ray. LC 86-31690. 224p. 1987. 116.00 (*0-8493-5407-2*, QH545, CRC Reprint) Franklin.

Pollutant Transfer & Transport in the Sea, 2 vols., Vol. I. Gunnar Kullenberg. 240p. 1982. 150.00 (*0-8493-5601-6*, GC1085, CRC Reprint) Franklin.

Pollutant Transfer & Transport in the Sea, 2 vols., Vol. II. Gunnar Kullenberg. 248p. 1982. 142.00 (*0-8493-5602-4*, GC1085, CRC Reprint) Franklin.

Pollutants & Their Ecotoxicological Significance. Ed. by H. W. Nurnberg. LC 84-7540. (Wiley-Interscience Publications). (Illus.). 529p. reprint ed. pap. 164.00 (*0-7837-3413-1*, 204338000008) Bks Demand.

Pollutants in a Multimedia Environment. Ed. by Yoram Cohen. LC 86-22704. 340p. 1986. 79.50 (*0-306-42405-3*, Plenum Trade) Perseus Pubng.

Polluted Air. John M. Patten, Jr. LC 94-38616. (Read All about Eye on the Environment Ser.). 24p. (J). (gr. 1-4). 1995. lib. bdg. 18.60 (*1-55916-098-5*) Rourke Bk Co.

Polluted Poems: An Anthology of Environmental Poetry. Ed. & Illus. by G. Murray Thomas. LC 94-65984. 86p. (Orig.). 1994. pap. 10.00 (*1-885021-03-8*) Orange Ocean.

***Polluted Sites: Remediation of Soils & Groundwater.** Paul Lecomte. (Illus.). 220p. 1999. 58.50 (*90-5410-784-7*, Pub. by A A Balkema) Ashgate Pub Co.

Polluters: A Community Fights Back. Susan Uarlamoff. Ed. by Donald E. Montgomery. (Illus.). 301p. (Orig.). 1993. pap. 14.95 (*0-938577-07-7*) St Johns Pub.

Polluting for Pleasure. Audre Mele. LC 92-43498. 224p. 1993. 22.95 (*0-393-03510-7*) Norton.

Polluting Sacred Faith: A Study on Communalism & Violence. Pramod Kumar. (C). 1992. 17.50 (*0-945921-22-5*, Pub. by Ajanta) S Asia.

Polluting the Censorship Debate: A Summary & Critique of the Final Report of the Attorney General's Commission on Pornography. Barry W. Lynn. 188p. 1986. 5.00 (*0-86566-040-9*) ACLU DC.

Pollution. Janine Amos. 32p. (J). (gr. 1-4). 1993. pap. 4.95 (*0-8114-4917-3*) Raintree Steck-V.

Pollution. Nicola Barber. (Illus.). 44p. (J). (gr. 5-8). 1996. write for info. (*0-237-51513-X*) EVN1 UK.

***Pollution.** Rosemary Border. (Illus.). 24p. 1999. pap. 6.95 (*0-19-422868-1*) OUP.

Pollution. Central Office of Info. (Aspects of Britain Ser.). (Illus.). 1997. pap. 10.00 (*0-11-701777-9*, Pub. by Statnry Office) Bernan Associates.

Pollution. Alan Collinson. LC 91-24081. (Repairing the Damage Ser.). (Illus.). 48p. (J). (gr. 4-6). 1992. lib. bdg. 21.00 (*0-02-722995-5*, Mac Bks Young Read) S&S Childrens.

Pollution. Ed. by Charles P. Cozic. LC 93-4552. (Current Controversies Ser.). 224p. 1994. pap. 16.20 (*1-56510-075-1*); lib. bdg. 26.20 (*1-56510-076-X*) Greenhaven.

Pollution. Claudia G. Ferrari & Manlio Brusatin. (Illus.). 72p. 1998. pap. 19.95 (*88-8158-151-5*, Pub. by Charta) Dist Art Pubs.

Pollution. Sharron McEldowney et al. LC 92-36776. (C). 1993. pap. text 52.50 (*0-582-08655-8*) Longman.

Pollution. Snape & Rowlands. (Science at Work Ser.). 1992. pap. text. write for info. (*0-582-07828-8*, Pub. by Addison-Wesley) Longman.

Pollution: Examining Cause & Effect Relationships. Robert Anderson. LC 92-25958. (Opposing Viewpoints Juniors Ser.). (Illus.). 36p. (J). (gr. 4-7). 1992. lib. bdg. 16.20 (*0-89908-574-1*) Greenhaven.

***Pollution: Opposing Viewpoints.** Tamara L. Roleff. LC 99-17677. (Opposing Viewpoints Ser.). 192p. (YA). (gr. 9-12). 2000. lib. bdg. 27.45 (*0-7377-0135-8*) Greenhaven.

***Pollution: Opposing Viewpoints.** Ed. by Tamara L. Roleff. LC 99-17677. (Opposing Viewpoints Ser.). 312p. (YA). (gr. 9-12). 2000. pap. 17.45 (*0-7377-0134-X*) Greenhaven.

***Pollution: Problems & Solutions.** National Wildlife Federation Staff. LC 98-39954. (Ranger Rick's Naturescope Ser.: Vol. 1). (Illus.). 96p. (J). (gr. 1-7). 1999. lib. bdg. 19.95 (*0-7910-4882-9*) Chelsea Hse.

Pollution: Problems & Solutions. National Wildlife Federation Staff. LC 97-36214. (Ranger Rick's Naturescope Ser.). 96p. 1998. pap. 12.95 (*0-07-047105-3*) McGraw.

Pollution: Problems & Solutions. National Wildlife Federation Staff. (J). (gr. k-8). 1991. pap. 7.95 (*0-945051-40-9*, 75045) Natl Wildlife.

Pollution? No Problem! David Morichon. LC 98-5690. (J). 1998. pap. write for info. (*0-7613-0434-7*); lib. bdg. 21.90 (*0-7613-1260-9*) Millbrook Pr.

Pollution Abatement Strategies in Central & Eastern Europe. Ed. by Michael A. Toman. 89p. 1994. pap. 15.95 (*0-915707-73-X*) Resources Future.

Pollution, Air Quality Research, Memorandum of Understanding Between the U. S. of America & Mexico. 1994. lib. bdg. 250.00 (*0-8490-8534-9*) Gordon Pr.

Pollution & Contamination: How Will Property Insurers Respond? American Bar Association, Tort & Insurance Practic. LC 87-70246. 192p. 1987. pap. 29.95 (*0-89707-285-5*, 519-0067) Amer Bar Assn.

Pollution & Freshwater Fish. Richard Lloyd. (Illus.). 1992. 59.95 (*0-85238-187-5*) Blackwell Sci.

Pollution & Personal Injury: Toxic Torts II. Charles Pugh & Martyn Day. 297p. 1995. 84.00 (*1-874698-16-3*, Pub. by Cameron May) Gaunt.

Pollution & the Death of Man. Francis A. Schaeffer. LC 92-74125. 160p. 1992. pap. 11.99 (*0-89107-686-7*) Crossway Bks.

Pollution & the Environmental Law. Satish Shastri. (C). 1990. 100.00 (*0-89771-155-6*) St Mut.

Pollution & the Firm. Robert E. Kohn. LC 97-14364. (New Horizons in Environmental Economics Ser.). 272p. 1998. 90.00 (*1-85898-639-7*) E Elgar.

***Pollution & the Forests of Developing & Rapidly Industrializing Regions.** John L. Innes & A. H. Hassan. LC 00-23662. (IUFRO Research Ser.). 2000. write for info. (*0-85199-481-4*) C A B Intl.

Pollution & the Powerless: The Movement for Environmental Justice. Kathlyn Gay. (Impact Bks.). (Illus.). 112p. (YA). (gr. 7-12). 1994. lib. bdg. 24.00 (*0-531-11190-3*) Watts.

Pollution & the Struggle for the World Product: Multinational Corporations, Environment, & International Comparative Advantage. H. Jeffrey Leonard. (Illus.). 272p. 1988. text 85.00 (*0-521-34042-X*) Cambridge U Pr.

Pollution & the Use of Chemicals in Agriculture. Ed. by David E. Irving & Brian Knights. LC 74-180914. 146p. reprint ed. pap. 45.30 (*0-608-14829-6*, 202573600046) Bks Demand.

Pollution & Waste. Rosie Harlow & Sally Morgan. LC 95-6369. (Young Discoverers Ser.). (Illus.). 32p. (J). (gr. 2-5). 1995. 12.90 (*1-85697-614-9*, Kingfisher) LKC.

Pollution by Dumping: Pollution by Dumping. (The Law of the Sea Ser.). 77p. pap. 11.50 (*92-1-133274-5*, E.85.V.12) UN.

Pollution Control & Conservation. Ed. by M. Kovacs. LC 83-23172. 398p. 1986. text 143.00 (*0-470-27509-X*) P-H.

Pollution, Control & Energy Needs. J. Jimenson. 256p. (C). 1991. text 400.00 (*0-89771-552-7*, Pub. by Intl Bk Distr) St Mut.

Pollution Control & Energy Needs: A Symposium. Ed. by Robert M. Jimeson & Roderick S. Spindt. LC 73-92108. (Advances in Chemistry Ser.: No. 127). (Illus.). 264p. reprint ed. pap. 81.90 (*0-7837-4082-4*, 205247900011) Bks Demand.

Pollution Control & Environmental Protection. M. Terry Frederick. LC 83-198. (Papers: No. P-3). 1983. pap. text 4.00 (*0-88090-043-1*) Intl Fertilizer.

Pollution Control & the Patterns of Trade. Sezai Demiral. LC 90-3683. (Environment: Problems & Solutions Ser.). 214p. 1990. text 15.00 (*0-8240-0463-9*) Garland.

***Pollution Control & Waste Management in Developing Countries.** Ed. by Rogers W'O Okut-Uma et al. 160p. 2000. pap. 45.00 (*0-85092-557-6*, Pub. by Comm Sec) Stylus Pub VA.

Pollution Control, Economic Adjustment & Long-Run Equilibrium. G. Stephan. (Microeconomic Studies). (Illus.). 155p. 1989. 49.00 (*0-387-50987-9*) Spr-Verlag.

Pollution Control Engineer's Handbook. Pollution Engineering Staff. 205p. 1988. 34.95 (*0-934165-02-5*, 65029) Gulf Pub.

Pollution Control Engineer's Handbook. Ed. by Edward J. Shields. (Illus.). 206p. 1988. 34.95 (*0-685-43456-7*, Pollution Eng) Cahners Busn Des Plaines.

Pollution Control Equipment in Austria: A Strategic Entry Report, 1996. Compiled by Icon Group International Staff. (Illus.). 110p. 1999. ring bd. 1100.00 incl. audio compact disk (*0-7418-1400-5*) Icon Grp.

Pollution Control Equipment in Bolivia: A Strategic Entry Report, 1997. Compiled by Icon Group International Staff. (Country Industry Report). (Illus.). 115p. 1999. ring bd. 1150.00 incl. audio compact disk (*0-7418-0309-7*) Icon Grp.

***Pollution Control Equipment in Canada: A Strategic Entry Report, 1995.** Compiled by Icon Group International Staff. (Illus.). 137p. 1999. ring bd. 1370.00 incl. audio compact disk (*0-7418-1643-1*) Icon Grp.

Pollution Control Equipment in China: A Strategic Entry Report, 1996. Compiled by Icon Group International Staff. (Illus.). 174p. 1999. ring bd. 1740.00 incl. audio compact disk (*0-7418-1401-3*) Icon Grp.

***Pollution Control Equipment in Ecuador: A Strategic Entry Report, 1995.** Compiled by Icon Group International Staff. (Illus.). 137p. 1999. ring bd. 1370.00 incl. audio compact disk (*0-7418-1644-X*) Icon Grp.

***Pollution Control Equipment in Kuwait: A Strategic Entry Report, 1995.** Compiled by Icon Group International Staff. (Illus.). 126p. 1999. ring bd. 1260.00 incl. audio compact disk (*0-7418-1645-8*) Icon Grp.

***Pollution Control Equipment in Kuwait: A Strategic Entry Report, 1998.** Compiled by Icon Group International Staff. (Country Industry Report). (Illus.). 123p. 1999. ring bd. 1230.00 incl. audio compact disk (*0-7418-0541-3*) Icon Grp.

***Pollution Control Equipment in Pakistan: A Strategic Entry Report, 1999.** Compiled by Icon Group International. (Illus.). 185p. 1999. ring bd. 1850.00 incl. audio compact disk (*0-7418-1705-5*) Icon Grp.

Pollution Control Equipment in Peru: A Strategic Entry Report, 1996. Compiled by Icon Group International Staff. (Illus.). 143p. 1999. ring bd. 1430.00 incl. audio compact disk (*0-7418-1402-1*) Icon Grp.

Pollution Control Equipment in Peru: A Strategic Entry Report, 1997. Compiled by Icon Group International Staff. (Illus.). 145p. 1999. ring bd. 1450.00 incl. audio compact disk (*0-7418-0895-1*) Icon Grp.

***Pollution Control Equipment in Russia: A Strategic Entry Report, 1999.** Compiled by Icon Group International. (Illus.). 140p. 1999. ring bd. 1400.00 incl. audio compact disk (*0-7418-1864-7*) Icon Grp.

***Pollution Control Equipment in Saudi Arabia: A Strategic Entry Report, 1998.** Compiled by Icon Group International Staff. (Country Industry Report). (Illus.). 135p. 1999. ring bd. 1350.00 incl. audio compact disk (*0-7418-0542-1*) Icon Grp.

Pollution Control for Agriculture. 2nd ed. Raymond C. Loehr. 1984. text 83.00 (*0-12-455270-6*) Acad Pr.

Pollution Control in Fertilizer Production. Ed. by Charles A. Hodge & Neculai N. Popovici. LC 94-4798. (Environmental Science & Pollution Ser.: Vol. 10). (Illus.). 520p. 1994. text 210.00 (*0-8247-9188-6*) Dekker.

Pollution Control in Indian Industry. D. H. Panandiker. (C). 1991. 14.50 (*81-7018-633-1*, Pub. by BR Pub) S Asia.

Pollution Control in the European Community: Guide to the Ec Texts & Their Implementation by the Member States. S. Ercman. LC 96-47694. 1996. 244.50 (*90-411-0889-0*) Kluwer Law Intl.

***Pollution Control in the Paper Industry in India: A Strategic Entry Report, 1995.** Compiled by Icon Group International Staff. (Illus.). 194p. 1999. ring bd. 1940.00 incl. audio compact disk (*0-7418-1646-6*) Icon Grp.

Pollution Control in the South & North: A Comparative Assessment of Environmental Policy Approaches in India & the Netherlands. Onno Kuik. LC 97-27314. (Indo-Dutch Studies on Development Alternatives). 1997. 38.00 (*0-7619-9204-9*) Sage.

Pollution Control in the United States: Evaluating the System. J. Clarence Davies & Jan Mazurek. LC 97-49246. (Illus.). 319p. 1998. 48.00 (*0-915707-87-X*); pap. text 32.95 (*0-915707-88-8*) Resources Future.

Pollution Control Instrumentation for Oil & Effluents. H. Parker & G. D. Pitt. 272p. (C). 1987. reprint ed. lib. bdg. 163.00 (*0-86010-368-4*, Pub. by Graham & Trotman) Kluwer Academic.

Pollution Control Specialist. Jack Rudman. (Career Examination Ser.: C-3738). 1994. pap. 29.95 (*0-8373-3738-0*) Nat Learn.

Pollution Coverage Issues, 2 vols. Edward J. O'Gorman. LC 98-204276. 1290p. 1998. 198.00 (*1-886813-35-3*) Intl Risk Mgt.

Pollution Ecology: A Practical Approach. A. Dafni. LC 92-15944. (Practical Approach Ser.). 272p. 1993. 79.00 (*0-19-963299-5*) OUP.

Pollution Ecology of Freshwater Invertebrates. C. W. Hart & Samuel Fuller. 1974. text 90.00 (*0-12-328450-3*) Acad Pr.

Pollution Engineering Flow Sheets: Hazardous Waste Treatment & Unit Operations. Pollution Engineering Staff. 225p. 1988. 34.95 (*0-934165-23-8*, 65239) Gulf Pub.

Pollution Evaluation: The Quantitative Aspects. William F. Pickering. LC 77-12910. (Environmental Science & Technology Ser.: Vol. 2). (Illus.). 207p. reprint ed. pap. 64.20 (*0-608-08974-5*, 206960900005) Bks Demand.

Pollution for Sale: Emissions Trading & Joint Implementation. Ed. by Steve Sorrell & Jim Skea. LC 98-42885. 432p. 1999. 95.00 (*1-84064-010-3*) E Elgar.

Pollution Formation & Destruction in Flames see Progress in Energy & Combustion Science

Pollution from Offshore Installations. Maria Gavouneli. LC 95-2374. (International Environmental Law & Policy Ser.). 1995. lib. bdg. 119.00 (*1-85966-186-6*, Pub. by Graham & Trotman) Kluwer Academic.

Pollution Impacts on Marine Biotic Communities. Michael J. Kennish. LC 97-14857. (Marine Science Ser.). 336p. 1997. boxed set 94.95 (*0-8493-8428-1*) CRC Pr.

Pollution in America: The Trouble with Trash. S. Charles Maurice & Charles W. Smithson. Ed. by Steve Pejovich & Henry Dethloff. (Series on Public Issues: No. 7). (Illus.). 27p. (Orig.). (C). 1984. pap. 2.00 (*0-86599-017-4*) PERC.

Pollution in Livestock Production Systems. Ed. by I. A. Dewi et al. (Illus.). 464p. 1994. text 130.00 (*0-85198-857-1*) OUP.

Pollution in Space see Isaac Asimov's New Library of the Universe

Pollution in the U. K. Denise Franklin & Mark Lowe. 300p. 1993. 80.00 (*0-421-45690-6*, Pub. by Sweet & Maxwll) Gaunt.

Pollution in Tropical Aquatic Systems. Des W. Connell. 224p. 1991. lib. bdg. 149.00 (*0-8493-6581-3*, QH545) CRC Pr.

Pollution Insurance: International Survey of Coverages & Exclusions. Ed. by Werner Pfenningstorf. LC 93-32141. (International Environmental Law & Policy Ser.). 272p. (C). 1993. lib. bdg. 132.50 (*1-85333-941-5*, Pub. by Graham & Trotman) Kluwer Academic.

Pollution Knows No Frontier: A Reader. Ed. by Klaus Schleicher. (Illus.). 334p. 1992. 25.95 (*0-89226-127-7*) Prof World Peace.

Pollution Law & Insurance: A Comparison of the Legal Regimes of European States & the U. S. A. Anthony Fitzsimmons. LC 97-37210. 240p. 1997. 104.50 (*90-411-0895-5*) Kluwer Law Intl.

Pollution Law Handbook: A Guide to Federal Environmental Laws. Sidney M. Wolf. LC 87-13094. 294p. 1988. 72.95 (*0-89930-141-X*, WFP/, Quorum Bks) Greenwood.

Pollution Markets in a Green Country Town: Urban Environmental Management in Transition. Roger K. Raufer. LC 97-32945. 288p. 1998. 65.00 (*0-275-96174-5*, Praeger Pubs) Greenwood.

Pollution Microbiology: A Laboratory Manual. Melvin S. Finstein. LC QR0048.F5. (Illus.). 181p. reprint ed. pap. 56.20 (*0-7837-0791-6*, 204110500019) Bks Demand.

Pollution of Ganga River. N. C. Ghosh & C. B. Sharma. (C). 1989. 34.00 (*81-7024-245-2*, Pub. by Ashish Pub Hse) S Asia.

Pollution of International Watercourses. Johan G. Lammers. 1984. lib. bdg. 283.00 (*90-247-2955-6*) Kluwer Academic.

Pollution of Lakes & Resevoirs. (UNEP/GEMS Environment Library: No. 12). 40p. pap. 10.00 (*92-1-100584-1*) UN.

***Pollution of Lakes & Rivers: A Palaeoenvironmental Perspective.** John P. Smol. 224p. 2000. text 72.00 (*0-340-74146-5*, Pub. by E A) OUP.

***Pollution of Lakes & Rivers: A Paleoenvironmental Perspective.** John P. Smol. (Key Issues in Environmental Change Ser.). (Illus.). 224p. 2000. pap. text 29.95 (*0-340-69167-0*, Pub. by E A) OUP.

Pollution of Outer Space: Scientific, Policy & Legal Aspects. Gijsbertha C. Reijnen & W. De Graaff. (C). 1989. lib. bdg. 94.50 (*90-247-3750-8*) Kluwer Academic.

Pollution of the Mediterranean Sea: Proceedings of An IAWPRC International Regional Conference Held in Split, Yugoslavia, 2-5 October 1985. Ed. by M. Miloradov. (Water Science & Technology Ser.: No. 18). (Illus.). 338p. 1987. pap. 52.00 (*0-08-035578-1*, Pergamon Pr) Elsevier.

Pollution of the Mediterranean Sea: Selected Proceedings of the International Symposium on Pollution of the Mediterranean Sea, Held in Nicosia, Cyprus, 2-4 November, 1994. Ed. by M. L. Nicolaou & A. D. Andreadakis. (Water Science & Technology Ser.). 368p. 1996. pap. text 109.25 (*0-08-042885-1*, Pergamon Pr) Elsevier.

Pollution of the North Sea: An Assessment. Ed. by W. Salomons et al. (Illus.). 705p. 1989. 193.95 (*0-387-19288-3*) Spr-Verlag.

An Asterisk (*) at the beginning of an entry indicates that the title is appearing for the first time.

Pollution of the Wadden Sea Area. Ed. by K. Essink & W. J. Wolff. 61p. 1978. pap. 60.00 (*90-6191-058-7*, Pub. by A A Balkema) Ashgate Pub Co.

Pollution Papers. Ed. by George E. Frakes & Curtis B. Solberg. LC 79-146364. (C). 1971. 32.00 (*0-89197-503-9*) Irvington.

Pollution, Politics, & Foreign Investment in Taiwan: The Lukang Rebellion. James Reardon-Anderson. LC 92-29888. (Taiwan in the Modern World). 134p. (C). (gr. 13). 1992. text 53.95 (*0-87332-702-0*, East Gate Bk) M E Sharpe.

Pollution Prevention. 1995. lib. bdg. 250.95 (*0-8490-7533-5*) Gordon Pr.

Pollution Prevention. LC 98-104794. (Hazardous, Nuclear & Solid Waste Environmental Management Ser.: No. 4). 1996. pap. 10.00 (*1-55516-514-1*, 4661) Natl Conf State Legis.

***Pollution Prevention.** R. Ryan Dupont et al. LC 99-47203. 498p. 1999. write for info. (*1-56670-495-2*) Lewis Pubs.

Pollution Prevention. Richard K. Miller & Christy H. Gunter. (Market Research Survey Ser.: No. 305). 50p. 1996. 200.00 (*1-55865-329-5*) Future Tech Surveys.

Pollution Prevention. Louis Theodore & Young C. McGuinn. (Illus.). 432p. 1992. text 76.95 (*0-442-00606-3*, VNR) Wiley.

Pollution Prevention. Barbara B. Wells. Ed. by Gerry Feinstein. 55p. (Orig.). 1992. pap. text 18.95 (*1-55877-162-X*) Natl Governor.

Pollution Prevention: A Guide for Local Government. Catherine R. Leining. (Special Reports). (Illus.). 107p. 1994. pap. 28.00 (*0-87326-073-2*) Intl City-Cnty Mgt.

Pollution Prevention: A Practical Guide for State & Local Government. David T. Wigglesworth. 240p. 1993. lib. bdg. 75.00 (*0-87371-654-X*, L654) Lewis Pubs.

Pollution Prevention: A Self-Instructional Problem Workbook. Louis Theodore & Robert Allen. 424p. 1994. pap. text 60.00 (*1-882767-10-1*) ETS.

***Pollution Prevention: Fundamentals & Practice** Paul L. Bishop. LC 99-16020. 768p. 1999. 81.88 (*0-07-366147-3*) McGraw.

Pollution Prevention: Homework & Design Problems for Engineering Curricula. CWRT Staff & Center for Waste Reduction & American Institute fo. 156p. 1992. pap. 40.00 (*0-8169-0581-9*, C-1) Am Inst Chem Eng.

Pollution Prevention: Methodology, Technologies & Practices. Kenneth Mulholland & J. A. Dyers. LC 98-40828. (AIChE Originals Ser.). 330p. 1999. 175.00 (*0-8169-0782-X*, Q-7) Am Inst Chem Eng.

Pollution Prevention: Problems & Solutions. Louis Theodore. v, 320p. 1994. text 92.00 (*2-88449-142-2*); pap. text 47.00 (*2-88449-129-5*) Gordon & Breach.

Pollution Prevention & Abatement Handbook, 1998: Toward Cleaner Production. United Nations Industrial Development Organization et al. LC 98-34574. 472p. 1999. pap. 125.00 (*0-8213-3638-X*, 13638) World Bank.

Pollution Prevention & Strategic Environmental Engineering. O'Brien. (C). 1997. text 79.95 (*0-442-02342-1*, VNR) Wiley.

Pollution Prevention & Waste Minimization. Jeffery P. Perl. (C). 2000. 48.00 (*0-13-369091-1*, Macmillan Coll) P-H.

Pollution Prevention & Waste Minimization in Laboratories. Ed. by Peter A. Reinhardt et al. 512p. 1995. lib. bdg. 85.00 (*0-87371-975-1*, L975) Lewis Pubs.

Pollution Prevention at Industrial Laundries: A Collaborative Approach in Southern California. (Illus.). 235p. 1998. pap. text 45.00 (*0-7881-4943-1*) DIANE Pub.

Pollution Prevention at Industrial Laundries: Assessment Observations & Waste Reduction Options. (Illus.). 70p. (C). 1998. pap. text 25.00 (*0-7881-4942-3*) DIANE Pub.

Pollution Prevention Case Studies Compendium. Johnny Springer, Jr. 99p. (Orig.). (C). 1993. pap. text 20.00 (*1-56806-236-2*) DIANE Pub.

Pollution Prevention Directory. Beth Anderson. 103p. (C). 1996. pap. text 35.00 (*0-7881-2913-9*) DIANE Pub.

Pollution Prevention Economics: Financial Impacts on Business & Industry. James R. Aldrich. (Illus.). 192p. 1995. 45.00 (*0-07-000993-7*) McGraw.

Pollution Prevention Evaluation Report. (Illus.). 79p. (Orig.). (C). 1994. pap. text 25.00 (*0-7881-1366-6*) DIANE Pub.

Pollution Prevention for Chemical Processes. David T. Allen & Kirsten S. Rosselot. LC 96-8438. 456p. 1996. 79.95 (*0-471-11587-8*) Wiley.

Pollution Prevention for Chemical Processes: A Handbook with Solved Problems from the Refining & Chemical Processing Industries. David T. Allen & Kirsten S. Rosselot. (Illus.). 144p. (Orig.). (C). 1994. pap. text 40.00 (*0-7881-1407-7*) DIANE Pub.

Pollution Prevention for Process Engineers. Ed. by Paul E. Richardson et al. (Engineering Foundation Conference Proceedings Ser.). 368p. 1996. 115.00 (*0-939204-53-3*, P-83) Eng Found.

Pollution Prevention Guide: A Common Sense Approach to Environmental Management. Sandy Day. Date not set. pap. 6.95 (*0-9650267-1-X*) SanDay Servs.

Pollution Prevention Handbook. rev. ed. 1990. ring bd. 179.95 (*1-55645-337-X*, 337) Busn Legal Reports.

Pollution Prevention in California: An Overview of California's Pollution Prevention Programs & Technologies. Kathryn Barwick. (Illus.). 108p. (Orig.). (C). 1995. pap. text 30.00 (*0-7881-2398-X*) DIANE Pub.

Pollution Prevention in Industrial Processes: The Role of Process Analytical Chemistry. Ed. by Joseph J. Breen & Michael J. Dellarco. LC 92-30288. (ACS Symposium Ser.: Vol. 508). (Illus.). 316p. 1992. text 85.00 (*0-8412-2478-1*, Pub. by Am Chemical) OUP.

***Pollution Prevention Opportunities Assessments.** Healey. 240p. 1998. 80.00 incl. disk (*0-471-29226-5*) Wiley.

Pollution Prevention Opportunity Assessments: A Practical Guide. Marcus J. Healey. LC 97-37397. (Illus.). 350p. 1998. 69.95 incl. disk (*0-442-02493-2*, VNR) Wiley.

Pollution Prevention Opportunity Assessments for Research & Development Laboratories. Jill Engel-Cox & Kim Fowler. LC 99-14313. 102p. 1999. pap. 29.95 (*1-57477-070-5*) Battelle.

Pollution Prevention, Progress on Reducing Industrial Pollutants. 1994. lib. bdg. 250.00 (*0-8490-5755-8*) Gordon Pr.

Pollution Prevention Research Program (EPA) Gregory Ondich. 67p. (Orig.). 1996. reprint ed. pap. text 25.00 (*0-7881-2957-0*) DIANE Pub.

Pollution Prevention Software Systems Handbook. Nicholas P. Cheremisinoff. LC 96-36451. 398p. 1996. 98.00 (*0-8155-1405-0*) Noyes.

Pollution Prevention Strategies & Technologies. Mark S. Dennison. 463p. 1996. text 79.00 (*0-86587-480-8*) Gov Insts.

Pollution Prevention Technology Handbook. Ed. by Robert Noyes. LC 92-32508. (Illus.). 683p. 1993. 145.00 (*0-8155-1311-9*) Noyes.

Pollution Prevention Through Proces Integration: Systematic Design Tools. Mahmoud El-Halwagi. LC 97-9789. (Illus.). 318p. 1997. text 59.95 (*0-12-236845-2*) Morgan Kaufmann.

Pollution Prevention Via Process & Product Modifications. Mahmoud M. El-Halwagi & Demetri P. Petrides. LC 95-15066. (AIChE Symposium Ser.: No. 303). 180p. 1995. 75.00 (*0-8169-0664-5*) Am Inst Chem Eng.

Pollution, Prices & Public Policy. Allen V. Kneese & Charles L. Schultze. LC 74-1432. 125p. 1975. 28.95 (*0-8157-4994-5*); pap. 10.95 (*0-8157-4993-7*) Brookings.

Pollution, Protection & Control of Groundwater: Proceedings of the IAWPRC International Seminar, Held in Porto Alegre, Brazil, 20-21 September 1990. Ed. by E. M. Goettems. LC 82-645900. (Water Science & Technology Ser.: No. 24). (Illus.). 296p. 1992. pap. 157.00 (*0-08-041850-3*, Pergamon Pr) Elsevier.

Pollution Reader: Based on the National Conference on "Pollution & Our Environment" Anthony Devos. Ed. by Norman H. Pearson et al. LC 68-31597. (Harvest House Environment Ser.). (Illus.). 264p. reprint ed. pap. 81.90 (*0-608-30096-9*, 202229300026) Bks Demand.

Pollution, Recycling, Trash, & Litter. Doris Roettger. 1991. 8.99 (*0-86653-981-6*) Fearon Teacher Aids.

Pollution Reduction & Contaminant Control. (Encyclopedia of Environmental Control Technology Ser.: Vol. 6). (Illus.). 712p. 1992. 155.00 (*0-87201-285-9*, 1285) Gulf Pub.

Pollution Research Index: A Guide to World Research in Environmental Pollution. 2nd ed. Ed. by Andrew I. Sors & David Coleman. LC 79-70831. 565p. reprint ed. pap. 175.20 (*0-608-17082-8*, 202771500056) Bks Demand.

Pollution Risk Assessment & Management. Peter E. Douben. LC 98-12078. (Ecological & Environmental Toxicology Ser.). 478p. 1998. 190.00 (*0-471-97297-5*) Wiley.

Pollution Science. Ed. by Ian L. Pepper et al. LC 96-12826. (Illus.). 397p. 1996. text 63.00 (*0-12-550660-0*) Acad Pr.

***Pollwatching, Elections & Civil Society in Southeast Asia.** William A. Callahan. LC 99-46215. (Leeds Studies in Democratization). 218p. 1999. text 70.95 (*1-84014-474-2*, Pub. by Ashgate Pub) Ashgate Pub Co.

Pollworker Training Handbook. Linda Trudel. Ed. & Tr. by International Foundation for Election Systems Staf from FRE. (Illus.). iii, 118p. 1997. pap. text. write for info. (*1-879720-50-7*) Intl Fndt Elect.

Polly. Mary C. Borntrager. LC 94-5645. (Ellie's People Ser.: Vol. 7). 144p. (Orig.). (J). 1994. pap. 7.99 (*0-8361-3670-5*) Herald Pr.

Polly. large type ed. Mary C. Borntrager. (Ellie's People Ser.: Vol. 7). 144p. (Orig.). (J). 1994. pap. 8.99 (*0-8361-9008-4*) Herald Pr.

Polly: The True Story Behind Whiskey Galore. Roger Hutchinson. (Illus.). 160p. 1998. 15.95 (*1-84018-071-4*, Pub. by Mainstream Pubng) Trafalgar.

Polly Ann. Glenn Waggoner. 220p. 1992. 24.95 (*0-9632597-0-9*, TXU 507630); pap. 18.95 (*0-9632597-2-5*); text 29.95 (*0-9632597-3-3*); lib. bdg. 29.95 (*0-9632597-1-7*) Monroe Ent Pub.

***Polly Borland: Australians.** (Illus.). 2000. pap. 29.95 (*1-85514-282-1*, Pub. by Natl Port Gall) Antique Collect.

Polly Bumpkin Plants Pumpkins. large type ed. S. Bernadine Riske. LC 95-94956. (Illus.). 15p. (Orig.). (J). (ps-12). 1995. pap. 9.95 (*1-885981-08-2*, Brisk Pubns) Brisk Pubng.

Polly Farmer: A Biography. Steve Hawke. LC 94-206212. 360p. 1994. write for info. (*1-86368-092-6*, Pub. by Fremantle Arts) Intl Spec Bk.

Polly Jumped over the Moon. Helen Solomon. LC 88-45475. (Illus.). 32p. (J). (ps-2). 1989. 9.95 (*0-397-32328-X*) HarpC Child Bks.

Polly Jumped over the Moon. Helen Solomon. LC 88-45475. (Illus.). 32p. (J). (ps-2). 1989. lib. bdg. 9.89 (*0-397-32329-8*) HarpC Child Bks.

Polly Klaas. Barry Bortnick. 1996. mass mkt. 5.99 (*0-7860-0408-8*) Kensgtn Pub Corp.

Polly Klaas: Murder of America's Child. Barry Bortnick. 1995. mass mkt. 4.99 (*0-7860-0195-X*) Kensgtn Pub Corp.

***Polly Molly Woof Woof: A Book about Being Happy.** David Lloyd. LC 99-34808. (Illus.). (J). 2000. 13.99 (*0-7636-0755-X*) Candlewick Pr.

Polly Oliver. Alfred E. Coppard. LC 70-132114. (Short Story Index Reprint Ser.). 1977. 17.95 (*0-8369-3671-X*) Ayer.

Polly Panic. Mary F. Shura. 128p. (J). (gr. 5 up). 1992. reprint ed. pap. 3.50 (*0-380-71334-9*, Avon Bks) Morrow Avon.

Polly Peablossom's Wedding & Other Tales. Ed. by T. A. Burke. 1972. reprint ed. lib. bdg. 32.00 (*0-8422-8157-6*) Irvington.

Polly Peachum: The Story of Lavinia Fenton - "The Beggar's Opera" Charles E. Pearce. LC 68-21222. (Illus.). 1972. reprint ed. 26.95 (*0-405-08846-9*) Ayer.

Polly Pelican & Her Big Beak: Includes Toy. Paul Flemming. (Snappy Fun Bks.: Vol. 3). (Illus.). 12p. (J). (gr. k-3). 1998. bds. 3.99 (*1-57584-173-8*, Pub. by Rdrs Digest) Random.

***Polly Penguin Helps Santa.** Faye Erhard. (Illus.). 32p. (J). 2000. pap. 8.00 (*0-8059-4974-7*) Dorrance.

Polly Pinder's Papercrafts Book. Polly Pinder. (Illus.). 128p. 1994. pap. 19.95 (*0-85532-661-1*, 661-1, Pub. by Srch Pr) A Schwartz & Co.

***Polly Plane, 1.** Andy Robb. 1999. 4.00 (*0-570-05570-9*) Concordia.

Polly Pocket: Just Like a Real Ballerina. Carol Thompson. (Illus.). (J). (gr. k-2). Date not set. 4.99 (*0-614-19188-2*) Scholastic Inc.

Polly Pocket Cookbook. Shirley Albert. LC 96-13578. (Step into Reading Ser.: A Step 2 Book). (Illus.). (J). (ps-3). 1996. lib. bdg. 11.99 (*0-679-97484-9*) Random.

Polly Pocket Cookbook. Shirley Albert & Gail Herman. (Step into Reading Ser.: A Step 2 Book). (Illus.). (J). (gr. 1-3). 1996. pap. 3.99 (*0-679-87484-4*) Random.

Polly Popcan. Donald F. Lippert. (Illus.). 32p. (J). (ps). 1989. write for info. (*0-318-64640-4*) Pastel Pubns.

Polly Pratt Paper Dolls. Sheila Young. (Illus.). (J). (gr. k-3). 1993. pap. 4.95 (*0-486-27374-1*) Dover.

Polly Wolly Doodle: 24 Fun Songs for the Young & Young at Heart. Ed. by Dietrich Erbelding & Kathleen Skinner-Saffas. (Illus.). 121p. 1996. spiral bd. 15.95 (*1-58126-971-4*, PWD-Bk) Pocket Coach.

Polly Wolly Swings. D. Karp. 8p. 1993. pap. 2.95 (*0-7935-3026-1*, 00372231) H Leonard.

Pollyanna. Peterson. (J). Date not set. write for info. (*0-06-028226-6*) HarpC Child Bks.

Pollyanna. Peterson. 32p. (J). (gr. k-4). Date not set. pap. 4.95 (*0-06-443536-9*) HarpC Child Bks.

Pollyanna. Eleanor H. Porter. (J). 21.95 (*0-8488-1445-2*) Amereon Ltd.

Pollyanna. Eleanor H. Porter. (Andre Deutsch Classics). 224p. (J). (gr. 5-8). 1996. 9.95 (*0-233-99094-1*, Pub. by Andre Deutsch) Trafalgar.

Pollyanna. Eleanor H. Porter. (Young Reader's Christian Library). (Illus.). 224p. (J). (gr. 3-7). 1994. pap. text 1.39 (*1-55748-660-3*) Barbour Pub.

Pollyanna. Eleanor H. Porter. (Illus.). 256p. (YA). (gr. 5 up). 1996. pap. 4.99 (*0-14-036682-2*, PuffinBks) Peng Put Young Read.

Pollyanna. Eleanor H. Porter. Ed. by Joshua Hanft. (Great Illustrated Classics Ser.: Vol. 43). (Illus.). 240p. (J). (gr. 3-6). 1995. 9.95 (*0-86611-994-9*) Playmore Inc.

Pollyanna. Eleanor H. Porter. (J). 1997. pap. 2.95 (*0-8167-1468-1*) Troll Communs.

Pollyanna. abr. ed. Eleanor Porter. Ed. by Michael J. Marshall. (Core Classics Ser.: Vol. 4). (Illus.). 160p. (J). (gr. 4-6). 1997. pap. 5.95 (*1-890517-06-2*); lib. bdg. 10.95 (*1-890517-07-0*) Core Knowledge.

***Pollyanna.** large type ed. Eleanor H. Porter. (Large Print Heritage Ser.). 305p. (YA). (gr. 7-12). 2000. lib. bdg. 29.95 (*1-58118-069-1*, 23663) LRS.

Pollyanna Grows Up. Eleanor H. Porter. (J). 21.95 (*0-8488-1447-9*) Amereon Ltd.

Pollyanna Grows Up. Eleanor H. Porter. (Illus.). (YA). (gr. 5 up). 1996. pap. 4.99 (*0-14-036758-6*) Viking Penguin.

Pollyanna Herself. Ruth I. Dowell. (Illus.). 44p. (J). (ps-6). 1988. pap. 6.00 (*0-945842-08-2*) Pollyanna Prodns.

Pollyanna in the Briar Patch: The Community Arts Movement. Joseph Golden. LC 87-9906. (Illus.). 216p. (C). 1987. text 29.95 (*0-8156-2408-5*) Syracuse U Pr.

Pollyanna 'n Hollywood. Eleanor H. Porter. (J). 17.95 (*0-8488-1448-7*) Amereon Ltd.

Pollyanna's Debt of Honor. Eleanor H. Porter. (J). 15.95 (*0-8488-1446-0*) Amereon Ltd.

Pollyanna's Debt of Honor. Eleanor H. Porter. 1980. lib. bdg. 16.95 (*0-89968-253-7*, Lghtyr Pr) Buccaneer Bks.

Pollyanna's Debt of Honor. Harriet Smith. (J). 17.95 (*1-56723-091-1*) Yestermorrow.

Polly's Birth Book: Obstetrics for the Home. Polly Block. LC 96-68998. (Illus.). 563p. 1996. reprint ed. pap. 21.95 (*1-57636-019-9*) SunRise Pbl.

***Polly's Ghost.** large type ed. Abby Frucht. LC 00-28643. (Basic Ser.). 620p. 2000. write for info. (*0-7862-2564-5*) Thorndike Pr.

***Polly's Ghost: A Novel.** Abby Frucht. LC 99-35883. 368p. 2000. 24.00 (*0-684-83589-4*) Scribner.

Polly's Guide to Fitting & Costuming an Antique Doll for Those Who Would Like to Be Finished by Lunch. Polly Ford. (Polly's Guides to Costuming Ser.: Bklt. No. 1). (Illus.). 32p. 1997. reprint ed. pap. 6.50 (*0-9631893-4-4*) Sloane Pubns.

Polly's Guide to Fitting & Costuming Babies & Toddlers: Antique & Collectible Book, No. 2. Polly Ford. (Polly's Guides to Costuming Ser.). (Illus.). 32p. 1997. reprint ed. pap. 6.50 (*0-9631893-5-2*) Sloane Pubns.

Polly's Guides to French & German Dresses: Designing & Constructing for Girl Dolls 1880-1920. Polly Ford. (Polly's Guides to Costuming Ser.: No. 3). (Illus.). 32p. 1997. reprint ed. pap. 6.50 (*0-9631893-6-0*) Sloane Pubns.

Polly's Magic Games: A Child's View of Obsessive-Compulsive Disorder. Constance H. Foster. LC 93-74548. (Illus.). 24p. (J). 1995. pap. 12.95 (*0-9639070-8-5*) ebooksonthe.

Polly's Oats. Marc Simont. (Dell Young Yearling Ser.). 1994. 8.70 (*0-606-06675-6*, Pub. by Turtleback) Demco.

***Polly's Running Away Book.** Frances Thomas. 2001. mass mkt. (*0-385-72902-2*) BDD Bks Young Read.

Pollywog Is So Unique see Short Story Longs

Polnaya Istoriya Iskhoda (The Complete Story of the Exodus) Hagada-Skazaniye of Iskhode (The Passover Haggadah) B. Haskelevich. LC 90-60685. (RUS., Illus.). 192p. (Orig.). 1990. pap. text 5.00 (*1-878860-00-3*) Noviysvet.

Polnij Russkij Orthograficheskij Slovar' Ed. by P. A. Romashkevitch.Tr. of Complete Russian Orthographic Dictionary. 264p. reprint ed. pap. 10.00 (*0-317-29290-0*) Holy Trinity.

Polnisch. (Glossare Ser.). (GER.). 24p. 1997. pap. write for info. (*3-468-49108-5*); pap. write for info. (*3-468-49128-X*); pap. write for info. (*3-468-49148-4*) Langenscheidt.

Polnische Verfassung Vom 3. Mai 1791 Vor Dem Hintergrund der Europaischen Aufklarung. Reihalter Leisching. 99p. 1996. 29.95 (*3-631-30509-5*) P Lang Pubng.

Polnoe Sobranie Socinenij, 3 bande. Aleksandr S. Griboedova. (Akademiceskaja Biblioteka Russkich' Pisatelej-Vypusk' Ser.: No. 7). (GER., Illus.). 1257p. 1977. reprint ed. write for info. (*3-487-06081-7*) G Olms Pubs.

Polnoe Sobranie Socinenij, 24 bde. in 6 banden. Dmitrij S. Merezkovskij. (GER.). xii, 6043p. 1973. reprint ed. write for info. (*3-487-04808-6*) G Olms Pubs.

Polo. Susan Barrantes. LC 98-172791. (Illus.). 208p. 1998. 60.00 (*0-8478-5778-6*, Pub. by Rizzoli Intl) St Martin.

Polo. Jilly Cooper. LC 91-58983. 608p. 1992. 20.00 (*0-345-37557-2*) Ballantine Pub Grp.

Polo. Jilly Cooper. 768p. 1992. pap. 8.99 (*0-552-13552-6*) Bantam.

Polo: The Manual for Coach & Player. Ed. by Peter Cutino & Dennis Bledsoe. LC 75-20710. (Illus.). 225p. 1975. pap. 13.45 (*0-685-56491-6*) Swimming.

Polo a Way of Life. William G. Langdon, Jr. LC 93-206495. (Illus.). 219p. 1964. spiral bd. 29.95 (*1-883714-00-1*) Langdon Ent.

Polo Is a Four Letter Word. Fred Dailey. pap. 7.95 (*0-914916-77-7*) Ku Paa.

***Polo Is My Life.** 2000. audio compact disk 25.00 (*0-7435-0049-0*) S&S Audio.

Polo Is My Life. Hunter S. Thompson. 1998. write for info. (*0-679-40694-8*) McKay.

Polo Vision. rev. ed. Hugh Dawnay. 171p. 1990. 90.00 (*0-85131-539-9*, Pub. by J A Allen) Trafalgar.

Pologne dans l'Eglise Medievale. Jerzy Kloczowski. (Collected Studies: No. CS 417). 336p. 1993. 124.95 (*0-86078-359-6*, Pub. by Variorum) Ashgate Pub Co.

Polonais sans Peine: Polish for French Speakers. Assimil Staff. (FRE & POL.). 28.95 (*0-8288-4386-4*, F77660) Fr & Eur.

Polonaise: Stories. Anthony Bukoski. LC 98-26101. 192p. 1998. 19.95 (*0-87074-434-8*) SMU Press.

***Polonaises.** Frederic Chopin. (Music Scores Ser.). (Illus.). 1998. pap. text 7.98 (*963-8303-80-8*) Kone Music.

Polonia - i - Czlowiek, Ktory Zobaczyl Boga. rev. ed. Ansara Ali. Tr. by Magdalena Czyzycka from ENG. (POL., Illus.). 384p. 1995. 24.95 (*0-9636170-6-0*) Royal Rags.

Polonia & the Man Who Saw God. deluxe ed. Ansara Ali. Ed. by James J. McRae. LC 94-43178. (ENG & POL., Illus.). 384p. 1995. 45.00 incl. audio (*0-9636170-8-7*) Royal Rags.

Polonia & the Man Who Saw God. rev. ed. Ansara Ali. Ed. by James J. McRae. LC 94-43178. (Illus.). 384p. 1995. 24.95 (*0-9636170-5-2*) Royal Rags.

Polonians Listed in Baltimore City Directories, 1875-1895. Ed. by Thomas L. Hollowak. 94p. 1992. pap. 4.95 (*1-887124-03-9*, PG 104) Historyk Pr.

"Polovtsian Dances" & "In the Steppes of Central Asia" in Full Score. Borodin. 1998. pap. 9.95 (*0-486-29556-7*) Dover.

Polpop: Politics & Popular Culture in America. James Combs. LC 83-73574. 1984. 25.95 (*0-87972-276-2*) Bowling Green Univ Popular Press.

Polpop 2: Politics & Popular Culture in America Today. James Combs. LC 83-73574. 200p. (C). 1991. 39.95 (*0-87972-541-9*); pap. 19.95 (*0-87972-542-7*) Bowling Green Univ Popular Press.

Polska - Art, Architecture, Design, 1966-1970. Stefan Muthesius. (ENG, FRE, GER & POL.). lib. bdg. 39.95 (*3-7845-7612-5*, Pub. by Langewche) Abaris Bks.

Polska Walczaca W Oczaca CIA or "Freedom Fighters of Poland in the Eyes of CIA" (POL., Illus.). 325p. (Orig.). 1995. pap. 20.00 (*0-9654819-0-5*) A Tworkowski.

Polski Instytut Naukowy w Ameryce w Trzydziesta Rocznice, 1942-1972. Ed. by Damian Wandycz. 80p. 1974. 4.00 (*0-940962-35-7*) Polish Inst Art & Sci.

POLSSS - Policy for Sea Shipping Safety: Executive Summary. W. Walker et al. 73p. 1999. pap. 10.00 (*0-8330-2734-4*, MR1043-RE/VW) Rand Corp.

Poltava Museum of Art. K. G. Skalatskii. (Illus.). 1982. 103.00 (*0-7855-0811-2*) St Mut.

Poltava, 1709. Angus Konstam. (Campaign Ser.). 96p. 1994. pap. 14.95 (*1-85532-416-4*, 9533, Pub. by Osprey) Stackpole.

POLTCL IDLGY ENG1603 40. Intro. by Johann P. Sommerville. 254p. (C). 1989. pap. 45.00 (*0-582-49432-X*, 73617) Longman.

POLTCS RACE CLASS NATL20. Shula Marks & Stanley Trapido. LC 86-27554. (Illus.). (C). 1987. pap. text 33.50 (*0-582-64490-9*, 74623) Longman.

Poltergeist: A Study in Destructive Haunting. Colin Wilson. LC 92-38152. (Fate Presents Ser.). 448p. 1999. mass mkt. 5.95 (*0-87542-883-5*) Llewellyn Pubns.

Poltergeist: The Legacy. Kevin Anderson & Mitchell Kaufman. 224p. Date not set. pap. 12.95 (*1-58185-702-0*) Quadrillion Media.

P

Poltergeist Experience. D. Scott Rogo. 1990. 12.95 (*0-85030-887-9*, Pub. by Aqrn Pr) Harper SF.

Poltergeist Phenomenon: An Investigation into Psychic Disturbance. John Spencer & Ann Spencer. (Illus.). 311p. 1997. pap. 13.95 (*0-7472-5492-3*, Pub. by Headline Bk Pub) Trafalgar.

Poltergeists. Ed. by Anna Claybourne. (Paranormal Guides Ser.). (Illus.). 48p. (YA). (gr. 5 up). 1999. text 5.95 (*0-7460-3058-4*, Usborne) EDC.

Poltergeists? G. Harvey. (Paranormal Guides Ser.). (Illus.). 48p. (J). 1999. 13.95 (*1-58086-198-9*) EDC.

Poltergeists: An Annotated Bibliography of Works in English, Circa 1880-1975. Compiled by Michael Goss. LC 78-11492. 389p. 1979. 37.00 (*0-8108-1181-2*) Scarecrow.

Poltergeists: Opposing Viewpoints. 2nd ed. Adam Woog. (Opposing Viewpoints Juniors Ser.). (Illus.). 128p. (J). (gr. 5-12). 1995. lib. bdg. 22.45 (*1-56510-261-4*, 2614) Greenhaven.

Poltergeists & the Paranormal: Fact Beyond Fiction. Philip Stander & Paul Schmolling. LC 96-36205. 240p. 1999. pap. 12.95 (*1-56718-682-3*) Llewellyn Pubns.

Poltikverdrossenheit der Parteienstaat in der Historichen und Gegenwartigen Diskussion. (Prince Albert Studies: vol. 12). 1995. 60.00 (*3-598-21412-X*) K G Saur Verlag.

Poluprovodnikovye Sensory v Fiziko-Khimicheskikh Issledovaniiakh see Semiconductor Sensors in Physico-Chemical Studies

Polvo de Oro (Gold Dust) Geraldine McCaughrean. (SPA., Illus.). (YA). 1995. pap. 6.99 (*968-16-4720-3*, Pub. by Fondo) Continental Bk.

Polvos De Arroz see Rice Powder

Poly: New Speculative Writing. Ed. by Lee Ballentine. LC 87-19827. (Illus.). 336p. 1989. 59.95 (*0-938075-08-X*); pap. 24.95 (*0-938075-05-5*) Ocean View Bks.

***Poly Adp-Ribosylation Reactions: From DNA Damage & Stress Signalling to Cell Death.** Ed. by Gilbert De Murcia & Sydney Shall. (Illus.). 240p. 2000. text 125.00 (*0-19-850633-3*) OUP.

Poly Rhythms for the Drum Set. Peter Magadini. 60p. (Orig.). 1995. pap. text 21.95 (*0-89724-821-X*, EL9591CD) Wrner Bros.

Poly (Tetrahydrofuran) P. Dreyfuss. (Polymer Monographs: Vol. 8). xiv, 306p. 1982. text 274.00 (*0-677-03330-3*) Gordon & Breach.

Poly-X-Amino Acids: Protein Models for Conformational Studies. Ed. by Gerald D. Fasman. LC 66-27704. (Biological Macromolecules Ser.: No. 1). (Illus.). 780p. reprint ed. pap. 200.00 (*0-7837-0891-2*, 204119700019) Bks Demand.

Polya, Krutetskii & the Restaurant Problem. M. A. Clements & Nerida F. Ellerton. 93p. (C). 1991. pap. 66.00 (*0-7300-1253-0*, ECT405, Pub. by Deakin Univ) St Mut.

Polya Picture Album. Ed. by Gerald Alexanderson. 140p. 1987. 29.50 (*0-8176-3352-9*) Birkhauser.

Polyacetal Resins. Marshall Sittig. LC 63-12717. (Illus.). 159p. reprint ed. pap. 49.30 (*0-608-18161-7*, 203286200081) Bks Demand.

Polyacetylene & Polyarylenes: Synthesis & Conductive Properties, Vol.10. I. V. Krivoshei. (Polymer Monographs). 402p. 1991. text 283.00 (*2-88124-756-3*) Gordon & Breach.

Polyaeni Indices, Pars Altera: Indices Excerptarum Polyaeni Leonisque Imperatoris Strategematum. Ed. by Francisco M. Garcia & Alfredo R. Lopez. (Alpha-Omega, Reihe A Ser.: Bd. CXXVIII/2). (GER.). viii, 174p. 1992. write for info. (*3-487-09541-6*) G Olms Pubs.

Polyaeni Indices, Pars Prior: Index Polyaeni Strategematum. Ed. by Francisco M. Garcia & Alfredo R. Lopez. (Alpha-Omega, Reihe A Ser.: Bd. CXXVIII). (GER.). vi, 404p. 1993. write for info. (*3-487-09639-0*) G Olms Pubs.

Polyaenus: Strategems of War, 2 vols., Vol. I. rev. ed. Polyaenus. Ed. & Tr. by Peter Krentz & Everett L. Wheeler from GEC. (GRE.). xxxil, 549p. (Orig.). (C). 1994. pap. text 22.50 (*0-89005-503-3*) Ares.

Polyaenus: Strategems of War, 2 vols., Vol. II. rev. ed. Ed. by P. Krentz & E. Wheeler. 400p. (Orig.). (C). 1992. pap. 22.50 (*0-89005-504-1*) Ares.

Polyaldehydes: Papers Presented at the...Winter Meeting of the American Chemical Society. Symposium on Polymerization of Aldehydes & Structu. Ed. by Otto Vogl. LC 67-18891. 147p. reprint ed. pap. 45.60 (*0-608-16982-X*, 202710800054) Bks Demand.

***Polyalterity: New Cyberworks by Ron Hutt, Joseph Nechvatal & Jan Piribeck.** Sarah Maline et al. (Illus.). 24p. 2000. pap. write for info. (*0-9677432-0-6*) UMF Art Gallery.

Polyamic Acids & Polyimides Synthesis Transformations Structures. M. I. Bessonov. 1993. lib. bdg. 219.00 (*0-8493-6704-2*, TP1180) CRC Pr.

Polyamine-Chelated Alkali Metal Compounds: A Symposium Co-Sponsored by the Division of Polymer Chemistry & the Organometallic Subdivision of the Division of Inorganic Chemistry at the 164th Meeting of the American Chemical Society, New York, NY, August 28, 1972. Ed. by Arthur W. Langer. LC 74-75334. (Advances in Chemistry Ser.: No. 130). (Illus.). 302p. 1974. reprint ed. pap. 93.70 (*0-608-06775-X*, 206697200009) Bks Demand.

Polyamine Protocols. Ed. by David M. L. Morgan. LC 97-37499. (Methods in Molecular Biology Ser.: Vol. 79). (Illus.). 208p. 1997. 79.50 (*0-89603-448-8*) Humana.

Polyamines. Ed. by Herbert Tabor & Celia W. Tabor. (Methods in Enzymology Ser.: Vol. 94). 1983. text 188.00 (*0-12-181994-9*) Acad Pr.

Polyamines: Basic & Clinical Aspects: Proceedings of a Satellite Symposium of the 3rd International Congress on Cell Biology, Japan, 1984. Ed. by K. Imahori et al. 544p. 1985. lib. bdg. 145.00 (*90-6764-042-5*, Pub. by VSP) Coronet Bks.

Polyamines & Ethylene: Biochemistry, Physiology & Interactions. Ed. by Héctor E. Flores et al. LC 90-84611. (Current Topics in Plant Physiology: an American Society of Plant Physiologists Ser.: Vol. 5). (Illus.). 300p. (Orig.). 1990. pap. 25.00 (*0-943088-19-4*) Am Soc of Plan.

Polyamines As Biochemical Markers of Normal & Malignant Growth. fac. ed. Diane H. Russell & Brian G. Durie. LC 75-43340. (Progress in Cancer Research & Therapy Ser.: No. 8). (Illus.). 192p. pap. 59.60 (*0-7837-7352-8*, 204716100005) Bks Demand.

Polyamines in Biology & Medicine. Ed. by David R. Morris & Laurence J. Marton. LC 81-9757. (Biochemistry of Disease Ser.: No. 8). 477p. reprint ed. pap. 147.90 (*0-7837-3362-3*, 204332000008) Bks Demand.

Polyamines in Biomedical Research. Ed. by Joseph M. Gaugas. LC 79-40651. 490p. reprint ed. pap. 151.90 (*0-7837-0193-4*, 204048900017) Bks Demand.

Polyamines in Cancer: Basic Mechanisms & Clinical Approaches. Kenji Nishioka. LC 96-15935. (Medical Intelligence Unit Ser.). 278p. 1996. 99.00 (*1-57059-346-9*) Landes Bioscience.

Polyamines in Plants. Ed. by Arthur W. Galston & Terence A. Smith. (Advances in Agricultural Biotechnology Ser.). 1986. text 153.00 (*90-247-3245-X*) Kluwer Academic.

Polyamino Acids, Polypeptides & Proteins: Proceedings of an International Symposium Held at the University of Wisconsin, 1961. Ed. by Mark A. Stahmann. LC 62-12893. 416p. reprint ed. pap. 129.00 (*0-608-13919-X*, 202114900021) Bks Demand.

Polyamory: The New Love Without Limits. 2nd rev. ed. Deborah M. Anapol. LC 91-77439. 182p. 1997. pap. 16.00 (*1-880789-08-6*) IntiNet Res Ctr.

Polyanalytic Functions. M. B. Balk. (Mathematical Research Ser.: Vol. 63). 1991. pap. text 73.45 (*3-05-501292-5*, Pub. by Akademie Verlag) Wiley.

Polyandry in Ancient India. Sarva D. Singh. (C). 1987. 21.50 (*81-208-0487-2*, Pub. by Motilal Bnarsidass) S Asia.

Polyandry in India. Manis K. Raha. (C). 1987. 61.00 (*81-212-0105-5*, Pub. by Gian Publng Hse) S Asia.

Polyanna. Porter. (Classics Library). pap. 3.95 (*1-85326-145-9*, 1459WW, Pub. by Wrdsworth Edits) NTC Contemp Pub Co.

Polyanna's New Rules of Order. Julie A. Waterman. 7p. (Orig.). 1982. pap. 1.25 (*0-943334-02-0*) Carmonelle Pubns.

Polyarchy: Participation & Opposition. Robert A. Dahl. LC 70-140534. 1971. pap. 17.00 (*0-300-01565-8*, Y254) Yale U Pr.

Polyarchy: The Political Theory of Robert A. Dahl. Donald J. Lee. LC 91-32764. (Political Theory & Political Philosophy Ser.). 224p. 1991. text 10.00 (*0-8153-0202-9*) Garland.

Polybenzine Hydrocarbons & Their Derivatives see Rodd's Chemistry of Carbon Compounds

Polybii, Vol. I. Ed. by Dindorf et al. (GRE.). 1993. reprint ed. 57.50 (*3-519-01715-6*, T1715, Pub. by B G Teubner) U of Mich Pr.

Polybii, Vol. II. Ed. by Dindorf et al. (GRE.). 1995. reprint ed. 69.50 (*3-519-01716-4*, T1716, Pub. by B G Teubner) U of Mich Pr.

Polybii, Vol. III. Ed. by Dindorf et al. (GRE.). 1995. reprint ed. 62.50 (*3-519-01717-2*, T1717, Pub. by B G Teubner) U of Mich Pr.

Polybii, Vol. IV. Ed. by Dindorf et al. (GRE.). 1995. reprint ed. 79.50 (*3-519-01718-0*, T1718, Pub. by B G Teubner) U of Mich Pr.

Polybii Vol. V: Appendix: Indices et Historiarum Conspectus. Ed. by Dindorf et al. (GRE.). 1987. reprint ed. 43.50 (*3-519-01719-9*, T1719, Pub. by B G Teubner) U of Mich Pr.

Polybius. F. M. Walbank. 1990. pap. 16.95 (*0-520-06981-1*, Pub. by U CA Pr) Cal Prin Full Svc.

Polybius on Roman Imperialism. Polybius. Ed. by Alvin H. Bernstein. Tr. by E. S. Shuckburgh. LC 79-66479. 540p. (Orig.). 1980. pap. text 10.95 (*0-89526-902-3*) Regnery Pub.

Polybrominated Biphenyls. Ed. by World Health Organization Staff. (Environmental Health Criteria Ser.: No. 152). (ENG, FRE & SPA.). 577p. 1994. pap. text 103.00 (*92-4-157152-7*, 1160152) World Health.

Polybrominated Biphenyls (PBBS) Health & Safety Guide. (Health & Safety Guides Ser.: No. 83). 36p. 1993. pap. text 5.00 (*92-4-151083-8*, 1860083) World Health.

Polycarbonate-Workshop Amsterdam, September 1985. Ed. by L. W. Henderson et al. (Journal: Blood Purification: Vol. 4, No. 1-3, 1986). (Illus.). 184p. 1986. pap. 128.00 (*3-8055-4352-2*) S Karger.

Polycarp & John: The Harris Fragments & Their Challenge to the Literary Traditions. Frederick W. Weidmann. LC 98-50200. (Christianity & Judaism in Antiquity Ser.: No. 12). 244p. 1999. 35.00 (*0-268-03851-1*) U of Notre Dame Pr.

***Polycarp & the Second Century Church.** Stephen Long. 112p. 2000. pap. 8.99 (*0-9629550-3-5*) Word in Action.

Polycentric Games & Institutions: Readings from the Workshop in Political Theory & Policy Analysis. Michael McGinnis. (Institutional Analysis Ser.). 448p. 1999. text 69.50 (*0-472-09714-8*, 09714); pap. text 24.95 (*0-472-06714-1*, 06714) U of Mich Pr.

Polycentric Governance & Development: Readings from the Workshop in Political Theory & Policy Analysis. Michael McGinnis. LC 99-24422. 448p. 1999. text 69.50 (*0-472-11039-X*, 11039); pap. text 24.95 (*0-472-08623-5*, 08623) U of Mich Pr.

***Polycentricity: The Multiple Scenes of Law.** Ed. by Ari Hirvonen. LC 98-24899. (Law & Social Theory Ser.). 250p. 1998. pap. 24.95 (*0-7453-1363-9*) Pluto GBR.

Polycentricity: The Multiple Scenes of Law. Ari Hirvonen. LC 98-24899. (Law & Social Theory Ser.). 1998. write for info. (*0-7453-1368-X*, Pub. by Pluto GBR) Stylus Pub VA.

Polycentricity & Local Public Economies: Readings from the Workshop in Political Theory & Policy Analysis. Ed. by Michael McGinnis. LC 99-48673. 424p. 1999. text 69.50 (*0-472-11038-1*, 11038) U of Mich Pr.

Polycentricity & Local Public Economies: Readings from the Workshop in Political Theory & Policy Analysis. Ed. by Michael McGinnis. LC 99-48673. 424p. 1999. pap. text 24.95 (*0-472-08622-7*, 08622) U of Mich Pr.

Polycentrism: Growing Dissidence in the Communist Bloc. Ed. by Edward M. Bennett. LC 67-2568. 69p. reprint ed. pap. 30.00 (*0-608-18352-0*, 203303300083) Bks Demand.

Polychaeta Errantia of Antarctica. Ed. by O. Hartman. LC 64-60091. (Antarctic Research Ser.: Vol. 3). (Illus.). 131p. 1964. 12.00 (*0-87590-103-4*) Am Geophysical.

Polychaeta from Hawaii. M. Holly. (BMB Ser.: No. 129). 1974. reprint ed. pap. 25.00 (*0-527-02235-7*) Periodicals Srv.

Polychaeta Myzostomidae & Sedentaria of Antarctica. Ed. by O. Hartman. LC 66-61601. (Antarctic Research Ser.: Vol. 7). (Illus.). 158p. 1966. 13.00 (*0-87590-107-7*) Am Geophysical.

Polychaete Worms, Definitions & Keys to the Orders, Families & Genera. Kristian Fauchald. (Science Ser.: No. 28). (Illus.). 188p. 1977. 15.00 (*0-938644-08-4*) Nat Hist Mus.

Polychaetes: British Phyllodocoideans, Typhloscolecoideans & Tomopteroideans. F. Pleijel & R. P. Dales. (Synopses of the British Fauna Ser.: No. 45). (Illus.). 210p. 1991. pap. 65.00 (*90-73348-12-9*, Pub. by Backhuys Pubs) Balogh.

Polychaetes: Interstitial Families. W. Westheide. (Synopses of the British Fauna Ser.: No. 44). (Illus.). 160p. 1990. pap. 65.00 (*90-73348-08-0*, Pub. by Backhuys Pubs) Balogh.

Polychlorierte Biphenyle (PCB) Im Lebensraum Wasser (Aufnahme und Anreicherung Durch Organismen) - Probleme der Weitergabe in der Nahrungspyramide) Ein Literaturbericht Fuer die Jahre, 1972-1979. R. Faulkner et al. (Advances in Limnology Ser.: Vol. 17). (GER., Illus.). 74p. 1982. pap. text 25.00 (*3-510-47015-X*, Pub. by E Schweizerbartsche) Balogh.

Polychlorinated Biphenyls & Polybrominated Biphenyls. IARC Working Group on Evaluation of Carcinogenic R. LC RC0268.6.I54. (IARC Monographs on the Evaluation of the Carcinogenic Risk of Chemicals to Humans: No. 18). 140p. 1978. reprint ed. pap. 43.40 (*0-608-04398-2*, 206517900001) Bks Demand.

Polychlorinated Biphenyls & Terphenyls. 2nd ed. (Environmental Health Criteria Ser.: No. 140). (ENG, FRE & SPA.). 682p. 1993. pap. text 110.00 (*92-4-157140-3*, 1160140) World Health.

Polychlorinated Biphenyls (PCBS) & Polychlorinated Terphenyls (PCTS) Health & Safety Guide. (Health & Safety Guides Ser.: No. 68). 52p. 1992. pap. text 5.00 (*92-4-151068-4*, 1860068) World Health.

Polychlorinated Biphinyls (PCBS) Mammalian & Environmental Toxicology. S. Safe. (Environmental Toxin Ser.: Vol. 1). 160p. 1987. 101.95 (*0-387-15550-3*) Spr-Verlag.

Polychlorinated Dibenzo-Paradioxins & Dibenzofurans. (Environmental Health Criteria Ser.: No. 88). 409p. 1990. pap. text 63.00 (*92-4-154288-8*, 1160088) World Health.

Polychromatic Decoration As Applied to Buildings in the Medieval Styles see Victorian Sourcebook of Medieval Decoration: With 166 Full-Color Designs

Polychromatic Layering Technique. Ludwig A. Rinn. (Illus.). 155p. 1990. text 88.00 (*0-86715-225-7*) Quint Pub Co.

Polychromatic Screen Printing. rev. ed. Joy Stocksdale. (Illus.). 128p. 1991. reprint ed. pap. 12.95 (*0-9613331-0-3*) Oreg Street Pr.

Polychrome Historical Haggadah. Meir Ai-Nai-Yim. (Illus.). 1974. 40.00 (*0-686-10317-3*) J Freedman Liturgy.

Polychronicon Ranulphi Higden, Monachi Cestrenis, Together with the English Translation of John of Trevisa & of an Unknown Writer in the 15th Century, 9 vols. Ed. by Churchill Babington & Joseph R. Lumby. (Rolls Ser.: No. 41). 1974. reprint ed. 630.00 (*0-8115-1100-6*) Periodicals Srv.

***Polycrystalline Metal & Magnetic Thin Filming -- 2000: Materials Research Society Symposium Proceedings, Vol. 615.** Ed. by L. Gignac et al. 2000. text 73.00 (*1-55899-523-4*) Materials Res.

Polycrystalline Metal & Magnetic Thin Films Vol. 562: Materials Research Society Symposium Proceedings. Ed. by K. P. Rodbell et al. LC 99-49143. 348p. 1999. text 69.00 (*1-55899-469-6*) Materials Res.

Polycrystalline Semiconductors. Ed. by G. C. Harbeke. (Solid-State Sciences Ser.: Vol. 57). (Illus.). viii, 245p. 1985. 68.95 (*0-387-15143-5*) Spr-Verlag.

***Polycrystalline Semiconductors V: Bulk Materials, Thin Films & Devices.** Ed. by J. H. Werner et al. (Solid State Phenomena Ser.: 67-68). (Illus.). 616p. (C). 1999. 182.00 (*3-908450-43-8*, Pub. by Scitec Pubns) Enfield Pubs NH.

Polycrystalline Semiconductors IV: Physics, Chemistry & Technology. Ed. by S. Pizzini et al. (Solid State Phenomena Ser.: Vols. 51 & 52). 656p. 1996. 200.00 (*3-908450-19-5*, Pub. by Scitec Pubns) Enfield Pubs NH.

Polycrystalline Semiconductors Grain Boundaries & Interfaces. H. J. Moller et al. (Proceedings in Physics Ser.: Vol. 35). (Illus.). 380p. 1989. 85.95 (*0-387-50887-2*) Spr-Verlag.

Polycrystalline Semiconductors III: Physics & Technology. H. P. Strunk et al. Ed. by B. Fortin & O. Bonnaud. (Solid State Phenomena Ser.: Vols. 37-8). (Illus.). (C). 1994. text 200.00 (*3-908450-04-7*, Pub. by Trans T Pub) Enfield Pubs NH.

Polycrystalline Semiconductors II: Proceedings of the Second International Workshop Schwabisch-Hall, Fed. Republic of Germany July 30 - August 3, 1990. Ed. by J. H. Werner & H. P. Strunk. (Proceedings in Physics Ser.: Vol. 54). (Illus.). xvi, 547p. 1991. 93.00 (*0-387-53613-2*) Spr-Verlag.

Polycrystalline Silicon for Integrated Circuit Applications. Ted Kamins. (C). 1988. reprint ed. text 152.50 (*0-89838-259-9*) Kluwer Academic.

Polycrystalline Silicon for Integrated Circuit Applications. 2nd ed. Theodore I. Kamins. LC 98-27506. 378p. 1998. 115.00 (*0-7923-8224-2*) Kluwer Academic.

Polycrystalline Thin Films: Structure, Texture, Properties & Applications II. Ed. by Harold J. Frost et al. (MRS Symposium Proceedings Ser.: Vol. 403). 753p. 1996. 65.00 (*1-55899-306-1*, 403) Materials Res.

Polycrystalline Thin Films - Structure, Texture, Properties & Applications III: Materials Research Society Symposium Proceedings, Vol. 472. Ed. by J. Im et al. LC 97-32265. 474p. 1997. text 75.00 (*1-55899-376-2*) Materials Res.

Polycyclic Aromatic Hydrocarbon Carcinogenesis: Structure-Activity Relationships, Vol. I. Ed. by Shen K. Yang & B. D. Silverman. 256p. 1988. 129.00 (*0-8493-6730-1*, RC268, CRC Reprint) Franklin.

Polycyclic Aromatic Hydrocarbon Carcinogenesis: Structure-Activity Relationships, Vol. II. Ed. by Shen K. Yang & B. D. Silverman. 256p. 1988. 128.00 (*0-8493-6731-X*, CRC Reprint) Franklin.

Polycyclic Aromatic Hydrocarbon Structure Index. Lane C. Sander. 108p. 1998. per. 9.00 (*0-16-054771-7*) USGPO.

Polycyclic Aromatic Hydrocarbons. Ronald G. Harvey. LC 96-19742. 300p. 1996. write for info. (*1-56081-686-4*, Wiley-VCH) Wiley.

Polycyclic Aromatic Hydrocarbons. Ronald G. Harvey. LC 96-19742. 667p. 1997. 150.00 (*0-471-18608-2*) Wiley.

Polycyclic Aromatic Hydrocarbons: Index of New Information & Research Reference Book. Thomas E. Komarr. 181p. 1997. 47.50 (*0-7883-1246-4*); pap. 44.50 (*0-7883-1247-2*) ABBE Pubs Assn.

Polycyclic Aromatic Hydrocarbons & Astrophysics. Ed. by A. Leger et al. 1986. text 184.00 (*90-277-2361-3*) Kluwer Academic.

Polycyclic Aromatic Hydrocarbons, Distribution, Exposure & Effects: A Symposium. Otto Hutzinger & Roland W. Frei. (Toxicology & Environmental Chemistry Ser.: Vol. 16, No. 4). 80p. 1988. pap. text 261.00 (*0-677-25650-7*) Gordon & Breach.

Polycyclic Aromatic Hydrocarbons in Water Systems. Ruven et al. 200p. 1981. 117.00 (*0-8493-6255-5*, QD341, CRC Reprint) Franklin.

Polycyclic Compounds Excluding Steroids see Rodd's Chemistry of Carbon Compounds

Polycyclic Hydrocarbons & Carcinogenesis. Ed. by Ronald G. Harvey. LC 85-13384. (ACS Symposium Ser.: Vol. 283). 416p. 1985. reprint ed. pap. 129.00 (*0-608-03912-8*, 206435900009) Bks Demand.

Polycyclic Hydrocarbons & Carcinogens. Ronald G. Harvey. (ACS Symposium Ser.: No. 283). 406p. 1985. lib. bdg. 82.95 (*0-8412-0924-3*) Am Chemical.

Polycystic Kidney Disease. Ed. by M. H. Breuning et al. (Contributions to Nephrology Ser.: Vol. 97). (Illus.). vi, 142p. 1992. 49.75 (*3-8055-5586-5*) S Karger.

Polycystic Kidney Disease. Ed. by Michael L. Watson & Vicente E. Torres. LC 95-31363. (Oxford Clinical Nephrology Ser.). (Illus.). 606p. (C). 1996. text 125.00 (*0-19-262578-0*) OUP.

Polycystic Ovarian Disease. W. Futterweit. (Clinical Perspectives in Obstetrics & Gynecology Ser.). (Illus.). 155p. 1984. 87.00 (*0-387-90981-8*) Spr-Verlag.

Polycystic Ovaries: A Disorder or a Symptom?, Vol. 3. Ed. by Robert W. Shaw. (Advances in Reproductive Endocrinology Ser.). (Illus.). 222p. (C). 1991. 68.00 (*1-85070-343-4*) Prthnon Pub.

***Polycystic Ovary Syndrome.** Gabor Kovacs. LC 99-52561. 2000. write for info. (*0-521-66073-4*) Cambridge U Pr.

Polycystic Ovary Syndrome: Proceedings of the Symposium, Sponsored by Serono Symposia U S A, Inc., Held in Boston, Massachusetts, May 18-21, 1995. Ed. by R. Jeffrey Chang. LC 96-11919. 392p. 1996. 135.00 (*0-387-94741-8*) Spr-Verlag.

Polycythemia Vera & the Myleoproliferative Disorders. Louis R. Wasserman et al. LC 94-1680. (Illus.). 416p. 1994. text. write for info. (*0-7216-4213-6*, W B Saunders Co) Harcrt Hlth Sci Grp.

Polydiacetylenes. Ed. by H. J. Cantow. (Advances in Polymer Science Ser.: Fortschritte der Hochpolymerenforschung: Vol. 63). (Illus.). 160p. 1984. 79.95 (*0-387-13414-X*) Spr-Verlag.

Polydiacetylenes: Synthesis, Structure & Electronic Properties. Ed. by D. M. Bloor & R. R. Chance. 1985. text 233.00 (*90-247-3251-4*) Kluwer Academic.

Polydiagnostic Approach in Psychiatry. Ed. by G. Lenz & G. Pakesch. (Journal: Psychopathology: Vol. 19, No. 5, 1986). (Illus.). 76p. 1987. pap. 38.50 (*3-8055-4540-1*) S Karger.

An Asterisk (*) at the beginning of an entry indicates that the title is appearing for the first time.

Polydore Vergil's English History, from an Early Translation. Polydorus Vergilius. Ed. by Henry Ellis. (Camden Society, London. Publications, First Ser.: No. 36). reprint ed. 85.00 (*0-404-50136-2*) AMS Pr.

Polydoxy: Explorations in a Philosophy of Liberal Religion. Alvin J. Reines. LC 87-2259. 219p. 1987. 32.95 (*0-87975-399-4*) Prometheus Bks.

Polyelectrolyte Gels: Properties, Preparation, & Applications. Ed. by Ronald S. Harland & Robert K. Prud'homme. LC 91-37617. (ACS Symposium Ser.: No. 480). (Illus.). 450p. 1992. text 89.00 (*0-8412-2176-6*, Pub. by Am Chemical) OUP.

Polyelectrolytes. Fumio Oosawa. LC 70-134786. (Illus.). 167p. reprint ed. pap. 51.80 (*0-608-30542-1*, 205501000007) Bks Demand.

Polyelectrolytes: Formation, Characterization & Application. B. Philipp et al. LC 94-26915. 1994. 99.50 (*1-56990-127-9*) Hanser-Gardner.

Polyelectrolytes: Science & Technology. Masanori Hara. LC 90-32254. (Illus.). 416p. 1992. text 199.00 (*0-8247-8759-5*) Dekker.

Polyelectrolytes for Water & Wastewater Treatment. Ed. by William L. Schwoyer. 288p. 1981. 163.00 (*0-8493-5439-0*, TD455, CRC Reprint) Franklin.

Polyester: Fifty Years of Achievement, Tomorrow's Ideas & Profit. Ed. by D. Brunnschweiler & John W. Hearle. (C). 1993. 135.00 (*1-870812-50-6*, Pub. by Textile Inst) St Mut.

Polyester: The Indestructible Fashion. Matthew B. Smith. LC 98-84543. (Illus.). 160p. 1998. pap. 29.95 (*0-7643-0424-0*) Schiffer.

Polyester Grandpa. Martha Freeman. LC 98-15815. 160p. (J). (gr. 3-7). 1998. 15.95 (*0-8234-1398-5*) Holiday.

Polyester Molding Compounds. Burns. (Plastics Engineering Ser.: Vol. 2). (Illus.). 352p. 1982. text 160.00 (*0-8247-1280-3*) Dekker.

Polyester Prince: The Rise of Dhirubhai Ambani. Hamish McDonald. (Illus.). 296p. 1999. pap. 15.95 (*1-86448-468-3*, Pub. by Allen & Unwin Pty) IPG Chicago.

Polyester Textiles. Shirley Inst. Staff. (C). 1988. 400.00 (*0-7855-6078-5*, Pub. by British Textile Tech) St Mut.

Polyesters to Polypeptide Synthesis see Encyclopedia of Polymer Science & Engineering

Polyether Antibiotics Vol. 1: Naturally Occurring Acid Ionophores. Ed. by John W. Westley. LC 82-10004. (Illus.). 487p. reprint ed. pap. 151.00 (*0-608-06266-9*, 206659500001) Bks Demand.

Polyether Antibiotics Vol. 2: Naturally Occurring Acid Ionophores: Chemistry. J. Westley. (Illus.). 432p. 1983. text 165.00 (*0-8247-1888-7*) Dekker.

Polyethnicity & National Unity in World History. William H. McNeill. 1986. pap. 10.95 (*0-8020-6643-7*) U of Toronto Pr.

Polyethnicity & National Unity in World History. William H. McNeill. LC 88-128714. (Donald G. Creighton Lectures: No. 1985). 97p. reprint ed. pap. 30.10 (*0-7837-1791-1*, 204199200001) Bks Demand.

Polyethnicity in India & Canada: Possibilities for Exploration. G. Palanithural. LC 97-906773. 120p. 1997. pap. 90.00 (*81-7533-039-2*, Pub. by Print Hse) St Mut.

Polyethylene Glycol: Chemistry & Biological Applications. J. Milton Harris et al. LC 97-42150. (ACS Symposium Ser.: Vol. 680). 500p. 1997. text 134.95 (*0-8412-3537-6*, Pub. by Am Chemical) OUP.

Poly(ethylene Glycol) Chemistry: Biotechnical & Biomedical Applications. J. M. Harris. (Topics in Applied Chemistry Ser.). (Illus.). 408p. (C). 1992. text 110.00 (*0-306-44078-4*, Kluwer Plenum) Kluwer Academic.

Polyeucte. Corneille. (FRE.). (C). pap. 7.95 (*0-8442-1985-1*, VF1985-1) NTC Contemp Pub Co.

Polyeucte. Pierre Corneille. 1965. pap. 5.95 (*0-7859-0608-8*, FC1728) Fr & Eur.

PolyForm: WebForms Construction Kit & Booklet. John R. Boynton. (Illus.). 150p. (Orig.). 1996. pap. 149.95 (*1-56592-182-8*) Thomson Learn.

Polyform, Inc. A Computerized Decision Case in Cost & Managerial Accounting. Kirk Tennant & Galen Rupp. (C). 1991. text, teacher ed. 11.56 (*0-395-57765-9*) HM.

Polyfunctional Cytokines: IL-6 & LIF. Ed. by Gregory R. Bock & Kate Widdows. LC 92-5732. (CIBA Foundation Symposium Ser.: Vol. 167). 290p. 1992. 128.00 (*0-471-93439-9*) Wiley.

Polyfunctionality of Hemopoietic Regulators Suppl. 1: The Metcalf Forum, Vol. 12. Ed. by Martin J. Murphy, Jr. LC 94-73349. (Illus.). 326p. (C). 1994. text 69.00 (*1-880854-19-8*) AlphaMed Pr.

Polyfunctionality of Hemopoietic Regulators Suppl. 2: The Metcalf Forum, Vol. 12. Ed. by Martin J. Murphy, Jr. LC 94-73349. (Illus.). 326p. (C). 1994. pap. text 49.00 (*1-880854-20-1*) AlphaMed Pr.

Polygamist. Ndabaningi Sithole. LC 79-169156. 160p. 1972. 24.95 (*0-89388-036-1*) Okpaku Communications.

Polygamous Families in Contemporary Society. Irwin Altman & Joseph Ginat. (Illus.). 527p. (C). 1996. pap. text 27.95 (*0-521-56731-9*) Cambridge U Pr.

Polygamous Families in Contemporary Society. Irwin Altman & Joseph Ginat. (Illus.). 527p. (C). 1996. text 69.95 (*0-521-56169-8*) Cambridge U Pr.

Polygamy & Purdah: Women & Society among Rajputs. Ed. by Varsha Joshi. (C). 1995. 28.00 (*81-7033-275-3*, Pub. by Rawat Pubns) S Asia.

Polygamy in Islamic Law. Jamal Badawi. 20p. 1994. pap. 3.00 (*1-56744-191-2*) Kazi Pubns.

Polygamy in Mainstream America. Michelle Saka El. 100p. (Orig.). 1992. pap. text 7.00 (*0-9628788-2-0*) Alkebu-Lan & Assocs.

Polygamy, Prostitutes & Death: The Hellenistics Dynasties. Ed. by Daniel Ogden. 1999. 49.50 (*0-7156-2930-1*, Pub. by Classical Pr) David Brown.

Polygamy Reconsidered: African Plural Marriage & the Christian Churches. Eugene Hillman. LC 74-19967. 276p. reprint ed. pap. 85.60 (*0-8357-8991-8*, 203352600086) Bks Demand.

Polygamy Was Better Than Monotony: To My Grandfathers & Their Plural Wives. Paul Bailey. LC 72-83538. (Illus.). 24.95 (*0-87026-027-8*) Westernlore.

Polyglot Dictionary of Plant Names. (ARM, ENG, FRE, GER & LAT.). 180p. 1981. 29.95 (*0-8288-0065-0*, M15342) Fr & Eur.

Polyglot of Foreign Proverbs. Henry G. Bohn. LC 68-55796. (Bohn's Antiquarian Library). reprint ed. 27.50 (*0-404-50004-8*) AMS Pr.

Polygnotos & Vase Painting in Classical Athens. Susan B. Matheson. LC 95-9683. (Studies in Classics). 558p. 1995. 60.00 (*0-299-13870-4*) U of Wis Pr.

***Polygon Wood: Ypres.** Peter Taylor. (Battleground Europe Ser.). 1998. pap. text 16.95 (*0-85052-606-X*, Pub. by Leo Cooper) Trans-Atl Phila.

Polygonal Interface Problems. Serge Nicaise. LC 93-30137. (Methoden und Verfahren der Mathematischen Physik Ser.: Bd. 39). (Illus.). 250p. 1993. 49.00 (*3-631-46380-4*) P Lang Pubng.

Polygons see Discovering Shapes

Polygot Dictionary of Musical Terms. 2nd ed. Horst Leuchtmann. (ENG, FRE, GER, ITA & POL.). 805p. 1980. 195.00 (*0-8288-2186-0*, M9436) Fr & Eur.

Polygraph: Issues & Answers. 1996. 10.00 (*0-317-01468-4*) Am Polygraph.

Polygraph Defeats: How to Tell the "Truth" to a "Lie Detector" John J. Williams & Clifford Wiliams. 30p. (Orig.). 1997. pap. 25.00 (*0-934274-12-6*) Consumertronics.

Polygraph Dictionary for the Graphic Arts: English - German - Italian - French. Michael Nitsche. 642p. (C). 128.00 (*0-911126-09-0*, 1-245) Perfect Graphic.

Polygraph Dictionary of the Graphic Arts. Michael Nitsche. (ENG & GER.). 327p. 1987. 125.00 (*0-8288-7916-8*) Fr & Eur.

Polygraph Dictionary of the Graphic Arts. Michael Nitsche & Leonhard Trondt. (ENG & GER.). 334p. 1987. 95.00 (*0-8288-0691-8*, M 15136) Fr & Eur.

Polygraph Dictionary of the Graphic Arts: German-English, English-German. 6th rev. ed. Michael Nitsche & Leonhard Trondt. 339p. 1995. 65.00 (*0-911126-08-2*, 1-158) Perfect Graphic.

Polygraph Examinations. 1995. lib. bdg. 259.95 (*0-8490-7400-2*) Gordon Pr.

Polygraph Profession. Norman Ansley & Stanley Abrams. LC HV8078.A6. 56p. reprint ed. pap. 30.00 (*0-608-12943-7*, 202468100038) Bks Demand.

***Polygraph Secrets.** unabridged ed. John J. Williams. (Illus.). 63p. 1999. pap. 29.00 (*0-934274-77-0*) Consumertronics.

Polygraph Test: Lies, Truth & Science. Ed. by Anthony Gale. 256p. (C). 1988. text 35.00 (*0-8039-8122-8*) Sage.

Polygyny: A Cross-Cultural Study. Peter Bretschneider. LC 96-171037. (Uppsala Studies in Cultural Anthropology: No. 20). 229p. (Orig.). 1995. pap. 46.50 (*91-554-3607-2*) Coronet Bks.

Polygyny & Sexual Selection in Red-Winged Blackbirds. William A. Searcy & Ken Yasukawa. LC 94-19415. (Monographs in Behavior & Ecology). 320p. 1995. text 60.00 (*0-691-03686-1*, Pub. by Princeton U Pr); pap. text 29.95 (*0-691-03687-X*, Pub. by Princeton U Pr) Cal Prin Full Svc.

Polygyny in Pre-Christian Bafut & New Moral Theological Perspectives: A Thesis Presented in Partial Fulfilment of the Requirements for the Doctorate in Moral Theology. Engelbert N. Kofon. (European University Studies: Series 23, Vol. 453). 212p. 1992. pap. 41.80 (*3-631-44822-8*) P Lang Pubng.

***Polyhedra.** Peter R. Cromwell. (Illus.). 465p. (C). 1999. pap. 34.95 (*0-521-66405-5*) Cambridge U Pr.

Polyhedra: A Visual Approach. Anthony Pugh. LC 92-227036. 15.95 (*0-86651-538-0*) Seymour Pubns.

Polyhedra Primer. Peter Pearce. 1997. pap. text 14.95 (*0-86651-419-8*) Seymour Pubns.

Polyhedral Boranes. Earl L. Muetterties & Walter H. Knoth. LC 68-11437. 205p. reprint ed. pap. 63.60 (*0-608-18703-8*, 202710900054) Bks Demand.

Polyhedral Combinatorics: Proceedings of the DIMACS Workshop. Ed. by W. Cook & P. Seymour. LC 90-49139. (DIMACS Series in Discrete Mathematics & Theoretical Computer Science: Vol. 1). 288p. 1991. text 57.00 (*0-8218-6591-9*, DIMACS/1) Am Math.

Polyhedral Virions & Bipartate RNA Genomes. Ed. by B. D. Harrison & A. F. Murant. (Viruses Ser.: Vol. 5). (Illus.). 378p. (C). 1996. text 132.00 (*0-306-45225-1*, Kluwer Plenum) Kluwer Academic.

Polyhedron Models. Magnus J. Wenninger. LC 69-10200. (Illus.). 220p. 1974. pap. text 38.95 (*0-521-09859-9*) Cambridge U Pr.

Polyhedron Models for the Classroom. 2nd ed. Magnus J. Wenniger. (Illus.). 80p. 1975. 13.95 (*0-87353-083-7*) NCTM.

Polyhistory: Studies in the History & Historiography of Ancient Philosophy. Keimpe Algra et al. LC 96-30613. (Philosophia Antiqua Ser.). x, 438p. 1996. 161.00 (*90-04-10417-8*) Brill Academic Pubs.

Polyhymnia: The Rhetoric of Horatian Lyric Discourse. Gregson Davis. LC 90-49630. 293p. 1991. 50.00 (*0-520-07077-1*, Pub. by U CA Pr) Cal Prin Full Svc.

Polyimides. Ed. by D. Wilson et al. (Illus.). 352p. 1990. 149.50 (*0-412-02181-1*, A3616, Chap & Hall NY) Chapman & Hall.

Polyimides: Materials, Characterization & Application: Abstracts of the Fourth International Conference on Polyimides, October 30-November 1, 1991, the Nevele Country Club, Ellenville, NY. Society of Plastics Engineers Staff. LC TP1180.. 340p. reprint ed. pap. 105.40 (*0-7837-2152-8*, 204243800004) Bks Demand.

Polyimides: Synthesis, Characterization & Application: Proceedings - Third International Conference on Polyimides, November 2-4, 1988, Ellenville, NY, Sponsored by Mid-Hudson Section, Society of Plastics Engineers. International Conference on Polyimides Staff. LC TP0156.P6I68. (Illus.). 263p. reprint ed. pap. 81.60 (*0-8357-6273-4*, 203417900089) Bks Demand.

Polyimides: Synthesis, Characterization & Application: Proceedings of Second International Conference on Polyimides, the Nevele Country Club, Ellenville, NY, October 30-November 1985. International Conference on Polyimides. LC QD0382.H4T4. 759p. reprint ed. pap. 200.00 (*0-608-17122-0*, 202769400056) Bks Demand.

Polyimides: Synthesis, Characterization & Applications, 2 vols., Vol. 1. Ed. by K. L. Mittal. (Illus.). 650p. (C). 1984. text 174.00 (*0-306-41670-0*, Kluwer Plenum) Kluwer Academic.

Polyimides: Synthesis, Characterization & Applications, 2 vols., Vol. 2. Ed. by K. L. Mittal. (Illus.). 600p. (C). 1984. text 174.00 (*0-306-41673-5*, Kluwer Plenum) Kluwer Academic.

Polyimides: Thermally Stable Polymers. M. I. Bessonov et al. Ed. by W. W. Wright. Tr. by L. V. Backinowsky & M. A. Chlenov from RUS. LC 86-25155. (Macromolecular Compounds Ser.). (Illus.). 332p. (C). 1987. text 132.00 (*0-306-10993-X*, Kluwer Plenum) Kluwer Academic.

Polykleitos, the Doryphoros, & Tradition. Ed. by Warren G. Moon. LC 94-30288. (Wisconsin Studies in Classics). (Illus.). 1995. 50.00 (*0-299-14310-4*) U of Wis Pr.

Polylepis-Waelder Boliviens: Taxa, Oekologie, Verbreitung und Geschichte. Michael Kessler. (Dissertationes Botanicae Ser.: Band 246). (Illus.). x, 303p. 1995. pap. 89.00 (*3-443-64158-X*, Pub. by Gebruder Borntraeger) Balogh.

Polymer Adsorption & Dispersion Stability. Ed. by E. D. Goddard & B. Vincent. LC 83-25787. (ACS Symposium Ser.: No. 240). 477p. 1984. lib. bdg. 87.95 (*0-8412-0820-4*) Am Chemical.

Polymer Adsorption & Dispersion Stability. Tadros. 1995. write for info. (*0-8493-5835-3*) CRC Pr.

Polymer Adsorption & Dispersion Stability. Ed. by E. D. Goddard & B. Vincent. LC 83-25787. (ACS Symposium Ser.: Vol. 240). 487p. 1984. reprint ed. pap. 151.00 (*0-608-03071-6*, 206352400007) Bks Demand.

Polymer Alloys & Blends: Thermodynamics & Rheology. Leszek A. Utracki. 367p. 1990. 115.00 (*1-56990-104-X*) Hanser-Gardner.

Polymer Analysis. Stuart. 1969. text. write for info. (*0-471-89926-7*) Wiley.

Polymer Analysis & Characterization. J. L. Viovy et al. (Advances in Polymer Science Ser.: Vol. 114). (Illus.). 250p. 1994. 202.95 (*0-387-57238-4*) Spr-Verlag.

Polymer Analysis/Polymer Physics. (Advances in Polymer Science Ser.: Vol. 128). (Illus.). 194p. 1996. 154.00 (*3-540-61218-1*) Spr-Verlag.

Polymer & Composite Rheology. 2nd expanded rev. ed. R. K. Gupta. (Plastics Engineering Ser.). (Illus.). Date not set. write for info. (*0-8247-9922-4*, 9922-4) Dekker.

Polymer & Fiber Science: Recent Advances. Ed. by R. E. Fornes & R. D. Gilbert. 403p. 1991. 174.00 (*0-471-18823-9*, Wiley-VCH) Wiley.

Polymer Association Structures: Microemulsion & Liquid Crystals. Ed. by Magda A. El-Nokaly. LC 88-39192. (ACS Symposium Ser.: No. 384). (Illus.). 440p. 1989. 79.95 (*0-8412-1561-8*) Am Chemical.

Polymer Association Structures: Microemulsion & Liquid Crystals. Ed. by Magda A. El-Nokaly. LC 88-39192. (ACS Symposium Ser.: No. 384). (Illus.). 376p. 1989. reprint ed. pap. 116.60 (*0-608-03140-2*, 206359300007) Bks Demand.

Polymer Based Molecular Composites Vol. 171: Materials Research Society Symposium Proceedings. Ed. by D. W. Schaefer & J. E. Mark. 432p. 1990. text 17.50 (*1-55899-059-3*) Materials Res.

Polymer Biomaterials in Solution, As Interfaces & As Solids. Ed. by S. L. Cooper et al. 1100p. 1995. 260.00 (*90-6764-180-4*, Pub. by VSP) Coronet Bks.

Polymer Blends: Processing, Morphology & Properties, Vol. 2. Ed. by Marian Kryszewski et al. LC 80-22862. 296p. 1984. 85.00 (*0-306-41802-9*, Plenum Trade) Perseus Pubng.

***Polymer Blends & Alloys** Gabriel O. Shonaike & George P. Simon. LC 99-14999. (Plastics Engineering Ser.: 52). (Illus.). 768p. 1999. text 225.00 (*0-8247-1980-8*) Dekker.

Polymer Blends & Composites in Multiphase System. Ed. by C. D. Han. LC 83-24362. (Advances in Chemistry Ser.: Vol. 206). 396p. 1984. reprint ed. pap. 122.80 (*0-608-03510-6*, 206422900008) Bks Demand.

Polymer Blends & Composites in Multiphase Systems. Paul C. D. Han. LC 83-24362. (Advances in Chemistry Ser.: No. 206). 286p. 1984. lib. bdg. 65.95 (*0-8412-0783-6*) Am Chemical.

Polymer Blends & Mixtures. Ed. by D. J. Walsh et al. 1985. text 220.00 (*90-247-3152-6*) Kluwer Academic.

Polymer Blends & Polymer Composites: Proceedings of the International Workshop on Polymer Blends & Polymer Composites, Sydney, Australia, July 1997. Ed. by L. Ye & Y. W. Mai. (Key Engineering Materials Ser.: Vol. 137). (Illus.). 240p. (C). 1997. text 96.00 (*0-87849-766-8*, Pub. by Trans T Pub) Enfield Pubs NH.

Polymer Blends Set: Formulation & Performance. Paul Bucknall. LC 99-36533. 1189p. 1999. 300.00 (*0-471-24825-8*) Wiley.

Polymer Characteristics. Ed. by B. Hammouda et al. (Advances in Polymer Science Ser.: Fortschritte der Hochpolymerenforschung: Vol. 106). (Illus.). 208p. 1993. 109.00 (*0-387-56140-4*) Spr-Verlag.

Polymer Characterization. Elisabeth Schroder et al. 344p. 1989. 67.50 (*1-56990-093-0*) Hanser-Gardner.

Polymer Characterization. 2nd rev. ed. Donald Campbell et al. (Illus.). 400p. 2000. pap. 67.50 (*0-7487-4005-8*, Pub. by S Thornes Pubs) Trans-Atl Phila.

Polymer Characterization: Laboratory Techniques & Analysis. Nicholas P. Cheremisinoff. LC 96-10912. 251p. 1996. 98.00 (*0-8155-1403-4*) Noyes.

Polymer Characterization: Physical Property, Spectroscopic, & Chromatographic Methods Developed from a Symposium Sponsored by the Division of Polymeric Materials: Science & Engineering at the 196th National Meeting of the American Chemical Society, Los Angeles, CA, September 25-30, 1988. Ed. by Clara D. Craver & Theodore Provder. LC 90-47157. (Advances in Chemistry Ser.: No. 227). (Illus.). 536p. 1990. reprint ed. pap. 166.20 (*0-608-06792-X*, 206698900009) Bks Demand.

Polymer Characterization: Spectroscopic, Chromatographic & Physical Instrumental Methods. Ed. by Clara D. Craver. LC 82-24496. (Advances in Chemistry Ser.: Vol. 203). 808p. 1983. reprint ed. pap. 200.00 (*0-608-03508-4*, 206422700008) Bks Demand.

Polymer Characterization & Analysis. Jacqueline I. Kroschwitz. LC 89-27918. (Encyclopedia Reprints Ser). 992p. 1990. 210.00 (*0-471-51325-3*) Wiley.

Polymer Characterization by ESR & NMR. Ed. by Arthur E. Woodward & Frank A. Bovey. LC 80-21840. (ACS Symposium Ser.: No. 142). 1980. 43.95 (*0-8412-0594-9*) Am Chemical.

Polymer Characterization by ESR & NMR. Ed. by Arthur E. Woodward & Frank A. Bovey. LC 80-21840. (ACS Symposium Ser.: No. 142). (Illus.). 319p. 1980. reprint ed. pap. 98.90 (*0-608-03230-1*, 206374900007) Bks Demand.

Polymer Characterization by Liquid Chromatography. G. Glockner. (Journal of Chromatography Library: No. 34). 588p. 1987. 270.00 (*0-444-99507-2*) Elsevier.

Polymer Characterization by Thermal Methods of Analysis: Selected Papers. Symposium on Polymer Characterization by Thermal M. Ed. by Jen Chiu. LC 74-77063. 262p. reprint ed. pap. 81.30 (*0-608-15910-7*, 203085900071) Bks Demand.

Polymer Characterization, Spectroscopic, Chromatographic, & Physical Instrumental Methods. Ed. by Clara D. Craver. LC 82-24496. (Advances in Chemistry Ser.: No. 203). 791p. 1982. lib. bdg. 38.95 (*0-8412-0700-3*, Pub. by Am Chemical) OUP.

Polymer Chemistry: A Teaching Package for Pre-College Teachers. rev. ed. (Illus.). 244p. 1989. pap. 21.95 (*0-87355-058-7*) Natl Sci Tchrs.

Polymer Chemistry: An Introduction. Ger Challa. 170p. (C). 1993. 50.00 (*0-13-682519-2*) P-H.

Polymer Chemistry: An Introduction. 3rd ed. Malcolm P. Stevens. (Illus.). 576p. (C). 1998. text 72.00 (*0-19-512444-8*) OUP.

Polymer Chemistry: The Basic Concepts. Paul C. Hiemenz. (Illus.). 752p. 1984. text 65.00 (*0-8247-7082-X*) Dekker.

Polymer Chemistry & Physics, Vol. I. Edward T. Samulski. 1991. write for info. (*0-318-68472-1*, CRC Reprint) Franklin.

***Polymer Clay.** Irene Dean. LC 00-25776. (Weekend Crafter Ser.). (Illus.). 2000. pap. 14.95 (*1-57990-168-9*, Pub. by Lark Books) Sterling.

***Polymer Clay for the First Time.** Syndee Holt. LC 99-53579. (Illus.). 112p. 2000. 19.95 (*0-8069-6827-3*, Chapelle) Sterling.

Polymer-Clay Nanocomposites. T. J. Pinnavaia. text. write for info. (*0-471-63700-9*) Wiley.

***Polymer Clay Techniques Book.** Sue Heaser. (Illus.). 128p. 1999. pap. 22.99 (*1-58180-008-8*, 31503, North Lght Bks) F & W Pubns Inc.

Polymer Claywork. Mary McGuire. (New Crafts Ser.). (Illus.). 96p. 1996. 15.95 (*1-85967-298-1*, Lorenz Bks) Anness Pub.

Polymer Colloids: A Comprehensive Introduction. Ed. by Robert M. Fitch. LC 97-6619. (Illus.). 364p. 1997. text 125.00 (*0-12-257745-0*) Morgan Kaufmann.

Polymer Compatibility & Incompatibility, Principles & Practice, Vol. 2. Ed. by K. Solc. (MMI Press Symposium Ser.: Vol. 3). x, 464p. 1982. text 428.00 (*3-7186-0046-3*) Gordon & Breach.

Polymer Composite Processing: Second Industry Workshop. (Illus.). 120p. (Orig.). (C). 1992. pap. text 35.00 (*0-941375-68-4*) DIANE Pub.

Polymer Composites: Proceedings of the 28th Microsymposium on Macromolecules, Prague, Czechoslovakia, July 8-11, 1985. Ed. by Blahoslav Sedlacek. (Illus.). xii, 627p. 1986. lib. bdg. 234.65 (*3-11-010994-8*) De Gruyter.

Polymer Composites & Polymeric Materials. 103p. 1998. 59.00 (*0-7680-0171-4*) Soc Auto Engineers.

Polymer Composites & Polymeric Materials for Energy Management & Occupant Safety. (Special Publications). 110p. 1999. pap. 49.00 (*0-7680-0380-6*, SP-1448) Soc Auto Engineers.

Polymer Concrete. 136p. 1993. 59.95 (*0-685-72320-8*, SP-137BOW6) ACI.

Polymer Concretes & Their Structural Uses. K. V. Mikhailov et al. Ed. by V. S. Parameswaran. (Russian Translation Ser.: No. 91). (Illus.). 326p. (C). 1991. text 123.00 (*90-6191-110-9*, Pub. by A A Balkema) Ashgate Pub Co.

***Polymer Crystallization: The Development of Crystalline Order in Thermoplastic Polymers.** Jerold M. Schultz. LC 99-53366. 2000. write for info. (*0-8412-3669-0*) Am Chemical.

Polymer Data Handbook. Ed. by James E. Mark. LC 98-46567. (Illus.). 1040p. 1999. text 250.00 (*0-19-510789-6*) OUP.

P

An Asterisk (*) at the beginning of an entry indicates that the title is appearing for the first time.

Polymer Degradation: Principles & Practical Applications. Wolfram Schnabel. 228p. 1982. 67.50 (*1-56990-092-2*) Hanser-Gardner.

Polymer Devolatilization. Ramon J. Albalak. (Plastics Engineering Ser.: Vol. 33). (Illus.). 736p. 1996. text 250.00 (*0-8247-9627-6*) Dekker.

Polymer Durability: Degradation, Stabilization, & Lifetime Prediction. Ed. by Roger L. Clough et al. (Advances in Chemistry Ser.: Vol. 249). 728p. 1996. text 145.00 (*0-8412-3134-6*, Pub. by Am Chemical) OUP.

Polymer Electrolytes. F. M. Gray. (RSC Materials Monographs). 190p. 1997. 89.00 (*0-85404-557-0*) Am Chemical.

Polymer Engineering Principles: Properties, Processes, & Tests for Design. Richard C. Progelhof & James L. Throne. LC 93-34614. 720p. 1993. 159.00 (*1-56990-150-3*) Hanser-Gardner.

Polymer Engineering Principles: Properties, Processes, & Tests for Design. Richard C. Progelhof & James L. Throne. LC 93-34614. 720p. (C). 1993. pap. 79.95 (*1-56990-151-1*) Hanser-Gardner.

Polymer Engineering Principles: Properties, Processes, & Tests for Designs. Richard C. Progelhof & James L. Throne. LC 92-26915. 1993. write for info. (*0-19-520977-X*) OUP.

Polymer Extrusion. 3rd rev. ed. Chris J. Rauwendaal. 1994. 84.50 (*1-56990-140-6*) Hanser-Gardner.

***Polymer Extrusion: Theory & Practice.** Chan I. Chung. LC 00-35079. 2000. write for info. (*1-56990-288-7*) Hanser-Gardner.

Polymer Films in Sensor Applications. Gabor Harsanyi. LC 94-61559. 425p. 1994. text 154.95 (*1-56676-201-4*) Technomic.

Polymer Flow Interaction, No. 137. Sue Rabin. LC 85-73915. 302p. 1986. lib. bdg. 53.75 (*0-88318-336-6*) Am Inst Physics.

Polymer Fractionation. F. Francuskiewicz. LC 94-8283. (Laboratory Ser.). (Illus.). 224p. 1994. 79.95 (*0-387-57539-1*) Spr-Verlag.

Polymer Fracture. H. H. Kausch. (Polymers, Properties & Applications Ser.: Vol. 2). (Illus.). 430p. 1987. 230.95 (*0-387-13250-3*) Spr-Verlag.

Polymer Gels: Fundamentals & Biomedical Applications. D. DeRossi et al. LC 91-2631. (Illus.). 354p. (C). 1991. text 110.00 (*0-306-43805-4*, Kluwer Plenum) Kluwer Academic.

Polymer Grafts in Biochemistry. Ed. by Harry F. Hixson, Jr. & Eugene P. Goldberg. LC 76-17431. (Illus.). 382p. reprint ed. pap. 118.50 (*0-7837-0674-X*, 204100900019) Bks Demand.

Polymer Handbook. Brewis. 1997. write for info. (*0-582-03409-4*, Pub. by Addison-Wesley) Longman.

***Polymer Handbook.** 4th ed. Ed. by J. Brandrup et al. 2336p. 1999. 350.00 (*0-471-16628-6*) Wiley.

Polymer Handbook, Vol. 1. 3rd ed. Ed. by J. Brandrup & Edmund H. Immergut. LC 88-1258. 1904p. 1989. 295.00 (*0-471-81244-7*) Wiley.

Polymer Handbook Electronic Version. J. Brandrup. write for info. (*0-471-53205-3*) Wiley.

Polymer-Inorganic Interfaces II. Ed. by Nicholas A. Peppas et al. (Symposium Proceedings Ser.: Vol. 385). 255p. 1995. text 74.00 (*1-55899-288-X*) Materials Res.

Polymer Interface & Adhesion. Souheng Wu. (Illus.). 688p. 1982. text 215.00 (*0-8247-1533-0*) Dekker.

Polymer Interfaces: Structure & Strength. Richard P. Wool. 1994. 128.00 (*1-56990-133-3*) Hanser-Gardner.

***Polymer Interfaces & Emulsions.** Kunio Esumi. LC 99-35927. (Illus.). 584p. 1999. text 195.00 (*0-8247-1975-1*) Dekker.

Polymer Latexes, Epoxide Resins, Polyampholytes. M. Ballauff. LC 99-177490. (Advances in Polymer Science Ser.). 212 p. 1998. 149.00 (*3-540-64911-5*) Spr-Verlag.

Polymer Latices Science & Technology: Applications Latices. 2nd ed. Chapman & Hall Staff. text 248.00 (*0-412-62890-2*) Chapman & Hall.

Polymer Literature Review. Mary Stroup-Gardiner & David E. Newcomb. (Illus.). 218p. (C). 1998. reprint ed. pap. text 40.00 (*0-7881-4300-X*) DIANE Pub.

Polymer Materials for Electronic Applications. Ed. by Eugene D. Feit & Cletus Wilkins, Jr. LC 82-1670. (ACS Symposium Ser.: No. 184). 1982. 54.95 (*0-8412-0715-1*) Am Chemical.

Polymer Materials for Electronic Applications. Ed. by Eugene D. Feit & Cletus W. Wilkins, Jr. LC 82-1670. (ACS Symposium Ser.: Vol. 184). 266p. 1982. reprint ed. pap. 82.50 (*0-608-03109-7*, 206356200007) Bks Demand.

Polymer Materials Science. Jerold M. Schultz. (International Physical & Chemical Engineering Sciences Ser). (Illus.). 496p. 1973. 37.95 (*0-685-03900-5*) P-H.

Polymer Mechanochemistry see Macromolecular Mechanochemistry

Polymer Melt Rheology: A Guide for Industrial Practice. F. N. Cogswell. 190p. 1995. 135.00 (*1-85573-198-3*, Pub. by Woodhead Pubng) Am Educ Systs.

Polymer Membranes for Gas & Vapor Separation: Chemistry & Materials Science. Ingo Pinnau. Ed. by Benny D. Freeman. LC 99-25293. (ACS Symposium Ser.: No. 733). 320p. 1999. text 120.00 (*0-8412-3605-4*, Pub. by Am Chemical) OUP.

Polymer Microscopy. Linda C. Sawyer & David T. Grubb. 350p. 1987. text 115.00 (*0-412-25710-6*) Chapman & Hall.

Polymer Mixing: Technology & Engineering. James L. White et al. LC 98-34151. 2000. write for info. (*1-56990-237-2*) Hanser-Gardner.

Polymer Mixing & Extrusion Technology. Nicholas P. Cheremisinoff. (Plastics Engineering Ser.). (Illus.). 456p. 1987. text 185.00 (*0-8247-7793-X*) Dekker.

Polymer Modification: Principles, Techniques, & Applications. J. J. Meister. (Plastics Engineering Ser.). (Illus.). Date not set. text. write for info. (*0-8247-0078-3*) Dekker.

Polymer Modification: Proceedings of an ACS-PMSE Division Symposium Held in Orlando, Florida, August 21-25, 1996. Graham Swift et al. LC 97-35159. 222p. 1997. 95.00 (*0-306-45714-8*, Kluwer Plenum) Kluwer Academic.

Polymer Modified Asphalt Binders. Ed. by Kenneth R. Wardlaw & Scott Shuler. LC 92-8624. (Special Technical Publication Ser.: No. 1108). (Illus.). 400p. 1992. text 58.00 (*0-8031-1413-3*, STP1108) ASTM.

Polymer Modified Concrete. 220p. 1987. pap. 71.95 (*0-318-35477-2*, SP99BOW6) ACI.

Polymer-Modified Hydraulic-Cement Mixtures. Ed. by Louis A. Kuhlmann & D. Gerry Walters. LC 93-11049. (Special Technical Publication Ser.: No. STP 1176). (Illus.). 165p. 1993. text 46.00 (*0-8031-1490-7*, STP1176) ASTM.

Polymer Modifiers & Additives. J. T. Lutz & Richard F. Grossman. (Plastics Engineering Ser.). Date not set. write for info. (*0-8247-9949-6*) Dekker.

Polymer Molecular Weight Methods: A Symposium Co-Sponsored by the Division of Analytical Chemistry & the Division of Polymer Chemistry at the 162nd Meeting of the American Chemical Society, Washington, D. C., September 14-16, 1971. Ed. by Myer Ezrin. LC 73-89047. (Advances in Chemistry Ser.: No. 125). (Illus.). 360p. 1973. reprint ed. pap. 111.60 (*0-608-06776-8*, 206697300009) Bks Demand.

Polymer Molecular Weights, Pt. 2. Ed. by Philip E. Slade, Jr. LC 74-80625. (Illus.). 350p. reprint ed. pap. 108.50 (*0-7837-0882-3*, 204118800002) Bks Demand.

Polymer Molecular Weights, Pt.1. Ed. by Philip E. Slade, Jr. (Techniques & Methods of Polymer Evaluation Ser.: Vol. 4). (Illus.). 304p. 1975. text 160.00 (*0-8247-6227-4*) Dekker.

Polymer Motion in Dense Systems. Ed. by D. Richter & Timothy A. Springer. (Proceedings in Physics Ser.: Vol. 29). (Illus.). 305p. 1988. 70.00 (*0-387-19167-4*) Spr-Verlag.

Polymer Networks. Ed. by K. Dusek. (Advances in Polymer Science Ser.: Vol. 44). (Illus.). 164p. 1982. 73.95 (*0-387-11471-8*) Spr-Verlag.

Polymer Networks: Structure & Mechanical Properties: Proceedings. ACS Symposium on Highly Cross-Linked Polymer Networks. Ed. by A. J. Chompff & S. Newman. LC 73-163286. (Illus.). 507p. 1971. reprint ed. pap. 157.20 (*0-608-05460-7*, 206592900006) Bks Demand.

***Polymer Networks Group Review, Vol. 2.** B. T. Stokke. LC 99-26510. 272p. 2000. text 250.00 (*0-471-98713-1*) Wiley.

Polymer Networks, 1991. S. I. Kuchanov. 206p. 1992. 115.00 (*90-6764-145-6*) Coronet Bks.

Polymer Photonic Devices, Vol. 3281. Ed. by Bernard Kippelen & Donal D. Bradley. 366p. 1998. 89.00 (*0-8194-2720-9*) SPIE.

Polymer Photophysics: Luminescence, Energy Migration & Molecular Motion in Synthetic Polymers. Ed. by David Phillips. 250p. (C). 1985. text 79.95 (*0-412-16510-4*, NO. 9309) Chapman & Hall.

Polymer Physics. (Advances in Polymer Science Ser.: Vol. 95). (Illus.). 224p. 1990. 100.00 (*0-387-52159-3*) Spr-Verlag.

Polymer Physics. Ulf W. Gedde. (Illus.). 320p. 1995. text 77.95 (*0-412-59020-4*, Chap & Hall NY) Chapman & Hall.

Polymer Physics: Concepts, Methods & Open Problems. M. Muthukumar. (Lecture Notes in Physics Ser.: Vol. 22). 250p. (C). 1997. text 61.00 (*9971-5-0594-0*); pap. text 38.00 (*9971-5-0595-9*) World Scientific Pub.

Polymer Physics: Twenty-Five Years of the Edwards Model: Proceedings of the Workshop - Puri, India, 2-9 January 1991. Ed. by S. M. Bhattacharjee. LC 92-11873. 400p. (C). 1992. text 104.00 (*981-02-0741-7*); pap. text 61.00 (*981-02-1985-7*) World Scientific Pub.

Polymer Pioneers: A Popular History of the Science & Technology of Large Molecules. Peter J. Morris. (BCHOC Publication Ser.: No. 5). (Illus.). 88p. (Orig.). 1986. pap. 12.00 (*0-941901-03-3*, TP1116.M67 1986) Chem Heritage Fnd.

Polymer-Plastics Technology & Engineering, Vol. 2. Ed. by Louis Naturman. LC 73-9411. (Illus.). 270p. reprint ed. pap. 83.70 (*0-608-18026-2*, 202900600002) Bks Demand.

Polymer-Plastics Technology & Engineering, Vol. 3. Ed. by Louis Naturman. LC 73-94111. (Illus.). 268p. reprint ed. pap. 83.10 (*0-608-18027-0*, 202900700003) Bks Demand.

Polymer Powder Technology. Ed. by M. Narkis & N. Rosenzweig. LC 95-3061. 644p. 1995. 305.00 (*0-471-93872-6*) Wiley.

Polymer Process Engineering. Richard G. Griskey. 1992. text. write for info. (*0-442-00731-0*) Chapman & Hall.

***Polymer Process Engineering, 99.** Ed. by P. D. Coates. 200p. 1999. 80.00 (*1-86125-094-0*, Pub. by Inst Materials) Ashgate Pub Co.

Polymer Process Engineering 97. Ed. by Phil D. Coates. (Illus.). 324p. 1997. 100.00 (*1-86125-044-4*, Pub. by Inst Materials) Ashgate Pub Co.

Polymer Processing. Ed. by M. L. Fridman. (Advances in Polymer Science Ser.: Vol. 93). (Illus.). 192p. 1990. 107.95 (*0-387-51376-0*) Spr-Verlag.

Polymer Processing: Analysis & Innovation: Presented at the Design Conference of ASME, Washington, D. C., September 13-15, 1982. Design Conference Staff. Ed. by Nam P. Suh et al. LC 82-72702. (PED Ser.: Vol. 5). 169p. reprint ed. pap. 52.40 (*0-8357-8751-6*, 203364400087) Bks Demand.

Polymer Processing: Principles & Design. Donald G. Baird. 346p. 1995. text 145.00 (*0-7506-9105-0*) Buttrwrth-Heinemann.

Polymer Processing: Principles & Design. Donald G. Baird & Dimitris I. Collias. LC 98-2551. 360p. 1998. 94.95 (*0-471-25453-3*) Wiley.

Polymer Processing: Principles & Modeling. J. F. Agassant et al. 599p. 1991. 79.50 (*1-56990-000-0*) Hanser-Gardner.

Polymer Processing & Polymerization. Rakesh Gupta & Anil Kumar. LC 97-6035. (Illus.). 560p. (C). 1997. 85.00 (*0-07-025224-6*) McGraw.

Polymer Processing Fundamentals. Tim A. Osswald. LC 98-33644. 229p. 1998. pap. 34.95 (*1-56990-262-3*) Hanser-Gardner.

Polymer Products & Waste Management: A Multidisciplinary Approach. Ed. by Martijntje Smits. 256p. 1996. 79.00 (*90-6224-974-4*, Pub. by Uitgeverij Arkel); pap. 49.00 (*90-6224-977-9*, Pub. by Uitgeverij Arkel) LPC InBook.

Polymer Properties at Room & Cryogenic Temperatures. G. Hartwig. LC 94-43387. (International Cryogenics Monographs). (Illus.). 286p. (C). 1995. text 95.00 (*0-306-44987-0*, Kluwer Plenum) Kluwer Academic.

Polymer Reactions. Ed. by Geoffrey Allen & J. C. Bevington. (Comprehensive Polymer Science Ser.: Vol. 6). (Illus.). 664p. 1990. 440.00 (*0-08-036210-9*, Pergamon Pr) Elsevier.

Polymer Reactor Engineering. Ed. by C. McGreavy. LC 93-21352. 1993. write for info. (*0-7514-0083-1*, Pub. by B Acad & Prof) Routldge.

Polymer Reactor Engineering. Ed. by C. McGreavy. LC 93-21352. 1994. 95.00 (*1-56081-595-7*, Wiley-VCH) Wiley.

Polymer Recycling: Science, Technology, & Applications. John Scheirs. LC 98-9177. (Wiley Series in Polymer Science). 614p. 1998. 325.00 (*0-471-97054-9*) Wiley.

Polymer Recycling & Its Impact. Hamerton. text. write for info. (*0-471-87740-9*); pap. text. write for info. (*0-471-87741-7*) Wiley.

Polymer Regradeation. Mick Mars. 1982. 35.00 (*0-02-949640-3*) Macmillan.

Polymer Rheology. Nielsen. (Illus.). 216p. 1977. text 135.00 (*0-8247-7550-3*) Dekker.

Polymer Rheology. Lawrence E. Nielsen. LC 77-24187. (Illus.). 217p. Date not set. reprint ed. pap. 67.30 (*0-608-20717-9*, 207181500002) Bks Demand.

Polymer Science: Recent Advances, 2 vols., Set. Ed. by I. S. Bhardwaj. (Illus.). 1038p. (C). 1994. 560.00 (*2-7108-0670-3*, Pub. by Edits Technip) Enfield Pubs NH.

Polymer Science & Engineering. R. Byron Bird & Sigmund Floyd. LC 94-42316. (Technical Japanese Supplements Ser.). 96p. 1995. pap. 22.95 (*0-299-14694-4*) U of Wis Pr.

Polymer Science & Engineering: The Shifting Research Frontiers. National Research Council Polymer Science & Engine. 192p. (C). 1994. text 34.95 (*0-309-04998-9*) Natl Acad Pr.

Polymer Science & Technology. Robert O. Ebewele. LC 95-32995. 504p. 2000. boxed set 89.95 (*0-8493-8939-9*) CRC Pr.

Polymer Science & Technology. Joel R. Fried. 509p. (C). 1995. 89.00 (*0-13-685561-X*, 520302) P-H.

Polymer Science Dictionary. M. Alger. 544p. 1989. mass mkt. 175.95 (*1-85166-220-0*) Elsevier.

Polymer Science Overview: A Tribute to Herman F. Mark. Ed. by G. Allan Stahl. LC 81-17647. (ACS Symposium Ser.: No. 175). 1983. 43.95 (*0-8412-0668-6*); pap. 27.95 (*0-8412-0703-8*) Am Chemical.

Polymer Science Overview: A Tribute to Herman F. Mark. Ed. by G. Allan Stahl. LC 81-17647. (ACS Symposium Ser.: No. 175). (Illus.). 368p. 1981. reprint ed. pap. 114.10 (*0-608-03241-7*, 206376000007) Bks Demand.

Polymer Science Progress, 11. Jenkins. (Progress in Polymer Science: Vol # 11). Date not set. 144.00 (*0-08-034842-4*, Pergamon Pr) Elsevier.

Polymer Science, Recent Advances, 2 vols., Set. Ed. by Editions Technip Staff. 1994. 560.00 (*2-7708-0670-X*, Pub. by Edits Technip) Enfield Pubs NH.

Polymer Science Study Guide. Gerald S. Kirshenbaum. LC 73-80661. x, 136p. (Orig.). (C). 1973. pap. text 101.00 (*0-677-04515-8*) Gordon & Breach.

***Polymer Sensors & Actuators: With Contributions by Various Experts.** Ed. by Yoshihito Osada & Danilo E. De Rossi. LC 99-16715. (Macromolecular Systems - Materials Approach Ser.). (Illus.). 430p. 1999. 159.00 (*3-540-65487-9*) Spr-Verlag.

Polymer Single Crystals. Philip H. Geil. LC 63-19663. (Polymer Reviews Ser: Vol. 5). 572p. 1973. reprint ed. text 62.50 (*0-88275-088-7*) Krieger.

Polymer Solution Data Collection: Solvent Activity Coefficients at Infinite Dilution - Liquid-Liquid Equilibrium. Wen Hao et al. Ed. by Reiner Eckermann & Gerhard Kreysa. LC 98-137028. (Dechema Chemistry Data Ser.: Vol. 14, Pt. 2 & 3). (Illus.). 544p. 1992. text 230.00 (*3-926959-32-0*, Pub. by Dechema) Scholium Intl.

Polymer Solution Data Collection: Vapor Liquid Equilibrium. Wen Hao et al. Ed. by Reiner Eckermann. LC 98-137028. (Dechema Chemistry Data Ser.: Vol. 14, Pt. 1). (Illus.). 582p. 1992. text 270.00 (*3-926959-31-2*, Pub. by Dechema) Scholium Intl.

Polymer Solutions. Hisao Fujita. (Studies in Polymer Science: No. 9). xviii,370p. 1990. 203.00 (*0-444-88339-8*) Elsevier.

***Polymer-Solvent Complexes & Inthcalates: Macromolecular Symposia, Vols. 138.** Vittoria & Gaetano Guerra. 262p. 1999. 125.00 (*3-527-29806-1*) Wiley.

Polymer Spectroscopy. Ed. by Allan H. Fawcett. 410p. 1996. 295.00 (*0-471-96029-2*) Wiley.

***Polymer Spectroscopy Macromolecular Symposia Volume 141.** Ed. by J. M. Chalmers. 312p. 1999. 140.00 (*3-527-29809-6*) Wiley.

Polymer Stabilization & Degradation. Ed. by Peter P. Klemchuk. LC 85-9011. (ACS Symposium Ser.: No. 280). 446p. 1985. lib. bdg. 87.95 (*0-8412-0916-2*) Am Chemical.

Polymer Stabilization & Degradation. Ed. by Peter P. Klemchuk. LC 85-9011. (ACS Symposium Ser.: Vol. 280). 456p. 1985. reprint ed. pap. 141.40 (*0-608-03911-X*, 206435800009) Bks Demand.

Polymer, Structures & Spectrum see Atlas of Polymer & Plastics Analysis

Polymer-Supported Reactions in Organic Synthesis. Ed. by Philip G. Hodge & D. C. Sherrington. LC 79-41482. (Illus.). 498p. reprint ed. pap. 154.40 (*0-8357-8992-6*, 203333700085) Bks Demand.

Polymer Surface Dynamics. Ed. by Joseph D. Andrade. LC 87-35942. (Illus.). 190p. (C). 1988. text 102.00 (*0-306-42788-5*, Kluwer Plenum) Kluwer Academic.

Polymer Surface Modification: Relevance to Adhesion. Ed. by K. L. Mittal. (Illus.). 552p. 1996. 145.00 (*90-6764-201-0*, Pub. by VSP) Coronet Bks.

Polymer Surface Modification & Characterization. Chi-Ming Chan. LC 93-37465. 295p. 1993. 99.50 (*1-56990-158-9*) Hanser-Gardner.

Polymer Surfaces. Ed. by David T. Clark & W. J. Feast. LC 77-17426. (Illus.). 457p. reprint ed. pap. 141.70 (*0-608-30010-1*, 202210100024) Bks Demand.

Polymer Surfaces: From Physics to Technology. F. Garbassi et al. LC 97-24708. 510p. 1997. pap. 94.95 (*0-471-97100-6*) Wiley.

Polymer Surfaces & Interfaces: Characterization, Modification & Application. Ed. by K. L. Mittal & K. W. Lee. (Illus.). 435p. 1997. 127.50 (*90-6764-217-7*, Pub. by VSP) Coronet Bks.

Polymer Surfaces & Interfaces II. Ed. by W. J. Feast et al. LC 92-30939. 314p. 1993. 295.00 (*0-471-93456-9*) Wiley.

Polymer Surfaces & Interfaces III. R. Richards & S. Peace. LC 98-37165. 316p. 1999. 200.00 (*0-471-98286-5*) Wiley.

Polymer Surfaces from Physics to Technology. rev. ed. Fabio Garbassi et al. 474p. 1994. 275.00 (*0-471-93817-3*) Wiley.

Polymer Surfaces, Interfaces & Thin Films. Alamgir Karim. 250p. 1999. 84.00 (*981-02-3864-9*) World Scientific Pub.

Polymer-Surfactant Systems. Jan C. Kwak. LC 98-39464. (Surfactant Science Ser.). (Illus.). 504p. 1998. text 195.00 (*0-8247-0232-8*) Dekker.

Polymer Syntheses, No. II. 2nd ed. Stanley R. Sandler & Wolf Karo. (Organic Chemistry Ser.). (Illus.). 427p. 1993. text 117.00 (*0-12-618512-3*) Acad Pr.

Polymer Syntheses, No. 3. 2nd ed. Ed. by Stanley R. Sandler & Wolf Karo. (Illus.). 424p. 1996. text 99.00 (*0-12-618513-1*) Morgan Kaufmann.

Polymer Syntheses, Vol. 1. 2nd ed. Stanley R. Sandler & Wolf Karo. (Organic Chemistry Ser.: Vol. 29-I). (Illus.). 512p. 1991. text 71.00 (*0-12-618511-5*) Acad Pr.

Polymer Synthesis. R. Arshady et al. (Advances in Polymer Science Ser.: Vol. 111). (Illus.). 234p. 1994. 136.95 (*0-387-57198-1*) Spr-Verlag.

***Polymer Synthesis.** P. Rempp. 1998. 54.95 (*3-527-29721-9*) Wiley.

Polymer Synthesis - Polymer Engineering. (Advances in Polymer Science Ser.: Vol. 121). 176p. 1995. 149.95 (*3-540-58733-0*) Spr-Verlag.

Polymer Synthesis & Characterization: A Laboratory Manual. Stanley R. Sandler et al. (Illus.). 212p. 1998. lab manual ed. 39.95 (*0-12-618240-X*) Morgan Kaufmann.

Polymer Synthesis/Polymer-Polymer Complexation. Contrib. by S. Inoue et al. (Advances in Polymer Science Ser.: Vol. 146). (Illus.). 220p. 1999. 159.00 (*3-540-65313-9*) Spr-Verlag.

Polymer Technology. 3rd ed. D. C. Miles & J. H. Briston. (Illus.). 720p. 1996. 155.00 (*0-8206-0344-9*) Chem Pub.

Polymer Toughening. Charles B. Arends. (Plastics Engineering Ser.: Vol. 30). (Illus.). 432p. 1996. text 185.00 (*0-8247-9474-5*) Dekker.

***Polymer Viscoelasticity: Stress & Strain in Practice.** Evaristo Riande. LC 99-40874. (Plastics Engineering Ser.). (Illus.). 904p. 1999. text 235.00 (*0-8247-7904-5*) Dekker.

Polymer Wear & Its Control. Ed. by Huang L. Lieng. LC 85-15755. (ACS Symposium Ser.: Vol. 287). 432p. 1985. reprint ed. pap. 134.00 (*0-608-03915-2*, 206436200009) Bks Demand.

Polymer Yearbook, Vol. 1. Ed. by Hans-George Elias & Richard A. Pethrick. xii, 338p. 1984. text 117.00 (*3-7186-0177-X*); pap. text 58.00 (*3-7186-0178-8*) Gordon & Breach.

Polymer Yearbook, Vol. 2. Richard A. Pethrick. xii, 414p. 1985. text 129.00 (*3-7186-0274-1*); pap. text 50.00 (*3-7186-0276-8*) Gordon & Breach.

Polymer Yearbook, Vol. 3. Ed. by Richard A. Pethrick. xiv, 378p. 1986. text 189.00 (*3-7186-0342-X*); pap. text 71.00 (*3-7186-0341-1*) Gordon & Breach.

Polymer Yearbook, Vol. 4. Ed. by Richard A. Pethrick. xii, 410p. 1987. text 231.00 (*3-7186-0406-X*); pap. text 68.00 (*3-7186-0408-6*) Gordon & Breach.

Polymer Yearbook, Vol. 5. Richard A. Pethrick. xii, 466p. 1989. pap. 96.00 (*3-7186-4858-X*); text 291.00 (*3-7186-4857-1*) Gordon & Breach.

Polymer Yearbook, Vol. 14. Ed. by Richard A. Pethrick. 304p. 1997. text 162.00 (*90-5702-169-2*, Harwood Acad Pubs) Gordon & Breach.

An Asterisk (*) at the beginning of an entry indicates that the title is appearing for the first time.

Polymer Yearbook, Vol.6. Richard A. Pethrick. (Polymer Yearbook Ser.). 373p. 1990. text 351.00 (*3-7186-4997-7*, Harwood Acad Pubs) Gordon & Breach.

Polymer Yearbook 8, Vol. 8. 8th ed. Ed. by Richard A. Pethrick. 424p. 1991. text 444.00 (*3-7186-5154-8*) Gordon & Breach.

Polymer Yearbook 11. Ed. by Richard A. Pethrick. (Polymer Yearbook Ser.). 428p. 1994. text 303.00 (*3-7186-5481-4*, Harwood Acad Pubs) Gordon & Breach.

Polymer Yearbook 15. Ed. by Richard A. Pethrick. (Polymer Yearbook Ser.: Vol. 15). (Illus.). 352p. 1998. text 162.00 (*90-5702-320-2*, ECU208) Gordon & Breach.

Polymer Yearbook 7, Vol. 7. Richard A. Pethrick. (Polymer Yearbook Ser.). 384p. 1991. text 462.00 (*3-7186-5075-4*, Harwood Acad Pubs) Gordon & Breach.

***Polymer Yearbook 16.** Ed. by Richard A. Pethrick. (Polymer Yearbook Ser.: Vol. 16). 392p. 1999. text 250.00 (*90-5702-473-X*, Harwood Acad Pubs) Gordon & Breach.

Polymer Yearbook 10, Vol. 10. Ed. by Richard A. Pethrick. (Polymer Yearbook Ser.). 430p. 1993. text 347.00 (*3-7186-5334-6*) Gordon & Breach.

Polymer Yearbook 13, No. 13. Ed. by Richard A. Pethrick. 432p. 1996. text 193.00 (*3-7186-5914-X*, Harwood Acad Pubs) Gordon & Breach.

Polymer Yearbook 12. Richard A. Pethrick. v, 332p. 1995. text 275.00 (*3-7186-5712-0*, Harwood Acad Pubs) Gordon & Breach.

Polymerase Chain Reaction. Kary B. Mullis. (Illus.). 458p. 1994. 49.50 (*0-8176-3750-8*) Birkhauser.

Polymerase Chain Reaction. Henry A. Erlich. Ed. by Richard Gibbs & Haig H. Kazazian, Jr. LC 90-112524. (Current Communications in Molecular Biology Ser.). 255p. 1989. reprint ed. pap. 79.10 (*0-608-05665-0*, 206618100006) Bks Demand.

Polymerase Chain Reaction: A Textbook. Ed. by Kary B. Mullis & Richard Gibbs. (Illus.). xxii, 458p. (C). 1994. 79.00 (*0-8176-3607-2*) Birkhauser.

Polymerase Chain Reaction & the Analysis of the T Cell Receptor Repertoire. Jorge R. Oksenberg et al. (Medical Intelligence Unit Ser.). 125p. 1992. 99.00 (*1-879702-47-9*) Landes Bioscience.

Polymerase Chain Reaction (PCR) The Technique & Its Application. Rosalind A. Eeles & Alasdair Stamps. LC 93-4961. (Molecular Biology Intelligence Unit Ser.). 1993. 99.00 (*1-879702-58-4*) Landes Bioscience.

Polymerase Chain Reaction (PCR) for Human Viral Diagnosis. Jonathan P. Clewley. 240p. 1994. lib. bdg. 79.95 (*0-8493-4833-1*) CRC Pr.

Polymerge. Dan Raphael. 24p. (Orig.). 1979. pap. text 4.00 (*0-686-35895-3*) Skydog OR.

Polymeric Additives for High Performing Detergents. Paolo Zini. LC 94-60736. 275p. 1994. pap. text 84.95 (*1-56676-143-3*) Technomic.

Polymeric Biomaterials. Severian Dumitriu. (Illus.). 864p. 1993. text 250.00 (*0-8247-8969-5*) Dekker.

Polymeric Biomaterials. Ed. by Erhan Piskin & Allan S. Hoffman. 1986. text 175.00 (*90-247-3303-0*) Kluwer Academic.

***Polymeric Building Materials.** Ed. by D. Feldman. 576p. (C). (gr. 13). 1998. text 250.00 (*0-419-16020-5*) Chapman & Bkman.

Polymeric Carbons: Carbon Fibre, Glass & Char. Gwyn M. Jenkins & K. Kawamura. LC 74-16995. 186p. reprint ed. pap. 53.10 (*0-608-14084-8*, 2024480) Bks Demand.

Polymeric Compatibilizers: Uses & Benefits in Polymer Blends. Sudhin Datta & David J. Lohse. LC 96-14531. 542p. 1996. 139.00 (*1-56990-194-5*) Hanser-Gardner.

Polymeric Composites. Raymond B. Seymour. (New Concepts in Polymer Science Ser.). viii, 194p. 1990. 130.00 (*90-6764-121-9*, Pub. by VSP) Coronet Bks.

Polymeric Delivery Systems: Properties & Applications. Ed. by Magda A. El-Nokaly et al. LC 92-40099. (Symposium Ser.: Vol. 520). (Illus.). 420p. 1993. text 110.00 (*0-8412-2624-5*, Pub. by Am Chemical) OUP.

Polymeric Dental Materials, Vol. XIV. Michael Braden et al. LC 97-457. (Macromolecular Systems - Materials Approach Ser.). (Illus.). 150p. 1997. 149.00 (*3-540-61646-2*) Spr-Verlag.

Polymeric Dispersions: Principles & Applications. Ed. by Jose M. Asua. LC 97-10630. (NATO ASI Series, Applied Sciences: Series E). 1997. text 301.00 (*0-7923-4549-5*) Kluwer Academic.

Polymeric Drugs & Drug Administration. Ed. by Raphael M. Ottenbrite. LC 93-48086. (ACS Symposium Ser.: No. 545). 278p. 1994. text 78.00 (*0-8412-2744-6*, Pub. by Am Chemical) OUP.

Polymeric Drugs & Drug Delivery Systems. Ed. by Richard L. Dunn & Raphael M. Ottenbrite. LC 91-23423. (ACS Symposium Ser.: No. 469). (Illus.). 313p. 1991. text 85.00 (*0-8412-2105-7*, Pub. by Am Chemical) OUP.

Polymeric Foams. (Report Ser.: No. P-120U). 233p. 1996. 2950.00 (*1-56965-266-X*) BCC.

Polymeric Foams. Daniel Klempner & Kurt C. Frisch. 454p. (C). 1991. 159.00 (*1-56990-049-3*) Hanser-Gardner.

Polymeric Foams: Science & Technology. American Chemical Society Staff. Ed. by Kishan C. Khemani. LC 97-8468. (ACS Symposium Ser.: No. 669). (Illus.). 236p. 1997. text 105.00 (*0-8412-3516-3*, Pub. by Am Chemical) OUP.

Polymeric Foams, a Huge Sub-Industry, No. P-120R. 180p. 1994. 2650.00 (*1-56965-255-4*) BCC.

Polymeric Gas Separation Membranes. Robert E. Kesting & A. K. Fritzsche. LC 92-43556. 432p. 1993. 89.95 (*0-471-56931-3*, Pub. by Interscience) Wiley.

Polymeric Gas Separation Membranes. Donald R. Paul. 640p. 1993. boxed set 178.95 (*0-8493-4415-8*) CRC Pr.

Polymeric Layers. Ed. by P. Wunsche. (Progress in Colloid & Polymer Science Ser.: Vol. 85). 250p. 1992. 87.00 (*0-387-91400-5*) Spr-Verlag.

Polymeric Liquid Crystals: Polymer Science & Technology. Ed. by Alexandre Blumstein. (Polymer Science & Technology Ser.: Vol. 28). 450p. 1985. 115.00 (*0-306-41814-2*, Plenum Trade) Perseus Pubng.

Polymeric Materials: Chemistry for the Future. Joseph Alper & Gordon L. Nelson. LC 89-293. (Other Technical Bks.). (Illus.). 103p. (C). 1989. text 29.95 (*0-8412-1622-3*, Pub. by Am Chemical); pap. text 17.95 (*0-8412-1613-4*, Pub. by Am Chemical) OUP.

Polymeric Materials: Relationships Between Structure & Mechanical Behavior: Papers Presented at a Seminar of the American Society for Metals. American Society for Metals Staff. LC 74-20127. 626p. reprint ed. pap. 194.10 (*0-608-10143-5*, 201549400094) Bks Demand.

Polymeric Materials - Industrial Laminates, Filament Wound Tubing, Vulcanized Fibre, & Materials Used in Printed Wiring Boards, UL 746E. 2nd ed. (C). 1994. pap. text 95.00 (*1-55989-500-4*) Underwrtrs Labs.

Polymeric Materials - Long Term Property Evaluations, UL 746B. 3rd ed. (C). 1996. pap. text 95.00 (*0-7629-0065-2*) Underwrtrs Labs.

Polymeric Materials & Artificial Organs. Ed. by Charles G. Gebelein. LC 84-9297. (ACS Symposium Ser.: No. 256). 208p. 1984. lib. bdg. 40.95 (*0-8412-0854-9*) Am Chemical.

Polymeric Materials & Artificial Organs. Ed. by Charles G. Gebelein. LC 84-9297. (ACS Symposium Ser.: Vol. 256). 216p. 1984. reprint ed. pap. 67.00 (*0-608-03129-1*, 206358200007) Bks Demand.

Polymeric Materials & Flame Retardants for Wire, Cable & Fiber Optics, No. P-146. 127p. 1993. 2450.00 (*1-56965-301-1*) BCC.

Polymeric Materials & Processing: Plastics, Elastomers & Composites. Jean-Michel Charrier. 655p. (C). 1991. 59.95 (*1-56990-010-8*) Hanser-Gardner.

Polymeric Materials-Coil Forms, UL 1692. 2nd ed. (C). 1999. pap. text 95.00 (*1-55989-599-3*) Underwrtrs Labs.

Polymeric Materials for Corrosion Control. Ed. by Ray A. Dickie & F. Louis Floyd. LC 86-20646. (ACS Symposium Ser.: No. 322). (Illus.). ix, 359p. 1986. 76.95 (*0-8412-0998-7*) Am Chemical.

Polymeric Materials for Corrosion Control. Ed. by Ray A. Dickie & F. Louis Floyd. LC 86-20646. (ACS Symposium Ser.: Vol. 322). 384p. 1986. reprint ed. pap. 119.10 (*0-608-03526-2*, 206424500008) Bks Demand.

Polymeric Materials for Electronics Packaging & Interconnection. Ed. by John H. Lupinski & Robert S. Moore. (ACS Symposium Ser.: No. 407). 512p. 1989. text 110.00 (*0-8412-1679-7*, Pub. by Am Chemical) OUP.

Polymeric Materials for Microelectronic Applications: Science & Technology. Ed. by Hiroshi Ito et al. LC 94-38922. (ACS Symposium Ser.: No. 579). (Illus.). 540p. 1995. text 115.95 (*0-8412-3055-2*, Pub. by Am Chemical) OUP.

Polymeric Materials-Short Term Property Evaluations, UL 746A. 4th ed. (C). 1995. pap. text 95.00 (*1-55989-936-0*) Underwrtrs Labs.

Polymeric Materials Use in Electrical Equipment Evaluations, UL 746C. 4th ed. (C). 1995. pap. text 95.00 (*1-55989-949-2*) Underwrtrs Labs.

Polymeric Metals Encyclopedia. Salamone. 1996. lib. bdg. 9200.00 incl. cd-rom (*0-8493-2404-1*) CRC Pr.

Polymeric Multicomponent Materials: An Introduction. L. H. Sperling. LC 97-6509. 416p. 1997. 74.95 (*0-471-04138-6*) Wiley.

Polymeric Nanoparticles & Microspheres. Ed. by Pierre Guiot & Patrick Couvreur. 216p. 1986. 126.00 (*0-8493-5696-2*, RS201, CRC Reprint) Franklin.

Polymeric Reagents & Catalysts. Ed. by Warren T. Ford. LC 86-3521. (ACS Symposium Ser.: No. 308). (Illus.). viii, 295p. 1986. 63.95 (*0-8412-0972-3*, Pub. by Am Chemical) OUP.

Polymeric Reagents & Catalysts. Ed. by Warren T. Ford. LC 86-3521. (ACS Symposium Ser.: Vol. 308). 304p. 1986. reprint ed. pap. 94.30 (*0-608-03514-9*, 206423300008) Bks Demand.

Polymeric Site-specific Pharmacotherapy. Ed. by A. J. Domb. LC 93-39724. 476p. 1994. 350.00 (*0-471-93824-6*) Wiley.

Polymeric Surfactants. Ed. by Irja Piirma. (Surfactant Science Ser.: Vol. 42). (Illus.). 302p. 1992. text 185.00 (*0-8247-8608-4*) Dekker.

***Polymeric Systems: Proceedings ASME International Mechanical Engineering Congress & Exposition, Nashville, Tennesse, 1999.** Ed. by A. Saigal & K. Ramani. (MD Ser.: Vol. 88). 93p. 1999. 70.00 (*0-7918-1660-5*) ASME Pr.

Polymer/Inorganic Interfaces. Ed. by R. L. Opila et al. (Symposium Proceedings Ser.: Vol. 304). 235p. 1993. text 30.00 (*1-55899-200-6*) Materials Res.

Polymerization & Polycondensation Processes: A Collection of Papers Based on the Symposium on Polymerization & Polycondensation Processes; Division of Industrial & Engineering Chemistry, 140th Meeting of the American Chemical Society, Chicago, IL, September 5-6, 1961. Symposium on Polymerization & Polycondensation Pro. LC 62-15813. (Advances in Chemistry Ser.: Vol. 34). 266p. 1962. reprint ed. pap. 82.50 (*0-608-06901-9*, 206710900009) Bks Demand.

Polymerization by Organometallic Compounds. Leo Reich & A. Schindler. LC 65-14732. (Polymer Rev. Ser.: Vol. 12). 750p. reprint ed. pap. 200.00 (*0-608-30438-7*, 201196500080) Bks Demand.

Polymerization in Biological Systems. CIBA Foundation Staff. LC 72-86558. (CIBA Foundation Symposium: New Ser.: No. 7). 322p. reprint ed. pap. 99.90 (*0-608-13510-0*, 202213900024) Bks Demand.

Polymerization in Organized Media. Constantinos M. Paleos. 376p. 1992. text 161.00 (*2-88124-538-2*) Gordon & Breach.

Polymerization Kinetics & Technology: A Symposium Co-Sponsored by the Division of Industrial & Engineering Chemistry & the Division of Polymer Chemistry at the 163rd Meeting of the American Chemical Society, Boston, MA, April 10-14, 1972. Ed. by Norbert A. Platzer. LC 73-91733. (Advances in Chemistry Ser.: No. 128). (Illus.). 304p. 1973. reprint ed. pap. 94.30 (*0-608-06777-6*, 206697400009) Bks Demand.

Polymerization of Heterocyclics: Papers Presented at the XXIII IUPAC Congress. Ed. by Otto Vogl & Junji Furukawa. LC 73-76028. 227p. reprint ed. pap. 70.40 (*0-608-30377-1*, 205502300008) Bks Demand.

Polymerization Process Modeling. N. A. Dotson & R. Galvan. 371p. 1995. 115.00 (*0-471-18615-5*, Wiley-VCH) Wiley.

Polymerization Process Modeling. Neil A. Dotson et al. Ed. by D. Fennell Evans. LC 95-14939. (Center for Interfacial Engineering Ser.). (Illus.). 350p. 1995. 95.00 (*1-56081-693-7*, Wiley-VCH) Wiley.

Polymerization Reactions. Incl. Cationic Isomerization: Polymerization of Three-Methyl-One-Butene & Four-Methyl-One-Penene. J. P. Kennedy & J. E. Johnston. 1976. Grafting on Polyamides. E. B. Mano & F. M. Coutinho. 1976. Rigid Rods & the Characterization of Polyisozyanides. F. Millich. 1976. Stable Organic Cation Salts: Ion Pair Equilibria & Use in Cationic Polymerization. A. Ledwith & D. C. Sherrington. 1976. (Advances in Polymer Science Ser.: Vol. 19). (Illus.). 150p. 1976. 42.00 (*0-387-07460-0*) Spr-Verlag.

Polymerization Reactions & New Polymers: A Symposium Co-Sponsored by the Division of Industrial & Engineering Chemistry & the Division of Polymer Chemistry at the 163rd Meeting of the American Chemical Society, Boston, MA, April 10-14, 1972. Ed. by Norbert A. Platzer. LC 73-91734. (Advances in Chemistry Ser.: No. 129). (Illus.). 302p. 1973. reprint ed. pap. 93.70 (*0-608-06774-1*, 206697100009) Bks Demand.

Polymerization Technology Trends & Markets for Upgraded Commodities, No. YP-143: Highlighting Polyolefins & Polystyrene. Melvin Schlecter. (Illus.). 141p. 1993. 2550.00 (*1-56965-250-3*) BCC.

Polymers: Chemistry & Physics of Modern Materials. 2nd enl. rev. ed. J. M. Cowie. 448p. 1991. pap. 39.95 (*0-412-03121-3*, A6369, Chap & Hall NY) Chapman & Hall.

Polymers: Inside Out. A. E. Tonelli. text. write for info. (*0-471-38138-1*) Wiley.

Polymers: Structure & Properties. Carole A. Daniels. LC 88-50948. 112p. 1989. 69.95 (*0-87762-552-2*) Technomic.

Polymers: The Origins & Growth of a Science. unabridged ed. Herbert Morawetz. LC 95-6700. (Illus.). xiv, 306p. 1995. reprint ed. pap. text 11.95 (*0-486-68732-5*) Dover.

Polymers: Their Properties & Blood Compatibility. Ed. by Steen Dawids. (Developments in Hematology & Immunology Ser.). (C). 1989. text 251.00 (*0-7923-0491-8*) Kluwer Academic.

Polymers All Around You! Linda Woodward. (Illus.). 21p. (Orig.). 1993. pap. 4.00 (*1-883822-02-5*) Terrific Sci.

Polymers, an Encyclopedic Sourcebook of Engineering Properties. Ed. by Jacqueline I. Kroschwitz. LC 87-21693. 692p. 1987. 199.00 (*0-471-85652-5*) Wiley.

Polymers & Biomaterials: Proceedings of the Conference, Beijing, PR China, 18-22 June, 1990, 5 vols., Set. Ed. by H. Feng et al. (Chinese Materials Research Society Symposia Ser.: No. 3). 508p. 1991. 728.50 (*0-685-40619-9*, North Holland) Elsevier.

Polymers & Biomolecules see Singlet 02 Series

Polymers & Co-Polymers of Higher - Olefins: Chemistry, Technology, Applications. B. A. Krentsel. LC 97-4197. 375p. 1997. 147.50 (*1-56990-220-8*) Hanser-Gardner.

Polymers & Composites: Recent Trends Proceedings of National Seminar Organized by Dept. of Sci. & Tech. (C). 1989. 62.00 (*81-204-0425-4*, Pub. by Oxford IBH) S Asia.

Polymers & Fiber Science: Recent Advances. Ed. by R. E. Fornes et al. 403p. 1992. 125.00 (*1-56081-536-1*, Wiley-VCH) Wiley.

Polymers & Neutron Scattering. Julia S. Higgins & Henry C. Benoit. (Oxford Series on Neutron Scattering in Condensed Matter: No. 8). (Illus.). 456p. 1997. pap. text 55.00 (*0-19-850063-7*) OUP.

Polymers & Other Advanced Materials: Emerging Technologies & Business Opportunities. P. N. Prasad et al. (Illus.). 740p. (C). 1996. text 191.00 (*0-306-45210-3*, Kluwer Plenum) Kluwer Academic.

Polymers & People: An Informal History. Eric Elliot. (BCHOC Publication: No. 6). (Illus.). 32p. (Orig.). 1986. pap. 8.00 (*0-941901-04-1*, QD281.P6 E44 19) Chem Heritage Fnd.

Polymers & Plastics. Roberts. 1997. 1.20 (*0-7167-9216-8*) W H Freeman.

Polymers & Polymer Composites in Construction. Ed. by L. C. Hollaway. 275p. 1990. text 136.50 (*0-7277-1521-6*, Pub. by T Telford) RCH.

Polymers & the Environment. G. Scott. 144p. 1999. pap. 35.00 (*0-85404-578-3*) Royal Soc Chem.

Polymers As Biomaterials. Ed. by Shalaby W. Shalaby et al. 400p. 1985. 105.00 (*0-306-41886-X*, Plenum Trade) Perseus Pubng.

Polymers As Electrooptical & Photooptical Active Media. Ed. by V. B. Shibaev. LC 96-17847. (Macromolecular Systems, Materials Approach Ser.). 208p. 1996. 119.00 (*3-540-59486-8*) Spr-Verlag.

Polymers As Materials for Packaging. Jiri Stepek. (Polymer Science & Technology Ser.). 480p. 1988. text 84.00 (*0-470-20720-5*) P-H.

Polymers As Rheology Modifiers. Ed. by Donald N. Schultz. LC 91-11687. (ACS Symposium Ser.: No. 462). (Illus.). 357p. 1991. text 89.00 (*0-8412-2009-3*, Pub. by Am Chemical) OUP.

Polymers at Surfaces & Interfaces. Richard A. Jones & Randal W. Richards. LC 98-6554. (Illus.). 400p. (C). 1998. 90.00 (*0-521-47440-X*) Cambridge U Pr.

***Polymers at Surfaces & Interfaces.** Richard A. Jones & Randal W. Richards. LC 98-6554. (Illus.). 400p. (C). 1998. pap. 39.95 (*0-521-47965-7*) Cambridge U Pr.

Polymers, Biomaterials & Medical Applications: Biomaterials & Medical Applications. Ed. by Jacqueline I. Kroschwitz. LC 89-32479. (Encyclopedia Reprints Ser). 555p. 1989. 199.00 (*0-471-51207-9*) Wiley.

Polymers for Advanced Technologies: IUPAC International Symposium. Menachem Lewin. LC 88-177. 953p. 1988. 150.00 (*0-89573-293-9*, Wiley-VCH) Wiley.

Polymers for Controlled Drug Delivery. Peter J. Tarcha. 296p. 1990. lib. bdg. 295.00 (*0-8493-5652-0*, RS201) CRC Pr.

Polymers for Electronic & Photonic Applications. Ed. by C. P. Wong. (Illus.). 661p. 1992. text 82.00 (*0-12-762540-2*) Acad Pr.

Polymers for Electronic Applications. Juey H. Lai. LC 89-9860. 272p. 1989. 140.00 (*0-8493-4704-1*, TK7871) Franklin.

Polymers for Engineering Applications. Raymond B. Seymour. LC 87-70003. 208p. reprint ed. pap. 64.50 (*0-7837-2768-2*, 204315900006) Bks Demand.

Polymers for Fibers & Elastomers. Ed. by Jett C. Arthur, Jr. LC 84-14635. (ACS Symposium Ser.: No. 260). (Illus.). 444p. 1984. reprint ed. pap. 137.70 (*0-608-03137-2*, 206359000007) Bks Demand.

Polymers for Gas Separation. Ed. by N. Toshima & E. Tsuchida. 245p. 1992. 124.00 (*0-471-18805-0*, Wiley-VCH) Wiley.

Polymers for Gas Separation. Naoki Toshima. 245p. 1992. 85.00 (*1-56081-093-9*, Wiley-VCH) Wiley.

Polymers For High Technology: Electronics & Photonics. Ed. by Murrae J. Bowden & Richard S. Turner. LC 87-14573. (ACS Symposium Ser.: No. 346). x, 631p. 1987. 104.95 (*0-8412-1406-9*, Pub. by Am Chemical) OUP.

Polymers for High Technology: Electronics & Photonics. Ed. by Murrae J. Bowden & S. Richard Turner. LC 87-14573. (ACS Symposium Ser.: Vol. 346). 640p. 1987. reprint ed. pap. 198.40 (*0-608-03539-4*, 206425800008) Bks Demand.

Polymers for Lightwave & Integrated Optics. 1996. 225.00 (*0-614-18421-5*) Info Gatekeepers.

Polymers for Lightwave & Integrated Optics: Technology & Applications. Ed. by Lawrence A. Hornak. LC 92-19331. (Optical Engineering Ser.: Vol. 32). (Illus.). 768p. 1992. text 199.00 (*0-8247-8697-1*) Dekker.

Polymers for Microelectronics: Resists & Dielectrics. Ed. by Larry F. Thompson et al. LC 93-33955. (Symposium Ser.: No. 537). (Illus.). 554p. 1994. text 135.00 (*0-8412-2721-7*, Pub. by Am Chemical) OUP.

Polymers for Microelectronics Science & Technology: Proceedings of the International Symposium on Polymers for Microelectronics--Science & Technology, Tokyo, Japan, Oct. 29-November 2, 1989. Ed. by Yoneho Tabata et al. 870p. 1990. 230.00 (*3-527-26168-0*, Wiley-VCH) Wiley.

Polymers for Second-Order Nonlinear Optics. Ed. by Geoffrey A. Lindsay & Kenneth D. Singer. LC 95-30598. (ACS Symposium Ser.: Vol. 601). (Illus.). 560p. 1995. text 150.00 (*0-8412-3263-6*, Pub. by Am Chemical) OUP.

Polymers from Agricultural Coproducts. Ed. by Marshall L. Fishman et al. LC 94-31143. (Symposium Ser.: No. 575). (Illus.). 262p. 1994. text 78.00 (*0-8412-3041-2*, Pub. by Am Chemical) OUP.

Polymers from Biobased Materials. Ed. by Helena L. Chum. LC 90-23203. (Illus.). 169p. 1991. 109.00 (*0-8155-1271-6*) Noyes.

Polymers from Renewable Resources. Richard Gross et al. (ACS Synposium Ser.). 130.00 (*0-8412-3645-3*, Pub. by Am Chemical) OUP.

Polymers from Renewable Resources. Gary Leatham et al. (ACS Symposium Ser.). 110.00 (*0-8412-3647-X*, Pub. by Am Chemical) OUP.

Polymers from Renewable Resources: Biopolyesters & Biocatalysis. Carmen Scholz & Rich Gross. (ACS Symposium Ser.). 135.00 (*0-8412-3646-1*, Pub. by Am Chemical) OUP.

Polymers in Aqueous Media: Performance Through Association Developed from a Symposium Sponsored by the Division of Polymeric Materials: Science & Engineering at the 194th National Meeting of the American Chemical Society, New Orleans, LA, August 30-September 4, 1987. Ed. by J. Edward Glass. LC 89-15136. (Advances in Chemistry Ser.: No. 223). (Illus.). 592p. 1989. reprint ed. pap. 183.60 (*0-608-06783-0*, 206698000009) Bks Demand.

Polymers in Aqueous Media Performance Through Association. Ed. by J. Edward Glass. LC 89-15136. (Advances in Chemistry Ser.: No. 223). (Illus.). 551p. 1989. text 115.00 (*0-8412-1548-0*, Pub. by Am Chemical) OUP.

Polymers in Concrete. American Concrete Institute Staff. LC 73-86176. (American Concrete Institute Publication: No. SP-40). (Illus.). 368p. reprint ed. pap. 114.10 (*0-608-18574-4*, 200429400040) Bks Demand.

Polymers in Concrete: Advances & Applications. 110p. 1989. pap. 35.50 (*0-685-45549-1*, SP-116BOW6) ACI.

Polymers in Concrete: An Introduction. Satish Chandra. 224p. 1994. boxed set 173.95 (*0-8493-4815-3*, TA443) CRC Pr.

P

An Asterisk (*) at the beginning of an entry indicates that the title is appearing for the first time.

Polymers in Concrete: International Symposium. American Concrete Institute Staff. LC 78-73077. (American Concrete Institute Publication: SP-58). 426p. reprint ed. pap. 132.10 (*0-608-13002-8*, 202508200042) Bks Demand.

Polymers in Concrete: Proceedings of the 2nd East Asia Symposium on Polymers in Concrete (II-EASPIC), College of Engineering, Nihon University, Koriyama, Japan May 11-13, 1997. East Asia Symposium on Polymers in Concrete et al. LC 97-158094. (Illus.). 1997. 0.00 (*0-419-22330-4*, E & FN Spon) Routledge.

Polymers in Confined Environments. Ed. by S. Granick et al. LC 99-165901. (Advances in Polymer Science Ser.: Vol. 138). (Illus.). 270p. 1998. 189.00 (*3-540-64266-8*) Spr-Verlag.

Polymers in Electronics. Ed. by Theodore Davidson. LC 83-25782. (ACS Symposium Ser.: No. 242). 616p. 1984. lib. bdg. 87.95 (*0-8412-0823-9*) Am Chemical.

Polymers in Electronics. Ed. by Theodore Davidson. LC 83-25782. (ACS Symposium Ser.: Vol. 242). 616p. 1984. reprint ed. pap. 191.00 (*0-608-03123-2*, 206357600007) Bks Demand.

Polymers in Friction Assemblies of Machines & Devices: A Handbook. Ed. by A. V. Chichinadze. xii, 280p. 1984. 68.50 (*0-89864-010-5*) Allerton Pr.

Polymers in Improved Oil Recovery. Kenneth S. Sorbie. 1991. 110.00 (*0-8493-7137-6*, TN871) CRC Pr.

Polymers in Information Storage Technology. Ed. by K. L. Mittal. (Illus.). 466p. (C). text 156.00 (*0-306-43390-7*, Kluwer Plenum) Kluwer Academic.

Polymers in Injection Molding. Piaras V. De Cleir. LC 85-51316. 170p. (C). 1991. reprint ed. pap. 52.00 (*0-938648-25-X*) T-C Pr CA.

Polymers in Medicine. Ed. by G. E. Zaikov. LC 95-24679. 207p. 1995. 125.00 (*1-56072-252-5*) Nova Sci Pubs.

Polymers in Medicine: Biomedical & Pharmaceutical Applications. Ed. by Raphael M. Ottenbrite & Emo Chiellini. LC 92-60021. 265p. 1992. text 69.95 (*0-87762-929-3*) Technomic.

Polymers in Medicine & Pharmacy: Materials Research Society Symposium Proceedings. Ed. by Antonios G. Mikos et al. (MRS Symposium Proceedings Ser.: Vol. 394). 208p. 1995. text 90.00 (*1-55899-297-9*, 394) Materials Res.

Polymers in Medicine I: Biomedical & Pharmacological Applications. Ed. by Emo Chiellini & P. Giusti. 425p. 1983. 105.00 (*0-306-41360-4*, Plenum Trade) Perseus Pubng.

Polymers in Medicine II: Biomedical & Pharmaceutical Applications. Ed. by Luigi Nicolais et al. (Polymer Science & Technology Ser.: Vol. 34). 440p. 1986. 105.00 (*0-306-42390-1*, Plenum Trade) Perseus Pubng.

Polymers in Microelectronics: Fundamentals & Applications. David S. Soane & Z. Martynenko. 308p. 1989. 192.00 (*0-444-87290-6*) Elsevier.

Polymers in Microlithography: Materials & Processes. Ed. by Takao Iwayanagi et al. LC 89-17931. (Symposium Ser.: No. 412). (Illus.). 433p. 1989. text 105.00 (*0-8412-1701-7*, Pub. by Am Chemical) OUP.

Polymers in Nature. Elizabeth A. MacGregor & C. T. Greenwood. LC 79-41787. (Illus.). 399p. reprint ed. pap. 123.70 (*0-8357-3737-3*, 203646300003) Bks Demand.

Polymers in Optics: Physics, Chemistry, & Applications. Roger A. Lessard et al. LC 96-22980. (Critical Reviews of Optical Science & Technology Ser.). 1996. pap. 70.00 (*0-8194-2255-X*) SPIE.

Polymers in Sensors: Theory & Practice. Ed. by Naim Akmal & Arthur M. Usmani. LC 98-13989. (Symposium Ser.: No. 690). (Illus.). 320p. 1998. text 110.95 (*0-8412-3550-3*, Pub. by Am Chemical) OUP.

Polymers in Solar Energy Utilization. Ed. by Charles G. Gebelein et al. LC 83-6367. (Symposium Ser.: No. 220). 510p. 1983. lib. bdg. 65.95 (*0-8412-0776-3*) Am Chemical.

Polymers in Solar Energy Utilization. Ed. by Charles G. Gebelein et al. LC 83-6367. (ACS Symposium Ser.: No. 220). (Illus.). 534p. 1983. reprint ed. pap. 165.60 (*0-608-03210-7*, 206372900007) Bks Demand.

Polymers in Solution: Theoretical Considerations & Newer Methods of Characterization. Ed. by William C. Forsman. (Illus.). 316p. (C). 1986. text 132.00 (*0-306-42146-1*, Kluwer Plenum) Kluwer Academic.

Polymers in Space Research: Papers Presented at the Symposium. Symposium on Polymers in Space Research Staff. Ed. by Charles L. Segal et al. LC 76-119601. (Illus.). 480p. reprint ed. pap. 148.80 (*0-7837-0890-4*, 204119600019) Bks Demand.

Polymers, Laminations & Coatings Conference Bk. 1: 1984 Proceedings. Technical Association of the Pulp & Industry Staff. LC TS1118.F5. 357p. 1984. reprint ed. pap. 110.70 (*0-608-09971-6*, 202477900001) Bks Demand.

Polymers, Laminations & Coatings Conference Bk. 2: 1984 Proceedings. Technical Association of the Pulp & Industry Staff. LC TS1118.F5. 350p. 1984. reprint ed. pap. 108.50 (*0-608-09972-4*, 202477900002) Bks Demand.

Polymers, Laminations & Coatings Conference, 1986 Bk. 1: Proceedings of TAPPI, Opryland Hotel, Nashville, TN, September 15-17. Technical Association of the Pulp & Paper Industry. LC TS1118.I5. 187p. 1986. reprint ed. pap. 58.00 (*0-608-09973-2*, 202928100001) Bks Demand.

Polymers, Laminations & Coatings Conference, 1986 Bk. 2: Proceedings of TAPPI, Opryland Hotel, Nashville, TN, September 15-17. Technical Association of the Pulp & Paper Industry. LC TS1118.I5. 393p. 1986. reprint ed. pap. 121.90 (*0-608-09974-0*, 202928100002) Bks Demand.

Polymers, Laminations & Coatings Conference, 1989: Buena Vista Palace, Orlando, FL, Sept. 5-8, Bk. 1. Technical Association of the Pulp & Paper Industry. LC TS0198.3.F5. (TAPPI Proceedings Ser.). (Illus.). 473p. 1989. reprint ed. pap. 146.70 (*0-8357-6337-4*, 203561000001) Bks Demand.

Polymers, Laminations & Coatings Conference, 1989: Buena Vista Palace, Orlando, FL, Sept. 5-8, Bk. 2. Technical Association of the Pulp & Paper Industry. LC TS0198.3.F5. (TAPPI Proceedings Ser.). (Illus.). 422p. reprint ed. pap. 130.90 (*0-8357-6338-2*, 203561000002) Bks Demand.

Polymers, Laminations & Coatings Conference, 1990: Boston Marriott Copley Place, Boston, MA, September 4-7, 2 bks., Bk. 1. Technical Association of the Pulp & Paper Industry. LC TS1171.T43. (TAPPI Proceedings Ser.). (Illus.). 485p. reprint ed. pap. 150.40 (*0-8357-2937-0*, 203918100001) Bks Demand.

Polymers, Laminations & Coatings Conference, 1990: Boston Marriott Copley Place, Boston, MA, September 4-7, 2 bks., Bk. 2. Technical Association of the Pulp & Paper Industry. LC TS1171.T43. (TAPPI Proceedings Ser.). (Illus.). 547p. reprint ed. pap. 169.60 (*0-8357-2938-9*, 203918100002) Bks Demand.

Polymers, Laminations & Coatings Conference, 1991: San Diego Marriott, San Diego, CA, September 3-6, 2 bks., Bk. 1. Technical Association of the Pulp & Paper Industry. LC TS0198.3.F5P. (TAPPI Proceedings Ser.). (Illus.). 499p. reprint ed. pap. 154.70 (*0-7837-1139-5*, 204166900001) Bks Demand.

Polymers, Laminations & Coatings Conference, 1991: San Diego Marriott, San Diego, CA, September 3-6, 2 bks., Bk. 2. Technical Association of the Pulp & Paper Industry. LC TS0198.3.F5P. (TAPPI Proceedings Ser.). (Illus.). 544p. reprint ed. pap. 168.70 (*0-7837-1140-9*, 204166900002) Bks Demand.

Polymers, Laminations & Coatings Conference, 1992: Hilton at Walt Disney World Village, Lake Buena Vista, FL, September 8-11. Technical Association of the Pulp & Paper Industry. LC TS0198.3.F5P. (TAPPI Proceedings Ser.). (Illus.). 473p. reprint ed. pap. 146.70 (*0-7837-3571-5*, 204342900009) Bks Demand.

Polymers, Laminations & Coatings Conference, 1994: Opryland Hotel, Nashville, TN, August 28-September 1. Technical Association of the Pulp & Paper Industry. LC TS1171.T43. (TAPPI Proceedings Ser.). (Illus.). 548p. 1994. pap. 169.90 (*0-608-05367-8*, 208241600010) Bks Demand.

Polymers, Laminations & Coatings Conference, 1995: Chicago Marriott Downtown, Chicago, IL, August 27-31, Bk. 1. Technical Association of the Pulp & Paper Industry. LC TS1171.T43. (TAPPI Proceedings Ser.). (Illus.). 338p. reprint ed. pap. 104.80 (*0-608-09144-8*, 208248500001) Bks Demand.

Polymers, Laminations & Coatings Conference, 1995: Chicago Marriott Downtown, Chicago, IL, August 27-31, Bk. 2. Technical Association of the Pulp & Paper Industry. LC TS1171.T43. (TAPPI Proceedings Ser.). (Illus.). 348p. reprint ed. pap. 107.90 (*0-608-09145-6*, 208248500002) Bks Demand.

Polymers, Liquid Crystals & Low-Dimensional Solids. Ed. by Norman H. March & Mario P. Tosi. (Physics of Solids & Liquids Ser.). (Illus.). 648p. (C). 1984. text 174.00 (*0-306-41641-7*, Kluwer Plenum) Kluwer Academic.

Polymers Near Surfaces: Conformation Properties & Relation to Critical Phenomena 1992. E. Elsenriegler. 250p. (C). 1993. text 44.00 (*981-02-0595-3*) World Scientific Pub.

Polymers of Biological & Biomedical Significance. Ed. by Shalaby W. Shalaby et al. LC 93-34697. (Symposium Ser.: No. 540). (Illus.). 334p. 1994. text 98.00 (*0-8412-2732-2*, Pub. by Am Chemical) OUP.

Polymers or Fibers & Elastomers. Ed. by Jett C. Arthur, Jr. LC 84-14635. (Symposium Ser.: No. 260). 434p. 1984. lib. bdg. 76.95 (*0-8412-0859-X*) Am Chemical.

Polymers, Paint, Colour Yearbook. FMJ Intl. Publ. Ltd. Staff. 400p. (C). 1990. 245.00 (*0-7855-4938-2*, Pub. by Fuel Metallurgical Jrnl) St Mut.

Polymers-Plastics Market 1994. Market Intelligence Staff. 239p. 1994. 545.00 (*0-7889-0033-1*) Frost & Sullivan.

Polymers with Chemomechanical Function see Macromolecular Mechanochemistry

Polymethylmethacrylate: A Flexible Membrane for a Tailored Dialysis. Ed. by Claudio V. Ronco. LC 98-42558. (Contributions to Nephrology Ser.: Vol. 125). (Illus.). viii, 246p. 1998. 198.25 (*3-8055-6760-X*) S Karger.

Polymetic Materials Encyclopedia. Ed. by Joseph C. Salamone. 6900p. 1996. pap. 6294.95 (*0-8493-2652-4*) CRC Pr.

Polymetric Materials Encyclopedia, 12 vols. Ed. by Joseph C. Salamone. (Illus.). 9600p. 1996. boxed set 4414.95 (*0-8493-2470-X*) CRC Pr.

Polymide Membranes: Applications, Fabrications, & Properties. H. Ohya et al. 328p. 1996. text 78.00 (*90-5699-024-1*, ECU100) Gordon & Breach.

Polymides. Ed. by Malay K. Ghosh & K. L. Mittal. LC 96-18710. (Plastics Engineering Ser.: Vol. 36). (Illus.). 912p. 1996. text 250.00 (*0-8247-9466-4*) Dekker.

Polymodal Receptor: A Gateway to Pathological Pain. Takao Kumazawa et al. LC 96-41062. (Progress in Brain Research Ser.). 560p. 1996. 243.75 (*0-444-82473-1*) Elsevier.

Polymorphic Programming Languages: Design & Implementation. D. M. Harland. (Computers & Their Applications Ser.). 251p. 1984. text 65.95 (*0-470-20029-4*) P-H.

Polymorphism in Molecular Crystal. Bernstein. text. write for info. (*0-471-48972-7*) Wiley.

Polymorphism in Pharmaceutical Solids. Ed. by Brittain. LC 99-11315. (Drugs & the Pharmaceutical Sciences Ser.). (Illus.). 448p. 1999. text 185.00 (*0-8247-0237-9*) Dekker.

Polymorphisms & Fertility. Ed. by M. Adinolfi. (Journal: Experimental & Clinical Immunogenetics Ser.: Vol. 2, No. 2). (Illus.). 88p. 1985. pap. 35.00 (*3-8055-4066-3*) S Karger.

Polyn: Jewish Life in the Old Country. Alter Kacyzne. LC 99-14178. (Illus.). 192p. 1999. 65.00 (*0-8050-5097-3*); 50.00 (*0-8050-5907-5*) H Holt & Co.

Polynesia. 3rd ed. Charles E. Wood. LC 94-9947. (Illus.). 184p. 1994. pap. 125.00 (*0-9697265-0-3*, Pub. by Laurie Norie & Wilson Ltd) St Mut.

***Polynesia French: A Country Study Guide, 110 vols.** International Business Publications, USA Staff & Global Investment Center, USA Staff. (World Country Study Guides Library Ser.: Vol. 219). (Illus.). 350p. 2000. pap. 69.95 (*0-7397-1042-7*) Intl Business Pubns.

Polynesian & American Linguistic Connections. Mary R. Key. LC 85-101. (Edward Sapir Monographs in Language, Culture & Cognition: No. 12). xii, 80p. (Orig.). 1984. pap. 18.00 (*0-933104-17-0*) Jupiter Pr.

***Polynesian & Oceanian Designs.** Gregory Mirow. LC 00-31462. (Pictorial Archive Ser.). 2000. pap. write for info. (*0-486-41227-X*) Dover.

Polynesian Barkcloth. Simon Kooijman. (Ethnography Ser.: No. 7). (Illus.). 64p. 1989. pap. 10.50 (*0-85263-943-0*, Pub. by Shire Pubns) Parkwest Pubns.

Polynesian Botanical Bibliography, 1773-1935. E. D. Merrill. (BMB Ser.: No. 144). 1937. 30.00 (*0-527-02252-7*) Periodicals Srv.

Polynesian Canoes & Navigation. Judi Thompson & Alan Taylor. (Pamphlets Polynesia Ser.: No. 2). 32p. 1980. pap. 3.50 (*0-939154-15-3*) Inst Polynesian.

Polynesian Concept of Mana & the Greek Concept of Menos. Roland F. Perkins. (Monograph Ser.: No. 3). 41p. 1980. pap. write for info. (*1-892174-13-8*) Kamalu uluolele.

Polynesian Crafts. June Sasaki. (Illus.). 1978. pap. 6.95 (*0-912180-33-1*) Petroglyph.

Polynesian Cultural Center - English. Illus. by William Mahoni. 50p. 1995. pap. write for info. (*0-9644640-0-4*) Polynesian Cult.

Polynesian Cultural Center - Japanese. Tr. by PR Japan Staff. (JPN., Illus.). 50p. 1995. pap. write for info. (*0-9644640-1-2*) Polynesian Cult.

Polynesian Culture History: Essays in Honor of Kenneth P. Emory. Ed. by Genevieve A. Highland & Roland W. Force. LC 67-29172. (Bernice P. Bishop Museum Special Publications: No. 56). (Illus.). 614p. reprint ed. pap. 190.40 (*0-608-18797-6*, 203032000068) Bks Demand.

***Polynesian Dance Directory: Includes Suppliers & Musicians.** Karen I. Marks. 115p. 1998. spiral bd. 59.95 (*0-9673569-0-3*) Marks Designs.

***Polynesian Dance Directory: Includes Suppoiers & Musicians.** Karen I. Marks. 210p. 1998. pap. 39.95 (*0-9673569-2-X*) Marks Designs.

Polynesian Dancing for Men, Vol. II, Bk. 26. Vicki Corona. (Celebrate the Cultures Ser.). (Illus.). 34p. 1989. pap. 14.95 (*1-58513-016-8*) Dance Fantasy.

Polynesian Decorative Designs. R. H. Greiner. (BMB Ser.: No. 7). 1974. reprint ed. 30.00 (*0-527-02110-5*) Periodicals Srv.

Polynesian Family System in Ka-'u, Hawaii. E. S. Handy & Mary K. Pukui. LC 75-171998. 259p. 1972. pap. 9.95 (*0-8048-1031-1*) Tuttle Pubng.

Polynesian Family System in Ka'u, Hawai'i. E. S. Craighill Handy & Mary K. Pukui. 288p. 1999. mass mkt. 7.95 (*1-56647-232-6*) Mutual Pub HI.

Polynesian Herbal Medicine. W. Arthur Whistler. (Illus.). 238p. 1993. pap. text 33.00 (*0-915809-16-8*) Natl Trop Bot.

Polynesian Journal of Captain Martin. Martin. (Australian National University press Ser.). 1996. write for info. (*0-08-033033-9*, Pergamon Pr) Elsevier.

Polynesian Journal of Henry Byam Martin. Henry B. Martin. Ed. by Edward Dodd. (Illus.). 200p. 1981. 16.95 (*0-87577-060-6*, PEMP149, Peabody Museum) Peabody Essex Mus.

Polynesian Languages: A Survey of Research. Viktor Krupa. (Janua Linguarum, Series Critica: No. 11). 1973. pap. text 33.85 (*90-279-2423-6*) Mouton.

Polynesian Mythology & Ancient Traditional History of the New Zealanders As Furnished by Their Priests & Chiefs. George Grey. LC 75-35253. reprint ed. 37.50 (*0-404-14425-X*) AMS Pr.

Polynesian Peasants & Proletarians. Ben R. Finney. 150p. 1973. boxed set 34.95 (*0-87073-732-5*) Transaction Pubs.

Polynesian Religion (BMB) E. S. Handy. (Bayard Dominick Expedition Publication: No. 12 & 34). 1974. reprint ed. 60.00 (*0-527-02137-7*) Periodicals Srv.

Polynesian Seafaring & Navigation: Ocean Travel in Anutan Culture & Society. Richard Feinberg. LC 87-22572. (Illus.). 228p. 1988. 30.00 (*0-87338-352-4*) Kent St U Pr.

Polynesian Sound-Producing Instruments. Richard Moyle. (Ethnography Ser.: No. 20). (Illus.). 64p. 1990. pap. 10.50 (*0-7478-0095-2*, Pub. by Shire Pubns) Parkwest Pubns.

Polynesian Species of Hedyotis. F. R. Fosberg. (BMB Ser.: No. 174). 1974. reprint ed. 25.00 (*0-527-02282-9*) Periodicals Srv.

Polynesian Tattooing. Alan Taylor. (Pamphlets Polynesia Ser.: No. 3). 1981. pap. 3.50 (*0-939154-21-8*) Inst Polynesian.

Polynesian Wanderings. William A. Churchill. LC 75-35186. reprint ed. 45.00 (*0-404-14215-X*) AMS Pr.

Polynesians. Stephen Currie. LC 98-39780. (Endangered Cultures Ser.). (Illus.). 32p. (YA). (gr. 4 up). 1999. lib. bdg. 21.30 (*1-887068-94-5*) Smart Apple.

Polynesiens: Leur Origine, Leurs Migrations, Leur Langage, 4 vols., Set. Pierre A. Lesson. LC 75-35201. reprint ed. 162.50 (*0-404-14270-2*) AMS Pr.

Polyneuropathies Associated with Plasma Cell Dyscrasias. John J. Kelly et al. (Topics in the Neurosciences Ser.). (C). 1987. text 104.50 (*0-89838-884-8*) Kluwer Academic.

Polynomes Orthogonaux et Applications. Ed. by C. Brezinski et al. (Lecture Notes in Mathematics Ser.: Vol. 1171). (FRE & GER.). 584p. 1985. 77.95 (*0-387-16059-0*) Spr-Verlag.

Polynomial Algorithms in Computer Algebra. Franz Winkler. LC 96-7170. (Texts & Monographs in Symbolic Computation Ser.). 264p. 1996. pap. 69.00 (*3-211-82759-5*) Spr-Verlag.

Polynomial & Matrix Computations Vol. 1: Fundamental Algorithms. Dario Bini & Victor Pan. LC 94-27577. (Progress in Theoretical Computer Science Ser.). xvi, 415p. 1994. 71.00 (*0-8176-3786-9*) Birkhauser.

Polynomial & Spline Approximation. Ed. by Badri N. Sahney. (NATO Advanced Study Institutes Ser.: No. C-49). 1979. text 121.50 (*90-277-0984-X*) Kluwer Academic.

Polynomial Approach to Linear Algebra. P. A. Fuhrmann. LC 95-49237. (Universitext Ser.). 360p. 1996. pap. 39.00 (*0-387-94643-8*) Spr-Verlag.

Polynomial Approximation of Differential Equations. D. Funaro. (Lecture Notes in Physics Ser.: Vol. M8). x, 305p. 1992. 68.95 (*0-387-55230-8*) Spr-Verlag.

***Polynomial Completeness in Algebraic Systems.** Kalle Kaarli & Alden F. Pixley. LC 00-34538. 2000. write for info. (*1-58488-203-4*, Chap & Hall CRC) CRC Pr.

Polynomial Identities & Variants of n x n Matrices. Edward Formanek. LC 90-22966. (CBMS Regional Conference Series in Mathematics: Vol. 78). 55p. 1991. pap. 23.00 (*0-8218-0730-7*, CBMS/78C) Am Math.

Polynomial Invariant of Finite Groups. D. J. Benson. (London Mathematical Society Lecture Note Ser.: No. 190). 1993. pap. write for info. (*0-521-45866-8*) Cambridge U Pr.

Polynomial Invariants of Finite Groups. Larry Smith. LC 94-46590. (Research Notes in Mathematics Ser.). 376p. (C). 1995. text 64.00 (*1-56881-053-9*) AK Peters.

Polynomial Mappings. Wladyslaw Narkiewicz. LC 95-18957. (Lecture Notes in Mathematics Ser.: Vol. 1600). 1995. write for info. (*0-387-59435-3*) Spr-Verlag.

Polynomial Mappings. Wladyslaw Narkiewicz. Ed. by A. Dold & F. Takens. (Lecture Notes in Mathematics Ser.: Vol. 1600). vii, 130p. 1995. pap. 29.95 (*3-540-59435-3*) Spr-Verlag.

Polynomial Methods for Control Systems Design. Michael J. Grimbke & Vladimir Kucera. LC 96-27441. (Illus.). x, 255p. 1996. pap. 59.95 (*3-540-76077-6*) Spr-Verlag.

Polynomial Methods in Optimal Control & Filtering. Ed. by Kenneth J. Hunt. (IEE Control Engineering Ser.: No. 49). xv, 309p. 1993. boxed set 89.00 (*0-86341-295-5*) INSPEC Inc.

Polynomial Operator Equations in Abstract Spaces & Applications. Ioannis K. Argyros. LC 98-6373. 592p. 1998. boxed set 94.95 (*0-8493-8702-7*) CRC Pr.

Polynomial Rings & Affine Spaces. M. Nagata. LC 78-8264. (CBMS Regional Conference Series in Mathematics: No. 37). 33p. 1978. reprint ed. pap. 17.00 (*0-8218-1687-X*, CBMS/37) Am Math.

Polynomials. E. J. Barbeau. LC 96-29451. (Problem Books in Mathematics). (FRE., Illus.). 465p. 1995. 59.95 (*0-387-96919-5*) Spr-Verlag.

Polynomials. 7th ed. (C). 1995. text (*0-201-41555-0*) S&S Trade.

Polynomials see Key to Algebra Series

Polynomials: Addition Subtraction Inter 5.1. 7th ed. (C). 1995. text 0.66 (*0-201-41451-1*) Addison-Wesley.

Polynomials: An Algorithmic Approach. M. Mignotte & D. Stefanescu. (Series in Discrete Mathematics & Theoretical Computer Science). 320p. 1999. pap. 49.00 (*981-4021-51-2*) Spr-Verlag.

Polynomials: Patterns, Factors, Solutions & Connections - Real World Applications. Abigail Silver & Carl Carozza. (Textworks Ser.). (Illus.). ix, 76p. (YA). (gr. 9-12). 1995. ring bd. 39.95 (*1-58284-019-9*, Thoughtful Educ) Silver Strong.

Polynomials & Equations. K. T. Leung et al. 240p. (C). 1992. pap. text 20.00 (*962-209-271-3*, Pub. by HK Univ Pr) Coronet Bks.

Polynomials & Linear Control Systems. Stephen Barnett. LC 83-5309. (Monographs & Textbooks in Pure & Applied Mathematics: Vol. 77). 471p. reprint ed. pap. 146.10 (*0-608-08911-7*, 206954600005) Bks Demand.

Polynomials & Polynomial Inequalities. Peter Borwein & Tamas Erdelyi. LC 95-8374. (Graduate Texts in Mathematics Ser.: Vol. 160). 482p. 1995. 64.95 (*0-387-94509-1*) Spr-Verlag.

Polynomials in Several Variables & Fractional Equations. rev. ed. Mervin L. Keedy & Marvin L. Bittinger. (Algebra, a Modern Introduction Ser.). (gr. 7-9). 1981. pap. text. write for info. (*0-201-03987-7*) Addison-Wesley.

Polynomials Orthogonal over a Region & Bieberbach Polynomials: Proceedings. P. K. Suetin. LC 74-7346. (Proceedings of the Steklov Institute of Mathematics Ser.: No. 100). 91p. 1974. pap. 49.00 (*0-8218-3000-7*, STEKLO/100) Am Math.

***Polynomials with Special Regard to Reducibility.** Andrzej Schinzel. (Encyclopedia of Mathematics & Its Applications Ser.: Vol. 77). 500p. 2000. text 90.00 (*0-521-66225-7*) Cambridge U Pr.

Polynuclear Aromatic Compounds: Developed from a Symposium Sponsored by the Division of Petroleum Chemistry, Inc. at the 192nd Meeting of the American Chemical Society, Anaheim, CA, September 7-12, 1986. Ed. by Lawrence B. Ebert. LC 87-22973. (Advances in Chemistry Ser.: No. 217). (Illus.). 416p. 1988. reprint ed. pap. 129.00 (*0-608-06786-5*, 206698300009) Bks Demand.

An Asterisk (*) at the beginning of an entry indicates that the title is appearing for the first time.

Polynuclear Aromatic Compounds Pt. 1: Chemical, Environmental & Experimental Data. IARC Working Group on Evaluation of Carcinogenic Risk of Chemicals to Humans (1983: France) Staff. (IARC Monographs on the Evaluation of the Carcinogenic Risk of Chemicals to Humans: No. 32). 483p. 1983. reprint ed. pap. 149.80 (*0-608-04424-5*, 2043838) Bks Demand.

Polynuclear Aromatic Compounds - Bitumens, Coal-Tars & Derived Products, Shale-Oils & Soots: The Evaluation of Carcinogenic Risks to Humans. (IARC Monographs: No. 35). 271p. 1985. text 77.00 (*92-832-1235-5*) World Health.

Polynuclear Aromatic Compounds, Industrial Exposures in Aluminium Production, Coal Gasification, Coke Production & Iron & Steel Founding: The Evaluation of Carcinogenic Risks to Humans. (IARC Monographs: No. 34). 219p. 1984. text 53.00 (*92-832-1234-7*) World Health.

Polynuclear Aromatic Compounds, Part 1, Chemical, Environmental & Experimental Data: The Evaluation of Carcinogenic Risks to Humans. (IARC Monographs). 477p. 1983. text 88.00 (*92-832-1232-0*) World Health.

Polynuclear Aromatic Compounds, Synthesis, Properties, Analytical Measurements, Occurrence, & Biological Effects: Proceedings of the Thirteenth International Symposium on Polynuclear Aromatic Hydrocarbons, October 1-4, 1991, Bordeaux, France. Ed. by Philippe Garrigues & Michel Lamotte. LC 92-38976. 1264p. 1993. text 253.00 (*2-88124-545-5*) Gordon & Breach.

Polynuclear Aromatic Hydrocarbons: A Decade of Progress. Ed. by Marcus Cooke & Anthony J. Dennis. LC 79-642622. (Proceedings of the Tenth Polynuclear Aromatic Hydrocarbons International Symposiums Ser.). 960p. 1987. text 75.00 (*0-935470-34-4*) Battelle.

Polynuclear Aromatic Hydrocarbons: Chemical Analysis & Biological Fate. Ed. by Marcus Cooke & Anthony J. Dennis. LC 81-3669. (Fifth International Symposium on Polynuclear Aromatic Hydrocarbons Ser.). 770p. 1981. 65.00 (*0-935470-09-3*) Battelle.

Polynuclear Aromatic Hydrocarbons: Chemistry & Biological Effects. Ed. by Alf Bjorseth & Anthony J. Dennis. LC 80-17877. (Fourth International Symposium on Polynuclear Aromatic Hydrocarbons Ser.). (Illus.). 1097p. 1980. 65.00 (*0-935470-05-0*) Battelle.

Polynuclear Aromatic Hydrocarbons: Chemistry, Characterization & Carcinogenesis. M. Cooke & A. J. Dennis. LC 86-18430. (Ninth International Symposium on Polynuclear Aromatic Hydrocarbons Ser.). 987p. 1986. 75.00 (*0-935470-25-5*) Battelle.

Polynuclear Aromatic Hydrocarbons: Formation, Metabolism & Measurement. Marcus Cooke & Anthony J. Dennis. LC 83-12734. (Seventh International Polynuclear Aromatic Symposium on Hydrocarbons Ser.). 1301p. 1983. 65.00 (*0-935470-16-6*) Battelle.

Polynuclear Aromatic Hydrocarbons: Measurements, Means, & Metabolism: Proceedings of the 11th PAH International Symposium. Ed. by M. Cooke et al. LC 90-39041. 1220p. 1990. text 82.50 (*0-935470-58-1*) Battelle.

Polynuclear Aromatic Hydrocarbons: Mechanisms, Methods & Metabolism. Marcus Cooke & Anthony J. Dennis. LC 84-24254. (Eighth International Symposium on Polynuclear Aromatic Hydrocarbons Ser.). 1464p. 1984. 75.00 (*0-935470-22-0*) Battelle.

Polynuclear Aromatic Hydrocarbons: Physical & Biological Chemistry. Ed. by Marcus Cooke et al. LC 82-16439. (Sixth International Symposium on Polynuclear Aromatic Hydrocarbons Ser.). 947p. 1982. 65.00 (*0-935470-13-1*) Battelle.

Polynuclear Aromatic Hydrocarbons Pt. 2: Carbon Blacks, Mineral Oils (Lubricant Base Oils & Derived Products) & Some Nitroarenes. IARC Working Group on the Evaluation of the Carcin. LC RC0268.I57. (IARC Monographs on the Evaluation of Carcinogenic Risk of Chemicals to Humans: No. 33). (Illus.). 252p. reprint ed. pap. 78.20 (*0-7837-4008-5*, 204383800011) Bks Demand.

Polynuclear Aromatic Hydrocarbons Nomenclature Guide. C. Wright et al. LC 90-39042. 96p. 1990. pap. text 19.95 (*0-935470-59-X*) Battelle.

Polyol Paradigm & Complications of Diabetes. M. P. Cohen. (Illus.). xii, 143p. 1986. 99.00 (*0-387-96418-5*) Spr-Verlag.

Polyolefin Insulated Communications Cables for Outdoor Use. 1991. 60.00 (*0-614-18712-5*, S-56-434-1983) Insulated Cable.

Polyolefins VIII: Eighth International Conference on Polyolefins, February 21-24, 1993, Houston, Texas, Jointly Sponsored by the South Texas Section & Thermoplastic Materials & Foams Division of SPE. Society of Plastics Engineers Staff. LC TP1180.P67S6. 744p. reprint ed. pap. 200.00 (*0-7837-5729-8*, 204538900006) Bks Demand.

Polyolefins IV: Technical Papers, Regional Technical Conference, 1984. Society of Plastics Engineers Staff. LC TA0455.P5. 460p. reprint ed. pap. 142.60 (*0-608-12963-1*, 202472900038) Bks Demand.

Polyolefins IX: Ninth International Conference, February 26-March 1, 1995, Houston, TX. Society of Plastics Engineers Staff. LC TP1180.P67S6. (Illus.). 796p. 1995. reprint ed. pap. 200.00 (*0-7837-9716-8*, 206044700005) Bks Demand.

Polyolefins VI: Sixth International Conference on Polyolefins, February, 1989, Houston Texas. Society of Plastics Engineers Staff. LC TP1180.P67. 559p. reprint ed. pap. 173.30 (*0-8357-8575-0*, 203494100091) Bks Demand.

Polyoma Virus. B. E. Eddy. (Virology Monographs: Vol. 7). (Illus.). iv, 174p. 1969. 51.00 (*0-387-80934-1*) Spr-Verlag.

Polyominoes. 2nd ed. Solomon Golomb. 198p. 1994. pap. 14.95 (*0-691-02444-8*, Pub. by Princeton U Pr) Cal Prin Full Svc.

Polyominoes: A Guide to Puzzles & Problems in Tiling. George Martin. (Spectrum Ser.). (Illus.). 172p. 1991. pap. text 14.95 (*0-88385-501-1*, POLY) Math Assn.

Polyominoes: Solomon W. Golomb. Solomon W. Golomb. LC 93-41756. (Illus.). 248p. 1994. text 29.95 (*0-691-08573-0*, Pub. by Princeton U Pr) Cal Prin Full Svc.

Polyoxometalates: From Platonic Solids to Anti-Retroviral Activity. Ed. by Michael T. Pope & Achim Muller. LC 93-27849. (Topics in Molecular Organization & Engineering Ser.). 411p. (C). 1994. text 251.00 (*0-7923-2421-8*) Kluwer Academic.

Polypeptide Hormone Receptors. Barry I. Posner. LC 84-28677. (Receptors & Ligands in Intercellular Communication Ser.: No. 4). 621p. 1985. reprint ed. pap. 192.60 (*0-608-01328-5*, 206207100001) Bks Demand.

Polypeptide Hormones. Ed. by Roland F. Beers, Jr. & Edward G. Bassett. LC 79-66512. (Miles International Symposium Ser.: No. 12). (Illus.). 544p. 1980. reprint ed. pap. 168.70 (*0-608-00591-6*, 206117800007) Bks Demand.

Polypeptide Hormones: Molecular & Cellular Aspects. CIBA Foundation Staff. LC 76-2666. (CIBA Foundation Symposium: New Ser.: No. 41). 400p. reprint ed. pap. 124.00 (*0-608-14315-4*, 202216900024) Bks Demand.

Polyphase Flow & Transport Technology: Presented at the Symposium on Polyphase Flow & Transport Technology, Century 2--Emerging Technology Conferences, San Francisco, CA, August 13-15, 1980. Symposium on Polyphase Flow & Transport Technology. Ed. by R. A. Bajura. LC 80-130665. (Illus.). 278p. reprint ed. pap. 86.20 (*0-8357-2895-1*, 203913100011) Bks Demand.

Polyphase Induction Motors: Analysis, Design, & Application. Paul L. Cochran. (Electrical Engineering & Electronics Ser.: Vol. 59). (Illus.). 704p. 1989. text 215.00 (*0-8247-8043-4*) Dekker.

Polyphemes: Strange Adventures among Strange Beings. F. Hernaman Johnson. LC 74-15981. (Science Fiction Ser.). 318p. 1975. reprint ed. 26.95 (*0-405-06297-4*) Ayer.

Polyphonia Byzantina: Studies in Honour of Willem J. Aerts. Ed. by Hero Hokwerda et al. x, 383p. 1993. pap. 55.00 (*90-6980-054-3*, Pub. by Egbert Forsten) Hod1der & Stoughton.

Polyphonic Period II, 1400-1600 see Oxford History of Music

Polyphonic Sequence in Wolfenbuttel 677. Bryan Gillingham. (Wissenschaftliche Abhandlungen-Musicological Studies: Vol. 35). 80p. 1982. lib. bdg. 40.00 (*0-931902-14-2*) Inst Mediaeval Mus.

Polyphonie und Improvisation: Zur Offenen Form in Gunter Grass' Die Rattin. Klaus-Jurgen Roehm. LC 91-31480. (Studies in Modern German Literature: Vol. 47). (GER.). 185p. (C). 1992. text 36.95 (*0-8204-1693-2*) P Lang Pubng.

Polyphony & Symphony in Prophetic Literature: Rereading Jeremiah 7-20. Mark E. Biddle. (Studies in Old Testament Interpretation: Vol. 2). 160p. 1996. text 30.00 (*0-86554-503-0*, MUP/H394) Mercer Univ Pr.

Polyphony in Portugal, c. 1530-c. 1620: Sources from the Monastery of Santa Cruz, Coimbra. Owen Rees. LC 95-16153. (Outstanding Dissertations in Music from British Universities Ser.). (Illus.). 482p. 1995. text 127.00 (*0-8153-2029-9*) Garland.

Polyphony of Saint Martial & Santiago de Compostela, 2 vols. Theodore Karp. LC 91-2873. (C). 1992. 165.00 (*0-520-04744-3*, Pub. by U CA Pr) Cal Prin Full Svc.

Polyploidie Bei Pilzen: Unter Besonderer Beruecksichtigung der Boletales - Moeglichkeiten eines Cytofluorometrischen Nachweises. Birgit Wittmann-Meixner. (Bibliotheca Mycologica: Vol. 131). (GER., Illus.). iv, 163p. 1989. 48.00 (*3-443-59032-2*, Pub. by Gebruder Borntraeger) Balogh.

Polypodiaceous Ferns of India. C. K. Satija & S. S. Bir. (Aspects of Plant Sciences Ser.: Vol. VIII). (Illus.). 120p. 1985. 19.00 (*1-55528-044-7*) Scholarly Pubns.

Polyporaceae, Contribuicao Rara a Sua Bio-Taxonomia (Broteriana 8) J. Pinto-Lopez. (Illus.). 1968. reprint ed. pap. 48.00 (*3-7682-0555-X*) Lubrecht & Cramer.

Polyporaceae of North America: The Genus Fomes. 1957. 1.00 (*0-686-20693-2*) SUNY Environ.

Polyporaceae of North Europe, 2 vols., Set. Leif Ryvarden. (Illus.). 1988. pap. text. write for info. (*0-945345-13-5*) Lubrecht & Cramer.

Polyporaceae of Wisconsin. J. J. Neumann. 1971. reprint ed. 36.00 (*3-7682-0704-8*) Lubrecht & Cramer.

Polypores, Boletes & Agarica. Meinhard Moser. Tr. by Geoffrey Kibby & R. Rayner from GER. (Illus.). 355p. (C). 1983. text 72.50 (*0-916422-43-7*) Mad River.

Polypores of China. Ji-Ding Zhao & Xiao-Qing Zhang. Ed. by Rong Xiang. (Bibliotheca Mycologica: Vol. 145). (GER., Illus.). 524p. 1992. 112.00 (*3-443-59046-2*, Pub. by Gebruder Borntraeger) Balogh.

Polypores of Papua New Guinea: A Preliminary Conspectus. E. Quanten. (Opera Botanica Belgica Ser.: Vol. 11). (Illus.). 352p. 1997. 100.00 (*90-72619-34-X*, Pub. by Natl Botanic Grdn Belgium) Balogh.

Polypropylene. H. P. Frank. LC 68-24786. (Polymer Monographs: Vol. 2). (Illus.). x, 134p. 1968. text 156.00 (*0-677-01540-2*) Gordon & Breach.

***Polypropylene.** J. Karger-Kocsis. 988p. 1999. 265.50 (*0-412-80200-7*, Kluwer Plenum) Kluwer Academic.

Polypropylene: The Definitive User's Guide. Ed. by Clive Maier. LC 97-76233. (PDL Handbook Ser.). 425p. 1998. 285.00 (*1-884207-58-8*) William Andrew.

Polypropylene & Other Polyolefins: Polymerization & Characterization. S. Van der Ven. (Studies in Polymer Science: No. 7). 618p. 1990. 304.50 (*0-444-88690-7*) Elsevier.

Polypropylene Fibers & Films. Anthony V. Galanti & Charles L. Mantell. LC 65-26813. 190p. reprint ed. pap. 58.90 (*0-608-13255-1*, 205578700038) Bks Demand.

Polypropylene Handbook: Polymerization, Characterization, Properties, Processing, Applications. Edward P. Moore. 419p. 1996. 140.00 (*1-56990-208-9*) Hanser-Gardner.

Polypropylene Textiles. Shirley Inst. Staff. (C). 1982. 125.00 (*0-7855-4575-1*, Pub. by British Textile Tech) St Mut.

Polyquinane Chemistry Synthesis & Reactions. Leo A. Paquette & A. M. Doherty. (Reactivity & Structure Ser.: Vol. 26). (Illus.). 250p. 1987. 142.95 (*0-387-17703-5*) Spr-Verlag.

Polyrhythmic Studies for Snare Drum. Fred Albright. 72p. (YA). 1997. pap. text 14.95 (*0-7692-0946-7*, 0105B) Wrner Bros.

Polyrhythms. rev. ed. P. Magadini. 68p. 1988. pap. 19.95 (*0-7935-2124-6*, 06620611) H Leonard.

Polyrhythms, Bk. 1. rev. ed. P. Magadini. 68p. 1988. pap. 14.95 (*0-7935-2123-8*, 06620612) H Leonard.

Polysaccharide Applications: Cosmetics & Pharmaceuticals. Magda A. El-Nokaly & Helena A. Soini. LC 99-30375. (ACS Symposium Ser.: No. 737). (Illus.). 464p. 1999. text 135.00 (*0-8412-3641-0*, Pub. by Am Chemical) OUP.

Polysaccharide Association Structures in Food. Reginal H. Walter. LC 98-2762. (Food Science & Technology Ser.). (Illus.). 352p. 1998. text 165.00 (*0-8247-0164-X*) Dekker.

Polysaccharide Dispersions: Chemistry & Technology in Foods. Ed. by Reginald H. Walter. LC 97-74420. (Food Science & Technology International Ser.). (Illus.). 236p. 1997. text 99.95 (*0-12-733865-9*) Morgan Kaufmann.

Polysaccharides. Ed. by Dumitriu. LC 98-16717. (Illus.). 1176p. 1998. text 250.00 (*0-8247-0127-5*) Dekker.

Polysaccharides. George L. Innes & Business Communications Co Staff. LC 99-175713. (Opportunity Report Ser.). xx, 160 p. 1998. write for info. (*1-56965-550-2*) BCC.

Polysaccharides, No. C-186. LC 96-125127. 1994. 2450.00 (*1-56965-015-2*) BCC.

Polysaccharides & Glycoconjugates in Invertebrates & Polysaccharides & Glycoconjugates in Non-Mammalian Vertebrates. Maria G. Manfredi-Romanini & Anna M. Bolognani-Fantin. (Handbook of Histochemistry, Poly-Saccharides Ser.: Vol. 11, Pt. 5). (Illus.). 450p. 1991. text 255.00 (*1-56081-324-5*, Pub. by Gustav Fischer) Balogh.

Polysaccharides in Medicinal Applications. Severian Dumitiu. LC 96-15856. (Illus.). 816p. 1996. text 225.00 (*0-8247-9540-7*) Dekker.

***Polysemy: Theoretical & Computational Approaches.** Ed. by Yael Ravin & Claudia Leacock. (Illus.). 256p. 2000. text 75.00 (*0-19-823842-8*) OUP.

***Polysemy in Cognitive Linguistics: Selected Papers from the International Cognitive Linguistics Conference, Amsterdam, 1997.** Ed. by Hubert Cuyckens & Britta Zawada. (Current Issues in Linguistic Theory Ser.: Vol. 177). 330p. 2000. write for info. (*1-55619-894-9*) J Benjamins Pubng.

Polysexuality. Ed. by Francois Peraldi. 300p. Date not set. 12.00 (*1-57027-011-2*) Autonomedia.

PolyShrink Jewelry Techniques. Kit Zimmerman & Jo Rebeka. (PolyShrink Ser.). 49p. 1995. spiral bd. 14.95 (*0-9650993-0-X*) Lucky Squirrel.

Polysialic Acid: From Microbes to Men. Ed. by J. Roth et al. LC 92-48982. (Advances in Life Sciences Ser.). xxiii, 350p. 1992. 109.50 (*0-8176-2803-7*, Pub. by Birkhauser) Princeton Arch.

Polysilicon Films & Interfaces. Ed. by King N. Tu et al. (Symposium Proceedings Ser.: Vol. 106). 1988. text 17.50 (*0-931837-74-X*) Materials Res.

Polysilicon Thin Films & Interfaces. Ed. by T. Kamins et al. (Symposium Proceedings Ser.: Vol. 182). 405p. 1990. text 17.50 (*1-55899-071-2*) Materials Res.

Polysoaps/Stabilizers/Nitrogen-15 NMR. (Advances in Polymer Science Ser.: Vol. 124). (Illus.). 257p. 1995. 195.95 (*3-540-58983-X*) Spr-Verlag.

Polystochastic Models in Chemical Engineering. O. Iordache. vii, 231p. 1986. lib. bdg. 107.00 (*90-6764-063-8*, Pub. by VSP) Coronet Bks.

Polysubstance Abuse see Drug Abuse Prevention Library: The Risks of Drug Use

Polysymetrics: The Art of Making Geometric Patterns. June Oliver. 40p. 1982. pap. 3.95 (*0-685-05678-3*) P-H.

Polysymetrics: The Art of Making Geometric Patterns. June Oliver. (Illus.). 32p. (J). (gr. 5-9). 1986. pap. 7.95 (*0-906212-09-X*, Pub. by Tarquin Pubns) Parkwest Pubns.

Polysynthesis Parameter. Mark C. Baker. (Oxford Studies in Comparative Syntax). (Illus.). 576p. 1996. text 95.00 (*0-19-509307-0*) OUP.

Polytechnic Dictionary of Spanish & English Languages - English-Spanish. 2nd ed. F. Beigbeder Atienza. (ENG & SPA.). 1543p. 1997. 180.00 (*84-7978-299-4*, Pub. by Ediciones Diaz) IBD Ltd.

Poly Experiment. P. Pratt. LC 96-38318. 1997. 134.00 (*0-335-19564-4*) OpUniv Pr.

Polytechnical Dictionary, 2 vols. Incl. Vol. 1. English-German. 1967. 550.00 (*0-08-012435-6*); Vol. 2. German-English. 1967. 459.00 (*0-08-013223-5*); write for info. (*0-318-55187-X*, Pub. by Pergamon Repr) Franklin.

Polytechnical Dictionary. 3rd ed. A. Belov. 656p. (C). 1989. 175.00 (*0-7855-6692-9*, Pub. by Collets) St Mut.

Polytechnical Dictionary, Vol 1, English-German. 7th ed. Rudolf Walther. (ENG & GER.). 1126p. 1990. 195.00 (*0-7859-7058-4*) Fr & Eur.

Polytechnical Dictionary: Polytechnisches Woerterbuch der Technik Deutsch - Franzoesisch. 5th ed. Albert Schlegelmich. (FRE & GER.). 831p. 1988. 150.00 (*0-8288-2112-7*, M7591) Fr & Eur.

Polytechnical Dictionary of the English & Spanish Languages, English-Spanish, Vol. 1. F. Beigbeder Atienza. (ENG & SPA.). Date not set. 395.00 (*0-7859-9589-7*) Fr & Eur.

Polytechnical Railroad Dictionary, Basque, Catalan, English, French, German, Spanish. Mario Leon. (BAQ, CAT, ENG, FRE & GER.). 717p. 1997. 295.00 (*0-7859-9577-3*) Fr & Eur.

Polytechnical Russian-German Dictionary: Polytechnishes Woerterbuch Russisch-Deutsch. 5th ed. Paul Huter & Horst Gorner. (GER & RUS.). 1756p. 1989. lib. bdg. 125.00 (*0-8288-3838-0*, M9907) Fr & Eur.

Polytechnisches Woerterbuch: German-Portuguese. Lutz Franzke. (GER & POR.). 640p. 1991. 250.00 (*0-7859-8316-3*, 3341007695) Fr & Eur.

Polytene Chromosomes in Genetic Research. V. Sorsa. 272p. 1988. text 57.95 (*0-470-21215-2*) P-H.

Polytetrafluoroethylene (Teflon, Gore-Tex, Polytef, PTFE) Index of New Information with Authors, Subjects & References. Leslie N. Cooke. 150p. 1996. 47.50 (*0-7883-1254-5*); pap. 44.50 (*0-7883-1255-3*) ABBE Pubs Assn.

Polytheism of the Bible & the Mystery of Lucifer. 2nd rev. ed. Frank T. De Angelis. Ed. by William Strickfaden et al. LC 97-91766. (Illus.). (C). 1997. pap. 15.95 (*0-9657834-6-4*) Spartacus Pubns.

Polytheistic Systems. Ed. by Glenys Davies. 1991. pap. text 35.00 (*0-7486-0135-X*, Pub. by Edinburgh U Pr) Col U Pr.

Polythiophenes - Electrically Conductive Polymers. G. Kobmehl & G. Schopf. LC 97-108053. (Advances in Polymer Science Ser.: Vol. 129). (Illus.). 176p. 1996. 129.50 (*3-540-61483-4*) Spr-Verlag.

Polythlene Glycol as an Embedment for Microscopy & Histochemistry. Ed. by Kuixiong Gao. 144p. 1993. lib. bdg. 79.95 (*0-8493-4323-2*, QH324) CRC Pr.

***Polytopes: Combinatorics & Computation.** Gil Kalai & Ghunter M. Ziegler. LC 00-34237. (DMV Seminar Ser.). 2000. write for info. (*0-8176-6351-7*) Birkhauser.

Polytopes - Abstract, Convex & Computational: Proceedings of the NATO Advanced Study Institute, Scarborough, Ontario, Canada, August 20-September 3, 1993. Ed. by T. Bisztriczky. (NATO ASI Series C). 528p. (C). 1994. text 309.50 (*0-7923-3016-1*) Kluwer Academic.

Polytrauma: Diagnostik, Therapie. Ed. by W. A. Kozuschek & H. B. Reith. (Illus.). xii, 540p. 1993. 115.00 (*3-8055-5796-5*) S Karger.

Polytyque de l'Abbaye de Saint-Germain-des-Pres, 2 vols. Auguste Longnon. 852p. reprint ed. write for info. (*0-318-71374-8*) G Olms Pubs.

Polyunsaturated Acids see Progress in the Chemistry of Fats & Other Lipids

Polyunsaturated Fatty Acids in Human Nutrition. Nestle Company Staff. Ed. by Umberto Bracco & Richard J. Deckelbaum. LC 92-11920. (Nestle Nutrition Workshop Ser.: Vol. 28). (Illus.). 255p. 1992. reprint ed. pap. 79.10 (*0-608-07259-1*, 206748700009) Bks Demand.

Polyunsaturated Fatty Acids in Nutrition: Proceedings of a Round Table in Polyunsaturated Fatty Acids in Nutrition, Milan, Italy, April 1979. Ed. by Corraldo L. Galli & P. Avogaro. (Progress in Food & Nutrition Science Ser.: Vol. 4, No. 5). (Illus.). 80p. 1980. pap. 32.00 (*0-08-027362-9*, Pergamon Pr) Elsevier.

Polyunsaturated MAD. Mad Magazine Editors. 192p. 1976. mass mkt. 3.50 (*0-446-86179-0*, Pub. by Warner Bks) Little.

Polyurethane Foam Sorbents in Separation Science & Technology. Ed. by Tibor Braun et al. 232p. 1985. 132.00 (*0-8493-6597-X*, TP1180, CRC Reprint) Franklin.

Polyurethane Handbook. 2nd ed. Ed. by Gunter Oertel. LC 93-33469. 688p. (C). 1993. 230.00 (*1-56990-157-0*) Hanser-Gardner.

Polyurethane Sealants: Technology & Applications. Robert Evans. LC 93-60364. 190p. 1993. 84.95 (*0-87762-998-6*) Technomic.

Polyurethane Technology. Ed. by Paul F. Bruins. LC 68-54598. (Polymar Engineering & Technology Ser.). 299p. reprint ed. pap. 92.70 (*0-608-13424-4*, 205576300037) Bks Demand.

Polyurethanes: Chemistry, Technology, & Applications. Zygmunt Wirpsza. Tr. by T. J. Kemp from POL. LC 93-47369. (Ellis Horwood Series in Polymer Science & Technology).Tr. of Poliuretany Chemia Technologia Zastosowanie. 1993. text 119.00 (*0-13-683186-9*, Pub. by Tavistock-E Horwood) Routldge.

Polyurethanes: Index of New Information with Authors, Subjects & References. Paul D. Aloes. 150p. 1996. 47.50 (*0-7883-1270-7*); pap. 44.50 (*0-7883-1271-5*) ABBE Pubs Assn.

Polyurethanes: Index of New Information with Authors, Subjects & References. rev. ed. Paul D. Aloes. 155p. 1998. 47.50 (*0-7883-1986-8*); pap. 44.50 (*0-7883-1987-6*) ABBE Pubs Assn.

Polyurethanes in Biomedical Devices. Stuart L. Cooper. LC 97-41911. 1997. boxed set 139.95 (*0-8493-4517-0*) CRC Pr.

Polyurethanes in Medicine. Michael D. Lelah & Stuart L. Cooper. 256p. 1986. 136.00 (*0-8493-6307-1*, R857, CRC Reprint) Franklin.

Polyurethanes, 1994: Proceedings of the Society of the Plastics Industry, Inc., Polyurethane Division's 35th Annual Technical/Marketing Conference, Boston, MA, October 9-12, 1994. Ed. by Fran Lichtenberg. LC 94-61290. 692p. 1994. pap. 149.95 (*1-56676-208-1*, 762081) Technomic.

P

An Asterisk (*) at the beginning of an entry indicates that the title is appearing for the first time.

Polyurethanes, 92. Ed. by Society of the Plastics Industry, Inc. Staff. LC 92-61933. 700p. 1992. pap. text 54.95 (*0-87762-981-1*) Technomic.

Polyurethanes World Congress, 1993: Proceedings of the Polyurethanes World Congress, Vancouver BC, Canada, October 10-13, 1993. LC 93-60942. 632p. 1993. pap. 54.95 (*1-56676-079-8*, 760798) Technomic.

Polyurethanes World Congress '97. LC 97-61697. 725p. 1997. pap. text 199.95 (*1-56676-600-1*) Technomic.

Polyverse. Lee A. Brown. (New American Poetry Ser.: No. 31). 189p. (Orig.). 1999. pap. 11.95 (*1-55713-290-9*, Pub. by Sun & Moon CA) Consort Bk Sales.

Poly(Vinyl Alcohol), Vol. 10. John G. Pritchard. (Polymer Monographs). (Illus.). xii, 140p. 1970. text 190.00 (*0-677-01670-0*) Gordon & Breach.

Polyvinyl Alcohol: Properties & Applications. Ed. by C. A. Finch. LC 72-8599. (Illus.). 640p. 1973. reprint ed. pap. 198.40 (*0-608-06825-X*, 206702200009) Bks Demand.

Polyvinyl Alcohol: Properties & Applications. 2nd ed. C. A. Finch. LC 91-25583. 870p. 1992. 725.00 (*0-471-99850-8*) Wiley.

Polyvinyl Alcohol Fibers. I. Sakurada. (International Fiber Science & Technology Ser.: Vol. 6). (Illus.). 472p. 1985. text 225.00 (*0-8247-7434-5*) Dekker.

Polyvinyl Chloride, Polyethelene, & Rubber Insulating Tape, UL 510. 7th ed. (C). 1994. pap. text 95.00 (*1-55989-623-X*) Underwrtrs Labs.

Polyvinyl Chloride (PVC) Products in Mexico: A Strategic Entry Report, 1997. Compiled by Icon Group International Staff. (Illus.). 143p. 1999. ring bd. 1430.00 incl. audio compact disk (*0-7418-1068-9*) Icon Grp.

Polyvinyl Esters to Reduction see Ullmann's Encyclopedia of Industrial Chemistry

Polyvinylidene Chloride, Vol.5. Ed. by R. A. Wessling. (Polymer Monographs). xii, 200p. 1977. text 190.00 (*0-677-01700-6*) Gordon & Breach.

Pom - Pom's Big Win, No. 2904. Margaret Allen. Ed. by Joel Kupperstein. (Dr. Maggie's Phonics Readers Ser.). (Illus.). 16p. (J). (ps-1). 1999. pap. 2.99 (*1-57471-564-X*) Creat Teach Pr.

*__POM for Windows Version 2.__ Howard J. Weiss. 1999. cd-rom 25.20 (*0-13-022744-7*) P-H.

Pom-Pom Wars. Created by Francine Pascal. (Sweet Valley High Ser.: No. 113). 208p. (YA). (gr. 7 up). 1995. mass mkt. 3.99 (*0-553-56631-8*) Bantam.

Pom-Pom Wars. Kate William. (Sweet Valley High Ser.: No. 113). (YA). (gr. 7 up). 1995. 9.09 (*0-606-08218-2*) Turtleback.

Pom Pon U. S. A. rev. ed. Lynda Haller. 98p. (YA). (gr. 6-12). 1988. spiral bd. 10.95 (*0-9614174-1-2*) Cheertime USA.

Pomanders, Posies & Pot-Pourri. Jessica Houdret. 1989. pap. 25.00 (*0-85263-967-8*, Pub. by Shire Pubns) St Mut.

Pomba-Gira: Enchantments to Invoke the Formidable Powers of the Female Messenger of the Gods. Teixeira A. Neto. Tr. & Intro. by Carol L. Dow. (Illus.). 84p. 1992. pap. 11.95 (*1-878738-04-6*) Tech Sacred.

Pombal, Paradox of the Enlightenment. Kenneth Maxwell. (Illus.). 218p. (C). 1995. text 54.95 (*0-521-45044-6*) Cambridge U Pr.

Pombo: A Man of Che's Guerrilla - With Che Guevara in Bolivia, 1966-68. Harry Villegas. LC 97-65977. (Illus.). 365p. 1997. pap. 21.95 (*0-87348-833-4*) Pathfinder NY.

Pombo: A Man of Che's Guerrilla: With One Guevara in Bolivia, 1966-68. Harry Villegas. Ed. by Mary-Alice Waters. LC 97-65977. (Illus.). 365p. 1997. lib. bdg. 60.00 (*0-87348-834-2*) Pathfinder NY.

Pomegranate House. large type ed. Madeleine A. Polland. (Charnwood Large Print Ser.). 1994. 27.99 (*0-7089-8794-X*) Ulverscroft.

Pomegranate Pendant. Dvora Waysman. 223p. 1995. 16.95 (*0-87306-724-X*) Feldheim.

Pomegranate Princess & Other Tales from India. Illus. by O. O. Joshi. LC 90-47284. 134p. reprint ed. pap. 41.60 (*0-608-10596-1*, 207121700009) Bks Demand.

Pomegranate Seeds. Joyce Dunbar. LC 98-14046. (Panda & Gander Stories Ser.). (Illus.). (J). 1998. pap. write for info. (*0-7636-0707-X*) Candlewick Press.

Pomegranate Seeds. Laura Geringer. LC 94-11772. (Illus.). 48p. (J). (gr. 2-4). 1995. 15.95 (*0-395-68192-8*) HM.

Pomegranate Tree Speaks from the Dictator's Garden: Poems. J. P. White. LC 87-81569. (Illus.). 104p. (C). 1988. pap. 8.95 (*0-930100-29-8*) Holy Cow.

Pomegranate Tree Speaks to the Dictator's Garden: Poems. J. P. White. LC 87-81569. (Illus.). 104p. (C). 1988. 14.00 (*0-930100-30-1*) Holy Cow.

Pomegranates & Golden Bells: Studies in Biblical, Jewish, & Near Eastern Ritual, Law, & Literature in Honor of Jacob Milgrom. Ed. by David P. Wright et al. LC 95-19422. xxxii, 861p. 1995. text 65.00 (*0-931464-87-0*) Eisenbrauns.

Pomeranian. Ed. by Ian Dunbar. LC 99-12404. (Howell Book House's Essential Ser.). (Illus.). 92p. 1999. pap. 7.95 (*1-58245-074-9*) Howell Bks.

Pomeranian: An Owner's Guide to a Happy Healthy Pet. Happeth A. Jones. 160p. 1996. 12.95 (*0-87605-479-3*) Howell Bks.

Pomeranian Champions, 1987-1994. Camino E. E. & Bk. Co. Staff. (Illus.). 115p. 1997. pap. 32.95 (*1-55893-044-2*) Camino E E & Bk.

Pomeranian Champions, 1982-1986. Jan L. Freund. (Illus.). 89p. 1987. pap. 28.95 (*0-940808-56-0*) Camino E E & Bk.

Pomeranian Champions, 1952-1981. Jan L. Freund. (Illus.). 208p. 1987. pap. 36.95 (*0-940808-13-7*) Camino E E & Bk.

Pomeranians. Beverly Pisano. (Illus.). 1997. pap. 9.95 (*0-7938-2322-6*, KW-091S) TFH Pubns.

Pomeranians: A Complete Pet Owner's Manual. Joe Stahlkuppe. 64p. 1991. pap. 6.95 (*0-8120-4670-6*) Barron.

*__Pomeranians: Everything about Purchase, Care, Nutrition, Breeding, Behavior & Training.__ Joe Stahlkuppe. LC 99-43592. (Complete Pet Owner's Manual Ser.). (Illus.). 64-104p. 2000. pap. 6.95 (*0-7641-1046-2*) Barron.

Pomeranians: The Persistent Pioneers. Myron E. Gruenwald. (Illus.). 99p. 1987. pap. 7.00 (*0-9601536-6-7*) G J OConnell.

Pomeroy, Pt. 3. Albert A. Pomeroy. (Illus.). 342p. 1994. reprint ed. lib. bdg. 63.00 (*0-8328-4372-5*) Higginson Bk Co.

Pomeroy: History & Genealogy of the Pomeroy Family & Collateral Lines, England - Ireland - America, Comprising the Ancestors & Descendants of George Pomeroy of Pennsylvania. Ed. by William M. Pomeroy & John N. Pomeroy. (Illus.). 1454p. 1995. reprint ed. pap. 175.00 (*0-8328-4822-0*); reprint ed. lib. bdg. 185.00 (*0-8328-4821-2*) Higginson Bk Co.

Pomeroy: Romance & History of Eltweed Pomeroy's Ancestors in Normandy & England. Albert A. Pomeroy. (Illus.). 81p. 1992. reprint ed. pap. 16.00 (*0-8328-6573-7*); reprint ed. lib. bdg. 26.00 (*0-8328-2612-X*) Higginson Bk Co.

Pomeroy Pt. 3, Pt. 3. Albert A. Pomeroy. (Illus.). 342p. 1994. reprint ed. pap. 53.00 (*0-8328-4373-3*) Higginson Bk Co.

Pomeroy Family - House of De La Pomerai: Annals of the Family Which Was, from the Conquest to 1548. Edward E. Powley. (Illus.). 144p. 1999. 32.00 (*0-8328-9827-9*); pap. 22.00 (*0-8328-9828-7*) Higginson Bk Co.

Pomeroy, History & Genealogy of the Pomeroy Family: Collateral Lines in Family Groups, Nrmandy, Great Britain & America, Comprising the Ancestors & Descedants of Eltweed Pomeroy, from Beaminster, Co. Dorset, England, 1630. Albert A. Pomeroy. (Illus.). 962p. 1994. reprint ed. pap. 149.00 (*0-8328-4272-9*); reprint ed. lib. bdg. 159.50 (*0-8328-4271-0*) Higginson Bk Co.

Pomeroy's Equity Jurisprudence, 5 vols., Set. 5th ed. John N. Pomeroy. 1994. reprint ed. 450.00 (*0-88636-305-5*, 308730) W S Hein.

Pomes All Sizes. Jack Kerouac. LC 92-1204. (Pocket Poets Ser.: No. 48). x, 175p. 1992. pap. 10.95 (*0-87286-269-0*) City Lights.

Pomestnaya Tserkov. John Halsey. Tr. by Slavic Christian Publishing Staff & Vitaly Michka from ENG. (RUS.). 58p. (C). 1994. pap. write for info. (*0-9641805-1-0*) Baptist Intl.

Pomfret the Golden Decade. George Poulos. (Illus.). xii, 320p. (Orig.). 1988. pap. 9.95 (*0-917651-50-2*) Holy Cross Orthodox.

Pomfret Towers. Angela M. Thirkell. 272p. 1986. mass mkt. 4.95 (*0-88184-276-1*) Carroll & Graf.

Pomme. Illus. by Pierre-Marie Valat. (Gallimard - Mes Premieres Decouvertes Ser.: No. 3). (FRE.). (J). (ps-1). 1989. 13.95 (*2-07-035702-3*) Schoenhof.

*__Pommel Horse & the Rings.__ Joanne Mattern. LC 99-27924. 48p. (J). 1999. write for info. (*0-86593-568-8*) Rourke Corp.

Pomo. Edward D. Castillo. LC 99-23200. (Indian Nations Ser.). (Illus.). 48p. (ps-3). 1999. 25.69 (*0-8172-5455-2*) Raintree Steck-V.

Pomo. Suzanne Freedman. LC 97-9094. (Native American People Ser.: Set V). (Illus.). 32p. (J). (gr. 5-8). 1997. lib. bdg. 21.27 (*0-86625-606-7*) Rourke Pubns.

Pomo. Elaine Landau. LC 93-23264. (First Bks.). (Illus.). 64p. (J). (gr. 4-6). 1994. pap. 6.95 (*0-531-15687-7*) Watts.

Pomo Basketmaking: A Supreme Art for the Weaver. Elsie Allen. Ed. by Vinson Brown. (Illus.). 67p. 1972. pap. 6.95 (*0-87961-016-6*) Naturegraph.

Pomo Bear Doctors. fac. ed. Samuel A. Barrett. (University of California Publications in American Archaeology & Ethnology: Vol. 12: 11). 22p. (C). 1917. reprint ed. pap. text 2.81 (*1-55567-208-6*) Coyote Press.

Pomo Dawn of Song. Contrib. by Lois P. Stevens & Jewel M. Newburn. (Local History Studies: Vol. 33A). 1987. pap. 15.95 (*0-935089-14-4*) CA History Ctr.

Pomo Doctors & Poisoners. fac. ed. L. S. Freeland. (University of California Publications in American Archaeology & Ethnology: Vol. 20: 4). 18p. (C). 1923. reprint ed. pap. text 2.19 (*1-55567-240-X*) Coyote Press.

Pomo Folkways. fac. ed. Edwin Loeb. (University of California Publications in American Archaeology & Ethnology: Vol. 19: 2). 265p. (C). 1926. reprint ed. pap. text 28.13 (*1-55567-236-1*) Coyote Press.

Pomo Geography. fac. ed. Fred B. Kniffen. (University of California Publications in American Archaeology & Ethnology: Vol. 36: 6). 54p. (C). 1939. reprint ed. pap. text 6.56 (*1-55567-307-4*) Coyote Press.

Pomo Indian Basketry. Samuel A. Barrett & Sherrie Smith-Ferri. LC 96-41513. 1996. write for info. (*0-936127-07-4*) P A Hearst Mus.

Pomo Indians see Native Peoples Series

Pomo Indians. Bill Lund. (Native Peoples Ser.). (Illus.). (J). 1997. lib. bdg. 14.00 (*0-516-20525-0*) Childrens.

Pomo Indians of California & Their Neighbors. Vinson Brown. Ed. by Albert B. Elsasser. LC 78-13946. (American Indian Map Book: Vol. 1). (Illus.). 64p. (Orig.). 1969. pap. 8.95 (*0-911010-30-0*) Naturegraph.

Pomo Lands on Clear Lake. fac. ed. E. W. Gifford. (University of California Publications in American Archaeology & Ethnology: Vol. 20: 5). 16p. (C). 1923. reprint ed. pap. text 2.19 (*1-55567-241-8*) Coyote Press.

Pomo Myths. fac. ed. Samuel A. Barrett. Ed. by Ira Edwards. (Public Museum of the City of Milwaukee Ser.: Bulletin 15). 702p. (C). 1933. reprint ed. pap. text 62.50 (*1-55567-661-8*) Coyote Press.

*__Pomona Queen.__ Kem Nunn. 236p. 2000. pap. 12.95 (*1-56858-176-9*, Pub. by FWEW) Publishers Group.

Pomona Queen. Kem Nunn. Ed. by Maryanne Sacco. 240p. 1993. reprint ed. mass mkt. 10.00 (*0-671-79877-4*, WSP) PB.

Pomona's Travels. Frank Stockton. (Notable American Authors Ser.). 1999. reprint ed. lib. bdg. 125.00 (*0-7812-8932-7*) Rprt Serv.

Pomone see Chefs-d'Oeuvre Classiques de l'Opera Francais

PoMoSexuals: Challenging Assumptions about Gender & Sexuality. Carol Queen. LC 97-37703. 180p. 1997. pap. text 14.95 (*1-57344-074-4*) Cleis Pr.

Pomp & Circumstance. Noel Coward. 24.95 (*0-89190-219-8*) Amereon Ltd.

*__Pomp & Circumstance: Novel.__ Noel Coward. 304p. 2000. pap. 12.95 (*0-413-56370-7*) Methn.

Pomp & Circumstance (P&C) Personnel Services Software. Advantage International, Inc. Staff. 1992. student ed. 35.00 (*0-685-66143-1*); disk 99.00 (*1-56756-014-8*, OD430I) Advant Intl.

Pomp & Other Plays. Sada Cowan. LC 79-50024. (One-Act Plays in Reprint Ser.). 1980. reprint ed. 25.00 (*0-8486-2048-8*) Roth Pub Inc.

Pomp And Sustenance: Twenty Five Centuries Of Sicilian Food. Mary T. Simeti. LC 98-4834. (Illus.). 352p. 1998. pap. 19.95 (*0-88001-610-8*) HarpC.

Pomp of Yesterday: The Defence of India & the Suez Canal: 1798-1918. William Jackson. (Illus.). 288p. 1995. 50.00 (*1-85753-008-X*, Pub. by Brasseys) Brasseys.

Pompa Introitus: Ferdinandi Austriaci Cum Antiverpiam Adventu Suo Bearet, 15 Kal. Maii Anno 1665. Peter Paul Rubens. LC 68-21225. (LAT., Illus.). 1972. 71.95 (*0-405-08902-3*) Ayer.

Pompadour & Pearls: A Patchwork of Poetry. 62p. (Orig.). 1995. pap. 4.95 (*0-9628023-2-8*) Lillium Pr.

Pompadours. Mikhail Evgrafovich Saltykov-Shchedrin. Tr. & Intro. by David Magarshack. Orig. Title: Pompadury. 300p. 1984. pap. 12.95 (*0-88233-744-0*) Ardis Pubs.

Pompadury see Pompadours

Pompeian Herbal: Ancient & Modern Medicinal Plants. Wilhelmia Mary F. Jashemski. LC 98-51226. 112p. 1999. 35.00 (*0-292-74061-1*); pap. 17.95 (*0-292-74060-3*) U of Tex Pr.

Pompeii. Ian Andrews. (Cambridge Introduction to World History Topic Bks.). (Illus.). 48p. (YA). (gr. 7 up). 1978. pap. 12.95 (*0-521-20973-0*) Cambridge U Pr.

*__Pompeii.__ Piero Giovanni Guzzo & Antonio d'Ambrosio. (Getty Trust Publications). (Illus.). 160p. 2000. pap. 24.95 (*88-8265-026-X*) OUP.

Pompeii. Peter Connolly. (The Roman World Ser.). (Illus.). 78p. (J). (gr. 4-8). 1994. reprint ed. pap. 12.95 (*0-19-917158-0*) OUP.

Pompeii: An Architectural History. L. Richardson, Jr. (Illus.). 445p. 1997. reprint ed. pap. text 24.95 (*0-8018-5661-2*) Johns Hopkins.

Pompeii: Its Life & Art. 2nd ed. August Mau. Tr. by Francis W. Kelsey from GER. (Illus.). xxv, 557p. (C). 1982. reprint ed. lib. bdg. 60.00 (*0-89241-346-8*) Caratzas.

*__Pompeii: Monuments Past & Present.__ A. de Franciscus. (Illus.). 56p. 2000. pap. 21.95 (*88-8162-075-8*, Pub. by Vision Srl) J P Getty Trust.

Pompeii: Nightmare at Midday. Kathryn L. Humphrey. (J). (gr. 6). 1995. 9.28 (*0-395-73265-4*) HM.

Pompeii: Nightmare at Midday. large type ed. Kathryn L. Humphrey. 86p. (J). (gr. 6). 21.50 (*0-614-20611-1*, L-38213-00 APHB) Am Printing Hse.

Pompeii: Public & Private Life. Paul Zanker. Tr. by Deborah L. Schneider from GER. LC 98-24720. (Revealing Antiquity Ser.). (Illus.). 336p. 1999. 49.95 (*0-674-68966-6*) HUP.

Pompeii: Public & Private Life. Paul Zanker. Tr. by Deborah L. Schneider. LC 98-24720. (Revealing Antiquity Ser.). (Illus.). ix, 251 p. 1999. pap. 22.95 (*0-674-68967-4*) HUP.

Pompeii: The Day a City Died. Robert Etienne. (Discoveries Ser.). (Illus.). 226p. 1992. pap. 12.95 (*0-8109-2855-8*, Pub. by Abrams) Time Warner.

Pompeii: The Day a City Was Buried. LC 98-20336. 48p. (J). 1998. 14.95 (*0-7894-3419-9*) DK Pub Inc.

Pompeii: The Vanished City see Lost Civilizations Series

Pompeii: The Vanished City. Ed. by Dale Brown. (Lost Civilizations Ser.). (Illus.). 168p. 1992. lib. bdg. 19.45 (*0-8094-9863-4*) Time-Life.

Pompeii & Herculaneum. Peter Hicks. (Digging up the Past Ser.). (Illus.). 48p. (J). (gr. 4-6). 1995. lib. bdg. 24.26 (*1-56847-398-2*) Raintree Steck-V.

Pompeii & Herculaneum. John Seely & Elizabeth Seely. LC 99-25555. (Visiting the Past Ser.). 1999. lib. bdg. write for info. (*1-57572-859-1*) Heinemann Lib.

Pompeii... Buried Alive! Edith Kunhardt. LC 87-4512. (Step into Reading Ser.: A Step 3 Book). (Illus.). 48p. (J). (gr. 2-3). 1987. pap. 3.99 (*0-394-88866-9*, Pub. by Random Bks Yng Read) Random.

Pompeii... Buried Alive! Edith Kunhardt. (Step into Reading Ser.: A Step 3 Book). (J). (gr. 2-3). 1987. 9.19 (*0-606-03366-1*, Pub. by Turtleback) Demco.

Pompeii Difficile Est: Studies in the Political Life of Imperial Pompeii. James L. Granklin. LC 99-52255. 300p. 1999. text 47.50 (*0-472-11056-X*, 11056) U of Mich Pr.

Pompeii in Color see Travel Guides in Color

Pompeii, Its Life & Art. August Mau. 1982. 64.95 (*0-8434-0138-9*) McGrath NH.

Pompeo Leoni: Work in Marble & Alabaster in Relation to Spanish Sculpture. Beatrice G. Proske. (Illus.). 1956. 5.00 (*0-87535-088-7*) Hispanic Soc.

Pompes Funebres. Jean Genet. (Imaginaire Ser.). (FRE.). pap. 13.95 (*2-07-027919-7*) Schoenhof.

Pompey Poems... Celebrating a Cat. Ellen Langill. LC 86-91603. (Illus.). 64p. (YA). (gr. 7-12). 1986. 10.25 (*0-943864-28-3*) Davenport.

Pompey the Great. John Leach. (Classical Lives Ser.). 256p. (Orig.). 1986. reprint ed. pap. 14.95 (*0-7099-4127-7*, Pub. by C Helm) Routldge.

*__Pompidou Years, 1969-1974.__ Serge Bernstein & Jean-Pierre Rioux. Tr. by Christopher Woodall. (Cambridge History of Modern France Ser.: No. 9). (Illus.). 296p. (C). 2000. text 59.95 (*0-521-58061-7*) Cambridge U Pr.

Pompidou/Guggenheim: A Rendezvous. Yve-Alain Bois. (Illus.). 550p. 1998. 75.00 (*0-8109-6916-5*, Pub. by Abrams) Time Warner.

Pompiers - The Fire Station. Robert Munsch. (Droles D'Histories Ser.). (FRE., Illus.). 24p. (J). (ps up). 1988. pap. 6.95 (*2-89021-076-6*, Pub. by La Courte Ech) Firefly Bks Ltd.

Pompilia: A Feminist Reading of Robert Browning's the Ring & the Book. Ann P. Brady. LC 88-1733. 158p. (C). 1988. text 26.95 (*0-8214-0886-0*) Ohio U Pr.

Pompilidae (Insecta: Hymenoptera) see Fauna of New Zealand Series

Pompinea. Thomas Bailey Aldrich. (Works of Thomas Bailey Aldrich). 1989. reprint ed. lib. bdg. 79.00 (*0-685-27379-2*) Rprt Serv.

Pomponi Porfyrionis Commentum in Horatium Flaccum. Horace. Ed. by W. R. Connor & Alfred Holder. LC 78-67137. (Latin Texts & Commentaries Ser.). (LAT.). 1979. reprint ed. lib. bdg. 46.95 (*0-405-11606-3*) Ayer.

Pomponius Mela - Concordantia in Libros Pomponii Melae De Chorographia. Ed. by Carmen Guzman & Miguel E. Perez. (Alpha-Omega, Reihe A Ser.: Bd. LVI). 614p. 1989. write for info. (*3-487-09181-X*) G Olms Pubs.

Pomponius Mela's Description of the World. F. E. Romer & Pomponius Mela. LC 97-40709. (Illus.). 184p. (C). 1998. pap. text 21.95 (*0-472-08452-6*, 08452) U of Mich Pr.

Pomprey Train: The Portsmouth Line Explored. Picton Publishing (Chippenham) Ltd. Staff. (C). 1987. 30.00 (*0-948251-45-X*, Pub. by Picton) St Mut.

Pomps of Satan. Edgar E. Saltus. LC 70-116008. reprint ed. 42.50 (*0-404-05537-0*) AMS Pr.

Pon Jordan's Far Shore. Jean E. Holmes. LC 94-29293. (Weldon Oaks Ser.: No. 4). 1995. pap. 4.97 (*0-8163-1227-3*) Pacific Pr Pub Assn.

'Pon Top Edisto: Cookin' 'Tweenst the Rivers. Trinity Episcopal Church Members & Friends. LC 97-90451. (Illus.). 288p. 1997. spiral bd. 16.95 (*0-9658723-0-0*) Trinty Episcop.

Pon un Cuentito en Orden. Joy Evans & Jo E. Moore. Tr. by Liz Wolfe & Dora Ficklin from ENG. (SPA., Illus.). 20p. (J). (gr. 1-2). 1990. pap. text 5.95 (*1-55799-184-7*, EMC 026) Evan-Moor Edu Pubs.

Ponape: A Pacific Economy in Transition. William Bascom. LC 65-64597. (University of California, Anthropological Records: Vol. 22). 166p. reprint ed. pap. 51.50 (*0-608-13953-X*, 202132200021) Bks Demand.

Ponapean-English Dictionary. Kenneth L. Rehg & Damian G. Sohl. LC 79-19451. (PALI Language Texts, Micronesia Ser.). 278p. 1979. pap. text 17.00 (*0-8248-0562-3*) UH Pr.

Ponapean Reference Grammar. Kenneth L. Rehg & Damian G. Sohl. LC 80-13276. (PALI Language Texts Micronesia Ser.). 420p. 1981. pap. text 19.00 (*0-8248-0718-9*) UH Pr.

Ponca Chief see Standing Bear & the Ponca Chiefs

Ponca Tribe. James H. Howard. LC 95-22492. (Illus.). xvi, 215p. 1995. pap. 12.00 (*0-8032-7279-0*, Bison Books) U of Nebr Pr.

Ponce: Rebirth of a Valuable Heritage. Loretta Phelps De Cordova. 88p. 1991. pap. 19.95 (*0-89825-001-3*) Pub Resces PR.

Ponce: Rebirth of a Valuable Heritage. deluxe ed. Loretta Phelps De Cordova. 88p. 1991. 34.95 (*0-89825-002-1*) Pub Resces PR.

Ponce: Renacimiento De una Valiosa Herencia. Loretta Phelps De Cordova. Tr. by Carmen Bizjack from ENG. (SPA.). 88p. 1991. pap. 19.95 (*0-89825-003-X*) Pub Resces PR.

Ponce: Renacimiento De una Valiosa Herencia. deluxe ed. Loretta Phelps De Cordova. Tr. by Carmen Bizjack from ENG. (SPA.). 88p. 1991. 34.95 (*0-89825-004-8*) Pub Resces PR.

Ponce de Leon see Discovery Biographies

Ponce de Leon: An Intimate Portrait of Atlanta's Most Famous Avenue. George Mitchell. (Illus.). 160p. (Orig.). 1983. pap. 12.95 (*0-915063-01-8*) Argonne Bks.

Ponce de Leon & the Discovery of Florida: The Man, the Myth, & the Truth. Douglas R. Peck. LC 93-89738. (Illus.). 160p. (Orig.). 1993. pap. 13.95 (*1-880654-02-4*) Pogo Pr.

Ponce de Leon Sails Again. Susan Grohmann. (Time Travel Adventure Ser.). (Illus.). 80p. (gr. 4 up). 1999. pap. 14.95 (*1-892629-02-X*) Tail Tours.

Pond. Janice Boland. (Books for Young Learners). (Illus.). 8p. (J). (gr. k-2). 1997. pap. text 5.00 (*1-57274-070-1*, A2185) R Owen Pubs.

*__Pond.__ Lizi Boyd. LC 98-8435. (Illus.). 12p. (J). 1999. 5.95 (*0-8118-2118-8*) Chronicle Bks.

Pond. Paul Fleisher. LC 97-38071. (Webs of Life Ser.). (J). (gr. 2-4). 1998. lib. bdg. 22.79 (*0-7614-0835-5*, Benchmark NY) Marshall Cavendish.

Pond. Alan M. Hofmeister et al. (Reading for All Learners Ser.). (Illus.). (J). pap. write for info. (*1-56861-131-5*) Swift Lrn Res.

Pond. Brenda Parke. Ed. by Don Curry. (Guided Reading Ser.). 8p. (J). (gr. k). 1997. pap. text 2.75 (*1-56784-920-2*) Newbridge Educ.

Pond. Donald M. Silver. LC 97-5709. (Illus.). 48p. (J). (gr. 1-4). 1997. pap. 7.95 (*0-07-057932-6*) McGraw.

P

An Asterisk (*) at the beginning of an entry indicates that the title is appearing for the first time.

Pond & Brook: A Guide to Nature in Freshwater Environments. Michael J. Caduto. LC 89-38056. (Illus.). 288p. 1990. reprint ed. pap. 19.95 (*0-87451-509-2*) U Pr of New Eng.

***Pond & River.** Steve Parker. (Eyewitness Books). (Illus.). (J). (gr. 4-7). 2000. 19.99 (*0-7894-6555-8*) DK Pub Inc.

***Pond & River.** Steve Parker. (Eyewitness Books). (J). (gr. 4-7). 2000. 15.95 (*0-7894-5838-1*) DK Pub Inc.

***Pond & River Life.** Barron's Educational Editors. (Natural World Ser.). 32p. (J). (gr. 5). 2000. mass mkt. 5.95 (*0-7641-1075-6*) Barron.

Pond & Stream Safari: A Guide to the Ecology of Aquatic Invertebrates. 2nd rev. ed. Karen Edelstein. (Experience 4-H Natural Resources Ser.). (Illus.). 56p. (J). (gr. 5-7). 1996. 15.75 (*1-57753-039-X*, 147L24) Corn Coop Ext.

Pond Aquaculture Water Quality Management. Claude E. Boyd & C. S. Tucker. LC 97-48251. 720p. 1998. write for info. (*0-412-07181-9*) Kluwer Academic.

***Pond Basics: A Step-by-Step Guide for Water Gardeners.** Peter Robinson. (Illus.). 2000. pap. 11.95 (*0-8069-2287-7*) Sterling.

Pond Birds - Gator Basketball: The Whole Story from the Inside. Bill Koss. LC 96-44067. (Illus.). 258p. 1996. 24.95 (*0-8130-1523-5*) U Press Fla.

Pond Book. Sandra Jordan. LC 98-22795. (J). 1999. write for info. (*0-7894-2565-3*) DK Pub Inc.

Pond Book & Tadpole Tank. Storey Publishing Staff. 1997. pap. 14.95 (*0-676-57245-6*) Random.

Pond Book & the Tadpole Tank. Karen Dawe. (Hand in Hand with Nature Ser.). (Illus.). 80p. (J). (gr. k-5). 1998. pap. 14.95 (*1-895897-18-1*) Somerville Hse.

Pond Book & the Tadpole Tank. Karen Dawe. LC 95-3289. (Illus.). 80p. (J). (gr. 2-6). 1999. pap. 14.95 (*1-56305-921-5*, 3921) Workman Pub.

Pond Doctor. Storey Publishing Staff. 1997. pap. 17.95 (*0-676-57209-X*) Random.

Pond Doctor: Planning & Maintaining a Healthy Water Garden. Helen Nash. (Illus.). 160p. (Orig.). 1995. pap. 17.95 (*0-8069-0687-1*) Sterling.

Pond Dwellers: A History of the Freshwater-People of Mass, 1620-1676. Kelly Savage. 368p. (Orig.). 1996. pap. 13.95 (*1-57502-191-9*) Morris Pubng.

Pond Fisheries. F. G. Martyshev. (Russian Translation Ser.: No. 4). 462p. 1983. 162.00 (*90-6191-410-8*, Pub. by A A Balkema) Ashgate Pub Co.

Pond Fisheries in China. Lin Zhong. (International Academic Publishers Ser.). (Illus.). 300p. 1991. 58.00 (*0-08-036146-3*, Pergamon Pr) Elsevier.

Pond in the Meadow see Life In...

Pond (La Charca) Puerto Rico's Classic 19th Century Novel. Manuel Zeno-Ganolia. Tr. by Kal Woyenheim from SPA. LC 99-34418. Orig. Title: La Charca. 216p. 1999. reprint ed. pap. text 16.95 (*1-55876-092-X*) Wiener Pubs Inc.

Pond Lake River Sea. Maryjo Kock. (Illus.). 144p. 1995. pap. 15.00 (*0-00-649218-5*) Collins SF.

Pond Life. Trevor J. Beebee. (Illus.). 128p. text 19.95 (*0-905483-99-5*, Pub. by Whittet Bks) Diamond Farm Bk.

Pond Life. Deni Bown. (Look Closer Ser.). 32p. (J). (gr. 3-6). 1998. pap. 4.95 (*0-7894-2970-5*) DK Pub Inc.

Pond Life. Gerald Cox. (Illus.). 88p. (Orig.). 1988. pap. 5.95 (*0-935576-24-X*) Kesend Pub Ltd.

Pond Life. James Kavanagh. (Pocket Naturalist Ser.). (Illus.). 1997. 5.95 (*1-889903-27-2*, Pub. by Waterford WA) Falcon Pub Inc.

Pond Life. Barbara Taylor. LC 91-58196. (Look Closer Ser.). (Illus.). 32p. (J). (gr. 1-4). 1992. 9.95 (*1-879431-94-7*) DK Pub Inc.

Pond Monster, Bk. 5A. Groves. (J). Date not set. pap. text. write for info. (*0-582-18796-6*, Pub. by Addison-Wesley) Longman.

Pond Mountain Chronicle: Self-Portrait of a Southern Appalachian Community. Ed. by Leland R. Cooper & Mary L. Cooper. LC 97-38306. 252p. 1997. pap. 25.00 (*0-7864-0391-8*) McFarland & Co.

Pond of Stars. Karl Kempton. 52p. (Orig.). 1989. pap. 3.00 (*0-926935-11-9*) Runaway Spoon.

Pond Owner's Problem Solver. John Dawes. (Illus.). 208p. 29.95 (*1-56465-196-7*) Tetra Pr.

Pond Planting: Practical Designs for Water Gardens. Helen Nash. 2000. write for info. (*0-8069-9757-5*) Sterling.

Pond Plants. Ernestine Giesecke. LC 98-44522. (Plants Ser.). 32p. (J). 1999. 19.92 (*1-57572-826-5*) Heinemann Lib.

Pond Scum & Vultures: America's Sportswriters Talk about Their Glamorous Profession. Gene Wojciechowski. 256p. 1990. text 18.95 (*0-02-630851-7*) Macmillan.

Pond Seasons. Sue A. Alderson. LC 96-932115. (Illus.). 32p. (J). 1997. 15.95 (*0-88899-283-1*) Publishers Group.

***Pond Story.** Barbie Marsh. (Illus.). 26p. (J). (ps-2). 1998. pap. 5.95 (*0-9665222-5-7*) Lve to Read.

Pond Watchers Guide to Ponds & Vernal Pools of Eastern North America. Betsy Colburn & Tom Tyning. Ed. by Christopher Leahy. (Habitat Ser.). (Illus.). 8p. 1995. 3.95 (*0-932691-14-5*) MA Audubon Soc.

***Pond Watching with Ann Morgan.** Michael Elsohn Ross. LC 99-24953. (Naturalist's Apprentice Biographies Ser.). (Illus.). 48p. (J). (gr. 3-6). 2000. 19.93 (*1-57505-385-3*, Carolrhoda) Lerner Pub.

Pond Water Zoo: An Introduction to Microscopic Life. Peter H. Loewer. LC 93-18468. (Illus.). 96p. (J). (gr. 3-7). 1996. 16.00 (*0-689-31736-0*) Atheneum Yung Read.

Pond Woman. Charlotte Gafford. 70p. (Orig.). 1989. pap. 9.95 (*0-9623495-0-X*) Kudzu Pr.

Pond Woman: Poems by Charlotte Gafford. Charlotte Gafford. 75p. (C). 1989. text 12.95 (*0-685-26756-3*); pap. text 6.00 (*0-685-26757-1*) Kudzu Pr.

Pond Year. Kathryn Lasky. LC 94-14834. (Illus.). 32p. (J). (ps-3). 1995. 14.99 (*1-56402-187-4*) Candlewick Pr.

Pond Year. Kathryn Lasky. 1997. 11.19 (*0-606-12794-1*, Pub. by Turtleback) Demco.

Pond Year. Kathryn Lasky. LC 94-14834. (Illus.). 32p. (J). (gr. k-3). 1997. reprint ed. pap. 5.99 (*0-7636-0112-8*) Candlewick Pr.

Ponder Heart. Eudora Welty. 18.95 (*0-8488-0661-1*) Amereon Ltd.

Ponder Heart. Eudora Welty. LC 77-92140. (Illus.). 168p. 1967. pap. 9.00 (*0-15-672915-6*, Harvest Bks) Harcourt.

***Ponder Meets the Polka-Dots.** Richard Hays. (Illus.). (J). 2000. pap. 8.99 (*0-7814-3377-0*) Cook Communs Minist.

Ponder on This: A Compilation. Alice A Bailey. 1971. pap. 14.00 (*0-85330-131-X*) Lucis.

Ponder over Polacco. Sheila Winnick & Mary Rosenberg. (Illus.). 54p. 1998. pap. text 14.95 (*0-605-63277-4*, 390302) Perma-Bound.

Ponder the Path. 2nd rev. ed. Gary H. Wiles & Delores M. Brown. LC 96-71065. (Talking History of America Ser.: Vol. 1). 279p. 1996. pap. 12.95 (*1-889252-02-6*) Photosensitive.

Ponderables. Jay Hall. LC 82-83907. 93p. 1982. pap. text. write for info. (*0-937932-02-7*) Teleometrics.

Ponderables: Essays on Managerial Choice-Past & Future. Jay Hall. 1988. pap. 9.95 (*0-945804-23-7*) Woodstead Pr.

Pondered in Her Heart: Hannah's Book: Inside & Outside. Elaine S. Rich. LC 98-84134. 136p. 1998. pap. 12.95 (*0-945530-20-X*) Wordsworth KS.

***Pondering Another Passage.** A. C. Gray. LC 00-102410. 144p. 2000. pap. 10.00 (*1-57921-299-9*) WinePress Pub.

Pondering Postinternationalism: A Paradigm for the Twenty-First Century? Ed. by Heidi H. Hobbs. LC 99-39747. (C). 2000. text 62.50 (*0-7914-4507-0*); pap. text 20.95 (*0-7914-4508-9*) State U NY Pr.

Pondering Things Over... Short Stories & Poetry. Ron James. LC 90-91677. 77p. (C). 1990. 14.95 (*0-9619837-3-6*); pap. 9.95 (*0-9619837-2-8*) Ron James.

Ponderings. Fran Parker. 50p. 1976. pap. 3.50 (*0-686-40981-7*) TarPar.

Ponderings. Bobbi Sims. Ed. by Jan Williams. 1990. write for info. (*1-879521-00-8*) Elan Pub TX.

Ponderings: To Ponder is to Live Life on a Deeper Level. Bobbi Sims. (Illus.). 74p. 1991. spiral bd. write for info. (*0-318-68428-4*) Elan Pub TX.

Ponderings for the Potty. Bobbi Sims. Ed. by Jan Williams. 1990. write for info. (*1-879521-01-6*) Elan Pub TX.

Ponderings from the Precipice: Soulwork for the New Millennium. James A. Conlon. LC 98-6246. 143p. 1998. pap. 11.95 (*0-939516-40-3*) Forest Peace.

Ponderosa Country: A Scenic & Historic Guide to Reno & Vicinity. Stanley W. Paher. LC 72-87135. (Illus.). 1972. 14.95 (*0-913814-02-4*) Nevada Pubns.

***Ponder's Bible: All You Need to Know to Build Your Own Pond.** Gosta H. Lovgren. (Illus.). 177p. 2000. pap. 14.95 (*1-929741-08-1*) Carolelle.

***Pondfire.** Bill Maynard. LC 99-20082. 96p. (J). (gr. 4-8). 2000. 14.99 (*0-399-23439-X*, G P Putnam) Peng Put Young Read.

Pondlarker. Fred Gwynne. LC 90-9524. (Illus.). 40p. (J). (gr. k-4). 1990. pap. 14.00 (*0-671-70846-5*) S&S Bks Yung.

***Pondoro: Last of the Ivory Hunters.** John Taylor. 354p. 1999. 29.95 (*1-57157-164-7*) Safari Pr.

Ponds: Planning, Design, Construction. Clifton Deal. 92p. 1998. pap. 7.50 (*0-16-049350-1*, Agriculture Dept) USGPO.

Ponds & Creeks: Parables of Spiritual Growth. Jeffrey J. Pound. LC 96-69311. 64p. (Orig.). 1996. pap. 8.95 (*1-57736-005-2*) Providence Hse.

Ponds & Lakes of the White Mountains: A Four-Season Guide for Hikers & Anglers. 2nd ed. Steven D. Smith. LC 97-47491. (Illus.). 352p. 1998. pap. 16.00 (*0-88150-413-0*, Pub. by Countryman) Norton.

Ponds & Streams. John Stidworthy. LC 89-20331. (Nature Club Ser.). (Illus.). 32p. (J). (gr. 3-6). 1990. lib. bdg. 17.25 (*0-8167-1963-2*) Troll Communs.

Ponds & Water Features. Peter Robinson. LC 98-37316. (AHS Practical Guides Ser.). 80p. 1999. 8.95 (*0-7894-4156-X*) DK Pub Inc.

Ponds & Water Gardens. rev. ed. Bill Heritage. (Illus.). 176p. (Orig.). 1994. pap. 9.95 (*0-304-34366-8*, Pub. by Cassell) Sterling.

Ponds of Kalambayi: An African Sojourn. Mike Tidwell. 1990. 19.95 (*1-55821-078-4*) Lyons Pr.

Poneys Sauvages. Michel Deon. (FRE.). 1972. pap. 11.95 (*0-7859-1692-X*, 2070360717) Fr & Eur.

Ponga Orden en Su Mundo Interior. Gordon MacDonald. Tr. by Juan S. Araujo from ENG.Tr. of Ordering Your Private World. (SPA.). 176p. (C). 1989. pap. 7.99 (*0-88113-246-2*) Caribe Betania.

Pongee Goes to Paris. Rhya N. Cawley. (Illus.). 70p. (Orig.). (J). 1996. pap. 4.95 (*1-57502-282-6*, PO985) Morris Pubng.

***Pongo & Jeeves.** R. N. Varhaug. 166p. 2000. pap. 18.00 (*0-7388-2110-1*) Xlibris Corp.

Pongo to the Rescue. Justine Korman. (Golden Super Shape Bks.). (Illus.). 24p. (J). (ps-3). 1994. pap. 3.29 (*0-307-10014-6*, 10014, Goldn Books) Gldn Bks Pub Co.

Pongo's in Love. Mouseworks Staff. (101 Dalmations Ser.). 9p. (J). 1998. 8.98 (*1-57082-539-4*, Pub. by Mouse Works) Time Warner.

Poniendo el Cascabel Al Gato (Belling the Cat) Eugenia De Hoogh. (Bilingual Ser.). (ENG & SPA.). (J). 1977. 10.15 (*0-606-01429-2*, Pub. by Turtleback) Demco.

Poniendo el Cascabel al Gato. Dorothy S. Bishop et al.Tr. of Belling the Cat. (SPA., Illus.). 64p. 6.95 (*0-8442-7282-5*, 72825) NTC Contemp Pub Co.

***Poniendo los Puntos Sobre Lasies: Consideraciones Acerca del Liderazgo de Grupos.** Pablo Polischuk. (SPA.). 1998. pap. 13.99 (*0-8297-0353-5*) Vida Pubs.

Ponies. DK Editors. LC 97-34425. (Illus.). 64p. (J). (gr. 3-7). 1998. 15.95 (*0-7894-2810-5*) DK Pub Inc.

***Ponies.** Kindersley Publishing Dorling. (Touch & Feel Ser.). (Illus.). 12p. (ps-k). 1999. 6.95 (*0-7894-4748-7*) DK Pub Inc.

Ponies. Herta E. Kraupa-Tuskany. 1984. pap. 6.95 (*0-8120-2856-2*) Barron.

Ponies: A Complete Pet Owner's Manual. Herta F. Kraupa-Tuskany. 1984. 12.15 (*0-606-01110-2*, Pub. by Turtleback) Demco.

Ponies & Foals. Kate Petty. (Baby Animals Ser.). (Illus.). 24p. (J). (gr. k-3). 1993. pap. 3.95 (*0-8120-1487-1*) Barron.

Ponies at the Point, Vol. 10. Ben M. Baglio. (Animal Ark Ser.: No. 10). 144p. (J). (gr. 3-6). 1999. pap. 3.99 (*0-590-66231-7*) Scholastic Inc.

Ponies in the Wild. Elaine Gill. (Illus.). 128p. text 19.95 (*1-873580-11-8*, Pub. by Whittet Bks) Diamond Farm Bk.

Ponies, Patriots & Powder Monkeys: A History of Children in America's Armed Forces, 1776-1916. Eleanor C. Bishop. (Illus.). 180p. 1983. 14.95 (*0-911329-00-5*) Bishop Pr.

Ponkapog Papers. Thomas Bailey Aldrich. LC 70-84293. (Essay Index Reprint Ser.). 1977. 15.95 (*0-8369-1073-7*) Ayer.

Ponkapog Papers. Thomas Bailey Aldrich. (Works of Thomas Bailey Aldrich). 1989. reprint ed. lib. bdg. 79.00 (*0-7812-1681-8*) Rprt Serv.

Ponography, Feminism & Individual. Assiter. 192p. (C). pap. 15.95 (*0-7453-0521-0*) Pluto GBR.

Pons Dictionary (Das Pons Worterbuch) German-Italian--Italian-German. Tr. of Das Pons Woterbuch. (GER & ITA.). 1696p. 95.00 (*0-7859-8867-X*) Fr & Eur.

Pons English-German, German-English Business Dictionary. P. Collin. (ENG & GER.). 370p. 1990. 95.00 (*0-8288-7568-5*, 3125179300) Fr & Eur.

Pons English-German, German-English Dictionary of Agriculture. P. Collin & Alan Stephens. (ENG & GER.). 383p. 1992. 95.00 (*0-8288-7569-3*, 3125178509) Fr & Eur.

Pons, English-German, German-English Dictionary of Data Processing. S. M. Collin. (ENG & GER.). 410p. 1991. 95.00 (*0-8288-7564-2*, 3125179602) Fr & Eur.

Pons English-German, German-English Dictionary of Publishing & Printing. S. Klett & P. Collin. (ENG & GER.). 296p. 1990. 95.00 (*0-8288-3393-1*, F105870) Fr & Eur.

Pons English-German, German-English Law Dictionary. P. Collin. (ENG & GER.). 340p. 1990. 95.00 (*0-8288-7566-9*, 3125179505) Fr & Eur.

***Pons Fachwhorterbuch Recht: Englisch-Deutsch, Deutsch-Englisch.** 2nd ed. P. H. Collin. LC 99-194397. 499p. 1998. 53.00 (*3-12-517951-3*) Intl Bk Import.

Pons Fachwoerterbuch der Kraftfahrtechnik: English-German, German-English, 2 vols., Set. Peter A. Schmitt. (ENG & GER.). 1462p. 1992. 395.00 (*0-7859-6861-X*) Fr & Eur.

Pons Fachwoerterbuch Marketing. Pons. (ENG & GER.). 1991. 75.00 (*0-8288-7269-4*, 3125179807) Fr & Eur.

Pons Fachwoeterbuch Umwelt. Pons. (ENG & GER.). 1991. 75.00 (*0-8288-7268-6*, 3125179408) Fr & Eur.

Pons Fachworterbuch Recht. P. Von Collin. (ENG & GER.). 1990. lib. bdg. 85.00 (*0-8288-3888-7*, F129740) Fr & Eur.

Pons Fachworterbuch Wirtschafts. P. Von Collin. (ENG & GER.). 1990. lib. bdg. 85.00 (*0-8288-3889-5*, F131640) Fr & Eur.

Pons German / English - English / German Dictionary of Data Processing. Simon Collins. (ENG & GER.). 1997. 95.00 (*0-320-03706-1*) Fr & Eur.

Pons German-English, English-German Dictionary of Marketing. P. Collin. (ENG & GER.). 269p. 1991. 95.00 (*0-8288-7565-0*, 3125179807) Fr & Eur.

Pons German/English/German Dictionary of Data Processing. S. Collin. (ENG & GER.). 500p. 1997. 95.00 (*0-320-00451-1*) Fr & Eur.

Pons German/English/German Law Dictionary. P. Collin. (ENG & GER.). 340p. 1997. 95.00 (*0-320-00463-5*) Fr & Eur.

Pons Global Dictionary, English-German: Pons Global Woerterbuch Klett Englisch-Deutsch, Vol. 1. Peter Terrel. 1389p. 1986. 45.00 (*0-8288-0338-2*, M7015) Fr & Eur.

Pons Global Dictionary, German-English: Pons Global Woerterbuch Klett Deutsch-Englisch, Vol. 2. Peter Terrel. (ENG & GER.). 1986. 49.95 (*0-8288-4406-2*, M7014) Fr & Eur.

Pons Globalwoerterbuch Vol. 1: French-German. 2nd ed. Erich Weis & Heinrich Mattutat. (GER.). 1055p. 1985. 45.00 (*0-8288-1442-2*, M7004) Fr & Eur.

Pons Globalwoerterbuch Vol. 2: German-French. 2nd ed. Erich Weis & Heinrich Mattutat. (FRE & GER.). 1250p. 1985. 45.00 (*0-8288-4410-0*, M7003) Fr & Eur.

Pons-Kompakt Klett English-German-English Dictionary. Erich Weis. (ENG & GER.). 639p. 1985. 45.00 (*0-8288-1440-6*, M9361) Fr & Eur.

Pons Pictorial Dictionary: German-English-French-Spanish. J. C. Corbeil. (ENG, FRE, GER & SPA., Illus.). 959p. 1992. 117.00 (*0-7859-8917-X*) Fr & Eur.

PONS (Profile of Nonverbal Sensitivity) Test Manual. Robert Rosenthal et al. (Illus.). 1979. pap. text 19.95 (*0-89197-647-7*) Ardent Media.

Pont aux Trois Arches. Ismail Kadare. (FRE.). 1990. pap. 11.95 (*0-7859-2597-X*, 2070382850) Fr & Eur.

Pont de Brooklyn. Leslie Kaplan. (FRE.). 250p. 1991. pap. 15.95 (*0-7859-2613-5*, 2070383687) Fr & Eur.

Pont de la Riviere Kwai. Pierre Boulle. 9.95 (*0-686-54111-1*, M11077); pap. 11.95 (*0-8288-7623-1*, 2266023055) Fr & Eur.

Pont-de-Montvert: Social Structure & Politics in a French Village 1700-1914. Patrice L. Higonnet. LC 70-133209. (Historical Studies: No. 85). (Illus.). 233p. 1971. 20.00 (*0-674-68960-7*) HUP.

Pont Neuf. 4th ed. Edward M. Stack & Lydia Stack. (C). 1991. pap. text, wbk. ed. 18.40 (*0-13-530049-5*) P-H.

Pont Neuf: French Grammar in Review. 4th ed. Edward M. Stack. LC 90-49101. 352p. (C). 1990. pap. text 63.00 (*0-13-530031-2*) P-H.

Ponteach: Or The Savanges of America. Robert Roger. (Notable American Authors Ser.). 1999. reprint ed. lib. bdg. 125.00 (*0-7812-8834-7*) Rprt Serv.

Pontiac. William L. Johnston. Ed. by Robert Bensen. (Chapbook Ser.: No. 8). 21p. 1981. pap. 3.00 (*0-932884-07-5*) Red Herring.

Pontiac. Marie Tolbert. (Illus.). 116p. (Orig.). 1984. pap. 8.00 (*0-935787-00-3*) Freedom Pubs.

Pontiac . . . The Making of a U. S. Automobile Capital, 1818-1950. rev. ed. Esmo Woods. (Illus.). 240p. 1991. pap. 15.00 (*0-9641636-0-8*) New Pontiac.

Pontiac - Ottawa Rebel see North American Indians of Achievement

Pontiac & the Indian Uprising. Howard H. Peckham. LC 93-36864. 376p. 1994. pap. 16.95 (*0-8143-2469-X*) Wayne St U Pr.

Pontiac, Chief of the Ottawas. Jane Fleischer. (J). 1979. 8.70 (*0-606-01707-0*, Pub. by Turtleback) Demco.

Pontiac Dream Cars, Show Cars & Prototypes 1928-1998 Photo Album. Jesse Thomas. LC 98-75271. 1999. pap. 19.95 (*1-882256-93-X*) Iconografix.

Pontiac Fiero, 1984-88. Chilton Automotive Editorial Staff. LC 88-43193. (Illus.). 344p. (C). 1989. pap. text 17.95 (*0-8019-7949-8*) Thomson Learn.

Pontiac-Fiero, 1984-1988. Chilton Automotive Editorial Staff. 488p. (C). 1997. pap. 22.95 (*0-8019-9064-5*) Thomson Learn.

Pontiac Fiero, 1984-88. R. M. Clarke. (Brooklands Bks.). (Illus.). 100p. 1988. pap. 16.95 (*1-870642-01-5*, Pub. by Brooklands Bks) Motorbooks Intl.

Pontiac Firebird. Michael Burgan. LC 98-48709. (On the Road Ser.). 1999. 19.00 (*0-7368-0182-0*, Rivr Front Bks); 19.00 (*0-531-11813-4*) Capstone Pr.

Pontiac Firebird, 1982-92. Haynes Editors. (Automobile Repair Manuals Ser.). (Illus.). pap. 17.95 (*1-56392-065-4*, MBI 104290AM) Haynes Manuals.

***Pontiac Firebird, 1967-2000.** George W. Scala. (Illus.). 120p. 2000. pap. 24.95 (*1-58388-028-3*, 130631AE, Pub. by Iconografix) Motorbooks Intl.

Pontiac Firebird, Trans Am & GTO. (Best of Hot Rod Ser.: Vol. 7). (Illus.). 130p. 2000. pap. 18.95 (*1-884089-41-0*, Pub. by CarTech) Voyageur Pr.

Pontiac Firebird Trans Am 1969-1999 Photo Album. George Scala & Wallace Wyss. LC 98-75269. (Photo Album Ser.). (Illus.). 112p. (Orig.). 1999. pap. 19.95 (*1-882256-95-6*, 128237AE) Iconografix.

Pontiac Firebird, 1982-94: All U.S. & Canadian Models. Chilton Automotive Editorial Staff. (Chilton's Repair & Tune-up Guides Ser.). (Illus.). 492p. (C). 1995. pap. 16.95 (*0-8019-8598-6*) Thomson Learn.

***Pontiac GTO: The Great One.** Steve Statham. LC 00-26284. (Illus.). 156p. 2000. 29.95 (*0-7603-0828-4*, 129996AP) MBI Pubg.

Pontiac GTO Restoration Guide, 1964-1972. 2nd ed. Paul Zazarine & Charles Roberts. LC 94-44465. (Authentic Restoration Ser.). (Illus.). 544p. 1995. pap. 29.95 (*0-87938-953-2*) MBI Pubg.

***Pontiac, Michigan: A Postcard Album.** Gottfried Brieger. (Postcard History Ser.). (Illus.). 128p. 2000. pap. 18.99 (*0-7385-0714-8*) Arcadia Publng.

Pontiac Muscle Cars. Mike Mueller. (Enthusiast Color Ser.). (Illus.). 96p. 1994. pap. 13.95 (*0-87938-863-3*) MBI Pubg.

Pontiac Power. Thomas DeMauro et al. (Illus.). 162p. (Orig.). 1994. pap. 19.95 (*1-57913-002-X*) CSK Pub.

***Pontiaka Anecdota: Anecdotes from Asia Minor.** J. Tsopanides. (GRE.). 224p. 2000. pap. 15.00 (*1-885778-52-X*) Seaburn.

Pontifes de L'Ancienne Rome: Etudes Historique sur les Institutions Religieuses de Rome. Auguste Bouche-Leclercq. LC 75-10630. (Ancient Religion & Mythology Ser.). (FRE.). 1976. reprint ed. 36.95 (*0-405-07006-3*) Ayer.

Pontiffs: Popes Who Shaped History. John J. Hughes. LC 94-66025. 320p. (Orig.). 1994. text 16.95 (*0-87973-479-5*, 479) Our Sunday Visitor.

***Pontifical Mission for Palestine: 50 Years of Papal Concern.** Michael J. L. La Civita et al. Ed. by Helen C. Packard & Margaret Maron. (Illus.). 250p. 1999. write for info. (*0-9676262-0-X*) Cath Nr E Welfare.

Pontifications: Interviews. Norman Mailer & Michael J. Lennon. LC 82-82201. xv, 192 p. 1982. write for info. (*0-316-54419-1*) Little.

***Pontifikat Erzbischof Boemunds II von Trier, 1354-1362: Studien zur Reichs, Territorial-Und Verwaltungsgeschichte.** Michael Petzold. (Europaische Hochschulschriften Geschichte und Ihre Hilfswissenschaften Ser.). XXXVIII, 44p. 1999. 67.95 (*3-631-32298-4*) P Lang Pubng.

Pontius Family Letters, 1861-1933. James A. Thorson. LC 98-61481. (Illus.). 108p. 1999. 60.00 (*0-9631371-2-3*) James A Thorson.

Pontius Pilate: A Biographical Novel. Paul L. Maier. 384p. 1995. pap. 12.99 (*0-8254-3296-0*) Kregel.

***Pontius Pilate: A Biography.** Ann Wroe. LC 99-43000. 352p. 2000. 26.95 (*0-375-50305-6*) Random Hse Value.

Pontius Pilate in History & Interpretation. Helen K. Bond. LC 97-45970. (Society for New Testament Studies Monograph Ser.: No. 100). 276p. (C). 1998. text 59.95 (*0-521-63114-9*) Cambridge U Pr.

P

An Asterisk (*) at the beginning of an entry indicates that the title is appearing for the first time.

Pontius Pilate, 20 B. C.-A. D. 36. Adrian Johns. 199p. 1988. 40.00 (*0-7223-1960-6*, Pub. by A H S Ltd) St Mut.

Pontmercy's of Paris. William J. Read. (Illus.). 148p. (Orig.). 1996. pap. 12.95 (*1-57502-339-3*, P01127) Morris Pubng.

Pontoon: An Anthology of Washington State Poets. Ed. by Peter Pereira et al. (Number One Ser.). 80p. 1997. pap. 7.00 (*0-9647199-3-2*) Floating Bridge Pr.

***Pontoon No. 3: An Anthology of Washington State Poets.** Ed. by Peter Pereira et al. 96p. 1999. pap. 7.00 (*0-9647199-8-3*) Floating Bridge Pr.

***Pontoon, Number Two: An Anthology of Washington State Poets.** Ed. by Peter Pereira et al. 96p. 1998. pap. 7.00 (*0-9647199-5-9*) Floating Bridge Pr.

Pontoon/Deck Style Boats: Owner's Manual. TAL Marketing Services Staff. (Illus.). 93p. (Orig.). 1996. pap. 6.95 (*1-887960-05-8*, 596-207C) TotalConcepts.

Pontormo. Doris Krystof. (Masters of Italian Art Ser.). (Illus.). 140p. 1998. 19.95 (*3-8290-0254-8*, 520535) Konemann.

Pontormo: Paintings. Salvatore S. Nigro. LC 93-31283. (Illus.). 160p. 1994. 75.00 (*0-8109-3727-1*) Abrams.

Pontormo: Portrait of a Halberdier. Elizabeth Cropper. LC 97-19822. (Getty Museum Studies on Art). 138p. 1997. pap. 17.50 (*0-89236-366-5*, Pub. by J P Getty Trust) OUP.

***Pontormo: The Deposition.** Federico Zeri. (One Hundred Paintings Ser.). (Illus.). 48p. 2000. 14.95 (*1-55321-016-6*, Pub. by NDE Pub) IPG Chicago.

Pontormo-Rosso Fiorentino. Elisabetta M. Letta. Tr. by Anthony Brierly from ITA. (Library of Great Masters). (Illus.). 80p. (Orig.). 1995. pap. 12.99 (*1-878351-48-6*) Riverside NY.

Pontormo's Diary. Rosemary Mayer. (Illus.). 200p. (C). 1983. 26.95 (*0-915570-17-3*); pap. 16.95 (*0-686-86541-3*) Oolp Pr.

***Pontormos Diary.** Elizabeth Pilliod. 1999. 32.00 (*0-226-66827-4*); pap. 20.00 (*0-226-66828-2*) U Ch Pr.

Pontos Essenciais Do Portugues Comercial. Jose I. Suarez. 112p. (Orig.). 1987. pap. text 15.00 (*0-917129-06-7*) SLUSA.

Pony. Carolyn S. Baber. (Illus.). 22p. (J). 1990. pap. 9.95 (*0-9628937-0-6*, TX2910777) Richmond Saddlery.

Pony. Deni Bown. (Ultimate Sticker Books Ser.). (Illus.). 20p. (J). (ps-3). 1996. pap. 6.95 (*0-7894-1101-6*) DK Pub Inc.

Pony. DK Publishing Staff. 10p. (J). 1998. 3.95 (*0-7894-3714-7*) DK Pub Inc.

***Pony Activity Book.** Langton. 2000. pap. 8.95 (*0-85131-678-9*, Pub. by J A Allen) Trafalgar.

***Pony & the Bear,** Jeanne Betancourt. (Pony Pals Ser.: No. 23). (Illus.). 85p. (J). (gr. 3-5). 1999. mass mkt. 3.99 (*0-439-06489-9*) Scholastic Inc.

Pony Bob's Daring Ride: A Pony Express Adventure. Joe Bensen. LC 94-46348. (Highlights from American History Ser.). (Illus.). 32p. (J). 1995. pap. 5.95 (*1-56044-263-8*) Falcon Pub Inc.

Pony Breeder's Companion: A Practical Guide for Owners & Breeders. Caroline Nesbitt. LC 95-15647. (Illus.). 288p. 1995. pap. 29.95 (*0-87605-996-5*) Howell Bks.

Pony Club Quiz Book. Pony Club Staff. 112p. (C). 1990. pap. 21.00 (*0-900226-29-3*, Pub. by J A Allen) St Mut.

Pony Crazy. Bonnie Bryant. (Pony Tails Ser.: No. 1). (Illus.). (J). (gr. 3-5). 1995. pap. 4.50 (*0-553-54206-0*) BDD Bks Young Read.

Pony Crazy. Bonnie Bryant. (Pony Tails Ser.: No. 1). (Illus.). (J). (gr. 3-5). 1998. 9.09 (*0-606-08029-5*, Pub. by Turtleback) Demco.

***Pony Crosswords: 30 Fact-Filled Crosswords.** Roy Preston & Sue Preston. 96p. (J). 2000. mass mkt. 3.99 (*0-330-34107-3*) Mcm Child Bks.

Pony Express. Peter Anderson. (Cornerstones to Freedom Ser.). (Illus.). 32p. (J). (gr. 4-6). 1996. lib. bdg. 19.50 (*0-516-20002-X*) Childrens.

Pony Express. Peter Anderson. (Cornerstones to Freedom Ser.). (Illus.). 32p. (J). (gr. 3-7). 1998. pap. text 5.95 (*0-516-26286-6*) Childrens.

Pony Express. Allison Estes. (Short Stirrup Club Ser.: No. 10). (J). 1997. per. 3.99 (*0-671-00435-2*) PB.

Pony Express. Arlen Gould. (J). 1997. write for info. (*0-517-59825-6*); lib. bdg. write for info. (*0-517-59826-4*) Crown Bks Yng Read.

***Pony Express!** Steve Kroll-Smith. (Illus.). 40p. (J). (gr. 4-7). 2000. pap. 5.99 (*0-590-20240-5*) Scholastic Inc.

Pony Express. A. L. Lake. (Wild West in American History Ser.). (Illus.). 32p. (J). (gr. 3-8). 1989. lib. bdg. 23.93 (*0-86625-368-8*) Rourke Pubns.

Pony Express. Fred Reinfeld. LC 64-21330. (Illus.). 135p. 1973. pap. 7.00 (*0-8032-5786-4*, Bison Books) U of Nebr Pr.

Pony Express: A Thrilling & Truthful History. William L. Visscher. Ed. by William R. Jones. (Illus.). 64p. 1977. pap. 4.95 (*0-89646-062-2*) Vistabooks.

***Pony Express: Hands-On Projects about Early Communication.** Jennifer Quasha. LC 00-26676. (Great Social Studies Projects). (Illus.). (J). 2000. write for info. (*0-8239-5702-0*, PowerKids) Rosen Group.

***Pony Express: Voyage of Discovery.** Anthony Godfrey & Roy Webb. LC 99-60060. (Illus.). 64p. 1999. pap. 7.95 (*0-88714-147-1*) KC Pubns.

***Pony Express Christmas.** Sigmund Brouwer. 2000. 12.99 (*0-8423-4018-1*) Tyndale Hse.

Pony Express Guidebook. Jamison Station Press Staff. (Desert Rat Guidebook Ser.: No. 3). (Illus.). 57p. 1984. 2.95 (*0-317-01481-1*) Jamison Stn.

Pony Express in American History. Sue Hurwitz. LC 97-18045. (In American History Ser.). (J). 1998. write for info. (*0-89490-989-4*) Enslow Pubs.

Pony Express Riders of the Wild West. Jeff Savage. LC 94-43795. (Trailblazers of the Wild West Ser.). (Illus.). 48p. (J). (gr. 4-10). 1995. lib. bdg. 16.95 (*0-89490-602-X*) Enslow Pubs.

Pony Fish's Glow: And Other Clues to Plan & Purpose in Nature. George C. Williams. (Science Masters Ser.). (Illus.). 176p. 1998. pap. 11.00 (*0-465-07283-6*, Pub. by Basic) HarpC.

Pony for Jeremiah. Robert H. Miller. LC 96-3473. (Illus.). 64p. (J). 1996. pap. 4.95 (*0-382-39460-7*); lib. bdg. 12.95 (*0-382-39459-3*) Silver Burdett Pr.

Pony for Keeps. Jeanne Betancourt. (Pony Pals Ser.: No. 2). (Illus.). 96p. (J). (gr. 4-7). 1995. pap. 2.99 (*0-590-48584-9*) Scholastic Inc.

Pony for Keeps. Jeanne Betancourt. (Pony Pals Ser.: No. 2). (Illus.). (J). (gr. 2-5). 1995. 8.60 (*0-606-08027-9*, Pub. by Turtleback) Demco.

Pony for Luke. Kathryn Cocquyt. LC 97-29749. (Illus.). (J). Date not set. 14.95 (*1-56554-277-0*) Pelican.

Pony Games. Rosie Heywood. (Riding School Ser.). (Illus.). 32p. (J). (gr. 3 up). 1998. lib. bdg. 13.95 (*0-88110-993-2*, Usborne) EDC.

Pony Games: The Usborne Riding School. Rosie Heywood. (Illus.). 32p. (gr. 4-7). 1998. pap. text 5.95 (*0-7460-2921-7*, Usborne) EDC.

***Pony Hobby Book.** Karen Bush & Claire Colvin. 2000. pap. 8.95 (*0-85131-639-5*, Pub. by J A Allen) Trafalgar.

Pony in the Porch. Lucy Daniels. 1998. pap. text 16.95 (*0-7540-6038-1*) Chivers N Amer.

Pony in Trouble see Eclair Est Malade

Pony in Trouble. Jeanne Betancourt. LC 95-209004. (Pony Pals Ser.: No. 3). (Illus.). 96p. (J). (gr. 4-7). 1995. pap. 2.99 (*0-590-48585-7*) Scholastic Inc.

Pony in Trouble. Jeanne Betancourt. (Pony Pals Ser.: No. 3). (Illus.). (J). (gr. 2-5). 1995. 8.60 (*0-606-08028-7*, Pub. by Turtleback) Demco.

Pony Kids. Photos by Perry Ogden. LC 98-89094. (Illus.). 136p. 1999. 29.95 (*0-89381-859-3*, 193851) Aperture.

Pony Named Midnight. Susan T. Brown. (Illus.). 24p. 1998. boxed set 9.99 (*1-885101-94-5*) Writers Pr ID.

***Pony on the Porch.** Ben M. Baglio. (Animal Ark Ser.: No. 2). (J). (gr. 3-5). 1998. 9.09 (*0-606-13130-2*, Pub. by Turtleback) Demco.

***Pony Parade.** Lucy Daniels. (Animal Ark Pets Ser.: No. 7). (Illus.). 128p. (J). (gr. 2-5). 1999. pap. text 3.99 (*0-439-05164-9*) Scholastic Inc.

Pony Player. F. M. Cotolo. Ed. by Chuck Taylor. 175p. (Orig.). 1989. 16.95 (*0-941720-54-3*); pap. 8.95 (*0-941720-55-1*) Slough Pr TX.

Pony Promise. Lois Szymanski. 1996. pap. 3.99 (*0-380-78266-9*, Avon Bks) Morrow Avon.

Pony Puzzle Book. Mandy Langton & Anne Pilgrim. 86p. (J). 1990. 21.00 (*0-85131-535-6*, Pub. by J A Allen) Trafalgar.

***Pony Puzzles: Test Your Pony Knowledge.** Diana Kimpton. (Illus.). 128p. (J). 2000. mass mkt. 3.99 (*0-330-33640-1*) Mcm Child Bks.

Pony Riders. Guy N. Smith. 384p. 1997. mass mkt. 4.99 (*0-7860-0369-3*, Pinncle Kensgtn) Kensgtn Pub Corp.

Pony Riders Book. George Wheatley. 1970. 12.50 (*0-87556-407-0*) Saifer.

Pony-Sitters, Jeanne Betancourt. (Pony Pals Ser.: No. 14). (Illus.). 96p. (gr. 2-5). 1997. pap. 3.50 (*0-590-86601-X*, Little Apple) Scholastic Inc.

Pony Soldiers. James Axler. (Christmas Slipcase Ser.: No. 4). 1997. per. 5.99 (*0-373-89004-4*, 1-89004-5) Harlequin Bks.

Pony Stock/Mini Stock Racing Technology. Steve Smith. LC 99-161883. (Illus.). 112p. 1998. pap. 24.95 (*0-936834-97-8*) S S Autosports.

Pony Talk: A Complete Learning Guide for Young Riders. Judy Richter. (Illus.). 192p. 1993. 22.00 (*0-87605-849-7*) Howell Bks.

Pony to the Rescue see Perdue Dans les Bois

Pony to the Rescue. Jeanne Betancourt. (Pony Pals Ser.: No. 5). (Illus.). 96p. (J). (gr. 2-5). 1995. pap. 2.99 (*0-590-25244-5*) Scholastic Inc.

Pony to the Rescue. Jeanne Betancourt. (Pony Pals Ser.: No. 5). (Illus.). (J). (gr. 2-5). 1995. 8.09 (*0-606-08031-7*, Pub. by Turtleback) Demco.

Perdue Dans les Bois. Jeanne Betancourt. Tr. by Jocelyne Henri from ENG. (Pony Pals (Le Cercle des Poneys) Ser.: No. 5). Orig. Title: Pony to the Rescue. (FRE., Illus.). 120p. (J). (gr. 2-5). 1996. mass mkt. 6.99 (*0-590-16041-9*) Scholastic Inc.

Pony Tracks. Frederic Remington. 22.95 (*0-89190-780-7*) Amereon Ltd.

Pony Tracks. Frederic Remington. (Western Frontier Library: No. 19). (Illus.). 1975. reprint ed. 12.95 (*0-8061-1248-4*) U of Okla Pr.

Pony Trekking. Glenda Spooner. 150p. (C). 1990. pap. 30.00 (*0-85131-246-2*, Pub. by J A Allen) St Mut.

Pony Trouble. Dale Gasque. LC 97-18047. (Hyperion Chapters Ser.). (Illus.). 64p. (J). (gr. 2-4). 1998. pap. 3.99 (*0-7868-1218-4*, Pub. by Hyprn Ppbks) Little.

Pony Trouble. Dale Gasque. (Hyperion Chapters Ser.). 1998. 9.05 (*0-606-13714-9*, Pub. by Turtleback) Demco.

Pony Trouble. Dale Blackwell Gasque. LC 97-18047. (Illus.). 64p. (J). (gr. 2-4). 1998. lib. bdg. 14.49 (*0-7868-2267-8*, Pub. by Hyprn Child) Little.

Pony Trouble, Tessa Krailing. LC 99-20183. (Petsitters Club Ser.: No. 9). (Illus.). 96p. (J). (gr. 1-4). 1999. pap. 3.95 (*0-7641-0736-4*) Barron.

Pony Wife. Beverly Bird. 464p. (Orig.). 1995. mass mkt. 5.99 (*0-515-11629-7*, Jove) Berkley Pub.

Poo: Poems from Hollywood. Mark Dunster. 11p. 1998. pap. 5.00 (*0-89642-564-9*) Linden Pubs.

Poo, You & the Potoroo's Loo. David Bellamy. Ed. by Fran Balkwill. (Making Sense of Science Ser.). (Illus.). 32p. (J). 1997. pap. 12.00 (*1-85578-095-X*, Pub. by Portland Pr Ltd) Ashgate Pub Co.

Pooches & Small Fry: Parenting Skills for Dogs (& Kids!) Jack McDaniel & Colleen McDaniel. Ed. by Luana Luther. LC 94-69540. (Parenting Skills for Dogs & Kids Ser.). (Illus.). 174p. 1995. pap. 14.95 (*0-944875-37-8*) Doral Pub.

Poodle. Bruce Fogle. LC 96-46077. (Dog Breed Handbks.). 80p. 1997. 14.95 (*0-7894-1612-3*) DK Pub Inc.

Poodle. Bruce Fogle. LC 96-46077. (Dog Breed Handbks.). 80p. 1999. pap. 7.95 (*0-7894-4197-7*) DK Pub Inc.

Poodle. Anna K. Nicholas. (Illus.). 288p. 1984. text 24.95 (*0-86622-033-X*, PS-814) TFH Pubns.

Poodle: An Owner's Guide to a Happy, Healthy Pet. Virginia Guidry. (Owner's Guide to a Happy, Healthy Pet Ser.). (Illus.). 160p. 1995. 12.95 (*0-87605-387-8*) Howell Bks.

Poodle Collectibles of the 50's & 60's. Elaine Butler. (Illus.). 151p. (Orig.). 1995. pap. 19.95 (*0-89538-038-2*) L-W Inc.

Poodle Owners' Medical Manual. Robert M. Brown. LC 87-71345. 288p. (Orig.). 1988. pap. 17.00 (*0-938681-02-8*) Breed Manual Pubns.

Poodle Springs. Raymond Chandler & Robert B. Parker. 1990. mass mkt. 5.99 (*0-425-12343-X*) Berkley Pub.

Poodle Springs. large type ed. Raymond Chandler & Robert B. Parker. 303p. 1990. reprint ed. lib. bdg. 11.95 (*0-89621-977-1*) Thorndike Pr.

Poodle: The Other White Meat: The Second Sherman's Lagoon Collection. Jim Toomey. 1999. pap. text 9.95 (*0-8362-8287-6*) Andrews & McMeel.

***Poodle Who Barked at the Moon.** Charlotte Zolotow. 2001. text 15.95 (*0-8050-6306-4*) H Holt & Co.

Poodle Who Barked at the Wind. Charlotte Zolotow. LC 86-42992. (Charlotte Zolotow Bk.). (Illus.). 32p. (J). (ps-3). 1987. 12.95 (*0-06-026965-0*) HarpC Child Bks.

Poodles. Ariel Books Staff. LC 96-85911. 80p. 1997. 4.95 (*0-8362-2649-6*, Arie Bks) Andrews & McMeel.

Poodles. Stuart A. Kallen. LC 95-927. (Dogs Ser.). (Illus.). 24p. (J). (ps-4). 1995. lib. bdg. 13.99 (*1-56239-451-7*) ABDO Pub Co.

Poodles, AKC Rank No. 5. Kerry Donnelly. (KW Dog Ser.). (Illus.). 1996. pap. 9.95 (*0-7938-2363-3*, KW010S) TFH Pubns.

Poodles: Everything about Purchase, Care, Nutrition, Breeding, Behavior, & Training. Joe Stahlkuppe. LC 96-28312. (Complete Pet Owner's Manual Ser.). 1997. pap. 6.95 (*0-8120-9738-8*) Barron.

Poodle's Grave. large type ed. Howard C. Davis. (Linford Mystery Library). 1989. pap. 16.99 (*0-7089-6750-7*, Linford) Ulverscroft.

Poof! John O'Brien. (Illus.). 32p. (J). (ps). 1999. 14.95 (*1-56397-815-6*) Boyds Mills Pr.

Poof Tales: Poems from Hollywood. Mark Dunster. 11p. 1998. pap. 5.00 (*0-89642-547-9*) Linden Pubs.

Poof Wolf's New House. Marcus Porus et al. LC 95-92693. (Gribich & Friends Ser.). (Illus.). 32p. (J). (ps). 1996. 14.95 (*0-9646125-2-6*) Doog Pub Grp.

Poofin: The Cloud That Cried on Christmas. 5th ed. Richard M. Wainwright. (Illus.). 40p. (J). 1989. reprint ed. 16.00 (*0-9619566-1-5*) Family Life.

Pooh. Illus. by Diaz, Jamie, Studios Staff. (Look & Find Ser.). 24p. (J). 1996. lib. bdg. 14.95 (*1-56674-168-8*) Forest Hse.

Pooh. Golden Books Staff. (J). 1997. pap. text 1.79 (*0-307-07117-0*, 07117, Goldn Books) Gldn Bks Pub Co.

***Pooh.** Mouseworks Staff. (My Very First Cloth Book Ser.). (J). 1999. 6.99 (*0-7364-0177-6*, Pub. by Disney Pr) Little.

Pooh. Walt Disney Productions. (Pooh Songbook Ser.). (Illus.). 274p. (ps up). 1998. pap. 14.95 (*0-7935-9375-1*, HL00824130) H Leonard.

***Pooh: Coloring, Paint with Water, Activities.** Golden Books Staff. (Pooh Ser.). (Illus.). (J). 2000. pap. 3.99 (*0-307-25401-1*, Goldn Books) Gldn Bks Pub Co.

Pooh: Cook with Components. Mouseworks Staff. (J). 1996. write for info. (*1-57082-459-2*, Pub. by Mouse Works) Little.

Pooh: Eeyore Friendly Tales. Mouse Works Staff. LC 99-159402. (Friendly Tales Ser.). (Illus.). 5p. (J). 1997. 6.99 (*1-57082-690-0*, Pub. by Mouse Works) Time Warner.

Pooh: Good Friends-The Perfect Picnic Spot-A Walk in the Woods-Who Hid the Honey? Mouse Works Staff. (Pooh Ser.). (J). 1998. 9.98 (*1-57082-725-7*, Pub. by Mouse Works) Time Warner.

Pooh: Paint with Water. (J). pap. 1.79 (*0-307-08263-6*, 08263) Gldn Bks Pub Co.

Pooh: Special Edition Coloring Book. (J). 2.99 (*0-307-05545-0*, 05545) Gldn Bks Pub Co.

Pooh: Trace & Color. (J). 2.49 (*0-307-02117-3*, 02117) Gldn Bks Pub Co.

Pooh ABC. A. A. Milne, pseud. 32p. 1999. pap. 4.99 (*0-14-055750-4*) Viking Penguin.

Pooh & Piglet Go Hunting. A. A. Milne, pseud. (Slide & Peek Ser.). (ps-k). 1999. pap. 5.99 (*0-525-46117-5*) Peng Put Young Read.

Pooh & Piglet Snow Globe. 1999. text. write for info. (*1-57082-891-1*) Mouse Works.

Pooh & Some Bees. A. A. Milne, pseud. (Illus.). 24p. (J). 1996. pap. 3.99 (*0-525-45526-4*, Dutton Child) Peng Put Young Read.

Pooh & Some Bees. A. A. Milne, pseud. (Winnie-the-Pooh Collection). (J). 1998. pap. 5.99 (*0-525-46093-4*, Dutton Child) Peng Put Young Read.

Pooh & the Dragon. Golden Books Staff. (Little Golden Bks.). (Illus.). 24p. (J). 1997. 2.29 (*0-307-98798-1*, 98798, Goldn Books) Gldn Bks Pub Co.

Pooh & the Millennium. John Tyerman Williams. LC 98-44162. (Illus.). 224p. 1999. 20.00 (*0-525-45950-2*, Dutton Child) Peng Put Young Read.

Pooh & the Philosophers. John T. Williams. LC 95-40254. (Illus.). 240p. (J). 1996. 15.99 (*0-525-45520-5*, Dutt) Dutton Plume.

Pooh & the Storm That Sparkled. Isabel Gaines. LC 98-86648. (Winnie the Pooh First Readers Ser.: No. 14). (Illus.). 37p. (J). (gr. k-3). 1999. pap. 3.99 (*0-7868-4313-6*, Pub. by Disney Pr) Time Warner.

Pooh Anytime, Vol. 1. Mouse Works Staff. LC 96-227568. 61p. (J). 1996. 9.98 (*1-57082-409-6*) Little.

Pooh Bedtime Book. A. A. Milne, pseud. (Illus.). 48p. (ps-3). 1997. pap. 5.99 (*0-14-038793-5*) Viking Penguin.

Pooh Bedtime Stories: Two Tigger Tales. Ann Braybrooks. 24p. 1999. pap. text 3.29 (*0-307-13196-3*) Gldn Bks Pub Co.

Pooh Board Book. A. A. Milne, pseud. (J). 1999. pap. 4.50 (*0-525-45521-3*) NAL.

Pooh Board Book. 2nd ed. A. A. Milne, pseud. (J). 1999. pap., bds. 4.50 (*0-525-45522-1*) NAL.

Pooh Board Book. 3rd ed. A. A. Milne, pseud. (J). 1999. pap., bds. 4.50 (*0-525-45524-8*) NAL.

Pooh Board Book. 4th ed. A. A. Milne, pseud. (J). 1999. pap. 4.50 (*0-525-45525-6*) NAL.

Pooh Board Book Collection. A. A. Milne, pseud. 1995. text 14.99 (*0-525-45509-4*) NAL.

Pooh Book of Quotations. Illus. by Ernest H. Shepard. LC 91-2628. 128p. (J). (gr. 2 up). 1991. 14.99 (*0-525-44824-1*, Dutton Child) Peng Put Young Read.

Pooh Can, Can You?, Vol. 1. Disney Press Staff. (Learn & Grow Ser.). 12p. (J). 1999. 6.99 (*0-7364-0135-0*, Pub. by Mouse Works) Time Warner.

Pooh (Christmas) (Super Coloring Book Ser.). (J). pap. text 2.29 (*0-307-08538-4*, 08538) Gldn Bks Pub Co.

Pooh Christmas Days. Sparky Moore et al. LC 96-227808. (J). 1996. write for info. (*0-7853-1784-8*) Pubns Intl Ltd.

Pooh Christmas Songs A. A. Milne, pseud et al. LC 98-234873. 1998. write for info. (*0-7853-2729-0*) Pubns Intl Ltd.

Pooh Christmas with Friends. (J). pap. 3.29 (*0-307-09193-7*, 09193) Gldn Bks Pub Co.

***Pooh Clip & Read.** abr. ed. A. A. Milne, pseud. (Illus.). 24p. (ps-3). 1999. pap. 2.99 (*0-525-46203-1*, Dutton Child) Peng Put Young Read.

Pooh Colors the World: Paint Box Book. (J). pap. 3.99 (*0-307-09202-X*, 09202) Gldn Bks Pub Co.

Pooh Counting. Mouseworks Staff. LC 98-235635. (J). 1997. 9.98 (*1-57082-620-X*, Pub. by Mouse Works) Time Warner.

Pooh Counts to Five. Disney Publishing Group Staff. (Pooh's Learn & Grow Ser.: Vol. 4). (Illus.). 12p. (J). 1999. 3.49 (*1-57973-038-8*) Advance Pubs.

Pooh Dictionary: The Complete Guide to the Words of Pooh & All the Animals in the Forest. A. R. Melrose. LC 95-6033. (Illus.). 252p. (J). (gr. 4 up). 1995. 18.99 (*0-525-45395-4*, Dutton Child) Peng Put Young Read.

Pooh Flat Pack: Flndr Pb. Mouseworks Staff. 9.98 (*1-57082-744-3*, Pub. by Mouse Works) Time Warner.

Pooh Flip Book. Mouse Works Staff. 40p. (J). 1997. 2.98 (*1-57082-411-8*) Little.

***Pooh Friendly Tales.** Mouseworks Staff. (J). 1999. boxed set 27.96 (*0-7364-0041-9*, Pub. by Mouse Works) Time Warner.

Pooh Friendly Tales With Plush. Mouse Works Staff. LC 99-159402. (Pooh Ser.). (Illus.). 5p. (J). 1997. bds. 6.99 (*1-57082-692-7*, Pub. by Mouse Works) Time Warner.

Pooh Friendship Book. A. A. Milne, pseud. 1999. pap. write for info. (*0-14-037596-1*) Viking Penguin.

Pooh Gets Stuck, No. 1. Gaines. 48p. (J). (gr. k-2). 1998. pap. 3.95 (*0-7868-4184-2*, Pub. by Disney Pr) Time Warner.

Pooh Goes Visiting. A. A. Milne, pseud. (Illus.). 24p. (J). (ps-k). 1996. pap. 3.99 (*0-525-45527-2*, Dutton Child) Peng Put Young Read.

***Pooh Goes Visiting.** A. A. Milne, pseud. (Illus.). 32p. (J). (ps-3). 2000. 9.99 (*0-525-46457-3*, Dutton Child) Peng Put Young Read.

***Pooh Goes Visiting: And Other Stories.** A. A. Milne, pseud. (J). 1998. mass mkt. incl. audio (*1-84032-047-8*) HOD2.

Pooh Goes Visiting Puzzle. A. A. Milne, pseud. (Illus.). 14p. 1999. 7.99 (*0-525-46272-4*, Dutt) Dutton Plume.

Pooh Has Ears. Golden Staff. LC 94-77230. (Shaped Little Nugget Bks.). (Illus.). 14p. (J). (ps). 1995. bds. 3.99 (*0-307-12726-5*, 12726, Goldn Books) Gldn Bks Pub Co.

***Pooh Loves Christmas! A Winnie the Pooh Photo Album & Storybook.** Mouseworks Staff. (Keepsake Photo Storybks.). 10p. (J). 2000. bds. 6.99 (*0-7364-0191-1*, Pub. by Mouse Works) Time Warner.

Pooh Loves You: Pooh Friendly Tale Ser., 1. Mouse Works Staff. LC 99-195600. 10p. 1999. 6.99 (*0-7364-0102-4*, Pub. by Mouse Works) Time Warner.

***Pooh Movie Tree House Book: Freindship Book.** Mouseworks Staff. 8p. (J). (ps-3). 2000. 16.99 (*0-7364-1049-X*, Pub. by Hyperion) Time Warner.

Pooh on Management. Roger E. Allen. 192p. 1999. pap. 9.95 (*0-452-27336-6*, Plume) Dutton Plume.

Pooh on Problem Solving. Roger E. Allen. 164p. 1999. pap. 9.95 (*0-452-27526-1*, Plume) Dutton Plume.

***Pooh Party Time.** Golden Books Publishing Company Staff. (Illus.). 16p. (J). (ps-3). 2000. pap. text 2.99 (*0-307-08557-0*, 08557) Gldn Bks Pub Co.

Pooh Perplexed. Frederick C. Crews. (Winnie-the-Pooh Collection). 1999. 19.99 (*0-525-45602-3*) NAL.

Pooh Plays Doctor. Kathleen W. Zoehfeld. LC 96-71038. (Illus.). 32p. (J). (ps). 1997. 11.95 (*0-7868-3124-3*, Pub. by Disney Pr) Time Warner.

Pooh Plays Doctor. Kathleen W. Zoehfeld. (J). (ps-k). 1999. pap. 4.99 (*0-7868-4341-1*, Pub. by Disney Pr) Time Warner.

P

An Asterisk (*) at the beginning of an entry indicates that the title is appearing for the first time.

Pooh Plays Doctor Book & Kit. Disney Press Staff. (Learn & Grow Ser.). 32p. (J). 1999. boxed set 11.99 (*0-7364-0144-X*, Pub. by Mouse Works) Time Warner.
Pooh Reading Fun. 192p. (J). 1998. 19.95 (*0-7868-3224-X*, Pub. by Disney Pr) Time Warner.
Pooh Says Please! Disney Press Staff. 16p. (J). 1999. 3.50 (*0-7364-0150-4*, Pub. by Mouse Works) Time Warner.
Pooh Solves a Mystery: A Slide & Peek Book. A. A. Milne, pseud. LC 99-190546. 12p. (J). 1998. 5.99 (*0-525-45987-1*, Dutton Child) Peng Put Young Read.
Pooh Song Book. unabridged ed. A. A. Milne, pseud. (J). (gr. 4 up). 1984. audio 50.00 (*0-89845-558-8*, SSBC 702) HarperAudio.
Pooh Story Book. A. A. Milne, pseud. LC 65-19580. (Illus.). 80p. (J). (gr. k-4). 1965. 14.99 (*0-525-37546-5*, Dutton Child) Peng Put Young Read.
Pooh Story Book. A. A. Milne, pseud. LC 96-154709. (Illus.). 80p. (J). (ps-3). 1996. pap. 5.99 (*0-14-038168-6*, PuffinBks) Peng Put Young Read.
Pooh Story Book. A. A. Milne, pseud. 1996. 11.19 (*0-606-09761-9*, Pub. by Turtleback) Demco.
Pooh Storybook Treasury. Mouseworks Staff. LC 97-170388. (Illus.). (J). 1997. 14.98 (*1-57082-722-2*, Pub. by Mouse Works) Time Warner.
Pooh to Grow on. A. A. Milne, pseud. (Illus.). 48p. (ps-3). 1999. 9.99 (*0-525-46163-9*) NAL.
Pooh to the Rescue. A. A. Milne, pseud. (Illus.). (J). 1997. pap. 14.99 (*0-525-45689-9*) NAL.
Pooh Touch & Feel. A. A. Milne, pseud. (Illus.). 12p. (J). 1998. 9.99 (*0-525-45830-1*) NAL.
***Pooh Unplugged: A Parody: An Unauthorized Memoir.** Karen Finley. (Illus.). 64p. 1999. 19.95 (*1-889195-26-X*, Pub. by Smart Art Pr) RAM Publications.
Pooh Welcomes Winter. Kathleen Zoehfeld. 32p. (J). 1999. pap. 4.99 (*0-7868-4355-1*, Pub. by Disney Pr) Time Warner.
Pooh Welcomes Winter. Kathleen W. Zoehfeld. LC 96-72459. (My Very First Winnie the Pooh Ser.). (Illus.). 32p. (J). (ps). 1997. 11.95 (*0-7868-3146-4*, Pub. by Disney Pr) Time Warner.
***Pooh's Bad Dream.** Kathleen Zoehfeld. (My Very First Winnie the Pooh Ser.). 32p. (J). 2000. pap. 4.99 (*0-7868-4377-2*, Pub. by Disney Pr) Time Warner.
Pooh's Bad Dream. Kathleen W. Zoehfeld. LC 97-80237. (My Very First Winnie the Pooh Ser.). (Illus.). 32p. (J). (ps-k). 1998. 11.95 (*0-7868-3137-5*, Pub. by Disney Pr) Time Warner.
Pooh's Bedtime Book. A. A. Milne, pseud et al. LC 80-65523. (Illus.). 48p. (J). (ps-3). 1980. 13.99 (*0-525-44895-0*, Dutton Child) Peng Put Young Read.
Pooh's Best Friend. Isabel Gaines. LC 98-73265. (Winnie the Pooh First Readers Ser.: No. 7). (Illus.). 40p. (J). (gr. 2-4). 1998. pap. 3.95 (*0-7868-4265-2*, Pub. by Disney Pr) Time Warner.
Pooh's Best Friend Book & Friendship Bracelet. Ann Braybrooks. LC 97-65954. (Illus.). 32p. (J). (gr. 1-4). 1998. 7.95 (*0-7868-3152-9*, Pub. by Disney Pr) Time Warner.
***Pooh's Birthday Surprise: Learn & Grow.** Kathleen Zoehfeld. (Lift the Flaps Bks.). 14p. (J). 2000. 5.99 (*0-7364-1007-4*, Pub. by Mouse Works) Time Warner.
Pooh's Book of ABCs: My First Activity Book. Golden Books Staff. (Pooh Ser.). (Illus.). (J). 1997. pap. text 1.19 (*0-307-09335-2*, 09335, Goldn Books) Gldn Bks Pub Co.
Pooh's Book of Quotations. Brian Sibley. 1999. pap. 6.99 (*0-14-038114-7*) Viking Penguin.
***Pooh's Busy Bay.** A. A. Milne, pseud. (Illus.). 10p. (J). (ps-k). 2000. 5.99 (*0-525-46461-1*, Dutton Child) Peng Put Young Read.
***Pooh's Christmas Gift.** Isabel Gaines. 40p. (J). 1999. pap. 3.99 (*0-7868-4402-7*, Pub. by Disney Pr) Time Warner.
Pooh's Christmas Gifts. Isabel Gaines. 40p. (J). (gr. k-3). 1999. pap. 3.99 (*0-7868-4315-2*, Pub. by Disney Pr) Time Warner.
Pooh's Colorful Shapes. Disney Publishing Group Staff. (Pooh's Learn & Grow Ser.: Vol. 1). (Illus.). 12p. (J). 1999. 3.49 (*1-57973-035-3*) Advance Pubs.
Pooh's Easter Egg Hunt. Isabel Gaines. 40p. (J). (gr. 2-4). 1999. pap. 3.99 (*0-7868-4352-7*, Pub. by Disney Pr) Little.
Pooh's Easter Egg Hunt. Isabel Gaines. LC 98-86077. (Winnie the Pooh First Readers Ser.: No. 10). (Illus.). 40p. (J). (gr. 2-4). 1999. pap. 3.95 (*0-7868-4268-7*, Pub. by Disney Pr) Time Warner.
Pooh's Etiquette Book. Illus. by Ernest H. Shepard. LC 95-221589. 96p. (J). (ps up). 1995. 8.99 (*0-525-45501-9*, Dutton Child) Peng Put Young Read.
***Pooh's Fall Harvest.** Isabel Gaines. (Winnie the Pooh First Readers Ser.: No. 23). 40p. (J). 2000. pap. 3.99 (*0-7868-4370-5*, Pub. by Disney Pr) Time Warner.
***Pooh's Family Tree, Vol. 20.** Isabel Gaines. (Winnie the Pooh First Readers Ser.). 40p. (J). 2000. pap. 4.00 (*0-7868-4367-5*, Pub. by Disney Pr) Time Warner.
***Pooh's Fast & Slow Days.** Disney Publishing Group Staff. (Illus.). 12p. (J). 2000. pap. text 6.99 (*0-7364-1005-8*, Pub. by Mouse Works) Time Warner.
***Pooh's FavoriteThings about Spring.** Kathleen Zoehfeld. (My Very First Winnie the Pooh Reader Ser.). 32p. (J). 2000. 17.99 (*0-7868-3251-7*, Pub. by Disney Pr) Time Warner.
Pooh's First Clock With Other. A. A. Milne, pseud. LC 98-210004. (Illus.). 6p. (J). (ps-3). 1998. pap. 12.99 (*0-525-45983-9*, Dutton Child) Peng Put Young Read.
Pooh's First Day of School. Kathleen W. Zoehfeld. LC 96-71039. (My Very First Winnie the Pooh Ser.: Vol. 1). (Illus.). 32p. (J). (ps). 1997. 11.95 (*0-7868-3125-1*, Pub. by Disney Pr) Time Warner.
Pooh's First Day of School. Kathleen Weidner Zoehfeld. (My Very First Winnie the Pooh Bk.). (Illus.). 32p. (J). 1999. pap. 4.99 (*0-7868-4348-9*, Pub. by Disney Pr) Time Warner.
Pooh's Garden. Disney Publishing Group Staff. (Pooh's Learn & Grow Ser.: Vol. 11). (Illus.). 12p. (J). 1999. 3.49 (*1-57973-045-0*) Advance Pubs.
***Pooh's Graduation.** 22nd ed. Isabel Gaines. (Illus.). 40p. (J). (gr. k-3). 2000. pap. 3.99 (*0-7868-4369-1*, Pub. by Disney Pr) Time Warner.
Pooh's Grand Adventure. Leonard, Hal, Corporation Staff. 56p. 1998. pap. 9.95 (*0-7935-8968-1*) H Leonard.
Pooh's Grand Adventure: The Search for Christopher Robin. Justine Korman. LC 97-71021. (Little Golden Bks.). (J). 1997. 2.29 (*0-307-98841-4*, 98841, Goldn Books) Gldn Bks Pub Co.
Pooh's Grand Adventure: The Search for Christopher Robin, Vol. 1. Bruce Talkington. LC 97-65374. Vol. 1. (Illus.). 32p. (J). (gr. k-2). 1997. 12.95 (*0-7868-3135-9*, Pub. by Disney Pr) Time Warner.
***Pooh's Great Big Word Book.** A. A. Milne, pseud. (Illus.). 32p. (J). 2000. pap. 11.99 (*0-525-46335-6*, Dutton Child) Peng Put Young Read.
Pooh's Halloween Parade. Isabel Gaines. (Illus.). (J). (gr. k-3). 1999. pap. 3.99 (*0-7868-4314-4*, Pub. by Disney Pr) Time Warner.
Pooh's Hero Party, No. 12. Disney Press Staff. LC 98-86075. (Winnie the Pooh First Readers Ser.: No. 12). (Illus.). 40p. (J). (gr. k-3). 1999. pap. 3.99 (*0-7868-4270-9*, Pub. by Disney Pr) Time Warner.
Pooh's Honey Adventure. Kathleen Weidner Zoehfeld. (Read-Aloud Storybook Ser.). 64p. (J). 1999. pap. 5.99 (*0-7364-0133-4*, Pub. by Mouse Works) Time Warner.
Pooh's Honey Bee Counting Book. LC 96-124487. (Touch & Play Ser.). (Illus.). 24p. (J). 1994. 8.98 (*1-57082-149-6*, Pub. by Mouse Works) Time Warner.
Pooh's Honey Tree, No. 5. Isabel Gaines. LC PZ7.G1277Poh 1998. (Winnie the Pooh First Readers Ser.: No. 3). (Illus.). 40p. (J). (gr. k-2). 1998. pap. 3.50 (*0-7868-4253-9*, Pub. by Disney Pr) Time Warner.
***Pooh's Jingle Bells.** Kathleen Zoehfeld. (Illus.). 32p. (J). (ps-k). 2000. pap. 4.99 (*0-7868-4419-1*, Pub. by Disney Pr) Time Warner.
Pooh's Jingle Bells. Kathleen W. Zoehfeld. LC 98-84081. (My Very First Winnie the Pooh Ser.). (Illus.). 32p. (J). (ps). 1998. 11.95 (*0-7868-3204-5*, Pub. by Disney Pr) Time Warner.
Pooh's Leaf Pile. Isabel Gaines. (Illus.). 40p. (J). (gr. k-3). 1999. pap. 3.99 (*0-7868-4316-0*, Pub. by Disney Pr) Time Warner.
***Pooh's Leaf Pile Book Club: Special Sales Edition.** Isabel Gaines. 40p. (J). 1999. pap. 3.99 (*0-7868-4387-X*, Pub. by Disney Pr) Time Warner.
Pooh's Letters from the Hundred Acre Wood. A. A. Milne, pseud. LC 97-38862. (Illus.). 48p. (J). 1998. 16.99 (*0-525-45890-5*) NAL.
Pooh's Library, 4 bks., Set. A. A. Milne, pseud. (Illus.). (J). (ps up). 1988. pap. 44.00 (*0-525-44451-3*, Dutton Child) Peng Put Young Read.
Pooh's Library, 4 bks., Set. A. A. Milne, pseud. (Illus.). 48p. (J). (ps-3). 1992. pap. 20.00 (*0-14-095560-7*, PuffinBks) Peng Put Young Read.
***Pooh's Little Book of Feng Shui.** A. A. Milne, pseud. LC 99-89793. (Illus.). 96p. (YA). 2000. 9.99 (*0-525-46331-3*, Dutton Child) Peng Put Young Read.
Pooh's Little Instruction Book. Illus. by Ernest H. Shepard. (Winnie-the-Pooh Collection). 80p. (J). 1995. 10.99 (*0-525-45366-0*) NAL.
Pooh's Neighborhood. Kathleen Zoehfeld. 32p. (J). (ps-k). 1999. pap. 4.99 (*0-7868-4340-3*, Pub. by Disney Pr) Time Warner.
Pooh's Neighborhood, No. 3. Kathleen W. Zoehfeld. LC 96-86051. Vol. 1. (Illus.). 32p. (J). (ps). 1997. 11.95 (*0-7868-3136-7*, Pub. by Disney Pr) Time Warner.
Pooh's Noisy Book. Disney Press Staff. (Learn & Grow Ser.). 12p. (J). 1999. 6.99 (*0-7364-0136-9*, Pub. by Mouse Works) Time Warner.
Pooh's Pitter Patter Splash. Mouseworks Staff. (Pooh Busy Bks.). (Illus.). 12p. (J). 1999. bds. 6.99 (*1-57082-943-8*, Pub. by Mouse Works) Time Warner.
Pooh's Playful Pond. Disney Publishing Group Staff. (Pooh's Learn & Grow Ser.: Vol. 6). (Illus.). 12p. (J). 1999. 3.49 (*1-57973-040-X*) Advance Pubs.
Pooh's Popping Opposites, Pop-Up Book. Mouse Works Staff. (Illus.). 5p. (J). 1996. 7.98 (*1-57082-328-6*, Pub. by Mouse Works) Time Warner.
Pooh's Pumpkin. Isabel Gaines. LC 97-81434. (Winnie the Pooh First Readers Ser.: No. 6). (Illus.). 32p. (J). 1998. pap. 3.95 (*0-7868-4256-3*, Pub. by Disney Pr) Time Warner.
Pooh's Pumpkin Problem. Mary Hogan. 5p. (J). 1999. 4.99 (*0-7364-0158-X*, Pub. by Mouse Works) Time Warner.
Pooh's Pumpkin School Market Edition. Isabel Gaines. (Winnie the Pooh First Readers Ser.: No. 3). (Illus.). 48p. (J). (gr. k-2). 1998. pap. 3.95 (*0-7868-4304-7*, Pub. by Disney Pr) Time Warner.
Pooh's Rainy Day. Disney Publishing Group Staff. (Pooh's Learn & Grow Ser.: Vol. 10). (Illus.). 12p. (J). 1999. 3.49 (*1-57973-044-2*) Advance Pubs.
Pooh's Scavenger Hunt. Isabel Gaines. (Illus.). 40p. (J). (gr. k-3). 1999. pap. 3.99 (*0-7868-4317-9*, Pub. by Disney Pr) Time Warner.
***Pooh's Scavenger Hunt: Special Sales Edition.** Isabel Gaines. 40p. (J). 1999. pap. 3.99 (*0-7868-4386-1*, Pub. by Disney Pr) Time Warner.
Pooh's Scrapbook. Kathleen Zoehfeld. (My Very First Winnie the Pooh Ser.: No. 11). (Illus.). 32p. (J). 1999. 11.99 (*0-7868-3226-6*, Pub. by Disney Pr) Little.
***Pooh's Sled Ride, No. 24.** Isabel Gaines. 40p. (J). 2000. pap. 3.99 (*0-7868-4371-3*, Pub. by Disney Pr) Time Warner.
Pooh's Sunny Day. Disney Publishing Group Staff. (Pooh's Learn & Grow Ser.: Vol. 3). (Illus.). 12p. (J). 1999. 3.49 (*1-57973-037-X*) Advance Pubs.
Pooh's Surprise Basket. Isabel Gaines. (Winnie the Pooh First Readers Ser.: No. 13). (J). (gr. k-2). 1999. pap. 3.99 (*0-7868-4332-2*, Pub. by Disney Pr) Time Warner.
Pooh's Surprise Party Surprise. Marilyn Bollinger. LC 97-202427. (Magic Touch Talking Bks.). (Illus.). 22p. (J). (ps-2). 1996. 19.99 (*1-888208-15-5*) Hasbro.
Pooh's Treehouse. A. A. Milne, pseud. (J). 1999. write for info. (*0-525-45518-3*) NAL.
Pooh's Trick or Treat! Ann Braybrooks. LC 97-71235. (Little Golden Bks.). (J). 1997. 2.29 (*0-307-98838-4*, 98838, Goldn Books) Gldn Bks Pub Co.
Pooh's Wishing Star. Bruce Talkington. 32p. (J). 1999. 5.99 (*0-7868-4360-8*, Pub. by Disney Pr) Time Warner.
Pooh's Xmas Collection. A. A. Milne, pseud. (J). 1999. pap. 9.99 (*0-525-45500-0*) NAL.
Pookies ABC's Coloring Book. Etheridge G. Lovett. (Illus.). 32p. (J). (ps-6). 1998. pap. 3.00 (*0-9671805-0-3*) Lovett & Brown.
Pookie's Kinsman. Peter Wynn. LC 98-72113. 179 p. (J). 1998. write for info. (*0-9645170-1-9*) Ituri Forest Pr.
Pookins Gets Her Way. Helen Lester. (Illus.). 32p. (J). (ps-3). 1990. pap. 7.95 (*0-395-53965-X*) HM.
Pooks. Elizabeth Isele. LC 82-48462. (Illus.). 32p. (J). (ps-3). 1983. 8.95 (*0-397-32044-2*) HarpC Child Bks.
Pool: A Novel. Ajay Sahgal. LC 94-37213. 224p. 1995. pap. 10.00 (*0-8021-3343-6*, Grove) Grove-Atltic.
Pool: History, Strategies, & Legends. Michael I. Shamos. LC 95-223089. 128p. 1994. pap. 11.95 (*1-56799-061-4*, Friedman-Fairfax) M Friedman Pub Grp Inc.
Pool & Irving Villages: A Study of Hopewell Occupation in the Illinois River Valley. John C. McGregor. LC 58-5605. (Illus.). 244p. reprint ed. 75.70 (*0-8357-9694-9*, 201586400097) Bks Demand.
Pool Bar Jims Famous Frozen Drinks. 150p. 1988. 6.95 (*0-318-33267-1*) Am Bartenders.
***Pool Birds.** James Leonard. (Illus.). 24p. 2000. pap. 8.00 (*0-8059-4761-2*) Dorrance.
Pool Book: Living with a Swimming Pool. LC 93-61032. 104p. (Orig.). 1993. pap. 10.00 (*1-881818-01-2*) TBL.
Pool Book, 1994-95 Vol. 2: Knowing Your Swimming Pool. rev. ed. TBL Staff. (Illus.). 186p. 1994. pap. 10.00 (*1-881818-04-7*) TBL.
Pool Cookbook: Cool Recipes for Lazy Summer Days - Whether You Have a Pool or Not. Carole Marsh. (Carole Marsh Cookbooks Ser.). (Illus.). 1998. pap. 19.95 (*0-7933-8997-6*, C Marsh); lib. bdg. 29.95 (*0-7933-8996-8*, C Marsh) Gallopade Intl.
Pool Critical Assembly Pressure Vessel Facility Benchmark. I. Remec. 50p. 1997. pap. 4.50 (*0-16-054689-3*) USGPO.
Pool Cue Book. Stephen Mayhew. Ed. by Tina Rocha. LC 97-74026. (Illus.). 100p. 1998. 15.95 (*0-9660794-0-X*) Merrimack Pub.
Pool Cues, Beer Bottles & Baseball Bats: Animal's Guide to Improvised Weapons for Self-Defense & Survival. Marc A. MacYoung. (Illus.). 152p. 1990. pap. 20.00 (*0-87364-545-6*) Paladin Pr.
Pool Light. Ed. by Howard Schatz. (Illus.). 256p. 1998. 70.00 (*1-888001-47-X*) Graphis US.
Pool Maintenance Manual. Terry Tamminen. (Illus.). 468p. 1996. pap. 27.95 (*0-07-061408-3*) McGraw.
Pool of Aphrodite: The New Tristan. Patrick M. Thomas. LC 94-48865. 56p. 1997. pap. 14.95 (*0-7734-2758-9*, Mellen Poetry Pr) E Mellen.
Pool of Fire. large type ed. John Christopher. 280p. (J). (gr. 3 up). 1990. 18.95 (*0-7451-1176-9*, G K Hall Lrg Type) Mac Lib Ref.
Pool of Fire. 2nd ed. John Christopher. LC 88-16117. (Tripods Trilogy Ser.). 192p. (YA). (gr. 5-9). 1988. mass mkt. 4.50 (*0-02-042721-2*) Macmillan.
Pool of Fire. 2nd ed. John Christopher. (Tripods Triology Ser.). (J). 1988. 9.05 (*0-606-04360-8*, Pub. by Turtleback) Demco.
***Pool of Light.** Graphis. 1998. 70.00 (*0-688-16484-6*, Wm Morrow) Morrow Avon.
***Pool of Memory: The Autobiography of an Unwilling Intuitive** Michal Levin. LC 99-194274. x, 269 p. 1998. write for info. (*0-7171-2757-5*, Pub. by Gill & MacMill) St Mut.
***Pool of Radiance: Attack on Myth Drannor.** Shawn Carnes. (Forgotten Realms Ser.). 2000. pap. text 17.95 (*0-7869-1710-5*) Wizards Coast.
***Pool of Radiance: The Ruins of Myth Drannor.** Carrie A. Bebris. (Forgotten Realms Ser.). 2000. mass mkt. 6.99 (*0-7869-1387-8*) Wizards Coast.
Pool of Two Moons. Kate Forsyth. (The Witches of Eileanan Ser.: Bk. 2). 416p. 1999. mass mkt. 6.99 (*0-451-45690-4*, ROC) NAL.
Pool of Water: New Age Reflections. Barbara S. Mikolas. (Illus.). 128p. (Orig.). 1989. pap. 7.95 (*1-877633-01-1*) Luthers.
Pool on Otter Creek. J. David Loeb. (Illus.). 28p. (Orig.). (J). (ps-5). 1994. pap. 5.95 (*1-885744-00-5*) Otter Creek.
Pool Party see Ready, Set... Grow!
Pool Party. 1997. pap. 1.75 (*0-8289-1011-1*) Viking Penguin.
Pool Party. Linda Cargill. 211p. (YA). (gr. 7 up). 1996. mass mkt. 3.99 (*0-590-58111-2*) Scholastic Inc.
Pool Party. Linda Cargill. (YA). 1996. 9.09 (*0-606-09762-7*, Pub. by Turtleback) Demco.
Pool Party. Gary Soto. LC 92-34407. (Illus.). 112p. (J). 1993. 13.95 (*0-385-30890-6*) Delacorte.
Pool Party. Gary Soto. (J). 1995. 8.60 (*0-606-08032-5*) Turtleback.
Pool Party Panic! V. E. Mitchell. (Secret World of Alex Mack Ser.: No. 28). (J). (gr. 3-6). 1998. pap. 3.99 (*0-671-01428-5*) PB.
Pool Party Thief, Vol. 1. Gilbert Morris. (Too Smart Jones Ser.: Vol. 1). (Illus.). 115p. (J). (gr. 2-7). 1999. pap. 5.99 (*0-8024-4025-8*) Moody.
Pool Players Bible. Ray Langley. (Illus.). 1981. 6.00 (*0-686-29667-2*) Langley.
Pool Player's Road Atlas. Ed. by James R. Lawson. 200p. (Orig.). 1994. pap. 34.95 (*0-945071-80-9*) Lawco.
Pool Pointers. Billie Billing & Megan Ratner. 96p. 1992. pap. 10.00 (*0-380-76136-X*, Avon Bks) Morrow Avon.
***Pool Simplified, Somewhat.** George Fels. LC 00-38413. (Illus.). 2000. pap. write for info. (*0-486-41368-3*) Dover.
Poolbeg Book of Children's Verse. Ed. by Sean McMahon. 240p. (J). 1987. pap. 9.95 (*0-905169-88-3*, Pub. by Poolbeg Pr) Dufour.
Poolbeg Book of Children's Verse. Sean McMahon. 240p. (J). 1987. pap. 10.95 (*1-85371-080-6*, Pub. by Poolbeg Pr) Dufour.
Poolbeg Book of Irish Ballads. Sean McMahon. 188p. (Orig.). 1992. pap. 9.95 (*1-85371-127-6*, Pub. by Poolbeg Pr) Dufour.
Poolbeg Book of Irish Ghost Stories David Marcus. LC 91-114282. 302 p. 1990. write for info. (*1-85371-112-8*) Poolbeg Pr.
Poolbeg Book of Irish Heraldry. Micheal O. Comain. (Illus.). 173p. 1991. pap. 12.95 (*1-85371-126-8*, Pub. by Poolbeg Pr) Dufour.
Poolbeg Book of Irish Placenames. Sean McMahon. 113p. (Orig.). (YA). (gr. 10-12). 1990. pap. 8.95 (*1-85371-087-3*, Pub. by Poolbeg Pr) Dufour.
Poolbeg Book of Irish Poetry for Children. Shaun Traynor. LC 97-224323. 140p. (J). (gr. 5-7). 1997. pap. 9.95 (*1-85371-726-6*, Pub. by Poolbeg Pr) Dufour.
Poolbeg Book of Traditional Irish Cooking. Biddy W. Lennon. 186p. 1990. pap. 9.95 (*1-85371-092-X*, Pub. by Poolbeg Pr) Dufour.
Poolbeg Golden Treasury of Well Loved Poems. Ed. by Sean McMahon. 208p. 1989. pap. 8.95 (*1-85371-008-3*, Pub. by Poolbeg Pr) Dufour.
Poolbeg Quiz Book. Robert Duffy. 129p. 1988. pap. 6.95 (*1-85371-004-0*, Pub. by Poolbeg Pr) Dufour.
Poole: Harbour, Health & Islands. R. M. Bloomfield. 108p. 1984. 30.00 (*0-7212-0664-6*, Pub. by Regency Pr GBR) St Mut.
Poole Collection. Kurt E. Schon. LC 52-932. (Illus.). 116p. 1980. 18.00 (*0-9603880-0-1*) K E Schon.
Poole Harbour. Imray, Laurie, Norie & Wilson Ltd. Staff. (Illus.). (C). 1989. text 60.00 (*0-7855-5782-2*, Pub. by Laurie Norie & Wilson Ltd) St Mut.
Poole Pottery. rev. ed. Ed. by Leslie Hayward & Paul Atterbury. (Illus.). 200p. 1998. 95.00 (*0-903685-62-0*, Pub. by R Dennis) Antique Collect.
Poole Pottery: Carter & Company & Their Successors 1873-1995. Leslie Hayward. (Illus.). 192p. 1995. 95.00 (*0-903685-41-8*, Pub. by R Dennis) Antique Collect.
Pooled Cross-Sectional & Time Series Data Analysis. Terry E. Dielman. (Statistics: Textbooks & Monographs: Vol. 97). (Illus.). 264p. 1988. text 135.00 (*0-8247-7864-2*) Dekker.
Pooled Time Series Analysis. Lois W. Sayrs. (Quantitative Applications in the Social Sciences Ser.: Vol. 70). 80p. (C). 1989. pap. text 10.95 (*0-8039-3160-3*) Sage.
Poole's Index to Periodical Literature, 5 vols. Incl. Vol. 2. 1882-1887. 1963. 36.50 (*0-8446-1354-1*); Vol. 3. 1887-1892. 1963. 36.50 (*0-8446-1355-X*); Vol. 4. 1892-1896. 1963. 36.50 (*0-8446-1356-8*); Vol. 5. 1897-1902. 1963. 36.50 (*0-8446-1357-6*); Vol. 6. 1902-1906. 1963. 36.50 (*0-8446-1358-4*); 1963. 182.50 (*0-685-73409-9*) Peter Smith.
Poole's Index to Periodical Literature, Author Index. Ed. by C. Edward Wall. LC 77-143237. (Cumulative Author Index Ser.: No. 1). 1971. 110.00 (*0-87650-006-8*) Pierian.
Pooles of Pismo Bay. Howard Rose. 430p. 1990. 20.00 (*1-878352-04-0*); pap. 10.00 (*1-878352-05-9*) R Saroff Pub.
***Pooling Health Insurance Risks.** Mark V. Pauly & Bradley Herring. LC 99-46267. 115p. 1999. 39.95 (*0-8447-4119-1*, Pub. by Am Enterprise); pap. 19.95 (*0-8447-4120-5*, Pub. by Am Enterprise) Pub Resources Inc.
Pools of Ancient Evil. Eric E. Little. 446p. mass mkt. 4.99 (*1-55197-008-2*) Picasso Publ.
Pools of Water, Pillars of Fire: The Literature of Ibuse Masuji. John W. Treat. (Illus.). 328p. 1988. 30.00 (*0-295-96625-4*) U of Wash Pr.
***Poolside Tycoon: More Great Tips for Making Money on the Stock Market for Those Without a Clue.** Malcolm Stacey. 184p. 2000. pap. 12.95 (*1-86105-196-4*) Robson.
***Poombah of Badoombah.** Dee Lillegard. (Illus.). (J). 2000. pap. 5.99 (*0-698-11823-5*) Putnam Pub Group.
Poona in the Eighteenth Century: An Urban History. Balkrishna G. Gokhale. (Illus.). 240p. 1988. 19.95 (*0-19-562137-9*) OUP.
Poop Decks & Periwinkles: Emily & Jason Explore San Diego. Don White. LC 91-66464. 112p. (J). (gr. 3-6). 1991. pap. 12.95 (*0-942259-06-8*) Westerfield Enter.
Poop with Flies Drawing Contest! Rick Casteel. (Illus.). 112p. 1998. per. 10.95 (*0-9663633-0-2*) Cream Corn.
Pooped Troop. Judy Delton. (Pee Wee Scouts Ser.: No. 10). (Illus.). 96p. (J). (ps-3). 1989. pap. 3.99 (*0-440-40184-4*, YB BDD) BDD Bks Young Read.
Pooped Troop. Judy Delton. (Pee Wee Scouts Ser.). (J). 1989. 9.19 (*0-606-04302-0*, Pub. by Turtleback) Demco.
Poopoo: Poems from Hollywood. Mark Dunster. 11p. 1998. pap. 5.00 (*0-89642-563-0*) Linden Pubs.
Poopsie Pomerantz, Pick up Your Feet. Patricia Reilly Giff. 160p. (J). (gr. k-6). 1998. pap. 3.99 (*0-440-40287-5*, YB BDD) BDD Bks Young Read.
Poopsie Pomerantz, Pick up Your Feet. Patricia Reilly Giff. 1998. 9.09 (*0-606-13715-7*, Pub. by Turtleback) Demco.
***Poor.** unabridged ed. George Simmel. Ed. by Simona Draghici.Tr. of Arme. 80p. 2000. pap. text 5.95 (*0-943045-17-7*) Plutarch Pr OR.
Poor - A Rich Labial! The 1997 Dung Annual. Lyn Lifshin et al. (Illus.). 100p. 1997. lib. bdg. 13.30 (*0-9644321-6-1*) Camel Dung Writ.

P

Poor - Poore Family Gatherings, 1881-1888 (With Genealogy) (Illus.). 442p. 1998. reprint ed. pap. 67.00 (*0-8328-9491-5*); reprint ed. lib. bdg. 77.00 (*0-8328-9490-7*) Higginson Bk Co.

Poor Americans: How the White Poor Live. Ed. by Marc Pilisuk & Phyllis Pilisuk. 192p. 1971. reprint ed. pap. text 18.95 (*0-87855-569-2*) Transaction Pubs.

Poor among Us: Jewish Tradition & Social Policy. Elliot N. Dorff et al. LC 86-72482. 63p. (Orig.). 1986. pap. 7.50 (*0-87495-084-8*) Am Jewish Comm.

Poor & Minority Health Care. Ed. by Gary E. McCuen. LC 87-91953. (Ideas in Conflict Ser.). (Illus.). 202p. (YA). (gr. 7-12). 1988. lib. bdg. 15.95 (*0-86596-065-8*) G E M.

Poor & Pregnant in Paris: Strategies for Survival in the Nineteenth Century. Rachel G. Fuchs. (Illus.). 405p. (C). 1992. text 47.00 (*0-8135-1779-6*); pap. text 20.00 (*0-8135-1780-X*) Rutgers U Pr.

Poor & the Good News: A Call to Evangelize. Tom Scheuring et al. LC 92-37976. 176p. 1993. pap. 9.95 (*0-8091-3359-8*) Paulist Pr.

Poor & the Hard-Core Unemployed: Recommendations for New Approaches. Ed. by Wil J. Smith. LC 77-632182. 1970. pap. text 5.00 (*0-87736-311-0*) U of Mich Inst Labor.

Poor & the Powerless: Economic Policy & Change in the Caribbean. Clive Y. Thomas. 416p. (C). 1988. pap. 17.00 (*0-85345-744-1*, Pub. by Monthly Rev) NYU Pr.

***Poor & Their Money: Essays on Financial Services for Poor People.** Ed. by Stuart Rutherford. 100p. 2000. text 10.95 (*0-19-565255-X*) OUP.

Poor Angels: And Other Stories. Chris Dolan. 192p. (Orig.). 1995. pap. 15.95 (*0-7486-6206-5*, Pub. by Polygon) Subterranean Co.

***Poor Angus.** Robin Jenkins. 2000. pap. 15.00 (*1-84195-002-5*, Pub. by Canongate Books) Interlink Pub.

***Poor Are Not Us: Poverty & Pastoralism in Eastern Africa.** Ed. by David M. Anderson & Vigdis Broch-Due. LC 99-88156. (Eastern African Studies). 356p. 2000. text 44.95 (*0-8214-1312-0*, Ohio U Ctr Intl); pap. text 22.95 (*0-8214-1313-9*, Ohio U Ctr Intl) Ohio U Pr.

Poor Arnolds Almanac. Arnold Roth. (Illus.). 112p. 1998. pap. 12.95 (*1-56097-322-6*) Fantagraph Bks.

***Poor as Church Mice.** Roselyn Ogden Miller. LC 00-34070. (Illus.). 2000. write for info. (*1-886225-57-5*) MG-Hill OH.

Poor Bastard. Joe Matt. 172p. 1997. pap. 12.95 (*1-896597-04-1*, Pub. by Drawn & Quarterly) LPC InBook.

***Poor Belong to Us: Catholic Charities & American Welfare.** Dorothy M. Brown. 304p. 2000. pap. 18.95 (*0-674-00401-9*) HUP.

Poor Belong to Us: Catholic Charities & American Welfare. Dorothy M. Brown & Elizabeth McKeown. LC 97-25736. 352p. 1998. 45.00 (*0-674-68973-9*) HUP.

Poor Black & in Real Trouble. J. D. Wright. 256p. 1992. mass mkt. 3.95 (*0-87067-392-0*) Holloway.

Poor Black & in Real Trouble. J.D. Wright. 256p. 1992. mass mkt. 5.99 (*0-87067-890-6*, Holloway House) Holloway.

Poor Black Welfare. Cox. (C). Date not set. write for info. (*0-415-03238-5*) Routledge.

Poor Black Women Untitled. Mitchell Duneier. Date not set. text. write for info. (*0-374-23582-1*) FS&G.

Poor Bloody Murder: Personal Memoirs of the First World War. Ed. by Gordon Reid. 260p. 1992. 19.95 (*0-88962-123-3*); pap. 12.95 (*0-88962-122-5*) Mosaic.

Poor Boy, Rich Boy. Clyde R. Bulla. LC 79-2685. (I Can Read Bks.). (Illus.). 64p. (J). (ps-3). 1982. 9.95 (*0-06-020896-1*) HarpC Child Bks.

Poor but Proud: Alabama's Poor Whites. Wayne Flynt. LC 88-20859. 488p. (C). 1989. text 34.95 (*0-8173-0424-X*) U of Ala Pr.

Poor Butterfly. Stuart M. Kaminsky. (Toby Peters Mystery Ser.). 1991. mass mkt. 4.95 (*0-446-40011-4*, Pub. by Warner Bks) Little.

Poor Carolina: Politics & Society in Colonial North Carolina, 1729-1776. A. Roger Ekirch. LC 80-39889. 325p. reprint ed. pap. 100.80 (*0-608-06011-9*, 206633900008) Bks Demand.

Poor Caroline. Elizabeth Mansfield. 224p. (Orig.). 1995. mass mkt. 4.50 (*0-515-11659-9*, Jove) Berkley Pub.

Poor Caroline, the Indiaman's Daughter: All's Well That Ends Well. Alexander L. Stimson. LC 72-2037. (Black Heritage Library Collection). 1977. reprint ed. 18.95 (*0-8369-9066-8*) Ayer.

Poor Children & Welfare Reform. Olivia Golden. LC 92-886. 208p. 1992. 55.00 (*0-86569-045-6*, T045, Auburn Hse) Greenwood.

Poor Christ of Bomba. Mongo Beti. (African Writers Ser.). 219p. (C). 1971. pap. 9.95 (*0-435-90088-9*, 90088) Heinemann.

Poor Citizens. David Vincent. 1991. text. write for info. (*0-582-08451-2*) Longman.

Poor Dancer's Almanac: A Survival Manual for Choreographers, Managers & Dancers. Dance Theater Workshop Staff. Ed. by David R. White & Mindy N. Levine. LC 83-72080. 320p. (Orig.). 1984. pap. 15.00 (*0-9611382-0-3*) Dance Theater.

Poor Dancer's Almanac: Managing Life & Work in the Performing Arts. Ed. by David R. White et al. LC 92-21499. (Illus.). 384p. 1993. text 49.95 (*0-8223-1305-7*); pap. text 16.95 (*0-8223-1319-7*) Duke.

Poor Davie. unabridged ed. Alistair Ferguson. Ed. by William A. Landes. LC 98-50442. 55p. 1999. pap. 5.00 (*0-88734-772-X*) Players Pr.

Poor, Dear Margaret Kirby & Other Stories. Kathleen Norris. (Collected Works of Kathleen Norris). 393p. 1999. reprint ed. lib. bdg. 98.00 (*1-58201-798-0*) Classic Bks.

Poor Discipline: Parole & Control of the Underclass, 1890-1990. Jonathan Simon. LC 93-15876. (Studies in Crime & Justice). (Illus.). 296p. 1993. pap. text 15.95 (*0-226-75857-5*) U Ch Pr.

Poor Discipline: Parole & Control of the Underclass, 1890-1990. Jonathan Simon. LC 93-15876. (Studies in Crime & Justice). (Illus.). 296p. 1993. lib. bdg. 55.00 (*0-226-75856-7*) U Ch Pr.

Poor Eaters: Helping Children Who Refuse to Eat. J. Macht. LC 89-26514. (Illus.). 328p. (C). 1990. 19.95 (*0-306-43451-2*, Plenum Trade) Perseus Pubng.

Poor Fisherman. Park H. Bong. (Illus.). 88p. (Orig.). 1995. pap. text 9.95 (*0-9639999-3-1*) Jay St Pubs.

Poor Folk. Fyodor Dostoyevsky. Tr. by Robert Dessaix.Tr. of Bednye Liudi. 143p. 1983. pap. 12.50 (*0-88233-755-6*) Ardis Pubs.

Poor Folk & Other Stories. Fyodor Dostoyevsky. Tr. & Intro. by David-McDuff. 288p. 1989. pap. 9.95 (*0-14-044505-6*, Penguin Classics) Viking Penguin.

Poor Folk & the Gambler. Fyodor Dostoyevsky. Ed. by A. D. Briggs. Tr. by C. J. Hogarth. 320p. 1994. 5.50 (*0-460-87331-8*, Everyman's Classic Lib) Tuttle Pubng.

Poor Fool: Novel. Erskine Caldwell. LC 94-11456. (Voices of the South Ser.). 155p. 1994. pap. 12.95 (*0-8071-1947-4*) La State U Pr.

***Poor George: A Novel.** Paula Fox. 230p. 2000. pap. 13.00 (*0-393-32131-2*) Norton.

Poor Girl, Rich Girl. Johnniece M. Wilson. 192p. (J). (gr. 4-6). 1992. 13.95 (*0-590-44732-7*, Scholastic Hardcover) Scholastic Inc.

Poor Girl, Rich Girl. Johnniece M. Wilson. 192p. (J). (gr. 4-6). 1994. pap. 3.25 (*0-590-44733-5*) Scholastic Inc.

Poor Have Faces: Loving Your Neighbor in the Twenty-First Century. John Ronsvalle & Sylvia Ronsvalle. LC 92-916. 160p. (gr. 10). 1992. pap. 8.99 (*0-8010-7764-8*) Baker Bks.

Poor in a Hostile Society: Glimpses of Changing Poverty Scenario in India. Ed. by V. M. Rao. LC 98-908691. 1998. 28.00 (*81-259-0615-0*, Pub. by Vikas) S Asia.

Poor in Great Cities: Their Problems & What Is Doing to Solve Them. Robert A. Woods et al. LC 77-137195. (Poverty U. S. A. Historical Record Ser.). 1975. reprint ed. 26.95 (*0-405-03131-9*) Ayer.

Poor in the Ecclesiology of Juan Luis Segundo. Mary K. Nealen. LC 91-3910. (American University Studies: Theology & Religion: Ser. VII, Vol. 113). 190p. (C). 1992. text 35.95 (*0-8204-1595-2*) P Lang Pubng.

Poor in the Middle Ages: An Essay in Social History. Michel Mollat. Tr. by Arthur Goldhammer from FRE. LC 86-1686. 336p. 1986. 47.50 (*0-300-02789-3*) Yale U Pr.

Poor in the Middle Ages: An Essay in Social History. Michel Mollat. (FRE.). 1990. pap. 20.00 (*0-300-04605-7*) Yale U Pr.

Poor in Western Europe in the Eighteenth & Nineteenth Centuries. Stuart J. Woolf. 220p. 1986. text 59.50 (*0-416-39330-6*, 1039) Routledge.

Poor Jews: An American Awakening. Ed. by Naomi Levine & Martin Hochbaum. LC 73-85097. 206p. 1974. 32.95 (*0-87855-073-9*); pap. 18.95 (*0-87855-570-6*) Transaction Pubs.

Poor John Fitch: Inventor of the Steamboat. Thomas A. Boyd. LC 75-150171. (Select Bibliographies Reprint Ser.). 1977. reprint ed. 23.95 (*0-8369-5684-2*) Ayer.

Poor John Fitch, Inventor of the Steamboat. Thomas A. Boyd. 1993. reprint ed. lib. bdg. 89.00 (*0-7812-5432-9*) Rprt Serv.

Poor Jonny's Cookbook: A Natural Foods Vegetarian Survivalist Cookbook. Suellen Ocean. (Illus.). 130p. 1999. pap. 16.00 (*0-9651140-3-1*) Ocean Hose.

***Poor Kevin.** Kate Margam. LC 98-86425. 1999. pap. 12.99 (*1-85242-600-4*, Pub. by Serpents Tail) Consort Bk Sales.

Poor Law. Ros Franey. 1983. 20.00 (*0-7855-1464-3*, Pub. by NCCL) St Mut.

Poor Law: The English Citizen: His Rights & Responsibilities. 2nd ed. T. W. Fowle. vi, 175p. 1979. reprint ed. 30.00 (*0-8377-0534-7*, Rothman) W S Hein.

Poor Law & Settlement Documents of the Church of St. Mary, Oldswinford, Worcestershire., 1651-1794. (C). 1987. 50.00 (*0-7855-2109-7*, Pub. by Birmingham Midland Soc) St Mut.

Poor Law of Lunacy: The Administration of Pauper Lunatics in Mid-Nineteenth-Century England. Peter Bartlett. LC 98-51388. 310p. 1999. 85.00 (*0-7185-0104-7*) Bks Intl VA.

Poor Law Settlement Documents of the Church of St. John, Hagley, Worcestershire. (C). 1987. 35.00 (*0-7855-2097-X*, Pub. by Birmingham Midland Soc) St Mut.

Poor Laws of Massachusetts & New York. John Cummings. 135p. 1993. reprint ed. lib. bdg. 69.00 (*0-7812-5246-6*) Rprt Serv.

Poor Lila! Jamie Suzanne. (Sweet Valley Twins Ser.: No. 63). (J). (gr. 3-7). 1992. 8.60 (*0-606-00662-1*, Pub. by Turtleback) Demco.

Poor Little Butterflies. Kathryn Pippin. 280p. (Orig.). 1999. pap. write for info. (*0-9654213-2-5*) Cheston on Wye.

Poor Little Neil. Keith M. Brown. LC 98-61023. 176p. 1998. 5.95 (*1-56550-082-2*) Vis Bks Intl.

Poor Little Rich Boy: The Saga of America's Foremost Newspaper Dynasty - Col. Robert R. McCormick. Gwen Morgan & Arthur Veysey. LC 85-70124. (Illus.). 500p. 1985. pap. 15.00 (*0-916445-11-9*) Crossroads Comm.

Poor Little Rich Girl. Joan Smith. (Romance Ser.). 1993. per. 2.75 (*0-373-08972-4*, 5-08972-7) Silhouette.

Poor Mallory! Ann M. Martin. (Baby-Sitters Club Ser.: No. 39). 160p. (J). 1990. pap. 3.25 (*0-590-43568-X*); mass mkt. 3.99 (*0-590-73451-2*) Scholastic Inc.

Poor Mallory! Ann M. Martin. (Baby-Sitters Club Ser.: No. 39). 1990. 9.09 (*0-606-04775-1*, Pub. by Turtleback) Demco.

Poor Man Called Jesus: Reflections on the Gospel of Mark. Jose C. Pallares. Tr. by Robert R. Barr from SPA. LC 85-15339. 144p. reprint ed. pap. 44.70 (*0-7837-6974-1*, 204678500004) Bks Demand.

Poor Man's Atomic Bomb? Biological Weapons in the Middle East. W. Seth Carus. LC 91-10600. (Policy Papers: No. 23). 66p. 1991. pap. 8.00 (*0-944029-08-6*) Wash Inst NEP.

Poor Man's Cookbook: Old-Fashioned Country Cooking for Today's Budget. George Cook. 144p. 1995. pap. 9.95 (*0-943231-95-7*) Howell Pr VA.

Poor Man's Explanation of Kalman Filtering: or How I Stopped Worrying & Learned to Love Matrix Inversion. Roger Du Plessis. (Illus.). 57p. 1997. pap. 19.95 (*0-9661016-0-X*) Taygeta Sci.

Poor Man's Fort Knox: Home Security with Inexpensive Safes. Duncan Long. (Illus.). 48p. 1991. pap. 10.00 (*0-87364-645-2*) Paladin Pr.

Poor Man's Guardian, 4 vols. H. Hetherington. (C). 1969. text. write for info. (*0-85036-000-5*, Pub. by MRLN) Paul & Co Pubs.

Poor Man's Guide to Self Publishing. Ford F. Ruggieri. LC 84-1107. 164p. 1984. 24.95 (*0-931588-15-4*) Allegany Mtn Pr.

Poor Man's James Bond, Vol. 2. rev. ed. Kurt Saxon. (Illus.). 1987. pap. text 25.00 (*1-881801-02-0*) Atlan Formularies.

Poor Man's James Bond, Vol. 3. Kurt Saxon. 411p. 1988. pap. text 25.00 (*1-881801-03-9*) Atlan Formularies.

Poor Man's James Bond, Vol. 4. Kurt Saxon. 464p. 1991. pap. text 25.00 (*1-881801-04-7*) Atlan Formularies.

Poor Man's Legacy: An Anthology of Franciscan Poverty. Ed. by Cyprian J. Lynch. (Franciscan Pathway Ser.). 759p. 1988. pap. 45.00 (*1-57659-069-0*) Franciscan Inst.

Poor Man's Morning & Evening Portions. Robert Hawker. 934p. 1995. 19.00 (*1-892777-05-3*) Reform Heritage Bks.

Poor Man's Notebook. Shawn K. Records. Ed. by Tom Trusky. (Illus.). (Orig.). 1994. pap. 6.95 (*0-916272-60-5*) Ahsahta Pr.

Poor Man's Pittance, Vol. 2, Pt. 1. Richard Williams. Ed. by F. J. Furnivall. (Ballad Society Ser.). 57.50 AMS Pr.

Poor Man's U-Build Handbook: Lawn & Garden Tools. Johnny S. Blackwell. (U-Build Ser.: No. 7). (Illus.). 64p. 1993. 32.95 (*1-883964-07-5*) Poor Mans Pubns.

Poor Man's U-Build Handbook: Metal Turning Lathes & Accessories. Johnny S. Blackwell. (U-Build Ser.: No. 1). 70p. 1993. 37.95 (*1-883964-01-6*) Poor Mans Pubns.

Poor Man's U-Build Handbook: Metal Working Tools. Johnny S. Blackwell. (U-Build Ser.: No. 3). (Illus.). 64p. 1993. 34.95 (*1-883964-03-2*) Poor Mans Pubns.

Poor Man's U-Build Handbook: Photographic Equipment. Johnny S. Blackwell. (U-Build Ser.: No. 8). (Illus.). 64p. 1993. 34.95 (*1-883964-08-3*) Poor Mans Pubns.

Poor Man's U-Build Handbook: Power Sanders & Accessories. Johnny S. Blackwell. (U-Build Ser.: No. 6). (Illus.). 64p. 1993. 30.95 (*1-883964-06-7*) Poor Mans Pubns.

Poor Man's U-Build Handbook: Power Saws & Accessories. Johnny S. Blackwell. (U-Build Ser.: No. 5). (Illus.). 64p. 1993. 30.95 (*1-883964-05-9*) Poor Mans Pubns.

Poor Man's U-Build Handbook: Wood Turning Lathes & Accessories. Johnny S. Blackwell. (U-Build Ser.: No. 2). (Illus.). 64p. 1993. 36.95 (*1-883964-02-4*) Poor Mans Pubns.

Poor Man's U-Build Handbook: Wood Working Tools & Accessories. Johnny S. Blackwell. (U-Build Ser.: No. 4). (Illus.). 64p. 1993. 32.95 (*1-883964-04-0*) Poor Mans Pubns.

Poor Man's Weapon. David Drury. LC 97-91320. 1998. pap. 11.95 (*0-533-12639-8*) Vantage.

Poor Me & the Magic of Christmas. rev. ed. Cathy L. Crabtree & Joanne Fowler. LC 89-84463. (Poor Me Collections). (Illus.). 20p. (J). (gr. 2-3). 1989. pap. text 5.95 (*0-9622719-0-X*) Lavender Pr.

Poor Miss Finch. Wilkie Collins. Ed. by Catherine Peters. (The World's Classics Ser.). 480p. 1995. pap. 11.95 (*0-19-282322-1*) OUP.

Poor Miss Finch. Wilkie Collins. (Oxford World Classics Ser.). 480p. 2000. pap. 12.95 (*0-19-283699-4*) OUP.

Poor Miss Finch. Wilkie Collins. (Pocket Classics Ser.). 384p. 1994. pap. 10.95 (*0-7509-0655-3*, Pub. by Sutton Pub Ltd) Intl Pubs Mktg.

Poor Miss Finch: A Domestic Story see Works of Wilkie Collins

Poor Miss Finch: A Novel. Wilkie Collins. LC 77-131672. (Literature Ser.). (Illus.). 454p. 1972. reprint ed. 69.00 (*0-403-00559-0*) Scholarly.

Poor Mouth: A Bad Story about the Hard Life. Flann O'Brien. Tr. by Patrick C. Power from GAE. LC 95-26579. (Illus.). 128p. 1996. reprint ed. pap. 10.95 (*1-56478-091-0*) Dalkey Arch.

Poor Nation of the Pacific: Australia's Future. Ed. by Jocelynne A. Scutt. (C). 1986. text 42.95 (*0-86861-653-2*, Pub. by Allen & Unwin Pty) Paul & Co Pubs.

Poor No More. Robert Ruark. 1994. reprint ed. lib. bdg. 39.95 (*1-56849-329-0*) Buccaneer Bks.

Poor of the Land: A Christian Case for Land Reform. Roy H. May, Jr. LC 90-46980. 160p. reprint ed. pap. 49.60 (*0-608-20248-7*, 207150700012) Bks Demand.

Poor Old Tired Horse, Nos. 1-25. reprint ed. lib. bdg. 85.00 (*0-404-19543-1*) AMS Pr.

Poor Paris! Kierkegaard's Critique of the Spectacular City. George Pattison. LC 99-11509. xvi, 152p. 1999. 63.25 (*3-11-016388-8*) De Gruyter.

Poor Pearl, Poor Girl! The Murdered Girl Stereotype in Ballad & Newspaper. Anne B. Cohen. LC 73-7919. (Publications of the American Folklore Society, Bibliographical & Special Ser.: No. 58). 149p. reprint ed. pap. 46.20 (*0-7837-0089-X*, 204036400016) Bks Demand.

Poor People. Shelby Stephenson. 48p. 1998. pap. 9.95 (*1-879205-73-4*) Nightshade Pr.

Poor People & Library Services. Ed. by Karen M. Venturella. LC 98-21071. 200p. 1998. pap. 28.50 (*0-7864-0563-5*) McFarland & Co.

Poor Peoples' Movements. rev. ed. Frances F. Piven. 1999. pap. 0.00 (*0-375-70647-X*) Knopf.

Poor People's Movements: Why They Succeed, How They Fail. Frances F. Piven & Richard A. Cloward. LC 78-54652. 1979. pap. 7.96 (*0-394-72697-9*) Vin Bks.

***Poor Peoples Politics: Peonist Survival Networks & the Legacy of Evita.** Javier Auyero. (Illus.). 296p. 2000. lib. bdg. 54.95 (*0-8223-2627-2*) Duke.

***Poor Peoples Politics: Peronist Survival Networks & the Legacy of Evita.** Javier Auyero. (Illus.). 296p. 2000. pap. 18.95 (*0-8223-2621-3*) Duke.

Poor People's Social Movement Organizations: The Goal Is to Win. Melvin F. Hall. LC 95-6938. 168p. 1995. 55.00 (*0-275-94704-1*, Praeger Pubs) Greenwood.

Poor Polidor: A Critical Biography of the Author of the Vampyre. D. L. Macdonald. 400p. 1991. text 60.00 (*0-8020-2774-1*) U of Toronto Pr.

***Poor Polly Pig.** School Zone Publishing Staff. (Start to Read Board Bks.). (Illus.). (J). 2000. bds. 4.99 (*0-88743-812-1*) Sch Zone Pub Co.

Poor Preschool-Aged Children: Numbers Increase but Most Not in Preschool. (Illus.). 81p. (Orig.). (C). 1994. pap. text 30.00 (*0-7881-0213-3*) DIANE Pub.

Poor Quality Cost: Implementing, Understanding, & Using the Cost of Poor Quality. Harrington. (Quality & Reliability Ser.: Vol. 11). (Illus.). 224p. 1987. text 55.00 (*0-8247-7743-3*) Dekker.

Poor Reception: Misunderstanding & Forgetting Broadcast News. Barrie Gunter. (Communication Ser.). 384p. 1990. text 89.95 (*0-8058-1010-2*) L Erlbaum Assocs.

Poor Relations: The Children of the State in Illinois, 1818-1990. Joan Gittens. LC 93-10945. (Illus.). 312p. 1994. text 49.95 (*0-252-02064-2*); pap. text 18.95 (*0-252-06411-9*) U of Ill Pr.

Poor Relations: The Making of a Eurasian Community in British India, 1773-1833. C. J. Hawes. (Illus.). 220p. (C). 1996. text 35.00 (*0-7007-0425-6*, Pub. by Curzon Pr Ltd) UH Pr.

Poor Relief in Durham, Lee, & Medbury, NH, 1732-1891. Timothy Dodge. 135p. (Orig.). 1995. pap. text 14.00 (*0-7884-0150-5*) Heritage Bk.

Poor Relief in Elizabethan Ipswich. John Webb. (Suffolk Records Society Ser.: No. IX). 167p. 1970. 45.00 (*0-900716-03-7*) Boydell & Brewer.

Poor Relief in Scotland: Its Statistics & Development, 1791-1891. C. S. Loch. LC 75-38137. (Demography Ser.). 1976. reprint ed. 17.95 (*0-405-07990-7*) Ayer.

Poor, Rich & Happy. Joseph D. Ossorio et al. (Life's Roadmap Ser.). (Illus.). 60p. (J). (gr. 4-6). 1994. pap. 6.95 (*1-56721-043-0*) Twnty-Fifth Cent Pr.

Poor Richard Improved. Benjamin Franklin. (Notable American Authors Ser.). 1992. reprint ed. lib. bdg. 75.00 (*0-7812-2889-1*) Rprt Serv.

Poor Richard's Almanac. Benjamin Franklin. 1993. reprint ed. lib. bdg. 89.00 (*0-7812-5458-2*) Rprt Serv.

Poor Richard's Almanac, 1733. Benjamin Franklin. 24p. 1977. pap. 4.00 (*0-939084-07-4*) R Mus & Lib.

Poor Richard's Almanack. Benjamin Franklin. (Classics Ser.). 96p. 1952. 9.95 (*0-88088-918-7*) Peter Pauper.

Poor Richard's Books: An Exhibition of Books Owned by Benjamin Franklin Now on the Shelves of the Library Company of Philadelphia. James Green. 32p. (Orig.). 1990. pap. 5.00 (*0-914076-75-2*) Lib Co Phila.

***Poor Richard's Building Online Communities: Create a Web Community for Your Business, Club, Association.** Margaret Levine Young & John Levine. LC 00-105577. (Poor Richard's Ser.). (Illus.). 400p. 2000. pap. 29.95 (*0-9661032-9-7*) Top Floor Pub.

Poor Richard's Economic Survival Manual. Alfred W. Munzert. Ed. by Christina A. Pepper. (Illus.). 272p. (C). 1982. 11.95 (*0-917292-03-0*) H-U Public.

Poor Richard's Email Publishing: Newsletters, Bulletins, Discussion Groups & Other Powerful... Chris Pirillo. LC 98-96891. (Poor Richard's Ser.). (Illus.). 352p. 1999. pap. 29.95 (*0-9661032-5-4*) Top Floor Pub.

Poor Richards Horse Keeper. Susan McBane. 1993. 27.95 (*0-914327-52-6*) Breakthrgh NY.

Poor Richard's Internet Marketing & Promotions: How to Promote Yourself, Your Business, Your Ideas. Peter Kent & Tara Calishain. LC 98-96392. 404p. 1999. pap. 29.95 (*0-9661032-7-0*) Top Floor Pub.

***Poor Richard's Internet Marketing & Promotions: How to Promote Yourself, Your Business, Your Ideas Online.** 2nd ed. Tara Calishain. (Illus.). 352p. 2000. pap. 29.95 (*1-930082-00-2*, Pub. by Top Floor Pub) IPG Chicago.

***Poor Richard's Internet Recruiting: How to Promote Yourself, Your Business, Your Ideas Online.** Barbara Ling. 400p. 2000. pap. 29.95 (*1-930082-01-0*, Pub. by Top Floor Pub) IPG Chicago.

Poor Richard's Politicks: Benjamin Franklin & His New American Order. Paul W. Conner. LC 80-21490. 285p. 1980. reprint ed. lib. bdg. 65.00 (*0-313-22695-4*, COPRP, Greenwood Pr) Greenwood.

Poor Richard's Principle. Robert Wuthnow. 444p. 1996. pap. text 17.95 (*0-691-05895-4*, Pub. by Princeton U Pr) Cal Prin Full Svc.

An Asterisk (*) at the beginning of an entry indicates that the title is appearing for the first time.

Poor Richard's Principle: Restoring the American Dream by Recovering the Moral Dimension of Work, Business, & Money. Robert Wuthnow. LC 96-6799. 445p. 1996. text 49.50 (*0-691-02892-3*, Pub. by Princeton U Pr) Cal Prin Full Svc.

Poor Richard's Web Site: Geek-Free, Commonsense Advice on Building a Low-Cost Web Site. 2nd ed. Peter Kent. LC 99-60718. (Poor Richard's Ser.). (Illus.). 448p. 1999. pap. 29.95 (*0-9661032-0-3*, Pub. by Top Floor Pub) IPG Chicago.

Poor Roger. Bill Gross. LC PZ7.G8993Po 1998. (Doug Chronicles: No. 7). (Illus.). (J). (gr. 2-4). 1998. pap. 3.95 (*0-7868-4260-1*, Pub. by Disney Pr) Time Warner.

Poor, Sinning Folk: Confession & Conscience in Counter-Reformation Germany. W. David Myers. LC 95-46885. (Illus.). 224p. (C). 1996. text 37.50 (*0-8014-3081-X*) Cornell U Pr.

Poor Stainless. Mary Norton. LC 70-140781. (Borrowers Ser.). (Illus.). 32p. (J). (gr. 3-7). 1985. 7.95 (*0-15-263221-2*, Harcourt Child Bks) Harcourt.

Poor Store. Victor C. Klein. (Illus.). 1982. spiral bd. 100.00 (*0-9661812-9-8*, A-1) Lycanthrope Pr.

Poor Support: Poverty in the American Family. David T. Ellwood. LC 87-47779. 1988. write for info. (*0-465-06050-1*) Basic.

Poor Support: Poverty in the American Family. David T. Ellwood. LC 87-47779. 288p. 1989. pap. 13.50 (*0-465-05995-3*, Pub. by Basic) HarpC.

***Poor, Therefore Rich: Carthusian Novice Conferences on Poverty.** (Cistercian Studies: Vol. CS184). 1999. pap. 14.95 (*0-87907-784-0*) Cistercian Pubns.

Poor White. Sherwood Anderson. (Collected Works of Sherwood Anderson). 371p. 1998. reprint ed. lib. bdg. 98.00 (*1-58201-505-8*) Classic Bks.

Poor White. Sherwood Anderson. LC 92-44725. (New Directions Classics Ser.). 384p. 1993. reprint ed. pap. 12.95 (*0-8112-1242-4*, NDP763, Pub. by New Directions) Norton.

Poor White: or The Rebel Conscript. Emily C. Pearson. LC 72-1822. (Illus.). 326p. 1977. reprint ed. 28.95 (*0-8369-9042-0*) Ayer.

Poor Whites of the Antebellum South: Tenants & Laborers in Central North Carolina & Northeast Mississippi. Charles C. Bolton. LC 93-25978. (Illus.). 272p. 1994. text 49.95 (*0-8223-1428-2*); pap. text 18.95 (*0-8223-1468-1*) Duke.

Poor Wise Man. Mary Roberts Rinehart. 27.95 (*0-8488-0314-0*) Amereon Ltd.

Poor Women & Children in the European Past. Ed. by John Henderson & Richard Wall. LC 93-47314. 368p. (C). (gr. 13). 1994. 110.00 (*0-415-07716-8*, B2257) Routledge.

Poor Women, Poor Children: American Poverty in the 1990's. 3rd ed. Harrell R. Rodgers, Jr. LC 89-24372. 216p. (C). (gr. 13). 1996. text 64.95 (*1-56324-607-4*); pap. text 28.95 (*1-56324-608-2*) M E Sharpe.

Poor Women, Poor Families: The Economic Plight of America's Female-Headed Households. 2nd ed. Harrell R. Rodgers, Jr. LC 90-41481. 204p. (C). (gr. 13). 1990. text 66.95 (*0-87332-594-X*) M E Sharpe.

Poor Women, Poor Families: The Economic Plight of America's Female-Headed Households. 2nd rev. ed. Harrell R. Rodgers, Jr. LC 89-24372. 204p. (C). (gr. 13). 1990. pap. text 34.95 (*0-87332-595-8*) M E Sharpe.

Poor Women's Lives: Gender, Work & Poverty in Late-Victorian London. Andrew August. LC 98-54806. 1999. write for info. (*0-8386-3807-4*) Fairleigh Dickinson.

Poor Work: Disadvantages & the Division of Labor. Ed. by Philip Brown & Richard Scase. 176p. 1991. pap. 34.95 (*0-335-09940-8*) OpUniv Pr.

Poor You Have with You Always. Alan Keith-Lucas. Ed. by David A. Sherwood. 169p. (Orig.). (C). 1989. pap. text 18.00 (*0-9623634-0-5*) N American Assn.

Poor You Will Always Have, & the Ten Percent Will Never Fall, Vol. 2. David Jedidiah. Ed. & Illus. by Rael Jedidiah. (YA). 1999. pap. write for info. incl. audio (*1-892981-01-7*, BK02PA) Divinity Seven.

Poore Hunter: A Mad Fable. Lance Hazzard. 119p. (Orig.). 1986. pap. 7.95 (*0-933515-09-X*) Exile Pr.

Poore-Mans Plaster-Box, No. 664. Richard Hawes. LC 74-80183. 44p. 1974. reprint ed. 10.00 (*90-221-0664-0*) Walter J Johnson.

Poore Orphans Court. LC 72-6025. (English Experience Ser.: No. 551). 1973. reprint ed. 75.00 (*90-221-0551-2*) Walter J Johnson.

Poore Vicars Plea. Declaring That a Competencie of Means Is Due to Them Out of the Tithes..Notwithstanding the Impropriations. Thomas Ryves. LC 79-84135. (English Experience Ser.: No. 953). 164p. 1979. reprint ed. lib. bdg. 20.00 (*90-221-0953-4*) Walter J Johnson.

Poorest of the Poor: Female-Headed Households in Nonmetro America. Housing Assistance Council Staff. 48p. 1995. 8.50 (*1-58064-032-X*) Housing Assist.

***Poorest of the Poor? The Peoples of the West African Sahel.** Glenn Myers. (Briefings Ser.). (Illus.). 64p. 1998. reprint ed. pap. 6.99 (*1-85078-299-7*, Pub. by O M Pubng) OM Literature.

Poorhouse: Subsidized Housing in Chicago, 1895-1976. Devereux Bowly, Jr. LC 77-28271. (Illus.). 267p. 1978. 26.95 (*0-8093-0831-2*) S Ill U Pr.

Poorhouse Fair. John Updike. 128p. 1986. mass mkt. 5.99 (*0-449-21213-0*, Crest) Fawcett.

Poorhouse Fair. John Updike. 185p. 1977. reprint ed. 25.00 (*0-394-41050-5*) Knopf.

Poorhouse Fugitives: Self-Taught Poets & Poetry in Victorian Britain. Ed. by Brian Maidment. pap. write for info. (*0-85635-970-X*, Pub. by Carcanet Pr) Paul & Co Pubs.

Poorhouse Waif & His Divine Teacher. Isabel Byrum. 223p. pap. 4.00 (*0-686-29161-1*) Faith Pub Hse.

Poorly Performing Staff & How to Manage them: Capability, Competence, & Motivation. Tessa Atton & Brian Fidler. LC 98-37420. 1999. pap. write for info. (*0-415-19817-8*) Routledge.

Poorna Trupti. Lilaben Shah. (GUJ., Illus.). 156p. 1980. 19.95 (*0-318-36300-3*) Asia Bk Corp.

Poor's Register of Corporations, Directors & Executives. rev. ed. 1985. write for info. (*0-07-051881-5*) McGraw.

Pop. Judy Borger. LC 94-74040. (Illus.). 32p. (Orig.). (J). (gr. k-3). 1995. pap. 4.95 (*0-9642086-9-5*) Popular Press.

***Pop.** Bradley. LC 99-57794. 40p. (J). (ps-1). 2001. 15.95 (*0-06-028700-4*) HarpC.

Pop. Rachel Hadas. (Poets on Poetry Ser.). (Illus.). 136p. (C). pap. 14.95 (*0-472-06719-2*, 06719) U of Mich Pr.

***Pop.** David McCarthy. (Movements in Modern Art Ser.). (Illus.). 100p. 2000. 39.95 (*0-521-79014-X*); pap. 15.95 (*0-521-79363-7*) Cambridge U Pr.

***Pop.** David Thompson. (20th Century Rock & Roll Ser.). 2000. pap. 13.95 (*1-896522-25-4*) CN06.

***Pop: A Book about Bubbles.** Kimberly Brubaker Bradley. LC 99-57794. 2001. write for info. (*0-06-028701-2*); write for info. (*0-06-445208-5*) HarpC Child Bks.

***Pop! A Popcorn Party.** Pleasant Company Staff. 1999. pap. text 1.95 (*1-56247-778-1*) Pleasant Co.

Pop & Bud. Fern M. Wood. 191p. 1981. 10.25 (*0-9606922-0-7*) F M Wood.

Pop & Other New York Tales. Ruth Jespersen. 96p. (Orig.). 1987. pap. 6.95 (*0-9617134-1-0*) Biblia Candida.

Pop Annual: 1955-1994. Joel Whitburn. 880p. 1995. 69.95 (*0-89820-108-X*) Record Research.

Pop Annual, 1955-1994. Joel Whitburn. 880p. 1995. pap. 59.95 (*0-89820-109-8*) Record Research.

Pop Annual, 1955-1994. Billboard Staff & Joel Whitburn. 850p. pap. 39.95 (*0-7935-5016-5*, 00330153) H Leonard.

***Pop Annual, 1955-1999.** 6th rev. ed. Joel Whitburn. 900p. 2000. 79.95 (*0-89820-141-1*); pap. 69.95 (*0-89820-142-X*) Record Research.

Pop Architecture: Architecture Design Profile 98. Academy Editions Staff. 1992. pap. 26.95 (*0-312-08108-1*) St Martin.

Pop Architecture: Kanner Architects, Los Angeles. Contrib. by Kanner Architects Staff. LC 99-232752. (Illus.). 160p. 1998. 55.00 (*3-927258-63-6*) Gingko Press.

Pop Art. (Illus.). 72p. 1996. pap. 14.95 (*90-6918-145-2*, 620833, Pub. by Boymans Mus) Dist Art Pubs.

Pop Art. 1992. pap. 26.95 (*0-312-07898-6*) St Martin.

Pop Art. (Prestel Postcard Bks.). (Illus.). 18p. 1994. pap. 8.95 (*3-7913-1410-6*) te Neues.

***Pop Art.** Linda Bolton. LC 99-86941. (Art Revolutions Ser.). 32p. 2000. 16.95 (*0-87226-614-1*, 66141B, P Bedrick Books) NTC Contemp Pub Co.

Pop Art. Lucy R. Lippard. (World of Art Ser.). (Illus.). 216p. 1985. pap. 14.95 (*0-500-20052-1*, Pub. by Thames Hudson) Norton.

Pop Art. Tilman Osterwold. 1994. pap. 19.99 (*3-8228-0294-8*) Taschen Amer.

Pop Art. Tilman Osterwold. (SPA.). 1996. pap. 19.99 (*3-8228-0667-6*) Taschen Amer.

***Pop Art.** Tilman Osterwold. 1999. 19.99 (*3-8228-7014-5*) Taschen Amer.

***Pop Art.** Tilman Osterwold. (Big Art Ser.). (Illus.). 240p. 1999. reprint ed. 19.99 (*3-8228-7021-8*) Taschen Amer.

***Pop Art: A Continuing History.** 2nd ed. Marco Livingstone. LC 00-100788. (Illus.). 272p. 2000. reprint ed. pap. 29.95 (*0-500-28240-4*, Pub. by Thames Hudson) Norton.

Pop Art: A Critical History. Ed. by Steven H. Madoff. LC 97-2587. (Documents of Twentieth Century Art Ser.). (Illus.). 413p. 1997. 55.00 (*0-520-21018-2*, Pub. by U CA Pr); pap. 24.95 (*0-520-21243-6*, Pub. by U CA Pr) Cal Prin Full Svc.

Pop Art: The Critical Dialogue. Ed. by Carol A. Mahsun. LC 88-39868. (Studies in the Fine Arts: Criticism: No. 29). Orig. Title: Pop Art: The Critical Dialogue. 258p. reprint ed. 80.00 (*0-8357-1922-7*, 207073500004) Bks Demand.

Pop Art & Consumer Culture: American Super Market. Christin J. Mamiya. LC 91-18892. (American Studies Ser.). (Illus.). 230p. 1992. pap. 71.30 (*0-608-05105-5*, 206566600005) Bks Demand.

Pop Art & the Critics. Carol A. Mahsun. Ed. by Donald Kuspit. LC 87-6032. (Studies in the Fine Arts: Criticism: No. 23). (Illus.). 156p. reprint ed. pap. 48.40 (*0-8357-1960-X*, 207067200016) Bks Demand.

Pop Art: The Critical Dialogue see Pop Art: The Critical Dialogue

Pop Book Glover, Level 1. 28p. (Orig.). (J). 1994. pap. 6.95 (*0-89898-820-9*, FDL01051) Wrner Bros.

Pop Book Glover Primer. 32p. (Orig.). (J). 1994. pap. 6.95 (*0-89898-819-5*, FDL01050) Wrner Bros.

Pop Classic Hits Ii, 2. 44p. 1994. pap. 29.95 incl. disk (*0-7935-6432-8*) H Leonard.

Pop Classic Hits I, 1. 44p. 1994. pap. 29.95 incl. disk (*0-7935-6431-X*) H Leonard.

Pop Culture. Jim VanZyl. 1976. pap. 1.99 (*0-85234-068-0*, Pub. by Evangelical Pr) P & R Pubng.

Pop Culture. Legs McNeil. LC 98-17847. 208p. 2000. 24.95 (*0-671-01187-1*) S&S Trade.

***Pop Culture Florida.** James P. Goss. LC 99-52922. (Illus.). 160p. 2000. pap. 9.95 (*1-56164-199-5*) Pineapple Pr.

Pop Culture into Art: The Novels of Manuel Puig. Norman Lavers. LC 88-4807. 80p. 1988. pap. 12.95 (*0-8262-0685-9*) U of Mo Pr.

Pop Culture Landmarks: A Travelers Guide. Ed. by George Cantor. LC 94-29924. 401p. 1994. 55.00 (*0-8103-9399-9*, 102250) Gale.

Pop Culture Legends, 16 bks. Incl. Bruce Springsteen. Ron Frankl. LC 93-1850. (Illus.). 120p. (YA). (gr. 5 up). 1994. lib. bdg. 19.95 (*0-7910-2327-3*, Chelsea Juniors); David Letterman. Frances Lefkowitz. (Illus.). 120p. (YA). (gr. 5 up). 1995. lib. bdg. 19.95 (*0-7910-3252-3*); Elvis Presley. Tony Gentry. LC 93-28486. (Illus.). 120p. (YA). (gr. 5 up). 1994. lib. bdg. 19.95 (*0-7910-2329-X*); Grateful Dead. Intro. by Leeza Gibbons. LC 96-39425. (Illus.). 120p. (YA). (gr. 5 up). 1997. 19.95 (*0-7910-3250-7*); Grateful Dead. Sean Piccoli. LC 96-39425. 120p. (YA). (gr. 5 up). 1997. pap. 8.95 (*0-7910-4454-8*); Groucho Marx. Peter Tyson. LC 94-4797. (Illus.). 120p. (YA). (gr. 5 up). 1995. lib. bdg. 19.95 (*0-7910-2341-9*); James Dean. Alan Schroeder. (Illus.). 120p. (YA). (gr. 5 up). 1994. lib. bdg. 19.95 (*0-7910-2326-5*); John Lennon. Bruce W. Conord. LC 92-39113. (Illus.). 120p. (YA). (gr. 5 up). 1993. lib. bdg. 19.95 (*0-7910-1739-7*); John Wayne. Don Nardo. LC 94-17328. (Illus.). 120p. (YA). (gr. 5 up). 1994. lib. bdg. 19.95 (*0-7910-2348-6*); Johnny Cash. Sean Dolan. (Illus.). 120p. (YA). (gr. 5 up). 1994. lib. bdg. 19.95 (*0-7910-2328-1*); Madonna. Nicole Claro. LC 93-30227. (Illus.). 120p. (YA). (gr. 5 up). 1994. lib. bdg. 19.95 (*0-7910-2330-3*); Marilyn Monroe. Frances Lefkowitz. (Illus.). 120p. (YA). (gr. 5 up). 1995. lib. bdg. 19.95 (*0-7910-2342-7*); Stephen King. Amy Keyishan & Marjorie Keyishian. LC 94-37510. (Illus.). 120p. (YA). (gr. 5 up). 1995. lib. bdg. 19.95 (*0-7910-2340-0*); Steven Spielberg. Elizabeth Ferber. (Illus.). 128p. (YA). (gr. 5 up). 1996. lib. bdg. 19.95 (*0-7910-3256-6*); Three Stooges. Mark Scordato & Ellen Scordato. LC 94-19343. (Illus.). 120p. (YA). (gr. 5 up). 1995. lib. bdg. 19.95 (*0-7910-2344-3*); 1997. Set 5.25 hd 319.20 (*0-7910-2325-7*) Chelsea Hse.

Pop Culture Legends. Intro. by Leeza Gibbons. Incl. Bob Dylan. Susan Richardson. (Illus.). 120p. (YA). (gr. 5 up). 1995. pap. 8.95 (*0-7910-2360-5*); Bruce Springsteen. Ron Frankl. LC 93-1850. (Illus.). 120p. (YA). (gr. 5 up). 1994. pap. 8.95 (*0-7910-2352-4*); Elvis Presley. Tony Gentry. LC 93-28486. (Illus.). 120p. (YA). (gr. 5 up). 1994. pap. 8.95 (*0-7910-2354-0*, Chelsea Juniors); John Lennon. Bruce W. Conord. LC 92-39113. (Illus.). 120p. (YA). (gr. 5 up). 1993. pap. 8.95 (*0-7910-1740-0*); Johnny Cash. (Illus.). 120p. (YA). (gr. 5 up). 1996. pap. 8.95 (*0-7910-2353-2*); Madonna. Nicole Claro. LC 93-30227. (Illus.). 120p. (YA). (gr. 5 up). 1994. pap. 8.95 (*0-7910-2355-9*); Marilyn Monroe. Frances Lefkowitz. (Illus.). 120p. (YA). (gr. 5 up). 1995. pap. 8.95 (*0-7910-2367-2*); Steven Spielberg. Elizabeth Ferber. (Illus.). 120p. (YA). (gr. 6 up). 1996. pap. 8.95 (*0-7910-3257-4*); Three Stooges. Mark Scordato & Ellen Scordato. LC 94-19343. (Illus.). 120p. (YA). (gr. 5 up). 1995. pap. 8.95 (*0-7910-2369-9*); 1995. Set 5.25 hd 79.50 (*0-7910-3753-3*) Chelsea Hse.

Pop Culture Presents the Story of... Five. Jenni Hart. (Illus.). 32p. 1999. pap. text 9.95 (*0-7119-6896-9*, OZ100078) Music Sales.

Pop Culture Wars: Religion & the Role of Entertainment in American Life. William D. Romanowski. LC 96-16490. 380p. (Orig.). 1996. pap. 19.99 (*0-8308-1988-6*, 1988) InterVarsity.

POP 11 Comes of Age. Anderson. 1990. boxed set. write for info. (*0-318-68277-X*) P-H.

Pop Favorites. (Harmonica Fun Ser.). 48p. 1983. pap. 5.95 (*0-7935-2421-0*, 00850105) H Leonard.

***Pop Fleyes: Bob Popovics's Approach to Saltwater Fly Design.** Ed Jaworowski & Bob Popovics. 2001. 39.95 (*0-8117-1247-8*) Stackpole.

***Pop Goes Latin!** Nancy E. Krulik. LC 99-42124. (Illus.). 1999. pap. 4.99 (*0-448-42197-6*) Putnam Pub Group.

Pop Goes the Gospel. rev. ed. John Blanchard. 1983. pap. 6.99 (*0-85234-263-2*, Pub. by Evangelical Pr) P & R Pubng.

Pop Goes the Question. Carla Cassidy. (Yours Truly Ser.). 1997. per. 3.50 (*0-373-52037-9*, 1-52037-8) Silhouette.

***Pop Goes the Story! Canadian Fiction Anthology.** Ed. by Rob Payne. 256p. 1999. pap. 12.95 (*1-55082-233-0*) Quarry Pr.

Pop Goes the Weasel. James Patterson. LC 99-21473. 432p. (gr. 8). 1999. 26.95 (*0-316-69328-6*) Little.

***Pop Goes the Weasel.** James Patterson. 480p. 2000. mass mkt. 7.99 (*0-446-60881-5*) Warner Bks.

***Pop Goes the Weasel.** large type ed. James Patterson. LC 99-28491. 1999. 25.00 (*0-375-40854-1*) Wheeler Pub.

***Pop Goes the Weasel.** large type ed. James Patterson. 2000. pap. 13.95 (*0-375-72793-0*) Random.

Pop! Goes the Weasel & Yankee Doodle: New York in 1776 & Today, with Songs & Pictures. Robert Quackenbush. LC 75-28312. (Illus.). 40p. (J). (ps up). 1988. lib. bdg. 13.89 (*0-397-32265-8*) HarpC Child Bks.

Pop Hits for Organ. pap. 16.95 (*0-943748-67-4*) Ekay Music.

Pop Hits, 1940-1954. Joel Whitburn & Billboard Staff. 416p. 1995. 29.95 (*0-7935-5014-9*, 00330055) H Leonard.

Pop Hits: 1940-1954. Joel Whitburn. 416p. 1994. 44.95 (*0-89820-106-3*) Record Research.

***Pop Impressions: Europe - U. S. A. Prints & Multiples.** Wendy Weitman. 129p. 1999. pap. 24.95 (*0-87070-077-4*, Pub. by Mus of Modern Art) Abrams.

Pop Impressions: Prints & Multiples of Europe & USA. Wendy Weitman. (Illus.). 128p. 1999. pap. text 24.95 (*0-8109-6195-4*, Pub. by Abrams) Time Warner.

Pop Internationalism. Paul R. Krugman. (Illus.). 240p. 1997. reprint ed. pap. text 14.95 (*0-262-61133-3*) MIT Pr.

Pop Melodies Plus. 24p. 1993. pap. 14.95 (*0-7935-2185-8*, 00697270) H Leonard.

Pop Melodies Plus. 24p. 1997. pap. 4.95 (*0-7935-7383-1*) H Leonard.

Pop Melodies Plus, Set, Bks. 2 & 3. W. Schmid. 24p. 1983. pap., suppl. ed. 5.95 (*0-7935-3235-3*, 00699154) H Leonard.

Pop Memories: 1890-1954. Joel Whitburn. 660p. 1992. 59.95 (*0-89820-083-0*) Record Research.

Pop Memories, 1890-1954. 660p. 34.95 (*0-7935-5045-9*, 00330163) H Leonard.

Pop Memories, 1890-1954. Joel Whitburn. 658p. 1991. 34.95 (*0-7935-0829-0*, 00183002) H Leonard.

Pop Music: (Christians Must Choose) 1989. write for info. (*1-877784-07-9*) T Scott Pub.

Pop Music Connection: Piano. 79p. (Orig.). 1996. pap. 10.95 (*1-57623-547-5*, AF9670) Wrner Bros.

Pop-N Kimchi. Christina Lochmann & Soo-Young Chin. LC 98-12049. (J). 1998. write for info. (*1-879965-17-8*) Polychrome Pub.

Pop-O-Mania. Barbara Valenta. LC 96-45109. (Illus.). 16p. (gr. 1 up). 1997. 16.99 (*0-8037-1947-7*, Dial Yng Read) Peng Put Young Read.

Pop Out: Queer Warhol. Ed. by Jennifer Doyle et al. LC 95-35410. (Series Q). (Illus.). 296p. 1996. text 49.95 (*0-8223-1732-X*); pap. text 17.95 (*0-8223-1741-9*) Duke.

Pop-Out Play-Pak: Bats. Orig. Title: Child's Play. (Illus.). 14p. (J). (ps-4). reprint ed. write for info. (*1-881469-81-6*) Safari Ltd.

Pop-Out Play-Pak: Butterfly. Orig. Title: Child's Play. (Illus.). 14p. (J). (ps-4). reprint ed. write for info. (*1-881469-78-6*) Safari Ltd.

Pop-Out Play-Pak: Frogs. Orig. Title: Child's Play. (Illus.). 14p. (J). (ps-4). reprint ed. write for info. (*1-881469-82-4*) Safari Ltd.

Pop-Out Play Pak: Solar System. Orig. Title: Child's Play. (Illus.). 24p. (J). (ps-4). reprint ed. write for info. (*1-881469-77-8*) Safari Ltd.

Pop-Out Play-Pak: Spider. Orig. Title: Child's Play. (Illus.). 14p. (J). (ps-4). reprint ed. write for info. (*1-881469-79-4*) Safari Ltd.

Pop-Out Play-Pak: Time Tunnel. Orig. Title: Child's Play. (Illus.). 24p. (J). (ps-4). write for info. (*1-881469-76-X*) Safari Ltd.

***Pop Piano Book.** 512p. 1998. otabind 39.95 (*0-7935-9878-8*) H Leonard.

Pop Piano Library - B'ways Best: Piano. 40p. (Orig.). 1996. pap. 8.95 (*1-57623-396-0*, AF9613) Wrner Bros.

Pop Piano Library - Gershwin: Piano. 40p. (Orig.). 1996. pap. 8.95 (*1-57623-395-2*, AF9612) Wrner Bros.

Pop Piano Library - Love Songs: Piano. 40p. (Orig.). 1996. pap. 8.95 (*1-57623-394-4*, AF9611) Wrner Bros.

Pop Piano Library - Movie Magic: Piano. 40p. (Orig.). 1996. pap. 8.95 (*1-57623-397-9*, AF9614) Wrner Bros.

Pop Piano Library - Standards: Piano. 40p. (Orig.). 1996. pap. 8.95 (*1-57623-398-7*, AF9615) Wrner Bros.

Pop Piano Studio. Matt Dennis. 1996. pap. 19.95 incl. cd-rom (*0-943748-75-5*) Ekay Music.

Pop Poems & Selections. Mike Napoliello. 120p. pap. text 4.50 (*0-9640052-0-4*) US Mrkting.

Pop Pop: What Do Armadillos Eat? Jeannine D. Bray. Ed. by Imani Kenyatta. LC 98-66317. (Illus.). 56p. (J). (gr. k-6). 1998. 13.95 (*1-886580-87-1*) Pinnacle-Syatt.

***Pop Princesses.** Beth Peters. 2000. mass mkt. 5.50 (*0-345-43829-9*) Ballantine Pub Grp.

Pop! Prints from the Milwaukee Art Museum. Sue Taylor. (Illus.). 16p. (Orig.). 1993. pap. 4.95 (*0-944110-34-7*) Milwauk Art Mus.

Pop Quiz. Nancy Krulik. (Illus.). (J). (gr. 4 up). 1998. mass mkt. 3.99 (*0-671-02623-2*, Archway) PB.

***Pop-Rock Guitar Favorites.** 64p. 1998. pap. 8.95 (*0-7935-8031-5*) H Leonard.

Pop Songs: A Comprehensive Index. Roy Hemming. 1996. text 85.00 (*0-02-871037-1*) Macmillan.

Pop Songs for the Wedding. 1994. pap. 14.95 (*1-57560-378-0*, Pub. by Cherry Lane) H Leonard.

Pop Songs for the Wedding. Ed. by Milton Okun. 1994. pap. 14.95 (*0-89524-822-0*) Cherry Lane.

Pop Standards: Flute. 1985. pap. 10.95 incl. audio (*0-7935-2804-6*, 00844861) H Leonard.

Pop Standards for Two Pianos. Ed. by Tony Esposito. 56p. (Orig.). 1994. pap. 9.95 (*0-89724-291-2*, PF0914) Wrner Bros.

Pop Stars. Jeremy Reed et al. (Illus.). 94p. 1995. pap. 17.95 (*1-870612-29-9*, Pub. by Enitha Pr) Dufour.

Pop Surrealism. Ingrid Schaffner et al. (Illus.). 160p. (Orig.). 1998. pap. 9.95 (*1-888332-08-5*, Pub. by Aldrich Mus) Dist Art Pubs.

***Pop Synthetics & Metropolis Film.** Nick Luedde. (Illus.). 130p. 1999. pap. 12.00 (*0-9652528-9-2*, Pub. by Neshui Pubng) Booksource.

***Pop Tart: A Fresh, Frosted Sugar Rush Through Our Pre-Packaged Culture.** Liz Langley. 188p. 2000. pap. text 9.95 (*0-9673380-0-X*) Octavo Design.

Pop This a Behind the Scenes Look at the Best of Pop Up Video. Low. 1999. pap. 18.00 (*0-671-02724-7*) S&S Trade.

***Pop Tics with Other.** Die Gestalten Verlag Staff. 1999. pap. text 19.99 (*3-931126-30-7*, Pub. by Die Gestalten) Consort Bk Sales.

Pop. 1280. Jim Thompson. LC 90-50252. 224p. 1990. pap. 10.00 (*0-679-73249-7*) Vin Bks.

Pop-Up! A Manual of Paper Mechanisms. Duncan Birmingham. 1997. pap. 12.95 (*1-899618-09-0*, Pub. by Tarquin Pubns) Parkwest Pubns.

Pop-Up & Movable Books: A Bibliography. Ann R. Montanaro. (Illus.). 588p. 1993. 62.50 (*0-8108-2650-X*) Scarecrow.

***Pop-Up & Movable Books Supplement 1: A Bibliography: 1991-1997.** Ann R. Montanaro. 960p. 2000. 95.00 (*0-8108-3728-5*) Scarecrow.

Pop-Up Atlas of the World. Theodore Rowland-Entwistle. (Illus.). 18p. (J). (gr. 3 up). 1988. pap. 12.95 (*0-671-65898-0*) S&S Bks Yung.

Pop-Up Ballerina Bear. Dana Kubick. (Illus.). 16p. (J). (ps up). 1993. 12.95 (*0-590-46753-0*, Cartwheel) Scholastic Inc.

Pop-Up Best Greeting Cards. Keiko Nakazawa. (Illus.). 92p. (Orig.). 1995. pap. 17.00 (*0-87040-964-6*) Japan Pubns USA.

P

An Asterisk (*) at the beginning of an entry indicates that the title is appearing for the first time.

Pop-Up Book. Paul Jackson. 1995. pap. 16.95 (*0-8050-2884-6*) H Holt & Co.

Pop-Up Book of Big Trucks. Peter Seymour. (Illus.). 14p. (J). (gr. k-3). 1989. 14.95 (*0-316-78197-5*) Little.

Pop-Up Book of Ghost Tales. Korky Paul. (Illus.). 24p. (J). (gr. 3 up). 1991. 14.95 (*0-15-200589-7*, Harcourt Child Bks) Harcourt.

Pop-Up Book of Phobias. Gary Greenberg. LC 99-34370. 22p. 1999. 24.95 (*0-688-17195-8*, Wm Morrow) Morrow Avon.

Pop-Up Buck Rogers: Strange Adventures in the Spider Ship. Phil Nolan. LC 94-71381. (Illus.). 24p. (J). (gr. 4-7). 1994. 14.95 (*1-55709-236-2*) Applewood.

Pop-Up Caterpillar to Butterfly. Elizabeth Rodger. (J). (ps-1). 1996. 4.95 (*0-614-15771-4*, Cartwheel) Scholastic Inc.

Pop-Up Cinderella Cat. Illus. by Dana Kubick. 16p. (J). (ps-3). 1994. 12.95 (*0-590-48391-9*, Cartwheel) Scholastic Inc.

Pop-Up Geometric Origami. Masahiro Chatani & Keiko Nakazawa. (Illus.). 86p. 1994. pap. 15.00 (*0-87040-943-3*) Japan Pubns USA.

Pop-Up Gift Cards. Masahiro Chatani. LC 88-80140. (Illus.). 92p. (Orig.). 1988. pap. 15.00 (*0-87040-768-6*) Japan Pubns USA.

Pop-Up Goldilocks & the Three Bears. Harold B. Lentz. LC 95-77080. (Illus.). 24p. (J). (ps-5). 1995. 14.95 (*1-55709-239-7*) Applewood.

Pop-Up Greeting Cards. Paul Jackson. 128p. 1993. 12.98 (*1-55521-897-0*) Bk Sales Inc.

Pop-up Greeting Cards: A Creative Personal Touch for Every Occasion. Masahiro Chatani. (Illus.). 96p. (Orig.). 1986. pap. 15.00 (*0-87040-733-3*) Japan Pubns USA.

***Pop-Up Jungle.** Rod Campbell. (Illus.). 8p. (J). (ps-k). 2000. 7.99 (*1-85292-247-8*) Campbell Bks Ltd.

Pop up Just Ben. Joan Bowden. (J). 1989. 4.95 (*0-671-67555-9*) S&S Trade.

Pop-Up Kingdom of the Sea. (J). 1989. 9.95 (*0-8167-1295-6*) Troll Communs.

Pop-Up Little Duck. Peggy Tagel. (Springtime Pop-Ups Ser.). (Illus.). 14p. (J). (ps). 1991. 4.95 (*0-448-40056-1*, G & D) Peng Put Young Read.

Pop-Up London. Anne Wild. (Tarquin Pop-up Ser.). (Illus.). 32p. (J). (gr. 4-7). 1985. pap. 8.95 (*0-906212-30-8*, Pub. by Tarquin Pubns) Parkwest Pubns.

Pop-Up Merry Christmas. Illus. by Benrei Huang. (Christmas Mini Pop-Ups Ser.). 14p. (J). (ps-1). 1992. 3.95 (*0-448-40253-X*, G & D) Peng Put Young Read.

Pop-Up Mice of Mr. Brice. Theo LeSieg, pseud. LC 89-60507. (Illus.). 20p. (J). (ps-3). 1989. 16.00 (*0-679-80132-4*, Pub. by Random Bks Yng Read) Random.

Pop-Up Monster Party. Illus. by Benrei Huang. (Halloween Mini-Pops Ser.). 14p. (J). (ps-1). 1992. 3.95 (*0-448-40255-6*, G & D) Peng Put Young Read.

Pop-Up Mother Goose. Harold B. Lentz. LC 94-71382. (Illus.). 24p. (J). (ps-3). 1994. 14.95 (*1-55709-237-0*) Applewood.

Pop up My First Book of Dinosaurs. Roma Bishop. (J). 1993. pap. 13.00 (*0-671-86723-7*) S&S Bks Yung.

Pop-Up Night Before Christmas. (J). 1997. pap. 9.95 (*0-8167-1292-1*) Troll Communs.

Pop-Up Number of Bears. (J). 1989. pap. 9.95 (*0-8167-1294-8*) Troll Communs.

Pop-Up Origamic Architecture. Masahiro Chatani. (Illus.). 87p. (Orig.). 1985. pap. 15.00 (*0-87040-656-6*) Japan Pubns USA.

Pop-Up Paper Engineering: Cross-Curricular Activities in Design Engineering Technology, English & Art. Paul Johnson. 184p. 1992. pap. 29.95 (*1-85000-909-0*, Falmer Pr) Taylor & Francis.

***Pop-Up Parables & Other Bible Stories.** Carmen R. Sorvillo & Helen H. Moore. LC 99-209713. 48p. 1999. teacher ed. 9.00 (*0-570-05353-6*, 12-3404GJ) Concordia.

Pop-Up Paris. David Griffiths. (Illus.). 36p. 1986. pap. 8.95 (*0-906212-31-6*, Pub. by Tarquin Pubns) Parkwest Pubns.

Pop-Up! Pop-Up! The History of the Moveable Book. Albert Tillman. 60p. 1997. pap. 9.95 (*1-888345-05-5*, Whalestooth Farm) Paper Jam.

Pop-Up Puss-in-Boots. Harold B. Lentz. (Illus.). 24p. (J). (ps-3). 1995. 14.95 (*1-55709-238-9*) Applewood.

Pop-Up Spooky Night. Illus. by Benrei Huang. (Halloween Mini-Pops Ser.). 14p. (J). (ps-1). 1992. 3.95 (*0-448-40254-8*, G & D) Peng Put Young Read.

Pop-Up Tadpole to Frog. Elizabeth Rodger. (J). (ps-1). 1996. 4.95 (*0-614-15772-2*, Cartwheel) Scholastic Inc.

***Pop-up 3-D Time Scape.** Richard Platt. (Illus.). (YA). (gr. 3 up). 1999. 19.95 (*0-7894-4716-9*) DK Pub Inc.

Pop-Up Tiny Chick. Peggy Tagel. (Springtime Pop-Ups Ser.). (Illus.). 14p. (J). (ps). 1991. 4.95 (*0-448-40055-3*, G & D) Peng Put Young Read.

Pop-Up Trucks. Richard Fowler. LC 97-3979. (Illus.). 10p. (J). 1998. pap. 14.95 (*0-15-201681-3*) Harcourt.

Pop-Up Visit to Haunted House. (J). 1989. 9.95 (*0-8167-1291-3*) Troll Communs.

Pop Vocabulary Book. Nick Camas. Ed. by Robin Quinn. (Illus.). 246p. (Orig.). 1996. reprint ed. pap. 9.95 (*0-9645851-1-1*) Pennhills.

Pop Warner: Football's Greatest Teacher. Mike Bynum. (Illus.). 240p. 1992. pap. 9.95 (*1-878839-03-9*) Gridiron Football.

Pop Wiener: Naive Painter. Joanne Bock. LC 72-90409. (Illus.). 176p. 1974. lib. bdg. 25.00 (*0-87023-122-7*) U of Mass Pr.

Pop World of Henry James: From Fairy Tales to Science Fiction. Adeline R. Tintner. Ed. by A. Walton Litz. LC 88-27725. (Studies in Modern Literature: No. 89). 343p. reprint ed. 106.40 (*0-8357-1855-7*, 207077200004) Bks Demand.

POP 11 PROGRAM ART INTEL. Mike Burton & Nigel Shadbolt. 225p. (C). 1987. pap. text 23.75 (*0-201-18049-9*) Addison-Wesley.

***Popaganda: The Art & Subversion of Ron English.** Ron English. (Illus.). 2000. pap. 16.00 (*1-887128-60-3*) Soft Skull Pr.

Popanilla & Other Tales. fac. ed. Benjamin D. Beaconsfield. LC 79-113649. (Short Story Index Reprint Ser.). 1977. 23.95 (*0-8369-3378-8*) Ayer.

POPC: The First 10 Years Proceedings Compentium, 1973-1983. 1997. write for info. (*0-89791-947-5*, 549971) Assn Compu Machinery.

Popcorn! Scott Deschaine. (Illus.). 68p. (J). 1993. pap. 4.95 (*1-878181-06-8*) Discovery Comics.

Popcorn. Ben Elton. LC 97-23024. 298p. 1997. text 22.95 (*0-312-16965-5*) St Martin.

Popcorn. Ben Elton. 304p. 1998. pap. 13.95 (*0-312-19472-2*) St Martin.

Popcorn! Frances T. Geidt. LC 95-23951. (Illus.). 112p. 1995. 15.00 (*0-684-81190-1*) Simon & Schuster.

Popcorn. Alex Moran. LC 98-15566. (Green Light Readers Ser.). (Illus.). 20p. (J). 1999. pap. 3.95 (*0-15-201998-7*) Harcourt.

***Popcorn.** Alex Moran. (Green Light Readers Ser.). (J). 2000. 10.95 (*0-15-202375-5*) Harcourt.

Popcorn. Sterling Publishing Company, Inc. Staff. (The Magnet Gourmet Ser.). 10p. 1997. pap. text 5.95 (*0-8069-0619-7*) Sterling.

Popcorn, Vol. 3. Susana Abbs. 1996. pap. write for info. (*0-582-25558-9*) Addison-Wesley.

Popcorn: A Thematic Unit. Janet Hale. (Thematic Units Ser.). (Illus.). 80p. (Orig.). (gr. 1-3). 1992. student ed. 9.95 (*1-55734-263-6*) Tchr Create Mat.

***Popcorn: Hollywood Stories.** Julia Cameron. 256p. 2000. pap. 14.95 (*1-893329-12-7*, Pub. by Really Great Bks) SCB Distributors.

***Popcorn: Poems.** Illus. by James Stevenson. LC 97-6320. 64p. (J). (gr. 3-7). 1998. 14.95 (*0-688-15261-9*, Grenwillow Bks) HarpC Child Bks.

Popcorn at the Palace. Emily Arnold McCully. LC 96-17592. (Illus.). 40p. (J). (gr. k-3). 1997. 16.00 (*0-15-277699-0*, Harcourt Child Bks) Harcourt.

Popcorn Book. Tomie De Paola. LC 77-21456. (Illus.). 32p. (J). (ps-3). 1978. pap. 6.95 (*0-8234-0533-8*); lib. bdg. 15.95 (*0-8234-0314-9*) Holiday.

Popcorn Clouds & Bubblegum Trees: Devotions for Young Children. Sue Damon. LC 94-40241. (J). 1994. pap. 7.95 (*1-56212-076-X*) CRC Pubns.

Popcorn Commodity Exchange Encyclopaedia. Ed. by Barter Publishing Staff. 1984. ring bd. 49.95 (*0-911617-06-X*) Prosperity & Profits.

Popcorn Days & Buttermilk Nights. Gary Paulsen. 112p. (J). (gr. 5-9). 1989. pap. 4.99 (*0-14-034204-4*, PuffinBks) Peng Put Young Read.

Popcorn Days & Buttermilk Nights. Gary Paulsen. (J). 1989. 10.09 (*0-606-02250-3*, Pub. by Turtleback) Demco.

Popcorn Dragon. rev. ed. Jane Thayer. LC 88-39855. (Illus.). 32p. (J). (ps-3). 1989. 16.95 (*0-688-08340-4*, Wm Morrow) Morrow Avon.

Popcorn Is Missing. Zeno Zeplin. (Katy & Beth Mystery Ser.: No. 1). (Illus.). 48p. (J). (gr. 2-4). 1990. pap. text 6.95 (*1-877740-02-0*); boxed set 11.95 (*1-877740-01-2*) Nel-Mar Pub.

Popcorn King: How Orville Redenbacher & His Popcorn Charmed America. Len Sherman. LC 96-25359. (Illus.). 112p. 1996. pap. 12.95 (*1-56530-222-2*) Summit TX.

Popcorn Lover's Book. Sue Spitler & Nao Hauser. (Illus.). 96p. (Orig.). 1983. pap. 8.95 (*0-8092-5542-1*, 554210, Contemporary Bks) NTC Contemp Pub Co.

Popcorn Magic. (Illus.). (J). (ps-2). 1991. pap. 5.10 (*0-8136-5695-8*); lib. bdg. 7.95 (*0-8136-5195-6*) Modern Curr.

Popcorn Millionaire & Other Tales of Saugatuck. Kit Lane. LC 91-60187. (Illus.). 94p. (Orig.). 1991. pap. 5.50 (*1-877703-20-6*) Pavilion Pr.

Popcorn, Paris, & Paper Napkins. Natalie B. Hart. Ed. & Illus. by Mary H. Stancil. 270p. 1998. pap. 8.95 (*1-892212-05-6*) Love Pubg Co.

Popcorn Park Zoo. Wendy Pfeffer. LC 91-3273. (Illus.). 64p. (J). (gr. 2-5). 1992. 14.95 (*0-671-74587-5*, Julian Messner); pap. 16.95 (*0-671-74589-1*, Julian Messner) Silver Burdett Pr.

Popcorn Pimps. Pat Moriarity. 72p. 1996. pap. 8.95 (*1-56097-254-8*, Pub. by Fantagraph Bks) Seven Hills Bk.

Popcorn Plants. Kathleen V. Kudlinski. LC 97-1122. (Early Bird Nature Bks.). (Illus.). 48p. (J). (gr. 2-4). 1997. lib. bdg. 19.95 (*0-8225-3014-7*, Lerner Publctns) Lerner Pub.

Popcorn Report: Faith Popcorn on the Future of Your Company, Your World, Your Life. Faith Popcorn. LC 92-52682. 256p. 1992. pap. 14.00 (*0-88730-594-6*, HarpBusn) HarpInfo.

Popcorn Science. Natalie Lunis & Nancy White. (Thinking Like a Scientist Ser.). (Illus.). 20p. (J). Date not set. pap. 16.95 (*1-58273-370-8*) Newbridge Educ.

Popcorn Shop. Alice Low. LC 92-21423. (Hello Reader! Ser.). (Illus.). 32p. (J). (ps-3). 1994. 2.95 (*0-590-47121-X*) Scholastic Inc.

Popcorn, the Peraly Gates, & Other Kernels of Truth. E. Lonnie Melashenko & David B. Smith. LC 96-13827. 1996. pap. 1.97 (*0-8163-1347-4*) Pacific Pr Pub Assn.

Popcorn Tree. Carolyn Mamchur. LC 99-162384. (Illus.). 32p. (J). (ps-3). 1998. 15.95 (*0-7737-2896-1*) STDK.

Popcorn Use As Food, Crafts, Ornaments, Etc. & More with Select Recipes. rev. ed. Carrol, Frieda, Research Division Staff. 1992. student ed., ring bd. 24.95 (*0-911569-98-7*) Prosperity & Profits.

Popcorn 3: Activities. 1996. pap. write for info. (*0-582-25564-3*) Addison-Wesley.

Pope. Mark Dunster. (Borgia Ser.: Pt. 1). 36p. (Orig.). 1984. pap. 4.00 (*0-89642-112-0*) Linden Pubs.

***Pope.** JO GARCIA-COBB. LC 99-39621. 120p. 1999. pap. text 19.98 (*1-56799-827-5*, MetroBooks) M Friedman Pub Grp Inc.

Pope. Bream Hammond. (C). 1996. pap. text. write for info. (*0-583-25538-8*) Addison-Wesley.

Pope. Ed. by Brean Hammond. (Critical Readers Ser.). 264p. (C). 1996. pap. 29.06 (*0-582-25538-4*) Addison-Wesley.

Pope. Ed. by Brean Hammond. (Critical Readers Ser.). 264p. (C). 1996. text 67.00 (*0-582-25539-2*) Longman.

Pope. Leslie Stephen. Ed. by John Morley. LC 68-58397. (English Men of Letters Ser.). reprint ed. lib. bdg. 27.50 (*0-404-51730-7*) AMS Pr.

Pope: An Analysis of the Office of the Pope & the Roman Church & City. Jean Carrere. 1977. lib. bdg. 59.95 (*0-8490-2453-6*) Gordon Pr.

Pope: An Essay on Criticism: The Rape of the Lock & Epistles to Several Persons. 2nd ed. Ed. by Raymond Southall. (Annotated Student Texts Ser.). 352p. (Orig.). 1988. pap. 22.50 (*1-85373-086-6*, Pub. by Northcote House) Trans-Atl Phila.

***Pope' Architect of the First American Revolution.** Joe S. Sando. 96p. 2001. 9.95 (*1-57416-016-8*) Clear Light.

Pope: New Concepts. David Fairer. 272p. (C). 1991. text 74.50 (*0-389-20936-8*) B&N Imports.

Pope: Poems & Prose. Alexander Pope. (Poetry Library). 224p. 1985. pap. 11.95 (*0-14-058508-7*, Penguin Bks) Viking Penguin.

Pope: Recent Essays by Several Hands. Ed. by Maynard Mack & James A. Winn. LC 79-26345. (Essential Articles Ser.). iv, 768p. (C). 1979. lib. bdg. 57.50 (*0-208-01769-0*, Archon Bks) Shoe String.

Pope: The Critical Heritage. Ed. by John Barnard. (Critical Heritage Ser.). 550p. 1973. 69.50 (*0-7100-7390-9*, Routledge Thoemms) Routledge.

Pope Alexander the Seventh & the College of Cardinals. John Bargrave. Ed. by James C. Robertson. LC 78-160001. (Camden Society, London. Publications, First Ser.: No. 92). reprint ed. 37.50 (*0-404-50192-3*) AMS Pr.

Pope & His Critics. Wilbert L. MacDonald. LC 74-30369. (English Literature Ser.: No. 33). 1974. lib. bdg. 75.00 (*0-8383-1990-4*) M S G Haskell Hse.

Pope & His Poetry. Edward W. Edmunds. LC 73-18098. (English Biography Ser.: No. 31). 1974. lib. bdg. 75.00 (*0-8383-1735-9*) M S G Haskell Hse.

Pope & His Poetry. Edward W. Edmunds. LC 77-120969. (Poetry & Life Ser.). reprint ed. 27.50 (*0-404-52510-5*) AMS Pr.

Pope & Horace: Studies in Imitation. Frank Stack. 336p. 1985. text 80.00 (*0-521-26695-5*) Cambridge U Pr.

Pope & the Context of Controversy: The Manipulation of Ideas in an Essay on Man. Douglas H. White. LC 70-120009. 1970. lib. bdg. 15.00 (*0-226-89494-0*) U Ch Pr.

Pope & the Early Eighteenth-Century Book Trade. rev. ed. David Foxon. (Lyell Lectures in Bibliography, 1975-76). (Illus.). 288p. 1991. text 100.00 (*0-19-818402-6*) OUP.

Pope & the New Apocalypse: The Holy War Against Family Planning. Stephen D. Mumford. (Illus.). 82p. (Orig.). 1986. 6.95 (*0-937307-00-9*); pap. 3.95 (*0-937307-01-7*) CRPS.

Pope & the Witch. Dario Fo. (Oberon Bks.). 148p. 1997. pap. 10.95 (*1-870259-58-0*) Theatre Comm.

Pope Answers: John Paul II's Encyclical Letter "The Mission of Christ the Redeemer" adapted ed. Adapted by Juliette Baker. 70p. (C). 1990. 29.00 (*0-85439-405-2*, Pub. by St Paul Pubns) St Mut.

Pope Chronology. Reginald Berry. 192p. 1988. 40.00 (*0-8161-8951-X*, Hall Reference) Macmillan.

Pope County, Arkansas Census & Marriage, 1850, Bk. 1. Bobbie J. McLane & Capitola Glazner. 95p. (Orig.). 1966. pap. 15.00 (*0-929604-03-2*) Arkansas Ancestors.

Pope County, Arkansas Census, 1860. Bobbie J. McLane & Capitola Glazner. 139p. (Orig.). 1967. pap. 15.00 (*0-929604-04-0*) Arkansas Ancestors.

Pope County Arkansas Marriages, 1860-1892. Bobbie J. McLane & Capitola Glazner. 307p. (Orig.). 1972. pap. 25.00 (*0-929604-24-5*) Arkansas Ancestors.

Pope County III Pictorial. Turner Publishing Company Staff. LC 88-51190. 176p. 1994. 49.95 (*1-56311-154-3*) Turner Pub KY.

Pope Fiction: Answers to 30 Myths & Misconceptions about the Papacy. Patrick Madrid. 345p. 1999. pap. 14.99 (*0-9642610-0-6*) Basilica Pr.

Pope Gelasius I & the Lupercalia. A. W. Holleman. 197p. 1974. pap. 56.00 (*90-256-0690-3*, Pub. by AM Hakkert) BookLink Distributors.

***Pope Gregory VII, 1073-1085.** H. E. Cowdrey. 760p. 1998. text 150.00 (*0-19-820646-1*) OUP.

Pope, His Banker & Venice. Felix Gilbert. (Illus.). 176p. (C). 1990. pap. 15.50 (*0-674-68976-3*) HUP.

Pope in America. Ed. by Brian C. Anderson. (Illus.). 164p. (Orig.). 1996. pap. 13.95 (*1-883357-24-1*, Crisis Bks) Dumb Ox Bks.

Pope in Britain. St. Paul Publications Staff. (C). 1988. 60.00 (*0-85439-217-3*, Pub. by St Paul Pubns) St Mut.

Pope in Ireland. Veritas Publications Staff. 1989. pap. 22.00 (*0-7855-7046-2*, Pub. by Veritas Pubns) St Mut.

***Pope Innocent III & His World.** Ed. by John Moore. LC 99-20427. 408p. 1999. text 87.95 (*1-84014-646-X*, Pub. by Ashgate Pub) Ashgate Pub Co.

***Pope Joan.** Alain Boureau. 1999. pap. text 19.00 (*0-226-06745-9*); lib. bdg. 58.00 (*0-226-06744-0*) U Ch Pr.

Pope Joan. Donna W. Cross. 432p. 1997. pap. 12.95 (*0-345-41626-0*) Ballantine Pub Grp.

Pope Joan. Donna W. Cross. 432p. 1996. 25.00 (*0-614-18301-4*) Crown Pub Group.

Pope Joan. Lawrence Durrell. Tr. & Adapted by Emmanuel Royidis. LC 82-81088. 176p. 1984. 22.50 (*0-87951-963-0*, Pub. by Overlook Pr) Penguin Putnam.

Pope Joan. Lawrence Durrell. LC 84-7116. 160p. 1997. reprint ed. pap. 13.95 (*0-87951-786-7*, Pub. by Overlook Pr) Penguin Putnam.

Pope John Paul II: In My Own Words. abr. ed. John Paul, II, pseud. Ed. & Compiled by Anthony F. Chiffolo. LC 98-7743. (Illus.). 128p. 1998. 12.95 (*0-7648-0264-X*) Liguori Pubns.

Pope John Paul II on Jews & Judaism, 1979-1986. John Paul, II, pseud. Ed. by Eugene J. Fisher & Leon Klenicki. LC 87-406571. 97p. (Orig.). 1987. pap. 3.95 (*1-55586-151-2*) US Catholic.

Pope John Paul II on the Genius of Women. John Paul, II, pseud. LC 97-215289. 84p. 1997. pap. text 5.95 (*1-57455-113-2*) US Catholic.

Pope John Paul II's Theological Journey to the Prayer Meeting of Religions at Assisi Pt. 2, Vol. 1: The Trinitarian Trilogy: "Redemptor Hominis", "Dives in Misericordia", "Dominum et Vivificantem" Johannes Dormann. Tr. by Christopher Brandler from GER. 243p. (Orig.). 1996. pap. 11.45 (*0-935952-33-0*) Angelus Pr.

Pope John Paul II's Theological Journey to the Prayer Meeting of Religions in Assisi Pt. 1: From the Second Vatican Council to the Papal Election. Johannes Dormann. Ed. by Society of St. Pius X Staff. LC 94-25185. 8p. (Orig.). 1994. pap. 9.45 (*0-935952-52-7*) Angelus Pr.

Pope John Paul on Inculturation: Theory & Practice. S. Iniobong Udoidem. LC 96-3333. 168p. 1996. lib. bdg. 32.00 (*0-7618-0502-8*) U Pr of Amer.

***Pope John Paul II: Pope for the People.** Peggy Burns. LC 00-36935. (Famous Lives Ser.). (Illus.). 2000. write for info. (*0-8172-5714-4*) Raintree Steck-V.

***Pope John Paul II.** Life Magazine Editors. (Illus.). 128p. 2000. 29.95 (*0-8212-2677-0*, Pub. by Bulfinch Pr) Little.

Pope John Paul II. Patricia Cronin Marcello. LC 98-85420. (Little Bks.). (Illus.). 80p. 1998. 4.95 (*0-8362-7160-2*) Andrews & McMeel.

Pope John Paul II. John Moody. LC 96-36219. (Illus.). 208p. 1997. 20.00 (*0-517-20081-3*) Random Hse Value.

Pope John Paul II, Vol. 181. Tom Tierney. 1984. pap. 4.95 (*0-486-24648-5*) Dover.

Pope John Paul II: An American Celebration. Intro. by Theodore McCarrick. (Illus.). 128p. 1994. pap. 17.95 (*0-9642957-0-9*) Jersey Photo Project.

Pope John Paul II: The Biography. Tad Szulc. 1996. mass mkt. 6.99 (*0-671-00047-0*) PB.

Pope John Paul II: The Biography. Tad Szulc. (Illus.). 542p. 1995. 27.50 (*0-684-80416-6*) S&S Trade.

Pope John Paul II: The People's Pope. George A. Sullivan. LC 83-40395. (Illus.). 120p. (J). (gr. 7 up). 1984. 11.95 (*0-8027-6523-8*) Walker & Co.

Pope John Paul II & the Church. Peter Hebblethwaite. 320p. (Orig.). 1995. pap. 16.95 (*1-55612-814-2*) Sheed & Ward WI.

Pope John Paul II & the Family. John Paul, II, pseud. LC 82-13308. 379p. 1983. 15.00 (*0-8199-0851-7*, Frncscn Herld) Franciscan Pr.

Pope John Paul II Prays the Litany of the Sacred Heart of Jesus. John Paul, II, pseud. Ed. & Intro. by Carl J. Moell. LC 91-66666. (Illus.). 205p. (Orig.). 1992. pap. 5.95 (*0-87973-478-7*, 478) Our Sunday Visitor.

Pope John Paul II's Theological Journey to the Prayer Meeting of Religions at Assisi Pt. II, Vol. 2: The "Trinitarian Trilogy": Dives in Misericordia. Johannes Dormann. Tr. by Sebastian Wall from GER. 200p. 1998. pap. 10.95 (*0-935952-72-1*) Angelus Pr.

***Pope John Paul XXIII: In My Own Words.** Ed. & Compiled by Anthony F. Chiffolo. LC 99-26792. 128p. 1999. 13.95 (*0-7648-0498-7*) Liguori Pubns.

Pope John XXIII & Master John Hus of Bohemia. Eustace J. Kitts. LC 77-84726. reprint ed. 64.50 (*0-404-16127-8*) AMS Pr.

***Pope John XXIII: A Spiritual Biography.** Christian Feldman. (Lives & Legacies Ser.). 192p. 2000. 19.95 (*0-8245-2356-3*) Crossroad NY.

Pope Marcellus Mass. rev. ed. Giovanni P. Palestrini. Ed. by Lewis C. Lockwood. (Critical Scores Ser.). (C). 1975. pap. text 15.50 (*0-393-09242-9*) Norton.

Pope of Dreamers see Papa de los Sonadores

Pope or Church? Essays on the Infallibility of the Ordinary Magisterium. Paul Nau & Rene Berthod. 72p. 1998. pap. 5.45 (*0-935952-90-X*) Angelus Pr.

Pope, or President? Startling Disclosures of Romanism As Revealed by Its Own Writers : Facts for Americans. Ed. by Gerald N. Grob. LC 76-46094. (Anti-Movements in America Ser.). 1977. lib. bdg. 30.95 (*0-405-09967-3*) Ayer.

***Pope Pius XII: Architect for Peace.** Margherita Marchione. LC 99-58456. 368p. 2000. pap. 22.95 (*0-8091-3912-X*) Paulist Pr.

Pope St. Pius X. F. A. Forbes. LC 87-51072. 134p. 1992. reprint ed. pap. 8.00 (*0-89555-328-7*) TAN Bks Pubs.

Pope Speaks: Pope Plus XII on Purity. Nazareno Camilleri. 79p. 1985. pap. 1.25 (*0-911988-18-1*, 44808) AMI Pr.

Pope, Swift, & Women Writers. Ed. by Donald C. Mell. LC 96-16288. 256p. 1996. 39.50 (*0-87413-590-7*) U Delaware Pr.

Pope, the Council, & the Mass. James Likoudis & K. D. Whitehead. 1981. 13.95 (*0-8158-0400-8*) Chris Mass.

Pope to Burns, Vol. 12. Intro. by John W. Cunliffe. Date not set. 30.95 (*0-8369-4803-3*) Ayer.

Pope Urban II, the Collectio Britannica, & the Council of Melfi (1089) Robert Somerville. LC 97-142338. (Illus.). 340p. (C). 1996. text 110.00 (*0-19-820569-4*) OUP.

Popeiana, 25 vols. Incl. Vol. 1. Early Criticism, Seventeen Eleven to Seventeen Sixteen. 1974. lib. bdg. 61.00 (*0-8240-1239-9*); Vol. 2. Pope's Homer, One. 1974. lib. bdg. 61.00 (*0-8240-1240-2*); Vol. 4. On Literary Farces. 1974. lib. bdg. 61.00 (*0-8240-1242-9*); Vol. 6. Dunciad,

P

An Asterisk (*) at the beginning of an entry indicates that the title is appearing for the first time.

One. 1974. reprint ed. lib. bdg. 61.00 (*0-8240-1244-5*); Vol. 7. Dunciad, Two. 1974. reprint ed. lib. bdg. 61.00 (*0-8240-1245-3*); Vol. 8. Dunciad, Three. 1974. reprint ed. lib. bdg. 61.00 (*0-8240-1246-1*); Vol. 9. Attack of Thomas Cooke. 1974. lib. bdg. 61.00 (*0-8240-1247-X*); Vol. 10. Dunciad & Other Matters. 1974. reprint ed. lib. bdg. 61.00 (*0-8240-1248-8*); Vol. 11. On Taste, 1732 to 1735. 1974. lib. bdg. 61.00 (*0-8240-1249-6*); Vol. 12. Essay on Man, Crousaz. 1974. 61.00 (*0-8240-1250-X*); Vol. 13. Essay on Man, Crousaz 2. 1974. lib. bdg. 61.00 (*0-8240-1251-8*); Vol. 14. Essay on Man, Warburton, Etc. 1974. lib. bdg. 61.00 (*0-8240-1252-6*); Vol. 15. Cibber & the Dunciad. 1974. lib. bdg. 61.00 (*0-8240-1253-4*); Vol. 16. Dunciad. 1974. reprint ed. lib. bdg. 61.00 (*0-8240-1254-2*); Vol. 22. Biography. 1974. lib. bdg. 61.00 (*0-8240-1258-5*); Vol. 23. Biography. 1974. lib. bdg. 61.00 (*0-8240-1259-3*); Vol. 24. Biography. 1974. lib. bdg. 61.00 (*0-8240-1260-7*); Vol. 25. Folio Verse: Attacks, Defences, & Imitations. 1974. lib. bdg. 61.00 (*0-8240-1261-5*); Vols. 18-19. Warton on Pope., **2 vols.** 1974. lib. bdg. (*0-8240-1256-9*); Vols. 20-21. Biography. 1974. lib. bdg. 61.00 (*0-8240-1257-7*); (Life & Times of Seven Major British Writers Ser.). 1974. lib. bdg. write for info. (*0-318-52600-X*) Garland.

***Popes Against Modern Errors: 16 Famous Papal Documents.** Ed. by Anthony J. Mioni, Jr. LC 98-61396. 365p. 1999. pap. 16.50 (*0-89555-643-X*, 1588) TAN Bks Pubs.

Popes & Church Reform in the 11th Century. H. E. Cowdrey. 101.95 (*0-86078-797-4*) Ashgate Pub Co.

Popes & European Revolution. Owen Chadwick. (Oxford History of the Christian Church Ser.). 656p. 1981. 105.00 (*0-19-826919-6*) OUP.

Popes & Heresy in the Thirteenth Century. Albert C. Shannon. LC 78-63192. (Heresies of the Early Christian & Medieval Era Ser.: Second Ser.). reprint ed. 39.50 (*0-404-16228-2*) AMS Pr.

Popes & Princess, 1417-1517: Politics & Polity in Late Medieval Church. J. A. Thomson. (Early Modern Europe Today Ser.). 256p. 1980. text 16.95 (*0-04-901027-1*) Routledge.

Popes & Science. James J. Walsh. 1977. lib. bdg. 59.95 (*0-8490-2454-4*) Gordon Pr.

Popes & Slavery. Joel S. Panzer. LC 96-22753. 137p. (Orig.). 1996. pap. 7.95 (*0-8189-0764-9*) Alba.

Pope's Armada. G. Urquhart. 489p. 1996. 34.95 (*0-593-03388-4*) Bantam.

Pope's Armada. G. Urquhart. 1996. mass mkt. 9.99 (*0-552-14114-3*) Bantam.

Pope's Armada. Gordon Urquhart. LC 99-22326. 450p. 1999. 26.95 (*1-57392-699-X*) Prometheus Bks.

***Pope's Body.** Paravicini Bagliani, Agostino. LC 99-36181. (Illus.). 352p. 2000. 28.00 (*0-226-03437-2*) U Ch Pr.

Popes, Canonists, & Texts, 1100-1550. Kenneth Pennington. (Collected Studies: Vol. 412). 352p. 1993. 122.95 (*0-86078-387-1*, Pub. by Variorum) Ashgate Pub Co.

Pope's Confessor & Other Stories. Denis Murphy. 115p. (Orig.). 1985. pap. 8.75 (*971-10-0188-8*, Pub. by New Day Pub) Cellar.

Pope's Elephant. Silvio A. Bedini. LC 98-121003. (Illus.). 320p. 1998. 55.00 (*1-85754-277-0*, Pub. by Carcanet Pr) Paul & Co Pubs.

Pope's Elephant. Silvio A. Bedini. LC 98-36227. (Illus.). 312p. 1998. 29.95 (*1-879941-41-4*, Pub. by J S Sanders) Natl Bk Netwk.

***Pope's Elephant.** Silvio A. Bedini. (Illus.). 320p. 2000. pap. 14.95 (*0-14-028862-7*, Penguin Bks) Viking Penguin.

Pope's Essay on Man. A. D. Nuttall. LC 83-22298. (Unwin Critical Library). 250p. (C). 1984. text 55.00 (*0-04-800017-5*) Routledge.

Pope's Homer, One see Popeiana

Pope's Men: The Papal Civil Service in the Renaissance. Peter Partner. 288p. 1990. text 75.00 (*0-19-821995-4*) OUP.

Popes, Monks & Crusaders. H. E. Cowdrey. 400p. (C). 1983. 60.00 (*0-907628-34-6*) Hambledon Press.

Pope's Nose: Short Comic Plays & Sketches. Howard Korder. 1991. pap. 5.25 (*0-8222-0902-0*) Dramatists Play.

Popes of Vatican Council II. Peter Wigginton. 320p. 1983. 7.49 (*0-8199-0828-2*, Frncscn Herld) Franciscan Pr.

Pope's Once & Future Kings: Satire & Politics in the Early Career. John M. Aden. LC 78-16618. 232p. reprint ed. pap. 72.00 (*0-8357-6538-5*, 203590000097) Bks Demand.

Pope's Plan for Social Reconstruction. Charles P. Bruehl. 10.00 (*0-8159-6507-9*) Devin.

Pope's Puns & Other Air Force Cartoons. W. C. Pope. (Illus.). 96p. 1998. pap. 8.95 (*0-9671229-0-2*) Paradox Prods NY.

Pope's Rhinoceros. Lawrence Norfolk. LC 97-23401. 592p. 1997. 15.00 (*0-8050-5475-8*, Owl) H Holt & Co.

Pope's Taste in Shakespeare. John Butt. LC 74-100736. 1970. reprint ed. pap. 39.95 (*0-8383-0011-1*) M S G Haskell Hse.

Popes, Teachers, & Canon Law in the Middle Ages. Ed. by James R. Sweeney & Stanley Chodorow. LC 88-47930. 352p. 1989. 55.00 (*0-8014-2264-7*) Cornell U Pr.

Popes, Teachers & Canon Law in the Middle Ages. Ed. by James R. Sweeney & Stanley Chodorow. LC 88-47930. (Illus.). 357p. reprint ed. pap. 110.70 (*0-608-20952-X*, 207205100003) Bks Demand.

Popescu, Theory of Categories. 1979. lib. bdg. 93.00 (*90-286-0168-6*) Kluwer Academic.

Popeye: An Illustrated History of E. C. Segar's Character in Print, Radio, Television & Film Appearances, 1929-1993. Fred M. Grandinetti. LC 94-123. (Illus.). 288p. 1994. pap. 35.00 (*0-89950-982-7*) McFarland & Co.

Popeye: Sixtieth Anniversary Collection. Ed M. Higgs. 1995. 15.98 (*0-7858-0397-1*) Bk Sales Inc.

Popeye Postcard Book. Created by E. C. Segar. (Illus.). 30p. 1997. pap. 10.95 (*1-55670-582-4*) Stewart Tabori & Chang.

***Popeye Puzzle Book.** DOHERTY. 1999. mass mkt. 1.95 (*0-8125-7547-4*) Tor Bks.

Popful Mail. Zach Meston & J. Douglas Arnold. (Gaming Mastery Ser.). (Illus.). 160p. (Orig.). 1995. pap. 16.95 (*1-884364-18-7*) Sandwich Islands.

Popism: The Warhol Sixties. Andy Warhol. LC 76-40899. (Illus.). 336p. 1990. pap. 17.00 (*0-15-672960-1*, Harvest Bks) Harcourt.

Popkins. rev. ed. Murray Schisgal. 1990. pap. 5.25 (*0-8222-1436-9*) Dramatists Play.

POPL 98: POPL: Annual Symposium on Principles of Programming Languages. 1998. 70.00 (*0-89791-979-3*, 549981) Assn Compu Machinery.

POPL 95: 22nd Annual ACM SIGACT-SIGPLAN on Principles of Programming Languages. 415p. 1995. pap. text 58.00 (*0-89791-692-1*, 549950) Assn Compu Machinery.

POPL 94: 1st ACM Symposium on Principles of Programming Languages. 500p. 1994. pap. text 70.00 (*0-89791-636-0*, 549940) Assn Compu Machinery.

POPL 97: 24th Annual ACM SIGPLAN-SIGACT Symposium on Principles of Programming Languages. 497p. 1997. pap. 70.00 (*0-89791-853-3*, 549970) Assn Compu Machinery.

POPL 96: 23rd Annual ACM SIGPLAN-SIGACT Symposium on Principles of Programming Languages. 432p. 1996. pap. text 60.00 (*0-89791-769-3*, 549960) Assn Compu Machinery.

POPL 93: 20th ACM Symposium on Principles of Programming Languages. 520p. 1993. pap. text 72.00 (*0-89791-560-7*, 549930) Assn Compu Machinery.

Poplar Forest & Thomas Jefferson. S. Allen Chambers, Jr. LC 93-90066. (Illus.). 256p. 1998. reprint ed. 39.95 (*0-9667169-0-6*, Corp Poplar Forest) T J Poplar Forest.

Poplar Island - My Memories As a Boy. Peter K. Bailey. (Illus.). viii, 158p. 1996. 19.50 (*0-9655453-0-X*) P K Bailey.

Poplars & Willows in Wood Production & Land Use. F. A. O. Staff. 328p. 1987. 195.00 (*0-7855-3061-4*, Pub. by Intl Bk Distr) St Mut.

Poplars & Willows in Wood Production & Land Use. F. A. O. Staff. 328p. 1989. pap. 475.00 (*81-7089-085-3*, Pub. by Intl Bk Distr) St Mut.

Poplars & Willows in Wood Production & Land-Use. FAO Staff. 328p. 1987. pap. 275.00 (*81-7089-300-3*, Pub. by Intl Bk Distr) St Mut.

Poplars of the British Isles. P. A. Robertson. (Natural History Ser.: No. 58). (Illus.). 24p. 1989. pap. 5.25 (*0-7478-0093-6*, Pub. by Shire Pubns) Parkwest Pubns.

***PopLit, PopCult & the X-Files: A Critical Explanation.** Jan Delasara. 253p. 2000. lib. bdg. 39.95 (*0-7864-0789-1*) McFarland & Co.

Poplore: Folk & Pop in American Culture. Gene Bluestein. LC 93-43614. 184p. 1994. 35.00 (*0-87023-903-1*); pap. 15.95 (*0-87023-904-X*) U of Mass Pr.

Popmap: Integrated Software Package for Geographical Information, Maps & Graphics Database: User's Guide & Reference Manual. 325p. 1994. 280.00 incl. disk (*92-1-161370-1*, E.94.XVII.12) UN.

Popo & Fifina. Arna W. Bontemps & Langston Hughes. (Iona & Peter Opie Library of Children's Literature). (Illus.). 128p. (YA). (gr. 3 up). 1993. 16.95 (*0-19-508765-8*) OUP.

***Popo & Fifina: Children of Haiti.** Arna Bontemps & Langston Hughes. (The Iona & Peter Opie Library of Children's Literature). (Illus.). 128p. (YA). 2000. pap. 8.95 (*0-19-513939-9*) OUP.

Popol Vuh: A Sacred Book of the Maya. Tr. by David Unger. (Illus.). 85p. (YA). (gr. 2-7). 1999. text 19.95 (*0-88899-334-X*, Pub. by Gro1undwood-Douglas) Publishers Group.

Popol Vuh: Las Antiguas Historias Del Quiche (Indigenous Legends) Adrian Recinos. (SPA.). 187p. 1960. pap. 9.99 (*968-16-0327-3*, Pub. by Fondo) Continental Bk.

Popol Vuh: Las Antiguas Historias Del Quiche (Indigenous Legends) Tr. by Adrian Recinos. 268p. 1997. 9.95 (*84-8377-093-8*) Piedra Santa Editorial.

Popol Vuh: Mayan Book Dawn of Life. rev. ed. Dennis Tedlock. 384p. 1996. per. 15.00 (*0-684-81845-0*) S&S Trade.

Popol Vuh: Mythic & Heroic Sagas of the Kiches of Central America. Lewis Spence. LC 75-139178. (Popular Studies in Mythology, Romance & Folklore: No. 16). reprint ed. 12.50 (*0-404-53516-X*) AMS Pr.

Popol Vuh: The Definitive Edition of the Mayan Book of the Dawn of Life & the Glories of Gods & Kings. Dennis Tedlock. 380p. 1986. pap. 12.00 (*0-671-61771-0*, Touchstone) S&S Trade Pap.

Popol Vuh: The Mythic & Heroic Sagas of the Kiches of Central America. Lewis Spence. 66p. 1997. reprint ed. pap. 10.50 (*0-7661-0071-5*) Kessinger Pub.

***Popol Vuh: The Mythic Sections, Tales of First Beginnings from the Ancient Kbicheb-Maya.** Allen J. Christenson. LC 00-25329. (Ancient Texts & Mormon Studies). 2000. write for info. (*0-934893-52-7*, F A R M S) Brigham.

Popol Vuh: The Sacred Book of the Ancient Quiche Maya: Spanish Version of the Original Maya. Tr. by Adrian Recinos et al. LC 50-6643. (Civilization of the American Indian Ser.: No. 29). 288p. 1991. 29.95 (*0-8061-0205-5*) U of Okla Pr.

Popol Vuh: The Sacred Book of the Ancient Quiche Maya: Spanish Version of the Original Maya. Tr. by Adrian Recinos et al. LC 50-6643. (Civilization of the American Indian Ser.: No. 29). 288p. 1991. reprint ed. pap. 13.95 (*0-8061-2266-8*) U of Okla Pr.

Popol Vuh of the Jaguar Priests: Ancient Maya Book of Creation. Charles R. Barnett. Tr. by Silvia Devilliers De Knight. LC 89-84739. (ENG & SPA., Illus.). 100p. (Orig.). 1994. pap. 9.95 (*0-944482-31-7*) Except Bks NM.

***Popol Vuj: Libro Sagrado de los Maya.** Tr. by David Unger. (SPA., Illus.). 96p. (YA). (gr. 4 up). 1999. text 19.95 (*0-88899-344-7*, Pub. by Grndwd Bks) Publishers Group.

***Popol Vuj: Libro Sagrado de los Mayas.** Tr. by David Unger. (SPA., Illus.). 96p. (YA). (gr. 4 up). 1999. pap. 12.95 (*0-88899-362-5*, Pub. by Grndwd Bks) Publishers Group.

Popolazione Nella Storia D'Europa see Populations of Europe: A History

Poppa & Elizabeth: A Bobtail Romance. Robert E. May. (Bobtail Chronicles Ser.). (Illus.). 32p. (Orig.). (J). (ps-3). 1988. pap. 5.95 (*0-87397-313-5*, Strode Pubs); lib. bdg. 11.89 (*0-87397-314-3*, Strode Pubs) Circle Bk Service.

Poppa John. Larry Woiwode. 204p. 1981. 10.95 (*0-374-23630-5*) FS&G.

Poppa Psychology: The Role of Fathers in Children's Mental Well Being. Vicky Phares. LC 98-33614. 168p. 1999. 35.00 (*0-275-96367-5*, Praeger Pubs) Greenwood.

Poppa's Itchy Christmas. Angela S. Medearis. LC 96-40170. (Illus.). (J). (gr. k-3). 1998. 15.95 (*0-8234-1298-9*) Holiday.

Poppa's New Pants. Angela S. Medearis. LC 94-20489. (Illus.). 32p. (J). (ps-3). 1995. lib. bdg. 15.95 (*0-8234-1155-9*) Holiday.

PopPaw's Magic Garden. unabridged ed. Helen P. Miller. (Illus.). 28p. (J). (ps-3). 1997. pap. 6.95 (*0-9653084-3-X*) Mtn Hse Pub.

Popped. Willard Gellis. (Satan's Suckhole Ser.). 100p. 1992. pap. 20.00 (*0-917455-21-5*) Big Foot NY.

Popped Culture: The Social History of Popcorn in America. Andrew F. Smith. LC 98-40193. 256p. 1999. 24.95 (*1-57003-300-5*) U of SC Pr.

Popper. Bobby Markels. (Nonny Ser.). 80p. (Orig.). Date not set. pap. 6.50 (*1-880991-07-1*) Stone Pub.

Popper: Great Philosophers. Frederic Raphael. LC 99-22646. (Great Philosophers Ser.). 64p. 1999. pap. 6.00 (*0-415-92391-3*) Routledge.

Popper: Philosophy, Politics & Scientific Method. Geoff Stokes. LC 98-29547. (Key Contemporary Thinkers Ser.). 197p. 1999. 54.95 (*0-7456-0321-1*); pap. 21.95 (*0-7456-0322-X*) Blackwell Pubs.

Popper & After: Four Modern Irrationalists. David Stove. 192p. 1982. 59.00 (*0-08-026792-0*, Pub. by Pergamon Repr) Franklin.

Popper & the Human Sciences. Ed. by Gregory Currie & Alan E. Musgrave. 225p. 1985. pap. text 34.00 (*90-247-3141-0*, Pub. by M Nijhoff) Kluwer Academic.

Popper-Carnap Controversy. Alex C. Michalos. 133p. 1971. pap. text 71.00 (*90-247-5127-6*) Kluwer Academic.

Popper Selections. Karl R. Popper. Ed. by David Miller. LC 83-43084. 480p. 1985. pap. text 18.95 (*0-691-02031-0*, Pub. by Princeton U Pr) Cal Prin Full Svc.

Popper vs. Einstein: On the Philosophical Foundations of Physics. Christoph Von Mettenheim. LC 98-180167. 243p. 1998. 67.50 (*3-16-146910-0*, Pub. by JCB Mohr) Coronet Bks.

Popper's Open Society after Fifty Years: The Continuing Relevance of Karl Popper. Ian Jarvie. LC 98-47993. 1999. 40.00 (*0-415-16502-4*) Routledge.

Popper's Views on Natural & Social Science. Colin G. Simkin. LC 92-30556. (Brill's Studies in Epistemology, Psychology & Psychiatry: Vol. 3). viii, 208p. 1993. pap. 59.00 (*90-04-09680-9*) Brill Academic Pubs.

Poppie Nongena: A Novel of South Africa. Elsa Joubert. LC 87-14. 368p. 1995. pap. 8.95 (*0-8050-0230-8*, Owl) H Holt & Co.

Poppies. Judith Harris. LC 81-50428. (Series Six). 50p. (Orig.). 1981. pap. text 7.00 (*0-931846-19-6*) Wash Writers Pub.

Poppies. Floyd Skloot. LC 96-152760. 1994. pap. 6.00 (*1-878851-05-5*) Silverfish Rev Pr.

Poppies: The Poppy Family in the Wild & in Cultivation. Christopher Grey-Wilson. (Illus.). 239p. 1993. 37.95 (*0-88192-232-3*) Timber.

Poppies & Mandragora. Edgar E. Saltus. LC 74-182710. reprint ed. 37.50 (*0-404-05553-2*) AMS Pr.

Poppies & Mandragora: Poems. Edgar E. Saltus. (BCL1-PS American Literature Ser.). 57p. 1992. reprint ed. lib. bdg. 59.00 (*0-7812-6850-8*) Rprt Serv.

Poppies & Other Poems. Roger E. Egan. (Illus.). 80p. (Orig.). 1992. pap. 10.00 (*0-9632687-0-8*) PenRose Pub.

Poppies in the Wind. Louise O'Flaherty. 448p. (Orig.). 1981. mass mkt. 2.95 (*0-345-29201-4*) Ballantine Pub Grp.

Popping Corn. Beth Esh. (Big Bks.). (Illus.). 8p. (J). (ps-k). 1994. pap. text 10.95 (*1-57332-002-1*) HighReach Lrning.

Popping the Question: Real-Life Stories of Marriage Proposals from the Romantic to the Bizarre. Sheree Bykofsky & Laurie Viera. LC 96-28867. (Illus.). 128p. (Orig.). 1997. pap. 8.95 (*0-8027-7500-4*) Walker & Co.

Popping with Power. rev. ed. Ann Wiebe. Ed. by Betty Cordel & Judith A. Hillen. (Illus.). 111p. (J). (gr. 3-5). 1996. pap., teacher ed., wbk. ed. 16.95 (*1-881431-68-1*, 1205) AIMS Educ Fnd.

Poppin's Cut & Paste with 1000 Plus DynaSyms. Faith Carlson. (Illus.). 74p. 1994. pap. 15.00 (*1-886498-00-8*, 8-0002) Poppin & Co.

Poppin's DynaSyms 1700+ Faith Carlson. 47p. 1995. pap. 20.00 (*1-886498-01-6*, 8-0005) Poppin & Co.

Poppin's DynaSyms Test-Probe. Faith Carlson & Nancy T. Harlan. (Illus.). 1332p. 1997. ring bd. 50.00 (*1-886498-06-7*, 8-0015) Poppin & Co.

Poppin's Mini DynaSyms 1700+ Faith Carlson. (Illus.). 27p. (Orig.). 1996. pap. 17.00 (*1-886498-03-2*, 8-0012) Poppin & Co.

Poppleton. Cynthia Rylant. LC 96-3365. (Illus.). 56p. (J). (ps-2). 1997. 13.95 (*0-590-84782-1*, Blue Sky Press); pap. 3.99 (*0-590-84783-X*, Blue Sky Press) Scholastic Inc.

Poppleton. Cynthia Rylant. 1997. 9.19 (*0-606-11760-1*, Pub. by Turtleback) Demco.

Poppleton & Friends. Cynthia Rylant. LC 96-3366. (Illus.). 48p. (J). (ps-2). 1997. pap. 3.99 (*0-590-84788-0*, Blue Sky Press) Scholastic Inc.

Poppleton & Friends. Cynthia Rylant. LC 96-3366. (Illus.). 72p. (J). (ps-2). 1997. 13.95 (*0-590-84786-4*, Blue Sky Press) Scholastic Inc.

Poppleton & Friends. Cynthia Rylant. 1998. 9.19 (*0-606-13716-5*, Pub. by Turtleback) Demco.

***Poppleton Display.** Cynthia Rylant. (J). 1999. pap. text 95.76 (*0-439-05990-9*) Scholastic Inc.

Poppleton Everyday. Cynthia Rylant. LC 97-933. (Illus.). 48p. (J). (ps-2). 1998. 14.95 (*0-590-84845-3*, Blue Sky Press); pap. 3.99 (*0-590-84853-4*) Scholastic Inc.

Poppleton Everyday. Cynthia Rylant. 1998. 9.44 (*0-606-13717-3*) Turtleback.

Poppleton Forever. Cynthia Rylant. (Illus.). 56p. (J). (ps-2). 1998. pap. 3.99 (*0-590-84844-5*) Scholastic Inc.

Poppleton Forever. Cynthia Rylant. LC 97-14047. (Illus.). 56p. (J). (ps-2). 1998. 14.95 (*0-590-84843-7*, Blue Sky Press) Scholastic Inc.

Poppleton Forever. Cynthia Rylant. 1998. 9.19 (*0-606-13718-1*, Pub. by Turtleback) Demco.

***Poppleton Has Fun.** Cynthia Rylant. (Illus.). 56p. (J). (ps-2). 2000. pap. 3.99 (*0-590-84841-0*) Scholastic Inc.

Poppleton in Fall. Cynthia Rylant. LC 98-31791. (Illus.). 56p. (J). (ps-2). 1999. 14.95 (*0-590-84789-9*, Pub. by Scholastic Inc); pap. 3.99 (*0-590-84794-5*, Pub. by Scholastic Inc) Penguin Putnam.

Poppleton in Spring. Cynthia Rylant. LC 98-12858. (Illus.). 48p. (ps-2). 1999. pap. 3.99 (*0-590-84822-4*) Scholastic Inc.

Poppleton in Spring. Cynthia Rylant. LC 98-12858. (Poppleton Ser.). (Illus.). 48p. (J). (ps-2). 1999. 15.95 (*0-590-84818-6*, Blue Sky Press) Scholastic Inc.

***Poppleton Through & Through.** Illus. by Cynthia Rylant & Mark Teague. LC 99-29039. (J). 2000. 15.95 (*0-590-84839-9*, Blue Sky Press) Scholastic Inc.

Popposites: A Lift, Pull, & Pop Book of Opposites. Jung-Huyn Yoon. (Illus.). 14p. (J). 16.99 (*0-590-24937-1*) Scholastic Inc.

***Poppy.** (J). 1999. 9.95 (*1-58130-568-0*) Novel Units.

***Poppy.** (J). 2000. 11.95 (*1-58130-569-9*) Novel Units.

Poppy. Avi. (Illus.). 176p. (J). 1997. mass mkt. 4.99 (*0-380-72769-2*, Avon Bks) Morrow Avon.

Poppy. Avi. LC 95-6040. (Illus.). 160p. (J). (gr. 4-6). 1995. 15.95 (*0-531-09483-9*) Orchard Bks Watts.

Poppy. Illus. by Brian Floca. LC 95-6040. 160p. (J). (gr. 4-6). 1995. lib. bdg. 16.99 (*0-531-08783-2*) Orchard Bks Watts.

Poppy. Sam M. Itaya. 220p. 1993. pap. 7.50 (*0-9638592-5-0*) Woodhse Bks.

Poppy. Rosie Rushton. 224p. (J). (gr. 5-9). 2000. mass mkt. 3.99 (*0-7868-1391-1*, Pub. by Hyprn Ppbks) Little.

Poppy: The Genus Papaver. Jeno Bernath. (Medicinal & Aromatic Plants-Industrial Profiles Ser.). 360p. 1998. text 100.00 (*90-5702-271-0*, Harwood Acad Pubs) Gordon & Breach.

***Poppy & Ella.** Jeff Kaminsky. LC 99-28505. (Illus.). 48p. (J). 2000. 15.49 (*0-7868-2447-6*, Pub. by Hyprn Child) Time Warner.

Poppy & Ella. Jeff Kaminsky. LC 99-28505. (Illus.). 48p. (J). (ps-1). 2000. 14.99 (*0-7868-0511-0*, Pub. by Hyprn Ppbks) Little.

Poppy & Me. Robert Riche. 220p. mass mkt. 4.99 (*1-896329-67-5*) Picasso Publ.

***Poppy & Rye.** Avi. LC 97-31000. (Illus.). 182p. (J). (gr. 4-7). 1998. 14.95 (*0-380-97638-2*, Avon Bks) Morrow Avon.

***Poppy & Rye.** Avi. (Illus.). 208p. (J). (gr. 3-7). 1999. mass mkt. 4.95 (*0-380-79717-8*, Avon Bks) Morrow Avon.

Poppy & Rye. Avi. (J). 1997. 9.60 (*0-606-10906-4*, Pub. by Turtleback) Demco.

***Poppy Field.** Joseph Oleski. LC 98-90934. 1999. pap. 12.95 (*0-533-12992-3*) Vantage.

Poppy Flower: A Journey Thru Addiction. Penny Jones. Ed. by Barbara McCaig. (Illus.). 40p. (Orig.). 1987. pap. text 4.95 (*0-935201-18-1*) Affordable Adven.

Poppy Girl. large type ed. Jacqueline Gilbert. 268p. 1994. 27.99 (*0-7505-0635-0*, Pub. by Mgna Lrg Print) Ulverscroft.

Poppy, 1927. Georgia O'Keeffe. (Fine Art Jigsaw Puzzles Ser.). 1989. 9.95 (*0-934967-49-0*) Battle Rd Pr.

***Poppy Path.** large type ed. T. R. Wilson. 432p. 1999. 31.99 (*0-7089-9080-0*, Linford) Ulverscroft.

Poppy Penhaligon's Progress. Genevieve Lyons. 288p. 1996. 22.00 (*0-7278-4894-1*) Severn Hse.

Poppy Seed Cakes. Margery Clark. (Books for Young Readers). (J). (ps-1). 1986. 9.95 (*0-385-07457-3*) Doubleday.

Poppy Seeds. Clyde R. Bulla. (Illus.). 48p. (J). (gr. 2-5). 1994. pap. 3.99 (*0-14-036731-4*, PuffinBks) Peng Put Young Read.

***Poppy Seeds, Class Set.** unabridged ed. Clyde R. Bulla. (J). 1998. boxed set 70.70 incl. audio (*0-7887-2534-3*, 46704) Recorded Bks.

***Poppy Seeds, Homework.** unabridged ed. Clyde R. Bulla. (J). (gr. 2). 1998. boxed set 22.24 incl. audio (*0-7887-2229-8*, 40713) Recorded Bks.

Poppy Seeds, Etc. Fontaine M. Falkoff. LC 97-80786. (Illus.). 52p. 1997. pap. 5.00 (*1-886467-27-7*) WJM Press.

P

***Poppykettle Papers.** Michael Lawrence. (Illus.). 128p. (J). (gr. 3-7). 1999. 22.95 (*1-86205-282-4*, Pub. by Pavilion Bks Ltd) Trafalgar.

***Poppy's Babies.** Jill Barklem. 32p. (J). 2000. 9.95 (*0-689-83172-2*) S&S Trade.

Poppy's Chair. Karen Hesse. LC 91-47708. (Illus.). 32p. (J). (gr. k-3). 1993. lib. bdg. 14.95 (*0-02-743705-1*, Mac Bks Young Read) S&S Childrens.

***Poppy's Chair.** Karen Hesse. (Illus.). 32p. (J). (ps-3). 2000. pap. 5.99 (*0-439-16130-4*) Scholastic Inc.

Poppy's Clouds. Sharon C. Hare. LC 98-49050. (Illus.). 20p. (J). 1998. pap. 10.00 (*1-885938-16-0*) Cathdrl Fndtn Pr.

Poppy's Passion. large type ed. Helen Shelton. (Mills & Boon Large Print Ser.). 288p. 1998. 24.99 (*0-263-15412-2*, Pub. by Mills & Boon) Ulverscroft.

Poppy's Puppet. Patricia Lee Gauch. LC 98-51130. (Illus.). 32p. (J). (gr. k-3). 1999. 16.95 (*0-8050-5291-7*) H Holt & Co.

Poppy's Whale. Marie-Francine Hebert. 48p. 1996. pap. 5.95 (*0-929005-90-2*, Pub. by Sec Story Pr) LPC InBook.

Poppyseed. Stephen Cosgrove. (Serendipity Bks.). (Illus.). 32p. (Orig.). (J). (ps-3). 1996. pap. 4.99 (*0-8431-3924-2*, Price Stern) Peng Put Young Read.

Pop/Rock Ballads. (Easy Piano Ser.). 160p. 1995. otabind 14.95 (*0-7935-4890-X*, 00310072) H Leonard.

***Pop/Rock Collection.** 40p. 1999. pap. 19.95 (*0-7935-9357-3*) H Leonard.

***Pop/rock Hits.** 72p. 1999. pap. 7.95 (*1-57560-299-7*, Pub. by Cherry Lane) H Leonard.

***Pop/rock Hits.** 208p. 1999. otabind 14.95 (*1-57560-295-4*, Pub. by Cherry Lane) H Leonard.

***Pop/Rock Love Songs.** Contrib. by Cherry Lane Music Staff. 88p. 1999. otabind 10.95 (*1-57560-297-0*, Pub. by Cherry Lane) H Leonard.

Pops. Romulus Linney. 65p. 1987. pap. 5.25 (*0-8222-0906-3*) Dramatists Play.

Pops, No. 2. 48p. 1980. pap. 5.95 (*0-7935-0532-1*, 00276500) H Leonard.

Pops: Paul Whiteman, King of Jazz. Thomas A. Delong. LC 83-19291. (Illus.). 352p. 1983. 17.95 (*0-8329-0264-0*) New Win Pub.

Pops, Chops, & Crops. 2nd ed. Bobby L. Jackson. LC 89-51297. (Illus.). 32p. (J). (gr. k-4). 1994. reprint ed. 15.95 (*0-9634932-4-8*); reprint ed. pap. 7.95 (*0-9634932-5-6*) Multicult Pubns.

Pops of the 60's & 70's, Vol. 191. 1984. per. 10.95 (*0-7935-0703-0*, 00101865) H Leonard.

Pop's Secret. Maryann Townsend. LC 84-40773. (J). 1980. 11.95 (*0-201-07707-8*) HarpC Child Bks.

Pop's Truck. Honey Andersen & Bill Reinholdt. LC 93-18050. (Illus.). (J). 1994. write for info. (*0-383-03709-3*) SRA McGraw.

Popsicle Fish: Tales of Fathering. Michael Murphy. LC 96-22929. (Illus.). 180p. (Orig.). 1996. pap. 13.95 (*0-929173-23-6*) Health Press.

Popsicle Pony. Jill Stover. LC 93-79774. (J). (ps-3). 1994. 14.00 (*0-688-12392-9*, Wm Morrow) Morrow Avon.

Popsicles & Poems. Alan M. Hofmeister et al. (Reading for All Learners Ser.). (Illus.). (J). pap. write for info. (*1-56861-194-3*) Swift Lrn Res.

Popsicles Are Cold: Storybook for Young Children in Sign Languages. Sue Johnson. (Talking Fingers Bks.). (Illus.). 30p. (Orig.). (J). (ps-3). 1984. pap. 4.50 (*0-916708-12-8*) Modern Signs.

PopTerm - NVT for MS-DOS User's Guide. Rational Data Systems, Inc. Staff. 40p. 1992. pap. 5.50 incl. disk (*1-881378-04-7*) Rational Data.

PopTerm - NVT for Windows User's Guide. Rational Data Systems, Inc. Staff. 30p. 1992. pap. 5.50 incl. disk (*1-881378-05-5*) Rational Data.

PopTerm User's Guide. Rational Data Systems, Inc. Staff. 84p. 1992. pap. 4.00 incl. disk (*1-881378-00-4*) Rational Data.

Popula Literature in Ancient Egypt. A. Wiedemann. (African Studies). reprint ed. 10.00 (*0-938818-40-6*) ECA Assoc.

Populace. Elizabeth Treadwell. 68p. 1999. pap. 10.00 (*1-880713-16-0*, Pub. by AVEC Bks) SPD-Small Pr Dist.

***Popular.** Photos by Thierry Le Goues. (Illus.). 2000. 75.00 (*1-57687-075-8*, pwerHse Bks) pwerHse Cultrl.

Popular Abstracts. Ed. by Ray B. Browne & Christopher D. Geist. 1978. 13.95 (*0-87972-166-9*); pap. 7.95 (*0-87972-165-0*) Bowling Green Univ Popular Press.

Popular Account of the Ancient Egyptians. J. Gardner Wilkinson. (African Heritage Classical Research Studies). 419p. reprint ed. 40.00 (*0-938818-67-8*) ECA Assoc.

Popular Activities & Games for Blind, Visually Impaired & Disabled People. large type ed. Peter Rickards. (Illus.). 64p. 1986. pap. 19.95 (*0-9599747-8-4*) Am Foun Blind.

Popular Advertising Cuts of the Twenties & Thirties. Leslie E. Cabarga. LC 96-11365. (Pictorial Archive Ser.). 1996. pap. 8.95 (*0-486-29228-2*) Dover.

Popular Alienation: A Steamshovel Press Reade. Ed. by Kenn Thomas. LC 95-34668. (Illus.). 352p. (Orig.). 1995. pap. 19.95 (*1-881532-07-0*) IllumiNet Pr.

Popular American Housing: A Reference Guide. Ed. by Ruth Brent & Benyamin Schwarz. LC 94-47420. (American Popular Culture Ser.). 272p. 1995. lib. bdg. 79.50 (*0-313-28032-0*, Greenwood Pr) Greenwood.

Popular American Hymns/Spirituals: Piano. 28p. (Orig.). 1987. pap. 5.95 (*0-7692-1017-1*, PF0459) Wrner Bros.

***Popular American Literature of the 19th Century.** Ed. by Paul C. Gutjahr. (Illus.). 1488p. (C). 2000. pap. text 37.50 (*0-19-514140-7*) OUP.

***Popular American Recording Pioneers, 1895-1925.** Tim Gracyk & Frank Hoffmann. LC 99-49825. 444p. 2000. pap. 39.95 (*0-7890-1220-0*) Haworth Pr.

***Popular American Recording Pioneers, 1895-1925.** Tim Gracyk & Frank Hoffmann. LC 99-49825. 444p. 2000. 69.95 (*1-56024-993-5*) Haworth Pr.

Popular Amusements. Richard H. Edwards. LC 75-22812. (America in Two Centuries Ser.). 1976. reprint ed. 20.95 (*0-405-07686-X*) Ayer.

Popular Amusements: A Discourse. 2nd ed. Charles P. Krauth. 38p. 1997. reprint ed. pap. 2.50 (*1-891469-09-6*) Repristination.

Popular Amusements in Horse & Buggy America. Ed. by William L. Slout. LC 84-12310. (Clipper Studies in the Theater: No. 2). 208p. 1995. pap. 23.00 (*0-89370-461-X*) Millefleurs.

Popular Anatomy. Keath Fraser. LC 95-183798. 584p. 1995. pap. write for info. (*0-88984-149-7*) Porcup Quill.

Popular & Collectible Neckties: 1955 to the Present. Roseann Ettinger. LC 98-84541. (Illus.). 160p. 1998. pap. 29.95 (*0-7643-0516-6*) Schiffer.

Popular & Jazz Harmony. Daniel A. Ricigliano. 1967. 25.00 (*0-935058-03-6*) Donato Music.

Popular & Practical Introduction to Law Studies & to Every Department of the Legal Profession, 2 vols., Set. 3rd ed. Samuel Warren. LC 88-45751. (Warren's Law Studies). 1622p. 1988. reprint ed. 275.00 (*0-912004-68-1*) Gaunt.

Popular & Practical Science of Medieval England. Ed. by Lister M. Matheson. LC 93-72666. (Medieval Texts & Studies: No. 11). (Illus.). 425p. 1994. 68.00 (*0-937191-30-2*) Mich St U Pr.

Popular & the Serious in Select Twentieth-Century American Novels. Patrick D. Morrow. LC 92-4342. 162p. 1992. lib. bdg. 79.95 (*0-7734-9496-0*) E Mellen.

Popular Annuals of Eastern North America, 1865-1914. Peggy C. Newcomb. LC 84-1674. (Illus.). 208p. (Orig.). 1985. pap. 15.00 (*0-88402-138-6*) Dumbarton Oaks.

Popular Anti-Catholicism in Mid-Victorian Britain. Frank H. Wallis. LC 93-1752. (Texts & Studies in Religion: Vol. 60). 292p. 1993. 89.95 (*0-7734-9324-7*) E Mellen.

Popular Anti-Catholicism in Mid-Victorian England. D. G. Paz. 368p. (C). 1992. 47.50 (*0-8047-1984-5*) Stanford U Pr.

Popular Arias for Piano: Piano. 34p. (Orig.). 1996. pap. 10.95 (*1-57623-480-0*, AF9620) Wrner Bros.

Popular Art Deco: Depression Era Style & Design. Robert Heide & John Gilman. (Illus.). 228p. 1991. 39.95 (*1-55859-030-7*) Abbeville Pr.

Popular Arthurian Traditions. Ed. by Sally Slocum. LC 92-72942. 1992. 39.95 (*0-87972-561-3*); pap. 19.95 (*0-87972-562-1*) Bowling Green Univ Popular Press.

Popular Arts in America: A Reader. 2nd ed. Ed. by William M. Hammel. 501p. (C). 1977. pap. text 18.75 (*0-15-570742-6*) Harcourt Coll Pubs.

Popular Arts of Mexico: 1850-1950. Donna McMenamin. 240p. 1996. 59.95 (*0-7643-0026-1*) Schiffer.

Popular Astronomy. Simon Newcomb. (Notable American Authors Ser.). 1999. reprint ed. lib. bdg. 125.00 (*0-7812-4618-0*) Rprt Serv.

Popular Autocracy in Greece, 1936-41: A Political Biography of General Metaxas. P. J. Vatikiotis. LC 97-39080. 232p. 1998. 57.50 (*0-7146-4869-8*, Pub. by F Cass Pubs); pap. 25.00 (*0-7146-4445-5*) F Cass Pubs.

Popular Ballads for Classical Singers: High Voice. 1992. pap. 18.95 incl. audio (*0-7935-1057-0*, 00660204) H Leonard.

Popular Ballads for Classical Singers: Low Voice. 80p. 1992. pap. 18.95 (*0-7935-1058-9*, 00660205) H Leonard.

Popular Bands & Performers. Charles E. Claghorn. LC 94-42655. 480p. 1995. 79.00 (*0-8108-2976-2*) Scarecrow.

Popular Bear Art School Packages: Paint Kit, Countryside. Andy Cooke. (Illus.). 12p. (J). 1995. pap. 8.95 (*0-8120-8380-6*) Barron.

Popular Beliefs & Folklore Tradition in Siberia. Ed. by Vilmos Dioszegi. (Uralic & Altaic Ser.: No. 57). 1968. text 78.50 (*3-11-000041-5*) Mouton.

Popular Beliefs & Superstitions from North Carolina, Pt. 2 see **Frank C. Brown Collection of North Carolina Folklore**

Popular Beliefs & Superstitions from Utah. Anthon S. Cannon et al. Ed. by Wayland D. Hand & Jeannine E. Talley. LC 84-5286. 530p. reprint ed. pap. 164.30 (*0-7837-5538-4*, 204531200005) Bks Demand.

Popular Bible Dictionary see **Diccionario Popular de la Biblia**

Popular Bible Dictionary see **Diccionario. Popular De la Biblia**

Popular Bible Dictionary see **Diccionario Popular de la Biblia**

Popular Buddhism in China. Shao-ch'Ang Li. lib. bdg. 79.95 (*0-87968-539-5*) Krishna Pr.

Popular Buddhism in Japan: Shin Buddhist Religion & Culture. Esben Andreasen. LC 97-33209. 248p. 1997. text 39.00 (*0-8248-2027-4*, Latitude Twenty); pap. text 22.95 (*0-8248-2028-2*, Latitude Twenty) UH Pr.

Popular Card Games: How to Play & Win. Foulsham Editors. 83p. (Orig.). 1995. pap. 6.95 (*0-572-00161-4*, Pub. by Foulsham UK) Assoc Pubs Grp.

Popular Card Games: How to Play & Win. B. H. Wood & F. R. Ings. 83p. (Orig.). 1994. pap. 7.95 (*0-572-02001-5*, Pub. by W Foulsham) Trans-Atl Phila.

Popular Careers. Marilyn Funes & Alan Lazarus. Ed. by Benjamin Piltch. (Skyview Ser.). (Illus.). 64p. (YA). (gr. 7 up). 1980. 6.95 (*0-934618-01-1*) Learning Well.

Popular Carol Book: Music Edition, Words Edition. Cassell Publishing Staff. Ed. by Coleman et al. (Illus.). 1998. pap. text 23.95 (*0-264-67481-2*) A R Mowbray.

Popular Carol Book: Music Edition, Words Edition. Ed. by Coleman et al. (Illus.). 1998. pap. 9.50 (*0-264-67480-4*, Pub. by A R Mowbray) Cassell & Continuum.

Popular Catholicism in a World Church: Seven Case Studies in Inculturation. Ed. by Thomas Bamat & Jean-Paul Wiest. LC 98-55523. (Faith & Cultures Ser.). xii, 315p. 1999. pap. 24.00 (*1-57075-252-4*) Orbis Bks.

***Popular Chess Variants: Tournament.** David Pritchard. (Chess Bks.). (Illus.). 112p. 2000. pap. text 14.95 (*0-7134-8578-7*) B T B.

Popular Chinese Fables. Tr. by Wu Jingyu. (Illus.). 100p. 1996. 9.95 (*981-3029-95-1*, Pub. by Asiapac) China Bks.

Popular Chord Instructor. Brimhall. (Keyboard Chords Ser.). 1990. 6.95 (*0-685-32022-7*, T059) Hansen Ed Mus.

Popular Classics for Easy Piano. Robert Benedict. 40p. 1989. pap. 5.95 (*0-87166-567-0*, 94265) Mel Bay.

Popular Classics of the Great Composers Bk. 3: Arranged for Classical Guitar. Jason Waldron. 1997. pap. 14.95 (*0-947183-66-3*) Koala Pubns.

Popular Classics of the Great Composers Bk. 4: Arranged for Classical Guitar. Jason Waldron. 1997. pap. 14.95 (*0-947183-67-1*) Koala Pubns.

Popular Classics of the Great Composers Bk. 5: Arranged for Classical Guitar. Jason Waldron. 1997. pap. 14.95 (*0-947183-89-2*) Koala Pubns.

Popular Classics of the Great Composers Arranged for Classical Guitar, Bk. 2. Jason Waldron. (Progressive Ser.). 1997. pap. 14.95 incl. cd-rom (*0-947183-21-3*) Koala Pubns.

Popular Classics of the Great Composers Arranged for Classical Guitar, Bk. 6. Jason Waldron. (Progressive Ser.). (Illus.). 1997. pap. text 14.95 incl. audio compact disk (*1-875726-47-0*) Koala Pubns.

Popular Classics of the Great Composers Arranged for Classical Guitar Book. Jason Waldron. (Progressive Ser.). 1997. pap. text 14.95 incl. cd-rom (*0-947183-20-5*) Koala Pubns.

Popular Collecting & the Everyday Self: The Reinvention of Museums? Paul Martin. LC 98-17887. 1998. 85.00 (*0-7185-0170-5*) Bks Intl VA.

Popular Contention in Great Britain, 1758-1834. Charles Tilly. LC 94-48325. (Illus.). 512p. (C). 1995. 56.00 (*0-674-68980-1*) HUP.

Popular Culture. Iain Chambers. 1986. pap. 10.95 (*0-416-37680-0*) Routledge.

Popular Culture. Ed. by Roger Clestin & Eliane Dalmolin. 200p. 1997. pap. text 23.00 (*90-5699-551-0*) Gordon & Breach.

Popular Culture. Anne C. Francis. 87p. (C). 1995. pap. 44.00 (*0-949823-38-4*, Pub. by Deakin Univ) St Mut.

Popular Culture. Albert Goldbarth. LC 89-32882. (OSU Press - The Journal Award in Poetry Ser.). 95p. 1989. text 35.00 (*0-8142-0498-8*) Ohio St U Pr.

Popular Culture. Albert Goldbarth. LC 89-32882. (OSU Press - The Journal Award in Poetry Ser.). 95p. 1989. pap. 15.00 (*0-8142-0499-6*) Ohio St U Pr.

***Popular Culture.** C. Lee Harirngton & Diane D. Bielby. (Readings in Sociology Ser.). 368p. 2000. 62.95 (*0-631-21709-6*) Blackwell Pubs.

***Popular Culture.** C. Lee Harirngton & Diane D. Bielby. (Readings in Sociology Ser.). 368p. 2000. pap. 29.95 (*0-631-21710-X*) Blackwell Pubs.

Popular Culture. Isaac Sequeira. (C). 1991. 11.00 (*81-7018-654-4*, Pub. by BR Pub) S Asia.

Popular Culture. Ed. by David M. White. 1975. 27.95 (*0-405-06649-X*) Ayer.

Popular Culture: An Introduction. Carla Freccero. LC 99-6112. 1999. pap. 16.95 (*0-8147-2670-4*); text 50.00 (*0-8147-2669-0*) NYU Pr.

Popular Culture: An Introductory Text. Ed. by Jack Nachbar & Kevin Lause. LC 92-73539. (Illus.). 502p. (C). 1992. pap. 23.95 (*0-87972-572-9*) Bowling Green Univ Popular Press.

Popular Culture: Cavespace to Cyberspace. Marshall W. Fishwick. LC 98-42781. (Illus.). 304p. 1999. lib. bdg. 29.95 (*0-7890-0643-X*) Haworth Pr.

Popular Culture: Past & Present. Ed. by Bernard Waites et al. 326p. 1982. pap. 16.95 (*0-7099-1909-3*, Pub. by C Helm) Routldge.

Popular Culture: Schooling & Everyday Life. Henry A. Giroux et al. LC 89-35822. (Critical Studies in Education). 256p. (Orig.). 1989. pap. 18.95 (*0-89789-186-4*, G186, Bergin & Garvey) Greenwood.

Popular Culture: The Metropolitan Experience. Iain Chambers. (Communication Ser.). (Illus.). 256p. (C). 1986. pap. 18.99 (*0-415-02551-6*, 1022) Routledge.

Popular Culture & Acquisitions. Ed. by Allen Ellis. LC 92-17522. (Acquisitions Librarian Ser.: Vol. 8). 146p. 1993. 39.95 (*1-56024-299-X*) Haworth Pr.

Popular Culture & American Life: Selected Topics in the Study of Twentieth Century American Popular Culture. Martin W. Laforse & James A. Drake. LC 80-27809. 264p. (C). 1981. pap. text 24.95 (*0-88229-778-3*) Burnham Inc.

***Popular Culture & Corrections.** Robert M. Freeman. LC 00-32759. 2000. pap. write for info. (*1-56991-126-6*) Am Correctional.

Popular Culture & Critical Pedagogy: Reading, Constructing, Connecting. Ed. by Toby Daspit & John A. Weaver. LC 98-8645. (Pedagogy & Popular Culture Ser.: Vol. 2). 280p. 1998. 60.00 (*0-8153-2870-2*, SS1163) Garland.

***Popular Culture & Critical Pedagogy: Reading, Constructing, Connecting.** Ed. by Toby Daspit & John A. Weaver. (Pedagogy & Popular Culture Ser.: Vol. 2). 232p. (C). 2000. pap. 24.99 (*0-8153-3864-3*, Falmer Pr) Taylor & Francis.

Popular Culture & Elite Culture in France, 1400-1750. Robert Muchembled. LC 84-25078. 336p. reprint ed. pap. 104.20 (*0-7837-8813-4*, 204945900011) Bks Demand.

Popular Culture & High Art: An Analysis & Evaluation of Taste. 2nd rev. ed. Herbert J. Gans. LC 99-40910. 272p. 1999. pap. 16.00 (*0-465-02609-5*, Pub. by Basic) HarpC.

Popular Culture & High Culture: An Analysis & Evaluation of Taste. 2nd ed. Herbert J. Gans. LC 74-79287. 192p. 1977. pap. 15.00 (*0-465-09717-0*, Pub. by Basic) HarpC.

Popular Culture & Mass Communication in Twentieth-Century France. Ed. by Nicholas Hewitt & Rosemary Chapman. LC 92-8511. (Illus.). 300p. 1992. lib. bdg. 89.95 (*0-7734-9499-5*) E Mellen.

Popular Culture & Media Events. Ed. by Vincent Mosco & Janet Wasko. LC 82-11592. (Critical Communications Review Ser.: Vol. 3). 336p. 1985. text 78.50 (*0-89391-279-4*) Ablx Pub.

Popular Culture & Performance in the Victorian City. Peter Bailey. LC 99-174955. (Illus.). 320p. (C). 1998. text 59.95 (*0-521-57417-X*) Cambridge U Pr.

Popular Culture & Political Change in Modern America. Ed. by Ronald W. Edsforth & Larry Bennett. LC 90-47621. (SUNY Series in Popular Culture & Political Change in Modern America). 232p. (C). 1991. pap. text 21.95 (*0-7914-0766-7*) State U NY Pr.

Popular Culture & Political Change in Modern America. Ed. by Ronald W. Edsforth & Larry Bennett. LC 90-47621. (SUNY Series in Popular Culture & Political Change in Modern America). 232p. (C). 1991. text 65.50 (*0-7914-0765-9*) State U NY Pr.

Popular Culture & Popular Movements in Reformation Germany. R. W. Scribner. 380p. 1988. 60.00 (*0-907628-81-8*) Hambledon Press.

Popular Culture & Popular Protest in Late Medieval & Early Modern Europe. Michael Mullett. 256p. 1987. lib. bdg. 49.95 (*0-7099-3566-8*, Pub. by C Helm) Routldge.

Popular Culture & Social Relations. Tony Bennett et al. 224p. 1986. pap. 34.95 (*0-335-15107-8*) OpUniv Pr.

Popular Culture & the Motor Car. David W. Thoms et al. LC 97-35619. 307p. Date not set. text 78.95 (*1-85928-461-2*, Pub. by Ashgate Pub) Ashgate Pub Co.

Popular Culture as Metaphor. 2nd ed. Lawrence E Sneden. 120p. (C). 1994. 23.80 (*0-536-58579-2*) Pearson Custom.

Popular Culture As Method: An Approach to Social Studies Instruction. 2nd ed. George Chilcoat. 288p. (C). 1995. pap. text, per. 30.95 (*0-8403-9725-9*) Kendall-Hunt.

Popular Culture, Crime & Justice. Frankie Y. Bailey & Donna C. Hale. LC 97-24853. (Criminal Justice Ser.). 450p. (C). 1997. 36.95 (*0-534-51975-X*) Wadsworth Pub.

Popular Culture, Educational Discourse, & Mathematics. Peter M. Appelbaum. LC 94-46206. (SUNY Series, Education & Culture: Critical Factors in the Formation of Character & Community in American Life). 309p. (C). 1995. text 57.50 (*0-7914-2269-0*); pap. text 18.95 (*0-7914-2270-4*) State U NY Pr.

Popular Culture Genres: Theories & Texts. Arthur A. Berger. (Foundations of Popular Culture Ser.: Vol. 2). 160p. (C). 1992. text 42.00 (*0-8039-4725-9*); pap. text 18.95 (*0-8039-4726-7*) Sage.

Popular Culture in America: 1960. Loss. LC 98-72416. (C). 1998. pap. text 23.50 (*0-15-504146-0*, Pub. by Harcourt Coll Pubs) Harcourt.

Popular Culture in America, 1800-1925, 27 vols. David M. White. 1975. 759.50 (*0-405-06360-1*) Ayer.

***Popular Culture in American History.** Jim Cullen. 2000. 64.95 (*0-631-21957-9*); pap. 29.95 (*0-631-21958-7*) Blackwell Pubs.

Popular Culture in Early Modern Europe. rev. ed. Peter Burke. (Illus.). 416p. 1994. pap. 31.95 (*1-85928-102-8*, Pub. by Scolar Pr) Ashgate Pub Co.

Popular Culture in England, c. 1500-1850. Ed. by Tim Harris. LC 94-32994. 1995. pap. 19.95 (*0-312-12464-3*); text 55.00 (*0-312-12463-5*) St Martin.

Popular Culture in England 1550-1750. Barry Reay. LC 98-16046. (Themes in British Social History Ser.). 288p. (C). 1998. pap. 24.60 (*0-582-48954-7*) Longman.

Popular Culture in Medieval Cairo. Boaz Shoshan. LC 92-34084. (Studies in Islamic Civilization). (Illus.). 164p. (C). 1993. text 59.95 (*0-521-43209-X*) Cambridge U Pr.

Popular Culture in the Classroom: Teaching & Researching Critical Media Literacy. Donna E. Alvermann et al. LC 98-54821. (Literacy Studies Ser.). 1999. pap. 21.95 (*0-87207-245-2*, 245) Intl Reading.

Popular Culture in the Middle Ages. Ed. by Josie P. Campbell. LC 86-71408. 157p. 1986. 20.95 (*0-87972-339-4*) Bowling Green Univ Popular Press.

Popular Culture in the 20th Century. (Twentieth Century Ser.). (Illus.). (YA). (gr. 6 up). 29.95 (*0-614-21968-X*) Random.

Popular Culture of Modern Art: Picasso, Duchamp, & Avant-Gardism c. 1909-1917. Jeffrey S. Weiss. LC 94-892. (Illus.). 256p. 1994. 52.00 (*0-300-05895-0*) Yale U Pr.

Popular Culture, Schooling, & Everyday Life. Henry A. Giroux et al. LC 89-35822. (Critical Studies in Education). 256p. (Orig.). 1989. 59.95 (*0-89789-187-2*, H187, Bergin & Garvey) Greenwood.

Popular Cultures: Rock Music, Sport & the Politics of Pleasure. David Rowe. (Media Culture & Society Ser.). 224p. 1995. 69.95 (*0-8039-7700-X*); pap. 25.95 (*0-8039-7701-8*) Sage.

Popular Defense & Ecological Struggles. Paul Virilio. 120p. 1990. pap. 6.00 (*0-936756-05-5*) Autonomedia.

Popular Deities, Emblems & Images of Nepal. Dhurba K. Deep. x, 170p. 1993. 20.00 (*81-85693-25-0*, Pub. by Nirala Pubns) Nataraj Bks.

P

Popular Democracy & the Creation Imagination: The Writings of C. L. R. James 1950-1963. Anna Grimshaw. 50p. 1991. pap. 10.00 (*0-918266-28-9*) Smyrna.

Popular Development: Rethinking the Theory & Practice of Development. James Brohman. LC 95-42639. 352p. (C). 1996. 66.95 (*1-55786-315-6*); pap. text 28.95 (*1-55786-316-4*) Blackwell Pubs.

Popular Devotionals, Set. Incl. Epistles-Now. Leslie F. Brandt. (Illus.). 187p. 1986. pap. 8.99 (*0-570-04427-8*, 12-3032); Jesus-Now. Leslie Brandt. 192p. 1986. pap. 8.99 (*0-570-04428-6*); 1986. Set boxed set 28.99 (*0-570-04425-1*, 12-3030) Concordia.

Popular Dictionary of Buddhism. Christmas Humphreys. LC 97-24605. (Illus.). 240p. 1997. pap. 14.95 (*0-8442-0419-6*, 04196) NTC Contemp Pub Co.

Popular Dictionary of Hinduism. Karel Werner. LC 94-165541. 228p. (C). 1996. pap. text 20.00 (*0-7007-0279-2*, Pub. by Curzon Pr Ltd) UH Pr.

Popular Dictionary of Hinduism. Karel Werner. LC 97-24420. (Illus.). 192p. 1997. pap. 14.95 (*0-8442-0421-8*, 04218) NTC Contemp Pub Co.

Popular Dictionary of Islam. Ian R. Netton. LC 92-13600. 288p. (C). 1992. pap. 19.95 (*0-7007-0233-4*, Pub. by Curzon Pr Ltd) Paul & Co Pubs.

Popular Dictionary of Islam. Ian R. Netton. LC 92-13600. 244p. 1992. pap. 18.50 (*0-391-03756-0*) Humanities.

Popular Dictionary of Islam. Ian R. Netton. LC 97-23830. (Illus.). 288p. 1997. pap. 14.95 (*0-8442-0422-6*, 04226) NTC Contemp Pub Co.

Popular Dictionary of Judaism. Lavinia Cohn-Sherbok & Dan Cohn-Sherbok. LC 95-229166. 216p. (C). 1995. 45.00 (*0-7007-0366-7*); pap. 19.95 (*0-7007-0357-8*, Pub. by Curzon Pr Ltd) Paul & Co Pubs.

Popular Dictionary of Judaism. Lavinia Cohn-Sherbok & Dan Cohn-Sherbok. LC 97-21950. (Illus.). 208p. 1997. pap. 14.95 (*0-8442-0423-4*, 04234) NTC Contemp Pub Co.

Popular Dictionary of Judaism. Hugh J. Schonfield. 1966. pap. 1.75 (*0-8065-0075-1*, 232, Citadel Pr) Carol Pub Group.

Popular Dictionary of Shinto. Brian Bocking. LC 97-21947. (Illus.). 288p. 1997. pap. 14.95 (*0-8442-0425-0*, 04250) NTC Contemp Pub Co.

Popular Diplomacy & War. Sisley Huddleston. 9.00 (*0-8159-6508-7*) Devin.

***Popular Dissent, Human Agency & Global Politics.** Roland Bleiker. (Cambridge Studies in International Relations: No. 70). 313p. (C). 2000. text 59.95 (*0-521-77099-8*); pap. text 22.95 (*0-521-77829-8*) Cambridge U Pr.

Popular Disturbances in England, 1832-1939. Stevenson. 1999. pap. text. write for info. (*0-582-08099-1*, Pub. by Addison-Wesley) Longman.

Popular Dogs Stickers & Seals: 48 Full Color Pressure Sensitive Designs. John Green. (Illus.). (J). (gr. 4-7). 1991. pap. 5.95 (*0-486-26900-0*) Dover.

Popular Education in Quebec: Strengthening Social Movements. Adele Chene & Michael Chervin. 1991. 13.95 (*0-88379-051-3*) A A A C E.

Popular Elizabethan Tunes for Recorder & Guitar. Frederick M. Noad. (Ensemble Ser.). (Illus.). 1977. pap. 9.95 (*0-8256-9963-0*, AY15133, Ariel) Music Sales.

Popular Encyclopaedia of Art, Vol. 1. V. Polevoi. (RUS.). 447p. (C). 1986. 160.00 (*0-7855-6472-1*, Pub. by Collets) St Mut.

Popular Encyclopaedia of Art, Vol. 2. V. Polevoi. (RUS.). 432p. (C). 1986. 160.00 (*0-7855-6471-3*, Pub. by Collets) St Mut.

Popular Encyclopedia of Natural Sciences. W. B. Carpenter. 584p. 1991. 300.00 (*81-7041-245-5*, Pub. by Scientific Pubs) St Mut.

Popular English - Russian & Russian - English Dictionary. Ed. by L. P. Popova. (ENG & RUS.). 432p. 1995. 12.95 (*0-8285-5206-1*) Firebird NY.

Popular English Ballads, Vol. 1. Ed. by R. Brimley Johnson. LC 72-152151. (Granger Index Reprint Ser.). (Illus.). 1977. reprint ed. 24.95 (*0-8369-6257-5*) Ayer.

Popular English Ballads, Vol. 2. Ed. by R. Brimley Johnson. LC 72-152151. (Granger Index Reprint Ser.). (Illus.). 1977. reprint ed. 24.95 (*0-8369-6258-3*) Ayer.

Popular English Ballads, Vol. 3. Ed. by R. Brimley Johnson. LC 72-152151. (Granger Index Reprint Ser.). (Illus.). 1977. reprint ed. 23.95 (*0-8369-6259-1*) Ayer.

Popular English Ballads, Vol. 4. Ed. by R. Brimley Johnson. LC 72-152151. (Granger Index Reprint Ser.). (Illus.). 1977. reprint ed. 23.95 (*0-8369-6260-5*) Ayer.

Popular English-Hebrew-Russian Dictionary. 409p. 1994. 15.00 (*0-8285-5124-3*) Firebird NY.

Popular Entertainment, Class & Politics in Munich, 1900-1923. Robert E. Sackett. 206p. 1982. 36.50 (*0-674-68985-2*) HUP.

Popular Entertainment Research: How to Do It & How to Use It. Barbara J. Pruett. LC 92-3800. 593p. 1992. 66.00 (*0-8108-2501-5*) Scarecrow.

Popular Entertainments Through the Ages. Samuel McKechnie. LC 78-79998. (Illus.). 1972. reprint ed. 23.95 (*0-405-08768-3*) Ayer.

Popular European Cinema. Ed. by Richard Dyer & Ginette Vincendeau. LC 91-40138. (Illus.). 280p. (C). 1992. pap. 22.99 (*0-415-06803-7*, A9576) Routledge.

***Popular Evolution: Life-Lessons from Anthropology.** Joseph L. Popp. LC 00-105072. (Illus.). xviii, 300p. 2000. 39.95 (*0-9701255-7-7*) Man & Nature.

Popular Exposition of Methodist Theology. Charles O. Eldridge. pap. 7.99 (*0-88019-081-7*) Schmul Pub Co.

Popular Expression & National Identity in Puerto Rico: The Struggle for Self, Community, & Nation. Lillian Guerra. LC 98-16217. (Illus.). 432p. 1998. 49.95 (*0-8130-1594-4*) U Press Fla.

Popular Favorites. Ed. by Carol Cuellar. (Grand Duets for Piano Ser.). 112p. (Orig.). (YA). 1997. pap. text 12.95 (*0-7692-0108-3*) Wrner Bros.

Popular Fiction. Ed. by Hoppenstand. LC 97-35011. 800p. (C). 1997. pap. text 49.00 (*0-321-01164-3*) Addison-Wesley Educ.

Popular Fiction. Gary Hoppenstand. 18.00 (*0-321-01974-1*) Addison-Wesley Educ.

Popular Fiction. James Sherry. LC 85-61017. (Roof Bks.). 86p. (Orig.). 1985. pap. text 6.00 (*0-937804-15-0*) Segue NYC.

Popular Fiction by Women 1660-1730: An Anthology. Ed. by Paula R. Backsheider & John J. Richetti. LC 96-31093. (Illus.). 368p. 1997. text 90.00 (*0-19-871136-0*); pap. text 19.95 (*0-19-871137-9*) OUP.

Popular Fiction in England, 1914-1918. Harold Orel. LC 91-36651. 256p. 1992. 29.95 (*0-8131-1789-5*) U Pr of Ky.

Popular Fictions: Essays in Literature & History. Ed. by Peter Humm et al. (New Accents Ser.). 224p. 1987. 27.50 (*0-416-90040-2*, 1168); pap. 13.95 (*0-416-90050-X*, 9921) Routledge.

Popular '50s & '60s Glass: Color along the River. Leslie A. Pina. LC 95-11909. (Books for Collectors Ser.). (Illus.). 176p. 1995. 29.95 (*0-88740-829-X*) Schiffer.

Popular Film & Television Comedy. Steve Neale & Frank Krutnik. 304p. (C). 1990. pap. 20.99 (*0-415-04692-0*, A4315) Routledge.

Popular Financial Delusions. Robert L. Smitley. LC 63-18275. 1963. reprint ed. pap. 21.00 (*0-87034-004-2*) Fraser Pub Co.

Popular Folks Songs 1. Carmela Mercuri. (Dear Teacher. I've Always Wanted to Play the Piano Ser.), (Illus.). 32p. (Orig.). 1982. pap. 5.95 (*0-935474-02-1*, CAR1100) Carousel Pubns Ltd.

Popular French Romanticism: Authors, Readers, & Books in the 19th Century. James S. Allen. LC 80-27129. (Illus.). 307p. 1981. reprint ed. pap. 95.20 (*0-608-07588-4*, 205990300010) Bks Demand.

Popular Front & the Progressive Tradition: Socialists, Liberals & the Quest for Unity, 1884-1939. David Blaazer. 263p. (C). 1992. text 59.95 (*0-521-41383-4*) Cambridge U Pr.

Popular Fronts: Chicago & African-American Cultural Politics, 1935-46. Bill Mullen. LC 98-19740. 248p. 1999. pap. 16.95 (*0-252-06748-7*) U of Ill Pr.

Popular Fronts: Chicago & African-American Cultural Politics, 1935-46. Bill Mullen. LC 98-19740. (Illus.). 242p. 1999. 39.95 (*0-252-02440-0*) U of Ill Pr.

Popular Furniture of the 1920s & 1930s. LC 97-80769. (Illus.). 226p. 1998. pap. 29.95 (*0-7643-0431-3*) Schiffer.

Popular Games for Positive Players. Sher. 192p. 1998. pap. text 42.00 (*0-12-784565-8*) Acad Pr.

Popular Garden Birds: How to Identify Them, Attract Them, & Make Them Welcome. Joe Firmin. (Illus.). 96p. (Orig.). 1988. pap. 17.95 (*0-572-01445-7*, Pub. by W Foulsham) Trans-Atl Phila.

Popular German Stories. Ed. by F. W. Lieder. (GER.). (Orig.). pap. text 9.95 (*0-89197-351-6*) Irvington.

Popular Government. Henry S. Maine. LC 76-26329. 1977. reprint ed. 8.50 (*0-913966-14-2*) Liberty Fund.

Popular Government & the Supreme Court: Securing the Public Good & Private Rights. Lane V. Sunderland. LC 95-31164. 374p. (C). 1995. 40.00 (*0-7006-0743-9*) U Pr of KS.

Popular Government in an African Town: Kita, Mali. Nicholas S. Hopkins. LC 70-162528. 1995. lib. bdg. 30.00 (*0-226-35173-4*) U Ch Pr.

Popular Guide Through the Old Testament. Mary Reed Newland. 280p. 1999. pap. 16.95 (*0-88489-544-0*) St Marys.

Popular Guide to Classical Music. Anne Gray. LC 92-21111. 1993. 19.95 (*1-55972-165-0*, Birch Ln Pr) Carol Pub Group.

Popular Guide to Classical Music. Anne Gray. LC 92-21111. (Illus.). 368p. 1996. pap. 16.95 (*0-8065-1723-9*, Citadel Pr) Carol Pub Group.

Popular Guide to Garden Ponds. Compiled by Dick Mills. 1992. 17.95 (*1-56465-104-5*, 16012) Tetra Pr.

Popular Guide to Minority Rights. Ed. by Y. N. Kly. 224p. (Orig.). 1995. pap. 14.95 (*0-932863-19-1*) Clarity Pr.

Popular Guide to the Mass. William Marrevee. 174p. (Orig.). 1992. pap. 9.95 (*0-912405-93-7*, Pastoral Press) OR Catholic.

Popular Guide to Tropical Aquarium Fishes. Dick Mills. 320p. 1993. 22.95 (*1-56465-109-6*, 16016) Tetra Pr.

Popular Guitar Music. Barry Pollack. 256p. 1985. 16.95 (*0-13-685629-2*) P-H.

Popular History of American Invention, 2 vols., Set. Ed. by Waldemar B. Kaempffert. LC 74-9385. (Illus.). reprint ed. 125.00 (*0-404-11921-2*) AMS Pr.

Popular History of Astronomy in the Nineteenth Century. Agnes M. Clerke. LC 70-166614. 1908. reprint ed. 79.00 (*0-403-01492-1*) Scholarly.

Popular History of Greece: From the Earliest Period to the Roman Empire. D. Rose. Ed. by H. W. Dulcken. 30.00 (*0-8196-2866-2*) Biblo.

Popular History of Music from the Earliest Times until the Present. rev. ed. William S. Mathews. LC 74-173058. reprint ed. 49.50 (*0-404-07212-7*) AMS Pr.

Popular History of Philosophy. Contrib. by Teodoro De La Torre. 411p. 1998. 18.00 (*0-89555-481-X*) TAN Bks Pubs.

Popular History of Priestcraft in All Ages & Nations. William Howitt. 290p. 1998. reprint ed. pap. 19.95 (*0-7661-0216-5*) Kessinger Pub.

Popular History of the Archdiocese of New York. Florence D. Cohalan. LC 82-84246. (Monographs: Vol. 37). (Illus.). xviii, 354p. 1983. 15.00 (*0-930060-17-2*) US Cath Hist.

Popular History of the Catholic Church. Carl Koch. 304p. 1997. pap. 15.95 (*0-88489-395-2*) St Marys.

Popular Hits for Piano, Vol. 2. Ed. by Tony Esposito. 32p. (Orig.). 1997. pap. 5.95 (*0-7692-0074-5*, AF9749) Wrner Bros.

Popular Imagery of Moral Hysteria see Pedophiles on Parade

Popular Images--Personal Visions: The Art of William Hawkins, 1895-1990. Gary Schwindler. Ed. by Norma J. Roberts. (Illus.). 65p. (Orig.). 1990. pap. 8.95 (*0-918881-23-4*) Columbus Mus Art.

Popular Images of American Presidents. Ed. by William C. Spragens. LC 87-24944. 641p. 1988. lib. bdg. 125.00 (*0-313-22899-X*, SAP/, Greenwood Pr) Greenwood.

Popular Images of the Presidency: From Washington to Lincoln. Noble E. Cunningham, Jr. (Illus.). 328p. (C). 1991. 39.95 (*0-8262-0782-0*) U of Mo Pr.

Popular Indonesian Literature of the Qur'an, No. 72. Howard M. Federspiel. (Modern Indonesia Project Ser.). 172p. 1994. pap. 14.00 (*0-87763-038-0*) Cornell Mod Indo.

Popular Influence upon Public Policy: Petitioning in Eighteenth-Century Virginia, 10. Raymond C. Bailey. LC 78-73792. (Contributions in Legal Studies: No. 10). (Illus.). 203p. 1979. 49.95 (*0-313-20892-1*, BPP/, Greenwood Pr) Greenwood.

Popular Instrumental Hits for Tenor Sax. Ed. by Tony Esposito. 32p. (Orig.). 1997. pap. text 7.95 (*1-57623-999-3*, IF9710) Wrner Bros.

Popular Interset in Psychiatric Remedies: A Study in Social Control. Egon Bittner. Ed. by Harriet Zuckerman & Robert K. Merton. LC 79-8977. (Dissertations on Sociology Ser.). 1980. lib. bdg. 26.95 (*0-405-12953-X*) Ayer.

Popular Irish Poetry. Ed. & Intro. by Louis Bell. (Illus.). 96p. (Orig.). 1995. pap. 7.95 (*0-7171-2270-0*, Pub. by Gill & MacMill) Irish Bks Media.

Popular Irish Songs. Florence Leniston. 160p. 1992. pap. 9.95 (*0-486-26755-5*) Dover.

Popular Irish Songs & Ballads for Easy Piano. 48p. pap. 15.95 (*0-685-69132-2*, AM75110) Music Sales.

Popular Jamaican Sayings: Brawta Edition. Edna Bennett. (Wisdom Ser.). 96p. (Orig.). 1997. pap. 9.95 (*1-885778-18-X*) Seaburn.

Popular Jazz Songbook. Ed. by Tony Esposito. 100p. (YA). 1995. pap. text 14.95 (*0-89724-628-4*, MF9513) Wrner Bros.

Popular Jewelry of the 60s, 70s & 80s. Roseann Ettinger. LC 96-71095. (Illus.). 192p. 1997. pap. 29.95 (*0-88740-998-9*) Schiffer.

Popular Jewelry, 1840-1940. rev. ed. Roseann Ettinger. (Illus.). 176p. 1997. pap. 29.95 (*0-7643-0133-0*) Schiffer.

Popular Justice: A History of American Criminal Justice. 2nd ed. Samuel Walker. LC 97-8994. 304p. (C). 1997. text 49.95 (*0-19-507450-5*); pap. text 21.95 (*0-19-507451-3*) OUP.

Popular Justice & Community Regeneration: Pathways of Indigenous Reform. Kayleen M. Hazlehurst. LC 94-42815. 264p. 1995. 65.00 (*0-275-95131-6*, Praeger Pubs) Greenwood.

***Popular Law-Making: A Study of the Origin, History & Present Tendencies of Law.** fac. ed. Frederic Jesup Stimson. LC 00-22513. 2000. write for info. (*1-58477-094-5*) Lawbk Exchange.

Popular Law-Making: A Study of the Origin, History, & Present Tendencies of Law-Making by Statute. Frederic J. Stimson. xii, 390p. 1997. reprint ed. 120.00 (*1-56169-244-1*) Gaunt.

Popular Lectures on Mathematical Logic. Hao Wang. LC 93-4555. (Illus.). ix, 283p. 1993. reprint ed. pap. 8.95 (*0-486-67632-3*) Dover.

Popular Lectures on Theosophy, 1919. Annie W. Besant. 121p. 1996. reprint ed. pap. 16.95 (*1-56459-545-5*) Kessinger Pub.

***Popular Legacy: Studies in Cultural Practices & Poetics.** Ed. by John Trimbur. (Pittsburgh Ser. in Composition, Literacy, & Culture). 320p. 2001. 45.00 (*0-8229-4136-8*) U of Pittsburgh Pr.

Popular Legal Delusions. Mark Rollinson. viii, 169p. 1992. 22.95 (*0-9614303-6-2*) Summertown.

***Popular Literacy: Studies in Cultural Practices & Poetics.** Ed. by John Trimbur. (Pittsburgh Ser. in Composition, Literacy, & Culture). 320p. 2001. pap. 19.95 (*0-8229-5743-4*) U of Pittsburgh Pr.

Popular Literature: Poe's Not So Soon Forgotten Lore. J. Lasley Dameron. Ed. by Averil J. Kadis. 1980. pap. 2.50 (*0-910556-16-4*) Enoch Pratt.

Popular Literature & the Construction of British National Identity, 1707-1850. John A. Taylor. 224p. 1997. pap. 49.95 (*1-57309-199-5*) Intl Scholars.

Popular Literature & the Construction of British National Identity, 1707-1850. John A. Taylor. LC 96-45178. 224p. 1997. 69.95 (*1-57309-136-7*) Intl Scholars.

Popular Literature in Late Byzantium. Elizabeth Jeffreys & Michael Jeffreys. (Collected Studies: No. CS170). (Illus.). 342p. (C). 1983. reprint ed. lib. bdg. 124.95 (*0-86078-118-6*, Pub. by Variorum) Ashgate Pub Co.

Popular Literature in Victorian Scotland: Language, Fiction & the Press. Ed. by William Donaldson. (Illus.). 176p. 1986. text 27.95 (*0-08-034513-1*, Pub. by Aberdeen U Pr); pap. text 18.00 (*0-08-034515-8*, Pub. by Aberdeen U Pr) Macmillan.

Popular Literature of Ancient Egypt, 1902. A. Wiedemann. 52p. 1996. reprint ed. pap. 9.95 (*1-56459-604-4*) Kessinger Pub.

Popular Literature of Medieval England. Ed. by Thomas J. Heffernan. LC 84-26959. (Tennessee Studies in Literature: No. 28). (Illus.). 344p. 1985. reprint ed. pap. 106.70 (*0-608-02610-7*, 206326800004) Bks Demand.

Popular Literatures in Africa. Bernth Lindfors. per. 12.95 (*0-86543-221-X*) Africa World.

Popular Literatures in Africa. Bernth Lindfors. 1996. 45.00 (*0-86543-220-1*) Africa World.

Popular Management Books: How They Are Made & What They Mean for Organisations. Staffan Furusten. LC 99-18144. 1999. pap. write for info. (*0-415-21219-7*) Routledge.

***Popular Management Books: How They Are Made & What They Mean for Organisations.** Staffan Furusten. LC 99-18144. 192p. (C). 1999. text. write for info. (*0-415-21218-9*) Routledge.

Popular Manual for Wooden House Construction. 95p. 1990. 12.00 (*92-1-106244-6*, 90.III.E.6) UN.

Popular Mechanics: Houseworks :Guide to Understanding Your Home. Black & Decker Staff. LC 98-36739. (Illus.). 160p. 1998. pap. text 19.95 (*0-86573-772-X*) Creat Pub Intl.

Popular Mechanics Home How-To. Albert Jackson & David Day. Ed. by Ann Bramson. LC 88-17760. (Illus.). 512p. 2000. 30.00 (*0-688-08512-1*, Hearst) Hearst Commns.

Popular Mechanics Housewares. Ed. by Popular Mechanics Editors. 1924. write for info. (*0-688-16399-8*, Hearst) Hearst Commns.

***Popular Mechanics Kid's.** 2nd ed. Popular Mechanics Staff. 2000. pap. Morrow Avon.

***Popular Mechanics Kids.** 2nd ed. Popular Mechanics Staff. 64p. 2000. 16.95 (*0-688-17798-0*, Wm Morrow) Morrow Avon.

***Popular Mechanics 1998.** Popular Mechanics Editors. (Illus.). 160p. 1998. 24.95 (*0-688-16137-5*, Hearst) Hearst Commns.

Popular Mechanics Saturday Mechanic. Popular Mechanics Editors. LC 90-25333. 1994. 22.00 (*0-688-12963-3*, Hearst) Hearst Commns.

Popular Medical Encyclopedia. B. V. Petrovskih. (RUS.). 704p. 1984. 85.00 (*0-8288-1860-6*, M15422) Fr & Eur.

Popular Medicine in Puntarenas, Costa Rica: Urban & Societal Features see Community Culture & National Change

Popular Medicine in Seventeenth-Century England. Doreen E. Nagy. LC 88-70523. 140p. (C). 1988. 26.95 (*0-87972-435-8*); pap. 13.95 (*0-87972-436-6*) Bowling Green Univ Popular Press.

Popular Medicine in Thirteenth - Century England: Introduction & Texts. Tony Hunt. (Illus.). 478p. (C). 1994. reprint ed. 99.00 (*0-85991-290-6*) Boydell & Brewer.

***Popular Misconceptions about Instrumental Theory & Technique: And Other Published Articles - Tech - Theory & Philosophy of Music.** Donald W. Stauffer. (Illus.). 216p. 1999. pap. 19.95 (*1-929263-04-X*) Stauffer Pr.

Popular Mobilization in Mexico: The Teachers' Movement, 1977-87. Joe Foweraker. LC 92-33165. 220p. (C). 1993. text 74.95 (*0-521-44147-1*) Cambridge U Pr.

***Popular Modernity in America: Experience, Technology, Mythohistory.** Michael Thomas Carroll. (C). 2000. text 57.50 (*0-7914-4713-8*) State U NY Pr.

***Popular Modernity in America: Experience, Technology, Mythohistory.** Michael Thomas Carroll. 2000. pap. 18.95 (*0-7914-4714-6*) State U NY Pr.

Popular Mood of America, 1860-1890. Lewis O. Saum. LC 89-70493. 294p. 1990. reprint ed. pap. 91.20 (*0-608-03478-9*, 206418800008) Bks Demand.

Popular Movements & Political Change in Mexico. Ed. by Joe Foweraker & Ann L. Craig. LC 90-34593. 312p. 1990. pap. text 19.95 (*1-55587-219-0*) L Rienner.

***Popular Movements & State Formation in Revolutionary Mexico: The Agraristas & Cristeros of Michoacan.** Jennie Purnell. 1999. write for info. (*0-8223-2282-X*) Duke.

***Popular Movements & State Formation in Revolutionary Mexico: The Agraristas & Cristeros of Michoacan.** Jennie Purnell. LC 98-46237. (Illus.). 288p. 1999. pap. 17.95 (*0-8223-2314-1*) Duke.

***Popular Music.** Stephen Burt. LC 99-43627. 96p. 1999. pap. 14.95 (*0-87081-555-5*) Univ Pr Colo.

Popular Music, Vol. 13, 1988. Bruce Pollock. 1993. 75.00 (*0-8103-4945-0*) Gale.

Popular Music: An Annotated Index of Popular Songs. Ed. by Nat Shapiro. Incl. Vol. 10, 1986. 168p. 1986. 80.00 (*0-8103-0849-5*); Vol. 8, 1975-1979. 1984. 84.00 (*0-8103-0846-0*); Vol. 9, 1980-1984. 350p. 1986. 84.00 (*0-8103-0848-7*); Vol. 4, 1930-1939. Popular Music: An Annotated Index of Popular Songs. 1968. 75.00 (*0-8103-0842-8*); Vol. 5, 1920-1929. Popular Music: An Annotated Index of Popular Songs. 1969. 75.00 (*0-8103-0843-6*); Vol. 6, 1965-1969. Popular Music: An Annotated Index of Popular Songs. 1973. 84.00 (*0-8103-0844-4*); 1984. 75.00 (*0-8103-0840-1*) Gale.

Popular Music: An Annotated Index of Popular Songs, Vol. 1, 1950-1959. Ed. by Nat Shapiro. Incl. Vol. 10, 1986. 168p. 1986. 80.00 (*0-8103-0849-5*); Vol. 8, 1975-1979. 1984. 84.00 (*0-8103-0846-0*); Vol. 9, 1980-1984. 350p. 1986. 84.00 (*0-8103-0848-7*); Vol. 4, 1930-1939. Popular Music: An Annotated Index of Popular Songs. 1968. 75.00 (*0-8103-0842-8*); Vol. 5, 1920-1929. Popular Music: An Annotated Index of Popular Songs. 1969. 75.00 (*0-8103-0843-6*); Vol. 6, 1965-1969. Popular Music: An Annotated Index of Popular Songs. 1973. 84.00 (*0-8103-0844-4*); 1984. 70.00 (*0-8103-0839-8*) Gale.

Popular Music: An Annotated Index of Popular Songs see Popular Music: An Annotated Index of Popular Songs

Popular Music: An Annotated Index of Popular Songs, Vol. 7, 1970-74. Ed. by Nat Shapiro. Incl. Vol. 10, 1986. 168p. 1986. 80.00 (*0-8103-0849-5*); Vol. 8, 1975-1979. 1984. 84.00 (*0-8103-0846-0*); Vol. 9, 1980-1984. 350p. 1986. 84.00 (*0-8103-0848-7*); Vol. 4, 1930-1939. Popular Music: An Annotated Index of Popular Songs. 1968. 75.00 (*0-8103-0842-8*); Vol. 5, 1920-1929. Popular Music: An Annotated Index of Popular Songs.

P

An Asterisk (*) at the beginning of an entry indicates that the title is appearing for the first time.

1969. 75.00 (*0-8103-0843-6*); Vol. 6, 1965-1969. Popular Music: An Annotated Index of Popular Songs. 1973. 84.00 (*0-8103-0844-4*); 1984. 84.00 (*0-8103-0845-2*) Gale.

Popular Music & Communication. Ed. by James Lull. LC 91-30886. (Sage Focus Editions Ser.: Vol. 89). (Illus.). 256p. 1992. reprint ed. pap. 79.40 (*0-608-07686-4*, 206777600010) Bks Demand.

Popular Music & Communication. 2nd ed. Ed. by James Lull. (Focus Editions Ser.: Vol. 89). 334p. (C). 1991. text 59.95 (*0-8039-3916-7*); pap. text 26.00 (*0-8039-3917-5*) Sage.

Popular Music & Local Identity: Pop, Rock & Rap in Europe & Oceania. Tony Mitchell. (Illus.). 224p. (C). 1996. pap. 19.95 (*0-7185-0016-4*); text 99.90 (*0-7185-0019-9*) Bks Intl VA.

Popular Music & Society. Brian Longhurst. 278p. (C). 1995. text 61.95 (*0-7456-1437-X*); pap. text 28.95 (*0-7456-1464-7*) Blackwell Pubs.

***Popular Music & Youth Culture: Music, Identity & Place.** Andy Bennett. LC 99-16789. 2000. text 59.95 (*0-312-22753-1*) St Martin.

Popular Music Collection for the Advanced Player. Ed. by Carol Cuellar. 52p. (Orig.). 1997. pap. 14.95 (*0-7692-0127-X*, AF9754) Wrner Bros.

Popular-Music Culture in America. Prince Dorough. (Illus.). 352p. (C). 1992. text 39.95 (*1-880157-04-7*) Ardsley.

Popular Music, Gender & Postmodernism: Anger Is an Energy. Neil Nehring. LC 97-4590. 240p. 1997. 48.00 (*0-7619-0835-8*); pap. 21.95 (*0-7619-0836-6*) Sage.

Popular Music in England, 1840-1914: A Social History. 2nd ed. Dave Russell. (Illus.). 368p. 1998. pap. 29.95 (*0-7190-5261-0*, Pub. by Manchester Univ Pr) St Martin.

Popular Music in England, 1840-1914: A Social History. 2nd ed. Dave Russell. (Illus.). 368p. 1998. 79.95 (*0-7190-5310-2*, Pub. by Manchester Univ Pr) St Martin.

Popular Music in England, 1840-1914. Dave Russell. 320p. 1987. 65.00 (*0-7735-0541-5*, Pub. by McG-Queens Univ Pr) CUP Services.

Popular Music in India. (C). 1988. 34.00 (*81-85054-53-3*, Pub. by Manohar) S Asia.

Popular Music in Mexico. Claes Geijerstam. LC 75-17373. 209p. reprint ed. pap. 64.80 (*0-608-12047-2*, 202467700038) Bks Demand.

Popular Music in Theory: An Introduction. Keith Negus. LC 96-61301. (Music - Culture Ser.). 249p. 1996. pap. text 19.95 (*0-8195-6310-2*, Wesleyan Univ Pr) U Pr of New Eng.

Popular Music, 1989 Vol. 14: An Annotated Guide to American Popular Songs. Ed. by Bruce Pollock. LC 85-653754. 184p. 1990. 80.00 (*0-8103-4946-9*, 06516) Gale.

Popular Music, 1987, Vol. 12. annot. ed. Bruce Pollock. Ed. by Nat Shapiro. 350p. 1988. 80.00 (*0-8103-1810-5*) Gale.

Popular Music, 1986: An Annotated Index of American Popular Songs, Vol. 11. Ed. by Nat Shapiro & Bruce Pollock. (Popular Music Ser.). 179p. 1987. 80.00 (*0-8103-1809-1*) Gale.

Popular Music, 1980-1989: Cumulation. 80th ed. Ed. by Bruce Pollock. 911p. 1994. 132.00 (*0-7876-0205-1*) Gale.

Popular Music, 1900-1919. Ed. by Barbara Cohen-Stratyner. 656p. 1992. 104.00 (*0-8103-2595-0*, 006514-99584) Gale.

Popular Music, 1990, Vol. 15. Ed. by Bruce Pollock. 177p. 1991. 80.00 (*0-8103-4947-7*, 007101-M99348) Gale.

***Popular Music, 1998, Vol. 23.** 168p. 1999. 80.00 (*0-7876-1507-2*, 00156759) Gale.

Popular Music, 1995, Vol. 20. Pollock. 150p. 1996. 80.00 (*0-8103-6428-X*) Gale.

Popular Music, 1994 Vol. 19, 1994: An Annotated Guide to American Popular Songs, Including Introductory Essays, Lyricists & Composer Index, Important Performances Index, Awards Index & List of Publishers, Vol. 19. Ed. by Bruce Pollock. 160p. 1995. 80.00 (*0-8103-9057-4*) Gale.

Popular Music, 1991, Vol. 16. Bruce Pollock. 1992. 80.00 (*0-8103-7485-4*) Gale.

Popular Music, 1997, Vol. 22. 1998. 80.00 (*0-7876-1392-4*, 00156598) Gale.

Popular Music, 1996, Vol. 21. 150p. 1997. 80.00 (*0-7876-0069-5*, 0010870з) Gale.

Popular Music, 1993, Vol. 18. 93rd ed. Bruce Pollock. 1994. 80.00 (*0-8103-8498-1*, 007105) Gale.

Popular Music, 1992, Vol. 17. 1993. 80.00 (*0-8103-8234-2*) Gale.

Popular Music, 1920-1979: Cumulation, 3 vols. 20th ed. Ed. by Bruce Pollock. 2827p. 1985. 270.00 (*0-8103-0847-9*) Gale.

***Popular Music on Screen: From Hollywood Musical to Music Video.** John H. Mundy. 1999. 69.95 (*0-7190-4028-0*, Pub. by Manchester Univ Pr); pap. text 19.95 (*0-7190-4029-9*, Pub. by Manchester Univ Pr) St Martin.

Popular Music Perspectives: Ideas, Themes, & Patterns in Contemporary Lyrics. B. Lee Cooper. LC 90-83700. 216p. (C). 1991. 39.95 (*0-87972-505-2*); pap. 19.95 (*0-87972-506-0*) Bowling Green Univ Popular Press.

Popular Music Studies: A Select International Bibliography. Compiled by John Shepherd et al. LC 97-7515. 416p. 1996. 120.00 (*0-7201-2344-5*) Continuum.

***Popular Music 1999 Vol. 24.** 150p. 2000. 85.00 (*0-7876-3311-9*) Gale.

Popular Musicians 1999, 4 vols. Ed. by Steve Hochman & McCrea Adams. LC 99-11658. (Illus.). 1250p. (YA). (gr. 7 up). 1999. lib. bdg. 320.00 (*0-89356-986-0*) Salem Pr.

Popular Musics of the Non-Western World: An Introductory Survey. Peter Manuel. (Illus.). 314p. 1990. reprint ed. pap. text 19.95 (*0-19-506334-1*) OUP.

Popular Narrative Ballads of Modern Egypt. Pierre Cachia. 384p. 1989. text 86.00 (*0-19-826545-X*) OUP.

Popular Narratives Vol. 71-75: Chinese Children's Stories. Hwa-I Publishing Co., Staff. Ed. by Emily Ching et al. Tr. by Wonder Kids Publications Staff from CHI. (Popular Narratives Ser.). (Illus.). 28p. (J). (gr. 3-6). 1991. reprint ed. 39.75 (*1-56162-071-8*) Wonder Kids.

Popular Narratives & Ethnic Identity: Literature & Community in Die Abendschule. Brent O. Peterson. LC 91-55070. (Illus.). 320p. 1992. text 45.00 (*0-8014-2548-4*) Cornell U Pr.

Popular Nineteenth Century Painting. Philip Hook & Mark Poltimore. (Illus.). 632p. 1986. 89.50 (*1-85149-011-6*) Antique Collect.

Popular Nonfiction Authors for Children: A Biographical & Thematic Guide. Flora R. Wyatt et al. LC 97-32428. (Illus.). 207p. (YA). (gr. 5 up). 1998. 37.50 (*1-56308-408-2*) Libs Unl.

Popular Northern Sotho Dictionary: Sotho-English - English-Sotho. T. J. Kriel. (Hippocrene African Language Dictionaries Ser.). 335p. 1995. pap. 14.95 (*0-7818-0392-6*) Hippocrene Bks.

Popular Novel in England, 1770-1800. Joyce M. Tompkins. LC 61-16192. 396p. 1961. reprint ed. pap. 122.80 (*0-608-02145-8*, 206281400003) Bks Demand.

Popular Novel in England, 1770-1800. Joyce M. Tompkins. LC 76-174. 388p. 1976. reprint ed. lib. bdg. 65.00 (*0-8371-8656-0*, TOPN, Greenwood Pr) Greenwood.

Popular Opinion & Political Dissent in the Third Reich: Bavaria, 1933-1945. Ian Kershaw. (Illus.). 442p. 1985. pap. text 26.00 (*0-19-821971-7*) OUP.

Popular Opinion in Stalin's Russia: Terror, Propaganda & Dissent, 1934-1941. Sarah Davies. (Illus.). 256p. (C). 1997. text 59.95 (*0-521-56214-7*) Cambridge U Pr.

Popular Orchids. Brian Rittershausen & Wilma Rittershausen. 224p. 1982. 40.00 (*0-7223-0940-6*, Pub. by A H S Ltd) St Mut.

Popular Organ Classics. Albert De Vito. 1964. pap. 4.25 (*0-934286-43-4*) Kenyon.

Popular Organization & Democracy in Rio de Janeiro: A Tale of Two Favelas. Robert Gay. LC 93-11105. 208p. 1993. 69.95 (*1-56639-119-9*); pap. 22.95 (*1-56639-120-2*) Temple U Pr.

Popular Participation in Selected Upgrading Programmes in Urban Areas. 62p. 1987. pap. 8.50 (*92-1-130115-7*, E.86.IV.8) UN.

Popular Participation in Social Change: Cooperatives, Collectives, & Nationalized Industry. Ed. by June Nash et al. (World Anthropology Ser.). xviii, 622p. 1976. 73.10 (*90-279-7849-2*) Mouton.

Popular Participation in the Management of Natural Resources: Lessons from Baban Rafi, Niger. Kent M. Elbow. (Research Paper Ser.: Vol. 118). (Illus.). xii, 148p. (C). 1994. pap. 7.00 (*0-934519-29-3*, RP118) U of Wis Land.

Popular Participation Policies As Methods for Advancing Social Integration. 51p. pap. 10.00 (*92-1-130123-8*, E.87.IV.3) UN.

***Popular Patents: America's First Inventions from the Airplane to the Zipper.** Travis Brown. (Illus.). 224p. 2000. pap. 18.95 (*1-57886-010-5*, Pub. by Scarecrow) Natl Bk Netwk.

Popular Perception of Industrial History. Ed. by Robert Weible & Francis R. Walsh. (Business & Technology Ser.). 256p. 1989. pap. text 19.50 (*0-8026-0030-1*); lib. bdg. 39.00 (*0-8026-0029-8*) Univ Pub Assocs.

Popular Perception of Industrial History: (Essays from the 1985 Lowell Conference) Ed. by Robert Weible. (Illus.). 256p. 1989. pap. 15.00 (*0-937474-11-8*) Am Textile Hist.

Popular Physics & Astronomy: An Annotated Bibliography. Roger Smith. LC 96-3253. (Magill Bibliographies Ser.). 520p. 1996. 64.00 (*0-8108-3149-X*) Scarecrow.

Popular Physiology. R. T. Trall. 225p. 1996. reprint ed. spiral bd. 19.00 (*0-7873-0894-3*) Hlth Research.

Popular Physiology: An Application to the Preservation of Health (1884) R. T. Trall. 223p. 1996. reprint ed. pap. 17.95 (*1-56459-813-6*) Kessinger Pub.

Popular Piano Classics. Albert De Vito. 1964. pap. 4.25 (*0-934286-51-5*) Kenyon.

Popular Piano Solos: Level 4. 24p. 1997. pap. 4.95 (*0-7935-8585-6*) H Leonard.

Popular Piano Solos Level 3. 24p. 1997. pap. 4.95 (*0-7935-7725-X*) H Leonard.

Popular Piety in Late Medieval England: The Diocese of Salisbury, 1250-1550. Andrew Brown. (Oxford Historical Monographs). (Illus.). 308p. 1995. text 59.00 (*0-19-820521-X*) OUP.

Popular Plant Manager. Water Pollution Control Federation Staff. (Manual of Practice Ser.: No. MSM6). 92p. 1986. pap. 24.00 (*0-943244-70-6*) Water Environ.

Popular Poetic Pearls & Biographies of Poets. Frank McAlpine. LC 74-15745. (Popular Culture in America Ser.). (Illus.). 384p. 1975. reprint ed. 33.95 (*0-405-06380-6*) Ayer.

Popular Poetry in Puerto Rico: Origins & Themes. Maria C. De Martinez. (Puerto Rico Ser.). 1979. lib. bdg. 69.95 (*0-8490-2986-4*) Gordon Pr.

Popular Poetry in Soviet Russia. George Z. Patrick. LC 74-174378. 1972. reprint ed. 20.95 (*0-405-08841-8*, Pub. by Blom Pubns) Ayer.

Popular Poetry of the Finns. Charles J. Billson. (Popular Studies in Mythology, Romance & Folklore: No. 5). reprint ed. 27.50 (*0-404-53505-4*) AMS Pr.

Popular Political Economy: Four Lectures Delivered at the London Mechanics' Institution. Thomas Hodgskin. LC 66-19688. (Reprints of Economic Classics Ser.). xxxi, 268p. 1966. reprint ed. 45.00 (*0-678-00150-2*) Kelley.

Popular Politics: Renewing Democracy in a Sustainable World. George W. Shepard, Jr. LC 97-43947. 216p. 1998. 55.00 (*0-275-96007-2*, Praeger Pubs) Greenwood.

Popular Politics & British Anti-Slavery: The Mobilisation of Public Opinion Against the Slave Trade, 1787-1807. J. R. Oldfield. LC 98-29907. (Studies in Slave & Post-Slave Societies & Cultures). (Illus.). 216p. 1998. pap. 26.50 (*0-7146-4462-5*, Pub. by F Cass Pubs) Intl Spec Bk.

***Popular Politics & Political Culture in Upper Canada, 1800-1850.** Carol Wilton. 320p. 2000. text 65.00 (*0-7735-2053-8*, Pub. by McG-Queens Univ Pr) CUP Services.

Popular Politics & Religion in Civil War London. Keith Lindley. LC 96-34695. 464p. 1997. text 86.95 (*1-85928-343-8*, Pub. by Ashgate Pub) Ashgate Pub Co.

Popular Politics & the Irish Catholic Church: The Rise & Fall of the Independent Irish Party, 1850-1859. Steven R. Knowlton. LC 91-28574. (Modern European History II Ser.). 304p. 1991. text 20.00 (*0-8153-0669-5*) Garland.

Popular Politics in Nineteenth-Century England. Rohan McWilliam. LC 97-49376. (Historical Connections Ser.). 144p. (C). 1998. 60.00 (*0-415-18675-7*) Routledge.

Popular Politics in Nineteenth-Century England. Rohan McWilliam. LC 97-49376. (Historical Connections Ser.). 144p. (C). 1998. pap. 17.99 (*0-415-10841-1*) Routledge.

***Popular Pond Plants.** Philip Swindells. (Illus.). 144p. 2000. pap. 14.95 (*0-7645-6140-5*) IDG Bks.

Popular Potatoes Recipes. (Mini Cook Bks.). 148p. pap. 1.95 (*3-8290-0381-1*, 770118) Konemann.

Popular Practice of Fraud. T. Swann Harding. LC 75-39246. (Getting & Spending: The Consumer's Dilemma Ser.). 1976. reprint ed. 31.95 (*0-405-08020-4*) Ayer.

Popular Practice of Yoga. K. V. Mulbagala. 238p. 1996. pap. 17.00 (*0-89540-295-5*, SB-295) Sun Pub.

Popular Press Companion to Popular Literature. Victor Neuberg. LC 82-74162. 207p. 1983. 20.95 (*0-87972-233-9*) Bowling Green Univ Popular Press.

Popular Press, 1833-1865, 3. William E. Huntzicker. LC 98-22908. (History of American Journalism Ser.: Vol. 3). 224p. 1999. 65.00 (*0-313-30795-4*, Greenwood Pr) Greenwood.

Popular Prints, 1790-1870: Reading Popular Graphic Images. Fred H. Maidment. LC 95-43364. (Illus.). 240p. (C). 1997. text 69.95 (*0-7190-3370-5*, Pub. by Manchester Univ Pr) St Martin.

Popular Proverbs & Sayings. Gregory J. Titelman. LC 96-39602. 480p. 1997. 11.99 (*0-517-18658-6*) Random.

Popular Puppet Theatre in Europe, 1800-1914. John McCormick & Bennie Pratasik. LC 97-16552. (Illus.). 272p. (C). 1998. text 80.00 (*0-521-45413-1*) Cambridge U Pr.

***Popular Quimper.** Ann Marie O'Neill. (Illus.). 160p. 2000. pap. 19.95 (*0-7643-1099-2*) Schiffer.

Popular Quotations for All Uses. Lewis Copeland. 36.95 (*0-89190-474-3*) Amereon Ltd.

Popular Radicalism in Nineteenth-Century Britain. John Belchem. (Social History in Perspective Ser.). 160p. 1996. pap. 19.95 (*0-312-15806-8*); text 49.95 (*0-312-15799-1*) St Martin.

Popular Reading for Children: A Collection of the Booklist Columns. Barbara Elleman. LC 81-144124. 61p. reprint ed. pap. 30.00 (*0-608-14804-0*, 202560800045) Bks Demand.

***Popular Reading for Children IV: A Collection of Booklist Columns.** Ed. by Sally Estes. 64p. 1999. 8.95 (*0-8389-8010-4*) ALA.

Popular Reality. Ed. by David Crowbar. 224p. Date not set. 12.00 (*0-936756-72-1*) Autonomedia.

Popular Reality. Hartley. 1996. text 59.95 (*0-340-66294-8*, Pub. by E A) St Martin.

Popular Reality: Journalism, Modernity, Popular Culture. John Hartley. (Illus.). 288p. 1996. pap. text 19.95 (*0-340-58489-0*, Pub. by E A) OUP.

Popular Religion: Inspirational Books in America. Louis Schneider & Sanford M. Dornbusch. LC 58-11958. (Midway Reprint Ser.). 186p. reprint ed. pap. 57.70 (*0-608-16513-1*, 202674100051) Bks Demand.

Popular Religion & Liberation: The Dilemma of Liberation Theology. Michael R. Candelaria. LC 89-4573. (SUNY Series in Religion, Culture, & Society). 194p. (C). 1990. text 21.50 (*0-7914-0229-0*) State U NY Pr.

Popular Religion & Modernization in Latin America: A Different Logic. Cristian Parker. Tr. by Robert R. Barr from SPA. LC 96-11398. 325p. 1996. 45.00 (*1-57075-067-X*) Orbis Bks.

Popular Religion, Elites & Reform: Hook-Swinging & Its Prohibition in Colonial India. Geoffrey A. Oddie. LC 95-910445. (C). 1995. 28.00 (*81-7304-101-6*, Pub. by Manohar) S Asia.

Popular Religion in America: Symbolic Change & the Modernization Process in Historical Perspective. Peter W. Williams. 288p. 1989. reprint ed. pap. text 15.95 (*0-252-06073-3*) U of Ill Pr.

Popular Religion in America: The Evangelical Voice, 57. Erling Jorstad. LC 92-35919. (Contributions to the Study of Religion Ser.: No. 57). 240p. 1993. 62.95 (*0-313-27969-1*, JPB/) Greenwood.

Popular Religion in Germany & Central Europe, 1400-1800. Robert W. Scribner. LC 95-50826. 280p. 1996. text 49.95 (*0-312-12837-1*) St Martin.

Popular Religion in Late Saxon England: Elf Charms in Context. Karen L. Jolly. LC 95-38408. (Illus.). 256p. (C). 1996. pap. text 19.95 (*0-8078-4565-5*); lib. bdg. 49.95 (*0-8078-2262-0*) U of NC Pr.

Popular Religion in Restoration England. Charles J. Sommerville. LC 77-7618. (University of Florida Monographs: Social Sciences: No. 59). 162p. reprint ed. pap. 50.30 (*0-7837-5059-5*, 204474800004) Bks Demand.

Popular Religion in Sixteenth-Century England: Holding Their Peace. Christopher Marsh. LC 97-30787. (Social History in Perspective Ser.). 288p. 1998. pap. 19.95 (*0-312-21094-9*); text. write for info. (*0-312-21093-0*) St Martin.

Popular Religious Libraries in North America: A Statistical Examination. John F. Harvey. LC 98-20144. (Illus.). 768p. 1998. 110.00 (*0-8108-3342-5*) Scarecrow.

Popular Religious Magazines of the United States. Ed. by Mark P. Fackler & Charles H. Lippy. LC 94-7427. (Historical Guides to the World's Periodicals & Newspapers Ser.). 616p. 1995. lib. bdg. 125.00 (*0-313-28533-0*, Greenwood Pr) Greenwood.

Popular Reporting: Local Government Financial Reports to the Citizenry. Frances H. Carpenter et al. LC 92-70489. (Research Report Ser.). ix, 69p. 1992. write for info. (*0-910065-47-0*) Finan Acct Found.

***Popular Resistance Movements Against the British Rule.** Ed. by Raj Kumar. 1999. 38.50 (*81-261-0233-0*, Pub. by Anmol) S Asia.

Popular Rhymes & Nursery Tales. James O. Halliwell-Phillipps. LC 78-67715. (Folktale Ser.). reprint ed. 37.50 (*0-404-16092-1*) AMS Pr.

Popular Rhymes of Scotland. R. Chambers. 1972. 59.95 (*0-8490-0879-4*) Gordon Pr.

Popular Romances of the West of England. Ed. by Robert Hunt. LC 68-56495. 480p. 1972. reprint ed. 30.95 (*0-405-08643-1*, Pub. by Blom Pubns) Ayer.

Popular School. Ed. by Terence P. Logan & Denzell S. Smith. LC 74-81364. (Survey & Bibliography of Recent Studies in English Renaissance Drama). 313p. reprint ed. pap. 97.10 (*0-7837-1467-X*, 205716200016) Bks Demand.

Popular Science Complete Book of Power Tools. R. J. De Cristoforo. LC 98-11509. (Popular Science Ser.). 672p. 1998. 24.98 (*1-57912-026-1*) Blck Dog & Leventhal.

Popular Science Decks & Sun Spaces. Alfred Lees & Ernest V. Heyn. LC 90-10380. (Illus.). 256p. 1991. pap. 19.95 (*0-8069-7448-6*) Sterling.

Popular Secular Music in America Through 1800: A Preliminary Checklist of Manuscripts in North America Collections. Compiled by Kate Van Winkle Keller. (Music Library Association Index & Bibliography Ser.: No. 21). 140p. 1981. pap. 18.00 (*0-914954-22-9*) Scarecrow.

Popular Shakespearian Quotations. William Shakespeare. 1991. lib. bdg. 75.00 (*0-87700-951-1*) Revisionist Pr.

Popular Singers of the Twentieth Century: A Bibliography of Biographical Materials, 78. Robert H. Cowden. LC 99-22691. (Music Reference Collection: No. 78). 520p. 1999. lib. bdg. 85.00 (*0-313-29333-3*, GR9333, Greenwood Pr) Greenwood.

Popular Solos for Young Singers. 80p. 1994. pap. 9.95 (*0-7935-3444-5*, 00747077) H Leonard.

Popular Song Index. 3rd ed. Patricia P. Havlice. LC 89-6414. 879p. 1989. suppl. ed. 68.00 (*0-8108-2202-4*) Scarecrow.

Popular Song Index: First Supplement. Patricia P. Havlice. LC 77-25219. 386p. 1978. 52.00 (*0-8108-1099-9*) Scarecrow.

Popular Song Index: Second Supplement. Patricia P. Havlice. LC 83-7692. 534p. 1984. 55.00 (*0-8108-1642-3*) Scarecrow.

Popular Song Reader: A Sampler of Well-Known Twentieth-Century Songs. William E. Studwell. LC 92-44615. 273p. 1994. pap. 39.95 (*1-56023-029-0*, Harrington Park) Haworth Pr.

Popular Song Reader: A Sampler of Well-Known Twentieth-Century Songs. William E. Studwell. LC 92-44615. 273p. 1994. lib. bdg. 49.95 (*1-56024-369-4*) Haworth Pr.

Popular Songs & Ballads of Han China. Anne Birrell. 370p. 1988. 39.95 (*0-04-895028-9*) Routledge.

Popular Songs & Ballads of Han China. Anne Birrell. LC 93-18715. 240p. (C). 1993. reprint ed. pap. text 15.00 (*0-8248-1548-3*) UH Pr.

Popular Songs & Musical Word Puzzles. (Miscellaneous Ser.). 1990. 3.95 (*0-685-32018-9*, G195) Hansen Ed Mus.

Popular Songs for Guitar. 48p. 1990. pap. 7.95 (*0-7935-5524-8*, 50481309) H Leonard.

Popular Songs Inspiration: Easy Piano. 63p. (Orig.). 1996. pap. 8.95 (*0-7692-1018-X*, AF9666) Wrner Bros.

Popular Songs Inspiration: Piano/Vocal. 76p. (Orig.). 1996. pap. 9.95 (*0-7692-1046-5*, MF9610) Wrner Bros.

Popular Songs of Nineteenth Century America. Ed. by Richard Jackson. 290p. 1976. pap. 14.95 (*0-486-23270-0*) Dover.

***Popular Songs of the Twentieth Century: Chart Detail & Encyclopedia, 1900-1949.** Edward Foote Gardner. LC 00-20315. 528p. 2000. pap. 22.95 (*1-55778-789-1*) Paragon Hse.

Popular Souvenir Plates. Monica Lynn Clements & Patricia Rosser Clements. LC 98-84675. 176p. 1998. pap. 29.95 (*0-7643-0535-2*) Schiffer.

Popular Sovereignty & the Crisis of German Constitutional Law: The Theory & Practice of Weimar Constitutionalism. Peter Caldwell. LC 97-17282. 300p. 1997. pap. text 17.95 (*0-8223-1988-8*); lib. bdg. 49.95 (*0-8223-1979-9*) Duke.

Popular Standards. 95p. (Orig.). 1995. pap. 10.95 (*0-89724-959-3*, BP3344A) Wrner Bros.

Popular Standards 60's, 70's, 80's Easy Piano. (Easy Piano Ser.). 112p. 1997. per. 12.95 (*0-7935-7988-0*) H Leonard.

An Asterisk (*) at the beginning of an entry indicates that the title is appearing for the first time.

Popular Stories & Promised Lands: Fan Cultures & Symbolic Pilgrimages. Roger C. Aden. LC 98-19755. (Studies in Rhetoric & Communication). 26p. 1999. pap. 34.95 (*0-8173-0938-1*) U of Ala Pr.

Popular Stories of Ancient Egypt. Gaston C. Maspero. (African Studies). reprint ed. 40.00 (*0-938818-66-X*) ECA Assoc.

Popular Struggles in South Africa. Ed. by William Cobbett & Robin Cohen. LC 88-71831. 250p. (C). 1988. 35.00 (*0-86543-114-0*); pap. 11.95 (*0-86543-115-9*) Africa World.

Popular Studies in Mythology, Romance & Folklore, 15 vols. reprint ed. write for info. (*0-404-53500-3*) AMS Pr.

Popular Superstitions. Mary Hughes. LC 98-36081. (Costume, Tradition, & Culture Ser.). (Illus.). 64p. (YA). (gr. 5 up). 1999. lib. bdg. 16.95 (*0-7910-5172-2*) Chelsea Hse.

Popular Survey of the Old Testament. Norman L. Geisler. LC 77-78578. 304p. 1981. pap. 12.99 (*0-8010-3684-4*) Baker Bks.

Popular Tales. Charles Perrault. Ed. by Richard M. Dorson. LC 77-70607. (International Folklore Ser.). (Illus.). 1977. reprint ed. lib. bdg. 23.95 (*0-405-10118-X*) Ayer.

Popular Tales & Fictions, Their Migrations & Transformations, 2 vols. William A. Clouston. 1968. reprint ed. 95.00 (*1-55888-211-1*) Omnigraphics Inc.

Popular Tales of the West Highlands, Vol. 1. J. F. Campbell. 572p. pap. 25.95 (*1-874744-15-7*, Pub. by Birlinn Ltd) Dufour.

Popular Tales of the West Highlands, Vol. 2. J. F. Campbell. 612p. pap. 25.95 (*1-874744-16-5*, Pub. by Birlinn Ltd) Dufour.

Popular Teacher's Choice: Christmas Edition. Robert Schultz. Ed. by Carol Cuellar. 36p. (Orig.). 1993. pap. 8.95 (*0-7692-0133-4*, F3234P3X) Wrner Bros.

Popular Technology, 2 vols. Edward Hazen. LC 81-65737. 275p. 1981. 8.00 (*0-317-64495-5*) Early Am Indus.

Popular Television in Britain: Essays in Cultural History. Ed. by John Corner. (Illus.). 224p. 1991. 13.50 (*0-85170-269-4*, Pub. by British Film Inst); pap. 25.95 (*0-85170-270-8*, Pub. by British Film Inst) Ind U Pr.

Popular Theatre. 240p. 1994. write for info. (*92-806-3062-8*) U N I C E.

Popular Theatre. George J. Nathan. LC 75-120099. 236p. 1975. 25.00 (*0-8386-7945-5*) Fairleigh Dickinson.

***Popular Theatre in Political Culture: Britain & Canada in Focus.** Tim Prentki & Jan Selman. 224p. 2000. 35.95 (*1-84150-015-1*, Pub. by Intellect) Intl Spec Bk.

Popular Theatre Movement in Russia, 1862-1919. Gary J. Thurston. (Studies in Russian Literature & Theory). 416p. 1998. text 59.95 (*0-8101-1550-6*) Northwestern U Pr.

Popular Traditions & Learned Culture in France, 17th-20th Centuries. Ed. by Marc Bertrand. (Stanford French & Italian Studies: Vol. 35). (Illus.). 350p. 1986. pap. 56.50 (*0-915838-02-8*) Anma Libri.

Popular Trials: Rhetoric, Mass Media, & the Law. Ed. by Robert Hariman. LC 89-33736. 272p. 1993. pap. text 19.95 (*0-8173-0698-6*) U of Ala Pr.

Popular Tribunals. Hubert H. Bancroft. 1992. reprint ed. lib. bdg. 75.00 (*0-7812-5005-6*) Rprt Serv.

***Popular Tribunals, Pt. 1.** Hubert Howe Bancroft. (Works of Hubert Howe Bancroft: Vol. 36). 764p. 1999. reprint ed. lib. bdg. 90.00 (*0-7812-7829-5*) Rprt Serv.

***Popular Tribunals, Pt. 1.** Hubert Howe Bancroft. (Works of Hubert Howe Bancroft: Vol. 37). 782p. 1999. reprint ed. lib. bdg. 90.00 (*0-7812-7830-9*) Rprt Serv.

Popular Tribunals, 2 vols., Set. fac. ed. Hubert H. Bancroft. LC 67-29422. (Works of Hubert Howe Bancroft Ser.). 1967. reprint ed. 100.00 (*0-914888-39-0*) Bancroft Pr.

Popular Tropical Fish. Ed. by Cliff Harrison. 104p. 1995. pap. 8.95 (*0-572-01162-8*, Pub. by Foulsham UK) Assoc Pubs Grp.

Popular Variations in Ballroom Dancing. Alex Moore. (Ballroom Dance Ser.). 1984. lib. bdg. 79.95 (*0-87700-508-7*) Revisionist Pr.

Popular Variations in Latin-American Dancing. Ed. by Elizabeth Romain. 1984. lib. bdg. 79.95 (*0-87700-514-1*) Revisionist Pr.

Popular Verse. (Works). 540p. 1996. pap. 6.99 (*1-57215-202-8*, JG1201) World Pubns.

Popular View of the Doctrines of Charles Fourier. 2nd ed. Parke Godwin. LC 72-2951. reprint ed. 22.50 (*0-404-10716-8*) AMS Pr.

Popular View of the Doctrines of Charles Fourier: With the addition of Democracy, constructive & pacific. Parke Godwin. LC 77-187451. (American Utopian Adventure Ser.). 175p. 1972. reprint ed. lib. bdg. 35.00 (*0-87991-006-2*) Porcupine Pr.

Popular Voices in Latin American Catholicism. Daniel H. Levine. (Studies in Church & State). (Illus.). 424p. 1992. pap. text 22.95 (*0-691-02459-6*, Pub. by Princeton U Pr) Cal Prin Full Svc.

Popular Wedding Hits for Piano: Easy-Intermediate, Vol. 1. Ed. by Tony Esposito. 32p. (YA). 1995. pap. text 5.95 (*0-89724-688-8*, AF9516) Wrner Bros.

Popular Wedding Hits for Piano Vol. 2: Easy-Intermediate. Ed. by Tony Esposito. 32p. (YA). 1995. pap. text 5.95 (*0-89724-689-6*, AF9517) Wrner Bros.

Popular West: American Illustrators, 1900-1940. Phoenix Art Museum Staff. (Illus.). 55p. (Orig.). 1982. pap. 8.00 (*0-910407-08-8*) Phoenix Art.

Popular Writing in America: The Interaction of Style & Audience. 5th ed. Ed. by Donald McQuade & Robert Atwan. (Illus.). 96p. 1993. pap. text (*0-19-508283-4*) OUP.

Popular Young Adult Reading: A Collection of Booklist Columns. Sally Estes. 56p. 1996. pap. 7.95 (*0-8389-7835-5*) ALA.

Popularia Carmina: Index Popularium Carminum. Contrib. by Alfredo R. Lopez & Francisco M. Garcia. (Alpha-Omega Ser.: Reihe B, Bd. XI). (GER.). viii, 199p. 1997. 95.00 (*3-487-10301-X*) G Olms Pubs.

***Popularity Contest: Zoe.** Rachel Vail. (The Friendship Ring Ser.:). (Illus.). 240p. (J). (gr. 4-8). 2000. pap. 4.99 (*0-590-68911-8*, Apple Paperbacks) Scholastic Inc.

***Popularity Contest: Zoe, Vol. 5.** Rachel Vail. (The Friendship Ring Ser.). (J). (gr. 4-8). 2000. pap. 47.88 (*0-439-16067-7*) Scholastic Inc.

Popularity Has Its Ups & Downs. Meg F. Schneider. LC 91-1447. (J). (gr. 4-7). 1992. pap. 5.95 (*0-671-72849-0*, Julian Messner) Silver Burdett Pr.

Popularity of Middle English Romance. Velma B. Richmond. LC 75-21576. 1975. 14.95 (*0-87972-114-6*) Bowling Green Univ Popular Press.

Popularization of Images: Visual Culture under the July Monarchy. Ed. by Gabriel P. Weisberg. LC 93-47332. (Nineteenth-Century Art, Culture, & Society Ser.). 320p. 1994. text 42.50 (*0-691-03210-6*, Pub. by Princeton U Pr) Cal Prin Full Svc.

Popularization of Mathematics. Ed. by A. G. Howson & Jean-Pierre Kahane. (International Commission on Mathematical Instruction Study Ser.). (Illus.). 220p. (C). 1990. text 69.95 (*0-521-40319-7*); pap. text 22.95 (*0-521-40867-9*) Cambridge U Pr.

Popularizing Anthropology. Ed. by Jeremy MacClancy & Chris McDonaugh. 272p. (C). 1996. 85.00 (*0-415-13612-1*); pap. 25.99 (*0-415-13613-X*) Routledge.

Popularizing Classical Economics. Henry Brougham et al. LC 94-27002. (Studies in the History of Economics). 1994. text 65.00 (*0-312-12383-3*) St Martin.

Popularizing Pennsylvania: Henry W. Shoemaker & the Progressive Uses of Folklore & History. Simon J. Bronner. LC 95-15354. 272p. 1996. 50.00 (*0-271-01486-5*); pap. 19.50 (*0-271-01487-3*) Pa St U Pr.

Popularizing the Nation: Audience, Representation, & the Production of Identity in "Die Gartenlaube," 1853-1900. Contrib. by Kirsten Belgum. LC 97-29654. (Modern German Culture & Literature Ser.). (Illus.). xxxi, 237p. 1998. text 50.00 (*0-8032-1283-6*) U of Nebr Pr.

Populate & Perish: Australian Women's Fight for Birth Control. Stefania Siedlecky & Diana Wyndham. 240p. 1991. pap. text 18.95 (*0-04-442220-2*, Pub. by Allen & Unwin Pty) Paul & Co Pubs.

Population. Central Office of Info. LC 96-162400. (Aspects of Britain Ser.). (Illus.). 105p. 1995. pap. 12.00 (*0-11-702007-9*, Pub. by Statnry Office) Bernan Associates.

Population. Colin Clark. 30p. 1974. pap. 0.50 (*0-912414-19-7*) Lumen Christi.

***Population.** Charles Hohm. LC 99-36891. (Opposing Viewpoints Ser.). 360p. (YA). 2000. pap. 13.96 (*0-7377-0291-5*) Greenhaven.

Population. George Mosby, Jr. 1983. pap. 7.00 (*0-914610-35-X*) Hanging Loose.

Population. Don Nardo. LC 90-23525. (Overview Ser.). (Illus.). 112p. (YA). (gr. 5-8). 1991. lib. bdg. 22.45 (*1-56006-123-5*) Lucent Bks.

Population. Rafael M. Salas. 1981. write for info. (*0-08-026097-7*, Pergamon Pr); pap. write for info. (*0-08-026096-9*, Pergamon Pr) Elsevier.

Population. Wood. Date not set. pap. text. write for info. (*0-582-02424-2*, Pub. by Addison-Wesley) Longman.

Population. David Killingray & Margaret Killingray. Ed. by Edmund O'Connor. (World History Program Ser.). (Illus.). 32p. (YA). (gr. 6-11). 1980. reprint ed. pap. text 5.90 (*0-89908-116-9*) Greenhaven.

Population: A Study in Malthusianism. Warren S. Thompson. LC 74-76699. (Columbia University. Studies in the Social Sciences: No. 153). reprint ed. 37.50 (*0-404-51153-8*) AMS Pr.

Population: An International Directory of Organizations & Information Resources. Thaddeus C. Trzyna & Joan D. Smith. LC 76-4269. (Who's Doing What Ser.: No. 3). 160p. (Orig.). 1976. pap. 18.75 (*0-912102-22-5*) Cal Inst Public.

Population: An Introduction to Concepts & Issues. 3rd ed. John R. Weeks. 525p. (C). 1985. pap. write for info. (*0-534-06138-9*) Wadsworth Pub.

Population: An Introduction to Concepts & Issues. 4th ed. John R. Weeks. 552p. (C). 1989. pap. write for info. (*0-534-10122-4*) Wadsworth Pub.

Population: An Introduction to Concepts & Issues. 5th ed. John R. Weeks. 579p. (C). 1992. pap. 42.95 (*0-534-17346-2*) Wadsworth Pub.

Population: An Introduction to Concepts & Issues. 5th ed. John R. Weeks. 583p. 1993. mass mkt. 40.75 (*0-534-21120-8*) Wadsworth Pub.

Population: An Introduction to Concepts & Issues. 6th ed. John R. Weeks. LC 95-21581. 1995. 49.75 (*0-534-26460-3*) Wadsworth Pub.

Population: An Introduction to Concepts & Issues. 7th ed. Weeks. LC 98-39201. (Sociology-Upper Level Ser.). 1998. pap. 78.95 (*0-534-55305-2*) Wadsworth Pub.

Population: Contemporary Responses to Thomas Malthus. Ed. & Intro. by Andrew Pyle. (Key Issues Ser.). 320p. 1994. 72.00 (*1-85506-344-1*) Bks Intl VA.

Population: Contemporary Responses to Thomas Malthus. Ed. & Intro. by Andrew Pyle. (Key Issues Ser.). (Illus.). 320p. 1994. pap. 24.00 (*1-85506-345-X*) Bks Intl VA.

Population: Detecting Bias. Neal Bernards. LC 92-17419. (Opposing Viewpoints Juniors Ser.). (Illus.). 36p. (J). (gr. 4-7). 1992. lib. bdg. 16.20 (*0-89908-622-5*) Greenhaven.

Population: Dynamics, Ethics & Policy. Ed. by Priscilla Reining & Irene Tinker. LC 75-4498. (AAAS Miscellaneous Publications: No. 75-5). 192p. reprint ed. pap. 59.60 (*0-7837-0062-8*, 204030900016) Bks Demand.

Population: French-English Glossary & Glossaire Anglais-Francais. Contrib. by CE's Terminology Office Staff. 500p. (Orig.). 1994. pap. 56.00 (*92-871-2506-6*, Pub. by Council of Europe) Manhattan Pub Co.

Population: General Report & Analysis see Census of the United States: 13th Decennial Census, 1910

Population: Introduction to Concepts & Issues. 5th ed. Weeks. (Sociology - Intro Level Ser.). 1992. pap., teacher ed. write for info. (*0-534-17347-0*) Wadsworth Pub.

Population: Occupation Statistics see Census of the United States: 13th Decennial Census, 1910

***Population: Opposing Viewpoints.** Charles F. Hohm. LC 99-56750. (Opposing Viewpoints Ser.). 360p. (YA). 2000. 13.96 (*0-7377-0292-3*) Greenhaven.

Population: Opposing Viewpoints. Charles F. Hohm & Lori J. Jones. (Opposing Viewpoints Ser.). (Illus.). 240p. 1995. pap. text 16.20 (*1-56510-214-2*, 2142) Greenhaven.

***Population: Our Growing Planet.** rev. ed. Ed. by Virginia Peterson et al. (Information Plus Compact Ser.). (Illus.). 80p. (YA). 1998. pap. text 14.95 (*1-57302-104-0*) Info Plus TX.

Population: Reports by States Alabama-Montana see Census of the United States: 13th Decennial Census, 1910

Population: Reports by States Nebraska-Wyoming see Census of the United States: 13th Decennial Census, 1910

Population: The Complex Reality: A Report of the Population Summit of the World's Scientific Academies. Ed. by Frances Graham-Smith. LC 94-14992. 420p. (C). 1994. text 35.00 (*1-55591-926-X*) Fulcrum Pub.

Population: The First Essay. Thomas Robert Malthus. 160p. 1959. pap. text 13.95 (*0-472-06031-7*, 06031, Ann Arbor Bks) U of Mich Pr.

Population: The Growth of Metropolitan Districts in the United States, 1900-1940. Warren S. Thompson. LC 75-21958. (America in Two Centuries Ser.). 1976. reprint ed. 13.95 (*0-405-07736-X*) Ayer.

Population: The Human Race. Eric McGraw. 145p. 1990. pap. 14.95 (*1-85219-032-9*, Pub. by Bishopsgte Pr) Intl Spec Bk.

Population: Today & Tomorrow - Policies, Theories & Methodologies, 2 vols. 1989. 150.00 (*81-7018-588-2*, Pub. by BR Pub) S Asia.

Population - Control, Density, Dynamics, Growth, & Surveillance: Index of New Information with Authors, Subjects & Bibliography. rev. ed. James N. Palmerson. LC 94-34027. 136p. 1994. 47.50 (*0-7883-0382-1*); pap. 44.50 (*0-7883-0383-X*) ABBE Pubs Assn.

***Population Abstract of the U. S. A.** 2000. 175.00 (*0-7876-4968-6*, UXL) Gale.

Population Ageing, Migration & Social Expenditure. Jose Alvarado & John Creedy. LC 97-37218. 208p. (C). 1998. 75.00 (*1-85898-724-5*) E Elgar.

Population: Ages see Decennial Census Reports of the United States, 12th Census, 1900

Population Aging: International Perspectives. Ed. by Anita S. Harbert & Joan L. Roberts. 684p. (Orig.). 1993. 25.00 (*1-879167-01-8*) SDSU Coll Hlth Hum Servs.

Population Aging in the United States, 18. William J. Serow et al. LC 89-25699. (Contributions to the Study of Aging Ser.: No. 18). (Illus.). 240p. 1990. 55.00 (*0-313-27311-1*, SUU/, Greenwood Pr) Greenwood.

Population Ahead. Roy G. Francis. LC 58-7927. 170p. reprint ed. pap. 52.70 (*0-608-14771-0*, 205586900039) Bks Demand.

Population Analysis in Geography. Robert Woods. LC 78-41309. (Illus.). 288p. reprint ed. pap. 89.30 (*0-7837-5180-X*, 204491000004) Bks Demand.

Population & Community Ecology: Principles & Methods. E. C. Pielou. LC 72-86334. (Illus.). viii, 429p. 1974. text 225.00 (*0-677-03580-2*) Gordon & Breach.

Population & Community Ecology for Insect Management & Conservation: Proceedings of the Ecology & Population Dynamics Section, 20th International Congress Florence, 25-31 August, 1996. Ed. by J. Baumgartner et al. (Illus.). 253p. (C). 1998. text 85.00 (*90-5410-930-0*, Pub. by A A Balkema) Ashgate Pub Co.

Population & Community in Rural America. Lorraine Garkovich. LC 89-32805. 240p. 1989. pap. 17.95 (*0-275-93350-4*, B3550, Praeger Pubs) Greenwood.

Population & Community in Rural America, 84. Lorraine Garkovich. LC 89-11802. 251p. 1989. 65.00 (*0-313-26620-4*, GKM/, Praeger Pubs) Greenwood.

Population & Develop Reader. Demeny. LC 98-13495. 1998. pap. 26.95 (*0-312-21517-7*) St Martin.

Population & Development. Ed. by Geoffrey Hawthorn. 210p. 1978. 35.00 (*0-7146-3102-7*, Pub. by F Cass Pubs) Intl Spec Bk.

Population & Development. P. D. Malgavkar. 1982. 18.50 (*0-8364-0923-X*, Pub. by Somaiya) S Asia.

Population & Development: A Critical Introduction. Furedi. LC 97-16710. 208p. 1997. text 59.95 (*0-312-17656-2*) St Martin.

Population & Development: A Critical Introduction. Frank Furedi. LC 97-16710. 208p. 1997. pap. 19.95 (*0-312-17658-9*) St Martin.

Population & Development: A Message from the Cairo Conference. Robert Cliquet & Kristiaan Thienpont. LC 95-39653. (European Studies of Population: No. 3). 1995. lib. bdg. 88.00 (*0-7923-3763-8*) Kluwer Academic.

Population & Development: Implications for the World Bank. World Bank Staff. LC 94-31613. (Development in Practice Ser.). 144p. 1994. pap. 22.00 (*0-8213-2999-5*) World Bank.

Population & Development: Programme of Action Adopted at the International Conference on Population & Development, Cairo, Vol. I. (Population Studies: No. 149). 100p. pap. 10.00 (*92-1-151278-6*, E.95.XIII.12) UN.

Population & Development: The Search for Selective Interventions. Ronald G. Ridker. LC 76-16806. (Resources for the Future Ser.). (Illus.). 467p. 1976. 37.50 (*0-8018-1884-2*, Pub. by Resources Future) Johns Hopkins.

Population & Development Directory of Non-Governmental Organisations in OECD Countries. OECD Staff. 360p. (Orig.). 1994. pap. 73.00 (*92-64-04171-0*) OECD.

Population & Development in Poor Countries. Julian L. Simon. (Illus.). 446p. 1992. text 59.50 (*0-691-04256-X*, Pub. by Princeton U Pr) Cal Prin Full Svc.

Population & Development in the Third World. Allan M. Findlay & Anne M. Findlay. (Introductions to Development Ser.). (Illus.). 140p. 1987. pap. 10.95 (*0-416-91950-2*) Routledge.

Population & Development Planning. 285p. 20.00 (*92-1-151249-2*, E.92.XIII.13) UN.

Population & Development Planning: An Integrated Approach. O. Arowolo & I. Ekanem. 300p. 1992. 49.95 (*0-89388-228-3*); pap. 35.95 (*0-89388-229-1*) Okpaku Communications.

Population & Development Planning in China. Ed. by Wang Jiye & Terence H. Hull. 336p. 1991. pap. 24.95 (*0-04-442323-3*, Pub. by Allen & Unwin Pty) Paul & Co Pubs.

Population & Devlope Reader. Demeny. LC 98-13495. 363p. 1998. text 65.00 (*0-312-21516-9*) St Martin.

Population & Economic Change in Developing Countries. Ed. by Richard A. Easterlin. LC 79-12569. (National Bureau of Economic Research Ser.). 581p. 1979. lib. bdg. 56.00 (*0-226-18026-3*) U Ch Pr.

Population & Economic Change in Developing Countries. Richard A. Easterlin. LC 79-12569. (National Bureau of Economic Research Conference Report Ser.). x, 592p. (C). 1987. reprint ed. pap. text 40.00 (*0-226-18027-1*) U Ch Pr.

Population & Economic Development in Brazil, 1800 to the Present. Thomas W. Merrick & Douglas H. Graham. LC 78-20523. 408p. 1979. reprint ed. pap. 126.50 (*0-608-03671-4*, 206449700009) Bks Demand.

***Population & Economy: From Hunger to Modern Economic Growth.** Ed. by Tommy Bengtsson & Osamu Saito. 450p. 2000. text 95.00 (*0-19-829653-3*) OUP.

Population & Economy: From the Traditional to the Modern World. Ed. by Robert I. Rotberg & Theodore K. Robb. (Studies in Interdisciplinary History). (Illus.). 239p. 1986. pap. text 21.95 (*0-521-31055-5*) Cambridge U Pr.

Population & Energy: A Systems Analysis of Resource Utilization in the Dominican Republic. Gustavo A. Antonini et al. LC 75-2495. (Latin American Monographs: Vol. 14). (Illus.). 189p. 1975. reprint ed. pap. 58.60 (*0-608-04501-2*, 206524600001) Bks Demand.

***Population & Environment: A U. S. & International Perspective.** Joseph Siry. 224p. 2000. pap. 22.00 (*0-9655029-8-8*, Pub. by Acada Bks) Midpt Trade.

Population & Environment: Patterns, Problems, Some Pathways to Solutions. George J. Stolnitz. Ed. by Dennis Conway. (Series on Environment & Development). 21p. (Orig.). 1991. pap. 1.25 (*1-881157-05-9*) In Ctr Global.

Population & Environment Dynamics, Poverty & Quality of Life in Countries of the ESCAP Region. Economic & Social Commission for Asia & the Pacific Staff. (Asian Population Studies Ser.: No. 147). 195p. 1998. pap. 35.00 (*92-1-119813-5*) UN.

Population & Environment in Arid Regions. Ed. by John I. Clarke & Daniel Noin. LC 97-17028. (Man & the Biosphere Ser.: Vol. 19). (Illus.). 410p. 1998. 75.00 (*1-85070-962-9*) Prthnon Pub.

Population & Environment in Arid Regions. UNESCO Staff. 1998. 100.00 (*92-3-103410-3*, U4103, Pub. by UNESCO) Bernan Associates.

Population & Family in the Low Countries, No. 1. Ed. by Hein G. Moors et al. (Publications of the Netherlands Inter-University Demographic Institute & the Population & Family Study Centre Ser.). 1976. pap. text 85.50 (*90-247-1859-7*) Kluwer Academic.

Population & Family in the Low Countries, 1992: Family & Labour. Ed. by G. C. Beets et al. (NIDI-CBGS Publications: Vol. 26). viii, 272p. 1993. pap. 52.00 (*90-265-1342-9*) Swets.

Population & Family in the Low Countries, 1994: Selected Current Issues. Ed. by Hans Van Den Brekel. (European Studies of Population). 308p. (C). 1995. lib. bdg. 110.50 (*0-7923-3396-9*) Kluwer Academic.

Population & Family in the Low Countries, 1995: Selected Current Issues. Ed. by Hans Van Den Brekel. (European Studies of Population: No. 4). 176p. (C). 1996. lib. bdg. 102.50 (*0-7923-3945-2*) Kluwer Academic.

Population & Family Planning in India. G. C. Kendadamath. 1986. 20.00 (*0-8364-1557-4*, Pub. by Indian Doc Serv) S Asia.

Population & Family Planning in Nepal. J. M. Tuladhar et al. 125p. (C). 1978. 40.00 (*0-89771-055-X*, Pub. by Ratna Pustak Bhandar) St Mut.

Population & Family Planning in Nepal. T. Tuladhar et al. 1978. 20.00 (*0-7855-0234-3*, Pub. by Ratna Pustak Bhandar) St Mut.

P

An Asterisk (*) at the beginning of an entry indicates that the title is appearing for the first time.

Population & Fishery Statistics for Largemouth Bass, Smallmouth Bass, & Black Crappie, & Limnology of Owyhee Reservoir, Oregon, 1992. T. A. Rien et al. 64p. 1998. reprint ed. 12.40 (*0-89904-861-7*, Cascade Geog Soc); reprint ed. pap. 7.40 (*0-89904-862-5*, Cascade Geog Soc) Crumb Elbow Pub.

Population & Food: Global Trends & Future Prospects. Tim Dyson. LC 95-38227. (Global Environmental Change Ser.). 256p. (C). 1996. pap. 22.99 (*0-415-11975-8*) Routledge.

Population & Food in the Early Twenty-First Century: Meeting Future Food Demand of an Increasing Population. Ed. by Nurul Islam. (Occasional Papers). 1995. write for info. (*0-89629-331-9*) Intl Food Policy.

Population & Global Security. 2nd ed. Ed. by Nicholas Polunin. (Illus.). 328p. (C). 1998. text 74.95 (*0-521-56372-0*); pap. text 29.95 (*0-521-63539-X*) Cambridge U Pr.

Population & Global Warming. Ed. by Brian O'Neill et al. (Illus.). 300p. (C). 1999. write for info. (*0-521-66242-7*) Cambridge U Pr.

Population & Health Policy in the Peoples Republic of China. Peter Chan. 150p. 1978. pap. 12.00 (*0-686-76148-0*) Neo Pr.

Population & History: The Demographic Origins of the Modern Philippines. Ed. by Daniel F. Doeppers & Peter Xenos. (Wisconsin Monographs in Southeast Asian Studies: Vol. M16). (Illus.). 440p. 1998. 49.95 (*1-881261-22-0*); pap. 24.95 (*1-881261-23-9*) U Wisc Ctr SE Asian.

Population & Housing in Special Studies Zones. Claudia Grow. (Special Publications: No. 1). 51p. (Orig.). (C). 1981. pap. 20.00 (*0-685-28085-3*) Natural Hazards.

Population & Housing Problems in India, 2 vols., Set. S. D. Maurya. (C). 1989. 76.00 (*81-85076-79-0*, Pub. by Chugh Pubns) S Asia.

Population & Human Resources Development in the Sudan. Ed. by Omer S. Ertur & William J. House. LC 93-34547. (Illus.). 344p. 1994. text 72.95 (*0-8138-0699-2*) Iowa St U Pr.

Population & Human Rights. 230p. 1991. 25.00 (*92-1-151227-1*, 91.XIII.8) UN.

Population & Human Survival. Ed. by Gary E. McCuen. (Ideas in Conflict Ser.). (Illus.). 158p. (YA). (gr. 7-12). 1993. lib. bdg. 15.95 (*0-86596-089-5*) G E M.

Population & Income Change: Recent Evidence. Allen C. Kelley & Robert M. Schmidt. LC 94-27213. 130p. 1994. pap. 22.00 (*0-8213-2956-1*) World Bank.

Population & Land Use in Developing Countries: Report of a Workshop. National Research Council, Commission on Behaviora & National Research Council Staff. 172p. (Orig.). (C). 1993. pap. text 26.50 (*0-309-04838-9*) Natl Acad Pr.

Population & Peace in the Pacific. Warren S. Thompson. LC 79-1151. (Essay Index Reprint Ser.). 1977. reprint ed. 26.95 (*0-8369-2867-9*) Ayer.

Population & Political Systems in Tropical Africa. Robert F. Stevenson. LC 68-11435. 320p. reprint ed. pap. 99.20 (*0-8357-4587-2*, 203751800008) Bks Demand.

Population & Population Policy in Hungary. Ed. by Karoly Miltenyi et al. 231p. (C). 1984. 42.00 (*963-05-3870-9*, Pub. by Akade Kiado) St Mut.

Population & Poverty in the Developing World. Ed. by Massimo Livi-Bacci & Gustavo De Santis. LC 98-28485. (International Studies in Demography). (Illus.). 316p. 1999. text 70.00 (*0-19-829300-3*) OUP.

Population & Progress in the Far East. Warren S. Thompson. LC 59-10428. 453p. reprint ed. pap. 140.50 (*0-608-15112-2*, 202579300046) Bks Demand.

Population & Public Policy. Alan E. Nash. (C). 1996. pap. text 29.95 (*0-8133-7893-1*) Westview.

Population & Related Organizations: International Address List. Ed. by Thomas C. Putzer. LC 93-49526. (APLIC Special Publication Ser.: No. 6). (Orig.). 1994. pap. write for info. (*0-933438-20-6*) APLIC Intl.

Population & Related Organizations: International Address List. Ruth G. Sandor. LC 84-6302. (APLIC Special Publication Ser.: No. 5). 87p. (Orig.). 1984. pap. 45.00 (*0-933438-09-5*) APLIC Intl.

Population & Related Organizations: International Address List. Jane Vanderlin & Ruth G. Sandor. 87p. (Orig.). 1984. 45.00 (*0-317-00893-5*, LC 84-6302) Assn Pop Lib.

Population & Reproductive Rights: Feminist Perspectives from the South. Sonia Correa & Rebecca L. Reichmann. LC 94-32596. 136p. (C). 1994. text 19.95 (*1-85649-284-2*, Pub. by Zed Books) St Martin.

Population & Reproductive Rights: Gender & Development. Caroline Sweetman. (Gender & Development Ser.). (Illus.). 64p. (C). 1994. pap. 12.95 (*0-85598-278-0*, Pub. by Oxfam Pub) Stylus Pub VA.

Population & Resources in Western Intellectual Traditions: Based on Papers Presented at a Seminar Held at Pembroke College, University of Cambridge, August 1987. Ed. by Michael S. Teitelbaum & Jay M. Winter. LC 89-878. (Population & Development Review, Supplement Ser.: Vol. 14). 318p. reprint ed. pap. 98.60 (*0-7837-6745-5*, 204637300011) Bks Demand.

Population & Resources in Western Intellectual Traditions: Supplement to Population & Development Review, Vol. 14. Ed. by Michael S. Teitelbaum & Jay M. Winter. 310p. 1988. pap. text 14.00 (*0-614-00625-2*) Population Coun.

Population & Revenue in the Towns of Palestine in the Sixteenth Century. Amnon Cohen & Bernard Lewis. LC 78-51160. 228p. 1978. reprint ed. pap. 70.70 (*0-7837-9322-7*, 206006200004) Bks Demand.

Population & Rural Poor in India. Mahesh Pal. (C). 1991. 21.00 (*0-8364-2762-9*, Pub. by Chugh Pubns) S Asia.

Population & Social Change in an Indian Village. Kuttan Mahadevan & A. Aiyappan. (C). 1988. 40.00 (*81-7099-073-4*, Pub. by Mittal Pubs Dist) S Asia.

Population & Social Organization. Ed. by Moni Nag. (World Anthropology Ser.). x, 368p. 1975. 35.40 (*90-279-7589-2*) Mouton.

Population & Social Policy in France. Maire Cross & Sheila Perry. LC 96-45999. (Illus.). 192p. 1997. 85.00 (*1-85567-393-2*) Bks Intl VA.

Population & Society in India. B. Kuppuswamy. 136p. 1975. 14.95 (*0-318-36860-9*) Asia Bk Corp.

Population & Society in Norway, 1735-1865. Michael Drake. LC 69-14393. (Cambridge Studies in Economic History). 276p. reprint ed. pap. 78.70 (*0-608-12223-8*, 2024445) Bks Demand.

Population & Society in the Arab East. Gabriel Baer. Tr. by Hanna Szoke. LC 76-16835. (Illus.). 275p. 1976. reprint ed. lib. bdg. 35.00 (*0-8371-8963-2*, BAPSA, Greenwood Pr) Greenwood.

Population & Society in Twentieth Century France. Colin Dyer. LC 77-2908. (Illus.). 256p. (C). 1978. 42.00 (*0-8419-0308-5*) Holmes & Meier.

Population & Technological Change: A Study of Long-Term Trends. Ester Boserup. LC 80-21116. (Illus.). 268p. 1983. pap. text 12.95 (*0-226-06674-6*) U Ch Pr.

Population & the Environment: Rethinking the Debate. Ed. by Lourdes Arizpe et al. LC 94-2805. 352p. (C). 1994. pap. text 75.00 (*0-8133-8843-0*, Pub. by Westview) HarpC.

Population & the Environment: The Linacre Lectures, 1993-94. Ed. by Bryan Cartledge. LC 96-133283. (Illus.). 200p. 1995. text 45.00 (*0-19-854842-7*) OUP.

Population & the Environment in China. Qu Geping & Li Jinchang. LC 93-40821. 217p. 1994. lib. bdg. 49.95 (*1-55587-435-5*) L Rienner.

Population & the Family: The Development Process in Africa. Ed. by Aderanti Adepoju. 240p. (C). 1996. text 59.95 (*1-85649-465-9*, Pub. by Zed Books); text 22.50 (*1-85649-466-7*) Zed Books.

Population & the Population Explosion: A Bibliography for 1970. Stephen H. Goode. LC 72-87106. xxv, 361p. 1973. 17.00 (*0-87875-032-0*) Whitston Pub.

Population & the Population Explosion: A Bibliography for 1973. LC 72-87106. 1975. 13.00 (*0-87875-059-2*) Whitston Pub.

Population & the Population Explosion: A Bibliography for 1976. 1980. 38.50 (*0-87875-129-7*) Whitston Pub.

Population & the Social System. Francesco S. Nitti. LC 75-38140. (Demography Ser.). (Illus.). 1976. reprint ed. 19.95 (*0-405-07993-1*) Ayer.

Population & the Urban Future. Philip M. Hauser et al. LC 82-5529. 195p. reprint ed. pap. 60.50 (*0-8357-6582-2*, 203597700097) Bks Demand.

***Population & the World Bank: Adapting to Change.** World Bank Staff. LC 99-12962. 52p. 1999. pap. 22.00 (*0-8213-4430-7*) World Bank.

Population & the World Bank: Implications from Eight Case Studies. LC 92-13541. (Operations Evaluation Studies). 171p. 1992. 22.00 (*0-8213-2081-5*, 12081) World Bank.

Population & U. S. National Interests: A Framework for Thinking about the Connections. Ed. by David Wendt & Alene Gelbard. LC 95-42426. (CSIS Panel Reports: No. 899-0352). (C). 1996. pap. text 14.95 (*0-89206-278-9*) CSIS.

Population & Utilization of Land & Sea in Hawaii. J. W. Coulter. (BMB Ser.: No. 88). 1974. reprint ed. pap. 25.00 (*0-527-02194-6*) Periodicals Srv.

Population & Women. LC 96-215401. 459p. 35.00 (*92-1-151306-5*, HQ1240) UN.

Population Atlas of China. Ed. by People's Republic of China, State Council Staff & Chinese Academy of Sciences, Institute of the Hist. LC 87-675262. (Illus.). 216p. 1987. text 275.00 (*0-19-584092-5*) OUP.

***Population Balances: Theory & Applications to Particulate Systems in Engineering.** Doraiswami Ramkrishna. 400p. 2000. 115.00 (*0-12-576970-9*) Acad Pr.

Population-Based Medicine. Ed. by Mack Lipkin, Jr. & William A. Lybrand. LC 81-21116. 198p. 1982. 55.00 (*0-275-91370-8*, C1370, Praeger Pubs) Greenwood.

Population Biology. Ed. by H. I. Freedman & C. Strobeck. (Lecture Notes in Biomathematics Ser.: Vol. 52). 440p. 1983. pap. 46.60 (*0-387-12677-5*) Spr-Verlag.

Population Biology. Ed. by Subodh K. Jain & K. Wohrmann. (Illus.). xviii, 448p. 1990. 181.95 (*0-387-50802-3*) Spr-Verlag.

Population Biology. Ed. by Simon A. Levin. LC 83-21389. (Proceedings of Symposia in Applied Mathematics Ser.: Vol. 30). 101p. 1984. pap. 31.00 (*0-8218-0083-3*, PSAPM/30) Am Math.

***Population Biology: An Introduction to Mathematical Models.** Fred Brauer. (Illus.). 2000. 49.95 (*0-387-98902-1*) Spr-Verlag.

Population Biology: Concepts & Models. A. Hastings. LC 96-33165. 184p. 1996. 49.95 (*0-387-94862-7*) Spr-Verlag.

Population Biology: Concepts & Models. A. Hastings. LC 96-33165. 220p. 1997. pap. 21.95 (*0-387-94853-8*) Spr-Verlag.

***Population Biology: Concepts & Models.** 2nd ed. Alan Hastings. (Illus.). 2000. pap. 27.95 (*0-387-98847-5*) Spr-Verlag.

Population Biology & Evolution. Ed. by K. Woehrmann & V. Loschcke. (Proceedings in Life Sciences Ser.). (Illus.). 300p. 1984. 95.00 (*0-387-13278-3*) Spr-Verlag.

Population Biology & Evolution of Clonal Organisms. Jeremy B. Jackson. Ed. by Leo W. Buss & Robert E. Cook. LC 85-14186. 608p. (C). 1986. 80.00 (*0-300-03379-6*) Yale U Pr.

Population Biology of Animals: Amphibians & Invertebrates, Vol. 3. S. O. Sergievskii. iv, 86p. 1989. text 90.00 (*3-7186-4880-6*) Gordon & Breach.

Population Biology of Grasses. Ed. by G. P. Cheplick. LC 97-26257. (Illus.). 412p. (C). 1998. text 90.00 (*0-521-57205-3*) Cambridge U Pr.

Population Biology of Infectious Diseases: Berlin, 1982. Ed. by R. C. Anderson & Raoul M. May. (Dahlem Workshop Reports: Vol. 25). (Illus.). 320p. 1982. 35.00 (*0-387-11650-8*) Spr-Verlag.

Population Biology of Passerine Birds: An Integrated Approach. Ed. by Jean Blondel et al. (NATO ASI Series G: Ecological Sciences: Vol. 24). xv, 496p. 1991. 216.95 (*0-387-51759-6*) Spr-Verlag.

Population Biology of Plants. J. L. Harper. 1977. text 104.00 (*0-12-325850-2*) Acad Pr.

Population Biology of Plants. J. L. Harper. LC 76-16973. 1981. pap. text 58.00 (*0-12-325852-9*) Acad Pr.

Population Biology of Tropical Insects. Allen M. Young. LC 82-7562. 524p. 1982. 110.00 (*0-306-40843-0*, Plenum Trade) Perseus Pubng.

Population Bomb. Paul R. Ehrlich. 1997. reprint ed. 25.95 (*1-56849-587-0*) Buccaneer Bks.

Population Bomb. rev. ed. Paul R. Ehrlich. 201p. 1975. lib. bdg. 21.95 (*0-89190-861-7*, Rivercity Pr) Amereon Ltd.

Population Bulletin of ESCWA. 80p. 25.00 (*92-1-128177-6*) UN.

Population Bulletin of ESCWA, No. 3. 165p. 26.00 (*92-1-128135-0*, E.93.II.L.6); 26.00 (*92-1-128134-2*) UN.

Population Bulletin of ESCWA, No. 4. 195p. 34.00 (*92-1-128149-0*, E.95.II.L.2) UN.

Population Bulletin of ESCWA, No. 40. 128p. 26.00 (*92-1-128138-5*) UN.

Population Bulletin of ESCWA, No. 43. 126p. 26.00 (*92-1-128156-3*, DS101) UN.

Population Bulletin of the United Nations. 95p. 1988. pap. 10.00 (*0-685-74038-2*); write for info. (*92-1-151170-4*, 88.XIII.5) UN.

Population Bulletin of the United Nations, 25. 95p. 1988. write for info. (*92-1-151171-2*, 88.XIII.6) UN.

Population Bulletin of the United Nations, No. 3. 104p. pap. 17.00 (*92-1-151273-5*, E.94.XIII.16) UN.

Population Bulletin of the United Nations, No. 26. 18.00 (*92-1-151179-8*) UN.

Population Bulletin of the United Nations, No. 27. 135p. 11.50 (*92-1-151180-1*, E.89.XII.7) UN.

Population Bulletin of the United Nations, No. 29. 1990. 9.00 (*92-1-151190-9*, 90.XIII.5) UN.

Population Bulletin of the United Nations, No. 30. 125p. 1991. 15.00 (*92-1-151221-2*) UN.

Population Bulletin of the United Nations, No. 36. 110p. pap. 17.00 (*92-1-151269-7*, E.94.XIII.12) UN.

Population Bulletin of the United Nations, No. 39. 156p. pap. 17.00 (*92-1-151288-3*) UN.

Population Bulletin of the United Nations, 1986: A Special Issue in Commemoration of the 40th Anniversary of the Population Commission, Nos.19-20. 167p. 1987. 16.50 (*92-1-151162-3*, E.87.XIII.2) UN.

Population Bulletin of the United Nations, 1989, No. 28. 112p. 1989. 9.00 (*92-1-151189-5*, 90.XIII.3) UN.

Population Challenge. B. L. Raina. LC 94-900581. (C). 1994. 21.50 (*81-7018-763-X*, Pub. by BR Pub) S Asia.

Population Challenge: A Handbook for Non-Specialists, 19. Johannes Overbeek. LC 76-5328. (Contributions in Sociology Ser.: No. 19). (Illus.). 214p. 1976. 57.95 (*0-8371-8896-2*, OPC/, Greenwood Pr) Greenwood.

Population Change: Asia & Oceania, Proceedings of the Sydney Conference, Australia, 1967. International Union for the Scientific Study of Po. Ed. by W. D. Borrie & Morag Cameron. LC 73-168088. 216p. reprint ed. pap. 67.00 (*0-608-12386-2*, 205211900034) Bks Demand.

Population Change & Agricultural Development in 19th Century France. William H. Newell. Ed. by Stuart Bruchey. LC 77-77783. (Dissertations in European Economic History Ser.). (Illus.). 1978. lib. bdg. 29.95 (*0-405-10796-X*) Ayer.

Population Change & Crime Change. Deborah Caulfield. 15p. (Orig.). 1982. pap. 1.50 (*1-55719-040-2*) U NE CPAR.

Population Change & Social Continuity: Ten Years in a Coal Town. Harold W. Annand. LC 85-40506. (Illus.). 144p. 1986. 32.50 (*0-941664-14-7*) Susquehanna U Pr.

Population Change & Social Policy. Nathan Keyfitz. 288p. 1982. text 35.00 (*0-89011-568-0*) Abt Bks.

Population Change & the Economy. Andrew M. Isserman. 1985. lib. bdg. 126.00 (*0-89838-140-1*) Kluwer Academic.

Population Change in the Rural West, 1975-1990. Ed. by John M. Wardwell & James H. Copp. LC 96-34952. 306p. (C). 1996. 62.50 (*0-7618-0512-5*); pap. 34.50 (*0-7618-0513-3*) U Pr of Amer.

Population Change, Labor Supply, & Agriculture in Ausburg, 1480-1618: A Study of Early Demographic-Economic Interactions. Martha W. Paas. Ed. by Stuart Bruchey. LC 80-2821. (Dissertations in European Economic History Ser.). (Illus.). 1981. lib. bdg. 29.95 (*0-405-14005-3*) Ayer.

Population Change, Natural Resources & Regionalism. Ed. by Ann C. Reid. (Breaking New Ground Ser.: No. 1). 104p. 1986. pap. 15.00 (*0-938549-00-6*) Grey Towers Pr.

Population Changes in Omaha-Council Bluffs YMCA Branch Office Areas. Rebecca S. Fahrlander. 10p. (Orig.). 1981. pap. 1.00 (*1-55719-058-5*) U NE CPAR.

Population Consensus at Cairo, Mexico City & Bucharest. LC 96-114507. 172p. pap. 17.50 (*92-1-151300-6*) UN.

Population, Consumption, & the Environment: Religious & Secular Responses. Ed. by Harold Coward. LC 95-81019. 319p. (C). 1995. pap. text 21.95 (*0-7914-2672-6*) State U NY Pr.

Population, Contact & Climate in the New Mexican Pueblos. Ezra B. Zubrow. LC 73-86447. (Anthropological Papers of the University of Arizona: No. 24). 95p. reprint ed. pap. 30.00 (*0-608-12764-7*, 202432400037) Bks Demand.

Population Control & Family Planning in India. Mamta Lakshmana. (C). 1988. 24.00 (*81-7141-026-X*) S Asia.

Population Control & National Security: A Review of U. S. National Security Policy 1970-1988. Information Project for Africa, Inc. Staff. (IPFA Foreign Policy Ser.). 55p. 1991. pap. text 14.00 (*1-886719-00-4*) Info Proj for Afr.

Population Control & the Law. B. P. Sehgal. (C). 1990. 113.00 (*0-89771-295-1*) St Mut.

Population Control in China: Theory & Applications. Song Jian & Chi-Hsien Tuan. 310p. 1985. 49.95 (*0-275-90166-1*, C0166, Praeger Pubs) Greenwood.

Population Crisis in India. K. P. Bahadur. 180p. 1977. 15.95 (*0-318-36855-2*) Asia Bk Corp.

Population Data at a Glance: Shaded Contour Maps of Demographic Surfaces over Age & Time. James W. Vaupel et al. LC 98-207728. (Monographs on Population Aging Ser.: Vol. 4). (Illus.). 98p. 1998. 25.00 incl. 3.5 ld (*87-7838-338-2*, Pub. by Odense Univ) Intl Spec Bk.

Population-Demograph. M. E. Witherick. 1990. pap. text. write for info. (*0-582-35586-9*, Pub. by Addison-Wesley) Longman.

Population-Development-Environment: Understanding Their Interactions in Mauritius. Ed. by Wolfgang Lutz. LC 94-26937. 1994. 127.95 (*0-387-58301-7*); write for info. (*3-540-58301-7*) Spr-Verlag.

Population Dilemma. 2nd ed. Ed. by Philip M. Hauser. LC 73-96967. 1963. pap. 2.45 (*0-13-685669-1*) Am Assembly.

Population Dilemma in Latin America. Ed. by J. Mayone Stycos & Jorge R. Arias. LC 66-18575. 1966. 3.95 (*0-317-02961-4*); pap. 2.45 (*0-317-02962-2*) Am Assembly.

Population Dilemmas in the Middle East. Gad G. Gilbar. 141p. (C). 1997. text 42.50 (*0-7146-4706-3*, Pub. by F Cass Pubs); pap. text 19.50 (*0-7146-4244-4*, Pub. by F Cass Pubs) Intl Spec Bk.

Population, Disease & Land in Early Japan, 645-900. William W. Farris. (Harvard-Yenching Institute Monographs: No. 24). (Illus.). 400p. 1985. 20.00 (*0-674-69031-1*) HUP.

Population, Disease & Land in Early Japan, 645-900. William W. Farris. (Harvard-Yenching Institute Monographs: No. 24). (Illus.). 256p. 1995. pap. text 18.00 (*0-674-69005-2*, FARPOX) HUP.

Population Dispersal from Major Metropolitan Regions: An International Comparison. Daniel R. Vining, Jr. & Thomas Kontuly. (Discussion Papers: No. 100). 1977. pap. 10.00 (*1-55869-097-2*) Regional Sci Res Inst.

Population Displacement & Resettlement: Development & Conflict in the Middle East. Ed. by Seteney Shami. LC 94-24381. 326p. 1994. 17.50 (*0-934733-82-1*) CMS.

Population Distribution & Migration: Proceedings: United Nations Expert Group Meeting on Population Distribution & Migration (1993: Santa Cruz, Bolivia) Department of Economic and Social Affairs, Population Division Staff. LC 99-176675. 400p. 1998. pap. 45.00 (*92-1-151324-3*) UN.

Population Distribution in Colonial America. Stella H. Sutherland. LC 70-182725. reprint ed. 32.50 (*0-404-06306-3*) AMS Pr.

Population Distribution, Migration & Development. 513p. 1990. 45.00 (*92-1-151096-1*) UN.

***Population Diversity & the U. S. Army.** Ed. by Lloyd J. Matthews & Tinaz Pavri. 143p. 1999. pap. write for info. (*1-58487-002-8*) SSI US Army.

Population Dynamics: A New Economic Approach. C. Y. Cyrus Chu. LC 98-19032. (Illus.). 240p. 1998. text 60.00 (*0-19-512158-9*) OUP.

Population Dynamics: New Approaches & Synthesis. Ed. by Naomi Cappuccino & Peter W. Price. (Illus.). 429p. 1995. text 79.00 (*0-12-159270-7*) Acad Pr.

Population Dynamics & the Tribolium Model: Genetics & Demography. R. F. Costantino & R. A. Desharnais. Ed. by R. Frankel et al. (Monographs on Theoretical & Applied Genetics: Vol. 13). (Illus.). xii, 258p. 1991. 144.00 (*0-387-97581-0*) Spr-Verlag.

Population Dynamics in Ecological Space & Time. Ed. by Olin E. Rhodes, Jr. et al. (Illus.). 336p. 1996. lib. bdg. 50.00 (*0-226-71057-2*) U Ch Pr.

Population Dynamics in Ecological Space & Time. Ed. by Olin E. Rhodes et al. (Illus.). 336p. 1996. pap. text 18.00 (*0-226-71058-0*) U Ch Pr.

Population Dynamics in India. Prabha S. Ranade. 1990. 32.50 (*81-7024-307-6*, Pub. by Ashish Pub Hse) S Asia.

Population Dynamics in Indian States. Kuttan Mahadevan. 1989. 38.50 (*81-7099-178-1*, Pub. by Mittal Pubs Dist) S Asia.

Population Dynamics in Napal, Vol. 2. 1993. pap. 84.00 (*0-7855-7621-5*) St Mut.

Population Dynamics in Nepal, Vol. 3. 1993. pap. 84.00 (*0-7855-7622-3*) St Mut.

Population Dynamics in Nepal, Vol. 4. 1996. pap. 84.00 (*0-7855-7623-1*) St Mut.

Population Dynamics in Nepal, Vol. 5. 1996. pap. 84.00 (*0-7855-7624-X*) St Mut.

Population Dynamics in Variable Environments. Shripad Tuljapurkar. (Lecture Notes in Biomathematics Ser.: Vol. 85). ii, 154p. 1990. 38.95 (*0-387-52482-7*) Spr-Verlag.

Population Dynamics of a Philippine Rain Forest People: The San Ildefonso Agta. John D. Early & Thomas N. Headland. LC 97-41150. 224p. 1998. 39.95 (*0-8130-1555-3*) U Press Fla.

Population Dynamics of Commercial Fish in Inland Reservoirs. rev. ed. Ed. by L. A. Kuderskii. (Illus.). 166p. (C). 1996. text 91.00 (*90-5410-259-4*, Pub. by A A Balkema) Ashgate Pub Co.

An Asterisk (*) at the beginning of an entry indicates that the title is appearing for the first time.

Population Dynamics of Kenya. National Research Council Staff. Ed. by William Brass & Carole L. Jolly. (Population Dynamics of Sub-Saharan Africa Ser.). 200p. (Orig.). (C). 1993. pap. text 33.00 (*0-309-04943-1*) Natl Acad Pr.

Population Dynamics of Senegal. National Research Council Staff. Ed. by Gilles Pison et al. LC 95-68873. (Population Dynamics of Sub-Saharan Africa Ser.). 272p. (Orig.). (C). 1995. pap. text 35.00 (*0-309-05280-7*) Natl Acad Pr.

Population Dynamics on Staten Island: From Ethnic Homogeneity to Diversity. Nadia Youssef. 85p. 1991. 9.95 (*0-934733-62-7*) CMS.

Population Dynamics, Reproduction, & Activities of the Kangaroo Rat, Dipodomys ordii, in Western Texas. Herschel W. Garner. (Graduate Studies: No. 7). (Illus.). 28p. 1974. pap. 2.00 (*0-89672-014-4*) Tex Tech Univ Pr.

Population Ecology & Ecophysiology, Vol. 3. I. A. Shilov. iv, 64p. 1989. text 59.00 (*3-7186-4878-4*) Gordon & Breach.

Population, Ecology, & Social Evolution. Ed. by Steven Polgar. (World Anthropology Ser.). (Illus.). x, 354p. 1975. 35.40 (*0-685-18668-7*) Mouton.

Population Ecology of Cycles in Small Mammals: Mathematical Theory & Biological Fact. James P. Finerty. LC 79-23774. (Illus.). 248p. reprint ed. pap. 76.90 (*0-7837-3296-1*, 205769800006) Bks Demand.

Population Ecology of Human Survival. Ed. by Ryutaro Ohtsuka & Tsuguyoshi Suzuki. 300p. 1990. text 52.50 (*0-86008-456-6*, Pub. by U of Tokyo) Col U Pr.

Population Ecology of Individuals. Adam Lomnicki. LC 87-3439. (Monographs in Population Biology: No. 25). (Illus.). 236p. 1988. reprint ed. pap. 73.20 (*0-608-07127-7*, 206735300009) Bks Demand.

Population Ecology of Interest Representation: Lobbying Communities in the American States. Virginia Gray & David Lowery. (Illus.). 320p. (C). pap. text 21.95 (*0-472-08718-5*, 08718) U of Mich Pr.

Population Ecology of Interest Representation: Lobbying Communities in the American States. Virginia Gray & David Lowery. LC 96-4459. 320p. (C). 1996. text 47.50 (*0-472-10683-X*, 10683) U of Mich Pr.

Population Ecology of Raptors. Ian Newton. 1997. text 39.95 (*0-85661-023-2*) Acad Pr.

Population Ecology of Terrestrial Orchids. T. C. Wells & J. H. Willems. (Illus.). viii, 189p. 1991. pap. 50.00 (*90-5103-068-1*, Pub. by SPB Acad Pub) Balogh.

Population Ecology of the Bobwhite. John L. Roseberry & Willard D. Klimstra. LC 83-2481. (Illus.). 282p. 1984. 31.95 (*0-8093-1116-X*) S Ill U Pr.

Population Ecology of the Cooperatively Breeding Acorn Woodpecker. Walter D. Koenig & Ronald L. Mumme. LC 87-2385. (Monographs in Population Biology: No. 24). (Illus.). 454p. reprint ed. pap. 140.80 (*0-608-06353-3*, 206671400008) Bks Demand.

Population Ecology of the Gray Bat (Myotis Grisescens) Factors Influencing Early Growth & Development. Merlin D. Tuttle. (Occasional Papers: No. 36). 24p. 1975. pap. 1.00 (*0-317-04951-8*) U KS Nat Hist Mus.

Population Ecology of the Gray Bat (Myotis Grisescens) Philopatry, Timing & Patterns of Movement, Weight Loss During Migration, & Seasonal Adaptive Strategies. Merlin D. Tuttle. (Occasional Papers: No. 54). 38p. 1976. pap. 1.00 (*0-317-04955-0*) U KS Nat Hist Mus.

Population Ecology of the Little Brown Bat, Myotis Lucifugus, in Indiana & Northcentral Kentucky. Stephen R. Humphrey & James B. Cope. (ASM Special Publications: No. 4). (Illus.). vii, 81p. 1976. 7.50 (*0-943612-03-9*) Am Soc Mammalogists.

Population, Economic Development, & the Environment. Ed. by Partha Dasgupta. (Illus.). 312p. 1994. 35.00 (*0-19-828950-2*) OUP.

Population, Economic Development, & the Environment. Ed. by Kerstin Lindahl-Kiessling & Hans Landberg. (Illus.). 306p. 1998. reprint ed. pap. text 22.00 (*0-19-829242-2*) OUP.

Population Economics. Assaf Razin & Efraim Sadka. LC 94-27773. 285p. 1995. 34.50 (*0-262-18160-6*) MIT Pr.

Population Economics. T. Paul Schulz. LC 80-36830. (Perspectives on Economics Ser.). 224p. (C). 1981. pap. text. write for info. (*0-201-08371-X*) Addison-Wesley.

Population, Economy & Family Structure in Hertfordshire in 1851 Vol. 1: The Berkhamsted Region. Nigel Goose. (Illus.). 416p. 1996. pap. 29.95 (*0-900458-73-9*, Pub. by Univ of Herfordshire) Bold Strummer Ltd.

***Population, Economy & Family Structure in Hertfordshire in 1851 Vol. 2: St. Albans & Its Region.** Nigel Goose. (Illus.). 700p. 2000. 69.95 (*0-900458-84-4*, Pub. by Univ of Herfordshire); pap. 39.95 (*0-900458-83-6*, Pub. by Univ of Herfordshire) Bold Strummer Ltd.

Population, Economy, & Welfare in Sweden. Ed. by Tommy Bengtsson. LC 94-33960. 1994. write for info. (*0-387-58423-4*) Spr-Verlag.

Population, Economy, & Welfare in Sweden. Ed. by Tommy Bengtsson. LC 94-33960. (Population Economics Ser.). 1994. 78.95 (*3-540-58423-4*) Spr-Verlag.

Population Ecotoxicology. Newman. text 121.00 (*0-471-98818-9*) Wiley.

Population Education for Nepal. Daniel Taylor & Hem B. Hamal. 81p. 1974. pap. 4.00 (*0-89055-110-3*) Carolina Pop Ctr.

Population, Environment, & Development. E. Van Imhoff et al. (NIDI-CBGS Publications, Population & Family Study Center Ser.: Vol. 25). x, 90p. 1992. pap. 43.00 (*90-265-1305-4*) Swets.

Population, Environment & Development: Proceedings of the United Nations Expert Group Meeting on Population, Environment & Development. LC 94-213606. 285p. 30.00 (*92-1-151265-4*) UN.

Population, Environment & Resources, & Third World Development, 5. Ed. by Pradip K. Ghosh. LC 83-26430. (International Development Resource Bks.: No. 5). (Illus.). 634p. 1984. lib. bdg. 99.50 (*0-313-24141-4*, GPL/, Greenwood Pr) Greenwood.

Population, Environment, & the Quality of Life. Ed. by Dennis Hodgson. LC 74-579. (Studies in Modern Society: Political & Social Issues: No. 6). 1990. 32.50 (*0-404-10536-X*) AMS Pr.

Population Estimates: Methods for Small Area Analysis. Ed. by Everett S. Lee & Harold F. Goldsmith. LC 82-648. 248p. reprint ed. pap. 76.90 (*0-8357-8446-0*, 203471000091) Bks Demand.

Population Estimates for Counties & Metropolitan Areas. 1995. lib. bdg. 250.00 (*0-8490-5851-1*) Gordon Pr.

***Population Estimates, 1998: States & Counties, as of July 1, 1998.** Clark H. Bensen. 592p. 1999. ring bd. 98.00 (*1-57708-613-9*, BEC-98) Polidata.

***Population Estimates, 1999: States & Counties, as of July 1, 1999.** Clark H. Bensen. 592p. 2000. ring bd. 98.00 (*1-57708-614-7*, BEC-99) Polidata.

Population Estimation & Projection: Methods for Marketing, Demographic, & Planning Personnel. James C. Raymondo. LC 91-45709. 224p. 1992. 59.95 (*0-89930-663-2*, RPF, Quorum Bks) Greenwood.

Population Ethology, Vol. 3. E. N. Panov. iv, 104p. 1989. text 75.00 (*3-7186-4881-4*) Gordon & Breach.

Population Explosion. Paul R. Ehrlich & Anne H. Ehrlich. 320p. 1991. pap. 12.00 (*0-671-73294-3*, Touchstone) S&S Trade Pap.

Population Explosion. unabridged ed. Walter N. Kuhn, Jr. & Erika K. Putney. Ed. by Jean M. Kuhn. (Freddy Cricket & the Town of Corncob Ser.: Vol. 3). (Illus.). 20p. (J). (ps-10). 1996. spiral bd. 6.95 (*1-891547-04-6*) Hoppa Prodns.

Population Explosion (Explosion de Poblacion) unabridged ed. Walter N. Kuhn, Jr. Tr. by Norberto Rivera. (Freddy Cricket & the Town of Corncob Ser.: Vol. 3C). (ENG & SPA., Illus.). 20p. (J). (ps-10). 1997. spiral bd. 6.95 (*1-891547-22-4*) Hoppa Prodns.

Population Exposure from the Nuclear Fuel Cycle. Ed. by Edward L. Alpen et al. 370p. 1988. text 110.00 (*2-88124-278-2*) Gordon & Breach.

Population Family & Culture. Rabindra N. Pati. 1987. 31.95 (*81-7024-151-0*) Asia Bk Corp.

Population, Family, & Welfare: A Comparative Survey of European Attitudes, Vol. 1. Ed. by Hein Morrs & Rossella Palomba. (Illus.). 314p. 1995. text 69.00 (*0-19-828846-8*) OUP.

Population, Family, & Welfare: A Comparative Survey of European Attitudes, Vol. II. Ed. by Hein Moors & Rossella Palomba. (Illus.). 306p. 1999. text 82.00 (*0-19-828842-5*) OUP.

Population, Food & Rural Development. Ed. by Ronald D. Lee et al. (International Studies in Demography). (Illus.). 224p. 1992. pap. text 22.00 (*0-19-828391-1*) OUP.

Population Forecasting & Uncertainty at the National & Local Scale. R. Baxter & I. Williams. 1978. pap. 13.25 (*0-08-023112-8*, Pergamon Pr) Elsevier.

Population, Gender & Politics: Demographic Change in Rural North India. Roger Jeffery & Patricia Jeffery. LC 96-43848. (Contemporary South Asia Ser.: Vol. 3). 294p. (C). 1997. text 64.95 (*0-521-46116-2*); pap. text 22.95 (*0-521-46653-9*) Cambridge U Pr.

Population Genetics. Chapman & Hall Staff. (C). text 69.00 (*0-416-03160-9*) Chapman & Hall.

Population Genetics: A Concise Guide. John H. Gillespie. LC 97-19509. (Illus.). 184p. 1997. text 45.00 (*0-8018-5754-6*); pap. text 19.95 (*0-8018-5755-4*) Johns Hopkins.

Population Genetics: Diversity & Stability. Yu. P. Altukhov. xiii, 352p. 1990. text 305.00 (*3-7186-4984-5*, Harwood Acad Pubs) Gordon & Breach.

Population Genetics: The Nature & Causes of Genetic Variability in Populations. Cold Spring Harbor Symposia on Quantitative Biolog. LC 34-8174. (Cold Spring Harbor Symposia on Quantitative Biology Ser.: Vol. 20). (Illus.). 362p. 1955. pap. 112.30 (*0-7837-8976-9*, 204975700003) Bks Demand.

Population Genetics & Evolution. G. De Jong. (Illus.). 305p. 1988. 99.00 (*0-387-18452-X*) Spr-Verlag.

Population Genetics & Evolution. 2nd ed. Lawrence E. Mettler et al. (Illus.). 448p. (C). 1988. text 55.60 (*0-13-685678-0*) P-H.

Population Genetics & Fisheries. Ryman. Ed. by Fred Utter. 488p. 1987. 35.00 (*0-295-96435-9*) U of Wash Pr.

Population Genetics & Genetic Conservation of Forest Trees. P. H. Baradat et al. (Illus.). 479p. 1996. 150.00 (*90-5103-109-2*, Pub. by SPB Acad Pub) Balogh.

Population Genetics & Molecular Evolution. Ed. by T. Ohta & K. Aoki. 400p. 1986. 94.00 (*0-387-15584-8*) Spr-Verlag.

Population Genetics in Animal Breeding. 2nd ed. Franz Pirchner. Tr. by D. L. Frape from GER. LC 83-2164. 424p. 1983. 95.00 (*0-306-41201-2*, Plenum Trade) Perseus Pubng.

Population Genetics in Forestry. Ed. by H. R. Gregorius. (Lecture Notes in Biomathematics Ser.: Vol. 60). vi, 287p. 1985. 44.95 (*0-387-15980-0*) Spr-Verlag.

Population Genetics, Molecular Evolution & the Neutral Theory: Selected Papers. Motoo Kimura. Ed. by Naoyuki Takahata. (Illus.). 704p. 1994. pap. text 29.95 (*0-226-43563-6*); lib. bdg. 80.00 (*0-226-43562-8*) U Ch Pr.

Population Genetics of Bacteria. Ed. by S. Baumberg et al. (Society for General Microbiology Symposium Ser.: No. 52). (Illus.). 360p. (C). 1995. text 115.00 (*0-521-48052-3*) Cambridge U Pr.

Population Genetics of Forest Trees: Proceedings of the International Symposium on Population Genetics of Forest Trees, Corvallis, Oregon, U. S. A. July 31-August 2, 1990. Ed. by W. T. Adams et al. LC 92-18860. (Forestry Sciences Ser.: No. 42). 400p. (C). 1992. text 236.00 (*0-7923-1857-9*) Kluwer Academic.

***Population Genetics of Multiple Loci.** Freddy B. Christiansen. LC 99-41803. (Mathematical & Computational Biology Ser.). (Illus.). 380p. 1999. 170.00 (*0-471-97979-1*) Wiley.

Population Geography. Barrett. (J). 1992. pap. text. write for info. (*0-05-004507-5*) Addison-Wesley.

Population Geography. H. R. Jones. 336p. (C). 1981. 65.00 (*0-06-318189-4*, Pub. by P Chapman) St Mut.

Population Geography. 2nd ed. Huw Jones. LC 93-48975. 320p. 1990. pap. text 32.50 (*0-89862-464-9*) Guilford Pubns.

Population Geography. 6th ed. Gary L. Peters & Robert P. Larkin. LC 98-75500. 316p. 1999. per. 46.95 (*0-7872-5672-2*, 41567201) Kendall-Hunt.

Population Geography: Progress & Prospects. Ed. by Michael Pacione. (Progress in Geography Ser.). 336p. 1987. 49.95 (*0-7099-4045-9*, Pub. by C Helm) Routldge.

Population Geography of a Backward Region of Rohilkhand. N. P. Goel. 1989. 44.00 (*81-7169-029-7*, Pub. by Commonwealth) S Asia.

Population Growth. Judith E. Jacobsen. LC 95-61064. (Illus.). 58p. (Orig.). (C). 1996. pap. text 19.50 (*0-935702-81-4*) Univ Sci Bks.

Population Growth. Eric McGraw. (World Issues Ser.). (Illus.). 48p. (YA). (gr. 5 up). 1987. lib. bdg. 18.60 (*0-317-60380-9*) Rourke Corp.

Population Growth. Eric McGraw. (World Issues Ser.: Set II). (Illus.). 48p. (J). (gr. 5 up). 1988. lib. bdg. 25.27 (*0-86592-276-4*) Rourke Enter.

Population Growth: A Problem-Solving Approach. Darlene Southworth & Thomas M. Hursh. (gr. 11-12). 1979. pap. text 6.95 (*0-933694-01-6*, COM 4222A) COMPress.

Population Growth & Agricultural Change in Africa. Ed. by B. L. Turner, II et al. LC 93-2860. (Carter Lecture Series, Center for African Studies). (Illus.). 416p. (C). 1993. 49.95 (*0-8130-1219-8*) U Press Fla.

Population Growth & Agricultural Change in Nepal. Silwal U. Kant. LC 94-907328. (C). 1995. 32.00 (*0-7069-8826-4*, Pub. by Vikas) S Asia.

Population Growth & Balance. Joni Keating. 60p. 1988. pap., teacher ed. 14.99 (*0-89824-179-0*) Trillium Pr.

Population Growth & Development in India. R. S. Tripathi & R. P. Tiwari. (C). 1996. 52.00 (*81-7024-783-7*, Pub. by Ashish Pub Hse) S Asia.

Population Growth & Economic Development: Issues & Evidence. Ed. by D. Gale Johnson & Ronald D. Lee. LC 86-40447. 716p. reprint ed. pap. 200.00 (*0-8357-6800-7*, 203547900095) Bks Demand.

Population Growth & Economic Development: Policy Questions. National Research Council Staff. 120p. (Orig.). (C). 1986. pap. text 24.95 (*0-309-03641-0*) Natl Acad Pr.

Population Growth & Environmental Degradation in Southern Africa. Ed. by Ezekiel Kalipeni. LC 94-2569. 236p. 1994. lib. bdg. 49.95 (*1-55587-512-2*) L Rienner.

Population Growth & Environmental Issues. Ed. by Shridath Rampnal & Steven W. Sinding. LC 96-16279. (Environmental Literacy Ser.). 216p. 1996. 57.95 (*0-275-95371-8*, Praeger Pubs) Greenwood.

Population Growth & Its Demands upon Land for Housing in Evanston, Illinois. Albert G. Hinman. LC 73-2904. (Metropolitan America Ser.). (Illus.). 132p. 1974. reprint ed. 15.95 (*0-405-05395-9*) Ayer.

Population Growth & Justice: An Examination of Moral Issues Raised by Rapid Population Growth. Ronald M. Green. LC 76-44233. (Harvard Dissertations in Religion Ser.: Vol. 5). 288p. (Orig.). reprint ed. pap. 89.30 (*0-608-08679-7*, 206920200003) Bks Demand.

Population Growth & Mega-Cities: Sao Paulo. 36p. pap. 7.50 (*92-1-151254-9*, E.93.XIII.9) UN.

Population Growth & Migration in Jordon, 1950-1994. Onn Winkler. LC 97-202095. 152p. 1997. 55.00 (*1-898723-65-6*, Pub. by Sussex Acad Pr) Intl Spec Bk.

Population Growth & Planning Policy: Housing & Employment Location in the West Midlands. David E. Eversley et al. (Illus.). 88p. 1965. 24.00 (*0-7146-1583-8*, Pub. by F Cass Pubs) Intl Spec Bk.

Population Growth & Policies in Mega-Cities: Bangkok. 47p. pap. 7.50 (*92-1-151192-5*, 90.XIII.8) UN.

Population Growth & Policies in Mega-Cities: Bombay. 37p. pap. 7.50 (*92-1-151193-3*, 90.XIII.9) UN.

Population Growth & Policies in Mega-Cities: Cairo. 29p. pap. 7.50 (*92-1-151218-2*, E 90.XIII.31) UN.

Population Growth & Policies in Mega-Cities: Calcutta. 38p. pap. 7.50 (*92-1-151194-1*, E 90.XIII.10) UN.

Population Growth & Policies in Mega-Cities: Delhi. 38p. pap. 7.50 (*92-1-151196-8*, E 90.XIII.11) UN.

Population Growth & Policies in Mega-Cities: Dhaka. 38p. pap. 7.50 (*92-1-151197-6*, E 90.XIII.12) UN.

Population Growth & Policies in Mega-Cities: Jakarta. 46p. pap. 7.50 (*92-1-151198-4*, E 90.XIII.13) UN.

Population Growth & Policies in Mega-Cities: Karachi. 43p. pap. 7.50 (*92-1-151199-2*, E 90.XIII.14) UN.

Population Growth & Policies in Mega-Cities: Madras. 30p. pap. 7.50 (*92-1-151201-8*, E 90.XIII.15) UN.

Population Growth & Policies in Mega-Cities: Manila. 50p. pap. 7.50 (*92-1-151202-6*, E 90.XIII.16) UN.

Population Growth & Policies in Mega-Cities: Mexico City. 34p. pap. 7.50 (*92-1-151222-0*, 91.XIII.3) UN.

Population Growth & Policies in Mega-Cities: Seoul. 56p. pap. 7.50 (*92-1-151203-4*, E 90.XIII.17) UN.

Population Growth & Social Complexity: An Examination of Settlement & Environment in the Central Maya Lowlands. Anabel Ford. LC 85-52430. (Anthropological Research Papers: No. 35). (Illus.). xiii, 201p. (Orig.). 1986. pap. 17.50 (*0-9611932-5-5*) AZ Univ ARP.

Population Growth & Socioeconomic Progress in Less Developed Countries: Determinants of Fertility Transition. Peter N. Hess. LC 87-38472. 180p. 1988. 57.95 (*0-275-92979-5*, C2979, Praeger Pubs) Greenwood.

Population Growth & the Problems of Unemployment. S. P. Gupta. 1990. 48.50 (*81-7041-241-2*, Pub. by Anmol) S Asia.

Population Growth & Umemployment in India. N. R. Prabhakara & M. N. Usha. 1986. 15.00 (*81-7024-041-7*, Pub. by Ashish Pub Hse) S Asia.

Population Growth & Urban Systems Development. G. A. Van Der Knaap. (Studies in Applied Regional Science: Vol. 18). 245p. 1980. lib. bdg. 69.00 (*0-89838-024-3*) Kluwer Academic.

Population Growth & Urbanization in Latin America. Ed. by John M. Hunter et al. 310p. 1983. 22.95 (*0-87073-225-0*); pap. 17.95 (*0-87073-226-9*) Schenkman Bks Inc.

Population Growth, Economic Development & Social Change in Bavaria, 1750-1850. W. R. Lee. Ed. by Stuart Bruchey. LC 77-77194. (Dissertations in European Economic History Ser.). (Illus.). 1978. lib. bdg. 47.95 (*0-405-10806-0*) Ayer.

Population Growth, Energy Use, & Pollution: Understanding the Driving Forces of Global Change. Michael Kuby. (Active Learning Modules on the Human Dimensions of Global Change Ser.). (Illus.). 249p. (C). 1997. pap., teacher ed. 20.00 (*0-89291-235-9*); pap., student ed., wbk. ed. 8.75 (*0-89291-236-7*) Assn Am Geographers.

Population Growth in Latin America & U. S. National Security. Ed. by John Saunders. 224p. (C). 1986. text 44.95 (*0-04-497002-1*) Routledge.

Population Growth, Income Distribution, & Economic Development: Theory, Methodology, & Empirical Results. Nico Heerink. LC 93-38259. (Population Economics Ser.). 1994. 116.00 (*0-387-57323-2*) Spr-Verlag.

Population Growth, Poverty, & Environmental Stress: Frontier Migration in the Philippines & Costa Rica. enl. ed. Robert C. Repetto et al. 90p. 1992. pap. 20.00 (*0-915825-86-4*, MEPPP) World Resources Inst.

Population Growth, Resource Consumption, & the Environment: Seeking a Common Vision for a Troubled World. Rick Searle. 132p. (C). 1995. pap. 13.75 (*1-55058-064-7*) W Laurier U Pr.

Population Growth, Shifting Cultivatrion & Unsustainable Agricultural Development: A Case Study in Madagascar. Andrew Keck et al. LC 94-7419. (Discussion Paper, Africa Technical Department Ser.). 78p. 1994. pap. 22.00 (*0-8213-2793-3*) World Bank.

Population Growth, Society & Culture: An Inventory of Cross-Culturally Tested Causal Hypotheses. Richard G. Sipes. LC 80-81242. (Comparative Studies). 134p. 1980. 15.00 (*0-87536-337-7*); pap. 10.00 (*0-87536-338-5*) HRAFP.

Population Handbook. Arthur Haupt & Thomas T. Kane. 80p. 1997. 10.00 (*0-917136-09-8*) Population Ref.

Population Harvesting: Demographic Models of Fish, Forest, & Animal Resources. Wayne M. Getz & Robert G. Haight. LC 88-19950. (Monographs in Population Biology: Vol. 27). (Illus.). 408p. 1989. reprint ed. pap. 126.50 (*0-608-07659-7*, 205998000010) Bks Demand.

Population Health: Concepts & Methods. T. Kue Young. (Illus.). 328p. 1998. text 39.95 (*0-19-511972-X*) OUP.

***Population, Health & Nutrition: Selected Papers of Hector Correa.** Hector Correa et al. LC 00-28407. 2000. write for info. (*1-56072-785-3*) Nova Sci Pubs.

Population, Health & Nutrition in the Sahel: Issues in the Welfare of Selected West African Communities. Allan G. Hill. 394p. 29.95 (*0-7103-0099-9*) Routledge.

Population Health Research: Linking Theory & Methods. Ed. by Kathryn Dean. (Illus.). 256p. (C). 1993. text 62.00 (*0-8039-8751-X*); pap. text 23.95 (*0-8039-8752-8*) Sage.

Population History of Britain & Ireland 1500-1750. Rab A. Houston. (New Studies in Economic & Social History: No. 18). 105p. (C). 1995. text 34.95 (*0-521-55277-X*); pap. text 10.95 (*0-521-55776-3*) Cambridge U Pr.

Population History of England, 1541-1871. E. Anthony Wrigley & Roger S. Schofield. (Illus.). 830p. 1989. pap. text 39.95 (*0-521-35688-1*) Cambridge U Pr.

Population History of England, 1000-1540. Richard M. Smith. 224p. 1992. text. write for info. (*0-7190-3431-0*) Manchester Univ Pr.

Population History of New York City. Ira Rosenwaike. LC 75-39829. (New York State Bks.). (Illus.). 274p. 1972. 29.95 (*0-8156-2155-8*) Syracuse U Pr.

***Population History of North America.** Ed. by Michael R. Haines & Richard H. Steckel. (Illus.). 736p. (C). 2000. text 75.00 (*0-521-49666-7*) Cambridge U Pr.

Population in an Interacting World. Ed. by William Alonso. LC 86-20133. (Illus.). 296p. 1987. 49.95 (*0-674-69008-7*) HUP.

Population in Asia. Warren C. Sanderson & Jee-Peng Tan. (World Bank Regional & Sectoral Studies). 264p. 1996. text 77.95 (*1-85972-309-8*, Pub. by Avebry) Ashgate Pub Co.

Population in Asia. Warren C. Sanderson & Jee-Peng Tan. LC 94-41460. 264p. 1995. pap. 22.00 (*0-8213-3131-0*, 13131) World Bank.

Population in Development Planning: Background & Bibliography. Richard E. Bilsborrow. 1976. pap. 5.00 (*0-89055-048-4*) Carolina Pop Ctr.

***Population in Europe & North America on the Eve of the Millennium: Dynamics & Policy Responses.** United Nations. Economic Commission for Europe. 284p. 1999. 45.00 (*92-1-116718-3*) UN.

P

Population Index Bibliography Cumulated 1935 to 1968 by Authors & Geographical Areas. Princeton University Staff. 1971. 500.00 (*0-8161-1437-4*, G K Hall & Co) Mac Lib Ref.

Population Index Bibliography Cumulated, 1935 to 1968 by Geographical Areas. Princeton University Staff. 1971. 520.00 (*0-8161-1398-X*, G K Hall & Co) Mac Lib Ref.

Population Information: Resources & Activities in the Asia & the Pacific Region. LC 80-39639. 1980. pap. 8.00 (*0-933438-04-4*, SP 4) APLIC Intl.

Population Issues see Social Science Skills: Activities for the Secondary Classroom, Grades 9-12

***Population Issues: An Interdisciplinary Focus.** Ed. by Leo J. G. Van Wissen & Pearl A. Dykstra. LC 99-39025. (Plenum Series on Demographic Methods & Population Analysis). 292p. 1999. 59.95 (*0-306-46196-X*, Kluwer Plenum) Kluwer Academic.

Population, Labor Force & Long Swings in Economic Growth. Richard A. Easterlin. LC 68-26504. (National Bureau of Economic Research. General Ser.: No. 86). 318p. reprint ed. pap. 98.60 (*0-8357-3246-0*, 205714000011) Bks Demand.

Population, Labor Force & Long Swings in Economic Growth: The American Experience. Richard A. Easterlin. (General Ser.: No. 86). (Illus.). 318p. 1968. 82.70 (*0-87014-474-X*) Natl Bur Econ Res.

Population, Labour & Migration in 19th & 20th-Century Germany. Ed. by Klaus J. Bade. LC 86-24470. (German Historical Perspectives Ser.: Vol. 1). 212p. 1987. 37.50 (*0-85496-503-3*) Berg Pubs.

Population Land Management & Environment Change. 104p. pap. 15.00 (*92-808-0956-3*) UN.

Population, Land Values & Government: Studies of Growth & Population & Land Values & Problems of Government, Vol. 4. (Metropolitan America Ser.). 326p. 1974. 41.95 (*0-405-05417-3*) Ayer.

Population Law & Policy: Source Materials & Issues. Stephen L. Isaacs. LC 80-24549. 431p. (C). 1981. 54.95 (*0-89885-000-2*, Kluwer Acad Hman Sci) Kluwer Academic.

Population, Law & the Environment. Robert M. Hardaway. LC 93-44501. 192p. 1994. 57.95 (*0-275-94570-7*, Praeger Pubs) Greenwood.

Population Limitation in Birds. Ian Newton. (Illus.). 624p. 1998. boxed set 79.95 (*0-12-517365-2*) Acad Pr.

Population Limitation in Birds. Ian Newton. (Illus.). 624p. (C). 1998. pap. text 49.95 (*0-12-517366-0*) Acad Pr.

Population Management for Survival & Recovery. Ed. by J. D. Ballou et al. LC 94-25126. (Methods & Cases in Conservation Science Ser.). (Illus.). 512p. 1995. 72.00 (*0-231-10176-7*); pap. 32.50 (*0-231-10177-5*) Col U Pr.

Population Matters: People, Resources, Environment, & Immigration. Ed. by Julian L. Simon. 577p. 1990. 44.95 (*0-88738-300-9*) Transaction Pubs.

Population Matters: People, Resources, Environment, & Immigration. Ed. by Julian L. Simon. 589p. 1996. pap. text 29.95 (*1-56000-895-4*) Transaction Pubs.

Population Matters: The Local Dimension. Ed. by Tony Champion. LC 93-10934. 189p. 1993. pap. 33.00 (*1-85396-201-5*, Pub. by P Chapman) Taylor & Francis.

Population Migration & Displacement in the Sudan: A Reassessment. Gamal H. Hamid. LC 96-26307. (Illus.). 250p. 1996. 19.50 (*0-934733-96-1*) CMS.

Population Migration & the Changing World Order. Ed. by W. T. Gould & Anne M. Findlay. LC 93-49629. (Belhaven Series in Population Studies). 304p. 1994. 115.00 (*0-471-94916-7*) Wiley.

Population Migration in the European Union. Ed. by Philip H. Rees. LC 95-24756. 410p. 1997. 140.00 (*0-471-94968-X*) Wiley.

Population Mobility in Developing Countries: A Reinterpretation. Ronald Skeldon. LC 89-28629. 274p. 1993. text 125.00 (*0-471-94771-7*) Wiley.

Population Movements & the Third World. Mike Parnwell. LC 92-13687. (Introductions to Development Ser.). (Illus.). 160p. (C). 1993. pap. 17.99 (*0-415-06953-X*, A4477) Routledge.

Population Movements in the Caribbean. Malcolm J. Proudfoot. LC 75-109359. 187p. 1970. reprint ed. lib. bdg. 35.00 (*0-8371-3634-2*, PCA&, Greenwood Pr) Greenwood.

Population, 1960, Vol. 1. U. S. Bureau of the Census Staff. LC 75-22863. (America in Two Centuries Ser.). (Illus.). 1976. reprint ed. 93.95 (*0-405-07729-7*) Ayer.

Population of Athens in the Fifth & Fourth Centuries B. C. Arnold W. Gomme. LC 86-18344. 97p. 1987. reprint ed. lib. bdg. 65.00 (*0-313-22001-8*, GOPL, Greenwood Pr) Greenwood.

Population of Britain in the 1990s: A Social & Economics Atlas. Tony Champion et al. (Illus.). 164p. (C). 1996. text 49.95 (*0-19-874174-X*); pap. text 26.00 (*0-19-874175-8*) OUP.

Population of Britain in the Nineteenth Century. 2nd ed. Robert Woods. (New Studies in Economic & Social History: No. 20). 86p. (C). 1995. text 34.95 (*0-521-55279-6*); pap. text 10.95 (*0-521-55774-7*) Cambridge U Pr.

Population of Central Mexico in the Sixteenth Century. Sherburne F. Cook & Lesley B. Simpson. LC 76-29408. (Ibero-Americana Ser.: No. 31). reprint ed. 37.50 (*0-404-15333-X*) AMS Pr.

Population of India: Census Results & Methodology, 1991. Ashish Bose. (C). 1991. 9.50 (*81-7018-667-6*, Pub. by BR Pub) S Asia.

Population of Mauritius. S. Chandrasekhar. (C). 1990. 20.00 (*81-85182-31-0*, Pub. by Indus Pub) S Asia.

Population of Mauritius: Fact, Problem & Policy. S. Chandrasekhar. 95p. 1990. 20.00 (*0-9609080-5-6*) Popl Rev Bks.

Population of Mexico: Trends, Issues, & Policies. Francisco Alba. LC 81-1432. (Illus.). 150p. (C). 1981. 34.95 (*0-87855-359-2*) Transaction Pubs.

Population of Modern China. D. L. Poston, Jr. & D. Yaukey. LC 92-15525. (Demographic Methods & Population Analysis Ser.). (Illus.). 770p. (C). 1992. pap. 54.50 (*0-306-44138-1*, Plenum Trade) Perseus Pubng.

Population of Modern China. Ed. by Dudley L. Poston, Jr. & David Yaukey. LC 92-15525. (Demographic Methods & Population Analysis Ser.). (Illus.). 770p. (C). 1992. 90.00 (*0-306-44235-3*, Plenum Trade) Perseus Pubng.

Population of North Korea. Nicholas Eberstadt & Judith Banister. LC 91-76771. (Korea Research Monographs: No. 17). 1992. pap. 12.00 (*1-55729-030-X*) IEAS.

Population of PA Municipalities, 1960-1990. Diane Shoop et al. (Illus.). 180p. 1998. 35.00 (*1-58036-052-1*) Penn State Data Ctr.

Population of Palestine: Population Statistics of the Late Ottoman Period & the Mandate. Justin McCarthy. (Institute for Palestine Studies). 496p. 1990. text 69.50 (*0-231-07110-8*) Col U Pr.

Population of Peninsular Malaysia. Saw Swee-Hock. (Southeast Asian Studies). (Orig.). 1996. pap. 42.95 (*9971-69-126-4*) Intl Spec Bk.

Population of Peninsular Malaysia. Saw Swee-Hock. 356p. (Orig.). 1989. pap. 56.50 (*9971-69-131-0*, Pub. by Sngapore Univ Pr) Coronet Bks.

Population of Selves: A Therapeutic Exploration of Personal Diversity. Erving Polster. LC 94-42595. (Social & Behavioral Sciences Ser.). 271p. 1995. 30.95 (*0-7879-0076-1*) Jossey-Bass.

Population of States & Counties of the United States: 1790-1990, from the Twenty-one Decennial Censuses. Richard L. Forstall. 235p. 1996. per. 22.00 (*0-16-061061-3*) USGPO.

Population of States & Counties of the United States, 1790-1990. 1997. lib. bdg. 250.95 (*0-8490-6254-3*) Gordon Pr.

Population of the Soviet Union: History & Prospects. Frank Lorimer. LC 76-29424. reprint ed. 55.00 (*0-404-15339-9*) AMS Pr.

Population of the United States. Bogue. 1996. 150.00 (*0-02-903712-3*) Free Pr.

Population of the United States. 3rd ed. Douglas L. Anderton et al. LC 96-48990. (Illus.). 736p. 1997. 150.00 (*0-684-82774-3*) Free Pr.

Population of Virginia: Past, Present & Future. William J. Serow. LC 77-10340. (Illus.). 340p. reprint ed. pap. 105.40 (*0-8357-3140-5*, 203940300012) Bks Demand.

Population-Oriented Psychiatry. Gerald Caplan. LC 87-30985. 244p. 1989. 38.95 (*0-89885-418-0*, Kluwer Acad Hman Sci) Kluwer Academic.

***Population Parameters: Estimation for Ecological Models.** Hamish McCallum et al. (Illus.). 2000. pap. 79.00 (*0-86542-740-2*) Blackwell Sci.

Population Pattern & Social Change in India. Sharat Chandra. (C). 1992. 42.00 (*81-85613-34-6*, Pub. by Chugh Pubns) S Asia.

Population Perils. Ed. by George W. Forell & William H. Lazareth. LC 78-54548. (Justice Bks.). 63p. reprint ed. pap. 30.00 (*0-608-18028-9*, 202910900058) Bks Demand.

Population Perils & the Churches' Response. James B. Martin-Scramm. LC 98-218173. xxiii, 56 p. 1997. write for info. (*2-8254-1226-0*) COE Pubns.

Population Persistence & Migration in Rural New York, 1855-1860. David P. Davenport. (Studies in Historical Demography). 264p. 1990. text 15.00 (*0-8240-3769-3*) Garland.

Population Perspectives on Organizations. Howard Aldrich et al. 110p. (Orig.). 1986. pap. text 37.50 (*91-554-1909-7*, Pub. by Uppsala Univ Acta Univ Uppsaliensis) Coronet Bks.

Population Planning in India: Policy Issues & Research Priorities. Ed. by Ashish Bose & P. B. Desai. 1990. 27.50 (*81-7018-575-0*, Pub. by BR Pub) S Asia.

Population Policies & Movements in Europe. P. V. Glass. 490p. 1967. 45.00 (*0-7146-1580-3*, Pub. by F Cass Pubs) Intl Spec Bk.

Population Policies & Movements in Europe. David V. Glass. LC 67-19728. (Reprints of Economic Classics Ser.). xvi, 490p. 1967. reprint ed. 49.50 (*0-678-05049-X*) Kelley.

Population Policies & Programmes. 267p. 20.00 (*92-1-151252-2*) UN.

Population Policies for a New Economic Era. Lester R. Brown. 1983. pap. write for info. (*0-916468-52-6*) Worldwatch Inst.

Population Policies Reconsidered: Health, Empowerment, & Rights. Gita Sen et al. LC 94-8443. (Harvard Series on Population & International Health). 350p. 1994. pap. 16.95 (*0-674-69003-6*) HUP.

Population Policy. Ed. by Mark Schneider & Michael E. Kraft. (C). 1977. pap. 15.00 (*0-918592-23-2*) Pol Studies.

Population Policy: A New Consensus. Robert Cassen. LC 94-28294. (Policy Essay Ser.: Vol. 12). 128p. (Orig.). 1994. pap. 13.95 (*1-56517-017-2*) Overseas Dev Council.

Population Policy: Contemporary Issues. Ed. by Godfrey Roberts. LC 89-36160. 232p. 1990. 59.95 (*0-275-93039-4*, C3039, Praeger Pubs) Greenwood.

Population Policy Analysis: Issues in American Politics. Michael E. Kraft & Mark Schneider. (Illus.). 224p. 1985. reprint ed. lib. bdg. 39.50 (*0-8191-5146-7*) U Pr of Amer.

Population Policy & Reproductive Health: Proceedings of the Seminar on Policy Direction & Strategy of Action of Population & Reproductive Health in India, New Delhi, December 1996. Ed. by K. Srinivasan. LC 96-904591. (C). 1996. 45.00 (*81-7075-042-3*, Pub. by Hindustan) S Asia.

Population Policy & Women's Rights: Transforming Reproductive Choice. Ruth Dixon-Mueller. LC 92-28547. 304p. 1993. 59.95 (*0-275-94504-9*, C4504, Praeger Pubs); pap. 21.95 (*0-275-94611-8*, B4611, Praeger Pubs) Greenwood.

Population Policy Diskette Documentation. 33p. 1997. 7.50 (*92-1-151322-7*) UN.

Population Policy in Western Europe: Responses to Low Fertility in France, Sweden, & West Germany. C. Alison McIntosh. LC 82-5840. 292p. 1983. reprint ed. pap. 90.60 (*0-8357-2616-9*, 204010300014) Bks Demand.

Population Politics: The Choices That Shape Our Future. V. D. Abernethy. LC 92-41791. (Illus.). 370p. (C). 1993. 26.50 (*0-306-44461-5*, Plen Insight) Perseus Pubng.

Population Politics: The Choices That Shape Our Future. Virginia D. Abernethy. LC 99-23301. 365p. 1999. pap. 26.95 (*0-7658-0603-7*) Transaction Pubs.

Population Politics in Twentieth Century Europe: Fascist Dictatorships & Liberal Democracies. Maria S. Quine. LC 95-8636. (Historical Connections Ser.). 160p. (C). 1995. pap. 17.99 (*0-415-08069-X*) Routledge.

Population, Poverty, & Politics in Middle East Cities. Ed. by Michael E. Bonine. LC 96-21377. 384p. 1997. 49.95 (*0-8130-1474-3*) U Press Fla.

Population Pressure & Agrarian Change. R. S. Dube. 1990. 22.00 (*81-7033-075-0*, Pub. by Rawat Pubns) S Asia.

Population Pressure & Cultural Adjustment. Virginia Abernethy. LC 78-11676. 189p. 1979. 35.95 (*0-87705-329-4*, Kluwer Acad Hman Sci) Kluwer Academic.

Population Pressure & Human Fertility Response: Ohio, 1810-1860. Don R. Leet. LC 77-14754. (Dissertations in American Economic History Ser.). 1978. 33.95 (*0-405-11046-4*) Ayer.

Population Pressure & Management of Natural Resources: Income-Sharing & Labor. Food & Agriculture Organization Staff. LC 98-111349. (Economic & Social Development Paper Ser.: No. 139). 62p. 1997. pap. 7.00 (*92-5-103920-8*, F39208, Pub. by FAO) Bernan Associates.

Population Pressures: Emigration & Government in Late Nineteenth-Century Britain. Howard L. Malchow. LC 79-64166. (Illus.). 335p. 1979. 18.00 (*0-930664-02-7*) SPOSS.

Population Problem: A Study in Human Evolution. A. M. Carr-Saunders. LC 73-14150. (Perspectives in Social Inquiry Ser.). 520p. 1974. reprint ed. 29.95 (*0-405-05496-3*) Ayer.

Population Problems: A Demographic Study. Birendra K. Jha. (C). 1989. 37.50 (*81-85076-61-8*, Pub. by Chugh Pubns) S Asia.

***Population Problems: Topical Issues.** Ed. by J. Rose. Vol. 8. 176p. 1999. text 55.00 (*90-5699-230-9*) Gordon & Breach.

Population Problems of the Age of Malthus. 2nd ed. Talbot Griffith. (Illus.). 280p. 1967. reprint ed. 40.00 (*0-7146-1155-7*, BHA-01155, Pub. by F Cass Pubs) Intl Spec Bk.

Population Problems of the Pacific. Stephen H. Roberts. LC 71-99884. reprint ed. 55.00 (*0-404-00599-3*) AMS Pr.

Population Production & Regulation in the Sea: A Fisheries Perspective. David Cushing. (Illus.). 366p. (C). 1995. text 80.00 (*0-521-38457-5*) Cambridge U Pr.

Population Profile of Religion in India: Districtwise Data from 1991 Census. Ashish Bose. LC 97-914471. (C). 1997. 48.50 (*81-7018-937-3*, Pub. by BR Pub) S Asia.

Population Profile of the U. S. 1994. lib. bdg. 250.00 (*0-8490-5728-0*) Gordon Pr.

Population Profile of the U. S., 1995. (Illus.). 68p. (Orig.). (C). 1995. pap. text 25.00 (*0-7881-2071-9*) DIANE Pub.

***Population Profile of the United States, 1997.** Andrea Curry et al. (Illus.). 60p. (C). 2000. reprint ed. pap. text 20.00 (*0-7881-8727-9*) DIANE Pub.

Population Profile U. S. '95. U. S. Census Bureau Staff. 1995. pap. 5.50 (*0-614-30813-5*, POP95P) Claitors.

Population Projections: What Do We Really Know? Stanley K. Smith. (Bureau of Economic & Business Research Monographs). 50p. (Orig.). 1984. pap. text 8.00 (*0-930885-01-5*) Bur Econ & Bus Res.

Population Projections for States, by Age, Sex, Race & Hispanic Origin: 1993-2020. Paul Campbell. (Illus.). 105p. (Orig.). (C). 1994. pap. text 40.00 (*0-7881-1007-1*) DIANE Pub.

Population Projections of the United States by Age, Sex, Race, & Hispanic Origin: 1995 to 2050. Jennifer C. Day. (Illus.). 127p. (Orig.). 1997. pap. text 45.00 (*0-7881-3837-5*) DIANE Pub.

Population Projections of the United States by Age, Sex, Race & Hispanic Origin to 2050. 1994. lib. bdg. 255.95 (*0-8490-5835-X*) Gordon Pr.

Population Projections to 2010 for U. S.-Mexico Border Counties & Municipios. James Williams et al. 147p. (Orig.). 1994. pap. text 15.00 (*0-937795-02-X*) Waste-Mgmt Educ.

Population Radiation Cytogenetics of Animals, Vol. 3. Vladimir N. Orlov & N. S. Bulatova. iv, 62p. 1989. text 59.00 (*3-7186-4882-2*) Gordon & Breach.

Population Redistribution & Development in South Asia. Ed. by Leszek A. Kosinski & Maudood K. Elahi. 1985. lib. bdg. 122.00 (*90-277-1938-1*) Kluwer Academic.

Population Redistribution & Economic Growth: United States, 1870-1950. Simon Smith Kuznets et al. LC 57-10071. (American Philosophical Society, Memoirs Ser.: Vol. 51). 305p. reprint ed. pap. 94.60 (*0-608-13504-6*, 201971100014) Bks Demand.

Population Redistribution in the U. S. S. R. Its Impact on Society, 1897-1977. Robert A. Lewis & Richard H. Rowland. LC 79-18076. (Praeger Special Studies). 485p. 1979. 95.00 (*0-275-90382-6*, C0382, Praeger Pubs) Greenwood.

Population Reference Bureau's Population Handbook: International Edition. 2nd ed. Arthur Haupt & Thomas T. Kane. (Illus.). 76p. (C). 1986. reprint ed. pap. 5.00 (*0-917136-10-1*) Population Ref.

Population Reference Bureau's Population Handbook: International Edition. 3rd ed. Arthur Haupt. (Illus.). 72p. 1991. pap. 7.00 (*0-917136-12-8*) Population Ref.

Population Research in Latin America & the Caribbean: A Reference Bibliography. Ed. by Barry Edmonston. LC 79-14653. (Monograph Publishing; Sponsor Ser.). 177p. reprint ed. pap. 54.90 (*0-8357-0414-9*, 202259400028) Bks Demand.

Population Research, Policy & Related Studies in Puerto Rico: An Inventory. Kent C. Earnhardt. LC 77-16466. (Planning Ser.: No. S-6). 132p. 1984. pap. 5.00 (*0-8477-2447-6*) U of PR Pr.

Population, Resources & Environment: The Critical Challenges. Norman Myers. 154p. 1991. pap. 24.75 (*0-89714-101-6*, E.91.III.H.1) UN.

Population-Sample Decomposition Method. A. M. Wesselman. (C). 1987. text 111.00 (*90-247-3603-X*) Kluwer Academic.

Population, Settlement, & Conflict: Israel & the West Bank. David Newman. (Update Ser.). (Illus.). 72p. (C). 1991. pap. text 18.95 (*0-521-40804-0*) Cambridge U Pr.

Population, Settlement & Development in Zambia. Prithvish Nag. 1990. 34.00 (*81-7022-268-0*, Pub. by Concept) S Asia.

Population Settlements: Development & Planning. K. M. Lal. 1988. 32.00 (*81-85076-48-0*, Pub. by Chugh Pubns) S Asia.

Population Shift: Mobility & Change in Australia. Ed. by P. W. Newton & M. Bell. 496p. 1996. 51.95 (*0-644-36118-2*, Pub. by Aust Gov Pub) Accents Pubns.

Population, Social Equity & Changing Production Patterns. (Libros de la CEPAL: No. 35). 153p. pap. 17.50 (*92-1-121186-7*, E.93.II.G.8) UN.

Population Statistics & History of Western U. S. Cities. Riley Moffat. LC 95-14583. 355p. 1996. 45.00 (*0-8108-3033-7*) Scarecrow.

Population Structure, Genetics & Taxonomy of Aphids & Thysanoptera. Ed. by J. Holman et al. (Illus.). xiv, 542p. 1987. 172.00 (*90-5103-001-0*, Pub. by SPB Acad Pub) Balogh.

Population Structure of Indian Cities. Ram D. Singh. 173p. 1985. 39.95 (*0-318-36861-7*) Asia Bk Corp.

Population Structure of Vegetation. Ed. by J. A. White. (Handbook of Vegetation Science Ser.). 1985. text 380.00 (*90-6193-184-3*) Kluwer Academic.

Population Structures & Models: Developments in Spatial Demography. Ed. by Robert I. Woods & Philip H. Rees. 400p. (C). text 85.00 (*0-04-301200-0*) Routledge.

Population Studies. Ed. by Royce E. Longton. (Advances in Bryology Ser.: Vol. 6). (GER., Illus.). viii, 302p. 1997. 106.00 (*3-443-52004-9*, Pub. by Gebruder Borntraeger) Balogh.

Population Studies of European Sparrows in North America. Ted R. Anderson. (Occasional Papers: No. 70). 58p. 1978. pap. 1.00 (*0-317-04581-4*) U KS Nat Hist Mus.

Population Studies on Human Adaptation & Evolution in the Peruvian Andes. Ed. by Robert B. Eckhardt & Terry W. Melton. (Occasional Papers in Anthropology: No. 14). (Illus.). 257p. (Orig.). 1992. pap. text. write for info. (*1-881968-00-6*) PA St U Matson Mus.

Population Study of the Prairie Vole (Microtus ochrogaster) in Northeastern Kansas. Edwin P. Martin. (Museum Ser.: Vol. 8, No. 6). 56p. 1956. pap. 3.00 (*0-317-04886-4*) U KS Nat Hist Mus.

Population System Control. J. Yu. (Illus.). 290p. 1988. 130.00 (*0-387-18288-8*) Spr-Verlag.

Population Systems: A General Introduction. Alan A. Berryman. LC 80-26167. 238p. 1981. 29.50 (*0-306-40589-X*, Plenum Trade) Perseus Pubng.

Population, Technology, & Lifestyle: The Transition to Sustainability. Ed. by Robert Goodland et al. LC 92-14403. 155p. 1992. text 22.00 (*1-55963-199-6*) Island Pr.

Population Theory in China. Ed. & Intro. by H. Yuan Tien. LC 79-57159. 139p. 1980. reprint ed. pap. 43.10 (*0-7837-9941-1*, 206066800006) Bks Demand.

Population Transition in India. Ed. by S. N. Singh. 1989. 105.00 (*81-7018-579-3*, Pub. by BR Pub) S Asia.

Population Transition in South Asia. Ed. by Ashish Bose. (C). 1992. 24.00 (*81-7018-623-4*, Pub. by BR Pub) S Asia.

Population Trends of Breeding Birds in Ohio. Susan L. Earnst & Brad A. Andres. LC 96-68822. (Miscellaneous Contributions Ser.: Vol. 3). (Illus.). 130p. (C). 1996. pap. text 15.00 (*0-86727-121-3*) Ohio Bio Survey.

Population under Duress: The Geodemography of Post-Soviet Russia. Ed. by George J. Demko et al. LC 98-54405. 304p. (C). 1999. pap. 69.00 (*0-8133-8939-9*, Pub. by Westview) HarpC.

Population, Urbanization & Quality of Life: Unchs (Habitat) Contribution to the International Conference on Population & Development, 1994. United Nations Centre for Human Settlements Staff. LC 94-982929. vi, 47p. 1994. write for info. (*92-1-131232-9*) UN.

Population, Urbanization, & Settlement in Ghana: A Bibliographic Survey, 8. Joseph A. Sarfoh. LC 87-19627. (African Special Bibliographic Ser.: No. 8). 140p. 1987. lib. bdg. 55.00 (*0-313-26073-7*, SPX/, Greenwood Pr) Greenwood.

Population Validity & College Entrance Measures. Hunter M. Breland. LC 79-51738. (Research Monographs: No. 8). 104p. (Orig.). 1979. pap. 7.50 (*0-87447-110-9*, 270501) College Bd.

Population Welfare Planning. Ed. by B. N. Sarkar. (C). 1988. 52.00 (*81-85109-82-6*, Pub. by Naya Prokash) S Asia.

P

An Asterisk (*) at the beginning of an entry indicates that the title is appearing for the first time.

Population/Family Planning Thesaurus: An Alphabetical & Hierarchical Display of Terms Drawn from Population-Related Literature in the Social Sciences Caroline Lucas et al. LC 74-25288. xx, 286p. 1975. write for info. (*0-89055-047-6*) Carolina Pop Ctr.

Populations- und Ausbreitungsbiologische Untersuchungen Zur Sukzession Auf Weinbergsbrachen Am Keuperstudenrand Des Remstals. Ulrich Grunicke. (Dissertationes Botanicae Ser.: Band 261). (Illus.). xvi, 210p. 1996. pap. 65.00 (*3-443-64173-3*, Pub. by Gebruder Borntraeger) Balogh.

Populations of Europe: A History. Massimo Livi-Bacci. Tr. by Ian Shaw from ITA. LC 99-29297. (Making of Europe Ser.).Tr. of Popolazione Nella Storia D'Europa. (Illus.). 288p. 1999. 59.95 (*0-631-20078-9*); pap. 26.95 (*0-631-21881-5*) Blackwell Pubs.

Populations of States & Counties of the U. S. (1790-1990) Ed. by Richard L. Forstall. 225p. (Orig.). 1996. pap. text 35.00 (*0-7881-3330-6*) DIANE Pub.

Populations of the World. Ed. by Scott Morris. LC 92-22283. (Using & Understanding Maps Ser.). (Illus.). 48p. (YA). (gr. 5 up). 1993. lib. bdg. 17.95 (*0-7910-1805-9*) Chelsea Hse.

Populations, Species, & Evolution: An Abridgment of Animal Species & Evolution. abr. ed. Ernst W. Mayr. LC 79-111486. 453p. 1970. pap. 18.50 (*0-674-69013-3*) Belknap Pr.

***Populism.** Paul A. Taggart. LC 99-86747. (Concepts in the Social Sciences Ser.). 2000. pap. 19.95 (*0-335-20045-1*) Taylor & Francis.

Populism: An Annotated Bibliography. 1994. lib. bdg. 256.75 (*0-8490-9069-5*) Gordon Pr.

Populism: Reaction or Reform? Ed. by Theodore Saloutos. LC 77-15587. (American Problem Studies). 128p. 1978. reprint ed. pap. text 10.50 (*0-88275-638-9*) Krieger.

Populism: The Humane Preference in America, 1890-1900. Gene Clanton. (Twayne's Social Movements Past & Present Ser.). 208p. 1991. pap. 15.95 (*0-8057-9744-0*, Twyne); text 24.95 (*0-8057-9743-2*, Twyne) Mac Lib Ref.

Populism & Bureaucracy: The Case of Greece under PASOK, 1981-1989. Dimitri A. Sotiropoulos. LC 95-50516. (From the Helen Kellogg Institute for International Ser.). 208p. (C). 1996. text 33.00 (*0-268-03815-5*) U of Notre Dame Pr.

Populism & Democratic Thought in the Canadian Prairies, 1910-1945. David Laycock. (State & Economic Life Ser.). 369p. 1990. pap. 19.95 (*0-8020-6681-X*); text 45.00 (*0-8020-2637-0*) U of Toronto Pr.

Populism & Elitism: Politics in the Age of Equality. Jeffrey Bell. LC 91-47497. 300p. 1992. 21.95 (*0-89526-517-6*) Regnery Pub.

Populism & Feminism in Iran: Women's Strugggle in a Male-Defined Revolutionary Movement. Haideh Moghissi. 232p. 1997. pap. 19.95 (*0-312-16469-6*) St Martin.

Populism & Feminism in Iran: Women's Struggle in a Male-Defined Revolutionary Movement. Haideh Moghissi. LC 93-47024. 1994. text 69.95 (*0-312-12068-0*) St Martin.

Populism & the Capra Legacy, 44. Wes D. Gehring. LC 94-44725. (Contributions to the Study of Popular Culture Ser.: No. 44). 152p. 1995. 55.00 (*0-313-26183-0*, Greenwood Pr) Greenwood.

Populism & the Election of 1896. Compiled by Robert W. Cherny. 39.00 (*1-56696-074-6*) Jackdaw.

Populism in Latin America. Michael L. Conniff. LC 98-40081. 272p. 1999. text 44.95 (*0-8173-0959-4*) U of Ala Pr.

Populism in Latin America. Michael L. Conniff. LC 98-40081. 1999. pap. 22.50 (*0-8173-0970-5*) U of Ala Pr.

Populism in Peru: The Emergence of the Masses & the Politics of Social Control. Steve Stein. LC 80-8315. (Illus.). 313p. reprint ed. pap. 97.10 (*0-608-09933-3*, 206927100003) Bks Demand.

Populism in the Mountain West. Robert W. Larson. LC 86-16160. 220p. reprint ed. pap. 68.20 (*0-7837-5854-5*, 204557300006) Bks Demand.

Populism in the Old Dominion: Virginia Farm Politics, 1885-1900. William Sheldon. 1990. 16.50 (*0-8446-1493-9*) Peter Smith.

Populism in the Western United States, 1890-1900. David B. Griffiths. LC 92-22906. 600p. 1992. text 119.95 (*0-7734-9482-0*) E Mellen.

Populism, Its Rise & Fall. annot. ed. William A. Peffer. LC 91-18795. (Illus.). viii, 208p. 1992. 25.00 (*0-7006-0509-6*) U Pr of KS.

Populism, Progressivism, & the Transformation of Nebraska Politics, 1885-1915. Robert W. Cherny. LC 80-11151. (Illus.). 245p. reprint ed. pap. 76.00 (*0-8357-3790-X*, 203652100003) Bks Demand.

Populism, Racism & Society in Eastern Europe. Ed. by Joseph Held. 250p. 1996. 35.00 (*0-88033-337-5*, 440, Pub. by East Eur Monographs) Col U Pr.

Populism vs. Plutocracy: Past Heroes & the Coming Twenty-First Century Struggle. 1996. lib. bdg. 251.95 (*0-8490-6350-7*) Gordon Pr.

Populist Assault: Sarah E. Van De Vort Emery on American Democracy 1862-1895. Pauline Adams & Emma S. Thornton. LC 82-60665. (Illus.). 146p. 1982. 14.95 (*0-87972-203-7*) Bowling Green Univ Popular Press.

Populist Challenge: Argentine Electoral Behavior in the Postwar Era. Lars G. Schoultz. LC 82-24831. (James Sprunt Studies in History & Political Science: Vol. 58). xii, 141p. (Orig.). (C). 1983. pap. text 16.95 (*0-8078-5059-4*) U of NC Pr.

Populist Context: Rural Versus Urban Power on a Great Plains Frontier, 22. Stanley B. Parsons. LC 72-824. (Contributions in American History Ser.: No. 22). (Illus.). 205p. 1973. 57.95 (*0-8371-6392-7*, PAC/, Greenwood Pr) Greenwood.

Populist Mind. Ed. by Norman Pollack. (Orig.). (C). 1967. pap. 8.50 (*0-672-60076-5*, AHS50, Bobbs) Macmillan.

Populist Moment: A Short History of the Agrarian Revolt in America. Lawrence Goodwyn. 380p. 1978. pap. text 14.95 (*0-19-502417-6*) OUP.

***Populist Nationalism: Republican Insurgency & American Foreign Policy Making, 1918-1925, 69.** Karen A. J. Miller. LC 98-41419. (Contributions in American History Ser.: Vol. 183). 216p. 1999. 57.95 (*0-313-30776-8*, Greenwood Pr) Greenwood.

Populist Paradox: Interest Group Influence & the Promise of Direct Legislation. Elisabeth R. Garbor. LC 98-54178. 176p. 1999. 45.00 (*0-691-00266-5*, Pub. by Princeton U Pr) Cal Prin Full Svc.

Populist Paradox: Interest Group Influence & the Promise of Direct Legislation. Elisabeth R. Gerber. LC 98-54178. 176p. 1999. pap. 17.95 (*0-691-00267-3*, Pub. by Princeton U Pr) Cal Prin Full Svc.

Populist Persuasion: An American History. rev. ed. Michael Kazin. LC 98-28106. (Illus.). 408p. 1998. pap. 17.95 (*0-8014-8558-4*) Cornell U Pr.

Populist Religion & Left-Wing Politics in France, 1830-1852. Edward Berenson. LC 83-42548. 333p. 1984. reprint ed. pap. 103.30 (*0-7837-9297-2*, 206003600004) Bks Demand.

Populist Response to Industrial America. Norman Pollack. 176p. 1976. pap. 12.50 (*0-674-69051-6*) HUP.

Populist Revolt: A History of the Farmer's Alliance & the People's Party. John D. Hicks. LC 81-3236. (Illus.). 473p. 1981. reprint ed. lib. bdg. 99.50 (*0-313-22567-2*, HIPR, Greenwood Pr) Greenwood.

***Populist Seduction in Latin America: The Ecuadorian Experience.** Carlos de la Torre. LC 99-58922. (Research in International Studies : No. 32). 192p. 2000. pap. text 22.00 (*0-89680-210-8*, Ohio U Ctr Intl) Ohio U Pr.

Populist Vanguard: A History of the Southern Farmers' Alliance. Robert C. McMath. LC 75-9751. 235p. reprint ed. pap. 72.90 (*0-7837-0294-9*, 204061500018) Bks Demand.

Populists & Patricians: Essays in Modern German History. David Blackbourn. 304p. (C). 1987. text 55.00 (*0-04-943047-5*) Routledge.

Populous III: Beginning. David Ladyman. 240p. 1999. per. 19.99 (*0-7615-1205-5*) Prima Pub.

Populuxe. Hine. (Illus.). 192p. 1999. 14.98 (*1-56731-316-7*, MJF Bks) Fine Comms.

Poquito Amigo: A Novel. George R. Prentice. LC 97-4253. 192p. 1998. pap. 10.95 (*1-56474-221-0*) Fithian Pr.

Poquosin: A Study of Rural Landscape & Society. Jack T. Kirby. LC 94-48141. (Studies in Rural Culture). 1995. pap. 19.95 (*0-8078-4527-2*); text 49.95 (*0-8078-2214-0*) U of NC Pr.

Por Amor: Yesterday's Bride. Alison Kelly. (Bianca Ser.: Vol. 120).Tr. of For Love. (SPA.). 1998. per. 3.50 (*0-373-33470-2*, 1-33470-5) Harlequin Bks.

Por Amor a Nuestra Tierra: For the Love of Our Earth. P. K. Hallinan. Tr. by Aida E. Marcuse. (SPA., Illus.). (gr. 2-4). 2000. pap. 6.95 (*1-880507-58-7*) Lectorum Pubns.

Por Amor a Nuestra Tierra (For the Love of Our Earth) P. K. Hallinan. Tr. by Aida E. Marcuse from ENG. (SPA., Illus.). 24p. (J). 1994. 8.95 (*1-880507-11-0*) Lectorum Pubns.

Por Amor a Ti. Sara Wood. 1999. per. 3.50 (*0-373-33517-2*, 1335173) Harlequin Bks.

Por Amor a una Mujer (For Love to a Woman) Rebecca Winters. (Bianca Ser.). (SPA.). 1998. per. 3.50 (*0-373-33452-4*, 1-33452-3) Harlequin Bks.

Por Amor Al Arte: Memorias de un Teatrista Cubano, 1940-1970. Francisco Morin. LC 98-86960. (Coleccion Cuba y sus Jueces). (SPA., Illus.). 378p. (Orig.). 1998. pap. 24.95 (*0-89729-874-8*) Ediciones.

Por Amor aos Cato'licos Romano. Rick Jones.Tr. of Understanding Roman Catholicism. (POR.). 224p. 1997. pap. 9.95 (*0-937958-55-7*) Chick Pubns.

***Por Arte de Magia.** Jennifer Greene.Tr. of By Magic. (SPA.). 2000. per. 3.50 (*0-373-35328-6*) Harlequin Bks.

Por Caminos Extranos. Beverly Barton. (Deseo Ser.: No. 218).Tr. of Along Strange Roads. (SPA.). 1997. per. 3.50 (*0-373-35218-2*, 1-35218-6) Harlequin Bks.

***Por Despecho.** Miranda Lee. (Bianca Ser.: No. 183).Tr. of Out of Despite. (SPA.). 1999. per. 3.50 (*0-373-33533-4*, 1-33533-0) Harlequin Bks.

Por el Alma de la Familia. Thomas W. Petrisko. Tr. by Rosa M. Estrada. (SPA., Illus.). 316p. (Orig.). 1997. pap. 9.95 (*1-57918-006-X*, 3452S) Queenship Pub.

Por Estas Calles Bravas. Piri Thomas.Tr. of Down These Mean Streets. (SPA.). 1998. pap. 12.00 (*0-679-77628-1*) Vin Bks.

Por Favor, Ayudame a Cambiar. Mario E. Rivera. (Serie Guia de Bolsillo - Pocket Guides Ser.).Tr. of Free to Be Me. (SPA.). 1989. pap. 2.79 (*0-945792-23-9*, 498046) Editorial Unilit.

Por Favor, Comprendeme: Tipos de Caracter y Temperamento. David West Keirsey. Ed. by Stephen E. Montgomery. Tr. by Modesto Diaz from ENG. (SPA.). 207p. (Orig.). (C). 1990. pap. 11.95 (*0-9606954-3-5*) Prometheus Nemesis.

Por Favor, Di! Un Cuento Para Ninos Sobre el Abuso Sexual. Jessie.Tr. of Please Tell!. (ENG., Illus.). 32p. (J). (ps-7). pap. 8.00 (*0-89486-943-4*, 1474A) Hazelden.

Por Favor, Dios. (Serie Pescaditos - Fish Book Ser.).Tr. of Please, God. (SPA.). 16p. (J). 1987. pap. write for info. (*0-614-27112-6*) Editorial Unilit.

Por Favor, Sea Feliz. Andrew Matthews. 1997. pap. text 7.98 (*968-403-545-4*) Selector.

Por Favor Vive Plenamente. Patron Lujan Roger. (SPA.). (gr. 7 up). 1997. pap. text 4.99 (*968-409-894-4*) Edamex.

Por Fin es Carnaval. Arthur Dorros.Tr. of Tonight Is Carnival. (SPA.). 1995. 10.44 (*0-606-08033-3*) Turtleback.

Por la Acera de la Sombra (Cuentos Cubanos) Pancho Vives. LC 81-69538. (Coleccion Caniqui). (Orig.). 1982. pap. 7.95 (*0-89729-300-2*) Ediciones.

Por la Gran Cuchara De Cuerno (By the Great Horn Spoon!) Sid Fleischman. Tr. by Carlos A. Bliffeld. (Illus.). 178p. (YA). (gr. 6 up). 1994. 13.95 (*1-880507-07-2*) Lectorum Pubns.

Por la Gran Cuchara De Cuerno (By the Great Horn Spoon!) Sid Fleischman. 1994. 14.05 (*0-606-10490-9*, Pub. by Turtleback) Demco.

Por la Gran Cuchara de Cuerno! (By the Great Horn Spoon!) Sid Fleischman. Tr. by Carlos A. Bliffeld. (Illus.). 1994. pap. text 8.95 (*1-880507-08-0*) Lectorum Pubns.

Por la Libertad de Cuba: Una Historia Inconclusa. Nestor C. Cortina. LC 95-83996. (Coleccion Cuba y sus Jueces). (SPA., Illus.). 513p. (Orig.). 1996. pap. 29.95 (*0-89729-786-5*) Ediciones.

Por la Senda del Perdon. Luis Palau. (Serie Cruzada - Crusade Ser.).Tr. of Walk of Forgiveness. (SPA.). 33p. 1991. pap. 1.99 (*1-56063-117-1*, 498011) Editorial Unilit.

Por la Union Latino Americana. University of Latin American Workers Staff. (Coleccion CLAT Ser.). (SPA.). 300p. (Orig.). 1987. pap. 10.00 (*0-917049-14-4*) Saeta.

Por Lo Que Toca a una Mujer. Sergio Fernandez.Tr. of What Moves a Woman. 104p. 1996. pap. 10.50 (*0-679-76655-3*) Random.

Por los Caminos del Universo - Along the Roads of the Universe. Amor Halperin. Tr. by Ida Halperin. LC 98-150561. (ENG & SPA., Illus.). 144p. 1997. pap. 12.95 (*1-882291-57-3*) Oyster River Pr.

***Por los Ninos.** John Paul, II, pseud. (J). 2000. 16.95 (*0-439-14718-2*) Scholastic Inc.

Por Primera Vez: First Time Father. Emma Richmond. (Bianca Ser.).Tr. of For the First Time. (SPA.). 1997. per. 3.50 (*0-373-33433-8*, 1-33433-3) Harlequin Bks.

Por Que? Nikolai Popov. LC 98-7153. (SPA., Illus.). 48p. (J). (gr. k-3). 1998. 15.95 (*1-55858-942-2*, Pub. by North-South Bks NYC); pap. 6.95 (*1-55858-683-0*, Pub. by North-South Bks NYC) Chronicle Bks.

Por Que Chiapas. Luis Pazos. LC 94-156100. (SPA., Illus.). 156p. 1997. pap. 9.98 (*968-13-2633-4*, Pub. by Edit Diana) Libros Fronteras.

Por Que Creo (Why I Believe) D. James Kennedy.Tr. of Why I Believe. (SPA.). 176p. 1982. pap. 6.99 (*0-8297-1259-3*) Vida Pubs.

Por Que Decir No al Sexo? Josh McDowell.Tr. of Why Say No to Sex?. (SPA.). 4.99 (*0-7899-0213-3*, 495030) Editorial Unilit.

Por Que Deja de Amarnos Nuestra Pareja? Estrada Inda Lauro. 1997. pap. text 14.98 (*970-05-0636-3*) Grijalbo Edit.

Por Que Esperar? Lo Que de Necesita Saber Sobre de Crisis Sexual. Josh McDowell.Tr. of Why Wait? What You Need to Know about the Teen Sexuality Crisis. (SPA.). 495p. 1987. pap. 12.99 (*0-945792-48-4*, 498402) Editorial Unilit.

Por Que Fracaso la Democracia en Cuba. Luis Fernandez-Caubi. LC 93-71035. (Coleccion Cuba y sus Jueces). 91p. (Orig.). 1993. pap. 9.95 (*0-89729-680-X*) Ediciones.

Por Que las Mujeres Necesitan Chocolate. D F Waterhouse. (SPA.). 1999. pap. text 11.95 (*84-8327-012-9*) E Martinez Roca.

***Por Que Lloras?** Jose Maria Cubells. 1999. pap. 14.95 (*84-270-2450-9*) Planeta.

Por Que Lo Permite Dios? D. Martyn Lloyd-Jones.Tr. of Why Does God Allow War?. (SPA.). 96p. 1992. mass mkt. 3.99 (*0-8254-1448-2*, Edit Portavoz) Kregel.

Por que luchamos tanto? Carol Richardson.Tr. of Why Do We Struggle So?. (SPA.). pap. 8.99 (*1-884369-93-6*) McDougal Pubng.

Por Que Mi Nombre Es Marisol? Un Cuento De la Republica Dominicana. Josefina Baez. (Marisol Ser.: Vol. 1). (SPA., Illus.). 24p. (Orig.). (J). (gr. k-3). 1993. pap. 12.95 (*1-882161-01-7*) Latinarte.

Por Que Nadie Aprende Mucho de Nada en la Iglesia y Como Remediarlo. Contrib. by Thom Schultz & Joani Schultz.Tr. of Why Nobody Learns Much of Anything at Church & How to Fix It. (SPA.). 1996. pap. 10.99 (*1-55945-663-9*) Group Pub.

Por Que no Canta el Petirro. Xabier Mendiguren. pap. text 5.95 (*84-246-5407-2*) Lectorum Pubns.

Por Que Noe Eligio la Paloma. Isaac Bashevis Singer. Tr. by Aida E. Marcuse. LC 91-43925.Tr. of Why Noah Chose the Dove. (SPA., Illus.). 32p. (J). (ps-3). 1992. 16.00 (*0-374-36085-5*) FS&G.

Por Que Orar por los Misioneros y Como Hacerlo. F. F. Bruce. (Serie Discipulado Ser.).Tr. of Why & How to Pray for Missionaries. (SPA.). 24p. 1996. 1.99 (*1-56063-894-X*, 498248) Editorial Unilit.

Por Que Preocuparse? John Haggai. (Serie Actualidades - Actualities Ser.).Tr. of Why Worry?. (SPA.). 46p. 1987. pap. 2.29 (*1-56063-166-X*, 498126) Editorial Unilit.

Por Que Sigue Preso Mark Curtis? (Why Is Mark Cortis Still in Prison?) El Caso Fabricado Contra un Sindicalista y Socialista y la Campana Por Su Libertad. Naomi Craine. (SPA.). 86p. 1995. pap. 6.00 (*0-87348-809-1*) Pathfinder NY.

Por Que Zumban los Mosquitos en los Oidos de la Gente. Verna Aardema.Tr. of Why Mosquitoes Buzz in People's Ears. (SPA., Illus.). 32p. (J). 1998. 16.99 (*0-8037-2298-2*, Dial Yng Read) Peng Put Young Read.

Por Segunda Vez: A Wedding to Remember. Emma Darcy. (Born in the U. S. A. Ser.). (SPA.). 1996. per. 3.50 (*0-373-33390-0*, 1-33390-5) Harlequin Bks.

Por Si Lo Querias Saber, 1vol. Max Lucado. 1992. 8.99 (*0-88113-566-6*) Caribe Betania.

Por Tierras De Espana. Giner de los Rios. (C). 1995. pap. text 8.00 (*0-03-017105-9*) Harcourt Coll Pubs.

Por un Estornudo. Bernice Myers. Tr. by Argentina Palacios. (Spanish Whole Language Big Bks.).Tr. of Because of a Sneeze. (SPA., Illus.). 16p. (Orig.). (J). (ps-2). 1993. pap. 16.95 (*1-56784-091-4*) Newbridge Educ.

Porcelain. Kathryn B. Hiesinger. LC 83-6228. (Guides to European Decorative Arts Ser.: No. 1). (Illus.). 48p. (Orig.). 1984. pap. 6.00 (*0-87633-050-2*) Phila Mus Art.

Porcelain. Chay Yew. LC 96-47068. 240p. 1997. 12.00 (*0-8021-3500-5*, Grove) Grove-Atltic.

Porcelain: Antiques Checklist. Gordon Lang. Ed. by Judith Miller & Martin Miller. (Illus.). 192p. 1991. 15.95 (*0-85533-894-6*, Pub. by Millers Pubns) Antique Collect.

Porcelain & Composite Inlays & Onlays: Esthetic Posterior Restorations. David Garber & Ronald E. Goldstein. (Illus.). 158p. 1993. text 68.00 (*0-86715-171-4*) Quint Pub Co.

Porcelain & Pottery Tea Tiles. Ralph Moore & Dinah Tanner. LC 95-126901. (Illus.). 48p. 1994. pap. 6.48 (*1-57080-004-9*, 4071) Antique Pubns.

Porcelain Butterfly. Tr. by Patrick Morrow. 1972. pap. 2.00 (*0-88031-005-7*) Invisible-Red Hill.

***Porcelain Doll Design & Creation.** Brigitte Von Messner. (Illus.). 1999. 29.95 (*0-942620-27-5*) Portfolio Pr.

Porcelain Doll Making. rev. ed. Debra Anderson & Peter Bell. (Illus.). 44p. 1997. pap. 13.95 (*0-916809-93-5*) Scott Pubns MI.

Porcelain Dollmaking in Detail. Helena R. Neimi. (Illus.). 60p. (Orig.). 1995. pap. text, student ed. 15.00 (*0-9607800-0-9*) H R Niemi.

Porcelain Dollmaking Without Tears. Maureen Wilkins. Ed. by Barbara Case. (Illus.). 32p. 1995. reprint ed. pap. text 13.95 (*1-879825-21-X*) Jones Publish.

Porcelain Draped Dolls. Ricky Macias. (Illus.). 40p. (Orig.). 1996. pap. text 4.95 (*0-916809-90-0*) Scott Pubns MI.

Porcelain for Palaces: The Fashion for Japan in Europe, 1650-1750. John Ayers et al. (Illus.). 328p. 1990. 70.00 (*0-903421-24-0*, Pub. by P Wilson) Scala Books.

Porcelain from the Sevres Museum, 1740-1996. Marie-Noelle De Villechenon. (Illus.). 152p. 1996. 49.95 (*0-85331-689-9*, Pub. by Lund Humphries) Antique Collect.

Porcelain God: A Social History of the Toilet. Julie L. Horan. (Illus.). 240p. 1996. 17.95 (*1-55972-346-7*, Birch Ln Pr) Carol Pub Group.

Porcelain God: A Social History of the Toilet. Julie L. Horan. (Illus.). 240p. 1997. pap. text 12.00 (*0-8065-1947-9*, Citadel Pr) Carol Pub Group.

***Porcelain God: A Social History of the Toilet.** Julie L. Horan. (Illus.). 216p. 2000. reprint ed. text 25.00 (*0-7881-6890-8*) DIANE Pub.

Porcelain in Dentistry: A Clinical Technique Manual. 2nd ed. Robert J. Fish. (Illus.). 76p. (C). 1988. student ed. 8.00 (*0-317-92515-6*) Resc Inc.

Porcelain in the Age of Mozart: From the Metropolitan Museum of Art & Elise & Henry Clay Hofheimer, II. Marvin D. Schwartz. LC 84-72357. (Illus.). 71p. 1984. pap. 15.00 (*0-940744-48-1*) Chrysler Museum.

Porcelain Laminate Veneers. David A. Garber et al. (Illus.). 136p. 1988. text 68.00 (*0-86715-194-3*, 1943) Quint Pub Co.

Porcelain Man. R. Kennedy. 32p. (J). (ps-3). 14.95 (*0-06-027215-5*); lib. bdg. 14.89 (*0-06-027216-3*) HarpC.

Porcelain Manufactory at Sevres, 1800-1847. Derek E. Ostergard. LC 97-61445. 416p. 1997. 75.00 (*0-300-07338-0*) Yale U Pr.

***Porcelain Painter's Handbook.** Aude Creuze & Veronique Habegre. (Illus.). 80p. 2000. pap. 19.95 (*0-233-99550-1*, Pub. by Andre Deutsch) Trafalgar.

***Porcelain Painting: The Latest Technique.** Catherine Bergoin. (Illus.). 80p. 2000. pap. 19.95 (*0-233-99547-1*, Pub. by Andre Deutsch) Trafalgar.

Porcelain Painting with Uwe Geissler: Instructions, Examples & Patterns. Uwe Geissler. Tr. by Ed Force from GER. LC 95-31098. (Illus.). 127p. (Orig.). 1995. pap. 24.95 (*0-88740-899-0*) Schiffer.

Porcelain Potpourri. Ed. by Rolf E. Ericson. 1990. 9.95 (*0-916809-47-1*) Scott Pubns MI.

***Porcelain Stories: From China to Europe.** Mimi Gardner Gates & Julie Emerson. LC 99-59508. (Illus.). 319p. 2000. 50.00 (*0-932216-52-8*) Seattle Art.

Porcelaines Francaises. P. Dupont. (FRE.). 192p. 1991. pap. 195.00 (*0-8288-7303-8*, 270590330) Fr & Eur.

Porcelainiers du Huitieme Siecle Francais. Connaissance des Arts Editorial Staff. (FRE., Illus.). 150.00 (*0-685-11208-X*) Fr & Eur.

Porcelainiers du Huitieme Siecle Francais: French Porcelain Makers of the 18th Century. Connaissance des Arts Editorial Staff. 1966. write for info. (*0-8288-7387-9*) Fr & Eur.

Porcelainiers du Twenty-Eight Siecle Francais. Hachette Staff. 1991. lib. bdg. 150.00 (*0-8288-2637-4*) Fr & Eur.

***Porcelains in Polychrome & Contrasting Colors.** (Illus.). 1999. 99.95 (*962-07-5225-2*, Pub. by Commercial Pr) Cheng & Tsui.

***Porcelains with Cloisonne Enamel Decoration & Famille Rose Decoration.** (Illus.). 1999. 99.95 (*962-07-5224-4*, Pub. by Commercial Pr) Cheng & Tsui.

Porch & Patio Essentials. Cowles Creative Publishing Staff. (Black & Decker Quick Steps Ser.). (Illus.). 80p. (Orig.). 1997. pap. 9.95 (*0-86573-645-6*) Creat Pub Intl.

Porch Lawn & Cottage Furniture. Rustic History Furniture Company Staff. (Illus.). 80p. 1990. pap. 8.95 (*0-486-26531-5*) Dover.

P

An Asterisk (*) at the beginning of an entry indicates that the title is appearing for the first time.

Porch Light Blues: Selected Poems, 1993-1994. Radomir V. Luza, Jr. LC 98-104090. 80p. 1995. pap. 12.95 (*0-9643783-3-7*) R Luza.

Porch, Patio & Deck Furnishings. DeCosse, Cy, Incorporated Staff. LC 95-49810. (Portable Workshop Ser.). (Illus.). 96p. 1996. spiral bd. 14.95 (*0-86573-690-1*) Creat Pub Intl.

*__Porch People.__ Marilynn F. Adams. Ed. by Leslie D. Schilling. LC 98-89233. (Illus.). 64p. (YA). 1999. 34.95 (*1-893465-00-4*) AuCajunal Pubg.

Porch Perfect. Barbara Ballinger Buchholz & Lisa Skolnik. LC 99-18741. 1999. write for info. (*1-56799-772-4*) M Friedman Pub Grp Inc.

*__Porch Style.__ Barbara B. Bucholz. 2000. 35.00 (*0-8478-2238-9*, Pub. by Rizzoli Intl) St Martin.

Porch Swings & Picket Fences: Love in a Small Town. Jane Orcutt et al. LC 99-22466. 352p. 1999. pap. 10.95 (*1-57856-226-0*) Waterbrook Pr.

Porch Talk with Ernest Gaines: Conversations on the Writer's Craft. Marcia Gaudet & Carl Wooton. LC 90-31985. (Southern Literary Studies). (Illus.). 168p. 1990. 22.50 (*0-8071-1589-4*) La State U Pr.

Porche du Mystere de la Deuxieme Vertu. Charles Peguy. (FRE.). 1986. pap. 11.95 (*0-7859-2850-2*) Fr & Eur.

Porches. Ed. by Carrie Neumann & Ginny Ballor. 40p. (C). 1997. pap. text 3.00 (*1-882294-27-0*) Green Gate.

Porches: Structure & Design. Sally F. Robbins. LC 95-12221. 144p. 1995. 15.95 (*1-56799-208-0*, Friedman-Fairfax) M Friedman Pub Grp Inc.

*__Porches & Other Outdoor Spaces: A Design Guide for Living Outdoor.__ James Grayson Trulove. 2000. pap. text 24.99 (*1-56496-654-2*) Rockport Pubs.

Porches & Patios. (Home Repair & Improvement Ser.). (Illus.). 136p. 1981. 14.60 (*0-8094-3476-8*); lib. bdg. 20.60 (*0-8094-3475-X*) Time-Life.

Porches & Sunrooms. Jessica E. Hirschman. 72p. 1996. pap. text 12.95 (*1-56799-274-9*, Friedman-Fairfax) M Friedman Pub Grp Inc.

Porches, Decks & Fences. (Fix-It-Yourself Ser.). (Illus.). 144p. 1988. 17.27 (*0-8094-6260-5*); lib. bdg. 23.27 (*0-8094-6261-3*) Time-Life.

Porches, Decks & Outbuildings. FHB Editors & Taunton Press Staff. LC 96-48867. (Builder's Library). (Illus.). 128p. 1997. 24.95 (*1-56158-206-9*, 070333) Taunton.

Porcine Canticles. David Lee. LC 84-71252. 120p. (Orig.). 1984. pap. 10.00 (*0-914742-83-3*) Copper Canyon.

Porcupine. Julian Barnes. LC 93-15506. 1993. pap. 10.00 (*0-679-74482-7*) Vin Bks.

Porcupine. John Paul. (Illus.). (J). pap. 3.00 (*1-55500-072-X*) Alaska Native.

Porcupine. Victoria Sherrow. (Remarkable Animals Ser.). (Illus.). 60p. (J). (gr. 4). 1995. pap. 5.95 (*0-382-39234-5*) Silver Burdett Pr.

Porcupine. Victoria Sherrow. LC 90-3278. (Remarkable Animals Ser.). (Illus.). 60p. (J). (gr. 3 up). 1991. lib. bdg. 13.95 (*0-87518-442-1*, Dillon Silver Burdett) Silver Burdett Pr.

Porcupine, Reading Level 3-4. Ann Marie Dalmais. (World Animal Library). (Illus.). 28p. (J). (gr. 2-5). 1983. 12.50 (*0-685-58824-6*) Rourke Corp.

Porcupine, Reading Level 3-4. Ann Marie Dalmais. (World Animal Library). (Illus.). 28p. (J). (gr. 2-5). 1983. lib. bdg. 21.27 (*0-86592-852-5*) Rourke Enter.

Porcupine Dilemma. Leopold Bellak. 1970. 10.95 (*0-8065-0223-1*) CPS Inc.

Porcupine Hunter & Other Stories: The Original Tshimshian Texts of Henry Tate. Ed. by Ralph Maud. 112p. 1994. pap. 13.95 (*0-88922-333-5*, Pub. by Talonbks) Genl Dist Srvs.

Porcupine Literary Arts Magazine. Ed. by W. A. Reed. (Illus.). 150p. 1998. pap. 8.95 (*0-9663121-0-4*) Porcupine Press.

Porcupine Mountains Wilderness State Park: A Backcountry Guide for Hikers, Backpackers, & Winter Visitors. 2nd rev. ed. Jim DuFresne. Orig. Title: Michigan's Porcupine Mountains Wilderness State Park. (Illus.). 160p. 1999. pap. 11.95 (*1-882376-64-1*) Thunder Bay Pr.

Porcupine Mouse. Bonnie Pryor. LC 87-12305. (Illus.). 32p. (J). (ps-2). 1988. 15.93 (*0-688-07154-6*, Wm Morrow) Morrow Avon.

Porcupine Named Fluffy, 001. Helen Lester. LC 85-24820. (Illus.). 32p. (J). (ps-3). 1986. 16.00 (*0-395-36895-2*) HM.

Porcupine Named Fluffy. Helen Lester. LC 85-24820. (Illus.). 32p. (J). (ps-3). 1989. pap. 6.95 (*0-395-52018-5*) HM.

Porcupine Named Fluffy. Helen Lester. (J). 1986. 11.15 (*0-606-02251-1*, Pub. by Turtleback) Demco.

Porcupine People: Learning to Love the Unlovable. Lee Ezell. LC 98-28979. 200p. 1998. pap. 10.99 (*1-56955-105-7*) Servant.

Porcupine Ranch. Sally Carleen. 1997. per. 3.25 (*0-373-19221-5*, 1-19221-0) Silhouette.

Porcupines. Peter Murray. LC 93-22833. (Nature Books Ser.). (Illus.). 32p. (J). (gr. 2-6). 1994. lib. bdg. 22.79 (*1-56766-019-3*) Childs World.

Porcupines. Lynn M. Stone. LC 94-47386. (Wild Animals of the Woods Ser.). (Illus.). (J). (gr. 2-6). 1995. lib. bdg. 14.60 (*1-57103-092-1*) Rourke Pr.

Porcupines & Pancakes. Mary Hall. (Illus.). 16p. (J). (gr. k-2). 1998. pap. 12.95 (*0-9668006-0-5*) Scoty One.

Porcupine's Pajama Party. Terry W. Harshman. (I Can Read Bks.). (Illus.). 64p. (J). (gr. 1-3). 1988. 9.95 (*0-06-022248-4*) HarpC Child Bks.

Porcupines Pajama Party. Terry W. Harshman. LC 87-45681. (I Can Read Bks.). (Illus.). 64p. (J). (ps-3). 1990. pap. 3.95 (*0-06-444140-7*, HarpTrophy) HarpC Child Bks.

Porcupine's Princess. Rosalind Neroni. (Cleveland Poets Ser.: No. 18). 29p. 1978. pap. 2.50 (*0-914946-12-9*) Cleveland St Univ Poetry Ctr.

Porcupine's Quill Reader. Ed. by Tim Inkster & John Metcalf. 224p. 1996. pap. write for info. (*0-88984-183-7*) Porcup Quill.

Pordage's Mundorum Explicatio. rev. ed. Harriet Blumenthal. LC 91-31758. (Renaissance Imagination Ser.: No. 2). 688p. 1991. text 20.00 (*0-8153-0451-X*) Garland.

Pordy's Prickly Problem, Vol. 11. Janette Oke. Ed. by Grace Pettifor. LC 96-738. (Illus.). 100p. (J). (gr. 3 up). 1993. pap. 5.99 (*0-934998-50-7*) Bethany Hse.

Pore Structure & Permeability of Cementitious Materials Vol. 137: Materials Research Society Symposium Proceedings. Ed. by J. P. Skalny & L. R. Roberts. 465p. 1989. text 17.50 (*1-55899-010-0*) Materials Res.

Porfirio Diaz. Jose F. Godoy. 1976. lib. bdg. 59.95 (*0-8490-0880-8*) Gordon Pr.

Porfirio Diaz: Mistico de la Autoridad. Enrique Krauze. (Political Biographies of the Mexican Revolution Ser.). (SPA., Illus.). 160p. 1997. pap. 9.99 (*968-16-2286-3*, Pub. by Fondo) Continental Bk.

Porfolio Latinamericano. Ed. by Michael Koetzle. (Illus.). 80p. 1998. 35.00 (*3-929078-66-X*, Kehayoff) te Neues.

Porgy see Famous American Plays of the Nineteen Twenties

Porgy. DuBose Heyward. Date not set. reprint ed. lib. bdg. 20.95 (*0-89190-684-3*, Am Repr) Amereon Ltd.

Porgy. DuBose Heyward. 196p. 1991. reprint ed. lib. bdg. 18.95 (*0-89966-768-6*) Buccaneer Bks.

Porgy. DuBose Heyward. (Illus.). 1985. reprint ed. pap. 20.00 (*0-317-38096-6*) Tradd St Pr.

Porgy. 2nd ed. DuBose Heyward. (Illus.). 192p. Date not set. reprint ed. pap. 20.00 (*0-937684-22-8*, P23.H1587PO) Tradd St Pr.

Porgy: A Gullah Version. Dubose Heyward & Dorothy Heyward. Tr. & Intro. by Virginia M. Geraty. 129p. 1990. pap. 8.95 (*0-941711-11-0*) Wyrick & Co.

Porgy & Bess. 576p. 1997. pap. 100.00 (*0-7692-0056-7*) Wrner Bros.

Porhyrins: Excited States & Dynamics. Ed. by Martin Gouterman et al. LC 86-14647. (ACS Symposium Ser.: No. 321). (Illus.). ix, 384p. 1986. 71.95 (*0-8412-0997-9*) Am Chemical.

Poridat de las Poridades. Aristotle. Ed. by Lloyd A. Kasten. 94p. 1957. pap. 4.00 (*0-942260-00-7*) Hispanic Seminary.

Porius: A Romance of the Dark Ages. John Cowper Powys. Ed. by Wilbur Albrecht. 900p. 1994. text 48.95 (*0-912568-16-X*) Colgate U Pr.

Pork. (Magnet Gourmet Ser.). 1997. 5.95 (*0-614-27960-7*) Sterling.

Pork & Beef's Great Adventure. Damon Burnard. LC 97-8817. 48p. (J). (gr. 2-3). 1998. 15.00 (*0-395-86765-7*) HM.

*__Pork & Beef's Great Adventure.__ Damon Burnard. (Illus.). (J). 2000. pap. 5.95 (*0-618-07037-0*) HM.

Pork & Lamb. Ed. by Chuck Williams. LC 94-48063. (Williams-Sonoma Kitchen Library). (Illus.). 108p. (gr. 11). 1999. 18.95 (*0-7835-0309-1*) Time-Life.

Pork & Other Perks: Corruption & Governance in the Philippines. Shelia S. Coronel et al. LC 98-947502. 293 p. 1998. write for info. (*971-8686-18-5*) PCFIJ.

*__Pork Bellies & the Saki Bottle.__ Arin Greenwood. (Illus.). 24p. 2000. pap. 2.00 (*0-9676660-1-5*, Pick Pocket Pr) Phony Lid Pubns.

Pork Butcher. David Hughes. LC 88-28918. 123p. (C). 1988. reprint ed. pap. 9.95 (*0-941533-49-2*, NAB) I R Dee.

*__Pork Chop Hill.__ S. L. A. Marshall. 256p. 2000. mass mkt. 6.99 (*0-425-17505-7*) Berkley Pub.

Pork Chop Hill: The American Fighting Man in Action: Korea, Spring 1953. Samuel L. Marshall. (Combat Arms Ser.). (Illus.). 313p. 1986. reprint ed. 29.95 (*0-89839-090-7*) Battery Pr.

Pork Chop Santa. Al Blair. 6p. 1990. pap. 3.95 (*0-930366-41-7*) Northcountry Pub.

Pork in Family Meals. 1986. lib. bdg. 79.95 (*0-8490-3786-7*) Gordon Pr.

Pork Quality: Genetic & Metabolic Factors. Ed. by E. Puolanne et al. (CAB International Publication). (Illus.). 336p. 1993. text 95.00 (*0-85198-836-9*) OUP.

Porkchop & Rosie. Susan Pearson. (J). 1998. 9.95 (*0-13-685793-0*) S&S Childrens.

Porkchop to the Rescue. Jim Rubin. LC PZ7.R83125Po 1998. (Doug Chronicles: No. 2). (Illus.). 64p. (J). (gr. 2-4). 1998. pap. 3.99 (*0-7868-4231-8*, Pub. by Disney Pr) Time Warner.

Porkchoppers. Ross Thomas. 224p. 1993. mass mkt. 4.99 (*0-446-40171-4*, Pub. by Warner Bks) Little.

Porkchop's Puppy Days Chunky. Linda K. Garvey. 16p. 1999. 3.50 (*0-7364-0010-9*, Pub. by Mouse Works) Time Warner.

*__Porkchop's Summer Book.__ Ray Nelson et al. Ed. by Joseph Siegel & Mary Beth Habecker. (Illus.). 32p. (J). (gr. k-3). 1999. pap. 9.95 (*1-883772-24-9*) Flying Rhino.

Porkopolis: Sue Coe's Jungle. Judith A. Barter & Anne Mochon. (Illus.). 40p. (Orig.). 1993. pap. text 5.00 (*0-914337-16-5*) Mead Art Mus.

Porky-Pie. Linwood E. Tuscan. (Illus.). 39p. (Orig.). (J). (ps-5). 1997. pap. 9.95 (*0-929537-05-X*) Herit Pub Inc.

Porn: Myths for the Twentieth Century. Robert J. Stoller. 237p. (C). 1993. pap. 16.00 (*0-300-05755-5*) Yale U Pr.

Porn in America: The Drift Toward Decadence in Our Society. Jame Lambert. LC 97-74264. 1997. pap. text 11.99 (*1-56384-145-2*) Huntington Hse.

Porn King: The John Holmes Story. John C. Holmes et al. (Illus.). 192p. 1998. pap. 19.95 (*1-880047-69-1*) J Holmes Inc.

Porn 101: Eroticism, Pornography, & the First Amendment. Ed. by James E. Elias et al. LC 99-46627. 616p. 1999. pap. 21.95 (*1-57392-750-3*) Prometheus Bks.

Porne. Chris Tysh. 24p. (Orig.). 1984. pap. 3.95 (*0-932597-00-9*) In Camera.

Pornegrafik. Photos by Ken Probst. (Illus.). 96p. 1998. 50.00 (*0-944092-52-7*) Twin Palms Pub.

Pornegrafik. limited ed. Photos by Ken Probst. (Illus.). 96p. 1998. 400.00 (*0-944092-53-5*) Twin Palms Pub.

*__Porno Diva/Numero Uno: An Anonymous Confession.__ Stephen Berg. (Profile Ser.). 88p. 2000. pap. 12.95 (*1-889097-39-X*) Hard Pr MA.

*__Pornocopia: Porn, Sex, Technology & Desire.__ Laurence J. O'Toole. 2000. pap. 15.00 (*1-85242-720-5*) Serpents Tail.

Pornographers. Akiyuki Nozaka. Tr. by Michael Gallagher. 312p. 1991. pap. 9.95 (*0-8048-1378-7*) Tuttle Pubng.

Pornography. Daniel Linz & Neil M. Malamuth. (Communication Concepts Ser.: Vol. 5). 88p. (C). 1993. text 28.00 (*0-8039-4480-2*); pap. text 11.95 (*0-8039-4481-0*) Sage.

Pornography. Susan S. Nash. (Chapbook Ser.). 24p. 1992. pap. 5.00 (*0-945112-15-7*) Generator Pr.

Pornography, Vol. 1. (J). 1995. pap. 15.98 (*0-8050-3881-7*) St Martin.

Pornography: Debating the Issues. Ted Gottfried. LC 96-34291. (Issues in Focus Ser.). (Illus.). 128p. (YA). (gr. 6 up). 1997. lib. bdg. 20.95 (*0-89490-907-X*) Enslow Pubs.

Pornography: Group Pressures & Individual Rights. Hugh Potter. 180p. 1996. pap. 34.00 (*1-86287-215-5*, Pub. by Federation Pr) Gaunt.

Pornography: Opposing Viewpoints. Ed. by Carol Wekesser. LC 96-28268. (Opposing Viewpoints Ser.). (Illus.). (J). (gr. 5-12). 1996. pap. 16.20 (*1-56510-517-6*); lib. bdg. 26.20 (*1-56510-518-4*) Greenhaven.

Pornography: Private Right or Public Menace? 2nd rev. ed. Ed. by Robert M. Baird & Stuart E. Rosenbaum. LC 98-5614. (Contemporary Issues Ser.). 286p. 1998. pap. 17.95 (*1-57392-207-2*) Prometheus Bks.

Pornography: Production & Consumption of Male Supremacy. Gail Dines & Bob Jensen. LC 97-18263. 224p. 1997. pap. 19.99 (*0-415-91813-8*) Routledge.

Pornography: Production & Consumption of Male Supremacy. Gail Dines & Bob Jensen. LC 97-18263. 224p. (C). 1997. 80.00 (*0-415-91812-X*) Routledge.

Pornography: Research Advances & Policy Considerations. Ed. by Dolf Zillmann & Jennings Bryant. (Communication Ser.). 432p. (C). 1989. pap. 49.95 (*0-8058-0615-6*); text 89.95 (*0-8058-0032-8*) L Erlbaum Assocs.

*__Pornography: Slaying the Dragon.__ David Powlison. (Resources for Changing Lives Ser.). 20p. 1999. pap. 1.75 (*0-87552-677-2*) P & R Pubng.

Pornography: The New Terrorism. Clodagh Corcoran. (C). 1989. 29.00 (*0-946211-84-1*) St Mut.

Pornography: The Other Side. F. M. Christensen. LC 89-26543. 208p. 1990. 35.00 (*0-275-93537-X*, C3537, Greenwood Pr) Greenwood.

Pornography: Women, Violence & Civil Liberties. Ed. by Catherine Itzin. (Illus.). 654p. (C). 1993. reprint ed. pap. 26.00 (*0-19-825755-4*) OUP.

Pornography & Censorship. Ed. by David Copp & Susan Wendell. LC 83-61031. 414p. 1983. pap. 24.95 (*0-87975-182-7*) Prometheus Bks.

Pornography & Censorship: A Bibliography. Ed. by Joan Nordquist. (Contemporary Social Issues: A Bibliographic Ser.: No. 7). 50p. 1987. pap. 20.00 (*0-937855-13-8*) Ref Rsch Serv.

*__Pornography & Democritization: Legislating Obscenity in Post-Communist Russia.__ Paul Goldschmidt. LC 98-51497. 288p. 1998. text 75.00 (*0-8133-3575-2*, Pub. by Westview) HarpC.

Pornography & Difference. Berkeley Kaite. LC 94-49090. 208p. 1995. 35.00 (*0-253-32907-8*); pap. 14.95 (*0-253-20979-X*) Ind U Pr.

Pornography & Representation in Greece & Rome. Ed. by Amy Richlin. (Illus.). 352p. (C). 1992. pap. text 27.95 (*0-19-506723-1*) OUP.

Pornography & Sexual Aggression. Neil M. Malamuth & Edward Donnerstein. 1984. text 84.95 (*0-12-466280-3*) Acad Pr.

Pornography & Sexual Aggression. Neil M. Malamuth & Edward Donnerstein. 1986. pap. text 55.00 (*0-12-466281-1*) Acad Pr.

Pornography & Sexual Deviance: A Report of the Legal & Behavioral Institute, Beverly Hills, California. Michael J. Goldstein & Harold S. Kant. LC 72-97735. (Illus.). 200p. reprint ed. pap. 62.00 (*0-7837-4801-9*, 204444800003) Bks Demand.

*__Pornography & Sexual Representation: A Reference Guide.__ Joseph W. Slade. LC 99-85695. (American Popular Culture Ser.). 2000. lib. bdg. write for info. (*0-313-27568-8*) Greenwood.

*__Pornography & Sexual Representation: A Reference Guide, Vol. 1.__ Joseph W. Slade. (American Popular Culture Ser.). 2000. lib. bdg. write for info. (*0-313-31519-1*) Greenwood.

*__Pornography & Sexual Representation: A Reference Guide, Vol. 2.__ Joseph W. Slade. LC 99-85695. (American Popular Culture Ser.). 2000. lib. bdg. write for info. (*0-313-31520-5*) Greenwood.

*__Pornography & Sexual Representation: A Reference Guide, Vol. 3.__ Joseph W. Slade. LC 99-85695. (American Popular Culture Ser.). 2000. lib. bdg. write for info. (*0-313-31521-3*) Greenwood.

Pornography & the Justices: The Supreme Court & the Intractable Obscenity Problem. Richard F. Hixon. LC 96-42412. (Illus.). 284p. (C). 1996. 29.95 (*0-8093-2057-6*) S Ill U Pr.

Pornography & the Sex Crisis. Cole. 184p. 1994. pap. 14.95 (*0-929005-46-5*, Pub. by Sec Story Pr) LPC InBook.

Pornography Controversy: Changing Moral Standards in American Life. Ed. by Ray C. Rist. LC 73-92813. (Social Policy Ser.). 290p. 1974. pap. 21.95 (*0-87855-587-0*) Transaction Pubs.

Pornography, Feminism & Individual. Assiter. 192p. (C). 44.95 (*0-7453-0319-6*, Pub. by Pluto GBR) Stylus Pub VA.

Pornography in a Free Society. Gordon J. Hawkins & Franklin E. Zimring. (Illus.). 256p. (C). 1989. text 44.95 (*0-521-36317-9*) Cambridge U Pr.

Pornography in a Free Society. Gordon J. Hawkins & Franklin E. Zimring. (Illus.). 250p. (C). 1991. pap. text 17.95 (*0-521-40600-5*) Cambridge U Pr.

*__Pornography in America.__ Joseph W. Slade. (Contemporary World Issues Ser.). (Illus.). 250p. 2000. 45.00 (*1-57607-085-9*) ABC-CLIO.

Pornography, Sex Work, & Hate Speech, Pt. 1. Ed. & Intro. by Karen Maschke. LC 96-51517. (Gender & American Law Ser.: Vol. 6). 464p. 1997. text 84.00 (*0-8153-2520-7*) Garland.

Pornography's Victims. Phyllis Schlafly. LC 86-72068. 282p. (Orig.). 1987. pap. 4.95 (*0-934640-08-4*) Pere Marquette.

*__Pornstar.__ Ian Gittler. LC 99-27281. (Illus.). 224p. 1999. 35.00 (*0-684-82715-8*) S&S Trade.

Pornucopia. Piers Anthony. 188p. 27.95 (*0-8488-1594-7*) Amereon Ltd.

Pornucopia. Piers Anthony. 188p. 1998. lib. bdg. 29.95 (*1-56723-120-9*) Yestermorrow.

Poromechanics: A Tribute to Maurice A. Biot - Proceedings of the Biot Conference on Poromechanics, Louvain-la-Nueve, Belgium, 14-16.09.1998. Ed. by J. F. Thimus et al. 666p. (C). 1998. text 104.00 (*90-5809-003-5*, Pub. by A A Balkema) Ashgate Pub Co.

Porose Integumental Organs of Oribatid Mites: Acari, Oribatida. Ed. by Gerd Alberti & Roy A. Norton. (Zoologica Ser.: Vol. 146). (Illus.). 143p. 1997. pap. 122.00 (*3-510-55033-1*) Lubrecht & Cramer.

Porosity in Carbons. Date not set. text 86.50 (*0-340-54473-2*, Pub. by E A) Routldge.

Porosity in Carbons Characterisation & Applications. Ed. by John W. Patrick. 331p. 1994. text 125.00 (*0-470-23454-7*) Halsted Pr.

Porosity of Ceramics. Rice. LC 97-52813. (Illus.). 560p. 1998. text 195.00 (*0-8247-0151-8*) Dekker.

Porous Asphalt Pavements: An International Perspective, 1990. (Transportation Research Record Ser.: No. 1265). 110p. 1990. 18.00 (*0-309-05022-7*) Transport Res Bd.

Porous, Cellular & Microcellular Materials: Proceedings International Mechanical Engineering Congress & Exposition 1998, Anaheim, CA. Ed. by Vipin Kumar. LC 98-74432. (MD Ser.: Vol. 82). 117p. 1998. 120.00 (*0-7918-1602-8*) ASME.

Porous Ceramic Materials: Fabrication, Characterization, Applications. Ed. by Dean-Mo Liu. (Key Engineering Materials Ser.: Vol. 115). (Illus.). 248p. 1996. text 100.00 (*0-87849-706-4*, Pub. by Trans T Pub) Enfield Pubs NH.

Porous Electrodes: Theory & Practice: Proceedings of the Symposium. Symposium on Porous Electrodes, Theory & Practice. Ed. by Hans C. Maru et al. LC 84-80544. (Electrochemical Society Proceedings Ser.: No. 84-8). 492p. reprint ed. pap. 152.60 (*0-8357-2528-6*, 205240700014) Bks Demand.

Porous Materials for Tissue Engineering. Ed. by Dean-Mo Liu & Vivek Dixit. (Materials Science Forum Ser.: Vol. 250). (Illus.). 252p. (C). 1998. text 94.00 (*0-87849-773-0*, Pub. by Trans T Pub) Enfield Pubs NH.

*__Porous Materials in Environmentally Friendly Processes: Proceedings of the 1st International Feza Conference, Eger, Hungary, September 1-4, 1999__ I. Kiricsi. LC 99-35576. (Studies in Surface Science & Catalysis). 1999. write for info. (*0-444-50244-0*) Elsevier.

*__Porous Media.__ Ed. by A. Dmitrievsky & M. Panfilov. 420p. 1999. 96.00 (*981-02-4126-7*) World Scientific Pub.

Porous Media: Fluid Transport & Pore Structure. 2nd ed. F. A. Dullien. (Illus.). 574p. 1991. text 82.00 (*0-12-223651-3*) Acad Pr.

Porous Media: Geometry & Transports. Pierre M. Adler. 560p. 1992. text 115.00 (*0-7506-9236-7*) Buttrwrth-Heinemann.

Porous Media: Theory & Experiments R. De Boer. LC 99-20352. 1999. write for info. (*0-7923-5692-6*) Kluwer Academic.

Porous Pavement Handbook. Ferguson. 2001. 89.95 (*0-07-134124-2*) McGraw.

Porous Silicon. Zhe C. Feng & R. Tsu. LC 95-134818. 400p. 1994. text 109.00 (*981-02-1634-3*) World Scientific Pub.

Porous Silicon: Proceedings of Symposium 1 on Porous Silicon: Material, Technology & Devices of the 1995 E-MRS Spring Conference, Strasbourg, France, 22-26 May 1995. Ed. by W. Lang et al. LC 96-229437. (European Materials Research Society Symposia Proceedings Ser.: No. 57). 344p. 1996. text 216.25 (*0-444-82414-6*, North Holland) Elsevier.

Porous Silicon & Related Materials: Proceedings of Symposium F on Porous Silicon & Related Materials of the 1994 E-MRS Spring Conference, Strasbourg, France, 24-27 May 1994. R. Herino & W. H. Lang. LC 95-158197. (European Materials Research Society Symposia Proceedings Ser.: Vol. 51). 356p. 1995. 223.50 (*0-444-82137-6*) Elsevier.

Porous Silicon Science & Technology. Ed. by J. C. Vial & J. Derrien. LC 95-168549. 335p. 1995. 97.95 (*3-540-58936-8*) Spr-Verlag.

Porphyria. Ed. by H. F. Merk. (Skin Pharmacology & Applied Skin Physiology Ser.: Vol. 11, No. 6). (Illus.). 98p. 1999. pap. 34.00 (*3-8055-6908-4*) S Karger.

Porphyria: The Unknown Disease. Diana Deats-O'Reilly. 1999. pap. 17.95 (*0-9670365-0-X*) Prophyrin Pr.

P

An Asterisk (*) at the beginning of an entry indicates that the title is appearing for the first time.

Porphyria: The Woman Who Has the "Vampire" Disease. Tammy Evans. (Illus.). 288p. 1997. 22.95 (*0-88282-156-3*) New Horizon NJ.

Porphyric Pesticides: Chemistry, Toxicology & Pharmaceutical Applications. Ed. by Stephen O. Duke & Constantin A. Rebeiz. LC 94-16418. (ACS Symposium Ser.: No. 559). 318p. 1994. text 85.00 (*0-8412-2923-6*, Pub. by Am Chemical) OUP.

***Porphyrin Handbook, 10 vols. Set.** Karl M. Kadish et al. LC 99-64628. 3936p. 1999. 3500.00 (*0-12-393200-9*) Acad Pr.

Porphyrins: Excited States & Dynamics. Ed. by Martin Gouterman et al. LC 86-14647. (ACS Symposium Ser.: Vol. 321). 384p. 1986. reprint ed. pap. 119.10 (*0-608-03525-4*, 20642440008) Bks Demand.

Porphyrins in Human Diseases: Proceedings of the International Porphyrin Meeting, 1st, Freiburg, Germany, May, 1975. International Porphyrin Meeting Staff. Ed. by M. Doss. (Illus.). 400p. 1976. 167.00 (*3-8055-2259-2*) S Karger.

Porphyrius (Philosophus), Kommentar Zur Harmonielehre Des Ptolemaios. Ed. by Ingemar During. xlii, 217p. 1978. reprint ed. write for info. (*3-318-71001-3*) G Olms Pubs.

Porphyry: Cave of Nymphs. Tr. by Robert Lamberton. LC 82-16969. 64p. 1983. 35.00 (*0-930794-71-0*) Station Hill Pr.

Porphyry: The Homeric Questions. Ed. & Tr. by Robin R. Schlunk from GEC. LC 92-35639. (Classical Studies: Vol. 2). XI, 98p. (C). 1994. text 35.95 (*0-8204-1606-1*) P Lang Pubng.

Porphyry's Against the Christians: The Literary Remains. Tr. & Intro. by R. Joseph Hoffmann. LC 94-6779. 181p. (C). 1994. 32.95 (*0-87975-889-9*) Prometheus Bks.

Porphyry's Letter to His Wife Marcella Concerning the Life of Philosophy & the Ascent to the Gods. Tr. by Alice Zimmern from GRE. LC 85-29718. (Orig.). 1986. pap. 6.00 (*0-933999-27-5*) Phanes Pr.

Porphyry's Place in the Neoplatonic Tradition: A Study in Postplotinian Neoplatonism. A. Smith. 191p. 1975. pap. text 107.00 (*90-247-1653-5*) Kluwer Academic.

Porpoises. Andrew Read. LC 98-51770. (WorldLife Library). (Illus.). 72p. (YA). (gr. 6 up). 1999. pap. 16.95 (*0-89658-420-8*) Voyageur Pr.

Porpoises among the Whales: Small Navies in Asia & the Pacific. Joseph R. Morgan. (Illus.). 48p. (Orig.). (C). 1994. pap. text 30.00 (*0-7881-0888-3*) DIANE Pub.

Porpoises & Sonar. Winthrop N. Kellogg. LC 61-11294. (Illus.). xiv, 178p. 1992. pap. text 2.25 (*0-226-43005-7*, P518) U Ch Pr.

Porpoises & Sonar. Winthrop N. Kellogg. LC 61-11294. (Illus.). 191p. reprint ed. pap. 59.30 (*0-608-09422-6*, 205422200004) Bks Demand.

Porque de Las Lenguas. Kenneth E. Hagin.Tr. of Why Tongues?. (SPA.). 1983. pap. 1.00 (*0-89276-151-2*) Faith Lib Pubns.

Porque Hay Silencio. Alba Ambert. (Pioneer Ser.).Tr. of Perfect Silence. 208p. 1998. pap. 11.95 (*1-55885-250-6*) Arte Publico.

***Porque Te Amo.** Max Lucado. (SPA.). 2000. 10.99 (*0-7899-0765-8*) Editorial Unilit.

Porques de Nuestro Mundo. Tr. by Maia Larios S & Maria L. Sanz. (Explora y Aprende Ser.). (SPA., Illus.). 96p. (YA). (gr. 3-8). 1993. 15.00 (*0-915741-48-2*) C D Stampley Ent.

Porrua Dictionary of the Spanish Language: Diccionario Porrua de la Lengua Espanola. 26th ed. Poudevida A. Raluy. (SPA.). 849p. 1985. 10.95 (*0-8288-2057-0*, S12281) Fr & Eur.

Porsche. Randy Leffingwell. LC 94-44211. (Enthusiast Color Ser.). (Illus.). 96p. 1995. pap. 13.95 (*0-87938-992-3*) MBI Pubg.

Porsche. A. T. McKenna. LC 98-29319. (Ultimate Cars Ser.). 2000. lib. bdg. 21.35 (*1-57765-124-3*) ABDO Pub Co.

Porsche. Jay Schleifer. LC 91-31534. (Cool Classics Ser.). (Illus.). 48p. (J). (gr. 5). 1992. lib. bdg. 17.95 (*0-89686-703-X*, Crstwood Hse) Silver Burdett Pr.

Porsche. David Sparrow & Andrea Sparrow. (Color Family Album Ser.). (Illus.). 19.95p. 1998. 19.95 (*1-901295-28-1*) Vloce Pub.

Porsche: Fast & Beautiful, Set I. Shirley Haines & Harry Haines. (Car Classics Ser.). 32p. (YA). (gr. 5-12). 1991. lib. bdg. 15.95 (*0-86593-143-7*) Rourke Corp.

Porsche: Fine Art of the Sports Car. rev. ed. Lucinda Lewis. LC 97-29136. (Illus.). 312p. 1997. 39.98 (*1-57145-135-8*, Thunder Bay) Advantage Pubs.

Porsche: Off-Road & Rally. Robert Butler. (Illus.). 60p. (Orig.). (C). 1989. pap. write for info. (*0-318-65901-8*) Butler & Assocs.

Porsche: Power, Performance & Perfection. Susann C. Miller. 160p. 1996. 19.98 (*1-56799-391-5*, MetroBooks) M Friedman Pub Grp Inc.

***Porsche: Precision, Balance & Style.** Paul W. Cockerham. 1998. pap. text 10.98 (*1-57717-042-3*) Todtri Prods.

Porsche: Road Car - Race Car. Roger W. Hicks. (Illus.). 128p. 10.99 (*1-57215-250-8*, JG2508) World Pubns.

Porsche: Six Cylinder Supercars. Photos & Text by Henry R. Rasmussen. (Top Ten Ser.). (Illus.). 132p. 1992. 29.95 (*1-879301-02-4*) Top Ten Pub.

Porsche: The Man & His Cars. rev. ed. Richard A. Von Frankenberg. LC 78-431737. ix, 236p. 1969. write for info. (*0-85429-090-7*) GT Foulis.

Porsche Book: A Definitive Illustrated History. Lothar Boschen & Jurgen Barth. LC 78-695. 472 p. 1978. 29.95 (*0-668-04576-0*, Arco) Macmillan Gen Ref.

Porsche Book: A Definitive Illustrated History. Lothar Boschen & Jurgen Barth. LC 78-394959. 472p. 1978. write for info. (*0-85059-301-8*) P Stephenson.

Porsche Boxster: Color Tech. John Lamm. LC 98-23723. (ColorTech Ser.). (Illus.). 128p. 1998. pap. 17.95 (*0-7603-0519-6*) Motorbooks Intl.

Porsche Brochures & Sales Literature: A Sourcebook, 1948-1965. rev. ed. Susann C. Miller & Richard F. Merritt. 312p. 1985. reprint ed. 49.95 (*0-915927-02-0*) M & M Pub Inc.

Porsche, Double World Champions, 1900-1977. Richard A. Frankenberg & Michael Cotton. LC 79-322876. 279p. 1977. write for info. (*0-85429-171-7*) GT Foulis.

Porsche Factory Tour: Summer, 1960. Intro. by E. A. Singer & Mike Meyer. (Illus.). 48p. (Orig.). 1982. pap. 29.95 (*0-685-33359-0*) Carrera Intl.

Porsche High-Performance Driving Handbook. Vic Elford. LC 93-34450. (Illus.). 160p. 1994. pap. text 21.95 (*0-87938-849-8*) MBI Pubg.

***Porsche in Motorsport: Fifty Years on Track.** Peter Morgan. (Illus.). 192p. 2000. 49.95 (*1-85960-659-8*, 130425AE, Pub. by Haynes Manuals) Motorbooks Intl.

***Porsche 911.** Richard A. Lentinello. LC 00-33568. (Illus.). 2000. write for info. (*1-58663-028-8*, Friedman-Fairfax) M Friedman Pub Grp Inc.

***Porsche 911.** Laurence Meredith. (Illus.). 160p. 2000. 24.95 (*0-7509-2281-8*) Sutton Publng.

Porsche 911: The Complete Story. David Vivian. (Crowood Autoclassics "Legend of the Road" Ser.). (Illus.). 208p. 1990. 35.95 (*1-85223-330-3*, Pub. by Cro1wood) Motorbooks Intl.

Porsche 911 & Derivatives Vol. 1: A Collector's Guide, 1963-1980. Michael Cotton. (Illus.). 128p. 1994. 19.98 (*0-947981-90-X*, Pub. by Motor Racing) Motorbooks Intl.

***Porsche 911 & Derivatives Vol. 2: 1981-1994: A Collector's Guide.** Michael Cotton. (Illus.). 128p. 2000. pap. 19.95 (*1-899870-49-0*, 130539AE, Pub. by Motor Racing) Motorbooks Intl.

***Porsche 911 Carrera Service Manual, 1984-1989: Coupe, Targa & Cabriolet.** Ed. by Robert Bentley Publishers Staff. LC 00-23006. (Illus.). 750p. 2000. pap. 119.95 (*0-8376-0291-2*, P989) Bentley Pubs.

Porsche 911 Forever Young. Tobias Aichele. Tr. by Peter Albrecht from GER. (Illus.). 400p. (C). 1995. 69.95 (*0-929758-11-0*) Beeman Jorgensen.

***Porsche 911 Gold Portfolio, 1990-1997.** 172p. 2000. pap. 24.95 (*1-85520-396-0*, Pub. by Brooklands Bks) Voyageur Pr.

***Porsche 911 Model by Model.** Laurence Meredith. (Illus.). 160p. 2000. 44.95 (*1-86126-346-5*, 130699AE, Pub. by Cro1wood) Motorbooks Intl.

Porsche 911, 1963-1986. Walter Zeichner. Tr. by Edward Force from GER. LC 88-63996. (Illus.). 96p. 1987. 19.95 (*0-88740-169-4*) Schiffer.

***Porsche 911 Red Book 1965-1999.** Patrick C. Paternie. (Red Bks.). (Illus.). 160p. 2000. pap. 11.95 (*0-7603-0723-7*, 129810AP, Pub. by MBI Pubg) Motorbooks Intl.

***Porsche 911 Restoration Manual.** Porter & Morgan. (Illus.). 256p. 2000. pap. 32.95 (*1-85960-612-1*, Pub. by Haynes Manuals) Motorbooks Intl.

Porsche 911 Road Cars. Dennis Adler. LC 97-45035. (Sports Car Color History Ser.). (Illus.). 128p. 1998. pap. 21.95 (*0-7603-0365-7*) MBI Pubg.

Porsche 911 Story. 6th ed. Paul Frere. LC 97-61074. (Illus.). 352p. 1997. 39.95 (*1-85260-590-1*) Haynes Manuals.

Porsche 914 & 914/6. Brian Long. (Speed Pro Ser.). (Illus.). 160p. 1997. 39.95 (*1-874105-84-7*, Pub. by Vloce Pub) Motorbooks Intl.

Porsche 911: Engine History & Development. Tobias Aichele. LC 99-34042. (Illus.). 708p. 1999. text 39.95 (*0-7603-0702-4*, Pub. by MBI Pubg) Motorbooks Intl.

Porsche 911: Guide to Purchase & DIY Restoration. Lindsay Porter. (Illus.). 256p. 1988. pap. 32.95 (*0-85429-475-9*, Pub. by GT Foulis) Haynes Manuals.

***Porsche 917: The Winning Formula.** Peter Morgan. (Illus.). 208p. 1999. 49.95 (*1-85960-633-4*, 129063AE, Pub. by Haynes Manuals) Motorbooks Intl.

Porsche 968. David Sparrow. (Color Library). (Illus.). 128p. 1994. pap. text 15.95 (*1-85532-437-7*, Pub. by Osprey) Motorbooks Intl.

***Porsche 924.** Brian Long. (Illus.). 192p. 2000. 49.95 (*1-901295-85-0*, 130692AE, Pub. by Vloce Pub) Motorbooks Intl.

***Porsche 924, 944 & 968: A Collector's Guide.** Michael Cotton. (Illus.). 144p. 2000. pap. 19.95 (*1-899870-47-4*, 130540AE, Pub. by Motor Racing) Motorbooks Intl.

Porsche 924, 928, 944, 968. David Vivian. (Illus.). 160p. 1993. 34.95 (*1-85223-483-0*, Pub. by Cro1wood) Motorbooks Intl.

Porsche 914/4 Workshop Maintenance & Repair Manual: Range: 1970-1972. Drake Publishers Editors. LC 72-185632. 1972. write for info. (*0-87749-298-0*) Crescent Pubng.

Porsche Owner's Companion: A Manual of Preservation & Theft Protection. Dan W. Post. LC 80-82464. (Illus.). 192p. 1981. 16.95 (*0-911160-64-7*) Post Group.

Porsche, Past & Present Denis Jenkinson. LC 82-74042. 208 p. 1983. 16.95 (*0-668-05802-1*, Arco) Macmillan Gen Ref.

Porsche Progress: Stuttgart's Modern Development Story Michael Cotton. LC 88-175132. 200p. 1988. write for info. (*0-85059-928-8*) P Stephenson.

Porsche Racing. David Sparrow & Andrea Sparrow. (Illus.). 160p. 1997. 29.95 (*1-85532-616-7*, Pub. by Osprey) Motorbooks Intl.

***Porsche Racing Cars.** Bill Oursler. (Illus.). 192p. 2000. 39.95 (*0-7603-0727-X*, 129811AP, Pub. by MBI Pubg) Motorbooks Intl.

Porsche Racing Cars of the 70s. Paul Frere. LC 80-23773. 164 p. 1981. 19.95 (*0-668-05113-2*, Arco) Macmillan Gen Ref.

Porsche Speedster: The Evolution of the Porsche Lightweight Sportster, 1947-94. Michel Thiriar. 1998. 49.95 (*0-929758-15-3*) Beeman Jorgensen.

Porsche Sport 73. Joe Rusz. LC 73-89096. (Illus.). 1974. pap. 5.95 (*0-393-60017-3*) Norton.

Porsche Sport 72. Joe Rusz. LC 72-97717. (Illus.). 1973. pap. 4.95 (*0-393-60016-5*) Norton.

Porsche Sport, 1974/1975 Joe Rusz. LC 75-663. 104 p. 1975. 7.95 (*0-9600832-1-9*) Ruszkiewicz Publishing.

Porsche Story. Julius Joseph Weitmann. LC 69-11868. 256 p. 1969. write for info. (*0-668-01843-7*, Arco) Macmillan Gen Ref.

Porsche Story. Julius Joseph Weitmann. LC 78-389774. 256p. 1968. write for info. (*0-85059-030-2*) P Stephens.

Porsche Story. 2nd rev. ed. Julius Joseph Weitmann & Michael Kettlewell. LC 72-185221. 288p. 1971. write for info. (*0-85059-091-4*) P Stephens.

Porsche 356. Denis Jenkinson. (Illus.). 144p. 1999. pap. text 19.95 (*1-85532-970-0*, 129151AE) Osprey.

Porsche 356. Brian Long. (Illus.). 160p. 1996. 39.95 (*1-874105-63-4*, Pub. by Vloce Pub) Motorbooks Intl.

Porsche 356. David Styles. (Illus.). 200p. 1998. 34.95 (*1-86126-085-7*, Pub. by Cro1wood) Motorbooks Intl.

Porsche 356: Driving in Its Purest Form. Dirk-Michael Conradt. (Illus.). 264p. (C). 1993. reprint ed. 64.95 (*0-929758-09-9*) Beeman Jorgensen.

Porsche 356 & 550: A Pictorial History. Photos & Text by Henry R. Rasmussen. (Illus.). 160p. 1992. 29.95 (*1-879301-03-2*) Top Ten Pub.

***Porsche 356 & RS Spyders.** Gordon Maltby. (Illus.). 160p. 2000. pap. 24.95 (*0-7603-0903-5*, 130530AP, Pub. by MBI Pubg) Motorbooks Intl.

Porsche 356 Defined: A Pictorial Guide. Brett Johnson. (Illus.). 144p. 1996. 29.95 (*0-929758-14-5*) Practice Ring.

Porsche 356, 1948-1965. Walter Zeichner. LC 89-63364. (Illus.). 96p. 1989. 19.95 (*0-88740-210-0*) Schiffer.

Porsche 356 1948-1965 Photo Album. Ed. by Wallace A. Wyss. LC 97-75280. (Photo Album Ser.). (Illus.). 112p. 1998. pap. 19.95 (*1-882256-85-9*) Iconografix.

Porsche Turbo Race Cars. Ian Bamsey. (Illus.). 160p. 1989. 49.95 (*0-85429-780-4*, F780, Pub. by GT Foulis) Haynes Manuals.

Porsche Year, 1982. Ed. by Susann C. Miller. (Illus.). 96p. 1982. 50.00 (*0-910597-00-6*); pap. 5.00 (*0-910597-01-4*) M & M Pub Inc.

Porsche Year, 1985-6. Ed. by Susann C. Miller. (Porsche Ser.). (Illus.). 96p. (Orig.). 1986. 50.00 (*0-915927-04-7*); pap. text 18.95 (*0-915927-03-9*) M & M Pub Inc.

Porsche 356 Carrera: Four Cam Production Car. Cole R. Scrogham. (Illus.). 120p. 1996. 29.95 (*0-929758-13-7*) Beeman Jorgensen.

Porsche 911. Michael Burgan. LC 98-48708. (On the Road Ser.). 1999. 19.00 (*0-7368-0183-9*); 19.00 (*0-531-11815-0*) Capstone Pr.

Porsche 911 Performance Handbook. 2nd ed. Bruce Anderson. LC 96-43706. (Performance Handbook Ser.). (Illus.). 272p. 1996. pap. 21.95 (*0-7603-0033-X*) MBI Pubg.

Porsche 924, 928, 944: The New Generation Jerry Sloniger. LC 81-192135. 168 p. 1981. 9.95 (*0-85045-415-8*) Osprey.

Porsche 956, 962 John Allen. LC 87-82838. (Motoring Bks.). 158p. 1988. write for info. (*0-85429-642-5*) GT Foulis.

***Porshe Turbo: The Full History of the Race & Production Cars.** Peter Vann. (Illus.). 160p. 2000. 39.95 (*0-7603-0965-5*, 130719AP, Pub. by MBI Pubg) Motorbooks Intl.

Port. Doug McIvor & Neil Mathieson. (Pocket Guide Ser.). (Illus.). 96p. 1999. 6.99 (*0-7858-1059-5*) Bk Sales Inc.

Port Adelaide Conservation Study. Elizabeth Vines & Port Adelaide Centre Joint Committee Staff. LC 80-500102. 109p. 1977. write for info. (*0-7243-5221-X*) Libs So Aus.

Port Administration in the United States. Marvin L. Fair. LC 54-8653. (Illus.). 233p. reprint ed. 72.30 (*0-8357-9074-6*, 201525900093) Bks Demand.

***Port Agency.** Malcolm Latarche. 200p. 1998. pap. 60.00 (*1-85609-157-0*, Pub. by Witherby & Co) St Mut.

Port & a Star Boarder. B. J. Morison. LC 84-24. 244p. 1984. 12.95 (*0-89621-081-2*) Nrth Country Pr.

Port & Development. Sachinandan Sau. LC 96-912026. (C). 1997. pap. 18.00 (*81-7102-065-8*, Pub. by Firma KLM) S Asia.

Port. & Eng. see Girl from Ipanema

Port. & Eng. see Girl from Ipanema: Mini

Port. & Eng. see Girl from Ipanema

Port & Harbour Engineering. Ed. by Adrian Jarvis. LC 97-30339. (Studies in the History of Civil Engineering: Vol. 6). 420p. 1998. text 153.95 (*0-86078-755-9*, Pub. by Ashgate Pub) Ashgate Pub Co.

Port & Ocean Engineering under Arctic Conditions: Selected Papers from the 3rd International Conference. Ed. by Michael E. McCormick. 1977. pap. 29.00 (*0-08-021421-5*, Pergamon Pr) Elsevier.

***Port & Shipbuilding Equipment in Pakistan: A Strategic Entry Report, 1999.** Compiled by Icon Group International. (Illus.). 175p. 1999. ring bd. 1750.00 incl. audio compact disk (*0-7418-1713-6*) Icon Grp.

Port & Shipbuilding Equipment in Vietnam: A Strategic Entry Report, 1997. Compiled by Icon Group International Staff. (Illus.). 159p. 1999. ring bd. 1590.00 incl. audio compact disk (*0-7418-0902-8*) Icon Grp.

***Port & the Douro.** Richard Mayson. (Illus.). 320p. 2000. pap. 16.00 (*0-571-19522-9*) Faber & Faber.

Port Angeles-Washington: A History, Vol. I. Paul Martin & Peggy Brady. LC 82-82187. (Illus.). 252p. 1983. pap. 18.95 (*0-918146-23-2*) Peninsula WA.

Port Architecture, Academy Edition. Peter Quartermaine. (Illus.). 128p. 1999. 45.00 (*0-471-98470-1*) Wiley.

Port Arrivals & Immigrants to the City of Boston, 1715-1716 & 1762-1769. William H. Whitmore. 111p. 1996. reprint ed. pap. 12.50 (*0-8063-0541-X*, 615) Clearfield Co.

Port Arthur: A Story of Strength & Courage. Margaret Scott. LC 97-159022. (Illus.). 1997. write for info. (*0-09-183521-6*) Trafalgar.

Port Arthur Built: An Illustrated History of Port Arthur Shipbuilding. David Benedet. (Great Lakes Marine History Ser.). (Illus.). 148p. 1994. pap. 21.95 (*0-9697778-0-9*, Pub. by RivT) Partners Pubs Grp.

Port Arthur Centennial History: Official Pictorial History of Port Arthur, Texas, 1898-1998, 2 vols. 2nd ed. Michael Cate et al. Ed. by Dub Brown. LC 96-77840. 488p. 1997. 65.00 (*1-886130-06-X*) Cate Media.

Port Authority Poetry Review, Vol. 1. Maurice Hart et al. 100p. (Orig.). 1985. pap. 6.00 (*0-935505-00-8*) Bank St Pr.

Port Authority Poetry Review, Vol. 2. Mary Y. Sampson & Maurice Hart. Ed. by Mary Bertschmann. (Illus.). 100p. (Orig.). 1986. pap. 6.00 (*0-935505-01-6*) Bank St Pr.

Port Authority Poetry Review, Vol. 3. Mary Y. Sampson & Maurice Hart. Ed. by Mary Bertschmann. 96p. (Orig.). 1986. pap. 6.00 (*0-935505-02-4*) Bank St Pr.

Port Authority Poetry Review, Vol. 4. Mary Y. Sampson & Maurice Hart. Ed. by Mary Bertschmann. (Illus.). 100p. (Orig.). 1987. pap. 6.00 (*0-935505-03-2*) Bank St Pr.

Port Bowles. Paul Bowles. 1999. pap. 22.00 (*0-670-84461-6*) Viking Penguin.

Port Carling: The Hub of the Muskoka Lakes. Richard Tatley. (Illus.). 120p. 1996. 28.95 (*1-55046-187-7*, Pub. by Boston Mills) Genl Dist Srvs.

Port Chicago Mutiny. Robert L. Allen. 224p. 1993. reprint ed. pap. 9.95 (*1-56743-010-4*, Amistad) HarperTrade.

Port Cities & Intruders: The Swahili Coast, India & Portugal in the Early Modern Era. Michael N. Pearson. LC 97-20627. (Symposia in Comparative History Ser.). (Illus.). 202p. 1998. text 35.95 (*0-8018-5692-2*) Johns Hopkins.

***Port Clinton, the Peninsula & the Bass Islands, Ohio.** Sally Sue Witten. (Images of America Ser.). (Illus.). 128p. 2000. pap. 18.99 (*0-7385-0702-4*) Arcadia Publng.

Port Companion: A Connoisseur's Guide. Godfrey D. Spence. LC 97-3205. (Illus.). 224p. 1997. 23.95 (*0-02-861781-9*) Macmillan.

***Port Companion: A Connoisseur's Guide.** Godfrey D. Spence. (Illus.). 224p. 2000. reprint ed. text 24.00 (*0-7881-6911-4*) DIANE Pub.

***Port Coquitlam: Where the Rivers Meet.** Chuck Davis. (Illus.). 196p. 2000. 39.95 (*1-55017-221-2*) Harbour Pub Co.

Port Dalhousie: Shoes & Ships & Sealing Wax. Dorothy Turcotte. (Illus.). 60p. (Orig.). 1991. pap. 9.95 (*0-919783-58-9*, Pub. by Boston Mills) Genl Dist Srvs.

Port Design: Guidelines & Recommendations. Carl A. Thoresen. (Illus.). 308p. (Orig.). 1988. pap. 197.50 (*0-685-28129-9*) Coronet Bks.

Port Development: A Handbood for Planners in Developing Countries. UNCTAD, Secretariat. 227p. 1985. 23.00 (*92-1-112160-4*, E.84.II.D.1) UN.

***Port Development in Russia: A Strategic Entry Report, 1995.** Compiled by Icon Group International Staff. (Illus.). 155p. 1999. ring bd. 1550.00 incl. audio compact disk (*0-7418-1654-7*) Icon Grp.

***Port Development in Turkey: A Strategic Entry Report, 1995.** Compiled by Icon Group International Staff. (Illus.). 149p. 1999. ring bd. 1490.00 incl. audio compact disk (*0-7418-1655-5*) Icon Grp.

***Port Development in United Arab Emirates: A Strategic Entry Report, 1998.** Compiled by Icon Group International Staff. (Country Industry Report). (Illus.). 96p. 1999. ring bd. 960.00 incl. audio compact disk (*0-7418-0549-9*) Icon Grp.

***Port Development Services in Egypt: A Strategic Entry Report, 1999.** Compiled by Icon Group International. (Illus.). 161p. 1999. ring bd. 1610.00 incl. audio compact disk (*0-7418-1778-0*) Icon Grp.

Port Economics. Jan O. Jansson & Dan Shneerson. (Transportation Studies). (Illus.). 208p. 1982. 40.00 (*0-262-10025-8*) MIT Pr.

Port Economics in Developing Countries & the Appraisal of Port Warehouse Extensions. ICHCA Staff. (C). 1974. 25.00 (*0-7855-5078-X*, Pub. by ICHCA) St Mut.

Port Engineering Vol. 1: Harbor Planning, Breakwaters & Marine Terminals. 4th ed. Per Bruun. 1464p. 1989. 195.00 (*0-87201-843-1*, 1843) Gulf Pub.

Port Engineering Vol. 2: Harbor Transportation, Fishing Ports, Sediment Transport, Geomorphology, Inlets, & Dredging. 4th ed. 1146p. 1989. 195.00 (*0-87201-847-4*) Gulf Pub.

Port Engineering & Operation: Proceedings of a Conference Organized by the Institution of Civil Engineers. 235p. 1985. 42.00 (*0-7277-0244-0*, Pub. by T Telford) RCH.

Port Engineering Seminar. Ed. by Cargo Systems Staff. 1986. 220.00 (*0-907499-54-6*, Pub. by Cargo Systs) St Mut.

Port Englouti. Jacques Cassabois. (Folio - Cadet Rouge Ser.: No. 204). (FRE., Illus.). 79p. (J). (gr. 3-7). 1989. pap. 8.95 (*2-07-031204-6*) Schoenhof.

Port Equipment in Brazil: A Strategic Entry Report, 1998. Compiled by Icon Group International Staff. (Country Industry Report). (Illus.). 153p. 1999. ring bd. 1530.00 incl. audio compact disk (*0-7418-0322-4*) Icon Grp.

Port Equipment in Taiwan: A Strategic Entry Report, 1998. Compiled by Icon Group International Staff. (Country Industry Report). (Illus.). 118p. 1999. ring bd. 1180.00 incl. audio compact disk (*0-7418-0323-2*) Icon Grp.

Port Eternity. C. J. Cherryh. 192p. 1987. pap. 5.99 (*0-88677-206-0*, Pub. by DAW Bks) Penguin Putnam.

***Port Facilities in Singapore: A Strategic Entry Report, 1995.** Compiled by Icon Group International Staff. (Illus.). 113p. 1999. ring bd. 1130.00 incl. audio compact disk (*0-7418-1656-3*) Icon Grp.

P

Port Facilities in Singapore: A Strategic Entry Report, 1996. Compiled by Icon Group International Staff. (Illus.). 113p. 1999. ring bd. 1130.00 incl. audio compact disk (0-7418-1421-8) Icon Grp.

*Port Facilities in Singapore: A Strategic Entry Report, 1999.** Compiled by Icon Group International. (Illus.). 117p. 1999. ring bd. 1170.00 incl. audio compact disk (0-7418-1867-1) Icon Grp.

Port Fuel Injection. Tom McKenna. 24p. 1988. pap., wbk. ed. 7.00 (0-8064-0875-8, A21) Bergwall.

Port Handling Equipment in China: A Strategic Entry Report, 1997. Compiled by Icon Group International Staff. (Country Industry Report). (Illus.). 182p. 1999. ring bd. 1820.00 incl. audio compact disk (0-7418-0324-0) Icon Grp.

Port Hudson Campaign, 1862-1863. Edward Cunningham. LC 63-16655. (Illus.). 200p. 1994. pap. 14.95 (0-8071-1925-3) La State U Pr.

Port Hudson, Confederate Bastion on the Mississippi. Lawrence L. Hewitt. LC 87-3198. (Illus.). 240p. 1994. pap. 12.95 (0-8071-1961-X) La State U Pr.

Port Huron Statement. (Studies in American Radicalism). 1992. lib. bdg. 75.00 (0-8490-5456-7) Gordon Pr.

Port Huron Statement: The Founding Manifesto of Students for a Democratic Society. Tom Hayden et al. (Sixties Ser.). 80p. (Orig.). (C). 1990. reprint ed. pap. 9.00 (0-88286-172-7); reprint ed. lib. bdg. 22.95 (0-88286-173-5) C H Kerr.

Port Jervis Diamond Jubilee Journal History, 1982. Orange County Genealogical Society Staff. 140p. 1986. 5.00 (0-937135-16-X) Orange County Genealog.

Port Jervis Industrial Record, 1902. Orange County Genealogical Society Staff. 42p. 1986. 4.00 (0-937135-17-8, 86-47) Orange County Genealog.

Port Jews of Habsburg Trieste: Absolutist Politics & Enlightenment Culture. Lois C. Dubin. (Studies in Jewish History & Culture). (Illus.). 2p. 1998. 49.50 (0-8047-3320-1) Stanford U Pr.

Port Kennedy: A Village in the Shadow of Valley Forge. Karen Sweeny-Justice. (Illus.). 42p. (C). 1994. pap. text 5.95 (0-939631-78-4) Thomas Publications.

Port Madison: Washington Territory, 1854-1889, 232p. 1989. 35.00 (0-9622337-0-6) Perry Pub WA.

Port of Albany & Ports on the Hudson River, New York. (Port Series : Vol. 6). per. 6.50 (0-16-001740-8) USGPO.

Port of Baltimore Maryland. Vol. 10. 108p. 1991. per. 9.00 (0-16-032128-X) USGPO.

Port of Boston, Massachusetts: Port Series No. 3. Vol. 3. 116p. 1994. per. 16.00 (0-16-061243-8) USGPO.

Port of Charleston & Georgetown, South Carolina. Vol. 13. 80p. 1987. per. 7.00 (0-16-001793-9) USGPO.

Port of Chicago, Illinois. (Port Series : Vol. 46). per. 8.50 (0-16-001765-3) USGPO.

Port of Chicago, Illinois: Port Series No. 46. Vol. 46. 176p. 1995. per. 23.00 (0-16-061247-0) USGPO.

Port of Cincinnati Ohio& Ports on the Ohio River. Vol. 62. per. 8.50 (0-16-001778-5) USGPO.

Port of Cleveland, Ohio. Vol. 43. 58p. 1989. pap. 8.00 (0-16-001800-5) USGPO.

Port of Coos Bay, Oregon & Ports on the Columbia Snake River System. Vol. 33. 164p. 1986. per. 13.00 (0-16-001784-X) USGPO.

Port of Corpus Christi, Texas. 25. per. 12.00 (0-16-061238-1) USGPO.

Port of Duluth, Minnesota, Superior, Wisconsin, Taconite Harbor, Silver Bay & Two Harbors, Minnesota & Ashland, Wisconsin. Vol. 49. 68p. 1987. pap. 7.50 (0-16-001792-0) USGPO.

*Port of Entry.** Richard Setlowe. 2001. write for info. (0-06-018392-6, HarpCollins) HarperTrade.

*Port of Gloucester: Photographs by Josh Reynolds.** Photos by Josh Reynolds. (New England Landmarks Ser.). (Illus.). 64p. 2000. 16.95 (1-889833-17-7, Commonwealth Eds) Memoirs Unltd.

Port of Hong Kong: A Survey of Its Development. T. N. Chiu. LC 73-88376. 158p. reprint ed. pap. 49.00 (0-8357-2744-0, 203985300013) Bks Demand.

Port of Houston, Texas. (Port Series : Vol. 24). per. 10.00 (0-16-001771-8) USGPO.

Port of Leith. Susan Mowat. 470p. (C). 1996. pap. 60.00 (0-85976-403-6, Pub. by J Donald) St Mut.

Port of London. R. Douglas Brown. 212p. (C). 1988. 50.00 (0-900963-87-5, Pub. by T Dalton) St Mut.

Port of Louisville, Kentucky & the Ports on the Ohio River, Cumberland & Green Rivers, Miles 560-980: Port Series. 63. 180p. 1993. per. 12.00 (0-16-061236-5) USGPO.

Port of Milwaukee. Edward Hamming. LC 55-3708. (Augustana College Library Publications: No. 25). 162p. 1953. pap. 6.00 (0-910182-20-5) Augustana Coll.

Port of Milwaukee: An Economic Review. Eric Schenker. LC 67-13553. 228p. reprint ed. pap. 70.70 (0-608-14770-2, 202371500033) Bks Demand.

Port of Mobile, Alabama. Vol. 18. 108p. 1986. per. 6.50 (0-16-001786-6) USGPO.

Port of Mobile, Alabama, Revised 1998: Port Series No. 18. Vol. 18. per. 9.00 (0-16-061263-2) USGPO.

Port of Natchez, Vickburg, Greenville & Ports on the Mississippi River. (Port Series : Vol. 72). 100p. 1991. per. 9.00 (0-16-033200-1) USGPO.

Port of New Orleans, Louisana. Vol. 20. 212p. 1990. per. 12.00 (0-16-022609-0) USGPO.

Port of New Orleans, Louisiana. Vol. 20. per. 10.00 (0-16-001748-3) USGPO.

Port of New York: A History of the Rail & Terminal System from the Grand Central Electrification to the Present, Vol. 2. Carl W. Condit. LC 79-16850. 412p. 1981. 48.00 (0-226-11461-9) U Ch Pr.

Port of New York Authority. Erwin W. Bard. LC 68-58547. (Columbia University. Studies in the Social Sciences: No. 468). reprint ed. 34.50 (0-404-51468-5) AMS Pr.

Port of Oakland, Alameda, Richmond & Ports on the CArquinez Strait, California. Vol. 31. 126p. 1991. per. 9.00 (0-16-032129-8) USGPO.

Port of Portland Oregon. VOL. 34. 80p. 1985. pap. 7.00 (0-16-001756-4) USGPO.

Port of Portland, Oregon & Ports on Columbia-snake River System: Port Series No. 34. Vol. 34. per. 36.00 (0-16-061252-7) USGPO.

Port of Portsmouth Ships & the Cotton Trade, 1783-1829. Ray Brighton. (Portsmouth Marine Society Ser.: No. 10). (Illus.). 236p. 1985. 24.95 (0-915819-09-0) Portsmouth Marine Soc.

Port of Sacremento, Stockton, Pittsburgh & Antioch California. Vol. 32. 92p. 1985. per. 7.00 (0-16-001783-1) USGPO.

Port of Saints. William S. Burroughs. LC 80-10309. 1980. 49.95 (0-912652-64-0); pap. 14.95 (0-912652-65-9) Blue Wind.

Port of San Diego, California: Port Series. 27. per. 23.00 (0-16-061264-0) USGPO.

Port of San Diego,California. (Port Series : Vol. 27). 68p. 1987. pap. 6.50 (0-16-001791-2) USGPO.

Port of Seattle, Washington: Port Series. 36. per. 22.00 (0-16-061240-3) USGPO.

Port of Toledo, Ohio. Vol. 44. pap. 7.00 (0-16-001799-8) USGPO.

Port on the Tennessee River, Tennessee, Tombigbee & Black Warrior Waterways on the Alabama River. Vol. 64. 228p. 1986. per. 11.00 (0-16-001785-8) USGPO.

*Port Orange.** Harold D. Cardwell, Sr. & Priscilla D. Cardwell. (Images of America Ser.). (Illus.). 128p. 2000. pap. 18.99 (0-7385-0618-4) Arcadia Publng.

Port Orford: A History. Patrick Masterson. LC 94-70323. (Illus.). 380p. 1994. 29.95 (1-885221-08-8) BookPartners.

Port Orford, Oregon, Meteorite Mystery. Ed. by Roy S. Clarke, Jr. LC 92-26788. (Smithsonian Contributions to the Earth Sciences Ser.: No. 31). 48p. reprint ed. pap. 30.00 (0-7837-4483-8, 204425800001) Bks Demand.

Port Phillip Bay Environment Study. (Illus.). 239p. 1996. pap. 60.00 (0-643-05927-X, Pub. by CSIRO) Accents Pubns.

Port Planning & Development. Ernst G. Frankel. 795p. 1987. 200.00 (0-471-83708-3) Wiley.

Port Project. 138p. 1996. pap. 14.00 (0-16-061981-5) USGPO.

Port Project: Market Segment Specialization Program - Audit Technique Guide. 140p. (Orig.). 1996. pap. 47.00 (1-57402-121-4) Athena Info Mgt.

Port-Related State Programs & Federal Legislative Issues. Leigh B. Boske. (Policy Research Project Report Ser.). 285p. 1995. pap. 15.00 (0-89940-725-0) LBJ Sch Pub Aff.

Port Royal. Linda L. Chaikin. LC 96-207804. (Buccaneers Ser.: No. 1). pap. 11.99 (0-8024-1071-5, 252) Moody.

Port-Royal. Henry De Montherlant. (FRE.). 1960. write for info. (0-318-63579-8) Fr & Eur.

Port Royal. Henry De Montherlant. (FRE.). 1972. pap. 10.95 (0-8288-3753-8, F115790) Fr & Eur.

Port-Royal, 3 vols. Charles-Augustin Sainte-Beuve. 1955. lib. bdg. 100.00 (0-7859-3789-7) Fr & Eur.

Port-Royal, 3 tomes, Vol. 1. deluxe ed. Charles-Augustin De Sainte-Beuve. (Pleiade Ser.). (FRE.). 1955. 63.95 (2-07-010495-8) Schoenhof.

Port-Royal, 3 vols., Vol. 2. Charles-Augustin Sainte-Beuve. 1955. lib. bdg. 105.00 (0-7859-3790-0) Fr & Eur.

Port-Royal, 3 tomes, Vol. 2. deluxe ed. Charles-Augustin De Sainte-Beuve. (Pleiade Ser.). (FRE.). 1955. 63.95 (2-07-010496-6) Schoenhof.

Port-Royal, 3 tomes, Vol. 3. deluxe ed. Charles-Augustin De Sainte-Beuve. (Pleiade Ser.). (FRE.). 1955. 59.95 (2-07-010497-4) Schoenhof.

Port-Royal, 3 vols., Vol.3. Charles-Augustin Sainte-Beuve. 1955. lib. bdg. 100.00 (0-7859-3791-9) Fr & Eur.

*Port-Royal & Jansenism in France.** John Mason Neale. Ed. by Jimmie R. Rankin. (Old Catholic Studies). 108p. 2000. pap. 14.95 (1-883938-74-0) Dry Bones Pr.

Port Royal & Notes de Theatre sur le Maitre de Santiago et Port-Royal. Henry De Montherlant. (Folio Ser.: No. 253). (FRE.). 192p. 1972. pap. 6.95 (2-07-036253-1) Schoenhof.

*Port Said Revisited.** Sylvia Modelski. LC 99-96961. (Illus.). 212p. 2000. pap. 14.95 (0-9676230-0-6, Pharos Bk) FAROS.

Port Series: Mississippi River Ports Above & Below New Orleans, Louisiana. 20a. 188p. 1991. per. 12.00 (0-16-061232-2) USGPO.

Port Series: Port of Cincinnati, Ohio & Ports on the Ohio River. 62. 120p. 1991. per. 10.00 (0-16-061231-4) USGPO.

Port Series: Ports of St. Louis, Missouri & Upper Mississippi River. 70. 128p. 1992. per. 11.00 (0-16-061233-0) USGPO.

*Port-Site & Wound Recurrences in Cancer Surgery: Incidence - Pathogenesis - Prevention.** M. A. Reymond et al. Tr. by A. Jack from GER. (Illus.). 210p. 2000. 104.00 (3-540-66929-9) Spr-Verlag.

Port State Control & Jurisdiction: Evolution of the Port State Regime. George C. Kasoulides. LC 93-10241. 1993. lib. bdg. 124.00 (0-7923-2281-9) Kluwer Academic.

Port-to-Port: A Complete Set of Safe Courses to All Harbor Destinations Covering Eastport, Maine to Block Island, Rhode Island. William R. Zolla. 200p. (Orig.). 1989. 75.00 (0-685-28925-7) Pilot Pub Assocs.

Port-to-Port: A Complete Set of Safe Courses to All Harbor Destinations Covering Eastport, Maine to Block Island, Rhode Island. William R. Zolla. 210p. (Orig.). 1989. 75.00 (0-685-28924-9); 75.00 (0-685-28923-0); 75.00 (0-685-28926-5); pap. 49.50 (1-878262-00-9); pap. 49.50 (1-878262-01-7) Pilot Pub Assocs.

Port-to-Port: A Complete Set of Safe Courses to All Harbor Destinations Covering Eastport, Maine to Block Island, Rhode Island. William R. Zolla. 230p. (Orig.). 1989. 75.00 (0-685-28927-3) Pilot Pub Assocs.

Port Valdez, Alaska: Environmental Studies, Nineteen Seventy-Six to Nineteen Seventy-Nine. Ed. by J. M. Colonell & H. K. Stockholm. (Occasional Publications: No. 5). (Illus.). 373p. 1980. 20.00 (0-685-04965-5) U of AK Inst Marine.

Port Vila Blues: A Wyatt Novel. Garry Disher. 232p. (Orig.). 1996. pap. 6.95 (1-86448-025-4, Pub. by Allen & Unwin Pty) IPG Chicago.

Port West. Rebecca West. 1999. pap. 14.95 (0-14-024710-6, Viking) Viking Penguin.

Port Wine. Andrew Jefford. 1988. 9.98 (0-671-10032-7) S&S Trade.

Port-Wine Sea: A Parody. Susan Wenger. LC 98-83015. 192p. 1999. pap. 12.95 (1-893162-00-1) Erica Hse.

Port Wine Stain: Partick Boyle's Best Short Stroies. Patrick Boyle. Ed. by Peter Fallon. (Classic Irish Fiction Ser.). 236p. 1983. 15.95 (0-8159-6524-9) Devin.

Porta Argentariorum. D. E. Haynes & P. E. Hirst. (Illus.). 43p. 1939. 45.00 (0-614-21817-9, Pub. by British Schl Rome) David Brown.

Portability & Performance for Parallel Processing. Ed. by Anthony J. Hey & Jeanne Ferrante. LC 94-2539. (Wiley Professional Computing Ser.). (Illus.). 282p. 1994. reprint ed. pap. 87.50 (0-608-05275-2, 206581300001) Bks Demand.

Portable Aaron Travis. Aaron Travis. 1999. pap. 12.95 (1-56333-680-4) Masquerade.

Portable Aaron Travis, 1. Aaron Travis. 1999. pap. text 10.95 (1-58419-013-2) Masq Bks.

Portable Abraham Lincoln. Intro. by Andrew Delbanco. 384p. 1993. pap. 13.95 (0-14-017031-6, Penguin Bks) Viking Penguin.

Portable Action Lab for Creating Quality: Student Projects for Health Careers. Anthony Alongi et al. (Illus.). 50p. 1997. pap. 25.00 (1-887410-91-0) Jobs for Future.

Portable American Realism Reader. Ed. by James Nagel & Tom Quirk. LC 97-12448. 1997. pap. 14.95 (0-14-026830-8) Viking Penguin.

Portable & Mine Power Feeders Plus Revision 1. Date not set. 46.00 (0-614-18709-5, NEMA WC 58) Insulated Cable.

Portable & Personal Digital Assistants in Mexico: A Strategic Entry Report, 1998. Compiled by Icon Group International Staff. (Country Industry Report). (Illus.). 156p. 1999. ring bd. 1560.00 incl. audio compact disk (0-7418-0455-7) Icon Grp.

Portable Apocalypse: A Quotable Companion to the End of the World. Ed. & Compiled by Allan Appel. LC 98-41789. 272p. 1999. pap. 12.00 (1-57322-714-5, Riverhd Trade) Berkley Pub.

Portable Architecture. Ed. by Robert Kronenburg. (Illus.). 114p. 1998. pap. 44.95 (0-471-98422-1) Wiley.

Portable Architecture. 2nd ed. Robert Kronenburg. LC 96-35761. (Butterworth Architecture New Technology Ser.). 160p. 2000. text 72.95 (0-7506-2388-8) Buttrwrth-Heinemann.

*Portable Architecture.** 2nd ed. Robert Kronenburg. LC 99-88493. (Illus.). 176p. 2000. pap. text 56.95 (0-7506-4472-9) Buttrwrth-Heinemann.

Portable Arthur Miller. Arthur Miller. Ed. & Intro. by Christopher W. Bigsby. LC 95-9485. 608p. 1995. pap. 16.95 (0-14-024709-2, Penguin Bks) Viking Penguin.

Portable Baker: Baking on Boat & Trail. Jean Spangenberg & Samuel Spangenberg. LC 96-23357. (Illus.). 166p. 1997. pap. 14.95 (0-07-059871-1) McGraw.

Portable Baker's Biographical Dictionary of Musicians. Nicolas Slonimsky. Ed. by Richard Kostelanetz. 293p. (Orig.). 1995. pap. 19.95 (0-8256-9394-2, GS 10034, Schirmer Books) Mac Lib Ref.

Portable Bamburak. Gary Bamburak. (Illus.). 72p. (Orig.). 1989. pap. 4.95 (0-9622560-0-5) Bamburak Designs.

Portable Bankruptcy Code & Rules. Ed. by Sally M. Henry. LC 96-11153. (Illus.). 1996. pap. 29.95 (1-57073-276-0) Amer Bar Assn.

Portable Battery Operated Tools: 745-3. 1995. write for info. (1-55989-784-8, UL 745-3) Underwrtrs Labs.

Portable Battery Powered Products Markets. LC 97-120229. (Report Ser.: No. GB-184). 327p. 1996. 2950.00 (1-56965-234-1) BCC.

Portable Beat Reader. Ed. by Ann Charters. 608p. 1992. reprint ed. pap. 15.95 (0-14-015102-8, Penguin Bks) Viking Penguin.

Portable Best Friend: Wit & Wisdom to Get Through Life's Rough Spots. Sandy Weinstein & Carol Wallace. 128p. (Orig.). 1996. mass mkt. 6.99 (0-446-67171-1, Pub. by Warner Bks) Little.

Portable Blake. William Blake. Ed. by Alfred Kazin. (Portable Library: No. 26). 728p. 1977. pap. 15.95 (0-14-015026-9, P26, Penguin Bks) Viking Penguin.

Portable Business Writer. William Murdick. LC 98-72065. (English Essentials Ser.). vi, 216 p. 1998. pap. text 8.07 (0-395-90921-X) HM.

Portable Businessaurus: A Treasury of Insight, Wit & Wisdom from Tomorrow's Captians of Industry. Steve J. Bennett. (Illus.). 96p. 1998. pap. 7.95 (1-886284-29-6, Pub. by Chandler Hse) Natl Bk Netwk.

Portable C. Henry Rabinowitz & Chaim Schaap. 288p. (C). 1990. pap. 29.95 (0-13-685967-4) P-H.

Portable Calibrator for Across-the-Road Radar Systems. Arthur J. Ondreka. 37p. 1998. pap. 3.50 (0-16-056690-8) USGPO.

Portable Cervantes. Miguel De Cervantes Saavedra. Tr. by Samuel Putnam. LC 76-44354. (Portable Library: No. 57). 854p. 1976. pap. 22.99 (0-14-015057-9, Penguin Bks) Viking Penguin.

Portable Charles Lamb. John M. Brown. LC 75-11488. 594p. 1975. reprint ed. lib. bdg. 38.50 (0-8371-8202-6, LAPCL, Greenwood Pr) Greenwood.

Portable Chaucer. rev. ed. Geoffrey Chaucer. Ed. by Theodore Morrison. LC 75-2224. (Portable Library: No. 81). 800p. 1977. pap. 15.95 (0-14-015081-1, Penguin Bks) Viking Penguin.

Portable Chekhov. Anton Chekhov. Ed. by Avrahm Yarmolinsky. (Portable Library: No. 35). 640p. 1977. pap. 15.95 (0-14-015035-8, Penguin Bks) Viking Penguin.

*Portable Coach: 28 Sure-Fire Strategies for Business & Personal Success.** Thomas J. Leonard & Byron Laursen. LC 98-26631. 336p. 1998. 23.00 (0-684-85041-9) Scribner.

Portable Coach: 28 Surefire Strategies for Business & Personal Success. abr. ed. Thomas J. Leonard. 1998. 17.00 incl. audio (0-671-58216-X, Audioworks) S&S Trade.

Portable Coleridge. Samuel Taylor Coleridge. Ed. by Ivor A. Richards. (Portable Library: No. 48). (J). (gr. 10 up). 1977. pap. 16.95 (0-14-015048-X, P48, Penguin Bks) Viking Penguin.

Portable College Adviser: A Guide for High School Students. Wendy H. Robbins. LC 95-47026. (Illus.). 160p. (YA). (gr. 9-12). 1996. lib. bdg. 24.00 (0-531-11257-8) Watts.

Portable College Adviser: A Guide for High School Students. Wendy H. Robbins. LC 95-47026. (Illus.). 160p. (YA). (gr. 9-12). 1996. pap. 9.00 (0-531-15790-3) Watts.

Portable Computers & Wireless Communications. 211p. 1991. 895.00 (0-614-18367-7, IGIC-68) Info Gatekeepers.

Portable Computing Official Laptop Field Manual. Sebastian Rupley. LC 90-84499. 205p. 1994. 14.95 (1-878058-10-X) IDG Bks.

Portable Conrad. rev. ed. Joseph Conrad. Ed. by Morton D. Zabel & Frederick R. Karl. (Portable Library: No. 33). 768p. 1976. pap. 15.95 (0-14-015033-1, P33, Penguin Bks) Viking Penguin.

Portable Conservative Reader. Ed. by Russell Kirk. 768p. 1982. pap. 17.95 (0-14-015095-1) Viking Penguin.

*Portable Creative Writing Workshop.** Pat Boran. LC 99-191098. 204 p. 1999. 16.95 (1-897648-51-0) Dufour.

Portable Curmudgeon. Compiled by Jon Winokur. LC 92-53550. (Illus.). 320p. 1992. reprint ed. pap. 11.95 (0-452-26668-8, Plume) Dutton Plume.

Portable Dante. Dante Alighieri. Ed. by Mark Musa. 752p. 1995. pap. 15.95 (0-14-023114-5, Penguin Bks) Viking Penguin.

Portable Darwin. Charles Darwin. Ed. by Duncan M. Porter & Peter W. Graham. LC 93-17106. 640p. (Orig.). 1993. pap. 14.95 (0-14-015109-5, Penguin Bks) Viking Penguin.

Portable Do It! rev. ed. Peter McWilliams. 1995. pap. text 5.95 (0-931580-42-0) Prelude Press.

Portable Doonesbury. Garry B. Trudeau. (Illus.). 256p. (Orig.). 1993. pap. 12.95 (0-8362-1734-9) Andrews & McMeel.

Portable Dorothy Parker. rev. ed. Dorothy R. Parker. (Portable Library: No. 74). 640p. 1976. pap. 14.95 (0-14-015074-9, Penguin Bks) Viking Penguin.

Portable Dublin. Arthur Frommer. (Frommer's Portable Guides Ser.). (Illus.). 176p. 1997. 9.95 (0-02-861578-6) Macmillan.

Portable Edgar Allan Poe. Edgar Allan Poe. Ed. & Selected by Phillip V. Stern. LC 76-54888. (Portable Library: No. 12). 704p. 1977. pap. 15.95 (0-14-015012-9, Penguin Bks) Viking Penguin.

Portable Edmund Burke. Edmund Burke & Isaac Kramnick. LC 98-41476. 544p. 1999. pap. 16.95 (0-14-026760-3, PuffinBks) Peng Put Young Read.

Portable Edmund Wilson see Edmund Wilson Reader

Portable Electric Hand Lamps, UL 298. 4th ed. (C). 1996. pap. text 95.00 (0-7629-0124-1) Underwrtrs Labs.

Portable Electric Lamps, UL 153. 11th ed. (C). 1995. pap. text 95.00 (1-55989-842-9) Underwrtrs Labs.

Portable Electric Lighting Units for Use in Hazardous (Classified) Locations, UL 781. 6th ed. (C). 1993. pap. text 215.00 (1-55989-297-8) Underwrtrs Labs.

Portable Electric Tools: 745-1. 1995. write for info. (1-55989-763-5, UL 745-1) Underwrtrs Labs.

Portable Electric Tools, UL 45. 8th ed. (C). 1997. pap. text 330.00 (1-55989-185-8) Underwrtrs Labs.

Portable Emerson. Ralph Waldo Emerson. Ed. by Carl Bode & Malcolm Cowley. 718p. 1981. pap. 15.95 (0-14-015094-3, Penguin Bks) Viking Penguin.

Portable Engineer - (Any Motive Power Except Steam) (AMPES) Jack Rudman. (Career Examination Ser.: C-599). 1994. pap. 29.95 (0-8373-0599-3) Nat Learn.

Portable Engineer (Steam) Jack Rudman. (Career Examination Ser.: C-600). 1994. pap. 29.95 (0-8373-0600-0) Nat Learn.

Portable English Handbook. 3rd ed. Herman. (C). 1986. pap. text, teacher ed. 27.50 (0-03-002138-3) Harcourt Coll Pubs.

Portable Enlightenment Reader. Ed. by Isaac Kramnick. 608p. 1995. pap. 15.95 (0-14-024566-9, Penguin Bks) Viking Penguin.

*Portable Ethicist: An A-Z Guide to Responsible Practice.** Barton E. Bernstein & Thomas L. Hartsell. 288p. 2000. pap. 39.95 (0-471-38265-5) Wiley.

Portable Executive: Building Your Own Job Security--from Corporate Dependancy to Self-Direction. John A. Thompson & Catherine A. Henningsen. 256p. 1995. 22.50 (0-671-86904-3) S&S Trade.

Portable Executive: Building Your Own Job Security From Corporate Dependency to Self-Direction. John A. Thompson & Catherine Henningsen. 272p. 1996. per. 12.00 (0-684-81891-4, Fireside) S&S Trade Pap.

P

An Asterisk (*) at the beginning of an entry indicates that the title is appearing for the first time.

Portable Father. Stacey Granger. (Illus.). 160p. (Orig.). 1997. pap. 7.95 (*1-888952-30-X*) Cumberland Hse.

Portable Faulkner. rev. ed. William Faulkner. Ed. by Malcolm Cowley. (Portable Library: No. 18). 768p. (J). (gr. 10 up). 1977. pap. 15.95 (*0-14-015018-8*, Penguin Bks) Viking Penguin.

Portable File-Folder Word Walls: 25 Reproducible Thematic Word Walls to Help Kids Become Better. Mary Beth Spann. (Illus.). 56p. 1999. pap. text 9.95 (*0-439-05181-9*) Scholastic Inc.

Portable Financial Analyst: What Practitioners Need to Know. Mark P. Kritzman. 200p. 1994. text 50.00 (*1-55738-831-8*, Irwn Prfssnl) McGraw-Hill Prof.

Portable Fire Extinguishers. National Fire Protection Association Staff. 56p. 1998. 26.00 (*0-317-63040-7*, 10-98) Natl Fire Prot.

Portable Gardens. Linda L. Davis & Terry M. Davis. (Illus.). 24p. 1999. pap. 14.95 (*0-9672536-0-8*, 100648) Lindas Creat Cents.

Portable Graham Greene. Graham Greene. LC 93-49078. 560p. 1994. pap. 23.99 (*0-14-023359-8*, Penguin Bks) Viking Penguin.

Portable Greek Historians. Ed. by Moses I. Finley. (Portable Library: No. 65). 1977. pap. 16.95 (*0-14-015065-X*, Penguin Bks) Viking Penguin.

Portable Greek Reader. Ed. by W. H. Auden. (Portable Library: No. 39). 726p. 1977. pap. 15.95 (*0-14-015039-0*, P39, Penguin Bks) Viking Penguin.

Portable GUI Development with C. Mark Watson. 1992. 45.00 (*0-07-068489-8*) McGraw.

Portable Guide to Federal Conspiracy Law. Joseph F. McSorley. LC 96-31821. 1996. pap. 64.95 (*1-57073-368-6*) Amer Bar Assn.

***Portable Handbook of Texas.** Roy R. Barkley et al. LC 00-36368. 2000. write for info. (*0-87611-180-0*) Tex St Hist Assn.

***Portable Hannah Arendt.** Hannah Arendt & P. R. Baehr. LC 99-38487. 2000. pap. 16.95 (*0-14-026974-6*) Penguin Putnam.

Portable Harlem Renaissance Reader. Ed. & Intro. by David L. Lewis. 816p. 1995. pap. 15.95 (*0-14-017036-7*) Viking Penguin.

Portable Hawthorne. rev. ed. Nathaniel Hawthorne. Ed. by Malcolm Cowley. (Portable Library: No. 38). 704p. 1977. pap. 16.95 (*0-14-015038-2*, P38, Penguin Bks) Viking Penguin.

Portable Henry James. rev. ed. Henry James. Ed. by Morton D. Zabel. (Portable Library: No. 55). 704p. 1977. pap. 15.95 (*0-14-015055-2*, Penguin Bks) Viking Penguin.

Portable Henry Rollins. Henry Rollins. 1998. write for info. (*0-679-45965-0*) Villard Books.

Portable Henry Rollins. Henry Rollins. LC 97-2931. 400p. 1998. pap. 19.95 (*0-375-75000-2*) Villard Books.

Portable India. Ed. by Jug Suraiya & Anurag Mathur. (C). 1994. 44.00 (*81-7223-089-3*, Pub. by Indus Pub) S Asia.

Portable Internist. Ed. by Anthony J. Zollo. (Illus.). 700p. 1994. pap. text 45.00 (*1-56053-066-9*) Hanley & Belfus.

Portable Jack Kerouac. Ed. by Ann Charters. 656p. 1996. pap. 15.95 (*0-14-017819-8*, Viking) Viking Penguin.

Portable Jack London. Jack London. Ed. by Earle G. Labor. LC 93-38740. 672p. 1994. pap. 15.95 (*0-14-017969-0*, Penguin Bks) Viking Penguin.

Portable James Joyce. James Joyce. (Portable Library: No. 30). 768p. 1976. pap. 23.99 (*0-14-015030-7*, Penguin Bks) Viking Penguin.

Portable Jung. C. G. Jung. Ed. by Joseph Campbell. Tr. by R. F. C. Hull. LC 76-44022. (Portable Library: No. 70). 659p. 1976. pap. 15.95 (*0-14-015070-6*, Penguin Bks) Viking Penguin.

Portable Karl Marx. Karl Marx. Ed. by Eugene Kamenka. 704p. (C). 1983. pap. 15.95 (*0-14-015096-X*) Viking Penguin.

Portable Kipling. Rudyard Kipling. Ed. & Intro. by Irving Howe. LC 81-15402. xlii, 687p. 1982. pap. 16.95 (*0-14-015097-8*, Penguin Bks) Viking Penguin.

Portable Kisses. Tess Gallagher. 94p. 1997. pap. 16.95 (*1-85224-365-1*, Pub. by Bloodaxe Bks) Dufour.

Portable Kobbe's Opera Guide. Ed. by Earl of Harewood. 512p. (Orig.). 1994. pap. 20.00 (*0-399-51872-X*, Perigee Bks) Berkley Pub.

Portable Kristeva. Julia Kristeva & Kelly Oliver. LC 96-34403. 1997. 41.50 (*0-231-10504-5*) Col U Pr.

Portable Kristeva. Kelly Oliver & Julia Kristeva. LC 96-34403. 464p. (C). 1997. pap. 18.50 (*0-231-10505-3*) Col U Pr.

Portable Labyrinth. 2nd ed. Karen Troiani & Kathleen M. Sewalk. (Illus.). 1997. 34.95 (*0-941461-32-7*) Tunnel Press.

Portable Ladders No. 4. J. Steven Kidd & John Czajkowski. 1995. teacher ed. write for info. (*0-8151-5090-3*) Mosby Inc.

Portable Lawyer for Mental Health Professionals: An A-Z Guide to Protecting Your Clients, Your Practice & Yourself. Barton E. Bernstein & Thomas L. Hartsell. LC 98-10048. 288p. 1998. pap. 39.95 (*0-471-24869-X*) Wiley.

Portable Leader. John Van Maurik. LC 96-41889. 1996. pap. write for info. (*0-07-709119-1*) McGraw.

Portable Life 101. rev. ed. Peter McWilliams. 1995. pap. text 5.95 (*0-931580-41-2*) Prelude Press.

Portable Lighting Handbook: For Architects & Interior Designers. John Traister & C. Keeler Chapman. (Illus.). 544p. 1998. 54.95 (*0-07-064800-X*) McGraw.

Portable Lowlife. Ed Brubaker. (Illus.). 48p. (Orig.). 1994. pap. 4.95 (*1-883847-16-8*) MU Press.

Portable M B A in Entreprenevrship Case Studies. Bill Bygrave. LC 98-136320. (Portable MBA Ser.). 336p. 1997. pap., student ed. 29.95 (*0-471-18229-X*) Wiley.

Portable Machiavelli. Niccolo Machiavelli. Tr. by Peter E. Bondanella & Mark Musa from ITA. (Portable Library: No. 92). 576p. (Orig.). 1979. pap. 15.95 (*0-14-015092-7*, Penguin Bks) Viking Penguin.

Portable Margaret Fuller. Intro. by Mary Kelley. LC 93-49079. 528p. 1994. pap. 16.95 (*0-14-017665-9*, Penguin Bks) Viking Penguin.

Portable Marine Fuel Tanks, UL 1185. 4th ed. (C). 1996. pap. text 330.00 (*1-55989-988-3*) Underwrtrs Labs.

Portable Mark Twain. Mark Twain, pseud. Ed. by Bernard A. De Voto. (Portable Library: No. 20). 790p. 1977. pap. 15.95 (*0-14-015020-X*, Penguin Bks) Viking Penguin.

***Portable MBA Desk Reference: An Essential Business Companion.** 2nd ed. Nitin Nohria. LC 98-3767. (Portable MBA Ser.). 680p. 1998. 35.00 (*0-471-24530-5*) Wiley.

Portable MBA in Economics. Philip K. Y. Young & John J. McAuley. 304p. 1994. 34.95 (*0-471-59526-8*) Wiley.

Portable MBA in Entrepreneurship. 2nd ed. William D. Bygrave. LC 96-43971. 528p. 1997. 34.95 (*0-471-16078-4*) Wiley.

Portable MBA in Finance & Accounting. 2nd ed. John L. Livingstone. LC 97-14095. 640p. 1997. 34.95 (*0-471-18425-X*) Wiley.

Portable MBA in Investment. Peter L. Bernstein. LC 95-18969. (Portable MBA Ser.). 448p. 1995. 34.95 (*0-471-10661-5*) Wiley.

Portable MBA in Management. Allan R. Cohen. LC 92-41917. 392p. 1993. 29.95 (*0-471-57379-5*) Wiley.

Portable MBA in Management. Allan R. Cohen. LC 92-41917. 400p. 1995. pap. 19.95 (*0-471-12723-X*) Wiley.

Portable MBA in Marketing. 2nd ed. Charles D. Schewe & Alexander Hiam. LC 97-38520. (Portable MBA Ser.). 512p. 1998. 34.95 (*0-471-19367-4*) Wiley.

Portable MBA in Strategy. Ed. by Liam Fahey & Robert Randall. 496p. 1994. 34.95 (*0-471-58498-3*) Wiley.

***Portable MBA in Strategy.** 2nd ed. Liam Fahey & Robert M. Randall. 400p. 2000. 34.95 (*0-471-19708-4*) Wiley.

Portable Medieval Reader. Ed. by James B. Ross & Mary M. McLaughlin. (Portable Library: No. 46). 704p. 1977. pap. 22.99 (*0-14-015046-3*, Penguin Bks) Viking Penguin.

Portable Metal Ladders: UL 184. 6th ed. (C). 1997. pap. text 95.00 (*0-7629-0208-6*) Underwrtrs Labs.

Portable Milton. John Milton. Ed. & Intro. by Douglas Bush. (Portable Library: No. 44). 704p. 1976. pap. 15.95 (*0-14-015044-7*, Penguin Bks) Viking Penguin.

Portable Mother. Stacey Granger. LC 96-28860. (Illus.). 160p. (Orig.). 1996. pap. 7.95 (*1-888952-02-4*) Cumberland Hse.

Portable Nabokov. Wallace Stegner. 1999. pap. 6.95 (*0-14-015106-0*) Viking Penguin.

***Portable New York City from $80 a Day.** Frommer's Staff. (Frommer's $-a-Day Guides Ser.). (Illus.). 208p. 2000. pap. text 9.99 (*0-02-863446-2*, Frommer) Macmillan Gen Ref.

Portable Nietzsche. Friedrich Wilhelm Nietzsche. Ed. by Walter Kaufmann. (Portable Library: No. 62). 704p. 1977. pap. 22.99 (*0-14-015062-5*, Penguin Bks) Viking Penguin.

Portable Nineteenth-Century Russian Reader. Ed. by George Gibian. 704p. (Orig.). 1993. pap. 15.95 (*0-14-015103-6*, Penguin Bks) Viking Penguin.

Portable North American Indian Reader. Ed. by Frederick W. Turner, 3rd. LC 72-12545. (Portable Library: No. 77). 640p. 1977. pap. 15.95 (*0-14-015077-3*, Penguin Bks) Viking Penguin.

Portable Oscar Wilde. Oscar Wilde. Ed. by Stanley Weintraub & Richard Aldington. 752p. 1981. pap. 15.95 (*0-14-015093-5*, Penguin Bks) Viking Penguin.

Portable Parallel Programming with the Message - Passing Interface see Using MPI

Portable Pediatrician. Ed. by Howard Markel et al. (Illus.). 396p. 1992. pap. text 39.00 (*1-56053-007-3*) Hanley & Belfus.

***Portable Pediatrician.** 2nd ed. Howard Markel et al. LC 99-40835. (Illus.). 450p. 2000. text. write for info. (*1-56053-362-5*, Pub. by Hanley & Belfus) Mosby Inc.

Portable Pediatrician for Parents. Laura W. Nathanson. LC 93-24395. (Illus.). 544p. 1994. pap. 23.00 (*0-06-273176-9*, Harper Ref) HarpC.

Portable Pediatrician's Guide to Kids: Your Child's Physical & Behavioral Development from... Laura W. Nathanson. LC 96-8801. 352p. 1996. pap. 21.00 (*0-06-273347-8*) HarpC.

Portable Pension Plans for Casual Labor Markets: Lessons from the Operating Engineers' Central Pension Fund. Garth L. Mangum et al. LC 95-7960. 216p. 1995. 67.95 (*0-89930-995-X*, Quorum Bks) Greenwood.

Portable Pep Talk: Motivational Morsels for Inspiring You to Succeed. Alexander Lockhart. 256p. (Orig.). 1997. pap. 8.95 (*0-9643035-7-4*) Zander Pr.

Portable Pilgrim: Seven Paths to Spiritual Enlightenment. Alex Witchel. LC 98-7074. 224p. 1998. pap. 9.95 (*0-440-50829-0*) Doubleday.

Portable Platanov: The Centenary of His Birth. Ed. & Tr. by Robert Chandler. (Glas Ser.: Vol. 20). (Illus.). 200p. 2000. pap. 14.95 (*1-56663-272-2*, Pub. by I R Dee) Natl Bk Netwk.

Portable Plato. Plato. Ed. by Scott Buchanan. (Portable Library: No. 40). 696p. 1977. pap. 15.95 (*0-14-015040-4*, Penguin Bks) Viking Penguin.

Portable Power Distribution Units: 1640. 1995. write for info. (*1-55989-906-9*, UL 1640) Underwrtrs Labs.

Portable Power Saw. Richard Hunter. LC 85-702249. 1985. student ed. 7.00 (*0-8064-0273-3*, 709) Bergwall.

Portable Power Tools see Art of Woodworking Series

Portable Power Tools. LC 92-25558. (Art of Woodworking Ser.). 144p. 1992. lib. bdg. 14.95 (*0-8094-9909-6*) Time-Life.

Portable Power Tools. 2nd ed. L. P. McDonnell. (Construction & Building Trades Ser.). 1978. teacher ed. 13.50 (*0-8273-1101-X*); mass mkt. 25.75 (*0-8273-1100-1*) Delmar.

Portable Queen: Elizabeth I & the Politics of Ceremony. Mary H. Cole. LC 99-27676. (Studies in Early Modern Culture). 288p. 2000. text 35.00 (*1-55849-214-3*) U of Mass Pr.

Portable Radio in American Life. Michael B. Schiffer. LC 91-11749. (Culture & Technology Ser.). (Illus.). 259p. 1992. reprint ed. pap. 26.95 (*0-8165-1284-1*) U of Ariz Pr.

Portable Relaxer. Fine Creative Media Staff & McKay. 128p. 1998. pap. 5.98 (*1-56731-272-1*) Fine Comms.

Portable Renaissance Reader. Ed. by James B. Ross & Mary M. McLaughlin. (Portable Library: No. 61). 1977. pap. 16.95 (*0-14-015061-7*, Penguin Bks) Viking Penguin.

Portable Roman Reader. Ed. by Basil Davenport. (Portable Library: No. 56). 656p. 1977. pap. 16.95 (*0-14-015056-0*, Penguin Bks) Viking Penguin.

Portable Romantic see Romantic Essentials: Hundreds of Ways to Show Your Love

Portable Router Book. R. J. De Cristoforo. (Illus.). 352p. (Orig.). 1987. 24.95 (*0-8306-0869-9*) McGraw-Hill Prof.

Portable Router Book. 2nd ed. R. J. De Cristoforo. (Orig.). 1993. pap. 16.95 (*0-8306-4461-X*); pap. 19.95 (*0-07-016337-5*) McGraw-Hill Prof.

***Portable 7 Habits: Choice: Choosing the Proactive Life You Want to Live.** Stephen R. Covey. 128p. 1999. 10.95 (*1-929494-02-5*) Franklin Covey.

Portable Shell Programming: An Extensive Collection of Bourne Shell Examples. Bruce Blinn. LC 95-39657. 288p. 1995. pap. 48.00 (*0-13-451494-7*) P-H.

Portable Skeletal X-Ray Library: An Atlas of Correlative Radiology. Marshall N. Deltoff & Peter L. Kogon. LC 97-3246. (Illus.). 384p. (gr. 13). 1997. text 67.95 (*0-8151-2244-6*, 24846) Mosby Inc.

Portable Spray Hose Nozzles for Fire-Protection Service, UL 401. 3rd ed. (C). 1993. pap. text 290.00 (*1-55989-428-8*) Underwrtrs Labs.

Portable Steam Engines. Lyndon R. Shearman. (Album Ser.: No. 163). (Illus.). 32p. pap. 4.75 (*0-85263-783-7*, Pub. by Shire Pubns) Parkwest Pubns.

Portable Stein. Fred F. Ferri. (Illus.). 368p. (C). (gr. 13). 1993. pap. text 32.95 (*0-8016-7825-0*, 07825) Mosby Inc.

Portable Steinbeck. John Steinbeck. Ed. by Pascal Covici, Jr. (Portable Library: No. 2). 736p. 1976. pap. 16.95 (*0-14-015002-1*, Penguin Bks) Viking Penguin.

Portable Stephen Crane. Stephen Crane. Ed. & Intro. by Joseph Katz. LC 77-8036. (Portable Library: No. 68). 576p. 1977. pap. 15.95 (*0-14-015068-4*, Penguin Bks) Viking Penguin.

Portable Sun-Heat Lamps, UL 482. 8th ed. (C). 1999. pap. text 95.00 (*1-55989-616-7*) Underwrtrs Labs.

Portable TA Vol. 1: Problem Solving Guide, Vol. 1. Andrew Elby. (C). 1995. pap. text, teacher ed. 26.67 (*0-13-231713-3*, Prentice Hall) P-H.

Portable TA Physics: A Physics Problem Solving Guide, Vol. 2. Andrew Elby. LC 98-140182. 1997. pap. text, student ed. 26.67 (*0-13-231721-4*) P-H.

***Portable Theater: American Literature & the Nineteenth-Century Stage.** Alan L. Ackerman, Jr. LC 99-19382. (Illus.). 304p. 1999. 45.00 (*0-8018-6161-6*) Johns Hopkins.

Portable Therapist. Donald C. Doyle. Ed. by Betty Doyle. LC 95-92394. 280p. (Orig.). (C). 1995. pap. 14.95 (*0-9648370-0-5*) D&D Publns.

Portable Therapist. Susanna McMahon. LC 93-30957. 256p. 1994. pap. 10.95 (*0-440-50603-4*) Dell.

Portable Thomas Jefferson. Thomas Jefferson. Ed. by Merrill D. Peterson. (Portable Library: No. 80). 640p. 1977. pap. 15.95 (*0-14-015080-3*, Penguin Bks) Viking Penguin.

Portable Thoreau. rev. ed. Henry David Thoreau. Ed. by Carl Bode. (Portable Library: No. 31). 704p. 1977. pap. 15.95 (*0-14-015031-5*, P31, Penguin Bks) Viking Penguin.

Portable Tolstoy. Leo Tolstoy. Ed. by John Bayley. Tr. by Louise Maude et al from RUS. (Portable Library: No. 91). 896p. 1978. pap. 17.95 (*0-14-015091-9*, Penguin Bks) Viking Penguin.

Portable Twentieth-Century Russian Reader. rev. ed. Ed. by Clarence Brown. LC 92-39863. 624p. 1993. pap. 15.95 (*0-14-015107-9*, Penguin Bks) Viking Penguin.

Portable UNIX. Douglas W. Topham. LC 92-24561. 288p. 1993. pap. 18.95 (*0-471-57926-2*) Wiley.

***Portable Ventilation Systems Handbook.** Neil McManus. LC 00-42320. 2000. write for info. (*1-56032-893-2*) Taylor & Francis.

Portable Victorian Reader. Ed. by Gordon S. Haight. (Portable Library). 704p. 1976. pap. 15.95 (*0-14-015069-2*, Penguin Bks) Viking Penguin.

Portable Video: ENG & EFP. 3rd ed. Norman J. Medoff & Tom Tanquary. LC 97-20550. (Illus.). 304p. 1997. pap. 39.95 (*0-240-80285-3*, Focal) Buttrwrth-Heinemann.

Portable Video: ENG & EFP. Norman J. Medoff & Tom Tanquary. (Professional Librarian Ser.). (Illus.). 191p. (C). 1988. 50.00 (*0-86729-147-8*, Hall Reference); pap., student ed. 27.95 (*0-86729-148-6*, Hall Reference) Macmillan.

Portable Voltaire. Voltaire. Ed. by Ben R. Redman. LC 77-4746. (Portable Library: No. 41). 1977. pap. 15.95 (*0-14-015041-2*, Penguin Bks) Viking Penguin.

Portable Walt Whitman. rev. ed. Walt Whitman. Ed. by Mark Van Doren. LC 73-2773. (Portable Library: No. 78). 688p. 1977. pap. 22.99 (*0-14-015078-1*, P78, Penguin Bks) Viking Penguin.

Portable Wealth: The Complete Guide to Precious Metals Investment. Adam Starchild. LC 98-147763. 80p. 1998. pap. 14.00 (*0-87364-959-1*) Paladin Pr.

Portable Wedding Consultant. Leah Ingram. LC 97-18253. 288p. 1997. pap. 15.95 (*0-8092-3086-0*, 308600, Contemporary Bks) NTC Contemp Pub Co.

Portable Western Reader. William Kittredge. LC 96-47243. 592p. 1997. pap. 14.95 (*0-14-023026-2*) Viking Penguin.

Portable World: A Complete Pocket Atlas. Ed. by B. M. Willett et al. (Illus.). 272p. 1990. pap. 9.95 (*0-380-76176-9*, Avon Bks) Morrow Avon.

Portable World Atlas. rev. ed. Ed. by B. M. Willett et al. LC 93-676419. (Illus.). 272p. 1993. pap. 12.00 (*0-380-77329-5*, Avon Bks) Morrow Avon.

Portable World Bible. Robert O. Ballou. (Portable Library). 1977. pap. 15.95 (*0-14-015005-6*, Penguin Bks) Viking Penguin.

Portable World Factbook. Keith Lye. 352p. (Orig.). 1996. pap. 12.00 (*0-380-78570-6*, Avon Bks); pap. 14.00 (*0-380-73051-0*, Avon Bks) Morrow Avon.

Portable Writer. 2nd ed. Hilary Russell. 128p. (YA). (gr. 9-12). 1998. pap. text 9.33 (*1-877653-47-0*) Wayside Pub.

Portable Writers' Conference: Your Guide to Getting & Staying Published. Ed. by Stephen B. Mettee. LC 96-45131. 464p. 1997. pap. 19.95 (*1-884956-23-8*) Quill Driver.

Portable Writing Lab. Vivian I. Davis et al. 352p. (C). 1990. pap. text 22.75 (*0-15-570779-5*) Harcourt Coll Pubs.

Portable Writing Lab. Hook. (C). 1996. pap. text 32.00 (*0-15-504455-9*) Harcourt Coll Pubs.

Portage Heritage. Ed. by James B. Holm. (Illus.). 824p. 1993. reprint ed. lib. bdg. 82.50 (*0-8328-2831-9*) Higginson Bk Co.

Portage into the Past: By Canoe along the Minnesota-Ontario Boundary. J. Arnold Bolz. LC 60-15895. (Illus.). 199p. reprint ed. pap. 61.70 (*0-8357-3298-3*, 203955400013) Bks Demand.

Portage Lake: Memories of an Ojibwe Childhood. Maude Kegg. Ed. & Tr. by John D. Nichols. LC 93-14353. (ENG & OJI.). 292p. 1993. reprint ed. pap. 17.95 (*0-8166-2415-1*) U of Minn Pr.

***Portage Lakes Then & Now.** Carolyn Vogenitz. (Illus.). 272p. 1999. pap. 19.95 (*0-9670779-0-7*) Waterside Pubg.

Portage Paths see Historic Highways of America...with Maps & Illustrations

Portage Pathways. Loris C. Troyer. LC 97-38126. (Illus.). 362p. 1998. 30.00 (*0-87338-600-0*) Kent St U Pr.

Portage to San Cristobal of A. H. George Steiner. LC 99-24007. 1999. pap. 12.00 (*0-226-77235-7*) U Ch Pr.

***Portal.** Max G. Harrington. (Illus.). vi, 148p. 2000. pap. 11.00 (*1-892571-02-1*) TDC Pr.

Portal. Joyce Jenkins. (Red Ser.). 1993. pap. 6.00 (*0-938631-18-7*) Pennywhistle Pr.

Portal. Sharon Pape. 1994. per. 3.50 (*0-373-27033-X*, 5-27033-5) Harlequin Bks.

Portal: A Dual-Language (Spanish-English) Activity Book for Senior Learners. Carlos Gaitan. (ENG & SPA.). 91p. 1997. spiral bd. 15.95 (*1-879633-31-0*, P217) Eldersong.

Portal - Pousette-Dart. Photos by David Finn. (Illus.). 100p. 1998. 29.95 (*0-8109-6352-3*, Pub. by Abrams) Time Warner.

Portal Design in Radiation Therapy. B. Dasher et al. 168p. 1994. pap. text 45.00 (*0-9642715-0-8*) D W V.

Portal Hypertension: A Multidisciplinary Approach to Current Clinical Management. Ed. by Stuart J. Knechtle. LC 98-25898. (Illus.). 298p. 1998. 150.00 (*0-87993-414-X*) Futura Pub.

Portal Hypertension: Clinical & Physiological Aspects. Ed. by Kunio Okuda & J. P. Benhamou. (Illus.). 592p. 1991. 336.00 (*0-387-70054-4*) Spr-Verlag.

***Portal Hypertension: Diagnostic Imaging & Imaging-Guided Therapy.** Ed. by P. Rossi et al. LC 99-55309. (Medical Radiology Ser.). (Illus.). 300p. 2000. 199.00 (*3-540-65797-5*) Spr-Verlag.

Portal Hypertension: Pathophysiology & Treatment. Ed. by Jaime Bosch & Roberto J. Groszmann. LC 94-5895. (Illus.). 190p. 1994. 70.00 (*0-86542-846-8*) Blackwell Sci.

Portal Hypertension: Proceedings of the 79th Falk Symposium (Part III of the Gastroenterology Week Freiburg 1994), Held in Freiburg-in-Breisgau, Germany, June 17-19, 1994. Falk Symposium 79 Staff. Ed. by A. Holstege et al. LC 95-20105. 1995. text 184.00 (*0-7923-8879-8*) Kluwer Academic.

Portal Hypertension II: Definitions, Methodology & Therapeutic Strategies, 2. Ed. by Roberto De Franchis. 336p. 1995. 75.00 (*0-86542-614-7*) Blackwell Sci.

Portal in Pensacola: The Real Thing Hits Brownsville. Renee DeLoriea. LC 97-149646. 182p. 1997. pap. 10.99 (*1-56043-189-X*, Revival Pr) Destiny Image.

PORTAL Language Description. A. Businger. (Lecture Notes in Computer Science Ser.: Vol. 198). viii, 186p. 1985. pap. 14.50 (*0-387-15682-8*) Spr-Verlag.

PORTAL Language Description. A. Businger. (Lecture Notes in Computer Science Ser.: Vol. 198). viii, 197p. 1988. 33.00 (*0-387-18960-2*) Spr-Verlag.

Portal of Initiation: A Rosicrucian Mystery Drama. 2nd ed. Rudolf Steiner. Ed. by Adam Bittleston. LC 61-9348. (Illus.). 288p. 1981. lib. bdg. 19.95 (*0-89345-012-X*, Spir Sci Lib) Garber Comm.

Portal of Initiation: A Rosicrucian Mystery Drama. 2nd ed. Rudolf Steiner & Johann W. Von Goethe. LC 61-9348. 288p. 1992. pap. 12.95 (*0-8334-0028-2*, Spir Lit Lib) Garber Comm.

Portal to Paradise: 11,537 Years, More or Less, on the Northeast. Alden C. Hayes. LC 98-40077. (Illus.). 424p. 1999. 29.95 (*0-8165-1785-1*) U of Ariz Pr.

Portale Hypertension. K. J. Paquet et al. Ed. by H. Denck & R. Berchtold. x, 282p. 1982. pap. 56.75 (*3-8055-3480-9*) S Karger.

Portales: Intermediate Spanish. (C). 2000. write for info. (*0-13-025795-8*) Aspen Law.

P

Portales de Esplendor. Elizabeth Elliot.Tr. of Through Gates of Splendor. (SPA., Illus.). 272p. 1959. pap. 8.99 (*0-8254-1200-5*, Edit Portavoz) Kregel.

Portals. Firestone. pap. text 49.99 incl. cd-rom (*0-471-37816-X*) Wiley.

Portals. Segall. (C). 1998. pap. text, teacher ed. 26.75 (*0-15-508113-6*) Harcourt.

Portals. Segall. LC 97-77787. (C). 1998. pap. text 35.50 (*0-15-505474-0*, Pub. by Harcourt Coll Pubs) Harcourt.

Portals: New England Doorways. Photos by William Morgan. (Illus.). 1981. pap. 4.75 (*0-87233-057-5*) Bauhan.

Portals of Entry: University Colleges & Undergraduate Divisions. Ed. by Diane W. Strommer. (Freshman Year Experience Monograph: No. 12). 134p. (Orig.). 1993. pap. 30.00 (*1-889271-09-8*) Nat Res Ctr.

Portals of Power: Shamanism in South America. Ed. by E. Jean Langdon & Gerhard Baer. LC 91-42609. (Illus.). 360p. 1992. reprint ed. pap. 111.60 (*0-608-04135-1*, 206486800011) Bks Demand.

Portals, Pilgrimage & Crusade in Western Tuscany. Dorothy F. Glass. LC 96-33486. 200p. 1997. text 39.50 (*0-691-01172-9*, Pub. by Princeton U Pr) Cal Prin Full Svc.

Portals to Adventure. 1992. 13.00 (*0-923763-55-4*) Mayfair Games.

Portals to Freedom. Howard C. Ives. 256p. 1937. pap. 13.25 (*0-87743-013-6*) G Ronald Pub.

Portals to Hell: Civil War Prisons. Lonnie Speer. LC 97-2719. (Illus.). 410p. 1997. 34.95 (*0-8117-0334-7*) Stackpole.

Portavoces del Eterno. Harold Ellison. Orig. Title: Old Testament Prophets. (SPA.). 216p. 1982. pap. 8.99 (*0-8254-1201-3*, Edit Portavoz) Kregel.

Portcawl, Newton & Nottage: A Concise Illustrated History. Alun Morgan. 120p. (C). 1989. 59.00 (*0-905928-73-3*, Pub. by D Brown & Sons Ltd) St Mut.

Porte. Georges Simenon. (FRE.). 1993. pap. 11.95 (*0-7859-3258-5*, 2266052683) Fr & Eur.

Porte du Fond. Christiane Rochefort. (FRE.). 1990. pap. 12.95 (*0-7859-3154-6*, 2253052779) Fr & Eur.

Porte Etroite see Strait Is the Gate

Porte Etroite. Gide. (FRE.). (C). pap. 7.95 (*0-8442-1839-1*, VF1839-1) NTC Contemp Pub Co.

Porte Etroite. Andre Gide. 192p. 1972. write for info. (*0-318-63580-1*) Fr & Eur.

Porte Etroite. Andre Gide. (FRE.). 1972. pap. 10.95 (*0-8288-3685-X*, F102761); pap. 10.95 (*0-7859-2281-4*, 2070362108) Fr & Eur.

Porte Etroite. Andre Gide. (Folio Ser.: No. 210). (FRE.). 192p. 1972. pap. 6.95 (*2-07-036210-8*) Schoenhof.

Porte Noir. Daniel Boulanger. (FRE.). 160p. 1981. pap. 10.95 (*0-7859-2220-2*, 207037324X) Fr & Eur.

Portent. James Herbert. LC 96-33809. 368p. 1996. 14.00 (*0-06-105211-6*, HarperPrism) HarpC.

Portent & Other Stories. George MacDonald. (George MacDonald Original Works Ser.: Series IV). 340p. 1999. reprint ed. 22.00 (*1-881084-24-8*) Johannesen.

Portentous Tales: Views Through the Third Eye. Ronald Blandon. LC 98-90896. 1999. pap. 9.95 (*0-533-12975-3*) Vantage.

Portents: Scares Old & New. Francis Neilson. 1979. lib. bdg. 39.00 (*0-685-96635-6*) Revisionist Pr.

Portents of the Air. Charles Norman. LC 77-187009. 64p. 1973. 5.95 (*0-672-51407-9*, Bobbs) Macmillan.

Portents of the Coming Millennium. Dudley F. Cates. LC 98-65629. 64p. 1999. pap. 9.95 (*1-57197-107-6*) Pentland Pr.

Porter. Terry Foster. (Classic Beer Style Ser.). (Illus.). 142p. 1992. pap. 11.95 (*0-937381-28-4*) Brewers Pubns.

Porter As a Portion of Maines: Its Settlement, Etc. Thomas Moulton. (Illus.). 96p. 1997. reprint ed. pap. 19.00 (*0-8328-5898-6*) Higginson Bk Co.

Porter Broadway Showstoppers. 160p. (Orig.). 1996. pap. 16.95 (*0-7692-1047-3*, MF9614) Wrner Bros.

Porter Cole Easy Piano Solos. Cole Porter. (Easy Piano Ser.). 144p. 1992. per. 20.95 (*0-7935-1516-5*, 00311576) H Leonard.

Porter Family. Philip Ferrato. LC 80-81265. (Illus.). 23p. (Orig.). 1980. pap. 2.00 (*0-943526-37-X*) Parrish Art.

Porter on Broadway. Ed. by Carol Cuellar. 260p. (Orig.). (C). 1995. pap. text 24.95 (*0-7692-0508-9*, SF0202) Wrner Bros.

Porter Rockwell: A Biography. Richard Lloyd Dewey. LC 65-63355. (Illus.). 612p. 1986. 22.95 (*0-9616024-0-6*) Paramount Bks.

***Porter Rockwell Chronicles, Vol. I.** Richard Lloyd Dewey. 490p. 1999. 21.95 (*0-9616024-6-5*) Paramount Bks.

Porter Township: or Now When Your Father Was a Boy: Or Now When Your Father Was a Boy. Illus. by Tad Barney. LC 88-61313. 278p. 1989. 15.95 (*0-9620797-0-7*) Rotabar Pub.

Porterfield: The Porterfields. Frank B. Porterfield. 345p. 1993. reprint ed. pap. 54.00 (*0-8328-3387-8*); reprint ed. lib. bdg. 64.00 (*0-8328-3386-X*) Higginson Bk Co.

Porterhouse Blue. Tom Sharpe. LC 88-38005. 224p. 1989. pap. 12.00 (*0-87113-279-6*, Atlntc Mnthly) Grove-Atltic.

Porterhouse Blue. large type ed. Tom Sharpe. 344p. 1990. reprint ed. 19.95 (*1-85089-308-X*, Pub. by ISIS Lrg Prnt) Transaction Pubs.

Portero. Reinaldo Arenas. LC 89-82738. (Coleccion Caniqui). (SPA.). 158p. (Orig.). 1990. pap. 16.00 (*0-89729-560-9*) Ediciones.

Porter's EMS Protocols. William Porter. 164p. 1997. ring bd. 595.00 (*1-882740-08-4*) Porter & Assocs.

Porter's Guide to Congressional Roll Call Votes, 6 vols. Allison I. Porter. Incl. Senate, 1985 (Serial & Annual) 1985. 80.00 (*0-916481-26-3*); Vol. 1. House, 1983 (Annual) 1984. 80.00 (*0-916481-07-7*); Vol. 2. Senate, 1983 (Annual) 1984. 80.00 (*0-916481-08-5*); Vol. 3. House, 1984 (Serial & Annual) 1984. 80.00 (*0-916481-09-3*); Vol. 4. Senate, 1984 (Serial & Annual) 1984. 80.00 (*0-916481-10-7*); Vol. 5. House, 1985 (Serial & Annual) 1985. 80.00 (*0-916481-25-5*); 435.00 (*0-916481-06-9*) Legis Info Pr.

Porter's pocket Guide to Emergency & Critical Care. 6th ed. Porter & Associates Staff. 127p. 1999. spiral bd. 16.95 (*1-882740-07-6*) Porter & Assocs.

Porter's Pocket Guide to Nursing. William Porter. (Illus.). 1999. pap. 18.95 (*1-882740-21-1*) Porter & Assocs.

Porter's Pocket Guide to Pediatrics. 3rd ed. William Porter. 1999. pap. 16.95 (*1-882740-20-3*) Porter & Assocs.

Portes Ouvertes. Haggstrom. 1997. 82.00 incl. cd-rom (*0-03-024176-6*) Harcourt.

Portes Ouvertes. Haggstrom. (C). 1997. pap. text, wbk. ed. 29.00 (*0-03-013833-7*) Harcourt Coll Pubs.

Portes Ouvertes: An Interactive Multimedia Approach to First "Year" French. Margaret Haggstrom. 1998. 107.00 (*0-03-024168-5*) Harcourt Coll Pubs.

Portes Ouvertes: An Interactive Multimedia Approach to First "Year" French. Margaret Haggstrom et al. LC 97-73490. (FRE., Illus.). 848p. (C). 1997. text 76.00 (*0-03-008627-2*) Harcourt Coll Pubs.

Porteus Maze Test: Fifty Years' Application. Stanley D. Porteus. LC 65-18125. (Illus.). viii, 320p. 1965. 27.95 (*0-87015-139-8*) Pacific Bks.

Portfel' Literaturnyi Sbornik. Ed. by Aleksandr Sumerkin. (RUS.). 420p. (Orig.). 1996. pap. 19.95 (*0-87501-116-0*) Ardis Pubs.

Portfolio. Paul Vangelisti. 1978. 4.00 (*0-88031-054-5*) Invisible-Red Hill.

Portfolio. deluxe ed. Paul Vangelisti. 1978. 15.00 (*0-88031-055-3*) Invisible-Red Hill.

Portfolio, Set. Margolis. 1468p. 1997. ring bd. 150.00 (*0-316-54742-5*, Aspen Law & Bus) Aspen Pub.

Portfolio: Essays for Critical Thinking & Writing. Anthology Staff. Ed. by Patrick Scanlan. LC 99-193995. 290p. 1998. pap. text 24.95 (*0-917962-44-3*) T H Peek.

Portfolio Activity Resource - Introduction to Design Technology. Todd. (TP - Technology Education Ser.). (J). (gr. k-12). 1996. 24.95 (*0-538-64468-0*) S-W Pub.

Portfolio & Its Use: A Road Map for Assessment. Sharon McDonald. (Illus.). 120p. 1997. pap. 19.95 (*0-942388-20-8*) So Early Chldhood Assn.

Portfolio & Its Use: Developmentally Appropriate Assessment of Young Children. 3rd ed. Cathy Grace & Elizabeth F. Shores. 58p. (C). 1994. pap. 10.00 (*0-942388-10-0*) So Early Chldhood Assn.

***Portfolio & Performance Assessment in Teacher Education.** Dorothy M. Campbell. LC 99-23805. 154p. 1999. pap. text 27.95 (*0-205-30850-3*) Allyn.

Portfolio & Performance Assessments. 2nd ed. Farr. LC 97-73098. (C). 1997. pap. text 39.00 (*0-15-505402-3*, Pub. by Harcourt Coll Pubs) Harcourt.

Portfolio As a Learning Strategy. Carol Porter & Janell Cleland. LC 94-3522. 164p. 1994. pap. text 19.00 (*0-86709-348-X*, 0348, Pub. by Boynton Cook Pubs) Heinemann.

Portfolio Assessment. Amy Seely. (Professional's Guide Ser.). 80p. 1995. pap., teacher ed. 9.95 (*1-55734-845-6*) Tchr Create Mat.

Portfolio Assessment: A Handbook for Educators. Ed. by James Barton et al. (Assessment Bookshelf Ser.). 113p. (Orig.). 1996. teacher ed. 16.50 (*0-201-49387-X*) Addison-Wesley.

Portfolio Assessment: A Handbook for Middle Level Teachers. Keith Lustig. LC 96-30253. 1996. pap. write for info. (*1-56090-111-X*) Natl Middle Schl.

Portfolio Assessment: A Handbook for Preschool & Elementary Educators. Sue C. Wortham et al. LC 98-20427. 1998. pap. write for info. (*0-87173-145-2*) ACEI.

Portfolio Assessment: Applications of Portfolio Analysis. Ed. by Michael E. Knight & Denise Gallaro. 146p. (C). 1994. lib. bdg. 34.00 (*0-8191-9415-8*) U Pr of Amer.

Portfolio Assessment: Getting Started. Scholastic, Inc. Staff. 1996. pap. 12.95 (*0-590-49183-0*) Scholastic Inc.

Portfolio Assessment Across the Curriculum. 1998. pap., teacher ed. 12.95 (*0-8167-3276-0*) Troll Communs.

Portfolio Assessment in the Reading-Writing Classroom. Robert J. Tierney et al. 216p. 1991. pap. 24.95 (*0-926842-08-0*) CG Pubs Inc.

Portfolio Book: A Step by Step Guide for Teachers. Cathy Grace & Elizabeth Shores. LC 98-20705. 256p. 1998. pap. 19.95 (*0-87659-194-2*) Gryphon Hse.

Portfolio Breeches: A Poem. Timothy M. Riordan. 21p. (Orig.). 1988. pap. 10.00 (*0-9625817-1-2*) In Hse Bks.

Portfolio Connection. Kay Burke. 196p. 1998. pap. 31.00 (*0-205-29267-4*) P-H.

Portfolio Connection. Kay Burke et al. LC 94-78532. (Mindful School Ser.). 196p. 1994. pap. 26.95 (*0-932935-78-8*) SkyLght.

Portfolio Construction, Management & Protection. Robert A. Strong. Ed. by Burvikovs. LC 92-24117. 600p. (C). 1992. mass mkt. 67.00 (*0-314-00918-3*) West Pub.

Portfolio Construction, Management & Protection. 2nd ed. Strong. LC 99-25144. (SWC-Finance). 599p. 1999. pap. 93.95 (*0-324-00619-5*) S-W Pub.

Portfolio Design. Harold Linton. (Illus.). 144p. 1996. 30.00 (*0-393-73008-5*) Norton.

***Portfolio Design.** 2nd ed. Harold Linton. (Illus.). 2000. 34.95 (*0-393-73059-X*) Norton.

Portfolio Development for Career Planning. Michael J. Pierson & Oscar L. Dorsey. 116p. 1987. pap. text 19.95 (*0-912855-71-1*) E Bowers Pub.

***Portfolio Experiment: A Study of Assessment, Instruction & Middle School Reform.** Terry Underwood. LC 99-42587. 259p. 1999. pap. 26.95 (*0-8141-3628-1*) NCTE.

Portfolio for Retirement. 1993. lib. bdg. 255.95 (*0-8490-8926-3*) Gordon Pr.

***Portfolio Guidance for Veterinary Nurses.** Ed. by College of Animal Welfare Staff. 112p. 2000. pap. text 24.50 (*0-7506-4809-0*) Buttrwrth-Heinemann.

***Portfolio Guide, United States History, Modern Times.** Christine Perkins. 36p. 2000. 15.95 (*1-930731-11-6*) DAC Ed Pubns.

***Portfolio Guidebook: Implementing Quality in an Age of Standards.** Richard Koch & Jean Schwartz-Petterson. LC 99-66214. (Bill Harp Professional Teachers Library). 140p. 1999. pap. 15.95 (*1-929024-01-0*) CG Pubs Inc.

Portfolio II. Ed. by Kathryn Stewart. (Illus.). 48p. 1988. write for info. (*0-318-64087-2*) Am Indian Contemp.

Portfolio in the Middle, Bk. 1. Tom Bye. 1995. pap. text 10.00 (*0-13-454232-0*) P-H.

Portfolio in the Middle Student, Bk. 3. Tom Bye. 1995. pap. text 10.00 (*0-13-454315-7*) P-H.

***Portfolio Indexing: Theory & Practice.** Harold Hutchins. LC 99-20545. 176p. 1999. 79.95 (*0-471-98868-5*) Wiley.

Portfolio Insurance: A Guide to Dynamic Hedging. Ed. by Donald L. Luskin. LC 88-37151. 322p. 1988. 99.95 (*0-471-85849-8*) Wiley.

Portfolio Investment in Developing Countries. Ed. by Stijn Claessens & Sudarshan Gooptu. LC 93-44215. (Discussion Papers: Vol. 228). 502p. 1993. pap. 26.00 (*0-8213-2747-X*) World Bank.

Portfolio Journey: A Creative Guide to Keeping Student-Managed Portfolios in the Classroom. Tom Crockett. LC 97-52984. 1998. 25.00 (*1-56308-454-6*) Teacher Ideas Pr.

Portfolio Keeping. Reynolds. 1999. pap. text, student ed. 6.95 (*0-312-19151-0*) St Martin.

***Portfolio Keeping: A Guide For Teachers.** Reynolds. 2000. pap. text, teacher ed. 13.95 (*0-312-19809-4*) St Martin.

***Portfolio Management.** Ed. by John N. Dunlevy. 2000. 75.00 (*1-883249-64-3*) F J Fabozzi.

Portfolio Management: New Models for Successful Investment Decisions. C. Kenneth Jones. LC 92-19257. 1992. 45.00 (*0-07-707583-8*) McGraw.

Portfolio Management: The Concept of Profit Potentials; Its Application. 3rd ed. F. F. Neubauer. 110p. 1990. 52.00 (*90-6544-500-5*) Kluwer Law Intl.

Portfolio Management Approach to Strategic Airline Planning: An Exploratory Investigative Study on Services Management. Mike L. Thomas. LC 97-3332. (European University Studies: Vol. 2052). 381p. (C). Date not set. pap. text 60.95 (*0-8204-3406-X*, Pub. by P Lang) P Lang Pubng.

Portfolio Management Approach to Strategic Airline Planning: An Exploratory Investigative Study on Services Management. Mike L. Thomas. (European University Studies, Series 5: Vol. 2052). (Illus.). 381p. 1997. pap. 60.95 (*3-906757-29-3*) P Lang Pubng.

Portfolio Management for New Products. Robert Cooper. LC 97-49937. 1998. 38.00 (*0-201-32814-3*) Addison-Wesley.

Portfolio Management Formulas: Mathematical Trading Methods for the Futures, Options & Stock Markets. Ralph Vince. LC 90-12145. 288p. 1990. 85.00 (*0-471-52756-4*) Wiley.

Portfolio Management Using the Directional Policy Matrix. Malcolm McDonald. Date not set. audio compact disk 65.95 (*0-7506-4891-0*) Buttrwrth-Heinemann.

Portfolio of a Dragon: Dunkelzahn's Secrets. Steve Kenson & Mike Colton. (Shadowrun Ser.). (Illus.). 96p. 1996. pap. 15.00 (*1-55560-306-8*) FASA Corp.

Portfolio of Basketball Drills from College Coaches. R. Haun. 178p. (C). 1985. text 27.95 (*0-13-685785-X*) P-H.

Portfolio of Bathroom Ideas. Cy DeCosse Incorporated Staff. LC 93-41245. (Illus.). 96p. 1994. pap. 9.95 (*0-86573-926-9*) Creat Pub Intl.

Portfolio of Bedroom Ideas. Cy DeCosse Incorporated Staff. LC 95-21129. (Illus.). 96p. 1995. pap. 9.95 (*0-86573-962-5*) Creat Pub Intl.

Portfolio of Benjamin Latrobe. R. Denney. (QRL Poetry Bks.: Vol. XXV). 300p. 1984. 20.00 (*0-614-06408-2*) Quarterly Rev.

Portfolio of Best Selling House Plans. Ed. by National Plan Service, Inc. Staff. (Illus.). 32p. reprint ed. pap. 3.95 (*0-934039-22-4*, A34) Hme Dsgn Altntves.

***Portfolio of Cartoons.com.** Charles Preston. (Illus.). 2000. pap. 12.00 (*1-881944-29-8*, Wall St Jrnl) Dow Jones & Co.

Portfolio of Ceramic & Natural Tile Ideas. Cy DeCosse Incorporated Staff. LC 96-15845. (Illus.). 96p. 1996. pap. 9.95 (*0-86573-991-9*) Creat Pub Intl.

***Portfolio of Contemporary Gardens.** Stephen Woodhams. 2000. 40.00 (*1-56496-754-9*) Rockport Pubs.

Portfolio of Deck Ideas: Your Practical Guide to Great Deck Design. De Cosse, Cy, Inc. Staff. LC 93-8175. (Illus.). 96p. 1993. pap. 9.95 (*0-86573-922-6*) Creat Pub Intl.

Portfolio of Fence & Gate Ideas. Cy DeCosse Incorporated Staff. LC 96-18889. (Illus.). 96p. (Orig.). 1996. pap. 9.95 (*0-86573-992-7*) Creat Pub Intl.

Portfolio of Fireplace Ideas. Cy DeCosse Incorporated Staff. LC 96-7947. (Illus.). 96p. 1996. pap. 9.95 (*0-86573-990-0*) Creat Pub Intl.

Portfolio of Flooring Ideas. Cy DeCosse Inc., Staff. LC 94-49672. (Illus.). 96p. 1995. pap. 9.95 (*0-86573-958-7*) Creat Pub Intl.

Portfolio of Home Entertainment Ideas. Cowles Creative Publishing, Inc. Staff & Black & Decker Staff. LC 98-7293. (Illus.). 96p. 1998. pap. 10.95 (*0-86573-891-2*) Creat Pub Intl.

Portfolio of Home Office Ideas. Creative Publishing International Staff. LC 98-7294. (Illus.). 96p. 1998. pap. 10.95 (*0-86573-889-0*) Creat Pub Intl.

Portfolio of Home Spa Ideas. Cowles Creative Publishing, Inc. Staff. LC 98-17225. (Illus.). 96p. 1998. pap. 10.95 (*0-86573-890-4*) Creat Pub Intl.

Portfolio of Kitchen Ideas. rev. ed. Cy DeCosse. LC 90-33946. (Illus.). 96p. 1995. pap. 9.95 (*0-86573-970-6*) Creat Pub Intl.

Portfolio of Landscaping Ideas. Cy DeCosse Incorporated Staff. LC 94-20074. (Illus.). 96p. 1994. pap. 9.95 (*0-86573-940-4*) Creat Pub Intl.

Portfolio of Lighting Ideas. Cy DeCosse Incorporated Staff. LC 95-40811. (Illus.). 96p. 1996. pap. 9.95 (*0-86573-963-3*) Creat Pub Intl.

Portfolio of Lunar Drawings. Harold Hill. (Practical Astronomy Handbooks Ser.). (Illus.). 264p. (C). 1991. text 57.95 (*0-521-38113-4*) Cambridge U Pr.

Portfolio of Outdoor Furnishing Ideas. Cy DeCosse Incorporated Staff. LC 96-31463. (Illus.). 96p. (Orig.). 1996. pap. 9.95 (*0-86573-885-8*) Creat Pub Intl.

Portfolio of Porch & Patio Ideas. DeCosse, Cy, Incorporated Staff. LC 95-49809. (Illus.). 96p. 1996. pap. 9.95 (*0-86573-983-8*) Creat Pub Intl.

Portfolio of Rose Hips. John C. MacGregor. (Illus.). 20p. 1981. 35.00 (*0-936736-01-1*); pap. 25.00 (*0-936736-02-X*) Sweetbrier.

Portfolio of Storage Ideas. Cy DeCosse Incorporated Staff. LC 96-1754. (Illus.). 96p. 1996. pap. 9.95 (*0-86573-964-1*) Creat Pub Intl.

***Portfolio of Teaching Ideas for High School Biology: Activities for Grades 9-12.** Don Galbraith et al. (Illus.). 117p. 2000. pap. text, teacher ed. 28.75 (*1-895579-91-0*, Pub. by Trifolium Inc) ACCESS Pubs Network.

Portfolio of the Earth. Thomas F. Lombardi. LC 94-32367. 64p. 1995. pap. 14.95 (*0-7734-0003-6*, Mellen Poetry Pr) E Mellen.

Portfolio of Unique Deck Ideas. Cy DeCosse Incorporated Staff. LC 95-20475. (Illus.). 96p. 1995. pap. 9.95 (*0-86573-974-9*) Creat Pub Intl.

Portfolio of Water Garden & Specialty Landscape Ideas. Cy DeCosse Incorporated Staff. LC 95-44655. (Illus.). 96p. 1996. pap. 9.95 (*0-86573-975-7*) Creat Pub Intl.

Portfolio of Window & Window Treatment Ideas. Cy DeCosse Incorporated Staff. LC 94-36571. (Illus.). 96p. 1995. pap. 9.95 (*0-86573-956-0*) Creat Pub Intl.

***Portfolio of Women in Business Cartoons.** Charles Preston. (Illus.). 2000. pap. 12.00 (*1-881944-27-1*, Wall St Jrnl) Dow Jones & Co.

Portfolio Optimisation. Adcock. text. write for info. (*0-471-49101-2*) Wiley.

***Portfolio Organizer: Succeeding with Portfolios in Your Classroom.** Noreen Carol Rolheiser-Bennett et al. LC 00-8817. 2000. write for info. (*0-87120-374-X*) ASCD.

Portfolio Papers. Philip G. Hamerton. LC 77-37148. (Essay Index Reprint Ser.). 1977. reprint ed. 25.95 (*0-8369-2504-1*) Ayer.

Portfolio Planner. Julia Jasmine. 1997. pap. text 12.95 (*1-55734-546-5*) Tchr Create Mat.

***Portfolio Planner.** Martin. LC 99-160578. viii, 87p. 1999. pap. text. write for info. (*0-13-081314-1*) S&S Trade.

Portfolio Policies of Commercial Banks in the United States, 1920-1939. Pearson Hunt. Ed. by Stuart Bruchey. LC 80-1187. (Rise of Commercial Banking Ser.). 1981. reprint ed. lib. bdg. 15.95 (*0-405-13657-9*) Ayer.

Portfolio Portraits. Ed. by Donald H. Graves & Bonnie S. Sunstein. LC 92-915. 202p. (C). 1992. pap. text 23.00 (*0-435-08727-4*, 08727) Heinemann.

Portfolio Power: The New Way to Showcase All Your Job Skills & Experiences. Martin Kimeldorf. Ed. by Karen Hansen. LC 97-3499. 232p. 1997. pap. 14.95 (*1-56079-761-4*) Petersons.

Portfolio Practices: Assessing & Thinking Through Children's Work. Project Zero, Harvard Graduate School of Education. 160p. (Orig.). 1997. pap. 16.95 (*0-8106-1858-3*, 1858-3) NEA.

***Portfolio Practices: Lessons from Schools, Districts & States.** Sandra Murphy & Terry Underwood. 350p. 2000. pap. text, teacher ed. 38.95 (*1-929024-18-5*, 795) CG Pubs Inc.

Portfolio Presentation for Fashion Designers. Linda Tain. (Illus.). 265p. 1997. pap. 38.95 (*1-56367-094-1*) Fairchild.

Portfolio Primer: Teaching, Collecting & Assessing Student Writing. Geof Hewitt. LC 94-24748. 215p. 1994. pap. text 23.00 (*0-435-08834-3*) Heinemann.

Portfolio Process. Servat. 2000. pap. text 36.50 (*0-07-057858-3*) McGraw.

Portfolio Process. Annabel Servat & Anne Bailey. 150p. (C). 1995. text, student ed. 17.20 (*0-536-59117-2*) Pearson Custom.

Portfolio Programs Guide. Reynolds. 2000. pap. text. write for info. (*0-312-19811-6*) St Martin.

***Portfolio Project: A Study of Assessment, Instruction & Middle School Reform: Learning the Hypothesis-Test Process.** Diane Stephens & Jennifer Story. LC 99-47462. 199p. 1999. pap. 19.95 (*0-8141-2785-1*, 27851-3050) NCTE.

Portfolio Risk Management: A Computer Simulation for Stock & Options. Peter H. Ritchken et al. (Illus.). (C). 1989. pap. text 41.95 (*0-201-06498-7*) Addison-Wesley.

Portfolio Selection: Efficient Diversification of Investments. Harry M. Markowitz. 1991. 52.95 (*1-55786-108-0*) Blackwell Pubs.

***Portfolio Standard: Teaching Students to Show Us What They Know & Are Able to Do.** Ed. by Bonnie Sunstein. LC 99-58143. 2000. pap. text 22.00 (*0-325-00234-7*) Heinemann.

Portfolio, Techknowledge Reference Series. Schmidt. (TP - Technology Education Ser.). (J). (gr. k-12). 1997. 19.95 (*0-538-64481-8*) S-W Pub.

Portfolio the Image of Man. Teneues Publishing Company Staff. (Illus.). 200p. 1999. pap. text 35.00 (*3-570-19167-2*) V C Bertelsman.

Portfolio Theory. Irvin B. Tucker. Date not set. pap. text, teacher ed. write for info. (*0-314-03416-1*) West Pub.

An Asterisk (*) at the beginning of an entry indicates that the title is appearing for the first time.

***Portfolio Theory & Asset Pricing.** Edwin J. Elton & Martin J. Gruber. LC 98-51526. (Investments Ser.: Vol. 1). (Illus.). 468p. 1999. 55.00 (*0-262-05059-5*) MIT Pr.

Portfolio Theory & Capital Markets: The Original Edition. William Sharpe. 209p. 2000. pap. 14.95 (*0-07-135230-9*) McGraw.

***Portfolio Theory & Capital Markets: The Original Edition.** William F. Sharpe. LC 00-265577. (Illus.). 316p. 1999. 34.95 (*0-07-135320-8*) McGraw.

Portfolio Theory & Investment Management: An Introduction to Modern Portfolio Theory. 2nd ed. Richard Dobbins et al. 208p. 1994. pap. 37.95 (*0-631-19182-8*) Blackwell Pubs.

Portfolio Verwaltung Excel Reihe Losungen. Michael Muller. (GER.). (C). 1991. text. write for info. (*0-201-55978-1*) Addison-Wesley.

Portfoliomanagement Offizieller Wahrungsbehorden Unter Wahrungsrisike: Die Strategie der Reservediversifizierung unter Berucksichtigung Portfoliotheoretischer Erklarungsansatze & Deren Konsequenzen fur ein Stabiles Weltwahrungssystem. Bastian Hepperle. (GER., Illus.). 448p. 1996. 63.95 (*3-631-30809-4*) P Lang Pubng.

Portfolios: African-American Artists. Teresa S. Unseld. Ed. by Rachel Farber & Geri Stewart. LC 94-162957. (Illus.). 56p. (Orig.). Date not set. pap. text 12.95 (*0-86651-758-8*, DS31300) Seymour Pubns.

Portfolios: African-Americans of the Old West. Teresa S. Unseld. Ed. by Bev Dana et al. LC 96-215214. (Illus.). 80p. (J). (gr. 4-8). Date not set. pap. 13.60 (*1-57232-359-0*, 31330); pap. text 24.95 (*1-57232-360-4*, 31331) Seymour Pubns.

Portfolios: Assessing Learning in the Primary Grades. Marianne L. Lescher. LC 95-4295. (What Research Says to the Teacher Ser.). 1995. pap. 5.95 (*0-8106-1094-9*) NEA.

Portfolios: Clarifying, Constructing & Enhancing. Nancy J. Johnson & Leonie M. Rose. LC 96-61634. 365p. 1997. pap. text 34.95 (*1-56676-476-9*, 764769) Scarecrow.

Portfolios: Enriching & Assessing All Students Identifying the Gifted Grades K-6. Bertie Kingore. (Illus.). 220p. (Orig.). 1993. pap. text, teacher ed. 30.00 (*0-911943-33-1*) Leadership Pub.

Portfolios: Process & Product. Patricia Belanoff & Marcia Dickson. LC 91-3804. 315p. (C). 1991. pap. text 25.00 (*0-86709-275-0*, 0275, Pub. by Boynton Cook Pubs) Heinemann.

Portfolios Across the Curriculum & Beyond. Donna J. Cole et al. Ed. by Janice L. Herman & Jerry J. Hernam. LC 95-22649. (Illus.). 104p. 1995. pap. 17.95 (*0-8039-6303-3*) Corwin Pr.

Portfolios Across the Curriculum & Beyond. Donna J. Cole et al. LC 95-22649. (Illus.). 104p. 1995. 41.95 (*0-8039-6403-X*) Corwin Pr.

***Portfolios Across the Curriculum & Beyond.** 2nd ed. Donna J. Cole et al. LC 99-6842. 104p. (C). 1999. pap. 18.95 (*0-7619-7534-9*); lib. bdg. 43.95 (*0-7619-7533-0*) Corwin Pr.

Portfolios & Beyond: Collaborative Assessment in Reading & Writing. Susan M. Glazer & Carol S. Brown. (Illus.). 200p. (J). (gr. k up). 1993. pap. text 23.95 (*0-926842-25-0*) CG Pubs Inc.

Portfolios & Other Assessments. Julia Jasmine. (Illus.). 176p. 1993. teacher ed. 15.95 (*1-55734-504-X*) Tchr Create Mat.

Portfolios & Performance Assessment. (C). 1996. 30.00 (*0-02-405275-2*, Macmillan Coll) P-H.

Portfolios for Development: A Guide for Trainers & Managers. Warren Redman. 192p. (Orig.). 1994. pap. text 27.95 (*0-89397-394-7*) Nichols Pub.

Portfolios for Development Guide for Trainers & Managers. Warren Redman. 224p. (C). 1994. pap. 45.00 (*0-7494-1158-9*, Pub. by IPM Hse) St Mut.

Portfolios in Teacher Education. MaryEllen Vogt & Maureen McLaughlin. LC 96-41258. 164p. 1996. pap. 21.95 (*0-87207-150-2*, 150) Intl Reading.

Portfolios in the Classroom. J. Clemmons et al. 1993. pap. text 18.95 (*0-590-49273-X*) Scholastic Inc.

Portfolios in the Classroom: Tools for Learning & Instruction. Beth Schipper & Joanne C. Rossi. LC 97-19440. (Illus.). viii, 120p. 1997. pap. text 12.50 (*1-57110-060-1*) Stenhse Pubs.

Portfolios of Ansel Adams. Ansel Adams. LC 77-71628. (Illus.). 1977. 45.00 (*0-8212-0723-7*, Pub. by Bulfinch Pr) Little.

Portfolios of Ansel Adams. Ansel Adams. 1981. 25.00 (*0-316-71395-3*) Little.

Portfolios Plus: A Critical Guide to Alternative Assessment. Linda Mabry. LC 99-6169. (1-Off Ser.). (Illus.). 136p. 1999. 61.95 (*0-8039-6610-5*); pap. 27.95 (*0-8039-6611-3*) Corwin Pr.

Portfolios Through the Year. Carol Coff. (Illus.). 112p. (J). 1997. pap., teacher ed. 11.95 (*1-57690-036-3*, TCM2036) Tchr Create Mat.

***Porthole to Time.** Michael Eugene Stoddard. 176p. (YA). 1999. pap. 19.95 (*0-9675924-0-2*) M E Stoddard.

Portia: A Unique Woman Who Touches the World. Denise Turney. (Illus.). 1997. pap. 15.00 (*0-9663539-0-0*) Chistell Publ.

Portia: The World of Abigail Adams. Edith B. Gelles. LC 92-7860. (Illus.). 256p. 1992. 25.95 (*0-253-32553-6*) Ind U Pr.

Portia: The World of Abigail Adams. Edith B. Gelles. (Illus.). 256p. 1995. pap. text 12.95 (*0-253-21023-2*) Ind U Pr.

Portia Munson: Paintings & Pink. Leslie Camhi. (Illus.). 8p. (Orig.). 1994. pap. 5.00 (*0-9626731-8-8*) Yoshii Gallery.

Portia Prinz of the Glamazons. Richard Howell. (Illus.). 196p. 1996. 22.95 (*1-56924-800-1*) Marlowe & Co.

Portia Prinz of the Glamazons. limited ed. Richard Howell. (Illus.). 196p. 1996. 50.00 (*1-56924-803-6*); pap. 14.95 (*1-56924-829-X*) Marlowe & Co.

Portia's Prank. Dave Sargent. LC 98-10133. (Animal Pride Ser.). (J). 1998. pap. 6.95 (*1-56763-351-X*) Ozark Pub.

Portia's Prank. David M. Sargent. LC 98-10133. (Illus.). (J). 1998. write for info. (*1-56763-350-1*) Ozark Pub.

Porticello Shipwreck: A Mediterranean Merchant Vessel of 415-385 B.C. Cynthia J. Eiseman & Brunhilde S. Ridgeway. LC 86-14503. (Nautical Archaeology Ser.: No. 2). (Illus.). 138p. 1987. 75.00 (*0-89096-244-8*) Tex A&M Univ Pr.

Portikus, 1987-1997. 336p. 1998. pap. 55.00 (*3-928071-34-3*, Pub. by Richter Verlag) Dist Art Pubs.

Porting to Win32, No. 32. Thomas Lauer. LC 95-23946. 504p. 1995. 43.95 (*0-387-94572-5*) Spr-Verlag.

Porting UNIX Applications to Windows NT. Andrew Lowe. LC 96-78993. 544p. 1997. 49.99 (*1-57870-004-3*) Macmillan Tech.

Porting UNIX Software: From Download to Debug. Greg Lehey. 538p. 1995. pap. 29.95 (*1-56592-126-7*) Thomson Learn.

Portion for Foxes. Kay Mitchell. 1997. per. 4.99 (*0-373-26235-3*, 1-26235-1, Wrldwide Lib) Harlequin Bks.

Portion of His Life: William Blake's Miltonic Vision of Woman. Eugene R. Freed. LC 92-56604. (C). 1995. 60.00 (*0-8387-5265-9*) Bucknell U Pr.

Portion of Labor. Mary E. Wilkins Freeman. LC 67-29267. (Americans in Fiction Ser.). (Illus.). 563p. reprint ed. pap. text 12.95 (*0-89197-897-6*); reprint ed. lib. bdg. 52.50 (*0-8398-0568-3*) Irvington.

Portion of Reason. Robert Hoffman. 394p. (Orig.). (C). 1992. lib. bdg. 62.50 (*0-8191-8766-6*) U Pr of Amer.

Portion of Reason. Robert Hoffman. 394p. (Orig.). (C). 1992. pap. text 38.00 (*0-8191-8767-4*) U Pr of Amer.

Portion of the Poor: Good News to the Poor in the Wesleyan Tradition. Ed. by M. Douglas Meeks. (Kingswood Ser.). 160p. (Orig.). 1995. pap. 12.95 (*0-687-15529-0*) Abingdon.

Portion Photos of Popular Foods. Ed. by Mary Abbott Hess. 128p. 1997. spiral bd. 129.95 (*0-88091-162-X*) Am Dietetic Assn.

Portion Savvy: The 30 Day Smart Plan for Eating Well. Carrie Latt Wiatt. 222p. 1998. 24.00 (*0-671-02416-7*) S&S Trade.

Portion Savvy: The 30-Day Smart Plan for Eating Well. Carrie Latt Wiatt. 240p. 2000. per. 15.95 (*0-671-02417-5*) PB.

Portland. Gousha, H. M., Editors. 1995. 4.95 (*0-671-53577-3*, H M Gousha) Prntice Hall Bks.

***Portland.** Paul Koberstein. (City Smart Ser.). (Illus.). 240p. 2000. pap. 14.95 (*1-56261-530-0*, Pub. by Avalon Travel) Publishers Group.

Portland. Frank H. Sleeper. (Images of America Ser.). 128p. 1996. pap. 16.99 (*0-7524-0263-3*) Arcadia Publng.

Portland. rev. ed. Patricia M. Anderson et al. Ed. by Lydia B. Summers. (Illus.). 229p. 1986. pap. 19.95 (*0-685-17690-8*) Greater Portland.

Portland: A Collection of 19th Century Engravings. Ed. by Bruce Nelson. (Illus.). 1976. pap. 6.95 (*0-9600612-6-6*) Greater Portland.

Portland: Planning, Politics & Growth in a Twentieth Century City. Carl Abbott. LC 82-21978. 360p. 1983. reprint ed. pap. 111.60 (*0-608-01404-4*, 206216700002) Bks Demand.

Portland: The Riches of a City. K. C. Cowan et al. LC 98-35379. (Illus.). 304p. 1998. 45.00 (*1-885352-70-0*) Community Comm.

Portland: The Rose City, Pictorial & Biographical. With Deluxe Supplement, 2 vols. (Illus.). 1072p. 1997. reprint ed. lib. bdg. 99.50 (*0-8328-6917-1*) Higginson Bk Co.

Portland & Vicinity. Edward H. Elwell. (Illus.). 138p. 1975. reprint ed. pap. 6.95 (*0-9600612-3-1*) Greater Portland.

Portland Art Museum: Selected Works. LC 96-694. (Illus.). 1996. write for info. (*0-614-98004-6*) Portland Art Mus.

Portland Baby Resource Guide. Kari Hazen & Amy Cavers. Ed. by Troy M. Smith. Date not set. pap. 10.95 (*0-9633777-6-0*) Im Expecting.

Portland Baby Resource Guide. Hazen Publishing Staff. 1998. pap. text 10.95 (*1-891506-01-3*) Im Expecting.

Portland Best Places: Restaurants, Lodgings, Shopping, Nightlife, Arts, Sights, Outings. 4th rev. ed. Ed. by Kim Carlson. (Best Places Ser.). 368p. 1998. pap. 16.95 (*1-57061-123-8*) Sasquatch Bks.

Portland Bill to Start Point. Imray, Laurie, Norie & Wilson Ltd. Staff. (Illus.). (C). 1986. text 60.00 (*0-7855-6526-4*, Pub. by Laurie Norie & Wilson Ltd) St Mut.

Portland Bridge Book. Sharon Wood. (Illus.). (Orig.). (J). (ps-7). 2000. pap. 16.95 (*0-87595-211-9*) Oregon Hist.

Portland Cement Association's Guide to Concrete Homes: Building Tomorrow's Homes Today. Pieter A. Vanderwerf & W. Keith Munsell. LC 94-22245. 304p. 1994. 42.95 (*0-07-067020-X*) McGraw.

Portland Cement Concrete Pavement Evaluation System (COPES) (National Cooperative Highway Research Program Report Ser.: No. 277). 175p. 1985. 12.80 (*0-309-03861-8*) Transport Res Bd.

Portland Cement Plaster (Stucco) Manual. rev. ed. 56p. 1996. pap. 15.00 (*0-89312-046-4*, EB049M) Portland Cement.

Portland Cheap Eats: 200 Terrific Bargain Eateries. Ed. by Carrie Floyd. (Illus.). 176p. 1999. pap. 14.95 (*1-57061-196-3*) Sasquatch Bks.

Portland Dine-a-Mate. 256p. 1994. pap. 30.00 (*1-57393-018-0*) Dine-A-Mate.

Portland Dine-a-Mate Book. 256p. 1996. pap. text 30.00 (*1-57393-063-6*) Dine-A-Mate.

Portland Dining Guide. Timothy D. Haft & Audrey Berman. 160p. (Orig.). 1996. pap. 10.00 (*0-9651806-9-7*) Trashproof.

***Portland Entertainment, 2000.** (Illus.). 806p. 1999. pap. 45.00 (*1-880248-99-9*, 0029) Enter Pubns.

***Portland from the Air.** Photos by Russ Heinl. LC 00-27924. (Illus.). 112p. 2000. 29.95 (*1-55868-526-X*) Gr Arts Ctr Pub.

Portland, Gateway to the Northwest. Carl Abbott. LC 97-74096. (Illus.). 264p. 1997. 39.95 (*0-9654754-3-3*) Am Historical Pr.

***Portland Head Light & Fort Williams: An Illustrated History with a Walking Guide Map.** Kenneth E. Thompson, Jr. (Illus.). 104p. 1998. pap. 11.50 (*0-9677650-0-5*) Thompson Grp.

Portland Hikes: The Best Day-Hikes in Oregon & Washington Within 100 Miles. 2nd ed. Art Bernstein & Andrew Jackman. LC 97-38136. (Illus.). 320p. 1998. pap. 18.00 (*1-879415-22-4*) Mtn n Air Bks.

Portland in the Past with Historical Notes of Old Falmouth. William Goold. (Illus.). 543p. 1997. reprint ed. pap. 37.50 (*0-7884-0688-4*, G556) Heritage Bk.

***Portland JobBank.** 3rd ed. (JobBank Ser.). 320p. 2000. pap. 16.95 (*1-58062-451-0*) Adams Media.

Portland Laugher. Earl Emerson. 1995. mass mkt. 5.99 (*0-345-39782-7*) Ballantine Pub Grp.

***Portland Maine & Vicinity: Street Atlas.** 2nd ed. 2000. pap. 9.95 (*0-89933-407-5*) DeLorme Map.

Portland Map Book, 15. G. M. Johnson Associates Staff. (Orig.). 1999. pap. 9.95 (*0-9698943-4-1*) GM Johnson Assocs.

***Portland Metro Area Combo, Vol. 1.** Thomas Brothers Maps Staff. 1999. pap. (*1-58174-207-X*) Thomas Bros Maps.

***Portland Metro Area; Street Guide & Directory, Zip ed., Vol. 1.** Thomas Brothers Maps Staff. 1999. pap. write for info. (*1-58174-143-X*) Thomas Bros Maps.

***Portland Metro Area; Street Guide & Directory, 85th Anniversary ed., Vol. 1.** 85th ed. Thomas Brothers Maps Staff. 1999. pap. write for info. (*1-58174-142-1*) Thomas Bros Maps.

***Portland Metro Area 2000, Vol. 1.** Thomas Brothers Maps Staff. (Thomas Guides Ser.). 1999. (*1-58174-206-1*) Thomas Bros Maps.

***Portland Metro Business Directory (2000-2001)** American Business Directories Staff et al. 3,568p. 2000. boxed set 550.00 incl. cd-rom (*0-7687-0201-1*) Am Busn Direct.

Portland Names & Neighborhoods: Their Historic Origins. Eugene E. Snyder. LC 79-55518. (Illus.). 256p. 1979. 14.95 (*0-8323-0347-X*) Binford Mort.

Portland, OR. (Streetfinder Ser.). (Illus.). 1995. pap. 15.95 (*0-528-91369-7*) Rand McNally.

Portland, OR JobBank. 2nd ed. Ed. by Adams Media Corporation Staff. (JobBank Ser.). 320p. 1998. pap. 16.95 (*1-58062-032-9*) Adams Media.

***Portland, Oregon.** Rand McNally Fact Books Staff. 1999. 3.95 (*0-528-98009-2*) Rand McNally.

***Portland, Oregon.** Rand McNally Staff. 1998. 5.95 (*0-528-94536-X*) Rand McNally.

Portland Painting Now: Major New Works. Paul Sutinen. (Illus.). 1985. pap. 2.00 (*0-914435-13-2*) Marylhurst Art.

Portland Potpourri: Art, Fountains, & Old Friends. Eugene E. Snyder. LC 91-76512. (Illus.). 208p. 1991. 19.95 (*0-8323-0493-X*); pap. 12.95 (*0-8323-0494-8*) Binford Mort.

Portland Rose Festival: For You a Rose in Portland Grows. Mike Donahue. LC 97-137014. (Illus.). 104p. (Orig.). 1996. pap. 19.95 (*1-56037-106-4*) Am Wrld Geog.

Portland Step-by-Step: A Walking Guide to Scenic & Historic Points of Interest. Joe Bianco. (Illus.). 88p. (Orig.). 1988. pap. 9.95 (*0-911518-79-7*) F Amato Pubns.

***Portland Street Map.** DeLorme US Staff. 2000. pap. 4.95 (*0-89933-305-2*) DeLorme Map.

Portland Symphony Cookbook. 5th ed. Ed. by Adele J. Robinson. LC 74-84052. 336p. 1974. 9.95 (*0-9601266-1-9*) Friends Portland Symphony.

Portland Trail Blazers see Pro Basketball Today

Portland Trail Blazers. Bob Italia. LC 96-52413. (Inside the NBA Ser.). (Illus.). 32p. (J). (gr. 3-8). 1997. lib. bdg. 16.95 (*1-56239-771-0*) ABDO Pub Co.

***Portland Undercover: How to Visit New England's Hippest City Without Looking Like a Tourist.** Chris Barry. (Illus.). 96p. 2000. pap. 9.95 (*0-9700303-0-4*) Maine Pubng.

Portland-Vancouver Bridal Guide, 1990. Mary L. Burton & Marion Clifton. (Illus.). 380p. (Orig.). 1989. pap. 12.95 (*0-685-29058-1*) Bravo Pubns.

***Portland West Suburban, Oregon, 1.** Rand McNally Staff. 1999. 3.95 (*0-528-98011-4*) Rand McNally.

Portland Woman's Exchange Cookbook, 1913. Intro. by James Beard. LC 73-89993. (Illus.). 380p. 1987. spiral bd. 9.95 (*0-87595-045-0*) Oregon Hist.

Portlandia. Wanda Z. Larson. (Illus.). 1991. pap. 8.95 (*0-9628584-0-4*) Blue Uncrn.

Portland's Best by Bus: A Public Transit Guide to Portland's 30 Most Interesting Places. Nancy J. DenDooven. LC 98-72104. (Illus.). 144p. 1998. pap. 10.95 (*0-9661854-1-2*) Around Town.

Portland's Public Art: A Guide & History. Norma C. Gleason & Chet Orloff. (Illus.). 82p. (Orig.). 1984. pap. 4.95 (*0-87595-059-0*) Oregon Hist.

Portmanteau Dictionary: Blend Words in the English Language, Including Trademarks & Brand Names. Dick Thurner. LC 92-51011. 190p. 1993. lib. bdg. 35.00 (*0-89950-687-9*) McFarland & Co.

Portmanteau Plays. Stuart Walker. Ed. & Intro. by Edward Hale Bierstadt. LC 77-70364. (One-Act Plays in Reprint Ser.). 1977. reprint ed. 20.00 (*0-8486-2024-0*) Roth Pub Inc.

Portmarnock: A Closer Look. Pref. by Barry Murphy. 128p. 1997. pap. 7.95 (*0-86327-100-6*, Pub. by Wolfhound Press) Irish Amer Bk.

Portnoy et Son Complexe. Philip Roth. (FRE.). 1973. pap. 10.95 (*0-7859-4017-0*) Fr & Eur.

Portnoy's Complaint. Philip Roth. LC 94-16661. 288p. 1994. pap. 13.00 (*0-679-75645-0*) Vin Bks.

***Porto.** Gheldere DeAlexis. (Illus.). 2000. pap. 12.95 (*2-89464-323-3*) Ulysses Travel.

Porto & Northern Portugal. 128p. text 14.95 (*88-7009-917-2*, Pub. by Bonechi) Eiron.

Porto Bello Gold. A. D. Smith. LC 99-14322. (Classics of Nautical Fiction Ser.). 320p. 1999. reprint ed. pap. 13.95 (*0-935526-57-9*) McBooks Pr.

Porto Rico, Past & Present: The Island after Thirty Years of American Rule. Cuesta J. Enamorado. LC 74-14231. (Puerto Rican Experience Ser.). (Illus.). 180p. 1975. reprint ed. 15.95 (*0-405-06220-6*) Ayer.

Portobello Cookbook. Jack Czarnecki. LC 96-47967. (Illus.). 84p. 1997. 14.95 (*1-885183-75-5*) Artisan.

Portobello Mushroom Cookbook. Ron Meyer. (Illus.). 78p. 1999. pap. 11.95 (*0-9671074-0-7*) R Meyer.

Portofino. Frank Schaeffer. 1996. mass mkt. 6.99 (*0-425-14981-1*) Berkley Pub.

Portofino. Frank Schaeffer. 288p. 1999. pap. text 12.00 (*0-425-16694-5*) Berkley Pub.

Portofino: A Novel. Frank Schaeffer. 256p. 1992. text 15.00 (*0-02-607051-0*) Macmillan.

Portofino PTA. Gerald Green. 1976. reprint ed. lib. bdg. 20.95 (*0-89190-124-8*, Rivercity Pr) Amereon Ltd.

Portolan-Atlas des Battista Agnese Von 1546. fac. limited ed. (GER., Illus.). 1993. reprint ed. boxed set 2515.00 (*3-201-01599-7*, Pub. by Akademische Druck-und) Balogh.

Portolan-Atlas des Battista Agnese von 1546. fac. ed. (GER., Illus.). 1993. reprint ed. 623.00 (*3-201-01658-6*, Pub. by Akademische Druck-und) Balogh.

Portolan Atlas of the Mediterranean Sea & Western European Waters, with a World Map. Contrib. by Juan Oliva. LC 87-675334. 12p. 1987. 15.95 (*0-8444-0572-8*) Lib Congress.

Portolan Charts: Carte Nautiche Italiane. P. Frabetti. (Illus.). 1983. pap. 65.00 (*0-87556-599-9*) Saifer.

Portones Del Diablo. De Santiago.Tr. of Gates of Hell. (SPA.). 245p. write for info. (*1-56063-953-9*) Editorial Unilit.

Portorium: Etude Sur L'Organisation Douaniere Chez les Romains, Surtout a L'Epoque Du Haut-Empire. Siegfried J. De Laet. LC 75-7312. (Roman History Ser.). (FRE.). 1975. reprint ed. 42.95 (*0-405-07194-9*) Ayer.

Portrait. Charles Atkinson. LC 98-11357. 272p. 1998. text 23.95 (*0-312-18652-5*) St Martin.

***Portrait.** Terry Brown. LC 00-20021. (Todaysgirls.Com Ser.: Vol. 2). (Illus.). 128p. (J). (gr. 5-9). 2000. pap. 5.99 (*0-8499-7561-1*) Tommy Nelson.

***Portrait.** Norbert Schneider. 1999. 19.99 (*3-8228-6522-2*) Benedikt Taschen.

Portrait, Bk. I. Maggie R. Stone. (Casa Valledorres - A Trilogy Ser.). 161p. (Orig.). (J). (gr. 5-12). 1990. pap. 5.95 (*0-685-38818-2*) M R Stone Minst.

Portrait, Vol. 1. Charles F. Atkinson. Date not set. write for info. (*0-312-96698-9*) Tor Bks.

Portrait: Professional Techniques & Practices in Portrait Photography. rev. ed. Eastman Kodak Company Staff. LC 95-68105. (Illus.). 120p. (Orig.). 1997. pap. 24.95 (*0-87985-513-4*, O-24, Kodak) Saunders Photo.

Portrait: Theory. Ed. by Kelly Wise. LC 81-80880. (Illus.). 176p. 1982. 35.00 (*0-912810-34-3*); pap. 19.95 (*0-912810-35-1*) Lustrum Pr.

Portrait Album of Four RI Leaders. Marguerite Appleton. 1978. 12.00 (*0-932840-00-0*) RI Hist Soc.

Portrait & Biographical Album of Barry & Eaton Counties: Containing Full Page Portraits & Biographical Sketches of Prominent & Representative Citizens of the County. (Illus.). 832p. 1997. reprint ed. lib. bdg. 85.00 (*0-8328-6747-0*) Higginson Bk Co.

Portrait & Biographical Album of Branch County: Containing Full Page Portraits & Biographical Sketches of Prominent & Representative Citizens of the County. (Illus.). 653p. 1997. reprint ed. lib. bdg. 65.00 (*0-8328-6751-9*) Higginson Bk Co.

Portrait & Biographical Album of Clinton & Shiawassee Counties: Containing Full Page Portraits & Biographical Sketches of Prominent & Representative Citizens of the County. (Illus.). 1001p. 1997. reprint ed. lib. bdg. 99.00 (*0-8328-6752-7*) Higginson Bk Co.

Portrait & Biographical Album of Coles County Illinois, Containing Portraits & Biographical Sketches of Prominent & Representative Citizens of the County. (Illus.). 580p. 1998. reprint ed. lib. bdg. 59.00 (*0-8328-7071-4*) Higginson Bk Co.

Portrait & Biographical Album of Dekalb County Illinois, Containing Portraits & Biographical Sketches of Prominent & Representative Citizens of the Counties. (Illus.). 721p. 1998. reprint ed. lib. bdg. 75.00 (*0-8328-7073-0*) Higginson Bk Co.

Portrait & Biographical Album of Des Moines County, Containing Full Page Portraits & Biographical Sketches of Prominent & Representative Citizens of the County. (Illus.). 778p. 1998. reprint ed. lib. bdg. 79.50 (*0-8328-9599-7*) Higginson Bk Co.

Portrait & Biographical Album of DeWitt & Piatt Counties: Containing Full Page Portraits & Biography. (Illus.). 968p. 1997. reprint ed. lib. bdg. 95.00 (*0-8328-5735-1*) Higginson Bk Co.

Portrait & Biographical Album of Genesee, Lapeer & Tuscola Counties: Containing Biographical Sketches of Prominent & Representative Citizens of the Counties. (Illus.). 1062p. 1997. reprint ed. lib. bdg. 99.50 (*0-8328-6756-X*) Higginson Bk Co.

P

Portrait & Biographical Album of Green Lake, Marquette & Waushura Counties, Wisconsin. (Illus.). 850p. 1994. reprint ed. lib. bdg. 89.50 (*0-8328-3868-3*) Higginson Bk Co.

Portrait & Biographical Album of Greene & Clark Counties: Containing Full-Page Portraits of Prominent & Representative Citizens. (Illus.). 924p. 1997. reprint ed. lib. bdg. 93.50 (*0-8328-6301-7*) Higginson Bk Co.

Portrait & Biographical Album of Henry County, IL. Chapman Brothers. (Illus.). 834p. 1993. reprint ed. lib. bdg. 85.00 (*0-8328-3081-X*) Higginson Bk Co.

Portrait & Biographical Album of Isabella County: Containing Portraits & Sketches of Prominent & Representative Citizens of the County. (Illus.). 590p. 1997. reprint ed. lib. bdg. 59.50 (*0-8328-6762-4*) Higginson Bk Co.

Portrait & Biographical Album of Jackson County: Containing Full Page Portraits & Biographical Sketches of Prominent & Representative Citizens of the County. (Illus.). 885p. 1997. reprint ed. lib. bdg. 89.00 (*0-8328-6764-0*) Higginson Bk Co.

Portrait & Biographical Album of Johnson & Pawnee Counties, Neb., Containing Full Page Portraits & Biographical Sketches of Prominent & Representative Citizens of the Cos. (Illus.). 626p. 1995. reprint ed. lib. bdg. 63.00 (*0-8328-4472-1*) Higginson Bk Co.

Portrait & Biographical Album of Lake County: Containing Full Page Portraits & Biographical Sketches of Prominent & Representative Citizens of the County. (Illus.). 785p. 1997. reprint ed. lib. bdg. 79.50 (*0-8328-5757-2*) Higginson Bk Co.

Portrait & Biographical Album of Lenawee County: Containing Full Page Portraits & Biographical Sketches of Prominent & Representative Citizens of the County. (Illus.). 1280p. 1997. reprint ed. lib. bdg. 119.00 (*0-8328-6766-7*) Higginson Bk Co.

Portrait & Biographical Album of Louisa County, Iowa. (Illus.). 653p. 1993. lib. bdg. 67.00 (*0-8328-3532-3*) Higginson Bk Co.

Portrait & Biographical Album of Mahaska County: Containing Full Page Portraits & Biographical Sketches of Prominent & Representative Citizens of the County. (Illus.). 552p. 1995. reprint ed. lib. bdg. 58.50 (*0-8328-5021-7*) Higginson Bk Co.

Portrait & Biographical Album of McLean County: Containing Full Page Portraits & Biographical Sketches of Prominent & Representative Citizens. With History of McLean County. Reprinted Without the Biographies of U. S. Presidents & Governors of Illinois. (Illus.). 1030p. 1995. reprint ed. lib. bdg. 105.00 (*0-8328-5008-X*) Higginson Bk Co.

Portrait & Biographical Album of Newatgo County: Containing Portraits & Biographical Sketches of Prominent & Representative Citizens. (Reprinted Without the First 174 Pages Which Contained Biographies of Presidents of the U. S. & Governor of Michigan) Ed. by Newaygo County Historical Society Staff. (Illus.). 478p. 1995. reprint ed. lib. bdg. 51.00 (*0-8328-5044-6*) Higginson Bk Co.

Portrait & Biographical Album of Oakland County: Containing Full Page Portraits & Biography. (Illus.). 964p. 1997. reprint ed. lib. bdg. 96.50 (*0-8328-6779-9*) Higginson Bk Co.

Portrait & Biographical Album of Peoria County, Illinois. (Illus.). 982p. 1994. lib. bdg. 99.00 (*0-8328-4367-9*) Higginson Bk Co.

Portrait & Biographical Album of Pike & Calhoun Counties Illinois, Containing Portraits & Biographical Sketches of Prominent & Representative Citizens of the Counties. (Illus.). 628p. 1998. reprint ed. lib. bdg. 65.00 (*0-8328-7088-9*) Higginson Bk Co.

Portrait & Biographical Album of Polk County: Containing Full Page Portraits & Biographical Sketches of Prominent & Representative Citizens (Reprinted Without Biographies of Presidents & Governors) (Illus.). 690p. 1995. reprint ed. lib. bdg. 74.00 (*0-8328-5025-X*) Higginson Bk Co.

Portrait & Biographical Album of Rock Island Co, IL. Chapman Brothers. (Illus.). 818p. 1993. reprint ed. lib. bdg. 82.50 (*0-8328-3082-8*) Higginson Bk Co.

Portrait & Biographical Album of Saint Joseph County: Containing Full Page Portraits & Biographical Sketches of Prominent & Representative Citizens of the County. (Illus.). 609p. 1997. reprint ed. lib. bdg. 63.00 (*0-8328-6787-X*) Higginson Bk Co.

Portrait & Biographical Album of Sangamon County Illinois, Containing Portraits & Biographical Sketches of Prominent & Representative Citizens of the County. (Illus.). 680p. 1998. reprint ed. lib. bdg. 69.50 (*0-8328-7089-7*) Higginson Bk Co.

Portrait & Biographical Album of Washington, Clay & Riley Counties: Containing Full Page Portraits & Biographical Sketches of Prominent & Representative Citizens of the Counties. (Illus.). 1233p. 1997. reprint ed. lib. bdg. 119.00 (*0-8328-6725-X*) Higginson Bk Co.

Portrait & Biographical Album of Whiteside County, Containing Full-Page Portraits & Biographical Sketches of Prominent & Representative Citizens of the County with...a History of the County, from Its Earliest Settlement to the Present (1885) (Illus.). 942p. 1995. reprint ed. lib. bdg. 95.00 (*0-8328-4597-3*) Higginson Bk Co.

Portrait & Biographical Record of Adams County, Ill. Containing Biographical Sketches of Prominent & Representative Citizens. (Illus.). 598p. 1997. reprint ed. lib. bdg. 62.50 (*0-8328-5711-4*) Higginson Bk Co.

Portrait & Biographical Record of Christian County Illinois, Containing Sketches of Prominent & Representative Citizens. (Illus.). 459p. 1998. reprint ed. lib. bdg. 47.50 (*0-8328-7070-6*) Higginson Bk Co.

Portrait & Biographical Record of Denver & Vicinity: Containing Portraits & Biographies of Many Well Known Citizens of the Past & Present. (Illus.). 1306p. 1998. reprint ed. lib. bdg. 124.50 (*0-8328-7017-X*) Higginson Bk Co.

Portrait & Biographical Record of Dubuque, Jones & Clayton Counties, Containing Biographical Sketches of Prominent & Representative Citizens of the Counties. (Illus.). 557p. 1998. reprint ed. lib. bdg. 59.00 (*0-8328-9600-4*) Higginson Bk Co.

Portrait & Biographical Record of Guernsey County, Containing Biographical Sketches of Prominent & Representative Citizens of the County. (Illus.). 541p. 1995. reprint ed. lib. bdg. 57.50 (*0-8328-5093-4*) Higginson Bk Co.

Portrait & Biographical Record of Hanock, McDonough & Henderson Counties: Containing Biographical Sketches of Prominent & Representative Citizens of the County. (Illus.). 602p. 1997. reprint ed. lib. bdg. 62.50 (*0-8328-5745-9*) Higginson Bk Co.

Portrait & Biographical Record of Kalamazoo, Allegan & Van Buren Counties: Containing Sketches of Prominent & Representative Citizens. (Illus.). 950p. 1997. reprint ed. lib. bdg. 95.00 (*0-8328-6765-9*) Higginson Bk Co.

Portrait & Biographical Record of Lackawanna County: Containing Portraits & Biographical Sketches of Prominent & Representative Citizens of the County. (Illus.). 1077p. 1997. reprint ed. lib. bdg. 105.00 (*0-8328-6418-8*) Higginson Bk Co.

Portrait & Biographical Record of LaFayette & Saline Counties: Containing Biographical Sketches of Prominent & Representative Citizens. (Illus.). 642p. 1997. reprint ed. lib. bdg. 67.50 (*0-8328-6847-7*) Higginson Bk Co.

Portrait & Biographical Record of Lancaster County, Pa. rev. ed. Ed. by William L. Iscrupe & Shirley G. Iscrupe. (Illus.). 608p. 1988. reprint ed. 39.95 (*0-944128-00-9*) SW PA Geneal Servs.

Portrait & Biographical Record of Lehigh, Northampton & Carbon Counties: Containing Biographical Sketches of Prominent & Representative Citizens of the Counties. (Illus.). 999p. 1997. reprint ed. lib. bdg. 97.50 (*0-8328-6425-0*) Higginson Bk Co.

Portrait & Biographical Record of Macoupin County: Containing Biographical Sketches of Prominent & Representative Citizens (Reprinted Without Biographies of Presidents & Governors) (Illus.). 720p. 1995. reprint ed. lib. bdg. 75.00 (*0-8328-5006-3*) Higginson Bk Co.

Portrait & Biographical Record of Madison County Illinois, Containing Biographical Sketches of Prominent & Representative Citizens of the County. (Illus.). 548p. 1998. reprint ed. lib. bdg. 57.50 (*0-8328-7082-X*) Higginson Bk Co.

Portrait & Biographical Record of Marion, Ralls & Pike Counties, Containing Biographical Sketches of Prominent & Representative Citizens of the Counties. (Illus.). 803p. 1997. reprint ed. lib. bdg. 82.50 (*0-8328-5966-4*) Higginson Bk Co.

Portrait & Biographical Record of Montgomery & Bond Counties: Containing Biographical Sketches of Prominent & Representative Citizens. (Illus.). 521p. 1997. reprint ed. lib. bdg. 55.00 (*0-8328-5774-2*) Higginson Bk Co.

Portrait & Biographical Record of Oklahoma. (Illus.). 1299p. 1994. reprint ed. lib. bdg. 135.00 (*0-8328-4024-6*) Higginson Bk Co.

Portrait & Biographical Record of Orange County, Containing Portraits & Biographical Sketches of Prominent & Representative Citizens of the County. (Illus.). 1547p. 1997. reprint ed. lib. bdg. 149.00 (*0-8328-6194-4*) Higginson Bk Co.

Portrait & Biographical Record of Orange County, NY. Ed. by Chapman Publishing Co. Staff. (Illus.). 1573p. (Orig.). 1995. pap. text 64.00 (*0-7884-0133-5*) Heritage Bk.

Portrait & Biographical Record of Portage & Summit Counties, Ohio. (Illus.). 988p. 1994. reprint ed. lib. bdg. 97.50 (*0-8328-3620-6*) Higginson Bk Co.

Portrait & Biographical Record of Randolph, Jackson, Perry & Monroe Counties: Containing Biographical Sketches of Prominent & Representative Citizens of the Counties. (Illus.). 694p. 1997. reprint ed. lib. bdg. 72.00 (*0-8328-5788-2*) Higginson Bk Co.

Portrait & Biographical Record of Seneca & Schuyler Counties. (Illus.). 508p. 1997. reprint ed. lib. bdg. 53.00 (*0-8328-6237-1*) Higginson Bk Co.

Portrait & Biographical Record of Shelby & Moultrie Counties: Containing Biographical Sketches of Prominent & Representative Citizens of the Counties, with Biographies of the Governors of Illinois & the Presidents of the U. S. (Illus.). 730p. 1997. reprint ed. lib. bdg. 76.50 (*0-8328-5798-X*) Higginson Bk Co.

Portrait & Biographical Record of Southeastern Kansas: Containing Biographical Sketches of Prominent & Representative Citizens of the Counties. (Illus.). 501p. 1997. reprint ed. lib. bdg. 53.00 (*0-8328-6715-2*) Higginson Bk Co.

Portrait & Biographical Record of Suffolk County (Long Island), Containing Portraits & Biographical Sketches of Prominent & Representative Citizens of the County. (Illus.). 1038p. 1997. reprint ed. lib. bdg. 69.50 (*0-8328-6253-3*) Higginson Bk Co.

Portrait & Biographical Record of Tazewell & Mason Counties: Containing Biographical Sketches of Prominent & Representative Citizens of the Counties. (Illus.). 712p. 1997. reprint ed. lib. bdg. 73.50 (*0-8328-5799-8*) Higginson Bk Co.

Portrait & Biographical Record of the Scioto Valley, Ohio. (Illus.). 429p. 1993. reprint ed. lib. bdg. 46.50 (*0-8328-3230-8*) Higginson Bk Co.

Portrait & Biographical Record of the Willamette Valley: Containing Original Sketches of Many Well Known Citizens of the Past & Present. (Illus.). 1571p. 1997. reprint ed. lib. bdg. 149.00 (*0-8328-6375-0*) Higginson Bk Co.

Portrait & Biographical Record of Western Oregon: Containing Original Sketches of Many Well Known Citizens of the Past & Present. (Illus.). 1033p. 1997. reprint ed. lib. bdg. 109.00 (*0-8328-6373-4*) Higginson Bk Co.

***Portrait & Biographical Record of Winnebago & Boone Cos., Illinois: Containing Biographical Sketches of Prominent & Representatives.** fac. ed. 1140p. 1999. reprint ed. 109.50 (*0-8328-9969-0*) Higginson Bk Co.

Portrait & Biographical Records of Lancaster County, Pennsylvania. (Illus.). 690p. 1994. reprint ed. lib. bdg. 69.50 (*0-8328-4010-6*) Higginson Bk Co.

Portrait & Story: Dramaturgical Approaches to the Study of Persons, 7. Larry Cochran. LC 85-12708. (Contributions in Psychology Ser.: No. 7). 203p. 1986. 52.95 (*0-313-24966-0*, CPS/, Greenwood Pr) Greenwood.

Portrait Bust: Renaissance to Enlightenment. Ed. by Carl Goldstein. (Illus.). 64p. (Orig.). 1969. pap. 10.00 (*0-933519-14-1*) D W Bell Gallery.

Portrait Cast in Steel: Buckeye International & Columbus, Ohio, 1881-1980, 49. Mansel G. Blackford. LC 82-6114. (Contributions in Economics & Economic History Ser.: No. 49). (Illus.). 225p. 1982. 45.00 (*0-313-23393-4*, BPC/) Greenwood.

Portrait Catalog, 5 vols. New York Academy of Medicine Staff. 1970. suppl. ed. 175.00 (*0-8161-0733-5*, G K Hall & Co) Mac Lib Ref.

Portrait Catalog, 5 vols. New York Academy of Medicine Staff. 1971. suppl. ed. 160.00 (*0-8161-0900-1*, G K Hall & Co) Mac Lib Ref.

Portrait Catalogue, 1959-1965. 1994. 175.00 (*0-7838-2318-5*, G K Hall & Co) Mac Lib Ref.

Portrait Drawing. Wendon Blake. (Artist's Painting Library). (Illus.). 80p. (Orig.). 1981. pap. 8.95 (*0-8230-4094-1*) Watsn-Guptill.

Portrait Drawings: Forty-Five Plates. Henri Matisse. (Illus.). 48p. 1990. pap. 4.95 (*0-486-26438-6*) Dover.

Portrait Dreams. Victoria Malvey. 1998. mass mkt. 6.50 (*0-671-02070-6*) S&S Trade.

Portrait du Joueur. Phillipe Sollers. (FRE.). 1986. pap. 12.95 (*0-7859-2913-4*) Fr & Eur.

Portrait du Vocabulaire Francais. Aurelien Sauvageot. 285p. 1964. 9.95 (*0-8288-7491-3*) Fr & Eur.

Portrait d'un Ami qui s'appelait Moi. Andre Maurois. (Coll. Les Auteurs Juges par leurs Oeuvres). pap. 17.50 (*0-685-36953-6*) Fr & Eur.

Portrait d'un Inconnu. Nathalie Sarraute. (FRE.). 1977. pap. 10.95 (*0-8288-3741-4*, M11120) Fr & Eur.

Portrait d'un Inconnu. Nathalie Sarraute. (Folio Ser.: No. 942). (FRE.). 1964. pap. 8.95 (*2-07-036942-0*) Schoenhof.

Portrait d'un Seducteur. Henriette Jelinek. (FRE.). 243p. 1977. pap. 10.95 (*0-7859-2393-4*, 2070369714) Fr & Eur.

Portrait for Posterity: Lincoln & His Biographers. Benjamin P. Thomas. LC 72-38318. (Biography Index Reprint Ser.). (Illus.). 1977. reprint ed. 20.95 (*0-8369-8130-8*) Ayer.

Portrait History of the Romans Emperors: Based on Coins & Medallions. William Hornyak. LC 98-71758. 183p. 1998. pap. 9.00 (*1-57502-823-9*, PO2268) Morris Pubng.

Portrait Hollywood: Gary Bernstein's Classic Celebrity Photographs. Gary Bernstein. Ed. by Jon Rochmis. LC 94-60747. (Illus.). 144p. 1994. 34.95 (*0-942627-02-4*) Woodford Pubng.

***Portrait Hollywood: Gary Bernstein[0012]s Classic Celebrity Photographs.** (Illus.). 160p. 2000. reprint ed. text 35.00 (*0-7881-9074-1*) DIANE Pub.

Portrait in a Spoon: Poems by James Cummins. James Cummins. LC 97-4723. 90p. 1997. pap. 9.95 (*1-57003-192-4*); text 15.95 (*1-57003-191-6*) U of SC Pr.

Portrait in America. Brooks Johnson. LC 89-82710. (Illus.). 74p. 1990. pap. 12.00 (*0-940744-60-0*) Chrysler Museum.

Portrait in Art. Ed. by Stephen Longstreet. (Master Draughtsman Ser.). (Illus.). (Orig.). 1965. pap. 4.95 (*0-87505-199-5*) Borden.

Portrait in Blue. L. Chester. mass mkt. 6.95 (*0-7472-5283-1*, Pub. by Headline Bk Pub) Trafalgar.

Portrait in Britain & America with a Dictionary of Portrait Painters, 1680-1914. Robin Simon. 256p. 1987. 65.00 (*0-8161-8795-9*, Hall Reference) Macmillan.

Portrait in British Art. John Hayes. LC 93-111938. (Illus.). 176p. 1991. 85.00 (*1-85514-050-0*, Pub. by Natl Port Gall); pap. 49.50 (*1-85514-051-9*, Pub. by Natl Port Gall) Antique Collect.

Portrait in Clay. Peter Rubino. LC 97-17653. (Illus.). 160p. 1997. pap. 24.95 (*0-8230-4102-6*) Watsn-Guptill.

Portrait in Eighteenth-Century America. Ed. by Ellen G. Miles. LC 90-50995. (Illus.). 168p. (C). 1993. 49.50 (*0-87413-437-4*) U Delaware Pr.

Portrait in Gold. large type ed. Patricia Ainsworth. 416p. 1986. 27.99 (*0-7089-1496-9*) Ulverscroft.

Portrait in Memory. Intro. by Bruce Aufhammer. 60p. 1990. pap. 6.00 (*1-879025-03-5*) Christopher-Burghardt.

Portrait in Reflections. Joseph C. Phillips. LC 97-66321. 96p. (Orig.). 1997. pap. 14.95 (*1-883122-11-2*) Pearce Pub.

Portrait in the Renaissance: The A. W. Mellon Lectures in the Fine Arts, 1963. John W. Pope-Hennessy. (Bollingen Ser.: Vol. XXXV, No. 12). (Illus.). 380p. (C). 1989. pap. text 35.00 (*0-691-01825-1*, Pub. by Princeton U Pr) Cal Prin Full Svc.

Portrait in Time. Priscilla Gurney. 111p. (C). 1992. pap. text 50.00 (*0-9519723-0-8*, Pub. by P Gurney) St Mut.

Portrait Index of North American Indians in Published Collections. 1995. lib. bdg. 250.00 (*0-8490-6549-6*) Gordon Pr.

Portrait Index of North American Indians in Published Collections. 1997. lib. bdg. 255.95 (*0-8490-6081-8*) Gordon Pr.

Portrait Index of North American Indians in Published Collections. Patrick Frazier. LC 90-13329. 142p. 1992. 16.00 (*0-8444-0707-0*, 030-000-00241-5) Lib Congress.

Portrait Index of North American Indians in Published Collections. Patrick Frazier. 219p. 1997. per. 23.00 (*0-16-059169-4*, Library of Cong) USGPO.

Portrait Inspirations: A Collection of Drawing & Painting Ideas for Artists. Rockport Publishers Editors. (Inspirations Ser.). (Illus.). 96p. 1997. pap. 12.99 (*1-56496-383-7*, Quarry Bks) Rockport Pubs.

Portrait Is Not a Likeness. Intro. by Terence Pitts. (Illus.). 48p. 1991. pap. 14.00 (*0-938262-22-X*) Ctr Creat Photog.

Portrait Life of Lincoln. Francis T. Miller. LC 76-133528. (Select Bibliographies Reprint Ser.). 1977. reprint ed. 28.95 (*0-8369-5560-9*) Ayer.

Portrait Medallions of David D'Angers: An Illustrated Catalogue of David's Contemporary & Retrospective Portraits. J. G. Reinis. (Illus.). 528p. 1999. text 285.00 (*0-937370-01-0*) Polymath Pr.

Portrait Miniature in England. Katherine Coombs. LC 99-215417. 1998. 50.00 (*1-85177-206-5*, Pub. by V&A Ent) Antique Collect.

Portrait Miniatures in Early American History, 1750-1840: 1750-1840. Norton, R. W., Art Gallery Staff. LC 76-11634. 1976. pap. 3.50 (*0-913060-09-7*) Norton Art.

Portrait Miniatures in Russia, 18th-19th Centuries. T. Selinova. 358p. (C). 1988. 170.00 (*0-7855-4514-X*, Pub. by Collets) St Mut.

Portrait Miniatures in the National Museum of American Art. Robin Bolton-Smith. LC 84-2692. (Chicago Visual Library: No. 46). (Illus.). 92p. 1984. lib. bdg. 72.00 (*0-226-68857-7*) U Ch Pr.

Portrait Mummies from Roman Egypt (I-IV Centuries A. D.) with a Catalog of Portrait Mummies in Egyptian Museums. L. H. Corcoran. LC 94-69121. (Studies in Ancient Oriental Civilization: No. 56). (Illus.). xxx, 250p. 1995. pap. text 55.00 (*0-918986-99-0*) Orient Inst.

Portrait Now. Robin Gibson. (Illus.). 128p. 1993. 19.95 (*1-85514-098-5*) Antique Collect.

Portrait of a Banker, James Stillman. Anna R. Burr. 1975. 36.95 (*0-405-06950-2*, 19126) Ayer.

Portrait of a Builder: William A. McIntyre. Clarence W. Hall. 1983. pap. 5.95 (*0-86544-020-4*) Salv Army Suppl South.

Portrait of a Chef. Helen Morris. (Midway Reprint Ser.). (Illus.). xii, 222p. 1993. reprint ed. pap. text 7.95 (*0-226-54000-6*) U Ch Pr.

Portrait of a Child: Capturing Your Childs Most Precious Sayings, 1. Carol Fitzgerald. 1998. 19.95 (*0-9641596-2-7*) Carobi Five.

Portrait of a Community: A Collection of Eulogies. Arthur W. Shaw. LC 93-79853. 52p. (Orig.). 1993. pap. text 4.00 (*0-9626308-7-X*) Haleys.

Portrait of a Dalai Lama: The Life & Times of the Great Thirteenth. Charles Bell. (Tibet Book - Yellow Ser.). (Illus.). 464p. 1987. pap. 22.95 (*0-86171-055-X*) Wisdom MA.

Portrait of a Dancer, Memories of Balanchine: An Autobiography. Alice Patelson. 1995. 17.95 (*0-533-11378-4*) Vantage.

Portrait of a Director: Satyajit Ray. Marie Seton. LC 75-108946. 350p. 1971. write for info. (*0-253-16815-5*) Ind U Pr.

Portrait of a Family. South California Consortium Staff. (Sociology - Introductory Level Ser.). 1988. pap. 13.75 (*0-534-09174-1*) Wadsworth Pub.

Portrait of a Family. 2nd ed. Southern California Consortium Staff. (Sociology - Introductory Level Ser.). 1991. pap. 15.00 (*0-534-12719-3*) Wadsworth Pub.

Portrait of a Family: Telecourse Guide. 3rd ed. Intelecom Staff. LC 93-233112. (Sociology Ser.). 1993. pap. 19.75 (*0-534-18751-X*) Wadsworth Pub.

Portrait of a Family: Telecourse Guide. 4th ed. Mary A. Lamanna. (Sociology Ser.). 1996. pap. 23.50 (*0-534-50562-7*) Wadsworth Pub.

Portrait of a Farm Family. Raymond Bial. (Illus.). 48p. (J). (gr. 3-7). 1995. 15.95 (*0-395-69936-3*) HM.

Portrait of a Father. Robert Penn Warren. LC 88-5. 96p. 1988. 17.00 (*0-8131-1655-4*) U Pr of Ky.

Portrait of a Flying Lady. George Menzel. LC 94-60145. (Illus.). 248p. 1994. 29.95 (*1-56311-136-5*) Turner Pub KY.

Portrait of a Friend. Gwen Watkins. 226p. (C). 1983. 21.00 (*0-85088-847-6*, Pub. by Gomer Pr) St Mut.

Portrait of a Fulfilled Woman, Reflections from Proverbs 31. Virginia Leih. 132p. 1979. 4.95 (*0-8423-4860-3*) Tesseract SD.

Portrait of a Girl. large type ed. Mary Williams. LC 95-17615. 1995. pap. 19.95 (*0-7862-0501-6*) Thorndike Pr.

Portrait of a Greek Imagination. Herzfeld. LC 97-24232. 320p. 1997. lib. bdg. 48.00 (*0-226-32909-7*) U Ch Pr.

***Portrait of a Hero, or a Theory of the Novel.** Arild Pedersen. (Acta Humaniora). 361p. 1998. pap. 48.00 (*82-00-12935-7*) Scandnvan Univ Pr.

P

An Asterisk (*) at the beginning of an entry indicates that the title is appearing for the first time.

Portrait of a Hill Town: A History of Washington, N. H., 1876-1976. Ronald Jager & Grace Jager. LC 76-62912. (Illus.). 1998. reprint ed. 18.00 (*0-9666475-1-3*) Town of WA.

Portrait of a Judge: And Other Stories see Henry Cecil Reprint Series

Portrait of a Killer: Crying Freeman. Kazuo Koike. (Illus.). 456p. 1996. pap. 19.95 (*1-56931-077-7*) Viz Commns Inc.

Portrait of a Know-Nothing Legislature: The Massachusetts General Court of 1855. Virginia C. Purdy. (Nineteenth Century American Political & Social History Ser.). 298p. 1989. reprint ed. 20.00 (*0-8240-4073-2*) Garland.

Portrait of a Lady. Henry James. 560p. (C). 1983. mass mkt. 4.95 (*0-553-21127-7*, Bantam Classics) Bantam.

Portrait of a Lady. Henry James. 1998. pap. 4.95 (*0-7910-4567-6*) Chelsea Hse.

Portrait of a Lady. Henry James. 598p. 1991. 18.95 (*0-679-40562-3*) Everymns Lib.

Portrait of a Lady, 001. Henry James. Ed. by Leon Edel. LC 56-13883. (YA). (gr. 9 up). 1972. pap. 13.96 (*0-395-05106-1*, RivEd) HM.

Portrait of a Lady. Henry James. 240p. 1998. 7.95 (*3-89508-454-9*) Konemann.

Portrait of a Lady. Henry James. (Modern Library College Editions). 591p. (C). 1966. pap. 8.44 (*0-07-553637-4*, T47) McGraw.

Portrait of a Lady. Henry James. 560p. 1995. mass mkt. 4.95 (*0-451-52597-3*, Sig Classics) NAL.

Portrait of a Lady. Henry James. 560p. 1996. mass mkt. 5.99 (*0-451-19130-7*, Sig Classics) NAL.

Portrait of a Lady. Henry James. Ed. & Intro. by Nicola Bradbury. (Oxford World's Classics Ser.). 668p. 1998. pap. 8.95 (*0-19-283369-3*) OUP.

Portrait of a Lady. Henry James. LC 99-461941. 692p. 1999. 17.00 (*0-19-210038-6*) OUP.

Portrait of a Lady. Henry James. Ed. by Priscilla L. Watson. 1995. pap. 4.95 (*0-460-87588-4*, Everyman's Classic Lib) Tuttle Pubng.

Portrait of a Lady. Henry James. Ed. & Intro. by Geoffrey Moore. (English Library). 688p. 1984. pap. 9.95 (*0-14-043223-X*, Penguin Classics) Viking Penguin.

Portrait of a Lady. Henry James. (Classics Library). 1997. pap. 3.95 (*1-85326-177-7*, 1777WW, Pub. by Wrdsworth Edits) NTC Contemp Pub Co.

Portrait of a Lady. Meyer. (Bedford Introduction to Literature Ser.). 2000. pap. text 35.10 (*0-312-13891-1*) St Martin.

Portrait of a Lady see Works of Henry James Jr.: Collected Works

Portrait of a Lady. Henry James. 1990. reprint ed. lib. bdg. 21.95 (*0-89966-651-5*) Buccaneer Bks.

Portrait of a Lady, Vol. I. large type ed. Henry James. LC 97-23389. (Perennial Ser.). 465p. 1997. lib. bdg. 24.95 (*0-7838-8266-1*, G K Hall Lrg Type) Mac Lib Ref.

Portrait of a Lady, Vol. 1. Henry James. LC 72-158782. (Novels & Tales of Henry James Ser.: Vol. 3). 437p. 1977. reprint ed. lib. bdg. 37.50 (*0-678-02803-6*) Kelley.

Portrait of a Lady, Vol. II. large type ed. Henry James. LC 97-23389. (Perennial Ser.). 469p. 1997. lib. bdg. 24.95 (*0-7838-8268-8*, G K Hall Lrg Type) Mac Lib Ref.

Portrait of a Lady, Vol. 2. Henry James. LC 72-158782. (Novels & Tales of Henry James Ser.: Vol. 4). xx, 427p. 1977. reprint ed. lib. bdg. 37.50 (*0-678-02804-4*) Kelley.

Portrait of a Lady: An Authoritative Text, Henry James & the Novel, Reviews & Criticism. 2nd ed. Henry James. Ed. by Robert D. Bamberg. (Critical Editions Ser.). (C). 1995. pap. text 18.25 (*0-393-96646-1*) Norton.

Portrait of a Lady: Maiden, Woman & Heroine. Lyall H. Powers. (Twayne's Masterwork Studies: No. 78). 128p. 1991. 23.95 (*0-8057-8066-1*, Twyne); pap. 18.00 (*0-8057-8550-7*, Twyne) Mac Lib Ref.

Portrait of a Lady: Sargent & Lady Agnew. Julia R. Rolfe. (Illus.). 96p. 1997. pap. 19.95 (*0-903598-71-X*, Pub. by Natl Galleries) Antique Collect.

Portrait of a Lady Notes. James L. Roberts. (Cliffs Notes Ser.). 80p. 1965. pap. 4.95 (*0-8220-1066-6*, Cliff) IDG Bks.

Portrait of a Lawman: U. S. Deputy Marshal Heck Thomas. Bonnie S. Speer. LC 95-72480. (Illus.). 172p. (Orig.). 1996. pap. 11.95 (*0-9619639-3-X*) Reliance Pr.

Portrait of a Legislature. Richard F. Proud. 413p. 1989. 15.95 (*0-9621473-0-3*) Duorp Pr.

Portrait of a Man Unknown. Nathalie Sarraute. Tr. by Maria Jolas. LC 58-7873. 223p. (Orig.). 1990. pap. 9.95 (*0-8076-1252-9*) Braziller.

Portrait of a Marriage. Pearl Synderstricker Buck. 21.95 (*0-8488-0791-X*) Amereon Ltd.

Portrait of a Marriage. P. G. Wodehouse. 316p. Date not set. 24.95 (*0-8488-2419-9*) Amereon Ltd.

Portrait of a Marriage: Vita Sackville-West & Harold Nicolson. Nigel Nicolson. LC 98-23343. (Illus.). 262p. 1998. pap. 15.00 (*0-226-58357-0*) U Ch Pr.

Portrait of a Mobster. Harry Grey. 180p. 1992. reprint ed. lib. bdg. 25.95 (*0-89966-884-4*) Buccaneer Bks.

***Portrait of a Mood on Stilts: Poems.** J. S. Venit. LC 00-190969. 124p. 2000. pap. 18.00 (*0-7388-2147-0*) Xlibris Corp.

Portrait of a Nude. Laura A. Shamas. LC 95-146509. 1995. 5.60 (*0-87129-475-3*, P22) Dramatic Pub.

Portrait of a Parish: Monsea & Killodiernan, Tipperary. Daniel Grace. (Illus.). 346p. (Orig.). 1996. pap. 23.95 (*0-946327-17-3*, Pub. by Relay Pubns) Irish Bks Media.

Portrait of a Patriot: Selected Writings by Mohammad Hatta. Mohammed Hatta. 1972. text 86.15 (*90-279-7015-7*) Mouton.

Portrait of a Place: San Luis Obispo. Barbara Seymour. (Illus.). 120p. (Orig.). 1986. pap. 12.95 (*0-9617522-0-3*) Garden Creek Pubns.

Portrait of a Port. L. G. Taylor. (C). 1987. 30.00 (*0-85174-312-9*) St Mut.

Portrait of a Port: Boston, 1852-1914. William H. Bunting. 544p. (C). 1994. pap. text 22.95 (*0-674-69076-1*) HUP.

Portrait of a Puddy. Richard B. Urban. 60p. 1991. pap. text 10.00 (*0-9632662-0-9*) FurSure Ent.

Portrait of a Quaker: A Biography of Levi T. Pennington. Donald McNichols. LC 80-66654. (Illus.). 180p. 1980. 12.50 (*0-913342-24-6*) Barclay Pr.

Portrait of a Racetrack: A Behind the Scenes Look at a Thoroughbred Horseracing Community. David G. Best. LC 92-97019. (Illus.). 96p. (Orig.). 1992. pap. 24.95 (*0-9634241-0-6*) Best Edits.

Portrait of a Racist. Reed Massengill. 1997. pap. 14.95 (*0-312-16725-3*) St Martin.

Portrait of a Region - a Pictorial Journey Along the Chattahoochee Trace of Alabama & Georgia. Historic Chattahoochee Commission Staff. (Illus.). 80p. 1982. pap. 5.00 (*0-945477-02-3*) Hist Chattahoochee.

Portrait of a Revolutionary. B. P. Koirala. (C). 1990. text 16.00 (*81-85195-34-X*, Pub. by Minerva) S Asia.

Portrait of a Revolutionary: General Richard Mulcahy & the Founding of the Irish Free State. Maryann G. Valiulis. LC 92-9800. (Illus.). 320p. (C). 1992. text 39.95 (*0-8131-1791-7*) U Pr of Ky.

Portrait of a Scholar, & Other Essays Written in Macedonia, 1916-1918. Robert W. Chapman. LC 68-29197. (Essay Index Reprint Ser.). 1977. reprint ed. 18.95 (*0-8369-0291-2*) Ayer.

Portrait of a Ship, the Benj. F. Packard. Paul C. Morris. LC 87-80164. (Illus.). 200p. 1987. 30.00 (*0-936972-09-2*) Lower Cape.

Portrait of a Small Town: A Pictorial & Personal History of Huntington Station. Alfred V. Sforza. (Illus.). 176p. 1997. 24.95 (*0-930545-16-8*) Maple Hill Pr.

Portrait of a Soap Star, the Emily McLaughlin Story. Mary Ann Anderson. (Illus.). 155p. (Orig.). 1994. pap. text 14.95 (*0-9643167-8-1*) Orchard Books.

Portrait of a Soviet School under Glasnost. James Muckle. LC 90-31927. 225p. 1990. text 39.95 (*0-312-04748-7*) St Martin.

Portrait of a Superstar: Humanizing the Jaguar. Monica Daddio. 235p. (Orig.). 1998. pap. 12.00 (*0-9667783-0-8*) Francella.

Portrait of a Survivor. Florence M. Soghoian. LC 96-71910. (Illus.). 128p. 1997. 14.95 (*0-8158-0526-8*) Chris Mass.

Portrait of a Thousand Punks: Hard Core Logo. Nick Craine. LC 99-192475. (Illus.). 128p. 1998. pap. 14.95 (*0-88784-606-8*, Pub. by Hse of Anansi Pr) Genl Dist Srvs.

Portrait of a Town: Alexandria, District of Columbia, Virginia 1820-1830. T. Michael Miller. 595p. (Orig.). 1995. pap. text 40.50 (*0-7884-0248-X*) Heritage Bk.

Portrait of a Village. Francis B. Young. LC 73-163050. (Short Story Index Reprint Ser.). (Illus.). 1977. reprint ed. 19.95 (*0-8369-3964-6*) Ayer.

Portrait of a Waldorf School. A. C. Harwood. (Illus.). 24p. 1977. reprint ed. pap. 1.50 (*0-913098-06-X*) Orion Society.

***Portrait of a Westmeath Tenant Community, 1879-85.** Ann-Janine Murtagh. LC 99-29356. (Maynooth Studies in Local History). 64p. 2000. pap. 10.95 (*0-7165-2673-5*, Pub. by Irish Acad Pr) Intl Spec Bk.

Portrait of a Woman. Michel Vinaver. Tr. by Donald Watson from FRE. 1992. pap. 5.95 (*0-87129-127-4*, P71) Dramatic Pub.

Portrait of a Woman: A Novel. Joseph Roccasalvo. LC 94-73066. 253p. (Orig.). 1995. pap. 12.95 (*0-89870-545-2*) Ignatius Pr.

Portrait of a Woman As Artist: Emilia Pardo Bazan & the Modern Novel in France & Spain. rev. ed. Francisca Gonzalez-Arias. LC 92-17442. (Harvard Dissertations in Romance Languages Ser.). 256p. 1992. text 45.00 (*0-8240-0687-9*) Garland.

Portrait of a Woman's Soul. Marjorie S. Broadhead. LC 98-90041. xvi, 64p. 1998. 17.95 (*0-9663074-7-X*, 1657725) Whippersnap OH.

Portrait of a Young Man Drowning. Charles Perry. LC 95-39541. (Old School Bks.). 296p. 1996. pap. 11.00 (*0-393-31462-6*) Norton.

Portrait of Alaska. Sarah Eppenbach. 1997. 85.00 (*0-9645701-2-2*) R Munoz Ltd.

Portrait of Alaska. Hilary Hilscher. 1997. pap. text 12.95 (*1-55868-356-9*) Gr Arts Ctr Pub.

Portrait of Alaska's Inside Passage. Kim Heacox. LC 97-70191. (Illus.). 70p. 1997. pap. 12.95 (*1-55868-316-X*) Gr Arts Ctr Pub.

Portrait of America, 6 vols. Stephen B. Oates. (C). Date not set. pap., teacher ed., suppl. ed. 31.56 (*0-395-71727-2*) HM.

Portrait of America, 6 vols. 6th ed. Oates. LC 94-76537. (C). 1994. pap. text 31.56 (*0-395-70887-7*) HM.

Portrait of America, 6 vols., Vol. 2. 6th ed. Stephen B. Oates. LC 94-76537. (C). 1994. pap. text 31.56 (*0-395-70888-5*) HM.

Portrait of American Jews: The Last Half of the Twentieth Century. Samuel C. Heilman. LC 95-13360. (Samuel & Althea Stroum Lectures in Jewish Studies). 208p. (C). 1995. 30.00 (*0-295-97470-2*); pap. 17.95 (*0-295-97471-0*) U of Wash Pr.

Portrait of American Mothers & Daughters. Photos by Raisa Fastman. LC 87-90682. (Illus.). 128p. 1987. pap. 22.95 (*0-939165-04-X*) NewSage Press.

Portrait of American Mothers & Daughters. limited ed. Photos by Raisa Fastman. LC 87-90682. (Illus.). 128p. 1987. 60.00 (*0-939165-05-8*) NewSage Press.

Portrait of American Politics, 2 vols. Murphy. LC 93-78690. (C). Date not set. pap., teacher ed., suppl. ed. 27.96 (*0-395-68640-7*) HM.

Portrait of an Abolitionist: A Biography of George Luther Stearns, 1809-1867, 167. Charles E. Heller. LC 95-35712. (Contributions in American History Ser.: No. 167). 264p. 1996. 65.00 (*0-313-29863-7*, Greenwood Pr) Greenwood.

Portrait of an Air Force: The Royal New Zealand Air Force 1937-1987. Ed. by Geoffrey Bentley & Maurice Conly. 212p. (C). 1988. 95.00 (*1-86934-010-8*, Pub. by Grantham Hse) St Mut.

Portrait of an Appeaser: Robert Hadow, First Secretary in the British Foreign Office, 1931-1939. Lindsay W. Michie. LC 95-42503. 184p. 1996. 59.95 (*0-275-95369-6*, Praeger Pubs) Greenwood.

Portrait of an Artist: A Biography of Georgia O'Keeffe. Laurie Lisle. 1997. per. 15.00 (*0-671-01666-0*) PB.

***Portrait of an Artist as an Old Man.** Joseph Heller. 240p. 2000. 22.50 (*0-7432-0200-7*) S&S Trade.

***Portrait of an Englishman in His Chateau.** Andre Pieyre De Mandiargues. Tr. by J. Fletcher. 1999. pap. text 12.99 (*1-873982-93-3*) Dedalus.

Portrait of an Estuary. Verle Barnes. Ed. by Aubrey R. McKinney. LC 86-81736. (Adventures in Science Ser.). (Illus.). 220p. 1986. 24.95 (*0-914587-04-8*) Helix Pr.

Portrait of an Expatriate: William Gardner Smith, Writer, 91. Leroy S. Hodges, Jr. LC 85-934. (Contributions in Afro-American & African Studies: No. 91). 130p. 1985. 55.00 (*0-313-24882-6*, HPO/, Greenwood Pr) Greenwood.

Portrait of an Eye: Three Novels. Kathy Acker. LC 97-35003. 320p. 1998. pap. 14.00 (*0-8021-3543-9*, Grove) Grove-Atltic.

Portrait of an Independent: Moorfield Storey, 1845-1929. Mark A. Howe. LC 76-37346. (Select Bibliographies Reprint Ser.). 1977. reprint ed. 26.95 (*0-8369-6693-7*) Ayer.

Portrait of an Island. Mildred Teal & John Teal. LC 81-7631. (Illus.). 184p. 1997. reprint ed. pap. 14.95 (*0-8203-1961-9*, Brown Thrasher) U of Ga Pr.

Portrait of an Italian American Neighborhoo: The North End of Boston. Anthony V. Riccio. LC 97-35581. (Illus.). 204p. 1998. 39.95 (*1-57703-006-0*) CMS.

Portrait of an Unknown Man: Manuel Azana & Modern Spain. Cipriano de Rivas Cherif. Tr. by Paul Stewart. LC 94-42956.Tr. of Retrato de un desconocido. 432p. 1995. 59.50 (*0-8386-3584-9*) Fairleigh Dickinson.

Portrait of Aphasia. David Knox. LC 85-8958. 124p. (Orig.). 1985. reprint ed. pap. 14.95 (*0-8143-1800-2*) Wayne St U Pr.

Portrait of Aristotle. Marjorie Grene. LC 63-5566. 1979. pap. text 14.00 (*0-226-30822-7*, Midway Reprint) U Ch Pr.

***Portrait of Aristotle, 1967 Edition.** Marjorie Grene. (Key Texts Ser.). 271p. 1998. pap. 20.00 (*1-85506-551-7*) Thoemmes Pr.

Portrait of Arizona. Fred Hirshmann. (Illus.). 80p. 1995. pap. 12.95 (*1-55868-239-2*) Gr Arts Ctr Pub.

Portrait of Bathsheba. Grimes. (J). 2000. write for info. (*0-15-100199-5*, Harcourt Child Bks) Harcourt.

Portrait of Breast Cancer: Expressions in Words & Art. Ed. by William D. Smith. (Illus.). 192p. 1996. 25.00 (*0-9655886-0-2*); pap. 12.95 (*0-9655886-1-0*) Project Woman.

Portrait of California. Judith Morgan. (Illus.). 80p. 1996. pap. text 12.95 (*1-55868-249-X*) Gr Arts Ctr Pub.

***Portrait of Chloe.** Elvi Rhodes. 2000. 27.95 (*0-593-04216-6*, Pub. by Transworld Publishers Ltd) Trafalgar.

Portrait of Christ. Steve Green. (Illus.). 48p. 1992. 15.95 (*0-917143-13-2*) Sparrow TN.

Portrait of Delmore: Journals & Notes of Delmore Schwartz, 1939-1959. Delmore Schwartz. Ed. & Intro. by Elizabeth Pollet. 1986. 35.00 (*0-374-23639-9*) FS&G.

Portrait of Desire. Cassie Edwards. 1982. mass mkt. 3.50 (*0-571-11839-9*, Zebra Kensgtn) Kensgtn Pub Corp.

Portrait of Desire. Cassie Edwards. 384p. 1998. mass mkt. 5.99 (*0-8217-5862-4*, Zebra Kensgtn) Kensgtn Pub Corp.

Portrait of Divorce: Adjustment to Marital Breakdown. Gay C. Kitson & William M. Holmes. LC 91-35431. (Perspectives on Marriage & the Family Ser.). 438p. 1992. lib. bdg. 45.00 (*0-89862-081-3*) Guilford Pubns.

Portrait of Dona Elena. Katherine Q. Ranck. LC 82-83842. 1982. pap. 2.95 (*0-89229-012-9*) TQS Pubns.

***Portrait of Dorian Gray.** Oscar Wilde. Ed. by Jeremy Reed. (Creation Classics). (Illus.). 192p. 2000. pap. 12.95 (*1-84068-017-2*, Pub. by Creation Books) Subterranean Co.

Portrait of Dr. Gachet: The Story of a Van Gogh Masterpiece, Money, Politics, Collectors, Greed & Loss. Cynthia Saltzman. (Illus.). 432p. 1999. pap. 14.95 (*0-14-025487-0*) Viking Penguin.

Portrait of Eccentricity: Arcimboldo & the Mannerist Grotesque. Giancario Maiorino. (Illus.). 160p. 1991. 35.00 (*0-271-00727-3*) Pa St U Pr.

***Portrait of Egypt: A Journey Through the World of Militant Islam.** Mary Anne Weaver. LC 00-29361. 288p. 2000. pap. 14.00 (*0-374-52710-5*) FS&G.

Portrait of Egypt: A Journey Through the World of Militant Islam. 374th ed. Mary Anne Weaver. LC 98-26375. 288p. 1999. 25.00 (*0-374-23542-2*) FS&G.

Portrait of Elgar. 3rd ed. Michael Kennedy. (Illus.). 394p. (C). 1993. pap. text 24.95 (*0-19-816365-7*, 432) OUP.

Portrait of Elmbury. large type ed. John Moore. (Isis Large Print Ser.). 1997. 25.95 (*0-7531-5432-3*) T T Beeler.

Portrait of France, 1. Lee Server. 1998. 17.98 (*1-57717-087-3*) Todtri Prods.

Portrait of Frances Hodgkins. Eric Hall McCormick. (Illus.). 1981. 34.95 (*0-19-647991-6*) OUP.

Portrait of Galveston Island: An Overview of the City's History A.D. 700/800-1995. (Illus.). 100p. (Orig.). (YA). (gr. 6-12). 1996. write for info. (*0-9654160-1-1*) M W Remmers.

Portrait of George Moore in a Study of His Work. John Freeman. 1988. reprint ed. lib. bdg. 49.00 (*0-7812-0299-X*) Rprt Serv.

Portrait of George Moore in a Study of His Work. John Freeman. LC 78-131711. 1971. reprint ed. 23.00 (*0-403-00598-1*) Scholarly.

Portrait of Greece, 1. Terri Hardin. 1998. 17.98 (*1-57717-088-1*) Todtri Prods.

Portrait of Greek Imagination. Michael Herzfeld. LC 97-24232. 320p. 1997. pap. text 18.95 (*0-226-32910-0*) U Ch Pr.

***Portrait of Hawaii.** Photos by Cliff Hollenbeck & Nancy Hollenbeck. (Illus.). 2000. pap. 12.95 (*1-55868-527-8*) Gr Arts Ctr Pub.

***Portrait of Health in the United States: Major Statistical Trends & Guide to Resources.** Daniel Melnick & Beatrice A. Rouse. 500p. 2000. pap. 89.00 (*0-89059-189-X*) Bernan Pr.

Portrait of Heaven's Love. Kirk Gilchrist. 150p. (Orig.). 1996. pap. 8.95 (*0-9647871-6-4*, Hope of Israel) Hebron Minist.

***Portrait of Hemingway.** Lillian Ross. LC 99-26195. 1999. pap. 9.95 (*0-375-75438-5*) Modern Lib NY.

Portrait of Historic Athens & Clarke County. Frances T. Thomas. LC 90-23435. (Illus.). 256p. 1992. 29.95 (*0-8203-1356-4*) U of Ga Pr.

Portrait of Homelessness. Phyllis F. Holmes. 104p. 1995. pap. 12.95 (*0-8059-3632-7*) Dorrance.

Portrait of Humankind: An Introduction to Human Biology & Prehistoric Cultures. Paul Driben. 456p. 1994. pap. 41.33 (*0-13-064015-8*) P-H.

Portrait of India. Ved Mehta. LC 92-83817. 544p. (C). 1993. reprint ed. pap. 20.00 (*0-300-05538-2*) Yale U Pr.

***Portrait of Ireland.** Dorling Kindersley. (Travel Guides Ser.). (Illus.). 368p. 2000. 29.95 (*0-7894-6361-X*) DK Pub Inc.

Portrait of Italy, 1. Dwight V. Gast. 1998. 17.98 (*1-57717-090-3*) Todtri Prods.

Portrait of Jennie. Robert Nathan. 1976. 19.95 (*0-8488-1096-1*) Amereon Ltd.

Portrait of Jennie. Robert Nathan. 10.00 (*0-89064-051-3*) NAVH.

Portrait of Jennie. Robert Nathan. 293p. (J). 1981. reprint ed. lib. bdg. 21.95 (*0-89966-356-7*); reprint ed. lib. bdg. 16.95 (*0-89967-030-X*, Harmony Rain) Buccaneer Bks.

***Portrait of Jennie.** Robert Nathan. 1998. reprint ed. pap. 14.00 (*1-892391-03-1*) Tachyon Pubns.

Portrait of Jesus. Joseph F. Girzone. 192p. 1999. pap. 10.95 (*0-385-48477-1*) Doubleday.

Portrait of Jesus. large type ed. Joseph F. Girzone. LC 98-49535. 1999. write for info. (*1-56895-598-7*) Wheeler Pub.

Portrait of John: The Midwest & the World, 1928-1984. Frederic Will. LC 89-49005. 164p. (C). 1990. 27.95 (*0-8143-2139-9*) Wayne St U Pr.

Portrait of John: The Midwest & the World, 1928-1984. Frederic Will. LC 89-49005. (Fall & the Gods Ser.: Vol. 2). 162p. reprint ed. pap. 50.30 (*0-608-10597-X*, 2071218) Bks Demand.

Portrait of John Milton at Princeton. John R. Martin. LC 61-14263. (Illus.). 42p. 1961. 15.00 (*0-87811-006-2*) Princeton Lib.

Portrait of John Paul II. Andre Frossard. Tr. by Mary E. Hamilton from FRE. LC 89-83259. (Illus.). 175p. (Orig.). 1990. pap. 10.95 (*0-89870-277-1*) Ignatius Pr.

Portrait of Jonathan. large type ed. Margaret Dickinson. (Magna Large Print Ser.). 272p. 1997. 27.50 (*0-7505-0785-3*) Thorndike Pr.

Portrait of Katherine Mansfield. Nora Crone. 348p. 1989. 110.00 (*0-7223-1862-6*, Pub. by A H S Ltd) St Mut.

Portrait of Leni Riefenstahl. Audrey Salkeld. 1996. 18.99 (*0-224-02480-9*, Pub. by Jonathan Cape) Macmillan.

Portrait of Life: Of Medicine & Technology, Love, Society & Our Past. Luis H. Toledo-Pereyra. 55p. 1994. pap. 9.95 (*0-9639806-2-9*) L H Toledo-Pereyra.

Portrait of Liszt. Adrian Williams. (Illus.). 756p. 1990. text 80.00 (*0-19-816150-6*) OUP.

Portrait of Lost Tibet. Rosemary J. Tung. LC 87-12986. (Illus.). 240p. (C). 1996. pap. 19.95 (*0-520-20461-1*, Pub. by U CA Pr) Cal Prin Full Svc.

Portrait of Lozana: The Lusty Andalusian Woman. Francisco Delicado. Tr. by Bruno M. Damiani. 1987. 45.50 (*0-916379-41-8*) Scripta.

Portrait of Mary. Nikki Grimes. 128p. 1994. 15.95 (*0-15-173199-3*) Harcourt.

Portrait of Me: Featuring Christine Kontos. Barbara Aiello & Jeffrey Shulman. (Kids on the Block Bks.). (Illus.). 48p. (J). (gr. 5-8). 1995. lib. bdg. 13.95 (*0-941477-05-3*) TFC Bks NY.

Portrait of Miranda. Karin N. Mango. LC 92-8191. (Charlotte Zolotow Bk.). 240p. (YA). (gr. 7 up). 1993. 16.00 (*0-06-021777-4*); lib. bdg. 15.89 (*0-06-021778-2*) HarpC Child Bks.

Portrait of Molokai: Collectors' Edition. James H. Brocker. LC 95-201358. 1994. pap. text 19.95 (*0-9642197-0-0*) Molokai Fish & Dive.

Portrait of Morris. Vern Haddick. LC 78-31684. 1981. 19.95 (*0-87949-152-3*) Ashley Bks.

Portrait of Mount St. Helens: A Changing Landscape. Chuck Williams. LC 97-70189. 1997. pap. 12.95 (*1-55868-310-0*) Gr Arts Ctr Pub.

Portrait of Mr. W. H. Oscar Wilde. LC 78-64000. (Gay Experience Ser.). reprint ed. 27.50 (*0-404-61519-8*) AMS Pr.

Portrait of My Body. Phillip Lopate. 240p. 1997. pap. 12.95 (*0-385-48377-5*, Anchor NY) Doubleday.

Portrait of My Father in an English Landscape. George Szirtes. 72p. 1998. pap. 12.95 (*0-19-288091-8*) OUP.

Portrait of My Heart. Patricia Cabot. 352p. 1999. mass mkt. 5.99 (*0-312-96814-0*) St Martin.

P

Portrait of Nantucket, 1659-1890: Paintings by Rodney Charman. Text by Robert F. Mooney. 45p. text 50.00 (*0-9638910-3-0*); pap. text 20.00 (*0-9638910-4-9*) Mill Hill Pr.

Portrait of New Canaan: The History of a Connecticut Town. Mary L. King. (Illus.). 352p. 1981. 21.50 (*0-939958-00-7*) New Canaan.

Portrait of Newport II. Leonard J. Panaggio. (Illus.). 160p. (Orig.). 1994. pap. text 9.95 (*0-9642783-0-8*) Bank of Newport.

Portrait of Obedience: The Biography of Robert T. Ketcham. J. Murray Murdoch. 328p. 1979. pap. 9.99 (*0-87227-070-X*, RBP5076) Reg Baptist.

Portrait of Oregon. Photos by Rick Schafer. LC 93-73316. (Illus.). 80p. 1994. pap. 12.95 (*1-55868-162-0*) Gr Arts Ctr Pub.

Portrait of Pay, 1970-82: An Analysis of the New Earnings Survey. Ed. by Mary B. Gregory & Andrew W. Thomson. (Illus.). 576p. 1990. 125.00 (*0-19-828576-0*) OUP.

Portrait of Perth. Jiri Lochman & Marie Lochman. (Panoramic Ser.). (Illus.). 128p. 1999. 24.95 (*1-86436-374-6*, Pub. by New Holland) BHB Intl.

Portrait of Philip in Acts: A Study of Roles & Relations. F. Scott Spencer. (JSNT Supplement Ser.: No. 67). 320p. (C). 1992. 85.00 (*1-85075-340-7*, Pub. by Sheffield Acad) CUP Services.

Portrait of Picasso as a Young Man: An Interpretive Biography. Norman Mailer. (Illus.). 400p. 1999. reprint ed. text 35.00 (*0-7881-6112-1*) DIANE Pub.

Portrait of Pierre. large type ed. Ivy Preston. (Linford Romance Library). 320p. 1992. pap. 16.99 (*0-7089-7136-9*, Linford) Ulverscroft.

Portrait of Portsea, 1840-1940. Joy Harwood. (C). 1989. 39.00 (*1-85455-044-6*, Pub. by Ensign Pubns & Print) St Mut.

Portrait of Richard Graves. Clarence Tracy. 200p. 1987. text 35.00 (*0-8020-5697-0*) U of Toronto Pr.

***Portrait of Roman Britain.** J. S. Wacher. LC 99-48121. 160p. 2000. 75.00 (*0-415-03321-7*) Routledge.

Portrait of Scotland. Colin Baxter. LC 97-1885. (Illus.). 96p. 1997. 19.95 (*0-89658-360-0*) Voyageur Pr.

***Portrait of Scotland.** Colin Baxter. (Illus.). 96p. 2000. pap. 16.95 (*0-89658-515-8*) Voyageur Pr.

Portrait of Seattle. rev. ed. Timothy Egan. LC 86-80096. (Portrait Ser.). (Illus.). 80p. 1980. pap. 12.95 (*1-55868-001-2*) Gr Arts Ctr Pub.

Portrait of Simone. Odie Hawkins. 176p. 1991. mass mkt. 3.50 (*0-87067-363-7*) Holloway.

***Portrait of Sister Nicola.** Sonia Deane. 320p. 1999. 20.99 (*1-85389-960-7*) Ulverscroft.

***Portrait of Southern Writers.** Curt P. Richter. 2000. 45.00 (*1-892514-83-4*) Hill St Pr.

Portrait of Spotted Deer's Grandfather. Amy Littlesugar. LC 96-2704. (Illus.). 32p. (J). (gr. 2-7). 1997. lib. bdg. 15.95 (*0-8075-6622-5*) A Whitman.

Portrait of Sri Ramakrishna: Sri Sri Ramakrishna Punthi. Akshay K. Sen. 888p. 1999. 29.95 (*81-85843-92-9*) Vedanta Pr.

Portrait of St. Lucie County, Florida. Lucille R. Rights. LC 94-32009. (Illus.). 1994. write for info. (*0-89865-917-5*) Donning Co.

Portrait of St. Paul. John Fletcher. 1979. pap. 11.99 (*0-88019-096-5*) Schmul Pub Co.

Portrait of T. E. Lawrence. Vyvyan Richards. LC 75-22043. (English Biography Ser.: No. 31). 1975. lib. bdg. 75.00 (*0-8383-2093-7*) M S G Haskell Hse.

***Portrait of Texture.** Karl Kempton. 20p. 1999. pap. 5.00 (*1-57141-047-3*) Runaway Spoon.

Portrait of Thailand, 1. David Devoss. 1998. 17.98 (*1-57717-092-X*) Todtri Prods.

Portrait of the American Jewish Community. Jerome Chanes. Ed. by Norman J. Linzer & David A. Schnall. LC 97-38800. 240p. 1998. 59.95 (*0-275-96022-6*, Praeger Pubs) Greenwood.

Portrait of the Artist As a Young Ape. Michel Butor. LC 94-36953. 1995. pap. 10.95 (*1-56478-089-9*) Dalkey Arch.

Portrait of the Artist As a Young Ape. Michel Butor. Tr. by Dominic Di Bernardi from FRE. LC 94-36953. 128p. 1995. 19.95 (*1-56478-077-5*) Dalkey Arch.

Portrait of the Artist as a Young Dog. Dylan Thomas. LC 40-34154. 1956. pap. 8.95 (*0-8112-0207-0*, NDP51, Pub. by New Directions) Norton.

Portrait of the Artist As a Young Man. Holt Staff. 1989. pap., student ed. 11.00 (*0-03-023462-X*) Holt R&W.

Portrait of the Artist As a Young Man. James Joyce. 22.95 (*0-89190-725-4*) Amereon Ltd.

Portrait of the Artist As a Young Man. James Joyce. 256p. 1992. mass mkt. 4.95 (*0-553-21404-7*, Bantam Classics) Bantam.

Portrait of the Artist As a Young Man. James Joyce. 288p. 1991. 17.00 (*0-679-40575-5*) Knopf.

Portrait of the Artist As a Young Man. James Joyce. LC 96-17279. 1996. 15.50 (*0-679-60232-1*) Modern Lib NY.

Portrait of the Artist As a Young Man. James Joyce. 256p. 1991. mass mkt. 4.95 (*0-451-52544-2*, Sig Classics) NAL.

Portrait of the Artist As a Young Man. James Joyce. 1998. per. 5.99 (*0-671-01538-9*) PB.

Portrait of the Artist As a Young Man. James Joyce. 1916. 14.05 (*0-606-02826-9*, Pub. by Turtleback) Demco.

Portrait of the Artist As a Young Man. James Joyce. Ed. & Intro. by Seamus Deane. LC 93-12395. 329p. 1993. pap. 8.95 (*0-14-018683-2*, Penguin Classics) Viking Penguin.

Portrait of the Artist As a Young Man. James Joyce. 1999. pap. 10.95 (*0-14-028328-5*) Viking Penguin.

Portrait of the Artist As a Young Man. James Joyce. 1993. pap. 10.00 (*0-679-73989-0*) Vin Bks.

Portrait of the Artist As a Young Man. James Joyce. (Classics Library). 196p. 1997. pap. 3.95 (*1-85326-006-1*, 0061WW, Pub. by Wrdsworth Edits) NTC Contemp Pub Co.

Portrait of the Artist as a Young Man. James Joyce. Ed. by Hans W. Gabler & Walter Hettche. LC 93-19733. 366p. 1993. text 61.00 (*0-8153-1278-4*) Garland.

***Portrait of the Artist as a Young Man.** James Joyce. (Literature Made Easy Ser.). 96p. 1999. pap. 4.95 (*0-7641-0825-5*) Barron.

Portrait of the Artist As a Young Man. Tessa Krailing. (Barron's Book Notes Ser.). 1985. pap. 2.95 (*0-8120-3535-6*) Barron.

***Portrait of the Artist as a Young Man.** Clarice Swisher. LC 99-55868. (Literary Companion Ser.). 224p. (YA). 2000. 17.45 (*0-7377-0360-1*) Greenhaven.

***Portrait of the Artist as a Young Man.** Clarice Swisher. LC 99-55868. (Literary Companion to British Literature Ser.). (Illus.). 224p. (YA). 2000. pap. 13.96 (*0-7377-0359-8*) Greenhaven.

Portrait of the Artist As a Young Man. large type ed. James Joyce. 410p. 1995. lib. bdg. 24.00 (*0-939495-86-4*) North Bks.

Portrait of the Artist As a Young Man. James Joyce. LC 93-48840. 192p. 1994. reprint ed. pap. 2.00 (*0-486-28050-0*) Dover.

Portrait of the Artist As a Young Man. James Joyce. 255p. 1998. reprint ed. lib. bdg. 24.00 (*1-58287-057-8*) North Bks.

Portrait of the Artist as a Young Man. James Joyce. 350p. 1992. reprint ed. lib. bdg. 26.95 (*0-89966-899-2*) Buccaneer Bks.

Portrait of the Artist As a Young Man: Curriculum Unit. Center for Learning Network Staff & James Joyce. (Novel Ser.). 75p. (YA). (gr. 9-12). 1991. spiral bd. 18.95 (*1-56077-189-5*) Ctr Learning.

***Portrait of the Artist As a Young Man: Reproducible Teaching Unit.** James Scott. (Illus.). 53p. (YA). (gr. 7-12). 1999. ring bd. 29.50 (*1-58049-186-3*, TU129) Prestwick Hse.

Portrait of the Artist As a Young Man: Text & Criticism. James Joyce. Ed. by Chester G. Anderson. (Critical Studies). 576p. 1977. pap. 15.95 (*0-14-015503-1*, Viking) Viking Penguin.

Portrait of the Artist As a Young Man: Voices of the Text. Marguerite Harkness. (Masterwork Studies: No. 38). 160p. 1989. 29.00 (*0-8057-8064-5*, MWS-38, Twyne); pap. 18.00 (*0-8057-8125-0*, Twyne) Mac Lib Ref.

Portrait of the Artist As a Young Man Notes. Valerie Zimbarro. (Cliffs Notes Ser.). 88p. 1964. pap. 4.95 (*0-8220-1057-7*, Cliff) IDG Bks.

Portrait of the Artist As a Young Patient: Psychodynamic Studies of the Creative Personality. Gerald Alper. LC 97-30453. 260p. 1997. pap. 19.95 (*1-57309-203-7*) Intl Scholars.

Portrait of the Artist as a Young Superman: A Study of Shaw's Novels. Richard F. Dietrich. LC 75-77613. 209p. reprint ed. pap. 64.80 (*0-7837-5094-3*, 204479300004) Bks Demand.

Portrait of the Artist As an Abominable Snowman. Gabriel Rosenstock. LC 89-82064. (ENG & IRI.). 112p. 1990. pap. 18.95 (*0-948259-56-6*, Pub. by Forest Bks) Dufour.

***Portrait of the Artist As an Abominable Snowman.** Gabriel Rosenstock. 108p. 2000. pap. 10.00 (*1-58345-124-2*) Domhan Bks.

Portrait of the Author As a Bibliography. Dan H. Laurence. LC 83-600082. (Engelhard Lecture on the Book). 19p. 1983. 3.95 (*0-8444-0426-8*, 030-000-0241-5) Lib Congress.

Portrait of the Blues: America's Blues Musicians in Their Own Words. Paul Trynka. LC 97-204066. (Illus.). 160p. 1997. pap. 25.00 (*0-306-80779-3*) Da Capo.

Portrait of the Caribbean. Margaret Zellers. LC 94-79353. (Illus.). 80p. 1995. pap. text 12.95 (*1-55868-204-X*) Gr Arts Ctr Pub.

Portrait of the Family Within the Total Economy: A Study in Longrun Dynamics, Australia 1788-1990. Graeme D. Snooks. (Illus.). 327p. (C). 1994. text 69.95 (*0-521-45203-1*) Cambridge U Pr.

Portrait of the Free State: A History of Maryland. Donald M. Dozer. LC 76-47023. (Illus.). 654p. 1976. reprint ed. pap. 200.00 (*0-7837-9085-6*, 204983500003) Bks Demand.

Portrait of the Immune System: Scientific Publications of Niels Kaj Jerne. Ivan Lefkovits. 1996. pap. text 48.00 (*981-02-2614-4*) World Scientific Pub.

Portrait of the Immune System Scientific Publications of Niels Kaj Jerne. 878p. 1996. 97.00 (*981-02-2605-5*) World Scientific Pub.

Portrait of the Independent Sector: The Activities & Finances of Charitable Organizations. Virginia A. Hodgkinson et al. 97p. (Orig.). 1993. pap. 20.00 (*0-929556-14-3*, P93) Ind Sector.

Portrait of the Israeli Soldier, 52. Reuven Gal. LC 85-27170. (Contributions in Military Studies Ser.: No. 52). (Illus.). 290p. 1986. 59.95 (*0-313-24315-8*, GIS/, Greenwood Pr) Greenwood.

***Portrait of the Lover.** Maurizio Bettini. LC 99-20905. 353p. 1999. 45.00 (*0-520-20850-1*, Pub. by U CA Pr) Cal Prin Full Svc.

Portrait of the Menopause: Expert Reports on Medical & Therapeutic Strategies for the 1990's. Ed. by H. Burger & M. Boulet. (Illus.). 110p. (C). 1991. 45.00 (*1-85070-357-4*) Prthnon Pub.

Portrait of the Outerbanks, N. C., Chapter 1. Photos by Robert V. Drapaca. (Illus.). 80p. Date not set. pap. 25.95 (*0-9660586-3-1*) Aerial Perspect.

Portrait of the Ozarks. Clay Anderson. 1995. pap. text 12.95 (*1-55868-205-8*) Gr Arts Ctr Pub.

Portrait of the Panama Canal. William Friar. (Portrait Ser.). (Illus.). 80p. 1996. pap. 15.95 (*1-55868-477-8*) Gr Arts Ctr Pub.

Portrait of the Past: A Photographic Journey Through Wisconsin, 1865-1920. Susan Smith et al. LC 72-185287. (Illus.). 176p. 1998. reprint ed. pap. 19.95 (*0-915024-61-6*) Trails Media.

Portrait of the Pastor: A Biblical Description of the Role of the Pastor. B. E. Underwood. 95p. 1995. pap. 5.95 (*0-911866-31-0*) LifeSprings Res.

Portrait of the Person: A Personality Theory for the Clinician. Zoltan Gross. 275p. 1992. 29.95 (*0-9632977-0-8*) Global Vil CA.

Portrait of the Psychopath As a Young Woman. Edward Lee & Elizabeth Steffen. 1998. pap. 12.95 (*1-889186-09-0*) Necro Publns.

Portrait of the Regions, 4 vols. 1995. 415.00 (*92-827-8735-4*, CA-74-95-000ENC, Pub. by Comm Europ Commun) Bernan Associates.

Portrait of the Regions, Vol. 4. Eurostat Staff. 227p. 1997. 105.00 (*92-827-0058-5*, CA85-94-389-ENC, Pub. by Comm Europ Commun) Bernan Associates.

Portrait of the Regions Vol. 5: Hungary. (Illus.). 165p. 1997. 50.00 (*92-827-8021-X*, CA-95-96-293ENC, Pub. by Comm Europ Commun) Bernan Associates.

***Portrait of the Savior's Love: Psalms & Poetry of a Prophet.** Scott Wallis. 160p. 2000. write for info. (*0-9642211-7-9*) Lghthouse Pubns.

Portrait of the Self after Postmodernity. Calvin O. Schrag. LC 96-38600. 176p. 1997. 30.00 (*0-300-06842-5*) Yale U Pr.

Portrait of the Stars & Stripes, 2 vols., I. 1990. 34.95 (*0-922564-00-0*) Seniram.

Portrait of the Stars & Stripes, 2 vols., Vol. II, 1919-1946. 1990. 50.00 (*0-922564-01-9*) Seniram.

Portrait of the Walrus by a Young Artist. Laurie Foos. LC 96-54052. 192p. 1997. 19.95 (*1-56689-057-8*) Coffee Hse.

Portrait of the Walrus by a Young Artist. Laurie Foos. LC 98-12910. 176p. 1998. pap. 11.00 (*0-15-600543-3*, Harvest Bks) Harcourt.

Portrait of Tradition: One Hundred Years of the Michigan Marching Band. (Illus.). 160p. 1998. 60.00 (*0-9667186-0-7*) U of MI Marching Band.

Portrait of Tsarist Russia: Unknown Photographs from the Soviet Archives. (Illus.). 1989. write for info. (*0-318-66744-4*) Pantheon.

Portrait of Twenty-Five Years. Ed. by Robert S. Cohen & Marx W. Wartofsky. 336p. 1985. pap. text 53.50 (*90-277-1971-3*, D Reidel) Kluwer Academic.

Portrait of Utah. Photos by David Muench. LC 98-89045. (Illus.). 1999. pap. 12.95 (*1-55868-423-9*) Gr Arts Ctr Pub.

Portrait of Venice. Giandomenico Romanelli. Tr. by Antony Shugaar from ITA. LC 97-65575. (Illus.). 324p. 1997. 95.00 (*0-8478-2035-1*, Pub. by Rizzoli Intl) St Martin.

Portrait of Vietnam. Lou Dematteis. (Illus.). 128p. 1996. 35.00 (*0-393-03948-X*); pap. 22.50 (*0-393-31429-4*) Norton.

Portrait of Walton. Michael Kennedy. (Illus.). 364p. 1998. pap. text 24.95 (*0-19-816705-9*) OUP.

Portrait of Washington. Photos by John Marshall. (Illus.). 80p. 1993. pap. 12.95 (*1-55868-154-X*) Gr Arts Ctr Pub.

Portrait of William Morris. E. Meynell. 1972. 59.95 (*0-8490-0881-6*) Gordon Pr.

Portrait of Wittgenstein As a Young Man: From the Diary of David Hume Pinsent 1912-1914. George H. Von Wright. (Illus.). 242p. (C). 1991. text 35.95 (*0-631-17511-3*) Blackwell Pubs.

Portrait of Zelide. Geoffrey Scott. (Illus.). 256p. (Orig.). 1997. pap. 13.95 (*1-885983-19-0*) Turtle Point Pr.

Portrait of 2. Lawrence A. Ringenberg. (Illus.). 42p. (YA). (gr. 10-12). 1995. reprint ed. pap. 8.50 (*0-87353-414-X*) NCTM.

Portrait on the Roof. 1988. 8.95 (*0-318-00148-9*) R Basu.

Portrait Painter's Pocket Palette. Ian Sidaway. 64p. 1996. 7.98 (*0-7858-0579-6*) Bk Sales Inc.

***Portrait Photographer's Handbook.** Bill Hurter. (Illus.). 120p. 2000. pap. 29.95 (*1-58428-043-3*, Pub. by Amherst Media) IPG Chicago.

Portrait Photographs. Jonathan Williams. LC 79-83754. (Illus.). 1979. pap. text 25.00 (*0-917788-15-X*) Gnomon Pr.

Portrait Prints from the Hope Collection. Richard Sharp. LC 98-158707. (Illus.). 32p. 1998. pap. 9.95 (*1-85444-107-8*, 1078, Pub. by Ashmolean Mus) A Schwartz & Co.

***Portrait Sculpture in the British Museum: A Catalogue.** Aileen Dawson. (Illus.). 240p. 1999. 150.00 (*0-7141-0598-8*, Pub. by British Mus Pr) Antique Collect.

Portrait the Wind the Chair. Y. York. 59p. 1996. pap. 5.60 (*0-87129-620-9*, P80) Dramatic Pub.

Portraits see Artists' Workshop Series

Portraits see Portraits

Portraits. Sonia Balassanian. (Illus.). 24p. (Orig.). 1983. pap. 10.00 (*0-9608388-1-3*) S Balassanian.

Portraits. Ernest A. Boyd. LC 79-93318. (Essay Index Reprint Ser.). 1977. 21.95 (*0-8369-1274-8*) Ayer.

Portraits. Kate Chopin. 4.95 (*0-7043-3844-0*, Pub. by Quartet) Charles River Bks.

Portraits. Ros Cuthbert. (Seeing Things Simply Ser.). 64p. 1994. 6.98 (*0-7858-0064-6*) Bk Sales Inc.

Portraits. Elaine Erickson. 64p. 1994. 7.95 (*0-932616-45-3*) Brick Hse Bks.

***Portraits.** John Hedgecoe. (Illus.). 2000. 45.00 (*1-85585-726-X*, Pub. by Collins & Br) Sterling.

Portraits. Stef Ann Holm. 336p. 1996. mass mkt. 5.99 (*0-671-51044-4*) PB.

Portraits. Penny King. LC 95-50853. (Artists' Workshop Ser.). 1996. 14.15 (*0-606-10287-6*, Pub. by Turtleback) Demco.

Portraits. Richard Martin. (Illus.). 80p. 2000. 75.00 (*2-84323-152-3*, Pub. by Assouline) Rizzoli Intl.

Portraits. Steve McCurry. (Contemporary Artists Ser.). 1999. 16.95 (*0-7148-3839-X*) Phaidon Press.

Portraits. Helmut Newton. (Illus.). 248p. 1998. pap. 35.00 (*3-8238-1711-6*) te Neues.

***Portraits.** Parramon's Editorial Team. LC 98-74719. (Art Handbooks). (Illus.). 96p. 1999. 9.95 (*0-7641-5108-8*) Barron.

Portraits. Tr. by Jennifer Riggs. LC 94-49121. (First Discovery Art Bk.).Tr. of Portraits. (ENG & FRE., Illus.). 24p. (J). (ps-2). 1995. 11.95 (*0-590-55200-7*, Cartwheel) Scholastic Inc.

Portraits. Photos by Danielle Weil. LC 95-22814. (Illus.). 60p. 1995. 15.00 (*1-885183-32-1*) Artisan.

Portraits. Kyffin Williams. (Illus.). 192p. 1996. 105.00 (*0-8464-4611-1*) Beekman Pubs.

Portraits. large type ed. Cynthia Freeman. 1092p. 1996. lib. bdg. 25.95 (*0-7862-0679-9*) Thorndike Pr.

Portraits. Desmond MacCarthy. LC 72-5613. (Essay Index Reprint Ser.). 1977. reprint ed. 21.95 (*0-8369-7299-6*) Ayer.

Portraits. 2nd ed. Mark Dunster. LC 76-358986. 140p. 1976. pap. 5.00 (*0-89642-031-0*) Linden Pubs.

Portraits: A Book of Photographs by Peter McWilliams. Peter McWilliams. (Illus.). 252p. 1992. 34.95 (*0-931580-77-3*) Prelude Press.

Portraits: A Face for Every Mask. Sarah K. Eiland. Ed. by Carolyn S. Zagury. LC 95-62363. 76p. 1996. pap. 12.95 (*1-880254-33-6*) Vista.

Portraits: A Gallery of Intellectuals. Edward Shils & Joseph Epstein. LC 96-33162. 1997. pap. text 17.95 (*0-226-75337-9*) U Ch Pr.

Portraits: A Gallery of Intellectuals. Edward Shils & Joseph Epstein. LC 96-33162. 1997. lib. bdg. 55.00 (*0-226-75336-0*) U Ch Pr.

Portraits: An Artist's Perception. (Shorewood Art Programs for Education Ser.). 8p. 1983. teacher ed. 107.00 (*0-88185-019-5*); 143.00 (*0-685-09218-6*) Shorewood Fine Art.

Portraits: Biographical Representation in the Greek & Latin Literature of the Roman Empire. Ed. by Simon Swain & M. J. Edwards. LC 97-9924. 278p. (C). 1997. text 75.00 (*0-19-814937-9*) OUP.

Portraits: Creative Conversations with Celebrities. Cork Millner. (Illus.). 224p. 1994. 25.00 (*1-56474-087-0*) Fithian Pr.

Portraits: Kith, Kin & Neighbors. Stan Proper. 40p. 1998. pap. 5.00 (*0-9619992-8-4*) Walden Sudbury.

Portraits: Lives of the Companions of Prophet Muhammad (Peace Be Upon Him) Abdur R. Al-Basha. Tr. by Alexandra S. Al-Osh. LC 93-18486.Tr. of Suwar Min Hayat Al-Sahabah. 1993. write for info. (*1-56923-003-X*) Inst Islamic.

Portraits: Lives of the Companions of Prophet Muhammad (Peace Be Upon Him), 1. Abdur R. Al-Basha. Tr. by Alexandra S. Al-Osh. LC 93-18486.Tr. of Suwar Min Hayat Al-Sahabah. 1993. write for info. (*1-56923-000-5*) Inst Islamic.

Portraits: Photographs by Mary Ellen Mark. Photos by Mary E. Mark. LC 97-1268. (Illus.). 1997. 24.95 (*1-56098-720-0*) Smithsonian.

Portraits: Poetry. Lize Stilma. Tr. by Lous Heshusius & Adrian Peetoom from DUT. pap. 9.95 (*0-88962-336-8*) Mosaic.

Portraits: Poetry. Lize Stilma. Tr. by Lous Heshusius & Adrian Peetoom from DUT. 1995. pap. 17.95 (*0-88962-337-6*) Mosaic.

Portraits: Real & Imaginary. Ernest A. Boyd. LC 77-126702. (BCL Ser. I). reprint ed. 31.50 (*0-404-00965-4*) AMS Pr.

Portraits: Real & Imaginary. Ernest A. Boyd. LC 71-131641. 1970. reprint ed. 8.00 (*0-403-00528-0*) Scholarly.

Portraits: Talking with Artists at the Met, the Modern, the Louvre, & Elsewhere. Michael Kimmelman. LC 98-9589. (Illus.). 256p. 1998. 25.95 (*0-679-45219-2*) McKay.

***Portraits: Talking with Artists at the Met, the Modern, the Louvre, & Elsewhere.** Michael Kimmelman. 288p. 1999. pap. 13.95 (*0-375-75483-0*) Modern Lib NY.

Portraits: The Portrait in Contemporary Photography. Ed. by Peter Weiermair. (Illus.). 160p. 1995. 45.00 (*3-905514-20-6*, Pub. by Edit Stemmle) Dist Art Pubs.

Portraits: Wooden Houses of Key West. Sharon Wells & Lawson Little. (Illus.). 64p. (C). 1991. reprint ed. pap. 14.95 (*0-943528-06-2*) Hist Fl Keys.

Portraits: Wooden Houses of Key West. rev. ed. Sharon Wells. LC 79-620056. (Illus.). 64p. 1982. reprint ed. pap. 10.95 (*0-943528-02-X*) Hist Fl Keys.

"Portraits" - Music, Art & Poetry. Martin Dahlgren et al. (Illus.). 34p. 1998. spiral bd. 20.00 (*1-893365-00-X*) Barefooted Friar.

Portraits & Backgrounds. Evangeline Blashfield. LC 73-134054. (Essay Index Reprint Ser.). 1977. 30.95 (*0-8369-2103-8*) Ayer.

Portraits & Biographical Album of Gage County: Containing Full Page Portraits & Biographical Sketches of Prominent & Representative Citizens of the County. (Illus.). 748p. 1997. reprint ed. lib. bdg. 81.00 (*0-8328-6866-3*) Higginson Bk Co.

Portraits & Biographical Album of Jefferson & Van Buren Counties: Containing Full Page Portraits & Biographical Sketches of Prominent & Representative Citizens of the County. (Illus.). 664p. 1997. reprint ed. lib. bdg. 69.00 (*0-8328-6683-0*) Higginson Bk Co.

Portraits & Biographical Album of Lancaster County: Containing Full Page Portraits & Biographical Sketches of Prominent & Representative Citizens of the County. (Illus.). 800p. 1997. reprint ed. lib. bdg. 82.50 (*0-8328-6869-8*) Higginson Bk Co.

P

An Asterisk (*) at the beginning of an entry indicates that the title is appearing for the first time.

Portraits & Biographical Album of Linn County: Containing Full Page Portraits & Biographical Sketches...of Prominent & Representative Citizens of the County. (Illus.). 972p. 1997. reprint ed. lib. bdg. 97.50 (*0-8328-6687-3*) Higginson Bk Co.

Portraits & Biographical Record of Leavenworth, Douglas & Franklin Counties: Containing Portraits, Biographies & Genealogies of Well Known Citizens of the Past & Present. (Illus.). 845p. 1997. reprint ed. lib. bdg. 86.50 (*0-8328-6719-5*) Higginson Bk Co.

Portraits & Biographical Record of Lee County: Containing Biographical Sketches of Prominent & Representative Citizens. (Illus.). 854p. 1997. reprint ed. lib. bdg. 87.50 (*0-8328-5759-9*) Higginson Bk Co.

Portraits & Daguerreotypes of Edgar Allan Poe. Michael Deas. LC 88-477. 208p. 1989. reprint ed. pap. 64.50 (*0-608-01442-7*, 206220500002) Bks Demand.

Portraits & Dreams. Wendy Ewald. (Illus.). 123p. 1985. 16.95 (*0-86316-087-5*); pap. 9.95 (*0-86316-088-3*) Writers & Readers.

Portraits & Elegies. Gjertrud Schnackenberg. 1986. pap. 6.95 (*0-374-51981-1*) FS&G.

***Portraits & Figures: Developing Style in Creative Photography.** Terry Hope. LC 00-24877. (Black & White Photography Ser.). (Illus.). 2000. write for info. (*1-883403-69-3*, Silver Pixel Pr) Saunders Photo.

Portraits & Landscapes. Phyllis Doyle. LC 96-53848. 52p. 1997. pap. 14.95 (*0-7734-2806-2*, Mellen Poetry Pr) E Mellen.

***Portraits & Maps.** Diane Ward. (Littoral Bks.). 72p. 1999. pap. 12.95 (*1-928801-02-1*, Pub. by Sun & Moon CA) Consort Bk Sales.

Portraits & Pamphlets. Karl Radek. LC 67-22113. (Essay Index Reprint Ser.). 1977. 21.95 (*0-8369-0804-X*) Ayer.

Portraits & Personalities. Gamaliel Bradford. Ed. by M. A. Bessey. LC 68-8440. (Essay Index Reprint Ser.). 1977. 21.95 (*0-8369-0242-4*) Ayer.

Portraits & Photographs from Nepal. Prakash A. Raj. 1994. pap. 40.00 (*0-7855-2760-5*, Pub. by Ratna Pustak Bhandar) St Mut.

Portraits & Portents. Alfred G. Gardiner. LC 79-167344. (Essay Index Reprint Ser.). 1977. reprint ed. 25.95 (*0-8369-2499-1*) Ayer.

Portraits & Profiles by Edmond Y. Axadian. Ed. by Agop J. Hacikyan et al. LC 94-33472. 1995. text 69.95 (*0-7734-9044-2*) E Mellen.

Portraits & Propaganda: Faces of Rome. Ed. by Rolf Winkes. (Illus.). (Orig.). 1989. pap. 20.00 (*0-933519-16-8*) D W Bell Gallery.

Portraits & Self-Portraits. Ed. by George Schreiber. LC 68-58812. (Essay Index Reprint Ser.). 1977. 19.95 (*0-8369-0053-7*) Ayer.

Portraits & Sketches. Edmund W. Gosse. LC 70-99699. (Essay Index Reprint Ser.). 1977. 23.95 (*0-8369-1411-2*) Ayer.

Portraits & Sketches. Edmund W. Gosse. (BCL1-PR English Literature Ser.). 297p. 1992. reprint ed. lib. bdg. 79.00 (*0-7812-7014-6*) Rprt Serv.

Portraits & Sketches. Edmund W. Gosse. 1971. reprint ed. 19.00 (*0-403-00994-4*) Scholarly.

Portraits & Statuary of Virginians. Katherine M. Smith & Ray O. Hummel, Jr. (Publication Ser.: No. 43). (Illus.). ix, 160p. 1977. pap. 7.95 (*0-88490-074-6*) Library of VA.

Portraits & the Poses. Edwin Brock. LC 73-78783. 64p. 1973. 6.95 (*0-8112-0486-3*, Pub. by New Directions); pap. 1.95 (*0-8112-0487-1*, NDP360, Pub. by New Directions) Norton.

***Portraits by Ingres: Image of an Epoch.** Jean-Auguste-Dominique Ingres et al. LC 98-48508. 1999. write for info. (*0-87099-891-9*) Metro Mus Art.

Portraits by Ingres: Image of an Epoch. Ed. by Gary Tinterow & Philip Conisbee. LC 98-48508. (Illus.). 596p. 1999. 85.00 (*0-8109-6536-4*, Pub. by Abrams) Time Warner.

Portraits by Ingres: Image of An Epoch. Jean-Auguste-Dominique Ingres. LC 98-48508. 1999. write for info. (*0-87099-890-0*) Metro Mus Art.

Portraits d'Inconnue. Jules Romains, pseud. (FRE.). 240p. 1962. pap. 10.95 (*0-7859-1620-2*, 2080506 20X) Fr & Eur.

Portraits Exposed. Nicole Andonov. LC 95-90214. 80p. 1995. pap. 6.95 (*0-9646048-0-9*) Westonian.

Portraits for a King: The British Military Paintings of A. J. Dubois Drahonet (1794-1834) Jenny Spencer-Smith. 96p. 1997. pap. 40.00 (*0-901721-21-2*, Pub. by Natl Army Mus) St Mut.

Portraits for Profits. 9.95 (*0-686-19135-8*) Triple B.

Portraits from an Uninhabited Land. Nicholas Adler. 1988. pap. write for info. (*0-318-63738-3*) Bantam.

Portraits from Germany. J. W. Jamieson. (Illus.). 156p. 2000. pap. 20.00 (*1-878465-30-9*) Scott-Townsend Pubs.

***Portraits from L. A. Don Bachardy, Dan McCleary, John Sonsini: Robert V. Fullerton Art Museum, California State University, San Bernardino, November 20, 1999-January 23, 2000.** Robert V. Fullerton Art Museum Staff. LC 99-52096. (Illus.). 1999. write for info. (*0-945486-15-4*) CSU SBRVFAM.

Portraits from Life by Edmund Gosse. Ann Thwaite. 176p. 1991. text 51.95 (*0-85967-796-6*, Pub. by Scolar Pr) Ashgate Pub Co.

Portraits from Life in 29 Steps. John Howard Sanden & Elizabeth R. Sanden. LC 98-55424. (Illus.). 144p. 1999. 28.99 (*0-89134-902-2*, 31434, North Lght Bks) F & W Pubns Inc.

Portraits from Memory. Richard Kostelanetz. 1975. 20.00 (*0-932360-21-1*); pap. 10.00 (*0-932360-20-3*) Archae Edns.

Portraits from Memory. deluxe limited ed. Richard Kostelanetz. 1975. 75.00 (*0-685-58447-X*) Archae Edns.

Portraits from North American Indian Life. Edward S. Curtis. 1989. 14.98 (*0-88394-004-3*) Promntory Pr.

Portraits from North American Indian Life: Original Portfolio Edition. Edward S. Curtis. 1990. 39.98 (*0-88394-077-9*) Promntory Pr.

Portraits from Paul's Pen. R. L. Rainey. 1994. pap. text 6.25 (*0-937396-96-6*) Walterick Pubs.

Portraits from the Age of Exploration: Selections from Andre Thevet's Les Vrais Pourtraits & Vies des Hommes Illustres. Ed. by Roger Schlesinger. Tr. by Edward Benson. (Illus.). 172p. (C). 1992. text 24.95 (*0-252-01943-1*) U of Ill Pr.

Portraits from the Desert: Bill Wright's Big Bend. Bill Wright. LC 97-9402. (Illus.). 176p. 1998. 40.00 (*0-292-79115-1*, WRIPOR); pap. 24.95 (*0-292-79116-X*, WRIPOP) U of Tex Pr.

Portraits in an Album. J. Glanfield. 1997. text 27.00 (*0-575-06482-X*, Pub. by V Gollancz) Trafalgar.

Portraits in Black. Becky Daniel. (Illus.). 96p. (J). (gr. 4-7). 1990. 11.99 (*0-86653-531-4*, GA1147) Good Apple.

Portraits in Black & White. Minnie I. Carter. 42p. (Orig.). 1996. pap. 10.00 (*0-9654392-0-8*) Carter Pubng.

Portraits in Cataloging & Classification: Theorists, Educators, & Practitioners of the Late Twentieth Century, Vol. 25. Ed. by Carolynne Myall & Ruth C. Carter. LC 98-18930. 344p. 1998. 59.95 (*0-7890-0543-3*) Haworth Pr.

Portraits in Color. Mary W. Ovington. 241p. 1977. 18.95 (*0-8369-2516-5*) Ayer.

Portraits in Conservation: Eastern & Southern Africa. Elisabeth Braun. (Illus.). 200p. (YA). (gr. 9 up). 1995. text 28.00 (*1-55591-914-6*) Fulcrum Pub.

Portraits in Courage: Extraordinary Lessons from Everyday Heroes. Dave Dravecky et al. LC 98-24703. 208p. 1998. 12.99 (*0-310-21664-8*) Zondervan.

Portraits in Homoeopathic Medicines Vol. 3: Expanding Views of the Materia Medica. Catherine R. Coulter. LC 97-30347. 338p. 1998. 33.00 (*1-57626-091-7*, QMP) Quality Med Pub.

Portraits in Miniature & Other Essays by Lytton Strachey. Giles L. Strachey. LC 77-10347. 214p. 1977. reprint ed. lib. bdg. 59.50 (*0-8371-9823-2*, STPM, Greenwood Pr) Greenwood.

Portraits in Oil. Annette A. Hanna. (How to Draw & Paint Ser.). (Illus.). 32p. 1992. pap. 6.95 (*1-56010-079-6*, HT238) W Foster Pub.

Portraits in Oil the Van Wyk Way. Helen Van Wyk. Ed. by Herbert Rogoff. (Illus.). 128p. (Orig.). 1998. 27.99 (*0-929552-14-8*) Art Instr Assocs.

Portraits in Oils. Phillippe Mailhebiau. pap. 23.95 (*0-8464-4484-4*) Beekman Pubs.

Portraits in Oils: The Personality of Aromatherapy Oils & Their Link with Human Temperament. Phillippe Mailhebiau. 304p. pap. 19.95 (*0-85207-237-6*, Pub. by C W Daniel) Natl Bk Netwk.

Portraits in Pastel. Ken Goldman. (How to Draw & Paint Ser.). (Illus.). 32p. (Orig.). 1992. pap. 6.95 (*1-56010-081-8*, HT240) W Foster Pub.

Portraits in Pen. Sari Mercedes. (Illus.). 100p. 1995. pap. 10.00 (*0-9647225-0-X*) Sari.

Portraits in Plaster. Laurence Hutton. (Notable American Authors Ser.). 1992. reprint ed. lib. bdg. 75.00 (*0-7812-3313-5*) Rprt Serv.

Portraits in Print: A Collection of Profiles & the Stories Behind Them. Helen Benedict. 176p. 1991. text 46.00 (*0-231-07226-0*) Col U Pr.

Portraits in Print: A Collection of Profiles & the Stories Behind Them. Helen Benedict. 176p. 1992. pap. 15.50 (*0-231-07227-9*) Col U Pr.

Portraits in Prose. Hugh Macdonald. LC 71-101830. (Biography Index Reprint Ser.). 1977. 30.95 (*0-8369-8004-2*) Ayer.

Portraits in Rhythm: 50 Studies for Snare Drum. Anthony J. Cirone. 56p. (Orig.). 1997. pap. 12.95 (*0-7692-1439-8*, HAB00101) Wrner Bros.

Portraits in Satire. Kenneth Hopkins. LC 71-161941. 290p. 1958. reprint ed. 59.00 (*0-403-01330-5*) Scholarly.

Portraits in Silicon. Robert Slater. 389p. 1989. pap. text 16.50 (*0-262-69131-0*) MIT Pr.

Portraits in Steel. Photos by Milton Rogovin & Michael Frisch. LC 92-56776. (Illus.). 288p. 1993. pap. text 29.95 (*0-8014-8102-3*) Cornell U Pr.

***Portraits in Steel: An Illustrated History of Jones & Laughlin Steel Corporation.** David H. Wollman. LC 98-44778. (Illus.). 344p. 1999. text 70.00 (*0-87338-624-8*) Kent St U Pr.

Portraits in Sun & Shadow. Maria Bakkum. (Illus.). 66p. 1995. pap. 5.00 (*0-614-24751-9*) Tesseract SD.

Portraits in the Massachusetts Historical Society. Andrew Oliver et al. LC 88-2936. (Illus.). 163p. 1988. 50.00 (*0-934909-26-1*, Pub. by Mass Hist Soc) NE U Pr.

Portraits in the Shadows of Crack. 2nd ed. Henry Hardee. 20p. (Orig.). 1998. reprint ed. pap. 5.00 (*1-884978-26-6*) Black Boys Dream.

Portraits in the Wild: Animal Behavior in East Africa. Cynthia Moss. LC 81-23092. (Illus.). 1996. pap. 15.95 (*0-226-54233-5*) U Ch Pr.

Portraits in Victorian Religious Thought. James Woelfel. LC 97-41215. (Texts & Studies in Religion: Vol. 77). 132p. 1997. 69.95 (*0-7734-8423-X*) E Mellen.

Portrait's Lifelines. Yolanda McCulloch. 40p. 1998. pap. 7.00 (*0-8059-4305-6*) Dorrance.

Portraits Litteraires. (Bibliotheque de la Pleiade Ser.). write for info. Schoenhof.

Portraits Litteraires: Texte etabli et presente. Anatole France, pseud. (Exeter French Texts Ser.: Vol. 32). (FRE.). 135p. Date not set. pap. text 19.95 (*0-85989-034-1*, Pub. by Univ Exeter Pr) Northwestern U Pr.

***Portraits Lost in Space.** George Condo. (Illus.). 96p. 1999. pap. write for info. (*1-878283-91-X*) PaceWildenstein.

Portraits of Adam in Early Judaism: From Sirach to 2 Baruch. John R. Levinson. (Journal for the Study of the Pseudepigrapha Supplement Ser.: No. 1). 254p. 1988. 75.00 (*1-85075-062-9*, Pub. by Sheffield Acad) CUP Services.

Portraits of Adjustment. Heesacker & Washington Post Writers Staff. LC 94-173813. 352p. 1994. pap. text 27.00 (*0-205-15808-0*) Allyn.

Portraits of African American Achievers. Doris H. Metcalf. 144p. teacher ed. 13.99 (*0-86653-815-1*, GA1507) Good Apple.

Portraits of Alaska's Wildlife. Tom Walker. LC 97-73083. 1998. pap. text 12.95 (*1-55868-364-X*) Gr Arts Ctr Pub.

***Portraits of Alice.** Stephanie Bolster & Carroll, Lewis Society of Canada Staff. (Illus.). 1998. pap. 8.00 (*1-55246-039-8*) Battered Silicon.

Portraits of American Cape Cod. Berman. (Illus.). 1998. 15.99 (*0-89009-881-6*) Bk Sales Inc.

***Portraits of American Continental Philosophers.** James R. Watson. LC 99-35079. 1999. pap. text 24.95 (*0-253-21337-1*) Ind U Pr.

Portraits of American Presidents - The Eisenhower Presidency: Eleven Intimate Perspectives of Dwight D. Eisenhower, Vol. 3. Ed. by Kenneth W. Thompson. LC 84-7368. 268p. (Orig.). 1984. pap. text 24.00 (*0-8191-3986-6*, Pub. by White Miller Center); lib. bdg. 52.00 (*0-8191-3985-8*, Pub. by White Miller Center) U Pr of Amer.

Portraits of American Women. Gamaliel Bradford. (Illus.). 276p. 1977. 19.95 (*0-8369-0004-9*) Ayer.

Portraits of American Women. Gamaliel Bradford. (BCL1 - U. S. History Ser.). 276p. 1991. reprint ed. lib. bdg. 79.00 (*0-7812-6030-2*) Rprt Serv.

Portraits of American Women: From Settlement to the Present. G. J. Barker-Benfield & Catherine Clinton. (Illus.). 624p. 1998. reprint ed. pap. 18.95 (*0-19-512048-5*) OUP.

Portraits of Anarchists. Casey Orr. (Illus.). (Orig.). 1997. pap. 24.95 incl. audio compact disk (*1-873176-37-6*) AK Pr Dist.

Portraits of Artists. Vivian Valvano Lynch. LC 99-19545. 296p. 1999. 52.00 (*1-57309-364-5*) Intl Scholars.

Portraits of Asian-Pacific Americans. Kim S. Steidl. 96p. (J). (gr. 4-8). 1991. 11.99 (*0-86653-598-5*, GA1323) Good Apple.

Portraits of Baha'i Women. O. Z. Whitehead. (Illus.). 368p. 1996. pap. 16.95 (*0-85398-403-4*) G Ronald Pub.

Portraits of Basques in the New World. Ed. by Richard W. Etulain & Jeronima Echeverria. LC 99-18318. (Illus.). 328p. 1999. 31.95 (*0-87417-332-9*) U of Nev Pr.

Portraits of Bible Men. George Matheson. LC 96-16868. (Bible Portrait Ser.: Vol. 1). 144p. 1996. pap. 9.99 (*0-8254-3292-8*) Kregel.

Portraits of Bible Men. George Matheson. LC 96-16868. (Bible Portrait Ser.: Vol. 2). 144p. 1996. pap. 9.99 (*0-8254-3293-6*) Kregel.

Portraits of Bible Men. George Matheson. LC 96-16868. (Bible Portrait Ser.: Vol. 3). 144p. 1996. pap. 9.99 (*0-8254-3294-4*) Kregel.

Portraits of Bible Men. George Matheson. LC 96-16868. (Bible Portrait Ser.: Vol. 4). 144p. 1996. pap. 9.99 (*0-8254-3295-2*) Kregel.

Portraits of Bible Women. George Matheson. LC 86-7429. 144p. 1993. reprint ed. pap. 9.99 (*0-8254-3250-2*) Kregel.

Portraits of Black Pride. Phyllis S. Jackson & Walter L. Brown. Ed. by Yvonne Fennick. LC 97-70163. (Illus.). 98p. (Orig.). 1997. pap. 12.95 (*0-9656473-3-1*) Brown Bear Pub.

Portraits of Canadian Women. Barbara Woodley. 152p. 1992. pap. 65.00 (*0-385-25309-5*) Doubleday.

Portraits of Celebrated Men. C. A. Sainte-Beuve. 1972. 59.95 (*0-8490-0882-4*) Gordon Pr.

Portraits of Celebrated Women. C. A. Sainte-Beuve. 1972. 59.95 (*0-8490-0883-2*) Gordon Pr.

Portraits of Charles V of France, 1338-1380. Claire R. Sherman. LC 69-18286. (College Art Association Monographs: Vol. 37). (Illus.). 168p. 1985. reprint ed. 35.00 (*0-271-00407-X*) Pa St U Pr.

Portraits of Chinese Women in Revolution. Agnes Smedley. Ed. by Jan MacKinnon & Steve MacKinnon. LC 76-18896. (Illus.). 208p. 1976. 35.00 (*1-55861-075-8*) Feminist Pr.

Portraits of Chinese Women in Revolution. Agnes Smedley. Ed. by Jan MacKinnon & Steve MacKinnon. LC 76-18896. (Illus.). 208p. 1976. reprint ed. pap. 14.95 (*0-912670-44-4*) Feminist Pr.

Portraits of Choreographers. Peggy J. Kaplan. (ENG & FRE., Illus.). 76p. 1988. 20.00 (*0-318-37950-3*) Feldman Fine Arts.

Portraits of Christ in Genesis. M. R. DeHaan. (M. R. De Haan Classic Library). 192p. 1995. pap. 10.99 (*0-8254-2476-3*) Kregel.

Portraits of Cities. Dong Kingman. LC 97-60668. (Illus.). vi, 133p. 1997. 39.95 (*0-9658333-5-6*) Twnty-Sec Cent Film.

Portraits of Civilization Pt. II: The Making of One World. Robert Garfield. 336p. (C). 1996. pap. text, per. 45.95 (*0-7872-2585-1*) Kendall-Hunt.

Portraits of Clay: Potters of Mata Ortiz. Smith. LC 97-51233. (Illus.). 64p. 1998. pap. 10.95 (*0-8165-1891-2*) U of Ariz Pr.

Portraits of Coleridge. Morton D. Paley. LC 98-49200. (Illus.). 190p. 1999. text 55.00 (*0-19-818469-7*) OUP.

Portraits of Community: African American Photography in Texas. Alan Govenar. (Illus.). 376p. 1996. 49.95 (*0-87611-153-3*) Tex St Hist Assn.

Portraits of Conflict: A Photographic History of Arkansas in the Civil War. Bobby Roberts & Carl H. Moneyhon. LC 87-5869. (Illus.). 256p. 1987. pap. 34.00 (*0-938626-84-1*) U of Ark Pr.

Portraits of Conflict: A Photographic History of Georgia in the Civil War. Anne J. Bailey & Walter J. Fraser, Jr. LC 96-21515. 1997. 75.00 (*1-55728-421-0*) U of Ark Pr.

Portraits of Conflict: A Photographic History of Louisiana in the Civil War. Bobby Roberts & Carl H. Moneyhon. (Illus.). 370p. 1990. 75.00 (*1-55728-158-0*); pap. 34.00 (*1-55728-159-9*) U of Ark Pr.

Portraits of Conflict: A Photographic History of Mississippi in the Civil War. Bobby Roberts & Carl H. Moneyhon. LC 92-21637. (Illus.). 424p. (C). 1993. 75.00 (*1-55728-260-9*) U of Ark Pr.

Portraits of Conflict: A Photographic History of North Carolina in the Civil War. Richard B. McCaslin. LC 97-1757. 1997. 75.00 (*1-55728-454-7*) U of Ark Pr.

Portraits of Conflict: A Photographic History of Texas in the Civil War. Carl Moneyhon & Bobby Roberts. LC 98-8827. (Illus.). 344p. 1998. 75.00 (*1-55728-533-0*) U of Ark Pr.

Portraits of Conflict Vol. 4: A Photographic History of South Carolina in the Civil War. Richard B. McCaslin. LC 94-5238. (Illus.). 416p. 1995. 75.00 (*1-55728-363-X*) U of Ark Pr.

Portraits of Contemporary African Americans. Doris H. Metcalf. 144p. teacher ed. 13.99 (*0-86653-723-6*, GA1442) Good Apple.

Portraits of Culture South & Mid America, Vol. 2. (Just in Time Ser.). (C). 1996. pap. write for info. (*0-536-59877-0*) Pearson Custom.

Portraits of Darkness. Stephen Doughty. (Orig.). 1989. pap. 2.50 (*1-55673-104-3*, 9815) CSS OH.

Portraits of Discovery: Profiles in Scientific Genius. George Greenstein. LC 97-6048. (Illus.). 240p. 1997. 24.95 (*0-471-19138-8*) Wiley.

Portraits of Dutch Painters & Other Artists of the Low Countries: Specime of an Iconography, Reportorium. H. Van Hall. 432p. 1963. pap. 132.25 (*90-265-0027-0*) Swets.

Portraits of Excellence: A Heritage of Athletic Achievement at the University of Kansas. Lyle Niedens & Steve Buckner. (Illus.). 256p. 1998. 39.50 (*1-885758-14-6*) Quality Sports.

Portraits of Exceptional African American Scientists. Doris H. Metcalf. (Illus.). 144p. (J). (gr. 4-8). 1994. 13.99 (*0-86653-800-3*, GA1492) Good Apple.

Portraits of Excess: Reading Character in the Modern in the Modern Spanish Novel. Juli Highfill. LC 98-61090. 184p. 1999. pap. 25.00 (*0-89295-093-5*) Society Sp & Sp-Am.

Portraits of Extraordinary Women. William F. Maestri. LC 96-53060. (Illus.). 120p. 1997. 19.95 (*1-56554-242-8*) Pelican.

***Portraits of Faithful Saints.** Herman Hanko. (Illus.). 450p. 1999. 32.95 (*0-916206-60-2*) Refrd Free Pub Assn.

Portraits of Famous American Women: An Analysis of Various Artists' Renderings of 13 Admired Figures. Robert Henkes. LC 97-21514. (Illus.). 180p. 1997. lib. bdg. 38.50 (*0-7864-0326-8*) McFarland & Co.

Portraits of Flowers. Patrick Lima. LC 95-181015. (Illus.). 160p. 1995. pap. write for info. (*0-88984-157-8*) Porcup Quill.

Portraits of Friends & Acquaintances. Marc Hauser. (Illus.). 96p. 1989. pap. 14.95 (*0-943981-01-8*); spiral bd. 25.00 (*0-318-23155-7*) Man Mtn Pub.

Portraits of Garden Bedfellows: The Gardeners Guide to Plants that Go - & Grow - Well Together. Elise Laurenzi & Gerald B. Levinson. LC 86-92069. (Illus.). 24p. 1987. pap. 5.95 (*0-9617942-0-8*) Corydalis Pr.

***Portraits of Grace: Stories of Salvation from Wesleyan World Missions.** Ed. by John Connor & Margie Connor. 255p. 1999. pap. text 9.95 (*0-89827-201-7*) Wesleyan Pub Hse.

Portraits of Guilt: The Woman Who Profiles the Faces of America's Deadliest Criminals. Jeanne Boylan. (Illus.). 336p. 2000. 24.95 (*0-671-03485-5*, PB Hardcover) PB.

Portraits of Historic St. Croix Before & after Hurricane Hugo. Dorene E. Carter. (Illus.). 88p. 1991. 39.95 (*0-9628507-0-5*) D E Carter.

Portraits of Homoeopathic Medicines Vol. 1: Psychophysical Analyses of Selected Constitutional Types. Catherine R. Coulter. LC 97-30347. 422p. 1997. 33.00 (*1-57626-089-5*) Quality Med Pub.

Portraits of Homoeopathic Medicines Vol. 2: Psychophysical Analyses of Selected Constitutional Types. Catherine R. Coulter. LC 97-30347. 300p. 1997. 33.00 (*1-57626-090-9*) Quality Med Pub.

Portraits of Hope: Conquering Breast Cancer, Vol. 2. Marcia S. Sherill. LC 98-229724. Vol. 2. (Illus.). 112p. 1998. 24.95 (*1-55670-855-6*) Stewart Tabori & Chang.

Portraits of Ideas. Guy A. D'Amato. (Illus.). 220p. 1977. 22.95 (*0-8369-8014-X*) Ayer.

***Portraits of Indian Trees: Arundhati Vartak.** J. J. White & L. B. Bruno. (Illus.). 44p. 1999. pap. 10.00 (*0-913196-66-5*) Hunt Inst Botanical.

Portraits of Japan. Adrian Waller. 258p. (Orig.). 1993. pap. 12.95 (*4-89684-230-8*, Pub. by Yohan Pubns) Weatherhill.

Portraits of Jesus: An Inductive Approach to the Gospels. Michael R. Cosby. LC 99-32672. 224p. 1999. pap. 22.95 (*0-664-25827-1*) Westminster John Knox.

Portraits of Jesus Through the Ages. George Drew. 1990. pap. 7.95 (*0-940754-94-0*) Ed Ministries.

Portraits of John Marshall. Andrew Oliver. LC 76-13648. (Illus.). 233p. reprint ed. pap. 72.30 (*0-7837-4355-6*, 204406500012) Bks Demand.

Portraits of John Quincy Adams & His Wife. Andrew Oliver. LC 70-128349. (Adams Papers: No. 4, Adams Family Portraits). (Illus.). 335p. 1970. 46.50 (*0-674-69152-0*) HUP.

***Portraits of Karen.** Karen Savage. (Squares Ser.: Vol. 3). (Illus.). 20p. 1999. pap. 15.00 (*1-888636-13-0*) Sara Ranchouse.

P

An Asterisk (*) at the beginning of an entry indicates that the title is appearing for the first time.

Portraits of Learning - K-8: America's Choice. (Illus.). 1998. 12.00 (*1-889630-73-X*) Natl Ctr & Econ.

Portraits of Life. Ed. by Rick Schaub. 1996. 69.95 (*1-57553-154-2*) Watermrk Pr.

Portraits of Little Women: Amy's Story. Susan Beth Pfeffer & Louisa May Alcott. LC 97-6137. 112p. (J). (gr. 3-7). 1997. 9.95 (*0-385-32529-0*) Delacorte.

Portraits of Little Women: Jo's Story. Susan Beth Pfeffer & Louisa May Alcott. LC 97-6142. (Portraits of Little Women Ser.). 112p. (J). (gr. 3-5). 1997. 9.95 (*0-385-32523-1*, Delacorte Pr Bks) BDD Bks Young Read.

Portraits of Little Women: Meg Makes a Friend. Susan Beth Pfeffer & Louisa May Alcott. LC 97-27855. (Portraits of Little Women Ser.). (Illus.). 112p. (J). 1998. 9.95 (*0-385-32580-0*) Delacorte.

Portraits of Little Women: Meg's Story. Susan Beth Pfeffer & Louisa May Alcott. LC 97-6141. 112p. (J). (gr. 3-7). 1997. 9.95 (*0-385-32520-7*) Delacorte.

Portraits of Livia: Imaging the Imperial Woman in Augustan Rome. Elizabeth Bartman. LC 97-46126. (Texts in the History of Philosophy Ser.). (Illus.). 288p. (C). 1998. text 95.00 (*0-521-58394-2*) Cambridge U Pr.

Portraits of Love. Scott B. Callahan. Ed. by Wayne D. Hogue. (Illus.). 81p. (Orig.). 1996. pap. 9.95 (*0-9651766-5-7*) Star-Lit Pub.

***Portraits of Madame de Pompadour; Celebrating the Femme Savante, Vol.7.** Elise Goodman. LC 99-41133. (Discovery Ser: Vol. 7). 200p. 2000. 45.00 (*0-520-21794-2*, Pub. by U CA Pr) Cal Prin Full Svc.

Portraits of Marriage in Literature. Ed. by Anne C. Hargrove & Maurine Magliocco. (Essays in Literature Bks.). 189p. 1984. pap. 8.00 (*0-934312-05-2*) WIU Essays Lit.

Portraits of Medieval & Renaissance Living: Essays in Memory of David Herlihy. Samuel K. Cohn, Jr. & Stephen A. Epstein. LC 96-5360. (Illus.). 480p. (C). 1996. text 64.00 (*0-472-10671-6*, 10671) U of Mich Pr.

Portraits of Men. Charles-Augustin Sainte-Beuve. Tr. by Forsyth Edereain. LC 72-4650. (Essay Index Reprint Ser.). 1977. reprint ed. 19.95 (*0-8369-2972-1*) Ayer.

Portraits of Mexican Americans. Nancy Marquez & Theresa Perez. 96p. (J). (gr. 4-8). 1991. 11.99 (*0-86653-605-1*, GA1324) Good Apple.

Portraits of Mount St. Helens: An Awesome Beauty. (Illus.). 32p. (Orig.). 1980. pap. 2.50 (*1-878395-00-9*) Smith-Western.

Portraits of Nathaniel Hawthorne: An Iconography. Rita K. Gollin. LC 83-12155. 122p. 1984. 35.00 (*0-87580-087-4*) N Ill U Pr.

Portraits of Native American Indians. Mary A. Mateo. (Illus.). 96p. (J). (gr. 4-7). 1992. 11.99 (*0-86653-669-8*, GA1322) Good Apple.

Portraits of Native Americans: Photographs from the 1904 Louisiana Purchase Exposition. Charles H. Carpenter. (Illus.). 48p. 1994. pap. 9.95 (*1-56584-160-3*, Pub. by New Press NY) Norton.

Portraits of Outstanding African American Women. Doris H. Metcalf. 96p. 1996. teacher ed. 10.99 (*1-56417-717-3*, GA1548) Good Apple.

Portraits of Outstanding Explorers. Doris H. Metcalf. 96p. 1996. teacher ed. 11.99 (*1-56417-845-5*, GA1552) Good Apple.

Portraits of Passion: Aging Defying the Myth. Marshall B. Stearn. Ed. by Terence Horne. (Illus.). 224p. (Orig.). 1991. pap. 10.95 (*0-9610480-4-2*) Park West.

Portraits of Paul: An Archaeology of Ancient Personality. Bruce J. Malina & Jerome H. Neyrey. LC 96-18497. 272p. (Orig.). 1996. pap. 29.95 (*0-664-25681-3*) Westminster John Knox.

Portraits of Perseverance. Henry Gariepy. 180p. 1991. pap. 9.99 (*0-89693-149-8*, 6-1149, Victor Bks) Chariot Victor.

Portraits of Pioneers in Psychology. Ed. by Gregory A. Kimble et al. LC 91-7226. (Illus.). 384p. 1991. 79.95 (*0-8058-0620-2*); pap. 29.95 (*0-8058-1136-2*) L Erlbaum Assocs.

Portraits of Pioneers in Psychology, Vol. II. Ed. by Gregory A. Kimble et al. LC 91-7226. (Illus.). 351p. (C). 1996. text 79.95 (*1-55798-344-5*, 431-7630); pap. text 29.95 (*1-55798-345-3*, 431-7631) Am Psychol.

Portraits of Pioneers in Psychology, Vol. 2. Ed. by Gregory A. Kimble et al. 300p. 1996. text 79.95 (*0-8058-2197-X*) L Erlbaum Assocs.

Portraits of Pioneers in Psychology, Vol. 2. Ed. by Gregory A. Kimble et al. 300p. 1996. pap. text 29.95 (*0-8058-2198-8*) L Erlbaum Assocs.

Portraits of Pioneers in Psychology, Vol. III. Ed. by Gregory A. Kimble et al. 363p. 1998. pap. 29.95 (*1-55798-479-4*) Am Psychol.

Portraits of Pioneers in Psychology, Vol. III. Ed. by Gregory A. Kimble & Michael Wertheimer. 360p. 1998. pap. 29.95 (*0-8058-2620-3*) L Erlbaum Assocs.

Portraits of Pioneers in Psychology, Vol. III. Ed. by Gregory A. Kimble & Michael Wertheimer. 370p. 1998. write for info. (*0-8058-2619-X*) L Erlbaum Assocs.

Portraits of Places see Works of Henry James Jr.: Collected Works

Portraits of Places. Henry James. LC 72-3300. (Essay Index Reprint Ser.). 1977. reprint ed. 22.95 (*0-8369-2910-1*) Ayer.

Portraits of Power. Norman D. Greenwald. LC 73-101828. (Biography Index Reprint Ser.). 1977. 20.95 (*0-8369-8001-8*) Ayer.

Portraits of Praise. Contrib. by Roger House. 1985. 8.99 (*0-8341-9718-9*, MB-547) Lillenas.

Portraits of Pride: The Mountaintop Remembers. Richard Winter. LC 95-35498. (Illus.). 208p. 1995. pap. 19.95 (*1-883789-06-0*) Blk Dome Pr.

***Portraits of "Primitives" Ordering Human Kinds in the Chinese Nation.** Susan D. Blum. 256p. 2000. 69.00 (*0-7425-0091-8*); pap. 24.95 (*0-7425-0092-6*) Rowman.

Portraits of Productive Schools: An Intermediate Study of Institutionalizing Activity-Based Practices in Elementary Science. Uwe Hameyer et al. LC 94-31526. (SUNY Series in Science Education). 177p. (C). 1995. text 44.50 (*0-7914-2499-5*); pap. text 14.95 (*0-7914-2500-2*) State U NY Pr.

Portraits of Recovery: Sixty Stories of Hope & Faith. Adam Gaynor. 96p. 1999. text 29.95 (*0-670-86964-3*) Viking Penguin.

Portraits of Russian Personalities Between Reform & Revolution. Richard Hare. LC 75-3735. 360p. 1975. reprint ed. lib. bdg. 75.00 (*0-8371-8063-5*, HAPR, Greenwood Pr) Greenwood.

Portraits of Sarajevo. Zlatko Dizdarevic. Tr. by Midhat Ridjanovic. LC 94-43620. 164p. 1995. 19.95 (*0-88064-167-3*) Fromm Intl Pub.

Portraits of Schooling: A Survey & an Analysis of Supplementary Schooling in Congregations. Samuel K. Joseph. LC 97-3359. (Illus.). 96p. (Orig.). 1997. pap. 8.00 (*0-8074-0636-8*, 243876) UAHC.

***Portraits of Spiritual Authority: Religious Power in Early Christianity, Byzantium & the Christian Orient.** Ed. by Jan Willem Drijvers. LC 99-45650. 137. 240p. 1999. text 130.00 (*90-04-11459-9*) Brill Academic Pubs.

Portraits of Spirituality in Recovery: The Use of Art in Recovery from Co-Dependency and-or Chemical Dependency. Nancy Barrett Chickerneo. LC 92-42194. (Illus.). 254p. 1993. text 54.95 (*0-398-05845-8*) C C Thomas.

Portraits of Spirituality in Recovery: The Use of Art in Recovery from Co-Dependency and/or Chemical Dependency. Nancy Barrett Chickerneo. LC 92-42194. (Illus.). 254p. 1993. pap. 37.95 (*0-398-06056-8*) C C Thomas.

Portraits of Success: Leaders Share Principles for Winning in the Nineties. Hal Donaldson & Kenneth M. Dobsen. 352p. 1994. pap. text 11.95 (*1-880689-03-0*) Onward Bks.

***Portraits of Successful Entrepreneurs & High-Flyers: A Psychological Perspective.** Syrine K. Lam. 270p. 1999. text 69.95 (*1-84014-791-1*, Pub. by Inst Materials) Ashgate Pub Co.

Portraits of Temperament. David West Keirsey. 124p. 1987. pap. 9.95 (*0-9606954-1-9*) Prometheus Nemesis.

Portraits of the Artist: Psychoanalysis of Creativity & Its Vicissitudes. John E. Gedo. 336p. 1989. pap. 24.95 (*0-88163-097-7*) Analytic Pr.

Portraits of the Artist in Contemporary Fiction. Lee T. Lemon. LC 84-22005. 281p. 1985. reprint ed. pap. 87.20 (*0-608-02382-5*, 206302400004) Bks Demand.

Portraits of the Bride. Ralph V. Reynolds. 142p. (Orig.). (C). 1985. pap. 5.95 (*0-685-27254-0*) Alpha Bible Pubns.

***Portraits of the Civil War: The Men & Women in Blue & Gray.** Leo Marriott. (Illus.). 128p. 1999. 14.98 (*0-7651-1691-X*) Smithmark.

Portraits of the Eighties. Horatio G. Hutchinson. LC 72-105020. (Essay Index Reprint Ser.). 1977. 29.95 (*0-8369-1441-4*) Ayer.

Portraits of The Game: Classic Photographs from The Turofsky Collection at The Hockey Hall of Fame. Andrew Podnieks. LC 98-127393. (Illus.). 176p. 1997. 50.00 (*0-385-25644-2*) Doubleday.

***Portraits of the Game: Classic Photographs from the Turofsky Collection at the Hockey Hall of Fame.** Andrew Podnieks. (Illus.). 176p. 1999. pap. 17.95 (*0-385-25801-1*) Doubleday.

Portraits of the Great 18th Century Revival. Paxton Hood. 224p. 1997. pap. 12.99 (*1-84030-009-4*) Emerald House Group Inc.

Portraits of the Greeks. Gisela Richter. Ed. by R. R. Smith. LC 83-73222. (Illus.). 272p. 1984. text 52.50 (*0-8014-1683-3*) Cornell U Pr.

Portraits of the Japanese Workplace: Labor Movements, Workers & Managers. Mark Selden. Ed. by Makoto Kumazawa. LC 96-15010. (Social Change in Global Perspective Ser.). 288p. 1996. text 75.00 (*0-8133-1709-6*, Pub. by Westview) HarpC.

***Portraits of the Nation: Stamps, Coins & Banknotes in Belgium & Switzerland, 1880-1945.** Alexis Schwarzenbach. LC 99-36362. (European University Studies: Series 3). (Illus.). 395p. (C). 1999. pap. text 60.95 (*0-8204-4614-9*) P Lang Pubng.

Portraits of the New Century. Edward R. Thompson. LC 74-117853. (Essay Index Reprint Ser.). 1977. 21.95 (*0-8369-1685-9*) Ayer.

Portraits of the Nineties. Edward R. Thompson. LC 78-117854. (Essay Index Reprint Ser.). 1977. 22.95 (*0-8369-1686-7*) Ayer.

Portraits of the Pecos Frontier. Patrick Dearen. LC 92-29829. 1993. pap. 14.95 (*0-89672-288-0*) Tex Tech Univ Pr.

***Portraits of the Pecos Frontier.** rev. ed. Patrick Dearen. LC 99-37212. 1999. pap. 19.95 (*0-89672-422-0*) Tex Tech Univ Pr.

***Portraits of the Presidents: The National Portrait Gallery.** Frederick S. Voss. (Illus.). 136p. 2000. 35.00 (*0-8478-2298-2*) Rizzoli Intl.

Portraits of the Seventeenth Century, Historic & Literary, 2 vols. C. A. Sainte-Beuve. 1972. lib. bdg. 200.00 (*0-8490-0884-0*) Gordon Pr.

Portraits of the Seventies. George W. Russell. LC 73-117834. (Essay Index Reprint Ser.). 1977. 24.95 (*0-8369-1717-0*) Ayer.

Portraits of the Sixties. Justin McCarthy. LC 79-142661. (Essay Index Reprint Ser.). 1977. reprint ed. 25.95 (*0-8369-2061-9*) Ayer.

Portraits of the South West: Aborigines, Women & the Environment. Brian K. De Garis. (Orig.). pap. 29.95 (*1-875560-12-2*, Pub. by Univ of West Aust Pr) Intl Spec Bk.

Portraits of the Spirit-Filled Personality: Guidelines for Holy Living from Philippians. Albert B. Simpson. LC 95-83830. 114p. 1996. pap. 8.99 (*0-87509-655-7*) Chr Pubns.

Portraits of the Whiteman. Keith H. Basso. LC 78-31535. 144p. 1979. pap. text 16.95 (*0-521-29593-9*) Cambridge U Pr.

Portraits of Tropical Birds see Retratos de Aves Tropicales

Portraits of Tropical Birds. John S. Dunning. LC 85-24552. (Illus.). 174p. 1985. reprint ed. 30.00 (*0-915180-27-8*) Harrowood Bks.

***Portraits of Type: An MBTI Research Compendium.** Arvil Thorne & Harrison Gough. 158p. 1999. pap. 14.99 (*0-935652-51-5*) Ctr Applications Psych.

Portraits of Unique Homes, Vol. 1. Shelley Nohowel. Ed. by Richard A. Goodwin. (Illus.). 224p. 1992. 90.00 (*1-56333-000-8*) Masquerade.

Portraits of Unique Homes Vol. 2: A Luxury Perspective. Shelley Nohowel. Ed. by Richard A. Goodwin. (Illus.). 208p. 1993. 90.00 (*1-56333-998-6*) Masquerade.

Portraits of Viruses: A History of Virology. Ed. by Frank Fenner & Adrian J. Gibbs. (Illus.). viii, 344p. 1988. 128.00 (*3-8055-4819-2*) S Karger.

Portraits of War: Civil War Photographers & Their Work. George A. Sullivan. LC 97-49005. 80p. (J). (gr. 5-8). 1998. lib. bdg. 24.40 (*0-7613-3019-4*, Copper Beech Bks) Millbrook Pr.

Portraits of White Racism. 2nd ed. David T. Wellman. LC 93-9812. 286p. (C). 1993. text 57.95 (*0-521-45183-3*); pap. text 16.95 (*0-521-45810-2*) Cambridge U Pr.

Portraits of Whole Language Classrooms: Learning for All Ages. Ed. by Heidi Mills & Jean A. Clyde. LC 89-35937. (Illus.). 307p. (Orig.). (C). (ps). 1990. pap. text 25.00 (*0-435-08510-7*, 08510) Heinemann.

Portraits of Wilderness: A Vision of Preservation. Bruce W. Heinemann et al. (Illus.). 64p. 1995. 14.95 (*0-945475-07-1*, Pub. by Mandala Pub Grp) Words Distrib.

Portraits of Wittgenstein, 4 Vol. Ludwig Josef Johann Wittgenstein. 1480p. 1999. 600.00 (*1-85506-601-7*) Thoemmes Pr.

Portraits of Women. Gamaliel Bradford. LC 75-90611. (Essay Index Reprint Ser.). 1977. 20.95 (*0-8369-1247-0*) Ayer.

Portraits of Women. Julie Fay. Ed. by Orvis C. Burmaster. LC 90-83249. (Ahsahta Press Modern & Contemporary Poets of the West Ser.). 70p. (Orig.). 1991. pap. 6.95 (*0-916272-47-8*) Ahsahta Pr.

Portraits of Women. Gamaliel Bradford. LC 75-90611. (Essay Index Reprint Ser.). (Illus.). 202p. reprint ed. lib. bdg. 20.00 (*0-8290-0469-6*) Irvington.

Portraits of Women: Gwen John & Her Forgotten Contemporaries. Alison Thomas. (Illus.). 272p. 1996. pap. 36.95 (*0-7456-1828-6*) Blackwell Pubs.

Portraits on the Wind: Robert Gonzales - A Retrospective Exhibition. 24p. 1990. 12.50 (*0-614-24041-7*) Mexican Museum.

Portraits Period. Ed. by Bennington Slaughter Associates Staff. (Illus.). 88p. 1990. per. write for info. (*0-9627710-0-7*) Prtrt Brkrs of Amer.

Portraits, Political & Personal. Leon Trotsky. Ed. by George Breitman & George Saunders. LC 77-50342. (Illus.). 237p. 1977. pap. 19.95 (*0-87348-504-1*); lib. bdg. 50.00 (*0-87348-503-3*) Pathfinder NY.

Portraits Souvenir, 1900-1914. Jean Cocteau. (FRE., Illus.). 216p. 1977. 16.95 (*0-8288-9132-X*, M96700) Fr & Eur.

Portraits, Tableaux, Dessins. Romaine Brooks. LC 75-12306. (Homosexuality Ser.). (Illus.). 1980. reprint ed. 13.95 (*0-405-07396-8*) Ayer.

Portraits to the Wall: Historic Lesbian Lives Unveiled. Rose Collis. (Women on Women Ser.). 224p. 1994. 69.95 (*0-304-32853-7*, Pub. by Cassell); pap. 19.95 (*0-304-32851-0*, Pub. by Cassell) LPC InBook.

Portraits U. S. A. Kelly Wise. (Illus.). 138p. (Orig.). 1989. pap. write for info. (*0-318-65394-X*) Heather Hse Pub.

Portraits U. S. A., 1776-1976. Harold E. Dickson. (Illus.). 133p. 1976. pap. 10.00 (*0-911209-07-7*) Palmer Mus Art.

Portraits with Backgrounds. Catherine Barjansky. (American Autobiography Ser.). 223p. 1995. reprint ed. lib. bdg. 79.00 (*0-7812-8450-3*) Rprt Serv.

Portraiture. Richard Brilliant. (Essays in Art & Culture Ser.). (Illus.). 192p. (C). 1992. 41.50 (*0-674-69175-X*) HUP.

Portraiture. Richard Brilliant. (Essays in Art & Culture Ser.). (Illus.). 192p. (C). 1993. pap. 22.95 (*0-674-69176-8*) HUP.

Portraiture: The Visual Construction of Identity. Joanna Woodall. LC 96-16844. (Critical Introductions to Art Ser.). (Illus.). 336p. 1997. text 29.95 (*0-7190-4614-9*, Pub. by Manchester Univ Pr) St Martin.

Portraiture: The Visual Construction of Identity. Ed. by Joanna Woodall. LC 96-16844. (Critical Introductions to Art Ser.). (Illus.). 336p. 1997. text 74.95 (*0-7190-4612-2*, Pub. by Manchester Univ Pr) St Martin.

Portraiture of Domestic Slavery in the United States. Jesse Torrey. LC 70-92446. (Illus.). 1970. reprint ed. 29.00 (*0-403-00184-6*) Scholarly.

Portraiture of Shakerism. Mary Marshall. LC 70-134420. reprint ed. 52.00 (*0-404-08461-3*) AMS Pr.

Portrat Meiner Selbst: Karl Krolow's Autobiographical Poems (1945-1958) & Their French Sources. Vera B. Profit. LC 90-22033. (American University Studies: Germanic Languages & Literature: Ser. I, Vol. 74). 214p. (C). 1991. text 37.95 (*0-8204-0851-4*) P Lang Pubng.

Portrayal of Community in Rabelais's "Quart Livre" Margaret B. Harp. LC 93-45753. (Contemporary Critical Concepts & Pre-Enlightenment Literature Ser.: No. 2). 130p. (C). 1997. text 36.95 (*0-8204-2363-7*) P Lang Pubng.

Portrayal of Life Stages in English Literature, 1500-1800: Infancy, Youth, Marriage, Aging, Death, Martyrdom: Essays in Memory of Warren W. Wooden. Ed. by Jeanie Watson & Phillip M. Pittman. LC 87-31521. (Studies in British History Ser.). (Illus.). 274p. 1989. 99.95 (*0-88946-462-6*) E Mellen.

Portrayal of Love: Botticelli's Primavera & Humanist Culture at the Time of Lorenzo the Magnificent. Charles Dempsey. 187p. 1992. pap. text 29.95 (*0-691-01573-2*, Pub. by Princeton U Pr) Cal Prin Full Svc.

Portrayal of Old Age in Twentieth Century Canadian Novels. Irina Sobkowska-Ashcroft & Lorna Berman. LC 91-2148. (Canadian Studies: Vol. 13). 328p. 1991. lib. bdg. 99.95 (*0-7734-9780-3*) E Mellen.

***Portrayal of Southeast Asian Refugees in Recent American Children's Books.** Michael M. Levy. LC 00-31041. (Studies in American Literature: Vol. 35). (Illus.). 116p. 2000. 59.95 (*0-7734-7753-5*) E Mellen.

Portrayals of Revolution: Images, Debates, & Patterns of Thought on the French Revolution. Noel Parker. LC 89-26365. (Illus.). 256p. (C). 1990. 31.95 (*0-8093-1684-6*) S Ill U Pr.

Portraying Analogy. James F. Ross. LC 81-15463. (Cambridge Studies in Philosophy). (Illus.). 255p. 1982. text 80.00 (*0-521-23805-6*) Cambridge U Pr.

Portraying Older People in Advertising: Magazine, Television, & Newspapers. Thomas E. Robinson, 2nd. (Garland Studies on the Elderly in America). 106p. 1998. 33.00 (*0-8153-3215-7*) Garland.

Portraying Persons with Disabilities: An Annotated Bibliography of Fiction for Children & Teenagers. Debra Robertson. (Serving Special Needs Ser.). 482p. 1992. 39.95 (*0-8352-3023-6*) Bowker.

Portraying Persons with Disabilities: An Annotated Bibliography of Nonfiction for Children & Teenagers. Joan B. Friedberg et al. (Serving Special Needs Ser.). 385p. 1992. 39.95 (*0-8352-3022-8*) Bowker.

Portraying the President: The White House & the News Media. Michael B. Grossman & Martha J. Kumar. LC 80-24634. 368p. reprint ed. pap. 114.10 (*0-608-17449-1*, 202991400066) Bks Demand.

Portraying the Self: Sean O'Casey & the Art of Autobiography. Michael Kenneally. (Irish Literary Studies: No. 26). 400p. 1987. 67.50 (*0-389-20714-4*, N8272) B&N Imports.

Ports & Their Hinterlands in India, 1700-1950. Indu Banga. (C). text 32.00 (*81-85425-86-8*, Pub. by Manohar) S Asia.

Ports As Nodal Points in a Global Transport System. Antony J. Dolman & Jan van Ettinger. 492p. 1992. 132.00 (*0-08-040994-6*, Pergamon Pr) Elsevier.

Ports Designated in Application of the International Health Regulations: Situation As on 1 April 1992. (ENG & FRE.). 40p. 1992. pap. text 10.00 (*92-4-058013-1*, 0150387) World Health.

Ports in the West. Ed. by Benjamin F. Gilbert & K. Jack Bauer. (Illus.). 100p. (Orig.). 1982. pap. text 15.00 (*0-89745-022-1*) Sunflower U Pr.

Ports, Inland Waterways & Civil Aviation. R. E. Baxter & C. Phillips. Ed. by W. F. Maunder. 1979. 143.00 (*0-08-022460-1*, Pub. by Pergamon Repr) Franklin.

Ports into the Next Century. Ed. by C. R. Ford. 276p. 1991. text 76.00 (*0-7277-1619-0*, Pub. by T Telford) RCH.

Ports, 1986. Ed. by Paul H. Sorenson. (Conference Proceedings Ser.). 1062p. 1986. 13.00 (*0-87262-538-9*) Am Soc Civil Eng.

Ports '95: Proceedings: Ports '95 Conference (1995: Tampa, FL), 2 vols., Set. Ed. by Michael A. Knott et al. LC 95-5439. 1510p. 1995. pap. 144.00 (*0-7844-0075-X*) Am Soc Civil Eng.

Ports '98: Proceedings of the Conference, 2 vols. Ed. by Michael A. Kraman et al. LC 98-11139. (Illus.). 1464p. 1998. pap. 159.00 (*0-7844-0329-5*, 40329-5) Am Soc Civil Eng.

Ports of Albany & Ports of the Hudson River: Port Series No. 6. Vol. 6. per. 14.00 (*0-16-061253-5*) USGPO.

Ports of Anchorage, Nikisi, Whittier, Seward, Valdez & Ketchkcan,Alalska. 38. per. 10.50 (*0-16-001760-2*) USGPO.

Ports of Baton Rogue & Lake Charles, Louisiana. Vol. 21. 208p. 1990. per. 13.00 (*0-16-029157-7*) USGPO.

Ports of Buffalo, Rochester, Oswego & Ogdensburg, New York. Vol. 41. 60p. 1990. pap. 7.50 (*0-16-019487-3*) USGPO.

***Ports of Call.** Sally Fairchild. 384p. (Orig.). 1999. mass mkt. 5.99 (*1-55166-505-0*, 1-66505-8, Mira Bks) Harlequin Bks.

Ports of Call. Amin Maalouf. Tr. by Alberto Manguel from FRE. LC 99-490291. 224p. 1999. 24.00 (*1-86046-446-7*, Pub. by Harvill Press) FS&G.

Ports of Call. Jack Vance. LC 97-31360. 1998. text 24.95 (*0-312-85801-9*) St Martin.

Ports of Call. Jack Vance. 304p. 1999. pap. 13.95 (*0-312-86474-4*) St Martin.

***Ports of Call: A Distinguished Companion to the Harbours & Marinas of the British Isles.** Ed. by Chris Perring. (Illus.). 224p. 2000. 24.95 (*1-871349-98-2*, Pub. by Kensington West) Midpt Trade.

Ports of Call: A Study of the American Nautical Novel. Gordon Milne. (Illus.). 132p. (C). 1987. pap. text 17.00 (*0-8191-5674-4*); lib. bdg. 35.50 (*0-8191-5673-6*) U Pr of Amer.

***Ports of Call: A Young Man's Odyssey on the Great Lakes Freighters.** Tad A. Pirmantgen. (Illus.). 176p. 2000. pap. 13.95 (*1-882376-76-5*, Pub. by Thunder Bay Pr) Partners Pubs Grp.

Ports of Call: Poems from Hollywood. Mark Dunster. 16p. 1998. pap. 5.00 (*0-89642-413-8*) Linden Pubs.

Ports of Call: The Caribbean & North America. rev. ed. Ed. by Arnie Weissmann. (Weissmann Travel Reports). ring bd. 329.00 (*0-945305-20-6*) Weissmann Travel.

An Asterisk (*) at the beginning of an entry indicates that the title is appearing for the first time.

Ports of Detroit & Monroe & Ports on the Saginaw River, Michigan: Port Series No. 45. Vol. 45. per. 25.00 (*0-16-061256-X*) USGPO.

Ports of Entry: Ethnic Impressions. Abelle Mason. 139p. (C). 1984. pap. text 15.50 (*0-15-570748-5*) Harcourt Coll Pubs.

Ports of Freeport, Port Isabel & Brownsville, Texas. Vol. 26. per. 7.00 (*0-16-001750-5*); per. 12.00 (*0-16-030326-5*) USGPO.

Ports of Galveston & Texas City, Texas: Port Series No. 23. Vol. 23. per. 17.00 (*0-16-061250-0*) USGPO.

Ports of Hampton Roads, Virginia (Norfolk, Newport News, Chesapeake, Portsmouth & Hampton) Port Series. 11. per. 30.00 (*0-16-061237-3*) USGPO.

Ports of Hawaii (Honolulu, Port Allen, Nawiliwili, Kahului, Kanaukakai, Kawaihee & Hilo) Vol. 50. 80p. 1987. per. 8.00 (*0-16-001795-5*) USGPO.

Ports of Huntington, West Virginia, Ohio River & Kanawha, West Virginia: Port Series. 61. 172p. 1992. per. 14.00 (*0-16-061234-9*) USGPO.

Ports of Jacksonville & Fernandina Beach, Florida. Vol. 15. 88p. 1986. pap. 7.00 (*0-16-001787-4*) USGPO.

Ports of Jacksonville & Fernandina Beach, Florida: Port Series No. 15. Vol. 15. per. 13.00 (*0-16-061258-6*) USGPO.

Ports of Long Beach, Los Angeles & Port Hueneme, California: Port Series No. 28. Vol. 28. per. 23.00 (*0-16-061254-3*) USGPO.

Ports of Los Angelos & Long Beach, California. (Port Series : Vol. 28). per. 8.50 (*0-16-001751-3*) USGPO.

Ports of Memphis, Tennessee, Helena, Arkansas & Lower Mississippi River. Vol. 71. per. 12.00 (*0-16-061242-X*) USGPO.

Ports of Miami, Port Everglades & Palm Beach, Florida. Vol. 16. 156p. 1991. per. 10.00 (*0-16-030104-1*) USGPO.

Ports of Milwaukee, Wisconsin & Ports on Lake Michigan: Port Series No. 48. Vol. 48. per. 26.00 (*0-16-061248-9*) USGPO.

Ports of Minneapolis, St. Paul & Port Port on the upper Mississippi River. (Port Series : Vol. 69). 164p. 1985. per. 8.50 (*0-16-001781-5*) USGPO.

Ports of Minneapolis St. Paul & Ports on the Upper Mississippi River: Port Series No. 69. Vol. 69. per. 38.00 (*0-16-061246-2*) USGPO.

Ports of Missouri, Arkansas, Verdigris, White & Ouachita Rivers. Vol. 68. pap. 12.00 (*0-16-001790-4*) USGPO.

Ports of Natchez, Vicksburg & Greenville, MS & Ports on the Lower Mississippi River, Miles 255 to 620 AHP rev. ed. Water Resources Support Center Staff & USGPO Staff. LC 92-209941. vi, 92 p. 1991. pap. 7.50 (*0-16-001774-2*) USGPO.

Ports of New York, New York, New Jersey & Long ISland, New York. Vol. 5. 364p. 1988. per. 18.00 (*0-16-001796-3*) USGPO.

Ports of Panama City & Pensacola, Florida: Port Series No. 19. Vol. 19. per. 21.00 (*0-16-061261-6*) USGPO.

Ports of Philadelphia, Pennsylvania: Port Series No. 8. Vol. 8. per. 21.00 (*0-16-061260-8*) USGPO.

Ports of Philadelphia, Pennsylvania, Camden New Jersey, Wilmingtond Delaware & Ports on the Delaware River. Vol. 8. per. 10.00 (*0-16-001741-6*) USGPO.

Ports of Pittsburgh, Pennsylvania & Ohio River: Port Series. 60. 148p. 1991. per. 14.00 (*0-16-061235-7*) USGPO.

Ports of Port Angeles, Port Townsend, Anacortes, Everett & Bellingham, Washington: Port Series No. 37. Vol. 37. per. 10.00 (*0-16-061262-4*) USGPO.

Ports of Port Angelos, Port Townsend, Everette, Anacortes & Bellingham, Washington. Vol. 37. 128p. 1987. per. 7.50 (*0-16-001794-7*) USGPO.

Ports of Port Arthur, Beaumont & Orange, Texas. Vol. 22. 130p. 1988. per. 9.00 (*0-16-001797-1*) USGPO.

Ports of Portland & Searsport, Maine & Portsmouth, New Hamshire. (Port Series : Vol. 1). per. 8.00 (*0-16-001736-X*) USGPO.

Ports of Sacramento, Stockton, Pittsburg & Antioch, California: Port Series No. 32. Vol. 32. per. 22.00 (*0-16-061255-1*) USGPO.

Ports of San Francisco & Redwood City. Vol. 30. per. 8.00 (*0-16-001752-1*) USGPO.

Ports of Sanfranciso & Redwood City, California. Vol. 30. per. 9.00 (*0-16-029894-6*) USGPO.

Ports of Savannah & Brunswick, Georgia. (Port Series : Vol. 14). 94p. 1990. pap. 8.50 (*0-16-020292-2*) USGPO.

Ports of Southeast Alaska: Port Series No. 38. Vol. 38. per. 23.00 (*0-16-061249-7*) USGPO.

Ports of Southern New England: Providence, Rhode Island, & Fall River. (Port Ser.: Vol. 4). per. 20.00 (*0-16-061241-1*) USGPO.

Ports of Southwest & Western Alaska: Port Series No. 39. Vol. 39. per. 23.00 (*0-16-061244-6*) USGPO.

Ports of Tacoma, Olympia & Grays Harbor, Washington: Port Series. 35. per. 15.00 (*0-16-061239-X*) USGPO.

Ports of Tampa & Port Manatee, Florida: Port Series No. 17. Vol. 17. per. 17.00 (*0-16-061251-9*) USGPO.

Ports of the World: Prints of Ports from the National Maritime Museum, 1700-1850. Cindy McCreery. 176p. 1999. 70.00 (*0-85667-505-9*, Pub. by P Wilson) Antique Collect.

Ports of Wilmington & Morehead City, North Carolina: Port Series No. 12. Vol. 12. per. 20.00 (*0-16-061257-8*) USGPO.

Ports on Tennessee River, Tennessee-Tombigbee & Black Warrior-Tombigbee Wateways: Port Series No. 64. Vol. 64. per. 38.00 (*0-16-061265-9*) USGPO.

Ports on the Illinois Waterway, Miles 0-291, Grafton To Lockport: Port Series No. 65. Vol. 65. per. 14.00 (*0-16-061245-4*) USGPO.

Ports, Waterways, Intermodal Terminals, & International Trade Transportation Issues. (Transportation Research Circular Ser.: No. 350). 72p. 1989. 7.00 (*0-685-38574-4*) Transport Res Bd.

Ports, Waterways, Rail, & International Trade Issues, 1990. (Transportation Research Record Ser.: No. 1263). 110p. 1990. 18.00 (*0-309-05019-7*) Transport Res Bd.

Ports, 1989. Ed. by Kenneth M. Childs, Jr. LC 89-6760. 750p. 1989. pap. text 76.00 (*0-87262-703-9*, 703) Am Soc Civil Eng.

Ports '80. Ed. by John Mascenik. LC 80-65719. 848p. 1980. pap. 8.00 (*0-87262-108-1*) Am Soc Civil Eng.

Ports '83. Ed. by Kong Wong. 842p. 1983. pap. 9.00 (*0-87262-352-1*) Am Soc Civil Eng.

Ports '92: Proceedings of the Conference, Seattle, Washington, July 20-22, 1992. Ed. by David Torseth. LC 92-19042. 1216p. 1992. pap. text 106.00 (*0-87262-874-4*) Am Soc Civil Eng.

Portsmouth. Nancy Jensen Devin & Richard Simpson. LC 97-158045. (Images of America Ser.). 1997. pap. 16.99 (*0-7524-0408-3*) Arcadia Publng.

Portsmouth. Gerald D. Foss. LC 95-163230. (Images of America Ser.). (Illus.). 1994. pap. 14.99 (*0-7524-0061-4*) Arcadia Publng.

Portsmouth: Architecture in an Ohio River Town. Sergio Sanabria et al. LC 82-82114. (Illus.). (Orig.). 1982. pap. 7.50 (*0-940784-01-7*) Miami Univ Art.

***Portsmouth & Coastal New Hampshire: A Photographic Portrait.** (Illus.). 128p. 2000. 24.95 (*1-885435-13-4*) Twin Lights.

***Portsmouth-Built: Submarines of the Portsmouth Naval Shipyard.** Richard E. Winslow, III. (Portsmouth Marine Society Ser.: Vol. 6). (Illus.). 2000. reprint ed. pap. 15.00 (*0-915819-28-7*, Pub. by Portsmouth Marine Soc) P E Randall Pub.

Portsmouth-Built Warships, 1497-1967. James Goss. 112p. 1987. 39.00 (*0-85937-278-2*, Pub. by K Mason Pubns Ltd) St Mut.

Portsmouth Built Warships, 1497-1967. Maritime Books Staff. (C). 1986. text 50.00 (*0-7855-5294-4*, Pub. by Maritime Bks) St Mut.

Portsmouth (NH) Records, 1645-1656: A Transcript of the First Thirty-Five Pages of the Earliest Town Book. Frank W. Hackett. 76p. 1985. reprint ed. pap. 9.00 (*0-935207-17-1*) Danbury Hse Bks.

Portsmouth Past & Present. Anthony Triggs. (C). 1989. 45.00 (*1-85455-009-8*, Pub. by Ensign Pubns & Print) St Mut.

Portsmouth People Famous Sons & Daughters. Geoffrey Stavert. (C). 1989. 39.00 (*0-7855-6616-3*, Pub. by Ensign Pubns & Print) St Mut.

Portsmouth Point: British Navy in Fiction, 1793-1815. C. Northcote Parkinson. 1979. 20.00 (*0-87556-509-3*) Saifer.

Portsmouth Project: A Documentary View of Portsmouth, 1740-1760. Charles E. Clark & Charles W. Eastman. LC 74-18701. (Illus.). 98p. 1974. pap. 10.00 (*0-912274-46-8*, 1249) Picton Pr.

Portugais: Guide de Conversation et Dictionnaire. Larousse Staff. (FRE & POR.). 192p. 1992. pap. 16.95 (*0-7859-7657-4*, 2034035054) Fr & Eur.

Portugais Sans Peine. Albert O. Cherel. 24.95 (*0-685-11505-4*); audio 125.00 (*0-685-01760-5*) Fr & Eur.

Portugal see Cultures of the World - Group 10

Portugal see Countries of the World

Portugal. 1997. lib. bdg. 257.99 (*0-8490-6131-8*) Gordon Pr.

Portugal. Deni Bown. LC 97-12455. (Eyewitness Travel Guides Ser.). 480p. 1997. 24.95 (*0-7894-1948-3*) DK Pub Inc.

Portugal. Neil Champion. (Modern Industrial World Ser.). (Illus.). 48p. (J). (gr. 6-8). 1995. lib. bdg. 24.26 (*1-56847-435-0*) Raintree Steck-V.

Portugal. Hugues Demeude. (Illus.). 160p. 1999. 19.99 (*3-8228-7065-X*) Taschen Amer.

Portugal. Jean Giraudoux. pap. 9.50 (*0-685-33924-6*) Fr & Eur.

Portugal. Insight Guides Staff. (Insight Guides). 1998. pap. text 7.95 (*0-88729-556-8*) Langenscheidt.

***Portugal.** Ed. by Langenscheidt Publishing Staff. (Langenscheidt Pocket Menu Reader Ser.). (POR & ENG., Illus.). 2000. pap. text 7.95 (*0-88729-314-X*, Insight Guides) Langenscheidt.

Portugal. NTC Publishing Group Staff. (Passport Essential Guide Ser.). (Illus.). 128p. 1998. pap. 8.95 (*0-8442-0125-1*, 01251, Passprt Bks) NTC Contemp Pub Co.

Portugal. Contrib. by Passport Books Staff. LC 97-40727. (Get Around in . . . Ser.). (POR., Illus.). 128p. 1998. pap. 8.95 (*0-8442-0158-8*, 01588) NTC Contemp Pub Co.

Portugal. Ed. by Pocket Books Staff. 1988. 5.95 (*0-671-84890-9*) PB.

Portugal. Joe Staines. (Exploring Rural Europe Ser.). (Illus.). 124p. 1993. pap. 12.95 (*0-8442-9467-5*, Passprt Bks) NTC Contemp Pub Co.

Portugal. U. S. Government Staff. (Country Studies). 1994. 19.00 (*0-87511-541-1*, UPORTU) Claitors.

Portugal. P. T. Unwin. (World Bibliographical Ser.: No. 71). 311p. 1987. lib. bdg. 50.50 (*1-85109-016-9*) ABC-CLIO.

Portugal. large type ed. Julia Wilkinson. (Guidebook Ser.). (Illus.). 1991. pap. 9.95 (*962-217-116-8*) L A Michaux.

Portugal. 2nd ed. Insight Guides Staff. (Insight Guides). 1998. pap. text 21.95 (*0-88729-742-0*) Langenscheidt.

Portugal. 2nd ed. Michelin Staff. 1998. pap. text 20.00 (*2-06-456702-X*) Michelin.

***Portugal.** 3rd ed. American Map Publishing Staff. 1999. pap. 21.95 (*0-88729-026-4*) Langenscheidt.

***Portugal.** 3rd ed. Marc Rigole & Claude-Victor Langlois. (Illus.). 448p. 2000. pap. 17.95 (*2-89464-245-8*, Pub. by Ulysses Travel) Globe Pequot.

Portugal. 4th ed. Fodor's Staff. 1998. pap. 17.50 (*0-679-00058-5*) Fodors Travel.

Portugal. 4th ed. Ian Robertson. (Blue Guide Ser.). (Illus.). 320p. 1996. pap. 19.95 (*0-393-31416-2*, Norton Paperbks) Norton.

***Portugal, Vol. 940.** 2nd ed. Michelin Staff. 1999. write for info. (*2-06-094003-6*) Michelin.

Portugal: A Companion History. Jose H. Saraiva. Ed. by Ian Robertson. Tr. by Ursula Fonss. LC 99-185309. (Illus.). 224p. 1998. 39.95 (*1-85754-201-0*, Pub. by Carcanet Pr); pap. 19.95 (*1-85754-211-8*, Pub. by Carcanet Pr) Paul & Co Pubs.

Portugal: A Country Study. Eric Solsten. 372p. 1994. boxed set 28.00 (*0-16-061160-1*) USGPO.

***Portugal: A Country Study Guide.** Global Investment & Business Center, Inc. Staff. (World Country Study Guides Library: Vol. 138). (Illus.). 350p. 2000. pap. 59.00 (*0-7397-2436-3*) Intl Business Pubns.

Portugal: Ancient Country, Young Democracy. Ed. by Kenneth Maxwell & Michael H. Haltzel. (Illus.). 136p. (C). 1990. lib. bdg. 22.25 (*0-943875-20-X*) W Wilson Ctr Pr.

Portugal: Birth of a Democracy. Robert Harvey. LC 78-4507. 1978. 24.00 (*0-312-63184-7*) St Martin.

Portugal: English Edition-Country, City & Regional Guides. (Green Guides). pap. 14.95 (*0-686-56388-3*) Fr & Eur.

Portugal: French Edition-Country & City Guide. (Green Guides). pap. 14.95 (*0-686-56405-7*) Fr & Eur.

Portugal: Investment & Growth. W. Chislett. (Euromoney Country Guide Ser.). 185p. 1997. 170.00 (*1-85564-565-3*, Pub. by Euromoney) Am Educ Systs.

Portugal: Major World Nations. Ronald Seth. LC 99-13781. (Major World Nations Ser.). (Illus.). 144p. 1999. 19.95 (*0-7910-5395-4*) Chelsea Hse.

Portugal: Revolutionary Change in an Open Economy. Rodney J. Morrison. LC 81-2099. 200p. (C). 1981. 39.95 (*0-86569-077-4*, Auburn Hse) Greenwood.

***Portugal: The Algarve.** 2nd ed. David J. J. Evans. (Guides Bks.). (Illus.). 2000. pap. 17.95 (*1-86011-957-3*) Cadgn Bks.

Portugal: The All-in-One Travel & Language Guide. NTC Publishing Staff. (Get Around in . . . Ser.). (POR., Illus.). 128p. 1998. pap. 19.95 incl. audio (*0-8442-0174-X*, 0174X) NTC Contemp Pub Co.

Portugal: The Impossible Revolution. Phil Mailer. 400p. 1977. 41.99 (*0-919618-34-0*, Pub. by Black Rose); pap. 12.99 (*0-919618-33-2*, Pub. by Black Rose) Consort Bk Sales.

Portugal: The Villages. Rosella Pace. 1977. 2.00 (*0-88031-039-1*) Invisible-Red Hill.

Portugal - A Country Study Guide: Basic Information for Research & Pleasure. Global Investment Center, USA Staff. (World Country Study Guide Library: Vol. 138). (Illus.). 350p. 1999. pap. 59.00 (*0-7397-1535-6*) Intl Business Pubns.

Portugal & Africa, 1815-1910: A Study in Uneconomic Imperialism. Birmingham. LC 99-11300. 1999. text 59.95 (*0-312-22319-6*) St Martin.

Portugal Business & Investment Opportunities Yearbook-98: Business, Investment, Export-Import. Contrib. by Russian Information & Business Center, Inc. Staff. (Business & Investment Opportunity Library-98). (Illus.). 350p. 1998. pap. 99.00 (*1-57751-962-0*) Intl Business Pubns.

***Portugal Business Intelligence Report, 190 vols.** Global Investment & Business Center, Inc. Staff. (World Business Intelligence Library: Vol. 138). (Illus.). 350p. 2000. pap. 99.95 (*0-7397-2636-6*) Intl Business Pubns.

***Portugal Business Law Handbook.** Global Investment & Business Center, Inc. Staff. (Global Business Law Handbooks Library: Vol. 138). (Illus.). 2000. pap. 99.95 (*0-7397-2036-8*) Intl Business Pubns.

PORTUGAL Business Law Handbook-98. Russian Information & Business Center, Inc. Staff. (World Business Law Library-98). (Illus.). 350p. 1998. pap. 99.00 (*1-57751-820-9*) Intl Business Pubns.

***Portugal Business Opportunity Yearbook.** Global Investment & Business Center, Inc. Staff. (Global Business Opportunity Yearbooks Library: Vol. 138). (Illus.). 2000. pap. 99.95 (*0-7397-2236-0*) Intl Business Pubns.

***Portugal Business Opportunity Yearbook: Export-Import, Investment & Business Opportunities.** International Business Publications, U. S. A. Staff & Global Investment Center, U. S. A. Staff. (Global Business Opportunity Yearbooks Library: Vol. 138). (Illus.). 350p. 1999. pap. 99.95 (*0-7397-1336-1*) Intl Business Pubns.

***Portugal Charming Inns & Itineraries 2000.** Karen Brown. LC 99-15248. (Guides Ser.). 1999. pap. 18.95 (*0-930328-94-9*) K Browns Guides.

***Portugal Country Review 2000.** Robert C. Kelly et al. (Illus.). 60p. 1999. pap. 39.95 (*1-58310-562-X*) CountryWatch.

Portugal Country Studies: Area Handbook. 2nd ed. Library of Congress Federal Research Division Staff. Ed. by Eric Solsten. LC 93-30722. (Area Handbook Ser.). 1994. 19.00 (*0-8444-0776-3*) Lib Congress.

***Portugal E Asaudade, Em Verso: Versos.** unabridged ed. Ed. by Jose Brites. (Poetas Populares Ser.: Vol. 4). (POR.). 128p. 2000. boxed set 12.95 (*1-889358-20-7*, 21) Peregrinacao.

***Portugal 1140-1660.** 2000. write for info. (*0-582-09233-7*) Pearson Educ.

Portugal Elite Forces Insignia, 1951-Present. Harry F. Pugh & Robert Bragg. LC 95-67552. (Elite Insignia Guides Ser.). (Illus.). 140p. (Orig.). 1995. pap. 16.00 (*0-9633231-4-8*) C&D Ent.

***Portugal Export-Import & Business Directory: Ultimate Directory for Conducting Export-Import Operations in the Country. largest Exporters * Importers, Strategic Government & Business Contacts, Selected xport-Import Regulations & More.** International Business Publications, USA Staff & Global Investment Center, USA Staff. (World Export-Import & Business Library: 25). (Illus.). 250p. 2000. pap. 99.95 (*0-7397-3382-6*) Intl Business Pubns.

***Portugal Foreign Policy & Government Guide.** Contrib. by Global Investment & Business Center, Inc. Staff. (World Foreign Policy & Government Library: Vol. 132). (Illus.). 350p. 1999. pap. 99.00 (*0-7397-3630-2*) Intl Business Pubns.

***Portugal Foreign Policy & Government Guide.** Global Investment & Business Center, Inc. Staff. (World Foreign Policy & Government Library: Vol. 132). (Illus.). 350p. 2000. 99.95 (*0-7397-3836-4*) Intl Business Pubns.

***Portugal Government & Business Contacts Handbook: Strategic Government & Business Contacts for Conducting Successful Business, Export-Import & Investment Activity.** International Business Publications, USA Staff & Global Investment Center, USA Staff. (World Export-Import & Business Library: 111). (Illus.). 250p. 2000. pap. 99.95 (*0-7397-6125-0*) Intl Business Pubns.

Portugal Green Guide. 5th ed. Michelin Staff. 1995. pap. 19.95 (*0-7859-7191-2*, 557) Fr & Eur.

Portugal Guide. 2nd ed. Ron Charles. 552p. 1997. pap. text 16.95 (*1-883323-52-5*) Open Rd Pub.

Portugal (Hotel & Restaurant Guide), 1996. Michelin Staff. 1996. 11.95 (*0-7859-9909-4*) Fr & Eur.

Portugal Hotel & Restaurant Guide 1998. Michelin. (ENG, FRE, GER, ITA & POR.). 1998. 11.95 (*0-7859-9613-3*) Fr & Eur.

***Portugal Hotels & Restaurants.** 100th ed. Michelin Staff. 1999. pap. text 12.00 (*2-06-972006-3*) Michelin.

Portugal in Africa, 24. Tarikh. Ed. by Jenny Lee. (Tarikh Ser.). 1981. pap. 6.95 (*0-582-65049-6*) Longman.

Portugal in Africa: The Last Hundred Years. Alan Rothman. LC 81-150129. 27.00 (*0-582-64379-1*) Longman.

Portugal in Pictures. Ed. by Lerner Geography Department Staff. (Visual Geography Ser.). (Illus.). 64p. (J). 1995. reprint ed. lib. bdg. 19.95 (*0-8225-1886-4*, Lerner Publctns) Lerner Pub.

Portugal in the Nineteen Eighties: Dilemmas of Democratic Consolidation, 138. Ed. by Kenneth Maxwell. LC 85-9872. (Contributions in Political Science Ser.: No. 138). (Illus.). 268p. 1986. 65.00 (*0-313-24889-3*, MPG/, Greenwood Pr) Greenwood.

***Portugal Investment & Business Guide.** Global Investment & Business Center, Inc. Staff. (Global Investment & Business Guide Library: Vol. 138). (Illus.). 2000. pap. 99.95 (*0-7397-1836-3*) Intl Business Pubns.

***Portugal Investment & Business Guide: Export-Import, Investment & Business Opportunities.** International Business Publications, USA Staff & Global Investment Center, USA Staff. (World Investment & Business Guide Library-99: Vol. 138). (Illus.). 350p. 1999. pap. 99.95 (*0-7397-0333-1*) Intl Business Pubns.

Portugal! Lingua e Cultura. Thomas A. Lathrop & Eduardo Dias. (Illus.). 510p. 1995. text 49.95 (*0-942566-19-X*) LinguaText.

Portugal: Lingua e Cultura: Writing & Langauage Lab Manual. Thomas Lathrop & Eduardo Dias. (Illus.). 440p. (Orig.). 1995. pap. text, wbk. ed. 20.95 (*0-942566-20-3*) LinguaText.

Portugal of Salazar. Michael Derrick. (Select Bibliographies Reprint Ser.). 1977. reprint ed. 15.95 (*0-8369-9959-2*) Ayer.

Portugal Pocket Guide, 1998. rev. ed. Berlitz Editors. (Pocket Guides Ser.). (Illus.). 144p. 1998. pap. 10.95 (*2-8315-6316-X*) Berlitz.

Portugal, 1716-1880: Joanine Pombaline & Rococo Portugal As Seen by British Diplomats & Traders. David Francis. (Monagrafias A Ser.: Vol. CIX). (Illus.). 300p. (C). 1985. 72.00 (*0-7293-0190-7*, Pub. by Tamesis Bks Ltd) Boydell & Brewer.

Portugal, Spain & the African Atlantic, 1343-1490: Chivalry & Crusade from John of Guant to Henry the Navigator & Beyond. P.E. Russell. (Collected Studies). 344p. 1995. 108.95 (*0-86078-474-6*, Pub. by Variorum) Ashgate Pub Co.

P

Portugal the Algarve: Cardogan Guides. David Evans & Kamin Mohammadi. (Cadogan Country Guides Ser.). (Illus.). 92p. 1996. pap. text 14.95 (*1-86011-066-5*, Pub. by Cadgn Bks) Globe Pequot.

Portugal the Pathfinder: Journeys from the Medieval Toward the Modern World, 1300-1600. George D. Winius. xii, 429p. 1995. 30.00 (*1-56954-008-X*) Hispanic Seminary.

Portugal's African Wars. Humbaraci & Mucnik. LC 72-93676. 1974. 29.95 (*0-89388-072-8*) Okpaku Communications.

***Portugal's Secret Jews, the End of an Era: Essays.** unabridged ed. Eduardo M. Dias. Ed. by Peregrinacao Publications Staff. (English Books, Essays Ser.: No. 2). (POR.). 112p. 1999. 12.00 (*1-889358-16-9*, 13) Peregrinacao.

Portugal's Wines & Winemakers: Port Madeira & Regional Wines. Richard Mayson. (Illus.). 224p. 1997. 34.95 (*0-932664-80-6*, 6679) Wine Appreciation.

Portugal's Wines & Winemakers: Port, Madeira & Regional Wines. 2nd rev. ed. Richard Mayson. (Illus.). 250p. 1999. 34.95 (*1-891267-01-9*) Wine Appreciation.

Portugiesisch. (Glossare Ser.). (GER.). 24p. 1997. pap. write for info. (*3-468-49113-1*); pap. write for info. (*3-468-49133-6*) Langenscheidt.

Portugiesisch Ohne Muhe. Albert O. Cherel. 24.95 (*0-685-11507-0*); audio 125.00 (*0-685-01761-3*) Fr & Eur.

Portugiesisch ohne Muhe: Portuguese for German Speakers. Assimil Staff. (GER & POR.). 28.95 (*0-8288-4349-X*, F49590) Fr & Eur.

Portugues? Sim, Obrigado, Vol. 1. (POR., Illus.). 100p. (J). 1996. pap. 12.95 (*88-8148-070-0*, Pub. by Europ Lang Inst) Distribks Inc.

Portugues? Sim, Obrigado, Vol. 2. (POR., Illus.). 100p. (J). 1996. pap. 12.95 (*88-8148-071-9*, Pub. by Europ Lang Inst) Distribks Inc.

Portugues Basico para Estrangeiros. 2nd rev. ed. Rejane De Oliveira Slade. 400p. 1999. pap. text 29.99 (*0-9638790-3-0*) BRAMINAS.

Portugues Basico para Estrangeiros: Livro de Excercicios. 2nd ed. Rejane De Oliveira Slade. 250p. 1999. pap. text, wbk. ed. 18.00 (*0-9638790-4-9*) BRAMINAS.

Portugues Basico para Estrangeiros: Manual Do Professor. Rejane De Oliveira Slade. 300p. (C). 1994. pap., teacher ed. 20.00 (*0-9638790-1-4*) BRAMINAS.

Portugues Contemporaneo, 2 vols. Maria I. Abreu & Clea Rameh. Incl. Vol. 1. Portugues Contemporaneo I. LC 66-25520. 256p. 1972. pap. 12.95 (*0-87840-026-5*); Vol. 2. Portugues Contemporaneo 2. LC 66-25520. 346p. 1973. pap. 14.95 (*0-87840-025-7*); LC 66-25520. 1971. write for info. (*0-318-52679-4*) Georgetown U Pr.

Portugues Contemporaneo I see Portugues Contemporaneo

Portugues Contemporaneo 2 see Portugues Contemporaneo

Portugues Para Principiantes. Claude E. Leroy et al. (POR., Illus.). xii, 422p. (C). 1993. text 18.00 (*0-9636612-0-5*) U WI Dept Span.

Portugues sans Peine: Portuguese for French Speakers. Assimil Staff. (FRE & POR.). 28.95 (*0-8288-4347-3*, F50560) Fr & Eur.

***Portuguese.** (Illus.). 160p. 2001. pap. 6.95 (*962-593-929-6*) Tuttle Pubng.

Portuguese. Barron's Educational Editors. LC 97-48406. (TravelWise Ser.). (ENG & POR.). 292p. 1998. pap. 16.95 incl. audio (*0-7641-7111-9*) Barron.

Portuguese. Barron's Educational Editors. Tr. by Kathleen Luft. LC 97-48408. (TravelWise Language Learning Ser.). (ENG & POR.). 290p. 1998. pap. 8.95 (*0-7641-0391-1*) Barron.

***Portuguese.** Kindersley Dorling. 144p. 2000. pap. 9.95 (*0-7894-6257-5*) DK Pub Inc.

***Portuguese.** 2nd ed. (Rough Guide Phrasebooks Ser.). 272p. 2000. pap. 5.00 (*1-85828-644-1*) Viking Penguin.

Portuguese: A Complete Course for Beginners. Manuela Cook. (POR., Illus.). 240p. 1995. pap. 12.95 (*0-8442-3819-8*, Teach Yrslf) NTC Contemp Pub Co.

***Portuguese: A Language Map.** Kristine K. Kershul. (Language Map Ser.). (Illus.). 8p. 2000. pap. 7.95 (*0-944502-11-3*) Bilingual Bks.

Portuguese: An Essential Grammar. Amelia P. Hutchinson & Janet Lloyd. (Essential Grammar Ser.). 208p. (C). 1996. 75.00 (*0-415-13707-1*); pap. 24.99 (*0-415-13708-X*) Routledge.

Portuguese: LANGUAGE/30. rev. ed. Educational Services Corporation Staff. (POR.). 1995. pap. 16.95 incl. audio (*0-910542-73-2*) Educ Svcs DC.

***Portuguese: The Land & Its People.** Marion Kaplan. 400p. 1998. pap. 16.95 (*0-14-026428-0*, Pub. by Pnguin Bks Ltd) Trafalgar.

Portuguese - English, English - Portuguese Legal Dictionary: Diccionario Juridico. 3rd ed. M. Chaves de Mello. (ENG & POR.). 515p. 1987. pap. 95.00 (*0-8288-0401-X*, F51280) Fr & Eur.

Portuguese - English Mini-Books Set with Audio, 11 bks. Claudia Schwalm. (ENG & POR., Illus.). (Orig.). (J). (gr. k-6). 1997. pap. 21.95 incl. audio (*0-614-24742-X*) Cultural Cnnect.

Portuguese - Italian Dictionary. Giuseppe Mea. (ITA & POR.). 2256p. 95.00 (*0-8288-9426-4*) Fr & Eur.

Portuguese - Russian Learners Dictionary. S. M. Starets & N. I. Voinova. (POR & RUS.). 472p. 1989. 12.95 (*0-8285-5429-3*) Firebird NY.

Portuguese - Spanish Dictionary see Dicionario de Portugues Espanhol

Portuguese Africa & the West. William Minter. LC 73-8054. 204p. reprint ed. pap. 63.30 (*0-608-15883-6*, 203076300070) Bks Demand.

Portuguese Americans & Spanish Americans: An Original Anthology. Ed. by Carlos E. Cortes. LC 79-6233. (Hispanics in the United States Ser.). 1981. lib. bdg. 31.95 (*0-405-13180-1*) Ayer.

Portuguese & Brazilian Balladry: A Thematic & Bibliographic Index see O Romanceiro Portugues e Brasileiro: Indice Tematico e Bibliografico

Portuguese & English Accounting Dictionary (Diccionario Tecnico Contabile) M. R. Altmann. (ENG & POR.). 126p. 1987. reprint ed. pap. 35.00 (*85-224-0254-X*, M9355) Fr & Eur.

Portuguese & Spanish Keyboard Music of the Eighteenth Century. Oswald Jonas. LC M 0020.J8. 48p. reprint ed. pap. 30.00 (*0-608-10743-3*, 203915000039) Bks Demand.

Portuguese & the Pacific Vol. 1: Proceedings of the International Colloquium, 1993. Ed. by Francis A. Dutra & Joao C. Dos Santos. LC 95-83243. (Publication Ser.: No. 10). 451p. (Orig.). (C). 1995. pap. 25.00 (*0-942208-29-3*) Bandanna Bks.

Portuguese at Your Fingertips. 1987. 5.95 (*0-7102-0727-1*, Routledge Thoemms) Routledge.

Portuguese Bible. 12.95 (*5-550-00764-9*) Nairi.

Portuguese, Brazilian, 2 vols., Vol. 1. Foreign Service Institute Staff. (POR.). 783p. pap. text 215.00 incl. audio (*0-88432-019-7*, AFP151) Audio-Forum.

Portuguese, Brazilian, 2 vols., Vol. 2. Foreign Service Institute Staff. (POR.). 618p. pap. text 245.00 incl. audio (*0-88432-100-2*, AFP994) Audio-Forum.

Portuguese, Brazilian & African Studies: Presented to Clive Willis on His Retirement. Ed. by T. F. Earle & Nigel Griffin. (Illus.). 242p. 1995. pap. 75.00 (*0-85668-667-0*, Pub. by Aris & Phillips) David Brown.

***Portuguese (Brazilian) Basic.** unabridged ed. Pimsleur International. (POR.). 1998. audio 29.95 (*0-671-31578-1*) S&S Audio.

Portuguese Cassette Pack. Berlitz Editors. (CD Pack Ser.). (POR., Illus.). 1999. pap. 19.95 incl. audio, cd-rom (*2-8315-6346-1*) Berlitz.

Portuguese Cassette Pack. rev. ed. Berlitz Editors. (Cassettepack Ser.). 1998. pap. 17.95 incl. audio (*2-8315-6334-8*) Berlitz.

Portuguese Colonial in America: Belmira Nunes Lopes: The Autobiography of a Cape Verdean-American. Maria L. Nunes. Ed. by Yvette E. Miller. LC 82-6569. 224p. 1982. 25.00 (*0-935480-08-0*); pap. 11.95 (*0-935480-07-2*) Lat Am Lit Rev Pr.

Portuguese Communist Party's Strategy for Power, 1921-1986. rev. ed. Carlos A. Cunha. LC 91-41523. (Modern European History Ser.: No. 2). 432p. 1992. text 25.00 (*0-8153-0676-8*) Garland.

Portuguese Conquest & Commerce in Southern Asia, 1500-1750. C. R. Boxer. (Collected Studies: No. CS208). (Illus.). 312p. (C). 1985. reprint ed. lib. bdg. 109.95 (*0-86078-156-9*, Pub. by Variorum) Ashgate Pub Co.

Portuguese Conversational. Hilary Fleming et al. (Conversational Ser.). (POR.). 96p. 1995. pap. 14.95 incl. audio (*0-8442-9139-0*, Natl Textbk Co) NTC Contemp Pub Co.

Portuguese Cooking. Hilarie Walden. 128p. 1995. 12.98 (*0-7858-0187-1*) Bk Sales Inc.

Portuguese Cooking: The Authentic & Robust Cuisine of Portugal. Carol Robertson. LC 93-1684. (Illus.). 166p. (Orig.). 1993. 24.95 (*1-55643-158-9*) North Atlantic.

Portuguese Decorative Tiles: Azulejos. Rioletta Sabo & Jorge N. Falcato. Tr. by Russell Stockman. LC 98-11563. (Illus.). 216p. 1998. 55.00 (*0-7892-0481-9*) Abbeville Pr.

Portuguese Dictionary. Allen. (Reference Library). 1997. pap. 6.95 (*1-85326-382-6*, 3826WW, Pub. by Wrdsworth Edits) NTC Contemp Pub Co.

Portuguese Dictionary. Bobby J. Chamberlain. 1991. pap. 6.99 (*0-679-40060-5*) McKay.

Portuguese Dictionary. Crown Publishing Group Staff. (POR.). 1998. pap. 5.00 (*0-609-80292-5*) Liv Lang.

Portuguese Economy Towards Nineteen Ninety-Two: Proceedings of a Conference Sponsored by Junta Nacional de Investigacao Cientifica e Tecnologica & Banco de Portugal. Ed. by Joao F. Do Amaral et al. 272p. 1992. lib. bdg. 101.00 (*0-7923-9193-4*) Kluwer Academic.

Portuguese Emigration to the U. S., 1820-1930. Charles R. Boxer. LC 79-65354. (Studies in Japanese History & Civilization). 172p. 1979. lib. bdg. 62.50 (*0-313-26982-3*, U6982) Greenwood.

Portuguese Emigration to the U. S. 1820-1930. Maria I. Baganha. LC 90-46975. (European Immigrants & American Society Ser.). 440p. 1990. reprint ed. text 30.00 (*0-8240-7421-1*) Garland.

Portuguese Empire Asia. Sanjay Subrahmanyam. LC 92-10236. (C). 1993. text 75.95 (*0-582-05069-3*, Pub. by Addison-Wesley) Longman.

Portuguese Empire, 1415-1808: A World on the Move. A. J. Russell-Wood. LC 98-3736. (Illus.). 289p. 1998. reprint ed. pap. 16.95 (*0-8018-5955-7*) Johns Hopkins.

Portuguese-English - English-Portuguese Legal Dictionary. 2nd ed. Durval De Noronha Goyos, Jr. LC 99-194721. (ENG & POR.). 551p. 1994. 70.00 (*85-85548-04-5*) Editora Observ Leg.

Portuguese-English - English-Portuguese Scientific & Technical Dictionary. (ENG & POR.). 871p. 1994. 60.00 (*972-22-1492-6*, Pub. by Edit Verbo) IBD Ltd.

Portuguese-English Banking Dictionary: Dicionario Bancario Portugues-Ingles. A. Correia Da Cunha. (ENG & POR.). 379p. 1984. pap. 39.95 (*0-8288-0322-6*, M8062) Fr & Eur.

Portuguese-English Dictionary see Dicionario Portugues-Ingles

Portuguese-English Dictionary. 2nd rev. ed. James L. Taylor. xxii, 662p. 1970. 49.50 (*0-8047-0480-5*) Stanford U Pr.

Portuguese-English Illustrated Dictionary (Brazilian) (New Michaelis) F. Wimmer. (ENG & POR.). 1328p. 1992. 55.00 (*0-7859-8918-8*) Fr & Eur.

Portuguese-English Medical Pocket Translator: Continantal, Brazilian, & Cape Verdean Dialects. Christopher Harding. (Medical Pocket Translator Ser.). 2000. pap. 9.95 (*0-9649425-2-6*) Intl Med Volntrs.

Portuguese-English Mini-Books Set with Audio, 11 bks. Claudia Schwalm. (ENG & POR., Illus.). (Orig.). (J). (ps-7). 1997. pap. 21.95 incl. audio (*0-614-24476-5*) Cultural Cnnect.

Portuguese-English/English-Portuguese Dictionary of Scientific & Technical Terms. Farinha dos Santos Tavares. (ENG & POR.). 876p. 1994. 295.00 (*0-7859-9319-3*) Fr & Eur.

Portuguese-English/English-Portuguese Dictionary of Scientific & Technical Terms. Farinha dos Santos Tavares. (ENG & POR.). 1995. 295.00 incl. audio compact disk (*0-7859-9539-0*) Fr & Eur.

Portuguese Expedition to Abyssinia in 1541-1543. Ed. by R. S. Whiteway. (Hakluyt Society Works: No. 2, Vol. 10). 1974. reprint ed. 60.00 (*0-8115-0332-1*) Periodicals Srv.

Portuguese Fado. Rough Guides Staff. 1998. audio compact disk 14.95 (*1-85828-369-8*) Penguin Putnam.

Portuguese Fast-Track European. Tr. by Leland Guyer. (ENG & POR., Illus.). 346p. 1996. pap. text 125.00 incl. audio (*0-88432-935-6*, FTPG20) Audio-Forum.

Portuguese Financial Markets. Ed. by Ricardo E. Salgado. (International Financial Markets Ser.). 192p. Date not set. write for info. (*1-85573-207-6*, Pub. by Woodhead Pubng) Am Educ Systs.

Portuguese Fluency & Culture One. Americo C. Araujo. (Illus.). xv, 217p. 1989. text 26.95 (*1-881495-00-0*) DAC Pubs.

Portuguese Fluency & Culture One: Testing - Activities Program. Americo C. Araujo. (Illus.). 85p. 1991. ring bd. 49.95 (*1-881495-01-9*) DAC Pubs.

Portuguese Fluency & Culture Two: Continuemos. Americo C. Araujo. (Illus.). x, 332p. 1991. text 28.95 (*1-881495-02-7*); text 28.95 (*1-881495-10-8*) DAC Pubs.

Portuguese Fluency & Culture 1: Workbook. 149p. 1992. pap., student ed. 8.95 (*1-881495-07-8*) DAC Pubs.

Portuguese Fluency & Culture 2: Testing - Activities Program. 1992. 49.59 (*1-881495-03-5*) DAC Pubs.

Portuguese Fluency & Culture 2: Testing - Activities Program. 142p. 1994. pap., student ed. 8.95 (*1-881495-08-6*) DAC Pubs.

Portuguese Folk-Tales. Pederoso Consiglieri. Tr. by H. Montfiro. 1974. reprint ed. pap. 25.00 (*0-8115-0503-0*) Periodicals Srv.

Portuguese Folk Tales. Z. Consigliere-Pedroso. LC 68-57186. 1972. reprint ed. 12.95 (*0-405-08375-0*, Pub. by Blom Pubns) Ayer.

Portuguese Gardens. Helder Carita & Homem Cardoso. (Illus.). 320p. 1991. 79.50 (*1-85149-101-5*) Antique Collect.

Portuguese Handy Dictionary. Davidovic Mladen. (Handy Dictionaries Ser.). 120p. (Orig.). 1991. pap. 8.95 (*0-87052-053-9*) Hippocrene Bks.

Portuguese-Hebrew, Hebrew-Portuguese Dictionary. Abraham Hatzamri. (HEB & POR.). 1991. 49.95 (*0-8288-8259-2*) Fr & Eur.

***Portuguese Homestyle Cooking.** Ana Patuleia Ortins. (Illus.). 2000. 25.00 (*1-56656-373-9*) Interlink Pub.

Portuguese-Hungarian Concise Dictionary. R. Kiraly. 728p. 1993. 60.00 (*963-05-6495-5*, Pub. by Akade Kiado) St Mut.

Portuguese-Hungarian Concise Dictionary. R. Kiraly. (HUN & POR.). 728p. 1978. 49.95 (*0-8288-5265-0*, M9326) Fr & Eur.

Portuguese in a Flash. 180p. 1999. 8.95 (*1-928804-04-7*) Avocado Pr.

Portuguese in India, 2 vols. Frederick C. Danvers. (Illus.). 1966. 95.00 (*0-7146-2005-X*, Pub. by F Cass Pubs) Intl Spec Bk.

Portuguese in India. M. N. Pearson. (New Cambridge History of India Ser.: I: 1). 202p. 1988. text 54.95 (*0-521-25713-1*) Cambridge U Pr.

Portuguese in India, 2 vols. Frederick C. Danvers. (C). 1988. reprint ed. 64.00 (*81-206-0391-5*, Pub. by Asian Educ Servs) S Asia.

Portuguese in India, 2 vols. Frederick C. Danvers. 1986. reprint ed. 84.00 (*0-685-14348-1*, Pub. by Usha) S Asia.

Portuguese in Rhode Island: A History. M. Rachel Cunha et al. Ed. by Patrick T. Conley. (Rhode Island Ethnic Heritage Pamphlet Ser.). (Illus.). 33p. (Orig.). 1985. pap. 6.75 (*0-917012-72-0*) RI Pubns Soc.

***Portuguese in 10 Minutes a Day.** Kristine K. Kershul. (Illus.). 134p. 2000. per. 17.95 (*0-944502-37-7*, Pub. by Bilingual Bks) Midpt Trade.

Portuguese in the United States: A Bibliography. Leo Pap. LC 76-9270. (Bibliographies & Documentation Ser.). 100p. 1976. pap. 9.95 (*0-913256-21-8*) CMS.

Portuguese in Three Months. Maria F. Allen. LC 98-48003. (Hugo Ser.). 256p. 1999. pap. 14.95 (*0-7894-4429-1*) DK Pub Inc.

Portuguese Language. J. Mattoso Camara, Jr. Tr. by Anthony J. Naro. LC 79-167939. (History & Structure of Languages Ser.). 208p. 1993. lib. bdg. 22.00 (*0-226-51121-9*) U Ch Pr.

Portuguese Language: With an Analytical Bibliography of the Writings of Joaquim Mattoso Camara, Jr. Joaquim M. Camara. Tr. & Compiled by Anthony J. Naro. Compiled by John Reighard. LC 79-167939. (History & Structure of Languages Ser.). 284p. reprint ed. pap. 88.10 (*0-608-09278-9*, 205415200004) Bks Demand.

Portuguese Language & Luso-Brazilian Literature: An Annotated Guide to Selected Reference Works. Bobby J. Chamberlain. LC 88-8409. (Selected Bibliographies in Language & Literature Ser.: No. 6). x, 95p. 1989. pap. 18.00 (*0-87352-957-X*, SB06P); lib. bdg. 32.00 (*0-87352-956-1*, SB06C) Modern Lang.

***Portuguese Language Pack.** HarperCollins Staff. (POR.). 1999. pap. 16.95 incl. audio (*0-00-472226-4*, Pub. by HarpC) Trafalgar.

Portuguese Language Phrase Book. Harrap Limited Staff. 1989. pap. 2.95 (*0-8442-9930-8*, Passprt Bks) NTC Contemp Pub Co.

Portuguese Letters: Love Letters of a Nun to a French Officer. 2nd ed. Donald E. Ericson. LC 86-71957. 78p. 1986. pap. 9.95 (*0-9617271-0-1*) Bennett-Edwards.

Portuguese Literature from Its Origins to 1990: A Bibliography Based on the Collections of Indiana University. Compiled by Hugo Kunoff. LC 93-49699. 507p. 1994. 56.00 (*0-8108-2844-8*) Scarecrow.

Portuguese Memory Book: A New Approach to Vocabulary Building. William F. Harrison & Dorothy W. Welker. LC 96-11038. (POR.). 112p. 1996. pap. 9.95 (*0-292-73106-X*); text 19.95 (*0-292-73105-1*) U of Tex Pr.

Portuguese Merchants & Missionaries in Feudal Japan, 1543-1640. C. R. Boxer. (Collected Studies: No. CS232). 338p. 1986. reprint ed. text 109.95 (*0-86078-180-1*, Pub. by Variorum) Ashgate Pub Co.

***Portuguese New Testament.** 1999. pap. text 5.95 (*5-550-00765-7*) Nairi.

***Portuguese Nun: Formation of a National Myth.** Anna Klobucka. LC 00-34224. 2000. write for info. (*0-8387-5465-1*) Bucknell U Pr.

Portuguese of the Arabian Coast. R. B. Serjeant. (Arab Background Ser.). 1968. 16.00 (*0-86685-027-9*) Intl Bk Ctr.

Portuguese Palissy Ware: A Survey of Ceramics from Caldas da Rainha, 1853-1920. Marshall P. Katz. LC 98-40056. (Illus.). 144p. 1999. 75.00 (*0-933920-63-6*, Pub. by Hudson Hills) Natl Bk Netwk.

***Portuguese Phrase Book.** rev. ed. Berlitz Editors. (Berlitz Phrase Book & Dictionary Ser.). (POR., Illus.). 192p. 1998. pap. text 7.95 (*2-8315-6243-0*) Berlitz.

***Portuguese Phrase Book & Dictionary.** (Collins Phrase Book & Dictionary Ser.). (POR & ENG.). 192p. 1999. pap. 7.50 (*0-00-472075-X*, Pub. by HarpC) Trafalgar.

***Portuguese Phrase Finder.** (Collins Gem Phrase Finder Ser.). 256p. 2000. pap. 6.50 (*0-00-470839-3*, Pub. by HarpC) Trafalgar.

Portuguese Pioneers. Edgar Prestage. xiv, 352p. 1985. reprint ed. lib. bdg. 49.00 (*0-932051-44-8*) Rprt Serv.

Portuguese Pioneers in India: Spotlight on Medicine. P. D. Gaitonde. 1983. 27.00 (*0-8364-1052-1*, Pub. by Popular Prakashan) S Asia.

Portuguese Primer. R. Anthony Castagnaro. (American University Studies: Foreign Language Instruction: Ser. VI, Vol. 9). (ENG & POR.). 415p. (C). 1989. text 47.95 (*0-8204-0870-0*) P Lang Pubng.

Portuguese Princess. Tibor Dery. 1996. pap. 14.95 (*0-7145-0485-8*) Riverrun NY.

Portuguese Programmatic, Vol. 2. Jack L. Ulsh. (Intensive Cassette Ser.). 618p. 1998. spiral bd. 240.00 incl. audio (*1-58214-003-0*) Mltilingl Bks.

Portuguese (SA)/English, Level 1. (VocabuLearn Ser.). (ENG & POR.). 1987. 15.95 incl. audio (*0-939001-80-2*) Penton Overseas.

Portuguese (SA)/English, Level 2. (Vocabulearn Ser.). (ENG & POR.). 1987. 15.95 incl. audio (*0-939001-64-0*) Penton Overseas.

Portuguese Scofield Bible. 1996. 32.34 (*1-56694-087-7*) Span Pubns.

***Portuguese Scofield Bible.** 1999. write for info. (*1-56694-090-7*) Span Pubns.

Portuguese Scofield Bible. Spanish Publications Inc. Staff. 1996. write for info. (*1-56694-088-5*); write for info. (*1-56694-084-2*); write for info. (*1-56694-063-X*); pap. text 47.94 (*1-56694-085-0*) Span Pubns.

Portuguese Short Fiction, Vol. I. Ed. by Eugenio Lisboa. LC 97-164484. 320p. 1997. pap. text 19.95 (*1-85754-206-1*, Pub. by Carcanet Pr) Paul & Co Pubs.

Portuguese Short Fiction, Vol. II. Ed. by Eugenio Lisboa. 320p. 1997. pap. text 19.95 (*1-85754-241-X*, Pub. by Carcanet Pr) Paul & Co Pubs.

Portuguese-Spanish Dictionary: Diccionario Portugues-Espanol. 4th ed. J. C. Fernandes. (POR & SPA.). 878p. 1984. 24.95 (*0-8288-1041-9*, S31570) Fr & Eur.

Portuguese-Spanish, Spanish-Portuguese Dictionary: Diccionario Portugues-Espanol-Portugues. 6th ed. J. C. Fernandes. (POR & SPA.). 1016p. 1985. 32.95 (*0-8288-1042-7*, S60686) Fr & Eur.

Portuguese Speakers: O Novo Ingles Sem Custo. (ENG & POR.). pap. 75.00 incl. audio (*2-7005-1329-0*, Pub. by Assimil) Distribks Inc.

Portuguese Spinner: An American Story. Ed. by Marsha McCabe & Joseph D. Thomas. LC 97-62313. (Illus.). 287 p. (Orig.). 1998. pap. 29.95 (*0-932027-39-3*) Spinner Pubns.

Portuguese Spinner: An American Story. Ed. by Marsha McCabe & Joseph D. Thomas. LC 97-62313. (Illus.). 250p. 1988. 45.00 (*0-932027-38-5*) Spinner Pubns.

Portuguese Supplement Technical Dictionary of Mechanics, Metallurgy, Hydraulics. Ed. by Michel Feutry et al. (ENG, FRE & GER.). 380p. 1981. suppl. ed. 46.00 (*2-85608-014-6*) IBD Ltd.

Portuguese Syntax: New Comparative Studies. Ed. by Joao Costa. LC 99-28002. 288p. 2000. text 75.00 (*0-19-512575-4*) OUP.

***Portuguese Syntax: New Comparative Studies.** Ed. by Juan G. Costa. LC 99-28002. (Oxford Studies in Comparative Syntax). 288p. 2000. pap. text 45.00 (*0-19-512576-2*) OUP.

Portuguese Tiles: From the National Museum of Azulejo, Lisbon. Joao C. Pereira. (Illus.). 128p. 1996. 35.00 (*0-302-00661-3*) Scala Books.

Portuguese Trade in Asia under the Habsburgs, 1580-1640. James C. Boyajian. LC 92-12042. 384p. 1993. text 50.00 (*0-8018-4405-3*) Johns Hopkins.

Portuguese Trade with India in the 16th Century. K. S. Mathew. 1983. 24.00 (*0-8364-0996-5*, Pub. by Manohar) S Asia.

Portuguese Verbs & Essentials of Grammar. Sue Tyson-Ward. LC 99-88831. (...Verbs & Essentials of Ser.). (Illus.). 128p. 1995. pap. 13.95 (*0-8442-4698-0*, 46980, Passprt Bks) NTC Contemp Pub Co.

Portuguese Vocables in Asiatic Languages. Anthony X. Soares. (C). 1988. reprint ed. 36.00 (*81-206-0413-X*, Pub. by Asian Educ Servs) S Asia.

***Portuguese Water Dog: A Guide for the New Owner.** Verne K. Foster. 48p. 1999. pap. 8.00 (*0-9674684-1-8*) VKFoster.

Portuguese Water Dog Champions, 1983-1986. Camino E. E. & Bk. Co. Staff & Dorothy L. Johnson. (Illus.). 49p. 1987. pap. 28.95 (*0-940808-40-4*) Camino E E & Bk.

Portuguese Word-Formation with Suffixes. J. H. D. Allen. (LD Ser.: No. 33). 1941. 25.00 (*0-527-00779-X*) Periodicals Srv.

***Portuguese Wrong Way, Jonah.** Kay Arthur & Scoti Domeij. Tr. by Eleni Leite. (Discover 4 Yourself Series for Children). (Illus.). 97p. (J). 1999. 7.99 (*1-888655-71-2*) Precept Ministries.

Portuguese/English Dictionary. Berlitz Editors. 368p. 1998. pap. 7.95 (*2-8315-6383-6*) Berlitz.

***Portugueses Na America Do Norte: Ensaios/Essays.** unabridged ed. Ed. by Eduardo Mayone Dias. (Documentos Ser.: Vol. 1). (POR & ENG.). 192p. 1999. boxed set 18.00 (*1-889358-08-8*, 16) Peregrinacao.

***Portugueses Na Guerra Do Vietname: Entrevistas.** unabridged ed. Ed. by Adalino Cabral & Eduardo Mayone Dias. (Documentos Ser.: Vol. 2). (POR., Illus.). 192p. 2000. boxed set 18.00 (*1-889358-15-0*, 19) Peregrinacao.

***Portulacaceae - Ranunculaceae.** Ed. by L. I. Kashina et al. (Flora of Siberia Ser.: Vol. 6). (Illus.). 2002. text. write for info. (*1-57808-105-X*) Science Pubs.

Portulacaceae Through Caryophyllaceae of New York State. Richard S. Mitchell. (New York State Museum Bulletin Ser.: No. 486). (Illus.). 124p. (Orig.). 1993. pap. 10.00 (*1-55557-228-6*) NYS Museum.

Porzellan im Vogelbauer. Wolfgang Hohne. (Illus.). 120p. 1995. pap. text 11.00 (*3-364-00253-3*) Gordon & Breach.

Pos Activity Book. Art Fettig. LC 86-83237. (Illus.). 48p. (J). (gr. k-7). 1984. pap. 5.95 (*0-9601334-5-3*) Growth Unltd.

Po's Magic Watering Can. Ed. by Scholastic, Inc. Staff. (Lift-the-Flap Bk.). (Illus.). 24p. (J). (ps-k). 1999. 6.99 (*0-590-98334-2*) Scholastic Inc.

Pos Parenting: A Guide to Greatness. Art Fettig. LC 85-80482. 1986. pap. 19.95 incl. audio (*0-685-10863-5*) Growth Unltd.

Pos Parenting: A Guide to Greatness. Art Fettig. LC 85-80482. (Illus.). 128p. 1986. pap. 5.95 (*0-916927-01-6*) Growth Unltd.

Po's Story. Peter Dickinson. LC 98-33908. (Kin Ser.). (Illus.). 224p. (J). (gr. 5 up). 1998. mass mkt. 3.99 (*0-448-41711-1*, G & D) Peng Put Young Read.

Posada. Jose Cruz Gonzalez.Tr. of Inn. 46p. 1998. pap. 3.50 (*0-87129-830-9*, No. L90) Dramatic Pub.

Posadas: A Bilingual Play. Jerome McDonough. Tr. by Betty Alderete from SPA. (Illus.). 26p. 1994. pap. 3.25 (*0-88680-398-5*) I E Clark.

Posadas: A Mexican-American Christmas Celebration. Diane Hoyt-Goldsmith. LC 99-17337. (Illus.). 32p. 1999. 16.95 (*0-8234-1449-3*) Holiday.

Posada's Broadsheets: Mexican Popular Imagery, 1890-1910. Patrick Frank. LC 98-5841. 264p. 1998. 50.00 (*0-8263-1903-3*); pap. 24.95 (*0-8263-1904-1*) U of NM Pr.

Posada's Popular Mexican Prints. Jose G. Posada. Ed. by Robert Berdecio & Stanley Appelbaum. LC 77-178994. (Illus.). 156p. (Orig.). 1972. pap. 11.95 (*0-486-22854-1*) Dover.

***Pose File Vol. 10: Dressing & Undressing.** Elite Publishers Staff. (Illus.). 160p. 2000. pap. 49.95 (*4-87199-064-8*, Pub. by Erute-Shuppan) Bks Nippan.

Pose for Me. Leo Francis. (Illus.). 44p. (Orig.). 1994. pap. 5.00 (*0-9644436-0-0*) Shagbark Pr.

Pose of Happiness. Gail Mazur. LC 85-45963. 96p. 1986. pap. 8.95 (*0-87923-616-7*) Godine.

Pose of Life. Henry C. Monk. 1998. pap. write for info. (*1-57553-759-1*) Watermrk Pr.

Pose Poems. Julie Siegel. LC 81-18422. (Lucky Heart Bk.). 26p. 1981. reprint ed. pap. 30.00 (*0-7837-9150-X*, 204985000003) Bks Demand.

***Poseido.** Tim F. LaHaye. (Left Behind Ser.: Vol. 7). (SPA.). 2000. pap. 9.99 (*0-7899-0755-0*) Editorial Unilit.

Poseidon Adventure. Paul Gallico. 1976. 24.95 (*0-8488-0270-5*) Amereon Ltd.

Poseidon, Apollo see Cults of the Greek States

Poseidon Awakened. Tom Gilmore. 64p. 1995. pap. text 3.95 (*1-879352-14-1*) Mini-Novel Pub.

Poseidonios, 2 vols. Karl Reinhardt. viii, 895p. 1976. write for info. (*3-487-06106-6*); write for info. (*0-318-71005-6*); write for info. (*0-318-71006-4*) G Olms Pubs.

Poseidonios' Metaphysische Schriften, 2 vols. Isaak Heinemann. vii, 714p. 1973. reprint ed. write for info. (*0-318-70932-5*) G Olms Pubs.

Poseidon's Gold. Lindsey Davis. 1995. mass mkt. 5.99 (*0-345-38025-8*) Ballantine Pub Grp.

***Poser 4 Handbook.** R. Shamms Mortier. (Illus.). 532p. 1999. pap. 49.95 incl. cd-rom (*1-886801-93-2*) Chrles River Media.

Poser 3 Handbook. Shamms Mortier. (Illus.). 450p. 1998. pap. 49.95 (*1-886801-90-8*, 1-886801-90-8) Chrles River Media.

***Posers Guide to the Internet & World Wide Web.** James E. Gaskin. 1998. pap. 9.95 (*0-9665370-3-3*) Ruby Moon Pr.

Poses: Poems from Hollywood. Mark Dunster. 1998. pap. 5.00 (*0-89642-515-0*) Linden Pubs.

Posesion Demoniaca: Un Manual Practico para la Iglesia de Hoy. Jorge A. Ovando.Tr. of Demonic Possession: Handbook for Today's Church. (SPA.). 96p. 1997. pap. text 7.99 (*0-311-05770-5*) Casa Bautista.

***Posesion Demoniaca y el Cristiano (Demon Possession & the Christian)** C. Fred Dickason. (SPA & ENG.). 368p. 1999. 12.99 (*0-88113-511-9*) Caribe Betania.

Posession: Cognitive Sources, Forces & Grammaticalization. Bernd Heine. (Cambridge Studies in Linguistics: No. 83). 290p. 1997. text 64.95 (*0-521-55037-8*) Cambridge U Pr.

Posey Carpentier's Master Plan for Real Estate Selling Success. Posey Carpentier. (Illus.). 186p. 1984. 19.95 (*0-13-687716-8*, Busn) P-H.

Posey County, Indiana 175th Anniversary, 1814-1989. Posey County, Indiana Historical Society Staff. LC 89-51786. 192p. 1989. 52.50 (*0-938021-72-9*) Turner Pub KY.

Posey's Spurs. Sandra Hirshkowith & Howard Greager. LC 99-61616. 172p. 1999. pap. 12.95 (*1-890437-30-1*) Western Reflections.

***Posh, Vol. 1.** Jean Carlton. 2000. pap. 15.95 (*0-9639632-6-0*) Stonehorse.

Posh Pancakes & Fancy Fritters: Light Meals with Flair. Helen V. Fisher. LC 93-7312. (Illus.). 128p. (Orig.). 1993. pap. 9.95 (*1-55561-052-8*) Fisher Bks.

Posh Parties: Theme Party Interpretation. Deborah Long. LC 96-96859. iv, 180p. 1996. pap. 15.95 (*0-9653705-1-8*) Delong Pub.

***Posia Borroca.** Et Al Quevedo. (SPA.). 1999. 13.00 (*84-481-0621-0*, McGrw-H College) McGrw-H Hghr Educ.

Posie Meets Sea Shells, Vol. 11. Alfreda Doyle. (Illus.). 25p. 1998. 8.95 (*1-56820-285-7*) Story Time.

Posie Meets the Butterflies, Vol. 12. Alfreda Doyle. (Illus.). 25p. 1998. 8.95 (*1-56820-286-5*) Story Time.

Posie Meets the Fabric Farm, Vol. 10. Alfreda Doyle. (Illus.). 25p. 1998. pap. 8.95 (*1-56820-284-9*) Story Time.

Posie Meets the Frogs, Vol. 13. Alfreda Doyle. (Illus.). 25p. 1998. pap. 8.95 (*1-56820-287-3*) Story Time.

Posie Meets the Junk Yard, Vol. 8. Alfreda Doyle. (Illus.). 25p. 1998. pap. 8.95 (*1-56820-282-2*) Story Time.

Posie Meets the Sugar Farm, Vol. 9. Alfreda Doyle. (Illus.). 25p. 1998. pap. 8.95 (*1-56820-283-0*) Story Time.

Posie Meets the Watermelon Patch, Vol. 7. Alfreda Doyle. (Illus.). 25p. 1998. pap. 8.95 (*1-56820-281-4*) Story Time.

Posie, Positive History: Reference Guide. Compiled by A. C. Doyle. 1983. pap. 6.95 (*0-317-00636-3*) Prosperity & Profits.

Posie the Positive Train: Illustrated Edition. A. C. Doyle. 60p. (J). (gr. 4-9). 1996. pap. 19.95 (*0-939476-96-7*) Prosperity & Profits.

Posie the Positive Train: Story Edition. Bibliotheca Press Staff. (J). (gr. 4-9). 1990. pap. 12.95 (*0-939476-28-2*) Prosperity & Profits.

Posie the Positive Train: Story Edition. Bibliotheca Press Staff. (J). (gr. 4-9). 1996. 17.95 (*0-939476-27-4*) Prosperity & Profits.

Posie the Positive Train Story Samphlet of Stories. Story Time Staff. (Illus.). (Orig.). 1997. pap., teacher ed. 17.95 (*1-56820-194-X*) Story Time.

Posies of G. Gascoigne, Corrected & Augmented. George Gascoigne. LC 79-84110. (English Experience Ser.: No. 929). 532p. 1979. reprint ed. lib. bdg. 50.00 (*90-221-0929-1*) Walter J Johnson.

***Posing a Threat: Flappers, Chorus Girls, & Other Brazen Performers of the American 1920s.** Angela J. Latham. LC 99-45571. (Illus.). 217p. 2000. pap. 19.95 (*0-8195-6401-X*, Wesleyan Univ Pr) U Pr of New Eng.

***Posing a Threat: Flappers, Chorus Girls & Other Brazen Performers of the American 1920s.** Angela J. Latham. LC 99-45571. (Illus.). 217p. 2000. text 50.00 (*0-8195-6400-1*, Wesleyan Univ Pr) U Pr of New Eng.

***Posing & Lighting Techniques for Studio Portrait Photography.** J. J. Allen. (Illus.). 120p. 2000. pap. 29.95 (*1-58428-031-X*, Pub. by Amherst Media) IPG Chicago.

Posing & Solving Problems with Story Boxes: First & Second Grade, Incl. blackline masters. Donna Burk & Allyn Snider. LC 94-75180. (Illus.). 218p. (C). 1994. teacher ed., spiral bd. 38.00 (*1-886131-25-2*, SB12) Math Lrning.

Posing Mathematically, 6 vols., Vol. 6. Brown. 1996. pap. text 20.00 (*0-435-07112-2*) Heinemann.

Posing Nude. Frederick A. Raborg, Jr. (Amelia Chapbooks Ser.). 64p. (Orig.). 1990. pap. 10.95 (*0-936545-14-3*) Amelia.

Posing of Questions: Logical Foundations of Erotetic Inferences. Andrzej Wisniewski. (Syntheses Library: Vol. 252). 262p. (C). 1995. lib. bdg. 118.00 (*0-7923-3637-2*, Pub. by Kluwer Academic) Kluwer Academic.

***Posing Questions for a Scientific Archaeology.** Sarah L. Sterling. Ed. by Terry L. Hunt & Carl P. Lipo. LC 00-37834. (Scientific Archaeology for the Third Millennium). 2000. write for info. (*0-89789-753-6*, Bergin & Garvey) Greenwood.

Posioned Water. John M. Patten, Jr. LC 94-37163. (Read All about Eye on the Environment Ser.). 24p. (J). (gr. 1-4). 1995. lib. bdg. 18.60 (*1-55916-097-7*) Rourke Bk Co.

Positeens: Empowerment for Today's Teens. Diane Howard & Connie Higgins. 123p. (Orig.). 1996. pap., teacher ed. 14.95 (*0-9647536-1-8*) Higgins & Howard.

***Position.** rev. ed. (Ironworking Lev 2 Ser.). 1999. teacher ed., ring bd. 12.00 (*0-13-019301-1*) P-H.

Position & Conditions of Intellectuals in Hungary. Ed. by Katalin S. Falusne. 188p. 1995. pap. 69.00 (*963-05-6870-5*, Pub. by Akade Kiado) St Mut.

Position & Pawn Tension in Chess. David H. Levin. (Illus.). 118p. (Orig.). 1993. pap. 13.95 (*0-9638001-0-8*) Syllogism Pr.

Position & Rights of a Bona Fide Purchaser for Value of Goods Improperly Obtained. J. Walter Jones. 128p. 1987. reprint ed. 35.00 (*0-8377-2303-5*, Rothman) W S Hein.

Position & Scale Studies Opus 8: Violin. Otakar Sevcik. 28p. 1986. pap. 7.95 (*0-7935-5437-3*) H Leonard.

Position & the Nature of Personhood: An Approach to the Understanding of Persons, 5. Larry Cochran. LC 84-12852. (Contributions in Psychology Ser.: No. 5). 191p. 1985. 49.95 (*0-313-24633-5*, CPN/, Greenwood Pr) Greenwood.

Position Available: A Comedy in One Act. Brad Gromelski. LC 98-211978. 31p. 1998. write for info. (*0-573-62622-7*) S French Trade.

Position Classification & Job Grading in the Federal Government: A Guide for Practitioners. David C. Knudsen. LC 98-119249. 164p. 1997. pap. 30.00 (*1-878810-40-5*) Dewey Pubns.

Position Classification for Wisconsin Public Libraries. Personnel & Professional Concerns Cmte Staff. (FRE.). 303p. 1994. 30.00 (*0-614-04669-6*) Wisc Lib Assn.

Position Classification Specialist. Jack Rudman. (Career Examination Ser.: C-601). 1994. pap. 29.95 (*0-8373-0601-9*) Nat Learn.

Position Descriptions in Special Libraries. 3rd rev. ed. Del Sweeney & Karin Zilla. LC 96-39359. 235p. 1996. pap. 41.00 (*0-87111-451-8*) SLA.

Position Descriptions in Special Libraries: A Collection of Examples. Special Libraries Association Staff. Ed. by Barbara Ivantcho. LC 83-10168. 160p. reprint ed. pap. 49.60 (*0-7837-4142-1*, 204387700011) Bks Demand.

Position Etudes. Shinichi Suzuki. (Suzuki Violin School Ser.). (JPN.). 32p. (gr. k-12). 1973. pap. text 5.95 (*0-87487-096-8*, Suzuki Method) Summy-Birchard.

Position for Success! Strategic Marketing for Group Practices. Andrea Eliscu. 148p. 1994. 49.00 (*1-56829-044-6*, 4812) Med Group Mgmt.

Position in Law of Women: A Concise & Comprehensive Treatise on the Position of Women at Common Law As Modified by the Doctrines of Equity & by Recent Legislation; Together with the Married Women's Property Acts, 1870, 1874, 1882: The Rules of the Supreme Court, 1883, Relating to Taking Acknowledgements & the Postal Regulations, 1883, Affecting Married Women. Thomas Barrett-Lennard. xxviii, 181p. 1983. reprint ed. 32.50 (*0-8377-0336-0*, Rothman) W S Hein.

***Position Method Handbook: Based on the Position Method of Learning Golf.** Po Chung. 20p. 1998. pap. 25.00 (*0-9667685-3-1*) Virtual Univ Educ Sys.

Position of America & Other Essays. Alfonso Reyes. Tr. by Harriet De Onis. LC 77-142690. (Essay Index Reprint Ser.). 1977. 19.95 (*0-8369-2067-8*) Ayer.

Position of Bernard Shaw in European Drama & Philosophy. Martin Ellehauge. LC 68-853. 1970. reprint ed. lib. bdg. 75.00 (*0-8383-0659-4*) M S G Haskell Hse.

Position of Christianity in the United States, in Its Relations with Our Political Institutions, & Specially with Reference to Religious Instruction in the Public Schools. Stephen Colwell. LC 78-38444. (Religion in America, Ser. 2). 180p. 1972. reprint ed. 19.95 (*0-405-04063-6*) Ayer.

Position of Ethnic Minorities: The 4th National Survey of Ethnic Minorities in Britain. Tariq Modood et al. LC 97-135979. 320p. (C). 1995. pap. 24.95 (*0-85374-671-0*) Brookings.

Position of Foreign Corporations in American Constitutional Law: A Contribution to the History & Theory of Juristic Persons in Anglo-American Law, 1918. Gerard C. Henderson. LC 99-18233. 1999. 50.00 (*1-886363-89-7*) Lawbk Exchange.

Position of Modern Science on the Beginning of Human Life. Scientists for Life Staff. 45p. (Orig.). 1983. pap. 1.75 (*0-937930-02-4*) Sun Life.

Position of Possessive & Demonstrative Adjectives in the Noctes Atticae of Aulus Gellius. Edward Yoder. (LD Ser.: No. 2). 1928. pap. 25.00 (*0-527-00748-X*) Periodicals Srv.

Position of the Author. Buzz Spector. 32p. (Orig.). 1993. pap. 7.00 (*0-89822-102-1*) Visual Studies.

Position of the Chief in the Modern Political System of Ashanti: A Study of the Influence of Contemporary Social Changes on Ashanti Political Institutions. Kofi A. Busia. LC 51-13932. 244p. reprint ed. pap. 75.70 (*0-8357-3220-7*, 205709200011) Bks Demand.

Position of the Laborer in a System of Nationalism: A Study in the Theories of the Later English Mercantilists. Edgar S. Furniss. LC 58-3121. (Reprints of Economic Classics Ser.). 260p. 1965. reprint ed. 35.00 (*0-678-00093-X*) Kelley.

Position of the Polynesian Languages within the (Austronesian Malayo-Polynesian) Language Family. George W. Grace. LC 59-7612. (Indiana University Publications in Anthropology & Linguistics Memoir: No. 16). 85p. reprint ed. pap. 30.00 (*0-608-13183-0*, 201520100094) Bks Demand.

Position of the "Roode En Witte Roos" in the Saga of "King Richard Third" Lambert Van Den Bos. Ed. by Oscar J. Campbell. LC 72-131494. reprint ed. 37.50 (*0-404-01375-9*) AMS Pr.

Position of Women. Frances M. Heidensohn. (Conflict & Change in Britain - A New Audit Ser.). 240p. (C). 1993. pap. 19.95 (*0-485-80106-X*, Pub. by Athlone Pr); text 50.00 (*0-485-80006-3*, Pub. by Athlone Pr) Humanities.

Position of Women As Considered by Representative American Authors Since 1800. C. B. Guest. 1972. 59.95 (*0-8490-0885-9*) Gordon Pr.

Position of Women in Hindu Civilization. A. S. Altekar. 384p. 1978. 17.95 (*0-318-37082-4*) Asia Bk Corp.

Position of Women in Indian Life. S. M. Mitra. (C). 1995. pap. 10.00 (*81-86142-38-X*, Pub. by Low Price) S Asia.

***Position of Women in Nineteenth-Century English Literature.** Veronica M. Boyle Churchich. LC 99-98745. 2000. 18.95 (*0-533-13346-7*) Vantage.

Position of Women in the U. S. S. R. George N. Serebrennikov. LC 72-137384. (Select Bibliographies Reprint Ser.). 1977. 18.95 (*0-8369-5585-4*) Ayer.

Position of Women on the Labour Market in the European Community. Daniele Meulders et al. 216p. 1993. 72.95 (*1-85521-419-9*, Pub. by Dartmth Pub) Ashgate Pub Co.

Position of Yana in the Hokan Stock. fac. ed. Edward Sapir. (University of California Publications in American Archaeology & Ethnology: Vol. 13: 1). 34p. (C). 1917. reprint ed. pap. text 3.75 (*1-55567-209-4*) Coyote Press.

Position Pieces for Cello. Rick Mooney. 64p. 1997. pap. text 8.95 (*0-87487-762-8*) Summy-Birchard.

Position Politique du Surrealisme. Andre Breton. (Bibliotheque Volante Ser.). 1991. pap. 10.95 (*0-7859-3163-5*, 2253056537) Fr & Eur.

Position Primer for the Guitar Student: An Easy, Fun, Systematic Approach to Learning the Fingerboard, Technique, Chords, Moveable Scale Forms, Keys & Improvising. Ralph L. Scicchitano. 61p. (Orig.). (J). (gr. 4-12). 1995. spiral bd. 8.95 (*0-9646652-9-8*) Anytime Pubns.

Position-Sensitive Detection of Thermal Neutrons. Ed. by Pierre Convert & J. Bruce Forsyth. 1984. text 123.00 (*0-12-186180-5*) Acad Pr.

Position Studies: Advance Position Study. Yoon-Il Auh. (Auh School of Violin Ser.). 35p. (J). (gr. 1-12). 1985. student ed. 10.00 (*1-882858-46-8*) Yoon-il Auh.

Position Studies: Scales & Shifting 1. Yoon-Il Auh. (Auh School of Violin Ser.). 30p. (YA). (gr. 5-12). 1990. student ed. 10.00 (*1-882858-11-5*) Yoon-il Auh.

Position Studies: Scales & Shifting 2. Yoon-Il Auh. (Auh School of Violin Ser.). 30p. (YA). (gr. 5-12). 1990. student ed. 10.00 (*1-882858-12-3*) Yoon-il Auh.

Position Studies: Third Position. Yoon-Il Auh. (Auh School of Violin Ser.). 35p. (YA). (gr. 5-12). 1986. student ed. 10.00 (*1-882858-45-X*) Yoon-il Auh.

Position to Command Respect: Women & the Eleventh Britannica. Gillian Thomas. LC 92-9857. 222p. 1992. 30.00 (*0-8108-2567-8*) Scarecrow.

Positional Chess Handbook. Israel Gelfer. (Chess Library). 224p. 1992. pap. 16.95 (*0-02-028831-X*) Macmillan.

Positional Cloning by Exon Trapping & CDNA Selection. Bernhard Korn. LC 98-13044. 77p. 1999. pap. 74.95 (*0-471-29797-6*) Wiley.

***Positional Faithfulness: An Optimality Theoretic Treatment of Phonological Asymmetries.** Jill N. Beckman. LC 99-27980. 250p. 1999. 69.00 (*0-8153-3348-X*) Garland.

Positional Release Technique. Chaitow. (C). 1998. pap. text 95.00 (*0-443-06129-7*) Church.

Positional Release Techniques. Chaitow. 1996. text 38.95 (*0-443-05299-9*, W B Saunders Co) Harcrt Hlth Sci Grp.

***Positional Release Techniques.** Denise Deig. (Illus.). 208p. 2000. 65.00 (*0-7506-7225-0*) Buttrwrth-Heinemann.

Positional Release Therapy: Assessment & Treatment of Musculoskeletol Dysfunction. Kerry J. D'Ambrogio & George B. Roth. (Illus.). 280p. (C). (gr. 13). 1997. text 79.95 (*0-8151-0096-5*, 26559) Mosby Inc.

Positional Sacrifices. Neil McDonald. 128p. 1995. pap. 15.95 (*1-85744-110-9*, Pub. by Cadgn Bks) Macmillan.

Positional Welding. Richard Hunter. (Series 904B). (Orig.). 1977. pap., student ed. 7.00 (*0-8064-0375-6*, 904B) Bergwall.

Positional Words. Barbara Gregorich. Ed. by Joan Hoffman. (I Know It! Book Ser.). (Illus.). 32p. (J). (ps-1). 1994. student ed. 2.49 (*0-938256-51-3*, 02051) Sch Zone Pub Co.

Positioneering. Charles N. Aronson. (Illus.). 347p. (C). 1969. 20.00 (*0-915736-01-2*) C N Aronson.

Positionen und Begriffe Im Kampf Mit Weimar-Genf-Versailles see Four Articles, 1931-1938

Positioning. Andrew Ries. 1993. 4.99 (*0-446-77692-0*) Warner Bks.

***Positioning.** 20th anniversary ed. Ries. 1999. pap. 24.95 (*0-07-135916-8*) McGraw.

Positioning: The Battle for Your Mind. rev. ed. Al Ries & Jack Trout. 1985. text 24.95 (*0-07-065264-3*) McGraw.

Positioning: The Battle for Your Mind. rev. ed. Al Ries & Jack Trout. 224p. 1987. mass mkt. 6.99 (*0-446-34794-9*, Pub. by Warner Bks) Little.

Positioning - The Logic of Sailboat Racing. Stuart H. Walker. 1992. 29.95 (*0-393-03339-2*) Norton.

Positioning Customer Support for the 21st Century: Theories & Technologies. Ed. by Keri E. Pearlson & Andrew B. Whinston. (C). 1995. pap. 14.95 (*1-887406-05-0*) ICTwo Inst.

Positioning Family & Consumer Sciences for the 21st Century. Pat Zito. 50p. 1998. pap. 8.00 (*0-911365-39-7*) Family & Consumer Sci Educ.

Positioning for Function: The Wheelchair & Other Assistive Technologies. Adrienne F. Bergen et al. (Illus.). (Orig.). (C). 1990. pap. text 49.95 (*0-911681-04-3*) Valhalla Rehab.

Positioning for Health & Function. Jody Winters. Ed. by Karen G. Mc Gowan. 144p. 1997. pap. 22.95 (*1-928752-09-8*) Mc Gowan Pubns.

***Positioning for Power: Kneeling Low in Prayer, Standing Tall in God.** Stuart Robinson. 1998. pap. 12.99 (*1-85240-228-8*) SOV5.

Positioning for Venture Capital: Mastering the Business Plan Presentation. Fernando L. Senior. Ed. by Amy N. Vroeland. LC 98-92313. 112p. (Orig.). 1998. pap. text 39.95 (*0-9669013-0-4*) Money Mktg.

Positioning in a Wheelchair: A Guide for Professional Caregivers of the Disabled Adult. 2nd ed. Jan K. Mayall & Guylaine Desharnais. LC 94-27090. 176p. 1995. pap. 23.00 (*1-55642-251-2*, 42512) SLACK Inc.

Positioning in Anesthesia & Surgery. 3rd ed. John T. Martin & Mark A. Warner. Ed. by Lesley Day. 352p. 1996. text 79.00 (*0-7216-6674-4*, W B Saunders Co) Harcrt Hlth Sci Grp.

Positioning of Tourist Destinations. Allen Z. Reich. (Advances in Tourism Applications Ser.: Vol. 4). (Illus.). 160p. 1999. pap. 16.95 (*1-57167-261-3*) Sagamore Pub.

Positioning Pensions for the Twenty-First Century. Ed. by Michael S. Gordon et al. LC 96-53837. 256p. 1997. text 42.50 (*0-8122-3391-3*) U of Pa Pr.

Positioning People in Space: Clip Art in Context for Architects & Designers. Mamdouh Fayek. LC 97-28554. (Illus.). 326p. 1997. pap. 39.95 (*0-07-021949-4*) McGraw.

Positioning Subjects: Psychoanalysis & Critical Educational Studies. Stephen Appel. LC 96-3624. (Critical Studies in Education & Culture: No. 1064-8615). 240p. 1996. 59.95 (*0-89789-442-1*, Bergin & Garvey) Greenwood.

P

Positioning Systems: A Unified Approach. C. R. Drane. LC 92-26470. (Lecture Notes in Control & Information Sciences: Vol. 181). 175p. 1992. 53.95 (*0-387-55850-0*) Spr-Verlag.

Positioning Systems in Intelligent Transportation Systems. Chris R. Drane & Chris Rizos. LC 97-42069. 392p. 1998. 89.00 (*0-89006-536-5*) Artech Hse.

Positioning the Missionary: John Booth Good & the Colonial Confluence of Cultures in Nineteenth-Century British Columbia. Brett Christophers. 224p. 1999. pap. 24.95 (*0-7748-0655-9*) U BC Pr.

Positioning Theory: Moral Contexts of International Action. Rom Harre & Van Langehove. LC 98-16534. 59.95p. 1998. 59.95 (*0-631-21138-1*); pap. 29.95 (*0-631-21139-X*) Blackwell Pubs.

Positioning Your Practice for the Managed Care Market. Ed. by J. Thomas Danzi. LC 95-44935. (Illus.). 328p. 1996. pap. 29.00 (*0-683-02373-X*) Lppncott W & W.

Positions see Let's Learn Set

Positions. (Home Workbooks Ser.). (Illus.). 64p. (J). (ps-1). 1995. pap., wbk. ed. 2.49 (*0-88724-307-X*, CD6804) Carson-Dellos.

Positions. Jacques Derrida. Tr. by Alan Bass from FRE. LC 80-17620. 1981. 11.95 (*0-226-14332-5*) U Ch Pr.

Positions. Jacques Derrida. Tr. by Alan Bass from FRE. LC 80-17620. 128p. 1982. pap. text 8.00 (*0-226-14331-7*) U Ch Pr.

Positions & Presuppositions in Science Fiction. Darko Suvin. LC 87-18352. 245p. 1988. 26.00 (*0-87338-356-7*) Kent St U Pr.

Positions Concerning the Training up of Children. Richard Mulcaster. Ed. by William Barker. 696p. 1993. text 80.00 (*0-8020-2987-6*) U of Toronto Pr.

Positions et Propositions, 2 vols. Jean Cocteau. (FRE.). 270p. 1983. pap. 22.95 (*0-7859-4717-5*) Fr & Eur.

Positions et Propositions, 2 vols., 1. Paul Claudel. (FRE.). 266p. 1934. pap. 12.95 (*0-685-73322-X*) Fr & Eur.

Positions et Propositions, 2 vols., 2. Paul Claudel. (FRE.). 266p. 1934. pap. 13.95 (*0-7859-1110-3*, 2070214958) Fr & Eur.

Positions in Art: A Round Table Discussion. Jan Hoet & James Turell. (Illus.). 208p. 1995. pap. 24.95 (*3-89322-279-0*) Dist Art Pubs.

Positions of German Design in the Late 1990's: International Design Conference Aspen, 1996. (Illus.). 320p. 1997. 49.95 (*3-931317-37-4*, Pub. by Art Bks Intl) Partners Pubs Grp.

Positions to Pray In. Barry Dempster. 96p. 1989. pap. 8.00 (*0-920717-08-X*) Guernica Editions.

Positions Wherein Those Primitive Circumstances Be Examined: Which Are Necessarie for the Training up of Children (1581 Edition) Richard Mulcaster. Ed. & Intro. by Jeffrey Stern. (Classics in Education Ser.). 308p. 1996. reprint ed. 80.00 (*1-85506-298-4*) Bks Intl VA.

Positions with White Roses. Ursule Molinaro. LC 82-24916. 104p. 1983. 12.95 (*0-914232-58-4*); 25.00 (*0-914232-59-2*) McPherson & Co.

Positions with White Roses. Ursule Molinaro. LC 82-24916. 104p. 1989. reprint ed. pap. 8.00 (*0-929701-00-3*) McPherson & Co.

Positive: HIV Affirmative Counseling. Craig Kain. 270p. 1996. pap. text 33.95 (*1-55620-147-8*, 72573) Am Coun Assn.

***Positive about Inspection.** Mike Tilling & Paul Nash. 40p. 2000. 59.95 (*0-566-08316-7*, Pub. by Ashgate Pub) Ashgate Pub Co.

Positive Accounting Theory. Ross L. Watts & Jerold L. Zimmerman. (Illus.). 432p. (C). 1985. text 41.20 (*0-13-686171-7*) P-H.

Positive Action No. WR5: Changing the Workplace for Women. Paddy Stamp & Sadie Robarts. 135p. (C). 1986. pap. 30.00 (*0-946088-25-X*, Pub. by NCCL) St Mut.

Positive Action Family Kit. Carol G. Allred. (Illus.). 372p. 1995. spiral bd. 54.95 (*1-57160-012-4*); ring bd. 59.95 (*1-57160-078-7*) Positive Action.

Positive Action in Action: Equal Opportunities & Declining Opportunities on Merseyside. Robert Moore. LC 97-71713. (Research in Ethnic Relations Ser.). (Illus.). 144p. 1997. text 59.95 (*1-84014-108-5*, Pub. by Ashgate Pub) Ashgate Pub Co.

Positive Actions for Living: A Guide for Learning Parent, Family, Community & Personal Positive Actions. Carol G. Allred. LC 95-72954. (Illus.). 381p. 1996. pap. 49.95 (*1-57160-082-5*); pap., wbk. ed. 4.00 (*1-57160-090-6*); pap. text 44.95 (*1-57160-087-6*) Positive Action.

Positive Addiction. William Glasser. LC 84-48643. 176p. 1976. pap. 12.50 (*0-06-091249-9*, CN 1249, Perennial) HarperTrade.

Positive African American Men-United: A Cultural Revolution. Sidney Wingfield. LC 93-7312. 118p. 1994. pap. text 19.95 (*1-883874-49-1*) African Am Positive.

Positive African Images for Children: CIBI: Social Studies Curriculum. Council of Independent Black Institutions Staff. LC 90-60173. (Illus.). 64p. 1990. pap. 7.95 (*0-932415-48-2*) Red Sea Pr.

Positive Aging: Essays In Educational & Social Groups. Percy. 52.95 (*1-84014-340-1*) Ashgate Pub Co.

Positive Aging: Every Woman's Quest for Wisdom & Beauty. Karen Kaigler-Walker. LC 97-1380. 250p. (Orig.). 1997. pap. 14.95 (*1-57324-084-2*) Conari Press.

Positive Aging A to Z. Kay Drikey. 164p. (Orig.). 1996. pap. 14.95 (*1-56550-038-5*) Vis Bks Intl.

***Positive Alternatives to Exclusion.** Paul Cooper. LC 00-28197. 2000. pap. write for info. (*0-415-19758-9*) Routledge.

Positive & Black: A Resource Directory of Famous Contemporary African Americans & Organizations. Karl P. Boyer. 31p. (J). (gr. 8). 1993. pap. text 6.00 (*0-9642154-0-3*) Positive & Black.

Positive & Negative Symptoms in Psychosis: Description, Research & Future Directions. Ed. by Philip D. Harvey & Elaine Walker. 351p. (C). 1987. text 49.95 (*0-89859-880-X*) L Erlbaum Assocs.

Positive & Negative Syndromes in Schizophrenia. Stanley R. Kay. LC 90-15113. (Einstein Clinical & Experimental Psychiatry Monograph Ser.: No. 5). 288p. 1991. text 45.95 (*0-87630-608-3*) Brunner-Mazel.

Positive & the Preventive Check: A Study of the Rate of Growth of Pre-Industrial Populations. Per G. Ohlin. Ed. by Stuart Bruchey. LC 80-2819. (Dissertations in European Economic History Ser.). (Illus.). 1981. lib. bdg. 54.95 (*0-405-14003-7*) Ayer.

***Positive Approach.** Frances James. (Kids' Stuff Ser.). (J). 1999. pap. text 15.95 (*0-947882-33-2*) Belair Pubns Ltd.

Positive Approach to Autism. Stella Waterhouse. LC 99-42605. 1999. pap. 23.95 (*1-85302-808-8*) Jessica Kingsley.

***Positive Approach to Occupation with People with Dementia.** Jackie Pool. LC 99-42840. (Bradford Dementia Group Good Practice Guide Ser.). 1999. pap. 22.95 (*1-85302-772-3*) Jessica Kingsley.

Positive Approach to the International Economic Order, 2 pts. Incl. Trade & Structural Adjustment. 82p. 1978. 3.00 (*0-902594-33-8*); Pt. 2. Nontrade Issues. V. N. Balasubramanyam & Alasdair I. MacBean. 1980. 5.00 (*0-902594-37-0*); write for info. (*0-318-59525-7*) Natl Planning.

Positive Approaches to Corrections: Research, Policy & Practice. Roger J. Lauen. LC 96-50994. 256p. 1997. pap. 29.95 (*1-56991-065-0*) Am Correctional.

Positive Approaches to Dementia Care. 3rd ed. U. P. Holden & R. T. Woods. (Illus.). 240p. 1995. pap. write for info. (*0-443-04970-X*) Church.

Positive Approaches to Living with End Stage Renal Disease: Psychosocial & Thanatalogic Aspects, 6. Ed. by Michael A. Hardy. LC 85-28334. 239p. 1986. 55.00 (*0-275-92019-4*, C2019, Praeger Pubs) Greenwood.

Positive As Sound: Emily Dickinson's Rhyme. Judy J. Small. LC 89-29073. 280p. 1990. 35.00 (*0-8203-1227-4*) U of Ga Pr.

Positive Assertions. Bonnie Seefeldt. 41p. 1988. pap. 6.00 (*1-884112-02-1*) See More Bks.

Positive Attitudes & Peacemaking for Younger Children: A Program to Enhance Positive Attitudes & Peacemaking Skills for Pre-School Through Third Grade. Michele Borba. Ed. by Marie Conte. (Character Builders Ser.: No. 5). (Illus.). 144p. 2000. pap. 19.95 (*1-880396-59-9*, JP9659-9) Jalmar Pr.

Positive Attitudes at Work. Sharon K. Ferrett. 104p. 1994. text 10.95 (*0-7863-0167-8*, Irwn Prfssnl) McGraw-Hill Prof.

Positive Attitudes for the 50+ Years: How Anyone Can Make Them Happy & Fulfilling. Willard A. Scofield. LC 98-67443. 160p. 1998. pap. 12.00 (*0-9654806-2-3*) Magnus Pr.

Positive Attitudes for the Physically Challenged. Hoyt Anderson. 20p. (Orig.). 1986. pap. 3.95 (*0-937743-00-3*) Successful Living.

Positive Background of Hindu Sociology, 2 vols., Set. Benoy K. Sarkar. LC 73-3807. (Sacred Books of the Hindus: Nos. 16 & 25). reprint ed. 74.50 (*0-404-57839-X*) AMS Pr.

Positive Background of Hindu Sociology: Introduction to Hindu Positivism. Benoy K. Sarkar. LC 74-17338. (Sacred Books of the Hindus: 32). reprint ed. 74.50 (*0-404-57850-0*) AMS Pr.

Positive Behavior Management Strategies for Physical Educators. Barry W. Lavay et al. LC 97-18733. (Illus.). 176p. (Orig.). 1997. pap. text 22.00 (*0-87322-880-4*, BLAV0880) Human Kinetics.

Positive Behavior Support in People with Developmental Disabilities: A Research Synthesis. Edward G. Carr. LC 99-22505. 108p. 1999. 31.95 (*0-940898-60-8*) Am Assn Mental.

Positive Behavioral Support: Including People with Difficult Behavior in the Community. Ed. by Lynn K. Koegel et al. 510p. 1995. 37.95 (*1-55766-228-2*) P H Brookes.

Positive Benefits of Astrology. Doane. 88p. 1992. 12.00 (*0-86690-410-7*) Am Fed Astrologers.

Positive Bible: From Genesis to Revelation: Scripture that Inspires, Nurtures & Heals. Compiled by Kenneth W. Caine. 320p. 1999. pap. 12.00 (*0-380-79180-3*, Avon Bks) Morrow Avon.

Positive Careers: The Rights & Responsibilities of HIV Positive Health Care Workers. Paul Mayho. 160p. 1997. pap. 27.50 (*0-304-33277-1*); text 79.50 (*0-304-33275-5*) Continuum.

Positive Caregiver Attitudes. James R. Sherman. (Illus.). 80p. 1994. pap. 9.95 (*0-935538-18-6*) Pathway Bks.

Positive Charges: 544 Ways to Stay Upbeat During Downbeat Times. Alexander Lockhart. 224p. (Orig.). 1994. pap. 6.95 (*0-9643035-5-8*) Zander Pr.

Positive Child: A Practical Parenting Guide. Tim Sponsler. Ed. by Pat Sponsler. LC 91-77852. 144p. (Orig.). 1992. pap. 6.95 (*0-9631832-0-6*) Judamarie Pub Hse.

Positive Child Guidance. Miller. (Early Childhood Education Ser.). 1990. 28.95 (*0-8273-3383-8*, VNR) Wiley.

Positive Child Guidance. 2nd ed. Darla F. Miller. 312p. (C). 1995. pap. 29.75 (*0-8273-5878-4*) Delmar.

Positive Child Guidance. 3rd ed. Darla F. Miller. LC 99-34456. (Early Childhood Education Ser.). 366p. (C). 1999. pap. 37.95 (*0-7668-0360-0*) Delmar.

Positive Child Guidance Instructor's Guide. 2nd ed. Miller. (Early Childhood Education Ser.). 1996. 14.00 (*0-8273-5879-2*, VNR) Wiley.

Positive Christian Living. J. J. Turner. 1983. pap. 7.15 (*0-89137-316-0*) Quality Pubns.

Positive Christologie Christian Hermann Weibes: Eine Untersuchung zur Hinwendung der Christologie zur Frage Nach Dem Historischen Jesus Als Antwort Auf das "Leben Jesu" von David Friedrich Straub. Volker Stumke. (Europäische Hochschulschriften Ser.: Reihe 23, Bd. 463). (GER.). VIII, 298p. 1992. 56.80 (*3-631-44495-8*) P Lang Pubng.

Positive Classroom Discipline. (Illus.). 368p. 1987. write for info. (*0-614-13414-5*) McGraw.

Positive Classroom Instruction. (Illus.). 250p. 1987. write for info. (*0-614-13415-3*) McGraw.

Positive Classroom Instruction. Fredric H. Jones. LC 86-18607. (Illus.). 1987. reprint ed. text 24.95 (*0-07-032782-3*) F H Jones.

Positive Classroom Management. Terri Breeden & Emalie Egan. Ed. by Anna Quinn. LC 96-78572. (Illus.). 144p. (Orig.). (J). (gr. 5-8). 1997. pap. text, teacher ed. 14.95 (*0-86530-355-X*, 349-4) Incentive Pubns.

Positive Classroom Management: A Step-by-Step Guide to Successfully Running the Show Without Destroying Student Dignity. Robert DiGiulio. LC 95-18298. (Illus.). 128p. 1995. pap. 19.95 (*0-8039-6289-4*) Corwin Pr.

Positive Classroom Management: A Step-by-Step Guide to Successfully Running the Show Without Destroying Student Dignity. Robert DiGiulio. LC 95-18298. (Illus.). 128p. 1995. 45.95 (*0-8039-6288-6*) Corwin Pr.

***Positive Classroom Management: A Step-by-Step Guide to Sucessfully Running the Show Without Destroying Student Dignity.** 2nd ed. Robert DiGiulio. LC 99-6664. (One-Off Ser.). (Illus.). 136p. 1999. pap. 21.95 (*0-8039-6816-7*); lib. bdg. 47.95 (*0-8039-6815-9*) Sage.

Positive Coaching: Building Character & Self-Esteem Through Sports. Jim Thompson. 397p. 1995. pap. 19.95 (*1-886346-00-3*) Warde Pubs.

Positive Confessions: A Prayer & Praise Workbook. Yvonne R. Dixon. 63p. 1996. wbk. ed. 8.95 (*0-9651838-0-7*) Dixon Solutions.

Positive Continental Afrikan Self-Knowledge Technology: or, To Know We Are Continental Afrikans, Is to Be Afrikans in Thoughts, Words & Deeds. Afrikadzata Deku. LC 91-72697. (Afrikan-Centric Self-Empowerment Ser.). 130p. 1998. 25.00 (*1-56454-035-9*) Cont Afrikan.

Positive Cooking: Cooking for People Living with HIV. Lisa McMillan et al. LC 96-33390. (Illus.). 264p. 1998. pap. 12.95 (*0-89529-734-5*, Avery) Penguin Putnam.

Positive Creativity: How to Enhance & Evaluate It. Jerry D. Jones & Billy Escue. (Illus.). 128p. (Orig.). (C). 1990. pap. 12.95 (*0-9627320-0-1*) Rowman.

Positive Criminology. Michael R. Gottfredson & Travis Hirschi. LC 87-16447. 189p. 1987. reprint ed. pap. 58.60 (*0-608-01455-9*, 205949900001) Bks Demand.

Positive Definite Unimodular Lattices with Trivial Automorhism Groups. E. Bannai. LC 90-31824. (Memoirs Ser.: No. 85/429). 70p. 1990. pap. 18.00 (*0-8218-2491-0*, MEMO/85/429) Am Math.

Positive Deviance in Child Nutrition. 153p. 30.00 (*92-808-0697-1*, 89.III.A.7) UN.

Positive Discipline. Didactic Systems Staff. (Study Units Ser.). 1978. pap. 9.00 (*0-89401-122-7*) Didactic Syst.

Positive Discipline. rev. ed. Jane Nelsen. 272p. 1996. pap. 11.00 (*0-345-40251-0*) Ballantine Pub Grp.

Positive Discipline. 2nd ed. Jane Nelsen. 242p. 1987. pap. 7.95 (*0-9606896-1-3*) Ballantine Pub Grp.

Positive Discipline: A Pocketful of Ideas. William W. Purkey & David B. Strahan. 50p. 1986. 9.00 (*1-56090-031-8*) Natl Middle Schl.

Positive Discipline: A Teacher's A-Z Guide: Turn Common Behavioral Problems into Learning Opportunities. Jane Nelsen et al. LC 95-47032. 384p. 1996. per. 14.95 (*0-7615-0499-0*) Prima Pub.

Positive Discipline: The First Three Years: From Infant to Toddler - Laying the Foundation for Raising a Capable, Confident Child. Jane Nelsen et al. LC 98-7750. 304p. 1998. pap. 16.00 (*0-7615-1505-4*) Prima Pub.

Positive Discipline A-Z. Jane Nelsen et al. 368p. 1993. pap. 14.95 (*1-55958-312-6*) Prima Pub.

Positive Discipline A-Z: From Toddlers to Teens - 1001 Solutions to Everyday Parenting Problems. 2nd expanded rev. ed. Lynn Lott et al. LC 98-51638. 384p. 1999. pap. 16.95 (*0-7615-1470-8*) Prima Pub.

Positive Discipline for Blended Families: Nurturing Harmony, Respect, & Unity in Your New Stepfamily. Jane Nelsen. LC 97-25126. 208p. 1997. per. 15.00 (*0-7615-1035-4*) Prima Pub.

Positive Discipline for Parenting in Recovery: A Guide to Help Recovering Parents. Jane Nelsen et al. LC 95-24341. 288p. 1995. pap. 12.95 (*0-7615-0130-4*) Prima Pub.

Positive Discipline for Preschoolers, Age Three to Six: For Their Early Years - Raising Children Who Are Responsible, Respectful & Resourceful. 2nd rev. ed. Jane Nelsen et al. LC 98-36006. 304p. 1998. pap. 16.00 (*0-7615-1515-1*) Prima Pub.

***Positive Discipline for Single Parents: A Practical Guide to Raising Children Who Are Responsibl.** 2nd rev. ed. Jane Nelsen et al. LC 99-27561. (Illus.). 288p. 1999. pap. 16.00 (*0-7615-2011-2*) Prima Pub.

Positive Discipline for Single Parents: A Practical Guide to Raising Children Who Are Responsible, Respectful, & Resourceful. Jane Nelsen et al. LC 93-17738. 208p. 1993. pap. 12.00 (*1-55958-355-X*) Prima Pub.

***Positive Discipline for Teenagers.** 2nd ed. Jane Nelson & Lynn Lott. LC 99-59674. (Positive Discipline Library). 2000. pap. 16.95 (*0-7615-2181-X*) Prima Pub.

Positive Discipline for Teenagers: Resolving Conflict with Your Teenager. Jane Nelsen & Lynn Lott. LC 93-36383. 448p. 1994. pap. 14.95 (*1-55958-441-6*) Prima Pub.

***Positive Discipline for Your Stepfamily.** 4th ed. Jane Nelsen et al. 2000. pap. 16.95 (*0-7615-2012-0*) Prima Pub.

Positive Discipline in the Classroom. 2nd expanded rev. ed. Jane Nelsen. LC 97-9016. 240p. 1997. per. 15.00 (*0-7615-1059-1*) Prima Pub.

***Positive Discipline in the Classroom.** 3rd ed. Jane Nelsen et al. LC 99-86308. (Positive Discipline Ser.). 272p. 2000. pap. text 16.95 (*0-7615-2421-5*) Prima Pub.

Positive Discipline in the Classroom: How to Effectively Use Class Meetings & Other Positive Discipline Strategies. Jane Nelsen et al. 192p. (Orig.). 1993. pap. 14.95 (*1-55958-311-8*) Prima Pub.

Positive Discrimination & Social Justice. John R. Edwards. 220p. 1987. pap. text 19.95 (*0-422-78990-9*, 1156, Pub. by Tavistock) Routldge.

Positive Displacement Pumps see Technical Engineering Training Series

Positive Displacement Pumps: European Positive Displacement (PD) Pump Markets. Market Intelligence Staff. 160p. 1993. 1700.00 (*1-56753-588-7*) Frost & Sullivan.

Positive Economics & Policy Objectives. T. W. Hutchinson. (Modern Revivals in Economics Ser.). 200p. 1992. 61.95 (*0-7512-0090-5*, Pub. by Gregg Pub) Ashgate Pub Co.

***Positive Encounters - A Guidebook for Professionals: Talking One-to-One with Teens about Contraceptive & Safer Sex.** Amy Vogelaar. (Illus.). 60p. 1999. 10.00 (*0-9609366-3-7*) Plan Parenthood.

***Positive Encounters - A Workshop for Professionals: Talking One-to-One with Teens about Contraceptive & Safer Sex.** Amy Vogelaar. 82p. 1999. 15.00 (*0-9609366-2-9*) Plan Parenthood.

Positive Environment: Physical & Social Influences on People with Senile Dementia in Residential Care. Ann Netten. LC 92-44396. 110p. 1993. pap. 28.95 (*1-85742-112-4*, Pub. by Arena) Ashgate Pub Co.

Positive Environment: Physical & Social Influences on People with Senile Dementia in Residential Care. Ann Netten. LC 92-44396. 110p. 1993. 54.95 (*1-85742-107-8*, Pub. by Arena) Ashgate Pub Co.

Positive Evolution of Religion. Frederic Harrison. LC 74-142641. (Essay Index Reprint Ser.). 1977. 20.95 (*0-8369-2053-8*) Ayer.

Positive Expectations of America's World Role: Historical Cycles of Realistic Idealism. Frank C. Klingberg. 506p. (C). 1996. pap. text 42.00 (*0-7618-0263-0*); lib. bdg. 64.00 (*0-7618-0262-2*) U Pr of Amer.

Positive Experiences in Retirement. Otto Pollak. (C). 1957. 6.50 (*0-256-00674-1*, Irwn McGrw-H) McGrw-H Hghr Educ.

Positive Experiential Awareness, Purposeful Relaxation, & Differentiated Bodily Feeling States, Set-PA. Russell E. Mason. (Train-Ascendance Cassettes Ser.). 1975. pap. 23.00 incl. audio (*0-89533-012-1*, GT-PA) F I Comm.

Positive Family. Arvella Schuller. 144p. 1984. mass mkt. 3.99 (*0-515-08091-8*, Jove) Berkley Pub.

Positive Feedback Economies. Agliardi. LC 97-38691. 160p. 1998. text 69.95 (*0-312-21248-8*) St Martin.

Positive Feedback in Natural Systems. Curtis C. Travis et al. (Biomathematics Ser.: Vol. 15). (Illus.). 305p. 1986. 164.95 (*0-387-15942-8*) Spr-Verlag.

Positive Filipino Values. Tomas D. Andres. xi, 196p. (Orig.). (C). 1990. pap. 17.50 (*971-10-0408-9*, Pub. by New Day Pub) Cellar.

Positive Flying: Flight-Tested Numbers & How to Fly Them for Precision Perfection. rev. ed. Richard L. Taylor & William M. Guinther. LC 92-14372. (Aviation Library). (Illus.). 223p. 1992. 24.95 (*1-56566-024-2*, Pub. by Thomasson-Grant) ASA Inc.

Positive Harmonic Functions & Diffusion. Ross G. Pinsky. (Studies in Advanced Mathematics: No. 45). 490p. (C). 1995. text 80.00 (*0-521-47014-5*) Cambridge U Pr.

Positive Health: Designs for Action. 2nd ed. Mary K. Beyrer. LC 76-22769. (Health Education, Physical Education, & Recreation Ser.). 195p. reprint ed. pap. 60.50 (*0-608-13433-3*, 201452500093) Bks Demand.

***Positive Hero in Russian Literature.** 2nd ed. Rufus W. Mathewson, Jr. LC 99-49407. 392p. 1999. pap. 22.95 (*0-8101-1716-9*) Northwestern U Pr.

Positive Hero in Russian Literature. 2nd ed. Rufus W. Mathewson, Jr. LC 72-97207. xviii, 366p. 1975. pap. 15.95 (*0-8047-0976-9*) Stanford U Pr.

Positive I. D. Dennis Allen et al. 60p. 1987. 6.99 (*0-8341-9160-1*, MB-580) Lillenas.

Positive Image: Toward a Multiracial Curriculum. Robert Jeffcoate. (Chameleon Education Ser.). 144p. 1981. pap. 4.95 (*0-906495-03-2*) Writers & Readers.

Positive Images: A Guide to 400 Non-Sexist Films for Young People. Linda Artel & Susan Wengraf. LC 75-46089. 1976. pap. 10.00 (*0-912932-03-1*) Booklegger Pubng.

Positive Images: Teaching Abstinence, Contraception & Sexual Health. Peggy Brick. 158p. 1995. 25.00 (*0-9609366-5-3*) Plan Parenthood.

Positive Imaging. Norman Vincent Peale. 1996. pap. 10.00 (*0-449-91164-0*) Fawcett.

Positive Imaging: Peale,&Norman Vincent. abr. ed. Norman Vincent Peale. 1992. audio 12.00 (*1-55994-472-2*, CPN 5002) HarperAudio.

Positive Influencing Skills. Ed. by Terry Gillen. 208p. 1995. pap. 90.00 (*0-85292-572-7*, Pub. by IPM Hse) St Mut.

Positive Insights on Education Guide. AIT-PDK Staff. 40p. (Orig.). 1997. pap. text 7.95 (*0-7842-0817-4*) Agency Instr Tech.

Positive Interactions Program of Activities for Persons with Alzheimer's Disease. Sylvia Nissenboim & Christine Vroman. LC 97-29098. 152p. 1997. pap. 28.95 (*1-878812-40-8*) Hlth Prof Pr.

P

An Asterisk (*) at the beginning of an entry indicates that the title is appearing for the first time.

Positive Interdependence: The Heart of Cooperative Learning. David W. Johnson & Roger T. Johnson. (Illus.). 35p. 1992. pap. text, teacher ed. 5.00 (*0-939603-17-9*) Interaction Bk Co.

Positive Involvement: How to Teach Your Child Habits for School Success. Jack Youngblood & Marsha Youngblood. 147p. (Orig.). 1995. pap. 14.95 (*0-9647295-0-4*) Brown Wood Pr.

Positive Leadership in "Skills for Growing" A Guide for Administrators. Linda Barr & Carole Gerber. Ed. by Hank Resnik. (Skills for Growing Ser.). (Illus.). 157p. 1990. pap. text 15.00 (*0-933419-47-3*) Quest Intl.

Positive Let-Off Motions. J. Foster. 1961. 70.00 (*0-7855-1019-2*) St Mut.

Positive Let-Off Motions. Wira Staff. (C). 1961. 125.00 (*0-900820-02-0*, Pub. by British Textile Tech) St Mut.

Positive Liberty: An Essay in Normative Political Philosophy. Lawrence H. Crocker. (Melbourne International Philosophy Ser.: Vol. 7). 156p. 1980. lib. bdg. 94.00 (*90-247-2291-8*, Pub. by M Nijhoff) Kluwer Academic.

Positive Life: Portraits of Women Living with HIV. Photos by Mary Berridge. LC 96-72481. (Illus.). 128p. 1997. 27.50 (*0-7624-0198-2*) Running Pr.

***Positive Linear Systems: Theory & Applications.** Loreza Farina & Sergio Rinaldi. 288p. 2000. 84.95 (*0-471-38456-9*) Wiley.

Positive Lives - Responses to HIV: A Photodocumentary. Ed. by Stephen Mayes & Lyndall Stein. LC 93-40472. 1993. 60.00 (*0-304-32846-4*) Continuum.

Positive Magic: Occult Self-Help. 3rd ed. Marion Weinstein. LC 94-70528. (Illus.). 289p. 1997. reprint ed. pap. 15.95 (*0-9604128-7-5*) Earth Magic.

Positive Management: Assertiveness for Managers. Paddy O'Brien. (People Skills for Professionals Ser.). (Illus.). 170p. 1995. reprint ed. pap. 17.95 (*1-85788-008-0*) Nicholas Brealey.

Positive Match. Tony Chiu. 480p. 1998. mass mkt. 6.50 (*0-553-57546-5*) Bantam.

Positive Measures: Panacea of Placebo in International Environmental Agreements Tema Nord 1998: 11. (Tema Nord Ser.). 80p. 1998. 18.00 (*92-893-0229-1*, NC2291) Nordic Coun Minsters.

Positive Measures Designed to Eradicate All Incitement to, or Acts of, Racial Discrimination. 39p. 1985. pap. text 7.00 (*92-1-154044-5*, 85.XIV.2) UN.

Positive Measures for Technology Transfer under the Climate Change Convention. Ed. by Tim Forsyth. 116p. 1998. pap. 14.95 (*1-86203-047-2*, Pub. by Royal Inst Intl Affairs) Brookings.

Positive Mental Attitude: A Guide for Personal Growth. Joe C. Harmon. (Hand Program Ser.: No. 2). 66p. Date not set. pap. text 9.95 (*1-928803-01-6*) Access Grp Inc.

Positive Mental Attitudes. Ed. by Bill FitzPatrick. 128p. (Orig.). 1995. pap. 6.00 (*1-884864-03-1*) Am Success Inst.

Positive Messages: For Young Men Growing up Without Their Fathers. Marc A. Butcher. 96p. (YA). (gr. 3-12). 1999. pap. 9.00 (*0-9622939-1-1*) Yamoo Pubs.

Positive Minute: Self-Esteem Skills. LC 98-96877. 272p. 1999. 23.95 (*1-892274-14-0*) W Whorton.

Positive Music for Today's Kids! Bright Smiles & Blue Skies. unabridged ed. Lisa M. Nelson. (Illus.). 16p. (J). (gr. k-6). 1990. pap. 9.95 incl. audio (*0-9627863-0-6*) Brght Ideas CA.

Positive Negatives: A Motif in Christian Tradition. Crerar Douglas. LC 91-31816. (American University Studies: Theology & Religion: Ser. VII, Vol. 103). 213p. (C). 1992. text 39.95 (*0-8204-1536-7*) P Lang Pubng.

Positive Neutrality: Letting Religious Freedom Ring, 69. Stephen V. Monsma. LC 92-25738. (Contributions in Legal Studies: No. 69). 304p. 1992. 59.95 (*0-313-27963-2*, MUY, Greenwood Pr) Greenwood.

Positive Nutrition for HIV Infection & AIDS: A Medically Sound Take Charge Plan to Maintain. Stacy Jane Bell. 192p. 1996. pap. 12.95 (*0-471-34696-9*) Wiley.

Positive Nutrition for HIV Infection & AIDS: A Medically Sound Take Charge Plan to Maintain. Stacey J. Bell. 192p. 1996. pap. 12.95 (*1-56561-089-X*) Wiley.

Positive Obedience: The Christian's Response to the Ten Commandments. John R. Bisagno. 80p. (Orig.). 1987. pap. 4.95 (*0-310-38141-X*, 9249P) Zondervan.

Positive Operators & Semigroups on Banach Lattices: Proceedings of the Caribbean Mathematics Foundation's Conference, 1990. Ed. by C. B. Huijsmans & W. A. Luxemburg. LC 92-26747. 168p. (C). 1992. text 132.00 (*0-7923-1964-8*) Kluwer Academic.

Positive Operators, Riesz Spaces, & Economics. Ed. by Charalambos D. Aliprantis et al. (Studies in Economic Theory: Vol. 2). vii, 229p. 1991. 79.95 (*0-387-54658-8*) Spr-Verlag.

Positive Options: A Handbook for People Living with HIV. Karin Timour & Kevin Armington. (Illus.). 152p. (Orig.). 1995. pap. 15.00 (*0-9653952-0-0*) Body Positive.

***Positive Options for Crohn's Disease: Self-Help & Treatment.** Joan Gomez. 160p. 2000. pap. 12.95 (*0-89793-278-1*, Pub. by Hunter Hse) Publishers Group.

***Positive Options for Crohn's Disease: Self-Help & Treatment.** Joan Gomez. 160p. 2000. 22.95 (*0-89793-279-X*, Pub. by Hunter Hse) Publishers Group.

***Positive Outcomes: Raising the Bar on Government Reinvention.** Ted A. Gaebler et al. (Illus.). xii, 306p. 1999. pap. 29.95 incl. cd-rom (*1-57420-093-3*) Chatelaine.

Positive Outcomes: Raising the Bar on Government Reinvention. Ted A. Gaebler et al. LC 99-6276. (Illus.). xii, 306p. 1999. 39.95 incl. cd-rom, disk (*1-57420-094-1*) Chatelaine.

***Positive Para: Helping Students Develop Positive Social Skills.** Linda P. Thurston. 30p. 2000. pap. text 12.50 (*1-893206-04-1*) Curriculum Solns.

Positive Parent-Child Communications. Edward W. Werz & Ron Kerner. (Family Forum Library). 16p. 1992. 1.95 (*1-56688-010-6*) Bur For At-Risk.

Positive Parental Discipline. Marvin Goldstein et al. (Family Forum Library). 16p. 1992. 1.95 (*1-56688-003-3*) Bur For At-Risk.

Positive Parenting. Jack M. Barnell. (Christian Living Ser.). 44p. 1990. pap. 3.50 (*0-8341-1366-X*) Beacon Hill.

Positive Parenting. Roger C. Rinn & Allan Markle. (Illus.). 1986. pap. text 8.95 (*0-89147-052-2*) CAS.

Positive Parenting. Abraham J. Twerski. 19.99 (*0-89906-644-5*); pap. 16.99 (*0-89906-645-3*) Mesorah Pubns.

Positive Parenting: A Survival Guide. Pat Rees. 1992. 50.00 (*1-85549-018-8*) St Mut.

Positive Parenting: Feeding. Beatrice Hollyer. LC 98-132853. 144p. 1998. pap. 10.95 (*0-7063-7645-5*, Pub. by WrLock) Sterling.

Positive Parenting Fitness: A Total Approach to Caring for the Physical & Emotional Needs of Your New Family. Sylvia K. Olkin. LC 91-28933. (Illus.). 344p. (Orig.). pap. 14.95 (*0-89529-481-8*, Avery) Penguin Putnam.

Positive Parenting for Teens. Karen R. Joslin. LC 96-49385. 1997. pap. 12.95 (*0-449-90996-4*) Fawcett.

Positive Parenting from A-Z. Karen R. Joslin. 400p. (Orig.). 1994. pap. 12.50 (*0-449-90780-5*, Columbine) Fawcett.

Positive Passage: Everyday Kwanzaa Poems. Johnnierenee Nelson. (Illus.). 48p. (Orig.). (J). (gr. 1 up). 1991. pap. 7.00 (*0-9623205-1-X*) House Nia.

Positive Peer Culture. 2nd ed. Harry H. Vorrath & Larry K. Brendtro. LC 84-21570. (Modern Applications of Social Work Ser.). (Illus.). 196p. (C). 1985. pap. text 24.95 (*0-202-36038-5*) Aldine de Gruyter.

Positive Peer Culture: A Selected Bibliography. Larry K. Brendtro et al. xxi, 172p. (Orig.). (C). 1994. pap. text 19.95 (*0-9639084-1-3*) S D A Pub.

Positive Peer Groups. Sharon Scott. 96p. 1988. pap. 9.95 (*0-87425-065-X*) HRD Press.

Positive Personalities: Joy, Significance, & Sexual Feelings & Values. Russell E. Mason. LC 70-167784. 1971. 16.00 (*0-89533-000-8*) F I Comm.

Positive Personality Fulfillment, Set-PPF. Russell E. Mason. (Train-Ascendance Cassettes Ser.). 1975. 16.00 incl. audio (*0-89533-048-2*, 71 GT-PF) F I Comm.

Positive Personality Profiles: Discover Personality Insights to Understand Yourself & Others. 4th ed. Robert A. Rohm. Ed. by Chris Carey & Nancy Enis. (Illus.). 200p. 1994. reprint ed. pap. 11.95 (*0-9641080-0-3*) Prsnality Insights.

Positive Perspectives - Youth. Scott. 1990. pap. text. write for info. (*0-582-05912-7*, Pub. by Addison-Wesley) Longman.

Positive Philosophy. Auguste Comte. Tr. by Hariet Martineau. LC 70-174979. reprint ed. 67.50 (*0-404-08209-2*) AMS Pr.

Positive Pleasures: Early Photography & Humor. Heinz K. Henisch & Bridget A. Henisch. LC 97-18490. 1998. 65.00 (*0-271-01671-X*) Pa St U Pr.

Positive Plus: The Practical Plan for Liking Yourself Better. Joyce Brothers. 288p. 1995. mass mkt. 5.99 (*0-425-14949-8*) Berkley Pub.

Positive Political Economy: Theory & Evidence. Ed. by Sylvester C. Eijffinger & Harry P. Huizinga. LC 96-43850. 400p. 1998. 59.95 (*0-521-57215-0*) Cambridge U Pr.

Positive Political Theory I: Collective Preference. David Austen-Smith & Jeffrey S. Banks. (Illus.). 224p. (C). pap. text 19.95 (*0-472-08721-5*, 08721) U of Mich Pr.

Positive Political Theory I: Collective Preference. David Austen-Smith & Jeffrey S. Banks. (Studies in Political Analysis). 224p. 1998. text 39.50 (*0-472-10480-2*, 10480) U of Mich Pr.

Positive Politics: Overcome Office Politics & Fast-Track Your Career. Mark Holden. (Illus.). 204p. 1999. pap. 19.95 (*1-875680-38-1*) Woodslane.

Positive Politics at Work. D. Douglas McKenna & Jeffrey J. McHenry. LC 93-24062. 144p. 1993. pap. 10.00 (*1-55623-879-7*, Irwn Prfssnl) McGraw-Hill Prof.

Positive Polynomials & Product Type Actions of Compact Groups. D. E. Handelman. LC 84-28463. (Memoirs of the AMS Ser.: No. 54/320). 79p. 1987. reprint ed. pap. 19.00 (*0-8218-2322-1*, MEMO/54/320) Am Math.

Positive Polynomials, Convex Integral Polytopes & a Random Walk Problem. D. E. Handelman. (Lecture Notes in Mathematics Ser.: Vol. 1282). xi, 136p. 1987. 30.95 (*0-387-18400-7*) Spr-Verlag.

Positive Potty Training: The Quick Guide to a Dry Floor in Three Weeks or Less, Vol. 1. September B. Morn. 16p. 1995. pap. text 3.75 (*0-9633884-2-8*) Pawprince Pr.

Positive Power of Criticism. Deborah Bright. 1990. wbk. ed. 79.95 incl. audio (*0-9615400-7-9*) Intl Ctr Creat Think.

Positive Power of Jesus Christ. Norman Vincent Peale. 266p. 1984. mass mkt. 5.99 (*0-8423-4914-6*) Tyndale Hse.

Positive Power of Praising People. Jerry D. Twentier. LC 98-9848. 224p. 1998. pap. 11.95 (*0-8092-2901-3*, 290130, Contemporary Bks) NTC Contemp Pub Co.

Positive Power Thinking. abr. ed. Robert A. Robinson. (Magic Magnifying Mind Ser.). 1991. pap. text 7.95 incl. audio (*1-884780-03-2*) Phoenix Pubng.

Positive Powerful Promotional Words: The Right-On Resource for Writers, Speakers & Creative Wordsmiths. Linda Surbeck. LC 96-75495. 400p. (Orig.). 1995. pap. 19.95 (*0-9628820-3-8*) Master Pubns.

Positive Practice: A Step-by-Step Approach to Family Therapy. Alan Carr. xiii, 264p. 1995. text 47.00 (*3-7186-5678-7*, Harwood Acad Pubs); pap. text 20.00 (*3-7186-5680-9*, Harwood Acad Pubs) Gordon & Breach.

Positive Preaching & the Modern World. 3rd ed. P. T. Forsyth. (Biblical & Theological Classics Library: Vol. 22). xvii, 237p. 1998. reprint ed. pap. 9.99 (*0-85364-876-X*, Pub. by Paternoster Pub) OM Literature.

Positive Pregnancy Fitness: A Guide to a More Comfortable Pregnancy & Easier Birth Through Exercise & Relaxation. Sylvia K. Olkin. LC 87-18844. (Illus.). 272p. pap. 12.95 (*0-89529-373-0*, Avery) Penguin Putnam.

Positive Prescriptions for Negative Parenting: The Counselor's Guide to Diagnosing & Assisting Troubled Parents & Children. John F. Taylor. (Illus.). 47p. 1991. 10.95 (*1-884063-81-0*) Mar Co Prods.

Positive Pressure Fire Tests of Door Assemblies, UL 10C. 1998. write for info. (*0-7629-0259-0*) Underwrtrs Labs.

Positive Principle Today: How to Renew & Sustain the Power of Positive Thinking. Norman Vincent Peale. LC 96-96658. 1996. pap. 10.00 (*0-449-91198-5*) Fawcett.

Positive Profiles: Building Community Together. Ernest Pancsofar. LC 98-34028. (Illus.). 86p. (Orig.). 1998. pap. 25.00 (*1-883302-26-9*) Trning Res.

***Positive Psychology of Buddhism & Yoga: Paths to Mature Happiness.** Marvin Levine. LC 00-22894. 2000. write for info. (*0-8058-3349-8*) L Erlbaum Assocs.

Positive Regard: Carl Rogers & Other Notables He Inspired. Mel Suhd. LC 93-87337. 457p. 1994. 26.95 (*0-8314-0081-1*) Sci & Behavior.

Positive Reinforcement Activities Grades K-6. Lee Canter. (Illus.). 48p. 1983. student ed. 5.95 (*0-9608978-3-6*) Canter & Assocs.

Positive Reinforcement Activities Grades 7-12. Lee Canter. (Illus.). 40p. 1987. student ed. 5.95 (*0-939007-02-9*) Canter & Assocs.

Positive Risks, Challenges & Other Paths to Success: Busing the Four Conditions of Self-Esteem in Elementary & Middle Schools. Reynold Bean. LC 92-19096. 1992. 21.95 (*1-56071-070-5*) ETR Assocs.

Positive Sciences of the Ancient Hindus. Brajendranath Seal. 313p. 1986. reprint ed. 19.00 (*0-8364-1575-2*, Pub. by Motilal Bnarsidass) S Asia.

Positive Self-Talk for Children: Teaching Self-Esteem Through Affirmations - A Guide for Parents, Teachers, & Counselors. Douglas Bloch & Jon Merritt. LC 93-21706. 352p. 1993. pap. 12.95 (*0-553-35198-2*) Bantam.

Positive Selfishness: Your Positive Motivations Are the Natural & Health Way to Persue a Life of Happiness & Success. Evan Porter. LC 95-92746. 252p. 1999. pap. 18.95 (*0-940683-51-2*) Sync Society Pubng.

Positive Semigroups of Operators, & Applications. Ed. by O. Bratteli & P. E. Jorgensen. 1984. text 84.00 (*90-277-1839-3*) Kluwer Academic.

Positive Sermon Outlines. Russell E. Spray. (Sermon Outline Ser.). 64p. 1991. pap. 4.99 (*0-8010-8318-4*) Baker Bks.

Positive Sermons That Encourage. J. J. Turner. 1984. pap. 7.75 (*0-89137-115-X*) Quality Pubns.

Positive Shooting. Michael Yardley. (Illus.). 160p. 1994. 30.00 (*1-57157-012-8*) Safari Pr.

Positive Shooting. Michael Yardley. (Illus.). 160p. 1997. pap. 19.95 (*1-57157-107-8*) Safari Pr.

Positive Solutions of Differential, Difference & Integral Equations. Ravi P. Agarwal et al. LC 98-49417. 12p. 1999. write for info. (*0-7923-5510-5*) Kluwer Academic.

Positive Steps Approach: A Parent's Guide to Teaching Youth to Be Responsible for Today! Cindy Phillips & Levi Williams. Ed. by June Ford. LC 93-48830. 240p. (Orig.). 1994. pap. 9.95 (*1-56530-124-2*) Summit TX.

Positive Strand RNA Viruses. 1996. text 234.00 (*3-211-82522-3*) Spr-Verlag.

Positive-Strand RNA Viruses. Ed. by M. A. Brinton et al. LC 94-3138. (Archives of Virology Ser.: Suppl. 9). (Illus.). 1996. 234.00 (*0-387-82522-3*) Spr-Verlag.

Positive Stress Factor. Rebecca J. Holmes & Mary L. Webb. 192p. 1995. pap. 16.95 (*0-9634383-9-5*) Lee Ross Pub.

Positive Stress Factor. deluxe ed. Rebecca J. Holmes & Mary L. Webb. 192p. 1995. pap. 16.95 (*0-9634383-7-9*) Lee Ross Pub.

Positive Strokes for Little Folks, Vols. 1-7. 2nd ed. Catherine Wiands. (Illus.). 32p. (Orig.). (J). (gr. 1-6). 1983. reprint ed. pap. 2.50 (*0-943262-00-3*) Transitions.

Positive Strokes for Single Folks. Catherine Wiands. Ed. by Pat Ziebarth. 24p. reprint ed. pap. 2.00 (*0-943262-10-0*) Transitions.

Positive Substitution, Purposeful Relaxation, & Goal Achievement Training: A Systematic Positive Beginning, Set-PS. Russell E. Mason. 1975. pap. 60.00 incl. audio (*0-89533-014-8*) F I Comm.

Positive Sum: Improving North-South Negotiations. Ed. by I. William Zartman. 262p. 1986. 39.95 (*0-88738-107-3*); pap. 24.95 (*0-88738-650-4*) Transaction Pubs.

Positive Teacher Appraisal Through Classroom Observation. Diane Montgomery. 1999. pap. text 29.95 (*1-85346-607-7*) David Fulton.

Positive Teaching. 1984. pap. text 17.95 (*0-04-370151-5*) Routledge.

Positive Teaching, Positive Learning. Rob Barnes. LC 98-49944. 1998. pap. write for info. (*0-415-18139-9*) Routledge.

Positive Theories of Congressional Institutions. Ed. by Kenneth A. Shepsle & Barry R. Weingast. LC 95-16956. 328p. 1995. text 49.50 (*0-472-10684-8*, 10684); pap. text 20.95 (*0-472-08319-8*, 08319) U of Mich Pr.

Positive Theory of Capital. Eugen Von Bohm-Bawerk. Tr. by William Smart. LC 70-175689. (Select Bibliographies Reprint Ser.). 1977. reprint ed. 29.95 (*0-8369-6604-X*) Ayer.

Positive Theory of Capital see Capital & Interest

Positive Thinker: Self-Motivating Strategies for Personal Success. Alice Potter. 240p. (Orig.). 1994. mass mkt. 5.99 (*0-425-14257-4*) Berkley Pub.

Positive Thinkers Daily Instruction Manual. Richard Starr. (Illus.). 220p. (Orig.). 1994. pap. text. write for info. (*0-9640217-7-3*) Results Now.

Positive Thinkers Secret Weapons Handbook. 230p. (Orig.). pap. 39.00 (*0-9640217-8-1*) Results Now.

Positive Thinking! A Guide to Business & Personal Success. Dee Frances. Date not set. pap. 10.00 (*1-885519-09-5*, Pub. by DDDD Pubns) Baker & Taylor.

Positive Thinking: Everything You Have Always Known about Positive Thinking but Were Afraid to Put into Practice. Vera Peiffer. 1994. pap. 7.95 (*1-85230-554-1*, Pub. by Element MA) Penguin Putnam.

Positive Thinking: Everything You Have Always Known about Positive Thinking But Were Afraid to Put into Practice. Vera Peiffer. 192p. 1999. pap. 12.95 (*1-86204-528-3*, Pub. by Element MA) Penguin Putnam.

Positive Thinking: Everything You Have Always Known about Positive Thinking But Were Afraid to Put into Practice. Vera Pfeiffer. LC 92-26000. 1993. pap. 12.95 (*1-85230-079-5*, Pub. by Element MA) Penguin Putnam.

Positive Thinking & Actions. Bruce Goldberg. 1995. 12.00 incl. audio (*1-885577-57-5*) B Goldberg.

Positive Thinking Cards for Children. Deborah Thornton. 52p. 1993. 13.99 (*0-9636638-1-X*) Inspirat Prayer.

Positive Thinking Easier Than You Think. rev. ed. Dee Frances. Ed. by Harry Koster. 102p. 1993. pap. 8.95 (*0-9635341-4-9*) DDDD Pubns.

Positive Thinking Everyday see Pensamiento Positivo para Cada Dia

Positive Thinking Everyday: An Inspiration for Each Day of the Year. Norman Vincent Peale. LC 93-22576. 384p. 1993. pap. 10.00 (*0-671-86891-8*, Fireside) S&S Trade Pap.

Positive Thought for Every Day. Windy Dryden. 1999. 12.95 (*0-85969-744-4*) S C K Pubns.

Positive Thoughts: Living Your Life to the Fullest. Ariel Books Staff. (Illus.). 374p. 1995. pap. 5.95 (*0-8362-0723-8*) Andrews & McMeel.

Positive Thoughts Attract Success. Mary A. Dodson & Ella E. Dodson. 64p. 1993. pap. 5.50 (*0-89540-299-8*, SB-299) Sun Pub.

Positive Thoughts for Daily Meditation. Yogaswami. 128p. 1993. pap. 9.95 (*1-85230-426-X*, Pub. by Element MA) Penguin Putnam.

Positive Thoughts for Successful Living. Jim Lewis. LC 80-50277. 138p. (Orig.). 1979. pap. 7.95 (*0-942482-00-X*) Unity Church Denver.

Positive Thoughts for Successful Living. unabridged ed. Gary Arnold. LC 97-90384. (Illus.). 239p. 1999. pap. write for info. (*1-57867-032-2*) Windhorse Corp.

Positive Transfer Operators & Decay of Correlations. Viviane Baladi. (Advanced Series in Nonlinear Dynamics). 230p. 1998. 48.00 (*981-02-3328-0*) World Scientific Pub.

***Positive Transitions for Student Athletes: Life Skills for Transitions in Sport, College & Career.** Darin J. Meeker et al. LC 99-27442. (Illus.). 224p. (C). 1999. pap. 23.95 (*1-890871-22-2*) Holcomb Hath.

Positive Turbulence: Developing Climates for Creativity, Innovation, & Renewal. Stanley S. Gryskiewicz. LC 99-6075. 224p. 1999. text 32.95 (*0-7879-1008-2*) Jossey-Bass.

***Positive under Pressure: How to Be Calm & Effective When the Heat Is On.** Malcom Vandeburg. 2000. pap. 12.00 (*0-7225-3817-0*) Thorsons PA.

Positive Use of Commercial Television with Children. Rosemary L. Potter. LC 81-9646. (Analysis & Action Ser.). (Illus.). 136p. reprint ed. pap. 42.20 (*0-8357-6414-1*, 203577800097) Bks Demand.

Positive Uses of Psychic Energy. Manly P. Hall. pap. 4.95 (*0-89314-343-X*) Philos Res.

Positive Visualizations: For People with Cancer & Those Who Love Them. Amy O. Carty. (Illus.). 40p. (Orig.). 1993. pap. 4.95 (*0-9635970-1-9*) Birchard Bks.

Positive Women: Voices of Women Living with AIDS. Ed. by Andrea Rudd & Darien Taylor. (Illus.). 276p. 1992. pap. 14.95 (*0-929005-30-9*, Pub. by Sec Story Pr) LPC InBook.

Positively Alive! 1994. pap. 8.95 (*0-9602166-3-4*) Golden Key.

Positively Bob Dylan: A Thirty-Year Discography, Concert & Recording Session Guide, 1960-1989. Michael Krogsgaard. LC 89-92336. (Rock & Roll Reference Ser.: No. 33). (Illus.). 512p. 1991. 55.00 (*1-56075-000-6*) Popular Culture.

Positively Connecticut. Diane Smith. LC 98-212258. 1998. pap. 19.95 (*0-7627-0340-7*) Globe Pequot.

Positively Connecticut. limited ed. Diane Smith. 1998. 29.95 (*0-7627-0429-2*) Globe Pequot.

Positively False. Joan Shenton. LC 99-202560. 192p. 1998. 29.95 (*1-86064-333-7*, Pub. by I B T) St Martin.

Positively Fearless: Breaking Free of the Fears That Hold You Back. Vera Peiffer. 1993. pap. 12.95 (*1-85230-389-1*, Pub. by Element MA) Penguin Putnam.

***Positively Fearless: Breaking Free of the Fears That Hold You Back.** Vera Peiffer. 176p. 1999. pap. 10.95 (*1-86204-622-0*, Pub. by Element MA) Penguin Putnam.

***Positively Final Appearance: A Journal 1996-98.** Alec Guinness. LC 99-14264. 224p. 1999. 24.95 (*0-670-88800-1*, Viking) Viking Penguin.

***Positively Final Appearance: A Journal, 1996-98.** large type ed. Alec Guinness. LC 99-41439. (General Ser.). 320p. 1999. 23.95 (*0-7862-2093-7*) Thorndike Pr.

P

An Asterisk (*) at the beginning of an entry indicates that the title is appearing for the first time.

Positively Forward: A Handbook for HIV-Infected Persons. AIDS Foundation Dayton Staff & Volunteers. Ed. by L. Ruggieri & L. Loper. (Illus.). 118p. (Orig.). 1989. pap. 5.00 (*0-685-30446-9*) AIDS Fndtn Dayton.

Positively Gay. rev. ed. Ed. by Betty Berzon. 288p. 1995. pap. 12.95 (*0-89087-676-2*) Celestial Arts.

Positively Kindergarten: A Classroom-Proven, Theme-Based, Developmental Guide for the Kindergarten Teacher. Beth Lamb & Phyllis Logsdon. 141p. (Orig.). 1991. pap. 14.95 (*0-935493-48-4*) Modern Learn Pr.

Positively Mother Goose. Diane Loomans et al. Ed. by Linda Kramer. LC 90-52634. (Illus.). 32p. (J). (ps-2). 1991. 14.95 (*0-915811-24-3*, Starseed) H J Kramer Inc.

Positively Negative: Reversing of the Magnetic Poles. Marvin N. Carr. LC 94-60567. 580p. (Orig.). 1994. per. 9.95 (*0-9641226-7-7*) Trom Pubng.

Positively Ordered Semigroups. M. Satyanarayana. LC 79-10077. (Lecture Notes in Pure & Applied Mathematics Ser.: Vol. 42). 112p. reprint ed. pap. 34.80 (*0-608-08982-6*, 206961700005) Bks Demand.

Positively Outrageous Service. T. Scott Gross. 256p. 1994. mass mkt. 13.95 (*0-446-39468-8*, Pub. by Warner Bks) Little.

*__Positively Page: The Diamond Dallas Page Journey.__ Diamond Dallas Page. 2000. 28.95 (*0-9679922-0-6*) Pos Pubns MD.

Positively Pasta. Sandra Bartiromo. Ed. by Mackie Keenan. LC 83-51536. (Illus.). 54p. (Orig.). 1983. spiral bd. 4.95 (*0-916005-00-3*) Silver Sea.

Positively Peachy. Gene Westbrook. Ed. by Isabelle Hanson. LC 90-70947. (Illus.). 52p. 1990. pap. 5.95 (*0-9614247-2-9*) Gene Westbrook.

Positively POS. Dee Frances. Date not set. pap. text 3.00 (*1-885519-66-4*) DDDD Pubns.

Positively Positive: Nuggets for a Good Life. Sara D. Trigg. (Illus.). 32p. 1998. pap. 5.95 (*1-56469-041-5*) Harmony Hse Pub.

Positively Posters, Vol. XXII. Jack Rennert. 1996. 40.00 (*0-9664201-7-9*) Pstr Auctns Intl.

Positively Postmodern Vol. 8: The Multi-Media Muse in America, Set. Nicholas Zurgrugg. (Post Modern Positions Ser.: Vol. 8). (Illus.). 600p. 1996. pap. text 29.95 (*0-944624-22-7*) Maisonneuve Pr.

Positively Pregnant. Steve Phillips. Ed. by Cliff Carle. 1995. pap. text 4.99 (*0-918259-81-9*) CCC Pubns.

Positively Primary. Susan Luke. 1996. pap. 7.95 (*1-55503-727-5*, 019412) Covenant Comms.

Positively Single: The Art of Being Single & Happy. Vera Peiffer. 176p. 1991. pap. 12.95 (*1-85230-241-0*, Pub. by Element MA) Penguin Putnam.

Positively Single: The Art of Being Single & Happy. Vera Peiffer. 160p. 1995. pap. 7.95 (*1-85230-712-9*, Pub. by Element MA) Penguin Putnam.

Positively Single: The Art of Being Single & Happy. Vera Peiffer. 160p. 1999. pap. 10.95 (*1-86204-578-X*, Pub. by Onewrld Pubns) Penguin Putnam.

Positively Speaking. Stoops. LC 99-218724. 112p. 1998. pap. text 12.25 (*0-536-01878-2*) S&S Trade.

Positively Women: Living with AIDS. Sue O'Sullivan. 336p. 1996. pap. 18.00 (*0-04-440943-5*, Pub. by Pandora) NYU Pr.

*__Positively You: Change Your Thinking, Change Your Life.__ Jinger Heath. 224p. 2000. pap. 12.95 (*0-312-25408-3*) St Martin.

*__Positively You! Discovery Journal.__ Jinger Heath. 256p. 2000. pap. 15.95 (*0-312-25465-2*) St Martin.

Positively Young! The How-to Live, Love, Laugh, Let Go & Erase Inner Wrinkles at Any Age Game Book for Men & Women. Julia M. Busch. LC 93-90244. (Illus.). 144p. (Orig.). 1993. per. 9.95 (*0-9632907-2-X*) Anti Aging Pr.

Positives: Verses by Thom Gunn. Thom Gunn. LC 66-29663. (Illus.). 1994. lib. bdg. 10.00 (*0-226-31067-1*) U Ch Pr.

Positivism & Christianity: A Study of Theism & Verifiability. K. H. Klein. 194p. 1974. pap. text 57.00 (*90-247-1581-4*, Pub. by M Nijhoff) Kluwer Academic.

Positivism & Imagination: Scientism & Its Limits in Emile Hennequin, Wilhelm Scherer, & Dmitrii Pisarev. Catherine LeGouis. LC 96-15046. 272p. 1997. 39.50 (*0-8387-5323-X*) Bucknell U Pr.

Positivism & Sociology: Explaining Social Life. Peter Halfpenny. (Modern Revivals in Sociology Ser.). 144p. 1992. 49.95 (*0-7512-0059-X*, Pub. by Gregg Revivals) Ashgate Pub Co.

Positivism in Psychology: Historical & Contemporary Problems. Ed. by Charles W. Tolman. (Recent Research in Psychology Ser.). 232p. 1991. 64.95 (*0-387-97700-7*) Spr-Verlag.

Positivism Today. Ed. by Stephen Guest. (Issues in Law & Society Ser.). 200p. 1996. pap. 33.95 (*1-85521-696-5*, Pub. by Dartmth Pub); text 82.95 (*1-85521-689-2*, Pub. by Dartmth Pub) Ashgate Pub Co.

Positivist Science of Law. Keekok Lee. 224p. 1989. text 82.95 (*0-566-07032-4*, Pub. by Avebry) Ashgate Pub Co.

Positivist Sociology & Its Critics, 3 vols. Ed. by Peter Halfpenny & Peter McMylor. LC 93-32025. (Schools of Thought in Sociology Ser.: Vol. 11). 1792p. 1994. 600.00 (*1-85278-182-3*) E Elgar.

Positivity in Lie Theory: Open Problems. Joachim Hilgert. LC 98-6433. (Expositions in Mathematics Ser.). 290p. 1998. 138.95 (*3-11-016112-5*) De Gruyter.

Positrends or Negatrends? Dealing Positively with the 3rd Millennium. Eric Butterworth. LC 98-72264. 120p. 1998. pap. 9.95 (*0-87516-721-7*) DeVorss.

Positrol Plans & Logs: A Plan for Controlling Variation During Production. Mario Perez-Wilson. (Illus.). 1999. pap. 45.00 (*1-883237-15-7*) Adv Systs Cnslts.

Positron & Positronium Chemistry: Proceedings of the 3rd International Workshop, Milwaukee, U. S. A., 16-18 July 1990. Ed. by Y. C. Jean. 672p. (C). 1990. text 118.00 (*981-02-0300-4*) World Scientific Pub.

Positron Annihilation. Ed. by Z. Kajcsos & C. Szeles. 2146p. 1992. text 516.00 (*0-87849-636-X*, Pub. by Trans T Pub) Enfield Pubs NH.

Positron Annihilation: ICPA-11. Ed. by Y. C. Jean et al. (Materials Science Forum Ser.: Vol. 255-257). (Illus.). 852p. (C). 1998. text 260.00 (*0-87849-779-X*, Pub. by Trans T Pub) Enfield Pubs NH.

Positron Annihilation: Proceedings of the 7th International Conference on Positron Annihilation, New Delhi, January 1985. Ed. by R. M. Singru et al. 1150p. 1985. 209.00 (*9971-978-39-3*) World Scientific Pub.

Positron Annihilation: Proceedings of the 8th International Conference. Ed. by L. Dorikens-Vanpraet et al. 1032p. (C). 1989. text 156.00 (*9971-5-0733-1*) World Scientific Pub.

Positron Annihilation-ICPA-10. Ed. by Y. J. He & B. S. Cao. (Materials Science Forum Ser.: Vols. 175-178). (Illus.). 1104p. (C). 1995. 366.00 (*0-87849-686-6*, Pub. by Trans T Pub) Enfield Pubs NH.

Positron Annihilation in Chemistry. O. E. Morgensen. LC 94-27490. (Chemical Physics Ser.). 1994. 108.95 (*0-387-57853-6*) Spr-Verlag.

Positron Annihilation in Semiconductors: Defect Studies. R. Krause-Rehberg. LC 98-53844. 1998. 59.95 (*3-540-64371-0*) Spr-Verlag.

Positron Annihilation Studies of Fluids: Proceedings of the International Symposium. Ed. by S. C. Sharma. 640p. (C). 1988. text 133.00 (*9971-5-0472-3*) World Scientific Pub.

Positron Beams & Their Applications. Ed. by Paul Coleman. LC 99-89198. 300p. 1998. 68.00 (*981-02-3394-9*) World Scientific Pub.

Positron Beams for Solids & Surfaces. Ed. by Peter J. Schultz et al. LC 90-56407. (AIP Conference Proceedings Ser.: No. 218). 292p. 1991. lib. bdg. 85.00 (*0-88318-842-2*) Am Inst Physics.

Positron (Electron) - Gas Scattering: Proceedings of the 3rd International Workshop. Ed. by E. Kauppila et al. 372p. 1986. text 85.00 (*9971-978-97-0*) World Scientific Pub.

Positron-Electron Pairs in Astrophysics: AIP Conference Proceedings No. 101, Goddard Space Flight Center, 1983. Ed. by M. L. Burns et al. LC 83-71926. 447p. 1983. lib. bdg. 38.50 (*0-88318-200-9*) Am Inst Physics.

Positron Emission Tomography: A Critical Assessment of Recent Trends. Ed. by Balazs Gulyas & Hans W. Muller-Gartner. LC 98-18460. (Nato Science Partnership Sub-Ser.: No. 3). 482p. 1998. 234.00 (*0-7923-5091-X*) Kluwer Academic.

Positron Emission Tomography: Applications in Oncology. Ed. by Nielson Tse & Carl Hoh. 123p. 1994. 89.95 (*1-57059-128-8*, LN9128) CRC Pr.

Positron Emission Tomography: Research & Clinical Applications. R. E. Coleman. Date not set. write for info. (*0-8247-9486-9*) Dekker.

Positron Emission Tomography & Autoradiography: Principles & Applications for the Brain & Heart. Ed. by Michael E. Phelps et al. LC 85-19602. (Illus.). 704p. 1986. reprint ed. pap. 200.00 (*0-608-07225-7*, 206745000009) Bks Demand.

Positron Emission Tomography in Clinical Research: Tracer Modelling & Radioreceptors. Ed. by C. Beckers et al. (C). 1989. text 171.00 (*0-7923-0254-0*) Kluwer Academic.

*__Positron Emission Tomography in the Millennium: Proceedings of the International PET Symposium Held in Hokkaido, Japan, 24-26th September, 1999.__ International PET Symposium Staff & Nagara Tamaki. LC 00-34075. 2000. write for info. (*0-444-50385-4*) Elsevier.

Positron Named Priscilla: Scientific Discovery at the Frontier. National Academy of Sciences Staff. Ed. by Marcia Bartusiak et al. 360p. (C). 1994. 29.95 (*0-309-04893-1*) Natl Acad Pr.

*__Positron Physics.__ Michael Charlton & John Watkin Humberson. (Cambridge Monographs on Atomic, Molecular, & Chemical Physics: Vol. 11). (Illus.). 464p. 2000. write for info. (*0-521-41550-0*) Cambridge U Pr.

Positron Spectroscopy of Solids. A. Dupasquier. LC 94-73354. 780p. (gr. 12). 1995. 170.00 (*90-5199-203-3*) IOS Press.

Positron Studies of Condensed Matter. R. N. West. 132p. 1974. pap. 44.00 (*0-85066-070-X*) Taylor & Francis.

Positron Studies of Solids, Surface & Atoms. A. Mills & K. F. Canter. 352p. 1986. text 68.00 (*9971-978-44-X*) World Scientific Pub.

Positronic Man. Isaac Asimov & Robert Silverberg. LC 93-15148. 272p. 1993. 22.50 (*0-385-26342-2*) Doubleday.

Positronium & Muonium Chemistry: Based on a Symposium Sponsored by the Division of Physical Chemistry of the Chemical Institute of Canada at the Second Joint CIC/ACS Conference, Montreal, Canada, May 31-June 2, 1977. Ed. by Hans J. Ache. LC 79-11709. (Advances in Chemistry Ser.: No. 175). (Illus.). 384p. 1979. reprint ed. pap. 119.10 (*0-608-06753-9*, 206695000009) Bks Demand.

Positrons at Metallic Surfaces. Ed. by A. Ishii. (Solid State Phenomena Ser.: Vols. 28-29). 388p. 1993. text 184.00 (*0-87849-648-3*, Pub. by Trans T Pub) Enfield Pubs NH.

POSIX Explored: Shell & Utilities. 2nd ed. Hal Jespersen. 51p. 1993. pap. 10.00 (*0-936593-26-1*) UniForum.

POSIX Programmer's Guide. Donald Lewine. Ed. by Dale Dougherty. LC 92-225989. (Computer Science Ser.). (Illus.). 640p. 1991. reprint ed. pap. 37.95 (*0-937175-73-0*) OReilly & Assocs.

POSIX Programming Environment. Stephen Walli. (C). 1996. text. write for info. (*0-201-63345-0*) Addison-Wesley.

POSIX Supercomputing Application Environment Profile, 1003.10-1995. 80p. 50.00 (*1-55937-546-9*, SH94321) IEEE Standards.

POSIX.4: Programming for the Real World. Bill Gallmeister. (Illus.). 570p. (Orig.). 1995. pap. 29.95 (*1-56592-074-0*) Thomson Learn.

Poslanie. Goslaw S. Misztal.Tr. of Message. (POL.). 160p. (Orig.). 1987. pap. 10.00 (*0-930401-15-8*) Artex Pub.

Poslanije Saviatago Ignatija Antiokhiskago i Sviatago Polykarpa Smirnskago. St. Ignatius of Antioch & St. Polycarp of Simirna.Tr. of Letters of St. Ignatius of Antioch & of St. Polycarp of Smirna. (RUS.). 80p. (Orig.). 1975. pap. 2.00 (*0-88465-023-5*) Holy Trinity.

Posle Razluki: Berlinskii Pesennik. Andrey Bely. (RUS.). 125p. 1989. reprint ed. pap. 8.00 (*0-933884-74-5*) Berkeley Slavic.

Posledni Stupen Duvernosti see Ultimate Intimacy

Posmodernidad y Mijail Batjin. Iris M. Zavala. Tr. by Epiteto Diaz Navarro. (Nueva Austral Ser.: No. 169). (SPA.). 1991. pap. text 24.95 (*84-239-1969-2*) Elliots Bks.

*__Possadh & Bainis: A Guide to the Traditional Irish Wedding.__ Conrad Jay Bladey. (Illus.). 96p. (J). 2000. pap. 15.00 (*0-9702386-3-0*) Hutman Prodns.

Posse from Poison Creek. Lewis B. Patten. 1981. mass mkt. 1.75 (*0-451-09577-4*, Sig) NAL.

Posse from Stratton Forks. large type ed. Lee F. Gregson. (Dales Large Print Ser.). 1995. pap. 18.99 (*1-85389-523-7*, Dales) Ulverscroft.

Possedes, Tome I. Fyodor Dostoyevsky. (FRE.). 512p. 1974. pap. 11.95 (*0-7859-1784-5*, 2070365743) Fr & Eur.

Possedes, Tome II. Fyodor Dostoyevsky. (FRE.). 512p. 1974. pap. 11.95 (*0-7859-1785-3*, 2070365751) Fr & Eur.

Possesions. Hale Chatfield. (Cleveland Poets Ser.: No. 36). 34p. (Orig.). 1984. pap. 4.00 (*0-914946-39-0*) Cleveland St Univ Poetry Ctr.

*__Possessed.__ Anthony Masters. 144p. 1999. pap. (*1-86039-816-2*, Pub. by Orchard Bks) Raincoast Bk.

Possessed! Raymond A. Montgomery. (Choose Your Own Adventure Ser.: No. 161). (J). (gr. 4-8). 1995. 8.60 (*0-606-08034-1*) Turtleback.

Possessed. Fyodor Dostoyevsky. 702p. 1989. reprint ed. lib. bdg. 49.95 (*0-89966-628-0*) Buccaneer Bks.

Possessed: True Stories of Demonic Possession. Brian McConnell. (Illus.). 448p. 1997. mass mkt. 13.95 (*0-7472-4720-X*, Pub. by Headline Bk Pub) Trafalgar.

Possessed & Other Stories. Arthur C. Clarke. 188p. reprint ed. lib. bdg. 20.95 (*0-89190-956-7*, Rivercity Pr) Amereon Ltd.

Possessed & the Dispossessed: Spirits, Identity, & Power in a Madagascar Migrant Town. Lesley A. Sharp. (Comparative Studies of Health Systems & Medical Care: No. 37). (Illus.). 366p. (C). 1996. pap. 18.95 (*0-520-20708-4*, Pub. by U CA Pr) Cal Prin Full Svc.

Possessed Individual: Technology & New French Theory. Arthur Kroker. 250p. (Orig.). 1991. pap. 14.95 (*0-312-07130-2*) St Martin.

Possessed: or The Secret of Myslotch. Witold Gombrowicz. Tr. by J. A. Underwood from POL. 224p. 1988. pap. 16.95 (*0-7145-2738-6*) M Boyars Pubs.

Possessed Possessions: Haunted Antiques, Furniture & Collectibles. Ed Okonowicz. 112p. (Orig.). 1996. pap. 9.95 (*0-9643244-5-8*) Myst & Lace.

Possessed Posessions 2: More Haunted Antiques, Furniture & Collectibles. Ed Okonowicz. 112p. 1998. pap. 9.95 (*1-890690-02-3*) Myst & Lace.

Possessed Space. Javier Vallhonrat. (SPA., Illus.). 72p. 1998. 45.00 (*3-929078-00-7*, Kehayoff) te Neues.

Possessed with Greatness: The Heroic Tragedies of Chapman & Shakespeare. fac. ed. Richard S. Ide. LC 79-25864. 269p. 1980. reprint ed. pap. 83.40 (*0-7837-8052-4*, 204780500008) Bks Demand.

Possessing Albany, 1630-1710: The Dutch & English Experiences. Donna Merwick. (Illus.). 324p. (C). 1990. text 80.00 (*0-521-37386-7*) Cambridge U Pr.

Possessing Elissa. Donna Sterling. 1997. per. 3.50 (*0-373-25728-7*, 1-25728-6) Harlequin Bks.

Possessing God's Promises. Billy J. Daugherty. 32p. (Orig.). 1992. pap. 0.50 (*1-56267-082-4*) Victory Ctr OK.

Possessing Nature: Museums, Collecting, & Scientific Culture in Early Modern Italy. Paula Findlen. (Studies on the History of Society & Culture: Vol. 20). (Illus.). 449p. (C). 1996. pap. 19.95 (*0-520-20508-1*, Pub. by U CA Pr) Cal Prin Full Svc.

Possessing the Gates of the Enemy see Conquistemos Las Puertas Del Enemigo

Possessing the Gates of the Enemy: A Training Manual for Militant Intercession. 2nd ed. Cindy Jacobs. LC 91-17925. 272p. 1994. pap. 9.99 (*0-8007-9223-8*) Chosen Bks.

*__Possessing the Impact of Banana Biotechnology in Kenya.__ Matin Qaim. (ISAAA Briefs Ser.: Vol. 10). (Illus.). viii, 38p. 1999. pap. 25.00 (*1-892456-12-5*) Agri-Biotch.

Possessing the Land: Aragon's Expansion into Islam's Ebro Frontier under Alfonso the Battler, 1104-1134. Clay Stalls. LC 95-11140. (Medieval Mediterranean Ser.: No. 7). 417p. 1995. 120.50 (*90-04-10367-8*) Brill Academic Pubs.

Possessing the Past: Treasures from the National Palace Museum, Taipei. Wen C. Fong & James C. Watt. LC 95-49102. (Illus.). 600p. 1996. 85.00 (*0-87099-765-3*) Metro Mus Art.

Possessing the Promise of God: A Study of Joshua & Judges. Jack W. Hayford. LC 98-145872. (Spirit-Filled Life Bible Discovery Guide Ser.: Bk. 3). 160p. 1998. pap. 6.99 (*0-7852-1242-6*) Nelson.

Possessing the Secret of Joy. Alice Walker. LC 92-6883. x, 286p. 1992. 25.00 (*0-15-173152-7*) Harcourt.

Possessing the Secret of Joy. Alice Walker. LC 96-42270. (Illus.). 304p. 1997. per. 14.00 (*0-671-78945-7*, PB Trade Paper) PB.

Possessing the Secret of Joy. large type ed. Alice Walker. LC 96-22460. 252p. 1996. 24.95 (*1-56895-351-8*, Compass) Wheeler Pub.

Possessing the Secret of Joy. Alice Walker. Ed. by Bill Grose. 304p. 1993. reprint ed. per. 6.99 (*0-671-78942-2*, Pocket Star Bks) PB.

Possessing the Secret of Joy. unabridged ed. Alice Walker. 1992. pap. 25.00 incl. audio (*0-671-79306-3*, 592128, Pub. by S&S Audio) Lndmrk Audiobks.

Possessing Truth in Balance & Anatomy of a Backslider. Victor Bentley. LC 89-8945. 128p. (Orig.). (YA). 1989. pap. 2.99 (*0-932581-48-X*) Word Aflame.

Possessing Your Inheritance: Moving Forward in God's Covenant Plan for Your Life. Chuck D. Pierce & Rebecca Wagner Sytsema. LC 98-56162. 216p. (Orig.). 1999. pap. 10.99 (*0-8307-2357-9*, Renew) Gospel Lght.

Possessing Your Prophetic Promise. Tim Bagwell. 160p. (Orig.). 1995. pap. 9.99 (*1-884369-12-X*) McDougal Pubng.

Possession. Angela Ball. 96p. 1995. pap. 9.95 (*0-9639528-6-2*, Red Hen Press) Valentine CA.

Possession. Louis Bromfield. 31.95 (*0-8488-0690-5*) Amereon Ltd.

Possession. K. Cavendish. mass mkt. 6.95 (*0-7472-5244-0*, Pub. by Headline Bk Pub) Trafalgar.

Possession. Wendy Corsi-Staub. 1996. mass mkt. 3.99 (*0-8217-5153-0*) NAL.

Possession. J. M. Dillard. (Star Trek Next Generation Ser.: No. 40). 1996. per. 5.99 (*0-671-86485-8*, PB Trade Paper) PB.

Possession. Maura Seger. 1998. per. 4.25 (*0-373-07843-9*, 1-078435) Silhouette.

Possession. Celia Fremlin. 158p. 1985. reprint ed. pap. 5.95 (*0-89733-169-9*) Academy Chi Pubs.

Possession: A Novel. Ann Rule. 1997. per. 5.99 (*0-671-52788-6*) PB.

*__Possession: A Romance.__ A. S. Byatt. LC 99-56297. 608p. 2000. 19.95 (*0-679-64030-4*) Modern Lib NY.

Possession: A Romance. A. S. Byatt. LC 91-50023. (Vintage International Ser.). 555p. 1991. pap. 14.00 (*0-679-73590-9*) Vin Bks.

Possession: Demoniacal & Other. Traugott K. Oesterreich. 400p. 1974. reprint ed. pap. 4.95 (*0-8065-0436-6*, Citadel Pr) Carol Pub Group.

Possession & Exorcism. Ed. by Brian P. Levack. LC 92-22857. (Witchcraft, Magic, & Demonology Ser.: Vol. 9). 352p. 1992. text 68.00 (*0-8153-1031-5*) Garland.

Possession du Monde. Georges Duhamel. (FRE.). 240p. 1963. pap. 18.95 (*0-7859-5425-2*) Fr & Eur.

Possession, Ecstasy, & Law in Ewe Voodoo. Judy Rosenthal. LC 98-9396. 320p. 1998. pap. 18.50 (*0-8139-1805-7*); text 52.50 (*0-8139-1804-9*) U Pr of Va.

Possession of Celia. M. S. Valentine. 1998. mass mkt. 6.95 (*1-56333-666-9*) Masquerade.

Possession of Delia Sutherland. large type ed. Barbara Neil. LC 94-25968. 453p. 1995. pap. 19.95 (*0-7862-0293-9*) Thorndike Pr.

Possession of Loudun. De Certeau. LC 99-88078. (Illus.). 264p. 1993. pap. text 15.00 (*0-226-10035-9*); lib. bdg. 40.00 (*0-226-10034-0*) U Ch Pr.

Possession of Tony Saurian. Justin Lloyd. LC 86-70176. (Illus.). 242p. (YA). (gr. 10). 1986. pap. 10.00 (*0-937059-00-5*) AM to PM.

Possessions. Julia Kristeva. Tr. by Barbara Bray from FRE. LC 97-29554. 256p. 1998. 29.00 (*0-231-10998-9*) Col U Pr.

Possessions. Judith Michael, pseud. Ed. by Bill Grose. 1989. mass mkt. 6.50 (*0-671-69383-2*) PB.

Possessions. Judith Michael, pseud. 1994. per. 6.99 (*0-671-89956-2*) PB.

Possessions: A Maris Middleton Mystery. Kaye Davis. LC 97-40375. 240p. (Orig.). 1998. pap. 11.95 (*1-56280-192-9*) Naiad Pr.

Possessions: Indigenous Art/Colonial Culture. Nicholas Thomas. LC 98-61288. (Interplay Ser.). (Illus.). 304p. 1999. pap. 24.95 (*0-500-28097-5*, Pub. by Thames Hudson) Norton.

Possessions: New & Selected Poems 1938-1985. Ben Belitt. LC 85-45969. 160p. 1986. 20.00 (*0-87923-626-4*) Godine.

Possessions: New & Selected Poems 1938-1985. Ben Belitt. LC 85-45969. 160p. 1986. pap. 12.95 (*0-87923-633-7*) Godine.

Possessions of a Lady. Jonathan Gash. 288p. 1997. pap. 5.95 (*0-14-025792-6*) Viking Penguin.

Possessions, Projections & Entities. John-Roger. 84p. 1976. pap. 5.00 (*0-914829-17-3*) Mandeville LA.

Possessive Descriptions. Chris Barker. (Dissertations in Linguistics Ser.). 200p. (C). 1996. 49.95 (*1-881526-73-9*); pap. 22.95 (*1-881526-72-0*) CSLI.

Possessive Investment in Whiteness: How White People Profit from Identity Politics. George Lipsitz. LC 97-53204. 320p. (C). 1998. text 59.95 (*1-56639-634-4*); pap. text 19.95 (*1-56639-635-2*) Temple U Pr.

Possessives, Contractions, Compound Words & Homophones. Scholastic, Inc. Staff. (Fun with Phonics Ser.). (J). 1997. pap. text 6.95 (*0-590-76702-X*) Scholastic Inc.

Possessives in English: An Exploration in Cognitive Grammar. John R. Taylor. (Illus.). 382p. 1996. text 90.00 (*0-19-823586-0*) OUP.

*__Possessives in English: An Exploration in Cognitive Grammar.__ John R. Taylor. (Illus.). 384p. 2000. pap. text 29.95 (*0-19-829982-6*) OUP.

P

An Asterisk (*) at the beginning of an entry indicates that the title is appearing for the first time.

Possessors, Predicates, & Movement in the Determiners Phrase. Ed. by Chris Wilder & Artemis Alexiadou. LC 98-35296. (Linguistik Aktuell/Linguistics Today Ser.: No. 22). vi, 388p. 1998. 79.00 (*1-55619-906-6*) J Benjamins Pubng Co.

Possessory Estates & Future Interests Primer. Charles I. Nelson & Peter T. Wendel. LC 96-185579. (Paralegal). 200p. (C). 1996. pap. text 16.00 (*0-314-09730-9*) West Pub.

Possibilistic Data Analysis for Operations Research. H. Tanaka & P. Guo. LC 99-19568. (Studies in Fuzziness & Soft Computing: Vol. 29). (Illus.). xii, 182p. 1999. 59.00 (*3-7908-1183-1*) Spr-Verlag.

Possibilities: A Supplemental Anthology for Career Choices. Ed. by Janet Goode & Mindy Bingham. (Illus.). 288p. (YA). (gr. 9 up). 1991. pap. 9.95 (*1-878787-05-5*) Acad Innovat.

***Possibilities: Awakening Your Leadership Potential.** 154p. 2000. pap. 12.95 (*0-9641240-8-4*) J Magee Intl.

Possibilities: Poems from Hollywood. Mark Dunster. 15p. 1998. pap. 5.00 (*0-89642-431-6*) Linden Pubs.

Possibilities & Limitations of Pragmatics: Proceedings of the Conference on Pragmatics, Urbino, Italy, July 8-14, 1979. Ed. by Herman Parret et al. (Studies in Language Companion Ser.: No. 7). x, 854p. 1981. 177.00 (*90-272-3006-4*) J Benjamins Pubng Co.

***Possibilities for over One Hundredfold More Spiritual Information: The Humble Approach in Theology & Science** / John Templeton. LC 00-29917. 2000. pap. write for info. (*1-890151-33-5*) Templeton Fnd.

Possibilities for the Improvement of Nitrogen Fertilizer Efficiency in Rice Production. D. H. Parish. (Papers: No. P-1). 1980. pap. text 4.00 (*0-88090-061-X*) Intl Fertilizer.

Possibilities of Blue Sky. Gary David. (Salt River Poetry Ser.). 80p. 1989. pap. write for info. (*1-882021-02-9*) Summer.

Possibilities of Empty Space: Poems. Pit M. Pinegar. LC 97-19113. 1997. pap. 12.95 (*0-916897-29-X*) Andrew Mtn Pr.

Possibilities of Hidden Things: Narrative Transgression in Victorian Fictional Autobiographies. Hsiao-Hung Lee. (Studies in Nineteenth-Century British Literature: Vol. 5). XIII, 178p. (C). 1996. text 42.95 (*0-8204-2872-8*) P Lang Pubng.

Possibilities of Order: Cleanth Brooks & His Work. Lewis P. Simpson. LC 75-18046. 280p. 1976. pap. 86.80 (*0-7837-8503-8*, 204931100011) Bks Demand.

Possibilities of Organization. Barry Oshry. 178p. (Orig.). (C). 1986. pap. text 19.95 (*0-910411-10-7*) Power & Sys.

Possibilities of Prayer. E. M. Bounds. 175p. 1994. mass mkt. 5.99 (*0-88368-315-6*) Whitaker Hse.

Possibilities of Society: Wordsworth, Coleridge, & the Sociological Viewpoint of English Romanticism. Regina Hewitt. LC 96-42546. (SUNY Series, The Margins of Literature). 231p. (C). 1997. text 57.50 (*0-7914-3419-2*); pap. text 18.95 (*0-7914-3420-6*) State U NY Pr.

Possibilities of the Negro in Symposium. LC 75-173610. (Black Heritage Library Collection). 1977. reprint ed. 19.95 (*0-8369-8902-3*) Ayer.

Possibilities of Theology: Studies in the Theology of Eberhard Jungel in His Sixtieth Year. Ed. by John Webster. 256p. 1994. text 47.95 (*0-567-09720-X*, Pub. by T & T Clark) Bks Intl VA.

Possibilities of Transcendence: Human Destructiveness & the Universality of Constructive Relations. Jolana Polakova. Tr. by Jan Valeska. LC 95-8655. (Problems in Contemporary Philosophy Ser.: Vol. 34). 104p. 1996. 59.95 (*0-7734-8896-0*) E Mellen.

Possibility. Scott M. Buchanan. LC 74-22904. 204p. reprint ed. pap. 63.30 (*0-8357-8993-4*, 205679100085) Bks Demand.

Possibility: An Essay in Utopian Vision. Francis Golffing & Barbara Gibbs. LC 90-21358. (American University Studies: Philosophy: Ser. V, Vol. 109). (Illus.). XX, 159p. (C). 1991. text 29.95 (*0-8204-1431-X*) P Lang Pubng.

Possibility Chalice Pt. 2: The Relics of Power Trilogy. (Torg Ser.). 64p. 12.00 (*0-87431-310-4*, 20552) West End Games.

Possibility Living. Billy J. Daugherty. 32p. (Orig.). 1993. pap. 0.50 (*1-56267-086-7*) Victory Ctr OK.

***Possibility Living: Add Years to Your Life & Life to Your Years with God's Health Plan.** Robert A. Schuller & Doug Di Siena. LC 00-32047. 2001. write for info. (*0-06-067085-1*) Harper SF.

Possibility Living: Add Years to Your Life & Life to Your Years with God's Health Plan. Robert A. Schuller & Douglas Di Siena. (Illus.). 240p. 2000. 24.00 (*0-06-067086-X*) Harper SF.

***Possibility Living: Add Years to Your Life & Life to Your Years with God's Health Plan.** large type ed. Robert A. Schuller. 390p. 2000. pap. 24.00 (*0-06-019914-8*) HarpC.

Possibility, Necessity & Existence: Abbagnano & His Predecessors. Nino Languilli. (Themes in the History of Philosophy Ser.). 250p. (C). 1992. 59.95 (*0-87722-921-X*) Temple U Pr.

Possibility of a Universal Language see Needed Words

Possibility of Altruism. Thomas Nagel. LC 78-4323. 150p. 1979. pap. text 13.95 (*0-691-02002-7*, Pub. by Princeton U Pr) Cal Prin Full Svc.

Possibility of Angels: A Literary Anthology. Sophie Biriotti & Peter Malone. LC 96-53498. (Illus.). 144p. 1997. 24.95 (*0-8118-1530-7*) Chronicle Bks.

Possibility of Being: Selected Poems. Rainer Maria Rilke. Tr. by J. B. Leishman from GER. LC 77-4656. 122p. 1977. pap. 8.95 (*0-8112-0651-3*, NDP436, Pub. by New Directions) Norton.

Possibility of Communication. William T. Scott. (Approaches to Semiotics Ser.: No. 87). (Illus.). xii, 303p. (C). 1990. lib. bdg. 106.15 (*3-11-011909-9*) Mouton.

Possibility of Cooperation. rev. ed. Michael Taylor. (Studies in Rationality & Social Change). 220p. 1987. pap. text 23.95 (*0-521-33990-1*) Cambridge U Pr.

Possibility of Criticism. Monroe C. Beardsley. LC 78-103416. (Criticism Monograph Ser.: No. 2). 124p. reprint ed. pap. 38.50 (*0-7837-3811-0*, 204363100010) Bks Demand.

Possibility of God: A Reconsideration of Religion in a Technological Society. James F. Drane. (Quality Paperback Ser.: No. 321). 194p. 1976. 9.95 (*0-8226-0321-7*) Littlefield.

Possibility of Knowledge: Nozick & His Critics. Ed. by Steven Luper-Foy. 352p. 1987. 65.00 (*0-8476-7446-0*); pap. 26.50 (*0-8476-7447-9*) Rowman.

Possibility of Language: A Discussion of the Nature of Language, with Implications for Human & Machine Translation. Alan K. Melby & Terry Warner. LC 95-45373. (Benjamins Translation Library Ser.: Vol. 14). xxvi, 276p. 1995. 49.00 (*1-55619-695-4*) J Benjamins Pubng Co.

Possibility of Living Two Hundred Years. Ed. by F. C. Havens. 1991. lib. bdg. 79.95 (*0-87700-978-3*) Revisionist Pr.

Possibility of Living Two Hundred Years. F. O. Havens. 98p. 1990. reprint ed. spiral bd. 11.00 (*0-7873-0384-4*) Hlth Research.

Possibility of Metaphysics: Substance, Identity & Time. E. J. Lowe. LC 98-27587. 286p. 1998. text 65.00 (*0-19-823683-2*) OUP.

Possibility of Naturalism: A Philosophical Critique of the Contemporary Human Sciences. 3rd ed. Roy Bhaskar. LC 98-35442. 1998. 85.00 (*0-415-19873-9*); pap. 24.99 (*0-415-19874-7*) Routledge.

Possibility of Popular Justice: A Case Study of Community Mediation in the United States. Ed. by Sally E. Merry & Neal Milner. LC 93-23588. (Law, Meaning, & Violence Ser.). 504p. (Orig.). (C). 1993. text 64.50 (*0-472-10426-8*, 10426) U of Mich Pr.

Possibility of Popular Justice: A Case Study of Community Mediation in the United States. Ed. by Sally E. Merry & Neal Milner. LC 93-24588. 504p. (Orig.). (C). 1995. pap. text 25.95 (*0-472-08344-9*, 08344) U of Mich Pr.

***Possibility of Practical Reason.** J. David Velleman. 280p. 2000. pap. 19.95 (*0-19-823826-6*) OUP.

***Possibility of Practical Reason.** J. David Velleman. 280p. 2000. text 65.00 (*0-19-823825-8*) OUP.

Possibility of Relative Truth. Peter Davson-Galle. LC 97-77551. (Avebury Series in Philosophy). 198p. 1998. text 59.95 (*1-84014-115-8*, Pub. by Ashgate Pub) Ashgate Pub Co.

Possibility of Resurrection & Other Essays in Christian Apologetics. Peter Van Inwagen. LC 97-17602. 1997. pap. 65.00 (*0-8133-2731-8*, Pub. by Westview) HarpC.

Possibility of Resurrection & Other Essays in Christian Apologetics. Peter Van Inwagen. 1997. pap. 17.95 (*0-8133-2732-6*) Westview.

Possibility of the Aesthetic Experience. Ed. by Michael H. Mitias. 180p. 1986. lib. bdg. 122.00 (*90-247-3278-6*, Pub. by M Nijhoff) Kluwer Academic.

Possibility of Transcendental Philosophy. Jitendra N. Mohanty. (Phaenomenologica Ser.: Vol. 98). 282p. 1985. pap. text 49.00 (*90-247-3146-1*, Pub. by M Nijhoff); lib. bdg. 132.00 (*90-247-2991-2*, Pub. by M Nijhoff) Kluwer Academic.

Possibility of Weakness of Will. Robert Dunn. LC 85-24784. 192p. (C). 1987. pap. 14.95 (*0-915145-98-7*); lib. bdg. 32.95 (*0-915145-99-5*) Hackett Pub.

Possibility Theory: An Approach to Computerized Processing of Uncertainty. D. Dubois & H. Prade. LC 87-32179. (Illus.). 280p. (C). 1988. text 75.00 (*0-306-42520-3*, Kluwer Plenum) Kluwer Academic.

Possibility Thinking. Robert H. Schuller. LC 93-20166. (Itty Bitty Bk.). 1993. 4.99 (*0-8407-6311-5*) Nelson.

Possible. Bruce Bond. 32p. 1995. pap. 6.00 (*1-878851-06-3*) Silverfish Rev Pr.

Possible & Actual. Fran Jacob. 1994. pap. 9.95 (*0-295-97341-2*) U of Wash Pr.

Possible & the Actual: Readings in the Metaphysics of Modality. Intro. by Michael J. Loux. LC 79-7618. 336p. 1979. pap. text 16.95 (*0-8014-9178-9*) Cornell U Pr.

Possible & the Improbable see Possible e l'Improbabile: Italian Novel

Possible Begetter of the Old English Beowulf & Widsith. Albert S. Cook. (Connecticut Academy of Arts & Sciences Ser., Trans.: Vol. 25). 1922. pap. 20.00 (*0-685-22825-8*) Elliots Bks.

Possible Begetter of the Old English Beowulf & Widsith. Albert S. Cook. (Beowulf & the Literature of the Anglo-Saxons Ser.: No. 2). (C). 1970. reprint ed. pap. 22.95 (*0-8383-0018-9*) M S G Haskell Hse.

Possible Cinema: The Films of Alain Tanner. Jim Leach. LC 84-10610. 220p. 1984. 25.00 (*0-8108-1714-4*) Scarecrow.

Possible Death on the Highway: Attempted Murder or an Accident, Example of a Logical Map. (Analysis Ser.: No. 11). 1983. pap. 12.50 (*0-686-42847-1*, 0686428463) Inst Analysis.

Possible Debris. Richard Hague. (Cleveland Poets Ser.: No. 43). 60p. (Orig.). 1988. pap. 6.00 (*0-914946-70-6*) Cleveland St Univ Poetry Ctr.

Possible Dream. Charles P. Conn. 1987. mass mkt. 4.99 (*0-425-10566-0*) Berkley Pub.

Possible Dream: Mainstream Experiences of Hearing-Impaired Students. Ed. by Mildred Oberkotter et al. (Centennial Celebration Ser.). 68p. (Orig.). (YA). 1990. pap. text 7.95 (*0-88200-171-X*) Alexander Graham.

Possible Dream: Saving George Washington's View. Robert W. Straus & Eleanor B. Straus. Ed. by Bonnie L. Walker. (Illus.). 144p. (Orig.). (C). 1988. pap. 8.00 (*0-317-92278-5*) Accokeek Fndtn.

Possible Dreams: Enthusiasm for Technology in America. John L. Wright. 128p. 1992. pap. 14.95 (*0-933728-35-2*) Henry Ford Mus.

Possible e l'Improbarile: Italian Novel. Salvatore Rosciglione.Tr. of Possible & the Improbable. (ITA.). 167p. 1988. pap. 10.00 (*0-89304-657-4*) Cross-Cultrl NY.

Possible Experience: Understanding Kant's Critique of Pure Reason. Arthur W. Collins. LC 98-33670. 219p. 1999. 40.00 (*0-520-21498-6*, Pub. by U CA Pr); pap. 15.95 (*0-520-21499-4*, Pub. by U CA Pr) Cal Prin Full Svc.

Possible Floor. George Albon. 1990. pap. 3.50 (*0-938979-35-3*) EG Bksellers.

Possible Future Oil Provinces of the United States & Canada: Proceedings of the American Association of Petroleum Geologists, 26th, Houston, 1941. American Association of Petroleum Geologists Staff. Ed. by Arville I. Levorsen. LC 41-23448. 160p. reprint ed. pap. 49.60 (*0-608-13920-3*, 202374400033) Bks Demand.

***Possible Futures: Science Fiction Art from the Frank Collection: Re-Reading Science Fiction Art.** Dorit Yaron. LC 99-68342. (Illus.). 96p. 2000. 20.00 (*0-937123-39-0*) Art Gal U MD.

Possible Health Effects of Exposure to Residential Electric & Magnetic Fields. Ed. by John B. Little. (Illus.). 356p. (Orig.). (C). 1997. text 60.00 (*0-7881-4516-9*) DIANE Pub.

Possible Health Effects of Exposure to Residential Electric & Magnetic Fields. NRC, Possible Effects of Electromagnetic Fields on. LC 96-51230. 384p. 1997. text 39.95 (*0-309-05447-8*) Natl Acad Pr.

Possible Human. Jean Houston. 256p. 1997. 15.95 (*0-87477-872-7*, Tarcher Putnam) Putnam Pub Group.

Possible Human: A Course in Enhancing Your Physical, Mental, & Creative Abilities. Jean Houston. (Illus.). 229p. 1998. pap. text 15.00 (*0-7881-5737-X*) DIANE Pub.

Possible India: Essays in Political Criticism. Partha Chatterjee. 316p. 1999. pap. text 11.95 (*0-19-564766-1*) OUP.

Possible Influence of Montaigne's Essais on Descartes' Treatise on the Passions. Michael G. Paulson. 138p. (Orig.). (C). 1988. lib. bdg. 38.00 (*0-8191-7027-5*) U Pr of Amer.

Possible Landscape. Maureen Harris. 64p. 1993. pap. 11.95 (*0-919626-67-X*, Pub. by Brick Bks) Genl Dist Srvs.

Possible Lives: The Promise of Public Education. Mike Rose. 1996. pap. 13.95 (*0-614-20717-7*) Viking Penguin.

Possible Lives: The Promise of Public Education in America. Mike Rose. 464p. (C). 1996. pap. 13.95 (*0-14-023617-1*) Viking Penguin.

Possible Palladian Villas: Plus a Few Instructively Impossible Ones. George Hersey & Richard Freedman. (Illus.). 198p. 1992. pap. text 18.50 (*0-262-58110-8*) MIT Pr.

Possible Palladian Villas: Plus a Few Instructively Impossible Ones. George L. Hersey & Richard Freedman. (Illus.). 181p. 1992. 37.50 (*0-262-08210-1*) MIT Pr.

***Possible Pasts: Becoming Colonial in Early America.** Robert B. St. George. LC 99-89817. (Illus.). 464p. 2000. pap. 19.95 (*0-8014-8392-1*) Cornell U Pr.

Possible Sibyls. Madeline DeFrees. 80p. 1991. 16.95 (*0-89924-079-8*); pap. 8.50 (*0-89924-080-1*) Lynx Hse.

Possible Solution of the Number Series on Pages Fifty-One to Fifty-Eight of the Dresden Codex. C. E. Guthe. (Harvard University Peabody Museum of Archaeology & Ethnology Papers: Vol. 6, No.2). 1974. reprint ed. pap. 25.00 (*0-527-01207-6*) Periodicals Srv.

Possible State Court Responses to the ALI's Proposed Restatement of Products Liability: Report of the 1996 Forum for State Court Judges. Roscoe Pound Foundation Staff. Ed. by James Rooks. 75p. 1997. pap. 35.00 (*0-933067-18-6*) Roscoe Pound Inst.

Possible Tree. Aldridge. LC 92-13704. (Illus.). 32p. (J). (gr. k-3). 1998. per. 5.99 (*0-689-82131-X*) S&S Childrens.

Possible Tree. Josephine H. Aldridge. LC 92-13704. (Illus.). 32p. (J). (gr. k-3). 1993. lib. bdg. 16.00 (*0-02-700407-4*, Mac Bks Young Read) S&S Childrens.

Possible Universe. 2nd ed. J. A. Tallet. LC 96-49238. 240p. 1997. 42.50 (*0-7618-0665-2*) U Pr of Amer.

Possible Urban Worlds: Urban Strategies at the End of the 20th Century. Inura. (Illus.). 280p. 1998. pap. 45.00 (*3-7643-5986-2*, Pub. by Birkhauser) Princeton Arch.

Possible Vision: Holistic New Age Education. George A. Jones. LC 80-52612. 104p. 1981. pap. 5.00 (*0-917610-02-4*) Peacehaven.

***Possible Woman: Exploring Feminine Wisdom, Spirit & Potential.** (Illus.). 220p. 1999. pap. 20.00 (*0-9677823-0-9*) Barlow Bks.

***Possible Worlds.** J. B. S. Haldane. 134p. 2000. pap. 24.95 (*0-7658-0715-7*) Transaction Pubs.

***Possible Worlds: Acting Edition.** John Mighton. 80p. 1998. pap. 10.00 (*0-929741-43-9*) Playsmith.

Possible Worlds: And Other Papers. John Burdon Sanderson Haldane. LC 75-167351. (Essay Index Reprint Ser.). 1977. reprint ed. 20.95 (*0-8369-2452-5*) Ayer.

Possible Worlds, Artificial Intelligence, & Narrative Theory. Marie-Laure Ryan. LC 91-6825. (Illus.). 308p. 1992. 14.95 (*0-253-35004-2*) Ind U Pr.

Possible Worlds in Humanities, Arts, & Sciences; Proceedings of Nobel Symposium 65. Ed. by Sture Allen. (Research in Text Theory Ser.: Vol. 14). x, 453p. (C). 1989. lib. bdg. 150.00 (*3-11-011220-5*) De Gruyter.

Possible Worlds in Literary Theory. Ruth Ronen. (Literature, Culture, Theory Ser.: No. 7). 256p. (C). 1994. text 64.95 (*0-521-45017-9*); pap. text 19.95 (*0-521-45648-7*) Cambridge U Pr.

Possibles. Christopher C. Cook. 56p. (Orig.). 1970. pap. 10.00 (*1-879886-20-0*) Addison Gallery.

Possibles. Vaunda Micheaux Nelson. LC 94-44386. (Illus.). 192p. (J). (gr. 5-8). 1997. pap. 5.99 (*0-698-11551-1*, PapStar) Peng Put Young Read.

Possibles. Vaunda Micheaux Nelson. (J). 1997. 11.05 (*0-606-10989-7*, Pub. by Turtleback) Demco.

Possibles. Lass Small. 1994. per. 3.59 (*0-373-45164-4*) Silhouette.

Posson Jone & Pere Raphael see Collected Works of George W. Cable

Posson Jone & Pere Raphael. George W. Cable. (Works of George Cable). 1988. reprint ed. 59.00 (*0-685-48941-8*) Rprt Serv.

Possum & Ole Ez in the Public Eye: Contemporaries & Peers on T. S. Eliot & Ezra Pound. Ed. by Burton Raffel. LC 84-24593. 143p. (C). 1985. lib. bdg. 26.00 (*0-208-02057-8*, Archon Bks) Shoe String.

Possum & the Peeper. Anne Hunter. LC 97-9470. 32p. (J). 1998. 15.00 (*0-395-84631-5*) HM.

***Possum & the Peeper.** Anne Hunter. (Illus.). 32p. (J). (ps-3). 2000. pap. 5.95 (*0-618-07030-3*) HM.

Possum, Clover & Hades: The 475th Fighter Group in World War II. John C. Stanaway. LC 93-84493. (Illus.). 336p. 1993. 45.00 (*0-88740-518-5*) Schiffer.

Possum Come A-Knockin' Nancy Van Laan. (J). 1992. 12.19 (*0-606-01557-4*, Pub. by Turtleback) Demco.

Possum Come A-Knocking. Nancy Van Laan. LC 88-12751. (Illus.). 32p. (J). (ps-3). 1990. lib. bdg. 14.99 (*0-394-92206-9*, Pub. by Knopf Bks Yng Read) Random.

***Possum Hollow, Bk. 1.** Levi B. Weber. (Illus.). 144p. 2000. pap. 7.99 (*0-8361-9126-9*) Herald Pr.

***Possum Hollow, Bk. 2.** Levi B. Weber. (Illus.). 144p. (YA). (gr. 4 up). 2000. pap. 7.99 (*0-8361-9131-5*) Herald Pr.

Possum Huts. Helga Tacreiter & Walter Hankinson. LC 84-70691. (Illus.). 68p. 1984. pap. 6.95 (*0-916949-01-X*) Amaya Pub.

Possum in Every Pot: Once upon a Time in the South. James M. Hanna. LC 94-70704. 135p. 1994. pap. 9.95 (*0-9640458-1-8*) Cherokee Bks DE.

Possum in the Pawpaw Tree: A Seasonal Guide to Midwestern Gardening. B. Rosie Lerner & Beverly S. Netzhammer. LC 94-12066. (Illus.). 300p. 1994. 27.95 (*1-55753-053-X*); pap. 24.95 (*1-55753-054-8*) Purdue U Pr.

Possum Magic. Mem Fox. LC 90-34864. (Illus.). 32p. (J). (ps-3). 1990. 15.00 (*0-15-200572-2*, Gulliver Bks) Harcourt.

Possum Magic. Mem Fox. LC 90-34864. (Illus.). 32p. (J). (ps-3). 1991. pap. 6.00 (*0-15-263224-7*, Gulliver Bks) Harcourt.

Possum Magic. Mem Fox. (J). 1983. 11.20 (*0-606-00695-8*, Pub. by Turtleback) Demco.

Possum Magic: Mini Book. Mem Fox. (J). Date not set. write for info. (*0-15-201678-3*) Harcourt.

Possum Play: A Play in Two Acts Benjie Aerenson. LC 98-213913. 96 p. 1998. write for info. (*0-573-62436-4*) S French Trade.

***Possums & Gliders.** Ed. by Surrey Beatty Staff. 593p. 1999. pap. 380.00 (*0-949324-74-4*, Pub. by Surrey Beatty & Sons) St Mut.

Possums & Opossums: Studies in Evolution, 2 vols. Ed. by Surrey Beatty Staff. 800p. (C). 1999. pap. text 592.00 (*0-949324-05-1*, Pub. by Surrey Beatty & Sons) St Mut.

Possum's Harvest Moon. Anne Hunter. LC 95-20833. (Illus.). 32p. (J). (ps-3). 1996. 15.00 (*0-395-73575-0*) HM.

Possum's Harvest Moon. Anne Hunter. (Illus.). 32p. (J). (ps-3). 1998. pap. 5.95 (*0-395-91824-3*) HM.

Post - Colonial Conditions: Exiles, Migrations, & Nomadisms, Vol. 1. Francoise Lionnett. Ed. by Ronnie Scharfman. (Yale French Studies: No. 82). 272p. (C). 1993. pap. 18.00 (*0-300-05270-7*) Yale U Pr.

Post - Colonial Conditions: Exiles, Migrations, & Nomadisms, Vol. 2. Francoise Lionnet. Ed. by Ronnie Scharfman. (Yale French Studies: No. 83). 272p. (C). 1993. pap. 18.00 (*0-300-05397-5*) Yale U Pr.

Post Abolished: One Woman's Struggle for Employment Rights in Tanzania. Laeticia Mukurasi. (Cornell International Industrial & Labor Relations Reports: No. 19). 144p. 1991. 27.50 (*0-87546-702-4*, ILR Press); pap. 12.95 (*0-87546-703-2*, ILR Press) Cornell U Pr.

Post-Abortion Aftermath: A Comprehensive Consideration. Michael T. Mannion. LC 94-21556. 190p. (Orig.). 1994. pap. 12.95 (*1-55612-708-1*) Sheed & Ward WI.

Post-Abortion Syndrome: Its Wide Ramifications. Ed. by Peter Doherty. 128p. 1995. pap. 15.00 (*1-85182-159-7*, Pub. by Four Cts Pr) Intl Spec Bk.

Post-Abortion Trauma. Jeanette Vought. 256p. 1991. pap. 10.99 (*0-310-53641-3*) Zondervan.

Post Accident Heat Removal, Vol. 2. V. Coen & H. Holtbecker. (European Applied Research Reports Special Topics Ser.). vi, 398p. 1979. text 607.00 (*3-7186-0025-0*) Gordon & Breach.

Post Acute Care Reimbursement Manual. Cherilyn G. Murer et al. LC 97-36013. 1997. write for info. (*0-7863-1248-3*) McGraw.

Post-Ality Vol. 1: Marxism & Postmodernism. Ed. by Mas'ud Zavarzadeh et al. LC HX44.5.P67. (Transformation Ser.). 300p. (Orig.). (C). 1995. pap. 14.95 (*0-944624-27-8*) Maisonneuve Pr.

Post-Anaesthetic Recovery. R. J. Eltringham et al. Ed. by M. Durkin & S. Andrewes. (Illus.). 130p. 1984. pap. 25.50 (*0-387-12631-7*) Spr-Verlag.

Post-Anaesthetic Recovery. R. J. Eltringham et al. (Illus.). 215p. 1990. 51.95 (*0-387-19555-6*) Spr-Verlag.

P

Post-Analytic Philosophy. Ed. by John Rajchman & Cornel West. LC 85-377. 304p. 1985. pap. text 22.50 (*0-231-06067-X*) Col U Pr.

Post & Park: A Brief Illustrated History of the Presidio of San Francisco. Stephen A. Haller. LC 96-78727. (Illus.). 48p. (Orig.). 1997. pap. 9.95 (*1-883869-23-4*) Gldn Gate Natl Parks Assoc.

Post Anesthesia Care Unit: A Critical Care Approach to Post Anesthesia Nursing. 3rd ed. Cecil B. Drain. LC 93-8029. (Illus.). 640p. 1994. text 52.50 (*0-7216-4571-2*, W B Saunders Co) Harcrt Hlth Sci Grp.

Post Anesthesia Care Unit Competencies. Barbara Godden. 126p. 1996. ring bd. 115.00 (*1-879575-37-X*) Acad Med Sys.

Post-Apartheid Education: Towards Non-Racial, Unitary & Democratic Socialisation in the New South Africa. Mandla P. Mncwabe. 276p. (C). 1993. lib. bdg. 54.00 (*0-8191-8969-3*) U Pr of Amer.

Post-Apartheid South Africa. Ed. by Eric Wainwright. 262p. 1989. pap. text 14.95 (*0-943852-83-8*) Prof World Peace.

Post-Apartheid Southern Africa? Ed. by Nancy Thede & Pierre Beaudet. LC 92-40355. (International Political Economy Ser.). 250p. 1993. text 55.00 (*0-312-09577-5*) St Martin.

Post-Apartheid Southern Africa: Economic Challenges & Policies for the Future: Proceedings of the 16th Arne Ryde Symposium, 23-24 August 1996, Lund, Sweden. Lennart Peterson. LC 97-23353. 376p. (C). 1998. 85.00 (*0-415-16184-3*) Routledge.

Post Apollo Space Exploration, 2 Vols, Pt. II. American Astronautical Society Staff. (Advances in the Astronautical Sciences Ser.: Vol. 20). 1966. 35.00 (*0-87703-023-5*) Univelt Inc.

Post-Audits of Environmental Programs & Projects. Ed. by Charles G. Gunnerson. LC 89-17958. 112p. 1989. pap. text 5.00 (*0-87262-735-7*, 735) Am Soc Civil Eng.

Post-Augustan Poetry from Seneca to Juvenal. Harold E. Butler. LC 70-99656. (Select Bibliographies Reprint Ser.). 1977. 30.95 (*0-8369-5085-2*) Ayer.

Post-Augustan Satire: Charles Churchill & Satirical Poetry, 1750-1800. Thomas Lockwood. LC 78-4366. 208p. 1979. 30.00 (*0-295-95612-7*) U of Wash Pr.

Post-Auschwitz Fragments. Lore Shelley. 304p. 1998. pap. text 24.95 (*1-57502-900-6*, P02470) Morris Pubng.

Post-Basic Nursing Education Programmes for Foreign Students. (Technical Report Ser.: No. 199). 48p. 1960. pap. text 3.00 (*92-4-120199-1*) World Health.

Post-Biblical Saints Art Index: A Locator of Paintings, Sculptures, Mosaics, Icons, Frescoes, Manuscripts, Illuminations, Sketches, Woodcuts & Engravings Created from the 4th Century to 1950, with a Directory of the Institutions Holding Them. Mercedes Rochelle. LC 94-10155. 367p. 1994. lib. bdg. 75.00 (*0-89950-942-8*) McFarland & Co.

Post-Boom in Spanish American Fiction. Donald L. Shaw. LC 97-34102. (SUNY Series in Latin American & Iberian Thought & Culture). (Illus.). 224p. (C). 1998. text 49.50 (*0-7914-3825-2*); pap. text 16.95 (*0-7914-3826-0*) State U NY Pr.

Post-Brezhnev Era. Silviu Brucan. LC 83-16158. 144p. 1983. 47.95 (*0-275-90953-0*, C0953, Praeger Pubs) Greenwood.

Post-Broadcasting Age. Lutton Staff. 1997. pap. 31.95 (*1-86020-502-X*, Pub. by U of Luton Pr) Bks Intl VA.

***Post-Bubble Blues: How Japan Responded to Asset Price Collapse.** Tamim A. Bayoumi & Charles Collyns. LC 99-58930. 1999. write for info. (*1-55775-872-7*) Intl Monetary.

Post-Bureaucratic Organization. Ed. by Charles C. Heckscher & Anne Donnellon. 360p. 1994. 54.00 (*0-8039-5717-3*); pap. 25.00 (*0-8039-5718-1*) Sage.

Post-Byzantine Ecclesiastical Personalities. Ed. by Nomikos M. Vaporis. LC 78-11037. 111p. 1978. pap. 4.95 (*0-916586-30-8*, Pub. by Holy Cross Orthodox) BookWorld.

Post-Capitalist Industrialization: Planning Economic Independence in Tanzania. William L. Luttrell. LC 86-9452. (Illus.). 208p. 1986. 57.95 (*0-275-92310-X*, C2310, Praeger Pubs) Greenwood.

***Post-Capitalist Society.** Peter F. Drucker. 1999. pap. 13.50 (*0-06-662025-2*, HarpBusn) HarpInfo.

Post-Capitalist Society. Peter F. Drucker. LC 92-54323. 240p. 1994. reprint ed. pap. 13.50 (*0-88730-661-6*, HarpBusn) HarpInfo.

Post Captain. Patrick O'Brian. (Aubrey-Maturin Ser.). 496p. 1990. pap. 13.95 (*0-393-30706-9*) Norton.

Post Captain. Patrick O'Brian. 1994. 24.00 (*0-393-03702-9*) Norton.

***Post Captain.** large type ed. Patrick O'Brian. LC 00-21929. (Famous Authors Ser.). 689p. 2000. 27.95 (*0-7862-1933-5*, MML06400-17053) Thorndike Pr.

Post Captivity Names of Israel. W. Pascoe Goard. (Illus.). 128p. 1989. reprint ed. pap. 6.50 (*0-934666-31-8*) Artisan Pubs.

Post Card: From Socrates to Freud & Beyond. Jacques Derrida. Tr. by Alan Bass. LC 86-27259. (Illus.). 552p. (C). 1987. pap. text 26.00 (*0-226-14322-8*) U Ch Pr.

Post Card Crossword Puzzles, Vol. 1. Joan L. Jay. (Illus.). 98p. (Orig.). 1989. pap. 9.95 (*0-9623528-0-2*) J L Jay.

***Post Card History of Kenyon, Minnesota: From the Post Card Collection of John L. Cole.** John L. Cole. (Illus.). x, 110p. 1999. pap. 16.95 (*0-9676652-0-5*) J L Cole MN.

Post Card Passages. Susan Joyce. LC 94-2949. (Illus.). (J). (gr. 4-7). 1994. 13.95 (*0-939217-27-9*) Peel Prod.

Post Card Views & Other Souvenirs: Poems. Marcia M. Miller. (Illus.). 64p. 1973. pap. 2.95 (*0-913270-24-5*) Sunstone Pr.

Post Cards from Old Kansas City. Sam Ray. LC 80-84468. (Illus.). 48p. 1980. pap. 9.50 (*0-685-02273-0*) Hist Kansas City.

Post-Cartesian Meditations: An Essay in Dialectical Phenomenology. James L. Marsh. LC 88-82135. xiii, 279p. 1988. pap. 17.00 (*0-8232-1217-3*) Fordham.

Post-Christian Mind. Harry Blamires. LC 99-14076. 218p. 1999. pap. 10.99 (*1-56955-142-1*) Servant.

Post-Classical Predicament: Essays on Music & Society. Joseph Horowitz. 224p. 1995. text 29.95 (*1-55553-218-7*) NE U Pr.

***Post-Cold War Armored Vehicle Industries In Britain, Germany & France: A Study in Political Economy & Transition, 217.** James L. Graves. LC 99-88213. (Contributions in Economics & Economic History Ser.: Vol. 217). 224p. 2000. 65.00 (*0-313-31246-X*, Greenwood Pr) Greenwood.

Post-Cold War Conflict Deterrence. National Research Council Staff. 244p. (Orig.). 1997. pap. 47.00 (*0-309-05639-X*, Joseph Henry Pr) Natl Acad Pr.

Post-Cold War Force Sizing Debate: Paradigms, Metaphors, & Disconnects. James A. Winnefeld. LC 92-41970. 1992. pap. 7.50 (*0-8330-1286-X*, R-4243-JS) Rand Corp.

Post Cold War Order. Richard Leaver & Jim Richardson. 192p. 1994. pap. 24.95 (*1-86373-399-X*, Pub. by Allen & Unwin Pty) Paul & Co Pubs.

***Post-Cold War Presidency.** Ed. by Anthony J. Eksterowicz & Glenn P. Hastedt. LC 99-11725. 192p. 1999. 49.00 (*0-8476-9158-6*) Rowman.

Post-Cold War Presidency. Ed. by Anthony J. Eksterowicz & Glenn P. Hastedt. LC 99-11725. 192p. 1999. pap. 16.95 (*0-8476-9159-4*) Rowman.

Post-Cold War Secrecy Policy. Greg S. Elkmann. (Illus.). 172p. (Orig.). 1994. pap. text. write for info. (*1-879716-07-0*, P-94-1) Ctr Info Policy.

Post-Cold War Security Issues in the Asia-Pacific Region. Ed. by Colin J. McInnes & Mark G. Rolls. 1994. pap. 22.50 (*0-7146-4131-6*, Pub. by F Cass Pubs) Intl Spec Bk.

Post-Cold War Trading System: Who's on First. Sylvia Ostry. LC 96-42495. 1997. pap. 17.95 (*0-226-63790-5*) U Ch Pr.

Post-Cold War Trading System: Who's on First. Sylvia Ostry. LC 96-42495. 296p. 1999. lib. bdg. 48.00 (*0-226-63789-1*) U Ch Pr.

Post Cold War U. S. Security Strategies for the Persian Gulf. Marcy Agmon. LC 92-45222. 1993. pap. 7.50 (*0-8330-1312-2*, R-4268-AF/A) Rand Corp.

Post-Colonial African Fiction: The Crisis of Consciousness. 141st rev. ed. Mala Pandurang. LC 97-900873. 251p. 1997. write for info. (*81-85753-14-8*, Pub. by Pencraft International) Advent Bks Div.

Post-Colonial African Writers. Ed. by Pushpa N. Parekh. 1998. lib. bdg. 85.00 (*1-57958-053-X*) Fitzroy Dearborn.

Post Colonial Condition: Contemporary Politics in Africa. Pal Ahluwalia & Paul Nursey-Bray. 247p. 1997. text 75.00 (*1-56072-485-4*) Nova Sci Pubs.

***Post-Colonial Condition of African Literature.** Daniel Gover et al. LC 99-15295. (Annual Selected Papers of the ALA). 1999. write for info. (*0-86543-771-8*) Africa World.

Post-Colonial Critic: Interviews, Strategies, Dialogues. Gayatri Chakravorty Spivak & Sarah Harasym. 224p. (C). (gr. 13). 1990. pap. 18.99 (*0-415-90170-7*, A3543) Routledge.

Post-Colonial Cultures in France. Alec G. Hargreaves & Mark McKinney. LC 97-7027. (Illus.). 272p. (C). 1997. pap. 25.99 (*0-415-14488-4*) Routledge.

Post-Colonial Cultures in France. Alec G. Hargreaves & Mark McKinney. LC 97-7027. (Illus.). 320p. (C). 1998. 80.00 (*0-415-14487-6*) Routledge.

***Post-Colonial Detective.** Edmund B. Christian. LC 99-43512. 2000. text 55.00 (*0-312-22831-7*) St Martin.

Post-Colonial Discourse in South Asia. Ed. by Stephen Alter. (Asian Studies: Vol. 18). (Illus.). 643p. 1999. pap. 20.00 (*977-424-486-9*, Pub. by Am Univ Cairo Pr) Col U Pr.

Post-Colonial Drama: Theory, Practice, Politics. Helen Gilbert & Joanne Tompkins. 360p. (C). 1996. 90.00 (*0-415-09023-7*); pap. 27.99 (*0-415-09024-5*) Routledge.

Post-Colonial English Drama: Commonwealth Drama since 1960. Ed. by Bruce King. 236p. (C). 1993. text 59.95 (*0-312-07969-9*) St Martin.

Post-Colonial Essays on South Pacific Literature. Patrick D. Morrow. LC 97-49145. 200p. 1998. text 79.95 (*0-7734-8474-4*) E Mellen.

Post-Colonial Insecurities. Ed. by Judith Squires. (New Formations Ser.: No. 21). 192p. (C). 1994. pap. 19.95 (*0-85315-762-6*, Pub. by Lawrence & Wishart) NYU Pr.

Post-Colonial Literature in English. Dennis Walder. LC 97-42235. 240p. 1998. 57.95 (*0-631-19491-6*); pap. 26.95 (*0-631-19492-4*) Blackwell Pubs.

Post-Colonial Literature of Lusophone Africa. Ed. by Patrick Chabal. LC 95-53848. 314p. (C). 1996. pap. 17.95 (*0-8101-1423-2*); text 49.95 (*0-8101-1422-4*) Northwestern U Pr.

Post-Colonial Literatures: Expanding the Canon Deborah L. Madsen. LC 99-21628. 1999. write for info. (*0-7453-1515-1*) Pluto GBR.

***Post-Colonial Literatures: Expanding the Canon.** Deborah L. Madsen. LC 99-21628. 1999. pap. 22.50 (*0-7453-1510-0*) Pluto GBR.

Post-Colonial Literatures in English: Australia, 1970-1992. Richard Lever et al. LC 95-44820. (Reference Publication in Literature Ser.). 361p. 1996. 60.00 (*0-8161-7375-3*, G K Hall & Co) Mac Lib Ref.

Post Colonial Literatures in English: General Theoretical Comparative, 1970-1993. Alan Lawson et al. LC 97-3559. 1997. 65.00 (*0-8161-7358-3*) Mac Lib Ref.

Post-Colonial Literatures in English: Southeast Asia, New Zealand, & the Pacific, 1970-1992. Mark Williams. LC 95-44859. (Reference Publication in Literature Ser.). 1996. 200.00 (*0-8161-7353-2*, G K Hall & Co) Mac Lib Ref.

Post-Colonial Middle Ages. Cohen. 1999. text 45.00 (*0-312-21929-6*) St Martin.

***Post-Colonial Mizo Politics, 1947-1998.** Chitta Ranjan Nag. 1999. 30.00 (*81-259-0800-5*, Pub. by Vikas) S Asia.

Post Colonial Pathologies. Kaiser. 59.95 (*1-85972-518-X*) Ashgate Pub Co.

Post-Colonial Question: Common Skies, Divided Horizons. Ed. by Iain Chambers & Lidia Curti. LC 95-475. (Illus.). 288p. (C). 1996. pap. 20.99 (*0-415-10858-6*) Routledge.

Post-Colonial Shakespeare. Ed. by Ania Loomba & Martin Orkin. LC 98-235188. (New Accents Ser.). (Illus.). 288p. (C). (gr. 13). 1998. 60.00 (*0-415-17386-8*, D6270); pap. 17.99 (*0-415-17387-6*, D6274) Routledge.

Post-Colonial Society: The Algerian Struggle for Economic, Social, & Political Change, 1965-1990. Mohamed H. Abucar. (American University Studies Series XXI: Regional Studies: Vol. 14). 188p. (Orig.). (C). 1996. pap. text 29.95 (*0-8204-2823-X*) P Lang Pubng.

***Post-Colonial States of South Asia: Democracy, Development & Identity.** Amita Shastri & A. Jeyaratnam Wilson. LC 00-34493. 2000. write for info. (*0-312-23852-5*) St Martin.

Post-Colonial Studies Reader. Ed. by Bill Ashcroft et al. LC 94-17829. 384p. (gr. 13). 1995. pap. 25.99 (*0-415-09622-7*, B3134) Routledge.

Post-Colonial Studies Reader. Ed. by Bill Ashcroft et al. LC 94-17829. 384p. (C). (gr. 13). 1995. 90.00 (*0-415-09621-9*, B3130) Routledge.

***Post-Colonial Theory & English Literature: A Reader.** Peter Childs. 2000. pap. 27.00 (*0-7486-1068-5*, Pub. by Edinburgh U Pr) Col U Pr.

Post-Colonial Translation: Theory & Practice. Susan Bassnett & Harish Trivedi. LC 98-12969. (Translation Studies). 240p. (C). 1999. 75.00 (*0-415-14744-1*); pap. 25.99 (*0-415-14745-X*) Routledge.

Post-Colonialism: Culture & Identity in Africa. Pal Ahluwalia & Paul Nursey-Bray. LC 98-101330. (Horizons in Post Colonial Africa Ser.). 239p. 1997. lib. bdg. 85.00 (*1-56072-453-6*) Nova Sci Pubs.

Post-Colonialism & the Politics of Kenya. D. Pal Ahluwalia. (Illus.). 257p. (C). 1996. lib. bdg. 85.00 (*1-56072-387-4*) Nova Sci Pubs.

Post Communication: Criticism & Evaluation. Robert Cathcart. LC 66-19701. (Orig.). 1966. pap. 5.95 (*0-672-61073-6*, SC2, Bobbs) Macmillan.

Post-Communism: An Introduction. Leslie Holmes. LC 96-39936. 380p. 1996. lib. bdg. 54.95 (*0-8223-1987-X*) Duke.

Post-Communism: An Introduction. Leslie Holmes. LC 96-39936. 384p. 1997. pap. text 18.95 (*0-8223-1995-0*) Duke.

Post Communism: Rethinking the Second World. Ed. by Greta Slobin. (New Formations Ser.: No. 22). (C). 1994. pap. 19.95 (*0-85315-763-4*, Pub. by Lawrence & Wishart) NYU Pr.

Post-Communism & the Media in Eastern Europe. Ed. by Patrick H. O'Neil. LC 96-39923. 152p. (Orig.). (C). 1997. 37.50 (*0-7146-4765-9*, Pub. by F Cass Pubs); pap. 19.50 (*0-7146-4311-4*, Pub. by F Cass Pubs) Intl Spec Bk.

Post-Communism, the Market & the Arts: First Sociological Assessments. Ed. by Robert H. Reichardt & George Muskens. LC 92-36724. 205p. 1992. 40.00 (*3-631-45313-2*) P Lang Pubng.

Post-Communist Capitalism & Capital: Foreign Investors in Transitional Economics. Tauno Tiusanen. 147p. (C). 1996. lib. bdg. 95.00 (*1-56072-301-7*) Nova Sci Pubs.

Post-Communist Czechoslovakia. John Bradley. 250p. Date not set. lib. bdg. 35.00 (*0-88033-386-3*, 489, Pub. by East Eur Monographs) Col U Pr.

Post-Communist Eastern Europe, Crisis & Reform. Andrew A. Michta. Ed. by Ilya Prizel. 240p. 1992. text 39.95 (*0-312-07564-2*) St Martin.

Post-Communist Economic Revolutions: How Big a Bang? Anders Aslund. LC 92-37848. (Significant Issues Series - Creating the Post-Communist Order: No. 3). 116p. (C). 1992. pap. text 9.95 (*0-89206-203-7*) CSIS.

Post-Communist Economic Transformation: Essays in Honor of Gregory Grossman. Ed. by Robert W. Campbell. LC 94-16359. 320p. (C). 1994. text 79.00 (*0-8133-8856-2*, Pub. by Westview) HarpC.

***Post-communist Era: Change & Continuity in Eastern Europe.** Ben Fowkes. LC 99-13906. 1999. text 65.00 (*0-312-22368-4*) St Martin.

Post-Communist Monetary Problems: Lessons from the End of the Austro-Hungarian Empire. Rudiger Dornbusch. LC 93-42767. (Occasional Papers: No. 49). 1994. pap. 9.95 (*1-55815-308-X*) ICS Pr.

Post-Communist Party Politics. Michael McFaul. LC 93-7396. (Significant Issues Series - Creating the Post-Communist Order: Vol. 15, No. 3). 151p. (C). 1993. pap. text 9.95 (*0-89206-208-8*) CSIS.

Post-Communist Party Systems: Competition, Representation & Inter-Party Cooperation. Herbert Kitschelt et al. LC 98-46760. (Cambridge Studies in Comparative Politics). 472p. (C). 1999. 64.95 (*0-521-65288-X*) Cambridge U Pr.

Post-Communist Party Systems: Competition, Representation & Inter-Party Cooperation. Herbert Kitschelt et al. LC 98-46760. (Cambridge Studies in Comparative Politics). (Illus.). 457p. (C). 1999. pap. 19.95 (*0-521-65890-X*) Cambridge U Pr.

Post-Communist Poland: From Totalitarianism to Democracy. Ed. by J. Coenen-Huther & B. Synak. (Illus.). 137p. (C). 1993. lib. bdg. 95.00 (*1-56072-146-4*) Nova Sci Pubs.

Post-Communist Politics: The Transformation of Europe. Karen Henderson. 304p. 1997. pap. 30.00 (*0-13-442039-X*) P-H.

Post-Communist Press in Eastern & Central Europe: New Studies. 1992. 12.95 (*0-943089-03-4*) U GA CFIMCTR.

Post-Communist Reform: Pain & Progress. Ed. by Oliver J. Blanchard et al. 134p. 1993. 21.95 (*0-262-02362-8*) MIT Pr.

***Post-Communist Romania.** Duncan Light & David Phinnemore. LC 00-42209. (Illus.). 2000. write for info. (*0-333-79187-8*) St Martin.

Post-Communist States in the World Economy: Selected Papers from the Fifth World Congress of Central & East European Studies. William E. Ferry & Roger E. Kanet. LC 97-22913. 322p. 1998. text 69.95 (*0-312-17734-8*) St Martin.

Post-Communist Transition: Emerging Pluralism in Hungary. Ed. by Andras Bozoki et al. LC 92-6508. 208p. 1992. text 49.95 (*0-312-08092-1*) St Martin.

Post-Compulsory Education for Disabled People in OECD Countries. Don Labon & Peter Evans. LC 97-224789. 92p. 1997. pap. 19.00 (*92-64-15601-1*, 96-97-06-1, Pub. by Org for Econ) OECD.

Post-Confessionals: Conversations with American Poets of the Eighties. Ed. by Earl W. Ingersoll et al. LC 87-46424. (Illus.). 288p. 1989. 42.50 (*0-8386-3330-7*) Fairleigh Dickinson.

Post-Conflict Eritrea: Prospects for Reconstruction & Development. Alemseged Tesfai. Ed. by Martin Doornbos. LC 98-55215. 362p. 1999. 79.95 (*1-56902-108-2*) Red Sea Pr.

Post-Conflict Eritrea: Prospects for Reconstruction & Development. Alemseged Tesfai & Martin Doornbos. LC 98-55215. 362p. 1999. pap. 21.95 (*1-56902-109-0*) Red Sea Pr.

Post-Conquest Old English Manuscripts. Treharne. 76.95 (*1-85928-123-0*) Ashgate Pub Co.

Post-Consonantal W in Indo-European. Francis A. Wood. (LM Ser.: No. 3). 1926. pap. 25.00 (*0-527-00807-9*) Periodicals Srv.

Post-Construction Liability & Insurance. Ed. by J. Knocke. LC 92-41908. (Illus.). 424p. (C). 1993. 100.00 (*0-419-15350-0*, E & FN Spon) Routledge.

Post Conviction Remedies. Larry W. Yackle. LC 80-84875. 1981. 120.00 (*0-685-59848-9*) West Group.

Post-Corporate World: Life after Capitalism. David C. Korten. 336p. 1999. 27.00 (*1-57675-051-5*) Berrett-Koehler.

Post-Corporate World: Life after Capitalism. David C. Korten. LC 98-51489. 1998. write for info. (*1-887208-02-X*) CoPublns.

***Post-Corporate World: Life after Capitalism.** David C. Korten. 300p. 2000. reprint ed. pap. 19.95 (*1-887208-03-8*, Pub. by Berrett-Koehler) Publishers Group.

Post-Coup Chilean Poetry: A Bilingual Anthology. Silverio Munoz. Tr. by Mary E. Acevedo & Jocelyn Paska from SPA. LC 86-80932. (Illus.). 88p. 1986. pap. text 7.50 (*0-937985-01-5*) Ediciones Arauco.

Post Dates: Chronology of the Mails & Philately. Kenneth A. Wood. LC 85-3253. 416p. 1996. 29.95 (*0-934466-08-4*) Krause Pubns.

Post-Development Reader. Compiled by Majid Rahnema & Victoria Bawtree. LC 96-25685. 384p. 1997. pap. 25.00 (*1-85649-474-8*, Pub. by Zed Books); text 65.00 (*1-85649-473-X*, Pub. by Zed Books) St Martin.

Post-Diagnosis. Sandra Steingraber. LC 94-49696. 1995. pap. 9.95 (*1-56341-057-5*); lib. bdg. 20.95 (*1-56341-058-3*) Firebrand Bks.

Post-Digital Electronics. F. R. Pettit. (Electrical & Electronic Engineering Ser.). 176p. 1982. text 71.95 (*0-470-27334-8*) P-H.

Post-Disaster Assessment, 2 vols., Vol. 1. John R. Campbell & Joseph Chung. (Pacific Disaster Preparedness Project Ser.). 40p. 1991. 3.00 (*0-86638-073-6*) EW Ctr HI.

Post-Disaster Assessment, 2 vols., Vol. 2. John R. Campbell & Joseph Chung. (Pacific Disaster Preparedness Project Ser.). 40p. 1991. 3.00 (*0-86638-075-2*) EW Ctr HI.

Post Divorce Reconstruction - Workbook: Reconstructing Your Life after Divorce. Christine Smith. Ed. by Richard Greenfield. (Illus.). vi, 63p. 1996. spiral bd. 24.95 (*0-9653423-2-8*) Post Dvrce Recon.

Post-Dryout Heat Transfer Multiphase. G. F. Hewitt. 448p. 1992. lib. bdg. 89.95 (*0-8493-9301-9*) CRC Pr.

***Post-Dykes to Watch Out For.** Alison Bechdel. (Illus.). 144p. 2000. pap. 11.95 (*1-56341-122-9*, Pub. by Firebrand Bks); lib. bdg. 24.95 (*1-56341-123-7*, Pub. by Firebrand Bks) LPC InBook.

Post-Earthquake Investigation & Field Guide. rev. ed. Ed. by Susan Tubbesing. Orig. Title: Earthquake Response Plan & Field Guide. 196p. 1996. ring bd. 15.00 (*0-943198-54-2*, 96-1) Earthquake Eng.

Post-Earthquake Projects in Kobe, Hyogo in Japan: A Strategic Entry Report, 1997. Compiled by Icon Group International Staff. (Illus.). 175p. 1999. ring bd. 1750.00 incl. audio compact disk (*0-7418-0948-6*) Icon Grp.

Post-Earthquake Rehabilitation & Reconstruction. Franklin Y. Cheng & Y. Y. Wang. LC 96-26972. 484p. 1996. 131.50 (*0-08-042825-8*, Pergamon Pr) Elsevier.

***Post-Ecologist Politics: Social Theory & the Abdication of the Ecological Paradigm.** Ingolfur Blhuhdorn. LC 00-32173. (Innovations in Political Theory Ser.). 2000. write for info. (*0-415-19203-X*) Routledge.

Post-Education Society: Towards a Democracy of Learners. Norman Evans. LC 84-12750. (Radical Forum on Adult Education Ser.). 160p. 1984. pap. 14.95 (*0-7099-0948-9*, Pub. by C Helm) Routldge.

***Post '86 Fiesta: Identification & Value Guide.** Richard G. Racheter. (Illus.). 176p. 2000. pap. 19.95 (*1-57432-203-6*) Collector Bks.

Post-Evangelical. Dave Tomlinson. 1995. pap. 8.95 (*0-687-06635-2*) Abingdon.

Post Exilic Prophets. Eileen M. Schuller. (Message of Biblical Spirituality Ser.: Vol. 4). 192p. 1988. pap. 12.95 (*0-8146-5570-X*) Liturgical Pr.

P

An Asterisk (*) at the beginning of an entry indicates that the title is appearing for the first time.

***Post Exposure.** 2nd ed. Ctein. 208p. 2000. pap. text 32.95 (*0-240-80437-6*, Focal) Buttrwrth-Heinemann.

Post-Exposure: Advanced Techniques for the Photographic Printer. Ctein. LC 97-24532. (Illus.). 208p. 1997. pap. 29.95 (*0-240-80299-3*, Focal) Buttrwrth-Heinemann.

Post-Fandom & the Millennial Blues: The Transformation of Soccer Culture. Steve Redhead. LC 97-2916. 176p. (C). 1997. 75.00 (*0-415-11527-2*); pap. 22.99 (*0-415-11528-0*) Routledge.

Post-Fascist Fantasies: Psychoanalysis, History, & the Literature of East Germany. Julia Hell. (Post-Contemporary Interventions Ser.). 408p. 1997. pap. text 19.95 (*0-8223-1963-2*); lib. bdg. 59.95 (*0-8223-1955-1*) Duke.

Post Flask Management of Tissue-Cultured Bananas. Ed. by Jeff Daniells & Mike Smith. 1991. pap. 45.00 (*1-86320-042-8*, Pub. by ACIAR) St Mut.

Post for Divers Partes of the World, to Travaile from One Notable Citie unto an Other, 2 pts. Richard Rowlands. LC 77-7422. (English Experience Ser.: No. 889). 1977. reprint ed. 20.00 (*90-221-0889-9*) Walter J Johnson.

Post-Fordism: A Reader. Ed. by Ash Amin. LC 94-10761. (Studies in Urban & Social Change). 432p. 1994. pap. 29.95 (*0-631-18857-6*) Blackwell Pubs.

Post-fordism Gender & Work. Wigfield. 61.95 (*0-7546-1087-X*) Ashgate Pub Co.

Post-Formal Reader: Cognition & Education. Joe Kincheloe et al. LC 98-52828. (Critical Education Practice Ser.: Vol. 20). 480p. 1999. text 100.00 (*0-8153-1415-9*) Garland.

Post-Formal Reader: Cognition & Education. Shirley R. Steinberg et al. LC 98-52828. 1999. 45.00 (*0-8153-3399-4*) Garland.

Post-Frame Building Design. Ed. by John N. Walker & Frank E. Woeste. LC 92-73143. 332p. 1992. 51.50 (*0-929355-29-6*, M1092) Am Soc Ag Eng.

Post-Franco, Postmodern: The Films of Pedro Almodovar, 43. Ed. by Kathleen M. Vernon & Barbara Morris. LC 94-32047. (Contributions to the Study of Popular Culture Ser.: Vol. 43). 232p. 1995. 57.95 (*0-313-29245-0*, Greenwood Pr) Greenwood.

***Post-Genome Informatics.** Minoru Kanehisa. LC 99-49584. (Illus.). 160p. 2000. text 70.00 (*0-19-850327-X*); pap. text 35.00 (*0-19-850326-1*) OUP.

***Post Gibran: Anthology of New Arab American Writing.** Ed. by Munir Akash & Khaled Mattawa. (Illus.). 460p. 2000. pap. 19.95 (*0-9652031-3-1*) Syracuse U Pr.

Post-Glacial Vegetation of Canada. J. C. Ritchie. (Illus.). 192p. 1987. text 105.00 (*0-521-30868-2*) Cambridge U Pr.

Post-Graduate Orthopaedic Fellowships, 1996. Ed. by American Academy of Orthopaedic Surgeons Staff. 370p. 1996. pap. 35.00 (*0-89203-149-2*) Amer Acad Ortho Surg.

Post Han see **Chinese Archaeological Abstracts**

Post-Harvest & Processing Technologies of African Staple Foods: A Technical Compendium. 360p. 1991. 40.00 (*92-5-103076-6*, F0766, Pub. by FAO) Bernan Associates.

Post-Harvest Fish Losses in the Tropics. G. Ames et al. 1991. pap. 25.00 (*0-85954-291-2*, Pub. by Nat Res Inst) St Mut.

Post-Harvest Food Crop Conservation: Association of Consulting Scientists Symposium on Post-Harvest Food Crop Conservation, Harrogate, 13-15 November, 1979. (Progress in Food & Nutrition Science Ser.: Vol. 4). (Illus.). 138p. 1980. pap. 48.00 (*0-08-025907-3*, Pergamon Pr) Elsevier.

Post-Harvest Losses in Quality of Food Grains. 110p. 1984. 14.00 (*92-5-101456-6*, F2596, Pub. by FAO) Bernan Associates.

Post-Harvest Physiology & Crop Preservation. Ed. by Morris Lieberman. LC 82-3645. (NATO ASI Series A, Life Sciences: Vol. 46). 586p. 1983. 125.00 (*0-306-40984-4*, Plenum Trade) Perseus Pubng.

Post-Harvest Physiology & Reservation of Forages. Kenneth J. Moore. LC 95-6087. (Special Publication Ser.: Vol. 22). 115p. 1995. 28.00 (*0-89118-539-9*) Crop Sci Soc Am.

Post Harvest Physiology of Vegetables. Ed. by J. Weichmann. (Food Science & Technology Ser.: Vol. 24). (Illus.). 616p. 1987. text 245.00 (*0-8247-7601-1*) Dekker.

Post Harvest Technology of Cereals: Pulses & Oilseeds. rev. ed. A. Chakraverty. (C). 1988. 9.50 (*81-204-0289-8*, Pub. by Oxford IBH) S Asia.

***Post-Hipparcos Cosmic Candles.** Ed. by A. Heck & F. Caputo. LC 98-40847. (Astrophysics & Space Science Library: Vol. 237). 284p. 1999. 135.00 (*0-7923-5348-X*) Kluwer Academic.

Post Hoc. Michael Davidson. (Orig.). 1990. pap. 7.50 (*0-939691-04-3*) Avenue B.

Post Hoc. limited ed. Michael Davidson. (Orig.). 1990. pap. 18.00 (*0-685-35601-9*) Avenue B.

Post-Holocaust Christianity: Paul Van Buren's Theology of the Jewish-Christianity Reality. James H. Wallis. LC 97-33540. 208p. (C). 1997. 49.00 (*0-7618-0899-X*); pap. 29.50 (*0-7618-0900-7*) U Pr of Amer.

Post-Holocaust Dialogues: Critical Studies in Modern Jewish Thought. Steven T. Katz. (C). 1985. pap. text 19.50 (*0-8147-4587-3*) NYU Pr.

Post Human. Jeffrey Deitch. LC 92-90272. (Illus.). 160p. 1994. 35.00 (*0-9633037-0-8*, Pub. by Deste Found) Dist Art Pubs.

Post-Hypnotic Instructions. Arnold Furst. 1979. pap. 10.00 (*0-87980-119-0*) Wilshire.

Post-Imperative Negative Variation in Schizophrenic Patients & Healthy Subjects. Christoph Klein. LC 96-53386. (Psychophysiologie in Labor und Feld Ser.: Bd. 3). (Illus.). 386p. 1996. pap. text 63.95 (*0-8204-3233-4*, RC514) P Lang Pubng.

Post-Imperative Negative Variation in Schizophrenic Patients & Healthy Subjects. Christoph Klein. (Psychophysiologie in Labor und Feld Ser.: Bd. 3). (Illus.). 386p. 1997. pap. 63.95 (*3-631-31078-1*) P Lang Pubng.

Post-Imperial Presidency. Ed. by Vincent Davis. LC 79-67064. 190p. 1980. 49.95 (*0-275-90466-0*, C0466, Praeger Pubs) Greenwood.

Post-Imperial Presidency. Ed. by Vincent Davis. LC 79-67064. 190p. 1980. pap. text 21.95 (*0-87855-747-4*) Transaction Pubs.

Post-Implantation Development in the Mouse. CIBA Foundation Staff. LC 92-113. (CIBA Foundation Symposium Ser.: No. 165). 326p. 1992. 128.00 (*0-471-93384-8*, Wiley-Interscience) Wiley.

Post-Impressionism. Bernard Denvir. LC 91-65995. (World of Art Ser.). (Illus.). 216p. 1992. pap. 14.95 (*0-500-20255-9*, Pub. by Thames Hudson) Norton.

Post-Impressionism. Belinda Thomson. LC 98-24392. (Movements in Modern Art Ser.). (Illus.). 96p. (C). 1998. pap. 13.95 (*0-521-64609-X*) Cambridge U Pr.

***Post-Impressionism: The Rise of Modern Art, 1880-1920.** Thomas Parsons & Iain Gale. (Illus.). 424p. 2000. 94.95 (*0-9684749-6-9*, Pub. by NDE Pub) IPG Chicago.

Post-Impressionism in England. Ed. by J. B. Bullen. 288p. 1989. text 75.00 (*0-415-00216-8*) Routledge.

Post-Impressionist Prints: Paris in the 1890s. John Ihmann. (Illus.). 80p. 1997. pap. 29.95 (*0-87633-119-3*) Phila Mus Art.

Post-Impressionists. (Shorewood Art Programs for Education Ser.). 16p. 1975. teacher ed. 107.00 (*0-88185-057-8*); 143.00 (*0-685-07233-9*) Shorewood Fine Art.

Post-Impressionists. Charles L. Hind. LC 75-102244. (Select Bibliographies Reprint Ser.). 1977. 11.95 (*0-8369-5129-8*) Ayer.

Post-Impressionists. 2nd ed. Belinda Thomson. (Illus.). 192p. (C). 1995. reprint ed. pap. 19.95 (*0-7148-2662-6*, Pub. by Phaidon Press) Phaidon Pr.

Post Impressions: Cancelling Out. JoAnna Poehlmann. (Illus.). 148p. 1991. 4.98 (*1-55859-233-4*) Abbeville Pr.

Post Impressions: Food for Thought. JoAnna Poehlmann. (Illus.). 148p. 1991. 4.98 (*1-55859-232-6*) Abbeville Pr.

Post Impressions: Love Letters. JoAnna Poehlmann. (Illus.). 74p. 1991. 10.95 (*1-55859-231-8*) Abbeville Pr.

Post-incunabula & Their Publishers in the Low Countries: A Selection Based on Wouter Nijhoff's L'art Typographique Published in Commemoration of the 125th Anniversary of Martinus Nijhoff on January 1, 1978. Hendrik D. Vervliet et al. LC 79-306119. xiii, 205p. 1978. write for info. (*90-247-2079-6*) M Nijhoff.

Post Independence India, 1947-1990 Booklet & Teacher's Guide. (J). (gr. 6-10). pap. text 4.95 (*1-878099-19-1*) Vidya Bks.

Post-Industrial America: A Geographic Perspective. David Clark. 192p. (Orig.). (C). 1985. pap. text 13.95 (*0-416-38260-6*, 9307) Routledge.

Post-Industrial Capitalism. Joel I. Nelson. 206p. (C). 1995. 52.00 (*0-8039-7332-2*); pap. 23.50 (*0-8039-7333-0*) Sage.

Post-Industrial Cities: Politics & Planning in New York, Paris, & London. H. V. Savitch. LC 88-2548. 386p. 1988. reprint ed. pap. 119.70 (*0-608-03296-4*, 206381400007) Bks Demand.

Post Industrial Lives: Roles & Relationships in the 21st Century. Gerald Hage. 256p. (C). 1992. text 49.95 (*0-8039-4494-2*); pap. text 23.50 (*0-8039-4495-0*) Sage.

Post-Industrial Philadelphia: Structural Changes in the Metropolitan Economy. William J. Stull & Janice F. Madden. LC 90-30440. 232p. (Orig.). (C). 1990. pap. text 23.95 (*0-8122-8218-3*) U of Pa Pr.

Post Industrial Socialism: Towards a New Politics of Welfare. Adrian Little. LC 98-169364. 232p. (C). 1998. 85.00 (*0-415-17193-8*); pap. 25.99 (*0-415-17194-6*) Routledge.

Post-Industrial Society. Ed. by A. Bruce Boenau & Katsuyuki Niiro. 508p. (Orig.). (C). 1984. pap. text 37.00 (*0-8191-3613-1*) U Pr of Amer.

Post-Industrial Utopians. Boris Frankel. LC 87-6147. 315p. reprint ed. pap. 97.70 (*0-608-20428-5*, 207168100002) Bks Demand.

Post-Intellectualism & the Decline of Democracy: The Failure of Reason & Responsibility in the Twentieth Century. Donald N. Wood. LC 96-10420. 320p. 1996. 69.50 (*0-275-95421-8*, Praeger Pubs) Greenwood.

Post-Intellectualism & the Decline of Democracy: The Failure of Reason & Responsibility in the Twentieth Century. Donald N. Wood. LC 96-10420. 320p. 1996. pap. 21.95 (*0-275-95661-X*, Praeger Pubs) Greenwood.

***Post-Invasion Panama: The Challenges of Democratization in the New World Order.** Ed. by Orlando J. Perez. LC 99-86082. 208p. 2000. 55.00 (*0-7391-0120-X*) Lxngtn Bks.

Post-Jungians Today: Key Papers in Contemporary Analytical Psychology. Ann Casement. LC 98-9829. 248p. (C). 1998. 90.00 (*0-415-16154-1*); pap. 25.99 (*0-415-16155-X*) Routledge.

Post-Keynesian Approach to Economics: An Alternative Analysis of Economic Theory & Policy. Philip Arestis. (New Directions in Modern Economics Ser.). 336p. 1992. 90.00 (*1-85278-154-8*) E Elgar.

Post-Keynesian Approach to Economics: An Alternative Analysis of Economic Theory & Policy. Philip Arestis. (New Directions in Modern Economics Ser.). 336p. 1994. pap. 30.00 (*1-85898-013-5*) E Elgar.

Post Keynesian Econometrics, Microeconomics & the Theory of the Firm: Beyond Keynes. Ed. by Sheila Dow & John Hillard. 256p. 1999. 85.00 (*1-85898-584-6*) E Elgar.

Post-Keynesian Economic Theory. Ed. by Paul Wells. LC 95-8144. (Recent Economic Thought Ser.). (C). 1995. lib. bdg. 72.50 (*0-7923-9570-0*) Kluwer Academic.

Post Keynesian Economics. Kenneth K. Kurihara. (Modern Revivals in Economics Ser.). 464p. (C). 1993. text 79.95 (*0-7512-0246-0*, Pub. by Gregg Revivals) Ashgate Pub Co.

Post-Keynesian Economics. Ed. by Malcolm C. Sawyer. (Schools of Thought in Economics Ser.: Vol. 2). 512p. 1989. text 215.00 (*1-85278-052-5*) E Elgar.

Post Keynesian Economics: An Annotated Bibliography. John E. King. LC 95-19497. 816p. 1995. 240.00 (*1-85278-801-1*) E Elgar.

Post Keynesian Macrodynamics: A More General Theory. Michael A. Salant. LC 82-99901. (Illus.). 174p. 1983. 24.00 (*0-9609288-1-2*); pap. 16.00 (*0-9609288-0-4*) M A Salant.

Post Keynesian Macroeconomic Theory: A Foundation for Successful Economic Policies for the Twenty-First Century. Paul Davidson. 320p. 1994. 95.00 (*1-85278-835-6*); pap. 30.00 (*1-85278-836-4*) E Elgar.

Post Keynesian Monetary Economics. 2nd ed. Stephen Rousseas. LC 92-9112. 136p. (Orig.). (C). (gr. 13). 1992. text 64.95 (*1-56324-052-3*) M E Sharpe.

Post Keynesian Monetary Economics. 2nd ed. Stephen Rousseas. LC 92-9112. 136p. (Orig.). (C). (gr. 13). 1992. pap. text 34.95 (*1-56324-095-5*) M E Sharpe.

Post-Keynesian Monetary Economics: New Approaches to Financial Modelling. Ed. by Philip Arestis. (New Directions in Modern Economics Ser.). 320p. 1988. text 95.00 (*1-85278-046-0*) E Elgar.

Post-Keynesian Theory of Growth & Distribution. Ed. by Carlo Panico & Neri Salvadori. (International Library of Critical Writings in Economics: Vol. 21). 484p. 1993. 210.00 (*1-85278-613-2*) E Elgar.

Post-Lesion Neural Plasticity. Ed. by H. Flohr. (Illus.). 650p. 1988. 133.00 (*0-387-19455-X*) Spr-Verlag.

Post-Liberalism. John Gray. 352p. (C). 1996. pap. 25.99 (*0-415-13553-2*) Routledge.

Post Liminium: Essays & Critical Papers. Lionel P. Johnson. LC 68-20312. (Essay Index Reprint Ser.). 1977. 20.95 (*0-8369-0573-3*) Ayer.

***Post-Mao China: From Totalitarianism to Authoritarianism?** Sujian Guo. LC 99-43110. 240p. 2000. write for info. (*0-275-96780-8*, Praeger Pubs) Greenwood.

Post-Mao China & U. S.-China Trade. Ed. by Shao-Chuan Leng. LC 77-20811. 168p. reprint ed. pap. 52.10 (*0-8357-2713-0*, 203982700013) Bks Demand.

Post-Marcos Politics, 1992. Carl H. Lande. LC 96-33213. 171p. 1997. text 49.95 (*0-312-16483-1*) St Martin.

***Post-Marxism: An Intellectual History.** Stuart Sim. LC 00-32312. 2000. write for info. (*0-415-21814-4*) Routledge.

Post-Marxism & the Middle East. Ed. by Faleh A. Jabar. LC 96-224969. 256p. 1997. 60.00 (*0-86356-961-7*, Pub. by Saqi) Intl Spec Bk.

Post-Marxist Marxism: Questioning the Answer: Difference & Realism after Lukacs & Adorno. John Baldacchino. LC 96-85191. (Avebury Series in Philosophy). 179p. 1996. text 62.95 (*1-85972-438-8*, Pub. by Avebury) Ashgate Pub Co.

Post-Medieval Archaeology in Britain, Vol. 1. rev. ed. David Crossley. 1995. pap. 25.00 (*0-7185-1937-X*) St Martin.

Post Merger Management. Lee Colby. 1989. pap. 19.95 (*0-88057-909-9*) Exec Ent Pubns.

***Post Meridian.** Mary Ruefle. LC 98-71943. (Poetry Ser.). 88p. 2000. 24.95 (*0-88748-315-1*, Pub. by Carnegie-Mellon); pap. 12.95 (*0-88748-302-X*, Pub. by Carnegie-Mellon) CUP Services.

Post Middle Age Power: An Older Beginner's Guide to Pumping Iron. Loren O. Taylor. Ed. by Dirk G. Taylor. LC 85-63400. (Illus.). 96p. (Orig.). 1986. pap. 8.50 (*0-9615195-1-7*) Nakii Ent.

Post Milan ASL & English Literacy: Issues, Trends & Research. (Illus.). iv, 323p. 1994. pap. 20.00 (*1-893891-14-3*) Gallaudet U Contin Ed.

Post-Military Coup Strategy in Uganda: Amin's Early Attempts to Consolidate Political Support in Africa. Jeffrey T. Strate. LC 73-620094. (Papers in International Studies: Africa Ser.: No. 18). 75p. reprint ed. pap. 30.00 (*0-608-18611-2*, 200742500062) Bks Demand.

Post-Military Society: Militarism, Demilitarization & War at the End of the Twentieth Century. Martin Shaw. 240p. (C). 1991. 54.95 (*0-87722-940-6*); pap. 22.95 (*0-87722-941-4*) Temple U Pr.

Post-Minoan Crete. Ed. by W. G. Cavanagh et al. (BSA Studies: Vol. 2). (Illus.). 143p. 1998. lib. bdg. 35.00 (*0-904887-29-4*, Pub. by Brit Sch Athens) David Brown.

Post Mishnaic Judaism in Transition: Samuel on Berakhot & the Beginnings of Gemara. Baruch M. Bokser. LC 80-19702. (Brown Judaic Studies: No. 17). 575p. reprint ed. pap. 178.30 (*0-7837-5418-3*, 204518200005) Bks Demand.

Post-Modern Algebra: Pure & Applied Mathematics. Jonathan D. Smith & Anna B. Romanaska. LC 98-23909. (Series of Texts, Monographs & Tracts). 384p. 1999. 79.95 (*0-471-12738-8*, Wiley-Interscience) Wiley.

Post-Modern Aura: The Act of Fiction in an Age of Inflation. Charles Newman. 203p. 1985. reprint ed. 39.95 (*0-8101-0668-X*); reprint ed. pap. 16.95 (*0-8101-0669-8*) Northwestern U Pr.

Post-Modern Bizarro. Dan Piraro. (Illus.). 96p. (Orig.). 1991. pap. 6.95 (*0-87701-854-5*) Chronicle Bks.

Post-Modern Condition: A Report on Knowledge. Jean-Francois Lyotard. Tr. by Geoff Bennington & Brian Massumi from FRE. LC 83-14717. (Theory & History of Literature Ser.: Vol. 10). 131p. (C). 1984. pap. 12.95 (*0-8166-1173-4*) U of Minn Pr.

***Post-Modern Electromagnetics.** Hafner. LC 98-53331. 320p. (C). 1999. 60.00 (*0-471-98711-5*) Wiley.

Post Modern Epistemology: Language, Truth & Body. Jerry H. Gill & Mari Sorri. LC 89-12434. (Problems in Contemporary Philosophy Ser.: Vol. 19). 250p. 1989. lib. bdg. 89.95 (*0-88946-324-7*) E Mellen.

Post-Modern Law: Enlightenment, Revolution & the Death of Man. Ed. by Anthony Carty. 166p. 1990. 70.00 (*0-7486-0156-2*, Pub. by Edinburgh U Pr) Col U Pr.

Post-Modern Law: Enlightenment, Revolution, & the Death of Man. Ed. by Anthony Carty. 166p. 1992. pap. 27.50 (*0-7486-0192-9*, Pub. by Edinburgh U Pr) Col U Pr.

Post-Modern Malpractice. Forrest Wilson. LC 83-71225. (Illus.). 1983. pap. 7.50 (*0-931228-07-7*) Arts & Arch.

Post-Modern Perspective on Curriculum. William E. Doll, Jr. 232p. 1993. pap. 19.95 (*0-8077-3447-0*) Tchrs Coll.

Post-Modern Presidency: The Office after Ronald Reagan. Ryan J. Barilleaux. LC 87-25861. 192p. 1988. 39.95 (*0-275-92721-0*, C2721, Praeger Pubs) Greenwood.

Post Modern Reader. Academy. 1992. 35.00 (*0-312-07896-X*) St Martin.

Post-Modern Reader. Ed. by Charles Jencks. (Illus.). 416p. 1992. pap. 35.00 (*1-85490-107-9*, Pub. by Wiley) Wiley.

Post Modern Triumphs in London, Vol. 91. Charles Jencks. 1991. 21.95 (*0-312-06730-5*) St Martin.

Post-Modernism & Discontinuity. (Architectural Design Profiles Ser.). (Illus.). 80p. 1987. pap. 19.95 (*0-312-00859-7*) St Martin.

Post-Modernism & the Social Sciences: Insights, Inroads, & Intrusions. Pauline M. Rosenau. 220p. 1992. text 45.00 (*0-691-08619-2*, Pub. by Princeton U Pr); pap. text 15.95 (*0-691-02347-6*, Pub. by Princeton U Pr) Cal Prin Full Svc.

Post Modernism for Beginners. Jim Powell. (For Beginners Ser.). (Illus.). 176p. 1998. pap. 11.00 (*0-86316-188-X*) Writers & Readers.

Post-Modernism on Trial. 1991. pap. 21.95 (*0-312-06144-7*) St Martin.

Post-Modernism on Trial. Academy Editions Staff. 1991. pap. 19.95 (*0-312-06032-7*) St Martin.

Post Modernist Fiction. Brian McHale. 300p. 1987. 42.50 (*0-416-36390-3*, A0751) Routledge.

Post Modernist Fiction. Brian McHale. 300p. (C). 1987. pap. 25.99 (*0-415-04513-4*, A0755) Routledge.

Post Modernity: State & Education. John Hinkson. 141p. (C). 1995. pap. 48.00 (*0-7300-1278-6*, ESA844, Pub. by Deakin Univ) St Mut.

***Post Mortem.** Guy Cullingford. 222p. 1999. 21.95 (*0-7540-8525-2*, Black Dagger) Chivers N Amer.

Post Mortem. Guy Gullingford. 337p. 1991. 24.95 (*1-85089-398-5*) ISIS Lrg Prnt.

Post-Mortem. Liam Mac Uistin. (Irish Play Ser.). 1977. pap. 2.50 (*0-912262-43-5*) Proscenium.

Post-Mortem. large type ed. Harry Carmichael. 1978. 27.99 (*0-7089-0142-5*) Ulverscroft.

Post-Mortem. large type ed. Peter Whalley. 384p. 1989. 27.99 (*0-7089-2002-0*) Ulverscroft.

Post-Mortem: JFK Assassination Cover-Up Smashed! Harold Weisberg. 1975. per. 18.00 (*0-911606-05-X*) Weisberg.

Post Mortem Estate Planning. 2nd ed. Albert Kalter & Lawrence Newman. write for info. (*0-318-72262-3*) PLI.

Post Mortem Estate Planning: Strategies for Executors & Beneficiaries. Albert Kalter & Lawrence Newman. 327p. 1989. text 15.00 (*0-685-45797-4*, D1-0158) PLI.

Post Mortem Estate Planning, 1989. Albert Kalter & Lawrence Newman. 300p. 1989. 15.00 (*0-685-69475-5*) PLI.

Post Mortem Journal. Jane Sherwood. 188p. 1992. pap. 15.95 (*0-85207-253-8*, Pub. by C W Daniel) Natl Bk Netwk.

Post-Mortem Journal. Jane Sherwood. 128p. (Orig.). pap. 23.95 (*0-8464-4272-8*) Beekman Pubs.

Post-Mortem Tax Planning. Jerry Kasner. 1594p. 1982. text 195.00 (*0-07-033322-X*) Shepards.

Post Mortem Tax Planning. 2nd ed. Jerry A. Kasner. LC 94-44881. (Tax & Estate Planning Ser.). 1994. write for info. (*0-614-32247-2*) McGraw.

Post Mortem Tax Planning, 2 vols. 3rd ed. Jerry A. Kasner. LC 97-81207. 1998. write for info. (*0-7913-3447-3*) Warren Gorham & Lamont.

***Post Mortem Technique Handbook.** Michael T. Sheaff & D. J. Hopster. LC 00-32982. (Illus.). 2000. write for info. (*1-85233-132-1*) Spr-Verlag.

Post-NAFTA Political Economy: Mexico & the Western Hemisphere. Carol Wise. LC 98-16941. 1998. 55.00 (*0-271-01822-4*); pap. 18.95 (*0-271-01823-2*) Pa St U Pr.

Post-Natal Depression: Psychology, Science, & the Transition to Motherhood. Paula Nicolson. LC 97-49218. (Women & Psychology Ser.). 160p. (C). 1998. 60.00 (*0-415-16362-5*); pap. 18.99 (*0-415-16363-3*) Routledge.

Post-Natal Depression: Your Questions Answered. Erika Harvey. LC 98-46429. (Element Guide Ser.). 128p. 1999. pap. 9.95 (*1-86204-330-2*, Pub. by Element MA) Penguin Putnam.

Post-National Arguments: The Politics of the Anglophone-Canadian Novel Since 1967. Frank Davey. LC 93-93081. 277p. 1993. text 45.00 (*0-8020-2785-7*) U of Toronto Pr.

***Post-National Patriotism & the Feasibility of Post-National Community in United Germany.** Donald G. Phillips. LC 00-35972. 2000. write for info. (*0-275-97049-3*) Greenwood.

***Post-Nationalist American Studies.** John Carlos Rowe. LC 99-56775. 280p. 2000. 45.00 (*0-520-22438-8*, Pub. by U CA Pr) Cal Prin Full Svc.

P

***Post-Nationalist American Studies.** John Carlos Rowe. LC 99-56775. (Illus.). 280p. 2000. pap. 17.95 (*0-520-22439-6*, Pub. by U CA Pr) Cal Prin Full Svc.

Post Nationalist Ireland: Politics, Literature, Philosophy. Richard Kearney. LC 96-5492. 272p. (C). 1996. 75.00 (*0-415-11502-7*); pap. 22.99 (*0-415-11503-5*) Routledge.

Post New Wave Cinema in the Soviet Union & Eastern Europe. Ed. by Daniel J. Goulding. LC 87-46247. (Midland Bks.). (Illus.). 331p. (Orig.). 1989. reprint ed. pap. 102.70 (*0-608-01062-6*, 205937000001) Bks Demand.

Post-1965 Immigration to the United States: Structural Determinants. Philip Q. Yang. LC 94-33262. 248p. 1995. 59.95 (*0-275-95001-8*, Praeger Pubs) Greenwood.

Post-Nuclear Collegian. Kit Kiefer. LC 83-90426. (Illus.). 200p. (Orig.). 1984. pap. 7.95 (*0-914585-00-2*) Halfcourt Pr.

Post Occupancy Evaluation & the Corporate Architect. Edward T. White. (Illus.). 50p. 1990. pap. 9.00 (*1-928643-18-3*) Archit Media.

Post Occupancy Evaluation from the Client's Perspective. Edward T. White. (Illus.). 14p. 1989. pap. 4.00 (*1-928643-17-5*) Archit Media.

Post Office. Charles Olson. LC 74-75456. (Illus.). 66p. 1975. pap. 4.95 (*0-912516-14-3*) Grey Fox.

Post Office. Rabindranath Tagore. 76p. 1988. 4.50 (*0-318-37013-1*) Asia Bk Corp.

Post Office. Charles Bukowski. 196p. 1998. reprint ed. 25.00 (*0-87685-087-5*); reprint ed. pap. 14.00 (*0-87685-086-7*) Black Sparrow.

***Post Office: A Complete Theme Unit Including Learning Centers: Grades PS-2.** Dana McMillan. Ed. by Judy Mitchell. (Illus.). 32p. 1999. pap., teacher ed. 5.95 (*1-57310-195-8*) Teachng & Lrning Co.

Post Office: Active Learning about Community Workers. Carol Wawrychuk & Cherie McSweeney. (Hands-On Projects Ser.). (Illus.). 48p. (J). (ps-k). 1998. pap. 7.95 (*1-57612-038-4*, MM2053) Monday Morning Bks.

Post Office: Basic Terms. Douglas Moore. (All about Language Ser.). (Illus.). 1987. pap. text 22.00 incl. audio (*0-939990-52-0*) Intl Linguistics.

Post Office Book. Gail Gibbons. LC 81-43888. (Illus.). 32p. (J). (gr. k-3). 1982. lib. bdg. 14.89 (*0-690-04199-3*) HarpC Child Bks.

Post Office Book: Mail & How It Moves. Gail Gibbons. LC 85-45397. (Trophy Nonfiction Bk.). (Illus.). 32p. (J). (ps-3). 1986. pap. 5.95 (*0-06-446029-0*, HarpTrophy) HarpC Child Bks.

Post Office Book: Mail & How It Moves. Gail Gibbons. 1982. 11.15 (*0-606-01928-6*, Pub. by Turtleback) Demco.

Post Office Clerk-Carrier. 19th ed. Steinberg. 1995. pap. 11.00 (*0-671-89917-1*) S&S Trade.

***Post Office Delivers: Humor - The Left-Footed Postman.** Mathew J. Bowyer. (Illus.). 121p. 1999. pap. 12.95 (*0-7414-0169-X*) Buy Books.

Post Office Department of the United States of America. Daniel D. Leech. LC 75-22825. (America in Two Centuries Ser.). 1976. reprint ed. 18.95 (*0-405-07696-7*) Ayer.

Post Office Jobs: How to Get a Job with the U. S. Postal Service. Dennis V. Damp. LC 95-52578. (Illus.). 224p. 1996. pap. 17.95 (*0-943641-14-4*) Bookhaven Pr.

Post Office Jobs: How to Get a Job with the U. S. Postal Service. 2nd rev. ed. Dennis V. Damp. LC 99-32727. (Illus.). 224p. 2000. pap. 17.95 (*0-943641-19-5*) Bookhaven Pr.

Post Office Murals Restored: Poems. Robert B. Shaw. LC 93-47142. 80p. (Orig.). 1994. pap. 11.00 (*0-914278-63-0*) Copper Beech.

Post Office Tragedy: The Shooting at Royal Oak. 354p. (Orig.). (C). 1993. pap. text 40.00 (*1-56806-180-3*) DIANE Pub.

Post Office War in Timpanogos Town. Clyde E. Weeks, Jr. (Illus.). 144p. (Orig.). 1995. pap. 6.95 (*0-9643423-2-4*) Magnif Mormon.

Post Office Worker: A Trade Union & Social History. Alan Clinton. (Illus.). 304p. 1984. text 75.00 (*0-04-331086-9*) Routledge.

Post Offices in Finland, 1638-1985. Ed. by George B. Koplowitz. Tr. by Anneli Hvidonov from FIN. (Illus.). 110p. (Orig.). 1989. pap. 20.00 (*0-936493-13-5*) Scand Philatelic.

Post-Operative Care of Ophtalmic Surgery. Epstein. 1999. pap. text. write for info. (*0-7216-1911-8*, W B Saunders Co) Harcrt Hlth Sci Grp.

Post Operative Complications in Intracranial Neurosurgery. Ed. by Emily Friedman et al. LC 92-49908. 1992. 95.00 (*0-86577-438-2*) Thieme Med Pubs.

Post-Operative Recovery & Pain Relief. Ed. by Roger J. Eltringham et al. LC 97-14221. (Illus.). xii, 199p. 1997. pap. 49.00 (*3-540-76078-4*) Spr-Verlag.

Post-Partum Document. Mary Kelly. LC 98-30424. 250p. 1999. 50.00 (*0-520-21940-6*, Pub. by U CA Pr); pap. 24.95 (*0-520-21941-4*, Pub. by U CA Pr) Cal Prin Full Svc.

Post-Passage Politics: Bicameral Resolution in Congress. Stephen D. Van Beek. (Policy & Institutional Studies). 227p. (C). 1994. text 34.95 (*0-8229-3852-9*) U of Pittsburgh Pr.

Post-Patriarchal Christology. David W. Odell-Scott. (American Academy of Religion Academy Ser.). 280p. (C). 1991. 29.95 (*1-55540-657-2*, 010178); pap. 19.95 (*1-55540-658-0*, 010178) OUP.

***Post-Pelleting Application of Liquid Additives.** G. M. A. Engelen. 70p. 1999. 30.00 (*90-74134-66-1*) Wageningen Pers.

Post-Physician Era: Medicine in the Twenty-First Century. Jerrold S. Maxmen. LC 80-13557. 256p. reprint ed. pap. 79.40 (*0-608-08653-3*, 206917600003) Bks Demand.

***Post-Polhran Nuclear Politics: Fresh Perspectives on Indo-U. S. Relations.** Pravin Sheth. 1999. 29.00 (*81-7033-514-0*, Pub. by Rawat Pubns) S Asia.

Post-Polio. Betty Garee. LC 87-71476. 48p. (Orig.). 1987. reprint ed. pap. text 3.95 (*0-915708-21-3*) Cheever Pub.

Post-Polio Syndrome. Ed. by Lauro S. Halstead & Gunnar Grimby. LC 94-42418. (Illus.). 300p. 1995. text 40.95 (*1-56053-117-7*) Hanley & Belfus.

Post-Polio Syndrome. Theodore L. Munsat. (Illus.). 144p. 1990. text 80.00 (*0-409-90153-9*) Buttrwrth-Heinemann.

Post-Polymerization Polymer Modification: Materials & Applications. 162p. 1994. 2550.00 (*1-56965-306-2*, P-147) BCC.

Post-Pop, Post-Pictures. Courtenay Smith. LC 98-156897. (Illus.). 31p. 1997. pap. text 10.00 (*0-935573-20-8*) D & A Smart Museum.

Post-Popperian Methodology of Economics: Recovering Practice. Ed. by Neil De Marchi. 400p. (C). 1992. lib. bdg. 120.50 (*0-7923-9241-8*) Kluwer Academic.

Post-Pre-Raphaelite Print: Etching, Illustration, Reproductive Engraving, & Photography in England in & Around the 1860s. Allen Staley et al. LC 95-80446. (Illus.). 168p. 1996. pap. 30.00 (*1-884919-01-4*) Wallach Art Gallery.

***Post-Process Theory: Beyond the Writing-Process Paradigm.** Thomas Kent. LC 98-44170. 272p. 1999. 22.95 (*0-8093-2244-7*) S Ill U Pr.

***Post-process Theory: Beyond The Writing-Process Paradigm.** Thomas Kent. LC 98-44170. 1999. 49.95 (*0-8093-2243-9*) S Ill U Pr.

Post Processing Treatment of Composites. Mel M. Schwartz. LC 97-120989. (Illus.). 250p. 1996. pap. 77.50 (*0-608-04967-0*, 206554600004) Bks Demand.

Post-Project Analysis in Environmental Impact Assessment. 54p. 1990. 19.00 (*92-1-116471-0*, 90.II.E.6) UN.

Post-Rapture Diner. Dorothy Barresi. (Poetry Ser.). 86p. (C). 1996. pap. 10.95 (*0-8229-5581-4*) U of Pittsburgh Pr.

Post-Rapture Diner. Dorothy Barresi. (Poetry Ser.). 86p. (C). 1996. text 24.95 (*0-8229-3896-0*) U of Pittsburgh Pr.

Post-Realism: The Rhetorical Turn in International Relations. Ed. by Francis A. Beer & Robert Hariman. 280p. (Orig.). 1996. 35.95 (*0-87013-422-1*); pap. 24.95 (*0-87013-461-2*, 0-87013-422-1) Mich St U Pr.

Post-Recombination Universe. Ed. by N. Kaiser & A. N. Lasenby. (C). 1988. text 201.00 (*90-277-2778-3*) Kluwer Academic.

Post-Release Assistance Programs for Prisoners: A National Directory. 2nd ed. Anthony J. Bosoni. LC 94-46308. 189p. 1995. pap. 34.50 (*0-7864-0025-0*) McFarland & Co.

Post-Revolutionary Society: Essays. Paul M. Sweezy. LC 80-8085. 160p. 1980. pap. 10.00 (*0-85345-551-1*, Pub. by Monthly Rev) NYU Pr.

Post-Robot Age(1994-?) As More of Us "Get a Life," Work Becomes Personal. Mary K. Murphy-Aivazian. 259p. 1995. 29.95 (*1-881705-25-0*) Antilles Pub.

***Post-Sabbatian Sabbatianism: Study of an Underground Messianic Movement.** Bezalel Naor. (Illus.). 224p. 1999. pap. 24.95 (*0-9674512-1-3*) Orot Inc.

Post-Scarcity Anarchism. rev. ed. Murray Bookchin. 265p. 1986. pap. 19.99 (*0-920057-39-X*, Pub. by Black Rose) Consort Bk Sales.

Post-Scarcity Anarchism. 2nd rev. ed. Murray Bookchin. 265p. 1986. 48.90 (*0-920057-41-1*, Pub. by Black Rose) Consort Bk Sales.

Post Scripts: The Writer's Workshop. Vincent Kaufmann. Tr. by Deborah Triesman. LC 93-34066. 208p. (C). 1994. 41.50 (*0-674-69330-2*) HUP.

Post-Secondary Education: Preparation for the World of Work. Ron Watts & Jeff Greenberg. 236p. 1990. text 72.95 (*1-85521-062-2*, Pub. by Dartmth Pub) Ashgate Pub Co.

Post-Secondary Education in a Technological Society. Nuffield Canadian Seminar Staff. Ed. by Thomas H. McLeod. LC 73-79099. (ENG & FRE., Illus.). 259p. reprint ed. pap. 80.30 (*0-7837-6895-8*, 204672500003) Bks Demand.

Post-Secondary Education in a Technological Society: L'enseignement post-secondaire dans une societe technologique. Ed. by Thomas H. McLeod. 260p. (C). 1973. 55.00 (*0-7735-0162-2*, Pub. by McG-Queens Univ Pr) CUP Services.

Post-Secondary Education Planning in Texas: Techniques for Policy Analysis. Kenneth W. Tolo. (Policy Research Project Report Ser.: No. 8). 83p. 1975. pap. 3.00 (*0-89940-604-1*) LBJ Sch Pub Aff.

Post Secondary Sampling Form. (C). 1987. 0.00 (*0-201-92282-7*) HEPC Inc.

Post-Secular Philosophy: Between Philosophy & Theology. Phillip Blond. LC 97-8952. 392p. (C). 1998. 85.00 (*0-415-09777-0*); pap. 25.99 (*0-415-09778-9*) Routledge.

Post-Separation Events in North Carolina Equitable Distribution. Cheryl D. Howell. (Special Ser.: No. 11). (Illus.). 32p. (Orig.). (C). 1993. pap. text 7.00 (*1-56011-260-3*, SS11) Institute Government.

Post-Service Employment Seminar, First Annual (1992) First Annual. 72p. (Orig.). 1992. pap. text 10.00 (*1-56986-231-1*) Federal Bar.

Post-Service Employment Seminar, Third Annual (1994) 183p. 1994. 25.00 (*1-56986-247-8*) Federal Bar.

Post-Service Employment Seminar, 2nd Annual (1993) Second Annual. 190p. (Orig.). 1993. pap. text 35.00 (*1-56986-232-X*) Federal Bar.

Post-Shoa Religious Metaphors: The Image of God in the Poetry of Nelly Sachs. Ursula Rudnick. LC 95-37056. XI, 296p. 1995. pap. 57.95 (*0-8204-2929-5*, 68702) P Lang Pubng.

***Post-Shopping Wink.** Morgan Bulkely. (Illus.). 2000. pap. 19.95 (*1-889097-38-1*) Hard Pr MA.

Post-Sixties Nocturne. Pier G. Di Cicco. 49p. 1985. pap. 5.95 (*0-86492-050-4*, Pub. by Goose Ln Edits) Genl Dist Srvs.

Post-Socialist Media: What Power the West?: The Changing Media Landscape in Poland, Hungary & the Czech Republic. Ed. by Liana Giorgi. 160p. 1995. 68.95 (*1-85628-654-1*, Pub. by Avebry) Ashgate Pub Co.

Post-Socialist Political Economy: Selected Essays. James M. Buchanan. LC 97-25019. 296p. 1997. 85.00 (*1-85898-534-X*) E Elgar.

Post-Socialist World Orders: Russia, China & the U. N. System. Robert Boardman. LC 93-31242. 1994. text 65.00 (*0-312-10671-8*) St Martin.

Post-Soeharto Indonesia Forrester. LC 99-11030. 1999. text 59.95 (*0-312-22374-9*) St Martin.

Post-Soviet Archives: Organization, Access & Declassification. Theodore W. Karasik. LC 93-9603. 1993. pap. 9.00 (*0-8330-1334-3*, MR-150-USDP) Rand Corp.

Post-Soviet Central Asia. Atabaki. 342p. 1998. text 59.50 (*1-86064-327-2*, Pub. by I B T) St Martin.

Post-Soviet Economy: Soviet & Western Perspectives. Ed. by Anders Aslund. LC 91-37376. 256p. 1992. text 39.95 (*0-312-07569-3*) St Martin.

Post-Soviet Eurasia: Anthropological Perspectives on a World in Transition. Kathryn Lyon et al. (Michigan Discussions in Anthropology Ser.). (Illus.). vi, 102p. (Orig.). (C). 1996. pap. 17.00 (*1-889480-00-2*) U MI Dept Anthropol.

Post-Soviet Euroslavia. Claudiu A. Secara. (Political Management Ser.). 60p. 1991. pap. 4.50 (*0-9646073-0-1*) Algora Pubng.

Post-Soviet Handbook: A Guide to Grassroots Organizations & Internet Resources. 2nd rev. ed. M. Holt Ruffin et al. LC 98-54115. 396p. 1999. pap. 19.95 (*0-295-97794-9*) U of Wash Pr.

Post-Soviet Moldova: A Borderland in Transition. Charles King. LC 99-192117. 1178p. 1997. 29.95 (*973-98091-1-1*, Pub. by Ctr Romanian Studies) Intl Spec Bk.

Post-Soviet Nations: Perspectives in the Demise of the U. S. S. R. Ed. by Alexander J. Motyl. 360p. 1992. text 50.00 (*0-231-07894-3*) Col U Pr.

Post-Soviet Nations: Perspectives on the Demise of the U. S. S. R. Alexander J. Motyl. 322p. 1995. pap. 19.50 (*0-231-07895-1*) Col U Pr.

Post-Soviet Perspectives on Russian Psychology, 31. Vera R. Koltsova et al. LC 95-571. (Contributions in Psychology Ser.: Vol. 31). 352p. 1996. 75.00 (*0-313-28796-1*, Greenwood Pr) Greenwood.

Post-Soviet Policy Perspectives. Veskressenski. LC 97-41235. 237p. 1997. 75.00 (*1-56072-495-1*) Nova Sci Pubs.

Post-Soviet Political Order: Conflict & State Building. Barnett R. Rubin & Jack L. Snyder. LC 97-36987. (Illus.). 224p. (C). 1998. 80.00 (*0-415-17068-0*); pap. 25.99 (*0-415-17069-9*) Routledge.

Post-Soviet Puzzles: Mapping the Political Economy of the Former Soviet Union, 4 vols. Stiftung Wissenschaft und Politik Staff et al. Ed. by Klaus Segbers & Stephan De Spiegeleire. LC 96-119194. (Aktuelle Materialien zur Internationalen Politik Ser.). 1995. write for info. (*3-7890-4045-2*) Nomos Verlags.

Post-Soviet Republics: A Systematic Geography. Ed. by Denis J. Shaw. 192p. (C). 1996. pap. text 48.00 (*0-582-30175-0*) Longman.

***Post-Soviet Russia: A Journey Through the Yeltsin Era.** Roy Medvedev. Tr. by George Shriver. (RUS.). 640p. 2000. text 37.50 (*0-231-10606-8*) Col U Pr.

***Post-Soviet Russia: A Journey Through the Yeltsin Era.** Roy Aleksandrovich Medvedev. LC 00-40443. (Illus.). 2000. write for info. (*0-231-10607-6*) Col U Pr.

Post Soviet States: Mapping the Politics of Transition. Graham Smith. (Illus.). 288p. 1999. pap. text 24.95 (*0-340-67791-0*, Pub. by E A) OUP.

Post-Soviet States: Mapping the Politics of Transition. Graham Smith. 224p. 1999. text 70.00 (*0-340-67790-2*, Pub. by E A) OUP.

Post-Soviet-Type Economies in Transition. Jan Winiecki. LC 93-16355. 200p. 1993. 72.95 (*1-85628-406-9*, Pub. by Avebry) Ashgate Pub Co.

Post-Soviet Women: From the Baltic to Central Asia. Ed. by Mary Buckley. 333p. (C). 1997. text 59.95 (*0-521-56320-8*); pap. text 22.95 (*0-521-56530-8*) Cambridge U Pr.

Post Stroke Hope: A Motivational Journey to Recovery. Marty O. Hopps. 144p. 1998. 15.95 (*1-887750-88-6*) Rutledge Bks.

Post-Stroke Rehabilitation: Clinical Practice Guideline. Glen E. Gresham. 266p. 1995. pap. text 11.00 (*0-16-045575-8*) USGPO.

Post-Stroke Rehabilitation: Clinical Practice Guideline. Post-Stroke Rehabilitation Guideline Panel Staff et al. LC 95-44619. 250p. 1996. pap. 21.00 (*0-8342-0811-3*) Aspen Pub.

Post-Stroke Rehabilitation: Clinical Practice Guideline. Glen E. Gresham et al. (Illus.). 248p. (C). 1997. reprint ed. pap. text 50.00 (*0-7881-4144-9*) DIANE Pub.

Post-stroke Rehabilitation 16: Assessment, Referral & Patient Management, Reference for Clinicians. Glen E. Gresham. 36p. 1995. pap. 28.00 (*0-16-061540-2*) USGPO.

Post-Structural Approaches to Language: Language Theory in a Japanese Context. J. V. Neustupny. LC 80-482694. 317p. 1978. reprint ed. pap. 98.30 (*0-608-01255-6*, 206194300001) Bks Demand.

Post-Structuralist & Post-Modernist Sociology. Ed. by Scott Lash. (Schools of Thought in Sociology Ser.: No. 9). 512p. 1991. text 195.00 (*1-85278-183-1*) E Elgar.

Post Structuralist Theory & Classroom Practice. Bronwyn Davies. 127p. (C). 1995. pap. 60.00 (*0-7300-1728-1*, Pub. by Deakin Univ) St Mut.

Post-Suburbia: Government & Politics in the Edge Cities. Jon C. Teaford. LC 96-24378. 224p. 1996. text 32.50 (*0-8018-5450-4*) Johns Hopkins.

Post-Synodal Apostolic Exhortations. Pat Burke. Ed. by J. Michael Miller. 1998. 49.95 incl. cd-rom (*0-87973-290-3*) Our Sunday Visitor.

Post-Synodal Apostolic Exhortations of John Paul II. John Paul, II, pseud. Ed. & Intro. by J. Michael Miller. LC 97-69354. 800p. 1998. 49.94 (*0-87973-928-2*) Our Sunday Visitor.

***Post Tension.** (Ironworking Lev 3 Ser.). 2000. teacher ed., ring bd. 12.00 (*0-13-031255-X*) P-H.

Post-Tensioned Concrete Floors. Sami Khan & Martin Williams. LC 94-36854. (Illus.). 256p. 1995. text 74.95 (*0-7506-1681-4*) Buttrwrth-Heinemann.

Post-Tensioning Details for Long-Span Concrete Bridges. (PCI Journal Reprints Ser.). 19p. 1985. pap. 14.00 (*0-318-19785-5*, JR268) P-PCI.

Post-Test: Scoring Set GED. Contemporary, Staff. 1987. pap. 16.20 (*0-8092-4567-1*) NTC Contemp Pub Co.

Post-Test: Starter Set GED. Contemporary, Staff. 1998. pap. 33.95 (*0-8092-4566-3*) NTC Contemp Pub Co.

***Post Test Analysis of P5 Experiment in Panda Facility With TRAC-BF1 Code.** J. Polo. 20p. 2000. pap. 2.50 (*0-16-059176-7*) USGPO.

***Post, the Ghost.** Fink Inc. Staff. (Fink, Inc. Presents Ser.: Vol. 2). (Illus.). 2000. 2.50 (*1-930281-04-8*) FINK Inc.

***Post-Theory: New Directions in Criticism.** Martin McQuillan. 224p. 2000. pap. 28.00 (*0-7486-1065-0*, Pub. by Edinburgh U Pr) Col U Pr.

Post-Theory: Reconstructing Film Studies. Ed. by David Bordwell & Noel Carroll. LC 95-37052. (Wisconsin Studies in Film). (Illus.). 582p. 1996. pap. 24.95 (*0-299-14944-7*) U of Wis Pr.

Post-Theory: Reconstructing Film Studies. Ed. by David Bordwell & Noel Carroll. LC 95-37052. (Wisconsin Studies in Film). (Illus.). 582p. (C). 1996. 45.00 (*0-299-14940-4*) U of Wis Pr.

Post-Theory, Games, & Discursive Resistance: The Bulgarian Case. Ed. by Alexander Kiossev. LC 94-33220. (SUNY Series, The Margins of Literature). 214p. (C). 1995. text 57.50 (*0-7914-2357-3*); pap. text 18.95 (*0-7914-2358-1*) State U NY Pr.

Post-Therapeutic Neurodiagnostic Imaging. J. Randy Jinkins. LC 96-42057. 320p. 1996. text 131.00 (*0-397-58406-7*) Lppncott W & W.

Post-Totalitarian Spanish Fiction. Robert C. Spires. 280p. (C). 1996. 39.95 (*0-8262-1071-6*) U of Mo Pr.

Post-Transcriptional Control of Gene Expression. Ed. by J. E. McCarthy & Mick F. Tuite. (NATO ASI Series H: Cell Biology: Vol. 49). xix, 652p. 1991. 238.95 (*0-387-51774-X*) Spr-Verlag.

Post-Transcriptional Control of Gene Expression: Proceedings of the NATO Advanced Study Institute, Held on the Island of Spetsai, Greece, August 1992. Ed. by Orna Resnekov & A. Von Gabain. LC 96-14087. (NATO ASI - Cell Biology Ser.: Vol. 97). 288p. 1996. 139.00 (*0-387-56847-6*) Spr-Verlag.

Post-Transcriptional Control of Gene Expression: Proceedings of the NATO Advanced Study Institute, Held on the Island of Spetsai, Greece, August 1992. Alexander Von Gabain. Ed. by Orna Resnekov. LC 96-14087. (NATO ASI Series H: Vol. 97). 1996. write for info. (*3-540-56847-6*) Spr-Verlag.

Post Transcriptional Control of Gene Expression in Plants. Ed. by Witold Filipowicz. LC 97-108327. 448p. (C). 1996. text 257.50 (*0-7923-4275-5*) Kluwer Academic.

Post-Transcriptional Processing & the Endocrine System. Ed. by S. L. Chew. LC 99-19309. (Frontiers of Hormone Research Ser.: Vol. 25). (Illus.). x, 146p. 1999. 147.00 (*3-8055-6849-5*) S Karger.

Post-Translational Modification of Proteins. Ed. by Syozo Tuboi et al. 1992. 99.00 (*0-8493-7753-6*, QH450) CRC Pr.

Post-Translational Modifications in Plants. Ed. by N. H. Battey et al. LC 92-28694. (Society for Experimental Biology Seminar Ser.: No. 53). (Illus.). 330p. (C). 1993. text 100.00 (*0-521-41181-5*) Cambridge U Pr.

Post-Translational Modifications of Proteins. John J. Harding. 264p. 1991. lib. bdg. 225.00 (*0-8493-4171-X*, QH450) CRC Pr.

Post-Translational Processing. Ed. by S. J. Higgins & B. D. Hames. LC 98-52159. (The Practical Approach Ser.: No. 203). (Illus.). 352p. 1999. text 120.00 (*0-19-963794-6*) OUP.

Post-Translational Processing: A Practical Approach. Ed. by S. J. Higgins & B. D. Hames. LC 98-52159. (The Practical Approach Ser.: Vol. 203). (Illus.). 352p. 1999. pap. text 55.00 (*0-19-963795-4*) OUP.

Post-Trauma Stress. Frank Parkinson. LC 93-35868. 192p. (Orig.). 1993. pap. 12.95 (*1-55561-058-7*) Fisher Bks.

***Post-Trauma Stress: Recovery from Hidden Emotional Damage Caused by Violence & Disaster.** Frank Parkinson. 192p. 2000. pap. 14.00 (*1-55561-249-0*) Fisher Bks.

Post-Traumatic Culture: Injury & Interpretation in the Nineties. Kirby Farrell. LC 97-44042. 424p. 1998. 49.00 (*0-8018-5786-4*); pap. 17.95 (*0-8018-5787-2*) Johns Hopkins.

Post-Traumatic Neurosis: From Railway Spine to Whiplash. fac. ed. Michael R. Trimble. LC 82-135121. (Wiley Medical Publication). (Illus.). 166p. 1981. reprint ed. pap. 51.50 (*0-608-00990-3*, 206184600012) Bks Demand.

Post-Traumatic Stree Disorder: A Comprehensive Text. Ed. by Philip A. Saigh & J. Douglas Bremer. LC 98-38799. 434p. 1998. 65.95 (*0-205-26734-3*) Allyn.

An Asterisk (*) at the beginning of an entry indicates that the title is appearing for the first time.

Post Traumatic Stress Disorder. Philip A. Saigh. (Practitioner Guidebook Ser.). 212p. (C). 1992. pap. text 40.00 (*0-205-14553-1*, H4553, Longwood Div) Allyn.

Post-Traumatic Stress Disorder: A Clinician's Guide. K. Peterson et al. LC 90-14309. (Stress & Coping Ser.). (Illus.). 276p. (C). 1990. 42.50 (*0-306-43542-X*, Plenum Trade) Perseus Pubng.

Post-Traumatic Stress Disorder: A Complete Treatment Guide. Aphrodite Matsakis. LC 93-87082. 384p. 1994. 49.95 (*1-879237-68-7*) New Harbinger.

Post-Traumatic Stress Disorder: A Lifespan Developmental Perspective. A. Maercker et al. LC 98-36649. viii, 264p. 1998. 39.00 (*0-88937-187-3*) Hogrefe & Huber Pubs.

***Post Traumatic Stress Disorder: A Police Officers Report.** L. Ken Rogers. LC 99-75954. 272p. 2000. pap. 14.95 (*1-882792-83-1*) Proctor Pubns.

Post-Traumatic Stress Disorder: Assessment, Differential Diagnosis, & Forensic Evaluation. Ed. by Carroll L. Meek. LC 89-43413. 264p. 1990. 30.95 (*0-943158-35-4*, PTSDBP) Pro Resource.

Post Traumatic Stress Disorder: Causes, Characteristics, & Cures. 165p. 1998. pap. text 24.95 (*0-9634079-1-0*) R W Peterson.

Post Traumatic Stress Disorder: Concepts & Therapy. William Yule. LC 98-24146. 344p. 1999. 85.00 (*0-471-96058-6*) Wiley.

Post-Traumatic Stress Disorder: Defining, Examining, Preventing & Treating. Charles R. Figley. (Innovations in Psychology Ser.). 200p. 1994. lib. bdg. 39.95 (*1-57444-166-3*, SL1663) St Lucie Pr.

Post-Traumatic Stress Disorder: Diagnosis, Treatment, & Legal Issues. 2nd ed. C. B. Scrignar. (Illus.). 344p. (C). 1988. pap. 32.95 (*0-945032-01-3*) Bruno Pr.

Post-Traumatic Stress Disorder: Diagnosis, Treatment, & Legal Issues. 2nd large type ed. C. B. Scrignar. (Illus.). 344p. (C). 1988. 49.95 (*0-945032-00-5*) Bruno Pr.

Post-Traumatic Stress Disorder: Diagnosis, Treatment, & Legal Issues. 3rd ed. C. B. Scrignar. 1996. text 59.95 (*0-945032-05-6*); pap. text 39.95 (*0-945032-06-4*) Bruno Pr.

Post-Traumatic Stress Disorder: Psychological & Biological Sequelae. Ed. by Bessel A. Van Der Kolk. LC 84-6375. (Clinical Insights Ser.). 148p. reprint ed. pap. 45.90 (*0-8357-7813-4*, 203618500002) Bks Demand.

***Post Traumatic Stress Disorder: The Latest Assessment & Treatment Strategies.** Matthew J. Friedman. 108p. 2000. pap. 14.95 (*1-887537-14-7*, Pub. by Compact Clinicals) Midpt Trade.

Post-Traumatic Stress Disorder: The Victim's Guide to Healing & Recovery. Raymond B. Flannery, Jr. 240p. 1995. reprint ed. pap. 16.95 (*0-8245-1445-9*) Crossroad NY.

Post Traumatic Stress Disorder & Dramatherapy. Linda Winn. 160p. 1993. 36.00 (*1-85302-183-0*) Taylor & Francis.

Post-Traumatic Stress Disorder Sourcebook: A Guide to Healing, Recovery & Growth. Glenn R. Schiraldi. LC 99-47837. 352p. 2000. pap. 16.95 (*0-7373-0265-8*, 02658W) NTC Contemp Pub Co.

Post-Traumatic Stress Disorders: Concepts & Therapy. William Yule. LC 98-24146. (Series in Clinical Psychology). 344p. 1999. pap. 45.00 (*0-471-97080-8*) Wiley.

***Post Traumatic Stress Theory, Research & Application.** Ed. by John Harvey & Brian E. Pauwels. LC 00-36113. 184p. 2000. pap. text 21.95 (*1-58391-014-X*) Brunner-Mazel.

Post-Traumatic Therapy & Victims of Violence. Frank M. Ochberg. LC 87-26877. (Psychosocial Stress Ser.: No. 11). 384p. 1988. text 47.95 (*0-87630-490-0*) Brunner-Mazel.

Post-Trib Alternative to the Pre-Trib Rapture. Douglas Chinn & Virginia Chinn. LC 91-77954. 140p. 1992. pap. 9.95 (*0-944788-95-5*) IBRI.

Post-Trib, Pre-Wrath Rapture. R. Rasmussn. LC 96-92137. 1998. pap. 12.00 (*0-9651789-0-0*) Post-Trib Res.

Post-Tribal Epics: The Native American Novel Between Tradition & Modernity. Giorgio Mariani. LC 96-31145. (Native American Studies). 280p. 1997. text 89.95 (*0-7734-8936-3*) E Mellen.

***Post-Uruguay Round Tariff Regimes: Achievements & Outlook.** Raed Safadi. 176p. 1999. pap. 38.00 (*92-64-17128-2*, 22 1999 03 1 P, Pub. by Org for Econ) OECD.

Post Victorians. Intro. by William R. Inge. LC 77-37791. (Essay Index Reprint Ser.). 1980. reprint ed. 34.95 (*0-8369-2618-8*) Ayer.

Post Viral Fatigue Syndrome. James F. Mowbray. Ed. by Rachel Jenkins. LC 90-13138. 502p. 1993. pap. 176.95 (*0-471-93879-3*, Wiley-Liss) Wiley.

Post-Viral Fatigue Syndrome. Ed. by Rachel Jenkins & James F. Mowbray. LC 90-13138. (Illus.). 501p. 1991. reprint ed. pap. 155.40 (*0-608-01636-5*, 206222100002) Bks Demand.

Post War Britain. (Sense of History Ser.). Date not set. pap. text. write for info. (*0-582-09209-4*, Pub. by Addison-Wesley) Longman.

Post War Britain. C. M. Woodhouse. LC 67-15646. 1967. 18.95 (*0-8023-1122-9*) Dufour.

Post War Britain: Political History. A. Sked & C. Cook. 1993. pap. 19.95 (*0-14-017912-7*, Pub. by Pnguin Bks Ltd) Trafalgar.

Post War Caribbean Migration to Britain: The Unfinished Cycle. Margaret Byron. (Research in Ethnic Relations Ser.). 233p. 1995. 72.95 (*1-85628-615-0*, Pub. by Avebry) Ashgate Pub Co.

Post-War Economic Development of Japan. B. P. Shreshtha. 93p. 1988. text 15.95 (*0-89891-029-3*, Pub. by Himalaya Pub) Advent Bks Div.

Post-War Generation & Establishment Religion: Cross-Cultural Perspectives. Ed. by Jackson W. Carroll et al. LC 94-24178. 291p. (C). 1994. text 77.50 (*0-8133-8914-3*, Pub. by Westview) HarpC.

Post-War Mothers: Childbirth Letters to Grantly Dick-Read, 1946-1956. Mary Thomas. LC 97-42313. 216p. 1998. 60.00 (*1-878822-87-X*) Univ Rochester Pr.

Post-War Novella in German-Language Literature: An Analysis. Bruce Plouffe. (Studies in German Literature & Culture: Vol. 5). 1996. write for info. (*0-404-64055-9*) AMS Pr.

Post-War Planning in the Inner-Town of Leiden: A Study of Changing Perception & Policies. Lisa Johnson. (C). 1978. 40.00 (*0-7855-3876-3*, Pub. by Oxford Polytechnic) St Mut.

Post-War Policy Issues in the Persian Gulf. 270p. (Orig.). (C). 1994. pap. text 50.00 (*0-7881-0637-6*) DIANE Pub.

Post-War Protection of Human Rights in Bosnia & Herzegovina. Michael O'Flaherty & Gregory Gisvold. LC 98-7588. (International Studies in Human Rights). 336p. 1998. 89.00 (*90-411-1020-8*) Kluwer Law Intl.

Post-War Reconstruction in Central America: Lessons from El Salvador, Guatemala, & Nicaragua. Patricia Ardon. Tr. & Adapted by Deborah Eade. (Oxfam Working Papers Ser.). 120p. 1998. pap. 15.95 (*0-85598-405-8*, Pub. by Oxfam Pub) Stylus Pub VA.

Post-War Riots in America, 1919 & 1946: How the Pressures of War Exacerbated American Urban Tensions to the Breaking Point. Lee E. Williams, II. LC 91-40313. 180p. 1991. lib. bdg. 79.95 (*0-88946-694-7*) E Mellen.

Post War Wales, 1945-1990. Ed. by Trevor Herbert & Gareth E. Jones. (Illus.). 200p. 1993. pap. 18.95 (*0-7083-1291-8*, Pub. by Univ Wales Pr) Paul & Co Pubs.

Post Work: Wages of Cybernation. Ed. by Stanley Aronowitz & Jonathan Cutler. LC 97-26548. 288p. 1997. pap. 19.99 (*0-415-91783-2*) Routledge.

Post Work: Wages of Cybernation. Ed. by Stanley Aronowitz & Jonathan Cutler. LC 97-26548. 288p. (C). 1997. 75.00 (*0-415-91782-4*) Routledge.

***Post-World War II M-1 Helmets, An Illustrated Study.** Mark A. Reynosa. (Illus.). 136p. 2000. 39.95 (*0-7643-1033-X*) Schiffer.

Post-Yield Fracture Mechanics. 2nd ed. Ed. by D. G. Latzko et al. (Illus.). 512p. 1985. mass mkt. 221.50 (*0-85334-276-8*) Elsevier.

Post-Zionism Debates: Knowledge & Power in Israeli Culture. Laurence Silberstein. LC 98-39895. 1999. write for info. (*0-415-91315-2*) Routledge.

***Post-Zionism Debates: Knowledge & Power in Israeli Culture.** Laurence Silberstein. LC 98-39895. 1999. pap. 19.99 (*0-415-91316-0*) Routledge.

Post-1945 Internationalization of Economics. A. W. Coats. (History of Political Economy Annual Supplement Ser.). 280p. 1996. text 40.00 (*0-8223-1876-8*) Duke.

Posta Anamalia. Illus. by Helen Buttfield. 30p. 1996. pap. 10.95 (*1-55670-526-3*) Stewart Tabori & Chang.

Posta Botanica. Illus. by Helen Buttfield. 30p. 1996. pap. 10.95 (*1-55670-525-5*) Stewart Tabori & Chang.

***Posta Frutta.** Helen Buttfield. (Illus.). 30p. 2000. pap. 10.95 (*1-55670-997-8*) Stewart Tabori & Chang.

Posta Insecta. Illus. by Helen Buttfield. 30p. 1996. pap. 10.95 (*1-55670-527-1*) Stewart Tabori & Chang.

***Posta Verdura.** Helen Buttfield. (Illus.). 30p. 2000. pap. 10.95 (*1-55670-998-6*) Stewart Tabori & Chang.

Postabortion Care: A Reference Manual for Improving the Quality of Care. Ed. by Judith Winkler et al. (Illus.). (Orig.). 1995. pap. text 15.00 (*0-929817-08-7*) JHPIEGO.

Postage Due. Jon Foyt & Lois Foyt. 220p. 1995. 19.95 (*1-85776-021-2*, Pub. by Book Guild Ltd) Gannon.

Postage Meters: Risk of Significant Financial Loss but Controls Are Being Strengthened. (Illus.). 50p. (Orig.). (C). 1995. pap. text 20.00 (*0-7881-2088-3*) DIANE Pub.

Postage Stamp Garden Book. 2nd rev. ed. Duane G. Newcomb & Karen Newcomb. LC 98-31918. 1999. 12.95 (*1-58062-123-6*) Adams Media.

Postage Stamp Kitchen Garden Book. Duane G. Newcomb & Karen Newcomb. LC 97-43184. 256p. 1998. 9.95 (*1-58062-001-9*) Adams Media.

Postage Stamp Recycling As Fundraising, Crafts & a Hobby. Carrol, Frieda, Research Division Staff. 1984. ring bd. 21.95 (*0-318-04346-7*) Prosperity & Profits.

Postage Stamps of Japan & Dependencies. Alphonse M. Woodward. LC 73-86773. (Illus.). 768p. 1976. reprint ed. 150.00 (*0-88000-020-1*) Quarterman.

Postage Stamps of Lithuania. Lithuanian Philatelic Societies of New York & Toro. 237p. 1978. 18.00 (*0-912574-33-X*) Collectors.

Postal Applications of Operations Research. J. N. Gupta. 1978. pap. 42.00 (*0-08-023011-3*, Pergamon Pr) Elsevier.

Postal Arithmetic. Jack Rudman. (General Aptitude & Abilities Ser.: No. CS-20). pap. 19.95 (*0-8373-6720-4*, CS-20) Nat Learn.

Postal Bulletin. Government Printing Office Staff. pap. 103.00 (*0-16-011614-7*) USGPO.

Postal Clerk & Carrier. 19th ed. E. P. Steinberg. 304p. 1995. 10.95 (*0-02-860023-1*) Macmillan.

Postal Clerk & Carrier. 20th ed. E. P. Steinberg. 288p. 1997. pap. 10.95 (*0-02-861524-7*, Arco) Macmillan Gen Ref.

Postal Clerk & Carrier. 21st ed. E. P. Steinberg. LC 98-88349. 304p. 1999. 10.95 (*0-02-862809-8*, Arc) IDG Bks.

***Postal Clerk & Carrier.** 22nd ed. John Gosney. (Illus.). 336p. 2000. pap. text 10.95 (*0-02-863737-2*, Arco) Macmillan Gen Ref.

Postal Clerk Carrier. 4th ed. 1981. pap. 12.00 (*0-910553-89-0*) Ken-Bks.

Postal Clerk-Carrier & Mail Handler Exams. 4th ed. Harry W. Koch. 1981. 8.00 (*0-913164-89-5*) Ken-Bks.

Postal Communication in China & Its Modernization, 1860-1896. Ying-Wan Cheng. LC 70-120316. (East Asian Monographs: No. 34). (Illus.). 162p. 1970. pap. 20.00 (*0-674-69320-5*) HUP.

Postal Confessions. Max Garland. LC 94-41649. 120p. 1995. pap. 10.95 (*0-87023-982-1*) U of Mass Pr.

Postal Entrance Battery Test 470. (Career Examination Ser.: C-3660). pap. 19.95 (*0-8373-3660-0*) Nat Learn.

Postal Exam Complete Study Program: Test Battery 470 & R$ural Cqrrier Exam 460 - Money BackGuarfantee for Score of 95-100, Audio Tapes & Text/Work Book. rev. ed. T. W. Parnell. 130p. 1997. pap. 39.95 incl. audio (*0-940182-06-8*) Pathfinder Dist.

Postal Exam Text/Work Book: Data Conversion Operator Exam 710. rev. ed. T. W. Parnell. 120p. 1995. pap. 19.95 (*0-940182-04-1*) Pathfinder Dist.

Postal Exam Text/Work Book: Test Battery 470 & Rural Carrier Exam 460 - Money Back Guarantee for Score of 95-100. rev. ed. T. W. Parnell. 107p. 1997. pap. 19.95 (*0-940182-05-X*) Pathfinder Dist.

***Postal Exam Training Guide: Free Live Support & Guaranteed Score of 95-1005th** rev. ed. T. W. Parnell. (Illus.). 380p. 2000. pap. 19.95 (*0-940182-11-4*) Pathfinder Dist.

Postal Examination - Test Battery 460/470, 2 cass. REA Staff. LC 98-65408. 320p. 1998. pap. 25.95 incl. audio (*0-87891-080-8*) Res & Educ.

Postal Examinations Preparation Guide. rev. ed. Jerry Bobrow et al. (Cliffs Test Preparation Ser.). (Illus.). 312p. 1991. pap. 10.95 (*0-8220-2076-9*, Cliff) IDG Bks.

Postal Exams Handbook. 3rd ed. Eve P. Steinberg. 1995. pap. 12.00 (*0-671-89916-3*) S&S Trade.

Postal Exams Handbook. 5th ed. Arco. 272p. 1999. pap. text 12.95 (*0-02-863538-8*, Arco) Macmillan Gen Ref.

Postal Exams Made Easy: Getting a Job in the Post Office. Dick Gahler. 128p. 1991. pap. 9.00 (*0-685-38937-5*) Artek Pr Inc.

Postal History & Markings of the Forwarding Agents. Kenneth E. Rowe. Ed. by Leonard H. Hartmann. LC 96-75098. (Illus.). 288p. 1996. 47.50 (*0-917528-12-3*) L H Hartmann.

Postal History & Postage Stamps of Serbia, 1841-1921. Mirko R. Rasic. (Illus.). 276p. 1979. 18.00 (*0-912574-25-9*) Collectors.

Postal History & Stamps of Tuva. 2nd ed. Samuel Blekhman. Tr. by Ron Hogg from RUS. (Illus.). 104p. 1998. pap. 30.00 (*1-58490-017-2*) Scientific Consulting.

Postal History & Usage of Nineteen Hundred Seven & Earlier Precancels. Charles C. Souder. LC 89-90756. (Illus.). 297p. 1989. pap. 24.95 (*1-877998-05-2*) D G Phillips.

Postal History-Cancellation Study of the U. S. Pacific Islands: Including the Trust Territories. Robert T. Murphy. (Illus.). 361p. 1983. 46.00 (*0-933580-11-8*) Am Philatelic Society.

Postal History of British Airmails. Proud-Bailey Co. Ltd., Staff. (C). 1989. 175.00 (*1-872465-72-2*, Pub. by Proud Bailey) St Mut.

Postal History of Burlington, Vermont: The First 100 Years. Donald B. Johnstone. (Illus.). 64p. 1992. pap. 6.00 (*0-9635562-1-5*) VT Philatelic.

Postal History of Christmas Seals. Douglas K. Lehmann. (Illus.). 40p. (Orig.). 1990. pap. 9.95 (*1-878770-00-4*) Paragon OK.

Postal History of Hong Kong. Proud Bailey Co. Ltd., Staff. 1989. 175.00 (*1-872465-07-2*, Pub. by Proud Bailey) St Mut.

Postal History of Indiana, 2 vols., Set. J. David Baker. Ed. by Leonard H. Hartmann. LC 76-10531. (Illus.). 1100p. 1976. 75.00 (*0-917528-03-4*) L H Hartmann.

Postal History of Indiana, Vol. 1. J. David Baker. Ed. by Leonard H. Hartmann. (Illus.). 1976. write for info. (*0-917528-01-8*) L H Hartmann.

Postal History of Indiana, Vol. 2. J. David Baker. Ed. by Leonard H. Hartmann. (Illus.). 1976. write for info. (*0-917528-02-6*) L H Hartmann.

Postal History of Kenya. 1989. 175.00 (*0-7855-2650-1*, Pub. by Proud Bailey) St Mut.

Postal History of Kenya. Proud Bailey Co. Ltd., Staff. 1989. 175.00 (*0-614-01353-4*, Pub. by Proud Bailey) St Mut.

Postal History of Tanganyika. Proud-Bailey Co. Ltd., Staff. 1989. 175.00 (*1-872465-06-4*, Pub. by Proud Bailey) St Mut.

Postal History of the Forwarding Agents. Kenneth E. Rowe. Ed. by Leonard H. Hartmann. LC 84-80011. (Illus.). 296p. 1984. 35.00 (*0-917528-06-9*) L H Hartmann.

Postal History of the Naval & R. A. F. Postal Services. Proud Bailey Co. Ltd., Staff. (C). 1989. 175.00 (*1-872465-62-5*, Pub. by Proud Bailey) St Mut.

Postal History of the Occupation of Malaya & British Borne. Proud Bailey Co. Ltd., Staff. (C). 1989. 175.00 (*1-872465-73-0*, Pub. by Proud Bailey) St Mut.

Postal History of Uganda & Zanzibar. Proud-Bailey Co. Ltd., Staff. 1989. 175.00 (*1-872465-08-0*, Pub. by Proud Bailey) St Mut.

Postal History of Yukon Territory, Canada. Robert G. Woodall. LC 76-15747. 1976. 35.00 (*0-88000-086-4*) Quarterman.

Postal Inspector (U. S. P. S.) Jack Rudman. (Career Examination Ser.: C-602). 1994. pap. 27.95 (*0-8373-0602-7*) Nat Learn.

Postal Jobs: How to Score 95+ on the Postal Exam. Ed. by Federal Jobs Digest Staff. (Illus.). 229p. (Orig.). 1994. pap. 19.95 (*0-914327-35-6*) Breakthrgh NY.

Postal Machines Mechanic (USPS) (Career Examination Ser.: C-3366). 1994. pap. 27.95 (*0-8373-3366-0*) Nat Learn.

Postal Markings of New Jersey Stampless Covers. William C. Coles, Jr. LC 83-72780. (Illus.). 287p. 1983. 35.00 (*0-318-41003-6*) Collectors Club IL.

Postal Markings of U. S. Expositions. 2nd ed. William T. Bomar. (Illus.). 300p. 1996. pap. 45.00 (*1-880065-20-7*) Machine Cancel Soc.

Postal Police Officer (U.S.P.S.) Jack Rudman. (Career Examination Ser.: C-2211). 1994. pap. 27.95 (*0-8373-2211-1*) Nat Learn.

Postal Powers of Congress: A Study in Constitutional Expansion. Lindsay Rogers. LC 78-63956. (Johns Hopkins University. Studies in the Social Sciences. Thirtieth Ser. 1912: 2). reprint ed. 37.50 (*0-404-61204-0*) AMS Pr.

Postal Precipice: Can the U. S. Postal Service Be Saved. Kathleen Conkey. 515p. 1983. pap. text 30.00 (*0-936758-09-0*) Ctr Responsive Law.

Postal Rape. (Kake Ser.: No. 25). 1997. pap. 11.00 (*1-879055-09-0*) Tom Finland.

Postal Reform in Canada: Canada Post Corporation's Universal Service & Ratemaking. (Illus.). 70p. 1997. pap. text 40.00 (*1-57979-226-X*) DIANE Pub.

Postal Reform in Canada: Canada Post Corporation's Universal Service & Ratemaking. Hazel Bailey. (Illus.). 68p. (C). 1999. pap. text 20.00 (*0-7881-7642-0*) DIANE Pub.

Postal Route Gazetteer Pt. 1: New York State, 1839. Intro. by Robert D. Harris. (Postilion Series of Primary Sources: Vol. 6). (Illus.). 100p. 1992. pap. 28.00 (*0-941480-11-9*, Postilion Pubns) Subway Stamp.

Postal Routes. Elizabeth Kirschner. LC 97-65560. (Poetry Ser.). 57p. 1998. pap. 11.95 (*0-88748-262-7*) Carnegie-Mellon.

***Postal Service Guide to U. S. Stamps.** U. S. Postal Service Staff. 2001. write for info. (*0-06-095855-3*, HarpRes) HarpInfo.

Postal Service Guide to U. S. Stamps. 14th ed. LC 87-656545. (Illus.). 320p. 1987. 5.00 (*0-9604756-6-4*) USPS.

Postal Service Guide to U. S. Stamps. 15th ed. LC 87-656545. (Illus.). 328p. 1988. 5.00 (*0-9604756-8-0*) USPS.

Postal Service Guide to U. S. Stamps. 17th ed. (Illus.). 336p. 1990. pap. 5.95 (*0-685-34657-9*) USPS.

Postal Service Guide to U. S. Stamps. 18th ed. Ed. by Bill Halstead. (Illus.). 344p. 1992. pap. 5.95 (*1-877707-01-5*) USPS.

***Postal Service Guide to U. S. Stamps, 2001.** U. S. Postal Service Staff. 528p. 2000. 19.95 (*0-06-095854-5*, HarpRes) HarpInfo.

***Postal Service Guide to U. S. Stamps, 2003.** U. S. Postal Service Staff. 2002. write for info. (*0-06-095856-1*, HarpRes) HarpInfo.

Postal Service in Boston, 1639-1893. Carl W. Ernst. 1975. 3.00 (*0-89073-004-0*) Boston Public Lib.

Postal Service Reform: Issues Relevant to Changing Restrictions on Private Letter Delivery, 2 vols. (Illus.). 152p. (Orig.). (C). 1996. pap. text 35.00 (*0-7881-3636-4*) DIANE Pub.

Postal Supervisor (U. S. P. S.) Jack Rudman. (Career Examination Ser.: C-603). 1994. pap. 29.95 (*0-8373-0603-5*) Nat Learn.

Postal System Examiner (U. S. P. S.) Jack Rudman. (Career Examination Ser.: C-2079). 1994. reprint ed. pap. 34.95 (*0-8373-2079-8*) Nat Learn.

Postal Technology & Management. Husain Mustafa. LC 73-165579. (Illus.). 240p. 1971. 23.50 (*0-912338-01-6*); fiche 9.50 (*0-912338-02-4*) Lomond.

Postal Transportation Clerk (U. S. P. S.) Jack Rudman. (Career Examination Ser.: C-604). 1994. pap. 23.95 (*0-8373-0604-3*) Nat Learn.

Postal Worker California. LC 96-1817. (Civil Service Library). 1996. pap. 30.00 (*1-57685-049-8*) LrningExprss.

***Postal Worker Exam.** 2nd ed. LC 00-40532. 288p. 2000. write for info. (*1-57685-331-4*) LrningExprss.

Postal Worker Florida. Learning Express Staff. LC 96-32721. (Civil Service Library). 1996. pap. 30.00 (*1-57685-063-3*) LrningExprss.

Postal Worker New Jersey. LearningExpress Staff. LC 96-32256. (Civil Service Library). 1996. pap. 30.00 (*1-57685-070-6*) LrningExprss.

Postal Worker Texas. LC 96-1850. (Civil Service Library). 1996. pap. 30.00 (*1-57685-051-X*) LrningExprss.

***Postal Workers.** Paulette Bourgeois. (Illus.). (J). 2000. 11.40 (*0-606-18227-6*) Turtleback.

***Postal Workers.** unabridged ed. Paulette Bourgeois. (In My Neighborhood Ser.). (Illus.). 32p. (J). (gr. k-3). 2000. pap. 5.95 (*1-55074-785-1*, Pub. by Kids Can Pr) Genl Dist Srvs.

Postal Workers. unabridged ed. Paulette Bourgeois & Kim LaFave. LC 98-93196. (In My Neighborhood Ser.). (Illus.). 32p. (J). (ps-2). 1998. 12.95 (*1-55074-504-2*, Pub. by Kids Can Pr) Genl Dist Srvs.

Postal Workers: A to Z. Jean Johnson. (Walker's Community Helpers Ser.). (Illus.). 48p. (J). (gr. 1-3). 1987. 11.95 (*0-8027-6663-3*); lib. bdg. 12.85 (*0-8027-6664-1*) Walker & Co.

Postal Workers Take Care of Mail. Carol Greene. LC 97-4239. (Community Helpers Ser.). (Illus.). 32p. (J). (gr. k-4). 1997. lib. bdg. 21.36 (*1-56766-403-2*) Childs World.

***Postbaccalaureate Futures: New Markets, Resources & Credentials.** Ed. by Kay J. Kohl & Jules B. LaPidus. LC 00-21939. (Series on Higher Education). 256p. 2000. boxed set 34.95 (*1-57356-360-9*) Oryx Pr.

Postbasic & Graduate Education for Nurses. (EURO Reports & Studies: No. 99). 38p. 1985. pap. text 6.00 (*92-890-1265-X*, 1330099) World Health.

Postbus Country: Glimpses of Rural Scotland. Joan Burnie. (Illus.). 128p. 1995. 24.95 (*0-86241-484-9*, Pub. by Canongate Books) Interlink Pub.

P

Postcard. Elizabeth Kerlikowske. Ed. & Illus. by Robert Bixby. 37p. (Orig.). 1990. pap. 6.00 (*0-9624453-1-2*) March Street Pr.

Postcard. Beverly Lewis. LC 99-6378. 1999. pap. 15.99 (*0-7642-2225-2*); text 15.99 (*0-7642-2224-4*) Bethany Hse.

Postcard. Beverly Lewis. LC 99-6378. 288p. 1999. pap. text 10.99 (*0-7642-2211-2*) Bethany Hse.

*__Postcard.__ Beverly R. Lewis. LC 00-42579. 2000. write for info. (*0-7862-2713-3*) Thorndike Pr.

Postcard Book #13, Best Of Tales, 13. Howard Roffman. 1999. pap. text 8.95 (*3-86187-138-6*) B Gmunder.

*__Postcard Century.__ Tom Phillips. LC 00-10117. (Illus.). 2000p. 2000. pap. 29.95 (*0-500-97590-6*, Pub. by Thames Hudson) Norton.

Postcard-Chesapeake Bay. BrownTrout Publishing Company Staff. (Illus.). 1996. pap. 7.95 (*1-56313-808-5*) BrownTrout Pubs Inc.

*__Postcard from Dublin.__ John McKernan. 32p. 1999. pap. 5.00 (*1-880743-13-2*, Pub. by Dead Metaphor) SPD-Small Pr Dist.

Postcard from Graceland. Angel T. August. Ed. by Martha R. Carr. 267p. (Orig.). 1994. pap. 14.95 (*0-9638639-1-6*) Nimrod Hse.

Postcard from Heaven. Phyllis J. Sloan. (Illus.). (J). 1990. 3.00 (*0-940248-81-6*) Guild Pr.

Postcard from Hell. Rex Dancer. LC 94-40420. 1995. 21.00 (*0-671-88009-8*) S&S Trade.

Postcard from Hell: Andy Derain Novel. Rex Dancer. 320p. 1995. 22.00 (*0-684-80362-3*) S&S Trade.

Postcard from Hong Kong. David B. Thurston. (Illus.). 99p. 1997. 26.00 (*962-7283-17-7*, Pub. by FormAsia) Weatherhill.

Postcard from Kashmir. Agha S. Ali. Ed. by Stanley H. Barkan. Tr. by Jagan N. Azed. (Review Chapbook Ser.: No. 23: Indian (Urdu) Poetry 1). (ENG & URD., Illus.). 32p. 1991. 15.00 (*0-89304-885-2*, CCC199); 15.00 (*0-89304-887-9*); pap. 5.00 (*0-89304-886-0*); pap. 5.00 (*0-89304-888-7*) Cross-Cultrl NY.

*__Postcard from Madison, Vol. 1.__ Stephanie Jutt. 1999. audio compact disk 14.95 (*0-9658834-3-4*) U of Wis Pr.

*__Postcard from Madison, Vol. 2.__ Stephanie Jutt. 1999. audio compact disk 14.95 (*0-9658834-4-2*) U of Wis Pr.

*__Postcard from Paul: The Letter of Paul to Philemon.__ Timothy Cross. 75p. 1999. pap. 8.99 (*1-84030-050-7*) Ambassador Prodns Ltd.

Postcard from the Shore. Luci Shaw. LC 85-14317. (Wheaton Literary Ser.). 95p. 1985. pap. 5.99 (*0-87788-686-5*, H Shaw Pubs) Waterbrook Pr.

Postcard Graphics: Designs from Around the World. Compiled by Rockport Publishers Staff. (Motif Design Ser.). (Illus.). 160p. 1997. 34.99 (*1-56496-334-9*) Rockport Pubs.

Postcard Home. Robert Minhinnick. Ed. by Meic Stephens. (Changing Wales Ser.). 36p. 1994. pap. 11.95 (*0-8464-4743-6*) Beekman Pubs.

Postcard Journey along the Upper Mississippi. Robert Stumm. LC 97-6093. (Illus.). 248p. 1997. pap. 16.95 (*0-87243-235-1*) Templegate.

*__Postcard Memoir.__ Lawrence Sutin. (Illus.). 228p. 2000. pap. 23.95 (*1-55597-304-3*, Pub. by Graywolf) SPD-Small Pr Dist.

Postcard-National Museum. Smithsonian Institute Press Staff. 1988. pap. 49.50 (*0-87474-773-2*) Smithsonian.

Postcard Pest. Patricia Reilly Giff. (Polk Street Special Ser.). 1994. 9.09 (*0-606-06677-2*, Pub. by Turtleback) Demco.

Postcard Pest: Polk Street Special, No. 3. Patricia Reilly Giff. 112p. (J). (ps-3). 1994. pap. 3.99 (*0-440-40973-X*) Dell.

Postcard Price Guide. 2nd ed. Joseph L. Mashburn. Ed. by Emma H. Mashburn. (Illus.). 464p. 1994. pap. 16.95 (*1-885940-00-9*) Colonial House.

Postcard Price Guide. 3rd ed. Joseph L. Mashburn. LC 96-38126. 1997. pap. 19.95 (*1-885940-03-3*) Colonial House.

Postcard Projects: Creative Ideas for Studying Our 50 States. Barbara Shepard & Linda Wilbur. 160p. teacher ed. 14.99 (*0-86653-836-4*, GA1527) Good Apple.

Postcard to Heaven. Duane Parrish. LC 93-84140. 150p. (Orig.). 1994. pap. 9.95 (*0-89221-235-7*) New Leaf.

Postcard to the Future. Paul Higbee. 24p. (Orig.). 1999. pap. 5.95 (*0-9646798-2-5*) Mt Rushmore.

Postcard Views of Louisville from 1900 to 1920: A Picture Postcard History. Gene Blasi. (Illus.). 107p. 1994. pap. write for info. (*0-9645406-1-4*) G Blasi.

Postcard-Washington. BrownTrout Publishing Company Staff. (Illus.). 1996. pap. 7.95 (*1-56313-857-3*) BrownTrout Pubs Inc.

Postcard-Wyoming. Browntrout Publishers Staff. 1996. pap. 7.95 (*1-56313-859-X*) BrownTrout Pubs Inc.

Postcardbook No. 2: With 30 Postcards. Bel Ami. (Illus.). 1997. pap. text 7.95 (*3-86187-109-2*) B Gmunder.

Postcardbook #1: With 30 Postcards. Thoma Benno. (Illus.). 1997. pap. 7.95 (*3-86187-108-4*) B Gmunder.

Postcards. Diane Allmen. 1991. pap. 9.95 (*0-87637-802-5*) Hse Collectbls.

Postcards. Barbara Cole. 24p. 1998. write for info. (*0-9667655-1-6*) Beautifulswimmer.

Postcards. C. S. Giscombe. LC 77-13756. 57p. 1977. 3.50 (*0-87886-089-4*, Greenfld Rev Pr) Greenfld Rev Lit.

Postcards. James Prideaux. 1970. pap. 3.25 (*0-8222-0907-1*) Dramatists Play.

Postcards. E. Annie Proulx. 320p. 1994. per. 12.00 (*0-684-80087-X*) S&S Trade.

Postcards. E. Annie Proulx. 1996. 21.50 (*0-684-83368-9*) S&S Trade.

Postcards: An Advanced Listening & Notetaking Workbook. Susanna L. Minton. LC 98-168408. (Illus.). 200p. (C). 1998. pap. text 18.95 (*0-472-08493-3*, 08493) U of Mich Pr.

Postcards Collector's Guide. Jane Wood. (Illus.). 176p. (Orig.). 1985. pap. 9.95 (*0-89145-241-9*, 1441) L-W Inc.

Postcards for People in Love. Claire Cloninger. LC 95-2866. 128p. 1995. 12.99 (*0-8499-1208-3*) Word Pub.

Postcards for People Who Hurt. Claire Cloninger. LC 95-2867. 128p. 1995. 12.99 (*0-8499-1197-4*) Word Pub.

Postcards from a "Mo Betta" Time: When We All Believed in Santa Claus. unabridged ed. Mary E. Goodman. (Illus.). 55p. (Orig.). 1996. pap. 8.00 (*0-927562-23-5*) Levite Apache.

*__Postcards from a Stranger.__ Sally Stewart. 224p. 1999. 25.00 (*0-7278-2252-7*, Pub. by Severn Hse) Chivers N Amer.

*__Postcards from a Stranger.__ large type ed. Sally Stewart. 320p. 2000. 31.99 (*0-7505-1468-X*, Pub. by Mgna Lrg Print) Ulverscroft.

Postcards from Alphaville. Raphael Rubenstein. 1999. pap. 13.95 (*1-889097-35-7*, Pub. by Hard Pr MA) Consort Bk Sales.

Postcards from America. Dan Perjovschi. (Illus.). 70p. (Orig.). 1995. pap. write for info. (*1-878635-02-6*) Pont La Vue Pr.

Postcards from America Series: The White House Mystery, High Time in New York, Windy City Whirl, Trouble in the Black Hills, San Francisco Adventure. Penn Mullin. Ed. by Betty Lou Kratoville. (Illus.). (Orig.). (J). (gr. 4-12). 1992. pap. 17.00 (*0-87879-957-5*, 957-5) High Noon Bks.

Postcards from Aunt Bee's Mayberry Cookbook. Jim Clark & Kenneth Beck. (Illus.). 1993. pap. 8.95 (*1-55853-231-5*) Rutledge Hill Pr.

Postcards from Brazil. Zoe Dawson. LC 95-10301. (Postcards From Ser.). (J). 1995. lib. bdg. 21.40 (*0-8172-4013-6*) Raintree Steck-V.

Postcards from Brazil. Zoe Dawson. LC 95-10301. (Postcards from... Ser.). (Illus.). 32p. (J). (gr. 2-4). 1995. pap. 4.95 (*0-8172-4234-1*) Raintree Steck-V.

Postcards from Charlie: Aboard, No. 2. K. Wallace. (Illus.). (J). 1997. mass mkt. 6.95 (*0-340-66475-4*, Pub. by Hodder & Stought Ltd) Trafalgar.

Postcards from Europe Series, 5 bks. Penn Mullin. Ed. by Betty Lou Kratoville. (Illus.). 48p. (J). (gr. 6-10). 1994. pap. text 17.00 (*0-87879-976-1*) High Noon Bks.

Postcards from Europe Workbook. Lucy Collingwood. Ed. by Betty Lou Kratoville. 64p. (Orig.). (J). (gr. 4 up). 1995. pap., student ed. 14.00 (*0-87879-995-8*) High Noon Bks.

*__Postcards from France.__ Megan M. Libby. LC 96-30924. 160p. 1998. mass mkt. 4.99 (*0-06-101170-3*) HarpC.

Postcards from Germany. Helen Arnold. LC 95-16215. (Postcards From Ser.). (J). 1995. lib. bdg. 21.40 (*0-8172-4008-X*) Raintree Steck-V.

Postcards from Germany. Helen Arnold. LC 95-16215. (Postcards from... Ser.). (Illus.). 32p. (J). (gr. 2-4). 1995. pap. 4.95 (*0-8172-4229-5*) Raintree Steck-V.

Postcards from God. Imtiaz Dharker. LC 97-223654. 160p. 1997. pap. 19.95 (*1-85224-407-0*, Pub. by Bloodaxe Bks) Dufour.

Postcards from Heaven. Claire Cloninger. 1997. pap. 12.99 (*0-8499-4074-5*) Word Pub.

Postcards from Life's Little Instruction Book. H. Jackson Brown, Jr. (Illus.). 30p. 1993. pap. 8.95 (*1-55853-233-1*) Rutledge Hill Pr.

Postcards from Live & Learn & Pass It On. H. Jackson Brown, Jr. (Illus.). 30p. 1994. pap. 8.95 (*1-55853-285-4*) Rutledge Hill Pr.

*__Postcards from Manhattan: Sights & Sentiments from the Last Century.__ George L. Lankevich. 2000. pap. 8.95 (*0-7570-0101-7*) Square One.

*__Postcards from Nebraska: The Stories Behind the Stories.__ (Illus.). 2000. pap. write for info. (*0-934904-40-5*, 40-5) J & L Lee.

Postcards from Paradise Vol. 1: Romancing Key West. 2nd rev. ed. June Keith. LC 94-69012. (Illus.). 256p. 1997. pap. 19.95 (*0-9643434-8-7*) Palm Island.

Postcards from Paul. H. Scrimshire. 1995. 4.99 (*1-85792-086-4*, Pub. by Christian Focus) Spring Arbor Dist.

Postcards from Pinsk. Larry Duberstein. LC 90-53324. 224p. 1991. 22.00 (*1-877946-04-4*) Permanent Pr.

Postcards from Pluto: A Tour of the Solar System. Loreen Leedy. (Illus.). 32p. (J). (gr. k-3). 1993. pap. 6.95 (*0-8234-1237-7*); lib. bdg. 16.95 (*0-8234-1000-5*) Holiday.

Postcards from P.S. I Love You. H. Jackson Brown, Jr. (Illus.). 1993. pap. 8.95 (*1-55853-232-3*) Rutledge Hill Pr.

Postcards from South America, 5 bks., Set. Penn Mullin. Ed. by Betty Lou Kratoville. (Postcards Ser.). (Illus.). 48p. (Orig.). (J). (gr. 3-10). 1995. pap. text 17.00 (*1-57128-014-6*, 014-6) Acad Therapy.

*__Postcards from the Basque Country: A Journey of Enchantment & Imagination.__ Beth Nelson. LC 98-55675. (Illus.). 104p. 1999. text 19.95 (*1-55670-893-9*) Stewart Tabori & Chang.

Postcards from the Edge. Carrie Fisher. 1990. mass mkt. 5.99 (*0-671-72473-8*) PB.

Postcards from the Ledge: Collected Mountaineering Writings of Greg Child. Greg Child. LC 98-21175. (Illus.). 224p. 1998. 22.95 (*0-89886-584-0*) Mountaineers.

*__Postcards from the Ledge: Collected Mountaineering Writings of Greg Child.__ Greg Child. (Illus.). 224p. 2000. reprint ed. pap. 16.95 (*0-89886-753-3*) Mountaineers.

Postcards from the Moon. William Steinkellner. LC 99-47969. (Illus.). 192p. 2000. pap. 12.00 (*1-880284-39-1*, Pub. by J Daniel) SCB Distributors.

Postcards from the Net. John Casimir. 1997. pap. text 16.95 (*1-86448-280-X*, Pub. by Allen & Unwin Pty) IPG Chicago.

Postcards from the Shoulder. Scott M. Snyder. 96p. 1999. pap. 11.00 (*0-8059-4746-9*) Dorrance.

Postcards from the Trenches: Negotiating the Space Between Modernism & the First World War. Allyson Booth. (Illus.). 200p. 1996. text 42.00 (*0-19-510211-8*) OUP.

Postcards from the Underground: Portraits of the Beat Era. Photos by Larry Keenan. LC 99-31706. (Illus.). 70p. 1999. pap. 8.95 (*0-87286-365-4*, Pub. by City Lights) Subterranean Co.

Postcards from the '80s: 80 Lists to Remember. Stephanie Bennett & Amy Hall. LC 98-53692. 1999. 10.95 (*0-8362-9270-7*) Andrews & McMeel.

*__Postcards from Times Square: Sights & Sentiments from the Last Century.__ George L. Lankevich. 2000. pap. 8.95 (*0-7570-0100-9*) Square One.

Postcards from Treasures in the Trunk. Mary B. Cross. (Illus.). 1993. pap. 8.95 (*1-55853-230-7*) Rutledge Hill Pr.

Postcards in the Library: Invaluable Visual Resources. Ed. by Norman D. Stevens. LC 95-46638. (Popular Culture in Libraries Ser.: Vol. 3, No. 2). 233p. 1996. 24.95 (*1-56024-776-2*) Haworth Pr.

Postcards of Hitler's Germany, 1923-1936, Vol. 1. R. James Bender. LC 98-202382. (Illus.). 368p. 1996. pap. 54.95 (*0-912138-60-2*) Bender Pub CA.

Postcards of Hitler's Germany 1937-1939, Vol. 2. R. James Bender. LC 98-202382. (Illus.). 360p. 1998. 54.95 (*0-912138-61-0*) Bender Pub CA.

*__Postcards of Maryland: Sports.__ Ray Frager. 50 p. 2000. pap. 9.95 (*1-893116-15-8*) Baltimore Sun.

*__Postcards of North Dakota.__ Larry Aosen. (Postcard History Ser.). 1999. pap. 18.99 (*0-7385-0161-1*) Arcadia Publng.

Postcards of Old Key West. Shelley B. Malone & Phyllis B. Strunk. (Illus.). 64p. (Orig.). 1989. pap. write for info. (*0-318-65765-1*) S B Malone & P B Strunk.

Postcards of the Falkland Islands: A Catalogue: 1900-1950. Ed. by Henry Heyburn & Frances Heyburn. (Illus.). 256p. (C). 1990. pap. 45.00 (*0-902633-99-6*, Pub. by Picton) St Mut.

Postcards of the Falkland Islands: Supplement to the Catalogue, 1900-1950. Henry Heyburn & Frances Heyburn. 107p. 1990. 39.00 (*0-7855-2715-X*, Pub. by Picton) St Mut.

Postcards on Parade. Kenward Elmslie. 138p. (Orig.). 1993. pap. 12.50 (*0-917453-30-1*) Bamberger.

*__Postcards to Father Abraham.__ Catherine Lewis. LC 99-27005. (Illus.). 304p. (J). 2000. 17.00 (*0-689-82852-7*) Atheneum Yung Read.

Postcolonial African Philosophy: A Critical Reader. Ed. by Emmanuel C. Eze. LC 96-24388. 320p. (C). 1996. text 60.95 (*0-631-20339-7*); pap. text 26.95 (*0-631-20340-0*) Blackwell Pubs.

Postcolonial African Writers: A Bio-Bibliographical Critical Sourcebook. Pushpa N. Parekh & Siga F. Jagne. LC 97-5856. 560p. 1998. lib. bdg. 85.00 (*0-313-29056-3*, Greenwood Pr) Greenwood.

*__Postcolonial America.__ C. Richard King. LC 99-6692. 2000. 23.95 (*0-252-06852-1*) U of Ill Pr.

Postcolonial Bible. Ed. by R. S. Sugirtharajah. (Bible & Postcolonialism Ser.: Vol. 1). 204p. 1998. pap. 19.95 (*1-85075-898-0*, Pub. by Sheffield Acad) CUP Services.

Postcolonial Crescent: Islam's Impact on Contemporary Literature. Ed. by John Hawley. LC 97-17131. X, 291p. (C). 1998. pap. text 32.95 (*0-8204-3794-8*) P Lang Pubng.

Postcolonial Criticism. B. J. Moore-Gilbert et al. LC 97-255. (Critical Readers Ser.). 312p. (C). 1997. pap. 29.06 (*0-582-23798-X*) Addison-Wesley.

Postcolonial Criticism. B. J. Moore-Gilbert et al. LC 97-255. (Critical Readers Ser.). (C). 1998. text 68.44 (*0-582-23797-1*) Longman.

Postcolonial Developments: Agriculture in the Making of Modern India. Akhil Gupta. LC 97-43036. 1998. 64.95 (*0-8223-2183-1*) Duke.

Postcolonial Developments: Agriculture in the Making of Modern India. Akhil Gupta. LC 97-43036. (Illus.). xv, 409p. 1998. pap. 21.95 (*0-8223-2213-7*) Duke.

Postcolonial Discourse & Changing Cultural Contexts: Theory & Criticism, 64. Ed. by Gita Rajan & Radhika Mohanram. LC 95-16019. (Contributions to the Study of World Literature Ser.: Vol. 64). 240p. 1995. 62.95 (*0-313-29693-6*, Greenwood Pr) Greenwood.

*__Postcolonial Feminist Interpretation of the Bible.__ Musa W. Dube Shomanah. LC 00-8998. 2000. pap. 29.99 (*0-8272-2963-1*) Chalice Pr.

Postcolonial Identities in Africa. Ed. by Richard P. Werbner & Terence Ranger. LC 96-8379. (Postcolonial Encounters Ser.). 256p. (C). 1996. text 65.00 (*1-85649-415-2*, Pub. by Zed Books); text 25.00 (*1-85649-416-0*) Zed Books.

Postcolonial Identities in Africa. Ed. by Richard Werbner & Terence Ranger. 304p. 1997. pap. 59.95 (*1-919713-04-2*, U Pr W Africa) Intl Scholars.

Postcolonial Insecurities: India, Sri Lanka & the Question of Nationhood. Sankaran Krishna. LC 99-16845. (Borderlines Ser.: Vol. 15). 296p. 1999. pap. 22.95 (*0-8166-3330-4*, Pub. by U of Minn Pr); lib. bdg. 57.95 (*0-8166-3329-0*, Pub. by U of Minn Pr) Chicago Distribution Ctr.

Postcolonial Literature & the Biblical Call for Justice. Ed. by Susan V. Gallagher. LC 94-17078. 288p. 1994. text 37.50 (*0-87805-723-4*) U Pr of Miss.

Postcolonial Literatures: Achebe, Ngugi, Desai, Walcott. Ed. by Michael Parker & Roger Starkey. LC 95-9734. (New Casebooks Ser.). 1995. text 45.00 (*0-312-12664-6*) St Martin.

*__Postcolonial Masquerades: Culture & Politics in Literature, Film, Video & Photography.__ Niti Sampat-Patel. LC 00-42950. (Literary Criticism & Cultural Theory Ser.). (Illus.). 2000. write for info. (*0-8153-3649-7*) Garland.

Postcolonial Representations: Women, Literature, Identity. Francoise Lionnet. (Reading Women Writing Ser.). 208p. 1995. text 35.00 (*0-8014-2984-6*); pap. text 13.95 (*0-8014-8180-5*) Cornell U Pr.

Postcolonial Space(s) Ed. by Gulsum B. Nalbantoglu & Wong C. Thai. LC 97-10109. (Illus.). 128p. (Orig.). 1997. pap. 19.95 (*1-56898-075-2*) Princeton Arch.

Postcolonial Subjects: Francophone Women Writers. Ed. by Mary J. Green et al. LC 95-43890. 1996. pap. 19.95 (*0-8166-2629-4*); text 49.95 (*0-8166-2628-6*) U of Minn Pr.

Postcolonial Theory: A Bibliography. Joan Nordquist. (Social Theory: Vol. 50). 72p. 1998. pap. 20.00 (*0-937855-99-5*) Ref Rsch Serv.

Postcolonial Theory: A Critical Introduction. Leela Gandhi. LC 97-32402. 192p. 1998. pap. 45.00 (*0-231-11272-6*) Col U Pr.

Postcolonial Theory: A Critical Introduction. Leela Gandhi. LC 97-32402. 192p. 1998. pap. 18.50 (*0-231-11273-4*) Col U Pr.

Postcolonial Theory: Contexts, Practices, Politics. Bart Moore-Gilbert. LC 97-16324. 1997. pap. 20.00 (*1-85984-034-5*, Pub. by Verso) Norton.

*__Postcolonial Theory & Criticism.__ Ed. by Laura Chrisman & Benita Parry. (Essays & Studies). 192p. 1999. 55.00 (*0-85991-554-9*, DS Brewer) Boydell & Brewer.

*__Postcolonial Theory & the United States: Race, Ethnicity & Literature.__ Ed. by Amritjit Singh & Peter Schmidt. 400p. 2000. text 50.00 (*1-57806-251-9*); pap. text 26.00 (*1-57806-252-7*) U Pr of Miss.

*__Postcolonial Theory II - Literature & the Arts: A Bibliography.__ Ed. by Joan Nordquist. (Social Theory: Vol. 55). 72p. 1999. pap. 20.00 (*1-892068-09-5*) Ref Rsch Serv.

Postcolonialism: An Historical Introduction. Robert J. Young. 208p. 1999. 59.95 (*0-631-20070-3*); pap. 24.95 (*0-631-20071-1*) Blackwell Pubs.

Postcolonialism: Theory, Practice of Process? Ato Quayson. LC 99-25741. 208p. (C). 2000. text 54.95 (*0-7456-1712-3*, Pub. by Polity Pr) Blackwell Pubs.

Postcolonialism: Theory, Practice or Process? Ato Quayson. LC 99-25741. 208p. (C). 2000. pap. text 22.95 (*0-7456-1713-1*, Pub. by Polity Pr) Blackwell Pubs.

Postcolonialism My Living. A. Mukherjee. 1998. pap. 21.95 (*0-920661-75-0*) TSAR Pubns.

*__Postcolonizing the Commonwealth: Studies in Literature & Culture.__ Ed. by Rowland Smith. 222p. 2000. 44.95 (*0-88920-352-0*) Wilfrid Laurier.

Postcolumbian Culture History in the Northern Columbia Plateau A. D. 1500-1900. Sarah K. Campbell. LC 90-48883. (Evolution of North American Indians Ser.). 246p. 1990. text 10.00 (*0-8240-2224-6*) Garland.

*__Postcommunism.__ Richard Sakwa. LC 99-29821. (Concepts in the Social Sciences Ser.). 153p. 1999. pap. 19.95 (*0-335-20057-5*) OpUniv Pr.

Postcommunism & the Body Politic: Genders 22. Ed. by Ellen E. Berry. 380p. (C). 1995. text 55.00 (*0-8147-1247-9*); pap. text 19.50 (*0-8147-1248-7*) NYU Pr.

Postcommunist Presidents. Ed. by Ray Taras. LC 96-50024. 260p. (C). 1997. text 59.95 (*0-521-58282-2*); pap. text 19.95 (*0-521-58765-4*) Cambridge U Pr.

Postconflict Elections, Democratization & International Assistance. Ed. by Krishna Kumar. LC 98-9423. ix, 265 p. 1998. pap. 22.00 (*1-55587-778-8*); lib. bdg. 49.95 (*1-55587-755-9*) L Rienner.

Postconquest Coyoacan: Nahua-Spanish Relations in Central Mexico, 1519-1650. Rebecca Horn. LC 96-49743. 352p. 1997. 55.00 (*0-8047-2773-2*) Stanford U Pr.

Postconventional Moral Thinking: A Neo-Kohlbergian Approach. James Rest et al. LC 98-43690. 240p. 1999. 49.95 (*0-8058-3285-8*) L Erlbaum Assocs.

Postcranial Adaptation in Nonhuman Primates. Ed. by Daniel L. Gebo. LC 93-16550. (Illus.). 342p. (C). 1993. pap. 35.00 (*0-87580-559-0*); lib. bdg. 50.00 (*0-87580-179-X*) N Ill U Pr.

Postcranial Descriptions of Ilaria & Ngapakaldia, Vombatiformes, Marsupialia, & the Phylogeny of the Vombatiforms Based on Postcranial Morphology. Carol J. Munson. (Publications in Zoology: Vol. 125). (C). 1992. pap. 12.00 (*0-520-09772-6*, Pub. by U CA Pr) Cal Prin Full Svc.

Postcultural Theory. Eve T. Bannett. 240p. 1994. pap. 15.95 (*1-56924-891-5*) Marlowe & Co.

Postdivorce Family: Children, Parenting & Society Ross A. Thompson & Paul R. Amato. LC 99-6018. 1999. write for info. (*0-7619-1490-0*) Sage.

Postdivorce Family: Children, Parenting & Society. Ed. by Ross A. Thompson & Paul R. Amato. LC 99-6018. 245p. 1999. 55.00 (*0-7619-1489-7*) Sage.

Postemotional Society. Stjepan G. Mestrovic. 224p. 1996. 69.95 (*0-7619-5128-8*); pap. 24.95 (*0-7619-5129-6*) Sage.

*__Poster Allure Vol. XXX: PAI XXX.__ Jack Rennert. (Illus.). 192p. 2000. 50.00 (*1-929530-15-3*) Pstr Auctns Intl.

Poster Annual 1999. B. Martin Pedersen. 256p. 1999. text 70.00 (*1-888001-62-3*, Pub. by Graphis US) Watsn-Guptill.

*__Poster Annual 2000.__ B. Martin Pedersen. (Illus.). 2000. pap. 70.00 (*1-888001-67-4*) Graphis US.

Poster Art. Compiled by Rockport Publishers Editorial Staff. (Design Library). (Illus.). 80p. 1996. pap. 14.99 (*1-56496-290-3*) Rockport Pubs.

P

An Asterisk (*) at the beginning of an entry indicates that the title is appearing for the first time.

Poster Art of the Airlines: Featuring Pan American Airways & Its Contemporaries. W. Donald Thomas. LC 88-90329. (Illus.). 64p. 1989. pap. 10.00 (0-9618642-2-2) D Thomas.

Poster Brochure Little. 6th ed. Ed. by College. 1997. pap. text 11.00 (0-673-54296-3) P-H.

Poster Catalogue. Vicki Wray. Ed. by Nancy McGaw. (Illus.). 447p. 1985. 40.00 (0-9613932-0-3) B McGaw Graphics.

Poster Classics, Vol. 17. Jack Rennert. (Illus.). 1993. 40.00 (1-929530-02-1) Pstr Auctns Intl.

Poster Delights, Vol. XXIII. Jack Rennert. (Illus.). 1996. 40.00 (0-9664201-6-0) Pstr Auctns Intl.

Poster in History. Max Gallo. 22.98 (1-55521-410-X) Bk Sales Inc.

Poster Jubilee, Vol. 13. Jack Rennert. (Illus.). 1991. 40.00 (1-929530-05-6) Pstr Auctns Intl.

Poster Paints. M. Angels Comella. LC 96-33018. (Painting & Drawing Ser.). (J). 1997. pap. 6.95 (0-382-39849-1, Silver Pr NJ); lib. bdg. 15.95 (0-382-39850-5, Silver Pr NJ) Silver Burdett Pr.

Poster Palette, Vol. 9. Jack Rennert. (Illus.). 1989. 40.00 (1-929530-09-9) Pstr Auctns Intl.

Poster Panache, Vol. 12. Jack Rennert. (Illus.). 1991. 40.00 (1-929530-06-4) Pstr Auctns Intl.

Poster Panorama, Vol. XX. Jack Rennert. 1995. 40.00 (0-9664201-9-5) Pstr Auctns Intl.

*Poster Papers: International Conference on Atomic & Molecular Data & Their Applications (Icamdata 97) at the National Institute of Standards & Technology, Gaithersburg, Maryland. Wolfgang L. Wiese. 287p. 1998. per. 23.00 (0-16-056744-0) USGPO.

Poster Parade, Vol. 16. Jack Rennert. (Illus.). 1993. 40.00 (1-929530-03-X) Pstr Auctns Intl.

Poster Passion, Vol. 11. Jack Rennert. (Illus.). 1990. 40.00 (1-929530-07-2) Pstr Auctns Intl.

Poster Pizzazz, Vol. 5. Jack Rennert. (Illus.). 1987. 40.00 (1-929530-11-0) Pstr Auctns Intl.

Poster Pleasures, Vol. XXIV. Jack Rennert. (Illus.). 1997. 40.00 (0-9664201-5-2) Pstr Auctns Intl.

Poster Presentations. (Conference Preprints Ser.). 1997. 51.00 (1-896742-15-7) Pulp & Paper.

*Poster Presentations, Vol. C. (Conference Preprints Ser.). 272p. 1998. 51.00 (1-896742-36-X) Pulp & Paper.

*Poster Presentations, Vol. B. (Conference Preprints Ser.). 259p. 1998. 51.00 (1-896742-35-1) Pulp & Paper.

Poster Price Almanac. John Kisch. (Illus.). 544p. 1997. 39.95 (0-9661482-0-7) Separate Cinema.

Poster Prices V. 152p. 1999. 50.00 (0-9664201-3-6) Pstr Auctns Intl.

*Poster Proceedings for the 9th International World Wide Web Conference. (Illus.). 140p. 2000. pap. write for info. (1-930792-01-8) Foretec Sem.

Poster Song Book. rev. ed. Ralph McCoy. Ed. by Sandra Sladkey. (Illus.). 60p. (J). (gr. 1-5). 1994. pap. 23.95 (1-885819-05-6) His Songs.

Poster Treasures, Vol. 8. Jack Rennert. (Illus.). 1989. 40.00 (1-929530-10-2) Pstr Auctns Intl.

Poster Vogue, Vol. XXVIII. Jack Rennert. (Illus.). 176p. Date not set. 40.00 (0-9664201-2-8) Pstr Auctns Intl.

Posterbook. Allan Weiss. (NHL Coolest Books on Earth Ser.). 16p. (J). (gr. 1 up). 1999. pap. 8.99 (1-58184-036-5) Somerville Hse.

*Posterbook: Goalies. Allan Weiss. (NHL Coolest Books on Earth Ser.). (Illus.). 16p. (YA). (gr. 1 up). 1999. pap. text 8.99 (1-58184-078-0) Somerville Hse.

Posterior Analytics. Aristotle. Tr. & Comment by Hippocrates G. Apostle. LC 81-80233. (Apostle Translations of Aristotle's Works: Vol. 4). 328p. (C). 1981. 35.00 (0-9602870-6-X); pap. 17.00 (0-9602870-7-8) Peripatetic.

Posterior Analytics. 2nd ed. Aristotle. Tr. & Comment by Jonathan Barnes. (Clarendon Aristotle Ser.). (Illus.). 326p. (C). 1994. 60.00 (0-19-824088-0, 6050); pap. text 26.00 (0-19-824089-9) OUP.

Posterior Analytics, Bks. 1 & 2. Aristotle. Tr. by E. S. Forster & Hugh Tredennick. (Loeb Classical Library: No. 391). (ENG & GRE.). (C). 15.50 (0-674-99430-2) HUP.

Posterior Cervical Spine Surgery. William Dillin & Frederick A. Simeone. LC 97-31574. (Principles & Techniques in Spine Surgery Ser.). 256p. 1997. text 120.00 (0-7817-1005-7) Lppncott W & W.

Posterior-Chamber Lens Implant Surgery. Henry K. Yang & Oram R. Kline, Jr. LC 81-40609. (Illus.). 119p. 1983. reprint ed. pap. 36.90 (0-7837-9535-1, 206028400005) Bks Demand.

Posterior Circulation Disease: Clinical Findings, Diagnosis, & Management. Louis R. Caplan. (Illus.). 700p. 1996. 165.00 (0-86542-298-2) Blackwell Sci.

*Posterior Cruciate Ligament Injuries: A Pratical Guide to Managemet. Ed. by G. Fanelli. (Illus.). 304p. 2000. 140.00 (0-387-98573-5) Spr-Verlag.

Posterior Fossa, Spinal Cord & Peripheral Nerve Disease see Operative Neurosurgery

Posterior Fossa Tumors. Ed. by Anthony J. Raimondi et al. LC 92-49986. (Principles of Pediatric Neurosurgery Ser.). 1993. 198.00 (0-387-97915-8) Spr-Verlag.

Posterior Pituitary: Hormone Secretion in Health & Disease. Ed. by Peter H. Baylis & Paul L. Padfield. LC 85-16315. (Basic & Clinical Endocrinology Ser.: No. 6). (Illus.). 411p. reprint ed. pap. 127.50 (0-7837-0865-3, 204117300019) Bks Demand.

Posterior Segment Intraocular Inflammation - Guidelines. John V. Forrester et al. Ed. by Shigeaki Ohno. (Illus.). xiii, 202p. 1998. 57.00 (90-6299-167-X) Kugler Pubns.

Posterior Uveitis, Pt. 2. Tabbara. 1995. 39.00 (0-316-06077-1, Little Brwn Med Div) Lppncott W & W.

Posterior Uveitis: Diagnosis & Management. Khalid F. Tabbara & Robert B. Nussenblatt. LC 94-32315. (Illus.). 160p. 1994. text 110.00 (0-7506-9599-4) Buttrwrth-Heinemann.

*Posteriori Error Estimation in Finite Element Analysis. Mark Ainsworth & J. Tinsley Oden. (Pure & Applied Mathematics: A Wiley-Interscience Series of Texts, Monographs & Tracts). 256p. 2000. 84.95 (0-471-29411-X) Wiley.

Posterity & Strategic Policy: A Moral Assessment of Nuclear Policy Options. Alison Bailey. Ed. by Jeanine Czubaroff & Robert N. Ginsburg. LC 89-33902. (Social Philosophy Research Institute Bks.: No. 7). 162p. (Orig.). (C). 1989. pap. text 26.00 (0-8191-7476-9); lib. bdg. 45.00 (0-8191-7475-0) U Pr of Amer.

Posterity Lost: Progress, Ideology, & the Decline of the American Family. Richard T. Gill. LC 96-49901. (Illus.). 352p. 1997. 29.95 (0-8476-8379-6) Rowman.

Posterity Lost: Progress, Ideology, & the Decline of the American Family. Richard T. Gill. 352p. 1999. pap. 14.95 (0-8476-8380-X, Pub. by Rowman) Natl Bk Netwk.

Postermania, No. XXVI. Jack Rennert. (Illus.). 160p. 1998. 50.00 (0-9664201-0-1) Pstr Auctns Intl.

Postern of Fate. Agatha Christie. 304p. 1991. mass mkt. 5.99 (0-06-100276-3, Harp PBks) HarpC.

*Postern of Fate. Agatha Christie. 224p. 2000. mass mkt. 5.99 (0-451-20053-5, Sig) NAL.

Postern of Fate. Agatha Christie. (General Ser.). 1991. 10.09 (0-606-12483-7, Pub. by Turtleback) Demco.

Postern of Fate. large type ed. Agatha Christie. (General Ser.). 376p. 1992. lib. bdg. 19.95 (0-8161-4593-8, G K Hall Lrg Type) Mac Lib Ref.

Posters. 2nd ed. Algimantas Kezys. LC 96-77374. (Illus.). 262p. 1996. 800.00 (1-886060-06-1) Galerija.

Posters: A Concise History. John Barnicoat. (World of Art Ser.). (Illus.). 288p. 1985. pap. 14.95 (0-500-20118-8, Pub. by Thames Hudson) Norton.

Posters a la Miss Piggy with Stickers. Jim Henson. (J). (ps-3). 1997. 5.95 (0-448-41572-0, 752667T, G & D) Peng Put Young Read.

Posters American Style. Therese T. Heyman. LC 97-38050. 1998. 12.34 (0-8109-2780-2, Pub. by Abrams) Time Warner.

Posters American Style. Therese T. Heyman. LC 97-38050. (Illus.). 191p. 1998. 35.00 (0-8109-3749-2, Pub. by Abrams) Time Warner.

*Posters American Style. Therese Thau Heyman. (Illus.). 192p. 2000. 17.98 (0-8109-8202-1) Abrams.

*Posters for the Millennium, Vol. XXIX. Jack Rennert. (Illus.). 378p. 1999. 50.00 (1-929530-13-7) Pstr Auctns Intl.

Posters of GDR Films, 1945-1990. Ed. by Helmut Morsbach & Babett Stach. (Film-Television-Sound Archive Ser.: Vol. 2). 149p. 1991. lib. bdg. 60.00 (3-598-22591-1) K G Saur Verlag.

Posters of Jules Cheret. Jules Cheret & Lucy Broido. (Illus.). 128p. (Orig.). 1980. pap. 10.95 (0-486-24010-X) Dover.

Posters of Jules Cheret: Forty Six Full-Color Plates & an Illustrated Catalogue Raisonne. 2nd enl. rev. ed. Jules Cheret & Lucy Broido. (Illus.). 144p. (Orig.). 1992. pap. 17.95 (0-486-26966-3) Dover.

Posters of the Belle Epoque: The Wine Spectator Collection. Jack Rennert. (Illus.). 256p. Date not set. 75.00 (0-9664202-1-7) Posters Please.

Posters of WPA. Chris DeNoon. (Illus.). 176p. 1987. 39.95 (0-295-96543-6) U of Wash Pr.

Posters, Understanding & Creating Art Book 1. 2nd ed. Goldstein et al. 1991. 135.00 (0-314-90182-5) Thomson Learn.

Posters, Understanding & Creating Art Book 2. 2nd ed. Goldstein et al. 1991. 135.00 (0-314-90349-6) Thomson Learn.

Postethnic America: Beyond Multiculturalism. David A. Hollinger. 224p. 1995. pap. 13.00 (0-465-05992-9, Pub. by Basic) HarpC.

Postethnic America: Beyond Multiculturalism. David A. Hollinger. LC 94-40366. 224p. 1995. 22.00 (0-465-05991-0, Pub. by Basic) HarpC.

Postfeminisms: Feminism, Cultural Theory, & Cultural Forms. Ann Brooks. LC 96-47498. 256p. (C). 1997. pap. 22.99 (0-415-11475-6) Routledge.

Postfeminisms: Feminism, Cultural Theory, & Cultural Forms. Ann Brooks. LC 96-47498. 256p. (C). 1997. 75.00 (0-415-11474-8) Routledge.

*Postfoundationalist Task of Theology: Wolfhart Pannenberg & the New Theological Rationality. F. LeRon Shults. LC 99-46840. xvi, 269p. 1999. pap. 25.00 (0-8028-4686-6) Eerdmans.

Postgastrectomy & Postvagatomy Syndromes. H. D. Becker & W. F. Caspary. (Illus.). 500p. 1980. 108.00 (0-387-09445-8) Spr-Verlag.

Postglacial Vegetational Changes along an Elevational Gradient in the Adirondack Mountains (New York) Stephen T. Jackson. (New York State Museum Bulletin Ser.: No. 465). (Illus.). 29p. 1989. pap. 6.00 (1-55557-182-4) NYS Museum.

Postgraduate Education & Training in Public Health: Proceedings of the WHO Expert Committee, Geneva, 1973. WHO Staff. (Technical Reports: No. 533). 1973. pap. text 5.00 (92-4-120533-4, 1100533) World Health.

Postgraduate Education & Training in the Social Sciences: Processes & Products. Ed. by Robert G. Burgess. (Higher Education Policy Ser.: No. 19). 240p. 1994. 59.95 (1-85302-533-X) Taylor & Francis.

Postgraduate Education for Medical Personnel in the U. S. S. R. Report Prepared by the Participants in a Study Tour Organized by the World Health Organization. (Public Health Papers: No. 39). 52p. 1970. pap. text 4.00 (92-4-130039-6, 1110039) World Health.

Postgraduate Haematology. 4th ed. Ed. by A. Victor Hoffbrand et al. LC 97-18995. 722p. 1998. text 165.00 (0-7506-0583-9) Buttrwrth-Heinemann.

Postgraduate Orthopaedic Fellowships, 1998. AAOS Staff. 400p. 1998. pap. 30.00 (0-89203-206-5) Amer Acad Ortho Surg.

*Postgraduate Psychiatry: Clinical & Scientific Foundations. 2nd ed. Lois Appleby et al. (Illus.). 624p. 2000. pap. 50.00 (0-7506-3503-7) Buttrwrth-Heinemann.

Postgraduate Studies in the Biological Sciences: A Researcher's Companion. R. J. Beynon. 150p. 1993. pap. 20.00 (1-85578-009-7, Pub. by Portland Pr Ltd) Ashgate Pub Co.

Postgraduate Study in the Physical Sciences: A Researcher's Companion. R. W. Munn & Rob J. Beynon. (Illus.). 150p. (Orig.). (C). Date not set. pap. 20.00 (1-85578-078-X, Pub. by Portland Pr Ltd) Ashgate Pub Co.

Postgraduate Surgery: The Candidate's Guide. 2nd ed. M. A. R. Al-Fallouji. LC 97-22534. 688p. 1998. pap. text 155.00 (0-7506-1591-5) Buttrwrth-Heinemann.

Postgraduate Textbook of Clinical Orthopaedics. 2nd ed. N. H. Harris & R. Birch. 1120p. 1995. 250.00 (0-632-02902-1) Blackwell Sci.

Postharvest: An Introduction to the Physiology & Handling of Fruit, Vegetables & Ornamentals. 4th ed. Ron Wills et al. (A CAB International Publication). (Illus.). 280p. 1998. pap. text 45.00 (0-85199-264-1) OUP.

Postharvest Biology & Biotechnology. Ed. by H. O. Hultin & M. Milner. 462p. 1979. 71.00 (0-917678-05-2) Food & Nut Pr.

Postharvest Biotechnology of Cereals. Ed. by D. K. Salunkhe et al. (Postharvest Biotechnology Ser.). 224p. 1985. 127.00 (0-8493-6288-1, SB189, CRC Reprint) Franklin.

Postharvest Biotechnology of Flowers & Ornamental Plants. D. K. Salunkhe et al. (Illus.). 216p. 1989. 112.95 (0-387-19406-1) Spr-Verlag.

Postharvest Biotechnology of Food Legumes. Ed. by D. K. Salunkhe et al. (Postharvest Biotechnology Ser.). 176p. 1985. 101.00 (0-8493-6287-3, SB177, CRC Reprint) Franklin.

Postharvest Biotechnology of Fruits, 2 vols., Vol. 1. D. K. Salunkhe & B. B. Desai. LC 83-7770. (Postharvest Biotechnology Ser.). 184p. 1984. 105.00 (0-8493-6121-4, SB630) Franklin.

Postharvest Biotechnology of Oilseeds. D. K. Salunkhe & B. B. Desai. 288p. 1986. 156.00 (0-8493-6289-X, SB298, CRC Reprint) Franklin.

Postharvest Biotechnology of Sugar Crops. D. K. Salunkhe & B. B. Desai. LC 87-22473. 224p. 1988. 132.00 (0-8493-4578-2, SB217, CRC Reprint) Franklin.

Postharvest Biotechnology of Vegetables. D. K. Salunkhe & B. B. Desai. (Postharvest Biotechnology Ser.). 1984. 119.95 (0-317-05984-X, SB324, CRC Reprint); write for info. (0-8493-6123-0, CRC Reprint); 119.00 (0-8493-6124-9, CRC Reprint) Franklin.

Postharvest Grain Loss Assessment Methods. Kenton Harris & Carl Lindblad. 193p. 1990. 13.50 (0-685-45920-9) Vols Tech Asst.

Postharvest Handling: A Systems Approach. Ed. by Robert L. Shewfelt & Stanley E. Prussia. (Food Science & Technology Ser.). (Illus.). 358p. 1992. text 94.00 (0-12-639990-5) Acad Pr.

Postharvest Handling of Tropical Fruits. B. R. Champ et al. 500p. 1994. pap. 240.00 (1-86320-101-7, Pub. by ACIAR) St Mut.

Postharvest Physiology & Handling of Perishable Plant Products. Stanley J. Kays. LC 90-44213. (Illus.). 544p. (gr. 13). 1991. text 91.95 (0-442-23912-2) Chapman & Hall.

Postharvest Physiology & Storage of Tropical & Subtropical Fruits. Ed. by S. K. Mitra. LC 97-13568. (Illus.). 452p. (C). 1998. text 120.00 (0-85199-210-2) OUP.

Postharvest Technology of Fruit & Vegetables. A. K. Thompson. LC 95-54. 1995. write for info. (0-582-10163-8, Pub. by Addison-Wesley) Longman.

Postharvest Technology of Horticultural Crops. 2nd ed. Ed. by Adel A. Kader. (Illus.). 304p. (Orig.). 1992. pap. 50.00 (0-931876-99-0, 3311) ANR Pubns CA.

Posthistoire: Has History Come to an End? Lutz Niethammer. 160p. (C). (gr. 13 up). 1994. pap. 19.00 (0-86091-697-9, Pub. by Verso) Norton.

Posthuman Bodies. Ed. by Judith Halberstam & Ira Livingston. LC 94-45934. (Unnatural Acts Ser.). 288p. 1995. 35.00 (0-253-32894-2) Ind U Pr.

*Posthumanism. Neil Badmington. LC 00-33320. 2000. pap. write for info. (0-312-23794-4) St Martin.

Posthumous see Prose Works

Posthumous Book in Two Parts (Plus a Postscript) The Collaboration of a Mother & Her Son. Toni Kranz & Tony Kranz. (Illus.). 8p. 1998. ring bd. 5.95 (0-9663986-1-0); ring bd., boxed set 595.00 (0-9663986-0-2) Pollage Pr.

Posthumous Humanity: A Study of Phantoms. Adolphe D'Assier. Ed. by Henry S. Olcott. LC 81-50204. (Secret Doctrine Reference Ser.). 384p. 1981. reprint ed. 17.00 (0-913510-36-X) Wizards.

Posthumous Life of Plato. Frantisek Novotny. Ed. by Ludvik Svoboda & J. L. Barton. Tr. by Jana Fabryova. 664p. 1978. lib. bdg. 296.00 (90-247-2060-5, Pub. by M Nijhoff) Kluwer Academic.

Posthumous Meditations: A Dialogue in Three Acts. W. A. McMullen. LC 82-916. (HPC Dialogues Ser.). 79p. (C). 1982. pap. text 3.95 (0-915145-35-9) Hackett Pub.

Posthumous Memoirs of Bras Cubas. Joaquim Maria Machado de Assis. Tr. by Gregory Rabassa. LC 96-44125. (Library of Latin America). 240p. 1997. 25.00 (0-19-510169-3) OUP.

Posthumous Memoirs of Bras Cubas. Joaquim Maria Machado de Assis. Tr. by Gregory Rabassa. (Library of Latin America). 240p. 1998. reprint ed. pap. 12.95 (0-19-510170-7) OUP.

Posthumous Papers of a Living Author. Robert Musil. Tr. by Peter Wortsman from GER. LC 87-83298.Tr. of Nachlass zu Lebzeiten. 149p. 1987. pap. 12.00 (0-941419-01-0, Eridanos Library) Marsilio Pubs.

Posthumous Papers of the Pickwick Club see Oxford Illustrated Dickens

Posthumous Papers of the Pickwick Club. Charles Dickens. LC 99-214739. 1999. 23.00 (0-375-40548-8) Everymns Lib.

*Posthumous Papers of the Pickwick Club. Charles Dickens. (Penguin Classics Ser.). (Illus.). 960p. 2000. pap. 9.95 (0-14-043611-1, Penguin Classics) Viking Penguin.

Posthumous Papers of the Pickwick Club. George Davis. LC 72-3167. (Studies in Dickens: No. 52). 1972. reprint ed. lib. bdg. 75.00 (0-8383-1533-X) M S G Haskell Hse.

Posthumous People: Vienna at the Turning Point. Massimo Cacciari. Tr. by Rodger Friedman. LC 96-14952. (Meridian: Crossing Aesthetics Ser.). 1979. 45.00 (0-8047-2709-0) Stanford U Pr.

Posthumous People: Vienna at the Turning Point. Massimo Cacciari. Tr. by Rodger Friedman. LC 96-14952. (Meridian: Crossing Aesthetics Ser.). 1997. pap. 16.95 (0-8047-2710-4) Stanford U Pr.

Posthumous Pieces by Wei Wu Wei. Terence J. Gray. LC BD0431.G7. 246p. reprint ed. pap. 76.30 (0-608-18118-8, 203276900081) Bks Demand.

Posthumous Poems. Algernon Charles Swinburne et al. 1977. 17.95 (0-8369-6993-6, 7870) Ayer.

Posthumous Poems, 1824. Percy Bysshe Shelley. LC 91-28507. (Revolution & Romanticism Ser.). 438p. 1991. reprint ed. 75.00 (1-85477-079-9) Continuum.

Posthumous Poet: A Suite for Pier Paolo Pasolini. Pasquale Verdicchio. 48p. (Orig.). 1993. pap. 7.95 (0-9629903-2-9) Jahbone Pr.

Posthumous Theological Works, 2 vols. Incl. Vol. 1. LC 38-24293. 575p. 1996. 20.00 (0-87785-287-1); Vol. 2. LC 38-24293. 635p. 1996. 20.00 (0-87785-289-8); LC 38-24293. 1996. 35.00 (0-87785-285-5) Swedenborg.

Posthumous Theological Works, 2 vols. Emanuel Swedenborg. Tr. by J. Whitehead. LC 38-24293. 1914. 20.00 (0-87785-075-5) Swedenborg.

Posthumous Theological Works, 2 vols, Vol. 1. Emanuel Swedenborg. Tr. by J. Whitehead. LC 38-24293. 616p. 1914. 12.00 (0-87785-073-9) Swedenborg.

Posthumous Theological Works, 2 vols, Vol. 2. Emanuel Swedenborg. Tr. by J. Whitehead. LC 38-24293. 602p. 1914. 12.00 (0-87785-074-7) Swedenborg.

Posthumous Works. Ann E. Bleecker. LC 70-104419. 375p. reprint ed. lib. bdg. 32.00 (0-8398-0167-X) Irvington.

Posthumous Works. Ann E. Bleeker. 375p. (C). 1986. reprint ed. pap. text 7.95 (0-8290-1888-3) Irvington.

Posthumous Works. Robert Hooke. (Illus.). 518p. 1971. reprint ed. 65.00 (0-7146-1600-1, Pub. by F Cass Pubs) Intl Spec Bk.

Posthumous Works of Charles Fearne, Esquire, Barrister at Law: Consisting of a Reading on the Statute of Inrolments, Arguments in the Singular Cafe of General Stanwix & a Collection of Cases & Opinions. Ed. by Thomas M. Shadwell. xxiv, 480p. 1994. reprint ed. lib. bdg. 70.00 (0-8377-2138-5, Rothman) W S Hein.

Postilla Vol. 209: A Type Catalog of Fossil Invertebrates (Arthropoda: Hexapoda) Russell D. White. 55p. 1995. pap. 10.00 (0-912532-38-6) Peabody Mus Nat Hist.

Postilla Vol. 210: A Type Catalog of Fossil Invertebrates Arthropoda: Crustacea. Russell D. White. 19p. 1996. pap. 6.25 (0-912532-40-8) Peabody Mus Nat Hist.

Postilla Vol. 211: A Type Catalog of Fossil Invertebrates Arthropoda: Chelicerata. Russell D. White. 13p. 1996. pap. 6.25 (0-912532-41-6) Peabody Mus Nat Hist.

Postilla Vol. 212: A Type Catalog of Fossil Invertebrates Graptolithina. Russell D. White. 24p. 1996. pap. 7.50 (0-912532-42-4) Peabody Mus Nat Hist.

Postilla Vol. 213: A Type Catalog of Fossil Invertebrates Archaeocyatha, Poritera, Receptaculitidae & Stromatoporoidea. Russell D. White. 24p. 1997. pap. 7.50 (0-912532-43-2) Peabody Mus Nat Hist.

Postilla Vol. 214: A Type Catalog of Fossil Invertebrates Arthropoda Trilobita. Russell D. White & Bruce S. Lieberman. 151p. 1998. pap. 14.00 (0-912532-44-0) Peabody Mus Nat Hist.

Postilla Vol. 215: A Type Catalog of Fossil Invertebrates Echinodermata. Russell D. White. 31p. 1998. pap. 8.00 (0-912532-45-9) Peabody Mus Nat Hist.

Postilla of Nicholas of Lyra on the Song of Songs. Nicholas & James G. Kiecker. LC 98-8884. (Reformation Texts with Translation (1350-1650) Ser.). 1998. 15.00 (0-87462-703-6) Marquette.

Postimperialism & World Politics. Ed. by David G. Becker & Richard L. Sklar. LC 98-56626. (Illus.). 408p. 1999. 69.50 (0-275-96613-5, C6613, Praeger Pubs) Greenwood.

Postindian Conversations. Gerald Vicenor & A. Robert Lee. LC 99-11411. (American Indian Lives Ser.). 200p. 1999. 25.00 (0-8032-4666-8) U of Nebr Pr.

Postindustrial Possibilities: A Critique of Economic Discourse. Fred L. Block. 1990. pap. 17.95 (0-520-06988-9, Pub. by U CA Pr) Cal Prin Full Svc.

Postinfectious Glomerulonephritis. Karin Sorger. (Progress in Pathology Ser.: Band 125). 110p. 1986. pap. 75.00 (0-89574-223-3, Pub. by Gustav Fischer) Balogh.

*Posting the Mail. Frank Reisner. 224p. 1999. pap. 16.00 (0-8059-4629-2) Dorrance.

Postischemic Myocardium: Energetic State & Its Relation to Contractile Failure. J. Anders. No. 7. 96p. (Orig.). 1988. pap. 29.50 (90-6186-291-4, Pub. by Leuven Univ) Coronet Bks.

P

An Asterisk (*) at the beginning of an entry indicates that the title is appearing for the first time.

Postively Page: The Diamond Dallas Page Journey. Diamond Dallas Page & Larry Genta. (Illus.). 480p. 27.95 (*1-880325-28-4*) Borderlnds NH.

Postivist Republic: Auguste Comte & the Reconstruction of American Liberalism. Gillis J. Harp. LC 93-30385. 1994. 35.00 (*0-271-01041-X*) Pa St U Pr.

Postkommunismus und Zivilrecht: Das Obligationenrecht Georgiens. Mario Pellegrino. 364p. 1997. 76.95 (*3-631-31679-8*) P Lang Pubng.

Postlabelling Methods for the Detection of DNA Adducts. Ed. by D. H. Phillips et al. (IARC Scientific Publications: No. 124). (Illus.). 404p. 1993. pap. text 85.00 (*92-832-2124-9*) OUP.

Postlingually Acquired Deafness: Speech Deterioration & the Wider Consequences. Roddy Cowie & Ellen Douglas-Cowie. LC 92-12793. (Trends in Linguistics, Studies & Monographs: Vol. 62). x, 304p. (C). 1992. lib. bdg. 106.15 (*3-11-012575-7*, 105-92) Mouton.

Postliteracy in the Age of Democracy: A Comparative Study of China & Tanzania. Ladislaus Semali. (Illus.). 225p. (Orig.). 1996. 69.95 (*1-57292-009-2*); pap. 49.95 (*1-57292-008-4*) Austin & Winfield.

Postlude, a Play for the Moment. Jerome McDonough. 32p. 1998. pap. 3.25 (*0-87440-067-8*) Bakers Plays.

Postlude in F: Orchestra Score Critical Edition. Charles Edward Ives. 1991. 12.00 (*0-7935-0912-2*, 50481195) H Leonard.

Postlude in F Orchestra: SC & PT Critical Edition. Charles Edward Ives. 1991. pap. text 45.00 (*0-7935-0427-9*, 50481114) H Leonard.

Postlude to the Kreutzer Sonata: Tolstoj & the Debate on Sexual Morality in Russian Literature in the 1890s. Peter U. Miller. LC 87-20980. xviii, 346p. 1988. write for info. (*90-04-08310-3*) Brill Academic Pubs.

Postman. David Brin. 336p. 1997. mass mkt. 6.99 (*0-553-27874-6*, Bantam Classics) Bantam.

Postman. David Brin. 1986. 11.60 (*0-606-03120-0*, Pub. by Turtleback) Demco.

Postman. Ed. by Teacher Created Materials, Inc. Staff. (Go Bks.). 8p. (J). (gr. k-1). 1997. pap. 2.49 (*1-57690-812-7*) Tchr Create Mat.

Postman. Roger Martin du Gard. Tr. by John Russell from FRE. LC 74-13052. 156p. 1975. reprint ed. 29.50 (*0-86527-333-2*) Fertig.

Postman Always Rings Twice. James M. Cain. 20.95 (*0-89190-815-3*) Amereon Ltd.

Postman Always Rings Twice. James M. Cain. 1992. pap. 8.00 (*0-679-74097-X*) Random.

Postman Always Rings Twice. James M. Cain. (Crime Ser.). 1989. pap. 9.00 (*0-679-72325-0*) Vin Bks.

Postman Always Rings Twice. James M. Cain. 1992. pap. 8.00 (*0-394-23899-0*) Vin Bks.

Postman Always Rings Twice. large type ed. James M. Cain. LC 94-28140. 188p. 1995. pap. 18.95 (*0-7862-0279-3*) Thorndike Pr.

Postman Always Rings Twice. James M. Cain. 457p. 1981. reprint ed. lib. bdg. 27.95 (*0-89968-234-0*, Lghtyr Pr) Buccaneer Bks.

Postman Always Rings Twice. James M. Cain. 200p. 1995. reprint ed. 35.00 (*1-883402-18-2*) S&S Trade.

Postman (Il Postino) Antonio Skarmeta. Tr. by Katherine Silver. LC 95-4459. 128p. (J). 1995. pap. 9.70 (*0-7868-8127-5*, Pub. by Hyperion) Time Warner.

Postman Pat: Follows a Trail. J. Cunliffe. (Illus.). (J). 1996. text 17.95 (*0-340-67809-7*, Pub. by Hodder & Stought Ltd) Trafalgar.

Postman Pat: Has the Best Village. J. Cunliffe. (Illus.). (J). 1996. text 17.95 (*0-340-67810-0*, Pub. by Hodder & Stought Ltd) Trafalgar.

Postman Pat: Hole in the Road. J. Cunliffe. (Illus.). (J). 1996. text 17.95 (*0-340-67294-3*, Pub. by Hodder & Stought Ltd) Trafalgar.

Postman Pat: In a Muddle. J. Cunliffe. (Illus.). (J). 1996. text 17.95 (*0-340-67807-0*, Pub. by Hodder & Stought Ltd) Trafalgar.

Postman Pat: Misses the Show. J. Cunliffe. (Illus.). (J). 1996. text 7.99 (*0-340-67808-9*, Pub. by Hodder & Stought Ltd) Trafalgar.

Postman Pat: Suit of Armour. J. Cunliffe. (Illus.). (J). 1996. text 17.95 (*0-340-67806-2*, Pub. by Hodder & Stought Ltd) Trafalgar.

***Postman Pat & Christmas Baby.** J. Cunliffe. (Illus.). (J). 1998. text 17.95 (*0-340-69811-X*, Pub. by Hodder & Stought Ltd) Trafalgar.

***Postman Pat & Frog Pie Dinner.** J. Cunliffe. (Illus.). (J). 1998. mass mkt. 7.95 (*0-340-71436-0*, Pub. by Hodder & Stought Ltd) Trafalgar.

***Postman Pat & Goat Supper.** J. Cunliffe. (Illus.). (J). 1998. mass mkt. 7.95 (*0-340-71438-7*, Pub. by Hodder & Stought Ltd) Trafalgar.

***Postman Pat & Mushroom Tea.** J. Cunliffe. (Illus.). (J). 1998. mass mkt. 7.95 (*0-340-71440-9*, Pub. by Hodder & Stought Ltd) Trafalgar.

***Postman Pat & Surprise Breakfast.** J. Cunliffe. (Illus.). (J). 1998. mass mkt. 7.95 (*0-340-71434-4*, Pub. by Hodder & Stought Ltd) Trafalgar.

Postman Pat & the Beast of Greendale, Bk. 12. J. Cunliffe. (Illus.). (J). text 17.95 (*0-340-67816-X*, Pub. by Hodder & Stought Ltd) Trafalgar.

Postman Pat & the Big Surprise. J. Cunliffe. (Illus.). (J). text 17.95 (*0-340-67813-5*, Pub. by Hodder & Stought Ltd) Trafalgar.

Postman Pat & the Cure for Hiccups. J. Cunliffe. (Illus.). (J). mass mkt. 8.95 (*0-340-71626-6*, Pub. by Hodder & Stought Ltd) Trafalgar.

Postman Pat & the Mystery Tour. J. Cunliffe. (Illus.). (J). text 17.95 (*0-340-67817-8*, Pub. by Hodder & Stought Ltd) Trafalgar.

Postman Pat & the Robot. J. Cunliffe. (Illus.). (J). text 17.95 (*0-340-67814-3*, Pub. by Hodder & Stought Ltd); mass mkt. 8.95 (*0-340-70915-4*, Pub. by Hodder & Stought Ltd) Trafalgar.

Postman Pat Follows a Trail. J. Cunliffe. (J). mass mkt. 8.95 (*0-340-70387-3*, Pub. by Hodder & Stought Ltd) Trafalgar.

Postman Pat Has Many Parcels. J. Cunliffe. (Illus.). (J). mass mkt. 8.95 (*0-340-70408-X*, Pub. by Hodder & Stought Ltd) Trafalgar.

Postman Pat Has Too Many Parcels. J. Cunliffe. (Illus.). (J). text 17.95 (*0-340-67812-7*, Pub. by Hodder & Stought Ltd) Trafalgar.

Postman Pat in a Muddle, No. 3. J. Cunliffe. (Illus.). (J). mass mkt. 8.95 (*0-340-70385-7*, Pub. by Hodder & Stought Ltd) Trafalgar.

Postman Pat Misses the Show. J. Cunliffe. (Illus.). (J). mass mkt. 8.95 (*0-340-70386-5*, Pub. by Hodder & Stought Ltd) Trafalgar.

Postman Pat 1: Hole in the Road. J. Cunliffe. (Illus.). (J). mass mkt. 8.95 (*0-340-70384-9*, Pub. by Hodder & Stought Ltd) Trafalgar.

Postman Pat Paints a Ceiling. J. Cunliffe. (Illus.). (J). mass mkt. 8.95 (*0-340-70407-1*, Pub. by Hodder & Stought Ltd) Trafalgar.

Postman Pat Paints the Ceiling. J. Cunliffe. (Illus.). (J). text 17.95 (*0-340-67811-9*, Pub. by Hodder & Stought Ltd) Trafalgar.

Postman Pat Takes Flight. J. Cunliffe. (Illus.). (J). mass mkt. 8.95 (*0-340-71331-3*, Pub. by Hodder & Stought Ltd) Trafalgar.

Postman Pat Takes Flight 11. J. Cunliffe. (Illus.). (J). text 17.95 (*0-340-67815-1*, Pub. by Hodder & Stought Ltd) Trafalgar.

Postman Roulin. James Sunwall. 12p. (Orig.). 1985. pap. 10.00 (*0-931956-19-6*) Water Mark.

Postman's Horn. Arthur Bryant. LC 77-119927. (Select Bibliographies Reprint Ser.). 1977. 24.95 (*0-8369-5370-3*) Ayer.

***Postmark.** LaJoyce Martin. 150p. 2000. pap. 8.99 (*1-56722-420-2*) Word Aflame.

Postmark: An Abstract Effect. David Pagel et al. LC 99-60968. (Illus.). 56p. 1999. pap. write for info. (*0-9650583-6-0*) Site Santa Fe.

Postmark Murder. Mignon G. Eberhart. 208p. 1983. mass mkt. 5.50 (*0-446-31181-2*, Pub. by Warner Bks) Little.

Postmark Vermont. Marguerite H. Wolf. LC 94-61332. 112p. (Orig.). 1994. pap. text 9.95 (*1-881535-12-6*) New Eng Pr VT.

Postmarked for Death. Jonathan Lowe. 312p. 1996. 22.95 (*1-885173-13-X*) Write Way.

Postmarked Washington: An Encyclopedia of Postal History of Eleven Countries of Eastern Washington. Ed. by Bert Webber. LC 86-22453. 366p. 1987. 22.95 (*0-87770-211-X*) Ye Galleon.

Postmarked Washington: Pierce County. Guy R. Ramsey. LC 81-620032. (Illus.). 123p. 1981. pap. 8.50 (*0-917048-54-7*) Wash St Hist Soc.

Postmas Pat Has the Best Village. J. Cunliffe. (Illus.). (J). mass mkt. 8.95 (*0-340-70388-1*, Pub. by Hodder & Stought Ltd) Trafalgar.

Postmaster, 1st, 2nd, & 3rd Classes (U. S. P. S.) Jack Rudman. (Career Examination Ser.: C-605). 1994. pap. 29.95 (*0-8373-0605-1*) Nat Learn.

Postmaster, 4th Class (U. S. P. S.) Jack Rudman. (Career Examination Ser.: C-606). 1994. pap. 27.95 (*0-8373-0606-X*) Nat Learn.

Postmetaphysical Thinking: Philosophical Essays. Jurgen Habermas. (Studies in Contemporary German Social Thought). (Illus.). 242p. 1994. pap. text 16.00 (*0-262-58130-2*) MIT Pr.

Postmetropolis: Studies of Cities & Regions. Edward W. Soja. LC 99-47607. (Illus.). 320p. 1999. 62.95 (*1-57718-000-3*) Blackwell Pubs.

Postmetropolis: Studies of Cities & Regions. Edward W. Soja. LC 99-47607. (Illus.). 320p. 2000. pap. 26.95 (*1-57718-001-1*) Blackwell Pubs.

Postmillennialism: An Eschatology of Hope; An Eschatology of Hope. Keith A. Mathison. LC 98-55539. 1999. pap. 14.99 (*0-87552-389-7*) P & R Pubng.

Postminimalism: American Art of the Decade. Robert Pincus-Witten. LC 77-77010. (Illus.). 1981. pap. text 25.00 (*0-915570-07-6*) Oolp Pr.

Postminimalism into Maximalism: American Art, 1966-1986. Robert Pincus-Witten. LC 86-24925. (Studies in the Fine Arts: Criticism: No. 22). 445p. reprint ed. pap. 138.00 (*0-8357-1763-1*, 207064800012) Bks Demand.

Postmistress of Saddlestring, Wyoming. Edgar M. Morsman, Jr. LC 98-205298. (Illus.). xi, 90p. 1998. pap. 14.95 (*0-9664438-0-2*) E M Morsman.

Postmobilization Traning Resource Requirements: Army National Guard Heavy Enhanced Brigades. Thomas F. Lippiatt et al. LC 96-20308. (Illus.). 192p. 1997. pap. 15.00 (*0-8330-2379-9*, MR-662-A) Rand Corp.

Postmodern After-Images: A Reader in Film, Television, & Video. Ed. by Peter Brooker & Will Brooker. LC 96-48152. (An Arnold Publication). 304p. 1997. text 60.00 (*0-340-67692-2*, Pub. by E A); pap. text 19.95 (*0-340-67691-4*, Pub. by E A) OUP.

Postmodern American Fiction: A Norton Anthology. Paula Geyh. LC 97-24446. 700p. 1997. pap. 24.95 (*0-393-31698-X*) Norton.

Postmodern American Poetry. fac. ed. Jerome Mazzaro. LC 79-11119. 215p. 1980. reprint ed. pap. 66.70 (*0-7837-8079-6*, 204783200008) Bks Demand.

Postmodern American Poetry: A Norton Anthology. Ed. by Paul Hoover. 750p. (C). 1994. pap. 24.95 (*0-393-31090-6*) Norton.

Postmodern American Poetry: A Norton Anthology. Ed. by Paul Hoover. 750p. (C). 1994. pap. text 24.95 (*0-393-96450-7*) Norton.

Postmodern Analysis. Jurgen Jost. LC 97-37167. (Universitext Ser.). xv, 340p. (C). 1998. pap. 39.95 (*3-540-63485-1*) Spr-Verlag.

Postmodern & Political Agency. Tuija Pulkkinen. 250p. pap. 24.95 (*951-39-0660-4*, Pub. by SoPhi Academic) Intl Spec Bk.

***Postmodern Animal.** Steve Baker. (Essays in Art & Culture Ser.). (Illus.). 224p. 2000. pap. 24.95 (*1-86189-060-5*, Pub. by Reaktion Bks) Consort Bk Sales.

Postmodern Apocalypse: Theory & Cultural Practice at the End. Richard Dellamora. LC 96-32542. (New Cultural Studies). (Illus.). 288p. 1995. text 39.95 (*0-8122-3320-4*); pap. text 16.95 (*0-8122-1558-3*) U of Pa Pr.

Postmodern Archipelago: Two Essays on Science Fiction & Fantasy. Michael Swanwick. 68p. 1997. pap. 7.50 (*0-9648320-6-2*) Tachyon Pubns.

Postmodern Art Education: An Approach to Curriculum. Arthur Efland et al. (Illus.). 146p. 1996. pap. text 20.00 (*0-937652-89-X*, 262) Natl Art Ed.

Postmodern Arts: An Introductory Reader. Ed. by Nigel Wheale. LC 94-42950. (Critical Readers in Theory & Practice Ser.). 320p. (C). 1995. pap. 25.99 (*0-415-12611-8*) Routledge.

Postmodern Arts: An Introductory Reader. Nigel Wheale. LC 94-42950. (Critical Readers in Theory & Practice Ser.). (Illus.). 320p. (C). (gr. 13). 1995. 90.00 (*0-415-07776-1*, B4655) Routledge.

Postmodern Auteurs: Coppola, Lucas, De Palma, Spielberg & Scorsese. Kenneth Von Gunden. LC 91-52594. (Illus.). 192p. 1991. lib. bdg. 32.50 (*0-89950-618-6*) McFarland & Co.

Postmodern Bank Safety Net: Lessons from Developed & Developing Economies. Calomiris. LC 98-137537. 1997. pap. 9.95 (*0-8447-7100-7*) Am Enterprise.

Postmodern Bible: The Bible & Culture Collective. 416p. 1997. pap. 17.00 (*0-300-06818-2*) Yale U Pr.

Postmodern Brain. Gordon G. Globus. LC 94-25296. (Advances in Consciousness Research Ser.: Vol. 1). xii, 188p. 1995. pap. 32.95 (*1-55619-181-2*) J Benjamins Pubng Co.

Postmodern Brecht: A Re-Presentation. Elizabeth Wright. (Critics of the Twentieth Century Ser.). 208p. 1989. 45.00 (*0-415-02329-7*); pap. 13.95 (*0-415-02330-0*) Routledge.

Postmodern Canadian Fiction & the Rhetoric of Authority. Glenn Deer. 160p. 1994. 49.95 (*0-7735-1159-8*, Pub. by McG-Queens Univ Pr) CUP Services.

Postmodern Cartographes: The Geographical Imagination Contemporary American Culture. Jarvis. LC 97-49258. 216p. 1998. pap. 19.95 (*0-312-21345-X*) St Martin.

Postmodern Cartographies: Geographical Imagination in Contemporary American Culture. Jarvis. 1998. 54.95 (*0-7453-1290-X*, Pub. by Pluto GBR); pap. 18.95 (*0-7453-1285-3*, Pub. by Pluto GBR) Stylus Pub VA.

Postmodern Cartographies: The Geographical Imagination Contemporary American Culture. Jarvis. LC 97-49258. 216p. 1998. text 55.00 (*0-312-21344-1*) St Martin.

Postmodern Church. Jeremiah Newman. 157p. 1990. 10.00 (*1-85182-064-7*) Lumen Christi.

Postmodern Cities & Spaces. Ed. by Sophie Watson & Katherine Gibson. LC 09-415841. (Illus.). 256p. 1995. pap. 29.95 (*0-631-19404-5*) Blackwell Pubs.

Postmodern Conditions. Ed. by Andrew Milner et al. LC 89-31934. 224p. 1990. 19.50 (*0-85496-591-2*) Berg Pubs.

Postmodern Consumer Research: The Study of Consumption As Text. Elizabeth C. Hirschman. 144p. (C). 1992. text 48.00 (*0-8039-4742-9*); pap. text 21.00 (*0-8039-4743-7*) Sage.

Postmodern Contentions: Epochs, Politics, Space. Ed. by John P. Jones, III et al. LC 92-30077. (Mappings). 224p. 1993. pap. text 18.95 (*0-89862-495-9*); lib. bdg. 42.00 (*0-89862-494-0*) Guilford Pubns.

Postmodern Criminology. Dragan Milovanovic. LC 97-10779. (Current Issues in Criminal Justice Ser.: No. 22). (Illus.). 288p. 1997. text 55.00 (*0-8153-2456-1*) Garland.

Postmodern Currents: Art & Artists in the Age of Electronic Media. 2nd ed. Margot Lovejoy. 319p. (C). 1996. pap. text 48.00 (*0-13-158759-5*) P-H.

Postmodern Desire Learning from India. Paul McCarthy. LC 94-904666. (C). 1995. 32.00 (*81-85002-41-X*, Pub. by Promilla) S Asia.

Postmodern Dilemmas: Outrageous Essays in Art & Art Education. Jan Jagodzinski. LC 97-13327. (Illus.). xvi, 270p. 1997. 95.00 (*0-8058-2604-1*); pap. write for info. (*0-8058-2605-X*) L Erlbaum Assocs.

Postmodern Ecology: Communication, Evolution, & Play. Daniel R. White. LC 97-5503. 258p. (C). 1997. pap. text 19.95 (*0-7914-3574-1*) State U NY Pr.

Postmodern Ecology: Communication, Evolution, & Play. Daniel R. White. LC 97-5503. 258p. (C). 1997. text 59.50 (*0-7914-3573-3*) State U NY Pr.

Postmodern Education: Politics, Culture, & Social Criticism. Stanley Aronowitz & Henry A. Giroux. 192p. (C). 1990. pap. 15.95 (*0-8166-1880-1*) U of Minn Pr.

***Postmodern Educator: Arts-Based Inquiries & Teacher Development.** Ed. by Carol A. Mullen & C. T. Diamond. LC 98-24674. (Counterpoints Ser.: Vol. 89). xxi, 466p. (C). 1999. pap. text 32.95 (*0-8204-4101-5*) P Lang Pubng.

Postmodern Environmental Ethics. Ed. by Max Oelschlaeger. LC 94-32139. 341p. (C). 1995. text 59.50 (*0-7914-2547-9*); pap. text 21.95 (*0-7914-2548-7*) State U NY Pr.

Postmodern Ethics. Zygmunt Bauman. LC 93-16048. 264p. 1993. pap. 28.95 (*0-631-18693-X*) Blackwell Pubs.

Postmodern Explained. Jean F. Lyotard. Ed. by Julian Pefanis & Morgan Thomas. Tr. by Don Barry et al from FRE. LC 92-10408.Tr. of Le/Postmoderne Explique Aux Enfants. 104p. (C). 1992. pap. 12.95 (*0-8166-2211-6*) U of Minn Pr.

Postmodern Fables. Jean F. Lyotard. Tr. by Georges Van Den Abbeele from ENG. LC 97-25953. 1997. 24.95 (*0-8166-2554-9*) U of Minn Pr.

Postmodern Fables. Jean-Francois Lyotard. 1999. pap. 16.95 (*0-8166-2555-7*) U of Minn Pr.

Postmodern Fairy Tales: Gender & Narrative Strategies. Cristina Bacchilega. LC 96-49318. 218p. 1997. text 32.50 (*0-8122-3392-1*) U of Pa Pr.

Postmodern Fairy Tales: Gender & Narrative Strategies. Cristina Bacchilega. 1999. pap. text 14.95 (*0-8122-1683-0*) U of Pa Pr.

Postmodern Fiction: A Bio-Bibliographical Guide, 2. Ed. by Lawrence F. McCaffery. LC 85-17723. (Movements in the Arts Ser.: No. 2). 632p. 1986. lib. bdg. 95.00 (*0-313-24170-8*, MML/, Greenwood Pr) Greenwood.

Postmodern Fuentes. Chalene Helmuth. LC 96-20484. 152p. 1997. 31.00 (*0-8387-5322-1*) Bucknell U Pr.

Postmodern Genres. Ed. by Marjorie Perloff. LC 89-40220. (Oklahoma Project for Discourse & Theory Ser.). (Illus.). 288p. 1995. pap. 14.95 (*0-8061-2715-5*) U of Okla Pr.

Postmodern Geographies: The Reassertion of Space in Critical Social Theory. Edward W. Soja. 300p. (C). 1989. pap. 19.00 (*0-86091-936-6*, Pub. by Verso) Norton.

Postmodern God: A Theological Reader. Graham Ward. LC 97-8620. (Readings in Modern Theology Ser.: Vol. 2). (C). 1997. text 68.95 (*0-631-20140-8*); pap. text 31.95 (*0-631-20141-6*) Blackwell Pubs.

Postmodern History Reader. Keith Jenkins. LC 96-42429. 464p. (C). 1997. pap. 24.99 (*0-415-13904-X*) Routledge.

Postmodern in Latin & Latino American Cultural Narratives: Collected Essays & Interviews. Claudia Ferman. Ed. by David W. Foster. LC 95-39197. (Reference Library of the Humanities: Vol. 1728). 264p. 1996. text 37.00 (*0-8153-1330-6*) Garland.

Postmodern Insurgencies. De Silva Munck. LC 99-15423. 2000. text 69.95 (*0-312-22629-2*) St Martin.

***Postmodern Interpretations of the Bible - A Reader.** Ed. by A. K. M. Adam. 2000. pap. 29.99 (*0-8272-2970-4*) Chalice Pr.

Postmodern Italian Fiction: The Crisis of Reason in Calvino, Eco, Sciascia, Malerba. JoAnn Cannon. LC 88-45733. 144p. 1989. 32.50 (*0-8386-3346-3*) Fairleigh Dickinson.

***Postmodern Journeys: Film & Culture 1996-1998.** Joseph P. Natoli. LC 00-20339. (C). 2000. text 57.50 (*0-7914-4771-5*) State U NY Pr.

***Postmodern Journeys: Film & Culture, 1996-1998.** Joseph P. Natoli. LC 00-20339. 2000. pap. 18.95 (*0-7914-4772-3*) State U NY Pr.

Postmodern Law & Disorder: Psychoanalytic Semiotics, Chaos & Juridic Exegeses. Dragan Milovanovic. (Legal Semiotics Monographs Ser.: Vol. 3). 280p. 1992. 72.00 (*0-9513793-3-X*) Gaunt.

Postmodern Legal Feminism. Mary J. Frug. 224p. (C). 1992. pap. 23.99 (*0-415-90620-2*, A7371) Routledge.

Postmodern Legal Movements: Law & Jurisprudence at Century's End. Gary Minda. LC 94-24934. 350p. (C). 1995. text 45.00 (*0-8147-5510-0*) NYU Pr.

***Postmodern Literary Theory: An Anthology.** Ed. by Niall Lucy. LC 99-31612. 480p. 1999. pap. text 29.95 (*0-631-21028-8*) Blackwell Pubs.

Postmodern Literary Theory: An Anthology. Ed. by Niall Lucy. LC 99-31612. 480p. (C). 1999. text 62.95 (*0-631-21027-X*) Blackwell Pubs.

Postmodern Literary Theory: An Introduction. Niall Lucy. LC 97-12841. 288p. (C). 1997. text 62.95 (*0-631-20000-2*); pap. text 26.95 (*0-631-20001-0*) Blackwell Pubs.

***Postmodern Magick: The Unnatural Sourcebook.** Ed. by John Tynes. (Unknown Armies Ser.). (Illus.). 190p. 2000. pap. 23.95 (*1-887801-81-2*, Atlas Games) Trident MN.

Postmodern Management: The Emerging Partnership Between Employees & Stockholders. William M. Wallace. LC 97-41004. 232p. 1998. 65.00 (*1-56720-181-4*, Quorum Bks) Greenwood.

Postmodern Management & Organization Theory. Ed. by David M. Boje et al. 320p. 1995. 52.00 (*0-8039-7004-8*); pap. 25.00 (*0-8039-7005-6*) Sage.

Postmodern Management Theory. Ed. by Linda Smircich & Marta B. Calas. LC 97-25265. (History of Management Thought Ser.). 510p. 1997. text 174.95 (*1-85521-452-0*, Pub. by Ashgate Pub) Ashgate Pub Co.

Postmodern Marketing. Brown. (ITBP Textbooks Ser.). 1998. pap. 19.99 (*1-86152-483-8*) Thomson Learn.

Postmodern Marketing. Stephen Brown. (Consumer Research & Policy Ser.). 208p. (C). 1995. pap. 28.95 (*0-415-10982-5*) Thomson Learn.

Postmodern Marketing. Stephen Brown. LC 94-39939. (Consumer Research & Policy Ser.). 240p. (C). (gr. 13). 1995. pap. 71.95 (*0-415-10155-7*) Thomson Learn.

Postmodern Marketing: Telling Tales. 2nd ed. Stephen Brown. LC 98-124021. 224p. 1998. pap. 22.00 (*1-86152-018-2*) Thomson Learn.

Postmodern Marx. Terrell Carver. LC 98-20426. 1999. 50.00 (*0-271-01867-4*); pap. 17.95 (*0-271-01868-2*) Pa St U Pr.

***Postmodern Media Culture.** Jonathan Bignell. 224p. 2000. text 62.00 (*0-7486-0987-3*); pap. text 25.00 (*0-7486-0988-1*) Col U Pr.

Postmodern Military: Armed Forces after the Cold War. Charles C. Moskos et al. LC 99-48791. 304p. (C). 1999. text 45.00 (*0-19-513328-5*); pap. text 29.95 (*0-19-513329-3*) OUP.

P

An Asterisk (*) at the beginning of an entry indicates that the title is appearing for the first time.

Postmodern Moment: A Handbook of Contemporary Innovation in the Arts, 1. Ed. by Stanley Trachtenberg. LC 85-5452. (Movements in the Arts Ser.: No. 1). (Illus.). 323p. 1985. lib. bdg. 75.00 (*0-313-23786-7*, TRP/, Greenwood Pr) Greenwood.

***Postmodern Music/Postmodern Thought.** Joseph Auner. (Studies in Contemporary Music & Culture Ser.). 2000. 75.00 (*0-8153-3819-8*); pap. 24.95 (*0-8153-3820-1*) Garland.

Postmodern Narrative Theory. Currie. LC 97-51294. 184p. 1998. text 55.00 (*0-312-21390-5*) St Martin.

Postmodern Narrative Theroy. Currie. LC 97-51294. 184p. 1998. pap. 19.95 (*0-312-21391-3*) St Martin.

Postmodern Novel in Latin America. Raymond L. Williams. 150p. 1996. pap. 16.95 (*0-312-16458-0*) St Martin.

Postmodern Nursing Redefining Nursing. Watson. LC 99-36289. (C). 1998. pap. text 40.00 (*0-443-05744-3*) Church.

Postmodern Organization: Mastering the Art of Irreversible Change. William H. Bergquist. LC 92-43606. (Management Ser.). 299p. 1993. text 32.95 (*1-55542-533-X*) Jossey-Bass.

Postmodern Paradigm: Challenges to the Evangelistic Ministry of the Church. Ricky D. Gosnell. 1998. 15.95 (*0-941037-61-4*) D & F Scott.

Postmodern Perspectives. 2nd ed. Howard Risatti. LC 97-36145. 318p. 1997. pap. text 36.80 (*0-13-614504-3*) P-H.

Postmodern Philosophical Critique & the Pursuit of Knowledge in Higher Education. Roger P. Mourad, Jr. LC 97-217. (Critical Studies in Education & Culture Ser.). 136p. 1997. 52.95 (*0-89789-488-X*, Bergin & Garvey); pap. 18.95 (*0-89789-554-1*, Bergin & Garvey) Greenwood.

Postmodern Philosophy & Christian Thought Merold Westphal. LC 99-28626. (Series in the Philosophy of Religion). 1999. 19.95 (*0-253-21336-3*) Ind U Pr.

Postmodern Philosophy & Law: Douglas E. Litowitz. Douglas E. Litowitz. LC 97-14922. 240p. 1997. 35.00 (*0-7006-0857-5*) U Pr of KS.

***Postmodern Philosophy & Law: Douglas E. Litowitz.** Douglas E. Litowitz. 240p. 1999. reprint ed. pap. 15.95 (*0-7006-0999-7*) U Pr of KS.

***Postmodern Pilgrims: First Century Passion for the 21st Century World.** Leonard I. Sweet. 224p. 2000. 19.99 (*0-8054-2137-8*) Broadman.

Postmodern Platos: Nietzsche, Heidegger, Gadamer, Strauss, Derrida. Catherine H. Zuckert. LC 95-35118. 360p. 1996. lib. bdg. 56.00 (*0-226-99330-2*) U Ch Pr.

Postmodern Platos: Nietzsche, Heidegger, Gadamer, Strauss, Derrida. Catherine H. Zuckert. LC 95-35118. 360p. 1996. pap. text 19.95 (*0-226-99331-0*) U Ch Pr.

Postmodern Pluralism & Concepts of Totality: The Twenty-Fourth Wisconsin Workshop. Ed. by Jost Hermand. LC 94-27373. (German Life & Civilization Ser.). VIII, 163p. (C). 1995. text 44.95 (*0-8204-2658-X*) P Lang Pubng.

Postmodern Poetry: The Talisman Interviews. Edward Foster. LC 93-51062. viii, 176p. (Orig.). 1994. pap. 12.95 (*1-883689-10-4*); lib. bdg. 33.95 (*1-883689-11-2*) Talisman Hse.

Postmodern Political Communication: The Fringe Challenges the Center. Ed. by Andrew King. LC 91-45612. (Series in Political Communication). 208p. 1992. 55.00 (*0-275-93840-9*, C3840, Praeger Pubs) Greenwood.

Postmodern Political Condition. Agnes Heller & Ferenc Feher. 200p. 1989. text 43.50 (*0-231-07022-5*) Col U Pr.

Postmodern Politics for a Planet in Crisis: Policy, Process, & Presidential Vision. Ed. by David R. Griffin & Richard A. Falk. LC 92-22104. (SUNY Series in Constructive Postmodern Thought). 232p. (C). 1993. text 59.50 (*0-7914-1485-X*); pap. text 19.95 (*0-7914-1486-8*) State U NY Pr.

Postmodern Politics in Germany: The Politics of Resentment. Hans-Georg Betz. LC 90-39843. 224p. 1991. text 45.00 (*0-312-04881-5*) St Martin.

***Postmodern Postures: Literature, Science & the Two Cultures Debate.** Daniel Cordle. LC 99-52631. 202p. 2000. 78.95 (*0-7546-0095-5*, Pub. by Ashgate Pub) Ashgate Pub Co.

Postmodern Presence: Readings on Postmodernism in American Culture & Society. Arthur A. Berger. LC 97-45393. 320p. 1998. 62.00 (*0-7619-8979-X*); pap. 24.95 (*0-7619-8980-3*) AltaMira Pr.

***Postmodern Presidency: Bill Clinton's Legacy in U. S. Politics.** Ed. by Steven E. Schier. (Political Science Ser.). 296p. 2000. 45.00 (*0-8229-4135-X*); pap. 19.95 (*0-8229-5742-6*) U of Pittsburgh Pr.

Postmodern President: George Bush Meets the World. 2nd ed. Richard Rose. LC 91-12614. 408p. (C). 1991. pap. text 24.95 (*0-934540-94-2*, Chatham House Pub) Seven Bridges.

Postmodern Proust. Margaret E. Gray. LC 92-16747. (Illus.). 200p. (C). 1992. 32.50 (*0-8122-3149-X*) U of Pa Pr.

Postmodern Public Administration: Toward Discourse. Charles F. Fox & Hugh T. Miller. 146p. 1994. 42.00 (*0-8039-5801-3*); pap. 18.50 (*0-8039-5802-1*) Sage.

Postmodern Reader. Ed. by Joseph P. Natoli & Linda Hutcheon. LC 92-39294. 584p. (C). 1993. pap. text 21.95 (*0-7914-1638-0*) State U NY Pr.

Postmodern Reader. Ed. by Joseph P. Natoli & Linda Hutcheon. LC 92-39294. 584p. (C). 1993. text 59.50 (*0-7914-1637-2*) State U NY Pr.

Postmodern Reason & Religion. Ernest Gellner. 108p. 1996. pap. 13.95 (*0-614-21167-0*, 969) Kazi Pubns.

Postmodern Representations: Truth, Power, & Minesis in the Human Sciences & Public Culture. Ed. by Richard H. Brown. LC 94-24083. 288p. 1995. text 49.95 (*0-252-02176-2*); pap. text 22.50 (*0-252-06465-8*) U of Ill Pr.

Postmodern Revelation: Signs of Astrology & the Apocalypse. Jacques M. Chevalier. LC 97-180034. (Illus.). 416p. 1997. pap. text 22.95 (*0-8020-7976-8*) U of Toronto Pr.

Postmodern Revelation: Signs of Astrology & the Apocalypse. Jacques M. Chevalier. LC 97-180034. (Illus.). 415p. 1997. text 60.00 (*0-8020-4172-8*, BS2825) U of Toronto Pr.

Postmodern Revisionings of the Political. Anna Yeatman. (Thinking Gender Ser.). 160p. (C). 1993. pap. 18.99 (*0-415-90198-7*, A3706) Routledge.

Postmodern Scene: Excremental Culture & Hyper-Aesthetics. Arthur Kroker & David Cook. 1986. pap. 16.95 (*0-312-63229-0*) St Martin.

Postmodern School Leadership: Meeting the Crisis in Educational Administration. Ed. by Spencer J. Maxcy. LC 93-2868. 200p. 1993. 55.00 (*0-275-94565-0*, C4565, Praeger Pubs) Greenwood.

Postmodern Semiotics: Material Culture & the Forms of Postmodern Life. M. Gottdiener. (Illus.). 240p. 1995. pap. 27.95 (*0-631-19216-6*) Blackwell Pubs.

Postmodern Sexualities. William Simon. LC 95-25972. 208p. (C). 1996. 80.00 (*0-415-10626-5*); pap. 22.99 (*0-415-10627-3*) Routledge.

Postmodern Social Analysis & Criticism, 79. John W. Murphy. LC 88-35774. (Contributions in Sociology Ser.: No. 79). 185p. 1989. 49.95 (*0-313-26683-2*, MMS/, Greenwood Pr) Greenwood.

Postmodern Social Theory. George Ritzer. LC 96-21073. 336p. (C). 1996. pap. 41.88 (*0-07-053019-X*) McGraw.

Postmodern Socialism: Romanticism, City & State. Peter Beilharz. (Interpretations Ser.). 160p. 1994. pap. 19.95 (*0-522-84535-5*, Pub. by Melbourne Univ Pr) Paul & Co Pubs.

Postmodern Society & Religion. Flanagan. LC 96-19544. 240p. 1996. text 59.95 (*0-312-16109-3*) St Martin.

Postmodern Sophistications: Philosophy, Architecture & Tradition. David Kolb. LC 89-38915. (Illus.). 228p. 1990. lib. bdg. 36.00 (*0-226-45027-9*) U Ch Pr.

Postmodern Sophistications: Philosophy, Architecture & Tradition. David Kolb. LC 89-38915. (Illus.). 228p. 1992. pap. text 15.95 (*0-226-45028-7*) U Ch Pr.

Postmodern Southern Culture: Perspectives on Southern Cultures. Ed. by Richard H. King & Helen Taylor. 272p. (C). 1996. text 50.00 (*0-8147-4683-7*); pap. text 19.50 (*0-8147-4684-5*) NYU Pr.

Postmodern Sublime: Technology & American Writing from Mailer to Cyberpunk. Joseph Tabbi. 256p. 1995. text 39.95 (*0-8014-3074-7*) Cornell U Pr.

Postmodern Sublime: Technology & American Writing from Mailer to Cyberpunk. Joseph Tabbi. 256p. 1996. pap. text 15.95 (*0-8014-8383-2*) Cornell U Pr.

Postmodern Theatric(k)s: Monologue in Contemporary American Drama. Deborah Geis. LC 93-30132. 216p. (Orig.). 1995. pap. text 18.95 (*0-472-08352-X*, 08352) U of Mich Pr.

Postmodern Theologies: The Challenge of Religious Diversity. Terrence W. Tilley. LC 94-47927. 196p. (Orig.). 1995. pap. 19.00 (*1-57075-005-X*) Orbis Bks.

Postmodern Theory. Steven Best & Douglas Kellner. LC 91-2634. (Critical Perspectives Ser.). 256p. 1991. pap. 18.95 (*0-89862-418-5*); lib. bdg. 42.00 (*0-89862-412-6*) Guilford Pubns.

Postmodern Theory: Critical Interrogations Steven Best & Douglas Kellner. LC 92-173607. (Communications & Culture Ser.). xi, 324 p. 1991. write for info. (*0-333-48844-X*) Trans-Atl Phila.

Postmodern Theory & Biblical Theology: Vanquishing God's Shadow. Brian D. Ingraffia. 300p. (C). 1996. text 64.95 (*0-521-47136-2*); pap. text 21.95 (*0-521-56840-4*) Cambridge U Pr.

Postmodern Times. Franklin Daugherty. LC 87-71793. 280p. (YA). 1988. 14.95 (*0-944284-00-0*) T C Deleon.

Postmodern Times: A Christian Guide to Contemporary Thought & Culture. Gene E. Veith, Jr. LC 93-23646. (Turning Point Christian Worldview Ser.). 256p. 1994. pap. 14.99 (*0-89107-768-5*) Crossway Bks.

Postmodern Times: A Critical Guide to the Contemporary. Ed. by Thomas Carmichael & Alison Lee. LC 99-28171. 250p. 1999. 36.00 (*0-87580-251-6*) N Ill U Pr.

Postmodern Turn. Steven Best & Douglas Kellner. LC 97-15234. (Critical Perspectives Ser.). 306p. 1997. pap. 18.95 (*1-57230-221-6*, 0221); lib. bdg. 40.00 (*1-57230-220-8*, 0220) Guilford Pubns.

Postmodern Turn. Bernd Magnus. (C). (gr. 13). 1999. 55.00 (*0-415-90726-8*) Routledge.

Postmodern Turn: New Perspectives on Social Theory. Ed. by Steven Seidman. LC 93-48758. (Illus.). 320p. (C). 1994. text 59.95 (*0-521-45235-X*); pap. text 18.95 (*0-521-45879-X*) Cambridge U Pr.

Postmodern University? Contested Visions of Higher Education in Society. Smith. LC 97-16128. 144p. 1997. 118.00 (*0-335-19959-3*); pap. 36.95 (*0-335-19958-5*) OpUniv Pr.

Postmodern University: Essays on the Deconstruction of the Humanities. Stan Fogel. 150p. (C). 1988. text 25.00 (*1-55022-005-5*, Pub. by ECW); pap. text 15.00 (*1-55022-004-7*, Pub. by ECW) Genl Dist Srvs.

Postmodern Urban Condition. Michael Dear. LC 99-43567. 250p. 1999. 64.95 (*0-631-20987-5*) Blackwell Pubs.

Postmodern Urban Condition. Michael Dear. LC 99-43567. 250p. 1999. pap. 26.95 (*0-631-20988-3*) Blackwell Pubs.

Postmodern Urbanism. rev. ed. Nan Ellin. LC 98-8327. (Illus.). 368p. 1999. reprint ed. pap. 21.95 (*1-56898-135-X*) Princeton Arch.

Postmodern War: The New Politics of Conflict. Chris H. Gray. LC 97-1538. (Critical Perspectives Ser.). 314p. 1997. lib. bdg. 38.95 (*1-57230-160-0*, 0160) Guilford Pubns.

Postmodern War: The New Politics of Conflict. Chris H. Gray. LC 97-1538. (Illus.). 314p. 1998. pap. text 18.95 (*1-57230-176-7*) Guilford Pubns.

Postmodern Welfare: Reconstructing & Empancipatory Project. Peter Leonard. LC 97-65514. 224p. 1997. text 69.95 (*0-8039-7609-7*); pap. text 23.95 (*0-8039-7610-0*) Sage.

Postmodern Wetlands: Culture, History, Ecology. Rod Giblett. LC 97-113104. (Postmodern Theory Ser.). 1997. pap. text 28.00 (*0-7486-0844-3*) Col U Pr.

Postmodern/Drama: Reading the Contemporary Stage. Stephen Watt. LC 98-8970. (Theater--Theory/Text/Performance Ser.). (Illus.). 232p. (C). 1998. text 42.50 (*0-472-10872-7*, 10872) U of Mich Pr.

***Postmoderne Metahistoriographische Fiktion und Andrej Bitovs Puskinskij Dom.** Dunja Kary. (GER.). 395p. 1999. 67.95 (*3-631-34717-0*) P Lang Pubng.

Postmoderne Textpraxis Im Heitigen Frankreich Am Beispiel von Denis Roche. Eva M. Regler. 291p. 1997. 54.95 (*3-631-30728-4*) P Lang Pubng.

Postmodernism. Lewis L. Fried. Ed. by William Cain. (Wellesley Studies in Critical Theory). 800p. 1997. text 120.00 (*0-8153-1339-X*) Garland.

Postmodernism. Glenn Ward. (Illus.). 192p. 1998. pap. 11.95 (*0-8442-0037-9*, 00379, Teach Yrslf) NTC Contemp Pub Co.

Postmodernism: A Reader. Ed. by Thomas Docherty. LC 92-28779. 544p. (C). 1993. pap. 23.00 (*0-231-08221-5*); text 67.00 (*0-231-08220-7*) Col U Pr.

Postmodernism: A Reader. Compiled by Patricia Waugh. LC 92-28220. 1995. text 59.95 (*0-340-57380-5*, Pub. by E A) St Martin.

Postmodernism: A Theory, Culture & Society Special Issue. Mike Featherstone. 384p. (C). 1988. pap. text 19.95 (*0-8039-8194-5*) Sage.

Postmodernism: Postmodernism, Women's Voice & Cupid & Psyche. Mary Nicholaou. LC 99-94832. (Illus.). 120p. 1999. pap. 14.95 (*1-890812-02-1*, Pub. by EROS) Brodart.

Postmodernism: The Twilight of the Real. Neville Wakefield. 144p. (C). 44.95 (*0-7453-0341-2*, Pub. by Pluto GBR); pap. 15.95 (*0-7453-0471-0*, Pub. by Pluto GBR) Stylus Pub VA.

Postmodernism - Jameson - Critique. Ed. & Intro. by Douglas Kellner. 414p. 1989. pap. text 15.95 (*0-944624-07-3*) Maisonneuve Pr.

Postmodernism - Jameson - Critique. Ed. & Intro. by Douglas Kellner. LC PN96.C6P67. (Post Modern Positions Ser.: Vol. 4). 414p. 1989. lib. bdg. 34.95 (*0-944624-06-5*) Maisonneuve Pr.

Postmodernism - Local Effects, Global Flows. Vincent B. Leitch. LC 95-38880. (SUNY Series in Postmodern Culture). 195p. (C). 1996. text 54.50 (*0-7914-3009-X*); pap. text 19.95 (*0-7914-3010-3*) State U NY Pr.

Postmodernism Across the Ages. Ed. by William Readings & Bennet Schaber. 320p. 1993. text 39.95 (*0-8156-2577-4*); pap. text 19.95 (*0-8156-2581-2*) Syracuse U Pr.

Postmodernism & a Sociology of the Absurd: And Other Essays on the "Nouvelle Vague" in American Social Science. Stanford M. Lyman. LC 96-50984. (Studies in American Sociology). 1997. 34.00 (*1-55728-453-9*) U of Ark Pr.

***Postmodernism & China.** Arif Dirlik. LC 99-42240. (A Boundary Book Ser.). 464p. 2000. 69.95 (*0-8223-2506-3*) Duke.

***Postmodernism & China.** Arif Dirlik. LC 99-42240. (Boundary Book Ser.). (Illus.). 464p. 2000. pap. 23.95 (*0-8223-2544-6*) Duke.

Postmodernism & Christian Philosophy. Ed. by Roman T. Ciapalo. LC 96-49919. 294p. 1997. pap. 15.00 (*0-8132-0881-5*) Cath U Pr.

Postmodernism & Continental Philosophy. Ed. by Hugh J. Silverman & Donn Welton. LC 86-30068. (Selected Studies in Phenomenology & Existential Philosophy). 259p. (C). 1988. text 64.50 (*0-88706-521-X*); pap. text 21.95 (*0-88706-522-8*) State U NY Pr.

Postmodernism & Democratic Theory. Aryeh Botwinick. LC 92-15679. 288p. 1993. 59.95 (*0-87722-997-X*) Temple U Pr.

Postmodernism & Education. Robin Usher & Richard Edwards. LC 94-8494. (Illus.). 240p. (C). 1994. pap. 25.99 (*0-415-10281-2*, B4294) Routledge.

Postmodernism & Interaction in Everyday Life: Reflections on Self & Society. Jon Epstein. Ed. by Peter Cookson. (New Directions in Sociology Ser.: 2). 350p. 1998. text 70.00 (*0-8153-1891-X*) Garland.

Postmodernism & Islam: Predicament & Promise. Akbar Ahmed. LC 91-39584. 304p. (C). (gr. 13). 1992. pap. 24.99 (*0-415-06293-4*, A7179) Routledge.

Postmodernism & Its Critics. John McGowan. LC 90-55758. 320p. 1991. text 47.50 (*0-8014-2494-1*); pap. text 15.95 (*0-8014-9738-8*) Cornell U Pr.

Postmodernism & Japan. Ed. by Masao Miyoshi & H. D. Harootunian. LC 89-7709. 322p. 1989. text 49.95 (*0-8223-0779-0*); pap. text 17.95 (*0-8223-0896-7*) Duke.

Postmodernism & Law. Dennis Patterson. Ed. by Tom D. Campbell. (International Library of Essays in Law & Legal Theory). 500p. (C). 1994. lib. bdg. 150.00 (*0-8147-6550-5*) NYU Pr.

Postmodernism & Organizations. John Hassard & Martin Parker. (Illus.). 256p. (C). 1993. text 55.00 (*0-8039-8879-6*); pap. text 21.95 (*0-8039-8880-X*) Sage.

Postmodernism & Performance. Nick Kaye. LC 93-32470. (New Directions in Theatre Ser.). 176p. 1994. pap. 20.95 (*0-312-12024-9*); text 49.95 (*0-312-12023-0*) St Martin.

Postmodernism & Political Change. Nancy C. Hartsock. (Thinking Gender Ser.). (C). (gr. 13). 1999. 65.00 (*0-415-90530-3*) Routledge.

Postmodernism & Politics. Ed. by Jonathan Arac. LC 85-28835. (Theory & History of Literature Ser.: Vol. 28). 224p. (Orig.). 1986. pap. 14.95 (*0-8166-1468-7*) U of Minn Pr.

Postmodernism & Popular Culture. Angela McRobbie. LC 93-41812. (Illus.). 232p. (C). 1994. pap. 20.99 (*0-415-07713-3*, B4295) Routledge.

Postmodernism & Popular Culture: A Cultural History. John Docker. (Illus.). 335p. (C). 1995. pap. text 19.95 (*0-521-46598-2*) Cambridge U Pr.

Postmodernism & Race. Eric M. Kramer. LC 96-26281. 200p. 1997. 57.95 (*0-275-95367-X*, Praeger Pubs) Greenwood.

Postmodernism & Social Inquiry. Ed. by David R. Dickens & Andrea Fontana. LC 93-50860. (Critical Perspectives Ser.). 259p. 1994. pap. 21.95 (*0-89862-422-3*, 2422); lib. bdg. 40.00 (*0-89862-415-0*, C2415) Guilford Pubns.

Postmodernism & Society. Ed. by Roy Boyne & Ali Rattansi. LC 90-8644. (Illus.). 309p. 1990. pap. 15.95 (*0-312-05223-5*) St Martin.

***Postmodernism & the Enlightenment: Theory & Practice in the Study of Eighteenth-Century Fren.** Daniel Gordon. 240p. 2000. 80.00 (*0-415-92796-X*) Routledge.

***Postmodernism & the Enlightenment: Theory & Practice in the Study of Eighteenth-Century French.** Daniel Gordon. 240p. 2000. pap. 22.99 (*0-415-92797-8*) Routledge.

Postmodernism & the Environmental Crisis. Arran Gare. 176p. (C). 1995. pap. 22.99 (*0-415-12479-4*) Routledge.

***Postmodernism & the New Enlightenment.** Hugo A. Meynell. LC 99-17999. 1999. 39.95 (*0-8132-0946-3*) Cath U Pr.

Postmodernism & the New Enlightenment. Hugo A. Meynell. LC 99-17999. 2000. pap. 19.95 (*0-8132-0947-1*) Cath U Pr.

Postmodernism & the Other: New Imperialism of Western Culture. Sardar. LC 97-32972. 1998. 59.95 (*0-7453-0748-5*, Pub. by Pluto GBR) Stylus Pub VA.

Postmodernism & the Other: New Imperialism of Western Culture. Ziauddin Sardar. 1998. pap. 20.95 (*0-7453-0749-3*, Pub. by Pluto GBR) Stylus Pub VA.

***Postmodernism & the Politics of 'Culture'** Adam Katz. (Cultural Studies). 310p. 2000. pap. 42.00 (*0-8133-6807-3*) Westview.

Postmodernism & the Quebec Novel. Janet M. Paterson. Tr. by David Homel & Charles Phillips. (Theory - Culture Ser.). 168p. 1994. text 35.00 (*0-8020-0530-6*); pap. text 14.95 (*0-8020-6968-1*) U of Toronto Pr.

Postmodernism & the Search for Enlightenment. Karlis Racevskis. LC 93-7338. 172p. reprint ed. pap. 53.40 (*0-608-20052-2*, 207132400011) Bks Demand.

Postmodernism & the Social Sciences: A Thematic Approach. Robert Hollinger. LC 94-11587. (Contemporary Social Theory Ser.: Vol. 4). 240p. 1994. 44.00 (*0-8039-4637-6*); pap. 22.50 (*0-8039-4638-4*) Sage.

Postmodernism Debate in Latin America. Ed. by John Beverley et al. LC 94-23975. (Boundary Two Book Ser.). 336p. 1995. text 49.95 (*0-8223-1586-6*); pap. text 17.95 (*0-8223-1614-5*) Duke.

Postmodernism, Feminism, & Cultural Politics: Rethinking Educational Boundaries. Ed. by Henry A. Giroux. LC 90-36679. (SUNY Series, Teacher Empowerment & School Reform). 308p. (C). 1991. text 59.50 (*0-7914-0576-1*); pap. text 19.95 (*0-7914-0577-X*) State U NY Pr.

Postmodernism in Islam. Akber Ahmed. 294p. 1996. pap. 15.95 (*0-614-21168-9*, 970) Kazi Pubns.

Postmodernism in the Cinema. Ed. by Cristina Degli-Esposti. LC 97-46857. 272p. 1998. 59.95 (*1-57181-105-2*); pap. 22.50 (*1-57181-106-0*) Berghahn Bks.

Postmodernism Is Not What You Think. Charles Lemert. (Twentieth-Century Social Theory Ser.). 240p. 1997. pap. 21.95 (*1-55786-286-9*) Blackwell Pubs.

Postmodernism, or, the Cultural Logic of Late Capitalism. Fredric Jameson. LC 90-34074. (Post-Contemporary Interventions Ser.). (Illus.). 461p. 1992. pap. text 19.95 (*0-8223-1090-2*) Duke.

Postmodernism, "Reality" & Public Administration: A Discourse. Ed. by Hugh T. Miller & Charles J. Fox. LC 96-35674. 213p. (Orig.). 1997. pap. 25.95 (*1-57420-060-7*) Chatelaine.

Postmodernism, Reason & Religion. Ernest Gellner. LC 91-43166. 128p. (C). 1992. pap. 18.99 (*0-415-08024-X*, A7664) Routledge.

Postmodernism, Religion & the Future of Social Work. Ed. by Roland Meinert et al. LC 98-16142. (Social Thought Monograph Ser.: Vol. 18, No. 3). 92p. 1998. 29.95 (*0-7890-0516-6*, Haworth Pastrl) Haworth Pr.

Postmodernism Rightly Understood: The Return to Realism in American Thought Peter A. Lawler. LC 99-13633. (American Intellectual Culture Ser.). 208p. 1999. 19.95 (*0-8476-9426-7*) Rowman.

Postmodernism Rightly Understood: The Return to Reason in American Thought. Peter A. Lawler. LC 99-13633. 208p. 1999. pap. 60.00 (*0-8476-9425-9*) Rowman.

Postmodernism, Sociology & Health. Nicholas J. Fox. LC 93-4286. 192p. 1993. 37.50 (*0-335-19046-4*); pap. 12.99 (*0-335-19045-6*) U of Toronto Pr.

Postmodernism, Sociology, & Health. Nicholas J. Fox. 160p. (C). 1994. text 55.00 (*0-8020-0437-7*); pap. text 19.95 (*0-8020-7227-5*) U of Toronto Pr.

Postmodernism, Unraveling Racism & Democratic Institutions. John W. Murphy & Jung Min Choi. LC 97-5589. 144p. 1997. 52.95 (*0-275-95664-4*, Praeger Pubs) Greenwood.

P

Postmodernisms Now: Essays on Contemporaneity in the Arts. Charles Altieri. LC 98-17143. (Literature & Philosophy Ser.). 1998. 50.00 (*0-271-01803-8*) Pa St U Pr.

Postmodernisms Now: Essays on Contemporaneity in the Arts. Charles Altieri. LC 98-17143. (Literature & Philosophy Ser.). (Illus.). 304p. 1998. pap. 22.50 (*0-271-01804-6*) Pa St U Pr.

Postmodernist Culture: An Introduction to Theories of the Contemporary. 2nd ed. Steven Connor. LC 96-16125. 304p. 1996. pap. 24.95 (*0-631-20052-5*) Blackwell Pubs.

Postmodernist Tao: A Guide to Apprehending Ways of Meaning in Pathless Lands. Jim Norwine. Ed. by Linda F. Winans. LC 92-40602. 172p. (Orig.). (C). 1993. pap. text 21.50 (*0-8191-8993-6*); lib. bdg. 46.00 (*0-8191-8992-8*) U Pr of Amer.

Postmodernity. David Lyon. Ed. by Frank Parkin. (Concepts in the Social Sciences Ser.). 112p. 1994. 9.00 (*0-335-19149-5*); pap. 2.00 (*0-335-19148-7*) OpUniv Pr.

Postmodernity. David Lyon. LC 94-14630. (Concepts in Social Thought Ser.). 112p. 1994. text 39.95 (*0-8166-2612-X*) U of Minn Pr.

Postmodernity. Barry Smart. LC 92-9969. (Key Ideas Ser.). 176p. (C). 1993. pap. 16.99 (*0-415-06961-0*, A9809) Routledge.

Postmodernity. 2nd ed. David Lyon. 1999. pap. text 18.95 (*0-335-20144-X*) OpUniv Pr.

***Postmodernity.** 2nd ed. David Lyon. 1999. pap. text 14.95 (*0-8166-3227-8*) U of Minn Pr.

Postmodernity 2nd ed. David Lyon. 1999. 69.95 (*0-335-20145-8*) OpUniv Pr.

Postmodernity: Christian Identity in a Fragmented Age. Paul Lakeland. LC 97-23817. (Guide to Theological Inquiry Ser.). 128p. 1997. pap. 14.00 (*0-8006-3098-X*, 1-3098, Fortress Pr) Augsburg Fortress.

Postmodernity & Its Discontents. Zygmont Bauman. LC 96-47838. 1997. text 50.00 (*0-8147-1303-3*) NYU Pr.

Postmodernity & Its Discontents. Zygmunt Bauman. LC 96-47838. 1997. pap. text 18.00 (*0-8147-1304-1*) NYU Pr.

Postmodernity & the Fragmentation of Welfare. John Carter. LC 97-26563. 304p. (C). 1998. pap. 27.99 (*0-415-16392-7*) Routledge.

Postmodernity & the Fragmentation of Welfare. John Carter. LC 97-26563. (Illus.). 304p. (C). 1998. 85.00 (*0-415-16391-9*) Routledge.

***Postmodernity Ethics & Novel: From Leavis to Levinas.** Andrew Gibson. 224p. (C). 1999. text 75.00 (*0-415-19895-X*) Routledge.

Postmodernity, Ethics & Novel: From Levis to Levinas. Andrew Gibson. LC 98-51149. 1999. pap. 24.99 (*0-415-19896-8*) Routledge.

Postmodernity in Latin America: The Argentine Paradigm. Santiago Colas. LC 94-11348. (Post-Contemporary Interventions Ser.). 240p. 1994. text 49.95 (*0-8223-1508-4*); pap. text 17.95 (*0-8223-1520-3*) Duke.

Postmodernity U. S. A. The Crisis of Modernism in Postwar America. Anthony Woodiwiss. (Illus.). 192p. (C). 1993. text 69.95 (*0-8039-8788-9*); pap. text 22.95 (*0-8039-8789-7*) Sage.

***Postmodernity's Histories: The Past As Legacy & Project.** Arif Dirlik. 288p. 2000. 67.00 (*0-7425-0166-3*); pap. 23.95 (*0-7425-0167-1*) Rowman.

Postmodernization: Change in Advance Society. Stephen Crook et al. 272p. (C). 1992. text 65.00 (*0-8039-8327-1*); pap. text 21.95 (*0-8039-8328-X*) Sage.

Postmodernizing the Faith: Evangelical Response to the Challenge of Postmodernism. Millard J. Erickson. LC 97-38493. 176p. (C). 1998. pap. text 14.99 (*0-8010-2164-2*) Baker Bks.

PostModerns: The Beliefs, Hopes & Fears of Young Americans (1965-81) Craig K. Miller. LC 95-83705. 192p. 1997. pap. 19.95 (*0-88177-157-0*, DR157) Discipleship Res.

Postmoderns: The New American Poetry Revisited. rev. ed. Ed. by Donald Allen & George F. Butterick. LC 79-52054. 448p. 1982. pap. 14.95 (*0-8021-5035-7*, Grove) Grove-Atltic.

***Postmortem.** Patricia Cornwell. (SPA.). 1999. pap. 14.95 (*970-05-0943-5*) Distribks Inc.

Postmortem. Patricia Cornwell. 352p. 1991. mass mkt. 6.49 (*0-380-71021-8*, Avon Bks) Morrow Avon.

Postmortem. Patricia Cornwell. (Kay Scarpetta Mystery Ser.). 352p. 2000. mass mkt. 7.99 (*0-671-02361-6*, Pocket Books) PB.

Postmortem. Mark Dunster. 19p. (Orig.). 1983. pap. 4.00 (*0-89642-099-X*) Linden Pubs.

Postmortem. Ken Ludwig. LC 91-144218. 131p. 1989. write for info. (*0-573-69133-9*) S French Trade.

Postmortem: New Evidence in the Case of Sacco & Vanzetti. William Young & David E. Kaiser. LC 84-24483. (Illus.). 208p. 1985. 30.00 (*0-87023-478-1*); pap. 16.95 (*0-87023-479-X*) U of Mass Pr.

Postmortem: Poems by Maurice Kilwein Guevara. Maurice Kilwein Guevara. LC 93-12346. (Contemporary Poetry Ser.). 88p. 1994. pap. 14.95 (*0-8203-1562-1*) U of Ga Pr.

Postmortem Administration. Daniel A. Collins. 476p. 1997. ring bd. 795.00 (*0-922943-06-0*) Esperti Petrsn.

Postmortem Change in Human & Animal Remains: A Systematic Approach. Marc S. Micozzi. (Illus.). 136p. 1991. pap. 23.95 (*0-398-06288-9*); text 34.95 (*0-398-05747-8*) C C Thomas.

Postmortem Change in the Rat: A Histologic Characterization. William J. Seaman. LC 87-3418. (Illus.). 128p. 1987. reprint ed. pap. 39.70 (*0-608-00053-1*, 206081900006) Bks Demand.

Postmortem for a Postmodernist. Arthur A. Berger. LC 97-4893. 176p. 1997. 18.95 (*0-7619-8911-0*); pap. 54.00 (*0-7619-8910-2*) AltaMira Pr.

Postmortem on Malaya. Virginia M. Thompson. 1977. text 21.95 (*0-8369-8194-4*, 8332) Ayer.

Postmyocardial Infarction Management & Rehabilitation. Ed. by John K. Vyden. LC 83-5179. (Basic & Clinical Cardiology Ser.: No. 3). (Illus.). 489p. reprint ed. pap. 151.60 (*0-7837-3358-5*, 204331600008) Bks Demand.

Postnatal Care. Ed. by Jo Alexander et al. 1993. pap. text 17.95 (*0-8020-7452-9*) U of Toronto Pr.

Postnatal Development, Aging & Degeneration of the TMJ. Hans U. Luder. (Craniofacial Growth Ser.: Vol. 32). (Illus.). 270p. 1996. 55.00 (*0-929921-28-3*) UM CHGD.

Postnatal Development of the Ovary in Homo Sapiens & Macaca Mulatta, & Induction of Ovulation in the Macaque. Gertrude Van Wagenen & Miriam E. Simpson. LC 72-91309. (Illus.). 328p. reprint ed. pap. 101.70 (*0-8357-8279-4*, 203390900087) Bks Demand.

Postnatal Exercise Program. Arthur Ulene. Ed. by Kukla Vera. (Illus.). 196p. 1995. 19.95 incl. audio (*0-932513-03-4*) ACOR Programs.

Postnatal Growth Vol. 2: Neurobiology. 2nd ed. F. Falkner & J. M. Tanner. LC 85-19397. (Human Growth Ser.). (Illus.). 578p. (C). 1986. text 125.00 (*0-306-41952-1*) Kluwer Academic.

***Postnatal Yoga.** Francoise Harbira. (Illus.). 2000. 17.95 (*0-7548-0499-2*, Lorenz Bks) Anness Pub.

Postnational Democracy. Curtin. LC 97-189159. 1997. pap. text 28.00 (*90-411-0447-X*) Kluwer Academic.

Postnational Identity: Critical Theory & Existential Philosophy in Habermas, Kierkegaard & Havel. Martin J. Matustik & Vaclav Havel. LC 92-42692. (Critical Perspectives Ser.). 328p. 1993. pap. text 18.95 (*0-89862-270-0*) Guilford Pubns.

Postnaupliar Development of a Looking-Glass Copepod, Pleuromamma Xiphias (Giesbrecht, 1889), with Analysis of Distributions of Sex & Asymmetry. Frank D. Ferrari. LC 85-600051. (Smithsonian Contributions to Zoology Ser.: No. 420). 59p. reprint ed. pap. 30.00 (*0-608-16394-5*, 202655900050) Bks Demand.

PostNegritude Visual & Literary Culture. Mark A. Reid. LC 96-20292. (SUNY Series, Cultural Studies in Cinema/Video). 192p. (C). 1997. text 54.50 (*0-7914-3301-3*); pap. text 17.95 (*0-7914-3302-1*) State U NY Pr.

Postoperative Care of the Critically Ill Patient. Ed. by T. James Gallagher. LC 94-40829. (Illus.). 528p. 1995. 95.00 (*0-683-03416-2*) Lppncott W & W.

Postoperative Critical Care of the Massachusetts General Hospital. 2nd ed. Massachusetts General Hospital, Department of Anesthesiology Staff. Ed. by William Hoffman et al. LC 92-15625. 528p. 1992. pap. text 45.95 (*0-316-36838-5*) Lppncott W & W.

Postoperative Critical Care Procedures of the Massachusetts General Hospital. W. Andrew Kofke & Gerold H. Levy. 544p. 1986. 27.00 (*0-316-50098-4*, Little Brwn Med Div) Lppncott W & W.

Postoperative Epidural Opioids. J. Chrubasik et al. LC 93-25591. 1993. 35.00 (*0-387-56871-9*) Spr-Verlag.

Postoperative Epidural Opioids. J. Chrubasik et al. (Illus.). 115p. 1993. pap. write for info. (*3-540-56871-9*) Spr-Verlag.

Postoperative Infections in Orthopedic Surgery: Prevention & Treatment. Ed. by Paul A. Lotke. 73p. 1992. pap. 35.00 (*0-89203-099-2*) Amer Acad Ortho Surg.

Postoperative Management of the Cardiac Surgical Patient. Ed. by John P. Williams. 435p. 1995. text 90.00 (*0-443-08932-9*) Church.

Postoperative Pain Management. Ed. by F. Michael Ferrante & Timothy R. VadeBoncouer. (Illus.). 300p. (Orig.). 1992. pap. text 89.00 (*0-443-08766-0*) Church.

Postoperative Thromboembolism: Frequency, Etiology, Prophylaxis. David Bergqvist. (Illus.). 248p. 1983. 71.95 (*0-387-12062-9*) Spr-Verlag.

Postoptimal Analyses, Parametric Programming & Related Topics: Degeneracy, Multicriteria Decision Making, Redundancy. 2nd ed. Thomas Gal. LC 94-12443. 464p. (C). 1994. lib. bdg. 124.95 (*3-11-014060-8*) De Gruyter.

Postpartum Depression. Sharon Roan. 1993. write for info. (*0-471-54678-X*) Wiley.

Postpartum Depression: A Comprehensive Approach for Nurses. Kathleen A. Kendall-Tackett & Glenda K. Kantor. (Clinical Nursing Research Ser.). (Illus.). 160p. (C). 1993. text 37.00 (*0-8039-5034-9*); pap. text 16.95 (*0-8039-5035-7*) Sage.

Postpartum Depression: A Research Guide & International Bibliography. Laurence Kruckman & Chris Asmann-Finch. LC 85-31136. (Reference Books on Family Issues: Vol. 8). 200p. 1986. text 52.00 (*0-8240-9121-3*, SS335) Garland.

Postpartum Depression: Causes & Consequences. M. W. O'Hara & L. B. Alloy. (Series in Psychopathology). 256p. 1994. 90.00 (*0-387-94261-0*) Spr-Verlag.

Postpartum Depression & Child Development. Ed. by Lynne Murray & Peter J. Cooper. LC 96-39987. 322p. 1997. lib. bdg. 40.00 (*1-57230-197-X*, 0197) Guilford Pubns.

***Postpartum Depression & Child Development.** Ed. by Lynne Murray & Peter J. Cooper. 322p. 1999. pap. text 21.00 (*1-57230-517-7*) Guilford Pubns.

Postpartum Mood Disorders. Ed. by Laura J. Miller. LC 98-24929. (Clinical Practice Ser.). 280p. 1998. text 39.50 (*0-88048-929-4*, 8929) Am Psychiatric.

Postpartum Nursing: Health Care of Women. Joellen W. Hawkins & Beverly Gorvine. (Illus.). 192p. 1984. pap. 25.95 (*0-8261-4690-2*) Springer Pub.

Postpartum Psychiatric Illness: A Picture Puzzle. Ed. by James A. Hamilton & Patricia N. Harberger. LC 91-30386. (Illus.). 384p. (C). 1992. text 35.00 (*0-8122-3137-6*) U of Pa Pr.

Postpartum Psychiatric Illness: A Picture Puzzle. Ed. by James A. Hamilton & Patricia N. Harberger. LC 91-30386. (Illus.). 383p. 1992. reprint ed. pap. 118.80 (*0-608-05706-1*, 206622100007) Bks Demand.

PostPartum Survival Guide. Ann Dunnewald & Diane G. Sanford. LC 94-67045. (Illus.). 288p. (Orig.). 1994. pap. 14.95 (*1-879237-80-6*) New Harbinger.

Postphenomenology. Don Ihde. (Studies in Phenomenology & Existential Philosophy). (Illus.). 160p. 1993. 29.95 (*0-8101-1098-9*) Northwestern U Pr.

Postphenomenology: Essays in the Postmodern Context. Don Ihde. 162p. 1995. pap. text 16.95 (*0-8101-1275-2*) Northwestern U Pr.

Postponements: Woman, Sensuality, & Death in Nietzsche. David F. Krell. LC 85-42933. (Studies in Phenomenology & Existential Philosophy). (Illus.). 128p. (C). 1986. 31.95 (*0-253-34560-X*) Ind U Pr.

Postponing the Heat Death of the Universe. Stephen Gregg. 1986. 3.50 (*0-87129-399-4*, P61) Dramatic Pub.

***Postpositivism & Educational Research.** D. C. Phillips & Nicholas C. Burbules. LC 99-49770. (Philosophy, Theory, & Educational Research Ser.). 150p. 2000. text 15.95 (*0-8476-9121-7*) Rowman.

***Postpositivism & Educational Research.** D. C. Phillips & Nicholas C. Burbules. LC 99-49770. (Illus.). 150p. 2000. pap. 15.95 (*0-8476-9122-5*) Rowman.

Postprincipia: Gravitation for Physicists & Astronomers. Peter Rastall. 300p. (C). 1991. text 48.00 (*981-02-0778-6*) World Scientific Pub.

Postpublication National Quarter Horses. Jack McBryde. 274p. 1998. spiral bd. 99.95 (*1-893033-02-3*) Loshadt Publishing.

Postreform Congress. Roger H. Davidson. LC 91-61134. 384p. (Orig.). (C). 1991. pap. text 22.00 (*0-312-05673-7*) St Martin.

Postreproductive Gynecology. Ed. by Hugh M. Shingleton & W. Glenn Hurt. (Illus.). 590p. 1990. text 114.00 (*0-443-08641-9*) Church.

Postrer Duelo de Espana. Pedro Calderon de la Barca. Ed. by Guy Rossetti. (Textos B Ser.: Vol. XXIII). 218p. (C). 1977. 51.00 (*0-7293-0045-5*, Pub. by Tamesis Bks Ltd) Boydell & Brewer.

Postres Mexicanos. Nieto Blanca. 1997. pap. text 7.98 (*968-403-960-3*) Selector.

Postretirement Health Benefits: Measuring Financial Liability. Izzet Sahin. Ed. by Mary E. Brennan. LC 91-76776. 112p. (Orig.). 1992. pap. 15.00 (*0-89154-435-6*) Intl Found Employ.

Postructuralism & the New Testament: Derrida & Foucault at the Foot of the Cross. Stephen D. Moore. LC 94-2954. 144p. 1994. pap. 17.00 (*0-8006-2599-4*, Fortress Pr) Augsburg Fortress.

Posts: Re Addressing the Ethical. Dawne McCance. LC 95-33677. (SUNY Series in Postmodern Culture). 169p. (C). 1996. text 46.50 (*0-7914-3001-4*); pap. text 14.95 (*0-7914-3002-2*) State U NY Pr.

Postscript & Acrobat/PDF: Applications, Trouble Shooting & Cross-Platform-Publishing. T. Merz. LC 96-42126. (Illus.). 424p. 1996. 69.50 (*3-540-60854-0*) Spr-Verlag.

***Postscript & Acrobat/PDF Bible: Applications, Troubleshooting & Cross-Platform-Publishing.** 2nd ed. Thomas Merz. (Illus.). 650p. 1999. 64.95 (*3-540-65534-4*) Spr-Verlag.

Postscript by Example. Henry McGilton. (C). 1993. pap. text. write for info. (*0-201-59481-1*) Addison-Wesley.

PostScript by Example. Henry McGilton & Mary Compione. LC 92-19743. 640p. (C). 1992. pap. text 36.95 (*0-201-63228-4*) Addison-Wesley.

PostScript Language Program Design. Glenn C. Reid, Ed. by Adobe Systems Inc. Staff. (Adobe Postscript Ser.: Bk. 3). 240p. (C). 1988. pap. text 26.95 (*0-201-14396-8*) Addison-Wesley.

Postscript Language Reference. 3rd ed. Adobe Systems Inc. Staff. LC 98-55489. 912p. (C). 1999. pap. text 49.95 (*0-201-37922-8*) Addison-Wesley.

PostScript Language Reference Manual. 2nd ed. Adobe Systems Inc. Staff. 784p. (C). 1990. pap. text 36.95 (*0-201-18127-4*) Addison-Wesley.

PostScript Language Tutorial & Cookbook. Adobe Systems Inc. Staff. 256p. (C). 1986. pap. text 26.95 (*0-201-10179-3*) Addison-Wesley.

PostScript Programmer's Reference Guide. David A. Holzgang. (C). 1989. pap. 27.66 (*0-673-38574-4*, Scott Frsmn) Addison-Wesley Educ.

Postscript to the Name of the Rose. Umberto Eco. 1995. reprint ed. lib. bdg. 29.95 (*1-56849-675-3*) Buccaneer Bks.

PostScript Typeface Library, Vol. 2. Tony Esposito. 1994. pap. 37.95 (*0-442-01494-5*, VNR) Wiley.

PostScript Typeface Library: Sans Serif Design, Outline & Ornaments, Vol. 2. Tony Esposito & Jean C. King. 496p. 1994. pap. 37.95 (*0-471-28567-6*, VNR) Wiley.

Postscript Typeface Library: Serif & Script, Vol. 1. Tony Esposito. 1994. pap. 37.95 (*0-442-01491-0*, VNR) Wiley.

Postscript Typeface Library: Serif & Script, Vol. 1. Tony Esposito & Jean C. King. 496p. 1994. pap. 37.95 (*0-471-28566-8*, VNR) Wiley.

PostScripts. Carl Cook. LC 94-23596. 80p. 1994. 10.00 (*1-880729-09-1*) Vega Pr.

Postscripts for Thinking Flutists: Self-Help Techniques for Individualized Optimum Beauty of Sound. Harriet Peacock-LeJeune. 1993. 12.95 (*0-533-10521-8*) Vantage.

Postsecondary Developmental Programs: A Traditional Agenda with New Imperatives. Louise M. Tomlinson. Ed. by Jonathan D. Fife. LC 89-63439. (ASHE-ERIC Higher Education Reports: No. 89-3). 109p. (Orig.). (C). 1989. pap. text 24.00 (*0-9623882-2-X*) GWU Grad Schl E&HD.

Postsecondary Education & the New Workforce. Esther M. Rodriguez. 29p. 1996. pap. 2.25 (*0-16-063598-5*) USGPO.

Postsecondary Enrollment Options Program: A Research Report. Susan Urahn. (Illus.). 70p. 1998. reprint ed. pap. text 25.00 (*0-7881-2810-8*) DIANE Pub.

***Postsecondary Financing Strategies: How Undergraduates Combine Work, Borrowing & Attendance.** Stephen Cuccaro-Alamin. 77p. 1998. pap. 6.00 (*0-16-063650-7*) USGPO.

Postsecondary Financing Strategies: How Undergraduates Combine Work, Borrowing & Attendance. Stephen Cuccaro-Alamin & Susan P. Choy. Ed. by C. Dennis Carroll. (Illus.). 67p. (C). 1999. pap. text 20.00 (*0-7881-7763-X*) DIANE Pub.

Postsecondary Institutions of the People's Republic of China: A Comprehensive Guide to Institutions of Higher Education in China. William Paver & Yiping Wan. (World Education Ser.). 627p. (Orig.). 1992. pap. text 50.00 (*0-929851-11-0*) Am Assn Coll Registrars.

Postsecondary Persistence & Attainment. Stephanie Cuccaro-Alamin. 34p. 1997. pap. 4.25 (*0-16-049222-X*) USGPO.

Postsecondary Students & the Courts in Canada: Cases & Commentary from the Common-Law Provinces. David A. Hannah. LC 98-13279. 1998. 54.50 (*0-912557-20-6*) Coll Admin Pubns.

***Postslavery Literatures in the Americas: Family Portraits in Black & White.** George B. Handley. 256p. 2000. 57.50 (*0-8139-1976-2*); pap. 18.50 (*0-8139-1977-0*) U Pr of Va.

Postsocialist Pathways: Transforming Politics & Property in East Central Europe. David Stark & Laszlo Bruszt. LC 97-21299. (Cambridge Studies in Comparative Politics). (Illus.). 296p. (C). 1998. text 59.95 (*0-521-58035-8*); pap. text 22.95 (*0-521-58974-6*) Cambridge U Pr.

***Poststructural Geographies: The Diabolical Art of Spatial Science.** Marcus Doel. (Illus.). 1999. pap. 28.95 (*0-8476-9819-X*) Rowman.

***Poststructuralism & International Relations: Bringing the Political Back In.** Jenny Edkins. LC 99-21481. (Critical Perspectives on World Politics Ser.). 1999. 49.95 (*1-55587-845-8*) L Rienner.

Poststructuralism, Citizenship, & Social Policy. Alan R. Petersen. LC 99-19521. 1999. pap. write for info. (*0-415-18288-3*) Routledge.

***Poststructuralism, Citizenship & Social Policy.** Alan R. Petersen. LC 99-19521. 1999. write for info. (*0-415-18287-5*) Routledge.

Poststructuralism, Politics & Education. Michael Peters. LC 95-36905. (Critical Studies in Education & Culture). 232p. 1996. 65.00 (*0-89789-418-9*, Bergin & Garvey); pap. 21.95 (*0-89789-420-0*, Bergin & Garvey) Greenwood.

Postsuburban California: The Transformation of Orange County since World War II. Ed. by Rob Kling et al. (Illus.). 307p. 1995. pap. 17.95 (*0-520-20160-4*, Pub. by U CA Pr) Cal Prin Full Svc.

***Posttest Analysis of the Steel Containment Vessel Model.** J. S. Ludwigsen. 37p. 2000. pap. 4.00 (*0-16-059113-9*) USGPO.

Posttranslational Modifications, Pt. A. Ed. by Sidney P. Colowick & Nathan O. Kaplan. (Methods in Enzymology Ser.: Vol. 106). 1984. text 188.00 (*0-12-182006-8*) Acad Pr.

Posttranslational Modifications, Vol. 107, Pt. B. Sidney P. Colowick & Nathan O. Kaplan. (Methods in Enzymology Ser.). 1984. text 179.00 (*0-12-182007-6*) Acad Pr.

Posttraumatic Growth: Positive Changes in the Aftermath of Crisis. Ed. by Richard Tedeschi et al. LC 97-26304. (Personality & Clinical Psychology Ser.). 225p. 1997. 34.50 (*0-8058-2319-0*) L Erlbaum Assocs.

Posttraumatic Nightmares: Psychodynamic Explorations. Melvin R. Lansky & Carol R. Bley. LC 94-43415. 208p. 1995. 34.50 (*0-88163-193-0*) Analytic Pr.

Posttraumatic Peripheral Nerve Regeneration: Experimental Basis & Clinical Implications. Alfredo Gorio. LC 81-40380. 658p. 1981. reprint ed. pap. 200.00 (*0-608-00379-4*, 206109300007) Bks Demand.

Posttraumatic Stress Disorder: Acute & Long-Term Responses to Trauma & Disaster. Ed. by Carol S. Fullerton & Robert J. Ursano. LC 96-24027. (Progress in Psychiatry Ser.: Vol. 51). 308p. 1997. text 42.50 (*0-88048-751-8*, 8751) Am Psychiatric.

Posttraumatic Stress Disorder: Additional Perspectives. Merrill I. Lipton. LC 93-37142. 258p. 1994. pap. 34.95 (*0-398-06242-0*) C C Thomas.

Posttraumatic Stress Disorder: Additional Perspectives. Merrill I. Lipton. LC 93-37142. 258p. (C). 1994. text 52.95 (*0-398-05899-7*) C C Thomas.

Posttraumatic Stress Disorder: DSM-IV & Beyond. Ed. by Jonathan R. Davidson & Edna B. Foa. LC 92-7052. 262p. 1992. text 35.00 (*0-88048-502-7*, 8502) Am Psychiatric.

Posttraumatic Stress Disorder: Etiology, Phenomenology, & Treatment. Ed. by Marion E. Wolf & Aron D. Mosnaim. LC 90-68. 270p. 1990. text 19.95 (*0-88048-299-0*, 8299) Am Psychiatric.

Posttraumatic Stress Disorder in Children. Spencer Eth & Robert S. Pynoos. LC 85-15762. (Progress in Psychiatry Ser.: No. 4). 186p. 1985. 19.95 (*0-88048-067-X*, 8067) Am Psychiatric.

Posttraumatic Stress Disorder in Litigation: Guidelines for Forensic Assessment. Ed. by Robert I. Simon. 192p. 1994. text 29.50 (*0-88048-687-2*, 8687) Am Psychiatric.

***Posttraumatic Stress Intervention: Challenges, Issues & Perspectives.** John M. Violanti et al. LC 00-25323. 2000. pap. write for info. (*0-398-07067-9*) C C Thomas.

An Asterisk (*) at the beginning of an entry indicates that the title is appearing for the first time.

*Posttraumatische Belastungsstorungen: Stand und Perspektiven des Wissens uber Effektive Therapien. A. Maercker. (Verhaltenstherapie Ser.). 60p. 1999. 35.00 (3-8055-7028-7) S Karger.
Postulates of Re-Evaluation Counseling. Harvey Jackins. Tr. by Ersi Zarangali from ENG. (GRE.). 1982. pap. 1.00 (0-911214-99-2) Rational Isl.
Postulates of Re-Evaluation Counseling. rev. ed. Personal Counselors, Inc. Staff. 1990. pap. 2.00 (0-913937-43-6) Rational Isl.
Postulates of Re-Evaluation Counseling: Arabic Translation. Harvey Jackins. 1987. pap. 1.00 (0-913937-21-5) Rational Isl.
Postulates of Re-Evaluation Counseling: Chinese Translation. Harvey Jackins. Tr. by Sun Jian-Min from ENG. 1987. pap. 1.00 (0-913937-27-4) Rational Isl.
Postulates of Re-Evaluation Counseling: Hungarian Translation. Harvey Jackins. Tr. by Molnar Gabriella. 1981. pap. 1.00 (0-911214-93-3) Rational Isl.
Postulates of Reevaluation Counseling. Harvey Jackins. Tr. by Mark Shtern from ENG. (RUS.). (Orig.). 1982. pap. 1.00 (0-911214-95-X) Rational Isl.
Postural Behavior in Newborn Infants. Paul Casear. (Clinics in Developmental Medicine Ser.: Vol. 72). (Illus.). 112p. (C). 1991. text 29.95 (0-521-41201-3, Pub. by Mc Keith Pr) Cambridge U Pr.
Posture: Sitting, Standing, Chair Design & Exercise. Dennis Zacharkow. (Illus.). 456p. 1988. pap. 49.95 (0-398-06510-1) C C Thomas.
Posture: Sitting, Standing, Chair Design & Exercise. Dennis Zacharkow. (Illus.). 456p. (C). 1988. text 72.95 (0-398-05418-5) C C Thomas.
Posture & Motility in Preterm Infants: A Clinical Approach. Laila De Groot. 160p. 1994. pap. 25.00 (90-5383-239-4, Pub. by VU Univ Pr) Paul & Co Pubs.
Posture, Get It Straight! Janice Novak. 1999. pap. 11.95 (0-399-52548-3, Perigee Bks) Berkley Pub.
Posture, Get It Straight! Janice S. Novak. LC 98-51991. 192p. 1999. pap. 11.95 (0-399-52500-9) Berkley Pub.
Posture Makes Perfect Health. Victor Barker. (Illus.). 206p. (Orig.). 1993. pap. 22.00 (0-87040-871-2) Japan Pubns USA.
Posture of Meditation: A Practical Guide for Meditators of All Traditions. Will Johnson. (Illus.). 112p. (Orig.). 1996. pap. 9.00 (1-57062-232-9, Pub. by Shambhala Pubns) Random.
*Posture Prescription: A Doctor's Rx for: Eliminating Back, Muscle & Joint Pain; Achieving Optimum Strength & Mobility; Living a Lifetime of Fitness & Well-Being. Arthur H. White & Kate Kelly. LC 00-34419. 2001. pap. 16.00 (0-609-80631-9, Three Riv Pr) Crown Pub Group.
Postures: Poems from Hollywood. Mark Dunster. 11p. 1998. pap. 5.00 (0-89642-521-5) Linden Pubs.
Postures for Non-Proliferation Arms Limitation & Security Policies to Minimize Nuclear Proliferation. 168p. 1979. 21.00 (0-85066-133-1) Taylor & Francis.
Postures of Assembly During Eucharistic Prayer. Nathan D. Mitchell & John Leonard. LC 94-31581. 120p. 1994. pap. 11.95 (0-929650-64-6, POSTUR) Liturgy Tr Pubns.
*Postville: A Clash of Cultures in Heartland America. Stephen G. Bloom. (Illus.). 324p. 2000. 25.00 (0-15-100652-0) Harcourt.
Postviral Fatigue Syndrome. Ed. by Peter Behan et al. (British Medical Bulletin Ser.: Vol. 47, No. 4). (Illus.). 264p. 1992. text. write for info. (0-443-04490-2) Church.
*Postwar America: A Student Companion. Harvard Sitkoff. LC 98-34183. (Student Companions to American History Ser.). (Illus.). 296p. (YA). (gr. 7 up). 2000. lib. bdg. 40.00 (0-19-510300-9) OUP.
Postwar America: The United States since 1945. Irwin Unger & Debi Unger. LC 89-60982. 233p. (Orig.). (C). 1989. pap. text 32.95 (0-312-03217-X) St Martin.
Postwar America: 1948 & the Incubation of Our Times. George H. Douglas. LC 97-31438. 295p. (C). 1998. pap. 28.50 (1-57524-041-6) Krieger.
Postwar America, 1945-1971. Howard Zinn. LC 72-88273. (History of American Society Ser.). 260p. (Orig.). 1973. pap. 7.74 (0-672-60936-3, Bobbs) Macmillan.
Postwar Britain, 1945-1964. Anthony Gorst et al. 256p. 1989. text 47.50 (0-86187-760-8) St Martin.
Postwar British Fiction. James Gindin. LC 76-6558. 246p. 1976. reprint ed. lib. bdg. 38.50 (0-8371-8800-8, GIPB, Greenwood Pr) Greenwood.
Postwar British Politics in Perspective. David Marsh et al. LC 98-47771. 300p. 1999. 59.95 (0-7456-2029-9); pap. 29.95 (0-7456-2030-2) Blackwell Pubs.
Postwar Catalan Poetry. David H. Rosenthal. LC 89-43048. (Illus.). 128p. 1991. 29.50 (0-8387-5178-4) Bucknell U Pr.
Postwar Cycles in Manufacturers' Inventories. Thomas M. Stanback, Jr. (Studies in Business Cycles: No. 11). 160p. 1962. reprint ed. 41.60 (0-87014-094-9) Natl Bur Econ Res.
Postwar Developments in Japan's Foreign Trade. U. S. Tariff Commission Staff. LC 75-90741. 242p. 1970. reprint ed. lib. bdg. 65.00 (0-8371-2503-0, PODJ, Greenwood Pr) Greenwood.
Postwar Developments of Japanese Studies in the United States. Helen Hardacre. LC 98-15232. (Japanese Studies Library). xxviii, 425p. 1998. 103.00 (90-04-10981-1) Brill Academic Pubs.
Postwar Economic Problems. Ed. by Seymour E. Harris. LC 71-39103. (Essay Index Reprint Ser.). 1977. reprint ed. 17.95 (0-8369-2694-3) Ayer.
Postwar Economic Reconstruction & Lessons for the East Today. Ed. by Rudiger Dornbusch et al. LC 92-34804. (Illus.). 263p. 1993. 35.00 (0-262-04136-7) MIT Pr.
Postwar Economic Trends in the United States. Ed. by Ralph E. Freeman. LC 72-10884. (Essay Index Reprint Ser.). 1977. reprint ed. 21.95 (0-8369-7216-3) Ayer.
Postwar Evolution of Development Thinking. Charles P. Oman & Ganeshan Wignaraja. LC 91-27768. 288p. 1991. pap. 19.95 (0-312-07185-X) St Martin.
*Postwar Figures of L'Ephemere: Yves Bonnefoy, Louis-Rene de Forets, Jacques Dupin, Andre du Bouchet. James Petterson. LC 00-23107. 248p. 2000. 42.50 (0-8387-5451-1) Bucknell U Pr.
Postwar Foreign Policy Preparation, 1939-1945. Harley Notter. (History - United States Ser.). 726p. 1993. reprint ed. lib. bdg. 109.00 (0-7812-4920-1) Rprt Serv.
Postwar German Literature: A Critical Introduction. Peter Demetz. LC 73-114169. 264p. 1970. 29.75 (0-8290-0198-0); pap. text 9.95 (0-8290-1889-1) Irvington.
Postwar Immigrant: The Story of Truth. unabridged ed. Karl-Heinz Kahl. vii, 353p. 1999. 24.00 (0-9668317-0-5) K Kahl.
Postwar Immigrant America: A Social History. Reed Ueda. 208p. 1994. text 39.95 (0-312-10279-8); pap. text 15.95 (0-312-07526-X) St Martin.
Postwar Indochina: Old Enemies & New Allies. 1995. lib. bdg. 250.99 (0-8490-6757-X) Gordon Pr.
Postwar Industrial Policy in Japan: An Annotated Bibliography. Karl Boger. LC 87-26535. 218p. 1988. 35.00 (0-8108-2080-3) Scarecrow.
Postwar Japan: 1945 to the Present. Paul J. Bailey. (Historical Association Studies). (Illus.). 224p. 1996. pap. 14.95 (0-631-17901-1) Blackwell Pubs.
Postwar Japan as History. Ed. by Andrew Gordon. 563p. (C). 1992. pap. 22.50 (0-520-07475-0, Pub. by U CA Pr) Cal Prin Full Svc.
Postwar Japanese Economy: Its Development & Structure. Takafusa Nakamura. 300p. 1995. pap. 34.00 (0-86008-514-7, Pub. by U of Tokyo) Col U Pr.
Postwar Japanese Economy: Its Development & Structure. Takafusa Nakamura. LC HC0462.9.N31. 291p. 1981. reprint ed. pap. 90.30 (0-608-01254-8, 206194200001) Bks Demand.
Postwar Japanese System: Cultural Economy & Economic Transformation. William K. Tabb. 424p. 1995. pap. text 24.95 (0-19-508950-2) OUP.
Postwar Kuwait - The Middle East: A Window of Opportunity. Diania Hanson. (Illus.). 118p. (Orig.). 1991. pap. 19.95 (0-9629852-0-1) Landmark TX.
Postwar Macroeconomic Developments. Compiled by John Sargent. (Collected Research Studies of the Royal Commission on the Economic Union & Development Prospects for Canada: Vol. 20). 351p. 1986. pap. text 22.95 (0-8020-7262-3) U of Toronto Pr.
Postwar Market for State & Local Government Securities. Roland I. Robinson. (Studies in Capital Formation & Financing: No. 5). 251p. 1960. reprint ed. 65.30 (0-87014-103-1) Natl Bur Econ Res.
Postwar Monetary Plans & Other Essays. John H. Williams. Ed. by Mira Wilkins. LC 78-3957. (International Finance Ser.). 1979. reprint ed. lib. bdg. 41.95 (0-405-11258-0) Ayer.
Postwar Novel in Canada: Narrative Patterns & Reader Response. Rosmarin Heidenreich. 248p. (C). 1989. text 34.95 (0-88920-980-4) W Laurier U Pr.
Postwar Polish Poetry: An Anthology. rev. ed. Czeslaw Milosz. LC 82-16084. 180p. (C). 1983. pap. 15.95 (0-520-04476-2, Pub. by U CA Pr) Cal Prin Full Svc.
Postwar Politician: The Life of Masayoshi Ohira. Shunpei Kumon et al. (Illus.). 680p. 1990. 39.95 (0-87011-999-0) Kodansha.
Postwar Politics in the G-7: Orders & Eras in Comparative Perspective. Ed. by Byron E. Shafer. LC 96-18066. 336p. 1996. pap. 19.95 (0-299-15104-2) U of Wis Pr.
Postwar Politics in the G-7: Orders & Eras in Comparative Perspective. Ed. by Byron E. Shafer. LC 96-18066. 336p. 1996. 50.00 (0-299-15100-X) U of Wis Pr.
Postwar Productivity Trends in the United States, 1948-1969. John W. Kendrick. (General Ser.: No. 98). 391p. 1973. 101.70 (0-87014-240-2) Natl Bur Econ Res.
Postwar Quality of State & Local Debt. George H. Hempel. (General Ser.: No. 94). 190p. 1971. reprint ed. 49.40 (0-87014-217-8) Natl Bur Econ Res.
*Postwar Rapprochement Of Malaya & Japan 1945-61. Junko Tomaru. LC 99-50168. 2000. text 65.00 (0-312-22777-9) St Martin.
Postwar Rearmament of Japanese Maritime Forces, 1945-1971. James E. Auer. LC 72-83564. (Special Studies in International Politics & Government). 1973. 40.50 (0-275-28633-9) Irvington.
Postwar Reconstruction of the Japanese Economy. Saburo Okita. 200p. 1992. text 44.50 (0-86008-478-7, Pub. by U of Tokyo) Col U Pr.
Postwar Residential Mortgage Market. Saul B. Klaman. (Studies in Capital Formation & Financing: No. 8). 334p. 1961. reprint ed. 86.90 (0-87014-106-6) Natl Bur Econ Res.
Postwar Rise in the Velocity of Money: A Sectoral Analysis. Richard T. Selden. (Occasional Papers: No. 78). 70p. 1962. reprint ed. 20.00 (0-87014-392-1) Natl Bur Econ Res.
Postwar Rise of Mortgage Companies. Saul B. Klaman. (Occasional Papers: No. 60). 118p. 1959. reprint ed. 30.70 (0-87014-374-3) Natl Bur Econ Res.
Postwar Taiwan in Historical Perspective. Ed. by Huang Chun-Chieh. LC 98-4313. (Studies in Global Chinese Affairs Ser.: No. 1). (Illus.). 350p. 1998. pap. 20.00 (1-883053-37-4) Univ Pr MD.
Postwar Trade in Divided Germany: The Internal & International Issue. Karel Holbik & Henry Myers. LC 64-10941. 157p. reprint ed. pap. 48.70 (0-608-10765-4, 200542100053) Bks Demand.
Postwar Transfer of Resources Abroad by Latin America. (Cuadernos de la CEPAL: No. 67). 90p. 20.00 (92-1-121175-1, E.91II.G.9) UN.
Postwar Transformation of Germany: Democracy, Prosperity & Nationhood. Ed. by John S. Brady et al. LC 99-6174. 544p. 1999. text 75.00 (0-472-10993-6, 10993); pap. text 29.95 (0-472-08591-3, 08591) U of Mich Pr.
Postwar Trends in U. S. Forest Products Trade: A Global, National & Regional View. Roger A. Sedjo & Samuel J. Radcliffe. LC 80-8886. 595p. 1980. pap. 30.00 (0-8018-2635-7) Resources Future.
Postwar Vietnam: Dilemmas in Socialist Development. Ed. by David Marr & Christine White. (Southeast Asia Program Ser.: No. 3). (Illus.). x, 254p. (Orig.). (C). 1988. pap. text 12.00 (0-87727-120-8) Cornell SE Asia.
Postwar Women's Writing in German: Feminist Critical Approaches. Ed. by Chris Weeden. LC 95-50634. 368p. 1997. 65.00 (1-57181-902-9); pap. 19.95 (1-57181-048-X) Berghahn Bks.
Postwar Years: The Cold War & the Atomic Age (1950-1959) Richard Steins. (First Person America Ser.). (Illus.). 64p. (J). (gr. 5-8). 1995. lib. bdg. 18.90 (0-8050-2587-1) TFC Bks NY.
Posy Bates, Again! Helen Cresswell. LC 93-5789. (Illus.). 112p. (J). (gr. k-4). 1994. mass mkt. 13.95 (0-02-725372-4, Mac Bks Young Read) S&S Childrens.
Posy of a Ring: A Cycle of Poems. limited ed. Francis K. Weaver. LC 86-71489. (Living Poets' Library: No. 36). (Illus.). 103p. 1986. pap. 10.00 (0-934218-36-6) Dragons Teeth.
Posy of Roses: Victorian Photograph Album. Nancy Akmon & Roni Akmon. (Illus.). 26p. 1996. 19.95 (1-884807-15-1) Blushing Rose.
Posy Ring. Ed. by Kate D. Wiggin & Nora A. Smith. LC 70-128164. (Granger Index Reprint Ser.). 1977. 18.95 (0-8369-6193-5) Ayer.
Pot: New Facts, Old Fictions. rev. ed. Jim Parker. 1999. pap. 0.50 (0-89230-162-7) Do It Now.
Pot: What It Is, What It Does. unabridged ed. Ann Tobias. (Illus.). (J). (gr. 2-4). 1992. pap. 15.95 incl. audio (0-87499-265-6); pap. 24.95 incl. audio (0-87499-266-4) Live Oak Media.
Pot: What It Is, What It Does, 4 bks., Set. unabridged ed. Ann Tobias. (Illus.). (J). (gr. 2-4). 1992. pap., teacher ed. 31.95 incl. audio (0-87499-267-2) Live Oak Media.
Pot Au Feu. Fraser & Whipple. 1975. pap. text 10.59 (0-88334-068-2, 76063) Longman.
Pot-Bellied Pet Pigs: Mini-Pig Care & Training Manual. Kayla Mull & Lorrie B. Boldrick. (Illus.). 154p. (Orig.). 1989. pap. 9.95 (0-9624531-0-2) All Pub.
Pot Bellied Pigs. Dennis Kelsey-Wood. (Illus.). 64p. 1997. 19.95 (0-7938-0143-5, WW-027) TFH Pubns.
Pot-Bellied Pigs: A Complete & Up-to-Date Guide. Dennis Kelsey-Wood & American Society for the Prevention of Cruelty to Animals Staff. LC 97-3624. (Basic Domestic Pet Library). 76p. (J). (gr. 3 up). 1997. 19.95 (0-7910-4616-8) Chelsea Hse.
Pot-Bellied Pigs & Other Miniature Pet Pigs. Lisa H. Huckaby. (Illus.). 144p. 1992. text 23.95 (0-86622-438-6, TS-181) TFH Pubns.
Pot-Bellied Pigs As Your New Family Pet. Michael Taylor. (TS Ser.). (Illus.). 192p. 1993. text 35.95 (0-86622-081-X, TS-188) TFH Pubns.
Pot-Bellied Pigs in Your Home. Dennis Kelsey-Wood. (Illus.). 160p. 1995. pap. 35.95 (0-7938-0075-7, TS208) TFH Pubns.
Pot Boiler: A One-Act Comedy. Alice Gerstenberg. 24p. 1983. pap. 3.00 (0-88680-206-7) I E Clark.
Pot-Bouille see Pot Luck
Pot-Bouille. Emile Zola. (Coll. Diamant). 12.95 (0-685-23949-7) Fr & Eur.
Pot-Bouille. Emile Zola. Ed. by Colette Becker. 4.95 (0-686-55798-0) Fr & Eur.
Pot-Bouille. Emile Zola. (FRE.). 1984. pap. 12.95 (0-7859-3409-X, 225300698X) Fr & Eur.
Pot-Bouille, 1 vol. Emile Zola. 288p. 1999. pap. 7.50 (0-460-87579-5) J M Dent & Sons.
Pot for Pennies. Mudd. 1998. pap. 19.95 (0-9647858-3-8) Trans-High Corp.
Pot Full of Tales. Vowery D. Carlile. (J). Date not set. teacher ed. 12.95 (1-56644-972-3, 011-4AP) Educ Impress.
Pot is Not... Mimi. LC 99-207952. (Jake's World Ser.). 12p. 1999. 9.95 (1-892780-00-3) Giggles Grp.
Pot Likker, Pulley Bones, & Pea Vine Hay. Faye Brown. (Illus.). 226p. (Orig.). 1987. pap. 9.95 (0-943487-02-1) Sevgo Pr.
Pot-Limit & No-Limit Poker. 2nd rev. ed. Bob Ciaffone & Stewart Reuben. 224p. 1999. pap. 25.00 (0-9661007-1-9) B Ciaffone.
Pot Liquor: Counseling/Africian American Divorce Women. Millicent Thompson. LC 99-166032. 1998. pap. 11.99 (1-56043-301-9, Treasure Hse) Destiny Image.
Pot-Liquor Hill. Charles E. Cravey. 1989. pap. 9.95 (0-938645-27-7) In His Steps.
Pot Luck. Emile Zola. Tr. & Intro. by Brian Nelson. LC 98-19514. (Oxford World's Classics Ser.).Tr. of Pot-Bouille. 406p. 1999. pap. 9.95 (0-19-283179-8) OUP.
Pot Luck: Adventures in Archaeology. F. Lister. LC 96-10006. (Illus.). 196p. 1997. pap. 19.95 (0-8263-1760-X) U of NM Pr.
Pot Luck: Recipes from the Stars. Ed. by Caroline Esdaile. (Illus.). 146p. 1996. 29.95 (1-85626-184-0, Pub. by Cathie Kyle) Trafalgar.
Pot Metal Plating on Video. R. L. Nyborg. (Illus.). 75p. 1995. pap. 35.00 incl. VHS (1-57002-061-2) Univ Publng Hse.
Pot of Gold. Judith Michael, pseud. 1994. pap. 209.70 (0-671-99160-4); mass mkt. 6.99 (0-671-88629-0) PB.
Pot of Gold. Judith Michael, pseud. LC 93-14336. 1993. 23.00 (0-671-70704-3) S&S Trade.
Pot of Gold. Ed. by Pocket Books Staff. 1994. mass mkt. 6.50 (0-671-88600-2) PB.
Pot of Gold. Illus. by Jerry Smath. (Jewel Sticker Stories Ser.). 24p. (J). (ps-2). 1997. mass mkt. 3.99 (0-448-41702-2, G & D) Peng Put Young Read.
Pot of Gold. abr. ed. Judith Michael, pseud. 1993. 17.00 incl. audio (0-671-87586-8) S&S Audio.
Pot of Gold. large type ed. Judith Michael, pseud. LC 94-6739. 1994. 26.95 (1-56895-060-8) Wheeler Pub.
Pot of Gold & Other Plays. Incl. Brothers Menaechmus. Plautus. Tr. by E. F. Watling. 1965. pap. Prisoner. Plautus. Tr. by E. F. Watling. 1965. pap. Pseudolus. Swaggering Soldier. Plautus. Tr. by E. F. Watling. 1965. pap. (Classics Ser.). 272p. (Orig.). 1965. Set pap. 15.99 (0-14-044149-2, Penguin Classics) Viking Penguin.
Pot of Gold & Other Stories. Mary E. Wilkins Freeman. LC 74-113661. (Short Story Index Reprint Ser.). 1977. 22.95 (0-8369-3390-7) Ayer.
Pot of Paint. John K. Rothenstein. LC 70-128303. (Essay Index Reprint Ser.). 1977. 20.95 (0-8369-1847-9) Ayer.
*Pot on the Fire: Further Confessions of a Renegade Cook. John Thorne & Matt Lewis Thorne. LC 00-38015. 400p. 2000. 25.00 (0-86547-564-4) N Point Pr.
*Pot Pies: Comfort Food under Cover. Diane Phillips. LC 99-36312. (Illus.). 224p. 2000. 24.95 (0-385-49458-0) Doubleday.
Pot Pies: Forty Savory Suppers. Beatrice A. Ojakangas. LC 92-16447. 112p. 1993. 14.00 (0-517-58573-1) C Potter.
Pot Pourri: A Practical Guide. Mary Lane. 100p. 1985. 60.00 (0-7855-2950-0, Pub. by Bishopsgate Pr Ltd) St Mut.
Pot Pourri: A Practical Guide. Mary Lane. 100p. 1985. pap. 21.00 (0-7855-2951-9) St Mut.
Pot-Pourri de Litterature Francaise. LC 96-190715. (FRE.). (C). 1982. pap. 6.99 (0-8442-1050-1, VF1050-1) NTC Contemp Pub Co.
Pot-Pourri Making. Margaret Roberts. LC 94-5873. (Illus.). 96p. 1994. pap. 10.95 (0-8117-2590-1) Stackpole.
Pot Puzzle Fun Book. Dana Larson & Dan Lowehndorf. (Illus.). 64p. 2000. pap. 12.95 (0-932551-34-3) Quick Am Pub.
Pot Safari: A Visit to the Top Marijuana Researchers. rev. ed. Peggy Mann. LC 82-91050. 133p. (Orig.). (YA). (gr. 9-12). 1987. pap. 6.95 (0-942493-01-X) Woodmere Press.
Pot Shots: Scribblings by an Unabashed Clinton Basher. Glenn McCoy. Ed. by Wesley Alexander. (Illus.). 144p. 1998. pap. 12.95 (0-9662637-0-7) Stormfield Pr.
*Pot Shots 2 Vol. 2: More Scribblings by an Unabashed Clinton Basher. rev. ed. Glenn McCoy. Ed. by Wesley Alexander. (Illus.). 100p. 1999. pap. 12.95 (0-9662637-1-5) Stormfield Pr.
Pot Stories for the Soul. Compiled by Paul Krassner. (Illus.). 128p. 1999. pap. 12.95 (1-893010-02-3, Pub. by Trans-High Corp) Publishers Group.
Potager: Fresh Garden Cooking in the French Style. Georgeanne Brennan & John Vaughan. (Illus.). 144p. 1992. pap. 19.95 (0-8118-0127-6) Chronicle Bks.
Potager: Fresh Garden Cooking in the French Style. Georgeanne Brennan & John Vaughn. (Illus.). 144p. 1992. 29.95 (0-8118-0134-9) Chronicle Bks.
Potaje y Otro Mazote de Estampas Cubanas. Jose Sanchez-Boudy. LC 88-82316. (Coleccion Caniqui). (SPA.). 148p. (Orig.). 1988. pap. 9.95 (0-89729-286-3) Ediciones.
Potala of Tibet. Ed. by Richard Kemp. (Illus.). 132p. Date not set. boxed set 35.00 (0-905743-48-2, Pub. by Stacey Intl) Intl Bk Ctr.
Potash. (Metals & Minerals Ser.). 1993. lib. bdg. 250.95 (0-8490-8993-X) Gordon Pr.
Potash & Perlmutter: Their Co-Partnership Ventures & Adventures. Montagu Glass. LC 74-27988. (Modern Jewish Experience Ser.). (Illus.). 1975. reprint ed. 39.95 (0-405-06715-1) Ayer.
Potassic Igneous Rocks & Associated Gold-Copper Mineralization. D. Muller. Ed. by H. J. Neugebauer et al. (Lecture Notes in Earth Sciences Ser.: Vol. 56). (Illus.). xiv, 210p. 1995. 75.95 (3-540-59116-8) Spr-Verlag.
Potassic Igneous Rocks & Associated Gold-Copper Mineralization. Daniel Muller & David I. Groves. LC 95-10058. (Lecture Notes in Earth Sciences Ser.: Vol. 56). 1995. write for info. (0-387-59116-8) Spr-Verlag.
Potassic Igneous Rocks & Associated Gold-Copper Mineralization. 2nd ed. Daniel Muller & David I. Groves. LC 96-40254. (Lecture Notes in Earth Sciences Ser.: Vol. 56). (Illus.). 238p. 1997. pap. 78.95 (3-540-62075-3) Spr-Verlag.
*Potassic Igneous Rocks & Associated Gold-Copper Mineralization. 3rd rev. enl. ed. Daniel Mueller & D. I. Groves. LC 99-40223. (Illus.). xiv, 252p. 1999. 79.95 (3-540-66371-1) Spr-Verlag.
Potassium. Horacio J. Adrogue & Donald E. Wesson. LC 94-17877. (Basics of Medicine Ser.). (Illus.). 248p. 1994. pap. 10.95 (0-86542-427-6) Blackwell Sci.
Potassium. Horacio J. Adrogue & Donald E. Wesson. (A & W Basics in Medicine Ser.). 250p. 1992. text 29.95 (0-9630670-1-X) Libra & Gemini.
Potassium: Its Biologic Significance. Robert Whang. 176p. 1983. 95.00 (0-8493-5872-8, QP535, CRC Reprint) Franklin.
Potassium, Calcium, & Magnesium in the Tropics & Subtropics. Robert D. Munson. Ed. by J. C. Brosheer. LC 82-11944. (Technical Bulletin Ser.: No. T-23). (Illus.). 70p. (Orig.). 1982. pap. text 4.00 (0-88090-041-5) Intl Fertilizer.
Potassium Channel Modulators, Pharmacological, Molecular & Clinical Aspects. A. H. Weston & T. C. Hamilton. (Frontiers in Pharmacology & Therapeutics Ser.). (Illus.). 528p. 1992. 175.00 (0-632-03044-5) Blackwell Sci.

P

An Asterisk (*) at the beginning of an entry indicates that the title is appearing for the first time.

Potassium Channel Protocols. Stephen Kurtz. (Methods in Molecular Biology Ser.). 1999. 79.50 (*0-89603-697-9*) Humana.

Potassium Channels: Basic Function & Therapeutic Aspects. Thomas J. Colatsky. (Progress in Clinical & Biological Research Ser.). 362p. 1990. 275.00 (*0-471-56714-0*) Wiley.

Potassium Channels: Structure, Classification, Function & Therapeutic Potential. Nigel S. Cook. 1990. text 123.00 (*0-470-21605-0*) P-H.

Potassium Channels & Their Modulators: From Synthesis to Clinical Experience. Ed. by John M. Evans et al. 416p. 1996. 192.00 (*0-7484-0557-7*) Taylor & Francis.

Potassium Channels in Normal & Pathological Conditions. Ed. by J. Vereecke et al. (Illus.). 447p. (Orig.). 1995. pap. 99.50 (*90-6186-701-0*, Pub. by Leuven Univ) Coronet Bks.

Potassium in Agriculture. R. D. Munson. (Illus.). 1123p. 1985. 58.00 (*0-89118-086-9*) Am Soc Agron.

Potassium in Cardiovascular & Renal Medicine: Arrhythmias, Myocardial Infarction & Hypertension. Ed. by Paul K. Whelton et al. LC 85-29383. (Kidney Disease Ser.: No. 6). (Illus.). 576p. reprint ed. pap. 178.60 (*0-7837-3350-X*, 204330800008) Bks Demand.

Potato. Ed. by Y. P. S. Bajaj. (Biotechnology in Agriculture & Forestry Ser.: Vol. 3). (Illus.). 535p. 1987. 309.95 (*0-387-17966-6*) Spr-Verlag.

Potato. Burton. 1989. pap. text. write for info. (*0-582-46229-0*, Pub. by Addison-Wesley) Longman.

Potato. Barrie Watts. LC 87-16702. (Stopwatch Ser.). (Illus.). 25p. (J). (gr. k-4). 1988. pap. 3.95 (*0-382-24018-9*, Silver Pr NJ); lib. bdg. 9.95 (*0-382-09527-8*, Silver Pr NJ) Silver Burdett Pr.

***Potato: A Tale from the Great Depression.** Kate Lied. (Illus.). 48p. (J). (gr. k-5). 1998. 16.00 (*0-7922-3521-5*, Pub. by Natl Geog) Publishers Group.

Potato: How the Humble Spud Rescued the Western World. Larry Zuckerman. LC 97-49107. (Illus.). 304p. 1998. 23.95 (*0-571-19951-8*) Faber & Faber.

***Potato: How the Humble Spud Rescued the Western World.** Larry Zuckerman. LC 99-25615. 320p. 1999. pap. 13.00 (*0-86547-578-4*) N Point Pr.

Potato: Production, Processing & Products. Kiran L. Kadam & D. K. Salunkhe. 304p. 1991. boxed set 229.00 (*0-8493-6876-6*, TP444) CRC Pr.

Potato: The Definitive Guide to Potatoes & Potato Cooking. Alex Barker & Sally Mansfield. 256p. 1999. 30.00 (*0-7548-0172-1*, Lorenz Bks) Anness Pub.

Potato & Its Wild Relatives: Section Tuberarium of the Genus Solanum. Donovan S. Correll. (Illus.). 606p. 1962. lib. bdg. 50.00 (*0-934454-93-0*) Lubrecht & Cramer.

Potato Antioxidant: Alpha Lipoic Acid. Beth M. Ley. LC 96-44738. 80p. (Orig.). 1996. pap. 6.95 (*0-9642703-6-6*) B L Pubns.

Potato Beetles. Richard L. Jacques, Jr. (Flora & Fauna Handbook Ser.: No. 3). (Illus.). 108p. 1988. pap. 25.50 (*90-04-08477-0*) Lubrecht & Cramer.

Potato Beetles: The Genus Leptinotarsa in North America. Richard L. Jacques, Jr. LC 87-15095. (Flora & Fauna Handbook Ser.: No. 3). (Illus.). 144p. 1988. pap. text 39.95 (*0-916846-40-7*) Sandhill Crane.

Potato Branch: Sketches of Mountain Memories. Joe R. Morgan. LC 92-24274. 176p. 1992. 14.95 (*0-914875-20-5*) Bright Mtn Bks.

Potato by Any Other Name. Helen L. McMullin. (Illus.). 50p. 1998. pap. 3.95 (*1-890535-01-X*) H & J Spec.

Potato Chip Cookies & Tomato Soup Cake: Recipes of Americana. Carole Eberly. (Illus.). 160p. (Orig.). 1992. pap. 8.95 (*0-932296-15-7*) Eberly Pr.

***Potato Chip Difference: How to Apply Leading Edge Marketing Strategies to Landing the Job You Want.** Micheal A. Goodman. LC 00-104975. (Illus.). 144p. 2001. pap. 16.95 (*0-9702088-0-4*) Dialogue Pr.

Potato Chips for Breakfast. Cynthia G. Scales. 150p. (Orig.). 1986. 13.95 (*0-934391-04-1*); pap. 8.95 (*0-934391-05-X*) Quotidian.

Potato Cyst Nematodes: Biology, Distribution & Control. R. J. Marks & B. B. Brodie. LC 98-14968. (CAB International Publication). (Illus.). 432p. 1998. text 120.00 (*0-85199-274-9*) OUP.

Potato Eaters. Leonard Nathan. LC 98-12926. 96p. 1999. pap. 12.95 (*0-914061-75-5*) Orchises Pr.

***Potato Eyes.** Ed. by Carolyn W. Page. (Illus.). 120p. 1999. pap. 9.95 (*1-879205-82-3*) Nightshade Pr.

Potato Eyes. Ed. by Roy Zarucchi et al. (Literary Arts Journal: No. 8). (Illus.). 88p. (Orig.). 1993. pap. 7.95 (*1-879205-44-0*) Nightshade Pr.

Potato Eyes. Ed. by Roy Zarucchi et al. (Literary Arts Journal: Vol. 13). (Illus.). 104p. (Orig.). 1996. pap. 7.95 (*1-879205-67-X*) Nightshade Pr.

Potato Eyes, No. 6. Ed. by Roy Zarucchi et al. (Illus.). 88p. (Orig.). 1991. pap. 6.00 (*1-879205-24-6*) Nightshade Pr.

Potato Eyes, No. 7. Ed. by Roy Zarucchi et al. (Illus.). 128p. (Orig.). 1992. pap. 7.95 (*1-879205-37-8*) Nightshade Pr.

Potato Eyes, No. 9. Ed. by Roy Zarucchi & Carolyn Page. (Literature Ser.). (Illus.). 112p. (Orig.). 1994. pap. 7.95 (*1-879205-52-1*) Nightshade Pr.

***Potato Eyes, No. 19.** Ed. by Karen Blomain. (Illus.). 128p. 1999. pap. 9.95 (*1-879205-79-3*) Nightshade Pr.

Potato Eyes, Vol. 10. Ed. by Roy Zarucchi & Carolyn Page. (Lieracy Arts Journal). (Illus.). 120p. (Orig.). 1995. pap. 7.95 (*1-879205-59-9*) Nightshade Pr.

Potato Eyes, Vol. 11 & 12. Ed. by Roy Zarucchi et al. (Lieracy Arts Journal). (Illus.). 140p. (Orig.). 1995. pap. 7.95 (*1-879205-64-5*) Nightshade Pr.

Potato Eyes, Vol. 14. Ed. by Edward M. Holmes & Carolyn Page. (Illus.). 112p. 1996. pap. 7.95 (*1-879205-70-X*) Nightshade Pr.

Potato Eyes, Vol. 17. Ed. by Ruth Moose & Carolyn Page. (Illus.). 96p. 1998. pap. 9.95 (*1-879205-76-9*) Nightshade Pr.

Potato Eyes, Vols. 15 & 16. Ed. by Edward M. Holmes & Carolyn Page. (Illus.). 148p. 1997. pap. 9.95 (*1-879205-74-2*) Nightshade Pr.

Potato Genetics. Ed. by J. E. Bradshaw & G. R. Mackay. (Illus.). 576p. 1994. text 170.00 (*0-85198-869-5*) OUP.

Potato Harvest Cookbook. Ashley Miller. LC 97-48533. (Illus.). 176p. 1998. pap. 19.95 (*1-56158-246-8*, 070369) Taunton.

Potato Health Management. Ed. by Randall C. Rowe. LC 93-70663. (Plant Health Management Ser.). (Illus.). 193p. 1993. pap. 55.00 (*0-89054-144-2*) Am Phytopathol Soc.

Potato Hill & Other Recollections. Fritz Updike. 212p. 1988. pap. 13.95 (*0-932052-71-1*) North Country.

Potato Kid. Barbara Corcoran. 176p. (J). 1993. pap. 3.50 (*0-380-71213-X*, Avon Bks) Morrow Avon.

Potato Man. Megan McDonald. LC 90-7758. (Illus.). 32p. (J). (ps-2). 1991. 15.95 (*0-531-05914-6*) Orchard Bks Watts.

Potato Man. Megan McDonald. LC 90-7758. (Illus.). 32p. (J). (ps-3). 1991. lib. bdg. 16.99 (*0-531-08514-7*) Orchard Bks Watts.

Potato Man. Megan McDonald. LC 90-7758. (Illus.). 32p. (J). (ps-2). 1994. pap. 5.95 (*0-531-07053-0*) Orchard Bks Watts.

Potato Man. Megan McDonald. 1994. 11.15 (*0-606-08847-4*, Pub. by Turtleback) Demco.

Potato Pancakes All Around: A Hanukkah Tale. Marilyn Hirsh. (Illus.). 34p. (J). (gr. k-3). 1982. pap. 4.95 (*0-8276-0217-0*) JPS Phila.

Potato Party & Other Troll Tales. Loreen Leedy. LC 89-1746. (Illus.). 32p. (J). (gr. k-3). 1989. lib. bdg. 14.95 (*0-8234-0761-6*) Holiday.

Potato Pleasures Recipe Book. Sue E. Willett. 107p. 1992. spiral bd. 8.50 (*1-882835-22-0*) STA-Kris.

Potato Production & Consumption in Developing Countries. 52p. 1991. 12.00 (*92-5-103072-3*, F0723, Pub. by FAO) Bernan Associates.

***Potato Production, Processing & Technology.** Wilbur A. Gould. LC 99-36722. (Illus.). 272p. 1999. 103.00 (*0-930027-30-2*) CTI Pubns.

Potato Research in India, 1901-1991 Vol. 2: A Bibliography: Dessertations & Thesis. Shree R. Yadava. 348p. 1999. pap. 150.00 (*81-7233-052-9*, Pub. by Scientific Pubs) St Mut.

Potato Storage Technology & Practice: Proceedings of an International Symposium. B. F. Cargill et al. LC 88-83722. 340p. (Orig.). 1989. pap. 44.00 (*0-916150-99-2*, C0189) Am Soc Ag Eng.

Potato Story & Other Missionary Stories. Illus. by Elynne Chudnovsky. LC 91-78295. (Missionary Stories Ser.: Bk. 3). (J). (gr. 1-5). 1992. pap. 3.99 (*0-87509-484-8*) Chr Pubns.

Potato Uses: Uses for the Potato. rev. ed. Recycling Consortium Staff. 1992. ring bd. 19.95 (*0-317-04797-3*) Prosperity & Profits.

Potatoes see NGA Garden Library

Potatoes see Foods Series

Potatoes. (Popular Brands Cookbooks Ser.). (Illus.). 24p. 1995. pap. write for info. (*1-56144-673-4*) Modern Pub NYC.

Potatoes. Ann L. Burckhardt. (Early-Reader Science Foods Ser.). (Illus.). 24p. (J). (gr. k-3). 1996. 13.25 (*0-516-20278-2*) Childrens.

Potatoes. Le Cordon Bleu Staff. LC 98-65969. (Cordon Bleu Home Collection: Vol. 5). 64p. 1998. 12.00 (*962-593-428-6*, Periplus Eds) Tuttle Pubng.

Potatoes. Claire Llewellyn. LC 97-34924. (What's for Lunch? Ser.). (J). 1998. lib. bdg. 20.00 (*0-516-20838-1*) Childrens.

Potatoes. Claire Llewellyn. Ed. by Helaine Cohen. (What's for Lunch? Ser.). (Illus.). 32p. (J). (ps-2). 1998. pap. 6.95 (*0-516-26223-8*) Childrens.

Potatoes. Barbara K. Morgan. 36p. (Orig.). 1990. pap. 3.25 (*0-940844-37-0*) Wellspring.

Potatoes. Annie Nichols. 1998. 24.95 (*0-8478-2077-7*, Pub. by Rizzoli Intl) St Martin.

Potatoes. Jillian Powell. LC 96-27731. (Everyone Eats Ser.). (Illus.). 32p. (J). (gr. 2-6). 1997. lib. bdg. 22.83 (*0-8172-4762-9*) Raintree Steck-V.

Potatoes. Diane R. Worthington. LC 93-28231. (Williams-Sonoma Kitchen Library). (Illus.). 108p. 1994. lib. bdg. write for info. (*0-7835-0276-1*) Time-Life.

Potatoes. Diane R. Worthington. LC 93-28231. (Williams-Sonoma Kitchen Library). (Illus.). 108p. (YA). (gr. 11). 1999. 18.95 (*0-7835-0275-3*) Time-Life.

Potatoes: Classical Essential. Koenemann Inc. Staff. (Mini Cook Bks.). (Illus.). 64p. 1999. pap. 1.95 (*3-8290-2377-4*) Konemann.

Potatoes Vol. 34: Recipes for America's Favorite Vegetable. Current Kitchens Staff. 64p. 1994. pap., per. 3.95 (*0-942320-46-8*) Am Cooking.

Potatoes As Food & Medicine. H. Valentine Knaggs. 1991. lib. bdg. 72.00 (*0-8490-4963-6*) Gordon Pr.

Potatoes As Food & Medicine: Epsom Salt, Its Value & Use & the Cleansing Saline Fast. H. Valentine Knaggs. 15p. 1996. reprint ed. spiral bd. 9.50 (*0-7873-0503-0*) Hlth Research.

Potatoes Australia. Ed. by HarperCollins Publishing Staff. 2000. 19.95 (*0-00-255455-0*) HarperTrade.

Potatoes Love Herbs. Ruth Bass. LC 96-36505. (Fresh from the Garden Cookbook Ser.). (Illus.). 64p. 1997. 9.95 (*0-88266-963-X*) Storey Bks.

Potatoes Not Prozac. Kathleen DesMaisons. LC 97-43174. 256p. 1998. 22.50 (*0-684-84953-4*) S&S Trade.

Potatoes Not Prozac: A Natural Seven-Step Plan to: Control Your Cravings & Lose Weight, Recognize How Foods Affect the Way You Feel & Stabilize the Level of Sugar in Your Blood. Kathleen DesMaisons. (Illus.). 256p. 1999. per. 12.00 (*0-684-85014-1*) S&S Trade.

Potatoes of Bolivia: Their Breeding Value & Evolutionary Relationships. J. G. Hawkes & J. P. Hjerting. (Illus.). 504p. 1989. text 89.00 (*0-19-854220-8*) OUP.

Potatoes of South America: Bolivia. Carlos M. Ochoa. Tr. by Donald Ugent. (Illus.). 570p. (C). 1991. text 155.00 (*0-521-38024-3*) Cambridge U Pr.

Potatoes on Tuesday see Papas el Martes

Potatoes on Tuesday. 2nd ed. Dee Lillegard. (Let Me Read Ser.). (Illus.). 8p. (J). (ps). 1995. pap. 2.95 (*0-673-36235-3*, GoodYrBooks) Addson-Wesley Educ.

Potatoes, Papitas, Patatas . . . Gifts from the Goddess. Helen L. McMullin. (Illus.). 120p. (Orig.). 1998. pap. 11.95 (*1-890535-02-8*) H & J Spec.

Potatoes, Sweet & Irish. D. Young. 1983. pap. 2.95 (*0-88266-178-7*, Storey Pub) Storey Bks.

Potatoes, Tomatoes, Corn, & Beans: How the Foods in America Changed the World. Sylvia A. Johnson. LC 96-7207. (Illus.). 144p. (J). (gr. 5-9). 1997. 16.00 (*0-689-80141-6*) Atheneum Yung Read.

Potawatomi see Indians of North America

Potawatomi. Suzanne I. Powell. LC 96-52133. (First Bk.). (Illus.). 64p. (J). (gr. 4-6). 1997. lib. bdg. 22.00 (*0-531-20268-2*) Watts.

Potawatomi Pony: A Potawatomi Fable. Jack Wooldridge. (Potawatomi Fables Ser.). 32p. (J). (gr. 1). 1995. pap. 7.00 (*1-887963-02-2*) Pota Pr.

Potawatomi Tears & Petticoat Pioneers: More of the Romance of Michigan's Past. 2nd ed. Larry B. Massie. (Illus.). 296p. 1992. pap. 12.50 (*0-9626408-3-2*) Priscilla Pr.

Potawatomis: Keepers of the Fire. R. David Edmunds. LC 78-5628. (Civilization of the American Indian Ser.: No. 145). (Illus.). 384p. 1978. pap. 19.95 (*0-8061-2069-X*) U of Okla Pr.

Potbellied Pig Caper. Georgette Livingston. LC 97-97275. (Jennifer Gray Veterinarian Mystery Ser.: Bk. 10). 192p. 1997. 18.95 (*0-8034-9269-3*, Avalon Bks) Bouregy.

Potbellied Stove. George D. Clabon. LC 97-60486. (Illus.). 64p. 1997. pap. 10.00 (*1-890459-00-3*) TA Pubns.

Potch & Polly. Steig. 14.95 (*0-06-205144-X*); lib. bdg. 14.89 (*0-06-205145-8*) HarpC Child Bks.

***Potch & Polly.** William Steig & Jon Agee. 2000. text. write for info. (*0-374-36090-1*) FS&G.

Potefeuille. De Villedieu. Ed. by Homand. (Exeter French Texts Ser.: Vol. 31). (FRE.). 67p. Date not set. pap. text 19.95 (*0-85989-029-5*, Pub. by Univ Exeter Pr) Northwestern U Pr.

Potemkin. George Soloveytchik. LC 72-7192. (Select Bibliographies Reprint Ser.). 1977. reprint ed. 35.95 (*0-8369-6954-5*) Ayer.

Potemkin Mutiny. Richard Hough. LC 96-15055. (Bluejacket Bks.). 192p. 1996. pap. 13.95 (*1-55750-370-2*) Naval Inst Pr.

Potencies of God(s) Schelling's Philosophy of Mythology. Edward A. Beach. LC 91-15128. (SUNY Series in Philosophy). 317p. (C). 1994. text 59.50 (*0-7914-0973-2*); pap. text 19.95 (*0-7914-0974-0*) State U NY Pr.

Potency of Life: Books in Society. Ed. by Nicolas Barker. (The British Library Studies in the History of the Book). (Illus.). 216p. 1993. 80.00 (*0-7123-0287-5*, Pub. by B23tish Library) U of Toronto Pr.

***Potent Charms.** Peggy Waide. 320p. 2000. pap. 4.99 (*0-8439-4694-6*, Leisure Bks) Dorchester Pub Co.

Potent College: The Effect of Organizational Structure upon Value & Attitude Information. Rebecca Stafford. LC 90-3938. (Harvard Studies in Sociology). 165p. 1990. text 22.00 (*0-8240-2757-4*) Garland.

Potent Fictions: Children's Literacy & the Challenge of Popular Culture. Ed. by Mary Hilton. LC 95-25983. 216p. (C). 1996. pap. 18.99 (*0-415-13530-3*) Routledge.

Potent Pleasures. Eloisa James. LC 99-21996. 384p. 1999. 21.95 (*0-385-33360-9*) Delacorte.

***Potent Pleasures.** Eloisa James. 592p. 2000. mass mkt. 6.50 (*0-440-23456-5*, Island Bks) Dell.

Potent Quotes. Myles Munroe. 76p. (Orig.). 1995. pap. 5.99 (*1-56043-161-X*) Destiny Image.

Potent Self: A Guide to Spontaneity. Moshe Feldenkrais. LC 84-48217. 256p. 1992. reprint ed. pap. 13.00 (*0-06-250324-3*, Pub. by Harper SF) HarpC.

***Potential.** Ariel Schrag. (Illus.). 224p. (C). 2000. pap. 24.95 (*0-943151-04-X*) Slave Labor Bks.

Potential: The Name Analysis Book. Paul Rice & Valeta Rice. 192p. (Orig.). 1987. pap. 8.95 (*0-87728-632-9*) Weiser.

Potential Applications of Concentrated Solar Energy: Proceedings of a Workshop. National Research Council, Commission on Physical. 164p. 1991. pap. 20.00 (*0-309-04577-0*) Natl Acad Pr.

Potential Applications of Concentrated Solar Photons. National Research Council Staff. 90p. 1991. pap. text 19.00 (*0-309-04576-2*) Natl Acad Pr.

Potential Benefits of Geosynthetics in Flexible Pavement Systems. (National Cooperative Highway Research Program Report Ser.: No. 315). 56p. 1989. 9.00 (*0-309-04612-2*, NR315) Transport Res Bd.

Potential Benefits of Integration of Environmental & Economic Policies: An Incentive Based Approach to Policy Integration. DRI Staff. 448p. (C). 1994. lib. bdg. 125.00 (*1-85966-108-4*, Pub. by Graham & Trotman) Kluwer Academic.

Potential Climate Change Effects on Great Lakes Hydrodynamics & Water Quality. David C. L. Lam & William M. Schertzer. LC 98-55322. 232p. 1999. 32.00 (*0-7844-0413-5*) Am Soc Civil Eng.

Potential Commercial Dairying with Buffalo. R. E. McDowell et al. (Illus.). 78p. (Orig.). 1995. pap. 10.00 (*1-880762-07-2*) Kinnic Pubs.

***Potential Consequences of Climate Variability & Change to Water Resources in the United States.** Ed. by D. Briane Adams. 424p. 1999. pap. 75.00 (*1-882132-45-9*, TPS-99-1) Am Water Resources.

Potential Credit Exposure on Interest Rate Swaps. Ian Bond et al. LC HG6024.5. (Bank of England, Economics Division. Working Paper Ser.: No. 25). (Illus.). 45p. reprint ed. pap. 30.00 (*0-608-20163-4*, 207142700011) Bks Demand.

Potential Dilution at S&P Super 1500 Companies in 1997. Robert L. Newbury. LC 99-174114. 57p. 1998. 95.00 (*1-879775-58-1*) IRRC Inc DC.

Potential Economies in the Reorganization of Local School Attendance Units. Harry A. Little. LC 72-177900. (Columbia University. Teachers College. Contributions to Education Ser.: No. 628). reprint ed. 37.50 (*0-404-55628-0*) AMS Pr.

Potential Effects of a North American Free Trade Agreement on Apparel Investment in CBERA Countries. William Warlick. (Illus.). 91p. (Orig.). (C). 1995. pap. text 35.00 (*0-7881-2429-3*) DIANE Pub.

Potential Effects of Global Climate Change on the United States, 3 vols. 1991. lib. bdg. 199.95 (*0-8490-4482-0*) Gordon Pr.

Potential Effects of Global Climate Change on the United States. Joel B. Smith & Dennis A. Tirpak. 690p. 1990. 132.00 (*1-56032-071-0*) Hemisp Pub.

Potential Effects of Oil Spills on Seabirds & Selected Other Oceanic Vertebrates Off the North Carolina Coast. David S. Lee & Mary C. Socci. (Occasional Papers of the North Carolina Biological Survey). (Illus.). 64p. (Orig.). 1989. pap. text 8.00 (*0-917134-18-4*) NC Natl Sci.

Potential Effects of Selective Fishing on Stock Composition Estimates from the Mixed-Stock Model: Application of a High-Dimension Selective Fisheries Model. Peter W. Lawson et al. 26p. 1997. reprint ed. pap. 3.60 (*0-89904-588-X*, Cascade Geog Soc) Crumb Elbow Pub.

Potential Energy Surfaces. Ed. by K. P. Lawley. LC 81-466015. 618p. reprint ed. pap. 191.60 (*0-608-12466-4*, 202519600042) Bks Demand.

Potential Energy Surfaces: Proceedings of the Mariapfarr Workshop in Theoretical Chemistry. A. F. Sax. LC 98-47150. (Lecture Notes in Chemistry Ser.). 1998. pap. 58.00 (*3-540-65106-3*) Spr-Verlag.

Potential Environmental Impacts of Bioenergy Crop Production. 1996. lib. bdg. 251.95 (*0-8490-6008-7*) Gordon Pr.

Potential Environmental Impacts of Bioenergy Crop Production: Background Paper. 1994. lib. bdg. 250.00 (*0-8490-8598-5*) Gordon Pr.

***Potential Extension of the Customs Union Between Turkey & the EU No. 5: A Report on Agricultural Policy & Economic Development.** FAO Staff. 140p. 2000. pap. 29.00 (*92-5-104363-9*, F43639, Pub. by FAO) Bernan Associates.

Potential Fields & Their Transformations in Applied Geophysics. Wladimir Baranov. Ed. by R. G. Van Nostrand & S. Saxov. (Geoexploration Monographs: No. 6). (Illus.). xv, 121p. 1975. 38.00 (*3-443-13008-9*, Pub. by Gebruder Borntraeger) Balogh.

Potential Flow of Fluids. Ed. by M. Rahman. 264p. 1995. 121.00 (*1-85312-356-0*) Computational Mech MA.

Potential Flow of Fluids. Ed. by M. A. Rahman. LC 95-68891. (Advances in Fluid Mechanics Ser.: Vol. 6). 264p. 1995. text 121.00 (*1-56252-279-5*, 3560) Computational Mech MA.

Potential Flows: Computer Graphic Solutions. R. Kirchhoff. (Mechanical Engineering Ser.: Vol. 37). (Illus.). 200p. 1985. text 125.00 (*0-8247-7307-1*) Dekker.

Potential for Collaboration in New Sciences & Technology Development Between San Antonio, Texas & Nancy, France. Edgard Bertrand. LC 90-63057. 170p. 1990. student ed. 8.50 (*0-945632-04-5*) St Marys Univ Pr.

Potential for Criticality Following Disposal of Uranium at Low Level Waste Facilities: Uranium Blended with Soil. L. E. Toran. 137p. 1997. per. 14.00 (*0-16-062853-9*) USGPO.

Potential for Electronic Traction in North American Cities. 695.00 (*0-7106-1385-7*) Janes Info Group.

Potential for Forage Legumes on Land in West Africa. FAO Staff. LC 98-110854. (World Soil Resources Reports: No. 82). 118p. 1996. pap. 14.00 (*92-5-103790-6*, F37906, Pub. by FAO) Bernan Associates.

***Potential for Health.** Kenneth Calman. LC 97-51536. (Illus.). 304p. 1998. text 36.00 (*0-19-262585-3*) OUP.

Potential for Health. Kenneth C. Calman. (Illus.). 292p. 1998. pap. text 32.50 (*0-19-262944-1*) OUP.

Potential for Increasing Clothing Productivity Within the EEC. Wira Staff. (C). 1979. 125.00 (*0-900820-12-8*, Pub. by British Textile Tech) St Mut.

***Potential for Industrial Energy-Efficiency Improvement in the Long Term.** Jeroen de Beer. LC 00-35746. (Eco-Efficiency in Industry & Science Ser.). 2000. write for info. (*0-7923-6282-9*) Kluwer Academic.

Potential for Nutritional Modulation of the Aging Process. Donald K. Ingram. 1991. text 123.00 (*0-917678-26-5*) Food & Nut Pr.

Potential for PVD Equipment in the U. S. Thin Film Resistor Industry. Dennis M. Zogbi. 37p. (Orig.). 1995. pap. 3500.00 (*0-929717-43-0*) Paumanok Pubns.

Potential for Reform of Criminal Justice. Ed. by Herbert Jacob. LC 73-77871. (Sage Criminal Justice System Annuals Ser.: Vol. 3). 352p. reprint ed. pap. 109.20 (*0-608-10089-7*, 202191500026) Bks Demand.

Potential Fulfilled, Vol. 1. Priscilla Gilbert. 105p. 1976. 8.50 (*0-86690-105-1*, G1145-014) Am Fed Astrologers.

Potential Fulfilled - What Saved Them, Vol. 2. Priscilla Gilbert. LC 76-26745. 104p. 1976. 8.50 (*0-86690-106-X*, G1146-014) Am Fed Astrologers.

P

An Asterisk (*) at the beginning of an entry indicates that the title is appearing for the first time.

Potential Groundwater Contamination from Intentional & Nonintentional Stormwater Infiltration. Robert Pitt et al. (Illus.). 120p. (Orig.). (C). 1994. pap. text 40.00 (*0-7881-1059-4*) DIANE Pub.

Potential Health & Safety Impacts of High-BTU Coal Gasification: Occupational. Flow Resources Corporation Staff. 200p. 1978. pap. 3.50 (*0-318-12669-9*, F00687) Am Gas Assn.

Potential Health Effects of Climatic Change: Report of a WHO Task Group. 58p. 1990. pap. text 13.50 (*0-614-08031-2*, 1930017) World Health.

Potential Health Hazards of Existing Chemicals. Ed. by Berufsgenossenschaft der Chemischen Industrie Staf & B. G. Heidelberg. (Toxicological Evaluations Ser.: Vol. 13). 256p. 1997. 52.00 (*3-540-62658-1*) Spr-Verlag.

Potential Health Hazards of Existing Chemicals. Ed. by B. G. Chemie. LC 90-10020. (Toxicological Evaluations Ser.: Vol. 1). (Illus.). 368p. 1990. 62.95 (*0-387-52577-7*) Spr-Verlag.

Potential Health Hazards of Existing Chemicals. Ed. by B. G. Heidelberg. (Toxicological Evaluations Ser.: Vol. 12). (Illus.). 200p. 1997. 52.00 (*3-540-62657-3*) Spr-Verlag.

Potential Impact of Telephone Regional Holding Companies' Diversification & Video Service Strategies on the Broadcasting Industry. Kenneth R. Donow & Suzanne G. Douglas. 112p. (Orig.). 1990. pap. 80.00 (*0-89324-088-5*) Natl Assn Broadcasters.

Potential Impact on the U. S. Economy & Industries of the GATT Uruguay Round Agreements, 2 vols., Set. Mark Estes & Karen Laney-Cummings. (Illus.). 700p. (Orig.). (C). 1994. pap. text 90.00 (*0-7881-1527-8*) DIANE Pub.

Potential Impact on the U. S. Economy & Selected Industries of the NAFTA. 256p. 1993. pap. text 45.00 (*1-57979-236-7*) DIANE Pub.

Potential Impact on the U. S. Economy & Selected Industries of the North American Free Trade Agreement. (Illus.). 300p. (Orig.). (C). 1995. pap. text 40.00 (*0-7881-2535-4*) DIANE Pub.

Potential Impact Telecommunication. Donow. 1992. pap. 34.50 (*0-8058-1362-4*) L Erlbaum Assocs.

Potential Impacts of Climate Change on Tropical Forest Ecosystems. Adam Markham. LC 98-35416. 1998. 141.00 (*0-7923-5124-X*) Kluwer Academic.

Potential Levels of Existence Series. Alan C. Walter. Ed. by Beverly Miles. 22p. (Orig.). 1995. pap. text 2.79 (*1-57569-022-5*) Wisdom Pubng.

Potential Long-Term Ecological Impact of Genetically Modified Organisms. (Nature & Environment Ser.: No. 65). 1993. 15.00 (*92-871-2285-7*, Pub. by Council of Europe) Manhattan Pub Co.

Potential Low-Grade Iron Ore & Hydraulic-Fracturing Sand in Cambrian Sandstones, Northwestern Llano Region, Texas. V. E. Barnes & D. A. Schofield. (Reports of Investigations: RI 53). (Illus.). 58p. 1964. pap. 2.00 (*0-686-29335-5*) Bur Econ Geology.

Potential Market Demand for Two-Way Information Services to the Home, 1970-1990. Paul Baran. 139p. 1971. 10.50 (*0-318-14418-2*, R26) Inst Future.

Potential of Deep Seismic Profiling for Hydrocarbon Exploration: 5th IFP Exploration & Production Research Conference, Arles, 1989. B. Pinet & C. Bois. (Illus.). 502p. (C). 1990. 615.00 (*2-7108-0590-1*, Pub. by Edits Technip) Enfield Pubs NH.

Potential of Fantasy & Imagination. A. A. Sheikh & John T. Shaffer. LC 79-88092. 1979. lib. bdg. 15.00 (*0-913412-31-7*) Brandon Hse.

Potential of Gene Therapy in Cancer: Journal: Natural Immunity, Vol. 13, Nos. 2-3, 1994. Ed. by Eva Lotzova. (Illus.). 104p. 1994. pap. 41.00 (*3-8055-5956-9*) S Karger.

Potential of Herbs As a Cash Crop. 2nd ed. Richard A. Miller. 230p. 1998. pap. 20.00 (*0-911311-55-6*) Acres USA.

Potential of Imagination What Your Eyes Behold Are Neither Thus Or so But Only What Your Heart Reflects It's All You Know: Use It Wisely & Well, for It Is Your Willing Servant. LC 97-91709. (Illus.). 85p. 1997. pap. 10.95 (*0-9608960-9-0*) Single Vision.

Potential of Nanotechnology for Molecular Manufacturing. Max Nelson & Calvin Shipbaugh. 62p. (Orig.). 1995. pap. text 7.50 (*0-8330-2287-3*, MR-615-RC) Rand Corp.

Potential of Orthodox Thinking. 2nd ed. Mother Maria Gysi. (Library of Orthodox Thinking). 24p. 1998. pap. 4.00 (*0-920669-21-2*, Pub. by Peregrina Pubng) Cistercian Pubns.

Potential of Picture Books: From Visual Literacy to Aesthetic Understanding. Barbara Z. Kiefer. LC 94-9782. 320p. (C). 1994. pap. text 35.00 (*0-02-363535-5*, Macmillan Coll) P-H.

Potential of Remote Sensing for the Study of Global Change: COSPAR Report to the International Council of Scientific Unions S. I. Rasool. S. I. Rasool. (Advances in Space Research Ser.: Vol. 7). 1988. pap. 63.00 (*0-08-036648-1*, Pergamon Pr) Elsevier.

Potential of the Kakadu National Park Region. LC 90-104629. (Parliamentary Papers). xxi, 363 p. 1988. write for info. (*0-644-07647-X*, Pub. by Aust Inst Criminology) Advent Bks Div.

Potential of the Redeemed Mind. Wayne C. Gwilliam. 101p. 1991. pap. 5.95 (*0-9631477-0-6*) Reach Out NY.

Potential of the Traditional Birth Attendant. Ed. by A. Mangay Maglacas & J. Simons. (WHO Offset Publications: No. 95). 105p. 1986. pap. text 16.00 (*92-4-170095-5*, 1120095) World Health.

***Potential of U. S. Grazing Lands to Sequester Carbon & Mitigate the Greenhouse Effect.** R. F. Follett et al. LC 00-42832. 2000. write for info. (*1-56670-554-1*) Lewis Pubs.

***Potential of Us Cropland to Sequester Carbon & Mitigate the Greenhouse Effect.** Rattan Lal et al. LC 99-184688. 1998. boxed set 54.95 (*1-57504-112-X*) CRC Pr.

Potential Radiation Exposure in Military Operations: Protecting the Soldier Before, During & After. Institute of Medicine Staff. 160p. 1999. pap. 34.75 (*0-309-06439-2*) Natl Acad Pr.

Potential Random. Keith Waldrop. 36p. 1999. pap. 5.00 (*0-945926-32-4*, Pub. by Paradigm RI) SPD-Small Pr Dist.

Potential Reuse of Petroleum-Contaminated Soil: A Directory of Permitted Recycling Facilities. 1996. lib. bdg. 251.95 (*0-8490-6026-5*) Gordon Pr.

Potential Role of Oil Shale in the U. S. Energy Mix: Questions of Development & Policy Formulation in an Environment Age. Theodore J. Ellis. Ed. by Stuart Bruchey. LC 78-22677. (Energy in the American Economy Ser.). (Illus.). 1979. lib. bdg. 25.95 (*0-405-11980-1*) Ayer.

Potential Role of T-Cells in Cancer Therapy. Ed. by Alexander Fefer & Allan L. Goldstein. LC 80-5901. (Progress in Cancer Research & Therapy Ser.: No. 22). (Illus.). 311p. 1982. reprint ed. pap. 96.50 (*0-608-00613-0*, 206120000007) Bks Demand.

Potential Socioeconomic Effect. Ed. by Nguyen H. Ninh. (C). 1996. pap. text 34.85 (*0-8133-8860-0*) Westview.

Potential Solidification - Stabilization Superfund Projects. 48p. 1995. pap. 20.00 (*0-89312-180-0*, IS501S) Portland Cement.

Potential Teachers - 1952. Eugen Rosenstock-Huessy. (Eugen Rosenstock-Huessy Lectures: Vol. 4). 34p. 1997. pap. 15.00 incl. audio (*0-912148-23-3*) Argo Bks.

Potential Theory. J. Bliedtner. (Universitext Ser.). xiv, 435p. 1986. 79.95 (*0-387-16396-4*) Spr-Verlag.

Potential Theory. Ed. by Jaroslav Kral et al. LC 88-5836. (Illus.). 376p. 1988. 85.00 (*0-306-42838-5*, Plenum Trade) Perseus Pubng.

Potential Theory: Proceedings of the International Conference on Potential Theory, Nagoya, Japan, Aug. 30-Sep. 4, 1990. Ed. by Masanori Kishi. xi, 403p. (C). 1992. lib. bdg. 115.95 (*3-11-012812-8*) De Gruyter.

Potential Theory: Selected Topics. Hiroaki Aikawa & Matts R. Essen. LC 96-27493. (Lecture Notes in Mathematics Ser.: Vol. 163). 200p. 1996. pap. 43.00 (*3-540-61583-0*) Spr-Verlag.

Potential Theory & Degenerate Partial Differential Operators. Ed. by Marco Biroli. LC 95-37538. 1995. text 99.50 (*0-7923-3596-1*) Kluwer Academic.

Potential Theory & Function Theory for Irregular Regions. Iurii D. Burago & V. G. Mazya. LC 69-15004. (Seminars in Mathematics Ser.: Vol. 3). 76p. reprint ed. pap. 30.00 (*0-608-10044-7*, 202069500018) Bks Demand.

Potential Theory ICPT-94: Proceedings of the International Conference Held in Kouty, Czech Republic, August 13-20, 1994. Ed. by J. Vesely et al. LC 96-11744. ix, 499p. (C). 1996. lib. bdg. 152.95 (*3-11-014654-1*) De Gruyter.

Potential Theory in Gravity & Magnetic Applications. Richard Blakely. 461p. 1996. pap. text 37.95 (*0-521-57547-8*) Cambridge U Pr.

Potential Theory in the Complex Plane. Thomas Ransford. (London Mathematical Society Student Texts Ser.: No. 28). 242p. (C). 1995. text 69.95 (*0-521-46120-0*); pap. text 24.95 (*0-521-46654-7*) Cambridge U Pr.

Potential Theory of Unsteady Supersonic Flow. John W. Miles. LC 59-564. (Cambridge Monographs on Mechanics & Mathematics). 234p. reprint ed. pap. 66.70 (*0-608-11117-1*, 2050772) Bks Demand.

Potential Theory on Harmonic Spaces. C. Constantinescu & A. Cornea. LC 72-86117. (Grundlehren der Mathematischen Wissenschaften Ser.: Vol. 158). 1973. 103.95 (*0-387-05916-4*) Spr-Verlag.

Potential Theory on Infinite-Dimensional Abelian Groups. Alexander Bendikov. LC 95-14980. (Studies in Mathematics: Vol. 21).Tr. of Veroiatnostnaia Teoriia Potentsiala na Beskonechnomernykh Abelevykh Gruppakh. vi, 184p. (C). 1995. lib. bdg. 89.95 (*3-11-014283-X*) De Gruyter.

Potential Theory on Infinite Networks. Paolo M. Soardi. LC 94-34403. (Lecture Notes in Mathematics Ser.: 1590). 1994. 29.00 (*0-387-58448-X*) Spr-Verlag.

Potential Theory on Infinite Networks. Paolo M. Soardi. LC 94-34403. (Lecture Notes in Mathematics Ser.: 1590). 1994. 35.95 (*3-540-58448-X*) Spr-Verlag.

Potential Theory on Locally Compact Abelian Groups. C. Berg & G. Forst. (Ergebnisse der Mathematik und Ihrer Grenzgebiete Ser.: Vol. 87). 240p. 1975. 59.95 (*0-387-07249-7*) Spr-Verlag.

Potential Theory Surveys & Problems. Ed. by J. Vesely et al. (Lecture Notes in Mathematics Ser.: Vol. 1344). viii, 271p. 1988. 43.95 (*0-387-50210-6*) Spr-Verlag.

Potential Threats to U. S. Soviet Deterrence: The Political Dimension. John Van Oudenaren. LC 83-116523. (Paper Ser.). 36p. 1982. pap. 4.00 (*0-8330-2313-6*, P-6826) Rand Corp.

Potential Transmission of Spongiform Encephalopathies to Humans: The Food & Drug Administration's (FDA) Ruminant to Ruminant Feed Ban & the Safety of Other Products. Ed. by Christopher Shays. 131p. (C). 1998. pap. text 30.00 (*0-7881-7300-6*) DIANE Pub.

Potential Use of Spread Spectrum Techniques in Non-Government Applications. Walter C. Scales. (Illus.). 205p. (C). 1986. pap. 26.80 (*0-89412-129-4*) Aegean Park Pr.

Potential Uses for Military-Related Resources for Protection of Environment. (Disarmament Studies: No. 25). 54p. 20.00 (*92-1-142191-8*, E.93.IX.12) UN.

Potential Uses of Military-Related Resources for Protection of the Environment. Carlos E. Garcia et al. 54p. (C). 1998. reprint ed. pap. text 25.00 (*0-7881-7400-2*) DIANE Pub.

***Potentialities: Collected Essays.** Giorgio Agamben. LC 99-39449. 1999. pap. text 18.95 (*0-8047-3278-7*) Stanford U Pr.

***Potentialities: Collected Essays in Philosophy.** Giorgio Agamben. LC 99-39449. (Meridian Ser.). 307p. 1999. 55.00 (*0-8047-3277-9*) Stanford U Pr.

Potentialities for Later Living. Southern Conference on Gerontology Staff. Ed. by O. Bruce Thomason. LC 72-190378. (Institute of Gerontology Ser.: No. 17). 159p. reprint ed. pap. 49.30 (*0-7837-4960-0*, 204462600004) Bks Demand.

Potentiality, Entanglement & Passion-at-a-Distance, Vol. 2. R. S. Cohen et al. LC 97-189206. 1997. lib. bdg. 136.00 (*0-7923-4453-7*) Kluwer Academic.

Potentially Discriminatory Criminal Justice Agency Policies. 1984. write for info. (*0-318-57723-2*) Univ Alaska.

Potentially Swelling Soil & Rock in the Front Range Urban Corridor, Colorado. Stephen S. Hart. (Environmental Geology Ser.: No. 7). (Illus.). 49p. (Orig.). 1974. pap. 15.00 (*1-884216-11-0*) Colo Geol Survey.

Potentially Violent Patient & the Tarasoff Decision in Psychiatric Practice. James C. Beck. LC 84-28241. 153p. reprint ed. pap. 47.50 (*0-8357-2806-4*, 203620200011) Bks Demand.

Potentials & Bottlenecks in Spatial Development: Festschrift in Honor of Yasuhiko Oishi. Ed. by Hirotada Kohno & Peter Kijkamp. LC 93-37075. 1993. 118.00 (*0-387-57350-X*) Spr-Verlag.

Potentials & Limitations of Ecosystem Analysis. Ed. by Ernst-Detlef Schulze & H. Zwolfer. (Ecological Studies: Vol. 61). (Illus.). 450p. 1987. 185.95 (*0-387-17138-X*) Spr-Verlag.

Potentials & Policy Implications of Energy & Material Efficiency Improvement. LC 97-172782. 112p. 1997. 15.00 (*92-1-104477-4*) UN.

Potentials for Ridesharing in Southwest Iowa. Jack J. Ruff & R. K. Piper. 66p. (Orig.). 1982. pap. 4.50 (*1-55719-036-4*) U NE CPAR.

Potentiating Health & the Crisis of the Immune System: Integrative Approaches to the Prevention & Treatment of Modern Diseases. Ed. by Avshalom Mizrahi et al. LC 97-16693. (Illus.). 300p. (C). 1997. text 114.00 (*0-306-45602-8*, Kluwer Plenum) Kluwer Academic.

Potentiometric Water Analysis. Derek Midgely & Kenneth E. Torrance. LC 77-7213. 421p. reprint ed. pap. 130.60 (*0-608-17653-2*, 203051200069) Bks Demand.

Potentiometric Water Analysis. 2nd ed. Derek Midgely & Kenneth E. Torrance. LC 90-25307. 600p. 1991. 495.00 (*0-471-92983-2*) Wiley.

Potentiometry & Potentiometric Titrations. E. P. Serjeant. 742p. (C). 1991. reprint ed. lib. bdg. 110.00 (*0-89464-549-8*) Krieger.

Potholes. Gus Kaikkonen. 1984. pap. 5.25 (*0-8222-0908-X*) Dramatists Play.

Potholes & Pigsties, a Prodigal's Journey Home. C. E. Lenamon. Ed. by Kathy D. Weber. LC 97-92182. (Illus.). 208p. (Orig.). 1997. pap. 14.95 (*0-9658964-0-4*) Pippin Publ.

Potholes in the Sky. Nona Freeman. Ed. by Nell Perry. (Illus.). 133p. (Orig.). 1996. pap. 7.00 (*1-878366-11-4*) Nonas Bk Sales.

Potiki. Patricia Grace. LC 94-45651. (Talanoa Ser.). 185p. 1995. pap. 12.95 (*0-8248-1706-0*) UH Pr.

Potion Magique de Georges Bouillon. Roald Dahl. (Folio - Junior Ser.: No. 463). (FRE., Illus.). 148p. (J). (gr. 5-10). 1990. pap. 8.95 (*2-07-033463-5*) Schoenhof.

Potions & Pictures. Alan M. Hofmeister et al. (Reading for All Learners Ser.). (Illus.). (J). pap. write for info. (*1-56861-183-8*) Swift Lrn Res.

Potions, Poisons, & Panaceas: An Ethnobotanical Study of Montserrat. David E. Brussell. LC 90-25873. (Illus.). 208p. (C). 1997. 69.95 (*0-8093-1552-1*) S Ill U Pr.

Potions to Pulsars: Women Doing Science. Sue Bursztynski. (True Stories Ser.). 96p. (J). (gr. 3-8). 1996. pap. text 6.95 (*1-86448-246-X*) IPG Chicago.

Potiphar Papers. George W. Curtis. LC 04-13872. 1995. 8.00 (*0-403-00098-X*) Scholarly.

Potiphar Papers. George W. Curtis. LC 72-121280. (BCL Ser. I). reprint ed. 32.50 (*0-404-01888-2*) AMS Pr.

Potiphar Papers. Harriot Curtis. (Works of Harriot Curtis). 1990. reprint ed. lib. bdg. 79.00 (*0-7812-2464-0*) Rprt Serv.

Potlatch: A Tsimshian Celebration. Diane Hoyt-Goldsmith. LC 96-41367. (Illus.). 32p. (J). (gr. 4-6). 1997. lib. bdg. 16.95 (*0-8234-1290-3*) Holiday.

***Potlatch at Gitsegukla: William Beynon's 1945 Field Notebooks.** Ed. by Margaret Anderson & Marjorie Halpin. (Illus.). 256p. 2000. text 75.00 (*0-7748-0743-1*) UBC Pr.

Potlatch Corp. A Report on the Company's Environmental Policies & Practices. (Illus.). 44p. (C). 1994. reprint ed. pap. text 40.00 (*0-7881-0966-9*, Coun on Econ) DIANE Pub.

Potlatch Papers: A Colonial Case History. Christopher Bracken. LC 97-9829. 224p. 1997. pap. text 16.95 (*0-226-06987-7*); lib. bdg. 40.00 (*0-226-06986-9*) U Ch Pr.

Potluck. Anne Shelby. LC 90-7757. (Illus.). 32p. (J). (ps-2). 1994. pap. 6.95 (*0-531-07045-X*) Orchard Bks Watts.

Potluck. Anne Shelby. 1994. 12.15 (*0-606-09763-5*, Pub. by Turtleback) Demco.

Potluck: Exploring American Foods & Meals. rev. ed. Raymond C. Clark. (Vocabureader Workbook Ser.: No. 2). (Illus.). 128p. (Orig.). 1994. pap. text 10.50 (*0-86647-084-0*) Pro Lingua.

***Potluck: Poems from Hollywood.** Mark Dunster. 11p. 1999. pap. 5.00 (*0-89642-738-2*) Linden Pubs.

Potluck . . . Southern Style. Linda G. Hatcher. (Illus.). 183p. 1997. pap. 12.95 (*0-942407-33-4*) Father & Son.

Potluck Adventures of Mrs. Marmalade: A Children's Cookbook. Patsy Swendson. Ed. by Melissa Roberts. (Illus.). 32p. (J). (gr. 4-5). 1989. 10.95 (*0-89015-718-9*) Sunbelt Media.

Potluck Cookbook: Bodega Cooks for the Bodega Land Trust. Ed. by Bodega Land Trust Committee Staff. (Illus.). 179p. (Orig.). 1997. pap. 13.50 (*0-614-29919-5*) Tannery Creek.

Potluck Dinner That Went Astray: And Other Tales of Christian Life. Bob Reed. 96p. 1996. pap. 11.00 (*1-57312-041-3*) Smyth & Helwys.

Potluck on the Pedernales. Community Garden Club of Johnson City, Texas Staff. 324p. 1991. 16.95 (*0-89015-829-0*) Sunbelt Media.

Potluck on the Pedernales, Second Helping. Community Garden Club of Johnson City Staff. 324p. 1993. 16.95 (*0-89015-909-2*) Sunbelt Media.

Potluck Plain & Fancy: Our Favorite Recipes from "Quick 'n' Easy" to Masterpieces. Susan M. Peery. LC 96-22085. 256p. 1996. pap. 14.95 (*0-911469-13-3*) A C Hood.

Potluck Supper. 24p. (J). (ps-2). 1997. pap. write for info. (*0-7814-3028-3*, Chariot Bks) Chariot Victor.

Potluck Supper. Barbara Davoll. (Christopher Churchmouse Classics Ser.). (Illus.). 24p. (J). (ps-2). 1988. 8.99 (*0-89693-406-3*, 6-1406, Victor Bks) Chariot Victor.

Potluck, 1923-1998. MN State Catholic Daughters of the Americas Member. (Illus.). 518p. 1996. spiral bd. 15.00 (*0-9653975-0-5*) MN Catholic Dghtrs.

Potlucks & Petticoats. Ed. by Jerry Cope & Becky Cope. 1986. 11.95 (*0-9617157-0-7*) Topside Pubs.

Potman Spoke Sooth. David Fulk. 1977. pap. 3.50 (*0-87129-290-4*, P41) Dramatic Pub.

***Potomac: A Nation's River.** Arnout Hyde. LC 99-29585. (Illus.). 128p. 1999. 15.99 (*0-517-19455-4*) Random Hse Value.

Potomac Chronicle. Harold C. Fleming & Virginia Fleming. LC 95-52513. xxvi, 285p. (C). 1997. 32.00 (*0-8203-1836-1*) U of Ga Pr.

***Potomac Fever.** Henry Horrock. 2000. mass mkt. 6.99 (*0-7860-1105-X*, Pinncle Kensgtn) Kensgtn Pub Corp.

Potomac Fever. Henry Horrock. LC 98-45240. 304p. (YA). (gr. 8). 1999. 24.00 (*0-316-35472-4*) Little.

***Potomac Fever.** large type ed. Henry Horrock. LC 99-37938. 1999. 27.95 (*0-7862-2175-5*, G K Hall Lrg Type) Mac Lib Ref.

Potomac Journey: Fairfax Stone to Tidewater. Richard L. Stanton. (Illus.). 256p. 1996. pap. 15.95 (*1-56098-660-3*) Smithsonian.

Potomac Squire. Elswyth Thane. 29.95 (*0-8488-0727-8*) Amereon Ltd.

***Potomac State College.** Dinah W. Courrier. (College History Ser.). (Illus.). 128p. 2000. pap. 19.99 (*0-7385-0621-4*) Arcadia Publng.

Potosi: Colonial Treasures & the Bolivian City of Silver. Pedro Querejazu & Elizabeth Ferrer. LC 97-74730. (Illus.). 152p. Date not set. pap. 29.95 (*1-879128-16-0*) Americas Soc.

Potosi Mita, 1573-1700: Compulsory Indian Labor in the Andes. Jeffrey A. Cole. LC 84-40331. (Illus.). 224p. 1985. 39.50 (*0-8047-1256-5*) Stanford U Pr.

Potosi, St. Augustin & Ouro Preto see Monumental Cities

Potosi, the First One Hundred Years. 2nd ed. Juanita D. Zachry. LC 49-7331. (Illus.). 168p. 1973. 5.95 (*0-686-05778-3*) Zachry Assocs.

Potpourri. R. Thomas Dickman. LC 88-91415. 1989. 12.95 (*0-87212-223-9*) Libra.

Potpourri. Contrib. by Larry Lukas. 24p. (Orig.). 1996. pap. text 6.95 (*1-889416-05-3*, LS40006) Lukasound.

Potpourri. Barbara Randolph. 72p. 1991. 15.00 (*0-385-25334-6*) Doubleday.

Potpourri. Grady-Sue L. Saxon. (Illus.). 57p. 1996. 15.00 (*0-9647959-1-4*) G S L Saxon.

Potpourri. Susan B. Sirkis. (Wish Booklets Ser.: Vol. 12). (Illus.). 56p. 1973. pap. 5.95 (*0-913786-12-8*) Wish Bklets.

Potpourri. Alice D. Smith. 44p. 1983. pap. 2.50 (*0-614-24775-6*) Tesseract SD.

Potpourri: A Medley of Poems. Michael R. Collings. 54p. (Orig.). Date not set. pap. 6.00 (*1-886405-59-X*, Zarahemla Motets) White Crow Pr.

Potpourri: Bouquet of Language Activities. M. Sherry Smith & Deena L. Cendejas. (J). (gr. 2-5). 1991. student ed. 17.95 (*0-937857-25-4*, 1587) Speech Bin.

Potpourri: Recipes & Crafts. Bertha Reppert & Pat Humphries. 40p. 1973. pap. 5.00 (*0-9617210-2-2*) Remembrance.

Potpourri - Appalachian Mountain Dulcimer. James H. Hall, Jr. (Illus.). 100p. 1984. pap. 6.95 (*0-9614762-0-6*) J M Hall.

Potpourri & Fragrant Crafts. Betsy Williams. LC 96-4835. (Illus.). 144p. 1996. 24.95 (*0-89577-866-1*, Pub. by RD Assn) Penguin Putnam.

Potpourri & Perfumery from Australian Gardens. Denise Greig. (Illus.). 80p. reprint ed. 9.95 (*0-86417-081-5*, Pub. by Kangaroo Pr) Seven Hills Bk.

Potpourri & Scented Gifts: Gifts from Nature. Joanne Rippin. (Illus.). 64p. 1997. 12.95 (*1-85967-499-2*, Lorenz Bks) Anness Pub.

***Potpourri from Kettle Land.** Irene I. Luethge. 200p. 2000. pap. 9.95 (*1-886028-46-X*, Pub. by Savage Pr) Bookmen Inc.

Potpourri in Glass. Terra Parma. Ed. by Stained Glass Images Inc. Staff. (Illus.). 52p. 1991. pap. 12.95 (*0-936459-16-6*) Stained Glass.

P

Potpourri, Incense & Other Fragrant Concoctions. Ann T. Fettner. LC 77-5931. (Illus.). 144p. 1977. pap. 5.95 (*0-911104-97-6*, 133) Workman Pub.

Potpourri Making Easy & Simple Workbook. Alpha Pyramis Research Division Staff. (Illus.). 75p. (Orig.). 1992. ring bd., wbk. ed. 24.95 (*0-913597-28-7*) Prosperity & Profits.

Potpourri of Land & Sea. Melbourne Z. Myerson. 192p. 1998. pap. 12.50 (*0-9665757-0-9*) Ponder Pubns.

Potpourri of Life's Challenges. Esther Lay Miller. 1998. pap. write for info. (*1-57553-835-0*) Watermrk Pr.

Potpourri of Music for Movement & Improvisational Study: Specially Composed or Selected from Piano Literature to Teach Rhythm & Musical Nuance. Joy Yelin. 1998. teacher ed. 30.00 (*0-9626150-3-X*) Musical Mosaics.

Potpourri of Nostalgia. Bonnie H. Falk. (Illus.). 224p. 1990. pap. 14.95 (*0-9614108-2-5*) BHF Memories.

Potpourri of Old St. John's. Fred Adams. (Illus.). 100p. 1991. pap. 9.55 (*0-920021-99-9*) Creative Bk Pub.

Potpourri of Pansies. Storey Publishing Staff. 1997. 15.00 (*0-676-57156-5*) Random.

Potpourri of Pansies. Emilie Tolley & Chris Mead. LC 92-41125. 1993. 15.00 (*0-517-59449-8*) C Potter.

Potpourri of Pattern: A Collection of Original Open Patterns for Canvas & Linen Use. Ann Strite-Kurz. (Illus.). 132p. (Orig.). 1995. pap. 30.00 (*0-9633259-2-2*) A Strite-Kurz.

Potpourri of Physics Teaching Ideas. Ed. by Donna B. Conner. (Illus.). 363p. (Orig.). 1987. spiral bd. 34.00 (*0-917853-27-X*, OP-57) Am Assn Physics.

Potpourri of Pleasantries. Gladys K. Morse. Ed. by Gail H. Bickford. (Illus.). 60p. (Orig.). 1993. pap. 6.00 (*0-945069-01-4*) Freedom Pr Assocs.

Potpourri of Poetry. Carol P. Farmer. Ed. by Janet Leih. 67p. (Orig.). 1989. pap. 5.95 (*1-877649-00-7*) Tesseract SD.

Potpourri of Poetry. Eveline V. Kiley. 60p. 1998. pap. 6.95 (*1-57502-682-1*, P01929) Morris Pubng.

Potpourri of Poetry. Kathleen B. Lievense. 1998. pap. write for info. (*1-57553-705-2*) Watermrk Pr.

*__Potpourri of Poetry.__ Marcia Minot. 1999. pap. write for info. (*1-58235-105-8*) Watermrk Pr.

Potpourri of Poetry. Helen Saulsman. 138p. Date not set. pap. 20.00 (*0-9668452-4-2*) Brown Bks TX.

Potpourri of Praise. Susan T. Osborn & Wightman Weese. LC 97-154583. 179p. (Orig.). 1995. pap. 9.95 (*1-883893-27-5*) WinePress Pub.

Potpourri of Praise. unabridged ed. Sally A. Kates. Ed. by Lana Wegeng. (Illus.). 66p. 1998. pap. 16.95 (*0-9659454-6-4*) Columbia Pubns.

Potpourri of the Mind: A Collection of Poems in the Limerick Style. Joel D. Ash. LC 97-92589. 109p. 1997. 20.00 (*0-9664047-0-X*) Old Pine Bks.

Potpourri of War: Labors of Love Remembered. Noonie Fortin. LC 98-14954. (Illus.). 320p. 1998. pap. 15.95 (*1-880292-24-6*) LangMarc.

Potpourri Recipe Encyclopedia. 115.00 (*1-890928-23-2*) Frieda Carrol.

Potpourri Recipe Encyclopedia. Bibliotheca Press Staff. 100p. 1991. ring bd. 115.00 (*0-317-04653-5*) Prosperity & Profits.

Potpourri Sachets & Air Fresheners. Story Time Staff. (Alfreda's Recipe Ser.: No. 7). (Illus.). 30p. (Orig.). (YA). (gr. 6 up). 1997. pap. 18.95 (*1-56820-224-5*) Story Time.

Potpourri Simple & Easy Notebook. rev. ed. Data Notes Staff. 83p. 1993. ring bd. 29.95 (*0-911569-22-7*) Prosperity & Profits.

Potpourri That Can Be Drank, Sipped or Served. Scentouri Staff. (Scentouri Recipe Bks.). 1984. ring bd. 43.95 (*0-318-01388-6*) Prosperity & Profits.

Potpourris: Poems from Hollywood. Mark Dunster. 17p. 1998. pap. 5.00 (*0-89642-400-6*) Linden Pubs.

Potrait of Picasso As a Young Man: An Interpretive Biography. Norman Mailer. (Illus.). 464p. 1996. mass mkt. 19.99 (*0-446-67266-1*, Pub. by Warner Bks) Little.

Pots & Containers. Warren Schultz. (For Your Garden Ser.). 72p. 1996. pap. text 12.95 (*1-56799-280-3*, Friedman-Fairfax) M Friedman Pub Grp Inc.

Pots & Containers. Sue Spielburg. (Gardening Ser.). (Illus.). 96p. 1998. pap. 15.95 (*0-7078-0283-0*, Pub. by Natl Trust) Trafalgar.

Pots & Palaces: The Earthenware Ceramics of the Noblemen's Quarter of Vijayanagara. Carla Sinopoli. (C). 1993. 44.00 (*81-85425-28-0*, Pub. by Manohar) S Asia.

Pots & Pans. Patricia Hubbell. LC 97-1426. (Illus.). 24p. (J). (ps up). 1998. 9.95 (*0-694-01072-3*) HarpC.

Pots & Pans. Anne Rockwell. LC 91-4976. (Illus.). 32p. (J). (ps-1). 1993. lib. bdg. 13.95 (*0-02-777631-X*, Mac Bks Young Read) S&S Childrens.

Pots & Pans: A Colloquium on Precious Metals & Ceramics in the Muslim, Chinese, & Greco-Roman Worlds, Oxford 1985. Ed. by Michael Vickers. (Oxford Studies in Islamic Art: Vol. III). (Illus.). 224p. 1987. 65.00 (*0-19-728005-6*) OUP.

Pots & Pans of Classical Athens. Lucy Talcott & Brian A. Sparkes. (Excavations of the Athenian Agora Picture Bks.: No. 1). (Illus.). 32p. 1959. pap. 3.00 (*0-87661-601-5*) Am Sch Athens.

Pots & People: That Have Shaped the Heritage of Medieval & Later England. Maureen Meaor. LC 97-186379. (Illus.). 80p. 1998. pap. 13.95 (*1-85444-080-2*, 0801, Pub. by Ashmolean Mus) A Schwartz & Co.

*__Pots & Planters in a Weekend: Simple Step-by-Step Projects for Maximum Effect with Minimum Effort.__ Julie London. LC 99-50255. 2000. pap. 14.95 (*1-58290-028-0*) Jrny Editions.

Potsdam. Gabriele Leuthauser & Peter Feierabend. (ENG, FRE & GER., Illus.). 300p. 1997. 39.95 (*3-89508-238-4*, 810049) Konemann.

Potsdam Bluff. Jack D. Hunter. 384p. 1992. mass mkt. 4.99 (*0-8125-1379-7*) Tor Bks.

Potsdam Bluff. Jack D. Hunter. 304p. 2000. mass mkt. 0.10 (*0-380-75356-1*, Avon Bks) Morrow Avon.

Potsdam Conference Documents. Harry S. Truman et al. LC 86-893390. (The Presidential Documents Ser.). 2p. 1980. write for info. (*0-89093-353-7*) U Pubns Amer.

Potshot. Gerry Boyle. (Jack McMorrow Mystery Ser.). 1998. mass mkt. 5.99 (*0-425-16233-8*) Berkley Pub.

Potshot Reviews: Of Southern Colorado Ghostowns. Thomas Mariano. Ed. by Laura O. Tate. (Illus.). 282p. (Orig.). 1991. pap. 10.00 (*1-877637-04-1*) Mariano Pub.

Potsy. Colene Copeland. (Priscilla Pig Ser.: Vol. 6). 103p. (J). (gr. 1-6). 1997. pap. 4.95 (*0-939810-20-4*) Jordan Valley.

Pottawatomie Baptist Manual Labor Training School. Thomas P. Barr. LC 84-80938. (Illus.). 57p. 1984. pap. 3.00 (*0-87726-029-X*) Kansas St Hist.

Pottawattamie County Population Projections, 1975-2020. John P. Zipay. 24p. (Orig.). 1974. pap. 2.00 (*1-55719-052-6*) U NE CPAR.

Potted Fiction: Being a Series of Extracts from the World's Best Sellers, Put up in Thin Slices for Hurried Consumers. Ed. by John K. Bangs. LC 70-178436. (Short Story Index Reprint Ser.). 1977. reprint ed. 15.95 (*0-8369-4036-9*) Ayer.

*__Potted Garden: Home Library Garden Guides.__ Home Library Editors. 128p. 1999. pap. 12.95 (*1-56426-300-2*, Pub. by Cole Group) ACCESS Pubs Network.

Potted Gardens. Rebecca Cole. LC 97-11235. 1997. 27.50 (*0-517-70457-9*) Crown Pub Group.

Potted Gardens. Storey Publishing Staff. 1997. 27.50 (*0-676-57144-1*) Random.

Potted Histories: How to Make House Plants Feel at Home. Paul Simons & John Ruthven. LC 95-83720. (Illus.). 144p. 1996. pap. 16.95 (*0-563-37124-2*, BBC-Parkwest) Parkwest Pubns.

Potted Plant Organic Care. 3rd ed. Nancy Portugal & Jody S. Main. LC 79-22173. (Living on This Planet Ser.). (Illus.). 80p. 1978. pap. 4.50 (*0-9601088-7-4*) Wild Horses.

Potted Tree: Essays in Venetian Art. Norman E. Land. LC 93-40775. (ARTHIS Ser.). xiv, 188p. 1994. 65.00 (*1-879751-85-2*) Camden Hse.

Pottenger Portfolio: Fifty-Five Reprints of Medical Papers of Dr. Francis M. Pottenger, Jr. 1974. 35.00 (*0-916764-03-6*) Price-Pottenger.

Pottengers' Cats: A Study in Nutrition. Francis M. Pottenger, Jr. LC 83-80360. (Illus.). 126p. 1983. 5.95 (*0-916764-06-0*) Price-Pottenger.

Potter. Jacolyn Caton. (Illus.). 32p. (J). (ps-3). 1992. 10.95 (*1-55050-037-6*, Pub. by Coteau) Genl Dist Srvs.

Potter. Iowa Valley Community College Staff. (Nursing Texts Ser.). (C). (gr. 13). 1996. text 87.00 (*0-8151-4455-5*, 30719) Mosby Inc.

Potter. Walter Wangerin, Jr. LC 94-28924. (Illus.). 56p. (J). (gr. 2 up). 1994. 16.99 (*0-8066-2775-1*, 9-2775, Augsburg) Augsburg Fortress.

Potter: Genealogy of the Potter Families & Their Descendants in America. C. W. Potter. (Illus.). 300p. 1990. reprint ed. pap. 47.00 (*0-8328-1521-7*); reprint ed. lib. bdg. 55.00 (*0-8328-1520-9*) Higginson Bk Co.

Potter Addition: Poverty, Family & Kinship in a Heartland Community. David L. Harvey. (Social Institutions & Social Change Ser.). 336p. 1993. pap. text 27.95 (*0-202-30442-6*); lib. bdg. 49.95 (*0-202-30441-8*) Aldine de Gruyter.

Potter County Leek Cookbook. Dottie Bajor. (Illus.). 80p. (Orig.). 1990. pap. 6.95 (*0-9621577-0-8*) D Bajor.

Potter Giselle. Thomas Aarrestad. LC 98-48021. (Illus.). 32p. (J). (ps-3). 2000. 14.95 (*1-57102-146-9*, Ideals Child) Hambleton-Hill.

*__Potter Guide to Higher Education: Quality of Life & Learning in U. K. Universities & Colleges.__ 12th ed. Shelia Potter & Philippa Clare. (Illus.). 486p. 1999. pap. 29.50 (*1-870892-13-5*, Pub. by Dalebank Bks) Trans-Atl Phila.

Potter Highlands Historic District. Diane Wilk. (Historic Denver Guides Ser.). (Illus.). 96p. 1997. pap. 8.95 (*0-914248-14-6*) Hist Denver.

Potter Needlework Library: Needlepoint. Karen Elder. (Orig.). 1996. pap. 18.00 (*0-614-20778-9*) C Potter.

*__Potter Pig in Control: Four Stories on Anger Management for Grades 1-3.__ Diane S. Kooser. (Illus.). 64p. 2000. pap. 12.95 (*1-57543-084-3*) Mar Co Prods.

Potter Story Collection 1. Beatrix Potter. (J). 1999. 6.95 (*0-453-00947-6*, NAL Bks) NAL.

Potter Story Collection 2. Beatrix Potter. (J). 1999. 6.95 (*0-453-00948-4*, NAL Bks) NAL.

Potter Story Collection 3. Beatrix Potter. (J). 1999. 6.95 (*0-453-00949-2*, NAL Bks) NAL.

Potter Story Collection 4. Beatrix Potter. (J). 1999. 6.95 (*0-453-00950-6*, NAL Bks) NAL.

Potter v. Shrackle: Wrongful Death. 4th rev. ed. Kenneth S. Broun & James H. Seckinger. 162p. 1992. pap. 22.95 (*1-55681-313-9*) Natl Inst Trial Ad.

Potteries. David Sekers. (Album Ser.: No. 62). (Illus.). 32p. 1998. pap. 6.25 (*0-85263-564-8*, Pub. by Shire Pubns) Parkwest Pubns.

*__Potters.__ Leonard Everett Fisher. (Colonial Craftsmen Ser.). (Illus.). (J). 2000. 21.36 (*0-7614-1149-6*, Benchmark NY) Marshall Cavendish.

Potters & Paintresses: Women Designers in the Pottery Industry 1870-1955. Ed. by Cheryl Buckley. 35.00 (*0-7043-4211-1*, Pub. by Womens Press) Trafalgar.

Potters & Potteries of New York State, 1650-1900. rev. ed. William C. Ketchum. (New York State Bks.). (Illus.). 632p. 1987. pap. 29.95 (*0-8156-0219-7*) Syracuse U Pr.

Potters & Potteries of New York State, 1650-1900. 2nd rev. ed. William C. Ketchum. (New York State Bks.). (Illus.). 632p. 1987. text 60.00 (*0-8156-2413-1*) Syracuse U Pr.

*__Potter's Art.__ Henry H. Glassie. LC 99-37064. (Material Culture Ser.). (Illus.). 152p. 2000. pap. 12.95 (*0-253-21356-8*); lib. bdg. 25.00 (*0-253-33732-1*) Ind U Pr.

Potter's Art: A Complete History of Pottery in Britain. Garth Clark. (Illus.). 240p. (C). 1995. text 59.95 (*0-7148-3202-2*, Pub. by Phaidon Press) Phaidon Pr.

Potter's Atlas of Fetal & Infant Pathology. Edith L. Potter & Enid Gilbert-Barness. LC 98-23495. 398p. 1998. text. write for info. (*0-323-00126-2*) Mosby Inc.

Potter's Book. Bernard Leach. (J). 1946. pap. 14.00 (*0-693-01157-2*) Transatl Arts.

Potters Book. Bernard Leach. 1988. pap. 29.95 (*0-571-10973-X*) Faber & Faber.

Potter's Companion: Imagination, Originality, & Craft. Ronald Larsen. (Illus.). 192p. (Orig.). 1992. pap. 19.95 (*0-89281-445-4*, Park St Pr) Inner Tradit.

Potter's Complete Book of Clay & Glazes: A Comprehensive Guide to Formulating, Mixing, Applying, & Firing Clay Bodies & Glazes. James Chappell. (Illus.). 400p. 1991. 50.00 (*0-8230-4203-0*) Watsn-Guptill.

Potter's Dictionary of Materials & Techniques. 4th ed. Frank Hamer & Janet Hamer. LC 96-49036. (Illus.). 416p. 1997. 49.95 (*0-8122-3404-9*) U of Pa Pr.

Potter's Dictionary of Materials & Techniques. 4th ed. Frank Hammer & Janet Hammer. 1997. text 85.00 (*90-5703-091-8*, Pub. by Craftsman House) Gordon & Breach.

Potter's Directory of Shape & Form: Over 600 at-a-Glance Designs. Neal French. LC 97-80614. (Illus.). 80p. 1998. pap. 19.95 (*0-87341-560-4*, PDSF) Krause Pubns.

Potter's Field. Ann C. Fallon. Ed. by Dana Isaacson. 256p. (Orig.). 1993. mass mkt. 4.99 (*0-671-75136-0*) PB.

*__Potter's Field.__ Olafur Gunnarsson. 490p. 2000. pap. 19.95 (*1-899197-55-9*, Pub. by Mares Nest Pub) Dufour.

Potter's Field. Ellis Peters. 1991. mass mkt. 5.99 (*0-446-40058-0*, Pub. by Warner Bks) Little.

Potter's Field: The Seventeenth Chronicle of Brother Cadfael. large type ed. Ellis Peters. LC 91-15480. (General Ser.). 303p. 1991. lib. bdg. 19.95 (*0-8161-5194-6*, G K Hall Lrg Type) Mac Lib Ref.

Potter's Fields. large type ed. Frank Roderus. LC 97-34314. (Wheeler Large Print Book Ser.). 1997. pap. 22.95 (*1-56895-492-1*) Wheeler Pub.

*__Potter's Freedom: A Defense of the Reformation & Reply Norman Geisler's Chosen But Free.__ James White. 350p. 2000. pap. 15.95 (*1-879737-43-4*) Calvary Press.

Potter's Guide to Raw Glazing & Oil Firing Dennis Parks. LC 79-17357. 112p. 1980. write for info. (*0-684-16392-6*) Scribner.

Potter's House: God Is the Master Potter. 2nd rev. ed. Wallace H. Heflin, Jr. 168p. 1997. pap. 8.99 (*1-884369-61-8*) McDougal Pubng.

Potter's Manual. Kenneth Clark. (Illus.). 208p. 1990. pap. 14.98 (*0-89009-674-0*) Bk Sales Inc.

Potter's New Cyclopaedia of Botanical Drugs & Preparations. R. C. Wren. 376p. pap. 28.50 (*0-85207-197-3*, Pub. by C W Daniel) Natl Bk Netwk.

Potter's New Cyclopaedia of Botanical Drugs & Preparations. rev. ed. R. C. Wren. (C). 1994. pap. 32.50 (*0-8464-1039-7*) Beekman Pubs.

Potter's Niece. large type ed. Rona Randall. 1990. 18.95 (*0-7089-2130-2*) Ulverscroft.

Potter's Notes on Tai Chi Chuan. Margy Emerson. (Illus.). 76p. 1988. reprint ed. pap. 9.95 (*0-9620690-0-0*) Artichoke OR.

Potter's Odyssey: A Guide to the Pottery Art. Willard Spence. LC 94-42857. (Illus.). 192p. (Orig.). 1995. pap. 12.95 (*0-86534-003-X*) Sunstone Pr.

Potters on Pottery. Elisabeth Cameron & Philippa Lewis. (Illus.). 1976. 11.95 (*0-312-63280-0*) St Martin.

Potter's Palette: A Practical Guide to Creating over 700 Illustrated Glazes & Slip Covers. Christine Constant & Steve Ogden. LC 96-142140. (Illus.). 80p. 1996. pap. 19.95 (*0-8019-8753-9*) Krause Pubns.

Potter's Pathology of the Fetus & Infant, 2 vols. Ed. by Enid Gilbert-Barnes. (Illus.). 1776p. (C). (gr. 13). 1996. text 310.00 (*0-8016-7870-6*, 07870) Mosby Inc.

Potter's Perinatal Pathology. Alan Blanc. 1991. write for info. (*0-8151-0868-0*) Mosby Inc.

Potter's Primer. Morgen Hall. LC 97-73021. (Illus.). 144p. 1997. pap. 24.95 (*0-87341-540-X*, POTPRI) Krause Pubns.

Potter's Professional Handbook: A Guide to Defining, Identifying & Establishing Yourself in the Craft Community. Steven Branfman. LC 98-84101. (Illus.). 240p. 1999. pap. 29.95 (*0-87341-678-3*, POTBUS) Krause Pubns.

Potters' Quarter: The Pottery. Agnes N. Stillwell & J. L. Benson. LC 49-1745. (Corinth Ser.: Vol. 15, Pt. 3). (Illus.). xv, 432p. 1984. 75.00 (*0-87661-153-6*) Am Sch Athens.

Potters' View of Canada: Canadian Scenes on Nineteenth-Century Earthenware. Elizabeth Collard. (Illus.). 196p. 1983. 55.00 (*0-7735-0421-4*, Pub. by McG-Queens Univ Pr) CUP Services.

Potters Wheel. Ed. by V. Roux. (C). 1989. 44.00 (*81-204-0436-X*) S Asia.

Potter's Wheel: Change in English Language Arts Classrooms. Ed. by Rosalie Rafter. 109p. (C). 1996. pap. text 10.00 (*0-930348-20-6*) NY St Eng Coun.

*__Potter's Wheel, 1996-1998.__ unabridged ed. iv, 82p. 1998. pap. write for info. (*1-929706-05-7*) Anderson Pubng.

Potters Wheel, 1994-1996. unabridged ed. 93p. 1996. pap. write for info. (*1-929706-02-2*) Anderson Pubng.

Potter's Wheel Projects. Ed. by Thomas Sellers. LC 68-58829. (Ceramics Monthly Handbooks Ser.). (Illus.). 64p. 1968. pap. 7.95 (*0-934706-04-2*) Am Ceramic.

Potter's Workbook. Clary Illian. LC 98-52161. (Illus.). 124p. 1999. pap., wbk. ed. 22.95 (*0-87745-671-2*) U of Iowa Pr.

*__Potter's Workshop: 20 Unique Ceramic Projects for the Small Home Studio.__ Jenny Rodwell. (Illus.). 144p. 2000. 27.95 (*0-7153-0928-5*, Pub. by D & C Pub) Sterling.

Pottery. (Americana Bks.). (Illus.). 1972. 3.00 (*0-911410-32-5*) Applied Arts.

Pottery. Boy Scouts of America. (Illus.). 64p. (YA). (gr. 6-12). 1969. pap. 2.90 (*0-8395-3314-4*, 33314) BSA.

Pottery. John Gale. (Teach Yourself Ser.). (Illus.). 256p. 1998. pap. 10.95 (*0-8442-0011-5*, 00115, Teach Yrslf) NTC Contemp Pub Co.

Pottery. T. Potter. (Practical Guides Ser.). (Illus.). 48p. (J). (gr. 6-12). 1986. pap. 8.95 (*0-86020-944-X*) EDC.

Pottery. T. Potter. (Practical Guides Ser.). (Illus.). 48p. (J). (gr. 6 up). 1999. lib. bdg. 16.95 (*0-88110-319-5*) EDC.

Pottery: A Guide to Advanced Techniques. Doug Wensley. (Illus.). 160p. 1996. 35.00 (*1-85223-781-3*, Pub. by Crolwood) Trafalgar.

Pottery: A Manual of Techniques. Doug Wensley. (Illus.). 188p. 1992. pap. 29.95 (*1-85223-717-1*, Pub. by Crolwood) Trafalgar.

Pottery: Form & Expression. Marguerite Wildenhain. LC 83-17806. (Illus.). 158p. 1986. reprint ed. pap. 17.95 (*0-87015-238-6*) Pacific Bks.

Pottery Analysis: A Sourcebook. Prudence M. Rice. LC 86-24958. (Illus.). xxiv, 584p. (C). 1987. 65.00 (*0-226-71118-8*) U Ch Pr.

Pottery & Ceramics. Liza Gardner. (Contemporary Crafts Ser.). (Illus.), 96p. 1998. pap. text 14.95 (*1-85368-868-1*, Pub. by New5 Holland) Sterling.

*__Pottery & Chronology at Angel.__ Sherri L. Hilgeman. LC 99-50763. 2000. pap. 29.95 (*0-8173-1035-5*) U of Ala Pr.

Pottery & People: A Dynamic Interaction. Ed. by James M. Skibo & Gary M. Feinman. LC 98-38075. 1999. 55.00 (*0-87480-576-7*); pap. 25.00 (*0-87480-577-5*) U of Utah Pr.

Pottery & Porcelain. 9th ed. Harvey Duke. 1999. write for info. (*0-676-60091-3*) Hse Collectbls.

Pottery & Porcelain Ceramics Price Guide. 2nd rev. ed. Ed. by Kyle Husfloen & Susan N. Cox. LC 97-72626. (Illus.). 406p. 1997. pap. 14.95 (*0-930625-73-0*, Antique Trader) Krause Pubns.

Pottery by American Indian Women: The Legacy of Generations. Susan Peterson. LC 97-12628. (Illus.). 224p. (J). 2000. 55.00 (*0-7892-0353-7*, Abbeville Kids) Abbeville Pr.

Pottery by American Indian Women: The Legacy of Generations. Susan Peterson et al. LC 97-12628. 1997. pap. 37.50 (*0-7892-0354-5*) Abbeville Pr.

Pottery by the Lagan: The Downshire China Manufactury. Peter Francis & Linda Canning. (Illus.). 200p. 1998. pap. 20.95 (*0-85389-694-1*, Pub. by Inst Irish Studies) Irish Bks Media.

Pottery Decoration: Contemporary Approaches. John Gibson. (Illus.). 160p. 1997. text. write for info. (*90-5703-801-3*, Harwood Acad Pubs) Gordon & Breach.

Pottery Decoration: Contemporary Approaches. John Gibson. LC 97-2406. (Illus.). 160p. 1997. 35.00 (*0-87951-788-3*, Pub. by Overlook Pr) Penguin Putnam.

Pottery Ethnoarchaeology in the Central Maya Highlands. Michael Deal. LC 98-12945. 1998. 55.00 (*0-87480-560-0*); pap. 25.00 (*0-87480-561-9*) U of Utah Pr.

Pottery for the Archaeologist. A. M. Gibson & A. J. Woods. 200p. 1990. text 49.00 (*0-7185-1274-X*, Pub. by Leicester U Pr) Cassell & Continuum.

Pottery from Arroyo Hondo Pueblo, New Mexico: Tribalization & Trade in the Northern Rio Grande. Judith A. Habicht-Mauche. (Arroyo Hondo Archaeological Ser.: Vol. 8). (Illus.). 280p. (Orig.). 1993. pap. 35.00 (*0-933452-34-9*) Schol Am Res.

Pottery From Diyala Region. Pinhas Delougaz. 1973. lib. bdg. 21.00 (*0-226-14233-7*) U Ch Pr.

Pottery from Spanish Shipwrecks, 1500-1800. Mitchell W. Marken. LC 93-34787. (Illus.). 280p. (C). 1994. 49.95 (*0-8130-1268-6*) U Press Fla.

Pottery from the Aleutian Islands. George I. Quimby. LC 46-2911. (Chicago Natural History Museum Anthropology Ser.: Vol. 36, No. 1, September 19, 1945). (Illus.). 13p. 1945. reprint ed. pap. 30.00 (*0-608-02730-8*, 206339500004) Bks Demand.

Pottery Function: A Use-Alteration Perspective. J. M. Skibo. (Interdisciplinary Contributions to Archaeology Ser.). (Illus.). 222p. (C). 1992. 39.50 (*0-306-44159-4*, Plenum Trade) Perseus Pubng.

Pottery in Archaeology. Clive Orton et al. LC 92-25814. (Manuals in Archaeology Ser.). (Illus.). 287p. (C). 1993. pap. text 23.95 (*0-521-44597-3*) Cambridge U Pr.

Pottery in Rajasthan: Ethnoarchaeology in Two Indian Cities. Carol Kramer. LC 96-53553. (Series in Archaeological Inquiry). (Illus.). 288p. 1997. text 49.95 (*1-56098-740-5*) Smithsonian.

Pottery in Roman Britain. Vivien G. Swan. 1989. pap. 50.00 (*0-85263-912-0*, Pub. by Shire Pubns) St Mut.

Pottery in the Making: Ceramic Traditions. Ed. by Ian Freestone & David Gaimster. LC 98-136330. 240p. 1998. pap. text 35.00 (*1-56098-797-9*) Smithsonian.

Pottery Industry of Trenton: A Skilled Trade in Transition 1850-1929. Marc J. Stern. LC 93-45518. (Class & Culture Ser.). 370p. (C). 1994. text 48.00 (*0-8135-2098-3*) Rutgers U Pr.

P

An Asterisk (*) at the beginning of an entry indicates that the title is appearing for the first time.

Pottery-Making in the Southwest. fac. ed. E. W. Gifford. (University of Caifornia Publications in American Archaeology & Ethnology: Vol. 23: 8). 25p. (C). 1928. reprint ed. pap. text 2.81 (*1-55567-264-7*) Coyote Press.

Pottery, Modern Wares, 1920-1960. Leslie A. Pina. LC 94-66781. (Illus.). 240p. 1994. 49.95 (*0-88740-692-0*) Schiffer.

Pottery of Acatlan: A Changing Mexican Tradition. Louana M. Lackey. LC 81-40280. (Illus.). 176p. 1991. pap. 19.95 (*0-8061-2301-X*) U of Okla Pr.

Pottery of Lerna IV. Jeremy B. Rutter. LC 75-324986. (Lerna Ser.: Vol. 3). (Illus.). xxxvi, 781p. 1995. 120.00 (*0-87661-303-2*) Am Sch Athens.

Pottery of Palestine: Neolithic to Modern. Jeffrey A. Blakely & W. J. Bennett, Jr. (Illus.). Date not set. text 24.95 (*0-931464-98-6*) Eisenbrauns.

***Pottery of the American Indians: Illustrated with Halftone Photographs, Endpapers, Jackets & Line Drawings by Marion Downer.** Helen E. Stiles. (LC History-America-E). (Illus.). 169p. 1999. reprint ed. lib. bdg. 69.00 (*0-7812-4291-6*) Rprt Serv.

Pottery of the Great Basin & Adjacent Areas. Ed. by Suzanne Griset. LC 86-217441. (University of Utah, Anthropological Papers: No. 111). (Illus.). 198p. reprint ed. pap. 61.40 (*0-8357-6848-1*, 203554300095) Bks Demand.

Pottery of the Islamic World: In the Tareq Rajab Museum. Fehervari. (Illus.). 128p. Date not set. pap. 18.95 (*1-86064-364-7*, Pub. by I B T) St Martin.

Pottery of the Islamic World: In the Tareq Rajab Museum. Fehervari. (Illus.). 128p. 1998. text 39.50 (*1-86064-363-9*, Pub. by I B T) St Martin.

Pottery of the Pajarito Plateau & of Some Adjacent Regions in New Mexico: American Anthropology Association Memoirs. Alfred V. Kidder. LC 16-15195. (American Anthropological Association Memoirs Ser.: No. 12). 1915. 25.00 (*0-527-00511-8*) Periodicals Srv.

Pottery of the Shenandoah Valley Region. H. E. Comstock. LC 93-80689. (The Frank L. Horton Ser.). (Illus.). 538p. 1994. 125.00 (*0-945578-04-0*) Mus South Deco.

Pottery on the Wheel. Elsbeth S. Woody. (Illus.). 205p. 1975. pap. 25.00 (*0-374-51234-5*) FS&G.

Pottery, People & Time: A Workshop in Action. Alan Caiger-Smith. (Illus.). 216p. 1995. 60.00 (*0-903685-39-6*, Pub. by R Dennis) Antique Collect.

Pottery Place. Gail Gibbons. LC 86-32790. (Illus.). 32p. (J). (ps-3). 1987. 12.95 (*0-15-263265-4*, Harcourt Child Bks) Harcourt.

Pottery, Poetry & Prophecy: Studies in Early Hebrew Poetry. David N. Freedman. LC 80-68378. xiii, 376p. 1980. text 40.00 (*0-931464-04-8*) Eisenbrauns.

Pottery Science: Materials, Processes & Products. Allen Dinsdale. LC 85-29573. 276p. 1986. text 36.95 (*0-470-20276-9*) P-H.

Pottery Techniques of Native North America: An Introduction to Traditional Technology. John K. White. LC 76-10710. 59p. 1976. lib. bdg. 46.00 (*0-226-69815-7*) U Ch Pr.

Pottery Technology: Principles & Reconstruction. Owen S. Rye. LC 80-53439. (Manuals on Archeology Ser.: No. 4). (Illus.). xi, 150p. 1981. 18.00 (*0-9602822-2-X*) Taraxacum.

Pottery Works: Potteries of New York State's Capital District & Upper Hudson Region. Warren F. Broderick & William Bouck. LC 92-55116. (Illus.). 288p. (C). 1995. 59.50 (*0-8386-3538-5*) Fairleigh Dickinson.

Potting Places. Teri Dunn. LC 99-17299. 1999. text 24.95 (*1-56799-768-6*) M Friedman Pub Grp Inc.

Potting Shed Postcard Book. Smith. (Illus.). 1996. pap. text 7.95 (*0-7611-0626-X*) Workman Pub.

Potts: Historical Collection Relating to the Potts Family in Great Britain & America. T. M. Potts. (Illus.). 735p. 1990. reprint ed. pap. 104.50 (*0-8328-1523-3*); reprint ed. lib. bdg. 112.50 (*0-8328-1522-5*) Higginson Bk Co.

Potts Models & Related Problems in Statistical Mechanics. Paul Martin. (Advanced Series in Stat Mechanics: Vol. 5). 360p. 1991. text 36.00 (*981-02-0075-7*) World Scientific Pub.

Potts Village Site (39C019), Oahe Reservoir, North Central South Dakota. Robert L. Stephenson. Ed. by Robert T. Bray. (Missouri Archaeologist Ser.: Vol. 33). (Illus.). 140p. (Orig.). 1971. pap. 3.00 (*0-943414-50-4*) MO Arch Soc.

Pottsville. Leo L. Ward. (Images of America Ser.). 1995. pap. 16.99 (*0-7524-0227-7*) Arcadia Publng.

Pottsville, PA. Historical Briefs, Inc. Staff. Ed. by Thomas Antonucci & Michael Antonucci. 176p. 1993. pap. 19.95 (*0-89677-050-8*) Hist Briefs.

Potty Book see When You've Got to Go!

***Potty Book - For Boys.** Alyssa Satin Capucilli. (Illus.). 32p. (J). 2000. 5.95 (*0-7641-5232-7*) Barron.

***Potty Book - For Girls.** Alyssa Satin Capucilli. (Illus.). 32p. (J). 2000. 5.95 (*0-7641-5231-9*) Barron.

Potty Chronicles: A Story to Help Children Adjust to Toilet Training. Annie Reiner. LC 91-86. (Illus.). 32p. (J). (ps-1). 1991. pap. 8.95 (*0-945354-35-5*) Am Psychol.

Potty Proud. unabridged ed. Patricia Giangrande & Stephanie Olen. (Illus.). 16p. (J). (gr. 6). 1991. 19.95 incl. audio (*0-9629701-0-7*) Anton Enter.

***Potty Tales: Lulu's a Big Girl Now; Now Wash Your Hands!; Where's Max's Potty; Lulu's Su, 4 bks.** Kate Brookes & Hazel Songhurst. (Carry Cases Ser.). (Illus.). 10p. (J). (ps-k). 1998. bds. 7.98 (*0-7651-0805-4*) Smithmark.

Potty Time. Illus. by Bettina Paterson. (Teddy Board Bks.). 12p. (J). (ps). 1993. bds. 4.95 (*0-448-40539-3*, G & D) Peng Put Young Read.

***Potty Time.** Ed. by Fiona Watt & Rachel Wells. (Baby's World Ser.). (Illus.). 16p. (YA). (ps). 2000. pap. 4.95 (*0-7460-3839-9*, Pub. by Usbrne Pbng UK) EDC.

Potty Time Book. Melissa Tyrrell. LC 98-67969. (Illus.). 12p. (J). (gr. k-3). 1999. bds. 8.99 (*1-57584-303-X*, Pub. by Rdrs Digest) S&S Trade.

Potty Training Your Baby: A Practical Guide for Easier Toilet Training. Katie Van Pelt. (Illus.). 144p. Date not set. mass mkt. 5.95 (*0-89529-692-6*, Avery) Penguin Putnam.

***Potus Speaks: Finding the Words that Defined the Clinton Presidency.** Michael Waldman. 224p. 2000. 25.00 (*0-7432-0020-9*) S&S Trade.

P(O)2 Euclidean (Quantum) Field Theory. Barry Simon. LC 73-16782. (Princeton Series in Physics). (Illus.). 413p. 1974. reprint ed. pap. 128.10 (*0-608-06609-5*, 206680600009) Bks Demand.

Potyviridae. D. D. Shukla et al. LC 96-170505. (Illus.). 448p. 1994. text 150.00 (*0-85198-864-4*) OUP.

Potyvirus Taxonomy. Ed. by O. W. Barnett. LC 92-25228. (Archives of Virology Ser.: Suppl. 5). (Illus.). 400p. 1992. 193.00 (*0-387-82353-0*) Spr-Verlag.

Pouce par Pouce. Leo Lionni. (FRE., Illus.). (J). (gr. k-1). 1961. 15.95 (*0-8392-3028-1*) Astor-Honor.

Pouces Verts: Level A. Tistou & Druon. text 7.95 (*0-8219-1217-8*) EMC-Paradigm.

Poucette. (French Language Editions Ser.: No. 600-6). (FRE., Illus.). (J). (gr. 1). 3.50 (*0-7214-1274-2*, Ladybrd) Penguin Putnam.

Pouche: Assistant to the Easter Bunny. rev. ed. Louise Brickey. (Illus.). 20p. (J). (gr. k-3). 1991. bds. write for info. (*0-9624767-1-4*) Cottontail Creations.

Pouche: The Assistant to the Easter Bunny. rev. ed. Louise Brickey. (Illus.). 36p. (J). (gr. k-3). 1989. reprint ed. write for info. (*0-9624767-0-6*) Cottontail Creations.

***Poucher's Perfumes, Cosmetics & Soaps.** 10th ed. Hilda Butler. 800p. 2000. 260.00 (*0-7514-0479-9*) Kluwer Academic.

Poucher's Perfumes, Cosmetics & Soaps The Raw Material of Prefume. 9th ed. Routledge, Chapman, Hall Ltd Staff. text 159.50 (*0-7514-0301-6*) Routledge.

Poudre: A Photo History. Stanley R. Case. (Illus.). 350p. 1994. write for info. (*0-9643000-0-1*) S R Case.

Poudre aux Yeux. Eugene Labiche. 9.95 (*0-686-54250-9*) Fr & Eur.

Poudre Canyon. Glen W. Gonder. Ed. by Sharon J. Gonder. LC 98-92210. (Adventures of Willy Whacker Ser.: Vol. 9). (Illus.). 161p. (YA). (gr. 6-8). Date not set. lib. bdg. 8.95 (*1-58389-004-1*) Osage Bend Pub.

Poudre Canyon Ski & Snowshoe Trails. Mary Hagen. (Illus.). 50p. (Orig.). 1996. pap. 7.95 (*0-9642441-0-1*) Azure Pubng.

Poudre River - Cameron Pass, CO. rev. ed. Ed. by Trails Illustrated Staff. 1997. 8.99 (*0-925873-33-0*) Trails Illustrated.

Pouf Pieces. Beauregard Houston-Montgomery. (Illus.). 111p. (Orig.). 1990. pap. 5.95 (*0-937815-37-3*) Hanuman Bks.

***Poughkeepsie.** Joyce Ghee & Joan Spence. (Images of America Ser.). 128p. 1999. pap. 18.99 (*0-7385-0236-7*) Arcadia Publng.

Poughkeepsie: Halfway up the Hudson. Joyce C. Ghee. (Images of America Ser.). 1997. pap. 16.99 (*0-7524-0564-0*) Arcadia Publng.

Poul Anderson - Myth-Maker & Wonder-Weaver: An Interim Bibliography (1947-1985) 4th ed. Ed. by Gordon Benson, Jr. 46p. 1982. pap. 3.50 (*0-912613-03-3*) Galactic Central.

Poul Jorgensen's Book of Fly Tying: A Guide to Flies for All Game Fish. Poul Jorgensen. LC 88-83072. (Illus.). 280p. 1988. pap. 24.95 (*1-55566-002-9*, Sprng Creek Pr) Johnson Bks.

***Poul Jorgensen's Favorite Flies & How to Tie Them.** Poul Jorgensen. LC 99-52545. (Illus.). 2000. 40.00 (*0-8117-0627-3*) Stackpole.

"Poulains" de Corinthe. O. E. Ravel. (Illus.). 1979. text 80.00 (*0-916710-47-5*) Obol Intl.

Poulakos Class of Rhetic & Theory. John Poulakos. LC 98-72074. 1999. pap. text 27.87 (*0-395-84995-0*) HM.

Poulet: A Rooster Who Laid Eggs. Robin Fox. (FRE., Illus.). (J). 3.50 (*0-685-11509-7*) Fr & Eur.

Pouliuli. Albert Wendt. LC 78-323283. 147p. 1977. write for info. (*0-582-71754-X*) P Lngmn NZ.

Pouliuli. Albert Wendt. LC 80-15158. Vol. 8. 147p. 1980. pap. text 9.00 (*0-8248-0728-6*) UH Pr.

Poultry. 218p. 1990. 10.75 (*0-333-52306-7*) Macmillan.

Poultry. Jason Cooper. LC 97-13233. (Farm to Market Discovery Library). 24p. (J). (gr. k-4). 1997. lib. bdg. 15.93 (*0-86625-618-0*) Rourke Pubns.

Poultry. Jillian Powell. LC 96-29686. (Everyone Eats Ser.). 32p. (J). (gr. 2-6). 1998. lib. bdg. 22.83 (*0-8172-4767-X*) Raintree Steck-V.

***Poultry.** Adele Richardson. LC 99-36194. (Let's Investigate Ser.). 2001. lib. bdg. write for info. (*1-58341-082-1*, Creat Educ) Creative Co.

Poultry: A Guide to Management. Carol Twinch. (Illus.). 128p. 1994. pap. 22.95 (*1-85223-755-4*, Pub. by Cro1wood) Trafalgar.

Poultry: Flying Delights. Ed. by G & R Publishing Staff. (Uni-Bks.). 160p. (Orig.). 1994. pap. text 3.00 (*1-56383-024-8*, 3200) G & R Pub.

Poultry Breeding & Genetics. Ed. by R. D. Crawford. (Developments in Animal & Veterinary Science Ser.: No. 22). 1123p. 1990. 205.00 (*0-444-88557-9*) Elsevier.

Poultry Coccidiosis: Diagnostic & Testing Procedures. 2nd ed. Donal P. Conway & M. Elizabeth McKenzie. (Illus.). 66p. (C). 1991. pap. text. write for info. (*0-9602652-2-8*) Pfizer Intl.

Poultry Diseases. 4th ed. Jordan. 1996. text 74.00 (*0-7020-1912-7*, W B Saunders Co) Harcrt Hlth Sci Grp.

Poultry Diseases & Meat Hygiene: A Color Atlas. Drago C. Herenda & Don A. Franco. LC 96-5731. (Illus.). 356p. 1996. text 99.95 (*0-8138-2463-X*) Iowa St U Pr.

Poultry Egg & Meat Production. G. J. Mountney. (Illus.). 300p. (C). 1987. text 54.95 (*0-442-27497-1*) Chapman & Hall.

***Poultry Farmer's & Manager's Veterinary Handbook.** Crowood Press Staff. 1999. 35.00 (*1-86126-261-2*, Pub. by Cro1wood) Trafalgar.

Poultry For Anyone. Victoria Roberts. 1998. 38.95 (*1-873580-38-X*) Whittet Bks.

***Poultry, Game & Eggs: Le Cordon Bleu: Techniques & Recipes.** Jeni Wright & Eric Treuille. 54p. 2000. reprint ed. pap. 15.00 (*0-7881-9288-4*) DIANE Pub.

***Poultry Hatching & Raising Using Non-Electric Incubators & Brooders You Can Build Yourself.** C. E. Thorne & P. H. Jacobs. Ed. by Nathan Griffith. (Illus.). 40p. 2000. pap. 5.00 (*0-9665103-1-3*) Cobblemead Publications.

***Poultry Health & Management: Chicken, Ducks, Turkeys, Geese, Quail.** 4th ed. David Sainsbury. LC 99-43235. (Illus.). 216p. 2000. pap. text 42.95 (*0-632-05172-8*, Pub. by Blckwell Science) Iowa St U Pr.

Poultry in the Pulpit. large type ed. Alexander Cameron. LC 90-29321. 433p. 1991. reprint ed. lib. bdg. 19.95 (*1-56054-126-1*) Thorndike Pr.

Poultry Inspection: The Basis for a Risk-Assessment Approach. National Research Council U. S. Staff. LC 87-60910. 177p. reprint ed. pap. 54.90 (*0-7837-2042-4*, 204230900003) Bks Demand.

Poultry Meat Science, Vol. 25. Ed. by R. I. Richardson & G. C. Mead. (Poultry Science Symposium Ser.). (Illus.). 456p. 1999. text 120.00 (*0-85199-237-4*) OUP.

Poultry Mental Hygiene. Bremner. 1996. text 72.00 (*0-7020-1893-7*, W B Saunders Co) Harcrt Hlth Sci Grp.

Poultry Production. Ed. by P. Hunton. LC 95-24458. (World Animal Science Ser.: Vol. C9). 600p. 1995. 321.00 (*0-444-88965-5*) Elsevier.

Poultry Production. 13th ed. Richard E. Austic & Malden C. Nesheim. LC 89-35186. (Illus.). 325p. 1990. pap. text 47.50 (*0-8121-1241-5*) Lppncott W & W.

Poultry Production in Hot Climates. N. J. Daghir. (CAB International Publication Ser.). (Illus.). 320p. 1995. text 100.00 (*0-85198-907-1*) OUP.

Poultry Products Technology. Pref. by George J. Mountney. (Illus.). 368p. 1989. reprint ed. pap. 39.95 (*1-56022-001-5*) Haworth Jrnl Co-Edits.

Poultry Products Technology. 3rd ed. Ed. by George J. Mountney & Carmen R. Parkhurst. LC 94-48542. (Illus.). 446p. (C). 1995. 129.95 (*1-56022-856-3*, TS1986) Haworth Jrnl Co-Edits.

Poultry Punch Lines: Heavenly Humor for Southern Fried Saints. John Honeycutt. 60p. (Orig.). 1996. pap. 4.99 (*0-9656159-0-1*) Jonquel Prodns.

Poultry Science. 3rd ed. M. E. Ensminger. (Illus.). 480p. (YA). (gr. 9-12). 1992. 69.95 (*0-8134-2929-3*, 2087) Interstate.

***Poultry Waste Management Handbook.** Eldridge Collins, Jr. et al. LC 99-31153. (NRAES Ser.: Vol. 132). (Illus.). 64p. 1999. pap. text 16.00 (*0-935817-42-5*) NRAES.

Pounce: Cochon's Billions. Tom Morison. 248p. 1997. pap. 12.95 (*1-55212-095-3*, No. 97-0017) Trafford Pub.

Pound. P. N. Furbank. 100p. 1985. 99.95 (*0-335-15088-8*); pap. 26.95 (*0-335-15079-9*) OpUniv Pr.

Pound: "The Cantos" George Kearns. (Landmarks of World Literature Ser.). (Illus.). 136p. (C). 1989. pap. text 11.95 (*0-521-33649-X*) Cambridge U Pr.

Pound: "The Cantos" George Kearns. (Landmarks of World Literature Ser.). (Illus.). 136p. (C). 1990. text 34.95 (*0-521-33373-3*) Cambridge U Pr.

Pound - Joyce: Letters & Essays. Ezra Pound. LC 66-27616. (Correspondence of Ezra Pound Ser.). 1970. pap. 10.95 (*0-8112-0159-7*, NDP296, Pub. by New Directions) Norton.

Pound - the Little Review: The Letters of Ezra Pound to Margaret Anderson. Ezra Pound & Margaret Anderson. Ed. by Thomas L. Scott et al. LC 88-3410. (Correspondence of Ezra Pound Ser.: Vol. 6). 384p. 1989. 37.50 (*0-8112-1059-6*, Pub. by New Directions) Norton.

Pound - Zukofsky. Ezra Pound & Louis Zukofsky. LC 86-19181. (Correspondence of Ezra Pound Ser.). 384p. 1987. 38.50 (*0-8112-1013-8*, Pub. by New Directions) Norton.

Pound & Kester Families, Containing an Account of the Ancestry of John Pound (Born in 1735) & a William Kester (Born in 1733) & a Genealogical Record of All Their Descendants. J. E. Hunt. 628p. 1989. reprint ed. pap. 94.00 (*0-8328-0983-7*); reprint ed. lib. bdg. 102.00 (*0-8328-0982-9*) Higginson Bk Co.

Pound Cake Cookbook. Bibb Jordan. LC 93-79667. 64p. 1994. 8.95 (*1-56352-107-5*) Longstreet.

Pound Cakes . . . with Love. Jeannine B. Browning. 1994. pap. write for info. (*0-9627729-6-8*) J B Browning.

Pound Connection. Peter Russell. 77p. pap. write for info. (*3-7052-0203-0*, Pub. by Poetry Salzburg) Intl Spec Bk.

Pound Era. Hugh Kenner. LC 72-138349. 1971. pap. 19.95 (*0-520-02427-3*, Pub. by U CA Pr) Cal Prin Full Svc.

Pound Fishing - Bay Head to South Seaside Park, New Jersey. Ferdinand F. Klebold. Ed. by Richard L. Strickler. (Illus.). 130p. (Orig.). 1994. write for info. (*0-941965-06-6*) Ocean Cnty Hist.

Pound for Pound. Steve Vance. 216p. 1999. pap. 9.99 (*0-88092-451-9*, 4519) Royal Fireworks.

Pound-Ford: The Story of a Literary Friendship. Ezra Pound & Ford Madox Ford. Ed. by Brita L. Seyersted. LC 82-2255. (Correspondence of Ezra Pound Ser.). 384p. (C). 1982. 22.95 (*0-8112-0833-8*, Pub. by New Directions) Norton.

Pound-Full of Puppies! Evan Skolnick. (Disney's Enchanting Stories Ser.). (J). 1998. pap. text 4.50 (*1-57840-218-2*) Acclaim Bks.

Pound in Purgatory: From Economic Radicalism to Anti-Semitism. Leon Surette. LC 99-6096. 384p. 1999. 39.95 (*0-252-02498-2*) U of Ill Pr.

Pound-Lewis: The Letters of Ezra Pound & Wyndham Lewis. Ezra Pound & Wyndham Lewis. Ed. by Timothy Materer. LC 85-3007. (Correspondence of Ezra Pound Ser.). 384p. 1985. 37.50 (*0-8112-0932-6*, Pub. by New Directions) Norton.

Pound of Flesh: Perilous Tales of How to Produce Movies in Hollywood. Art Linson. 208p. 1998. reprint ed. pap. 12.00 (*0-8021-3551-X*, Grove) Grove-Atltic.

Pound of Flesh: Producing in Hollywood--Perilous Tales from the Trenches. Art Linson. 208p. 1995. pap. 9.00 (*0-380-72401-4*, Avon Bks) Morrow Avon.

***Pound of Prevention.** (Destroyer Ser.: Bk. 121). 2000. mass mkt. 5.99 (*0-373-63236-3*, 1-63236-3, Wrldwide Lib) Harlequin Bks.

Pound of Prevention: The Case for Universal Maternity Care in the U. S. Ed. by Jonathan Kotch et al. 275p. 1992. 30.00 (*0-87553-206-3*) Am Pub Health.

Pound Sterling. Imre Devegh. Ed. by Mira Wilkins. LC 78-3908. (International Finance Ser.). 1979. reprint ed. lib. bdg. 17.95 (*0-405-11213-0*) Ayer.

Pound, Thayer, Watson, & The Dial: A Story in Letters. Ed. by Walter Sutton. LC 94-11298. (Illus.). 432p. 1994. 49.95 (*0-8130-1316-X*) U Press Fla.

Pound Wise. Osbert Sitwell. LC 74-134136. (Essay Index Reprint Ser.). 1977. reprint ed. 23.95 (*0-8369-2429-0*) Ayer.

Pound, Yeats, Eliot & the Modernist Movement. C. K. Stead. 300p. (C). 1985. text 45.00 (*0-8135-1075-9*) Rutgers U Pr.

Pound/Cummings: The Correspondence of Ezra Pound & e. e. Cummings. Ed. by Barry Ahearn. LC 96-19031. 442p. (C). 1996. text 62.50 (*0-472-10298-2*, 10298) U of Mich Pr.

Poundemonium. Julian Rios. Tr. by Richard A. Francis from SPA. LC 96-7665. (Larva Ser.: No. 2). (Illus.). 160p. (Orig.). 1997. pap. 13.50 (*1-56478-138-0*) Dalkey Arch.

Pounder's Marine Diesel Engines. 6th ed. C. Wilbur & D. Wight. 588p. 1984. 115.00 (*0-7506-0078-0*) Buttrwrth-Heinemann.

Pounder's Marine Diesel Engines. 7th ed. Doug Woodyard. LC 98-22009. 592p. 1997. text 114.95 (*0-7506-2583-X*) Buttrwrth-Heinemann.

Pounding. E. A. Guldenzopf. 160p. (Orig.). 1995. pap. 6.99 (*0-9646170-0-5*, ES Bks) ES Communs.

Pounding Nails in the Floor with My Forehead. Eric Bogosian. 80p. (Orig.). 1994. pap. 8.95 (*1-55936-096-8*) Theatre Comm.

Pounding Out the Profits - A Century of American Invention: The Development & Manufacture of Crank-Activated Open-Die Power Forging Hammers. Douglas Freund. LC 97-214651. (Illus.). 317p. 1997. 32.50 (*0-9657652-0-2*) Mingus.

Pound's Cantos. Peter Makin. Ed. by Claude Rawson. (Unwin Critical Library). 368p. 1985. pap. text 18.95 (*0-04-811002-7*) Routledge.

Pound's Cantos. Peter Makin. 352p. 1992. reprint ed. pap. text 15.95 (*0-8018-4371-5*) Johns Hopkins.

Pound's Cantos Declassified. Philip Furia. LC 83-43227. 160p. 1984. 30.00 (*0-271-00373-1*) Pa St U Pr.

Pound's Cavalcanti: An Edition of the Translations, Notes, & Essays. Guido Cavalcanti & David Anderson. LC 82-47581. 335p. 1983. reprint ed. pap. 103.90 (*0-7837-9293-X*, 206003200004) Bks Demand.

Pound's Epic Ambition: Dante & the Modern World. Stephen Sicari. LC 90-44139. (SUNY Series, The Margins of Literature). 265p. (C). 1991. pap. text 21.95 (*0-7914-0700-4*) State U NY Pr.

Pound/Williams: Selected Letters of Ezra Pound & William Carlos Williams. Ezra Pound & William Carlos Williams. Ed. by Hugh Witemeyer. LC 95-38462. (Correspondence of Ezra Pound Ser.). 480p. 1996. 39.95 (*0-8112-1301-3*, Pub. by New Directions) Norton.

Poupee. Jacques Audiberti. (FRE.). 112p. 1969. pap. 9.95 (*0-7859-0365-8*, F83872) Fr & Eur.

Poupee Blonde. Patrick Modiano. (FRE.). 1992. pap. 14.95 (*0-7859-2723-9*) Fr & Eur.

Poupliniere et la Musique de Chambre Au XVIII Siecle. G. Cucuel. LC 70-158961. (Music Ser.). (FRE.). 1971. reprint ed. lib. bdg. 55.00 (*0-306-70186-3*) Da Capo.

***Pour Applesauce in the Jars.** Marilyn J. Noltie. (J). (gr. k-3). 1999. pap. 5.95 (*0-533-13161-8*) Vantage.

Pour et le Contre: Correspondance Polemique sur le Respect de la Posterite. Pline et les Anciens Auteurs qui ont Parle de Peinture et de Sculpture. Denis Diderot et al. (FRE., Illus.). 384p. 1958. 10.95 (*0-8288-9963-0*, F47360) Fr & Eur.

Pour Finir Encore. Samuel Beckett. (FRE.). 56p. 1976. pap. 10.95 (*0-7859-0659-2*, M3063) Fr & Eur.

Pour It On: 52 Ways to Maximize Your Bar Profits. Andrea Stewart. (Illus.). 132p. 1996. pap. 19.95 (*1-879239-07-8*) Pencom.

Pour la Revolution Africaine. Frantz Fanon. (Petite Coll. Maspero Ser.). pap. 9.95 (*0-685-35634-5*) Fr & Eur.

Pour l'Amour de Finette. Remo Forlani. (FRE.). 275p. 1985. pap. 11.95 (*0-7859-2441-8*, 2070372681) Fr & Eur.

***Pour L'amour Et Liberte.** Wolf White Wolf Publishing Staff. 1999. pap. text. write for info. (*1-56504-723-0*) White Wolf.

Pour le Bonheur d'Un Enfant. Valerie Parv. (Horizon Ser.: No. 482). (FRE.). 1998. mass mkt. 3.50 (*0-373-39482-9*, 1-39482-4) Harlequin Bks.

Pour le Merite & Germany's First Aces. John R. Angolia & Clint R. Hackney. (Illus.). 288p. 1984. write for info. (*0-9613392-0-9*) Hackney Pubns.

Pour l'Effort (Aout 62-Dec. 65) see Discours et Messages

Pour l'Histoire de la Science Hellene. Paul Tannery. xxiv, 435p. reprint ed. write for info. (*0-318-71437-X*) G Olms Pubs.

P

An Asterisk (*) at the beginning of an entry indicates that the title is appearing for the first time.

Pour l'Honneur. Joseph Kessel. (FRE.). 1987. pap. 10.95 (*0-7859-3242-9*, 2266043838) Fr & Eur.

Pour l'Honneur de l'Esprit: Correspondance, 1898-1914. Charles Peguy & Jean Basstaire. (FRE.). 352p. 1973. pap. 13.95 (*0-7859-5392-2*) Fr & Eur.

Pour l'Honneur de l'Esprit: Correspondance, 1898-1914. Romain Rolland & Charles Peguy. (FRE., Illus.). 352p. 1973. pap. 12.95 (*0-7859-5458-9*) Fr & Eur.

Pour Louis Bouilhet - Gustave Flauvert. Ed. by Alan Raitt. (Exeter French Texts Ser.: Vol. 87). 141p. 1995. pap. text 19.95 (*0-85989-441-X*, Pub. by Univ Exeter Pr) Northwestern U Pr.

Pour Lucrece. Jean Giraudoux. pap. 11.50 (*0-685-33925-4*) Fr & Eur.

Pour Manet. Emile Zola. (FRE.). 1989. pap. 20.95 (*0-7859-3318-2*, 2870273061) Fr & Eur.

Pour Man's Friend: A Guide & Reference for Bar Personnel. rev. ed. John C. Burton. Ed. by Nanci L. Burton. LC 90-81198. (Illus.). 246p. 1990. per. 14.95 (*0-9624625-0-0*) Aperitifs Pub.

Pour Man's Friend: Supplementary Workbook. John C. Burton. Ed. by Nanci L. Burton. (Illus.). 96p. (C). 1992. ring bd. 14.95 (*0-9624625-1-9*) Aperitifs Pub.

Pour Piano Seul. Andre Maurois. pap. 19.50 (*0-685-36954-4*) Fr & Eur.

Pour Prendre Conge. Jean Vercors. 4.95 (*0-686-55132-X*) Fr & Eur.

Pour Qui Sonne le Glas. Ernest Hemingway. (FRE.). 1973. pap. 11.95 (*0-7859-2318-7*, 2070364550) Fr & Eur.

Pour Raison Garder, 3 vols., 1. Jules Romains, pseud. (FRE.). 272p. 1967. pap. 10.95 (*0-7859-1408-0*, 2080507486) Fr & Eur.

Pour Raison Garder, 3 vols., 2. Jules Romains, pseud. (FRE.). 272p. 1967. pap. 13.95 (*0-7859-1409-9*, 2080602098) Fr & Eur.

Pour Raison Garder, 3 vols., 3. Jules Romains, pseud. (FRE.). 272p. 1967. pap. 13.95 (*0-7859-1410-2*, 2080602101) Fr & Eur.

Pour Sganarelle. Romain Gary. (FRE.). 480p. 1965. 20.95 (*0-8288-9770-0*, F101640) Fr & Eur.

Pour Sganarelle Recherche d'un Personnage et d'un Roman see Frere Ocean

Pour Toi - Para Ti - for You. Louis Untermeyer. (FRE & SPA.). 19p. 1968. 3.95 (*0-8288-6978-2*) Fr & Eur.

Pour un Ajustement Reussi: Quelques Enseignements a Tirer de l'Experience du Ghana; La Restructuration Economique en Nouvelle Zelande Depuis 1984. J. L. Abbey & David Caygill. LC HC0517.G6A33. (Fondation Per Jacobsson Conference de 1989 Ser.). (FRE.). 53p. reprint ed. pap. 30.00 (*0-608-08776-9*, 206941500004) Bks Demand.

Pour un Nouveau Roman: Critique Litteraire. Alain Robbe-Grillet. (FRE.). 144p. 1963. pap. 17.95 (*0-7859-1505-2*, 2707300624) Fr & Eur.

Pour un Nouvel Ordre Economique International see Towards a New International Economic Order

Pour une Critique de l'Economie Politique du Signe. Jean Baudrillard. (Tel Ser.). (FRE.). 268p. 1972. pap. 14.95 (*2-07-029614-8*) Schoenhof.

Pour une Historire des Alpes, Moyen Age et Temps Modernes. Jean-Francois Bergier. LC 97-40359. (Variorum Collected Studies Ser.: Vol. 587). 350p. 1998. text 109.95 (*0-86078-653-6*, Pub. by Ashgate Pub) Ashgate Pub Co.

Pour une meilleure gouvernance comme fondement de la reforme de la fonction publicque en Afrique au sud du Sahara. (FRE.). 58p. 1994. pap. 22.00 (*0-8213-2764-X*) World Bank.

Pour une Morale de l'Ambiguite: Pyrrhus et Cineas. Simone de Beauvoir. (FRE.). 384p. 1963. pap. 10.95 (*0-8288-9682-8*, 2070350215) Fr & Eur.

Pour une Naissance sans Violence see Birth Without Violence: The Book that Revolutionized the Way We Bring Our Children into the World

Pour une Philosophie de l'Education. Jacques Maritain. (FRE.). 254p. 1960. 18.95 (*0-8288-9853-7*, F111830) Fr & Eur.

Pour une Relecture Africaine de Marx et d'Engels. 2nd ed. Leopold S. Senghor. (FRE.). 72p. 1976. pap. 13.95 (*0-7859-1546-X*, 2723601188) Fr & Eur.

Pour Your Heart into It. Howard Schultz & Dori Jone Yang. 1997. 24.45 (*0-7868-6397-8*, Pub. by Hyprn Child) Time Warner.

Pour Your Heart into It: How Starbucks Built a Company One Cup at a Time. Schultz. 368p. (J). 1998. pap. 14.45 (*0-7868-8356-1*, Pub. by Hyperion) Time Warner.

Pourin' down Rain. Cheryl Foggo. (Illus.). 119p. (Orig.). 1990. pap. write for info. (*1-55059-010-3*) Detselig Ents.

Pouring Iron: A Foundry Ghost Story. David L. Weitzman. LC 97-49085. (Illus.). (J). (gr. 4-6). 1998. 15.00 (*0-395-84170-4*) HM.

Pouring New Wine into Old Wineskins: How to Change a Church Without Destroying It. Aubrey Malphurs. LC 93-10368. 224p. 1993. pap. 12.99 (*0-8010-6301-9*) Baker Bks.

Pourparlers, 1972-1990 see Negotiations, 1972-1990

Pourquoi et le Comment du Langage Integre. Ken Goodman. (Choix et Defi).Tr. of Le Pourquoi et le Comment du Langage Integre. (FRE.). 1989. pap. 12.99 (*0-590-71985-8*) Scholastic Inc.

Pourrais-Tu Arreter Josephine? Stephane Poulin. LC 88-50261. (FRE., Illus.). 24p. (J). (ps-3). 1989. 12.95 (*0-88776-217-4*); pap. 6.95 (*0-88776-228-X*) Tundra Bks.

Pourrait Etre Continue. . . La Poetica dell' "Opera Aperta" e "les Faux=Monnayeurs" di Andre Gide. Giovanni Lanza. (GER.). 353p. 1998. 51.95 (*3-631-33575-X*) P Lang Pubng.

Poursuite a Quebec. (FRE.). (C). 1985. pap. 7.95 (*0-8442-1217-2*, VF1217-2) NTC Contemp Pub Co.

Poursuite inattendue: Teacher's guide. Christiane Szeps-Fralin. 5.95 (*0-8219-0023-4*) EMC-Paradigm.

Poursuite inattendue: Textbook. Christiane Szeps-Fralin. 5.95 (*0-8219-0021-8*) EMC-Paradigm.

Poursuite inattendue: Workbook. Christiane Szeps-Fralin. 4.95 (*0-8219-0022-6*) EMC-Paradigm.

Poussin. Christopher Wright. (Illus.). 320p. 1997. 180.00 (*3-9802205-1-6*, Pub. by Art Bks Intl) Partners Pubs Grp.

Poussin: Paintings. R. Rey. (Rhythem & Color One Ser.). 1970. 9.95 (*0-8288-9504-X*) Fr & Eur.

Poussin - The Early Years in Rome: The Origins of French Classicism. Konrad Oberhuber. LC 88-9173. (Illus.). 368p. 1988. 65.00 (*1-55595-002-7*); pap. 24.95 (*1-55595-003-5*) Kimbell Art.

Poussin, Nicholas. Zolotov Yu. (C). 1985. 60.00 (*0-7855-4513-1*, Pub. by Collets) St Mut.

Poussin's Paintings: A Study in Art-Historical Methodology. David Carrier. (Illus.). 288p. 1993. 40.00 (*0-271-00816-4*) Pa St U Pr.

Poustinia: Christian Spirituality of the East for Westerners. Catherine D. Doherty. 224p. 1993. pap. 13.95 (*0-921440-35-9*) Madonna Hse.

Pouvoic Islamique see Authority in Islam: From Muhammad to Khomeini

Pouvoir aux Enfants. Pierre Daninos. 8.95 (*0-686-55570-8*) Fr & Eur.

Pouvoirs de l'Horreur. Julia Kristeva. (FRE.). 1983. pap. 16.95 (*0-7859-2694-1*) Fr & Eur.

Poverello: St. Francis of Assisi. Mark Hegener. 92p. 1989. pap. 4.95 (*0-8199-0112-1*, Frncscn Herld) Franciscan Pr.

Poverta see Poverty

Poverty. Raniero Cantalamessa. Tr. by Charles Serignat from ITA. LC 97-2512.Tr. of Poverta. 96p. (Orig.). 1997. mass mkt. 5.50 (*0-8189-0788-6*) Alba.

Poverty. Richard Worth. LC 96-47850. (Overview Ser.). (Illus.). (YA). (gr. 4-12). 1997. lib. bdg. 22.45 (*1-56006-192-8*) Lucent Bks.

Poverty: A Global Review Handbook on International Poverty Research. UNESCO Staff. 620p. 1996. pap. 75.00 (*92-3-103269-0*, U3269, Pub. by UNESCO) Bernan Associates.

Poverty: A History. Bronislaw Geremek. Tr. by Agnreszka Kolakowska from POL. LC 94-8783. 320p. 1997. pap. 25.95 (*0-631-20529-2*) Blackwell Pubs.

Poverty: A Persistent Global Reality. John Dixon & David MacArov. LC 97-35431. 304p. (C). 1998. 85.00 (*0-415-14681-X*) Routledge.

Poverty: A Persistent Global Reality. John Dixon & David Macarov. LC 97-35431. 304p. (C). 1998. pap. 25.99 (*0-415-14682-8*) Routledge.

***Poverty: Changing Attitudes 1900-2000.** Teresa Garlake. LC 99-12578. 64p. 1999. 27.12 (*0-8172-5894-9*) Raintree Steck-V.

Poverty: Human Consciousness & the Amnesia of Development. Rajni Kothari. LC 95-50411. 192p. (C). 1995. text 62.50 (*1-85649-339-3*, Pub. by Zed Books); text 22.50 (*1-85649-340-7*, Pub. by Zed Books) St Martin.

Poverty: Its Illegal Causes & Legal Cure. L. Spooner. LC 78-156804. (Studies in American History & Government). 108p. 1971. reprint ed. lib. bdg. 22.50 (*0-306-70207-X*) Da Capo.

Poverty: Its Perpetuity, Causes & Relief. rev. ed. Charles P. Krauth. 42p. 1997. pap. 3.00 (*1-891469-06-1*) Repristination.

Poverty: Opposing Viewpoints. Ed. by Katie DeKoster & Bruno Leone. LC 93-22397. 288p. (YA). 1994. pap. 16.20 (*1-56510-065-4*) Greenhaven.

***Poverty: Opposing Viewpoints.** Ed. by Laura Egendorf. LC 98-17866. (Opposing Viewpoints Ser.). (Illus.). 232p. (YA). (gr. 9-12). 1998. pap. 16.20 (*1-56510-946-5*); lib. bdg. 26.20 (*1-56510-947-3*) Greenhaven.

Poverty: Rowntree Revisited. Sean Stitt & Dianne Grant. 136p. 1993. 61.95 (*1-85628-402-6*, Pub. by Avebry) Ashgate Pub Co.

Poverty: The Forgotten Englishmen. Ken Coates & Richard Siburn. 282p. 1988. 77.50 (*0-7855-2935-7*); pap. 25.00 (*0-7855-2936-5*) St Mut.

Poverty - A Framework for Understanding & Working with Students & Adults from Poverty see Framework for Understanding Poverty

Poverty a Global Review: Handbook on Poverty Research. Ed. by Else Oyen et al. LC 97-105691. 600p. 1996. 54.00 (*82-00-22649-2*) Scandnvan Univ Pr.

Poverty Agenda: Trends & Policy Options. Ed. by G. Rodgers & R. Van der Hoeven. (New Approaches to Poverty Analysis & Policy: No.III). 205p. (C). 1995. pap. 27.00 (*92-9014-569-2*) Intl Labour Office.

Poverty Agenda & the ILO: Issues For Research & Action. Ed. by G. Rodgers. (New Approaches to Poverty Analysis & Policy Ser.: Vol. I). 202p. 1995. pap. 24.75 (*92-9014-536-6*) Intl Labour Office.

Poverty, Agriculture & Reform in Iran. Mohammad J. Amid. 224p. (C). (gr. 13). 1990. text 69.95 (*0-415-03561-9*, A5538) Routledge.

Poverty Alleviation & Rural Harijans. V. Pushpa Kumari. (C). 1990. text 54.00 (*81-7141-131-2*) S Asia.

Poverty Alleviation & Social Investment Funds: The Latin American Experience, 261. Philip J. Glaessner. LC 94-33268. (World Bank Discussion Papers). 80p. 1994. pap. 22.00 (*0-8213-3025-X*, 13025) World Bank.

Poverty Alleviation & Sustainable Development: Goals in Conflict? The Committee for Development Planning Report. 69p. pap. 15.00 (*92-1-130154-8*, E.92.IV.1) UN.

Poverty Alleviation for Rural Women: Indian Voluntary Organizations & Village Development. Geoffrey Griffith. 325p. 1994. 66.95 (*1-85628-640-1*, Pub. by Avebry) Ashgate Pub Co.

Poverty Alleviation in India: Policies & Programmes. Abdul Aziz. (Illus.). viii, 173p. 1994. 20.00 (*81-7024-626-1*, Pub. by Ashish Pub Hse) Nataraj Bks.

Poverty Alleviation in India: Programmes & Action. V. M. Rao & Abdul Aziz. (C). 1989. 30.00 (*81-7024-255-X*, Pub. by Ashish Pub Hse) S Asia.

Poverty Alleviation Through Agricultural Projects: Report on a Seminar Held Jointly by the Asian Development Bank, the Centre on Integrated Rural Development for Asia & the Pacific, & the Economic Development Institute of the World Bank. Emmanuel H. D'Silva & Kaye Bysouth. LC 92-23284. (EDI Policy Seminar Reports: No. 30). 88p. 1992. pap. 22.00 (*0-8213-2200-1*, 12200) World Bank.

Poverty Amidst Affluence: Britain & the United States. Victor George & Irving Howards. 224p. 1991. text 80.00 (*1-85278-337-0*); pap. text 25.00 (*1-85278-338-9*) E Elgar.

Poverty Amidst Prosperity. Carl Chinn. 1995. text 22.95 (*0-7190-3990-8*, Pub. by Manchester Univ Pr) St Martin.

Poverty Amidst Prosperity: Immigration & the Changing Face of Rural California. J. Edward Taylor et al. LC 97-26340. 125p. 1997. 39.00 (*0-87766-669-5*); pap. 21.50 (*0-87766-670-9*) U Pr of Amer.

Poverty Amidst Prosperity: Survey of Slums. Pushpa Agnihotri. 261p. 1994. pap. 180.00 (*81-85880-47-6*, Pub. by Print Hse) St Mut.

Poverty & Beyond: The Effects of Changing Resources in the Family, Community & Workplace. (Children of Poverty Studies & Dissertations). 250p. 1996. text 50.00 (*0-8153-2429-4*) Garland.

Poverty & Charity: Europe, Italy, Venice, 1400-1700. Brian Pullan. LC 94-5846. (Collected Studies). 1994. 106.95 (*0-86078-446-0*, Pub. by Variorum) Ashgate Pub Co.

Poverty & Charity in Aix-en-Provence, 1640-1789. Cissie C. Fairchilds. LC 75-36938. (Johns Hopkins University Studies in Historical & Political Science: Ser. 94, No. 1). 209p. reprint ed. pap. 64.80 (*0-8357-8280-8*, 203412200088) Bks Demand.

Poverty & Charity in Roman Palestine, First Three Centuries C. E. Gildas H. Hamel. LC 89-4948. (University of California Publications: No. 23). 304p. 1990. reprint ed. pap. 94.30 (*0-7837-8133-4*, 204794000008) Bks Demand.

Poverty & Child Health. Nick Spencer. LC 95-52764. 1996. write for info. (*1-85775-068-3*, Radcliffe Med Pr) Scovill Paterson.

Poverty & Children's Adjustment. Suniya S. Luthar. LC 98-51240. (Developmental Clinical Psychology & Psychiatry Ser.). 158p. 1999. 21.95 (*0-7619-0519-7*) Sage.

Poverty & Children's Adjustment. Suniya S. Luthar. LC 98-51240. (Developmental Clinical Psychology & Psychiatry Ser.: Vol. 41). 131p. 1999. 52.00 (*0-7619-0518-9*) Sage.

Poverty & Compassion: The Moral Imagination of the Late Victorians. Gertrude Himmelfarb. LC 92-50066. 1992. pap. 19.00 (*0-679-74173-9*) Vin Bks.

Poverty & Cultural Deprivation: Index of New Information with Authors, Subjects & Bibliography. Hope S. Garber. 180p. 1993. 47.50 (*1-55914-770-9*); pap. 44.50 (*1-55914-771-7*) ABBE Pubs Assn.

***Poverty & Development: Into the 21st Century.** Ed. by Tim Allen & Alan Thomas. (Illus.). 460p. 2000. pap. 29.95 (*0-19-877626-8*) OUP.

Poverty & Development in the Nineteen Nineties. Ed. by Tim Allen & Alan Thomas. 432p. 1992. 65.00 (*0-19-877330-7*) OUP.

Poverty & Development in the Nineteen Nineties. Ed. by Tim Allen & Alan Thomas. (Illus.). 432p. 1992. pap. text 24.00 (*0-19-877331-5*) OUP.

Poverty & Deviance in Early Modern Europe. Robert Jutte. (New Approaches to European History Ser.: No. 4). (Illus.). 255p. (C). 1994. text 54.95 (*0-521-41169-6*); pap. text 16.95 (*0-521-42322-8*) Cambridge U Pr.

Poverty & Discrimination. Lester C. Thurow. LC 69-18825. (Studies in Social Economics). 228p. reprint ed. pap. 70.70 (*0-608-13531-3*, 202255700028) Bks Demand.

Poverty & Ecology. Ed. by Leonardo Boff & Virgilio P. Elizondo. 150p. (Orig.). 1995. pap. 15.00 (*0-88344-886-6*) Orbis Bks.

Poverty & Economic Development: Views from City Hall. 30p. 1994. 25.00 (*0-933729-96-0*, No. 3020) Natl League Cities.

Poverty & Economic Inequality in Industrialized Western Societies. Ed. by Nico Keilman et al. 334p. (C). 1998. text 46.00 (*82-00-22493-7*) Scandnvan Univ Pr.

***Poverty & Exclusion in a Global World.** A. S. Bhalla & Frederic Lapeyre. LC 98-38452. 256p. 1999. text 65.00 (*0-312-21825-7*) St Martin.

Poverty & Famines: An Essay on Entitlement & Deprivation. Amartya K. Sen. (Illus.). 270p. 1983. pap. text 19.95 (*0-19-828463-2*) OUP.

Poverty & Farm Size in India. Parkash Mehta & Anjala Kumari. 1990. 17.00 (*81-7099-199-4*, Pub. by Mittal Pubs Dist) S Asia.

Poverty & Food Consumption in Urban Zaire. Hamid Tabatabai. (Working Papers: No. 47). 67p. (C). 1993. pap. 7.00 (*1-56401-147-X*) Cornell Food.

***Poverty & Food Security of Small Farm Households in South India: Impact of Various Policy Instruments.** Punitha Narayanasamy. 280p. 1999. pap. 29.95 (*3-8258-2968-5*, Pub. by CE24) Transaction Pubs.

Poverty & Growth in a South China County: Anxi, Fujian, 1949-1992. Thomas P. Lyons. (Cornell East Asia Ser.: No. 72). (Illus.). 174p. 1994. pap. 11.90 (*0-939657-72-4*, 72); lib. bdg. 18.70 (*0-939657-81-3*, 72) Cornell East Asia Pgm.

Poverty & Health: A Sociological Analysis. Ed. by John Kosa. LC 75-82295. (Commonwealth Fund Book Ser.). (Illus.). 467p. reprint ed. pap. 144.80 (*0-7837-4164-2*, 205901200012) Bks Demand.

Poverty & Health: Working with Families. Clare Blackburn. 160p. 1991. pap. 37.95 (*0-335-09734-0*) OpUniv Pr.

Poverty & Health in New York City. United Hospital Fund Staff. Ed. by Melvin I. Krasner. 224p. 1989. 40.00 (*0-934459-52-5*) United Hosp Fund.

Poverty & Human Capital. Nicaise. 67.95 (*1-84014-533-1*) Ashgate Pub Co.

Poverty & Human Development. World Bank Staff. (Illus.). 96p. (C). 1982. pap. text 8.00 (*0-19-520389-5*) OUP.

Poverty & Income Distribution. Ed. by K. S. Krishnaswamy. (Illus.). 428p. 1991. 19.95 (*0-19-562680-X*) OUP.

Poverty & Income Distribution in Latin America: The Story of the 1980s. George Psacharopoulos et al. LC 96-36910. (Technical Paper Ser.: No. 351). 328p. 1997. pap. 22.00 (*0-8213-3831-5*) World Bank.

Poverty & Inequality: The Political Economy of Redistribution. Jon Neill. LC 97-32412. (C). 1997. pap. 14.00 (*0-88099-181-X*); text 33.00 (*0-88099-182-8*) W E Upjohn.

Poverty & Inequality in Latin America: Issues & New Challenges. Victor E. Tokman & Guillermo A. O'Donnell. LC 97-46841. (Helen Kellogg Institute for International Studies). 1998. 40.00 (*0-268-03824-4*) U of Notre Dame Pr.

Poverty & Inequality in Latin America: Past Evidence, Future Prospects, Vol. 13. Samuel A. Morley. LC 94-35166. (Policy Essay Ser.). (Orig.). 1994. pap. 13.95 (*1-56517-020-2*) Overseas Dev Council.

Poverty & Inequality in Latin America: The Impact of Adjustment & Recovery. Samuel A. Morley. 288p. 1995. text 42.50 (*0-8018-5064-9*) Johns Hopkins.

***Poverty & Inequality in South Africa: Meeting the Challenge.** Julian May. LC 99-54460. 320p. 1999. pap. 29.95 (*1-85649-808-5*) Zed Books.

Poverty & Inequality in the United States. Sullivan. 1999. text. write for info. (*0-312-22179-7*) St Martin.

***Poverty & Inequality South Africa: Meeting the Challenge.** Julian May. LC 99-54460. 320p. 1999. text 69.95 (*1-85649-807-7*) St Martin.

Poverty & Its Vicious Circles. Jamison B. Hurry. LC 73-14158. (Perspectives in Social Inquiry Ser.). 196p. 1974. reprint ed. 13.95 (*0-405-05504-8*) Ayer.

Poverty & Joy: The Franciscan Tradition. William J. Short. LC 99-24173. (Traditions of Christian Spirituality Ser.). 144p. (J). 1999. pap. 13.00 (*1-57075-295-8*) Orbis Bks.

***Poverty & Low Income in the Nordic Countries.** Ed. by Bjorn Gustafsson. 228p. 1999. text 61.95 (*1-84014-810-1*, Pub. by Inst Materials) Ashgate Pub Co.

Poverty & Malnutrition in Latin America: Early Childhood Intervention Programs. Ernesto Pollitt. LC 80-18811. 162p. 1980. 45.00 (*0-275-90538-1*, C0538, Praeger Pubs) Greenwood.

Poverty & Nations. Manley. 122p. (C). 44.95 (*0-7453-0314-5*, Pub. by Pluto GBR); pap. 14.95 (*0-7453-0449-4*, Pub. by Pluto GBR) Stylus Pub VA.

Poverty & Peasantry in Peru's Southern Andes, 1963-90. R. F. Watters. (Latin American Ser.). 384p. (C). 1993. text 75.00 (*0-8229-1182-5*) U of Pittsburgh Pr.

Poverty & Piety in an English Village: Terling, 1525-1700. rev. ed. Keith Wrightson & David Levine. LC 78-1102. (Illus.). 256p. 1995. pap. text 29.95 (*0-19-820321-7*) OUP.

Poverty & Place: Ghettos, Barrios, & the American City. Paul A. Jargowsky. 304p. (C). 1997. text 39.95 (*0-87154-405-9*) Russell Sage.

Poverty & Place: Ghettos, Barrios & the American City. Paul A. Jargowsky. LC 96-2109. (Illus.). 304p. (C). 1998. pap. 17.95 (*0-87154-406-7*) Russell Sage.

Poverty & Planning. Chandulal N. Vakil. LC 73-19310. 357p. 1974. reprint ed. lib. bdg. 69.50 (*0-8371-7320-5*, VAPP, Greenwood Pr) Greenwood.

Poverty & Policy in Tudor & Stuart England. Paul A. Slack. (Themes in British Social History Ser.). (Illus.). 229p. (C). 1988. pap. text 15.95 (*0-582-48965-2*, 73416) Longman.

Poverty & Politics in Harlem. Alphonso Pinkney & Roger R. Woock. 1970. 19.95 (*0-8084-0249-8*); pap. 15.95 (*0-8084-0250-1*) NCUP.

Poverty & Poor Relief: Concepts & Reality. Sean Stitt. 221p. 1994. 77.95 (*1-85628-684-3*, Pub. by Avebry) Ashgate Pub Co.

Poverty & Power: Energy & the South African State. Eberhard. 1996. pap. 18.95 (*0-7453-1062-1*, Pub. by Pluto GBR) Stylus Pub VA.

Poverty & Power: The Political Representation of Poor Americans. Douglas R. Imig. LC 95-17949. xvi, 161p. 1996. text 45.00 (*0-8032-2500-8*) U of Nebr Pr.

Poverty & Power: The Role of Institutions & the Market in Development. Ed. by John Cameron et al. (Illus.). 304p. 1995. text 24.95 (*0-19-563654-6*) OUP.

Poverty & Power: Widening Access to Energy Services in South Africa. Eberhard. LC 95-8720. 1995. 54.95 (*0-7453-1063-X*) Westview.

Poverty & Progress: Social Mobility in a Nineteenth Century City. Stephan A. Thernstrom. LC 64-21793. (Joint Center for Urban Studies). 301p. 1964. pap. 16.00 (*0-674-69501-1*) HUP.

Poverty & Public Policy: An Analysis of Federal Intervention Efforts, 3. Michael Morris & John B. Williamson. LC 86-398. (Studies in Social Welfare Policies & Programs: No. 3). 248p. 1986. 59.95 (*0-313-24942-3*, MPV/, Greenwood Pr) Greenwood.

Poverty & Public Policy: An Evaluation of Social Science Research. Ed. by Vincent Covello. 314p. 1980. pap. text 13.95 (*0-87073-355-9*) Schenkman Bks Inc.

Poverty & Single Parent Families. rev. ed. Trudi J. Renwick. LC 98-8511. (Children of Poverty Ser.). (Illus.). 156p. 1998. 40.00 (*0-8153-3172-X*) Garland.

P

*Poverty & Social Assistance in Transition Countries Jeanine Braithwaite et al. LC 99-37662. 1999. text 45.00 (0-312-22436-2) St Martin.

Poverty & Social Change. Kirsten A. Gronbjerg et al. LC 78-876. viii, 248p. 1994. pap. text 9.00 (0-226-30963-0) U Ch Pr.

Poverty & Social Change: With a Reappraisal. 2nd ed. Tarlok Singh. LC 74-33899. 352p. 1975. reprint ed. lib. bdg. 69.50 (0-8371-8000-7, SIPO, Greenwood Pr) Greenwood.

Poverty & Social Change in Southeast Asia: Selections from the Proceedings, Canadian Council for Southeast Asian Studies, 1978. Canadian Council for Southeast Asian Studies Staff. Ed. by Ozay Mehmet. LC 81-484905. 289p. 1979. reprint ed. pap. 89.60 (0-608-02183-0, 206285200003) Bks Demand.

Poverty & Social Developments in Peru, 1994-1997. LC 99-15988. (Country Study Ser.). 88p. 1999. pap. 22.00 (0-8213-4492-7, 14492) World Bank.

Poverty & Social Exclusion in Tanzania. Frederick Kaijage & Anna Tibaijuka. LC 97-145332. x, 102p. 1996. pap. 22.50 (92-9014-540-4) Intl Labour Office.

Poverty & Social Justice: Critical Perspectives. Ed. by Francisco Jimenez. 160p. 1987. 24.00 (0-916950-75-1); pap. 14.00 (0-916950-76-X) Biling Rev-Pr.

Poverty & Social Security: Concepts & Principles. Paul Spicker. LC 92-11699. 208p. 1993. pap. write for info. (0-415-05936-4) Routledge.

Poverty & Social Welfare, 4 vols. Intro. by David J. Gladstone. 1600p. (C). 1996. 655.00 (0-415-13746-2) Routledge.

*Poverty & Social Welfare Trends. Kathleen O'Leary Morgan. 100p. 1998. pap. 50.00 (1-56692-342-5, M Quitno Pr) Morgan Quitno Corp.

Poverty & Society: The Growth of the American Welfare State in International Comparison. Daniel Levine. 368p. (C). 1988. pap. text 19.00 (0-8135-1353-7) Rutgers U Pr.

Poverty & the Adequacy of Social Security in the EC: A Comparative Analysis. Herman Deleeck. 221p. 1992. 65.95 (1-85628-395-X) Ashgate Pub Co.

Poverty & the Environment: Reconciling Short-term Needs with Long-term Sustainability Goals. LC 95-980410. 156p. pap. 14.95 (92-807-1474-0, E.95.III.D.65) UN.

Poverty & the Environment: Reversing the Downward Spiral. Alan B. Durning. (Orig.). (C). 1989. pap. 5.00 (0-916468-93-3) Worldwatch Inst.

Poverty & the Human Condition: A Philosophical Inquiry. John D. Jones. LC 90-43809. (Problems in Contemporary Philosophy Ser.: Vol. 26). 396p. 1990. lib. bdg. 99.95 (0-88946-273-9) E Mellen.

Poverty & the Lone-Parent Family: The Challenge to Social Policy. Jane Millar. 216p. 1989. text 63.95 (0-566-05770-0) Ashgate Pub Co.

Poverty & the Minimum Wage. Donald O. Parsons. LC 80-24407. (AEI Studies: No. 300). (Illus.). 72p. reprint ed. pap. 30.00 (0-8357-4525-2, 203738700008) Bks Demand.

Poverty & the Political Culture: The Rhetoric of Social Welfare in the Netherlands & France, 1815-1854. Frances Gouda. 256p. 1994. pap. text 26.95 (0-8476-7934-9); lib. bdg. 66.00 (0-8476-7933-0) Rowman.

Poverty & the Transition to a Market Economy in Mongolia. Ed. by Keith Griffin. LC 94-46184. 182p. 1995. text 59.95 (0-312-12577-1) St Martin.

Poverty & the Underclass: Changing Perceptions of the Poor in America. William A. Kelso. 336p. (C). 1994. text 45.00 (0-8147-4658-6); pap. text 19.00 (0-8147-4661-6) NYU Pr.

Poverty & Transfers In-Kind: A Re-Evaluation of Poverty in the United States. Morton Paglin. LC 79-88586. (Publication Ser.: No. 219). 108p. 1980. pap. 2.78 (0-8179-7192-0) Hoover Inst Pr.

Poverty & Un-British Rule in India. Dadabhai Naoroji. 1990. reprint ed. 20.00 (81-85395-87-X, Pub. by Low Price) S Asia.

Poverty & Underdevelopment: New Challenges - A Global Survey. Attar Chand. 512p. 1988. 46.00 (81-212-0148-9, Pub. by Gian Publng Hse) S Asia.

*Poverty & Undernutrition: Theory, Measurement & Policy. Peter Svedberg. LC 98-45930. (WIDER Studies in Development Economics). 368p. 2000. text 110.00 (0-19-829268-6) OUP.

Poverty & Wealth. Adam Smith. LC 96-31296. (Lynchburg College Symposium Readings Ser.). 1996. pap. text. write for info. (0-7618-0459-5) U Pr of Amer.

Poverty & Wealth: Citizenship, Deprivation & Privilege. John Scott. LC 93-43275. (Sociology Ser.). 1993. pap. text. write for info. (0-582-08089-4, Pub. by Addison-Wesley) Longman.

Poverty & Wealth: Comparing Afro-Asian Development. E. Wayne Nafziger. (Contemporary Studies in Economic & Financial Analysis: Vol. 75). 1994. 78.50 (1-55938-761-0) Jai Pr.

Poverty & Wealth: Why Socialism Doesn't Work. Ronald H. Nash. LC 92-14204. 224p. (C). 1992. reprint ed. pap. 14.99 (0-945241-16-X) Probe Bks.

Poverty & Welfare In England 1700-1850: A Regional Perspective. Steven Kingsley. text. write for info. (0-7190-4939-3, Pub. by Manchester Univ Pr) St Martin.

Poverty & Welfare in England 1700-1850: A Regional Perspective. Steven Kingsley. pap. write for info. (0-7190-4940-7, Pub. by Manchester Univ Pr) St Martin.

Poverty & Welfare in Scotland, 1890-1948. Ian Levitt. 200p. 1989. 68.00 (0-85224-558-0, Pub. by Edinburgh U Pr) Col U Pr.

Poverty & Welfare in Scotland, 1890-1948. Ian Levitt. 256p. 1990. pap. text 28.00 (0-85224-583-1, Pub. by Edinburgh U Pr) Col U Pr.

Poverty Bay. Earl Emerson. 1997. mass mkt. 5.99 (0-345-41406-3) Ballantine Pub Grp.

Poverty Bay. Earl Emerson. 256p. 1985. mass mkt. 4.99 (0-380-89647-8, Avon Bks) Morrow Avon.

Poverty, Celibacy & Obedience: A Radical Option for Life. Diarmuid O'Murchu. LC 98-41199. (Orig.). 1999. pap. 14.95 (0-8245-1473-4) Crossroad NY.

Poverty, Charity & "Doing the Double" Options for Claimants. Eileen Evason & Roberta Woods. LC 95-179809. 162p. 1995. text 66.95 (1-85972-044-7, Pub. by Avebry) Ashgate Pub Co.

Poverty, Chastity & Change: Lives of Contemporary American Nuns. Carole G. Rogers. (Illus.). 256p. 1996. per. 28.95 (0-8057-9136-1, Twyne) Mac Lib Ref.

Poverty Comparisons. Martin Ravallion. LC 93-14943. 130p. 1994. pap. text 27.00 (3-7186-5402-4) Gordon & Breach.

Poverty Comparisons: A Guide to Concepts & Methods. Martin Ravallion. (Living Standards Measurement Study Ser.: No. 88). 134p. 1992. 22.00 (0-8213-2036-X, 12036) World Bank.

Poverty Comparisons: A Guide to Concepts & Methods. Martin Ravallion. (Living Standards Measurement Study Ser.: No. 122-F). (FRE.). 176p. 1996. 22.00 (0-8213-3546-4, 13546) World Bank.

*Poverty Comparisons: A Guide to Concepts & Methods. Martin Ravallion. (Living Standards Measurement Study Ser.: No. 88R). (RUS.). 144p. 1999. 22.00 (0-8213-4116-2, 14116) World Bank.

Poverty Comparisons & Household Survey Design. Steven Howes & Jean O. Lanjouw. LC 96-53397. (LSMS Working Papers). 56p. 1997. pap. 22.00 (0-8213-3862-5) World Bank.

Poverty Curtain: Choices for the Third World. Haq Mahbub Ul. LC 76-7470. 247p. 1976. pap. text 20.50 (0-231-04063-6) Col U Pr.

Poverty Debate: Politics & the Poor in America. C. Emory Burton. LC 92-15992. 200p. 1992. pap. 16.95 (0-275-94436-0, B4436, Praeger Pubs) Greenwood.

Poverty Debate: Politics & the Poor in America, 102. C. Emory Burton. LC 92-14353. (Contributions in Sociology Ser.: No. 102). 224p. 1992. 57.95 (0-313-28594-2, BYL, Greenwood Pr) Greenwood.

Poverty, Deprivation & Social Work. Ed. by Ralph Davidson & Angus Erskine. 175p. 1992. 39.95 (1-85302-043-5) Taylor & Francis.

Poverty, Development & Health Policy. B. Abel-Smith & A. Leiserson. (Public Health Papers: No. 69). 109p. 1978. pap. text 10.00 (92-4-130069-8, 1110069) World Health.

Poverty Dynamics: Issues & Examples. Robert Walker, Jr. & Karl Ashworth. 291p. 1994. 82.95 (1-85628-929-X, Pub. by Avebry) Ashgate Pub Co.

Poverty, Economic Reform, & Income Distribution in Latin America. Ed. by Albert Berry. LC 97-22276. (Critical Perspectives LA Ser.). 278p. 1998. lib. bdg. 58.00 (1-55587-746-X) L Rienner.

*Poverty, Equality & Growth: The Politics of Economic Need in Postwar Japan. Deborah J. Milly. LC 98-45936. (Harvard East Asian Monographs). 1999. 49.50 (0-674-69475-9) HUP.

Poverty, Equity, & Growth in Malawi & Madagscar. Frederic L. Pryor. (World Bank Publication). (Illus.). 488p. 1991. text 39.95 (0-19-520823-4) OUP.

*Poverty, Ethnicity, & Gender in Eastern Europe During the Market Transition. Ed. by Rebecca Jean Emigh & Ivan Szelenyi. LC 00-29839. 2000. write for info. (0-275-96881-2) Greenwood.

Poverty, Ethnicity & Violent Crime. James F. Short. LC 97-507. (Crime & Society Ser.). (C). 1997. pap. text 24.00 (0-8133-2014-3, Pub. by Westview) HarpC.

Poverty, Famine & Economic Development: The Selected Essays of Meghnad Desai, 2 vols., Vol. II. Meghnad Desai. (Economists of the Twentieth Century Ser.). 1995. 90.00 (1-85278-690-6) E Elgar.

Poverty, Female Headed Households & Sustainable Economic Development, 190. Nerina C. Vecchio & Kartik Roy. LC 97-8782. (Contributions in Economics & Economic History: Vol. 190). 144p. 1998. 55.00 (0-313-30191-3, Greenwood Pr) Greenwood.

Poverty, Food & Nutrition in India. S. P. Singh. (C). 1991. 48.00 (0-8364-2658-4, Pub. by Chugh Pubns) S Asia.

*Poverty from the Wealth of Nations: Integration & Polarization in the Global Economy since 1760. M. Shahid Alam. LC 99-46992. 224p. 2000. text 69.95 (0-312-23018-4) St Martin.

Poverty, Gender & Reproductive Choice: An Analysis of Linkages. Swapna Mukhopadhyay & R. Savithri. LC 98-900602. 126 p. 1998. write for info. (81-7304-106-7) Manohar.

Poverty Glossary. Spicker. LC 98-46655. 1999. pap. 17.50 (1-85649-688-0); text 49.95 (1-85649-687-2) St Martin.

Poverty, Household Food Security, & Nutrition in Rural Pakistan. Harold Alderman. LC 93-39211. (Research Report Ser.: Vol. 96). 1993. write for info. (0-89629-099-9) Intl Food Policy.

Poverty in a Land of Plenty: Tenancy in Eighteenth-Century Maryland. Gregory A. Stiverson. LC 77-4554. (Maryland Bicentennial Studies). 208p. 1977. reprint ed. pap. 64.50 (0-608-03748-6, 206457300009) Bks Demand.

Poverty in America. Steven Pressman. 313p. 1994. 42.00 (0-8108-2833-2) Scarecrow.

Poverty in America. Bradley R. Schiller. 1996. pap. text 6.56 (0-07-057753-6) McGraw.

Poverty in America. Conference on Poverty in America. Ed. by M. S. Gordon. (New Reprints in Essay & General Literature Index Ser.). 1977. reprint ed. 34.95 (0-518-10197-5, 10197) Ayer.

Poverty in America: The Welfare Dilemma, 39. Ralph Segalman & Asoke Basu. LC 79-6568. (Contributions in Sociology Ser.: No. 39). (Illus.). 418p. 1981. 69.50 (0-313-20751-8, BPO/, Greenwood Pr) Greenwood.

Poverty in Britain & the Reform of Social Security. Anthony B. Atkinson. LC 76-85711. (University of Cambridge, Dept. of Applied Economics, Occasional Papers: 18). 224p. reprint ed. pap. 63.90 (0-608-12313-7, 2024402) Bks Demand.

Poverty in Cambridgeshire. Michael J. Murphy. (Cambridge Town, Gown & County Ser.: Vol. 23). (Illus.). 1978. pap. 5.95 (0-900891-29-7) Oleander Pr.

Poverty in Central Appalachia: Underdevelopment & Exploitation. Ada F. Haynes. LC 96-9707. (Garland Studies in the History of American Labor). 234p. 1996. text 75.00 (0-8153-2546-0) Garland.

*Poverty in China in the Period of Globalization: New Evidence on Trend & Pattern. Azizur Rahman Khan & International Labour Office. LC 98-218887. vii, 58 p. 1998. write for info. (92-2-111037-0) Intl Labour Office.

Poverty in Colombia. International Bank for Reconstruction & Development Staff. LC 94-40255. (Country Study Ser.). 352p. 1994. pap. 22.00 (0-8213-3098-5) World Bank.

Poverty in Developing Countries: A Bibliography of Publications by the ILO's World Employment Programme, 1975-91. (Bibliography Ser.: No. 12). 155p. (Orig.). 1992. pap. 18.00 (92-2-108248-2) Intl Labour Office.

Poverty in Eighteenth-Century Spain: The Women & Children of the Inclusa. Joan Sherwood. 239p. 1988. text 35.00 (0-8020-2662-1) U of Toronto Pr.

Poverty in Europe. A. B. Atkinson. LC 98-11439. 192p. 1998. 44.95 (0-631-20909-3); pap. 22.95 (0-631-21029-6) Blackwell Pubs.

Poverty in India. V. M. Dandekar. 159p. 1971. 8.95 (0-318-37213-4) Asia Bk Corp.

Poverty in India: Data Base Issues. Ed. by G. K. Kadekodi & G. V. Murthy. (Illus.). 360p. (C). 1992. text 40.00 (0-7069-5982-5, Pub. by Vikas) S Asia.

Poverty in New York City, 1996: An Update & Perspectives. Stephanie Aaronson & Stephen V. Cameron. 92p. 1997. 12.00 (0-88156-204-1) Comm Serv Soc NY.

Poverty in Rural America: A Case Study. Janet M. Fitchen. (Special Studies in Contemporary Social Issues). 257p. (C). 1981. pap. text 21.90 (0-89158-901-5) Westview.

Poverty in Rural America: A Case Study. Janet M. Fitchen. 257p. (C). 1995. reprint ed. pap. text 13.95 (0-88133-869-9) Waveland Pr.

Poverty in Russia: Public Policy & Private Responses. Ed. by Jeni Klugman. (EDI Development Studies). 296p. 1997. pap. 22.00 (0-8213-3803-X, 13803) World Bank.

Poverty in the American Dream: Women & Children First. Karin Stallard et al. (Politics & Economics Ser.). (Illus.). 64p. (Orig.). 1983. pap. 6.00 (0-89608-197-4) South End Pr.

Poverty in the Soviet Union. Mervyn Matthews. (Illus.). 227p. 1986. text 64.95 (0-521-32544-7); pap. text 19.95 (0-521-31059-8) Cambridge U Pr.

Poverty in the U. S. A Statistical Profile. (Illus.). 290p. (Orig.). (C). 1994. pap. text 50.00 (0-7881-0238-9) DIANE Pub.

Poverty in the U. S. Problems & Policies. Daniel W. Woods. LC 87-25246. (YA). 1988. pap. 5.95 (0-8027-6765-6); lib. bdg. 14.85 (0-8027-6764-8) Walker & Co.

Poverty in the United States. 1994. lib. bdg. 250.00 (0-8490-8573-X) Gordon Pr.

Poverty in the United States, 1996. Leatha Lamison-White. (Illus.). 59p. (C). 1998. pap. text 25.00 (0-7881-3187-7) DIANE Pub.

Poverty in Transition. 224p. 45.00 (92-1-126100-7) UN.

Poverty in Transition: Studies in Countries-in-Transition: Hungary, Bulgaria, Romania, Georgia, Russia, Mongolia. Ed. by Yogesh Atal. LC 98-47226. 272p. 1999. 59.95 (1-57181-191-5); pap. 17.50 (1-57181-192-3) Berghahn Bks.

*Poverty in Transition Economies. Sandra Hutton & Gerry Redmond. LC 99-46080. (Studies of Societies in Transition). 368p. 2000. 110.00 (0-415-21550-1) Routledge.

Poverty in Western Asia: A Social Perspective. (Eradicating Poverty Studies: No. 1). 100p. 20.00 (92-1-128168-7) UN.

Poverty in World Politics. Owen. LC 99-11276. 272p. 1999. text 68.00 (0-312-22314-5) St Martin.

Poverty, Inc. Why the Poor Pay More & Who Really Profits. Ed. & Pref. by Mike Hudson. (Southern Exposure Ser.). (Illus.). 64p. (Orig.). (C). 1993. pap. 5.00 (0-943810-57-4) Inst Southern Studies.

*Poverty, Inequality & Health: An International Perspective. Ed. by David Leon & Gill Walt. (Illus.). 336p. 2001. pap. text 55.00 (0-19-263196-9) OUP.

Poverty, Inequality, & Human Capital Development in Latin America, 1950-2025 see Pobreza, Desigualdad y Formacion del Capital Humano en America Latina, 1950-2025

Poverty, Inequality, & Human Capital Development in Latin America, 1950-2025. Juan L. Londono. LC 96-16979. (World Bank Latin American & Caribbean Studies). 48p. 1996. pap. 22.00 (0-8213-3630-4, 13630) World Bank.

Poverty, Inequality & Prices in Rural India. Nikhilesh Bhattacharya et al. 220p. (C). 1991. 28.50 (0-8039-9685-3) Sage.

Poverty, Inequality, & Rural Development. Ed. by Tim Lloyd & Oliver Morrissey. LC 93-47023. 1994. text 75.00 (0-312-12099-0) St Martin.

Poverty, Inequality & Social Welfare in Australia. D. T. Johnson. 185p. 1996. pap. 59.00 (3-7908-0942-X) Spr-Verlag.

Poverty, Inequality, & the Future of Social Policy: Western States in the New World Order. Ed. by Katherine McFate et al. 704p. 1995. 70.00 (0-87154-510-1) Russell Sage.

Poverty, Inequality, & the Future of Social Policy: Western States in the New World Order. Ed. by Katherine McFate et al. 756p. (C). 1996. reprint ed. pap. text 24.95 (0-87154-593-4) Russell Sage.

Poverty, Inequality & the Law: Cases, Commentary & Analyses. Barbara E. Brudno. 934p. 1976. write for info. (0-318-57525-6) West Pub.

Poverty, Inequality & Unemployment in India: (Incorporating Their Regional - Inter-State Dimensions) K. N. Prasad. 1993. 44.00 (81-7022-459-4, Pub. by Concept) S Asia.

Poverty, Inequality, Discrimination. Wolff. LC 96-9701. (Economics Ser.). (C). 1996. mass mkt. 95.95 (0-538-84580-5) S-W Pub.

Poverty Is Not a Vice: Charity, Society, & the State in Imperial Russia. Adele Lindenmeyr. 304p. 1996. text 49.50 (0-691-04489-9, Pub. by Princeton U Pr) Cal Prin Full Svc.

*Poverty Knowledge: Social Science, Social Policy & the Poor in Twentieth-Century U. S. History. Alice O'Connor. LC 00-34682. (Politics & Society in Twentieth-Century America Ser.). 2000. write for info. (0-691-00917-1) Princeton U Pr.

Poverty Law & Social Change: The Story of the Fitzroy Legal Service. John Chesterman. LC 96-230377. (Illus.). 296p. 1997. pap. 24.95 (0-522-84739-0, Pub. by Melbourne Univ Pr) Paul & Co Pubs.

Poverty Law, Theory & Practice: Cases & Materials. Julie N. Trubeck. LC 97-120754. (American Casebook Ser.). 885p. (C). 1996. 60.00 (0-314-07210-1) West Pub.

Poverty Lines in Theory & Practice. Martin Ravallion. LC 98-4023. (Living Standards Measurement Study Ser.: No. 133). 52p. 1998. pap. 22.00 (0-8213-4226-6, 14226) World Bank.

Poverty Measurement: Adjusting for Geographic Cost-of-Living Difference. 76p. (Orig.). (C). 1995. pap. text 25.00 (0-7881-2034-4) DIANE Pub.

Poverty Measurement: Issues in Revising & Updating the Official Definition. 48p. 1998. pap. text 20.00 (0-7881-3855-3) DIANE Pub.

Poverty, Migration, & Settlement in the Industrial Revolution: Sojourners' Narratives. J. Stephen Taylor. LC 89-60546. (Illus.). 221p. 1989. 28.00 (0-930664-09-4) SPOSS.

Poverty: My Riches: A Life of St. Elizabeth of Hungary. Elizabeth R. Obbard. 106p. 1997. pap. 16.95 (1-901157-80-6) St Austin.

Poverty, Natural Resources, & Public Policy in Central America. Ed. by Sheldon Annis et al. (U. S. Third World Policy Perspectives Ser.: No. 17). 280p. (C). 1992. 32.95 (1-56000-015-5); pap. text 17.95 (1-56000-577-7) Transaction Pubs.

Poverty of a Rich Society. John Fentress Gardner. 32p. 1976. pap. 1.50 (0-913098-09-4) Orion Society.

Poverty of American Politics: A Theoretical Interpretation. H. Mark Roelofs. (C). 1992. 59.95 (0-87722-877-9); pap. 24.95 (0-87722-878-7) Temple U Pr.

Poverty of American Politics: A Theoretical Interpretation. 2nd ed. H. Mark Roelofs. LC 97-45554. 368p. (C). 1998. pap. text 22.95 (1-56639-606-9) Temple U Pr.

Poverty of Communism. Nick Eberstadt. 317p. 1989. 39.95 (0-88738-188-X); pap. 21.95 (0-88738-817-5) Transaction Pubs.

Poverty of "Development Economics" Deepak Lal. (Illus.). 144p. 1986. pap. 12.95 (0-674-69471-6) HUP.

*Poverty of Development Economics. Deepak Lal. LC 00-21974. (Illus.). 175p. 2000. 24.95 (0-262-12234-0) MIT Pr.

Poverty of Development Economics. 2nd ed. Deepak Lal. 193p. 1997. 27.50 (0-255-36410-5, Pub. by Inst Economic Affairs) Coronet Bks.

Poverty of Historicism. Karl R. Popper. 176p. (C). 1988. pap. 18.99 (0-415-06569-0) Routledge.

*Poverty of Imagination: Bootstrap Capitalism, Sequel to Welfare Reform. David Stoesz. LC 00-8036. 2000. 50.00 (0-299-16950-2); pap. 19.95 (0-299-16954-5) U of Wis Pr.

Poverty of Nations. A. M. Khusro. LC 99-17494. 1999. text 69.95 (0-312-22174-6) St Martin.

Poverty of Nations: A Guide to the Debt Crisis from Argentina to Zaire. Ed. by Elmara Altvater et al. Tr. by Terry Bond from GER. LC 90-46692. (Illus.). 272p. (C). 1991. pap. 19.95 (0-86232-949-3, Pub. by Zed Books); text 55.00 (0-86232-948-5, Pub. by Zed Books) St Martin.

Poverty of Nations: Quality Education & National Development, with Special Reference to South Asia. Namdar Khan. 254p. (Orig.). (C). 1989. pap. text 14.95 (0-9622136-0-8) Calif Indus.

Poverty of Nations: The Aid Dilemma at the Heart of Africa. James Morton. LC 95-62319. 272p. 1996. text 24.50 (1-86064-034-6, Pub. by I B T) St Martin.

Poverty of Nations: The Political Economy of Hunger & Population. William W. Murdoch. LC 80-16201. (Illus.). 398p. reprint ed. pap. 123.40 (0-608-08793-9, 206943200004) Bks Demand.

Poverty of Nations & New Economic Order. Usha Garg & Jagdish Vibhakar. 246p. 1985. 20.95 (0-317-39868-7) Asia Bk Corp.

Poverty of Objects: The Prose Poem & the Politics of Genre. Jonathan Monroe. LC 86-24026. 352p. 1987. 42.50 (0-8014-1967-0) Cornell U Pr.

Poverty of Objects: The Prose Poem & the Politics of Genre. Jonathan Monroe. LC 86-24026. 351p. reprint ed. pap. 108.90 (0-608-20925-2, 2072024) Bks Demand.

P

An Asterisk (*) at the beginning of an entry indicates that the title is appearing for the first time.

Poverty of Philosophy. Karl Marx. LC 63-10632. 160p. 1992. pap. 6.95 (*0-7178-0701-0*) Intl Pubs Co.

Poverty of Philosophy. Karl Marx. Tr. by H. Quelch from FRE. LC 95-11391. (Great Books in Philosophy). 227p. 1995. pap. 7.95 (*0-87975-977-1*) Prometheus Bks.

Poverty of Philosophy. Karl Marx. 205p. 1973. pap. 22.95 (*0-8464-1331-0*) Beekman Pubs.

Poverty of Postmodernism. John O'Neill. LC 94-7260. (Social Futures Ser.). 240p. (Orig.). (C). 1994. pap. 24.99 (*0-415-11687-2*, B4746) Routledge.

Poverty of Progress: Changing Ways of Life in Industrial Societies. Ed. by I. Miles & J. Irvine. LC 81-17779. (Illus.). 275p. 1982. 161.00 (*0-08-028906-1*, K110, Pub. by Pergamon Repr) Franklin.

Poverty of Progress: Latin America in the Nineteenth Century. E. Bradford Burns. LC 80-51236. 224p. 1980. pap. 17.95 (*0-520-05078-9*, Pub. by U CA Pr) Cal Prin Full Svc.

Poverty of Revolution: The State & the Urban Poor in Mexico. Susan Eckstein. LC 88-20961. (Princeton Paperbacks Ser.). (Illus.). 381p. reprint ed. pap. 118.20 (*0-608-06343-6*, 206670500008) Bks Demand.

Poverty of Spirit. rev. ed. Johannes B. Metz. Tr. by John Drury. LC 97-49919. 64p. 1998. pap. 6.95 (*0-8091-3799-2*) Paulist Pr.

Poverty of Theory. E. P. Thompson. 300p. (C). 1996. pap. write for info. (*0-85036-446-9*, Pub. by MRLN) Paul & Co Pubs.

Poverty of Welfare Reform. Joel F. Handler. LC 95-18630. 177p. 1995. pap. 14.00 (*0-300-06481-0*) Yale U Pr.

Poverty or Development: Global Restructuring & Regional Transformation in the U. S. South & the Mexican South. Richard Tardanico & Mark Rosenberg. LC 99-20479. 296p. 1999. pap. 24.99 (*0-415-92432-4*) Routledge.

***Poverty or Development: Global Restructuring & Regional Transformation in U. S. South & Mexican South.** Richard Tardanico & Mark Rosenberg. LC 99-20479. 296p. 1999. text 75.00 (*0-415-92431-6*) Routledge.

Poverty Pentagon see Triumphs of Joseph: How Today's Community Healers Can Revive Our Streets & Neighborhoods

Poverty Pentagon. Woodson. 1997. 25.00 (*0-02-874077-7*) Free Pr.

Poverty, Planning & Economic Change in Jammu & Kashmir. M. L. Misri & M. S. Bhat. 1994. 34.00 (*0-7069-7776-9*, Pub. by Vikas) S Asia.

Poverty Point Culture. 2nd rev. ed. Clarence H. Webb. LC 81-85992. (Geoscience & Man Ser.: Vol. 17). (Illus.). 96p. 1982. pap. 25.00 (*0-938909-16-9*) Geosci Pubns LSU.

Poverty Point Culture: Local Manifestations, Subsistence Practices, & Trade Networks. Ed. by Kathleen M. Byrd. LC 90-80205. (Geoscience & Man Ser.: Vol. 29). (Illus.). 206p. 1992. pap. 35.00 (*0-938909-50-9*) Geosci Pubns LSU.

Poverty, Policy, & Food Security in Southern Africa. Ed. by Coralie Bryant. LC 87-32243. 280p. 1988. lib. bdg. 40.00 (*1-55587-092-9*) L Rienner.

Poverty, Policy & Politics in Madras Slums: Dynamics of Survival, Gender & Leadership. Joop W. De Wit. LC 96-3336. 308p. 1997. 39.95 (*0-8039-9347-1*) Sage.

Poverty Policy & Poverty Research: The Great Society & the Social Sciences. Robert H. Haveman. LC 86-40453. 320p. 1987. pap. 24.95 (*0-299-11154-7*) U of Wis Pr.

Poverty Policy & Poverty Research: The Great Society & the Social Sciences. Robert H. Haveman. LC 86-40453. (Illus.). 320p. 1987. reprint ed. pap. 99.20 (*0-608-06996-5*, 206720400009) Bks Demand.

Poverty, Population & Sustainable Development: Essays in Honour of Professor Victor S. D'Souza. Ed. by S. R. Mehta. LC 97-904553. (Illus.). xii, 430p. 1997. 43.00 (*81-7033-407-1*, Pub. by Rawat Pubns) Nataraj Bks.

Poverty Profile of Cambodia. Nicholas M. Prescott & Menno Pradhan. LC 97-29733. (Discussion Paper Ser.: No. 373). 94p. 1997. pap. 22.00 (*0-8213-4020-4*, 14020) World Bank.

Poverty, Progress & Development. Ed. by Paul-Marc Henry. 320p. 1991. 49.95 (*0-7103-0402-1*, A4879) Routledge.

Poverty, Prosperity & the World Economy: Essays in Memory of Sidney Dell. Ed. by Gerry Helleiner et al. LC 95-1356. xii, 257p. 1995. text 90.00 (*0-312-12628-X*) St Martin.

Poverty Puzzle: What Should Be Done to Help the Poor. Public Agenda Foundation Staff. 45p. (C). 1993. 12.19 (*0-07-051548-4*) McGraw.

Poverty Puzzle: What Should Be Done to Help the Poor? abr. ed. National Issues Forum Institute Staff. 32p. 1995. 3.25 (*0-8403-8652-4*) Kendall-Hunt.

Poverty Reduction & Human Development in the Caribbean. Judy L. Baker. LC HC1551.Z9P613. (World Bank Discussion Papers: No. 366). 229p. 1997. pap. 22.00 (*0-8213-3970-2*, 13970) World Bank.

Poverty Reduction & the World Bank: Progress & Challenges in the 1990's. 160p. 1996. pap. 22.00 (*0-8213-3293-7*, 13293) World Bank.

Poverty Reduction & the World Bank: Progress in Fiscal 1994. 88p. 1995. pap. 22.00 (*0-8213-2928-6*, 12928) World Bank.

Poverty Reduction & the World Bank: Progress in Fiscal 1996 & 1997. LC 98-122616. 200p. 1998. pap. 22.00 (*0-8213-3801-3*, 13801) World Bank.

***Poverty Reduction & the World Bank: Progress in Fiscal 1998.** LC 99-16209. 128p. 1999. pap. 22.00 (*0-8213-4384-X*, 14384) World Bank.

Poverty Reduction in East Asia: The Silent Revolution. Frida Johansen. LC 93-24676. (Discussion Papers). 82p. 1993. pap. 22.00 (*0-8213-2489-6*, 12489) World Bank.

Poverty Reduction in South Asia: Promoting Participation by the Poor. LC 94-14150. 44p. 1994. pap. 22.00 (*0-8213-2810-7*) World Bank.

Poverty Reduction Strategies: A Review. Department of International Economic and Social Affairs Staff. LC 99-172462. vii, 58p. 1998. write for info. (*92-1-104484-7*) UN.

Poverty Reform in Canada, 1958-1978: State & Class Influences on Policy Making. Rodney S. Haddow. (Critical Perspectives on Public Affairs Ser.). 256p. 1993. 60.00 (*0-7735-0990-9*, Pub. by McG-Queens Univ Pr) CUP Services.

Poverty Reform in Canada, 1958-1978: State & Class Influences on Policy Making. Rodney S. Haddow. (Critical Perspectives on Public Affairs Ser.). 256p. 1997. pap. 24.95 (*0-7735-1638-7*, Pub. by McG-Queens Univ Pr) CUP Services.

Poverty, Revolution & the Church. M. Paget-Wilkes. 142p. (Orig.). 1982. pap. text 13.50 (*0-85364-285-0*) Attic Pr.

Poverty, Riches & Social Citizenship. Hartley Dean & Margaret Melrose. LC 98-7075. 1998. text 69.95 (*0-312-21684-X*) St Martin.

***Poverty Row HORRORS! Monogram, PRC & Republic Horror Films of the Forties.** Tom Weaver. LC 92-50324. (Illus.). 392p. 1999. per. 25.00 (*0-7864-0798-0*, McFarland Cls) McFarland & Co.

Poverty Row Studios, 1929-1940: An Illustrated History of 53 Independent Film Companies, with a Filmography for Each. Michael R. Pitts. LC 96-22311. (Illus.). 542p. 1997. lib. bdg. 75.00 (*0-7864-0168-0*) McFarland & Co.

Poverty, Rural Development & Public Policy. Dr. Amarendra. 1998. 30.00 (*81-7629-097-1*) Deep & Deep Pubns.

Poverty, Social Services, & Safety Nets in Vietnam. Nicholas M. Prescott. LC 97-28972. (Discussion Paper Ser.: No. 376). 76p. 1997. pap. 22.00 (*0-8213-4024-7*, 14024) World Bank.

Poverty, Society & Philanthropy in the Late Mediaeval Greek World. Demetrios J. Constantelos. (Studies in the Social & Religious History of the Mediaeval Greek World: Vol. II). 190p. (C). 1992. lib. bdg. 60.00 (*0-89241-401-4*) Caratzas.

Poverty Survival Handbook. Pat B. O'Grady. LC 86-62681. (Illus.). 72p. (Orig.). 1986. pap. 5.00 (*0-9601846-3-5*) PM Ent.

Poverty Theory & Policy: A Study of Panama. Gian S. Sahota. LC 89-37685. (Studies in Development). (Illus.). 368p. 1990. text 62.00 (*0-8018-3892-4*) Johns Hopkins.

Poverty Transitions among Elderly Widows. Hiroko H. Dodge. LC 95-46138. (Studies on the Elderly in America). (Illus.). 164p. 1996. text 58.00 (*0-8153-2280-1*) Garland.

Poverty Trends, 1980-88: Changes in Family Composition & Income Sources among the Poor. 113p. (Orig.). (C). 1993. pap. text 30.00 (*1-56806-494-2*) DIANE Pub.

Poverty Tribals & Development: A Rehabilitation Approach. Anil Bhatt. 1990. 14.00 (*81-85054-96-7*, Pub. by Manohar) S Asia.

Poverty U. S. A. The Historical Record, 44 vols. Ed. by David J. Rothman. 1971. reprint ed. 1064.50 (*0-405-03090-8*) Ayer.

Poverty, Urbanization & Development Policy: A Philippine Perspective. Arsenio M. Balisacan. LC 94-945501. 188p. (Orig.). (C). 1995. pap. text 15.00 (*971-542-041-9*, Pub. by U of Philippines Pr) UH Pr.

Poverty, Vulnerability, & the Value of Human Life: A Global Agenda for Bioethics. Ed. by Z. Bankowski & J. H. Bryant. (Highlights & Papers of the XXVIIIth CIOMS Conference, Ixtapa, Guerrero State, Mexico). xi, 246p. 1994. pap. text 25.00 (*92-9036-060-7*, 1830028) World Health.

Poverty, Wealth Dictatorship, Democracy: Resource Scarcity & the Origins of Dictatorship. Jack Barkstrom. LC 98-96403. 535p. 1998. pap. 21.95 (*0-9610224-0-X*) Pericles Pr.

Poverty, Welfare & the Disciplinary State. Chris Jones. LC 98-51642. 1999. write for info. (*0-415-18289-1*); pap. write for info. (*0-415-18290-5*) Routledge.

Poverty Who Needs It: The Baptized Christian's Call to Perfection. 2nd ed. David M. Knight. 20p. 1990. reprint ed. pap. text 4.00 (*0-942971-18-3*) His Way.

Povest' o Stikhakh. Iurii Ivask. LC 85-62144. 150p. (Orig.). (C). 1987. pap. 13.00 (*0-89830-102-5*) Russica Pubs.

Povestea Unei Analize de Copil: Conduita in Psihanaliza Copilor Bazata Pe Tratamentul Unui Baiat de Zece Ani. Melanie Klein. Ed. by F. V. Vladescu. Tr. by C. Popovici. (Scrierile Melanie Klein in Patru Volume Ser.: Vol. 4).Tr. of Writings of Melanie Klein, 4: Narrative of Child Analysis. The Conduct of the Psycho-Analysis of Children As Seen in the Treatment of a Ten-Year-Old Boy. (RUM.). 494p. 1994. pap. 34.00 (*1-883881-04-8*, 048) S Freud RT&PF.

Povesti. Mikhail Afanasevich Bulgakov. (Sobranie Sochineii Ser.: Vol. 3). (RUS.). 248p. 1983. 25.00 (*0-88233-698-3*) Ardis Pubs.

Povesti Belkina (Tales of Belkin) Aleksandr Pushkin. (Voices from Russia Ser.). (RUS.). 52p. 1996. pap. text 9.50 (*1-58085-009-X*) Interlingua VA.

Povesti de Adormit Copii. Florentin Smarandache. Ed. by Xiquan Publishing House Staff. (RUM.). 70p. (Orig.). 1992. pap. 5.99 (*1-879585-19-7*) Erhus Univ Pr.

***Povest'vremennykh Let: An Interlinear Collation & Paradosis, 3 vols.** Ed. by Donald Ostrowski & David J. Birnbaum. (Library of Early Ukrainian Literature: Vol. 10, Pts. 1-3). (SLO.). 2100p. 1999. text 125.00 (*0-916458-91-1*) Harvard Ukrainian.

Povezlo. Vladimir Torchilin. LC 97-2693. (RUS.). 176p. 1997. 12.00 (*1-55779-097-3*) Hermitage Pubs.

Povorina. Mary C. Hudson. (Illus.). 16p. (J). (gr. k-5). 1988. pap. 5.95 (*0-9627745-0-2*) M C Hudson.

Povratak Filipa Latinovicza see Return of Philip Latinowicz

***POW.** Robert Cotterell. LC 00-190157. 2000. 25.00 (*0-7388-1538-1*); pap. 18.00 (*0-7388-1539-X*) Xlibris Corp.

POW. Gil Hash. 210p. mass mkt. 4.99 (*1-896329-01-2*) Picasso Publ.

***POW: Prisoners of War.** L. A. Girouard. LC 99-95008. 1999. pap. 8.95 (*0-533-13262-2*) Vantage.

POW: Tears That Never Dry. Anthony S. Czerwien. LC 94-33329. (Illus.). 256p. 1994. 22.00 (*0-912526-69-6*) Lib Res.

POW - MIA Issues, Vol. I: The Korean War, 1. Paul M. Cole. LC 93-40829. 1994. pap. 15.00 (*0-8330-1482-X*, MR-351/1-USDP) Rand Corp.

POW Diary - My Father's Struggle. George J. Matta, Jr. (Illus.). 252p. (Orig.). 1997. pap. 12.00 (*0-9658080-0-9*) DarRyan Pr.

POW-83. John W. Wallace. 250p. 1999. pap. 14.95 (*0-9673733-0-1*) Gray Rider.

POW-MIA: "The Men We Left Behind" Chimp Robertson. LC 94-66614. 304p. 1995. 19.95 (*0-914984-64-0*) Starburst.

Pow Wow: And Other Yakima Indian Traditions. Helen W. Willard. (Illus.). 128p. (Orig.). 1990. 29.95 (*0-9627594-1-4*); pap. 19.95 (*0-9627594-0-6*) Roza Run.

Pow-Wow: Dancer's & Craftworker's Handbook. Adolf Hungry Wolf. 144p. 1999. pap. text 21.95 (*0-920698-62-X*) Can Cab Pr.

Pow Wow Activity Book. Sandy Hummingbird & Jesse Hummingbird. (Illus.). 28p. (J). (gr. 1-5). 1999. pap. 4.95 (*1-57067-078-1*) Book Pub Co.

Pow Wow Book: A Must for Every Pow Wow. 2nd rev. ed. Randy Redhawk. LC 94-92187. (Illus.). 22p. (J). (gr. 3 up). 1994. pap. 5.00 (*0-9641861-0-1*) Redhawk Pubng.

Pow Wow Country. Chris Roberts. LC 92-29966. (Illus.). 128p. (Orig.). 1992. pap. 19.95 (*1-56037-025-4*) Am Wrld Geog.

Pow Wow on the Red Road. 47p. 1994. 25.00 (*0-9610334-4-4*) Natl Native.

Pow Wow Trail. Julia White. (Illus.). 112p. (Orig.). 1996. pap. text 8.95 (*1-57067-029-3*) Book Pub Co.

Pow-Wows. G. Hohman. 8.95 (*0-685-22072-9*) Wehman.

Pow-Wows: Long Lost Friend, A Collection of Mysteries & Invaluable Arts & Remedies. John G. Hohman. 149p. 1996. reprint ed. spiral bd. 14.50 (*0-7873-0415-8*) Hlth Research.

***Powahatan's World & Colonial Virginia: A Conflict of Cultures.** Frederic W. Gleach. 2000. pap. text 19.95 (*0-8032-7091-7*) U of Nebr Pr.

***Powder & Ball Small Arms.** Martin Pegler. (Illus.). 128p. 1999. write for info. (*1-86126-185-3*, Pub. by Cro1wood) Trafalgar.

Powder & Bulk Solids & Handling & Processing: Proceedings of the Technical Program, 9th, Rosemont, Il. International Powder Technology & Bulk Solids Conf. LC TP0156.P3. 669p. reprint ed. pap. 200.00 (*0-608-14768-0*, 202318800032) Bks Demand.

Powder & Bulk Solids Conference - Exhibition: Fifteenth Annual Proceedings of the Technical Program, June 4-7, 1990, O'Hare Exposition Center, Rosemont, IL. Powder & Bulk Solids Conference - Exhibition Staff. LC TP0156.: 676p. reprint ed. pap. 200.00 (*0-7837-2610-4*, 204277400006) Bks Demand.

Powder & Bulk Solids Conference - Exhibition: Proceedings of the 1991 Technical Program, May 6-9, 1991, Rosemont O'Hare Exposition Center, Rosemont, IL. Powder & Bulk Solids Conference - Exhibition Staff. LC TP0156.. 584p. pap. 181.10 (*0-7837-0354-6*, 204067300018) Bks Demand.

Powder & Bulk Solids Conference - Exhibition: Proceedings of the 1993 Technical Program, May 3-6, 1993, Rosemont Convention Center, Rosemont, IL. Powder & Bulk Solids Conference - Exhibition Staff. LC TS0180.8.B8. (Illus.). 708p. reprint ed. pap. 200.00 (*0-7837-7033-2*, 204684800004) Bks Demand.

Powder & Bulk Solids Conference-Exhibition, 13th: Proceedings of the Technical Program, May 9-12, 1988, O'Hare Exposition Center, Rosemont, IL. Powder & Bulk Solids Conference-Exhibition Staff. LC TP0156.. 800p. reprint ed. pap. 200.00 (*0-608-18185-4*, 203291300081) Bks Demand.

Powder & Bulk Solids Handling & Processing: Proceedings of the Technical Program: May 12-14, 1987. Powder & Bulk Solids Handling & Processing Staff. LC TP0156.. (Illus.). 716p. pap. 200.00 (*0-608-17394-0*, 203023400067) Bks Demand.

Powder & Bulk Solids Handling & Processing: Proceedings of the Technical Program, 10th, May 7-9, 1985, Rosemont, IL. Powder & Bulk Solids Handling & Processing Staff. LC TP0156.. 929p. reprint ed. pap. 200.00 (*0-608-12341-2*, 202519200042) Bks Demand.

Powder & Bulk Solids Handling & Processing: Proceedings of the Technical Program: 11th, O'Hare Exposition Center, Rosemont, IL, May 13-15, 1986. Powder & Bulk Solids Handlings & Processing. LC TP0156.. 786p. reprint ed. pap. 200.00 (*0-608-15442-3*, 202936700060) Bks Demand.

Powder & Bulk Solids Handling Processes: Instrumentation & Control. Koichi Iinoya et al. (Chemical Industries Ser.: Vol. 34). (Illus.). 296p. 1988. text 155.00 (*0-8247-7971-1*) Dekker.

Powder & Echo: Poems about the American Revolutionary War on Long Island. Dan Giancola. LC 91-73296. 37p. (Orig.). 1991. pap. 9.95 (*0-9630164-0-7*) Canios Edit.

Powder & Grains '97: Proceedings of the 3rd International Conference, Durham, South Carolina, 18-23 May 1997. Ed. by R. P. Behringer & J. T. Jenkins. (Illus.). 584p. (C). 1997. text 168.00 (*90-5410-884-3*, Pub. by A A Balkema) Ashgate Pub Co.

Powder & Patch. Georgette Heyer. Date not set. 28.95 (*0-8488-2302-8*) Amereon Ltd.

Powder & Patch. Georgette Heyer. 1998. lib. bdg. 21.95 (*1-56723-055-5*) Yestermorrow.

Powder Burn. Carl Hiaasen. LC 99-166691. 272p. 1998. pap. 12.00 (*0-375-70068-4*) Vin Bks.

***Powder Burn: Arson, Money & Mystery in Vail Valley.** Daniel Glick. (Illus.). 2001. 25.00 (*1-58648-003-0*) PublicAffairs NY.

Powder Burns: Cocain, Contras & the Drug War. Celerino Castillo, III & Dave Harmon. 224p. 1994. pap. 16.95 (*0-88962-578-6*) Mosaic.

Powder Celestial: Snuff Boxes, 1700-1880. Catherine Jestin. LC 90-70305. (Illus.). 16p. (Orig.). 1990. pap. 6.95 (*0-930606-63-9*) Yale Ctr Brit Art.

Powder Coating. David D. Taft. LC 76-359611. 299p. reprint ed. pap. 92.70 (*0-608-15024-X*, 205216800048) Bks Demand.

Powder Coating: The Complete Finisher's Handbook. Ed. by Nicholas Liberto. LC 94-78590. (Illus.). 1994. 75.00 (*0-9643091-0-6*) Powder Coat Inst.

Powder Coating Applications. fac. ed. Ed. by Sam Dawson & Vishu Reddy. LC 89-64306. (Manufacturing Update Ser.). (Illus.). 300p. 1990. reprint ed. pap. 93.00 (*0-7837-8188-1*, 204789300008) Bks Demand.

Powder Coating Made Easy. R. L. Nyborg. 101p. 1992. pap. 14.95 (*1-57002-079-5*) Univ Publng Hse.

Powder Coating Technology. Charles I. Hester et al. 81p. 1990. 79.00 (*0-8155-1246-5*) Noyes.

Powder Coating to Recycling Rubber see Encyclopedia of Chemical Technology

Powder Coatings. Josef H. Jilek. (Illus.). 35p. 1991. pap. 30.00 (*0-934010-37-4*) Fed Soc Coat Tech.

Powder Coatings. 2nd ed. (Illus.). Date not set. pap. 30.00 (*0-934010-38-2*) Fed Soc Coat Tech.

Powder Flask Book. Ray Riling. 496p. 1992. 70.00 (*1-884849-04-0*) R&R Bks.

Powder Forging. H. A. Kuhn & B. L. Ferguson. LC 89-13889. (Illus.). 288p. (C). 1990. 50.00 (*0-918404-84-3*) Metal Powder.

Powder Hound's Guide to Alta. Brad Asmus. 160p. 1992. pap. write for info. (*0-9631113-0-2*) Four Mile Pr.

Powder Hound's Guide to Skiing Snowbird. Brad Asmus. (Illus.). 160p. (Orig.). 1992. pap. 12.95 (*0-9631113-1-0*) Four Mile Pr.

Powder Injection Molding. Randall M. German. LC 90-5428. (Illus.). 543p. reprint ed. pap. 168.40 (*0-7837-5158-3*, 204488700004) Bks Demand.

Powder Injection Molding Symposium - 1992: Proceedings of the 1992 Powder Injection Molding Symposium Sponsored by the Metal Powder Industries Federation & the American Powder Metallurgy Institute, June 21-26, 1992, San Francisco, California. Ed. by Philip H. Booker et al. LC 92-29757. 1992. 135.00 (*1-878954-18-0*) Metal Powder.

Powder Keg: An Intelligence Officer's Guide to Military Forces in the Middle East, 1996-2000. Edward B. Atkeson. 300p. (Orig.). (C). 1996. pap. 15.00 (*0-9638692-5-6*) NOVA Pubns.

Powder Keg in the Middle East: The Struggle for Gulf Security. Ed. by Geoffrey T. Kemp & Janice G. Stein. LC 95-4607. 350p. (Orig.). (C). 1995. pap. text 24.95 (*0-8476-8076-2*); lib. bdg. 66.00 (*0-8476-8075-4*) Rowman.

Powder Magazine at Fort Michilimackinac: Excavation Report. Donald P. Heldman & William L. Minnerly. Ed. by David A. Armour. (Reports in Mackinac History & Archaeology: No. 6). (Illus.). (Orig.). 1977. pap. 6.00 (*0-911872-22-1*) Mackinac St Hist Pks.

***Powder Materials: Current Research & Industrial Practices.** Ed. by F. D. S. Marquis. LC 99-75851. 354p. 1999. 116.00 (*0-87339-456-9*) Minerals Metals.

Powder Metallurgy, No. GB-041X. LC 97-145027. 220p. 1994. 2450.00 (*1-56965-208-2*) BCC.

Powder Metallurgy: A New Process for Manufacturing Gears. D. Lynch et al. (Technical Papers: Vol. P249.02). (Illus.). 17p. 1951. pap. text 30.00 (*1-55589-346-5*) AGMA.

Powder Metallurgy: Applications, Advantages & Limitations. Klare. LC 82-73609. (Illus.). 320p. reprint ed. pap. 99.20 (*0-608-16002-4*, 203307500083) Bks Demand.

Powder Metallurgy: Principles & Applications. Fritz V. Lenel. LC 80-81890. (Illus.). 602p. reprint ed. pap. 186.70 (*0-7837-1562-5*, 204185400024) Bks Demand.

Powder Metallurgy - an Overview. Ivor Jenkins & J. V. Wood. (Series on Powder Metallurgy). 385p. 1991. 110.00 (*0-901462-81-0*, Pub. by Inst Materials) Ashgate Pub Co.

Powder Metallurgy - Recent Applications. Ed. by V. S. Arunachalam & O. V. Roman. (C). 1989. 42.00 (*81-204-0424-6*, Pub. by Oxford IBH) S Asia.

Powder Metallurgy Alloys: Proceedings of the Symposium on Powder Metallurgy Alloys Held at I. I. T. Bombay on 11th October, 1980. Ed. by P. Ramakrishnan. 124p. (C). 1982. text 91.00 (*90-6191-406-X*, Pub. by A A Balkema) Ashgate Pub Co.

Powder Metallurgy & Related High Temperature Materials. Ed. by P. Ramakrishnan. 500p. 1988. text 316.00 (*0-87849-577-0*, Pub. by Trans T Pub) Enfield Pubs NH.

Powder Metallurgy Conference: Proceedings of the Twenty-Second Annual Conference Presented at the 1966 Design Engineering Conference, Chicago, Illinois, May 9-12. Powder Metallurgy Conference Staff. LC TN695.P681. (Progress in Powder Metallurgy Ser.: No. 22). 150p. reprint ed. pap. 46.50 (*0-8357-6987-9*, 205707100009) Bks Demand.

Powder Metallurgy Design Manual. (Illus.). 150p. 1995. pap. 75.00 (*0-87895-459-7*) Metal Powder.

P

Powder Metallurgy Design Manual. Metal Powder Staff. LC 98-37973. (Illus.). 175p. 1998. pap. 89.00 (*1-878954-67-9*, 5031) Metal Powder.

Powder Metallurgy Equipment Manual. 2nd ed. Powder Metallurgy Equipment Association Staff. LC 76-52333. 174p. reprint ed. pap. 54.00 (*0-8357-7858-4*, 203625400002) Bks Demand.

Powder Metallurgy Equipment Manual. 3rd ed. Ed. by Samuel Bradbury. LC 76-52333. 200p. 1986. 10.00 (*0-918404-68-1*) Metal Powder.

Powder Metallurgy for Full Density Products. Ed. by Kishor M. Kulkarni. LC 87-60119. (New Perspectives in Powder Metallurgy Ser.: Vol. 8). (Illus.). 625p. 1988. 60.00 (*0-918404-72-X*) Metal Powder.

Powder Metallurgy Gears - Expanding Opportunities. W. Brian James & Howard Sanderow. (Technical Papers: Vol. 95FTM13). (Illus.). 12p. 1995. pap. text 30.00 (*1-55589-662-6*) AGMA.

Powder Metallurgy in Automotive Applications. Ed. by P. Ramakrishnan & Indian Institute of Technology Staff. (Illus.). 318p. 1998. 85.00 (*1-57808-025-8*) Science Pubs.

Powder Metallurgy in Defense, 3 vols. Incl. Vol. 4: Aberdeen, MD. 100p. 1978. pap. 9.00 (*0-918404-46-0*); pap. write for info. (*0-318-59526-5*) Metal Powder.

Powder Metallurgy in Defense Technology, Vol. 6. Ed. by C. L. Freeby & W. J. Ullrich. (Illus.). 224p. 1984. pap. 15.00 (*0-918404-62-2*) Metal Powder.

Powder Metallurgy in Defense Technology, Vol. 7. Ed. by W. J. Ullrich. (Illus.). 208p. 1987. pap. 20.00 (*0-918404-75-4*) Metal Powder.

Powder Metallurgy in Defense Technology: Proceedings of the P-M in Defense Technology Seminar, Held at Yuma, AZ, November 13 & 14, 1979, Vol. 5. P-M in Defense Technology Seminar Staff. LC TN0695.P66. (Illus.). 128p. reprint ed. pap. 39.70 (*0-7837-1561-7*, 204185300005) Bks Demand.

Powder Metallurgy of Iron & Steel. Randall M. German. LC 97-31764. 496p. 1998. 98.50 (*0-471-15739-2*, Wiley-Interscience) Wiley.

Powder Metallurgy of Titanium Alloys: Proceedings of the Metallurgy Society of AIME, 109th, Las Vegas, Nevada, 1980. Metallurgy Society of AIME Staff. Ed. by F. H. Froes & John E. Smugenesky. LC 80-83013. 319p. reprint ed. pap. 98.90 (*0-608-15170-X*, 205606900045) Bks Demand.

***Powder Metallurgy Q & A, Consulting the Experts.** 1999. pap. write for info. (*1-878954-75-X*) Metal Powder.

Powder Metallurgy Science. Randall M. German. LC 84-60862. 280p. 1984. 10.00 (*0-918404-60-6*) Metal Powder.

Powder Metallurgy Science. 2nd expanded rev. ed. Randall M. German. LC 94-1972. (Illus.). 472p. (C). 1994. 60.00 (*1-878954-42-3*) Metal Powder.

Powder Metallurgy Technology. G. S. Upadhyaya. 165p. 1996. pap. 44.00 (*1-898326-40-1*, Pub. by CISP) Balogh.

Powder Monkey. Carol R. Campbell. LC 99-21655. (Young Americans Ser.: Vol. 4). (Illus.). 116p. (J). (gr. 4-12). 1999. pap. 5.99 (*1-57249-170-1*, WM Kids) White Mane Pub.

Powder Monkey. Bill Wall. 160p. 1997. pap. 7.95 (*1-85635-154-8*, Pub. by Mercier Pr) Irish Amer Bk.

Powder Preparation/Rapid Quenching: Materials Research Society International Symposium Proceedings-IMAM-3. Ed. by K. Akashi et al. 645p. 1989. text 17.50 (*1-55899-032-1*, IMAM-3) Materials Res.

Powder Processing of High TC Oxide Superconductors & Their Properties. A. C. Vajpei & G. S. Upadhyaya. (Key Engineering Materials Ser.: Vols. 75-76). 348p. 1992. text 176.00 (*0-87849-630-0*, Pub. by Trans T Pub) Enfield Pubs NH.

Powder Production & Spray Forming. 512p. 1992. 135.00 (*1-878954-20-2*) Metal Powder.

Powder, Profit & Privateers: A Documentary History of the Virgin Islands During the Era of the American Revolution. George F. Tyson, Jr. (Illus.). 114p. 1977. 15.00 (*0-318-14617-7*) Isl Resources.

Powder Puff Puzzle. Patricia Reilly Giff. (Polka Dot Private Eye Ser.: No. 4). 80p. (Orig.). (J). (gr. k-6). 1987. pap. 3.50 (*0-440-47180-X*, YB BDD) BDD Bks Young Read.

Powder Puff Puzzle. Patricia Reilly Giff. (Polka Dot Private Eye Ser.). (J). 1987. 8.70 (*0-606-03638-5*, Pub. by Turtleback) Demco.

Powder Puff Puzzle. Patricia Reilly Giff. 75p. pap. 3.99 (*0-8072-1275-X*) Listening Lib.

Powder River. Jack Ballas. 208p. 1995. mass mkt. 4.50 (*0-515-11727-7*, Jove) Berkley Pub.

Powder River. Gary McCarthy. 384p. (Orig.). 1998. mass mkt. 5.50 (*0-8439-4408-0*, Leisure Bks) Dorchester Pub Co.

Powder River. large type ed. Ralph W. Cotton. LC 96-19595. 570p. 1996. lib. bdg. 22.95 (*0-7862-0794-9*) Thorndike Pr.

Powder River: Let'er Buck. Struthers M. Burt. LC 73-144923. (Illus.). 1971. reprint ed. 39.00 (*0-403-00886-7*) Scholarly.

Powder River: 91st Infantry Division. Roy Livengood. LC 94-60146. (Illus.). 408p. 1994. 29.95 (*1-56311-135-7*) Turner Pub KY.

Powder River Expedition Journals of Colonel Richard Irving Dodge. Richard I. Dodge. Ed. by Wayne R. Kime. LC 97-9315. (Illus.). 208p. 1997. 28.95 (*0-8061-2983-2*) U of Okla Pr.

Powder River Reunion. Myrna Temte. (Family Continuity Program Ser.: No. 35). 1999. mass mkt. 4.50 (*0-373-82183-2*, 1-82183-4) Harlequin Bks.

Powder Surface Area & Porosity. 3rd ed. S. Lowell & J. E. Shields. (Powder Technology Ser.). (Illus.). 250p. (gr. 13). 1991. text 109.95 (*0-412-39690-4*, A5566) Chapman & Hall.

Powder Technology & Pharmaceutical Processes. Dominique Chulia et al. LC 93-41271. (Handbook of Powder Technology Ser.: 9). 584p. 1993. 288.50 (*0-444-81533-3*) Elsevier.

Powder Technology Handbook. 2nd rev. ed. Ed. by Keishi Gotoh et al. LC 97-22484. (Illus.). 968p. 1997. text 225.00 (*0-8247-0015-5*) Dekker.

Powdered Detergents. Michael S. Showell. LC 97-31100. (Surfactant Science Ser.: No. 71). (Illus.). 368p. 1997. text 145.00 (*0-8247-9988-7*) Dekker.

Powdered Metal Gear, What Can You Expect? H. R. Stephenson. (Technical Papers: Vol. P199.01). (Illus.). 8p. 1977. pap. text 30.00 (*1-55589-339-2*) AGMA.

***Powdered Water Poems.** 2000. pap. 8.95 (*0-533-12881-1*) Vantage.

***Powderhouse: Scientific Postscript & Last Protocol.** Jens Bjorneboe. Tr. by Esther G. Murer from NOR. LC 99-39925. (History of Bestiality Ser.: No. 2). 180p. 2000. pap. 15.95 (*0-8023-1331-0*) Dufour.

Powderkeg: A Novel. Leo V. Gordon & Richard Vetterli. LC 91-19515. 368p. 1993. pap. 9.95 (*0-89141-506-8*) Presidio Pr.

Powders & Grains: Proceedings of an International Congress on Micromechanics of Granular Media, Clermont-Ferrand, 4 - 8 September 1989. Ed. by Jean Biarez & R. Gourves. (Illus.). 528p. (C). 1989. text 220.00 (*90-6191-984-3*, Pub. by A A Balkema) Ashgate Pub Co.

Powders & Grains, 1993. Ed. by C. Thornton. 472p. 1993. 168.00 (*90-5410-323-X*, Pub. by A A Balkema) Ashgate Pub Co.

Powdersmoke Canyon. large type ed. Lew Smith. (Linford Western Library). 1991. pap. 16.99 (*0-7089-7036-2*, Linford) Ulverscroft.

Powdersmoke Feud. William M. Raine. 1980. mass mkt. 1.75 (*0-451-09076-4*, E9076, Sig) NAL.

Powdersmoke Range. large type ed. William C. MacDonald. LC 96-48190. (Nightingale Ser.). 283p. 1997. lib. bdg. 17.95 (*0-7838-2048-8*, G K Hall Lrg Type) Mac Lib Ref.

Powdery Mildews (Erysiphales) of Europe. Uwe Braun. LC 95-229039. (Illus.). 336p. 1995. 90.00 (*3-334-60994-4*) Balogh.

Powell: Family Records of the Powell & Griffiths, with Poetry of John Powell. Rachel Powell. 119p. 1994. reprint ed. pap. 19.50 (*0-8328-4111-0*); reprint ed. lib. bdg. 29.50 (*0-8328-4110-2*) Higginson Bk Co.

Powell Affair: Freedom Minus One. Andrew Jacobs, Jr. LC 72-88272. 256p. (Orig.). 1973. pap. 5.50 (*0-672-61183-X*, Bobbs) Macmillan.

Powell Canal: Baytown Period Occupation on Bayou Macon in Southeast Arkansas. John H. House. (Illus.). 109p. 1982. pap. 4.00 (*1-56349-043-9*, RS19) AR Archaeol.

Powell Family of Allegany County, Maryland: Descendants of William Powell & Ann (Chambers) Powell of Timsbury, Somersetshire, England. George E. Russell. (Illus.). 117p. (Orig.). 1990. pap. 16.00 (*0-914385-12-7*) Catoctin Pr.

Powell Family of Norfolk & Elizabeth City Cos. Virginia & Their Descendants, with Notes & Data on Collateral Families of Bush, Beckwith, Bowles, Cargill & Others. S. E. Lucas, Jr. 305p. 1992. reprint ed. pap. 46.00 (*0-8328-2461-5*); reprint ed. lib. bdg. 56.00 (*0-8328-2460-7*) Higginson Bk Co.

Powell, John Wesley: Voyage of Discovery. Dan Murphy. LC 91-60044. (Illus.). 64p. (Orig.). 1991. pap. 7.95 (*0-88714-059-9*) KC Pubns.

Powell on Real Property, 17 vols. Richard R. Powell & Patrick J. Rohan. 1949. ring bd. 2235.00 (*0-8205-1550-7*) Bender.

***Powell-Smith & Furmston's Building Contract Casebook.** 3rd ed. Vincent Powell-Smith & M. P. Furmston. LC 99-89276. 2000. write for info. (*0-632-03991-4*) Blackwell Sci.

Powell-Smith & Sims' Building Contract Claims. 3rd ed. David Chappell & Vincent Powell-Smith. LC 97-33481. 1998. 99.95 (*0-632-03646-X*) Blackwell Sci.

Powell vs. Alabama: The Scottsboro Boys & American Justice. Gerald Horne. LC 96-33602. (Historic Supreme Court Cases Ser.). (J). 1997. lib. bdg. 24.00 (*0-531-11314-0*) Watts.

Powell's Army No. 1: Unchained Lightning. Terence Duncan. 224p. 1987. mass mkt. 2.50 (*0-8217-1994-7*, Zebra Kensgtn) Kensgtn Pub Corp.

Powell's Army No. 2: Apache Raiders. Terence Duncan. 224p. 1987. mass mkt. 2.50 (*0-8217-2073-2*, Zebra Kensgtn) Kensgtn Pub Corp.

Powell's Canyon Voyage. W. L. Rusho. LC 70-64908. (Wild & Woolly West Ser., No. 11). (Illus.). 52p. 1969. pap. 4.00 (*0-910584-12-5*) Filter.

Power. Judd Biasiotto. 80p. (Orig.). 1988. pap. 6.00 (*0-933079-07-9*) World Class Enterprises.

Power. Collins1. 1998. mass mkt. 3.99 (*0-671-02458-2*) S&S Trade.

Power. D. Dowding. 112p. 1996. pap. 2.00 (*0-335-19440-0*) Taylor & Francis.

Power. Keith Dowding. 112p. 1996. 9.00 (*0-335-19441-9*) Taylor & Francis.

Power. Keith Dowding. (Concepts in Social Thought Ser.). 128p. 1996. pap. 14.95 (*0-8166-2941-2*); text 37.95 (*0-8166-2940-4*) U of Minn Pr.

Power. Frederick C. Hatfield. (Illus.). 256p. (Orig.). 1989. pap. 16.95 (*0-8092-4433-0*, 443300, Contemporary Bks) NTC Contemp Pub Co.

Power. Linda Hogan. LC 97-42997. 192p. 1998. 23.00 (*0-393-04636-2*) Norton.

Power. Linda Hogan. 248p. 1999. pap. 13.00 (*0-393-31968-7*, Norton Paperbks) Norton.

Power. Ed. by Steven Lukes. LC 86-8511. (Readings in Social & Political Theory Ser.). 256p. (C). 1986. text 45.00 (*0-8147-5030-3*); pap. text 17.50 (*0-8147-5031-1*) NYU Pr.

Power. Frank M. Robinson. 224p. 2000. pap. 12.95 (*0-312-86654-2*, Pub. by Tor Bks) St Martin.

Power. James C. Word. 312p. (Orig.). 1996. pap. 14.99 (*1-56043-255-1*, Treasure Hse) Destiny Image.

Power: A Conceptual Analysis. Valeri Ledyaev. LC 98-11746. 1998. 65.00 (*1-56072-536-2*) Nova Sci Pubs.

Power: A New Social Analysis. Bertrand Russell. 216p. (C). 1993. pap. 16.99 (*0-415-09456-9*, B2534) Routledge.

Power: A Repossession Manual--Organizing Strategies for Citizens. Greg L. Speeter. LC 79-624732. (Illus.). (Orig.). (C). 1978. pap. 10.00 (*0-934210-00-4*) Devlp Commy.

Power! Black Workers, Their Unions & the Struggle for Freedom in South Africa. Denis MacShane et al. 195p. 1984. 30.00 (*0-89608-245-8*) South End Pr.

Power: Critical Concepts, 3 vols., Set. John Scott. 1408p. (C). (gr. 13). 1994. 655.00 (*0-415-07938-1*, B3788) Routledge.

Power: Focus for a Biblical Theology. Hans R. Weber. LC BS0680.P5W4. 216p. 1989. reprint ed. pap. 67.00 (*0-608-00577-0*, 206146000009) Bks Demand.

***Power: Government by Consent & Majority Rule in America.** R. Randall Bridwell. LC 98-18655. 291p. 1998. 75.00 (*1-57292-114-5*) Austin & Winfield.

Power! How to Get It, How to Use It. Michael Korda. 1991. mass mkt. 5.99 (*0-446-36016-3*, Pub. by Warner Bks) Little.

***Power: How Women Just Like You Become Weight-Loss Winners.** Sue Ellin Browder. 272p. 2000. 22.95 (*0-471-37968-9*) Wiley.

Power: Infinite Game. Michael F. Broom & Donald Klein. LC 96-209693. 1995. pap. text 24.95 (*0-87425-296-2*) HRD Press.

Power: Its Forms, Bases & Uses. Dennis H. Wrong. LC 94-45957. 340p. 1995. pap. 24.95 (*1-56000-822-9*) Transaction Pubs.

Power: Its Forms, Bases & Uses. Dennis H. Wrong. xii, 326p. 1993. pap. text 12.95 (*0-226-91067-9*) U Ch Pr.

Power: Its Myths & Mores in American Art, 1961-1991. Holliday T. Day. LC 91-71454. (Illus.). 160p. 1991. pap. 27.50 (*0-936260-57-2*); lib. bdg. 47.50 (*0-253-31658-8*) Ind Mus Art.

Power: Its Use & Abuse. Terence F. Moore. 94p. (Orig.). 1997. pap. text 8.00 (*0-9633518-6-9*) Ivory Grp.

Power: Mechanics of Energy Control. 2nd ed. Bohm & MacDonald. 1983. teacher ed. 11.16 (*0-02-672470-7*) Glencoe.

Power: Mechanics of Energy Control. 2nd ed. Ralph C. Bohm & MacDonald. 1983. 39.47 (*0-02-672460-X*) Glencoe.

Power: Prime Mover of Technology. 2nd ed. Joseph W. Duffy. (Illus.). 571p. (C). 1996. reprint ed. 108.00 (*1-878907-33-6*, RAN) TechBooks.

Power: The Inner Experience. David C. McClelland. LC 75-35603. (Illus.). 441p. 1979. 39.50 (*0-8290-0686-9*); pap. text 24.95 (*0-8290-0101-8*) Irvington.

***Power: The Power to Create the Future.** Eric A. Mitchell. LC 89-13824. (New Age Ser.). (Illus.). 192p. 1999. mass mkt. 3.95 (*0-87542-499-6*) Llewellyn Pubns.

Power Vol. III: Essential Works of Foucault, 1954-1984. Michel Foucault. Ed. by Colin Gordon & Paul Rabinow. Tr. by Robert Hurley et al from FRE. Orig. Title: Dit et Ecrits. 488p. 2000. 30.00 (*1-56584-257-X*, Pub. by New Press NY) Norton.

Power Acol: The Art of Being Lucky in the Bidding. Ron Klinger. 128p. 1996. pap. 13.95 (*0-575-06114-6*, Pub. by V Gollancz) Trafalgar.

Power Across the Pacific: A History of America's Relations with Japan. William R. Nester. 480p. (C). 1996. text 55.00 (*0-8147-5788-X*) NYU Pr.

Power Adaptations & Changing Cultures. Thorne Deuel. (Scientific Papers: Vol. XV). (Illus.). 204p. 1976. pap. 4.00 (*0-89792-063-5*) Ill St Museum.

Power, Administration & Finance in Mughal India. John F. Richards. (Collected Studies: Vol. CS419). 336p. 1993. 115.95 (*0-86078-366-9*, Pub. by Variorum) Ashgate Pub Co.

Power Aging. Ted L. Edwards, Jr. (Illus.). 94p. 1996. pap. 19.95 (*0-614-30284-6*) Hills Med.

Power Analysis of a Congregation. Roy M. Oswald. pap. 6.25 (*1-56699-008-4*) Alban Inst.

Power & Accountability: Restoring the Balance of Power Between Corporations, Owners, & Society. Robert A. Monks & Nell Minow. 224p. 1991. 22.95 (*0-88730-512-1*, HarpBusn) HarpInfo.

Power & Accountability: Restoring the Balance of Power Between Corporations, Owners, & Society. Robert A. Monks & Nell Minow. LC 91-58519. 304p. 1992. reprint ed. pap. 12.00 (*0-88730-534-2*, HarpBusn) HarpInfo.

Power & Authority: Transformation of Campus Governance. Ed. by Harold L. Hodgkinson & Louis R. Meeth. LC 74-132821. (Jossey-Bass Higher Education Ser.). 231p. reprint ed. pap. 71.70 (*0-608-16999-4*, 202775500056) Bks Demand.

Power & Authority in Adolescence: The Origins & Resolutions of Intergenerational Conflict. Group for the Advancement of Psychiatry Staff. LC 78-55380. (Group for the Advancement of Psychiatry, Symposium Ser.: Vol. 10, No. 101). 227p. reprint ed. pap. 70.40 (*0-7837-2106-4*, 204238300004) Bks Demand.

Power & Beauty: Images of Women in Art. Georges Duby & Michelle Perrot. (Illus.). 192p. 1995. 50.00 (*1-85043-612-6*, Pub. by I B T) St Martin.

Power & Benefits of Afrikan-Centricity: or, How to Live in the Heaven of Self-Knowledge As Freedom from the Hell of Self-Igorance. Afrikadzata Deku. LC 91-72694. (Afrikan Centric Essay Ser.). 185p. 1995. 25.00 (*1-56454-032-4*) Cont Afrikan.

Power & Benefits of Continental Afrikan Culture: or, Why continental Afrikan Culture is the Mother of All Cultures on Earth. Afrikadzata Deku. LC 91-72673. (Afrikan Centric Essay Ser.). 10p. 1995. pap. 5.00 (*1-56454-017-0*) Cont Afrikan.

Power & Betrayal in the Canadian Media. David Taras. 256p. 1999. pap. 19.95 (*1-55111-141-1*) Broadview Pr.

Power & Blessing. Jack W. Hayford. LC 93-42746. 180p. 1994. 16.99 (*1-56476-199-1*, 6-3199, Victor Bks) Chariot Victor.

Power & Blessing. Jack W. Hayford. 240p. 1995. pap. 10.99 (*1-56476-481-8*, 6-3481, Victor Bks) Chariot Victor.

Power & Change: The Administrative History of the Office of the Chief of Naval Operations, 1946-1986. Thomas C. Hone. (Contributions to Naval History Ser.: No. 2). (Illus.). 168p. (C). 1989. pap. text 8.50 (*0-945274-02-5*) Naval Hist Ctr.

Power & Choice. 7th ed. Shively. 2000. 31.00 (*0-07-232252-7*) McGraw.

Power & Choice: An Introduction to Political Science. 5th ed. E. Phillips Shively. 400p. (C). 1996. pap. 42.50 (*0-07-057187-2*) McGraw.

Power & Choice: An Introduction to Political Science. 6th ed. W. Phillips Shively. LC 98-24366. 416p. 1998. pap. 39.69 (*0-07-303387-1*) McGraw.

Power & Christian Ethics. James P. Mackey. (New Studies in Christian Ethics: No. 3). 251p. (C). 1994. text 69.95 (*0-521-41595-0*) Cambridge U Pr.

Power & City Governance: Comparative Perspectives on Urban Development. Alan DiGaetano & John S. Klemanski. LC 99-31736. (Globalization & Community Ser.: Vol. 4). 256p. 1999. pap. 22.95 (*0-8166-3219-7*, Pub. by U of Minn Pr); lib. bdg. 57.95 (*0-8166-3218-9*, Pub. by U of Minn Pr) Chicago Distribution Ctr.

Power & Civil Society: Toward a Dynamic Theory of Real Socialism, 271. Leszek Nowak. LC 90-47324. (Contributions in Political Science Ser.: No. 271). 248p. 1991. 59.95 (*0-313-27505-X*, NDP/, Greenwood Pr) Greenwood.

Power & Class: The Italian American Experience Today. Ed. by Francis X. Femminella. 1971. 5.00 (*0-934675-04-X*) Am Italian.

***Power & Communication Cables: Theory & Applications.** Ed. by R. Bartnikas & K. D. Srivastava. LC 99-18442. 896p. 1999. 129.95 (*0-7803-1196-5*, PC5665-QOE) Inst Electrical.

***Power & Communication Cables Handbook.** R. Bartnikas. (Professional Engineering Ser.). 900p. 1999. 129.95 (*0-07-135385-2*) McGraw.

Power & Community: Organizational & Cultural Responses to AIDS. Dennis Altman. LC 94-5754. 1994. 69.95 (*0-7484-0193-8*); pap. 24.95 (*0-7484-0194-6*) Taylor & Francis.

Power & Compassion: Working with Difficult Adolescents & Abused Parents. Jerome A. Price. LC 96-29012. (Family Therapy Ser.). 196p. 1996. lib. bdg. 30.00 (*1-57230-141-4*, 0141) Guilford Pubns.

Power & Compassion: Working with Difficult Adolescents & Abused Parents. Jerome A. Price. (Family Therapy Ser.). 196p. 1999. pap. text 18.00 (*1-57230-470-7*) Guilford Pubns.

Power & Conflict: Toward a General Theory. Hubert M. Blalock. LC 89-10215. (Violence, Cooperation, Peace Ser.). (Illus.). 280p. 1989. pap. 86.80 (*0-608-05069-5*, 206562400005) Bks Demand.

Power & Conflict: Toward a General Theory. Hubert M. Blalock, Jr. (Violence, Cooperation, & Peace Ser.: Vol. 4). 280p. (C). 1989. text 55.00 (*0-8039-3594-3*); pap. text 24.95 (*0-8039-3595-1*) Sage.

Power & Conflict in Age of Transportation. Bernard I. Finel. text. write for info. (*0-312-22937-2*) St Martin.

Power & Conflict in the University: Research in the Sociology of Complex Organizations. J. Victor Baldridge. LC 70-140548. 254p. reprint ed. 78.80 (*0-8357-9957-3*, 201311300085) Bks Demand.

***Power & Control: Escape from Violence.** Donald W. Tiffany & Phyllis G. Tiffany. LC 99-48930. 192p. 2000. 49.00 (*0-7618-1553-8*); pap. 27.50 (*0-7618-1554-6*) U Pr of Amer.

Power & Corruption: The Rotten Core of Government & Big Business. Stephen Moore. (Illus.). 202p. 1999. pap. 14.95 (*1-883319-83-8*) Frog Ltd CA.

Power & Counterpower: The Union Response to Global Capital. ICEM. LC 95-52766. (International Labour Ser.). 80p. 1996. pap. 10.95 (*0-7453-1113-X*, Pub. by Pluto GBR) Stylus Pub VA.

Power & Criticism: Poststructural Investigations in Education. Cleo H. Cherryholmes. (Advances in Contemporary Educational Thought Ser.). 240p. 1988. pap. 18.95 (*0-8077-3107-2*) Tchrs Coll.

Power & Culture: Essays on the American Working Class. Herbert G. Gutman. 1992. pap. 14.95 (*1-56584-010-0*, Pub. by New Press NY) Norton.

Power & Culture: The Japanese-American War, 1941-1945. Akira Iriye. LC 80-23536. (Illus.). 318p. (C). 1981. pap. 24.50 (*0-674-69582-8*) HUP.

Power & Decision: The Control of Reproduction. Ed. by Gita Sen & Rachel C. Snow. 330p. 1994. pap. 16.95 (*0-674-69533-X*) HUP.

Power & Democracy Vol. 1: Essays in Political Theory. Brian Barry. (Illus.). 344p. 1991. pap. 32.00 (*0-19-827297-9*, 9272) OUP.

Power & Democracy in America. Peter F. Drucker et al. Ed. by William V. D'Antonio. LC 79-28576. 181p. 1980. reprint ed. lib. bdg. 55.00 (*0-313-22319-X*, PDAM, Greenwood Pr) Greenwood.

P

Power & Difference: Gender in Island Southeast Asia. Ed. by Jane M. Atkinson & Shelly Errington. LC 89-78330. 520p. 1990. 57.50 (*0-8047-1781-8*); pap. 18.95 (*0-8047-1779-6*) Stanford U Pr.

Power & Distribution Transformers - U. S. & Canadian Markets, Competitors, & Materials: 1989-1996 Analysis. Julie Perangelo. (Illus.). 300p. 1992. pap. text 3000.00 (*1-878218-28-X*) World Info Tech.

Power & Economic Institutions: Reinterpretations in Economic History. Ed. by Bo Gustafsson. 352p. 1991. text 100.00 (*1-85278-397-4*) E Elgar.

Power & Emotion in Infant-Toddler Day Care. Robin L. Leavitt. LC 93-28222. (SUNY Series, Early Childhood Education). 140p. (C). 1994. pap. text 17.95 (*0-7914-1886-3*) State U NY Pr.

Power & Empowerment: A Radical Theory of Participatory Democracy. Peter Bachrach & Aryeh Botwinick. 250p. (C). 1992. 59.95 (*0-87722-930-9*); pap. 22.95 (*0-87722-939-2*) Temple U Pr.

Power & Empowerment: The Power Principle. Lynn P. Atkinson. LC 88-80073. 128p. 1988. pap. 9.95 (*0-941404-77-3*) New Falcon Pubns.

Power & Empowerment in Higher Education: Studies in Honor of Louis Smith. Ed. by D. B. Robertson. LC 77-76333. 167p. reprint ed. pap. 51.80 (*0-7837-5792-1*, 204545800006) Bks Demand.

Power & Energy in Alternating-Current Circuits. Heinz Rieger. LC TK1141. (Siemens Programmed Instruction Ser.: No. 14). 68p. reprint ed. pap. 30.00 (*0-608-13139-3*, 205209000033) Bks Demand.

Power & Everyday Life: The Lives of Working Women in Nineteenth-Century Brazil. Maria O. Dias. Tr. by Ann Frost. (Illus.). 240p. 1995. text 45.00 (*0-8135-2204-8*) Rutgers U Pr.

Power & Everyday Life: The Lives of Working Women in Nineteenth-Century Brazil. Maria O. Dias. Tr. by Ann Frost. LC 94-47497. (Illus.). 240p. (C). 1995. pap. text 15.95 (*0-8135-2205-6*) Rutgers U Pr.

Power & Family Therapy: A Special Issue of Contemporary Family Therapy. Ed. by William C. Nichols. 75p. 1988. pap. 14.95 (*0-89885-430-X*, Kluwer Acad Hman Sci) Kluwer Academic.

Power & Form of Emerson's Thought. Jeffrey L. Duncan. LC 73-85043. 121p. reprint ed. pap. 37.60 (*0-7837-0200-0*, 204049600017) Bks Demand.

Power & Gender: Issues in Sexual Dominance & Harassment. Rosemarie Skaine. LC 96-3222. 480p. 1996. lib. bdg. 49.95 (*0-7864-0208-3*) McFarland & Co.

Power & Gender: Social Relations in Theory & Practice. Ed. by Lorraine Radtke & Henderikus J. Stam. LC 93-86424. 328p. (C). 1994. text 45.00 (*0-8039-8674-2*); pap. text 14.99 (*0-8039-8675-0*) Sage.

Power & Glory. Emily Rodda. LC 95-1842. (Illus.). 32p. (J). (gr. k-4). 1996. 15.00 (*0-688-14214-1*, Grenwillow Bks) HarpC Child Bks.

Power & Gold: Jewelry from Indonesia, Malaysia, & the Philippines from the Collection of the Barbier-Mueller Museum, Geneva. Susan Rodgers. (Illus.). 369p. 1988. 85.00 (*3-7913-0859-9*, Pub. by Prestel) te Neues.

Power & Grace: The Working Horse. Klaus Alvermann. LC 89-27969. (Illus.). 144p. 1990. 35.00 (*0-87701-723-9*) Chronicle Bks.

Power & Hand Tools in Thailand: A Strategic Entry Report, 1997. Compiled by Icon Group International Staff. (Illus.). 141p. 1999. ring bd. 1410.00 incl. audio compact disk (*0-7418-1104-9*) Icon Grp.

Power & Ideas: Milton Friedman & the Big U-Turn, 2 vols. William Frazer. (Illus.). (Orig.). (C). 1988. 70.00 (*0-9619206-0-2*); pap. 39.00 (*0-9619206-3-7*) Gulf-Atlan Pub.

Power & Ideas: Milton Friedman & the Big U-Turn, 2 vols., Vol. I. William Frazer. (Illus.). (Orig.). (C). 1988. 35.00 (*0-9619206-1-0*); pap. 19.50 (*0-9619206-4-5*) Gulf-Atlan Pub.

Power & Ideas: Milton Friedman & the Big U-Turn, 2 vols., Vol. II. William Frazer. (Illus.). (Orig.). (C). 1988. 35.00 (*0-685-22793-6*); pap. 19.50 (*0-685-22794-4*) Gulf-Atlan Pub.

Power & Ideas: North-South Politics of Intellectual Property & Antitrust. Susan K. Sell. LC 97-31486. 289p. (C). 1997. text 59.50 (*0-7914-3575-X*); pap. text 19.95 (*0-7914-3576-8*) State U NY Pr.

Power & Identity: Tribalism in World Politics. Harold R. Isaacs. LC 79-55304. (Headline Ser.: No. 246). (Orig.). 1979. pap. 5.95 (*0-87124-057-2*) Foreign Policy.

Power & Ideology: A Marxist Approach to Political Sociology. Gerald Chasin & Barbara M. Chasin. 312p. 1974. pap. 11.95 (*0-87073-277-3*) Schenkman Bks Inc.

Power & Ideology: A Marxist Approach to Political Sociology. Barbara H. Chasin & Gerald Chasin. LC 73-82376. 272p. 1974. reprint ed. pap. 84.40 (*0-608-05344-9*, 206504900012) Bks Demand.

Power & Ideology in American Sport: A Critical Perspective. 2nd rev. ed. George H. Sage. LC 98-17002. (Illus.). 352p. (C). 1998. pap. text 29.00 (*0-88011-660-9*, BSAG0660) Human Kinetics.

Power & Ideology in Brazil. Peter McDonough. LC 81-47147. 360p. 1981. reprint ed. pap. 111.60 (*0-608-02996-3*, 206322200004) Bks Demand.

Power & Ideology in Education. Ed. by Jerome Karabel & Albert H. Halsey. 672p. 1977. pap. text 34.95 (*0-19-502139-8*) OUP.

Power & Illness: The Failure & Future of American Health Policy. Daniel M. Fox. LC 93-2977. 1993. 30.00 (*0-520-08409-8*, Pub. by U CA Pr) Cal Prin Full Svc.

Power & Illness: The Failure & Future of American Health Policy. Daniel M. Fox. 1995. pap. 14.95 (*0-520-20151-5*, Pub. by U CA Pr) Cal Prin Full Svc.

Power & Imagination: City-States in Renaissance Italy. Lauro Martines. LC 87-29843. (Illus.). 400p. (C). 1988. reprint ed. pap. text 17.95 (*0-8018-3643-3*) Johns Hopkins.

Power & Inequality in Language Education. Ed. by James W. Tollefson. (Applied Linguistics Ser.). (Illus.). 222p. (C). 1995. text 54.95 (*0-521-46266-5*) Cambridge U Pr.

Power & Inequality in Language Education. Keith Tribe. (Ideas in Context Ser.: No. 33). (Illus.). 222p. (C). 1995. pap. text 20.95 (*0-521-46807-8*) Cambridge U Pr.

Power & Influence: Beyond Formal Authority. John P. Kotter. 212p. 1985. 32.95 (*0-02-918330-8*) Free Pr.

Power & Influence: Enhancing Information Services Within the Organization. Guy St. Clair. (Information Services Management Ser.). 208p. 1994. 34.95 (*1-85739-098-9*) Bowker-Saur.

***Power & Influence after the Cold War: Germany in East-Central Europe.** Ann L. Phillips. 272p. 2000. pap. 26.95 (*0-8476-9523-9*); text 69.00 (*0-8476-9522-0*) Rowman.

Power & Influence in Organizations. Roderick M. Kramer & Margaret Ann Neale. LC 98-19776. 392p. 1998. 39.00 (*0-7619-0860-9*); pap. 19.99 (*0-7619-0861-7*) Sage.

Power & Innocence: A Search for the Sources of Violence. Rollo May. 288p. 1998. pap. 13.00 (*0-393-31703-X*) Norton.

Power & Interdependence. 2nd ed. Robert O. Keohane, Jr. & Joseph S. Nye. 315p. (C). 1997. pap. text 47.00 (*0-673-39891-9*) Addson-Wesley Educ.

***Power & Interdependence.** 3rd ed. 368p. (C). 2000. pap. text 44.00 (*0-321-04857-1*) Addison-Wesley.

***Power & Intimacy in the Christian Philippines.** Fenella Cannell. LC 98-24883. (Studies in Social & Cultural Anthropology: No. 109). (Illus.). 275p. (C). 1999. text 64.95 (*0-521-64147-0*); pap. text 24.95 (*0-521-64622-7*) Cambridge U Pr.

Power & Invention: Situating Science. Isabelle Stengers. Tr. by Paul Bains from FRE. LC 97-21760. (Theory Out of Bounds Ser.). 1997. pap. 21.95 (*0-8166-2517-4*); text 54.95 (*0-8166-2516-6*) U of Minn Pr.

Power & Involvement in Organizations: An Empirical Examination of Etzioni's Compliance Theory. Helga Drummond. 247p. 1993. 72.95 (*1-85628-474-3*, Pub. by Avebry) Ashgate Pub Co.

Power & Its Consequences: A Rational Perspective. Frank R. Vivelo. LC 98-30201. 232p. (C). 1998. 54.00 (*0-7618-1228-8*); pap. 34.50 (*0-7618-1229-6*) U Pr of Amer.

Power & Its Disguises: Anthropological Perspectives on Politics. Gledhill. LC 93-36729. (Anthropology, Culture & Society Ser.). 256p. (C). 54.95 (*0-7453-0738-8*, Pub. by Pluto GBR); pap. 19.95 (*0-7453-0739-6*) Pluto GBR.

***Power & Its Disguises: Anthropological Perspectives on Politics.** 2nd ed. John Gledhill. LC 00-26069. (Anthropology, Culture & Society Ser.). 2000. write for info. (*0-7453-1686-7*, Pub. by Pluto GBR) Stylus Pub VA.

Power & Knowledge: Astrology, Physiognomics, & Medicine in the Roman Empire. Tamsyn S. Barton. (Body in Theory: Histories of Cultural Materialism Ser.). (Illus.). 272p. (C). 1995. text 49.50 (*0-472-10425-X*, 10425) U of Mich Pr.

Power & Law: American Dilemma in World Affairs, Papers of the Conference on Peace Research in History. Ed. by Charles A. Barker. LC 76-135660. 219p. 1971. reprint ed. pap. 67.90 (*0-608-05924-2*, 206626000008) Bks Demand.

Power & Leadership in International Bargaining: The Path to the Camp David Accords. Shibley Telhami. 360p. 1990. text 57.50 (*0-231-07214-7*) Col U Pr.

Power & Leadership in International Bargaining: The Path to the Camp David Accords. Shibley Telhami. 360p. 1992. pap. text 23.00 (*0-231-07215-5*) Col U Pr.

Power & Light. 7.40 (*0-687-60916-X*) Abingdon.

Power & Light. 1994. pap., teacher ed. 6.95 (*0-687-60917-8*) Abingdon.

Power & Light. Barry Hannah. LC 83-62166. 80p. 1983. 15.00 (*0-913773-04-2*) S Wright.

Power & Light Company: (Packet) John Carr & Adrienne Carr. 64p. 1994. pap. 13.95 (*0-8358-0698-7*) Upper Room Bks.

Power & Machinery Employed in Manufactures in the Nineteenth Century, 2 vols., Set. 1996. lib. bdg. 659.99 (*0-8490-7596-3*) Gordon Pr.

Power & Marginality in the Abraham Narrative. Hemchand Gossai. LC 94-49094. 230p. (C). 1995. pap. text 24.00 (*0-8191-9862-5*); lib. bdg. 52.00 (*0-8191-9861-7*) U Pr of Amer.

Power & Method: Political Activism & Educational Research. Andrew Gitlin. LC 94-15749. (Critical Social Thought Ser.). 256p. (C). 1994. pap. 18.99 (*0-415-90690-3*) Routledge.

Power & Money. unabridged ed. George Li Wang. LC 97-71358. ix, 356p. 1997. pap. 16.95 (*0-9675684-0-4*, Pub. by G L Wang) Heritage West.

Power & Morality: American Business Ethics, 1840-1914, 28. Saul Engelbourg. LC 79-8288. (Contributions in Economics & Economic History Ser.: No. 28). 181p. 1980. 52.95 (*0-313-20871-9*, ENP/, Greenwood Pr) Greenwood.

Power & Morality in Global Transformation. Soedjatmoko. (First Morgenthau Memorial Lectures). 20p. 1982. pap. 4.00 (*0-87641-219-3*) Carnegie Ethics & Intl Affairs.

Power & Need in Africa. Ben Wisner. 300p. (C). 1989. 35.00 (*0-86543-101-9*); pap. 12.95 (*0-86543-102-7*) Africa World.

***Power & Negotiation.** I. W. Zartman & Jeffrey Z. Rubin. LC 99-43531. (Illus.). 320p. (C). 2000. text 39.50 (*0-472-11079-9*, 11079) U of Mich Pr.

Power & Order: Henry Adams & the Naturalist Tradition in American Fiction. Harold M. Kaplan. LC 80-23414. 160p. 1997. 18.00 (*0-226-42424-3*) U Ch Pr.

Power & Order: Henry Adams & the Naturalist Tradition in American Fiction. Harold Kaplan. LC 80-23414. 158p. reprint ed. pap. 49.00 (*0-608-09419-6*, 205421900004) Bks Demand.

Power & Organization Development. Larry E. Greiner & Virginia E. Schein. (Organization Development Ser.). (Illus.). 184p. (C). 1988. pap. text 40.00 (*0-201-12185-9*) Addison-Wesley.

Power & Paper: Margaret Bourke-White, Modernity & the Documentary Mode. John Stomberg. LC 97-77774. (Illus.). 64p. (C). 1998. pap. 20.00 (*1-881450-09-0*) Boston U Art.

Power & Parenting. Bonner. LC 97-38324. 177p. 1998. text 65.00 (*0-312-21002-7*) St Martin.

Power & Participatory Development: Theory & Practice. Ed. by Susan Wright & Nici Nelson. 208p. (Orig.). 1995. pap. 18.95 (*1-85339-241-3*, Pub. by Intermed Tech) Stylus Pub VA.

Power & Partnering. Ed. by Barbara Jo Brothers. LC 95-3596. 1995. 39.95 (*1-56024-720-7*) Haworth Pr.

***Power & Passion: A History of Latin America.** Marshall C. Eakin. 1999. text. write for info. (*0-312-22307-2*) St Martin.

***Power & Passion, Honor & Glory: Five Heroes of Modern Golf.** Gerald Sprayregen. 1999. 34.95 (*0-9671933-0-3*) Sports-Poetry.

Power & Passion of M. Carey Thomas. Helen Lefkowitz Horowitz. LC 98-45535. (Women in American History Ser.). 526p. 1999. pap. text 23.95 (*0-252-06811-4*) U of Ill Pr.

Power & Pawn: The Female in Iberian Families, Societies & Cultures, 1. Ann M. Pescatello. LC 75-35352. (Council on Intercultural & Comparative Studies: No. 1). 281p. 1976. 38.50 (*0-8371-8583-1*, PPP/, Greenwood Pr) Greenwood.

Power & Peace: The Diplomacy of John Foster Dulles. Frederick W. Marks, III. LC 92-42442. 296p. 1993. 59.95 (*0-275-94497-2*, C4497, Praeger Pubs) Greenwood.

Power & Peace: The Diplomacy of John Foster Dulles. Frederick W. Marks, III. LC 92-42442. 296p. 1995. pap. 24.95 (*0-275-95232-0*, Praeger Pubs) Greenwood.

Power & Performance in Gros Ventre War Expedition Songs. Orin T. Hatton. (Mercury Ser.: CES No. 114). (Illus.). 79p. 1991. pap. 11.95 (*0-660-10792-9*, Pub. by CN Mus Civilization) U of Wash Pr.

Power & Personality. Harold D. Lasswell. LC 75-22644. 262p. 1976. reprint ed. lib. bdg. 59.75 (*0-8371-8374-X*, LAPOP, Greenwood Pr) Greenwood.

Power & Persuasion: Fiestas & Social Control in Rural Mexico. Stanley Brandes. LC 87-19205. (Illus.). 224p. (C). 1988. text 39.95 (*0-8122-8077-6*) U of Pa Pr.

***Power & Persuasion: Ideology & Rhetoric in Communist Yugoslavia, 1944-1953.** Carol S. Lilly. 2000. pap. 45.00 (*0-8133-3825-5*) Westview.

Power & Persuasion in Late Antiquity: Towards a Christian Empire. Peter Brown. LC 92-50245. (Curti Lectures: Vol. 1988). 192p. (C). 1992. pap. 15.95 (*0-299-13344-3*) U of Wis Pr.

Power & Perversion. Marjorie K. Hacker. LC 89-60353. 383p. 1989. 16.00 (*0-925861-00-6*) Quaint Pub Co.

Power & Place in the North American West. Richard White. (Emil & Kathleen Sick Lecture-Book Series in Western History & Biography). 1999. 19.95 (*0-295-97774-4*) U of Wash Pr.

Power & Place in the North American West. Ed. by Richard White & John M. Findlay. LC 98-31496. 336p. 1999. pap. text 19.95 (*0-295-97773-6*) U of Wash Pr.

Power & Pleasure: Louis Barthou & the Third French Republic. Robert J. Young. 352p. 1991. text 65.00 (*0-7735-0863-5*, Pub. by McG-Queens Univ Pr) CUP Services.

Power & Pluralism: A View from the Bottom. Michael J. Parenti. (Reprint Series in Social Sciences). (C). 1993. reprint ed. pap. text 5.00 (*0-8290-3569-9*, PS-528) Irvington.

Power & Pluralism in American Cities: Researching the Urban Laboratory, 165. Robert J. Waste. LC 86-19381. (Contributions in Political Science Ser.: No. 165). (Illus.). 192p. 1987. 49.95 (*0-313-25016-2*, WPM, Greenwood Pr) Greenwood.

Power & Policy. Thomas K. Finletter. LC 74-159718. 408p. 1972. reprint ed. lib. bdg. 75.00 (*0-8371-6189-4*, FIPP, Greenwood Pr) Greenwood.

Power & Policy in Liberal Democracies. Ed. by Martin Harrop. (Illus.). 319p. (C). 1992. text 64.95 (*0-521-34579-0*); pap. text 19.95 (*0-521-34798-X*) Cambridge U Pr.

Power & Policy in Quest of the Law: Essays in Honor of Eugene Victor Rostow. Eugene V. Rostow et al. LC 83-26502. 1985. lib. bdg. 204.00 (*90-247-2911-4*) Kluwer Academic.

Power & Policy in the Third World. 4th ed. Robert P. Clark. 224p. (C). 1990. pap. 42.00 (*0-02-322675-7*, Macmillan Coll) P-H.

Power & Policy in Transition: Essays Presented on the Tenth Anniversary of the National Committee on American Foreign Policy in Honor of Its Founder, Hans J. Morgenthau, 126. Ed. by Vojtech Mastny. LC 84-15778. (Contributions in Political Science Ser.: No. 126). (Illus.). 271p. 1985. 59.95 (*0-313-24498-7*, MAY/) Greenwood.

Power & Policy in Western European Democracies. 4th ed. David M. Wood. (C). 1990. pap. 29.00 (*0-02-429575-2*, Macmillan Coll) P-H.

Power & Political Theory: Some European Perspectives. Ed. by Brian Barry. LC 75-25556. 312p. reprint ed. pap. 96.80 (*0-608-17684-2*, 203040300069) Bks Demand.

Power & Politics: An Introduction to American Government. 3rd ed. Thompson. (C). 1993. pap. text. write for info. (*0-07-064463-2*) McGraw.

Power & Politics: Federal Higher Education Policymaking in the 1990s. Michael D. Parsons. LC 96-43399. 254p. (C). 1997. text 59.50 (*0-7914-3423-0*); pap. text 19.95 (*0-7914-3424-9*) State U NY Pr.

Power & Politics: The Story of Malaysia's Orang Asli. Roy D. Jumper. LC 96-29619. 164p. 1997. 36.50 (*0-7618-0700-4*) U Pr of Amer.

Power & Politics & the Seaside: The Development of Devon's Seaside Resorts in the Twentieth. Nigel J. Morgan & Annette Pritchard. (Illus.). 250p. 1998. text 75.00 (*0-85989-571-8*, Pub. by Univ Exeter Pr) Northwestern U Pr.

Power & Politics & the Seaside: The Development of Devon's Seaside Resorts in the Twentieth Century. Nigel J. Morgan & Annette Pritchard. (Illus.). 250p. 1998. pap. text 29.95 (*0-85989-572-6*) Univ Exeter Pr.

Power & Politics at the Department of Education & Science. Ian Lawrence. Ed. by John Sayer. (Education Management Ser.). 192p. 1992. text 80.00 (*0-304-32624-0*); pap. text 37.95 (*0-304-32607-0*) Continuum.

Power & Politics In America 3rd ed. Freedman. (Political Science Ser.). 1978. pap. 15.25 (*0-87872-159-2*) Thomson Learn.

Power & Politics in America. 7th ed. Freedman. (C). 1999. text 50.00 (*0-15-507164-5*, Pub. by Harcourt Coll Pubs) Harcourt.

***Power & Politics in California.** 6th ed. (C). 1999. 26.00 (*0-321-06973-0*) Addison-Wesley.

Power & Politics in Early Britain & Ireland. Ed. by S. T. Driscoll & M. R. Nieke. (Illus.). 200p. 1988. 45.00 (*0-85224-520-3*, Pub. by Edinburgh U Pr) Col U Pr.

Power & Politics in Education. Ed. by David Dawkins. (Deakin Studies in Education Ser.: No. 6). 220p. 1991. 75.00 (*1-85000-889-2*, Falmer Pr); pap. 34.95 (*1-85000-890-6*, Falmer Pr) Taylor & Francis.

Power & Politics in Organizations. Ed. by Cynthia Hardy. (International Library of Management). (Illus.). 560p. 1995. text 229.95 (*1-85521-559-4*) Ashgate Pub Co.

Power & Politics in Organizations. Samuel B. Bacharach & Edward J. Lawler. LC 79-92460. (Jossey-Bass Social & Behavioral Science Ser.). 269p. reprint ed. pap. 83.40 (*0-8357-4849-9*, 203778000009) Bks Demand.

Power & Politics in Palestine: The Jews & the Governing of Their Land 100 BC-AD 70. James S. McLaren. (Journal for the Study of the New Testament, Supplement Ser.: No. 63). 248p. (C). 1991. 70.00 (*1-85075-319-9*, Pub. by Sheffield Acad) CUP Services.

Power & Politics in Project Management. Jeffrey K. Pinto. (Illus.). 160p. (Orig.). 1996. pap. 32.95 (*1-880410-43-5*) Proj Mgmt Inst.

Power & Politics in the Community College. Mary L. Zoglin. LC 75-35618. (C). 1976. 23.95 (*0-88280-037-X*) ETC Pubns.

***Power & Politics in Tudor England.** G. W. Bernard. LC 00-34848. 2000. write for info. (*0-7546-0245-1*, Pub. by Ashgate Pub) Ashgate Pub Co.

Power & Polity among the Brethren: A Study of Church Governance. S. Loren Bowman. LC 87-6345. 169p. 1987. reprint ed. pap. 52.40 (*0-608-02154-7*, 206282300004) Bks Demand.

Power & Popular Protest: Latin American Social Movements. Ed. by Susan Eckstein. 390p. (C). 1988. pap. 18.95 (*0-520-06414-3*, Pub. by U CA Pr) Cal Prin Full Svc.

***Power & Popular Protest: Latin American Social Movements.** Ed. by Susan Eckstein. (Illus.). 390p. 2001. pap. 18.95 (*0-520-22705-0*, Pub. by U CA Pr) Cal Prin Full Svc.

Power & Position. Barry Oshry. LC 88-8848. (Notes on Power Ser.). (Orig.). 1977. pap. text 13.50 (*0-910411-04-2*) Power & Sys.

Power & Potential of Youth in Service to Communities. 97p. 1993. pap. text 16.00 (*1-881282-01-5*) MN Ofc Citizenship.

Power & Power PC: Principles, Architecture & Implementation. Sholom Weiss & James E. Smith. LC 94-26708. 408p. 1994. text 61.95 (*1-55860-279-8*) Morgan Kaufmann.

Power & Power Transmission; Diesel Engines & Electric Power see Diesel Engines & Electric Power

Power & Powerless in Industry: An Analysis of the Social Relations of Production. Rosemary Harris. 1987. text 57.50 (*0-422-60920-X*, 1074, Pub. by Tavistock) Routldge.

Power & Powerlessness: Quiescence & Rebellion in an Appalachian Valley. John Gaventa. LC 80-12988. (Illus.). 288p. 1982. pap. text 13.95 (*0-252-00985-1*) U of Ill Pr.

Power & Prayer: Anthropological Essays on Politics & Religion. Ed. by Mart Bax & Adrianus Koster. 200p. 1993. pap. 35.00 (*90-5383-209-2*, Pub. by VU Univ Pr) Paul & Co Pubs.

Power & Precision. Ed. by Michael Borenstein et al. 1997. 495.00 incl. disk (*1-56321-198-X*) LEA S&AM.

***Power & Precision: Cycling, Equestrian, Shooting & Lots, Lots More.** Jason Page. (Zeke's Olympic Pocket Guide Ser.). (Illus.). 32p. (YA). (gr. 3 up). 2000. 3.95 (*0-8225-5050-4*, LernerSports) Lerner Pub.

Power & Prejudice: The Reception of the Gospel of Mark. Brenda Deen Schildgen. LC 98-28981. 1999. 34.95 (*0-8143-2785-0*) Wayne St U Pr.

Power & Preparedness in Thucydides. June W. Allison. LC 88-46115. (American Journal of Philology Monographs: No. 5). 192p. 1989. text 30.00 (*0-8018-3821-5*) Johns Hopkins.

Power & Prestige: The Arts of Island Melanesia & the Polynesian Outliers. Norman Hurst. (Illus.). 88p. (Orig.). 1996. pap. 25.00 (*0-9628074-5-1*) Hurst Gal.

P

An Asterisk (*) at the beginning of an entry indicates that the title is appearing for the first time.

Power & Price: How Market Economies Really Work. Fred Haber. LC 98-33934. 160p. 1999. pap. 19.95 (*0-935047-25-5*) Americas Group.

Power & Principle: Armed Intervention in Wilsonian Foreign Policy. Frederick S. Calhoun. LC 85-24086. 345p. 1986. 28.00 (*0-87338-327-3*) Kent St U Pr.

Power & Principles in International Affairs. 2nd ed. Gordon C. Schloming. (C). 1996. pap. text. write for info. (*0-15-501126-X*) Harcourt Coll Pubs.

Power & Privatization: Choice & Competition in the Remaking of British Democracy. Joel D. Wolfe. 209p. 1996. text 65.00 (*0-312-15952-8*) St Martin.

Power & Privilege: A Theory of Social Stratification. Gerhard E. Lenski. LC 83-26049. 512p. 1984. reprint ed. pap. 22.50 (*0-8078-4119-6*) U of NC Pr.

Power & Privilege at an African University. Pierre L. Van den Berghe. 273p. 1973. boxed set 39.95 (*0-87073-968-9*) Transaction Pubs.

Power & Process: Gender & Development. Geraldine Reardon. LC 96-155018. (Gender & Development Ser.). 280p. (C). 1995. pap. 15.95 (*0-85598-297-7*, Pub. by Oxfam Pub) Stylus Pub VA.

Power & Profit: A History of the International Drug Trade. Kathryn Meyer & Terry Parssinen. LC 98-23716. (State & Society in East Asia Ser.). 304p. 1998. pap. 19.95 (*0-8476-9017-2*) Rowman.

Power & Profits: U. S. Policy Toward Central America. Ronald W. Cox. LC 93-41718. 200p. 1994. 29.95 (*0-8131-1865-4*) U Pr of Ky.

Power & Progress, 2015. Patrick M. Cronin. 173p. 1996. per. 16.00 (*0-16-048752-8*) USGPO.

***Power & Promise: Helping School Girls Hold onto Their Dreams.** 2nd rev. ed. Timothy Hinds Flinders & Carol Lee Flinders. 260p. 1999. pap. 20.00 (*0-9676173-0-8*) Two Rock.

Power & Promise of School Reform: Grass Roots Movements During the Progressive Era. William J. Reese. (Critical Social Thought Ser.). 320p. (C). 1986. text 39.95 (*0-7100-9952-5*, Routledge Thoemms); pap. text 14.95 (*0-7102-0767-0*, Routledge Thoemms) Routledge.

Power & Property in Inca Peru. Sally F. Moore. LC 72-5456. 190p. 1973. lib. bdg. 35.00 (*0-8371-6441-9*, MOPO, Greenwood Pr) Greenwood.

***Power & Prosperity.** Olson. 2000. pap. 18.00 (*0-465-05196-0*, Pub. by Basic) HarpC.

Power & Prosperity: Economics & Security Linkages in Asia-Pacific. Ed. by Susan L. Shirk & Christopher P. Twomey. 304p. 1996. text 39.95 (*1-56000-252-2*) Transaction Pubs.

***Power & Prosperity: Outgrowing Communist & Capitalist Dictatorships.** Mancur Olsen. LC 99-52774. 272p. 1999. 41.00 (*0-465-05195-2*, Pub. by Basic) HarpC.

Power & Protectionism: Strategies of the Newly Industrializing Countries. David B. Yoffie. LC 83-2125. (Political Economy of International Change Ser.). 304p. 1983. pap. text 25.50 (*0-231-05551-X*) Col U Pr.

Power & Protest: Frances Power Cobbe & Victorian Society. Lori Williamson. (Illus.). 320p. 1998. text 35.00 (*1-85489-100-6*) NYU Pr.

Power & Protest: Movements for Change in Australian Society. Verity Burgmann. 240p. (Orig.). 1992. pap. text 18.95 (*1-86373-211-X*, Pub. by Allen & Unwin Pty) Paul & Co Pubs.

***Power & Protest in England 1525-1640.** Alison Wall. (Reconstructing in Early Modern History Ser.). 224p. 2000. text 72.00 (*0-340-76122-9*, Pub. by E A) OUP.

***Power & Protest in England 1525-1640.** Alison Wall. (Reconstructing in Early Modern History Ser.). 224p. 2000. pap. 24.95 (*0-340-61022-0*) OUP.

Power & Protest in the Countryside: Studies of Rural Unrest in Asia, Europe, & Latine America. Robert P. Weller & Scott E. Guggenheim. LC 82-12991. (Duke Press Policy Studies). viii, 212p. (C). 1983. text 49.95 (*0-8223-0483-X*); pap. text 16.95 (*0-8223-0895-9*) Duke.

Power & Purity: Cathar Heresy in Medieval Italy. Carol Lansing. (Illus.). 288p. (C). 1998. text 45.00 (*0-19-506391-0*) OUP.

Power & Purpose after the Cold War. Ed. by Zaki Laidi. Tr. by Helen McPhail. (World Time Ser.). 256p. 1995. 47.50 (*0-85496-807-5*); pap. 19.50 (*1-85973-077-9*) Berg Pubs.

Power & Religiosity in a Post-Colonial Setting: Sinhala Catholics in Contemporary Sri Lanka. R. L. Stirrat. (Cambridge Studies in Social & Cultural Anthropology: No. 87). (Illus.). 258p. (C). 1992. text 85.00 (*0-521-41555-1*) Cambridge U Pr.

Power & Resistance in an African Society: The Ciskei Xhosa & the Making of South Africa. Les Switzer. LC 93-10085. (Illus.). 464p. (C). 1993. pap. text 29.95 (*0-299-13384-2*); lib. bdg. 72.95 (*0-299-13380-X*) U of Wis Pr.

Power & Resistance in an African Society: The Ciskei Xhosa & the Making of South Africa. Les Switzer. (Illus.). 472p. 1993. pap. write for info. (*0-86980-905-9*, Pub. by Univ Natal Pr) Intl Spec Bk.

Power & Responsibility: Multinational Managers & Developing Country Concerns, Vol. 5. Lee A. Tavis. LC 95-18779. 500p. 1999. pap. text 32.00 (*0-268-03862-7*) U of Notre Dame Pr.

Power & Responsibility: The Life & Times of Theodore Roosevelt. William H. Harbaugh. Ed. by Katherine E. Speirs. LC 97-73117. (Signature Ser.). 542p. 1997. 35.00 (*0-945707-13-4*) Amer Political.

Power & Responsibility in Education. Ed. by Keith Watson et al. LC 97-181157. (International Debates Ser.). 440p. 1996. text 130.00 (*0-304-32891-X*) Continuum.

Power & Restraint: The Moral Dimension of Police Work. Howard S. Cohen & Michael Feldberg. LC 90-28100. 184p. 1991. 49.95 (*0-275-93856-5*, C3856, Praeger Pubs); pap. 18.95 (*0-275-93857-3*, B3857, Praeger Pubs) Greenwood.

Power & Ritual in the Israel Labor Party: A Study in Political Anthropology. rev. ed. Myron J. Aronoff. LC 92-13466. (Comparative Politics Ser.). 288p. (C). (gr. 13). 1993. text 75.95 (*1-56324-105-6*); pap. text 35.95 (*1-56324-106-4*) M E Sharpe.

Power & Ruling Classes in Northeast Brazil: Juazeiro & Petrolina in Transition. Ronald H. Chilcote. (Cambridge Latin American Studies: No. 69). (Illus.). 400p. (C). 1990. text 89.95 (*0-521-37384-0*) Cambridge U Pr.

Power & Secret of the Jesuits. Renee Fulop-Miller. 636p. 1997. reprint ed. pap. 45.00 (*0-7661-0056-1*) Kessinger Pub.

Power & Seduction. Amii Lorin, pseud. 192p. 1995. pap. text, mass mkt. 3.99 (*0-8439-3736-X*) Dorchester Pub Co.

Power & Service: A Cross-National Analysis of Public Administration, 277. Hardy Wickwar. LC 91-180. (Contributions in Political Science Ser.: No. 277). 224p. 1991. 62.95 (*0-313-27755-9*, WPV, Greenwood Pr) Greenwood.

Power & Sex: Developing Inner Strength to Deal with the World. Scilla Elworthy. LC 95-43387. 1996. pap. 24.95 (*1-85230-788-9*, Pub. by Element MA) Penguin Putnam.

Power & Sex: Developing Inner Strength to Deal with the World. Scilla Elworthy. (Illus.). 384p. 1997. pap. 16.95 (*1-85230-956-3*, Pub. by Element MA) Penguin Putnam.

Power & Shared Values in the Corporate Culture. Cathy A. Enz. LC 86-4298. (Research for Business Decisions Ser.: No. 90). (Illus.). 189p. reprint ed. pap. 58.60 (*0-8357-1738-0*, 207037600088) Bks Demand.

Power & Society. 7th ed. Dye. (Political Science Ser.). (C). 1995. pap. text, student ed. 17.95 (*0-534-26071-3*) Wadsworth Pub.

Power & Society. 8th ed. Dye. (C). 1998. pap. text, student ed. 24.00 (*0-15-507233-1*) Harcourt.

Power & Society. 8th ed. Thomas R. Dye. LC 97-77100. 384p. (C). 1998. pap. text 57.00 (*0-15-508080-6*) Harcourt.

Power & Society: Greater New York at the Turn of the Century. David C. Hammack. LC 81-66977. (Illus.). 450p. (C). 1982. 42.50 (*0-87154-348-6*) Russell Sage.

Power & Stability in the Middle East. Ed. by Berch Berberoglu. LC 89-8966. 288p. (C). 1989. pap. 19.95 (*0-86232-809-8*, Pub. by Zed Books); text 55.00 (*0-86232-808-X*, Pub. by Zed Books) St Martin.

Power & Status: Officeholding in Colonial America. Ed. by Bruce C. Daniels. LC 84-21023. 333p. reprint ed. pap. 103.30 (*0-7837-0212-4*, 204052000017) Bks Demand.

Power & Style: A Critique of Twentieth-Century Architecture in the U. S. Robert Twombly. (Illus.). 130p. (C). 1998. text 20.00 (*0-7881-5515-6*) DIANE Pub.

Power & Style: A Critique of Twentieth-Century Architecture in the United States. Robert Twombly. (Illus.). 144p. 1997. pap. 11.00 (*0-8090-1597-8*) Hill & Wang.

Power & Surrender. Jenifer Levin. 1999. pap. 20.95 (*0-525-93907-5*) Viking Penguin.

Power & Tactics in International Negotiation: How Weak Nations Bargain with Strong Nations. William M. Habeeb. LC 87-46307. 182p. reprint ed. pap. 56.50 (*0-8357-6905-4*, 203796300009) Bks Demand.

Power & Television in Latin America: The Dominican Case. Antonio V. Menendez. LC 92-383. 208p. 1992. 55.00 (*0-275-94275-9*, C4275, Praeger Pubs) Greenwood.

Power & the Blessing see **Poder y la Bendicion**

Power & the Church: Ecclesiology in an Age of Transition. Martyn Percy. LC 98-203042. 224p. 1998. 49.95 (*0-304-70107-6*); pap. 24.95 (*0-304-70105-X*) Continuum.

Power & the Corporate Mind: How to Use Rather Than Misuse Leadership. Abraham Zaleznik & Manfred F. Kets De Vries. LC 85-71835. 288p. 1985. 17.95 (*0-933893-05-1*) Bonus Books.

Power & the Darkness: The Life of Josh Gibson in the Shadows of the Game. Mark Ribowsky. 322p. 1999. reprint ed. lib. bdg. 29.95 (*0-7351-0058-6*) Replica Bks.

Power & the Division of Labour. Dietrich Rueschemeyer. LC 85-51798. viii, 260p. 1986. pap. 14.95 (*0-8047-1325-1*) Stanford U Pr.

Power & the Glory. Graham Greene. 24.95 (*0-88411-656-5*) Amereon Ltd.

Power & the Glory. Graham Greene. 1977. 17.05 (*0-606-12485-3*, Pub. by Turtleback) Demco.

Power & the Glory. Graham Greene. (Twentieth-Century Classics Ser.). 222p. 1991. pap. 12.95 (*0-14-018499-6*, Penguin Classics) Viking Penguin.

Power & the Glory. Esmond Jefferies. (C). 1990. pap. text 59.00 (*0-85305-303-0*, Pub. by Arthur James) St Mut.

Power & the Glory. Clint Kelly. LC 99-6642. (In the Shadow of the Mountain Ser.). 1999. pap. 10.99 (*1-55661-956-1*) Bethany Hse.

Power & the Glory. Ilija Poplasen. (Illus.). 408p. 1990. 20.00 (*0-935352-24-4*) MIR PA.

Power & the Glory: Curriculum Unit. Center for Learning Network Staff & Graham Greene. (Novel Ser.). 68p. (YA). (gr. 9-12). 1991. spiral bd. 18.95 (*1-56077-168-2*) Ctr Learning.

Power & the Glory: The Pittsburgh Industrial Landscapes of Aaron H. Gorson, 1872-1933. Rina Youngner. (Illus.). 16p. 1989. pap. 5.00 (*0-945936-05-2*) Spanierman Gallery.

Power & the Glory: The Sculpture of the Warship Wasa. 2nd ed. Hans Soop. (Illus.). 279p. 1992. 87.50 (*91-7402-236-9*) Coronet Bks.

Power & the Glory Notes. Edward A. Kopper, Jr. (Cliffs Notes Ser.). 88p. (Orig.). 1986. pap. text 4.95 (*0-8220-1071-2*, Cliff) IDG Bks.

Power & the Money: Inside the "Wall Street Journal" Francis X. Dealy, Jr. (Illus.). 288p. 1992. 19.95 (*1-55972-118-9*, Birch Ln Pr) Carol Pub Group.

Power & the Papacy: The People & Politics Behind the Doctrine of Infallibility. Robert McClory. LC 97-10772. 256p. (Orig.). 1997. 25.00 (*0-7648-0141-4*, Liguori Triumph) Liguori Pubns.

Power & the Passion. Emma Darcy. (Presents Ser.: No. 1272). 1990. per. 2.50 (*0-373-11272-6*) Harlequin Bks.

Power & the People. V. Bogdanor. 1997. text 40.00 (*0-575-06491-9*, Pub. by V Gollancz) Trafalgar.

Power & the People: Executive Management of Public Opinion in Foreign Affairs, 1897-1921. Robert C. Hilderbrand. LC 79-28119. (Supplementary Volumes to the Papers of Woodrow Wilson). vii, 263p. 1980. 39.95 (*0-8078-1432-6*) U of NC Pr.

Power & the People: Executive Management of Public Opinion in Foreign Affairs, 1897-1921. Robert C. Hilderbrand. LC 79-28119. (Supplementary Volumes to The Papers of Woodrow Wilson). 271p. reprint ed. pap. 84.10 (*0-608-08611-8*, 206913400003) Bks Demand.

Power & the Police Chief: An Institutional & Organizational Analysis. Raymond G. Hunt & John M. Magenau, III. (Studies in Crime, Law, & Justice). (Illus.). 150p. (C). 1993. text 52.00 (*0-8039-4654-6*); pap. text 21.95 (*0-8039-4655-4*) Sage.

Power & the Praise Poem: South African Voices in History. Leroy Vail & Landeg White. (Carter G. Woodson Institute Series in Black Studies). 336p. 1991. pap. text 19.50 (*0-8139-1340-3*) U Pr of Va.

***Power & the Presidency.** Robert A. Wilson. LC 00-44853. (Illus.). 2000. write for info. (*0-7838-9154-7*, G K Hall & Co) Mac Lib Ref.

***Power & the Presidency.** Ed. by Robert A. Wilson. LC 99-55287. 240p. 2000. 25.00 (*1-891620-43-6*, Pub. by PublicAffairs NY) HarpC.

Power & the Profession of Obstetrics. William R. Arney. LC 82-8410. (Illus.). xii, 304p. (C). 1983. lib. bdg. 30.00 (*0-226-02728-7*) U Ch Pr.

Power & the Profession of Obstetrics. William R. Arney. LC 82-8410. (Illus.). xii, 290p. (C). 1993. pap. text 10.95 (*0-226-02729-5*) U Ch Pr.

***Power & the Professions in Britain, 1700-1850.** P. J. Corfield. LC 99-33041. 280p. 1999. pap. 29.99 (*0-415-22265-6*) Routledge.

Power & the Pulpit in Puritan New England. Emory Elliott. LC 74-29093. 253p. reprint ed. pap. 78.50 (*0-8357-8994-2*, 205228000085) Bks Demand.

***Power & the Purse: Economic Statecraft, Interdependence & National Security.** Ed. by Jean-Marc F. Blanchard et al. 354p. 2000. 59.50 (*0-7146-5067-6*, Pub. by F Cass Pubs); pap. 24.50 (*0-7146-8116-4*, Pub. by F Cass Pubs) Intl Spec Bk.

Power & the Sacred in Revolutionary Russia: Religious Activists in the Village. Glennys Young. LC 96-52408. 1997. 47.50 (*0-271-01720-1*) Pa St U Pr.

***Power & the Writing: The Early Scribes of Mesopotamia.** Giuseppe Visicato. 316p. 2000. 50.00 (*1-883053-47-1*) CDL Pr.

Power & Timing Modeling for Performance of Integrated Circuits. Ed. by Daniel Auvergne & Reiner Hartenstein. (Microsystems Engineering Ser.: No. 204). (Illus.). 248p. (Orig.). 1993. pap. 42.80 (*0-9639887-4-3*) IT Press.

Power & Value of Philosophical Skepticism. Jeffrey P. Whitman. LC 96-12527. 118p. 1996. 49.50 (*0-8476-8232-3*); pap. 19.50 (*0-8476-8233-1*) Rowman.

Power & Value of Political Skepticism. Jeffrey P. Whitman. 275p. (C). 1995. text 37.50 (*0-89341-727-0*) Hollowbrook.

Power & Violence in a Colonial City: Oruro from the Mining Renaissance to the Rebellion of Tupac Amaru (1740-1782) Oscar Cornblit. (Cambridge Latin American Studies: No. 76). (Illus.). 244p. (C). 1995. text 74.95 (*0-521-44148-X*) Cambridge U Pr.

Power & Virtue: The Horse in Chinese Art. Robert E. Harrist, Jr. Ed. by Emily Walter. (CHI & ENG., Illus.). 115p. (Orig.). 1997. pap. 40.00 (*0-9654270-1-3*) China Institute Gallery.

Power & Weakness. 2nd ed. William Breault. 69p. 1993. pap. 7.00 (*0-910845-51-4*, 594) Landmark Ent.

***Power & Wealth in Rural China: The Political Economy of Institutional Change.** Susan H. Whiting. (Cambridge Modern China Ser.). (Illus.). 328p. 2000. 59.95 (*0-521-62322-7*) Cambridge U Pr.

Power & Wealth of Your Own Business. Kenn Freel. Ed. by Laurel Blankenship. LC 90-90282. 1990. 49.95 (*1-878055-00-3*); lib. bdg. 39.95 (*1-878055-01-1*) Freel Pub.

Power & Wisdom: The New Path for Women, 1. Priscila Marrota. 254p. 1999. pap. text 17.95 (*0-9666339-0-3*) Women Wisdom.

***Power & Wisdom: The New Path for Women, Millennium Edition.** 2nd ed. Priscilla Marotta. 256p. 1999. pap. 17.95 (*0-9666339-1-1*, Pub. by Women Wisdom) BookWorld.

Power Architecture: A Specification for a New Family of RISC Processors. International Business Machines Staff. LC 94-26709. 518p. (C). 1994. text 63.95 (*1-55860-316-6*) Morgan Kaufmann.

Power Astrology: Make the Most of Your Sun Sign. Robin MacNaughton. 287p. 1990. mass mkt. 6.99 (*0-671-67181-2*) PB.

Power at Cost: Ontario Hydro & Rural Electrification, 1911-1958. Keith R. Fleming. 352p. 1991. 65.00 (*0-7735-0868-6*, Pub. by McG-Queens Univ Pr) CUP Services.

Power at Odds: The 1922 National Railroad Shopmen's Strike. Colin J. Davis. LC 96-35702. 272p. 1997. text 49.95 (*0-252-02312-9*); pap. text 19.95 (*0-252-06612-X*) U of Ill Pr.

Power at Play: A Memoir of Parties, Politicians, & the Presidents in My Bedroom. Betty Beale. LC 92-41187. (Illus.). 355p. 1993. 20.00 (*0-89526-503-6*) Regnery Pub.

Power at Play: Sports & the Problem of Masculinity. Michael A. Messner. 256p. 1995. pap. 18.00 (*0-8070-4105-X*) Beacon Pr.

Power at the Top. Clive Jenkins. LC 75-45383. 292p. 1976. reprint ed. lib. bdg. 65.00 (*0-8371-8661-7*, JEPT, Greenwood Pr) Greenwood.

Power, Authority & Restrictive Practices: A Sociological Essay on Industrial Relations Alan Aldridge. LC 77-358899. xviii, 135p. 1976. 5.00 (*0-631-17230-0*) Blackwell Pubs.

Power, Autonomy, Utopia: New Approaches Toward Complex Systems. Ed. by Robert Trappl. (Illus.). 176p. (C). 1986. 90.00 (*0-306-42361-8*, Plenum Trade) Perseus Pubng.

Power Baccarat: The Best Game in the Casino. Byron F. Hebert. 241p. (Orig.). 1994. pap. 19.95 (*0-9635999-3-3*) Hebert & Assocs.

***Power Baccarat 2: Beat the Casino Playing Baccarat.** Byron F. Hebert. Ed. by James R. Katona. LC 98-94140. 287p. 2000. pap. 19.95 (*0-9635999-4-1*) Hebert & Assocs.

Power Baking: A Contemporary American Baking Manual. Kenneth Power. LC 91-66742. 512p. (Orig.). 1991. pap. 149.95 (*1-880650-14-2*) YCart Pub.

Power Balance Therapy & Pattern Change Programing, Bk. 3. Rose A. Parvin. 288p. 1995. lib. bdg. 15.00 (*1-885917-02-3*) Univrsl Pubng.

Power Ballads - Five of the Best. (Play-It-Like-It-Is Guitar Ser.). pap. 9.95 (*0-89524-527-2*) Cherry Lane.

Power Bankers: Sales Culture Secrets of High Performance Banks. Michael F. Price. LC 91-35803. 224p. 1992. 89.95 (*0-471-55555-X*) Wiley.

Power Base Attribution & the Perceived Legitimacy of Managerial Accounting. Roger W. Bartlett. LC 82-23697. (Research for Business Decisions Ser.: No. 57). (Illus.). 145p. reprint ed. pap. 45.00 (*0-8357-1393-8*, 207035800088) Bks Demand.

Power Base Selling: Secrets of in Ivy League Street Fighteru. Jim Holden. 240p. 1992. pap. text 17.50 (*0-471-58297-2*) Wiley.

Power Baseball. Derenne. 1992. mass mkt. 20.00 (*0-314-01849-2*) West Pub.

Power Basics of Baseball. James Bryce et al. LC 84-22839. 109p. (C). 1984. pap. text 5.95 (*0-13-688292-7*, Busn) P-H.

Power Beam Processing: Electron, Laser, Plasma-Arc: Proceedings of the International Power Beam Conference Held May 2-4, 1988, San Diego, CA. Ed. by D. Hauser & Edward A. Metzbower. LC 88-70470. (Illus.). 228p. 1988. reprint ed. pap. 70.70 (*0-608-02647-6*, 206330600004) Bks Demand.

Power Before the Throne. Ruth Rieder. Ed. by Bethany Sledge. (Illus.). 100p. 1999. pap. write for info. (*0-7392-0121-2*, PO3022) Morris Pubng.

Power Behind Positive Thinking: Unlocking Your Spiritual Potential. Eric Fellman. LC 96-20399. 1996. pap. 12.00 (*0-06-062316-0*) Harper SF.

Power Behind the Wheel: Creativity & the Evolution of the Automobile. Walter J. Boyne. (Illus.). 240p. 1991. 19.98 (*0-89660-018-1*, Artabras) Abbeville Pr.

Power Behind Your Eyes see **Poder Detras de Sus Ojos**

Power Behind Your Eyes: Improving Your Eyesight with Integrated Vision Therapy. Robert-Michael Kaplan. (Illus.). 192p. 1995. pap. 16.95 (*0-89281-536-1*) Inner Tradit.

Power! Black Workers, Their Unions, & the Struggle for Freedom in South Africa. Denis MacShane et al. 195p. (Orig.). 1984. pap. 8.00 (*0-89608-244-X*) South End Pr.

Power Blackjack: Use Casino Secrets to Break the Rules & Win with Clump Card Blackjack. Steven Heller. LC 93-80643. 200p. 1994. student ed. 137.00 (*0-9639994-0-0*) H I Ent.

Power Block Ideas for Teachers. Richard Cossen. (Illus.). 87p. (Orig.). 1993. pap. 4.50 (*0-9614646-3-1*) Ctr Innovation.

Power Boat Guide: 1999 Edition. Ed McKnew & Mark Parker. (Illus.). 1700p. 1999. pap. 79.95 (*0-9622134-0-3*) Amer Marine Pub.

Power Boating: The Great Ideas Book: How to Buy & Sell, Equipment, Trailer, Operate, Maintain, Store, & Insure Your Power Boat Successfully! William S. Carpenter. Ed. by Brooke M. Borer. LC 94-78110. (Illus.). 261p. (Orig.). 1995. pap. 19.95 (*1-883818-09-5*) Gemini Marine.

***Power Boats.** Jason Cooper. LC 99-15114. (Boats Ser.). 24p. 1999. lib. bdg. write for info. (*0-86593-564-5*) Rourke Corp.

Power Body: Injury Prevention, Rehabilitation & Sports Performance Enhancement. Tom Seabourne. Ed. by James O'Leary. (Illus.). 160p. 1999. pap. 16.95 (*1-886969-76-0*, Pub. by YMAA Pubn) Natl Bk Netwk.

Power Boilers. Martin D. Bernstein & Lloyd W. Yoder. LC 98-43261. 282p. 1997. 59.95 (*0-7918-0056-3*, 800563) ASME Pr.

Power Branding. Ann Chambers. LC 98-30379. 1998. 74.95 (*0-87814-745-4*) PennWell Bks.

Power Brink: Con Edison, A Centennial of Electricity. Alexander Lurkis. (Illus.). 207p. (Orig.). (C). 1982. 13.95 (*0-9609492-1-6*); pap. 9.95 (*0-9609492-0-8*) ICARE Pr.

Power Broker: Robert Moses & the Fall of New York. Robert A. Caro. LC 73-20751. (Illus.). 1296p. 1974. 50.00 (*0-394-48076-7*) Knopf.

P

An Asterisk (*) at the beginning of an entry indicates that the title is appearing for the first time.

Power Broker: Robert Moses & the Fall of New York. Robert A. Caro. 1975. pap. 24.00 (*0-394-72024-5*) Vin Bks.

Power Brokers. James W. Fraley. LC 94-78058. 1995. pap. 10.95 (*1-885487-06-1*) Brownell & Carroll.

Power Brokers & Kingmakers & Usurpers Throughout History. Rupert O. Matthews. LC 89-31332. 336p. 1989. reprint ed. pap. 104.20 (*0-608-02857-6*, 206392100007) Bks Demand.

Power Builder: Intermediate Level. RuNan Wang. LC 99-173940. 1997. write for info. (*1-889554-38-3*) Yutopian Ent.

Power Builder: Intermediate Level. RuNan Wang & BaoXun Zhu. Tr. by James JyhRen Dee. LC 99-173940. 1997. pap. text 17.50 (*1-889554-39-1*) Yutopian Ent.

Power Builder 4.0: Secrets of the Power Builder Masters: Creating Mission Critical Applications in Power Builder 4. 0. Ed. by Michael MacDonald & Steve Benfield. (Power Engineering Ser.). (Illus.). 600p. 1995. pap. 49.95 (*1-886141-00-2*) SYS-Con Pubns.

Power Building in Documentation. Deborah Montone. Ed. by Adrianne Williams. LC 97-34986. 320p. (C). 1998. pap. text 18.95 (*0-7216-6933-6*, W B Saunders Co) Harcrt Hlth Sci Grp.

Power Building in Scheduling. Deborah Montone. Ed. by Margaret Biblis. 256p. 1997. pap. text 18.95 (*0-7216-6932-8*, W B Saunders Co) Harcrt Hlth Sci Grp.

Power Building in the Money Trail. Deborah Montone. Ed. by Adrianne Williams. LC 98-25996. (Illus.). 430p. (C). 1998. pap. text 24.95 (*0-7216-6931-X*, W B Saunders Co) Harcrt Hlth Sci Grp.

Power Building Medical Coding. Deborah Montone. LC 98-4061. (C). 1998. pap. text 19.95 (*0-7216-6930-1*) Harcourt.

Power Business Reading. Rutter Baumgerten. 1999. 13.95 (*0-538-69222-7*) Thomson Learn.

*__Power Business Writing, Set.__ Patricia Westheimer. (Learn in Your Car - Discovery Ser.). 2000. pap. 15.95 incl. audio (*1-56015-202-8*) Penton Overseas.

Power Buying: How to Get What You Expect Without Negotiations. Godfrey Harris & J. Harris. 128p. 1993. pap. 7.99 (*0-935047-15-8*) Americas Group.

Power by Design: Constitution-Making in Nationalist China. Suisheng Zhao. LC 95-23127. 1996. text 37.00 (*0-8248-1721-4*) UH Pr.

Power Cable Maintainer. Jack Rudman. (Career Examination Ser.: C-653). 1994. pap. 23.95 (*0-8373-0653-1*) Nat Learn.

Power Cables & Their Applications, Pt. 1. 3rd rev. ed. Ed. by L. Heinhold & R. Stubbe. 1990. 155.00 (*3-8009-1535-9*) Wiley.

Power Cables & Their Applications, Vol. 2. 3rd ed. Ed. by L. Heinhold & R. Stubbe. 420p. 1993. 90.00 (*3-8009-1575-8*) Wiley.

Power Calling. Joan Guiducci. 128p. 1992. pap. 14.95 (*1-881833-00-3*) Tonino.

Power Calling, Vol. 2. Joan Guiducci. 1996. pap. text 19.95 (*1-881833-01-1*) Tonino.

Power Capacitors: 1994 Edition. 272p. 107.00 (*1-55937-416-0*, SH17228) IEEE Standards.

Power Carving Birds, Fish & Penguins: Using Beautiful Hardwoods. Gene Larson & Jeffrey B. Snyder. LC 93-87058. (Illus.). 64p. (Orig.). 1994. pap. 12.95 (*0-88740-565-7*) Schiffer.

Power Carving House Spirits with Tom Wolfe. Tom James Wolfe & Jeffrey B. Snyder. LC 96-9896. 64p. (gr. 10). 1997. pap. 12.95 (*0-7643-0183-7*) Schiffer.

Power Carving Santas with Tom Wolfe. Tom James Wolfe & Jeffrey B. Snyder. LC 96-31762. (Illus.). 64p. (YA). (gr. 10). 1997. pap. 12.95 (*0-88740-963-6*) Schiffer.

Power, Caste & Law: Social Conflict in Fourteenth-Century Montpellier. Jan Rogozinski. LC 78-70247. (Medieval Academy Bks.: No. 91). 1982. 30.00 (*0-910956-72-3*) Medieval Acad.

Power Centers. 1994. 99.00 incl. audio PA Bar Inst.

Power Charged for Life! Designing a Championship Attitude. Jeffrey L. Magee. Ed. by Nancy Drissel. 80p. (Orig.). (C). 1994. pap. 12.95 (*0-9641240-1-7*) J Magee Intl.

P

Power Chess: Great Grandmaster Battles from Russia. Ed. by Paul Keres & Burt Hochberg. 320p. 1991. pap. 14.00 (*0-8129-1949-1*, Times Bks) Crown Pub Group.

*__Power Chess Program Bk. 2: The Ultimate Chess Workout.__ Nigel Davies. (Chess Bks). (Illus.). 256p. 1999. pap. text 18.95 (*0-7134-8420-9*) B T B.

Power Chess Program Book 1. N. Davies. 1999. pap. text 19.95 (*0-7134-8415-2*) B T B.

Power, Choice, Governing: A Reader. 2nd ed. Coyer & Smith. (C). 1994. pap. text 17.25 (*0-07-011406-4*) McGraw.

Power Chords for Rock & Blues Guitar. 40p. 1996. pap. 5.95 (*0-7935-4372-X*, 00695016) H Leonard.

Power Circuit Breaker Theory & Design. rev. ed. Ed. by C. H. Flurscheim. (Power Engineering Ser.: No. 1). 606p. 1985. pap. 125.00 (*0-906048-70-2*, P0001) INSPEC Inc.

Power CL. Ted Holt & Ernie Malaga. LC 97-206719. (Illus.). 320p. (Orig.). 1997. pap. 99.00 (*1-883884-41-1*, 570) Midrange Comput.

Power, Class & Foreign Capital in Egypt: The Rise of the New Bourgeoisie. Malak Zaalouk. LC 88-31886. 272p. (C). 1989. pap. 17.50 (*0-86232-223-5*, Pub. by Zed Books); text 55.00 (*0-86232-222-7*, Pub. by Zed Books) St Martin.

*__Power Collecting: Automation for Effective Asset Management.__ Frederick A. Piumelli & David A. Schmidt. LC 97-34854. 352p. 1998. 74.95 (*0-471-18043-2*) Wiley.

Power Color! How to Attract Romance, Wealth, Youth, Vitality, & More! Julia M. Busch & Hollye Davidson. LC 94-75321. (Illus.). 256p. (Orig.). 1994. pap. 14.95 (*0-9632907-1-1*, Kosmic Kurrents) Anti Aging Pr.

Power Communication. Thomas D. Clark. (C). 1993. mass mkt. 26.95 (*0-538-82299-6*, EH60AA) S-W Pub.

Power Communications: Positioning Yourself for High Visibility. Valerie Wiener. LC 93-47480. (C). 1994. text 27.50 (*0-8147-9273-1*) NYU Pr.

Power, Community, & the City: Comparative Urban & Community Research, Vol. 1. Ed. by Michael P. Smith. 196p. (Orig.). 1988. pap. 21.95 (*0-88738-734-9*) Transaction Pubs.

Power, Competition & the State: Britain in Search of Balance, 1940-1961, Vol. 1. Keith Middlemas. (Publication Ser.: No. 349). 404p. (C). 1987. text 14.78 (*0-8179-8491-7*) Hoover Inst Pr.

Power Concealed, Power Revealed: The Arts of Africa. Robin Poyner. Ed. by Gary R. Libby & Sandra L. Miller. (Illus.). 50p. (C). 1988. pap. 5.00 (*0-933053-01-0*) Museum Art Sciences.

Power-Conflict Story: A Dynamic Model of Interstate Rivalry. Kelly M. Kadera. (Illus.). 216p. (C). text 44.50 (*0-472-11191-4*) U of Mich Pr.

Power Connectors: How to Connect to the Spirit's Power & Presence. Siang-Yang Tan & Douglas H. Gregg. LC 96-46084. 208p. 1997. pap. 12.99 (*0-310-20515-8*) Zondervan.

Power, Conscience, & Opposition: Essays in German History in Honour of John A. Moses. Ed. by Martin Travers et al. XIV, 538p. (C). 1996. text 79.95 (*0-8204-2863-9*) P Lang Pubng.

Power Consumer. Robert W. Boyington. 93p. 1992. pap. text. write for info. (*0-9632365-0-4*) Blk Sheep.

Power Consumption & Human Welfare. Ed. by Michael Corr. 1975. write for info. (*0-318-57474-8*) Macmillan Info.

Power Control Exchange Framework of Accounting: Applications to Management Control Systems. Seleshi Sisaye. LC 97-2660. (Studies in Managerial & Financial Accounting: Vol. 5). 231p. 1997. 78.50 (*0-7623-0233-X*) Jai Pr.

Power Conversion Equipment, UL 508C. 2nd ed. (C). 1996. pap. text 95.00 (*0-7629-0093-8*) Underwrtrs Labs.

Power Converters. Brian Taylor. (Illus.). 240p. 1998. pap. text 56.95 (*0-7506-3428-6*, Newnes) Buttrwrth-Heinemann.

Power Converters/Inverters & Power Converter/Inverter Systems for Land Vehicles & Marine Crafts, UL 458. 4th ed. (C). 1993. pap. text 330.00 (*1-55989-212-9*) Underwrtrs Labs.

Power Cookies: The Most Important Day in the Life of Wendy Johnson, Good Girl Extraordinaire. Edward L. Callahan. (Orig.). pap. 6.95 (*0-9637180-0-2*) Groth Pub.

Power Copywriting. Herschell Gordon Lewis. 334p. 1992. pap. text 34.50 (*0-85013-187-1*) Dartnell Corp.

Power Copywriting. Herschell Gordon Lewis. 334p. 1994. pap. 34.50 (*0-85013-227-4*) Dartnell Corp.

Power! CP-M Version. Shari Steiner. (Power User's Manual Ser.). (Orig.). 1983. pap. write for info. (*0-913733-00-8*) Computing.

Power Crime & Mystification. Steven Box. 300p. (Orig.). (C). 1984. pap. 20.99 (*0-415-04572-X*) Routledge.

*__Power Cruising: The Complete Guide to Selecting, Outfitting & Maintaining Your Power Boat.__ 2nd ed. Claiborne S. Young. LC 98-54167. (Illus.). 240p. 1999. pap. 17.95 (*1-56554-635-0*) Pelican.

Power, Culture & Place: Essays on New York City. Ed. by John H. Mollenkopf. LC 88-39077. 320p. 1989. 40.00 (*0-87154-603-5*) Russell Sage.

Power, Culture & Religion in France, 1350-1550. Ed. by Christopher Allmand. (Illus.). 178p. 1989. 75.00 (*0-85115-514-6*) Boydell & Brewer.

Power Curve. Richard Herman, Jr. LC 96-45324. 416p. 1997. mass mkt. 23.00 (*0-380-97320-0*, Avon Bks) Morrow Avon.

Power Curve. Richard Herman. LC 96-45324. 496p. 1998. mass mkt. 6.99 (*0-380-78786-5*, Avon Bks) Morrow Avon.

Power Cycles: A Strategy for Business & Investing Excellence in the 1980's & Beyond. William Kirkland & Doulgas Kirkland. (Illus.). 263p. 1985. 19.95 (*0-9614654-0-9*) Brandt Pub.

Power Cycles & Energy Efficiency: The Enhancement of Efficiency. E. J. Hoffman. (Illus.). 356p. 1996. text 54.95 (*0-12-351940-3*) Acad Pr.

Power Data: Solving Business Problems with Microsoft Access. Bloom. (C). 1996. pap. text. write for info. (*0-201-48325-4*) Addison-Wesley.

Power Dating: How to Have the Power & Confidence You Need to Have Unlimited Success with Women. David Schorr. LC 92-97348. 164p. (Orig.). 1993. pap. 10.95 (*0-9635214-4-6*) Courtyard Pub.

Power Deck: The Cards of Wisdom. Lynn V. Andrews. LC 90-56474. (Illus.). 114p. (Orig.). 1991. pap., boxed set 30.00 (*0-06-250078-3*, Pub. by Harper SF) HarpC.

Power Density Development: The Role of Improved Line Contact Performance. Charles A. Moyer. (Nineteen Eighty-Nine Fall Technical Meeting Ser.: Vol. 89FTM3). (Illus.). 10p. 1989. pap. text 30.00 (*1-55589-538-7*) AGMA.

Power Development. Paul Sheriff. (Visual Basic Power Guides Ser.). 134p. 1994. spiral bd. 69.00 (*1-886213-01-1*) Bldg Blocks.

*__Power Dialogues: The Ultimate System for Personal Change, Vol. 1.__ rev. ed. Barry Neil Kaufman. 336p. 2000. 49.95 (*1-887254-06-4*) Epic Century.

Power Direct Marketing: How to Make It Work for You. Ray Jutkins. (Illus.). 320p. 1995. 39.95 (*0-8442-3254-8*, NTC Business Bks) NTC Contemp Pub Co.

Power Direct Marketing: How to Make It Work for You. 2nd ed. Ray Jutkins. LC 98-54274. 320p. 1999. 39.95 (*0-8442-4298-5*, 42985, NTC Business Bks) NTC Contemp Pub Co.

Power Discipleship. Patricia B. Craig. LC 98-90516. 1999. pap. 12.95 (*0-533-12828-5*) Vantage.

Power Distribution Engineering: Fundamentals & Applications. James J. Burke. LC 94-11103. (Electrical Engineering & Electronics Ser.: Vol. 88). (Illus.). 376p. 1994. text 125.00 (*0-8247-9237-8*) Dekker.

*__Power Distribution in Saudi Arabia: A Strategic Entry Report, 1999.__ Compiled by Icon Group International. (Illus.). 134p. 1999. ring bd. 1340.00 incl. audio compact disk (*0-7418-1818-3*) Icon Grp.

Power Distribution Maintainer. Jack Rudman. (Career Examination Ser.: C-1394). 1994. pap. 23.95 (*0-8373-1394-5*) Nat Learn.

Power Distribution Planning Reference Book. H. Lee Willis. LC 97-13116. (Illus.). 832p. 1997. text 165.00 (*0-8247-0098-8*) Dekker.

Power Divided: Essays on the Theory & Practice of Federalism: Papers from the Third Berkeley Seminar on Federalism. Berkeley Seminar on Federalism (3rd, 1988) Staff. Ed. by Harry N. Scheiber et al. LC 89-15593. 179p. reprint ed. pap. 55.50 (*0-608-20121-9*, 207139300011) Bks Demand.

Power Dome. Edward Packard. (Choose Your Own Adventure Ser.: No. 174). (J). (gr. 4-8). 1996. 8.60 (*0-606-09764-3*, Pub. by Turtleback) Demco.

Power, Dominance & Nonverbal Behavior. Ed. by S. L. Ellyson & J. F. Dovidio. (Social Psychology Ser.). (Illus.). 420p. 1985. 84.95 (*0-387-96133-X*) Spr-Verlag.

Power Dreamers: The Jocasta Complex. Ursule Molinaro. 128p. 1994. 16.00 (*0-929701-44-5*) McPherson & Co.

*__Power Drills for Team Tennis.__ Renata Marcin Kowska. 149p. 1999. pap. 14.95 (*1-893009-04-1*) Summertown.

*__Power-Dry-Cutting of Bevel Gears.__ H. J. Stadtfeld. (Technical Papers: Vol. 99FTM8). 10p. 1999. pap. 30.00 (*1-55589-746-0*) AGMA.

Power Eating. Susan M. Kleiner & Maggie Greenwood-Robinson. LC 97-43566. (Illus.). 240p. 1998. pap. 15.95 (*0-88011-702-8*, PKLE0702) Human Kinetics.

*__Power Eating: How to Play Hard & Eat Smart for the Time of Your Life.__ rev. ed. Frances Berkoff et al. LC TX361.A8B47. (Illus.). 240p. 2000. pap. 17.95 (*1-55263-111-7*, Pub. by Key Porter) Firefly Bks Ltd.

Power Eating Program: You Are How You Eat. Lino Stanchich. (Illus.). (Orig.). (C). 1989. write for info. (*0-318-65751-1*) Healthy Prods.

Power Economics for the Next Generation. David J. Pristash. Ed. by Catherine L. Yuschak. (Illus.). 266p. (C). 1997. pap. 29.95 (*0-9657318-0-4*) Pub Systs.

*__Power, Effectiveness & Spirit: A New Paradigm for Human Potential & Pratical Steps for Archiving It.__ Lynn Woodland. 336p. 1999. pap. 16.95 (*1-890676-46-2*) Beavers Pond.

Power Electronic Converter Harmonics: Multipulse Methods for Clean Power. Derek A. Paice. LC 95-33342. 224p. 1995. 69.95 (*0-7803-1137-X*, PC5604) Inst Electrical.

Power Electronic Converters: DC-AC Conversion. G. Seguier & F. Labrique. (Electric Energy Systems & Engineering Ser.). (Illus.). 450p. 1993. 158.95 (*0-387-54974-9*) Spr-Verlag.

Power Electronic Converters: DC-DC Conversion. R. Bausiere et al. Ed. by John G. Kassakian & D. H. Naunin. LC 92-10524. (Electric Energy Systems & Engineering Ser.).Tr. of Les/Convertisseurs de l'Electronique de Puissance. (Illus.). 360p. 1993. 158.95 (*0-387-54760-6*) Spr-Verlag.

Power Electronic Maintainer. Jack Rudman. (Career Examination Ser.: C-3180). 1994. pap. 23.95 (*0-8373-3180-3*) Nat Learn.

Power Electronic Systems: Theory & Design. Jai P. Agrawal. 704p. (C). 2000. 98.00 (*0-13-442880-3*, Macmillan Coll) P-H.

Power Electronics. F. Csaki et al. 708p. (C). 1983. 168.00 (*963-05-3530-0*, Pub. by Akade Kiado) St Mut.

Power Electronics. F. Czaki et al. 708p. 1980. 410.00 (*0-569-08185-8*, Pub. by Collets) St Mut.

*__Power Electronics.__ Jacob. (Student Material TV Ser.). (C). 2001. text 57.75 (*0-7668-2332-6*) Delmar.

Power Electronics. 2nd ed. D. A. Bradley. 1994. pap. 34.95 (*0-412-57100-5*, Chap & Hall NY) Chapman & Hall.

Power Electronics. 3rd ed. Cyril W. Lander. LC 92-44563. (C). 1994. text 49.38 (*0-07-707714-8*) McGraw.

Power Electronics: Circuits, Devices, & Applications. 2nd ed. Muhammed H. Rashid. 650p. 1993. text 95.00 (*0-13-678996-X*) P-H.

Power Electronics: Converters, Applications & Design. 2nd ed. Ned Mohan et al. 824p. 1995. text 99.95 (*0-471-58408-8*) Wiley.

Power Electronics: Principles & Applications. Joseph Vithayathil. 512p. (C). 1995. 80.94 (*0-07-067555-4*) McGraw.

Power Electronics & Motor Control. 2nd ed. W. Shepherd et al. (Illus.). 563p. (C). 1996. text 145.00 (*0-521-47241-5*); pap. text 57.95 (*0-521-47813-8*) Cambridge U Pr.

Power Electronics & Variable Frequency Drives: Technology & Applications. Ed. by Bimal K. Bose. LC 96-6092. 664p. 1996. 94.95 (*0-7803-1084-5*, PC4382) Inst Electrical.

Power Electronics & Variable-Speed Drives: Proceedings of the Fifth International Conference, Savoy Place, London, 1994. (Conference Publications: No. 399). 715p. 1994. pap. 232.00 (*0-85296-625-3*) INSPEC Inc.

Power Electronics Applied. Jai P. Agrawal. (C). 2001. 70.00 (*0-13-442872-2*, Macmillan Coll) P-H.

Power Electronics Design Handbook: Low-Power Components & Applications. Nihal Kularatna. LC 98-8326. 300p. 1998. text 59.95 (*0-7506-7073-8*, Newnes) Buttrwrth-Heinemann.

Power Electronics for Technology. Ashfaq Ahmed. LC 98-15732. 427p. 1998. 105.00 (*0-13-231069-4*) P-H.

Power Electronics for the Microprocessor Age. Takashi Kenjo. (Illus.). 360p. 1994. reprint ed. pap. text 50.00 (*0-19-856508-9*) OUP.

Power Electronics Handbook. 3rd ed. F. F. Mazda. LC 98-134644. 448p. 1999. pap. text 54.95 (*0-7506-2926-6*) Buttrwrth-Heinemann.

*__Power Electronics in Transportation: October 22-23, 1998, Dearborn, Michigan__ Institute of Electrical & Electronics Engineers Staff & IEEE, Power Electronics Society Staff. LC 97-80778. 1998. pap. write for info. incl. fiche (*0-7803-4399-9*) IEEE Standards.

Power Electronics Lab Using Spice. Muhammad Ho Rashid. Ed. by Richard Bass. 1996. lab manual ed. 349.00 (*0-7803-2309-2*, HL5721) Inst Electrical.

Power Electronics, Problems Manual. Ed. by F. Csaki et al. 474p. (C). 1979. 114.00 (*963-05-1671-3*, Pub. by Akade Kiado) St Mut.

Power Electronics, Problems Manual. F. Czaki et al. Ed. by A. Karpati & P. Magyar. 476p. 1979. 435.00 (*0-569-08554-3*, Pub. by Collets) St Mut.

Power Electronics Technology & Applications. Ed. by Pierre A. Thollot. LC 92-35704. (IEEE Technology Update Ser.). 1992. 49.95 (*0-7803-0880-8*) Inst Electrical.

Power Elite. 2nd ed. C. Wright Mills. LC 99-16200. (Illus.). 448p. 2000. pap. 17.95 (*0-19-513354-4*) OUP.

Power Elite & the State: How Policy Is Made in America. G. William Domhoff. LC 90-393. (Social Institutions & Social Change Ser.). 334p. 1990. pap. text 29.95 (*0-202-30373-X*) Aldine de Gruyter.

Power Elites & Organizations. Ed. by G. William Domhoff & Thomas R. Dye. LC 85-30432. (Sage Focus Editions Ser.: No. 82). 292p. (Orig.). 1987. reprint ed. pap. 90.60 (*0-608-01456-7*, 205950000001) Bks Demand.

Power Elites & State Building. Ed. by Wolfgang Reinhard. (The Origins of the Modern State in Europe Ser.). (Illus.). 332p. (C). 1996. text 85.00 (*0-19-820547-3*) OUP.

*__Power, Employment & Accumulation: Social Structures in Economic Theory & Practice.__ Ed. by Jim Stanford et al. (Illus.). 296p. 2000. text 74.95 (*0-7656-0630-5*) M E Sharpe.

Power Encounter see Enfrentamiento de Poderes

Power Encounters: Reclaiming Spiritual Warfare. David Powlison. 160p. 1994. pap. 9.99 (*0-8010-7138-0*, Hour Glass) Baker Bks.

Power Engineering Society Winter Meeting, 1999 IEEE. 1400p. 1999. audio compact disk 234.00 (*0-7803-4896-6*) IEEE Standards.

Power Engineering '84: Proceedings, IASTED Symposium, New Orleans, U. S. A., November 12-14, 1984. Ed. by M. H. Hamza. 86p. 1984. 45.00 (*0-88986-071-8*, 081) Acta Pr.

Power English & Word Command, Bk. 1. Ed. by Margaret M. Bynum. 64p. (Orig.). (YA). (gr. 10-12). 1986. student ed. 15.00 (*0-913286-97-4*) Learn Inc.

Power English & Word Command, Bk. 2. Ed. by Margaret M. Bynum. 96p. (Orig.). (gr. 10-12). 1986. pap., student ed. 15.00 (*0-913286-98-2*) Learn Inc.

Power English & Word Command, Bk. 3. Margaret M. Bynum. 32p. (Orig.). (gr. 10-12). 1986. pap., student ed. 15.00 (*0-913286-99-0*) Learn Inc.

Power English Eight: Basic Language Skills for Adults. Dorothy Rubin. (C). 1989. pap. text 5.85 (*0-13-688516-0*) P-H.

Power English Five: Basic Language Skills for Adults. Dorothy Rubin. (C). 1989. pap. text 5.85 (*0-13-688482-2*) P-H.

Power English Four: Basic Language Skills for Adults. Dorothy Rubin. (C). 1989. pap. text 5.85 (*0-13-688474-1*) P-H.

Power English Nine: Basic Language Skills for Adults. Dorothy Rubin. (C). 1990. pap. text 5.85 (*0-13-688524-1*) P-H.

Power English One: Basic Language Skills for Adults. Dorothy Rubin. 128p. (C). 1989. pap. text 5.85 (*0-13-688441-5*) P-H.

Power English Seven: Basic Language Skills for Adults. Dorothy Rubin. (C). 1989. pap. text 5.85 (*0-13-688508-X*) P-H.

Power English Six: Basic Language Skills for Adults. Dorothy Rubin. (C). 1989. pap. text 5.85 (*0-13-688490-3*) P-H.

Power English Three: Basic Language Skills for Adults. Dorothy Rubin. (C). 1989. pap. text 5.85 (*0-13-688466-0*) P-H.

Power English Two: Basic Language Skills for Adults. Dorothy Rubin. (C). 1989. pap. text 5.85 (*0-13-688458-X*) P-H.

Power Equity Group: A Guide for Understanding Equity & Acknowledging Diversity. Carol J. Pierce. 180p. 1998. pap. 24.00 (*0-929767-05-5*) New Dynam Pubns.

Power, Ethics, & Human Rights: Studies of Refugee Research & Action. Ed. by Ruth M. Krulfeld & Jeffery L. MacDonald. LC 98-28141. 275p. 1998. 60.00 (*0-8476-8897-6*) Rowman.

Power, Ethics & Human Rights: Studies of Refugee Research & Action. Ed. by Ruth M. Krulfeld & Jeffery L. MacDonald. LC 98-28141. 275p. 1998. pap. 22.95 (*0-8476-8898-4*) Rowman.

Power Etiquette: What You Don't Know Can Kill Your Career. Dana M. Casperson. LC 98-49831. 150p. 1999. pap. 21.95 (*0-8144-7998-7*) AMACOM.

Power Evangelism see Evangelizacion Poderosa

Power Excel for Windows 95. James G. Meade. 1995. pap. 29.95 (*1-55828-440-0*, MIS Pr) IDG Bks.

*__Power Factor Specialization: Abs & Legs.__ Peter Sisco & John R. Little. LC 99-41278. (Illus.). 256 p. 2000. pap. 17.95 (*0-8092-2827-0*, 282700, Contemporary Bks) NTC Contemp Pub Co.

An Asterisk (*) at the beginning of an entry indicates that the title is appearing for the first time.

Power Factor Specialization: Chest & Arms. Peter Sisco & John Little. LC 98-46770. (Illus.). 256p. 1999. pap. 17.95 (*0-8092-2829-7*, 282970, Contemporary Bks) NTC Contemp Pub Co.

Power Factor Specialization: Shoulders & Back. Peter Sisco & John Little. LC 99-38196. 256p. 1999. pap. 17.95 (*0-8092-2828-9*, 282890, Contemporary Bks) NTC Contemp Pub Co.

Power Factor Training. Peter Sisco & John Little. LC 97-2345. (Illus.). 256p. 1997. pap. 15.95 (*0-8092-3071-2*, 307120, Contemporary Bks) NTC Contemp Pub Co.

Power Failure. Mary O'Neill. LC 90-11148. (SOS Planet Earth Ser.). (Illus.). 32p. (J). (gr. 3-6). 1997. pap. 4.95 (*0-8167-2289-7*) Troll Communs.

Power Failure: New York City Politics & Policy since 1960. Charles Brecher et al. 416p. (C). 1993. 35.00 (*0-19-504427-4*) OUP.

Power Faith: Balancing Faith in Words & Work. Ed. by Jack W. Hayford. LC 97-216744. 1994. pap. 6.99 (*0-8407-2094-7*) Nelson.

Power-Filled Living. R. A. Torrey. LC 99-11399. Orig. Title: Torrey on Power-Filled Living. 713p. 1999. pap. 17.99 (*0-88368-550-7*) Whitaker Hse.

Power Flatpicking Guitar. Steve Kaufman. 68p. 1994. pap. 9.95 (*1-56222-999-0*, 95108) Mel Bay.

Power Focus: Reconstruction of Self Through Mental Imagery. Jerry D. Mathes, II. LC 94-24971. 1994. 16.95 (*1-885018-04-5*); pap. 9.95 (*1-885018-05-3*) Logo Press.

***Power Foods.** Ed. by Editors of Prevention Health Books. 256p. 2000. pap. 5.99 (*0-312-97519-8*, St Martins Paperbacks) St Martin.

***Power Foods: Good Food, Good Health with Phytochemicals, Nature's Own Energy Boosters.** Stephanie Beling. 372p. 2000. text 25.00 (*0-7881-9021-0*) DIANE Pub.

Power Foods: High-Performance Nutrition for High-Performance People. Liz Applegate. 304p. 1994. pap. 14.95 (*0-87596-219-X*) Rodale Pr Inc.

Power for God's Sake: Power & Abuse in the Local Church. Paul Beasley-Murray. xiv, 194p. 1998. reprint ed. pap. 14.99 (*0-85364-899-9*, Pub. by Paternoster Pub) OM Literature.

***Power for Good: The History of Trinity Parish, Columbus, Georgia.** Lynn Willoughby. LC 99-45016. 1999. write for info. (*1-57312-309-9*) Smyth & Helwys.

Power for Living. Melvin Banks. pap. 5.99 (*0-551-01881-X*) Zondervan.

Power for Living. F. B. Meyer. 126p. 1997. pap. 8.99 (*1-84030-006-X*) Emerald House Group Inc.

Power for Living: Christian Leaders Share Principles That Will Change Your Life. Hal Donaldson & Kenneth M. Dobson. 250p. 1996. pap. text 11.95 (*1-880689-06-5*) Onward Bks.

Power for Living: Through the Psalms. 80p. 1998. pap. 10.00 (*0-9662633-0-8*) March Faith.

***Power for Living in These Days.** Charles A. Swan. LC 99-93886. 2000. pap. 10.95 (*0-533-13184-7*) Vantage.

Power for Reading. 3rd ed. (C). 1991. write for info. (*0-8087-7355-0*) Pearson Custom.

***Power for Resurrection's Flight: Poems.** Albert Steffen. (Illus.). 172p. 1998. pap. 16.95 (*0-932776-23-X*) Adonis Pr.

Power for Sanity: Selected Editorials of William Cullen Bryant, 1829-1861. Ed. by William C. Bryant. LC 93-44266. (Illus.). 321p. (C). 1994. 30.00 (*0-8232-1543-1*); pap. 20.00 (*0-8232-1544-X*) Fordham.

Power for Service. rev. ed. Jessie Penn-Lewis. LC 98-210095. 94p. 1988. pap. 5.99 (*0-87508-732-9*, Discov Hse) Chr Lit.

Power for the Abandoned Woman: Confronting the Victim Illusion. Carolyn Gabriel. Ed. by Judith D. Shellabarger. (Illus.). 86p. (Orig.). 1995. pap. 8.95 (*1-888368-00-4*) RUSA.

***Power for the Abandoned Woman: Confronting the Victim Illusion, Vol. 1.** Carolyn Gabriel. (Orig.). 1999. pap. 9.95 incl. audio (*1-888368-04-7*) RUSA.

Power for the MTA. (Illus.). 90p. 1977. 10.00 (*0-318-16374-8*); 7.00 (*0-318-16375-6*) Regional Plan Assn.

Power for the People: A Public Interest Blueprint for Electricity Restructuring. Public Citizen Staff et al. 20p. (Orig.). 1996. pap. 20.00 (*0-937188-27-1*) Pub Citizen.

Power for the Use of Man. 127p. 1978. 26.00 (*0-7277-0067-7*, Pub. by T Telford) RCH.

Power for Victorious Christian Living. R. W. Scambach. (Pocket Classics Ser.). 45p. 1995. pap. 3.00 (*1-888361-07-7*) Power Publns.

Power for Yachts. Tom Cox. (Illus.). 1975. 29.95 (*0-8464-0739-6*) Beekman Pubs.

Power for You. Charles H. Spurgeon. LC 97-213270. 167p. 1996. pap. 6.99 (*0-88368-379-2*) Whitaker Hse.

Power for Your Life. Andrew Murray. Orig. Title: Spirit of Christ. 238p. 1984. mass mkt. 5.99 (*0-88368-396-2*) Whitaker Hse.

Power Forearms. Health for Life Staff. (Illus.). 32p. (Orig.). 1984. pap. 11.95 (*0-944831-06-0*) Health Life.

Power, Form & Mind. Arthur Berndtson. LC 80-65658. 296p. 1981. 38.50 (*0-8387-5010-9*) Bucknell U Pr.

Power Freelancing: Home-Based Careers for Writers, Designers, & Consultants. George Sorenson. LC 95-12291. 192p. (Orig.). 1995. pap. 14.95 (*0-922811-20-2*) Mid-List.

Power Frequency & Electromagnetic Fields. 1991. lib. bdg. 77.95 (*0-8490-4978-4*) Gordon Pr.

Power Frequency Magnetic Fields & Public Health. William F. Horton & Saul Goldberg. LC 95-23092. 288p. 1995. boxed set 89.95 (*0-8493-9420-1*, 9420) CRC Pr.

Power from Above: The Gift of the Holy Spirit to the Body of Christ. Rod Parsley. 48p. (Orig.). Date not set. 1.00 (*0-614-10667-2*) Wrld Harvest Church.

***Power From God to Forgive.** John L. Young. Ed. by Jim Chavez, Sr. (Illus.). 211p. 2000. pap. 14.95 (*0-9700141-0-4*) J L Young.

Power from on High. Charles G. Finney. 1989. pap. 5.99 (*0-87508-190-8*) Chr Lit.

Power from on High. Charles G. Finney. LC 97-207237. 160p. 1996. mass mkt. 5.99 (*0-88368-397-0*) Whitaker Hse.

Power from on High: The Development of Mormon Priesthood. Gregory A. Prince. LC 95-7802. 240p. 1995. 24.95 (*1-56085-071-X*) Signature Bks.

Power from on High: The Spirit in Israel's Restoration & Witness in Luke - Acts. Max Turner. (Journal of Pentecostal Theology Supplement Ser.: No. 9). 550p. 1996. pap. 49.50 (*1-85075-756-9*, Pub. by Sheffield Acad) CUP Services.

Power from on High: The Story of the Great Moravian Revival of 1727. John Greenfield. 96p. 1989. reprint ed. pap. 4.00 (*1-878422-03-0*) Moravian Ch in Amer.

Power from Plants: The Global Implications of New Technologies for Electricity from Biomass. Walt Patterson et al. 80p. (C). 1994. pap. 14.95 (*1-85383-208-1*) Brookings.

Power from Steam: A History of the Stationary Steam Engine. Richard Hills. (Illus.). 354p. (C). 1993. pap. text 33.95 (*0-521-45834-X*) Cambridge U Pr.

Power from the Appalachians: A Solution to the Northeast's Electricity Problems?, 89. Frank J. Calzonetti et al. LC 88-28399. (Contributions in Economics & Economic History Ser.: No. 89). 249p. 1989. 59.95 (*0-313-25797-3*, CZW, Greenwood Pr) Greenwood.

Power from the Sun: Principles of High Temperature Solar Thermal Technology. 1991. lib. bdg. 250.00 (*0-8490-4212-7*) Gordon Pr.

Power from the Waves. David Ross. (Illus.). 224p. 1996. 40.00 (*0-19-856511-9*) OUP.

Power Funding: Gaining Access to Power, Money & Influence in Your Community. David Emenhiser. 189p. 1992. 45.00 (*0-930807-33-2*, 600332) Fund Raising.

Power FX 5.0 Addendum. Alan Chan. 174p. (Orig.). 1996. pap. 24.95 (*0-9655313-1-7*) Lghtspeed.

Power Game. Perry Henzell. 1997. 27.95 (*0-8038-9402-3*) Hastings.

Power Game. Hedrick Smith. 1996. pap. 16.00 (*0-345-41048-3*) Ballantine Pub Grp.

Power Game. Hedrick Smith. 1988. mass mkt. (*0-394-20622-3*) Random.

***Power Game: The History of Formula 1 & the World Championship.** Ivan Rendall. 2000. 29.95 (*0-304-35399-X*) Continuum.

Power Games. Penny Jordan. 1996. per. 5.99 (*1-55166-162-4*, 1-66162-8, Mira Bks) Harlequin Bks.

Power Games: Why Winners Win & Losers Lose. Gerald Alper. 153p. 1999. pap. 24.95 (*1-57309-397-1*) Intl Scholars.

Power, Gender & Christian Mysticism. Grace M. Jantzen. (Studies in Ideology & Religion: No. 8). (Illus.). 403p. (C). 1996. pap. text 24.95 (*0-521-47926-6*) Cambridge U Pr.

Power Generation & Distribution Equipment in Germany: A Strategic Entry Report, 1997. Compiled by Icon Group International Staff. (Illus.). 101p. 1999. ring bd. 1010.00 incl. audio compact disk (*0-7418-1010-7*) Icon Grp.

Power Generation & the Environment. L. E. Roberts et al. (Science, Technology, & Society Ser.: No. 6). (Illus.). 224p. 1990. 55.00 (*0-19-858338-9*) OUP.

Power Generation Conference: Environmental Control/Fuels & Combustion Technologies/Nuclear Engineering, Proceedings. Ed. by Sanyal Anupam et al. LC 96-78524. 688p. 1997. pap. 170.00 (*0-7918-1577-3*) ASME.

Power Generation Conference, 1997: Power, Proceedings, Vol. 2. Larry Kielasa & Al Clary. LC 97-76701. 700p. 1997. pap. 170.00 (*0-7918-1578-1*) ASME.

Power Generation Conference, 1996 Vol. 2: Power; Proceedings, International Joint Power Generation Conference (1996: Houston, Tx) Ed. by Larry Kielasa & George E. Weed. LC 96-78523. (PWR Ser.: Vol. 30). 926p. 1997. pap. 230.00 (*0-7918-1796-2*) ASME Pr.

***Power Generation Conference, 1998: Fuels & Combustion Technologies, Gas Turbines, Environmental Engineering, Nuclear Engineering; Proceedings, Vol. 1.** Ed. by Ashwani K. Gupta. 910p. 1998. 200.00 (*0-7918-1877-2*) ASME.

***Power Generation Conference, 1998: Power, Proceedings.** J. Ledger. LC TK101.I62 1998. 972p. 1998. 200.00 (*0-7918-1878-0*) ASME.

***Power Generation, Distribution & Transportation Equipment in Mexico: A Strategic Entry Report, 1995.** Compiled by Icon Group International Staff. (Illus.). 179p. 1999. ring bd. 1790.00 incl. audio compact disk (*0-7418-1568-0*) Icon Grp.

Power Generation, Energy Management & Environmental Sourcebook. Association of Energy Engineers Staff & Fairmont Press Staff. Ed. by M. Jackson. 636p. 1991. pap. 75.00 (*0-13-678285-X*) P-H.

Power Generation, Energy Management & Environmental Sourcebook. Ed. by Marilyn Jackson. (Illus.). 620p. 1991. pap. 75.00 (*0-88173-147-1*, 0281) Fairmont Pr.

Power Generation Equipment & Services in Vietnam: A Strategic Entry Report, 1997. Compiled by Icon Group International Staff. (Illus.). 156p. 1999. ring bd. 1560.00 incl. audio compact disk (*0-7418-0830-7*) Icon Grp.

Power Generation Equipment in Japan: A Strategic Entry Report, 1998. Compiled by Icon Group International Staff. (Country Industry Report). (Illus.). 160p. 1999. ring bd. 1600.00 incl. audio compact disk (*0-7418-0471-9*) Icon Grp.

***Power Generation Equipment in Kazakhstan: A Strategic Entry Report, 1999.** Compiled by Icon Group International. (Illus.). 136p. 1999. ring bd. 1360.00 incl. audio compact disk (*0-7418-1819-1*) Icon Grp.

Power Generation in Saudi Arabia: A Strategic Entry Report, 1998. Compiled by Icon Group International Staff. (Country Industry Report). (Illus.). 132p. 1999. ring bd. 1320.00 incl. audio compact disk (*0-7418-0472-7*) Icon Grp.

***Power Generation Investment & Financing in China: A Strategic Entry Report, 1999.** Compiled by Icon Group International. (Illus.). 178p. 1999. ring bd. 1780.00 incl. audio compact disk (*0-7418-1822-1*) Icon Grp.

Power Generation Market in United Kingdom: A Strategic Entry Report, 1997. Compiled by Icon Group International Staff. (Illus.). 110p. 1999. ring bd. 1100.00 incl. audio compact disk (*0-7418-0833-1*) Icon Grp.

Power Generation, Operation & Control. 2nd ed. Allen J. Wood & Bruce F. Wollenberg. LC 95-10876. 592p. 1996. 89.95 (*0-471-58699-4*) Wiley.

Power Generation Options: Rehabilitation for Life Extension & Cogeneration. 59p. 20.00 (*92-1-104421-9*) UN.

***Power Generation Upgrading Equipment in Russia: A Strategic Entry Report, 1996.** Compiled by Icon Group International Staff. (Illus.). 139p. 1999. ring bd. 1390.00 incl. audio compact disk (*0-7418-1200-2*) Icon Grp.

***Power, Globalization & Democracy.** Marc F. Plattner & Aleksander Smolar. LC 00-33040. (Journal of Democracy Book Ser.). 180p. 2000. 16.95 (*0-8018-6568-9*) Johns Hopkins.

Power Golf. Ben Hogan. 1990. per. 6.50 (*0-671-72905-5*) PB.

Power Golf. Ian Woosnam. LC 98-14388. 128p. 1992. pap. 16.95 (*1-55821-196-9*) Burford Bks.

Power Golf for Women: How to Hit Longer & Straighter from Tee to Green. Jane Horn. LC 99-14069. (Illus.). 176p. 1999. pap. 18.95 (*0-8065-2070-1*, Citadel Pr) Carol Pub Group.

Power Grab: How the National Education Association Is Betraying our Kids. G. Gregory Moo. LC 99-28645. 308p. 1999. 24.95 (*0-89526-315-7*) Regnery Pub.

Power Graphics Using Turbo C. Namir C. Shammas & Keith Weiskamp. LC 88-35177. 367p. 1989. pap. 24.95 (*0-471-61909-4*) Wiley.

Power Graphics Using Turbo C Plus Plus. 2nd ed. Loren Heiny. LC 93-36768. 447p. 1994. pap. 27.95 (*0-471-30929-X*) Wiley.

Power Graphics Using Turbo Pascal 6.0: A Coriolis Group Book. Keith Weiskamp & Loren Heiny. LC 91-14337. 400p. 1991. pap. 26.95 (*0-471-54736-0*) Wiley.

***Power Grooves.** Dave Lombardo. 48p. 1999. pap. 14.95 incl. audio compact disk (*0-7935-8849-9*) H Leonard.

Power GUI Programming with Visual Age C++ Hiroshi Tsuji et al. LC 96-49964. 800p. 1996. pap. text 54.95 incl. cd-rom (*0-471-16482-8*) Wiley.

Power Guide: An International Catalog of Small-Scale Energy Equipment. Wim Hulscher & Peter Fraenkel. (Illus.). 240p. (Orig.). 1994. pap. 47.50 (*1-85339-192-1*, Pub. by Intermed Tech) Stylus Pub VA.

Power Handling & Electrostatics: Understanding & Preventing Hazards. T. B. Jones & J. L. King. 120p. 1991. lib. bdg. 110.00 (*0-87371-488-1*, L488) Lewis Pubs.

Power Harp. Phil Duncan & Charlie Musselwhite. 96p. 1997. spiral bd. 19.95 incl. cd-rom (*0-7866-2875-8*, 94359BCD) Mel Bay.

Power Healing see Sanidad Poderosa

Power Healing. John Wimber. 320p. 1991. pap. 13.00 (*0-06-069541-2*, Pub. by Harper SF) HarpC.

Power Healing: Use the New Integrated Medicine to Cure Yourself. Leo Galland. 352p. 1998. pap. 14.95 (*0-375-75139-4*) Random.

***Power Herbs: A Practical Guide to Fifty Healing Herbs from the East & West.** Louis J. Vanrenen. 192p. 2000. pap. 12.95 (*1-58542-033-6*, Tarcher Putnam) Putnam Pub Group.

Power House: Creative Youth Programs. Mark Boykin. LC 86-83180. (Illus.). 336p. 1987. teacher ed., ring bd. 29.95 (*0-88243-852-2*, 02-0852) Gospel Pub.

Power House: House of Prayer. Marilyn J. Wright. (Illus.). 60p. (C). 1995. pap. 12.50 (*1-886232-40-7*) Majesty Pubns.

Power Hungry. Howard Weinstein. Ed. by Dave Stern. (Star Trek: The Next Generation Ser.: No. 6). 1991. mass mkt. 5.50 (*0-671-74648-0*) PB.

Power Hybrid Circuit Design Manufacture. Haim Taraseiskey. (Electrical Engineering & Electronics Ser.: Vol. 96). (Illus.). 336p. 1996. text 135.00 (*0-8247-9749-3*) Dekker.

Power! IBM PC Version. Shari Steiner. (Power User's Manual Ser.). 1983. pap. write for info. (*0-913733-01-6*) Computing.

Power Ideas for a Happy Family. Robert H. Schuller. 128p. 1982. mass mkt. 3.99 (*0-515-06499-8*, Jove) Berkley Pub.

Power, Ideology, & Control. J. C. Oliga. (Contemporary Systems Thinking Ser.). (Illus.). 344p. (C). 1996. 69.50 (*0-306-45160-3*, Plenum Trade) Perseus Pubng.

Power, Ideology, & the War on Drugs: Nothing Succeeds Like Failure. Christina J. Johns. LC 91-35017. (Criminology & Crime Control Policy Ser.). 224p. 1992. 59.95 (*0-275-94167-1*, C4167, Praeger Pubs) Greenwood.

Power, Impartiality, & Justice. Peter G. Woolcock. (Avebury Series in Philosophy). 319p. (C). 1998. text 72.95 (*1-84014-505-6*, Pub. by Ashgate Pub) Ashgate Pub Co.

Power in American State Legislatures, Vol. 11. Ed. by Alex B. Lacy, Jr. LC 74-216. 1966. 11.00 (*0-930598-10-5*) Tulane Stud Pol.

Power in American State Legislatures: The Case Studies of the Arkansas, Louisiana, Mississippi, & Oklahoma Legislatures. Ed. by Alex B. Lacy, Jr. LC 74-216. (Tulane Studies in Political Science: No. 11). 187p. Date not set. reprint ed. pap. 58.00 (*0-608-20655-5*, 207209200003) Bks Demand.

Power in Buildings: An Artist's View of Contemporary Architecture. Hugh Ferriss. LC 98-6442. (Illus.). 102p. 1998. reprint ed. 37.50 (*0-940512-11-4*) Hennessey.

Power in Doing Something Different. V. Wendell Hylton. Ed. by O. M. Weatherspoon. 150p. 1994. pap. text 15.00 (*1-885390-00-9*) V W H & Assocs.

Power in Europe? Great Britain, France, Italy & Germany in a Postwar World, 1945-1950, Contributions to an International Colloquim at Augsburg, April 1984. Ed. by Josef Becker & Franz Knipping. viii, 583p. 1986. lib. bdg. 169.25 (*3-11-010608-6*) De Gruyter.

Power in Europe? II: Great Britain, France, Germany & Italy & the History of the EEC, 1952-1957. Ed. by Ennio Di Nolfo. viii, 598p. (C). 1992. lib. bdg. 183.10 (*3-11-012158-1*) De Gruyter.

Power in Family Discourse. Richard J. Watts. LC 91-39289. (Contributions to the Sociology of Language Ser.: No. 63). xiv, 302p. (C). 1992. lib. bdg. 104.65 (*3-11-013228-1*) Mouton.

Power in His Name: The Wonderful Names of Our Wonderful Lord. Charles E Hurlbut. LC 96-139540. 64p. 1995. 5.97 (*1-55748-736-7*) Barbour Pub.

Power in Language: Verbal Communication & Social Influence. Ng Sik Hung & James J. Bradac. LC 93-18762. (Language & Language Behaviors Ser.: Vol. 3). (Illus.). 227p. (C). 1993. text 48.00 (*0-8039-4422-5*); pap. text 22.95 (*0-8039-4423-3*) Sage.

Power in Management. John P. Kotter. LC 78-31558. 117p. reprint ed. pap. 36.30 (*0-608-14994-2*, 205609000047) Bks Demand.

Power in Motion: Capital Mobility & the Indonesian State. Jeffrey A. Winters. 264p. 1996. 35.00 (*0-8014-2925-0*) Cornell U Pr.

Power in Movement: Social Movements, Collective Action & Politics. 2nd rev. ed. Sidney Tarrow. LC 97-35137. (Cambridge Studies in Comparative Politics). (Illus.). 272p. (C). 1998. text 59.95 (*0-521-62072-4*); pap. text 18.95 (*0-521-62947-0*) Cambridge U Pr.

Power in Numbers: How to Manage for Profit. Brian Forst. LC 87-21555. 271p. reprint ed. pap. 84.10 (*0-7837-3511-1*, 205784400008) Bks Demand.

***Power in Numbers: Peer Effects on Adolescent Girls Sexual Debut & Pregnancy.** Peter S. Bearman & Hannah Bruckner. 65p. 1999. pap. 15.00 (*1-58671-011-7*) Natl Cpgn Teen Preg.

Power in Organizations. Jeffrey Pfeffer. LC 80-29883. 391p. 1986. pap. 21.00 (*0-88730-199-1*, HarpBusn) HarpInfo.

Power in Our Hands. Tony Gibson. 1997. pap. 17.95 (*1-897766-28-9*, Pub. by Jon Carpenter) Paul & Co Pubs.

Power in Our Hands: A Curriculum on the History of Work & Workers in the United States. Norman Diamond & William Bigelow. 256p. (Orig.). 1988. pap., teacher ed. 18.00 (*0-85345-753-0*, Pub. by Monthly Rev); pap., student ed. 10.00 (*0-85345-754-9*, Pub. by Monthly Rev) NYU Pr.

Power in Parliament: Back-Bench Parties & Policy. Jack Brand. (Illus.). 380p. 1992. text 85.00 (*0-19-827705-9*) OUP.

Power in Performance: The Creation of Textual Authority in Weyewa Ritual Speech. Joel C. Kuipers. LC 90-12529. (Conduct & Communication Ser.). (Illus.). 224p. (C). 1990. text 32.50 (*0-8122-8245-0*) U of Pa Pr.

***Power in Practice: Adult Education & the Struggle for Knowledge & Power in Society.** Ronald M. Cervero. 2000. 34.95 (*0-7879-4729-6*) Jossey-Bass.

Power in Praise. Merlin R. Carothers. 143p. 1972. pap. 6.95 (*0-943026-01-6*) Carothers.

Power in Praise: Giant Print. Merlin R. Carothers. 1992. 7.95 (*0-943026-23-7*) Carothers.

Power in Praising God. Charles H. Spurgeon. LC 98-13176. 171p. 1998. pap. 6.99 (*0-88368-526-4*) Whitaker Hse.

Power in Prayer. Charles H. Spurgeon. LC 97-213339. 170p. 1996. mass mkt. 5.99 (*0-88368-441-1*) Whitaker Hse.

Power in Psychotherapeutic Practice. David Heller. 197p. 1985. 29.95 (*0-89885-228-5*, Kluwer Acad Hman Sci) Kluwer Academic.

***Power in Reading.** Orsini Gonzalez. 126p. (C). 2000. per. 37.95 (*0-7872-6814-3*) Kendall-Hunt.

Power in Sex. Ivon Luster. Ed. by Michael Lattiboudeaine & Carlisle Peterson. 140p. (Orig.). (YA). (gr. 10). 1998. pap. 12.95 (*1-889448-50-8*) NBN Publishers Group.

Power in Struggle: Feminism, Sexuality & the State. Davina Cooper. LC 96-34339. 192p. (C). 1995. text 50.00 (*0-8147-1526-5*); pap. text 19.00 (*0-8147-1527-3*) NYU Pr.

Power in Struggle: Feminism, Sexuality & the State. Davina Cooper. LC 94-49576. 192p. 1995. pap. 22.95 (*0-335-19211-4*); text 88.00 (*0-335-19212-2*) OpUniv Pr.

Power in the Blood. Charles H. Spurgeon. 190p. (Orig.). 1996. mass mkt. 5.99 (*0-88368-427-6*) Whitaker Hse.

Power in the Blood: A Handbook on AIDS, Politics, & Communication. Ed. by William N. Elwood. LC 98-7516. (Communication Ser.). 480p. 1998. write for info. (*0-8058-2906-7*) L Erlbaum Assocs.

P

An Asterisk (*) at the beginning of an entry indicates that the title is appearing for the first time.

Power in the Blood: A John Jordan Mystery. Michael Lister. LC 97-26866. 326p. 1997. 18.95 (*1-56164-137-5*) Pineapple Pr.

Power in the Blood: Popular Culture & Village Discourse in Early Modern Germany. David W. Sabean. (Illus.). 260p. 1988. pap. text 18.95 (*0-521-34778-5*) Cambridge U Pr.

Power in the Blood: The Cross in the African American Experience. JoAnne M. Terrell. LC 98-27278. (Bishop Henry McNeal Turner/Sojourners Truth Series in Black Religion: Vol. 15). 192p. 1998. pap. 18.00 (*1-57075-216-8*) Orbis Bks.

Power in the Blood of Jesus. Frank Marzullo. 16p. 1985. pap. write for info. (*1-892363-02-X*) Christian Covenant.

Power in the Bread. Jude O. Mbukanma. 130p. 1994. pap. 7.95 (*1-885417-03-9*) MET Pubng.

Power in the Classroom: Communication, Control, & Concern. Ed. by Virginia P. Richmond & James C. McCroskey. (Communication Ser.). 224p. 1992. text 45.00 (*0-8058-1027-7*) L Erlbaum Assocs.

Power in the Dark. Barry Mathias. (Illus.). 256p. 1997. pap. 11.95 (*1-894012-00-3*, Pub. by SalPress) Firebird Dist.

Power in the Eye: An Introduction to Contemporary Irish Film. Terry Byrne. LC 97-5509. 1997. 34.00 (*0-8108-3296-8*) Scarecrow.

***Power in the Global Era: Grounding Globalization.** Theodore H. Cohn et al. LC 00-33300. 2000. write for info. (*0-312-23562-3*) St Martin.

Power in the Helping Professions. Adolf Guggenbuhl-Craig. Tr. by Myron B. Gubitz from GER. LC 86-17901. 158p. (Orig.). (C). 1971. pap. 15.00 (*0-88214-304-2*) Spring Pubns.

Power in the Highest Degree: Professionals, Capitalism, & the Rise of a New Mandarin Order. Charles Derber et al. 287p. 1990. text 19.95 (*0-19-503778-2*) OUP.

***Power in the Pain.** Marian Kennedy-Brooks. LC 00-104289. 160p. 2000. pap. 14.95 (*1-56167-620-9*, Five Star Spec Ed) Am Literary Pr.

Power in the Party. Gill. LC 96-34345. 234p. 1996. text 65.00 (*0-312-16550-1*) St Martin.

Power in the Pentagon: Tells the Power of Prayer. Nita Scoggan. (Illus.). 112p. (Orig.). 1997. pap. 8.95 (*0-910487-36-7*) Royalty Pub.

Power in the People: She Fought Senator Packwood, Now She Outlines a Grassroots Workbook for Political Change in Your Neighborhood, State, & Nation. Jeanette L. Fruen. LC 96-68925. 256p. 1996. pap. 13.95 (*0-88282-142-3*) New Horizon NJ.

Power in the Pulpit: How to Prepare & Deliver Expository Sermons. Jerry Vines & Jim Shaddix. 391p. 1999. 29.99 (*0-8024-7740-2*) Moody.

Power in the Southern Cone Borderlands: An Anthropology of Development Practice. Carmen A. Ferradas. LC 97-40997. 240p. 1998. 59.95 (*0-89789-560-6*, Bergin & Garvey) Greenwood.

Power in the Spoken Word. Frank Marzullo. 19p. 1985. pap. write for info. (*1-892363-03-8*) Christian Covenant.

Power in the Workplace: The Politics of Production at AT&T. Steven P. Vallas. LC 91-42558. (SUNY Series in the Sociology of Work). 250p. (C). 1993. text 21.50 (*0-7914-1273-3*) State U NY Pr.

Power in Tudor England. Loades. LC 96-25754. 256p. 1996. pap. 18.95 (*0-312-16392-4*); text 49.95 (*0-312-16391-6*) St Martin.

Power in Verse: Metaphor & Metonymy in the Renaissance Lyric. Jane Hedley. LC 87-43120. 199p. 1988. lib. bdg. 35.00 (*0-271-00623-4*) Pa St U Pr.

Power in Washington. Murphy. (C). 1997. pap. text. write for info. (*0-15-505379-5*) Harcourt Coll Pubs.

***Power in Weakness: The Second Letter of Paul to the Corinthians.** Sze-Kar Wan. LC 99-87136. (New Testament in Context Ser.). 178p. 2000. pap. 16.00 (*1-56338-315-2*) TPI PA.

Power in World Politics. Ed. by Richard J. Stoll & Michael D. Ward. LC 88-28337. 380p. 1989. lib. bdg. 42.00 (*1-55587-125-9*) L Rienner.

Power in You. Shorter. LC 97-190487. 1997. pap. 5.99 (*0-89274-978-4*) Harrison Hse.

Power in Your Hand see Poder en Tus Manos: God Doing Extraordinary Miracles Through Ordinary People

Power in Your Hand. 2nd ed. Heflin. 1997. pap. 7.99 (*1-884369-60-X*) McDougal Pubng.

Power Index Method for Profitable Futures Trading. Harold Goldberg. 1986. 50.00 (*0-930233-09-3*) Windsor.

Power Industry Dictionary. Ann Chambers & Susan D. Kerr. LC 96-19937. 1996. 69.95 (*0-87814-605-9*) PennWell Bks.

Power, Influence, & Your Effectiveness in Human Resources. Thomas L. Quick. 1988. 18.95 (*0-201-06649-1*) Addison-Wesley.

Power Interviews: Job-Winning Tactics from Fortune 500 Recruiters. expanded rev. ed. Neil Yeager & Lee Hough. LC 97-35196. 238p. 1998. pap. 14.95 (*0-471-17788-1*) Wiley.

Power, Intimacy, & the Life Story: Personological Inquiries into Identity. Dan P. McAdams. LC 88-5285. 336p. 1988. pap. text 25.00 (*0-89862-506-8*) Guilford Pubns.

Power into Pageantry: Spectacle Entertainments of Early Imperial Rome. Richard C. Beacham. LC 99-11449. (Illus.). 288p. 1999. 35.00 (*0-300-07382-8*) Yale U Pr.

Power Investing with Sector Funds. Madlem. 368p. 1998. boxed set 39.95 (*0-910944-09-1*) St Lucie Pr.

Power Investing with Sector Funds: Mutual Fund Timing & Allocation Strategies. Peter W. Madlem. LC 97-39485. 1997. write for info. (*0-910944-05-9*) St Lucie Pr.

Power Is Within You. Louise L. Hay. (SPA.). 267p. pap. 12.95 (*84-7953-013-8*, 136S) Hay House.

Power Is Within You. Louise L. Hay & Linda C. Tomchin. Ed. by Dan Olmos. LC 91-71179. 256p. 1991. pap. 12.95 (*1-56170-023-1*, 136T) Hay House.

Power Is You. Bernie Fass & Rosemary Caggiano. 48p. (J). (gr. 2-12). 1979. pap. 14.95 (*0-86704-005-X*) Clarus Music.

Power Japan: How & Why the Japanese Economy Works. William T. Ziemba & Sandra L. Schwartz. 300p. 1991. 27.50 (*1-55738-275-1*, Irwn Prfssnl) McGraw-Hill Prof.

Power Journalism. Miller. LC 97-73100. (C). 1997. pap. text 21.00 (*0-15-503976-8*, Pub. by Harcourt Coll Pubs) Harcourt.

***Power Juices, Power Drinks: Quick & Delicious Recipes to Prevent & Reverse Disease.** Steve Meyerowitz. 2000. pap. 16.00 (*1-57566-528-X*, Knsington) Kensgtn Pub Corp.

Power Kills: Democracy As a Method of Nonviolence. R. J. Rummel. LC 96-45040. 187p. 1997. text 32.95 (*1-56000-297-2*) Transaction Pubs.

Power Klingon, 1. abr. ed. Mark Okrand & Barry Levine. (Star Trek Original Ser.). 1993. audio 12.00 (*0-671-87975-8*, Pimsleur) S&S Trade.

Power-Knowledge: Selected Interviews & Other Writings, 1972-1977. Michel Foucault. 1980. pap. 14.00 (*0-394-73954-X*) Pantheon.

Power, Knowledge, & Aborigines. Ed. by Bain Attwood & John Arnold. (Orig.). (C). 1993. pap. 19.95 (*1-86324-013-6*, Pub. by LaTrobe Univ) Intl Spec Bk.

Power Lab. Irvine H. Millgate. (Illus.). 262p. (Orig.). 1992. pap. 24.00 (*0-938919-14-8*) Six Lights.

Power Lab: Creditability & Initiative. Irvine H. Millgate & Joel W. Weaver. (Illus.). 86p. (Orig.). 1994. pap. 18.00 (*0-938919-20-2*) Six Lights.

Power Lab: For Children to Nurture the Human Spirit Project Think. Irvine H. Millgate & Joel W. Weaver. (Illus.). 324p. (Orig.). 1993. pap. 24.00 (*0-938919-19-9*) Six Lights.

Power Lab: Seeking the Meaning of Mindsets. Irvine H. Millgate & Joel W. Weaver. (Illus.). 87p. (Orig.). (YA). (gr. 11 up). 1994. pap. 18.00 (*0-938919-28-8*) Six Lights.

Power Lab: Seeking the Meaning of Outward Passage. Irvine H. Millgate & Joel W. Weaver. (Illus.). 109p. (Orig.). (YA). (gr. 9 up). 1994. pap. 18.00 (*0-938919-25-3*) Six Lights.

Power Lab: Seeking Understanding. Irvine H. Millgate & Joel W. Weaver. (Illus.). 54p. (Orig.). (J). (gr. 4 up). 1994. pap. 18.00 (*0-938919-24-5*) Six Lights.

Power Lab: What Have We Learned about Thinking? Irvine H. Millgate & Joel W. Weaver. (Illus.). 96p. (Orig.). 1994. pap. 18.00 (*0-938919-23-7*) Six Lights.

Power Language: Getting the Most Out of Your Words. Jeffrey McQuain. LC 95-48830. 224p. 1996. pap. 13.00 (*0-395-71255-6*) HM.

Power Lasers. Eloy. (Electrical & Electronic Engineering Ser.). 160p. 1987. text 51.95 (*0-470-20851-1*) P-H.

Power Lasers & Their Applications. Ed. by V. S. Letokhov & N. D. Ustinov. viii, 128p. 1983. text 172.00 (*3-7186-0166-4*) Gordon & Breach.

Power, Law & Procedure: A Contemporary Guide to Industrial Relations. A. T. Trollip. 220p. 1992. pap. 61.00 (*0-409-05844-0*, SA, MICHIE) LEXIS Pub.

***Power Lawn.** Peter Jaeger. 48p. 1999. pap. 15.00 (*1-55245-050-3*, Pub. by Coach Hse Bks) SPD-Small Pr Dist.

Power Lawn Mowers: An Unreasonably Dangerous Product. Sevart & Hall. (Illus.). 207p. 1982. 59.95 (*0-938830-01-5*) Inst Product.

***Power Learning.** Feldman. LC 99-39465. 432p. 1999. pap. 31.88 (*0-07-365505-8*) McGraw.

Power Learning. Gawith. 1991. pap. text. write for info. (*0-582-87644-3*, Pub. by Addison-Wesley) Longman.

Power Learning: A Game Plan for Student Athletes & Other Active Learners. Mary M. Harris. LC 88-82128. (Illus.). 200p. (Orig.). 1988. pap. 14.95 (*0-9621082-0-0*) Harris Learn Systs.

Power Learning in the Classroom. Jamieson A. McKenzie. Ed. by Jerry J. Herman & Janice L. Herman. LC 93-10946. (Road Maps to Success Ser.). 72p. 1993. pap. 14.95 (*0-8039-6056-5*) Corwin Pr.

Power Letters for Service Executives. William J. Lynott. 109p. 1994. pap. 19.95 (*1-930797-30-3*) Appliance Univ.

Power-Limited Circuit Cables, UL 13. 2nd ed. (C). 1996. pap. text 215.00 (*1-55989-997-2*) Underwrtrs Labs.

Power Line Vol. 1: Know Your Communications Goal; Make It a Win-Win. Diana Morris. 1998. pap. write for info. (*1-891019-11-2*) Morris Communs.

Power Line Vol. 2: Power-Up Your Listening Skills. Diana Morris. 1998. pap. write for info. (*1-891019-06-6*) Morris Communs.

Power Line Vol. 3: Accentuate the Positive. Diana Morris. 1998. pap. write for info. (*1-891019-12-0*) Morris Communs.

Power Line Vol. 4: Beware the Power of Self-Talk. Diana Morris. 1998. pap. write for info. (*1-891019-13-9*) Morris Communs.

Power Line Vol. 5: Keep Your Cool in Hot Situations. Diana Morris. 1998. pap. write for info. (*1-891019-04-X*) Morris Communs.

Power Line Vol. 6: Build Your Credibility Muscle. Diana Morris. 1998. pap. write for info. (*1-891019-05-8*) Morris Communs.

Power Line Filter Design for Switched-Mode Power Supplies. Mark J. Nave. (Illus.). 224p. 1991. text 54.95 (*0-442-00453-2*, VNR) Wiley.

Power Line Interference: A Practical Handbook. Marvin O. Loftness. LC 92-27686. 1992. write for info. (*0-917599-07-1*) Natl Rural.

Power Line Interference: Problems & Solutions. rev. ed. Russ Gundrum. LC 73-85629. (ABC of the Telephone Ser.: Vol. 14). (Illus.). 56p. (C). 1988. pap. text 24.95 (*1-56016-013-6*) ABC TeleTraining.

Power Line Radiation. H. Kikuchi. 1983. text 135.00 (*90-277-1541-6*) Kluwer Academic.

Power Lines. Robert L. Burgers. 1984. pap. 6.55 (*0-89137-317-9*) Quality Pubns.

Power Lines. Anne McCaffrey & Elizabeth A. Scarborough. 1995. mass mkt. 6.99 (*0-345-38780-5*, Del Rey) Ballantine Pub Grp.

Power Lines: A Decade of Poetry from Chicago's Guild Complex. Ed. by Luis Rodriguez et al. 280p. 1999. pap. 14.95 (*1-882688-22-8*, Pub. by Tia Chucha Pr) Northwestern U Pr.

***Power Lines: Celtic Prayers about Work.** David Adam. LC 99-87388. 128p. 2000. pap. 10.95 (*0-8192-1838-3*, 6279) Morehouse Pub.

Power Lines: How to Communicate with Power & Precision. Diana Morris. LC 97-72784. 92p. (Orig.). 1997. pap. write for info. (*1-891019-00-7*) Morris Communs.

Power Lines: U. S. Domination in the New Global Order. Alejandro Bendana. (Voices & Visions Ser.). 320p. 1996. 39.95 (*1-56656-167-1*, Olive Branch Pr); pap. 18.95 (*1-56656-168-X*, Olive Branch Pr) Interlink Pub.

***Power Lines to Productivity & Profit.** Deborah Bartlett. 1999. 4.99 (*1-56229-484-9*) Pneuma Life Pub.

Power Linux. 1995. 43.00 (*3-540-14512-5*) Spr-Verlag.

Power LINUX: Linux 1.2 - LST Distribution 2.1. S. Probst & R. Flaxa. Tr. by A. Derieg. 200p. 1997. pap. text 49.95 incl. cd-rom (*3-540-14556-7*, AIP Pr) Spr-Verlag.

Power LINUX Kit. S. Probst et al. 1997. pap. 65.95 incl. audio compact disk (*0-387-98263-9*) Spr-Verlag.

Power Living: Everybody's Health & Diet Book. Ira A. Kellman. 224p. (Orig.). 1996. pap. 10.99 (*1-56043-792-8*, Treasure Hse) Destiny Image.

***Power Living: The Art of Mastering Self-Discipline.** Michael Anthony Janke. Ed. by Kathleen Marusak. LC 99-91240. (Illus.). 256p. 2000. pap. 19.95 (*0-9675139-3-6*) Special Opers.

Power Loss Regulation: The Origins of Deregulation & Restructuring in the American Electric Utility System. Richard F. Hirsh. LC 99-15443. (Illus.). 406p. 2000. 50.00 (*0-262-08273-X*) MIT Pr.

Power, Love & Wisdom. Friedhelm Hardy. 350p. 1989. 29.95 (*0-04-440118-3*) Routledge.

Power, Love, & Wisdom in the Religious Culture of India. Friedhelm Hardy. LC 93-12492. (Studies in Religious Traditions: No. 4). (Illus.). 627p. (C). 1994. text 85.00 (*0-521-44181-1*) Cambridge U Pr.

Power Lunch. Mayfair Games Staff. Date not set. 15.00 (*1-56905-055-4*) Mayfair Games.

Power Machines. Photos & Text by Ken Robbins. LC 92-30649. (Illus.). 32p. (J). (gr. k-3). 1995. 15.95 (*0-8050-1410-1*, Bks Young Read) H Holt & Co.

Power Machines. Ken Robbins. 1997. pap. text 6.95 (*0-8050-5297-6*) H Holt & Co.

Power Macintosh Programmer's Guide: A Road Map to Native PowerPC Application Development. Michael B. Bentley. 1995. pap. 28.95 (*0-201-40789-2*) Addison-Wesley.

Power Magic. Alison Alexander. (J). 1991. pap. 6.95 (*0-671-74130-6*) S&S Bks Yung.

Power Maintainer - Group A. Jack Rudman. (Career Examination Ser.: C-607). 1994. pap. 23.95 (*0-8373-0607-8*) Nat Learn.

Power Maintainer - Group B. Jack Rudman. (Career Examination Ser.: C-608). 1994. pap. 23.95 (*0-8373-0608-6*) Nat Learn.

Power Maintainer - Group C. Jack Rudman. (Career Examination Ser.: C-609). 1994. pap. 23.95 (*0-8373-0609-4*) Nat Learn.

Power Management That Works! James C. Bunnell. 92p. 1996. mass mkt. 24.95 (*0-929392-22-1*) Annabooks.

***Power Mandalas.** Klaus Holitzka. 2000. pap. 10.95 (*0-8069-2883-2*) Sterling.

Power Manual: The Revival of Praise & Worship in the Church. Frederick A. Drummond. (Illus.). 216p. (C). 1994. student ed., ring bd. 30.00 (*1-885042-00-0*) ESCA Triumphant.

Power, Marginality & African Oral Literature. Ed. by Graham Furniss & Liz Gunner. 299p. (C). 1995. text 69.95 (*0-521-48061-2*) Cambridge U Pr.

Power Marketers Yearbook 1997. 400p. 1997. pap. 249.00 incl. disk (*0-931032-13-X*, 409807) Edison Electric.

Power Marketing Administrations: Cost Recovery, Financing, & Comparison to NonFederal Utilities. (Illus.). 117p. (Orig.). (C). 1996. pap. text 35.00 (*0-7881-3587-2*) DIANE Pub.

***Power Marketing for Consultants.** Marjorie Brody. 1999. pap. 19.99 (*1-57472-310-3*) Archer-Ellison.

***Power Marketing for Small Business.** 2nd ed. Jody Hornor. (PSI Successful Business Library). 298p. 2000. reprint ed. pap. 19.95 (*1-55571-524-9*, Oasis Pr) PSI Resch.

***Power Marketing Your Novel: Marketing & Promoting Fiction & Nonfiction.** Joyce Spizer. LC 00-29566. 148p. 2000. 12.50 (*1-881164-88-8*, Pub. by Intercont VA) ACCESS Pubs Network.

Power Mates. Bruce Pandolfini. 1996. pap. 14.00 (*0-684-80120-5*) S&S Trade.

***Power, Meaning & Identity: Essays in Critical Educational Studies.** Michael W. Apple. LC 98-53525. (Counterpoints Ser.: Vol. 109). ix, 252p. (C). 1999. pap. text 29.95 (*0-8204-4427-8*) P Lang Pubng.

Power Mechanics. McKnight Staff & Wilbur R. Miller. LC 78-53394. (Basic Industrial Arts Ser.). (Illus.). 1978. pap. 7.72 (*0-02-672870-2*) Glencoe.

Power Mechanics/Small Engines. Questech Staff. (Illus.). 120p. (J). 1997. text 99.95 (*1-58100-013-8*) Beckley Cardy.

Power Metallurgy: A Source Guide. 1991. lib. bdg. 75.00 (*0-8490-4872-9*) Gordon Pr.

Power Ministry see Ministere de Puissance: Un Manuel pour les Predicateurs Pentecotistes

***Power Ministry: A Handbook for Pentecostal Preachers.** Denny Miller. (Discovery Ser.). 134p. 1999. pap. text. write for info. (*1-891110-06-3*, ATTS Pubns) Africa Theolog Trng.

Power Misses: Essays Across (Un)Popular Culture. David James. LC 96-39455. (C). 1996. pap. 19.00 (*1-85984-101-5*, Pub. by Verso) Norton.

Power, Modernity & Sociology: Selected Sociological Writings. Ed. by Dominique Schnapper. 240p. 1988. text 90.00 (*1-85278-030-4*) E Elgar.

Power Money: The International Business Executive's Guide to Government Resources. William A. Delphos. Ed. by Alan J. Beard et al. 211p. 1994. 35.00 (*1-883917-05-0*) Venture Pub NA.

***Power, Money, & Sex: How Success Almost Destroyed One of America's Great Athletes.** Deion Sanders. 192p. 1999. pap. 12.99 (*0-8499-3776-0*) Word Pub.

Power, Money & Sex: How Success Almost Ruined My Life. Deion Sanders & Jim Nelson Black. LC 98-39068. (Illus.). 194p. 1998. 21.99 (*0-8499-1499-X*) Word Pub.

***Power Money Fame Sex: A Users Guide.** Gretchen Craft Rubin. 304p. 2000. 25.95 (*0-671-04128-2*) PB.

Power Monitoring & Control Systems: Survey of Practices in Use. Kenneth E. Nicholson. Ed. by Helen Cripe. (Illus.). 40p. 1997. pap., spiral bd. 89.00 (*0-9643916-3-5*) Integ Tech Res.

Power Mosfets: Theory & Applications. Duncan A. Grant & John Gowar. LC 88-31169. 528p. 1989. 198.50 (*0-471-82867-X*) Wiley.

Power Multi-Level Marketing. Mark Yarnell. Date not set. pap. 15.95 (*1-879706-84-9*) Paper Chase.

Power Multi-Level Marketing. Mark Yarnell & Rene R. Yarnell. 152p. 1993. pap. 10.00 (*1-883599-01-6*) Quantum NV.

Power Music: Music & Trance in the Shamanic Universe. Brian Christman. 44p. (Orig.). 1993. pap. 8.25 (*0-933421-38-9*) Redwood Seed.

Power Negotiating: Strategies for Winning in Life & Business. John Ilich. LC 79-12646. 1980. 12.95 (*0-201-03149-3*) Addison-Wesley.

Power Negotiating Tactics & Techniques. David V. Lewis. LC 81-5164. 243p. 1984. 19.95 (*0-13-686808-8*, Busn); pap. 5.95 (*0-13-687740-0*, Busn) P-H.

Power Networking: Using the Contacts You Don't Even Know You Have to Succeed in the Job You Want. Marc Kramer. LC 97-15770. (Illus.). 160p. 1997. 12.95 (*0-8442-4494-5*, 44945) NTC Contemp Pub Co.

Power Networking: 55 Secrets for Personal & Professional Success. Donna Fisher & Sandy Vilas. 192p. 1991. 21.95 (*0-9627825-0-5*); pap. 14.95 (*0-9627825-4-8*) Discovery Seminars.

***Power Networking: 59 Secrets for Personal & Professional Success.** 2nd ed. Donna Fisher. 2000. pap. 14.95 (*1-885167-47-4*) Bard Pr.

Power, Norms, & Inflation: A Skeptical Treatment. Michael R. Smith. (Sociology & Economics Ser.). 317p. 1992. lib. bdg. 51.95 (*0-202-30429-9*) Aldine de Gruyter.

Power, Norms & Inflation: A Skeptical Treatment. Michael R. Smith. (Sociology & Economics Ser.). 317p. 1992. pap. text 30.95 (*0-202-30430-2*) Aldine de Gruyter.

Power Notes. 3rd ed. (C). 1997. write for info. (*0-13-755364-1*, Macmillan Coll) P-H.

Power Notes: Effective Communication for Every Business Occasion. Florence Isaacs. LC 97-27152. 1998. 17.00 (*0-517-70891-4*) C Potter.

Power Notes - Marketing. 6th ed. William G. Zikmund. 1998. pap. 13.50 (*0-538-88234-4*) Thomson Learn.

Power Notes & Forms: Managerial Acct:information for Decisions. Ingram. (SWC-Accounting Ser.). 1997. pap. 13.50 (*0-538-86932-1*) Sth-Wstrn College.

Power Notes for Management Accounting. Atkinson. 1996. text 19.75 (*0-13-266651-0*) P-H.

***Power Nuggets: 101 Reflections for Empowered Living.** Mark Bowser. 1999. pap. 11.95 (*0-7880-1424-2*, Fairway Pr) CSS OH.

Power Nutrition: How to Live Longer, Prevent Illness & Be Healthier with Good Nutrition. Ed Blonz. LC 99-171536. 272p. 1998. mass mkt. 5.99 (*0-451-19726-7*, Sig) NAL.

Power Nutrition for Your Chronic Illness. Kristine Napier. LC 98-5192. 320p. 1999. 19.95 (*0-02-862059-3*) Macmillan.

Power of . . . Approach 2.0 for Windows. Charles Seigel. 1995. pap. 27.95 (*1-55828-266-1*, MIS Pr) IDG Bks.

Power of . . . FoxPro 2.5 for Windows. Nelson King. 1995. pap. 34.95 (*1-55828-261-0*, MIS Pr) IDG Bks.

Power of a Consecrated Heart. Warren Hunter. Ed. by Richard Phillips. 96p. 1998. pap. 7.00 (*1-889816-18-3*) Sword Ministries.

Power of a Millionaire Mentality: The Best Kept Secret to Wealth. 3rd ed. Richard Solano. (Illus.). 89p. 1992. ring bd. 29.95 (*0-9671461-0-0*) Solano Grp.

Power of a Navajo: Carl Gorman, the Man & His Life. Henry Greenberg. LC 96-6244. 224p. (Orig.). 1996. pap. 24.95 (*0-940666-82-0*) Clear Light.

Power of a Navajo: Carl Gorman, the Man & His Life. Henry Greenberg & Georgia Greenberg. LC 96-6244. (Illus.). 224p. (Orig.). 1996. pap. 14.95 (*0-940666-80-4*) Clear Light.

***Power of a New Identity.** Dan Sneed. 2000. pap. 12.99 (*1-85240-255-5*, Pub. by SOV5) Gospel Lght.

Power of a Parent's Words see Palabras de los Padres y Su Asombroso Poder

Power of A Penny. Dromgoole. LC 99-15885. 1999. text 13.95 (*0-312-24422-3*) St Martin.

Power of a Praying Kid. Stormie Omartian. 80p. Date not set. pap. 7.99 (*0-7369-0122-1*) Harvest Hse.

Power of a Praying Parent. Stormie Omartian. LC 95-8627. 213p. 1995. pap. 9.99 (*1-56507-354-1*) Harvest Hse.

P

An Asterisk (*) at the beginning of an entry indicates that the title is appearing for the first time.

*Power of a Praying Parent Prayer & Study Guide. Stormie Omartian. 144p. 2000. pap., student ed. 6.99 (0-7369-0343-7) Harvest Hse.

Power of a Praying Wife. Stormie Omartian. LC 97-7436. 203p. 1997. pap. 9.99 (1-56507-572-2) Harvest Hse.

Power of a Praying Wife, Set. Stormie Omartian. audio 16.99 (0-7369-0054-3) Harvest Hse.

*Power of a Praying Wife Prayer & Study Guide. Stormie Omartian. 144p. 2000. pap. 6.99 (0-7369-0317-8) Harvest Hse.

*Power of a Praying Woman Prayer Journal. Stormie Omartian. 208p. 1999. 11.99 (0-7369-0130-2) Harvest Hse.

Power of a Promise, 5 vols. Charles R. Swindoll. 1998. mass mkt. 13.95 (1-57972-211-3) Insight Living.

Power of a Promise. Illus. by Rosalyn White. LC 88-33457. (Jataka Tales Ser.). 32p. (Orig.). (J). (gr. 1-5). 1989. 16.95 (0-89800-196-X); pap. 7.95 (0-89800-197-8) Dharma Pub.

Power of a Promise Kept see Poder de una Pormesa Cumplida

Power of a Promise Kept. Gregg Lewis. 1995. 17.99 (1-56179-350-7) Focus Family.

*Power of a Third Kind: The Western Attempt to Colonize the Global Village. Hisham M. Nazer. LC 98-47761. 200p. 1999. 23.95 (0-275-96489-2, C6489, Praeger Pubs) Greenwood.

Power of a Woman. Barbara Taylor Bradford. 432p. 1998. mass mkt. 7.50 (0-06-109440-4) HarpC.

Power of a Woman. large type ed. Barbara Taylor Bradford. LC 97-28016. 1997. 29.95 (0-7862-1223-3) Thorndike Pr.

*Power of a Woman. large type ed. Barbara Taylor Bradford. LC 97-28016. 1999. pap. 27.95 (0-7862-1224-1) Thorndike Pr.

Power of a Woman: Mcteer,&Janet, Set. abr. ed. Barbara Taylor Bradford. 1997. audio 25.00 (0-694-51861-1, 695440) HarperAudio.

Power of Acceptance: Building Meaningful Relationships in a Judgmental World. Bill Thatcher & Douglas P. Shadel. 192p. (Orig.). 1997. pap. 12.95 (0-87877-242-1) Newcastle Pub.

Power of Affirmations. Jerry Fankhauser. 56p. 1979. pap. 8.00 (0-9617006-1-0) J Fankhauser.

*Power of Affirmative Faith. Bruce G. Epperly. 2001. pap. 18.99 (0-8272-2968-2) Chalice Pr.

Power of Africentric Celebrations: Inspirations from the Zairean Liturgy. Nwaka C. Egbulem. 180p. 1996. pap. 14.95 (0-8245-1489-0) Crossroad NY.

Power of Agreement. Brian D. Molitor. LC 98-48100. 256p. 1999. 14.99 (0-8054-1836-9) Broadman.

Power of Aleph Beth, Vol. I. Philip S. Berg. (FRE.). 288p. 1989. 14.95 (0-924457-28-7); 14.95 (0-943688-94-9); 14.95 (0-924457-67-8); pap. 13.95 (0-924457-29-5); pap. 12.95 (0-943688-95-7); pap. 12.95 (0-924457-68-6) Res Ctr Kabbalah.

Power of Aleph Beth, Vol. II. Philip S. Berg. (SPA.). 256p. 1989. 12.95 (0-943688-96-5); 12.95 (0-924457-69-4); pap. 12.95 (0-943688-97-3); pap. 12.95 (0-924457-70-8) Res Ctr Kabbalah.

Power of Aleph Beth, Vol. II. Philip S. Berg. (FRE.). 224p. 1990. 12.95 (0-924457-30-9); pap. 11.95 (0-924457-31-7) Res Ctr Kabbalah.

Power of Alignment: How Great Companies Stay Centered & Accomplish Extraordinary Things. George Labovitz & Victor Rosansky. LC 97-12815. 256p. 1997. 27.95 (0-471-17790-3) Wiley.

Power of Allegiances: Identity, Culture & Representational Strategies. Marino Tuzi. LC 96-79288. 197p. 1997. pap. 18.00 (1-55071-029-X) Guernica Editions.

Power of an Encouraging Word. Ken Sutterfield. LC 97-68953. 146p. 1997. boxed set 10.95 (0-89221-357-4) New Leaf.

*Power of Animals: An Ethnography. Brian Morris. (Illus.). 2000. pap. 19.50 (1-85973-225-9, Pub. by Berg Pubs) NYU Pr.

*Power of Animals: Malawian Culture & Mammalian Life. Brian Morris. LC 99-165884. 4p. 1998. 65.00 (1-85973-220-8, Pub. by Berg Pubs) NYU Pr.

Power of Apartheid: State, Power, & Space in South African Cities. Jennifer Robinson. LC 95-39072. (Policy, Planning, & Critical Theory Ser.). (Illus.). 192p. 1996. pap. 29.95 (0-7506-2689-5) Buttrwrth-Heinemann.

Power of Aries: Myth & Reality in Karen Blixen's Life. Anders Westenholtz. Tr. by Lise Kure-Jensen. LC 86-18534. 121p. 1987. text 27.50 (0-8071-1261-5) La State U Pr.

Power of Art. Lewis. (C). 1994. pap. text, teacher ed., suppl. ed. 33.75 (0-15-501214-2) Harcourt Coll Pubs.

Power of Art. Richard Lewis & Susan Lewis. (Illus.). 528p. (Orig.). (C). 1994. pap. text 65.50 (0-15-500320-8, Pub. by Harcourt Coll Pubs) Harcourt.

Power of Association. Ford & Associates Staff. LC 96-132440. 160p. 1995. pap. text, per. 16.95 (0-7872-1789-1) Kendall-Hunt.

Power of Attorney: A Guide. 1992. lib. bdg. 74.95 (0-8490-5284-X) Gordon Pr.

Power of Attorney: Durable & General. LawPak Staff. 120p. (Orig.). 1994. pap. 14.95 (1-879421-02-X) LawPak.

Power of Attorney Handbook. Robert Norris. 80p. (Orig.). 1989. pap. 15.95 (0-317-93474-0) Peoples Birmingham.

Power of Attorney Handbook. 3rd ed. Edward A. Haman. LC 98-15492. (Legal Survival Guides Ser.). 140p. 1998. pap. 19.95 (1-57071-348-0) Sourcebks.

*Power of Attorney Kit. 8th rev. ed. M. Stephen Georgas. 56p. 1999. pap. 12.95 (1-55180-192-2) Self-Counsel Pr.

Power of Attorney Kit, Do It Yourself. Timothy J. Smith. (Illus.). 1991. 14.95 (0-9625456-4-3) SJT Enterprises.

Power of Awareness. Kenneth Mestre. Ed. by Joan Levine & Newton Levine. Tr. by Inlingua Translation Service Staff from SPA.Tr. of El Saber Es Poder. (Illus.). 110p. 1997. write for info. (0-9654059-0-7) Wrld Finan.

Power of Awareness. Victoria Goddard Neville. 124p. 1993. reprint ed. pap. 8.95 (0-87516-655-5) DeVorss.

Power of Babel: Language in the African Experience. Ali A. Mazrui & Alamin M. Mazrui. LC 97-32844. 256p. 1998. pap. text 19.00 (0-226-51429-3); lib. bdg. 40.00 (0-226-51428-5) U Ch Pr.

Power of Babel: Teaching & Learning in Multilingual Classrooms. Viv Edwards. (Illus.). 100p. 1998. pap. 18.95 (1-85856-095-0, Trentham Bks) Stylus Pub VA.

Power of Bacterial Genetics: A Literature-Based Course. Jonathan Beckwith & Thomas J. Silhavy. LC 92-11643. (Illus.). 842p. Date not set. reprint ed. pap. 200.00 (0-608-20710-1, 207180800002) Bks Demand.

*Power of Balance: A New Procss of Personal Transformation for the 21st Century. Jack Beauregard. 232p. 2000. pap. 14.95 (0-9662362-0-3) Innervision Pr.

Power of Balance: Transforming Self, Society, & Scientific Inquiry. William R. Torbert. (Illus.). 296p. 1991. 48.00 (0-8039-4067-X); pap. 21.95 (0-8039-4068-8) Sage.

Power of Being Debt-Free: How Eliminating the National Debt Can Improve the Standard of Living. 1992. lib. bdg. 75.00 (0-8490-5270-X) Gordon Pr.

*Power of Being Human. Kira Rosner. LC 00-91144. xii, 164p. 2000. pap. 15.00 (0-9679978-0-1, Pub. by Coherent Bks) Anthroposophic.

Power of Believing in Your Child: Unleash Your Power as a Parent to Help Your Kids Be All They Can Be. Miles McPherson. 28p. 1998. pap. 10.99 (0-7642-2078-0) Bethany Hse.

Power of Birthdays, Stars & Numbers. S. Crawford & G. Sullivan. LC 98-13941. 1998. pap. 0.24 (0-345-41819-0) Ballantine Pub Grp.

Power of Black Music: Interpreting Its History from Africa to the United States. Samuel A. Floyd, Jr. (Illus.). 336p. 1996. reprint ed. pap. 16.95 (0-19-510975-9) OUP.

Power of Blackness: Hawthorne, Poe, Melville. Harry Levin. LC 80-83221. 286p. 1980. reprint ed. pap. 14.95 (0-8214-0581-0) Ohio U Pr.

Power of Boldness: Ten Master Builders of American Industry Tell Their Success Stories. Ed. by Elkan Blout. 224p. 1996. pap. 18.95 (0-309-05445-1, Joseph Henry Pr) Natl Acad Pr.

Power of Brokenness. Don Nori. LC 97-170080. 168p. 1997. pap. 10.99 (1-56043-178-4) Destiny Image.

Power of Building Your Bright Side: Five Surprising Renewal Strategies to Personal & Business Success. Donna Rae Smith. 192p. (Orig.). (gr. 10). 1995. pap. 11.99 (0-922066-90-6) Wynwood.

Power of CalcResult For the Commodore 64. Robert E. Williams. (Power of Ser.). 1983. pap. 14.95 (0-685-08100-1) P-H.

Power of Call. Martha C. Pennington. (Illus.). 224p. 1996. 47.95 (0-940753-04-9); pap. 24.95 (0-940753-03-0) Athelstan Pubns.

Power of Cartilage: Discover the Amazing Benefits of Shark & Bovine Cartilage. Stephen S. Holt. LC 99-167162. 256p. 1998. pap. 14.00 (1-57566-340-6) Kensgtn Pub Corp.

Power of Character: Prominent Americans Talk about Life, Family, Work, Values & More. Ed. by Michael Josephson & Wes Hanson. LC 98-25534. (Health & Psychology Ser.). 320p. 1998. pap. 24.00 (0-7879-4172-7) Jossey-Bass.

Power of Charismatic Healing. Andy O'Neill. 120p. 1997. pap. 11.95 (0-85342-749-6, Pub. by Mercier Pr) Irish Amer Bk.

Power of Charitable Remainder Trusts in Estate Planning (After the Taxpayer Relief Act of 1997) Bill S. Wolfkiel. (Illus.). ix, 272p. 1998. pap. 79.95 (0-9665320-1-5) Guild Pubng CO.

Power of Ch'i: An Introduction to Chinese Mysticism & Philosophy. Michael Page. (Illus.). 128p. (Orig.). 1988. pap. 10.00 (0-85030-764-3, Pub. by Aqrn Pr) Harper SF.

Power of Choice. Todd B. Bailey. 94p. 1993. pap. 3.95 (1-883155-00-2) T Bailey Minist.

Power of Choice. Robert Fritz & Brian R. Smith. (Illus.). 21p. 1982. pap. 4.95 (0-943290-00-7) Fainshaw Pr.

Power of Choice: A Guide to Personal & Professional Self-Management. Ted Willey. 252p. 1988. 19.95 (0-929376-92-7) Berwick Hse.

Power of Choice: Create the Future You Desire Based on the Choices You Make. Sam Silverstein. LC 98-84653. 136p. 1998. pap. 12.00 (0-9639468-1-1) Star Pubng.

Power of Christ the Warrior. Charles H. Spurgeon. Ed. by Lance Wubbels. (Life of Christ Ser.). 200p. (Orig.). 1996. pap. 9.99 (1-883002-18-4) Emerald WA.

Power of Christlike Living; Me Be Like Jesus? see Jesus in the Image of God: A Challenge to Christlikeness

Power of Christ's Miracles. Charles H. Spurgeon. Ed. by Lance Wubbels. LC 96-157069. (Power Ser.). 192p. (Orig.). 1995. pap. 9.99 (1-883002-15-X) Emerald WA.

Power of Christ's Prayer Life. Charles H. Spurgeon. Ed. by Lance Wubbels. (Power Ser.). 204p. (Orig.). 1995. pap. 9.99 (1-883002-17-6) Emerald WA.

Power of Christ's Second Coming. Charles H. Spurgeon. Ed. by Lance Wubbels. (Life of Christ Ser.). 200p. (Orig.). 1996. pap. 9.99 (1-883002-20-6) Emerald WA.

Power of Christ's Tears. Charles H. Spurgeon. Ed. by Lance Wubbels. (Life of Christ Ser.). 200p. (Orig.). 1996. pap. 9.99 (1-883002-19-2) Emerald WA.

Power of Clan. Wolf. 192p. 1998. pap. text 21.95 (0-7658-0449-2) Transaction Pubs.

Power of Clan: The Influence of Human Relationships on Heart Disease. Stewart G. Wolf & John G. Bruhn. 192p. (C). 1992. 34.95 (1-56000-043-0) Transaction Pubs.

*Power of Collaborative Leadership: Lessons for the Learning Organization. Iva M. Wilson et al. (Illus.). 320p. 2000. pap. 19.95 (0-7506-7268-4) Buttrwrth-Heinemann.

Power of Collective Pursestrings: The Effects of Bank Hegemony on Corporation & the State. Davita S. Glasberg. 1989. 40.00 (0-520-06489-5, Pub. by U CA Pr) Cal Prin Full Svc.

Power of Color: Creating Healthy Interior Spaces. Sara O. Marberry & Laurie Zagon. LC 94-23831. (Construction Business & Management Library). 100p. 1995. 64.95 (0-471-07685-6) Wiley.

Power of Color: How It Can Reduce Fatigue, Relieve Monotony, Enhance Sexuality, & More. Faber Birren. LC 96-49751. 320p. 1997. pap. 14.95 (0-8065-1857-X, Citadel Pr) Carol Pub Group.

Power of Color: The Art & Science of Making Colors Work for You. Morton Walker. LC 90-19501. (Illus.). 208p. 1991. pap. 9.95 (0-89529-430-3, Avery) Penguin Putnam.

Power of Commerce: Economy & Governance in the First British Empire. Nancy F. Koehn. LC 94-4314. 256p. 1994. text 35.00 (0-8014-2699-5) Cornell U Pr.

Power of Commitment: How Ordinary People Can Make an Extraordinary Impact on the World. Jerry White. LC 96-233066. 1997. pap. text 12.00 (0-89109-985-9) NavPress.

Power of Concentration. Theron Dumont. reprint ed. 15.00 (0-911662-39-1) Yoga.

Power of Confidence: Genesis & Structure of the Way of "Spiritual Childhood" of St. Therese of Lisieux. Conrad De Meester. Tr. by Susan Conroy from FRE. LC 98-3989. 443p. 1998. pap. 22.95 (0-8189-0819-X) Alba.

Power of Conflict & Sacrifice: A Therapy Manual for Christian Marriage. Bettie P. Mitchell. 106p. (Orig.). 1988. pap. 5.00 (1-885193-01-7) Good Samaritan.

Power of Conscious Breathing in Hatha Yoga: Discover the Tremendous Benefits of Ancient Yoga Techniques to Relieve Stress, Improve Health, Prevent & Heal Ailments, Achieve Inner Peace. Vasanthi Bhat. Ed. by Amita Shenoi & Rich Slogar. (Illus.). xii, 244p. (Orig.). 1997. pap. 19.95 (0-9655499-0-9) Vasantha Yoga.

Power of Consciousness & the Force of Circumstances in Sartre's Philosophy. Thomas W. Busch. LC 89-45191. (Studies in Continental Thought). 128p. 1990. 8.95 (0-253-31283-3) Ind U Pr.

Power of Consultative Selling. Bryce Webster. (Illus.). 228p. (C). 1987. pap. text 11.95 (0-13-686270-5) P-H.

Power of Contemporary Architecture. Peter Cook. 128p. 1999. pap. 45.00 (0-471-98419-1) Wiley.

Power of Convening: Collaborative Policy Forums for Sustainable Development; Proceedings of an International Workshop Held in Claremont, California, October 5-7, 1989. Ed. by Thaddeus C. Trzyna & Ilze M. Gotelli. LC 90-32864. (Environmental Studies). 112p. (Orig.). 1990. pap. 20.00 (0-912102-92-6) Cal Inst Public.

Power of CorelDRAW! Version 4. James Karney. 1995. pap. 34.95 (1-55828-318-8, MIS Pr) IDG Bks.

Power of CorelDRAW! 5.0 for Windows. James Karney. LC 94-47611. 900p. 1995. pap. 34.95 incl. cd-rom (1-55828-376-5) IDG Bks.

*Power of Corporate Kinetics: Create the Self-Adjusting, Self-Renewing, Instant-Action Enterprise. Michael Fradette et al. 256p. 2001. pap. 15.00 (0-684-85590-9, Fireside) S&S Trade Pap.

*Power of Covenant. Kingsley Fletcher. 2000. pap. 10.99 (0-8307-2526-1, Renew) Gospel Lght.

Power of Covenant Prayer. Francis Frangipane. LC 98-3466. 1998. pap. 9.99 (0-88419-548-1) Creation House.

Power of Culture: Critical Essays in American History. Ed. by Richard W. Fox & Jackson T. Lears. LC 92-31011. (Illus.). 312p. (C). 1993. lib. bdg. 46.50 (0-226-25954-4) U Ch Pr.

Power of Culture: Critical Essays in American History. Ed. by Richard W. Fox & T. J. Lears. LC 92-31011. (Illus.). 312p. (C). 1993. pap. text 16.95 (0-226-25955-2) U Ch Pr.

Power of Culture: Studies in Chinese Cultural History. Ed. by Willard J. Peterson et al. LC 97-178510. 380p. (Orig.). (C). 1997. 44.50 (962-201-596-4, Pub. by Chinese Univ) U of Mich Pr.

Power of Darkness. Durwood L. Buchheim. 1985. 7.30 (0-89536-746-7, 5852, Fairway Pr) CSS OH.

Power of David's Key. Vincent M. Walsh. 192p. (Orig.). 1981. pap. 5.00 (0-943374-03-0) Key of David.

Power of Decimal, Decimating Prayer. David Thomas. 112p. 1997. spiral bd. 12.00 (1-891416-01-4) Intercessors.

Power of Decision. Raymond C. Barker. LC 87-32058. 165p. 1996. reprint ed. pap. 10.95 (0-87516-699-7) DeVorss.

Power of Delusion, Christian Life see Engano del Poder, Vida Cristiana

Power of Development. Ed. by Jonathan Crush. LC 94-40708. 304p. (C). 1995. pap. 27.99 (0-415-11177-3, C0062) Routledge.

Power of Development. Ed. by Jonathan Crush. LC 94-40708. 304p. (C). (gr. 13). 1995. 85.00 (0-415-11176-5, C0061) Routledge.

Power of Dialogue: Critical Hermeneutics after Gadamer & Foucault. Herbert Hans. 1999. pap. text 20.00 (0-262-61148-1) MIT Pr.

Power of Dialogue: Critical Hermeneutics after Gadamer & Foucault. Hans H. Kogler. (Studies in Contemporary German Social Thought). (Illus.). 350p. 1996. 40.00 (0-262-11216-7) MIT Pr.

Power of Discourse: An Introduction to Discourse Analysis. Moira Chimombo & Robert L. Roseberry. LC 97-14162. 350p. 1997. write for info. (0-8058-2635-1); pap. write for info. (0-8058-2636-X) L Erlbaum Assocs.

Power of Display: A History of Exhibition Installations at the Museum of Modern Art. Mary A. Staniszewski. LC 98-7880. (Illus.). 400p. 1998. 50.00 (0-262-19402-3) MIT Pr.

Power of Dreaming: Messages from Your Inner Self. D. Jason Cooper. LC 95-31175. (Llewellyn's Strategies for Success Ser.). 224p. 1999. pap. 12.00 (1-56718-175-9) Llewellyn Pubns.

*Power of Dreaming: Messages from Your Inner Self. D. Jason Cooper. 2000. 7.99 (0-7858-1195-8) Bk Sales Inc.

Power of Effective Speech. Augusta I. Barrick. (Orig.). 1959. pap. 14.95 (0-8084-0251-X) NCUP.

Power of Eloquence & English Renaissance Literature. Neil Rhodes. LC 92-14672. 1992. text 49.95 (0-312-08421-8) St Martin.

*Power of Empathy: A Practical Guide to Creating Intimacy, Self-Understanding & Lasting Love in Your Life. Arthur P. Ciaramicoli & Katherine Ketcham. LC 99-89849. 288p. 2000. 24.95 (0-525-94511-3, Dutt) Dutton Plume.

Power of Empowerment: What the Experts Say & 16 Actionable Case Studies. Ed. by Bill Ginnodo. LC 97-65436. (Illus.). viii, 264p. (Orig.). 1997. pap. 19.95 (0-9656587-0-8) Pride Pubns IL.

Power of Encouragement: Lift up the Defeated. David Jeremiah. LC 96-52136. 224p. 1997. pap. 12.99 (1-57673-135-9, Multnomah Bks) Multnomah Pubs.

*Power of Esoterics. Vernon Howard. 224p. 1999. pap. 11.95 (0-911203-43-5) New Life.

Power of Ethical Management. Norman Vincent Peale. 1996. pap. 10.00 (0-449-91975-7) Fawcett.

Power of Ethical Management: Why the Ethical Way Is the Profitable Way - in Your Life & in Your Business. Kenneth Blanchard & Norman Vincent Peale. LC 87-24210. 136p. 1988. 17.95 (0-688-07062-0, Wm Morrow) Morrow Avon.

Power of Ethical Persuasion: Winning Through Understanding at Work & at Home. Tom Rusk & D. Patrick Miller. 240p. 1994. pap. 9.95 (0-14-017214-9, Penguin Bks) Viking Penguin.

Power of Example. Leslie Horan. (Illus.). 24p. 1987. pap. 10.00 (0-944290-01-9) Light Speed.

Power of Exhibit Marketing: How to Make Money at Trade or Consumer Shows. 4th rev. expanded ed. Barry Siskind. (Illus.). 304p. 1997. 15.95 (1-55180-121-3) Self-Counsel Pr.

Power of Expectation. David M. Blunt. 56p. 1998. pap. write for info. (1-893716-05-8) Church Rk.

*Power of Extraordinary Prayer. Robert Bakke. LC 00-25256. 224p. 2000. pap. 10.99 (1-58134-154-7) Crossway Bks.

Power of Face Reading: For Sales, Self-Esteem, & Better Relationships. Rose Rosetree. LC 99-165374. (Illus.). 382p. 1998. pap. 18.95 (0-9651145-2-X) Womens Intuition.

Power of Faith. Ed. by Guideposts Editors. (Illus.). 400p. 1997. 12.99 (0-88486-161-9, Bristol Park Bks) Arrowood Pr.

Power of Faith: A Mother's Prayers for Her Dying Son. Connie M. Drummond. Ed. & Illus. by Sample Enterprises, Inc. 34p. 1997. mass mkt. 8.98 (1-930384-13-0, BB-42003) Sample Enter.

Power of Faith for Today's Christian. R. W. Schambach. (Legacy Ser.). 110p. 1995. pap. 5.00 (1-888361-03-4) Power Publns.

Power of Family Love: True Stories of Love & Courage. Samantha Glen & Mary Pesaresi. (Illus.). 288p. 1997. per. 12.00 (0-7615-1102-4) Prima Pub.

Power of Family Therapy. rev. ed. Michael Nichols. 464p. (C). 1993. reprint ed. pap. text 29.95 (0-89876-204-9, RC488.5.N5345) Gardner Pr.

Power of Fantasy: Illusion & Eroticism in Everyday Life. Gini Graham Scott. LC 94-12606. 288p. 1994. 19.95 (1-55972-239-8, Birch Ln Pr) Carol Pub Group.

Power of Fantasy: Illusion & Eroticism in Everyday Life. Gini Graham Scott. 244p. 1998. text 20.00 (0-7881-5938-0) DIANE Pub.

*Power of Feelings: Personal Meaning in Psychoanalysis, Gender & Culture. Nancy Julia Chodorow. (Illus.). 320p. 1999. 27.50 (0-300-07959-1) Yale U Pr.

Power of Femininity: Rediscovering the Art of Being a Woman. Michelle McKinney-Hammond. LC 99-24433. 1999. pap. 10.99 (0-7369-0142-6) Harvest Hse.

Power of Femininity in the New South: Women's Organizations & Politics in North Carolina, 1880-1930. Anastatia Sims. LC 97-4862. (Illus.). 260p. 1997. 29.95 (1-57003-178-9) U of SC Pr.

Power of Feminist Art: The American Movement of the 1970s, History & Impact. Ed. by Norma Broude & Mary D. Garrard. (Illus.). 320p. 1996. pap. 24.95 (0-8109-2659-8, Pub. by Abrams) Time Warner.

*Power of Feminist Theory. Amy Allen. LC 98-41071. (Feminist Theory & Politics Ser.). 160p. 1998. text 59.00 (0-8133-9072-9, Pub. by Westview) HarpC.

Power of Film Propaganda: Myth or Reality? Nicholas Reeves. LC 99-10122. 1999. 75.00 (0-304-33871-0); pap. 21.95 (0-304-33872-9) Continuum.

Power of Financial Innovation: Successful Corporate Solutions to Managing Interest Rate, Foreign Exchange Rate & Commodity Exposures on a World-Wide Basis. John Geanuracos & Bill Mi. 448p. 1991. 59.95 (0-88730-470-2, HarpBusn) HarpInfo.

Power of Five: Hundreds of 5-Second to 5-Minute Scientific Shortcuts to Ignite Your Energy, Burn Fat, Stop Aging & Revitalize Your Love Life. Harold H. Bloomfield & Robert K. Cooper. 524p. 1996. pap. 12.95 (0-87596-363-3) Rodale Pr Inc.

Power of Flow: Practical Ways to Transform Your Life with Meaningful Coincidence. Charlene Belitz & Meg Lundstrom. LC 98-25300. 304p. 1998. pap. 12.00 (0-609-80197-X) Crown Pub Group.

P

Power of Flow: Practical Ways to Transform Your Life with Meaningful Coincidence. Charlene Belitz & Meg Lundstrom. LC 97-183204. 276p. 1997. 22.00 (*0-517-70558-3*) Random.

***Power of Focus: How to Hit Your Business, Personal & Financial Targets with Absolute Certainty.** Jack Canfield et al. LC 99-89886. (Illus.). 300p. 2000. pap. 12.95 (*1-55874-752-4*) Health Comm.

Power of Focus: Your Future Depends upon It! Gary R. Blair. 48p. 1998. pap. 6.95 (*1-889770-10-8*) GoalsGuy.

Power of Focused Thinking. Edward De Bono. 1991. student ed. 99.95 incl. audio (*0-9615400-6-0*) Intl Ctr Creat Think.

***Power of Focusing.** Ann W. Cornell. 128p. 1999. 5.98 (*1-56731-297-7*, MJF Bks) Fine Comms.

Power of Focusing: A Practical Guide to Emotional Self-Healing. Ann W. Cornell. LC 95-72225. 120p. 1996. pap. text 12.95 (*1-57224-044-X*) New Harbinger.

Power of Forgiveness. Marilyn Hickey. 24p. (Orig.). pap. 1.00 (*1-56441-162-1*) M Hickey Min.

***Power of Forgiving.** Robert Strand. 96p. 2000. pap. 5.95 (*1-58169-050-9*, Evergrn Pr AL) Genesis Comm Inc.

Power of Form. Gilbert J. Rose & Andrew Farge. LC 79-53592. (Psychological Issues Monographs: No. 49, Vol. 13, No. 1). (Illus.). 252p. 1980. 35.00 (*0-8236-4171-6*) Intl Univs Pr.

Power of Form: A Psychoanalytic Approach to Aesthetic Form. 2nd ed. Gilbert J. Rose. 288p. (C). 1992. reprint ed. pap. 24.95 (*0-8236-8188-2*) Intl Univs Pr.

Power of Framework Business Profession. 19.95 (*0-13-686973-4*) P-H.

Power of Frameworks. (C). 1995. write for info. (*0-201-96648-4*) Addison-Wesley.

Power of Frameworks: For Windows & Os/2 Developers. Taligent Press Staff. 352p. 1995. pap. 44.95 (*0-201-48348-3*) Addison-Wesley.

Power of Freedom: First Baptist Church, Asheville, North Carolina, 1829-1997. Charles Deweese. LC 97-75413. (Illus.). 384p. 1997. 24.95 (*1-57736-076-1*) Providence Hse.

Power of Gems & Charms. George H. Bratley. 198p. 1988. pap. 9.95 (*0-87877-132-8*) Newcastle Pub.

Power of Gems & Crystals: How They Can Transform Your Life. Soozi Holbeche. (Illus.). 221p. 1995. pap. text 9.99 (*0-86188-954-1*, Pub. by Piatkus Bks) London Brdge.

Power of Gemstones. R. J. Walters. 160p. 1996. 17.98 (*0-7858-0642-3*) Bk Sales Inc.

***Power of Gemstones.** Raymond J. Walters. (Illus.). 160p. 2000. pap. 18.95 (*1-85868-729-2*, Pub. by Carlton Bks Ltd) Natl Bk Netwk.

Power of Gender in Religion. Farrell. 1996. pap. 22.81 (*0-07-021768-8*) McGraw.

Power of Geography: How Territory Shapes Social Life. Ed. by Jennifer R. Wolch & M. J. Dear. 352p. 1988. text 70.00 (*0-04-445228-4*) Routledge.

Power of Geography: How Territory Shapes Social Life. Ed. by Jennifer R. Wolch & M. J. Dear. 352p. (C). 1989. pap. 29.95 (*0-04-445056-7*) Routledge.

Power of Glamour: The Women Who Defined the Magic of Stardom. Annette Tapert. LC 97-46790. (Illus.). 256p. 1998. 40.00 (*0-517-70376-9*) Random Hse Value.

Power of Glass. Nomi Joval. (Illus.). 16p. (J). (ps-4). 1993. lib. bdg. 13.95 (*1-879567-21-0*, Valeria Bks) Wonder Well.

Power of Goals: Quotations to Strengthen Your Climb to New Heights. Career Press. LC 98-28304. 128p. 1998. pap. 7.99 (*1-56414-384-8*) Career Pr Inc.

Power of Goalsetting. Timothy L. Rogers. 96p. (Orig.). 1991. pap. 7.95 (*0-9630182-0-5*) T L Rogers.

Power of God. Craig W. Hagin. 84p. mass mkt. 2.95 (*0-89276-900-9*) Faith Lib Pubns.

***Power of God.** Chuck Klein. LC 99-88371. 188p. 1999. pap. 11.95 (*0-87714-456-7*) Denlingers.

Power of God. Mark A. Smith. 304p. 1997. 19.98 (*0-88290-612-7*, 1080) Horizon Utah.

Power of God: Dunamis in Gregory of Nyssa's Trinitarian Theology. Michel R. Barnes. LC 98-20197. 1999. 64.95 (*0-8132-0929-3*) Cath U Pr.

Power of God: Readings on Omnipotence & Evil. Ed. by Linwood P. Urban & Douglas Walton. 1978. text 10.95 (*0-19-502201-7*) OUP.

Power of God Against the Guns of Government: Religious Upheaval in Mexico at the Turn of the Century. Paul J. Vanderwood. LC 97-32506. 1998. 65.00 (*0-8047-3038-5*); pap. 24.95 (*0-8047-3039-3*) Stanford U Pr.

Power of God in a Broken World: Studies in Ephesians. Erwin Penner. (Luminaire Studies). 196p. (C). 1990. pap. 7.95 (*0-921788-11-8*) Kindred Prods.

Power of God Through the Dynamic of the Holy Spirit. Robert A. Hawkins. 125p. (Orig.). 1993. pap. 5.95 (*1-56794-035-8*, C2297) Star Bible.

Power of God to Heal. G. Garland. 1983. pap. 10.95 (*0-933062-08-7*) R H Sommer.

***Power of Gold: The History of an Obsession.** Peter L. Bernstein. 432p. 2000. 27.95 (*0-471-25210-7*) Wiley.

***Power of Gratitude.** Gordon Ferguson. 144p. 1999. pap. 9.99 (*1-57782-124-6*) Discipleshp.

Power of Health Care Teams: Strategies for Success. Kathleen Phillips. Ed. & Illus. by Joint Commission on Accreditation of Healthcare Organizations. LC 96-77364. 201p. 1997. pap. 50.00 (*0-86688-473-4*, HCT-100) Joint Comm Hlthcare.

Power of Her Sympathy: The Autobiography & Journals of Catharine Maria Sedgwick. Intro. by Mary Kelley. LC 93-29901. 1993. 25.00 (*0-934909-35-0*, Pub. by Mass Hist Soc) NE U Pr.

Power of His Presence see Poder de Su Presenciq

Power of His Presence. Adrian Rogers. LC 94-24968. 192p. 1995. 14.99 (*0-89107-841-X*) Crossway Bks.

Power of Historical Knowledge: Narrating the Past in Hawthorne, James & Dreiser. Susan L. Mizruchi. 336p. 1988. text 49.50 (*0-691-06725-2*, Pub. by Princeton U Pr) Cal Prin Full Svc.

Power of Holy Habits: A Discipline for Faithful Discipleship. William H. Hinson. 1991. pap. 10.95 (*0-687-33200-1*) Abingdon.

Power of Honor: What Love Looks Like. Fawn Parish. LC 99-25908. 224p. 1999. pap. 9.99 (*0-8307-2381-1*) Gospel Lght.

Power of Hope. Guideposts Editors. (Illus.). 384p. 1996. 12.99 (*0-88486-141-4*) Arrowood Pr.

Power of Hope. Maurice Lamm. 1997. per. 10.00 (*0-684-82547-3*, Fireside) S&S Trade Pap.

Power of Hope: A Doctor's Perspective. Howard Spiro. LC 98-18731. 320p. 1998. 40.00 (*0-300-07410-7*); pap. 18.00 (*0-300-07632-0*) Yale U Pr.

Power of Hope: The One Essential of Life & Love. Maurice Lamm. 288p. 1995. text 22.95 (*0-89256-361-3*, Rawson Assocs) Macmillan.

Power of Horses: Activity Book. Kim M. Wood. (Illus.). 68p. (YA). (gr. 3-12). 1999. pap. 14.95 (*0-9671978-1-3*) Syncopated Pr.

Power of Human Imagination: New Methods in Psychotherapy. J. L. Singer & K. S. Pope. LC 78-15392. (Emotions, Personality, & Psychotherapy Ser.). (Illus.). 426p. (C). 1978. 70.00 (*0-306-31140-2*, Plenum Trade) Perseus Pubng.

Power of Human Rights: International Norms & Domestic Change. Ed. by Thomas Risse et al. (Studies in International Relations: Vol. 66). (Illus.). 330p. 1999. pap. 19.95 (*0-521-65882-9*) Cambridge U Pr.

Power of Human Rights: International Norms & Domestic Change. Ed. by Thomas Risse et al. (Studies in International Relations: Vol. 66). (Illus.). 330p. (C). 1999. 54.95 (*0-521-65093-3*) Cambridge U Pr.

Power of Ideals in American History. Ephraim D. Adams. LC 75-98025. (BCL Ser.: No. II). reprint ed. 32.50 (*0-404-00285-4*) AMS Pr.

Power of Ideals in American History. Ephraim D. Adams. (BCL1 - U. S. History Ser.). 159p. 1991. reprint ed. lib. bdg. 69.00 (*0-7812-6027-2*) Rprt Serv.

***Power of Ideas.** Isaiah Berlin. Ed. by Henry Hardy. 2000. 24.95 (*0-691-05018-X*) Princeton U Pr.

Power of Ideas: The Heritage Foundation at 25 Years. Lee Edwards. LC 97-41296. (Illus.). 360p. 1998. 29.95 (*0-915463-77-6*) Jameson Bks.

***Power of Ideas: The University of Louisville Grawemeyer Awards in Music, Education, Religion & World Order.** Allan Dittmer. LC 99-58106. 1999. write for info. (*0-945084-78-1*) J Stuart Found.

***Power of Identification with Christ.** Mark Hankins. 202p. 1998. pap. 10.00 (*1-889981-04-4*) M Hankins Minist.

Power of Identity: Politics in a New Key. Kenneth R. Hoover et al. LC 96-51258. (Studies in Political Thinking). (Illus.). 176p. (C). 1997. pap. text 19.95 (*1-56643-051-8*, Chatham House Pub) Seven Bridges.

Power of Identity Vol. 2: The Information Age: Economy, Society & Culture. Manuel Castells. LC 96-36317. (Information Age Ser.). (Illus.). 352p. 1997. pap. text 27.95 (*1-55786-874-3*) Blackwell Pubs.

Power of Ideology. Istvan Meszaros. 640p. (C). 1990. pap. text 22.50 (*0-8147-5458-9*) NYU Pr.

Power of Images: Studies in the History & Theory of Response. David Freedberg. LC 88-27638. (Illus.). 560p. 1991. pap. 25.00 (*0-226-26146-8*) U Ch Pr.

Power of Images: Studies in the History & Theory of Response. David Freedberg. LC 88-27638. (Illus.). 560p. 1998. 47.95 (*0-226-26144-1*) U Ch Pr.

Power of Images in the Age of Augustus. Paul Zanker. Tr. by Alan Shapiro. 396p. 1990. pap. text 22.95 (*0-472-08124-1*, 08124) U of Mich Pr.

Power of Imagination. large type ed. Darwin L. Gross. 285p. 1998. pap. 16.95 (*0-931689-26-0*) Be Good To Your Self.

***Power of Impression Management: Strategies for Successful Interpersonal Communication.** Donald W. Slowik & Cara Cantarella. LC 97-90717. (Illus.). 305p. 2000. 69.95 (*1-883342-13-9*, 202); pap. text 29.95 (*1-883342-04-X*, 102) Evergrn Pr CO.

***Power of Indirect Influence.** Judith C. Tingley. 2000. pap. 17.95 (*0-8144-7050-5*) AMACOM.

***Power of Indirect Suggestion: Hypnosis, Genetics & Depression.** Oren B. Boyce. LC 99-93695. 2000. pap. 12.50 (*0-533-13104-9*) Vantage.

Power of Industrial Brands: An Effective Route to Competitive Advantage. Paul Hague & Peter Jackson. LC 94-21099. (Marketing for Professionals Ser.). 1994. write for info. (*0-07-707839-X*) McGraw.

***Power of Influence.** John Maxwell. 2000. pap. 6.99 (*1-56292-967-4*) Honor Bks OK.

Power of Influence: Intensive Influencing Skills at Work. Tom Lambert. (People Skills for Professionals Ser.). (Illus.). 214p. (Orig.). 1996. pap. 17.95 (*1-85788-115-X*) Nicholas Brealey.

Power of Information: Transforming the World, Professional Papers from the 86th Annual Conference of the Special Libraries Association, Montreal, Quebec, Canada, June 10-15, 1995. Special Libraries Association Staff. LC 95-17678. 99p. 1995. reprint ed. pap. 30.70 (*0-608-01999-2*, 206265500003) Bks Demand.

Power of Inner Peace. Diana Cooper. 234p. 1995. pap. 12.95 (*0-7499-1435-1*, Pub. by Piatkus Bks) London Brdge.

Power of Innovation: How to Make Innovation a Way of Life & How to Put Creative Solutions... Min Basadur. LC 95-19365. (Illus.). 330p. 1994. 28.95 (*0-273-61362-6*) F T P-H.

Power of Innovative Thinking: Let New Ideas Lead You to Success. Jim Wheeler. LC 98-5753. 128p. 1998. pap. 10.99 (*1-56414-365-1*) Career Pr Inc.

Power of Inspiration. Great Quotations Staff. 64p. 1995. 6.50 (*1-56245-214-2*) Great Quotations.

Power of Integrity: Building a Life Without Compromise. John F. MacArthur. LC 97-7861. 192p. 1997. pap. 10.99 (*0-89107-942-4*) Crossway Bks.

Power of Intercessory Prayer. Camille Nehmsmann. 104p. 1998. pap. text 6.95 (*0-9657682-3-6*) Moriah Pr.

Power of Internal Marketing: Building a Values-Based Corporate Culture. Lamar D. Berry. (Illus.). 140p. 1996. 22.00 (*1-888042-07-9*) Good Readng.

Power of Internal Martial Arts: Combat Secrets of Ba Gua, Tai Chi, & Hsing-I. Bruce K. Frantzis. LC 97-21285. (Illus.). 300p. (Orig.). 1997. pap. 24.95 (*1-55643-253-4*) North Atlantic.

Power of Intranets: Creating Workgroup Web Sites with Microsoft Office 2000 & FrontPage 2000. Evan Callahan. LC 99-21356. (Illus.). 300p. 1999. pap. 29.99 incl. cd-rom (*0-7356-0641-2*) Microsoft.

Power of Iron Man. John S. Romita et al. (Illus.). 160p. 1984. pap. 15.95 (*0-87135-599-X*) Marvel Entrprs.

***Power of It.** S. Braithwaite. 1998. pap. 88.00 (*81-86982-01-9*, Pub. by Business Pubns) St Mut.

Power of IT: Maximizing Your Technology Investments. Timothy Braithwaite. 150p. 1996. pap. 27.00 (*0-87389-349-2*, H0902) ASQ Qual Pr.

Power of Jewelry. Nancy Schiffer. LC 88-61467. (Illus.). 256p. 1988. 75.00 (*0-88740-135-X*) Schiffer.

Power of Jude. Jean B. Mirassou et al. 64p. (Orig.). 1993. pap. 5.95 (*0-9637572-0-2*) Deux Goudez.

Power of KI: How to Develop It & How to Use It. large type ed. Edgar Stiltner, Jr. Tr. by Bill Rouse. (Illus.). 50p. 1995. 9.95 (*0-9656596-0-7*) Toku-Kai Intl.

Power of Kindness. Harry M. Tippett. (Uplook Ser.). 32p. 1955. pap. 0.99 (*0-8163-0076-3*, 16415-2) Pacific Pr Pub Assn.

***Power of Kindness: Reconnecting to Friends, Family & the World.** Ed. by Random Acts. 336p. 2000. 6.98 (*1-56731-402-3*, MJF Bks) Fine Comms.

Power of Kings: Monarchy & Religion in Europe, 1589-1715. Paul K. Monod. LC 99-17815. (Illus.). 384p. 1999. 35.00 (*0-300-07810-2*) Yale U Pr.

Power of Kiowa Song: A Collaborative Ethnography. Luke E. Lassiter. LC 98-8866. 270p. 1998. lib. bdg. 40.00 (*0-8165-1834-3*) U of Ariz Pr.

Power of Kiowa Song: A Collaborative Ethnography. Luke E. Lassiter. LC 98-8866. (Illus.). 270p. 1998. pap. 17.95 (*0-8165-1835-1*) U of Ariz Pr.

Power of Knowing Who I Am in Christ. J. R. Reinhart. LC 82-73254. 220p. 1983. pap. 8.95 (*0-918060-04-4*) Burn Hart.

Power of Knowledge: George Eliot & Education. Linda K. Robertson. LC 96-33035. (University of Kansas Humanistic Studies: No. 61). VII, 191p. (C). 1997. text 43.95 (*0-8204-3064-1*) P Lang Pubng.

***Power of Large Numbers: Population, Politics & Gender in Nineteenth-Century France.** Joshua Cole. LC 99-46229. 2000. 39.95 (*0-8014-3701-6*) Cornell U Pr.

Power of Learning: A Guide to Gaining Competitive Advantage. Andrew Mayo & Elizabeth Lank. 280p. (C). 1994. pap. 60.00 (*0-85292-565-4*, Pub. by IPM Hse) St Mut.

Power of Learning: Fostering Employee Growth. Klas Mellander. LC 92-47432. 225p. 1993. 27.50 (*1-55623-893-2*, Irwn Prfssnl) McGraw-Hill Prof.

***Power of Learning: Gaining Competitive Advantage.** Mayo & Lank. 288p. 2000. pap. 59.95 (*0-8464-5132-8*) Beekman Pubs.

Power of Legitimacy among Nations. Thomas M. Franck. 320p. 1990. text 65.00 (*0-19-506178-0*) OUP.

Power of Letting Go: A Practical Approach to Releasing the Pressures in Your Life. Patricia Carrington. LC 98-46434. 1999. pap. 14.95 (*1-86204-329-9*, Pub. by Element MA) Penguin Putnam.

Power of Lies: Trangression in Victorian Fiction. John Kucich. LC 94-11987. 304p. 1994. text 45.00 (*0-8014-2842-4*); pap. text 17.95 (*0-8014-8089-2*) Cornell U Pr.

Power of Life or Death. Michael V. Disalle. LC 82-45662. (Capital Punishment Ser.). reprint ed. 28.50 (*0-404-62411-1*) AMS Pr.

***Power of Life or Death: Medical Coercion & the Euthanasia Debate.** Fabian Tassano. 1999. pap. 59.95 (*0-9536772-0-6*, Pub. by Inst Psychol Rsch) St Mut.

Power of Light: Eight Stories for Hanukkah. Isaac Bashevis Singer. LC 80-20263. (Illus.). 96p. (J). (ps-3). 1990. pap. 8.95 (*0-374-45984-3*, Sunburst Bks) FS&G.

Power of Light: Eight Stories for Hanukkah. Isaac Bashevis Singer. 80p. (J). (gr. 4 up). 1982. pap. 2.50 (*0-380-60103-6*, Avon Bks) Morrow Avon.

Power of Light: Eight Stories for Hanukkah, , Class Set. unabridged ed. Isaac Bashevis Singer. (J). (gr. 2). 1997. 129.30 incl. audio (*0-7887-2904-7*, 46402) Recorded Bks.

Power of Light: Eight Stories for Hanukkah, Homework Set. unabridged ed. Isaac Bashevis Singer. (J). 1997. pap., boxed set 36.20 incl. audio (*0-7887-1842-8*, 40622) Recorded Bks.

Power of Limits: Proportional Harmonies in Nature, Art & Architecture. Gyorgy Doczi. 1981. pap. 24.95 (*0-394-73580-3*, Pub. by Shambhala Pubns) Random.

Power of Limits: Proportional Harmonies in Nature, Art & Architecture. Gyorgy Doczi. LC 77-90883. (Illus.). 224p. 1994. pap. 27.00 (*0-87773-193-4*, Pub. by Shambhala Pubns) Random.

Power of Listening. Roberta Turnbull-Ray. 176p. (C). 1995. spiral bd. 20.95 (*0-8403-9127-7*) Kendall-Hunt.

Power of Literature & Its Connection with Religion. Francis S. Key. (Notable American Authors Ser.). 1999. reprint ed. lib. bdg. 125.00 (*0-7812-3675-4*) Rprt Serv.

Power of Little Words: Some Ideas to Improve Your Writing. John L. Beckley. (Illus.). 128p. 1984. 14.95 (*0-910187-02-9*) Economics Pr.

Power of Logic. Charles S. Layman. LC 98-13617. ix, 566p. 1998. text 51.95 (*1-55934-955-7*, 1955) Mayfield Pub.

***Power of Logic: Alternate Printing.** Charles S. Layman. LC 99-51536. ix, 566p. 1999. pap. text. write for info. (*0-7674-1773-9*, 1773-9) Mayfield Pub.

Power of Logic: Study Guide. C. Stephen Layman et al. vi, 164p. (C). 1999. pap. text, student ed. 17.95 (*0-7674-0690-7*, 0690-7) Mayfield Pub.

***Power of Logic Test Bank.** C. Stephen Layman & Edwin Martin. 92p. (C). 1999. pap. text. write for info. (*0-7674-1363-6*, 1363-6) Mayfield Pub.

Power of Logos. William L. Haig & Laurel Harper. LC 96-49074. (Illus.). 160p. (C). 1997. text 39.95 (*0-442-02313-8*, VNR) Wiley.

Power of Logos: How to Create Effective Company Logos. William L. Haig & Laurel Harper. 208p. 1997. 39.95 (*0-471-28778-4*, VNR) Wiley.

***Power of Love.** (Rock & Pop Classics: Vol. 1). (Illus.). 30p. 1999. write for info. (*1-892207-30-3*) Intl Masters Pub.

Power of Love. M. Baroin. 192p. 1989. 73.50 (*0-08-036562-0*, Pergamon Pr) Elsevier.

Power of Love. Ed. by Guidepost Editors. (Illus.). 400p. 1995. 12.99 (*0-88486-115-5*) Arrowood Pr.

Power of Love. Rosemary Hammond. (Romance Ser.). 1995. pap. 2.99 (*0-373-17218-4*, 1-17218-8) Harlequin Bks.

Power of Love. Jayne Ann Krentz et al. (Promo Ser.). 1998. per. 9.99 (*0-373-83399-7*, 1-83399-5) Harlequin Bks.

***Power of Love.** Stuart J. Levy. 1999. pap. 4.99 (*1-892213-13-3*, SMILE Bks) Mixx Enter Inc.

***Power of Love: A Promise Kept.** rev. ed. Marian Joan Yoest. Orig. Title: Love after Life. 222p. 2000. pap. 16.95 (*0-945105-17-7*) Yoest Expressions.

Power of Love: For Uncomplicated Christians. Emile Briere. 158p. 1990. pap. 11.95 (*0-921440-17-0*) Madonna Hse.

Power of Love: The Moral Use of Knowledge Amongst the Amuesha of Central Peru. Fernando Santos-Granero. LC 90-814. (Monographs on Social Anthropology: Vol. 62). (Illus.). 256p. (C). 1991. text 75.00 (*0-485-19562-3*, Pub. by Athlone Pr) Humanities.

***Power of Love to Transform Our Lives & Our World.** June Singer. (Illus.). 328p. 2000. pap. 18.95 (*0-89254-052-4*, Pub. by Nicolas-Hays) Weiser.

Power of Loving Your Church: Leading Through Acceptance & Grace. David Hansen. Ed. by David L. Goetz. LC 97-33847. (Pastor's Soul Ser.). 176p. 1998. text 16.99 (*1-55661-968-5*) Bethany Hse.

Power of Magic: Ancient Secrets & Modern Mysteries. Derek Parker. 1999. pap. text 17.95 (*1-84000-222-0*) Millers Pubns.

Power of Magic: Ancient Secrets & Modern Mysteries. Derek Parker & Julia Parker. LC 92-12175. 224p. 1993. 20.00 (*0-671-76921-9*) S&S Trade.

Power of Management Capital: Reconnecting the Disconnected Corporation. Armand V. Feigenbaum. 324p. 1997. 24.95 (*0-07-021733-5*) McGraw.

Power of Mantra & the Mystery of Initiation. Pandit Rajmani Tigunait. 248p. 1999. pap. text 14.95 (*0-89389-176-2*) Himalayan Inst.

Power of Maps. Denis Wood. LC 92-23443. (Mappings). (Illus.). 248p. 1992. pap. text 18.95 (*0-89862-493-2*); lib. bdg. 39.95 (*0-89862-492-4*) Guilford Pubns.

Power of Mastering Your Primal Sense. Charles R. Beam. LC 97-92221. (Illus.). 308p. 1997. 19.95 (*0-9653985-1-X*, 9702) StarSide Pr.

Power of Matter over Mind. Date not set. pap. write for info. (*1-893637-11-5*) Hlth & Hap.

Power of Meditation: Energize the Mind & Restore the Body. Christopher Titmuss. LC 99-20327. (Illus.). 128p. 1999. 19.95 incl. audio compact disk (*0-8069-2447-0*) Sterling.

Power of Meditation & Prayer. Michael Toms et al. LC 97-11492. 200p. (Orig.). 1997. pap. 12.95 (*1-56170-423-7*, 892) Hay House.

Power of Mental Imagery. Warren Hilton. LC 90-81217. (Applications of Psychology to the Problems of Personal & Business Efficiency Ser.: No. 5). 65p. 1990. reprint ed. pap. 10.00 (*0-87034-095-6*) Fraser Pub Co.

***Power of Mentoring.** Taking the Lead Staff. (Leadership Ser.). (Illus.). 40p. 2000. pap. text 11.95 (*1-930390-01-7*, Taking The Lead) Ctr for Career Dev in Educ.

***Power of Metaphor: Story Telling & Guided Journeys for Trainers & Therapists.** Michael Berman & David Brown. 160p. 2000. pap. 19.95 (*1-899836-43-8*, Pub. by Crown Hse) LPC Group.

Power of Metaphor in the Age of Electronic Media. Raymond Gozzi, Jr. LC 99-18902. (Communication Ser.). 256p. (C). 1999. 65.00 (*1-57273-122-2*); pap. 24.95 (*1-57273-123-0*) Hampton Pr NJ.

***Power of Microeconomics.** Navarro. 1999. cd-rom 21.56 (*0-07-228314-9*) McGraw.

Power of Mindful Learning. Ellen Langer. 1998. pap. 12.00 (*0-201-33991-9*) Addison-Wesley.

Power of Mindful Learning. Ellen J. Langer. 167p. 1997. 20.00 (*0-614-28237-3*) Addison-Wesley.

Power of Mindfulness. Nyanaponika Thera. 58p. 1986. 3.00 (*955-24-0002-3*, Pub. by Buddhist Pub Soc) Vipassana Res Pubns.

Power of Miracles: Stories of God in the Everyday. rev. ed. Joan W. Anderson. LC 98-13966. 1998. 23.00 (*0-345-39732-0*) Ballantine Pub Grp.

Power of Modern Greek: Basic Course I in the Modern Greek Language. 2nd ed. Strati Demertzis. 221p. (C). 1992. pap. text 22.22 (*0-685-72071-3*) Expressway Pubs.

Power of Modern Greek: Basic Course II in the Modern Greek Language. 2nd ed. Strati Demertzis. 231p. (C). 1993. pap. text 24.44 (*0-685-72072-1*) Expressway Pubs.

Power of Modern Greek: Intermediate Modern Greek, Level III & IV. Strati Demertzis. 217p. (Orig.). (C). 1992. pap. text 27.77 (*0-9618466-2-3*) Expressway Pubs.

Power of Money. Armand Van Dormael. LC 96-35577. 1997. text 27.50 (*0-8147-8791-6*) NYU Pr.

An Asterisk (*) at the beginning of an entry indicates that the title is appearing for the first time.

Power of Money: Coinage & Politics in the Athenian Empire. Thomas J. Figueira. LC 97-50265. 624p. 1998. 49.95 (*0-8122-3441-3*) U of Pa Pr.

*****Power of Mother Love: Transforming Both Mother & Child.** Brenda Hunter. LC 98-229053. 288p. 1998. 19.95 (*1-57856-001-2*) Waterbrook Pr.

*****Power of Mother Love: Transforming Both Mother & Child.** Brenda Hunter. 288p. 1999. pap. 12.95 (*1-57856-256-2*) Waterbrook Pr.

*****Power of Movement in Plants.** Charles Darwin. 592p. 2000. reprint ed. 79.95 (*1-930665-07-5*) Blackburn Pr.

Power of Movement in Plants. 2nd ed. Charles Darwin. LC 65-23402. 1966. reprint ed. lib. bdg. 55.00 (*0-306-70921-X*) Da Capo.

Power of Music: A Complete Music Activities Program for Older Adults. Bill Messenger. LC 95-18826. 96p. 1995. spiral bd. 25.95 incl. audio (*1-878812-27-0*) Hlth Prof Pr.

Power of Myth. Joseph Campbell. 320p. 1991. pap. 12.95 (*0-385-41886-8*) Doubleday.

Power of Myth. Joseph Campbell & Bill Moyers. LC 88-4218. (Illus.). 256p. 1988. pap. 29.95 (*0-385-24774-5*) Doubleday.

Power of Names: A Fascinating Study in the Psychology of Names. Judy Miller. Ed. by Barry Bernard. 211p. (Orig.). 1992. per. 11.95 (*0-9631327-0-9*) Cascade Spec.

Power of Naming: A Concilium Reader in Feminist Liberation Theology. Ed. by Elisabeth S. Fiorenza. LC 96-41166. (Concilium Ser.). 350p. (Orig.). 1996. pap. 20.00 (*1-57075-094-7*) Orbis Bks.

Power of Nations in the 1990s: A Strategic Assessment. Ray S. Cline. 152p. 1994. 48.50 (*0-8191-9150-7*); pap. 24.50 (*0-8191-9151-5*) U Pr of Amer.

Power of Natural Healing. Hua-Ching Ni. LC 90-60823. 232p. (Orig.). 1991. pap. 14.95 (*0-937064-31-9*) SevenStar Comm.

Power of Nature. Margie Burton et al. Ed. by Alison Adams. (Early Connections Ser.). 16p. (J). (gr. k-2). 1999. pap. 4.50 (*1-58344-078-X*) Benchmark Educ.

Power of Negative Thinking: Coming to Terms with Our Forbidden Emotions. Gerald Amada. LC 98-54369. 260p. 1999. 24.95 (*1-56833-125-8*) Madison Bks UPA.

Power of Negotiating: Strategies for Success. Mike R. Stark. LC 95-90945. 128p. 1996. pap. 12.95 (*0-9649453-0-4*) Trimrk Publng.

*****Power Of Networking: It's Not What You Know, I'ts Who You Know.** Hilton Catt. 1999. pap. text 17.95 (*0-7494-2975-5*, Kogan Pg Educ) Stylus Pub VA.

Power of News. Michael Schudson. LC 94-36194. 272p. 1995. text 35.95 (*0-674-69586-0*, SCHPOW) HUP.

Power of News. Michael Schudson. 288p. 1996. pap. 17.95 (*0-674-69587-9*) HUP.

Power of News: The History of Reuters. 2nd ed. Donald Read. LC 98-36926. (Illus.). 558p. 1999. 49.95 (*0-19-820768-9*) OUP.

*****Power of Nice.** Ronald M. Shapiro et al. LC 98-21033. 288p. 1998. 24.95 (*0-471-29377-6*) Wiley.

Power of Nonviolence. 3rd ed. Richard B. Gregg. 192p. (Orig.). 1984. pap. 15.00 (*0-934676-70-4*) Greenlf Bks.

*****Power of Now: A Guide to Spiritual Enlightment.** Eckhart Tolle & Russell DiCarlo. LC 99-42366. 224p. 1999. 21.95 (*1-57731-152-3*) New Wrld Lib.

*****Power of Now: How Winning Companies Sense & Respond to Change Using Real-Time Technology.** Vivek Ranadive. LC 00-271759. 214p. 1999. 29.99 (*0-07-135684-3*) McGraw.

Power of Numbers: A Teacher's Guide to Mathematics in a Social Studies Context. Fred Gross et al. (Illus.). 271p. (Orig.). 1993. pap. 28.00 (*0-942349-05-9*) Eductrs Soc Respons.

Power of Observation. Judy R. Jablon et al. (Illus.). 134p. (C). 1999. pap. text 19.95 (*1-879537-36-2*, Pub. by Tchng Strtgs) Gryphon Hse.

Power of One. 32p. 1991. 8.00 (*0-318-23891-8*) Future Home.

Power of One. John Baird. LC 97-70295. 300p. (C). 1997. text 35.00 (*0-943590-90-6*) Amer College.

Power of One. Bryce Courtenay. LC 96-96683. 518p. 1996. pap. 12.95 (*0-345-41005-X*) Ballantine Pub Grp.

Power of One: Authentic Leadership in Turbulent Times. Sharif M. Abdullah. 96p. 1991. pap. 10.00 (*0-9632184-0-9*) Forum Comm Trans.

Power of One: Authentic Leadership in Turbulent Times. Sharif M. Abdullah. 96p. 1995. pap. 10.00 (*0-86571-325-1*) New Soc Pubs.

Power of One: Recreating Your Life from the Source. Denise Gibel. 261p. 1998. pap. 12.95 (*0-9671717-0-9*) Enter Light.

*****Power of One: The Solo Play for Playwrights, Actors & Directors.** Louis E. Catron. LC 99-49233. 240p. 2000. pap. 18.95 (*0-325-00153-7*, Pub. by Heinemann) Natl Bk Netwk.

Power of Open Book Management: Releasing the True Potential of Peoples' Minds, Hearts & Hands. John P. Schuster et al. LC 95-42390. 320p. 1996. 24.95 (*0-471-13287-X*) Wiley.

Power of Open Book Management: Releasing the True Potential of People's Minds, Hearts & Souls. John P. Schuster et al. 256p. 1995. 25.00 (*0-939246-78-3*) Wiley.

Power of Optimism. Alan L. McGinnis. 1993. pap. 5.50 (*0-685-67757-5*, Harp PBks) HarpC.

Power of OS-2: A Comprehensive User's Manual. Judi N. Fernandez & Ruth Ashley. 1989. 21.95 (*0-8306-2693-X*, 2993); pap. 21.95 (*0-8306-2993-9*, 2993P) McGraw-Hill Prof.

Power of Our Ideas: Papers from the 1992 Principals Academy. Ed. by Regina Haney. 115p. 1993. pap. text 6.00 (*1-55833-096-8*) Natl Cath Educ.

Power of Paideia Schools: Defining Lives Through Learning. Terry Roberts & National Paideia Center Staff. LC 98-9049. 125p. 1998. pap. 17.95 (*0-87120-303-0*, 198034) ASCD.

Power of Participation: Improving Schools in a Democratic Society. Raymond J. Golarz & Marion J. Golarz. LC 95-129765. 129p. (Orig.). 1995. pap. 19.95 (*0-9636531-1-3*) Nat Trning.

Power of Partnership in the Church. John C. Maxwell. 1999. pap. text 3.99 (*0-8499-5535-1*) Countryman.

Power of Partnerships: The Next Step Beyond TQM, Reengineering & Lean Production : A Competitive Cornerstone for the 21st Century. John L. Mariotti. LC 95-1579. 1995. 24.95 (*1-55786-717-8*) Blackwell Pubs.

Power of Pascal. Larry Leff. 1986. text 39.95 (*0-13-687450-9*, Busn) P-H.

Power of Passion: Achieve Your Own Everests. 7th ed. Alan Hobson. 198p. 1997. pap. 18.95 (*0-9682430-0-2*) Inn3er Everests.

Power of Pasta. Olwen Woodier. LC 84-48812. (Illus.). 160p. 1985. pap. 6.95 (*0-88266-384-4*, Garden Way Pub) Storey Bks.

*****Power of Peaceful Thinking: How to Stop Creative Stress.** 2000. pap. write for info. (*0-9701303-0-9*) Pos People Part OH.

Power of Peervention: A Manual for the Trainers of Peer Facilitators. Robert D. Myrick & Betsy E. Folk. LC 90-86234. (Illus.). 226p. (C). 1991. teacher ed., spiral bd. 39.95 (*0-932796-36-2*) Ed Media Corp.

Power of People Skills: A Manager's Guide to Assessing & Developing Your Organization's Greatest Resource. Douglas Stewart. 296p. (C). 1993. reprint ed. pap. text 25.00 (*0-8191-8900-6*) U Pr of Amer.

Power of Perception. Marcus Bach. LC 73-5535. 156p. 1983. pap. 8.95 (*0-87516-523-0*) DeVorss.

*****Power of Performance Management: How Leading Companies Create Sustained Value.** Andre de Waal. 224p. 2001. 39.95 (*0-471-38347-3*) Wiley.

Power Of Perimenopause. Stephanie Bender. 1999. pap. 12.00 (*0-609-80416-2*) Random Hse Value.

Power of Personal Advertising: Self-Empowerment in the Search for Personal Relationships. Marlow P. Weaver. 130p. (Orig.). 1996. pap. 9.95 (*0-9654136-0-8*) MW Enter.

Power of Personal Influence. Richard Hale & Peter Whitlam. LC 95-24731. 1995. write for info. (*0-07-709131-0*) McGraw.

Power of Personal Integrity. Charles H. Dyer. LC 96-43750. 230p. 1997. pap. 9.99 (*0-8423-4884-0*) Tyndale Hse.

Power of Personal Presence: The Art of Cultivating a Dynamic Presence. Jane Hundley. 212p. (Orig.). 1993. pap. 14.95 (*0-9634511-0-3*) Centerpt Pr.

Power of Personal Storytelling. Jack Maguire. LC 98-21250. (Inner Workbook Ser.). 288p. 1998. 16.95 (*0-87477-930-8*, Tarcher Putnam) Putnam Pub Group.

Power of Personality. Orison S. Marden. 86p. 1997. pap. 8.00 (*0-89540-362-5*, SB-362) Sun Pub.

Power of Persuasion. Elizabeth Massie. (Buffy the Vampire Slayer Ser.: No. 7). 196p. (YA). (gr. 7 up). 1999. per. 4.99 (*0-671-02632-1*) PB.

Power of Persuasion. Betty L. Randolph. Ed. by Success Education Institute International. (Success Ser.). 1989. 14.98 incl. audio (*1-55909-231-9*, 190P); 14.98 incl. audio (*1-55909-232-7*, 190PM) Randolph Tapes.

Power of Persuasion. 2nd ed. Harry Hazel. 166p. (C). 1998. per. 27.95 (*0-7872-5009-0*) Kendall-Hunt.

Power of Photography: How Photographs Changed Our Lives. Vicki Goldberg. (Illus.). 280p. 1991. 45.00 (*1-55859-039-0*) Abbeville Pr.

Power of Photography: How Photographs Changed Our Lives. Vicki Goldberg. (Illus.). 280p. 1993. pap. 35.00 (*1-55859-467-1*) Abbeville Pr.

Power of Pinjarra. Sandy Dengler. LC 88-32756. (Australian Destiny Ser.: No. 2). 272p. (Orig.). 1989. pap. 8.99 (*1-55661-057-2*) Bethany Hse.

Power of Pittsburgh. Sharon K. Williams et al. LC 98-12633. (Urban Tapestry Ser.). (Illus.). 528p. 1998. 44.95 (*1-881096-11-4*) Towery Pub.

Power of Place. Winifred Gallagher. LC 93-41798. 240p. 1994. reprint ed. pap. 13.00 (*0-06-097602-0*, Perennial) HarperTrade.

Power of Place: Bringing Together Geographical & Sociological Imaginations. Ed. by John Agnew & James S. Duncan. 272p. 1989. 49.95 (*0-04-445281-0*) Routledge.

Power of Place: Landscape in New Zealand Children's Fiction. Diane Hebley. LC 98-197143. 250p. 1998. pap. 39.95 (*1-877133-47-7*, Pub. by Univ Otago Pr) Intl Spec Bk.

Power of Place: Sacred Ground in Natural & Human Environments. James A. Swan. (Illus.). 315p. 1993. pap. 14.95 (*0-8356-0670-8*, Quest) Theos Pub Hse.

Power of Place: Urban Landscapes As Public History. Dolores Hayden. LC 94-23424. (Illus.). 316p. 1995. 35.00 (*0-262-08237-3*) MIT Pr.

Power of Place: Urban Landscapes As Public History. Dolores Hayden. (Illus.). 320p. 1997. reprint ed. pap. text 17.50 (*0-262-58152-3*) MIT Pr.

Power of Place: World Regional Geography. Gil Latz. 235p. 1997. pap., student ed. 28.95 (*0-471-12841-4*) Wiley.

Power of Play: New Visions of Creativity. Ed. by Carol S. Lawson. (Chrysalis Reader Ser.: Vol. 3). 160p. (Orig.). 1996. pap. 12.95 (*0-87785-227-8*) Swedenborg.

Power of Poetry: Plateaus & Hurdles. Marbl Johnson. (Illus.). 160p. 1998. pap. 10.95 (*1-888106-77-8*) Agreka Bks.

*****Power of Political Art: The 1930s Literary Left Reconsidered.** Robert Shulman. LC 99-55916. 400p. 2000. lib. bdg. 49.95 (*0-8078-2540-9*) U of NC Pr.

*****Power of Political Art: The 1930s Literary Left Reconsidered.** Robert Shulman. LC 99-55916. 400p. 2000. pap. 19.95 (*0-8078-4853-0*) U of NC Pr.

Power of Positive Choices. Gail McMeekin. 37p. 1996. pap. 15.00 (*0-9678271-0-8*) Creative Suc.

Power of Positive Coaching. Raymond M. Nakamura. LC 96-4186. 1996. pap. 33.75 (*0-7637-0031-2*) Jones & Bartlett.

*****Power of Positive Confrontation.** Barbara Pachter & Susan F. Magee. LC 99-40096. 224p. 1999. 22.95 (*1-56924-679-3*) Marlowe & Co.

*****Power of Positive Criticism.** Hendrie Weisinger. LC 99-34293. 150p. 1999. pap. 15.00 (*0-8144-0483-9*) AMACOM.

*****Power of Positive Desire.** Ed. by Cynthia Hansen. 30p. 2000. pap. 4.00 (*0-9667225-2-3*) J Hernandez.

Power of Positive Doing: Twelve Strategies for Taking Control of Your Life. Ivan G. Burnell. (Orig.). 1990. pap. 14.95 (*0-9625806-0-0*) IPD Pubg.

Power of Positive Doing: 12 Strategies for Taking Control of Your Life. rev. ed. Ivan G. Burnell. LC 99-94026. 240p. (Orig.). 1999. pap. 14.95 (*0-9625806-3-5*) IPD Pubg.

Power of Positive Faith in God. large type ed. Wilson Hildreth. 181p. (Orig.). 1997. pap. 17.00 (*0-9660161-0-6*) W Hildreth Pub.

Power of Positive Living. Norman Vincent Peale. LC 96-96721. 1996. pap. 10.00 (*0-449-91166-7*) Fawcett.

Power of Positive Living: The Opportunity of a Lifetime. Hua C. Ni. (Course for Total Health Ser.). 1996. pap. 8.50 (*0-937064-90-4*) SevenStar Comm.

Power of Positive Parenting. Glenn I. Latham. 1994. pap. text 19.95 (*1-56713-175-1*) APP.

Power of Positive Praying. John R. Bisagno. 91p. 1965. mass mkt. 6.99 (*0-310-21212-X*, 9238P) Zondervan.

Power of Positive Praying. large type ed. John R. Bisagno. (Large Print Inspirational Ser.). 256p. 1987. pap. 8.95 (*0-8027-2580-5*) Walker & Co.

Power of Positive Prophecy: Finding the Hidden Potential in Everyday Life. Laurie Beth Jones. LC 99-20548. 288p. 1999. 21.95 (*0-7868-6350-1*, Pub. by Hyperion) Time Warner.

Power of Positive Prophecy: How to Envision & Create Your Best Future. Alan Vaughan. 1992. pap. 13.95 (*1-85538-099-4*, Pub. by Aqrn Pr) HarpC.

Power of Positive Resistance. Roy H. Hicks. 128p. 1983. mass mkt. 5.99 (*0-89274-294-1*, HH-294) Harrison Hse.

Power of Positive Shrinking: Appetite - Weight Control by Hypnosis & Behavior Modification. Richard U. Gunderson. 54p. (Orig.). 1981. 12.95 (*0-686-36697-2*) Gunderson.

Power of Positive Teaching. Floyd G. McCormick. LC 92-42276. 336p. 1994. 39.50 (*0-89464-831-4*) Krieger.

Power of Positive Thinking. Norman Vincent Peale. 210p. 1982. mass mkt. 5.99 (*0-449-21493-1*, Crest) Fawcett.

Power of Positive Thinking. Norman Vincent Peale. LC 96-96734. 1996. pap. 10.00 (*0-449-91147-0*) Fawcett.

Power of Positive Thinking. Norman Vincent Peale. 226p. 1987. 20.50 (*0-671-76470-5*) S&S Trade.

Power of Positive Thinking. large type ed. Norman Vincent Peale. 464p. 1985. reprint ed. pap. 15.95 (*0-8027-2465-5*) Walker & Co.

Power of Positive Thinking: From Poverty to Fame. Michael E. Akpan & Ememobong M. Akpan. LC 92-75966. 182p. 1992. pap. text 15.00 (*0-9634998-0-7*) Ebewos Afr-Am.

Power of Positive Thought: The Key to Attainment. Gilbert Oakley. 148p. 1995. pap. 7.95 (*0-572-01536-4*, Pub. by Foulsham UK) Assoc Pubs Grp.

Power of Positivity: 80 Ways to Energize Your Life. Joel Schroeder & Ruth Schroeder. Ed. by Kelly Scanlon. LC 96-69969. (Illus.). 190p. 1997. pap. 12.95 (*1-57294-068-9*, 12-0034) SkillPath Pubns.

Power of Power Politics: From Classical Realism to Neotraditionalism. John A. Vasquez. LC 98-20166. (Studies in International Relations: No. 63). (Illus.). 468p. (C). 1999. text 64.95 (*0-521-44235-4*); pap. text 24.95 (*0-521-44746-1*) Cambridge U Pr.

Power of PowerPoint 4.0 for Windows. James Karney. LC 94-40120. 473p. 1994. pap. 34.95 incl. disk (*1-55828-377-3*, MIS Pr) IDG Bks.

Power of Praise. Kenneth A. Erickson. 112p. 1984. pap. 6.99 (*0-570-03925-8*, 12-2859) Concordia.

Power of Praise, Vol. 3. Joy Haney. 1997. pap. 6.95 (*1-880969-25-4*) Schl Prophet.

Power of Praise & Worship. Terry Law. (Illus.). 256p. (Orig.). 1985. pap. 9.99 (*0-932081-01-0*) Victory Hse.

Power of Prayer. 192p. 1987. pap. 9.99 (*0-310-33311-3*, 10909P) Zondervan.

Power of Prayer. Ronnie Burch, pseud. (Illus.). 115p. (C). 1989. student ed. write for info. (*0-318-66288-4*) B T Burch.

Power of Prayer. Ed. by Dale Salwak. LC 98-24991. 240p. 1998. 20.00 (*1-880032-79-1*) New Wrld Lib.

*****Power of Prayer,** Dale Salwak. LC 98-24991. 240p. 1999. pap. 14.00 (*1-57731-123-X*, Pub. by New Wrld Lib) Publishers Group.

*****Power of Prayer.** R. A. Torrey. LC 00-8966. 2000. pap. write for info. (*0-88368-607-4*) Whitaker Hse.

Power of Prayer. Ellen Gould Harmon White. LC 94-78149. 224p. 1994. per. 7.95 (*1-57258-002-X*) Teach Servs.

Power of Prayer. rev. ed. Samuel Prime. 265p. 1998. pap. 12.50 (*0-85151-758-7*) Banner of Truth.

Power of Prayer, No. 6. Charles Stanley. 24p. 1995. pap. 2.50 (*1-56476-438-9*, 6-3438, Victor Bks) Chariot Victor.

Power of Prayer & Fasting: 10 Secrets of Spiritual Strength. Ronnie W. Floyd. LC 97-14644. 1997. pap. 12.99 (*0-8054-0164-4*) Broadman.

Power of Prayer in a Believer's Life. Charles H. Spurgeon. Ed. by Robert Hall. (Believer's Life Ser.). 192p. (Orig.). 1993. pap. 9.99 (*1-883002-03-6*) Emerald WA.

Power of Praying & Fasting. Marlin S. Hoffman. 1968. 4.35 (*0-89137-535-X*) Quality Pubns.

Power of Praying in Other Tongues: Mini Book. Terry Crist. Ed. by Jimmy Peacock. (Illus.). (Orig.). (C). 1990. 1.00 (*0-9623768-5-X*) SpiritBuilder.

*****Power of Praying Together: Forgotten Secrets of a Growing Prayer Group.** Oliver W. Price. LC 99-24711. 192p. 1999. pap. 10.99 (*0-8254-3552-8*) Kregel.

Power of Presidential Ideologies. Dennis Florig. LC 92-14726. 328p. 1992. 59.95 (*0-275-94304-6*, C4304, Praeger Pubs) Greenwood.

*****Power of Pride: The Man & Women Who Embodied the Spirit of the Harlem Renaissance.** Carole L. Marks & Diana Edkins. LC 98-31259. (Illus.). 272p. 1999. 35.00 (*0-609-60096-6*, Crown) Crown Pub Group.

Power of Prism: A Rigging & Jigging Breakthrough for the 90's. Reg Delwiche. (Illus.). 44p. (Orig.). 1989. pap. 2.95 (*0-9624936-0-0*) Prog Fisherman.

Power of Problem Solving: Practical Ideas & Teaching Strategies for Any K-8 Subject Area. Juanita S. Sorenson et al. LC 95-12679. 320p. (C). 1995. pap. text 40.00 (*0-205-15943-5*) Allyn.

Power of Product Platforms: Creating & Sustaining Robust Corporations. Mark H. Meyer & Alvin P. Lehnerd. LC 96-33508. 288p. 1997. 34.50 (*0-684-82580-5*) Free Pr.

Power of Professional Management. George S. Dively. LC 77-151052. 191p. reprint ed. pap. 59.30 (*0-608-13397-3*, 205574000034) Bks Demand.

Power of Prophecy. Wallace H. Heflin. 224p. 1996. pap. 10.99 (*1-884369-22-7*) McDougal Pubng.

Power of Prophetic Synergy. Carlisle J. Peterson. LC 98-91102. 200p. (gr. 8-12). 1999. pap. 12.95 (*1-889448-24-9*) NBN Publishers Group.

Power of Prosperous Thinking: A Practical & Inspirational Guide to Making, Managing, & Multiplying Your Money. Jack Johnstad & Lois Johnstad. (Illus.). 256p. 1982. 12.95 (*0-312-63431-5*) St Martin.

*****Power of Public Engagement: A Beacon of Hope for America's Schools.** Ed. by William G. O'Callaghan. xiv, 305p. 1999. text 24.95 (*0-914607-67-7*, 1747) Master Tchr.

Power of Public Ideas. Ed. by Robert B. Reich. 272p. 1990. pap. 15.95 (*0-674-69590-9*) HUP.

Power of Public Ideas. Ed. by Robert B. Reich. LC 87-1371. 264p. 1987. 24.95 (*0-88730-128-2*, HarpBusn) HarpInfo.

Power of Public Relations. Joseph F. Awad. LC 85-6258. 176p. 1985. 42.95 (*0-275-90054-1*, C0054, Praeger Pubs) Greenwood.

Power of Public Speaking. Marie Stuttard. LC 96-32955. 1997. pap. 10.95 (*0-8120-9794-7*) Barron.

Power of Public Speaking: Eloquence That Works. Carpenter. LC 99-182785. 180p. (C). 1998. pap. text 14.95 (*0-205-27124-3*) P-H.

Power of Purpose: Creating Meaning in Your Life & Work. Richard J. Leider. LC 97-15571. 200p. 1997. 20.00 (*1-57675-021-3*) Berrett-Koehler.

*****Power of Purpose: Creating Meaning in Your Life & Work.** Richard J. Leider. 176p. 2000. 6.98 (*1-56731-406-6*, MJF Bks) Fine Comms.

Power of Purpose: Your Pathway to Dynamic Living, Wealth, & Personal Success. Jack C. McDowell. LC 94-10904. 1993. pap. 14.95 (*0-9625485-1-0*) Epiphany GA.

Power of Pyruvate. Ronald T. Stanko & Laura O'Hare. LC 99-31539. 128p. 1999. pap. 14.95 (*0-87983-990-2*, 39902K, Keats Publng) NTC Contemp Pub Co.

Power of QuarkXPress for the Mac. David Brown. LC 94-39390. 900p. 1994. pap. 34.95 (*1-55828-381-1*, MIS Pr) IDG Bks.

Power of Raceless Thinking. William Mitchum. (Illus.). 189p. 1988. 9.95 (*0-9612120-4-7*); pap. 5.95 (*0-9612120-5-5*) Para-Bk-Pr.

Power of Raven, Wisdom of Serpent: Celtic Women's Spirituality. Noragh Jones. 240p. (Orig.). 1995. pap. 16.95 (*0-940262-66-5*, Lindisfarne) Anthroposophic.

Power of Reading: Insights from the Research. Stephen D. Krashen. LC 92-15096. x, 119p. 1993. pap. text 20.00 (*1-56308-006-0*) Libs Unl.

Power of Reason - 1988: An Autobiography. Lyndon H. LaRouche, Jr. LC 87-7894. (Illus.). 331p. (Orig.). 1987. pap. 10.00 (*0-943235-00-6*) Exec Intel Review.

Power of Reiki: An Ancient Hands-On Healing Technique. Tanmaya Honervogt. LC 97-31261. (Illus.). 144p. 1998. 16.95 (*0-8050-5559-2*) H Holt & Co.

Power of Relationships in a Changing World. Jenyce Johnson. 64p. (Orig.). 1997. pap. 10.00 (*0-9658894-4-0*) J Johnson & Assocs.

Power of Religion: A Comparative Introduction. Amanda Porterfield. (Illus.). 240p. (C). 1997. pap. text 21.95 (*0-19-509329-1*) OUP.

Power of Religious Publics: Staking Claims in American Society. Ed. by William H. Swatos, Jr. & James K. Wellman, Jr. LC 98-53393. (Religion in the Age of Transformation Ser.). 248p. 1999. 59.95 (*0-275-96478-7*, C6478, Praeger Pubs) Greenwood.

*****Power of Retelling: Developmental Steps for Building Comprehension.** Vicki Benson & Carrice Cummins. LC 00-31989. 2000. spiral bd. write for info. (*0-322-01541-3*) Wright Group.

Power of Ritual. Robbie Davis-Floyd. 1999. write for info. (*0-8052-4155-8*) Schocken.

Power of Ritual. Rachel Pollack. LC 99-38831. (Omega Institute Mind, Body & Spirit Bks.). 224p. 2000. pap. 12.95 (*0-440-50872-X*, Dell Trade Pbks) Dell.

Power of Rome, Vol. 3. Date not set. 30.95 (*0-8369-4794-0*) Ayer.

P

An Asterisk (*) at the beginning of an entry indicates that the title is appearing for the first time.

Power of Sacrifice. Ian Bradley. pap. write for info. (*0-232-52057-7*) S Asia.

Power of Self-Esteem. Samuel Cypert. 80p. 1993. pap. 10.95 (*0-8144-7798-4*) AMACOM.

Power of Self-Esteem: An Inspiring Look at Our Most Important Psychological Resource. Nathaniel Branden. 97p. (Orig.). 1992. pap. 7.95 (*1-55874-213-1*) Health Comm.

Power of Self Esteem: Using It All to Get It All. Willie H. Houseal. 8.95p. 1999. pap. 8.95 (*1-880710-36-6*) Monterey Pacific.

Power of Self-Hypnosis: The Key to Confidence. Gilbert Oakley. 144p. (Orig.). 1989. pap. text 14.95 (*0-572-01135-0*, Pub. by W Foulsham) Trans-Atl Phila.

Power of Self-Knowledge. Gene Davis. 107p. (Orig.). 1992. pap. 9.95 (*0-685-66138-5*) Life Res Found.

Power of Self-Love. Caren Croxen. 1981. audio 6.95 (*0-944955-01-0*) Wissmann Pub.

Power of Self-Love. Caren Croxen. 1987. pap. 6.95 (*0-944955-00-2*) Wissmann Pub.

Power of Self-Management: Achieving Success in Your Healthcare Career. Michael H. Cohen. (Illus.). 196p. (Orig.). 1992. pap. 7.95 (*0-9613768-1-3*) Canoe Press.

Power of Self-Suggestion. Samuel McComb. 1991. lib. bdg. 69.95 (*0-8490-4542-8*) Gordon Pr.

Power of Self-Suggestion. Samuel McComb. 53p. 1996. reprint ed. spiral bd. 10.00 (*0-7873-1241-X*) Hlth Research.

Power of Self Suggestion (1916) Samuel McComb. 60p. 1998. reprint ed. pap. 7.95 (*0-7661-0668-3*) Kessinger Pub.

Power of Separation: American Constitutionalism & the Myth of Legislative Veto. Jessica Korn. 188p. 1996. pap. text 16.95 (*0-691-05856-3*, Pub. by Princeton U Pr) Cal Prin Full Svc.

Power of Servant Leadership. Robert K. Greenleaf. Ed. by Larry C. Spears. LC 98-24143. 378p. 1998. pap. 17.95 (*1-57675-035-3*) Berrett-Koehler.

Power of Shame: A Rational Perspective. Agnes Heller. 352p. 1985. 65.00 (*0-7100-9922-3*, Routledge Thoemms) Routledge.

Power of Shazam! Jerry Ordway. Ed. by Mike Carlin. LC 94-158497. (Illus.). 96p. 1995. mass mkt. 7.50 (*1-56389-153-0*, Pub. by DC Comics) Time Warner.

Power of Silence. Carlos Castaneda. Ed. by Jane Rosenman. 288p. 1991. 14.00 (*0-671-73248-X*, WSP) PB.

Power of Silence: Social & Pragmatic Perspectives. Adam Jaworski. (Language & Language Behaviors Ser.: Vol. 1). 208p. (C). 1992. 48.00 (*0-8039-4966-9*); pap. 22.95 (*0-8039-4967-7*) Sage.

Power of Simplicity: A Management Guide to Cutting Through the Nonsense & Getting Things Right. Jack Trout & Steve Rivkin. LC 98-37927. 240p. 1998. 24.95 (*0-07-065362-3*) McGraw.

***Power of Social Skills & Character Development.** Jennifer L. Scully. (Illus.). 200p. 2000. pap. text 29.95 (*1-887943-42-0*, PSSC) Nat Prof Res.

Power of Solitude: My Life in the German Resistance. Marion Yorck von Wartenburg. Ed. & Tr. by Julie M. Winter from GER. LC 99-42656. (Illus.). 96p. 2000. pap. 15.00 (*0-8032-9915-X*, Bison Books); text 40.00 (*0-8032-4915-2*, Bison Books) U of Nebr Pr.

Power of Soul: Pathways to Psychological & Spiritual Growth for African Americans. Darlene Powell & Derek S. Powell. LC 97-18078. 256p. 1998. 23.00 (*0-688-15110-8*, Wm Morrow) Morrow Avon.

Power of Soul: Pathways to Psychological & Spiritual Growth for African Americans. Darlene P. Hopson & Derek S. Hopson. 240p. 1999. reprint ed. pap. 12.00 (*0-688-16630-X*, Wm Morrow) Morrow Avon.

***Power of Sound: Using Psychoacoustics for Improved Learning & Performance.** Joshua Leeds. 272p. 2001. pap. 19.95 incl. audio compact disk (*0-89281-768-2*) Inner Tradit.

Power of Speech. Marie Stuttard. LC 96-3187. 1997. pap. 10.95 (*0-8120-9795-5*) Barron.

***Power of Spirit: How Organizations Transform.** Harrison Owen. 260p. 2000. pap. 19.95 (*1-57675-090-6*, Pub. by Berrett-Koehler) Publishers Group.

Power of Statistical Thinking: Improving Industrial Processes. Mary G. Keubajer et al. 544p. (C). 1995. 56.00 (*0-201-63390-6*) Addison-Wesley.

Power of Steam: An Illustrated History of the World's Steam Age. Asa Briggs. LC 82-40321. (Illus.). 208p. Date not set. reprint ed. pap. 64.50 (*0-608-20609-1*, 205457700003) Bks Demand.

Power of Steam: An Illustrated History of the World's Steam Age. Asa Briggs. LC 82-40321. (Illus.). 208p. (C). 1983. reprint ed. pap. 10.00 (*0-226-07497-8*) U Ch Pr.

***Power of Still Waters: Living in the Enlightment Experience.** Vernon K. Turner. LC 99-71613. 208p. 1999. pap. 13.95 (*1-57174-134-8*) Hampton Roads Pub Co.

Power of Stone. Date not set. write for info. (*1-887822-05-4*) Around Snd Pr.

Power of Story: Rediscovering the Oldest, Most Natural Way to Reach People for Christ. Leighton Ford & Jim Denney. LC 94-14344. 192p. (Orig.). 1994. pap. 12.00 (*0-89109-851-8*) NavPress.

Power of Story: Teaching Through Storytelling. 2nd ed. Rives Collins & Pamela J. Cooper. 182p. (C). 1996. reprint ed. pap. text 23.00 (*0-13-776709-9*) Allyn.

Power of Storytelling: A Step-by-Step Guide to Dramatic Learning in K-12. Harriet Mason. LC 95-50176. (Illus.). 128p. 1996. pap. 19.95 (*0-8039-6414-5*) Corwin Pr.

Power of Storytelling: A Step-by-Step Guide to Dramatic Learning in K-12. Harriet Mason. LC 95-50176. (Illus.). 128p. 1996. 45.95 (*0-8039-6413-7*) Corwin Pr.

***Power of Strategic Costing: Uncover Your Competitors' & Suppliers' Costs. Set Your Company's Target Costs. Maximize Your Profits.** Dale M. Brethauer. LC 99-30854. 250p. 1999. 32.95 (*0-8144-0486-3*) AMACOM.

***Power of Strategic Thinking.** Robert. 206p. 1999. 24.95 (*0-07-135777-7*) McGraw.

Power of Style: The Women Who Defined the Art of Living Well. Annette Tapert & Diana Edkins. LC 93-31783. (Illus.). 224p. 1994. 40.00 (*0-517-58568-5*, Crown) Crown.

Power of Suffering: LGL John MacArthur. (MacArthur Study Ser.: No. 7). 192p. 1995. pap. 9.99 (*1-56476-429-X*, 6-3429, Victor Bks) Chariot Victor.

Power of Suggestion. Carolyn Keene. Ed. by Anne Greenberg. LC 93-127246. (Nancy Drew Files: No. 80). 152p. (Orig.). (J). (gr. 6 up). 1993. pap. 3.75 (*0-671-73084-3*, Archway) PB.

Power of Suggestion. J. Herman Randall. 71p. 1996. reprint ed. spiral bd. 9.00 (*0-7873-1066-2*) Hlth Research.

Power of Superfoods: 30 Days That Will Change Your Life. Sam Graci & Harvey Diamond. 304p. 1997. pap. text 29.95 (*0-13-673856-7*) P-H.

Power of Superfoods: 30 Days That Will Change Your Life. 2nd ed. Sam Graci. 304p. 1999. pap. text 15.99 (*0-13-021223-7*) P-H.

Power of Surrender. Joyce S. Dueker. (Illus.). 51p. 1998. pap. 8.25 (*0-9614638-1-3*) Diving Safety.

Power of Surrender. 2nd ed. Tom Johnson. 48p. 1984. reprint ed. pap. 3.25 (*0-941992-12-8*) Los Arboles Pub.

Power of Symbols Against the Symbols of Power: The Rise of Solidarity & the Fall of State Socialism in Poland. Jan Kubik. LC 93-9895. (Illus.). 344p. (C). 1994. 50.00 (*0-271-01083-5*); pap. 16.95 (*0-271-01084-3*) Pa St U Pr.

Power of Sympathy. William H. Brown. (Masterworks of Literature Ser.). 1970. write for info. (*0-8084-0345-1*); pap. 15.95 (*0-8084-0346-X*) NCUP.

Power of Sympathy: The Autobiography & Journals of Catharine Maria Sedgwick. Intro. by Mary Kelley. LC 93-29901. 1993. pap. 8.95 (*0-934909-36-9*, Pub. by Mass Hist Soc) NE U Pr.

Power of Sympathy & the Coquette. William H. Brown & Hannah W. Foster. Ed. & Intro. by Carla Mulford. LC 96-5347. (Penguin Classics Ser.). 384p. 1996. pap. 13.95 (*0-14-043468-2*, Penguin Bks) Viking Penguin.

Power of Tautology: The Roots of Literary Theory. Allen Thiher. LC 97-10196. 176p. 1997. 32.50 (*0-8386-3752-3*) Fairleigh Dickinson.

Power of Taxation under the Constitution. K. Parameshwaran. (C). 1987. 65.00 (*0-7855-5269-3*) St Mut.

Power of Team Building: Using Ropes Techniques. Harrison Snow. LC 91-44321. (Illus.). 206p. 1992. text 39.95 (*0-88390-306-7*, Pfffr & Co) Jossey-Bass.

Power of Ten Fold. Thomas P. Zoe. 1998. pap. write for info. (*1-57553-657-9*) Watermrk Pr.

Power of the Aleph Beth, Vol. 1. Philip S. Berg. 288p. 1988. 14.95 (*0-943688-11-6*); pap. 13.95 (*0-943688-10-8*) Res Ctr Kabbalah.

Power of the Aleph Beth, Vol. II. Philip S. Berg. 224p. 1988. 12.95 (*0-943688-56-6*); pap. 11.95 (*0-943688-57-4*) Res Ctr Kabbalah.

Power of the Bear: Paintings by Susan Seddon Boulet. Michael Babcock. LC 97-50126. (Illus.). 96p. 1998. 25.00 (*0-7649-0612-7*) Pomegranate Calif.

Power of the Blood see Power of the Blood: Church/Home Pac

Power of the Blood. Marilyn Hickey. 40p. (Orig.). pap. 1.00 (*1-56441-161-3*) M Hickey Min.

Power of the Blood. Andrew Murray. 1993. pap. 6.99 (*0-87508-381-1*) Chr Lit.

Power of the Blood. H. A. Whyte. 96p. 1973. mass mkt. 5.99 (*0-88368-027-0*) Whitaker Hse.

Power of the Blood: Church/Home Pac. Benny Hinn & Larry Keefauver. Incl. Power of the Blood. 120p. Date not set. pap., student ed. 7.99 (*0-88419-428-0*); 1997. (*0-88419-429-9*) Creation House.

Power of the Blood of Jesus. Andrew Murray. 182p. 1993. mass mkt. 5.99 (*0-88368-234-6*) Whitaker Hse.

Power of the Blood of Jesus. Andrew Murray. 144p. 1987. pap. 6.99 (*0-310-29701-X*, 10369P) Zondervan.

Power of the Bull. Michael Rice. LC 97-11049. (Illus.). 336p. (C). 1998. 60.00 (*0-415-09032-6*) Routledge.

Power of the Call. Henry T. Blackaby et al. LC 97-11964. 256p. 1997. 19.99 (*0-8054-6297-X*) Broadman.

Power of the Center: The New Version. Rudolf Arnheim. (Illus.). 256p. 1988. pap. 17.95 (*0-520-06242-6*, Pub. by U CA Pr) Cal Prin Full Svc.

Power of the Charlatan. Grete De Francesco. Tr. by Miriam Beard from GER. LC 79-8609. reprint ed. 31.50 (*0-404-18471-5*) AMS Pr.

Power of the City - The City of Power. Christel Holevoet et al. (Illus.). 80p. (Orig.). 1992. pap. 12.95 (*0-685-64945-8*) Whitney Mus.

Power of the Cross. Tim F. LaHaye. Date not set. pap. 8.99 (*0-8297-1686-6*) Vida Pubs.

Power of the Cross. Charles Stanley. LC 97-28983. 208p. 1998. 12.99 (*0-7852-7065-5*, Oliver-Nelson) Nelson.

Power of the Cross: A 30-Day Devotional. Steve Green. 1994. pap. 9.95 (*0-917143-27-2*) Sparrow TN.

Power of the Cross: Foundations for a Christian Feminist Ethic of Community. Sally Purvis. LC 92-41372. 160p. (Orig.). 1993. pap. 6.78 (*0-687-33206-0*) Abingdon.

Power of the Cross: Real Stories - Real People - a Real God. Tim F. LaHaye. LC 97-45539. 256p. 1998. 19.99 (*1-57673-212-6*) Multnomah Pubs.

***Power of the Cross: Theology & the Death of Christ in Paul, Luther & Pascal.** 2nd ed. Graham Tomlin. (Biblical & Theological Monographs). xiv, 343p. 1999. reprint ed. pap. text 40.00 (*0-85364-984-7*, Pub. by Paternoster Pub) Eisenbrauns.

Power of the Cross of Christ. Charles H. Spurgeon. Ed. by Lance Wubbels. (Power Ser.). 192p. (Orig.). 1995. pap. 9.99 (*1-883002-16-8*) Emerald WA.

Power of the Dead. Henry Williamson. 1999. pap. text 14.75 (*0-7509-2153-6*) A Sutton.

Power of the Dragon, Vol. 2. 2nd rev. ed. Louis Turi. (Illus.). 434p. 1999. pap. 29.95 (*0-9667312-2-0*) Startheme Pubns.

Power of the Dream: Looking Forward in the Later Years. Marie White Webb. LC 99-38468. 1999. pap. 10.00 (*0-687-07532-7*) Dimen for Liv.

Power of the Endless Blessing. Miriam Hellman. 90p. 1990. pap. 10.00 (*1-891309-00-5*) Prophetic DC.

Power of the Enneagram: A New Technology of Self-Discovery. Don Richard Riso. 1996. 18.00 incl. audio (*0-671-56797-7*) S&S Trade.

Power of the Financial Press: Journalism & Economic Opinion in Britain & America. Wayne Parsons. 272p. 1989. 95.00 (*1-85278-039-8*) E Elgar.

Power of the Financial Press: Journalism & Economic Opinion in Britain & America. Wayne Parsons. LC 89-43066. 300p. 1990. text 24.95 (*0-8135-1497-5*) Rutgers U Pr.

***Power of the Force: The Spirituality of the "Star Wars" Films.** David Wilkinson. 2000. pap. 13.95 (*0-7459-4402-7*, Pub. by Lion Pubng) Trafalgar.

Power of the Gun: The Emergence of Modern Chinese Warlordism. Edward A. McCord. LC 92-31375. 384p. 1993. 50.00 (*0-520-08128-5*, Pub. by U CA Pr) Cal Prin Full Svc.

Power of the Holy Spirit. 100p. 1999. 9.95 (*0-9671950-0-4*) Carswell Enter.

Power of the Holy Spirit. George Gillies & Harriet Gillies. 111p. 1997. mass mkt. 4.99 (*0-88368-511-6*) Whitaker Hse.

Power of the Holy Spirit. G. Earl Knight. LC 97-67168. 128p. 1998. per. 9.95 (*1-57258-141-7*) Teach Servs.

Power of the Holy Spirit, Vol. 1. 8th ed. Don DeWelt. 150p. (Orig.). (C). 1963. pap. 5.99 incl. VHS (*0-89900-123-8*) College Pr Pub.

Power of the Holy Spirit, Vol. 3. 3rd ed. Don Dewelt. 256p. (C). 1972. pap. 5.99 incl. VHS (*0-89900-125-4*) College Pr Pub.

Power of the Image. Louis Marin. (Illus.). (C). text. write for info. (*0-472-09585-4*); pap. text. write for info. (*0-472-06585-8*) U of Mich Pr.

Power of the Image: Essays on Representation & Sexuality. Annette Kuhn. 176p. (C). 1985. pap. 17.99 (*0-415-08460-1*) Routledge.

Power of the Image: Essays on Representation & Sexuality. Annette Kuhn. (Illus.). 176p. 1985. pap. 10.95 (*0-7100-9731-X*, Routledge Thoemms) Routledge.

Power of the Impossible: The Life Story of Percy & Marion MacKaye. Arvia M. Ege. (Illus.). 750p. (C). 1992. text 39.95 (*0-933858-16-7*) Adonis Pr.

***Power of the Inner Judge: Psychodynamic Treatment of the Severe Neuroses.** Leon Wurmser. 2000. 60.00 (*0-7657-0177-4*) Aronson.

Power of the Lamb. Edith Ratzleff. 48p. 1988. teacher ed. 1.50 (*0-919797-72-5*) Kindred Prods.

Power of the Lamb. John E. Toews et al. 184p. 1986. pap. 7.95 (*0-919797-50-4*) Kindred Prods.

Power of the Lord Is over All: The Pastoral Letters of George Fox. T. Canby Jones. LC 89-1258. 530p. 1989. 29.00 (*0-944350-08-9*) Friends United.

Power of the Lord Was Present to Heal. Mike Francen. (Illus.). 48p. (Orig.). 1995. pap. 4.00 (*1-888079-00-2*) Francen Wrld.

Power of the Middle Class. Joseph L. Grady. 1992. 21.95 (*0-9613178-2-5*) Erin Books.

Power of the Middle Class: Its Birth, Growth & Apparent Demise. Joseph L. Grady. 461p. 1992. 21.95 (*0-9613178-1-7*) Erin Books.

***Power of the Mind.** J. A. Spencer. 1999. pap. 12.95 (*1-57500-028-8*, Pub. by TV Bks) HarpC.

Power of the Mind over Matter: What You Think Is What You Get in Life - Think Rich, Get Rich. Maria Kuman. (Illus.). 200p. 1999. pap. 20.00 (*1-893637-09-3*) Hlth & Hap.

Power of the Mind to Heal: Renewing Body, Mind & Spirit. Joan Borysenko & Miroslav Borysenko. LC 94-31668. 272p. 1994. 19.95 (*1-56170-093-2*, 157) Hay House.

Power of the Mind to Heal: Renewing Body, Mind & Spirit. Joan Borysenko & Miroslav Borysenko. LC 94-31668. 240p. 1995. pap. 12.00 (*1-56170-144-0*, 157T) Hay House.

Power of the Mountain Man. William W. Johnstone. 256p. 1995. mass mkt. 3.99 (*0-8217-4871-8*, Zebra Kensgtn) Kensgtn Pub Corp.

Power of the Mountain Man. William W. Johnstone. 1995. mass mkt. 4.99 (*0-8217-5363-0*, Zebra Kensgtn) Kensgtn Pub Corp.

Power of the New York Court of Appeals, 1952-1993 Cumulative Supplement: Cumulative Supplement to Cohen & Karger. James R. Sahlem et al. LC 93-37987. vi, 214p. 1994. 62.50 (*0-89941-857-0*, 307760) W S Hein.

Power of the Page: Children's Books & Their Readers. Ed. by Pat Pinsent. 144p. 1993. pap. 27.50 (*1-85346-234-9*, Pub. by David Fulton) Taylor & Francis.

***Power of the Patriarch: Patriarchal Jurisdiction on the Verge of the Third Millennium** Francis J. Marini. LC 98-75170. (Maronite Rite Ser.). 413 p. 1998. write for info. (*1-885589-09-3*) St Maron Pubns.

Power of the Periodic Table: The Secret of Change in the Universe the Chemical Reaction. Roy S. Timmreck. (Illus.). 224p. (Orig.). 1991. pap. 32.50 (*1-878862-00-6*) Royal Palm Pub.

Power of the Poor in History: Selected Writings. Gustavo Gutierrez. Tr. by Robert R. Barr from SPA. LC 82-22252. 256p. 1983. reprint ed. pap. 79.40 (*0-608-02148-2*, 206281700003) Bks Demand.

Power of the Porch: Narrative Strategies in Works by Zora Neale Hurston, Gloria Naylor, & Randall Kenan. Trudier Harris. LC 96-3461. (Mercer University Lamar Memorial Lectures: No. 39). 1997. 22.95 (*0-8203-1857-4*) U of Ga Pr.

Power of the Poster. Ed. by Margaret Timmers. (Illus.). 252p. 1998. 50.00 (*1-85177-240-5*, Pub. by V&A Ent) Antique Collect.

Power of the Posterity Clause. Robert Whitelaw. pap. 0.39 (*0-87377-107-9*) GAM Pubns.

Power of the Powerless see Poder de los Debiles

Power of the Powerless. 2nd ed. Christopher De Vinck. 144p. 1995. pap. 10.99 (*0-310-48691-2*) Zondervan.

Power of the Powerless: Citizens Against the State in Central Eastern Europe. Vaclav Havel. Ed. by John Keane. LC 85-24978. 228p. 1985. reprint ed. text 43.95 (*0-87332-370-X*) M E Sharpe.

Power of the Powerless: Citizens Against the State in Central Eastern Europe. Vaclav Havel. Ed. by John Keane. LC 85-24978. 228p. (gr. 13). 1990. reprint ed. pap. text 30.95 (*0-87332-761-6*) M E Sharpe.

Power of the Presidency. James L. Fisher. (ACE-Oryx Series on Higher Education). 224p. 1983. 27.95 (*0-02-910520-X*, 2016) Free Pr.

Power of the Presidency. James L. Fisher. LC 83-15150. 224p. reprint ed. pap. 69.50 (*0-608-20855-8*, 207195400003) Bks Demand.

Power of the Presidency: Concepts & Controversy. 3rd ed. Ed. by Robert S. Hirschfield. 502p. 1982. pap. text 33.95 (*0-202-24160-2*) Aldine de Gruyter.

Power of the Press: The Birth of American Political Reporting. Denise M. Bonilla & Beth Levy. LC 99-21172. (Reference Shelf Ser.). 1999. write for info. (*0-8242-0962-1*) Wilson.

Power of the Professional Person. Ed. by Robert W. Clarke & Robert P. Lawry. LC 88-840. 250p. (Orig.). (C). 1988. lib. bdg. 48.00 (*0-8191-6955-2*) U Pr of Amer.

Power of the Prophetic. Elbert A. Dempsey. 1988. pap. 5.00 (*0-8309-0512-X*) Herald Pub Hse.

Power of the Pulpit. Gardiner Spring. 244p. 1986. reprint ed. 19.99 (*0-85151-492-8*) Banner of Truth.

Power of the Purse: A History of American Public Finance, 1776-1790. Elmer J. Ferguson. LC 61-325. 376p. reprint ed. pap. 116.60 (*0-8357-3856-6*, 203658900004) Bks Demand.

Power of the Purse Strings: Do Congressional Budget Procedures Restrain? Richard Forgette. LC 93-11865. 160p. 1994. 57.95 (*0-275-94738-6*) Greenwood.

Power of the Rays. S. G. Ouseley. 99p. 1996. reprint ed. pap. 11.00 (*0-7873-0648-7*) Hlth Research.

Power of the Renewed Mind. Bill Basansky. 48p. 1991. pap. 3.00 (*0-89274-021-3*, HH-021) Harrison Hse.

Power of the Rosary. Albert J. Shamon. LC 90-61011. 48p. 1990. pap. 3.00 (*1-877678-10-4*) CMJ Marian Pubs.

Power of the Sacraments. Briege McKenna. 32p. (Orig.). 1996. pap. 1.50 (*0-8198-5901-X*) Pauline Bks.

Power of the Sacred Name: V. Raghavan's Studies in Namasiddhanta & Indian Culture. Ed. by William J. Jackson. (C). 1994. text 28.50 (*81-7030-395-8*, Pub. by Sri Satguru Pubns) S Asia.

Power of the Secret Place. Bobbie J. Merck. 78p. (Orig.). 1990. pap. 5.95 (*0-929263-03-0*) Great Love Church Intl.

***Power of the Seed.** Lawerence Powell. 144p. 2000. pap. 8.99 (*1-890900-32-X*) Insight Intl.

Power of the Shadow. Nelson A. Ossorio. (Orig.). 1995. pap. 11.95 (*1-56721-119-4*) Twnty-Fifth Cent Pr.

Power of the Spirit. William Law. Ed. by D. Hunt. 1993. pap. 5.99 (*0-87508-247-5*) Chr Lit.

Power of the Spirit: In the Life of the Believer. Keith Hershey. (Christian Life Ser.). 30p. (Orig.). 1992. pap. 1.95 (*0-940487-05-5*) Jubilee CA.

Power of the Spoken Word. Florence Scovel Shinn. Ed. by Christine Schneider. 81p. 1978. pap. 6.95 (*0-87516-260-6*) DeVorss.

Power of the Star-Point. Takagawa Shukaku. 1988. pap. 14.95 (*4-87187-032-4*, G32) Ishi Pr Intl.

Power of the Story: Fiction & Political Change. Michael Hanne. LC 94-36032. 272p. (C). 1994. 29.95 (*1-57181-019-6*) Berghahn Bks.

Power of the Story: Fiction & Political Change. Michael Hanne. 272p. (C). 1996. pap. 19.95 (*1-57181-051-X*) Berghahn Bks.

Power of the Story: Fiction & Political Change. Michael Hanne. (Illus.). 272p. 1995. 29.95 (*0-8264-0784-6*) Continuum.

Power of the Sword. Wilbur Smith. 671p. Date not set. 36.95 (*0-8488-2394-X*) Amereon Ltd.

Power of the Sword. Wilbur Smith. 602p. 1987. mass mkt. 6.99 (*0-449-21414-1*, Crest) Fawcett.

Power of the Sword. Wilbur Smith. 1986. 19.95 (*0-316-80171-2*) Little.

Power of the Tongue. Kenneth Copeland. 1996. pap. text 1.00 (*1-57562-113-4*) K Copeland Pubns.

Power of the Tongue. Perry A. Gaspard. 1983. pap. 2.50 (*0-931867-04-5*) Abundant Life Pubns.

Power of the Weak: Studies on Medieval Women. Ed. by Jennifer Carpenter & Sally-Beth MacLean. LC 94-45063. (Illus.). 240p. (C). 1995. text 39.95 (*0-252-02169-X*); pap. text 14.95 (*0-252-06504-2*) U of Ill Pr.

Power of the Witch: The Earth, the Moon, & the Magical Path to Enlightenment. Laurie Cabot & Tom Cowan. 320p. 1990. pap. 12.95 (*0-385-30189-8*, Delta Trade) Dell.

Power of the Word. Ed J. Pinegar. pap. 12.98 (*1-55517-281-4*) CFI Dist.

P

An Asterisk (*) at the beginning of an entry indicates that the title is appearing for the first time.

Power of the Word: Holy Scripture in Orthodox Interpretation, Confession & Celebration. John Breck. LC 86-24773. 237p. 1987. pap. 10.95 (*0-88141-043-8*) St Vladimirs.

Power of the Word: Saving Doctrines from the Book of Mormon. Robert L. Millet. LC 93-44307. x, 342p. 1994. 14.95 (*0-87579-826-8*) Deseret Bk.

Power of the Word: The Story of Dorcas Camacho Byrd. Elizabeth Rivera. LC 98-176609. (Illus.). 118p. (YA). (gr. 7-12). 1998. pap. text 7.95 (*1-56309-235-2*, W986104) Womans Mission Union.

***Power of the Written Tradition.** Jack Goody. 200p. 2000. 45.00 (*1-56098-987-4*); pap. 18.95 (*1-56098-962-9*) Smithsonian.

Power of Their Ideas: Lessons for America from a Small School in Harlem. Deborah Meier. 208p. 1996. pap. 13.00 (*0-8070-3111-9*) Beacon Pr.

Power of Thetis: Allusion & Interpretation in the "Iliad" Laura M. Slatkin. LC 91-6712. 137p. (C). 1992. 30.00 (*0-520-07251-0*, Pub. by U CA Pr) Cal Prin Full Svc.

Power of Thetis: Allusion & Interpretation in the "Iliad" Laura M. Slatkin. LC 91-6712. 137p. (C). 1995. pap. 13.95 (*0-520-20355-0*, Pub. by U CA Pr) Cal Prin Full Svc.

Power of Thought: Ageless Secrets for Great Achievement. Glenn Bland. LC 95-36034. 176p. 1996. 16.95 (*0-7615-0341-2*) Prima Pub.

Power of Thought: How to Control What Happens to You. Eugene Maurey. (Illus.). 96p. (Orig.). 1990. pap. write for info. (*0-318-68473-X*) Midwest Bks.

Power of Thought: How to Control What Happens to You. Eugene Maurey. (Illus.). 95p. (Orig.). 1992. pap. text 5.95 (*0-9626906-2-7*) Midwest Bks.

***Power of Three.** Eliza Willard. (Charmed Ser.: No. 1). (YA). (gr. 7 up). 1999. per. 5.99 (*0-671-04162-2*) S&S Trade.

Power of Three: Parent, Student & Teacher Collaboration. Peter Coleman. LC 98-234102. 1998. pap. 29.95 (*1-85396-399-2*, Pub. by P Chapman) P H Brookes.

Power of 360 Degree Feedback. David A. Waldman & Leanne E. Atwater. LC 97-46343. (Improving Human Performance Ser.). 148p. 1998. 24.95 (*0-88415-412-2*, 5412) Gulf Pub.

***Power of Tiananmen.** Dingxin Zhao. 2000. 35.00 (*0-226-98260-2*) U Ch Pr.

Power of Tithing: The Tither Is the Greatest Benefactor. J. Owens Smith. 148p. 1994. reprint ed. pap. 16.95 (*0-9639442-0-7*) Gldn Star.

Power of Total Commitment: A Leader's Legacy. Frank Wagner. Ed. by Rebecca Atkinson. 160p. 1991. 18.95 (*0-9627785-4-0*) Praxis Pr.

Power of Total Perspective. R. E. McMaster, Jr. 496p. 1994. 29.95 (*0-9647861-2-5*) A N Inc Intl.

Power of Total Perspective. 2nd ed. R. E. McMaster, Jr. 523p. 1994. pap. 29.95 (*0-9643552-0-5*) A N Inc Intl.

Power of Touch: The Basis for Survival, Health, Intimacy & Emotional Well-Being. 2nd rev. ed. Phyllis K. Davis. LC 98-55707. xxviii; 238p. (Orig.). 1999. pap. 11.95 (*1-56170-574-8*, 576) Hay House.

Power of Travel: A Passport to Adventure, Discovery & Growth. Steve Zikman. LC 99-17351. 192p. 1999. 12.95 (*0-87477-981-2*, Tarcher Putnam) Putnam Pub Group.

Power of Trees: The Reforesting of the Soul. Michael Perlman. LC 94-4552. 266p. (Orig.). 1994. pap. 17.00 (*0-88214-362-X*) Spring Pubns.

Power of Truth. Herrymon Maurer. (C). 1950. pap. 4.00 (*0-87574-053-7*) Pendle Hill.

Power of Turbo: Programming. Leon A. Wortman. 1991. 24.95 (*0-8306-6653-2*) McGraw-Hill Prof.

Power of Turbo Basic: Programming with Applications. Leon A. Wortman. (Illus.). 290p. 1988. pap. 17.95 (*0-8306-2997-1*) McGraw-Hill Prof.

Power of Turbo Pascal. Sanjiva K. Nath & Philippe Kahn. 320p. 1986. pap. 19.95 (*0-89303-791-5*); disk 39.95 (*0-89303-794-X*) P-H.

Power of Turbo Prolog: The Natural Language of Artificial Intelligence. Ralph Roberts. (Illus.). 256p. 1987. 22.95 (*0-8306-0782-X*, 2782); pap. 14.95 (*0-8306-2782-0*) McGraw-Hill Prof.

***Power of Twelve: A New Approach to Personal Empowerment.** 2nd ed. Anne Brewer. LC 98-61429. (Illus.). 322p. 2000. pap. 17.95 (*1-887472-70-3*, Pub. by Sunstar Pubng) Midpt Trade.

Power of Twelve: Achieving 12-Stranded DNA Consciousness. unabridged ed. Anne Brewer. Ed. by Janice Mason. LC 97-62466. 256p. 1998. pap. 19.00 (*1-888604-07-7*) SunShine CO.

Power of Two. John Conlon. LC 98-9057. 193p. 1998. 25.50 (*0-7879-0946-7*) Que.

Power of Two. Annette Tapert. 1999. 40.00 (*0-517-70375-0*) Random Hse Value.

Power of Two: Secrets to a Strong & Loving Marriage. Susan Heitler. LC 96-71151. (Illus.). 304p. (Orig.). 1997. pap. 15.95 (*1-57224-059-8*) New Harbinger.

Power of Ula. Miles Sheldon-Williams. Ed. by R. Reginald & Douglas Melville. LC 77-84276. (Lost Race & Adult Fantasy Ser.). 1978. reprint ed. lib. bdg. 28.95 (*0-405-11014-6*) Ayer.

***Power of Un.** Nancy Etchemendy. LC 99-58281. 144p. (J). (gr. 3-7). 2000. 14.95 (*0-8126-2850-0*, Pub. by Front St-Cricket Bks) Publishers Group.

Power of Values. Polaris Associates Staff. 76p. 1996. per. 50.00 (*0-7872-2898-2*, 41289801) Kendall-Hunt.

***Power of Visual Presentation.** Visual Reference Publications Staff. 1999. 39.95 (*0-688-17666-6*, Wm Morrow) Morrow Avon.

Power of Visual Presentation: Retail Design/Kiosks/ Exhibit Design/Environmental Design. Ed. by Martin M. Pegler. (Illus.). 176p. 2000. 39.95 (*1-58471-007-1*) Visual Refer.

Power of Visualization: Notes from a Mathematica Course. Stan Wagon. 117p. (Orig.). (C). 1994. pap. 25.00 (*0-9631678-3-9*) Inst Computation.

Power of Welsh Witchcraft: Psychic Development & the Old Religion. Rhuddlwm Gawr. LC 85-73762. (Illus.). 144p. (Orig.). 10.95 (*0-931760-17-8*); pap. 12.95 (*0-931760-39-9*, CP 10117) Camelot GA.

Power of Will. Frank C. Haddock. 1988. pap. 13.95 (*0-912576-17-0*) R Collier.

Power of Will: A Practical Companion Book for the Unfoldment of the Powers of Mind (1907) Frank C. Haddock. 410p. 1998. reprint ed. pap. 30.00 (*0-7661-0289-0*) Kessinger Pub.

Power of Will: Key Strategies to Unlock Your Inner Strengths & Enjoy Success in All Aspects of Life. Anthony Parinello. LC 97-77505. 228p. 1998. 15.95 (*1-886284-09-1*, Pub. by Chandler Hse) Natl Bk Netwk.

Power of Windows & DOS Together: Work Faster & Smarter by Combining the Strengths of Both. Martin S. Matthews. LC 93-3791. 1993. pap. 24.95 (*1-55958-339-8*) Prima Pub.

Power of Women. Irene O. Ogbru. 104p. (Orig.). 1993. pap. 10.95 (*1-880365-49-9*) Prof Pr NC.

Power of Women: A Topos in Medieval Art & Literature. Susan L. Smith. LC 95-5626. 456p. 1995. text 45.95 (*0-8122-3279-8*) U of Pa Pr.

Power of Words. James Carroll. (Illus.). 192p. 1996. pap. 14.92 (*1-891897-02-0*) Mission Evangelism.

Power of Words: Documents in American History, Vol. 2. Ed. by T. H. Breen. LC 95-18487. Vol. 2. 347p. (C). 1997. pap. text 37.00 (*0-06-501113-9*) Addson-Wesley Educ.

Power of Words: Literacy & Revolution in South China, 1949-95. Glen Peterson. LC 97-228623. 352p. 1998. text 75.00 (*0-7748-0611-7*) U of Wash Pr.

Power of Words Vol. 2: Documents in American History. Ed. by T. H. Breen. LC 95-18487. Vol. 1. 331p. (C). 1997. pap. text 37.00 (*0-06-501112-0*) Addson-Wesley Educ.

Power of Writing. David W. Chapman & Preston L. Waller. LC 93-21676. 366p. (C). 1993. pap. text 35.95 (*1-55934-138-6*, 1138) Mayfield Pub.

Power of Writing. David W. Chapman & Preston L. Waller. (C). 1994. pap. text, teacher ed. write for info. (*1-55934-139-4*, 1139) Mayfield Pub.

Power of Writing with Additional Readings. David W. Chapman & Preston L. Waller. LC 94-32374. 568p. (C). 1994. pap. text 37.95 (*1-55934-453-9*, 1453) Mayfield Pub.

Power of Writing with Additional Readings. Preston L. Waller & David W. Chapman. 96p. (C). 1994. pap. text, teacher ed. write for info. (*1-55934-478-4*, 1478) Mayfield Pub.

Power of Your Actions. James R. Ball. Ed. by Vicki Shannon. (Illus.). 40p. 1993. pap. 2.75 (*0-9633184-2-X*) Goals Inst.

Power of Your Dreams. Soozi Holbeche. 192p. 1993. mass mkt. 4.50 (*0-380-77247-7*, Avon Bks) Morrow Avon.

Power of Your Other Hand: A Course in Channeling the Inner Wisdom of the Right Brain. Lucia Capacchione. 207p. (Orig.). 1988. pap. 12.95 (*0-87877-130-1*, 640) Newcastle Pub.

Power of Your Own Medicine. Robert G. Chaney. LC 95-75540. 192p. 1995. pap. 15.95 (*0-918936-30-6*) Astara.

Power of Your Plate: Eating Well for Better Health - 20 Experts Tell You How. rev. ed. Neal D. Barnard. LC 94-43222. 256p. (C). 1995. pap. 12.95 (*1-57067-003-X*) Book Pub Co.

Power of Your Subconscious Mind. Joseph Murphy. 1963. pap. 5.95 (*0-685-03917-X*, Reward) P-H.

Power of Your Subconscious Mind. Joseph Murphy. 224p. 1982. mass mkt. 6.99 (*0-553-27043-5*) Bantam.

Power of Your Subconscious Mind. Joseph Murphy. 224p. (C). 1988. pap. 10.95 (*0-13-687972-1*) P-H.

***Power of Your Subconscious Mind.** rev. expanded ed. Joseph Murphy & Ian McMahan. (Illus.). 288p. 2000. pap. 13.00 (*0-7352-0168-4*) PH Pr.

Power of Your Voice: Patterns of Psycho-Linguistics. Patrick K. Porter. Ed. by Jerry De Shazo. 180p. (Orig.). 1993. pap. 19.98 (*0-9637611-5-3*) Positive Chngs Hypnosis.

Power of Your Voice: Patterns of Psycho-Linguistics. Patrick K. Porter. Ed. by Paul K. Massengill. LC 93-86046. 180p. (Orig.). (C). reprint ed. pap. 19.98 (*1-887630-01-5*) Renaissnce Pub.

Power of Your Words. Don Gosset & E. W. Kenyon. 214p. 1984. mass mkt. 5.99 (*0-88368-348-2*) Whitaker Hse.

***Power of Youth: Understanding the Power of Youth God's Way.** Samuel Bass. 80p. (YA). 2000. pap. write for info. (*0-9671417-5-3*) BibleScope.

Power of 5: Hundreds of 5-Second to 5-Minute Techniques to Improve All of Your Life Without Wasting Any of Your Time. Harold H. Bloomfield. LC 94-33084. 1994. 24.95 (*0-87596-201-7*) Rodale Pr Inc.

Power On: New Tools for Teaching & Learning-Developments in the Use of Computer-Based Technologies. 1991. lib. bdg. 250.00 (*0-8490-4353-0*) Gordon Pr.

Power on Display: The Politics of Shakespeare's Genres. Leonard Tennenhouse. 220p. 1986. pap. text 13.50 (*0-416-01281-7*, 9212) Routledge.

***Power on Earth: Kubic's Observations IX.** unabridged ed. Frank Kubic. LC 99-75805. 56p. 1999. pap. 6.95 (*1-888958-23-5*) Nuggets Wisdom.

Power on the Job: The Legal Rights of Working People. Michael Yates. 320p. 1994. 30.00 (*0-89608-498-1*) South End Pr.

Power 101: A Basic Introduction to Electric Utility Power. Mark S. Shirilau. (Illus.). 230p. 1998. pap. 24.95 (*1-881568-12-1*) Healing Spirit.

Power-Operated Dispensing Devices for LP-Gas, UL 495. 2nd ed. (C). 1994. pap. text 230.00 (*1-55989-679-5*) Underwrtrs Labs.

Power-Operated Dispensing Devices for Petroleum Products, UL 87. 10th ed. (C). 1995. per. 95.00 (*1-55989-884-4*) Underwrtrs Labs.

Power-Operated Pumps for Anhydrous Ammonia & LP-Gas, UL 51. 8th ed. (C). 1995. pap. text 230.00 (*1-55989-287-0*) Underwrtrs Labs.

Power-Operated Pumps for Petroleum Dispensing Products, UL 79. 8th ed. (C). 1996. pap. text 135.00 (*1-55989-290-0*) Underwrtrs Labs.

***Power Optimization & Synthesis at Behavioral & System Levels Using Formal Methods** Jui-Ming Chang & Massoud Pedram. LC 99-31819. 1999. write for info. (*0-7923-8560-8*) Kluwer Academic.

Power or Authority? The Entelechy of Power. A. Khoshkish. 138p. (C). 1991. lib. bdg. 38.50 (*0-8191-8395-4*) U Pr of Amer.

Power or Pure Economics. Joseph Alois Schumpeter. LC 98-34978. 28p. 1999. text 75.00 (*0-312-21955-5*) St Martin.

Power Outlets, UL 231. 8th ed. (C). 1998. pap. text 290.00 (*1-55989-591-8*) Underwrtrs Labs.

Power over Demons. H. Maxwell Whyte. Orig. Title: Demons & Deliverance. 174p. 1993. mass mkt. 5.99 (*0-88368-460-8*) Whitaker Hse.

Power over Headaches. Linda Fowler. (Orig.). 1997. pap. 15.95 (*0-9654001-0-7*) Life Style Prods.

Power over Life Leads to Domination of Mankind. Michel Schooyans. Tr. & Pref. by John H. Miller. 80p. 1996. pap. 8.00 (*1-887567-01-1*) CBCCU Amer.

Power over Panic: Freedom from Panic-Anxiety Related Disorders. rev. ed. Bronwyn Fox. 110p. 1999. pap. 12.95 (*0-9627327-1-0*, 4082576241) Shakti River Pr.

Power over People. rev. ed. Louise B. Young. (Illus.). 272p. 1992. pap. 10.95 (*0-19-507578-1*) OUP.

Power over Rationality: The Bush Administration & the Gulf Crisis. Alex R. Hybel. LC 92-10663. (SUNY Series in the Making of Foreign Policy). 159p. (C). 1993. text 59.50 (*0-7914-1421-3*); pap. text 19.95 (*0-7914-1422-1*) State U NY Pr.

***Power over Satan.** Charles H. Spurgeon. LC 00-20322. 185p. 2000. pap. 7.99 (*0-88368-595-7*) Whitaker Hse.

Power over Temptation. R. W. Schambach. (Pocket Classics Ser.). 45p. 1995. pap. 3.00 (*1-888361-06-9*) Power Publns.

Power Pacing for Indoor Cycling. Kristopher Kory & Tom Seabourne. LC 98-45940. (Illus.). 200p. 1999. spiral bd. 15.95 (*0-88011-981-0*, PKOR0981) Human Kinetics.

***Power Pack: Cardiovascular System.** Sarah Angliss. 32p. (J). 1999. lib. bdg. 15.95 (*1-929298-19-6*, Pub. by Thameside Pr) Smart Apple.

Power Pack: Chemistry, 2 vols. 2nd ed. Barron's Educational Editors. 1998. pap. 14.95 (*0-7641-7162-3*) Barron.

Power Pack II: The Application of Power. John Hunkins et al. (Illus.). 170p. (Orig.). 1994. pap. 19.95 (*1-57913-001-1*) CSK Pub.

Power Pack 1: The Source of Power. John Hunkins et al. (Illus.). 92p. (Orig.). 1994. pap. 19.95 (*1-57913-000-3*) CSK Pub.

***Power Packaging.** David E. Carter. 1999. pap. text 35.00 (*0-8230-4261-8*) Watsn-Guptill.

Power-Packed Direct Mail: How to Get More Leads & Sales by Mail. Robert W. Bly. LC 94-32821. 1995. 25.00 (*0-8050-3505-2*) H Holt & Co.

Power-Packed Direct Mail: How to Get More Leads & Sales by Mail. Robert W. Bly. 1995. pap. 14.95 (*0-8050-3506-0*) H Holt & Co.

Power-Packed PR. 50p. 1988. 25.00 (*1-878604-19-8*) Briefings Pub Grp.

Power-Packed Writing That Works. 1989. 25.00 (*1-878604-20-1*) Briefings Pub Grp.

Power Packing: Principles of Lightweight Long Distance Backpacking. Illus. by Jason Ridley. ii, 68p. (Orig.). 1996. mass mkt. write for info. (*0-9655261-6-X*) TwoLB Ent.

Power, Paideia & Pythagoreanism: Greek Identity, Conceptions of the Relationship Between Philosophers & Monarchs & Political Ideas in Philostratus' Life of Apollonius. Jaap-Jan Flinterman. LC 96-102342. (Dutch Monographs on Ancient History & Archaeology: Vol. 13). vi, 276p. 1995. lib. bdg. 84.00 (*90-5063-236-X*, Pub. by Gieben) J Benjamins Pubng Co.

Power, Pain & Dentistry. Sarah Nettleton. 192p. 1992. 113.00 (*0-335-09723-5*); pap. 36.95 (*0-335-09722-7*) OpUniv Pr.

Power Pak of Games. 112p. (J). 1994. teacher ed., per. 11.95 (*1-57405-000-1*) CharismaLife Pub.

Power Pak of Object Lessons. 104p. (J). 1994. teacher ed., per. 11.95 (*1-57405-001-X*) CharismaLife Pub.

Power Paradigms in the Social Sciences. Charles R. Spruill. (Illus.). 196p. (Orig.). (C). 1983. pap. text 22.00 (*0-8191-3288-8*); lib. bdg. 50.50 (*0-8191-3287-X*) U Pr of Amer.

Power Paragraphs: Buildings Blocks for Eloquent Essays. Chris Robinson. 80p. 1997. pap. text 16.50 (*1-56226-372-2*) CAT Pub.

Power Parent: Taking Corporate Management Home. Miles McCall. 208p. 1995. teacher ed. 89.95 (*0-9648995-0-7*) C M & Assocs.

Power Parenting for Children with ADD-ADHD: A Practical Parent's Guide for Managing Difficult Behaviors of Children. Grad L. Flick. LC 95-5133. 256p. (C). 1996. pap. text 19.95 (*0-87628-877-8*) P-H.

Power Parenting for Children with ADD-ADHD: A Practical Parent's Guide for Managing Difficult Children. Grad L. Flick. 256p. (C). 1996. text 27.95 (*0-87628-885-9*) P-H.

Power, Parliament & the People. Michael Coper & George Williams. 223p. 1997. pap. 29.00 (*1-86287-247-3*, Pub. by Federation Pr) Gaunt.

Power Partnering: A Strategy for Business Excellence in the 21St Century. Sean Gadman. LC 96-26398. 200p. 1996. pap. text 17.95 (*0-7506-9809-8*) Buttrwrth-Heinemann.

Power, Passion & Pain of Black Love. rev. ed. Jawanza Kunjufu. 164p. 1994. per. 12.95 (*0-913543-36-5*) African Am Imag.

Power Passion & Persuasion: Advocacy Inside & Out. Dominic J. Gianna. 184p. 1996. pap. 185.00 incl. audio (*0-943380-96-0*) PEG MN.

Power, Passions & Purpose: Prospects for North-South Negotiations. Ed. by Jagdish N. Bhagwati & John G. Ruggie. (Illus.). 360p. (Orig.). (C). 1984. 37.50 (*0-262-02201-X*); pap. text 18.50 (*0-262-52091-5*) MIT Pr.

Power, Pasta & Politics: The World According to Senator Al D'Amato. Alfonse M. D'Amato. Orig. Title: Enough Is Enough. 384p. (J). 1995. 24.45 (*0-7868-6045-6*, Pub. by Hyperion) Time Warner.

Power, Pasta & Politics: The World According to Senator Al D'Amato. Al D'Amato. LC 95-9429. 384p. (J). 1996. reprint ed. pap. 12.45 (*0-7868-8182-8*, Pub. by Hyperion) Time Warner.

Power, Pathology, Paradox: The Dynamics of Evil & Good. Marguerite Shuster. 352p. 1987. 22.95 (*0-310-39750-2*, 18398) Zondervan.

Power, Patronage & Political Violence: State Building on a Brazilian Frontier, 1822-1889. Judy Bieber. LC 99-22581. (Illus.). 304p. 1999. text 45.00 (*0-8032-1297-6*) U of Nebr Pr.

Power Pattern Offenses for Winning Basketball. Jack Nagle. LC 85-32072. 192p. (C). 1986. 27.95 (*0-13-687708-7*, Parker Publishing Co) P-H.

Power PC. Michael Koerner. 1996. 39.95 (*0-614-14491-4*) P-H.

Power PC Compiler Writer's Guide. IBM Staff. 272p. 1996. pap. text. write for info. (*0-9649654-0-2*) Warthman Assocs.

Power PC Programmer's Toolkit. Tom Thompson. 1996. 45.00 incl. cd-rom (*0-614-14449-3*) Macmillan.

Power, Pedagogy & Practice. Norman Whitney. 410p. 1996. pap. text 24.95 (*0-19-437205-7*) OUP.

Power Penning: A Student's Guide to Letter Writing Success. Suze M. Kroeker. 80p. (YA). (gr. 8 up). 1996. pap. 12.95 (*0-9647923-0-3*) Manchester WA.

Power Performance for Singers: Transcending the Barriers. Shirlee Emmons & Alma Thomas. LC 97-31732. (Illus.). 336p. 1998. 29.95 (*0-19-511224-5*) OUP.

Power, Personalities, & Policies: Essays in Honour of Donald Cameron Watt. Ed. by Michael G. Fry. LC 92-13528. 344p. 1993. 45.00 (*0-7146-3428-X*, Pub. by F Cass Pubs) Intl Spec Bk.

Power Persuaders. 55p. 1978. 1.00 (*0-914389-08-4*) Common Cause.

Power Persuasion: Moving an Ancient Art into the Media Age. 2nd rev. ed. Martha D. Cooper & William L. Nothstine. 357p. (Orig.). 1997. pap. text 20.95 (*0-9616489-8-8*) Alistair Pr IN.

Power Pete Official Secrets & Solutions. Tuncer Deniz. 1995. pap. text 12.95 (*0-7615-0293-9*) Prima Pub.

Power Piping Data. Technical Association of the Pulp & Paper Industry. Ed. by Frank M. Tenore. LC TH6711.. 42p. reprint ed. pap. 30.00 (*0-608-18617-1*, 202529500043) Bks Demand.

Power Piping Data. 2nd rev. ed. Keith W. Smeal & Frank M. Tenore. 62p. 1992. pap. 31.00 (*0-89852-262-5*, 0101R118) TAPPI.

Power Pitches: How to Produce Winning Presentations Using Charts, Slides, Video & Multimedia. Alan L. Brown. LC 96-48063. 208p. 1997. text 39.95 (*0-7863-0972-5*, Irwn Prfssnl) McGraw-Hill Prof.

Power Place Study Guide. 3rd ed. Annenberg. 235p. 1999. pap. 38.95 (*0-471-35741-3*) Wiley.

Power Places of Kathmandu: Hindu & Buddhist Holy Sites in the Sacred Valley of Nepal. Photos by Kevin Bubriski. (Illus.). 144p. 1995. 39.95 (*0-89281-540-X*) Inner Tradit.

Power Planets: A Manual for Human Empowerment. Luisa De La Lama. LC 93-60378. 225p. 1993. pap. 17.95 (*1-883381-20-7*) White Dragon.

Power Planning Workbook. 29p. 1996. pap., wbk. ed. 10.00 (*1-886880-08-5*) Life Changers.

Power Plant Chemistry: A Practical Guide. Brad Buecker. LC 97-36403. 1997. 89.95 (*0-87814-619-9*) PennWell Bks.

***Power-Plant Control & Instrumentation: The Control of Boilers & Heat-Recovery Steam Generator Systems (HRSGs)** David Lindsley. (IEE Control Engineering Ser.: No. 58). 240p. 1999. boxed set 65.00 (*0-85296-765-9*) INSPEC Inc.

Power Plant Electrical Reference Series. Stone & Webster Engineering Corporation Staff. LC 90-114618. 1987. write for info. (*0-8033-0002-6*) Elec Power Res Inst.

Power Plant Engineers Guide. 3rd ed. Frank Graham & Charles Buffinghon. LC 83-17779. (Illus.). 816p. 1984. text 32.50 (*0-672-23329-0*) Macmillan.

Power Plant Equipment Design - Bolted Joints, Pumps, Valves, Pipe & Duct Supports. Ed. by E. C. Goodling, Jr. 184p. 1993. 45.00 (*0-7918-0982-X*, H00814) ASME.

Power Plant Fitting & Testing, 2 vols. 1982. 60.00 (*0-7855-2889-X*) St Mut.

Power Plant Instrumentation for Measurement of High-Purity Water Quality - STP 742. Ed. by R. W. Lane & G. Otten. 235p. 1981. 26.50 (*0-8031-0798-6*, STP742) ASTM.

Power Plant Operator. Jack Rudman. (Career Examination Ser.: C-1395). 1994. pap. 27.95 (*0-8373-1395-3*) Nat Learn.

P

An Asterisk (*) at the beginning of an entry indicates that the title is appearing for the first time.

Power Plant Permitting. Kimberly M. Evans & Harold A. Frediani. LC 96-44184. 1996. 74.95 (*0-87814-592-3*) PennWell Bks.

Power Plant Simulation, 1988. Ed. by David Hetrick. (Illus.). 112p. (Orig.). (C). 1988. pap. 40.00 (*0-911801-27-8*, MC88-3) Soc Computer Sim.

Power Plant Supervisor. Jack Rudman. (Career Examination Ser.: C-3403). 1994. pap. 29.95 (*0-8373-3403-9*) Nat Learn.

Power Plant System Design. Kam W. Li & A. Paul Priddy. LC 84-22177. 656p. 1985. text 111.95 (*0-471-88847-8*) Wiley.

Power Plant Theory & Design. 2nd ed. Philip J. Potter. LC 87-17348. 722p. 1989. reprint ed. 82.50 (*0-89464-236-7*) Krieger.

Power Plant Transients: 1994 International Mechanical Engineering Congress & Exposition, Chicago, Illinois - November 6-11, 1994. (FED Ser.: Vol. 204). 116p. 1994. 54.00 (*0-7918-1433-5*, G00928) ASME.

Power Plant Transients - 1992. Ed. by R. R. Schultz et al. (FED Ser.: Vol. 140). 188p. 1992. 50.00 (*0-7918-1100-X*, G00744) ASME.

Power Plant Utilization of Coal. D. W. Locklin & H. R. Hazard. LC TK1191.L6. (Battelle Energy Program Report Ser.: No. 3). 109p. reprint ed. pap. 33.80 (*0-608-10895-2*, 200513500050) Bks Demand.

Power Plant Writer: How to Put Power in Your Writing. Carol Blank. LC 86-33578. 104p. (Orig.). 1987. pap. 14.95 (*0-87683-888-3*, A888-3) GP Courseware.

Power Play see Prueba de Fuerza

Power Play. Edward J. Barbeau. LC 96-79983. (Spectrum Ser.). 212p. 1997. pap. text 31.95 (*0-88385-523-2*, POPL) Math Assn.

Power Play. Matt Christopher. (J). 1992. pap. write for info. (*0-316-14088-0*) Little.

Power Play. Delaney. mass mkt. 6.95 (*0-7472-5447-8*, Pub. by Headline Bk Pub) Trafalgar.

Power Play. Franklin W. Dixon. Ed. by Anne Greenberg. (Hardy Boys Casefiles Ser.: No. 50). (Illus.). 160p. (YA). (gr. 7 up). 1991. pap. 3.99 (*0-671-70047-2*, Archway) PB.

Power Play. Franklin W. Dixon. (Hardy Boys Casefiles Ser.: No. 50). (YA). (gr. 6 up). 1991. 9.09 (*0-606-05003-5*, Pub. by Turtleback) Demco.

Power Play. Stephen Fay. (Illus.). 416p. 1995. text 45.00 (*0-340-50844-2*, Pub. by Hodder & Stought Ltd) Trafalgar.

Power Play. Stephen Fay. 1996. mass mkt. 17.95 (*0-340-66633-1*, Pub. by Hodder & Stought Ltd) Trafalgar.

Power Play. Penny Jordan. 1990. mass mkt. 4.95 (*0-373-97108-7*) Harlequin Bks.

***Power Play.** Penny Jordan. 2000. mass mkt. 5.99 (*1-55166-587-5*, 1-66587-6, Mira Bks) Harlequin Bks.

Power Play. Anne McCaffrey & Elizabeth A. Scarborough. 1996. mass mkt. 5.99 (*0-345-38781-3*, Del Rey) Ballantine Pub Grp.

Power Play. Created by Francine Pascal. (Sweet Valley High Ser.: No. 4). 176p. (YA). (gr. 7 up). 1984. mass mkt. 3.99 (*0-553-27493-7*) Bantam.

Power Play. Kate William. (Sweet Valley High Ser.: No. 4). (YA). (gr. 7 up). 1984. 9.09 (*0-606-01264-8*, Pub. by Turtleback) Demco.

Power Play: An Inside Look at the Big Business of the National Hockey League. Gil Stein. LC 97-25994. (Illus.). 288p. 1997. 21.95 (*1-55972-422-6*, Birch Ln Pr) Carol Pub Group.

***Power Play: Sport, the Media & Popular Culture.** Raymond Boyle & Richard Haynes. LC 99-38838. 256p. 2000. pap. 23.00 (*0-582-36939-8*) Addison-Wesley.

Power Play: Who's in Control of the Energy Revolution? J. C. Whorton & Paulette Whitcomb. LC 98-8035. 1998. 59.95 (*0-87814-748-9*) PennWell Bks.

Power Play in Paraguay: The Rise & Fall of General Stroessner. Paul C. Sondrol. (Pew Case Studies in International Affairs). 50p. (Orig.). (C). 1996. pap. text 3.50 (*1-56927-612-9*, GU Schl Foreign) Geo U Inst Dplmcy.

Power Play-Individuals in Conflict: Liiterary Selections for Students of English. 2nd ed. Brenda Dyer. LC 97-157018. 256p. (C). 1996. pap. text 32.33 (*0-13-122046-2*) P-H.

Power Play Science: Grades 1-2. Mega Books Staff. 80p. (gr. 1-2). 1998. 6.95 (*0-684-84426-5*) S&S Trade.

Power Players. Michael P. Weinreb. LC 96-90721. 232p. 1996. pap. 5.95 (*0-614-23146-9*) M P Weinreb.

Power Plays. Brenda Schaeffer. 24p. (Orig.). 1986. pap. 3.25 (*0-89486-373-8*, 5205B) Hazelden.

Power Plays. Linda K. Sibley et al. (Next Level Preteen Electives). (Illus.). 128p. 1997. teacher ed. 14.99 (*0-7847-0645-X*, 42105) Standard Pub.

Power Plays. Collin Wilcox. 21.95 (*0-89190-582-0*) Amereon Ltd.

***Power Plays.** 2nd rev. ed. George F. Walker. 208p. 2000. 14.95 (*0-88922-414-5*) Talonbks.

Power Plays: Critical Events in the Institutionalization of the Tennessee Valley Authority. Richard A. Colignon. LC 95-39702. (SUNY Series in the Sociology of Work). 367p. (C). 1996. pap. text 24.95 (*0-7914-3012-X*) State U NY Pr.

Power Plays: Critical Events in the Institutionalization of the Tennessee Valley Authority. Richard A. Colignon. LC 95-39702. (SUNY Series in the Sociology of Work). 367p. (C). 1997. text 74.50 (*0-7914-3011-1*) State U NY Pr.

Power Plays: How Teens Can Pull the Plug on Sexual Harassment. Harriet Hodgson. LC 93-5171. 176p. (J). 1993. pap. 8.95 (*0-925190-67-5*) Fairview Press.

Power Plays: Primary School Children's Constructions of Gender, Power & Adult Work. Becky Francis. 170p. 1998. pap. 22.50 (*1-85856-097-7*, Trentham Bks) Stylus Pub VA.

Power Plays: Profiles of America's Independent Renewable Electricity Developers. 2nd rev. ed. Susan Williams & Brenda G. Bateman. 1995. 75.00 (*1-879775-25-5*) IRRC Inc DC.

Power Plays: Shakespeare's Lessons in Leadership & Management. John Whitney & Tina Packer. LC 00-29160. 320p. 2000. 25.50 (*0-684-86887-3*) Simon & Schuster.

Power Plays: Their Uses & Abuses in Human Relations. Gerald Alper. LC 97-51293. 294p. 1998. 34.95 (*1-57309-267-3*); pap. 16.95 (*1-57309-259-2*) Intl Scholars.

***Power + Action50.** Tom Peters. 240p. 2001. 15.95 (*0-375-40774-X*) Knopf.

Power Plus Assertiveness: Step-by-Step with the Magic Communication Wand. Jean W. Miller. (Illus.). 192p. 1998. pap. 12.00 (*0-9663030-0-8*) Commun Ents.

Power Pneumatics. Brian Callear & Michael Pinches. 368p. 1997. pap. 67.00 (*0-13-489790-0*) P-H.

Power Point. large type ed. Rowan Edwards. 352p. 1996. 27.99 (*0-7089-3496-X*) Ulverscroft.

***Power Point for Terrified Teachers.** Teacher Created Materials Staff & Elin K. Cook. 304p. 1999. pap., teacher ed. 24.95 (*1-57690-440-7*, TCM2440) Tchr Create Mat.

Power Point 4.0. Sarah E. Hutchinson & Glen J. Coulthard. (Advantage Series for Computer Education). 200p. 1995. text 17.00 (*0-7863-0444-8*, Irwn Prfssnl) McGraw-Hill Prof.

Power Point 4.0 for Windows Beginners. Richard Klivans & Monique Peterson. (Quicksteps to Learning Ser.). 254p. 1994. spiral bd. 22.95 (*1-56951-027-X*) Sftware Trng.

Power Politics. Margaret Atwood. 58p. 1971. pap. 4.95 (*0-88784-020-5*, Pub. by Hse of Anansi Pr) Genl Dist Srvs.

Power Politics. Martin Wight. Ed. by Hedley Bull & Carsten Holbraad. 320p. 1995. reprint ed. pap. 21.95 (*0-7185-1002-X*) Bks Intl VA.

Power Politics: Australia's Party System. Dean Jaensch. 272p. 1994. pap. 24.95 (*1-86373-638-7*, Pub. by Allen & Unwin Pty) Paul & Co Pubs.

Power Politics: Poems. 2nd rev. ed. Margaret Atwood. LC 96-930636. 76p. 1996. pap. 9.95 (*0-88784-579-7*, Pub. by Hse of Anansi Pr) Genl Dist Srvs.

***Power, Politics & Crime.** Chambliss. 2000. pap. 18.95 (*0-8133-3487-X*, Pub. by Westview) HarpC.

Power, Politics & Crime. William J. Chambliss. LC 99-32625. (Crime & Society Ser.). 224p. 1999. 25.00 (*0-8133-3486-1*, Pub. by Westview) HarpC.

Power, Politics, & Organizations: A Behavioural Science View. Andrew Kakabadse & Christopher Parker. LC 83-14523. (Illus.). 249p. reprint ed. pap. 77.20 (*0-8357-8517-3*, 203481400091) Bks Demand.

Power, Politics & Participation in the Firm. Steve Minett. 236p. 1992. 82.95 (*1-85628-331-3*, Pub. by Avebry) Ashgate Pub Co.

Power Politics & Peace Policies: Intra-state Conflict Resolution in Southern Africa. Thomas Ohlson. LC 98-224863. (Report / Dept. of Peace & Conflict Research). 199 p. 1998. write for info. (*91-506-1311-1*) Uppsala Universitet.

Power, Politics & Pentecostals in Latin America. Ed. by Edward L. Cleary & Hannah Stewart-Gambino. 272p. (C). 1996. pap. 26.00 (*0-8133-2129-8*, Pub. by Westview) HarpC.

Power, Politics & Pentecostals in Latin America. Ed. by Hannah W. Stewart-Gambino & Edward L. Cleary. LC 96-39896. 272p. 1996. pap. 79.00 (*0-8133-2128-X*, Pub. by Westview) HarpC.

Power, Politics & Policy in Nursing. Rita R. Wieczorek. 288p. 1984. 29.95 (*0-8261-4630-9*) Springer Pub.

***Power, Politics & Portraits: Art & Propaganda in the Fourteenth-Century Court of Charles IV of Bohemia.** I. J. M. Rosario. (Illus.). 288p. 2000. 75.00 (*0-85115-787-4*) Boydell & Brewer.

Power, Politics & Progress: Social Change in Rural Peru. William F. Whyte & Giorgio Alberti. (RDC Bks.). 307p. 1976. 4.00 (*0-86731-118-5*) Cornell CIS RDC.

Power, Politics & Progress: Social Change in Rural Peru. William F. Whyte & Giorgio Alberti. LC 76-25193. 321p. reprint ed. pap. 99.60 (*0-608-16303-1*, 202625800049) Bks Demand.

Power, Politics, & Public Policy: A Matter of Caring. Ed. by Anne Boykin. 260p. 1995. 32.95 (*0-88737-644-4*, 14-2684, NLN Pr) Natl League Nurse.

Power Politics & Social Change in National Socialist Germany: A Process of Escalation into Mass Destruction. John M. Steiner. (Issues in Contemporary Politics Ser.: No. 2). 1975. text 52.35 (*90-279-7651-1*) Mouton.

Power Politics & Social Justice: Backward Castes in Karnataka. G. Thimaiah. (Illus.). 204p. (C). 1993. text 26.00 (*0-8039-9124-X*) Sage.

Power, Politics & the Ego. Kenneth J. Comfort. LC 99-164645. v, 485p. 1997. 29.95 (*0-9659144-0-2*) PAINYS.

Power, Politics, & the Making of the Bible: An Introduction. Robert B. Coote & Mary P. Coote. LC 89-29954. 208p. (Orig.). 1990. pap. 18.00 (*0-8006-2441-6*, 1-2441) Augsburg Fortress.

Power, Politics & the Olympic Games. Alfred Erich Senn. LC 98-48879. 336p. 1999. pap. 21.95 (*0-88011-958-6*) Human Kinetics.

***Power Politics California.** 6th ed. Ken DeBow & John C. Syer. LC 99-42111. 241p. (C). 1999. pap. text 42.00 (*0-321-07043-7*) Addison-Wesley.

Power Politics, Diplomacy, & the Avoidance of Hostilities Between England & the United States in the Wake of the Civil War. Pia G. Baldelli. Tr. by Elena Bertozzi & Cynthia D. Ipsen from ITA. LC 98-17754. (Studies in American History: Vol. 21). 390p. 1998. 109.95 (*0-7734-8398-5*) E Mellen.

Power Politics in South Asia. Dinesh K. Singh. (C). 1995. 14.00 (*81-7027-211-4*, Pub. by Radiant Pubs) S Asia.

Power Pop-Up Book: Our Planet's Energy Resources: Production, Consumption, Conservation, & Innovation. Claudio Vita-Finzi. (Illus.). 10p. (J). (gr. 3 up). 1991. boxed set 13.95 (*0-671-73535-7*) S&S Bks Yung.

Power Positioning. Valerie Wiener. 224p. 1998. 24.95 (*0-9667082-6-1*) PowerMark Pubg.

Power, Poverty, & Poison: Disaster & Response in an Indian City. James Manor. LC 92-40655. (Illus.). 200p. 1993. 28.50 (*0-8039-9466-4*) Sage.

Power, Poverty & Urban Policy. Ed. by Warner Bloomberg & Henry J. Schmandt. LC 68-24710. (Urban Affairs Annual Reviews Ser.: Vol. 2). 604p. reprint ed. pap. 172.20 (*0-608-09935-X*, 2021871) Bks Demand.

Power, Powerlessness, & the Divine: New Inquiries in Bible & Theology. Ed. by Cynthia L. Rigby. LC 97-42124. (Studies in Theological Education). 314p. 1997. 39.95 (*0-7885-0422-3*, 000809); pap. 24.95 (*0-7885-0423-1*, 000809) Duke.

Power Praying: Prayer That Produces Results. Jennifer K. Dean. LC 96-61548. 112p. 1996. pap. 9.00 (*1-883893-61-5*, Pub. by WinePress Pub) BookWorld.

Power Preaching for Church Growth. David Eby. 1996. pap. 15.99 (*1-85792-252-2*, Pub. by Christian Focus) Spring Arbor Dist.

Power Presentations: How to Connect with Your Audience & Sell Your Ideas. Marjorie Brody & Shawn Kent. LC 92-10949. 224p. 1992. pap. 19.95 (*0-471-55961-X*) Wiley.

Power Press: Its Impact on America & What You Can Do about It. Paul Mongerson. LC 97-26223. 224p. (Orig.). 1997. pap. 22.95 (*1-55591-347-4*) Fulcrum Pub.

Power Press & Safety Manual. 2nd ed. National Safety Council Staff. LC TJ1450.N27. 96p. reprint ed. pap. 30.00 (*0-608-13917-3*, 202501100040) Bks Demand.

Power Press Safety Manual. 3rd ed. National Safety Council Staff. LC 79-63712. (Illus.). 107p. reprint ed. pap. 33.20 (*0-8357-6425-7*, 203579300097) Bks Demand.

Power Pricing: How Managing Price Transforms the Bottom Line. Robert J. Dolan & Hermann Simon. LC 96-28203. 384p. 1997. 40.00 (*0-684-83443-X*) Free Pr.

***Power Primer: A Nontechnical Guide from Generation to End Use.** Ann Chambers. LC 98-54440. 262p. 1999. 64.95 (*0-87814-756-X*) PennWell Bks.

Power Principle. Blaine Lee. LC 97-9793. 1997. 24.50 (*0-684-81058-1*) S&S Trade.

Power Principle. Blaine Lee. 384p. 1998. per. 14.00 (*0-684-84616-0*, Fireside) S&S Trade Pap.

Power Printing with PCL: For the HP LaserJet & Compatibles. William Barden, Jr. (Bantam Book-Software Library). 400p. 1988. pap. 39.95 incl. disk (*0-553-34588-5*) Bantam.

Power, Privilege & Law. Leslie Bender & Daan Braveman. (American Casebook Ser.). 193p. (C). 1994. pap. text. write for info. (*0-314-05931-8*) West Pub.

Power, Privilege & Law: A Civil Rights Reader. Daan Braveman & Leslie Bender. (American Casebook Ser.). 622p. 1994. pap. 45.50 (*0-314-04577-5*) West Pub.

Power, Privilege, & Place: The Geography of the American Upper Class. Stephen R. Higley. 208p. (C). 1995. lib. bdg. 57.50 (*0-8476-8020-7*) Rowman.

Power, Privilege, & the Post: The Katharine Graham Story. Carol Felsenthal. LC 98-35864. (Illus.). 512p. 1999. pap. 16.95 (*1-888363-86-X*) Seven Stories.

Power Process: An NLP Approach to Writing. Dixie Elsie Hickman & Sid Jacobson. 237p. 1998. pap. 19.95 (*1-899836-07-1*, Pub. by Crown Hse) LPC Group.

Power, Process, & Participation: Tools for Change. Ed. by Rachel Slocum et al. 252p. (Orig.). 1995. pap. 19.95 (*1-85339-303-7*, Pub. by Intermed Tech) Stylus Pub VA.

Power, Process & Popular Sovereignty. Julie Mostov. 256p. (C). 1992. 49.95 (*0-87722-970-8*) Temple U Pr.

***Power Process Control Instrumentation in France: A Strategic Entry Report, 1996.** Compiled by Icon Group International Staff. (Illus.). 127p. 1999. ring bd. 1270.00 incl. audio compact disk (*0-7418-1201-0*) Icon Grp.

***Power Producer: A Practical Guide to RV News Producing.** Dow C. Smith. (Illus.). 150p. 2000. spiral bd. 30.00 (*0-9678432-0-0*) Radio TV News.

Power Production: What Are the Risks? J. Fremlin. 328p. 1985. 71.00 (*0-85274-479-X*) Taylor & Francis.

Power, Production & the Unprotected Worker: The Social Relations of Subordination. Jeffrey Harrod. LC 86-26374. (Political Economy of International Change Ser.). 336p. 1987. text 68.50 (*0-231-05844-6*) Col U Pr.

Power, Production & World Order: Social Forces in the Making of History. Robert W. Cox. (Political Economy of International Change Ser.). 392p. 1987. text 80.00 (*0-231-05808-X*) Col U Pr.

***Power Professor.** Amy Rogers. (Powerpuff Girls Ser.: No. 1). (Illus.). 64p. (J). (gr. 1-4). 2000. mass mkt. 3.99 (*0-439-16019-7*) Scholastic Inc.

Power, Profit, & Urban Land: Landownership in Medieval & Early Modern Northern European Towns. Ed. by Fin-Einar Eliassen & Geir A. Ersland. LC 96-27876. (Historical Urban Studies). (Illus.). 296p. 1996. 86.95 (*1-85928-341-1*, Pub. by Scolar Pr) Ashgate Pub Co.

Power Program: Retire Wealthy Within 10 Years. Richard M. Greene, Jr. (Illus.). 227p. 1980. pap. 39.95 (*0-934487-52-9*) R M Greene.

Power Programming in HP Openview: Developing CMIS Applications. Raymond P. Caruso & Power Play Technology Staff. LC 96-24171. 400p. (C). 1996. pap. text 56.00 (*0-13-443011-5*) P-H.

Power Programming Motif. 2nd ed. Kevin Reichard. 1995. pap. 59.95 incl. disk (*1-55828-322-6*, MIS Pr) IDG Bks.

Power Programming with ADA for the IBM PC. John W. Winters. (Illus.). 220p. 1987. 24.95 (*0-8306-7902-2*); pap. 16.95 (*0-8306-2902-5*) McGraw-Hill Prof.

Power Programming with Mathematica. David B. Wagner. LC 96-18798. (Illus.). 434p. 1996. pap. 44.95 (*0-07-912237-X*) McGraw.

Power Programming with RPC. John Bloomer. (Computer Science). 522p. (Orig.). 1992. pap. write for info. (*0-937175-77-3*) Thomson Learn.

Power Programming with SQL Windows. Rajesh Lalwani. 1994. pap. 29.95 incl. disk (*0-13-179306-3*) P-H.

***Power Project Documentation.** rev. ed. Asia Law & Practice Staff. 292p. 1999. pap. text 260.00 (*962-936-057-8*, Pub. by Asia Law & Practice) Am Educ Systs.

Power Projection: A Net Assessment of the U. S. & Soviet Capabilities. Ed. by W. Scott Thompson. 89p. 1978. pap. text 14.95 (*0-87855-800-4*) Transaction Pubs.

Power Projection & the Long-Range Combat Aircraft: Missions, Capabilities & Alternative Designs. Jacquelyn K. Davis & Robert L. Pfaltzgraff, Jr. LC 81-82130. (Special Reports). 37p. 1981. 11.95 (*0-89549-033-1*) Inst Foreign Policy Anal.

Power Promoting: How to Market Your Business to the Top! Jeffrey Sussman. LC 96-13043. 215p. 1997. pap. 18.95 (*0-471-14254-9*) Wiley.

Power Promotions: Powerful, Low Cost Ways to Increase Your Sales. Jill Griffin. (Profit Generator Marketing Ser.). (Illus.). 193p. (Orig.). 1989. pap. text 35.00 (*0-317-93859-2*) J Griffin.

Power Prompts: Practice Every Kind of Writing. Murray Svid & Wanda Lincoln. (Illus.). 128p. 1999. pap. 14.95 (*1-57612-071-6*, MM2085) Monday Morning Bks.

Power Prospecting Series. Alan C. Walter. Ed. by Beverly Miles. 40p. (Orig.). 1995. pap. text 4.89 (*1-57569-017-9*) Wisdom Pubng.

Power, Protection, & Free Trade: International Sources of U. S. Commercial Strategy, 1887-1939. David A. Lake. LC 87-47869. (Cornell Studies in Political Economy). 264p. 1988. text 42.50 (*0-8014-2134-9*) Cornell U Pr.

Power, Protection, & Free Trade: International Sources of U. S. Commercial Strategy, 1887-1939. David A. Lake. LC 87-47869. (Cornell Studies in Political Economy). 264p. 1990. reprint ed. pap. text 17.95 (*0-8014-9753-1*) Cornell U Pr.

Power, Providence, & Personality: Biblical Insight into Life & Ministry. Walter Brueggemann. 120p. (Orig.). 1990. pap. 14.95 (*0-664-25138-2*) Westminster John Knox.

Power, Public Opinion, & Diplomacy. Ed. by Lillian P. Wallace & William C. Askew. LC 68-55861. (Essay Index Reprint Ser.). 1977. 22.95 (*0-8369-0969-0*) Ayer.

Power Public Relations: How to Get PR to Work for You. Leonard Saffir. (Illus.). 272p. 1994. pap. 27.95 (*0-8442-3260-2*) NTC Contemp Pub Co.

Power Public Relations: How to Get PR TOR to Work for You. Leonard Saffir. (Illus.). 848p. 1994. 39.95 (*0-8442-3259-9*, 32599, NTC Business Bks) NTC Contemp Pub Co.

Power Public Relations: How to Master the New Pr. 2nd ed. Leonard Saffir. LC 99-24839. 304p. 2000. 39.95 (*0-658-00060-8*, 000608) NTC Contemp Pub Co.

Power Publicity! A Simple, Comprehensive, Step-By-Step Program for Building Your Business Through Free Press Coverage. Sheila R. Danzig. Ed. by William Danzig. LC 89-92232. (How to Make People Buy Whatever You're Selling Whether They Know They Need It or Not Ser.). 107p. 1990. pap. 20.00 (*0-9624333-4-9*) Natl Success.

Power Publishing with Ventura (IBM) James F. Clark & Xerox Corporation Staff. 240p. (C). 1992. text 33.35 (*0-697-16511-6*) Bus & Educ Tech.

***Power Puff Sticker Book.** CEDCO Publishing Staff. (Illus.). (J). 2000. pap. 8.95 (*0-7683-2227-8*) CEDCO Pub.

Power Pups & Fat Cats. Duno. 1999. text. write for info. (*0-312-24531-9*) St Martin.

Power Purchasing: Supply Management in the 21st Century. Peter L. Grieco, Jr. & Carl R. Cooper. LC 95-18522. 205p. 1995. 39.95 (*0-945456-13-1*) PT Pubns.

Power, Purpose & Collective Choice: Economic Strategy in Socialist States. Ed. by Ellen Comisso & Laura D. Tyson. LC 86-47639. (Cornell Studies in Political Economy). 424p. 1986. pap. text 21.95 (*0-8014-9435-4*) Cornell U Pr.

Power Push. Randy Gilbert. 32p. 1994. 2.00 (*0-9642046-0-6*) Faith Landmark.

***Power Quality.** (Electronic Sys Technician Lev 2). 2000. pap. 12.00 (*0-13-031270-3*) P-H.

***Power Quality Measurement & Troubleshooting.** Glen A. Mazur. (Illus.). 192p. 1999. pap. text 29.96 (*0-8269-1425-X*) Am Technical.

Power Quality Measurement & Troubleshooting: Resource Guide. Glen A. Mazur. 192p. pap. 295.00 (*0-8269-1426-8*) Am Technical.

Power Quality Primer. Kennedy. 400p. 1999. 75.00 (*0-07-134416-0*) McGraw-Hill Prof.

Power Quality Program Guide. Electrotek Concepts, Inc. Staff. LC 92-20042. 1992. write for info. (*0-917599-06-3*) Natl Rural.

Power Quality Solutions: Case Studies for Troubleshooters. Greg Porter & Van Sciver. 283p. (C). 1998. 79.00 (*0-13-020730-6*) P-H.

An Asterisk (*) at the beginning of an entry indicates that the title is appearing for the first time.

Power Quality Solutions: 25 Case Studies for Troubleshooters. Greg Porter & Andy VanSciver. LC 98-8456. (Illus.). 277p. 1998. 79.00 (*0-88173-279-6*, 0420) Fairmont Pr.

Power Quest. Carol Batdorf. LC 90-91108. (Illus.). 224p. 1990. pap. 12.95 (*0-88839-240-0*) Hancock House.

Power Quiz Book of Cricket. Narottam Puri. (C). 1987. 14.00 (*81-220-0045-2*, Pub. by Konark Pubs) S Asia.

Power Quotes: 4,000 Trenchant Soundbites on Leadership & Liberty, Treason & Triumph, Sacrifice & Scandal, Risk & Rebellion, Weakness & War, & Other Affaires Politiques. Daniel B. Baker. 402p. 1992. 15.95 (*0-8103-9416-2*) Visible Ink Pr.

***Power, Race & Gender in Academe: Strangers in the Tower?** Shirley Lim et al. LC 99-44991. 1999. 18.00 (*0-87352-270-2*) Modern Lang.

Power Rangers Turbo: Simple Simon Says & Other Stories. Acclaim Comics Staff. 1997. mass mkt. 4.50 (*1-57840-070-8*, Pub. by Acclaim Bks) Penguin Putnam.

Power Rangers Turbo Vs. Big, Bad Beetleborgs. Evan Skolnick. (Power Rangers Turbo Ser.). 1997. pap. text 4.50 (*1-57840-154-2*, Pub. by Acclaim Bks) Penguin Putnam.

Power Rating for Helical & Herringbone Gearing for Rolling Mill Service. 2nd rev. ed. AGMA Technical Committee. (ANSI/AGMA Standard Ser.: Vol. 6005-B89). (Illus.). 33p. 1996. pap. text 75.00 (*1-55589-530-1*) AGMA.

Power Reactor Noise. Thie. 222p. 1983. 50.00 (*0-89448-025-1*, 300018) Am Nuclear Soc.

Power Reading. Rick Ostrov. 1978. pap. write for info. (*0-9601706-2-6*) Educ Pr CA.

Power Reading. Laurie Rozakis. 1996. 12.95 (*0-02-861367-8*) Macmillan.

Power Reading. Laurie E. Rozakis. 224p. 1995. 12.95 (*0-02-860562-4*, Arc) IDG Bks.

Power Reading. 2nd ed. P.A.R. Staff & Barry Smith. 64p. (C). 1986. per. 9.90 (*0-256-10551-0*, Irwn McGrw-H) McGrw-H Hghr Educ.

Power Reading. 2nd ed. Barry Smith & P.A.R. Staff. 370p. (C). 1986. teacher ed. 26.95 (*0-89702-053-7*, Irwn McGrw-H) McGrw-H Hghr Educ.

Power Reading: A Dynamic System for Mastering All Your Business Reading. Phyllis Mindell. 226p. 1998. reprint ed. (*0-13-020780-2*) P-H.

Power Reading 1: Reading for Power. P. A. R. Staff. (C). 1985. pap. text, teacher ed. 26.95 (*0-256-10596-0*, Irwn McGrw-H) McGrw-H Hghr Educ.

Power Reading 1: Reading for Power. P.A.R. Staff. (C). 1983. pap. text, suppl. ed. 9.90 (*0-256-10595-2*, Irwn McGrw-H) McGrw-H Hghr Educ.

Power Real Estate Letters. 3rd ed. Willian H. Pivar. LC 97-121392. 1997. pap. text 39.95 incl. disk (*0-7931-2474-3*, 1926-0303) Dearborn.

Power Recovery: The Twelve Steps for a New Generation. James Wiley. LC 94-43302. 192p. (Orig.). 1995. pap. 7.95 (*0-8091-3552-3*) Paulist Pr.

Power Relations in Nigeria: Ilorin Slaves & Their Successors. Ann O'Hear. LC 97-20263. (Rochester Studies in African History & the Diaspora: Vol. 1). (Illus.). 352p. 1997. 65.00 (*1-878822-86-1*) Univ Rochester Pr.

Power, Reproduction & Gender: The Intergenerational Transfer of Knowledge. Ed. by Wendy Harcourt. LC 96-34464. 240p. (C). 1997. text 65.00 (*1-85649-425-X*, Pub. by Zed Books) St Martin.

Power Research on the Internet: A Guide to Doing Research on the Internet. Cheryl Harris. 1995. 43.95 (*0-534-25851-4*) Wadsworth Pub.

Power Resource Theory & the Welfare State: A Critical Approach. Julia S. O'Connor. LC 98-205029. 368p. 1998. text 60.00 (*0-8020-0809-7*); pap. text 21.95 (*0-8020-7171-6*) U of Toronto Pr.

Power Resumes. 3rd ed. Ron Tepper. LC 97-46824. 272p. 1998. pap. 14.95 (*0-471-24781-2*) Wiley.

***Power Retail: Winning Strategies from Chapters & Other Leading Retailers in Canada.** Lawrence N. Stevenson. 288p. 1999. 24.95 (*0-07-560996-7*) McGraw.

Power Rhythm Chording. rev. ed. Ron Middlebrook. (Illus.). 56p. (YA). (gr. 8 up). 1995. pap. text 17.95 incl. audio compact disk (*0-931759-96-X*) Centerstream Pub.

Power Rock: Authentic Transcriptions with Lyrics. 64p. 1991. pap. 12.95 (*0-7935-1092-9*, 06621751) H Leonard.

Power RPG III: Advanced Concepts, Tips, & Techniques. Doug Pence & Ron Hawkins. (Illus.). 374p. (Orig.). 1995. pap. 99.00 (*1-883884-26-8*, 529) Midrange Comput.

Power RPG IV: Advanced Concepts, Tips, & Techniques, Including ILE. Doug Pence & Ron Hawkins. LC 98-105330. (Illus.). 500p. (Orig.). 1996. pap. 99.00 (*1-883884-32-2*, 560) Midrange Comput.

Power Rules: The Evolution of NATO's Conventional Force Posture. John S. Duffield. LC 94-25006. xi, 386p. 1995. 49.50 (*0-8047-2396-6*) Stanford U Pr.

Power Sales Presentations. 2nd rev. ed. Stephan Schiffman. 204p. 1993. pap. 7.95 (*1-55850-252-1*) Adams Media.

Power Sales Writing: What Every Sales Person Needs to Know to Turn Prospects into Buyers. Sue A. Hershkowitz. 1996. pap. text 15.95 (*0-9648464-0-3*) High Impct.

Power Scheduling. Power Scheduling Staff. 96p. 1995. pap. text, per. 14.95 (*0-7872-0516-8*) Kendall-Hunt.

Power Schmoozing: The New Etiquette for Social & Business Success. Terri Mandell. (First Books for Business Ser.). 173p. 1996. pap. 14.95 (*0-07-039887-9*) McGraw.

Power Searching the Internet for Your Next Job. Thomas E. Wright. Ed. by Donna J. Wright & Robert B. Wright. LC 98-96404. v, 200p. 1998. spiral bd. 24.95 (*0-9665257-0-1*) Whttney Grimm.

Power Secrets from a Sorcerer's Private Magnum Arcanum. 2nd unabridged ed. Gavin Frost & Yvonne Frost. (Illus.). 220p. 1980. reprint ed. pap. text 9.95 (*0-13-687251-4*) Godolphin Hse.

Power Secrets to Fast Money. John V. Kamin. 112p. 1979. 10.00 (*0-911353-06-2*) Forecaster Pub.

***Power Sector Controls & Instrumentation in Poland: A Strategic Entry Report, 1996.** Compiled by Icon Group International Staff. (Illus.). 180p. 1999. ring bd. 1800.00 incl. audio compact disk (*0-7418-1202-9*) Icon Grp.

***Power Sector Controls, Instrumentation in Finland: A Strategic Entry Report, 1996.** Compiled by Icon Group International Staff. (Illus.). 102p. 1999. ring bd. 1020.00 incl. audio compact disk (*0-7418-1356-4*) Icon Grp.

***Power Sector in Vietnam: A Strategic Entry Report, 1999.** Compiled by Icon Group International. (Illus.). 168p. 1999. ring bd. 1680.00 incl. audio compact disk (*0-7418-1726-8*) Icon Grp.

***Power Sector Reform in Subsaharan Africa.** John K. Turkson. LC 99-41122. 2000. text 79.95 (*0-312-22778-7*) St Martin.

Power Seekers. rev. ed. Michael C. Giammatteo. (Illus.). (Orig.). (C). 1999. pap. 8.95 (*0-918428-02-5*) Sylvan Inst.

Power Selling by Telephone. Barry Z. Masser & William M. Leeds. 240p. 1982. 19.95 (*0-13-686998-X*, Parker Publishing Co) P-H.

Power Semiconductor Control of AC Motor Drives. J. M. Murphy & F. G. Turnbull. (Illus.). 220p. 1988. 239.00 (*0-08-022683-3*, CRC Reprint) Franklin.

Power Semiconductor Devices. B. Jayant Baliga. (General Engineering Ser.). 528p. 1995. mass mkt. 109.95 (*0-534-94098-6*) PWS Pubs.

Power Semiconductor Devices: Theory & Applications. Vitezslav Benda et al. LC 98-22030. 432p. 1999. 149.95 (*0-471-97644-X*) Wiley.

Power Semiconductor Devices & Circuits. A. A. Jaecklin. LC 92-42064. (Brown Boveri Symposia Ser.). (Illus.). 408p. (C). 1993. text 115.00 (*0-306-44402-X*, Kluwer Plenum) Kluwer Academic.

Power Semiconductor Materials & Devices Vol. 483: Materials Research Society Symposium Proceedings. Ed. by S. J. Pearton et al. LC 98-2946. 456p. 1998. text 73.00 (*1-55899-388-6*) Materials Res.

Power Semiconductors in Germany: A Strategic Entry Report, 1997. Compiled by Icon Group International Staff. (Illus.). 97p. 1999. ring bd. 970.00 incl. audio compact disk (*0-7418-0823-4*) Icon Grp.

Power Sequencing with Master Tracks Pro-Pro 4. Craig Anderton. (Illus.). 112p. 1990. pap. 19.95 (*0-8256-2585-8*, AM76613) Music Sales.

Power Series from a Computational Point of View. K. T. Smith. (Universitext Ser.). (Illus.). viii, 132p. 1987. 48.95 (*0-387-96516-5*) Spr-Verlag.

Power Series over Commutative Rings. James W. Brewer. (Lecture Notes in Pure & Applied Mathematics Ser.: Vol. 64). (Illus.). 112p. 1981. pap. text 115.00 (*0-8247-6952-X*) Dekker.

***Power Sermons for Children Vol. 1: New Testament.** T. D. Hunt. 120p. 2000. spiral bd. 29.95 (*0-9679484-5-2*) Perform Bulder Pub.

***Power Sermons for Children Vol. 2: Old Testament.** T. D. Hunt. (Illus.). 120p. 2000. spiral bd. 29.95 (*0-9679484-6-0*, 0-9679484-6-0) Perform Bulder Pub.

Power Serve: 236 Inspiring Ideas on Servant Leadership. Byrd Baggett. (Illus.). 128p. 1998. 12.95 (*1-890651-00-1*, Saltillo Press); pap. 6.95 (*1-890651-03-6*, Saltillo Press) Williford Communs.

***Power Sewing Step-by-Step.** Sandra Betzina. LC 00-23431. (Illus.). 2000. 34.95 (*1-56158-363-4*) Taunton.

Power Sharing: Language, Rank, Gender, & Social Space in Pohnpei, Micronesia. Elizabeth Keating. LC 98-36857. (Studies in Anthropological Linguistics). (Illus.). 224p. 1998. text 75.00 (*0-19-511197-4*) OUP.

Power Sharing & International Mediation in Ethnic Conflicts. Timothy D. Sisk. LC 96-8127. (Perspectives Ser.). 143p. 1996. pap. text 7.95 (*1-878379-56-9*) US Inst Peace.

Power Sharing in South Africa. Arend Lijphart. LC 85-82195. (Policy Papers in International Affairs: No. 24). x, 179p. (C). 1985. pap. text 11.50 (*0-87725-524-5*) U of Cal IAS.

Power Shift in Germany: The 1998 Election & the End of the Kohl Era. Ed. by David P. Conradt et al. LC 99-87840. (Modern German Studies: Vol. 5). 336p. 2000. pap. 19.95 (*1-57181-200-8*) Berghahn Bks.

Power Shift in Germany: The 1998 Election & the End of the Kohl Era. Ed. by David P. Conradt et al. LC 99-87840. (Modern German Studies: Vol. 5). 336p. 2000. 69.95 (*1-57181-199-0*) Berghahn Bks.

***Power Shift to Gracious Abundance: Spirituality Made Practical for All Aspects of Life.** Beca Lewis. 250p. 2000. pap. 14.95 (*0-915009-71-4*, Pub. by World Leis Corp) Midpt Trade.

Power Shopping: A Guide for Building Owners & Managers to Prepare for the Deregulated Electricity Marketplace. Karen W. Penafiel. (Illus.). 108p. 1996. pap. 50.00 (*0-614-31137-3*, 135-PWRSHP) Build Own & Man.

Power Skills in Science. Philip Carona. 1979. pap. text 4.95 (*0-07-010134-5*) McGraw.

Power Slalom - Twenty-Eight Breakthrough Concepts for Mastering the Sport. Mike Kjellander. Ed. by Jo Robertson. (Illus.). 100p. (Orig.). (YA). 1989. pap. 14.95 (*0-944406-06-8*) World Pub FL.

Power Sleep. abr. ed. James B. Maas. 1998. 14.00 incl. audio (*0-375-40201-2*) Random.

Power Sleep: The Revolutionary Program That Prepares Your Mind for Peak Performance. James B. Maas. LC 98-34045. 304p. 1999. pap. 13.00 (*0-06-097760-4*) HarpC.

Power Snacks. Kate Schumann & Jennifer Raymond. (Illus.). 32p. 1996. pap. write for info. (*1-882330-49-8*) Magni Co.

Power So Great. Ruth A. Patrick. 40p. (Orig.). 1996. pap. 7.95 (*1-57502-276-1*, PO975) Morris Pubng.

Power Sonic & Ultrasonic Transducers Design. Ed. by B. F. Hamonic & J. N. Decarpigny. (Illus.). 255p. 1988. 72.95 (*0-387-18664-6*) Spr-Verlag.

Power Source. Larry Simpson. LC 97-94451. 177p. 1997. pap. 7.50 (*1-891429-00-0*) Armadillo Pubng.

Power Sources: Research & Development in Non-Mechanical Electrical Power Sources, No. 8. Ed. by J. Thompson. LC 74-18513. 1982. text 294.00 (*0-12-689155-9*) Acad Pr.

Power Sources for Biomedical Implantable Applications & Ambient Temperature Lithium Batteries: Proceedings of the Symposia. Symposium on Power Sources for Biomedical Implanta. Ed. by Boone B. Owens & Nehemiah Margalit. LC 80-66385. (Electrochemical Society Proceedings Ser.: Vol. 80-4). (Illus.). 650p. 1980. pap. 200.00 (*0-7837-8997-1*, 205926200002) Bks Demand.

Power Sources 9: Research & Development in Nonmechanical Power Sources. J. Thompson. 1983. text 294.00 (*0-12-689160-5*) Acad Pr.

Power Speaking: A Guide to Writing & Delivering Professional Speeches. Mark B. Yarnell. Ed. by Werner A. Riefling. LC 95-67581. 160p. (Orig.). 1995. pap. 14.95 (*1-879706-64-4*) Paper Chase.

***Power, Speed & Stamina for Tennis: A Complete Guide for the Player & Coach.** Jack Thompson & Gary Cook. 110p. 1999. per. 15.00 (*0-7872-6263-3*) Kendall-Hunt.

Power Spots. Jose Rosa & Nathaniel Altman. 96p. 1988. pap. 8.95 (*0-85030-474-1*, Pub. by Aqn Pr) Harper SF.

Power SQL Development with Visual Basic. Paul Sheriff. (Visual Basic Power Guides Ser.). 160p. 1994. spiral bd. 69.00 (*1-886213-02-X*) Bldg Blocks.

Power Stability & Contraband: The Inmate Economy. David B. Kalinich. (Illus.). 119p. (C). 1986. reprint ed. pap. text 11.95 (*0-88133-200-3*) Waveland Pr.

Power Start. Paul Sheriff. (Visual Basic Power Guides Ser.). 225p. 1994. spiral bd. 69.00 (*1-886213-00-3*) Bldg Blocks.

Power Station Developments & Local Planning. Ed. by J. Glasson. (C). 1983. 35.00 (*0-7855-3846-1*, Pub. by Oxford Polytechnic) St Mut.

Power Station Instrumentation. Ed. by Max W. Jervis. (Illus.). 750p. 1993. text 330.00 (*0-7506-1196-0*) Buttrwrth-Heinemann.

Power Steering: Global Automakers & the Transformation of Rural Communities. Michele M. Hoyman. LC 96-45944. (Studies in Government & Public Policy). 272p. 1997. 35.00 (*0-7006-0818-4*); pap. 17.95 (*0-7006-0819-2*) U Pr of KS.

***Power Stone.** Prima's Temp Authors Staff. (Official Strategy Guides Ser.). 1999. pap. 12.99 (*0-7615-2578-5*, Prima Games) Prima Pub.

Power Strategies of Jesus Christ: Principles of Leadership from the Greatest Motivator of All Time. Harry A. Olson. LC 98-47544. 192p. 1999. 5.99 (*0-517-20334-0*) Random Hse Value.

Power Strategies of Jesus Christ: Principles of Leadership from the Greatest Motivator of All Time. Harry A. Olson. LC 91-11891. 192p. 1991. reprint ed. pap. 9.95 (*0-89243-505-4*, Liguori Triumph) Liguori Pubns.

Power, Strategy, & Security: A World Politics Reader. Ed. by Klaus E. Knorr. LC 82-48561. 291p. 1983. reprint ed. pap. 90.30 (*0-7837-9360-X*, 206010200004) Bks Demand.

***Power Strokes I Vol. 3: Hibachi Papers III.** Mark St. George. LC 99-93357. (Illus.). 240p. 1999. pap. 12.95 (*0-9620541-9-4*) Proteus LA.

Power Stronger Itself. George Lewis. 1997. pap. 16.95 (*0-226-47696-0*); lib. bdg. 48.00 (*0-226-47695-2*) U Ch Pr.

Power Structure: Ownership, Integration, & Competition in the U. S. Electricity Industry. John E. Kwoka, Jr. LC 96-47148. 208p. (C). 1996. lib. bdg. 99.00 (*0-7923-9843-2*) Kluwer Academic.

Power Structure of American Business. Beth Mintz & Michael Schwartz. LC 84-8841. (Illus.). 348p. 1985. 33.00 (*0-226-53108-2*) U Ch Pr.

Power Structure of American Business. Beth Mintz & Michael Schwartz. LC 84-8841. (Illus.). 352p. 1987. pap. text 17.00 (*0-226-53109-0*) U Ch Pr.

Power Structure Research. Ed. by G. William Domhoff. LC 79-25255. (Sage Focus Editions Ser.: No. 17). 270p. reprint ed. pap. 83.70 (*0-8357-8456-8*, 203472000091) Bks Demand.

Power Struggle: An Exposition of the 27th Psalm. R. W. Schambach. (Legacy Ser.). 110p. 1995. pap. 5.00 (*1-888361-04-2*) Power Publns.

***Power Struggles.** Ethel S. Person. 2001. write for info. (*0-688-17577-5*, Wm Morrow) Morrow Avon.

***Power Sums, Gorenstein Algebras & Determinantal Loci.** A. Iarrobino & Vassil. (Lecture Notes in Mathematics Ser.: Vol. 1721). xxix, 345p. 2000. 69.80 (*3-540-66766-0*) Spr-Verlag.

***Power Supervising: Correcting Job Performance.** Joseph A. Antonelli. Ed. by Sally W. Antonelli. v, 71p. 1998. 12.95 (*0-9672586-0-X*) Mgmt Support.

Power Supplies. 2nd ed. David Lines. (Illus.). 124p. 1997. pap. 19.95 (*0-7906-1120-1*) Prompt Publns.

Power Supplies: Continuous Data & Network Service. 134p. 1993. 2650.00 (*0-89336-964-0*, E-050) BCC.

Power Supplies for Fire Protective Signaling Systems, UL 1481. 4th ed. (C). 1999. pap. text 95.00 (*1-55989-554-3*) Underwrtrs Labs.

Power Supplies, Switching Regulators, Inverters & Converters. Irving M. Gottlieb. (Illus.). 448p. (Orig.). 1984. pap. 21.95 (*0-8306-1665-9*) McGraw-Hill Prof.

Power Supplies, Switching Regulators, Inverters & Converters. 2nd ed. Irving Gottlieb. 496p. (Orig.). 1994. pap. 29.95 (*0-07-024007-8*) McGraw.

Power Supplies, Switching Regulators, Inverters, & Converters. 2nd rev. ed. Irving M. Gottlieb. LC 93-1029. 1993. reprint ed. text 32.95 (*0-8306-4405-9*); reprint ed. pap. text 21.95 (*0-8306-4404-0*) McGraw-Hill Prof.

Power Supply Cookbook. Marty Brown. 248p. 1997. pap. text 29.95 (*0-7506-7010-X*, Newnes) Buttrwrth-Heinemann.

Power Supply in Telecommunications. 3rd rev. ed. Hans Gumhalter. 1995. write for info. (*3-540-57068-3*) Spr-Verlag.

Power Supply in Telecommunications: Principles, Equipment, Engineering. 3rd ed. Hans Gumhalter. (Illus.). 450p. 1995. 141.95 (*0-387-57068-3*) Spr-Verlag.

Power Supply Regulators. Buck Engineering Staff. Ed. by Buck Engineering Tech. Writers Staff. (F. A. C. E. T. Ser.: Vol. 9). (Illus.). 100p. 1989. pap. text, teacher ed. 11.00 (*0-86657-025-X*); ring bd. 13.00 (*0-86657-024-1*) Lab-Volt.

Power Supply Testing: A Handbook for Making Strategic Choices. Earl Crandall. 1990. text 89.95 (*0-442-23845-2*, VNR) Wiley.

Power Supply Troubleshooting & Repair. Lanny Logan. (Illus.). 195p. 1998. pap. 24.95 (*0-7906-1138-4*) Prompt Publns.

Power Surfcasting. R. Arra. 1991. pap. 12.95 (*1-55821-112-8*) Lyons Pr.

Power Surge: Guide to the Coming Energy Revolution. Christopher Flavin & Nicholas Lenssen. 300p. 1994. pap. 10.95 (*0-393-31199-6*) Norton.

Power Surge: Sex, Violence & Pornography. Susan G. Cole & Susan G. Gail. 253p. 1995. pap. 14.95 (*0-929005-78-3*) Africa World.

***Power Surge: Six Marks of Discipleship for a Changing Church.** Michael W. Foss. LC 00-37119. 2000. write for info. (*0-8006-3264-8*, Fortress Pr) Augsburg Fortress.

Power-Switching Converters. Simon S. Ang. (Electrical Engineering & Electronics Ser.: Vol. 93). (Illus.). 432p. 1995. text 160.00 (*0-8247-9630-6*) Dekker.

Power System Analysis. Hadi Saadat. LC 98-21030. 672p. 1998. 65.75 (*0-07-012235-0*) McGraw-Hill Prof.

Power System Analysis. Hadi Sadaat. 1998. 97.19 (*0-07-561634-3*) McGraw.

Power System Analysis & Design. 2nd ed. J. Duncan Glover & Mulukutla S. Sarma. LC 93-34243. 592p. (C). 1993. mass mkt. 84.95 (*0-534-93960-0*) PWS Pubs.

Power System Commissioning & Maintenance Practice. R. J. Meredith. (Power Ser.: No. 24). 520p. 1998. 139.00 (*0-85296-909-0*, PO024) INSPEC Inc.

Power System Control & Stability. rev. ed. Paul M. Anderson & Aziz A. Fouad. LC 93-10958. 480p. 1993. 69.95 (*0-7803-1029-2*, PC0379-8) Inst Electrical.

Power System Control Technology. Torsten Cegrell. (Illus.). 352p. 1986. text 46.00 (*0-13-688433-4*) P-H.

Power System Design Applications for Alternative Energy Sources. Khalil Denno. 272p. (C). 1988. text 50.20 (*0-13-688004-5*) P-H.

Power System Dynamics: Stability & Control. K. R. Padiyar. LC 95-48240. 1999. pap. 45.00 (*0-471-19002-0*) Wiley.

Power System Dynamics & Stability. Jacques Bialek et al. LC 96-39033. 484p. 1997. 149.95 (*0-471-97174-X*) Wiley.

Power System Dynamics & Stability. Jan Machowski & Janusz Bialek. LC 96-39033. 484p. 1997. pap. 79.95 (*0-471-95643-0*) Wiley.

Power System Dynamics & Stability. Peter W. Sauer. LC 97-17360. 357p. 1997. 94.00 (*0-13-678830-0*) P-H.

Power System Grounding & Transients: An Introduction. A. P. Sakis Meliopoulos. (Electrical Engineering & Electronics Ser.: Vol. 50). (Illus.). 472p. 1988. text 185.00 (*0-8247-7908-8*) Dekker.

Power System Harmonic Analysis. J. Arrillaga. LC 97-309. 382p. 1997. 149.95 (*0-471-97548-6*) Wiley.

***Power System Harmonics.** 1998. 1689.00 (*0-7803-5301-3*) IEEE Standards.

Power System Harmonics. J. Arrillaga et al. LC 84-22097. 348p. reprint ed. pap. 107.90 (*0-7837-0110-1*, 20403870016) Bks Demand.

Power System Modeling, Analysis & Control. A. P. Melipoulos. (Electrical Engineering & Electronics Ser.). (Illus.). Date not set. text. write for info. (*0-8247-9734-5*) Dekker.

Power System Operation. 3rd ed. Robert H. Miller. 271p. 1994. 60.00 (*0-07-041977-9*) McGraw.

Power System Operation. 3rd ed. Robert H. Miller & James H. Malinowski. 271p. 1997. 50.00 (*0-7803-3461-2*, PC5720-QOE) Inst Electrical.

Power System Operation in Emergency. Knight. text. write for info. (*0-471-49016-4*) Wiley.

Power System Protection. Anderson. (Illus.). 1236p. 1998. 124.95 (*0-07-134323-7*) McGraw.

***Power System Protection.** Paul M. Anderson. LC 98-28659. (Power Engineering Ser.). 1998. 124.95 (*0-7803-3427-2*) IEEE Standards.

Power System Protection Vol. I: Principles & Components, 4 vols. rev. ed. Ed. by Electricity Training Association Staff. (Illus.). 544p. 1995. reprint ed. 395.00 (*0-85296-834-5*, PO905) INSPEC Inc.

Power System Protection Vol. II: Systems & Methods. rev. ed. (Illus.). 344p. 1995. reprint ed. boxed set 125.00 (*0-85296-836-1*, PO905B) INSPEC Inc.

Power System Protection Vol. III: Application. rev. ed. (Illus.). 496p. 1995. reprint ed. boxed set 132.00 (*0-85296-837-X*, PO905C) INSPEC Inc.

Power System Protection Vol. IV: Digital Protection & Signalling. 132p. 1995. 45.00 (*0-85296-838-8*, PO905D) INSPEC Inc.

P

***Power System Quality Assessment.** J. Arrillaga et al. LC 99-38990. 400p. 2000. text 120.00 (*0-471-98865-0*) Wiley.

Power System Reliability Evaluation. Roy Billinton. x, 300p. 1970. text 220.00 (*0-677-02870-9*) Gordon & Breach.

Power System Stability, 3 vols. Edward W. Kimbark. LC 94-42999. (Power Systems Engineering Ser.). 1008p. 1995. pap. 149.95 (*0-7803-1135-3*, PP5600) Inst Electrical.

Power System Stability & Control. P. Kundur & Neal J. Balu. 1176p. 1997. 95.00 (*0-7803-3463-9*, PC5718-QOE) Inst Electrical.

Power System Stability & Control. Prabha Kundur. 1176p. 1993. 95.00 (*0-07-035958-X*) McGraw.

Power System Transient Stability Analysis Using the Transient Energy Function Method. Abdel-Azia Fouad & Vijay Vittal. 384p. (C). 1991. text 69.80 (*0-13-682675-X*) P-H.

Power Systems: Analysis & Design. John J. Grainger. 784p. (C). 1994. 103.44 (*0-07-061293-5*) McGraw.

Power Systems: Modelling & Control Applications. Ed. by A. J. Calvaer. LC 89-31106. (IFAC Proceedings Ser.: IFPS 8909). (Illus.). 548p. 1989. 135.01 (*0-685-26444-0*) Elsevier.

***Power Systems Analysis.** 2nd ed. Bergen. LC 99-20875. 619p. 1999. 105.00 (*0-13-691990-1*) P-H.

Power Systems Analysis. 2nd ed. Charles A. Gross. LC 85-17995. 608p. 1986. text 108.95 (*0-471-86206-1*) Wiley.

Power Systems Analysis & Design 3rd ed. Sarma Glover. (Electrical Engineering Ser.). (C). 2001. pap. text 36.95 (*0-534-95367-0*) Brooks-Cole.

Power Systems Analysis & Planning. Ed. by A. H. El Abiad. LC 82-6228. (Arab School of Science & Technology Ser.). (Illus.). 350p. 1983. text 137.00 (*0-89116-272-0*) Hemisp Pub.

Power Systems Analysis Handbook. J. Schirra. (Electrical Engineering & Electronics Ser.). Date not set. write for info. (*0-8247-9424-9*) Dekker.

Power Systems & Engineering. Ed. by J. Hasegawa. (Series on Energy & Power Systems). 178p. 1994. 75.00 (*0-88986-204-4*, 213) Acta Pr.

***Power Systems, Biotechnological Processes, Fault Detection, Vol. O.** Ed. by T. McAvoy et al. 606p. 1999. pap. 126.00 (*0-08-042753-7*) Elsevier.

Power Systems of East European Countries: Problems & Methods for Control & Development. Ed. by Y. N. Rudenko. LC 93-23936. 353p. 1993. 110.00 (*1-56700-013-4*) Begell Hse.

Power Systems Restructuring: Engineering & Economics. Marija D. Ilic et al. LC 98-6642. (Power Electronics & Power System Engineering & Computer Science Ser.). 1998. 145.00 (*0-7923-8163-7*) Kluwer Academic.

Power Systems Stability Handbook. Anthony J. Pansini. 1991. 25.00 (*0-87814-647-4*) PennWell Bks.

Power Tactics of Jesus Christ. 2nd ed. Jay Haley. 1989. pap. 12.95 (*0-931513-05-7*) Norton.

Power Tactics of Jesus Christ, & Other Essays. 2nd ed. Jay Haley. 160p. 1986. 14.95 (*0-931513-04-9*) Triang Pr.

Power Taiji. Erle Montaigue & Michael Babin. (Illus.). 200p. 1995. pap. 25.00 (*0-87364-846-3*) Paladin Pr.

Power Talk, unabridged ed. Contrib. by Stephen R. Covey et al. (Professional Ser.). 1993. text 48.85 incl. audio (*1-55927-254-6*) Audio Renaissance.

Power Talk: How to Use Theater Techniques to Win Your Audience. Niki Flacks & Robert W. Rasberry. LC 81-69632. 256p. 1982. 32.95 (*0-02-910390-8*) Free Pr.

Power Talk: The Art of Effective Communication. Howard J. Rankin. LC 98-85059. 200p. 1999. pap. 11.95 (*0-9658261-3-9*) Stepwise Pr.

***Power Talk: Using Language to Build Authority & Influence.** Sarah Myers McGinty. 224p. 2001. 24.95 (*0-446-52537-5*) Warner Bks.

Power Talk: Standard American English: Your Ladder to Success! Bettye P. Zoller & John A. Watleins. 65p. (gr. 6-12). lib. bdg., teacher ed., student ed. 24.95 (*1-884643-11-6*, SPP95) ZWL Pubng.

Power Talk: Standard American English: Your Ladder to Success! Bettye P. Zoller et al. LC 93-94292. (Illus.). 160p. (C). (gr. 6-12). pap. 24.95 (*1-884643-04-3*, AMSP 2 PT) ZWL Pubng.

Power Talk: Standard American English: Your Ladder to Success! Bettye P. Zoller et al. LC 93-94292. (Illus.). 160p. (C). (gr. 6-12). pap. 39.95 incl. audio (*1-884643-02-7*, AMSP 2 PT) ZWL Pubng.

Power Talking. George R. Walther. 1992. mass mkt. 5.99 (*0-425-13328-1*) Berkley Pub.

Power Tarot. Trish McGregor. LC 97-46843. 288p. 1998. per. 12.00 (*0-684-84185-1*) S&S Trade.

Power Teaching. Benj Mahle. 1989. pap. 9.99 (*0-8224-5192-1*) Fearon Teacher Aids.

Power Teaching: A Primary Role of the School Library Media Specialist. Kay E. Vandegrift. LC 93-35565. (School Library Media Programs Ser.: No. 14). (Illus.). 187p. reprint ed. pap. 58.00 (*0-608-06022-4*, 206635000008) Bks Demand.

Power Technology. Theodore B. Sauselein. LC 93-5631. 144p. 1994. 17.95 (*0-912524-85-5*) Busn News.

Power Technology. 4th ed. George E. Stephenson. 544p. 1985. pap. 32.95 (*0-8273-2446-4*) Delmar.

Power Technology. 4th ed. George E. Stephenson. 96p. 1985. pap., teacher ed., suppl. ed. 12.95 (*0-8273-2424-3*) Delmar.

Power Technology. 4th ed. George E. Stephenson. 544p. 1986. teacher ed. 8.00 (*0-8273-2447-2*) Delmar.

Power Tennis. abr. ed. Roger W. Breternitz. 1985. pap. 9.95 incl. audio (*1-893417-24-7*) Vector Studios.

Power Tennis Training. Donald A. Chu. LC 94-21325. 176p. 1994. pap. 15.95 (*0-87322-616-X*, PCHU0616) Human Kinetics.

Power That Heals. Charles A. Ballough. 62p. 1996. reprint ed. spiral bd. 9.00 (*0-7873-0069-1*) Hlth Research.

Power That Heals: Love Healing & the Trinity. David J. Randolph. LC 93-31888. 160p. (Orig.). 1994. pap. 3.29 (*0-687-33207-9*) Abingdon.

Power That Heals & How to Use It. Charles A. Ballough. 1991. lib. bdg. 79.00 (*0-8490-4545-2*) Gordon Pr.

Power That Preserves. Stephen R. Donaldson. 528p. 1987. mass mkt. 6.99 (*0-345-34867-2*, Del Rey) Ballantine Pub Grp.

Power That Women Have: Keys to Unlock a Man's Heart. Christopher P. Johnson. Ed. by Robbi Hunt. iv, 216p. 1998. pap. 12.00 (*0-9667517-0-1*) Fishnet Pubns.

Power, the Press & the Technology of Freedom: The Coming Age of ISDN. Leonard R. Sussman. LC 89-16806. (Focus on Issues Ser.: No. 9). (Illus.). 514p. (C). 1990. 33.00 (*0-932088-39-2*) Freedom Hse.

Power Theory of Economics. Yasuma Takata. Tr. by Douglas Hunter. LC 95-1370. 1995. text 79.95 (*0-312-12626-3*) St Martin.

Power Therapy: Maximizing Health Through Self-Efficacy. Michael Aleksiuk. LC 96-17394. 392p. 1996. 22.50 (*0-88937-138-5*) Hogrefe & Huber Pubs.

Power Thinking: The Secret of Success. Robert L. Albee. 139p. (Orig.). 1989. pap. text 8.95 (*0-9624441-0-3*) Writers Express.

Power Thinking for Success. Cathy C. Block & John N. Mangieri. 238p. 1996. pap. text 16.95 (*1-57129-019-2*) Brookline Bks.

Power Thought Cards. Louise L. Hay. 1999. pap. 15.95 (*1-56170-612-4*, L441) Hay House.

Power Thought Cards. Louise L. Hay. 1999. 15.95 (*1-56170-655-8*) Hay House.

Power Thoughts. large type ed. Robert H. Schuller. 278p. 1995. 23.95 (*0-7838-1391-0*, G K Hall Lrg Type) Mac Lib Ref.

Power Thoughts: One Hundred Steps to Goal Achievement. David D. Thornburg. (Illus.). 219p. (Orig.). (C). 1988. pap. 12.95 (*0-942207-07-6*) Starsong CA.

Power Thoughts: Positive Messages for Everyday Life, Set. abr. ed. Robert H. Schuller. 1994. audio 17.00 (*1-55994-882-5*, CPN 2416) Zondervan.

Power Through Constructive Thinking. Emmet Fox. LC 89-45351. 288p. 1989. pap. 14.00 (*0-06-062861-8*, Perennial) HarperTrade.

Power Through Constructive Thinking. Emmet Fox. 1994. reprint ed. lib. bdg. 18.95 (*1-56849-520-X*) Buccaneer Bks.

Power Through Discourse. Leah Kedar. LC 86-32029. 192p. (C). 1987. text 73.25 (*0-89391-328-6*) Ablx Pub.

***Power Through People & Principles: Not Puppets & Prejudices.** Vipen Kapur. 2000. 29.95 (*0-07-116443-X*) McGraw.

Power Through Prayer. E. M. Bounds. (E. M. Bounds Classics on Prayer Ser.). 96p. (gr. 10). 1992. pap. 6.99 (*0-8010-1013-6*) Baker Bks.

Power Through Prayer. E. M. Bounds. (Classics Ser.). mass mkt. 4.99 (*0-8024-6729-6*, 393) Moody.

Power Through Prayer. E. M. Bounds. 105p. 1983. mass mkt. 5.99 (*0-88368-117-X*) Whitaker Hse.

Power Through Repose (1891) Annie P. Call. 178p. 1998. reprint ed. pap. 17.95 (*0-7661-0590-3*) Kessinger Pub.

Power Through the Written Word. Robin C. Scarcella. (J). 1994. audio 29.95 (*0-8384-4670-1*) Heinle & Heinle.

Power Through Weakness: Paul's Understanding of the Christian Ministry in 2 Corinthians. Timothy B. Savage. (Society for New Testament Studies Monographs: No. 86). 267p. (C). 1995. text 59.95 (*0-521-49640-3*) Cambridge U Pr.

Power Thyristor Physics. Adolph Blicher. (Applied Physics & Engineering Ser.: Vol. 12). 1976. 96.00 (*0-387-90173-6*) Spr-Verlag.

Power Ties: Economic Interdependence, Balancing & War. Paul Papayoanou. LC 98-40093. 216p. 1999. text 44.50 (*0-472-10960-X*, 10960) U of Mich Pr.

Power to Be a Continental Afrikan Again: or, Why We Can No Longer Destroy Ourselves with the Poison of Our Present Day Colonial/Slave Identities. Afrikadzata Deku. LC 91-72672. (Afrikan Centric Essay Ser.). 44p. 1966. pap. 13.00 (*1-56454-016-2*) Cont Afrikan.

Power to Be Forever Free. Kenneth Copeland. 11p. 1987. pap. 1.00 (*1-57562-058-8*) K Copeland Pubns.

Power to Be Forever Free. Kenneth Copeland. 1996. pap. text 1.00 (*0-88114-787-7*) K Copeland Pubns.

Power! To Be Your Best! Creating & Maintaining the Life You Deserve. Todd Duncan. (Illus.). xxi, 337p. 1998. 24.95 (*0-9665134-0-1*) T Duncan Grp.

***Power! To Be Your Best! Creating & Maintaining the Life You Deserve.** Todd Duncan. LC 99-36581. 1999. 21.99 (*0-8499-1621-6*) Word Pub.

***Power to Become.** Cornelius Sanders, II. LC 00-90068. 143p. 2000. pap. 14.95 (*1-58597-023-9*) Leathers Pub.

***Power to Bless.** rev. ed. Myron C. Madden. LC 99-33213. 130p. 1999. reprint ed. pap. 15.00 (*0-914520-39-3*) Insight Pr.

Power to Bring Them Back. Anne McReynolds & Jo Packer. pap. 11.98 (*1-55517-318-7*) CFI Dist.

Power to Burn: Michael Ovitz & the New Business of Show Business. Stephen Singular. LC 95-47830. (Illus.). 272p. 1996. 22.50 (*1-55972-335-1*, Birch Ln Pr) Carol Pub Group.

Power to Care? Norma Baldwin. 210p. 1990. text 66.95 (*1-85628-092-6*, Pub. by Avebry) Ashgate Pub Co.

Power to Care: Clinical Practice Effectiveness with Overwhelmed Clients. June G. Hopps et al. LC 94-41532. 1994. 35.00 (*0-02-925285-7*) Free Pr.

Power to Change. John Dan. LC 94-70391. (Illus.). 288p. 1994. 12.00 (*1-884898-00-9*); pap. 8.00 (*1-884898-01-7*) Eden Pubng OR.

Power to Change: How to Stay Slim, Sober, & Smokeless. Harold Hill & Liz Rogers. 319p. (Orig.). 1987. mass mkt. 5.99 (*0-88270-625-X*) Bridge-Logos.

Power to Change: Sermon for Lent-Easter: Cycle B, First Lesson Texts. Durwood L. Buchheim. LC 93-18008. 1993. pap. 11.50 (*1-55673-612-6*, 9337) CSS OH.

Power to Change: Third World Women Shaping Their Environment. Ed. by Women's Feature Service Staff. 256p. (C). 1993. text 49.95 (*1-85649-225-7*, Pub. by Zed Books) St Martin.

Power to Change: Third World Women Shaping Their Environment. Ed. by Women's Feature Service Staff. 256p. (C). 1993. text 22.50 (*1-85649-226-5*, Pub. by Zed Books) St Martin.

Power to Change Your Life. Rick Warren. 156p. 1990. pap. 9.99 (*0-89693-472-1*, 6-1472, Victor Bks) Chariot Victor.

Power to Choose. Haydn Sargent. 168p. (C). 1990. pap. 50.00 (*0-7316-7606-8*, Pub. by Boolarong Pubns) St Mut.

Power to Choose: Bangladeshi Women & Labor Market Decisions in London & Dhaka. Naila Kabeer. 1999. 29.00 (*1-85984-804-4*, Pub. by Verso) Norton.

Power to Choose: True Stories of Tragedy & Triumph. John Dan et al. (Illus.). 256p. (Orig.). 1995. pap. 8.00 (*1-884898-07-6*) Eden Pubng OR.

Power to Choose: Twelve Steps to Wholeness. Mike S. O'Neil. 209p. (Orig.). 1991. pap. 19.95 (*0-9633454-0-0*) Sonlight Pub.

Power 'to Coin' Money: The Exercise of Monetary Powers by the Congress. Thomas F. Wilson. LC 91-340. 272p. (C). (gr. 13). 1992. text 75.95 (*0-87332-794-2*) M E Sharpe.

Power 'to Coin' Money: The Exercise of Monetary Powers by the Congress. Thomas F. Wilson. LC 91-340. 272p. (C). (gr. 13). 1992. pap. text 40.95 (*0-87332-795-0*) M E Sharpe.

Power to Communicate: Gender Differences As Barriers. 3rd rev. ed. Deborah Borisoff & Lisa Merrill. LC 99-195446. 151p. 1998. pap. text 12.50 (*0-88133-989-X*) Waveland Pr.

Power to Create. Phillip Aaron. 1991. pap. 12.95 (*0-9630418-0-0*) Pennington TX.

***Power to Destroy: How the IRS Became America's Most Powerful Agency, How Congress Is Taking Control & What You Can Do to Protect Yourself under the New Law.** William V. Roth, Jr. & William H. Nixon. LC 98-52234. 288p. 1999. 23.00 (*0-87113-748-8*, Atlntc Mnthly) Grove-Atltic.

Power to Die. Robert H. Long. (CSU Poetry Ser.: Vol. XXIV). 108p. (Orig.). 1987. pap. 6.00 (*0-914946-63-3*) Cleveland St Univ Poetry Ctr.

Power to Dissolve: Lawyers & Marriages in the Courts of the Roman Curia. John T. Noonan. LC 75-176044. 510p. reprint ed. pap. 158.10 (*0-7837-3959-1*, 204378800011) Bks Demand.

Power to Dream: Interviews with Women in the Creative Arts. Nancy J. Hoy. LC 95-79768. 296p. 1996. pap. 14.00 (*0-9641292-9-9*) Global Cty Pr.

Power to Excel. Hubert E. Dobson. LC 81-90553. 273p. 1982. 10.95 (*0-9607256-0-1*); pap. 4.95 (*0-9607256-1-X*) Rich Pub Co.

***Power to Explore: A History of Marshall Space Flight Center, 1960-1990.** Andrew J. Dunar. 723p. 2000. boxed set 49.00 (*0-16-058992-4*) USGPO.

Power to Get In. Michael A. Boylan. 204p. 1998. pap. 14.95 (*0-312-19522-2*) St Martin.

Power to Get In: Using the Circle of Leverage System to Get in Anyone's Door Faster, More Effectively & with Less Expense. Michael Boylan. (Illus.). 296p. 1999. text 25.00 (*0-7881-5683-7*) DIANE Pub.

Power to Get Wealth. Luther Blackwell. 160p. 1995. pap. 11.99 (*0-927936-35-6*) Vincom Pubng Co.

Power to Get Wealth: Enjoying Prosperity. Luther Blackwell. 160p. 1996. pap. 8.99 (*1-880089-89-0*, AP-989, Pub. by Albury Pub) Appalach Bk Dist.

Power to Govern. W. H. Hamilton & D. Adair. LC 77-37759. (American Constitutional & Legal History Ser). 252p. 1972. reprint ed. lib. bdg. 32.50 (*0-306-70433-1*) Da Capo.

Power to Harm. John Cornwell. 336p. 1998. pap. 14.95 (*0-14-025471-4*) Viking Penguin.

Power to Harm: Mind, Medicine, & Murder on Trial. John Cornwell. LC 96-6722. xii, 321p. 1998. pap. 14.95 (*0-14-026996-7*) Viking Penguin.

Power to Heal. John Hagee. Ed. by Lucretia Hobbs & Connie Reece. 101p. (Orig.). 1991. per. 8.00 (*1-56908-008-9*) Global Evang.

Power to Heal. Francis S. MacNutt. LC 77-77845. 256p. 1977. pap. 9.95 (*0-87793-133-X*) Ave Maria.

Power to Heal. H. B. Wilson. 1991. lib. bdg. 75.00 (*0-8490-4519-3*) Gordon Pr.

Power to Heal. Henry B. Wilson. 92p. 1996. reprint ed. spiral bd. 14.00 (*0-7873-1065-4*) Hlth Research.

Power to Hurt. Darcy O'Brien. 528p. 1997. mass mkt. 6.50 (*0-06-109600-8*, Harp PBks) HarpC.

Power to Hurt: The Virtues of Alienation. William F. Monroe. LC 97-4639. 256p. 1997. text 36.95 (*0-252-02351-X*); pap. text 16.95 (*0-252-06657-X*) U of Ill Pr.

Power to Keep Peace, Today & in a World Without War. Lincoln P. Bloomfield. 1971. pap. 2.95 (*0-912018-12-7*) World Without War.

Power to Lead. Frank Siccone. 299p. (C). 1996. pap. text 36.00 (*0-205-14345-8*) Allyn.

Power to Lead In Diverse Classrooms. 256p. (C). 2000. pap. text 27.00 (*0-205-31364-7*) Allyn.

Power to Learn. Campbell. 1992. mass mkt., teacher ed. 11.50 (*0-534-19406-0*) Wadsworth Pub.

Power to Learn: Helping Yourself to College Success. 2nd ed. William E. Campbell. LC 96-21479. (Freshman Orientation Ser.). 235p. (C). 1996. 31.95 (*0-534-26352-6*) Wadsworth Pub.

***Power to Learn: Stories of Success in the Education of Asian & Other Bilingual Pupils.** Terry Wrigley. 160p. 2000. pap. 25.00 (*1-85856-210-4*) Stylus Pub VA.

Power to Live a New Life. Gloria Copeland. 15p. 1986. pap. 1.00 (*1-57562-056-1*) K Copeland Pubns.

Power to Live Through Nutrition. James W. McAfee. LC 80-82331. (Illus.). 196p. (Orig.). 1980. pap. 6.95 (*0-9604592-0-0*) Image Awareness.

Power to Make War: The Career of the Assyrian Who Will Rule the World. Zane C. Hodges. 135p. (Orig.). 1995. pap. 7.95 (*1-879534-01-0*) Redencion Viva.

Power to Parent. S. Smith. mass mkt. 15.95 (*0-340-71016-0*, Pub. by Hodder & Stought Ltd) Trafalgar.

Power to Persuade: A Rhetoric & Reader for Argumentative Writing. 3rd ed. Sally D. Spurgin. LC 93-2233. 389p. (C). 1993. pap. text 33.20 (*0-13-221185-8*) P-H.

Power to Prevent Suicide: A Guide for Teens Helping Teens. Richard E. Nelson. LC 94-5594. 1994. 17.05 (*0-606-06678-0*, Pub. by Turtleback) Demco.

Power to Prevent Suicide: A Guide for Teens Helping Teens. Richard E. Nelson & Judith C. Galas. Ed. by Pamela Espeland. LC 94-5594. (Illus.). 136p. (YA). (gr. 5 up). 1994. pap. 12.95 (*0-915793-70-9*) Free Spirit Pub.

Power to Prosper: The Inner Path to Success. Ruth Ross. 1992. 49.95 incl. audio (*0-9622313-3-9*) Prosper Natural.

Power to Punish. Garland. 1997. pap. 31.95 (*1-85742-104-3*) Ashgate Pub Co.

Power to Punish: A Social Inquiry into Coercion & Control in Urban Schools. Stanley W. Rothstein. 188p. (Orig.). (C). 1984. pap. text 23.00 (*0-8191-3732-4*) U Pr of Amer.

Power to Rise: The Story of the National Ballet of Canada. James Neufeld. (Illus.). 320p. 1996. text 45.00 (*0-8020-4109-4*) U of Toronto Pr.

Power to Rise & Succeed. unabridged ed. W. Lee Spurlock. Ed. by Lana Wegeng. 66p. 1998. pap. 9.95 (*0-9659454-8-0*) Columbia Pubns.

***Power to Serve: A Theology of Pentecost.** William W. Menzies & Robert P. Menzies. LC 00-28975. 2000. write for info. (*0-310-23507-3*) Zondervan.

Power to Soar. Charles Slagle & Paula Slagle. 192p. (Orig.). 1993. pap. 6.99 (*1-56043-101-6*) Destiny Image.

Power to Tax. G. Brennan & James M. Buchanan. LC 79-56862. (Illus.). 256p. 1980. text 59.95 (*0-521-23329-1*) Cambridge U Pr.

***Power to Tax: Analytical Foundations of a Fiscal Constitution.** Geoffrey Brennan & James M. Buchanan. LC 99-24061. (Collected Works of James M. Buchanan : Vol. 9). 2000. 20.00 (*0-86597-229-X*); pap. 12.00 (*0-86597-230-3*) Liberty Fund.

Power to the People: Democratization Around the World. Robert K. Schaeffer. 1998. 16.95 (*0-8133-2339-8*) Westview.

***Power to the People: Energy & the Cuban Nuclear Program.** Jonathan Benjamin-Alvarado. LC 99-55074. 192p. 2000. pap. write for info. (*0-415-92438-3*) Routledge.

***Power to the People: Energy & the Cuban Nuclear Program.** Jonathan Benjamin-Alvarado. LC 99-55074. 192p. 2000. 75.00 (*0-415-92437-5*) Routledge.

Power to the People: Essays on Russian History. John L. Keep. 439p. 1995. 63.00 (*0-88033-312-X*, 415, Pub. by East Eur Monographs) Col U Pr.

***Power to the People! Russian Strength Training Secrets for Every American.** Pavel Tsatsouline. (Illus.). 124p. 2000. pap. 34.95 (*0-938045-19-9*) Dragon Door.

***Power to the People: Sunlight to Electriciy Using Solar Cells.** Martin Green. 128p. 2000. pap. 19.95 (*0-86840-554-X*, Pub. by NSW U Pr) Intl Spec Bk.

Power to the People: The Rise & Fall of the Black Panther Party. James Haskins. LC 96-8824. (Illus.). 144p. (YA). (gr. 7 up). 1997. mass mkt. 16.00 (*0-689-80085-1*) S&S Bks Yung.

Power to the Schools: School Leader's Guidebook to Restructuring. William J. Bailey. LC 92-335. 160p. 1992. pap. 21.95 (*0-8039-6017-4*) Corwin Pr.

Power to the Teacher: How America's Educators Become Militant. Marshall O. Donley. LC 75-31421. (Illus.). 254p. reprint ed. pap. 78.80 (*0-8357-3952-X*, 205704800004) Bks Demand.

Power to the West! A Study in Nomocracy. Mario Gomez-Zimmerman. Tr. by Zusel Pordominsky from SPA. LC 92-94305. 650p. 1997. 21.95 (*0-533-10532-3*) Vantage.

Power to Win. Walter D. Staples. LC 93-43165. 224p. 1994. 17.95 (*1-56554-005-0*) Pelican.

Power Tool Box Praise & Worship, 4 vols., Set. (J). (gr. 1-6). 1993. ring bd., boxed set 599.95 incl. audio, trans. (*1-57405-042-7*) CharismaLife Pub.

Power Tool Kit. Ed. by Jerry Lenz. 84p. 1995. teacher ed., ring bd. 59.95 incl. audio, trans. (*1-57405-002-8*) CharismaLife Pub.

***Power Tool Safety & Operation.** rev. ed. Thomas Hoerner. 126p. 1998. spiral bd. 10.45 (*0-913163-30-9*) Hobar Pubns.

Power Tool Woodcarving: Projects & Techniques. Alan Bridgewater & Gill Bridgewater. LC 93-41044. (Illus.). 164p. 1994. pap. 14.95 (*0-8069-8710-3*) Sterling.

Power Tools: A Leader's Guide to the Latest Management Thinking. John Nirenberg. LC 96-30054. 460p. (C). 1997. pap. text 24.95 (*0-13-745845-2*) P-H.

Power Tools: Care & Use. William Veasey. LC 85-61523. (Illus.). 64p. 1985. pap. 7.95 (*0-88740-047-7*) Schiffer.

Power Tools: Newbridge Edition. Sam Deep. 1998. 22.95 (*0-201-36033-0*) Addison-Wesley.

An Asterisk (*) at the beginning of an entry indicates that the title is appearing for the first time.

Power Tools: Prop Ideas for Prayer, Praise & Worship. Marilyn J. Wright. (Illus.). 60p. (C). 1995. pap. 5.00 (1-886232-25-3) Majesty Pubns.
Power Tools: 100+ Essential Forms & Presentations for Your School Library Information Program. Joyce Kasman Valenza. LC 97-38414. 1997. 45.00 (0-8389-0717-2) ALA.
Power Tools: 50 Management Inventions You Can Use Today. Sam Deep. LC 97-39809. 256p. 1998. pap. 15.00 (0-201-77297-3) Addison-Wesley.
Power Tools & Equipment. (Fix-It-Yourself Ser.). (Illus.). 144p. 1989. lib. bdg. 23.27 (0-8094-6269-9) Time-Life.
Power Tools & Equipment. Time-Life Staff. (Fix-It-Yourself Ser.). (Illus.). 144p. 1989. 17.27 (0-8094-6268-0) Time-Life.
Power Tools for Bass: 4, 5 & 6 String Bass. 76p. 1996. spiral bd. 12.95 (0-7935-6067-5) H Leonard.
Power Tools for 4, 5, & 6 String Bass. Fred Cockfield. (Illus.). 80p. 1994. pap. 12.95 (1-886714-00-2) Acad Mus Publ.
***Power Tools for Guitar Book-CD Set.** Fred Cockfield & Michael Wilton. 80p. 1998. pap. 17.95 incl. cd-rom (0-7866-3318-2, 96913BCD) Mel Bay.
Power Tools for Long-Term Care Marketing. Clint Maun & Robert Haacker. 85p. 1992. 149.00 incl. audio (0-929442-15-6, 2221pp) Prof Prnting & Pub.
Power Tools for Teaching. Lefgren & Jackson. 1988. pap. 6.95 (0-88494-660-6) Bookcraft Inc.
Power Tools for Woodcarving. David Tippey. (Illus.). 144p. 1999. pap. 19.95 (1-86108-104-9, Pub. by Guild Master) Sterling.
Power Tower: Prayer Is the Tower to Power. Jacquelyn Bryant. 95p. (Orig.). 1995. pap. 8.99 (0-9634306-4-5) End-Time Wave.
Power, Trade, & War. Edward D. Mansfield. LC 93-13700. 300p. 1994. text 45.00 (0-691-03288-2, Pub. by Princeton U Pr) Cal Prin Full Svc.
Power Training for Sport: Plyometrics for Maximum Power Development. rev. ed. Tudor O. Bompa. LC 96-932270. 1998. pap. 14.95 (0-88962-629-4) Mosaic.
Power Training in Kung-Fu & Karate. Ronald L. Marchini & Leo Fong. Ed. by John Cocoran & John Scurra. LC 74-14128. (Specialties Ser.). (Illus.). 1974. pap. text 17.95 (0-89750-047-4, 400) Ohara Pubns.
Power Trains. 5th rev. ed. Ed. by Deere & Company Staff. (Fundamentals of Service Ser.). 130p. 1991. pap. 57.95 incl. trans. (0-614-24202-9, FOS4005M) Deere & Co.
Power Trains. 6th rev. ed. Ed. by Deere & Company Staff. (Fundamentals of Service Ser.). (Illus.). 176p. 1991. pap. text 21.95 (0-86691-241-X, FOS4006NC); pap. text, teacher ed. 14.95 (0-86691-163-4, FOS4006T); pap. text, student ed. 17.95 (0-86691-164-2, FOS4006W) Deere & Co.
Power Transducers for Sonics & Ultrasonics: Proceedings of the International Workshop Held in Toulon, France, June 12 & 13, 1990. Ed. by B. F. Hamonic et al. (Illus.). viii, 279p. 1991. 75.95 (0-387-53423-7) Spr-Verlag.
Power Transfer & Electoral Politics. Ed. by Hsin C. Kuan et al. (Illus.). 320p. (C). pap. text 26.00 (962-201-899-8, Pub. by Chinese Univ) U of Mich Pr.
***Power Transformers.** Martin Heathcote. 384p. 2002. 94.95 (0-7506-4903-8) Buttrwrth-Heinemann.
Power Transformers of the Oil Immersed Sealed Type. EEMUA Staff. 1982. 80.00 (0-85931-048-5, Pub. by EEMUA) St Mut.
Power Transitions: Strategies for the 21st Century. Ronald L. Tammen et al. LC 99-50686. 250p. 2000. pap. text 29.95 (1-889119-43-1, Chatham House Pub) Seven Bridges.
Power Transmission. Scott. LC 99-35154. 336p. 1999. text 91.00 (0-13-095386-5) S&S Trade.
Power Transmission & Gearing Conference: Proceedings, 7th International Power Transmission & Gearing Conference, San Diego, CA, 1996. Ed. by Albert Karvelis. LC 96-86510. (DE Ser.: Vol. 88). 828p. 1996. pap. 280.00 (0-7918-1514-5, TJ1045) ASME.
***Power Transmission & Motion Control: Proceedings Bath Workshop Bath, UK 1999.** Ed. by C.R. Burrows & K.A. Edge. 376p. 1999. 378.00 (1-86058-205-2) Prof Eng Pubng.
***Power Transmission Equipment in Germany: A Strategic Entry Report, 1996.** Compiled by Icon Group International Staff. (Illus.). 91p. 1999. ring bd. 910.00 incl. audio compact disk (0-7418-1203-7) Icon Grp.
Power Transmission Sourcebook. Market Intelligence Staff. 309p. 1994. 545.00 (0-7889-0008-0) Frost & Sullivan.
Power Trio: Mars, Jupiter, Saturn. Mae R. Wilson-Ludlam. 156p. 1976. 11.00 (0-86690-331-3, W1537-034) Am Fed Astrologers.
***Power Trip.** Jeffrey Nodelman. (Doug Chronicles: No. 5). (Illus.). (J). (gr. 2-4). 1998. pap. 3.99 (0-7868-4258-X, Pub. by Disney Pr) Time Warner.
Power Trips & Other Journeys: Essays in Feminism As Civic Discourse. Jean B. Elshtain. LC 90-50083. 192p. (C). 1991. pap. text 14.95 (0-299-12674-9) U of Wis Pr.
Power, Trust, & Meaning: Essays in Sociological Theory & Analysis. Samuel N. Eisenstadt. 414p. 1995. pap. text 22.50 (0-226-19556-2); lib. bdg. 65.00 (0-226-19555-4) U Ch Pr.
***Power, Truth, & Community in Modern Culture.** Charles C. West. LC 99-37888. (Christian Mission in Modern Culture Ser.). 160p. 1999. pap. 14.00 (1-56338-297-0) TPI PA.
Power Twins. Ken Follett. 96p. (J). (gr. 4-7). 1991. pap. 2.75 (0-590-42507-2) Scholastic Inc.
***Power U. S. Transformer Industry.** S. Moskowitz. 250p. 2000. ring bd. 2500.00 (0-317-55172-8) Lead Edge Reports.
Power Unbridled: The Nineteen Sixty-One Redistricting of California. T. Anthony Quinn. 50p. 1980. pap. text 12.50 (1-883638-05-4) Rose Inst.
Power Units Other Than Class 2, UL 1012. 6th ed. (C). 1994. pap. text 175.00 (1-55989-587-X) Underwrtrs Labs.
Power Unlimited. unabridged ed. Craig Tappe. 98p. 1983. pap. 6.55 (0-89137-575-9, 75759) Quality Pubns.
Power Unlimited: Relation of Man with God. D. N. Saraf. (C). 1996. 30.00 (81-7017-333-7, Pub. by Abhinav) S Asia.
Power Unlimited: The Corruption of Union Leadership. Sylvester Petro. LC 79-4432. (McClellan Committee Hearings). 323p. 1979. reprint ed. lib. bdg. 35.00 (0-313-20898-0, PEPU, Greenwood Pr) Greenwood.
Power Unseen: How Microbes Rule the World. Bernard Dixon. LC 93-37697. 1994. text 18.40 (0-7167-4504-6) W H Freeman.
Power Unseen: How Microbes Rule the World. Bernard Dixon. LC 95-44746. (Illus.). 272p. 1998. reprint ed. pap. text 16.95 (0-7167-4550-X) OUP.
Power Up! Energy. Sharon Franklin. (Explore! Science Ser.). (Illus.). 48p. (J). (gr. 3-6). 1995. pap. 4.95 (0-673-36216-7, GoodYrBooks) Addson-Wesley Educ.
Power Up! How to Make Battery Adapters for Military Radios. Dave Strom. (Illus.). 96p. (Orig.). 1994. pap. 14.95 (0-939780-22-4) CRB Res.
Power-Up: Kicking Your Faith to a New Level Student Journal. Randy Petersen et al. (Nineteen Ninety-Eight Fifty-Day Spiritual Adventure Ser.). 80p. (YA). (gr. 7-12). 1997. wbk. ed. 6.00 (1-57849-040-5) Mainstay Church.
Power Up: Student Leader's Guide. Jim Hancock. Ed. by Mitch Vander Vorst. (Nineteen Ninety-Eight Fifty-Day Spiritual Adventure Ser.). 64p. (YA). 1997. wbk. ed. 8.00 (1-57849-054-5) Mainstay Church.
Power Up: Transforming Organizations Through Shared Leadership. David L. Bradford & Allan R. Cohen. LC 97-35610. 364p. 1998. 27.95 (0-471-12122-3) Wiley.
Power Up: 101 Ways to Boost Your Energy. Daryn Eller. 240p. 1999. pap. 12.00 (0-380-79724-0, Avon Bks) Morrow Avon.
Power up for Success. Madeleine Singer. (Illus.). 192p. (Orig.). 1993. pap. 12.95 (1-56184-070-X) New Falcon Pubns.
Power up for the Recovery: Industrial Power Conference, 1983. Ed. by F. M. Rhodes. 104p. 1983. pap. text 25.00 (0-317-02641-0, I00159) ASME.
Power-Up Teams & Tools: For Process Improvement & Problem Solving. William L. Montgomery. LC 94-96139. 305p. 1995. pap. 39.95 (0-9641124-0-X) Montgomery.
***Power-Up Teams & Tools: For Process Improvement & Problem Solving.** 2nd rev. ed. William Montgomery. (Illus.). 280p. 1999. pap. text 39.95 (0-9641124-2-6) Montgomery.
Power up with Lotus 5 for Windows. Joseph C. Otto & Garry L. Nordenstam. 1996. pap. text 28.95 (1-56118-808-5) Paradigm MN.
Power up with Microsoft Office. Elizabeth Vogt & Eddie Platt. LC 96-13829. 1996. write for info. (1-56118-849-2); write for info. (1-56118-854-9); write for info. (1-56118-855-7) Paradigm MN.
Power up with Word 6 for Windows. Joseph W. Habraken. LC 95-12386. 1995. pap. text 28.95 (1-56118-813-1) Paradigm MN.
Power up with WordPerfect 6.1 for Windows. Mona French. LC 95-38812. 1995. pap. text 28.95 incl. 3.5 hd (0-614-08634-5); pap. text 28.95 (1-56118-859-X); pap. text 28.95 incl. 5.25 hd (1-56118-861-1) Paradigm MN.
Power-up with WordPerfect 6.1 for Windows: Instructor's Guide. Mona French. text 19.00 (1-56118-862-X) EMC-Paradigm.
Power up Your Library: Creating the New Elementary School Library Program. Sheila Salmon et al. LC 96-8836. (Illus.). 290p. 1996. pap. text 37.50 (1-56308-357-4) Libs Unl.
Power up Your People Skills: Communicating in the New Millenium. (Illus.). 140p. 1999. pap. 19.95 (1-875680-71-3) Woodslane.
Power User's Guide to Excel for Windows 95. Ed Martin. 1996. pap. text 72.00 (1-57576-022-3) Que Educ & Trng.
Power Vacuum Tubes Handbook. J. Whitaker. xviii, 609p. 1994. text 89.95 (0-442-30894-9, VNR) Wiley.
Power Vacuum Tubes Handbook. 2nd ed. Jerry C. Whitaker. LC 99-21062. 728p. 1999. boxed set 99.95 (0-8493-1345-7) CRC Pr.
Power, Value & Conviction: Theological Ethics in the Postmodern Age. William Schweiker. LC 98-36259. 224p. 1998. 29.95 (0-8298-1297-0); pap. 19.95 (0-8298-1290-3) Pilgrim OH.
Power VB4. (Visual Basic Power Guides Ser.). 174p. 1995. pap. 69.00 (1-886213-04-6) Bldg Blocks.
Power Vector. Gyla B. Seal & January Taylor. 236p. (J). 1998. pap. 9.99 (0-88092-441-1, 4411) Royal Fireworks.
Power Ventilators, UL 705. 5th ed. (C). 1994. pap. text 175.00 (1-55989-574-8) Underwrtrs Labs.
Power Versus Force: An Anatomy of Consciousness. David R. Hawkins. 320p. 1994. 24.95 (0-9643261-0-8); pap. 14.95 (0-9643261-1-6) Veritas AZ.
***Power Versus Liberty: Madison, Hamilton, Wilson, & Jefferson.** James H. Read. LC 99-34633. (Illus.). 224p. 2000. 47.50 (0-8139-1911-8) U Pr of Va.
Power Vested. deluxe ed. Harry Krenek. (Illus.). 1980. 40.00 (0-935978-09-7) Presidial.
Power, Violence, Decision W. J. MacKenzie. LC 76-361447. (Peregrine Bks.). 272 p. 1975. write for info. (0-14-055098-4) Penguin Putnam.
Power Vision: Featuring New High Definition 3D Images. Day. 1995. pap. 10.99 (1-57081-654-9) At-A-Glance Consumer.
Power Vision II: Featuring New High Definition 3D Images. Day. 1995. pap. 10.99 (1-57081-832-0) At-A-Glance Consumer.
Power Vocabulary Builder. 1998. mass mkt. 5.99 (0-345-91357-4) Ballantine Pub Grp.
Power Vocabulary Five: Basic Word Strategies for Adults. Dorothy Rubin. 128p. 1992. pap. text 5.55 (0-13-681214-7) P-H.
Power Vocabulary Four: Basic Word Strategies for Adults. Dorothy Rubin. 128p. 1992. pap. text 5.55 (0-13-681206-6) P-H.
Power Vocabulary One: Basic Word Strategies for Adults. Dorothy Rubin. 112p. (C). 1992. pap. text 12.50 (0-13-678244-2) P-H.
Power Vocabulary Three: Basic Word Strategies for Adults. Dorothy Rubin. 96p. (C). 1992. pap. text 12.50 (0-13-681198-1) P-H.
Power Vocabulary Two: Basic Word Strategies for Adults. Dorothy Rubin. 96p. (C). 1992. pap. text 5.55 (0-13-678251-5) P-H.
Power vs. Force: Synopsis & Study Guide. Teddy Carney & David R. Hawkins. 70p. (Orig.). 1998. pap., wbk. ed. 10.95 (0-9643261-6-7) Veritas AZ.
Power vs. Profit: Multinational Corporation-Nation State Interaction. Reza Bassiry. Ed. by Stuart Bruchey. LC 80-566. (Multinational Corporations Ser.). 1981. lib. bdg. 31.95 (0-405-13363-4) Ayer.
***Power Washer's Guidebook.** Ed. by Allison McGraw. (Illus.). 241p. 1999. pap. 30.00 (0-944352-31-6) Cleaning Cons.
Power Weight Loss. Betty L. Randolph. Ed. by Success Education Institute International. (Health Ser.). 1989. 14.98 incl. audio (1-55909-209-2, 2P); 14.98 incl. audio (1-55909-210-6, 2PM); 14.98 incl. audio (1-55909-207-6, 1P); 35.00 incl. audio (1-55909-208-4, 1PM) Randolph Tapes.
Power Windows 96. Jonathan Ramin. 600p. 1995. pap. 29.95 incl. disk (1-55828-380-3, MIS Pr) IDG Bks.
Power with People. James K. Van Fleet. 1970. pap. 4.95 (0-13-686964-5, Reward) P-H.
Power Within: Living with Your Full Potential. Jerald H. Reckner & Jeni F. Norton. LC 87-71541. (Illus.). (Orig.). (C). 1987. pap. 8.95 (0-943889-00-6) Assoc Beta Cos.
Power Within! Tap Your Inner Force & Program Youself for Success. James K. Van Fleet. 1994. pap. 11.95 (0-13-042996-1) P-H.
***Power Within: The Five Disciplines of Personal Effectiveness.** Allen Johnson. LC 00-8345. 2001. write for info. (1-890009-82-2) Exec Excell.
Power Within Henry Washe. William G. Dallavo. (Illus.). 51p. 1983. pap. 6.00 (0-942494-74-1) Coleman Pub.
Power Within the Land: The Roots of Celtic & Underworld Traditions Awakening the Sleepers & Regenerating the Earth. rev. ed. Robert John Stewart. LC 99-16134. (Illus.). 164p. 1998. pap. 15.95 (1-892137-00-3) Mercury NC.
Power Within Us. Charles Baudouin. LC 68-16905. (Essay Index Reprint Ser.). 1977. 18.95 (0-8369-0176-2) Ayer.
Power Within Us. Cabeza De Vaca. Ed. & Tr. by Haniel Long. (Illus.). 50p. 1976. 75.00 (0-933861-06-0) H Berliner.
Power Within Us. Russell M. Nelson. LC 88-20299. ix, 160p. 1988. 15.95 (0-87579-154-9) Deseret Bk.
Power Within You. John-Roger. 86p. 1984. pap. 10.00 (0-914829-24-6) Mandeville LA.
***Power Within You Pt. 1: Through the MetaSpherian Principal.** William S. Bradford. (Illus.). 90p. 2000. pap. 12.99 (1-56411-236-5) Untd Bros & Sis.
Power Without Force: The Political Capacity of Nation States. Robert W. Jackman. (Analytical Perspectives on Politics Ser.). 208p. (C). 1993. text 49.50 (0-472-10463-2, 10463); pap. text 18.95 (0-472-08236-1, 08236) U of Mich Pr.
Power Without Pollution: A Home Electric Plant. 2nd unabridged ed. Jack Hedger. LC 92-96987. (Illus.). 182p. (Orig.). 1992. pap. 19.95 (1-882416-08-2) Akela West Pubs.
Power Without Responsibility: How Congress Abuses the People Through Delegation. David Schoenbrod. LC 93-13260. 264p. 1993. 32.50 (0-300-05363-0) Yale U Pr.
Power Without Responsibility: How Congress Abuses the People Through Delegation. David Schoenbrod. 1995. pap. 15.00 (0-300-06518-3) Yale U Pr.
Power Without Responsibility: The Press & Broadcasting in Britain. 5th ed. James Curran & Jean Seaton. LC 97-7921. 432p. (C). 1997. 80.00 (0-415-16810-4); pap. 21.99 (0-415-11407-1) Routledge.
Power Word. Kate Edson. LC 95-37725. 1995. pap. 29.95 incl. disk (1-55828-395-1, MIS Pr) IDG Bks.
Power Words for Prosperous Living! 120p. 1984. pap. 6.95 (0-9602166-1-8) Golden Key.
Power Workout. abr. ed. Roger W. Breternitz. 1985. pap. 9.95 incl. audio (1-893417-25-5) Vector Studios.
Power Write! A Practical Guide to Words That Work. Helene Hinis. viii, 54p. (Orig.). 1989. pap. 12.95 (1-878542-00-1, 12-0002) SkillPath Pubns.
Power Writing. rev. ed. Robert R. Max & Sarah P. Cerny. 167p. reprint ed. spiral bd. 120.00 incl. audio, VHS (1-55678-006-0, 3000) Learn Inc.
Power Writing. rev. ed. Robert R. Max & Sarah P. Cerny. 167p. 1988. reprint ed. teacher ed. 75.00 (1-55678-008-7) Learn Inc.
Power Writing for Professionals. R. E. Hine. LC 92-25577. 124p. (Orig.). (C). 1992. pap. text 19.50 (0-8191-8842-5) U Pr of Amer.
Power Writing Reflects You: An Executive Writing Style Handbook. Janna L. Hugo. 96p. 1994. ring bd. 12.95 (0-9643706-0-3) Educ Dialogues.
Power Yachts. Rosemary Mudie & Colin Mudie. (Illus.). 1977. 29.95 (0-8464-1298-5) Beekman Pubs.
***Power Yoga: Connect to the Core with Astanga Yoga.** Liz Lark. (Illus.). 160p. 2000. pap. 19.95 (1-55209-502-9) Firefly Bks Ltd.
Power Yoga: The Total Strength & Flexibility Workout. Beryl B. Birch. 286p. 1995. per. 15.00 (0-02-058351-6) Macmillan.
Power Your Golf Swing with Centrifugal Force: Science of Circle Swing. Bill Dale. Ed. by Elsa Larson. (Illus.). 123p. (Orig.). 1996. pap. text 23.00 (0-944972-07-1) Dale Publishing Co.
***Power Your Way Through Y2K.** P. J. Wylie. 152p. 1999. pap. 29.95 (1-929275-00-5) P J W Enterprises Inc.
***Power Your Way Through Y2K: City Plan 2000.** P. S. Wiley. 148p. 1999. pap. 14.95 (1-892873-08-7, Torn Tree Pr) Ginger Pubns.
Power Zone: Jesus' Model for a New Humanity. Larry Calvin. Ed. by Patty Crowley. LC 95-67132. (Faith Focus Ser.). 181p. (Orig.). 1995. pap. 9.95 (0-8344-0242-4, FFSBH) Sweet Pub.
Power-Zoning. Woody Bates. (Illus.). 30p. 1999. spiral bd. 14.95 (0-9671118-1-1) Woodys Ways.
Power 3D: High Speed Graphics in Windows 95-NT. Kyle Lussier. LC 96-45698. 552p. 1997. 54.95 (1-884777-33-3) Manning Pubns.
Power 95. Friedrichsen. Date not set. pap. text, student ed. write for info. (0-314-09465-2) West Pub.
Powerboat Buyer's Guide. (Illus.). 504p. (Orig.). 1996. pap. 49.95 (1-879620-37-5) Belvoir Pubns.
Powerboat Guide: 2000 Edition. Mark Parker & Ed McKnew. (Illus.). 1650p. 1999. pap. 89.95 (0-9622134-1-1, Pub. by Amer Marine Pub) R Hale & Co.
Powerboat Maintenance Manual. LC 95-75758. (Illus.). 344p. 1996. pap. 36.95 (0-89287-654-9, B700) Intertec Pub.
Powerboat Racing see MotorSports
Powerboat Racing. Jay H. Smith. (Motorsports Ser.). (Illus.). 48p. (J). (gr. 3-6). 1995. 19.00 (0-516-35231-8) Childrens.
Powerboat Racing on the Chesapeake. William W. Mowbray. LC 95-44185. (Illus.). 127p. 1995. pap. 16.95 (0-87033-473-5, Tidewtr Pubs) Cornell Maritime.
Powerboater's Guide to Electrical Systems: Maintenance, Troubleshooting & Improvements. Ed Sherman. (Illus.). 160p. 2000. 22.95 (0-07-134326-1, Ragged Mntain) McGraw-Hill Prof.
***Powerboating.** Sandy Lindsey. (Woman's Guides Ser.). (Illus.). 160p. 2000. pap. 14.95 (0-07-135702-5) McGraw.
Powerboating: A Guide to Sportsboat Handling. Peter White. 96p. (C). 1990. text 80.00 (0-906754-59-3, Pub. by Fernhurst Bks) St Mut.
***PowerBook: A Novel.** Jeanette Winterson. 304p. 2000. 24.00 (0-375-41111-9) Knopf.
Powerbook: The Digital Nomad's Guide. Andrew Gore & Mitch Ratcliffe. 1993. disk 24.00 (0-679-74601-3) Random.
PowerBuilder: Best of PBDJ: PowerBuilder Developer's Journal. Michael Griffith. (PowerBuilder Training Ser.). (Illus.). 480p. (Orig.). 1996. pap. 37.75 (1-886141-03-7) SYS-Con Pubns.
PowerBuilder CD Tutor. T. Hubbard & Ahern. (Illus.). 512p. (Orig.). 1995. 49.99 (0-7897-0281-9) Que.
Powerbuilder Classwizard: How to Build Class Libraries?: PowerBuilder Developer's Journal. Sean Rhody. (PowerBuilder Training Ser.). (Illus.). 384p. (Orig.). 1996. pap. 37.75 (1-886141-04-5) SYS-Con Pubns.
Powerbuilder Construction Kit. John Ribar. 512p. 1994. pap. text 24.95 (0-07-882079-0) Osborne-McGraw.
Powerbuilder Developers Resource. Robin Schumacher. LC 97-143994. 672p. (C). 1996. pap. text 49.95 incl. cd-rom (0-13-271156-7) P-H.
PowerBuilder 5: Object-Oriented Design & Development. William Green & Millard F. Brown. (Illus.). 631p. 1996. pap. 49.95 (0-07-024469-3) McGraw.
Powerbuilder 5.0 Fundamentals. Steve Erlank & Craig Levin. LC 96-8569. (Illus.). 400p. 1996. mass mkt. 41.95 (1-85032-283-X) ITCP.
Powerbuilder for Xbase Programmers. abr. ed. Greg Nunemacher. 1995. pap. 39.95 incl. disk (1-55851-453-8, M&T Bks) IDG Bks.
Powerbuilder Foundation Class Library: Professional Reference. Howard Block et al. LC 97-22705. (Client/Server Computing Ser.). (Illus.). 448p. 1997. pap., pap. text 49.95 incl. cd-rom (0-07-913267-7) McGraw.
Powerbuilder Questions & Answers. Tim Hattan. LC 97-15946. (Illus.). 392p. 1997. pap. text 43.95 (1-884777-43-0) Manning Pubns.
PowerBuilder Questions & Answers 6.0. Tim Hatton. LC 97-15946. 447p. 1998. pap. 43.95 (1-884777-70-8) Manning Pubns.
***PowerBuilder 7.0 Unleashed.** Simon Herbert. (Unleashed Ser.). 1999. pap. 49.99 (0-672-31782-6) Sams.
PowerBuilder 4 Expert Solutions. Victor Rasputnis & Anatole Tartakosky. (Illus.). 1000p. (Orig.). 1995. 60.00 (0-7897-0346-7) Que.
PowerBuilder 4 Program for Dummies. James Coombs & Ted Coombs. 384p. 1995. pap. 19.99 (1-56884-325-9) IDG Bks.
Powerbuilder 4.0: Developer's Guide. David McClanahan. 1995. pap. 44.95 incl. disk (1-55851-417-1, M&T Bks) IDG Bks.
PowerBuilder 5 How-To: The Definitive PowerBuilder 5 Problem-Solver. Daryl Biberdorf & Keith Glidden. 800p. (Orig.). 1996. pap. 49.99 incl. cd-rom (1-57169-055-7) Sams.
Powerbuilder 5.0, Set. D. William Reynolds. LC 94-37381. 448p. 1995. 39.95 incl. disk (0-201-40886-4) Addison-Wesley.

P

PowerBuilder 5.0: Secrets of the PowerBuilder Masters: PowerBuilder Developer's Journal. 2nd rev. ed. Michael MacDonald & Michael Griffith. (PowerBuilder Training Ser.). (Illus.). 1104p. 1996. pap. 59.95 incl. cd-rom (*1-886141-01-0*) SYS-Con Pubns.

PowerBuilder 6 Unleashed. 3rd ed. Simon Gallagher & Simon Herbert. LC 97-68002. 1296p. 1997. 59.99 (*0-672-31179-8*) Sams.

Powerbuilder 6: A Developer's Guide. David McClanahan. LC 97-46340. 1024p. 1998. pap. 59.99 (*1-55851-581-X*, M&T Bks) IDG Bks.

Powerchicks: How Women Will Dominate America. Matt Towery. LC 98-66356. 240p. 1998. 22.00 (*1-56352-521-6*) Longstreet.

***Powercon '98: 1998 International Conference on Power System Technology, Proceedings, August 18-2, 2 vols.** World Scientific Staff. LC 98-84360. xx, 1578 p. 1999. 308.00 (*7-80003-425-9*) World Scientific Pub.

***Powerdown.** Peter Tonkin. 2000. pap. 11.00 (*0-7472-6187-3*, Pub. by Headline Bk Pub) Trafalgar.

Powerdraw Users Manual Vol. 1: Version 3.0. Bill Stanley et al. (Powercadd Ser.). (Illus.). 1989. 795.00 (*1-878250-00-0*) Eng Soft NC.

Powereading, 3 vols. rev. ed. Barry M. Smith et al. (Powereading Program Ser.: Bk. 1). (Illus.). (C). 1986. teacher ed. 18.95 (*0-685-03948-X*, Irwn McGrw-H); pap. text 28.50 (*0-685-03947-1*, Irwn McGrw-H) McGrw-H Hghr Educ.

Powereading, 3 vols. 2nd rev. ed. Barry M. Smith et al. (Powereading Program Ser.: Bk. 1). (Illus.). 384p. (C). 1986. 27.95 (*0-89702-050-2*, Irwn McGrw-H) McGrw-H Hghr Educ.

Powereading, 3 vols., Bk. 2. 2nd rev. ed. Barry M. Smith et al. (Powereading Program Ser.: Bk. 1). (Illus.). 112p. (C). 1986. 12.50 (*0-89702-051-0*, Irwn McGrw-H) McGrw-H Hghr Educ.

Powereading, 3 vols., Bk. 3. 2nd rev. ed. Barry M. Smith et al. (Powereading Program Ser.: Bk. 1). (Illus.). 128p. (C). 1986. 11.25 (*0-89702-052-9*, Irwn McGrw-H) McGrw-H Hghr Educ.

Powered by Coalition: The Story of Independent Sector. Brian O'Connell. LC 96-51318. 236p. 1997. 26.95 (*0-7879-0954-8*) Jossey-Bass.

Powered by Honda: Developing Excellence in the Global Enterprise. Dave Nelson et al. LC 97-45106. 272p. 1998. 29.95 (*0-471-18182-X*) Wiley.

Powered Endoscopic Sinus Surgery. John H. Krouse & Dewey A. Christmas. LC 97-677. 1997. write for info. (*4-260-14347-6*); write for info. (*0-89640-347-5*) Igaku-Shoin.

Powered Endoscopic Sinus Surgery. John H. Krouse & Dewey A. Christmas, Jr. LC 97-677. 162p. 1997. 59.00 (*0-683-30351-1*) Lppncott W & W.

***Powered Instrumentation in Otolaryngology: Head & Neck Surgery.** Yanagisawa. 2001. pap. 140.00 (*0-7693-0123-1*, Pub. by Singular Publishing) Thomson Learn.

***Powered Metal Applications.** (Special Publications). 174p. 2000. 99.00 (*0-7680-0585-X*, SP-1535) Soc Auto Engineers.

Powered Ultralight Flying. Dennis Pagen. (Illus.). 190p. (Orig.). 1983. pap. 11.95 (*0-936310-06-5*, Sport Aviation Pubns) Black Mntn.

Powered Ultralight Training Course. rev. ed. Dennis Pagen. (Illus.). 112p. 1991. pap. 9.95 (*0-936310-04-9*, Sport Aviation Pubns) Black Mntn.

PowerFoods: Good Food, Good Health with Phytochemicals, Nature's Own Energy Boosters. Stephanie Beling. 384p. 1998. pap. 15.00 (*0-06-092954-5*, Perennial) HarperTrade.

Powerful! God Enabling You. Churches Alive, Inc. Staff. (God in You Bible Study Ser.). (Illus.). 72p. (Orig.). 1986. pap. 5.00 (*0-89109-095-9*) NavPress.

Powerful Amulets of Santeria. Carlos Montenegro. 90p. 1997. pap. 9.95 (*0-942272-46-3*) Original Pubns.

Powerful Black Women. Jessie C. Smith. (Illus.). 420p. 1996. 18.95 (*0-7876-0882-3*) Visible Ink Pr.

***Powerful Bodies: Performance in French Cultural Studies.** Ed. by Victoria Best & Peter Collier. LC 99-40046. (Modern French Identities Ser.: Vol. 1). 220p. (C). 1999. pap. text 32.95 (*0-8204-4239-9*) P Lang Pubng.

Powerful Budgeting for Better Planning & Management. Robert G. Finney. 224p. 1993. 24.95 (*0-8144-5046-6*) AMACOM.

***Powerful Classroom Management Strategies: Motivating Students to Learn.** Paul R. Burden. LC 99-50711. (One-Off Ser.). 160p. 2000. pap. 21.95 (*0-7619-7563-2*); lib. bdg. 49.95 (*0-7619-7562-4*) Corwin Pr.

Powerful Communication Skills: How to Communicate with Confidence. Colleen McKenna. Ed. by Career Press Staff. LC 98-5752. 128p. 1998. pap. 10.99 (*1-56414-356-2*) Career Pr Inc.

Powerful Conceptions: A Series on Bishops & Birth Control. Denise Shannon & Maggie Hume. 1991. pap. 10.00 (*0-915365-17-0*) Cath Free Choice.

Powerful Conversations: How High Impact Leaders Communicate. Philip J. Hawkins. LC 99-26326. 224p. 1999. pap., student ed. 24.95 (*0-07-135321-6*) McGraw.

Powerful Evangelism for the Powerless. 2nd rev. ed. C. John Miller. LC 97-6827. Orig. Title: Evangelism & Your Church. 176p. 1997. pap. 9.99 (*0-87552-383-8*) P & R Pubng.

Powerful Expressions: Recent American Drawings. Jack Flam et al. LC 96-70089. (Illus.). 84p. (Orig.). 1996. pap. 18.95 (*1-887149-02-3*) Nat Acad of Des.

Powerful Faith. R. A. Torrey. 173p. (Orig.). 1996. mass mkt. 5.99 (*0-88368-417-9*) Whitaker Hse.

***Powerful Girls Adventures.** Anthony DiGiacomo. (Illus.). 50p. (J). (gr. 5-7). 2000. pap. 6.00 (*1-58265-025-X*, 0112) Orphan Press.

Powerful Good News. Robert J. Wieland. 146p. 1993. reprint ed. pap. text 6.95 (*0-9635077-0-2*) Glad Tidngs.

Powerful Ideas for Text Processing. Gary F. Simons. LC 83-51795. 200p. (Orig.). 1984. pap. 10.00 (*0-88312-930-2*) S I L Intl.

Powerful Ideas in Physical Science. American Institute Physics Staff & American Association Physics Teachers Staff. (Illus.). 1200p. 1996. teacher ed. 500.00 (*0-917853-66-0*) Am Assn Physics.

Powerful Images: Portrayals of Native America. Sarah E. Boehme & Gerald T. Conaty. LC 97-40098. (Illus.). 160p. 1998. pap. text 30.00 (*0-295-97675-6*) U of Wash Pr.

Powerful Images: Portrayals of Native America. Sarah Boehme et al. (Illus.). 160p. 1998. 50.00 (*0-295-97697-7*) U of Wash Pr.

Powerful Inspirational Thoughts: Reach for the Stars. 2nd ed. Lorenza Bedgood. LC 91-72524. (Illus.). 96p. 1991. pap. 7.95 (*1-879926-05-9*) D M K D Pubns.

Powerful Is the Light. Hazel Deane. (Illus.). 206p. 1987. reprint ed. text 20.00 (*0-685-34706-0*); reprint ed. lib. bdg. 12.95 (*0-685-34705-2*) First Divine Sci Ch Denver.

Powerful Learning. Ron Brandt. LC 98-17715. 94p. 1998. pap. 8.95 (*0-87120-305-7*, 198179) ASCD.

Powerful Love Spells. 1999. pap. 5.95 (*0-942272-54-4*) Original Pubns.

Powerful Memory: A Key to Success. Steve Aldrich. 1989. 5.00 (*0-9622229-0-9*) Zauberman Pr.

Powerful Multimedia Presentations: Interactive Video Production. Reza Azarmas. 352p. (C). 1995. pap. 50.95 (*0-534-25416-0*) Wadsworth Pub.

Powerful Paragraphs. Bruce Ross-Larson. LC 98-35265. (Effective Writing Ser.). 107p. 1999. pap. 10.00 (*0-393-31794-3*) Norton.

Powerful Parent Letters for K-3. Mary A. Duggan. LC 97-4818. 152p. 1997. 61.95 (*0-8039-6585-0*); pap. 27.95 (*0-8039-6586-9*) Corwin Pr.

***Powerful Partnerships: Twenty Crime Prevention Strategies that Work for Refugees, Law Enforcement & Communities.** Ed. by Judy Kirby. 149p. (Orig.). 1998. pap. 14.95 (*0-934513-74-0*) Natl Crime DC.

Powerful Passages: True Stories of People Whose Lives Were Changed by a Single Scripture. Ron Watts & Dorothy E. Watts. LC 95-50714. 1996. pap. 10.99 (*0-8163-1337-7*) Pacific Pr Pub Assn.

***Powerful Peace: The Integrative Thinking Classroom.** Warren Heydenberk. 255p. 2000. pap. 28.00 (*0-205-29360-3*) Allyn.

Powerful Percent: Student at the Heart of the Great Commission. Patricia Burgin. 141p. (C). Date not set. pap. 7.95 (*0-9629245-0-4*) WSN Pr.

Powerful Perceptions. W. T. Buchanan. (Illus.). 280p. 1994. 24.00 (*0-9640175-0-4*) Value Concepts.

Powerful Performance Appraisals: How to Set Expectations & Work Together to Improve. Karen McKirchy. LC 98-13954. Orig. Title: How to Conduct Win-Win Performance Appraisals. 128p. 1998. pap. 12.99 (*1-56414-367-8*) Career Pr Inc.

Powerful Personalities. Tim Kimmel. LC 93-6795. 1993. 14.99 (*1-56179-093-1*) Focus Family.

Powerful Placebo: From Ancient Priest to Modern Physician. Arthur K. Shapiro & Elaine Shapiro. LC 97-6754. 312p. 1997. text 39.95 (*0-8018-5569-1*) Johns Hopkins.

***Powerful Planning Skills: Envisioning the Future & Making It Happen.** National Seminars Staff. LC 99-56825. 128p. 1999. pap. 10.99 (*1-56414-441-0*) Career Pr Inc.

Powerful Points for Preaching. John R. Terry. 150p. 1982. pap. 4.95 (*0-933704-44-5*) Dawn Pr.

***Powerful Positive Pep Talks to Live By.** William J. Bond. (YA). (gr. 9). 1999. pap. 5.99 (*0-918694-05-1*) Career Pub MA.

***Powerful Positive Pep Talks to Live By.** William J. Bond. 1999. 12.99 (*0-918694-04-3*) Career Pub MA.

***Powerful Potential of Learning Communities: Improving Education for the Future.** Oscar T. Lenning & Larry H. Ebbers. LC 98-88007. (ASHE-ERIC Higher Education Report: Vol. 26, No. 6). 100p. 1999. pap. 24.00 (*1-878380-86-9*) GWU Grad Schl E&HD.

Powerful Prayer Secrets! How to Get What You Need Every Day! Julia Busch & Hollye Davidson. LC 95-94783. 128p. 1996. pap. 9.95 (*1-886369-00-3*, Kosmic Kurrents) Anti Aging Pr.

Powerful Prayers. Irwin Katsof & Larry King. 256p. pap. 15.95 (*1-58063-086-3*) Renaissance.

Powerful Prayers. large type ed. Larry King. LC 99-21721. 327p. 1999. 26.95 (*0-7838-8604-7*) Mac Lib Ref.

Powerful Prayers: Conversations on Faith, Hope & the Human Spirit. Larry King & Irwin Katsof. LC 98-38169. 254p. 1998. 22.95 (*1-58063-034-0*) Renaissance.

Powerful Presentation Skills. Dennis Becker & Paula B. Becker. LC 93-16149. (Business Skills Express Ser.). 96p. 1993. pap. 10.95 (*1-55623-870-3*, Irwn Prfssnl) McGraw-Hill Prof.

Powerful Presentation Skills: A Quick & Handy Guide for Any Manager or Business Owner. Ed. by Career Press Staff. LC 93-22387. (Business Desk Reference Ser.). 128p. (Orig.). 1993. pap. 8.95 (*1-56414-109-8*) Career Pr Inc.

Powerful Principles of Increase. John F. Avanzini. LC 93-206075. (POR.). 230p. (Orig.). 1990. pap. 7.95 (*0-89274-579-7*, HH579) Harrison Hse.

***Powerful Products: Strategic Management of Successful New Product Development.** Roger Bean & Russell Radford. LC 00-24828. 300p. 2000. 39.95 (*0-8144-0566-5*) AMACOM.

***Powerful Program Keys: Successful Church Programs for All Occasions.** Christine Butler. 132p. 1998. reprint ed. pap. text 6.95 (*0-940955-47-4*) Urban Ministries.

Powerful Proofreading Skills: Tips, Techniques & Tactics. Debra Smith & Helen Sutton. Ed. by Elaine Brett. LC 93-73201. (Fifty-Minute Ser.). (Illus.). 94p. (Orig.). 1994. pap. 10.95 (*1-56052-259-3*) Crisp Pubns.

Powerful Reading, Efficient Learning. Eleanor Leo. LC 93-886. 462p. (C). 1993. pap. text 38.00 (*0-02-369762-8*, Macmillan Coll) P-H.

Powerful Relations: Kinship, Status, & the State in Sung China (960-1279) Beverly J. Bossler. LC 97-27130. (Harvard-Yenching Institute Monograph Ser.). 370p. 1998. 45.00 (*0-674-69592-5*) HUP.

Powerful Schools Handbook: Starting & Running a Collaborative School Improvement Program. Photos by Jeffrey High. (Illus.). 152p. (Orig.). 1995. pap. 19.95 (*0-9647444-0-6*) Court St Pr.

Powerful Telephone Skills: A Quick & Handy Guide for Any Manager or Business Owner. Ed. by Career Press Staff. (Business Desk Reference Ser.). 128p. 1993. pap. 8.95 (*1-56414-107-1*) Career Pr Inc.

Powerful Voltage of Christ's Humility. 4th rev. ed. B. R. Hicks. (Illus.). 178p. 1995. pap. 9.95 (*1-58363-066-X*, MD-4013) Christ Gospel.

Powerful Waves. D. M. Souza. (J). (gr. 1-4). 1992. lib. bdg. 19.95 (*0-87614-661-2*, Carolrhoda) Lerner Pub.

Powerful Wisdom: Voices of Distinguished Women Psychotherapists. Lourene A. Nevels & Judith M. Coche. LC 93-3621. (Social & Behavioral Science Ser.). 190p. 1993. 33.95 (*1-55542-570-4*) Jossey-Bass.

Powerful Witness Preparation. Ronald J. Cohen & Paula M. Demore. 223p. 1995. pap. 185.00 incl. audio (*0-943380-97-9*) PEG MN.

Powerful Writing: Helping Students Organize & Share Ideas. Marcia Treat. 33p. 1998. pap. text 12.50 (*0-9659517-9-0*) Curriculum Solns.

Powerful Writing Skills: A Quick & Handy Guide for Any Manager or Business Owner. National Seminars Staff. LC 94-3751. (Business Desk Reference Ser.). 128p. 1994. pap. 8.95 (*1-56414-145-4*) Career Pr Inc.

***Powerful Writing/Responsible Teaching.** Timothy J. Lensmire. LC 00-21070. (Critical Issues in Educational Leadership Ser.). 2000. write for info. (*0-8077-3957-X*) Tchrs Coll.

Powerfully Fit: Dozens of Ways to Boost Strength, Increase Endurance, & Chisel Your Body. Men's Health Books Staff et al. LC 95-25484. (Men's Health Life Improvement Guides Ser.). (Illus.). 176p. (Orig.). 1996. pap. 14.95 (*0-87596-279-3*) Rodale Pr Inc.

Powerfully Positive Self-Talk: Cool Things to Say to Yourself. Joanna Giordano-Whelton. 52p. (J). (gr. 4 up). 1998. spiral bd. 4.95 (*0-9663762-3-4*) Playful Pr.

Powerholders. David Kipnis. LC 75-43230. (Illus.). 1996. pap. text 11.00 (*0-226-43732-9*, P820) U Ch Pr.

Power/Holiness/Evangelism: Rediscovering God's Purity, Power... Randy Clark. 1999. pap. 11.99 (*1-56043-345-0*) Destiny Image.

Powerhouse. Robert L. Sumner. 1978. pap. 3.95 (*0-914012-18-5*) Sword of Lord.

Powerhouse. Wojkowski. (C). 1994. text. write for info. (*0-318-70370-X*) S-W Pub.

Powerhouse: Inside a Nuclear Power Plant. Charlotte Wilcox. (Illus.). 48p. (J). (gr. 3-7). 1996. pap. 7.95 (*0-87614-979-4*, Carolrhoda); lib. bdg. 16.95 (*0-87614-945-X*, Carolrhoda) Lerner Pub.

***Powerhouse Intermediate Business English Coursebook.** (C). 2000. pap., student ed. 7.75 (*0-582-32560-9*) Pearson Educ.

***Powerhouse Intermediate Business English Coursebook.** (C). 2000. pap. 16.50 (*0-582-29879-2*); pap., teacher ed. 11.95 (*0-582-32558-7*) Pearson Educ.

Powerhouse of the Atom. K. Gladkov. (Illus.). 303p. 1972. 22.95 (*0-8464-0741-8*) Beekman Pubs.

Powerhouse of the Atom. K. A. Gladkov. Tr. by S. M. Semenov & H. C. Creighton from RUS. LC QC0173.G43. (Illus.). 304p. reprint ed. pap. 94.30 (*0-8357-2915-X*, 203915500011) Bks Demand.

PowerHouse Official Secrets & Solutions. Bruce Shelley. 96p. 1995. pap. text 12.95 (*0-7615-0231-9*) Prima Pub.

Powerhouse Pepper. Basil Wolverton. 104p. 1994. pap. 11.95 (*1-56097-148-7*) Fantagraph Bks.

Powering Apollo: James E. Webb of NASA. W. Henry Lambright. LC 94-29063. (New Series in NASA History). (Illus.). 296p. 1995. text 39.95 (*0-8018-4902-0*) Johns Hopkins.

Powering Asia: Is Gas the Answer?: 14th Annual Pacific Rim Workshop. Loren Cox et al. LC 98-191720. iii, 23 p. 1998. 8.00 (*0-89843-231-6*) The Aspen Inst.

Powering the Future: Blueprint for a Sustainable Electricity Industry. Christopher Flavin & Nicholas Lenssen. 64p. (Orig.). 1994. pap. 5.00 (*1-878071-20-3*) Worldwatch Inst.

***Powering the Future: The Ballard Fuel Cell & the Race to Change the World.** Tom Koppel. LC 99-931896. 288p. 1999. 29.95 (*0-471-64421-8*) Wiley.

***Powering up Performance Management: An Integrated Approach to Getting the Best from Your People.** Richard Hale & Peter Whitlam. LC 99-46261. 200p. 2000. 78.95 (*0-566-08189-X*, Pub. by Gower) Ashgate Pub Co.

Powering War: Modern Land Force Logistics. P. D. Foxton. (Land Warfare: Brassey's New Battlefield Weapons & Technology Ser.: Vol. 11). 182p. 1993. 40.00 (*1-85753-053-5*, Pub. by Brasseys); pap. 25.00 (*1-85753-048-9*, Pub. by Brasseys) Brasseys.

Powering Your Web Site with Windows NT Server. Nik Simpson. LC 96-51200. (Illus.). 661p. (Orig.). 1997. pap. 44.95 (*1-882419-51-0*) News Four-Hund.

***PowerJ Developer's Professional Reference: Featuring Version 2.0.** Peter J. Horwood. LC 98-2750. (Team Powersoft Ser.). (Illus.). 480p. 1998. pap., pap. text 49.95 incl. cd-rom (*0-07-913660-5*) McGraw.

PowerKids Readers Set 1: My World, 6 bks. Heather L. Feldman. Incl. My Bedtime: A Book about Getting Ready for Bed. LC 98-49480. (Illus.). 24p. (J). (ps-2). 1998. lib. bdg. 14.60 (*0-8239-5522-2*, PowerKids); My Best Friend: A Book about Friendship. LC 98-31955. (Illus.). 24p. (J). (ps-2). 1998. lib. bdg. 14.60 (*0-8239-5526-5*, PowerKids); My Breakfast: A Book about a Great Morning Meal. LC 98-31956. (Illus.). 24p. (J). (ps-2). 1998. lib. bdg. 14.60 (*0-8239-5527-3*, PowerKids); My Day at the Baseball Game: A Book about a Special Day. LC 98-31954. (Illus.). 24p. (J). (ps-2). 1998. lib. bdg. 14.60 (*0-8239-5525-7*, PowerKids); My Dog: A Book about a Special Pet. LC 98-49397. (Illus.). 24p. (J). (ps-2). 1998. lib. bdg. 14.60 (*0-8239-5524-9*, PowerKids); My School Bus: A Book about School Bus Safety. LC 98-31957. (Illus.). 24p. (J). (ps-2). 1998. lib. bdg. 14.60 (*0-8239-5523-0*, PowerKids); (J). (ps-2). Set lib. bdg. 87.60 (*0-8239-7002-7*, PowerKids) Rosen Group.

PowerKids Readers Set 2: Nature Books, 6 bks. Kristin Ward. Incl. Apples. LC 98-52680. (Illus.). 24p. (J). (ps-2). 2000. lib. bdg. 14.60 (*0-8239-5528-1*, PowerKids); Leaves. LC 99-14630. (Illus.). 24p. (J). (ps-2). 1999. lib. bdg. 14.60 (*0-8239-5533-8*, PowerKids); Oceans. LC 98-49733. (Illus.). 24p. (J). (ps-2). 1999. lib. bdg. 14.60 (*0-8239-5532-X*, PowerKids); Rain. LC 98-53866. (Illus.). 24p. (J). (ps-2). 1999. lib. bdg. 14.60 (*0-8239-5531-1*, PowerKids); Sand. LC 98-49732. (Illus.). 24p. (J). (ps-2). 1999. lib. bdg. 14.60 (*0-8239-5530-3*, PowerKids); Snow. LC 98-49734. (Illus.). 24p. (J). (ps-2). 1999. lib. bdg. 14.60 (*0-8239-5529-X*, PowerKids); (Illus.). (J). (ps-2). Set lib. bdg. 87.60 (*0-8239-7003-5*, PowerKids) Rosen Group.

Power/Knowledge/Pedagogy: The Meaning of Democratic Education in Unsettling Times. Ed. by Dennis Carlson & Michael W. Apple. (Edge Ser.). 368p. 1999. pap. 28.00 (*0-8133-9138-5*, Pub. by Westview) HarpC.

Powerlearning: Memory & Learning Techniques for Personal Power. 4th rev. ed. Donald J. Lofland. Ed. by Pamela Altschul. (Illus.). v, 243p. 1997. pap. 13.95 (*0-9660348-1-3*) Powerlrning Systs.

Powerless: Selected Poems, 1973-1990. Tim Dlugos. Ed. by David Trinidad. (High Risk Ser.). 150p. (Orig.). 1996. pap. 12.99 (*1-85242-407-9*, High Risk Bks) Serpents Tail.

***Powerless by Design: The Age of the International Community.** Michael Feher. 152p. 2000. lib. bdg. 14.95 (*0-8223-2605-1*) Duke.

***Powerless by Design: The Age of the International Community.** Michel Feher. LC 00-39382. (Public Planet Ser.). 152p. 2000. pap. 14.95 (*0-8223-2613-2*) Duke.

Powerless It's a Fraud see Impotencia es un Fraude

Powerless Position: The Commanding General of the Army of the United States, 1864-1903. Robert F. Stohlman, Jr. 184p. 1975. pap. text 32.95 (*0-89126-022-6*) MA-AH Pub.

Powerlift - Getting to Desert Storm: Strategic Transportation & Strategy in the New World Order. Douglas Menarchik. LC 93-2857. 216p. 1993. 55.00 (*0-275-94642-8*, C4642, Praeger Pubs) Greenwood.

***Powerlifting: Technique & Training for Athletic Muscular Development.** Barney Groves. LC 00-24484. (Illus.). 160p. 2000. pap. 18.95 (*0-88011-978-0*) Human Kinetics.

Powerlifting Basics, Texas-Style: The Adventures of Lope Delk. Paul Kelso. LC 96-76289. 96p. (Orig.). 1996. pap. 14.95 (*0-926888-04-8*) IronMind Enterprises.

Powerline: The First Battle of America's Energy War. Barry M. Casper & Paul D. Wellstone. LC 80-25903. (Illus.). 328p. 1981. lib. bdg. 35.00 (*0-87023-320-3*) U of Mass Pr.

***Powerline Ampacity System: Theory, Modeling & Applications.** Anjan K. Deb. LC 00-36093. 2000. write for info. (*0-8493-1306-6*) CRC Pr.

Powerlines: A Completely Practical Guide to Communicating with Confidence & Power. 2nd ed. Diana Morris. LC 98-65602. Orig. Title: Powerlines - How to Communicate with Power & Precision. 150p. 1998. pap. 16.95 (*1-891019-08-2*) Morris Communs.

***PowerLines: Breakthrough Communication Strategies for People Moving into Leadership: A Manager's Orientation Program.** (Management Excellence Library: Vol. 2). 65p. 1999. ring bd. write for info. (*1-891019-17-1*) Morris Communs.

Powerlines: What Great Evangelicals Believed about the Holy Spirit, 1850-1930. Leona Choy. LC 90-81459. 321p. (Orig.). (C). 1990. pap. 12.99 (*0-87509-434-1*) Chr Pubns.

Powerlines - How to Communicate with Power & Precision see Powerlines: A Completely Practical Guide to Communicating with Confidence & Power

Powerliving: Practical Principles for Living in the Spirit. Raymond F. Culpepper. 143p. 1997. pap. 9.99 (*0-87148-974-0*) Pathway Pr.

Powermatics: A Discursive Critique of New Technology. Marike Finlay. (International Library of Phenomenology & Moral Sciences). 376p. 1987. lib. bdg. 69.95 (*0-7102-0761-1*, Routledge Thoemms) Routledge.

Powermind System: Twelve Lessons on the Psychology of Success. Michael M. Kiefer. Ed. by Carol A. Kennedy. LC 95-94200. (Illus.). 435p. (Orig.). 1995. pap. 13.95 (*0-9645934-0-8*) Kiefer Enterprises.

Powermonger: The Authorized Strategy Book. Paula Spiese. (Secrets of the Games Ser.). (Illus.). 352p. (Orig.). 1992. pap. 18.95 (*1-55958-128-X*) Prima Pub.

Powernomics: Economics & Strategy after the Cold War. Clyde V. Prestowitz. 1991. pap. 16.95 (*0-8191-8039-4*) Madison Bks UPA.

Powernotes: Accounting, Vol. 1, Chapters 1-13. 18th ed. Carl S. Warren. (AB - Accounting Principles Ser.). 1996. pap. 13.95 (*0-538-86532-6*) S-W Pub.

P

An Asterisk (*) at the beginning of an entry indicates that the title is appearing for the first time.

Powernotes: Accounting, Vol. 3, Chapters 1-17. 18th ed. Carl S. Warren. (AB - Accounting Principles Ser.). 1996. pap. 13.95 (*0-538-86534-2*) S-W Pub.

Powernotes: Chapters 12-24 Accounting. 19th ed. Warren et al. (SWC-Accounting). 1998. pap. 12.00 (*0-538-87420-1*) S-W Pub.

PowerNotes Vol. I: Strategy: New Mandates, New Ideas, New Possibilities. Charles Tombazian & William Heitzman. (Leadership & Team Handbks.). 60p. 1997. pap. 19.95 (*1-891889-00-1*) PowerNotes.

PowerNotes Vol. II: Actuating Your Firm's Service Culture. Charles Tombazian et al. (Leadership & Team Handbks.). 80p. 1998. pap. 19.95 (*1-891889-01-X*) PowerNotes.

PowerNotes Vol. III: Innovate or Die. Charles Tombazian & William Heitzman. (Leadership & Team Handbks.). 1998. pap. 19.95 (*1-891889-02-8*) PowerNotes.

***Powernotes Chapters 1-16 Accounting.** 20th ed. Warren et al. 2001. pap. 13.00 (*0-324-05191-3*) Thomson Learn.

***Powernotes Chapters 11-24 Accounting.** 20th ed. Warren et al. 2001. pap. 13.00 (*0-324-05192-1*) Thomson Learn.

Powernotes-strategic Mgt 2e. 2nd ed. Hitt et al. (SWC-Management). 1996. pap. 12.00 (*0-314-20759-7*) S-W Pub.

Powernotes Vol 2 Ch 14-26 -accounting, Vol. 2, Chapters 14-26. 18th ed. Carl S. Warren. (SWC-Accounting). 1996. pap. 13.95 (*0-538-86533-4*) S-W Pub.

PowerPak of Scripture Memory Fun. 112p. (J). 1999. 11.95 (*1-57405-448-1*) CharismaLife Pub.

PowerPC Macintosh Book. Stephan Somogyi & Brita Meng. LC 93-38276. 256p. (C). 1994. pap. 19.95 (*0-201-62650-0*) Addison-Wesley.

PowerPC Microprocessor Common Hardware Reference Platform: A System Architecture. Apple Computer, Inc. Staff et al. LC 95-49032. 309p. (C). 1996. pap. text 43.95 (*1-55860-394-8*) Morgan Kaufmann.

PowerPC Programming for Intel Programmers. Kip McLanahan. 720p. 1995. pap. 49.99 (*1-56884-306-2*) IDG Bks.

PowerPC System Architecture. Tom Shanley. (PC System Architecture Ser.). 656p. (C). 1995. pap. text 34.95 (*0-201-40990-9*) Addison-Wesley.

PowerPC System Architecture: A New Family of RISC Processors. International Business Machines Staff. 320p. 1994. text 63.95 (*1-55860-344-1*) Morgan Kaufmann.

***Powerplant Guide for Certification of Part 23, Airplanes, September 21, 1999.** 134p. 2000. pap. 14.00 (*0-16-059089-2*) USGPO.

Powerplant Handbook. 372p. reprint ed. 24.95 (*0-614-13164-2*, 21-13470) EAA Aviation.

Powerplant Technology. M. M. El-Wakil. 544p. (C). 1984. 107.19 (*0-07-019288-X*) McGraw.

Powerplant Test Guide, 2000: Fast-Track Guide 2000. rev. ed. FAA Staff. Ed. by Dale Crane. (Fast-Track Guides for Aviation Mechanics Ser.). (Illus.). 196p. 1999. pap. 12.95 (*1-56027-349-6*, ASA-AMP-99) ASA Inc.

Powerplants of the Future, 4 vols. 1996. 36.00 (*1-56091-838-1*, SP-1187) Soc Auto Engineers.

Powerplay: Toys as Popular Culture. Dan Fleming. LC 95-43362. (Illus.). 224p. 1997. pap. 27.95 (*0-7190-4717-X*) St Martin.

Powerplay in Tibullus: Reading Elegies, Bk. 1. Parshia Lee-Stecum. LC 99-161355. (Cambridge Classical Studies). 330p. (C). 1998. 64.95 (*0-521-63083-5*) Cambridge U Pr.

PowerPoint: Student Guide. Gronbeck. 24p. (C). 1999. pap. text, student ed. 13.00 (*0-321-04926-8*) Addson-Wesley Educ.

PowerPoint: The Visual Learning Guide. Grace J. Beatty. LC 94-65674. (Illus.). 272p. 1994. pap. 19.95 (*1-55958-550-1*) Prima Pub.

***Powerpoint Social Psychology 9/e: Powerpoint Presentation.** 9th ed. 1999. write for info. (*0-205-29806-0*) Benjamin-Cummings.

PowerPoint Electronic Transparencies. 7th ed. Ed. by Prentice-Hall Staff. (C). 2000. write for info. (*0-13-084705-4*) P-H.

PowerPoint Essentials. Suzanne Weixel. 1995. pap. text 22.99 (*1-57576-048-7*) Que Educ & Trng.

PowerPoint for Windows 95 Smartstart. Que Education & Training Staff. LC 95-74886. 332p. 1996. pap. text 29.99 (*1-57576-038-X*) Que Educ & Trng.

PowerPoint for Windows Smartstart. 1995. pap. text, teacher ed. 39.99 incl. disk (*1-56529-821-7*) Que Educ & Trng.

PowerPoint for Windows 4.0 Quick Reference Guide. DDC Publishing Staff. LC 94-216277. 1994. spiral bd. 12.00 (*1-56243-178-1*, OPPW4) DDC Pub.

PowerPoint for Windows 95: The Visual Learning Guide. David Gardner. 1995. pap. text 19.95 (*0-7615-0210-6*) Prima Pub.

Powerpoint for Windows 95 Essentials. 2nd ed. Linda Bird. 181p. (C). 1997. pap. text 18.67 (*1-58076-029-5*) Que Educ & Trng.

PowerPoint for Windows 95 for Busy People. Ron Mansfield. (Busy People Bks.). 304p. 1996. pap. text 22.95 (*0-07-882204-1*) McGraw.

PowerPoint for Windows 95 for Dummies. Doug Lowe. 368p. 1996. pap. 19.99 (*1-56884-931-1*) IDG Bks.

Powerpoint for Windows 95 Made Simple. Stephen. 160p. Date not set. pap. text 19.95 (*0-7506-2817-0*) Buttrwrth-Heinemann.

PowerPoint for Windows 95 Virtual Tutor. Que Education & Training Staff. 1997. pap. text 25.00 (*1-57576-491-1*) Que Educ & Trng.

PowerPoint 4 for Windows VisiRef. Susan Stover & Que Development Group Staff. LC 94-66543. (Illus.). 158p. 1994. 12.99 (*1-56529-862-4*) Que.

PowerPoint 4 for Windows SmartStart. Que Corporation Staff. LC 94-68012. 278p. 1994. 29.99 (*1-56529-795-4*) Que.

PowerPoint 4/7: Byte by Bite. Glenda Friesen. (Byte by Bite Ser.). (Illus.). 44p. 1997. pap. 10.00 (*1-891412-02-7*) Training Solut.

***PowerPoint 98 in One Hour: Macintosh Version.** Vicki Sharp. (Illus.). 171p. (YA). (gr. 5-12). 1999. spiral bd. 29.95 (*1-56484-148-0*) Intl Society Tech Educ.

PowerPoint 95 Essentials. Kathy Elliott. 1996. text, teacher ed. 49.99 (*1-57576-256-0*) Que Educ & Trng.

***PowerPoint 97.** ENI Publishing Ltd. Staff. (Triunfar Con Ser.). 2000. pap. 7.95 (*2-84072-875-3*) ENI Publng.

PowerPoint 97: Blue Ribbon Edition. 2nd ed. Duffy. 112p. (C). 1998. pap. text 25.00 (*0-201-44852-1*, Prentice Hall) P-H.

PowerPoint 97: Byte by Bite. Glenda Friesen. (Byte by Bite Ser.). (Illus.). iv, 51p. 1997. pap. 10.00 (*1-891412-00-0*) Training Solut.

***Powerpoint 97: Module 2.** Niit. (CT Course Instructor Training Ser.). 2000. 8.00 (*0-619-02297-3*) Course Tech.

PowerPoint 97 - Intermediate. Ed. by Ron Pronk. (Illus.). 180p. 1997. pap. 20.00 (*1-58264-004-1*, 119) ActiveEd.

PowerPoint 97 - Introduction. Ed. by Ron Pronk. (Illus.). 180p. 1997. pap. 20.00 (*1-58264-068-8*, 112) ActiveEd.

PowerPoint 97 - Introduction. rev. ed. Ed. by Ron Pronk. (Illus.). 180p. 1997. pap. 20.00 (*1-58264-039-4*, 158) ActiveEd.

PowerPoint 97 Advanced. Computer Confidence Staff. (Illus.). xviii, 126p. 1998. spiral bd. 29.00 incl. disk (*1-57533-069-5*, 07753) Comput Confidence.

***PowerPoint 97 Advanced.** deluxe ed. Computer Confidence Staff. (Illus.). xviii, 126p. 1998. spiral bd. 25.95 incl. disk (*1-57533-116-0*, 7753D) Comput Confidence.

PowerPoint 97 Essentials. Bird. LC 97-67229. (Illus.). 240p. 1997. 22.99 (*1-57576-824-0*) Sams.

PowerPoint 97 Essentials, Level 1. Linda Bird. LC 97-65586. 192p. 1997. 22.99 (*1-57576-785-6*) Sams.

PowerPoint 97 Exam Prep. 10th ed. David W. Beskeen. 264p. (C). 1997. pap. 29.99 (*1-57610-233-5*) Coriolis Grp.

PowerPoint 97 Expert Test Preparation. Ed. by Ron Pronk. (Illus.). 120p. 1997. pap. 20.00 (*1-58264-027-0*, 145) ActiveEd.

PowerPoint 97 for Windows for Dummies. Doug Lowe. LC 96-79270. (For Dummies Ser.). (Illus.). 384p. 1997. pap. 19.99 (*0-7645-0051-1*) IDG Bks.

***PowerPoint 97 for Teachers.** Pamela W. Adams & Sara R. Pressley. Ed. by Jennell L. Davis. (Educator's Ser.). (Illus.). 200p. 1999. pap. text 49.95 (*1-58163-080-8*) CPI Train.

***PowerPoint 97 for Windows for Dummies Quick Reference.** McCue. LC T385.M377999 1998. (Illus.). 224p. 1998. spiral bd. 12.99 (*0-7645-0494-0*) IDG Bks.

***PowerPoint 97 for Windows 95: Teacher Materials.** annot. ed. 1999. teacher ed. write for info. incl. disk (*0-02-803358-2*) Glencoe.

***PowerPoint 97 in One Hour: Windows Version.** Vicki Sharp. (Illus.). 183p. (YA). (gr. 5-12). 1999. spiral bd. 29.95 (*1-56484-149-9*) Intl Society Tech Educ.

PowerPoint 97 Introduction. Computer Confidence Staff. (Illus.). xviii, 164p. 1997. spiral bd. 29.00 incl. disk (*1-57533-068-7*, 07751) Comput Confidence.

PowerPoint 97 Introduction. deluxe ed. Computer Confidence Staff. (Illus.). xviii, 164p. 1997. spiral bd. 25.95 incl. disk (*1-57533-115-2*, 7951D) Comput Confidence.

PowerPoint 97 (MOUS) - Intermediate. Ed. by Ron Pronks. (Illus.). 180p. 1997. pap. 20.00 (*1-58264-021-1*, 137) ActiveEd.

PowerPoint 97 (MOUS) - Introduction. Ed. by Ron Pronk. (Illus.). 180p. 1997. pap. 20.00 (*1-58264-020-3*, 136) ActiveEd.

PowerPoint 97 Smartstart. Sally M. Preston et al. LC 97-65618. (Smartstart Ser.). (Illus.). 364p. 1997. 29.99 incl. disk (*1-57576-820-8*) Sams.

Powerpoint Presentation. 2nd ed. (C). 1999. text. write for info. (*0-205-29547-9*) Allyn.

Powerpoint Presentation. 9th ed. Ed. by Prentice-Hall Staff. (C). 2000. write for info. (*0-13-022417-0*) P-H.

***PowerPoint 7 for Windows 95: Teacher Material.** annot. ed. 1999. teacher ed. write for info. incl. disk (*0-02-803345-0*) Glencoe.

PowerPoint 7.0 for Windows. Glencoe Staff. (Illus.). 448p. 1999. pap. text 60.76 (*0-02-803304-3*) Glencoe.

PowerPoint 7.0 for Windows 95 - Introduction. Ed. by Ron Pronk. (Illus.). 180p. 1996. pap. 20.00 (*1-58264-049-1*, 84) ActiveEd.

PowerPoint 7.0 for Windows 95 - Intermediate. Ed. by Ron Pronk. (Illus.). 180p. 1996. pap. 20.00 (*1-58264-051-3*, 86) ActiveEd.

PowerPoint 7.0 for Windows 95 Introduction. Computer Confidence Staff. (Illus.). xviii, 166p. 1996. spiral bd. 29.00 incl. disk (*1-57533-077-6*, 07747) Comput Confidence.

***PowerPoint Simple Projects: Intermediate.** Corinne Burton. (Illus.). 96p. 2000. pap., teacher ed. 8.95 (*1-57690-441-5*, TCM 2441) Tchr Create Mat.

PowerPoint Slides for Introductory Psychology Series I. 2nd ed. (C). 1998. Price not set. (*0-13-012353-6*) P-H.

PowerPoint Starter Kit for Macintosh. Barrie Sosinsky & Hayden Development Group Staff. (Illus.). 325p. (Orig.). 1995. pap. text 25.00 (*1-56830-121-9*) Hayden.

Powerpoint Trans. Introduction to Management Accounting. 11th ed. Horngren. 1998. text. write for info. (*0-13-274383-3*) P-H.

***PowerPoint 2000.** Johnson Toliver. 224p. (C). 1999. pap. text 25.00 (*0-201-45902-7*, Prentice Hall) P-H.

***PowerPoint 2000! I Didn't Know You Could Do That...** Michael Miller. 2000. pap. 19.99 (*0-7821-2787-8*) Sybex.

***PowerPoint 2000: Module II.** Frank Davenhauer. Ed. by Linnea Nigro & Kathleen DeFlippo. (Illus.). 205p. (C). 1999. pap. write for info. (*0-7423-0301-2*) ComputerPREP.

***PowerPoint 2000 - Intermediate.** Ed. by Ron Pronk. (Illus.). 154p. 1999. pap. 20.00 (*1-58264-101-3*) ActiveEd.

***PowerPoint 2000 Advanced.** Computer Confidence Inc. Staff. (Illus.). xx, 132p. 1999. pap. 29.95 (*1-57533-093-8*); pap. 25.95 incl. disk (*1-57533-105-5*, 7758D) Comput Confidence.

Microsoft Powerpoint 2000 Bible. Wempen. LC 98-73782. 648p. 1999. 34.99 (*0-7645-3252-9*) IDG Bks.

***PowerPoint 2000 Core.** ENI Publishing Ltd. Staff. (MOUS Exam Ser.). (Illus.). 2000. pap. 20.95 (*2-7460-0981-1*) ENI Publng.

***PowerPoint 2000 Essentials Advanced.** Linda Bird. 2000. pap. text 14.00 (*1-58076-286-7*) Que Educ & Trng.

Powerpoint 2000 Expert. Carol M. Cram. (C). 1999. 15.00 (*0-619-00124-0*) Course Tech.

PowerPoint 2000 Fast & Easy. Coletta Witherspoon & Richard Cravens. LC 98-68148. (Fast & Easy Ser.). 371p. 1999. pap. 16.99 (*0-7615-1763-4*, Prima Tech) Prima Pub.

***PowerPoint 2000 for Windows for Dummies.** Camille McCue. LC 98-88741. (Windows for Dummies Ser.). (Illus.). 224p. 1999. spiral bd. 12.99 (*0-7645-0451-7*) IDG Bks.

***PowerPoint 2000 Guia Rapida.** Claudio Sanchez. (PC Users Express Ser.).Tr. of PowerPoint 2000 Express Guide. (SPA., Illus.). 2000. pap. 13.90 (*987-526-025-8*) MP Ediciones.

***PowerPoint 2000 Introduction.** Computer Confidence Inc. Staff. (Computer Confidence Ser.). (Illus.). xxii, 164p. 1999. pap. 25.95 (*1-57533-104-7*, 7756D) Comput Confidence.

***PowerPoint 2000 Introduction.** Computer Confidence Inc. Staff. (Illus.). xxii, 164p. 1999. spiral bd. 29.95 incl. disk (*1-57533-092-X*, 7756) Comput Confidence.

***PowerPoint 2000 MOUS Cheat Sheet.** Doug Klippert. 300p. 1999. pap. text 19.99 (*0-7897-2118-X*) Que.

Powerpoint 2000 Professional. Finkelstein. 480p. 1999. pap. 29.99 (*0-07-211993-4*) McGraw.

PowerPoint 2000/98 for Windows & Macintosh: Visual QuickStart Guide. Rebecca Bridges Altman. 250p. 1999. pap. text 17.99 (*0-201-35441-1*) Peachpit Pr.

PowerPoint 2.0 for Windows: Beginners. 1993. 29.95 (*1-56877-059-6*); teacher ed. 49.95 (*1-56877-060-X*) Catapult WA.

***PowerPoint 2000.** ENI Publishing Ltd. Staff. (On Your Side Ser.). 2000. pap. 15.95 (*2-7460-0797-5*) ENI Publng.

***PowerPoint 2000.** ENI Publishing Ltd. Staff. (By Example Ser.). (Illus.). 2000. pap. 28.95 (*2-7460-0800-9*) ENI Publng.

***PowerPoint 2000.** ENI Publishing Ltd. Staff. (Pasaporte Ser.). 2000. pap. 15.95 (*2-7460-0994-3*); pap. 7.95 (*2-7460-0996-X*) ENI Publng.

***PowerPoint 2000.** ENI Publishing Ltd. Staff. (Finding Your Way Ser.). (Illus.). 2000. pap. 12.95 (*2-7460-0975-7*) ENI Publng.

***PowerPoint 2000.** ENI Publishing Staff. (Straight to the Point Ser.). 2000. pap. 7.95 (*2-7460-0793-2*) ENI Publng.

***PowerPoint 2000 Essentials Advanced.** 1999. 18.67 (*0-13-026641-8*) P-H.

***Powerpoint 2000 Essentials Basic with CD-ROM.** Linda Bird. 300p. (C). 1999. spiral bd. 21.33 (*1-58076-095-3*) Que Educ & Trng.

PowerPoint 2000 Express Guide see PowerPoint 2000 Guia Rapida

***Powerpoint 2000 for Dummies.** Doug Lowe. LC T385.L6923 1999. (Windows for Dummies Ser.). (Illus.). 384p. 1999. pap. 19.99 (*0-7645-0450-9*) IDG Bks.

PowerPoint 3.0. (Illus.). xvii, 180p. 1993. teacher ed., spiral bd., wbk. ed. 29.00 (*0-7402-0297-9*, MSPPW3011G) Accelerated Comput Train.

PowerPoint 3.0 for Windows: Beginners. 1993. 29.95 (*1-56877-061-8*); teacher ed. 49.95 (*1-56877-062-6*) Catapult WA.

PowerPoint 4 - Win 3.1/3.11. (Quick Study Computer Ser.). 4p. pap. 3.95 (*1-57222-162-3*) Barcharts.

Powerpoint 4 Smartstart. 1997. 19.99 (*0-7686-0087-1*) Quest Custom.

PowerPoint 4.0 for Windows. Rick Sullivan. (Computer Traning Ser.). (C). pap. 18.95 (*0-538-64139-8*) S-W Pub.

PowerPoint 4.0 for Windows. Rick Sullivan. (Computer Training Ser.). 180p. (C). 1995. spiral bd. 21.95 (*0-538-64144-4*) S-W Pub.

PowerPoint 4.0 Windows Advanced. Computer Confidence Staff. (Illus.). 160p. 1995. spiral bd. 29.95 incl. disk (*1-57533-021-0*) Comput Confidence.

PowerPoint 4.0 Windows Introduction. Computer Confidence Staff. (Illus.). 160p. 1994. spiral bd. 29.95 incl. disk (*1-57533-020-2*) Comput Confidence.

PowerPoint 7 - Win 95/NT. (Quick Study Computer Ser.). 4p. pap. 3.95 (*1-57222-170-4*) Barcharts.

PowerPoint 7.0 for Windows. Sean C. Feeney & Douglas M. Finney. (Illus.). (Orig.). 1996. pap., spiral bd. 29.95 incl. disk (*1-56435-104-1*) Finney Lrng Systs.

PowerPoint 9 - 97. Kenneth Laudon. LC 97-46808. 128p. (C). 1998. pap. 14.69 (*0-07-038439-8*) McGraw.

PowerPoint 95 Essentials. Linda Bird. 1996. 22.99 (*1-57576-257-9*) Que Educ & Trng.

***PowerPoint 97.** Daniel Speers. (Lazy Way Ser.). 304p. 1999. pap. text 12.95 (*0-02-863019-X*) Macmillan.

PowerPoint 97: Day 2. DDC Publishing Staff. (One-Day Course Ser.). 1998. pap. text 22.00 (*1-56243-581-7*, DC31) DDC Pub.

PowerPoint 97: Just the Basics. D D C Publishing Staff. (One-Day Course Ser.). 1997. pap. text 22.00 incl. cd-rom (*1-56243-531-0*, DC-14) DDC Pub.

PowerPoint 97 - What's New. Ron Pronk. 70p. 1997. 20.00 (*1-58264-029-7*) ActiveEd.

PowerPoint 97 - Win 95/NT. (Quick Study Computer Ser.). 4p. pap. 3.95 (*1-57222-210-7*) Barcharts.

PowerPoint 97 Essentials: Level II. Linda Bird. 1997. teacher ed. 49.99 (*1-57576-810-0*) Que Educ & Trng.

PowerPoint 97 Essentials (Academic) Imperative Programming Languages, Ii. Que Education & Training Staff. 1997. teacher ed. 39.99 (*1-57576-870-4*) Que Educ & Trng.

PowerPoint 97 Essentials Level I Level 1. 189p. 1997. teacher ed., spiral bd. 49.99 (*1-57576-786-4*) Que Educ & Trng.

PowerPoint 97 Essentials Level II. Linda Bird. LC 97-65621. 192p. 1997. 22.99 (*1-57576-802-X*) Sams.

PowerPoint 97 Smartstart. Que Education & Training Staff. 1997. teacher ed. 39.99 (*1-57576-821-6*) Que Educ & Trng.

PowerPoint97 Quick Reference. Que Development Group Staff. 300p. 1997. 16.99 (*0-7897-1268-7*) Que.

***PowerPoints.** Simon & Schuster Staff. (C). 2000. write for info. (*0-13-013388-4*) S&S Trade.

PowerPoints. 2nd ed. Ed. by Prentice-Hall Staff. (C). 1999. text. write for info. (*0-13-010289-X*) P-H.

***PowerPoints.** 8th ed. Simon & Schuster Staff. (C). 1999. write for info. (*0-13-013663-8*) S&S Trade.

***Powerprep Software: Test Preparation for the Computer-Adaptive GMAT, Version 3.0.** 2000. pap. write for info. (*0-446-39659-1*) Warner Bks.

***Powerprep Software: Test Preperation for the GRE General Test, Version 2.0.** Educational Testing Service Staff. 1999. pap. text 45.00 incl. cd-rom (*0-446-39656-7*) Warner Bks.

***Powerpuff Girls.** CEDCO Publishing Staff. (Illus.). (J). 2000. 14.95 (*0-7683-2229-4*) CEDCO Pub.

***Powerpuff Girls.** Golden Books Staff. 2000. pap. text 2.99 (*0-307-20212-7*); pap. text 2.99 (*0-307-25736-3*) Gldn Bks Pub Co.

***Powerpuff Girls.** Golden Books Staff. (Illus.). (J). 2000. pap. 2.99 (*0-307-28328-3*, Goldn Books) Gldn Bks Pub Co.

***Powerpuff Girls: Super Shape Book.** (Illus.). 24p. (J). 2000. pap. text. write for info. (*0-307-13330-3*) Gldn Bks Pub Co.

***Powerpuff Girls Ruff n' Tuff Tattoo Book.** Scholastic Books Staff. (Powerpuff Girls Ser.). (Illus.). 32p. (J). (ps-3). 2000. mass mkt. 5.99 (*0-439-16016-2*) Scholastic Inc.

***Powerpuff Girls Save the Day.** Scholastic Books Staff. (Powerpuff Girls Ser.). (Illus.). 32p. (J). (ps-3). 2000. mass mkt. 5.99 (*0-439-16015-4*) Scholastic Inc.

Power/Resistance: Local Politics & the Chaotic State. Andrew Kirby. LC 92-41702. 212p. 1993. 27.50 (*0-253-33144-7*) Ind U Pr.

Power/Resistance: Local Politics & the Chaotic State. Andrew Kirby. LC 92-41702. 199p. Date not set. reprint ed. pap. 61.70 (*0-608-20554-0*, 2054468) Bks Demand.

***Powers & Activities of Man's Spirit.** Harold R. Eberle. Ed. by Annette Bradley & Dennis Bradley. LC 97-60374. (Spiritual Realities Ser.: Vol. 4). 146p. 1998. pap. 9.95 (*1-882523-12-1*) Winepress Pubng.

Powers & Duties Cases. 20p. 1993. 15.00 (*0-317-05922-X*, PB-03) Natl Attys General.

Powers & Duties of Magistrates. B. R. Beotra. (C). 1990. 175.00 (*0-89771-188-2*) St Mut.

Powers & Duties of Police Officers & Coroners. Robert H. Vickers. LC 74-156034. (Foundations of Criminal Justice Ser.). reprint ed. 34.50 (*0-404-09136-9*) AMS Pr.

Powers & Duties of Women. Horace Mann. (Notable American Authors Ser.). 1999. reprint ed. lib. bdg. 125.00 (*0-7812-3938-9*) Rprt Serv.

Powers & Jurisdiction of Criminal Courts & Criminal Trials. 1034p. 1973. 130.00 (*0-7855-7564-2*) St Mut.

Powers & Pantheons Lorebook. Eric L. Boyd. (Forgotten Realms Game World Ser.). 1997. 21.95 (*0-7869-0657-X*, Pub. by TSR Inc) Random.

Powers & Prospects: Reflections on Human Nature & the Social Order. Noam Chomsky. 244p. 1996. 40.00 (*0-89608-536-8*); pap. 16.00 (*0-89608-535-X*) South End Pr.

Powers & the Middle East: The Ultimate Strategic Arena. Ed. by Bernard Reich. LC 86-21266. 361p. 1986. 49.95 (*0-275-92304-5*, C2304, Praeger Pubs) Greenwood.

Powers at Play. Bliss Perry. LC 74-110209. (Short Story Index Reprint Ser.). 1977. 20.95 (*0-8369-3360-5*) Ayer.

Powers, Duties & Operations of State Attorneys General, 5 pts. (Illus.). 404p. 1977. 10.00 (*0-318-15221-5*) Natl Attys General.

Powers, Duties, Liabilities of Corporate Officers & Directors. 32p. 1983. 2.00 (*0-686-89213-5*, 68687-3) P-H.

Powers Latent in Man. Douglas M. Baker. 1977. pap. 12.00 (*0-906006-76-7*, Pub. by Baker Pubns) New Leaf Dist.

Powers Matchless: The Pontificate of Urban VIII, the Baldachin, & Gian Lorenzo Bernini. Chandler W. Kirwin. LC 95-13793. (Hermeneutics of Art Ser.: No. 6). (Illus.). XXVIII, 476p. (C). 1997. pap. text 45.95 (*0-8204-2822-1*) P Lang Pubng.

Powers Northeast Golf Guide, 1993. William Anderson. 250p. 1992. pap. 14.95 (*0-9631658-1-X*) Briarcliff NY.

Powers Northeast Region Golf Guide, 1994. Briarcliff Press Staff. 1993. pap. 14.95 (*0-9631658-2-8*) Briarcliff NY.

Powers of Art: Patronage in Indian Culture. Ed. by Barbara S. Miller. (Illus.). 364p. 1992. text 19.95 (*0-19-562842-X*) OUP.

Powers of Attorney. Mimi Latt. Ed. by Julie Rubenstein. 544p. 1994. reprint ed. per. 5.99 (*0-671-86916-7*) PB.

Powers of Attorney: A Practical Guide. John Thurston. 217p. 1991. 60.00 (*1-85190-135-3*, Pub. by Tolley Pubng) St Mut.

Powers of AutoCAD. Milt McGrew. (CAD/CAM Ser.). 1990. pap., teacher ed. 16.00 (*0-8273-3695-0*) Delmar.

P

Powers of Being: David Holbrook & His Work. Ed. by Edwin Webb. LC 94-23698. (Illus.). 288p. 1995. 39.50 (*0-8386-3529-6*) Fairleigh Dickinson.

***Powers of Charlotte.** Jane Lazarre. LC 00-21649. (Orig.). 2000. write for info. (*1-891305-53-0*) Painted Leaf.

Powers of Congress. R. Conrad Stein. LC 94-36913. (Cornerstones to Freedom Ser.). (Illus.). 32p. (J). (gr. 4-7). 1995. lib. bdg. 19.50 (*0-516-06696-X*) Childrens.

***Powers of Darkness.** (In Classical Mood Ser.: Vol. 58). (Illus.). 30p. 1999. write for info. (*1-892207-11-7*) Intl Masters Pub.

Powers of Darkness: Principalities & Powers in Paul's Letters. Clinton E. Arnold. LC 91-33075. 234p. (Orig.). 1992. pap. 13.99 (*0-8308-1336-5*, 1336) InterVarsity.

Powers of Desire: The Politics of Sexuality. Ed. by Ann Snitow et al. LC 82-48037. (New Feminist Library). 448p. 1983. pap. 22.00 (*0-85345-610-0*, Pub. by Monthly Rev) NYU Pr.

Powers of Evil: A Biblical Study of Satan & Demons. Sydney H. T. Page. LC 95-18467. 296p. 1994. pap. 19.99 (*0-8010-7137-2*) Baker Bks.

Powers of Expression, Expressions of Power: Speech Presentation in Latin Literature. Andrew Laird. LC 98-52497. (Oxford Classical Monographs Ser.). 382p. 2000. text 85.00 (*0-19-815276-0*) OUP.

Powers of Freedom: Reframing Political Thought. Nikolas Rose. LC 98-40306. 320p. (C). 1999. text 59.95 (*0-521-65075-5*); pap. text 22.95 (*0-521-65905-1*) Cambridge U Pr.

Powers of Genre: Interpreting Haya Oral Literature. Peter Seitel. LC 98-47851. (Oxford Studies in Anthropological Linguistics: No. 22). 264p. 1999. text 55.00 (*0-19-511700-X*) OUP.

Powers of Healing. (Mysteries of the Unknown Ser.). (Illus.). 160p. 1989. lib. bdg. 23.27 (*0-8094-6369-5*) Time-Life.

Powers of Horror: An Essay on Abjection. Julia Kristeva. Tr. by Leon S. Roudiez from FRE. LC 82-4481. (European Perspectives Ser.). 248p. 1984. reprint ed. pap. text 20.00 (*0-231-05347-9*) Col U Pr.

Powers of Hypnosis. Jean Dauven. (Illus.). 254p. 1980. pap. 5.95 (*0-8128-1391-X*, Scrbrough Hse) Madison Bks UPA.

Powers of Imagining: Ignatius de Loyola: A Philosophical Hermeneutic of Imagining Through the Collected Works of Ignatius de Loyola. Antonio T. de Nicolas. LC 85-2739. 390p. (C). 1986. pap. text 19.95 (*0-88706-110-9*) State U NY Pr.

Powers of Investigation in Revenue, Companies & Trade Practices Law. J. B. Kluver & R. H. Woellner. 1983. 94.00 (*0-409-49381-3*, AT, MICHIE) LEXIS Pub.

Powers of Knowledge. Ronald E. Puhek. 83p. 1998. pap. 10.00 (*1-892590-04-2*) Out Your Bk.

Powers of Literacy: A Genre Approach to Teaching Writing. Ed. by Bill Cope & Mary Kalantzis. (Series in Composition, Literacy, & Culture). 296p. (C). 1993. pap. 19.95 (*0-8229-6104-0*); text 49.95 (*0-8229-1179-5*) U of Pittsburgh Pr.

Powers of Music: Aesthetic Theory & the Invention of Opera. rev. ed. Ruth Katz. LC 94-1960. 224p. (C). 1994. pap. 21.95 (*1-56000-747-8*) Transaction Pubs.

Powers of Observation: Alternative Views in Archeology. Ed. by Sarah M. Nelson & Alice B. Kehoe. 1990. write for info. (*0-913167-42-8*) Am Anthro Assn.

Powers of Observation: Familiar Essays. George Woodcock. 128p. 1989. pap. 12.95 (*0-919627-15-3*, Pub. by Quarry Pr) LPC InBook.

Powers of Persuasion: The Malaysian Media in the Pergau Dam Affair. Roger Kershaw. LC 98-146671. (Monographs on South-East Asian Politics & International Relations). iii, 57 p. 1997. write for info. (*0-85958-907-2*) Univ of Hull Pr.

Powers of Preservation: New Life for Historic Structures. Arthur C. Moore. LC 98-2784. (Illus.). 256p. 1998. 59.95 (*0-07-043394-1*) McGraw.

Powers of Speech: The Politics of Culture in the GDR. David Bathrick. LC 95-2354. (Modern German Culture & Literature Ser.). x, 303p. 1995. text 50.00 (*0-8032-1258-5*) U of Nebr Pr.

Powers of Tamil Women. Intro. by Susan S. Wadley. (South Asian Ser.). 192p. (Orig.). (C). 1991. reprint ed. text 9.00 (*0-915984-42-3*) Maxwell Schl Citizen.

Powers of Ten: About the Relative Size of Things in the Universe. Philip Morrison et al. LC 82-5504. (Illus.). 159p. (C). 1994. pap. 19.95 (*0-7167-6008-8*) W H Freeman.

Powers of Ten: About the Relative Size of Things in the Universe. Morrison et al. LC 82-5504. (Scientific American Library). (Illus.). 164p. (C). 1991. VHS 39.95 (*0-7167-5029-5*) W H Freeman.

Powers of the Crown: A. D. 1600 - 1700 see TimeFrame Series

Powers of the Crown: Time Frame: AD 1600-1700. Time-Life Books Editors. (Time Frame Ser.). (Illus.). 176p. 1990. lib. bdg. write for info. (*0-8094-6455-1*) Time-Life.

Powers of the Holy: Religion, Politics, & Gender in Late Medieval English Culture. David Aers & Lynn Staley. LC 95-25309. 1996. 55.00 (*0-271-01541-1*); pap. 19.95 (*0-271-01542-X*) Pa St U Pr.

Powers of the Mind. Brian Innes. LC 98-30154. (Unsolved Mysteries Ser.). 1999. 24.26 (*0-8172-5488-9*) Raintree Steck-V.

Powers of the Mind. Brian Innes. (Unsolved Mysteries Ser.). 48p. (J). (gr. 3). 1999. pap. 6.95 (*0-8172-5850-7*) Raintree Steck-V.

Powers of the New York Court of Appeals. Henry Cohen & Arthur Karger. LC 92-81351. 1026p. 1992. reprint ed. 125.00 (*0-89941-790-6*, 307510) W S Hein.

Powers of the Orishas. Migene Gonzalez-Wippler. 136p. 1992. 8.95 (*0-942272-25-0*) Original Pubns.

Powers of the Past: Reflections on the Crisis & the Promise of History. Harvey J. Kaye. 224p. (C). 1992. pap. 15.95 (*0-8166-2121-7*) U of Minn Pr.

Powers of the Presidency. 2nd ed. LC 97-503. 294p. (YA). (gr. 11). 1997. text 29.95 (*1-56802-310-3*) Congr Quarterly.

Powers of the President As Commander-in-Chief of the Army & Navy of the United States. Dorothy Schaffter & Dorothy Mathews. LC 76-172099. (American Constitution & Legal History Ser.). xi, 145p. 1974. reprint ed. lib. bdg. 24.50 (*0-306-70615-6*) Da Capo.

Powers of the Press: Newspapers, Power & the Public in Nineteenth-Century England. Aled Jones. LC 95-53260. 1996. 86.95 (*1-85928-132-X*, Pub. by Scolar Pr) Ashgate Pub Co.

Powers of the Press: Twelve of the World's Influential Newspapers. Martin Walker. LC 84-10975. 416p. 1984. reprint ed. pap. 12.95 (*0-915361-10-8*) Lambda Pubs.

Powers of the Psalms. Anna Riva. 128p. (Orig.). 1982. pap. 4.95 (*0-943832-07-1*) Intl Imports.

Powers of the Rational: Science, Technology, & the Future of Thought. Dominique Janicaud. Tr. by Peg Birmingham & Elizabeth Birmingham from FRE. LC 94-6693. (Studies in Continental Thought).Tr. of Puissance du Rationnel. 308p. 1995. 39.95 (*0-253-33108-0*) Ind U Pr.

Powers of the Supreme Court. R. Conrad Stein. LC 94-38266. (Cornerstones to Freedom Ser.). (Illus.). 32p. (J). (gr. 5-7). 1995. lib. bdg. 19.50 (*0-516-06697-8*) Childrens.

Powers of the Word. Rene Daumal. Tr. by Mark Polizzotti from FRE. 192p. (Orig.). 1991. pap. 12.95 (*0-87286-259-3*) City Lights.

Powers of Their Own. McLaughlin. 1999. 27.50 (*0-06-016781-5*) HarperTrade.

Powers of Thought. 2nd ed. Omraam M. Aivanhov. LC 91-70253. (Izvor Collection: No. 224). 230p. 1991. reprint ed. pap. 7.95 (*0-911857-08-7*) Prosveta USA.

Powers, Possessions, & Freedom: Essays in Honour of C. B. Macpherson. Ed. by Alkis Kontos. LC 80-45716. 186p. reprint ed. pap. 57.70 (*0-7837-4289-4*, 204398100012) Bks Demand.

***Powers That Be.** David Halberstam. 792p. 2000. 24.95 (*0-252-06941-2*) U of Ill Pr.

Powers That Be. Anne McCaffrey & Elizabeth A. Scarborough. 384p. 1994. mass mkt. 5.99 (*0-345-38779-1*, Del Rey) Ballantine Pub Grp.

***Powers That Be: Discover the Amazing Powers of the Energies Around You.** Deborah Cannarella. (Illus.). 120p. 1999. pap. 25.00 (*0-88363-931-9*, Pub. by H L Levin) Publishers Group.

***Powers That Be: Pridi Banomyong Through the Rise & Fall of Thai Democracy.** Sulak Sivaraksa. 2000. pap. 12.00 (*974-7449-18-8*, Pub. by CPNCOCAPB) Lantern Books.

Powers That Be: Theology for a New Millennium. Walter Wink. 240p. 1999. pap. 12.95 (*0-385-48752-5*) Doubleday.

Powers That Be (1935) Alexander Cannon. 210p. 1998. reprint ed. pap. 19.95 (*0-7661-0376-5*) Kessinger Pub.

Powers That Make Us Human: The Foundations of Medical Ethics. Ed. by Kenneth Vaux. LC 84-28028. 152p. 1986. text 21.95 (*0-252-01187-2*) U of Ill Pr.

Powers That Punish: Prison & Politics in the Era of the "Big House," 1920-1955. Charles Bright. LC 96-9954. (Law, Meaning, & Violence Ser.). 336p. (C). 1996. text 49.50 (*0-472-10732-1*, 10732) U of Mich Pr.

Powers That Shape: Memories, Images, & Fables. Bill Thrash. 240p. 1995. 22.00 (*0-9645061-3-0*) Billy Arts.

Powers That Turn Failure into Success. Brown Landone. 73p. 1985. reprint ed. spiral bd. 11.00 (*0-7873-1250-9*) Hlth Research.

Powers Which We Do Not Know: The Gods & Spirits of the Inuit. Daniel Merkur. LC 91-6394. 288p. (C). 1991. pap. 22.95 (*0-89301-148-7*) U of Idaho Pr.

***Powers Within.** Sri Aurobindo. 196p. 1999. pap. text 5.95 (*0-941524-96-5*) Lotus Pr.

Powers 1995 Northeast Region Golf Guide. Briarcliff Press Staff. 1994. pap. 16.95 (*0-9631658-3-6*) Briarcliff NY.

Powers 1996 Northeast Region Golf Guide. Briarcliff Press Staff. 1995. pap. text 16.95 (*0-9631658-4-4*) Briarcliff NY.

Powersharing: White House-Cabinet Relations in the Modern Presidency. Shirley Anne Warshaw. LC 95-16871. (SUNY Series on the Presidency). 380p. (C). 1996. pap. text 24.95 (*0-7914-2870-2*) State U NY Pr.

Powersharing: White House-Cabinet Relations in the Modern Presidency. Shirley Anne Warshaw. LC 95-16871. (SUNY Series on the Presidency). 380p. (C). 1996. text 74.50 (*0-7914-2869-9*) State U NY Pr.

Powershift: Knowledge, Wealth, & Violence at the Edge of the 21st Century. Alvin Toffler. 640p. 1991. mass mkt. 7.99 (*0-553-29215-3*) Bantam.

***Powerskills: Building Top-Level Relationships for Bottom-Line Results.** James P. Masciarelli. LC 99-69863. 336p. 2000. 29.95 (*0-9677111-1-8*) Nimbus Pr MA.

Powerspeak. Dorothy Leeds. 1991. mass mkt. 6.99 (*0-425-12489-4*) Berkley Pub.

PowerSpeaking: How Ordinary People Can Make Extraordinary Presentations. 3rd ed. Frederick Gilbert. 1998. pap. 15.95 (*0-9629272-7-9*) F Gilbert Assocs.

Powerstones. Linda Ching & Robin Stephens. 25.00 (*0-9619891-4-9*) Hawaiian Goddesses.

Powertalk. Therese Halscheid. 68p. 1995. pap. 8.95 (*0-9654798-0-3*) T Halscheid.

PowerTalk, Bk. 1. Edwin T. Cornelius, Jr. (PowerTalk Video Ser.). (Illus.). 150p. 1988. pap. text 9.95 (*0-89209-970-4*); audio 12.00 (*0-89209-947-X*); audio 12.00 (*0-89209-948-8*); digital audio 12.00 (*0-89209-946-1*); VHS 59.95 (*0-89209-916-X*); VHS 59.95 (*0-89209-917-8*); VHS 59.95 (*0-89209-918-6*) Pace Grp Intl.

PowerTalk, Bk. 2. Edwin T. Cornelius. (PowerTalk Video Ser.). (Illus.). 133p. 1988. pap. text 9.95 (*0-89209-971-2*); audio 12.00 (*0-89209-950-X*); audio 12.00 (*0-89209-951-8*); digital audio 12.00 (*0-89209-949-6*); VHS 59.95 (*0-89209-919-4*); VHS 59.95 (*0-89209-920-8*); VHS 59.95 (*0-89209-921-6*) Pace Grp Intl.

PowerTalk, Bk. 3. Edwin T. Cornelius, Jr. (PowerTalk Video Ser.). (Illus.). 133p. 1988. pap. text 9.95 (*0-89209-972-0*); audio 12.00 (*0-89209-952-6*); audio 12.00 (*0-89209-953-4*); audio 12.00 (*0-89209-954-2*); VHS 59.95 (*0-89209-922-4*); VHS 59.95 (*0-89209-923-2*); VHS 59.95 (*0-89209-924-0*) Pace Grp Intl.

PowerTalk, Bk. 4. Edwin T. Cornelius, Jr. (PowerTalk Video Ser.). (Illus.). 197p. 1988. pap. 9.95 (*0-89209-973-9*); audio 12.00 (*0-89209-955-0*); audio 12.00 (*0-89209-956-9*); audio 12.00 (*0-89209-957-7*); audio 12.00 (*0-89209-958-5*); VHS 59.95 (*0-89209-925-9*); VHS 59.95 (*0-89209-926-7*); VHS 59.95 (*0-89209-927-5*) Pace Grp Intl.

Powerticians: Politics & Social Life in Jersey City. Thomas F. Smith. (Illus.). 256p. 1982. 15.00 (*0-8184-0328-4*) Carol Pub Group.

Powertown. Michael Lind. 1997. mass mkt. write for info. (*0-06-101219-X*, Harp PBks) HarpC.

PowerTrace: User Manual. 247p. 1998. pap. write for info. (*1-892267-01-2*) AccelSoft.

***Powertrain Systems NVH.** (Special Publications). 124p. 2000. 69.00 (*0-7680-0565-5*, SP-1515) Soc Auto Engineers.

Powertrain Tribology. 100p. 1998. pap. 45.00 (*0-7680-0229-X*, SP-1372) Soc Auto Engineers.

PowerUp with Excel 5 for Windows. 5th ed. Joseph Otto & Garry L. Nordenstam. 448p. 1994. text 28.95 incl. 3.5 hd (*1-56118-617-1*) Paradigm MN.

PowerUp with Lotus 5 for Windows. 5th ed. Joseph Otto & Garry L. Nordenstam. 428p. 1996. text 28.95 incl. 3.5 hd (*1-56118-615-5*) Paradigm MN.

Powerwalking. Steve Reeves & James A. Peterson. LC 81-18184. 1982. pap. write for info. (*0-672-52713-8*) Macmillan.

Powerwebb. Sylvia Sieling. Date not set. pap. 10.99 (*1-56813-201-8*) Madera Cinevideo.

PowerWords SAT Cartoon Verbal Prep. 2nd ed. Edith L. Sennet & Carole L. Sarnoff. (Illus.). 78p. 1992. reprint ed. 9.95 (*1-879871-05-X*) Sennet Lrn Sys.

PowerWords SAT Cartoon Verbal Prep, Bk. 2. 2nd ed. Edith L. Sennet & Carole L. Sarnoff. (Illus.). 78p. 1992. reprint ed. 9.95 (*1-879871-06-8*) Sennet Lrn Sys.

PowerWords SAT Cartoon Verbal Prep, Vol. 3. 2nd ed. Edith L. Sennet & Carole L. Sarnoff. (Illus.). 78p. 1992. reprint ed. 9.95 (*1-879871-07-6*) Sennet Lrn Sys.

PowerWriting. Marlene Caroselli. LC 88-92374. 74p. (Orig.). (C). 1988. pap. 9.95 (*0-922411-00-X*) CPD NY.

Powerwus. Jason Marcy & Jeremy Kaposy. Ed. by Ron Gravelle. (Illus.). 104p. (YA). 1999. pap. 12.95 (*0-9662984-4-6*) Landwaster Bks.

***Powhatan Cemetery Internment & Lot Records of Powhatan Point, Ohio.** Tr. by Ellen Carpenter Massey. LC 99-61483. 344p. 1999. pap. 19.95 (*0-89725-370-1*) Picton Pr.

Powhatan County Marriages, 1777-1830. Catherine L. Knorr. 110p. 1983. reprint ed. 15.00 (*0-89308-258-9*, VA 21) Southern Hist Pr.

Powhatan County, Virginia Marriages, 1777-1850. John Vogt & T. William Kethley, Jr. 161p. 1985. pap. 12.95 (*0-935931-12-0*) Iberian Pub.

Powhatan Foreign Relations, 1500-1722. Ed. by Helen C. Rountree. LC 92-21942. (Illus.). 328p. 1993. text 35.00 (*0-8139-1409-4*) U Pr of Va.

Powhatan Indians see Junior Library of American Indians

Powhatan Indians. Bill Lund. (Native Peoples Ser.). (J). 1998. 14.00 (*0-516-21356-3*) Childrens.

Powhatan Indians of Virginia: Their Traditional Culture. Helen C. Rountree. LC 88-27905. (Civilization of the American Indian Ser.: Vol. 193). (Illus.). 232p. 1992. pap. 13.95 (*0-8061-2455-5*) U of Okla Pr.

Powhatan People. Kim Covert. LC 98-7269. (Native Peoples Ser.). (J). 1998. 14.00 (*0-7368-0078-6*, Bridgestone Bks) Capstone Pr.

Powhatan, Salem & Courtney Henrico Artillery. Richard L. Nicholas & Joseph Servis. (Virginia Regimental Histories Ser.). (Illus.). 246p. 1998. 25.00 (*1-56190-104-0*) H E Howard.

Powhatan's Mantle: Indians in the Colonial Southeast. Ed. by Peter H. Wood et al. LC 88-20630. (Indians of the Southeast Ser.). (Illus.). xviii, 355p. 1989. reprint ed. pap. text 30.00 (*0-8032-9727-0*, Bison Books) U of Nebr Pr.

Powhatan's World & Colonial Virginia: A Conflict of Cultures. Frederic W. Gleach. LC 96-32723. (Studies in the Anthropology of North American Indians). (Illus.). ix, 243p. 1997. text 65.00 (*0-8032-2166-5*) U of Nebr Pr.

Powles: The Mareva Injunction & Associated Orders. David G. Powles. 1985. boxed set 48.00 (*0-86205-069-3*, MICHIE) LEXIS Pub.

***Pownall: Plays One.** David Pownall. 340p. 2000. pap. 20.95 (*1-84002-076-8*) Theatre Comm.

Powstanie Warszawskie W Walce I Dyplomacji. J. K. Zawodny. 303p. 1944. pap. 16.00 (*0-614-02656-3*) Szwede Slavic.

Powtech 75: Proceedings of the International Powder Technology & Bulk Solids Conference, 3rd, 1975. 3rd ed. International Powder Technology & Bulk Solids Conf. LC TA0418.78.I5. (Powder Technology Publication: No. 6). 94p. reprint ed. pap. 30.00 (*0-608-12553-9*, 202403800035) Bks Demand.

Powtech, 71: Proceedings of the International Powder Technology & Bulk Solids Conference, 1st, Harrogate, England, 1971. International Powder Technology & Bulk Solids Conf. Ed. by A. S. Goldberg. LC TA0418.78.I5. (Powder Technology Publication: No. 1). 277p. reprint ed. pap. 85.90 (*0-608-12653-5*, 202403600035) Bks Demand.

Powtech 73 Papers-Particulate Matter: Proceedings of the International Powder Technology & Bulk Solids Conference, Harrogate, England, 1973. International Powder Technology & Bulk Solids Conf. Ed. by A. S. Goldberg. LC TA0418.78.I5. (Powder Technology Publication: No. 2). 110p. reprint ed. pap. 34.10 (*0-608-12658-6*, 202403700035) Bks Demand.

Powwow. Photos by George Ancona. LC 92-15912. (Illus.). 48p. (J). (gr. 1-7). 1993. 17.00 (*0-15-263268-9*) Harcourt.

Powwow. George Ancona. LC 92-15912. (Illus.). 48p. (C). (gr. 1-7). 1993. pap. 9.00 (*0-15-263269-7*) Harcourt.

Powwow. Terry Behrens. LC 83-7274. (Special Holiday Bks.). (Illus.). 32p. (J). (gr. k-4). 1983. pap. 4.95 (*0-516-42387-8*) Childrens.

Powwow. George P. Capture. LC 90-80178. (Illus.). 64p. 1989. pap. 7.50 (*0-931618-29-0*) Buffalo Bill Hist Ctr.

Powwow: A Good Day to Dance. Jacqueline D. Greene. LC 97-32392. (First Bks.). (Illus.). 63p. (YA). (gr. 1-5). 1998. lib. bdg. 22.00 (*0-531-20337-9*) Watts.

Powwow: A Good Day to Dance. Jacqueline D. Greene. LC 97-32392. (Illus.). 64p. (J). (gr. 4-6). 1999. pap. text 6.95 (*0-531-15926-4*) Watts.

Powwow: Images along the Red Road. Photos by Ben Marra. LC 96-6093. (Illus.). 112p. 1996. pap. 16.95 (*0-8109-2680-6*, Pub. by Abrams) Time Warner.

***Powwow ABC.** Sandy Hummingbird. (ps-3). 2000. pap. 4.95 (*1-57067-096-X*) Book Pub Co.

***Powwow Calendar: Guide to Native American Gatherings in the U. S. A. & Canada, 2000.** Liz Campbell. 112p. 1999. pap. 9.95 (*1-57067-084-6*) Book Pub Co.

Powwow Country: People of the Circle. Chris Roberts. 128p. 1998. pap. text 21.95 (*1-56037-124-2*) Am Wrld Geog.

Powwow Highway. David Seals. (Illus.). 230p. (Orig.). 1983. pap. 4.50 (*0-9612274-0-0*) Sky & Sage Bks.

Powwow Highway. rev. ed. David Seals. (Seven Council Fires of Sweet Medicine Ser.: Act 1). (Orig.). 1996. audio 17.00 (*1-887786-27-9*) Sky & Sage Bks.

Powwow Power. James D. Beissel, Sr. Ed. by Joseph M. Rogers. LC 97-94645. 1998. 33.95 (*0-9623159-3-1*) Crystal Educn.

Powwow Summer: A Family Celebrates the Circle of Life. Marcie R. Rendon. (Illus.). (J). (gr. k-3). 1996. pap. 7.95 (*1-57505-011-0*, Carolrhoda) Lerner Pub.

Powwow Summer: A Family Celebrates the Circle of Life. Marcie R. Rendon. LC 95-36777. (Illus.). 1996. lib. bdg. 16.95 (*0-87614-986-7*, Carolrhoda) Lerner Pub.

Powwowing in Union County: A Study of Pennsylvania German Folk Medicine in Context. Barbara L. Reimensnyder. LC 88-35082. (Immigrant Communities & Ethnic Minorities in the U. S. & Canada Ser.: No. 31). 1989. 55.00 (*0-404-19441-9*) AMS Pr.

Powwows: or The Long Lost Friend. rev. ed. John G. Hohman. (Illus.). 80p. (Orig.). reprint ed. pap. 7.95 (*0-9620251-5-1*) Yardbird Bks.

Powys Family. Littleton C. Powys. LC 74-7023. (English Biography Ser.: No. 31). 1974. lib. bdg. 39.00 (*0-8383-1995-5*) M S G Haskell Hse.

***Pox.** Hayden. 2000. 27.50 (*0-465-02881-0*, Pub. by Basic); pap. 17.00 (*0-465-02882-9*, Pub. by Basic) HarpC.

Pox. Robert Hinson. (Illus.). 109p. (YA). (gr. 6-12). 1998. pap. 6.95 (*1-890424-09-9*) Dyn-Novel.

Poyais Bubble. Intro. by James C. Andrews. (Quarterly Review Ser.: Vol. XXVIII). 2157p. 1987. reprint ed. pap. 3.25 (*0-913129-16-X*) La Tienda.

***Poyson Garden: An Elizabethan Mystery.** Karen Harper. 320p. 2000. mass mkt. 5.99 (*0-440-22592-2*) Dell.

Poyson Garden: An Elizabethan Mystery. Karen Harper. LC 99-25694. 1999. write for info. (*1-57490-191-5*, Beeler LP Bks) T T Beeler.

***Pozdnie Ztoety.** Suetlana Boguslavskaya.Tr. of Late Flowers. (RUS., Illus.). 1999. text. write for info. (*0-9673753-3-9*) Gelany.

Poziadavky Na Prijimacie Skusky Pre Osemrocne Gymnazia - Matematika (The Requirements for the Admittance Examinations for 8-Year-Gymnasiums) M. Hanula. (SLO.). 112p. 1997. pap. write for info. (*80-08-02465-8*, Pub. by Slov Pegagog Naklad) IBD Ltd.

Poziadavky Na Prijimacie Skusky Pre Osemrocne Gymnazia - Slovensky Jazyk a Literatura (The Requirements for Admittance Examinations for 8-Year-Gymnasiums) M. Poliakova. (SLO.). 96p. 1996. pap. write for info. (*80-08-02476-3*, Pub. by Slov Pegagog Naklad) IBD Ltd.

***Pozieres.** Graham Keech. 1998. pap. 16.95 (*0-85052-589-6*, Pub. by Leo Cooper) Trans-Atl Phila.

Pozitivny Krestan. Vladimir Uhri. (SLO.). 108p. (Orig.). 1996. pap. 5.50 (*1-56983-024-X*) New Creat WI.

***Pozor: Rozhdenni Molchaniem Upruzhyeskoye Nasiliye v Yevreiskoi Obshchinye.** Abraham J. Twerski. Tr. by Tatyana Margolin.Tr. of Shame Borne in Silence: Spouse Abuse in the Jewish Community. (RUS.). 155p. 2000. pap. 14.95 (*0-9648508-5-0*) Mirkov Pubns.

Pozzolanic & Cementitious Materials. V. M. Malhotra. (Advances in Concrete Technology Ser). 136p. 1996. pap. text 27.00 (*2-88449-211-9*) Gordon & Breach.

P

An Asterisk (*) at the beginning of an entry indicates that the title is appearing for the first time.

Pozzolanic & Cementitious Materials. P. Kumar Mehta & V. M. Malhotra. (Advances in Concrete Technology Ser). 136p. 1996. text 39.00 (*2-88449-235-6*) Gordon & Breach.

PP&L: 75 Years of Powering the Future: An Illustrated History of Pennsylvania Power & Light Co. Bill Beck. 450p. 1995. text. write for info. (*0-9645915-0-2*); pap. text. write for info. (*0-9645915-1-0*) PA Power & Light.

PPC Controller's Tax Guide, 3 vols. Douglas L. Weinbrenner et al. Incl. Vol. 1. 1997. ring bd. Not sold separately (*0-7646-0234-9*); Vol. 2. 1997. ring bd. Not sold separately (*0-7646-0235-7*); Vol. 3. 1997. ring bd. Not sold separately (*0-7646-0236-5*); 145.00 (*0-7646-0233-0*) Prctnrs Pub Co.

PPC GuideWare for Windows. Practitioners Publishing Company Staff. 1996. 72.00 incl. disk (*1-56433-519-4*) Prctnrs Pub Co.

PPC Library Viewer for Windows Learning Guide, Vol. 1. Practitioners Publishing Co. Staff. 1996. write for info. (*0-7646-0076-1*) Prctnrs Pub Co.

***PPC Medical Focus.** Practitioners Publishing Co. Staff. 1998. ring bd. write for info. (*0-7646-0476-7*, HLCN 98) Prctnrs Pub Co.

PPC Tax Planning Guide - Closely Held Corporations, 3 vols. Albert L. Grasso et al. Incl. Vol. 1. PPC Tax Planning Guide - Closely Held Corporations. 1998. ring bd. 180.00 (*0-7646-0480-5*); Vol. 2. PPC Tax Planning Guide - Closely Held Corporations. 1998. ring bd. 180.00 (*0-7646-0481-3*); Vol. 3. PPC Tax Planning Guide - Closely Held Corporations. 1998. ring bd. 180.00 (*0-7646-0482-1*); 180.00 (*0-7646-0479-1*) Prctnrs Pub Co.

PPC Tax Planning Guide - Closely Held Corporations, 3 vols. Albert L. Grasso et al. Incl. Vol. 1. 1997. ring bd. (*0-7646-0206-3*); Vol. 2. 1997. ring bd. (*0-7646-0207-1*); Vol. 3. 1997. ring bd. (*0-7646-0208-X*); 170.00 (*0-7646-0205-5*) Prctnrs Pub Co.

PPC Tax Planning Guide - Closely Held Corporations see PPC Tax Planning Guide - Closely Held Corporations

PPC Tax Planning Guide - Partnerships, 3 vols. Grover A. Cleveland et al. Incl. Vol. 1. PPC Tax Planning Guide - Partnerships. 1998. ring bd. (*0-7646-0474-0*); Vol. 2. PPC Tax Planning Guide - Partnerships. 1998. ring bd. 180.00 (*0-7646-0501-1*); Vol. 3. PPC Tax Planning Guide - Partnerships. 1998. 180.00 (*0-7646-0502-X*); Vol. 1. 1997. ring bd. (*0-7646-0168-7*); Vol. 2. 1997. ring bd. (*0-7646-0169-5*); Vol. 3. 1997. ring bd. (*0-7646-0170-9*); 170.00 (*0-7646-0167-9*); 180.00 (*0-7646-0473-2*) Prctnrs Pub Co.

PPC Tax Planning Guide - Partnerships see PPC Tax Planning Guide - Partnerships

PPC Tax Planning Guide - S Corporations, 3 vols. Andrew R. Biebl et al. Incl. Vol. 1. PPC Tax Planning Guide - S Corporations. George M. Carefoot & John B. Esch. 1998. ring bd. (*0-7646-0470-8*); Vol. 2. PPC Tax Planning Guide - S Corporations. George M. Carefoot & John B. Esch. 1998. ring bd. 180.00 (*0-7646-0471-6*); Vol. 3. PPC Tax Planning Guide - S Corporations. George M. Carefoot & John B. Esch. 1998. ring bd. 180.00 (*0-7646-0472-4*); Vol. 1. Gerorge M. Carefoot & Richard L. Burris. 1997. ring bd. (*0-7646-0176-8*); Vol. 2. Gerorge M. Carefoot & Richard L. Burris. 1997. ring bd. (*0-7646-0177-6*); Vol. 3. George M. Carefoot & Richard L. Burris. 1997. ring bd. (*0-7646-0178-4*); 170.00 (*0-7646-0175-X*); 180.00 (*0-7646-0469-4*) Prctnrs Pub Co.

PPC Tax Planning Guide - S Corporations see PPC Tax Planning Guide - S Corporations

PPC Tax Planning Guide-Closely Held Corporations, 3 vols. Albert L. Grasso et al. Incl. Vol. 1. 1996. ring bd. (*1-56433-957-2*); Vol. 2. 1996. ring bd. (*1-56433-958-0*); Vol. 3. 1996. ring bd. (*1-56433-959-9*); 150.00 (*1-56433-956-4*) Prctnrs Pub Co.

PPC's Accounting Staff Guide. David A. Tolson et al. 1997. ring bd. 99.00 (*0-7646-0224-1*) Prctnrs Pub Co.

PPC's Accounting Staff Guide. David A. Tolson et al. 1998. ring bd. 99.00 (*0-7646-0504-6*) Prctnrs Pub Co.

***PPC'S Business Compliance Guide, Vol. 1.** G. Evan Loper et al. 1998. ring bd. 195.00 (*0-7646-0386-8*) Prctnrs Pub Co.

***PPC'S Business Solutions, Vol. 1.** Stephen W. Lindsey et al. 1999. ring bd. write for info. (*0-7646-0947-5*) Prctnrs Pub Co.

***PPC'S College Financial Aid Seminar Package, Vol. 1.** Rick G. Darvis et al. 1998. ring bd. write for info. (*0-7646-0546-1*) Prctnrs Pub Co.

PPC's Controllership Guide, 4 vols. David A. Tolson et al. Incl. Vol. 1. 1997. ring bd. 170.00 (*0-7646-0370-1*); Vol. 2. 1997. ring bd. 170.00 (*0-7646-0371-X*); Vol. 3. 1997. ring bd. 170.00 (*0-7646-0372-8*); Vol. 4. 1997. ring bd. 170.00 (*0-7646-0373-6*); 140.00 (*0-7646-0369-8*) Prctnrs Pub Co.

***PPC's Controllership Guide, 4 vols.** David A. Tolson et al. 1998. ring bd. 179.00 (*0-7646-0641-7*) Prctnrs Pub Co.

***PPC's Controllership Guide, Vol. 2.** David A. Tolson et al. 1998. ring bd. write for info. (*0-7646-0643-3*) Prctnrs Pub Co.

***PPC's Controllership Guide, Vol. 3.** David A. Tolson et al. 1998. ring bd. write for info. (*0-7646-0644-1*) Prctnrs Pub Co.

***PPC's Controllership Guide, Vol. 4.** David A. Tolson et al. 1998. ring bd. write for info. (*0-7646-0645-X*) Prctnrs Pub Co.

***PPC's Controllership Guide, Vols. 1.** David A. Tolson et al. 1998. ring bd. write for info. (*0-7646-0642-5*) Prctnrs Pub Co.

***PPC'S Eldercare Services Client Seminar, Vol. 1.** Mimi Blanco-Best & Terry W. Lovelace. 1998. ring bd. write for info. (*0-7646-0576-3*) Prctnrs Pub Co.

PPC's 1120 Deskbook, 2 vols. Incl. Vol. 1. PPC's 1120 Deskbook. Michael I. Bernstein. 1999. ring bd. (*0-7646-0938-6*); Vol. 2. PPC's 1120 Deskbook. Michael I. Bernstein. 1999. ring bd. (*0-7646-0939-4*); Vol. 1. 1998. ring bd. (*0-7646-0621-2*); Vol. 2. 1998. ring bd. (*0-7646-0622-0*); 1998. Set ring bd. 150.00i (*0-7646-0620-4*) Prctnrs Pub Co.

***PPC's 1120 Deskbook, 2 vols.** Incl. Vol. 1. PPC's 1120 Deskbook. Michael I. Bernstein. 1999. ring bd. (*0-7646-0938-6*); Vol. 2. PPC's 1120 Deskbook. Michael I. Bernstein. 1999. ring bd. (*0-7646-0939-4*); Vol. 1. 1998. ring bd. (*0-7646-0621-2*); Vol. 2. 1998. ring bd. (*0-7646-0622-0*); 1999. Set ring bd. 150.00i (*0-7646-0937-8*) Prctnrs Pub Co.

PPC's 1120 Deskbook see PPC's 1120 Deskbook

***PPC's 1120S Deskbook, 2 vols.** Andrew R. Biebl et al. Incl. Vol. 1. PPC's 1120S Deskbook. 1999. ring bd. (*0-7646-0908-4*); Vol. 2. PPC's 1120S Deskbook. 1999. ring bd. (*0-7646-0909-2*); 1999. Set ring bd. 150.00 (*0-7646-0907-6*) Prctnrs Pub Co.

PPC's 1120S Deskbook see PPC's 1120S Deskbook

PPC's 1120S Deskbook, Vol. 1. Andrew R. Biebl et al. 1998. ring bd. write for info. (*0-7646-0561-5*) Prctnrs Pub Co.

PPC's 1120S Deskbook, Vol. 2. Andrew R. Biebl et al. 1998. ring bd. write for info. (*0-7646-0562-3*) Prctnrs Pub Co.

PPC's 1120S Deskbook, Vols. 1 & 2. Andrew R. Biebl et al. 1998. ring bd. 150.00 (*0-7646-0560-7*) Prctnrs Pub Co.

***PPC's Engagement Manager Learning Guide.** Practitioners Publishing Co. Staff. 1999. ring bd. 149.00 (*0-7646-0825-8*) Prctnrs Pub Co.

PPC's 5500 DeskBook, 2 vols. Nancy K. Black et al. Incl. Vol. 1. 1998. ring bd. 150.00 (*0-7646-0394-9*); Vol. 2. 1998. ring bd. 150.00 (*0-7646-0395-7*); 150.00 (*0-7646-0393-0*) Prctnrs Pub Co.

***PPC's Financial Advisory Services College.** Practitioners Publishing Co. Staff. 1999. ring bd. write for info. (*0-7646-0869-X*, CURP 99) Prctnrs Pub Co.

PPC's Guide To Audits of Small Businesses, 4 vols. Douglas R. Carmichael et al. Incl. Vol. 1. 1998. ring bd. 164.00 (*0-7646-0427-9*); Vol. 2. 1998. ring bd. 164.00 (*0-7646-0428-7*); Vol. 3. 1998. ring bd. 164.00 (*0-7646-0429-5*); Vol. 4. 1998. ring bd. 164.00 (*0-7646-0430-9*); 164.00 (*0-7646-0426-0*) Prctnrs Pub Co.

PPC's Guide to Audits of Small Businesses, 4 vols. Douglas R. Carmichael et al. Incl. Vol. 1. 1997. ring bd. (*0-7646-0180-6*); Vol. 2. 1997. ring bd. (*0-7646-0181-4*); Vol. 3. 1997. ring bd. (*0-7646-0182-2*); Vol. 4. 1997. ring bd. (*0-7646-0183-0*); 150.00 (*1-56433-947-5*); 156.00 (*0-7646-0179-2*) Prctnrs Pub Co.

***PPC'S Guide to Roth IRAs.** G. Douglas Puckett et al. 1998. ring bd. 153.00 (*0-7646-0619-0*) Prctnrs Pub Co.

PPC's Homeowners' Association Tax Library. Gary A. Porter et al. 1997. ring bd. 125.00 (*0-7646-0210-1*) Prctnrs Pub Co.

***PPC's Homeowners' Association Tax Library.** Gary A. Porter et al. 1999. ring bd. 138.00 (*0-7646-0817-7*) Prctnrs Pub Co.

PPC's 990 DeskBook, 2 vols. Edward K. Kitrosser et al. Incl. Vol. 1. 1998. ring bd. 150.00 (*0-7646-0397-3*); Vol. 2. 1998. ring bd. 150.00 (*0-7646-0398-1*); 150.00 (*0-7646-0396-5*) Prctnrs Pub Co.

PPC's Nonprofit Bookkeepers Guide. Cheryl A. Hartfield et al. 1997. ring bd. 78.00 (*0-7646-0307-8*) Prctnrs Pub Co.

PPC's Nonprofit Financial & Accounting Manual. Cheryl A. Hartfield et al. 1998. ring bd. 85.00 (*0-7646-0483-X*) Prctnrs Pub Co.

***PPC's Nonprofit Financial & Accounting Manual.** Cheryl A. Hartfield et al. 1999. ring bd. 85.00 (*0-7646-0885-1*) Prctnrs Pub Co.

PPC's Payroll Tax Deskbook see PPC's Payroll Tax Deskbook

PPC's Payroll Tax Deskbook, 2 vols. Douglas L. Weinbrenner et al. 1998. ring bd. 150.00i (*0-7646-0528-3*) Prctnrs Pub Co.

***PPC's Payroll Tax Deskbook, 2 vols.** Douglas L. Weinbrenner et al. Incl. PPC's Payroll Tax Deskbook. 1999. ring bd. (*0-7646-0918-1*); Vol. 2. PPC's Payroll Tax Deskbook. 1999. ring bd. (*0-7646-0919-X*); 1999. Set ring bd. 150.00i (*0-7646-0917-3*) Prctnrs Pub Co.

PPC's Payroll Tax Deskbook, 2 vols. Douglas L. Weinbrenner et al. Incl. Vol. 1. 1997. 150.00 (*0-7646-0333-7*); Vol. 2. 1997. 150.00 (*0-7646-0334-5*); Set ring bd. 150.00 (*1-56433-804-5*); Set ring bd. 150.00 (*0-7646-0073-7*); Set ring bd. 150.00 (*0-7646-0332-9*) Prctnrs Pub Co.

PPC's Personal Compliance Guide, 2 vols. Van A. Thaxton et al. Incl. Vol. 1. 1997. ring bd. (*0-7646-0113-X*); Vol. 2. 1997. ring bd. (*0-7646-0114-8*); 170.00 (*0-7646-0112-1*) Prctnrs Pub Co.

PPCs Personnel Compliance Guide, 2 vols. Van A. Thaxton et al. Incl. Vol. 1. 1998. ring bd. 179.00 (*0-7646-0412-0*); Vol. 2. 1998. ring bd. 179.00 (*0-7646-0413-9*); 179.00 (*0-7646-0411-2*) Prctnrs Pub Co.

***PPC's Practitioners Update, Vol. 1.** Don Pallais et al. 1998. ring bd. 135.00 (*0-7646-0601-8*) Prctnrs Pub Co.

PPC's 706/709 Deskbook, 2 vols. Blake T. Smith et al. Incl. Vol. 1. 1997. ring bd. (*0-7646-0156-3*); Vol. 2. 1997. ring bd. (*0-7646-0157-1*); 150.00 (*0-7646-0155-5*) Prctnrs Pub Co.

***PPC's 706/709 Deskbook, 2 vols.** Blake T. Smith et al. 1999. ring bd. 150.00 (*0-7646-0904-1*) Prctnrs Pub Co.

PPC's 706/709 Deskbook, Vol. 1. Blake T. Smith et al. 1998. ring bd. write for info. (*0-7646-0613-1*) Prctnrs Pub Co.

***PPC's 706/709 Deskbook, Vol. 1.** Blake T. Smith et al. 1999. ring bd. write for info. (*0-7646-0905-X*) Prctnrs Pub Co.

PPC's 706/709 Deskbook, Vol. 2. Blake T. Smith et al. 1998. ring bd. write for info. (*0-7646-0614-X*) Prctnrs Pub Co.

***PPC's 706/709 Deskbook, Vol. 2.** Blake T. Smith et al. 1999. ring bd. write for info. (*0-7646-0906-8*) Prctnrs Pub Co.

PPC's 706/709 Deskbook, Vols. 1 & 2. Blake T. Smith et al. 1998. ring bd. 150.00 (*0-7646-0612-3*) Prctnrs Pub Co.

PPC's Small Business Tax Guide, Vol. 1. Douglas L. Weinbrenner et al. 1998. ring bd. write for info. (*0-7646-0515-1*) Prctnrs Pub Co.

PPC's Small Business Tax Guide, Vol. 2. Douglas L. Weinbrenner et al. 1998. ring bd. write for info. (*0-7646-0516-X*) Prctnrs Pub Co.

PPC's Small Business Tax Guide, Vols. 1 & 2. Douglas L. Weinbrenner et al. 1998. ring bd. 125.00 (*0-7646-0514-3*) Prctnrs Pub Co.

PPC's Tax Elections Deskbook. Anthony J. DeChellis et al. LC 98-114127. 1997. ring bd. 150.00 (*0-7646-0351-5*) Prctnrs Pub Co.

***PPC's Tax Elections Deskbook.** Anthony J. DeChellis et al. 1998. ring bd. 150.00i (*0-7646-0654-9*) Prctnrs Pub Co.

***PPC's Tax Elections Deskbook.** Anthony J. DeChellis et al. 1999. ring bd. 150.00i (*0-7646-0927-0*) Prctnrs Pub Co.

PPC's 1040 Deskbook, 2 vols. Andrew R. Biebl et al. Incl. Vol. 1. 1997. ring bd. 150.00 (*0-7646-0263-2*); Vol. 2. 1997. ring bd. 150.00 (*0-7646-0264-0*); 150.00 (*0-7646-0052-4*); 150.00 (*0-7646-0262-4*) Prctnrs Pub Co.

***PPC's 1040 Deskbook, 2 vols.** Andrew R. Biebl et al. 1999. ring bd. 150.00 (*0-7646-0850-9*) Prctnrs Pub Co.

***PPC's 1040 Deskbook, Vol. 1.** Andrew R. Biebl et al. 1999. ring bd. write for info. (*0-7646-0851-7*) Prctnrs Pub Co.

***PPC's 1040 Deskbook, Vol. 2.** Andrew R. Biebl et al. 1999. ring bd. write for info. (*0-7646-0852-5*) Prctnrs Pub Co.

***PPC's 1065 Deskbook, 2 vols.** Incl. Vol. 1. 1998. ring bd. (*0-7646-0552-6*); Vol. 2. 1998. ring bd. (*0-7646-0553-4*); 1998. Set ring bd. 150.00i (*0-7646-0551-8*) Prctnrs Pub Co.

***PPC's 1065 Deskbook, 2 vols.** William R. Bischoff et al. 1999. ring bd. 150.00 (*0-7646-0871-1*) Prctnrs Pub Co.

***PPC's 1065 Deskbook, Vol. 1.** William R. Bischoff et al. 1999. ring bd. write for info. (*0-7646-0872-X*) Prctnrs Pub Co.

***PPC's 1065 Deskbook, Vol. 2.** William R. Bischoff et al. 1999. ring bd. write for info. (*0-7646-0873-8*) Prctnrs Pub Co.

PPC's Trackker Quick Guide. 1997. per. 237.00 incl. cd-rom (*0-7646-0348-5*) Prctnrs Pub Co.

***PPC's 1040 Deskbook, 2 vols.** 1998. ring bd. 150.00i (*0-7646-0557-7*) Prctnrs Pub Co.

PPC's 1041 Deskbook, 2 vols. Hugh H. Sprunt et al. Incl. Vol. 2. PPC's 1041 Deskbook. 1997. ring bd. 150.00 (*0-7646-0330-2*); Vol. 2. 1996. ring bd. Not sold separately (*0-7646-0047-8*); Vol. 1. 1997. ring bd. 150.00 (*0-7646-0329-9*); 150.00 (*0-7646-0045-1*); 150.00 (*0-7646-0328-0*) Prctnrs Pub Co.

PPC's 1041 Deskbook, Vol. 1. Hugh H. Sprunt et al. 1998. ring bd. write for info. (*0-7646-0616-6*) Prctnrs Pub Co.

***PPC's 1041 Deskbook, Vol. 1.** Hugh H. Sprunt et al. 1999. ring bd. write for info. (*0-7646-0786-3*) Prctnrs Pub Co.

PPC's 1041 Deskbook see PPC's 1041 Deskbook

PPC's 1041 Deskbook, Vol. 2. Hugh H. Sprunt et al. 1998. ring bd. write for info. (*0-7646-0617-4*) Prctnrs Pub Co.

***PPC's 1041 Deskbook, Vol. 2.** Hugh H. Sprunt et al. 1999. ring bd. write for info. (*0-7646-0787-1*) Prctnrs Pub Co.

PPC's 1041 Deskbook, Vols. 1 & 2. Hugh H. Sprunt et al. 1998. ring bd. 150.00 (*0-7646-0615-8*) Prctnrs Pub Co.

PPC's 1065 Deskbook, 2 vols. William R. Bischoff et al. Incl. Vol. 1. 1997. 150.00 (*0-7646-0226-8*); Vol. 2. 1997. ring bd. 150.00 (*0-7646-0227-6*); 150.00 (*0-7646-0026-5*); 150.00 (*0-7646-0225-X*) Prctnrs Pub Co.

PPC's 1120 Deskbook, 2 vols. James R. Allen et al. Incl. Vol. 1. 1997. ring bd. 150.00 (*0-7646-0311-6*); Vol. 2. 1997. ring bd. 150.00 (*0-7646-0312-4*); Set ring bd. 150.00 (*0-7646-0041-9*); Set ring bd. 150.00 (*0-7646-0310-8*) Prctnrs Pub Co.

PPC's 1120S Deskbook, 2 vols. Andrew R. Biebel et al. Incl. Vol. 1. 1997. ring bd. 150.00 (*0-7646-0345-0*); Vol. 2. 1997. ring bd. 150.00 (*0-7646-0346-9*); Set ring bd. 150.00 (*0-7646-0344-2*) Prctnrs Pub Co.

PPC's 5500 Deskbook, 2 vols. Andrea L. Dyer et al. Incl. Vol. 1. 1997. ring bd. (*0-7646-0135-0*); Vol. 2. 1997. ring bd. (*0-7646-0136-9*); 150.00 (*1-56433-895-9*); 150.00 (*0-7646-0134-2*) Prctnrs Pub Co.

PPC's 990 Deskbook, 2 vols. Edward W. Kitrosser et al. Incl. Vol. 1. 1997. ring bd. (*0-7646-0120-2*); Vol. 2. 1997. ring bd. (*0-7646-0121-0*); 150.00 (*1-56433-863-0*); 150.00 (*0-7646-0119-9*) Prctnrs Pub Co.

PPE Made Easy: A Comprehensive Checklist Approach to Selecting & Using Personal Protective Equipment. Jeffrey O. Stull. 614p. 1998. pap. text 79.00 (*0-86587-558-8*, 558) Gov Insts.

PPI Detailed Report. Government Printing Office Staff. per. 34.00 (*0-16-011471-3*) USGPO.

PPK 16 CIG Dog Assortment Display. write for info. (*0-02-863520-5*) Macmillan Gen Ref.

PPK 16 CIG Fish-Reptile Assortment Display. write for info. (*0-02-863522-1*) Macmillan Gen Ref.

PPK 16 CIG Pet Assortment Display. write for info. (*0-02-863521-3*) Macmillan Gen Ref.

PPK 12 Pocket Idiot's Guide to Beanie Babies CD. write for info. (*0-02-863081-5*) Macmillan Gen Ref.

PPM Drafting & CAD. 2nd abr. ed. Larkin. 64p. 1996. pap. text, student ed. 12.00 (*0-8273-4625-5*) Delmar.

Ppm For Automotive Technicians 4e. 4th ed. George Moore. (Business Math). (C). 1991. mass mkt. 14.75 (*0-8273-4622-0*) Delmar.

***PPM for Carpenters.** 7th ed. Huth. (C). 2000. pap. 17.25 (*0-7668-2250-8*) Delmar.

PPM for Electronics Technicians. R. Sullivan. (Business/Vocational Math Ser.). 1982. 12.00 (*0-8273-2087-6*) Delmar.

PPM for Electronics Technicians. 3rd ed. Herman. 96p. 1995. text, teacher ed. 17.95 (*0-8273-6762-7*) Delmar.

***PPM for Environmental Technology.** Myers. (Business Math). (C). 2000. pap. 14.25 (*0-7668-0222-1*) Delmar.

PPM for Graphic Communications. 2nd ed. Dennis. 32p. (C). 1998. pap. text, teacher ed. 12.00 (*0-8273-7947-1*); mass mkt. 22.95 (*0-8273-7946-3*) Delmar.

PPM for Heating & Cooling Technicians. 3rd ed. Devore. LC 97-37160. 304p. (C). 1998. mass mkt. 18.95 (*0-8273-7948-X*) Delmar.

PPM for Heating & Cooling Technicians - IML. 3rd ed. Devore. 32p. (C). 1998. teacher ed. 12.00 (*0-8273-7949-8*) Delmar.

PPM for Manufacturing. 4th ed. Davis. 96p. 1995. teacher ed. 21.00 (*0-8273-6711-2*) Delmar.

PPM for Sheet Metal Technicians. F. W. Schumacher. (Business/Vocational Math Ser.). 1973. teacher ed. 12.00 (*0-8273-0288-6*) Delmar.

PPM for Welders. 4th ed. Frank R. Schell. 96p. 1995. text, teacher ed. 17.95 (*0-8273-6707-4*) Delmar.

PPM Industrial Technology. 2nd rev. ed. Donna D. Boatwright. 64p. 1996. pap. text, teacher ed. 12.00 (*0-8273-6975-1*) Delmar.

PPO Directory. Ed. by Medical Economics Staff. (Illus.). 340p. 1999. 215.00 (*1-56363-352-3*, PDR) Med Econ. The 2000 HMO/PPO Directory is an invaluable resource which provides detailed information on over 600 HMO's & more than 1,000 PPO's with listings organized alphabetically by state & city - including name, address, phone number & key decision makers by title & name, plus e-mail addresses whenever available. 100 verified by our Data Verification Group, the book also contains difficult to find details such as: current member enrollments, number of affiliated physicians & affiliated hospitals, average claim compensation categories for both physicians & hospitals; year founded; employer references; federal qualifications; profit or non-profit status; type of HMO/PPO (staff, IPA, group, network) Six cross referenced indexes that include listings alphabetically by organization, by personnel, & by the number of members enrolled. 340 pages, Available: November 1999. (Special combo package of WinHMO/PPO on CD-ROM & print edition also available. ISBN: 1-56363-354-X. $499.00 Call for details.)** ***Publisher Paid Annotation.

***PPO Guide.** Thomas G. Goddard. Ed. by Garry Carneal & Guy D'Andrea. 332p. 1999. 195.00 (*1-930104-01-4*) U R A C.

PPOPP 93: 4th ACM-SIGPLAN Symposium on Principles & Practices of Parallel Programming. 268p. 1993. pap. text 38.00 (*0-89791-589-5*, 551930) Assn Compu Machinery.

PPOPP 97: ACM-SIGPLAN Symposium on Principles & Practices of Parallel Programming. 1997. pap. 42.00 (*0-89791-906-8*, 551970) Assn Compu Machinery.

***PPP & L2TP: Remote Access Communications.** Uyless Black. LC 99-47025. 240p. 1999. 39.99 (*0-13-022462-6*) P-H.

PPP Debugging. James Carlson. LC 97-41553. 240p. (C). 1997. pap. text 29.95 (*0-201-18539-3*) Addison-Wesley.

***PPPPPP: Poems, Performance, Pieces, Prose, Plays Poetics.** Kurt Schwitters. Ed. & Tr. by Pierre Joris & Jerome Rothenberg from GER. 288p. 2000. reprint ed. pap. 15.95 (*1-878972-35-9*, Pub. by Exact Change) Consort Bk Sales.

***PPST: Praxis 1-Pre-Professional Skills Test.** Learning Express Staff. LC 98-24093. 272p. 1998. pap. 18.95 (*1-57685-136-2*) LrningExprss.

PPST: Pre-Professional Skills Test. Ed. by ARCO Editorial Board Staff. 224p. 1991. pap. 14.00 (*0-13-691130-7*, Arco) Macmillan Gen Ref.

PPST - Pre-Professional Skills Test. Research & Education Association Staff. 350p. 2000. pap. text 21.95 (*0-87891-867-1*) Res & Educ.

PPST Essay Guide: A Practice Book for College-Level Standardized Achievement Tests in Writing. Educational Testing Service Staff. (Educational Testing Service Ser.). 1994. pap. 16.00 (*0-446-39573-0*, Pub. by Warner Bks) Little.

PPST Guide: A Practice Book for College-Level Standardized Achievement Tests in Reading, Mathematics, & Writing. rev. ed. Educational Testing Service Staff. 1994. pap. 16.00 (*0-446-39575-7*, Pub. by Warner Bks) Little.

PQLS Math Start Set. 79.75 (*0-06-028854-X*) HarpC.

PQMI: Tips, Experiences & Lessons Learned. 2nd rev. ed. Alfred Watkins. Ed. by Mari-Lynn Hankinson. (AT&T Quality Library). (Illus.). 101p. (Orig.). 1990. pap. 19.95 (*0-932764-33-9*, 500-446) AT&T Customer Info.

PQQ & Quinoproteins. Ed. by J. A. Jongejan & J. A. Duine. (C). 1989. text 202.50 (*0-7923-0248-6*) Kluwer Academic.

PR! A Social History of Spin. Stuart Ewen. 1998. pap. 17.00 (*0-465-06179-6*, Pub. by Basic) HarpC.

P

PR & Communications. Ed. by Jill Muehrcke. (Leadership Ser.). 93p. 1993. spiral bd. 35.00 (*0-614-07104-6*) Soc Nonprofit Org.

PR Client Service Manual: Managing for Results & Profits. 2nd ed. Ed. by Tom Gable. (Illus.). 224p. (Orig.). 1994. pap. 85.00 (*0-9639708-0-1*) Gable Grp.

***PR Cracking the GED 2001.** Princeton Review Publishing Staff. 608p. 2000. pap. 18.00 (*0-375-75619-1*, Pub. by PRP NY) Random.

***PR Cracking the GMAT- CAT 2001.** Princeton Review Publishing Staff. 416p. 2000. pap. 18.00 (*0-375-75623-X*, Pub. by PRP NY) Random.

***PR Cracking the GMAT CAT.** Princeton Review Publishing Staff. 432p. 2000. pap. 34.95 incl. cd-rom (*0-375-75624-8*, Pub. by PRP NY) Random.

***PR Cracking the GRE CAT 2001.** Princeton Review Publishing Staff. 400p. 2000. pap. 20.00 (*0-375-75625-6*, Pub. by PRP NY); pap. 31.00 incl. audio compact disk (*0-375-75626-4*, Pub. by PRP NY) Random.

***PR Cracking the LSAT 2001.** Princeton Review Publishing Staff. 400p. 2000. pap. 20.00 (*0-375-75628-0*, Pub. by PRP NY); pap. 34.95 incl. cd-rom (*0-375-75629-9*, Pub. by PRP NY) Random.

***PR Cracking the SSAT/ISEE 2001.** Princeton Review Publishing Staff. 576p. 2000. pap. 18.00 (*0-375-75630-2*, Pub. by PRP NY) Random.

***PR Crash Course for the GMAT.** Princeton Review Publishing Staff. 208p. 2000. pap. 9.95 (*0-375-75618-3*, Pub. by PRP NY) Random.

***PR Guide to Your Career.** 4th ed. Princeton Review Publishing Staff. 464p. 2000. pap. 21.00 (*0-375-75620-5*, Pub. by PRP NY) Random.

PR Mini Graduate School Guide. 1999. pap. 0.00 (*0-375-75328-1*) Random.

PR News Casebook. Denny Griswold. Ed. by David Bianco. 1796p. (C). 1993. 99.00 (*0-8103-8905-3*, 101568) Gale.

***PR 1996 English Session Laws.** 3600p. 1999. Price not set. (*0-327-09768-X*, 4757917) LEXIS Pub.

***PR 1996 English Session Laws, Vol. 1.** 1150p. 1999. Price not set. (*0-327-09785-X*, 8465517) LEXIS Pub.

***PR 1996 English Session Laws, Vol. 2.** 1050p. 1999. Price not set. (*0-327-09786-8*, 8465617) LEXIS Pub.

***PR 1996 English Session Laws, Vol. 3.** 800p. 1999. Price not set. (*0-327-09787-6*, 8465917) LEXIS Pub.

***PR 1996-1998 Opinions of the Secretary of Justice.** 290p. 1999. Price not set. (*0-327-09769-8*, 4758018) LEXIS Pub.

PR Notebook for School Librarians. Ed. by Robert Graef & Renee Naughton. (Professional Growth Ser.). (Illus.). 244p. 1990. ring bd. 39.95 (*0-938865-01-3*) Linworth Pub.

PR Prototypes: A Guidebook for Promoting Foreign Language Study to the Public. Rosanne G. Royer et al. LC 81-15482. (Language in Education Ser.). vii, 98p. 1981. write for info. (*0-87281-161-1*) Ctr Appl Ling.

PR Set a - Intermediate Acct. 5th ed. Williams et al. 104p. (C). 1995. pap. text, student ed. 22.50 (*0-03-007393-6*) Dryden Pr.

PR Set 1 Financial Accounting. Gary Porter et al. 64p. (C). 1995. student ed. 28.50 (*0-15-501680-6*) Dryden Pr.

Pr-Sl see Milton Encyclopedia

PR 101: The Funniest Course in College. Jim Weakley. LC 77-85116. (Illus.). 144p. 1977. pap. 10.00 (*0-912760-54-0*) Valkyrie Pub Hse.

Prabhakara School of Purva Mimamsa. 2nd rev. ed. Ganganatha Jha. 1978. 12.50 (*0-89684-016-6*, Pub. by Motilal Bnarsidass) S Asia.

Prabhupada Saraswati Thakura: Life & Precepts of Srila. Phillip Murphy. Ed. by Raoul Goff. (Illus.). 164p. 1997. 60.00 (*0-945475-10-1*, 1046, Pub. by Mandala Pub Grp) Words Distrib.

Prabodhasudhakara: The Nectar Ocean of Enlightenment of Sri Sankaracharya. Sri Sankaracharya. Tr. by Samvid from SAN. 94p. 1989. 9.95 (*0-910261-09-1*, Arcana Pubng) Lotus Pr.

Prac Quantitative Doppler, 001. John H. Phillips. (Illus.). 152p. 1991. boxed set 99.95 (*0-8493-4921-4*, RC683) CRC Pr.

Praca S Umeleckym Textom: Metodicka Prirucka Pre Ucitelov 1. Stupna ZS. Rosslerova-Slavikova. (SLO.). 256p. 1997. write for info. (*80-08-01434-2*, Pub. by Slov Pegagog Naklad) IBD Ltd.

Pracatical Sgml. Eric Van Herwijnen. 336p. (C). 1990. pap. text 76.00 (*0-7923-0635-X*) Kluwer Academic.

Prace I Pisma Ksiedza Biskupa Franciszka Hodura, 2 vols. Tom Drugi. (POL.). 145p. (Orig.). (C). 1986. pap. 20.00 (*0-944497-03-9*) Polish Natl Cath Ch.

***Pracl Miracles for Mars & Venus.** John Gray. 2000. pap. 13.00 (*0-06-095827-8*) HarpC.

Pract Compiling w/ Pascal. Mike Rees & David Robson. (Illus.). 256p. (C). 1988. pap. text 29.25 (*0-201-18487-7*) Addison-Wesley.

Pract Real Estate Law/calif 2e. 2nd ed. Daniel F. Hinkel. LC 94-44139. (Paralegal). 666p. (C). 1995. mass mkt. 92.95 (*0-314-04582-1*) West Pub.

Pract Real Estate Law/florida 2e. 2nd ed. Daniel F. Hinkel. LC 94-44138. (Paralegal). 668p. (C). 1995. mass mkt. 58.00 (*0-314-04570-8*) West Pub.

Pract Real Estate Law/new York 2e. 2nd ed. Daniel F. Hinkel. LC 94-44140. (Paralegal). 714p. (C). 1995. mass mkt. 95.95 (*0-314-04571-6*) West Pub.

Pract Real Estate Law/texas 2e. 2nd ed. Daniel F. Hinkel. LC 94-44141. (Paralegal). 672p. (C). 1995. mass mkt. 58.00 (*0-314-04572-4*) West Pub.

Pract Reasoning Ntrl Lang. 3rd ed. S. 1985. pap. text 16.95 (*0-13-692152-3*) P-H.

Pract Test Cassette. D. Phillips. 1988. audio 37.95 (*0-8013-0032-0*, 75697) Longman.

Practcl Gd Neural Netwrk. Marilyn M. Nelson. 368p. 1991. pap. text 39.95 (*0-201-52376-0*) Addison-Wesley.

Practial Design of Masonry Structures. 396p. 1987. 75.00 (*0-7277-0382-X*, Pub. by T Telford) RCH.

Practial Eventing. rev. ed. Sally O'Connor. LC 98-44329. (Illus.). 160p. 1998. 28.95 (*0-939481-52-9*) Half Halt Pr.

Practica Copiosa. Caspar Stromayr. Ed. by Brunn. Tr. & Intro. by Donald Blanchard. (Illus.). 70p. (C). 1989. text 50.00 (*0-9624399-1-6*) Blanchards Brook.

Practica de Jesus see Practice of Jesus

Practica de la Presencia de Dios. Hermano Lawrence.Tr. of Practice of the Presence of God. (SPA.). 96p. 1997. mass mkt. 5.99 (*0-88368-012-2*) Whitaker Hse.

Practica de los Circulos de Control de Calidad. Kaoru Ishikawa. (SPA., Illus.). 248p. (Orig.). 1988. pap. 40.00 (*84-87022-50-2*) Productivity Inc.

Practica Forense Federal. 1992. suppl. ed. 22.00 (*1-56257-114-1*, 84263-10, MICHIE) LEXIS Pub.

Practica Forense Federal. Ed. by Butterworth Staff. 390p. 1992. 40.00 (*0-88063-506-1*, MICHIE) LEXIS Pub.

Practica Forense Puertorriquena, Vols. 1-3. Ed. by LLP Staff. (SPA.). 2260p. 1998. pap. 125.00 (*0-327-05128-0*, 47526-11) LEXIS Pub.

Practica Forense Puertorriquena: Evidencia, Tomo 3. Ed. by Butterworth Staff. 380p. 1993. 35.00 (*0-614-05947-X*, MICHIE) LEXIS Pub.

***Practica Forense Puertorriquena: Evidencia y Disposiciones Procesales Especiales y Reglamentarias, Comentadas y Anotadas.** (SPA.). 659p. 1999. pap. write for info. (*0-327-09503-2*, 4752312) LEXIS Pub.

Practica Forense Puertorriquena: Evidencia y Reglas Miscelaneas, Comentadas y Anotadas. Ed. by Lexis Law Publishing Staff. (SPA.). 670p. 1998. pap. write for info. (*0-327-05127-2*, 47523-11) LEXIS Pub.

Practica Forense Puertorriquena: Procedimiento Civil, Tomo 1. Ed. by Butterworth Staff. 880p. 1993. 35.00 (*0-614-05948-8*, MICHIE) LEXIS Pub.

***Practica Forense Puertorriquena: Procedimiento Civil y Disposiciones Procesales Especiales y Reglamentarias, Comentadas.** (SPA.). 871p. 1999. pap. write for info. (*0-327-09192-4*, 4752112) LEXIS Pub.

Practica Forense Puertorriquena: Procedimiento Criminal, Tomo 2. Ed. by Butterworth Staff. 510p. 1993. 35.00 (*0-614-05949-6*, MICHIE) LEXIS Pub.

Practica Forense Puertorriquena: Procedimiento Criminal, Comentado 7 Anotado. Ed. by Lexis Law Publishing Staff. (SPA.). 670p. 1998. pap. write for info. (*0-327-05126-4*, 47522-11) LEXIS Pub.

***Practica Forense Puertorriquena: Procedimiento Criminal y Disposiciones Procesales Especiales y Reglamentarias, Comentadas.** 726p. 1999. pap. write for info. (*0-327-09193-2*, 4752212) LEXIS Pub.

Practica Forense Puertorriquena No. 1: Procedimiento Civil, Comentado 7 Anotado. Ed. by Lexis Law Publishing Staff. (SPA.). 810p. 1998. pap. write for info. (*0-327-05125-6*, 47521-11) LEXIS Pub.

Practica Forense Puertorriquena, Tomo 1: Tres Tomos Comentados y Anotados, Procedimiento Civil. 880p. 1985. boxed set 35.00 (*0-88063-594-0*, MICHIE) LEXIS Pub.

Practica Forense Puertorriquena, Tomo 1: Tres Tomos Comentados y Anotados, Procedimiento Civil. 1993. suppl. ed. 30.00 (*0-685-74396-9*, MICHIE) LEXIS Pub.

***Practica Forense Puertorriquena Tomo 1 Procedimiento Civil.** 850p. 2000. write for info. (*0-327-11136-4*, 4752113, Lexis Law PR) LEXIS Pub.

Practica Forense Puertorriquena, Tomo 2: Tres Tomos Comentados y Anotados, Procedimiento Criminal. 510p. 1986. boxed set 35.00 (*0-88063-590-8*, MICHIE) LEXIS Pub.

Practica Forense Puertorriquena, Tomo 2: Tres Tomos Comentados y Anotados, Procedimiento Criminal. 1993. suppl. ed. 30.00 (*0-685-74397-7*, MICHIE) LEXIS Pub.

***Practica Forense Puertorriquena Tomo 2 Procedimiento Criminal.** 700p. 2000. write for info. (*0-327-11137-2*, 4752213, Lexis Law PR) LEXIS Pub.

Practica Forense Puertorriquena, Tomo 3: Tres Tomos Comentados y Anotados, Evidencia. 380p. 1983. boxed set 35.00 (*0-88063-595-9*, MICHIE) LEXIS Pub.

Practica Forense Puertorriquena, Tomo 3: Tres Tomos Comentados y Anotados, Evidencia. 1993. suppl. ed. 30.00 (*0-685-74398-5*, MICHIE) LEXIS Pub.

***Practica Forense Puertorriquena Toro 3 Evidencia.** 800p. 2000. write for info. (*0-327-11138-0*, 4752313) LEXIS Pub.

***Practica Juridica - Derecho Procesal Civil.** (SPA.). 1999. pap. write for info. (*0-327-09190-8*, 8290111) LEXIS Pub.

Practica Jurmdica De Puerto Rico -- Derecho Procesal Civil. Rafael Hernandez Colsn. 89.00 (*0-327-12499-7*) LEXIS Pub.

Practica Musicae of Franchinus Gafurius. Franchinus Gafurius. Ed. & Tr. by Irwin Young. LC 69-16113. 311p. reprint ed. pap. 96.50 (*0-8357-3500-1*, 203428200089) Bks Demand.

Practica Musice. fac. ed. Franchinus Gafurius. (Monuments of Music & Music Literature in Facsimile Ser., Series II: Vol. 99). (Illus.). 1979. lib. bdg. 65.00 (*0-8450-2299-7*) Broude.

Practica Para el Examen de Cuidadania. 3rd ed. Carlos F. Paz. (SPA.). 128p. 1990. pap. 8.95 (*0-685-54072-3*, Arco) Macmillan Gen Ref.

Practicable Socialism: Essays on Social Reform. Samuel A. Barnett & Henrietta O. Barnett. LC 72-3394. (Essay Index Reprint Ser.). 1977. reprint ed. 18.95 (*0-8369-2891-1*) Ayer.

***Practical Accelerated Life Testing: Practical Approaches (Tools & Techniques)** James A. McLinn. Ed. & Illus. by Harold W. Williams, Jr. 132p. 2000. 28.00 (*0-9701923-0-4*) Reliability Div.

Practical Account of General Paralysis, Its Mental & Physical Symptoms, Statistics, Causes, Seat, & Treatment. Thomas J. Austin. LC 75-16681. (Classics in Psychiatry Ser.). 1976. reprint ed. 20.95 (*0-405-07413-1*) Ayer.

Practical Accounting & Global Management Kazuo Inamori. 2000. 16.95 (*0-07-135566-9*) McGraw.

Practical Accounting for Business Studies. V. N. Newcomb. LC 82-11103. 380p. reprint ed. pap. 117.80 (*0-608-14908-X*, 202598400048) Bks Demand.

Practical Accounting for Farm & Rural Business. Ben Brown. 192p. 1991. text 34.95 (*0-85236-224-2*, Pub. by Farming Pr) Diamond Farm Bk.

Practical Acoustics. Stephen Kamichik. LC 98-67779. 249p. 1998. pap. text 29.95 (*0-7906-1169-4*) Prompt Publns.

***Practical Action Research: A Collection of Articles.** 2000. write for info. (*1-57517-267-4*) SkyLght.

Practical Action Research for Change. 176p. (C). 1998. pap. 30.00 (*0-205-29268-2*, Longwood Div) Allyn.

Practical Action Research for Change. Richard Schmuck. LC 97-73841. 160p. 1997. pap. 25.95 (*1-57517-041-8*) SkyLght.

Practical Actions for the Social Protection of Homeworkers in Indonesia Lucita Lazo. LC 98-949262. (Out of the Shadows Ser.). iii, 109 p. 1996. write for info. (*92-2-110193-2*) Intl Labour Office.

Practical Actions for the Social Protection of Homeworkers in Indonesia. Lucita Lazo & ILO Regional Office for Asia & the Pacific Staff. LC 98-947402. (From the Shadows to the Fore Ser.). ii, 86p. 1993. write for info. (*92-2-109068-X*) Intl Labour Office.

Practical Actions for the Social Protection of Homeworkers in Thailand. ILO Regional Office for Asia & the Pacific Staff. LC 98-949261. (From the Shadows to the Fore Ser.). ii, 95 p. 1993. write for info. (*92-2-109069-8*) Intl Labour Office.

Practical Actions for the Social Protection of Homeworkers in Thailand Lucita Lazo. LC 98-949260. (Out of the Shadows Ser.). iii, 139p. 1996. write for info. (*92-2-110195-9*) Intl Labour Office.

Practical Actions for the Social Protection of Homeworkers in the Philippines. ILO Regional Office for Asia & Pacific Staff. LC 98-949267. (From the Shadows to the Fore Ser.). ii, 129 p. 1993. write for info. (*92-2-109070-1*) Intl Labour Office.

Practical Activated Sludge Process Control Operator's Guide. Ronald G. Schuyler. Date not set. 59.95 (*0-87371-639-6*, L639) Lewis Pubs.

Practical Activities for Practically Everything. Carole Cook & Jody Carlisle. 1990. 12.99 (*0-8224-5576-5*) Fearon Teacher Aids.

Practical Administrative Law Paralegals. Anne Cohen. LC 95-37729. (Paralegal). 450p. (C). 1996. mass mkt. 87.95 (*0-314-06505-9*) West Pub.

Practical Advice for Meditators. Bhikkhu Khantipalo. 36p. 1986. 1.50 (*955-24-0014-7*, Pub. by Buddhist Pub Soc) Vipassana Res Pubns.

***Practical Advice to Teachers.** rev. ed. Rudolf Steiner. Tr. by Johanna Collis from GER. (Foundations of Waldorf Education Ser.: Vol. 2).Tr. of Erziehungskunst Methodisch-Didaktisches. 224p. 2000. pap. 16.95 (*0-88010-467-8*) Anthroposophic.

Practical Aerodynamics. A. Martynov & V. Brix. LC 63-10019. (International Series of Monographs in Aeronautics & Astronautics: Vol. 4). 1965. 179.00 (*0-08-010137-2*, Pub. by Pergamon Repr) Franklin.

Practical Aircraft Electronic Systems. Albert D. Helfrick. LC 94-26978. 352p. (C). 1994. text 60.80 (*0-13-118803-8*) P-H.

Practical Algebra: A Self-Teaching Guide. 2nd ed. Steven L. Slavin. LC 90-43296. (Self-Teaching Guides Ser.). 336p. 1991. pap. 17.95 (*0-471-53012-3*) Wiley.

Practical Algorithms for Image Analysis: Description, Examples & Code. Michael Seul et al. LC 99-18752. (Illus.). 350p. 2000. 59.95 (*0-521-66065-3*) Cambridge U Pr.

Practical Algorithms for Programmers. Andrew Binstock & John Rex. 592p. (C). 1995. pap. text 34.95 (*0-201-63208-X*) Addison-Wesley.

Practical Algorithms in Pediatric Endocrinology. Ed. by Ze'va Hochberg. LC 98-29290. (Illus.). iv, 104p. 1998. pap. 48.00 (*3-8055-6693-X*) S Karger.

Practical Algorithms in C++ Bryan Flamig. LC 94-32688. 464p. 1995. pap. text 54.99 incl. disk (*0-471-00955-5*) Wiley.

***Practical Allergy.** Milgrom. 2001. pap. text. write for info. (*0-323-01236-1*) Mosby Inc.

Practical Anaesthesia & Analgesia for Day Surgery. J. Millar et al. (Illus.). 256p. (Orig.). 1997. pap. 39.90 (*1-85996-081-2*, Pub. by Bios Sci) Bks Intl VA.

Practical Analog Design Techniques. Ed. by Walt Kester. (Analog Devices Technical Reference Bks.). (Illus.). 428p. (Orig.). 1995. pap. text 30.00 (*0-916550-16-8*) Analog Devices.

Practical Analog Electronics for Technicians. W. A. Kimber. LC 97-172612. 256p. 1997. pap. text 26.95 (*0-7506-2952-5*, Newnes) Buttrwrth-Heinemann.

Practical Analysis & Design for Client-Server & GUI Systems. David A. Ruble. LC 97-9895. 542p. (C). 1997. 54.67 (*0-13-521758-X*) P-H.

Practical Analysis of Advanced Electronic Circuits Through Experimentation. 2nd ed. Lorne MacDonald. 384p. 1984. pap. text 20.00 (*0-911908-18-8*) Tech Ed Pr.

Practical Analysis of Composite Laminates. J. N. Reddy & Antonio Miravete. LC 95-34343. 336p. 1995. boxed set 99.95 (*0-8493-9401-5*, 9401) CRC Pr.

Practical Analysis of Extreme Values. Jan Beirlant et al. (Illus.). 170p. (Orig.). 1996. pap. 52.50 (*90-6186-768-1*, Pub. by Leuven Univ) Coronet Bks.

Practical Analysis of High-Loaded Gears by Using the Modified-Scoring-Index Calculation Method. Manfred Hirt & T. Weib. (1985 Fall Technical Meeting Ser.: Vol. 85FTM3). (Illus.). 28p. 1985. pap. text 30.00 (*1-55589-096-2*) AGMA.

Practical Anatomy of the Rabbit: An Elementary Laboratory Textbook in Mammalian Anatomy. 8th ed. Benjamin A. Bensley. Ed. by E. Horne Craigie. LC 68-9247. 405p. reprint ed. pap. 125.60 (*0-7837-0029-6*, 203401500016) Bks Demand.

Practical & Cost Saving Tips for Parents of Infants & Toddlers. Elizabeth Nordhausen. 1994. pap. 1.99 (*0-614-15343-3*) Dageforde Pub.

Practical & Needful: Dutch Lace Schools, 1850-1940. Patricia Wardle. 1993. 27.50 (*90-6918-096-0*, Pub. by Boymans Mus) U of Wash Pr.

Practical & Organic Building Up of the Church. Witness Lee. 100p. 1989. per. 5.50 (*0-87083-462-2*, 08-019-001) Living Stream Ministry.

Practical & Perplexing Questions Answered see Preguntas Practicas y Dificiles Contestadas

Practical & Simple Guide to a Home Mortgage: A Step-by-Step Guide to Finding & Financing Your Next House. Gary J. Bass. LC 87-82025. 66p. (Orig.). 1987. pap. text 6.95 (*0-944319-00-9*) G & P Pub.

Practical & the Pious: Essays on Thomas Chalmers (1780-1847) A. C. Cheyne. (C). 1988. text 75.00 (*0-7152-0582-X*) St Mut.

Practical & Theological Study of the Book of Acts. 2nd ed. Samuel C. Gipp. ii, 333p. 1994. reprint ed. pap. 15.00 (*1-890120-03-0*) DayStar Pub.

***Practical & Theological Study of the Gospel of John.** 2000. pap. write for info. (*1-890120-11-1*) DayStar Pub.

Practical & Theoretical Aspects of Psychoanalysis. rev. ed. Lawrence S. Kubie. LC 74-6433. 361p. 1975. 55.00 (*0-8236-4181-3*); pap. 24.95 (*0-8236-8193-9*, 24180) Intl Univs Pr.

Practical Anesthesia Information Guide. Raymond Jerome. 127p. 1992. pap. 12.95 (*0-929240-21-9*) EMIS.

Practical Angioplasty. Ed. by David P. Faxon. LC 93-18672. (Illus.). 244p. 1994. reprint ed. pap. 75.70 (*0-608-07228-1*, 206745300009) Bks Demand.

Practical Animal Handling. Andrew T. Edney. (Veterinary Handbook Ser.). (Illus.). 300p. 1991. text 130.00 (*0-08-036151-X*, Pergamon Pr); pap. text 45.00 (*0-08-036152-8*, Pergamon Pr) Elsevier.

Practical Animal Husbandry. T. K. Ewer. (Illus.). 272p. 1982. text 39.95 (*0-85608-026-8*) Blackwell Sci.

Practical Answers to Common Questions about Sex in Marriage. Tim F. LaHaye & Beverly LaHaye. 72p. (Orig.). 1984. pap. 1.70 (*0-310-27042-1*, 18340P) Zondervan.

Practical Antenna Design & Analysis: Computer Programs for the Radio Amateur. R. P. Haviland. (Illus.). (Orig.). 1988. disk 59.95 (*0-685-35368-0*); disk. write for info. (*0-9621208-2-0*); disk. write for info. (*0-9621208-3-9*); disk. write for info. (*0-9621208-4-7*); disk. write for info. (*0-9621208-5-5*) MiniLab Bks.

Practical Antenna Design & Analysis: Computer Programs for the Radio Amateur. Robert P. Haviland. (Illus.). (Orig.). (C). 1988. pap. text 39.95 (*0-9621208-0-4*) MiniLab Bks.

Practical Antenna Handbook. Joseph J. Carr. (Illus.). 416p. 1989. 31.95 (*0-8306-9270-3*); pap. 21.95 (*0-8306-3270-0*) McGraw-Hill Prof.

Practical Antenna Handbook. 2nd ed. Joseph J. Carr. LC 93-44428. 1994. 49.95 (*0-07-011104-9*); pap. 29.95 (*0-07-011105-7*) McGraw-Hill Prof.

Practical Antenna Handbook. 3rd ed. Joseph J. Carr. LC 98-5964. 650p. 1998. pap. 49.95 incl. cd-rom (*0-07-012026-9*) McGraw.

Practical Antenna Handbook. 3rd ed. Joseph J. Carr. LC 98-5964. 574p. 1998. 54.95 incl. cd-rom (*0-07-012027-7*) McGraw.

Practical Anthropometry. 2nd ed. Ales Hrdlicka. LC 71-137243. reprint ed. 41.50 (*0-404-03372-5*) AMS Pr.

***Practical Apartment Management.** 4th ed. Edward N. Kelley. LC 99-34879. (Illus.). 374p. 2000. text 56.95 (*1-57203-032-1*, 909); pap. text 49.99 (*1-57203-033-X*, 910) Inst Real Estate.

Practical Application of Azolla for Rice Production. Ed. by W. S. Silver & E. C. Schroder. (Development in Plant & Soil Sciences Ser.). 1984. text 122.00 (*90-247-3068-6*) Kluwer Academic.

Practical Application of Computer-Aided Drug Design. Paul S. Charifson. LC 97-20897. (Illus.). 564p. 1997. text 150.00 (*0-8247-9885-6*) Dekker.

Practical Application of Futures Trading for Oil Industry: Papers Presented at the Joint Seminar Between the Institute of Petroleum Energy Economics Group & the International Petroleum Exchange of London Limited, 9th May 1985. Institute of Petroleum, London Staff. LC 89-23896. (Illus.). 107p. reprint ed. pap. 33.20 (*0-7837-6845-1*, 204667400003) Bks Demand.

Practical Application of Meridian-Style Acupuncture. John E. Pirog. LC 95-69801. (Illus.). 392p. (Orig.). 1996. pap. 70.00 (*1-881896-13-7*) Pacific View Pr.

Practical Application of Object-Oriented Techniques to Relational Databases. Donald K. Burleson. 250p. 1994. 64.99 (*0-471-61225-1*) Wiley.

Practical Application of Remote Sensing in Forestry. Ed. by Sune Sohlberg & Viatcheslav E. Sokolov. (Forestry Sciences Ser.). 1986. text 161.50 (*90-247-3392-8*) Kluwer Academic.

Practical Application of Science of Mind. Ernest Holmes & Willis H. Kinnear. 96p. 1958. pap. 5.95 (*0-911336-24-9*) Sci of Mind.

Practical Application of SPC in the Flexible Packaging Industry. Douglas B. Relyea. 176p. 1992. pap. text 21.50 (*0-527-91645-5*, 916455) Productivity Inc.

P

An Asterisk (*) at the beginning of an entry indicates that the title is appearing for the first time.

Practical Application of SPC in the Wire & Cable Industry. Douglas B. Relyea. (Illus.). 176p. 1990. pap. 21.50 (*0-527-91643-9*, 916439) Productivity Inc.

Practical Applications for Criminal Justice Statistics. Mark L. Dantzker et al. LC 97-9588. 196p. 1997. 26.95 (*0-7506-9830-6*, BH Security) Buttrwrth-Heinemann.

Practical Applications for Federal Agencies: A Summary Report. unabridged ed. (HRM Series II). 1996. pap. 15.00 (*1-57744-016-1*) Nat Acad Public Admin.

***Practical Applications for the Seven Laws of Teaching: Lessons for Staff Training.** Tom Spencer. 26p. 1998. spiral bd. 10.00 (*1-930443-16-1*, B080, Pub. by Logos Schl) Veritas Pr PA.

Practical Applications of Accounting Standards: A Decade of Comment on Accounting & Auditing Problems. Carman G. Blough. Ed. by Richard P. Brief. LC 80-1472. (Dimensions of Accounting Theory & Practice Ser.). 1980. reprint ed. lib. bdg. 49.95 (*0-405-13502-5*) Ayer.

***Practical Applications of Approximate Equations in Finance & Economics.** Manuel Tarrazo. LC 00-37266. 300p. 2000. 69.00 (*1-56720-393-0*) Greenwood.

Practical Applications of Clinical Neurophysiological Testing. Thoru Yamada & Mark Ross. (Advances In Pulp & Paper Chemistry Ser.). 1999. 89.95 (*0-8493-7692-0*) CRC Pr.

***Practical Applications of Computational Intelligence for Adaptive Control.** Charles Karr. LC 99-10490. 21p. 1999. lib. bdg. 89.95 (*0-8493-2069-0*) CRC Pr.

Practical Applications of Dynamic Symmetry. Jay Hambidge. 1965. 12.95 (*0-8159-6509-5*) Devin.

Practical Applications of Ergonomics. Joyce. (KU - Office Proceures Ser.). (C). 1988. mass mkt., wbk. ed. 16.50 (*0-538-07643-7*) S-W Pub.

Practical Applications of Fiberoptics in Critical Care Monitoring. Ed. by F. R. Lewis & U. J. Pfeiffer. 204p. 1990. 55.95 (*0-387-51718-9*) Spr-Verlag.

***Practical Applications of Fuzzy Technologies.** H. J. Zimmermann. LC 99-40742. (Fuzzy Sets Ser.). 1999. pap. write for info. (*0-7923-8628-0*) Kluwer Academic.

Practical Applications of GIS for Archaelogists: A Predictive Modeling Kit. Konnie Westcott & R. Joe Brandon. LC 99-13217. 1999. 29.95 (*0-7484-0830-4*) Taylor & Francis.

Practical Applications of Infrared Thermal Sensing & Imaging Equipment. Herbert Kaplan. LC 92-47462. (Tutorial Texts in Optical Engineering Ser.: Vol. TT 13). 1993. 20.00 (*0-8194-1207-4*) SPIE.

***Practical Applications of Infrared Thermal Sensing & Imaging Equipment.** 2nd ed. Herbert Kaplan. LC 98-47919. (Tutorial Texts in Optical Engineering Ser.: Vol. TT34). 180p. 1999. pap. 48.00 (*0-8194-3138-9*) SPIE.

Practical Applications of Ion Trap Mass Spectrometry. Ed. by Raymond E. March & John F. Todd. (Modern Mass Spectrometry Ser.). 448p. 1995. boxed set 159.95 (*0-8493-4452-2*, 4452) CRC Pr.

Practical Applications of Ion Trap Mass Spectrometry. Ed. by Raymond E. March & John F. Todd. (Modern Mass Spectrometry Ser.). 544p. 1995. boxed set 129.95 (*0-8493-8251-3*, 8251) CRC Pr.

Practical Applications of Linear Programming Duality. Semen Gdalevitch. LC 94-2442. (Approximation & Optimization Ser.: Vol. 6). (Illus.). 181p. 1994. write for info. (*3-631-46716-8*) P Lang Pubng.

Practical Applications of Management Principles in the Pulp & Paper Industry Staff: May 23-24 Atlanta Hilton, Atlanta, GA. Technical Association of the Pulp & Paper Industry. LC HD9820.65. 342p. reprint ed. pap. 106.10 (*0-608-13332-9*, 202556600044) Bks Demand.

Practical Applications of Neutron Radiography & Gaging - STP 586. 330p. 1976. 25.50 (*0-8031-0535-5*, STP582) ASTM.

Practical Applications of Psychology. 4th ed. (C). 1997. text 24.00 (*0-673-54185-1*, GoodYrBooks) Addson-Wesley Educ.

Practical Applications of Psychology. 4th ed. Anthony F. Grasha. LC 94-29604. 528p. (C). 1997. pap. text 74.00 (*0-673-52340-3*) Addson-Wesley Educ.

Practical Applications of Psychotropic Drugs & Other Biological Treatments. Ed. by Herman M. Van Praag et al. LC 81-7786. (Handbook of Biological, Experimental & Clinical Psychiatry Ser.: Pt. 6, No. 1). (Illus.). 573p. 1981. pap. 177.70 (*0-7837-8346-9*, 204913500010) Bks Demand.

Practical Applications of Quantitative Metallography - STP 839. Ed. by J. L. McCall & J. H. Steele, Jr. LC 83-73230. 190p. 1984. text 34.00 (*0-8031-0220-8*, STP839) ASTM.

Practical Applications of Quantitative Structure- Activity Relationships (QSAR) in Environmental Chemistry & Toxicology. Ed. by Walter Karcher & J. Devillers. (C). 1990. text 248.50 (*0-7923-0827-1*) Kluwer Academic.

Practical Applications of Residual Stress Technology: Proceedings of the Third International Conference Held May 15-17, 1991, Indianapolis, IN. Ed. by Clayton Ruud. LC 91-74086. (ASM International Conference Proceedings Ser.). (Illus.). 189p. 1991. reprint ed. pap. 58.60 (*0-608-02648-4*, 206330700004) Bks Demand.

Practical Applied Optometry. A. M. Skeffington. Ed. by Sally M. Coringold. (Illus.). 114p. (C). 1991. reprint ed. lib. bdg. 18.00 (*0-943599-18-0*) OEPF.

Practical Appraisal of Industrial Projects-Application of Social Cost-Benefit Analysis in Pakistan. 181p. 1980. pap. 13.00 (*92-1-106100-8*, E.79.11.B.5) UN.

Practical Approach. 2nd ed. Kate Lorig. LC 95-36414. 256p. 1995. pap. 26.95 (*0-7619-0074-8*) Sage.

Practical Approach: Patient Education. 2nd ed. Kate Lorig. LC 95-36414. 1995. 58.00 (*0-7619-0073-X*) Sage.

Practical Approach Pediatric I. Isaacs. 1996. text 83.00 (*0-443-05142-9*, W B Saunders Co) Harcrt Hlth Sci Grp.

Practical Approach to Acupuncture. Prabha Borwanker. (C). 1988. 34.00 (*0-8364-2396-8*, Pub. by Popular Prakashan) S Asia.

***Practical Approach to Arbitration Law.** Keren Tweeddale & Andrew Tweeddale. 446p. 1999. pap. 60.00 (*1-85431-974-4*, 18460, Pub. by Blackstone Pr) Gaunt.

Practical Approach to Assessment of Liability & Damages in Tort. Nathan. 1986. 148.00 (*9971-70-051-4*, MICHIE) LEXIS Pub.

Practical Approach to Bank Lending. L. S. Dyer. 243p. (C). 1990. pap. 125.00 (*0-85297-181-8*, Pub. by Chartered Bank) St Mut.

Practical Approach to Bank Lending. 2nd ed. L. S. Dyer. 232p. 1980. 130.00 (*0-85297-084-6*, Pub. by Chartered Bank) St Mut.

Practical Approach to Breast Cancer. Ed. by Lois F. O'Grady et al. LC 94-26205. (Illus.). 328p. 1995. pap. text 54.00 (*0-316-63377-1*) Lppncott W & W.

Practical Approach to C + + Todd Knowlton. LC 96-6974. 1999. pap. 35.95 (*0-538-66928-4*) S-W Pub.

Practical Approach to Cardiac Anesthesia. 2nd rev. ed. Ed. by Frederick A. Hensley, Jr. & Donald E. Martin. LC 94-42512. 736p. 1995. pap. text 65.00 (*0-316-35786-3*) Lppncott W & W.

Practical Approach to Cardiac Arrhythmias. 2nd rev. ed. Stephen C. Vlay. 464p. 1995. pap. text 54.00 (*0-316-91483-5*, Little Brwn Med Div) Lppncott W & W.

Practical Approach to Civil Procedure. Stuart Sime. 520p. 1994. pap. 46.00 (*1-85431-280-4*, Pub. by Blackstone Pr) Gaunt.

Practical Approach to Civil Procedure. 2nd ed. Stuart Sime. 602p. 1995. pap. 44.00 (*1-85431-481-5*, Pub. by Blackstone Pr) Gaunt.

Practical Approach to Civil Procedure. 3rd ed. Stuart Sime. 551p. 1997. pap. 52.00 (*1-85431-654-0*, Pub. by Blackstone Pr) Gaunt.

Practical Approach to Clinical Paediatrics. J. M. Gupta & D. W. O'Gorman-Hughes. 250p. 1996. text 53.00 (*981-02-1849-4*) World Scientific Pub.

Practical Approach to Clinical Pediatrics. J. M. Gupta & D. W. O'Gorman-Hughes. 250p. 1996. pap. text 30.00 (*981-02-2136-3*) World Scientific Pub.

Practical Approach to Computing. fac. ed. W. Y. Arms et al. LC 75-15787. 365p. pap. 113.20 (*0-7837-7375-7*, 204718500005) Bks Demand.

Practical Approach to Conveyancing. Robert Abbey & Mark Richards. 466p. 1998. pap. 54.00 (*1-85431-732-6*, Pub. by Blackstone Pr) Gaunt.

***Practical Approach to Conveyancing.** 2nd ed. Robert Abbey & Mark Richards. 504p. 2000. pap. 50.00 (*1-85431-915-9*, Pub. by Blackstone Pr) Gaunt.

Practical Approach to Corel WordPerfect 7.0 for Windows 95. Eisch. 1997. mass mkt. 56.95 (*0-538-67650-7*) S-W Pub.

Practical Approach to Criminal Procedure. Christopher Emmins. 538p. 1988. pap. 36.00 (*1-85431-015-1*, Pub. by Blackstone Pr) Gaunt.

Practical Approach to Data Structures: Related Algorithms in Pascal with Applications. Kit Lester. 1990. text 49.95 (*0-470-21504-6*) P-H.

Practical Approach to Database Systems. Pal Quittner. LC 94-181853. 291p. 1994. pap. 90.00 (*963-05-6636-2*, Pub. by Akade Kiado) St Mut.

Practical Approach to dBase 5.0 for Windows: Complete Course. Denise Hayward. LC 95-14480. 1995. mass mkt. 41.95 (*0-538-63540-1*) S-W Pub.

Practical Approach to Dealing with Children's Misbehavior. Lawrence Zuckerman & Fred Gladish. 23p. (Orig.). 1979. pap. 3.00 (*0-918560-23-3*) Adler Sch Prof Psy.

***Practical Approach to Digital Electronics.** James L. Antonakos & Alan C. Dixon. LC 99-26192. (Illus.). 376p. (C). 1999. text 76.00 incl. audio compact disk (*0-13-727595-1*, Macmillan Coll) P-H.

Practical Approach to Eighteenth-Century Counterpoint. Robert Gauldin. (Illus.). 335p. (C). 1995. pap. text 32.95 (*0-88133-853-2*) Waveland Pr.

Practical Approach to Emergency Medicine. Robert J. Stine. Ed. by Robert H. Marcus. (C). 1987. pap. 29.50 (*0-685-17583-9*, Little Brwn Med Div) Lppncott W & W.

Practical Approach to Epilepsy. Ed. by Mogens Dam. 300p. 1991. 49.50 (*0-08-041171-1*, Pub. by PPI) McGraw.

Practical Approach to Evidence. Peter Murphy. 637p. 1992. pap. 48.00 (*1-85431-223-5*, Pub. by Blackstone Pr) Gaunt.

Practical Approach to Evidence in Malaysia & Singapore. R. K. Nathan. 500p. 1993. 160.00 (*0-409-99646-7*, SI, MICHIE) LEXIS Pub.

Practical Approach to Family Law. 4th ed. Jill Black et al. LC 95-157702. 560p. 1994. pap. 46.00 (*1-85431-326-6*, Pub. by Blackstone Pr) Gaunt.

Practical Approach to Family Law. 5th ed. Jill Black et al. 357p. 1998. pap. 48.00 (*1-85431-653-2*, Pub. by Blackstone Pr) Gaunt.

Practical Approach to Head & Neck Tumors. Jack Gluckman et al. LC 94-26061. 224p. 1994. text 82.00 (*0-7817-0228-3*) Lppncott W & W.

Practical Approach to Infectious Diseases. 4th ed. Ed. by Richard E. Reese & Robert F. Betts. 1200p. 1996. pap. text 74.95 (*0-316-73721-6*, Little Brwn Med Div) Lppncott W & W.

Practical Approach to Instructional Design. Elizabeth Jared. LC 99-181766. 82p. (C). 1998. per. 23.95 (*0-7872-2246-1*, 41224601) Kendall-Hunt.

Practical Approach to International Operations. Michael Gendron. LC 88-6698. 200p. 1988. 57.95 (*0-89930-252-1*, GNO/, Quorum Bks) Greenwood.

Practical Approach to Investing. Robert W. Kolb. (C). 1989. text 56.50 (*0-673-18904-X*, Scott Frsmn) Addson-Wesley Educ.

Practical Approach to Land Law. Judith-Anne MacKenzie & Mary Phillips. 332p. (C). 1989. 160.00 (*1-85431-046-1*, Pub. by Blackstone Pr) St Mut.

Practical Approach to Land Law. 5th ed. Judith-Anne MacKenzie & Mary Phillips. 374p. 1994. text 36.00 (*1-85431-354-1*, Pub. by Blackstone Pr) Gaunt.

Practical Approach to Land Law. 6th ed. Judith-Anne MacKenzie & Mary Phillips. 380p. 1996. pap. 38.00 (*1-85431-550-1*, Pub. by Blackstone Pr) Gaunt.

Practical Approach to Land Law. 7th rev. ed. Judith-Anne MacKenzie & Mary Phillips. LC 99-160193. 399p. 1997. pap. 38.00 (*1-85431-683-4*, Pub. by Blackstone Pr) Gaunt.

Practical Approach to Landlord & Tenant. Simon Garner. 390p. 1995. pap. 40.00 (*1-85431-462-9*, Pub. by Blackstone Pr) Gaunt.

Practical Approach to Legal Advice & Drafting. 4th ed. Susan Blake. 472p. 1993. 44.00 (*1-85431-253-7*, Pub. by Blackstone Pr) Gaunt.

Practical Approach to Legal Advice & Drafting. 5th ed. Susan Blake. 412p. 1997. pap. 46.00 (*1-85431-541-2*, Pub. by Blackstone Pr) Gaunt.

***Practical Approach to Liens on Real Estate.** 1998. 99.00 incl. audio 99.00 incl. audio PA Bar Inst.

Practical Approach to Lilly Vol. 1: Traditional Horary Study Guide. Bobby Bratcher-Nelson & Carol A. Wiggers. (Illus.). 114p. (Orig.). (C). 1990. pap. 20.00 (*1-878935-04-6*) JustUs & Assocs.

Practical Approach to Local Government Law. John Sharland. LC 97-181076. 277p. 1997. pap. 40.00 (*1-85431-503-X*, Pub. by Blackstone Pr) Gaunt.

Practical Approach to Logical Access Control. Ernst & Young Staff & Young. LC 93-4624. 1993. write for info. (*0-07-707807-1*) McGraw.

Practical Approach to Lotus 1-2-3 for Windows. large type ed. Nancy J. Groneman. 1995. 95.50 (*0-614-09603-0*, L-83779-00) Am Printing Hse.

Practical Approach to Lotus 1-2-3 for Windows Releases 4 & 5. Groneman. (DF - Computer Applications Ser.). (C). 1995. mass mkt. 41.95 (*0-538-71282-1*) S-W Pub.

Practical Approach to Microsoft Office for Mac: Complete Course. Murphy. 1997. pap. 53.95 (*0-538-67962-X*) Thomson Learn.

Practical Approach to Microsoft 97 for Windows. Morrison. (DF - Computer Applications Ser.). 1997. mass mkt. 53.95 (*0-538-71927-3*) S-W Pub.

***Practical Approach to Neurooncology.** Leslie D. McAllister et al. 350p. 2000. pap. 47.50 (*0-7506-7180-7*) Buttrwrth-Heinemann.

Practical Approach to Occupational & Environmental Medicine. 2nd rev. ed. Ed. by Robert J. McCunney & Paul W. Brandt-Rauf. LC 94-11269. Orig. Title: Handbook of Occupational Medicine. 856p. 1994. reprint ed. pap. text 65.00 (*0-316-55534-7*, Little Brwn Med Div) Lppncott W & W.

Practical Approach to Pain Management. Ed. by Mathew Lefkowitz et al. 310p. 1996. pap. text 40.00 (*0-316-51958-8*, Little Brwn Med Div) Lppncott W & W.

Practical Approach to Permanent Pacemaker Implantation, Set. Peter H. Belott. LC 94-39121. (Illus.). 152p. 1996. wbk. ed. 95.00 incl. VHS (*0-87993-594-4*) Futura Pub.

Practical Approach to Planning Law. Victor Moore. 368p. (C). 1987. 190.00 (*1-85185-070-8*, Pub. by Blackstone Pr) St Mut.

Practical Approach to Planning Law. 4th ed. Victor Moore. 415p. 1994. pap. 42.00 (*1-85431-355-X*, Pub. by Blackstone Pr) Gaunt.

Practical Approach to Planning Law. 5th ed. Victor Moore. 562p. 1995. pap. 38.00 (*1-85431-483-1*, Pub. by Blackstone Pr) Gaunt.

Practical Approach to Planning Law. 6th ed. Victor Moore. LC 98-226958. 576p. 1997. pap. 44.00 (*1-85431-685-0*, Pub. by Blackstone Pr) Gaunt.

Practical Approach to Professional Writing: Technical & Business. Douglas Brooks. 240p. (C). 1996. per. 37.95 (*0-7872-2894-X*, 41289401) Kendall-Hunt.

Practical Approach to Pulmonary Medicine. Ronald H. Goldstein et al. LC 97-9420. 624p. 1997. text 59.95 (*0-7817-1237-8*) Lppncott W & W.

Practical Approach to Pulmonary Medicine. Joel Karlinsky et al. 600p. 1997. text 69.95 (*0-316-54884-7*) Lppncott W & W.

Practical Approach to Quality Improvement. Karen Parsley & Philomena Corrigan. LC 93-36305. 1993. write for info. (*0-412-48360-2*) Chapman & Hall.

Practical Approach to Quality Improvement. Karen Parsley & Philomena Corrigan. LC 93-36305. 176p. 1993. pap. 54.25 (*1-56593-236-6*, 0556) Singular Publishing.

Practical Approach to Road Traffic Law. Richard McMahon. 358p. 1993. 40.00 (*1-85431-260-X*, Pub. by Blackstone Pr) Gaunt.

Practical Approach to RSP: A Handbook for the Resource Specialist Program. 2nd ed. Leslie A. Williams & Lucile S. Arntzen. LC 94-525. (Illus.). 120p. 1994. pap. 20.95 (*0-398-06498-9*) C C Thomas.

Practical Approach to RSP: A Handbook for the Resource Specialist Program. 2nd ed. Leslie A. Williams & Lucile S. Arntzen. LC 94-525. (Illus.). 120p. (C). 1994. text 33.95 (*0-398-05908-X*) C C Thomas.

Practical Approach to Saliva. Johnson. (C). 1998. pap. text 36.00 (*0-12-784572-0*) Acad Pr.

Practical Approach to Sedimentology. Roy Lindholm. (Illus.). 192p. 1987. text 45.00 (*0-04-551131-4*); pap. text 21.95 (*0-04-551132-2*) Routledge.

Practical Approach to Sentencing. Christopher Emmins. 370p. (C). 1985. text 42.00 (*0-906322-66-9*, Pub. by Blackstone Pr); pap. text 36.00 (*0-906322-71-5*, Pub. by Blackstone Pr) Gaunt.

Practical Approach to Serials Cataloging. Lynn S. Smith. Ed. by Robert D. Stueart. LC 77-25282. (Foundations in Library & Information Science: Vol. 2). 424p. 1979. 78.50 (*0-89232-007-9*) Jai Pr.

Practical Approach to Sixteenth-Century Counterpoint. Robert Gauldin. (Illus.). 312p. (C). 1995. pap. text 26.95 (*0-88133-852-4*) Waveland Pr.

Practical Approach to Strength Training. 3rd rev. ed. Matt Brzycki. (Illus.). 256p. 1995. pap. 17.95 (*1-57028-018-5*, 80185H, Mstrs Pr) NTC Contemp Pub Co.

Practical Approach to Teaching Physical Education. David L. Kizer et al. 1984. pap. 24.95 (*0-932392-18-0*) Mouvement Pubns.

Practical Approach to Teaching Reading. 2nd ed. Dorothy Rubin. LC 92-21969. 512p. 1992. 79.00 (*0-205-14215-X*) Allyn.

***Practical Approach to Technical Writing.** 4th ed. (C). 2000. write for info. (*0-13-027390-2*) P-H.

Practical Approach to the Drumset. Beck. 48p. 1985. pap. 7.95 (*0-7935-2320-6*, 00123245) H Leonard.

Practical Approach to the Greek New Testament. Richard P. Belcher. 58p. 1993. reprint ed. pap. 10.00 (*1-883265-03-7*) Richbarry Pr.

Practical Approach to the Study of Form in Music. Peter Spencer & Peter M. Temko. (Illus.). 215p. (C). 1994. pap. text 28.95 (*0-88133-806-0*) Waveland Pr.

Practical Approach to the Use of Radiation in Molecular Biology. Gillian Scott-Wood. 1998. pap. 150.00 (*0-948237-33-3*, Pub. by H&H Sci Cnslts) St Mut.

Practical Approach to Total Flexibility Through Stretching. Richard Trestrail. 118p. (C). 1996. pap. text, per. 17.95 (*0-7872-2713-7*) Kendall-Hunt.

Practical Approach to Using Learning Styles in Math Instruction. Ruby B. Midkiff & Rebecca D. Thomasson. LC 93-5643. (Illus.). 132p. 1993. pap. 25.95 (*0-398-06289-7*) C C Thomas.

Practical Approach to Using Learning Styles in Math Instruction. Ruby B. Midkiff & Rebecca D. Thomasson. LC 93-5643. (Illus.). 132p. (C). 1993. text 36.95 (*0-398-05888-1*) C C Thomas.

Practical Approach to Word Perfect 6.0 for Windows - Complete Course: Complete Course. Mary Alice Eisch. (DF - Computer Applications Ser.). (C). 1994. mass mkt. 46.95 (*0-538-71321-6*) S-W Pub.

Practical Approach to Wordperfect 6.0: Complete Course. Mary Alice Eisch. (DF - Computer Applications Ser.). (C). 1994. mass mkt. 41.95 (*0-538-63485-5*) S-W Pub.

Practical Approach to Wordperfect 6.0 for Windows: Standard Course. Mary Alice Eisch. (DF - Computer Applications Ser.). (C). 1994. mass mkt. 37.95 (*0-538-71291-0*) S-W Pub.

Practical Approach to WordPerfect 6.1 for Windows: Complete Course. (Computer Applications Ser.). 680p. 1995. mass mkt. 53.95 (*0-538-71402-6*) S-W Pub.

Practical Approach to Wp 6 /6.1 Dos. 2nd ed. Eisch. 1996. pap. 40.25 (*0-538-66804-0*) Thomson Learn.

Practical Approach Utilities for Maple: Maple V, Release 3. Darren Redfern & D. Doherty. (Illus.). 328p. 1995. 75.95 incl. disk (*0-387-14221-5*) Spr-Verlag.

Practical Approach Utilities for Maple: Maple V, Release 4. Darren Redfern. 1996. pap. text 69.00 incl. disk (*0-387-14225-8*) Spr-Verlag.

Practical Approach, Version 3.0. Charles Siegel. LC 94-26167. 89p. 1994. pap. 27.95 (*1-55828-350-1*) IDG Bks.

Practical Approaches. (Space & Society Ser.). Date not set. pap. text. write for info. (*0-582-35352-1*, Pub. by Addison-Wesley) Longman.

Practical Approaches for Building Study Skills & Vocabulary. 2nd ed. Gary Funk et al. 384p. (C). 1996. per. 42.95 (*0-7872-2189-9*, 41218901) Kendall-Hunt.

***Practical Approaches for Teaching Reading & Writing in Middle Schools.** Teresa M. Morretta & Michelle Ambrosini. 2000. pap., teacher ed. 19.95 (*0-87207-266-5*, 266) Intl Reading.

Practical Approaches in the Treatment of Women Who Abuse Alcohol & Other Drugs. 1995. lib. bdg. 252.99 (*0-8490-6808-8*) Gordon Pr.

Practical Approaches in the Treatment of Women Who Abuse Alcohol & Other Drugs. 301p. 1994. per. 20.00 (*0-16-045254-6*) USGPO.

Practical Approaches in Treating Adolescent Chemical Dependency: A Guide to Clinical Assessment & Intervention. Ed. by Paul B. Henry. LC 89-1660. (Journal of Chemical Dependency Treatment: Vol. 2, No. 1). 284p. 1989. text 49.95 (*0-86656-709-7*); pap. text 17.95 (*0-86656-813-1*) Haworth Pr.

Practical Approaches to Alcoholism Psychotherapy. 2nd ed. Ed. by Sheldon Zimberg et al. LC 84-24922. (Illus.). 432p. 1985. 39.50 (*0-306-41762-6*, Kluwer Plenum) Kluwer Academic.

Practical Approaches to Cancer Invasion & Metastases: A Compendium of Radiation Oncologists' Responses to 40 Histories. Ed. by A. Robert Kagan & Richard J. Steckel. LC 93-42006. (Medical Radiology, Diagnostic Imaging & Radiation Oncology Ser.). (Illus.). 144p. 1994. 115.00 (*0-387-56375-X*) Spr-Verlag.

Practical Approaches to Development Planning: Korea's Second Five-Year Plan. Ed. by Irma Adelman. LC 69-19467. (Illus.). 320p. 1969. reprint ed. pap. 99.20 (*0-608-04079-7*, 206481100011) Bks Demand.

Practical Approaches to Earthquake Prediction & Warning. Ed. by C. Kisslinger & Tsuneji Rikatake. 1985. text 259.00 (*90-277-2168-8*) Kluwer Academic.

Practical Approaches to Individualizing Staff Development for Adults. Ed. by Rita Dunn & Kenneth Dunn. LC 97-33710. 160p. 1998. 49.95 (*0-275-96066-8*, Praeger Pubs) Greenwood.

P

Practical Approaches to Legal Research. Kent C. Olson & Robert C. Berring. LC 88-6800. (Legal Reference Services Quarterly Ser.: Supp. No. 1). 143p. 1988. text 39.95 (*0-86656-253-2*); pap. text 19.95 (*0-86656-853-0*) Haworth Pr.

Practical Approaches to Pediatric Radiology. Andrew K. Poznanski. LC 75-16022. 478p. reprint ed. pap. 148.20 (*0-608-13468-6*, 202272800029) Bks Demand.

Practical Approaches to Rightsizing. Ed. by Deirdre M. Greene. LC 92-11195. 1992. 52.95 (*0-915164-84-1*) NACUBO.

Practical Approaches to Scheduling & Planning: Papers from the 1992 Spring Symposium. Ed. by Mark Drummond et al. (Technical Reports). (Illus.). 164p. (Orig.). 1993. spiral bd. 25.00 (*0-929280-32-6*) AAAI Pr.

Practical Approaches to Teaching Shakespeare. Peter Reynolds. Ed. by Roma Gill. (Oxford School Shakespeare Ser.). 128p. (YA). (gr. 6 up). 1992. pap. text 12.95 (*0-19-831954-1*) OUP.

Practical Approaches to the Conservation of Biological Diversity. Ed. by Richard K. Baydack et al. LC 98-25753. 320p. 1998. text 65.00 (*1-55963-543-6*); pap. text 35.00 (*1-55963-544-4*) Island Pr.

Practical Approaches to the Treatment of Heart Failure. Roger M. Mills, Jr. & James B. Young. LC 97-41999. 352p. 1997. 45.00 (*0-683-18104-1*) Lppncott W & W.

Practical Approaches to Usability Testing for Technical Documentation. Karen Wilson et al. Ed. by Judith Ramey & Christopher Velotta. (Anthology Ser.). (Illus.). 105p. (C). 1995. per. 45.00 (*0-914548-81-6*, 157-95) Soc Tech Comm.

*__Practical Approaches to Using Learning Styles in Higher Education.__ Rita Stafford Dunn & Shirley A. Griggs. LC 99-40321. 280p. 2000. write for info. (*0-89789-703-X*, Bergin & Garvey) Greenwood.

Practical Arabic. George Scott. (ARA.). 419p. 1979. 22.00 (*0-86685-050-3*, LDL0533, Pub. by Librairie du Liban) Intl Bk Ctr.

Practical Arabic-French Dictionary: Dictionnaire Pratique Arabe-Francais. Zaki Coussa. (ARA & FRE.). 440p. 1986. pap. 26.95 (*0-8288-0997-6*, M15721) Fr & Eur.

Practical Archaeologist: How We Know What We Know About the Past. Jane McIntosh. (Illus.). 192p. 1986. 26.95 (*0-8160-1400-0*) Facts on File.

Practical Archaeologist: How We Know What We Know About the Past. Jane McIntosh. (Illus.). 192p. 1988. pap. 15.95 (*0-8160-1814-6*) Facts on File.

*__Practical Archaeologist: How We Know What We Know About the Past.__ 2nd ed. Jane McIntosh. LC 98-48595. 1999. 16.95 (*0-8160-3951-8*, Checkmark) Facts on File.

Practical Archaeologist: How We Know What We Know About the Past. 2nd ed. Jane McIntosh. LC 98-48595. (Illus.). 192p. 1999. 35.00 (*0-8160-3950-X*) Facts on File.

Practical Archaeology: An Introduction to Archaeological Field Work Excavations. Graham Webster. LC 74-82133. (C). 1975. 25.00 (*0-312-63455-2*) St Martin.

Practical Archaeology: Field & Laboratory Techniques & Archaeological Logistics. 3rd ed. Ed. by Brian D. Dillon. LC 93-43422. (UCLA Institute of Archaeology Publications: No. 2). (Illus.). 85p. 1993. pap. 15.00 (*0-917956-80-X*) UCLA Arch.

Practical Architecture. William Halfpenny & John Halfpenny. LC 68-8317. (Illus.). 1968. reprint ed. 19.95 (*0-405-08590-7*, Pub. by Blom Pubns) Ayer.

Practical Argument: An Introduction to Reasoning, Comm. & Commitment. 2nd ed. William M. Keith. 138p. (C). 1997. spiral bd. 27.95 (*0-7872-4455-4*, 41445501) Kendall-Hunt.

Practical Argument: An Introduction to Reasoning, Communication, & Commitment. William Keith. 198p. (C). 1996. 36.95 (*0-7872-2892-3*) Kendall-Hunt.

*__Practical Aromatherapy: How to Use Essential Oils to Restore Health & Vitality.__ Shirley Price. 2000. pap. 12.00 (*0-7225-3906-1*, Pub. by Thorsons PA) HarpC.

Practical Aromatherapy: How to Use Essential Oils to Restore Health & Vitality. 3rd ed. Shirley Price. 1994. pap. 11.00 (*0-7225-2850-7*) Thorsons PA.

Practical Aromatherapy: The Complete Beginner's Guide to Choosing, Massaging & Relaxing with Essential Oils. Penny Rich. (Illus.). 128p. 1999. reprint ed. text 25.00 (*0-7881-6195-4*) DIANE Pub.

Practical Aromatherapy: Understanding & Using Essential Oils to Heal the Mind & Body. Robyn M. Feller. LC 97-143887. 256p. 1997. mass mkt. 5.99 (*0-425-15576-5*) Berkley Pub.

Practical Art Criticism. Edmund B. Feldman. LC 93-17880. 84p. (C). 1993. pap. text 28.00 (*0-13-706674-0*) P-H.

Practical Art of Aromatherapy. Random House Value Publishing Staff. Date not set. write for info. (*0-517-20325-1*) Random Hse Value.

Practical Art of Motion Picture Sound: Professional Techniques of Motion Picture & Television Audio. David L. Yewdall. LC 99-30428. (Illus.). 267p. 1999. pap. 39.95 incl. cd-rom (*0-240-80288-8*, Focal) Buttrwrth-Heinemann.

*__Practical Art of Suicide Assessment: A Guide for Mental Health Professionals & Substance Abuse Counselors.__ Shawn C. Shea. LC 98-55218. 272p. 1999. 45.00 (*0-471-18363-6*) Wiley.

*__Practical Art School: Twelve Lessons in Painting, Drawing & Sketching.__ Ian Simpson. 1999. 24.99 (*1-84100-218-6*) Quadrillion Pubng.

Practical Artificial Intelligence Systems. N. J. Cercone. (Computers & Mathematics with Applications Ser.). 1985. pap. 30.00 (*0-08-032598-X*, Pergamon Pr) Elsevier.

*__Practical Asic Design & Verification.__ (C). 2000. pap. 75.00 (*0-13-026366-4*) HEPC Inc.

Practical Aspects of Authentic Assessment: Putting the Pieces Together. Bonnie C. Hill & Cynthia Ruptic. (Illus.). 268p. (J). (gr. k-6). 1994. pap. text 41.95 (*0-926842-36-6*) CG Pubs Inc.

*__Practical Aspects of Declarative Languages: Proceedings of Second International Workshop, PADL 2000, Boston, MA, U. S. A., January 17-18, 2000.__ Ed. by PADL 2000 Staff et al. LC 00-20529. (Lecture Notes in Computer Science Ser.: Vol. 1753). x, 323p. 2000. pap. 56.00 (*3-540-66992-2*) Spr-Verlag.

Practical Aspects of Declarative Languages: 1st International Workshop, PADL '99, San Antonio, Texas, U. S. A., January 18-19, 1999, Proceedings. Ed. by G. Gupta et al. LC 99-11972. (Lecture Notes in Computer Science Ser.: Vol. 1551). viii, 367p. 1999. pap. 62.00 (*3-540-65527-1*) Spr-Verlag.

Practical Aspects of Drug Enforcement: Procedures & Administration. M. Lyman. (Practical Aspects of Criminal & Forensic Investigations Ser.). iix, 450p. 1989. 49.50 (*0-444-01455-1*) CRC Pr.

Practical Aspects of Finite Element Methods. Nassehi. text. write for info. (*0-471-49042-3*) Wiley.

Practical Aspects of Gambling Investigation Techniques. Kevin B. Kinnee. LC 92-16682. (Series in Practical Aspects of Criminal & Forensic Investigations). 228p. 1992. boxed set 78.95 (*0-444-01649-X*, HV8079) CRC Pr.

Practical Aspects of Gas Chromotography-Mass Spectrometry. Gordon M. Message. LC 83-23475. 368p. 1984. 195.00 (*0-471-06277-4*, Wiley-Interscience) Wiley.

Practical Aspects of Ground Water Modeling. 3rd ed. W. Walton. LC 85-29755. 588p. 1985. 31.25 (*1-56034-037-1*, T165) Natl Grnd Water.

Practical Aspects of Gynaecourology: Proceedings of the 9th Annual Meeting of IUGA, Budapest, Hungary, 9-11 Sept. 1985. Ed. by Attila Tanko et al. (Illus.). 469p. 1986. 150.00 (*963-05-4440-7*, Pub. by Akade Kiado) St Mut.

Practical Aspects of International Management & Processing. Ed. by G. E. McClelland et al. LC 95-73104. (Illus.). 124p. (Orig.). 1996. pap. 49.00 (*0-87335-143-6*, 143-6) SMM&E Inc.

Practical Aspects of Interview & Interrogation. Douglas E. Wicklander & David E. Zulawski. 508p. 1991. 34.95 (*0-444-01632-5*, HV8073) CRC Pr.

Practical Aspects of Interview & Interrogation. David E. Zulawski. 368p. 1998. per. 19.95 (*0-8493-8132-0*) CRC Pr.

Practical Aspects of Interview & Interrogation. Ed. by David E. Zulawski & Douglas E. Wicklander. LC 93-21679. 368p. (C). 1992. reprint ed. boxed set 68.95 (*0-8493-9520-8*, HV8073) CRC Pr.

Practical Aspects of Intravenous Drug Administration: Principles for Nurses, Pharmacists, & Physicians. Richard D. Leff & Robert J. Roberts. 64p. (C). 1992. pap. text 15.00 (*1-879907-23-2*) Am Soc Hlth-Syst.

Practical Aspects of Ion Trap Mass Spectrometry Vol. II: Ion Trap Instrumentation, Vol. 2. Ed. by Raymond E. March & John F. Todd. LC 95-14146. (Modern Mass Spectrometry Ser.). 352p. 1995. boxed set 159.95 (*0-8493-8253-X*, 8253) CRC Pr.

Practical Aspects of Memory - Current Research & Issues Vol. 1: Memory of Everyday Life, Vol. 1, Memory of Everyday Life. Ed. by Michael M. Gruneberg et al. 580p. 1988. 165.00 (*0-471-91234-4*) Wiley.

Practical Aspects of Memory - Current Research & Issues Vol. 2: Clinical & Educational Implications, Vol. 2, Clinical and Educational Implications. Ed. by Michael M. Gruneberg et al. 584p. 1988. 659.00 (*0-471-91867-9*) Wiley.

Practical Aspects of Munchausen by Proxy & Munchausen Syndrome Investigation. Kathryn Artingstall. LC 98-13159. (Practical Aspects of Criminal & Forensic Investigation Ser.). 384p. 1998. boxed set 74.95 (*0-8493-8162-2*, 8162) CRC Pr.

Practical Aspects of Ophthalmic Optics: Third Edition. 3rd ed. Margaret Dowaliby. (Illus.). 581p. 1988. text 49.50 (*0-7506-9661-3*) Buttrwrth-Heinemann.

Practical Aspects of Pressing & Drying Seminar: 1984 Notes. Technical Association of the Pulp & Paper Industry. LC TS1118.D7T4. 200p. reprint ed. pap. 62.00 (*0-608-12034-0*, 202279800030) Bks Demand.

Practical Aspects of Pressing & Drying Seminar, Atlanta, March 14-18, 1988. Technical Association of the Pulp & Paper Industry. LC TS1118.. (TAPPI Notes Ser.). (Illus.). 255p. reprint ed. pap. 79.10 (*0-608-18429-2*, 203227500079) Bks Demand.

Practical Aspects of Pressing & Drying Seminar, 1985: Notes of TAPPI, The Waverly, Atlanta, GA, March 18-22. Technical Association of the Pulp & Paper Industry. LC TS1118.. 234p. reprint ed. pap. 72.60 (*0-608-12803-1*, 202528400043) Bks Demand.

Practical Aspects of Pressing & Drying Seminar, 1986: Notes of TAPPI, the Waverly Hotel, Atlanta, GA, March 17-21. Technical Association of the Pulp & Paper Industry. LC TS1118.. 265p. pap. 82.20 (*0-608-15251-X*, 202917800059) Bks Demand.

Practical Aspects of Pressing & Drying Seminar, 1987: Notes of TAPPI, Intercontinental Hotel, Geneva, Switzerland, March 16-20. Technical Association of the Pulp & Paper Industry. LC TS1118.. (Illus.). 267p. pap. 82.80 (*0-608-17489-0*, 202998500067) Bks Demand.

Practical Aspects of Pressing & Drying Seminar, 1989: Ritz-Carlton, Buckhead, Atlanta, GA, March 19-23. Technical Association of the Pulp & Paper Industry. LC TS1118.P74P7. (TAPPI Notes Ser.). (Illus.). 233p. pap. 72.30 (*0-8357-6339-0*, 203561100096) Bks Demand.

Practical Aspects of Pressing & Drying Seminar, 1994: Perdido Beach Hotel, Orange Beach, AL, Marsh 14-18. Technical Association of the Pulp & Paper Industry. LC 86-645208. (TAPPI Course Notes Ser.). (Illus.). 476p. 1994. reprint ed. pap. 147.60 (*0-608-05355-4*, 208240300004) Bks Demand.

Practical Aspects of Pressing & Drying Short Course, 1990: Ritz-Carlton, Buckhead, Atlanta, GA, March 18-23. Technical Association of the Pulp & Paper Industry. LC TS1118.P6T4. (TAPPI Notes Ser.). (Illus.). 282p. reprint ed. pap. 87.50 (*0-8357-3933-3*, 203666800004) Bks Demand.

Practical Aspects of Pressing & Drying Short Course, 1991: Ritz-Carlton, Buckhead, Atlanta, GA, March 25-28. Technical Association of the Pulp & Paper Industry. LC TS1118.P6.T4. (TAPPI Notes Ser.). 284p. pap. 88.10 (*0-7837-0260-4*, 204056900017) Bks Demand.

Practical Aspects of Pressing & Drying Short Course, 1992: The Peabody Hotel, Orlando, FL, March 23-27. Technical Association of the Pulp & Paper Industry. LC TS1118.P6T4. (TAPPI Notes Ser.). 297p. reprint ed. pap. 92.10 (*0-7837-2442-X*, 204259300005) Bks Demand.

Practical Aspects of Pressing & Drying Short Course, 1995: Fairmont Hotel, New Orleans, LA, March 27-31. Technical Association of the Pulp & Paper Industry. LC TS1118.P74P7. (TAPPI Course Notes Ser.). (Illus.). 594p. reprint ed. pap. 184.20 (*0-608-09133-2*, 208246100007) Bks Demand.

Practical Aspects of Rape Investigation: A Multidisciplinary Approach. Ed. by Robert R. Hazelwood & Ann W. Burgess. LC 86-29326. (Practical Aspects of Criminal & Forensic Investigations Ser.). 589p. 1987. 44.95 (*0-444-01144-7*, HV8079) CRC Pr.

Practical Aspects of Rape Investigation: A Multidisciplinary Approach. Robert R. Hazelwood & A. W. Burgess. LC 86-29326. (Series in Practical Aspects of Criminal & Forensic Investigations). 392p. 1992. reprint ed. lib. bdg. 211.00 (*0-8493-9509-7*, HV8079, CRC Reprint) Franklin.

Practical Aspects of Rape Investigation: A Multidisciplinary Approach. 2nd ed. Ed. by Robert R. Hazelwood & Ann W. Burgess. 416p. 1995. boxed set 84.95 (*0-8493-8152-5*, 8152) CRC Pr.

*__Practical Aspects of SPIN Model-Checking: 6th International Workshop, SPIN'99, Held As FM'99 User Group Meeting, Toulouse, France, September 21 & 24, 1999, Proceedings.__ Ed. by D. Dams et al. LC 99-49725. (Lecture Notes in Computer Science Ser.: Vol. 1680). x, 277p. 1999. pap. 52.00 (*3-540-66499-8*) Spr-Verlag.

Practical Aspects of Staged Therapy Defibrillators. Ed. by Lukas Kappenberger & Fred W. Lindemans. LC 92-14637. (Bakken Research Center Ser.: Vol. 5). (Illus.). 156p. 1992. 35.00 (*0-87993-531-6*) Futura Pub.

Practical Aspects of the Transfusion Service. Harold B. Anstall & Robert C. Blylock. LC 95-40102. 335p. 1996. pap. 55.00 (*0-89189-396-2*) Am Soc Clinical.

Practical Aspects of Tip Releif. T. R. Rideout. (Technical Paper Ser.: Vol. P78). (Illus.). 22p. 1931. pap. 30.00 (*1-55589-177-2*) AGMA.

Practical Aspects of Trading with the U. S. S. R., Vol. 2. Robert Starr. (Business Studies on the U. S. S. R.). x, 202p. 1990. text 262.00 (*2-88316-002-3*) Gordon & Breach.

Practical Aspects of Urinary Incontinence. Ed. by F. M. Debruyne & E. V. Van Kerrebroeck. (Developments in Surgery Ser.). 1986. text 111.00 (*0-89838-752-3*) Kluwer Academic.

Practical Assessment. Adele Fiderer. 1996. pap. 15.95 (*0-590-48458-3*) Scholastic Inc.

Practical Astrology. A. Leo. 228p. 1988. 10.95 (*0-318-36378-X*) Asia Bk Corp.

Practical Astrology. Alan Leo. 224p. 1996. reprint ed. spiral bd. 16.00 (*0-7873-1059-X*) Hlth Research.

Practical Astrology: A Simple Method of Casting Horoscope. rev. ed. Comte C. De Saint-Germain. 224p. 1996. reprint ed. spiral bd. 16.50 (*0-7873-0552-9*) Hlth Research.

Practical Astrology: A Simple Method of Casting Horoscopes. Comte C. De Saint-Germain. 1991. lib. bdg. 75.00 (*0-8490-4309-3*) Gordon Pr.

Practical Astrology: A Simple Method of Casting Horoscopes, the Language of the Stars, Easily Comprehended. De Saint Germain. 260p. 1993. reprint ed. pap. 15.95 (*1-56459-371-1*) Kessinger Pub.

Practical Astronomer. Brian Jones. Ed. by Stephen Edberg. (Illus.). 160p. 1990. per. 15.00 (*0-671-69303-4*) S&S Trade Pap.

Practical Astronomy: A User-Friendly Handbook for Skywatchers. H. Robert Mills. (Illus.). 240p. 1994. 29.95 (*1-898563-02-0*) Paul & Co Pubs.

Practical Astronomy During the Seventeenth Century: Almanac Makers in America & England. John T. Kelly. LC 90-26672. (Harvard Dissertations in the History of Science Ser.). (Illus.). 344p. 1991. reprint ed. text 45.00 (*0-8240-7445-9*) Garland.

Practical Astronomy with Your Calculator. 3rd ed. Peter J. Duffett-Smith. (Illus.). 200p. 1989. text 54.95 (*0-521-35629-6*) Cambridge U Pr.

Practical Astronomy with Your Calculator. 3rd ed. Peter J. Duffett-Smith. (Illus.). 200p. 1989. pap. 16.95 (*0-521-35699-7*) Cambridge U Pr.

Practical Atlantean Magic: A Study of the Science, Mysticism & Theurgy of Ancient Atlantis. Murry Hope. (Illus.). 1992. pap. 15.00 (*1-85538-069-2*, Pub. by Aqrn Pr) Harper SF.

Practical Atlas of Refractive Surgery. Lee Nordan. 300p. 1997. text 130.00 (*0-397-51641-X*) Lppncott W & W.

Practical Atlas of Retinal Disease & Therapy. 2nd ed. Ed. by William R. Freeman. LC 97-14106. (Illus.). 384p. 1997. text 199.00 (*0-397-51841-2*) Lppncott W & W.

*__Practical Audio Amplifier Circuit Projects.__ Andrew Singmin. LC 99-36689. 160p. 1999. pap. 19.95 (*0-7506-7149-1*, Newnes) Buttrwrth-Heinemann.

Practical Audiology for Speech-Language Therapists. Janet Doyle et al. LC 98-205045. xi, 292p. 1998. write for info. (*1-86156-059-1*) Whurr Pub.

Practical Audiometry Manual, Vol. 1. Stig Arlinger. 226p. 1989. 64.50 (*1-56593-554-3*, 0002) Singular Publishing.

Practical Audiometry Manual, Vol. 2. Stig Arlinger. 248p. 1991. pap. 64.50 (*1-56593-555-1*, 0003) Singular Publishing.

Practical Aural Habilitation: For Speech-Language Pathologists & Educators of Hearing-Impaired Children. Pratibha Srinivasan. LC 95-46954. (Illus.). 382p. 1996. 65.95 (*0-398-06573-X*); pap. 46.95 (*0-398-06574-8*) C C Thomas.

Practical Autolisp. Thomas A. Stellman. (CAD/CAM Ser.). (C). 1990. mass mkt. 41.75 (*0-8273-3663-2*) Delmar.

Practical Avian Medicine. Ed. by Heidi L. Hoefer. (Illus.). 240p. 1997. pap. text 48.00 (*1-884254-34-9*) Vet Lrn Syst.

Practical Aviation Law. 2nd ed. J. Scott Hamilton. 86p. 1995. pap. text, teacher ed. 14.95 (*0-8138-0978-9*) Iowa St U Pr.

Practical Aviation Law. 2nd ed. J. Scott Hamilton. LC 95-44295. (Illus.). 224p. 1995. text 32.95 (*0-8138-0971-1*) Iowa St U Pr.

Practical Aviation Law. 2nd ed. J. Scott Hamilton. (Illus.). 72p. 1996. pap., wbk. ed. 14.95 (*0-8138-0982-7*) Iowa St U Pr.

Practical Aviation Vibration & Noise Handbook. Jack E. Foster. Ed. by Maryanna J. Foster. (Illus.). xii, 276p. 1995. 69.95 (*1-888638-00-1*) Arrow Pr WA.

Practical Ayurveda: Secrets to Physical, Sexual & Spiritual Health. Atreya. LC 97-48967. (Illus.). 256p. 1998. pap. 14.95 (*1-57863-029-0*) Weiser.

Practical Bakery. Paul Connelly. 342p. 1998. 44.95 (*0-470-25522-6*) Wiley.

Practical Baking. 2nd ed. William J. Sultan. 832p. 1989. 69.95 (*0-471-28982-5*) Wiley.

Practical Baking. 5th ed. William J. Sultan. 822p. 1990. text 55.95 (*0-442-31956-8*, VNR) Wiley.

Practical Balance & Hair-Spring Work. Walter J. Kleinlein. (Illus.). 115p. 1992. pap. 11.95 (*0-930163-46-X*) Arlington Bk.

Practical Bank Operation, 2 vols. L. H. Langston. Ed. by Stuart Bruchey. LC 80-1159. (Rise of Commercial Banking Ser.). (Illus.). 1981. reprint ed. lib. bdg. 71.95 (*0-405-13666-8*) Ayer.

Practical Banking. Albert S. Bolles. Ed. by Stuart Bruchey. LC 80-1136. (Rise of Commercial Banking Ser.). 1981. reprint ed. lib. bdg. 30.95 (*0-405-13636-6*) Ayer.

Practical Banking & Building Society Law. Anu Arora. 430p. 1997. pap. 54.00 (*1-85431-628-1*, Pub. by Blackstone Pr) Gaunt.

Practical Bankrptcy Law/paralegals 2e. 2nd rev. ed. Pamela Webster. LC 95-44757. (Paralegal). 500p. (C). 1996. pap. 81.95 (*0-314-06664-0*) West Pub.

Practical Basketball for Teacher & Coach. Connie Johnson. (Illus.). 160p. (Orig.). (C). 1989. spiral bd. 13.80 (*0-87563-332-3*) Stipes.

Practical Bazar Medicines with over 200 Useful Prescriptions. G. T. Birdwood. 220p. 1986. reprint ed. 15.00 (*0-8364-1768-2*, Pub. by Manohar) S Asia.

Practical Beauty Culture, No. I. Milady Publishing Company Staff. (Standard Texts of Cosmetology Ser.). (SPA.). 1990. pap. 24.95 (*0-87350-384-8*, VNR) Wiley.

Practical Beauty Culture Workbook. Milady Editors. (Illus.). 1984. pap. 16.00 (*0-87350-378-3*) Milady Pub.

Practical Beauty Culture Workbook. 2nd ed. Milady Editors. (Illus.). 1988. pap., teacher ed. 23.95 (*0-87350-351-1*) Milady Pub.

Practical Beekeeping. Clive De Bruyn. (Illus.). 288p. 1997. 50.00 (*1-86126-049-0*, Pub. by Crolwood) Trafalgar.

Practical Beekeeping. Roger Griffith & Enoch Tompkins. LC 76-51401. (Illus.). 224p. 1983. pap. 9.95 (*0-88266-091-8*) Storey Bks.

Practical Beginning Theory. 7th ed. Bruce Benward & Barbara Jackson. 1992. teacher ed. 14.68 (*0-697-10636-5*, WCB McGr Hill) McGrw-H Hghr Educ.

Practical Beginning Theory. 7th ed. Bruce Benward & Barbara S. Jackson. (C). 1991. audio. write for info. (*0-697-10637-3*) Brown & Benchmark.

Practical Beginning Theory. 8th ed. Benward. 1999. 31.00 (*0-07-234797-X*) McGraw.

Practical Beginning Theory: A Fundamentals Worktext. 7th ed. Bruce Benward & Barbara S. Jackson. 320p. (C). 1991. text. write for info. (*0-697-10635-7*) Brown & Benchmark.

Practical Beginning Theory: A Fundamentals Worktext. 8th ed. Bruce Benward & Jackson. 336p. 1999. pap. 38.75 (*0-697-34397-9*) McGraw.

Practical Benchwork for Horologists. 8th rev. ed. Louis Levin & Samuel Levin. (Illus.). 382p. 1988. reprint ed. pap. 19.95 (*0-930163-12-5*) Arlington Bk.

Practical Bengali Grammar. W. S. Milne. (BEN & ENG.). 1992. 49.95 (*0-8288-8469-2*) Fr & Eur.

Practical Bible Dictionary & Concordance. 288p. 1985. pap. 3.97 (*0-916441-28-8*) Barbour Pub.

Practical Bible Doctrine. Keith L. Brooks. (Teach Yourself the Bible Ser.). pap. 5.99 (*0-8024-6733-4*, 543) Moody.

Practical Bible Illustrations from Yesterday & Today. Compiled by Charles H. Spurgeon. (Bible Illustrations Ser.). (Illus.). pap. 9.99 (*0-89957-231-6*) AMG Pubs.

Practical Bible Illustrations from Yesterday & Today. Ed. by Rick Steele & Evelyn Stoner. LC 96-86820. (Bible Illustration Ser.). (Illus.). 416p. 1996. 19.99 (*0-89957-228-6*) AMG Pubs.

*__Practical Bible Study Handbook: Personal & Small Group Bible Studies.__ Stephen Hsu. (CHI., Illus.). 166p. 2000. pap. 6.95 (*1-930490-00-3*, 05A-104) CCM Pubs.

P

An Asterisk (*) at the beginning of an entry indicates that the title is appearing for the first time.

Practical Bifurcation & Stability Analysis: From Equilibrium to Chaos. Rudiger Seydel. LC 94-18005. (Interdisciplinary Applied Mathematics Ser.). 1994. 65.95 (*0-387-94316-1*) Spr-Verlag.

Practical Bilevel Optimization: Algorithms & Applications. Jonathan F. Bard. LC 98-45182. (Nonconvex Optimization & Its Applications Ser.). 19p. 1999. 225.00 (*0-7923-5458-3*) Kluwer Academic.

Practical Biochemistry for Advanced Biology. 160p. 1994. pap. text 22.95 (*0-521-43781-4*) Cambridge U Pr.

Practical Biochemistry for Advanced Biology. 80p. 1995. spiral bd. 59.95 (*0-521-43782-2*) Cambridge U Pr.

Practical Biomechanics for the Orthopaedic Surgeon. 2nd ed. Eric L. Radin et al. (Illus.). 216p. 1991. text 62.00 (*0-443-08702-4*) Church.

Practical Biostatistical Methods. S. Selvin. LC 94-30582. 503p. 1994. text, mass mkt. 95.95 incl. 3.5 ld (*0-534-23802-5*) PWS Pubs.

Practical Black Bass Fishing see Field & Stream Bass-Fishing Handbook

Practical Blacksmithing, Vols. I & II, Pt. I. Ed. by M. T. Richardson. LC 98-163049. (Illus.). 262p. 1998. reprint ed. pap. 24.95 (*1-879335-81-6*) Astragal Pr.

Practical Blacksmithing, Vols. III & IV, Pt. II. Ed. by M. T. Richardson. LC 98-163049. (Illus.). 284p. 1998. reprint ed. pap. 27.95 (*1-879335-82-4*) Astragal Pr.

Practical Blacksmithing & Metalworking. 2nd ed. Percy W. Blandford. 368p. 1988. pap. 19.95 (*0-07-155644-3*) McGraw.

Practical Blacksmithing & Metalworking. 2nd ed. Percy W. Blandford. (Illus.). 368p. 1988. 24.95 (*0-8306-0394-8*); pap. 17.95 (*0-8306-2894-0*) McGraw-Hill Prof.

Practical Blood Transfusion. 4th ed. Douglas W. Huestis et al. 489p. 1988. 85.00 (*0-316-37953-0*, Little Brwn Med Div) Lppncott W & W.

Practical Boat Buying. 4th ed. Practical Sailor Staff. 1996. pap. text 47.95 (*0-07-069869-4*) McGraw.

Practical Boat Buying, 2 vols., Set. 4th ed. Practical Sailor Editors. 728p. 1996. 59.95 (*1-879620-41-3*) Belvoir Pubns.

Practical Boat Canvas Work. Lisa Carr. (Illus.). 1996. 25.95 (*1-85310-567-8*) Waterline.

Practical Boating Skills. Katie Hamilton & Gene Hamilton. LC 94-28750. (Illus.). 144p. 1995. pap. 15.95 (*0-688-13205-7*) Hearst Marine Bks.

Practical Boiler Water Treatment: Including Air-Conditioning Systems. Leo I. Pincus. LC 80-29604. 284p. 1981. reprint ed. lib. bdg. 33.50 (*0-89874-255-2*) Krieger.

Practical Bonsai. Colin Lewis. (Illus.). 64p. 1992. pap. 8.95 (*1-85223-661-2*, Pub. by Crolwood) Trafalgar.

Practical Book of American Antiques. Harold D. Eberlein & Abbot McClure. (Paperback Ser.). (Illus.). 1977. reprint ed. pap. 7.95 (*0-306-80062-4*) Da Capo.

Practical Book of Greenhouse Gardening. Ronald H. Menage. 168p. 1983. 7.95 (*0-312-63461-7*) St Martin.

Practical British Two-Stroke: Lightweight Motorcycles. Steve Wilson. (Illus.). 112p. 1990. 29.95 (*0-85429-709-X*, Pub. by GT Foulis) Haynes Manuals.

Practical Buddhism: The Kagyu Path. Ole Nydahl & Carol Aronoff. 48p. (Orig.). 1989. pap. 5.00 (*0-931892-63-5*) B Dolphin Pub.

Practical Builders Estimating. Ed. by W. Wood & W. Howard Wainwright. (C). 1989. 165.00 (*0-09-144931-6*, Pub. by S Thornes Pubs) St Mut.

Practical Building Conservation. Catt. (Illus.). 192p. 1997. text. write for info. (*0-419-21660-X*, E & FN Spon) Routledge.

Practical Building Conservation, Vol.2. John Ashurst & Nicola Malnic. 1988. 51.95 (*0-291-39746-8*) Ashgate Pub Co.

Practical Building Conservation, Vol.4. John Ashurst & Nicola Malnic. 1988. 51.95 (*0-291-39748-4*) Ashgate Pub Co.

Practical Building Conservations, Vol.5. Ashurst. 128p. 1988. 51.95 (*0-291-39776-X*) Ashgate Pub Co.

Practical Business Chinese. Wei Hong. (CHI & ENG.). 180p. 1997. 16.95 (*0-8351-2590-4*); 24.95 incl. audio (*0-8351-2591-2*) China Bks.

Practical Business Communication. Tim J. Saben. LC 93-33173. (Business Skills Express Ser.). (Illus.). 104p. 1993. pap. 10.95 (*0-7863-0227-5*, Irwn Prfssnl) McGraw-Hill Prof.

Practical Business Conversations. Chen-Ch'Ing Li & Te-Ming Yeh. (CHI.). 225p. (Orig.). 1992. pap. text 18.95 (*0-88710-172-0*) Yale Far Eastern Pubns.

Practical Business English. Colleen Vawdrey et al. LC 92-17684. 512p. 1992. teacher ed. write for info. (*0-256-11562-1*, Irwn McGrw-H) McGrw-H Hghr Educ.

Practical Business Ethics. Warren A. French. LC 93-50588. (Illus.). 256p. (C). 1994. pap. text 45.00 (*0-02-338863-3*, Macmillan Coll) P-H.

Practical Business Forecasting. J. Saunders et al. 250p. 1986. text 87.95 (*0-566-02516-7*, Pub. by Gower) Ashgate Pub Co.

Practical Business Forecasting. Jae K. Shim. 248p. 1998. ring bd. 65.00 (*1-882312-34-1*) Delta Pub CA.

Practical Business Law. 3rd ed. John J. Moran. LC 94-25594. 480p. 1994. 62.00 (*0-13-138660-3*) P-H.

Practical Business Math. 5th ed. Slater. 1996. student ed. 54.50 (*0-256-24362-X*) McGraw.

Practical Business Math. 7th ed. Michael D. Tuttle. LC 97-16215. 492p. 1997. pap. text 72.00 (*0-13-615916-8*) P-H.

Practical Business Math: An Applications Approach. 5th ed. Michael D. Tuttle. 528p. (C). 1989. text 51.25 (*0-697-08487-6*, WCB McGr Hill) McGrw-H Hghr Educ.

Practical Business Math: An Applications Approach. 5th ed. Michael D. Tuttle. 528p. 1989. text 14.38 (*0-697-11321-3*, WCB McGr Hill) McGrw-H Hghr Educ.

Practical Business Math: An Applications Approach. 6th ed. Michael D. Tuttle. 384p. (C). 1993. text 27.50 (*0-697-12448-7*, WCB McGr Hill) McGrw-H Hghr Educ.

***Practical Business Math: An Applications Approach.** 8th ed. Michael D. Tuttle. LC 99-89103. 512p. 2000. pap. 57.33 (*0-13-025667-6*) P-H.

***Practical Business Math: An Applications Approach, Brief Edition.** 8th ed. Michael D. Tuttle. 400p. 2000. pap. 36.00 (*0-13-025660-9*) P-H.

***Practical Business Math: Applications Approach.** 8th ed. 608p. (C). 2000. write for info. (*0-13-026486-5*) P-H.

Practical Business Math Procedures. Jeffrey Slater. (C). 1982. 48.95 (*0-256-02832-X*, Irwn McGrw-H) McGrw-H Hghr Educ.

Practical Business Math Procedures. 4th ed. Jeffrey Slater. LC 92-44528. 1993. text. write for info. (*0-256-11791-8*, Irwn McGrw-H) McGrw-H Hghr Educ.

Practical Business Math Procedures. 4th ed. Jeffrey Slater. LC 92-44528. 640p. (C). 1993. per. 49.95 (*0-256-11217-7*, Irwn McGrw-H) McGrw-H Hghr Educ.

Practical Business Math Procedures. 5th ed. Jeffrey Slater. 656p. (C). 1996. text 50.00 (*0-256-19381-9*, Irwn McGrw-H) McGrw-H Hghr Educ.

Practical Business Math Procedures. 5th ed. Jeffrey Slater. (C). 1996. text, student ed. 56.20 incl. disk (*0-256-24249-6*, Irwn McGrw-H) McGrw-H Hghr Educ.

Practical Business Math Procedures. 5th ed. Jeffrey Slater. 80p. (C). 1996. text, student ed. 20.00 (*0-256-21546-4*, Irwn McGrw-H) McGrw-H Hghr Educ.

Practical Business Math Procedures. 5th abr. ed. Jeffrey Slater. 400p. (C). 1996. text 38.00 (*0-256-21085-3*, Irwn McGrw-H) McGrw-H Hghr Educ.

Practical Business Math Procedures. 6th ed. Slater. LC 99-15438. 1999. 54.50 (*0-07-366064-7*) McGraw.

***Practical Business Math Procedures.** 6th ed. Jeffrey Slater. 88p. (C). 1999. pap., student ed. 22.19 (*0-07-233149-6*) McGrw-H Hghr Educ.

***Practical Business Math Procedures** 6th ed. Jeffrey Slater. LC 99-15438. 2000. write for info. (*0-07-366065-5*) McGrw-H Hghr Educ.

Practical Business Math Procedures: Business Math Handbook. 5th ed. Jeffrey Slater. (C). 1996. pap. text 9.88 (*0-256-23874-X*, Irwn McGrw-H) McGrw-H Hghr Educ.

***Practical Business Math Procedures: Electronic Calculator Guide.** 6th ed. Jeffrey Slater. 112p. (C). 1999. pap. 17.50 (*0-07-233157-7*) McGrw-H Hghr Educ.

Practical Business Math Procedures: Selected Material. 4th ed. Jeffrey Slater. (C). 1994. pap. text 27.95 (*0-256-18011-3*, Irwn McGrw-H) McGrw-H Hghr Educ.

Practical Business Math Procedures: The Electronic Calculator Guide. 5th ed. Jann Underwood. 104p. (C). 1996. text 13.00 (*0-256-22661-X*, Irwn McGrw-H) McGrw-H Hghr Educ.

***Practical Business Math Procedures: With Business Math Handbook, Wall Street Journal Insert & CD-ROM.** 6th ed. Jeffrey Slater. (C). 1999. student ed. 68.44 incl. cd-rom (*0-07-233759-1*) McGrw-H Hghr Educ.

Practical Business Math Procedures & Metric. 4th ed. Jeffrey Slater. 16p. (C). 1996. text 50.00 (*0-256-19105-0*, Irwn McGrw-H) McGrw-H Hghr Educ.

Practical Business Math Procedures Package: With Electronic Calculator Guide & Business Math Handbook. 5th ed. Jeffrey Slater & Jann Underwood. (C). 1996. text 54.50 (*0-256-23835-9*, Irwn McGrw-H) McGrw-H Hghr Educ.

Practical Business Negotiations in French-English-Spanish. B. Lapeyre. (ENG, FRE & SPA.). 174p. 1992. 24.95 (*0-7859-7513-6*, 8428319464); pap. 22.00 (*0-7859-8919-6*) Fr & Eur.

Practical Business Negotiations in French-English-Spanish. B. Lapeyre & P. Sheppard. (ENG, FRE & SPA.). 174p. 1992. pap. 23.25 (*84-283-1946-4*, Pub. by Paraninfo) IBD Ltd.

Practical Business Re-Engineering: Tools & Techniques for Achieving Effective Change. Nick Obolensky. LC 95-12523. 346p. 1995. 29.95 (*0-88415-646-X*, 5646) Gulf Pub.

Practical Business Statistics. 2nd ed. Andrew F. Siegel. 128p. (C). 1994. text, student ed. 11.25 (*0-256-16787-7*, Irwn McGrw-H) McGrw-H Hghr Educ.

Practical Business Statistics. 3rd ed. Siegel. (C). 1996. text, student ed. 73.74 (*0-256-26674-3*) McGraw.

Practical Business Statistics. 3rd ed. Andrew F. Siegel. 120p. (C). 1996. text, student ed. 11.25 (*0-256-21490-5*, Irwn McGrw-H) McGrw-H Hghr Educ.

Practical Business Statistics. 3rd ed. Andrew F. Siegel. 880p. (C). 1996. text 71.25 (*0-256-25739-6*, Irwn McGrw-H); text 82.75 (*0-256-24217-8*, Irwn McGrw-H) McGrw-H Hghr Educ.

Practical Business Statistics. 3rd ed. Andrew F. Siegel. 456p. (C). 1996. text, student ed. 24.37 (*0-256-21489-1*, Irwn McGrw-H) McGrw-H Hghr Educ.

Practical Business Statistics. 3rd ed. Andrew F. Siegel. 880p. (C). 1996. text 68.50 (*0-256-19407-6*, Irwn McGrw-H) McGrw-H Hghr Educ.

Practical Business Statistics. 3rd annot. ed. Andrew F. Siegel. 1996. teacher ed. write for info. (*0-256-21492-1*, Irwn McGrw-H) McGrw-H Hghr Educ.

Practical Business Statistics. 4th ed. Siegel. LC 99-462499. 1999. 67.50 (*0-07-366061-2*) McGraw.

***Practical Business Statistics.** 4th ed. Andrew F. Siegel. LC 99-462499. (Illus.). 2000. write for info. (*0-07-117788-4*, Irwn Prfssnl) McGraw-Hill Prof.

***Practical Business Statistics.** 4th ed. Andrew F. Siegel. (C). 1999. 87.81 incl. cd-rom (*0-07-233755-9*); pap., student ed. 20.31 (*0-07-233617-X*) McGrw-H Hghr Educ.

Practical Business Statistics: Statpad Manual. 3rd ed. Andrew F. Siegel & Skyline Technologies. 88p. (C). 1996. pap., text 16.87 incl. disk (*0-256-22478-1*, Irwn McGrw-H) McGrw-H Hghr Educ.

Practical Business Statistics Minitab Guide. 2nd ed. Andrew F. Siegel. 144p. (C). 1993. text 10.50 (*0-256-11942-2*, Irwn McGrw-H) McGrw-H Hghr Educ.

Practical Business Statistics Minitab Guide. 3rd ed. Andrew F. Siegel. LC 96-213485. 160p. (C). 1996. text 12.50 (*0-256-22481-1*, Irwn McGrw-H) McGrw-H Hghr Educ.

Practical C++ Rob McGregor. 900p. 1999. pap. 29.99 (*0-7897-2144-9*) Que.

Practical C++ Programming. Steve Oualline. Ed. by Adrian Nye. LC 96-137928. 584p. 1995. reprint ed. pap. 34.95 (*1-56592-139-9*) Thomson Learn.

Practical C Programming. 2nd ed. Steven Qualline. (Computer Science). (Illus.). 396p. 1993. pap. 29.95 (*1-56592-035-X*) Thomson Learn.

Practical C Programming. 3rd rev. ed. Steve Oualline. Ed. by Andy Oram. (Illus.). 454p. (Orig.). 1997. pap. 34.95 (*1-56592-306-5*) OReilly & Assocs.

Practical Cacti Growing. Patrick Johns. (Illus.). 64p. 1993. pap. 8.95 (*1-85223-730-9*, Pub. by Crolwood) Trafalgar.

Practical CAD Training, CAD CAM: Design & Planning Data for Production. Paul Gunnar. 227p. 1991. pap. 19.95 (*1-56990-036-1*) Hanser-Gardner.

Practical CAD Training, CAD 3D Pt. 2: Introduction to Three-Dimensional Design. Christian Bohler. 212p. 1990. pap. 19.95 (*1-56990-005-1*) Hanser-Gardner.

Practical CAD Training, CAD 2D Pt. 1: Introduction to Two-Dimensional Design. Paul Gunnar. 202p. 1990. pap. 19.95 (*1-56990-035-3*) Hanser-Gardner.

Practical Calculation of Interionic Potentials in Solids, Set, Pts. 1 & 2. Ed. by A. H. Harker. iv, 192p. 1990. pap. text 361.00 (*2-88124-739-3*) Gordon & Breach.

Practical Calculations for Business Studies: Problems & Applications for Students in Africa. V. N. Newcomb. LC 80-42019. 164p. reprint ed. pap. 50.90 (*0-608-15631-0*, 203176000076) Bks Demand.

Practical Camp Cook. Fred Bouwman. 218p. 1988. 17.98 (*0-88290-328-4*) Horizon Utah.

Practical Canadian Mortgage Guide. Richard Steacy. 164p. 1986. pap. 9.95 (*0-7737-5057-6*) Genl Dist Srvs.

Practical Candleburning Rituals. 3rd ed. Raymond Buckland. LC 86-20915. (Practical Magick Ser.). (Illus.). 210p. 1982. pap. 7.95 (*0-87542-048-6*) Llewellyn Pubns.

Practical Capillary Electrophoresis. Robert Weinberger. (Illus.). 312p. 1993. text 59.00 (*0-12-742355-9*) Acad Pr.

***Practical Capillary Electrophoresis.** 2nd ed. Robert Weinberg. (Illus.). 2000. 89.95 (*0-12-742356-7*) Acad Pr.

Practical Capital Allowances. Peter Newbold & Martin Wilson. 220p. 1994. boxed set 88.00 (*0-406-03484-2*, UK, MICHIE) LEXIS Pub.

***Practical Cardiology.** A. H. Khan. (Illus.). 550p. 1999. text 47.50 (*0-340-74111-2*, Pub. by E A) OUP.

Practical Cardiology. C. V. Shah. (Illus.). 246p. 1985. 23.50 (*0-318-36367-4*) Asia Bk Corp.

Practical Cardiovascular Pathology. Mary N. Sheppard & Michael J. Davies. (An Arnold Publication). (Illus.). 240p. 1998. text 125.00 (*0-340-67749-X*) OUP.

Practical Care of the Ambulatory Patient. Kenneth Stults & Dere. 592p. 1989. text 80.00 (*0-7216-2474-X*, W B Saunders Co) Harcrt Hlth Sci Grp.

Practical Carriage & Wagon Painting. M. C. Hillick. LC 97-70455. (Illus.). 180p. 1997. reprint ed. pap. 17.95 (*1-879335-77-8*) Astragal Pr.

Practical Carriage Building, Set, Vols. I & II. Ed. by M. T. Richardson. LC 94-70620. (Illus.). 512p. 1994. reprint ed. pap. 24.95 (*1-879335-50-6*) Astragal Pr.

Practical Case Analysis. Linda L. Edwards. LC 95-26178. 250p. (C). 1996. mass mkt. 44.95 (*0-314-06434-6*) West Pub.

Practical Casting. rev. ed. 128p. 1994. spiral bd. 13.95 (*0-9615984-5-X*) Brynmorgen.

Practical Catalan-Castilian, Castilian-Catalan Dictionary: Diccionari Practic Catila-Castella-Catala. 9th ed. Miguel Arimany Coma. 232p. 1981. pap. 14.95 (*0-7859-4940-2*) Fr & Eur.

Practical Catalan Dictionary of Synonyms, Words & Phrases see Diccionari Practic de Sinonims Catalans: Mots i Frases

Practical Catechism, 3 vols. Henry Hammond. LC 79-168238. (Library of Anglo-Catholic Theology: No. 8). reprint ed. 87.50 (*0-404-52090-1*) AMS Pr.

Practical Celestial Navigation. rev. ed. Susan P. Howell. Ed. by Donald Treworgy. (Illus.). 272p. 1987. pap. 19.95 (*0-939510-05-7*) Mystic Seaport.

Practical Cell Culture Techniques. Ed. by Alan A. Boulton et al. LC 92-1518. (Neuromethods Ser.: Vol. 23). 380p. 1992. 69.50 (*0-89603-214-0*); pap. 79.50 (*0-89603-348-1*) Humana.

Practical Cellular & PCS Design. Clint Smith. LC 97-33009. (Telecommunications Ser.). (Illus.). 400p. 1997. 69.95 (*0-07-059287-X*) McGraw.

Practical Chemistry in the Twelfth Century. Muhammad Ibn Zakariya. Ed. by Robert R. Steele. Tr. by Gerard Of Cremona. LC 79-8590. reprint ed. 37.50 (*0-404-18444-8*) AMS Pr.

Practical Chemotherapy of Malaria: Report of a WHO Scientific Group. (Technical Reports: No. 805). (ENG, FRE & SPA.). 158p. 1990. pap. text 16.00 (*92-4-120805-8*, 1100805) World Health.

Practical Chess Analysis. 3rd ed. Mark Buckley. (Illus.). 200p. 1998. pap. text 19.95 (*0-938650-88-2*) Thinkers Pr.

Practical Chess Endings. Paul Kerns. 1985. pap. 12.95 (*0-8011-4418-3*) Calif Education.

Practical Chess Endings. Irving Chernev. LC 69-15362. (Illus.). 318p. 1969. reprint ed. pap. 8.95 (*0-486-22208-X*) Dover.

Practical Child Support Collection Workbook. Gary L. Callahan. 65p. (Orig.). 1991. pap., wbk. ed. 10.00 (*1-890471-00-3*) Charis Pubns.

Practical Child Support Collection Workbook. rev. ed. Gary L. Callahan. 75p. (Orig.). 1997. pap., wbk. ed. 14.95 (*1-890471-01-1*) Charis Pubns.

Practical Chin Na. Zhao Da Yuan. (Illus.). 211p. 1993. pap. 17.95 (*0-86568-175-9*) Unique Pubns.

Practical Chin Na: A Detailed Analysis of the Art of Seizing & Locking. Zhao D. Yun. Tr. by Tim Cartnell from CHI. (Illus.). 224p. (Orig.). 1993. pap. 17.95 (*1-883175-02-X*) High View Pubns.

Practical Chinese Dialogues Two. Ching-yi Li et al. Ed. by Chen-ch'ing Li & Te-ming Yeh. (Mandarin Training Center Ser.). (CHI.). 619p. (Orig.). 1991. pap. text 28.95 (*0-88710-166-6*) Yale Far Eastern Pubns.

Practical Chinese Dialogues Two: Student Workbook. (Mandarin Training Center Ser.). (CHI.). 57p. (Orig.). 1991. student ed. 9.95 (*0-88710-167-4*) Yale Far Eastern Pubns.

Practical Chinese Grammar. Hung-nin S. Cheung et al. 550p. 1997. pap. text 39.50 (*962-201-595-6*, Pub. by Chinese Univ) U of Mich Pr.

Practical Chinese Grammar for Foreigners. Compiled by Li Dejin & Cheng Meizhen. 742p. 1988. 22.95 (*0-8351-1917-3*) China Bks.

Practical Chinese Reader, Bk. 1. 551p. 1981. pap. 16.95 (*7-100-00088-2*) China Bks.

Practical Chinese Reader, Bk. 2. 506p. 1981. pap. 16.95 (*7-100-00089-0*) China Bks.

Practical Chinese Reader, No. 5. (Illus.). (C). 1989. pap. 16.95 (*7-100-00036-X*) China Bks.

Practical Chinese Reader, Elementary Course Bk. 1: Traditional Character Edition. Beijing Language Institute Staff. (C & T Asian Language Ser.). 394p. (C). 1990. pap. text 18.95 (*0-88727-229-0*) Cheng & Tsui.

Practical Chinese Reader I: Patterns & Exercises (Simplified Character Edition) rev. ed. Madeline M. Chu. LC 89-51123. (C & T Asian Language Ser.). (CHI.). 200p. (Orig.). 1992. pap., student ed. 14.95 (*0-88727-233-9*) Cheng & Tsui.

Practical Chinese Reader I: Patterns & Exercises, Traditional Character Edition. rev. ed. Madeline M. Chu. LC 90-91839. (C & T Asian Language Ser.). 224p. (Orig.). (C). 1993. pap. text, student ed. 14.95 (*0-88727-187-1*) Cheng & Tsui.

Practical Chinese Reader II: Patterns & Exercises, Simplified Character Edition. expanded ed. Ling-hsia Yeh. (C & T Asian Language Ser.). 171p. (Orig.). (C). 1995. pap. text, student ed. 14.95 (*0-88727-208-8*) Cheng & Tsui.

Practical Chinese Reader II: Patterns & Exercises, Traditional Character Edition. expanded rev. ed. Ling-hsia Yeh. LC 93-74711. (C & T Asian Language Ser.). 171p. (Orig.). (C). 1995. pap., student ed. 14.95 (*0-88727-200-2*) Cheng & Tsui.

Practical Chinese Reader III. Li Xun et al. (Illus.). 393p. 1986. pap. 16.95 (*0-8351-1788-X*) China Bks.

Practical Chinese Reader IV. Liu Xun et al. (Illus.). 381p. (Orig.). (C). 1987. pap. 16.95 (*0-8351-1814-2*) China Bks.

Practical Chinese Reader 1 & 2: Writing Workbook, Traditional Character Edition. rev. ed. Ed. by Shou-hsin Teng. (C & T Asian Language Ser.). 150p. (C). 1993. pap. text 8.95 (*0-88727-191-X*) Cheng & Tsui.

Practical Christian (James) Gordon J. Keddie. 1989. pap. 11.99 (*0-85234-261-6*, Pub. by Evangelical Pr) P & R Pubng.

Practical Christian Living. Wayne Taylor. Ed. by Chuck Smith. (Calvary Basics Ser.). 161p. 1995. pap. 3.50 (*0-936728-57-4*) Word for Today.

Practical Christian Living: Teacher's Guide. Priority Associates Staff. 149p. Date not set. pap., teacher ed. 15.00 (*1-57902-082-8*, 5401g) Integrtd Res.

Practical Christian Living Vol. 1: Lessons 1-9, Nos. 1-9. Priority Associates Staff. 106p. Date not set. 11.00 (*1-57902-080-1*) Integrtd Res.

Practical Christian Living Vol. 2: Lessons 10-18, Nos. 10-18. Priority Associates Staff. 218p. Date not set. 6.00 (*1-57902-081-X*) Integrtd Res.

Practical Christian Socialism. Adin Ballou. LC 72-2936. (Communal Societies in America Ser.). reprint ed. 61.50 (*0-404-10702-8*) AMS Pr.

Practical Christian Socialism, 2 vols. Adin Ballou. 655p. 1985. reprint ed. lib. bdg. 79.00 (*0-932051-86-3*) Rprt Serv.

Practical Christian Theology: Examining the Great Doctrines of the Faith. 3rd ed. Floyd H. Barackman. LC 97-49304. 576p. 1998. pap. text 22.99 (*0-8254-2374-0*) Kregel.

Practical Christianity. Arthur W. Pink. 232p. (gr. 10). 1995. pap. 9.99 (*0-8010-6990-4*) Baker Bks.

Practical Christianity: Divine Lessons for Daily Living from the Book of James. Albert B. Simpson. LC 95-83826. 117p. 1996. pap. 9.99 (*0-87509-658-1*) Chr Pubns.

Practical Christianity: Studies in the Book of James. David L. Roper. 148p. 1987. pap. 6.99 (*0-89225-291-X*, G5291X) Gospel Advocate.

Practical Church Computing. Ed. by Stoker Wilson. (C). 1989. 49.00 (*0-7855-4421-6*, Pub. by Jay Bks) St Mut.

***Practical Cinematography.** Paul Wheeler. LC 99-57567. 178p. 2000. pap. 34.95 (*0-240-51555-2*, Focal) Buttrwrth-Heinemann.

Practical Circuit Analysis of Amplifiers. Lorne MacDonald. 544p. 1994. pap. text 25.00 (*0-911908-22-6*) Tech Ed Pr.

***Practical Cisco Routers.** Joe Habraken. 350p. 1999. pap. 29.99 (*0-7897-2103-1*) Que.

P

Practical Classroom Applications of Language Experience: Looking Back, Looking Forward. Olga G. Nelson et al. LC 98-21656. 280p. 1998. pap. text 34.00 (*0-205-26156-6*) Allyn.

Practical Cleanroom Design. rev. ed. Raymond K. Schneider. LC 94-40439. 1995. 34.95 (*1-885863-03-9*) Busn News.

Practical Clematis Growing. Ian Murray. (Illus.). 64p. 1993. pap. 8.95 (*1-85223-656-6*, Pub. by Crolwood) Trafalgar.

Practical Clinical Biochemistry. 6th ed. Alan H. Gowenlock Varley. 1988. 105.00 (*0-8493-0156-4*) CRC Pr.

Practical Clinical Psychopharmacology. 3rd ed. William Appleton. 224p. 1988. pap. 33.00 (*0-683-00239-2*) Lppncott W & W.

Practical Clinical Ultrasonic Diagnosis. 300p. 1997. 54.00 (*981-02-2922-4*) World Scientific Pub.

***Practical Clock Escapements.** Laurie Penman. (Illus.). 245p. 1998. 42.50 (*0-9523270-4-X*) Clockwks Pr.

Practical Clock Repairing. 2nd ed. Donald De Carle. (Illus.). 243p. 1987. 35.00 (*0-7198-0000-5*, Pub. by NAG Press) Antique Collect.

Practical CM. unabridged ed. David D. Lyon. (Illus.). 301p. 1996. spiral bd. 45.00 (*0-9661248-7-1*) Raven Publ.

***Practical CM: Best Configuration Management Practices for the 21st Century.** David D. Lyon. 208p. 2000. 59.95 (*0-7506-4724-8*) Buttrwrth-Heinemann.

Practical CM: Best Configuration Management Practices for the 21st Century. 2nd rev. ed. David D. Lyon. (Illus.). 210p. 1999. spiral bd. 55.00 (*0-9661248-4-7*) Raven Publ.

Practical CNC-Training for Planning & Shop: Working Transparencies for Part 1: Fundamentals. Josef Franz. 130p. 1985. 159.95 (*1-56990-021-3*) Hanser-Gardner.

Practical CNC-Training for Planning & Shop: Working Transparencies for Part 2: Examples & Exercises. Josef Franz. 96p. 1989. 159.95 (*1-56990-020-5*) Hanser-Gardner.

Practical CNC-Training for Planning & Shop Pt. 1: Fundamentals. Josef Franz. 184p. 1985. pap. 59.95 (*1-56990-023-X*) Hanser-Gardner.

Practical CNC-Training for Planning & Shop Pt. 2: Examples & Exercises. Josef Franz. 191p. 1988. pap. 59.95 (*1-56990-022-1*) Hanser-Gardner.

Practical CNC-Training for Planning & Shop Pt. 3: Turning & Complete Machining on Single & Twin-Slide Turning Centers. Hans G. Frommer. 281p. 1990. pap. 69.95 (*1-56990-024-8*) Hanser-Gardner.

Practical Coaching Techniques, 10 bks., Set. Mel Rosen et al. 1981. 39.95 (*0-932741-95-9*) Championship Bks & Vid Prodns.

Practical Coal Mine Management. Scott G. Britton. LC 81-11426. 248p. 1986. reprint ed. 40.50 (*0-471-09035-2*, (JW)) Krieger.

Practical College Reading. Gene Wintner. LC 94-9321. 480p. (C). 1994. text 19.90 (*0-256-15451-1*, Irwn McGrw-H) McGrw-H Hghr Educ.

Practical Color Magick. Raymond Buckland. LC 83-80173. (Practical Magick Ser.). (Illus.). 160p. 1983. pap. 6.95 (*0-87542-047-8*) Llewellyn Pubns.

Practical Color Measurement: A Primer for the Beginner, a Reminder for the Expert. Anni Berger-Schunn. Tr. by Max Saltzman from GER. 192p. 1994. 79.95 (*0-471-00417-0*) Wiley.

Practical Communication Antennas with Wireless. Leo Setian. LC 97-36373. 608p. (C). 1997. 82.00 (*0-13-652355-2*) P-H.

Practical Communication Theory. Dave Adamy. 160p. 1994. 49.95 (*1-885897-04-9*) Lynx Pubng.

Practical Companion to Ethics. Anthony Weston. 128p. (C). 1996. pap. text 14.95 (*0-19-510534-6*) OUP.

Practical Companion to Reservoir Simulation. Michael J. Economides. (Developments in Petroleum Science Ser.: Vol. 34). xii,226p. 1992. 104.00 (*0-444-89324-5*) Elsevier.

Practical Compendium of Colorpuncture. Peter Mandel. Tr. by Christopher Baker from GER. (Illus.). 269p. 1986. text 98.00 (*3-925806-08-3*) Medicina Bio.

***Practical Compendium of the Law of Master & Servant in General & Especially of Employers & Workmen under the Acts of 1875 with Suggestions for Its Improvement.** Charles Petersdorff. vii, 147p. 1999. reprint ed. 48.00 (*1-56169-548-3*, 18112) Gaunt.

Practical Competencies: An HVAC-R Lab Book. Cecil Johnson. 928p. 1998. lab manual ed. 35.95 (*0-8273-8458-0*) Delmar.

Practical Comprehensive Treatment of Anorexia Nervosa & Bulimia. Arnold E. Andersen. LC 84-47958. (Johns Hopkins Series in Contemporary Medicine & Public Health). 224p. 1985. reprint ed. pap. 69.50 (*0-608-03639-0*, 206446500009) Bks Demand.

Practical Computer Data Communications. W. J. Barksdale. (Applications of Communications Theory Ser.). (Illus.). 470p. (C). 1986. 110.00 (*0-306-42323-5*, Plenum Trade) Perseus Pubng.

Practical Computer Engineering Skills. Ronald Ayling. LC 96-26970. (Illus.). 149p. (Orig.). 2000. pap. 18.95 (*1-56072-366-1*, Nova Kroshka Bks) Nova Sci Pubs.

Practical Computer Ethics. Duncan Langford. LC 95-2503. 1995. pap. write for info. (*0-07-709012-8*) McGraw.

Practical Computer Exercises. Bradley. 1997. pap. write for info. (*0-7299-0261-7*) Addison-Wesley.

Practical Computer Network Security. Mike Hendry. LC 95-23939. 203p. 1995. 69.00 (*0-89006-801-1*) Artech Hse.

Practical Computer Vision Using C. J. R. Parker. LC 93-549. 1993. 32.00 (*0-471-59411-3*); pap. 74.99 incl. disk (*0-471-59262-5*) Wiley.

Practical Computer Vision Using C. James R. Parker. 476p. 1993. pap. 37.95 (*0-471-59259-5*) Wiley.

Practical Concerns about Siblings: Bridging the Research-Practice Gap. Ed. by Frances F. Schachter & Richard K. Stone. LC 87-31095. (Journal of Children in Contemporary Society: Vol. 19, Nos. 3-4). (Illus.). 211p. 1988. text 6.95 (*0-86656-647-3*) Haworth Pr.

Practical Concrete Quality Assurance: Computer Aided Statistical Analysis Approach. Clifford Gordon et al. 1999. 65.00 (*0-8493-2707-5*, 2707) CRC Pr.

Practical Conduct of Play. Henry S. Curtis. 1982. 26.95 (*0-8434-0429-9*, Pub. by McGrath NH) Ayer.

Practical Conservation in English, Bk. 2. Eugene J. Hall. 176p. (C). 1987. pap. text 17.20 (*0-13-689159-4*) Prentice ESL.

Practical Conservation in English 2. Eugene J. Hall. 158p. (gr. 9-12). 1981. pap. text 4.75 (*0-88345-439-4*, 20064) Prentice ESL.

Practical Conservation in English 2. Eugene J. Hall. 158p. (YA). (gr. 9-12). 1981. audio 45.00 (*0-686-86691-6*, 40028) Prentice ESL.

Practical Considerations of RF. Bernardin. text. write for info. (*0-471-49183-7*) Wiley.

Practical Construction Science. Brian J. Smith. LC 79-40562. (Longman Technician Series, Construction & Civil Engineering). 348p. reprint ed. pap. 107.90 (*0-608-13166-0*, 202523500043) Bks Demand.

Practical Container Gardening. David Carr. (Illus.). 64p. 1992. pap. 8.95 (*1-85223-621-3*, Pub. by Crolwood) Trafalgar.

Practical Contemporary Home Plans. Ed. by National Plan Service, Inc. Staff. (Illus.). 32p. (Orig.). reprint ed. pap. 3.95 (*0-934039-09-7*, A52) Hme Dsgn Altntves.

Practical Continous Improvement for Professional Services. Clive Shearer. LC 94-28615. (Illus.). 312p. 1994. 30.00 (*0-87389-281-X*, H0837) ASQ Qual Pr.

Practical Conversation in English, Bk. 1. Eugene Hall. (C). 1987. 98.67 (*0-13-689175-6*, PH Regents) P-H.

Practical Conversation in English, Bk. 1. Eugene J. Hall. (Practical Conversations in English Ser.). 176p. (YA). (gr. 9-12). 1987. pap. text 17.20 (*0-13-689142-X*, 20052) Prentice ESL.

Practical Conversation in English 1. Eugene J. Hall. (Practical Conversations in English Ser.). (YA). (gr. 9-12). 1987. 40.00 (*0-685-04297-9*, 40016) Prentice ESL.

Practical Conversational English, Bk. 3. Eugene J. Hall. 176p. 1987. pap. text 17.20 (*0-13-689167-5*) P-H.

Practical Cook Book. J. H. Tilden. 222p. 1996. reprint ed. spiral bd. 17.50 (*0-7873-0876-5*) Hlth Research.

Practical Cook Book Including Suggestions Regarding Proper Food Combinations with Illustrative Menus (1926) J. H. Tilden. (Illus.). 218p. 1996. reprint ed. pap. 15.95 (*1-56459-872-1*) Kessinger Pub.

Practical Cookery. 7th ed. Victor Ceserani & Ronald Kinton. 570p. 1993. text 39.95 (*0-470-23351-6*) Halsted Pr.

Practical Cooling Technology. Johnson. (Heating, Ventilation/Air Conditioning Ser.). 1997. pap., teacher ed. 14.95 (*0-8273-6815-1*, VNR) Wiley.

Practical Cooling Technology. William M. Johnson. LC 96-41093. (Heating, Ventilation & Air Conditioning Ser.). 672p. 1996. mass mkt. 92.95 (*0-8273-6814-3*) Delmar.

Practical Cooling Technology Lab Manual. Johnson. 160p. 1997. lab manual ed. 15.95 (*0-8273-7603-0*) Delmar.

Practical Corporate Planning. 3rd ed. John Argenti. 434p. 1989. pap. 14.99 (*0-415-09100-4*) Routledge.

Practical Corrosion Control Methods for Gas Utility Piping. 2nd ed. Lindsay Enloe. LC 76-5317. (Illus.). 80p. 1994. 68.00 (*1-877914-79-7*) NACE Intl.

Practical Cost Estimating for Fabricated Weldments for Welding Shops. George Kuprianczyk & Hans Ceisel. LC 97-207331. (Illus.). 1997. write for info. (*0-912914-72-6*) Practical Pubns.

Practical Cost Estimating for Machining Operations for Machine Shops. George Kuprianczyk & Hans Ceisel. LC 97-207324. (Illus.). 1997. write for info. (*0-912914-71-8*) Practical Pubns.

Practical Cost Estimating for Metal Fabrication. Richard S. Budzik & George Kuprianczyk. 1988. 84.95 (*0-912914-70-X*) Practical Pubns.

Practical Cost-Saving Techniques for Housing Construction. Bart Jahn. LC 94-30226. 1994. text 50.00 (*0-07-005208-5*) McGraw.

Practical Counseling Principles for the Christian: Biblical Counseling & How to Give It. Jeffery A. Owens. Ed. by Linda Stubbelfield. LC 97-95058. 384p. 1998. pap. 13.95 (*0-9649393-1-2*) Owens Publns.

Practical Counseling Tools for Pastoral Workers. Dan Montgomery. LC 96-1949. 144p. (Orig.). 1996. pap. 10.95 (*0-8198-5899-4*) Pauline Bks.

Practical Counselling & Helping. Philip Burnard. LC 98-49632. 1999. pap. write for info. (*0-415-18883-0*) Routledge.

Practical Counselor: Elements of Effective Helping. Philip Lauver & David R. Harvey. LC 96-12007. 277p. (C). 1996. mass mkt. 45.95 (*0-534-34349-X*) Brooks-Cole.

Practical Course in Functional Programming Using ML. Richard Bosworth. LC 95-51. 1995. 19.95 (*0-07-707625-7*) McGraw.

Practical Course in Terminology Processing. Juan C. Sager. LC 90-1018. xii, 252p. 1990. 65.00 (*1-55619-112-X*); pap. text 19.95 (*1-55619-113-8*) J Benjamins Pubng Co.

Practical Critical Care in Cardiology. Zab Mohsenifar & P. K. Shah. LC 97-45024. (Fundamental & Clinical Cardiology Ser.). (Illus.). 472p. 1997. text 165.00 (*0-8247-0097-X*) Dekker.

Practical Criticism - Chinese Edition: Giving It & Taking It. John W. Alexander. Tr. by Samuel E. Kao. (CHI.). 19p. 1986. pap. 1.50 (*1-56582-015-0*) Christ Renew Min.

Practical Criticism, a Study of Literary Judgment. Ivor A. Richards. LC 56-13740. 378p. 1956. pap. 9.95 (*0-15-673626-8*, Harvest Bks) Harcourt.

Practical Cross Country: A Rider's Guide to Hunter Trials. Jane Holderness-Roddam. (Illus.). 176p. (Orig.). 1996. pap. 19.95 (*0-7063-7505-X*, Pub. by WrLock) Sterling.

Practical Cross Infection Control in Dentistry. Peter R. Wood. (Illus.). 207p. (C). (gr. 13). 1992. text 55.95 (*0-8151-9439-0*, 21903) Mosby Inc.

Practical CT Techniques. W. Gedroyc & S. C. Rankin. (Illus.). viii, 100p. 1992. 42.95 (*0-387-19726-5*) Spr-Verlag.

Practical Current Awareness Services from Libraries. Ed. by Tom Whitehall. 120p. 1986. text 39.95 (*0-566-03519-7*, Pub. by Gower) Ashgate Pub Co.

Practical Cytopathology. Robert W. Astarita. (Illus.). 472p. 1989. text 160.00 (*0-443-08469-6*) Church.

Practical Czech Course for English-Speaking Students. Milos Sova. (CZE & ENG.). 325p. 1962. pap. text 25.00 (*0-87415-294-1*, SOVA) Foreign Lang.

Practical Data Analysis: Case Studies in Business Statistics. Peter G. Bryant & Marlene A. Smith. LC 94-21385. 96p. (C). 1994. text 26.75 (*0-256-15827-4*, Irwn McGrw-H) McGrw-H Hghr Educ.

Practical Data Analysis: Case Studies in Business Statistics, Vol. 2. Peter G. Bryant & Marlene A. Smith. 112p. (C). 1994. text 26.75 (*0-256-15828-2*, Irwn McGrw-H) McGrw-H Hghr Educ.

Practical Data Analysis I. 2nd ed. Smith Bryant. 112p. (C). 1998. pap. 13.75 (*0-256-23871-5*) McGraw.

Practical Data Analysis II. 2nd ed. Smith Bryant. 128p. (C). 1998. pap. 13.75 (*0-256-23872-3*) McGraw.

Practical Data Communications. Roger L. Freeman. LC 94-48318. (Telecommunications & Signal Processing Ser.). 656p. 1995. 98.95 (*0-471-31021-2*) Wiley.

***Practical Data Communications.** Roger L. Freeman. 850p. 2001. 150.00 (*0-471-39302-9*) Wiley.

Practical Data Communications. Mari Rettke. 256p. (C). 1990. text 32.50 (*0-07-067667-4*) McGraw.

Practical Data Handling Bk. A: Activities for Stages 1 & 2, Bk. A. Glyn Davies. 162p. 1993. pap., teacher ed. 35.00 (*0-340-55389-8*, Pub. by Hodder & Stought Ltd) Lubrecht & Cramer.

Practical Data Security. Ed. by John Gordon. (UNICOM Applied Information Technology Ser.). 166p. 1993. 97.95 (*1-85742-145-0*, Pub. by Avebury Technical) Ashgate Pub Co.

Practical Data Structures in C Plus Plus. Bryan Flaming. 448p. 1993. pap., pap. text 54.99 incl. disk (*0-471-55863-X*) Wiley.

Practical Decision Maker: A Handbook for Decision Making & Problem Solving in Organizations. Thomas R. Harvey et al. LC 97-61004. 300p. 1999. ring bd. 49.95 (*1-56676-547-1*) Scarecrow.

***Practical Decision Making in Health Care Ethics: Cases & Concepts.** 2nd rev. ed. Raymond J. Devettere. LC 99-38611. 656p. 2000. pap. text 35.00 (*0-87840-763-4*) Georgetown U Pr.

Practical Decorator & Ornamentalist. Ed. by Barbara Delius. (ENG, FRE & GER.). 260p. 2000. 39.95 (*3-89508-228-7*) Konemann.

Practical Dehydration. 2nd ed. Greensmith. 1998. boxed set 162.00 (*1-85573-394-3*, Pub. by Woodhead Pubng) Am Educ Systs.

Practical Dehydration. 2nd ed. Maurice Greensmith. LC 98-18881. (Woodhead Publishing Series In Food Science & Technology). 1998. ring bd. 139.95 (*0-8493-1175-6*) CRC Pr.

Practical Delivery of Sports Medicine Services: A Conceptual Approach. Jerald D. Hawkins. Ed. by PRC Publishing, Inc. Staff. (Illus.). 425p. (Orig.). 1993. pap. text 39.95 (*0-944183-16-6*) PRC Pub.

Practical Dementia Care. Peter V. Rabins et al. LC 98-49715. (Illus.). 304p. 1999. text 34.95 (*0-19-510625-3*) OUP.

Practical Demonkeeping. Christopher Moore. 320p. 1999. mass mkt. 6.99 (*0-380-73037-5*, Avon Bks) Morrow Avon.

***Practical Demonkeeping.** Christopher Moore. 256p. 2000. pap. 13.00 (*0-380-81655-5*, Avon Bks) Morrow Avon.

Practical Demonstrations: Interpreting vs. Transliterating, 5 cass.; set. LindaLee Massoud. 299p. 1996. spiral bd. 130.00 incl. VHS (*1-878819-51-8*) SignQuest Pubs.

Practical Dentofacial Orthopedics. Frans Van der Linden. LC 96-205290. (Illus.). 708p. 1997. pap. 120.00 (*1-85097-041-6*) Quint Pub Co.

Practical Dermatology. 2nd ed. Beth G. Goldstein. LC 96-28852. (Illus.). 448p. (C). (gr. 13). 1997. pap. text 59.95 (*0-8151-3764-8*, 26815) Mosby Inc.

Practical Descriptive Geometry. Samuel E. Rusinoff. LC 47-24789. 268p. 1947. reprint ed. pap. 83.10 (*0-608-11843-5*, 200456200043) Bks Demand.

Practical Design: Using Programmable Logic. Dave Pellerin. 400p. 1991. text 43.60 (*0-13-723834-7*) P-H.

Practical Design & Evaluation of Biomedical Research. Rasmussen. Date not set. text. write for info. (*0-397-51660-6*) Lppncott W & W.

Practical Design & Production of Optical Thin Films. Contrib. by Ronald R. Willey. LC 96-25978. (Optical Engineering Ser.: Vol. 56). (Illus.). 304p. 1996. text 135.00 (*0-8247-9428-1*) Dekker.

Practical Design Calculations for Groundwater & Soil Remediation. Jih-Fen Kuo. LC 98-28646. 272p. 1998. lib. bdg. 69.95 (*1-56670-238-0*, L1238) Lewis Pubs.

Practical Design Compiler. Parker & Wyatt. (C). 2001. pap. text 42.67 (*0-13-246117-X*) P-H.

Practical Design of Power Supplies. Ron Lenk. 288p. 1998. 69.95 (*0-7803-3458-2*, PC5715-QOE) Inst Electrical.

Practical Design of Reinforced Concrete. Russell S. Fling. LC 86-11158. 516p. 1987. text 49.95 (*0-471-80827-X*) P-H.

Practical Design of Ships, 2 vols., 2. Ed. by J. B. Caldwell & G. Ward. LC 92-13190. 1992. write for info. (*1-85166-862-4*) Elsevier.

Practical Design of Ships & Mobile Units: Proceedings Of The 7th International Symposium on Practical Design of Ships & Mobile Units, The Netherlands, September, 1998. Marinus W. Oosterveld. LC 98-37581. 1998. write for info. (*0-444-82918-0*) Elsevier.

Practical Design of Structural Elements in Aluminium. John W. Bull. 201p. 1994. 78.95 (*0-291-39798-0*, Pub. by Avebury Technical) Ashgate Pub Co.

Practical Design of Structural Elements in Timber. 2nd ed. John W. Bull. LC 94-7967. 1994. 78.95 (*0-291-39802-2*) Ashgate Pub Co.

Practical Design Power Supplies. Lenk. 1998. 69.95 (*0-07-134324-5*) McGraw.

***Practical Design Solutions & Strategies: Key Advice for Sound Construction from Fine Woodworking.** LC 99-53024. (Woodworker's Library). (Illus.). 2000. write for info. (*1-56158-346-4*) Taunton.

***Practical Design Solutions & Strategies: Key Advice for Sound Construction from Fine Woodworking.** Fine Woodworking Magazine Staff. LC 99-47526. (Illus.). 192p. 2000. pap. 17.95 (*1-56158-344-8*) Taunton.

Practical Design Techniques for Power & Thermal Management. Walt Kester. (Illus.). 374p. 1998. pap. 30.00 (*0-916550-19-2*) Analog Devices.

Practical Detail of the Cotton Manufacture of the United States of America. James Montgomery. LC 68-56266. (Library of Early American Business & Industry: No. 32). (Illus.). 219p. 1969. reprint ed. 39.50 (*0-678-00572-9*) Kelley.

Practical Developments in Inherited Metabolic Diseases. Ed. by G. M. Addison et al. 1986. text 206.50 (*0-85200-690-X*) Kluwer Academic.

Practical Diabetes Çare. Rowan Hillson. (Illus.). 240p. 1996. pap. text 49.50 (*0-19-261859-8*) OUP.

Practical Diagnosis in Traditional Chinese Medicine. Tieh-Tao Teng & Kevin Ergil. LC 98-37012. 1999. 99.00 (*0-443-04582-8*) Church.

Practical Diagnosis of Hematologic Disorders. 4th ed. Ed. by Carl R. Kjeldsberg. LC 95-15075. 1995. 75.00 (*0-89189-442-X*) Am Soc Clinical.

Practical Diagnosis of Viral Infections. Ed. by George J. Galasso et al. LC 92-49524. (Illus.). 334p. 1993. reprint ed. pap. 103.60 (*0-608-05823-8*, 205978800007) Bks Demand.

Practical Dictionary of Acupuncture & Accupressure see Dictionnaire Pratique de l'Acupuncture et de l'Acupressure

Practical Dictionary of Adult Emergency Medicine: Diccionario Practico de Urgencias Medicas del Adulto. Arnaud Cenac et al. (SPA.). 368p. 1982. 69.95 (*0-8288-1864-9*, S39898) Fr & Eur.

Practical Dictionary of Cardiology: Dizionario Pratico Di Cardiologia. Giuseppe Folli & Erminio Vitolo. (ITA.). 432p. 1986. 125.00 (*0-8288-1847-9*, F45090) Fr & Eur.

Practical Dictionary of Chinese Medicine. Nigel Wiseman & Feng Ye. LC 94-18575. 944p. (C). 1998. 125.00 (*0-912111-54-2*) Ashgate Pub Co.

Practical Dictionary of Clinical Medicine: Dictionnaire Pratique de Medecine Clinique. 2nd ed. Leon Perlemuter. (FRE.). 1856p. 1982. 195.00 (*0-8288-1821-5*, M6440) Fr & Eur.

Practical Dictionary of Diet & Nutrition: Dictionnaire Pratique de Dietetique et de Nutrition. Marian Apfelbaum & Leon Perlemuter. (FRE.). 736p. 1981. 150.00 (*0-8288-1298-5*, M15571) Fr & Eur.

Practical Dictionary of English for Biologists, Chemists & Doctors: Dictionnaire Pratique de l'Anglais pour les Biologistes, Chimistes, Medecins. J. G. Bieth et al. (ENG & FRE.). 272p. 1983. 89.95 (*0-8288-0560-1*, M14532) Fr & Eur.

Practical Dictionary of German Usage. K. B. Beaton. (GER.). 938p. 1997. text 153.00 (*0-19-824002-3*, Clarendon Pr) OUP.

Practical Dictionary of Guadeloupe Creole: Dictionnaire Pratique du Creole de Guadeloupe. Henry Tourneux & Maurice Barbotin. (CRP & FRE.). 488p. 1990. lib. bdg. 125.00 (*0-8288-4042-3*, M30550) Fr & Eur.

Practical Dictionary of Homonyms see Dictionnaire Practique des Homonymes

Practical Dictionary of Journalism - Dizionario Pratico Di Giornalismo. C. DeMartino. 1991. 75.00 (*0-8288-8434-X*) Fr & Eur.

Practical Dictionary of Medical Therapy (Dictionnaire Pratique de Therapeutique Medicale) 6th ed. Leon Perlemuter. (FRE.). 1824p. 1990. ring bd. 150.00 (*0-7859-4566-0*) Fr & Eur.

Practical Dictionary of Music: English/French/German/Italian. 2nd ed. Roberto Braccini. (ENG, FRE, GER & ITA.). 1994. 65.00 (*0-320-00566-6*) Fr & Eur.

Practical Dictionary of Music Composers. Sandy Feldstein. (Alfred Handy Guide Ser.). (Illus.). 64p. 1984. pap. 4.95 (*0-88284-332-X*, 2240) Alfred Pub.

Practical Dictionary of Music Theory. Sandy Feldstein. (Alfred Handy Guide Ser.). 48p. 1983. pap. text 5.50 (*0-88284-226-9*, 2330) Alfred Pub.

Practical Dictionary of Musical Terms. Sandy Feldstein. (Alfred Handy Guide Ser.). 1982. pap. 4.95 (*0-88284-199-8*, 5327) Alfred Pub.

Practical Dictionary of Odontology & Stomatology: Dictionnaire Pratique d'Odontologie et de Stomatologie. Michel Goudaert & Michel Danhiez. 342p. 1983. 65.00 (*0-8288-1807-X*, M886) Fr & Eur.

Practical Dictionary of Pediatric Therapeutics see Dictionnaire Pratique de Therapeutique Pediatrique

Practical Dictionary of Shipping Business: Japanese-English; English-Japanese. (ENG & JPN.). 236p. 1978. 125.00 (*0-8288-5266-9*, M9340) Fr & Eur.

An Asterisk (*) at the beginning of an entry indicates that the title is appearing for the first time.

Practical Dictionary of the Spanish of the New World see Diccionario Practico de la Lengua Espanola del Nuevo Mundo

Practical Dictionary of Therapeutic Pediatrics: Diccionario Practico de Terapeutica Pediatrica. Robert Steinschneider. 768p. 1982. 85.00 (*0-8288-1879-7*, S39897) Fr & Eur.

Practical Dictionary to Understand the Study of Cancer: Dictionnaire Pratique du Cancer: Pour Comprendre le Langage du Cancerologue. Philippe Lagarde. (FRE.). 1984. 59.95 (*0-8288-1812-6*, M404) Fr & Eur.

***Practical Differential Diagnosis in Surgical Neuropathology.** Ed. by Richard A. Prayson & Mark L. Cohen. 192p. 2000. 125.00 (*0-89603-817-3*) Humana.

Practical Digital Data & Data Communication with LSI Applications. Paul Bates. (Illus.). (C). 1987. write for info. (*0-318-61640-8*) P-H.

Practical Digital Design Using ICS. 3rd ed. Joseph D. Greenfield. 656p. (C). 1993. text 78.80 (*0-13-689894-7*) P-H.

Practical Digital Electronics. Pierre Pelloso. Tr. by John C. Nelson from FRE. LC 85-15524. 229p. reprint ed. pap. 71.00 (*0-7837-4408-0*, 204415100012) Bks Demand.

***Practical Digital Imaging & PACs: 1999 AAPM Summer School Proceedings.** Ed. by J. Anthony Seibert et al. (Illus.). 562p. 2000. pap. text 65.00 (*0-944838-92-8*) Med Physics Pub.

Practical Digital Libraries: Books, Bytes, & Bucks. Michael Lesk. LC 97-22069. (Illus.). 300p. 1997. text 49.95 (*1-55860-459-6*) Morgan Kaufmann.

Practical Digital Logic Design & Testing. Parag K. Lala. LC 95-20486. 420p. (C). 1995. 96.00 (*0-02-367171-8*, Macmillan Coll) P-H.

Practical Digital Video Programming with Examples in C. Phillip E. Mattison. LC 94-215942. 522p. 1994. pap. write for info. (*0-471-31015-8*) Wiley.

Practical Director. 2nd ed. Mike Crisp. LC 97-105432. (Illus.). 224p. 1996. pap. 39.95 (*0-240-51448-3*, Focal) Buttrwrth-Heinemann.

Practical Dispersion: A Guide to Understanding & Formulating Slurries. R. F. Conley. 464p. 1996. 165.00 (*0-471-18640-6*) Wiley.

Practical Dispersion: A Guide to Understanding & Formulating Slurries. Robert F. Conley. LC 95-38037. (Illus.). 500p. 1996. 135.00 (*1-56081-931-6*, Wiley-VCH) Wiley.

Practical Distiller. 1996. lib. bdg. 256.99 (*0-8490-8318-4*) Gordon Pr.

Practical Distiller. Monzert. 1987. reprint ed. pap. 8.95 (*0-917914-58-9*) Lindsay Pubns.

Practical Divining. Richard Foord. (Illus.). (Orig.). 1997. pap. 22.95 (*1-898307-78-4*, Pub. by Capall Bann Pubng) Holmes Pub.

Practical Divinity: The Works & Life of Reverend Richard Greenham. Kenneth L. Parker & Eric J. Carlson. LC 97-38530. (St. Andrews Studies in Reformation History). 250p. 1998. 105.95 (*1-84014-200-6*, BX9339.G74P37, Pub. by Ashgate Pub) Ashgate Pub Co.

Practical Divinity Vol. 1: Theology in the Wesleyan Tradition, Vol. 1. rev. ed. Ed. by Thomas A. Langford. LC 98-27227. 320p. 1998. pap. 25.00 (*0-687-07382-0*) Abingdon.

Practical Divinity Vol. 2: Readings in Wesleyan Theology, Vol. 2. Ed. by Thomas A. Langford. 1999. pap. 25.00 (*0-687-01247-3*) Abingdon.

Practical Divorce Solutions: How to Settle Out of Court. Charles E. Sherman. LC 88-60307. (Illus.). 144p. (Orig.). 1994. pap. 14.95 (*0-944508-13-8*) Nolo Occidental.

Practical Doppler Ultrasound for the Clinician. Raymond L. Powis & Robert A. Schwartz. (Illus.). 208p. 1991. 60.00 (*0-683-06958-6*) Lppncott W & W.

Practical DOS, Set. 3rd ed. Ruth Schmitz. (C). 1995. pap. text 42.50 (*0-07-911987-5*) McGraw.

Practical Drafting for the HVAC Trades. 274p. (C). 1996. text 49.00 (*0-536-59622-0*) Pearson Custom.

***Practical Drainage for Golf, Sportsturf & Horticultural.** Keith McIntyre. Ed. by Bent Jakobsen. LC 99-53388. (Illus.). 210p. 2000. 49.95 (*1-57504-139-1*, Ann Arbor Press) Sleepng Bear.

Practical Dreamer. Richard P. Olsen. 1990. pap. 8.95 (*0-687-60906-2*) Abingdon.

Practical Dreamer: Israel Friedlander & the Shaping of American Judaism. Baila R. Shargel. (Moreshet Ser.: No. X). 1985. 20.00 (*0-87334-027-2*) Jewish Sem.

***Practical Dreamer's Handbook: Finding the Time, Money & Energy to Live Your Dream.** Paul Edwards & Sarah Edwards. 240p. 2000. 21.95 (*1-58542-055-7*, Tarcher Putnam) Putnam Pub Group.

***Practical Dreaming: Awakening the Power of Dreams in Your Life.** Lillie Weiss. (Illus.). 144p. 1999. pap. 12.95 (*1-57224-164-0*) New Harbinger.

Practical Dredging. H. R. Cooper. (C). 1987. 90.00 (*0-85174-079-0*) St Mut.

Practical Dressage Manual. Bengt Ljungquist. (Illus.). 164p. 1983. 22.95 (*0-939481-36-7*) Half Halt Pr.

Practical Drilling & Well Planning Manual. Steve Devereaux. LC 97-47327. 1998. 89.95 (*0-87814-696-2*) PennWell Bks.

Practical Drug Enforcement: Procedures & Administration. Michael D. Lyman. LC 93-19071. 416p. 1992. boxed set 83.95 (*0-8493-9514-3*, HV8079) CRC Pr.

Practical DSP Modeling Techniques, 1 vol. 1994. disk 13.00 (*0-471-00613-0*) Wiley.

Practical DSP Modeling, Techniques & Programming in C. Don Morgan. 442p. 1994. pap. 36.95 (*0-471-00606-8*); pap. 49.95 incl. disk (*0-471-00434-0*) Wiley.

Practical Earth Science Exercises. David Berry & Jonathan Nourse. 88p. (C). 1996. pap. text, per. 23.95 (*0-7872-2853-2*, 41285301) Kendall-Hunt.

Practical Echocardiography & Doppler. Mark J. Monaghan. 154p. 1990. 284.95 (*0-471-92069-X*) Wiley.

Practical Echocardiography in the Adult: With Doppler & Color-Doppler Flow Imaging. J. P. Hamer. (C). 1990. text 221.50 (*0-7923-0670-8*) Kluwer Academic.

Practical Echocardiology. Joseph R. Roelandt. LC 77-1619. (Ultrasound in Biomedicine Ser.: No. 1). (Illus.). 330p. reprint ed. pap. 102.30 (*0-8357-4554-6*, 203745300008) Bks Demand.

Practical Economics for the Real Economist. Peter Bowbrick. (C). 1988. lib. bdg. 96.50 (*1-85333-076-0*, Pub. by Graham & Trotman) Kluwer Academic.

Practical Education Program for the Diabetic Client Within the Rehabilitation Setting. Nancy Dyer & Pat Homeyer. LC RC0660.D84. (American Foundation for the Blind Practice Ser.). 153p. reprint ed. pap. 47.50 (*0-7837-0144-6*, 204043400016) Bks Demand.

Practical Education, 1801, 3 vols. Richard L. Edgeworth & Maria Edgeworth. LC 95-41947. (Revolution & Romanticism, 1789-1834 Ser.). 1996. 225.00 (*1-85477-179-5*) Continuum.

Practical Egyptian Magic. 5th ed. Murry Hope. 192p. 1986. pap. 10.95 (*0-312-63474-9*) St Martin.

Practical Electric Motor Handbook. Gottlieb. 220p. 1997. pap. text 39.95 (*0-7506-3638-6*) Buttrwrth-Heinemann.

Practical Electrical Safety. D. C. Winburn. (Occupational Safety & Health Ser.: Vol. 15). (Illus.). 296p. 1988. text 99.75 (*0-8247-7948-7*) Dekker.

Practical Electrical Wiring. 17th ed. W. C. Schwan & Herbert P. Richter. (Illus.). 656p. 1996. pap. 44.95 (*0-07-052395-9*) McGraw.

Practical Electrical Wiring: Residential, Farm & Industrial. 16th ed. Herbert P. Richter & W. Creighton Schwan. LC 92-35995. 643p. 1992. 35.00 (*0-07-052394-0*) McGraw.

Practical Electricity. Cook. 1996. pap. text, lab manual ed. 38.20 (*0-13-268210-9*) P-H.

Practical Electricity. Nigel P. Cook. 464p. (C). 1996. 63.00 (*0-13-243296-X*) P-H.

Practical Electricity & Electronics: Electronics Fundamentals for Career Preparation. F. Coit Butler. (Illus.). 178p. (Orig.). 1982. pap. text 8.00 (*0-86657-006-3*) Lab-Volt.

Practical Electricity & Electronics: Electronics Fundamentals for FM Communications. (Illus.). 178p. (Orig.). 1982. pap. text 8.00 (*0-86657-001-2*) Lab-Volt.

Practical Electricity & Electronics Vol. 11: Fundamentals for Digital Communication: Pulse Modulation. Lab-Volt Systems, Inc. Staff. (Illus.). 92p. (Orig.). (C). 1985. pap. text. write for info. (*0-86657-054-3*, TM19616-00) Lab-Volt.

Practical Electromyography. 2nd ed. Ernest W. Johnson. 620p. 1988. 75.00 (*0-683-04463-X*) Lppncott W & W.

Practical Electromyography. 3rd ed. Ernest W. Johnson & William S. Pease. LC 96-17610. (Illus.). 416p. 1996. 59.95 (*0-683-04457-5*) Lppncott W & W.

Practical Electron Microscopy: A Beginner's Illustrated Guide. 2nd ed. Elaine E. Hunter. (Illus.). 185p. (C). 1993. spiral bd. 36.95 (*0-521-38539-3*) Cambridge U Pr.

Practical Electron Microscopy for Biologists. 2nd ed. Geoffrey A. Meek. LC 75-4955. 550p. reprint ed. pap. 170.50 (*0-608-17744-X*, 205224200069) Bks Demand.

Practical Electron Microscopy in Materials Science. J. W. Edington. (Illus.). 356p. (C). 1991. reprint ed. 135.00 (*1-878907-35-2*) TechBooks.

Practical Electronic Fault Finding & Troubleshooting. Robin Pain. LC 95-18106. (Illus.). 240p. 1996. pap. text 39.95 (*0-7506-2461-2*) Buttrwrth-Heinemann.

Practical Electronic Reliability Engineering: Getting the Job Done from Requirement Through Acceptance. Jerome Klion. (Illus.). 608p. 1992. text 74.95 (*0-442-00502-4*, VNR) Wiley.

Practical Electronics. Nigel P. Cook. 447p. (C). 1996. 63.00 (*0-13-243304-4*) P-H.

Practical Electronics for Inventors. Paul Scherz. (Illus.). 600p. 1998. pap. 39.95 (*0-07-058078-2*) McGraw-Hill Prof.

Practical Electronics Handbook. Sinclair. 1988. 22.00 (*0-434-91841-5*) CRC Pr.

***Practical Electronics Handbook.** 4th ed. Ian Sinclair. (Illus.). 480p. 2000. pap. 36.95 (*0-7506-4585-7*, Newnes) Buttrwrth-Heinemann.

Practical Electronics Handbook. 4th ed. Ian R. Sinclair. LC 94-26865. (Illus.). 439p. 1995. text 36.95 (*0-7506-2168-0*) Buttrwrth-Heinemann.

Practical Electronics Microprocessor Handbook. Coles. 1988. 32.00 (*0-408-01583-7*) CRC Pr.

Practical Electronics Troubleshooting. James Perozzo. LC 84-28626. 256p. (C). 1985. pap. 36.95 (*0-8273-2433-2*) Delmar.

Practical Electronics Troubleshooting. James Perozzo. LC 84-28626. 256p. (C). 1985. teacher ed. 16.00 (*0-8273-2434-0*) Delmar.

Practical Electronics Troubleshooting. 2nd ed. James Perozzo. 1990. pap., teacher ed. 16.00 (*0-8273-4054-0*) Delmar.

Practical Electronics Troubleshooting. 2nd rev. ed. James Perozzo. 448p. 1992. pap. text 38.50 (*0-8273-4053-2*) Delmar.

Practical Elements of Rhetoric: With Illustrative Examples. John F. Genung. LC 95-6796. (American Linguistics, 1700-1900 Ser.: Vol. 493). (Illus.). 534p. 1995. 60.00 (*0-8201-1493-6*) Schol Facsimiles.

Practical Elements of Thorough-Bass. Wolfgang Amadeus Mozart. LC 76-27136. 1976. reprint ed. pap. 3.00 (*0-915282-04-6*) J Patelson Mus.

Practical Embryology. C. H. Barnett. 124p. 1969. pap. 19.95 (*0-8464-1326-4*) Beekman Pubs.

Practical Encyclopedia of East European Cooking: The Definitive Collection of Traditional Recipes, from the Baltic to the Black Sea. Lesley Chamberlain. (Illus.). 256p. 1999. 40.00 (*0-7548-0071-7*, Lorenz Bks) Anness Pub.

Practical Encyclopedia of Feng Shui: A Complete Guide to the Ancient Chinese Art of Feng Shui. Gill Hale. (Illus.). 256p. 1999. 30.00 (*1-85967-880-7*, Lorenz Bks) Anness Pub.

Practical Encyclopedia of Keeping & Breeding Tortoises & Freshwater Turtles. Andy C. Highfield. LC 96-154749. (Illus.). 295p. (C). 1996. pap. 49.95 (*1-873943-06-7*, Pub. by Carapace Press) Serpents Tale.

***Practical Encyclopedia of Mexican Cooking.** Jane Milton. (Illus.). 2000. 35.00 (*0-7548-0500-X*, Lorenz Bks) Anness Pub.

Practical Encyclopedia of Natural Healing. Mark Bricklin. 1992. 10.98 (*1-56731-005-2*, MJF Bks) Fine Comms.

Practical Encyclopedia of Natural Healing. Mark Bricklin. (Illus.). 592p. 1990. pap. 14.95 (*0-14-013864-1*, Penguin Bks) Viking Penguin.

Practical Encyclopedia of Pedagogy, 6 vols., Set. Planeta Staff. (SPA.). 695.00 (*0-8288-8254-1*) Fr & Eur.

***Practical Encyclopedia of Sewing: A Complete Guide to Sewing, Patchwork & Embroidery.** Dorothy Wood. 1999. 40.00 (*0-7548-0277-9*, Pub. by Anness Pub) Random.

Practical Encyclopedia of Sex & Health: From Aphrodisiacs & Hormones to Potency, Stress, Vasectomy, & Yeast Infection. Prevention Magazine Editors & Stefan Bechtel. LC 92-35043. 352p. 1993. text 27.95 (*0-87596-163-0*) Rodale Pr Inc.

Practical Endgame Play. Neil McDonald. 160p. 1996. pap. 17.95 (*1-85744-176-1*, Pub. by Cadgn Bks) Macmillan.

Practical Endodontics: A Clinical Atlas. Edward Besner et al. LC 93-7003. (Illus.). 296p. (C). (gr. 13). 1993. text 77.95 (*0-8016-7798-X*, 07798) Mosby Inc.

Practical Endoscopic Sinus Surgery. Ed. by Vijay K. Anand & William R. Panje. LC 92-49884. (Illus.), 186p. 1992. text 129.00 (*0-07-105419-7*) McGraw-Hill HPD.

Practical Endoscopy. Ed. by Shephard & J. Mason. LC 97-224771. (Illus.). 352p. 1997. pap. text 45.00 (*0-412-54000-2*, Pub. by E A) OUP.

Practical Engine Swapping. John Thawley. (Illus.). 128p. 1976. pap. text 15.95 (*0-936834-11-0*) S S Autosports.

Practical Engineering, 6 vols. Watkins. (C). 1995. pap., teacher ed., wbk. ed. 11.96 (*0-395-73336-7*) HM.

Practical Engineering, 6 vols. 6th ed. Watkins. (C). 1995. pap. text, wbk. ed. 17.96 (*0-395-73335-9*) HM.

Practical Engineering Handbook, 9 vols. Watkins. (C). 1991. pap. 20.36 (*0-395-59018-3*) HM.

Practical Engineering Handbook, 9 vols. 9th ed. Watkins. (C). 1992. pap. text, suppl. ed. 0.76 (*0-395-60631-4*) HM.

Practical Engineering Handbook, 10 vols. 10th ed. Watkins. (C). 1995. pap. text 23.96 (*0-395-73333-2*) HM.

Practical Engineering Handbook, 10 vols. 10th ed. Watkins. (C). 1995. pap. text 11.96 (*0-395-76561-7*) HM.

Practical Engineering Statistics. Daniel B. Schiff & Ralph B. D'Agostino. LC 95-23303. 328p. 1995. 99.00 (*0-471-54768-9*) Wiley.

Practical English: Activities Book. (Illus.). 120p. 1987. pap. 9.82 (*0-8325-0328-2*); pap., teacher ed. 5.58 (*0-8325-0329-0*) NTC Contemp Pub Co.

Practical English: Learning Cards with Teacher's Manual. (Illus.). 1988. pap., teacher ed. 84.71 (*0-8325-0324-X*) NTC Contemp Pub Co.

Practical English: Teacher's Manual. (Illus.). 1987. pap., teacher ed. 8.41 (*0-8325-0326-6*) NTC Contemp Pub Co.

Practical English-Chinese Dictionary. (CHI & ENG.). 1880p. 1996. 39.95 (*7-80052-242-3*) China Bks.

Practical English-Chinese Dictionary. Commercial Press Staff. (CHI & ENG.). 1674p. 1979. 29.95 (*0-8288-4831-9*, M9291) Fr & Eur.

Practical English-Chinese Pronouncing Dictionary. Janey Chen. LC 78-77122. (CHI & ENG.). 602p. 1992. pap. 19.95 (*0-8048-1877-0*) Tuttle Pubng.

Practical English-Chinese Pronouncing Dictionary. Janey Chen. (CHI & ENG.). 601p. 1980. 39.95 (*0-8288-1605-0*, M9545) Fr & Eur.

Practical English for People Working in Chinese Restaurant. Yuan Dai. 108p. 1994. pap. text 29.99 (*0-9644008-0-4*) GBE Pubng.

Practical English Grammar. Leonid Kossman. (ENG & RUS.). 134p. 1992. 29.95 (*0-7859-1082-4*, 5710500275) Fr & Eur.

Practical English Grammar. 4th ed. A. J. Thomson. 384p. (Orig.). 1986. pap. text 13.95 (*0-19-431342-5*) OUP.

Practical English Grammar: A Sentence-to-Paragraph Approach. Jean Anderson Embree. LC 95-10619. (Illus.). 336p. 1996. pap. text 38.95 (*1-55934-348-6*, 1348) Mayfield Pub.

Practical English Grammar: Exercises 1. 3rd ed. A. J. Thompson & A. V. Martinet. 181p. 1986. pap. 8.95 (*0-19-431343-3*) OUP.

Practical English Grammar: Exercises 2, Exercises 2. 3rd ed. A. J. Thompson & A. V. Martinet. 208p. 1986. pap. text 8.95 (*0-19-431344-1*) OUP.

Practical English Handbook. 8th ed. Floyd C. Watkins & William B. Dillingham. 1988. teacher ed. write for info. (*0-318-63340-X*) HM.

Practical English Handbook. 8th annot. ed. Floyd C. Watkins & William B. Dillingham. LC 88-81366. 1988. teacher ed., student ed. 17.96 (*0-318-36904-4*) HM.

Practical English Handbook, 9 vols. 9th ed. Floyd C. Watkins & William B. Dillingham. (C). 1991. pap. 23.96 (*0-395-59017-5*) HM.

Practical English Handbook, 10 vols. 10th annot. ed. Floyd C. Watkins & William B. Dillingham. (C). 1995. text, teacher ed. 25.16 (*0-395-73334-0*) HM.

Practical English-Japanese Dictionary. Noah S. Brannen. (ENG & JPN.). 412p. (Orig.). 1991. pap. 12.95 (*0-8348-0187-6*) Weatherhill.

Practical English 1. 2nd ed. Tim Harris & Allan Rowe. (Illus.). (C). 1986. pap. text, student ed. 15.50 (*0-15-570912-7*) Harcourt Coll Pubs.

Practical English 1. 2nd ed. Tim Harris & Allan Rowe. (C). 1989. pap. text 9.00 (*0-15-570918-6*) Harcourt Coll Pubs.

Practical English One, Set. 2nd ed. Tim Harris & Allan Rowe. (C). 1986. audio 32.00 (*0-15-570919-4*) Harcourt Coll Pubs.

Practical English-Polish Dictionary. J. Stanislawski. (ENG & POL.). 913p. 1981. 35.00 (*0-8288-0479-6*, M9328) Fr & Eur.

Practical English 3. 2nd ed. Tim Harris & Allan Rowe. (C). (ps). 1988. pap. text 50.00 incl. audio (*0-15-570935-6*) Harcourt.

Practical English 3. 2nd ed. Tim Harris & Allan Rowe. (Illus.). 350p. (C). 1988. pap. text 15.50 (*0-15-570928-3*) Harcourt Coll Pubs.

Practical English 3. 2nd ed. Tim Harris & Allan Rowe. (Illus.). 350p. (C). 1989. pap. text 9.00 (*0-15-570934-8*) Harcourt Coll Pubs.

Practical English Usage. 2nd ed. Michael Swan. 688p. 1995. pap. text 18.95 (*0-19-431197-X*) OUP.

Practical English Writing Skills. Mona Scheraga. (Illus.). 224p. 1995. pap. 19.95 (*0-8442-7591-3*, Natl Textbk Co) NTC Contemp Pub Co.

Practical English Writing Skills: A Handbook with Practice. 2nd ed. Mona Scheraga. 192p. 1998. pap., student ed. 15.95 (*0-8442-0477-3*, 04773, Natl Textbk Co) NTC Contemp Pub Co.

Practical English Writing Skills: A Handbook with Practice. 2nd ed. Mona Shraga. 1998. pap., teacher ed. 7.00 (*0-8442-0478-1*) NTC Contemp Pub Co.

Practical English 2. 2nd ed. Tim Harris & Allan Rowe. 300p. (C). 1987. pap. text 15.50 (*0-15-570920-8*) Harcourt Coll Pubs.

Practical English 2. 2nd ed. Tim Harris & Allan Rowe. 300p. (C). 1989. pap. text, teacher ed. 9.00 (*0-15-570926-7*) Harcourt Coll Pubs.

Practical English/Spanish Maritime Dictionary. Carl W. Glasgow. (SPA & ENG.). 208p. 2000. pap. text 12.95 (*0-87033-523-5*) Cornell Maritime.

Practical Entomologist. Rick Imes. (Illus.). 160p. 1992. pap. 16.00 (*0-671-74695-2*, Fireside) S&S Trade Pap.

Practical Environmental Analysis. M. Radojevic & V. Bashkin. 480p. 1999. pap. 65.00 (*0-85404-594-5*, Pub. by Royal Soc Chem) Spr-Verlag.

Practical Environmental Bioremediation. R. Barry King et al. 176p. 1992. lib. bdg. 85.00 (*0-87371-437-7*, L437) Lewis Pubs.

Practical Environmental Bioremediation. 2nd ed. Barry King et al. LC 97-37142. 1997. lib. bdg. 79.95 (*1-56670-208-9*) Lewis Pubs.

Practical Environmental Forensics: Process & Case Histories, Vol. 1. Sullivan. 750p. 89.95 (*0-471-35398-1*) Wiley.

Practical Epidemiology. 4th ed. D. J. Barker & A. J. Hall. (Illus.). 176p. 1991. pap. text 19.95 (*0-443-03787-6*) Church.

***Practical Equine Dermatology.** David Lloyd et al. (Illus.). 160p. 2001. pap. text 76.95 (*0-632-04807-7*, Pub. by Blckwell Science) Iowa St U Pr.

Practical Ergonomics. Mark A. Ousnamer. LC 98-2851. (Illus.). 1998. 29.95 (*0-89806-184-9*, PRERGO) Eng Mgmt Pr.

Practical Error Correction Design for Engineers. 2nd ed. Neal Glover & Trent Dudley. 469p. (C). 1988. 45.00 (*0-927239-00-0*) DST Corp.

Practical ESD Control for Small & Medium Companies. Laie. (Electrical Engineering Ser.). 1991. write for info. (*0-442-23815-0*, VNR) Wiley.

Practical ESP & Clairvoyance. Beverly C. Jaegers. (Illus.). 125p. 1973. pap. text 7.00 (*0-318-41026-5*) Aries Prod.

Practical Essays. Alexander Bain. LC 72-4533. (Essay Index Reprint Ser.). 1977. reprint ed. 21.95 (*0-8369-2935-7*) Ayer.

Practical Essays on American Government. Albert B. Hart. LC 73-19152. (Politics & People Ser.). 320p. 1974. reprint ed. 23.95 (*0-405-05874-8*) Ayer.

Practical Ethics. Thomas Reid. Ed. by Knud Haakonssen. (Illus.). 544p. 1990. text 79.50 (*0-691-07350-3*, Pub. by Princeton U Pr) Cal Prin Full Svc.

Practical Ethics. Ron Yezzi. iv, 251p. (Orig.). (C). 1993. pap. 15.00 (*0-9619368-4-3*) G Bruno.

Practical Ethics. 2nd ed. Peter Albert David Singer. LC 92-23819. 411p. (C). 1993. pap. text 16.95 (*0-521-43971-X*) Cambridge U Pr.

Practical Ethics: A Collection of Addresses & Essays. Henry Sidgwick. 1977. 17.95 (*0-8369-7122-1*, 7956) Ayer.

Practical Ethics: A Collection of Addresses & Essays. Henry Sidgwick. LC 97-7574. (Practical & Professional Ethics: No. 1). 168p. 1998. text 39.95 (*0-19-511288-1*) OUP.

Practical Ethics: What Every Lawyer Needs to Know about Professional Responsibility. 87p. 1994. pap. 30.00 (*0-614-26755-2*, 1022); pap. 175.00 incl. VHS (*0-614-26756-0*, 3022); pap. 92.00 incl. audio (*0-614-26757-9*, 2022) NYS Bar.

Practical Ethics for Our Time. Eiji Uehiro. Tr. by Carl L. Becker. 184p. 1998. 24.95 (*0-8048-2106-2*) Tuttle Pubng.

Practical Ethics for Roman Gentlemen: The Works of Valerius Maximus. Clive Skidmore. 176p. 1996. text 60.00 (*0-85989-477-0*, Pub. by Univ Exeter Pr) Northwestern U Pr.

P

Practical Ethics for Students, Interns, & Residents: A Short Reference Manual. 2nd rev. ed. C. Junkerman & D. Schiedermayer. 77p. 1998. pap. text 6.95 (*1-55572-054-4*) Univ Pub Group.

Practical Ethics for the Federal Employee: Staking Out the High Ground. 3rd rev. ed. Susan McGuire Smith. (Illus.). 85p. pap. 14.95 (*1-930542-03-8*) FPMI Comns.

Practical Ethics for the Federal Employee: Staking Out the High Ground. 3rd rev. ed. Susan McGuire Smith. (Illus.). 93p. 1998. pap. 14.95 (*0-936295-15-5*) FPMI Comns.

Practical Evaluation. Michael Q. Patton. (Illus.). 320p. 1982. 48.00 (*0-8039-1904-2*); pap. 22.50 (*0-8039-1905-0*) Sage.

Practical Evaluation & Management of the Shoulder. Fredrick A. Matsen, III et al. LC 93-41664. 1994. text 85.00 (*0-7216-4819-3*, W B Saunders Co) Harcrt Hlth Sci Grp.

***Practical Evaluation Guide: Tools for Museums & Other Informal Educational Settings.** Judy Diamond. LC 98-40238. (American Association for State & Local History Book Ser.). 200p. 1999. 59.00 (*0-7619-8939-0*); pap. 21.95 (*0-7619-8940-4*) AltaMira Pr.

Practical Everyday Spelling Workbook: Patterns & Principles of English Spelling. H. Elaine Kim. (Illus.). 1988. pap., teacher ed. 6.99 (*0-8442-7488-7*); pap., wbk. ed. 8.46 (*0-8442-7487-9*) NTC Contemp Pub Co.

Practical Evidence Manual. Mark B. Simons. 530p. 1994. pap. 65.00 (*0-614-05950-X*, MICHIE) LEXIS Pub.

Practical Evidence Manual, 1995 Edition. 3rd ed. Mark B. Simons. 500p. 1995. pap. 65.00 (*0-250-47247-3*, 82335-11, MICHIE) LEXIS Pub.

Practical Evidence, 1993. Wake Forest University School of Law Continuing Le. 240p. 1993. pap. 65.00 (*0-942225-65-1*) Wake Forest Law.

Practical Examples for HP48 Calculator. Donald R. Mackenroth. 1992. pap. text 24.95 (*0-201-56325-8*) Addison-Wesley.

Practical Executive: Leadership. Dayle M. Smith. LC 96-38713. (Practical Executive Ser.). (Illus.). 192p. 1997. pap. 14.95 (*0-8442-2980-6*, NTC Business Bks) NTC Contemp Pub Co.

Practical Executive: Workforce Density. William H. Sonnenschein. LC 96-35853. (Practical Executive Ser.). (Illus.). 192p. 1997. pap. 14.95 (*0-8442-2981-4*, NTC Business Bks) NTC Contemp Pub Co.

Practical Exercise Therapy. 4th ed. Margaret Hollis & Phil F. Cook. LC 98-53120. 1999. write for info. (*0-632-04973-1*) Blackwell Sci.

Practical Exercises for Bar Students. Ed. by K. J. Reddy. 300p. (C). 1991. 80.00 (*1-85352-893-5*, Pub. by HLT Pubns) St Mut.

Practical Exercises for Inner Harmony. Vernon Howard. 1980. pap. 2.00 (*0-911203-02-8*) New Life.

Practical Exercises in Business Communications. Hill. 1996. pap. 17.95 (*0-87393-561-6*) Dame Pubns.

Practical Exercises in Probability & Statistics: With Answers & Hints on Solutions. N. A. Rahman. 1972. 30.00 (*0-85264-217-2*) Lubrecht & Cramer.

Practical Exotic Animal Medicine. LC 97-178478. (Illus.). 275p. 1997. pap. text 51.00 (*1-884254-33-0*) Vet Lrn Syst.

Practical Experience in Building Expert Systems. Ed. by Max A. Bramer. LC 89-27241. (Illus.). 238p. 1990. reprint ed. pap. 73.80 (*0-608-05297-3*, 206583500001) Bks Demand.

***Practical Experience with the OECD Transfer Pricing Guidelines.** International Fiscal Association Staff. LC 99-50121. (IFA Congress Seminar Ser.). 1999. pap. 36.00 (*90-411-1298-7*) Kluwer Law Intl.

Practical Experiences of Control & Automation in Wastewater Treatment & Water Resources Management, Vol. 13, 8-12. S. H. Jenkins et al. 1982. pap. 180.00 (*0-08-029086-8*, Pergamon Pr) Elsevier.

Practical Experiment Designs. 2nd ed. William J. Diamond. 1989. text 60.95 (*0-442-31849-9*, VNR) Wiley.

Practical Experiment Designs for Engineers & Scientists. 2nd ed. William J. Diamond. (Competitive Manufacturing Ser.). 408p. 1989. 75.00 (*0-471-28971-X*, VNR) Wiley.

Practical Experimental Design & Optimization Methods for Chemists. C. K. Bayne & I. B. Rubin. (Illus.). 205p. 1987. 60.00 (*0-89573-136-3*, Wiley-VCH) Wiley.

Practical Explanatory Dictionary of Magical Items & Related Articles. J. Bersez.Tr. of Dictionnaire Pratique des Explicatif des Produits Magiques et Articles Usuels. (FRE.). 125p. 1985. pap. 75.00 (*0-7859-4847-3*, M6732) Fr & Eur.

Practical Expression of the Church. Witness Lee. 188p. 1970. per. 8.25 (*0-87083-015-5*, 08-020-001) Living Stream Ministry.

Practical Family Law Desk Book-Form Book. Wake Forest University School of Law Continuing Le. 1106p. 1993. pap. 110.00 (*0-942225-76-7*) Wake Forest Law.

Practical Family Law Form Book. Wake Forest University School of Law Continuing Le. 510p. 1993. pap. 65.00 (*0-942225-72-4*) Wake Forest Law.

Practical Farm Buildings: A Text & Handbook. 3rd ed. James S. Boyd. LC 78-179872. 1993. teacher ed. 9.95 (*0-8134-2964-1*); pap. 43.75 (*0-8134-2940-4*, 2054) Interstate.

Practical Farmer: Being a New & Compendious System of Husbandry, Adapted to the Different Soils & Climates of America. John Spurrier. LC 72-89091. (Rural America Ser.). 1973. reprint ed. 32.00 (*0-8420-1499-3*) Scholarly Res Inc.

Practical Faster Reading. Gerald Mosback & Vivienne Mosback. 132p. 1977. pap. text 12.95 (*0-521-21346-0*) Cambridge U Pr.

Practical Feeding of Horses & Ponies. Sarah Pilliner. LC 97-27543. 1998. pap. 29.95 (*0-632-04828-X*) Blackwell Sci.

Practical Feminist Criticism. Maggie Humm. 256p. (C). 1995. pap. text 29.00 (*0-13-355371-X*) P-H.

Practical Feng Shui: Arrange, Decorate & Accessorize Your Home to Promote Health, Wealth & Happiness. Simon Brown. LC 98-128278. (Illus.). 160p. 1998. 19.95 (*0-7063-7634-X*, Pub. by WrLock) Sterling.

Practical Feng Shui: The Chinese Art of Living in Harmony with Your Surroundings. Richard Craze. (New Life Library). (Illus.). 64p. 1997. 9.95 (*1-85967-510-7*, Lorenz Bks) Anness Pub.

***Practical Feng Shui Astrology: Using the Nine Ki System to Make Important Decisions in Your Life.** Simon Brown. (Illus.). 128p. 1999. pap. 17.95 (*0-7063-7825-3*, Pub. by WrLock) Sterling.

Practical Feng Shui for Business. Simon Brown. LC 99-209806. 1999. pap. 19.95 (*0-7063-7768-0*, Pub. by WrLock) Sterling.

***Practical Feng Shui Solutions: Easy-to-Follow Practical Advice on Making the Most of Modern Living.** Simon Brown. 2000. pap. 19.95 (*0-304-35476-7*, Pub. by Cassell) Sterling.

Practical Fibreoptic Endoscopy & Inhibation. Popat. 226p. pap. text 63.00 (*0-7506-4496-6*) Buttrwrth-Heinemann.

Practical Film Criticism - An Enlightened Approach to Moviegoing. Bert Cardulle. LC 99-15808. (Studies in History & Criticism of Film: Vol. 1). 324p. 1999. text 99.95 (*0-7734-7967-8*) E Mellen.

Practical Financial Management. Micah Lasher. (FN - Financial Mangement Ser.). (C). 1996. mass mkt. 17.95 (*0-314-20753-8*) S-W Pub.

Practical Financial Management. William Lasher. LC 96-41519. 600p. 1996. mass mkt. 68.00 (*0-314-20186-6*) West Pub.

***Practical Financial Management.** 2nd ed. Lasher. (SWC-Finance Ser.). (C). 2000. pap. 19.00 (*0-324-05598-6*) Sth-Wstrn College.

Practical Financial Management. 2nd ed. Lasher. LC 99-25138. (SWC-Finance). 650p. 1999. pap. 95.95 (*0-324-00674-8*) Thomson Learn.

Practical Financial Management. 2nd ed. Micah Lasher. (SWC-Finance Ser.). 1999. pap., student ed. 19.75 (*0-324-00797-3*) Thomson Learn.

***Practical Financial Management.** 2nd ed. Lewellen & Halloran. 2001. pap. 51.00 (*0-324-07173-6*) Sth-Wstrn College.

Practical Financial Management: New Techniques for Local Governments. Ed. by John Matzer, Jr. (Practical Management Ser.). (Illus.). 207p. 1984. pap. text 23.95 (*0-87326-043-0*) Intl City-Cnty Mgt.

Practical Fire & Arson Investigation. O'Connor. 3p. 1992. lib. bdg. 54.95 (*0-8493-9518-6*) CRC Pr.

Practical Fire & Arson Investigation. J. J. O'Connor. (Practical Aspects of Criminal & Forensic Investigations Ser.). 400p. 1986. 44.95 (*0-444-00874-8*) CRC Pr.

Practical Fire & Arson Investigation. 2nd ed. David R. Redsicker & John J. O'Connor. LC 96-16777. (Practical Aspects of Criminal & Forensics Investigations Ser.). (Illus.). 432p. 1996. boxed set 74.95 (*0-8493-8155-X*, 8155) CRC Pr.

Practical Fire Precautions. G. W. Underdown. (C). 1979. 450.00 (*0-7855-4062-8*, Pub. by Witherby & Co) St Mut.

***Practical Firewalls.** Terry Ogletree. 450p. 2000. pap. 34.99 (*0-7897-2416-2*) Que.

***Practical Fishing Encyclopedia.** Tony Miles & Martin Ford. 256p. 2000. 40.00 (*0-7548-0283-3*) Anness Pub.

Practical Fishing Knots. Mark Sosin & Lefty Kreh. (Illus.). 144p. 1991. pap. 10.95 (*1-55821-102-0*) Lyons Pr.

***Practical Fishkeeping.** Mary Bailey & Gina Sanford. 2000. pap. 12.95 (*1-84215-055-3*) Anness Pub.

Practical Flexible Sigmoidoscopy. Basuk Cohen & Waye Cohen. (Illus.). 192p. 1995. 54.95 (*0-89640-272-X*) Igaku-Shoin.

Practical Flow Cytometry. 3rd ed. Howard M. Shapiro. (Illus.). 588p. 1994. 165.00 (*0-471-30376-3*) Wiley.

Practical Fluid Mechanics for Engineering Applications. J. J. Bloomer. LC 99-39935. (Mechanical Engineering Ser.). 392p. 1999. 150.00 (*0-8247-9575-X*) Dekker.

Practical Fluorescence. 2nd expanded rev. ed. Ed. by George G. Guilbault. (Modern Monographs in Analytical Chemistry: Vol. 3). (Illus.). 824p. 1990. text 275.00 (*0-8247-8350-6*) Dekker.

Practical Fly Fisherman. A. J. McClane. 240p. 1983. pap. 7.95 (*0-13-689380-5*, Reward) P-H.

Practical Folk Medicine of Hawaii. L. R. McBride. (Illus.). 1975. pap. 8.95 (*0-912180-27-7*) Petroglyph.

Practical Food & Beverage Cost Control. Ojugo. LC 98-25767. (Food & Hospitality Ser.). 432p. (C). 1998. text 57.95 (*0-7668-0038-5*) Delmar.

Practical Food Inspection. 9th ed. Martin. (Illus.). 827p. (C). 1978. text 80.95 (*0-7186-0435-0*) Chapman & Hall.

Practical Food Microbiology & Technology. 3rd ed. George J. Mountney & Wilbur A. Gould. 364p. (C). 1992. reprint ed. lib. bdg. 74.50 (*0-89464-673-7*) Krieger.

Practical Food Service Spreadsheets with Lotus 1-2-3. 2nd ed. Joel Chaban. LC 93-3346. 1993. text 44.95 (*0-442-01304-3*, VNR) Wiley.

Practical Foodservice Spreadsheets with LOTUS 1-2-3. 2nd ed. Joel Chaban. 256p. 1993. 54.95 (*0-471-29011-4*, VNR) Wiley.

Practical Footcare for Nurse Practitioners: A Training Manual & Clinical Handbook. Ronald A. Nicholson. LC 94-66314. (Illus.). 192p. (Orig.). (C). 1994. pap. text 69.95 (*1-885421-01-X*) Practical Footcare.

Practical Footcare for Physician Assistants: A Training Manual & Clinical Handbook. Ronald A. Nicholson. LC 94-66313. (Illus.). 192p. (Orig.). (C). 1994. pap. text 69.95 (*1-885421-00-1*) Practical Footcare.

Practical Footcare for Primary Care Physicians: A Training Manual & Clinical Handbook. Ronald A. Nicholson. LC 94-66215. (Illus.). 192p. (Orig.). (C). 1994. pap. text 69.95 (*1-885421-02-8*) Practical Footcare.

Practical Forage Concepts. Donald M. Ball. LC 98-97018. (Illus.). viii, 160p. 1999. pap. 10.00 (*0-9616023-1-7*) AL Cattlemen.

Practical Forecasting. Ed. by Martin P. Edelman. LC 88-82742. (Illus.). 34p. 1985. 35.00 (*1-55822-012-7*) Am Prod & Inventory.

Practical Forensic Anthropology of Human Skeletal Remains Recovery Analysis & Resolution. William D. Haglund et al. 1999. 54.95 (*0-8493-8157-6*, 8157) CRC Pr.

Practical Forensic Pathology. Charles V. Wetli. LC 87-35275. (Illus.). 160p. 1988. 63.00 (*0-89640-144-8*) Igaku-Shoin.

Practical Forestry for the Agent & Surveyor. 3rd rev. ed. Cyril Hart. (Illus.). 688p. (C). 1991. text 53.95 (*0-86299-962-6*, Pub. by Sutton Pub Ltd) Intl Pubs Mktg.

Practical Formal Methods for Hardware Design. Ed. by C. Delgado Kloos & W. Damm. LC 97-17153. (Research Reports ESPRIT, Project 6128, FORMAT). 300p. 1997. pap. 43.00 (*3-540-62007-9*) Spr-Verlag.

Practical Formation Evaluation. Robert C. Ransom. LC 95-11161. (Illus.). 490p. 1995. 140.00 (*0-471-10755-7*) Wiley.

Practical Foundation Accounting. 4th ed. Johnson. 1992. pap. write for info. (*0-415-07864-4*) Thomson Learn.

Practical Foundation Costing. Wright. 1994. pap. write for info. (*0-415-11240-0*) Thomson Learn.

Practical Foundation Engineering Handbook. Robert W. Brown. 1120p. 1995. 99.95 (*0-07-008194-8*) McGraw.

***Practical Foundation Engineering Handbook.** 2nd ed. Robert Wade Brown. (Illus.). 1104p. 2000. 115.00 (*0-07-135139-6*) McGraw.

Practical Foundation in Accounting. 5th ed. Harry Johnson et al. LC 98-199999. 509p. 1998. pap. 19.99 (*1-86152-259-2*) Thomson Learn.

Practical Foundation in Costing. David Wright. LC 93-25485. 1994. pap. 29.95 (*0-415-09875-0*) Thomson Learn.

Practical Foundations of Mathematics. Paul Taylor. LC 98-39472. (Studies in Advanced Mathematics: No. 59). (Illus.). 528p. (C). 1998. text 80.00 (*0-521-63107-6*) Cambridge U Pr.

***Practical FPGA: Designer's Guide to VHDL & Verilog.** Ken Coffman. 320p. 2001. 79.00 incl. cd-rom (*0-13-028026-7*) P-H.

Practical Fracture Mechanics. Alexander Blake. (Mechanical Engineering Ser.: Vol. 102). (Illus.). 456p. 1996. text 140.00 (*0-8247-9678-0*) Dekker.

Practical Fracture Treatment. 3rd ed. Ronald K. McRae. LC 93-7651. 384p. 1994. pap. text 60.00 (*0-443-04809-6*) Church.

Practical French-Arabic Dictionary (Dictionnaire Pratique Francais-Arabe) Zaki Coussa. 440p. 1986. 24.95 (*0-7859-4851-1*) Fr & Eur.

Practical Fuchsia Growing. Alan Toogood. (Illus.). 64p. 1992. pap. 8.95 (*1-85223-632-9*, Pub. by Cro1wood) Trafalgar.

Practical Fungal Physiology. Peter M. Robinson. LC 78-4243. 131p. reprint ed. pap. 40.70 (*0-608-18821-2*, 203047300069) Bks Demand.

Practical Gambling Investigation Techniques. Kevin B. Kinnee. (Practical Aspects of Criminal & Forensic Investigations Ser.). 238p. 1992. 52.95 (*0-8493-9512-7*) CRC Pr.

Practical Gamma-Ray Spectrometry. Gordon Gilmore & John D. Hemingway. LC 94-24760. 322p. 1995. 195.00 (*0-471-95150-1*) Wiley.

Practical Gamuts & Differential Diagnosis in Pediatric Radiology. Kook S. Oh et al. LC 81-19832. 243p. reprint ed. pap. 75.40 (*0-8357-7597-6*, 205691800096) Bks Demand.

***Practical Garden Companion: How to Design, Plan & Create the Perfect Garden.** Peter McHoy. (Illus.). 2000. 40.00 (*1-85967-922-6*, Lorenz Bks) Anness Pub.

***Practical Garden Companion: How to Design, Plan & Create the Perfect Garden.** Peter McHoy. (Illus.). 2000. 40.00 (*1-84038-351-8*) Hermes Hse.

Practical Garden Design. Yvonne Rees. (Illus.). 64p. pap. 8.95 (*1-85223-624-8*, Pub. by Cro1wood) Trafalgar.

Practical Garden Designs. Guy Farthing & Donald Farthing. (Illus.). 112p. (Orig.). 1988. pap. 19.95 (*0-572-01478-3*, Pub. by W Foulsham) Trans-Atl Phila.

Practical Garden of Eden: Beautiful Landscaping with Fruits & Vegetables. Fred Hagy. LC 87-7623. (Illus.). 320p. 1990. 35.00 (*0-87951-208-3*, Pub. by Overlook Pr) Penguin Putnam.

Practical Gardener. Reader's Digest Editors. LC 93-19529. (Successful Gardening Ser.). (Illus.). 176p. 1993. 18.98 (*0-89577-539-5*) RD Assn.

Practical Gardener: An A-Z Guide to Techniques & Tips. Ann R. Dines. LC 94-27977. (Illus.). 192p. 1995. 15.95 (*1-56799-157-2*, Friedman-Fairfax) M Friedman Pub Grp Inc.

Practical Gardener: Mastering the Elements of Good Growing. Roger B. Swain. (Illus.). 288p. 1997. 9.99 (*0-88365-986-7*) Galahad Bks.

Practical Gardener: Mastering the Elements of Good Growing. Roger B. Swain. (Illus.). 288p. 1998. 12.95 (*1-57866-002-5*) Galahad Bks.

Practical Gardener: Understanding the Elements of Good Growing. Roger B. Swain. (Illus.). 88p. 1995. pap. 12.95 (*0-8050-1741-0*, Owl) H Holt & Co.

***Practical Gardener's Encyclopedia: The Essential Guide to Creating a Beautiful Garden.** Fog City Press Staff. LC 99-57153. (Illus.). 2000. 40.00 (*1-875137-70-X*) Weldon Owen.

Practical Gas Metal & Flux Cored Arc Welding. Mike Gellerman. LC 98-23219. 183p. 1998. pap. text 48.00 (*0-13-639238-5*) P-H.

Practical Gastrointestinal Endoscopy. 3rd ed. Ed. by P. B. Cotton & C. B. Williams. (Illus.). 288p. 1990. 54.95 (*0-632-02435-6*) Mosby Inc.

Practical Gastrointestinal Endoscopy. 4th ed. Peter B. Cotton & Christopher B. Williams. LC 95-25737. (Illus.). 352p. 1996. 145.00 (*0-86542-851-4*) Blackwell Sci.

Practical Gemmology. Robert Webster. (Illus.). 209p. 1987. 29.50 (*0-7198-0011-0*, Pub. by NAG Press) Antique Collect.

Practical Gemmology. Robert Webster. (Illus.). 216p. 24.95 (*0-7198-0131-1*, Pub. by R Hale Ltd) Seven Hills Bk.

Practical Genetic Counselling. 4th ed. Peter S. Harper. LC 93-8275. (Illus.). 348p. 1993. pap. 65.00 (*0-7506-0928-1*) Buttrwrth-Heinemann.

Practical Genetic Counselling. 4th ed. Peter S. Harper. (Illus.). 306p. 1988. 39.95 (*0-7506-0342-9*, Pub. by John Wright) Buttrwrth-Heinemann.

Practical Genetic Counselling. 5th ed. Peter S. Harper. LC 98-28065. 376p. 1998. pap. text 67.00 (*0-7506-3368-9*) Buttrwrth-Heinemann.

Practical Genetics. R. N. Jones & G. K. Richards. 232p. 1991. 216.50 (*0-471-93235-3*, Wiley-Liss); pap. 84.95 (*0-471-93234-5*, Wiley-Liss) Wiley.

Practical Genetics for Primary Care. Peter W. Rose & Anneke Lucassen. LC 99-35034. (Oxford General Practice Ser.: 45). (Illus.). 384p. 1999. pap. text 65.00 (*0-19-262931-X*) OUP.

Practical Gentic Algorithms. Randy L. Haupt & Sue E. Haupt. LC 97-13172. 177p. 1997. 54.95 (*0-471-18873-5*) Wiley.

Practical Geodesy: Using Computers. Marrten Hooijberg. LC 97-30416. 290p. 1997. write for info. (*3-540-61826-0*) Spr-Verlag.

Practical Geography Africa. Pritchard. 1984. pap. text. write for info. (*0-582-60366-8*, Pub. by Addison-Wesley) Longman.

Practical Geologist. Dougal Dixon. Ed. by Raymond I. Bernor. (Illus.). 160p. (Orig.). 1992. per. 15.00 (*0-671-74697-9*) S&S Trade Pap.

***Practical Geostatistics: Modeling & Spatial Analysis.** S. W. Houlding. 120p. 2000. 84.00 incl. cd-rom (*3-540-66820-9*) Spr-Verlag.

Practical Geriatrics. Ed. by H. P. Hahn. (Illus.). 448p. 1975. 28.00 (*3-8055-1768-8*) S Karger.

Practical German for the Tourist. Cathrine O. Gekker. 1976. per. 5.00 (*0-686-00543-0*) Huffman Pr.

Practical German-Polish Dictionary: Podreczny Slownik Niemiecko-Polski. J. Chodera. (GER & POL.). 1023p. 1984. 39.95 (*0-8288-0482-6*, F33230) Fr & Eur.

***Practical Goat Packing.** Carolyn Eddy. Ed. by Kaye Phaneuf. (Illus.). 144p. 1999. pap. 17.95 (*0-9677097-0-9*) ECPG.

Practical Golf. John Jacobs & Ken Bowden. LC 82-73277. 192p. 1983. pap. 15.95 (*0-689-70634-0*) Atheneum Yung Read.

Practical Golf. 2nd ed. John Jacobs & Ken Bowden. LC 98-17318. (Illus.). 144p. 1998. pap. 16.95 (*1-55821-738-X*) Lyons Pr.

Practical Golf Course Maintenance: The Magic of Greenkeeping. Gordon Witteveen & Michael Bavier. LC 98-9691. (Illus.). 262p. 1999. 49.95 (*1-57504-047-6*) Sleepng Bear.

Practical Government Budgeting: A Workbook for Public Managers. Susan L. Riley & Peter W. Colby. LC 89-26374. (SUNY Series in Public Administration). 138p. (C). 1990. pap. text 17.95 (*0-7914-0392-0*) State U NY Pr.

***Practical Government Subcontracting.** R. Jones. 44p. (C). (gr. 13). 1998. pap. text 32.99 (*1-85032-012-8*) ITCP.

Practical Grammar. Ed. by Charlotte Lyons. 1980. 4.95 (*1-55708-325-8*, MCR459) McDonald Pub Co.

Practical Grammar: The No-Frills Basics. Peter Hartley. 45p. 1983. pap. 4.98 (*0-9611790-1-5*) Devco Pr.

Practical Grammar for Classical Hebrew. 2nd ed. Jacob Weingreen. 328p. 1959. text 31.95 (*0-19-815422-4*) OUP.

Practical Grammar of Basic Biblical Hebrew. Laurence M. Vance. LC 97-90417. 134p. 1997. ring bd. 9.95 (*0-9628898-3-0*) Vance FL.

***Practical Grammar of Sanskrit Language.** M. Monier-Williams. 2000. reprint ed. 34.50 (*81-215-0939-4*, Pub. by M Manoharial) Coronet Bks.

Practical Grammar of the Arabic Language. F. El-Shidiac. 160p. (C). 1987. pap. 75.00 (*1-85077-187-1*, Pub. by Darf Pubs Ltd) St Mut.

Practical Grammar of the Central Alaskan Yup'ik Eskimo Language. Steven A. Jacobson & Anna W. Jacobson. LC 94-16979. xii, 524p. 1995. pap. 26.00 (*1-55500-062-2*) Alaska Native.

Practical Grammar of the English Language. Thomas W. Harvey. LC 87-26850. 280p. 1987. 50.00 (*0-8201-1427-8*) Schol Facsimiles.

Practical Grammar of the St. Lawrence Island/Siberian Yupik Eskimo Language: Preliminary. Steven A. Jacobson. iv, 103p. (C). 1990. pap. text 12.50 (*1-55500-034-7*) Alaska Native.

Practical Grammar of the Turkish Language. Charles Wells. (ENG & TUR.). 286p. 1992. 79.95 (*0-8288-8527-3*) Fr & Eur.

Practical Grounding: Theory & Design. Myron L. Brewer. LC 73-85629. (ABC of the Telephone Ser.: Vol. 12). (Illus.). 180p. (Orig.). (C). 1987. pap. text 24.95 (*1-56016-011-X*) ABC TeleTraining.

Practical Groundwater Hydrology. Michael E. Renz. 1995. 49.95 (*0-87371-643-4*, L643) Lewis Pubs.

An Asterisk (*) at the beginning of an entry indicates that the title is appearing for the first time.

Practical Group Therapy: A Guide for Clinicians. William H. Friedman. LC 88-46082. (Social & Behavioral Science Ser.). 304p. 1989. 39.95 (*1-55542-139-3*) Jossey-Bass.

Practical Guidance for Parents of the Visually Handicapped Preschooler. Patricia L. Maloney. (Illus.). 88p. 1981. pap., spiral bd. 23.95 (*0-398-04583-6*) C C Thomas.

Practical Guide Classroom Observer. Sandu. (C). 1991. pap. text 32.80 (*0-536-57945-8*) Pearson Custom.

Practical Guide for Advanced Writers. Munsell & Clough. 1984. teacher ed. 5.00 (*0-8384-3280-8*) Heinle & Heinle.

Practical Guide for Conducting Extra-Territorial Discovery for Use in U. S. Litigation. 62p. 1992. pap. 32.00 (*0-9621989-4-3*) IADC IL.

Practical Guide for Developing Agency/School Partnerships for Service-Learning. (Illus.). 150p. 1995. pap. write for info. (*1-58534-006-5*) Points of Light.

Practical Guide for Employer & Employee to the Industrial Relations Act 1971. Alan Pardoe. xx, 319p. 1972. pap. 6.50 (*0-85308-024-0*); pap. 6.50 (*0-8377-1022-7*, Rothman) W S Hein.

Practical Guide for Experimental Microvascular Surgery: A Practical Guide. Kenneth E. Korber & Jeanne G. Halpern. (Illus.). 311p. (C). 1990. pap. 47.50 (*0-87527-470-6*) Green.

Practical Guide for Feeding Captive Reptiles. rev. ed. Fredric L. Frye. 186p. 1996. 26.50 (*0-89464-966-3*) Krieger.

Practical Guide for Groundwater Sampling. M. J. Barcelona et al. 156p. (C). 1988. 160.00 (*0-7855-6712-7*, Pub. by Scientific) St Mut.

Practical Guide for Hazardous Waste Management, Administration, & Compliance. James L. Lieberman. Ed. by Gary Gauiter. LC 94-12877. 256p. 1994. lib. bdg. 75.00 (*1-56670-115-5*, L1115) Lewis Pubs.

Practical Guide for Hazardous Waste Management, Administration & Compliance: RCRA Compliance Guide. James L. Lieberman. (Environmental Regulatory Compliance Ser.). 240p. (C). 1993. pap. text. write for info. (*0-9638274-0-5*) Envir Info Srvs.

Practical Guide for Implementing Secure Intranets & Extranets. Kaustubh M. Phaltankar. LC 99-45834. (Telecommunications Library). 401p. 1999. 83.00 (*0-89006-447-4*) Artech Hse.

Practical Guide for Improving Your Metal Fabricating Shop Layout with Easy to Use Suggestions & Aids. Richard S. Budzik. 1988. 84.95 (*0-912914-23-8*) Practical Pubns.

Practical Guide for Mariners English-Italian. Fernando Picchi. (ENG & ITA.). 319p. 1980. pap. 29.95 (*0-8288-4713-4*, M9193) Fr & Eur.

Practical Guide for Notaries Public in Pennsylvania. 20th ed. 1985. pap. write for info. (*0-318-56916-7*) Penn Assoc Not.

Practical Guide for Performing, Teaching & Singing "Messiah" Leonard Van Camp. Ed. by Scott Foss. 240p. (Orig.). (C). 1993. pap. text 29.00 (*0-89328-104-2*, 30-1004) Lorenz Corp.

***Practical Guide for Policy Analysis: The Eightfold Path to More Effective Problem Solving.** 2nd ed. Eugene Bardach. LC 99-50621. (Illus.). 144p. (C). 2000. pap. text 12.95 (*1-889119-29-6*) Seven Bridges.

Practical Guide for Private Investors. Ed Smith. 1982. pap. 14.00 (*0-87364-553-7*) Paladin Pr.

Practical Guide for Royal Arch Chapter Officers & Companions. rev. ed. Elmer T. Reid. (Illus.). x, 92p. 1980. reprint ed. pap. 6.95 (*0-88053-015-4*, M-063) Macoy Pub.

Practical Guide for Supervisory Training & Development. 2nd ed. David L. Kirkpatrick. (Illus.). 224p. 1983. text. write for info. (*0-201-13435-7*) Addison-Wesley.

Practical Guide for Teachers of Elementary Japanese. Mutsuko E. Simon. LC 83-21075. (Illus.). xvi, 101p. (Orig.). (C). 1984. pap. text 10.95 (*0-939512-16-5*) U MI Japan.

Practical Guide for Teaching Science to Students with Special Needs in Inclusive Settings. Margo A. Mastropieri & Thomas E. Scruggs. (Illus.). 371p. (C). 1993. spiral bd. 34.00 (*0-89079-611-4*, 6817) PRO-ED.

Practical Guide for Teaching Self-Determination. Sharon Field & Council for Exceptional Children Staff. LC 97-36908. 184p. 1997. pap. 39.95 (*0-86586-301-6*, P5231) Coun Exc Child.

Practical Guide for Teaching the Mentally Retarded to Swim. Council for National Cooperation in Aquatics Staff. LC 74-9727. (Illus.). 160p. reprint ed. pap. 49.60 (*0-7837-5568-6*, 204534300005) Bks Demand.

Practical Guide for Technical & Skills Trainers Vols. 1 & 2, 2 vols., Set. Ed. by Barbara Darraugh. LC 94-79054. 418p. 1994. pap. text 165.00 (*1-56286-014-3*) Am Soc Train & Devel.

Practical Guide for the Bilingual Classroom. 2nd rev. ed. Bertha E. Segal-Cook. (SPA.). 80p. 1994. 12.99 (*0-938395-32-7*) B Segal.

Practical Guide for the Obstetric Team. M. D. Read & Diana Wellby. LC 84-15257. 197p. reprint ed. pap. 61.10 (*0-7837-1879-9*, 204208000001) Bks Demand.

Practical Guide for the Prearation of Specimens for X-Ray Fluorescence & X-Ray Diffraction Analysis. Victor E. Buhrke et al. LC 97-16687. 360p. 1997. 89.95 (*0-471-19458-1*) Wiley.

Practical Guide for Translators. Geoffrey Samuelsson-Brown. LC 92-45761. 1993. 49.00 (*1-85359-189-0*, Pub. by Multilingual Matters); pap. 18.90 (*1-85359-188-2*, Pub. by Multilingual Matters) Taylor & Francis.

Practical Guide for Translators. 2nd ed. Geoffrey Samuelsson-Brown. LC 95-13175. (Topics in Translation Ser.: Vol. 2). 160p. 1995. 59.00 (*1-85359-304-4*, Pub. by Multilingual Matters); pap. 19.95 (*1-85359-303-6*, Pub. by Multilingual Matters) Taylor & Francis.

Practical Guide for Translators. 3rd ed. Geoffrey Samuelsson-Brown. LC 98-29779. (Topics in Translation Ser.). 1998. pap. 19.95 (*1-85359-428-8*, Pub. by Multilingual Matters) Taylor & Francis.

***Practical Guide for Translators.** 3rd ed. Geoffrey Samuelsson-Brown. LC 98-29779. (Topics in Translation Ser.). 201p. 1998. 69.00 (*1-85359-429-6*) Taylor & Francis.

Practical Guide for Writing Goals & Objectives. rev. ed. Fran S. Gelb. LC 73-88787. 112p. 1973. pap. 13.50 (*0-87879-274-0*) Acad Therapy.

Practical Guide in Handling Your Own Traffic Cases in Honolulu. Vicente F. Aquino. pap. 7.95 (*0-681-27238-4*) Booklines Hawaii.

Practical Guide Medical & Surgical Procedures. Alan Dudley. 179p. 1989. pap. text 49.50 (*0-433-00058-9*) Buttrwrth-Heinemann.

Practical Guide of Authentic Assessment for Elementary Teachers. Kathleen Montgomery. 128p. (C). 2000. pap. 29.33 (*0-321-03782-0*) Addison-Wesley.

Practical Guide on Implementing Suggestion Systems. Andrew E. Marx. 118p. (C). 1992. pap. text 22.00 (*0-7021-2794-9*, Pub. by Juta & Co) Intl Spec Bk.

Practical Guide to a CASE Tool Selection Process. Steven C. Hill & Lee A. Robinson. 64p. (C). 1995. 15.00 (*1-886717-01-X*) Enter Tech Concepts.

Practical Guide to Academic Research. Graham Birley & Neil Moreland. 192p. 1998. pap. 25.00 (*0-7494-2277-7*, Kogan Pg Educ) Stylus Pub VA.

Practical Guide to Achieving Excellence in the Practice of Law: Standards, Methods, & Self-Evaluation. Institutional Staff. 524p. 1992. pap. text 75.00 (*0-8318-0683-4*, B683) Am Law Inst.

Practical Guide to Acquisitions: How to Make a Success of the Most Risky Business Activity. Denzil Rankine. LC 97-9427. 170p. 1997. pap. 49.95 (*0-471-97598-2*) Wiley.

Practical Guide to Activities for Young Children. Christine Hobart & Jill Frankel. 128p. 1995. pap. 22.50 (*0-7487-1924-5*, Pub. by S Thornes Pubs) Trans-Atl Phila.

***Practical Guide to Activities for Young Children.** 2nd ed. Christine Hobart & Jill Frankel. 1999. 24.50 (*0-7487-4503-3*, Pub. by S Thornes Pubs) Trans-Atl Phila.

Practical Guide to ADA & Visual Impairment. Elga Joffee. LC 98-15740. 1998. 39.95 (*0-89128-318-8*) Am Foun Blind.

***Practical Guide to Aging: What Everyone Needs to Know.** Ed. by Christine Cassel. 2001. pap. 17.95 (*0-8147-1516-8*) NYU Pr.

Practical Guide to Aging: What Everyone Needs to Know. Ed. by Christine K. Cassel. LC 97-21571. (Illus.). 352p. (C). 1999. 24.95 (*0-8147-1515-X*) NYU Pr.

Practical Guide to Air Quality Compliance. 2nd ed. Russell E. Erbes. LC 95-46166. 434p. 1996. 120.00 (*0-471-15006-1*) Wiley.

Practical Guide to Airplane Performance & Design. Donald R. Crawford. LC 81-67801. (Illus.). 200p. 1981. pap. text 18.95 (*0-9603934-0-4*) Crawford Aviation.

Practical Guide to Algol 68. Frank G. Pagan. LC 75-6925. (Wiley Series in Computing). 223p. reprint ed. pap. 69.20 (*0-7837-4388-2*, 204412800012) Bks Demand.

Practical Guide to Alterations & Extensions. A. Williams. LC 95-67605. (Illus.). 224p. (Orig.). (C). 1995. pap. 39.99 (*0-419-20080-0*, E & FN Spon) Routledge.

***Practical Guide to Alterations & Improvements.** R. Cooper. 170p. (C). (gr. 13). 1998. pap. text 29.99 (*1-85032-006-3*) ITCP.

Practical Guide to Alternative Assessment. Joan L. Herman et al. LC 92-30244. 1992. pap. 13.95 (*0-87120-197-6*) ASCD.

Practical Guide to American 19th Century Color Plate Books, Set only. Whitman Bennett. 162p. 1996. reprint ed. 45.00 (*1-888262-14-1*) Martino Pubng.

Practical Guide to Analog Behavioral Modeling for IC System Design. Paul A. Duran. LC 98-33840. 1998. 115.00 (*0-7923-8276-5*) Kluwer Academic.

Practical Guide to Anorectal Testing. 2nd ed. Ed. by Lee E. Smith. LC 95-1315. (Illus.). 344p. 1995. pap. 69.50 (*0-89640-278-9*) Igaku-Shoin.

Practical Guide to Antibacterial Agents. Don J. Maurio. 40p. (Orig.). Date not set. pap. 15.95 (*0-9657721-1-X*) Grp Tech.

Practical Guide to Applying, Installing, & Maintaining Transformers. rev. ed. Ed. by Alfred Berutti & Robert B. Morgan. (Practical Guide to Ser.). (Illus.). 88p. 1994. pap. 23.95 (*0-87288-585-2*) Intertec Pub.

Practical Guide to Applying Low-Voltage Fuses. 2nd rev. ed. John A. Dedad. Ed. by Hermann W. Reichenstein. (Practical Guide to Ser.). (Illus.). 113p. 1992. pap. 23.95 (*0-87288-479-1*) Intertec Pub.

Practical Guide to Applying Treatment Outcomes & Efficacy Research. Ed. by Roberta Kreb. LC 98-114042. 1997. 28.00 (*0-910329-99-0*, 0112030) Am Speech Lang Hearing.

Practical Guide to Archaeological Photography. 2nd ed. Carol L. Howell & Warren Blanc. LC 95-33494. (UCLA Institute of Archaeology Publications: No. 6). (Illus.). 106p. 1995. pap. 25.00 (*0-917956-85-0*) UCLA Arch.

Practical Guide to Arrest & Detention. Christopher J. Lethem. (Waterlow Procedure Notes Ser.). 128p. 1991. pap. 33.90 (*0-08-036919-7*) Macmillan.

Practical Guide to Art Therapy Groups. Diane Fausek. LC 96-34526. 115p. 1997. 39.95 (*0-7890-0136-5*) Haworth Pr.

Practical Guide to Art Therapy Groups. Diane Fausek. LC 96-34526. 115p. 1997. pap. 22.95 (*0-7890-0186-1*) Haworth Pr.

Practical Guide to Arts Participation Research. Compiled by AMS Planning & Research Corp. Staff. LC 95-12004. (Research Division Reports: No. 30). 1995. write for info. (*0-614-32291-X*) Natl Endow Arts.

***Practical Guide to Augmentative & Alternative Communication: Assessment & Intervention Strategies.** Patricia D. Quattlebaum & Lily N. Nalty. (Illus.). 48p. (J). 1998. spiral bd., wbk. ed. 14.95 (*1-58650-071-6*, BK-269) Super Duper.

Practical Guide To Autocad Autolisp. Trevor Bousfield. 200p. (C). 1999. pap. text 57.95 (*0-582-32673-7*) Addison-Wesley.

Practical Guide to Autocad 3-D Design. Trevor Bousfield. 400p. (C). 1999. pap. 44.00 (*0-582-36935-5*) Addison-Wesley.

Practical Guide to Autos: Operation, Safety & Maintenance. Frank L. Bouquet. (Illus.). 100p. (C). 1991. 45.00 (*1-56216-050-8*); pap. 25.00 (*1-56216-051-6*) Systems Co.

Practical Guide to Autos - 1992. 2nd ed. Frank L. Bouquet. (Illus.). 150p. (Orig.). 1992. pap. 30.00 (*1-56216-103-2*); text 50.00 (*1-56216-102-4*) Systems Co.

Practical Guide to Avoiding Steam Purity Problems in Industrial Plants Vol. 35: A Practical Guide to Avoiding Steam Purity Problems in Industrial Plants. ASME Research & Technology Committee on Water & St. (CRTD Ser.: Vol. 35). 40p. 1995. pap. 10.00 (*0-7918-1220-0*, I00383) ASME.

***Practical Guide to Bankruptcy Law.** Matthew S. Cornick. (Paralegal Ser.). (C). 2000. pap. 32.00 (*0-7668-0437-2*) Delmar.

Practical Guide to Beauty Therapy. 2nd ed. Janet Simms. (Illus.). 324p. 1998. pap. 37.50 (*0-7487-3278-0*, Pub. by S Thornes Pubs) Trans-Atl Phila.

Practical Guide to Behavioral Research: Tools & Techniques. 4th ed. Barbara B. Sommer & Robert Sommer. LC 96-35531. (Illus.). 400p. (C). 1997. text 62.95 (*0-19-510418-8*); pap. text 34.95 (*0-19-510419-6*) OUP.

Practical Guide to Behavioral Research No. 4: Tools & Techniques. 4th ed. Barbara Sommer & Robert Sommer. 108p. 1998. pap., teacher ed. write for info. (*0-19-512443-X*) OUP.

Practical Guide to Better Concentration. Melvin Powers. (Orig.). 1980. pap. 5.00 (*0-87980-120-4*) Wilshire.

Practical Guide to Bone Marrow Transplantation. Edward D. Ball & John Lister. (Illus.). 795p. 2000. text. write for info. (*0-443-07622-7*, W B Saunders Co) Harcrt Hlth Sci Grp.

Practical Guide to Borehole Geophysics in Environmental Investigations. W. Scott Keys. LC 96-27449. 176p. 1996. lib. bdg. 65.00 (*1-56670-232-1*) Lewis Pubs.

***Practical Guide to Bryan-College Station.** 2nd rev. ed. Diane Oswald. Ed. by Alma Maxwell. (Illus.). 1999. pap. 8.95 (*0-9659698-2-7*, LW5003) Lacewing Pr.

Practical Guide to Bryan-College Station: Your Indespensable Reference. Diane L. Oswald. (Illus.). 112p. 1998. pap. 7.95 (*0-9659698-1-9*, LW5002) Lacewing Pr.

Practical Guide to Building Your New Home: Decisions to Live With. Esther DiMarzio & Gail Jacky. (Illus.). 40p. (Orig.). 1996. pap. 12.00 (*0-9654464-0-9*) Sycamore Pr IL.

Practical Guide to Building Your New Home: The Financing Process. Esther DiMarzio & Gail D. Jacky. 20p. 1997. pap. 6.00 (*0-9654464-1-7*) Sycamore Pr IL.

Practical Guide to Business Process Re-Engineering. Mike Robson & Philip Ullah. LC 95-40204. 169p. 1996. 74.95 (*0-566-07577-6*, Pub. by Gower) Ashgate Pub Co.

Practical Guide to Business Process Reengineering Using IDEF0. Clarence G. Feldmann. LC 98-20236. (Illus.). 240p. 1998. pap. 34.95 (*0-932633-37-4*) Dorset Hse Pub Co.

Practical Guide to Calligraphy. Rosemary Sassoon. (Illus.). 1982. pap. 10.95 (*0-500-27251-4*, Pub. by Thames Hudson) Norton.

***Practical Guide to Capacity Planning & Management.** Harry K. Jackson & Normand L. Frigon. LC 97-37064. 240p. 1998. 79.00 (*0-471-18092-0*) Wiley.

Practical Guide to Cardiac Pacing. 4th ed. H. Weston Moses et al. LC 94-3383. 256p. 1995. pap. text 39.00 (*0-316-58552-1*, Little Brwn Med Div) Lppncott W & W.

Practical Guide to Cardiac Pacing. 5th ed. H. Weston Moses et al. 224p. pap. text 39.95 (*0-7817-1956-9*) Lppncott W & W.

Practical Guide to Career Planning. Joseph H. Horton. (Orig.). (YA). (gr. 7-12). 1993. pap. 19.95 (*0-9652418-2-3*) Horton Pubng.

Practical Guide to Catching More Crappie. Buck Taylor. (Illus.). 238p. (Orig.). 1983. pap. 9.95 (*0-940022-02-8*) Outdoor Skills.

Practical Guide to CCD Astronomy. Patrick Martinez & Alain Klotz. Tr. by Andre Demers. LC 96-54304. (Practical Astronomy Handbooks Ser.: Vol. 8). (Illus.). 264p. (C). 1997. pap. 30.95 (*0-521-59950-4*); text 80.00 (*0-521-59063-9*) Cambridge U Pr.

Practical Guide to Centronic, RS232 & Game Ports. Pei An. (Illus.). 352p. 1998. pap. text 32.95 (*0-7506-3637-8*, Newnes) Buttrwrth-Heinemann.

Practical Guide to Chemical Spill Response. John W. Hosty & Patricia E. Foster. (Industrial Health & Safety Ser.). 193p. 1992. 59.95 (*0-471-28415-7*, VNR) Wiley.

Practical Guide to Chemical Spill Response. John W. Hosty & Patricia E. Foster. (Illus.). 193p. 1992. text 48.95 (*0-442-00569-5*, VNR) Wiley.

Practical Guide to Chemometrics. Ed. by Haswell. (Illus.). 344p. 1992. text 145.00 (*0-8247-8597-5*) Dekker.

Practical Guide to Child-Care Employment. Christine Hobart & Jill Frankel. 136p. 1998. pap. 25.50 (*0-7487-2576-8*) St Mut.

Practical Guide to Child Development. Valda Reynolds. (Teacher's Books ser.). 48p. (C). 1988. pap., teacher ed. 27.50 (*0-85950-525-1*, Pub. by S Thornes Pubs) Trans-Atl Phila.

Practical Guide to Child Development, 2 vols., Vol. 1. Valda Reynolds. 302p. (C). 1987. pap. 29.50 (*0-85950-221-X*, Pub. by S Thornes Pubs) Trans-Atl Phila.

Practical Guide to Child Development, 2 vols., Vol. 2. Valda Reynold. 134p. (C). 1987. pap. 27.50 (*0-85950-240-6*, Pub. by S Thornes Pubs) Trans-Atl Phila.

Practical Guide to Child Nutrition. Angela Dare & Margaret O'Donovan. 128p. 1996. pap. 22.50 (*0-7487-2375-7*, Pub. by S Thornes Pubs) Trans-Atl Phila.

***Practical Guide to Child Observation & Assessment.** Christine Hobart & Jill Frankel. (Illus.). 143p. 1999. pap. 23.50 (*0-7487-4500-9*, Pub. by S Thornes Pubs) Trans-Atl Phila.

Practical Guide to Childbirth on Shabbos & Yom Tov. S. Wagschal. 1994. 7.95 (*0-87306-679-0*) Feldheim.

Practical Guide to Chorion Villus Sampling. Ed. by David T. Liu. (Illus.). 168p. 1991. 62.00 (*0-19-262006-1*) OUP.

Practical Guide to Client/Server Computing. 98th ed. Hugh W. Ryan et al. LC 97-209141. 816p. 1997. boxed set 160.00 (*0-8493-9951-3*) CRC Pr.

Practical Guide to Client/Server Computing 1999. 99th ed. Hugh W. Ryan. 19p. 1998. boxed set 95.00 (*0-8493-9967-X*) CRC Pr.

Practical Guide to Clinical Data Management. Susanne Prokscha. LC 99-21232. 1999. 189.00 (*1-57491-100-7*) Interpharm.

Practical Guide to Clinical Documentation in Behavioral Health Care. Joint Commission on Accreditation of Healthcare Organizations. LC 96-79319. (Illus.). 131p. 1997. pap. 40.00 (*0-86688-505-6*, BH-200) Joint Comm Hlthcare.

Practical Guide to Clinical Laboratory Testing. Daniel Cowan. LC 96-46197. 356p. (Orig.). 1997. pap. 34.95 (*0-86542-470-5*) Blackwell Sci.

Practical Guide to Clinical Teaching in Medicine. Kaaren Douglas et al. (Medical Education Ser.). 208p. 1988. 29.95 (*0-8261-5940-0*) Springer Pub.

Practical Guide to Clinical Virology. Ed. by G. C. Haukenes et al. LC 89-14767. 218p. 1989. pap. 59.95 (*0-471-91978-0*) Wiley.

Practical Guide to Cognitive Therapy. Dean Schuyler. 180p. 1991. 22.95 (*0-393-70105-0*) Norton.

Practical Guide to Combinatorial Chemistry. Ed. by Anthony W. Czarnik & Sheila H. DeWitt. LC 97-36358. (ACS Professional Reference Bks.). 360p. 1997. text 89.95 (*0-8412-3485-X*, Pub. by Am Chemical) OUP.

Practical Guide to Community Assessment. Vicki Luther & Milan Wall. 120p. 1999. pap. 10.00 (*0-9666699-1-6*) Heartland Ctr.

***Practical Guide to Competency Related Pay.** D. Brown. (Financial Times Management Briefings Ser.). 1998. pap. 89.50 (*0-273-63751-7*, Pub. by F T P-H) Trans-Atl Phila.

Practical Guide to Comprehensive Planning. Cori F. Traub & David Church. (Illus.). 94p. 1996. pap. 14.00 (*0-8113-0004-8*) NY Plan Fed.

Practical Guide to Compressor Technology. Heinz P. Bloch. LC 95-22898. 518p. 1995. 62.50 (*0-07-005937-3*) McGraw.

Practical Guide to Computers in Education. 2nd ed. Peter Coburn. 1985. text 18.30 (*0-201-10593-4*) Addison-Wesley.

Practical Guide to Conducting Customized Work Force Training. Ed. by Sherrie L. Kantor. LC 85-644753. (New Directions for Community Colleges Ser.: No. CC 85). 112p. (Orig.). 1994. pap. 22.00 (*0-7879-9957-1*) Jossey-Bass.

***Practical Guide to Container Gardening.** Susan Berry & Steve Bradley. 160p. 2000. pap. 16.95 (*1-58017-329-2*) Storey Bks.

Practical Guide to Contemporary Pharmacy Practice. Judith E. Thompson. LC 98-15843. 340p. 1998. pap. 32.95 (*0-683-30538-7*) Lppncott W & W.

Practical Guide to Contracts of Affreightment & Hybrid Contracts. 2nd enl. ed. Lars Gorton & Rolf Ihre. 126p. 1990. 90.00 (*1-85044-276-2*, 341.75668) LLP.

Practical Guide to Cooperative Learning in Collegiate Mathematics. Ed. by Nancy L. Hagelgans et al. LC 95-76289. (MAA Notes Ser.: No. 37). 190p. 1995. pap. 28.95 (*0-88385-095-8*, NTE-37) Math Assn.

Practical Guide to Corals for the Reef Aquarium. 2nd rev. ed. Ed Puterbaugh & Eric Borneman. LC 96-86765. (Illus.). 112p. 1997. 34.95 (*0-945738-99-4*) Crystal KY.

Practical Guide to Course Portfolios. Karen Vaught-Alexander. LC 98-142938. 128p. (YA). (gr. 9-13). 1996. pap. text 17.95 (*1-881641-48-1*) Pencil Point.

Practical Guide to Cranial Adjustment. Harvey Getzoff. LC 98-10405. (Illus.). 85p. 1996. pap., spiral bd. 39.95 (*0-938198-02-5*) Weidner & Sons.

***Practical Guide to Creating a Garden Pond.** Gina Sandford. (Tankmasters Ser.). (Illus.). 80p. 2000. 9.95 (*0-7641-5269-6*) Barron.

Practical Guide to Creative Senility. Donovan Bess. LC 88-9551. (Illus.). 176p. (Orig.). 1988. pap. 9.95 (*0-931892-16-3*) B Dolphin Pub.

Practical Guide to Credit & Collection. George O. Bancroft. LC 88-83151. 276p. 1989. 29.95 (*0-8144-5953-6*) AMACOM.

P

Practical Guide to Cross-Cultural Communication. Gregory Barnard. (Illus.). 144p. 1995. 90.00 (*0-304-33152-X*); pap. 25.95 (*0-304-33154-6*) Continuum.

Practical Guide to Customer Relations. Highfield Publications Staff. (C). 1989. 60.00 (*0-89771-810-0*, Pub. by Highfield Pubns) St Mut.

Practical Guide to Customer Service Management & Operations. E. Patricia Birsner & Ronald D. Balsley. LC 81-69366. 224p. reprint ed. pap. 69.50 (*0-608-12403-6*, 205214000040) Bks Demand.

Practical Guide to Data Analysis for Physical Science Students. Louis Lyons. (Illus.). 107p. (C). 1991. text 49.95 (*0-521-41415-6*); pap. text 16.95 (*0-521-42463-1*) Cambridge U Pr.

Practical Guide to DBMS Selection. Lindsay Peat. 340p. 1982. 138.50 (*3-11-008167-9*) De Gruyter.

***Practical Guide to Decorative Antique Effects.** Annie Sloan. (Illus.). 128p. 1999. pap. 17.95 (*1-85585-257-8*, Pub. by Collins & Br) Sterling.

***Practical Guide to Decorative Antique Effects: Paints, Waxes, Varnishes.** Annie Sloan. (Illus.). 128p. 1999. reprint ed. text 27.00 (*0-7881-6555-0*) DIANE Pub.

Practical Guide to Dental Equipment. Nicholas M. Jedyakiewicz. LC 92-12792. (Illus.). 193p. (C). (gr. 13). 1992. text 29.95 (*0-8151-4867-4*, 21945) Mosby Inc.

Practical Guide to Designing Expert Systems. Sholom M. Weiss & Casimir A. Kulikowski. (Illus.). 186p. 1984. text 53.00 (*0-86598-108-6*) Rowman.

Practical Guide to Diagnostic Imaging. Ed. by Neil T. Specht. LC 97-23636. (Illus.). 650p. (C). (gr. 13). 1997. spiral bd. 32.95 (*0-8151-9356-4*, 29194) Mosby Inc.

Practical Guide to Diagnostic Imaging: Radiography & Ultrasonography. C. M. Ham et al. LC 94-71186. 300p. 1994. pap. text 31.00 (*0-939674-54-8*) Am Vet Pubns.

Practical Guide to Diagnostic Parasitology. Lynne S. Garcia. LC 99-12315. (Illus.). 320p. 1999. pap. 49.95 (*1-55581-154-X*) ASM Pr.

Practical Guide to Directors Report. R. K. Agarwal. (C). 1989. 140.00 (*0-7855-6128-5*) St Mut.

Practical Guide to Disputes Between Adjoining Landowners Easements, 2 vols. James Backman & David Thomas. 1989. ring bd. 165.00 (*0-8205-1060-2*) Bender.

Practical Guide to Divorce in Hawaii. 2nd ed. Peter J. Herman. LC 90-48159. 144p. 1991. pap. 9.95 (*0-8248-1360-X*, Kolowalu Bk) UH Pr.

***Practical Guide to Document Authentication: Legalization of Notarized & Certified Documents (Millennium Edition 2000)** John P. Sinnott. 637p. 1999. text 150.00 (*0-379-21221-8*, 7925123) Oceana.

Practical Guide to Dog & Puppy Care. Andrew T. Edney. (Illus.). 119p. 10.95 (*1-56465-164-9*, 16022) Tetra Pr.

Practical Guide to Dog Care. Consumer Guide Editors. 192p. 1995. mass mkt. 4.99 (*0-451-18575-7*, Sig) NAL.

Practical Guide to Drafting Pleading. Anthony Radevsky. 214p. 1991. 70.00 (*1-85190-141-8*, Pub. by Tolley Pubng) St Mut.

Practical Guide to Drafting Pleading. Anthony Radevsky & Quentin Edwards. (Lawyers Practice & Procedure Ser.). 227p. 1995. pap. 195.00 (*0-85459-948-7*, Pub. by Tolley Pubng) St Mut.

Practical Guide to DSM-IV Diagnosis & Treatment. 2nd ed. Carol J. Cole. 173p. 1998. 39.95 (*1-890961-03-5*) C Communs.

***Practical Guide to Ear Candling: A New Twist on an Ancient Practice.** 5th rev. ed. Russell Sheppard. (Illus.). 64p. 1999. pap. 6.98 (*0-9672708-0-4*) Wallys Nat Prods.

Practical Guide to Early Childhood Curriculum. 5th ed. 1993. teacher ed. 6.00 (*0-02-332224-1*, Macmillan Coll) P-H.

Practical Guide to Early Childhood Curriculum. 6th ed. Claudia Fuhriman-Eliason et al. LC 98-17011. 584p. (C). 1998. pap. text 46.00 (*0-13-685538-5*, Scribners Ref) Mac Lib Ref.

Practical Guide to Early Childhood Planning Methods & Materials: The What, Why & How of Lesson Plans. Evelyn Petersen. 224p. (C). 1995. pap. text 30.00 (*0-205-17404-3*) Allyn.

Practical Guide to ECG Interpretation. 2nd ed. Ken Grauer. 1998. pap. text 34.95 (*1-55664-557-0*) Mosby Inc.

Practical Guide to Echocardiography & Cardiac Doppler Ultrasound. 2nd ed. Ibrahim A. Jawad. LC 95-43199. 432p. 1996. pap. text 43.00 (*0-316-45837-6*) Lppncott W & W.

Practical Guide to Effective Hearing Conservation Programs in the Workplace. (Illus.). 105p. (Orig.). (C). 1994. pap. text 30.00 (*0-7881-0510-8*) DIANE Pub.

Practical Guide to Effective Presentation. Rex P. Gatto. LC 90-83272. (Illus.). 177p. (Orig.). (C). 1990. pap. text 9.95 (*0-945997-20-5*) GTA Pr.

Practical Guide to Effective Protection at the Land Registry. Stephen R. Convey & Andrew J. Pain. 232p. 1991. 75.00 (*1-85190-121-3*, Pub. by Tolley Pubng) St Mut.

Practical Guide to Electrical Energy Efficiency & Reduced Costs. Ed. by Alfred Berutti & Robert J. Lawrie. (Practical Guide to Ser.). (Illus.). 136p. 1994. pap. 23.95 (*0-87288-584-4*) Intertec Pub.

Practical Guide to Elementary Instruction: From Plan to Delivery. Suzanne Borman & Joel M. Levine. LC 96-38717. 396p. 1997. pap. text 57.00 (*0-205-14188-9*) Allyn.

Practical Guide to Elementary Instruction: From Plan to Delivery. Suzanne Borman & Joel M. Levine. (C). 1997. pap., teacher ed. write for info. (*0-205-26516-2*, T6516-3) Allyn.

Practical Guide to ELISA. D. M. Kemeny. (Illus.). 128p. 1991. pap. text 26.75 (*0-08-037507-3*, Pergamon Pr) Elsevier.

Practical Guide to Emergency & Protective Crisis Intervention: Dealing with the Violent & Self-Destructive Person. Joel Foxman. 320p. 1990. pap. 44.95 (*0-398-06127-0*) C C Thomas.

Practical Guide to Emergency & Protective Crisis Intervention: Dealing with the Violent & Self-Destructive Person. Joel Foxman. 320p. (C). 1990. text 66.95 (*0-398-05621-8*) C C Thomas.

Practical Guide to Emergency, Standby & Other Auxiliary Power Systems. LC 99-162939. 132p. 1996. 23.95 (*0-87288-603-4*) Intertec Pub.

Practical Guide to Enrollment & Retention Management in Higher Education. Marguerite J. Dennis. LC 98-9532. 160p. 1998. 55.00 (*0-89789-591-6*, Bergin & Garvey) Greenwood.

Practical Guide to Environmental Community Relations. Carol J. Forrest & Renee H. Mays. LC 96-41858. 342p. 1997. 90.00 (*0-471-16388-0*) Wiley.

Practical Guide to Environmental Impact Assessment. Paul A. Erickson. (Illus.). 266p. 1994. text 73.00 (*0-12-241555-8*) Acad Pr.

***Practical Guide to Environmental Management.** 8th ed. Frank B. Friedman. LC 97-209655. 472p. 2000. 39.95 (*0-911937-72-2*) Environ Law Inst.

***Practical Guide to Environmental Management.** 8th ed. Frank Friedman & Environmental Law Institute Staff. LC 00-33168. 2000. write for info. (*1-58576-007-2*) Environ Law Inst.

Practical Guide to Equal Employment Opportunity, 2 vols. Walter B. Connolly, Jr. & Michael J. Connolly. 1100p. 1979. 135.00 (*0-317-01348-3*) NY Law Pub.

Practical Guide to Equal Opportunities. Hyacinth Malik. 128p. 1998. pap. 26.00 (*0-7487-3652-2*, Pub. by S Thornes Pubs) Trans-Atl Phila.

Practical Guide to Estate Planning in Massachusetts, 2 vols. Jon E. Steffensen et al. LC 96-77821. 952p. 1996. ring bd. 125.00 (*1-57589-020-8*, 97-08.12-BK) Mass CLE.

Practical Guide to Estimating for Alterations & Repairs. G. Chrystal-Smith. (Illus.). 168p. (C). (gr. 13). 1988. pap. 29.99 (*0-7198-2545-8*, E & FN Spon) Routledge.

Practical Guide to Etching & Other Intaglio Printmaking Techniques. Manly Banister. 128p. 1986. reprint ed. pap. 7.95 (*0-486-25165-9*) Dover.

Practical Guide to European Travel. M. N. Polfen. 200p. 1981. pap. 7.95 (*0-934036-07-1*) PMF Research.

Practical Guide to Evidence. Christopher Allen. xlii, 395p. 1998. pap. 38.00 (*1-85941-316-1*, Pub. by Cavendish Pubng) Gaunt.

Practical Guide to Exotic Pets: How to Keep & Enjoy a Wide Range of Unusual Pets. Chris Mattison. 1999. pap. 9.99 (*1-84100-244-5*) Quadrillion Media.

Practical Guide to Experimental Design. Normand L. Frigon & David Mathews. LC 96-23728. 342p. 1996. 90.00 (*0-471-13919-X*) Wiley.

***Practical Guide to Facilitation: A Self-Study Resource.** John D. Farrell & Richard G. Weaver. 150p. 2000. pap. 33.95 (*1-57675-095-7*, Pub. by Berrett-Koehler) Publishers Group.

Practical Guide To Family Law. Matthew S. Cornick. LC 94-46248. (Paralegal). 422p. (C). 1995. mass mkt. 63.95 (*0-314-04451-5*) West Pub.

Practical Guide to Fares & Ticketing. 2nd ed. Jeanne Semer-Purzycki. LC 93-25702. (C). 1994. mass mkt. 35.75 (*0-8273-6088-6*) Delmar.

Practical Guide to Fares & Ticketing. 2nd ed. Jeanne Semer-Purzycki. 125p. 1994. teacher ed. 17.00 (*0-8273-6089-4*) Delmar.

Practical Guide to Fares & Ticketing. 3rd ed. Semer-Purzyc. (C). 2000. pap. text 47.95 (*0-7668-1582-X*) Delmar.

Practical Guide to Federal Evidence: Objections, Responses, Rules, & Practice Commentary. 3rd ed. Anthony J. Bacchina & David A. Sonenshein. LC 98-106575. 298p. 1997. 32.95 (*1-55681-557-3*) Natl Inst Trial Ad.

***Practical Guide to Federal Evidence: Objections, Responses, Rules & Practice Commentary.** 4th ed. Anthony J. Bocchino & David A. Sonenshein. 2000. 39.95 (*1-55681-650-2*) Natl Inst Trial Ad.

Practical Guide to Ferret Care. 2nd large type rev. ed. Deborah Jeans. (Illus.). 176p. 1996. pap. 22.95 (*0-9642589-1-9*) Ferrets.

Practical Guide to Fetal Echocardiography. Alfred Abuhamad. LC 97-2780. (Illus.). 185p. 1997. text 63.00 (*0-397-51674-6*) Lppncott W & W.

***Practical Guide to Finance & Accounting.** (C). 2001. text 49.95 (*0-13-026502-0*) P-H.

Practical Guide to Finite Elements: A Solid Mechanics Approach. Steven M. Lepi. LC 97-52825. (Mechanical Engineering Ser.: Vol. 115). (Illus.). 544p. 1998. text 165.00 (*0-8247-0075-9*) Dekker.

Practical Guide to Finite Risk Insurance & Reinsurance. R. George Monti & Andrew Barile. LC 95-20443. 341p. 1995. 220.00 (*0-471-12818-X*) Wiley.

Practical Guide to Fishing. (Illus.). 172p. 1999. 19.95 (*3-8290-2132-1*, 521045) Konemann.

Practical Guide to Florida Retirement. 2nd ed. Betty McGarry. LC 88-31220. 250p. 1989. pap. 9.95 (*0-910923-61-2*) Pineapple Pr.

Practical Guide to Food & Drug Law & Regulation. Ed. by Kenneth R. Pina & Wayne L. Pines. LC 98-203165. 354p. (C). 1998. pap. 129.00 (*1-885259-55-7*) Food & Drug Law.

Practical Guide to Foreign Direct Investment in the European Union: The Green Book. 2nd ed. (Euroconfidential Collection). 360p. 1998. 220.00 (*2-930066-46-6*, Pub. by Euroconfidential) Paul & Co Pubs.

Practical Guide to Forensic Psychotherapy. Ed. by Estela V. Welldon & Cleo Van Velsen. 300p. 1996. pap. 34.95 (*1-85302-389-2*, Pub. by Jessica Kingsley) Taylor & Francis.

Practical Guide to Fourth Generation Programming Languages. Jeff Bernknopf. (Illus.). 320p. 1989. text 39.95 (*0-07-004960-2*) McGraw.

Practical Guide to French Pronunciation. H. S. McKellar. LC PC2137.. 157p. reprint ed. pap. 48.70 (*0-608-16298-1*, 202653100050) Bks Demand.

Practical Guide to Front Office Management. Hatch. (Food & Hospitality Ser.). 1998. teacher ed. 9.24 (*0-8273-7776-2*); wbk. ed. 11.51 (*0-8273-7775-4*); 23.06 (*0-8273-7774-6*); 30.76 (*0-8273-7777-0*) Delmar.

***Practical Guide to Fund-Raising in Schools.** Paul Morris. LC 99-87277. 208p. 2000. write for info. (*0-415-22957-X*) Routledge.

Practical Guide to Garden Design. Time-Life Books Editors. Ed. by Janet Cave. LC 96-157. (Complete Gardener Ser.). (Illus.). 160p. (gr. 11). 1999. pap. 16.95 (*0-7835-4111-2*) Time-Life.

Practical Guide to Gastrointestinal Function Testing. C. Stendal. (Illus.). 1997. 74.95 (*0-632-04918-9*) Blackwell Sci.

Practical Guide to Graduate Research. M. Stock. 176p. (C). 1985. text. write for info. (*0-07-061583-7*) McGraw.

Practical Guide to Grand Opera. M. N. Polfen. 200p. (Orig.). 1981. pap. 7.95 (*0-934036-08-X*) PMF Research.

Practical Guide to Graphite Furnace Atomic Absorption Spectrometry. David J. Butcher & Joseph Sneddon. LC 97-29336. (Chemical Analysis). 272p. 1998. 79.95 (*0-471-12553-9*, Wiley-Interscience) Wiley.

Practical Guide to Ground Fault Protection. Ed. by Alfred Berutti. (Practical Guide to Ser.). (Illus.). 78p. 1995. pap. 23.95 (*0-87288-608-5*) Intertec Pub.

Practical Guide to Groundwater & Solute Transport Modeling. Karlheinz Spitz & Joanna Moreno. LC 95-35407. (Illus.). 461p. 1996. 99.00 (*0-471-13687-5*, Wiley-Interscience) Wiley.

Practical Guide to Grouting of Underground Structures. Raymond W. Henn. LC 96-3135. 200p. 1996. 42.00 (*0-7844-0140-3*) Am Soc Civil Eng.

Practical Guide to Growing Healthy Houseplants. Matthew Biggs. 1997. 16.95 (*1-85833-525-6*, Pub. by CLib Bks) Whitecap Bks.

Practical Guide to Handling IRS Income Tax Audits. Ralph L. Guyette. LC 86-4905. 1986. text 39.95 (*0-13-690876-4*) P-H.

Practical Guide to Handwriting Analysis. Kirsten Hall. (Illus.). 156p. 1999. 17.98 (*1-57912-072-5*) Blck Dog & Leventhal.

Practical Guide to Hazardous (classified) Locations. LC 96-78406. 108 p. 1996. 23.95 (*0-87288-640-9*) Intertec Pub.

Practical Guide to Head Injury Management. Ed. by Paul V. Marks & Christopher B. Lavy. (Illus.). 168p. 1992. text 30.00 (*0-7020-1615-2*, Pub. by W B Saunders) Saunders.

Practical Guide to Head Injury Rehabilitation: A Focus on Postacute Residential Treatment. Michael D. Wesolowski & Arnie H. Zencius. LC 93-30642. (Critical Issues in Neuropsychology Ser.). 254p. 1994. 39.50 (*0-306-44427-5*, Kluwer Plenum) Kluwer Academic.

Practical Guide to Health & Diseases: Health Is Bliss. Alice K. Wong & Gary C. Lee. (CHI., Illus.). 375p. (Orig.). pap. write for info. (*0-9641190-1-3*) Beacon Hlth.

Practical Guide to Health Assessment. Shelly Leasia. Ed. by Barbara N. Cullen. LC 96-41703. (Illus.). 464p. 1997. pap. text 24.95 (*0-7216-1468-X*, W B Saunders Co) Harcrt Hlth Sci Grp.

Practical Guide to Health Assessment Through the Lifespan. 2nd ed. Mildred O. Hogstel. (Illus.). 411p. 1996. pap. 22.95 (*0-8036-0130-1*) Davis Co.

Practical Guide to Health Promotion after Spinal Cord Injury. Indira S. Lanig & Teresa Chase. 300p. 1995. 62.00 (*0-8342-0628-5*) Aspen Pub.

Practical Guide to Heavy Tails. Ed. by R. Adler et al. LC 97-8731. 533p. 1997. 64.50 (*0-8176-3951-9*) Birkhauser.

Practical Guide to Heavy Tails: Statistical Techniques for Analyzing Heavy Tailed Distributions. Robert J. Adler et al. LC 97-8731. 1997. write for info. (*3-7643-3951-9*) Birkhauser.

Practical Guide to High-Risk Pregnancy & Delivery. 2nd ed. Fernando Arias. (Illus.). 496p. (C). (gr. 13). 1992. pap. text 62.00 (*0-8016-0057-X*, 00057) Mosby Inc.

Practical Guide to HO Model Railroading: The Practical Guide to HO Model Railroading. Ed. by Bob Hayden. (Illus.). 88p. 1986. pap. 12.95 (*0-89024-086-8*, 12075, Kalmbach Books) Kalmbach.

Practical Guide to Holistic Health. rev. ed. Swami Rama. LC 80-81598. 110p. 1999. pap. 14.95 (*0-89389-174-6*) Himalayan Inst.

Practical Guide to Horseshoeing. Wilshire Staff. 1981. pap. 5.00 (*0-87980-239-1*) Wilshire.

Practical Guide to Hospital Dental Practice see Oral Medicine & Hospital Practice

Practical Guide to HPLC Detection. Ed. by Donald Parriott. LC 92-13082. (Illus.). 293p. 1992. text 71.00 (*0-12-545680-8*) Acad Pr.

Practical Guide to Human Cancer Genetics. S. V. Hodgson & E. R. Maher. LC 92-49932. (Illus.). 258p. (C). 1993. text 105.00 (*0-521-40128-3*); pap. text 42.95 (*0-521-40951-9*) Cambridge U Pr.

Practical Guide to Human Cancer Genetics. 2nd expanded rev. ed. Shirley V. Hodgson & Eamonn R. Maher. (Illus.). 260p. (C). 1998. text 100.00 (*0-521-64025-3*) Cambridge U Pr.

***Practical Guide to Human Cancer Genetics.** 2nd expanded rev. ed. Shirley V. Hodgson & Eamonn R. Maher. (Illus.). 260p. (C). 1999. pap. text 42.95 (*0-521-64961-7*) Cambridge U Pr.

Practical Guide to Implementing the Family & Medical Leave Act. Robert L. Duston & Scott Robbins. 153p. 1993. 85.00 (*1-878240-29-3*) Coll & U Personnel.

Practical Guide to Implementing the Family & Medical Leave Act, 1996 Supplement. Robert L. Duston & Scott Robins. 1997. 65.00 (*1-878240-56-0*) Coll & U Personnel.

Practical Guide to Import-Export. Arthur C. Simon. LC 78-55996. (Illus.). 1978. pap. 12.95 (*0-930490-14-2*) Future Shop.

Practical Guide to Impractical Pets. Barbara Burn. LC 97-1822. 352p. 1997. 27.95 (*0-87605-724-5*) Howell Bks.

***Practical Guide to Impractical Pets: 84 Exotic Pets & How to Live with Them Successfully.** rev. ed. Barbara Burn. (Illus.). 372p. 1999. reprint ed. text 28.00 (*0-7881-6663-8*) DIANE Pub.

Practical Guide to Industrial Metal Cleaning. David S. Peterson. LC 96-41044. 1997. 49.95 (*1-56990-216-X*) Hanser-Gardner.

Practical Guide to Information System Strategic Planning. Anita Cassidy. LC 98-13359. 304p. 1998. boxed set 44.95 (*1-57444-133-7*) St Lucie Pr.

***Practical Guide to Information Systems Process Improvement.** Anita Cassidy & Keith Guggenberger. LC 00-9370. 2000. write for info. (*1-57444-281-3*) St Lucie Pr.

Practical Guide to Infrared Microspectroscopy. Howard J. Humecki. (Practical Spectroscopy Ser.: Vol. 19). (Illus.). 488p. 1995. text 165.00 (*0-8247-9449-4*) Dekker.

Practical Guide to Inmate Discipline. 2nd ed. William C. Collins. 120p. 1997. ring bd. 97.50 (*1-887554-04-1*) Civic Res Inst.

Practical Guide to Inspecting Electrical, No. 5. Roy Newcomer. (Illus.). 91p. 1996. pap. 49.00 (*1-928545-04-1*) Am Home Inspect.

Practical Guide to Inspecting Exteriors, No. 2. Roy Newcomer. (Illus.). 82p. 1996. pap. 49.00 (*1-928545-01-7*) Am Home Inspect.

Practical Guide to Inspecting Heating & Cooling, No. 6. Roy Newcomer. (Illus.). 150p. 1996. pap. 49.00 (*1-928545-05-X*) Am Home Inspect.

Practical Guide to Inspecting Interiors, Insulation, Ventilation, No. 7. Roy Newcomer. (Illus.). 128p. 1996. pap. 49.00 (*1-928545-06-8*) Am Home Inspect.

Practical Guide to Inspecting Plumbing, No. 4. Roy Newcomer. (Illus.). 95p. 1996. pap. 49.00 (*1-928545-03-3*) Am Home Inspect.

Practical Guide to Inspecting Roofs, No. 3. Roy Newcomer. (Illus.). 85p. 1996. pap. 49.00 (*1-928545-02-5*) Am Home Inspect.

Practical Guide to Inspecting Structure, No. 1. Roy Newcomer. (Illus.). 116p. 1996. pap. 49.00 (*1-928545-00-9*) Am Home Inspect.

Practical Guide to Instrumental Analysis. Erno Pungor. 400p. 1994. boxed set 99.95 (*0-8493-8681-0*) CRC Pr.

Practical Guide to Integral Yoga. 7th ed. Sri Aurobindo. Ed. by Manibhai. 1979. pap. 7.95 (*0-89744-942-8*) Auromere.

Practical Guide to Integral Yoga. 7th ed. Sri Aurobindo & Mother. Ed. by Manibhai. (Illus.). 338p. 1995. pap. 7.95 (*81-7058-034-X*, Pub. by SAA) E-W Cultural Ctr.

Practical Guide to Integrated Circuits. 2nd ed. Alfred W. Barber. write for info. (*0-318-58193-0*) P-H.

Practical Guide to Integrated Marketing Communication. 2nd ed. Tom Brannan. 1998. pap. 30.00 (*0-7494-2703-5*) Kogan Page Ltd.

***Practical Guide to Interest Based Bargaining.** 2nd ed. (Illus.). 43p. 2000. pap. 14.95 (*1-930542-02-X*) FPMI Comns.

Practical Guide to International Business. 2nd rev. ed. Abdol S. Soofi. LC 96-75341. (Illus.). 250p. 1997. pap. text 44.95 (*0-9630486-1-9*) Intercont Trad.

***Practical Guide to International Commercial Arbitration.** Henry D. Gabriel. LC 99-50150. 2000. 85.00 (*0-379-21396-6*) Oceana.

Practical Guide to Internet Filters: A Neal-Schuman Special Report. Karen G. Schneider. LC 98-100425. (Neal-Schuman Net Guide Ser.). 164p. 1997. pap. 55.00 (*1-55570-322-4*) Neal-Schuman.

Practical Guide to Intranet Client-Server Applications. Norman E. Smith. LC 97-20680. (Illus.). 500p. 1997. pap. 49.95 incl. cd-rom (*1-55622-549-0*) Wordware Pub.

Practical Guide to Introducing Evidence. Ed. by Harold W. Potter, Jr. & Paul E. Troy. 1998. ring bd., suppl. ed. 95.00 (*1-57589-096-8*, 98-05.55-SP) Mass CLE.

Practical Guide to Introducing Evidence. rev. ed. Harold W. Potter, Jr. et al. LC 93-86126. 508p. 1993. ring bd. 95.00 (*0-944490-55-7*) Mass CLE.

Practical Guide to Introducing Evidence, 1996 Supplement. Harold W. Potter, Jr. et al. LC 93-86126. 368p. 1996. ring bd., suppl. ed. 95.00 (*1-57589-037-2*, 96-05.59-SP) Mass CLE.

Practical Guide to Introducing Evidence, 2000 Supplement. write for info. (*1-57589-178-6*) Mass CLE.

Practical Guide to Irrigation Systems. D. Raes & J. Feyen. 1994. pap. 150.00 (*0-7855-2751-6*, Pub. by Scientific Pubs) St Mut.

Practical Guide to ISO 9000: Implementation, Registration, & Beyond. Richard C. Randall. (Engineering Process Improvement Ser.). 464p. (C). 1995. 47.00 (*0-201-63379-5*) Addison-Wesley.

Practical Guide to Japanese-English Onomatopoeia & Mimesis. Hideichi Ono. 408p. 1997. boxed set 42.95 (*4-590-00722-3*, Pub. by Hokuseido Pr) Book East.

Practical Guide to Japan's Overseas Development Assistance Program & Getting in on It. (Illus.). 120p. (Orig.). (YA). (gr. 12 up). 1993. pap. text 350.00 (*0-7881-0838-7*) DIANE Pub.

An Asterisk (*) at the beginning of an entry indicates that the title is appearing for the first time.

Practical Guide to Joint Ventures & Corporate Alliances: How to Form How to Organize How to Operate. Robert P. Lynch. LC 89-8893. 416p. 1989. 158.95 (*0-471-62456-X*) Wiley.

Practical Guide to Kashruth. rev. ed. Rabbi S. Wagschal. 1991. 19.95 (*0-87306-561-1*) Feldheim.

Practical Guide to Keeping Out of Crime's Way. 1992. lib. bdg. 199.95 (*0-8490-8880-1*) Gordon Pr.

Practical Guide to Knowledge Acquisition. A. Carlisle Scott et al. (Illus.). 528p. (C). 1991. 47.95 (*0-201-14597-9*) Addison-Wesley.

Practical Guide to Labour Law. 2nd ed. M. A. Fouche et al. LC 97-197853. (Digma Ser.). xiv, 359 p. 1996. pap. write for info. (*0-409-02835-5*, MICHIE) LEXIS Pub.

Practical Guide to Landfill Tax. J. Clay. LC 98-215892. 48p. 1998. write for info. (*0-7277-2687-0*) T Telford.

Practical Guide to Language Learning: A Fifteen Week Program of Strategies for Success. H. Brown & A. Douglas. (C). 1989. text 22.50 (*0-07-008208-1*) McGraw.

Practical Guide to Leasing: A Survey of Lease Accounting, Taxation, & Regulation. Alfred W. Fink. LC 94-5753. 1994. write for info. (*0-07-707969-8*) McGraw.

Practical Guide to Legal Issues Affecting College Teachers. Donald D. Gehring et al. LC 85-16644. (Higher Education Administration Ser.). 56p. 1994. pap. 12.95 (*0-912557-02-8*) Coll Admin Pubns.

Practical Guide to Legal Writing & Legal Method. 2nd ed. John C. Dernbach et al. LC 94-16472. xxiii, 399p. 1994. pap. 19.95 (*0-8377-0561-4*, Rothman) W S Hein.

Practical Guide to Libel Law. Neil J. Rosini. LC 91-9566. 256p. 1991. 52.95 (*0-275-93782-8*, C3782, Praeger Pubs) Greenwood.

Practical Guide to Lifeboat Survival. Center for the Study & Practice of Survival at Sea. Tr. by David S. Jeffs & David Keating from FRE. LC 95-50503. (ENG., Illus.). 160p. 1997. 29.95 (*1-55750-121-1*) Naval Inst Pr.

Practical Guide to LINUX. Mark G. Sobell. 1072p. (C). 1997. pap. 42.95 (*0-201-89549-8*) Addison-Wesley.

***Practical Guide to Living in Japan: Everything You Need to Know to Successfully Settle In.** Jarrell D. Sieff. (Illus.). 288p. 2000. pap. 16.95 (*1-880656-50-7*) Stone Bridge Pr.

Practical Guide to Local Government Liability in North Carolina. Anita R. Brown-Graham. (C). 1999. ring bd. 45.00 (*1-56011-347-2*, 99.05) Institute Government.

Practical Guide to Logic. G. Tillmann. 1998. 45.00 (*0-07-064763-1*) McGraw.

Practical Guide to Managing Acidic Surface Waters - Fisheries. Robert W. Brocksen. 208p. 1992. lib. bdg. 79.95 (*0-87371-755-4*, L755) Lewis Pubs.

Practical Guide to Managing Information for Competitive Positioning in Economic Development. Keith Harman. Ed. by Peter Hernon & Charles R. McClure. (Information Management, Policies & Services Ser.: Vol. 4). 136p. (C). 1990. pap. 39.50 (*0-89391-585-8*) Ablx Pub.

***Practical Guide to Managment 24 Hours Operations.** Martin C. Moore-Ede. 131p. 1998. pap. 69.95 (*0-9648893-1-5*) Circadian Info.

Practical Guide to Massachusetts Limited Liability Companies. Peter M. Rosenblum et al. LC 96-77819. 566p. 1996. ring bd. 125.00 (*1-57589-043-7*, 97-04.36-BK) Mass CLE.

Practical Guide to Massachusetts Limited Liability Companies, 2000 Supplement. write for info. (*1-57589-179-4*) Mass CLE.

Practical Guide to Medical Billing. Denna L. Holmes. 155p. pap. 89.00 (*0-934213-53-4*, PB98-114374) Natl Tech Info.

Practical Guide to Medical Mycology: Diagnosis & Patient Management. Alan M. Sugar. 224p. 1996. pap. text 49.00 (*0-397-51772-6*) Lppncott W & W.

Practical Guide to Medical-Surgical Nursing in the Home. Marianne Neighbors. 670p. 1997. pap. write for info. (*0-7216-7331-7*, W B Saunders Co) Harcrt Hlth Sci Grp.

Practical Guide to Medically Important Fungi & the Diseases They Cause. Alan M. Sugar & Caron A. Lyman. LC 96-29896. 174p. 1997. pap. text 49.00 (*0-397-51686-X*, Lippncott) Lppncott W & W.

Practical Guide to Medications: Guide Pratique des Medicaments. 13th ed. P. Dorosz. 1624p. 1993. 125.00 (*0-685-64733-1*, M15473) Fr & Eur.

Practical Guide to Medicine & the Law. Ed. by J. P. Jackson. (Illus.). 320p. 1991. 54.95 (*0-387-19677-3*) Spr-Verlag.

Practical Guide to Meetings. O. Britzius. 125p. 1991. pap. 39.00 (*0-409-01340-4*, SA, MICHIE) LEXIS Pub.

Practical Guide to Membrane Protein Purification. Ed. by Gebhard Von Jagow & Hermann Schagger. LC 94-14643. (Separation, Detection, & Characterization of Biological Macromolecules Ser.). (Illus.). 166p. 1994. pap. 53.00 (*0-12-725550-8*) Acad Pr.

Practical Guide to Modern Hematology Analyzers. Warren Groner & Elkin Simson. LC 95-3302. 258p. 1995. 176.95 (*0-471-95712-7*) Wiley.

Practical Guide to Modern Lighting Techniques. Ed. by Joe Knisley. (Practical Guide to Ser.). (Illus.). viii, 92 p. 1993. pap. 23.95 (*0-87288-478-3*) Intertec Pub.

Practical Guide to Molecular Cloning. 2nd ed. Bernard Prebal. 811p. 1988. 385.00 (*0-471-85071-3*); pap. 215.00 (*0-471-85070-5*) Wiley.

Practical Guide to Monoclonal Antibodies. J. Eryl Liddell & A. Cryer. LC 90-13056. 206p. 1991. pap. 147.00 (*0-471-92905-0*) Wiley.

Practical Guide to Motors & Motor Controls. Ed. by Alfred Berutti. (Practical Guide to Ser.). (Illus.). 88p. 1991. pap. 23.95 (*0-87288-457-0*) Intertec Pub.

***Practical Guide to Movement Disorders: Diagnosis, Investigation & Treatment.** Roger A. Barker. (Illus.). 224p. 2000. pap. text 57.50 (*0-7506-4469-9*) Buttrwrth-Heinemann.

Practical Guide to Multi-Risk Crop Insurance for Developing. P. K. Ray. (C). 1991. text 21.50 (*81-204-0604-4*, Pub. by Oxford IBH) S Asia.

Practical Guide to Multi-Risk Crop Insurance for Developing Countries. P. K. Ray. (Illus.). 180p. 1998. 40.00 (*1-57808-028-2*) Science Pubs.

Practical Guide to Municipal Budgeting in Nebraska. John W. Swain. (Illus.). 131p. (C). 1988. ring bd. 19.95 (*1-55719-180-8*) U NE CPAR.

***Practical Guide to National Hospital Fraud Investigations.** 354p. 1999. ring bd. 179.00 (*0-929156-56-0*) Atlantic Info Services Inc.

Practical Guide to Needs Assessment: A Publication of the American Society for Training & Development. Kavita Gupta. LC 98-25370. (Business & Management Ser.). 224p. 1998. 39.95 incl. disk (*0-7879-3988-9*, Pfffr & Co) Jossey-Bass.

Practical Guide to Neural Networks. Marilyn M. Nelson. 352p. (C). 1994. pap. 40.00 (*0-201-63378-7*) Addison-Wesley.

Practical Guide to Newsletter Editing & Design: Instructions for Printing by Mimeograph or Offset for the Inexperienced Editor. 2nd ed. LaRae H. Wales. LC 76-1753. (Illus.). 52p. reprint ed. pap. 30.00 (*0-608-18765-8*, 202977800065) Bks Demand.

Practical Guide to Noise & Vibration Control for HVAC Systems. Ed. by Mildred Geshwiler. 190p. (C). 1991. pap. 63.00 (*0-910110-76-X*) Am Heat Ref & Air Eng.

Practical Guide to Nursing Home Advocacy. Legal Counsel for the Elderly Staff. 245p. 1991. pap. 30.00 (*0-933945-02-7*) Legal Coun Elderly.

Practical Guide to Object-Oriented Systems Development. Page-Jones. (C). 1999. pap. text 53.33 (*0-13-619966-6*, Prentice Hall) P-H.

Practical Guide to Occupational Health & Safety. Paul A. Erickson. (Illus.). 282p. 1996. text 49.95 (*0-12-240570-6*) Acad Pr.

Practical Guide to On-Line Particle Counting. (Illus.). 152p. 1995. pap. 53.00 (*0-89867-785-8*, 90674) Am Water Wks Assn.

Practical Guide to On-Site in Situ Remedial Technology. Richard A. Brown et al. Date not set. 69.95 (*0-87371-348-6*, L348) Lewis Pubs.

Practical Guide to Open Shop Construction. 71p. 1982. 9.00 (*0-318-17988-1*) Assn Gen Con.

Practical Guide to Out of Court Restructurings & Prepackaged Plans of Reorganization. 2nd ed. Nicholas P. Saggese & Alesia Ranney-Marinelli. 772p. 1993. ring bd. 145.00 (*0-13-108507-7*) Aspen Law.

Practical Guide to Overcurrent Protection. LC 96-78404. 91p. 1996. 23.95 (*0-87288-636-0*) Intertec Pub.

Practical Guide to Package Holiday Law & Contracts. John Nelson-Jones & Peter Stewart. 1987. 120.00 (*1-85190-041-1*, Pub. by Fourmat Pub) St Mut.

Practical Guide to Package Holiday Law & Contracts. John Nelson-Jones & Peter Stewart. 300p. 1993. 105.00 (*0-85459-810-3*, Pub. by Tolley Pubng) St Mut.

Practical Guide to Particle Counting: A Guide for Drinking Water Treatment. John M. Broadwell. 224p. 1999. 49.95 (*1-56670-306-9*) Lewis Pubs.

Practical Guide to Past Life Regression. Florence W. McClain. LC 84-45285. 160p. (Orig.). 1999. pap. 7.95 (*0-87542-510-0*) Llewellyn Pubns.

Practical Guide to Pediatric Intensive Care, 3. 3rd ed. Jeffery L. Blumer. (Illus.). 1120p. (C). (gr. 13). 1990. pap. text 69.00 (*0-8016-2854-7*, 02854) Mosby Inc.

Practical Guide to Pediatric Respiratory Diseases. Ed. by Daniel V. Schidlow & David S. Smith. LC 94-14803. (Illus.). 400p. 1994. text 57.00 (*1-56053-009-X*) Hanley & Belfus.

***Practical Guide to Pennsylvania Evidence: Objections, Responses, Rules & Practice Commentary.** Anthony J. Bocchino. LC 99-189425. 241 p. 1998. 39.95 (*1-55681-622-7*) Natl Inst Trial Ad.

Practical Guide to Percussion Terminology. Russ Girsberger & Cirone. LC 98-67352. 106 p. 1998. write for info. (*1-57463-059-8*) Meredith Music.

***Practical Guide to Peripheral Nerve & Neuromuscular Disorders.** David J. Dick. (Illus.). 320p. 2002. pap. 67.50 (*0-7506-4895-3*) Buttrwrth-Heinemann.

Practical Guide to Pharmaceutical Care. Ed. by John P. Rovers. LC 98-8812. 242p. 1998. pap. 40.00 (*0-917330-90-0*) Am Pharm Assn.

Practical Guide to Pharmacovigilance: Diagnosis & Reporting of Adverse Drug Reactions. Ed. by Christian Benichou. LC 94-6102. 320p. 1994. pap. 148.95 (*0-471-94211-1*) Wiley.

Practical Guide to Phytotherapy: Guide Pratique de Phytotherapie. R. Fauron. (FRE.). 840p. 1984. 99.50 (*0-8288-1805-3*, M15431) Fr & Eur.

Practical Guide to Planned Giving. 96th ed. Len C. Clough et al. Ed. by Taghrid Barron. 950p. 1995. 120.00 (*0-930807-47-2*) Taft Group.

Practical Guide to Planned Giving, 1991. 1990. 95.00 (*0-914977-31-8*, 00008677) Taft Group.

Practical Guide to Planned Giving, 1995. 95th ed. A. B. Tueller. Ed. by Taghrid Barron. 944p. 1994. 120.00 (*0-930807-46-4*) Taft Group.

Practical Guide to Planned Giving, 1997. 97th ed. A. B. Tueller. 950p. 1997. 130.00 (*1-56995-054-7*) Taft Group.

Practical Guide to Planned Giving, 1992. 92nd ed. Alden B. Tueller. 717p. 1991. 95.00 (*1-879784-31-9*, 600348) Taft Group.

Practical Guide to Planned Giving, 1993. 93rd ed. Alden B. Tueller, Jr. Ed. by Mark W. Scott. 824p. 1992. 99.00 (*1-879784-30-0*, 600398) Taft Group.

Practical Guide to Planned Giving, 1994. 94th ed. A. B. Tueller. Ed. by Mark W. Scott. 2000p. 1993. 105.00 (*0-930807-45-6*, 600468) Taft Group.

Practical Guide to Planned Giving, 1999. 8th ed. 930p. 1999. 130.00 (*1-56995-339-2*, 00157933) Taft Group.

Practical Guide to Planned Giving 2000. 100th ed. 1999. 130.00 (*1-56995-340-6*) Taft Group.

Practical Guide to Planning a Family Reunion. Emma J. Wisdom. LC 88-90539. (Illus.). 1988. pap. 8.95 (*0-9620115-0-9*) Post Oak Pubns.

Practical Guide to Planning a Family Reunion. rev. ed. Emma J. Wisdom. (Illus.). 96p. 1997. pap. 10.95 (*0-9620115-8-4*) Post Oak Pubns.

Practical Guide to Power Distribution Systems for Information Technology Equipment. 2nd rev. ed. Ed. by Raymond Waggoner. (Illus.). 118p. 1997. pap. 23.95 (*0-87288-654-9*) Intertec Pub.

Practical Guide to Prepare for & Survive Widowhood. Rachel L. Carpenter. 1990. pap. 5.95 (*0-9628080-0-8*) Carpenter Ventures.

Practical Guide to Preservation in School & Public Libraries. Maxine K. Sitts. 49p. 1990. 6.50 (*0-937597-31-7*, IR-90) ERIC Clear.

Practical Guide to Productivity Measurement. Leon Greenberg. LC 73-75981. 77p. reprint ed. pap. 30.00 (*0-608-16703-7*, 202679400052) Bks Demand.

Practical Guide to Project Planning. Celia Burton & Norma Michael. 160p. 1994. pap. 27.95 (*0-89397-396-3*) Nichols Pub.

Practical Guide to Prosperous Living. J. Douglas Bottorff. LC 97-52696. 172p. 1998. pap. 11.95 (*0-87159-220-7*) Unity Bks.

Practical Guide to Protein & Peptide Purification for Microsequencing. 2nd ed. Ed. by Paul T. Matsudaira. (Illus.). 188p. 1993. 42.00 (*0-12-480282-6*) Acad Pr.

Practical Guide to Pseudospectral Methods. Bengt Fornberg. (Cambridge Monographs on Applied & Computational Mathematics: No. 1). (Illus.). 243p. (C). 1996. text 59.95 (*0-521-49582-2*) Cambridge U Pr.

Practical Guide to Pseudospectral Methods. Bengt Fornberg. (Monographs on Applied & Computational Mathematics: No. 1). (Illus.). 243p. (C). 1998. pap. 29.95 (*0-521-64564-6*) Cambridge U Pr.

Practical Guide to Purchasing Groups: A Comprehensive Reference Source on Formation, Operation & Regulation of Purchasing Groups Formed under the Liability Risk Retention Act. Karen Cutts. LC 96-112043. 245p. 1995. text 495.00 (*0-9625840-9-6*) Insure Commns.

Practical Guide to Qabalistic Symbolism. Gareth Knight. LC 66-71818. 640p. 1978. reprint ed. 37.50 (*0-87728-397-4*) Weiser.

Practical Guide to Quality Assurance. Sherry Peterson. 1990. 39.95 (*0-944496-09-1*) Precept Pr.

Practical Guide to Quality Assurance in Medical Imaging. B. M. Moores et al. LC 86-24529. 139p. reprint ed. pap. 43.10 (*0-7837-6390-5*, 204610300010) Bks Demand.

Practical Guide to Quality Power for Sensitive Electronic Equipment. 2nd ed. R. M. Waggoner. LC 97-74773. vii, 144 p. 1997. 23.95 (*0-87288-667-0*) Intertec Pub.

Practical Guide to Rapid High Efficiency Dialysis. rev. ed. Prakash Keshaviah et al. 132p. 1989. reprint ed. spiral bd. 75.00 (*1-56488-001-X*) Dialyrn.

Practical Guide to Real-Time Office Sonography in Obstetrics & Gynecology. Robert V. Giglia et al. LC 85-12033. (Illus.). 236p. (C). 1986. spiral bd. 78.00 (*0-306-41865-7*, Kluwer Plenum) Kluwer Academic.

Practical Guide to Real-Time Systems Development. 350p. 1993. pap. 57.00 (*0-13-718503-0*) P-H.

Practical Guide to Regulatory Systems Hardware Qualifications. (Illus.). 26p. Date not set. 39.50 (*1-930114-15-X*) Serentec Pr.

Practical Guide to Releasing Tension & Increasing Energy. Robinne Comissiona. LC 91-25701. (Illus.). 110p. 1992. pap. 10.95 (*0-944957-07-2*) Rivercross Pub.

Practical Guide to Reproductive Medicine. Ed. by Paul A. Rainsbury & D. A. Viniker. LC 96-38763. (Illus.). 542p. 1997. text 85.00 (*1-85070-727-8*) Prthnon Pub.

Practical Guide to Research Methods. 4th ed. Gehard Lang & George D. Heiss. 204p. (Orig.). (C). 1990. pap. text 22.00 (*0-8191-7974-4*); lib. bdg. 43.50 (*0-8191-7973-6*) U Pr of Amer.

Practical Guide to Research Methods. 5th ed. Gerhard Lang & George D. Heiss. LC 93-40438. 202p. (C). 1994. pap. text 25.00 (*0-8191-9384-4*); lib. bdg. 51.00 (*0-8191-9383-6*) U Pr of Amer.

Practical Guide to Research Methods. 6th ed. Gerhard Lang & George D. Heiss. LC 97-44434. 200p. (C). 1997. 54.00 (*0-7618-0979-1*); pap. 27.00 (*0-7618-0980-5*) U Pr of Amer.

Practical Guide to Respirator Usage in Industry. David S. Blackwell & Gyan S. Rajhans. (Illus.). 144p. 1985. 42.95 (*0-7506-9232-4*) Buttrwrth-Heinemann.

Practical Guide to Retail Security. David H. Sells, Jr. 187p. 1992. pap., teacher ed. 8.00 (*0-8273-4731-6*) Delmar.

Practical Guide to Retail Security. David H. Sells, Jr. 187p. (C). 1993. mass mkt. 30.00 (*0-8273-4730-8*) Delmar.

***Practical Guide to Risk Assessment & Decision Making.** Glenn R. Koller. LC 98-43655. (Illus.). 256p. 1999. boxed set 39.95 (*0-8493-0268-4*) CRC Pr.

Practical Guide to Road Traffic Accident Claims. R. Thorn & N. Airey. (C). 1987. 250.00 (*0-7855-4061-X*, Pub. by Witherby & Co) St Mut.

Practical Guide to SABRE Reservations & Ticketing. Jeanne Semer-Purzycki. 416p. (C). 1992. mass mkt. 35.75 (*0-8273-4196-2*) Delmar.

Practical Guide to SABRE Reservations & Ticketing. Jeanne Semer-Purzycki. 1992. pap., teacher ed. 13.95 (*0-8273-4197-0*) Delmar.

***Practical Guide to Sales & Use Tax Book.** 99th ed. Delta Staff. 1999. pap. text 159.00 (*0-15-606631-9*) Harcourt.

Practical Guide to Scanning Probe Microscopy. Rebecca Howland & Lisa Benatar. Ed. by Christy Symanski. (Illus.). 74p. (C). 1998. pap. text 30.00 (*0-7881-7126-7*) DIANE Pub.

Practical Guide to SEC Proxy & Compensation Rules. Ed. by Amy L. Goodman & John F. Olson. 898p. 1993. ring bd. 126.00 (*0-13-122763-7*) Aspen Law.

Practical Guide to SEC Proxy & Compensation Rules. 2nd ed. Ed. by Amy L. Goodman & John F. Olson. 898p. 1998. ring bd. 185.00 (*1-56706-286-5*) Aspen Law.

Practical Guide to Section 16: Reporting & Compliance. 2nd ed. Goodman. 1996. write for info. (*0-13-720152-4*) Aspen Law.

Practical Guide to Section 16: Reporting & Compliance. 3rd ed. Goodman. LC 96-45427. 520p. 1997. ring bd. 185.00 (*1-56706-340-3*) Aspen Law.

Practical Guide to Selecting a Cat. Dorothy S. Richards. (Illus.). 162p. 1995. 10.95 (*1-56465-150-9*, 16014) Tetra Pr.

Practical Guide to Selecting a Large Dog. Joan Palmer. (Illus.). 119p. 1995. 10.95 (*1-56465-135-5*, 16018) Tetra Pr.

Practical Guide to Selecting a Small Dog. Joan Palmer. (Illus.). 119p. 1996. 10.95 (*1-56465-124-X*, 16019) Tetra Pr.

Practical Guide to Self Defense Thru Tang Soo Do. Ron J. Tramontano. LC 95-90278. (Illus.). 192p. (Orig.). 1995. pap. 48.00 (*0-9646263-0-6*) R Tramontano.

Practical Guide to Self Defense Thru the Martial Arts. rev. ed. Ron J. Tramontano. LC 95-90278. (Illus.). 192p. 1995. reprint ed. pap. 23.95 (*0-9646263-1-4*) R Tramontano.

Practical Guide to Self-Hypnosis. Melvin Powers. (Orig.). 1960. pap. 10.00 (*0-87980-122-0*) Wilshire.

Practical Guide to Self Managed Teams. abr. ed. Kenneth A. Burger & Alvin E. Ray. (Illus.). 62p. 1997. pap. text 14.95 (*0-936295-76-7*) FPMI Comns.

Practical Guide to Sermon Preparation. Jerry Vines. 18.99 (*0-8024-6744-X*, 254) Moody.

***Practical Guide to Setting up Your Tropical Freshwater Aquarium.** Gina Sandford. (Tankmasters Ser.). (Illus.). 80p. 2000. 9.95 (*0-7641-5266-1*) Barron.

Practical Guide to SGML Filters. Norman E. Smith. LC 96-38405. (Illus.). 450p. (Orig.). (C). 1996. pap. 49.95 incl. disk (*1-55622-511-3*) Wordware Pub.

Practical Guide to SGML/XML Filters. Norman E. Smith. LC 98-23432. 1998. pap. text 69.95 (*1-55622-587-3*) Wordware Pub.

***Practical Guide to Single Story House Extensions.** A. Williams. 67p. (C). (gr. 13). 1998. pap. text 37.99 (*1-85032-033-0*) ITCP.

Practical Guide to SNMPv3 & Network Management. David Zeltserman. LC 99-24579. (Prentice Hall Series in Computer Networking & Distributed). (Illus.). 352p. (C). 1999. 60.00 (*0-13-021453-1*) P-H.

Practical Guide to Software Localization. Bert Esselink. LC 98-30385. (Language International World Directory Ser.: Vol. 3). x, 310p. 1998. 63.00 (*1-55619-742-X*) J Benjamins Pubng Co.

***Practical Guide to Software Localization.** Bert Esselink. LC 98-30385. (Language International World Directory Ser.: Vol. 3). x, 310p. 1998. pap. 24.95 (*1-55619-743-8*) J Benjamins Pubng Co.

Practical Guide to Software Quality Management. John W. Horch. LC 96-19493. 259p. 1996. pap. 66.00 (*0-89006-865-8*) Artech Hse.

Practical Guide to Solaris. Mark G. Sobell. LC 99-21057. 1168p. (C). 1999. pap. text 44.95 (*0-201-89548-X*) Addison-Wesley.

Practical Guide to Solving Preschool Behavior. 4th ed. Essa. LC 98-28392. (Early Childhood Education Ser.). 416p. 1998. text 41.95 (*0-7668-0033-4*) Delmar.

Practical Guide to Solving Preschool Behavior Problems. 2nd ed. Eva Essa. (Illus.). 288p. 1989. pap. 22.00 (*0-8273-3965-8*) Delmar.

Practical Guide to Solving Preschool Behavior Problems. 3rd ed. Eva Essa. LC 94-31042. 400p. (C). 1994. pap. 22.50 (*0-8273-5812-1*) Delmar.

Practical Guide to Spiritual Reading. rev. ed. Susan A. Muto. LC 94-19939. 328p. 1994. reprint ed. pap. 29.95 (*1-879007-09-6*) St Bedes Pubns.

Practical Guide to Splines. C. De Boor. (Applied Mathematical Sciences Ser.: Vol. 27). (Illus.). 1994. 59.95 (*0-387-90356-9*) Spr-Verlag.

***Practical Guide to Splines.** 2nd ed. Carl De Boor. LC 99-42676. (Applied Mathematical Sciences Ser.). 2000. write for info. (*0-387-98922-6*) Spr-Verlag.

***Practical Guide to Sports Injuries.** Malcolm Read. (Illus.). 336p. 2000. pap. 45.00 (*0-7506-3251-8*) Buttrwrth-Heinemann.

Practical Guide to Stage Lighting. Shelley. LC 98-43725. 304p. 1999. pap. 36.95 (*0-240-80353-1*) Buttrwrth-Heinemann.

Practical Guide to Structured Systems Design. 2nd ed. Meilir Page-Jones. (Illus.). 384p. 1988. pap. 75.00 (*0-13-690769-5*) P-H.

Practical Guide to Student Teaching & Field Experience: Through the Looking Glass. M. Carrol Tama. 176p. 1991. per. 24.95 (*0-8403-6660-4*) Kendall-Hunt.

***Practical Guide to Successful Estate Planning: Iowa, Minnesota, North Dakota, South Dakota, Wisconsin.** Mark R. Alvig & Thomas M. Petracek. (User-Friendly Financial Ser.). (Illus.). 148p. 2000. pap. 18.95 (*1-58007-021-3*, Pub. by Specialty Pr) Voyageur Pr.

Practical Guide to Successful Interviewing. Philip Hodgson. 104p. 1987. pap. text 10.95 (*0-07-084941-2*) McGraw.

Practical Guide to Surgical Pathology with Cytologic Correlation: A Text & Color Atlas. K. Kim & B. Naylor. (Illus.). xiii, 359p. 1991. 189.00 (*0-387-97538-1*) Spr-Verlag.

P

Practical Guide to Syntactic Analysis. Georgia M. Green & Jerry L. Morgan. (CSLI Lecture Notes Ser.). 250p. 1996. pap. 22.95 (*1-57586-016-3*) CSLI.

Practical Guide to Syntactic Analysis. Georgia M. Green & Jerry L. Morgan. (CSLI Lecture Notes Ser.). 120p. 1996. 64.95 (*1-57586-017-1*) CSLI.

***Practical Guide to Tax Issues in Employment.** Julia K. Brazelton. (Illus.). 336p. 1999. reprint ed. text 95.00 (*0-8080-0385-2*, 0-5300-100) CCH INC.

Practical Guide to Tax Shelter Litigation. Edward Brodsky. 600p. 1985. ring bd. 70.00 (*0-318-21434-2*, 00577) NY Law Pub.

Practical Guide to Teacher Education Evaluation. Ed. by Jerry B. Ayers & Mary F. Berney. (C). 1989. lib. bdg. 86.00 (*0-7923-9042-3*) Kluwer Academic.

Practical Guide to Teaching Adults. Henry Morse. LC 98-37515. (Electrical Trades Ser.). 65p. 1998. pap. text 12.95 (*0-7668-1134-4*) Delmar.

Practical Guide to Teaching in the Fire Service. Morse. LC 98-14459. 1998. pap. 12.95 (*0-7668-0432-1*) Delmar.

Practical Guide to Teshuvah. Shaul Wagshal. 80p. 1991. pap. 7.95 (*0-944070-32-9*, Pub. by Targum Pr) Feldheim.

Practical Guide to Testing Object-Oriented Software. John D. McGregor. (C). Date not set. pap. text. write for info. (*0-201-32564-0*) Addison-Wesley.

Practical Guide to Texas Civil Evidence: Objections, Responses, Rules, & Practice Commentary. Gerald R. Powell et al. 1995. 28.95 (*1-55681-487-9*) Natl Inst Trial Ad.

Practical Guide to Texas Evidence: Objections, Responses, Rules & Practice Commentary. 2nd ed. Gerald Reading Powell. LC 99-29254. 1999. 35.95 (*1-55681-600-6*) Natl Inst Trial Ad.

Practical Guide to the Bankruptcy Reform Act, 2 vols. Harvey R. Miller & Michael L. Cook. 1400p. 1979. write for info. (*0-318-65476-8*, C00191) P-H.

Practical Guide to the Care, Maintenance, & Troubleshooting of Capillary Gas Chromatographic Systems. 2nd ed. Dean Rood. LC 95-226863. (Chromatographic Methods Ser.). 323p. 1995. 60.00 (*3-7785-2319-8*, Pub. by Huethig BRD) U Pr of Amer.

Practical Guide to the Care, Maintenance & Troubleshooting of Capillary Gas Chromatographic Systems. 3rd ed. Dean Rood. LC 99-192528. 344p. 1999. 115.00 (*3-527-29750-2*) Wiley.

Practical Guide to the Care of Children on Shabbos & the Laws of Yom Tov & Chol Ha-Mo'ed. S. Wagschal. 1994. 19.95 (*1-58330-115-1*) Feldheim.

Practical Guide to the Care of Geriatric Patient. 2nd ed. Fred F. Ferri & Marsha D. Fretwell. LC 97-106715. (Illus.). 624p. (C). (gr. 13). 1996. spiral bd. 29.95 (*0-8151-3194-1*, 29178) Mosby Inc.

Practical Guide to the Care of the Ambulatory Patient. Tom J. Wachtel & Michael D. Stein. (Illus.). 560p. (C). (gr. 13). 1995. spiral bd. 32.95 (*0-8016-8063-8*, 08063) Mosby Inc.

Practical Guide to the Care of the Ambulatory Patient. 2nd ed. (Illus.). 625p. 1999. spiral bd. 29.95 (*0-8151-7888-3*, 30954) Mosby Inc.

Practical Guide to the Care of the Critically Ill Parent. Joseph Varon. LC 94-19744. (Illus.). 424p. (C). (gr. 13). 1994. spiral bd. 32.00 (*0-8016-8106-5*, 08106) Mosby Inc.

Practical Guide to the Care of the Gynecologic-Obstetric Patient. George T. Danakas. (Illus.). 1072p. (C). (gr. 13). 1996. pap. text 39.95 (*0-8151-2316-7*, 25553) Mosby Inc.

Practical Guide to the Care of the Medical Patient, No. 4. 4th ed. Fred F. Ferri. (Illus.). 1168p. (C). (gr. 13). 1998. spiral bd. 32.95 (*0-8151-3668-4*, 32806) Mosby Inc.

Practical Guide to the Care of the Pediatric Patient. Anthony J. Alario. (Illus.). 800p. (C). (gr. 13). 1997. spiral bd. 35.95 (*0-8151-0150-3*, 26341) Mosby Inc.

Practical Guide to the Care of the Psychiatric Patient. 2nd ed. Richard J. Goldberg. LC 99-181154. (Illus.). 496p. (C). (gr. 13). 1998. spiral bd. 29.95 (*0-8151-7892-1*, 30955) Mosby Inc.

Practical Guide to the Comprehensive Crime Control Act of 1984. B. James George. 1985. 55.00 (*0-317-29417-2*, #H43864) Harcourt.

Practical Guide to the Design & Implementation of Information Systems Measurement Programs. Howard Rubin. (C). 2001. boxed set 38.00 (*0-13-681784-X*) P-H.

Practical Guide to the Determination of Human Exposure to Radio Frequency Fields. Intro. by Charles B. Meinhold. LC 93-45910. (Report Ser.: No. 119). 233p. (Orig.). 1993. pap. 40.00 (*0-929600-35-5*) NCRP Pubns.

Practical Guide to the Development Bank Business: How to Identify It, Market to It, & Win It; A Comprehensive Guide for Exporters of Goods & Services. Nicholas H. Ludlow. LC 88-71941. (Illus.). 312p. 1988. pap. text 193.00 (*0-943781-00-0*) Develop Bank.

Practical Guide to the Employment Function. Ed. by Dick Cottrill et al. 112p. 1988. 15.00 (*0-910402-80-9*) Coll & U Personnel.

Practical Guide to the English Kindergarten: 1858 Edition. F. Froebel et al. Ed. & Intro. by Jeffrey Stern. (Classics in Education Ser.). 292p. 1996. reprint ed. 80.00 (*1-85506-281-X*) Bks Intl VA.

Practical Guide to the Evaluation of Child Physical Abuse & Neglect. Angelo P. Giardino et al. LC 96-35623. 352p. 1997. 85.00 (*0-8039-5426-3*) Sage.

Practical Guide to the Evaluation of Sexual Abuse in the Prepubertal Child. Angelo P. Giardino et al. (Illus.). 128p. (C). 1992. 49.95 (*0-8039-4815-8*) Sage.

***Practical Guide to the Genetic Family History.** Robin Bennett. LC 98-37273. 251p. 1999. pap. 49.95 (*0-471-25154-2*) Wiley.

***Practical Guide to the I Ching.** Kim-anh Lim. 304p. 2000. pap. 16.95 (*90-74597-40-8*, Pub. by Binkey Kok) Weiser.

Practical Guide to the IBM Personal Computer AT. Dennis L. Foster. LC 85-1249. 1985. write for info. (*0-201-12040-2*) Addison-Wesley.

Practical Guide to the Law of Secured Lending. Eric M. Holmes & Peter J. Shedd. LC 85-25568. 1986. text 59.95 (*0-13-690942-6*, Busn) P-H.

Practical Guide to the Lecturer's Guide to Quality & Standards in Colleges & Universities. Kate Ashcroft. LC 95-3430. 210p. 1995. 85.00 (*0-7507-0338-5*, Falmer Pr); pap. 32.95 (*0-7507-0339-3*, Falmer Pr) Taylor & Francis.

Practical Guide to the Low Voltage Directive. Gregg Kervill. LC 98-229429. (Illus.). 256p. 1998. pap. text 52.95 (*0-7506-3745-5*, Newnes) Buttrwrth-Heinemann.

Practical Guide to the Machinery Directive. H. P. Van Ekelenburg et al. 520p. 1996. ring bd. 370.00 (*0-85298-973-3*, 989733) ASME Pr.

Practical Guide to the Management of Nasal & Sinus Disorders. Hueston C. King & Richard L. Mabry. LC 92-48498. (Illus.). 264p. 1993. 59.00 (*0-86577-482-X*) Thieme Med Pubs.

Practical Guide to the Marine Animals of Northeastern North America. Leland W. Pollock. LC 96-39284. (Illus.). 272p. 1997. text 70.00 (*0-8135-2398-2*); pap. text 29.00 (*0-8135-2399-0*) Rutgers U Pr.

***Practical Guide to the Microsoft OLAP Server.** John Shumate. (Illus.). 448p. 2000. pap. 39.95 (*0-201-48557-5*) Addison-Wesley.

Practical Guide to the "Mistakes" Made in Census Indexes. Ed. by Richard H. Saldana. 63p. 1989. reprint ed. pap. 10.95 (*1-877677-81-7*) Herit Quest.

Practical Guide to the "Mistakes" Made in Census Indexes. Ed. by Richard H. Saldana. (Illus.). 63p. 1996. reprint ed. lib. bdg. 10.95 (*1-877677-01-9*) Herit Quest.

Practical Guide to the MPI Clean-Up: Step One in Creating Your Enterprise MPI. Maida R. Herbst & June Muniz. (Illus.). 150p. 1998. pap. text. write for info. (*1-57839-037-0*) Opus Communs.

Practical Guide to the New York Equitable Distribution Divorce Law. Ed. by Henry H. Foster, Jr. 771p. 1980. 35.00 (*0-686-89094-9*, C00566) Harcourt.

Practical Guide to the Occupational Safety & Health Act. Walter B. Connolly, Jr. & Donald R. Crowell. 650p. 1982. 90.00 (*0-317-03299-2*, 00578) NY Law Pub.

Practical Guide to the Oregon Evidence Code: Objections, Responses, Rules & Practice Commentary. Wayne T. Westling et al. 302p. 1994. 39.95 (*1-55681-430-5*) Natl Inst Trial Ad.

Practical Guide to the Original Issue Discount Regulations. David C. Garlock. LC 87-6990. write for info. (*0-15-004431-3*) P-H.

Practical Guide to the Persian Alphabet. Ahmad Jabbari. LC 83-50569. (Illus.). 74p. (Orig.). 1983. pap. text 6.50 (*0-939214-12-1*) Mazda Pubs.

Practical Guide to the Real Estate Settlement Procedures Act. Laurence E. Platt & Phillip L. Schulman. 624p. 1995. pap. 175.00 (*0-7913-2202-5*) Warren Gorham & Lamont.

Practical Guide to the Runes: Their Uses in Divination & Magic. Lisa Peschel. LC 89-2246. (New Age Ser.). (Illus.). 192p. (Orig.). 1999. mass mkt. 4.99 (*0-87542-593-3*) Llewellyn Pubns.

Practical Guide to the Script & Pronunciation of the Nepali Language. Krishna Bhai Pradhan. 53p. 1989. pap. text 5.00 (*0-9659801-2-X*) U Wisconsin-Madison.

Practical Guide to the Selection of High-Temperature Engineering Thermoplastics. A. A. Collyer. viii, 104p. 1990. 105.00 (*0-946395-87-X*, Pub. by Elsvr Adv Tech) Elsevier.

Practical Guide to the Small Claims Court: A Guide to Suing & Defending. George Applebey. 223p. 1994. pap. 150.00 (*0-85459-767-0*, Pub. by Tolley Pubng) St Mut.

Practical Guide to the Structure of English for the English Teacher. Joe E. Pierce. LC 87-80359. 100p. (Orig.). 1987. pap. 7.50 (*0-913244-67-8*) Hapi Pr.

Practical Guide to the Tax Act of 1984. Ed. by Law & Business Inc. Staff. LC 84-27795. 243p. 1985. 60.00 (*0-15-004375-9*) Harcourt.

Practical Guide to the Teaching of English As a Foreign Language. Robert J. Dixson. (C). 1987. pap. text 9.00 (*0-13-691032-7*, 18132) Prentice ESL.

Practical Guide to the Teaching of English As a Second or Foreign Language. Wilga M. Rivers & Mary S. Temperley. 416p. 1978. pap. text 15.95 (*0-19-502210-6*) OUP.

Practical Guide to the Treatment of Bulimia Nervosa. Johan Vanderlinden et al. LC 91-40876. (Brunner-Mazel Eating Disorders Monographs: No. 6). 224p. 1992. text 33.95 (*0-87630-656-3*) Brunner-Mazel.

Practical Guide to the UNIX System. 3rd ed. Mark G. Sobell. 800p. (C). 1994. pap. text 38.44 (*0-8053-7565-1*) Benjamin-Cummings.

Practical Guide to the Use of Elastomeric Linings. (MTI Manual Ser.: No. 7). (Illus.). 74p. 1983. pap. 27.00 (*0-685-47796-7*) NACE Intl.

Practical Guide to the Use of Elastomeric Linings. A. F. Hall. LC TA0455.E4H34. (MTI Manual Ser.: No. 7). (Illus.). 90p. 1983. reprint ed. pap. 30.00 (*0-608-06695-8*, 206689200009) Bks Demand.

***Practical Guide to the Use of the High-Resolution Electrocardiogram.** Edward J. Berbari & Jonathan S. Steinberg. LC 99-52567. (Illus.). 192p. 1999. 52.00 (*0-87993-445-X*) Futura Pub.

Practical Guide to the Wiring Regulations. 2nd ed. Geoffrey Stokes. LC 98-34672. 12p. 1998. pap. write for info. (*0-632-04141-2*) Blackwell Sci.

Practical Guide to Therapeutic Plasma Exchange. Andre A. Kaplan & University of Connecticut Health Center Staff. LC 98-33622. (Illus.). 253p. 1998. pap. 43.95 (*0-632-04395-4*) Blackwell Sci.

Practical Guide to Three Days in Paris: English Edition. Casa Bonechi. 96p. text 10.95 (*88-7009-368-9*, Pub. by Bonechi) Eiron.

Practical Guide to TIG (GTA) Welding. P. W. Muncaster. 144p. 1991. 108.00 (*1-85573-020-0*, Pub. by Woodhead Pubng) Am Educ Systs.

Practical Guide to Torah Learning. Dovid Landesman. LC 94-32902. 248p. 1996. 30.00 (*1-56821-320-4*) Aronson.

Practical Guide to Tropical Aquarium Fish. Richard Crow. 1999. pap. 9.99 (*1-84100-242-9*) Quadrillion Media.

Practical Guide to U. S. Taxation of International Transactions. Robert E. Meldman & Michael S. Schadewald. LC 98-117568. 400p. 1998. 125.00 (*90-411-0622-7*) Kluwer Law Intl.

Practical Guide to U. S. Taxation of International Transactions. Meldman & Schadewald. LC 96-158623. 384p. 1996. 89.00 (*0-8080-0090-X*, 26595BLS01) CCH INC.

Practical Guide to U. S. Taxation of International Transactions. 2nd ed. Robert E. Meldman & Michael S. Schadewald. LC 98-117568. 400p. 1996. 95.00 (*0-8080-0171-X*) CCH INC.

***Practical Guide to U. S. Taxation of International Transactions.** 3rd ed. Robert E. Meldman & Michael S. Schadewald. 496p. (C). 2000. text 99.00 (*0-8080-0491-3*) CCH INC.

Practical Guide to UCC Article 4A Funds Transfer. 232p. 1990. per. 55.00 (*1-55520-179-2*, Irwn Prfssnl) McGraw-Hill Prof.

Practical Guide to Ultrasound in Obstetrics & Gynecology. 2nd ed. Eric E. Sauerbrei et al. LC 97-11902. (Illus.). 400p. 1997. pap. text 52.95 (*0-397-51698-3*) Lppncott W & W.

Practical Guide to Ultrasound of Fetal Anomalies. Frederick N. Hegge. 256p. 1991. pap. text 50.00 (*0-88167-845-7*) Lppncott W & W.

***Practical Guide to Understanding, Managing & Reviewing Risk Assessment Reports.** David A. Belluck. (Illus.). 350p. 1999. text 69.95 (*0-8493-4111-6*) CRC Pr.

Practical Guide to Understanding, Managing & Reviewing Risk Assessment Reports. Sally Benjamin. ring bd. 69.95 (*1-56670-448-0*) Lewis Pubs.

Practical Guide to Urban & Environmental Movies: Educational Orientation, No. 780. rev. ed. Ed. by Ambrose Klain & Dennis M. Phelan. 1975. 5.00 (*0-686-20349-6*, Sage Prdcls Pr) Sage.

***Practical Guide to Usability Testing.** 2nd ed. Joseph S. Dumas & Janice C. Redish. 416p. 1999. pap. 34.95 (*1-84150-020-8*, Pub. by Intellect) Intl Spec Bk.

Practical Guide to Using Video in the Behavioral Sciences. Peter W. Dowrick. LC 90-19418. 335p. 1991. 125.00 (*0-471-63613-4*) Wiley.

Practical Guide to Valuation for Rating. F. H. Gladwin. (C). 1982. pap. 53.00 (*0-7219-0251-0*, Pub. by Scientific) St Mut.

***Practical Guide to Vertebrate Mechanics.** Christopher McGowan. LC 98-29462. (Illus.). 320p. (C). 1999. text 90.00 (*0-521-57194-4*); pap. text 39.95 (*0-521-57673-3*) Cambridge U Pr.

Practical Guide to Veterinary Microbiology. Quinn. 1993. 112.00 (*0-8151-6975-2*) Mosby Inc.

Practical Guide to Visiting Amsterdam. 96p. text 9.95 (*88-7009-608-4*, Pub. by Bonechi) Eiron.

Practical Guide to Visiting Vienna. Casa Bonechi. 96p. text 10.95 (*88-7009-495-2*, Pub. by Bonechi) Eiron.

Practical Guide to Winning: Land Use Approvals & Permits. Nyal Deems & Jennette Stevenson, 3rd. 1989. ring bd. 170.00 (*0-8205-1847-6*) Bender.

Practical Guide to Winning the Lottery. Nathan Mitchell. 102p. 1998. pap. 8.95 (*1-57502-981-2*, PO2682) Morris Pubng.

Practical Guide to Wisconsin Evidence: Objections, Responses, Rules, & Practice Commentary. Jeffrey S. Kinsler et al. 302p. 1995. 39.95 (*1-55681-469-0*) Natl Inst Trial Ad.

Practical Guide to Working in an Equipment Rental Business. Dick Detmer. 114p. 1986. pap. 45.00 (*0-685-19239-3*) Am Rent Assn.

Practical Guide to Working with Babies. 2nd ed. Angela Dare & Margaret O'Donovan. (Illus.). 192p. 1998. pap. 23.50 (*0-7487-3635-2*, Pub. by S Thornes Pubs) Trans-Atl Phila.

Practical Guide to Working with Babies 0-1. Margaret O'Donovan & Angela Dare. 128p. (C). 1994. pap. 32.00 (*0-7478-1743-X*, Pub. by S Thornes Pubs) Trans-Atl Phila.

Practical Guide to Working with Diversity: The Process, the Tools, the Resources. Joy Leach. LC 94-44293. 320p. 1995. 55.00 (*0-8144-0244-5*) AMACOM.

Practical Guide to Working with Young Children. 2nd ed. Christine Hobart & Jill Frankel. 128p. 1996. pap. 22.50 (*0-7487-2242-4*, Pub. by S Thornes Pubs) Trans-Atl Phila.

***Practical Guide to Working with Young Children.** 3rd ed. Christine Hobart & Jill Frankel. (Illus.). 160p. 1999. pap. 24.50 (*0-7487-4504-1*, Pub. by S Thornes Pubs) Trans-Atl Phila.

Practical Guide to World Class Buying. Brian Farrington & Derek W. Waters. 256p. 1994. mass mkt. 35.00 (*0-412-72210-0*) Chapman & Hall.

Practical Guide to Writing Poetry. (Connecting Scholarship Ser.). 61p. 1997. pap. text 9.00 (*0-9648943-3-5*) Serenus Pr.

***Practical Guide to Writing with Readings.** 8th ed. 2000. teacher ed. 26.00 (*0-321-05813-5*) Addison-Wesley.

Practical Guide to Writing with Readings. 8th ed. Barnet. LC 99-40170. 588p. (C). 1999. pap. text 49.00 (*0-321-02391-9*) Addson-Wesley Educ.

Practical Guide to X Window Programming. Ed. by Keller. 349p. 1990. boxed set 83.95 (*0-8493-7406-5*, Q) CRC Pr.

Practical Guide to XML. Norman Smith. 1999. pap. text 29.95 (*1-55622-635-7*) Wordware.

Practical Guide to Your Unemployment Insurance Rates. Howard Dressman. 76p. 1984. pap. 4.95 (*0-317-70028-6*) H Dressman.

Practical Guide, Vienna. 96p. 11.95 (*88-476-0014-6*, Pub. by Bonechi) Eiron.

Practical Guidelines for Corrosion Protection in the Mining & Metallurgy Industry. R. H. Andrew. 1997. pap. 97.00 (*1-57590-025-4*, 37547) NACE Intl.

Practical Guidelines for Minimizing Tort Liability. (National Cooperative Highway Research Program Report Ser.: No. 106). 40p. 1983. 6.80 (*0-309-03567-8*) Transport Res Bd.

Practical Guidelines for Reducing the Risk of Communicable Disease in a School Setting. MESD School Health Services Staff. 1992. 7.50 (*1-880118-06-8*) MESD Pr.

***Practical Guidelines for Transfusion Medicine.** (Illus.). 2000. pap. text. write for info. (*1-56395-128-2*) Am Assn Blood.

Practical Guilt: Moral Dilemmas, Emotions & Social Norms. P. S. Greenspan. LC 93-40067. 264p. 1995. reprint ed. pap. text 24.95 (*0-19-509090-X*) OUP.

Practical Gunsmithing. American Gunsmith Editors Staff. LC 96-83883. (Illus.). 256p. 1996. pap. 19.95 (*0-87349-187-4*, PG, DBI Bks) Krause Pubns.

Practical Gynecologic Oncology. 2nd ed. Jonathan S. Berek & Neville F. Hacker. 721p. 1994. text 90.00 (*0-614-32078-X*) Lppncott W & W.

Practical Gynecologic Oncology. 2nd ed. Jonathan S. Berek & Neville F. Hacker. (Illus.). 608p. 1994. 94.00 (*0-683-00597-9*) Lppncott W & W.

Practical Gynecologic Oncology. 3rd ed. Jonathan S. Berek & Neville F. Hacker. 752p. text 129.00 (*0-683-30719-3*) Lppncott W & W.

Practical Gynecology: Clinical Manual. Allan Jacobs & Michael Gast. (Illus.). 528p. (C). 1994. pap. text 29.95 (*0-8385-1336-0*, A1336-5, Apple Lange Med) McGraw.

***Practical Handbook for Bacterial Identification.** D. Roy Cullimore. (Illus.). 232p. (C). 2000. boxed set 79.95 (*1-56670-392-1*) Lewis Pubs.

Practical Handbook for Bank Directors. Martin Lowy. LC 95-95284. 160p. 1995. pap. 19.95 (*0-9649801-0-X*) Finan Srvs Pr.

Practical Handbook for Hospital Epidemiologists. Loreen Herwaldt & Michael Decker. LC 97-10168. (Illus.). 448p. 1998. pap. text 65.00 (*1-55642-302-0*, 13020) SLACK Inc.

***Practical Handbook for Interpersonal Skills Training.** Y. Barry Chung. 98p. 2000. write for info. (*1-58692-024-3*) Copyright Mgmt.

Practical Handbook for Ministry: From the Writings of Wayne E. Oates. Ed. by Thomas W. Chapman. LC 92-2317. 624p. 1993. text 39.95 (*0-664-21975-6*) Westminster John Knox.

Practical Handbook for Software Development. N. D. Birrell & Martyn A. Ould. (Illus.). 272p. 1988. pap. text 37.95 (*0-521-34792-0*) Cambridge U Pr.

Practical Handbook for the Actor. Melissa Bruder. 1986. pap. 9.00 (*0-394-74412-8*) Random.

Practical Handbook for the Emerging Artist. Margaret R. Lazzari. 302p. (C). 1995. pap. text 24.00 (*0-15-501498-6*, Pub. by Harcourt Coll Pubs) Harcourt.

Practical Handbook for Underground Rock Mechanics. T. R. Stacey & C. H. Page. (Series on Rock & Soil Mechanics: Vol. 12). 150p. 1986. text 70.00 (*0-87849-056-6*, Pub. by Trans T Pub) Enfield Pubs NH.

Practical Handbook for Wetland Identification & Delineation. John Grimson Lyon. (Mapping Sciences Ser.). 176p. 1993. boxed set 85.00 (*0-87371-590-X*, L590) Lewis Pubs.

Practical Handbook of Agricultural Science. Ed. by Angus A. Hanson. 427p. 1989. lib. bdg. 97.50 (*0-8493-3706-2*, S501) CRC Pr.

Practical Handbook of Basic Letter, Memo & Report Formats. Peter Hartley. (Illus.). 136p. (C). 1982. pap. 24.95 (*0-9611790-0-7*) Devco Pr.

Practical Handbook of Biochemistry & Molecular Biology. Ed. by Gerald D. Fasman. 616p. 1989. boxed set 115.95 (*0-8493-3705-4*, QP514) CRC Pr.

Practical Handbook of British Beetles. N. H. Joy. 622p. 1932. 75.00 (*0-7855-0670-5*) St Mut.

Practical Handbook of Clinical Gerontology. Ed. by Laura L. Carstensen et al. LC 96-9986. 688p. 1996. 65.00 (*0-8039-5237-6*) Sage.

Practical Handbook of Compost Engineering. Roger T. Haug. 752p. 1993. lib. bdg. 95.00 (*0-87371-373-7*, L373) Lewis Pubs.

Practical Handbook of Curves & Graphics. Seggern. 288p. 1994. boxed set 89.95 (*0-8493-8916-X*) CRC Pr.

Practical Handbook of Digital Mapping Concepts & Terminology. Sandra L. Arlinghaus. 352p. 1994. boxed set 104.95 (*0-8493-0131-9*, GA139) CRC Pr.

Practical Handbook of Disturbed Land Revegetation. Frank F. Munshower. LC 93-21625. 288p. 1993. boxed set 95.00 (*1-56670-026-4*, L1026) Lewis Pubs.

Practical Handbook of Elementary Foreign Language Programs. 2nd ed. Gladys C. Lipton. 1991. pap. text 19.95 (*0-8442-9338-5*) NTC Contemp Pub Co.

Practical Handbook of Estuarine & Marine Pollution. Michael J. Kennish. LC 96-14030. (Marine Science Ser.). 544p. 1996. boxed set 104.95 (*0-8493-8424-9*) CRC Pr.

An Asterisk (*) at the beginning of an entry indicates that the title is appearing for the first time.

Practical Handbook of Genetic Algorithm Complex Coding System. Lance D. Chambers. 592p. 1998. boxed set 84.95 (*0-8493-2539-0*) CRC Pr.

Practical Handbook of Genetic Algorithms Vol. 2: New Frontiers, Vol. II. Ed. by Lance D. Chambers. 448p. 1995. boxed set 94.95 (*0-8493-2529-3*, 2529) CRC Pr.

Practical Handbook of Genetic Algorithms (GAs) Applications. Ed. by Lance D. Chambers. 568p. 1995. boxed set 99.95 (*0-8493-2519-6*, 2519) CRC Pr.

Practical Handbook of Ground Water Monitoring. Ed. by David M. Nielsen. (Illus.). 728p. (C). 1991. boxed set 115.00 (*0-87371-124-6*, L124) Lewis Pubs.

Practical Handbook of Human Biologic Age Determination. Ed. by Arthur K. Balin. 544p. 1994. lib. bdg. 165.00 (*0-8493-0129-7*, QP86) CRC Pr.

Practical Handbook of Joint Fluid Analysis. 2nd ed. Robert A. Gatter & H. Ralph Schumacher. (Illus.). 122p. 1991. text 44.50 (*0-8121-1377-2*) Lppncott W & W.

Practical Handbook of Language Teaching. David Cross. 296p. (C). 1992. pap. 20.25 (*0-13-380957-9*) P-H.

Practical Handbook of Marine Science. Ed. by Michael J. Kennish. 744p. 1988. 72.95 (*0-8493-3700-3*, GC11) CRC Pr.

Practical Handbook of Marine Science. 2nd ed. Ed. by Michael J. Kennish. LC 93-3715. 576p. 1994. boxed set 136.95 (*0-8493-3712-7*, GC11) CRC Pr.

Practical Handbook of Materials Science. Ed. by Charles T. Lynch. 648p. 1989. boxed set 110.00 (*0-8493-3702-X*, TA403) CRC Pr.

Practical Handbook of Medical Physics. Robert G. Waggener. 1990. 49.95 (*0-8493-3701-1*) CRC Pr.

Practical Handbook of Microbiology. Ed. by William O'Leary. 688p. 1989. boxed set 115.95 (*0-8493-3704-6*, QR72) CRC Pr.

Practical Handbook of Nutrition in Clinical Practice. Ed. by Donald F. Kirby & Stanley J. Dudrick. LC 93-45906. (Modern Nutrition Ser.). 320p. 1994. boxed set 104.95 (*0-8493-7847-8*) CRC Pr.

Practical Handbook of Physical Properties of Rocks & Minerals. Robert S. Carmichael. 744p. 1988. lib. bdg. 89.95 (*0-8493-3703-8*, QE431) CRC Pr.

Practical Handbook of Plant Alchemy: An Herbalist's Guide to Preparing Medicinal Essences, Tinctures, & Elixirs. 2nd ed. Manfred M. Junivs. LC 92-47111. (Illus.). 272p. 1993. pap. 19.95 (*0-89281-485-3*, Heal Arts VT) Inner Tradit.

Practical Handbook of Processing & Recycling of Municipal Waste. A. G. Manser & Alan A. Keeling. 560p. 1996. lib. bdg. 85.00 (*1-56670-164-3*, L1164) Lewis Pubs.

Practical Handbook of Psychophanmacology. Edward A. Workman. 192p. 1993. per. 73.95 (*0-8493-8638-1*, RC483) CRC Pr.

Practical Handbook of Sample Size Guidelines for Clinical Trials. Jonathan J. Shuster. 224p. 1992. boxed set 115.95 (*0-8493-4487-5*, R853); boxed set 115.95 (*0-8493-8678-0*, R853) CRC Pr.

Practical Handbook of Soil, Vadose Zone, & Ground Water Contamination: Assessment, Prevention, & Remediation. J. Russell Boulding. 960p. 1995. lib. bdg. 99.95 (*1-56670-051-5*, L1051) Lewis Pubs.

Practical Handbook of Solid State Troubleshooting. Robert C. Genn, Jr. LC 80-23897. 256p. 1981. 12.95 (*0-13-691303-2*, Parker Publishing Co) P-H.

Practical Handbook of Soybean Processing & Utilization. Ed. by David R. Erickson. LC 95-8610. 584p. 1995. 80.00 (*0-935315-63-2*) Am Oil Chemists.

Practical Handbook of Spatial Statistics. Ed. by Sandra L. Arlinghaus & Daniel A. Griffith. 336p. 1995. boxed set 84.95 (*0-8493-0132-7*, 132) CRC Pr.

***Practical Handbook of Speech Codes.** A T & T Staff. (Discrete Mathematical & Applications Ser.). 256p. 2000. boxed set 79.95 (*0-8493-8525-3*) CRC Pr.

Practical Handbook of Spreadsheet Curves & Geometric Constructions. Deane Arganbright. LC 93-7960. 224p. 1993. boxed set 94.95 (*0-8493-8938-0*, QA483) CRC Pr.

***Practical Handbook of Stainless Steels & Nickel Alloys.** Ed. by Stephen Lamb. 360p. 1999. 90.00 (*1-894038-23-1*, 06819G, Pub. by Csti Pubng); 166.00 incl. cd-rom (*1-894038-24-X*, 06817AZ, Pub. by Csti Pubng) ASM.

Practical Handbook of the Oriya Language. T. J. Maltby. (ENG & ORI.). 214p. 1986. 39.95 (*0-8288-8464-1*) Fr & Eur.

Practical Handbook of Warehousing. 3rd ed. K. Ackerman. (Illus.). 612p. (C). (gr. 13). 1990. mass mkt. 84.95 (*0-412-09701-X*) Chapman & Hall.

Practical Handbook on Image Processing for Scientific Applications. Bernd Jaehne. LC 96-47399. 608p. 1997. boxed set 99.95 (*0-8493-8906-2*, 8906) CRC Pr.

Practical Handbook on Stress in the Russian Language. V. Klepko. (RUS.). 1985. 13.95 (*0-87557-072-0*) Saphrograph.

Practical Handbook on Year Around Back Yard Gardening: You Can Be an Expert in Your Own Back Yard. Norman Martin & Katheryn Martin. 58p. 1996. spiral bd. 8.95 (*0-9646489-3-8*) Martain Pub.

Practical Handbook Rock Mass Classification Systems: Modes of Ground Failure. Andy A. Afrouz. 208p. 1992. boxed set 136.95 (*0-8493-3711-9*, QE431) CRC Pr.

Practical Handbook Spectroscopy. James W. Robinson. (Illus.). 944p. 1991. boxed set 147.95 (*0-8493-3708-9*, QD95) CRC Pr.

Practical Handbook to Elementary Foreign Language Programs. 2nd ed. Gladys C. Lipton. 224p. 1995. pap. 19.95 (*0-8442-9332-6*, Natl Textbk Co) NTC Contemp Pub Co.

Practical Handbook to Elementary Foreign Language Programs (FLES*) (FLES) Including FLES, FLEX & IMM. 3rd ed. Gladys C. Lipton. LC 97-69971. 288p. 1998. pap. 19.95 (*0-8442-9330-X*, VS9330-X) NTC Contemp Pub Co.

Practical Handbook to Your New Grandchild: From Pregnancy Through Toddlerhood. Therese Weston. LC 97-92867. 384p. 1999. pap. 14.95 (*0-9660553-0-6*) PenWorks Pub.

***Practical HapKiDo Textbook.** Hui Son Choe. (Illus.). 206p. 1999. pap. 29.95 (*0-9668254-1-1*) World Hap Ki Do.

Practical Harmonist at the Harpsichord. Francesco Gasparini. Ed. by David L. Burrows. Tr. by Frank S. Stillings from ITA. LC 79-26854. (Music Reprint Ser.: 1980). (Illus.). 1980. reprint ed. lib. bdg. 27.50 (*0-306-76017-7*) Da Capo.

***Practical Head & Neck Ultrasound.** Ed. by Rhodri Evans & Anil Ahuja. (Greenwich Medical Media Ser.). (Illus.). 208p. 2000. pap. text 69.50 (*1-900151-99-5*) OUP.

Practical Healing. Fenwicke L. Holmes. 105p. 1997. pap. 8.00 (*0-89540-391-9*) Sun Pub.

***Practical Health & Safety Management for Small Businesses.** Jacqueline Jeynes. LC 00-33745. 2000. pap. write for info. (*0-7506-4680-2*) Buttrwrth-Heinemann.

Practical Hearing Aid Selection & Fitting. Henry Tobin. (Illus.). 143p. (C). 1998. pap. text 30.00 (*0-7881-4770-6*) DIANE Pub.

Practical Heat Treating. Howard E. Boyer. 243p. 1984. 97.00 (*0-87170-178-2*, 6518) ASM.

Practical Heating Technology. Johnson. 96p. 1994. text, teacher ed. 16.50 (*0-8273-4882-7*) Delmar.

Practical Heating Technology. William M. Johnson. LC 94-251. 481p. 1994. mass mkt. 65.50 (*0-8273-4881-9*) Delmar.

Practical Heating Technology. William M. Johnson. 92p. 1994. pap., lab manual ed. 18.50 (*0-8273-4883-5*) Delmar.

Practical Heating, Ventilation, Air Conditioning, & Refrigeration. Henry Puzio & Jim Johnson. LC 94-30878. 1995. pap. 45.75 (*0-8273-5591-2*) Delmar.

Practical Heating, Ventilation, & Air Conditioning. Henry Puzio & Johnson. 96p. 1995. teacher ed. 14.95 (*0-8273-5592-0*) Delmar.

Practical Hebrew to English Dictionary. Y. Lazar. (ENG & HEB.). 538p. 1997. 95.00 (*0-320-00694-8*) Fr & Eur.

Practical Help for New Supervisors. 3rd ed. Joan Giesecke & Library Administration & Management Association Pr. LC 96-35907. vi, 117 p. 1996. 24.00 (*0-8389-3467-6*) ALA.

***Practical Helps for a Hurting Church: 1 Cor.6:12-11:34.** Charles R. Swindoll. 1998. pap., student ed. 5.95 (*1-57972-194-X*) Insight Living.

Practical Hematology. 7th ed. Ed. by John V. Dacie & S. M. Lewis. (Illus.). 556p. 1991. text 59.00 (*0-443-03952-6*) Church.

Practical Hematology. 8th ed. John V. Dacie & S. M. Lewis. 1995. pap. text 83.00 (*0-443-04931-9*) Church.

Practical Herb Gardening. Anne Chamberlain. (Illus.). 128p. (Orig.). 1993. pap. 15.95 (*0-572-01701-4*, Pub. by W Foulsham) Trans-Atl Phila.

Practical High-Performance Liquid Chromatography. Ed. by Colin F. Simpson. LC QD0079.C454P. 327p. reprint ed. pap. 101.40 (*0-608-13869-X*, 205206500033) Bks Demand.

Practical Hindi-English Dictionary. Mahendra Chaturvedi & Nath T. Bhola. (ENG & HIN.). 700p. 1974. 16.00 (*0-88386-380-4*) S Asia.

Practical Hindi-English Dictionary. 9th ed. Mahendra Chaturvedi & B. N. Tiwari. 875p. 1987. 49.95 (*0-8288-1741-3*, M14105) Fr & Eur.

Practical Hints & Tips: Household. Consumer Guide Editors. 256p. 1995. mass mkt. 4.99 (*0-451-18358-4*, Sig) NAL.

Practical Histochemistry. Joseph Chayen & Lucille Bitensky. LC 90-19606. 336p. 1991. 240.00 (*0-471-92931-X*, Wiley-Interscience) Wiley.

Practical Histochemistry. Joseph Chayen et al. LC 72-8596. 285p. reprint ed. pap. 88.40 (*0-608-18840-9*, 203049500069) Bks Demand.

Practical History of a New Epidemical Eruptive Military Fever . . . in Boston New England in the Years 1735 & 1736. William Douglass. (Notable American Authors Ser.). 1992. reprint ed. lib. bdg. 75.00 (*0-7812-2678-3*) Rprt Serv.

Practical Holiness. Evan H. Hopkins. (Vital Ser.). 1997. pap. 0.75 (*0-87508-549-0*) Chr Lit.

Practical Holiness: A Second Look. David K. Bernard. LC 86-119761. 336p. (Orig.). 1985. pap. 9.99 (*0-912315-91-1*) Word Aflame.

***Practical Holography XIII.** Ed. by Stephen A. Benton. 264p. 1999. pap. text 72.00 (*0-8194-3108-7*) SPIE.

Practical Holography XI & Holographic Materials III, Vol. 3011. Ed. by Stephen A. Benton & T. John Trout. LC 97-175316. 378p. 1997. 69.00 (*0-8194-2422-6*) SPIE.

Practical Holography XII, Vol. 3293. Ed. by Stephen A. Benton. 276p. 1998. 69.00 (*0-8194-2733-0*) SPIE.

***Practical Home Care Medicines: A Natural Approach.** Ed. by Christine Murphy. 96p. 2000. pap. 10.00 (*1-930051-09-3*) Lantern Books.

Practical Home Modification. Karen G. Mc Gowan & Jim Mc Gowan. (Illus.). 128p. 1993. pap. 19.95 (*1-928752-10-1*) Mc Gowan Pubns.

Practical Home-Office Solutions. Marilyn Zelinsky. LC 98-24786. (Illus.). 1998. pap. 24.95 (*0-07-063365-7*) McGraw.

Practical Home Restoration: Stained Glass & Ceramics. Yvonne Rees. (Illus.). 96p. 1996. pap. 14.95 (*0-7063-7468-1*, Pub. by WrLock) Sterling.

Practical Homeopathy: A Beginner's Guide. Vinton McCabe. LC 99-26936. 594p. 2000. pap. 18.95 (*0-312-20669-0*) St Martin.

Practical Homicide Investigation: Tactics, Procedures, & Forensic Techniques. 3rd ed. Ed. by Vernon J. Geberth. (Practical Aspects of Criminal & Forensic Investigations Ser.). (Illus.). 960p. (C). 1996. boxed set 74.95 (*0-8493-8156-8*) CRC Pr.

Practical Homicide Investigation Checklist & Field Guide. Vernon J. Geberth. LC 96-41157. (Practical Aspects of Criminal & Forensic Investigations Ser.). 96p. (C). 1996. spiral bd. 24.95 (*0-8493-8160-6*) CRC Pr.

Practical Homiletics Manual see Manual Practico de Homiletica

Practical Hooked Rugs. Stella H. Rex. (Illus.). 1975. 20.00 (*0-89166-004-6*); pap. 15.00 (*0-89166-003-8*) Cobblesmith.

Practical Horary Astrology. Gayatri D. Vasudev. (C). 1992. 4.50 (*81-85273-88-X*, Pub. by Ranjan Pubs) S Asia.

***Practical Horse & Pony Nutrition.** McCarthy. 2000. pap. 22.95 (*0-85131-697-2*, Pub. by J A Allen) Trafalgar.

Practical Horse Psychology. Moyra Williams. 1978. pap. 10.00 (*0-87980-247-2*) Wilshire.

***Practical Horticulture.** 4th ed. Rice. LC 99-23130. (Illus.). 455p. (C). 1999. 89.00 (*0-13-020610-5*) P-H.

Practical House Carpenter. Asher Benjamin. 119p. reprint ed. 49.00 (*0-318-04471-4*) Rprt Serv.

Practical House Carpenter: Being a Complete Development of the Grecian Orders of Architecture. Asher Benjamin. 1988. reprint ed. lib. bdg. 39.00 (*0-685-44268-3*) Rprt Serv.

Practical House Carpenter: Being a Complete Development of the Grecian Orders of Architecture. Asher Benjamin. 1976. reprint ed. 59.00 (*0-403-06633-6*, Regency) Scholarly.

Practical House Carpenter, 1830 see Works of Asher Benjamin: Boston, 1806-1843

Practical House Officer. 2nd ed. Imogen Mitchell & G. R. Teale. LC 96-31455. (Illus.). 352p. 1997. pap. 34.95 (*0-86542-769-0*) Blackwell Sci.

Practical House Officer. 3rd ed. I. A. Mitchell & G. R. Teale. (Illus.). 272p. 1992. pap. 24.95 (*0-632-03309-6*) Blackwell Sci.

Practical How-Tos of Dental Infection Control. R. R. Runnells. 82p. (C). 1987. pap. text. write for info. (*0-936751-03-7*) Infection Control.

Practical HPLC Method Development. 2nd ed. Lloyd R. Snyder et al. LC 96-34296. 765p. 1997. 89.95 (*0-471-00703-X*) Wiley.

Practical HPLC Methodology & Applications. Brian A. Bidlingmeyer. LC 92-4680. 464p. 1993. 89.95 (*0-471-57246-2*) Wiley.

***Practical HRT.** P. G. Van Der Weijer. 2001. write for info. (*1-84214-028-0*) Prthnon Pub.

Practical HTML: A Self-Paced Tutorial. Roy Tennant. LC 96-188410. (Internet Workshop Ser.: Vol. 6). 106p. 1996. pap. text 54.00 incl. disk (*1-882208-19-6*) Library Solns.

***Practical HTML 4.** Lee Anne Phillips. 850p. 1999. pap. 29.99 (*0-7897-2148-1*) S&S Trade.

Practical Human Biology. J. S. Weiner & J. A. Lourie. LC 81-66372. 1981. text 79.95 (*0-12-741960-8*) Acad Pr.

Practical Hunter's Dog Book. John R. Falk. LC 91-9317. (Illus.). 352p. 1994. pap. 9.95 (*0-89658-260-4*) Voyageur Pr.

Practical Hydraulics. Melvyn Kay. LC 98-30901. (Illus.). 240p. (C). (gr. 13). 1998. pap. 32.99 (*0-419-22880-2*, E & FN Spon) Routledge.

Practical Hydraulics. 3rd ed. Andrew L. Simon. LC 85-20273. 493p. 1986. text 42.50 (*0-471-88488-X*) P-H.

Practical Hydraulics Handbook. Barbara A. Hauser. 360p. 1991. 66.95 (*0-87371-548-9*, L548) Lewis Pubs.

Practical Hydraulics Handbook. 2nd ed. Barbara A. Hauser. 368p. 1995. lib. bdg. 75.00 (*1-56670-038-8*, L1038) Lewis Pubs.

Practical Hydrology. Jack D. Keen. 85p. (C). 1995. pap. text 35.00 (*1-56569-045-1*) Land Survey.

Practical Hydromet 'Eighty-Three: Annual Symposium on Uranium & Precious Metals, 7th, Lakewood, CO, August 22-24, 1983. Symposium on Uranium & Precious Metals Staff. LC 84-70650. (Illus.). 132p. reprint ed. pap. 41.00 (*0-7837-1218-9*, 204174900023) Bks Demand.

Practical Hymnology. Hubert M. Poteat. LC 72-1693. reprint ed. 29.50 (*0-404-09912-2*) AMS Pr.

Practical Hypnotism. Philip Magonet. 1976. pap. 3.00 (*0-87980-123-9*) Wilshire.

Practical Hypnotism: Theories & Experiments (1901) Comte C. Saint-Germain. 264p. 1996. reprint ed. pap. 15.95 (*1-56459-929-9*) Kessinger Pub.

Practical Hypnotism, Theories & Experiments. Comte C. De Saint-Germain. 1996. reprint ed. spiral bd. 17.00 (*0-7873-0268-6*) Hlth Research.

Practical Hysteroscopy. P. J. Taylor & A. G. Gordon. (Illus.). 128p. 1993. 65.00 (*0-632-03672-9*) Blackwell Sci.

Practical IBM Personal Computer Programs for Beginners. Michael Fox. 96p. 1984. 8.95 (*0-86668-045-4*) ARCsoft.

Practical Idealism (1908) William D. Hyde. 350p. 1998. reprint ed. pap. 24.95 (*0-7661-0534-2*) Kessinger Pub.

Practical Ideas. American Machinist Staff. (Illus.). 116p. 1998. pap. 22.95 (*0-932905-13-7*) Penton Pub.

Practical Ideas . . . for Metalworking Operations, Tooling, & Maintenance. Ed. by American Machinist & Automated Manufacturing Magaz. (Illus.). 330p. 1988. reprint ed. 32.50 (*0-932905-05-6*) Penton Pub.

***Practical Ideas for Addressing Challenging Behaviors.** Ed. by Susan R. Sandall & Michaelene Ostrosky. (Young Exceptional Children Monograph Ser.). 88p. 1999. pap. 12.00 (*1-57035-264-X*, 143MONO1) Sopris.

***Practical Ideas for Celebrating Liturgies with Children: A Seasonal Guide.** Carolyn Deitering-Ancell. Ed. by Jean Larkin. (Illus.). 108p. 1999. pap. 19.95 (*0-937997-48-X*) Hi-Time Pflaum.

Practical Ideas for Teaching Writing As a Process. Carol B. Olson. (Illus.). 224p. (C). 1996. reprint ed. pap. text 30.00 (*0-7881-2718-7*) DIANE Pub.

Practical Ideas for Teaching Writing As a Process, Elementary & Middle Grade Levels. Carol B. Olson. (Illus.). 320p. 1996. pap. 18.00 (*0-8011-1221-4*) Calif Education.

***Practical Ideas That Really Work for Students with ADHD.** Kathleen McConnell et al. LC 99-41748. (Illus.). 2000. pap. write for info. (*0-89079-837-0*) PRO-ED.

***Practical Ideas That Really Work for Students with Autism Spectrum Disorders.** Kathleen McConnell & Gail Ryser. LC 00-32803. 2000. write for info. (*0-89079-858-3*) PRO-ED.

Practical Identification of Wood Pulp Fibers. Russell A. Parham & Richard L. Gray. LC 82-50114. 220p. 1982. 118.00 (*0-89852-400-8*, 0101R100) TAPPI.

Practical Identification of Wood Pulp Fibers. Russell A. Parham & Richard L. Gray. LC 82-50114. reprint ed. pap. 55.00 (*0-608-12028-6*, 2022820) Bks Demand.

Practical Idioms - Using Phrasal Verbs in Everyday Contexts: Intermediate Through Advanced. Louis A. Berman. (Illus.). 192p. 1994. pap. 12.95 (*0-8442-0672-5*, 06725, Natl Textbk Co) NTC Contemp Pub Co.

Practical Ifa Divination Vol. 3: Ifa Reference Manual for the Beginner & Professional. large type unabridged ed. S. Solagbade Popoola. (ENG & YOR., Illus.). 594p. 1997. pap. 49.95 (*1-890157-02-3*, Pub. by Athelia-Henrietta) BookWorld.

Practical Illustrated Dictionary of Pottery: Diccionario Ilustrado de Alfareria Practica. Robert Fournier. (SPA., Illus.). 320p. 1981. 49.95 (*0-8288-1425-2*, S40513) Fr & Eur.

Practical Illustrations of Bible Truths: Ideas for Children, Youth & Adults. Muriel Davis. LC 89-4006. 80p. 1989. pap. 5.99 (*0-87227-131-5*, RBP5161) Reg Baptist.

Practical Illustrations of Rhetorical Gesture & Action. Henry Siddons. LC 67-18425. (Illus.). 1972. reprint ed. 30.95 (*0-405-08971-6*) Ayer.

Practical Image Processing in C: Acquisition Manipulation Storage. Craig A. Lindley. Ep. 1990. disk 49.95 (*0-471-53240-1*) Wiley.

Practical Image Processing in C: Acquisition Manipulation Storage. Craig A. Lindley. LC 90-41054. 553p. 1991. pap. 51.95 (*0-471-53062-X*); pap. text 94.90 incl. disk (*0-471-54377-2*) Wiley.

Practical Imagination: Stories, Poems, Plays. Northrop Frye et al. LC 86-22788. 1465p. reprint ed. pap. 200.00 (*0-7837-3953-2*, 204378200011) Bks Demand.

Practical Imagination: The German Sciences of State in the Nineteenth Century. David F. Lindenfeld. LC 96-43699. 1997. pap. text 19.95 (*0-226-48242-1*); lib. bdg. 57.00 (*0-226-48241-3*) U Ch Pr.

Practical Immunisation. G. Dick. 1986. text 82.00 (*0-85200-925-9*) Kluwer Academic.

Practical Immunoassay. Wilfrid Butt. (Clinical & Biochemical Analysis Ser.: Vol. 14). (Illus.). 328p. 1984. text 175.00 (*0-8247-7094-3*) Dekker.

Practical Implementation of New Management Strategies: Managing Your Processes. Tom Dark. (C). 1994. 97.50 (*0-7478-1839-8*, Pub. by S Thornes Pubs) Trans-Atl Phila.

Practical Implementation of Software Metrics. Paul Goodman. 240p. 1993. 50.00 (*0-07-707665-6*) McGraw.

Practical Implications of Calvinism. Albert N. Martin. 1979. pap. 2.00 (*0-85151-296-8*) Banner of Truth.

Practical Implications of Grain Market Liberalization in Southern Africa. J. A. Conway & P. S. Tyler. 194p. 1995. pap. 60.00 (*0-85954-398-6*, Pub. by Nat Res Inst) St Mut.

Practical Implications of the Health Care Quality Improvement Act: Antitrust Analysis. LC 94-70083. 80p. 1994. pap. 40.00 (*0-89707-929-9*, 503-0235, ABA Antitrust) Amer Bar Assn.

***Practical In Situ Hybridization.** T. Schwarchzacher & P. Heslop-Harrison. 216p. 1999. pap. 39.95 (*0-387-91596-6*) Spr-Verlag.

Practical Incubation. Rob Harvey. 136p. 1993. pap. 17.95 (*0-88839-310-5*) Hancock House.

Practical Indonesian: A Communication Guide. John Baker. (IND.). 70p. 1992. pap. 2.95 (*0-945971-52-4*) Periplus.

Practical Indonesian: A Communication Guide. John Baker. Tr. by Michael Stachels from IND. (GER.). 70p. 1992. pap. 2.95 (*0-945971-53-2*) Periplus.

Practical Indonesian: A Communication Guide. John Baker. (DUT.). 70p. 1992. pap. 2.95 (*0-945971-54-0*); pap. 2.95 (*0-945971-55-9*) Periplus.

Practical Induction. Elijah Millgram. LC 96-41362. 192p. 1997. 47.50 (*0-674-69597-6*) HUP.

Practical Induction. Elijah Millgram. 184p. 1999. pap. 17.95 (*0-674-00073-0*) HUP.

Practical Infection Control in Dentistry. James A. Cottone et al. LC 90-5643. (Illus.). 286p. 1990. pap. 36.95 (*0-8121-1326-8*) Lppncott W & W.

Practical Infection Control in Dentistry. 2nd ed. James A. Cottone et al. LC 95-2678. (Illus.). 456p. 1996. pap. 37.50 (*0-683-02138-9*) Lppncott W & W.

***Practical Information for Cabinet-Makers & Furniture Men.** John Phin. 130p. 2000. pap. 15.95 (*1-892836-09-2*, Pub. by Cambium Pr) IPG Chicago.

***Practical Information Policies.** 2nd ed. Elizabeth Orna. LC 98-40510. 200p. 1999. 87.95 (*0-566-07693-4*, Pub. by Gower) Ashgate Pub Co.

P

An Asterisk (*) at the beginning of an entry indicates that the title is appearing for the first time.

Practical Information Policies: How to Manage Information Flow in Organizations. Elizabeth Orna. 263p. 1991. text 76.95 (0-566-03632-0, Pub. by Gower) Ashgate Pub Co.

Practical Inheritance Tax Planning. 3rd ed. Ralph P. Ray & John E. Redman. LC 95-135359. 416p. 1994. pap. 45.00 (0-406-02417-0, UK, MICHIE) LEXIS Pub.

Practical Insight Meditation: Basic & Progressive Stages. Mahasi Sayadaw. 70p. 1991. 4.74 (955-24-0089-9, Pub. by Buddhist Pub Soc) Vipassana Res Pubns.

Practical Instructional Design for Open Learning Materials: A Modular Course Covering Open Learning, Computer-Based Training, Multimedia. 2nd ed. Nigel Harrison. LC 94-34853. (Training Ser.). 1994. write for info. (0-07-709055-1) McGraw.

Practical Insurance Security Analysis. Jim Bannister. (DYP Textbook Ser.). 134p. 1993. pap. 155.00 (1-870255-51-8) LLP.

Practical Intake Aerodynamic Design. Ed. by E. L. Goldsmith & John Seddon. LC 93-97. (Education Ser.). 448p. 1993. 79.95 (1-56347-064-0, 64-0) AIAA.

Practical Intellect: Computers & Skills. Bo Goranzon. LC 92-19987. (Artificial Intelligence & Society Ser.). 1993. 43.95 (0-387-19759-1) Spr-Verlag.

***Practical Intelligence in Everyday Life.** Robert J. Sternberg et al. (Illus.). 304p. 2000. pap. text 17.95 (0-521-65958-2) Cambridge U Pr.

***Practical Intelligence in Everyday Life.** Robert J. Sternberg et al. (Illus.). 304p. (C). 2000. text 49.95 (0-521-65056-9) Cambridge U Pr.

***Practical Intensive Care Medicine: Problem Solving in the ICU.** Charlie Corke. (Illus.). 160p. 2000. pap. text 32.50 (0-7506-4752-3) Buttrwrth-Heinemann.

Practical International Tax Planning. 3rd ed. Marshall J. Langer. 1050p. 1988. 195.00 (0-685-69476-3, J6-1461) PLI.

***Practical Internet.** Barbara Kasser. 592p. 1999. 37.95 (0-7897-2226-7) Que.

Practical Internet Groupware. Jon Udell. Ed. by Mark Stone. (Illus.). 400p. 1999. pap. 29.95 (1-56592-537-8) OReilly & Assocs.

Practical Internetworking with TCP - IP & Unix. Smoot Carl-Mitchell & John S. Quarterman. LC 92-41015. (Illus.). 496p. (C). 1993. 54.95 (0-201-58629-0) Addison-Wesley.

Practical Interventional Radiology of the Hepatobiliary System & Gastrointestinal Tract. Ed. by Andy Adam & Robert Gibson. 224p. 1994. text 98.50 (0-340-55166-6, Pub. by E A) OUP.

Practical Interventional Radiology of the Musculoskeletal System. David Wilson. (Practical Interventional Radiology Series). (Illus.). 160p. 1995. text 120.00 (0-340-57645-6, Pub. by E A) OUP.

Practical Interventional Radiology of the Peripheral Vascular System. Ed. by Anna-Maria Belli. 136p. 1994. text 85.00 (0-340-55865-2, Pub. by E A) OUP.

***Practical Intranet Security: Overview of the State of the Art & Available Technologies.** Paul Ashley. LC 98-49719. 16p. 1999. write for info. (0-7923-8354-0) Kluwer Academic.

Practical Introduction: Alexander Technique. Richard Brennan. LC 98-24793. (Illus.). 144p. 1998. pap. 14.95 (1-86204-158-X, Pub. by Element MA) Penguin Putnam.

Practical Introduction: Reflexology. Inge Dougans. LC 98-24940. (Illus.). 208p. 1998. pap. 14.95 (1-86204-160-1, Pub. by Element MA) Penguin Putnam.

Practical Introduction: Shiatsu. Oliver Cowmeadow. LC 98-4676. 1998. pap. 14.95 (1-86204-162-8, Pub. by Element MA) Penguin Putnam.

Practical Introduction: Tai Chi. Paul Crompton. LC 97-45125. 1998. pap. 14.95 (1-86204-163-6, Pub. by Element MA) Penguin Putnam.

Practical Introduction: Yoga. Swami Purna. LC 97-39389. 96p. 1998. pap. 14.95 (1-86204-164-4, Pub. by Element MA) Penguin Putnam.

Practical Introduction to Copyright. 2nd ed. G. McFarlane. (Waterflow Practitioner's Library). 448p. 1990. reprint ed. pap. 59.95 (0-08-033074-6, Pergamon Pr) Elsevier.

Practical Introduction to Data Structures & Algorithm Analysis. (C). 1997. text. write for info. (0-13-017375-4) P-H.

Practical Introduction to Data Structures & Algorithm Analysis. Clifford Shaffer. LC 96-27210. (Illus.). 494p. (C). 1996. 71.33 (0-13-190752-2) P-H.

Practical Introduction to Data Structures & Algorithms: Java Edition. Clifford A. Shaffer. LC 98-106835. 488p. (C). 1997. 71.33 (0-13-660911-2, Prentice Hall) P-H.

Practical Introduction to Denotational Semantics. L. Allison. (Cambridge Computer Science Texts Ser.: No. 23). (Illus.). 144p. 1987. pap. text 21.95 (0-521-31423-2) Cambridge U Pr.

Practical Introduction to Electronic Circuits. 3rd ed. Martin H. Jones. (Illus.). 544p. (C). 1996. text 100.00 (0-521-47286-5); pap. text 36.95 (0-521-47879-0) Cambridge U Pr.

Practical Introduction to Electronic Instrumentation. 3rd ed. Giorgio Rizzoni. 136p. (C). 1997. spiral bd. 29.95 (0-7872-3576-8, 41357601) Kendall-Hunt.

Practical Introduction to ENT Disease. N. B. Solomons. (Illus.). 96p. 1990. 21.95 (0-387-19566-1) Spr-Verlag.

Practical Introduction to Greek Accentuation. 2nd rev. ed. H. W. Chandler. (College Classical Ser.). xxxiii, 292p. (C). 1983. reprint ed. lib. bdg. 35.00 (0-89241-112-0) Caratzas.

Practical Introduction to Health Information Management. Sara N. Di Lima et al. LC 98-34764. 1998. write for info. (0-8342-1231-5) Aspen Pub.

Practical Introduction to Impedence Matching. Robert L. Thomas. LC 75-31378. 175p. reprint ed. pap. 54.30 (0-608-15012-6, 205608500047) Bks Demand.

Practical Introduction to Literacy Theory & Criticism. M. Keith Booker. LC 95-20852. 512p. (C). 1995. pap. 41.40 (0-8013-1765-7) Longman.

Practical Introduction to Major Chinese Herbal Formulas. Hong-yen Hsu. 1993. pap. 4.95 (0-941942-00-7) Orient Heal Arts.

Practical Introduction to Management Science. 2nd ed. Donald Waters. (C). 1998. pap. text. write for info. (0-201-17847-8) Addison-Wesley.

Practical Introduction to Optical Mineralogy. Colin D. Gribble & A. J. Hall. (Illus.). 200p. 1985. text 70.00 (0-04-549007-4); pap. text 24.95 (0-04-549008-2) Routledge.

Practical Introduction to Pascal. 2nd ed. I. R. Wilson & A. M. Addyman. 236p. 1990. 33.95 (0-387-91210-X, BSI 6192) Spr-Verlag.

Practical Introduction to Phonetics. J. C. Catford. (Illus.). 255p. (C). 1988. pap. text 24.00 (0-19-824217-4) OUP.

Practical Introduction to Pumping Technology. Uno Wahren. LC 97-18401. 200p. 1997. pap. 44.95 (0-88415-686-9, 5686) Gulf Pub.

Practical Introduction to Research Methods. 2nd ed. Eugene B. Zechmeister & John J. Shaughnessy. LC 94-117668. (C). 1993. pap. text 18.50 (0-07-072703-1) McGraw.

Practical Introduction to Research Methods in Psychology. 3rd ed. John J. Shaughnessy & Eugene B. Zechmeister. LC 97-104644. 276p. (C). 1996. pap. 25.63 (0-07-072705-8) McGraw.

Practical Introduction to Standard PASCAL. I. D. Chivers. (Computers & Their Applications Ser.). 276p. 1986. text 36.95 (0-470-20359-5) P-H.

Practical Introduction to Systems Analysis & Design. M. J. Hughes. 400p. 1995. pap. 59.95 (1-85805-132-0, Pub. by DP Publns) St Mut.

Practical Introduction to the Simulation of Molecular Systems. Martin Field. LC 98-37540. 350p. (C). 1999. write for info. (0-521-58129-X) Cambridge U Pr.

Practical Introduction to Videohistory: The Smithsonian Institution & Alfred P. Sloan Foundation. Ed. by Terri A. Schorzman. LC 92-6784. 256p. (C). 1994. lib. bdg. 33.50 (0-89464-725-3) Krieger.

Practical Introduction to Zoning. 86p. 1993. 30.00 (0-933729-89-8, 6703) Natl League Cities.

Practical Introductory Quantitative Analysis. rev. ed. Phoebe K. Dea & Hendrick Keyzer. (C). 1986. pap. text, student ed. 13.50 (0-685-29053-0) Occidental Coll.

***Practical Intrusion Detection Handbook.** 500p. (C). 2000. 49.99 (0-13-025960-8) S&S Trade.

Practical Intuition: How to Harness the Power of Your Instinct & Make It Work for You. abr. ed. Laura Day. 1996. audio 18.00 (0-694-51748-8, CPN 2644) HarperAudio.

Practical Intuition: How to Harness the Power of Your Instinct & Make It Work for You. Laura Day. LC 97-19482. 208p. 1997. reprint ed. pap. 14.00 (0-7679-0034-0) Broadway BDD.

Practical Intuition for Success: A Step-by-Step Program to Increase Your Wealth Today. Laura Day. 216p. 1998. text 22.00 (0-7881-5812-0) DIANE Pub.

Practical Intuition for Success: Let Your Interests Guide You To the Career of Your Dreams. Laura Day. 256p. 1999. pap. 13.00 (0-06-093022-5, Perennial) HarperTrade.

Practical Intuition for Success: Trust Your Gut & Increase Your Bottom Line in Ten Days. abr. ed. Laura Day. 1997. audio 18.00 (0-694-51864-6, CPN 2675) HarperAudio.

Practical Intuition in Love: Start a Journey through Pleasure to the Love of Your Life. Laura Day. LC 98-34520. 256p. 1998. 23.00 (0-06-017578-8) HarpC.

Practical Intuition in Love: Start a Journey Through Pleasure to the Love of Your Life. Laura Day. LC 99-89316. 256p. 2000. pap. 12.95 (0-06-093110-8) HarpC.

***Practical Intuition in Love: Start a Journey Through Pleasure to the Love of Your Life, Set.** Laura Day. 1998. audio 18.00 (0-694-51980-4) HarperAudio.

Practical Intuition/Business. Laura Day. 22.00 (0-375-50026-X) Villard Books.

Practical Inverse Analysis in Engineering. David M. Trujillo & Henry R. Busby. LC 97-16868. (CRC Mechanical Engineering Ser.). 256p. 1997. 79.95 (0-8493-9659-X, No. 9659) CRC Pr.

Practical Investigation Techniques. Kevin B. Kinnee. LC 93-51085. (Practical Aspects of Criminal & Forensic Investigations Ser.). 416p. 1994. boxed set 73.95 (0-8493-8151-7) CRC Pr.

Practical Investment Appraisal. Ralph Tiffin & Hannah Ellis. 200p. 1992. 133.00 (0-406-00736-5, U.K., MICHIE) LEXIS Pub.

Practical Investment Management. Robert A. Strong. LC 96-50330. 600p. 1997. mass mkt. 93.95 (0-314-20335-4) S-W Pub.

***Practical Investment Management.** 2nd ed. Strong. (SWC-Finance Ser.). (C). 2000. text, student ed. 18.96 (0-324-05981-7) Sth-Wstrn College.

***Practical Investment Management.** 2nd ed. Robert A. Strong. LC 00-38777. 2001. write for info. (0-324-01914-9) Sth-Wstrn College.

Practical Iridology. Donald Bamer. 1996. pap. text 18.95 (1-885670-02-8) Woodland UT.

Practical ISDN. Jeffrey Merritt. 1997. pap. text 24.95 (1-55828-520-2, MIS Pr) IDG Bks.

Practical Isozyme Genetics. Nicole Pasteur et al. 215p. 1988. text 52.95 (0-470-21155-5) P-H.

Practical Issues in Cointegration Analysis. Ed. by Leslie Oxley & Michael McAleer. LC 99-19757. (Journal of Economic Surveys Ser.). 274p. 1998. pap. 39.95 (0-631-21198-5) Blackwell Pubs.

Practical Issues in Collection Development & Collection Access: The 1993 Charleston Conference. Ed. by Katina Strauch et al. LC 95-16712. (Collection Management: Vol. 19, Nos. 3-4). 193p. 1995. 49.95 (1-56024-733-9) Haworth Pr.

***Practical Issues in Database Management: A Reference for the Thinking Practitioner.** Fabian Pascal. LC 00-22984. 304p. 2000. pap. 39.95 (0-201-48555-9) Addison-Wesley.

Practical Issues in Employment Testing. Robert G. Rose. LC 93-27798. 156p. 1993. pap. 27.00 (0-911907-09-2) Psych Assess.

Practical Issues in the Application of Double Tax Conventions: Problemes Pratiques D'Application des Conventions Contre la Double Imposition. International Fisco Associates Staff. LC 98-21912. (Studies on International Fiscal Law). (FRE & GER.). 1998. 130.00 (90-411-1002-X) Kluwer Law Intl.

Practical Issues of This Life. Watchman Nee. Tr. by Stephen Kaung. 163p. 1975. pap. 5.00 (0-935008-29-2) Christian Fellow Pubs.

Practical Jaguar Ownership - How to Extend the Life of a Well-Worn "Cat" Martin Cross. 128p. 1998. 29.95 (1-899870-24-5, Pub. by Motor Racing) Motorbooks Intl.

Practical Japanese Cooking: Easy & Elegant. Shizuo Tsuji & Koichiro Hata. LC 85-45706. (Illus.). 152p. 1991. 35.00 (0-87011-762-9) Kodansha.

Practical Japanese-English Dictionary. Noah S. Brannen. LC 97-9665. (ENG & JPN.). 416p. 1997. pap. text 14.95 (0-8348-0342-9) Weatherhill.

Practical Japanese Made Simple. Iwaki. 1964. pap. 8.00 (0-87505-147-2) Borden.

Practical Java. Ken Arnold. (C). 2001. pap. 29.95 (0-201-31005-8) Addison-Wesley.

Practical Java: Programming Language Guide. Peter Haggar. LC 99-57905. 288p. (C). 2000. pap. text 32.95 (0-201-61646-7) Addison-Wesley.

Practical Jewelry Rendering. Tim McCreight. (Illus.). 96p. (C). 1993. pap. text 24.95 (0-9615984-4-1) Brynmorgen.

Practical Jewelry Repair. James Hickling. (Illus.). 192p. 1987. 29.50 (0-7198-0082-X, Pub. by NAG Press) Antique Collect.

Practical Joint Assessment: Upper Quadrant. 2nd ed. Anne Hartley. LC 94-11608. (Illus.). 368p. (C). (gr. 13). 1994. spiral bd. 46.00 (0-8151-4238-2, 24264) Mosby Inc.

Practical Joint Assessment Upper Quadrant: A Sports Medicine Manual. 2nd ed. Anne Hartley. LC 94-18031. (Illus.). 368p. (C). (gr. 13). 1994. spiral bd. 46.00 (0-8151-4237-4, 24265) Mosby Inc.

Practical Joke War. Alane Ferguson. 96p. (J). (gr. 4-8). 1993. pap. 3.50 (0-380-71721-2, Avon Bks) Morrow Avon.

Practical Joke War. Stephanie St. Pierre. LC 93-73812. (Little Mermaid Novels Ser.: No. 9). (Illus.). 80p. (J). (gr. 1-4). 1994. pap. 3.50 (1-56282-641-7, Pub. by Disney Pr) Time Warner.

Practical Jokes: Pocket Entertainment. Lorenz Staff. (Illus.). 96p. 1998. 7.95 (1-85967-769-X) Anness Pub.

Practical Judaism. Yisrael Meir Lau. 404p. 1997. 29.95 (0-87306-827-0) Feldheim.

Practical Jung: Nuts & Bolts of Jungian Psychotherapy. Harry A. Wilmer. LC 87-18233. 296p. 1987. pap. 19.95 (0-933029-16-0) Chiron Pubns.

Practical Junk Rig. H. G. Hasler & J. K. McLeod. 1996. 49.95 (1-888671-01-7) Tiller.

Practical Junk Rig: Design, Aerodynamics & Handling. H. G. Hasler & J. K. McLeod. 1996. text 49.95 (0-07-027029-5) McGraw.

Practical Jurisprudence: A Comment on Austin. E. C. Clark. xii, 403p. 1980. reprint ed. 42.50 (0-8377-0427-8, Rothman) W S Hein.

Practical Justice of the Peace & Parish-Officer, of His Majesty's Province of South Carolina. William Simpson. LC 70-37985. (American Law: The Formative Years). 288p. 1972. reprint ed. 23.95 (0-405-04028-8) Ayer.

Practical Kabbala. Laibl Wolf. LC 99-13940. 1999. pap. 14.00 (0-609-80378-6) Crown.

Practical Karate for the Streets. 1991. lib. bdg. 79.95 (0-8490-4749-8) Gordon Pr.

Practical Key to the Kannada Language. F. Ziegler. 112p. 1986. reprint ed. 22.00 (0-8364-1844-1, Pub. by Usha) S Asia.

***Practical Kick-Boxing: Strategy in Training & Technique.** rev. ed. Benny Urquidez. Ed. by Stuart Sobel. Tr. by Kumiko Abe from JPN. LC 97-76067. (Illus.). 189p. 1998. reprint ed. pap. 16.95 (0-9615126-9-5) Pro Action Pub.

***Practical Kinesiology for Physical Therapist Assistants: Laboratory Manual.** Jeff G. Konin. (Illus.). 80p. 1999. pap. text 12.00 (1-55642-419-1) SLACK Inc.

Practical Kinesiology for the Physical Therapist Assistant. Jeff Konin. LC 99-20311. 240p. 1999. pap. 35.00 (1-55642-299-7, 42997) SLACK Inc.

***Practical Kinesiology for the Physical Therapist Assistant: Instructor's Manual.** Jeff G. Konin. 80p. (C). 1999. pap. text, teacher ed. write for info. (1-55642-420-5) SLACK Inc.

Practical Kitten Care. James Depoitetto. LC 96-24293. (Illus.). 192p. 1996. 12.95 (0-87605-763-6) Howell Bks.

Practical Knight Endings. Edmar Mednis. 188p. (Orig.). 1993. pap. 12.95 (0-945470-35-5) Chess Ent.

Practical Knowledge. Yves Simon. Ed. by Robert Mulvaney. LC 90-85757. xiii, 163p. 1991. 35.00 (0-8232-1316-1); pap. 19.95 (0-8232-1317-X) Fordham.

Practical Knowledge: Applying the Social Sciences. Nico Stehr. (Illus.). 208p. (C). 1992. 65.00 (0-8039-8699-8) Sage.

Practical Knowledge Based Systems in Conceptual Design. John Miles & Carolynne Moore. LC 92-46682. 1993. 142.95 (0-387-19823-7) Spr-Verlag.

Practical Knowledge for a Private Security Officer. 2nd ed. John L. Coleman. LC 93-11147. (Illus.). 258p. 1993. pap. 32.95 (0-398-06066-5) C C Thomas.

Practical Knowledge for a Private Security Officer. 2nd ed. John L. Coleman. LC 93-11147. (Illus.). 258p. (C). 1993. text 51.95 (0-398-05875-X) C C Thomas.

Practical Knowledge for Interstate Drivers & Independent Truckers, Vol. 2: The Interstate Driver. Lewis J. Grill. (Independent Operator Training Ser.). 78p. (C). 1992. pap. text 9.95 (1-881912-02-7) Atlantic Pac Res.

Practical Knowledge of the Soul. Eugen Rosenstock-Huessy. Ed. by Clinton C. Gardner. Tr. by Mark Huessy & Freya Von Moltke. 66p. 1988. pap. 6.00 (0-912148-00-4) Argo Bks.

Practical Knowledge, Tradition & Technique. Ed. by J. C. Nyiri & Barry Smith. 224p. 1987. lib. bdg. 62.50 (0-7099-4477-2, Pub. by C Helm) Routldge.

Practical Korean Cooking. Chin-hwa Noh. (Illus.). 192p. 1998. 46.95 (0-930878-37-X) Hollym Intl.

Practical Laboratory Andrology. David Mortimer. LC 92-48921. (Illus.). 416p. 1994. text 75.00 (0-19-506595-6) OUP.

Practical LAN Interconnection: Featuring FDDI. Daniel Minoli. 1993. text 40.00 (0-07-042524-8) McGraw.

Practical Lans Analysed. Franz J. Kauffels. 352p. 1989. text 44.95 (0-470-21229-2) P-H.

Practical Laparoscopy. A. G. Gordon & P. J. Taylor. (Illus.). 160p. 1993. 65.00 (0-632-03658-3) Blackwell Sci.

Practical Laser Safety. 2nd rev. ed. D. C. Winburn. (Occupational Safety & Health Ser.: Vol. 18). (Illus.). 256p. 1989. text 95.00 (0-8247-8240-2) Dekker.

Practical Law for Correctional Personnel: A Resource Manual & a Training Curriculum (by the National Street Law Institute) Edward L. O'Brien et al. (Illus.). 249p. (C). 1986. reprint ed. pap. text 16.50 (0-8299-1034-4) West Pub.

Practical Law Office Mgmt. Brent D. Roper. LC 94-19945. (Paralegal). 520p. (C). 1994. mass mkt. 36.50 (0-314-04305-5) West Pub.

Practical Law Office Mgmt- Study Guide. Roper. (Paralegal). (C). 1994. student ed. 14.25 (0-314-04851-0) Delmar.

Practical Lawyer's Manual on Divorce & Separation. Institutional Staff. LC 85-72055. 173p. 1985. pap. 7.50 (0-685-13475-X, F128) Am Law Inst.

Practical Lawyer's Manual on Labor Law, No. 1. Institutional Staff. LC 82-74526. 216p. 1983. pap. 7.50 (0-686-40800-4, F124) Am Law Inst.

Practical Lawyer's Manual on Labor Law, No. 2. Institutional Staff. LC 82-74526. 214p. 1988. pap. 13.00 (0-318-35989-8, F137) Am Law Inst.

Practical Lawyer's Manual on Lawyer-Client Relations. Institutional Staff. 197p. 1983. pap. 7.50 (0-317-12708-X, F127) Am Law Inst.

Practical Lawyer's Manual on Memoranda of Law, No. 2. F. Trowbridge Vom Baur. 128p. 1991. pap. 40.00 (0-685-66314-0, F139) Am Law Inst.

Practical Lawyer's Manual on Pretrial Preparation, No. 2. Institutional Staff. 188p. 1986. pap. 7.50 (0-317-65909-X, F134) Am Law Inst.

Practical Lawyer's Manual on Trade Regulation. Michael G. Walsh. LC 85-72345. 210p. 1985. pap. 7.50 (0-685-13476-8, F133) Am Law Inst.

Practical Lawyer's Real Property Law Manual, No. 2. Institutional Staff. 209p. 1983. 7.50 (0-685-31337-9, F126) Am Law Inst.

Practical LCP: A Direct Approach to Structured Programming. Albert C. Gardner. (Illus.). 256p. 1982. 32.50 (0-07-084561-1) McGraw.

Practical Leadership Skills: Accident-Incident Investigation. Ed. by M. Douglas Clark. 1986. ring bd. 180.00 (0-88061-056-5) Intl Loss Cntrl.

Practical Leadership Skills: Causes & Effects of Loss. Ed. by M. Douglas Clark. 1986. ring bd. 180.00 (0-88061-055-7) Intl Loss Cntrl.

Practical Leadership Skills: Group Meetings. Ed. by M. Douglas Clark. 1986. ring bd. 180.00 (0-88061-060-3) Intl Loss Cntrl.

Practical Leadership Skills: Job Pride Development. Ed. by M. Douglas Clark. 1986. ring bd. 180.00 (0-88061-074-3) Intl Loss Cntrl.

Practical Leadership Skills: Job-Task Analysis & Procedures. Ed. by M. Douglas Clark. 1986. ring bd. 180.00 (0-88061-059-X) Intl Loss Cntrl.

Practical Leadership Skills: Management Control. Ed. by M. Douglas Clark. 1986. ring bd. 180.00 (0-88061-075-1) Intl Loss Cntrl.

Practical Leadership Skills: Personal Communications. Ed. by M. Douglas Clark. 1986. ring bd. 180.00 (0-88061-061-1) Intl Loss Cntrl.

Practical Leadership Skills: Planned Inspections. Ed. by M. Douglas Clark. 1986. ring bd. 180.00 (0-88061-057-3) Intl Loss Cntrl.

Practical Leadership Skills: Planned Job-Task Observation. Ed. by M. Douglas Clark. 1986. ring bd. 180.00 (0-88061-058-1) Intl Loss Cntrl.

Practical Leadership Skills-Fire Loss Control, 12 vols., Set. Date not set. ring bd. 180.00 (0-88061-085-9) Intl Loss Cntrl.

Practical Leadership Skills-Occupational Health, Set. Date not set. 180.00 (0-88061-087-5) Intl Loss Cntrl.

Practical Leadership Skills-Special Problems Solution, 12 vols., Set. Date not set. 180.00 (0-88061-086-7) Intl Loss Cntrl.

Practical Leather Technology. 4th ed. Thomas C. Thorstensen. LC 91-39162. 350p. (C). 1993. lib. bdg. 42.50 (0-89464-689-3) Krieger.

P

An Asterisk (*) at the beginning of an entry indicates that the title is appearing for the first time.

Practical Legal Ethics, 1993. Wake Forest University School of Law Continuing Le. 233p. 1993. pap. 65.00 (*0-942225-64-3*) Wake Forest Law.

Practical Legal Guidelines for the Private Security Officer: The Essential Consequences of the Laws Regarding Private Security & the Affective Social Trends of Today. John L. Coleman. 324p. 1990. pap. 40.95 (*0-398-06067-3*) C C Thomas.

Practical Legal Guidelines for the Private Security Officer: The Essential Consequences of the Laws Regarding Private Security & the Affective Social Trends of Today. John L. Coleman. 324p. (C). 1990. text 59.95 (*0-398-05694-3*) C C Thomas.

Practical Legal Writing for Legal Assistants. Celia C. Elwell & Robert B. Smith. LC 95-32136. 400p. (C). 1996. mass mkt. 49.95 (*0-314-06115-0*) West Pub.

Practical Lessons for Africa from East Asia in Industrial & Trade Policies. Peter Harrold et al. (World Bank Discussion Papers: Vol. 310). 134p. 1996. pap. 22.00 (*0-8213-3484-0*, 13484) World Bank.

Practical Lessons from the Loma Prieta Earthquake. Ed. by National Research Council's Geotechnical Board. (Illus.). 274p. (C). 1994. 25.00 (*0-309-05030-8*, LP-93) Natl Acad Pr.

Practical Lessons in Endodontic Surgery. Donald E. Arens et al. (Illus.). 216p. 280.00 incl. VHS (*0-86715-336-9*) Quint Pub Co.

Practical Lessons in Endodontic Surgery. Donald E. Arens et al. LC 98-15844. (Illus.). 216p. 1998. spiral bd. 82.00 (*0-86715-333-4*) Quint Pub Co.

Practical Lessons to Promote a Global Perspective in Elementary Education. Ed. by Elaine Jarchow et al. 1998. 15.00 (*0-89333-161-9*) AACTE.

***Practical Life of Faith: Hebrews 11-13.** Charles R. Swindoll. 1998. pap., student ed. 5.95 (*1-57972-195-8*) Insight Living.

Practical Lighting Tips for Video Productions. 1989. 4.95 (*0-89816-132-0*) Embee Pr.

***Practical Linux.** Que Corporation Staff. 704p. 2000. 29.99 (*0-7897-2251-8*) Que.

Practical Liturgies for the School Year. Mary Fearon. 1998. pap. text 25.75 (*0-697-02999-9*, WCB McGr Hill) McGrw-H Hghr Educ.

Practical Liver Biopsy Interpretation: A Manual of Diagnostic Tables. Jurgen Ludwig. 248p. 1992. 75.00 (*0-89189-347-4*) Am Soc Clinical.

Practical Liver Biopsy Interpretation: Diagnostic Algorithms. 2nd ed. Jurgen Ludwig & Kenneth P. Batts. LC 98-9870. 1998. 105.00 (*0-89189-431-4*) Am Soc Clinical.

Practical Logic. 2nd ed. Ron Yezzi. LC 92-73813. Orig. Title: A Primer of Practical Logic. 367p. (C). 1992. pap. text 19.00 (*0-9619368-3-5*) G Bruno.

Practical Logic. 4th ed. Soccio. (C). 1997. pap. text 54.00 (*0-15-517769-9*) Harcourt Coll Pubs.

Practical Logic. 4th ed. Douglas J. Soccio. (C). 1992. pap. text, teacher ed. 4.75 (*0-03-079566-4*) Harcourt Coll Pubs.

Practical Logic. 5th ed. Soccio. (C). 1997. pap. text 44.50 (*0-15-503036-1*, Pub. by Harcourt Coll Pubs) Harcourt.

Practical Logic: An Antidote for Uncritical Thinking. 4th ed. Vincent E. Barry & Douglas J. Soccio. Ed. by JoAnn Weaver. (Illus.). 512p. (C). 1992. text 50.25 (*0-03-073907-1*, Pub. by Harcourt Coll Pubs) Harcourt.

Practical Logic: With the Appendix on Deontic Logic. Zygmunt Ziembinski. Tr. by Leon Ter-Oganian & Szslaw Ziemba. LC 75-45254. 452p. 1976. text 199.00 (*90-277-0557-7*, D Reidel) Kluwer Academic.

Practical Longitudinal Data Analysis. David Hand & Martin Crowder. 1998. 69.95 (*0-412-59940-6*) Thomson Learn.

Practical Loss Control Leadership. F. E. Bird, Jr. & George L. Germain. (Illus.). ix, 446p. 1986. pap. text 65.00 (*0-88061-054-9*) Intl Loss Cntrl.

Practical Loss Control Leadership: French Home Study. Frank E. Bird, Jr. & George L. Germain. (FRE.). Date not set. student ed. 35.00 (*0-88061-152-9*) Intl Loss Cntrl.

Practical Loss Control Leadership: French Version. Frank E. Bird, Jr. & George L. Germain. (FRE.). Date not set. 65.00 (*0-88061-151-0*) Intl Loss Cntrl.

Practical Loss Control Leadership: German Version. Frank E. Bird, Jr. & George L. Germain. (GER.). Date not set. 65.00 (*0-88061-150-2*) Intl Loss Cntrl.

Practical Loss Control Leadership: Spanish Home Study. Frank E. Bird, Jr. & George L. Germain. (SPA.). Date not set. student ed. 35.00 (*0-88061-154-5*) Intl Loss Cntrl.

Practical Loss Control Leadership: Spanish Version. Frank E. Bird, Jr. & George L. Germain. (SPA.). (C). Date not set. 65.00 (*0-88061-153-7*) Intl Loss Cntrl.

Practical LotusScript. Anthony Patton. LC 99-13034. (Illus.). 488p. 1999. pap. 43.95 (*1-884777-76-7*) Manning Pubns.

Practical Low Fat Cooking: From Nancy's Kitchen. Nancy B. Scheer. Ed. by Linda J. Stewart. vi, 158p. 1997. spiral bd. 15.00 (*0-9652159-9-7*) Quillan Pub.

Practical Low Power Digital VLSI Design. Gary K. Yeap. LC 97-33994. 232p. 1997. text 108.00 (*0-7923-8009-6*) Kluwer Academic.

Practical LSD Manufacture. 2nd rev. ed. Uncle Fester. LC 96-79425. 1997. pap. text 20.00 (*1-55950-161-8*) Loompanics.

***Practical Lubrication for Industrial Facilities.** Heinz P. Bloch. LC 99-34016. 612p. 2000. 150.00 (*0-88173-296-6*) Fairmont Pr.

Practical Machine Vision. Julie Pingry. 140p. student ed. 77.00 (*0-943779-00-6*) Cutter Information.

Practical Machinery Management. 3rd ed. Heinz P. Block. LC 98-26184. (Practical Machinery Management for Process Plants Ser.: No. 1). 600p. 1998. 95.00 (*0-88415-661-3*, 5661) Gulf Pub.

Practical Macromolecular Organic Chemistry, Vol. 2. Ed. by Dietrich Braun et al. (MMI Press Polymer Monographs). xiv, 332p. 1984. text 335.00 (*3-7186-0059-5*) Gordon & Breach.

Practical Magic. Alice Hoffman. 304p. 1998. pap. 13.00 (*0-425-16320-2*); mass mkt. 7.50 (*0-425-16846-8*) Berkley Pub.

Practical Magic. abr. ed. Alice Hoffman. 1995. 17.00 incl. audio (*0-671-53540-4*) S&S Audio.

Practical Magic. Alice Hoffman. 352p. 1996. reprint ed. mass mkt. 7.99 (*0-425-15249-9*) Berkley Pub.

Practical Magic: A Translation of Basic Neuro-Linguistic Programming into Clinical Psychotherapy. Stephen Lankton. LC 80-50148. 1980. pap. 19.95 (*0-916990-08-7*) META Pubns.

Practical Magic in the Northern Tradition. Nigel Pennick. (Illus.). 288p. 1988. pap. 14.95 (*0-85030-757-0*, Pub. by Aqrn Pr) Harper SF.

Practical Malay. Wendy Hutton & Thomas G. Oey. (Illus.). 70p. 1994. pap. 3.95 (*0-945971-84-2*) Periplus.

Practical Management. Colwill & Birchall. 1992. pap. text. write for info. (*0-582-86980-3*, Pub. by Addison-Wesley) Longman.

Practical Management. 3rd ed. Tim Clark & John Rees. 176p. (C). 1998. text. write for info. (*1-85317-587-0*, Pub. by Martin Dunitz) Mosby Inc.

Practical Management Development: Strategies for Management Resourcing & Development in the 1990s. Gordon McBeath. (Illus.). 350p. 1994. pap. text 31.95 (*0-631-19346-4*) Blackwell Pubs.

Practical Management for Supervisors. Lester R. Bittel. 1993. teacher ed. 16.12 (*0-02-802485-0*) Glencoe.

Practical Management for Supervisors. 2nd ed. Lester R. Bittel. LC 92-36417. 1992. 20.00 (*0-02-802484-2*) Glencoe.

Practical Management of Asthma. 2nd ed. Tim Clark. 176p. (C). 1996. text. write for info. (*1-85317-199-9*, Pub. by Martin Dunitz) Mosby Inc.

Practical Management of Cardiac Arrhythmias. Ed. by Nabil El-Sherif & Jean Lekieffre. LC 96-36935. (Illus.). 348p. 1997. 95.00 (*0-87993-652-5*) Futura Pub.

***Practical Management of Chemicals & Hazardous Waste.** Lee Kuhre. (Illus.). xxi, 341p. 1999. pap. 49.00 (*1-929609-00-0*, ES 7655) Stadler Burgess.

Practical Management of Emotional Problems in Medicine. enl. rev. ed. Hugh J. Lurie. LC 81-40019. 272p. 1982. pap. 84.40 (*0-7837-8357-4*, 204914700010) Bks Demand.

Practical Management of Hypertension. Ed. by William H. Birkenhager. (Developments in Cardiovascular Medicine Ser.). (C). 1991. lib. bdg. 124.50 (*0-7923-0918-9*) Kluwer Academic.

Practical Management of Hypertension. Francisco Leyva-Leon & Andrew J. Coats. LC 98-32240. 1999. write for info. (*0-632-05045-4*) Blackwell Sci.

Practical Management of Hypertension. 2nd ed. Ed. by Willem H. Birkenhager. LC 96-115. (Developments in Cardiovascular Medicine Ser.: Vol. 184). 224p. 1996. text 100.50 (*0-7923-3952-5*) Kluwer Academic.

Practical Management of Low-Grade Primary Brain Tumors. Jack P. Rock. LC 98-44542. 1999. write for info. (*0-7817-1101-0*) Lppncott W & W.

Practical Management of Pain. 2nd ed. P. Prithvi Raj. (Illus.). 1120p. (C). (gr. 13). 1991. text 190.00 (*0-8151-7012-2*, 22126) Mosby Inc.

Practical Management of Pain, Vol. 3. 3rd ed. P. Prithvi Raj. (Illus.). 1312p. (C). (gr. 13). 2000. text 190.00 (*0-8151-2569-0*, 31308) Mosby Inc.

Practical Management of Skin Cancer. Ronald L. Moy. LC 98-30093. (Illus.). 288p. 1998. text 125.00 (*0-397-51604-5*) Lppncott W & W.

Practical Management of Spasticity in Children & Adults. Mel B. Glenn & John Whyte. LC 89-13414. 325p. 1990. text 49.50 (*0-8121-1297-0*) Lppncott W & W.

Practical Management of the Balance Disorder Patient. Ed. by Neil T. Shepard & Steven A. Telian. 240p. (Orig.). 1996. pap. 55.00 (*1-879105-84-5*, 0347) Thomson Learn.

Practical Management of the Dizzy Patient. Joel A. Goebel. 288p. text 65.00 (*0-7817-1820-1*) Lppncott W & W.

Practical Management of the Newborn. 5th ed. I. M. Balfour-Lynn & H. B. Valman. LC 92-49491. 304p. 1993. pap. 36.95 (*0-632-03571-4*, Pub. by Blckwll Scitfc UK) Blackwell Sci.

***Practical Management of the Side Effects of Psychotropic Drugs.** Ed. by Richard Balon. LC 98-44760. (Medical Psychiatry Ser.: Vol. 12). (Illus.). 304p. 1998. text 150.00 (*0-8247-1926-3*) Dekker.

Practical Management of Therapeutic Fasting see Prakticheskoe Rukovodstvo K Lecheniiu Golodom

Practical Management of Therapeutic Fasting. Lew Strogat, pseud. Tr. by Jack E. Evans from RUS. LC 92-70789. 64p. 1992. pap. 10.00 (*0-911971-68-8*) Effect Pub.

Practical Management Principles: Management Insights for Any Organization. Charles J. Washington. LC 98-74322. 280p. 1998. pap. 18.95 (*0-9667775-0-6*) Advantage Consult Enter.

Practical Management Science. Winston & Albright. 1996. mass mkt. 78.75 (*0-534-21777-X*) Duxbury Syst.

Practical Management Science. 2nd ed. Albright Winston. (Business Statistics Ser.). 2000. pap. text. write for info. (*0-534-37135-3*) Brooks-Cole.

Practical Management Science: Spreadsheet Modeling & Applications. Wayne L. Winston & S. Christian Albright. LC 96-18224. (Business Statistics Ser.). (C). 1997. pap. 99.95 (*0-534-21774-5*) Wadsworth Pub.

Practical Management Skills for Engineers & Scientists. William C. Giegold. LC 91-25890. 454p. (C). 1992. reprint ed. lib. bdg. 49.50 (*0-89464-654-0*) Krieger.

Practical Manager's Guide to Excellence in Management. Ronald Brown. LC 79-11883. 128p. reprint ed. pap. 39.70 (*0-608-12855-4*, 202358700033) Bks Demand.

Practical Manual & Workbook on Computer Science. V. B. Aggarwal & P. C. Bagga. 124p. 1996. pap. 35.00 (*81-209-0443-5*, Pub. by Pitambar Pub) St Mut.

Practical Manual for a Basic Approach to Clinical Electrodynography. Sheldon Langer et al. 68p. 1988. pap. text 24.00 (*0-317-91266-6*); pap. text 24.00 (*0-936445-02-5*) Langer Found BSMR.

Practical Manual for Coup D'Etat. 1991. lib. bdg. 66.00 (*0-8490-4424-3*) Gordon Pr.

Practical Manual for Network Planning, 1997. APEC Telecommunications Working Group. LC 97-944112. 165p. 1997. write for info. (*981-00-9291-1*) AgBe Pub.

Practical Manual for the Piano & Harmonium Tuner: A Treatise on the Tuning & Repair of These Instruments. E. Nugues et al. (Illus.). vi, 146p. 1913. pap. text 20.00 (*0-913746-30-4*) Organ Lit.

Practical Manual for Zebra Mussel Monitoring & Control. Renata Claudi & Gerald L. Mackie. LC 93-5031. 240p. 1993. lib. bdg. 85.00 (*0-87371-985-9*, L985) Lewis Pubs.

Practical Manual of Brachytherapy. Ed. by Bernard Pierquin & Ginette Marinello. Tr. by Frank Wilson et al from FRE. LC 96-49909.Tr. of Manuel Pratique de Curietherapie. (Illus.). 300p. 1997. text 109.95 (*0-944838-73-1*) Med Physics Pub.

***Practical Manual of Captive Animal Photography.** Michael Havelin. (Illus.). 120p. 2000. pap. 29.95 (*1-58428-023-9*) Amherst Media.

Practical Manual of Land Development. 3rd ed. Barbara Colley. LC 98-34765. (Illus.). 352p. 1998. 59.95 (*0-07-011967-8*) McGraw-Hill Prof.

Practical Manual of Mechanical Ventilation. Pierson. 1998. pap. text 27.95 (*0-7216-6072-X*, P1231, W B Saunders Co) Harcrt Hlth Sci Grp.

Practical Manual of Medical Translation English-French. Hoof. Orig. Title: Precis Pratique de Traduction Medicale. 309p. 1996. 98.00 (*2-224-01183-0*, Pub. by Maloine) IBD Ltd.

Practical Manual of Operative Laparoscopy & Hysteroscopy. 2nd ed. Ricardo Azziz & Ana A. Murphy. LC 96-21229. 347p. 1997. 85.00 (*0-387-94696-9*) Spr-Verlag.

Practical Manual of Wastewater Chemistry. Barbara A. Hauser. 250p. (C). 1996. ring bd. 54.95 (*1-57504-012-3*) CRC Pr.

Practical Manual on Lipid Analysis I: Fatty Acids. J. G. Alvarez & J. C. Touchstone. 104p. 1991. student ed. 29.95 (*0-945537-02-6*) Norell Pr.

Practical Manual on Microbiologically Influenced Corrosion. Ed. by G. Kobrin. (Illus.). 233p. 1993. 89.00 (*1-877914-56-8*) NACE Intl.

Practical Marine Electrical Knowledge. Dennis T. Hall. 132p. 1984. 175.00 (*0-900886-87-0*, Pub. by Witherby & Co) St Mut.

Practical Marine Engineering. 2nd ed. Reno C. King, Jr. (Illus.). 555p. (C). 1985. pap. text 28.50 (*0-934114-60-9*, BK-448) Marine Educ.

Practical Mariner's Book of Knowledge: 420 Rules of Thumb That Define the Limits Within. John Vigor. 1994. pap. 17.95 (*0-07-067475-2*) Intl Marine.

Practical Marketing: An Asian Perspective. Chow Wee. LC 96-25487. 1996. 19.95 (*0-201-62857-0*) Addison-Wesley.

Practical Marketing Research. Paul Scipione. 272p. (C). 1992. spiral bd. 35.95 (*0-8403-8101-8*) Kendall-Hunt.

Practical Marketing Research. 2nd rev. ed. Jeffrey L. Pope. 314p. 1993. 32.95 (*0-8144-5086-5*) AMACOM.

Practical Marriage. Dallas Schulze. (Here Come the Grooms Ser.: No. 16). 1996. per. 3.99 (*0-373-30116-2*, 1-30116-7) Harlequin Bks.

Practical Martial Arts for Special Forces. William Beaver. (Illus.). 112p. 1996. pap. 17.00 (*0-87364-866-8*) Paladin Pr.

Practical Mastitis Control in Dairy Herds. W. H. Giesecke et al. (Illus.). 328p. 1999. pap. 39.95 (*0-409-10923-1*) Buttrwrth-Heinemann.

Practical Math. Roslyn Snow & Lois DallaRiva. 24p. 1981. pap. 5.00 (*0-9679093-9-2*) Easy Guides.

Practical Math. 3rd ed. American Technical Publishers Staff. LC 94-6617. 352p. 1994. pap. 22.96 (*0-8269-2244-9*) Am Technical.

Practical Math: Skills & Conceptions. Frederick & Fredrick. 1990. 49.95 (*0-03-012757-2*) Harcourt Schl Pubs.

Practical Math Applications. Burton. (MB - Business/Vocational Math Ser.). (C). 1995. mass mkt. 29.95 (*0-538-70726-7*) S-W Pub.

Practical Math for Business, 4 vols. 4th ed. Alan R. Curtis. (C). 1987. trans. 101.56 (*0-395-42401-1*) HM.

Practical Math for Health Fitness Professionals. Dennis K. Flood. LC 95-36602. (Illus.). 224p. 1995. pap. text 24.00 (*0-87322-758-1*, BFLO0758) Human Kinetics.

Practical Math for Respiratory Care. Ray Sibberson. (Illus.). 304p. (gr. 13). 1995. pap. text, wbk. ed. 22.00 (*0-8151-8001-2*, 25934) Mosby Inc.

Practical Math for the Technician: The Basics. Barbara Bode-Snyder. 592p. 1990. pap. text 100.00 (*0-13-251513-X*) P-H.

Practical Math Handbook for the Building Trades. Paul Calter. (Illus.). 288p. 1983. pap. 17.25 (*0-13-692228-7*) P-H.

Practical Math Skills - Intermediate Level. Jim Duncan. (Illus.). 64p. (J). (gr. 4-6). 1989. student ed. 8.99 (*0-86653-465-2*, GA1070) Good Apple.

Practical Math Skills - Junior High Level. Jim Duncan. (Illus.). 64p. (J). (gr. 7-9). 1989. student ed. 8.99 (*0-86653-466-0*, GA1071) Good Apple.

Practical Math Skills - Primary Level. Jim Duncan. (Illus.). 64p. (J). (gr. 1-3). 1989. student ed. 8.99 (*0-86653-464-4*, GA1069) Good Apple.

Practical Math Success in 20 Minutes a Day. Judith Robinovitz. LC 98-6120. (Skill Builders Ser.). 208p. 1998. pap. 15.95 (*1-57685-129-X*) LrningExprss.

Practical Mathematics. 7th ed. Claude I. Palmer & L. A. Mrachek. 560p. 1985. text 68.50 (*0-07-048254-3*) McGraw.

Practical Mathematics for Environmental Engineers Vol. 1: Basic Calculations. SciTech Publishers Staff. (Illus.). 136p. 1990. 17.95 (*0-925760-15-3*) SciTech Pubs.

Practical Mathematics for Environmental Engineers Vol. 2: Calculations Using Geometry. SciTech Publishers Staff. (Illus.). 149p. 1990. 17.95 (*0-925760-16-1*) SciTech Pubs.

Practical Mathematics for Environmental Engineers Vol. 3: Solutions by Algebra. SciTech Publishers Staff. (Illus.). 176p. 1990. 21.95 (*0-925760-17-X*) SciTech Pubs.

Practical Mathematics for Environmental Engineers Vol. 4: Trigonometry & Logarithms. SciTech Publishers Staff. (Illus.). 136p. 1990. 17.95 (*0-925760-18-8*) SciTech Pubs.

Practical Mathematics for Metalworking Trainees. rev. ed. William E. Hardman. 272p. 1982. teacher ed. 16.95 (*0-910399-19-0*, 5112); pap. text 19.50 (*0-910399-03-4*, 5012) Natl Tool & Mach.

Practical Mathematics in Nuclear Medicine Technology. Patricia C. Wells. LC 99-34617. 373p. 1999. write for info. (*0-932004-67-9*, Pub. by Soc Nuclear Med) Matthews Medical Bk Co.

Practical Measurement in Physical Education & Sport. 4th ed. Harold M. Barrow et al. LC 88-34035. (Illus.). 364p. 1989. text 39.95 (*0-8121-1216-4*) Lppncott W & W.

Practical Measurement of Physical Performance. Helen M. Eckert. LC 73-16292. (Health Education, Physical Education, & Recreation Ser.). 307p. reprint ed. pap. 95.20 (*0-608-16665-0*, 205618500055) Bks Demand.

Practical Meat Inspection. Wilson. 1987. 31.00 (*0-632-01449-0*) CRC Pr.

Practical Meat Inspection. 6th ed. Andrew Wilson & William Wilson. LC 97-20711. 1997. 62.95 (*0-632-04898-0*) Blackwell Sci.

Practical Media Relations. Judith Ridgway. 232p. 1996. pap. 26.95 (*0-566-07702-7*, Pub. by Gower) Ashgate Pub Co.

Practical Medical Ethics. David Seedhouse & Lisetta Lovett. 142p. 1993. pap. 65.00 (*0-471-92843-7*, Wiley-Liss) Wiley.

Practical Medical Halachah. 3rd ed. Fred Rosner & Moshe Tendler. LC 97-28714. 192p. 1997. pap. 40.00 (*0-7657-9990-1*) Aronson.

Practical Medical Microbiology. 14th ed. Collee. (C). 1997. text 127.00 (*0-443-04721-9*, W B Saunders Co) Harcrt Hlth Sci Grp.

Practical Meditation. Steve Hounsome. (Orig.). 1996. pap. 22.95 (*1-898307-58-X*, Pub. by Capall Bann Pubng) Holmes Pub.

***Practical Meditation: Spiritual Yoga for the Mind.** Sister Jayanti. 150p. 2000. pap. 10.95 (*1-55874-827-X*) Health Comm.

Practical Meditator. Harry C. Meserve. LC 80-15631. 137p. 1981. 27.95 (*0-87705-506-8*, Kluwer Acad Hman Sci) Kluwer Academic.

Practical Mental Influence (1908) William W. Atkinson. 96p. 1998. reprint ed. pap. 16.95 (*0-7661-0197-5*) Kessinger Pub.

Practical Mental Magic. Theodore Annemann. (Illus.). 310p. (Orig.). 1983. pap. 8.95 (*0-486-24426-1*) Dover.

Practical Merchandising Math. Leo Gafney. LC 95-37072. (National Retail Federation Ser.). 300p. 1995. pap. 69.95 (*0-471-14518-1*) Wiley.

***Practical Meta-Analysis.** Mark W. Lipsey & David B. Wilson. LC 00-35379. (Applied Social Research Methods Ser.). 2000. write for info. (*0-7619-2168-0*) Sage.

Practical Metal Plate Work. 1996. lib. bdg. 250.99 (*0-8490-8333-8*) Gordon Pr.

Practical Metallography. S. P. Rockwell. (Technical Papers: Vol. P79). (Illus.). 6p. 1924. pap. text 30.00 (*1-55589-320-1*) AGMA.

***Practical Metallurgy & Materials of Industry.** 154p. (C). 1999. text 25.00 (*0-536-02738-2*) Pearson Custom.

Practical Metallurgy & Materials of Industry. 2nd ed. John E. Neely. 406p. 1984. pap. text 6.00 (*0-471-80125-9*) P-H.

Practical Metallurgy & Materials of Industry. 3rd ed. John E. Neely. 1989. text 40.95 (*0-471-60923-4*) P-H.

***Practical Metallurgy & Materials of Industry.** 5th ed. John Neely. 461p. 1999. 90.00 (*0-13-624552-8*) P-H.

Practical Method Pt. 2: Violin in Four Parts. N. Laoureux. 64p. 1986. pap. 7.95 (*0-7935-5454-3*, 50326960) H Leonard.

Practical Method for Violin, Pt. 1. N. Laoureux. 60p. 1986. pap., suppl. ed. 8.95 (*0-7935-5107-2*, 50326940) H Leonard.

Practical Method of Italian Mezzo-Soprano for Alto or Baritone. N. Vaccai. 48p. 1986. pap. 3.95 (*0-7935-5120-X*, 50262810) H Leonard.

Practical Method of Italian Singing High Soprano. N. Vaccai. 48p. 1986. pap. 3.95 (*0-7935-3908-0*, 50262820) H Leonard.

Practical Method of Italian Singing Soprano or Tenor. N. Vaccai. 48p. 1986. pap. 3.95 (*0-7935-5318-0*, 50262800) H Leonard.

Practical Method of Vovi Esoteric Science. rev. ed. Luong Si Hang. Ed. by Mai Nguyen et al. Tr. by Hoang Vinh from VIE. (Illus.). 104p. 1994. pap. 5.00 (*0-9633690-4-0*) VoVi LED.

P

An Asterisk (*) at the beginning of an entry indicates that the title is appearing for the first time.

Practical Method Violin, Pt. 1 A Cappella. N. Laoureux. 68p. 1986. pap. 7.95 (*0-7935-5440-3*, 50326950) H Leonard.

Practical Methodology of Forensic Photography. Ed. by David R. Redsicker. (Illus.). 292p. 1991. 44.95 (*0-444-01597-3*, TR822) CRC Pr.

Practical Methodology of Forensic Photography. David R. Redsicker. 304p. 1992. boxed set 69.95 (*0-8493-9519-4*) CRC Pr.

Practical Methodology of Forensic Photography. 2nd ed. David R. Redsicker. (Practical Aspects of Criminal & Forensic Investigation Ser.). 328p. ring bd. 79.95 (*0-8493-2004-6*) CRC Pr.

Practical Methods for Design & Analysis of Complex Surveys. Risto Lehtonen & Erkki J. Pahkinen. LC 94-20917. (Statistics in Practice Ser.). 348p. 1995. 125.00 (*0-471-93934-X*) Wiley.

Practical Methods for Reliability Data Analysis. J. I. Ansell & M. J. Phillips. (Oxford Statistical Science Ser.: No. 14). (Illus.). 256p. 1994. text 65.00 (*0-19-853664-X*) OUP.

Practical Methods for Self Development. Elizabeth Towne. 159p. 1996. reprint ed. spiral bd. 12.00 (*0-7873-0884-6*) Hlth Research.

Practical Methods for Your Year 2000 Problem: The Lowest Cost Solution. Robert Chapman. LC 97-37378. 236p. 1998. pap. 55.00 incl. cd-rom (*1-884777-52-X*) Manning Pubns.

Practical Methods in Advanced Protein Chemistry. Gary C. Howard & William E. Brown. 2000. 59.95 (*0-8493-9453-8*) CRC Pr.

Practical Methods in Choral Speaking. Marguerite E. DeWitt et al. 1973. text 2.50 (*0-686-09411-5*) Expression.

Practical Methods in Molecular Biology. Robert F. Schleif & P. C. Wensink. (Illus.). 220p. 1987. 105.00 (*0-387-90603-7*) Spr-Verlag.

Practical Methods of Optimization. 2nd ed. R. Fletcher. LC 87-8126. 450p. 1988. 144.95 (*0-471-91547-5*) Wiley.

Practical Microprocessor Interfacing. S. A. Money. LC 87-23204. 247p. 1987. 125.00 (*0-471-63788-2*) Wiley.

Practical Microscopic Hematology. 4th ed. Fritz Heckner. (Illus.). 124p. 1994. 34.95 (*0-8121-1711-5*) Lppncott W & W.

***Practical Microsoft SQL Server 7.** Brad McGehee & Robert A. Kraft. 750p. 1999. pap. 29.99 (*0-7897-2147-3*) S&S Trade.

***Practical Microsoft Windows 98.** 2nd ed. Joe Kraynak. (Illus.). 600p. 1999. pap. 24.99 (*0-7897-2202-X*) Que.

Practical Microwave Electron Devices. T. Koryu Ishii. 407p. 1990. text 88.00 (*0-12-374700-7*) Acad Pr.

Practical Microwave Oven Repair. Homer L. Davidson. (Illus.). 364p. (Orig.). 1984. pap. 15.95 (*0-8306-1667-5*) McGraw-Hill Prof.

Practical Microwaves. Thomas S. Laverghetta. LC 95-10971. 484p. (C). 1995. 63.80 (*0-13-186875-6*) P-H.

Practical Middlegame Technique. Daniel Kopec. 1997. text 21.95 (*1-85744-142-7*) Macmillan.

Practical MIDI Handbook. 3rd ed. R. A. Penfold. (Illus.). 135p. 1995. pap. 15.95 (*1-870775-36-8*) Cimino Pub Grp.

Practical Mind Reading. William W. Atkinson. reprint ed. pap. 3.00 (*0-911662-43-X*) Yoga.

Practical Ministry in the Real World. Robert Shannon & J. Michael Shannon. LC 97-24824. 1997. pap. 7.99 (*0-89900-785-6*) College Pr Pub.

Practical Minor Surgery. David Crawford & Chris Khoo. (Illus.). 1996. audio compact disk 350.00 (*90-5702-006-8*); audio compact disk 70.00 (*90-5702-007-6*) Gordon & Breach.

***Practical Miracles for Mars & Venus: Eight Principles for Lasting Love, Increasing Success & Vibrant Health in the 21st Century.** John Gray. 192p. 2000. 24.00 (*0-06-019859-1*, HarpCollins) HarperTrade.

***Practical Miracles for Mars & Venus: Eight Principles for Lasting Love, Increasing Success & Vibrant Health in the 21st Century.** large type ed. John Gray. 250p. 2000. 24.00 (*0-06-019950-4*) HarpC.

Practical Missiology: The Life & Mission Methods of John L. Nevius, 1829-1893. Samuel H. Chao. LC 93-37649. (American University Studies: Vol. 151). 1994. write for info. (*0-8204-2355-6*) P Lang Pubng.

Practical Mock Scene Manual. Timothy A. Perry. 60p. 1986. student ed. 59.95 (*0-915837-02-1*) T Perry.

Practical Model Management Using CASE Tools. Debra L. Hudson. 298p. (Orig.). 1993. 64.99 (*0-471-56734-5*, GD440X) Wiley.

Practical Modern Basketball. 3rd ed. John Wooden. LC 99-184373. 452p. 1998. pap. 27.00 (*0-205-29125-2*) Allyn.

Practical Mold Installation. William J. Tobin. 45p. (Orig.). 1993. pap. text 15.00 (*0-936994-09-6*) W J T Assocs.

Practical Molecular Virology. Ed. by Mary K. Collins. LC 91-7049. (Methods in Molecular Biology Ser.: Vol. 8). (Illus.). 340p. 1991. 54.50 (*0-89603-191-8*); pap. 59.50 (*0-89603-299-X*) Humana.

Practical, Moral, & Personal Sense of Nursing: A Phenomenological Philosophy of Practice. Anne H. Bishop & John R. Scudder, Jr. LC 89-11480. 185p. (C). 1990. pap. text 21.95 (*0-7914-0252-5*) State U NY Pr.

Practical, Moral, & Political Economy: Or the Government, Religion & Institutions Most Conducive to Individual Happiness & National Power. Thomas R. Edmonds. LC 68-55706. (Reprints of Economic Classics Ser.). viii, 304p. 1969. reprint ed. 45.00 (*0-678-00564-8*) Kelley.

***Practical Motion Planning in Robotics.** Kamal Gupta. LC 98-16161. 368p. 1998. 105.00 (*0-471-98163-X*) Wiley.

***Practical MR Imaging of the Foot & Ankle.** Alison R. Spouge & Thomas Lee Pope. LC 00-39845. (Illus.). 2000. write for info. (*0-8493-0281-1*) CRC Pr.

Practical MRI: A Teaching File. Jeffrey J. Brown & Franz J. Wippold, II. (Illus.). 592p. 1995. text 135.00 (*0-7817-0200-3*) Lppncott W & W.

Practical MRI Atlas of Neonatal Brain Development. A. James Barkovich & Charles L. Truwit. LC 90-8860. (Illus.). 83p. 1990. reprint ed. pap. 30.00 (*0-608-07234-6*, 206745900009) Bks Demand.

Practical MRI, Magnetic Resonance Imaging: A Case Study Approach. Wilson S. Wong et al. LC 86-22337. 463p. 1987. reprint ed. pap. 143.60 (*0-608-03459-2*, 206416000008) Bks Demand.

Practical Multiservice LANs: ATM & RF Broadband. Ernest O. Tunmann. LC 99-17793. (Telecommunications Library). (Illus.). 346p. 1999. 89.00 (*0-89006-408-3*) Artech Hse.

Practical Muse: Pragmatist Poetics in Hulme, Pound, & Stevens. Patricia Rae. LC 97-11896. 320p. 1997. 46.50 (*0-8387-5352-3*) Bucknell U Pr.

Practical Musical Criticism. Oscar Thompson. (Music Reprint Ser.: 1979). 1979. reprint ed. lib. bdg. 29.50 (*0-306-79514-0*) Da Capo.

Practical Musical Instrument Owner's Guide Series, 4 bks. Patrick F. McLaughlin. (Illus.). 40p. (J). (gr. 7 up). 1992. pap. text 5.95 (*1-881158-00-4*); pap. text 5.95 (*1-881158-02-0*); pap. text 5.95 (*1-881158-01-2*); pap. text 5.95 (*1-881158-03-9*) Instrument Pr.

Practical Musical Instrument Owner's Guide Series, 4 bks., Set. Patrick F. McLaughlin. (Illus.). 40p. (J). (gr. 7 up). 1992. pap. text. write for info. (*1-881158-04-7*) Instrument Pr.

Practical Musicianship: A Learning Package in Twenty Stages. Catherine Dale & Shiela McQuattie. 112p. (Orig.). 1992. pap. text 12.95 (*0-85958-499-2*, Pub. by Univ of Hull Pr) Paul & Co Pubs.

Practical Muskrat Raising. E. J. Dailey. (Illus.). 136p. pap. 4.00 (*0-936622-17-2*) A R Harding Pub.

Practical MVS-JCL Examples: An Introduction to MVS-ESA. James G. Janossy. LC 92-28504. 400p. 1993. pap. 54.99 (*0-471-57316-7*) Wiley.

Practical Mystic or How to Make Perfection Appear (1915) Katharine F. Pedrick. 224p. 1998. reprint ed. pap. 17.95 (*0-7661-0573-3*) Kessinger Pub.

Practical Mysticism. Evelyn Underhill. 128p. 1991. pap. 9.99 (*0-86347-036-X*, Pub. by Eagle Bks) Shaw Pubs.

Practical Mysticism. Evelyn Underhill. 192p. 1988. reprint ed. pap. 9.95 (*0-89804-143-0*) Ariel GA.

Practical Mysticism: A Little Book for Normal People (1914) Evelyn Underhill. 160p. 1998. reprint ed. pap. 16.95 (*0-7661-0141-X*) Kessinger Pub.

Practical Mysticism: Business Success & Balanced Living Through Ancient & Modern Spiritual Teachings. David Samuel. LC 99-90376. 208p. 2000. pap. 14.95 (*0-9671384-0-X*, Pub. by Bakshi Pubns) ACCESS Pubs Network.

Practical Nature Cure. 13th ed. K. Lakshmana Sarma. 743p. 1986. 29.95 (*0-318-36368-2*) Asia Bk Corp.

Practical Navigation. John Seller. LC 93-24424. 556p. 1993. reprint ed. 75.00 (*0-8201-1484-7*) Schol Facsimiles.

Practical Navigation for Second Mates. rev. ed. T. G. Jones. (C). 1987. 84.00 (*0-85174-397-8*) St Mut.

Practical Negotiations of Government Contracts: Course Manual. Timothy Sullivan. write for info. (*0-318-61726-9*) Fed Pubns Inc.

Practical Negotiator. I. William Zartman et al. LC 81-40435. 263p. 1983. reprint ed. pap. 18.00 (*0-300-03097-5*, Y-467) Yale U Pr.

Practical Neonatal Respiratory Care. Ed. by Richard L. Schreiner & Jeffrey A. Kisling. LC 81-23482. (Illus.). 481p. 1982. reprint ed. pap. 149.20 (*0-608-00578-9*, 206116500007) Bks Demand.

Practical Network Analysis & Design. James D. McCabe. LC 97-34934. 450p. (C). 1997. text 54.95 (*1-55860-498-7*) Morgan Kaufmann.

***Practical Network Cabling.** 400p. 1999. 29.99 (*0-7897-2247-X*) Que.

***Practical Networking.** 650p. 1999. text 29.99 (*0-7897-2252-6*) Que.

Practical Networking with Fast Ethernet. Kyas. (ITCP-UK Computer Science Ser.). (C). 1997. pap. 39.99 (*1-85032-322-4*) ITCP.

Practical Networking with Token Ring: Improving Network Operations with Dedicated & Base Token Ring. James Carlo et al. (ITCP-US Computer Science Ser.). 350p. 1997. pap. 39.99 (*1-85032-884-6*) ITCP.

Practical Neural Network Recipes in C++ Timothy Masters. (Illus.). 493p. 1993. pap. text 59.00 (*0-12-479040-2*) Acad Pr.

Practical Neuro-Urology: Genitourinary Complications in Neurologic Disease. Michael B. Chancellor & Jerry G. Blaivas. LC 95-2117. 390p. 1995. text 95.00 (*0-7506-9556-0*, Focal) Buttrwrth-Heinemann.

Practical Neuroangiography. Pearse Morris. LC 97-3874. (Illus.). 400p. 1997. 99.00 (*0-683-30020-2*) Lppncott W & W.

Practical Neurology. Jose Biller. LC 97-4327. 752p. 1997. pap. text 59.95 (*0-316-09483-8*) Lppncott W & W.

Practical Neurology of the Elderly. Ed. by Jacob I. Sage & Margery H. Mark. (Neurological Disease & Therapy Ser.: Vol. 41). (Illus.). 1176p. 1996. text 250.00 (*0-8247-9506-7*) Dekker.

Practical Neutron Radiography. Ed. by J. C. Domanus. LC 92-18023. 288p. (C). 1992. text 193.50 (*0-7923-1860-9*) Kluwer Academic.

Practical New Thought: Several Things That Have Helped People. William W. Atkinson. 96p. 1997. reprint ed. pap. 16.95 (*0-7661-0049-9*) Kessinger Pub.

Practical Newspaper Readings. rev. ed. Chen-Ch'Ing Li. (CHI., Illus.). 279p. 1989. 26.95 (*0-318-42726-5*) Yale Far Eastern Pubns.

Practical Newspaper Reporting. 2nd rev. ed. Geoffrey T. Harris et al. 360p. 1993. pap. 36.95 (*0-7506-0030-6*) Buttrwrth-Heinemann.

Practical Newspaper Reporting. 3rd ed. Geoffrey Harris & David Spark. LC 97-214939. 360p. 1997. pap. 36.95 (*0-240-51511-0*, Focal) Buttrwrth-Heinemann.

Practical NIR Spectroscopy: With Applications in Food & Beverage Analysis. 2nd rev. ed. B. G. Osborne et al. LC 92-36734. Orig. Title: Near Infrared Spectroscopy in Food Analysis. 1993. 144.15 (*0-582-09946-3*) Longman.

Practical NLP for Managers. Ian McDermott & Joseph O'Connor. 200p. 1996. 61.95 (*0-566-07671-3*, Pub. by Gower) Ashgate Pub Co.

Practical NMR Imaging. Ed. by M. A. Foster & J. M. Hutchinson. 328p. 1987. 72.00 (*1-85221-011-7*) OUP.

Practical NMR Spectroscopy. Maryvonne L. Martin et al. LC QD0096.N8M37. 492p. reprint ed. pap. 152.60 (*0-608-12455-9*, 202520200042) Bks Demand.

Practical Nomad: How to Travel Around the World. Edward Hasbrouck. LC 97-208361. (Illus.). 580p. 1997. pap. 17.95 (*1-56691-076-5*, Moon Handbks) Avalon Travel.

***Practical Nomad: How to Travel Around the World.** 2nd rev. ed. Edward Hasbrouck. (Illus.). 580p. 2000. pap. 19.95 (*1-56691-214-8*, Pub. by Avalon Travel) Publishers Group.

Practical Nonparametric & Semiparametric Bayesian Statistics, Vol. 133. Dipak Dey et al. LC 98-16460. (Lecture Notes in Statistics). 1998. pap. 49.95 (*0-387-98517-4*) Spr-Verlag.

Practical Nonparametric Statistics. 3rd ed. W. J. Conover. LC 98-8521. 584p. 1998. text 100.95 (*0-471-16068-7*) Wiley.

Practical Nuclear Medicine. Edwin L. Palmer et al. (Illus.). 409p. 1992. text 94.00 (*0-7216-7030-X*, W B Saunders Co) Harcrt Hlth Sci Grp.

Practical Nuclear Medicine. 2nd ed. P. F. Sharp. (Illus.). 362p. 1998. text (*0-19-262842-9*) OUP.

Practical Nuclear Medicine. 2nd ed. Ed. by Peter F. Sharp et al. LC 97-34661. (Illus.). 362p. 1998. pap. text 59.50 (*0-19-262841-0*) OUP.

Practical Nuclear Power Plant Technology, 2 vols. Robert W. Deutsch et al. (Illus.). 1973. ring bd. 175.00 (*0-87683-295-8*) GP Courseware.

Practical Numerical Algorithms for Chaotic Systems. T. S. Parker & L. O. Chua. (Illus.). xiv, 348p. 1991. reprint ed. 60.95 (*0-387-96689-7*) Spr-Verlag.

Practical Numerical Analysis. Gwynne A. Evans. 470p. 1996. text 175.00 (*0-471-95535-3*) Wiley.

Practical Nurse. Jack Rudman. (Career Examination Ser.: C-642). 1994. pap. 27.95 (*0-8373-0642-6*) Nat Learn.

Practical Nursing. 14th ed. M. Clark. (Illus.). 416p. 1991. pap. text 19.95 (*0-7020-1411-7*) Bailliere Tindall.

Practical Nymph Fishing. Dan Wright. (Illus.). 224p. 1998. 24.95 (*0-07-072100-9*) McGraw.

Practical Object-Oriented Design. Mark Priestley. LC 96-8873. 1996. write for info. (*0-07-709176-0*) McGraw.

Practical Object-Oriented Design. Mark Priestley. (Illus.). 350p. 1996. pap., pap. text 45.00 incl. disk (*0-07-913018-6*) McGraw.

Practical Object-Oriented Development in C++ & Java. Cay S. Horstmann. LC 97-1736. 576p. 1997. pap. 39.99 (*0-471-14767-2*) Wiley.

Practical Obstetric Anesthesia. David M. Dewan. Ed. by David D. Hood & Lesley Day. 320p. 1996. text 58.00 (*0-7216-3658-6*, W B Saunders Co) Harcrt Hlth Sci Grp.

Practical Obstetrics & Gynecology. Bikash C. Basu. (C). 1983. 150.00 (*0-89771-340-0*, Pub. by Current Dist) St Mut.

Practical Obstetrics & Gynecology. 2nd ed. Bikash C. Basu. (C). 1982. 75.00 (*0-7855-6114-5*, Pub. by Current Dist) St Mut.

Practical Obstetrics & Gynecology. 3rd ed. Bikash C. Basu. 1982. 59.00 (*0-7855-0824-4*, Pub. by Current Dist) St Mut.

Practical Obstetrics & Gynecology: Manual of Selected Procedures & Treatments. Vaclav Insler & Roy Homburg. (Illus.). 1979. 71.50 (*3-8055-2945-7*) S Karger.

Practical Occultism. Ernest Loomis. 73p. 1996. reprint ed. spiral bd. 10.00 (*0-7873-0569-3*) Hlth Research.

Practical Occultism. 3rd ed. Helena P. Blavatsky. 1989. 4.95 (*81-7059-076-0*, Pub. by Theos Pub Hse) Natl Bk Netwk.

Practical Occultism: From the Private Letters of William Q. Judge. William Q. Judge. LC 78-63320. 314p. 1979. reprint ed. 20.95 (*0-911500-29-4*); reprint ed. pap. 13.95 (*0-911500-30-8*) Theos U Pr.

Practical Occupational Medicine. Anthony Seaton et al. 288p. 1994. pap. text 42.50 (*0-340-55936-5*, Pub. by E A) OUP.

Practical Odyssey. 2nd ed. Johnson. (Mathematics Ser.). 1995. pap., teacher ed. 26.50 (*0-534-94376-4*) Brooks-Cole.

***Practical Office Procedures.** Oja Parsons. (New Perspectives Ser.). (C). 2000. text 40.95 (*0-619-01919-0*) Course Tech.

Practical Oil-Field Metallurgy & Corrosion. 2nd ed. Bruce D. Craig. LC 92-33961. 270p. 1993. 35.00 (*0-87814-388-2*) PennWell Bks.

Practical On-the-Job Training. Didactic Systems Staff. (Study Units Ser.). 1977. pap. 9.00 (*0-89401-114-6*) Didactic Syst.

Practical Oncology. Robert B. Cameron. (Illus.). 720p. (C). 1995. pap. text 34.95 (*0-8385-1326-3*, A1326-6, Apple Lange Med) McGraw.

Practical Open Systems for the 1990s: An Essential Guide for IS Managers. Michaela Howard & Russell Meredith. 416p. (C). 1991. 995.00 (*1-85271-178-7*, Pub. by IBC Tech Srvs) St Mut.

Practical Opening Tips. Edmar Mednis. 144p. 1997. pap. text 19.95 (*1-85744-186-9*, Pub. by Cadgn Bks) Macmillan.

Practical Operations & Management of a Bank. 2nd ed. Marshall C. Corns. LC 68-17247. (Illus.). 979p. reprint ed. pap. 200.00 (*0-608-18753-4*, 205222700065) Bks Demand.

Practical Ophthalmic Lenses. Mohammed Jalie & Len Wray. (C). 1989. 175.00 (*0-900099-25-9*, Pub. by Assn Brit Dispen Opticians) St Mut.

Practical Ophthalmic Microsurgery. A. Lim Siew Ming. (Illus.). 1980. 34.00 (*3-8055-3036-6*) S Karger.

Practical Ophthalmic Problems for Allied Health Professionals. Wayne F. March. (Allied Health Professions Monograph). 148p. 1984. pap. 12.50 (*0-87527-329-7*) Green.

Practical Ophthalmology: A Manual for Beginning Residents. 4th ed. Fred M. Wilson & Judith E. Gurland. LC 96-41408. 1996. pap. write for info. (*1-56055-034-1*) Am Acad Ophthal.

Practical Optics see Optics & Optical Instruments

Practical Optics. William P. Ewald et al. Ed. by Richard H. Roberts. (Illus.). 280p. (C). 1983. pap. text 56.00 (*0-911705-00-7*) Image Makers.

Practical Optics. Ernest Zebrowski, Jr. (Illus.). 30p. (Orig.). (C). 1982. pap. text 2.95 (*0-943908-00-0*) ITEC.

Practical Optimization. Margaret H. Wright. LC 81-66366. 1982. pap. text 63.00 (*0-12-283952-8*) Acad Pr.

Practical Optimization Methods with Mathematics Applications. M. A. Bhatti. (Illus.). 592p. 1999. 64.95 incl. cd-rom (*0-387-98631-6*) Spr-Verlag.

Practical Oral Surgery. 3rd ed. Henry B. Clark. LC 65-19426. 503p. reprint ed. pap. 156.00 (*0-608-13438-4*, 201453400094) Bks Demand.

Practical Organic Chemistry. Mann. 1979. pap. 34.95 (*0-582-44407-1*, Pub. by Addison-Wesley) Longman.

Practical Organic Mass Spectrometry. Chapman. text. write for info. (*0-471-48981-6*); pap. text. write for info. (*0-471-48982-4*) Wiley.

Practical Organic Mass Spectrometry: A Guide for Chemical & Biochemical Analysis. J. R. Chapman. LC 93-9129. 352p. 1995. pap. 74.95 (*0-471-95831-X*) Wiley.

***Practical Orthodontic Assessment.** Stephens. 1999. cd-rom 175.00 (*0-7236-1075-4*) Buttrwrth-Heinemann.

Practical Orthodontic Assessment. C. D. Stephens & K. G. Isaacson. 144p. 1990. 65.00 (*0-7236-1064-9*) Buttrwrth-Heinemann.

Practical Orthodontic Assessment. C. D. Stephens & K. G. Isaacson. 144p. 1997. reprint ed. pap. text 65.00 (*0-7236-0251-4*, RK522, Pub. by John Wright) Buttrwrth-Heinemann.

Practical Orthopedic Medicine. Brian Corrigan & G. D. Maitland. 432p. 1985. pap. text 70.00 (*0-7506-0494-8*) Buttrwrth-Heinemann.

Practical Orthopedics. 4th ed. Lonnie R. Mercier. LC 95-12842. (Illus.). 528p. (C). (gr. 13). 1995. pap. text 74.95 (*0-8151-5903-X*, 24430) Mosby Inc.

Practical Orthopedics. 5th ed. Lonnie R. Mercier. (Illus.). 560p. Date not set. pap. text. write for info. (*0-323-00827-5*) Mosby Inc.

Practical Oscillator Handbook. Irving Gottlieb. LC 97-190255. (Illus.). 292p. 1997. pap. text 42.95 (*0-7506-3102-3*) Buttrwrth-Heinemann.

Practical Oscilloscope Handbook. John Douglas-Young. (Illus.). 1979. 14.95 (*0-13-693549-4*, Parker Publishing Co) P-H.

Practical Otology. Daniel J. Pender. (Illus.). 348p. 1992. text 45.00 (*0-397-51016-0*) Lppncott W & W.

Practical Outdoor Survival: A Modern Approach. Len McDougall. (Illus.). 148p. 1993. pap. 11.95 (*1-55821-228-0*) Lyons Pr.

Practical Paediatric Haematology: A Laboratory Worker's Guide to Blood Disorders in Children. Ed. by John S. Lilleyman & R. F. Hinchliffe. LC 86-32497. (Wiley Medical Publication). 422p. 1987. reprint ed. pap. 130.90 (*0-608-01639-X*, 206222400002) Bks Demand.

Practical Paediatrics. 2nd ed. Ed. by M. J. Robinson. (Illus.). 668p. 1990. pap. text 52.00 (*0-443-04053-2*) Church.

Practical Paediatrics. 4th ed. M. J. Robinson & D. M. Roberton. LC 97-42805. 1998. text 70.00 (*0-443-05893-8*) Church.

Practical Paganism. Anthony Kemp & J. M. Sertori. (Illus.). 192p. 1999. 24.95 (*0-7090-5787-3*, Pub. by R Hale Ltd) Seven Hills Bk.

Practical Pain Management: A Guide for Practitioners. S. W. Coniam & A. W. Diamond. (Illus.). 116p. 1995. text 65.00 (*0-19-262405-9*); pap. text 29.95 (*0-19-262404-0*) OUP.

Practical Paleontologist. Steve Parker. Ed. by Raymond L. Bernor. (Illus.). 160p. 1991. per. 15.00 (*0-671-69307-7*, Fireside) S&S Trade Pap.

Practical Palmistry. Comte C. De Saint-Germain. 273p. 1996. reprint ed. spiral bd. 18.00 (*0-7873-0266-X*) Hlth Research.

Practical Parallel Computing: Status & Prospects. fac. ed. Ed. by Paul C. Messina & Almerico Murli. LC 91-44139. 253p. 1991. reprint ed. pap. 78.50 (*0-7837-8279-9*, 204906000009) Bks Demand.

Practical Parallel Programming. Gregory V. Wilson. LC 95-9800. (Scientific & Engineering Computation Ser.). (Illus.). 600p. (C). 1995. 55.00 (*0-262-23186-7*) MIT Pr.

Practical Parenting: A Jewish Perspective. Gail J. Lipsitz. LC 96-40372. 1997. 29.50 (*0-88125-538-6*); pap. 17.95 (*0-88125-536-X*) Ktav.

Practical Parenting: Successful Strategies for Solving Your Child's Behavior Problems. Glen Stenhouse. (Illus.). 170p. 1996. pap. text 21.95 (*0-19-558333-7*) OUP.

Practical Parenting: 1-5 Years, Child & Youth Health, SA. Ed. by Pam Linke. 1996. 75.00 (*0-86431-199-0*, Pub. by Aust Council Educ Res); teacher ed. 110.00 (*0-86431-198-2*, Pub. by Aust Council Educ Res) St Mut.

Practical Parenting for the 21st Century: The Manual You Wish Had Come with Your Child. Julie A. Ross. LC 92-55103. 160p. (Orig.). 1993. pap. 10.95 (*0-9627226-6-9*) Excalibur Pub.

Practical Parenting Tips. enl. rev. ed. Vicki Lansky. LC 92-17149. (Illus.). 192p. 1992. pap. 8.00 (*0-88166-192-9*) Meadowbrook.

Practical Parenting Tips for the First Five Years. rev. ed. Vicki Lansky. LC 92-17149. (Illus.). 192p. 1992. 8.00 (*0-671-79205-9*) S&S Trade.

Practical Parent's Handbook on Teaching Children with Learning Disabilities. Shelby Holley. (Illus.). 308p. 1994. pap. 41.95 (*0-398-06150-5*) C C Thomas.

Practical Parent's Handbook on Teaching Children with Learning Disabilities. Shelby Holley. (Illus.). 308p. (C). 1994. text 65.95 (*0-398-05903-9*) C C Thomas.

Practical Pathology & Microbiology. 11th ed. Ed. by N. C. Dey. (C). 1982. 55.00 (*0-7855-4662-6*, Pub. by Current Dist) St Mut.

Practical Patience. Marc Royer. 99p. 1999. pap. 8.95 (*0-7392-0083-6*, P02950) Morris Pubng.

Practical PC-2-PC-1500 Pocket Computer Programs. Jim Cole. 96p. 1983. 7.95 (*0-86668-028-4*) ARCsoft.

Practical Peacemaking: A Mediator's Handbook. Mark Anstey. 178p. 1993. pap. 24.00 (*0-7021-2966-6*, Pub. by Juta & Co) Intl Spec Bk.

Practical Peacemaking in the Middle East Vol. 1: Arms Control & Regional Security. David J. Pervin & Steven L. Spiegel. LC 94-40942. 262p. 1995. text 15.00 (*0-8153-1999-1*, SS1026) Garland.

Practical Peacemaking in the Middle East Vol. II: The Environment, Water, Refugees, & Economic Cooperation & Development. Ed. by Steven L. Spiegel & David J. Pervin. LC 94-40942. (Illus.). 434p. 1995. text 25.00 (*0-8153-2000-0*) Garland.

Practical Pedagogy for the Jewish Classroom: Classroom Management, Instruction & Curriculum Development. Daniel B. Kohn. LC 98-29676. (Greenwood Educators' Reference Collection). 224p. 1999. lib. bdg. 49.95 (*0-313-30931-0*, Greenwood Pr) Greenwood.

Practical Pediatric & Adolescent Gynecology. John Dewhurst. LC 80-24015. (Reproductive Medicine Ser.: Vol. 1). (Illus.). 288p. reprint ed. pap. 89.30 (*0-608-08928-1*, 206956300005) Bks Demand.

Practical Pediatric Dermatology. William L. Weston. 1985. 78.00 (*0-316-93167-5*, Little Brwn Med Div) Lppncott W & W.

Practical Pediatric Gastroenterology. 2nd ed. J. A. Walker-Smith. LC 97-8965. 313p. 1996. 49.95 (*1-55009-025-9*) DEKR.

Practical Pediatric Imaging. Donald Kirks. 811p. 1984. 125.00 (*0-316-49471-2*, Little Brwn Med Div) Lppncott W & W.

Practical Pediatric Imaging: Diagnostic Radiology of Infants & Children. 3rd ed. Ed. by Donald R. Kirks. LC 97-18901. 1100p. 1997. text 225.00 (*0-316-49473-9*) Lppncott W & W.

Practical Pediatric Oncology. write for info. (*0-340-50632-6*, Pub. by E A) Routldge.

Practical Pediatric Oncology. Ed. by Giulio J. D'Angio et al. 320p. 1992. 145.00 (*0-471-58835-0*) Wiley.

Practical Pediatric Ophthalmology. David Conrad Taylor & Creig S. Hoyt. LC 96-18413. (Illus.). 800p. (Orig.). 1996. pap. text 65.00 (*0-86542-720-8*) Blackwell Sci.

Practical Pediatric Ophthalmology: A Clinical Guide. Gallin. (Illus.). 350p. 2000. 99.00 (*0-86577-768-3*) Thieme Med Pubs.

Practical Pediatric Otolaryngology. Ed. by Robin T. Cotton & Charles M. Myer, 3rd. LC 98-17722. (Illus.). 900p. 1998. text 245.00 (*0-397-51720-3*) Lppncott W & W.

Practical Pediatric Radiology. 2nd ed. Ed. by Saskien von Waldenburg Hilton & David K. Edwards. LC 93-39227. 1994. text 150.00 (*0-7216-3553-9*, W B Saunders Co) Harcrt Hlth Sci Grp.

Practical Pediatric Therapy. Heinz F. Eichenwald & J. Stoder. 1190p. 1985. lib. bdg. 64.95 (*0-89573-323-4*, Wiley-VCH) Wiley.

Practical Pediatric Therapy. Heinz F. Eichenwald & Josef Stroder. 1985. 64.95 (*0-8016-1543-7*) Mosby Inc.

Practical Pediatrician: The A to Z Guide to Your Child's Health, Behavior, & Safety. Howard Markel & Frank A. Oski. (Illus.). 350p. 1996. pap. text 16.95 (*0-7167-2896-6*) W H Freeman.

Practical Pediatrics. 3rd ed. Robinson. 1994. pap. text 66.00 (*0-443-04869-X*, W B Saunders Co) Harcrt Hlth Sci Grp.

Practical Pediatrics in Less-Developed Countries. Karen Olness. 1980. pap. 9.95 (*0-9602790-2-4*) Hlth Frontiers.

Practical Pedology. Stuart G. McRae. 300p. 1988. text 52.95 (*0-470-21062-1*) P-H.

Practical Pendulum Book. D. Jurriaanse. LC 85-45051. (Illus.). 96p. 1986. pap. 6.95 (*0-87728-517-9*) Weiser.

Practical Pentatonics: An Introduction to Pentatonic Patterns, Theory, & Usage. Askold Buk. 1996. pap. 5.95 (*0-8256-1495-3*, AM931326) Music Sales.

Practical Performance Analyst: Performance-by-Design Techniques for Distributed Systems. Neil J. Gunther. LC 97-27470. (Illus.). 416p. 1998. text 74.00 incl. disk (*0-07-912946-3*) McGraw.

Practical Performance Appraisal. V. Stewart & A. Stewart. 182p. 1978. text 61.95 (*0-566-02081-5*, Pub. by Gower) Ashgate Pub Co.

Practical Perinatal Care: The Baby under 1000 Grams. Harvey. 375p. 1999. text 165.00 (*0-7506-1717-9*) Buttrwrth-Heinemann.

Practical Petroleum Engineers' Handbook. 5th ed. Joseph Zaba & W. T. Doherty. LC 58-12306. (Illus.). 961p. 1970. reprint ed. pap. 200.00 (*0-608-07290-7*, 206751800009) Bks Demand.

Practical Petroleum Geology. Jeff Morris et al. Ed. by Jodie Leecraft. (Illus.). 234p. (Orig.). 1985. pap. text 35.00 (*0-88698-097-6*, 1.00210) PETEX.

Practical Petroleum Tables for Ship Use. J. A. Janssens. (C). 1987. 84.00 (*0-85174-103-7*) St Mut.

Practical Pharmaceutical Chemistry, Vol. 1, Part I. 4th rev. ed. A. H. Beckett & J. B. Stenlake. LC 87-14470. 382p. (C). 1988. text 55.00 (*0-485-11322-8*, Pub. by Athlone Pr) Humanities.

Practical Pharmaceutical Chemistry, Vol. 2, Part II. 4th rev. ed. A. H. Beckett & J. B. Stenlake. LC 87-14470. 560p. (C). 1988. text 75.00 (*0-485-11323-6*, Pub. by Athlone Pr) Humanities.

Practical Pharmacology in Dentistry. Geza Terezhalmy & Les Felpel. 352p. 39.95 (*0-683-30570-0*) Lppncott W & W.

Practical Phased-Array Antenna Systems. Ed. by Eli Brookner. (Antenna Library). 258p. 1991. text. write for info. (*0-89006-563-2*) Artech Hse.

Practical Philosophy. R. L. Dabney. 1992. 23.99 (*0-87377-980-0*) GAM Pubns.

Practical Philosophy. Immanuel Kant. Ed. by Mary J. Gregor. (Edition of the Works of Immanuel Kant in Translation). 668p. (C). 1999. pap. text 27.95 (*0-521-65408-4*) Cambridge U Pr.

Practical Philosophy: Practical Theory. Immanuel Kant. Ed. by Mary J. Gregor. (The Cambridge Edition of the Works of Immanuel Kant). 704p. (C). 1996. text 85.00 (*0-521-37103-1*) Cambridge U Pr.

Practical Philosophy & Action Theory. Ed. by Timo Airaksinen & Wojciech W. Gasparski. LC 92-34585. (Praxiology: the International Annual of Practical Philosophy & Methodology Ser.: Vol. 2). 319p. (C). 1993. text 49.95 (*1-56000-094-5*) Transaction Pubs.

Practical Philosophy for the Life Sciences. Wim J. Van der Steen. LC 92-27319. (SUNY Series in Philosophy & Biology). 208p. (C). 1993. text 59.50 (*0-7914-1615-1*); pap. text 19.95 (*0-7914-1616-X*) State U NY Pr.

Practical Philosophy of Oswald Schwemmer. Patrick Riordan. 128p. (Orig.). (C). 1991. pap. text 19.50 (*0-8191-8181-1*); lib. bdg. 44.00 (*0-8191-8180-3*) U Pr of Amer.

Practical Philosophy of Sport. R. Scott Kretchmar. LC 93-27142. 304p. 1994. text 39.00 (*0-87322-619-4*, BKRE0619) Human Kinetics.

Practical Phonetics for Students of African Languages. D. Westermann & Ida C. Ward. (Published in Association with the International Frican Institute Ser.). 169p. 1988. pap. 15.95 (*0-7103-0295-9*) Routledge.

Practical Photojournalism: A Professional Guide. 2nd ed. Martin Keene. (Illus.). 264p. 1995. pap. text 42.95 (*0-240-51432-7*, Focal) Buttrwrth-Heinemann.

Practical Photovoltaics: Electricity from Solar Cells. 3rd ed. Richard J. Komp. LC 95-22580. (Illus.). 216p. 1995. pap. 18.95 (*0-937948-11-X*) aatec Pubns.

Practical Physical Chemistry. 3rd ed. Arthur M. James & F. Elizabeth Prichard. LC 73-85687. 358p. reprint ed. pap. 111.00 (*0-608-13211-X*, 202525400043) Bks Demand.

Practical Physical Geology: Problems & Solutions. John A. Ciciarelli. x, 264p. 1986. text 195.00 (*2-88124-098-4*); pap. text 75.00 (*2-88124-065-8*) Gordon & Breach.

Practical Physics. 3rd ed. G. L. Squires. 227p. 1985. pap. text 34.95 (*0-521-27095-2*) Cambridge U Pr.

Practical Physics: How Things Work. David Lazarus & Manfred Raether. (Illus.). 1984. pap. text 15.80 (*0-87563-167-3*) Stipes.

Practical Physics Dictionary: Dictionnaire Pratique de Physique. R. Ferry. (FRE.). 280p. 1981. 29.95 (*0-8288-2235-2*, M15602) Fr & Eur.

Practical Physiotherapy with Older People. Lucinda Smyth et al. Ed. by Jo Campling. (Therapy in Practice Ser.: No. 14). 160p. 1990. pap. 23.00 (*0-412-33580-8*, A4448) Chapman & Hall.

Practical Piano Skills. 5th ed. Constance Starr & William J. Starr. 208p. (C). 1991. text. write for info. (*0-697-10437-0*) Brown & Benchmark.

***Practical Picture Restoration.** Peter Oldale. (Illus.). 160p. 2000. pap. 35.00 (*1-86126-239-6*, Pub. by Crolwood) Trafalgar.

Practical Pigeon Shooting. Peter Hall. (Illus.). 112p. 1996. 29.95 (*1-85223-864-X*, Pub. by Crolwood) Trafalgar.

Practical Pilot: Coastal Navigation by Eye, Intuition, & Common Sense. Leonard A. Eyges. 244p. 1989. pap. 22.95 (*0-07-157274-0*) McGraw.

Practical Pilot: Coastal Navigation by Eye, Intuition, Common Sense, & Cunning. Leonard A. Eyges. (Illus.). 192p. 1989. pap. text 22.95 (*0-87742-969-3*) Intl Marine.

Practical Pistol Manual: How to Use a Handgun for Self Defense. Bill Clede. LC 98-226176. (Illus.). 176p. 1998. pap. 7.95 (*0-915463-74-1*) Jameson Bks.

Practical Placer Mining. Ed. by L. Cope & L. Rice. LC 91-66951. (Illus.). 112p. (Orig.). 1992. pap. 47.00 (*0-87335-105-3*, 105-3) SMM&E Inc.

Practical Planning: A How-To Guide for Solos & Small Law Firms. Henry W. Ewalt. 113p. 1985. 36.95 (*0-89707-196-4*, 511-0098) Amer Bar Assn.

Practical Planning: Extending the Classical AI Planning Paradigm. David E. Wilkins. (Representation & Reasoning Ser.). 205p. (C). 1988. text 44.95 (*0-934613-94-X*) Morgan Kaufmann.

Practical Plant Physiology. A. Adharyya & G. Gupta. (C). 1989. 50.00 (*0-89771-416-4*, Pub. by Current Dist) St Mut.

Practical Plant Physiology. J. Roberts & D. G. Whitehouse. LC 75-46566. 171p. reprint ed. pap. 53.10 (*0-608-13081-8*, 202521300043) Bks Demand.

Practical Plant Virology: Protocols & Exercises. Jeanne Dijkstra & C. P. De Jager. LC 98-5845. (Illus.). 350p. 1998. pap. text 69.95 (*3-540-63759-1*) Spr-Verlag.

Practical Plants. Joyce Pope. (Plant Life Ser.). 64p. (YA). 1990. 15.95 (*0-8160-2424-3*) Facts on File.

Practical Plays. Pamela Marx. (Illus.). 128p. (Orig.). (J). (gr. 1-5). 1993. pap. 9.95 (*0-673-36049-0*, GoodYrBooks) Addson-Wesley Educ.

Practical Playwriting. David Copelin. LC 98-36275. 204p. 1998. pap. 12.95 (*0-87116-185-0*) Writer.

Practical Plumbing Engineering. rev. ed. Ed. by Cyril M. Harris. (Illus.). 504p. 1998. 79.95 (*1-891255-04-5*) Am Soc Plumb Eng.

Practical Pneumatics. 1997. pap. text 23.95 (*0-340-66219-0*, Pub. by E A) Routldge.

Practical Poetry: A Guide for Poets. rev. ed. Laverne Frith & Carol Frith. 60p. 1998. pap. 8.00 (*0-9648232-4-1*) Frith Pr.

Practical Poetry Coarse. Alison Chisholm. 144p. 1995. pap. 9.95 (*0-7490-0114-3*) Allison & Busby.

Practical Pointers for Training Your Child. Lloy A. Kniss. 1975. pap. 3.50 (*0-87813-509-X*) Christian Light.

Practical Pointers to Personal Prayer. Carrol J. Shewmake. 128p. 1989. pap. 7.99 (*0-8280-0486-2*) Review & Herald.

Practical Points Concerning Blending. Witness Lee. 47p. 1994. pap. 4.25 (*0-87083-783-4*, 08-040-001) Living Stream Ministry.

PRACTICAL POINTS CONCERNING THE BLENDING see Puntos Practicos en Cuanto a la Compenetracion

Practical Pole Building Construction: With Plans for Barns, Cabins, & Outbuildings. Leigh Seddon. Ed. by Susan Williamson. LC 85-9248. (Illus.). 186p. 1985. pap. 10.95 (*0-913589-16-0*) Williamson Pub Co.

Practical Polish-English Dictionary. J. Stanislawski & M. Szercha. 1036p. (C). 1986. 95.00 (*0-7855-6681-3*, Pub. by Collets) St Mut.

Practical Polish-English Dictionary. J. Stanislawski et al. (ENG & POL.). 1036p. 1981. 35.00 (*0-8288-0480-X*, M 7670) Fr & Eur.

Practical Polish-German Dictionary: Podreczny Slownik Polsko-Niemiecki. J. Chodera. (GER & POL.). 1018p. 1984. 39.95 (*0-8288-0483-4*, F46690) Fr & Eur.

Practical Politics: Five Principles for a Community That Works. Michael K. Briand. LC 98-58010. 320p. 1999. 44.95 (*0-252-02460-5*); pap. text 15.95 (*0-252-06766-5*) U of Ill Pr.

Practical Politics: Social Work & Political Responsibility. Ed. by Maryann Mahaffey & John W. Hanks. LC 82-80273. 260p. (C). 1982. 23.95 (*0-87101-099-2*) Natl Assn Soc Wkrs.

Practical Politics: Twentieth-Century Views on Politics & Economics. George Bernard Shaw. Ed. by Lloyd J. Hubenka. LC 75-3571. 294p. reprint ed. pap. 91.20 (*0-7837-1826-8*, 204202600001) Bks Demand.

Practical Polymer Analysis. T. R. Crompton. (Illus.). 842p. (C). 1993. text 195.00 (*0-306-44524-7*, Kluwer Plenum) Kluwer Academic.

Practical Polymer Analysis. John Scheirs. LC 99-56526. 2000. pap. text. write for info. (*0-471-62572-8*) Wiley.

Practical Polyphenolics: From Structure to Molecular Recognition & Physiological Action. Edwin Haslam. LC 97-8686. (Illus.). 438p. (C). 1998. text 100.00 (*0-521-46513-3*) Cambridge U Pr.

Practical Portfolios: Reading, Writing, Math, & Life Skills, Grades 3-6. Susan Mundell & Karen DeLario. (Illus.). vii, 149p. 1994. pap. text 22.00 (*1-56308-197-0*) Teacher Ideas Pr.

Practical Portrait Painting. Slater. (Illus.). 236p. pap. 7.95 (*0-486-26133-6*) Dover.

Practical Poultry Keeping. David Bland. (Illus.). 160p. 1996. 29.95 (*1-86126-010-5*, Pub. by Crolwood) Trafalgar.

Practical PR for School Library Media Centers. Marian S. Edsall. LC 83-4086. 178p. 1984. 27.95 (*0-918212-77-4*) Neal-Schuman.

Practical Practice of Marriage & Family Therapy: Things My Training Supervisor Never Told Me. Mark Odell & Charles E. Campbell. LC 97-19857. 276p. (C). 1997. 49.95 (*0-7890-0063-6*); pap. 24.95 (*0-7890-0431-3*) Haworth Pr.

***Practical PRAM Programming.** Joerg Keller et al. 400p. 2000. 99.95 (*0-471-35351-5*) Wiley.

Practical Prayer. Derek Prime. Date not set. 6.99 (*1-871676-51-7*, Pub. by Christian Focus) Spring Arbor Dist.

***Practical Prayers for Generational & Family Deliverance & Restoration.** large type ed. Uwem Inyang. Ed. by Benita Gilliard. (Spiritual Warfare Prayer Ser.: Vol. 4). 25p. 1999. spiral bd. 10.00 (*1-929623-03-8*) Jesus Recon Min.

Practical Prayers for Practically Everything. Jay Steele. LC 97-38006. (Illus.). 96p. 1997. pap. 5.95 (*0-7611-0398-8*) Workman Pub.

Practical Praying. Linette Martin. LC 96-49760. (Illus.). 128p. 1997. pap. 10.00 (*0-8028-4233-X*) Eerdmans.

Practical Preacher: Handy Hints for Hesitant Homilists. Paul Edwards. 176p. (Orig.). 1994. pap. 11.95 (*0-8146-2334-4*, Liturg Pr Bks) Liturgical Pr.

Practical Prescribing. Ed. by Martin J. Brodie & P. Ian Harrison. LC 85-20926. (Illus.). 295p. 1986. text 51.00 (*0-443-03304-8*) Church.

Practical Primary Drama. Geoff Davies. 63p. (C). 1983. pap. text 17.50 (*0-435-18236-6*) Heinemann.

Practical Primer for Developing a Business German Program. Maria Egbert & Andrea Vlatten. (Illus.). 127p. 1997. pap. 23.00 (*0-942017-55-2*, 04-64358) Amer Assn Teach German.

Practical Principles for Everyday Management: A Practical, Sound, Easy-to-Use Primer on Effective Management & Leadership. Westinghouse Electric Corp. Staff. 96p. 1996. pap. 14.95 (*1-880470-39-X*) Creative Des.

Practical Principles for Public Speaking. Vitall. (C). 1997. pap. text 18.25 (*0-07-066683-0*) McGraw.

Practical Principles of Cytopathology. Richard M. DeMay. LC 98-32155. 1999. 150.00 (*0-89189-437-3*) Am Soc Clinical.

Practical Principles of Ion-Exchange Water Treatment. 2nd rev. ed. Dean L. Owens. LC 85-51869. 210p. 1995. 55.00 (*0-927188-00-7*) Tall Oaks Pub.

Practical Print Making. P. Quarto. 160p. 1996. 15.98 (*0-7858-0655-5*) Bk Sales Inc.

Practical Privacy Strategies for Windows 95 see Practical Privacy Strategies for Windows 95/98

***Practical Privacy Strategies for Windows 95/98.** 2nd ed. Mark Nestmann. Orig. Title: Practical Privacy Strategies for Windows 95. 45p. 2000. spiral bd. 25.00 (*1-891266-17-9*, Pub. by Asset Protection Intl) Pathway Bk Serv.

Practical Problem Solver: Substitutes, Shortcuts & Ingenious Solutions to Make Life Easier. Digest Readers Staff. 1997. pap. text 16.95 (*0-89577-935-8*, Pub. by RD Assn) Penguin Putnam.

***Practical Problem Solving in HPLC.** Stavros Kromidas. 194p. 2000. 54.95 (*3-527-29842-8*) Wiley.

Practical Problems for Math for Carpenters. Harry Huth. 32p. (C). 1995. pap., teacher ed. 12.00 (*0-8273-6988-3*) Delmar.

Practical Problems in Banking & Currency. Ed. by Walter Hull & Stuart Bruchey. LC 80-1151. (Rise of Commercial Banking Ser.). 1981. reprint ed. lib. bdg. 60.95 (*0-405-13656-0*) Ayer.

Practical Problems in Clinical Psychiatry. Ed. by Keith E. Hawton & Philip Cowen. LC 92-49369. (Illus.). 272p. (C). 1993. 34.50 (*0-19-262333-8*); text 65.00 (*0-19-262334-6*) OUP.

Practical Problems in Dermatology. Ronald Marks. 264p. 1996. pap. write for info. (*1-85317-050-X*) Martin Dunitz.

Practical Problems in Exploration Geochemistry. A. A. Levinson et al. LC 86-72694. (Illus.). 269p. 1987. 80.00 (*0-915834-05-7*) Applied Pub.

Practical Problems in Financial Management. Baber et al. 160p. (C). 1997. spiral bd. 17.95 (*0-7872-4279-9*, 41427901) Kendall-Hunt.

Practical Problems in Math: Machinists. 3rd ed. Edward G. Hoffman. (Business/Vocational Math Ser.). 1986. pap., teacher ed. 14.00 (*0-8273-2560-6*) Delmar.

Practical Problems in Math for Welders. 4th ed. Frank R. Schell & Bill J. Matlock. LC 95-12431. 256p. (C). 1995. mass mkt. 21.95 (*0-8273-6706-6*) Delmar.

Practical Problems in Mathematics for Auto Technologies. 5th ed. George Moore. LC 97-11280. 256p. (C). 1997. pap. 19.95 (*0-8273-7944-7*) Delmar.

Practical Problems in Mathematics for Auto Technologies. 5th ed. George Moore. (C). 1998. pap. text, teacher ed. 12.00 (*0-8273-7945-5*) Delmar.

Practical Problems in Mathematics for Automotive Technicians Instructors Guide. 4th ed. George Moore. 1991. teacher ed. 13.00 (*0-8273-4623-9*) Delmar.

Practical Problems in Mathematics for Business & Marketing. Mandava. (C). 1996. pap. text 14.95 (*0-8273-6769-4*); pap. text, teacher ed. 12.00 (*0-8273-6770-8*) Delmar.

Practical Problems in Mathematics for Carpenters. 5th ed. Harry C. Huth. 214p. 1991. pap., teacher ed. 14.00 (*0-8273-4580-1*) Delmar.

Practical Problems in Mathematics for Carpenters. 6th ed. Harry Huth. 224p. 1995. mass mkt. 21.95 (*0-8273-6987-5*) Delmar.

Practical Problems in Mathematics for Drafting & CAD. 2nd ed. John C. Larkin. LC 95-22533. (Business/Vocational Math Ser.). 320p. (C). 1995. mass mkt. 21.95 (*0-8273-4624-7*) Delmar.

Practical Problems in Mathematics for Electricians. 4th ed. Crawford G. Garrard et al. 192p. 1986. pap. 15.95 (*0-8273-2553-3*) Delmar.

Practical Problems in Mathematics for Electricians. 4th ed. Crawford G. Garrard et al. 192p. 1986. teacher ed. 14.00 (*0-8273-2554-1*) Delmar.

Practical Problems in Mathematics for Electricians. 5th ed. Herman. 400p. 1996. 16.00 (*0-8273-6709-0*) Delmar.

Practical Problems in Mathematics for Electricians. 5th ed. Stephen L. Herman & Crawford G. Garrard. LC 95-21874. (Practical Problems in Mathematics Ser.). 256p. 1995. mass mkt. 21.95 (*0-8273-6708-2*) Delmar.

Practical Problems in Mathematics for Electronics Technicians. 2nd ed. Richard Sullivan. LC 90-3060. (Practical Problems in Mathematics Ser.). (Illus.). 212p. (Orig.). 1990. pap. 15.95 (*0-8273-4033-8*) Delmar.

Practical Problems in Mathematics for Electronics Technicians. 2nd ed. Richard Sullivan. (Practical Problems in Mathematics Ser.). (Illus.). 212p. (Orig.). 1991. pap., teacher ed. 14.00 (*0-8273-4034-6*) Delmar.

Practical Problems in Mathematics for Electronics Technicians. 3rd ed. Stephen L. Herman & Richard L. Sullivan. LC 95-3236. (C). 1995. mass mkt. 25.95 (*0-8273-6761-9*) Delmar.

Practical Problems in Mathematics for Health Occupations. Louise M. Simmers. LC 95-15972. 304p. (C). 1995. mass mkt., suppl. ed. 21.95 (*0-8273-6771-6*) Delmar.

Practical Problems in Mathematics for Health Occupations. Louise M. Simmers. 64p. 1996. text, teacher ed. 12.95 (*0-8273-6772-4*) Delmar.

Practical Problems in Mathematics for Heating & Cooling Technicians. 2nd ed. Russell De Vore. (Business Math). 200p. (C). 1991. mass mkt. 14.75 (*0-8273-4062-1*) Delmar.

Practical Problems in Mathematics for Industrial Technology. Donna D. Boatwright. LC 95-37205. (Practical Problems in Mathematics Ser.). 288p. 1996. mass mkt. 25.95 (*0-8273-6974-3*) Delmar.

P

Practical Problems in Mathematics for Manufacturing. 4th ed. Dennis D. Davis. LC 95-5979. (Practical Problems in Mathematics Ser.). (C). 1995. mass mkt. 21.95 (*0-8273-6710-4*) Delmar.

Practical Problems in Mathematics for Masons. 2nd ed. John E. Ball. LC 78-74431. (Mathematics - Construction Ser.). 200p. (C). 1980. teacher ed. 14.00 (*0-8273-1284-9*); pap. text 15.75 (*0-8273-1283-0*) Delmar.

Practical Problems in Mathematics for Mechanical Drafting. J. Larkin. LC 77-78236. (C). 1979. pap. 15.00 (*0-8273-1670-4*) Delmar.

Practical Problems in Mathematics for Welders. 3rd ed. Frank R. Schell & Bill J. Matlock. (Practical Problems in Mathematics Ser.). (Illus.). (Orig.). 1988. pap. 15.00 (*0-8273-3294-7*) Delmar.

Practical Problems in Research Methods: A Casebook with Questions for Discussion. Estabrook D. Verdugo. LC 99-229046. 120p. (C). 1998. pap. text 19.95 (*1-884585-11-6*) Pyrczak Pub.

Practical Problems in Soil Mechanics & Foundation Engineering, 2 vols., 2. G. Sanglerat. (Developments in Geotechnical Engineering Ser.). 254p. 1985. 175.75 (*0-444-42123-8*) Elsevier.

Practical Problems to Accompany College Physics. 5th ed. Serway. (C). 1998. pap. text 12.00 (*0-03-022488-8*) Harcourt Coll Pubs.

Practical Procedures for Children with Language . . . C. Donald Nelson. 94p. 1991. pap. text 27.00 (*0-7506-9734-2*) Buttrwrth-Heinemann.

Practical Procedures for the Gynecological Oncologist. A. Peter Heintz & D. G. Allen. LC 97-28523. 300p. 1997. 250.00 (*0-444-82617-3*) Elsevier.

Practical Procedures in Aesthetic Plastic Surgery. Tolbert S. Wilkinson. LC 93-41835. (Illus.). 496p. 1994. 179.00 (*0-387-94082-0*) Spr-Verlag.

Practical Procedures in Anesthesia & Critical Care. Peter J. F. Baskett et al. (Illus.). 298p. (C). (gr. 13). 1994. 71.00 (*1-56375-606-4*) Gower-Mosby.

Practical Procedures in Nephrology. L. R. I. Baker et al. (Illus.). 160p. 1999. text 45.00 (*0-340-74083-3*, Pub. by E A) OUP.

*__Practical Procedures in the Emergency Department.__ John Bache et al. (Illus.). 184p. 1998. pap. write for info. (*0-7234-3013-6*) Mosby Inc.

Practical Process Control. A. M. Seal. LC 98-205036. 168p. 1998. 49.95 (*0-340-70590-6*, Pub. by Coronet) Trafalgar.

Practical Process Control. A. M. Seal. LC 98-205036. 160p. 1998. 59.95 (*0-470-28321-1*) Wiley.

Practical Process Engineering: A Working Approach to Plant Design. rev. ed. Edward T. Luckiewicz & Henry J. Sandler. (Illus.). 639p. 1993. reprint ed. pap. text 55.00 (*0-9650257-0-5*) XIMIX.

*__Practical Process Research & Development.__ Neal G. Anderson. 360p. 2000. 89.95 (*0-12-059475-7*) Acad Pr.

*__Practical Process Simulation Using Object-Oriented Techniques & C++__ Jose Garrido. LC 98-41883. 1998. 77.00 (*0-89006-655-8*) Artech Hse.

Practical Product Assurance Management. John Bieda. LC 97-27776. 350p. 1997. 41.00 (*0-87389-375-1*, H0966) ASQ Qual Pr.

Practical Professional Cookery. 3rd ed. H.L. Cracknell & R.J. Kaufmann. 908p. 1994. pap. 49.95 (*0-470-23411-3*) Wiley.

Practical Profiling. Moyra Evans. LC 88-3979. 192p. reprint ed. pap. 59.60 (*0-608-20336-X*, 207158900002) Bks Demand.

Practical Program Development Using JSP: A Manual of Program Design Using the Design Method Developed by M. A. Jackson Ralph Storer & M. A. Jackson. LC 86-26368. (Computer Science Texts Ser.). xi, 339 p. 1987. write for info. (*0-632-01699-X*) Blackwell Sci.

Practical Program Evaluation: Examples from Child Abuse Prevention. Jeanne Pietrzak et al. (Sourcebooks for the Human Services Ser.: Vol. 9). 320p. (C). 1989. pap. text 26.00 (*0-8039-3496-3*) Sage.

Practical Program Evaluation: Examples from Child Abuse Prevention. 9th ed. Jeanne Pietrzak et al. (Sourcebooks for the Human Services Ser.: Vol. 9). 320p. (C). 1989. text 56.00 (*0-8039-3495-5*) Sage.

P

Practical Program for America. Ed. by Henry Hazlitt. LC 67-23229. (Essay Index Reprint Ser.). 1977. 17.95 (*0-8369-0523-7*) Ayer.

Practical Program for Cardiovascular Health Enhancement. Illus. by Fuzzy Duck Productions Staff. 63p. 1999. pap., wbk. ed. 14.95 (*0-9672646-1-8*) Wth U In Mind.

Practical Program for Health Enhancement. Illus. by Fuzzy Duck Productions Staff. 66p. 1999. pap., student ed. 14.95 (*0-9672646-0-X*) Wth U In Mind.

Practical Programmable Circuits: A Guide to PLDs, State Machines, & Microcontrollers. James D. Broesch. (Illus.). 286p. (C). 1991. text 65.00 (*0-12-134885-7*) Acad Pr.

Practical Programming in Continuing Professional Education: Examples for Understanding & Improving Practice. Ed. by Sue D. Orem & Deborah F. Brue. 1991. 13.95 (*0-88379-050-5*) A A A C E.

Practical Programming in TCL & TK. 2nd ed. Brent B. Welch. LC 97-16392. 688p. (C). 1997. pap. 42.00 (*0-13-616830-2*, Prentice Hall) P-H.

*__Practical Programming in TCL & TK.__ 3rd ed. Brent Welch. LC 99-47206. 832p. 1999. pap. text 45.00 (*0-13-022028-0*) P-H.

*__Practical Project: Guidelines for Project Engineers.__ 2nd rev. ed. David D. Lyon. (Illus.). 210p. 1999. spiral bd. 55.00 (*0-9661248-5-5*) Raven Publ.

Practical Project: Guidelines for Project Engineers & Program Management Personnel. David D. Lyon. (Illus.). 210p. 1999. spiral bd. 55.00 (*0-9661248-1-2*) Raven Publ.

*__Practical Project Leadership.__ Svein Arne Jessen. 253p. 1998. pap. 37.00 (*82-00-12914-4*, Pub. by Scand Univ Pr) IBD Ltd.

Practical Project Management. B. Graham. (Financial Times Management Briefings Ser.). 1997. pap. 89.50 (*0-273-63236-1*) F T P-H.

Practical Project Management. B. Graham. 1996. pap. 129.00 (*1-85953-066-4*, Pub. by Tech Comm) St Mut.

Practical Project Management: Restoring Quality to DP Projects & Systems. Meilir Page-Jones. LC 85-71101. (Illus.). 248p. (Orig.). 1985. pap. 34.95 (*0-932633-00-5*) Dorset Hse Pub Co.

Practical Project Management: Secrets of Managing Any Project on Time & on Budget. Michael Dobson. Ed. by Kelly Scanlon. LC 96-67864. (Lifelong Learning Library). (Illus.). 292p. 1996. pap. 18.95 (*1-57294-015-8*, 17-0002) SkillPath Pubns.

Practical Projects for the Blacksmith. Ted Tucker. (Illus.). 228p. 1996. reprint ed. pap. 18.95 (*0-9650755-0-8*) Larson Publng.

Practical Promotion: Strategies for Improving Services & Image. Randall Stoner. (Special Reports). 257p. 1992. pap. 36.00 (*0-87326-803-2*) Intl City-Cnty Mgt.

*__Practical Proofreading.__ Matthew Willen. LC 99-67689. (Illus.). 104p. (C). 2000. pap. text (*0-88362-297-1*) GATFPress.

Practical Propagation. Alan Toogood. (Illus.). 64p. 1993. pap. 8.95 (*1-85223-631-0*, Pub. by Crolwood) Trafalgar.

Practical Protein Chemistry: A Handbook. A. Darbre. LC 84-26942. 640p. 1986. reprint ed. pap. 198.40 (*0-7837-8317-5*, 204910300010) Bks Demand.

Practical Protein Chromatography. Ed. by Andrew Kenney & Susan Fowell. LC 92-3609. (Methods in Molecular Biology Ser.: Vol. 11). (Illus.). 352p. 1992. 69.50 (*0-89603-213-2*) Humana.

Practical Protein Crystallography. Duncan E. McRee. (Illus.). 386p. 1993. text 73.00 (*0-12-486050-8*) Acad Pr.

Practical Protein Crystallography. 2nd ed. Duncan E. McRee. 500p. 1999. 75.00 (*0-12-486052-4*) Acad Pr.

Practical Protein Electrophoresis for Genetic Research. George Acquaah. LC 92-4755. (Illus.). 136p. 1992. pap. 26.95 (*0-931146-22-4*, Dioscorides) Timber.

Practical Protocol: A Guide to International Courtesies. James E. Lott. LC 73-75393. (Illus.). 208p. reprint ed. pap. 64.50 (*0-608-18169-2*, 203287500081) Bks Demand.

Practical Protocols in Molecular Biology. LC 97-70267. 400p. (gr. 12). Date not set. 69.50 (*90-5199-317-X*) IOS Press.

Practical Protocols in Molecular Biology. Contrib. by Li Yongming & Zhao Yuqi. 312p. 1996. 49.95 (*7-03-005077-0*, Pub. by Sci Pr) Lubrecht & Cramer.

Practical Protocols in Molecular Biology. Li Yongming et al. (Illus.). 312p. (C). 1996. text 64.45 (*1-880132-14-1*) Sci Pr NY.

Practical Psychiatric Practice: Forms & Protocols for Clinical Use. Richard J. Wyatt. LC 93-21731. 192p. reprint ed. pap. 59.60 (*0-608-20024-7*, 207129600010) Bks Demand.

Practical Psychiatric Practice: Forms & Protocols for Clinical Use. 2nd ed. Richard J. Wyatt. LC 97-41043. 312p. 1998. spiral bd. 49.50 (*0-88048-943-X*, 8943) Am Psychiatric.

Practical Psychiatry. Tim Betts & Claire Kenwood. 576p. 1993. 49.95 (*0-19-263027-X*) OUP.

Practical Psychiatry for the Health Professional. Carlos E. Climent & Barbara J. Burns. LC 84-4926. (Illus.). 223p. 1984. text 29.50 (*0-88331-182-8*) R B Luce.

*__Practical Psychiatry in the Long Term Care Facility.__ 2nd rev. ed. D. Conn et al. 350p. 2000. 34.50 (*0-88937-222-5*) Hogrefe & Huber Pubs.

Practical Psychiatry in the Nursing Home: A Handbook for Staff. Ed. by D. Conn et al. (Illus.). 300p. 1992. text 34.50 (*0-88937-042-7*) Hogrefe & Huber Pubs.

Practical Psychiatry of Old Age. 2nd ed. John P. Wattis. 264p. 1993. pap. 47.75 (*1-56593-150-5*, 0462) Singular Publishing.

Practical Psychic. John Freidlander & Cynthia Pearson. LC 90-23601. 160p. (Orig.). 1991. pap. 9.95 (*0-87728-728-7*) Weiser.

Practical Psychological Guide to the Interrogation of Criminal Suspects. 2nd rev. ed. Edward I. Gelb. 94p. 1997. 39.00 (*0-9659479-0-4*) Intercept.

Practical Psychology for Diabetes Clinicians: How to Deal with the Key Behavioral Issues Faced by Patients & Health Care Teams. Barbara J. Anderson et al. LC 96-15937. (Practical Approaches in Diabetes Care Ser.). (Orig.). 1996. pap. 24.95 (*0-945448-73-2*, PPPDC) Am Diabetes.

Practical Psychology for Pastors. 2nd ed. William R. Miller & Kathleen A. Jackson. LC 94-34115. 448p. 1994. pap. text 86.00 (*0-13-171829-0*) P-H.

Practical Psychology in Character Development. abr. ed. Rudolf Allers. 190p. 1999. reprint ed. 22.95 (*0-912141-72-7*) Roman Cath Bks.

Practical Psychomancy & Crystal Gazing. (Lyal Ser.). 93p. 1997. pap. 8.00 (*0-89540-324-2*, SB-324) Sun Pub.

Practical Psychomancy & Crystal Gazing (1907) William W. Atkinson. 100p. 1998. reprint ed. pap. 6.95 (*0-7661-0247-5*) Kessinger Pub.

Practical Psychometry: Its Value & How It Is Mastered. O. Hashnu Hara. 1993. reprint ed. pap. 16.95 (*1-872736-42-4*, Pub. by Mandrake Pr) Holmes Pub.

Practical Public affairs in an Era of Change: A Cutting-Edge Communications Guide for Government, Business, & College. Ed. by Lloyd B. Dennis. 450p. (C). 1995. pap. text 29.50 (*0-7618-0086-7*); lib. bdg. 62.50 (*0-7618-0085-9*) U Pr of Amer.

Practical Public Management. Robert T. Golembiewski. (Public Administration & Public Policy Ser.: Vol. 57). (Illus.). 408p. 1994. text 145.00 (*0-8247-9261-0*) Dekker.

Practical Publicity: How to Boost Any Cause. David Tedone. LC 82-23364. (Illus.). 176p. 1983. pap. 8.95 (*0-916782-35-2*) Harvard Common Pr.

Practical Pulmonary Pathology. Ed. by Mary N. Sheppard. (Illus.). 304p. 1995. text 75.00 (*0-340-57318-X*, Pub. by E A) OUP.

Practical Qabalah. Charles Fielding. LC 89-9188. 184p. (Orig.). 1989. pap. 11.00 (*0-87728-654-X*) Weiser.

Practical QC. Lawrence H. Keith. 1p. 1994. 99.00 (*1-885844-04-2*) Instant Ref Srvs.

Practical Quality Management in the Chemical Process Industry. Morton E. Bader. (Industrial Engineering Ser.: Vol. 7). (Illus.). 160p. 1983. text 75.00 (*0-8247-1903-4*) Dekker.

Practical Quantum Mechanics. S. Fluegge. LC 74-23732. (Illus.). xiv, 623p. 1994. 53.95 (*0-387-07050-8*) Spr-Verlag.

Practical Quantum Mechanics. 2nd ed. Siegfried Flugge. LC 98-45580. (Classics in Mathematics Ser.). 1999. 45.00 (*3-540-65035-0*) Spr-Verlag.

Practical Queuing Analysis. Mike Tanner. LC 94-27972. (IBM Ser.). 1994. 39.95 (*0-07-709078-0*) McGraw.

*__Practical Quilting.__ 72p. 2000. per. 12.00 (*0-7432-0580-4*) S&S Trade.

Practical Rabbit-Keeping. Katie Thear. (Concorde Country Bks.). (Illus.). 95p. 1981. pap. 14.95 (*0-8464-1214-4*) Beekman Pubs.

Practical Radiation Protection. Dowd. 1994. 260.00 (*0-7216-4920-3*) Harcourt.

Practical Radiation Protection & Applied Radiobiology. Steven B. Dowd. LC 93-22594. 1994. text 34.50 (*0-7216-4917-3*, W B Saunders Co); text, teacher ed. write for info. (*0-7216-4918-1*, W B Saunders Co); 231.00 (*0-7216-4919-X*, W B Saunders Co) Harcrt Hlth Sci Grp.

Practical Radiation Protection & Applied Radiobiology. 2nd ed. Steven B. Dowd & Elwin R. Tilson. Ed. by Andrew Allen. LC 98-43925. (Illus.). 365p. 1999. text 32.95 (*0-7216-7523-9*, W B Saunders Co) Harcrt Hlth Sci Grp.

Practical Radio Frequency Handbook. 2nd ed. Ian Hickman. LC 97-223261. (Illus.). 320p. 1997. pap. text 39.95 (*0-7506-3447-2*, Newnes) Buttrwrth-Heinemann.

*__Practical Radio Frequency Test & Measurement: A Technician's Handbook.__ Joseph J Carr. LC 99-28220. 320p. 1999. pap. text 34.95 (*0-7506-7161-0*, Newnes) Buttrwrth-Heinemann.

Practical Radio Promotions. Ted E. Roberts. (Electronic Media Guide Ser.). 104p. 1992. pap. 24.95 (*0-240-80090-7*, Focal) Buttrwrth-Heinemann.

Practical Radiography: A Hand-Book of the Application of the X-Rays. H. Snowden Ward. (Illus.). 112p. 1995. pap. 16.95 (*0-944838-49-9*) Med Physics Pub.

Practical Radiography: Principles, Applications. 11th ed. Erwin A. Hoxter. LC 82-14200. 216p. reprint ed. pap. 67.00 (*0-608-16012-1*, 203308900083) Bks Demand.

Practical Radiotherapy Planning. 2nd ed. Jane Dobbs & Ann Barrett. 320p. 1992. pap. text 48.00 (*0-340-54557-7*, Pub. by E A) OUP.

Practical Radiotherapy Planning. 3rd ed. LC 99-34126. (Illus.). 416p. 1999. pap. text 49.50 (*0-340-70631-7*, Pub. by E A) OUP.

Practical Raman Spectroscopy. Ed. by D. J. Gardiner & P. R. Graves. (Illus.). 170p. 1989. 79.95 (*0-387-50254-8*) Spr-Verlag.

Practical Ray Tracing in C. Craig A. Lindley. LC 92-30223. 528p. 1992. pap. 49.95 incl. disk (*0-471-57301-9*) Wiley.

Practical Reader in Contemporary Literary Theory. Peter Widdowson & Peter Brooker. 580p. 1997. pap. text 42.00 (*0-13-442567-7*, Prentice Hall) P-H.

Practical Readings in Financial Derivatives. Ed. by Robert W. Kolb. LC 97-23202. (Illus.). 300p. (C). 1997. pap. 36.95 (*1-57718-084-4*) Blackwell Pubs.

Practical Real Estate: Legal, Tax & Business Strategies. Robert K. Lifton. 702p. 1983. 60.00 (*0-15-004280-9*, H42809) Harcourt.

Practical Real Estate Law. Daniel F. Hinkel. Ed. by Hannan. 611p. (C). 1991. text 58.25 (*0-314-76645-6*) West Pub.

Practical Real Estate Law 2e. 2nd ed. Daniel F. Hinkel. LC 94-37593. (Paralegal). 650p. (C). 1994. mass mkt. 54.50 (*0-314-04583-X*) West Pub.

Practical Real Estate Lawyer Forms Manual, No. 1. Institutional Staff. ix, 216p. 1991. pap. 22.00 (*0-685-51829-9*, F203) Am Law Inst.

Practical Real Estate Lawyer's Manual, No. 1. Institutional Staff. LC 87-70534. 218p. 1987. pap. 10.00 (*0-317-65913-8*, F201) Am Law Inst.

Practical Real Estate Lawyer's Manual, No. 2. Institutional Staff. LC 87-70534. 286p. 1989. pap. 11.00 (*0-318-42485-1*, F202) Am Law Inst.

Practical Real Estate Math. 2nd ed. Betty J. Armbrust & Hugh H. Bradley. 306p. (Orig.). (C). 1995. pap. text 32.67 (*0-13-777707-8*) P-H.

Practical Realism & Moral Psychology. Jonathan Jacobs. LC 94-37060. 200p. 1995. 42.50 (*0-87840-583-6*) Georgetown U Pr.

*__Practical Reality.__ Jonathan Dancy. 195p. 2000. 29.95 (*0-19-824115-1*) OUP.

Practical Reason: On the Theory of Action. Pierre Bourdieu. Tr. by Randal Johnson et al. 162p. 1998. 14.95 (*0-8047-3363-5*); pap. 39.50 (*0-8047-3362-7*) Stanford U Pr.

Practical Reason: Papers & Discussions by G. E. M. Anscombe . . . et al. Bristol Conference on Critical Philosophy Staff. Ed. by Stephan Khorner. LC 74-77066. 272p. reprint ed. pap. 84.40 (*0-8357-8281-6*, 203378900087) Bks Demand.

Practical Reason: Philosophical Papers, Vol. 1. George H. Von Wright. LC 83-71775. 192p. 1983. text 39.95 (*0-8014-1673-6*) Cornell U Pr.

*__Practical Reason & Norms.__ Joseph Raz. 224p. 1999. pap. text 29.95 (*0-19-826834-3*) OUP.

Practical Reasoning: ACPA Proceedings, 1984, Vol. 58. Ed. by Daniel O. Dahlstrom. 250p. 1985. pap. 20.00 (*0-918090-18-0*) Am Cath Philo.

Practical Reasoning: Goal-Driven, Knowledge-Based, Action Guiding Argumentation. Douglas N. Walton. LC 96-3026. 272p. (C). 1990. lib. bdg. 59.50 (*0-8476-7605-6*) Rowman.

Practical Reasoning: International Conference on Formal & Applied Practical Reasoning, FAPR 96, Bonn, Germany, June 1996, Proceedings, Vol. 108. D. M Gabbay & Hnas J. Ohlbach. LC 96-22590. (Lecture Notes in Artificial Intelligence). 721p. 1996. pap. 106.00 (*3-540-61313-7*) Spr-Verlag.

Practical Reasoning about Final Ends. Henry S. Richardson. (Cambridge Studies in Philosophy). 342p. (C). 1994. text 69.95 (*0-521-46472-2*) Cambridge U Pr.

Practical Reasoning about Final Ends. Henry S. Richardson. (Cambridge Studies in Philosophy). 340p. 1997. pap. text 21.95 (*0-521-57442-0*) Cambridge U Pr.

Practical Reasoning in Bioethics. James F. Childress. LC 96-25001. (Medical Ethics Ser.). 1997. 39.95 (*0-253-33218-4*) Ind U Pr.

Practical Reasoning in Human Affairs. Ed. by James L. Golden & Joseph J. Pilotta. 416p. 1986. text 193.50 (*90-277-2255-2*, D Reidel) Kluwer Academic.

Practical Reasoning in Natural Language. 4th ed. Stephen N. Thomas. LC 96-18454. 504p. (C). 1998. pap. text 57.00 (*0-13-678269-8*) P-H.

Practical Recognition of the Brotherhood of Man: John G. Fee & the Camp Nelson Experience. Richard D. Sears. LC 86-71186. (Illus.). 94p. (Orig.). 1986. pap. 8.00 (*0-938211-01-3*) Berea College Pr.

Practical Record Keeping - Working Papers. 5th ed. (BB - Record Keeping I Ser.). 1982. mass mkt. 36.95 (*0-538-02056-3*) S-W Pub.

Practical Record Keeping & Bookkeeping. 4th ed. Harold Baron & Steinfeld. (BB - Record Keeping I Ser.). 1988. mass mkt. 36.25 (*0-538-02110-1*) S-W Pub.

Practical Record Keeping & Bookkeeping. 4th ed. Harold Baron & Steinfeld. (BB - Record Keeping I Ser.). 1988. mass mkt. 23.95 (*0-538-02112-8*) S-W Pub.

Practical Record Keeping & Bookkeeping, Units 1-7. 4th ed. Harold Baron & Steinfeld. (BB - Record Keeping I Ser.). 1987. mass mkt., wbk. ed. 22.95 (*0-538-02111-X*) S-W Pub.

Practical Record Keeping & Bookkeeping Units 1-5 - Working Papers. 4th ed. Harold Baron & Steinfeld. (BB - Record Keeping I Ser.). 1988. mass mkt. 34.95 (*0-538-02116-0*) S-W Pub.

Practical Record Keeping & Bookkeeping Units 1-7, Tests. 4th ed. Harold Baron & Steinfeld. (BB - Record Keeping I Ser.). 1988. 1.95 (*0-538-02113-6*) S-W Pub.

Practical Record Keeping & Bookkeeping Units 8-15, Tests. 4th ed. Harold Baron & Steinfeld. (BB - Record Keeping I Ser.). 1988. 1.95 (*0-538-02114-4*) S-W Pub.

Practical Record Keeping Working Papers. 5th ed. (BB - Record Keeping I Ser.). 1981. mass mkt. 18.95 (*0-538-02051-2*) S-W Pub.

Practical Recording Techniques: The Step-by-Step Approach to Professional Audio Recording. 2nd ed. Bruce Bartlett & Jenny Bartlett. LC 97-41861. 488p. 1998. pap. text 29.95 (*0-240-80306-X*, Focal) Buttrwrth-Heinemann.

Practical Recycling Handbook. Kindred Association Staff. 184p. 1994. 6.00 (*0-7277-1990-4*) Am Soc Civil Eng.

Practical Reference to SNA. Mike Oxborrow. LC 92-43138. 1993. 24.95 (*0-07-707791-1*) McGraw.

Practical Reference Work. 2nd ed. Denis J. Grogan. LC 93-13902. 206p. 1992. reprint ed. pap. 63.90 (*0-608-02473-2*, 206311700004) Bks Demand.

Practical Reflections on Figured Song. rev. ed. Giambattista Mancini. Tr. by Edward V. Foreman from ITA. (Masterworks on Singing Ser.: Vol. VII). 1996. reprint ed. pap. 15.00 (*1-887117-04-0*) Pro musica pr.

Practical Reformation: A Realistic Approach to the Reformation of the Self. Calbraith MacLeod. 1999. pap. 10.95 (*1-879418-68-1*, Pub. by Audenreed Pr) Baker & Taylor.

Practical Rehabilitation Techniques for Geriatric Aides. 2nd ed. Ruth L. Di Domenico & Wilma Z. Ziegler. LC 93-39450. (Illus.). 220p. 1994. 88.00 (*0-8342-0548-3*) Aspen Pub.

Practical Reiki: A Personal Step by Step Guide to This Ancient Healing Art. Mari Hall. (Illus.). 128p. (Orig.). 1997. pap. 15.00 (*0-7225-3465-5*) Thorsons PA.

Practical Reiki: Focus Your Body's Energy for Deep Relaxation & Inner Peace. Richard Ellis. (Illus.). 128p. 1999. pap. text 17.95 (*0-8069-6807-9*) Sterling.

Practical Reliability Eng 3e R. 3rd rev. ed. P. D. O'Connor. LC 90-13082. 456p. 1996. pap. 64.95 (*0-471-95767-4*) Wiley.

Practical Reliability Engineering. 3rd rev. ed. P. D. O'Connor. LC 90-13082. (Quality & Reliability Engineering Ser.). 456p. 1996. 125.00 (*0-471-96025-X*) Wiley.

Practical Religion: Being Plain Papers on Daily Duties, Experience Dangers, & Privileges of Professing Christianity. J. C. Ryle. 495p. 1998. pap. text 11.99 (*0-85151-743-9*) Banner of Truth.

Practical Renal Medicine. Ed. by Roger Gabriel. LC 93-2823. 372p. 1993. 115.00 (*0-632-02809-2*) Blackwell Sci.

*__Practical Research.__ 7th ed. Leedy. 352p. 2000. pap. text. write for info. (*0-13-960360-3*) P-H.

An Asterisk (*) at the beginning of an entry indicates that the title is appearing for the first time.

Practical Research: A Guide for Therapists. Sally French. LC 93-14002. (Skills for Practice Ser.). (Illus.). 232p. 1993. pap. text 34.50 (*0-7506-0618-5*) Buttrwrth-Heinemann.

Practical Research: Planning & Designing. 6th ed. Paul D. Leedy. LC 96-9917. 304p. (C). 1996. pap. 53.00 (*0-13-241407-4*) P-H.

Practical Research Methods for Physiotherapists. Carolyn M. Hicks. (Illus.). 312p. (Orig.). 1988. pap. text 29.00 (*0-443-03757-4*) Church.

Practical Researcher: A Student Guide to Conducting Psychological Research. Dana Dunn. LC 98-26089. 408p. 1998. pap. 48.13 (*0-07-018323-6*) McGraw.

Practical Reservoir Engineering, Vol. 1. E. H. Timmerman. 376p. 1982. 25.00 (*0-87814-168-5*) PennWell Bks.

Practical Reservoir Engineering, Vol. 2. E. H. Timmerman. 367p. 1982. 25.00 (*0-87814-181-2*) PennWell Bks.

***Practical Resources for Adult ESL: A Selection Guide to Materials for Adult ESL & ESL/ESOL Literacy.** Anna Silliman & Abigail Tom. LC 00-100876. 176p. 2000. pap. text. write for info. (*1-882483-80-4*) Alta Bk Ctr.

Practical Review of German Grammar. Gerda Dippman. 514p. (C). 1987. teacher ed. write for info. (*0-318-59094-8*) P-H.

Practical Review of German Grammar. 3rd ed. Dippmann. 397p. (C). 1999. 49.00 (*0-13-938143-0*) P-H.

Practical Revolutionaries: A New Interpretation of the French Anarchosyndicalists, 5. Barbara Mitchell. LC 86-15028. (Contributions to the Study of World History Ser.: No. 5). 325p. 1987. 65.00 (*0-313-25289-0*, MLE/, Greenwood Pr) Greenwood.

Practical RF Design Manual. 2nd ed. Doug DeMaw. (Illus.). 246p. 1997. reprint ed. pap. 19.95 (*1-891237-00-4*, MFJ-3507) MFJ Ent.

Practical RF Power Design Techniques. Irving M. Gottlieb. 304p. 1993. pap. 29.95 (*0-07-023986-X*) McGraw.

Practical RF Power Design Techniques. Irving M. Gottlieb. LC 92-5599. (Illus.). 320p. 1993. 32.95 (*0-8306-4130-0*, 4228); pap. 19.95 (*0-8306-4129-7*, 4228) McGraw-Hill Prof.

Practical Risk Analysis: An Approach Through Case Histories. David B. Hertz & Howard Thomas. LC 81-16056. (Illus.). 326p. 1984. reprint ed. pap. 101.10 (*0-608-01634-9*, 206221900002) Bks Demand.

Practical Risk Assessment for Project Management. Stephen Grey. LC 94-46422. (Software Engineering Practice Ser.). 158p. 1995. 80.00 (*0-471-93979-X*) Wiley.

Practical Risk Management. Jim E. Banninster & Paul A. Bawcutt. 240p. (C). 1981. 140.00 (*0-900886-22-6*, Pub. by Witherby & Co) St Mut.

Practical Risk Management in the Construction Industry. Leslie Edwards. 132p. 1995. 33.60 (*0-7277-2064-3*, Pub. by T Telford) RCH.

Practical Robotics. unabridged ed. Bill Davies. LC 98-106773. (Illus.). 330p. Date not set. 39.95 (*0-9681830-0-X*, Pub. by Werd Tech) Mondo-tronics.

Practical Rock Gardening. Patrick Jones. (Illus.). 64p. 1993. pap. 8.95 (*1-85223-660-4*, Pub. by Crolwood) Trafalgar.

Practical Rook Endings. Edmar Mednis. (Illus.). 71p. (Orig.). 1982. pap. 6.00 (*0-931462-16-9*) Chess Ent.

Practical Rules for the Management & Medical Treatment of Negro Slaves, in the Sugar Colonies. D. A. Collins. LC 70-153484. (Black Heritage Library Collection). 1977. 24.95 (*0-8369-8773-X*) Ayer.

Practical Ruskin: Economics & Audience in the Late Work. Linda M. Austin. LC 90-23911. 264p. 1991. text 42.00 (*0-8018-4162-3*) Johns Hopkins.

Practical Russian-French Dictionary: Dictionnaire Pratique Russe-Francais. G. Dontchenko. (FRE & RUS.). 272p. 1984. 29.95 (*0-8288-0791-4*, F47270) Fr & Eur.

Practical Safety & Reliability Assessment. K. C. Hignett. 208p. (C). (gr. 13). 1996. 80.00 (*0-419-21330-9*) Routledge.

Practical Sailing: The Modern Cruising Yacht. Timothy Jeffery. 112p. 10.99 (*1-57215-231-1*, JG2311) World Pubns.

Practical Sales Forecasting. E. J. Davis. 256p. 1989. text 13.95 (*0-07-707080-1*) McGraw.

Practical Saltwater Fly Fishing. Mark Sosin. (Cortland Library). (Illus.). 96p. 1989. pap. 12.95 (*1-55821-043-1*) Lyons Pr.

Practical Sampling. Gary T. Henry. (Applied Social Research Methods Ser.: Vol. 21). (Illus.). 160p. (C). 1990. 42.00 (*0-8039-2958-7*); pap. 18.95 (*0-8039-2959-5*) Sage.

Practical Sampling Techniques. 2nd expanded rev. ed. Ranjan K. Som. LC 95-35436. (Statistics: Textbooks & Monographs: Vol. 148). (Illus.). 672p. 1995. text 165.00 (*0-8247-9676-4*, HA31) Dekker.

Practical Sampling Techniques for Infrared Analysis. Patricia B. Coleman. 320p. 1993. boxed set 136.95 (*0-8493-4203-1*, QD96) CRC Pr.

Practical Sanitation in the Food Industry. Ian S. Maddox. xii, 182p. 1994. text 73.00 (*2-88449-005-1*); pap. text 29.00 (*2-88124-992-2*) Gordon & Breach.

Practical Sanskrit Dictionary. Arthur A. MacDonell. (C). 1996. 46.00 (*81-215-0715-4*, Pub. by M Manoharial) Coronet Bks.

Practical Sanskrit Dictionary: With Transliteration Accentuation & Etymological Analysis Throughout. Arthur A. MacDonnell. (SAN.). 396p. 1984. reprint ed. text 95.00 (*0-19-864303-9*) OUP.

***Practical Sanskrit-English Dictionary.** Vama Shivaram Apte. 1998. 40.00 (*81-208-1568-8*) Motilal Bnarsidass.

Practical Sanskrit-English Dictionary. rev. ed. Vaman S. Apte. 112p. 1987. 95.00 (*0-8288-1779-0*, M14250) Fr & Eur.

Practical Sanskrit-English Dictionary Containing Appendices on Sanskrit Prosody & Important Literary & Geographical Names of Ancient India. vii, 1166p. 1989. reprint ed. 64.00 (*81-208-0567-4*, Pub. by Motilal Bnarsidass) S Asia.

Practical Scanning Electron Microscopy: Electron & Ion Microprobe Analysis. Ed. by Joseph I. Goldstein & Harvey Yakowitz. LC 74-34162. (Illus.). 582p. 1975. 79.50 (*0-306-30820-7*, Plenum Trade) Perseus Pubng.

Practical Scent Dog Training. Lue Button. LC 90-184. (Illus.). 160p. 1990. pap. 11.95 (*0-931866-47-2*) Alpine Pubns.

Practical School Security: Basic Guidelines for Safe & Secure Schools. Kenneth S. Trump. LC 97-33725. 120p. 1997. 43.95 (*0-8039-6353-X*); pap. 18.95 (*0-8039-6354-8*) Corwin Pr.

Practical Schooling: Improving the Horse & Rider. Michael J. Stevens. (Illus.). 128p. 1995. 34.95 (*1-872082-76-9*) Half Halt Pr.

Practical Science: The Role & Reality of Practical Work in School Science. Ed. by Brian E. Woolnough. 192p. 1990. 113.00 (*0-335-09390-6*) OpUniv Pr.

Practical Scientific Russian. S. Kaganoff. vi, 342p. (Orig.). 1967. text 137.00 (*0-677-40030-6*) Gordon & Breach.

Practical Seal Design. Leonard J. Martini. (Mechanical Engineering Ser.: Vol. 29). (Illus.). 312p. 1984. text 125.00 (*0-8247-7166-4*) Dekker.

Practical Secrets of the Spiritual Life: How-To Revealed. Harold M. Richards. LC 89-2198. 160p. (Orig.). 1989. pap. 9.00 (*0-922615-05-5*) Hampton Hill.

Practical Security in a Networked Environment - Course Notes. M. Abrams et al. (Illus.). 427p. (Orig.). (C). 1995. pap. 46.97 (*0-942891-62-7*) Comp Educ.

Practical Security in Networks: Course Notes. Marshall Abrams et al. 452p. 1998. pap. 49.72 (*0-942891-75-9*) Comp Educ.

Practical Security Training. Patrick Kane. LC 99-26836. 255p. 1999. pap. text 34.95 (*0-7506-7159-9*) Buttrwrth-Heinemann.

Practical Self-Help: or How to Make the Full & Effective Use of the Greatest & Best That Is in You. Christian D. Larson. 223p. 1997. pap. 20.00 (*0-89540-400-1*, SB-400) Sun Pub.

Practical Selling: A Case Approach. Maurice G. Clabaugh, Jr. et al. Ed. by Leyh. 528p. (C). 1992. pap. text 27.75 (*0-314-93311-5*) West Pub.

Practical Selling: A Relationship Approach. Maurice G. Clabaugh, Jr. & Jesse L. Forbes. Ed. by Leyh. 535p. (C). 1992. text 61.50 (*0-314-88422-X*) West Pub.

Practical Semantics: A Study in the Rules of Speech & Action. H. J. Heringer. (Trends in Linguistics, Studies & Monographs: No. 3). 1978. pap. text 62.35 (*90-279-7736-4*) Mouton.

Practical SGML. 2nd ed. Eric Van Herwijnen. LC 93-47579. 312p. (C). 1994. pap. text 76.00 (*0-7923-9434-8*) Kluwer Academic.

Practical Sheet Metal Projects-130 Graded Projects with Drawings, Forming Information & Sequences. 2nd ed. Richard S. Budzik. LC 79-93132. (Illus.). (gr. 7-12). 1986. 29.95 (*0-912914-28-9*) Practical Pubns.

Practical Shielded Metal Arc Welding. Mike Gellerman. LC 97-10375. 181p. (C). 1997. pap. text 53.00 (*0-13-601931-5*) P-H.

Practical Ship Design. D. G. Watson. LC 98-13994. (Ocean Engineering Ser.). 350p. 1998. 125.00 (*0-08-042999-8*) Elsevier.

Practical Ship Handling. M. C. Armstrong. (C). 1987. 60.00 (*0-85174-387-0*) St Mut.

***Practical Ship Hydrodynamics.** Volker Bertram. 224p. 2000. pap. 54.95 (*0-7506-4851-1*) Buttrwrth-Heinemann.

Practical Shipbuilding, 2 vols. A. C. Holms. LC 76-49170. 1977. lib. bdg. 200.00 (*0-8490-2461-7*) Gordon Pr.

Practical Shooting: Beyond Fundamentals. Brian Enos. (Illus.). 208p. (Orig.). 1990. pap. 16.95 (*0-9626925-0-6*) Zediker Pub.

Practical Shop Mathematics Vol. 1: Elementary. 4th ed. John H. Wolfe & E. R. Phelps. 1958. text 25.20 (*0-07-071358-8*) McGraw.

***Practical Short Story Writing.** John Paxton Sheriff. 160p. 1999. 14.95 (*0-7090-6326-1*, Pub. by R Hale Ltd) Seven Hills Bk.

Practical Sign Shop Operation. 7th rev. ed. Bob Fitzgerald. (Illus.). 1992. pap. 19.95 (*0-911380-93-0*) ST Pubns.

***Practical Skeptic: Care Concepts in Sociology.** Ed. by Lisa J. McIntyre. LC 98-22180. xiii, 313p. 1998. pap. text 24.95 (*0-7674-0685-0*) Mayfield Pub.

Practical Skeptic: Core Concepts in Sociology. Lisa J. McIntyre. LC 98-19599. xiv, 313p. 1998. pap. text 24.95 (*1-55934-954-9*, 1954) Mayfield Pub.

Practical Skeptic Instructor's Manual. Lisa J. McIntyre. v, 205p. (C). 1998. pap. text, teacher ed. write for info. (*0-7674-0636-2*, 0636-2) Mayfield Pub.

Practical Skills: Basic Criminal Practice. 297p. 1995. pap. 30.00 (*0-614-26676-9*, 1073) NYS Bar.

Practical Skills: Estate Planning & Will Drafting. 365p. 1997. pap. 30.00 (*0-614-26726-9*, 1069); pap. 175.00 incl. VHS (*0-614-26727-7*, 30691); pap. 92.00 incl. audio (*0-614-26728-5*, 20691) NYS Bar.

Practical Skills: Probate & Administration of Estates. 395p. 1996. pap. 30.00 (*0-614-26739-0*, 1029); pap. 92.00 incl. audio (*0-614-26740-4*, 20297) NYS Bar.

Practical Skills Guide for Midwifery: A Tool for Midwives & Students. Pam Weaver & Sharon K. Evans. (Illus.). (C). 1994. 33.00 (*0-9642387-0-5*) Mrningstar Pubng.

Practical Skills Guide for Midwifery: A Tool for Midwives & Students. 2nd ed. Pam Weaver & Sharon K. Evans. (Illus.). 277p. (C). 1997. lab manual ed. 39.95 (*0-9642387-1-3*) Mrningstar Pubng.

Practical Skills in Biology. Allan Jones. LC 92-36775. (C). 1994. pap. text 40.00 (*0-582-06699-9*, Pub. by Addison-Wesley) Longman.

***Practical Skills in Biology.** 2nd ed. Allan Jones. 292p. (C). 1998. pap. text 64.00 (*0-582-29885-7*) Longman.

Practical Skills in Biomolecular Sciences. Reed. 328p. (C). 1998. pap. text 64.00 (*0-582-29826-1*) Longman.

Practical Skills in Bobbin Lace. Bridget M. Cook. (Illus.). 192p. 1987. pap. 16.95 (*0-486-25561-1*) Dover.

Practical Slam Bidding: The Self-Help Guide to Better Slam Bidding. Ron Klinger. 96p. 1998. pap. 13.95 (*0-575-06604-0*, Pub. by V Gollancz) Trafalgar.

Practical Small Animal Internal Medicine. Michael S. Leib & William E. Monroe. Ed. by Ray Kersey. 1008p. 1996. text 94.00 (*0-7216-4839-8*, W B Saunders Co) Harcrt Hlth Sci Grp.

Practical Small Gardening: The Complete Step-by-Step Guide to Planning, Planting & Maintaining a Small Garden. Peter McHoy et al. (Illus.). 192p. 1997. pap. 16.95 (*1-85967-384-8*, Lorenz Bks) Anness Pub.

Practical Soccer Tactics. Larry Maisner. LC 78-64382. (Illus.). 144p. 1979. pap. 4.95 (*0-89037-157-1*) Anderson World.

Practical Sociology. 3rd ed. Hale. (C). 1997. pap. text. write for info. (*0-201-32235-8*) Addison-Wesley.

Practical Sociology: Postempiricism & the Reconstruction of Theory & Application. Christopher G. Bryant. (Illus.). 186p. (C). 1996. 70.95 (*0-7456-1492-2*); pap. 30.95 (*0-7456-1493-0*) Blackwell Pubs.

Practical Software Configuration. Tim Mikkelson & Suzanne Pherigo. 1997. pap. 39.00 incl. cd-rom (*0-614-28521-6*) P-H.

Practical Software Configuration Management: The Latenight Developer's Handbook. Tim Mikkelson & Suzanne Pherigo. LC 97-173384. 336p. (C). 1997. pap. text 44.99 (*0-13-240854-6*) P-H.

Practical Software Maintenance: Best Practices for Managing Your Software Investment. Thomas M. Pigoski. LC 96-25884. 384p. 1996. 59.99 (*0-471-17001-1*) Wiley.

***Practical Software Measurement: Measuring for Process Management & Improvement.** William A. Florac. LC 99-20519. 272p. (C). 1999. 54.95 (*0-201-60444-2*) Addison-Wesley.

Practical Software Metrics for Project Management & Process Improvement. Robert B. Grady. 304p. (C). 1992. 59.00 (*0-13-720384-5*) P-H.

Practical Software Requirements: A Manual of Content & Style. Benjamin L. Kovitz. LC 98-29162. 448p. 1998. pap. 47.95 (*1-884777-59-7*) Manning Pubns.

Practical Solar Energy Technology. Martin L. Greenwald & Thomas K. McHugh. LC 84-23721. (Illus.). 256p. (C). 1985. text 45.00 (*0-13-693979-1*) P-H.

Practical Solaris Administration: System Configuration & File Systems. 400p. 1920. 39.99 (*1-57870-204-6*) Macmillan Tech.

Practical Solaris System Administration. Peter Galvin. (C). 1998. pap. text. write for info. (*0-201-84526-1*) Addison-Wesley.

Practical Solitary Magic. Nancy B. Watson. 272p. (Orig.). 1996. reprint ed. pap. 14.95 (*0-87728-874-7*) Weiser.

Practical Solutions: Sustainable Self-Reliance Skills Emergency Energy Survival Choices. Heather Gurley & Bob Larson. (Illus.). 92p. (Orig.). 1981. pap. text 10.00 (*0-9634694-3-6*) Sun Light Wks.

***Practical Solutions for Assessing Human Performance.** John Walker. 1999. pap. 26.95 (*1-57879-007-7*) E Bowers Pub.

Practical Solutions for Everyday Work Problems. Liz Chesla. LC 99-11368. 224p. 1999. pap. 14.95 (*1-57685-203-2*) LrningExprss.

Practical Solutions for Potters: Your Top 465 Questions with Thousands of Practical Solutions. Gill Bliss. LC 98-48456. (Illus.). 192p. 1998. 29.95 (*0-8069-6307-7*) Sterling.

Practical Solutions for Practically Every Problem: The Early Childhood Teacher's Manual. Steffen Saifer. LC 90-42636. (Illus.). 190p. (Orig.). 1990. pap. 25.95 (*0-934140-61-8*, 1526) Redleaf Pr.

Practical Solutions in Occupational Medicine. Dosman. 1997. write for info. (*0-87371-618-3*, L618) Lewis Pubs.

Practical Sonography in Obstetrics & Gynecology. 2nd ed. John W. Seeds et al. LC 95-11323. (Illus.). 240p. 1995. text 72.00 (*0-7817-0335-2*) Lppncott W & W.

Practical Sourcebook on National Identity: Writing Englishness, 1900-1950. Ed. by Judy Giles & Tim Middleton. LC 95-767. 304p. (C). 1995. pap. 25.99 (*0-415-11442-X*) Routledge.

Practical Sourcebook on National Identity: Writing Englishness, 1900-1950. Ed. by Judy Giles & Tim Middleton. LC 95-767. 304p. (C). (gr. 13). 1995. 90.00 (*0-415-11441-1*) Routledge.

Practical Spanish Dictionary & Phrasebook. Marguerite D. Bomse. (SPA.). 1978. pap. text 18.00 (*0-08-023020-2*, Pergamon Pr) Elsevier.

Practical Spanish for Medical & Hospital Personnel. 2nd ed. Marguerite D. Bomse & Julian H. Alfaro. 1978. pap. text 16.00 (*0-08-023001-6*, Pergamon Pr) Elsevier.

Practical Spanish for School Personnel, Firemen, Policemen & Community Agencies. 2nd ed. Marguerite D. Bomse & Julian H. Alfaro. 1978. pap. text 16.00 (*0-08-023002-4*, Pergamon Pr) Elsevier.

Practical Spanish Grammar. Marguerite D. Bomse. 1978. pap. text 18.00 (*0-08-021859-8*, Pergamon Pr) Elsevier.

Practical Spanish Grammar: A Self-Teaching Guide. 2nd ed. Marcial Prado. LC 96-39865. 368p. 1997. pap. 17.95 (*0-471-13446-5*) Wiley.

Practical Spanish-Polish Dictionary. 3rd rev. ed. S. Wawzkowicz. (POL & SPA.). 1992. 35.00 (*0-8288-7274-0*, F47390) Fr & Eur.

***Practical Spectroscopy of High-Frequency Discharges.** S. A. Kazantsev et al. LC 97-40604. (Physics of Atoms & Molecules Ser.). 352p. (C). 1998. 115.00 (*0-306-45676-1*, Plenum Trade) Perseus Pubng.

Practical Speech for Modern Business. Robert C. Martin et al. LC 63-7333. 1963. 32.50 (*0-89197-353-2*) Irvington.

Practical Speech Handbook. Nancy Hauer & Ed Martley. LC 92-29447. (Illus.). 112p. (C). 1993. text 13.20 (*0-256-13057-4*, Irwn McGrw-H) McGrw-H Hghr Educ.

Practical Spelling. Anna Castley. LC 97-39166. (Basics Made Easy Ser.). 208p. 1998. pap. 13.95 (*1-57685-083-8*) LrningExprss.

Practical Spelling Book. Deborah Muirhead. (Illus.). 60p. 1998. pap. write for info. (*0-89822-149-8*) Visual Studies.

Practical Spiritual Gifts. James W. Zackrison. LC 96-3336. 1996. 3.97 (*0-8163-1357-1*) Pacific Pr Pub Assn.

Practical Spirituality. pap. 4.95 (*81-85843-13-9*) Vedanta Pr.

Practical Spirituality. Steve Hounsome. 1997. pap. 22.95 (*1-86163-015-8*, Pub. by Capall Bann Pubng) Holmes Pub.

Practical Spirituality. Torkom Saraydarian. LC 96-60649. 69p. 1996. 6.00 (*0-929874-54-4*) TSG Pub Found.

Practical Spirituality. John R. Price. LC 96-38831. 160p. (Orig.). 1996. reprint ed. pap. 10.95 (*1-56170-351-6*, 834) Hay House.

Practical Spoken Spanish. 7th ed. F. M. Kercheville. LC 35-4432. 154p. 1959. reprint ed. pap. 10.95 (*0-8263-0059-6*) U of NM Pr.

Practical Spread Spectrum: Frequency Hopping, Bk. II. Charles O. Phillips. 187p. 1994. pap. 48.80 (*0-89412-224-X*) Aegean Park Pr.

Practical Spread Spectrum Bk. IV: Detection, Recognition & Recording of Spread Spectrum Signals. Charles O. Phillips. 154p. 1993. pap. 48.80 (*0-89412-220-7*) Aegean Park Pr.

Practical SQL Handbook: Using Structured Query Language. 3rd ed. Judith S. Bowman et al. LC 96-20301. 496p. (C). 1996. pap. text 39.95 incl. cd-rom (*0-201-44787-8*) Addison-Wesley.

Practical SSADM: Version 4+ 2nd ed. Philip L. Weaver. 403p. 1998. pap. 54.50 (*0-273-62675-2*, Pub. by Pitman Pub) Trans-Atl Phila.

Practical Stability of Nonlinear Systems. V. Lakshmikantham et al. 220p. (C). 1990. text 53.00 (*981-02-0351-9*); pap. text 36.00 (*981-02-0356-X*) World Scientific Pub.

***Practical Standards for Microsoft Visual Basic Programmers.** James D. Foxall. LC 99-56695. (gr. 8). 2000. pap. 49.99 (*0-7356-0733-8*) Microsoft.

Practical Statistical Sampling for Auditors. A. J. Wilburn. (Statistics Ser.: Vol. 52). (Illus.). 424p. 1984. text 137.50 (*0-8247-7124-9*) Dekker.

Practical Statistics. Simon S. Cohen. (Illus.). 224p. (Orig.). 1988. pap. text 17.95 (*0-7131-3648-0*, Pub. by E A) Routldge.

***Practical Statistics by Example Using Microsoft Excel.** Terry Sincich. LC 98-43919. 846p. 1999. 91.00 (*0-13-096083-7*) P-H.

Practical Statistics for Analytical Chemists. Robert L. Anderson. (Illus.). 352p. 1987. text 52.95 (*0-442-20973-8*, Chap & Hall CRC) CRC Pr.

Practical Statistics for Educators. Ruth Ravid. LC 94-4720. 366p. 1994. lib. bdg. 57.50 (*0-8191-9498-0*) U Pr of Amer.

***Practical Statistics for Educators.** 2nd ed. Ruth Ravid. LC 99-57337. 384p. 2000. pap. 37.50 (*0-7618-1594-5*) U Pr of Amer.

Practical Statistics for Engineers & Scientists. Nicholas P. Cheremisinoff. LC 86-72352. 224p. 1986. 29.95 (*0-87762-505-0*) Technomic.

***Practical Statistics for Experimental Biologists.** 2nd ed. A. C. Wardlaw. 260p. 2000. 95.00 (*0-471-98821-9*) Wiley.

***Practical Statistics for Experimental Biologists** 2nd ed. A. C. Wardlaw. LC 99-35926. 260p. 2000. pap. 40.00 (*0-471-98822-7*) Wiley.

Practical Statistics for Field Biology. Jim Fowler & Lou Cohen. 220p. 1990. 88.00 (*0-335-09208-X*); pap. 33.00 (*0-335-09207-1*) Wiley.

Practical Statistics for Field Biology. 2nd ed. Jim Fowler et al. LC 98-9178. 259p. 1998. 110.00 (*0-471-98295-4*); pap. 44.95 (*0-471-98296-2*) Wiley.

Practical Statistics for Students. Louis Cohen & Mike Holliday. LC 96-226109. 408p. 1996. pap. text 26.95 (*1-85396-329-1*, Pub. by P Chapman) Taylor & Francis.

Practical Statistics for the Analytical Scientist: A Bench Guide. T. J. Farrant. 1997. write for info. (*0-85404-442-6*) Am Chemical.

Practical Statistics for the Physical Sciences. Ed. by Larry L. Havlicek & Ronald D. Crain. LC 88-10573. (Professional Reference Book Ser.). (Illus.). 512p. 1988. text 65.00 (*0-8412-1453-0*, Pub. by Am Chemical) OUP.

Practical Statistics Simply Explained. 2nd ed. Russell A. Langley. 399p. 1971. pap. 9.95 (*0-486-22729-4*) Dover.

Practical Steps for Aligniny Information Technology with Business Strategy: How to Achieve a Competitive Analysis. Bernard H. Boar. 368p. 1994. 59.99 (*0-471-07637-6*) Wiley.

Practical Steps for Informing Literacy Instruction: A Diagnostic Decision-Making Model. Michael W. Kibby. LC 95-18246. 1995. pap. 13.50 (*0-87207-133-2*) Intl Reading.

***Practical Steps to the Research Process for High School.** Deborah B. Stanley. LC 99-50169. (Information Literacy Ser.). 250p. (YA). 1999. pap. 29.00 (*1-56308-762-6*) Libs Unl.

***Practical Steps to the Research Process for High School.** Deborah B. Stanley. (Information Literacy Ser.). 255p. 2000. 33.00 (*1-56308-763-4*) Libs Unl.

Practical Stereology. J. C. Russ. (Illus.). 194p. (C). 1986. text 59.50 (*0-306-42460-6*, Kluwer Plenum) Kluwer Academic.

P

Practical Stock Investor: The Single Source of Tools & Techniques for Individual Investors. (Illus.). 182p. (Orig.). 1997. pap. text 19.95 (*0-9640600-0-0*) ARDI Res Pr.

Practical Stonemasonry Made Easy. Stephen M. Kennedy. (Illus.). 256p. 1988. 24.95 (*0-8306-1115-0*, 2915H) McGraw-Hill Prof.

Practical Strategic Planning: A Guide & Manual for Line Managers. William P. Anthony. LC 85-9489. (Illus.). 217p. 1985. 62.95 (*0-89930-102-9*, ANT/, Greenwood Pr) Greenwood.

Practical Strategies for Critical Thinking: A Student's Handbook. Jan Rehner. (C). 1993. text, teacher ed. 2.36 (*0-395-67341-0*); pap. text 9.16 (*0-395-67340-2*) HM.

Practical Strategies for Developing Large Software Systems Ellis Horowitz. LC 74-28818. xiii, 226p. 1975. write for info. (*0-201-02977-4*) Addison-Wesley.

Practical Strategies for Electronic Structure Calculations. Warren J. Hehre. 255p. 1995. 25.00 (*0-9643495-1-5*) Wavefunction.

***Practical Strategies for Experimenting.** G. K. Robinson. LC 00-27336. (Series in Probability & Statistics). 2000. write for info. (*0-471-49055-5*) Wiley.

Practical Strategies for Family-Centered Early Intervention. P. J. McWilliam et al. (Early Childhood Intervention Ser.). (Illus.). 212p. (Orig.). 1996. pap. 39.95 (*1-879105-94-2*, 0355) Thomson Learn.

Practical Strategies for Improving Instruction. Karen Wood. 118p. (C). 1994. pap. text 19.00 (*1-56090-082-2*) Natl Middle Schl.

Practical Strategies for Individual Behaviour Difficulties. Geraldine Mitchell. LC 98-149254. 96p. 1997. pap. 24.95 (*1-85346-518-6*, Pub. by David Fulton) Taylor & Francis.

***Practical Strategies for Mathematics Instruction.** Gail Bornfield. (Illus.). 120p. (C). 1999. pap. 15.95 (*1-886979-13-8*) Practicl Pr.

Practical Strategies for Reading Instruction. Gail Bornfield. (Illus.). 88p. (Orig.). 1997. pap. text 13.95 (*1-886979-11-1*) Practicl Pr.

Practical Strategies for School Improvement. National School Services Staff. (C). 1991. teacher ed. 95.00 (*0-932957-56-0*) Natl School.

Practical Strategies for School Improvement: Guidebook. National School Services Staff. (C). 25.00 (*0-932957-58-7*) Natl School.

Practical Strategies for Stock Options. Fred Bailey. 20p. 1997. pap. 3.00 (*0-915513-82-X*) Ctr Futures Ed.

Practical Strategies for Written Language Instruction. Gail Bornfield. (Illus.). 40p. (Orig.). 1996. pap. 8.95 (*1-886979-08-1*) Practicl Pr.

Practical Strategies in OB/GYN. Ransom. LC 99-33413. (C). 1999. text 105.00 (*0-7216-7854-8*, W B Saunders Co) Harcrt Hlth Sci Grp.

Practical Strategies in Outpatient Medicine. 2nd ed. Brendan M. Reilly. (Illus.). 1328p. 1990. text 155.00 (*0-7216-2821-4*, W B Saunders Co) Harcrt Hlth Sci Grp.

Practical Strategies in Pediatric Diagnosis & Therapy. Robert M. Kliegman et al. Ed. by Lisette Bralow & Judy Fletcher. LC 95-10279. 1184p. 1996. text 79.00 (*0-7216-5161-5*, W B Saunders Co) Harcrt Hlth Sci Grp.

Practical Strategies When Johnny Can't Learn or Behave. Linda Culbreth. 54p. 1999. spiral bd. 9.95 (*1-893784-00-2*) Aunt Matilda.

Practical Strategist. Robert J. Allio. 1990. pap. text 16.95 (*0-88730-399-4*, HarpBusn) HarpInfo.

Practical Strategist: Business & Corporate Strategy for the 1990s. Robert J. Allio. 240p. 1988. text 32.95 (*0-88730-319-6*, HarpBusn) HarpInfo.

Practical Stress Analysis for Design Engineers: Design & Analysis of Aerospace Vehicle Structures. Jean-Claude Flabel. LC 95-94570. xvi, 685 p. 1997. write for info. (*0-9647014-0-5*) Lake City Publng.

Practical Stress Analysis in Engineering Design. 2nd rev. ed. Blake. (Mechanical Engineering Ser.: Vol. 69). (Illus.). 712p. 1989. text 85.00 (*0-8247-8152-X*) Dekker.

***Practical Stress Management: A Comprehensive Workbook for Managing Change & Promoting Health.** 2nd ed. John A. Romas. LC 99-25928. 304p. 1999. pap. text 34.00 incl. cd-rom, audio compact disk (*0-205-31132-6*) P-H.

Practical Study of Argument. Trudy Govier. (C). 1984. pap. write for info. (*0-534-03333-4*) Wadsworth Pub.

Practical Study of Argument. 2nd ed. Trudy Govier. 376p. (C). 1987. pap. write for info. (*0-534-08262-9*) Wadsworth Pub.

Practical Study of Argument. 3rd ed. Govier. (Philosophy Ser.). 1991. teacher ed. write for info. (*0-534-14713-5*) Wadsworth Pub.

Practical Study of Argument. 3rd ed. Trudy Govier. 433p. (C). 1991. mass mkt. 31.25 (*0-534-14712-7*) Wadsworth Pub.

Practical Study of Argument. 4th ed. Trudy Govier. LC 96-21491. (Philosophy Ser.). (C). 1996. 58.95 (*0-534-50523-6*) Wadsworth Pub.

Practical Study of Argument. 5th ed. Govier. (Philosophy Ser.). 2000. pap. 36.00 (*0-534-51976-8*) Wadsworth Pub.

Practical Stylist. 7th ed. A. Baker. (C). 1997. pap. text 11.00 (*0-06-360430-2*) HarpC.

***Practical Stylist.** 8th ed. Baker. (C). 2000. pap. text. write for info. (*0-321-05507-1*) Addison-Wesley.

Practical Stylist. 8th ed. Sheridan Warner Baker. LC 97-22126. 268p. (C). 1997. pap. text 40.00 (*0-321-01975-X*) Addison-Wesley.

***Practical Stylist: Canadian.** 4th ed. 1998. teacher ed. write for info. (*0-201-37889-2*) Addison-Wesley.

Practical Stylist: Canadian Edition. 3rd ed. Sheridan Baker. (C). 1991. pap. 20.93 (*0-06-040449-3*) Addson-Wesley Educ.

Practical Stylist with Readings & Handbook. 8th ed. Sheridan W. Baker. LC 96-49817. 540p. (C). 1997. pap. text 49.00 (*0-321-01182-1*) Longman.

Practical Suggestions for Successful Ministry. Frederick K. Price. 112p. (Orig.). 1991. pap. 6.99 (*0-89274-880-X*, HH880) Harrison Hse.

Practical Suggestions for the Learning of an African Language in the Field. Ida C. Ward. LC PL8005.W28. (International African Institute Memorandum Ser.: Vol. 14). 40p. reprint ed. pap. 30.00 (*0-608-11073-6*, 205539000017) Bks Demand.

Practical Sun Power. 2nd rev. ed. William H. Rankins, III & David A. Wilson. (Illus.). 132p. 1999. pap. 12.00 (*0-934852-13-8*, LH-13) Lorien Hse.

Practical Supervision: How to Organize for Effectiveness. Anthony M. Micolo. Ed. by Stephen E. Bruce. 322p. 1987. ring bd. 63.71 (*1-55645-427-9*, 427) Busn Legal Reports.

Practical Surface Analysis: Auger & X-Ray Photoelectron Spectroscopy, Vol. 1, Auger and X-ray Photoelectron Spectroscopy. 2nd ed. Ed. by D. Briggs & M. P. Seah. 674p. 1996. pap. 175.00 (*0-471-95340-7*) Wiley.

Practical Surface Analysis, 2E, Vol. 2, Ion & Neutral Spectroscopy, Vol. 2, Ion and Neutral Spectroscopy. 2nd ed. Ed. by D. Briggs & M. P. Seah. LC 90-12172. 756p. 1992. 438.00 (*0-471-92082-7*) Wiley.

Practical Surveying & Computations. 2nd ed. A. L. Allan. LC 98-105135. (Illus.). 592p. 1997. pap. text 49.95 (*0-7506-3655-6*, Butterwrth Archit) Buttrwrth-Heinemann.

Practical Surveying for Technicians. Robert P. Landon. 36p. 1992. teacher ed. 14.95 (*0-8273-3942-9*) Delmar.

Practical Surveying Guide to Celestial Observations: A Compendium of Notes, Examples, Tables, Figures, Helpful Hints & HP41 Programs for Accurate Directions from Celestial Observations. Richard L. Elgin et al. (Illus.). 168p. 1989. pap. 40.00 (*0-9624124-0-6*) Busn News.

Practical Switching Power Supply Design. Marty Brown. (Professional & Technical Ser.). 240p. 1990. text 48.00 (*0-12-137030-5*) Acad Pr.

Practical Synthesis of High-Performance Analog Circuits. Emil S. Ochotta. LC 98-33724. 1998. 120.00 (*0-7923-8237-4*) Kluwer Academic.

Practical System of Rhetoric: or The Principles & Rules of Style. Samuel P. Newman. LC 95-31654. 334p. 1995. 50.00 (*0-8201-1496-0*) Schol Facsimiles.

Practical Systems Thinking. Alan Waring. 272p. 1996. mass mkt. 31.95 (*0-412-71750-6*) Chapman & Hall.

Practical Sytlistics: An Approach to Poetry. H. G. Widdowson. 244p. 1992. pap. text 18.95 (*0-19-437184-0*) OUP.

***Practical, Tactical & Legal Perspectives of Terrorism & Hostage-Taking.** James M. Poland & Michael J. McCrystle. LC 99-52435. (Criminology Studies: Vol. 9). 248p. 2000. 89.95 (*0-7734-7877-9*) E Mellen.

Practical Tae Kwon Do. Y. D. Choi. 414p. 1997. write for info. (*0-9658285-0-6*) Martial Arts.

Practical Talmud Dictionary. Yitzchak Frank. (ARC & HEB.). 1991. student ed. 22.95 (*0-87306-588-3*) Feldheim.

Practical Talmud Dictionary. enl. ed. Yitzchak Frank. (ARC & HEB.). 1991. 33.95 (*0-87306-587-5*) Feldheim.

Practical Taoism. Tr. by Thomas Cleary. LC 95-23894. 112p. 1996. pap. 12.95 (*1-57062-200-0*, Pub. by Shambhala Pubns) Random.

Practical Tatting. Phyllis Sparks. 94p. 1994. 20.00 (*0-916896-55-2*) Lacis Pubns.

Practical Tax: Individual & Estate Taxation for the Non-Tax Lawyer. John E. Moore. 313p. 1998. pap. 185.00 incl. audio (*0-943380-98-7*) PEG MN.

Practical Tax Administration. Dennis Frampton. 130p. (C). 1993. pap. 175.00 (*0-9515157-1-3*, Pub. by Fiscal Pubns) St Mut.

Practical Taxidermy. 2nd ed. John W. Moyer. LC 92-4770. 158p. 1992. reprint ed. lib. bdg. 23.50 (*0-89464-743-1*) Krieger.

Practical Taxonomic Computering. Richard J. Pankhurst. (Illus.). 160p. 1991. 45.00 (*0-340-55149-6*, A5557, Pub. by E A) Routldge.

Practical Techniques for Groundwater & Soil Remediation. Evan Nyer. 224p. 1992. lib. bdg. 85.00 (*0-87371-731-7*, L731) Lewis Pubs.

Practical Techniques for Laboratory Analysis. James A. Poppiti. 208p. 1994. lib. bdg. 75.00 (*0-87371-361-3*, L361) Lewis Pubs.

Practical Techniques of Business Forecasting: Fundamentals & Applications for Marketing, Production, & Financial Managers. George J. Kress. LC 85-6361. (Illus.). 257p. 1985. 65.00 (*0-89930-107-X*, KSU/, Quorum Bks) Greenwood.

Practical Techniques of Electronic Circuit Design. Robert L. Bonebreak. LC 81-11394. (Illus.). 324p. reprint ed. pap. 100.50 (*0-7837-3526-X*, 205786200008) Bks Demand.

Practical Techniques of Psychic Self-Defense. Murry Hope. 96p. 1985. pap. 7.95 (*0-312-63552-4*) St Martin.

Practical Technology Forecasting. James R. Bright. 110p. 1978. pap. 25.00 (*1-884154-09-3*) Tech Futures.

Practical Telepathy (1924) Joseph Ouette. 116p. 1998. reprint ed. pap. 14.95 (*0-7661-0634-9*) Kessinger Pub.

Practical Teratology. Pamela Taylor. 1986. text 73.00 (*0-12-683860-7*) Acad Pr.

Practical Thai Cooking. Puangkram C. Schmitz. 1997. pap. text 19.95 (*4-7700-2181-X*, Pub. by Kodansha Intl) Kodansha.

Practical Theology. Gerben Heintink. LC 99-11227. 360p. 1999. pap. 45.00 (*0-8028-4294-1*) Eerdmans.

Practical Theology: A New Approach. Marcel Viau. LC 99-24525. (Empirical Studies in Theology). 224p. 1999. 68.00 (*90-04-11440-8*) Brill Academic Pubs.

***Practical Theology: A View from the Plains.** Ed. by Michael G. Lawler & Gail S. Risch. 440p. 2000. 25.00 (*1-881871-36-3*, Pub. by Creighton U Pr); pap. 17.00 (*1-881871-37-1*, Pub. by Creighton U Pr) BookMasters.

Practical Theology: International Perspectives. Ed. by Friedrich Schweitzer & Johannes A. Van der Ven. LC 99-31599. (Erfahrung und Theologie Ser.: Vol. 34). 456p. 1999. pap. 56.95 (*0-8204-4329-8*) P Lang Pubng.

Practical Theology & the Ministry of the Church, 1952-1984: Essays in Honor of Edmund P. Clowney. Ed. by Harvie M. Conn. 328p. 1990. pap. 16.99 (*0-87552-207-6*) P & R Pubng.

Practical Theology of Spirituality. Lawrence O. Richards. 288p. 1987. 19.95 (*0-310-39140-7*, 18301) Zondervan.

Practical Theorist: The Life & Work of Kurt Lewin. Alfred J. Marrow. LC 77-1400. 319p. reprint ed. pap. 98.90 (*0-608-13533-X*, 202255100028) Bks Demand.

Practical Theory. Ed. by Aaron Stang. 164p. (Orig.). (C). 1993. audio 21.95 (*0-89898-692-3*, F3339GTXAT) Wrner Bros.

Practical Theory, Vol. 1. Sandy Feldstein. 32p. 1982. pap. text 5.95 (*0-88284-216-1*, 2280) Alfred Pub.

Practical Theory, Vol. 2. Sandy Feldstein. 32p. 1982. pap. 5.95 (*0-88284-217-X*, 2281) Alfred Pub.

Practical Theory, Vol. 3. Sandy Feldstein. 32p. 1982. pap. text 5.95 (*0-88284-218-8*, 2282) Alfred Pub.

Practical Theory: Complete. Sandy Feldstein. 96p. 1982. pap. text 10.95 (*0-88284-225-0*, 1998) Alfred Pub.

Practical Theory in Composition. Recchio & Spellmen. pap. text. write for info. (*0-312-07528-6*) St Martin.

Practical Theory of Programming. Eric C. Hehner. LC 93-5269. (Texts & Monographs in Computer Science). (Illus.). 243p. 1993. 58.95 (*0-387-94106-1*) Spr-Verlag.

Practical Theory of Tanning Leather, 1890-1987. J. Naylor. (Illus.). 150p. 1991. pap. 20.00 (*0-87556-359-7*) Saifer.

Practical Therapeutics for Older Patients. Denis O'Mahony & Una Martin. LC 98-36751. 284p. 1999. pap. 50.00 (*0-471-98594-5*) Wiley.

Practical Therapeutics of Traditional Chinese Medicine. Wu Yan & Warren Fischer. Ed. by Jake P. Fratkin. LC 97-4808. 700p. 1997. text 70.00 (*0-912111-39-9*) Paradigm Publns.

Practical Therapist Series: Metaphor in Psychotherapy, Rational Emotive Behavior Therapy, Meditative Therapy, Integrative Brief Therapy, 4 vols., Set. Michael L. Emmons et al. 1999. 99.95 (*1-886230-99-4*) Impact Pubs CA.

Practical Thermal Design for Electronic Equipment. Sung Jin Kim & Sanjeev B. Sathe. 1999. write for info. (*0-8493-1689-8*) CRC Pr.

Practical Thermocouple Thermometry. Thomas W. Kerlin. LC 98-38818. 1998. 50.00 (*1-55617-644-9*) ISA.

Practical Thermoforming. 2nd ed. Florian. (Plastics Engineering Ser.: Vol. 39). (Illus.). 480p. 1996. text 175.00 (*0-8247-9762-0*) Dekker.

Practical Thermoforming: Principles & Applications. John Florian. LC 86-29296. (Plastics Engineering Ser.: Vol. 14). (Illus.). 381p. reprint ed. pap. 118.20 (*0-608-08934-6*, 206956900005) Bks Demand.

Practical Thin-Layer Chromatography: A Multidisciplinary Approach. Ed. by Bernard Fried & Joseph Sherma. 288p. 1996. spiral bd. 79.95 (*0-8493-2660-5*) CRC Pr.

Practical Thinking. Edward De Bono. 1990. 25.00 (*0-317-90560-0*) Intl Ctr Creat Think.

Practical Thoracoscopy. Ed. by C. Boutin et al. (Illus.). 112p. 1992. 163.00 (*0-387-52369-3*) Spr-Verlag.

Practical Timber Formwork. B. Peters. 1991. pap. 44.95 (*0-442-31386-1*) Chapman & Hall.

Practical Time. C. Gilles-Brown. Ed. by Cindy Drolet. (Language for Living Ser.). 207p. 1993. spiral bd. 44.00 (*1-883315-03-4*, 8005) Imaginart Intl.

Practical Time-Frequency Analysis: Gabor & Wavelet Transforms with an Implementation in Wavelet Analysis & Its Applications, Vol. 9. R. Carmona et al. LC 98-22862. (Wavelet Analysis And Its Applications ;). (Illus.). 490p. (C). 1998. text 65.00 (*0-12-160170-6*) Acad Pr.

Practical Time Management: How to Get More Things Done in Less Time. 2nd ed. Bradley C. McRae. (Business Ser.). 144p. 1992. pap. 7.95 (*0-88908-281-2*) Self-Counsel Pr.

Practical Time Management: How to Make the Most of Your Most Perishable Resource. Marion E. Haynes. LC 84-20742. 122p. 1991. pap. 14.95 (*1-56052-018-3*) Crisp Pubns.

***Practical Time Series.** Gareth Janacek. 256p. 2000. pap. text 34.95 (*0-340-71999-0*) E A.

Practical Timeshare & Group Ownership. Colin Jenkins. 192p. 1987. pap. 74.00 (*0-406-10328-3*, UK, MICHIE) LEXIS Pub.

Practical Timex-Sinclair Computer Programs for Beginners. Edward Page. 96p. 1983. 7.95 (*0-86668-027-6*) ARCsoft.

Practical Tips for Americans Traveling Abroad: Ignore Them at Your Own Risk. Gladson I. Nwanna. LC 97-19149. 255p. (Orig.). 1998. pap. 19.99 (*1-890605-09-3*) Wld Trvl Inst.

Practical Tips for Turners & Carvers. (Illus.). 80p. 1996. pap. 9.95 (*0-946819-91-2*, Pub. by Guild Master) Sterling.

Practical Tips for Woodturners: The Best from Woodturning Magazine. Woodturning Magazine Editors. (Illus.). 64p. 1995. pap. 9.95 (*0-946819-74-2*) Sterling.

Practical to the EMEA. William J. Currie & Monica Lofgren. 203p. (Orig.). 1996. pap. 175.00 (*1-882615-27-1*) Parexel Intl.

Practical Tools & Techniques for Managing Time. Myrna Lebov. 1981. pap. 5.95 (*0-917386-38-8*) Exec Ent Pubns.

Practical Tourism Forecasting. Douglas C. Frechtling. LC 97-130584. (Illus.). 256p. 1996. pap. text 46.95 (*0-7506-0877-3*) Buttrwrth-Heinemann.

Practical Tourist: or Sketches of the State of the Useful Arts, & of Society, Scenery in Great Britain, France & Holland, 2 vols. Zachariah Allen. LC 73-38258. (Evolution of Capitalism Ser.). 896p. 1972. reprint ed. 57.95 (*0-405-04111-X*) Ayer.

***Practical Training Strategies for the Future.** S. Brelade et al. (Financial Times Management Briefings Ser.). 1998. pap. 89.50 (*0-273-63395-3*, Pub. by F T P-H) Trans-Atl Phila.

Practical Transfer Handbook. 2nd ed. Lowdon. 1996. text 59.50 (*0-07-038860-1*) McGraw.

Practical Transformer Design Handbook. Eric Lowden. LC 80-50057. 1980. pap. 23.95 (*0-672-21657-4*) Sams.

Practical Transformer Handbook for Electronics, Radio & Communications Engineers. Irving Gottlieb. LC 98-229027. (Illus.). 192p. 2000. pap. text 39.95 (*0-7506-3992-X*, Newnes) Buttrwrth-Heinemann.

***Practical Transfusion Medicine.** Michael F. Murphy & Derwood H. Pamphilon. (Illus.). 328p. 2000. 110.00 (*0-632-05114-0*) Blackwell Sci.

Practical Treatise of Astral Medicine & Therapeutics. M. D. Duz. 252p. 1996. reprint ed. pap. 16.00 (*0-7873-0304-6*) Hlth Research.

Practical Treatise of Astral Medicine & Therapeutics. M. D. Duz. 257p. 1996. reprint ed. pap. 14.95 (*1-56459-684-2*) Kessinger Pub.

Practical Treatise of Cast & Wrought Iron Bridges & Girders: As Applied to Railway Structures & to Buildings Generally. William Humber. (Industrial Antiquities Ser.). (Illus.). 236p. 1998. reprint ed. pap. 405.00 (*1-85297-018-9*, Pub. by Archival Facs) St Mut.

Practical Treatise of Powers. 8th ed. Edward Sugden. xxii, 1000p. 1993. reprint ed. 125.00 (*0-8377-1172-X*, Rothman) W S Hein.

Practical Treatise of Powers, 2 vols., Set. Edward Sugden. LC 93-78307. 1186p. 1993. reprint ed. 125.00 (*0-89941-844-9*, 307880) W S Hein.

Practical Treatise on Business. Edwin T. Freedley. LC 73-2508. (Big Business; Economic Power in a Free Society Ser.). 1973. reprint ed. 25.95 (*0-405-05089-5*) Ayer.

Practical Treatise on Coal, Petroleum & Other Distilled Oils. 2nd ed. Abraham Gesner. LC 67-29511. (Library of Early American Business & Industry: No. 33). (Illus.). 181p. 1968. reprint ed. 37.50 (*0-678-00440-4*) Kelley.

Practical Treatise on Fractures & Dislocations. Frank H. Hamilton. (American Civil War Medical Ser.: No. 3). (Illus.). 757p. 1991. reprint ed. 95.00 (*0-930405-32-3*) Norman SF.

Practical Treatise on Military Surgery. Frank H. Hamilton. LC 88-60873. (American Civil War Surgery Ser.: No. 5). 232p. 1989. reprint ed. 65.00 (*0-930405-05-6*) Norman SF.

Practical Treatise on Nullities & Irregularities in Law: Their Character, Distinctions, & Consequences. H. MacNamara. xx, 231p. 1996. reprint ed. 37.50 (*0-8377-2481-3*, Rothman) W S Hein.

Practical Treatise on Organ - Building, 2 vols. F. E. Robertson. (Illus.). 370p. 1997. reprint ed. pap. 75.00 (*0-913746-04-5*) Organ Lit.

Practical Treatise on the Diseases of the Eye. deluxe ed. William Mackenzie. LC 78-31614. 732p. 1979. reprint ed. 49.50 (*0-88275-947-7*) Krieger.

Practical Treatise on the Diseases of the Eye. William Mackenzie. LC 78-31614. 732p. 1979. reprint ed. 44.50 (*0-88275-841-1*) Krieger.

Practical Treatise on the Domestic Management & Most Important Diseases of Advanced Life. George E. Day. Ed. by Robert J. Kastenbaum. LC 78-22198. (Aging & Old Age Ser.). 1979. reprint ed. lib. bdg. 19.95 (*0-405-11815-5*) Ayer.

Practical Treatise on the Law of Auctions: With Forms, Tables, Statutes & Cases, & Directions to Auctioneers. xii, 360p. 1994. reprint ed. 47.50 (*0-8377-2524-0*, Rothman) W S Hein.

Practical Treatise on the Law of Corporations: In General, As Well Aggregate As Sole. James Grant. LC 93-78461. 797p. 1993. reprint ed. 160.00 (*1-56169-041-4*) Gaunt.

Practical Treatise on the Law of Covenants for Title. 3rd enl. rev. ed. William H. Rawle. LC 97-28843. xliii, 832p. 1997. reprint ed. 97.50 (*0-8377-2583-6*, Rothman) W S Hein.

***Practical Treatise on the Law of Partnership: First American, from the Last London Edition with Notes & References...** Niel Gow & Edward D. Ingraham. LC 99-58121. xxvii, 518p. 2000. 75.00 (*1-57588-570-0*) W S Hein.

***Practical Treatise on the Law of Replevin.** J. E. Cobbey. 993p. 1999. 210.00 (*1-56169-451-7*) Gaunt.

Practical Treatise on the Law of Slavery. Jacob D. Wheeler. LC 68-58073. 476p. 1969. reprint ed. lib. bdg. 75.00 (*0-8371-0748-2*, WHL&) Greenwood.

Practical Treatise on the Office of Sheriff: Comprising the Whole of the Duties, Remuneration, & Liabilities of Sheriffs, in the Execution & Return of Writs, & in the Election of Knights of the Shire. 2nd ed. William H. Watson. LC 94-19792. xvi, 577p. 1994. reprint ed. 67.50 (*0-8377-2776-6*, Rothman) W S Hein.

Practical Treatise on the Settling of Evidence for Trials at Nisi Prius: And on the Preparing & Arranging the Necessary Proofs. 2nd ed. Isaac 'Espinasse. LC 98-10638. xxii, 550p. 1998. reprint ed. 75.00 (*0-8377-2111-3*, Rothman) W S Hein.

Practical Treatise on the Use of the Microscope. John Quekett. (History of Microscopy Ser.). 512p. 1987. reprint ed. 72.00 (*0-940095-05-X*) Sci Heritage Ltd.

Practical Treatise upon the Authority & Duty of Justices of the Peace in Criminal Prosecutions. Daniel Davis. iv, 687p. 1994. reprint ed. 67.50 (*0-8377-2040-0*, Rothman) W S Hein.

An Asterisk (*) at the beginning of an entry indicates that the title is appearing for the first time.

Practical Treatise upon the Law of Railways. 2nd ed. Isaac F. Redfield. LC 70-37982. (American Law Ser.: The Formative Years). 850p. 1972. reprint ed. 53.95 (*0-405-04025-3*) Ayer.

Practical Treatment of Backache & Sciatica. D. N Golding & J. Barrett. 1984. text 88.00 (*0-85200-773-6*) Kluwer Academic.

Practical Tree Management: An Arborists Handbook. Trevor Lawrence & Paul Norquay. 132p. 1997. pap. 44.95 (*0-909605-72-6*) Buttrwrth-Heinemann.

Practical Troubleshooting for Microprocessors. James W. Coffron. (Illus.). 256p. 1981. text 47.00 (*0-13-694273-3*) P-H.

Practical Troubleshooting with the Advanced Video Analyzer. Robert L. Goodman. 384p. 1993. pap. 24.95 (*0-07-023999-1*) McGraw.

Practical Troubleshooting with the Advanced Video Analyzer. Robert L. Goodman. LC 92-43107. 1993. pap. 24.60 (*0-8306-4353-2*) McGraw-Hill Prof.

Practical Trust Administration. Michael Sladen. 448p. 1990. pap. 125.00 (*0-85297-328-4*, Pub. by Chartered Bank) St Mut.

Practical Truth Series, 6 Vols. Incl. Elisha. Ed. by Alfred Edersheim. 1986. Israel's Wanderings. Ed. by Alfred Edersheim. 1986. Pastoral Epistles. Thessalonians. Ed. by Alfred Edersheim. 1986. 1940p. 1986. 75.95 (*0-8254-3529-3*) Kregel.

Practical Truths from the Pastoral Epistles. Eugene Stock. LC 83-6113. 352p. 1983. 14.99 (*0-8254-3746-6*, Kregel Class) Kregel.

Practical Tutor. Emily Meyer & Louise Z. Smith. (Illus.). 368p. 1987. pap. text 29.95 (*0-19-503865-7*) OUP.

Practical Tv/video Systems Repair. Ross. LC 99-46635. (C). 1999. pap. text 54.95 (*0-8273-8547-1*) Delmar.

Practical Twinework for Fisherman & Gear Technologists. Joseph T. DeAlteris. Ed. by Kathleen M. Castro. 172p. (Orig.). (C). 1990. 5.00 (*1-882027-02-7*) URI ICMRD.

Practical Typecasting. Theo Rehak. (Illus.). 240p. 1993. 64.95 (*0-938768-33-6*) Oak Knoll.

Practical Understanding of Capability by Implementing Statistical Process Control. 2nd rev. ed. James C. Abbott. LC 95-69102. (Illus.). 338p. 1996. boxed set 39.95 (*1-887355-02-2*) R H Smith Pubs.

Practical Understanding of Capability by Implementing Statistical Process Control. 3rd ed. James C. Abbott. LC 98-89305. (Illus.). 406p. 1999. 49.95 (*1-887355-03-0*) R H Smith Pubs.

***Practical Understanding of Pre- & Poststack Migraitons Vol. 2: (Prestack)** John C. Bancroft. Ed. by Roger A. Young. (Course Notes Ser.: No. 9). (Illus.). 388p. 1998. pap. text 60.00 (*1-56080-084-4*) Soc Expl Geophys.

Practical Understanding of Pre- & Poststack Migrations Vol. 1: (Poststack) John C. Bancroft. Ed. by Roger A. Young. (Course Notes Ser.: No. 7). (Illus.). 380p. 1997. pap. text 47.00 (*1-56080-045-3*) Soc Expl Geophys.

***Practical Unix.** 650p. 1999. 29.99 (*0-7897-2250-X*) Que.

Practical UNIX & Internet Security. 2nd ed. Simson Garfinkel & Gene Spafford. 1004p. 1996. pap. 39.95 (*1-56592-148-8*) Thomson Learn.

Practical UNIX Programming: A Guide to Concurrency, Communication, & Multithreading. Kay A. Robbins & Steven Robbins. LC 95-39618. 672p. 1996. 62.00 (*0-13-443706-3*) P-H.

Practical Upholstering: And the Cutting of Slip Covers. Frederick Palmer. LC 80-51766. (Illus.). 288p. 1982. pap. 11.95 (*0-8128-6170-1*, Scrbrough Hse) Madison Bks UPA.

Practical Urodynamics. Victor W. Nitti. Ed. by Stephanie Donley. LC 97-37848. (Illus.). 352p. (C). 1998. text 115.00 (*0-7216-3806-6*, W B Saunders Co) Harcrt Hlth Sci Grp.

Practical Urogynecology. L. Lewis Wall et al. LC 93-9416. (Illus.). 416p. 1993. 75.00 (*0-683-08645-6*) Lppncott W & W.

Practical Urology in Spinal Cord Injury. K. F. Parsons & J. M. Fitzpatrick. (Clinical Practice in Urology Ser.). (Illus.). xii, 145p. 1991. 126.00 (*0-387-19676-5*) Spr-Verlag.

Practical U.S. Resource Guide to the European Union. Christian D. De Fouloy. LC 98-235197. 280 p. 1998. 75.00 (*90-411-0641-3*) Kluwer Law Intl.

Practical Usage of ISPF Dialog Manager. Anthony S. Rudd. 1989. text 32.95 (*0-470-21574-7*) P-H.

Practical Usage of ISPF Dialog Manager. 2nd rev. ed. Anthony Rudd. 381p. 1996. pap. 69.95 (*3-540-19950-0*) Spr-Verlag.

Practical Usage of MVS REXX. 2nd rev. ed. Anthony S. Rudd. (Illus.). xiv, 310p. 1996. pap. 59.95 (*3-540-19952-7*) Spr-Verlag.

***Practical Usage of TSO REXX.** 3rd rev. ed. Anthony S. Rudd. LC 00-20844. (Illus.). xvi, 362p. 2000. pap. 79.95 (*1-85233-261-1*) Spr-Verlag.

Practical Use of Fracture Mechanics. David Broek. (C). 1988. lib. bdg. 216.00 (*90-247-3707-9*) Kluwer Academic.

Practical Use of Fracture Mechanics. David Broek. (C). 1989. pap. text 75.00 (*0-7923-0223-0*) Kluwer Academic.

***Practical Use of Mathcad: Solving Mathematical Problems with a Computer Algebra System.** Hans Benker. Tr. by A. Rudd from GER. LC 99-33922. xiv, 506p. 1999. 54.00 (*1-85233-166-6*, Pub. by Spr-Verlag) Spr-Verlag.

Practical Use of Speech Communication. 6th ed. Barrett. (C). 1995. pap. write for info. (*0-03-017068-0*) Harcourt Coll Pubs.

Practical Use of Theory in Fluid Flow Bk. 1: Inertial Flows. S. W. Churchill. 155p. 1988. text 66.95 (*0-936282-01-0*) Buttrwrth-Heinemann.

Practical User Interface Design: Developing Software Within Real World Constraints. Debra Herschmann. 350p. 1999. pap. 44.95 (*1-55860-501-0*, Pub. by Morgan Kaufmann) Harcourt.

Practical User Interface Design: Making GUIs Work. Carl Zetie. LC 95-34164. 1995. pap. 45.00 (*0-07-709167-1*) McGraw.

Practical User's Guide to the Trust Territory Archives. Sam McPhetres. (Educational Ser.: No. 14). 45p. 1992. pap. 7.50 (*1-878453-12-2*) Univ Guam MAR Ctr.

Practical Uses of Open VMS System Services: Emulating DCL in Fortran & C Programs. Mike Taylor & Retha Taylor. (Illus.). 408p. 1998. spiral bd. 50.00 (*0-9650944-5-6*) Taylor Made Sftwre.

Practical Uses of Speech Communication. 6th ed. Harold Barrett. 320p. (C). 1987. pap. text 23.50 (*0-03-003272-5*) Harcourt Coll Pubs.

Practical Utility Safety: A Collection of Discussions & Calculation Aids for Power, Telephone & CATV Utilities. Ed. by Allan L. Clapp. (Illus.). 360p. 1999. pap. write for info. (*0-7392-0162-X*, PO3116) Morris Pubng.

Practical Vascular Surgery. Yao & Pearce. 600p. 1999. 155.00 (*0-8385-8164-1*, Apple Lange Med) McGraw.

Practical VCR Repair. David T. Ronan. LC 94-20858. 592p. 1994. pap. 69.95 (*0-8273-6583-7*) Delmar.

Practical Vedanta. Swami Vivekananda. 112p. 2002. pap. 2.50 (*81-7505-087-X*, Pub. by Advaita Ashrama) Vedanta Pr.

Practical Vedic Astrology: A Complete Self Learning Treatise. Ed. by G. S. Agarwal. 1998. pap. 20.00 (*0-8364-5537-1*) S Asia.

Practical Vedic Dictionary. Suryakanta. 1981. 75.00 (*0-8288-1784-7*) Fr & Eur.

Practical Vedic Dictionary. Suryakanta. (C). 1981. 55.00 (*0-19-561298-1*) OUP.

Practical Veterinary Ultrasound. Robert E. Cartee et al. LC 94-44192. (Lea & Febiger Ser.). (Illus.). 352p. 1995. (*0-683-01483-8*) Lppncott W & W.

Practical View of Christianity. William Wilberforce. Ed. by Kevin Belmonte. 288p. 1996. 16.95 (*1-56563-176-5*) Hendrickson MA.

Practical View of the Present State of Slavery in the West Indies. Alexander Barclay. LC 74-83955. (Black Heritage Library Collection). 1977. 36.95 (*0-8369-8508-7*) Ayer.

Practical Visionaries: A Study of Community Aid Abroad. Susan Blackburn. 272p. (Orig.). 1993. pap. 29.95 (*0-522-84562-2*, Pub. by Melbourne Univ Pr) Paul & Co Pubs.

***Practical Visionaries: Women, Education & Social Progress, 1790-1930.** Mary Hilton & Pamela Hirsch. LC 99-44986. (Women & Men in History Ser.). 264p. 2000. pap. 25.00 (*0-582-40431-2*) Longman.

Practical Visions of Ya'qub Sanu' Irene L. Gendzier. LC 66-28047. (Middle Eastern Monographs: No. 15). 179p. 1966. pap. 4.50 (*0-674-69650-6*) HUP.

Practical Visual Basic 6. Bob Reselman. 850p. 1999. pap. 29.99 (*0-7897-2145-7*) Que.

Practical Visual C++ 6. Jonathan B. Bates & Timothy J. Tompkins. 1999. pap. 29.99 (*0-7897-2142-2*) Que.

Practical Visual InterDev 6. Michael Amundsen & Susan Warren. 750p. 1999. pap. 29.99 (*0-7897-2143-0*) Que.

Practical Vocabulary. Judith Meyers. LC 97-47189. (Basics Made Easy Ser.). 208p. 1998. pap. 13.95 (*1-57685-082-X*) LrningExprss.

Practical Vocational Neuropsychological & Psychotherapy Interventions. Robert T. Fraser & David C. Clemmons. LC 99-30237. 264p. 1999. boxed set 59.95 (*0-8493-3315-6*) CRC Pr.

Practical Waste Management. Ed. by John R. Holmes. LC 82-8633. (Illus.). 583p. 1990. reprint ed. pap. 180.80 (*0-7837-6383-2*, 204609600010) Bks Demand.

Practical Watch Adjusting. Donald De Carle. (Illus.). 162p. 21.95 (*0-7198-0050-1*, Pub. by R Hale Ltd) Seven Hills Bk.

Practical Watch Adjusting. Donald De Carle. (Illus.). 242p. 1987. reprint ed. 29.50 (*0-7198-0051-X*, Pub. by NAG Press) Antique Collect.

Practical Watch Repairing. 3rd ed. Donald De Carle. 1986. 35.00 (*0-7198-0030-7*, Pub. by NAG Press) Antique Collect.

Practical Wax Modeling: Advanced Techniques for Wax Modelers. Hiroshi Tsuyuki & Yoko Ohba. Tr. by Susumu Satow from JPN. (Illus.). 143p. 1993. pap. 29.95 (*0-9637463-0-8*) ASQ.

PRACTICAL WAY TO LIVE A LIFE ACCORDING TO THE HIGH PEAK OF THE DIVINE REVELATION IN THE HOLY SCRIPTURES see Manera Practica de Llevar una Vida Conforme a la Cumbre de la Revelacion Divinae Contenida En Las Santas Escrituras

Practical Way To Live a Life According to the High Peak of the Divine Revelation in the Holy Scriptures. Witness Lee. 50p. 1994. pap. 4.50 (*0-87083-818-0*, 04-033-001) Living Stream Ministry.

Practical Ways to Improve Your Communication. Robert Phillips & Rob Phillips. 38p. pap. text 49.50 incl. audio (*0-88432-182-7*, S08100) Audio-Forum.

Practical Welding Technology. Rudy Mohler. LC 83-23298. (Illus.). 220p. (C). 1983. 30.95 (*0-8311-1143-7*) Indus Pr.

Practical Well Control. Jim Fitzpatrick. Ed. by Ron Baker. LC 98-24790. (Illus.). 354p. 1998. pap. 40.00 (*0-88698-183-2*, 2.80040) PETEX.

Practical Western Training. 2nd rev. ed. Dave Jones. LC 85-40476. (Illus.). 288p. 1985. 24.95 (*0-8061-1949-7*) U of Okla Pr.

***Practical Wildlife Care: For Veterinary Nurses, Animal Care Students & Rehabilitators.** Les Stocker. LC 99-461977. (Illus.). 304p. 2000. pap. text 34.95 (*0-632-05245-7*, Pub. by Blckwell Science) Iowa St U Pr.

Practical Wills Drafting. W. A. McIntyre. 236p. 1992. 67.00 (*0-409-89762-0*, MICHIE) LEXIS Pub.

***Practical Windows Millennium.** 2nd ed. Faithe Wempen. (Illus.). 600p. 2000. pap. 24.99 (*0-7897-2405-7*) Que.

***Practical Windows Peer Networking: Networking 2-10 PCs in Your Home or Office.** Jerry Ford. (Illus.). 500p. 1999. pap. 29.99 (*0-7897-2233-X*) Que.

***Practical Windows 2000 Professional.** Ed Bott. 600p. 2000. pap. text 24.99 (*0-7897-2124-4*) Que.

***Practical Windows 2000 Server.** Robert Reinstein. 700p. 2000. pap. text 29.99 (*0-7897-2141-4*) Que.

Practical Wine Knowledge. Bruce H. Axler. 1974. pap. 3.95 (*0-672-96119-9*, Bobbs) Macmillan.

Practical Wireless Data Modem Design. Jonathon Cheah. LC 99-27667. (Artech House Mobile Communications Library). 427p. 1999. 97.00 (*1-58053-047-8*) Artech Hse.

Practical Wisdom: Making the Most of Every Moment. Dan Millman. 1995. 16.00 incl. audio (*0-671-52904-8*) S&S Trade.

Practical Wisdom & Timely Advice. Richard Reed. LC 98-93856. x, 342p. 1998. pap. 14.95 (*0-9666197-0-6*) Catawba Pr.

***Practical Wisdom of Proverbs.** Louis Goldberg. LC 99-57599. 224p. 1999. pap. 10.99 (*0-8254-2733-9*) Kregel.

Practical Witchcraft. unabridged ed. Mellisa Swaim. (Modern Witchcraft Ser.: Vol. 1). (Illus.). 115p. 1997. 29.95 (*1-57179-066-7*) Intern Guild ASRS.

Practical Wood Patternmaking. 1996. lib. bdg. 263.95 (*0-8490-8338-9*) Gordon Pr.

Practical Woodturner. F. Pain. 1990. pap. 12.95 (*0-8273-5384-7*) Delmar.

***Practical Woodworker.** rev. ed. Bernard E. Jones. (Illus.). 600p. 2000. pap. 16.95 (*1-58008-146-0*) Ten Speed Pr.

Practical Woody Plant Propagation for Nursery Growers, Vol. I. Bruce Macdonald. (Illus.). 660p. 1987. 69.95 (*0-88192-062-2*) Timber.

***Practical Word Studies in the New Testament, Vol. 2.** LC 98-75730. 1300p. 1999. write for info. (*1-57407-108-4*) Ldrship Minist Wrldwide.

***Practical Word Studies in the New Testament: A-Z.** LC 98-75730. 2600p. 1999. write for info. (*1-57407-106-8*); write for info. (*1-57407-107-6*) Ldrship Minist Wrldwide.

Practical Work in Elementary Astronomy. M. J. Minnaert. 247p. 1969. text 88.00 (*90-277-0133-4*) Kluwer Academic.

Practical Work in Planning Education. Eric Reade. (C). 1981. 35.00 (*0-7855-3863-1*, Pub. by Oxford Polytechnic) St Mut.

Practical Work in School Science: Which Way Now? J. J. Wellington. LC 98-3969. 288p. (C). 1998. 80.00 (*0-415-17492-9*) Routledge.

Practical Work in School Science: Which Way Now? J. J. Wellington. LC 98-3969. xvi, 293 p. (C). 1998. pap. 25.99 (*0-415-17493-7*) Routledge.

***Practical Work in Science Education: Recent Research Studies.** John Leach & Albert Chr. Paulsen. 331p. 1999. pap. 96.00 (*87-7867-079-9*) Kluwer Academic.

Practical Work of a Bank. William H. Kniffin, Jr. Ed. by Stuart Bruchey. LC 80-1157. (Rise of Commercial Banking Ser.). (Illus.). 1981. reprint ed. lib. bdg. 55.95 (*0-405-13664-1*) Ayer.

Practical Work on Self. E. J. Gold. LC 89-1377. (Illus.). 210p. (Orig.). 1989. pap. 15.95 (*0-89556-056-9*) Gateways Bks & Tapes.

Practical Works of Richard Baxter, 23 vols. Richard Baxter. Ed. by William Orme. LC 72-161735. reprint ed. lib. bdg. write for info. (*0-404-00700-7*) AMS Pr.

Practical Works of Richard Baxter. Richard Baxter. (Giant Summit Bks.). 1000p. 1981. reprint ed. pap. 14.95 (*0-8010-0804-2*) Baker Bks.

Practical Works of Richard Baxter, 4 vols. 2nd ed. Richard Baxter. Incl. . Call to the Unconverted: Volume 2 of the Practical Works. 2nd ed. 1063p. 2000. reprint ed. text 60.00 (*1-877611-15-8*); . Christian Directory: Volume 1 of the Practical Works. 2nd ed. Frwd. by J. I. Packer. 1023p. 2000. reprint ed. text 60.00 (*1-877611-13-1*); No. 3. Saints' Everlasting Rest: Volume 3 of the Practical Works. 2nd ed. 1068p. 2000. reprint ed. text 60.00 (*1-877611-28-X*); No. 4. Reformed Pastor: Volume 4 of the Practical Works. 2nd ed. 1047p. 2000. reprint ed. text 60.00 (*1-877611-36-0*); 4201p. 2000. reprint ed. Set text 240.00 (*1-877611-37-9*) Soli Deo Gloria.

Practical Writer. 6th ed. Bailey. (C). 1995. pap. text, teacher ed. 33.75 (*0-15-501789-6*) Harcourt Coll Pubs.

Practical Writer. 7th ed. Bailey. (C). 1998. pap. text 32.50 (*0-15-505509-7*, Pub. by Harcourt Coll Pubs) Harcourt.

Practical Writer with Readings. 3rd ed. Edward P. Bailey, Jr. et al. 390p. (C). 1992. teacher ed. write for info. (*0-03-055842-5*) Harcourt Coll Pubs.

Practical Writer's Guide. Susan X. Day & Elizabeth McMahan. LC 96-7026. 466p. 1996. pap. text 40.00 (*0-205-17386-1*) Allyn.

Practical Writer's Guide: Examination Copy. Susan X. Day et al. 496p. (C). 1996. pap. text. write for info. (*0-205-26429-8*, T6429-9) Allyn.

Practical Writer's Guide with Additional Readings: Examination Copy. Susan X. Day et al. 576p. (C). 1996. pap. text. write for info. (*0-205-26430-1*, T6430-7) Allyn.

Practical Writer's Guide with Readings. Susan X. Day & Elizabeth McMahan. LC 96-1201. 546p. 1996. pap. text 42.00 (*0-205-17389-6*) Allyn.

Practical Writing Techniques. 2nd ed. 208p. (C). 1992. 35.60 (*0-536-58177-0*) Pearson Custom.

Practical Writing Techniques. 4th ed. Zan Dale Robinson. 218p. (C). 1994. text 34.00 (*0-536-58565-2*) Pearson Custom.

Practical Writing Techniques. 5th ed. Zan Dale Robinson. 218p. (C). 1995. text 34.00 (*0-536-58887-2*) Pearson Custom.

Practical Writing Techniques. 6th ed. 218p. (C). 1996. 29.00 (*0-536-59454-6*) Pearson Custom.

Practical Writing Techniques. 7th ed. Robinson. 330p. 1998. pap. text 24.00 (*0-536-01225-3*) Pearson Custom.

***Practical Writing Techniques.** 8th ed. 340p. (C). 1999. 28.20 (*0-536-60259-X*) Pearson Custom.

Practical Writing with Readings. 5th ed. Bailey. (C). 1998. pap. text 34.00 (*0-15-505502-X*, Pub. by Harcourt Coll Pubs) Harcourt.

Practical Xilinx Designer. David E. Van Den Bout. 384p. (C). 1997. pap. text, lab manual ed. 41.00 (*0-13-095502-7*, Prentice Hall) P-H.

***Practical Xilinx Designer Lab Book: Version 1.5.** David E. Van Den Bout. LC 99-12146. 1999. write for info. (*0-13-021617-8*) P-H.

Practical XView Programming. Kenneth D. Bibb & Larry Wake. LC 92-30943. 480p. 1993. pap. 34.95 (*0-471-57460-0*) Wiley.

Practical Yoga. 6th ed. O. Hashnu Hara. 79p. 1996. reprint ed. spiral bd. 10.00 (*0-7873-0373-9*) Hlth Research.

Practical Youth Ministry. Bert Jones. 217p. 1993. ring bd. 24.95 (*0-917851-23-4*) Bristol Hse.

Practical Youth Ministry Handbook: 43 No-Fail Ways to Energize Your Ministry! Michael D. Warden. LC 92-43278. 1993. 14.99 (*1-55945-175-0*) Group Pub.

Practical Zone System. 3rd ed. Chris Johnson. 208p. 1998. pap. text 29.95 (*0-240-80328-0*, Focal) Buttrwrth-Heinemann.

Practical Zone System: A Guide to Photographic Control. 2nd ed. Chris Johnson. LC 93-39251. (Illus.). 176p. 1994. pap. text 29.95 (*0-240-80178-4*, Focal) Buttrwrth-Heinemann.

Practical Zoology (Hons) G. Ghosh & M. Manna. (C). 1989. 60.00 (*0-89771-421-0*, Pub. by Current Dist) St Mut.

Practical Zuni Orthography see Zuni Law: A Field of Values, with an Appendix

Practicalities. Marguerite Duras. LC 89-77419. (Illus.). 143p. 1992. pap. 9.95 (*0-8021-3311-8*, Grove) Grove-Atltic.

***Practicality of Pulsed Fast Neutron Transmission Spectroscopy for Aviation Security.** National Research Council Staff. 58p. 1999. pap. 18.00 (*0-309-06449-X*) Natl Acad Pr.

Practically Married. Christine Rimmer. 1998. per. 4.25 (*0-373-24174-7*, 1-24174-0) Silhouette.

***Practically Minimal.** Maggie Toy. LC 00-101017. (Illus.). 192p. 2000. 40.00 (*0-500-51010-5*, Pub. by Thames Hudson) Norton.

Practically Painless English. 2nd ed. Sally F. Wallace. (English Composition Ser.). 212p. (C). 1989. pap. text 45.00 (*0-13-692781-5*) P-H.

***Practically Perfect.** Caroline Anderson. 288p. 2000. 26.99 (*0-263-16330-X*, Pub. by Mills & Boon) Ulverscroft.

Practically Perfect. Janet Lambert. 20.95 (*0-8488-0130-X*) Amereon Ltd.

***Practically Perfect Pajamas.** Erik Brooks. LC 99-16879. (Illus.). 32p. (J). (ps-3). 2000. 16.95 (*1-890817-22-8*, Pub. by Winslow Pr) Publishers Group.

Practically Popular Crowd: Pretty Enough. Meg F. Schneider. 192p. (J). (gr. 4-6). 1992. 2.95 (*0-590-44804-8*, Apple Paperbacks) Scholastic Inc.

Practically Religious: Worldly Benefits & the Common Religion of Japan. Ian Reader & George J. Tanabe, Jr. LC 98-4192. (Illus.). 328p. 1998. text 45.00 (*0-8248-2065-7*); pap. text 22.95 (*0-8248-2090-8*) UH Pr.

Practically Speaking: A Dictionary of Quotations on Engineering, Technology & Architecture. Carl C. Gaither & Alma E. Cavazos-Gaither. LC 98-46032. (Illus.). 367p. 1998. 24.99 (*0-7503-0594-0*) IOP Pub.

Practically Speaking: A Sourcebook for Instructional Consultants. Kathleen Brinko & Robert J. Menges. (Faculty Development Ser.). 360p. 1997. pap. 39.95 (*0-913507-87-3*) New Forums.

Practicals for Psychology. Cara Flanagan. (Illus.). 184p. (C). 1998. pap., wbk. ed. 32.99 (*0-415-15774-9*) Routledge.

Practicar Es Ganar. Larry Jones.Tr. of Practice to Win. (SPA.). 1983. 2.99 (*0-8423-6188-X*, 498412); pap. write for info. (*0-614-27113-4*) Editorial Unilit.

Practicas de Oficina, Vol. 89. Carmen E. Diaz Zayas. (SPA.). (C). 1997. pap. 11.66 (*0-673-19283-0*) HEPC Inc.

Practicas y Teorias para Bomberos. 347p. Date not set. 80.00 (*0-614-11241-9*) Inter-Am Safety.

Practicas y Teorias para Bomberos. 6th ed. Ed. by Gene P. Carlson & William J. Vandevort. Tr. & Intro. by Mitch Ventura. LC 91-72468. (SPA., Illus.). 347p. 1991. pap. text 23.00 (*0-87939-095-6*) IFSTA.

Practice, Vol. I. (C). 2000. 10.00 (*0-13-021490-6*) P-H.

Practice: Architecture, Technique & Representation. Contrib. by Stan Allen. (Illus.). 170p. 1999. text 22.00 (*90-5701-032-1*, 810593); pap. text 18.00 (*90-5701-072-0*, 810594) Gordon & Breach.

Practice Almost Perfect: The Early Days at Arnold, Fortas & Porter. Norman Diamond. LC 96-47284. 376p. 1997. text 29.95 (*0-7618-0627-X*) U Pr of Amer.

Practice & Drill for the Clerk, Typist & Stenographer Examinations. Jack Rudman. (General Aptitude & Abilities Ser.: No. CS-19). pap. 23.95 (*0-8373-6719-0*, CS-19) Natl Learn.

Practice & Improve Plus: Advanced. (GER.). (C). 13.25 (*0-8442-2571-1*, X2571-1) NTC Contemp Pub Co.

Practice & Improve Plus: Advanced. 1988. teacher ed. 13.25 (*0-8442-2570-3*, X2570-3) NTC Contemp Pub Co.

Practice & Improve Your English. Saxon Menne. 208p. 1988. pap. 9.95 (*0-8442-5683-8*); pap. 9.95 (*0-8442-5697-8*) NTC Contemp Pub Co.

P

Practice & Improve Your English. Saxon Penne. (Practice & Improve Ser.). pap. 39.95 incl. audio (*0-8442-5682-X*, 5682X, Natl Textbk Co) NTC Contemp Pub Co.

Practice & Improve Your English Plus. Saxon Penne. (Practice & Improve Ser.). pap. 39.95 incl. audio (*0-8442-5696-X*, 5696X, Natl Textbk Co) NTC Contemp Pub Co.

Practice & Improve Your French. Chantal Marsden. (Practice & Improve Ser.). (FRE.). 1995. pap. 39.95 incl. audio (*0-8442-1664-X*, 1664X, Natl Textbk Co) NTC Contemp Pub Co.

Practice & Improve Your French: Intermediate. (FRE.). (C). 1988. pap. 13.25 (*0-8442-1666-6*, VF1666-6) NTC Contemp Pub Co.

Practice & Improve Your French: Listening Guide. (FRE.). (C). 1988. pap. 13.25 (*0-8442-1665-8*, VF1665-8) NTC Contemp Pub Co.

Practice & Improve Your French Plus. Chantal Marsden. (Practice & Improve Ser.). (FRE.). 1995. pap. 39.95 incl. audio (*0-8442-1678-X*, 1678X, Natl Textbk Co) NTC Contemp Pub Co.

Practice & Improve Your French Plus: Advanced. (FRE.). (C). 1988. pap. 13.25 (*0-8442-1680-1*, VF1680-1) NTC Contemp Pub Co.

Practice & Improve Your French Plus: Listening Guide. (FRE.). (C). 1988. pap. 13.25 (*0-8442-1679-8*, VF1679-8) NTC Contemp Pub Co.

Practice & Improve Your German. Ruth Rach. (Practice & Improve Ser.). 1995. pap. 39.95 incl. audio (*0-8442-2555-X*, Natl Textbk Co) NTC Contemp Pub Co.

Practice & Improve Your German: Intermediate. (GER.). (C). 1988. 13.25 (*0-8442-2557-6*, X2557-6) NTC Contemp Pub Co.

Practice & Improve Your German: Intermediate, Listening Guide. (GER.). (C). 1988. 13.25 (*0-8442-2556-8*, X2556-8) NTC Contemp Pub Co.

Practice & Improve Your German Plus. Ruth Rach. (Practice & Improve Ser.). 1995. pap. 39.95 incl. audio (*0-8442-2569-X*, Natl Textbk Co) NTC Contemp Pub Co.

Practice & Improve Your Italian. Paola Tite. (Practice & Improve Ser.). (ITA.). 1995. pap. 39.95 incl. audio (*0-8442-8002-X*, 8002X, Natl Textbk Co) NTC Contemp Pub Co.

Practice & Improve Your Italian: Intermediate Handbook. (ITA.). (C). 13.25 (*0-8442-8003-8*, X8003-8) NTC Contemp Pub Co.

Practice & Improve Your Italian: Intermediate Listening Guide & Course Book. (ITA.). (C). 13.25 (*0-8442-8001-1*, X8001-1) NTC Contemp Pub Co.

Practice & Improve Your Italian Plus. Paola Tite. (Practice & Improve Ser.). (ITA.). 1995. pap. 39.95 incl. audio (*0-8442-8033-X*, Natl Textbk Co) NTC Contemp Pub Co.

Practice & Improve Your Italian Plus: Advanced Handbook. (ITA.). (C). 13.25 (*0-8442-8026-7*, X8026-7) NTC Contemp Pub Co.

Practice & Improve Your Italian Plus: Advanced Listening Guide Course Book. (ITA.). (C). 13.25 (*0-8442-8025-9*, X8025-9) NTC Contemp Pub Co.

Practice & Improve Your Spanish: A Complete Listening Program to Help You Master Conversational Spanish. Jose Amodia Gomez et al. (Practice & Improve Ser.). pap. 39.95 incl. audio (*0-8442-7660-X*, 7660X, Natl Textbk Co) NTC Contemp Pub Co.

Practice & Improve Your Spanish: Additional Handbooks. (SPA.). Date not set. 13.25 (*0-8442-7662-6*, VS7662-6) NTC Contemp Pub Co.

Practice & Improve Your Spanish: Additional Listening Guide Course Books. (SPA.). Date not set. 13.25 (*0-8442-7661-8*, VS7661-8) NTC Contemp Pub Co.

Practice & Improve Your Spanish Plus. (SPA.). Date not set. 13.25 (*0-8442-7682-0*, VS7682-0) NTC Contemp Pub Co.

Practice & Improve Your Spanish Plus. Jose A. Gomez. (Practice & Improve Ser.). (SPA.). 1995. pap. 39.95 incl. audio (*0-8442-7688-X*, Natl Textbk Co) NTC Contemp Pub Co.

Practice & Improve Your Spanish Plus: Additional Handbooks. (SPA.). Date not set. 13.25 (*0-8442-7683-9*, VS7683-9) NTC Contemp Pub Co.

Practice & Inquiry for Nursing Administration: Intradisciplinary & Interdisciplinary Perspectives. LC 91-33134. 1993. 10.00 (*1-55810-066-0*, G-184) Am Nurses Pub.

Practice & Law of International Banking. Graham Penn. 1985. 114.00 (*0-85297-137-0*, Pub. by Chartered Bank) St Mut.

***Practice & Learn.** Karen Froloff. (Illus.). 304p. (J). (gr. 2). 1999. pap., teacher ed. 14.95 (*1-57690-712-0*, TCM2712) Tchr Create Mat.

***Practice & Learn.** Dona Herweck Rice. (Illus.). 304p. (J). (gr. 3). 1999. pap., teacher ed. 14.95 (*1-57690-713-9*, TCM2713) Tchr Create Mat.

***Practice & Learn.** J. L. Smith. (Illus.). 304p. (J). (gr. 1). 1999. pap., teacher ed. 14.95 (*1-57690-711-2*, TCM2711) Tchr Create Mat.

***Practice & Learn.** Ed. by Teacher Created Materials Staff. (Illus.). 1999. pap. 14.95 (*1-57690-721-X*) Tchr Create Mat.

Practice! & Learn! Alphabet Fun! Ed. by Phillip Rosenbaum. (Illus.). 144p. (J). (ps-1). 1997. pap., teacher ed., wbk. ed. 10.95 (*1-57882-016-2*, TF-4003) Teachers Friend Pubns.

Practice! & Learn! Colors, Numbers & Shapes. Ed. by Phillip Rosenbaum. (Illus.). 144p. (J). (ps-1). 1997. pap., teacher ed., wbk. ed. 10.95 (*1-57882-014-6*, TF-4001) Teachers Friend Pubns.

Practice! & Learn! Learning to Trace & Write. Ed. by Phillip Rosenbaum. (Illus.). 144p. (J). (ps-1). 1997. pap., teacher ed., wbk. ed. 10.95 (*1-57882-017-0*, TF-4004) Teachers Friend Pubns.

Practice! & Learn! Numbers & Counting 1-20. Ed. by Phillip Rosenbaum. (Illus.). 144p. (J). (ps-1). 1997. pap., teacher ed., wbk. ed. 10.95 (*1-57882-015-4*, TF-4002) Teachers Friend Pubns.

***Practice & Learn: What Every Kindergartner Needs to Know to Ensure Success.** J.L. Smith. (Illus.). 304p. 1999. pap., teacher ed. 14.95 (*1-57690-710-4*, TCM2710) Tchr Create Mat.

***Practice & Learn: What Every 4th Grader Needs to Know.** Dona Herweck Rice. (Illus.). 304p. (J). (gr. 4). 1999. pap., teacher ed. 14.95 (*1-57690-714-7*, TCM2714) Tchr Create Mat.

***Practice & Learn: What Every 5th Grader Needs to Know to Ensure Success.** Char-Lee L. Hill. 304p. (J). (gr. 5). 1999. pap., teacher ed. 14.95 (*1-57690-715-5*, TCM2715) Tchr Create Mat.

***Practice & Learn: What Every 6th Grader Needs to Know to Ensure Success.** Sheila Greenberg & Betty Weiss. (Illus.). 304p. (J). (gr. 6). 1999. pap., teacher ed. 14.95 (*1-57690-716-3*, TCM2716) Tchr Create Mat.

Practice & Perspective in Validation. Ed. by Clive H. Church. 180p. 1983. 38.00 (*0-900868-94-5*) Taylor & Francis.

Practice & Problems in Advanced Mathematics. 75p. 1994. pap. text 11.95 (*0-521-45561-8*) Cambridge U Pr.

Practice & Procedure Before the National Labor Relations Board. 2nd ed. Betty S. Murphy & Elliot S. Azoff. (Corporate Practice Ser.: No. 41). 1989. 95.00 (*1-55871-104-X*) BNA.

Practice & Procedure Before the National Labor Relations Board. 5th ed. Stanley R. Strauss & John E. Higgins, Jr. LC 96-84424. 293p. 1996. text 95.00 (*0-8318-0698-2*, B698) Am Law Inst.

Practice & Procedure for the Quantity Surveyor. 7th ed. A. J. Willis & C. J. Willis. (Illus.). 1976. pap. 42.95 (*0-8464-0744-2*) Beekman Pubs.

Practice & Procedure for the Quantity Surveyor. 10th ed. Christopher J. Willis et al. LC 94-16578. 256p. 1994. pap. 34.95 (*0-632-03831-4*, Pub. by Blckwll Scitfc UK) Blackwell Sci.

Practice & Procedure in District Registries. Roger Bird. 165p. 1991. 65.00 (*1-85190-143-4*, Pub. by Tolley Pubng) St Mut.

Practice & Procedure in Magistrates Courts. C. H. Mosier. 216p. 1986. 104.00 (*1-85190-013-6*, Pub. by Fourmat Pub) St Mut.

Practice & Procedure in Magistrates Courts. 3rd ed. C. H. Moiser & V. A. Philips. 268p. 1992. 75.00 (*1-85190-163-9*, Pub. by Tolley Pubng) St Mut.

***Practice & Procedure in Pa.'s Appellate Courts.** 1999. 99.00 incl. audio PA Bar Inst.

Practice & Procedure in the Crown Court. Kris Gledhill. 200p. 1993. 75.00 (*0-85459-753-0*, Pub. by Tolley Pubng) St Mut.

Practice & Procedure in the Sheriff Ordinary Court. Duncan B. White. 174p. 1988. 60.00 (*1-85190-037-3*, Pub. by Tolley Pubng) St Mut.

Practice & Procedure of International Conferences. Frederick S. Dunn. LC 70-158959. reprint ed. 31.50 (*0-404-02221-9*) AMS Pr.

Practice & Procedure of the Commercial Court. 3rd enl. ed. Anthony Coleman. 252p. 1990. 105.00 (*1-85044-287-8*) LLP.

Practice & Procedure of the Commercial Court. 4th ed. Coleman. (Lloyd's Commercial Law Library). 300p. 1995. 175.00 (*1-85044-859-0*) LLP.

Practice & Procedure of the Companies Court. Contrib. by Alan Boyle et al. (Lloyd's Commercial Law Library). 400p. 1995. write for info. (*1-85044-502-8*) LLP.

Practice & Procedures of the IRS Hearing. 364p. 1997. per. 20.00 (*0-16-063245-5*, Congress) USGPO.

Practice & Progress in Cardiac Pacing & Electrophysiology. Ed. by Ali M. Oto. LC 96-116. (Developments in Cardiovascular Medicine Ser.: Vol. 183). 416p. (C). 1996. text 217.50 (*0-7923-3950-9*) Kluwer Academic.

Practice & Prospects of the Ombudsmen in the United Kingdom. Ed. by Roy Gregory et al. LC 94-17941. 240p. 1995. text 89.95 (*0-7734-9081-7*) E Mellen.

Practice & Realization: Studies in Kant's Moral Philosophy. Nathan Rotenstreich. 163p. 1979. lib. bdg. 121.00 (*90-247-2112-1*, Pub. by M Nijhoff) Kluwer Academic.

Practice & Representation of Reading in England. Ed. by James Raven et al. (Illus.). 331p. (C). 1996. text 59.95 (*0-521-48093-0*) Cambridge U Pr.

***Practice & Research in Social Work: Postmodern Feminist Perspectives.** Ed. by Barbara Fawcett et al. LC 99-31189. 224p. (C). 1999. text. write for info. (*0-415-19511-X*) Routledge.

***Practice & Research in Social Work: Postmodern Feminist Perspectives.** Barbara Fawcett. LC 99-31189. 224p. 2000. pap. 25.99 (*0-415-19512-8*) Routledge.

Practice & Science of Drawing. Harold Speed. (Illus.). 296p. 1972. reprint ed. pap. 8.95 (*0-486-22870-3*) Dover.

Practice & Theory of Automated Timetabling: First International Conference, Edinburgh, U.K., August 29-Septmber 1, 1995:Selected Papers, Vol. 115. Edmund Burke & Ross. LC 96-35279. (Lecture Notes in Computer Science Ser.). xiii, 381p. 1996. 62.00 (*3-540-61794-9*) Spr-Verlag.

Practice & Theory of Automated Timetabling II: Second International Conference, PATAT/97, Toronto, Canada, August 20-22, 1997, Selected Papers. Edmund Burke & Michael Carter. Ed. by G. Goos et al. LC 98-39445. (Lecture Notes in Computer Science Ser.: Vol. 1408). xii, 273p. 1998. pap. 49.00 (*3-540-64979-4*) Spr-Verlag.

Practice & Theory of Enzyme Immunoassays. Ed. by P. Tijssen et al. 575p. 1985. pap. 39.50 (*0-444-80633-4*) Elsevier.

Practice & Theory of Psychoanalysis, 2 vols., Vol. 1. Herman Nunberg. 218p. 1961. 32.50 (*0-8236-4220-8*) Intl Univs Pr.

Practice & Theory of Psychoanalysis, Vol. 2. Herman Nunberg. 219p. 1961. 32.50 (*0-8236-4240-2*) Intl Univs Pr.

***Practice Anesthesia for Infants & Children.** 3rd ed. Charles J. Cote et al. (Illus.). 605p. (C). 1999. text. write for info. (*0-7216-7286-8*, W B Saunders Co) Harcrt Hlth Sci Grp.

Practice-Based Epidemiology: An Introduction. Stanley H. Schuman. xiv, 258p. 1986. text 147.00 (*2-88124-047-X*); pap. text 59.00 (*2-88124-046-1*) Gordon & Breach.

Practice-Based Learning. Howard S. Barrows. 145p. 1994. pap. 19.95 (*0-931369-27-4*) Southern IL Univ Sch.

Practice Before Federal Magistrates. Kent Sinclair. 1984. 220.00 (*0-8205-1557-4*) Bender.

Practice Before the Massachusetts State Ethics Committee. Thomas Zampino. LC 90-63120. 91p. 1990. pap. 45.00 (*0-944490-41-7*) Mass CLE.

Practice Before U. S. Claims Court & U. S. Court of Appeals for Federal Circuit (1987) 459p. 1987. pap. text 15.00 (*1-56986-057-2*) Federal Bar.

***Practice Being Godly.** Gospel Light Publications Staff. 2000. pap. 14.99 (*5-550-03158-2*) Nairi.

Practice Book A see Crane Reading System

Practice Book Annotated, 2 vols. 4th ed. Wesley W. Horton et al. LC 98-60997. (Connecticut Practice Ser.). 1998. write for info. (*0-314-23556-6*) West Pub.

Practice Book B see Crane Reading System

Practice Book C see Crane Reading System

Practice Book D see Crane Reading System

Practice Book E see Crane Reading System

Practice Book F see Crane Reading System

Practice Book for the Degrees of Reading Power Test. Sylvia Blake & Sy Kaufman. 1981. 4.95 (*0-9602800-6-5*) Comp Pr.

Practice Book for the RCT in U. S. History & Government. Jay Becker et al. 157p. 1990. student ed. 8.95 (*0-910307-23-7*) Comp Pr.

Practice Book for the Regents Competency Test in Global Studies. Alexander Dummer. 167p. 1990. student ed. 8.95 (*0-910307-22-9*) Comp Pr.

Practice Book for the Regents Competency Test in Reading. Sylvia Blake & Sy Kaufman. 103p. 1981. 4.50 (*0-9602800-0-6*) Comp Pr.

Practice Book G see Crane Reading System

Practice Book H see Crane Reading System

Practice Book I see Crane Reading System

Practice Book J see Crane Reading System

Practice Book on English Stress & Intonation. Kenneth Croft. 81p. 1961. pap. 5.50 (*0-87789-013-7*); audio 90.00 (*0-87789-125-7*) ELS Educ Servs.

Practice Builder: Complete Marketing Library of $1,000,000 Strategies. Alan Bernstein & Donna Freiermuth. 400p. 1992. text 69.95 (*0-13-678798-3*) P-H.

Practice Building Shell Floor Plans. Mark Karlen. 1992. text 27.95 (*0-442-01345-0*, VNR) Wiley.

Practice Building Shell Floor Plans. Mark Karlen. 1992. pap. 39.95 (*0-471-28534-X*, VNR) Wiley.

Practice Business Math Process Brief 6th ed. Slater. 1999. pap., wbk. ed. 54.06 (*0-07-233761-3*) McGraw.

Practice by Foreign Lawyers in Japan. 344p. 1989. pap. 95.00 (*0-89707-476-9*, 521-0064) Amer Bar Assn.

Practice Case in Financial Statement Preparation & Analysis: The Keller Corporation. Francis S. Kearns et al. 1991. pap. 23.95 (*0-87393-134-3*) Dame Pubns.

Practice Compliance with the EPA Risk Management Program. R. J. Walters. LC 98-49791. 21p. 1999. 69.00 (*0-8169-0748-X*, G-53) Am Inst Chem Eng.

Practice Data Analysis, Vol. 3. 2nd ed. Bryant. 128p. 1998. pap. 13.75 (*0-07-365488-4*) McGraw.

Practice Development: Creating the Marketing Mindset. M. Riskin & McKenna. 224p. 1989. pap. 63.00 (*0-409-80636-6*, MICHIE) LEXIS Pub.

Practice, Drill, & Review for Reading Hebrew. Lillian W. Adler & C. Castberg. 1972. pap., wbk. ed. 4.95 (*0-87441-216-1*) Behrman.

Practice Drills for Japanese Swordsmanship. Nicklaus Suino. LC 95-11130. (Illus.). 112p. 1995. pap. 14.95 (*0-8348-0339-9*) Weatherhill.

Practice Effect. David Brin. 288p. (Orig.). 1995. mass mkt. 6.99 (*0-553-26981-X*, Bantam Classics) Bantam.

Practice Essay Exams. America's Bar Review Staff. (C). 1992. pap. text 16.95 (*1-879563-28-2*) Lexicon CA.

Practice Ethical Behavior Module, Connections: School & Work Transitions - Work Skills-Work Maturity Skills. National Center for Research in Vocational Educati. 1987. write for info. (*0-318-67182-4*, SP100CB10) Ctr Educ Trng Employ.

Practice Evaluation for the 21st Century. Hudson & Nugent. (Social Work). 2000. mass mkt. 49.95 (*0-534-34867-X*) Brooks-Cole.

Practice Exams & Answer Keys for Basic CV Science & Invasive Cardiovascular Technology. 2nd rev. ed. J. Wesley Todd. (Illus.). 300p. 1996. pap. 60.00 (*0-9653568-6-8*) Cardiac Self Assessmnt.

Practice Exercise Book "A" Component of Self-Tutoring Math Kit. Mary Powell. (ENG & SPA.). 1986. pap., wbk. ed. 5.00 (*1-892302-01-2*) MATHCO Educ.

Practice Exercise Book "B" Componet of Self-Tutoring Math Kit. Mary Powell. (ENG & SPA.). 1986. pap., wbk. ed. 5.00 (*1-892302-02-0*) MATHCO Educ.

Practice Exercises for the TOEFL, Set. 4th ed. P. Sharpe. pap. text 29.95 incl. audio (*0-7641-7301-4*) Barron.

***Practice Field Instruction in Social Work: Theory & Process: Theory & Practice.** 2nd ed. Marion Bogo & Elaine J. Vayda. LC 97-48592. 288p. 1998. pap. 24.50 (*0-231-11319-6*) Col U Pr.

Practice for Air Force Placement Tests. 7th ed. Eve P. Steinberg. 256p. 1989. pap. 13.95 (*0-13-689423-2*, Arc) IDG Bks.

Practice for Clerical, Typing & Stenographic Tests. 8th ed. Maryhelen H. Hoffman. 256p. 1993. per. 12.95 (*0-671-84668-X*, Arc) IDG Bks.

Practice for Enclosed Cylindrical Wormgear Speed Reducers & Gearmotors. 2nd rev. ed. AGMA Technical Committee. (ANSI/AGMA Standard Ser.: Vol. 6034-B92). (Illus.). 37p. 1999. pap. text 53.00 (*1-55589-494-1*) AGMA.

Practice for Helical & Herringbone Speed Reducers for Oilfield Pumping Units. rev. ed. AGMA Technical Committee. (AGMA Standard Ser.: Vol. 422.03 (R1992)). 44p. 1998. pap. text 60.00 (*1-55589-050-4*) AGMA.

***Practice for Operational Procedures/Inspection & Quality Control of First-Generation Silver-Gelatin Microfilm of Documents: ANSI/AIIM MS23-1998.** Association for Information & Image Management Staff. 108p. 1998. spiral bd. 52.00 (*0-89258-347-9*, MS23) Assn Inform & Image Mgmt.

Practice for the Armed Forces Test. pap. 7.95 (*0-685-17145-0*) P-H.

Practice for the Armed Forces Test. Eve P. Steinberg. write for info. (*0-318-59584-2*) S&S Trade.

Practice for the Armed Forces Test. 11th rev. ed. LC 81-10799. (Illus.). 336p. 1982. lib. bdg. 12.00 (*0-668-05558-8*, Arco) Macmillan Gen Ref.

Practice for the ASVAB. 14th ed. Solomon Wiener. 640p. 1994. pap. 12.00 (*0-671-84786-4*, Arco) Macmillan Gen Ref.

Practice for the U. S. Citizenship & Legalization of Status Tests. 3rd ed. Carlos F. Paz. 128p. 1991. pap. 9.00 (*0-13-691288-5*, Arco) Macmillan Gen Ref.

Practice for the U.S. Citizenship & Legalization of Status. 3rd ed. Carlos F. Paz. (SPA.). 144p. 1991. per. 9.95 (*0-13-677097-5*, Arc) IDG Bks.

Practice for Understanding & Using English. 576p. (C). 1972. pap. 30.00 (*0-02-310130-X*, Macmillan Coll) P-H.

Practice Forms for School Litigation in Federal Courts. Ed. by Naomi E. Gittens. 420p. 1992. ring bd. 190.00 incl. disk (*0-88364-136-4*, 06-138) Natl Sch Boards.

Practice Games for Winning Soccer. rev. ed. Ed. by J. Malcolm Simon & John A. Reeves. LC 97-2612. (Illus.). 184p. 1997. 14.95 (*0-88011-631-5*, PSTM0631) Human Kinetics.

Practice Geograph. Anne Buttimer. LC 82-13091. (Illus.). (C). 1984. text 31.95 (*0-582-30087-8*) Longman.

Practice Good Work Habits Module, Connections: School & Work Transitions - Work Skills-Work Maturity Skills. National Center for Research in Vocational Educati. 1987. write for info. (*0-318-67181-6*, SP100CB09) Ctr Educ Trng Employ.

Practice Grammar of German: English Language Edition Of The Famous Lehr- & Ubungsbuch Der Deutsc. Distribooks, Inc. Staff. 1999. pap. text 48.95 (*3-88532-630-2*) Distribks Inc.

***Practice Guide for Conducting Extra-Territorial Discovery for Use in U. S. Litigation.** 2nd expanded rev. ed. Graig J. Alvarez et al. 130p. 1999. 42.50 (*0-327-01593-4*, 6995010) LEXIS Pub.

Practice Guide to Language Learning. 2nd ed. Brown. 2001. 11.50 (*0-07-365518-X*) McGraw.

Practice Guide to the Nutrition-Labeling Laws for the Restaurant Industry. 60p. 1996. pap. 15.95 (*0-614-31133-0*, MG760) Natl Restaurant Assn.

***Practice Guideline for the Treatment of Patients with Delirium.** 14p. 1999. pap. 24.50 (*0-89042-313-X*) Am Psychiatric.

Practice Guidelines & Standards for Providers of Biofeedback & Applied Psychophysiological Services, 1999. rev. ed. Sebastian Striefel. 56p. Date not set. ring bd. 28.00 (*1-887114-05-X*) AAPB.

Practice Guidelines for Extended Psychiatric Residential Care: From Chaos to Collaboration. Patrick W. Corrigan et al. (Illus.). 176p. 1995. 47.95 (*0-398-06535-7*) C C Thomas.

Practice Guidelines for Extended Psychiatric Residential Care: From Chaos to Collaboration. Patrick W. Corrigan et al. (Illus.). 176p. (C). 1995. pap. text 31.95 (*0-398-06536-5*) C C Thomas.

Practice Guidelines for Family Nurse Practitioners. Karen Fenstermacher & Barbara T. Hudson. Ed. by Barbara N. Cullen. LC 96-37237. 416p. 1997. pap. text 39.00 (*0-7216-6861-5*, W B Saunders Co) Harcrt Hlth Sci Grp.

***Practice Guidelines for Family Nurse Practitioners.** 2nd ed. Karen Fenstermacher. LC 99-49764. (Illus.). 430p. 2000. text 41.00 (*0-7216-8696-6*, W B Saunders Co) Harcrt Hlth Sci Grp.

Practice Guidelines for Obstetrics & Gynecology. Janet Scoggin & Geri Morgan. LC 96-31549. (Illus.). 352p. 1997. spiral bd. 37.95 (*0-397-55426-5*) Lppncott W & W.

***Practice Guidelines in Primary Care.** Ralph Gonzales & Jean Kutner. (Illus.). 208p. 2000. pap. 14.95 (*0-8385-3417-1*) McGraw.

Practice Husband. Judith McWilliams. (Desire Ser.). 1997. per. 3.50 (*0-373-76062-0*, 1-76062-8) Silhouette.

P

An Asterisk (*) at the beginning of an entry indicates that the title is appearing for the first time.

Practice in Christianity. Soren Kierkegaard. Ed. & Tr. by Edna H. Hong. Tr. by Howard V. Hong. (Illus.). 464p. 1991. text 62.50 (*0-691-07396-1*, Pub. by Princeton U Pr); pap. text 18.95 (*0-691-02063-9*, Pub. by Princeton U Pr) Cal Prin Full Svc.

Practice in Civil Actions & Proceedings in the Law of Courts of the State of Delaware, 2 vols., Set. Victor B. Woolley. LC 85-70092. 1350p. 1985. reprint ed. 195.00 (*0-912004-26-6*) Gaunt.

Practice in English Vol. I: The Art of Composition. S. N. Ritzvi et al. 206p. 1996. pap. 35.00 (*81-209-0772-8*, Pub. by Pitambar Pub) St Mut.

Practice in English Vol. II: The Art of Comprehension. S. N. Ritzvi et al. 128p. 1996. pap. 25.00 (*81-209-0757-4*, Pub. by Pitambar Pub) St Mut.

Practice in English Vol. III: Grammar, Usage & Vocabulary. S. N. Ritzvi et al. 268p. 1996. pap. 25.00 (*81-209-0870-8*, Pub. by Pitambar Pub) St Mut.

Practice in German Grammar. Alan G. Jones & Gudrun Lawlor. (GER.). 214p. 1994. pap. 24.00 (*1-85234-451-2*, Pub. by S Thornes Pubs) Trans-Atl Phila.

Practice in the Case of School Children. Thomas J. Kirby. LC 70-176955. (Columbia University. Teachers College. Contributions to Education Ser.: No. 58). reprint ed. 37.50 (*0-404-55058-4*) AMS Pr.

Practice Issues for the Acute Care Nurse Practitioner. Ed. by Ruth M. Kleinpell & Mariann Piano. LC 98-27636. (Illus.). 200p. 1998. 34.95 (*0-8261-1204-8*) Springer Pub.

Practice Issues in Occupational Therapy: Intraprofessional Team Building. Ed. by Sally E. Ryan. LC 92-50459. (Illus.). 408p. 1993. pap. 30.00 (*1-55642-179-6*) SLACK Inc.

Practice Issues in Social Welfare Administration, Policy & Planning. Ed. by Milton M. Lebowitz. LC 82-6269. (Administration in Social Work Ser.: Vol. 6, Nos. 2 & 3). 157p. 1982. text 49.95 (*0-86656-142-0*, B142); pap. text 17.95 (*0-86656-166-8*) Haworth Pr.

*__Practice Knowledge & Expertise.__ Joy Higgs & Angie Titchen. 256p. 2000. pap. text 49.50 (*0-7506-4688-8*) Buttrwrth-Heinemann.

Practice Learning in the Caring Professions. Dave Evans. LC 98-52027. 1999. write for info. (*1-85742-423-9*) Ashgate Pub Co.

Practice Learning in the Caring Professions. Dave Evans. LC 98-52027. 300p. 1999. text 65.95 (*1-85742-422-0*) Ashgate Pub Co.

Practice Made Perfect: The Physician's Guide to Communication & Marketing. Edna Kaplan. (Illus.). 261p. 1990. 29.95 (*0-9616920-1-4*) Barrington MA.

Practice Made Perfect: The Seven Secrets of Successful Lawyering. Paul M. Lisnek. 208p. 1998. pap. 9.95 (*0-15-900392-X*, Pub. by Harcourt Legal) Natl Bk Netwk.

Practice Makes Perfect. Paul M. Lisnek. 120p. 1995. pap. text 10.00 (*0-910095-02-7*) Law Bulletin.

Practice Makes Perfect. large type ed. Caroline Anderson. (Dales Large Print Ser.). 265p. 1998. pap. 19.99 (*1-85389-805-8*, Dales) Ulverscroft.

Practice Makes Perfect, Vol. 1. Ralph Bosman. 116p. 1989. pap. 12.50 (*0-933704-80-1*) Dawn Pr.

Practice Makes Perfect, Vol. 2. Ralph Bosman. 144p. 1990. pap. 12.50 (*0-933704-89-5*) Dawn Pr.

Practice Makes Perfect, Vol. 3. Ralph Bosman. 200p. 1993. pap. 12.50 (*0-933704-95-X*) Dawn Pr.

Practice Makes Perfect: Applications for WordPerfect. Johnson. (Computer Applications Ser.). 1995. 83.95 (*0-538-71057-8*); pap. 33.95 (*0-538-71056-X*) S-W Pub.

Practice Makes Perfect: Idiomatic English. Loretta S. Gray. LC 99-49998. 288p. 2000. pap. 12.95 (*0-8442-2394-8*, 23948) NTC Contemp Pub Co.

Practice Makes Perfect: Spanish Pronouns & Prepositions. Dorothy Richmond. LC 97-69977. (Practice Makes Perfect Ser.). (Illus.). 160p. 1998. pap. 9.95 (*0-8442-7311-2*, 73112) NTC Contemp Pub Co.

Practice Makes Perfect: Spanish Verb Tenses. Dorothy M. Devney. (Illus.). 320p. 1995. pap. 9.95 (*0-8442-7334-1*, 73341) NTC Contemp Pub Co.

Practice Makes Perfect: The Professional's Guide to Sales Success. Marvin Montgomery. LC 95-24239. 144p. 1995. pap. 12.95 (*1-886939-02-0*, Pub. by OakHill Pr VA) ACCESS Pubs Network.

Practice Makes Practice: A Critical Study of Learning to Teach. Deborah P. Britzman. LC 90-37229. (SUNY Series, Teacher Empowerment & School Reform). 283p. (C). 1991. pap. text 24.95 (*0-7914-0569-9*) State U NY Pr.

Practice Management. K. J. Bolden et al. (Illus.). 144p. 1992. pap. 32.95 (*0-632-03319-3*) Blackwell Sci.

Practice Management: New Perspectives for the Construction Professional. Ed. by Peter Barrett & R. Males. (Illus.). 366p. (C). 1991. 85.00 (*0-419-17150-9*, E & FN Spon) Routledge.

Practice Management Compendium Pt. 1: Understanding the Contract. J. Fry et al. (C). 1990. pap. text 49.00 (*0-7923-8940-9*) Kluwer Academic.

Practice Management Compendium Pt. 2: Organising the Practice. J. Fry et al. (C). 1990. pap. text 49.00 (*0-7923-8942-5*) Kluwer Academic.

Practice Management Compendium Pt. 3: Finance & Reports. J. Fry et al. (C). 1991. pap. text 49.00 (*0-7923-8943-3*) Kluwer Academic.

Practice Management Compendium Pt. 4: Clinical Practices. J. Fry et al. (C). 1991. pap. text 49.00 (*0-7923-8944-1*) Kluwer Academic.

*__Practice Management for Complementary Therapists.__ Paul M. Baker. (Illus.). 256p. 2000. pap. 45.00 (*0-7506-4510-5*) Buttrwrth-Heinemann.

Practice Management for Design Professionals: A Practical Guide to Avoiding Liability & Enhancing Profitability. John P. Bachner. LC 90-47916. 400p. 1991. 110.00 (*0-471-52205-8*) Wiley.

Practice Management for Land, Construction & Property Professionals. Ed. by B. Greenhalgh. (Illus.). 320p. (C). 1996. 115.00 (*0-419-21370-8*, E & FN Spon) Routledge.

Practice Management for Physicians. Donald L. Donohugh. (Illus.). 365p. 1986. pap. text 55.00 (*0-7216-1889-8*, W B Saunders Co) Harcrt Hlth Sci Grp.

Practice Management for the Dental Team. 4th ed. Betty L. Finkbeiner & Charles A. Finkbeiner. 588p. 1995. spiral bd. 47.00 (*0-8151-3241-7*) Taylor & Francis.

Practice Management for the Young Orthopaedic Surgeon. Ed. by Michael F. Schafer. (Managed Care Series for the Orthopaedic Surgeon). 200p. 1998. pap. 45.00 (*0-89203-203-0*) Amer Acad Ortho Surg.

Practice Management Portfolio. 95th ed. Fowler. 1995. pap. text 312.00 (*0-15-601894-2*) Harcourt Legal.

Practice Management/Communication Skills. Bittel. (SPA.). 395.00 incl. VHS (*0-8068-8289-1*, 8289) AIMS Multimedia.

Practice Management/Difficult Situations. Bittel. 395.00 incl. VHS (*0-8068-8187-9*, 8187) AIMS Multimedia.

Practice Management/Leadership Skills. Bittel. (SPA.). 395.00 incl. VHS (*0-8068-8290-5*, 8290) AIMS Multimedia.

Practice Math: Consumer Applications. Fredrick. 1993. pap. text, teacher ed. 75.25 (*0-03-076792-X*) Holt R&W.

Practice Math: Skills & Concepts. Fredrick. 1993. pap. text, teacher ed. 75.25 (*0-03-076789-X*) Holt R&W.

Practice Mathematics: Consumer Applications. Fredrick. 1989. pap. text, teacher ed. 75.25 (*0-03-012769-6*); pap. text, teacher ed. 9.75 (*0-03-012777-7*) Holt R&W.

Practice Mathematics: Consumer Applications Testbook. Fredrick. 1989. pap. text, teacher ed., suppl. ed. 13.50 (*0-03-012778-5*) Holt R&W.

Practice Mathematics: Skills & Concepts. Fredrick. 1989. pap. text, teacher ed. 75.25 (*0-03-012758-0*); pap. text, teacher ed. 9.75 (*0-03-012764-5*) Holt R&W.

Practice Mathematics: Skills & Concepts Testbook. Fredrick. 1989. pap. text, teacher ed., suppl. ed. 13.50 (*0-03-012763-7*) Holt R&W.

Practice Nurse. 2nd ed. P. Jeffree. (Illus.). 416p. 1994. pap. text 47.75 (*1-56593-294-3*, 0618) Singular Publishing.

Practice of Advertising. 4th ed. Ed. by Norman A. Hart. (Marketing Ser.). 287p. 1995. pap. text 41.95 (*0-7506-2239-3*) Buttrwrth-Heinemann.

Practice of Anaesthesia & Resuscitation. P. K. Gupta. 1985. 59.00 (*0-7855-0747-7*, Pub. by Current Dist) St Mut.

Practice of Anasthesia. P. K. Gupta. (C). 1989. 55.00 (*0-89771-351-6*, Pub. by Current Dist) St Mut.

Practice of Anesthesia & Resuscitation. 2nd ed. A. K. Gupta. (C). 1989. 60.00 (*0-7855-4664-2*, Pub. by Current Dist) St Mut.

Practice of Anesthesia for Infants & Children. 2nd ed. Charles J. Cote et al. (Illus.). 558p. 1992. text 96.00 (*0-7216-3198-3*, W B Saunders Co) Harcrt Hlth Sci Grp.

Practice of Archipelagic States. (The Law of the Sea Ser.). 257p. 32.00 (*92-1-133423-3*) UN.

Practice of Architecture, 1833 see Works of Asher Benjamin: Boston, 1806-1843

Practice of Aromatherapy. Jean Valnet. write for info. (*0-85207-143-4*, Pub. by C W Daniel) Natl Bk Netwk.

Practice of Aromatherapy. 7th ed. Jean Valnet. 280p. pap. 20.95 (*0-8464-4273-6*) Beekman Pubs.

Practice of Aromatherapy: A Classic Compendium of Plant Medicines & Their Healing Properties. Jean Valnet. Ed. by Robert Tisserand. 279p. 1990. pap. 14.95 (*0-89281-398-9*) Inner Tradit.

Practice of Art History: Reflections on Method. Otto Pacht. Tr. by David Britt. (Illus.). 152p. 1999. text 29.95 (*1-872501-26-5*); pap. text 14.95 (*1-872501-31-1*) Gordon & Breach.

Practice of Artistic Therapy. Eva Mees-Christeller. Tr. by Margreet Vunderink from DUT. (Illus.). 78p. (Orig.). 1985. pap. 8.00 (*0-936132-77-9*) Merc Pr NY.

Practice of Autonomy: Patients, Doctors & Medical Decisions. Carl E. Schneider. LC 98-12178. 336p. 1998. text 39.95 (*0-19-511397-7*) OUP.

Practice of Autosuggestion by the Method of Emile Coue. C. Harry Brooks. 120p. 1981. pap. 12.00 (*0-89540-076-6*, SB-076) Sun Pub.

Practice of Aviation Safety: Observations from Flight Safety Foundation Safety Audits. E. R. Arbon et al. LC TL0553.5. 45p. reprint ed. pap. 30.00 (*0-7837-7031-6*, 204684600004) Bks Demand.

Practice of Banking. Fitzgerald. 1986. pap. text 25.00 (*0-86010-589-X*) Kluwer Academic.

Practice of Banking: Quiz Book, No. 1. Ed. by Institute of Bankers Staff. 1985. 40.00 (*0-85297-131-1*, Pub. by Chartered Bank) St Mut.

Practice of Banking 1. Michael Marsden. 225p. 1985. pap. text 36.00 (*0-86010-563-6*); lib. bdg. 50.00 (*0-86010-580-6*) G & T Inc.

Practice of Banking 1, Vol. 5. Michael Marsden. 150p. 1985. pap. text, student ed. 25.00 (*0-86010-588-1*) G & T Inc.

Practice of Bayesian Analysis. Ed. by Simon French & Jim Q. Smith. LC 97-190223. (An Arnold Publication). 304p. 1997. 65.00 (*0-340-66240-9*, Pub. by E A) OUP.

Practice of Behavior Therapy. 3rd ed. Joseph Wolpe. (Illus.). 425p. 1982. text 96.00 (*0-08-027165-0*, J115, Pergamon Pr); pap. text 31.00 (*0-08-027164-2*, Pergamon Pr) Elsevier.

Practice of Behavior Therapy, No. 1. 4th ed. Joseph Wolpe. 448p. (C). 1992. pap. text 53.00 (*0-205-14514-0*, H4514) Allyn.

Practice of Behavioral & Cognitive Psychotherapy. Richard Stern & Lynne M. Drummond. (Illus.). 264p. (C). 1991. pap. text 37.95 (*0-521-38742-6*) Cambridge U Pr.

*__Practice of Breast Ultrasound: Techniques, Findings, Differential Diagnosis.__ H. Madjar & Jack Jellins. LC 99-52543. (Illus.). 2000. 99.00 (*0-86577-898-1*) Thieme Med Pubs.

Practice of Brief Psychotherapy. 2nd ed. Sol L. Garfield. LC 98-9987. 320p. 1998. 49.95 (*0-471-24251-9*) Wiley.

*__Practice of Business Statistics.__ Moore et al. 2001. pap. text. write for info. (*0-7167-4111-3*, Pub. by W H Freeman) VHPS.

Practice of Cardiac Pacing. 3rd ed. rev. ed. Seymour Furman & David L. Hayes. Ed. by David R. Holmes, Jr. (Illus.). 816p. 1993. 95.00 (*0-87993-538-3*) Futura Pub.

Practice of Cardiology. Ed. by Robert A. Johnson et al. 1980. 82.00 (*0-316-46945-9*, Little Brwn Med Div) Lppncott W & W.

Practice of Case Management. David P. Moxley. (Human Services Guides Ser.: Vol. 58). 188p. (C). 1989. pap. text 18.95 (*0-8039-3205-7*) Sage.

*__Practice of Chemistry: Class Test Version.__ 3rd ed. Wink. 2000. pap. text. write for info. (*0-7167-4093-1*, Pub. by W H Freeman) VHPS.

*__Practice of Chemistry Class Test Version.__ Wink. 1999. pap. text. write for info. (*0-7167-3887-2*) W H Freeman.

Practice of Child Therapy. Ed. by Richard J. Morris & Thomas R. Kratochwill. (General Psychology Ser.: No. 124). (Illus.). 360p. 1983. text 100.00 (*0-08-028033-1*, Pergamon Pr); pap. text 40.00 (*0-08-028032-3*, Pergamon Pr) Elsevier.

*__Practice of Child Therapy.__ 3rd ed. Ed. by Richard J. Morris & Thomas R. Kratochwill. LC 97-18367. 496p. (C). 1998. pap. text 79.00 (*0-205-16818-3*) Allyn.

Practice of Chinese Buddhism, 1900-1950. Holmes H. Welch. LC 67-13256. (Illus.). 568p. 1967. pap. 19.50 (*0-674-69701-4*) HUP.

Practice of Classical Palmistry. Madame La Roux. LC 92-5951. (Illus.). 288p. 1993. pap. 14.95 (*0-87728-720-1*) Weiser.

*__Practice of Clinical Neuropsychiatry & Behavioural Neurology.__ Moore. (Illus.). 450p. 2001. 100.00 (*0-7506-4940-2*) Buttrwrth-Heinemann.

Practice of Clinical Psychology in Great Britain. Ed. by Andree Liddell. LC 82-20030. 277p. reprint ed. pap. 85.90 (*0-7837-3219-8*, 204323700007) Bks Demand.

Practice of Clinical Sociology & Sociotherapy. L. Alex Swan. 127p. 1984. 18.95 (*0-87073-402-4*); pap. 12.95 (*0-87073-403-2*) Schenkman Bks Inc.

Practice of Confessional Subscription. David W. Hall. 348p. (C). 1995. lib. bdg. 47.50 (*0-8191-9907-9*) U Pr of Amer.

Practice of Conscious Dying: Off-Ramp to Liberation & Freeway to Conscious Immortality. Benito F. Reyes. 134p. (Orig.). 1990. pap. 6.75 (*0-939375-16-8*) World Univ Amer.

Practice of Conservation of Library Materials in Sub-Saharan Africa. M. E. Ojo-Igbinoba. 61p. 1993. 7.00 (*0-941934-65-9*) Indiana Africa.

Practice of Construction Management. 3rd ed. Barry Fryer & Marilyn Fryer. LC 96-42440. 294p. 1996. pap. 39.95 (*0-632-04142-0*) Blackwell Sci.

Practice of Constructivism in Science Education. Ed. by Kenneth G. Tobin. 360p. 1994. pap. 36.00 (*0-8058-1878-2*) L Erlbaum Assocs.

Practice of Coronary Disease Prevention. Michael Miller & Robert A. Vogel. LC 95-45490. (Illus.). 352p. 1996. pap. 24.95 (*0-683-18045-2*) Lppncott W & W.

Practice of Court Interpreting. Alicia Betsy Edwards. LC 95-15376. (Benjamins Translation Library Ser.: No. 6). xiii, 192p. 1995. pap. 24.95 (*1-55619-684-9*); lib. bdg. 65.00 (*1-55619-683-0*) J Benjamins Pubng Co.

Practice of Crime Scene Investigation. John Horswell. 300p. 1997. 99.00 (*0-7484-0609-3*, Pub. by Tay Francis Ltd) Taylor & Francis.

Practice of Cultural Analysis: Exposing Interdisciplinary Interpretation. Mieke Bal & Bryan Gonzales. LC 98-35018. (Cultural Memory in the Present Ser.). 1999. 65.00 (*0-8047-3066-0*); pap. 24.95 (*0-8047-3067-9*) Stanford U Pr.

Practice of Data Analysis: Essays in Honor of John W. Tukey. John W. Tukey et al. LC 97-19695. 352p. 1998. text 49.50 (*0-691-05782-6*, Pub. by Princeton U Pr) Cal Prin Full Svc.

Practice of Decision Making. Ed. by S. R. Watson. 100p. 1983. pap. 17.00 (*0-08-028162-1*, Pergamon Pr) Elsevier.

Practice of Diplomacy: Its Evolution, Theory & Administration. Richard Langhorn & Keith Hamilton. LC 94-15093. 288p. (C). 1994. pap. 27.99 (*0-415-10475-0*, B4100) Routledge.

*__Practice of Dramaturgy.__ Tori Haring-Smith. 2001. pap. write for info. (*0-325-00298-3*) Heinemann.

Practice of Dzogchen. 2nd ed. Tulka T. Rinpoche et al. Ed. by Harold Talbott. LC 88-39545. Vol. 3. 488p. 1989. pap. 22.95 (*1-55939-054-9*) Snow Lion Pubns.

Practice of Earthquake Hazard Assessment. 284p. pap. text 75.00 (*0-7881-1592-8*) DIANE Pub.

Practice of Econometrics. Ernst R. Berndt. LC 96-21200. (Illus.). 720p. (C). 1991. text 45.25 (*0-201-17628-9*) Addison-Wesley.

Practice of Econometrics. Ernst R. Berndt. (Illus.). 222p. (C). 1994. pap. text 26.73 (*0-201-17629-7*) Addison-Wesley.

Practice of Econometrics: A Computer Handbook Using Shazam. Kenneth J. White & Linda T. Bui. (Illus.). 180p. (C). 1991. pap. text 34.60 (*0-201-50048-5*) Addison-Wesley.

Practice of Econometrics: Classic & Contemporary. Ernst R. Berndt. 702p. 1996. 98.00 (*0-201-49900-2*) Addison-Wesley.

Practice of Econometrics: Classic & Contemporary. Ernst R. Berndt. LC 96-21200. (Illus.). (C). 1996. text. write for info. (*0-201-51488-5*) Addison-Wesley.

Practice of Econometrics: Classic & Contemporary. 2nd ed. Ernst R. Berndt. (C). 1998. text. write for info. (*0-201-82393-4*) Addison-Wesley.

Practice of Economics: Economic Systems & Decision Making in Western Societies. Alex N. McLeod. 368p. (C). 1992. 44.95 (*1-56000-083-X*) Transaction Pubs.

Practice of Electrocardiography: A Problem-Solving Guide to Confident Interpretation. 5th ed. Thomas M. Blake. LC 93-39587. (Illus.). 336p. 1994. 59.50 (*0-89603-292-2*); pap. 39.00 (*0-89603-261-2*) Humana.

Practice of Emergency Care. 2nd ed. James H. Cosgriff, Jr. & Diann L. Anderson. (Illus.). 652p. 1984. text 39.75 (*0-397-54357-3*, 64-02994, Lippnctt) Lppncott W & W.

Practice of Emotionally Focused Marital Therapy: Creating Connection. Susan M. Johnson. (Basic Principles into Practice Ser.: Vol. 11). 256p. 1996. pap. 27.95 (*0-87630-817-5*) Brunner-Mazel.

Practice of Empowerment. Dennis C. Kinlaw. 180p. 1995. 69.95 (*0-566-07570-9*, Pub. by Gower) Ashgate Pub Co.

Practice of English: Language Teaching. 2nd ed. J. Hormer. (Handbooks for Language Teachers Ser.). (C). 1991. pap. 28.81 (*0-582-04656-4*, 79110) Longman.

Practice of English Fundamentals: V. Form. A. Bachelor & J. Haley. 1945. pap. text 12.95 (*0-685-03901-3*) P-H.

Practice of English Language Teaching. Jeremy Harmer. (Handbooks for Language Teachers Ser.). 252p. (Orig.). 1985. pap. text 16.46 (*0-582-74612-4*, 74758) Longman.

Practice of Entrepreneurship. Philip A. Neck et al. ix, 196p. 1982. text 27.00 (*92-2-102839-9*); pap. text 20.25 (*92-2-102846-1*) Intl Labour Office.

Practice of Everyday Life. Michel De Certeau. Tr. by Steven F. Rendall from FRE. LC 83-18070. 260p. 1984. pap. 16.95 (*0-520-06168-3*, Pub. by U CA Pr) Cal Prin Full Svc.

Practice of Everyday Life. Luce Giard & Pierre Mayol. LC 98-10876. 296p. 1998. write for info. (*0-8166-2876-9*); pap. 19.95 (*0-8166-2877-7*) U of Minn Pr.

Practice of Facilitation: Managing Group Process & Solving Problems. Harry Webne-Behrman. LC 97-32989. 232p. 1998. 55.00 (*1-56720-067-2*, Quorum Bks) Greenwood.

Practice of Family Therapy. 2nd ed. Hanna. (Counseling Ser.). 342p. 1998. mass mkt. 60.95 (*0-534-35768-7*) Brooks-Cole.

Practice of Family Therapy: Key Elements Across Models. Suzanne M. Hana & Joseph H. Brown. LC 94-16803. 248p. 1994. 51.75 (*0-534-25098-X*) Brooks-Cole.

Practice of Family Therapy: Key Elements Across Models. Suzanne M. Hanna & Joseph H. Brown. 1994. mass mkt., teacher ed. write for info. (*0-534-25099-8*) Brooks-Cole.

Practice of Field Instruction in Social Work: Theory & Process. 2nd ed. Marion Bogo & Elaine Vayda. (Illus.). 288p. 1998. pap. text 18.95 (*0-8020-7979-2*) U of Toronto Pr.

Practice of Field Instruction in Social Work Theory & Process. Marion Bogo & Elaine Vayda. 176p. (C). 1987. pap. text 17.95 (*0-8020-6689-5*) U of Toronto Pr.

Practice of Foreign Language Teaching. Wasyl Cajkler & Ron Addelman. 160p. 1992. pap. 29.95 (*1-85346-205-5*, Pub. by David Fulton) Taylor & Francis.

Practice of Forensic Neuropsychology: Meeting Challenges in the Courtroom. Robert J. McCaffrey et al. LC 96-37015. (Critical Issues in Neuropsychology Ser.). (Illus.). 235p. (C). 1996. text 47.00 (*0-306-45256-1*, Kluwer Plenum) Kluwer Academic.

Practice of Freedom. Banerjea Benoyendranath. 1983. 9.00 (*0-8364-0918-3*, Pub. by Minerva) S Asia.

Practice of Geriatrics. 3rd ed. Edmund H. Duthie, Jr. & Paul R. Katz. Ed. by Ray Kersey. LC 97-22941. (Illus.). 544p. (C). 1998. text 85.00 (*0-7216-6599-3*, W B Saunders Co) Harcrt Hlth Sci Grp.

Practice of Godliness. Jerry Bridges. (NavClassics Ser.). 1996. pap. 10.00 (*0-89109-941-7*) NavPress.

Practice of Godliness: Bible Study. Jerry Bridges. 72p. 1996. pap. 5.00 (*0-89109-498-9*) NavPress.

*__Practice of God's Presence.__ Andrew Murray. LC 00-21013. 567p. 2000. pap. 16.99 (*0-88368-590-6*) Whitaker Hse.

Practice of Graduate Research in Hospitality & Tourism. Ed. by K. S. Chon. LC 99-32018. 240p. (C). 1999. 39.95 (*0-7890-0727-4*) Haworth Pr.

Practice of Group Therapy. Ed. by S. R. Slavson. 272p. 1965. 40.00 (*0-8236-4200-3*) Intl Univs Pr.

Practice of Group Work. Ed. by William Schwartz & Serapio R. Zalba. LC 75-127101. 1971. text 58.00 (*0-231-03241-2*) Col U Pr.

Practice of Happiness: Exercises & Techniques for Developing Mindfulness, Wisdom, & Joy. Mirko Fryba. 192p. 1996. pap. 14.00 (*1-57062-123-3*, Pub. by Shambhala Pubns) Random.

Practice of Harmony. 4th ed. (C). 2000. write for info. (*0-13-022894-X*) S&S Trade.

*__Practice of Harmony.__ 4th ed. Peter Spencer. LC 99-37586. 422p. 1999. spiral bd. 42.00 (*0-13-022350-6*) P-H.

Practice of Health Services Research. Ong. 174p. 1993. pap. 54.25 (*1-56593-214-5*, 0567) Singular Publishing.

Practice of High Performance Liquid Chromatography. Ed. by H. Tristram Engelhardt. (Illus.). 480p. 1989. text 163.95 (*0-387-12589-2*) Spr-Verlag.

Practice of Human Resource Strategy. Ed. by Shaun Tyson. 1997. pap. 67.50 (*0-273-62824-0*, Pub. by Pitman Pub) Trans-Atl Phila.

Practice of Hypnotherapy see Medical Hypnosis

Practice of Hypnotic Suggestion. Sylvain A. Lee. 160p. 1996. reprint ed. spiral bd. 13.50 (*0-7873-0548-0*) Hlth Research.

Practice of Hypnotism, 2 vols. Andre M. Weitzenhoffer. 800p. 1989. 320.00 (*0-471-62199-4*) Wiley.

Practice of Hypnotism. 2nd ed. Andre M. Weitzenhoffer. LC 99-27109. 646p. 1999. 85.00 (*0-471-29790-9*) Wiley.

P

An Asterisk (*) at the beginning of an entry indicates that the title is appearing for the first time.

Practice of Hypnotism: Traditional & Semi-Traditional Techniques & Phenomenology, Vol. 1, Traditional and Semi-Traditional Technique. Andre M. Weitzenhoffer. 448p. 1989. 145.00 (0-471-62167-6) Wiley.

Practice of Intercession. Zacharias T. Fomum. 1991. 23.95 (0-533-08779-1) Vantage.

Practice of International Litigation. Lawrence W. Newman & Michael Burrows. 870p. 1993. 125.00 (1-56425-005-9) Juris Pubng.

Practice of Interventional Cardiology. King, III et al. Ed. by Morton J. Kern. (Illus.). 1000p. (C). (gr. 13). 1998. text 159.00 (0-8151-4945-X, 30379) Mosby Inc.

Practice of Interventional Neuroradiology. J. J. Connors & Joan C. Wojak. LC 97-28810. (Illus.). xxiv, 795p. (C). 1999. text 190.00 (0-7216-7147-0, W B Saunders Co) Harcrt Hlth Sci Grp.

Practice of Ion Chromatography. Frank C. Smith, Jr. & Richard C. Chang. 234p. (C). 1990. reprint ed. 77.00 (0-89464-502-1) Krieger.

Practice of Japan in International Law, 1961-1970. Ed. by Shigeru Oda et al. LC 82-193177. 503p. 1982. reprint ed. pap. 156.00 (0-608-01257-2, 206194500001) Bks Demand.

Practice of Jesus. Hugo Echegaray. Tr. by Matthew J. O'Connell from SPA. LC 83-19341. Orig. Title: La Practica de Jesus. 144p. (Orig.). reprint ed. pap. 44.70 (0-8357-2673-8, 204020900015) Bks Demand.

Practice of Justice: A Theory of Lawyers Ehtics. William H. Simon. LC 97-40929. 1998. 35.00 (0-674-69711-1) HUP.

***Practice of Justice: A Theory of Lawyers' Ethics.** William H. Simon. 2000. pap. text 18.95 (0-674-00275-X) HUP.

Practice of Kabbalah: Meditation in Judaism. Steven A. Fisdel. LC 95-51820. 232p. 1996. 40.00 (1-56821-508-8) Aronson.

Practice of Kalachakra. Glenn H. Mullin. LC 91-27945. 352p. 1991. pap. 16.95 (0-937938-95-5) Snow Lion Pubns.

Practice of Kindness: Meditations for Bringing More Peace, Love, & Compassion into Daily Life. Conari Press Editors. 290p. (Orig.). 1996. pap. 9.95 (1-57324-028-1) Conari Press.

Practice of Kinetics see Comprehensive Chemical Kinetics

Practice of Language Rights in Canada. C. Michael MacMillan. LC 99-179457. (Illus.). 272p. 1998. text 50.00 (0-8020-4279-1); pap. text 19.95 (0-8020-8115-0) U of Toronto Pr.

Practice of Local Government Planning. Ed. by Frank S. So et al. LC 79-21380. (Municipal Management Ser.). (Illus.). 676p. 1979. text 39.95 (0-87326-020-1) Intl City-Cnty Mgt.

Practice of Local Government Planning. 2nd ed. Ed. by Frank S. So & Judith Getzels. (Municipal Management Ser.). (Illus.). 554p. 1988. text 39.95 (0-87326-077-5) Intl City-Cnty Mgt.

***Practice of Local Government Planning.** 3rd ed. Charles Hoch et al. LC 00-35070. (Municipal Management Ser). 2000. write for info. (0-87326-171-2) Intl City-Cnty Mgt.

Practice of Love: Lesbian Sexuality & Perverse Desire. Teresa De Lauretis. LC 93-44453. 352p. 1994. 36.95 (0-253-31681-2); pap. 15.95 (0-253-20878-5) Ind U Pr.

Practice of Loving Kindness. Nagabodhi. 32p. (Orig.). 1995. pap. 3.95 (0-904766-51-9) Windhorse Pubns.

Practice of Loving Kindness. Bhikkhu Nanamoli. 28p. 1987. 1.50 (955-24-0005-8, Pub. by Buddhist Pub Soc) Vipassana Res Pubns.

Practice of M-Mode & Two-Dimensional Echocardiagraphy. Jos R. Roelandt. 1983. text 191.50 (90-247-2745-6) Kluwer Academic.

Practice of Machine Design. Yotaro Hatamura. LC 98-12013. (Series on Advanced Manufacturing: Vol. 14). (Illus.). 352p. 1999. text 125.00 (0-19-856560-7) OUP.

Practice of Macro Social Work. William G. Brueggemann. LC 95-30670. (Illus.). 1996. text 61.95 (0-8304-1368-5) Thomson Learn.

Practice of Magic: An Introductory Guide to the Art. Draja Mickaharic. LC 94-49078. 176p. (Orig.). 1995. pap. 9.95 (0-87728-807-0) Weiser.

P

Practice of Magical Evocation. 4th ed. Franz Bardon. Tr. by Peter A. Dimai from GER. (Illus.). 435p. 1984. 44.00 (0-914732-11-0) Bro Life Inc.

Practice of Mahamudra: The Teachings of His Holiness, the Drikung Kyabgon, Chetsang Rinpoche. H. H. Chetsang Rinpoche. Ed. by Ani T. Chodron & D. Emmerich. Tr. by Robert Clark & Khenpo K. Gyaltshen from TIB. LC 99-27858. 135p. 1999. pap. 12.95 (1-55939-124-3) Snow Lion Pubns.

***Practice of Management.** Peter F. Drucker. 1999. pap. 17.00 (0-06-662026-0, HarpBusn) HarpInfo.

Practice of Management. Peter Ferdinand Drucker. LC 85-45189. 404p. 1986. pap. 17.00 (0-88730-613-6, HarpBusn) HarpInfo.

Practice of Management: Bookspan,&Martin. abr. ed. Peter Drucker. 1990. audio 12.00 (1-55994-278-9, CPN 1866) HarperAudio.

Practice of Management Development. Ed. by Sidney Mailick et al. LC 88-2398. 226p. 1988. 59.95 (0-275-92357-6, C2357, Praeger Pubs) Greenwood.

Practice of Mathematics. Yvette Solomon. (International Library of Psychology). 224p. 1989. 57.50 (0-415-03038-2) Routledge.

Practice of Medical Radiesthesia. Vernon D. Wethered. 160p. (C). 1977. 14.95 (0-8464-1040-0) Beekman Pubs.

Practice of Medicinal Chemistry. Ed. by Camile G. Wermuth. (Illus.). 600p. 1996. text 169.00 (0-12-744640-0) Acad Pr.

Practice of Medicine among the Burmese. Keith N. MacDonald. LC 77-87505. reprint ed. 42.50 (0-404-16837-X) AMS Pr.

Practice of Mental Health Consultation. Fortune V. Mannino. 1975. 24.95 (0-89876-082-8) Gardner Pr.

Practice of Moral Judgment. Barbara Herman. LC 92-20915. 264p. (C). 1993. 37.95 (0-674-69717-0) HUP.

Practice of Moral Judgment. Barbara Herman. 272p. 1996. pap. 18.00 (0-674-69718-9) HUP.

Practice of Multinational Banking: Macro-Policy Issues & Key International Concepts. 2nd ed. Dara M. Khambata. LC 95-38766. 320p. 1996. 69.50 (0-89930-971-2, Quorum Bks) Greenwood.

Practice of Municipal Administration. Lent D. Upson. LC 73-11912. (Metropolitan America Ser.). 604p. 1974. reprint ed. 41.95 (0-405-05432-7) Ayer.

Practice of Neural Science. John C. Brunst. LC 99-43399. (C). 1999. pap. text 29.95 (0-8385-8117-X, A-8117-2) Appleton & Lange.

Practice of Neurosurgery, 3 vols. George Tindall et al. 4,000p. 599.00 (0-683-30003-2) Lppncott W & W.

Practice of Neurosurgery, 3 vols., Set. George N. Tindall et al. (Illus.). 3297p. 1996. 595.00 (0-683-08266-3) Lppncott W & W.

Practice of Newpaper Management. W. Parkman Rankin. LC 85-28099. 176p. 1986. 55.00 (0-275-92051-8, C2051, Praeger Pubs) Greenwood.

Practice of Nursing Research. 3rd ed. Nancy Burns. 1997. text 59.00 (0-7216-7572-7, W B Saunders Co) Harcrt Hlth Sci Grp.

Practice of Nursing Research: Conduct, Critique & Utilization. 3rd ed. Nancy Burns & Susan K. Grove. Ed. by Thomas Eoyang. (Illus.). 715p. 1997. text 43.95 (0-7216-3054-5, W B Saunders Co) Harcrt Hlth Sci Grp.

Practice of Nursing Research: Conduct, Critique & Utilization. 3rd ed. Nancy Burns & Susan K. Grove. (Illus.). 1997. teacher ed. write for info. (0-7216-3057-X, W B Saunders Co) Harcrt Hlth Sci Grp.

Practice of Obstetrics & Gynecology. Geoffrey V.P. Chamberlain & C. J. Dewhurst. (Illus.). 271p. 1977. 34.95 (0-8464-1120-2) Beekman Pubs.

Practice of Obstetrics & Gynecology. 3rd ed. Geoffrey Chamberlain & J. Friend. LC 98-32449. (Illus.). 250p. 1998. pap. write for info. (0-443-05103-8) Church.

Practice of Ocean Rescue. R. E. Sanders. (C). 1987. 45.00 (0-85174-294-7) St Mut.

Practice of Operational Research. George Mitchell. LC 93-7352. 256p. 1993. 115.00 (0-471-93982-X) Wiley.

***Practice of Oxygen Measurement for Divers.** J. S. Lamb. LC 98-86313. (Illus.). 120p. 1999. pap. 19.95 (0-941332-68-3, B0990) Best Pub Co.

Practice of Palmistry. Comte C. De Saint-Germain. 410p. 1973. pap. 12.95 (0-87877-019-4, P-19) Newcastle Pub.

Practice of Patient Education. 8th ed. Barbara K. Redman & Barbara Klug. (Illus.). 304p. (C). (gr. 13). 1996. pap. text 34.00 (0-8151-9357-2, 29203) Mosby Inc.

Practice of Patriarchy: Gender & the Politics of Household Authority in Early Modern France. Julie Hardwick. LC 97-49175. 240p. 1998. 55.00 (0-271-01782-1); pap. 19.95 (0-271-01783-X) Pa St U Pr.

Practice of Peace. Ed. by Judith Rafaela & Nancy Fay. LC 98-21101. 208p. 1998. pap. 15.00 (0-9644196-7-X) Sherman Asher Pub.

Practice of Peptide Synthesis. M. Bodanszky et al. (Reactivity & Structure, Concepts in Organic Chemistry Ser.: Vol. 21). 240p. 1992. 113.00 (0-387-13471-9) Spr-Verlag.

Practice of Peptide Synthesis. 2nd rev. ed. Miklos Bodanszky & Agnes Bodanszky. Ed. by Barry M. Trost. LC 94-890. (Laboratory Ser.). (Illus.). 280p. (C). 1994. 49.00 (0-387-57505-7) Spr-Verlag.

Practice of Perfection: The Paramitas from a Zen Buddhist Perspective. Robert Aitken. LC 97-5488. 240p. 1997. pap. text 13.50 (1-887178-40-6, Pub. by Counterpt DC) HarpC.

Practice of Performance: Studies in Musical Interpretation. Ed. by John Rink. (Illus.). 304p. (C). 1996. text 69.95 (0-521-45374-7) Cambridge U Pr.

***Practice of Persuasion: Politics & Paradox in Art History.** Keith Moxey. 2001. 39.95 (0-8014-3801-2); pap. 15.95 (0-8014-8675-0) Cornell U Pr.

Practice of Pharmacy: Institutional & Ambulatory Pharmaceutical Services. Ed. by Donald C. McLeod & William A. Miller. LC 81-51777. (Illus.). 502p. 1981. text 9.00 (0-9606488-0-1) H W Bks.

Practice of Philosophy: A Handbook for Beginners. 3rd ed. Jay F. Rosenberg. LC 95-12865. 133p. 1995. pap. text 23.60 (0-13-230848-7) P-H.

Practice of Photography. 2nd ed. Philip H. Delamotte. LC 72-9193. (Literature of Photography Ser.). 1973. reprint ed. 18.95 (0-405-04903-X) Ayer.

Practice of Piety. Lewis Bayly. 343p. 1994. reprint ed. 24.95 (1-877611-66-2) Soli Deo Gloria.

Practice of Piety: Puritan Devotional Disciplines in Seventeenth-Century New England. Charles E. Hambrick-Stowe. LC 81-19806. (Illus.). 314p. 1982. pap. 97.40 (0-608-05210-8, 206574700001) Bks Demand.

Practice of Poetry: Reconsiderations of Louis Zukofsky's a Test of Poetry. Cid Corman. 52p. 1998. pap. 10.00 (0-9620575-4-1) Origin Pr.

Practice of Poetry: Writing Exercises from Poets Who Teach. Ed. by Robin Behn & Chase Twichell. LC 92-52535. 320p. 1992. pap. 15.00 (0-06-273024-X, Harper Ref) HarpC.

Practice of Policy Analysis: Forty Years of Art & Technology. Peter W. House & Roger D. Shull. LC 91-24363. (Illus.). 188p. 1991. 36.00 (0-929590-03-1); pap. 16.00 (0-929590-04-X) Compass Pr.

Practice of Political Authority: Authority & the Authoritative. Richard E. Flathman. LC 79-26431. 228p. 1995. 24.00 (0-226-25319-8) U Ch Pr.

Practice of Political Authority: Authority & the Authoritative. Richard E. Flathman. LC 79-26431. (Illus.). 286p. reprint ed. pap. 88.70 (0-608-08833-1, 206947200004) Bks Demand.

Practice of Power: U. S. Relations with China since 1949. Rosemary Foot. 304p. 1997. reprint ed. pap. text 19.95 (0-19-829292-9) OUP.

Practice of Praise: How to Develop the Habit of Abundant, Continual Praise in Your Daily Life. Charles H. Spurgeon. LC 97-193637. 170p. 1995. mass mkt. 5.99 (0-88368-296-6) Whitaker Hse.

Practice of Prayer. Margaret Guenther. LC 98-25255. (New Church's Teaching Ser.: Vol. 4). 160p. 1998. 11.95 (1-56101-152-5) Cowley Pubns.

Practice of Prayer. G. Campbell Morgan. 1997. pap. text 7.99 (1-898787-49-2) Emerald House Group Inc.

Practice of Preaching. Paul S. Wilson. (Orig.). 20.00 (0-687-08593-4) Abingdon.

Practice of Preaching. Paul S. Wilson. 256p. (Orig.). 1995. 20.95 (0-687-19506-3) Abingdon.

Practice of Prediction: The Astrologer's Handbook of Techniques Used to Accurately Forecast the Future. Nancy A. Hastings. LC 89-33879. (Illus.). 316p. (Orig.). 1989. pap. 16.95 (0-87728-684-1) Weiser.

Practice of Primary Nursing. Marie Manthey. LC 79-92975. 96p. 1980. 10.00 (1-886624-10-0, B240) Creative Nursing.

***Practice of Principle: Defence of the Pragmatic Approach to Legal Theory.** Jules Coleman. (Clarendon Law Lectures). 280p. 2000. 39.95 (0-19-829814-5) OUP.

Practice of Printing, 1971. Ralph Weiss Polk. 1986. 19.96 (0-02-665410-5) Macmillan.

Practice of Private Investigation. Ralph D. Thomas. 70p. (Orig.). 1992. pap. 19.95 (0-918487-56-0) Thomas Investigative.

***Practice of Programming.** Brian W. Kernighan & Rob Pike. LC 99-10131. 288p. (C). 1999. pap. text 24.95 (0-201-61586-X) Addison-Wesley.

Practice of Prolog. Ed. by Leon S. Sterling. (Logic Programming Ser.). 342p. 1990. 42.50 (0-262-19301-9) MIT Pr.

Practice of Prophesying. Witness Lee. 46p. 1990. pap. 3.50 (0-87083-543-2, 12-028-001) Living Stream Ministry.

Practice of Psycho-Social Occupational Therapy. 2nd ed. Linda Finlay. 224p. 1997. 39.95 (1-56593-931-X, 1848) Singular Publishing.

Practice of Psychoanalytic Criticism. Ed. by Leonard Tennenhouse. LC 76-26079. 280p. reprint ed. pap. 86.80 (0-608-16052-0, 203318200084) Bks Demand.

Practice of Psychoanalytic Therapy. Karl Konig. Tr. by Paul Foulkes. LC 94-29292. (GER.). 342p. 1995. 50.00 (1-56821-353-0) Aronson.

Practice of Psychological Assessment. Norman Tallent. 416p. (C). 1991. text 58.33 (0-13-678111-X) P-H.

Practice of Psychosocial Occupational Therapy. 2nd ed. Linda Finlay. (Orig.). 1997. pap. 24.95 (0-7487-3342-6, Pub. by S Thornes Pubs) Trans-Atl Phila.

Practice of Public Relations. 4th ed. Ed. by Sam Black. (Marketing Ser.). 186p. 2000. pap. text 49.95 (0-7506-2318-7) Buttrwrth-Heinemann.

Practice of Public Relations. 7th ed. Fraser P. Seitel. LC 97-29845. 556p. 1997. 92.00 (0-13-613811-X) P-H.

***Practice of Public Relations.** 8th ed. Fraser P. Seitel. 582p. 2000. write for info. (0-13-027679-0) P-H.

Practice of Public Speaking: A Practical Guide for Beginning Speakers. 3rd ed. Ed. by Deanna D. Sellnow. 176p. (C). 1995. pap. text, per. 16.58 (0-8403-9705-4) Kendall-Hunt.

Practice of Public Speaking: A Practical Guide for Beginning Speakers. 4th ed. Deanna D. Sellnow et al. 192p. (C). 1996. pap. text, per. 19.95 (0-7872-2533-9, 41253301) Kendall-Hunt.

Practice of Quality. Donald Irvine & Sally Irvine. LC 95-51478. 206p. 1996. 28.95 (1-85775-073-X, Radcliffe Med Pr) Scovill Paterson.

Practice of Quality Management. Uday S. Karmarkar. Ed. by Phillip J. Lederer. LC 96-52832. 328p. (C). 1997. lib. bdg. 137.50 (0-7923-9864-5) Kluwer Academic.

Practice of Rational Emotive Behavior Therapy. 2nd ed. Albert Ellis & Windy Dryden. LC 96-32061. 280p. 1997. 42.95 (0-8261-5471-9) Springer Pub.

Practice of Reading. Derek Alsop & Walsh. LC 98-49468. 1999. pap. 21.95 (0-312-22157-6) St Martin.

Practice of Reading. Denis Donoghue. LC 97-42549. 320p. 1998. 35.00 (0-300-07466-2) Yale U Pr.

***Practice of Reading.** Denis Donoghue. LC 97-42549. 320p. 2000. pap. 15.95 (0-300-08264-9) Yale U Pr.

Practice of Reservoir Engineering. L. Dake. LC 93-35471. (Developments in Petroleum Science Ser.: No. 36). 556p. 1994. 242.00 (0-444-88538-2) Elsevier.

Practice of Reservoir Engineering. L. P. Dake. (Developments in Petroleum Science Ser.: Vol. 36). 556p. 1994. pap. 100.00 (0-444-82094-9) Elsevier.

Practice of Risk Management. SBC Warburg Dillon Read Staff & Goldman Sachs Staff. 264p. 1998. 225.00 (1-85564-627-7, Pub. by Euromoney) Am Educ Systs.

Practice of Ritual Magic: Powerful Aids to Concentration & Visualization. 3rd rev. ed. Gareth Knight. (Illus.). 96p. (Orig.). 1996. pap. 9.95 (0-9650839-8-5) Sun Chalice.

Practice of Shrimp Culture. rev. ed. Nobuo Matsui. (Illus.). 166p. (C). 1997. text 104.00 (90-5410-277-2, Pub. by A A Balkema) Ashgate Pub Co.

Practice of Silviculture. 9th ed. David M. Smith. LC 96-25883. 560p. 1996. text 102.95 (0-471-10941-X) Wiley.

***Practice of Social Influence in Multiple Cultures.** Ed. by Wilhelmina Wosinska et al. (A Volume in the Applied Social Research Series). 336p. 2000. write for info. (0-8058-3279-3) L Erlbaum Assocs.

Practice of Social Inquiry. G. Moore. 136p. 1984. text 23.00 (0-08-030369-2, Pergamon Pr); pap. text 14.50 (0-08-030370-6, Pergamon Pr) Elsevier.

Practice of Social Research. Babbie. (Sociology - Introductory Level Ser.). 1975. pap. 13.00 (0-534-00381-8) Wadsworth Pub.

Practice of Social Research. 2nd ed. Babbie. (Sociology - Introductory Level Ser.). 1979. pap. 20.00 (0-534-00630-2) Wadsworth Pub.

Practice of Social Research. 4th ed. Earl Babbie. 577p. (C). 1985. pap. write for info. (0-534-05658-X) Wadsworth Pub.

Practice of Social Research. 5th ed. Earl Babbie. 501p. (C). 1988. pap. write for info. (0-534-09726-X) Wadsworth Pub.

Practice of Social Research. 6th ed. Earl Babbie. 493p. (C). 1991. pap. 48.95 (0-534-15576-6) Wadsworth Pub.

Practice of Social Research. 7th ed. Earl Babbie. LC 94-25048. 476p. 1994. mass mkt. 60.95 (0-534-18744-7) Wadsworth Pub.

Practice of Social Research. 8th ed. Babbie. (Sociology Ser.). 1997. 50.25 (0-534-50507-4) Wadsworth Pub.

Practice of Social Research. 8th ed. Earl Babbie. LC 97-25892. (Sociology Ser.). 672p. (C). 1997. pap. 50.25 (0-534-50468-X) Brooks-Cole.

***Practice of Social Research.** 9th ed. Babbie. (Sociology - Intro Level Ser.). 2001. 50.25 (0-534-57474-2) Wadsworth Pub.

Practice of Social Research: Study Guide. 8th ed. Earl Babbie & Wagenaar. 1997. student ed. 16.50 (0-534-50469-8) Brooks-Cole.

Practice of Social Work. 2nd ed. Charles H. Zastrow. 545p. (C). 1985. pap. 36.25 (0-534-11277-3) Brooks-Cole.

Practice of Social Work. 2nd ed. Charles H. Zastrow. (Social Work Ser.). Date not set. pap. write for info. (0-534-11278-1) Brooks-Cole.

Practice of Social Work. 3rd ed. Charles H. Zastrow. 581p. (C). 1989. pap. 41.25 (0-534-10933-0) Brooks-Cole.

Practice of Social Work. 3rd ed. Charles H. Zastrow. (Social Work Ser.). 1989. pap., teacher ed. write for info. (0-534-10934-9) Brooks-Cole.

Practice of Social Work. 4th ed. Charles H. Zastrow. 599p. (C). 1991. text 48.95 (0-534-17004-8) Brooks-Cole.

Practice of Social Work. 5th ed. Charles H. Zastrow. LC 94-8987. 714p. 1994. pap. 50.25 (0-534-23844-0) Brooks-Cole.

Practice of Social Work. 5th ed. Charles H. Zastrow. 1995. pap., teacher ed. write for info. (0-534-23845-9) Brooks-Cole.

Practice of Social Work. 6th ed. Charles H. Zastrow. LC 98-10398. (Social Work Ser.). 1998. mass mkt. 62.95 (0-534-35657-5) Brooks-Cole.

Practice of Social Work in Schools. Wendy G. Winters & Freda Easton. LC 83-47655. (C). 1983. 29.95 (0-02-935660-1) Free Pr.

Practice of Sociology. 5th ed. Babbie. (Sociology - Introductory Level Ser.). 1988. pap., teacher ed. write for info. (0-534-09728-6) Wadsworth Pub.

Practice of Sociology. 6th ed. Babbie. (Sociology Ser.). 1992. teacher ed. write for info. (0-534-15578-2) Wadsworth Pub.

Practice of Soil Reinforcing in Europe: Proceedings of the Symposium Organized by the Tenax Group under the Auspices of the International Geosynthetics Society, & Held at the Institution of Civil Engineers, May 18, 1995. Ed. by T. S. Ingold. LC 96-133639. 318p. 1995. 105.00 (0-7277-2083-X) Am Soc Civil Eng.

Practice of Soil Reinforcing in Europe: Proceedings of the Symposium Organized by the Tenax Group under the Auspices of the International Geosynthetics Society, & Held at the Institution of Civil Engineers, May 18, 1995. Ed. by T. S. Ingold. 318p. 1995. 105.60 (0-614-14263-6, Pub. by T Telford) RCH.

Practice of Solidarity: American Hat Finishers in the Nineteenth Century. David Bensman. LC 83-6592. (Working Class in American History Ser.). (Illus.). 264p. 1985. text 27.50 (0-252-01093-0) U of Ill Pr.

***Practice of Speech Language Pathology: A Study of Clinical Activities & Knowledge Areas for the Certified SLP.** Michael Rosenfeld & Gregory B. Kocher. 2000. 30.00 (1-58041-065-0) Am Speech Lang Hearing.

Practice of Spinal Surgery. Henry V. Crock. (Illus.). 340p. 1983. 153.00 (0-387-81738-7) Spr-Verlag.

Practice of Spiritual Direction. William A. Barry & William G. Connolly. 224p. (Orig.). 1986. pap. 17.00 (0-86683-951-8, Pub. by Harper SF) HarpC.

Practice of State & Regional Planning. Frank S. So et al. LC 84-72732. (Illus.). 637p. 1986. lib. bdg. 47.00 (0-918286-38-7, Planners Press) Am Plan Assn.

Practice of States at the Time of Entry into Force of the United Nations Convention on the Law of the Sea. LC 94-219808. (The Law of the Sea Ser.). 243p. 25.00 (92-1-133474-8) UN.

Practice of Statistics: Putting the Pieces Together. John D. Spurrier. LC 99-21479. 1999. 38.95 (0-534-36490-X) Dorsey.

Practice of Steelmaking. 1984. 1520.00 (0-387-93495-2) Spr-Verlag.

Practice of Steelmaking. 2nd ed. 1984. 1215.00 (0-387-93514-2) Spr-Verlag.

Practice of Strategic Environmental Assessment. Riki Therivel & Maria R. Paridario. 224p. 1997. 70.00 (1-85383-374-6, Pub. by Escan Pubns); pap. 36.00 (1-85383-373-8, Pub. by Escan Pubns) Island Pr.

Practice of Supportive Psychotherapy. David S. Werman. LC 84-12740. 208p. 1988. text 32.95 (0-87630-365-3) Brunner-Mazel.

Practice of Surgery. Ronald A. Malt. LC 92-22929. (Illus.). 512p. 1993. text 240.00 (0-7216-1811-1, W B Saunders Co) Harcrt Hlth Sci Grp.

An Asterisk (*) at the beginning of an entry indicates that the title is appearing for the first time.

Practice of Teaching. Philip W. Jackson. 176p. (C). 1986. pap. text 14.95 (*0-8077-2810-1*) Tchrs Coll.

Practice of Teaching in the Secondary School. rev. ed. Henry C. Morrison. LC 31-9855. 698p. reprint ed. pap. 200.00 (*0-608-13401-5*, 202410100035) Bks Demand.

Practice of Technical & Scientific Communication: Writing in Professional Contexts. Jean A. Lutz & C. Gilbert Storms. LC 97-30772. (ATTW Studies in Technical Communication). 250p. 1998. 73.25 (*1-56750-361-6*); pap. 24.95 (*1-56750-362-4*) Ablx Pub.

Practice of Technology: Exploring Technology, Ecophilosophy, & Spiritual Disciplines for Vital Links. Alan R. Drengson. LC 95-1305. 218p. (C). 1995. text 59.50 (*0-7914-2669-6*); pap. text 19.95 (*0-7914-2670-X*) State U NY Pr.

Practice of Tempera Painting. Daniel V. Thompson. (Illus.). 141p. 1962. pap. 6.95 (*0-486-20343-3*) Dover.

Practice of the Crown Side of the Court of King's Bench & the Practice of the Sessions: The General Rules of Court, from the Reign of James I to the Present Time & the Statutes Relating to the Practice: Together with a Table of Fees, & Bills of Costs - Also, an Appendix of Forms & Precedents, 2 vols., Set. Richard Gude. 1990. reprint ed. 145.00 (*0-8377-2212-8*, Rothman) W S Hein.

Practice Of The Group Meetings. Witness Lee. 68p. 1990. pap. 4.00 (*0-87083-551-3*, 12-027-001) Living Stream Ministry.

Practice of the ICT for Yugoslavia & Rwanda. John R. Jones. LC 97-29257. 1997. 95.00 (*1-57105-079-5*) Transnatl Pubs.

***Practice of the International Criminal Tribunals for the Former Yugoslavia & Rwanda.** 2nd ed. John R. Jones. LC 99-53177. 690p. 1999. 125.00 (*1-57105-124-4*) Transnatl Pubs.

Practice of the Love of Jesus Christ. rev. ed. Alphonsus Leguori. Tr. by Peter Heinegg from ITA. LC 96-37868. 256p. 1997. pap. 13.00 (*0-7648-0031-0*) Liguori Pubns.

Practice of the Presence of God see Practica de la Presencia de Dios

Practice of the Presence of God. Brother Lawrence. Ed. by Conrad DeMeester. Tr. by Salvatore Sciurba from FRE. LC 93-2444. (Illus.). 240p. (Orig.). 1994. pap. 9.95 (*0-935216-21-9*) ICS Pubns.

Practice of the Presence of God. Brother Lawrence. 112p. (YA). (gr. 10). 1989. mass mkt. 4.99 (*0-8007-8599-1*, Spire) Revell.

Practice of the Presence of God. Tr. by John Delaney. 144p. 1996. pap. 6.00 (*0-385-48240-X*) Doubleday.

Practice of the Presence of God. Lawrence. Ed. by Donald E. Demaray. LC 96-53201. 81p. 1997. mass mkt. 4.50 (*0-8189-0770-3*) Alba.

Practice of the Presence of God. Lawrence. LC 99-32606. (Nelson's Royal Classic Ser.: Vol 6). 320p. 1999. 18.99 (*0-7852-4227-9*) Nelson.

Practice of the Presence of God. Brother Lawrence. Ed. by Hal M. Helms. LC 84-61019. (Living Library). 158p. 1984. pap. 8.95 (*0-941478-29-7*, 930-008, Pub. by Paraclete MA) BookWorld.

Practice of the Presence of God. Brother Lawrence. Tr. by Donald Attwater. (Illus.). 128p. 1981. pap. 9.95 (*0-87243-104-5*) Templegate.

Practice of the Presence of God. Brother Lawrence. 95p. 1982. mass mkt. 5.99 (*0-88368-105-6*) Whitaker Hse.

Practice of the Presence of God. large type ed. Brother Lawrence. LC 85-61019. 144p. 1985. reprint ed. pap. 7.95 (*0-8027-2510-4*) Walker & Co.

Practice of the Presence of God. Brother Lawrence. 60p. 1996. reprint ed. pap. 8.00 (*0-7873-1325-4*) Hlth Research.

Practice of the Presence of God. Brother Lawrence. 114p. 1990. reprint ed. 9.95 (*0-910261-12-1*, Arcana Pubng) Lotus Pr.

***Practice of the Presence of God.** rev. ed. Brother Lawrence. Ed. by Harold J. Chadwick. (Pure Gold Classics). (Illus.). 2000. pap. 9.99 (*0-88270-793-0*) Bridge-Logos.

Practice of the Presence of God: Conversations & Letters of Brother Lawrence. Brother Lawrence. (Mystical Classics of the World Ser.). 112p. 1999. reprint ed. text 7.99 (*1-85168-198-1*, Pub. by Onewrld Pubns) Penguin Putnam.

Practice of the Presence of God: The Best Rule of a Holy Life. Brother Lawrence. Ed. by Epworth Press Staff. 96p. 1996. pap. 4.95 (*1-888813-04-0*) Brghtside.

Practice of the Presence of God: Updated in Today's Language. Brother Lawrence. 64p. 1998. 5.97 (*1-57748-243-3*) Barbour Pub.

Practice of the Wild. Gary Snyder. 200p. 1990. pap. 11.00 (*0-86547-454-0*) N Point Pr.

Practice of Theory. Ed. by Stacey Herbert. (Theory@Buffalo Ser.: No. 5). 200p. (C). 1999. pap. 8.00 (*0-922668-20-5*) SUNYB Poetry Rare Bks.

Practice of Theory: Poststructuralism, Cultural Politics, & Art History. Keith Moxey. LC 93-27229. (Illus.). 208p. 1994. text 35.00 (*0-8014-2933-1*); pap. text 13.95 (*0-8014-8153-8*) Cornell U Pr.

Practice of Theory: Rhetoric, Knowledge, & Pedagogy in the Academy. Michael Bernard-Donals. LC 97-8796. (Literature, Culture, Theory Ser.: Vol. 26). 256p. (C). 1998. pap. 19.95 (*0-521-59506-1*); text 59.95 (*0-521-59433-2*) Cambridge U Pr.

Practice of Thin Layer Chromatography. 3rd ed. Joseph C. Touchstone. LC 91-23496. 400p. 1992. 110.00 (*0-471-61222-7*) Wiley.

Practice of Thoracic Anesthesia: Principles in Clinical Practice. Edmund Cohen. 608p. 1995. text 72.50 (*0-397-51078-0*) Lppncott W & W.

Practice of Time Series Analysis. Ed. by H. Akaike & G. Kitagawa. LC 98-31331. (Statistics in Engineering & Physical Science Ser.). 400p. 1999. 49.95 (*0-387-98658-8*) Spr-Verlag.

Practice of Tranquility & Insight: A Guide to Tibetan Buddhist Meditation. Khenchen Thrangu. Tr. by Peter Roberts from TIB. LC 98-28051. (Illus.). 170p. 1998. pap. 14.95 (*1-55939-106-5*, Snow Lion) Snow Lion Pubns.

Practice of Translating: Drills for Training Translators. Jacob A. Loewen. (Helps for Translators Ser.). xiv, 260p. 1981. pap. 19.99 (*0-8267-0028-4*, 102703) Untd Bible Soc.

Practice of Typography. Theodore L. De Vinne. LC 68-25308. (Reference Ser.: No. 44). 1972. reprint ed. lib. bdg. 75.00 (*0-8383-0935-6*) M S G Haskell Hse.

Practice of Uncertainty: Medicine & Malpractice Claims Through the Voices of Physicians & Patients. Stephen L. Fielding. LC 98-31028. 256p. 1999. 65.00 (*0-86569-284-X*, Auburn Hse) Greenwood.

***Practice of University History.** Alan Booth. 2000. pap. 27.95 (*0-7190-5492-3*, Pub. by Manchester Univ Pr); text 79.95 (*0-7190-5491-5*, Pub. by Manchester Univ Pr) St Martin.

Practice of Urology, Vol. 1. Barry Stein. Date not set. write for info. (*0-393-71002-5*) Norton.

Practice of Urology, Vol. 2. Barry Stein. Date not set. 0.01 (*0-393-71003-3*) Norton.

Practice of Vajrakilaya: Oral Teachings Given by Khenpo Namdrol Rinpoche at Kunzang Palyul Choling Poolesville, MD USA June 1995. Khenpo Namdrol Rinpoche. LC 99-10883. (Illus.). 90p. 1998. pap. 12.95 (*1-55939-103-0*, Snow Lion) Snow Lion Pubns.

Practice of Veterinary Dentistry: A Team Effort. Jan Bellows. LC 98-33711. (Illus.). 216p. (C). 1999. text 64.95 (*0-8138-2617-9*) Iowa St U Pr.

Practice of Wakefullness see Wakeful

***Practice of Wholeness: Spiritual Transformation in Everyday Life.** Lorena Monda. (Illus.). xxvi, 286p. 2000. pap. 16.95 (*0-9678137-0-0*) Golden Flower.

Practice of Witchcraft Today: An Introduction to Beliefs & Rituals. Robin Skelton. 216p. 1995. pap. 10.95 (*0-8065-1674-7*, Citadel Pr) Carol Pub Group.

Practice of Workplace Participation: Management-Employee Relations at Three Participatory Firms. S. Lance Denning. LC 97-32990. 192p. 1998. 55.00 (*1-56720-195-4*, Quorum Bks) Greenwood.

Practice of Writing. David Lodge. 1997. pap. 13.95 (*0-14-026106-0*) Viking Penguin.

Practice of Writing. 4th ed. Robert Scholes et al. 360p. 1994. pap. text 38.95 (*0-312-10312-3*) St Martin.

Practice of Writing. 5th ed. Scholes. 2000. pap. text 36.95 (*0-312-20105-2*) St Martin.

Practice of Yoga for Health, Happiness & Development of Body, Mind & Emotions. Ed. by Health Research Staff. 89p. 1996. reprint ed. spiral bd. 12.00 (*0-7873-0398-4*) Hlth Research.

Practice of Zen Meditation. Hugo M. Enomiya-Lassalle. 1991. pap. 16.00 (*1-85274-059-0*, Pub. by Aqrn Pr) Harper SF.

Practice Oriented Nutrition Research: An Outcomes Measurement Guide. Carol S. Ireton-Jones et al. LC 97-23618. 272p. 1997. 49.00 (*0-8342-0885-7*, 20885) Aspen Pub.

***Practice Pack.** Brenda K. Murphy. (Sail Away Ser.). (Illus.). 86p. (J). (ps-5). 1999. pap. text, wbk. ed. 15.95 (*1-58504-002-9*) UTW Res Inc.

***Practice Pack: A Teacher's Guide.** Brenda K. Murphy. (Sail Away Ser.). 24p. 1999. pap. text 8.95 (*1-58504-003-7*) UTW Res Inc.

Practice Pages for Statistics CV. Summers. (C). 1996. pap. write for info. (*0-03-018347-2*) Harcourt Coll Pubs.

Practice Parameters from the American Academy of Pediatrics: A Compilation of Evidence-Based Guidelines for Pediatric Practice. American Academy of Pediatrics Staff. 396p. 1997. pap. 39.95 (*0-910761-78-7*) Am Acad Pediat.

***Practice Parameters in Medicine & Primary Care: 1999-2000 Edition.** rev. ed. Paul D. Chan. (Current Clinical Strategies Ser.). 235p. 1999. pap. 36.95 incl. cd-rom (*1-881528-64-2*) Current Clin Strat.

Practice Parameters in Medicine & Primary Care, 1999-2000 Edition: Current Clinical Strategies. rev. ed. Paul D. Chan. (Current Clinical Strategies Ser.). 88p. 1998. pap. 18.95 (*1-881528-35-9*) Current Clin Strat.

Practice Performance Tests. America's Bar Review Staff. (C). 1992. pap. text 34.95 (*1-879563-29-0*) Lexicon CA.

Practice, Politics & Power in Social Services: Social Work, Local Government & Politics. Roger Clough. (Issues in Social Work Ser.). 308p. 1990. text 72.95 (*1-85628-060-8*, Pub. by Avebry) Ashgate Pub Co.

***Practice Power Practice Book Addition.** (Illus.). 16p. (J). (gr. k-2). 2000. spiral bd., wbk. ed. write for info. (*1-930355-03-3*) Scentex.

***Practice Power Practice Book Cursive Letters.** (Illus.). 16p. (J). (gr. k-4). 2000. spiral bd., wbk. ed. write for info. (*1-930355-00-9*) Scentex.

***Practice Power Practice Book Division.** (Illus.). 16p. (J). (gr. 2-5). 2000. spiral bd., wbk. ed. write for info. (*1-930355-02-5*) Scentex.

***Practice Power Practice Book Manuscripts Letters.** (Illus.). 16p. (J). (ps-2). 2000. spiral bd., wbk. ed. write for info. (*1-930355-05-X*) Scentex.

***Practice Power Practice Book Multiplication.** (Illus.). 16p. (J). (gr. 2-5). 2000. spiral bd., wbk. ed. write for info. (*1-930355-01-7*) Scentex.

***Practice Power Practice Book Subtraction.** (Illus.). 16p. (J). (gr. k-2). 2000. spiral bd., wbk. ed. write for info. (*1-930355-04-1*) Scentex.

Practice Power Practice Pal Addition & Subtraction. (Illus.). 24p. (J). (gr. k-2). 1996. spiral bd., wbk. ed. write for info. (*1-930355-06-8*) Scentex.

Practice Power Practice Pal Counting 1-20. (Illus.). 24p. (J). (ps-k). 1996. spiral bd., wbk. ed. write for info. (*1-930355-07-6*) Scentex.

Practice Power Practice Pal Cursive Writing. (Illus.). 24p. (J). (gr. k-4). 1996. spiral bd., wbk. ed. write for info. (*1-930355-09-2*) Scentex.

Practice Power Practice Pal Manuscript Letters. (Illus.). 24p. (J). (ps-1). 1996. spiral bd., wbk. ed. write for info. (*1-930355-08-4*) Scentex.

Practice Power Practice Pal Multiplication & Division. (Illus.). 24p. (J). (gr. 2-5). 1996. spiral bd., wbk. ed. write for info. (*1-930355-10-6*) Scentex.

***Practice Power Practice Pal Safety for Children.** (Illus.). 24p. (J). (ps-6). 1999. spiral bd., wbk. ed. write for info. (*1-930355-11-4*) Scentex.

***Practice Power Workbook Addition.** (Illus.). 16p. (J). (gr. k-2). 1999. wbk. ed. write for info. (*1-930355-13-0*) Scentex.

***Practice Power Workbook Cursive Letters.** (Illus.). 16p. (J). (gr. k-4). 1999. wbk. ed. write for info. (*1-930355-15-7*) Scentex.

***Practice Power Workbook Division.** (Illus.). 16p. (J). (gr. 2-5). 1999. wbk. ed. write for info. (*1-930355-17-3*) Scentex.

***Practice Power Workbook Manuscript Letters.** (Illus.). 16p. (J). (ps-1). 1999. wbk. ed. write for info. (*1-930355-14-9*) Scentex.

***Practice Power Workbook Multiplication.** (Illus.). 16p. (J). (gr. 2-5). 1999. wbk. ed. write for info. (*1-930355-16-5*) Scentex.

***Practice Power Workbook Subtraction.** (Illus.). 16p. (J). (gr. k-2). 1999. wbk. ed. write for info. (*1-930355-12-2*) Scentex.

Practice! Practice! A Latin Via Ovid Workbook. Norma Goldman. LC 74-183525. (Illus.). 166p. reprint ed. pap. 51.50 (*0-608-10598-8*, 207121900009) Bks Demand.

Practice! Practice! A Latin Via Ovid Workbook. rev. ed. Norma Goldman & Michael Rossi. 150p. (YA). (gr. 10-12). 1995. pap., student ed. 9.95 (*0-8143-2611-0*) Wayne St U Pr.

Practice, Practice, Practice, Bk. II+ Proportions, Percents, Integers, Rationals, Equations, Area, Volume, Problem Solving, Combinations. 2nd ed. Timothy Trinkle et al. 224p. (YA). 1990. teacher ed. 3.00 (*0-943542-03-0*); pap. 14.50 (*0-943542-04-9*) ST Two.

Practice Practice Practice, Bk. 1+ Whole Numbers, Decimals & Fractions. Timothy Trinkle et al. 208p. 1982. teacher ed. 3.00 (*0-943542-01-4*) ST Two.

Practice Practice Practice, Bk. 1+ Whole Numbers, Decimals & Fractions. Timothy Trinkle et al. 208p. (J). (gr. 4-9). 1982. text 14.50 (*0-943542-00-6*) ST Two.

Practice Preventive Corporate Law. Ronald L. Jones. LC 85-71419. 273p. 1985. 19.00 (*0-8318-0477-7*, B477) Am Law Inst.

Practice Pro. Mike Cowan. 98p. (C). 1996. spiral bd. 18.95 (*0-7872-2449-9*, 41244901) Kendall-Hunt.

Practice Problem Financial Accounting: Billy's Video. rev. ed. Strawser. 1997. pap. 10.95 (*0-87393-673-6*) Dame Pubns.

Practice Problem in Financial Statement Analysis. Holmes & Strawser. 1998. pap. 9.95 (*0-87393-746-5*) Dame Pubns.

Practice Problem in Intermediate Accounting II: Rainy Day Books. 3rd ed. Edmonds & Grossman. 1998. pap. 18.95 (*0-87393-823-2*) Dame Pubns.

Practice Problems for Dosage Calculations. Kathryn A. Melson. 1991. pap., teacher ed. 11.00 (*0-8273-4401-5*) Delmar.

Practice Problems for the Civil Engineering PE Exam: A Companion to the Civil Engineering Reference Manual. 7th ed. Michael R. Lindeburg. 592p. 1999. pap., student ed. 34.95 (*1-888577-41-X*, CESL7) Prof Pubns CA.

***Practice Problems for the Mechanical Engineering PE Exam: A Companion to the Mechanical Engineering Reference Manual.** 10th ed. Michael R. Lindeburg. 480p. 2000. pap. 29.95 (*1-888577-49-5*) Prof Pubns CA.

***Practice Problems for the P. E. Examination in Environmental Engineering.** 2nd ed. Michael J. McFarland et al. Ed. by William Anderson. LC 99-23154. 120p. 1999. 69.95 (*1-883767-30-X*) Am Acad Environ.

Practice Problems with Solutions. 4th ed. Raymond A. Serway. (C). 1995. pap. text, wbk. ed. 18.50 (*0-03-018238-7*) Harcourt Coll Pubs.

Practice Questions & Solutions Based on Formwork for Concrete Structures (Tables Only) for Florida Contractor's Tests. Robert Lash. 62p. 1977. pap. 7.00 (*0-935715-08-8*, 0477) Construct Bkstore.

Practice Questions for the Registered Professional Reporter & Registered Merit Reporter Exams. 317p. 1996. pap. text 24.95 (*1-881859-15-0*) Natl Ct Report.

Practice RCT Reading Exam. Marie Lackner & Cynthia Paterno. 1998. pap. 11.95 (*0-937820-34-2*); pap. 11.95 (*0-937820-35-0*) WestSea Pub.

Practice Reality. Herbert L. Beierle. 1982. pap. 2.00 (*0-940480-27-1*) UNIPress.

Practice Reality. rev. ed. Herbert L. Beierle. 1995. pap. 2.00 (*0-940480-35-2*) UNIPress.

Practice Record & Assignment Book. 32p. 1982. pap. 1.95 (*1-56222-020-9*, 93865) Mel Bay.

***Practice Safe Stress: A Guide to Using Your Inner Sense of Humor to Minimize Day to Day Stress.** Barry Roberts. (Illus.). 88p. 2000. pap. 12.00 (*0-9700246-0-6*) HAHA.

Practice Set-Basic Accounting. 2nd ed. Calvin Engler. 1969. pap. 6.00 (*0-672-26020-4*, Bobbs) Macmillan.

Practice Set for Intermediate 1: Acme Box Company. Meixner. 1997. pap. 19.95 (*0-87393-733-3*) Dame Pubns.

***Practice Southwestern Geometry.** South-Western Educational Publishing Staff. 1999. 3.75 (*0-538-69221-9*) Thomson Learn.

Practice Standards of ASHP, 1997-1998. Professional Practice Division Staff. 424p. 1997. reprint ed. pap. text 38.00 (*1-879907-75-5*, P510) Am Soc Hlth-Syst.

Practice Standards of ASHP, 1996-1997. rev. ed. Ed. by Joe Deffenbaugh. 400p. 1996. pap. 38.00 (*1-879907-65-8*) Am Soc Hlth-Syst.

Practice Standards of ASHP, 1995-1996. rev. ed. Ed. by Wanda E. Hicks. (Illus.). 364p. 1995. pap. 20.00 (*1-879907-58-5*) Am Soc Hlth-Syst.

Practice Standards of ASHP, 1998-1999. rev. ed. Professional Practice Division Staff. 552p. 1998. pap. text 38.00 (*1-879907-87-9*) Am Soc Hlth-Syst.

Practice Success! The Physician's Guide to Survival & Success in the Medical Practice. 3rd ed. Coker Group Staff. Ed. by Kay B. Stanley. 500p. 1997. 195.00 (*0-9655304-0-X*) Coker Publishing.

Practice Test Psychiatry. 11th ed. Chan & Prosen. 1998. pap. 19.95 (*0-8385-0360-8*) Appleton & Lange.

Practice Tests for Nursing Students. Bourque. 160p. (C). (gr. 13). 1990. pap. text 15.95 (*0-8016-0737-X*, 00737) Mosby Inc.

***Practice Tests for Sociology: US in a Global Community.** 4th ed. Ferrante. (Sociology Ser.). 1999. pap. 5.25 (*0-534-57057-7*) Wadsworth Pub.

Practice Tests for the FCC General Radiotelephone Operator's License Exam. Victor F. Veley. 304p. 1993. 27.95 (*0-07-067371-3*) McGraw.

Practice Tests for the FCC General Radiotelephone Operator's License Examination. Victor F. Veley. LC 92-30651. 1993. pap. text 24.95 (*0-8306-2578-X*) McGraw-Hill Prof.

Practice Therapeutic Endoscopy. Tytgat. 1995. text 166.00 (*0-443-04832-0*, W B Saunders Co) Harcrt Hlth Sci Grp.

Practice These Principles. Bill Pittman. LC 99-188657. 1997. pap. 9.95 (*1-56838-150-6*, 1059 A) Hazelden.

Practice Tips. 2nd ed. John Murtagh. (Illus.). 224p. 1995. 49.00 (*0-07-470180-0*) McGraw-Hill HPD.

Practice Tips for Litigators. LC 83-71990. 64p. 1983. pap. 21.00 (*0-89707-113-1*, 519-0034-01) Amer Bar Assn.

Practice Tips for Litigators, No. 2. LC 83-71990. 160p. 1986. pap. 29.95 (*0-89707-256-1*, 519-0060-01) Amer Bar Assn.

***Practice to Deceive.** David Housewright. (Holland Taylor Mystery Ser.). 2000. mass mkt. 5.99 (*0-425-17312-7*) Berkley Pub.

Practice to Deceive: A Holland Taylor Mystery. David Housewright. LC 97-12864. (Holland Taylor Mystery Ser.). 256p. 1997. 22.00 (*0-88150-404-1*, Foul Play) Norton.

***Practice to Deceive: The Amazing Stories of Literary Forgery's Most Notorious Practices.** Joseph Rosenblum. LC 99-48636. (Illus.). 370p. 2000. 39.95 (*1-58456-010-X*) Oak Knoll.

Practice to Win see Practicar Es Ganar

Practice under Florida Probate Code. Florida Bar Members. LC 94-61156. 1228p. 1997. ring bd. 125.00 incl. disk (*0-945979-62-2*, 201) FL Bar Legal Ed.

Practice under Florida Usury Law: 1993 Supplement. 2nd ed. Florida Bar Members. LC 89-80982. 264p. 1993. ring bd. 25.00 (*0-945979-04-5*, 287) FL Bar Legal Ed.

Practice under the California Corporate Securities Laws, 3 vols. Harold W. Marsh & Robert H. Volk. 1972. 580.00 (*0-8205-1552-3*) Bender.

Practice under the California Environmental Quality Act, Set, Vols. 1 & 2. Stephen L. Kostka & Michael H. Zischke. Ed. by Craig H. Scott & Mary Gerber. LC 93-73950. 1500p. 1994. 275.00 (*0-88124-690-5*, RE-32060) Cont Ed Bar-CA.

Practice under the California Environmental Quality Act: 11/97 Update. Stephen L. Kostka & Michael H. Zischke. Ed. by John K. Chaplin. LC 93-73950. 1006p. 1997. ring bd. 117.00 (*0-7626-0157-4*, RE-32063) Cont Ed Bar-CA.

***Practice under the California Environmental Quality Act - 8/99 Update, 2 vols.** Stephen L. Kostka & Michael H. Zischke. Ed. by Donald R. Briggs. LC 93-73950. 1264p. 1999. ring bd. 118.00 (*0-7626-0352-6*, RE-32064) Cont Ed Bar-CA.

***Practice under the California Family Code, 2000.** M. Dee Samuels & Frederick A. Mandabach. Ed. by Elizabeth M. Johnson. LC 92-70751. 1186p. 2000. 99.00 (*0-7626-0407-7*, FA-31958) Cont Ed Bar-CA.

Practice under the Federal Sentencing Guidelines, 3 vols. 3rd ed. Ed. by Phylis S. Bamberger & David J. Gottlieb. 2690p. 1993. ring bd. 260.00 (*0-13-126905-4*) Aspen Law.

Practice under the Occupational Safety & Health Act. 3rd ed. Charles M. Chadd & Jerome K. Bowman. (Corporate Practice Ser.: No. 9). 1992. ring bd. 95.00 (*1-55871-289-5*) BNA.

Practice Using Excel 5 for Windows. John Preston. LC 94-68008. 1994. wbk. ed. 27.99 (*1-56529-873-X*) Que.

Practice Using Lotus 1-2-3 R 2.X. Deryk Marien. LC 93-86101. 1994. wbk. ed. 27.99 (*1-56529-668-0*) Que.

Practice Using MS-DOS 6.2. Que E & T Staff. (C). 1994. 35.33 (*1-56529-718-0*) Que.

Practice Using MS-DOS 6.2 Wkbk. Lynda Ambruster. LC 93-86967. 262p. 1994. 27.99 (*1-56529-674-5*) Que.

Practice Using NetWare 3.12. Guy Yost. LC 95-70076. 277p. 1997. pap. 37.99 (*0-7897-0495-1*) Que Educ & Trng.

Practice Using PowerPoint 4. 1994. teacher ed. 39.99 (*1-56529-804-7*) Que.

Practice Using PowerPoint 4. 1994. 59.90 (*1-56529-797-0*) Que.

Practice Using Windows 3.1 Wkbk. John Preston. LC 93-86493. 269p. 1993. 27.99 (*1-56529-669-9*) Que.

Practice Using Word 6 for Windows. Lawson. 1995. pap. text, teacher ed. 39.99 (*1-56529-814-4*) Que Educ & Trng.

P

An Asterisk (*) at the beginning of an entry indicates that the title is appearing for the first time.

Practice Using Word 6 for Windows Wkbk. John Preston. LC 94-68006. 343p. 1995. pap. text, wbk. ed. 27.99 (*1-56529-878-0*) Que Educ & Trng.

***Practice What You Preach.** James F. Keenan & Joseph J. Kotva, Jr. LC 99-16894. 150p. 1999. pap. 15.95 (*1-58051-064-7*) Sheed & Ward WI.

***Practice What You Preach: The Need for Ethics in Church Leadership.** James F. Keenan. LC 00-8461. (Annual Jesuit Lecture in Human Values Ser.). 2000. pap. write for info. (*0-87462-032-5*) Marquette.

Practice What You Preached. Ron DeBock. LC 93-90373. (Illus.). 231p. 1993. 21.95 (*0-9636750-1-X*); pap. 9.95 (*0-9636750-0-1*) Fireball Pubns.

***Practice Wife.** large type ed. Margaret O'Neill. 1999. 25.99 (*0-263-15992-2*, Pub. by Mills & Boon) Ulverscroft.

Practice Wisdom: A Guide for Helping Professionals. Donald F. Krill. LC 90-8606. (Sage Human Services Guides Ser.: No. 62). (Illus.). 134p. 1990. reprint ed. pap. 41.60 (*0-7837-9905-5*, 206063100006) Bks Demand.

Practice Wisdom: A Program of Learning for Helping Professionals. Donald F. Krill. (Human Services Guides Ser.: Vol. 62). (Illus.). 155p. (C). 1990. pap. 18.95 (*0-8039-3606-0*) Sage.

Practice with Idioms. Ronald E. Feare. 188p. 1980. pap. text 14.95 (*0-19-502782-5*) OUP.

Practice with Spreadsheets. Sandra T. Myers. 254p. (C). 1997. pap. text 32.00 (*0-13-456682-3*) P-H.

Practice with Your Partner: Dictation Activities for Student-Student Interaction. Linda Mrowicki. 46p. 1987. pap. text 19.95 (*0-9655910-9-3*) Linmore Pub.

Practice Workbook. 1994. pap. text, wbk. ed. 14.75 (*0-15-305109-4*) Harcourt Schl Pubs.

Practice Workbook for Matematicas Sin Limites. Fennell. (SPA.). 1988. pap., student ed. 9.25 (*0-03-009168-3*); pap., student ed. 10.00 (*0-03-009169-1*); pap., student ed. 10.00 (*0-03-009172-1*) Harcourt Schl Pubs.

Practice Workbook for Math Plus. (J). (gr. k). 1992. pap. text, teacher ed. 14.75 (*0-15-300953-5*) Harcourt Schl Pubs.

Practice Workbook for Math Plus. (J). (gr. 3). 1992. pap. text, teacher ed. 18.25 (*0-15-300956-X*) Harcourt Schl Pubs.

Practice Workbook for Math Plus. (J). (gr. 4). 1992. pap. text 11.00 (*0-15-300948-9*); pap. text, teacher ed. 18.25 (*0-15-300957-8*) Harcourt Schl Pubs.

Practice Workbook for Math Plus. (J). (gr. 5). 1992. pap. text 11.00 (*0-15-300949-7*); pap. text, teacher ed. 18.75 (*0-15-300958-6*) Harcourt Schl Pubs.

Practice Workbook for Math Plus. (J). (gr. 6). 1992. pap. text 11.50 (*0-15-300950-0*); pap. text, teacher ed. 18.75 (*0-15-300959-4*) Harcourt Schl Pubs.

Practice Workbook for Math Plus. (J). (gr. 7). 1992. pap. text 12.00 (*0-15-300951-9*); pap. text, teacher ed. 20.00 (*0-15-300960-8*) Harcourt Schl Pubs.

Practice Workbook for Math Plus. (J). (gr. 8). 1992. pap. text 12.00 (*0-15-300952-7*) Harcourt Schl Pubs.

Practice Workbook for Math Plus, 1992. HBJ Staff. 1992. pap., wbk. ed. 20.00 (*0-15-300961-6*) Harcourt Schl Pubs.

Practice Workbook for Mathematics Today. Abbott. 1987. pap., teacher ed. 20.50 (*0-15-350077-8*); pap., teacher ed. 15.50 (*0-15-350070-0*); pap., teacher ed. 18.75 (*0-15-350071-9*); pap., teacher ed. 18.75 (*0-15-350072-7*); pap., teacher ed. 20.50 (*0-15-350073-5*); pap., teacher ed. 20.50 (*0-15-350074-3*); pap., teacher ed. 20.50 (*0-15-350075-1*); pap., teacher ed. 20.50 (*0-15-350076-X*); pap., teacher ed. 20.50 (*0-15-350078-6*); pap., student ed. 9.00 (*0-15-350060-3*); pap., student ed. 9.75 (*0-15-350062-X*); pap., student ed. 11.25 (*0-15-350063-8*); pap., student ed. 11.25 (*0-15-350065-4*); pap., student ed. 11.25 (*0-15-350066-2*); pap., student ed. 12.25 (*0-15-350067-0*); pap., student ed. 12.25 (*0-15-350068-9*); pap., student ed. 9.75 (*0-15-350061-1*) Harcourt Schl Pubs.

Practice Workbook Math Plus. 1994. pap. text 18.00 (*0-15-305111-6*); pap. text 18.25 (*0-15-305112-4*); pap. text 18.75 (*0-15-305114-0*); pap. text 18.75 (*0-15-305115-9*) Harcourt Schl Pubs.

Practice Workbook Math Plus: Grade 1. 1994. pap. text 10.00 (*0-15-305101-9*) Harcourt Schl Pubs.

Practice Workbook Math Unlimited, 1991: Grade K. 1991. pap. text, teacher ed. 13.75 (*0-15-351597-X*) Harcourt Schl Pubs.

Practice Workbook Math Unlimited, 1991: Grade 1. 1991. pap. text, teacher ed. 17.00 (*0-15-351598-8*); pap. text, student ed. 9.50 (*0-15-351589-9*) Harcourt Schl Pubs.

Practice Workbook Math Unlimited 1991: Grade 2. 1991. pap. text, student ed. 9.50 (*0-15-351590-2*) Harcourt Schl Pubs.

Practice Workbook Math Unlimited, 1991: Grade 2. 1991. pap. text, teacher ed. 17.00 (*0-15-351599-6*) Harcourt Schl Pubs.

Practice Workbook Math Unlimited, 1991: Grade 3. 1991. pap. text, teacher ed. 17.50 (*0-15-351600-3*); pap. text, student ed. 11.25 (*0-15-351591-0*) Harcourt Schl Pubs.

Practice Workbook Math Unlimited, 1991: Grade 4. 1991. pap. text, teacher ed. 17.50 (*0-15-351601-1*); pap. text, student ed. 11.25 (*0-15-351592-9*) Harcourt Schl Pubs.

Practice Workbook Math Unlimited, 1991: Grade 5. 1991. pap. text, teacher ed. 17.75 (*0-15-351602-X*); pap. text, student ed. 11.25 (*0-15-351593-7*) Harcourt Schl Pubs.

Practice Workbook Math Unlimited, 1991: Grade 6. 1991. pap. text, teacher ed. 17.75 (*0-15-351603-8*); pap. text, student ed. 11.25 (*0-15-351594-5*) Harcourt Schl Pubs.

Practice Workbook Math Unlimited, 1991: Grade 7. 1991. pap. text, teacher ed. 18.00 (*0-15-351604-6*); pap. text, student ed. 12.00 (*0-15-351595-3*) Harcourt Schl Pubs.

Practice Workbook Math Unlimited, 1991: Grade 8. 1991. pap. text, teacher ed. 18.00 (*0-15-351605-4*); pap. text, student ed. 12.00 (*0-15-351596-1*) Harcourt Schl Pubs.

Practice Writer with Readings. 3rd ed. Bailey. (C). 1992. pap. text, teacher ed. 40.50 (*0-03-055844-1*, Pub. by Harcourt Coll Pubs) Harcourt.

Practice Your Comparative. Adrian-Vallance. 1990. pap. write for info. (*0-582-01443-3*) Addison-Wesley.

Pratice Your Comprehension Skills 4. McCartne. 1994. pap. text. write for info. (*0-582-87520-X*, Pub. by Addison-Wesley) Longman.

Practice Your Comprehension Skills 3. McCartne. 1994. pap. text. write for info. (*0-582-87519-6*, Pub. by Addison-Wesley) Longman.

Practice Your Comprehension Skills 6. McCartne. 1994. pap. text. write for info. (*0-582-87522-6*, Pub. by Addison-Wesley) Longman.

Practice Your Conprehension Skills 5. McCartne. 1994. pap. text. write for info. (*0-582-87521-8*, Pub. by Addison-Wesley) Longman.

PracticeCards for Golfers: Problem Solving Instructional Cards for Use on the Practice Range & Practice Green. Ed. by Joseph Davidson & Thomas Strang. (PracticeCard Ser.). (Illus.). 128p. 1992. 19.95 (*0-9633090-0-5*) PracticeCard.

Practiced in the Presence: Essays in Honor of T. Canby Jones. Ed. by D. N. Snarr & Daniel Smith-Christopher. LC 94-12654. 266p. 1994. 19.00 (*0-944350-32-1*) Friends United.

Practices & Policies Regarding Broadcasting of Opinions About Controversial Issues by Radio & Television Stations in the United States. Joseph M. Ripley, Jr. Ed. by Christopher H. Sterling. LC 78-21734. (Dissertations in Broadcasting Ser.). 1980. lib. bdg. 20.95 (*0-405-11771-X*) Ayer.

***Practices & Principles: Approaches to Ethical & Legal Judgement.** Mark Tunick. 272p. 2001. pap. 19.95 (*0-691-07079-2*) Princeton U Pr.

Practices & Principles: Approaches to Ethical & Legal Judgment. Mark Tunick. LC 97-29599. 233p. 1998. text 35.00 (*0-691-01560-0*, Pub. by Princeton U Pr) Cal Prin Full Svc.

Practices & Procedures of the Investigating Services of the Deparment of Defense & the Military Departments Concerning the Investigations into the Deaths of Military Personnel Which May Have Resulted from Self-Inflicted Causes. Ed. by Strom Thurmond. (Illus.). 268p. 1998. pap. text 40.00 (*0-7881-4236-4*) DIANE Pub.

***Practices & Proceedings of the Internal Revenue Service: Government Hearings.** Ed. by William V. Roth, Jr. 357p. (C). 1999. reprint ed. pap. text 45.00 (*0-7881-8239-0*) DIANE Pub.

Practices & Products for Clean Marinas: A Best Management Practice Handbook. (Illus.). 143p. (Orig.). write for info. (*0-614-10782-2*) Intl Marina Inst.

Practices for Evaluation of Concrete in Existing Massive Structures for Service Conditions. 15p. 1994. 30.25 (*0-614-02500-1*, 207.3R94BOW6) ACI.

Practices in Archaeological Stratigraphy. Ed. by Edward C. Harris et al. (Illus.). 296p. 1993. text 69.95 (*0-12-326445-6*) Acad Pr.

Practices in Veterinary Public Health & Preventative Medicine. Ed. by George T. Woods. LC 86-10459. (Illus.). 365p. 1986. reprint ed. pap. 113.20 (*0-608-06891-8*, 2067099) Bks Demand.

Practices in Veterinary Public Health & Preventative Medicine in the United States. Ed. by George T. Woods. LC 86-10459. (Illus.). 365p. 1986. reprint ed. pap. 113.20 (*0-608-00054-X*, 206082000006) Bks Demand.

Practices of a Healthy Church: Biblical Strategies for Vibrant Church Life & Ministry. Donald J. MacNair & Esther L. Meek. LC 99-26138. 256p. 1999. pap. 11.99 (*0-87552-390-0*) P & R Pubng.

Practices of Freedom: Selected Writings on HIV-AIDS. Simon Watney. LC 94-11033. (Series Q). 312p. 1994. pap. 16.95 (*0-8223-1564-5*); text 49.95 (*0-8223-1553-X*) Duke.

Practices of Human Genetics Michael Fortun & Everett Mendelsohn. LC 98-49927. (Sociology of the Sciences Ser.). 17p. 1999. write for info. (*0-7923-5333-1*) Kluwer Academic.

Practices of Hybridity. Mireille Rosello. 96p. 1996. pap. 22.50 (*0-7486-0638-6*, Pub. by Edinburgh U Pr) Col U Pr.

***Practices of Painting in Japan, 1475-1500.** Quitman Eugene Phillips. (Illus.). 259p. 2000. 49.50 (*0-8047-3446-1*) Stanford U Pr.

Practices of Reason: Aristotle's Nicomachean Ethics. C. D. C. Reeve. 240p. 1995. pap. text 24.95 (*0-19-823565-8*) OUP.

Practicing. Jamie MacInnis. 88p. (Orig.). 1980. pap. 5.00 (*0-939180-13-8*) Tombouctou.

Practicing Adolescent Medicine: A Collection of Resources. American Academy of Pediatrics Staff. LC 94-70994. 362p. 1994. pap. 44.95 (*0-910761-56-6*) Am Acad Pediat.

Practicing American English. Grant Taylor. (Saxon Series in English As a Second Language). (C). 1962. 25.31 (*0-07-062943-9*) McGraw.

Practicing American Politics. David Edwards & Alessandra Lippucci. (Illus.). (C). 1998. text 43.00 (*1-57259-143-9*) Worth.

Practicing American Politics. David V. Edwards & Alessandra Lippucci. (Illus.). 880p. 1998. write for info. (*1-57259-528-0*); pap. write for info. (*1-57259-534-5*) Worth.

Practicing American Politics. Edwards & Alessandra Lippucci. pap. text. write for info. (*0-312-24147-X*) St Martin.

Practicing American Politics: Instructor's Resource Manual. David V. Edwards & Alessandra Lippucci. 1998. teacher ed. write for info. (*1-57259-530-2*) Worth.

Practicing American Politics Chapters 1-16: Basic Edition. David Edwards & Alessandra Lippucci. (Illus.). (C). 1997. pap. text 35.00 (*1-57259-533-7*) Worth.

Practicing American Politics Basic Dummy. Edwards & Alessandra Lippucci. pap. text. write for info. (*0-312-24075-9*) St Martin.

Practicing American Politics Dummy. Edwards & Alessandra Lippucci. pap. text. write for info. (*0-312-24074-0*); pap. text, student ed. write for info. (*0-312-24146-1*) St Martin.

***Practicing Amnesia.** Heather Thomas. (Philadelphia Publishing Project Ser.). (Illus.). 76p. 2000. pap. 12.50 (*0-935162-20-8*, Pub. by Singing Horse) SPD-Small Pr Dist.

Practicing Anthropology in a Postmodern World: Lessons & Insights from Federal Contract Research. Michael C. Reed. LC 97-6539. (NAPA Bulletin Ser.). 1997. write for info. (*0-913167-81-9*) Am Anthro Assn.

Practicing Anthropology in Corporate America: Consulting on Organizational Culture. Ed. by Ann T. Jordan. LC 94-8980. (NAPA Bulletin Ser.: Vol. 14). 1994. write for info. (*0-913167-64-9*) Am Anthro Assn.

Practicing Anthropology in the South. James M. Wallace. LC 96-10267. (Southern Anthropological Society Proceedings Ser.: No. 30). 1997. 40.00 (*0-8203-1860-4*) U of Ga Pr.

***Practicing Basic Spiritual Disciplines.** Charles F. Stanley. (In Touch Study Ser.: Vol. 23). 2000. pap. 7.99 (*0-7852-7294-1*) Nelson.

Practicing Business. James Vanoosting. (C). Date not set. pap. text, teacher ed., suppl. ed. write for info. (*0-395-60815-5*) HM.

Practicing Business. James Vanoosting. (C). 1991. pap., teacher ed. 2.76 (*0-395-60165-7*) HM.

Practicing California Judicial Arbitration. LC 82-74525. 243p. 1983. 70.00 (*0-88124-104-0*, CP-30660) Cont Ed Bar-CA.

***Practicing California Judicial Arbitration - 12/99 Update.** William A. Robinson. Ed. by Linda A. Compton. LC 82-74525. 216p. 1999. pap. text 58.00 (*0-7626-0376-3*, CP-30666) Cont Ed Bar-CA.

Practicing Catholic. Daniel E. Pilarczyk. 88p. 1998. pap. text 6.95 (*0-86716-361-5*) St Anthony Mess Pr.

Practicing Catholic: The Search for a Liveable Catholicism. Penelope J. Ryan. LC 97-51624. 256p. 1995. 22.95 (*0-8050-4663-1*) H Holt & Co.

Practicing Chemists: A History of the Society for Analytic Chemistry. Royal Society of Chemistry Staff. 1989. 22.00 (*0-85990-100-9*) CRC Pr.

Practicing Cognitive Therapy: A Guide to Interventions. Ed. by Robert L. Leahy. LC 97-5689. 504p. 1997. text 60.00 (*1-56821-824-9*) Aronson.

Practicing Community: Class, Culture, & Power in an Urban Neighborhood. Rhoda H. Halperin. LC 97-33917. 336p. (C). 1998. 40.00 (*0-292-73118-3*, HALPRA); pap. 19.95 (*0-292-73117-5*, HALPRP) U of Tex Pr.

Practicing Compassion for the Stranger. Nancy Alexander. LC 86-63727. 1987. pap. 4.00 (*0-87574-271-8*) Pendle Hill.

Practicing Conceptual Physical Science. 2nd ed. Paul G. Hewitt. 224p. (C). 1998. 19.00 (*0-321-03531-3*) Addison-Wesley.

Practicing Conceptual Physical Science to Accompany Conceptual Physical Science. Paul G. Hewitt et al. LC 93-4561. (C). 1997. pap. text, student ed. 22.00 (*0-673-46380-X*) Addson-Wesley Educ.

Practicing CPA on Developing & Marketing Services. Ed. by Graham Goddard. LC 97-210530. 176p. (Orig.). 1997. pap. 34.00 (*0-87051-186-6*) Am Inst CPA.

Practicing Daily Prayer in the Orthodox Christian Life. Theodora D. Argue. 1989. pap. 4.95 (*0-937032-64-6*) Light&Life Pub Co MN.

Practicing Democracy. 2nd ed. Isaac. LC 95-73205. 123p. 1996. pap. text 13.95 (*0-312-15272-8*) St Martin.

Practicing Desire: Homosexual Sex in Era of AIDS. Gary W. Dowsett. LC 96-10879. 1996. 49.50 (*0-8047-2711-2*); pap. 16.95 (*0-8047-2712-0*) Stanford U Pr.

Practicing Disciplined Coping & the (Co) American Dream: Life & Pursuit of Successful Living, Vol. 2. Homer Wells. LC 92-73386. 256p. 1992. pap. 19.95 (*0-942963-32-6*) Distinctive Pub.

Practicing Econometrics: Essays in Method & Application. Zvi Griliches. LC 97-50276. (Economists of the Twentieth Century Ser.). 688p. 1998. 125.00 (*1-85278-659-0*) E Elgar.

Practicing Economic Development. Ed. by Robert L. Koepke. 109p. (Orig.). 1991. pap. 10.00 (*0-9616567-0-0*) Amer Econ Dev Council.

Practicing Economic Development. 2nd ed. Ed. by Robert L. Koepke. 188p. (Orig.). 1993. pap. 45.00 (*0-9616567-5-1*) Amer Econ Dev Council.

Practicing Economic Development. 3rd ed. Ed. by Robert L. Koepke. (Illus.). 296p. (Orig.). 1996. pap. text 50.00 (*0-9616567-8-6*) Amer Econ Dev Council.

Practicing Economic Development in Texas. Ed. by Sherman M. Wyman & Robert R. Weaver. 77p. 1990. pap. text 40.00 (*0-936440-82-1*) U TX SUPA.

Practicing Ecumenism. Ed. by Blair G. Meeks. (Liturgy Ser.). 80p. (Orig.). 1992. pap. 10.95 (*0-918208-57-2*) Liturgical Conf.

Practicing Effective Leadership. Mescon Group Staff. (Performance Through Participation Ser.). 1996. text, teacher ed. 23.95 (*0-538-84939-8*); text, suppl. ed. 14.95 (*0-538-84938-X*) S-W Pub.

Practicing Enlightenment: Hume & the Formation of a Literary Career. Jerome Christensen. LC 95-18996. 336p. 1986. pap. 19.95 (*0-299-10754-X*) U of Wis Pr.

Practicing Enlightenment: Hume & the Formation of a Literary Career. Jerome Christensen. LC 86-40048. 299p. 1987. reprint ed. pap. 92.70 (*0-608-07000-9*, 206720800009) Bks Demand.

Practicing Environmental Archaeology: Methods & Interpretations. Roger W. Moeller. LC 82-73087. (Occasional Papers: No. 3). (Illus.). 112p. 1982. pap. text 10.00 (*0-936322-00-4*) Inst Amer Indian.

Practicing Eternity. Carol Givens & L. Diana Fortier. Ed. by Adele Gorelick. LC 91-66757. 171p. (Orig.). 1992. pap. 10.95 (*0-9628595-2-4*) Paradigm San Diego.

Practicing Ethical Engineering. Charles E. Harris, Jr. (IEEE Engineers Guides to Business Ser.). 100p. 1997. pap. text 19.95 (*0-7803-2333-5*, EG115) Inst Electrical.

Practicing Family Therapy in Diverse Settings. Michael Berger & Gregory J. Jurkovic. LC 94-70555. 396p. 1994. pap. 50.00 (*1-56821-238-0*) Aronson.

Practicing Family Therapy in Diverse Settings. Michael Berger et al. LC 83-49256. (Jossey-Bass Social & Behavioral Science Ser.). 396p. reprint ed. pap. 122.80 (*0-8357-4817-0*, 203775400009) Bks Demand.

Practicing Feminisms, Reconstructing Psychology: Notes on a Liminal Science. Jill G. Morawski. LC 94-10786. (Critical Perspectives on Women & Gender Ser.). 288p. (C). 1994. text 44.50 (*0-472-09481-5*, 09481); pap. text 18.95 (*0-472-06481-9*, 06481) U of Mich Pr.

***Practicing Feminist Ethics in Psychology.** Ed. by Mary M. Brabeck. LC 99-41175. 285p. 1999. 39.95 (*1-55798-623-1*, 431-2300); pap. 29.95 (*1-55798-635-5*) Am Psychol.

Practicing Financial Planning: A Complete Guide for Professionals. Sitansu S. Mittra. (Illus.). 658p. (C). 1993. pap. 29.95 (*0-9636527-0-2*) Mittra & Assocs.

Practicing for Heaven. Julia B. Levine. (Anhinga Prize for Poetry Ser.). 96p. 1999. pap. 12.00 (*0-938078-62-3*) Anhinga Pr.

Practicing for Young Musicians: You Are Your Own Teacher!!! 2nd rev. ed. Harvey R. Snitkin. LC 96-94279. (Illus.). 151p. (Orig.). (J). (gr. 4 up). 1996. pap. 14.95 (*1-888732-00-8*) HMS Pubns CT.

Practicing French Grammar: A Workbook. Roger Hawkins et al. (Practicing...Grammar Ser.). (ENG & FRE., Illus.). 256p. 1998. pap., wbk. ed. 15.95 (*0-8442-1630-5*, 16305) NTC Contemp Pub Co.

Practicing German Grammar: A Workbook. 2nd ed. Martin Durrell. (GER & ENG., Illus.). 256p. 1997. pap., wbk. ed. 15.95 (*0-8442-2209-7*, 22097) NTC Contemp Pub Co.

Practicing Golf: A System for Generating the Best Golf You Can Play. Chuck Hogan. Ed. by Mike Altman. (Illus.). 58p. (Orig.). 1991. write for info. (*0-685-39424-7*); audio 24.95 (*0-9624504-2-1*) Sports Enhance.

***Practicing Grammar & Usage.** 4th ed. Harris. 240p. 1999. pap. 13.33 (*0-13-023127-4*) P-H.

***Practicing Harm Reduction Psychotherapy: An Alternative Approach to Addictions.** Patt Denning. 270p. 2000. lib. bdg. 35.00 (*1-57230-555-X*, C0555) Guilford Pubns.

Practicing His Presence. 3rd ed. Brother Lawrence & Frank C. Laubach. Ed. by Gene Edwards. 1973. pap. 8.95 (*0-940232-01-4*) Seedsowers.

Practicing History: Selected Essays. Barbara W. Tuchman. 1982. pap. 12.95 (*0-345-30363-6*) Ballantine Pub Grp.

Practicing Identities. Sasha Roseneil & Seymour. LC 99-18649. 257p. 1999. text 65.00 (*0-312-22227-0*) St Martin.

Practicing in the New Mental Health Marketplace: Ethical, Legal & Moral Issues. Ed. by Richard F. Small & Laurence R. Barnhill. LC 98-15627. 277p. 1998. 39.95 (*1-55798-494-8*, 431-709A) Am Psychol.

Practicing Insanity. Alfred J. Bruey. 21p. 1982. pap. 7.95 (*0-944754-02-3*) Pudding Hse Pubns.

Practicing Judicious Discipline: An Educator's Guide to a Democratic Classroom. 2nd ed. Ed. by Barbara McEwan. 128p. (C). 1994. pap. text 14.95 (*1-880192-09-8*) Caddo Gap Pr.

***Practicing Judicious Discipline: An Educator's Guide to a Democratic Classroom.** 3rd rev. ed. Ed. by Barbara McEwan. 224p. 1999. pap. 24.95 (*1-880192-29-2*) Caddo Gap Pr.

Practicing Law in Frontier California. Gordon M. Bakken. LC 90-40646. (Law in the American West Ser.). (Illus.). xviii, 192p. 1991. text 50.00 (*0-8032-1219-4*) U of Nebr Pr.

Practicing Law in New York City. Ed. by Council of New York Law Associates Staff et al. 195p. 1975. pap. 3.75 (*0-318-03111-6*) Coun NY Law.

Practicing Law Without Clients: Making a Living As a Freelance Lawyer. LC 96-86562. 116p. 1996. pap. 59.95 (*1-57073-403-8*, 511-0376) Amer Bar Assn.

Practicing Leadership: Principles & Applications. Arthur Shriberg et al. LC 96-36096. 242p. 1996. pap. 49.95 (*0-471-11374-3*) Wiley.

Practicing Linguistic Historiography: Selected Papers. Konrad Koerner. LC 89-36613. (Studies in the History of the Language Sciences: Vol. 50). (FRE, GER & ITA.). xiv, 455p. (C). 1989. 94.00 (*90-272-4533-9*) J Benjamins Pubng Co.

Practicing Mass Media Research. 2nd ed. Wimmer. (Mass Communication Ser.). 1987. pap., student ed. 10.00 (*0-534-06705-0*) Wadsworth Pub.

***Practicing Neurology: What You Need to Know, What You Need to Do.** Rahman Pourmand. LC 98-54985. 369p. 1999. pap. text 30.00 (*0-7506-9970-1*) Buttrwrth-Heinemann.

Practicing New Historicism? Catherine Gallagher & Stephen Greenblatt. LC 99-42410. 1993. 25.00 (*0-226-27934-0*) U Ch Pr.

Practicing Nursing. MacLeod. 1996. text 29.95 (*0-443-05279-4*, W B Saunders Co) Harcrt Hlth Sci Grp.

An Asterisk (*) at the beginning of an entry indicates that the title is appearing for the first time.

Practicing Organization Development: A Guide for Consultants. William J. Rothwell et al. LC 94-69887. 512p. 1995. text 59.95 (*0-88390-379-5*) Jossey-Bass.

Practicing Our Faith: A Guide for Conversation, Learning & Growing. Dorothy C. Bass. LC 96-80241. 56p. 1998. pap., student ed. 6.00 (*0-7879-0365-5*) Jossey-Bass.

Practicing Our Faith: A Way of Life for a Searching People. Ed. by Dorothy C. Bass. LC 96-45782. (Religion in Practice Ser.). 1997. mass mkt. 22.50 (*0-7879-0336-1*) Jossey-Bass.

Practicing Our Faith: A Way of Life for a Searching People. Ed. by Dorothy C. Bass. (Religion in Practice Ser.). 256p. 1998. pap. 14.00 (*0-7879-3883-1*) Jossey-Bass.

Practicing Our Sighs: The Collected Poems of Richard Snyder. Richard Snyder. Ed. by Mary Snyder & Robert McGovern. 155p. 1989. 35.00 (*0-912592-26-5*); pap. 10.00 (*0-912592-27-3*) Ashland Poetry.

Practicing Peace: Ten Spiritual Exercises That Heal. W. Glyn Evans. 160p. 1987. pap. 6.95 (*0-310-29381-2*, 10463P) Zondervan.

Practicing Philosophy: Pragmatism & the Philosophical Life. Richard Shusterman. LC 96-30438. 240p. (C). 1996. pap. 19.99 (*0-415-91395-0*) Routledge.

Practicing Philosophy: Pragmatism & the Philosophical Life. Richard Shusterman. LC 96-30438. 240p. (C). 1997. 70.00 (*0-415-91394-2*) Routledge.

Practicing Physician's Approach to Headache. 5th ed. Seymour Diamond & Donald J. Dalessio. 320p. 1991. 49.00 (*0-683-02506-6*) Lppncott W & W.

Practicing Physics (Workbook) to Accompany Conceptual Physics, 7/E. 7th ed. Geoffrey F. Hewitt. (C). 1993. pap. text, student ed. 22.00 (*0-673-52319-5*) Addson-Wesley Educ.

Practicing Postmodernism/Reading Modernism. Patricia Waugh. (Interrogating Texts Ser.). 224p. 1995. pap. text 16.95 (*0-340-55050-3*, A7050, Pub. by E A) OUP.

Practicing Process. (C). 1989. pap. text 11.00 (*0-673-47053-9*) S&S Trade.

Practicing Psychiatry in the Community: A Manual. Ed. by Jerome V. Vaccaro & Gordon H. Clark, Jr. 560p. 1996. text 69.50 (*0-88048-663-5*, 8663) Am Psychiatric.

Practicing Psychology in Hospitals & Other Health Care Facilities. American Psychological Association Practice Direct. LC 97-51278. (Illus.). 156p. 1998. pap. 29.95 (*1-55798-491-3*) Am Psychol.

Practicing Psychology in Rural Settings: Hospital Privileges & Collaborative Care. Jerry A. Morris. LC 97-25216. (Illus.). 159p. 1997. pap. text 19.95 (*1-55798-452-2*) Am Psychol.

Practicing Psychotherapy: A Casebook. Michael F. Basch. LC 91-55601. 224p. 1992. 42.00 (*0-465-06175-3*, Pub. by Basic) HarpC.

Practicing Psychotherapy: Basic Techniques & Practical Issues. Edmund C. Neuhaus & William Astwood. LC 79-25464. 208p. 1980. 35.95 (*0-87705-467-3*, Kluwer Acad Hman Sci); pap. 22.95 (*0-89885-230-7*, Kluwer Acad Hman Sci) Kluwer Academic.

Practicing Public Management. 3rd ed. Meyer & Brown. pap. text. write for info. (*0-312-06745-3*) St Martin.

Practicing Public Management: A Casebook. 2nd ed. C. Kenneth Meyer & Charles H. Brown. LC 88-60537. 250p. (C). 1988. pap. text 34.95 (*0-312-00329-3*) St Martin.

Practicing Public Speaking: A Student Coursebook. Leigh Makay. 288p. (C). 1994. per. 18.36 (*0-8403-9368-7*) Kendall-Hunt.

Practicing Racial Reconciliation in Your Church. Michelle L. Paige. 20p. 1998. pap. 1.95 (*1-56212-345-9*, 1930-0322) CRC Pubns.

***Practicing Radical Honesty.** Brad Blanton. 2000. 25.00 (*0-9630921-3-8*); pap. 15.00 (*0-9630921-9-7*) Sparrowhawk.

Practicing Recursion in Pascal. Irena Pevac & Joan M. Calvert. 84p. (C). 1996. text 22.80 (*0-536-59300-0*) Pearson Custom.

Practicing Rehabilitation with Geriatric Clients. Ed. by J. Dermot Frengley et al. 256p. 1990. 36.95 (*0-8261-6980-5*) Springer Pub.

***Practicing Renaissance Scholarship: Plays & Pageants, Patrons & Politics.** David M. Bergeron. LC 99-50701. (Medieval & Renaissance Literary Studies). (Illus.). 240p. 2000. text 55.00 (*0-8207-0313-3*) Duquesne.

Practicing Responsible Tourism: International Case Studies in Tourism Planning, Policy & Developement. Lynn Harrison & Winston Husbands. LC 96-14316. 590p. 1996. 69.95 (*0-471-12236-X*) Wiley.

Practicing Safety in the Organic Chemistry Laboratory. Michael W. Rapp. Ed. by J. Jeffers. (Modular Laboratory Program in Chemistry Ser.). 12p. (C). 1997. pap. text 1.75 (*0-87540-700-5*) Chem Educ Res.

***Practicing Self-Inquiry: The Teaching of Sri Ramana Maharshi.** V. Ganesan. 17p. 2000. pap. 1.95 (*1-888599-16-2*) AHAM Pubns.

Practicing Sentence Options. William Strong. LC 93-44854. 128p. (C). 1984. pap. 22.81 (*0-07-554481-4*) McGraw.

Practicing Social. 5th ed. Babbie. (Sociology - Introductory Level Ser.). 1988. pap. 12.00 (*0-534-09727-8*) Wadsworth Pub.

Practicing Social Research. 3rd ed. Babbie. (Sociology - Introductory Level Ser.). 1983. pap., student ed. 8.75 (*0-534-01256-6*) Wadsworth Pub.

Practicing Social Research. 4th ed. Babbie. (Sociology - Introductory Level Ser.). 1985. pap., student ed. 9.50 (*0-534-05659-8*) Wadsworth Pub.

Practicing Social Research. 6th ed. Babbie. (Sociology-Introduction Level Ser.). 1991. pap., student ed. 12.75 (*0-534-15577-4*) Wadsworth Pub.

Practicing Social Research. 7th ed. Earl R. Babbie. (Sociology Ser.). 1994. pap., student ed. 18.95 (*0-534-18746-3*) Wadsworth Pub.

***Practicing Social Research: Guided Activities.** 9th ed. Babbie. 2000. pap. 18.75 (*0-534-57480-7*) Wadsworth Pub.

Practicing Sub-Regional Economic Development in Texas: New Approaches & Techniques. Ed. by Sherman M. Wyman. 151p. 1991. pap. text 4.00 (*0-936440-84-8*) U TX SUPA.

Practicing Texas Politics. 6th ed. Eugene W. Jones et al. 576p. (C). 1985. disk. write for info. (*0-318-60191-5*) HM.

Practicing Texas Politics. 7th ed. Eugene W. Jones et al. 1988. teacher ed., student ed. write for info. (*0-318-63310-8*); student ed. write for info. (*0-318-63309-4*); trans. write for info. (*0-318-63311-6*) HM.

Practicing Texas Politics. 10th ed. Jones Staff. LC 97-72496. (C). 1997. text 41.96 (*0-395-87004-6*) HM.

Practicing Texas Politics: A Brief Survey, 2 vols. 2nd ed. Eugene W. Jones et al. LC 86-81541. 272p. (C). 1986. pap. text 25.16 (*0-395-42324-4*) HM.

Practicing Texas Politics: A Brief Survey, 3 vols. 3rd ed. Eugene W. Jones et al. (C). 1989. 25.96 (*0-395-54000-3*) HM.

Practicing Texas Politics: A Brief Survey, 3 vols. 3rd ed. Eugene W. Jones et al. (C). 1990. pap. text 2.76 (*0-395-52680-9*) HM.

Practicing Texas Politics: A Brief Survey, 5 vols. 5th ed. Eugene W. Jones et al. 352p. (C). 1995. pap. text 36.36 (*0-395-74606-X*) HM.

Practicing Texas Politics: A Brief Survey, 5 vols. 5th ed. Eugene W. Jones et al. (C). 1996. text, teacher ed. 11.96 (*0-395-74607-8*) HM.

Practicing the Application of Health Education Skill & Competencies. Marilyn Morrow et al. (Health Science Ser.). 400p. 1997. pap. 28.75 (*0-7637-0533-0*) Jones & Bartlett.

Practicing the Cosmic Science: Key Insights in Modern Astrology. 2nd rev. ed. Stephen Arroyo. LC 99-28073. 210p. 1999. pap. 13.95 (*0-916360-62-8*) CRCS Pubns CA.

Practicing the Guidance of God: Daily Readings to Guide You to the Life You Want to Live. Harold J. Wickey. 388p. 1997. pap. 16.95 (*0-9640643-1-6*) Hal-Vat Pub.

Practicing the Prayer of Presence. rev. ed. Susan A. Muto & Adrian Van Kaam. LC 93-83751. 190p. 1993. pap. 8.95 (*1-878718-14-2*, Resurrection Pr) Catholic Bk Pub.

Practicing the Presence. Joel S. Goldsmith. LC 97-19887. 155p. 1997. reprint ed. 15.95 (*1-889051-11-X*, I Lvl) Acrpls Bks CO.

Practicing the Presence: A Course in Meditation. Tom Pritscher. LC 95-90643. (Illus.). 108p. (YA). (gr. 11 up). 1999. pap. 19.95 (*0-9648165-1-2*) Thou Art.

Practicing the Presence: The Inspirational Guide to Regaining Meaning & a Sense of Purpose in Your Life. Joel S. Goldsmith. LC 90-56462. 144p. 1991. reprint ed. pap. 13.00 (*0-06-250399-5*, Pub. by Harper SF) HarpC.

Practicing the Presence Bk. 1: A Course in Meditation. Tom Pritscher. LC 95-90643. (Illus.). 108p. (Orig.). 1996. pap. 13.00 (*0-9648165-0-4*) Thou Art.

Practicing the Presence of God: Conversations & Letters of Nicholas Herman of Lorraine. Lawrence. Ed. by Robert E. Coleman. (Collection of Classics Ser.). 56p. 1996. pap. text 2.95 (*1-879089-23-8*) B Graham Ctr.

***Practicing the Presence of People: How We Learn to Love.** Mike Mason. LC 99-33834. 288p. 1999. pap. 11.95 (*1-57856-265-1*) Waterbrook Pr.

***Practicing the Presence of the Goddess: Everyday Rituals to Personal Power.** Barbara Ardinger. (Illus.). 128p. 2000. 16.00 (*1-57731-173-6*, Pub. by New Wrld Lib) Publishers Group.

Practicing the Principles: Continuing the Journey. Carol Hibler. 32p. Date not set. pap. text, wbk. ed. 15.00 (*1-890896-51-9*) Passion Pub.

Practicing the Process: A Basic Text. Marlene Martin. (C). 1989. text 30.00 (*0-673-18759-4*) Addson-Wesley Educ.

Practicing Theory & Reading Literature: An Introduction. Raman Selden. LC 89-8992. 218p. 1989. 27.00 (*0-8131-1705-4*); pap. 15.00 (*0-8131-0191-3*) U Pr of Ky.

Practicing Therapy: Exercises for Growing Therapists. Anne H. Rambo et al. 180p. (C). 1993. pap. 14.95 (*0-393-70161-1*) Norton.

Practicing to Be a Woman: New & Selected Poems. Rochelle Ratner. Ed. by Robert B. Peters. LC 81-21472. (Poets Now Ser.: No. 2). 152p. 1982. 14.50 (*0-8108-1510-9*) Scarecrow.

Practicing to Take the GRE Biology Test. (Orig.). 1983. pap. 6.95 (*0-88685-001-0*) Educ Testing Serv.

Practicing to Take the GRE Chemistry Test. (Orig.). 1983. pap. 6.95 (*0-88685-002-9*) Educ Testing Serv.

Practicing to Take the GRE Chemistry Test. 3rd ed. Educational Testing Service Staff. 1996. pap. 13.00 (*0-446-39616-8*, Pub. by Warner Bks) Little.

Practicing to Take the GRE Education Test. 1983. pap. 6.95 (*0-88685-003-7*) Educ Testing Serv.

Practicing to Take the GRE Education Test. Educational Testing Service Staff. 1986. mass mkt. 6.95 (*0-446-38459-3*) Warner Bks.

Practicing to Take the GRE Engineering Test. (Orig.). 1983. pap. 6.95 (*0-88685-004-5*) Educ Testing Serv.

Practicing to Take the GRE General Test. (Orig.). 1983. pap. 7.95 (*0-88685-000-2*) Educ Testing Serv.

Practicing to Take the GRE General Test. 2nd ed. 170p. (Orig.). 1984. pap. text 7.95 (*0-88685-023-1*) Educ Testing Serv.

Practicing to Take the GRE General Test, No. 3. Educational Testing Service Staff. 1986. pap. 7.95 (*0-446-38441-0*, Pub. by Warner Bks) Little.

Practicing to Take the GRE General Test, No. 4. Educational Testing Service Staff. 1986. pap. 7.95 (*0-446-38439-9*, Pub. by Warner Bks) Little.

Practicing to Take the GRE General Test, No. 5. Educational Testing Service Staff. 1987. pap. 7.95 (*0-446-38594-8*, Pub. by Warner Bks) Little.

Practicing to Take the GRE General Test, No. 6. (Orig.). 1988. mass mkt. 7.95 (*0-446-35307-8*) Warner Bks.

Practicing to Take the GRE General Test, No. 9. Educational Testing Service Staff. 1992. pap. 15.00 (*0-446-39469-6*, Pub. by Warner Bks) Little.

Practicing to Take the GRE General Test No. 4: APPLE Software Edition. Educational Testing Service Staff. 1986. boxed set 55.00 (*0-446-38443-7*) Warner Bks.

Practicing to Take the GRE General Test No. 4: IBM Software Edition. Educational Testing Service Staff. 1986. pap. 55.00 (*0-446-38445-3*, Pub. by Warner Bks) Little.

Practicing to Take the GRE History Test. 48p. 1986. pap. text 6.95 (*0-685-13217-X*) Educ Testing Serv.

Practicing to Take the GRE Literature in English. Educational Testing Service Staff. 1986. pap. 9.00 (*0-446-38465-8*) Warner Bks.

Practicing to Take the GRE Literature in English Test. (Orig.). 1983. pap. 6.95 (*0-88685-005-3*) Educ Testing Serv.

Practicing to Take the GRE Literature in English Test. 3rd ed. Educational Testing Service Staff. LC 98-125203. 1996. pap. 13.00 (*0-446-39618-4*, Pub. by Warner Bks) Little.

Practicing to Take the GRE Mathematics Test. 2nd ed. Educational Testing Service Staff. 1993. pap. 11.00 (*0-446-39540-4*, Pub. by Warner Bks) Little.

Practicing to Take the GRE Political Science Test. 2nd ed. 1994. pap. write for info. (*0-446-39569-2*) Warner Bks.

Practicing to Take the GRE Psychology Test. (Orig.). 1983. pap. 6.95 (*0-88685-006-1*) Educ Testing Serv.

Practicing to Take the GRE Revised Education Test. 3rd ed. Educational Testing Service Staff. LC 98-125178. 1996. pap. 13.00 (*0-446-39589-7*, Pub. by Warner Bks) Little.

Practicing to Take the GRE Sociology Test. Educational Testing Service Staff. 1987. mass mkt. 6.95 (*0-446-38652-9*) Warner Bks.

Practicing to Take the GRE Sociology Test. 2nd ed. Educational Testing Service Staff. 1993. pap. 11.00 (*0-446-39542-0*, Pub. by Warner Bks) Little.

Practicing Truth in the Family of God, Hebrews Chapter 11-13. Eva Gibson. (Discovering the Heart of God Ser.). 120p. 1995. pap. 5.95 (*1-56616-012-X*, 524003) Aglow Communs.

Practicing Universal Design: An Interpretation of the ADA. William L. Wilkoff & Laura W. Abed. LC 93-8488. 210p. 1994. pap. 36.95 (*0-442-01376-0*, VNR) Wiley.

Practicing Virtues: Moral Traditions at Quaker & Military Boarding Schools. Kim Hays. LC 92-42858. (C). 1994. 38.00 (*0-520-08237-0*, Pub. by U CA Pr) Cal Prin Full Svc.

Practicing Vivaldi. Mary Shumway. (W.N.J. Ser.: No. 15). 1981. pap. 6.00 (*1-55780-064-2*) Juniper Pr ME.

Practicing What We Know: Informed Reading Instruction. National Council of Teachers of English Staff. Ed. by Constance Weaver. LC 98-10262. 587p. 1998. pap. 26.95 (*0-8141-3675-3*) NCTE.

Practicing What We Teach: Confronting Diversity in Teacher Education. Ed. by Renee J. Martin. LC 94-32933. (Social Context of Education Ser.). 282p. (C). 1995. pap. text 21.95 (*0-7914-2550-9*) State U NY Pr.

Practicing Wholeness: Analytical Psychology & Jungian Thought. Murray Stein. LC 76-15659. 256p. 1996. pap. 27.50 (*0-8264-0905-9*) Continuum.

Practicing Writing & Learning. 3rd ed. Carolyn E. Foster. (Illus.). 160p. (Orig.). (C). 1992. pap. text, wbk. ed. 28.00 (*0-02-338970-2*, Macmillan Coll) P-H.

***Practicum Companion for Social Work: Integrating Class & Field Work.** Marla Berg-Weger & Julie Birkenmaier. LC 99-16837. 305p. (C). 1999. pap. text 36.00 (*0-321-04519-X*) Addison-Wesley Educ.

Practicum Economics. Osullivan & Sheffrin. (C). 1998. pap. text 30.60 (*0-13-975269-2*) P-H.

Practicum in Healthcare Management: HSM 489. California College for Health Sciences Staff. 10p. (C). 1994. pap., student ed. write for info. (*0-933195-56-7*) CA College Health Sci.

Practicum in Healthcare Management: HSM 489. rev. ed. M. Cronin. 10p. (C). 1994. spiral bd. write for info. (*0-933195-71-0*) CA College Health Sci.

Practioners Get Psychoactive Drive. Bassuk. 1977. 19.95 (*0-306-30953-X*) Da Capo.

***Practioner's Handbook to Software Project Management.** 700p. 2000. 60.00 (*1-57870-224-0*) Macmillan Tech.

Practiquemos Mas! 2nd ed. Terri A. Gebel & Hildegard Morales-Gomez. 118p. (C). 1996. pap. text, per. 17.95 (*0-7872-0301-7*) Kendall-Hunt.

Practise to Deceive. Sally Wentworth. 1994. per. 2.99 (*0-373-11701-9*, 1-11701-9) Harlequin Bks.

Practise to Deceive. large type ed. Sally Wentworth. (Harlequin Ser.). 1994. lib. bdg. 19.95 (*0-263-13725-2*) Mac Lib Ref.

Practise Writing. Stephens. Date not set. pap. text. write for info. (*0-582-79107-3*, Pub. by Addison-Wesley) Longman.

Practise Your Conjunctions & Infinitives. Adamson. 1995. pap. text. write for info. (*0-582-09669-3*, Pub. by Addison-Wesley) Longman.

Practise Your Gerunds & Infinitives. Kinsbury. 1995. pap. text. write for info. (*0-582-09666-9*, Pub. by Addison-Wesley) Longman.

Practise Your Modal Verbs. Watkins. 1990. pap. text. write for info. (*0-582-00993-6*, Pub. by Addison-Wesley) Longman.

Practise Your Phrasal Verbs. Heaton. 1995. pap. text. write for info. (*0-582-09667-7*, Pub. by Addison-Wesley) Longman.

Practise Your Preposition. Keane. 1990. pap. text. write for info. (*0-582-00994-4*, Pub. by Addison-Wesley) Longman.

Practise Your Skills Book, Vol. 1. Kavanagh. 1994. pap. text. write for info. (*0-582-66169-2*, Pub. by Addison-Wesley) Longman.

Practise Your Skills Book, Vol. 2. Kavanagh. 1994. pap. text. write for info. (*0-582-66170-6*, Pub. by Addison-Wesley) Longman.

Practise Your Skills Book, Vol. 3. Kavanagh. 1994. pap. text. write for info. (*0-582-66171-4*, Pub. by Addison-Wesley) Longman.

Practise Your Skills Book, Vol. 4. Kavangh. 1994. pap. text. write for info. (*0-582-66172-2*, Pub. by Addison-Wesley) Longman.

Practise Your Tenses. Adamson. 1990. pap. text. write for info. (*0-582-01446-8*, Pub. by Addison-Wesley) Longman.

Practising Development: Social Science Perspectives. Ed. by Johan Pottier. LC 92-13084. (European Inter-University Development Opportunity Study Group Ser.). 240p. (C). (gr. 13). 1993. pap. 25.99 (*0-415-08911-5*, A9872) Routledge.

Practising Ethics in Schools. Felicity Haynes. LC 97-25911. 224p. (C). 1998. pap. 25.99 (*0-415-14185-0*) Routledge.

Practising Faith in a Pagan World see Faithful Living in a Faithless World

Practising Femininity: Domestic Realism & the Performance of Gender in Early Canadian Fiction. Misao Dean. LC 99-165740. (Theory/Culture Ser.). 160p. 1998. text 40.00 (*0-8020-4312-7*); pap. text 16.95 (*0-8020-8138-X*) U of Toronto Pr.

Practising Feminism: Identity, Difference & Power. Ed. by Felicia Hughes-Freeland & Nickie Charles. LC 95-19337. 240p. (C). 1996. pap. 24.99 (*0-415-11109-9*) Routledge.

***Practising Global Journalism.** John Herbert. 224p. 2000. pap. 42.95 (*0-240-51602-8*, Focal) Buttrwrth-Heinemann.

Practising Grammar 1 Without Key. Blundell. 1992. pap. text, wbk. ed. write for info. (*0-17-555744-6*) Addison-Wesley.

Practising Grammar 3 Without Key. Blundell. 1992. pap. text, wbk. ed. write for info. (*0-17-555746-2*) Addison-Wesley.

Practising Health Promotion. Naidoo. (C). 1998. pap. text 35.00 (*0-7020-2122-9*, W B Saunders Co) Harcrt Hlth Sci Grp.

***Practising Reflexivity in Health & Welfare: Making Knowledge.** Carolyn Taylor & Susan White. LC 00-36733. 2000. pap. write for info. (*0-335-20518-6*) Taylor & Francis.

***Practising Reform in Montaigne's Essays.** Dorothea Heitsch. LC 99-52997. (Studies in Intellectual History). 208p. 2000. 56.00 (*90-04-11630-3*) Brill Academic Pubs.

Practising Translation in Renaissance France: The Example of Etienne Dolet. Valerie Worth. (Oxford Modern Languages & Literature Monographs). 252p. 1989. text 69.00 (*0-19-815818-1*) OUP.

***Practitioner-Based Enquiry.** Louisa Murray & Brenda Lawrence. LC 99-28142. (Social Research & Educational Studies). 1999. write for info. (*0-7507-0771-2*, Falmer Pr) Taylor & Francis.

Practitioner Manual for Introductory Patterns of Neuro Linguistic Programming. Maryann Reese & Carol L. Yancar. 245p. 1986. 30.00 (*0-9615502-1-X*) Southern Inst Pr.

Practitioner Research: Critical Appreciation of Practice As a Basis for Professional Development. Della Fish. LC 98-20551. (Illus.). 288p. 1998. pap. text 32.00 (*0-7506-3001-9*) Buttrwrth-Heinemann.

Practitioner Research: The Reflexive Social Worker. Roger Fuller & Alison Petch. LC 95-8638. 224p. 1995. 98.95 (*0-335-19323-4*); pap. 31.95 (*0-335-19322-6*) OpUniv Pr.

Practitioner Research in Health Care. Ed. by Jan Reed & Sue Procter. 208p. 1995. pap. 34.95 (*0-412-49810-3*) Chapman & Hall.

Practitioner Research in Health Care: The Inside Story. J. Reed & S. Proctor. (Illus.). 224p. 1994. pap. text 42.50 (*1-56593-189-0*, 0504) Singular Publishing.

Practitioner Research in the Primary School. Ed. by Rosemary Webb. 224p. 1990. 79.95 (*1-85000-807-8*, Falmer Pr); pap. 39.95 (*1-85000-808-6*, Falmer Pr) Taylor & Francis.

***Practitioner-Researcher: Developing Theory from Practice.** Peter Jarvis. LC 98-25320. (Higher & Adult Education Ser.). 1998. 29.95 (*0-7879-3880-7*) Jossey-Bass.

Practitioner-Researcher Partnerships: Building Knowledge from, in, & for Practice. Ed. by Peg M. Hess & Edward J. Mullen. LC 94-47527. 286p. (C). 1995. lib. bdg. 31.95 (*0-87101-252-9*, 2529) Natl Assn Soc Wkrs.

Practitioner's Approach to Indoor Air Quality Investigations: Proceedings of the Indoor Air Quality International Symposium. Ed. by Donald M. Weekes & Richard B. Gammage. 179p. 1990. 50.00 (*0-932627-38-2*) Am Indus Hygiene.

Practitioner's Guide for Improving an Organization. Kenneth D. Mackenzie. LC 95-94247. 159p. (Orig.). 1995. pap. text 39.95 (*0-9646185-0-8*) Mackenzie & Co.

***Practitioner's Guide to Advanced Pension Topics.** 2nd ed. David A. Littell & Kenn B. Tacchino. LC 99-73063. 375p. (C). 1999. text 56.00 (*1-57996-015-4*) Amer College.

Practitioner's Guide to Audit Sampling: A Guide for Auditors. Dan M. Guy et al. LC 97-38263. 195p. 1998. text 69.95 incl. disk (*0-471-24635-2*) Wiley.

P

An Asterisk (*) at the beginning of an entry indicates that the title is appearing for the first time.

Practitioner's Guide to Clinical Neuropsychology. Robert M. Anderson, Jr. LC 94-2057. (Critical Issues in Neuropsychology Ser.). 406p. (C). 1994. spiral bd. 49.50 (0-306-44616-2, Kluwer Plenum) Kluwer Academic.

Practitioner's Guide to Consumer Bankruptcy. Lee. E. Woodard. LC 96-77085. 317p. 1996. 95.00 (1-55834-347-4, 68553, MICHIE) LEXIS Pub.

Practitioner's Guide to Consumer Bankruptcy: 1998 Cumulative Supplement. 85p. 1998. suppl. ed. write for info. (0-327-00273-5, 68554-11) LEXIS Pub.

Practitioner's Guide to Cross-Border Insolvencies, 2 vols. Ed. by Jon Yard Arnason & Ian M. Fletcher. LC 99-48141. 2000. ring bd. 300.00 (0-379-01280-4, 0517011) Oceana.

Practitioner's Guide to Development Impact Fees. James C. Nicholas et al. LC 90-80606. (Illus.). 300p. (Orig.). 1991. lib. bdg. 56.00 (0-918286-70-0, Planners Press) Am Plan Assn.

Practitioner's Guide to Developmental & Psychological Testing. G. P. Aylward. (Critical Issues in Developmental & Behavioral Pediatrics Ser.). (Illus.). 276p. (C). 1994. spiral bd. 39.50 (0-306-44689-8, Kluwer Plenum) Kluwer Academic.

Practitioner's Guide to Dynamic Assessment. Carol S. Lidz. LC 91-13657. (School Practitioner Ser.). 210p. 1991. pap. text 24.00 (0-89862-242-5); lib. bdg. 49.95 (0-89862-363-4) Guilford Pubns.

***Practitioner's Guide to Empirically-Based Measures.** Arthur M. Nezu et al. 362p. 2000. 69.95 (0-306-46246-X) Kluwer Academic.

Practitioner's Guide to GAAS '99: Covering All SAS's, SSAE's SSAR's & Interpretations. Dan M. Guy & D. R. Carmichael. 131.00 incl. cd-rom (0-471-32052-8) Wiley.

Practitioner's Guide to Kansas Family Law, 2 vols. Illus. by Steve Leben. 1400p. 1997. write for info. (1-890452-03-3) KS Bar.

Practitioner's Guide to Liquor Liability Litigation. Institutional Staff. Ed. by Ronald S. Beitman. 261p. 1987. suppl. ed. 40.00 (0-8318-0556-0, B556/B668) Am Law Inst.

Practitioner's Guide to Liquor Liability Litigation: 1991 Supplement. Ronald S. Beitman. LC 87-71248. 89p. 1991. pap. 15.00 (0-8318-0668-0, B668) Am Law Inst.

Practitioner's Guide to Litigating Insurance Coverage Actions, 3 vols. Jerold Oshinsky et al. LC 94-11950. 2254p. 1998. ring bd. 295.00 (0-13-128166-6) Aspen Law.

Practitioner's Guide to Litigating Insurance Coverage Actions, Set. 2nd ed. Jerold Oshinsky & Theodore A. Howard. LC 97-39117. 1998. 360.00 (1-56706-678-X) Aspen Law.

Practitioner's Guide to Managerial Economics. 2nd ed. Semoon Chang. LC 94-28353. 1994. pap. 24.50 (0-8191-9652-5) U Pr of Amer.

***Practitioner's Guide to Mediation: A Client-Centered Approach.** Stephen K. Erickson & Marilyn S. McKnight. 224p. 2000. 45.00 (0-471-35368-X) Wiley.

***Practitioner's Guide to Professional Development.** Margaret Atwood & Robin White. 224p. 2000. pap. 39.95 (0-632-05629-0) Blackwell Sci.

Practitioner's Guide to Prospective Financial Statements. Frank J. Kopczynski. LC 95-44559. 279p. 1996. 89.00 (0-471-13455-4) Wiley.

Practitioner's Guide to Psychoactive Drugs. 3rd ed. Ed. by Alan J. Gelenberg et al. 486p. 1991. spiral bd. 45.00 (0-306-43461-X, Plenum Trade) Perseus Pubng.

Practitioner's Guide to Psychoactive Drugs. 4th rev. ed. Ed. by Alan J. Gelenberg & Ellen L. Bassuk. LC 97-29885. 568p. 1997. spiral bd. 49.50 (0-306-45468-8, Kluwer Plenum) Kluwer Academic.

Practitioner's Guide to Psychoactive Drugs for Children & Adolescents. Ed. by John S. Werry & Michael G. Aman. LC 93-7044. (Illus.). 472p. (C). 1993. spiral bd. 39.50 (0-306-44389-9, Kluwer Plenum) Kluwer Academic.

Practitioner's Guide to Psychoactive Drugs for Children & Adolescents. 2nd ed. Ed. by John S. Werry & Michael G. Aman. LC 98-29332. (Illus.). 528p. (C). 1998. spiral bd. 39.50 (0-306-45885-3, Kluwer Plenum) Kluwer Academic.

P

Practitioner's Guide to Rational-Emotive Therapy. 2nd ed. Windy Dryden et al. (Illus.). 400p. (C). 1992. pap. text 33.95 (0-19-507169-7) OUP.

Practitioner's Guide to Reflexology. Kevin Kunz & Barbara Kunz. 1985. 17.95 (0-13-694324-1) P-H.

Practitioner's Guide to RISC Microprocessor Architecture. Patrick H. Stakem. LC 95-4732. 400p. 1996. 91.50 (0-471-13018-4) Wiley.

Practitioner's Guide to Suspension & Debarment. LC 95-104610. 200p. 1994. pap. 40.00 (1-57073-046-6, 539-0132, ABA Pub Contract) Amer Bar Assn.

Practitioner's Guide to Suspension & Debarment. 2nd ed. LC 96-175875. 134p. 1995. pap. 45.00 (1-57073-332-5, 539-0158, ABA Pub Contract) Amer Bar Assn.

***Practitioners' Guide to the EC-Turkey Association Agreement.** Nicola Rogers & Immigration Law Practitioners' Association Staff. LC 99-48000. 256p. 1999. 111.00 (90-411-1281-2) Kluwer Law Intl.

Practitioner's Guide to the Economics of the Antitrust Merger Guidelines. Samuel C. Thompson, Jr. LC 97-71744. 404p. 1997. text 145.00 (0-8318-0771-7) Am Law Inst.

Practitioners Guide to the Enterprise Investment Scheme. Mavis Seymour. 1994. pap. 39.95 (0-406-04472-4, MICHIE) LEXIS Pub.

Practitioner's Guide to the Family Law Act, 1996. David Burrows. 170p. 1996. pap. 43.00 (1-85811-116-1, Pub. by CLT Prof) Gaunt.

Practitioner's Guide to the Impact of the Human Rights Act of 1998. Ed. by Murray Hunt & Rabinder Singh. 400p. 1999. pap. 45.00 (1-901362-49-3, Pub. by Hart Pub) Intl Spec Bk.

Practitioners Guide to the Joint Physical Custody of Children. Michelle Virzi. LC 89-2012. (Legal Research Guides Ser.: Vol. 7). 58p. 1989. lib. bdg. 32.00 (0-89941-667-5, 305770) W S Hein.

Practitioner's Guide to the Neuropsychiatric Aspects of HIV-AIDS. Ed. by Wilfred G. Van Gorp & Stephan L. Buckingham. LC 97-42478. 280p. 1998. lib. bdg. 40.00 (1-57230-309-3) Guilford Pubns.

Practitioner's Guide to the Oklahoma Uniform Consumer Credit Code, 1990-1992. Frederick H. Miller et al. 490p. 1990. ring bd. 95.00 (0-409-25146-1, MICHIE) LEXIS Pub.

Practitioner's Guide to the Recordation of Trademarks with Customs in the U. S. & E. E. C. Ed. by June G. Kolbert & David A. Latham. 82p. 1993. pap. 30.00 (0-939190-06-0) Intl Trademark.

Practitioner's Guide to the Trusts of Land & Appointment of Trustees Act, 1996. Hugh Barraclough & Paul Matthews. 234p. 1996. pap. 46.50 (1-85811-115-3, Pub. by CLT Prof) Gaunt.

Practitioner's Guide to Trusts. John Thurston. 265p. (C). 1994. pap. 190.00 (0-85459-920-7, Pub. by Tolley Pubng) St Mut.

Practitioner's Guide to Understanding Indigenous & Foreign Cultures: An Analysis of Relationships Between Ethnicity, Social Class & Therapeutic Intervention Strategies with Third World Peoples from Other Countries. 2nd ed. George Henderson & Dorscine Spigner-Littles. 262p. 1996. 58.95 (0-398-06593-4); pap. 40.95 (0-398-06594-2) C C Thomas.

Practitioner's Guide to Veterinary Dentistry. Anthony D. Shipp & Peter Fahrenkrug. (Illus.). 288p. 1992. text 69.00 (0-9635578-0-7) Dr Shipps Lab.

Practitioner's Guide to Wills. Meryl Thomas. 371p. 1992. 120.00 (1-85190-165-5, Pub. by Tolley Pubng) St Mut.

Practitioner's Handbook Electrical Installation & Maintenance in Potentially Explosive Atmospheres. EEMUA Staff. 1998. pap. 135.00 (0-85931-145-7, Pub. by EEMUA) St Mut.

Practitioner's Handbook for Appeals to the Court of Appeals of the State of New York. 2nd ed. Rev. by David D. Siegel & Donald M. Sheraw. 169p. 1991. pap. 40.00 (0-614-26656-4, 4190) NYS Bar.

Practitioner's Handbook for Institutional Effectiveness & Student Outcomes Assessment: Assessment Implementation. 3rd rev. ed. James O. Nichols et al. LC 95-40857. (Illus.). 296p. 1996. text 36.00 (0-87586-113-X) Agathon.

Practitioner's Handbook for Real-Time Analysis: Guide to Rate Monotonic Analysis for Real-Time Systems. Mark Klein et al. LC 93-10744. (International Series in Engineering & Computer Science, VLSI, Computer Architecture, & Digital Screen Processing). 712p. (C). 1993. reprint ed. text 148.50 (0-7923-9361-9) Kluwer Academic.

Practitioners intro Early Childhood Education. (C). 1999. Price not set. (0-13-022223-2) P-H.

Practitioners Manual. Ed. by Herbert L. Beierle et al. LC 96-137657. 1995. pap. 12.95 (0-940480-26-3) UNIPress.

***Practitioner's Pocket Pal: Ultra Rapid Medical Reference.** Jim Hancock. (Illus.). 96p. 2000. pap. text 15.95 (0-940780-43-7) MedMaster.

Practitioner's Power of Choice in Staff-Development & Inservice Training. Ed. by H. K. Letiche et al. 184p. 1991. pap. 23.50 (90-265-1124-8) Swets.

Practitioners' Probate Manual. 22nd ed. Ed. by R. F. Yeldham & A. Plumb. (Waterlow Practitioner's Library). 320p. 1985. 29.00 (0-08-039242-3, Pergamon Pr) Elsevier.

Practitioner's Trademark Manual of Examining Procedure. James E. Hawes. LC 98-185187. (Intellectual Property Library). 1064p. 1998. write for info. (0-8366-1244-2) West Group.

Pradeeps Standard Oxford Dictionary: English to English, Panjabi & Hindi. 1983. 16.50 (0-8364-0991-4, Pub. by Pradeep Co) S Asia.

Prader-Willi Syndrome. Ed. by M. L. Caldwell & R. L. Taylor. (Illus.). 120p. 1988. 94.95 (0-387-96699-4) Spr-Verlag.

Prader Willi Syndrome. James et al. LC 92-49609. 240p. 1992. pap. write for info. (1-56593-046-0, 0294) Singular Publishing.

Prader-Willi Syndrome: A Guide for Parents & Professionals. Merlin G. Butler. (Prader-Willi Syndrome Information Ser.: No. 4). (Illus.). 53p. (Orig.). 1995. pap. text 7.50 (0-9646533-0-3) P-W Perspect.

Prader-Willi Syndrome: A Practical Guide, Vol. 1. Jackie Waters. (Resource Materials for Teachers Ser.). 1999. pap. 26.95 (1-85346-614-X) David Fulton.

Prader-Willi Syndrome & Other Chromosome 15q Deletion Disorders. Ed. by S. B. Cassidy. (NATO ASI Series H: Cell Biology: Vol. 61). (Illus.). xvi, 265p. 1992. 181.95 (0-387-53095-9) Spr-Verlag.

Pradestination, Zeit und Kontingenz: Philosophisch-Historische Untersuchungen zu Wilhelm von Ockhams. Tractatus de pradestinatione et de praescientia dei Repectu Futurorum Contingentium. Dominik Perler. (Bochumer Studien zur Philosophie Ser.: Vol. 12). (GER.). x, 322p. 1988. 63.00 (90-6032-310-6, Pub. by B R Gruner) Humanities.

Pradikate und Satzmodelle in Zeitungstexten. Harry Anttila. (Studies in the Humanities & Social Sciences: Bd. 12). (GER.). 569p. 1996. 88.95 (3-631-31105-2) P Lang Pubng.

Prado. Santiago A. Blanch. LC 96-3896. (Illus.). 474p. 1996. pap. 39.98 (0-8109-8147-5, Pub. by Abrams) Time Warner.

Prado de Valencia. Francisco A. Tarrega. Ed. by Jose L. Valles. (Textos B Ser.: Vol. XXVI). (SPA.). 210p. 1985. pap. 51.00 (0-7293-0214-8, Pub. by Tamesis Bks Ltd) Boydell & Brewer.

Prado Museum. Text by Alessandro Bettagno et al. LC 97-215454. (Illus.). 670p. 1997. 175.00 (0-8109-6346-9, Pub. by Abrams) Time Warner.

Prae-Italic Dialects of Italy, 3 vols. Robert S. Conway et al. (Illus.). xlvii, 1277p. 1967. reprint ed. 400.00 (0-318-71103-6) G Olms Pubs.

Prae-Italic Dialects of Italy, 3 vols., Set. Robert S. Conway et al. (Illus.). 1967. reprint ed. 400.00 (0-685-66454-6, 05101889) G Olms Pubs.

Praecepta Book. Paramhansa Yogananda & Swami Dhirananda. 44p. 1993. pap. 7.95 (0-937134-07-4) Amrita Found.

Praefationem et Scholia Ad Libros A-D Continens see Scholia Graeca in Homeri Iliadem: Scholia Vetera

Praeter Caesarum Libros Reliquiae. C. Suetonius. Ed. by Augustus Reifferscheid. (GER.). xx, 566p. 1971. reprint ed. write for info. (0-318-70526-5) G Olms Pubs.

Praeterita & Dilecta see Complete Works of John Ruskin

Praetorian Guard. Boris Rankov. (Elite Ser.). (Illus.). 64p. 1994. pap. 12.95 (1-85532-361-3, 9465, Pub. by Ospry) Stackpole.

Praetorian Guard: The U. S. Role in the New World Order. John Stockwell. 200p. (Orig.). 1991. 30.00 (0-89608-396-9); pap. 11.00 (0-89608-395-0) South End Pr.

***Praetorship in the Roman Republic.** T. Corey Brennan. LC 99-35017. 2000. write for info. (0-19-511459-0); write for info. (0-19-511460-4) OUP.

***Praetorship in the Roman Republic, 2 vol.** T. Corey Brennan. 912p. 2000. text 150.00 (0-19-513867-8) OUP.

Praetransfusionelle Untersuchungen Vol. 2: Ueberarbeitete Auflage. Diether Schoenitzer. (Illus.). xiv, 264p. 1997. pap. 49.75 (3-8055-6581-X) S Karger.

Praeventive Aspekte in der Paediatrie. Ed. by G. Stalder & C. P. Fliegel. (Paediatrische Fortbildungskurse fuer die Praxis Ser.: Vol. 52). (Illus.). vi, 182p. 1981. 64.50 (3-8055-1980-X) S Karger.

Praferenzen & Zahlungsbereitschaft fur Eine Verbesserte Umweltqualitat im Agrarbereich. Martina Jung. (GER., Illus.). 229p. 1996. 44.95 (3-631-31022-6) P Lang Pubng.

Praga. 1999. pap. text 9.95 (2-06-661301-0) Michelin.

***Praga.** DK Publishing Staff. (Eyewitness Travel Guides Ser.). (SPA.). 2000. pap. text 19.95 (0-7894-6215-X) DK Pub Inc.

Pragmalinguistics: East European Approaches. Jan Prucha. (Pragmatics & Beyond: An Interdisciplinary of Language Studies: Vol. IV:5). v, 103p. 1983. pap. 38.00 (0-915027-28-3) J Benjamins Pubng Co.

Pragmalinguistics: Theory & Practice. Ed. by Jacob L. Mey. (Janua Linguarum, Series Major: No. 85). 1979. text 80.80 (90-279-7757-7) Mouton.

Pragmatic a Priori: A Study on the Epistemology of C. E. Lewis. Sandra B. Rosenthal. LC 75-41707. 104p. 1975. 10.00 (0-87527-142-1) Green.

Pragmatic Analysis of Norwegian Modal Particles. Erik E. Andvik. LC 92-60901. (Publications in Linguistics Ser.: Vol. 113). x, 140p. 1992. pap. 11.00 (0-88312-188-3) S I L Intl.

Pragmatic Approach to Business Ethics. Alex C. Michalos. LC 94-45244. 248p. 1995. text 36.95 (0-8039-7084-6); pap. text 17.95 (0-8039-7085-4) Sage.

Pragmatic Approach to Group Psychotherapy. Henry I. Spitz & Susan T. Spitz. LC 98-18652. 1998. 34.95 (0-87630-896-5) Brunner-Mazel.

Pragmatic Approach to Low-Back Pain Including Manual Therapy & Steroid Injections: A Multicentre Study in Primary Health Care. Stefan Blomberg. 146p. (Orig.). 1993. pap. 45.00 (91-554-3030-9) Coronet Bks.

Pragmatic Approaches to Aphasia Therapy. Sergio Carlomagno. (Illus.). 170p. (Orig.). (C). 1994. pap. text 42.50 (1-56593-244-7, 0568) Singular Publishing.

Pragmatic Approaches to Shakespeare: Essays on Othello, Coriolanus & Timon of Athens. Juhani Rudanko. 222p. (C). 1993. lib. bdg. 43.00 (0-8191-9107-8) U Pr of Amer.

Pragmatic Aspects of Human Communication. Ed. by Colin Cherry. LC 73-91427. (Theory & Decision Library: No. 4). 176p. 1974. lib. bdg. 93.00 (90-277-0432-5) Kluwer Academic.

Pragmatic Basis of Aphasia: A Neurolinguistic Study of Morphosyntax among Bilinguals. Marc L. Schnitzer. 224p. 1988. 49.95 (0-8058-0191-X) L Erlbaum Assocs.

Pragmatic Bioethics. Ed. by Glenn McGee. LC 98-25317. (Vanderbilt Library of American Philosophy). 344p. 1999. lib. bdg. 49.95 (0-8265-1320-4) Vanderbilt U Pr.

Pragmatic Choral Procedures. Russell A. Hammar. LC 84-5332. 377p. 1984. 34.50 (0-8108-1698-9) Scarecrow.

Pragmatic Construction of the Self in English Composition Theory. Joseph Zeppetello. LC 99-32391. 156p. 1999. text 69.95 (0-7734-7993-7) E Mellen.

Pragmatic Disability in Children: Studies in Disorders of Communication. Ed. by Michael F. McTear & Gina Conti-Ramsden. (Illus.). 246p. (C). 1991. pap. 45.00 (1-879105-56-X, 0237) Thomson Learn.

Pragmatic Entente: Israeli-Iranian Relations, 1948-1988. Sohrab Sobhani. LC 89-3557. 206p. 1989. 55.00 (0-275-93337-7, C3337, Praeger Pubs) Greenwood.

Pragmatic-Existential Psychotherapy with Personality Disorders. Herbert M. Potash. 300p. (C). 1993. text 35.00 (0-940524-05-8) G Handwerk.

Pragmatic Functions in Functional Grammar of Arabic. Ahmed Moutaouakil. (Functional Grammar Ser.: No. 8). xi, 156p. 1989. pap. 38.50 (90-6765-271-7) Mouton.

Pragmatic Fund-Raising for College Administrators & Development Officers. Ralph L. Lowenstein. LC 97-15573. 128p. 1997. 24.95 (0-8130-1525-1) U Press Fla.

Pragmatic God: On the Nihilism of Reinhold Niebuhr. Harry J. Ausmus. LC 90-34440. (American University Studies: Theology & Religion: Ser. VII, Vol. 80). XIV, 308p. (C). 1990. text 57.95 (0-8204-1379-8) P Lang Pubng.

Pragmatic Guide to Advertising. Donald E. Leonard. 336p. (C). 1992. pap. text, per. 37.95 (0-8403-7429-1) Kendall-Hunt.

***Pragmatic Guide to Bartering.** James Harvey Stout. LC 99-67759. 120p. 2000. pap. 24.00 (1-891628-12-7) Interlingua Pubns.

Pragmatic Guide to Consumer Behavior. Donald E. Leonard. 308p. 1993. per. 34.95 (0-8403-8256-1) Kendall-Hunt.

Pragmatic Guide to Marketing. Donald E. Leonard. 272p. (C). 1990. per. 32.95 (0-8403-6371-0) Kendall-Hunt.

***Pragmatic Historicism: A Theology for the Twenty-first Century.** Sheila G. Davaney. LC 99-57803. (C). 2000. pap. text 20.95 (0-7914-4694-8) State U NY Pr.

***Pragmatic Historicism: A Theology for the Twenty-first Century.** Sheila G. Davaney. LC 99-57803. (C). 2000. text 62.50 (0-7914-4693-X) State U NY Pr.

Pragmatic Humanism of F. C. S. Schiller. Reuben Abel. LC 70-158220. reprint ed. 24.50 (0-404-00275-7) AMS Pr.

Pragmatic Idealism: Canadian Foreign Policy, 1945-1995. Costas Melakopides. 248p. 1998. text 39.95 (0-7735-1722-7, Pub. by McG-Queens Univ Pr) CUP Services.

Pragmatic Inversion of Geophysical Data. Sven-Erik Hjelt. LC 92-30938. (Lecture Notes in Earth Sciences Ser.: Vol. 39). 1992. 76.95 (0-387-55622-2) Spr-Verlag.

Pragmatic Language Intervention: Interactive Activities. Lynn S. Bliss. LC 93-25192. 1993. 51.00 (0-930599-85-3) Thinking Pubns.

Pragmatic Legal Expert System. James Popple. (Applied Legal Philosophy Ser.). (Illus.). 416p. 1996. text 91.95 (1-85521-739-2, Pub. by Dartmth Pub) Ashgate Pub Co.

Pragmatic Liberalism. Charles W. Anderson. LC 90-30177. 234p. 1990. 33.00 (0-226-01801-6) U Ch Pr.

Pragmatic Liberalism. Charles W. Anderson. 234p. 1994. pap. text 14.95 (0-226-01802-4) U Ch Pr.

Pragmatic Liberalism & the Critique of Modernity. Gary Gutting. LC 98-36501. (Modern European Philosophy Ser.). 240p. (C). 1999. text 49.95 (0-521-64013-X); pap. text 17.95 (0-521-64973-0) Cambridge U Pr.

Pragmatic Literacy, East & West, 1200-1330. Ed. by Richard Britnell. LC 96-38238. (Illus.). 274p. 1997. 90.00 (0-85115-695-9) Boydell & Brewer.

Pragmatic Logic. K. Ajdukiewicz. Tr. by Olgierd Wojtasiewicz. (Synthese Library: Vol. 62). 475p. 1974. text 176.50 (90-277-0326-4, D Reidel) Kluwer Academic.

Pragmatic Logic for Commands. Melvin J. Adler. (Pragmatics & Beyond Ser.: No. I-3). viii, 131p. 1980. pap. 29.00 (90-272-2501-X) J Benjamins Pubng Co.

Pragmatic Magics: Grimoire of Sorcery. Darren Fox. Ed. & Intro. by Thor Templar. (Illus.). 158p. 1994. 45.00 (1-57179-043-8) Intern Guild ASRS.

***Pragmatic Markers & Propositional Attitude.** Gisle Andersen & Thorstein Fretheim. LC 00-28921. (Pragmatics & Beyond Ser.). vi, 279p. 2000. 69.00 (1-55619-797-7) J Benjamins Pubng Co.

Pragmatic Markers in English: Grammaticalization & Discourse Functions. Laurel J. Brinton. LC 96-5401. (Topics in English Linguistics Ser.: Vol. 19). xvi, 412p. (C). 1996. lib. bdg. 124.45 (3-11-014872-2) Mouton.

***Pragmatic Meaning & Cognition.** Ed. by Sophia Marmaridou. LC 99-462345. (Pragmatics & Beyond New Ser.: No. 72). xii, 322p. 2000. pap. 24.95 (1-55619-837-X) J Benjamins Pubng Co.

***Pragmatic Meaning & Cognition.** Ed. by Sophia S. A. Marmaridou. LC 99-462345. (Pragmatics & Beyond New Ser.: No. 72). xii, 322p. 2000. 65.00 (1-55619-919-8) J Benjamins Pubng Co.

Pragmatic Meaning of God. Robert O. Johann. LC 66-20282. (Aquinas Lectures). 1966. 15.00 (0-87462-131-3) Marquette.

Pragmatic Mind: Emerson, James, Peirce, & the Psychology of Belief. Mark Bauerlein. LC 97-6289. 176p. 1997. lib. bdg. 45.95 (0-8223-2004-5) Duke.

Pragmatic Mind: Emerson, James, Peirce, & the Psychology of Belief. Mark Bauerlein. LC 97-6289. xix, 136p. 1997. pap. text 15.95 (0-8223-2013-4) Duke.

Pragmatic Perspective: Selected Papers from the 1985 International Pragmatics Conference. Ed. by Jef Verschueren & Marcella Bertucelli-Papi. LC 87-18409. (Pragmatics & Beyond Companion Ser.: No. 5). xiii, 836p. 1987. 206.00 (1-55619-011-5) J Benjamins Pubng Co.

Pragmatic Philosophy of C. S. Peirce. Manley H. Thompson. LC 53-10445. 336p. reprint ed. pap. 104.20 (0-608-10205-9, 200728400063) Bks Demand.

Pragmatic Philosophy of William James. Ellen K. Suckiel. LC 81-21993. 177p. (C). 1984. reprint ed. pap. text 14.00 (0-268-01555-4) U of Notre Dame Pr.

Pragmatic Presidency: Effective Leadership in the Two-Year College. Edwin E. Vineyard. 232p. 1993. text 34.95 (0-9627042-4-5) Anker Pub.

***Pragmatic Programmer Thoughts: From Journeyman to Master; 50 Tips to Make You a Better Developer & Improve Your Career.** Andrew Hunt. LC 99-43581. 352p. 1999. pap. text 34.95 (0-201-61622-X) Addison-Wesley.

Pragmatic Prophet: The Life of M. R. Zigler. Donald F. Durnbaugh. LC 89-34973. 416p. 1989. pap. 12.95 (0-87178-717-2, 8172) Brethren.

Pragmatic Prophet: The Life of M. R. Zigler. Donald F. Durnbaugh. LC 89-34973. (Illus.). 440p. 1989. 24.95 (0-87178-715-6, 8156) Brethren.

An Asterisk (*) at the beginning of an entry indicates that the title is appearing for the first time.

Pragmatic Theology: Negotiating the Intersections of an American Philosophy of Religion & Public Theology. Victor Anderson. LC 97-12086. (SUNY Series, Religion & American Public Life). 224p. (C). 1998. pap. text 19.95 (*0-7914-3638-1*) State U NY Pr.

Pragmatic Theology: Negotiating the Intersections of an American Philosophy of Religion & Public Theology. Victor Anderson. LC 97-12086. (SUNY Series, Religion & American Public Life). 224p. (C). 1998. text 59.50 (*0-7914-3637-3*) State U NY Pr.

Pragmatic Theory of Fallacy. Douglas N. Walton. LC 94-23534. (Studies in Rhetoric & Communication). (FRE, GRE & LAT., Illus.). 344p. (C). 1995. text 39.95 (*0-8173-0798-2*) U of Ala Pr.

Pragmatic Theory of Rhetoric. Walter H. Beale. LC 86-11807. 186p. 1987. text 21.95 (*0-8093-1300-6*) S Ill U Pr.

Pragmatic Women & Body Politics. Ed. by Margaret Lock & Patricia Kaufert. LC 97-10263. (Studies in Medical Anthropology: No. 5). 376p. (C). 1998. text 64.95 (*0-521-62099-6*); pap. text 22.95 (*0-521-62929-2*) Cambridge U Pr.

Pragmatics. Stephen C. Levinson. LC 82-14701. (Cambridge Textbooks in Linguistics Ser.). 434p. 1983. pap. text 29.95 (*0-521-29414-2*) Cambridge U Pr.

Pragmatics Jean S. Peccei. LC 99-10322. (Language Workbooks Ser.). 1999. pap. write for info. (*0-415-20523-9*) Routledge.

Pragmatics, 4 vols., Set. Asa Kasher. Incl. LC 97-39445. 1997. Not sold separately (*0-415-16934-8*); LC 97-39445. 1997. pap. Not sold separately (*0-415-16935-6*); LC 97-39445. 1997. pap. Not sold separately (*0-415-16936-4*); LC 97-39445. 1997. Not sold separately (*0-415-16937-2*); LC 97-39445. 1997. (*0-415-16938-0*); LC 97-39445. 1997. (*0-415-16993-3*); (Critical Concepts in Linguistics Ser.). 2653p. (C). 1998. 905.00 (*0-415-11734-8*) Routledge.

Pragmatics: A Reader. Steven I. Davis. 608p. (C). 1991. pap. text 49.95 (*0-19-505898-4*) OUP.

Pragmatics: An Annotated Bibliography. Jef Verschueren. (Library & Information Sources in Linguistics: No. 4). xvi, 270p. 1978. 59.00 (*90-272-0995-2*) J Benjamins Pubng Co.

Pragmatics: From Theory to Practice. Ed. by Judith F. Duchan et al. LC 93-10009. 214p. 1993. pap. 55.00 (*0-13-678988-9*) P-H.

Pragmatics & Education. Ed. by F. Lowenthal & Fernand Vandamme. 352p. 1986. 75.00 (*0-306-42374-X*, Plenum Trade) Perseus Pubng.

Pragmatics & Fiction. Jon K. Adams. LC 86-26883. (Pragmatics & Beyond Ser.: VI-2). vi, 77p. 1986. pap. 29.00 (*0-915027-64-X*) J Benjamins Pubng Co.

Pragmatics & Grammatical Theory, Vol. 2. 1986. 8.00 (*0-318-35423-3*) Chicago Ling.

Pragmatics & Natural Language Understanding. 2nd ed. Georgia M. Green. LC 96-18566. (Tutorial Essays in Cognitive Science Ser.). 200p. 1996. pap. 21.00 (*0-8058-2166-X*) L Erlbaum Assocs.

Pragmatics & Natural Language Understanding. 2nd ed. Georgia M. Green. LC 96-18566. (Tutorial Essays in Cognitive Science Ser.). 200p. 1996. text 45.00 (*0-8058-2165-1*) L Erlbaum Assocs.

Pragmatics & Semantics: An Empiricist Theory. Carol A. Kates. 304p. 1980. 45.00 (*0-8014-1288-9*) Cornell U Pr.

Pragmatics & Semiotics of Standard Languages. Albert M. Sweet. LC 87-43180. 226p. 1988. lib. bdg. 28.50 (*0-271-00630-7*) Pa St U Pr.

Pragmatics & the Philosophy of Mind Vol. 1: Thought in Language. Marcelo Dascal. (Pragmatics & Beyond Ser.: iv: 1). xii, 207p. 1983. pap. 59.00 (*90-272-2503-6*) J Benjamins Pubng Co.

Pragmatics at Issue, 3 vols., Set. Ed. by Jan Blommaert & Jef Verschueren. 900p. 1991. 236.00 (*1-55619-101-4*) J Benjamins Pubng Co.

Pragmatics in Neurogenic Communication Disorders. Michel Paradis & International Association of Logopedics & Phoniatr. LC 98-6486. 1998. 122.50 (*0-08-043065-1*, Pergamon Pr) Elsevier.

***Pragmatics in Speech & Language Pathology: Studies in Clinical Applications.** Ed. by Nicole Muller. LC 00-21033. (Studies in Speech Pathology & Clinical Linguistics: Vol. 7). viii, 173p. 2000. 60.00 (*1-55619-274-6*) J Benjamins Pubng Co.

Pragmatics of Chinese As Native & Target Language. Ed. by Gabriele Kasper. (Technical Reports: No. 5). 312p. (Orig.). 1995. pap. text 15.00 (*0-8248-1733-8*) Sec Lang Tching.

Pragmatics of Conditional Marking: Implicature, Scalarity, & Exclusivity. Sandra Hirshkowith. LC 98-51950. (Outstanding Dissertations in Linguistics Ser.). 275p. 1999. 63.00 (*0-8153-3309-9*) Garland.

***Pragmatics of Defining Religion: Contexts, Concepts & Contests.** Jan Platvoet & Arie L. Molendijk. LC 99-33639. (Studies in the History of Religions). 496p. 1999. 118.00 (*90-04-11544-7*) Brill Academic Pubs.

Pragmatics of Discourse Anaphora in English: Evidence from Conversational Repair. Ronald Geluykens. LC 94-12629. (Topics in English Linguistics Ser.: Vol. 14). ix , 203p. 1994. 90.80 (*3-11-013416-0*) Mouton.

Pragmatics of Human Communication. Paul Watzlawick et al. (Illus.). 1967. 27.00 (*0-393-01009-0*) Norton.

Pragmatics of Human Relationships. Dorothy S. Beevar & Raphael J. Beevar. (C). 1998. pap. text 29.95 (*1-884228-26-7*) Geist & Russell.

Pragmatics of Insignificance: Chekhov, Zoshchenko, Gogol. Cathy Popkin. LC 93-7021. (Illus.). 304p. (C). 1993. 42.50 (*0-8047-2209-9*) Stanford U Pr.

Pragmatics of Intercultural & International Communication Vol. 3: Selected Papers of the International Pragmatics Conference, Antwerp, August 17-22, 1987. Ed. by Jan Blommaert & Jef Verschueren. LC 91-22067. (Pragmatics & Beyond New Ser.: Vol. 6: 3). viii, 249p. 1991. 80.00 (*1-55619-108-1*) J Benjamins Pubng Co.

Pragmatics of Japanese As Native & Target Language. Ed. by Gabriele Kasper. (Technical Report Ser.: No. 3). 144p. 1992. pap. text 10.00 (*0-8248-1462-2*) Sec Lang Tching.

Pragmatics of Language: Clinical Practice Issues. Ed. by Tanya M. Gallagher. (Illus.). 384p. (Orig.). (C). 1991. pap. 49.50 (*1-879105-10-1*, A074); pap. text 49.95 (*1-879105-13-6*, 0074) Thomson Learn.

Pragmatics of Mathematics Education: Vagueness in Mathematical Discourse. Tim Rowland. LC 99-26513. (Studies in Mathematics Education). (Illus.). 242p. 1999. 90.00 (*0-7507-1012-8*, Pub. by Falmer Pr UK); pap. 28.95 (*0-7507-1013-6*, Pub. by Falmer Pr UK) Taylor & Francis.

***Pragmatics of Propositional Attitude Reports.** Ed. by K. M. Jaszczolt. (Current Research in the Semantics/Pragmatics Interface Ser.). 226p. 2000. 97.00 (*0-08-043635-8*) Elsevier.

Pragmatics of Psychotherapy: A Survey of Theories & Practices. William Schofield. 272p. 1987. 34.95 (*0-88738-174-X*) Transaction Pubs.

Pragmatics of Style. Ed. by Leo Hickey. 260p. 1989. 65.00 (*0-415-02617-2*, A3468) Routledge.

Pragmatics of the Human Heritage. Jasper Blystone. 92p. (Orig.). 1997. 19.95 (*0-941910-13-X*) Long Beach Pubns.

Pragmatics of the Left Detachment in Spoken Standard French. Betsy K. Barnes. LC 85-26773. (Pragmatics & Beyond Ser.: VI-3). viii, 123p. (Orig.). 1986. pap. 46.00 (*0-915027-65-8*) J Benjamins Pubng Co.

Pragmatics of Translation. Leo Hickey. LC 98-21842. 242p. 1998. 95.00 (*1-85359-405-9*); pap. 39.95 (*1-85359-404-0*) Multilingual Matters.

Pragmatics of Word Order: Typological Dimensions of Verb Initial Languages. Doris L. Payne. (Empirical Approaches to Language Typology Ser.: No. 7). xiv, 298p. (C). 1990. lib. bdg. 113.85 (*3-11-012207-3*) Mouton.

Pragmatics of Word Order Flexibility. Ed. by Doris L. Payne. LC 92-5354. (Typological Studies in Language: No. 22). viii, 320p. 1992. 103.00 (*1-55619-408-0*); pap. 29.95 (*1-55619-409-9*) J Benjamins Pubng Co.

Pragmatics, Truth, & Language. Richard M. Martin. (Boston Studies in the Philosophy of Science: No. XXXVIII). 325p. 1979. pap. text 62.50 (*90-277-0993-9*, D Reidel); lib. bdg. 104.50 (*90-277-0992-0*, D Reidel) Kluwer Academic.

***Pragmatische Schriftlichkeit in Englischen Arthurischen Romanzen.** Bianca Melis-Spielkamp. 357p. 1999. 52.00 (*3-631-34400-7*) P Lang Pubng.

Pragmatism. Ed. by Robert Hollinger & David Depew. LC 94-22657. 368p. 1999. pap. 24.95 (*0-275-96524-4*, Praeger Pubs) Greenwood.

Pragmatism. William James. Ed. by Bruce Kuklick. LC 80-21788. (HPC Classics Ser.). 152p. (C). 1980. pap. text 5.95 (*0-915145-05-7*); lib. bdg. 24.95 (*0-915145-04-9*) Hackett Pub.

Pragmatism. William James. LC 90-63046. (Great Books in Philosophy). 144p. (C). 1991. pap. 7.95 (*0-87975-633-0*) Prometheus Bks.

Pragmatism. Harry K. Wells. LC 74-128331. (Essay Index Reprint Ser.). 1977. 18.95 (*0-8369-2084-8*) Ayer.

Pragmatism. William James. (Notable American Authors Ser.). 1992. reprint ed. lib. bdg. 75.00 (*0-7812-3477-8*) Rprt Serv.

Pragmatism. David L. Murray. LC 75-3292. reprint ed. 22.50 (*0-404-59278-3*) AMS Pr.

Pragmatism. unabridged ed. William James. 128p. 1995. pap. text 1.50 (*0-486-28270-8*) Dover.

Pragmatism: A Contemporary Reader. Ed. by Russell B. Goodman. 288p. (C). 1995. pap. 19.99 (*0-415-90910-4*, B3513) Routledge.

Pragmatism: A New Name for Some Old Ways of Thinking; the Meaning of Truth: a Sequel to Pragmatism. William James. LC 77-28535. 399p. reprint ed. pap. 123.70 (*0-7837-3856-0*, 204367800010) Bks Demand.

Pragmatism: A Reader. Louis Menand. LC 97-9328. 1997. pap. 16.00 (*0-679-77544-7*) Random.

Pragmatism: An Open Question. Hilary Putnam. 128p. 1995. pap. 20.95 (*0-631-19343-X*) Blackwell Pubs.

Pragmatism: From Progressivism to Postmodernism. Ed. by Robert Hollinger & David Depew. LC 94-22657. 368p. 1995. 69.50 (*0-275-94882-X*, Praeger Pubs) Greenwood.

Pragmatism: The Classic Writings. Ed. by H. Standish Thayer. LC 82-2944. 384p. (C). 1982. reprint ed. lib. bdg. 34.95 (*0-915145-38-3*) Hackett Pub.

Pragmatism: The Classic Writings. Ed. & Text by H. Standish Thayer. LC 82-2944. 384p. (C). 1982. reprint ed. pap. text 12.95 (*0-915145-37-5*) Hackett Pub.

Pragmatism & Classical American Philosophy: Essential Readings & Interpretive Essays. 2nd ed. John J. Stuhr. LC 98-41475. (Illus.). 720p. (C). 1999. text 55.00 (*0-19-511829-4*); pap. text 29.95 (*0-19-511830-8*) OUP.

Pragmatism & Development: The Prospect for Pluralist Transformation in the Third World. Murray J. Leaf. LC 98-9534. 256p. 1998. 59.95 (*0-89789-573-8*, Bergin & Garvey) Greenwood.

Pragmatism & Feminism: Reweaving the Social Fabric. Charlene H. Seigfried. LC 95-46879. 296p. 1996. pap., pap. text 16.95 (*0-226-74558-9*); lib. bdg. 55.00 (*0-226-74557-0*) U Ch Pr.

***Pragmatism & Other Writings.** William James & Giles B. Gunn. LC 99-36952. 2000. pap. 14.95 (*0-14-043735-5*) Penguin Putnam.

Pragmatism & Phenomenology: A Philosophic Encounter. Sandra B. Rosenthal & Patrick L. Bourgeois. viii, 199p. (Orig.). 1980. pap. write for info. (*90-6032-179-0*) B R Gruner.

Pragmatism & Philosophical Anthropology: Understanding Our Human Life in a Human World. Sami Pihlstrom. (American University Studies: Vol. 186, No. V). XV, 287p. (C). 1998. text 47.95 (*0-8204-4076-0*) P Lang Pubng.

Pragmatism & Political Theory: From Dewey to Rorty. Matthew Festenstein. LC 97-26617. 248p. 1997. pap. text 19.00 (*0-226-24502-0*); lib. bdg. 50.00 (*0-226-24501-2*) U Ch Pr.

Pragmatism & Purpose: Essays Presented to Thomas A. Goudge. Ed. by L. W. Sumner et al. LC 81-147737. 366p. reprint ed. pap. 113.50 (*0-8357-4149-4*, 203692200007) Bks Demand.

Pragmatism & Realism. Frederick L. Will. Ed. by Kenneth R. Westphal. LC 96-32048. (Studies in Epistemology & Cognitive Theory: No. 35). 272p. 1996. 66.00 (*0-8476-8349-4*); pap. 25.95 (*0-8476-8350-8*) Rowman.

Pragmatism & Social Theory. Hans Joas. LC 92-19533. 280p. (C). 1993. pap. text 18.95 (*0-226-40042-5*); lib. bdg. 49.50 (*0-226-40041-7*) U Ch Pr.

Pragmatism & the Meaning of Truth. William James. 400p. 1978. pap. 17.50 (*0-674-69737-5*) HUP.

Pragmatism & the Political Economy of Cultural Revolution, 1850-1940. James Livingston. 416p. (C). 1994. pap. 19.95 (*0-8078-4664-3*) U of NC Pr.

Pragmatism & the Political Economy of Cultural Revolution, 1850-1940. James Livingston. LC 94-5736. (Cultural Studies of the United States). 416p. 1997. 49.95 (*0-8078-2157-8*) U of NC Pr.

Pragmatism As a Principle & Method of Right Thinking: The 1903 Harvard Lectures on Pragmatism. Charles Sanders Peirce. Ed. by Patricia A. Turrisi. LC 96-14144. 305p. (C). 1997. text 57.50 (*0-7914-3265-3*); pap. text 19.95 (*0-7914-3266-1*) State U NY Pr.

Pragmatism Considers Phenomenology. Ed. by Robert S. Corrington et al. LC 87-22995. (Current Continental Research Ser.). 256p. 1987. 52.50 (*0-8191-6581-6*); pap. 26.00 (*0-8191-6582-4*) U Pr of Amer.

Pragmatism in the Age of Jihad: The Precolonial State of Bundu. Michael Gomez. (African Studies: No. 75). (Illus.). 268p. (C). 1993. text 69.95 (*0-521-41940-9*) Cambridge U Pr.

Pragmatism, Neo-Pragmatism, & Religion: Conversations with Richard Rorty. Ed. by Charles Hardwick & Don Crosby. LC 97-12507. (American Liberal Religious Thought Ser.: Vol. 6). X, 473p. (C). 1998. pap. text 49.95 (*0-8204-3730-1*) P Lang Pubng.

Pragmatism, Reason & Norms: A Realistic Assessment. Kenneth R. Westphal. LC 97-38942. (American Philosophy Ser.: No. 10). xv, 353p. 1998. 39.00 (*0-8232-1818-X*); pap. 19.95 (*0-8232-1819-8*) Fordham.

Pragmatism, Rights, & Democracy. Beth J. Singer. LC 98-23028. (American Philosophy Ser.: No. 11). 192p. 1998. 30.00 (*0-8232-1867-8*) Fordham.

Pragmatism, Rights, & Democracy. Beth J. Singer. LC 98-23028. (American Philosophy Ser.: No. 11). 192p. 1999. pap. 18.00 (*0-8232-1868-6*) Fordham.

Pragmatism Versus Marxism: An Appraisal of John Dewey's Philosophy. George Novack. LC 75-10032. 320p. 1975. reprint ed. lib. bdg. 55.00 (*0-87348-452-5*) Pathfinder NY.

Pragmatism Versus Marxism: An Appraisal of John Dewey's Philosophy. George Novack. LC 75-10032. 320p. 1975. reprint ed. pap. 19.95 (*0-87348-453-3*) Pathfinder NY.

Pragmatism's Freud: The Moral Disposition of Psychoanalysis. Ed. by Joseph H. Smith & William Kerrigan. LC 85-45867. (Psychiatry & the Humanities Ser.: Vol. 9). 224p. 1986. text 35.00 (*0-8018-3324-8*) Johns Hopkins.

***Pragmatist Aesthetics: Living Beauty, Rethinking Art.** 2nd ed. Richard Shusterman. LC 99-56792. 384p. 2000. pap. 19.95 (*0-8476-9765-7*); text 65.00 (*0-8476-9764-9*) Rowman.

Pragmatist Philosophy of Life in Ortega y Gasset. John T. Graham. LC 94-6736. 440p. 1994. 44.95 (*0-8262-0938-6*) U of Mo Pr.

Pragmatist's Progress? Richard Rorty & American Intellectual History. Ed. by John Pettegrew. (American Intellectual Culture Ser.: No. 108). 240p. 2000. pap. 24.95 (*0-8476-9062-8*); text 60.00 (*0-8476-9061-X*) Rowman.

Prague. (FRE.). 1999. 9.95 (*2-06-655501-0*) Michelin.

Prague. (Baedeker's Ser.). (Illus.). 1991. pap. 16.95 (*0-13-094806-3*, P-H Travel) Prntice Hall Bks.

Prague. Caroline Crawford. LC 95-94140. 160p. 1995. pap. 12.50 (*0-9645891-0-9*) Green Trees CA.

Prague. DK Publishing Staff. LC 93-34987. (Eyewitness Travel Guides Ser.). (Illus.). 264p. 1994. pap. 22.95 (*1-56458-503-4*) DK Pub Inc.

Prague. Globetrotter Staff. (Globetrotter Travel Packs Ser.). 1998. pap. text 14.95 (*1-85368-963-7*, Pub. by New5 Holland) Globe Pequot.

Prague. Insight Guides Staff. 1998. pap. 9.95 (*0-8416-0601-3*) Insight.

Prague. Insight Guides Staff. (Insight Guides). 1998. pap. text 7.95 (*0-88729-557-6*) Langenscheidt.

Prague. Michael Jacobs. (Blue Guide Ser.). (Illus.). 224p. 1999. pap. 19.95 (*0-393-31933-4*) Norton.

***Prague.** Konemann Inc. Staff. 2000. 14.95 (*3-8290-3403-2*) Konemann.

Prague. Susie Lunt. LC 97-180598. (World Bibliographical Ser.). 204p. 1997. lib. bdg. 60.00 (*1-85109-252-8*) ABC-CLIO.

Prague. Ivan Margolius. (Architecture Guides Ser.). (Illus.). 320p. 1997. pap. 5.95 (*3-89508-282-1*, 520191) Konemann.

Prague. Ed. by John Miller & Kirsten Miller. LC 93-48953. (Chronicles Abroad Ser.). (Illus.). 256p. 1994. 12.95 (*0-8118-0649-9*) Chronicle Bks.

Prague. NTC Publishing Group Staff. (Passport Essential Guide Ser.). (Illus.). 128p. 1998. pap. 8.95 (*0-8442-0134-0*, 01340, Passprt Bks) NTC Contemp Pub Co.

Prague. Nicholas Parsons. (Illustrated Travel Guides from Thomas Cook Ser.). (Illus.). 192p. 1994. pap. 12.95 (*0-8442-9065-3*, Passprt Bks) NTC Contemp Pub Co.

Prague. Rand McNally Staff. pap. 6.95 (*0-528-95972-7*) Rand McNally.

Prague. Photos by Alfred Seiland. (Illus.). 108p. 1995. 60.00 (*3-905514-31-1*, Pub. by Edit Stemmle) Dist Art Pubs.

Prague. Ed. by Paul Wilson. (Travelers' Literary Companions Ser.: Vol. 2). 256p. 1995. pap. 13.95 (*1-883513-01-4*) Whereabouts.

***Prague.** Petr Wittlich. 1999. 29.99 (*3-8228-6530-3*) Benedikt Taschen.

Prague. 2nd ed. Thomas Cook. LC 96-70698. (Passport's Illustrated Travel Guides Ser.). (Illus.). 192p. 1998. pap. 14.95 (*0-8442-4842-8*, 48428, Passprt Bks) NTC Contemp Pub Co.

***Prague.** 2nd ed. Globe Pequot Press Staff. (Globetrotter Travel Packs Ser.). (Illus.). 2000. pap. 14.95 (*1-85974-414-1*) New5 Holland.

Prague. 2nd ed. Insight Guides Staff. (Insight Guides). 1998. pap. text 12.95 (*0-88729-927-X*) Langenscheidt.

***Prague.** 2nd ed. New Holland Publishing Staff. (Globetrotter Travel Guides Ser.). 2000. pap. 10.95 (*1-85974-412-5*) New5 Holland.

Prague. 3rd ed. (Time Out Travel Guides Ser.). 288p. 1999. pap. 14.95 (*0-14-027444-8*, Penguin Classics) Viking Penguin.

Prague. 4th ed. Insight Guides Staff. (Insight Guides). 1998. pap. text 21.95 (*0-88729-743-9*) Langenscheidt.

***Prague.** 4th ed. Rough Guides Staff. (Illus.). 320p. 2000. pap. 14.95 (*1-85828-525-9*, Rough Guides) Viking Penguin.

Prague. 5th ed. Insight Guides Staff. 2000. pap. 22.95 (*0-88729-042-6*) Langenscheidt.

Prague: An Architectural Guide. Radomira Sedlakova. (Illus.). 144p. 1996. pap. 17.95 (*88-7743-160-1*, Pub. by Arsenale Editrice) Antique Collect.

Prague: Cadogan City Guides. 3rd ed. Sadakat Kadri. (Cadogan City Guides Ser.). (Illus.). 432p. 1996. pap. text 19.95 (*1-86011-015-0*, Pub. by Cadgn Bks) Globe Pequot.

***Prague: Insiders' Guide for Cosmopolitan Travelers.** 2nd ed. Dan Levine. (Avant-Guide Bks.). (Illus.). 2000. pap. 19.95 (*1-891603-09-4*) Empire Pr.

Prague: The Travel Notebook. Pascale Loiseau. 104p. 1997. 14.95 (*2-911141-13-X*, Pub. by Les Edtns Pascale) Assoc Pubs Grp.

Prague: The Turbulent Century. Ed. by Jan Kaplan. (ENG, FRE & GER., Illus.). 360p. 1997. 24.95 (*3-89508-528-6*, 810092) Konemann.

Prague: 20th Century Architecture. Ed. by Stefan Templ et al. (Illus.). 200p. 1999. pap. 32.50 (*3-211-83229-7*, Pub. by Spr-Verlag) Princeton Arch.

Prague - Czech Republic. 2nd rev. ed. Nelles Verlag Staff. (Nelles Guides Ser.). (Illus.). 256p. 1999. pap. 15.95 (*3-88618-907-4*) Hunter NJ.

Prague - the Czech Republic: Nelles Guide. (Nelles Guides Ser.). (Illus.). 256p. (Orig.). 1995. pap. 14.95 (*3-88618-408-0*, Pub. by Nelles Verlag) Seven Hills Bk.

Prague & Budapest. Fodor's Staff. 272p. 1999. pap. 15.00 (*0-679-00096-8*) Fodors Travel.

Prague & the Czech Republic. Tim Nollen. 1996. pap. 19.95 (*1-895907-92-6*) ITMP Pub.

Prague Blues: The Fiction of Josef Skvorecky. Sam Solecki. 286p. (C). 1990. text 26.00 (*1-55022-108-6*, Pub. by ECW); pap. text 16.00 (*1-55022-110-8*, Pub. by ECW) Genl Dist Srvs.

Prague Counterpoint. Bodie Thoene. LC 89-37345. (Zion Covenant Ser.: Vol. 2). 384p. (Orig.). 1989. pap. 11.99 (*1-55661-078-5*) Bethany Hse.

***Prague Counterpoint.** Bodie Thoene. Vol. 2. 400p. (Orig.). 2000. mass mkt. 7.99 (*0-7642-2428-X*) Bethany Hse.

Prague Essays, Presented by a Group of British Historians to the Caroline University of Prague on the Occasion of Its Six-Hundredth Anniversary. Ed. by Robert W. Seton-Watson. LC 76-76915. (Essay Index Reprint Ser.). 1977. 19.95 (*0-8369-0030-8*) Ayer.

Prague for Less. (For Less Compact Guides Ser.). 1999. pap. 9.95 (*1-901811-70-0*) IPG Chicago.

***Prague Guide.** 2nd ed. Ted Brewer. (Illus.). 280p. 1999. pap. 14.95 (*1-892975-21-1*) Open Rd Pub.

Prague in Black & Gold: Scenes from the Life of a European City. Peter Demetz. LC 96-52216. 1997. 27.50 (*0-8090-7843-0*) Hill & Wang.

Prague in Black & Gold: Scenes from the Life of a European City. Peter Demetz. (Illus.). 432p. 1998. pap. text 15.00 (*0-8090-1609-5*) Hill & Wang.

Prague in Your Pocket Guide. Michelin Staff. (In Your Pocket Guides Ser.). 1996. per. 9.95 (*2-06-650501-3*, 6505) Michelin.

Prague Linguistic Circle Papers (Travaux Du Cercle Linguistique De Prague, Vol. 1. Ed. by Eva Hajicova et al. (Prague Linguistic Circle Papers: No. 1). 330p. 1995. lib. bdg. 79.00 (*1-55619-674-1*) J Benjamins Pubng Co.

Prague Linguistic Circle Papers (Travaux du Cercle Linguistique de Prague), Vol. 2. Ed. by Eva Hajicova et al. (Prague Linguistic Circle Papers Ser.: Vol. 2). viii, 346p. 1996. lib. bdg. 79.00 (*1-55619-673-3*) J Benjamins Pubng Co.

P

An Asterisk (*) at the beginning of an entry indicates that the title is appearing for the first time.

***Prague Linguistic Circle Papers (Travaux du Cercle Linguistique de Prague), Vol. 3.** Ed. by Eva Hajicova et al. (Prague Linguistic Circle Papers Ser.: Vol. 3). viii, 310p. 1999. 84.00 (*1-55619-672-5*) J Benjamins Pubng Co.

Prague, 1962 see Chemistry of Natural Products: Proceedings

Prague Orgy. Philip Roth. LC 95-24898. 96p. 1996. pap. 10.00 (*0-679-74903-9*) Knopf.

Prague Pocket Guide. rev. ed. Berlitz Editors. (Illus.). 144p. 1998. pap. 8.95 (*2-8315-6317-8*) Berlitz.

Prague School & Its Legacy: In Linguistics, Literature, Semiotics, Folklore & the Arts. Yishai Tobin. LC 88-2899. (Linguistic & Literary Studies in Eastern Europe: Vol. 27). xxix, 317p. (C). 1988. 97.00 (*90-272-1532-4*) J Benjamins Pubng Co.

Prague School of Structural & Functional Linguistics: A Short Introduction. Ed. by Philip A. Luelsdorff. LC 94-31089. (Linguistic & Literary Studies in Eastern Europe: No. 41). vii, 385p. 1994. lib. bdg. 95.00 (*1-55619-266-5*) J Benjamins Pubng Co.

Prague Slav Congress of 1848. Lawrence D. Orton. (East European Monographs: No. 46). 187p. 1978. text 60.00 (*0-914710-39-7*, Pub. by East Eur Monographs) Col U Pr.

***Prague Slav Congress 1848: Slavic Identities.** Horst Haselsteiner. 2000. 38.00 (*0-88033-450-9*, 552, Pub. by East Eur Monographs) Col U Pr.

Prague Spring: A Mixed Legacy. Ed. by Jiri Pehe. LC 88-16261. (Perspectives on Freedom Ser.: No. 10). (Illus.). 236p. (Orig.). (C). 1988. pap. text 20.50 (*0-932088-28-7*); lib. bdg. 45.50 (*0-932088-27-9*) Freedom Hse.

***Prague Spring--Prague Fall: Blank Spots of 1968.** Miklos Kun. Tr. by Hajnal Csatorday from HUN. LC 99-236764. (Illus.). 252p. 1999. 60.00 (*963-05-7608-2*, Pub. by Akade Kiado) Intl Spec Bk.

Prague Spring & Its Aftermath: Czechoslovak Politics, 1968-1970. Kieran Williams. 283p. (C). 1997. text 59.95 (*0-521-58226-1*) Cambridge U Pr.

***Prague Spring, 1968.** Ed. by Jaromir Navratil. LC 98-44001. 700p. (C). 1998. 59.95 (*963-9116-15-7*) Ctrl Europ Univ.

Prague Spring, 1968: A National Security Archive Documents Reader. Ruth Tosek. 1994. 40.00 (*1-56584-068-2*, Pub. by New Press NY) Norton.

Prague Sprung: Notes & Voices from the New World. David Leviatin. LC 93-2869. 160p. 1993. 57.95 (*0-275-94536-7*, C4536, Praeger Pubs) Greenwood.

Prague Studies in Mathematical Linguistics, No. 9. Ed. by Eva Hajicova et al. LC 86-16432. (Linguistic & Literary Studies in Eastern Europe: No. 22). 200p. 1987. 59.00 (*90-272-1527-8*) J Benjamins Pubng Co.

Prague Studies in Mathematical Linguistics, Vol. 7. Ed. by Josef Machek et al. (Linguistic & Literary Studies in Eastern Europe: No. 9). 255p. 1981. 65.00 (*90-272-1511-1*) J Benjamins Pubng Co.

Prague Studies in Mathematical Linguistics, Vol. 8. Ed. by Eva Hajicova et al. (Linguistic & Literary Studies in Eastern Europe: No. 17). 224p. 1983. 65.00 (*90-272-1521-9*) J Benjamins Pubng Co.

Prague Studies in Mathematical Linguistics, Vol. 10. Ed. by Eva Hajicova et al. (Linguistic & Literary Studies in Eastern Europe: Vol. 34). 199p. 1990. 65.00 (*90-272-1541-3*) J Benjamins Pubng Co.

***Prague Sunset.** Carvel De Bussy. LC 98-74966. 240p. 1998. text 33.50 (*0-88033-419-3*, 521, Pub. by East Eur Monographs) Col U Pr.

Prague Tales. Jan Neruda. (Central European Classics). 1993. pap. text 16.95 (*963-9116-23-8*) Ctrl Europ Univ.

Prague Tales. Jan Neruda. Tr. by Michael H. Heim. (Central European Classics Ser.). 368p. (C). 1996. pap. 16.95 (*1-85866-058-0*) Ctrl Europ Univ.

***Prague Territories: National Conflict & Cultural Innovation in Kafka's Fin de Siecle.** Scott P. Spector. LC 99-41955. (Weimar & Now Ser.: Vol. 21). (Illus.). 345p. 2000. 45.00 (*0-520-21909-0*, Pub. by U CA Pr) Cal Prin Full Svc.

Prague Trial: The First Anti-Zionist Show Trial in the Communist Bloc. Meir Cotic. LC 87-47555. 288p. 1987. 19.50 (*0-317-59699-3*, Cornwall Bks) Assoc Univ Prs.

Prague Trial: The First Anti-Zionist Show Trial in the Communist Bloc. Meir Kotik. LC 87-47555. 1987. 19.50 (*0-8453-4814-0*, Cornwall Bks) Assoc Univ Prs.

Prague, U. S. A. Richard Katrovas. 144p. (Orig.). 1996. pap. 10.00 (*0-916620-96-4*) Portals Pr.

Praguewalks: Five Ultimate Walking Tours of Prague. Ivana Edwards. (Illus.). 272p. 1995. pap. 14.95 (*0-8050-2360-7*) H Holt & Co.

Praguiana: Some Basic & Less Known Aspects of the Prague Linguistic School. Ed. by Josef Vachek & Libuse Duskova. (Linguistic & Literary Studies in Eastern Europe: No. 12). xxxi, 321p. 1983. 107.00 (*90-272-1514-6*) J Benjamins Pubng Co.

Praguiana 1945-1990. Ed. by Philip A. Luelsdorff et al. LC 93-44739. (Linguistic & Literary Studies in Eastern Europe: No. 40). x, 250p. 1994. 75.00 (*1-55619-265-7*) J Benjamins Pubng Co.

Praier & Complaynte of the Ploweman into Christe. Douglas H. Parker. LC 98-116769. 256p. 1997. text 60.00 (*0-8020-4268-6*) U of Toronto Pr.

Praire Dog Primer. Pat Storer & Lynda Watson. (Illus.). 76p. 1997. pap. 15.50 (*1-888144-13-0*) Country Storer Ent.

Praire Night Before Christmas see Cowboy Night Before Christmas

Praire see Images

Prairie. James Fenimore Cooper. 411p. Date not set. 27.95 (*0-8488-2546-2*) Amereon Ltd.

Prairie. James Fenimore Cooper. 1976. lib. bdg. 28.95 (*0-89968-160-3*, Lghtyr Pr) Buccaneer Bks.

***Prairie.** James Fenimore Cooper. Ed. by Donald A. Ringe. (Oxford World's Classics Ser.). 432p. 2000. pap. 10.95 (*0-19-283766-4*) OUP.

Prairie. James Fenimore Cooper. Ed. by James P. Elliott. LC 84-24096. 566p. (C). 1985. pap. text 19.95 (*0-87395-672-9*) State U NY Pr.

Prairie. James Fenimore Cooper. Ed. & Intro. by James P. Elliott. LC 84-24096. 566p. (C). 1985. text 59.50 (*0-87395-363-0*) State U NY Pr.

Prairie. James Fenimore Cooper. Ed. & Intro. by Blake Nevius. 384p. 1987. pap. 11.95 (*0-14-039026-X*, Penguin Classics) Viking Penguin.

Prairie. Alison Ormsby. LC 97-39444. (Ecosystems of North America Ser.). (Illus.). (YA). (gr. 6 up). 1998. lib. bdg. 27.07 (*0-7614-0897-5*, Benchmark NY) Marshall Cavendish.

Prairie. Lynn M. Stone. LC 95-46186. (Biomes Discovery Library). 24p. (J). (gr. k-4). 1996. lib. bdg. 10.95 (*0-86593-420-7*) Rourke Corp.

Prairie. James Fenimore Cooper. (Works of James Fenimore Cooper). 1990. reprint ed. lib. bdg. 79.00 (*0-7812-2375-X*) Rprt Serv.

Prairie: The Land & Its People. Mil Penner & Carol Schmidt. Ed. by Mary Nielsen. LC 89-91644. (Illus.). 224p. 1990. 39.95 (*0-9615597-1-3*) Sounds Kansas.

Prairie: The Legend of Charles Burton Irwin & the Y6 Ranch. Anna Lee Waldo. 1216p. 1986. pap. 8.99 (*0-515-10696-8*, Jove) Berkley Pub.

Prairie Adventures of Turk & the Gobblers. Barry Clay. Ed. by Myrna Kemnitz. 190p. (YA). (gr. 7 up). 1995. pap. 9.99 (*0-88092-324-5*) Royal Fireworks.

***Prairie Albion: An English Settlement in Pioneer Illinois.** Contrib. by Charles Boewe. LC 99-21403. (Shawnee Classics). (Illus.). 320p. 1999. pap. 16.95 (*0-8093-2283-8*) S Ill U Pr.

Prairie Alphabet. Jo Bannatyne-Cugnet. LC 92-80414. (Illus.). 32p. (J). (gr. k up). 1992. 19.95 (*0-88776-292-1*) Tundra Bks.

Prairie Alphabet. Jo Bannatyne-Cugnet. LC 92-80414. (Illus.). 32p. (J). (gr. 1-3). 1994. pap. 7.95 (*0-88776-323-5*) Tundra Bks.

Prairie Alphabet. Jo Bannatyne-Cugnet. LC 92-80414. 1992. 13.15 (*0-606-06679-9*, Pub. by Turtleback) Demco.

Prairie Architect: The Life & Work of F. C. W. Kuehn. Jeannette Kinyon. (Illus.). 144p. 1984. 2.00 (*0-931170-23-0*) Ctr Western Studies.

Prairie Avenue Cookbook: Recipes & Recollections from Prominent 19th-Century Chicago Families. Compiled by Carol Callahan. LC 92-23088. (Illus.). 224p. (C). 1993. 36.95 (*0-8093-1814-8*); pap. 18.95 (*0-8093-1815-6*) S Ill U Pr.

Prairie Birds. large type ed. Chris C. Fisher. (Illus.). 128p. 1995. pap. 11.95 (*1-55105-051-X*) Lone Pine.

Prairie Born. Dave Bouchard. (Illus.). 32p. (ps-3). 1999. pap. 6.95 (*1-55143-152-1*) Orca Bk Pubs.

Prairie Boy on the Trail. Neil Meili. 48p. (Orig.). 1997. pap. 7.00 (*1-890636-02-9*) New Tex Pr.

Prairie Boy's Springtime. Neil Meili. 24p. (Orig.). 1994. pap. 5.00 (*1-890636-00-2*) New Tex Pr.

Prairie Boy's Summer. William Kurelek. LC 98-61092. (Illus.). 48p. (YA). (gr. 5 up). 1996. reprint ed. pap. 7.95 (*0-88776-116-X*) Tundra Bks.

Prairie Boy's Winter, 001. William Kurelek. LC 73-8913. (Illus.). 48p. (J). (gr. k-3). 1984. pap. 8.95 (*0-395-36609-7*) HM.

***Prairie Bride.** Julianne MacLean. (Historical Ser.). 2000. mass mkt. 4.99 (*0-373-29126-4*, 1-29126-9) Harlequin Bks.

***Prairie Brides: Four New Inspirational Love Stories from the American Prairie.** JoAnn A. Grote et al. 352p. 2000. pap. 4.97 (*1-57748-712-5*) Barbour Pub.

Prairie Canyon Member, a New Unit of the Upper Cretaceous Mancos Shale, West-Central Colorado & East-Central Utah. Rex D. Cole et al. (Miscellaneous Publication of the Utah Geological Survey Ser.: Vol. 97-4). (Illus.). 23p. 1997. pap. 3.00 (*1-55791-603-9*, MP-97-4) Utah Geological Survey.

Prairie Chicken Kill: A Truman Smith Mystery. Bill Crider. (Truman Smith Mystery Ser.). 216p. 1996. 20.95 (*0-8027-3282-8*) Walker & Co.

***Prairie Chief.** R. M. Ballantyne. (Illus.). 256p. 2000. reprint ed. 18.00 (*1-889128-72-4*) Mantle Ministries.

***Prairie Child: 1848.** 1999. VHS 95.00 (*1-877933-87-2*) Her Own Words.

Prairie Child, 1848. Jocelyn Riley. 114p. 1999. teacher ed. 45.00 (*1-877933-90-2*, 24002) Her Own Words.

***Prairie Christmas.** Catherine Palmer et al. LC 00-37783. (Illus.). (J). 2000. pap. write for info. (*0-8423-3562-5*) Tyndale Hse.

Prairie Chronicles. Mike Blair. (Illus.). 176p. (Orig.). 1993. pap. 12.95 (*0-9637862-3-7*) Creator Pub.

Prairie City: The Story of an American Community. Angie Debo. LC 98-15864. (Illus.). 276p. 1998. pap. 12.95 (*0-8061-3094-6*) U of Okla Pr.

Prairie City, Iowa: Three Seasons at Home. Douglas Bauer. LC 88-13121. (Iowa Heritage Collection). 330p. 1988. reprint ed. pap. 10.95 (*0-8138-1328-X*) Iowa St U Pr.

Prairie Collection Cookbook Centennial Edition. Barbara Larson. Ed. by Helga Gonzalez. (Illus.). 224p. 1988. 17.95 (*0-318-35132-3*) Bismarck Mandan.

Prairie Conservation: Preserving North America's Most Endangered Ecosystem. Ed. by Fred B. Samson & Fritz L. Knopf. 352p. 1996. text 55.00 (*1-55963-427-8*); pap. text 28.00 (*1-55963-428-6*) Island Pr.

Prairie Cooks: Glorified Rice, Three-Day Buns, & Other Reminiscences. Carrie Young & Felicia Young. LC 93-17414. (Bur Oak Original Ser.). (Illus.). 148p. 1993. 15.95 (*0-87745-436-1*) U of Iowa Pr.

***Prairie Cooks: Glorified Rice, Three-Day Buns & Other Reminiscences.** Carrie Young. LC 93-17414. (Illus.). 148p. 2000. reprint ed. pap. 12.95 (*0-87745-717-4*) U of Iowa Pr.

Prairie Coulee. Thomas Willock. 1990. pap. 6.95 (*0-919433-56-1*) Lone Pine.

Prairie County Arkansas Census, 1850. Courtney York & Gerlene York. 51p. (Orig.). 1969. pap. 12.00 (*0-916660-07-9*) Hse of York.

Prairie Crossings: Illinois' Exciting Rail Junctions in the 1990s. Stanley A. Chanenon. LC 98-93264. (Illus.). 500p. 1998. 55.00 (*0-9631811-2-2*); pap. 45.00 (*0-9631811-3-0*) S A Changnon.

Prairie Dawn's Purple Book: Activity Book. 1986. pap. text 5.75 (*0-19-434163-1*) OUP.

Prairie Dawn's Purple Book: Student Book. 1986. pap. text, student ed. 8.50 (*0-19-434161-5*) OUP.

Prairie Dawn's Purple Book: Teacher's Book. 1986. pap. text, teacher ed. 15.95 (*0-19-434162-3*) OUP.

Prairie Day. Laura Ingalls Wilder. (My First Little House Bks.). (Illus.). (J). (ps-1). 1998. 10.15 (*0-606-13719-X*, Pub. by Turtleback) Demco.

***Prairie Day.** adapted ed. Laura Ingalls Wilder. (My First Little House Bks.). (Illus.). 32p. (J). (ps-1). 1998. pap. 5.95 (*0-06-443504-0*, HarpTrophy) HarpC Child Bks.

Prairie Designs for Stained Glass Windows. Alex Spatz. 40p. 1994. pap. 9.95 (*0-9641597-0-8*) Cliffside Studio.

***Prairie Designs II.** (Illus.). 38p. 1999. pap. 5.67 (*0-9641597-5-9*) Cliffside Studio.

Prairie Dog. Sabrina Crewe. LC 96-4828. (Life Cycles Bks.). (Illus.). 32p. (J). (ps-4). 1996. lib. bdg. 21.40 (*0-8172-4365-8*) Raintree Steck-V.

Prairie Dog Dreams: And Other Poems from Navajoland. Sigmund A. Boloz. Ed. by Karen Snow. (Illus.). 36p. (Orig.). (J). (gr. 4-12). 1995. pap. text 6.00 (*1-886635-00-5*) Wooded Hill AZ.

Prairie Dog Pets. 3rd rev. ed. Pat Storer. (Illus.). 218p. 1996. 27.00 (*1-888144-04-1*) Country Storer Ent.

Prairie Dog Pioneers see Como los Perros de la Pradera

***Prairie Dog Pioneers.** Jo Harper. 2000. pap. 8.95 (*1-890515-23-X*) Turtle Bks.

***Prairie Dog Pioneers.** Jo Harper & Josephine Harper. LC 98-9678. (Illus.). 48p. (YA). (gr. k up). 2000. 16.95 (*1-890515-10-8*, Pub. by Turtle Bks) Publishers Group.

Prairie Dog Town. Rae Oetting. LC 68-56829. (Illus.). 48p. (J). (gr. 2-5). 1968. lib. bdg. 10.95 (*0-87783-030-4*) Oddo.

***Prairie Dog Town.** Janette Oke. (Illus.). 140p. (J). (gr. 3 up). 1998. pap. 5.99 (*0-934998-31-0*) Bethany Hse.

Prairie Dog Town. Bettye Rogers. (Smithsonian Wild Heritage Collection). 1993. 10.15 (*0-606-08035-X*, Pub. by Turtleback) Demco.

Prairie Dog Town. deluxe ed. Rae Oetting. LC 68-56829. (Illus.). 48p. (J). (gr. 2-5). 1968. pap. 3.94 (*0-87783-157-2*) Oddo.

Prairie Dogs. Emery Bernhard. LC 96-22849. (Illus.). 40p. (J). (ps-3). 1997. 15.00 (*0-15-201286-9*) Harcourt.

Prairie Dogs. Dorothy Hinshaw Patent. (Illus.). 64p. (YA). (gr. 4-9). 1999. pap. 6.95 (*0-395-52601-9*, Clarion Bks) HM.

***Prairie Dogs.** Dorothy H. Patent. LC 92-34724. (Illus.). 64p. (J). 1999. 16.00 (*0-395-56572-3*, Clarion Bks) HM.

Prairie Dogs. Frank J. Staub. LC 97-48260. (Early Bird Nature Bks.). (Illus.). 48p. (J). (gr. 2-4). 1998. 14.95 (*0-8225-3038-4*) Lerner Pub.

Prairie Dogs. Lynn M. Stone. LC 93-19463. (Unusual Animals Discovery Library). 24p. (J). (gr. k-4). 1993. lib. bdg. 10.95 (*0-86593-282-4*) Rourke Corp.

Prairie Dogs Kiss & Lobsters Wave: How Animals Say Hello. Marilyn Singer & Normand Chartier. LC 96-44255. (J). (gr. k-3). 1995. 15.95 (*0-8050-3703-9*) H Holt & Co.

Prairie du Chien: French, British, American. Peter L. Scanlan. 258p. 1998. reprint ed. pap. write for info. (*0-9668004-0-0*) Prairie du Chien.

Prairie Dust see Across the Wide & Lonesome Prairie: The Oregon Trail Diary of Hattie Campbell, 1847

Prairie Echoes. Pauline N. Diede. Ed. by C. Jane Brandt. Tr. by New Salem Journal Printing Staff. Vol. V. (Illus.). (Orig.). 1989. pap. text. write for info. (*0-318-65406-7*) P Neher Diede.

Prairie en Nouvelle-France, 1647-1760: Itude d'histoire sociale. Louis Lavallee. (FRE.). 304p. 1992. 65.00 (*0-7735-0933-X*, Pub. by McG-Queens Univ Pr); pap. 29.95 (*0-7735-1108-3*, Pub. by McG-Queens Univ Pr) CUP Services.

Prairie Experiences in Handling Cattle & Sheep. William Shepherd. LC 70-165807. (Select Bibliographies Reprint Ser.). 1977. reprint ed. 20.95 (*0-8369-5964-7*) Ayer.

Prairie Falcon. Stanley H. Anderson & John R. Squires. LC 96-41375. (Corrie Herring Hooks Ser.). (Illus.). 168p. 1997. 29.95 (*0-292-70473-9*); pap. 16.95 (*0-292-70474-7*) U of Tex Pr.

Prairie Falcon. Jim Cohn. 96p. (Orig.). 1989. pap. 7.95 (*1-55643-058-2*) North Atlantic.

Prairie Farmer's Directory of Grundy & Kendall Counties: Complete Directory of the Farmers of Grundy & Kendall Cos...Breeders' Directory...& Business Directory. (Illus.). 224p. 1997. reprint ed. pap. 25.00 (*0-8328-5744-0*) Higginson Bk Co.

Prairie Farmer's Directory of Hancock County: Complete Directory of Farmers... Business Directory... Valuable Statistics & General Information. 267p. 1998. reprint ed. pap. 27.00 (*0-8328-9596-2*); reprint ed. lib. bdg. 35.00 (*0-8328-9595-4*) Higginson Bk Co.

Prairie Farming in America: With Notes by the Way on Canada & the United States. James Caird. LC 72-89090. (Rural America Ser.). 1973. reprint ed. 16.00 (*0-8420-1479-9*) Scholarly Res Inc.

***Prairie Fire.** Marilynn Reynolds. LC 98-89928. (Illus.). 32p. (J). (ps-3). 1999. 14.95 (*1-55143-137-8*) Orca Bk Pubs.

Prairie Fire. Mark K. Roberts. LC 94-121842. 288p. 1993. mass mkt. 3.50 (*0-8217-4167-5*, Zebra Kensgtn) Kensgtn Pub Corp.

Prairie Fire. Val H. Usle. (Illus.). 272p. 1999. pap. 18.00 (*0-8059-4763-9*) Dorrance.

Prairie Fire: The 1885 North-West Rebellion. Bob Beal & Rod Macleod. (Illus.). 384p. (Orig.). 1994. pap. 19.99 (*0-7710-1109-1*) McCland & Stewart.

Prairie Fires: John Slocum. Jake Logan. (Slocum Ser.: Vol. 225). 192p. 1997. mass mkt. 4.99 (*0-515-12190-8*, Jove) Berkley Pub.

***Prairie Firestorm.** Jon Sharpe. (Trailsmen Ser.: Vol. 225). 2000. mass mkt. 4.99 (*0-451-20072-1*, Sig) NAL.

Prairie Flower: Adventure in the Far West. Emerson Bennett. LC 79-104416. 126p. (C). 1986. reprint ed. pap. text 5.95 (*0-8290-2390-9*); reprint ed. lib. bdg. 22.50 (*0-8398-0163-7*) Irvington.

Prairie Folks. enl. rev. ed. Hamlin Garland. LC 76-98403. reprint ed. 29.50 (*0-404-02684-2*) AMS Pr.

Prairie Folks see Collected Works of Hamlin Garland

Prairie Folks. Hamlin Garland. (Collected Works of Hamlin Garland). 1988. reprint ed. lib. bdg. 59.00 (*0-7812-1220-0*) Rprt Serv.

Prairie Folks: or Pioneer Life on the Western Prairies. enl. rev. ed. Hamlin Garland. 1972. reprint ed. lib. bdg. 18.00 (*0-8422-8057-X*) Irvington.

Prairie Frontier. Ed. by Sandra Looney et al. (Illus.). 166p. (Orig.). 1984. pap. text 6.00 (*0-9604816-1-3*) Nordland Her Found.

Prairie Garden: Seventy Native Plants You Can Grow in Town or Country. J. Robert Smith & Beatrice S. Smith. (Illus.). 232p. 1980. pap. text 15.95 (*0-299-08304-7*) U of Wis Pr.

Prairie Garden Planner: A Personal Journal. Jan Mather. (Prairie Garden Bks.). (Illus.). 256p. 1996. pap. 22.95 (*0-88995-144-6*, Pub. by Red Deer) Genl Dist Srvs.

Prairie Gold: By Iowa Authors & Artists. LC 77-150560. (Short Story Index Reprint Ser.: Vol. 1). 1977. reprint ed. 23.95 (*0-8369-3857-7*) Ayer.

Prairie Grass Roots: An Iowa Small Town in the Early Twentieth Century. Thomas J. Morain. LC 88-652. (Henry A. Wallace Series on Agricultural History & Rural Studies). (Illus.). 306p. 1988. 27.95 (*0-8138-0068-4*) Iowa St U Pr.

Prairie Hardball. Alison Gordon. (Kate Henry Mystery Ser.: Bk. 5). 288p. 1998. mass mkt. 6.95 (*0-7710-3413-X*) McCland & Stewart.

***Prairie Hardball: A Kate Henry Mystery.** Alison Gordon. 288p. 1998. 20.95 (*0-7710-3412-1*) McCland & Stewart.

Prairie Hearts: Women View the Midwest. Marilyn Coffey & Kathleen Bogan. Ed. by Whitney Scott. (Illus.). 208p. (Orig.). 1996. pap. 14.95 (*0-9621039-3-4*) Outrider Pr.

Prairie Heat. Madeline Baker. 448p. 1991. pap. text 4.99 (*0-8439-3161-2*) Dorchester Pub Co.

Prairie Heat. Madeline Baker. 448p. 1995. mass mkt. 5.99 (*0-8439-4036-0*) Dorchester Pub Co.

Prairie Heritage: A Pictorial History of Kossuth County. Joanne Walker. LC 95-30222. 1995. write for info. (*0-89865-946-9*) Donning Co.

Prairie Home Commonplace Book 25 Years on the Air. Garrison Keillor. 1999. pap. text 19.95 (*1-56511-291-1*) Higby Fam Trust.

Prairie Home Commonplace Book: 25 Years on the Air. Garrison Keillor. 1999. 29.95 (*1-56511-345-4*) Higby Fam Trust.

Prairie Home Cooking: 400 Recipes That Celebrate the Bountiful Harvests, Creative Cooks, & Comforting Foods of the American Heartland. Judith M. Fertig. LC 99-14392. (Illus.). 528p. 1999. pap. 16.95 (*1-55832-145-4*) Harvard Common Pr.

Prairie Homestead. Arleta Richardson. LC 94-27086. (Orphans' Journey Ser.: Vol. 3). 144p. (J). (gr. 1-8). 1994. pap. 4.99 (*0-7814-0091-0*) Chariot Victor.

Prairie Homestead: Meet the Browns & Their Neighbors. Keith Crew & Douglas Heck. (Illus.). 40p. (Orig.). 1996. mass mkt. 3.95 (*0-9651386-0-7*) Prairie Homestead.

Prairie in My Pocket. Arthur K. Drackley. LC 92-80681. (Illus.). 64p. (Orig.). 1992. pap. 12.95 (*0-88100-076-0*) Natl Writ Pr.

Prairie in Nineteenth-Century American Poetry. Steven Olson. LC 93-32550. (Illus.). 224p. 1995. pap. 15.95 (*0-8061-2640-X*) U of Okla Pr.

***Prairie in Your Pocket: A Guide to Plants of the Tallgrass Prairie.** Mark Muller. (Illus.). 2000. pap. 8.95 (*0-87745-683-6*) U of Iowa Pr.

Prairie Jungle: Songs, Poems & Stories for Children. Ed. by Wenda Mcarthur. LC 85-91257. (Illus.). 120p. (J). (ps-5). 1998. pap. 9.95 (*0-919926-45-2*, Pub. by Coteau) Genl Dist Srvs.

Prairie Keepers: Secrets of the Grasslands. Mary Houle. 272p. 1996. pap. 11.00 (*0-201-40821-X*) Addison-Wesley.

***Prairie Kingdom of the West.** M. B. Good. LC 99-91297. 176p. (J). 2000. pap. 16.95 (*1-56167-566-0*) Am Literary Pr.

Prairie Kitchen Sampler. E. Mae Fritz. Ed. by Krista F. Rogers. LC 88-92599. (Illus.). 435p. 1988. 16.95 (*0-9620404-0-1*) Prairie Wnds AZ.

Prairie Lamps. Alex Spatz. (Illus.). 44p. (Orig.). 1995. pap. 9.95 (*0-9641597-2-4*) Cliffside Studio.

Prairie Laureate: The Collected Poems of Robert Lee Brothers. Susan F. Wiltshire. LC 97-14511. 160p. (Orig.). 1998. pap. write for info. (*1-57168-169-8*, Eakin Pr) Sunbelt Media.

***Prairie Legacy: Tender Years; Searching Heart; Quiet Strength; Like Gold Refined, Vols. 1-4.** Janette Oke. 2000. pap., boxed set 43.99 (*0-7642-8650-1*) Bethany Hse.

Prairie Legends. Monica F. Earring et al. (Indian Culture Ser.). (Illus.). (J). (gr. 6-9). 1978. pap. 1.95 (*0-89992-069-1*) Coun India Ed.

P

An Asterisk (*) at the beginning of an entry indicates that the title is appearing for the first time.

Prairie Liberalism: The Liberal Party in Saskatchewan. David E. Smith. LC 74-78676. (Canadian Government Ser.: No. 18). 365p. reprint ed. pap. 113.20 (*0-7837-4281-9*, 204397300012) Bks Demand.

Prairie Logbooks: Dragoon Campaigns to the Pawnee Villages in 1844, & to the Rocky Mountains in 1845. James H. Carleton. Ed. & Intro. by Louis Pelzer. LC 82-24755. 311p. 1983. reprint ed. pap. 96.50 (*0-608-03489-4*, 206420400008) Bks Demand.

Prairie Man. Steven Porter. LC 89-92532. 62p. (YA). 1990. pap. text 6.00 (*0-9625372-0-9*) Phantom Pubns.

Prairie Man. 2nd rev. ed. Steven Porter. LC 92-80226. (Illus.). 70p. 1992. pap. 9.95 (*0-9625372-3-3*, Pub. by Phantom Pubns) Empire Pub Srvs.

Prairie Memories: An Eighteen Ninety-One Iowa Album in Painting & Verse. Izanna L. Chamberlain. Ed. by Lowell Chamberlain & Mary Sherinian. LC 91-66691. (Illus.). 64p. 1991. 35.00 (*0-945213-04-2*) Rudi Pub.

Prairie Memories from the Bauhs House. Marguerite Livesay. (Illus.). 247p. 1991. pap. 14.95 (*0-9662144-0-4*) Shuab Bks.

Prairie Mirth: Crowson Cartoons from Wichita, Kansas. Richard Crowson. (Illus.). 160p. (Orig.). 1992. pap. 9.95 (*1-880652-10-2*) Wichita Eagle.

Prairie Needles. Helen S. Pederson. (Illus.). 57p. 1997. pap. 7.95 (*0-942323-27-0*) N Amer Heritage Pr.

Prairie Night: Black-Footed Ferrets & the Recovery of Endangered Species. Brian Miller et al. (Illus.). 320p. 1996. 37.50 (*1-56098-603-4*) Smithsonian.

Prairie Nightmare. Pierre Berton. (Canada Moves West Ser.). (Illus.). 88p. (J). (gr. 6-9). pap. 4.99 (*0-7710-1440-6*) McCland & Stewart.

Prairie Nights to Neon Lights: The Story of Country Music in West Texas. Joe Carr & Alan Munde. (Illus.). 224p. 1995. text 35.00 (*0-89672-349-6*) Tex Tech Univ Pr.

Prairie Nights to Neon Lights: The Story of Country Music in West Texas. Joe Carr & Alan Munde. LC 95-51753. (Illus.). 234p. 1997. pap. 18.95 (*0-89672-365-8*) Tex Tech Univ Pr.

Prairie Passage: The Illinois & Michigan Canal Corridor. Edward Ranney. LC 98-8906. 224p. 1998. 24.95 (*0-252-06714-2*); text 49.95 (*0-252-02411-7*) U of Ill Pr.

Prairie Patrimony: Family, Farming, & Community in the Midwest. Sonya Salamon. LC 92-53622. (Studies in Rural Culture). xx, 298p. (C). 1992. 59.95 (*0-8078-2045-8*) U of NC Pr.

Prairie Patrimony: Family, Farming, & Community in the Midwest. Sonya Salamon. LC 92-53622. (Studies in Rural Culture). 318p. (C). 1995. pap. text 19.95 (*0-8078-4553-1*) U of NC Pr.

Prairie Patterns: Folk Arts in North Dakota. Christopher Martin. (Illus.). 126p. (Orig.). 1989. pap. 18.00 (*0-911205-03-9*) N Dak Coun Arts.

Prairie Peninsula Proceedings, Sixth, Ohio State University, Columbus, Ohio, August 12-17, 1978: In the "Shadow" of Transeau. North American Prairie Conference Staff. Ed. by Ronald L. Stuckey & Karen J. Reese. LC 81-82059. (Biological Notes Ser.: No. 15). (Illus.). 1981. pap. text 15.00 (*0-86727-090-X*) Ohio Bio Survey.

Prairie People: Continuity & Change in Potawatomi Indian Culture, 1665-1965. James A. Clifton. LC 98-24997. (Illus.). 568p. 1998. pap. text 24.95 (*0-87745-644-5*) U of Iowa Pr.

Prairie People: Forgotten Anabaptists. Rod Janzen. LC 98-18711. (Illus.). 342p. 1999. pap. 25.00 (*0-87451-931-4*); text 50.00 (*0-87451-930-6*) U Pr of New Eng.

Prairie Pictures. Shirlee S. Matheson. 128p. (J). (gr. 4-7). pap. 9.99 (*0-7710-5857-8*) McCland & Stewart.

Prairie Plants & Their Environment: A Fifty-Year Study of the Midwest. J. E. Weaver. LC 90-20848. (Illus.). xiv, 276p. 1991. reprint ed. pap. text 15.00 (*0-8032-9730-0*, Bison Books) U of Nebr Pr.

Prairie Plants of the Midwest: Identification & Ecology. Russell R. Kirt & Roberta L. Simonds. (Illus.). 137p. (Orig.). (C). 1995. pap. text 13.95 (*0-87563-573-3*) Stipes.

Prairie Poems Revisited. 2nd rev. ed. Arnold H. Marzolf. 201p. 1997. pap. 9.95 (*0-9658463-0-X*) A H Marzolf.

Prairie Poetry. Audrae Visser. LC 98-90988. 100p. 1998. pap. write for info. (*1-57579-138-2*) Pine Hill Pr.

Prairie Poetry: Cowboy Verse of Kansas. Jim Hoy. (Illus.). 1995. pap. 15.95 (*1-880652-49-8*) Wichita Eagle.

Prairie Populism: The Fate of Agrarian Radicalism in Kansas, Nebraska, & Iowa, 1880-1892. Jeffrey Ostler. LC 93-14828. (Rural America Ser.). 272p. 1993. 29.95 (*0-7006-0606-8*) U Pr of KS.

Prairie Populist: The Memoirs of Luna Kellie. Ed. by Jane T. Nelsen. LC 91-41361. (Singular Lives: The Iowa Series in North American Autobiography). (Illus.). 209p. 1992. pap. text 13.95 (*0-87745-369-1*) U of Iowa Pr.

Prairie Potpourri. (Illus.). 348p. 1991. 16.99 (*0-9645275-0-2*) Alegent Immanuel Med Ctr.

Prairie Practitioners: 20th Century South Dakota Veterinarians. Janice L. Kitzler. Ed. & Intro. by Thomas B. Ludgate. 288p. (Orig.). 1996. pap. write for info. (*1-57579-033-5*) Pine Hill Pr.

Prairie Primer. Margie Gray. Ed. by Mei Leslie. (Literature Based Unit Studies Utilizing the "Little House" Ser.). (Illus.). 341p. 1993. teacher ed., spiral bd. 45.00 (*0-9652511-0-1*) Cadron Creek.

Prairie Primer. Stan Nichols et al. (Illus.). 59p. (C). 1999. pap. text 15.00 (*0-7881-7758-3*) DIANE Pub.

Prairie Print Makers. 2nd ed. Barbara T. O'Neil & George C. Foreman. Ed. by Howard W. Ellington. (Illus.). 60p. 1984. reprint ed. pap. 10.00 (*0-9614307-0-2*) Gallery Ellington.

***Prairie Prose... And Cons.** 2nd ed. Illus. by Antoinette Clark. 1999. reprint ed. 13.00 (*0-9700848-1-1*) J Hilderbrant Enter.

***Prairie Prose... And Cons.** 2nd ed. Illus. by Antoinette Clark. 53p. 1999. reprint ed. pap. 8.00 (*0-9700848-0-3*) J Hilderbrant Enter.

Prairie Provinces. Ed. by P. J. Smith. (Studies in Canadian Geography). 1972. pap. text 7.95 (*0-8020-6161-3*) U of Toronto Pr.

Prairie Queen. Cynthia Haseloff. 1999. 20.00 (*0-7862-1165-2*); 30.00 (*0-7862-1579-8*) Thorndike Pr.

Prairie Queen. large type ed. Cynthia Haseloff. 275p. 2000. 30.00 (*0-7838-0315-X*, G K Hall Lrg Type) Mac Lib Ref.

***Prairie Queen.** large type ed. Cynthia Haseloff. 2000. 30.00 (*0-7862-1177-6*, G K Hall Lrg Type) Mac Lib Ref.

Prairie Recipes & Kitchen Antiques: Tasty, Healthy Dishes from Simpler Days. Wilma Kurtis & Anita Gold. (Illus.). 131p. 1992. 14.95 (*0-929387-81-3*) Bonus Books.

Prairie Relics in California: A Guidebook Based on Dr. James Barry's 1971 Survey & Maps. James Barry. Ed. by Craig C. Dremann. (Illus.). 1989. pap. 5.50 (*0-933421-31-1*) Redwood Seed.

Prairie Reunion. Barbara J. Scot. LC 95-13111. 220p. 1995. 21.00 (*0-374-23686-0*) FS&G.

***Prairie Reunion.** Barbara J. Scot. (Bur Oak Bks.). (Illus.). 310p. 2001. reprint ed. pap. 14.95 (*0-87745-738-7*) U of Iowa Pr.

***Prairie Rock Garden.** Donna Balzer. (Prairie Garden Bks.). (Illus.). 96p. 2000. pap. 9.95 (*0-88995-195-0*, Pub. by Red Deer) Genl Dist Srvs.

Prairie Rose. Susan Kirby. 1997. mass mkt. 5.99 (*0-380-78503-X*, Avon Bks) Morrow Avon.

Prairie Rose. Catherine Palmer. LC 97-23018. (Town Called Hope Ser.: Vol. 1). 272p. 1997. pap. 10.99 (*0-8423-7056-0*) Tyndale Hse.

Prairie Rose Garden. Jan Mather. LC 96-910777. (Prairie Garden Bks.). (Illus.). 80p. 1997. pap. 10.95 (*0-88995-163-2*, Pub. by Red Deer) Genl Dist Srvs.

***Prairie Runways: The History of Wichita's Original Municipal Airport.** Kansas Aviation Museum Staff. LC 99-64965. (Illus.). 127p. 1999. 30.00 (*0-9666451-0-3*) Air Capital Pr.

Prairie School. Lois Lenski. LC 51-11169. (Illus.). 208p. (J). (gr. 4-7). 1951. lib. bdg. 15.89 (*0-397-30194-4*) HarpC Child Bks.

Prairie School: Frank Lloyd Wright & His Midwest Contemporaries. Harold A. Brooks. LC 72-151363. 398p. reprint ed. pap. 123.40 (*0-608-16930-7*, 202641900049) Bks Demand.

Prairie School: Frank Lloyd Wright & His Midwest Contemporaries. rev. ed. H. Allen Brooks. (Illus.). 400p. 1996. pap. 22.50 (*0-393-31439-1*, Norton Paperbks) Norton.

Prairie School Architecture: Studies from "The Western Architect" Ed. by Harold A. Brooks. LC 73-91567. 351p. reprint ed. pap. 108.90 (*0-608-13717-0*, 202045900018) Bks Demand.

Prairie Schoolhouse. Campbell. LC 95-4357. (Illus.). 151p. 1996. pap. 29.95 (*0-8263-1660-3*) U of NM Pr.

"Prairie Schooner" Anthology of Contemporary Jewish American Writing: Fiction & Poetry. Ed. by Hilda Raz. LC 97-41201. iv, 293p. 1998. pap. 20.00 (*0-8032-8971-5*, Bison Books) U of Nebr Pr.

Prairie Schooner Detours. 2nd ed. Irene D. Paden. (Illus.). 310p. 1990. reprint ed. pap. 12.95 (*0-935284-77-X*) Patrice Pr.

Prairie Schooners. Glen Rounds. (Illus.). (J). (gr. 4-7). 1994. pap. 6.95 (*0-8234-1087-0*) Holiday.

Prairie Schooners. Glen Rounds. (Illus.). 96p. (J). (gr. 4-6). 1994. reprint ed. 15.95 (*0-8234-1086-2*) Holiday.

Prairie Sketches. Raymond S. Nelson. LC 92-73894. (Illus.). 96p. (Orig.). 1992. pap. 8.95 (*0-9627947-8-3*) Hearth KS.

***Prairie Skies.** C. Milne. 1999. pap. 16.95 (*1-895618-25-8*) Fifth Hse Publ.

Prairie Small-Town Survival: The Challenge of Agro-Manitoba. John S. Brierley & Daniel Todd. LC 89-13551. (Canadian Studies: Vol. 7). 88p. 1990. lib. bdg. 49.95 (*0-88946-211-9*) E Mellen.

Prairie Smoke. Melvin R. Gilmore. LC 78-168148. (Illus.). reprint ed. 27.50 (*0-404-02776-8*) AMS Pr.

Prairie Smoke. Melvin R. Gilmore. LC 86-31205. xxviii, 225p. (gr. 4-12). 1987. reprint ed. pap. 7.95 (*0-87351-207-3*, Borealis Book) Minn Hist.

Prairie Son. Dennis M. Clausen. LC 98-46831. (First Series). (Illus.). 239p. 1999. pap. 16.00 (*0-922811-39-3*) Mid-List.

***Prairie Song.** Cheryl Anne Porter. 352p. 2000. mass mkt. 5.99 (*0-312-97291-1*) St Martin.

Prairie Song & Western Story. Hamlin Garland. LC 73-163026. (Short Story Index Reprint Ser.). (Illus.). 1977. reprint ed. 23.95 (*0-8369-3940-9*) Ayer.

Prairie Songs. Pam Conrad. 176p. (J). (gr. 7 up). 1985. lib. bdg. 15.89 (*0-06-021337-X*) HarpC.

Prairie Songs. Pam Conrad. (Illus.). (J). (gr. 4-7). 1985. 14.00 (*0-06-021336-1*, 236070) HarpC.

Prairie Songs. Pam Conrad. LC 85-42633. (Trophy Bk.). (Illus.). 176p. (J). (gr. 4-7). 1987. pap. 4.95 (*0-06-440206-1*, HarpTrophy) HarpC Child Bks.

Prairie Songs. Pam Conrad. 1995. 19.25 (*0-8446-6812-5*) Peter Smith.

Prairie Songs. Pam Conrad. LC 85-42633. (J). 1987. 9.60 (*0-606-03639-3*, Pub. by Turtleback) Demco.

Prairie Songs see Collected Works of Hamlin Garland

Prairie Songs. Hamlin Garland. (Collected Works of Hamlin Garland). 1988. reprint ed. lib. bdg. 59.00 (*0-7812-1221-9*) Rprt Serv.

Prairie Songs: A Study Guide. Toni Albert. Ed. by J. Friedland & R. Kessler. (Novel-Ties Ser.). (J). (gr. 4-6). 1993. pap. text, student ed. 15.95 (*0-88122-882-6*) Lrn Links.

Prairie Soul: Poems. Hazel C. Crosswhite. 136p. 1998. pap. 12.95 (*1-57087-373-9*) Prof Pr NC.

Prairie State: The Civil Rights of Administrators. Richard W. Hostrop. LC 94-35091. (Effective School Administration Ser.: No. 5). 1995. 35.00 (*0-88280-125-2*) ETC Pubns.

Prairie State College in Its First Quarter- Century, 1957-1982: A Community College History. Richard G. Sherman. 464p. 1992. pap. 16.50 (*0-9632760-0-X*); 11.00 (*0-9632760-1-8*) Prairie State Coll.

Prairie Stationmaster: The Story of One Man's Railroading Career in Nebraska 1917-1963. Barbara B. Clayburn. LC 78-78305. (Illus.). 128p. 1979. 6.50 (*0-8187-0034-3*) Harlo Press.

Prairie Stories of the West. Elizabeth Ballinger. (Illus.). 124p. (Orig.). (J). (gr. k-8). 1993. reprint ed. pap. text 8.95 (*1-879331-39-X*, Classc Pub) Marciel Pub & Print.

Prairie Storm, Vol. 3. Catherine Palmer. LC 98-31508. 300p. 1999. pap. text 9.99 (*0-8423-7058-7*) Tyndale Hse.

Prairie Style: Houses & Gardens by Frank Lloyd Wright & the Prairie School. Dixie Legler. LC 99-15471. (Illus.). 208p. 1999. text 45.00 (*1-55670-931-5*) Stewart Tabori & Chang.

Prairie Summer. Nancy Hundal. (Illus.). 40p. (J). (gr. k-3). 1999. text 16.95 (*1-55041-403-8*, Pub. by Fitzhenry & W Ltd) Genl Dist Srvs.

Prairie Summer. Alina Roberts. (Great Escapes Ser.). 1994. per. 1.99 (*0-373-83274-5*, 1-83274-0) Harlequin Bks.

Prairie Summer: The Goose River Settlement. Marie Gleason. 1998. pap. 4.00 (*1-57514-288-0*) Encore Perform Pub.

Prairie Summer: The Mourning Dove. Marie Gleason. 1998. pap. 4.00 (*1-57514-289-9*) Encore Perform Pub.

Prairie Sunset. Irma B. King. (Illus.). 31p. 1989. pap. 3.00 (*0-614-24762-4*) Tesseract SD.

Prairie Tales II: A History of Bowman County, N. D. Bowman County Historical Society Staff. (Illus.). 652p. 1989. 42.50 (*0-317-93516-X*) Bowman County.

***Prairie Thunder.** Taylor Brady. LC 99-28411. (Romances Ser.). 1999. pap. 24.95 (*0-7862-2085-6*, Five Star MI) Mac Lib Ref.

Prairie Time: The Leopold Reserve Revisited. John Ross & Beth Ross. LC 97-5268. (Illus.). 240p. 1998. 24.95 (*0-299-15660-5*) U of Wis Pr.

***Prairie to Mountain Explorer User's Guide.** Ed. by Patricia McClurg. 64p. 1999. pap. text, teacher ed. 55.00 incl. cd-rom (*0-941570-19-3*) U of Wyoming.

***Prairie Town.** Ryan Durney. (Illus.). 8p. (J). (gr. k-2). 2000. pap. 3.75 (*1-58323-014-9*) Seedling Pubns.

Prairie Town. Bonnie Geisert. LC 97-40049. 32p. (J). (gr. 1-4). 1998. 16.00 (*0-395-85907-7*) HM.

Prairie-Town Boy. Carl Sandburg. LC 55-5239. (Illus.). 208p. (J). (gr. 3-7). 1990. pap. 4.95 (*0-15-263332-4*, Odyssey) Harcourt.

Prairie Trails & Cow Towns. Floyd B. Streeter. (Illus.). 1963. 16.95 (*0-8159-6510-9*) Devin.

Prairie Traveler. Randolph B. Marcy. LC 92-38878. 288p. 1988. reprint ed. pap. 10.95 (*0-918222-89-3*) Applewood.

Prairie Traveler: The Classic Handbook for American Pioneers. Randolph P. Marsi. (Illus.). 240p. 1994. pap. 11.95 (*0-399-51865-7*, Perigee Bks) Berkley Pub.

Prairie Tree. Marilyn G. Komechak. LC 87-91064. (Illus.). 80p. (Orig.). 1987. pap. 7.00 (*0-9619277-0-4*) Clear Fork Cafe.

Prairie University: A History of the University of Nebraska. Robert E. Knoll. LC 94-367729. (Illus.). xviii, 309p. 1995. text 50.00 (*0-8032-2717-5*) U of Nebr Pr.

Prairie Vengeance. large type ed. Wayne C. Lee. LC 97-44867. (Nightingale Ser.). 199p. 1998. pap. 18.95 (*0-7838-8379-X*, G K Hall & Co) Mac Lib Ref.

Prairie View Summer Science Academy. Ed. by John F. Krizmanic. (AIP Conference Proceedings Ser.: No. 291). (Illus.). 224p. 1993. text 95.00 (*1-56396-133-4*, AIP Pr) Spr-Verlag.

Prairie Visions: The Life & Time of Solomon Butcher. Pam Conrad. 1998. write for info. (*0-397-32482-0*); write for info. (*0-397-32483-9*) Lppncott W & W.

Prairie Voices: Iowa's Pioneering Women. Ed. by Glenda Riley. LC 96-24258. 300p. (Orig.). (C). 1996. pap. text 24.95 (*0-8138-2595-4*) Iowa St U Pr.

Prairie Voices: Process Anthropology in Family Medicine. Howard F. Stein. LC 95-44321. 160p. 1996. 57.95 (*0-89789-429-4*, Bergin & Garvey) Greenwood.

Prairie Waltz: Poetry, Art, & "Receipts"...from the Heart of a West Texan. Madelaine Lowe. (Illus.). 32p. (Orig.). 1995. pap. 7.95 (*0-9641166-1-8*) Flatland Pubng.

Prairie Wanderings: The Land & Creatures of the Grasslands. Paul Jantzen. LC 93-79794. (Illus.). 154p. (Orig.). 1993. pap. 9.95 (*1-882420-05-5*) Hearth KS.

Prairie Was Home. Pauline N. Diede. Tr. by Abbey Press Printing Staff. (Pioneer Life Bks.: Vol. II). (Illus.). 154p. (Orig.). 1986. pap. text 6.95 (*0-685-26960-4*) P Neher Diede.

***Prairie Wetland Ecology: The Contribution of the Marsh Ecology Research Program.** Ed. by Henry R. Murkin et al. (Illus.). 488p. 2000. 79.95 (*0-8138-2752-3*) Iowa St U Pr.

Prairie Wife. Arthur Stringer. 1976. lib. bdg. 14.85 (*0-89968-122-0*, Lghtyr Pr) Buccaneer Bks.

Prairie Wildflowers. Dee Strickler. LC 86-90566. (Illus.). 80p. (Orig.). 1986. pap. 9.95 (*0-934318-99-9*) Falcon Pub Inc.

Prairie Willow. Maxine Trottier. LC 99-229703. (Illus.). 24p. (J). (gr. k-3). 1998. 15.95 (*0-7737-3067-2*) STDK.

***Prairie Willow.** Maxine Trottier. (Illus.). 24p. (J). (gr. k-5). 2000. pap. 6.95 (*0-7737-6100-4*) Stoddart Publ.

Prairie Wind, Blow Me Back. Evelyn D. Iverson. LC 88-63282. (Illus.). 158p. (Orig.). 1988. pap. 7.95 (*0-942323-03-3*) N Amer Heritage Pr.

Prairie Winds. Irma B. King. (Illus.). 32p. 1988. pap. 3.00 (*0-614-24763-2*) Tesseract SD.

Prairie Wings. Edgar M. Queeny. (Illus.). 256p. 1979. reprint ed. 50.00 (*0-916838-21-8*) Schiffer.

Prairie Winnows Out Its Own: The West River Country of South Dakota in the Years of Depression & Dust. Paula M. Nelson. LC 95-24904. (Illus.). 276p. 1996. text 27.95 (*0-87745-525-2*) U of Iowa Pr.

Prairie Year. Jo Bannatyne-Cugnet. LC 93-61792. (Illus.). 32p. (J). (gr. 3-6). 1994. 16.95 (*0-88776-334-0*) Tundra Bks.

Prairies. Tanya Lloyd. LC 96-910741. (Illus.). 96p. 14.95 (*1-55110-522-5*) Whitecap Bks.

Prairies. Peter Murray. LC 96-17569. (Biomes of Nature Ser.). (Illus.). 32p. (J). (gr. 2-6). 1996. lib. bdg. 22.79 (*1-56766-277-3*) Childs World.

Prairies. Dorothy H. Patent. LC 96-14125. (Illus.). 40p. (J). (gr. 4-6). 1996. lib. bdg. 15.95 (*0-8234-1277-6*) Holiday.

Prairies. Lynn M. Stone. (Ecozones Ser.). (Illus.). 48p. (J). (gr. 4-8). 1989. 11.95 (*0-685-58573-5*) Rourke Corp.

Prairies. Lynn M. Stone. (Ecozones Ser.). (Illus.). 48p. (J). (gr. 4-8). 1989. lib. bdg. 22.60 (*0-86592-446-5*) Rourke Enter.

Prairies & the Pampas: Agrarian Policy in Canada & Argentina, 1880-1930. Carl E. Solberg. LC 86-27854. (Comparative Studies in History, Institutions & Public Policy). 320p. 1987. 45.00 (*0-8047-1346-4*) Stanford U Pr.

Prairies & Their People. Flint. (And Its People Ser.). 48p. (J). (gr. 5-6). 1994. 24.26 (*0-8172-4673-8*) Raintree Steck-V.

Prairies, Forests, & Wetlands: The Restoration of Natural Landscape Communities in Iowa. Janette R. Thompson. LC 92-9457. (Bur Oak Original Ser.). (Illus.). 151p. 1992. text 24.95 (*0-87745-372-1*) U of Iowa Pr.

Prairies of Fever. Ibrahim Nasrallah. Tr. by M. Jayyusi & J. Reed from ARA. LC 92-23386. (Emerging Voices: New International Fiction Ser.). 160p. 1993. 22.95 (*1-56656-103-5*); pap. 9.95 (*1-56656-106-X*) Interlink Pub.

Prairies Within: The Tragic Trilogy of Ole Rolvaag. Harold P. Simonson. LC 85-32294. 112p. 1987. 20.00 (*0-295-96388-3*) U of Wash Pr.

Prairiescapes. Photos by Larry Kanfer. LC 87-14807. (Visions of Illinois Ser.). (Illus.). 120p. 1987. 34.95 (*0-252-01482-0*) U of Ill Pr.

Prairieton Raid. Lauran Paine. 192p. 1994. 19.95 (*0-8027-4139-8*) Walker & Co.

Prairieton Raid. large type ed. Lauran Paine. LC 94-32216. 245p. 1995. 19.95 (*0-7862-0328-5*) Thorndike Pr.

Prairieville Storekeeper. Don L. Taylor. (Illus.). 354p. 1989. 19.00 (*0-9639286-0-0*) Prairieville Pr.

Prairyerth (A Deep Map) An Epic History of the Tallgrass Prairie County. William Least Heat-Moon. 640p. 1999. pap. 17.00 (*0-395-92569-X*) HM.

Praise, Vol.1. 80p. 1984. per. 8.95 (*0-634-00967-2*) H Leonard.

Praise. David C. Cook Publishing Co., Staff. (J). Date not set. pap. text 7.90 (*1-55513-207-3*) Cook.

Praise. Robert Hass. LC 78-16016. (American Poetry Ser.: Vol. 17). 1990. pap. 11.00 (*0-88001-242-0*) HarpC.

Praise. McGahan. LC 98-17596. 288p. 1998. pap. 13.95 (*0-312-18754-8*) St Martin.

Praise: A Matter of Life & Breath. R. Allen. Tr. by Silas Chan. (CHI.). 204p. 1982. pap. write for info. (*0-941598-04-7*) Living Spring Pubns.

Praise a la Carte: Nourishment for Body & Soul from My Kitchen to Yours. Kay D. Rizzo. LC 96-1940. 1997. 6.97 (*0-8163-1353-9*) Pacific Pr Pub Assn.

Praise & Thanksgiving. Billy J. Daugherty. 32p. (Orig.). 1992. pap. 0.50 (*1-56267-070-0*) Victory Ctr OK.

Praise & Worship. (Cross Training Ser.: Vol. 1). 64p. (YA). (gr. 10-12). 1994. pap. 29.95 incl. VHS (*1-57405-009-5*) CharismaLife Pub.

***Praise & Worship.** (POR.). 107p. 1999. spiral bd. 12.95 (*0-941975-52-5*) Powerhouse.

Praise & Worship. A. L. Gill & Joyce Gill. (KOR.). 147p. 1993. spiral bd. 12.95 (*0-941975-15-0*) Powerhouse.

Praise & Worship. Rod Parsley. 128p. 1993. pap. 6.99 (*0-89274-637-8*, HH-637) Harrison Hse.

Praise & Worship. Ed. by Zondervan Publishing Staff. LC 99-233014. (God's Light Ser.). (Illus.). 160p. 2000. 9.99 (*0-310-97426-7*) Zondervan.

Praise & Worship, Vol. 1. 2nd rev. ed. E. Bernard Jordan. Ed. by Deborah Jones. 128p. (Orig.). 1990. pap. text 20.00 (*0-939241-13-7*) Faith Print.

Praise & Worship: A Devotional for Little Ones. Angela Abraham & Ken Abraham. LC 95-13343. (Illus.). 224p. (J). (ps-3). 1996. 14.99 (*0-8499-1191-5*) Tommy Nelson.

Praise & Worship: Becoming Worshipers of God. 112p. 1999. spiral bd. 12.95 (*0-941975-43-6*) Powerhouse.

Praise & Worship: Becoming Worshipers of God. A. L. Gill & Joyce Gill. (RUS.). (Orig.). 1994. spiral bd. 12.95 (*0-941975-29-0*) Powerhouse.

Praise & Worship: Becoming Worshipers of God. A. L. Gill & Joyce Gill. 112p. (Orig.). 1995. reprint ed. pap. 9.95 (*0-941975-33-9*) Powerhouse.

Praise & Worship: Becoming Worshippers of God. A. L. Gill & Joyce Gill. 110p. (C). 1996. spiral bd. 12.95 (*0-941975-19-3*) Powerhouse.

Praise & Worship Favorites. 1996. 6.99 (*0-8341-9534-8*, MB-743) Lillenas.

***Praise & Worship for Guitar.** 64p. 2000. pap. 8.95 (*0-634-00226-0*) H Leonard.

***Praise & Worship Guitar: Advancing Guitar Skills for the Glory of God.** Steve Turley. 92p. 1999. pap. write for info. (*0-9671749-1-0*) Fretboard Fellow.

***Praise & Worship Hymn Solos: Book/cd Packs.** 48p. 1998. pap. 8.95 (*0-7935-9730-7*) H Leonard.

***Praise & Worship Hymn Solos: Book/cd Packs.** 16p. 1998. pap. 12.95 incl. audio compact disk (*0-7935-9685-8*); pap. 12.95 incl. audio compact disk

P

(0-7935-9756-0); pap. 12.95 incl. audio compact disk (0-7935-9758-7); pap. 12.95 incl. audio compact disk (0-7935-9759-5); pap. 12.95 incl. audio compact disk (0-7935-9760-9); pap. 12.95 incl. audio compact disk (0-7935-9761-7); pap. 12.95 incl. audio compact disk (0-7935-9762-5) H Leonard.

Praise & Worship Hymnal. ring bd. 19.99 (0-8341-9641-7) Lillenas.

Praise & Worship Hymnal. 1968. pap. 9.99 (0-8341-9640-9, MB-152) Nazarene.

Praise & Worship: Hymns of Praise see Alabanza y Adoracion: Canciones de Alabanza

Praise & Worship Piano. Arranged by Fred Bock. (Piano Collection Ser.: No. 2). 1997. pap. 10.95 (0-7935-9992-X) H Leonard.

Praise & Worship Songbook. 112p. 1993. 9.98 (1-57919-068-5) Randolf Prod.

Praise & Worship: Songs of Faith see Alabanza y Adoracion: Canciones de Fe

Praise & Worship: Songs of Joy see Alabanza y Adoracion: Canciones de Alegria

***Praise, Anxiety, & Other Symptoms of Grace.** Joey Earl Horstman. 2000. pap. 16.99 (0-8272-2967-4) Chalice Pr.

Praise Be to the Name of God Forever. 1994. pap. 1.30 (0-8341-9227-6, AN-8097) Lillenas.

Praise Bible: 52 Stories for Enjoying God's Goodness & Greatness. Mack Thomas. LC 99-215992. (Illus.). 464p. (J). (ps-2). 1998. 15.95 (1-57856-037-3) Waterbrook Pr.

Praise Classic, Vol. 1. 1988. 11.95 (0-943026-14-8) Carothers.

Praise Disjoined: Changing Patterns of Salvation in 17th-Century English Literature. William P. Shaw. LC 90-19214. (Seventeenth-Century Texts & Studies: Vol. 2). X, 306p. (C). 1991. text 50.95 (0-8204-1460-3) P Lang Pubng.

Praise-Easy Arrangements for Piano & Organ see Alabadle-Arreglos Faciles para el Teclado

Praise Every Morning: Intermediate-Advanced Level. Laurindo Almeida. 40p. 1996. pap. 19.95 incl. audio compact disk (0-7866-2100-1, 95983BCD) Mel Bay.

Praise Favorite I: For Worship. Evan Chen. 150p. 1991. pap. 5.75 (0-9631789-0-3) Evan Formosan.

Praise God. Gunvor Edwards & Joan Brown. 56p. 1994. pap. 4.95 (0-8146-2327-1) Liturgical Pr.

***Praise God with All Creation: A Book of Prayer for Morning & Evening.** Michael Kwatera. LC 99-86151. 72p. 2000. pap. 11.95 (0-89390-504-6) Resource Pubns.

***Praise Guitar Made Easy: Learning to Play Guitar for the Glory of God.** Steve Turley. 84p. 1999. pap. write for info. (0-9671749-0-2) Fretboard Fellow.

***Praise Her in the Gates: The Calling of Christian Motherhood.** Nancy Wilson. LC 00-9453. 2000. write for info. (1-885767-70-6) Canon Pr.

Praise Him. Ruled. 1997. 7.98 (0-7824-7906-5) Antioch Pub Co.

Praise Him. Les Sussman. LC 98-9600. 192p. 1998. text 19.95 (0-312-18653-3) St Martin.

***Praise Him! Christian Music Stars Share Their Favorite Verses from the Scriptures.** Lee Sussman. 192p. (Orig.). 1999. pap. 11.00 (0-425-16867-0) Berkley Pub.

Praise Him: Psalm Selections for Singing. 170p. 1987. spiral bd. 8.00 (1-884527-03-5) Crown & Covenant.

Praise His Holy Name. Don Szobodi. 1998. pap. write for info. (1-57553-919-5) Watermrk Pr.

Praise His Holy Names. 1992. 1.25 (0-8341-9012-5) Nazarene.

Praise in Crisis see Crisis en la Alabanza

Praise in Many Colors. 1996. pap. 9.99 (0-8341-9564-X, MB-752) Lillenas.

Praise in St. Augustine: Readings & Reflections. John M. Quinn. 220p. 1987. pap. 8.95 (0-8158-0430-X) Chris Mass.

Praise in "The Faerie Queene" Thomas H. Cain. LC 78-8962. 245p. reprint ed. pap. 76.00 (0-7837-0227-2, 204053500017) Bks Demand.

***Praise Islands.** John J. Slevkoff. (Illus.). 46p. 1999. pap. 19.95 (0-9675173-0-3) Praise Islands.

Praise Jerusalem! Augusta Trobaugh. LC 96-52628. (Literary Fiction Ser.). 288p. (gr. 10 up). 1998. pap. 12.99 (0-8010-5814-7) Baker Bks.

Praise, My Soul, the King of Heaven. 1994. pap. 1.30 (0-8341-9069-9, AN-2641) Lillenas.

Praise of Folie by Sir Thomas Chaloner. Ed. by C. H. Miller. (EETS Original Ser.: Vol. 257). 1965. 30.00 (0-19-722257-9, Pub. by EETS) Boydell & Brewer.

Praise of Folly. Desiderius Erasmus. Ed. by Leonard F. Dean. (University Classics Ser.). 182p. 1983. pap. 10.95 (0-87532-105-4) Hendricks House.

Praise of Folly. Desiderius Erasmus. Tr. by John Wilson. LC 94-5475. (Great Minds Ser.). 196p. (C). 1994. pap. 9.95 (0-87975-885-6) Prometheus Bks.

Praise of Folly. Desiderius Erasmus. LC 78-13575. 184p. 1979. pap. 13.00 (0-300-02373-1) Yale U Pr.

Praise of Folly. Desiderius Erasmus. 160p. 1958. pap. text 14.95 (0-472-06023-6, 06023, Ann Arbor Bks) U of Mich Pr.

Praise of Folly: And, Letter to Maarten Van Dorp, 1515. Desiderius Erasmus. Tr. by Betty Radice. LC 94-142502. 256p. 1994. pap. 10.95 (0-14-044608-7, Penguin Classics) Viking Penguin.

Praise of Folly: And Other Papers. Bliss Perry. (BCL1-PS American Literature Ser.). 230p. 1992. reprint ed. lib. bdg. 79.00 (0-7812-6829-X) Rprt Serv.

Praise of Folly & Other Writings: A New Translation with Critical Commentary. Desiderius Erasmus. Tr. by Robert M. Adams. 340p. (C). 1989. pap. text 12.50 (0-393-95749-7) Norton.

Praise of Lincoln. Ed. by A. Dallas Williams. LC 77-108590. (Granger Index Reprint Ser.). 1977. 21.95 (0-8369-6118-8) Ayer.

Praise of "Sons of Bitches" James V. Schall. (C). 1988. 39.00 (0-85439-145-2, Pub. by St Paul Pubns) St Mut.

Praise of the Needle: John Taylor's Poem of 1631. John Taylor. Ed. & Intro. by Kathleen A. Epstein. 58p. (Orig.). 1995. pap. 7.95 (0-9633331-6-X) Curious Works.

Praise of Theory: Speeches & Essays. Hans-Georg Gadamer. Tr. by Chris Dawson. LC 98-7115. (Yale Studies in Hermeneutics). 256p. 1998. 30.00 (0-300-07310-0) Yale U Pr.

Praise Past Due: A Memoir of Richard Ellis, Designer & Printer, 1894-1982. Frank G. Harrington. 80p. 1991. 45.00 (0-930126-34-3) Typographeum.

Praise Poems: The Katherine White Collection. Pamela McClusky. LC 83-51840. (Illus.). 122p. 1984. 34.95 (0-932216-16-1); pap. 22.95 (0-932216-15-3) Seattle Art.

Praise Poems: The Katherine White Collection. Pamela McClusky. LC 83-51840. (Illus.). xiv, 122p. 1993. pap. 20.00 (0-226-73446-3, 73446-3) U Ch Pr.

Praise Poems: The Katherine White Collection. Pamela McClusky. LC 83-51840. (Illus.). xiv, 134p. 1997. 54.00 (0-226-73445-5, 73445-5) U Ch Pr.

***Praise Prayers, 1.** James S Yagow. 1999. 10.00 (0-570-05572-5) Concordia.

Praise Releases Faith. Terry Law. 252p. (Orig.). 1987. pap. 9.99 (0-932081-15-0) Victory Hse.

Praise Songs. Dianne Tittle-deLaet. Vol. 1. 80p. (Orig.). 1987. pap. text. write for info. (0-318-62270-X) Arete.

Praise the Bridge That Carries You Over: The Life of Joseph Sutton. Shepard Krech, 3rd. 238p. 1981. pap. text 18.95 (0-87073-650-7) Schenkman Bks Inc.

Praise the Day: Visionary Poems & Paintings. A. Whitwell. 1994. pap. 22.95 (1-85230-467-7, Pub. by Element MA) Penguin Putnam.

Praise the High Grass. Peter Carlos. 1977. 1.50 (0-918476-01-1) Cornerstone Pr.

Praise the Lord: Litanies, Prayers & Occasional Services. Gennifer B. Brooks. LC 96-10672. (Orig.). 1996. pap. 12.75 (0-7880-0851-X) CSS OH.

Praise the Lord & Rub It Out. Ralph Gross. (Illus.). 30p. (Orig.). (C). 1981. pap. 5.00 (0-686-32010-7) Karma Pub.

Praise the Lord Anyway. Frances Hunter. 1978. reprint ed. pap. 4.95 (0-87162-131-2) Hunter Bks.

Praise the Lord with Bells, Bk. I. Nikki Bronstein. 31p. (J). (gr. k-7). 1992. spiral bd. 15.00 (1-880892-14-6) Com Sense FL.

Praise the Lord with Bells, Bk. II. Nikki Bronstein. 38p. (J). (gr. k-7). 1992. spiral bd. 15.00 (1-880892-15-4) Com Sense FL.

Praise, the Ultimate Experience: Worship, The Ultimate Relationship. Rod Parsley & Clint Brown. 124p. (Orig.). 1992. pap. 7.99 (1-880244-10-1) Wrld Harvest Church.

Praise to the Man. Larry Barkdull. LC 97-39831. viii, 134p. 1997. pap. 6.95 (1-57345-320-X) Deseret Bk.

Praise with Understanding. David Wright & Jill Wright. 64p. 1983. pap. 4.95 (0-85364-355-5, Pub. by Paternoster Pub) McClelland & Stewart.

Praise Works. Merlin R. Carothers. 161p. (Orig.). 1973. pap. 6.95 (0-943026-06-7) Carothers.

Praise! Worship! Ed. by Dave Anderson. (Other Choices Ser.). 66p. 1990. pap. 5.00 (0-9628303-1-3) Fellow Minist.

Praise Ye the Lord: Haiku Written to Psalm 148. Lesley Einer. 15p. (Orig.). 1988. pap. 3.50 (0-9620822-0-1) Sage Shadow Pr.

Praises. Elizabeth Jennings. LC 99-196456. 64p. 1999. pap. 14.95 (1-85754-399-8, Pub. by Carcanet Pr) Paul & Co Pubs.

Praises: Three Decades of Inspirational Song 27 Stirring Classics & Exciting New Standards. Des. by Tom Fettke. 1994. suppl. ed. 350.00 (0-614-01704-1, OR-9177) Lillenas.

Praises for All Seasons: The Hymns of James Quinn, SJ. James Quinn. 124p. 1995. pap. text 12.00 (0-9622553-8-6, 125-408) Selah Pub Co.

Praises for the King of Kings. Walter J. Chantry. 114p. (Orig.). 1991. pap. 5.99 (0-85151-587-8) Banner of Truth.

Praises of Dingana. Ed. by D. K. Rycroft & A. B. Ngcobo. (Killie Campbell Africana Library Publication). (Illus.). 272p. 1988. 23.00 (0-86980-629-7, Pub. by Univ Natal Pr) Intl Spec Bk.

Praises to a Formless God: Nirguni Texts from North India. David N. Lorenzen. LC 95-20931. (SUNY Series in Religious Studies). 303p. (C). 1996. text 49.50 (0-7914-2805-2); pap. text 16.95 (0-7914-2806-0) State U NY Pr.

Praises We Sing. Elmina Yoder & Lula Miller. 1980. pap. 6.95 (0-87813-515-4) Christian Light.

Praisesong for the Widow. Paule Marshall. (Contemporary Fiction Ser.). 256p. 1984. pap. 12.95 (0-452-26711-0, Plume) Dutton Plume.

Praisesong of Survival: Lectures & Essays, 1957-89. Richard K. Barksdale. 280p. (C). 1992. text 45.00 (0-252-01898-2); pap. text 18.95 (0-252-06286-8) U of Ill Pr.

Praising God: The Trinity in Christian Worship. Ruth C. Duck et al. LC 99-22981. 224p. 1999. pap. 22.00 (0-664-25777-1) Westminster John Knox.

***Praising God in Carmel: Studies in Carmelite Liturgy** James John Boyce. LC 99-21601. 1999. write for info. (0-9656910-1-2) Carmelite Inst.

Praising in Black & White: Unity & Diversity in Christian Worship. Brenda E. Aghahowa. LC 96-34339. 232p. (Orig.). 1996. pap. 16.95 (0-8298-1134-6) Pilgrim OH.

Praising the Lord. N. A. Woychuk. (Service Adult Ser.: Memory Bk. 2). (Illus.). 164p. (Orig.). 1980. pap. 5.00 (1-880960-14-1) Script Memory Fl.

Praising the Lord Through Poetry. Ruth Gibbons. 28p. 1988. pap. text 4.00 (0-935369-14-7) In Tradition Pub.

Prajapati & the Year. J. Gonda. (Verhandelingen der Koninklijke Nederlandse Akademie van Wetenschappen, Afd. Letterkunde, Nieuwe Reeks Ser.: No. 123). 100p. 1984. pap. 40.75 (0-444-85594-7) Elsevier.

Prajapati's Relations with Brahman, Brhaspati & Brahma. J. Gonda. (Verhandelingen der Koninklijke Nederlandse Akademie van Wetenschappen, Afd. Letterkunde, Nieuwe Reeks Ser.: No. 138). 78p. 1989. pap. 47.00 (0-444-85695-1) Elsevier.

Prajapati's Rise to Higher Rank. Jan Gonda. (Orientalia Rheno-Traiectina Ser.: Vol. 21). x, 208p. 1986. 116.00 (90-04-07734-0) Brill Academic Pubs.

Prajnaparamita: The Six Perfections. 2nd ed. Venerable Khenpo Palden Sherab Rinpoche. Ed. by Joan Kaye. Tr. by Venerable Khenpo Tsewang Dongyal Rinpoche from TIB. (Illus.). 106p. (Orig.). (C). 1991. reprint ed. pap. 15.00 (1-880975-00-9) Sky Dancer Pr.

Prajnaparamita & Related Systems: Studies in Honor of Edward Conze. Ed. by Luis O. Gomez & Lewis R. Lancaster. (Berkeley Buddhist Studies). xvi, 451p. 1977. 20.00 (0-87725-311-0) U of Cal IAS.

Prajnaparamita in Tibetan Buddhism. Ed. by Harcharan S. Sobti. (C). 1988. 35.00 (81-85132-05-4) S Asia.

***Prajnaparamitra in Tibetan Buddhism.** E. Obermiller. LC 99-939907. 1998. 21.00 (81-86230-13-0, Pub. by Paljor Pubns) S Asia.

Prakashika. Ahmad Nawaz. LC 98-70826. (BEN.). xiv, 102p. 1998. pap. 10.00 (1-58225-144-4) Ananta Prakashani.

Prakrit Dhammapada. Suttapitaka. LC 78-70127. reprint ed. 31.50 (0-404-17386-1) AMS Pr.

Prakriti: Your Ayurvedic Constitution. 2nd rev. ed. Robert E. Suoboda. Ed. by Margaret Mahan & John Clancy. (Illus.). 208p. 1988. pap. 15.00 (0-9656208-3-2, Pub. by Sadhana Pubns) Lotus Pr.

Prakrti the Integral Vision Vol. 1: Primal Elements the Oral Tradition. Ed. by Kapila Vatsyayan & Baidyanath Saraswati. 1995. 52.00 (81-246-0037-6, Pub. by DK Pubs Ind) S Asia.

Prakrti the Integral Vision Vol. 2: Vedic, Buddhist, & Jain Traditions. Ed. by Kapila Vatsyayan & Sampat Narayanan. (C). 1995. 52.00 (81-246-0038-4, Pub. by DK Pubs Ind) S Asia.

Prakrti the Integral Vision Vol. 4: Agamic Tradition & the Arts. Ed. by Kapila Vatsyayan & Bettina Baumer. (C). 1995. 52.00 (81-246-0039-2, Pub. by DK Pubs Ind) S Asia.

Prakrti the Integral Vision Vol. 4: Nature of Matter. Ed. by Kapila Vatsyayan & Jayant V. Narlikar. (C). 1995. 52.00 (81-246-0040-6, Pub. by DK Pubs Ind) S Asia.

Prakrti the Integral Vision Vol. 5: Man in Nature. Ed. by Kapila Vatsyayan & Baidyanath Saraswati. (C). 1995. 52.00 (81-246-0041-4, Pub. by DK Pubs Ind) S Asia.

Prakruti: Your Ayurvedic Constitution. Robert E. Svoboda. (Illus.). 206p. (Orig.). 1988. pap. 12.00 (0-945669-00-3) Geocom Ltd.

Prakticheskaia Metodika Prepodavaniia Russkogo Iazyka Dlia Nachinaiushchikh Prepodavatelei. Serafima Gettys.Tr. of Learning to Teach Russian: Effective Classroom Techniques. (RUS.). 189p. (C). 1998. pap. text 15.00 (1-57201-051-7) Berkeley Slavic.

Prakticheskoe Rukovodstvo K Lecheniiu Golodom. Lew Strogat, pseud. LC 92-72887.Tr. of Practical Management of Therapeutic Fasting. (RUS.). 64p. (Orig.). 1992. pap. 10.00 (0-911971-71-8) Effect Pub.

Prakticka Laska: Minibook. Vladimir Uhri. (SLO.). 26p. 1996. 1.25 (1-56983-023-1) New Creat WI.

Prakticka Slovencina (Practical Slovak) J. Mistrik et al. (SLO.). 290p. 1997. pap. write for info. (80-08-02402-X, Pub. by Slov Pegagog Naklad) IBD Ltd.

Praktiese Boedelbeplanning. P. A. Olivier & G. P. Van Den Berg. 307p. 1991. pap. write for info. (0-7021-2623-3, Pub. by Juta & Co) Gaunt.

Praktikos & Chapters on Prayer. Tr. by John E. Bamberger from GRE. LC 76-152483. (Cistercian Studies: No. 4). xciv, 88p. 1972. pap. 6.95 (0-87907-904-5) Cistercian Pubns.

Praktische Anleitung Zur Interpretation Von Dichtung. Doris F. Merrifield. LC 81-40127. 246p. (Orig.). 1982. pap. text 21.50 (0-8191-2054-5) U Pr of Amer.

Praktische Ansatze Zur Verwirklichung Einer Umweltgerechten Landnutzung: Beispiele fur Eine Konstruktive Zusammenarbeit Zwischen Angewandter Forschung, Beratung und Praxis in den Landkreisen Schmalkalden-Meiningen (Thuringen), Saalkreis (Sachsen-Anhalt) und Ausgewahlten Vergleichsregionen in Hessen. Ed. by Karlheinz Knickel & Hermann Priebe. (Illus.). XXVI, 298p. 1997. pap. 57.95 (3-631-31553-8) P Lang Pubng.

Praktische Aspekte der Onkologie. Ed. by U. R. Kleeberg. (Journal: Onkologie: Vol. 7, Suppl. 1). (Illus.). 64p. 1984. pap. 77.50 (3-8055-3918-5) S Karger.

Praktische Handreichung Fur Fremdsprachenlehrer: Zweite, Verbesserte und Erweiterte Auflage Unter Mitarbeit von Heidrun Jung. 2nd ed. Udo O. Jung. (Bayreuther Beitrage zur Glottodidaktik Ser.: Bd. 2). (GER., Illus.). VIII, 456p. 1998. 67.95 (3-631-31499-X) P Lang Pubng.

Praktische Lexikon der Naturheilkunde: Practical Lexicon of Natural Healing. Ernst Meyer-Camberg. (GER.). 1977. pap. 45.00 (0-8288-5514-5, M7594) Fr & Eur.

Praktische Methode der Vovi Kontemplation. Luong Si Hang. Ed. by Mai Nguyen et al. Tr. by Hua Bach Mai from ENG. (GER., Illus.). 76p. (Orig.). 1993. pap. 5.00 (0-9633690-2-4) VoVi LED.

Praktische Neonatologie. Ed. by E. Bossi. (Paediatrische Fortbildungskurse fuer die Praxis Ser.: Vol. 57). (Illus.). xii, 208p. 1983. pap. 85.25 (3-8055-3657-7) S Karger.

Praktische Rationalitaet: Grundlagenprobleme und Ethische Anwendungen Des Rational Choice-Paradigmas. Ed. by Julian Nida-Ruemelin. (Perspektiven der Analytischen Philosophie - Perspectives in Analytical Philosophy Ser.: No. 2). (GER.). viii, 458p. 1993. lib. bdg. 167.70 (3-11-013656-2) De Gruyter.

Praktische Statistik Fuer Meteorologen und Geowissenschaftler. C. D. Schoenwiese. vi, 231p. 1992. 20.00 (3-443-01029-6, Pub. by Gebruder Borntraeger) Balogh.

Praktischer Leitfaden fuer die Therapeutische Anwendung von Cefotiam. Ed. by H. C. Neu & L. D. Sabath. (Pharmanual Ser.: Vol. 3). (Illus.). vi, 182p. 1983. pap. 48.75 (3-8055-3694-1) S Karger.

Praktisches Woerterbuch der Musik, Italian-English-German-French. Roberto Braccini. (ENG, GER & ITA.). 65.00 (0-7859-6943-8) Fr & Eur.

Praktrti in Samkhya-Yoga: Material Principle, Religious Experience, Ethical Implications. Knut A. Jacobsen. LC 96-32937. (Asian Thought & Culture Ser.: Vol. 7). XV, 427p. (C). 1999. 67.95 (0-8204-3465-5) P Lang Pubng.

Praktykshandleiding Oor Die Invordering van Skuld. M. De Jong & J. C. Du Plessis. (AFR.). 384p. 1995. pap. write for info. (0-409-02277-2, MICHIE) LEXIS Pub.

Pralekhan aur Abhivechan. 2nd ed. Ed. by Murli Manohar. (HIN.). (C). 1991. 95.00 (0-7855-5609-5) St Mut.

***Pralingual Gehorlose Im Alter.** Wilhelm Koch-Bode. 145p. 1999. 28.95 (3-631-34451-1) P Lang Pubng.

***Prallel Solution of Partial Differential Equation.** Ed. by P. Bjorstad & M. Luskin. (IMA Volumes in Mathematics & Its Applications Ser.: Vol. 120). (Illus.). 316p. 2000. 79.95 (0-387-95008-7) Spr-Verlag.

Pramanavarttika of Dharmakirti (with Dharmaakirti's Own Commentary on the Third Chapter & Manorathanandin's Commentary on the Entire Text. Ed. by R. C. Pandeya. (C). 1989. 42.00 (81-208-0546-1, Pub. by Motilal Bnarsidass) S Asia.

Pran Swen Ko Ou: Public Health Information in Haitian Creole. Maude Heurtelou, Ed. by Fequiere Vilsaint. (Illus.). 82p. Date not set. pap. 12.00 (1-881839-40-0) Educa Vision.

Prana: The Secret of Yogic Healing. Atreya. LC 96-15586. (Illus.). 176p. (Orig.). 1996. pap. 12.95 (0-87728-885-2) Weiser.

Prancer. Stephen Cosgrove. LC 89-83843. (Illus.). 32p. (J). (gr. k-7). 1990. 14.95 (1-55868-019-5); pap. 12.95 incl. audio (1-55868-041-1) Gr Arts Ctr Pub.

Prances: Poems from Hollywood. Mark Dunster. 24p. (Orig.). 1997. pap. 5.00 (0-89642-363-8) Linden Pubs.

Prancing Through the Zodiac Calendar - Almanac - Directory. Stacey Dean. (Illus.). 50p. (C). 1989. pap. text 9.99 (0-317-93882-7) MY Las Vegas.

Praneshacharya's Dilemma. Marilyn Turkovich. (Passages to India Ser.). (C). 1989. spiral bd. 20.00 (1-56709-016-8) Indep Broadcast.

Pranks. Steve Kowit. (Bloody Twin Press Ser.). (Illus.). 24p. (Orig.). 1990. pap. 25.00 (1-886350-34-5) Bloody Twin Pr.

Pranks! Ed. by Vale Vale. (RE-Search Ser.: Vol. 11). (Illus.). 240p. (Orig.). 1987. pap. 19.99 (0-9650469-8-2) RE Search.

Pranks 'An Enlightenment of Frank 'An Me. Robert Wolley. (Illus.). 212p. 1997. 16.95 (1-884707-49-1) Lifestyles.

Pranksters. Dennis Alexander. 4p. 1990. pap. 1.95 (0-7390-0875-7, 3673) Alfred Pub.

Prankster's Ultimate Handbook. Erik L. Buckman. (Illus.). 103p. 1996. pap. 13.95 (0-9656356-0-0) E L Buckman.

Prankster's Ultimate Handbook. Erik L. Buckman. (Illus.). 140p. 1996. pap. 13.95 (0-9656356-1-9) E L Buckman.

Prarieblomman: The Prairie Blossoms for An Immigrant's Daughter. Linda K. Hubalek. LC 94-74376. (Butter in the Well Ser.: Bk. 2). (Illus.). 144p. 1994. reprint ed. pap. 9.95 (1-886652-01-5) Butterfld Bks.

***Prarthana: Songs of Sirla Narottama Dasa Thakura Mahasaya.** (Illus.). 164p. 1999. pap. 12.95 (0-9653858-9-2, Pub. by Mandala Pub Grp) Words Distrib.

Prasanta Chandra Mahalanobis: A Biography. Ashok Rudra. LC 96-906245. (Illus.). 510p. (C). 1997. 45.00 (0-19-563679-1) OUP.

Prasanthi Vahini (Writings on Divine Peace) Sathya Sai Baba. 1986. pap. 2.00 (1-57836-065-X, BA-307) Sathya Sai Bk Ctr.

Prasenzwirkung: Heilung Durch Kontakt see History of Energy Transference: Exploring the Foundations of Modern Healing

Prash & Ras. N. D. Williams. 192p. 1997. pap. 12.95 (1-900715-00-7, Pub. by Peepal Tree Pr) Paul & Co Pubs.

Prashad Cooking with Indian Masters. J. Inder Kalra & Pradeep Das Gupta. 1986. 18.00 (81-7023-006-3, Pub. by Allied Pubs) S Asia.

Prasna Marga, Pt. 2. Bangalore V. Raman. (ENG & SAN.). (C). 1992. text 17.50 (81-208-1034-1, Pub. by Motilal Bnarsidass); pap. text 11.50 (81-208-1035-X, Pub. by Motilal Bnarsidass) S Asia.

Prasna Marga, Part 1: English Translation with Original Text in Devanagri & Notes. Bangalore V. Raman. (C). 1991. reprint ed. 12.50 (81-208-0918-1, Pub. by Motilal Bnarsidass); reprint ed. 12.52 (81-208-0914-9, Pub. by Motilal Bnarsidass) S Asia.

***Prasna Upanisad: With the Original Text in Sanskrit & Roman Transliteration.** Narayana Prasad. LC 99-936802. 1999. pap. 14.00 (81-246-0129-1, Pub. by D K Printwrld) S Asia.

P

An Asterisk (*) at the beginning of an entry indicates that the title is appearing for the first time.

Prasnopanisad. Tr. by Swami Sarvananda from SAN. (Upanishads with Shankara's Commentary Ser.). 104p. (C). 1979. pap. 2.00 (*0-87481-204-6*, Pub. by Advaita Ashrama) Vedanta Pr.

Prasnothara Vahini (Stream of Questions & Answers) Sathya Sai Baba. 1983. pap. 2.00 (*1-57836-066-8*, BA-308) Sathya Sai Bk Ctr.

Prat la Grammaire Intereractive. 2nd ed. Favrod. (C). 1999. pap. text. write for info. (*0-201-65423-7*) Addison-Wesley.

Prateechi: A Literary Digest of West Indian Languages 1987. Ed. by Suresh Dalal. (C). 1992. pap. text 10.00 (*81-7201-089-3*, Pub. by National Sahitya Akademi) S Asia.

Prater-Prather, Genealogy & History, 2 vols. John W. Prather, Jr. Incl. Vol. I. Praters in Wiltshire, 1480-1670. (Illus.). 215p. 1987. 30.00 (*0-9619434-1-6*); Vol. II. Prator, Prather, Prator, Praytor, in America, 1620-1800: 1-5 Generations. LC 88-129646. 489p. 1994. 50.00 (*0-9619434-2-4*); 80.00 (*0-9619434-0-8*) J W Prather.

Prater the Prairie Dog. Dave Sargent & Pat Sargent. LC 97-27203. (Illus.). (J). 1998. write for info. (*1-56763-384-6*); pap. write for info. (*1-56763-385-4*) Ozark Pub.

Prater Violet: A Novel. Christopher Isherwood. LC 87-8610. (Michael di Capua Bks.). 4494p. 1987. pap. 10.00 (*0-374-52053-4*) FS&G.

Praters in Wiltshire, 1480-1670 see Prater-Prather, Genealogy & History

Pratice Workbook for Mathematics Today Level 4. Abbott. 1987. pap., student ed. 11.25 (*0-15-350064-6*) Harcourt Schl Pubs.

Pratidanam, Indian, Iranian & Indo-European Studies Presented to Franciscus Bernardus Jacobus Kuiper on His 60th Birthday. J. C. Heesterman et al. (Janua Linguarum, Ser. Major: No. 34). 1968. text 149.35 (*90-279-0686-6*) Mouton.

Pratioue du Neerlandais: Intermediate Dutch for French Speakers. Assimil Staff. (DUT & FRE.). 28.95 (*0-8288-4489-5*, M11925) Fr & Eur.

Pratique de la grammaire see Basic French

Pratique de la Grammaire, Niveau Intermediaire 1. Simonne Venisse-Fam. (C). 1996. pap. text 15.46 (*0-201-83602-5*) Addison-Wesley.

Pratique De La Lecture. 2nd ed. Favrod Walker. (C). 2000. pap. text. write for info. (*0-201-65422-9*) Addison-Wesley.

Pratique de la Lecture, Niveau Intermediaire 1. Muriel Walker. (FRE.). (C). 1996. pap. text 15.46 (*0-201-83663-7*) Addison-Wesley.

Pratique de la Lecture, Niveau Intermediaire 2: High/Intermediate Reading Skills. David Walker & Muriel Walker. (FRE.). (C). 1996. pap. text 15.46 (*0-201-83620-3*) Addison-Wesley.

Pratique de l'Ecriture: Niveau Intermediaire 2. Diane B. Woody. (C). 1996. pap. text 15.46 (*0-201-83601-7*) Addison-Wesley.

Pratique du Francais de A a Z. Benedicte Gaillard. (FRE.). 384p. 1995. pap. 24.95 (*2-218-05496-5*, Pub. by Ed Hatier) Hatier Pub.

Pratique la Correction Ecrite. Favrod. (C). 1997. pap. text. write for info. (*0-201-68132-3*) Addison-Wesley.

***Pratique, Pratique: Manuel de Conversation Guidee.** L. Gary Lambert. 256p. 1999. pap. 34.50 (*0-7618-1468-X*) U Pr of Amer.

Pratiques Culturelles. Ed. by Jean Carduner. LC 81-50963. (Michigan Romance Studies: Vol. 3). 188p. 1983. pap. 15.00 (*0-939730-02-2*) Mich Romance.

Pratiques de Gestion des Ressources Naturelles, Avantages et Inconvenients des Regimes Fonciers dans le Bassin Versant de Diafore, Fouta Djallon, Guinee. Julie E. Fischer et al. (Research Paper Ser.: Vol. 122-F). (Illus.). xii, 66p. (C). 1995. pap. 7.00 (*0-934519-35-8*, RP122-F) U of Wis Land.

Pratiques et Methodes (1911-1971) see Historie Mondiale de L'architecture et de L'urbanisme Modernes

Pratiques Sociales et Mediations Symboliques. Ed. by Michele Grossen & Bernard Py. (Sciences pour la Communication Ser.: Vol. 50). (FRE.). 265p. 1997. 46.95 (*3-906758-04-4*, Pub. by P Lang) P Lang Pubng.

Prator, Prather, Prator, Praytor, in America, 1620-1800: 1-5 Generations see Prater-Prather, Genealogy & History

Pratt & Kulsrud Tax Series: Corporate, Partnership, Estate & Gift Taxation - 1999 Edition. Pratt et al. 1998. 78.95 (*0-87393-755-4*) Dame Pubns.

Pratt & Kulsrud Tax Series: Corporate, Partnership, Estate & Gift Taxation - 1999 Edition (Study Guide) Pratt et al. 1998. pap., student ed. 24.95 (*0-87393-771-6*) Dame Pubns.

Pratt & Kulsrud Tax Series: Corporate, Partnership, Estate & Gift Taxation - 2000 Edition. Ed. by Pratt & Kulsrud. 1999. 78.95 (*0-87393-858-5*); pap., student ed. 24.95 (*0-87393-859-3*) Dame Pubns.

Pratt & Kulsrud Tax Series: Federal Taxation. Ed. by Pratt & Kulsrud. 1999. 80.95 (*0-87393-850-X*); pap., student ed. 24.95 (*0-87393-851-8*) Dame Pubns.

Pratt & Kulsrud Tax Series: Federal Taxation - 1999 Edition. Pratt et al. 1998. 80.95 (*0-87393-753-8*) Dame Pubns.

Pratt & Kulsrud Tax Series: Federal Taxation - 1999 Edition (Study Guide) Pratt et al. 1998. pap., student ed. 24.95 (*0-87393-772-4*) Dame Pubns.

Pratt & Kulsrud Tax Series: Individual Taxation - 1999 Edition. Pratt et al. 1998. 77.95 (*0-87393-754-6*) Dame Pubns.

Pratt & Kulsrud Tax Series: Individual Taxation - 1999 Edition (Study Guide) Pratt et al. 1998. pap., student ed. 23.95 (*0-87393-770-8*) Dame Pubns.

Pratt & Kulsrud Tax Seriesd: Individual Taxation - 2000 Edition. Ed. by Pratt & Kulsrud. 1999. 77.95 (*0-87393-854-2*); pap., student ed. 23.95 (*0-87393-855-0*) Dame Pubns.

Pratt & Whitney Gear-Shaving Process. H. D. Tanner. (Technical Papers: Vol. P35). (Illus.). 6p. 1928. pap. text 30.00 (*1-55589-219-1*) AGMA.

Pratt Creative Arts Therapy Review, Vol. 17. Pratt Institute Art Therapy Staff & Auther Robins. (Illus.). 100p. 1997. pap. 8.00 (*0-614-31246-9*) Pratt Inst.

Pratt Families of Virginia. William N. Hurley, Jr. LC 96-228064. (Illus.). 320p. (Orig.). 1996. pap. 28.00 (*0-7884-0512-8*, H871) Heritage Bk.

Pratt Family: or the Descendants of Lt. William Pratt One of the First Settlers of Hartford & Saybrook; with Genealogical Notes of John of Hartford, Peter of Lyme, & John Pratt. F. W. Chapman. (Illus.). 421p. 1989. reprint ed. pap. 63.00 (*0-8328-0985-3*); reprint ed. lib. bdg. 71.00 (*0-8328-0984-5*) Higginson Bk Co.

Pratt Institute Creative Arts Therapy Review, Vol. 16. Ed. by Arthur Robbins. (Orig.). 1995. pap. text 8.00 (*1-884870-01-5*) Pratt Inst.

Pratt Institute Creative Arts Therapy Review, Vol. 17. Ed. by Arthur Robbins. (Illus.). (Orig.). 1997. pap. text 8.00 (*1-884870-02-3*) Pratt Inst.

Pratt Portraits. Anna Fuller. LC 79-94725. (Short Story Index Reprint Ser.). 1977. 21.95 (*0-8369-3104-1*) Ayer.

Pratt Ware. John Lewis & Griselda Lewis. (Album Ser.: No. 296). (Illus.). 32p. (C). 1989. pap. 4.75 (*0-7478-0220-3*, Pub. by Shire Pubns) Parkwest Pubns.

Pratt Ware, 1780-1840: English & Scottish Relief Decorated & Underglaze Coloured Earthenware, 1780-1840. John Lewis & Griselda Lewis. (Illus.). 320p. 1993. 69.50 (*1-85149-191-0*) Antique Collect.

Pratt's Guide to Venture Capital Sources. 18th ed. Ed. by Daniel Bokser & Ted Weissberg. 900p. 1996. 295.00 (*0-914470-70-1*) Venture Econ.

Pratt's Guide to Venture Capital Sources, 1997. 21st ed. Daniel Bokser. 968p. 1997. 325.00 (*0-914470-84-1*) SD Pub.

***Pratt's Guide to Venture Capital Sources 1999.** 23rd ed. Stanley E. Pratt. 1999. 385.00 (*0-914470-97-3*) Venture Econ.

Pratt's Landing. Martha Kirkland. 272p. 1997. mass mkt. 5.99 (*0-515-12180-0*, Jove) Berkley Pub.

Prattsburgh Correspondence. Ruth M. Kempher. (Illus.). 103p. 1993. pap. 15.95 (*0-9637483-0-0*) Kings Estate.

Pratyutpanna Samadhi Sutra/The Surangama Samadhi Sutra. Numata Center for Buddhist Translation & Research. Ed. by Mayeda Sengaku & Kenneth Inada. Tr. by Paul Harrison & John McRae from CHI. LC 97-69169. (BDK English Tripitaka Ser.: Vol. 25-II, III). 288p. (C). 1998. text 35.00 (*1-886439-06-0*) Numata Ctr.

Praugasastra. J. Gonda. (Mededelingen der Koninklijke Nederlandse Akademie van Wetenschappen, Afd. Letterkunde Ser.: No. 44(3)). 82p. 1981. pap. 28.25 (*0-444-85523-8*) Elsevier.

Pravargya Brahmana of the Taittiriya Aranyaka: An Ancient Commentary on the Pravargya Ritual. Ed. by Jan E. M. Houben. (C). 1991. 15.00 (*81-208-0868-1*, Pub. by Motilal Bnarsidass) S Asia.

Pravatica. Ahmad Nawaz. LC 98-70827. (BEN.). xiv, 115p. 1998. pap. 10.00 (*1-58225-145-2*) Ananta Prakashani.

Pravda: A Fleet Street Comedy. Howard Brenton & David Hare. (Methuen Modern Plays Ser.). 113p. (Orig.). (C). 1988. pap. 9.95 (*0-413-58480-1*, A0228) Heinemann.

***Pravention Von Lese- Und Rechtschreiswierigkeiten: Evaluation Einer Vorschulischen Forderung der Phonologischen Bewusstheit und der Buchstaenkenntnis.** Ellen Rothenberg. (Europaische Hochschulschriften Ser.). (Illus.). 288p. 1999. 48.95 (*3-631-34145-8*) P Lang Pubng.

Pravidla Slovenskej Vyslovnosti. Kral. (SLO.). 632p. 1996. write for info. (*80-08-00305-7*, Pub. by Slov Pegagog Naklad) IBD Ltd.

Pravo Na Blizost. Vladimir Isaev. LC 93-49678. (RUS.). 252p. (Orig.). 1994. pap. 7.00 (*0-916201-15-5*) M I P Co.

Pravoslavie see Orthodox Church

Pravoslavije, Rimo-Katolichestvo, Protenstatizm i Sektantstvo. Mitrophan Znoskovo-Borovsky.Tr. of Orthodoxy, Roman-Catholicism, Protenstatism & Sectarianism. 156p. 1972. pap. text 5.00 (*0-317-30254-X*) Holy Trinity.

Pravoslavno-Khristijanskaja Apologetika. I. M. Andreyev.Tr. of Orthodox-Christian Apologetics. 92p. 1965. pap. text 5.00 (*0-317-30249-3*) Holy Trinity.

Pravoslavno-Khristijanskoe Nravstvennoje Bogoslovije. I. M. Andreyev.Tr. of Orthodox-Christian Moral Theology. 148p. 1966. pap. text 5.00 (*0-317-30264-7*) Holy Trinity.

Pravoslavnoe Dogmaticheskoe Bogoslovie see Theologie Dogmatique Orthodoxe - Expose Concis (Orthodox Dogmatic Theology - A Concise Exposition)

Prawn Ascot: A Pawn in Aspic. Charles E. Gould, Jr. (Illus.). 8p. (Orig.). 1987. pap. write for info. (*0-9618531-0-7*) C E Gould Jr.

Prawns & Prawn Fisheries of India. C. V. Kurian. (C). 1993. 44.00 (*81-7075-032-6*, Pub. by Hindustan) S Asia.

Prawns & Prawn Fisheries of India. 3rd ed. C. V. Kurian & V. O. Sebastian. 1986. 38.50 (*0-8364-2289-9*, Pub. by Hindustan) S Asia.

Praxapostolos see Orthodox New Testament, No. 2, Acts, Epistles, & Revelation: Praxapostolos

Praxedes: Wife, Mother, Widow, & Lay Dominican. Martin-Maria Olive. LC 87-50548. 203p. 1992. pap. 12.00 (*0-89555-309-0*) TAN Bks Pubs.

Praxeology & Understanding: An Analysis of the Controversy in Austrian Economics. George A. Selgin. 78p. (Orig.). 1990. pap. text 6.95 (*0-945466-09-9*) Ludwig von Mises.

Praxiological Studies. Wojciech Gasparski. 432p. 1983. text 255.50 (*90-277-1258-1*, D Reidel) Kluwer Academic.

Praxiologies & the Philosophy of Economics: The Learned Society of Praxiology, Vol. 1. Ed. by Wojciech W. Gasparski & Marek K. Mlicki. 707p. (C). 1992. text 89.95 (*1-56000-003-1*) Transaction Pubs.

Praxis. Ed. by Mihailo Markovic & Gajo Petrovic. (Boston Studies in the Philosophy of Science: No. XXXVI; Synthese Library, No. 134). 441p. 1979. pap. text 78.00 (*90-277-0968-8*, D Reidel); lib. bdg. 141.50 (*90-277-0727-8*, D Reidel) Kluwer Academic.

Praxis: Marxist Criticism & Dissent in Socialist Yugoslavia. Gerson S. Sher. LC 77-72193. 380p. reprint ed. pap. 117.80 (*0-608-13224-1*, 205605900044) Bks Demand.

***PRAXIS Administrative.** Ada Burnette et al. (Praxis Ser.). (C). 2000. per. 40.00 (*1-58197-050-1*) XAM.

Praxis & Computer. 1995. 127.00 (*3-540-60071-X*) Spr-Verlag.

***PRAXIS Biology.** abr. ed. Lynn Sly. Ed. by Sharon Wynne. (Praxis Ser.). (Illus.). 125p. (C). 2000. per. 22.50 (*1-58197-020-X*) XAM.

***PRAXIS Educational Media Specialist.** abr. ed. Marilyn Rinear. (Praxis Ser.). 125p. (C). 2000. per. 22.50 (*1-58197-022-6*) XAM.

***PRAXIS Elementary Competency & Skills.** Marilyn Ranier et al. (Praxis Ser.). (C). 2000. per. 40.00 (*1-58197-010-2*) XAM.

***PRAXIS Elementary Education & Middle Grade Teacher Certification.** Roberta Ramsey. (Praxis Ser.). (C). 2000. per. 40.00 (*1-58197-009-9*); per. 30.00 (*1-58197-008-0*) XAM.

***PRAXIS Emotionally Handicapped.** Kathy Sohnirman. (Praxis Ser.: Vol. 3). (C). 2000. per. 22.50 (*1-58197-002-1*) XAM.

***PRAXIS Emotionally Handicapped.** Kathy Schnirman. (Praxis Ser.: Vol. 4). (C). 2000. per. 50.00 (*1-58197-003-X*) XAM.

***PRAXIS English High School.** Joyce Kelly et al. (Praxis Ser.). (Illus.). 100p. (C). 2000. per. 22.50 (*1-58197-023-4*) XAM.

***PRAXIS English Middle School.** Marilyn Ranier et al. (Praxis Ser.). (C). 2000. per. 22.50 (*1-58197-055-2*) XAM.

***PRAXIS Guidance Counceling.** Sandra Loewenstein. (Praxis Ser.). (C). 2000. per. 22.50 (*1-58197-052-8*) XAM.

Praxis II. 13th ed. Joan U. Levy & Norman Levy. 325p. 1997. 15.95 (*0-02-862198-0*, Arc) IDG Bks.

***Praxis in Manuscripts of the Greek Testament.** 3rd rev. ed. Charles F. Sitterly. 80p. 1999. pap. 15.00 (*1-57074-381-9*) Greyden Pr.

***PRAXIS Math Middle School.** Arlene Schlessinger. (Praxis Ser.). (C). 2000. per. 22.50 (*1-58197-015-3*) XAM.

***PRAXIS Mathematics High School.** Patty J. White Rosario. (Praxis Ser.). (C). 2000. per. 50.00 (*1-58197-051-X*) XAM.

Praxis of My System see Chess Praxis

Praxis of Suffering: An Interpretation of Liberation & Political Theologies. Rebecca S. Chopp. LC 86-824. 190p. (Orig.). 1986. reprint ed. pap. 58.90 (*0-608-02150-4*, 206281900003) Bks Demand.

Praxis I: A Faculty Casebook on Community Service Learning. Ed. by Jeffrey Howard. (Praxis Ser.). (Illus.). 208p. (C). 1993. text. write for info. (*0-9638136-0-9*) OCSL Pr.

***PRAXIS I Language Arts - English - Writing.** Marilyn Rinear. (Praxis Ser.). (C). 2000. per. 22.50 (*1-58197-053-6*) XAM.

***PRAXIS I PPST Math.** Nabil Husni. (Praxis Ser.: No. 14). 225p. (C). 2000. per. 50.00 (*1-58197-013-7*) XAM.

***PRAXIS I PPST Math.** Nabil Husni. (Praxis Ser.: Vol. 13). 225p. (C). 2000. per. 22.50 (*1-58197-012-9*) XAM.

***PRAXIS I Reading.** Marta Yeara. (Praxis Ser.). (C). 2000. per. 22.50 (*1-58197-057-9*) XAM.

***PRAXIS Physical Education High School.** Sharon Wynne & Alexandria Luchawich. Ed. by Jerry Holt. (Praxis Ser.). (Illus.). 150p. (C). 2000. per. 22.50 (*1-58197-019-6*) XAM.

***PRAXIS Political Science.** Evan Siedman. (Praxis Ser.). (C). 2000. per. 22.50 (*1-58197-018-8*) XAM.

***PRAXIS Principles of Learning & Teaching: One Guide Covers All Three Levels Elementary - Middle - High School.** Jerry Holt. (Praxis Ser.: Vol. 5). (C). 2000. per. 22.50 (*1-58197-004-8*) XAM.

***PRAXIS Principles of Learning & Teaching: One Guide Covers All Three Levels Elementary - Middle - High School.** Jerry Holt. (Praxis Ser.: Vol. 6). (C). 2000. per. 50.00 (*1-58197-005-6*) XAM.

***PRAXIS Psychology.** Roy Dawson. (Praxis Ser.). (C). 2000. per. 10.00 (*1-58197-025-0*) XAM.

Praxis Schulleben in der Weimarer Republik, 1918-1933. Ed. by Helmut Heiland & Karl H. Sahmel. (Documenta Paedagogica Ser.: Bd. 3). (GER.). viii, 216p. 1986. write for info. (*3-487-07626-8*) G Olms Pubs.

***PRAXIS Social Studies High School.** Jeanne Armistead. (Praxis Ser.). (C). 2000. per. 22.50 (*1-58197-016-1*) XAM.

***PRAXIS Social Studies Middle School.** Jerry Holt et al. (Praxis Ser.). (C). 2000. per. 22.50 (*1-58197-017-X*) XAM.

Praxis Spagyrica Philosophica & From One to Ten, 2 vols. in 1. Frater Albertus. LC 97-48438. (Illus.). 144p. 1998. reprint ed. 37.95 (*0-87728-892-5*) Weiser.

***PRAXIS Spanish.** Janette Harker. (Praxis Ser.). (C). 2000. per. 22.50 (*1-58197-058-7*) XAM.

***PRAXIS Special Education.** Roberta Ramsey. (Praxis Ser.: Vol. 2). Orig. Title: Special Education Teacher Competency Tests - Revised. (Illus.). 328p. (C). 2000. per. 50.00 (*1-58197-001-3*) XAM.

***PRAXIS Special Education.** rev. ed. Roberta Ramsey. (Praxis Ser.). Orig. Title: Special Education Teacher Competency Tests - Revised. (Illus.). 328p. (C). 2000. spiral bd. 40.00 (*1-58197-000-5*, 569-245-6080) XAM.

***PRAXIS Subject Area Assessment General Science.** Kelly Benson et al. (Praxis Ser.). (C). 2000. spiral bd. 22.50 (*1-58197-054-4*) XAM.

***PRAXIS Subject Area Assessment Home Economics.** abr. ed. Barbra Teman. (Praxis Ser.). (Illus.). 125p. (C). 2000. spiral bd. 22.50 (*1-58197-024-2*) XAM.

Praxis System: Guitar Compendium, Vol. 1: Technique, Improvisation, Musicianship & Theory. Howard Roberts & Garry Hagberg. (Illus.). 163p. (C). 1989. 35.00 (*3-89221-019-5*, Pub. by Advance Mus); pap. text 19.95 (*0-317-04756-6*, Pub. by Advance Mus) McClelland & Stewart.

Praxis System: Guitar Compendium, Vol. 2: Technique, Improvisation, Musicianship & Theory. Howard Roberts & Garry Hagberg. (Illus.). 237p. 1989. 40.00 (*3-89221-021-7*, Pub. by Advance Mus); pap. text 19.95 (*0-317-04626-8*, Pub. by Advance Mus) McClelland & Stewart.

Praxis System: Guitar Compendium, Vol. 3: Technique, Improvisation, Musicianship & Theory. Howard Roberts & Garry Hagberg. (Illus.). 227p. 1989. 40.00 (*3-89221-020-9*, Pub. by Advance Mus); pap. text 24.95 (*0-317-04757-4*, Pub. by Advance Mus) McClelland & Stewart.

Praxis II: NTE & MSAT Cassette. write for info. (*0-02-861201-9*, Arc) IDG Bks.

PRAXIS II: NTE with Computer Adaptive Software (CAT) REA Staff. (TESTware Ser.). Date not set. pap. 34.95 incl. disk (*0-87891-134-0*) Res & Educ.

Praxis II: Service-Learning Resources for University Students, Staff & Faculty. Ed. by J. Galura et al. (Praxis Ser.). (Illus.). 448p. (C). 1993. text. write for info. (*0-9638136-2-5*) OCSL Pr.

***PRAXIS II Elementary Education Competency & Skill.** Marilyn Ranier et al. (Praxis Ser.). (C). 2000. per. 40.00 (*1-58197-011-0*) XAM.

***PRAXIS II French.** Mary Mellgren. (Praxis Ser.). (C). 2000. per. 10.00 (*1-58197-059-5*) XAM.

Praxis II, NTE, MSAT. 12th ed. Joan U. Levy. 416p. 1995. 14.95 (*0-02-860601-9*) Macmillan.

Praxis II Preparation Kit. 13th ed. Joan U. Levy & Norman Levy. 336p. 1998. pap. 19.95 incl. audio (*0-02-862197-2*, Arc) IDG Bks.

***PRAXIS II Professional Knowledge.** Jerry Holt & Debbie McCray. (Praxis Ser.: Vol. 8). (C). 2000. per. 50.00 (*1-58197-007-2*) XAM.

Praxis 2: NTE 1999-2000. Kaplan Educational Centers. 1999. pap. 29.95 (*0-684-85672-7*) S&S Trade.

PRAXIS/NTE, 1998. Kaplan Staff. 1997. 24.95 incl. audio (*0-684-83685-8*) S&S Trade.

Pray: God Is Listening. enl. ed. Richard DeHaan. 96p. 1989. mass mkt. 5.99 (*0-310-23541-3*, 9479P) Zondervan.

Pray All Ways. Edward Hays. LC 81-69329. (Illus.). 166p. 1981. pap. 10.95 (*0-939516-01-2*) Forest Peace.

Pray Always. Lawrence G. Lovasik. (Saint Joseph Picture Bks.). (Illus.). 1987. pap. 1.25 (*0-89942-309-4*, 309-00) Catholic Bk Pub.

Pray & Grow Rich: Seven Overlooked Secrets from the Bible That Control Your Wealth, Success & Happiness. Richard G. Briley. 145p. 1998. pap. 12.99 (*1-882988-07-8*) Pub-in-the-Glen.

Pray & Play Bible for Young Children. Ed. by Jody Brolsma. LC 96-40288. 176p. (Orig.). (J). 1997. pap. 16.99 (*0-7644-2024-0*) Group Pub.

Pray As You Go: A Travel Guide for Prayerful Living. Johnny R. Almond. 369p. 1998. pap. 12.95 (*1-57087-383-6*) Prof Pr NC.

Pray As You Go: On Living Your Faith in the Nineties. Robert Meneilly. 160p. 1996. 19.95 (*0-8362-2170-2*) Andrews & McMeel.

Pray Away Pounds. Lisa R. Turner. 210p. 1993. pap. 7.95 (*0-9624049-5-0*) Hatrack River.

Pray by the Book. Robert B. Emrick. Ed. by Judith M. Emrick. 40p. (Orig.). 1996. pap. 6.00 (*0-9655492-1-6*) Reveal Pub MT.

Pray, Christian Pray! Arthur J. Clement. LC 93-84931. 123p. (Orig.). 1993. pap. 8.99 (*0-8100-0499-2*, 06N0697) Northwest Pub.

Pray for a Brave Heart. Helen MacInnes. LC 55-5241. 1955. 24.95 (*0-15-173901-3*) Harcourt.

Pray for All the Children of the Universe & Death Ends Desire. Bob Madden. 126p. (Orig.). 1995. pap. 6.99 (*0-9608256-1-4*) R Madden.

Pray for Justice: On the Trail with Ornin Porter Rockwell. Marc Otte. LC 97-69007. (Illus.). 172p. 1997. pap. 12.95 (*1-888125-19-5*) Publ Consult.

***Pray for Me... I'll Pray for You.** Magnolia Holiday. LC 99-96243. 80p. 2000. pap. 6.95 (*0-9611952-4-X*) Magnolia Prodns.

***Pray for Our Nation: Scriptural Prayers to Revive Our Country.** Harrison House Publishing Staff. 2000. pap. 4.99 (*1-57794-254-X*) Harrison Hse.

Pray for Ricky Foster. Jane Johnston. 224p. 1991. per. 3.50 (*0-373-26068-7*) Harlequin Bks.

Pray for Ricky Foster. Jane Johnston. 200p. 1985. 12.95 (*0-312-63555-9*) St Martin.

***Pray for Texas.** Cotton Smith. 272p. 2000. mass mkt. 4.50 (*0-8439-4710-1*, Leisure Bks) Dorchester Pub Co.

Pray for the World see Alcanzando el Mundo a Traves de la Oracion

Pray for the World. Ed. by Zondervan Publishing Staff. 1996. pap. 4.99 (*0-310-40039-2*) Zondervan.

Pray for Us. Philip Luber. LC 97-97040. (Orig.). 1998. mass mkt. 5.99 (*0-449-18329-7*, GM) Fawcett.

P

An Asterisk (*) at the beginning of an entry indicates that the title is appearing for the first time.

Pray for Your Child: A Perpetual Calendar to Use Year after Year to Help You . . . Bob Guinter & Dee Guinter. (Illus.). 372p. 1998. ring bd. 15.00 (*1-890651-05-2*, FamilyFinds) Williford Communs.

Pray for Yourself & Other Stories. Anne Calcagno. (TriQuarterly Bks.). 104p. 1993. 26.95 (*0-8101-5000-X*); pap. 12.95 (*0-8101-5003-4*) Northwestern U Pr.

Pray God & Keep Walking: Stories of Women Refugees. Beatrice N. Hackett. LC 95-36699. 174p. 1995. lib. bdg. 27.50 (*0-7864-0089-7*) McFarland & Co.

Pray God to Die. Carey Roberts. 320p. 1994. mass mkt. 4.99 (*0-380-72259-3*, Avon Bks) Morrow Avon.

***Pray Hard.** Pamela Walker. LC 00-36579. (Illus.). (J). 2001. write for info. (*0-439-21586-2*) Scholastic Inc.

Pray in the Spirit. Arthur Wallis. 1992. mass mkt. 5.99 (*0-87508-561-X*) Chr Lit.

Pray in This Way: Sermons on the Lord's Prayer. John A. Stroman. (Protestant Pulpit Exchange Ser.). 96p. (Orig.). 1994. pap. 8.95 (*0-687-00234-6*) Abingdon.

Pray ing with Meister Eckhart. Wayne Simsic. Ed. by Carl Koch. (Companions for the Journey Ser.). (Illus.). 120p. 1998. pap. 8.95 (*0-88489-516-5*) St Marys.

Pray It Again, Sam. Kenneth J. Roberts. Ed. by Anna Marie Ruskin. LC 83-61243. 116p. (Orig.). 1983. pap. 3.95 (*0-9610984-0-6*) PAX Tapes.

Pray Like Jesus: Sermons & Bible Study on Prayer. John R. Brokhoff. LC 94-227. (Orig.). 1994. pap. 14.50 (*0-7880-0105-1*) CSS OH.

Pray Like the Hunted. David Lerner. 91p. (Orig.). 1992. pap. 6.00 (*0-929730-38-0*) Zeitgeist Pr.

Pray Love, Remember. Elaine Fox. 368p. 1998. mass mkt. 5.50 (*0-8439-4374-2*, Leisure Bks) Dorchester Pub Co.

Pray Love, Remember. Elaine Fox. 368p. 1998. mass mkt. 5.50 (*0-8439-4384-X*, Leisure Bks) Dorchester Pub Co.

Pray, Love, Remember. large type ed. Margaret Yorke. 432p. 1996. 27.99 (*0-7089-3622-9*) Ulverscroft.

Pray, Pray, Pray. Betsy War. LC 93-87011. 252p. 1995. pap. text 6.95 (*1-882972-21-X*, 3321) Queenship Pub.

***Pray Tell: The Containment of the Prince of Darkness.** C. Bryan Moore. 1998. pap. 11.95 (*0-9665299-2-8*) Coomansingh.

Pray Tell Vol. 2: The Shining Light, 2 vols. C. Bryan Moore. 79p. (YA). (gr. 11 up). 1999. pap. 11.95 (*0-9665299-3-6*) Coomansingh.

***Pray the Bible.** Page M. Zyromski. 104p. 2000. pap. text 6.95 (*0-86716-342-9*) St Anthony Mess Pr.

Pray the Price: United Methodist United in Prayer. Terry Teykl. Ed. by Lynn Ponder. 176p. (Orig.). 1997. pap. 10.00 (*1-57892-041-8*) Prayer Pt Pr.

Pray the Price Resource Kit. Terry Teykl. Ed. by Lynn Ponder. (Illus.). 55p. 1997. ring bd. 49.00 (*1-57892-042-6*) Prayer Pt Pr.

Pray the Promises. Cecil Culbreth. 168p. 1999. ring bd. 10.00 (*0-9671852-1-1*) Book of Hope.

Pray the Rosary. Joseph Mary Leleu. (Illus.). 1980. pap. 0.85 (*0-89942-040-0*, 40/05) Catholic Bk Pub.

Pray the Rosary. Press Regina. 1993. pap. text 25.00 (*0-88271-325-6*) Regina Pr.

***Pray the Rosary: 131 Questions for a Deeper, More Profound Rosary.** George Twigg-Porter. 20p. 1999. pap. text 1.95 (*1-57918-059-0*) Queenship Pub.

Pray to Love - Love to Pray: Good Thoughts from Good People - Prayers, Reflections, & Life Stories of 14 Great Pray-ers. Compiled by Carol A. Graser. 64p. 1996. pap. 5.95 (*0-937997-33-1*) Hi-Time Pflaum.

Pray to Win! A Blueprint for Success. Alfred A. Montapert. LC 86-73037. 235p. 1986. per. 10.00 (*0-9603174-4-9*) Bks of Value.

Pray Today: A Scriptural Guide to Daily Prayer. Stephen C. Johnson. (Carpenter's Tools Ser.). 200p. 1997. pap. 10.00 (*0-9659699-0-8*) Lambs Blood.

***Pray Together Now: How to Find or Form a Prayer Group.** Cay Randall-May. LC 99-36500. 208p. 1999. text 16.95 (*1-86204-497-X*, Pub. by Element MA) Penguin Putnam.

Pray with All Your Senses: Discovering the Wholeness Jesus Brings. Lo-Ann Trembley & David Trembley. 96p. (Orig.). 1997. pap. 8.95 (*0-87946-160-8*) ACTA Pubns.

Pray with Me Daddy-Portable: Heartfelt Prayers for Dads & Daughters. Robert Wolgemuth. 160p. 1998. pap. 6.99 (*1-56292-533-4*) Honor Bks OK.

Pray with the Heart see Oren Con el Corazon

Pray with the Heart. rev. ed. Slavko Barbaric. 235p. (C). 1990. 4.50 (*0-940535-34-3*, UP112) Franciscan U Pr.

Pray with Your Eyes Open. rev. ed. Richard L. Pratt, Jr. (Devotional Ser.). 224p. 1998. pap. 7.95 (*1-885216-21-1*) Evan Formosan.

Pray with Your Eyes Open: Looking at God, Ourselves & Our Prayers. Richard L. Pratt, Jr. LC 87-2762. 1987. pap. 8.99 (*0-87552-378-1*) P & R Pubng.

***Pray without Ceasing: Mindfulness of God in Daily Life.** Wayne Simsic. LC 99-50788. 120p. 2000. pap. 7.95 (*0-88489-668-4*) St Marys.

Pray Without Ceasing: Prayer for Morning & Evening. Joyce Zimmermann. 672p. (Orig.). 1993. 24.95 (*0-8146-2294-1*) Liturgical Pr.

Pray Your Way. Bruce Duncan. pap. write for info. (*0-232-52019-4*) S Asia.

Pray Your Way Through It. Joseph Murphy. 171p. 1973. pap. 8.50 (*0-87516-190-1*) DeVorss.

Pray Yuba/Sutter. 1995. 19.95 incl. VHS (*1-890553-03-4*, CV 603 VSN) Double Vision.

***Prayball: A Religion for All Seasons: The Spiritual Insights of a Jewish Sportsfan.** James M. Gordon. LC 99-36607. 180p. 1999. 21.95 (*965-229-219-2*) Gefen Bks.

Prayer see IVP Booklets

Prayer. 1988. pap. 1.35 (*0-8474-0779-9*) Back to Bible.

Prayer. 1996. pap. text 10.99 (*0-8474-1153-2*) Back to Bible.

Prayer. (Little Lessons for Little Learners Ser.). (J). 1996. 4.95 (*0-88271-488-0*) Regina Pr.

Prayer. Saint Aphraates. 1993. pap. 1.00 (*0-89981-072-1*) Eastern Orthodox.

Prayer. Charles Gallagher. (Celebrate Love Ser.). 70p. (Orig.). 1990. pap. text 3.95 (*0-911905-30-8*) Past & Mat Rene Ctr.

***Prayer.** Alfonso Galvez & Society of Jesus Christ the Priest Staff. Tr. by Michael Adams from SPA. 116p. 2000. text. write for info. (*0-9641108-8-1*) Shoreless Lake.

***Prayer.** Mohandas Karamchand Gandhi. (Illus.). 256p. 2000. pap. 14.00 (*1-893163-09-1*, Pub. by Berkeley Hills) Publishers Group.

Prayer. Kahlil Gibran. 1999. 4.95 (*0-375-40460-0*) Knopf.

Prayer. Bill Hybels. (Christian Basics Bible Studies). 64p. (Orig.). 1994. pap., wbk. ed. 4.99 (*0-8308-2004-3*, 2004) InterVarsity.

Prayer. Illus. by Patricia R. Mattozzi. (Little Lessons for Little Learners Ser.). (J). 4.95 (*0-614-22068-8*) Regina Pr.

Prayer. Walter Russell & Lao Russell. Ed. by Laara Lindo. 39p. 1997. pap. text 6.00 (*1-879605-48-1*) U Sci & Philos.

Prayer. Charles H. Spurgeon. (Spurgeon Collection: Vol. 5). 228p. 1998. pap. 9.99 (*1-889893-17-X*) Emerald House Group Inc.

Prayer. Lester Sumrall. 71p. (C). 1982. pap. text 12.00 (*0-937580-53-8*) Sumrall Pubng.

Prayer. Hans U. Von Balthasar. Tr. by Graham Harrison from GER. LC 85-82172. Orig. Title: Das Betrachtende Gebet. 311p. 1986. pap. 14.95 (*0-89870-074-4*) Ignatius Pr.

***Prayer.** Nee Watchman. 1998. pap. 2.00 (*0-7363-0132-1*) Living Stream Ministry.

***Prayer, 5 vols.** John White. 32p. (Orig.). 1999. pap. 4.95 (*0-8308-6567-5*) InterVarsity.

Prayer. Zondervan Publishing Staff. LC 99-230155. (God's Light Ser.). (Illus.). 160p. 2000. 9.99 (*0-310-97428-3*) Zondervan.

Prayer. expanded ed. O. Hallesby. LC 93-44780. 208p. 1994. pap. 6.99 (*0-8066-2700-X*, 9-2700) Augsburg Fortress.

Prayer. John Bunyan. (Puritan Paperbacks Ser.). Orig. Title: Praying in the Spirit. 172p. 1989. reprint ed. pap. 6.99 (*0-85151-090-6*) Banner of Truth.

Prayer, Vol. 2. Darryl Pearson. Ed. by Kara Eckmann Powell. (True Life Ser.: No. 2). 1999. pap. 14.99 (*0-8307-2408-7*, Gospel Light) Gospel Lght.

Prayer: A Baha'i Approach. William Hellaby & Madeline Hellaby. 117p. 1985. pap. 8.95 (*0-85398-213-9*) G Ronald Pub.

Prayer: A Cry of the Heart. Marilyn Kirk. 176p. (Orig.). 1994. pap. 5.95 (*0-910487-31-6*) Royalty Pub.

Prayer: A Discovery of Life. Alexandra Kovats. (Nazareth Bks). 128p. 1984. 1.95 (*0-86683-714-0*, AY8361) Harper SF.

Prayer: A Handbook for Today's Catholic. Eamon Tobin. LC 88-83981. 160p. 1989. pap. 4.95 (*0-89243-300-0*) Liguori Pubns.

Prayer: A Holy Occupation. Oswald Chambers. LC 92-35949. 192p. 1993. 12.99 (*0-929239-59-8*) Discovery Hse Pubs.

Prayer: A Study in the History & Psychology of Religion. Friedrich Heiler. 420p. 1997. pap. 19.95 (*1-85168-143-4*, Pub. by Onewrld Pubns) Penguin Putnam.

Prayer: A 31-Day Plan to Enrich Your Prayer Life. Andrew Murray. (Little Library Ser.). 48p. 1995. spiral bd. 0.99 (*1-55748-646-8*) Barbour Pub.

Prayer: An Adventure with God. David Healey. (LifeGuide Bible Studies). 64p. (Orig.). 1994. pap., wbk. ed. 4.99 (*0-8308-1053-6*, 1053) InterVarsity.

Prayer: Beginning Conversations with God. Richard J. Beckmen. LC 94-42239. (Face to Face with God Ser.). 80p. 1995. pap. text 8.99 (*0-8066-2768-9*, 10-27689) Augsburg Fortress.

Prayer: Beholding God's Glory. 1991. pap. 2.50 (*0-89109-549-7*) NavPress.

Prayer: Bible Study Kit-HWML. Kenneth A. Cherney. 1998. 37.99 (*0-8100-0765-7*, 22N0965) Northwest Pub.

***Prayer: Bringing Heaven to Earth.** (SPA.). 122p. 1999. spiral bd. 12.95 (*0-941975-64-9*) Powerhouse.

Prayer: Communicating with God. Carol E. Wilson. 96p. 1998. pap. 5.99 (*1-880266-30-X*) Neighborhood Bible.

Prayer: Discovering What Scripture Says. Timothy Jones & Jill Zook-Jones. (Fisherman Bible Studyguide Ser.). 80p. (Orig.). 1993. pap. text 4.99 (*0-87788-709-8*, H Shaw Pubs) Waterbrook Pr.

Prayer: Finding the Heart's True Home. Richard J. Foster. LC 92-58908. 288p. 1992. 22.00 (*0-06-062846-4*, Pub. by Harper SF) HarpC.

Prayer: From Children & Young Men & Women. (Illus.). 144p. 2000. pap. 7.95 (*0-8146-2579-7*) Liturgical Pr.

Prayer: God's Time & Ours! Warren F. Groff. LC 84-19913. 124p. 1984. reprint ed. pap. 38.50 (*0-608-02161-X*, 206283000004) Bks Demand.

Prayer: How to Talk to God. (BMC Teaching Bks.). (Illus.). (J). (gr. 1-8). 1970. pap. text 4.50 (*0-86508-153-0*) BCM Pubn.

Prayer: Integration of Faith & Life. Bernard Haring. (C). 1988. 60.00 (*0-85439-107-X*, Pub. by St Paul Pubns) St Mut.

Prayer: Its Nature & Technique. 4th ed. Kirpal Singh. LC 81-50727. (Illus.). 149p. 1982. reprint ed. pap. 10.00 (*0-918224-10-1*) S K Pubns.

Prayer: Kirpal Singh. 153p. 1989. pap. 5.00 (*0-942735-50-1*) Ruhani Satsang.

Prayer: Language of the Soul. Peter Lorie & Manuela Dunn Mascetti. LC 97-13472. (Illus.). 320p. 1997. 24.95 (*0-87596-428-1*) Rodale Pr Inc.

Prayer: Learning How to Talk to God. J. L. Groth. (Concept Books for Children: No. 4). (Illus.). 24p. (J). (gr. 1 up). 1983. pap. 3.99 (*0-570-07799-0*, 56-1395) Concordia.

Prayer: My Soul's Adventure with God. Robert H. Schuller. 190p. 1996. pap. 5.99 (*0-385-48505-0*); pap. 5.99 (*0-614-19799-6*) Doubleday.

Prayer: My Soul's Adventure with God. Robert H. Schuller. 224p. 1995. 19.99 (*0-7852-7777-3*) Nelson.

Prayer: My Soul's Adventure with God. abr. ed. Robert H. Schuller & Sandra Hirshkowith. 1995. audio 19.99 (*0-7852-7623-8*) Nelson.

Prayer: Opening Your Heart to God. Bill Hybels. (Small Group Ser.). 96p. (Orig.). 1997. pap. 5.99 (*0-310-21714-8*) Zondervan.

Prayer: The Compulsive Word. Gladys A. Reichard. LC 84-45512. (American Ethnological Society Monographs: No. 7). 1988. reprint ed. 29.50 (*0-404-62907-5*) AMS Pr.

Prayer: The Cornerstone. Helen G. Hole. LC 62-19073. (Orig.). 1962. pap. 4.00 (*0-87574-123-1*) Pendle Hill.

Prayer: The Cry for the Kingdom. Stanley J. Grenz. 112p. 1988. pap. 9.95 (*0-913573-92-2*) Hendrickson MA.

***Prayer: The Foundation for Growing Closer to God.** Karyn Henley. Ed. by Jim Eichenberger. (Foundations). (Illus.). 96p. 2000. pap. 10.99 (*0-7847-1216-6*, 42065) Standard Pub.

Prayer: The Global Experience. Francis A. Eigo. LC 97-14146. 1997. write for info. (*0-87723-090-0*) Villanova U Pr.

Prayer: The Great Adventure. David Jeremiah. 263p. 1999. pap. 12.99 (*1-57673-486-2*) Multnomah Pubs.

Prayer: The Great Conversation. Peter Kreeft. LC 91-75444. 178p. 1991. reprint ed. pap. 10.95 (*0-89870-357-3*) Ignatius Pr.

***Prayer: The Hidden Fire.** Tom Harpur. 2000. pap. 16.95 (*1-896836-40-2*, Pub. by NStone Publ) Logos Prods.

Prayer: The Hidden Fire: A Practical & Personal Approach. Tom Harpur. 256p. 1998. 24.95 (*1-896836-22-4*) NStone Publ.

Prayer: The Hidden Fire Journal & Companion Guide, 1. Tom Harpur. 224p. 1999. pap. 11.95 (*1-896836-32-1*) NStone Publ.

Prayer: The Master Key. James D. Freeman. LC 68-11793. 255p. 1968. 7.95 (*0-87159-128-6*) Unity Bks.

Prayer: The Missing Link. C. E. Glover. 96p. 1996. pap. text 9.95 (*1-885066-31-7*) Four-G Pubs.

Prayer: The Mission of the Church. Jean Danielou. LC 96-9103. (Ressourcement Ser.). 140p. 1996. 15.00 (*0-8028-4105-8*) Eerdmans.

Prayer: The Voice of Faith. Charles B. Hodge, Jr. 1996. 5.95 (*0-945441-23-1*) Res Pubns AR.

Prayer: Three Beautiful Adaptations of Artwork by Francis Hook (Cross-Stitch) Jean D. Crowther. 1984. 6.98 (*0-88290-268-7*) Horizon Utah.

Prayer: Your Foundation for Success. 1983. pap. 4.99 (*0-88114-273-5*) K Copeland Pubns.

***Prayer: Your Foundation for Success.** Kenneth Copeland. 1999. pap. 8.99 (*1-57794-155-1*) Harrison Hse.

***Prayer - Bringing Heaven to Earth.** Tr. of Oracao. (POR.). 122p. 1999. spiral bd. 12.95 (*0-941975-54-1*) Powerhouse.

Prayer - Bringing Heaven to Earth. A. L. Gill & Joyce Gill. 112p. 1997. pap. 9.95 (*0-941975-41-X*) Powerhouse.

Prayer - Cushions of the Flesh. Robert Irwin. (Original Fiction in Paperback Ser.). 140p. 1999. pap. 11.99 (*1-873982-63-1*, Pub. by Dedalus) Subterranean Co.

Prayer - Key to Revival see Oracion - Clave del Avivamiento

Prayer - Living with God. Simon Tugwell. 144p. 1980. pap. 10.95 (*0-87243-100-2*) Templegate.

Prayer - Songs for the Very Young & Their Families. Louise Reinecke. LC 98-93396. (Illus.). vi, 22p. (J). (ps-6). 1998. pap. write for info. (*0-9665302-0-9*) Garm Co.

Prayer: A Biblical Perspective see Oracion la una Perspectiva Biblica: La una Perspectiva Biblica

Prayer a Day: 365 Prayers - One for Every Day of the Year. Illus. by Caroline Ewen. LC 99-208700. 96p. (J). (gr. k-3). 1999. 9.99 (*0-7847-0973-4*, 03724) Standard Pub.

Prayer, a Lifestyle. Dennis B. Harris. Ed. by Kay Harris. (Illus.). 44p. 1997. 19.95 (*1-890022-47-0*) Lfestyle Min.

Prayer-a-Phrases. Anthony Ruspantini. 112p. 1997. pap. 9.99 (*1-56043-286-1*, Treasure Hse) Destiny Image.

***Prayer, a Story, a Guide: The Complete High Holiday Prayer Book Companion.** Zalman Goldstein. 196p. 2000. pap. 12.95 (*1-891293-10-9*, JLG03, Pub. by Jewish Lrning) IPG Chicago.

Prayer, a Taste of Glory. Helen Tadlock. 232p. 1993. pap. 10.00 (*0-939513-77-3*) Joy Pub SJC.

Prayer, a Weekly Outline. Martha Mayfield. 122p. 1997. pap. 16.50 (*0-9657149-1-8*) Stress Pr TX.

Prayer According to the Scriptures. Jean Laplace. 85p. 1991. pap. 8.95 (*1-85390-167-9*, Pub. by Veritas Pubns) St Mut.

Prayer & a Promise. Marian Edwards. 384p. 1997. mass mkt. 4.99 (*0-8217-5786-5*, Zebra Kensgtn) Kensgtn Pub Corp.

Prayer & Christian Ethics. Sergio Bastianel. (C). 1988. 39.00 (*0-7855-3218-8*, Pub. by St Paul Pubns) St Mut.

Prayer & Community: The Benedictine Tradition. Stewart Columba. LC 98-21362. (Traditions of Christian Spirituality Ser.). 128p. 1998. pap. 13.00 (*1-57075-219-2*) Orbis Bks.

Prayer & Community: The Havurah in American Judaism. Riv-Ellen Prell. LC 88-25107. (Illus.). 336p. reprint ed. pap. 104.20 (*0-608-10599-6*, 2071220) Bks Demand.

Prayer & Community: The Havurah Movement in American Judaism. Riv-Ellen Prell. LC 88-25107. (Illus.). 336p. 1989. pap. 21.95 (*0-8143-1935-1*) Wayne St U Pr.

Prayer & Devotional Life of United Methodists. Steve Harper. LC 99-41013. 128p. 1999. pap. 5.00 (*0-687-08432-6*) Abingdon.

Prayer & Evangelism. Jessie Penn-Lewis. 1979. mass mkt. 5.99 (*0-87508-960-7*) Chr Lit.

Prayer & Fasting. Kingsley A. Fletcher. 168p. (Orig.). 1999. pap. 11.99 (*0-88368-543-4*) Whitaker Hse.

Prayer & Fasting. Gordon Lindsay. 1960. 3.95 (*0-89985-076-6*) Christ for the Nations.

Prayer & Fasting. W. E. McCumber. 36p. 1990. pap. 3.25 (*0-8341-1379-1*) Beacon Hill.

Prayer & Healing. Alvin B. Kuhn. 50p. 1993. reprint ed. pap. 7.95 (*1-56459-327-4*) Kessinger Pub.

Prayer & Intercession. Debbie Bentley. (Basic Christian Doctrine Ser.: No. 9). 16p. (Orig.). (YA). 1995. pap. 1.00 (*1-885090-08-0*) Cosecha Latina.

***Prayer & Japa.** 4th ed. Sri Aurobindo & Mother. Ed. by Vijay. 28p. 1998. pap. 1.00 (*81-7060-027-8*, Pub. by SAA) E-W Cultural Ctr.

Prayer & Joy. large type ed. write for info. (*0-318-68662-7*, 7010) LBW.

Prayer & Our Bodies. Flora S. Wuellner. 1987. pap. 8.95 (*0-687-60911-9*) Abingdon.

Prayer & Our Bodies. Flora S. Wuellner. LC 87-50705. 144p. 1987. pap. 10.00 (*0-8358-0568-9*) Upper Room Bks.

Prayer & Peanut Butter. Shirley Lueth. (Illus.). 147p. (Orig.). 1986. reprint ed. pap. 7.95 (*0-937911-01-1*) Lueth Hse Pub.

Prayer & Penitence: A Commentary on the High Holy Day Machzor. Jeffrey M. Cohen. LC 94-3077. 336p. 1994. 40.00 (*1-56821-046-9*) Aronson.

Prayer & Personal Religion. large type ed. John B. Coburn. LC 85-10477. 160p. 1985. reprint ed. pap. 8.95 (*0-8027-2509-0*) Walker & Co.

Prayer & Piety in the Poems of Gerard Manley Hopkins: The Landscape of a Soul. John Delli-Carpini. LC 98-17419. (Studies in British Literature). 1998. 79.95 (*0-7734-8380-2*) E Mellen.

***Prayer & Play in Late Tokugawa Japan: Asakusa Sensoji & EDO Society.** Nam-lin Hur. (Harvard East Asian Monographs: Vol. 185). 2000. 40.00 (*0-674-00240-7*) HUP.

Prayer & Power: George Herbert & Renaissance Courtship. Michael C. Schoenfeldt. (Illus.). 358p. 1991. pap. text 19.95 (*0-226-74002-1*) U Ch Pr.

Prayer & Power: George Herbert & Renaissance Courtship. Michael C. Schoenfeldt. (Illus.). 328p. 1994. lib. bdg. 49.95 (*0-226-74001-3*) U Ch Pr.

Prayer & Power in Byzantine & Papal Imagery. Christopher Walter. (Collected Studies: No. CS 396). (ENG & FRE.). 320p. 1993. 154.95 (*0-86078-363-4*, Pub. by Variorum) Ashgate Pub Co.

Prayer & Power in the Capital: With Prayers of the Presidents. Ed. by Pauline B. Innis. LC 82-156801. (Illus.). 120p. 1982. 7.50 (*0-941402-02-9*) Devon Pub.

***Prayer & Practice in the American Catholic Community.** Ed. by Joseph P. Chinnici & Angelyn Dries. (American Catholic Identities Ser.). 300p. 2000. 50.00 (*1-57075-346-6*) Orbis Bks.

***Prayer & Practice in the American Catholic Community.** Ed. by Joseph P. Chinnici & Angelyn Dries. (American Catholic Identities Ser.). (Illus.). 300p. 2000. pap. 30.00 (*1-57075-342-3*) Orbis Bks.

Prayer & Praying Men. E. M. Bounds. (E. M. Bounds Classics on Prayer Ser.). 160p. (gr. 10). 1992. pap. 6.99 (*0-8010-1006-3*) Baker Bks.

Prayer & Renewal: Proceedings & Communications of Regional Meetings of the Sister-Formation Conferences, 1969. Sister Formation Conferences Staff. Ed. by Mary H. Valentine. LC 58-10465. (Sister Formation Ser.). 160p. reprint ed. pap. 49.60 (*0-7837-0476-3*, 204079900018) Bks Demand.

Prayer & Selfknowledge. rev. ed. Anselm Gruen. Ed. by Alphonse M. Lauer. Tr. by M. Frances Market from GER. (Schuyler Spiritual Ser.: No. 7). 72p. 1993. pap. text 4.50 (*1-56788-009-6*, 10-007) BMH Pubns.

Prayer & Spirituality: Adult Workshops. Center for Learning Network Staff. (Adult Workshops Ser.). 88p. 1989. spiral bd. 15.95 (*1-56077-037-6*) Ctr Learning.

Prayer & Temperament: Different Prayer Forms for Different Personality Types. rev. ed. Chester P. Michael & Marie C. Norrisey. 208p. (Orig.). 1991. pap. 7.95 (*0-940136-02-3*) Open Door Inc.

***Prayer & the Art of Volkswagen Maintenance.** Don Miller. LC 99-41916. 300p. 2000. pap. 10.99 (*0-7369-0160-4*) Harvest Hse.

Prayer & the Christian Life: C-4 Devotional Journal II. Ed. by Steve Clapp. (C-4 Journals Ser.). 126p. (Orig.). 1982. pap. 6.00 (*0-317-11522-7*) C-Four Res.

Prayer & the Christian's Devotional Life. G. Raymond Carlson. LC 80-83522. (Radiant Life Ser.). 124p. 1981. pap. 3.95 (*0-88243-878-6*, 02-0878); pap., teacher ed. 5.50 (*0-88243-190-0*, 32-0190) Gospel Pub.

***Prayer & the Coming Rivial.** Andrew Murray. 1999. pap. 9.99 (*1-84030-053-1*) Ambassador Prodns Ltd.

Prayer & the Five Stages of Healing. Ron Roth. LC 98-43146. 272p. (C). 1999. text 23.00 (*1-56170-551-9*, 575) Hay House.

***Prayer & the Five Stages of Healing.** Ron Roth. (SPA., Illus.). 256p. 2001. pap. 13.95 (*1-56170-799-6*) Hay House.

***Prayer & the Five Stages of Healing.** Ron Roth & Peter Occhiogrosso. 272p. 2000. reprint ed. pap. 13.95 (*1-56170-678-7*, 575T) Hay House.

***Prayer & the New Testament.** Robert J. Karris. 232p. 2000. pap. 25.95 (*0-8245-1874-8*, Pub. by Crossroad NY) Natl Bk Netwk.

P

An Asterisk (*) at the beginning of an entry indicates that the title is appearing for the first time.

Prayer & the Prayer Meeting see Oracion y los Cultos de Oracion

***Prayer & the Quest for Healing: Our Personal Transformation & Cosmic Responsibility.** Barbara Fiand. LC 99-12732. 1999. pap. 14.95 (*0-8245-1812-8*) Crossroad NY.

Prayer & the Will of God. Hubert Van Zeller. 124p. 1978. pap. 6.95 (*0-87243-084-7*) Templegate.

Prayer & Worship: Workshop Models for Gr. 7-8. Center for Learning Network Staff. (Junior High Religion Ser.). 111p. 1992. teacher ed., spiral bd. 15.95 (*1-56077-185-2*) Ctr Learning.

Prayer Asking & Receiving. 1980. mass mkt. 2.95 (*0-87398-655-5*) Sword of Lord.

Prayer, Aspiration & Contemplation. Venard Poslusney. 212p. 1994. pap. 6.50 (*1-890137-27-8*) One Hund-One Fnd.

Prayer Assemblies for Primary Schools. Raymond Topley. 144p. 1989. pap. 27.00 (*1-85390-146-6*, Pub. by Veritas Pubns) St Mut.

Prayer at Bedtime see Oraciones a la Hora de Dormir

***Prayer at Day's Dawning.** Jim Cotter. 208p. 1999. 40.00 (*0-85305-459-2*, Pub. by Arthur James) St Mut.

***Prayer at Night's Approaching.** Jim Cotter. 1999. 40.00 (*0-85305-419-3*, Pub. by Arthur James) St Mut.

Prayer at Night's Approaching. Jim Cotter. 208p. 1998. 16.95 (*0-8192-1772-7*) Morehouse Pub.

Prayer at the Ruins of Jerusalem. Charles B. Chavel. 32p. 1978. pap. 2.50 (*0-88328-031-0*) Shilo Pub Hse.

Prayer Attitude in the Eastern Church. Gabriele Winkler. 1978. pap. 2.95 (*0-937032-01-8*) Light&Life Pub Co MN.

Prayer Before an Awesome God: The Psalms for Teenagers. David Haas. 128p. (YA). 1998. pap. 7.95 (*0-88489-600-5*) St Marys.

Prayer Book see Siddur Tenillat Hashem with Tenillim

Prayer Book see Siddur Tenillat Hashem with Tehillim

Prayer Book. 368p. (Orig.). 1979. 10.00 (*0-317-30304-X*) Holy Trinity.

Prayer Book. Tr. by Ben Z. Bokser from HEB. 430p. 1983. 18.00 (*0-87441-368-0*); pap. 15.00 (*0-87441-372-9*) Behrman.

Prayer Book. Ed. by Anna Riva et al. 128p. (Orig.). 1984. pap. 4.95 (*0-943832-09-8*) Intl Imports.

Prayer Book. large type ed. (Orig.). pap. 5.00 (*0-317-01858-2*) Cath Guild Blind.

Prayer Book & People in Elizabethan & Early Stuart England. Judith Maltby. LC 97-15776. (Cambridge Studies in Early Modern British History). (Illus.). 328p. (C). 1998. text 64.95 (*0-521-45313-5*) Cambridge U Pr.

***Prayer Book & People in Elizabethan & Early Stuart England.** Judith Maltby. (Cambridge Studies in Early Modern British History). (Illus.). 331p. 2000. pap. write for info. (*0-521-79387-4*) Cambridge U Pr.

Prayer Book & the Lord's Prayer. Frederick D. Maurice. 416p. 1977. reprint ed. 14.00 (*0-87921-038-9*) Attic Pr.

Prayer Book Concordance. Ed. by Galen Bushey. 977p. 1988. 49.95 (*0-89869-150-8*) Church Pub Inc.

Prayer Book for Australia: Short Edition. abr. ed. Anglican Church of Australia Staff. 493p. 1996. 19.95 (*0-85574-190-2*, Pub. by E J Dwyer) Morehouse Pub.

Prayer Book for Catholic Families. Ed. by Christopher Anderson et al. LC 97-49896. (Illus.). 218p. 1998. 14.95 (*0-8294-1076-7*) Loyola Pr.

***Prayer Book for Catholic Families.** Christopher Anderson. 186p. 1999. pap. 9.95 (*0-8294-1528-9*) Loyola Pr.

Prayer Book for Earnest Christians: A Spiritually Rich Anabaptist Resource. Ed. & Tr. by Leonard Gross from GER. LC 96-8616.Tr. of Ernesthafte Christenpflicht. 152p. 1997. pap. 9.99 (*0-8361-9044-0*) Herald Pr.

Prayer Book for Summer Camps. Morris Silverman & Hillel Silverman. (J). (gr. 3-12). 8.95 (*0-87677-060-X*); pap. 6.95 (*0-87677-061-8*) Prayer Bk.

***Prayer Book for Today's Catholic.** Michael Buckley. LC 99-86139. 154p. 2000. pap. 9.99 (*1-56955-183-9*, Charis) Servant.

Prayer Book for Young Catholics. deluxe ed. Robert J. Fox. LC 82-81318. 146p. (J). (gr. 4-8). 1982. pap. 5.95 (*0-87973-370-5*, 370) Our Sunday Visitor.

Prayer Book in the Church. Charles P. Price. 24p. (Orig.). 1997. pap. 1.95 (*0-88028-195-2*, 1452) Forward Movement.

Prayer Book of Michelino Da Besozzo. Patricia Corbett. (Illus.). 1995. 45.00 (*0-8076-1389-4*) Braziller.

Prayer Book of Michelino Da Besozzo. Patricia Corbett. LC 81-68186. (Illus.). 1981. boxed set 65.00 (*0-8076-1016-X*) Braziller.

Prayer Book Parallels: The Public Services of the Church Arranged for Comparative Study, Vol. 1. Paul V. Marshall. 701p. 1989. 44.95 (*0-89869-181-8*) Church Pub Inc.

Prayer Book Parallels: The Public Services of the Church Arranged for Comparative Study, Vol. 2. Paul V. Marshall. 576p. 1990. 39.95 (*0-89869-209-1*) Church Pub Inc.

Prayer Book Rubrics Expanded. Byron D. Stuhlman. 248p. 1987. 19.95 (*0-89869-160-5*) Church Pub Inc.

Prayer Book Spirituality: A Devotional Companion to the Book of Common Prayer Compiled from Classical Anglican Sources. Ed. by J. Robert Wright. (Illus.). 473p. 1989. 32.95 (*0-89869-171-0*) Church Pub Inc.

Prayer Book Through the Ages: A Revised Edition of the Story of the Real Prayer Book. 3rd rev. ed. William Sydnor. LC 89-35852. Orig. Title: The Real Prayer Book. 144p. 1997. reprint ed. pap. 11.95 (*0-8192-1509-0*) Morehouse Pub.

Prayer Box: Time Management for Your Prayer Life. Dru S. Decker. 1998. 12.95 (*0-9660527-4-9*) Bridgecross Pr.

Prayer Box Gift: Answers from God - Questions Busy People Ask about Guidance & Prayer. Dru S. Decker. 1998. write for info. (*0-9660527-0-6*); pap. write for info. (*0-9660527-1-4*) Bridgecross Pr.

Prayer Box Gift Time Management for Your Spiritual Life. Dru S. Decker. 1998. write for info. (*0-9660527-9-X*) Bridgecross Pr.

Prayer Bubbles. Kymn Chapman. 140p. (Orig.). 1997. pap. 10.00 (*0-9660043-0-2*) K Chapman Ent.

Prayer Bundle. Toons Hermans. Tr. by John F. Jansen Inde Wal from DUT. 80p. (Orig.). 1993. pap. 6.95 (*1-55612-459-7*, LL1459) Sheed & Ward WI.

Prayer Can Change Your Marriage. rev. ed. Ron Auch. LC 90-63496. 176p. 1990. pap. 8.95 (*0-89221-118-0*) New Leaf.

Prayer Celebrations for the Liturgical Year. Thomas H. Morris. LC 98-119997. (Illus.). 64p. (J). (gr. 7-9). 1998. pap. text 6.00 (*0-8215-5640-1*) Sadlier.

***Prayer-Centered Healing: Finding the God Who Heals.** Rick Mathis. LC 00-29603. 2000. pap. 14.95 (*0-7648-0660-2*) Liguori Pubns.

Prayer Centered Life: Living in Conversation with the Father. Dudley J. Delffs. LC 96-50346. 191p. (Orig.). 1997. pap. 9.00 (*0-89109-997-2*) NavPress.

***Prayer Changes Things.** Eunice Alfred. 200p. 1999. 15.00 (*0-9670227-1-1*) E Alfred.

Prayer Companion: For the Federal Association, U. S. A, the Sovereign Military Hospitaller Order of St. John of Jerusalem, of Rhodes, & of Malta. Federal Association, U. S. A., Staff. LC 97-23736. 1997. pap. write for info. (*0-8091-3774-7*) Paulist Pr.

Prayer Companion for MOMS. V. LoPiccolo Jennett & Paula Hagen. LC 93-19670. (Illus.). 104p. (C). 1993. pap. 7.95 (*0-89390-265-9*) Resource Pubns.

***Prayer Connection: A True Story of Miracles.** Gloria Mascarelli & Robert Mascarelli. LC 99-74732. x, 230p. 1999. 21.95 (*0-9673376-1-5*); pap. 14.95 (*0-9673376-0-7*) Miracle Bk Pubs.

Prayer Conversing with God. Rosalind Rinker. 128p. 1986. mass mkt. 9.99 (*0-310-32171-9*) Zondervan.

Prayer Country: A Tour Guide to the Wonders of Prayer. Dorothy E. Watts. LC 92-14847. 1993. pap. 8.99 (*0-8163-1112-9*) Pacific Pr Pub Assn.

Prayer, Despair, & Drama: Elizabethan Introspection. Peter I. Kaufman. LC 95-32477. (Studies in Anglican History). 160p. 1996. text 24.95 (*0-252-02222-X*) U of Ill Pr.

Prayer Doll. (Illus.). 4p. (J). (ps-1). 1996. 14.99 (*1-888074-35-3*) Pckts Lrning.

***Prayer-Driven Church: Releasing God's Power to Every Member.** Ray Fulenwider. LC 00-21434. 2000. pap. write for info. (*0-89900-864-X*) College Pr Pub.

Prayer Factor. Sammy Tippit. pap. 9.99 (*0-8024-6678-8*, 255) Moody.

***Prayer, Faith & Healing: Cure Your Body, Heal Your Mind & Restore Your Soul.** Kenneth Winston Caine & Brian Paul Kaufman. 544p. 2000. pap. 19.95 (*1-57954-265-4*) Rodale Pr Inc.

Prayer, Faith & Healing: Cure Your Body, Heal Your Mind & Restore Your Soul. Kenneth Winston Caine et al. LC 98-31577. (Illus.). 512p. 1999. 29.95 (*1-57954-006-6*) Rodale Pr Inc.

Prayer, Fear, & Our Powers: Finding Our Healing, Release, & Growth in Christ. Flora S. Wuellner. LC 89-50643. 144p. 1989. pap. 10.00 (*0-8358-0597-2*) Upper Room Bks.

Prayer, Fear, & Our Powers: Stories of the Days Between Ascensiontide & Advent. Flora S. Wuellner. 1989. pap. 9.95 (*0-687-60912-7*) Abingdon.

Prayer for a Child. Rachel Field. LC 84-70991. (Illus.). 32p. (J). 1984. mass mkt. 4.99 (*0-02-043070-1*) Macmillan.

Prayer for a Child. Rachel Field. LC 44-47191. (Illus.). 32p. (J). (ps-1). 1968. lib. bdg. 14.00 (*0-02-735190-4*, Mac Bks Young Read) S&S Childrens.

Prayer for a Child. Rachel Field. (Illus.). 32p. (J). (ps-k). 1997. 6.99 (*0-689-81319-8*) S&S Childrens.

***Prayer for Beginners.** Peter Kreeft. 130p. 2000. pap. 9.95 (*0-89870-775-7*) Ignatius Pr.

Prayer for Children. Ina Hughs. LC 96-39944. 189p. 1997. per. 10.00 (*0-684-82993-2*, Fireside) S&S Trade Pap.

Prayer for Daybreak & Day's End, 2 vols., Set. Mary S. Taylor. 848p. 1993. pap. 19.95 (*0-86716-215-5*) St Anthony Mess Pr.

Prayer for Daybreak & Day's End, Vol. 1. Mary S. Taylor. 428p. 1993. pap. 15.95 (*0-86716-147-7*) St Anthony Mess Pr.

Prayer for Daybreak & Day's End, Vol. 2. Mary S. Taylor. 432p. 1993. pap. 15.95 (*0-86716-148-5*) St Anthony Mess Pr.

***Prayer for Deliverance from the Spirit of Fear.** large type ed. Uwem Inyang. Ed. by Benita Gilliard. (Spiritual Warfare Prayer Ser.: Vol. 3). 12p. 1999. spiral bd. 10.00 (*1-929623-02-X*) Jesus Recon Min.

Prayer for Divine Love, by Jesus of Nazareth. James E. Padgett. 1989. pap. write for info. (*1-887621-18-0*) Found Ch Divine Truth.

Prayer for Fair Weather. John Broderick. LC 83-6341. 192p. 1984. 13.95 (*0-7145-2796-3*) M Boyars Pubs.

Prayer for Guidance. Elbert Willis. 1977. 2.00 (*0-89858-012-9*) Fill the Gap.

***Prayer for Healing of the Heart & Mind.** large type ed. Uwem Inyang. Ed. by Benita Gilliard. (Spiritual Warfare Prayer Ser.: Vol. 5). 16p. 1999. spiral bd. 10.00 (*1-929623-04-6*) Jesus Recon Min.

***Prayer for Monica: A Little Ditty for a Child of the City, 1999.** Radomir Luza, Jr. (Illus.). 13p. 1999. pap. 5.00 (*0-9643783-6-1*) R Luza.

***Prayer for My Child: A Guide for the Precious Prayer of Parents.** Tim Spilman. Ed. by Stephanie Spilman. (Illus.). 1999. pap. write for info. (*0-9674948-0-X*) Pictures of Life.

Prayer for Owen Meany. John Irving. 640p. 1991. mass mkt. 6.99 (*0-345-36179-2*) Ballantine Pub Grp.

Prayer for Owen Meany. John Irving. 1999. pap. 12.95 (*0-345-41797-6*) Ballantine Pub Grp.

***Prayer for Owen Meany.** John Irving. 1999. 7.99 (*0-345-91555-0*); pap. 12.95 (*0-345-91556-9*) Ballantine Pub Grp.

Prayer for Owen meany: Curriculum Unit. Center for Learning Network Staff & John Irving. (Novel Ser.). 86p. (YA). (gr. 9-12). 1996. spiral bd. 18.95 (*1-56077-414-2*) Ctr Learning.

Prayer for Parish Groups: Preparing & Leading Prayer for Group Meetings. Julie Kavanagh & Donal Harrington. 252p. 1998. pap. 12.95 (*0-88489-620-X*) St Marys.

Prayer for Patient Waiting. Elbert Willis. 1977. 2.00 (*0-89858-002-1*) Fill the Gap.

***Prayer for People Who Think Too Much: A Guide to Everyday, Anywhere Prayer from the World's Faith Traditions.** Mitch Finley. LC 99-24027. 224p. 1999. 21.95 (*1-893361-00-4*) SkyLight Paths.

***Prayer for People Who Think Too Much: A Guide to Everyday, Anywhere Prayer from the World's Faith Traditions.** Mitch Finley. 2000. pap. 16.95 (*1-893361-21-7*) SkyLight Paths.

Prayer for Peter: The Story of Peter in Prison. Patricia L. Nederveld. LC 98-16961. (God Loves Me Ser.). (Illus.). 24p. (J). (ps). 1998. pap. 2.45 (*1-56212-315-7*, 1105-0146) CRC Pubns.

Prayer for Relief: The Constitutional Infirmities of the Military Academies' Conduct, Honor & Ethics Systems. Michael T. Rose. vii, 194p. 1973. pap. 17.50 (*0-8377-1025-1*, Rothman) W S Hein.

Prayer for Revelation. Watchman. 43p. 1998. pap. 1.00 (*1-57593-875-8*, 18-067-001) Living Stream Ministry.

***Prayer for the Children of Zimbabwe.** LC 00-101250. (Illus.). 32p. 2000. pap. 8.95 (*1-57736-183-0*) Providence Hse.

Prayer for the City: The True Story of a Mayor & Five Heroes in a Race Against Time. Buzz Bissinger. (Illus.). 448p. 1999. pap. 15.00 (*0-679-74494-0*) Vin Bks.

Prayer for the Dead. Orthodox Eastern Church Staff. 1991. pap. 1.50 (*0-89981-045-4*) Eastern Orthodox.

Prayer for the Dead. David Wiltse. 352p. 1992. mass mkt. 6.50 (*0-425-13398-2*) Berkley Pub.

Prayer for the Dying. large type ed. Jack Higgins. 302p. 1995. lib. bdg. 22.95 (*0-7862-0359-5*) Thorndike Pr.

Prayer for the Dying: A Novel. Stewart O'Nan. LC 98-39613. 195p. 1999. 22.00 (*0-8050-6147-9*) H Holt & Co.

***Prayer for the Dying: A Novel.** Stewart O'Nan. LC 99-85964. 208p. 2000. pap. 13.00 (*0-312-25501-2*, Picador USA) St Martin.

***Prayer for the Dying: A Novel.** large type ed. Stewart O'Nan. LC 99-86694. 2000. 25.95 (*1-56895-841-2*) Wheeler Pub.

Prayer for the Earth: The Story of Naamah, Noah's Wife. Sandy Eisenberg Sasso. LC 96-42065. (Illus.). 32p. (J). (ps up). 1996. 16.95 (*1-879045-60-5*) Jewish Lights.

Prayer for the Government: Ukrainians & Jews in Revolutionary Times, 1917-1920. Henry Abramson. (Harvard Series in Ukrainian Studies; Harvard Center for Jewish Studies). (Illus.). 310p. (C). 1999. pap. 18.95 (*0-916458-87-3*) Harvard Ukrainian.

Prayer for the Government: Ukrainians & Jews in Revolutionary Times, 1917-1920. Henry Abramson. (Harvard Series in Ukrainian Studies; Harvard Center for Jewish Studies). (Illus.). 320p. (C). 1999. text 34.95 (*0-916458-88-1*) Harvard Ukrainian.

Prayer for the Opening of the Little League Season. Willie Morris. LC 94-14471. (Illus.). 32p. 1995. 15.00 (*0-15-200892-6*) Harcourt.

Prayer for the Opening of the Little League Season. Willie Morris. LC 94-14471. (Illus.). 32p. (J). 1999. pap. 5.00 (*0-15-201724-0*) Harcourt.

***Prayer for the Planet.** Joseph Nolan. 128p. 2000. pap. 14.95 (*0-88347-464-6*, 661-239) T More.

Prayer for the Seasons of God's People Year C: Worship Aids for the Revised Common Lectionary. B. David Hostetter. 192p. 1997. pap. 14.95 (*0-687-33601-5*) Abingdon.

Prayer for the Ship. Douglas Reeman. pap. 3.75 (*0-09-907890-2*) Arrow Bks.

Prayer for the Twenty-First. John Marsden. LC 99-70749. (Illus.). 40p. (YA). (gr. 6-12). 1998. 15.95 (*1-887734-42-2*) Star Brght Bks.

Prayer for Tiger. Roxana F. Sinex. LC 97-26033. (Illus.). (J). 1997. write for info. (*0-87743-265-1*) Bellwood Pr.

Prayer for Today's People: Sermons on Prayer by Carl Michalson (1915-1965) Ed. by Edward J. Wynne, Jr. & Henry O. Thompson. LC 82-17583. 88p. (Orig.). 1983. pap. text 15.00 (*0-8191-2772-8*) U Pr of Amer.

***Prayer for Total Deliverance.** large type ed. Uwem Inyang. Ed. by Benita Gilliard. (Spiritual Warfare Prayer Ser.: Vol. 2). 27p. 1999. spiral bd. 10.00 (*1-929623-01-1*) Jesus Recon Min.

Prayer from Alexander to Constantine: Critical Anthology. Ed. by Mark Kiley. LC 97-183216. 320p. (C). 1997. 85.00 (*0-415-13234-7*); pap. 27.99 (*0-415-13235-5*) Routledge.

Prayer Groups. Joseph E. McNamara. LC 94-65550. 94p. (Orig.). 1994. pap. 1.95 (*1-882972-25-2*, 3201) Queenship Pub.

Prayer Guide. Andrew Murray. Orig. Title: Prayer Topics. 75p. 1992. mass mkt. 5.99 (*0-88368-475-6*) Whitaker Hse.

***Prayer Guide for the Brokenhearted.** Michelle McKinney-Hammond. LC 00-34939. 2000. write for info. (*1-56955-252-5*, Vine Bks) Servant.

***Prayer Guide for the Brokenhearted: Comfort & Healing on the Way to Wholeness.** Michelle McKinney Hammond. 2000. pap. 10.99 (*1-56955-222-3*) Servant.

***Prayer Heals: Miracles That Cannot Be Denied.** Irene Jenkins. 138p. 2000. pap. 8.95 (*0-9701472-0-1*) Temple Of God.

Prayer-Hymns: A New & Different Hymnal for Church & Home. W. Armstrong. LC 73-101347. pap. write for info. (*0-686-08988-X*) Gonzaga U Pr.

***Prayer Ideas for Ministry with Young Teens.** Joseph Grant. LC 00-8082. (Help Ser.). 120p. (YA). 2000. pap. 19.95 (*0-88489-570-X*) St Marys.

Prayer in Catholic Life see Basic Book of Catholic Prayer: How to Pray & Why

Prayer in Christian Moral Life. Ed. by Sergio Bastianel. 112p. (C). 1988. 49.00 (*0-7855-2322-7*, Pub. by St Paul Pubns) St Mut.

Prayer in Christian Moral Life. Sergio Bastianel. 128p. (C). 1990. 60.00 (*0-85439-283-1*, Pub. by St Paul Pubns) St Mut.

Prayer in Greek Religion. Simon Pulleyn. LC 97-20423. (Oxford Classical Monographs). (Illus.). 260p. 1998. text 75.00 (*0-19-815088-1*) OUP.

Prayer in Judaism: Continuity & Change. Ed. by Gabriel H. Cohn & Harold Fisch. LC 95-51821. 272p. 1996. pap. 35.00 (*1-56821-501-0*) Aronson.

Prayer in Practice see Art of Praying: The Principles & Methods of Christian Prayer

Prayer in Practice. Abudus-Samad Sharafuddin. 14p. 1996. pap. 2.00 (*0-614-21472-6*, 972) Kazi Pubns.

Prayer in Practice. Simon Tugwell. 152p. 1980. pap. 7.95 (*0-87243-099-5*) Templegate.

Prayer in Sixteenth-Century England. Faye L. Kelly. LC 66-64090. (University of Florida Humanities Monographs: No. 22). 76p. reprint ed. pap. 30.00 (*0-7837-5007-2*, 204467400004) Bks Demand.

Prayer in the Black Tradition. 1986. pap. 7.95 (*0-687-60910-0*) Abingdon.

Prayer in the Contemporary World. Douglas V. Steere. LC 80-82942. 32p. 1990. pap. 4.00 (*0-87574-291-2*) Pendle Hill.

Prayer in the Hebrew Bible: The Drama of Divine-Human Dialogue. Samuel E. Balentine. LC 92-20553. (Overtures to Biblical Theology Ser.). 328p. 1993. pap. 21.00 (*0-8006-2615-X*, 1-2615) Augsburg Fortress.

Prayer in the New Age. White Eagle Staff. 112p. 1957. 6.95 (*0-85487-041-5*, Pub. by White Eagle) DeVorss.

Prayer in the New Age. large type ed. White Eagle Staff. 112p. 1984. reprint ed. (*0-85487-064-4*) White Eagle.

Prayer in the New Testament. Oscar Cullman. Tr. by John Bowden. (Overtures to Biblical Theology Ser.). 244p. 1995. pap. 20.00 (*0-8006-2944-2*) Augsburg Fortress.

Prayer in the Public Schools & the Constitution, 1961-1992: Government Sponsored Religious Activities in Public Schools & the Constitution. Robert Sikorski. LC 92-42959. (Controversies in Constitutional Law Ser.). 512p. 1993. text 88.00 (*0-8153-1272-5*) Garland.

Prayer in the Talmud: Forms & Patterns. Joseph Heinemann. (Studia Judaica: Vol. 9). (C). 1977. 115.40 (*3-11-004289-4*) De Gruyter.

Prayer in the Unseen Warfare. Jack N. Sparks. LC 96-37840. (Orig.). 1997. pap. 9.95 (*1-888212-03-9*) Conciliar Pr.

Prayer in World Religions. Denise L. Carmody & John T. Carmody. LC 89-48198. 176p. reprint ed. pap. 54.60 (*0-608-20188-X*, 207144700012) Bks Demand.

Prayer in Your Life. Santan Pinto. 63p. 1995. pap. 10.00 (*1-888080-02-7*) ABCD Prnting.

Prayer Is a Gentle Way of Being with God. Joan W. Anglund. LC 98-40504. 48p. 1999. 11.99 (*0-87788-708-X*, H Shaw Pubs) Waterbrook Pr.

Prayer Is a Hunger. Edward Farrell. 1971. pap. 11.95 (*0-87193-031-5*) Dimension Bks.

***Prayer Is a Welcome Place: A User-Friendly Guide to Prayer.** Betsy Lee. Ed. by Terry McDowell. LC 99-93354. (Illus.). 120p. 1999. pap. 10.00 (*0-9673557-0-2*) Prayer Vent.

Prayer Is Good Medicine: How to Reap Healing Benefits of Prayer. Larry Dossey. LC 96-12273. 272p. 1997. pap. 13.00 (*0-06-251424-5*, Pub. by Harper SF) HarpC.

Prayer Is Invading the Impossible see Oracion Invade lo Imposible

Prayer Is Invading the Impossible. Jack W. Hayford. LC 77-71684. 150p. 1994. 11.99 (*0-88270-721-3*) Bridge-Logos.

Prayer Is Invading the Impossible. rev. ed. Jack W. Hayford. LC 77-71684. 170p. 2000. pap. 9.99 (*0-88270-218-1*) Bridge-Logos.

Prayer Is More Than Saying "Please" John H. Hampsch. 16p. 1997. pap. 1.25 (*1-57918-028-0*, 7156) Queenship Pub.

Prayer Is the Answer. Joseph Murphy. 190p. 1973. pap. 7.50 (*0-87516-189-8*) DeVorss.

***Prayer Is the Key--Faith Unlocks the Door.** Becky A. Gray. LC 93-93884. 1999. 12.95 (*0-533-10669-9*) Vantage.

Prayer is Warfare. Mickey Bonner. LC 96-122443. 105p. 1987. pap. 7.00 (*1-878578-00-6*) M Bonner Evan Assn.

***Prayer Journal.** Mary Ann P. DiEdwardo & Patricia J. Pasda. (Illus.). 75p. (J). 2000. spiral bd. 19.95 (*0-9641468-5-1*) M DiEdwardo Pubng.

Prayer Journal. Jubilee Staff. 1996. pap. text 5.95 (*1-57727-020-7*) Jubilee Pub Grp.

Prayer Journal, 1. Patricia Burnette. 63p. 1998. ring bd. 14.99 (*0-9668295-0-6*) Word of Wis.

Prayer Journal, Ivory Cover/Burgundy Ink. Allan Wolf. 1996. pap. 5.95 (*0-89841-055-X*) Zoe Pubns.

P

An Asterisk (*) at the beginning of an entry indicates that the title is appearing for the first time.

*__Prayer Journal for Busy Women: Convenient Easy to Use Guide for Personal Growth & Practical Application.__ Susan A. Lund. Ed. by Jenny Schlagenhaft. 208p. 1999. pap. 14.95 (*0-9676629-0-7*) Learn By Design.

Prayer Journal-IVR CVR/PR. Allan Wolf. 1996. pap. 5.95 (*0-89841-069-X*) Zoe Pubns.

*__Prayer Journal 2000: Jubilee 2000.__ (Illus.). 208p. 1999. 12.95 (*0-932085-28-8*) Word Among Us.

Prayer Journey. Fredi Trammell. 105p. (Orig.). 1991. pap. write for info. (*0-9629286-0-7*) Harmony Min.

Prayer Journey for Persons with AIDS. Robert Nugent. 49p. 1990. pap. text 3.95 (*0-86716-127-2*) St Anthony Mess Pr.

*__Prayer KJV: Matthew 6:5-24.__ 27p. 1999. pap. 4.95 (*1-57407-074-6*) Ldrship Minist Wrldwide.

Prayer Life see Prayer Power

Prayer Life. Andrew Murray. pap. 3.99 (*0-551-00027-9*) Zondervan.

Prayer Life: A Guide to the Inner Chamber. Andrew Murray. 128p. 1987. pap. 3.95 (*0-310-55072-6*, 19007P) Zondervan.

Prayer Life for the Beginner. Ignatius Brianchaninov. 1994. pap. 0.50 (*0-89981-156-6*) Eastern Orthodox.

Prayer Life of Jesus. D. M. McIntyre. 5.99 (*1-85792-010-4*, Pub. by Christian Focus) Spring Arbor Dist.

Prayer Life of Jesus: Shout of Agony, Revelation of Love, a Commentary. William D. Spencer & Alda B. Spencer. 308p. (C). 1991. pap. text 29.50 (*0-8191-7779-2*) U Pr of Amer.

Prayer Made Easy. Mark Water. 64p. 1999. pap. 5.95 (*1-56563-102-1*) Hendrickson MA.

Prayer Made Practical. Frederick Pelser. 1998. pap. 9.99 (*1-873796-65-X*) Review & Herald.

Prayer Medicine: How to Dance, Cry, Sing, Meditate, Wrestle, Love & Pray Your Way to Healing. Louis M. Savary. LC 96-20766. 176p. 1995. pap. 12.95 (*0-88268-199-0*) Station Hill Pr.

Prayer Ministry of the Church. (SPA.). 89p. 1998. per. 7.00 (*1-57593-908-8*, 04-038-002) Living Stream Ministry.

Prayer Ministry of the Church. Watchman Nee. Tr. by Stephen Kaung. 128p. 1973. pap. 4.50 (*0-935008-30-6*) Christian Fellow Pubs.

Prayer Ministry of the Church. Watchman Nee. 84p. 1995. per. 6.00 (*0-87083-860-1*, 04-038-001) Living Stream Ministry.

Prayer-Moments for Every Day of the Year. M. Kathleen Glavich. LC 97-61822. 80p. 1998. pap. 7.95 (*0-89622-748-0*) Twenty-Third.

*__Prayer Mountain: Exploring the High Places of Prayer.__ Brother Ramon. 144p. 1999. 12.95 (*1-85311-225-9*, 6112, Pub. by Canterbury Press Norwich) Morehouse Pub.

*__Prayer NIV: Matthew 6:5-24.__ 27p. 1999. pap. 4.95 (*1-57407-099-1*) Ldrship Minist Wrldwide.

Prayer of Daily Confession for a Person Entering on the Way of Salvation. Dimitry of Rostov. 1996. pap. 0.50 (*0-89981-165-5*) Eastern Orthodox.

Prayer of Faith. Leonard S. Boase. 126p. 1985. reprint ed. pap. 5.95 (*0-8294-0493-7*) Loyola Pr.

Prayer of Heart & Body: Meditation & Yoga As Christian Spiritual Practice. Thomas P. Ryan. LC 94-32996. (Illus.). 336p. 1995. pap. 12.95 (*0-8091-3523-X*) Paulist Pr.

*__Prayer of Jabez: Breaking Through to the Blessed Life.__ Bruce Wilkenson. LC 00-8406. 93p. 2000. 7.99 (*1-57673-733-0*) Multnomah Pubs.

Prayer of St. Francis. Carol A. McClure. 1.25 (*0-687-02774-8*) Abingdon.

Prayer of St. Patrick. 1976. pap. 1.00 (*0-89981-073-X*) Eastern Orthodox.

Prayer of the Bone. Paul Bryers. 288p. 1999. 23.95 (*1-58234-022-6*) Bloomsbury Pubg.

*__Prayer of the Bone.__ Paul Bryers. 2000. pap. 13.95 (*1-58234-075-7*) Bloomsbury Pubg.

Prayer of the Faithful: Understanding & Creatively Leading Corporate Intercessory Prayer. Walter C. Huffman. LC 92-12757. 80p. 1992. pap. 10.99 (*0-8066-2645-3*, 10-26453) Augsburg Fortress.

*__Prayer of the Faithful, 2000: Resource for Sundays, Feasts, Holidays, Parish Events & Weekdays.__ Ed. by James Wilde. 112p. 1999. pap. 5.95 (*1-57992-072-1*) OR Catholic.

Prayer of the Heart. Carol R. Knox. Ed. by Carolyn Cogan. LC 92-74522. 250p. (C). 1992. pap. 15.50 (*0-9628400-0-9*) C R Knox Fndtn.

*__Prayer of the Righteous.__ Mark Templer. 150p. 2000. 10.99 (*1-57782-126-2*) Discipleshp.

Prayer of the Warrior. Michael H. Brown. LC 93-72630. (Illus.). 248p. (Orig.). 1993. pap. 11.00 (*1-880033-10-0*) Queenship Pub.

*__Prayer 101: What It Is. What It Isn't. How to Do It.__ Don M. Aycock. LC 98-11175. 144p. 1998. 9.99 (*0-8054-1500-9*) Broadman.

Prayer Organizer. rev. ed. James B. Richards. 114p. 1990. ring bd. 20.00 (*0-924748-01-X*) Impact Ministries.

Prayer Organizer: Making a Difference Through Personal Prayer. unabridged ed. Creative Encouragers Staff. 110p. 1996. reprint ed. ring bd. 24.95 (*1-890533-00-9*, Prayer Organizer) Creat Encouragers.

Prayer Organizer: Making a Difference Through Personal Prayer. 2nd rev. ed. Creative Encouragers Staff. (Illus.). xii, 116p. 1999. ring bd. 24.95 (*1-890533-03-3*); ring bd. 24.95 (*1-890533-04-1*) Creat Encouragers.

Prayer Organizer: Making a Difference Through Personal Prayer Adult Edition. 2nd abr. rev. ed. Creative Encouragers Staff. (Illus.). 110p. ring bd. 24.95 (*1-890533-02-5*, Prayer Organizer) Creat Encouragers.

Prayer Organizer: Making a Difference Through Personal Prayer Youth Edition. rev. ed. Creative Encouragers Staff. (Illus.). 110p. (YA). (gr. 7-12). 1997. ring bd. 24.95 (*1-890533-01-7*, Prayer Organizer) Creat Encouragers.

Prayer Partners Prayer Book. Zondervan Publishing Staff. 1998. 3.99 (*0-310-96368-0*) Zondervan.

Prayer Patterns. Lin Johnson. LC 93-19786. (Tapestry Collection). 96p. (Orig.). 1993. pap. 6.50 (*1-56476-193-2*, 6-3193, Victor Bks) Chariot Victor.

Prayer Perspectives. Ed. by Edward Carter. LC 86-28675. 108p. (Orig.). 1987. pap. 5.95 (*0-8189-0513-1*) Alba.

Prayer Planner: A Daily Journal. Ann Moore. (Illus.). 384p. 1995. spiral bd. 36.00 (*1-888041-00-5*, Prayer Planner) Frnds of God.

Prayer Poems. Ed. by O. V. Armstrong & Helen J. Armstrong. LC 72-86793. (Granger Index Reprint Ser.). 1977. 18.95 (*0-8369-6094-7*) Ayer.

Prayer Portraits. Catherine Hoesterey. 1995. 10.99 (*0-7852-7986-5*) Nelson.

Prayer Power. George M. Brown. 160p. (Orig.). 1992. pap. 8.95 (*0-940999-94-3*, C2264) Star Bible.

Prayer Power. Janice T. Connell. LC 98-19205. 1999. 13.00 (*0-06-061523-0*) HarpC.

*__Prayer Power.__ Jim Gallery & Criswell Freeman. 128p. 2000. pap. 4.95 (*1-58334-082-3*, Pub. by Walnut Gr Pr) Midpt Trade.

Prayer Power. Andrew Murray. LC 98-43717. Orig. Title: The Prayer Life. 159p. 1999. pap. 6.99 (*0-88368-567-1*) Whitaker Hse.

Prayer Power: Secrets of Healing & Protection. Janice T. Connell. LC 98-19205. 320p. 1998. 18.00 (*0-06-061522-2*, Pub. by Harper SF) HarpC.

Prayer, Power, & Prosperity: Three Keys to a Move of God. Mark Brazee. 119p. 1998. pap. 7.00 (*0-934445-05-2*) Eternal Word.

Prayer Power Unlimited: Achieving Intimacy with God Through Prayer. J. Oswald Sanders. LC 97-4943. 176p. 1997. reprint ed. pap. 9.99 (*1-57293-023-3*) Discovery Hse Pubs.

Prayer Powerpoints. Randall D. Roth. LC 95-1640. 192p. 1995. 11.99 (*1-56476-433-8*, 6-3433, Victor Bks) Chariot Victor.

Prayer, Praise, & Glory. Jean Beyer. 54p. 1991. pap. 6.95 (*1-85390-172-5*, Pub. by Veritas Pubns) St Mut.

Prayer, Praise & Promises: A Daily Walk Through the Psalms. Warren W. Wiersbe. 1992. pap. 10.95 (*0-8474-0701-2*) Back to Bible.

*__Prayer, Praise & Promises: A Daily Walk Through the Psalms.__ Warren W. Wiersbe. 1999. pap. text 10.99 (*0-8474-6620-5*) Back to Bible.

Prayer Primer: A Philosophy Book. Patty Jo Cornish. Ed. by Roberto Quintero. LC 84-81741. 68p. (Orig.). pap. 5.95 (*0-9613717-0-6*) Hilltop Hse.

Prayer Primer for Catechists & Teachers: For Personal & Classroom Use. Gwen Costello. LC 97-62565. 64p. 1998. pap. 5.95 (*0-89622-922-X*) Twenty-Third.

Prayer Primer for Catholic Families. Christopher Anderson. 1998. pap. 3.15 (*0-8294-1015-5*) Loyola Pr.

Prayer Request - Answer Log. (Believer's Life System Women's Edition Ser.). 1998. ring bd. 3.50 (*0-8024-6975-2*) Moody.

Prayer Room Counselor's Handbook. Cathy Jakobcic. 47p. 1983. pap. 2.25 (*0-88144-015-9*) Christian Pub.

*__Prayer Room Intercessor's Handbook.__ Prayer Point Press Staff. 1999. 5.00 (*1-57892-049-3*) Prayer Pt Pr.

Prayer Rugs. Richard Ettinghausen et al. LC 74-15703. (Illus.). 139p. 1974. 25.00 (*0-685-56677-3*); pap. 18.50 (*0-614-25022-6*) Textile Mus.

Prayer Rugs from Private Collections. Patricia Fiske. (Illus.). 139p. 1974. pap. 2.50 (*0-87405-003-0*) Textile Mus.

Prayer Secrets. 136p. 1997. reprint ed. pap. text 6.95 (*0-942889-11-8*) Christ Life Pubns.

Prayer Secrets. 2nd ed. Kenneth E. Hagin. 1967. pap. 2.95 (*0-89276-005-2*) Faith Lib Pubns.

Prayer Service Models. Center for Learning Network Staff. (Parish Ministry Manuals Ser.). 108p. 1989. spiral bd. 15.95 (*1-56077-035-X*) Ctr Learning.

Prayer Service to St. Tikhon of Zadonsk. (SLA.). 1994. pap. 3.00 (*0-89981-151-5*) Eastern Orthodox.

Prayer Services for Catechist & Teacher Meetings. Gwen Costello. LC 96-60347. 72p. (Orig.). 1996. pap. 12.95 (*0-89622-696-4*) Twenty-Third.

Prayer Services for Parish Councils. Robert D. Eimer & Sarah A. O'Malley. 40p. (Orig.). 1995. pap. 2.95 (*0-8146-2304-2*, Liturg Pr Bks) Liturgical Pr.

*__Prayer Services for Teens: 34 Resources for Special Reasons & Church Seasons.__ Kass P. Dotterweich. Ed. by Jean Larkin. (Illus.). 96p. 1999. pap. 19.95 (*0-937997-47-1*) Hi-Time Pflaum.

Prayer Services for the Elderly. Sandra DeGidio. LC 95-61900. 112p. (Orig.). 1996. pap. 19.95 (*0-89622-685-9*) Twenty-Third.

Prayer Services for Young Children: Thirty Ten-Minute Celebrations. Gayle Schreiber. LC 92-82674. 72p. (Orig.). 1993. pap. 9.95 (*0-89622-542-9*) Twenty-Third.

Prayer-Shaped Disciple: Learn How Prayer Can Enrich Your Spiritual Life. Dan R. Crawford. 230p. 1999. 17.95 (*1-56563-092-0*) Hendrickson MA.

Prayer Shield see Escudo de Oracion

Prayer, Stress & Our Inner Wounds. Flora S. Wuellner. LC 84-51830. 94p. 1985. pap. 10.00 (*0-8358-0501-8*) Upper Room Bks.

Prayer Stress, Our. Flora S. Wuellner. 1985. pap. 9.95 (*0-687-60925-9*) Abingdon.

*__Prayer Takes Wings: How God Sends His Angels as We Pray.__ Thetus Tenney. LC 99-56929. 2000. pap. 9.99 (*0-8307-2465-6*, Regal Bks) Gospel Lght.

Prayer-Texts of Luke Acts. Steven F. Plymale. LC 91-18623. (American University Studies: Theology & Religion: Ser. VII, Vol. 118). 134p. (C). 1992. text 35.95 (*0-8204-1658-4*) P Lang Pubng.

Prayer That Brings Revival: Interceding for God to Move in Your Family, Church & Community. David Yonggi Cho. LC 98-44139. 204p. 1998. pap. 12.99 (*0-88419-580-5*) Creation House.

*__Prayer That God Answers: Experiencing the Power & Fullness of the Lord's Prayer.__ Michael Youssef. LC 99-59066. 240p. 2000. pap. 12.99 (*0-7852-7105-8*) Nelson.

Prayer That Heals: Praying for Healing in the Family. Francis S. MacNutt. LC 80-69770. 120p. (Orig.). 1981. pap. 6.95 (*0-87793-219-0*) Ave Maria.

Prayer That Moves Mountains. Gordon Lindsay. 1960. per. 5.95 (*0-89985-078-2*) Christ for the Nations.

Prayer That Moves Mountains. Gordon Lindsay. (Literature Crusade Ser.). 1965. pap. 0.95 (*0-89985-352-8*) Christ for the Nations.

Prayer That Moves Mountains (La Oracion Que Nueve las Montanas) Gordon Lindsay. (Literature Crusade Ser.). (SPA.). 1965. pap. 0.95 (*0-89985-365-X*) Christ for the Nations.

Prayer That Produces Results see Oracion Que da Resultados

Prayer That Releases Power: How to Pray the Scriptures. Glenn Egli. LC 81-71753. 119p. 1991. mass mkt. 4.99 (*0-88270-506-7*) Bridge-Logos.

Prayer That Shapes the Future. Bradley J. Longfield & Doug McMurry. LC 99-18212. 1999. pap. 12.99 (*0-310-22540-X*) HarpC.

*__Prayer That Works.__ Jill Briscoe. LC 00-21837. 2000. pap. 10.99 (*0-8423-1919-0*) Tyndale Hse.

Prayer the Key to Purpose. Al T. Henry. 16p. (Orig.). 1996. pap. text 3.00 (*1-886861-00-5*) Hosanna Pub Hse.

Prayer-the Key to Salvation. Michael Muller. LC 85-52207. 226p. 1992. reprint ed. pap. 7.50 (*0-89555-287-6*) TAN Bks Pubs.

Prayer, the Remedy That Always Works. Joanna R. Light. Ed. by Leo Love. 185p. 1997. pap. 13.00 (*1-891109-36-7*) Peace Mind.

Prayer Themes & Guided Meditations for Children. Barbara A. Bretherton. LC 97-62343. 96p. (J). 1998. pap. 9.95 (*0-89622-896-7*) Twenty-Third.

Prayer Therapy. Keith McClellan. LC 89-82664. (Illus.). 76p. (Orig.). 1990. pap. 4.95 (*0-87029-225-0*, 20206-9) Abbey.

Prayer to a Purple God: Poems. Constance Studer. LC 95-53288. (Illus.). 64p. 1996. pap. 14.95 (*0-7734-2682-5*, Mellen Poetry Pr) E Mellen.

Prayer to Fish. James Iody. 15p. 1983. pap. 2.00 (*0-941720-11-X*) Slough Pr TX.

Prayer to Our Lady of La Vang see Hoa Kinh Dang Me La Vang

*__Prayer to Thank You.__ Karen Kaslov Burr. Ed. by Noreen Wise. (Book-a-Day Collection). (Illus.). 32p. (J). (ps up). 2000. pap. 5.95 (*1-58584-385-7*) Huckleberry CT.

Prayer to the Great Mystery: The Uncollected Writings & Photography of Edward S. Curtis. abr. ed. Ed. by Gerald Hausman & Bob Kapoun. (Illus.). 228p. 1997. pap. 17.95 (*0-312-16969-8*) St Martin.

Prayer Topics see Prayer Guide

Prayer Treasures: Discover the Riches of Prayer. Dorothy E. Watts. LC 95-18289. 1995. pap. 3.97 (*0-8163-1271-0*) Pacific Pr Pub Assn.

*__Prayer Treasury, 1 vol.__ Victor Publishing Chariot. LC 99-203970. 1999. 12.99 (*0-7459-4085-4*) Lion USA.

Prayer Tree. Annie Jones. LC 98-13073. 369p. 1998. pap. 11.99 (*1-57673-239-8*) Multnomah Pubs.

Prayer Voices. H. Robert Cowles & K. Neill Foster. 308p. 1996. mass mkt. 5.99 (*0-87509-677-8*) Chr Pubns.

Prayer-Walking: A Simple Path to Body & Soul Fitness. Linus Mundy. LC 93-72446. 55p. (Orig.). 1994. pap. 4.95 (*0-87029-264-1*, 201772) Abbey.

*__Prayer Walking: Step by Step Prayer Walking Instructions.__ Henry Gruver. 77p. 1998. pap. 10.00 (*1-58538-005-9*) Prophecy Club.

Prayer Warriors: A Story. Celeste P. Walker. LC 96-21113. 1996. pap. 12.99 (*0-8163-1359-8*) Pacific Pr Pub Assn.

Prayer Warriors: Powerful Portraits of Men & Women on God's Front Lines. Compiled by Christian Publications Staff. 200p. 1998. mass mkt. 5.99 (*0-87509-702-2*) Chr Pubns.

Prayer Warriors: The True Story of a Gay Son, His Fundamentalist Christian Family & Their Battle for His Soul. Stuart H. Miller. LC 98-55996. 304p. 1999. pap. 13.95 (*1-55583-445-0*, Pub. by Alyson Pubns) Consort Bk Sales.

*__Prayer Way to Health, Wealth & Happiness.__ rev. ed. Lowell Fillmore. LC 99-36564. 360p. 2000. 12.95 (*0-87159-255-X*, 140) Unity Bks.

Prayer Wheels of Bluewater. Loss P. Glazier. (Doubles Ser.). (Illus.). 64p. 1993. 39.95 (*0-938075-33-0*); pap. 11.95 (*0-938075-34-9*) Ocean View Bks.

Prayer When It's Hard to Pray. Martin Helldorfer. LC 94-60351. 80p. (Orig.). 1994. pap. 7.95 (*0-89622-602-6*) Twenty-Third.

Prayer with Searchers & Saints. Edward F. Gabriele. LC 98-232662. (Illus.). 92p. 1998. pap. 13.95 (*0-88489-526-2*) St Marys.

Prayer Without Ceasing: Breath Prayers. Kathleen S. Lewis. LC 97-69269. 1998. pap. text 8.99 (*0-933451-37-7*) Prescott Pr.

Prayer Words: An Exercise in Meditative Prayer. Graham Smith. 120p. (Orig.). 1994. pap. 30.00 (*0-86012-185-2*, Pub. by Srch Pr) St Mut.

Prayer Works! Robert Collier. 1985. pap. 6.95 (*0-912576-01-4*) R Collier.

Prayer Works! True Stories of Answered Prayer. Rosemary Guiley. LC 97-28382. 192p. 1998. pap. 12.95 (*0-87159-218-5*) Unity Bks.

*__Prayer Works: True Stories of Answered Prayer.__ Rosemary Ellen Guiley. (Illus.). 192p. 1999. pap. 12.95 (*0-87159-243-6*, Unity Hse) Unity Bks.

Prayer Works for Teens, Bk. 1. Lisa-Marie Calderone-Stewart. Ed. by Robert Samschror. (Resources for Parishes, Schools & Families Ser.: Vol. 1). (Illus.). 72p. (YA). 1997. pap. 12.95 (*0-88489-432-0*) St Marys.

Prayer Works for Teens, Bk 2. Lisa-Marie Calderone-Stewart. Ed. by Robert Samschror. Vol. 2. (Illus.). 64p. (YA). 1997. pap. 12.95 (*0-88489-433-9*) St Marys.

Prayer Works for Teens, Bk. 3. Lisa-Marie Calderone-Stewart. (Resources for Parishes, Schools & Families Ser.: Vol. 3). (Illus.). 72p. (YA). 1997. pap. 12.95 (*0-88489-434-7*) St Marys.

Prayer Works for Teens, Bk. 4. Lisa-Marie Calderone-Stewart. (Resources for Parishes, Schools & Families Ser.: Vol. 4). (Illus.). 72p. (YA). 1997. pap. 12.95 (*0-88489-435-5*) St Marys.

Prayer, Your Foundation for Success. Kenneth Copeland. 112p. 1983. pap. 5.95 (*0-88114-704-4*) K Copeland Pubns.

Prayerbook: Book of Hours. Monks of New Skete Staff. Tr. by Laurence Mancuso from GRE. (Illus.). 752p. 1976. 35.00 (*0-9607924-3-0*) Monks of New Skete.

Prayerbook: Service of the Heart. (Home Study Program Ser.: No. 302). 6.00 (*0-686-96123-4*) USCJE.

Prayerbook for Catechists. Gwen Costello. 41p. 1999. pap. 5.95 (*0-89622-979-3*) Twenty-Third.

Prayerbook for Catholics. Robert J. Fox. 112p. (Orig.). 1982. pap. 3.95 (*0-931888-08-5*) Christendom Pr.

Prayerbook for Engaged Couples. Austin Fleming. 85p. 1990. pap. 5.95 (*0-929650-23-9*, PWED) Liturgy Tr Pubns.

Prayerbook (for Hospitals) rev. ed. James Toal & Ann Redig. 48p. 1992. pap. 0.30 (*0-8199-0503-8*, Frncscn Herld) Franciscan Pr.

*__Prayerbook for Husbands & Wives: Partners in Prayer.__ Ruthanne Wangerin & Walter Wangerin. LC 00-41623. 2000. pap. 11.99 (*0-8066-4062-6*, Augsburg) Augsburg Fortress.

*__Prayerbook for Spiritual Friends: Partners in Prayer.__ Madeleine L'Engle & Luci Shaw. LC 99-25817. (Illus.). 96p. 1999. pap. 10.99 (*0-8066-3892-3*) Augsburg Fortress.

Prayerbook for the Days of Awe see Kol Haneshamah: Mahzor LeYamim Nora'im

Prayerbook Hebrew Answer Book & Teacher's Guide. Joseph Anderson. Ed. by Ethelyn Simon & Victoria Kelman. 110p. (Orig.). (C). 1994. pap. text 8.95 (*0-939144-19-0*) EKS Pub Co.

*__Prayerbook Hebrew the Easy Way.__ 3rd ed. Joseph Anderson et al. 312p. 2000. pap. 18.95 (*0-939144-32-8*) EKS Pub Co.

Prayerbook of Favorite Litanies: 116 Favorite Catholic Litanies & Responsory Prayers. Compiled by Albert Hebert. LC 84-51818. 192p. 1985. pap. 10.00 (*0-89555-252-3*) TAN Bks Pubs.

Prayerbook of the King: The Psalms: A Commentary. Charles J. Dollen. LC 97-20173. 320p. 1998. pap. 16.95 (*0-8189-0751-7*) Alba.

*__Prayer/Classic Guitar Duo.__ Frederic Hand. 16p. 1999. pap. 5.95 (*0-7866-4795-7*, 98189) Mel Bay.

Prayerful Journey with Mary - Lift up Your Hearts. Anthony A. Petrusic. Ed. by Sue H. Parker. (Illus.). 1999. 7.95 (*0-937739-43-X*, 10041) Roman IL.

Prayerful Responsibility: Prayer & Social Responsibility in the Religious Thought of Douglas Steere. John D. Copenhaver. 216p. (Orig.). (C). 1992. lib. bdg. 44.00 (*0-8191-8530-2*) U Pr of Amer.

Prayerfully Sinning. Bryan A. Floyd. LC 83-63239. 92p. 1985. 22.00 (*0-932966-49-7*); pap. 16.00 (*0-932966-48-9*) Permanent Pr.

Prayerlike Poems. 2nd ed. Carol Lauman. LC 96-96992. (Illus.). ix, 55p. 1996. reprint ed. pap. 7.95 (*0-9654672-0-1*) Chriss Pub.

*__Prayerpath to Jesus Through Mary: Sequel to the Scriptural Rosary.__ rev. ed. Christianica Staff. Orig. Title: The Christianica. (Illus.). 160p. 2000. 9.95 (*0-911346-15-5*) Christianica.

*__Prayers.__ Marian Edelman. 96p. (J). 1999. pap. 5.99 (*0-7868-1438-1*, Pub. by Hyperion) Time Warner.

*__Prayers.__ Marian Edelman. 96p. (J). 2000. lib. bdg. 15.49 (*0-7868-2513-8*, Pub. by Hyperion) Little.

*__Prayers.__ Marian Elderman. 96p. (J). 2000. 15.99 (*0-7868-0597-8*, Pub. by Disney Pr) Time Warner.

Prayers. Theodore P. Ferris. 1984. 7.20 (*0-8164-0483-6*) Harper SF.

Prayers. Bruno Forte. 47p. (Orig.). 1992. pap. 3.95 (*0-8198-5884-6*) Pauline Bks.

*__Prayers.__ Havoc Publishing Staff. 1999. pap. 5.00 (*0-7416-1102-3*) Havoc Pub.

Prayers. Peter Washington. LC 96-223595. 256p. 1995. 10.95 (*0-679-44466-1*) Knopf.

Prayers. Soren Kierkegaard. 246p. (C). 1996. reprint ed. pap. 12.00 (*0-226-47057-1*) U Ch Pr.

Prayers. Michel Quoist. LC 63-17141. 190p. 1985. reprint ed. pap. 8.95 (*0-934134-46-4*) Sheed & Ward WI.

Prayers: For Daily & Occasional Use. Victor Hoagland. 1969. pap. 2.50 (*0-8091-5158-8*) Paulist Pr.

Prayers: From Adoration to Zeal. C. Welton Gaddy. LC 93-9254. 128p. 1993. pap. 12.00 (*0-8170-1190-0*) Judson.

Prayers: Poems from Hollywood. Mark Dunster. 11p. 1998. pap. 5.00 (*0-89642-557-6*) Linden Pubs.

Prayers about Everyday Stuff: Off the Cuff & from the Heart. Jack Van Bemmel. LC 98-61594. 87p. 1999. pap. 7.95 (*0-89622-968-8*) Twenty-Third.

Prayers Across the Centuries. Ed. by Vinita H. Wright. LC 92-32268. 176p. (Orig.). 1993. pap. 8.99 (*0-87788-646-6*, H Shaw Pubs) Waterbrook Pr.

An Asterisk (*) at the beginning of an entry indicates that the title is appearing for the first time.

Prayers, Activities, Celebrations (& More) for Catholic Families. Bridget M. Meehan. LC 94-61850. 80p. (Orig.). 1995. pap. 7.95 (*0-89622-641-7*) Twenty-Third.

Prayers Against Depression. Lance Martin & Carol Martin. 124p. 1996. pap. 8.95 (*0-914733-21-4*) Desert Min.

Prayers & Beliefs for Children. (J). Date not set. 1.50 (*0-88271-544-5*, 10358) Regina Pr.

***Prayers & Blessings.** 32p. 2000. 9.95 (*1-929669-02-X*) Vinings Pubng.

Prayers & Blessings. Lois R. Beverly. 53p. 1998. pap. 5.95 (*1-55630-833-7*) Brentwood Comm.

Prayers & Blessings. John T. Ferrier. 64p. 1985. text 7.00 (*0-900235-41-1*) Order Of The Cross.

Prayers & Blessings for Daily Life in Christ. enl. rev. ed. Michael Scanlan & John Bertolucci. 83p. (Orig.). 1989. pap. 3.95 (*0-940535-00-9*, UP101) Franciscan U Pr.

Prayers & Code of Conduct on the Path. Albert Gani. LC 99-184217. 200p. 1998. pap. 10.00 (*1-882853-05-9*) A Gani.

Prayers & Devotion. John Paul, II, pseud. 1998. pap. 9.95 (*0-14-024725-4*) Viking Penguin.

Prayers & Devotions. Hoagland. (Catholic Classics Ser.). (J). 1997. pap. 3.95 (*0-88271-478-3*) Regina Pr.

Prayers & Devotions for Teachers. Martha W. Hickman. LC 88-8188. 1989. pap. 6.95 (*0-687-33631-7*) Abingdon.

Prayers & Fables: Meditating on Aesop's Wisdom. William Cleary. LC 97-47387. (Illus.). 180p. 1997. pap. 14.95 (*1-55612-960-2*, LL1960) Sheed & Ward WI.

Prayers & Graces. Alice J. Davidson. (Alice in Bibleland Storybooks). (Illus.). 32p. (J). (gr. 3 up). 1986. 5.95 (*0-8378-5078-9*) Gibson.

Prayers & Graces. Compiled by Michael Jones. 96p. 1990. 10.95 (*0-86315-063-2*, 404, Pub. by Floris Bks) Anthroposophic.

Prayers & Graces. Random House Value Publishing Staff. (Illus.). 1999. 5.99 (*0-517-20327-8*) Random Hse Value.

Prayers & Heavenly Promises. Compiled by Joan C. Cruz. LC 90-70225. (Illus.). 130p. (Orig.). 1990. pap. 5.00 (*0-89555-397-X*) TAN Bks Pubs.

Prayers & Inspiration for Senior Children of God. Anne Kunath & Lillian Riegert. 1979. pap. 5.50 (*0-87516-369-6*) DeVorss.

Prayers & Journey of Faith. Thomas Lion. 1995. 12.95 (*0-7459-3358-0*, Pub. by Lion Pubng) Trafalgar.

Prayers & Litanies for the Christian Seasons. Sharlande Sledge. LC 98-37031. 1999. 14.00 (*1-57312-192-4*) Smyth & Helwys.

Prayers & Mantras. Sri Aurobindo & Mother. Ed. by Vijay. 120p. 1996. 4.95 (*81-7060-022-7*, Pub. by SAA) E-W Cultural Ctr.

Prayers & Meditation for Healing. 2nd ed. Charles R. Toye. 96p. 1988. reprint ed. pap. 6.95 (*0-9619732-0-X*) Send Your Spirit Pub.

***Prayers & Meditations.** Sa Ashram. 1998. 17.50 (*81-7058-110-9*) SAA.

Prayers & Meditations. Baha'u'llah. Tr. by Shoghi Effendi. LC 53-10767, 347p. 1955. 15.95 (*0-87743-024-1*, 103-010) Bahai.

Prayers & Meditations. Baha'u'llah. Tr. by Shoghi Effendi. 262p. 1984. 17.50 (*0-900125-39-X*) Bahai.

Prayers & Meditations. Baha'u'llah. 347p. 1987. pap. 3.95 (*0-87743-181-7*) Bahai.

Prayers & Meditations. rev. ed. Tr. by Aurobindo from FRE. 380p. (Orig.). (C). 1979. pap. 13.00 (*0-89744-998-3*, Pub. by Sri Aurob Ashram Trust); text 16.00 (*0-89744-219-9*, Pub. by Sri Aurob Ashram Trust) Acrpls Bks CO.

Prayers & Meditations. 2nd ed. Mother.Tr. of Prieres et Meditations. (FRE.). 381p. 1997. pap. 14.50 (*81-7058-052-8*, Pub. by SAA) E-W Cultural Ctr.

Prayers & Meditations for Children. Greer Lawrence. 1998. pap. text 7.98 (*1-57717-061-X*) Todtri Prods.

Prayers & Meditations for Our Little Angels. Hafeesa Nettles. LC 96-5895. (Illus.). (J). 1996. 14.95 (*1-881316-49-1*); pap. 7.95 (*1-881316-33-5*) A&B Bks.

Prayers & Meditations from Around the World. Tracy Baumgardner. (Illus.). 80p. 1997. 6.95 (*0-87573-065-5*) Jain Pub Co.

Prayers & Meditations of St. Anselm. St. Anselm. Tr. by Benedicta Ward. (Classics Ser.). 288p. 1979. pap. 12.95 (*0-14-044278-2*, Penguin Classics) Viking Penguin.

Prayers & Meditations of Therese of Lisieux. Ed. by Cindy Cavnar. 186p. 1993. pap. 9.99 (*0-89283-749-7*, Charis) Servant.

Prayers & Poems. (Children's Bible Stories Ser.). (Illus.). 24p. (J). 1993. 4.98 (*1-56173-723-2*) Pubns Intl Ltd.

Prayers & Poems for Christmas. Ideals Publications Editors. 160p. 1996. 24.95 (*0-8249-4074-1*) Ideals.

Prayers & Poems from the Leeward Side. Lucia Christian. Ed. by Richard A. Schrader, Sr. LC 97-91269. (Illus.). 108p. 1998. pap. write for info. (*0-9622987-7-8*) R A Schrader.

***Prayers & Praises.** Ed. by Jennifer Stewart. (Illus.). 48p. (J). (ps-2). 1999. pap. 2.49 (*0-7847-0985-8*, 22055) Standard Pub.

Prayers & Proclamations. 1990. pap., spiral bd. 6.95 (*0-934920-97-4*, B-58) Derek Prince.

Prayers & Proclamations. (ENG & IND.). 1993. pap. write for info. (*0-934920-46-X*, B-58IN) Derek Prince.

Prayers & Proclamations. Derek Prince & Ruth Prince. 77p. 1999. reprint ed. mass mkt. 5.99 (*0-88368-226-5*, B-59) Whitaker Hse.

***Prayers & Promises.** Leslie Eckard. 2001. 10.99 (*0-8054-2039-8*) Broadman.

Prayers & Promises for Every Day. large type ed. Corrie Ten Boom. 272p. 1985. pap. 13.95 (*0-8027-2505-8*) Walker & Co.

Prayers & Readings for Worship, Vol. 2. Ed. by Peter Judd. (Illus.). 96p. (Orig.). 1996. pap. text 16.00 (*0-8309-0719-X*) Herald Pub Hse.

Prayers & Recommended Practices. 2nd ed. Jerome F. Coniker. LC 78-66374. (Living Meditation & Prayerbook Ser.). (Illus.). 91p. pap. text 3.00 (*0-932406-01-7*) AFC.

Prayers & Reflections. 112p. 1993. teacher ed., spiral bd. 15.95 (*1-56077-247-6*) Ctr Learning.

Prayers & Sermons from the City Pulpit. Joseph Parker. (Bible Sermon Ser.: Pulpit Legends Colletions). 1996. 19.99 (*0-89957-208-1*) AMG Pubs.

Prayers & Tears of Jacques Derrida: Religion Without Religion. John D. Caputo. LC 96-47839. (Indiana Series in the Philosophy of Religion). 1997. 39.95 (*0-253-33268-0*); pap. 19.95 (*0-253-21112-3*) Ind U Pr.

Prayers & Thoughts for Peace. Illus. by Jacqueline Craske. 60p. 1986. pap. 5.95 (*0-900125-67-5*) Bahai.

Prayers Around the Family Table. Vinita H. Wright & Carol Plueddemann. (Pocketpac Bks.). 144p. (Orig.). 1992. pap. text 3.99 (*0-87788-691-1*, H Shaw Pubs) Waterbrook Pr.

Prayers at Christmastime. Pamela Kennedy. (Illus.). 24p. (J). (ps-1). 1996. reprint ed. 6.95 (*1-57102-098-5*, Ideals Child) Hambleton-Hill.

Prayers at Eastertime. Pamela Kennedy. (Illus.). 24p. (J). (ps-1). 1996. 6.95 (*1-57102-073-X*, Ideals Child) Hambleton-Hill.

Prayers at Meals. Michael Kwatera & Dietrich Reinhart. 44p. 1983. pap. 0.95 (*0-8146-1318-7*) Liturgical Pr.

***Prayers by Children: In Their Own Words.** Ed. by Good Books Editors. 96p. (J). 1999. 7.95 (*1-56148-299-4*) Good Bks PA.

***Prayers Daytime/Nighttime.** Havoc Publishing Staff. 1999. pap. 9.00 (*0-7416-1005-1*) Havoc Pub.

Prayers Encircling the World: An International Anthology. Westminister Publishing Staff. Ed. by SPCK Staff. LC 98-53720. 284p. 1999. pap. 15.00 (*0-664-25821-2*) Westminster John Knox.

Prayers Everyone Should Know. St. Pauls Publications Staff. 1996. pap. 39.95 (*0-85439-506-7*, Pub. by St Paul Pubns) St Mut.

Prayers for a Child's Day. Ed. by Laura Ring. (Happy Day Bks.). (Illus.). 24p. (J). (ps-2). 1999. pap. 1.99 (*0-7847-0891-6*, 04264) Standard Pub.

Prayers for a Fragile World. Carol Watson. 12.95 (*0-7459-1949-9*) Lion USA.

Prayers for a Lifetime. Karl Rahner. 1994. pap. 24.95 (*0-567-29132-4*, Pub. by T & T Clark) Bks Intl VA.

Prayers for a New Millennium. Mary L. Kownacki. 48p. 1998. pap. 1.95 (*0-7648-0232-1*) Liguori Pubns.

Prayers for a Planetary Pilgrim: A Personal Manual for Prayer & Ritual. Edward Hays. LC 88-83763. (Illus.). 292p. 1989. kivar 15.95 (*0-939516-10-1*) Forest Peace.

Prayers for a Quiet Heart. Date not set. 5.95 (*0-88271-549-6*, 10126) Regina Pr.

Prayers for a Small Child. Illus. by Eloise Wilkin. 1995. 4.99 (*0-679-86656-6*, Pub. by Random Bks Yng Read) Random.

Prayers for a Sojourning People: A Collection of Pastoral Prayers. Susan Gregg-Schroeder. 150p. 1997. pap. 11.95 (*1-57438-015-X*, 3535) Ed Ministries.

Prayers for a Thousand Years: Blessings & Expressions of Hope for the New Millennium. Ed. by Elizabeth Roberts & Elias L. Amidon. LC 98-43252. 384p. 1999. pap. 15.00 (*0-06-066875-X*, Pub. by Harper SF) HarpC.

Prayers for a Woman of Faith, NIV. (Women of Faith Ser.). 128p. 1998. 7.99 (*0-310-97336-8*, Zondervan Gifts) Zondervan.

Prayers for All Occasions. 96p. 1951. pap. 1.65 (*0-88028-006-9*, 977) Forward Movement.

Prayers for All Occasions. Ed. by Francis Evans. 160p. (Orig.). 1988. pap. 5.25 (*0-89942-917-3*, 917/09) Catholic Bk Pub.

Prayers for All Occasions. large type ed. Compiled by Francis J. Moore. 96p. 1987. pap. 2.50 (*0-88028-100-6*, 883) Forward Movement.

Prayers for All Occasions. Stuart R. Oglesby. 180p. 1989. reprint ed. pap. 14.95 (*0-8042-2485-4*) Westminster John Knox.

Prayers for All Occasions: For Pastors & Lay Leaders. Roy Pearson. 144p. (Orig.). 1990. pap. 14.00 (*0-8170-1127-7*) Judson.

Prayers for All Occasions: My Voice to the Lord. John A. Shalhoub. 200p. (Orig.). 1996. pap. 9.95 (*1-880971-25-9*) Light&Life Pub Co MN.

Prayers, for All People, for All Occasions. Leander M. Zimmerman. LC BV0245.Z5. 68p. reprint ed. pap. 30.00 (*0-608-17173-5*, 202787700056) Bks Demand.

Prayers for Bedtime, No. 2. Alan Parry & Linda Parry. LC 97-66276. (Time to Pray Ser.). (Illus.). 12p. (J). (ps). 1997. 4.99 (*0-8499-1466-3*) Tommy Nelson.

Prayers for Bobby: A Mother's Coming to Terms with the Suicide of Her Gay Son. Leroy Aarons. LC 94-45141. 288p. 1996. pap. 14.00 (*0-06-251123-8*, Pub. by Harper SF) HarpC.

Prayers for Boys & Girls. Scovil. (Precious Moments Ser.). 1983. 10.99 (*0-7667-0404-1*) Gibson.

Prayers for Caregivers. Ed. by David Philippart. (Prayer Book Ser.). 64p. 2000. pap. 4.00 (*1-56854-264-X*, PCARE) Liturgy Tr Pubns.

Prayers for Catholics Experiencing Divorce: Prayers for Healing. William Rabior & Vicki W. Bedard. LC 93-78434. 96p. 1993. pap. 4.95 (*0-89243-528-3*) Liguori Pubns.

Prayers for Children. (Little Golden Storybks.). (Illus.). (J). 1998. 3.99 (*0-307-16085-8*, 16085, Goldn Books) Gldn Bks Pub Co.

Prayers for Children. Ed. by Dietz. (Illus.). (J). (gr. 1-6). 1990. pap. 0.99 (*0-87509-121-0*) Chr Pubns.

Prayers for Children. S. First. (J). 1996. bds. 4.95 (*0-88271-454-6*) Regina Pr.

Prayers for Children. Terry Teykl. (Keys to the Kingdom Ser.). 40p. 1996. ring bd. 6.00 (*1-57892-008-6*) Prayer Pt Pr.

Prayers for Children: North American Edition. Compiled by Christopher Herbert. 272p. 1994. pap. 10.95 (*0-88028-149-9*, 1247) Forward Movement.

Prayers for Contemporary Worship. Church of Scotland - Committee on Public Worship &. 1977. pap. 4.95 (*0-7152-0351-7*) Outlook.

Prayers for Contemporary Worship. Church of Scotland Panel on Worship Staff. 128p. 1993. pap. 22.00 (*0-86153-091-8*, Pub. by St Andrew) St Mut.

Prayers for Dark People. W. E. B. Du Bois. Ed. by Herbert Aptheker. LC 80-12234. 88p. 1980. pap. 10.95 (*0-87023-303-3*) U of Mass Pr.

Prayers for Dark People. unabridged ed. W. E. B. Debois. 1997. 16.95 incl. audio (*0-9645593-9-0*) MasterBuy Audio Bks.

Prayers for Each Day. Taiz Communities Staff. LC 98-22356. 174p. 1998. pap. 12.00 (*1-57999-029-0*) GIA Pubns.

Prayers for Everyday. Lawrence G. Lovasik. (Saint Joseph Picture Bks.). (Illus.). (J). 1987. pap. 1.25 (*0-89942-381-7*, 381-00) Catholic Bk Pub.

Prayers for Everyday. Ed. by Elaine S. Rich. LC 90-80749. 95p. 1990. pap. 6.95 (*0-87303-137-7*) Faith & Life.

Prayers for Everyday Use. Josephine Bunch. 128p. 1994. pap. 7.95 (*1-85311-059-0*, 854, Pub. by Canterbury Press Norwich) Morehouse Pub.

Prayers for Everyone. (Illus.). 16p. (J). (gr. k-3). 1982. reprint ed. 0.99 (*0-86683-653-5*, AY8232) Harper SF.

Prayers for Expectant Mothers: Celebrating the Miracle of Life. Angela Guffey. 208p. 1998. 12.99 (*1-56292-538-5*) Honor Bks OK.

Prayers for Girlfriends & Sisters & Me. Evelyn Bence. LC 98-53805. 1999. 6.97 (*1-56955-118-9*) Servant.

Prayers for Healing. 1.50 (*0-87677-096-0*) Prayer Bk.

Prayers for Healing. Terry Teykl. (Keys to the Kingdom Ser.). 40p. 1996. ring bd. 6.00 (*1-57892-009-4*) Prayer Pt Pr.

Prayers for Healing: 365 Blessings, Poems & Meditations from Around the World. Ed. by Maggie Oman. LC 97-19158. 294p. 1997. 14.95 (*1-57324-089-3*) Conari Press.

***Prayers for Healing: 365 Blessings, Poems & Meditations from Around the World.** Ed. by Maggie Oman. 2000. reprint ed. pap. 13.95 (*1-57324-522-4*) Conari Press.

Prayers for Healing & Strength - Lift up Your Hearts. Anthony A. Petrusic. Ed. by Sue H. Parker. (Illus.). 1999. 7.95 (*0-937739-45-6*, 10043) Roman IL.

***Prayers for Health & Healing.** LC 00-24084. 128p. 2000. 18.95 (*0-8264-1264-5*) Continuum.

Prayers for Help & Healing. William Barclay. LC 94-39634. 1994. pap. 10.99 (*0-8066-2784-0*, 9-2784, Augsburg) Augsburg Fortress.

Prayers for Home & School. M. Doney. (Illus.). 16p. (J). 1982. reprint ed. 0.99 (*0-86683-652-7*, AY8231) Harper SF.

Prayers for Inner Strength. large type ed. John P. Beilenson. (Large Print Inspirational Ser.). 1987. pap. 5.95 (*0-8027-2582-1*) Walker & Co.

***Prayers for Jubilee.** Liturgy Training Publications Staff. 1999. pap. 3.00 (*1-56854-282-8*) Liturgy Tr Pubns.

Prayers for Later Years. Ed. by David Philippart. 64p. (Orig.). 1996. pap. 4.00 (*1-56854-146-5*, ELDER) Liturgy Tr Pubns.

Prayers for Little Hearts see Oraciones para Corazoncitos

Prayers for Little Hearts. Illus. by Elena Kucharik. LC 95-40114. (J). 1996. 9.99 (*0-8423-4970-7*) Tyndale Hse.

Prayer's for Little Hearts: Praise You, God/Thank You, God/I Love You, God/ Help Me, God, 1. Illus. by Elena Kucharik. 1999. 12.99 (*0-8423-3690-7*) Focus Family.

Prayers for Little People. Sarah Fletcher. (Illus.). 32p. (J). (ps-2). 1974. pap. 2.89 (*0-570-03429-9*, 56-1184) Concordia.

Prayers for Married Couples. Renee Bartkowski. LC 89-80027. 96p. (Orig.). 1989. pap. 4.95 (*0-89243-301-9*) Liguori Pubns.

Prayers for Midday. Ed. by David Philippart. LC 98-89934. (Prayer Book Ser.). 64p. 1999. pap. 4.00 (*1-56854-263-1*, MDAY) Liturgy Tr Pubns.

Prayers for My Family, No. 1. Alan Parry & Linda Parry. LC 97-66278. (Time to Pray Ser.). (Illus.). 12p. (J). (ps). 1997. 4.99 (*0-8499-1465-5*) Tommy Nelson.

Prayers for My Husband. Terry Teykl. (Keys to the Kingdom Ser.). 40p. 1996. ring bd. 6.00 (*1-57892-007-8*) Prayer Pt Pr.

Prayers for My Pastor. Terry Teykl. (Keys to the Kingdom Ser.). 40p. 1996. ring bd. 6.00 (*1-57892-005-1*) Prayer Pt Pr.

Prayers for My Village. Michel Bouttier. 1994. pap. 7.95 (*0-687-60887-2*) Abingdon.

Prayers for My Village. Michel Bouttier. Tr. by Lamar Williamson from FRE. 96p. 1994. pap. 8.00 (*0-8358-0711-8*) Upper Room Bks.

Prayers for My Wife. Terry Teykl. (Keys to the Kingdom Ser.). 40p. 1996. ring bd. 6.00 (*1-57892-006-X*) Prayer Pt Pr.

***Prayers for New Mothers.** Angela T. Guffey. 2000. 12.99 (*1-56292-776-0*) Honor Bks OK.

Prayers for One Voice: Two Hundred Prayers Based on the Revised Common Lectionary. Phyllis Cole & Everett Tilson. LC 92-42141. 176p. 1993. pap. 12.95 (*0-687-30339-7*) Abingdon.

Prayers for Parents & Children. Rudolf Steiner. 80p. 2000. reprint ed. pap. text 9.95 (*1-85584-036-7*) R Steiner Pr.

Prayers for Pastor & People. Ed. by Carl G. Carlozzi. 310p. 1984. 19.95 (*0-89869-108-7*) Church Pub Inc.

Prayers for Peace of Mind & Heart. Joseph P. Laruffa. 60p. pap. 1.25 (*0-8198-5866-8*) Pauline Bks.

Prayers for People in Hospital. Neville Smith. 200p. 1994. pap. 20.00 (*0-19-110009-9*) OUP.

Prayers for People Like Me. Robert St. Clair. LC 89-7206. 1989. pap. 6.95 (*0-941037-09-6*, BIBAL Press) D & F Scott.

Prayers for People under Pressure. Donald Deffner. LC 92-60994. 120p. (Orig.). 1992. pap. 8.99 (*0-8100-0429-1*, 06N0692) Northwest Pub.

Prayers for Pre-Schoolers. Beverly C. Burgess. (Illus.). (Orig.). (J). (ps-2). 1991. pap. 4.98 (*1-879470-02-0*) Burgess Pub.

Prayers for Priests Thomas R. Haney. LC 99-23018. 1999. write for info. (*0-8245-1816-0*) Crossroad NY.

Prayers for Prisoners. M. Countryman. 224p. 1989. pap. 12.95 (*0-937347-30-2*) C & D Intl.

Prayers for Public Worship. Ed. by Edward K. Ziegler. LC 86-6777. 72p. reprint ed. pap. 30.00 (*0-7837-5930-4*, 204572900007) Bks Demand.

Prayers for Puppies: Aging Autos, & Sleepless Nights. Robert Jones. (Illus.). 96p. (Orig.). 1993. pap. 9.95 (*0-664-25356-3*) Westminster John Knox.

***Prayers for Rain.** Dennis Lehane. 416p. 2000. mass mkt. 6.99 (*0-380-73036-7*) Morrow Avon.

Prayers for Rain. A Novel. Dennis Lehane. LC 99-22048. 352p. 1999. 25.00 (*0-688-15333-X*, Wm Morrow) Morrow Avon.

***Prayers for Rain: A Novel.** large type ed. Dennis Lehane. LC 99-46176. (G. K. Hall Core Ser.). 570p. 1999. 28.95 (*0-7838-8786-8*, G K Hall Lrg Type) Mac Lib Ref.

Prayers for Sunday Services. Church of Scotland - Committee on Public Worship &. 1980. pap. 6.95 (*0-7152-0456-4*) Outlook.

Prayers for Sunday Services. Church of Scotland Panel on Worship Staff. 144p. 1993. pap. 22.00 (*0-86153-088-8*, Pub. by St Andrew) St Mut.

Prayers for Sundays & Seasons: Year A. Peter Scagnelli. 170p. (Orig.). 1998. pap. 15.00 (*1-56854-225-9*, PRAYSA) Liturgy Tr Pubns.

Prayers for Sundays & Seasons: Year B. Peter Scagnelli. LC 96-34767. 208p. 1996. pap. 15.00 (*1-56854-112-0*, PRAYSB) Liturgy Tr Pubns.

Prayers for Sundays & Seasons: Year C. Peter Scagnelli. 208p. 1997. pap. 15.00 (*1-56854-212-7*, PRAYSC) Liturgy Tr Pubns.

Prayers for Teenagers. Nick Aiken. 104p. (YA). 1992. pap. 5.99 (*0-551-01931-X*) Zondervan.

Prayers for the Age of Technology. Haskell M. Miller. LC 97-29583. 64p. 1998. pap. 7.50 (*0-7880-1172-3*) CSS OH.

Prayers for the Age of Technology. Haskell M. Miller. 1998. pap. 7.50 (*0-7880-1175-8*) CSS OH.

Prayers for the Beginning of Life. National Conference of Catholic Bishops & United States Catholic Conference Administrative B. 16p. (Orig.). 1989. pap. 1.95 (*1-55586-297-7*) US Catholic.

Prayers for the Blessing & Sanctification of Icons of Various Kinds, & of an Iconostasis. Tr. by Isaac E. Lambertsen from SLA. 24p. (Orig.). 1993. pap. 3.00 (*0-912927-51-8*, D014) St John Kronstadt.

Prayers for the Breaking of Bread: Reflections on the Collects of the Church Year. Herbert O'Driscoll. LC 91-19446. 184p. 1991. pap. 9.95 (*1-56101-045-6*) Cowley Pubns.

Prayers for the Classroom. Ed. by Philip A. Verhalen. LC 97-27348. 248p. 1998. 19.95 (*0-8146-2456-1*) Liturgical Pr.

Prayers for the Common Good. Ed. by A. Jean Lesher. LC 97-47076. 208p. 1998. 18.95 (*0-8298-1248-2*) Pilgrim OH.

Prayers for the Dead: A Peter Decker & Rina Lazarus Novel. Faye Kellerman. LC 96-7494. (Peter Decker & Rina Lazarus Ser.). 424p. 1997. mass mkt. 6.99 (*0-380-72624-6*, Avon Bks) Morrow Avon.

Prayers for the Dead: A Peter Decker & Rina Lazarus Novel. large type ed. Faye Kellerman. LC 96-31420. (Large Print Bks.). 586p. 1996. 26.95 (*0-7838-1910-2*, G K Hall Lrg Type) Mac Lib Ref.

Prayers for the Dead: Sunday's Hollow Stories. Dennis Vannatta. 196p. 1994. pap. 14.00 (*1-877727-39-3*) White Pine.

Prayers for the Dead Ventriloquist. D. J. Smith. Ed. by Dale K. Boyer. 60p. (Orig.). 1995. pap., per. 6.95 (*0-916272-62-1*) Ahsahta Pr.

Prayers for the Dedication of a Church. Ed. by David Philippart. LC 97-39787. 84p. 1997. pap. 5.00 (*1-56854-197-X*, CHURCH) Liturgy Tr Pubns.

Prayers for the Domestic Church: A Handbook for Worship in the Home. rev. ed. Edward Hays. LC 82-72077. (Illus.). 215p. 1979. kivar 14.95 (*0-939516-11-X*) Forest Peace.

***Prayers for the Family.** John Woolley. 96p. 1999. 22.00 (*0-85305-449-5*, Pub. by Arthur James) St Mut.

Prayers for the Gathered Community: Resources for the Liturgical Year. Don C. Skinner. LC 98-13953. (Illus.). 256p. (Orig.). 1997. pap. 16.95 (*0-8298-1217-2*) Pilgrim OH.

Prayers for the Later Years. Josephine Robertson. LC 74-187591. 60 p. 1972. write for info. (*0-687-33628-7*) Abingdon.

Prayers for the Little Church in the Home: A Guidebook for Personal & Family Worship. S. Nicholas George. (Illus.). 87p. (Orig.). (C). 1995. pap. text 24.99 (*1-884090-21-4*) Ecumenics Intl.

Prayers for the Little Ones. Julia Cameron. LC 98-51023. 112p. 1999. 11.95 (*1-58063-048-0*, Pub. by Renaissance) St Martin.

Prayers for the New Babel: A Criticism of the Alternative Service Book, 1980. Ed. by Brynmill Press Ltd. Staff. 106p. (C). 1989. 45.00 (*0-907839-04-5*, Pub. by Brynmill Pr Ltd); pap. 30.00 (*0-907839-31-2*, Pub. by Brynmill Pr Ltd) St Mut.

Prayers for the No Longer Young. large type rev. ed. Mary C. White & Rollo M. Boas. 80p. 1997. pap. 2.95 (*0-88028-179-0*, 352) Forward Movement.

P

***Prayers for the Road: Psalm Meditations for College Students.** Thomas W. Currie. LC 00-35370. 115p. 2000. pap. write for info. (0-664-50129-X, Pub. by Geneva Press) Presbyterian Pub.

Prayers for the Seasons of God's People Year A: Worship Aids for the Revised Common Lectionary. B. David Hostetter. LC 98-52205. 192p. 1998. pap. 14.95 (0-687-33749-6) Abingdon.

Prayers for the Seasons of God's People Year B: Worship Aids for the Revised Common Lectionary. B. David Hostetter. 1999. pap. 14.95 (0-687-33664-3) Abingdon.

Prayers for the Seasons of Life. Sue K. Downing. (Illus.). 96p. 1997. 14.95 (1-57736-041-9) Providence Hse.

Prayers for the Servants of God. Edward Hays. (Illus.). 143p. 1980. pap. 7.95 (0-939516-03-9) Forest Peace.

Prayers for the Sick. Orthodox Eastern Church Staff. 1993. pap. 1.00 (0-89981-114-0) Eastern Orthodox.

Prayers for the Sickroom. William A. Lauterbach. 64p. 1968. pap. 1.95 (0-570-03524-4, 14-1236) Concordia.

Prayers for the Tongue-Tied: Ways to Pray When You Can't Find the Words. Ray W. Smith. 155p. 1994. write for info. (0-9639576-0-0) Christian Counsel.

Prayers for the Twelve Steps - A Spiritual Journey. Friends in Recovery. LC 93-15978. (Illus.). 128p. (Orig.). 1993. pap. 8.95 (0-941405-28-1) RPI Pubng.

Prayers for Today. Terence Cooke. 190p. 1991. pap. 6.95 (0-8189-0628-6) Alba.

Prayers for Urgent Occasions. Bernard Marie. 1990. pap. 5.25 (0-89942-918-1, 918/04) Catholic Bk Pub.

Prayers for Use in Church. Jack Masterton. 152p. 1993. pap. 24.00 (0-7152-0680-X, Pub. by St Andrew) St Mut.

Prayers for Worship: Alternate Collects for the Three Year Lectionary Ser. Ed. by Gregory J. Wismar. LC 93-12515. 80p. 1993. pap. 10.00 (0-570-04610-6, 12-3194) Concordia.

Prayers for Worship: Prayers of the Church for Every Sunday. Arnold G. Kuntz. LC 93-2946. 80p. 1993. pap. 10.00 (0-570-04607-6, 12-3193) Concordia.

Prayers for Young Bahais. LC 93-40941. (J). 1993. pap. 14.95 (0-933770-09-X) Kalimat.

Prayers for Young People. William Barclay. LC 92-38164. (Abingdon Classics Ser.). 96p. (Orig.). (YA). 1993. pap. 1.49 (0-687-33328-8) Abingdon.

Prayers for Your Husband. W. T. Whalin. LC 99-12295. 64p. 1999. 5.99 (0-8054-1856-3) Broadman.

***Prayers for Your Son.** W. T. Whalin. LC 98-54411. 64p. 1999. 5.99 (0-8054-1854-7) Broadman.

Prayers for Your Wife. W. T. Whalin. LC 99-12296. 64p. 1999. 5.99 (0-8054-1857-1) Broadman.

***Prayers from a Child's Heart Gift Book: A Delightful Read-a-Long Book That Will Help Young Children Learn.** Joni Eareckson Tada. (Illus.). 64p. (J). (ps-7). 1999. 14.99 (1-58375-474-1) Garborgs.

Prayers from a Mother's Heart. Ruth Bell Graham. LC 98-31551. (Illus.). 126p. 1999. 12.99 (0-7852-7304-2) Nelson.

Prayers from Grandma Gift Book. Compiled by Becky L. Amble. (Illus.). 96p. 1998. 12.99 (1-58375-421-0) Garborgs.

***Prayers from My Heart.** Pino Madero. Tr. by Mary David Wickenhiser. (Illus.). 32p. (J). (gr. 2-5). 2000. pap. 3.95 (0-8198-5916-8) Pauline Bks.

Prayers from the Ancient World: Greco-Roman, Jewish & Christian Prayers. Ed. by Gregory E. Sterling & Peter W. Van der Horst. (Christianity & Judaism in Antiquity Ser.: Vol. 13). 200p. 2000. 29.95 (0-268-03853-8, Pub. by U of Notre Dame Pr) Chicago Distribution Ctr.

***Prayers from the Ancient World: Greco-Roman, Jewish & Christian Prayers.** Ed. by Pieter W. Van der Horst & Gregory E. Sterling. (Christianity & Judaism in Antiquity Ser.: Vol. 13). 200p. 2000. pap. 18.00 (0-268-03855-4, Pub. by U of Notre Dame Pr) Chicago Distribution Ctr.

Prayers from the Ark. Carmen Bernos de Gasztold. (FRE.). (J). (gr. 3-8). 29.95 (0-685-11511-9) Fr & Eur.

Prayers from the Ark. Carmen Bernos de Gasztold. 1976. pap. 11.95 (0-14-058677-6) NAL.

Prayers from the Ark: Selected Poems. Carmen Bernos de Gasztold. (J). 1995. 11.19 (0-606-08589-0, Pub. by Turtleback) Demco.

Prayers from the Bible, No. 3. Alan Parry & Linda Parry. LC 97-66277. (Time to Pray Ser.). (Illus.). 12p. (J). (ps). 1997. 4.99 (0-8499-1467-1) Tommy Nelson.

Prayers from the East. Bryan D. Spinks. (Worship Ser.). 125p. (C). 1993. pap. text 14.95 (1-56929-000-8, Pastoral Press) OR Catholic.

Prayers from the Faithful. Ed Greenwood. (Forgotten Realms Game World Ser.). 1997. 19.95 (0-7869-0682-0, Pub. by TSR Inc) Random.

Prayers from the Flowers. Ann Qiray. LC 98-72425. (Illus.). 64p. 1998. pap. 11.95 (0-9665301-0-1) Essa Bks.

Prayers from the Heart. Carl Mays. LC 95-75424. (Illus.). 128p. (Orig.). 1995. pap. 9.95 (1-879111-49-7) Lincoln-Bradley.

Prayers from the Heart. Foster Rich. 144p. 1994. 19.00 (0-06-062847-2, Pub. by Harper SF) HarpC.

***Prayers from the Heart.** gif. ed. Conover Swofford. (Inspire Charming Petites Ser.). (Illus.). 80p. 1999. 4.95 (0-88088-137-2) Peter Pauper.

Prayers from the Heart: Simple Conversations with God. Honor Books Staff. 208p. 1999. 14.99 (1-56292-636-5) Honor Bks OK.

Prayers from the Imitation of Christ. Thomas, a Kempis. Ed. by Ronald Klug. (Classic Prayer Ser.). 96p. 1996. pap. 10.99 (0-8066-2989-4, 9-2989, Augsburg) Augsburg Fortress.

Prayers from the Psalms: With Other Prayers from Scripture. 2nd unabridged ed. Compiled by Hubert McEvoy. (Marian Ser.: Vol. 7). 152p. 1995. 13.95 (0-940147-39-4) Source Bks CA.

Prayers, Given to Mankind Abd-Ru-Shin. Abd-ru-shin. 1966. pap. 5.00 (3-87860-138-7) Grail Fndtn-Amer.

***Prayers God Always Answers: How His Faithfulness Surprises, Delights, & Amazes.** Nancy Kennedy. LC 99-26108. 224p. 1999. pap. 11.95 (1-57856-197-3) Waterbrook Pr.

Prayers, Graces, & Hymns for Children. Gail Harvey. LC 92-39152. (Illus.). 96p. (J). (gr. 2 up). 1993. 8.99 (0-517-09276-X) Random Hse Value.

***Prayers I Love.** 2nd rev. ed. Ed. by David A. Redding. (Illus.). 128p. 1999. pap. 15.95 (0-9671701-0-9, 1-A) Starborne Hse.

Prayers in Dialogue, Series C. David C. Godshall. (Common & Lutheran Ser.). 1985. 10.75 (0-89536-759-9, 5866) CSS OH.

Prayers in Stone: Christian Science Architecture in the United States, 1894-1930. Paul E. Ivey. LC 98-25358. 296p. 1999. 49.95 (0-252-02445-1) U of Ill Pr.

Prayers in Stone: Greek Architectural Sculpture 600-100 BC. Brunilde S. Ridgway. LC 98-3583. (Sather Classical Lectures: Vol. 63). 363p. 1999. 50.00 (0-520-21556-7, Pub. by U CA Pr) Cal Prin Full Svc.

***Prayers in the Precincts: The Christian Right in the 1998 Elections.** Ed. by John C. Green et al. LC 99-36840. 416p. 2000. pap. 23.95 (0-87840-775-8); text 65.00 (0-87840-774-X) Georgetown U Pr.

Prayers in Time of Sorrow. Mayhew. 1996. 5.95 (0-88271-497-X) Regina Pr.

Prayers, Meditations, & Thought for Health. Felicia Franks. Date not set. pap. write for info. (1-886583-09-9) SeaStar Pub.

Prayers New & Old. large type ed. Compiled by Gilbert P. Symons. 128p. 1987. pap. 3.25 (0-88028-101-4, 882) Forward Movement.

Prayers New & Old. rev. ed. Ed. by Priscilla Martin. 96p. 1993. pap. 1.50 (0-88028-140-5, 375) Forward Movement.

Prayers of a Christian Educator. Mobby Larson. (Greeting Book Line Ser.). 32p. (Orig.). 1985. pap. 1.95 (0-89622-277-2) Twenty-Third.

Prayers of a Mystic. Flower A. Newhouse. LC 86-71083. 102p. (Orig.). 1986. pap. 9.00 (0-910378-21-5) Christward.

Prayers of a Woman. 3rd rev. ed. Tracy Voigt. 55p. 1982. reprint ed. spiral bd. 4.00 (0-686-37419-3) T Voigt.

Prayers of a Working Mother. Judy Esway. (Greeting Book Line Ser.). 32p. (Orig.). 1985. pap. 1.95 (0-89622-269-1) Twenty-Third.

***Prayers of a Young Man.** Roch Carrier & Sheila Fischman. 192p. 1999. text. write for info. (0-670-88587-8) Studio Bks.

Prayers of an Accidental Nature. Debra Di Blasi. LC 98-56287. 224p. 1999. pap. 13.95 (1-56689-083-7, Pub. by Coffee Hse) Consort Bk Sales.

Prayers of an Omega: Facing the Transitions of Aging. Katie F. Wiebe. LC 93-43266. 104p. (Orig.). 1994. pap. 8.99 (0-8361-3658-6) Herald Pr.

Prayers of Consolation. Morris Silverman. 1972. 8.95 (0-87677-062-6); pap. 6.95 (0-87677-063-4) Prayer Bk.

Prayers of David: Psalms 51-72. Studies in the Psalter, II. Michael Goulder. (JSOT Supplement Ser.: No. 102). 264p. 1990. 75.00 (1-85075-258-3, Pub. by Sheffield Acad) CUP Services.

Prayers of Faith: On Learning to Trust God. Faith A. Sand. LC 95-47070. 206p. (Orig.). 1996. pap. 12.95 (0-932727-78-6); lib. bdg. 18.95 (0-932727-79-4) Hope Pub Hse.

Prayers of Jesus for Children. (J). write for info. (0-88271-162-8) Regina Pr.

Prayers of John Donne. John Donne. Ed. by Herbert H. Umbach. 1962. pap. 7.95 (0-8084-0252-8) NCUP.

Prayers of John of the Cross. 3rd ed. Alphonse Ruiz. 128p. 1994. pap. 9.95 (1-56548-073-2) New City.

Prayers of John Paul II. St. Paul Publications Staff. (C). 1988. 39.00 (0-85439-214-9, Pub. by St Paul Pubns) St Mut.

Prayers of Kierkegaard. Ed. by Perry D. LeFevre. LC 56-11000. (Midway Reprint Ser.). 246p. 1996. pap. text 20.50 (0-226-47059-8) U Ch Pr.

Prayers of Man. Ed. by Alfonso Di Nola. 1960. 27.95 (0-8392-1152-X) Astor-Honor.

Prayers of Mohammad. 1993. pap. 16.50 (1-56744-183-1) Kazi Pubns.

Prayers of Noons & Evenings see Tefillat Minchah U'Tefillat Aruit

Prayers of Noons & Evenings see Tefillat Minona Utefillat Aruit

Prayers of Peter Marshall. Ed. & Compiled by Catherine Marshall. LC 54-11762. 252p. (gr. 11). 1988. pap. 11.99 (0-8007-9141-X) Chosen Bks.

Prayers of Praise. Alan Parry & Linda Parry. LC 94-3641. (Little Prayers Ser.). (Illus.). 12p. (J). (ps-k). 1995. 3.99 (0-8499-1159-1) Tommy Nelson.

Prayers of Robert Louis Stevenson. Robert Louis Stevenson. 25p. (Orig.). 1983. pap. 2.50 (0-914005-00-6) Yokefellow Pr.

Prayers of Saint Francis. 6th rev. ed. Tr. by Alan Neame from GER. LC 94-10222. 112p. 1994. pap. 7.95 (1-56548-066-X) New City.

Prayers of Saint Paul. W. H. Thomas. 1989. pap. 3.99 (0-88019-252-6) Schmul Pub Co.

Prayers of Saint Therese of Lisieux. Guy Gaucher & Therese of Lisieux. Tr. by Aletheia Kane from FRE. LC 96-50347. (Critical Edition of the Complete Works (Texts And Words) of Saint Therese of the Child Jesus & of the Holy Face Ser.). 162p. 1997. pap. 8.95 (0-935216-60-X) ICS Pubns.

Prayers of St. Augustine: A Contemporary Anthology. Augustine, Saint. Ed. by Barry Ulanov. 160p. 1985. pap. 7.95 (0-86683-881-3, 7460) Harper SF.

Prayers of Susanna Wesley. Ed. by W. L. Doughty. 80p. 1984. reprint ed. pap. 4.95 (0-310-36351-9, 12368P) Zondervan.

Prayers of Teresa of Avila. 5th ed. Ed. by Thomas Alvarez. 136p. 1990. pap. 9.95 (1-56548-065-1) New City.

Prayers of the Bible. John E. McFadyen. LC 95-83608. (Bible Study Ser.: Pulpit Legends Collection). 375p. 1996. 14.99 (0-89957-213-8) AMG Pubs.

Prayers of the Bible. John E. McFadyen. (Classic Library). 350p. 1996. reprint ed. 15.99 (0-529-10483-0, POTB) World Publng.

Prayers of the Cosmos: Meditations on the Aramaic Words of Jesus. Neil Douglas-Klotz. LC 89-46456. 112p. 1993. pap. 12.00 (0-06-061995-3, Pub. by Harper SF) HarpC.

Prayers of the Eucharist: Early & Reformed. 3rd ed. Ronald C. Jasper & Geoffrey J. Cuming. 314p. 1992. pap. 19.95 (0-8146-6085-1, Pueblo Bks) Liturgical Pr.

Prayers of the Faithful. annuals spiral bd. write for info. (0-8146-2216-X) Liturgical Pr.

Prayers of the Faithful, Cycles A, B, C. 217p. 1992. pap. 19.95 (0-8146-6029-0, Pueblo Bks) Liturgical Pr.

***Prayers of the Faithful, 1999: Resource for Sundays, Feasts, Holidays, Parish Events & Weekdays.** rev. ed. Ed. by James A. Wilde. (Illus.). 112p. 1998. pap. 5.95 (1-57992-020-9) OR Catholic.

Prayers of the Faithful, 1997: Resource for Sundays, Feasts, Holidays, Parish Events & Weekdays. rev. ed. Ed. by Jim Wilde. (Illus.). 111p. 1996. pap. 5.95 (0-915531-51-8) OR Catholic.

Prayers of the Faithful 1998: Resource for Sundays, Feasts, Holidays, Parish Events & Weekdays. rev. ed. Ed. by Jim Wilde. (Illus.). 111p. 1997. pap. 5.95 (0-915531-92-5) OR Catholic.

***Prayers of the Heart.** Stormie Omartian. (Moment Meditations Ser.). 64p. 1999. pap. 7.99 (0-7369-0207-4) Harvest Hse.

Prayers of the Hours: Morning, Midday, & Evening. James R. Lahman. LC 95-61503. 136p. (Orig.). 1996. pap. 9.95 (0-89622-677-8) Twenty-Third.

Prayers of the Lenten & Easter Seasons. National Conference of Catholic Bishops & United States Catholic Conference Administrative B. 63p. (Orig.). 1989. pap. 2.95 (1-55586-301-9) US Catholic.

Prayers of the Martyrs. Duane W. Arnold. 144p. 1991. 12.99 (0-310-31450-X) Zondervan.

Prayers of the Old Testament. Clarence E. Macartney. LC 95-8722. 120p. 1995. pap. 9.99 (0-8254-3279-0) Kregel.

Prayers of the Orthodox Christian Church. large type ed. 1993. pap. 5.00 (0-89981-302-X) Eastern Orthodox.

Prayers of the Orthodox Church. 1992. pap. 1.00 (0-89981-075-6) Eastern Orthodox.

Prayers of the OT: Faith of Fathers. Stephen D. Eyre. (Truthseed Ser.). 80p. 1995. pap. 4.99 (1-56476-368-4, 6-3368, Victor Bks) Chariot Victor.

Prayers of the People: Ways to Make Them Your Own. David E. Johnson. 64p. (Orig.). 1988. pap. 1.90 (0-88028-083-2, 944) Forward Movement.

Prayers of the Prophet with Arabic Text. Abdul H. Siddiqui. 1991. pap. 3.75 (1-56744-184-X) Kazi Pubns.

Prayers of the Women Mystics. Ronda De Sola Chervin. 260p. (Orig.). 1992. pap. 8.99 (0-89283-750-0, Charis) Servant.

Prayers of the World. Compiled by Richard L. Polese. 96p. 2000. pap. 8.00 (0-943734-00-2) Ocean Tree Bks.

Prayers of Those Who Make Music. 2nd rev. ed. Ed. by David Philippart. 64p. (Orig.). 1996. pap. 4.00 (1-56854-131-7, MUSICR) Liturgy Tr Pubns.

Prayers of Those Who Mourn. 2nd ed. David Philippart. 64p. (Orig.). 1996. reprint ed. pap. 4.00 (1-56854-132-5, MOURNR) Liturgy Tr Pubns.

Prayers on My Pillow: Prayers for Girls on the Threshold of Change. Celia Straus. LC 98-21643. 224p. (J). (gr. 4-7). 1998. 18.50 (0-345-42673-8) Ballantine Pub Grp.

Prayers or Meditations, Where the Mind Is Stirred Patiently to Suffer All Afflictions Here. Catharine Parr. LC 76-57370. (English Experience Ser.: No. 788). 1977. reprint ed. lib. bdg. 20.00 (90-221-0788-4) Walter J Johnson.

Prayers Plainly Spoken. Stanley Hauerwas. LC 99-18735. 132p. 1999. 12.99 (0-8308-2209-7, 2209) InterVarsity.

***Prayers, Poems & Praise.** Katina Kefalos. (Illus.). 24p. 1999. pap. 4.95 (1-929172-08-7) Emerald Prodns.

Prayers, Praises & Professing. Arrie Lewallen. 1988. pap. write for info. (0-938645-03-X) In His Steps.

Prayers That Avail - Fathers Gift. G. E. Copeland. mass mkt. 19.99 (0-89274-965-2) Harrison Hse.

Prayers That Avail - Mothers Gift. G. E. Copeland. mass mkt. 17.99 (0-89274-840-0) Harrison Hse.

Prayers That Avail Much see Oraciones con Poder

***Prayers That Avail Much.** Germaine Copeland. 576p. 1999. 24.99 (1-57794-263-9) Harrison Hse.

Prayers That Avail Much. Word Ministries Staff. 1998. pap. text 9.99 (1-57794-125-X) Harrison Hse.

Prayers That Avail Much, Vol. 1. Germaine Copeland. 1999. pap. 9.99 (1-57794-064-4) Dake Pub.

***Prayers That Avail Much, Vol. 1.** Germaine Copeland. 2000. pap. 7.99 (1-57794-282-5) Harrison Hse.

Prayers That Avail Much, Vol. 1. Harrison House, Inc., Editors. 160p. 1995. mass mkt. 5.99 (0-89274-960-1, HH-960) Harrison Hse.

Prayers That Avail Much, Vol. I. rev. ed. Word Ministries, Staff. 180p. 1989. pap. 7.99 (0-89274-590-8, HH590) Harrison Hse.

Prayers That Avail Much, Vol. 2. Germaine Copeland. 1999. pap. 9.99 (1-57794-062-8) Dake Pub.

***Prayers That Avail Much, Vol. 2.** Germaine Copeland. 2000. pap. 7.99 (1-57794-283-3) Harrison Hse.

Prayers That Avail Much, Vol. 3. Germaine Copeland. 1999. pap. 9.99 (1-57794-063-6) Dake Pub.

***Prayers That Avail Much, Vol. 3.** Germaine Copeland. 2000. pap. 7.99 (1-57794-284-1) Harrison Hse.

Prayers That Avail Much, Vol. 3. Word Ministries Staff & Germaine Copeland. LC 97-188492. 192p. 1996. pap. 9.99 (0-89274-939-3, HH939) Harrison Hse.

Prayers That Avail Much: Special Edition. rev. ed. Word Ministries, Staff. 320p. 1989. ring bd. 19.99 (0-89274-556-8, HH556) Harrison Hse.

Prayers That Avail Much: Three Bestselling Works Complete in One Volume. gif. ed. Word Ministries Staff. LC 97-162529. (Prayers That Avail Much Ser.). 464p. 19.99 (0-89274-950-4) Harrison Hse.

Prayers That Avail Much: WWJD. Copeland. 101p. 1994. pap. 6.99 (1-57794-119-5) Harrison Hse.

Prayers That Avail Much Vol. 2: Portable Gift Book. Word Ministries Staff. 160p. 1995. mass mkt. 5.99 (0-89274-963-6, HH-963) Harrison Hse.

Prayers That Avail Much - Business Edition. Word Ministries, Staff. 207p. 1995. pap. 9.99 (0-89274-958-X) Harrison Hse.

Prayers That Avail Much for Children. Angela Brown. (Illus.). 32p. (Orig.). (J). (gr. 1-3). 1983. pap. 4.99 (0-89274-296-8) Harrison Hse.

Prayers That Avail Much for Kids: Short & Simple Prayers Packed with the Power of God's Word. Word Ministries Staff. (Prayers That Avail Much Ser.), 48p. (J). 9.99 (0-89274-956-3, HH956) Harrison Hse.

***Prayers That Avail Much for Kids II.** Ministries Word Ministries Staff. 1999. 9.99 (1-57794-112-8) Harrison Hse.

Prayers That Avail Much for Men. gif. ed. Germaine Copeland. 1999. 14.99 (1-57794-182-9) Harrison Hse.

Prayers That Avail Much for Mothers. Germaine Copeland. 1998. mass mkt. 10.99 (1-57794-120-9) Harrison Hse.

Prayers That Avail Much, for Mothers. deluxe ed. Word Ministries, Staff. 320p. (Orig.). 1990. bond lthr. 14.99 (0-89274-754-4, HH754) Harrison Hse.

Prayers That Avail Much for Teens. (YA). 14.99 (0-89274-902-4) Harrison Hse.

Prayers That Avail Much, for Teens. Word Ministries Staff. 144p. 1995. mass mkt. 5.99 (0-89274-843-5, HH-843) Harrison Hse.

Prayers That Avail Much for Women. 1998. 14.99 (1-57794-127-6) Harrison Hse.

Prayers That Avail Much for Women. Copeland. 19.99 (1-57794-124-1) Harrison Hse.

Prayers That Avail Much Journal: Mens's Edition. Word Ministries, Staff. (Prayers That Avail Much Ser.). 160p. 1995. 9.99 (0-89274-830-3, HH-830) Harrison Hse.

Prayers That Avail Much Journal: Women's Edition. Word Ministries, Staff. 160p. 1995. 9.99 (0-89274-831-1, HH-831) Harrison Hse.

Prayers That Avail Much Mother. Word Ministries Staff. 320p. 1994. mass mkt. 6.99 (0-89274-954-7, HH-954) Harrison Hse.

Prayers That Avail Much, Special Edition. deluxe rev. ed. Word Ministries, Staff. 352p. 1990. bond lthr. 19.99 (0-89274-866-4, HH-866) Harrison Hse.

Prayers That Bring Miracles. rev. ed. Stephen M. Bird. LC 97-44694. 176p. 1997. reprint ed. 15.95 (1-56236-238-0, Pub. by Aspen Bks) Origin Bk Sales.

Prayers That Prevail. Victory House Staff. 1990. pap. 9.99 (0-932081-25-8) Victory Hse.

Prayers That Prevail for Your Children. Cliff Richards. 1994. pap. 9.99 (0-932081-39-8) Victory Hse.

Prayers Through the Centuries. Nancy Martin. (C). 1988. 45.00 (1-85219-018-3, Pub. by Bishopsgate Pr Ltd) St Mut.

Prayers to Mary. Virgilio Noe. Ed. by Anthony M. Buono.Tr. of Preghiere a Maria. 96p. 1988. pap. 3.95 (0-89942-210-1, 210/04) Catholic Bk Pub.

***Prayers to Move Your Mountains: Powerful Prayers for the Spirit-Led Life.** Thomas M. Freiling & Michael A. Klassen. 224p. 2000. 14.99 (0-7852-6864-2) Nelson.

Prayers to Protest: Poems That Center & Bless Us. Ed. by Jennifer Bosveld. xii, 227p. 1998. pap. 19.95 (0-944754-46-5) Pudding Hse Pubns.

Prayers to She Who Is. William Cleary. 132p. 1995. pap. 15.95 (0-8245-1527-7) Crossroad NY.

Prayers to Sophia: A Companion to "The Star in My Heart" Joyce Rupp. LC 99-56817. (Illus.). 128p. 2000. pap. 12.95 (1-880913-42-9) Innisfree Pr.

Prayers to the Boy Jesus. Lawrence G. Lovasik. (Saint Joseph Picture Bks.). (Illus.). 1987. pap. text 1.25 (0-89942-388-4, 388-00) Catholic Bk Pub.

Prayers to the Little Flower with Novena. Francis Broome. 21p. 1973. 1.25 (0-911988-95-5, 48789) AMI Pr.

Prayers to the Most Holy Theotokos (The Virgin Mary) Schema-Hieromonk Nilus. 1992. pap. 1.00 (0-89981-134-5) Eastern Orthodox.

Prayers to the Nature Spirits. Julia Cameron. LC 98-51022. 112p. 1999. 11.95 (1-58063-047-2, Pub. by Renaissance) St Martin.

Prayers to the Other Life: Poems. Christopher Seid. LC 97-25988. (Winner of the 1997 Marianne Moore Poetry Prize Ser.). 72p. (Orig.). 1997. pap. 9.95 (1-884235-20-4) Helicon Nine Eds.

Prayers to the Saints. Lawrence G. Lovasik. (Saint Joseph Beginner Ser.). (J). 1993. 3.50 (0-89942-216-0, 216/22) Catholic Bk Pub.

Prayers, Verses & Devotions. John Henry Newman. LC 88-81571. 766p. 1989. 31.95 (0-89870-217-8) Ignatius Pr.

Prayers with Pizzazz for Junior High Teens. Judi Lanciotti. Ed. by Robert P. Stamschror. 76p. (YA). 1996. spiral bd. 12.95 (0-88489-376-6) St Marys.

Prayers with the Dying. David Philippart. 64p. (Orig.). 1997. pap. 4.00 (1-56854-115-5, DYING) Liturgy Tr Pubns.

An Asterisk (*) at the beginning of an entry indicates that the title is appearing for the first time.

Prayers Without Words. Phyllis Anderson & Harriet T. Statz. (Illus.). 40p. 1993. pap. 12.00 (*0-9636957-0-3*) Bethel Luth.

Prayers Women Pray: Intimate Moments with God. Ruthanne Garlock. LC 97-46403. 1998. pap. 9.99 (*1-56955-087-5*) Servant.

***Prayers Written at Vailima.** Robert Louis Stevenson. LC 00-103845. (Illus.). 48p. 2000. 18.95 (*0-9700689-0-5*) Calamus.

***Prayers Written at Vailima, Vol. 1.** Robert Louis Stevenson. 24p. 1999. 10.99 (*0-570-05220-3*, 12.-4027) Concordia.

PrayerStarters for Busy People. Daniel Grippo. LC 99-72386. (Prayerstarters Ser.). 72p. 1999. pap. 4.95 (*0-87029-328-1*, 20109) Abbey.

***PrayerStarters for Dealing with Anger.** Linus Mundy. LC 00-100684. (Prayerstarters Ser.). 72p. 2000. pap. 4.95 (*0-87029-338-9*) Abbey.

Prayerstarters in Times of Pain or Illness. Alaric Lewis. LC 99-72387. (Prayerstarters Ser.). 72p. 1999. pap. 4.95 (*0-87029-327-3*, 20110) Abbey.

***PrayerStarters in Times of Sadness or Depression.** Molly Wigand. LC 00-100742. (Prayerstarters Ser.). 72p. 2000. pap. 4.95 (*0-87029-339-7*) Abbey.

***PrayerStarters on the Way to Forgiveness.** Denise Robinson. LC 00-100740. (Prayerstarters Ser.). 72p. 2000. pap. 4.95 (*0-87029-340-0*) Abbey.

PrayerStarters to Handle Stress. Molly Wigand. LC 99-72413. (Prayerstarters Ser.). 72p. 1999. pap. 4.95 (*0-87029-330-3*, 20107) Abbey.

PrayerStarters to Help You Heal after Loss. Elizabeth Stalling. LC 99-72385. (Prayerstarters Ser.). 72p. 1999. pap. 4.95 (*0-87029-329-X*, 20108) Abbey.

***PrayerStarters When You're Worried.** Daniel Grippo. LC 00-100748. (Prayerstarters Ser.). 72p. 2000. pap. 4.95 (*0-87029-337-0*) Abbey.

***PrayerTime Cycle C Vol. 3: Faith-Sharing Reflections.** Jean Marie Hiesberger et al. Ed. by Robert J. Heyer. 208p. 2000. pap. 9.95 (*1-930978-00-6*) RENEW Intl.

Prayertimes with Mother Teresa: Involving Scripture, Mother Teresa & You. Ed. by Eileen Egan & Kathleen Egan. 176p. 1989. pap. 8.95 (*0-385-26231-0*, Image Bks) Doubleday.

Prayerwalking see Caminata en Oracion

Prayerwalking: Praying on Site with Insight. Steve Hawthorne & Graham Kendrick. 1993. pap. 11.99 (*0-88419-268-7*) Creation House.

PrayerWays. Carl Koch et al. Ed. by Barbara Allaire & Julia Ahlers. (Illus.). 160p. 1995. teacher ed., spiral bd. 24.95 (*0-88489-259-X*) St Marys.

PrayerWays. Carl Koch et al. Ed. by Barbara Allaire & Julia Ahlers. (Illus.). 208p. (YA). (gr. 11-12). 1995. pap. text 14.00 (*0-88489-258-1*) St Marys.

Prayerwheels. Meredith Luyten. Ed. by Peter Kaplan. LC 76-14544. 1976. 3.00 (*0-915176-14-9*) Pourboire.

Praying. Dolores Ready. Ed. by Thomas Zanzig. (Discovering Program Ser.). (Illus.). 43p. 1989. teacher ed. 6.00 (*0-88489-195-X*); text 3.00 (*0-88489-194-1*) St Marys.

Praying: A Book for Children. Nancy L. Roth. (Illus.). 55p. (J). (gr. 3-7). 1991. pap. 8.95 (*0-89869-189-3*) Church Pub Inc.

Praying All Ways. Judith Dunlap & Carleen Suttman. Ed. by Marilyn Kielbasa. (Horizons Ser.: Level 1, Minicourse 6). (Illus.). 56p. (Orig.). (YA). (gr. 9). 1996. pap. text, student ed. 9.95 (*0-88489-364-2*) St Marys.

Praying Alone & Together: An 11-Session Prayer Module for Small Faith Communities. Arthur Baranowski. 107p. 1988. pap. 6.95 (*0-86716-897-8*) St Anthony Mess Pr.

Praying Always. Frans Bakker. Tr. by Cornelis Pronk & Fredrika Pronk from DUT. 114p. 1987. reprint ed. pap. 7.99 (*0-85151-514-2*) Banner of Truth.

Praying Always: A Self-Directed Bible Study for Christian Service. Peggy Musgrove. 80p. 1993. pap. text 3.95 (*0-88243-684-8*, 02-0684) Gospel Pub.

Praying & Doing the Stations of the Cross with Children. Diane Abajian. (Illus.). 24p. (J). (gr. 1-3). 1980. pap. 1.95 (*0-89622-118-0*) Twenty-Third.

Praying As Believing: The Lord's Prayer & the Christian Doctrine of God. Timothy Bradshaw. LC 98-17455. (Regent's Study Guides). 224p. 1998. pap. 15.00 (*1-57312-198-3*) Smyth & Helwys.

Praying Beyond God's Ability. Roy H. Hicks. 96p. 1977. pap. 5.99 (*0-89274-052-3*) Harrison Hse.

Praying Body & Soul: Spiritual Living in a Secular World. Anthony De Mello. Tr. by Phillip Berryman. LC 97-566. 168p. 1997. pap. 12.95 (*0-8245-1673-7*) Crossroad NY.

Praying by Hand: Rediscovering the Rosary As a Way of Prayer. M. Basil Pennington. LC 90-55775. 144p. 1995. pap. 10.00 (*0-06-066541-6*, Pub. by Harper SF) HarpC.

Praying by Heart: Prayers for Personal Devotion & Public Worship. Kay B. Northcutt. LC 98-35075. 144p. 1998. pap. 12.95 (*0-8298-1285-7*) Pilgrim OH.

Praying Christ: A Study of Jesus' Doctrine & Practice of Prayer. James G. Thomson. 155p. (C). 1995. reprint ed. pap. 16.95 (*1-57383-049-6*) Regent College.

Praying Church. Sue Curran. 160p. 1991. 10.99 (*1-56043-442-2*, Treasure Hse) Destiny Image.

Praying Church Profile. Terry Teykl. 49p. (Orig.). 1999. pap. 9.95 (*1-57892-013-2*) Prayer Pt Pr.

Praying Church Sourcebook. 2nd ed. Alvin Vander Griend & Edith Bajema. 367p. 1997. pap. 24.95 (*1-56212-258-4*, 1940-0406) CRC Pubns.

Praying Daily with Paul. Eldon Degge. (Horizon Ser.). 1997. pap. 9.99 (*1-56570-016-3*) Meridian MI.

Praying Drunk. Andrew Hudgins. 6p. 1991. pap. 15.00 (*1-891472-12-7*) Dim Gray.

***Praying Effectively.** Dorothy Mason-Raley. 221p. 1999. spiral bd. 12.00 (*1-930479-01-8*) C R Pubs.

Praying Effectively. Bennie S. Triplett. LC 90-60886. 1991. pap. 8.99 (*0-87148-952-X*) Pathway Pr.

Praying for a Cure: Medical Ethics in Conflict with Religious Freedom. Margaret Battin et al. (Point/Counterpoint Ser.). 224p. 1998. 57.00 (*0-8476-8773-2*) Rowman.

Praying for a Cure: When Medical & Religious Practices Conflict. Peggy DesAutels et al. LC 98-45358. (Point/Counterpoint Ser.). 160p. 1999. 57.00 (*0-8476-9262-0*); pap. 17.95 (*0-8476-9263-9*) Rowman.

***Praying for a Whole New World: Gospel Sermons for Advent/Christmas/Epiphany, Cycle C.** William G. Carter. LC 00-35798. 126p. 2000. pap. 11.95 (*0-7880-1728-4*); disk 11.95 (*0-7880-1729-2*) CSS OH.

Praying for Base Hits: An American Boyhood. Bruce Clayton. LC 98-21276. (Illus.). 280p. 1998. pap. 16.95 (*0-8262-1189-5*) U of Mo Pr.

Praying for End. Baumgartner. LC 99-14214. 1999. text 26.95 (*0-312-21092-2*) St Martin.

Praying for Fishhooks: Understanding Intercessory Prayer. Mary Caldwell. 108p. 1994. pap. 11.00 (*1-880837-75-7*) Smyth & Helwys.

Praying for Friends & Enemies: Intercessory Prayer. Jane E. Vennard. LC 95-3487. (Face to Face with God Ser.). 80p. 1995. pap. 8.99 (*0-8066-2769-7*, 10-27697, Augsburg) Augsburg Fortress.

Praying for Guidance: How to Discover God's Will. Ron Kincaid. LC 95-48960. 178p. (Orig.). 1996. pap. 9.99 (*0-8308-1689-5*, 1689, Saltshaker Bk) InterVarsity.

Praying for Justice: Faith, Order & Community in an American Town. Carol J. Greenhouse. LC 86-47642. (Anthropology of Contemporary Issues Ser.). 264p. 1986. text 37.50 (*0-8014-1971-9*); pap. text 14.95 (*0-8014-9678-0*) Cornell U Pr.

***Praying for Koreans 1 (Yang Min Sim Sur 1)** Richard Kim. (KOR.). xxxvi, 348p. 1999. pap. 19.00 (*0-9669981-0-3*) Rich Zeus.

Praying for Missionary Kids see Orando por los Hijos de los Misioneros

Praying for One Another see Orondo los Unos por los Otros

Praying for One Another see Orando los Unos por los Otros

Praying for Others: Quotations from the Writings of Ellen G. White. Kenneth R. Wade et al. LC 97-24843. 143p. 1997. pap. 5.99 (*0-8163-1405-5*) Pacific Pr Pub Assn.

Praying for Power: Buddhism & the Formation of Gentry Society in Late-Ming China. Timothy Brook. LC 93-5407. (Harvard-Yenching Institute Monographs: No. 38). 400p. 1994. 35.00 (*0-674-69775-8*) HUP.

Praying for Rain: Timothy Findley's Not Wanted on the Voyage. Donna Pennee. (Canadian Fiction Studies: No. 21). 120p. (C). 1993. pap. text 14.95 (*1-55022-121-3*, Pub. by ECW) Genl Dist Srvs.

***Praying for Recovery: Psalms & Meditations.** Eli Ezry. LC 99-88436. 100p. 2000. pap. 7.95 (*1-55874-788-5*, Simcha Press) Health Comm.

Praying for Sheetrock. Melissa F. Greene. 1991. 21.95 (*0-201-55048-2*) Addison-Wesley.

Praying for Sheetrock. Melissa F. Greene. 325p. 1992. pap. 11.00 (*0-449-90753-8*, Columbine) Fawcett.

Praying for Sleep. Jeffery Deaver. 432p. 1994. mass mkt. 7.50 (*0-451-18146-8*, Sig) NAL.

Praying for the Harvest. rev. ed. Guy Duininck. (Illus.). 163p. 1997. pap. 8.00 (*0-929400-04-6*) Masters Touch Pub Co.

***Praying for the World's 365 Most Influential People.** David Kopp & Heather Kopp. LC 99-20323. 1999. pap. 12.99 (*0-7369-0047-0*) Harvest Hse.

Praying for Time & Other Top Recorded Hits. (Chartbuster Ser.). 72p. (Orig.). 1990. pap. 12.95 (*0-7935-0327-2*, HL00490525) H Leonard.

Praying for Wholeness & Healing. Richard J. Beckmen. LC 95-4053. (Face to Face with God Ser.). 80p. 1995. pap. 8.99 (*0-8066-2770-0*, 10-27700) Augsburg Fortress.

Praying for You: A Workbook for Reaching Others Through Prayer. Howard A. Tryon, Jr. 144p. 1996. pap. 7.99 (*0-8254-3848-9*) Kregel.

Praying for Your Unborn Child. Francis S. MacNutt. 176p. 1989. pap. 10.00 (*0-385-23282-9*) Doubleday.

Praying from God's Heart: Experiencing the Power of God-Focused Prayer. Lee Brase. 96p. (Orig.). 1994. pap. 6.00 (*0-89109-792-9*) NavPress.

***Praying from the Free-Throw Line.** Minka S. Sprague. LC 99-44125. (Journeybook Ser.). 1999. pap. write for info. (*0-89869-317-9*) Church Pub Inc.

Praying God's Promises. Victory House Staff. 1998. pap. 5.99 (*0-932081-64-9*) Victory Hse.

Praying God's Will for My Daughter. Lee Roberts. 320p. 1998. 4.99 (*0-7852-7543-6*) Nelson.

Praying God's Will for My Husband. Lee Roberts. 320p. 1998. 4.99 (*0-7852-7544-4*) Nelson.

Praying God's Will for My Marriage. Lee Roberts. LC 93-34311. 1994. pap. 11.99 (*0-8407-9223-9*) Nelson.

Praying God's Will for My Son. Lee Roberts. 320p. 1998. 4.99 (*0-7852-7545-2*) Nelson.

Praying God's Word. Ed Dufresne. 96p. 1992. mass mkt. 5.99 (*0-88368-240-0*) Whitaker Hse.

***Praying God's Word: Breaking Free from Spiritual Strongholds.** Beth Moore. LC 99-55801. 256p. 2000. 16.99 (*0-8054-2351-6*) Broadman.

Praying Hyde. Francis A. McGaw et al. pap. 4.99 (*1-56632-009-7*) Revival Lit.

Praying Hyde: The Life of John "Praying" Hyde. E. G. Carre. LC 82-73972. 187p. 1983. pap. 9.99 (*0-88270-541-5*) Bridge-Logos.

Praying in His Presence: Enjoying Constant Communication with God. Ken Bible. 160p. (Orig.). 1993. pap. 4.99 (*1-882854-02-0*) Allegis.

Praying in the Catholic Tradition. Peter Schineller. LC 92-81359. 64p. 1992. pap. 3.95 (*0-89243-416-3*) Liguori Pubns.

Praying in the Presence of Our Lord: Players for Eucharistic Adoration. Benedit J. Groeschel. LC 98-68199. 123p. 1999. pap. 6.95 (*0-87973-586-4*) Our Sunday Visitor.

Praying in the Spirit see Prayer

Praying in the Spirit: Heavenly Resources for Praise & Intercession. Ed. by Jack W. Hayford. LC 96-228197. (Spirit-Filled Life Bible Ser.). 160p. 1996. pap. 6.99 (*0-7852-1141-1*) Nelson.

***Praying in the Spirit of Catherine McAuley: A Collection of Prayers.** 1999. pap. 9.00 (*1-56854-336-0*) Liturgy Tr Pubns.

***Praying in the Will of God.** David J. Swisher. 1999. pap. 1.50 (*1-929168-01-2*) Lasting Impr KS.

Praying in Your Own Voice...Through Writing. Virginia Phelan. LC 94-78949. 64p. (Orig.). 1994. pap. 3.95 (*0-89243-682-4*) Liguori Pubns.

Praying Jesus' Way: A Guide for Beginners & Veterans. Brian J. Dodd. LC 96-48376. 129p. (Orig.). 1997. pap. 9.99 (*0-8308-1993-2*, 1993) InterVarsity.

Praying Life: Living Beyond Your Limits. Jennifer K. Dean. Ed. by Becky Nelson. 96p. (Orig.). 1994. pap. text 8.99 (*1-56309-091-0*, N944105, New Hope) Womans Mission Union.

Praying Like Jesus. Howard W. Roberts. LC 98-45513. 160p. 1999. pap. 15.95 (*0-8298-1326-8*) Pilgrim OH.

Praying Mantids. Frederick R. Prete. LC 99-44360. 560p. 1999. 89.95 (*0-8018-6174-8*) Johns Hopkins.

Praying Mantis see Living Things - Group 1

Praying Mantis King-Fu Vol. 3: Steals the Peach. Paul Eng. Ed. by David Nakahara. LC 93-71092. (CHI & ENG., Illus.). 188p. (Orig.). 1993. pap. 13.95 (*0-939427-30-3*) Alpha Pubns OH.

Praying Mantis Kung Fu. Un Ho Bun. 96p. 1998. pap. 17.95 (*0-901764-09-4*, 93328) P H Crompton.

Praying Mantis Kung-Fu Vol. 4: Plum Blossom Hand. Paul Eng. Ed. by David Nakahara. LC 93-79320. (CHI & ENG., Illus.). 136p. (Orig.). 1993. pap. 13.95 (*0-939427-31-1*) Alpha Pubns OH.

Praying Mantises. Larry Dane Brimner. LC 99-13837. (Animals Ser.). (J). 1999. 21.50 (*0-516-21163-3*) Childrens.

***Praying Mantises.** Larry Dane Brimner. (True Bks.). (J). 2000. pap. text 6.95 (*0-516-26769-8*) Childrens.

***Praying Mantises.** Helen Frost. LC 00-9676. (Insects Ser.). (Illus.). (J). 2001. write for info. (*0-7368-0853-1*, Pebble Bks) Capstone Pr.

Praying My Identity in Christ. Terry Teykl. (Keys to the Kingdom Ser.). 40p. 1998. ring bd. 6.00 (*1-57892-047-7*) Prayer Pt Pr.

Praying on the Journey with Christ: A Commitment to Encounter Christ Through the Gospel of John. Richard F. Bansemer. 1997. pap. text 19.25 (*0-7880-1179-0*) CSS OH.

Praying on the Journey with Christ: A Committment to Encounter Christ Through the Gospel of John. Richard F. Bansemer. LC 97-39506. 222p. 1997. pap. 19.25 (*0-7880-1176-6*) CSS OH.

Praying Our Experiences. rev. ed. Joseph Schmidt. 64p. 1989. pap. 3.95 (*0-88489-113-5*) St Marys.

***Praying Our Experiences.** 20th anniversary ed. Joseph F. Schmidt. 96p. 2000. pap. 5.95 (*0-88489-649-8*) St Marys.

Praying Our Goodbyes. Joyce Rupp. LC 87-72291. 184p. 1988. pap. 9.95 (*0-87793-370-7*) Ave Maria.

Praying Our Goodbyes. Joyce Rupp. 1992. reprint ed. mass mkt. 4.99 (*0-8041-1060-3*) Ivy Books.

Praying Our Prayers. H. P. Lyons. 72p. 1976. 4.95 (*0-8199-0598-4*, Frncscn Herld) Franciscan Pr.

Praying Our Way Through Life. M. Basilea Schlink. 48p. 1991. pap. 0.95 (*3-87209-636-2*) Evang Sisterhood Mary.

***Praying Peace: A Mystic, a Scientist & a Psychologist Examine the Most Powerful Force in the Universe.** James F. Twyman. 2000. pap. 12.95 (*1-899171-48-7*) Findhorn Pr.

Praying People: Massachusett Acculturation & the Failure of the Puritan Mission, 1600-1690. 2nd rev. ed. Dane Morrison. (American Indian Studies: Vol. 2). XXXI, 273p. (C). 1998. reprint ed. pap. text 32.95 (*0-8204-4191-0*) P Lang Pubng.

Praying Prince. C. Mackenzie. (Biblewise Ser.). (J). 1995. 2.99 (*1-85792-155-0*, Pub. by Christian Focus) Spring Arbor Dist.

Praying Santa. Linda Frederiksen. (Illus.). 52p. (J). 1996. pap. 8.95 (*0-7880-0685-1*, Fairway Pr) CSS OH.

Praying Shapes Believing: A Theological Commentary on the Book of Common Prayer. Leonel L. Mitchell. 220p. 1984. 24.50 (*0-86683-494-X*) Harper SF.

Praying Shapes Believing: A Theological Commentary on the Book of Common Prayer. Leonel L. Mitchell. LC 90-28624. 352p. 1991. reprint ed. pap. 19.95 (*0-8192-1553-8*) Morehouse Pub.

Praying Successfully. Charles H. Spurgeon. LC 97-30553. 112p. 1997. pap. 6.99 (*0-88368-443-8*) Whitaker Hse.

***Praying That Receives Answers.** E. M. Bounds. Orig. Title: Obtaining Answers to Prayer. 140p. 1999. mass mkt. 6.99 (*0-88368-594-9*) Whitaker Hse.

***Praying the Angelus.** Jean Fournee. 64p. 2000. pap. 8.95 (*0-8245-1864-0*, Pub. by Crossroad NY) Natl Bk Netwk.

Praying the Beatitudes: A Retreat on the Sermon on the Mount. Max Oliva. 126p. 1989. pap. 30.00 (*1-85390-039-7*, Pub. by Veritas Pubns) St Mut.

Praying the Bible: An Introduction to Lectio Divina. Mariano Magrassi. Tr. by Edward Hagman. LC 97-52992. 144p. 1998. pap. 11.95 (*0-8146-2446-4*) Liturgical Pr.

Praying the Bible for Your Baby. Heather Harpham Kopp. 160p. 1998. 11.95 (*1-57856-086-1*) Waterbrook Pr.

***Praying the Bible for Your Children.** David Kopp & Heather Kopp. LC 98-229080. 208p. 1998. 14.95 (*1-57856-009-8*) Waterbrook Pr.

***Praying the Bible for Your Life.** David Kopp. LC 99-21781. 224p. 1999. 14.95 (*1-57856-136-1*) Waterbrook Pr.

***Praying the Bible for Your Marriage.** David Kopp & Heather Kopp. LC 98-228470. 208p. 1998. 14.95 (*1-57856-051-9*) Waterbrook Pr.

***Praying the Bible with Your Family.** David Kopp & Heather Kopp. 224p. 2000. 14.95 (*1-57856-384-4*) Waterbrook Pr.

***Praying the Catechism: Opening Your Heart to Divine Wisdom.** Louise Perrotta. 174p. 2000. pap. 9.99 (*1-56955-207-X*) Servant.

Praying the Daily Gospels: A Guide to Meditation. Philip St. Romain. LC 95-76472. 256p. (Orig.). 1995. pap. 9.95 (*0-89243-841-X*) Liguori Pubns.

Praying the Divine Mercy Chaplet During Adoration for the Sick & Dying. write for info. (*0-944203-44-2*) Marian Pr.

Praying the Eucharist: Reflections on the Eucharistic Experience of God. Charles Miller. LC 96-3465. 128p. 1996. pap. 9.95 (*0-8192-1670-4*) Morehouse Pub.

***Praying the Hours.** Suzanne Guthrie. LC 00-23053. (Cloister Bks.). 144p. 2000. pap. 9.95 (*1-56101-177-0*) Cowley Pubns.

Praying the Labyrinth: A Journal for Spiritual Exploration. Jill Kimberly Geoffrion. LC 99-34495. 160p. 1999. pap. 16.95 (*0-8298-1343-8*) Pilgrim OH.

Praying the Lord's Prayer see Orando la Oracion del Senor, el Padre Nuestro

Praying the Lord's Prayer. Glaphre Gilliland. (Fast Lane Bible Studies Ser.). 40p. (J). (gr. 7-9). 1995. pap. 9.95 (*0-87303-232-2*) Faith & Life.

***Praying the Lord's Prayer: An Ageless Prayer for Today.** Herman C. Waetjen. LC 99-25004. 144p. 1999. pap. 14.00 (*1-56338-276-8*) TPI PA.

Praying the Name of Jesus: The Ancient Wisdom of the Jesus Prayer. Wilfrid Stinissen. Tr. by Joseph B. Board from SWE. LC 99-33765. 144p. 1999. reprint ed. pap. 13.95 (*0-7648-0496-0*) Liguori Pubns.

Praying the Our Father Today. Brother John of Taize. 64p. 1992. pap. 7.95 (*0-912405-91-0*, Pastoral Press) OR Catholic.

Praying the Parables: A Spiritual Journey Through the Stories of Jesus. Joyce Huggett. LC 97-17076. 120p. 1997. pap. 8.99 (*0-8308-1355-1*, 1355) InterVarsity.

Praying the Psalms. Thomas Merton. 48p. 1956. pap. 3.95 (*0-8146-0548-6*) Liturgical Pr.

Praying the Psalms. rev. ed. Walter Bruggemann. LC 94-154133. 72p. 1993. pap. 5.95 (*0-88489-322-7*) St Marys.

Praying the Right Way. Elbert Willis. 1977. 2.00 (*0-89858-011-0*) Fill the Gap.

Praying the Rosary: New Reflections on the Mysteries. Gloria Hutchinson. 65p. 1991. pap. text 3.95 (*0-86716-143-4*) St Anthony Mess Pr.

Praying the Rosary: The Companion Volume to the Catholic Prayer Book. large type ed. Ron Lengwin. LC 92-410. 96p. 1995. pap. 6.95 (*0-8027-2671-2*) Walker & Co.

Praying the Rosary: The Joyful, Fruitful, Sorrowful & Glorious Mysteries. Warren F. Dicharry. LC 97-34281. 1998. pap. 4.95 (*0-8146-2484-7*) Liturgical Pr.

Praying the Sacraments. Peter E. Fink. (Worship Ser.). 220p. 1991. reprint ed. pap. 14.95 (*0-912405-86-4*, Pastoral Press) OR Catholic.

***Praying the Sacred in Secular Settings.** Gail E. Bowman. 2000. pap. text. write for info. (*0-8272-2962-3*) Chalice Pr.

Praying the Scriptures: A Field Guide for Your Spiritual Journey. Evan B. Howard. LC 99-10870. 180p. 1999. pap. 10.99 (*0-8308-2201-1*, 2201) InterVarsity.

Praying the Scriptures: Communicating with God in His Own Words. Judson Cornwall. LC 89-82724. 223p. (C). 1998. pap. 11.99 (*0-88419-266-0*) Creation House.

***Praying the Tradition.** Mark J. Boda. LC 99-47146. 1999. 108.35 (*3-11-016433-7*) De Gruyter.

Praying the Way: Reflections on the Stations of the Cross. Gloria Hutchinson. 133p. 1995. pap. 6.95 (*0-86716-212-0*) St Anthony Mess Pr.

Praying the Word: An Introduction to Lectio Divina. Enzo Bianchi. Ed. by E. Rozanne Elder. Tr. by James W. Zona from ITA. LC 98-55938. (Cistercian Studies: Vol. CS182). 119p. 1999. pap. 11.95 (*0-87907-682-8*) Cistercian Pubns.

Praying Through Crisis: Lessons in Prayer. Don Gilmore. 104p. (Orig.). 1990. mass mkt. 5.99 (*0-87508-171-1*, 171) Chr Lit.

Praying Through Grief: Healing Prayer Services for Those Who Mourn. Mauryeen O'Brien. LC 97-17053. 112p. 1997. pap. 12.95 (*0-87793-629-3*) Ave Maria.

Praying Through Scripture. Ken Gire. Date not set. 14.99 (*0-310-21213-8*) HarpC.

Praying Through Scriptures. Ken Gire. Date not set. 19.99 (*0-310-21197-2*); 14.99 (*0-310-21211-1*) HarpC.

Praying Through The. Steve Harper. 10.35 (*0-687-60921-6*) Abingdon.

Praying Through the Lord's Prayer. Steve Harper. LC 91-67166. 112p. 1992. pap. 9.00 (*0-8358-0656-1*) Upper Room Bks.

Praying Through the 100 Gateway Cities see Orando por las 100 Ciudades de Acceso

Praying Through the 100 Gateway Cities of the 10 - 40 Window. Ed. by C. Peter Wagner et al. 148p. (Orig.). 1995. pap. 8.99 (*0-927545-80-2*) YWAM Pub.

Praying to A. L. Judith Caseley. LC 99-22045. 160p. (YA). (gr. 5-9). 2000. 15.95 (*0-688-15934-6*, Greenwillow Bks) HarpC Child Bks.

P

An Asterisk (*) at the beginning of an entry indicates that the title is appearing for the first time.

Praying to a Laughing God: A Novel. Kevin McColley. LC 97-48720. 336p. 1998. 23.50 (*0-684-83761-7*) S&S Trade.

Praying to Change the World. Gordon Lindsay. (School of Prayer Ser.). 200p. 1960. per. 6.95 (*0-89985-956-9*) Christ for the Nations.

Praying to Get Results. 2nd ed. Kenneth E. Hagin. 1969. pap. 2.95 (*0-89276-013-3*) Faith Lib Pubns.

Praying to God. D. Brumi. (J). 1996. bds. 3.95 (*0-88271-451-1*) Regina Pr.

***Praying Twice: The Music & Words of Congregational Song.** Brian Wren. LC 99-88810. 272p. 2000. pap. 22.95 (*0-664-25670-8*, Pub. by Westminster John Knox) Presbyterian Pub.

Praying up a Storm. Daniel Bernard. 112p. (Orig.). 1997. pap. 7.00 (*1-57892-050-7*, Pastors In Print) Prayer Pt Pr.

Praying While You Work see Holiness for Housewives: And Other Working Women

Praying with a Passionate Heart. Bridget M. Meehan & Regina M. Oliver. LC 98-35989. 128p. 1999. pap. 12.95 (*0-7648-0212-7*) Liguori Pubns.

Praying with & for Your Wife. abr. ed. E. Glenn Wagner. 20p. 1.95 (*1-57229-020-X*) FamilyLife.

Praying with Anthony of Padua. Madeline P. Nugent. (Companions for the Journey Ser.). (Illus.). 120p. 1996. pap. 7.95 (*0-88489-397-9*) St Marys.

Praying with Benedict. Katherine Howard. Ed. by Carl Koch. (Companions for the Journey Ser.). (Illus.). 128p. 1997. pap. 8.95 (*0-88489-379-0*) St Marys.

Praying with Body & Soul: A Way to Intimacy with God. Jane E. Vennaro. LC 98-28752. (Illus.). 144p. 1998. pap. 12.99 (*0-8066-3614-9*, 9-3614) Augsburg Fortress.

Praying with C. S. Lewis. Charles C. Taliaferro. Ed. by Carl Koch. (Companions for the Journey Ser.). (Illus.). 120p. 1998. pap. 8.95 (*0-88489-318-9*) St Marys.

Praying with Cancer. Sherry Hunt. (Illus.). 44p. 1998. pap. 1.95 (*0-88028-198-7*, 1476) Forward Movement.

Praying with Catherine McAuley. Helen Marie Burns & Sheila Carney. Ed. by Carl Koch. (Companions for the Journey Ser.). (Illus.). 128p. 1996. pap. 7.95 (*0-88489-334-0*) St Marys.

Praying with Catherine of Siena. Patricia Mary Vinje. Ed. by Carol Koch. LC 90-888346. (Companions for the Journey Ser.). (Illus.). 112p. 1990. pap. 7.95 (*0-88489-230-1*) St Marys.

Praying with Children, Bk. 1. Center for Learning Network Staff. 119p. (J). (gr. 1-3). 1991. spiral bd. 12.95 (*1-56077-028-7*) Ctr Learning.

Praying with Children, Bk. 2. Center for Learning Network Staff. 107p. (J). (gr. 4-6). 1991. spiral bd. 12.95 (*1-56077-029-5*) Ctr Learning.

Praying with Christ-Sophia: Services for Healing & Renewal. Jann Aldredge-Clanton. LC 96-60419. 160p. (Orig.). 1996. pap. 19.95 (*0-89622-697-2*) Twenty-Third.

Praying with Clare of Assisi. Ingrid Peterson & Ramona Miller. Ed. by Carl Koch. (Companions for the Journey Ser.). (Illus.). 120p. (Orig.). 1994. pap. 8.95 (*0-88489-333-2*) St Marys.

***Praying with Dante.** James J. Collins. LC 00-8145. (Companions for the Journey Ser.). (Illus.). 120p. (C). 2000. pap. 8.95 (*0-88489-674-9*) St Marys.

Praying with Dominic. Michael Monshau. Ed. by Carl Koch. (Companions for the Journey Ser.). (Illus.). 120p. (Orig.). 1993. pap. 8.95 (*0-88489-288-3*) St Marys.

Praying with Dorothy Day. James Allaire & Rosemary Broughton. Ed. by Carl Koch. (Companions for the Journey Ser.). (Illus.). 128p. (Orig.). 1995. pap. 8.95 (*0-88489-306-5*) St Marys.

Praying with Elizabeth Seton. Margaret Alderman & Josephine Burns. Ed. by Carl Koch. LC 93-143874. (Companions for the Journey Ser.). (Illus.). 120p. 1992. pap. 8.95 (*0-88489-282-4*) St Marys.

Praying with Francis of Assisi. Joseph Stoutzenberger & John D. Bohrer. Ed. by Carl Koch. (Companions for the Journey Ser.). (Illus.). 112p. 1989. pap. 8.95 (*0-88489-222-0*) St Marys.

Praying with Frederic Ozanam. Ronald Ramson. Ed. by Carl Koch. LC 98-234036. (Companions for the Journey Ser.). (Illus.). 128p. 1998. pap. 8.95 (*0-88489-504-1*) St Marys.

Praying with Hildegard of Bingen. Gloria Durka. Ed. by Carl Koch. (Companions for the Journey Ser.). (Illus.). 120p. (Orig.). 1991. pap. 8.95 (*0-88489-254-9*) St Marys.

Praying with Icons. Jim Forest. LC 96-37303. (Illus.). 175p. (Orig.). 1997. pap. 16.00 (*1-57075-112-9*) Orbis Bks.

Praying with Ignatius of Loyola. Jacqueline Syrup Bergan & S. Marie Schwan. Ed. by Carl Koch. (Companions for the Journey Ser.). (Illus.). 120p. 1991. pap. 8.95 (*0-88489-263-8*) St Marys.

Praying with Jesus see Enseigne - Nous A Prier

Praying with Jesus see Orando con Cristo

Praying with Jesus see Orando Con Jesus

Praying with Jesus: A Year of Daily Prayers & Reflections on the Words & Actions of Jesus. Eugene H. Peterson. LC 92-54533. 400p. 1993. pap. 12.00 (*0-06-066566-1*, Pub. by Harper SF) HarpC.

***Praying with Jesus: What the Gospels Tell Us about How to Pray.** George Martin. LC BV229.M28 2000. 127p. 2000. pap. 11.95 (*0-8294-1476-2*) Loyola Pr.

Praying with John Baptist de La Salle. Carl Koch. LC 91-169110. (Companions for the Journey Ser.). (Illus.). 112p. 1990. pap. 8.95 (*0-88489-240-9*) St Marys.

Praying with John Cardinal Newman. Halbert Weidner. Ed. by Carl Koch. LC 97-214656. (Companions for the Journey Ser.). (Illus.). 120p. (Orig.). 1997. pap. 7.95 (*0-88489-409-6*) St Marys.

Praying with John Donne & George. Date not set. pap. 7.95 (*0-281-04552-6*) Society Prom Christ Know.

Praying with John of the Cross. Wayne Simsic. Ed. by Carl Koch. (Companions for the Journey Ser.). (Illus.). 104p. (Orig.). 1993. pap. 8.95 (*0-88489-290-5*) St Marys.

Praying with Julian of Norwich. Gloria Durka. Ed. by Carl Koch. (Companions for the Journey Ser.). (Illus.). 107p. 1989. pap. 8.95 (*0-88489-221-2*) St Marys.

Praying with Julian of Norwich: Selections from "A Revelation of Love" with Commentary by Ritamary Bradley. Ritamary Bradley. LC 94-60353. 192p. (Orig.). 1994. pap. 12.95 (*0-89622-601-8*) Twenty-Third.

Praying with Louise de Marillac. Audrey Gibson & Kieran Kneaves. Ed. by Carl Koch. LC 95-238093. (Companions for the Journey Ser.). (Illus.). 120p. (Orig.). 1995. pap. 7.95 (*0-88489-329-4*) St Marys.

Praying with Martin Luther. Peter E. Bastien. Ed. by Carl Koch. (Companions for the Journey Ser.). (Illus.). 128p. 1999. pap. 8.95 (*0-88489-580-7*) St Marys.

Praying with Mary: A Treasury for All Occasions. Janice T. Connell. 192p. 1999. pap. 12.00 (*0-06-061521-4*) HarpC.

Praying with Mary: Sacred Prayers to the Blessed Mother for All Occasions. Janice T. Connell. LC 97-41337. 192p. 1997. 18.00 (*0-06-061520-6*, Pub. by Harper SF) HarpC.

***Praying with Mother Teresa.** Jean Maalouf. LC 99-50865. (Companions for the Journey Ser.). (Illus.). 136p. (C). 2000. pap. 8.95 (*0-88489-640-4*) St Marys.

Praying with One Another for Healing. Dennis Linn et al. 1984. pap. 11.95 (*0-8091-2619-2*) Paulist Pr.

Praying with Our Eyes Open: Engendering Feminist Liturgical Prayer. Marjorie Proctor-Smith. LC 95-38861. 256p. 1995. pap. 16.95 (*0-687-39122-9*) Abingdon.

***Praying with Our Hands: Twenty-One Practices of Embodied Prayer from the World's Spiritual Traditions.** Jon M. Sweeney. (Illus.). 2000. pap. 14.95 (*1-893361-16-0*) SkyLight Paths.

Praying with Paul: A Year of Daily Prayers & Reflections on the Words of Paul. Eugene H. Peterson. 400p. 1995. pap. 12.00 (*0-06-066433-9*, Pub. by Harper SF) HarpC.

Praying with Pope John XXIII. Bill Huebsch. Ed. by Carl Koch. (Companions for the Journey Ser.). 120p. 1999. pap. 8.95 (*0-88489-596-3*) St Marys.

Praying with Power. Lowell Lundstrom. Orig. Title: How You Can Pray with Power & Get Results. 263p. 1984. mass mkt. 5.99 (*0-88368-470-5*) Whitaker Hse.

Praying with Power. C. Peter Wagner. LC 97-10999. (Prayer Warrior Ser.). 1997. pap. 12.99 (*0-8307-1919-9*, Regal Bks) Gospel Lght.

Praying with Power As Jesus Taught. Ron Roth. 92p. 1989. pap. 4.00 (*1-893869-14-8*) Celbrtng Life.

***Praying with Sacred Beads.** Joan Hutson. LC 99-57763. (Illus.). 128p. 2000. 14.95 (*0-7648-0569-X*, Liguori Triumph) Liguori Pubns.

Praying with Saint Augustine. Paula Clifford. (Praying With...Ser.). 1987. pap. 5.95 (*0-687-86040-7*) Abingdon.

Praying with Scriptures. Center for Learning Network Staff. (Spiritual Growth Ser.). 61p. 1993. teacher ed., spiral bd. 15.95 (*1-56077-273-5*) Ctr Learning.

Praying with Smith Wigglesworth. Larry Keefauver. LC 96-85029. 1999. pap. 13.99 (*0-88419-444-2*) Dake Pub.

Praying with Spirituality. Sol Scharfstein. LC 98-184959. 128 p. 1995. pap. 8.95 (*0-88125-517-3*) Ktav.

Praying with St. Teresa of Avila. Tr. by Paula Clifford. LC 97-7859. (Praying with...Ser.). 116p. 1997. reprint ed. pap. 10.00 (*0-8028-4314-X*) Eerdmans.

Praying with Teresa of Avila. Rosemary Broughton. Ed. by Carl Koch. (Companions for the Journey Ser.). (Illus.). 120p. (Orig.). 1990. pap. 8.95 (*0-88489-249-2*) St Marys.

Praying with the Anabaptists: The Secret of Bearing Fruit. Marlene Kropf & Eddy Hall. LC 94-71733. 176p. 1994. pap. 12.95 (*0-87303-246-2*); pap., boxed set 19.95 incl. audio (*0-87303-248-9*) Faith & Life.

***Praying with the Celtic Saints.** Mary C. Earle & Sylvia Maddox. (Companions for the Journey Ser.). 112p. (C). 1999. pap. 8.95 (*0-88489-616-1*) St Marys.

Praying with the Church. Anthony M. Buono. LC 90-33607. 152p. (Orig.). 1990. pap. 6.95 (*0-8189-0579-4*) Alba.

Praying with the Church Through the Christian Year. Rachel Hales. 1989. pap. 7.95 (*0-937032-62-X*) Light&Life Pub Co MN.

Praying with the English Hymn Writers. Timothy Dudley-Smith. (Praying With...Ser.). 1990. pap. 5.95 (*0-687-86039-3*) Abingdon.

Praying with the English Poets. Ruth Etchells. (Praying With...Ser.). 1990. pap. 6.95 (*0-687-86045-8*) Abingdon.

Praying with the Holy Spirit. Robert B. Burnette. (Holy Spirit Ser.: Vol. 3). 64p. 1990. pap. 3.95 (*1-881202-04-6*) Anointed Pubns.

Praying with the Jewish Tradition. Tr. by Paula Clifford. LC 97-7871. (Praying with...Ser.). 250p. 1997. reprint ed. pap. 10.00 (*0-8028-4317-4*) Eerdmans.

Praying with the New Catechism. Michael Hollings. 96p. 1994. pap. 29.00 (*0-85597-539-3*) St Mut.

Praying with the One You Love. Arthur Hunt. 196p. 1996. pap. 9.99 (*0-88070-891-3*, Multnomah Bks) Multnomah Pubs.

Praying with the Orthodox Tradition. Tr. by Paula Clifford from GRE. 101p. (Orig.). 1996. pap. 5.95 (*0-88141-156-6*) St Vladimirs.

Praying with the Psalms: A Year of Daily Prayers & Reflections on the Words of David. Eugene H. Peterson. LC 92-54532. 400p. 1993. pap. 13.00 (*0-06-066567-X*, Pub. by Harper SF) HarpC.

Praying with the Saints: Julian of Norwich & Saint Francis of Assissi. Jerry Moye. (Reclaiming the Sacred Ser.: No. 1). 128p. 1996. pap. 13.00 (*1-57312-036-7*) Smyth & Helwys.

Praying with the Saints: Saints' Lives & Prayers. William Lane. 67p. (Orig.). 1989. pap. 5.95 (*1-85390-034-6*, Pub. by Veritas Pubns) St Mut.

Praying with the Saints: 30 Classroom Services for Children. Gwen Costello. (Illus.). 95p. (J). (gr. 3-6). 1999. pap. 12.95 (*0-89622-982-3*) Twenty-Third.

Praying with the Word: Advent, Christmas & Epiphany. David Haas. 128p. (Orig.). 1996. pap. 8.95 (*0-86716-299-6*, B2996) St Anthony Mess Pr.

Praying with the Word: Lent, Easter & Holy Week. David Haas. LC 97-150849. 208p. (Orig.). 1997. pap. 11.95 (*0-86716-300-3*, B3003) St Anthony Mess Pr.

Praying with Therese of Lisieux. Joseph F. Schmidt. Ed. by Carl Koch. LC 93-190187. (Companions for the Journey Ser.). (Illus.). 128p. 1992. pap. 8.95 (*0-88489-250-6*) St Marys.

***Praying with Thomas Aquinas.** Mary Mercy Houle et al. Ed. by Carl Koch. (Companions for the Journey Ser.). (Illus.). 128p. (C). 2000. pap. 8.95 (*0-88489-561-0*) St Marys.

Praying with Thomas Merton. Wayne Simsic. Ed. by Carl Koch. (Companions for the Journey Ser.). (Illus.). 125p. (Orig.). 1994. pap. 8.95 (*0-88489-303-0*) St Marys.

Praying with Vincent de Paul. Thomas McKenna. Ed. by Carl Koch. (Companions for the Journey Ser.). (Illus.). 120p. (Orig.). 1994. pap. 8.95 (*0-88489-316-2*) St Marys.

***Praying with Visionary Women.** Bridget Meehan. LC 99-35188. 200p. 1999. pap. 12.95 (*1-58051-063-9*) Sheed & Ward WI.

Praying with Women of the Bible. Bridget M. Meehan. LC 98-3176. 176p. 1998. pap. 12.95 (*0-7648-0231-3*, Liguori Triumph) Liguori Pubns.

Praying...God You Can Trust. Leith Anderson. 28p. 1998. pap. 9.99 (*0-7642-2119-1*, 212119) Bethany Hse.

Praywell: A Holistic Guide to Health & Renewal. Walter L. Weston. (Illus.). 442p. (Orig.). 1996. pap. 19.95 (*1-884537-06-5*) Transit Press.

PRC Joint Ventures: Capital Contributions, Asset Valuation & Financing. 2nd ed. Asia Law & Practice Staff. 276p. 1997. pap. 330.00 (*962-360-007-0*, Pub. by Asia Law & Practice) Am Educ Systs.

PRC Joint Ventures: Drafting & Negotiating Contracts. Asia Law & Practice Staff. 220p. 1997. pap. 330.00 (*962-7708-89-5*) Am Educ Systs.

PRC Joint Ventures: Financial Management. Asia Law & Practice Staff. 250p. 1997. pap. 330.00 (*962-360-010-0*) Am Educ Systs.

Pre: The Story of America's Greatest Running Legend, Steve Prefontaine. Tom Jordan. LC 97-153178. 176p. 1997. pap. 14.95 (*0-87596-457-5*) Rodale Pr Inc.

Pre- & Perinatal Psychology: An Introduction. Thomas R. Verny. LC 86-27222. 296p. 1986. text 44.95 (*0-89885-327-3*, Kluwer Acad Hman Sci) Kluwer Academic.

Pre- & Post-Anesthesia Nursing Knowledge Base & Clinical Competencies. Ed. by Deborah B. Atsberger & Monica T. Zichuhr. (Illus.). 158p. 1994. pap. text 47.00 (*0-7216-5645-5*, W B Saunders Co) Harcrt Hlth Sci Grp.

Pre- & Post-Operative Care of the Cataract Patient. Paul C. Ajamian. LC 92-16080. (Illus.). 134p. 1992. spiral bd. 47.50 (*0-7506-9073-9*) Buttrwrth-Heinemann.

Pre- & Postmodern Discourses on the Enlightenment, 3 vols., Set. G. S. Rousseau. LC 90-19452. 976p. 1991. text 200.00 (*0-7190-3549-X*, Pub. by Manchester Univ Pr) St Martin.

Pre- & Postsynaptic Receptors: Proceedings of a Study Group Held at the Thirteenth Annual Meeting of the American College of Neuropsychopharmacology, San Juan, Puerto Rico. Ed. by Earl Usdin & William E. Bunney, Jr. LC 75-4238. (Modern Pharmacology-Toxicology Ser.: No. 3). (Illus.). 357p. reprint ed. pap. 110.70 (*0-7837-0970-6*, 204127600019) Bks Demand.

Pre- & Proto- Historic Finns, Both Eastern & Western, with the Magic Songs of the West Finns, 2 vols. John Abercromby. LC 70-144523. (Grimm Library: Nos. 9-10). reprint ed. 74.50 (*0-404-53590-9*) AMS Pr.

Pre-Adamite Man: Demonstrating the Existence of the Human Race. 6th ed. Paschal B. Randolph. 408p. 1996. reprint ed. spiral bd. 21.50 (*0-7873-0695-9*) Hlth Research.

Pre-Adamite Man: Demonstrating the Existence of the Human Race upon This Earth 100,000 Thousand Years Ago! (1888) Paschal B. Randolph. 408p. 1996. reprint ed. pap. 19.95 (*1-56459-825-X*) Kessinger Pub.

Pre-Ahom Assam. Nayanjot Lahiri. (C). 1991. 16.00 (*0-685-50019-5*, Pub. by M Manoharial) S Asia.

Pre-Algebra. Thomas Camilli. (Mathematics Ser.). (Illus.). 32p. (J). (gr. 4-6). 1997. pap., teacher ed. 2.95 (*1-55799-481-1*, 4083) Evan-Moor Edu Pubs.

Pre-Algebra. William K. Carter & Eatherly. (MA - Academic Math Ser.). 1991. mass mkt. 54.95 (*0-538-61375-0*) S-W Pub.

Pre-Algebra. Dolc. (C). 1991. pap., teacher ed., suppl. ed. 29.28 (*0-395-59675-0*) HM.

Pre-Algebra. Frank Schaffer Publications, Inc. Staff. (Middle School Bks.). (Illus.). 1996. wbk. ed. 12.95 (*0-86734-922-0*, FS-10219) Schaffer Pubns.

Pre-Algebra. Dawn T. Jacobi. Ed. by Patricia Pedigo & Roger DeSanti. (Kelley Wingate Ser.). 128p. (YA). (gr. 5-8). 1996. pap. text 10.95 (*0-88724-449-1*, CD-3731) Carson-Dellos.

Pre-Algebra. Phares O'Daffer. (SPA.). 592p. (C). 1992. text 33.33 (*0-201-51868-6*) Addison-Wesley.

Pre-Algebra. Price. 1997. 41.99 (*0-02-825031-1*) McGraw.

***Pre-Algebra.** Price et al. 1999. student ed. 43.99 (*0-02-833240-7*); wbk. ed. 7.47 (*0-02-825041-9*) Glencoe.

Pre-Algebra. Myrl Shireman. (Illus.). 80p. (YA). (gr. 5). 1994. pap. text 9.95 (*1-58037-064-0*, Pub. by M Twain Media) Carson-Dellos.

Pre-Algebra. Robert E. Slavin. (TAI Mathematics Ser.). (J). 1995. pap. text 6.50 (*0-88106-165-4*, M013) Charlesbridge Pub.

Pre-Algebra. Trivieri. 1993. teacher ed. 64.37 (*0-07-065226-0*) McGraw.

Pre-Algebra. Alan Wise & Carol Wise. (College Outline Ser.). 400p. (C). 1991. pap. text 14.50 (*0-15-601518-8*) Harcourt Coll Pubs.

Pre-Algebra. 3rd ed. Van Dyke et al. 928p. (C). 1998. pap. 48.50 (*0-03-019638-8*, Pub. by SCP) Harcourt.

Pre-Algebra, Bk. 1. S. Harold Collins. (Straight Forward Math Ser.). (Illus.). 34p. (YA). (gr. 6-12). 1989. pap. 3.95 (*0-931993-28-8*, GP-028) Garlic Pr OR.

Pre-Algebra, Bk. 2. S. Harold Collins. (Straight Forward Math Ser.). (Illus.). 34p. (YA). (gr. 6-12). 1989. pap. 3.95 (*0-931993-29-6*, GP-029) Garlic Pr OR.

Pre-Algebra: A Laboratory Workbook. 3rd ed. Patricia J. Newell & Kevin R. Lavrack. 64p. (C). 1996. pap. text, per. 15.95 (*0-7872-3471-0*, 41347101) Kendall-Hunt.

***Pre-Algebra: An Integrated Transition to Algebra & Geometry, Teacher's Wraparound Edition.** Price et al. 1999. teacher ed. 56.51 (*0-02-833241-5*) Glencoe.

Pre-Algebra: Answer Key. Jocelyn Walton & Cheryl Klein. 150p. 1995. text, teacher ed. 19.95 (*1-886292-14-0*) CEO Sftware.

Pre-Algebra: Basic Mathematics Skills. Thomas Camilli. Ed. by Bob DeWeese. (Illus.). 32p. (J). (gr. 5-6). 1995. pap., wbk. ed. 2.50 (*1-58610-102-1*, Learn on the Go) Learn Horizon.

Pre-Algebra: Instructor's Solutions Manual. Lial & Hestwood. 144p. 1999. 25.20 (*0-321-02989-5*) Addson-Wesley Educ.

***Pre-Algebra: Inventive Exercises to Sharpen Skills & Raise Achievement.** Imogene Forte & Marjorie Frank. Ed. by Jennifer Streams. (Basic Not Boring Ser.). (Illus.). 64p. (YA). (gr. 6-8). 2000. pap. text 6.95 (*0-86530-447-5*, IP 401-5) Incentive Pubns.

Pre-Algebra: Teacher's Resource File. Eatherly Carter. 1991. teacher ed. 395.00 (*0-538-61654-7*) Sth-Wstrn College.

Pre-Algebra Bk. 5: Series E. Jocelyn C. Walton & Sheryl Klein. 151p. (J). (gr. 7-10). 1995. text, wbk. ed. 19.95 (*1-886292-08-6*) CEO Sftware.

***Pre-Algebra & Algebra.** Lucille Caron & Phil St. Jacques. (Math Success Ser.). (Illus.). 64p. (YA). (gr. 4-10). 2000. lib. bdg. 17.95 (*0-7660-1434-7*) Enslow Pubs.

Pre-Algebra Brain Teasers. Teacher Created Materials Staff. (Brain Teasers Ser.). 80p. (J). (gr. 5-8). 1998. pap. 11.95 (*1-57690-039-8*) Tchr Create Mat.

Pre-Algebra by Design. Russell F. Jacobs. Ed. by Abbey L. Naughton. 53p. (J). (gr. 7-9). 1998. pap. text, wbk. ed. 17.95 (*0-918272-29-7*) Jacobs.

Pre-Algebra Homework. 1996. pap. 2.95 (*0-88012-866-6*) Instruct Fair.

Pre Algebra, 1986. Nichols. 1986. 48.50 (*0-03-001858-7*) Harcourt Schl Pubs.

Pre-Algebra, 1992. Nichols. 1992. text, teacher ed. 78.25 (*0-03-047069-2*); text, student ed. 48.50 (*0-03-047068-4*) H Holt & Co.

Pre-Algebra Step-by-Step. Frank Schaffer Publications, Inc. Staff. (Middle School Bks.). (Illus.). 1996. wbk. ed. 10.95 (*0-7647-0059-6*, FS-10211) Schaffer Pubns.

Pre-Algebra Student's Solutions Manual. Tom Clark Tom. 54p. 1995. pap. text 27.40 incl. VHS (*0-201-88978-1*) Addison-Wesley.

Pre Algebra Text. Symons. 1995. text 34.74 (*0-07-062167-5*) McGraw.

Pre-Alphabet Days: The History of the Letters of the Alphabet. Otto F. Ege. 1977. lib. bdg. 59.95 (*0-8490-2464-1*) Gordon Pr.

Pre & Perinatal Massage Therapy. Carole Osborne-Sheets. (Illus.). 200p. 1998. pap. text 23.95 (*0-9665585-0-2*) Body Therapy.

Pre & Post-Natal Development of the Human Brain: Proceedings of the 1972 International Children's Center Conference, Vol. 13. International Children's Center Conference Staff. Ed. by Samuel R. Berenberg & N. P. Masse. (Illus.). 300p. 1974. 112.25 (*3-8055-1667-3*) S Karger.

Pre-Apprentice Training: Basic Skills. 2nd ed. Jack Martin & Mary Serich. (Illus.). 223p. (YA). (gr. 10 up). 1995. reprint ed. pap. text 27.95 (*0-9649530-0-5*) J Martin & Assocs.

Pre-Aryan Tamil Culture. P. T. Iyengar. 88p. 1986. reprint ed. 16.00 (*0-8364-1720-8*, Pub. by Manohar) S Asia.

Pre-Astronauts: Manned Ballooning on the Threshold of Space. Craig Ryan. (Illus.). 368p. 1995. 31.95 (*1-55750-732-5*) Naval Inst Pr.

Pre-Award Construction Contract Auditing. J. W. Knowles & J. Postel. Ed. by Lee A. Campbell. (Self-Study Ser.). 93p. 1992. pap. text 130.00 (*0-89413-271-7*, A6051) Inst Inter Aud.

Pre-Band Instrument Method. John Brimhall. Ed. by Debbie Cavalier. 32p. (YA). 1997. pap. text 4.95 (*0-7692-1695-1*, 0189B) Wrner Bros.

Pre-Band Instrument Method. John Brimhall. Ed. by Debbie Cavalier. (C). 1997. pap. text. write for info. (*0-7692-1776-1*, 0196B) Wrner Bros.

Pre-Budget Report, November 1997: Securing Britain's Long-Term Economic Future, Command Paper 3804. (Command Papers (All) Ser.: No. 81011068). 1997. 45.00 (*0-10-138042-9*, HM80429, Pub. by Statnry Office) Bernan Associates.

Pre-Bukulu of Ertakasenti No. 1: Sili-Sili: The Kaffric Epoch. Dibinga W. Said. LC 94-6981. 200p. (Orig.). (C). 1995. pap. text 18.00 (*0-943324-33-5*) Omenana.

Pre-Bukulu of Ertakasenti No. 2: Sili: The Kushanic Epoch. Dibinga W. Said. LC 94-89481. 200p. (Orig.). (C). 1995. pap. text 18.00 (*0-943324-35-1*) Omenana.

Pre-Bukulu of Ertakasenti No. 3: Kale-Kale: The Anic Epoch. Dibinga W. Said. LC 94-6981. 200p. (Orig.). (C). 1995. pap. text. write for info. (*0-943324-37-8*) Omenana.

An Asterisk (*) at the beginning of an entry indicates that the title is appearing for the first time.

Pre-Bukulu of Ertakasenti No. 4: Zamani-Kale: The Kemetic Epoch. Dibinga W. Said. LC 94-6981. 200p. (C). 1995. pap. text 18.00 (*0-943324-76-9*) Omenana.

Pre Bukulu of Ertakasenti No. 5: Zamani-Zamani: The Ptolemic Epoch. Dibinga W. Said. LC 94-69481. (Bukulu of Ertakasenti Ser.: No. 5). 200p. (Orig.). (C). 1995. pap. text 18.00 (*0-614-08517-9*) Omenana.

Pre-Caddoan Cultures in the Trans-Mississippi South: A Beginning Sequence. Frank F. Schambach. LC 98-11231. (Arkansas Archeological Survey Research Ser.: No. 53). (Illus.). 142p. 1998. pap. 20.00 (*1-56349-084-6*) AR Archaeol.

Pre-Calculus. Page. (Mathematics Ser.). 2002. mass mkt. 64.95 (*0-534-34137-3*) Brooks-Cole.

***Pre-Calculus.** Robert Sadler. (Illus.). 128p. (YA). (gr. 5). 1999. pap. text 11.95 (*1-58037-093-4*, Pub. by M Twain Media) Carson-Dellos.

Pre-Calculus. Stan Vernooy. (Straight Forward Math Ser.). (Illus.). 160p. (YA). (gr. 8-12). 1993. pap., student ed. 7.95 (*0-931993-53-9*, GP-053) Garlic Pr OR.

Pre-Calculus & Calculus Workbook & Videotape. Barry Reichman. (Pre-Calculus Ser.). 100p. (J). (gr. 6-12). 1990. 225.00 (*0-685-38398-9*) Video Tutorial Serv.

Pre-Calculus Problem Solver: A Complete Solution Guide to Any Textbook. rev. ed. Research & Education Association Staff. LC 84-61812. (Illus.). 960p. 2000. pap. text 23.95 (*0-87891-556-7*) Res & Educ.

Pre-Capitalist Economic Formations. Karl Marx. Tr. by Jack Cohen. LC 65-16393. 160p. 1989. pap. 4.95 (*0-7178-0165-9*) Intl Pubs Co.

Pre-Capitalist Economic Thought: Three Modern Interpretations. LC 70-38469. (Evolution of Capitalism Ser.). 142p. 1972. reprint ed. 19.95 (*0-405-04132-2*) Ayer.

Pre-Capitalist Iran: A Theoretical History. Abbas Vali. LC 93-23837. (C). 1993. text 50.00 (*0-8147-8773-8*) NYU Pr.

***Pre-Carboniferous Geology of the Northern Part of the Arctic Islands: Northern Heiberg Fold Belt, Clements Markham Fold Belt, & Pearya, Northern Axel Heiberg & Ellesmere Islands** Hans P. Trettin. LC 99-204003. (Bulletin/Geological Survey of Canada Ser.). (ENG & FRE.). 401p. 1998. write for info. (*0-660-17013-2*, Pub. by Can7 Govern Pub) Intl Spec Bk.

Pre-Chappel Conodonts of the Llano Region, Texas. G. Seddon. (Reports of Investigations: RI 68). (Illus.). 130p. 1970. pap. 7.50 (*0-318-03170-1*) Bur Econ Geology.

Pre-Christian Ireland: From the First Settlers to the Early Celts. Peter Harbison. LC 87-51301. (Ancient Peoples & Places Ser.). (Illus.). 208p. 1995. pap. 16.95 (*0-500-27809-1*, Pub. by Thames Hudson) Norton.

Pre-Civil War Black Nationalism. William McAdoo. LC 83-60956. (Illus.). 96p. (Orig.). (C). 1983. 12.95 (*0-912135-01-8*); pap. 6.95 (*0-912135-00-X*) D Walker Pr.

Pre-Classical Economists: Pierre le Pesant Boisquilbert (1645-1714), George Berkeley (1685-1753), Baron de Montesquieu (1689-1755), Ferdinando Galiani (1727-1787), James Anderson (1739-1808), Dugald Stewart (1753-1828) Ed. by Mark Blaug. (Pioneers in Economics Ser.: Vol. 7). 192p. 1991. text 110.00 (*1-85278-469-5*) E Elgar.

Pre-Classical Economists Vol. 1: Charles Davenant (1656-1714) & William Petty (1623-1687) Ed. by Mark Blaug. (Pioneers in Economics Ser.: Vol. 6). 272p. 1991. text 125.00 (*1-85278-468-7*) E Elgar.

Pre-Classical Economists Vol. 3: John Law (1671-1729), & Bernard Mandeville (1660-1733) Ed. by Mark Blaug. (Pioneers in Economics Ser.: Vol. 8). 272p. 1991. text 135.00 (*1-85278-470-9*) E Elgar.

Pre-Classical Period, 1610-1634 see History of French Dramatic Literature in the Seventeenth Century

Pre-Clinical Assessment Manual. California College for Health Sciences Staff. 106p. (C). 1985. write for info. (*0-933195-52-4*) CA College Health Sci.

Pre-Code Hollywood: Sex, Immorality & Insurrection in American Cinema, 1930-1934. Thomas Doherty. LC 99-11956. 416p. 1999. 49.50 (*0-231-11094-4*); pap. 19.50 (*0-231-11095-2*) Col U Pr.

Pre-Colonial West Africa. Davidson. LC 97-48911. 272p. (C). 1998. 74.00 (*0-582-31852-1*) Addison-Wesley.

Pre-Columbian America. Incl. Araucanians. 1971. pap. 1.00 (*0-8270-4895-5*); Aztecs. 1972. pap. 1.00 (*0-8270-4890-4*); Incas. 1975. pap. 1.00 (*0-8270-4885-8*); Mesoamerica. (ENG & SPA.). 1979. pap. 1.00 (*0-8270-4270-1*); Mesoamerica. (ENG & SPA.). 1979. pap. 1.00 (*0-8270-4265-5*); pap. write for info. (*0-318-54741-4*) OAS.

***Pre-Columbian America: Ritual Arts of the New Continent.** (Illus.). 400p. 2000. 67.50 (*88-8118-326-9*, Pub. by Skira IT) Abbeville Pr.

Pre-Columbian Architecture, Art, & Artifacts Slide Catalog. H. L. Murvin. 99p. 1988. pap. 3.95 (*0-9608498-2-3*) H L Murvin.

Pre-Columbian Art. Dumbarton Oaks Collection Staff. Ed. by Elizabeth P. Benson. LC 76-8176. 21p. 1976. lib. bdg. 30.00 (*0-226-68981-6*) U Ch Pr.

Pre-Columbian Art. Esther Pasztory. (Illus.). 176p. 1999. pap. 18.95 (*0-521-64551-4*) Cambridge U Pr.

Pre-Columbian Art: Investigations & Insights. Hilda D. Pang. LC 91-23661. (Illus.). 330p. 1992. 70.00 (*0-8061-2379-6*) U of Okla Pr.

***Pre-Columbian Art & the Post-Columbian World: Ancient American Sources of Modern Art.** Barbara Braun. (Illus.). 340p. 2000. pap. 34.95 (*0-8109-2947-3*, Pub. by Abrams) Time Warner.

Pre-Columbian Art & the Post-Columbian World: Ancient Sources of Modern Art. Barbara Braun. LC 92-29047. (Illus.). 340p. 1993. 75.00 (*0-8109-3723-9*, Pub. by Abrams) Time Warner.

Pre-Columbian Art in the Barakat Collection. (Illus.). 120p. 30.00 (*0-685-37761-X*) Barakat.

Pre-Columbian Art of Mexico & Central America. George A. Kubler. 1988. 23.00 (*0-89467-039-5*) Yale Art Gallery.

Pre-Columbian Contact with the Americas Across the Oceans: An Annotated Bibliography, 2 vols. John L. Sorenson & Martin H. Raish. 1340p. (C). 1990. 89.00 (*0-934893-14-4*) Res Press UT.

Pre-Columbian Designs from Panama: 591 Illustrations of Cocle Pottery. Samuel K. Lothrop. LC 75-17177. (Pictorial Archive Ser.). (Illus.). 108p. 1976. pap. 7.95 (*0-486-23232-8*) Dover.

***Pre-Columbian Discovery of America by the Northmen.** 229p. 1999. pap. 40.00 (*1-57074-379-7*) Greyden Pr.

Pre-Columbian Literatures of Mexico. Miguel Leon-Portilla. Tr. by Grace Lobanov. LC 79-32551. (Civilization of the American Indian Ser.: Vol. 92). (Illus.). 256p. (Orig.). 1986. pap. 15.95 (*0-8061-1974-8*) U of Okla Pr.

Pre-Columbian Man Finds Central America: The Archaeological Bridge. Doris Stone. LC 72-801668. (Peabody Museum Papers). (Illus.). 256p. 1972. reprint ed. pap. text 18.00 (*0-87365-776-4*) Peabody Harvard.

Pre-Columbian Metallurgy of South America, Proceedings: A Conference at Dumbarton Oaks, October 18 & 19, 1975. Ed. by Elizabeth P. Benson. LC 79-49261. (Illus.). 107p. 1979. 24.00 (*0-88402-094-0*) Dumbarton Oaks.

***Pre-Columbian Painting: Murals of the Mesoamerica.** (Illus.). 272p. 1999. 95.00 (*88-16-69003-8*, Pub. by Jaca) Antique Collect.

Pre-Columbian Plant Migration from Lowland South America to Mesoamerica. Ed. by Doris Stone. LC 84-61138. (Peabody Museum Papers: Vol. 76). (Illus.). 183p. (Orig.). 1984. pap. 32.00 (*0-87365-202-9*, P76) Peabody Harvard.

Pre-Columbian Shell Engravings from the Craig Mound at Spiro, Oklahoma, 6 vols. limited ed. Philip Phillips et al. LC 74-77557. (Illus.). 1990. 360.00 (*0-87365-777-2*) Peabody Harvard.

Pre-Columbian Shell Engravings from the Craig Mound at Spiro, Oklahoma, Pt. 1, Vols. I-III. limited ed. Philip Phillips & James A. Brown. LC 78-56050. (Illus.). 530p. 1978. pap. 35.00 (*0-87365-795-0*) Peabody Harvard.

Pre-Columbian Shell Engravings from the Craig Mound at Spiro, Oklahoma, Pt. 2, Vols. IV-VI. limited ed. Philip Phillips & James A. Brown. LC 78-56050. (Illus.). 596p. 1984. pap. 35.00 (*0-87365-802-7*) Peabody Harvard.

***Pre-Columbian States of Being.** Ed. by Francesco Pellizzi. (RES Journal Monographs: Vol. 33). (Illus.). 256p. 1998. pap. 30.00 (*0-87365-826-4*) Peabody Harvard.

Pre-Columbian Stories. Robert Hull. LC 93-48468. (Tales from Around the World Ser.). (Illus.). 48p. (J). 1994. lib. bdg. 24.26 (*1-56847-181-5*) Raintree Steck-V.

Pre-Commission Cleaning of Water Systems. C. J. Parsloe. 1991. pap. 100.00 (*0-86022-291-8*, Pub. by Build Servs Info Assn) St Mut.

Pre-Confederation Premiers: Ontario Government Leaders 1841 to 1867. Ed. by J. M. Careless. (Ontario Historical Studies). 368p. 1985. pap. 16.95 (*0-8020-6590-2*) U of Toronto Pr.

Pre-Confederation Premiers: Ontario Government Leaders, 1841-1867. Ed. by James M. Careless. LC 80-501684. (Ontario Historical Studies). 358p. reprint ed. pap. 111.00 (*0-608-16708-8*, 205611900050) Bks Demand.

Pre-Conquest Charter-Bounds of Devon & Cornwall. Della Hooke. LC 93-48923. (Illus.). 265p. (C). 1994. 75.00 (*0-85115-354-2*, Boydell Pr) Boydell & Brewer.

Pre-Contract Practice for the Building Team. 8th rev. ed. Aqua Group Staff. LC 92-12075. (Illus.). 128p. 1992. pap. 32.95 (*0-632-02817-3*) Blackwell Sci.

Pre-Contract Studies. Ashworth. 1996. pap. text. write for info. (*0-582-24984-8*) Addison-Wesley.

Pre-Delivery & Set-Up Guides for Sales & Service Departments in Case-IH & John Deere: Equipment Dealerships. James P. Beal. Ed. by Lenore A. Beal. (Managed Approach to time & Costs Ser.). 6p. 1987. wbk. ed. 150.00 (*0-9634476-4-5*) Taking Care Of Busn.

Pre-Development Handbook: The Permit Process for Multi-Family Housing: New Construction & Rehabilitation. Leon A. Frechette. LC 91-38934. 1991. pap. 14.95 (*0-929489-01-2*) CRS Inc.

Pre-Drama Curriculum Guide & Teacher's Edition: Drama for Elementary Schools. Travis Tyre. (Illus.). 150p. (Orig.). 1994. pap., teacher ed. 26.50 (*1-887710-00-0*, ArtCan Drama) Promise Prodns.

Pre-Drama Student Manual: Drama for Elementary Schools. Travis Tyre. (Illus.). 110p. (Orig.). 1994. pap. text 16.50 (*1-887710-01-9*, ArtCan Drama) Promise Prodns.

Pre-Dressing Skills. rev. ed. Marsha D. Klein. 152p. 1983. pap. text 34.00 (*0-7616-4689-2*) Commun Skill.

Pre-Earthly Deeds of Christ. Rudolf Steiner. 16p. 1976. reprint ed. pap. 3.95 (*0-919924-01-8*, Pub. by Steiner Book Centre) Anthroposophic.

Pre Echo. Murray. 336p. (C). 1995. pap. text 29.95 (*0-13-320714-5*) P-H.

Pre-1841 Census & Population Listings in the British Isles. 92p. pap. 12.95 (*1-873686-00-5*) Lochin.

***Pre-1841 Censuses & Population Listings in the British Isles.** 5th ed. Colin R. Chapman. LC 99-71501. 84p. 1999. pap. 15.00 (*0-8063-1613-6*) Genealog Pub.

Pre 1870 American Seed Trade Catalogs of the National Agricultural Library Index. 110p. 1993. write for info. (*0-88736-219-2*) Chadwyck-Healey.

Pre-Election Polling: Sources of Accuracy & Error. Irving Crespi. LC 88-15770. 208p. 1988. 24.95 (*0-87154-208-0*) Russell Sage.

***Pre-Election Technical Assessment: Papua, New Guinea, February 1999.** James A. Heilman. iv, 176p. 1999. pap. 20.00 (*1-879720-78-7*) Intl Fndt Elect.

Pre-Emergency Planning. William F. Jenaway. (Illus.). 164p. 1986. pap. text 21.87 (*0-9615990-2-2*) Intl Soc Fire Serv.

Pre-Employment Counselor. Jack Rudman. (Career Examination Ser.: C-1396). 1994. pap. 29.95 (*0-8373-1396-1*) Nat Learn.

Pre Employment Interview: Hiring the Right People. rev. ed. James C. Campbell. (Skill Centered Leadership Ser.). 30p. 1997. pap., wbk. ed. 12.95 incl. audio (*1-891161-53-9*) ClamShell Pub.

Pre Employment Investigation. Ralph D. Thomas. 105p. (Orig.). 1992. pap. 35.00 (*0-918487-47-1*) Thomas Investigative.

Pre-Employment Screening for Psychopathology: A Guide to Professional Practice. Rodney L. Lowman. Ed. by Harold H. Smith, Jr. LC 88-43546. (Practitioner's Resource Ser.). 86p. 1989. pap. 16.45 (*0-943158-34-6*, PESPB) Pro Resource.

Pre-Employment Testing & the ADA. Mary A. Nester. (ADA Practice Ser.). 16p. 1994. pap. 9.00 (*0-685-72821-8*) LRP Pubns.

Pre End Stage Renal Disease: A Guide for the Professional Nutritionist. Mary Denny et al. 218p. (C). pap. text 22.50 (*1-883146-52-6*) Coun Renal Nutrit.

***Pre-Engagement: Five Questions to Ask Yourselves.** David Powlison. (Resources for Changing Lives Ser.). 40p. 2000. pap. 2.25 (*0-87552-679-9*) P & R Pubng.

Pre-Engineered Dry Chemical Extinguishing Systems Units, UL 1254. 2nd ed. (C). 1996. pap. text 330.00 (*1-55989-066-5*) Underwrtrs Labs.

Pre-Equilibrium Nuclear Reactions. Ettore Gadioli & P. E. Hodgson. (Studies in Nuclear Physics: No. 15). (Illus.). 536p. 1992. 135.00 (*0-19-851734-3*) OUP.

Pre-Eternal Rest. Frank E. Stranges. 12p. 1985. pap. text 2.00 (*0-933470-07-X*) Intl Evang.

Pre-Exam for Nursing Home Administrator Examinees Preparing for the Licensure Examination. 4th ed. Edmond Boudreaux. 44p. (C). 1991. pap. text 10.00 (*1-878199-01-3*) Pro Exam Review.

Pre-Exam for Nursing Home Administrator Examinees Preparing for the Licensure Examination. 4th ed. Edmond Boudreaux. 40p. (C). 1995. pap. text 10.00 (*1-878199-08-0*) Pro Exam Review.

Pre-Exercise, Competition & Post-Exercise Nutrition for Maximum Performance. Edmund R. Burke. LC 98-168656. (Sports Nutrition Guides Ser.). 48p. 1998. pap. 3.95 (*0-87983-850-7*, 38507K, Keats Publng) NTC Contemp Pub Co.

Pre-Exercise Health Screening Guide. Timothy Olds & Kevin Norton. LC 99-24274. 85p. 1999. pap. write for info. (*0-7360-0210-3*) Human Kinetics.

Pre-Existence of Man, No. 1. Hilton Hotema. 23p. 1998. reprint ed. spiral bd. 10.00 (*0-7873-0453-0*) Hlth Research.

Pre-Existence of Man, No. 2. Hilton Hotema. 58p. 1998. reprint ed. spiral bd. 13.00 (*0-7873-0449-2*) Hlth Research.

Pre-Faces & Other Writings. Jerome Rothenberg. LC 80-24031. 224p. 1981. 14.95 (*0-8112-0785-4*, Pub. by New Directions); pap. 6.95 (*0-8112-0786-2*, NDP511, Pub. by New Directions) Norton.

Pre-failure Deformation of Geomaterials, Vol. 1. Shibuya. 1994. 110.00 (*90-5410-400-7*) Ashgate Pub Co.

Pre-failure Deformation of Geomaterials, Vol. 2. Shibuya. 1995. 110.00 (*90-5410-501-1*) Ashgate Pub Co.

***Pre-Failure Deformation of Geomaterials: Proceedings International Symposium, Torino, Italy, 1999.** Ed. by J. Jamiolkowski. 1999. 70.00 (*90-5809-076-0*, Pub. by A A Balkema) Ashgate Pub Co.

Pre-Failure Deformation of Geomaterials: Proceedings of the International Symposium on Pre-Failure Deformation Characteristics of Geomaterials, Sapporo, Japan, 12-14 September 1994, 2 vols. Ed. by S. Shibuya et al. (Illus.). 1200p. (C). 1995. text 175.00 (*90-5410-399-X*, Pub. by A A Balkema) Ashgate Pub Co.

Pre-Feeding Skills. Morris. 1998. pap. 65.00 (*0-12-784568-2*) Acad Pr.

Pre-Feeding Skills: A Comprehensive Resource for Feeding Development. Suzanne E. Morris & Marsha D. Klein. (Illus.). 414p. 1987. pap. text 65.00 (*0-7616-7406-3*) Commun Skill.

Pre-GED Critical Reading Skills. Patricia Benner. 1987. pap. 10.57 (*0-8092-4844-1*) NTC Contemp Pub Co.

Pre-GED Critical Reading Skills Exercises. Ed. by Lowe. 1992. pap., wbk. ed. 7.65 (*0-8092-3885-3*) NTC Contemp Pub Co.

Pre-GED Guide to Literature. 1995. pap. 9.96 (*0-8114-4485-6*) Raintree Steck-V.

Pre-GED Interpreting Literature & the Arts. Elizabeth Chesla. LC 97-67680. (GED Test Ser.). 192p. 1998. pap. 10.95 (*0-87891-797-7*) Res & Educ.

Pre-GED Intrepretive Literature & Arts Exercise Book. McClanahan. (YA - Adult Education Ser.). 1996. pap. 6.95 (*0-538-63996-2*) S-W Pub.

Pre-GED Literature & The Arts. Contemporary Book Editors. 1995. pap. 11.93 (*0-8092-3491-2*) NTC Contemp Pub Co.

Pre-GED Math Exercise Book. McClanahan. (YA - Adult Education Ser.). 1996. pap. 6.95 (*0-538-63997-0*) S-W Pub.

Pre-GED Math Problem Solving Skills Exercises. Ed. by Karen Gibbons. 1992. pap., wbk. ed. 7.65 (*0-8092-3886-1*) NTC Contemp Pub Co.

Pre-GED Mathematics. Contemporary Book Editors. 1995. pap. 11.93 (*0-8092-3490-4*) NTC Contemp Pub Co.

Pre-GED Mathematics. Michael Lanstrum. LC 97-65278. (GED Test Ser.). 256p. 2000. pap. 11.95 (*0-87891-798-5*) Res & Educ.

***Pre-GED Mathematics.** Raintree Steck-Vaughn Publishing Staff. 2000. pap. 11.94 (*0-7398-0983-0*) Raintree Steck-V.

Pre-GED Mathematics & Problem-Solving Skills, 2 Vols., 2. Robert Mitchell. 1987. pap. 10.57 (*0-8092-5150-7*) NTC Contemp Pub Co.

***Pre-GED Reading.** Raintree Steck-Vaughn Publishers Staff. 1999. pap. text 11.94 (*0-7398-0982-2*) Raintree Steck-V.

Pre-GED Science. Contemporary Books, Inc., Staff. LC 95-9123. 1995. pap. 11.93 (*0-8092-3492-0*) NTC Contemp Pub Co.

***Pre-GED Science.** Raintree Steck-Vaughn Publishers Staff. 1999. pap. text 11.94 (*0-7398-0984-9*) Raintree Steck-V.

Pre-GED Science. Arthur Wagner. (GED Test Ser.). 192p. 2000. pap. 10.95 (*0-87891-799-3*) Res & Educ.

Pre-GED Science Exercies Book. McClanahan. (YA - Adult Education Ser.). 1996. pap. 6.95 (*0-538-63995-4*) S-W Pub.

Pre-GED Science Skills. Ed. by Nancy L. Knapp. 1987. pap. 10.57 (*0-8092-4897-2*) NTC Contemp Pub Co.

Pre-GED Science Skills Exercise. Van. 1992. pap., wbk. ed. 7.65 (*0-8092-3883-7*) NTC Contemp Pub Co.

Pre-GED Science Skills Exercises. Ed. by Van. 1992. pap. 12.70 (*0-8092-3880-2*) NTC Contemp Pub Co.

Pre GED Social Studies. 1994. pap. text 9.96 (*0-8114-4488-0*) Raintree Steck-V.

Pre-GED Social Studies. Lynne-Elizabeth Karren. LC 97-65276. (GED Test Ser.). 192p. 1998. pap. 10.95 (*0-87891-800-0*) Res & Educ.

***Pre-GED Social Studies.** Raintree Steck-Vaughn Publishing Staff. 2000. pap. 11.94 (*0-7398-0985-7*) Raintree Steck-V.

Pre-GED Social Studies Exercise Book. McClanahan. (YA - Adult Education Ser.). 1996. pap. 6.95 (*0-538-63994-6*) S-W Pub.

Pre-GED Social Studies Skills. Contemporary Book Editors. 1995. pap. 11.93 (*0-8092-3493-9*) NTC Contemp Pub Co.

Pre-GED Social Studies Skills. Kenneth Tamarkin. 1987. pap. 10.57 (*0-8092-5026-8*) NTC Contemp Pub Co.

Pre-GED Social Studies Skills Exercises. Ed. by Weiss. 1992. pap., wbk. ed. 7.65 (*0-8092-3888-8*) NTC Contemp Pub Co.

***Pre-GED Writing.** Raintree Steck-Vaughn Publishers Staff. 2000. pap. 11.94 (*0-7398-0981-4*) Raintree Steck-V.

Pre-GED Writing. Lynda Spiegel. LC 97-65280. (GED Test Ser.). 192p. 1998. pap. 10.95 (*0-87891-801-9*) Res & Educ.

Pre-GED Writing & Language Skills. Ed. by Joan Mott. 1987. pap. 10.57 (*0-8092-4898-0*) NTC Contemp Pub Co.

Pre-GED Writing & Language Skills Exercises. Ed. by Elizabeth Romanek. 1992. pap., wbk. ed. 7.65 (*0-8092-3884-5*) NTC Contemp Pub Co.

Pre-GED Writing Exercise Book. McClanahan. (YA - Adult Education Ser.). 1996. pap. 6.95 (*0-538-63993-8*) S-W Pub.

Pre-GED Writing Skills. Contemporary Book Editors. 1995. pap. 11.93 (*0-8092-3494-7*) NTC Contemp Pub Co.

Pre-Geography of Snow. Lyn King. 1987. pap. 8.50 (*0-919626-34-3*, Pub. by Brick Bks) Genl Dist Srvs.

Pre-Geometry. Sharon Vogt. (Illus.). 80p. (YA). (gr. 5). 1995. pap. text 9.95 (*1-58037-027-6*, Pub. by M Twain Media) Carson-Dellos.

Pre-Geometry, Bk. 1. S. Harold Collins. (Straight Forward Math Ser.). (Illus.). 29p. (YA). (gr. 6-12). 1990. pap. 3.95 (*0-931993-30-X*, GP-030) Garlic Pr OR.

Pre-Geometry, Bk. 2. S. Harold Collins. (Straight Forward Math Ser.). (Illus.). 33p. (YA). (gr. 8-12). 1990. pap. 3.95 (*0-931993-31-8*, GP-031) Garlic Pr OR.

Pre-Geometry Brain Teasers. Sylvia Connolly. (Brain Teasers Ser.). 80p. (J). (gr. 5-8). 1998. pap. 9.95 (*1-57690-218-8*) Tchr Create Mat.

Pre-Harvest Sprouting in Cereals, 1995. Ed. by Kaz Noda & D. J. Mares. 495p. 1996. pap. 93.50 (*4-906417-09-4*, Pub. by Jap Sci Soc Pr) Intl Spec Bk.

Pre-Harvest Sprouting in Cereals, 1992. Ed. by J. L. Ried. LC 93-71502. (Illus.). xiv, 480p. 1993. pap. 99.00 (*0-913250-81-3*, BEF 2345) Am Assn Cereal Chem.

Pre-Hispanic Occupance in the Valley of Sonora, Mexico: Archaeological Confirmations of Early Spanish Reports. William E. Doolittle. LC 87-30040. (Anthropological Papers: No. 48). 88p. 1988. pap. 28.50 (*0-8165-1010-5*) U of Ariz Pr.

***Pre-Hispanic Settlement Patterns in the Upper Mantaro & Tarma Drainages, Junbin, Peru.** Jeffrey R. Parsons et al. LC 00-30886. (Memoirs of the Museum of Anthropology, University of Michigan Ser.). 2000. write for info. (*0-915703-49-1*) U Mich Mus Anthro.

Pre-Historic Archaelogy of Madhya Pradesh. Pandeez. (C). 1987. 62.50 (*81-85067-04-X*, Pub. by Sundeep Prak) S Asia.

Pre-Historic Background of Indian Culture. D. H. Gordon. (C). 1997. 48.00 (*81-215-0731-6*, Pub. by M Manoharial) Coronet Bks.

Pre-Historic Background of Indian Culture. Douglas H. Gordon. Ed. by D. Barrett & Desai Madhuri. LC 75-31825. (Illus.). 199p. 1975. lib. bdg. 75.00 (*0-8371-8440-1*, GOIC, Greenwood Pr) Greenwood.

Pre-Historic Graves As a Source of Information. Ed. by Berta Stjernquist. (Konferenser Ser.: No. 29). (Illus.). 267p. 1994. pap. 48.50 (*91-7402-243-1*) Coronet Bks.

Pre-Historic Nations. John D. Baldwin. (Works of John D. Baldwin). vii, 411p. reprint ed. lib. bdg. 59.00 (*0-932051-07-3*) Rprt Serv.

Pre-Historic Nations: or Inquiries Concerning Some of the Great People: The Works of John D. Baldwin. John D. Baldwin. 414p. reprint ed. text 79.00 (*0-7812-0734-7*) Rprt Serv.

P

Pre-Historic Nations: or Inquiries Concerning Some of the Great Peoples & Civilizations of Antiquity. John D. Baldwin. 414p. 1988. reprint ed. spiral bd. 41.50 (*0-7873-1280-0*) Hlth Research.

Pre-Historic Nations or Inquiries Concerning Some of the Great Peoples & Civilizations of Antiquity & Their Probable Relation to a Still Older Civilization of the Ethiopians or Cushites of Arabia (1869) John D. Baldwin. 400p. 1998. reprint ed. pap. 29.95 (*0-7661-0143-6*) Kessinger Pub.

***Pre-Historic Races of America & Other Lands As Disclosed Thru Indian Traditions, Comprehending Also the Origin of Matter & the Formation of the World, the Periodic Changes of the Earth, the Glacial Periods, & Astronomy Solving the Chronological Problems, Etc., Etc.** Erastus S. Curry. (LC History-America-E). 373p. 1999. reprint ed. lib. bdg. 89.00 (*0-7812-4320-3*) Rprt Serv.

Pre-Historic Times. John Lubbock. LC 74-169771. (Select Bibliographies Reprint Ser.). 1977. reprint ed. 42.95 (*0-8369-5991-4*) Ayer.

Pre-History of the Armenian People. LC 83-15429. (Anatolian & Caucasian Studies). 258p. 1985. 50.00 (*0-88206-039-2*) Caravan Bks.

Pre-Hospital Emergency Care by Ambulance Services. Dorothy J. Douglas & Julian A. Roth. 300p. 1989. text 39.50 (*0-8290-2391-7*) Irvington.

***Pre Hospital Pediatric Life Support.** Ed. by Advanced Paediatric Life Support Group Staff. 203p. 1999. pap. 39.95 (*0-7279-1419-7*, Pub. by Brit Med Assn) Amer Coll Phys.

Pre-Hospital Trauma Life Support. rev. ed. National Association of EMT's Pre-Hospital Life Su et al. Ed. by Alexander M. Butman et al. 358p. 1990. reprint ed. pap. text 22.50 (*0-940432-07-2*) Educ Direction.

Pre-Imperial Coinage of Roman Antioch. Edward T. Newell. 45p. 1980. reprint ed. pap. 5.00 (*0-916710-66-1*) Obol Intl.

Pre-Incident Planning. 9th ed. Kidd-Czajkowski & First Due Engine Company Staff. 66p. (C). (gr. 13). 1995. teacher ed. 37.00 (*0-8151-5058-X*) Mosby Inc.

Pre-Industrial Britain see Industrial Revolutions

Pre-Industrial Cities Reader. Colin Chant. LC 98-26901. (Cities & Technology Ser.). 1999. write for info. (*0-415-20077-6*); pap. write for info. (*0-415-20078-4*) Routledge.

Pre-Industrial Population Changes. Ed. by Tommy Bengtsson et al. 420p. 1984. text 77.50 (*91-22-00741-5*) Coronet Bks.

Pre-Industrial Urban System: France, 1740-1840. Bernard Lepetit. Tr. by Godfrey Rogers. LC 93-26676. (Themes in International Urban History Ser.: No. 2). (Illus.). 503p. (C). 1994. text 80.00 (*0-521-41734-1*) Cambridge U Pr.

Pre-Intermediate Choice Workbook Without Key. Mohamed Acklam. 1993. pap. write for info. (*0-582-07104-6*) Addison-Wesley.

Pre-Interpreting Survey: Introduction to Interpreting. LindaLee Massoud. 25p. 1993. 34.00 incl. VHS (*1-878819-23-2*) SignQuest Pubs.

Pre-Interpreting Survey: Peer Evaluation. LindaLee Massoud. 13p. 1993. 28.00 incl. VHS (*1-878819-24-0*) SignQuest Pubs.

Pre-Invasion Bombing Strategy: General Eisenhower's Decision of March 25, 1944. W. W. Rostow. 166p. 1997. reprint ed. pap. text 15.00 (*0-7881-5023-5*) DIANE Pub.

***Pre-Islamic Middle East.** Martin Sicker. LC 99-54421. 240p. 2000. 65.00 (*0-275-96890-1*) Greenwood.

Pre-Jurassic Rocks in Western North American Suspect Terrances. Ed. by Calvin H. Stevens. (Illus.). 142p. (Orig.). 1983. pap. 6.00 (*1-878861-40-9*) Pac Section SEPM.

***Pre-k: Lost & Found in Jumpstart Town.** Scholastic Teacher Editors. (Jumpstart Ser.). (Illus.). (J). (ps-k). 2000. pap. text 3.99 (*0-439-08789-9*) Scholastic Inc.

Pre-K Gourmet: Children's Recipes & Related Activities to Encourage Learning. Jennifer Y. Carroll. Ed. by Dianne Young. (Illus.). 140p. (J). 1998. pap. text 14.95 (*0-9645202-1-4*) Commun Counts.

Pre-K Math: Concepts from Global Sources. Cynthia M. Manthey. LC 95-51841. (Illus.). 162p. (Orig.). 1996. lib. bdg. 29.95 (*0-89334-246-7*, 2477054, Humanics Lrng) Humanics Ltd.

***Pre-Kindergarten Readiness Curriculum.** Shannon. 2000. pap. 22.50 (*0-7668-2249-4*) Delmar.

***Pre-Kindergarten Screen Manual.** Raymond E. Webster. 2000. pap. 22.00 (*1-57128-151-7*) Acad Therapy.

Pre-Lab Exercises to Accompany Experimental Organic Chemistry: A Miniscale & Microscale Approach. 2nd ed. Gilbert. 160p. 1997. pap. text, student ed. 15.00 (*0-03-024748-9*) SCP.

Pre-Law Equivalency Examination (PL) Jack Rudman. (Admission Test Ser.: Vol. 40). 49.95 (*0-8373-5140-5*) Nat Learn.

Pre-Law Equivalency Examination (PL) Jack Rudman. (Admission Test Ser.: ATS-40). 1994. pap. 29.95 (*0-8373-5040-9*) Nat Learn.

Pre-Malthusian Doctrines of Population. Charles E. Stangeland. LC 05-7910. (Columbia University. Studies in the Social Sciences: No. 56). reprint ed. 32.50 (*0-404-51056-6*) AMS Pr.

Pre-Malthusian Doctrines of Population. Charles E. Stangeland. LC 66-21372. (Reprints of Economic Classics Ser.). 356p. 1966. reprint ed. 30.00 (*0-678-00159-6*) Kelley.

Pre-Marital Agreement Kit, Do-It-Yourself. John C. Howell. 14.95 (*1-880398-05-2*, 01015) SJT Enterprises.

Pre-Med Handbook. Howard Levitin. 336p. (Orig.). 1986. mass mkt. 12.95 (*0-446-38291-4*, Pub. by Warner Bks) Little.

Pre-Meiji Works in the Library of Congress: Japanese Literature, Performing Arts, & Reference Books. Compiled by Shojo Honda. LC 95-10036. (Asian Division Bibilographics Ser.: No. 2). 1995. write for info. (*0-8444-0877-8*) Lib Congress.

Pre-Meiji Works in the Library of Congress: Japanese Literature, Performing Arts & Reference Books, Bibliography. Shojo Honda. 109p. 1997. boxed set 18.00 (*0-16-061812-6*, Library of Cong) USGPO.

Pre-Mesozoic Geology in France & Related Areas. Ed. by J. D. Keppie. LC 93-44603. 1994. write for info. (*3-540-56502-7*) Spr-Verlag.

Pre-Mesozoic Geology in France & Related Areas. Ed. by J. D. Keppie. LC 93-44603. 1994. 318.95 (*0-387-56502-7*) Spr-Verlag.

Pre-Mesozoic Geology in the Alps. Ed. by J. F. Von Raumer & F. Neubauer. LC 93-18444. (Illus.). 672p. 1993. 318.95 (*0-387-54757-6*) Spr-Verlag.

Pre-Mesozoic Geology of Iberia: IGCP-Project 233. Ed. by R. D. Dallmeyer & E. Martinez-Garcia. (Illus.). 550p. 1991. 214.95 (*0-387-51792-8*) Spr-Verlag.

***Pre-Mesozoic Ice Ages: Their Bearing on Understanding the Climate System.** John C. Crowell. (Geological Society of America. Memoir Ser.: Vol. 192). 106p. 1999. 46.00 (*0-8137-1192-4*) Geol Soc.

Pre-Modern & Modern National Identity in Russia & Eastern Europe. Wendy Bracewell et al. 236p. 1993. pap. text 53.00 (*2-88124-625-7*) Gordon & Breach.

Pre-Modern Encyclopedia Texts: Proceedings of the Second COMERS Congress, Groningen, 1-4 July 1996. Ed. by Peter Binkley. LC 97-18515. (Studies in Intellectual History: Vol. 79). (Illus.). 400p. 1997. 131.00 (*90-04-10830-0*) Brill Academic Pubs.

Pre-Morning. Yevgeny Yevtushenko. Ed. by Albert C. Todd. LC 95-61263. (ENG & RUS., Illus.). 152p. 1995. pap. 15.00 (*1-885563-04-3*) VIA Press MD.

Pre-Mortem Estate Planning Checklist. Edward S. Schlesinger & Adam M. Schenck. 165.00 (*0-8318-0813-6*) Am Law Inst.

Pre-Mughal Persian in Hindustan, 2 vols., Set. Muhammad A. Ghani. LC 96-900961. (C). 1994. reprint ed. 54.00 (*81-85326-84-3*, Pub. by Vintage) S Asia.

Pre-Natal Injuries & Wrongful Life: Practice Guide. Lawyers Cooperative Publishing Staff. LC 92-74951. 1993. ring bd. 105.00 (*0-317-05381-7*) West Group.

Pre-Nineteen Hundred Dog License Tags. William J. Bone. LC 93-90483. (Illus.). 218p. 1993. pap. text 27.50 (*0-9638012-0-1*) W J Bone Ent.

Pre-Nineteen Sixty Developments in the Bill of Rights Area, 2 vols. Ed. by Paul L. Murphy. (Bill of Rights & American Legal History Ser.). 1472p. 1990. reprint ed. text 40.00 (*0-8240-5859-3*) Garland.

***Pre 19th Century British Bibliographers.** Ward W. Briggs. LC 99-33325. (Dictionary of Literary Biography Ser.). 400p. 1999. text 155.00 (*0-7876-3105-1*) Gale.

Pre-Nursing Reviews in Arithmetic. 2nd ed. Mary E. Stehman. 33p. 1961. pap. 3.95 (*0-8036-8140-2*) Davis Co.

Pre-Object Relatedness: Early Attachment & the Psychoanalytic Situation. Ivri Kumin. LC 95-19657. (Psychoanalysis Ser.). 240p. 1995. lib. bdg. 40.00 (*1-57230-015-9*) Guilford Pubns.

***Pre-Occupation of Postcolonial Studies.** Fawzia Afzal-Khan & Kalpana Seshadri-Crooks. LC 99-53103. 448p. 2000. 21.95 (*0-8223-2521-7*) Duke.

***Pre-Occupation of Postcolonial Studies.** Ed. by Fawzia Afzal-Khan & Kalpana Seshadri-Crooks. (Illus.). 448p. 2000. text 64.95 (*0-8223-2486-5*) Duke.

***Pre-Paid Legal Story: The Story of One Man, His Company & Its Mission to Provide Affordable Legal Protection for Everyone.** Harland C. Stonecipher. (Illus.). 288p. 2000. pap. 25.00 (*0-7615-2221-2*) Prima Pub.

Pre-Palatial: The Foundations of Palatial Crete: A Survey of Crete in the Early Bronze Age. K. Branigan. xvi, 232p. (Orig.). 1988. pap. 50.00 (*90-256-0954-6*, Pub. by AM Hakkert) BookLink Distributors.

Pre-Permian Geology of Central & Eastern Europe. Ed. by R. D. Dallmeyer et al. (Illus.). 608p. 1995. 433.95 (*0-387-55472-6*) Spr-Verlag.

Pre-Pleiade Poetry. Ed. by Jerry C. Nash. LC 84-81851. (French Forum Monographs: No. 57). 148p. (Orig.). 1985. pap. 12.95 (*0-917058-57-7*) French Forum.

Pre-Prison Writings. Antonio Gramsci. Ed. by Richard Bellamy. Tr. by Virginia Cox. LC 92-47069. (Cambridge Texts in the History of Political Thought Ser.). (ENG & ITA.). 404p. (C). 1994. text 59.95 (*0-521-41143-2*) Cambridge U Pr.

Pre-Prison Writings. Antonio Gramsci. Ed. by Richard Bellamy. Tr. by Virginia Cox. LC 92-47069. (Cambridge Texts in the History of Political Thought Ser.). (ENG & ITA.). 404p. (C). 1994. pap. text 19.95 (*0-521-42307-4*) Cambridge U Pr.

Pre-Production Planning for Video, Film, & Multimedia. Steve R. Cartwright. LC 96-17689. 224p. 1996. pap. 39.95 (*0-240-80271-3*, Focal) Buttrwrth-Heinemann.

Pre-Production Quality Assurance for Healthcare Manufacturers. G. W. Hough et al. LC 97-2869. (Illus.). 308p. 1997. 169.00 (*1-57491-045-0*) Interpharm.

Pre-Professional Skills Test (PPST) (Admission Test Ser.: ATS-95). 1994. pap. 23.95 (*0-8373-5095-6*) Nat Learn.

Pre Professional Skills Test (PPST) Jack Rudman. (Admission Test Ser.: Vol. 95). 43.95 (*0-8373-5195-2*) Nat Learn.

Pre-Prosthetic Surgery: A Self-Instructional Guide, Bk. 7. 3rd rev. ed. James R. Hooley & Robert J. Whitacre. (Illus.). 58p. 1983. pap. 5.95 (*0-89939-071-4*) Stoma Pr.

***Pre-Psychoanalytic Writings of Sigmund Freud.** Ed. by Flip Geerardyn & Gertrudis Van De Vijver. 300p. 2000. 49.99 (*1-900877-21-X*, Pub. by Rebus Pr Ltd) Intl Spec Bk.

***Pre-Qin Civilization in the Jianghan Region.** Ed. by Yau Hok-wa. 192p. 1999. 78.00 (*962-7101-44-3*, Pub. by Chinese Univ of Hong Kong) St Mut.

Pre-Raphaelite, & Other Poets. Lafcadio Hearn. Ed. by John Erskine. LC 68-22096. (Essay Index Reprint Ser.). 1977. 23.95 (*0-8369-0526-1*) Ayer.

Pre-Raphaelite Art in Its European Context. Ed. by Susan P. Casteras & Alicia C. Faxon. LC 94-15619. 1995. write for info. (*0-8386-4850-9*) Fairleigh Dickinson.

Pre-Raphaelite Art in Its European Context. Susan P. Casteras & Alicia C. Faxon. LC 92-55114. 248p. 1995. 80.00 (*0-8386-3539-3*) Fairleigh Dickinson.

Pre-Raphaelite Body: Fear & Desire in Painting, Poetry & Criticism. J. B. Bullen. (Illus.). 256p. (C). 1998. text 65.00 (*0-19-818257-0*) OUP.

Pre-Raphaelite Cats. Susan Herbert. LC 98-75343. (Illus.). 64p. 1999. 19.95 (*0-500-01912-6*, Pub. by Thames Hudson) Norton.

Pre-Raphaelite Circle. National Portrait Gallery Staff. LC 99-215291. (Character Sketches Ser.). 1997. 11.95 (*1-85514-231-7*, Pub. by Lund Humphries) Antique Collect.

Pre-Raphaelite Drawings of Edward Burne-Jones. Edward Burne-Jones. (Art Library). (Illus.). 44p. (Orig.). 1981. pap. 4.95 (*0-486-24113-0*) Dover.

Pre-Raphaelite Friendship: The Correspondence of William Holman Hunt & John Lucas Tupper. Ed. by James H. Coombs et al. LC 86-1486. (Nineteenth-Century Studies). 357p. reprint ed. 110.70 (*0-8357-1745-3*, 207047200095) Bks Demand.

***Pre-Raphaelite Illustrators: The Published Graphic Art of the English Pre-Raphaelites & Their Associates with Critical Biographical Essays, Catalogues of the Works & Galleries of Their Engraved Illustraions.** Gregory R. Suriano. LC 99-87847. 2000. write for info. (*1-58456-021-5*) Oak Knoll.

Pre-Raphaelite Paintings & Drawings in the Birmingham Museum & Art Gallery. (Microfiche Ser.). (Illus.). 2500p. (C). 1990. 730.00 (*0-8161-1760-8*, G K Hall & Co) Mac Lib Ref.

Pre-Raphaelite Photography. Ed. by Graham Ovenden. (Illus.). 84p. 1984. pap. 14.95 (*0-312-63736-5*) St Martin.

Pre-Raphaelite Prints: Millais, Holman Hunt, Rosetti & Their Followers. Rodney Engen. (Illus.). 129p. 1995. 50.00 (*0-85331-656-2*, Pub. by Lund Humphries) Antique Collect.

Pre-Raphaelite Sculpture: Nature & Imagination in British Sculpture 1848-1914. Ed. by Bendict Read. (British Sculptors & Sculpture Ser.). (Illus.). 176p. (C). 1991. 70.00 (*0-85331-609-0*, Pub. by Lund Humphries) Antique Collect.

Pre-Raphaelite Sisterhood. Jan Marsh. (Illus.). 416p. 1995. pap. 19.95 (*0-7043-0169-5*, Pub. by Quartet) Interlink Pub.

Pre-Raphaelite to Arts & Crafts Jewellery. Charlotte Gere. (Illus.). 244p. 1989. 69.50 (*1-85149-257-7*) Antique Collect.

Pre-Raphaelite Twilight: The Story of Charles Augustus Howell. Helen R. Angeli. 1988. reprint ed. lib. bdg. 49.00 (*0-7812-0026-1*) Rprt Serv.

Pre-Raphaelite Twilight: The Story of Charles Augustus Howell. Helen R. Angeli. LC 72-158494. (Illus.). 1971. reprint ed. 39.00 (*0-403-01312-7*) Scholarly.

Pre-Raphaelite Vision. Phaidon Staff. LC 99-495105. (Miniature Editions Ser.). (Orig.). (C). 1994. pap. 8.95 (*0-7148-3252-9*, Pub. by Phaidon Press) Phaidon Pr.

Pre-Raphaelite Women Artists. Jan Marsh & Pamela Gerrish Nun. LC 98-61449. (Illus.). 157p. 1999. pap. 24.95 (*0-500-28104-1*, Pub. by Thames Hudson) Norton.

Pre-Raphaelites. (Illus.). 12p. 1997. 4.98 (*0-7858-0693-8*) Bk Sales Inc.

Pre-Raphaelites. Book Sales Staff. 1998. pap. text 6.99 (*0-7858-0988-0*) Bk Sales Inc.

Pre-Raphaelites. Timothy Hilton. (World of Art Ser.). (Illus.). 216p. 1985. pap. 14.95 (*0-500-20102-1*, Pub. by Thames Hudson) Norton.

Pre-Raphaelites. Ed. by Leslie Parris. (Illus.). 312p. 1995. pap. 60.00 (*1-85437-144-4*) U of Wash Pr.

Pre-Raphaelites. Random House Value Publishing Staff. 1999. 9.99 (*0-517-16116-8*) Random Hse Value.

Pre-Raphaelites. Andrea Rose. (Color Library). (Illus.). 128p. (C). 1994. pap. 14.95 (*0-7148-2907-2*, Pub. by Phaidon Press) Phaidon Pr.

Pre-Raphaelites: An Anthology. Ed. by Jerome H. Buckley. 503p. 1987. reprint ed. pap. 12.00 (*0-89733-237-7*) Academy Chi Pubs.

***Pre-Raphaelites Inspiration from the Past, 1.** Terri Hardin. 1998. 16.95 (*1-880908-76-X*) Todtri Prods.

***Pre-Raphaelites: Romance & Realism.** Laurence Des Cars. LC 99-45854. (Discoveries Ser.). 128p. 2000. pap. 12.95 (*0-8109-2891-4*, Pub. by Abrams) Time Warner.

Pre-Raphaelites: Their Lives in Letters & Diaries. Jan Marsh. LC 96-220485. (Illus.). 160p. 1997. 24.95 (*1-85585-246-2*, Pub. by Collins & Br) Trafalgar.

Pre-Raphaelites: Writings & Sources, 4 vols. Inga Bryden. LC 98-14090. (Illus.). 1160p. (C). 1998. reprint ed. 655.00 (*0-415-16908-9*) Routledge.

Pre-Raphaelites & Their Circle. 2nd ed. Cecil Y. Lang. LC 75-12233. xxix, 592p. 1975. pap. text 16.95 (*0-226-46866-6*, P651) U Ch Pr.

Pre-Raphaelites & Their World. Rachel Barnes. LC 98-158608. (Illus.). 112p. 1997. pap. 25.95 (*1-85437-220-3*, Pub. by Tate Gallery) U of Wash Pr.

Pre-Raphaelites in Context. Malcolm Warner et al. LC 91-47549. 259p. reprint ed. pap. 80.30 (*0-608-03463-0*, 206416800008) Bks Demand.

Pre-Raphaelites in Literature & Art. Ed. by D. S. Welland. LC 72-76949. (Granger Index Reprint Ser.). 1977. 18.95 (*0-8369-6046-7*) Ayer.

Pre-Raphaelites Re-Viewed. Ed. by Marcia Pointon. (Cultural Politics Ser.). 192p. 1989. text 29.95 (*0-7190-2821-3*, Pub. by Manchester Univ Pr) St Martin.

Pre-Raphaelitism & Medievalism in the Arts. Ed. by Liana De Girolami Cheney. LC 92-5491. (Illus.). 328p. 1992. lib. bdg. 99.95 (*0-7734-9491-X*) E Mellen.

Pre-Raphaelitism & the Pre-Raphaelite Brotherhood, 2 vols. William H. Hunt. LC 05-40801. reprint ed. 125.00 (*0-404-03437-3*) AMS Pr.

Pre-Referral Intervention Manual: The Most Common Learning & Behavior Problems Encountered in the Educational Environment. Stephen B. McCarney & Kathy C. Wunderlich. 504p. (Orig.). 1993. pap. 33.00 (*1-878372-11-4*) Hawthorne Educ Servs.

Pre-Reform Coinage of Diocletian. Percy H. Webb. (Illus.). 1977. 6.50 (*0-915018-29-2*) Attic Bks.

Pre Reformatn Church Eng. (C). 1989. pap. text 13.50 (*0-582-35555-9*, 78422) Longman.

Pre Reformatn Church Eng. rev. ed. Christopher Harper-Bill. LC 96-4175. (Seminar Studies in History). 152p. (C). 1996. pap. text 14.06 (*0-582-28989-0*, Pub. by Addison-Wesley) Longman.

***Pre-Release: Managing the Legal Aspects of Technology.** 2nd ed. Lee B. Burgunder. (SWC-General Business Ser.). 1999. pap. 35.00 (*0-324-04077-6*) Thomson Learn.

Pre-Republican Rome: An Analysis of the Cultural & Chronological Relations, 1000-500 B.C. Jorgen C. Meyer. (Analecta Romana Ser.: Suppl. XI). 210p. (Orig.). 1983. pap. 43.50 (*87-7492-434-6*, Pub. by Odense Universitets Forlag) Coronet Bks.

Pre-Requisites for the Study of Jacob Boehme. C. J. Barker. 1987. reprint ed. pap. 6.95 (*1-55818-104-0*, Sure Fire) Holmes Pub.

Pre-Requisites for the Study of Jacob Boehme. C. J. Barker. 34p. 1997. reprint ed. pap. 4.95 (*0-7661-0062-6*) Kessinger Pub.

Pre-Restoration Stage Studies. William J. Lawrence. LC 67-23857. 1972. reprint ed. 30.95 (*0-405-08738-1*, Pub. by Blom Pubns) Ayer.

Pre-Retirement Planning for Women: Program Design & Research. Ed. by Christopher L. Hayes & Jane M. Deren. LC 89-26332. 192p. 1990. 33.95 (*0-8261-6350-5*) Springer Pub.

Pre-Retirement Workbook. Charles D. Tellalian. 117p. 1988. student ed. 19.95 (*0-929743-11-3*) Sequoia Retire Servs.

Pre-Revolutionary Dutch Houses & Families in Northern New Jersey & Southern New York. Rosalie Bailey. 612p. 1993. reprint ed. lib. bdg. 109.00 (*0-7812-5292-X*) Rprt Serv.

Pre-Revolutionary Writings. Edmund Burke. Ed. by Ian Harris. (Cambridge Texts in the History of Political Thought Ser.). 406p. (C). 1993. text 59.95 (*0-521-36227-X*); pap. text 19.95 (*0-521-36800-6*) Cambridge U Pr.

Pre-Roman & Roman Winchester Pt. 2: The Roman Cemetary at Lankhills. Giles Clarke. (Winchester Studies). (Illus.). 510p. 1980. text 105.00 (*0-19-813177-1*) OUP.

Pre-Roman Urnfields in the North of the Netherlands. P. B. Kooi. Tr. by B. M. Van der Maulen-Melrose from DUT. (Illus.). viii, 203p. 1979. 43.00 (*90-6243-012-0*, Pub. by Boumas Boekhuis) Gen Publ ON.

Pre-Romantic Attitudes to Landscape in the Writings of Friedrich Schiller. Sheila M. Benn. (Quellen und Forschungen zur Sprach und Kulturgeschichte der Germanischen Voelker: Vol. 99-223). xiv, 242p. (C). 1991. lib. bdg. 92.35 (*3-11-012825-X*) De Gruyter.

Pre-Sargonid Temples in Diyala. Pinhas Delougaz. 1992. lib. bdg. 8.00 (*0-226-14232-9*) U Ch Pr.

Pre-School, Bk. 1. Schaffer, Frank, Publications Staff. (Reproducible Workbooks Ser.). (Illus.). 48p. (J). (ps). 1983. student ed. 4.98 (*0-86734-022-3*, FS-2651) Schaffer Pubns.

Pre-School, Bk. 2. Schaffer, Frank, Publications Staff. (Reproducible Workbooks Ser.). (Illus.). 48p. (J). (ps). 1983. student ed. 4.98 (*0-86734-023-1*, FS-2652) Schaffer Pubns.

Pre-School & Kindergarten: Individual Sets. Marion W. Stuart. text. write for info. (*0-943343-06-2*) Lrn Wrap-Ups.

Pre-School & Kindergarten Skills see Let's Learn Set

Pre-School Behavior Checklist (PBCL) Jacqueline McGuire & Naomi Richman. 1988. 16.00 (*0-87879-639-8*); teacher ed., ring bd. 55.00 (*0-87879-638-X*); 6.00 (*0-685-44973-4*) Acad Therapy.

Pre-School Provision for Children with Special Needs. B. Robson. Ed. by Peter Mittler. (Special Needs in Ordinary Schools Ser.). 208p. 1989. pap. text 29.95 (*0-304-31559-1*) Continuum.

Pre-School to School: A Behavioural Study. Naomi Richman et al. (Behavioral Development Monographs). 1982. text 110.00 (*0-12-587940-7*) Acad Pr.

Pre-School Virtuoso, Bk. I. Yoon-Il Auh. (Auh School of Violin Ser.). 40p. (J). (gr. k-5). 1988. student ed. 10.00 (*1-882858-03-4*) Yoon-il Auh.

Pre-School Virtuoso, Bk. II. Yoon-Il Auh. (Auh School of Violin Ser.). 40p. (J). (gr. k-5). 1988. student ed. 10.00 (*1-882858-04-2*) Yoon-il Auh.

Pre-School Virtuoso, Bk. III. Yoon-Il Auh. (Auh School of Violin Ser.). 40p. (J). (gr. k-5). 1988. student ed. 10.00 (*1-882858-05-0*) Yoon-il Auh.

Pre-School Virtuoso, Bk. IV. Yoon-Il Auh. (Auh School of Violin Ser.). 40p. (J). (gr. k-5). 1988. student ed. 10.00 (*1-882858-06-9*) Yoon-il Auh.

Pre-Scissor Skills. 3rd ed. Marsha D. Klein. (Illus.). 1990. 34.00 (*0-7616-3101-1*) Commun Skill.

Pre-Seminole Florida: Spanish Soldiers, Friars, & Indian Missions, 1513-1763. Robert M. Matter. LC 90-21600. (Evolution of North American Indians Ser.: Vol. 13). 208p. 1991. reprint ed. text 10.00 (*0-8240-2508-3*) Garland.

P

Pre-Shave Gear Cutting Tools. A. D. Moncrieff. (Technical Papers: Vol. P129.07). (Illus.). 31p. 1949. pap. text 30.00 (*1-55589-155-1*) AGMA.

***Pre-Shipment Inspection Services No. 2: Policies & Country Experiences.** Unod Rege. (Trade & Enterprise Papers Ser.). 90p. 2000. pap. 9.95 (*0-85092-619-X*, Pub. by Comm Sec) Stylus Pub VA.

Pre-Slinging & Strapping of Cargo. ICHCA Staff. (C). 1977. 95.00 (*0-7855-5091-7*, Pub. by ICHCA) St Mut.

Pre-Slinging & Strapping of Cargo. ICHCA Staff. (C). 1988. 65.00 (*0-7855-6168-4*, Pub. by ICHCA) St Mut.

Pre-Socratics: A Collection of Critical Essays. Ed. by Alexander P. Mourelatos. 580p. 1993. pap. text 22.95 (*0-691-02088-4*, Pub. by Princeton U Pr) Cal Prin Full Svc.

"Pre-Stage" Guitar Book- Learn How to Get a Grip on Your First Guitar!- Learn How to Play Guitar!! Chris Lopez. 1999. spiral bd. 14.95 (*0-9667719-5-8*) C Winkle Prods.

Pre-Sung Dynasty Chinese Stonewares in the Royal Ontario Museum. Y. Mino. (Illus.). 104p. 25.71 (*0-88854-155-4*) Brill Academic Pubs.

Pre-Surfaced Boards. 1973. 39.00 (*0-7855-1087-7*) St Mut.

Pre-Task Briefing: A Prescription for Accident Prevention. H. C. Howlett, 2nd. (Illus.). 7p. 1994. pap. 3.50 (*1-57614-011-3*) TECHSTAR.

***Pre-Teen & Teenagers Guide to Personal Growth, Health, Safety, Sex, & Survival: A Parents & Teenagers Guide to Better Understanding.** Debrah Harris-Johnson. Ed. by Tony Rose. LC 99-29200. 250p. 1999. pap. 19.95 (*0-9655064-4-4*) Amber Books.

Pre-Teen Means Inbetween. Linda Lewis. Ed. by Pat MacDonald. 160p. (Orig.). (J). (gr. 3-6). 1993. per. 2.99 (*0-671-74535-2*, Minstrel Bks) PB.

Pre-Test: Scoring Set GED. 1987. pap. 16.20 (*0-8092-4572-8*) NTC Contemp Pub Co.

Pre-Test: Starter Set GED. 1987. pap. 33.95 (*0-8092-4570-1*) NTC Contemp Pub Co.

Pre-Test Clinical Vignettes for USMLE Step I. McGraw-Hill Inc Staff. LC 99-13440. 304p. 1999. 24.95 (*0-07-135133-7*) McGraw-Hill HPD.

Pre-Text: The First Decade. Ed. by Victor J. Vitanza. LC 93-1007. (Series in Composition, Literacy, & Culture). 352p. (C). 1993. pap. 19.95 (*0-8229-5513-X*); text 49.95 (*0-8229-3763-8*) U of Pittsburgh Pr.

***Pre-Theories & Theories of Foreign Policy-Making.** Emmanuel N. Amadife. LC 99-13537. 192p. 1999. 35.00 (*0-7618-1364-0*) U Pr of Amer.

Pre-Trial & Pre-Hearing Procedures Worldwide. Ed. by Charles Platto. (C). 1990. lib. bdg. 181.50 (*1-85333-458-8*, Pub. by Graham & Trotman) Kluwer Academic.

Pre-Trial Discovery in Canada: International Litigation in Canadian & German Forums. Georg A. Wittuhn. (European University Studies: Law: Ser. 2, Vol. 922). XXIII, 123p. 1990. pap. 38.00 (*3-631-42509-0*) P Lang Pubng.

Pre-Trial Litigation: Law, Policy & Practice. R. Lawrence Dessem. (American Casebook Ser.). 190p. (C). 1991. pap. text, teacher ed. write for info. (*0-314-90908-7*) West Pub.

Pre-Trial Litigation: Law, Policy & Practice. R. Lawrence Dessem. (American Casebook Ser.). 608p. 1993. reprint ed. pap. text 35.50 (*0-314-81932-0*) West Pub.

Pre-Trial Manual. IPDC Staff. 628p. 1995. ring bd. 30.00 (*0-7872-0945-7*) Kendall-Hunt.

Pre-Victorian Book Illustration In Britain & Europe, 8 Vol. 3776p. 1998. 1350.00 (*1-85506-594-0*) Thoemmes Pr.

Pre-Victorian British Typography & Printers' Manuals, 8 vols. (First Collection). (Illus.). 3550p. 1998. 1225.00 (*1-85506-593-2*) Thoemmes Pr.

Pre-View of Policy Sciences. Harold D. Lasswell. LC 78-165801. (Policy Sciences Book Ser.). 187p. reprint ed. pap. 58.00 (*0-608-16307-4*, 202625900049) Bks Demand.

Pre-Visit Expectations & Post-Visit Impressions of Japanese Holiday Visitors to New Zealand Jane Edmondston. LC 87-214035. (NZTP Overseas Market Research Ser.). 93 p. 1986. 35.00 (*0-477-02419-X*, Pub. by Manaaki Whenua) Balogh.

Pre-Vocational Franchise: Organising Community-Linked Education for Adult & Working Life. Bill Law. 224p. (C). 1986. pap. 50.00 (*0-06-318354-4*, Pub. by P Chapman) St Mut.

Pre-War Business Cycle, 1907-1914. William C. Schluter. LC 68-57580. (Columbia University. Studies in the Social Sciences: No. 243). reprint ed. 20.00 (*0-404-51243-7*) AMS Pr.

Pre-Wrath Rapture of the Church. Marvin J. Rosenthal. 320p. 1990. pap. 15.99 (*0-8407-3160-4*) Nelson.

Pre-Wrath Rapture of the Church: Is It Biblical? Paul S. Karleen. 102p. (Orig.). 1991. pap. 7.95 (*0-9628612-0-0*) BF Press.

Pre-Writing Skills. rev. ed. Marsha D. Klein. 119p. 1990. 34.00 (*0-7616-2089-3*) Commun Skill.

Preach for a Year. Roger Campbell. LC 87-29400. (Preach for a Year Ser.: No. 2). 224p. 1993. pap. 11.99 (*0-8254-2330-9*) Kregel.

Preach for a Year. Roger Campbell. (Preach for a Year Ser.: No. 3). 224p. 1995. pap. 11.99 (*0-8254-2321-X*) Kregel.

Preach for a Year. Roger F. Campbell. LC 87-29400. (Preach for a Year Ser.: No. 1). 224p. 1988. pap. 11.99 (*0-8254-2329-5*) Kregel.

Preach for a Year, No. 4. Roger Campbell. 224p. 1996. pap. 11.99 (*0-8254-2318-X*) Kregel.

Preach for a Year No. 5: Two Complete Outlines for Every Sunday of the Year. Roger F. Campbell. (Preach for a Year Ser.). 224p. 1998. pap. 11.99 (*0-8254-2347-3*) Kregel.

***Preach It! Messages of the Bible.** James Benedict. (Good Ground Ser.: Vol. 2:1). 41p. 1999. pap. 5.95 (*0-87303-359-0*) Faith & Life.

Preach Liberty: Selections from the Bible for Progressives. Ed. by Steve Bachmann. LC 89-35507. (Illus.). 120p. (Orig.). 1989. pap. 10.95 (*0-941423-29-8*) FWEW.

Preach Life Change. Willow Creek Resources Staff. (Defining Moments Ser.: Vol. 20). 9.99 (*0-310-20442-9*) Zondervan.

Preach the Gospel. Joel C. Gerlach & Richard Balge. 186p. 1982. 19.99 (*0-8100-0153-5*, 15NO387) Northwest Pub.

Preach the Word. Billy Apostolon. (Sermon Outline Ser.). 64p. 1958. pap. 4.99 (*0-8010-0039-4*) Baker Bks.

Preach the Word. Charles R. Gresham. LC 83-71917. 200p. (Orig.). 1983. pap. 4.99 (*0-89900-198-X*) College Pr Pub.

Preach the Word. D. Lane. 1994. pap. 3.99 (*0-85234-247-0*, Pub. by Evangelical Pr) P & R Pubng.

Preacher. Carol Duerksen & Maynard Knepp. LC 96-61387. (Jonas Ser.: Vol. 3). (Illus.). 136p. (Orig.). 1996. pap. 9.95 (*0-9648525-2-7*) Willowsprng.

Preacher. Martin. 1999. write for info. (*0-316-54710-7*) Little.

Preacher: A Novel. Luther Butler. Ed. by Laura Ware. LC 91-42294. 212p. (Orig.). 1992. pap. 14.95 (*0-86534-171-0*) Sunstone Pr.

***Preacher: All Hell's A-Coming.** Garth Ennis. (Illus.). 192p. (YA). 2000. pap. text 17.95 (*1-56389-617-6*, Pub. by DC Comics) Time Warner.

Preacher: Ancient History. Garth Ennis. Ed. by Bob Kahan. LC 98-153207. (Illus.). 224p. 1998. pap. text 14.95 (*1-56389-405-X*, Pub. by DC Comics) Time Warner.

Preacher: Dixie Fried. Garth Ennis. LC 99-211478. (Illus.). 224p. 1998. pap. text 14.95 (*1-56389-428-9*, Pub. by DC Comics) Time Warner.

Preacher: Gone to Texas. Garth Ennis. Ed. by Bob Kahan. LC 96-164708. (Illus.). 200p. 1996. mass mkt. 14.95 (*1-56389-261-8*, Pub. by DC Comics) Time Warner.

Preacher: Proud Americans. Garth Ennis. LC 98-106459. (Preachers Ser.: Vols. 18-26). (Illus.). 232p. 1997. pap. text 14.95 (*1-56389-327-4*, Pub. by DC Comics) Time Warner.

Preacher: Salvation. Garth Ennis. (Illus.). 256p. 1999. pap. text 14.95 (*1-56389-519-6*, Pub. by DC Comics) Time Warner.

Preacher: Until the End of the World. Garth Ennis. LC 97-177014. (Preacher Ser.). 1997. pap. text 14.95 (*1-56389-312-6*, Pub. by DC Comics) Time Warner.

Preacher: War in the Sun. Garth Ennis. 240p. 1999. pap. text 14.95 (*1-56389-490-4*, Pub. by DC Comics) Time Warner.

Preacher among the Prophets. George B. Duncan. 176p. 1985. reprint ed. pap. 5.95 (*0-930577-00-0*) N Burleson.

Preacher & Cross: Person & Message in Theology & Rhetoric. Andre Resner, Jr. LC 98-53604. 205p. 1999. pap. 18.00 (*0-8028-4640-8*) Eerdmans.

Preacher & His Audience: Studies in the Early Christian & Byzantine Homiletics. Mary B. Cunningham et al. LC 98-17575. 275p. 1998. 103.00 (*90-04-10681-2*) Brill Academic Pubs.

Preacher & His Preaching. A. P. Gibbs. 1947. pap. 15.00 (*0-937396-30-3*) Walterick Pubs.

***Preacher & His Preaching.** Albert W. Pettet, Sr. LC 99-75572. 256p. 1999. pap. 12.95 (*1-58597-004-2*) Leathers Pub.

Preacher & Preaching: Reviving the Art in the Twentieth Century. Ed. by Samuel T. Logan, Jr. LC 85-32558. 480p. 1986. 22.99 (*0-87552-294-7*) P & R Pubng.

Preacher & Teacher. Macmill. 1997. 24.99 (*1-85792-240-9*, Pub. by Christian Focus) Spring Arbor Dist.

***Preacher & the Mountain Caesar.** William W. Johnstone. (First Mountain Man Ser.). 2000. mass mkt. 5.99 (*0-8217-6585-X*, Zebra Kensgtn) Kensgtn Pub Corp.

Preacher & the Mountain Caesar No. 6: First Mountain Man. William W. Johnstone. 416p. 1997. reprint ed. mass mkt. 4.99 (*0-8217-5636-2*, Zebra Kensgtn) Kensgtn Pub Corp.

Preacher & the Mountain Ceaser. William W. Johnstone. 1995. mass mkt. 4.50 (*0-8217-5144-1*, Zebra Kensgtn) Kensgtn Pub Corp.

Preacher Bird. Robert C. Wallace. LC 96-114801. (Illus.). 224p. (Orig.). 1995. pap. 8.00 (*0-9634992-2-X*) Pretani.

Preacher Boy. Irvin Scheel. 300p. (Orig.). 1996. pap. text 19.00 (*1-57502-091-2*) Morris Pubng.

Preacher Called David. Delores Bean. 120p. 1998. pap. 11.95 (*1-880047-50-0*) Creative Des.

Preacher from Liberty Hill. Ophelia R. Wade. LC 96-90380. (Illus.). 392p. (Orig.). 1996. pap. 19.95 (*0-934426-68-6*) NAPSAC Reprods.

Preacher from the Black Lagoon. Rob Suggs. LC 91-33657. (Illus.). 104p. (Orig.). 1991. pap. 6.99 (*0-8308-1333-0*, 1333) InterVarsity.

Preacher, I've Got a Question: Clarifying Confusing Doctrines. Maralene Wesner & Miles Wesner. LC 88-51862. 134p. (Orig.). 1989. pap. 8.95 (*0-936715-21-9*) Diversity Okla.

Preacher Joke Book: Religious Anecdotes from the Oral Tradition. Loyal Jones. (Illus.). 128p. (Orig.). 1989. pap. 7.95 (*0-87483-087-7*) August Hse.

Preacher King: Martin Luther King, Jr. & the Word That Moved America. Richard Lischer. 360p. 1995. 30.00 (*0-19-508779-8*) OUP.

Preacher King: Martin Luther King, Jr. & the Word That Moved America. Richard Lischer. 368p. 1997. reprint ed. pap. 15.95 (*0-19-511132-X*) OUP.

Preacher Named Emma. George W. Rice. 70p. 1995. pap. 2.49 (*0-8341-1564-6*) Beacon Hill.

Preacher of Cedar Mountain: A Tail of the Open Country. Ernest Thompson Seton. 426p. 1995. pap. 24.95 (*1-885529-06-6*) Stevens Pub.

Preacher of Cedar Mountain: A Tale of the Open Country. Ernest Thompson Seton. (BCL1-PS American Literature Ser.). 428p. 1992. reprint ed. lib. bdg. 99.00 (*0-7812-6854-0*) Rprt Serv.

Preacher on the Run (Jonah) Gordon J. Keddie. 1986. pap. 8.99 (*0-85234-231-4*, Pub. by Evangelical Pr) P & R Pubng.

***Preacher, Politician, Patriot: A Life of John Dunmore Lang.** D. W. Baker. LC 98-201228. 240p. 1999. pap. 29.95 (*0-522-84822-2*, Pub. by Melbourne Univ Pr) Paul & Co Pubs.

Preacher-Prophet in Mass Society. rev. ed. Jesse J. McNeil, Sr. Ed. by Amos Jones, Jr. LC 93-40626. 1994. text 7.95 (*0-910683-12-3*) Townsnd-Pr.

Preacher Sisters & Their Famous Biblical Women's Quiz. Julie A. Waterman. 11p. 1989. 2.00 (*0-943334-11-X*) Carmonelle Pubns.

Preacher Special: Cassidy: Blood & Whiskey. Garth Ennis. LC 98-195100. (Dc Comics Vertigo Ser.). 48p. 1998. 5.95 (*1-56389-340-1*) DC Comics.

Preacher Woman. unabridged ed. S. Gianinazzi. 1998. pap. 14.95 (*1-893336-04-2*) B Newton.

***Preacher Woman Sings the Blues: The Autobiographies of Nineteenth-Century African American Evangelists.** Richard J. Douglass-Chin. 288p. 2001. 34.95 (*0-8262-1311-1*) U of Mo Pr.

Preachers & Teachers. Nancy Hevly. (Settling the West Ser.). (Illus.). 96p. (J). (gr. 5-8). 1995. lib. bdg. 20.40 (*0-8050-2996-6*) TFC Bks NY.

Preachers Are People Too! Gerald Loyd. 266p. (Orig.). 1994. pap. 10.99 (*1-56043-817-7*, Treasure Hse) Destiny Image.

***Preacher's Boy.** Katherine Paterson. LC 98-50083. 160p. (YA). (gr. 5-9). 1999. 15.00 (*0-395-83897-5*, Clarion Bks) HM.

***Preacher's Boy.** Katherine Paterson. 176p. (YA). (gr. 7 up). 2001. mass mkt. 4.95 (*0-06-447233-7*, HarpTrophy) HarpC Child Bks.

Preacher's Daughter: Could Rachael Live Within the Constraints of the Church? Al Tarvin. 300p. Date not set. pap. 12.95 (*0-9643250-8-X*) CJH Ent.

Preacher's Demons: Bernardino of Siena & the Social Underworld of Early Renaissance Italy. Franco Mormando. LC 98-40505. 1999. 29.00 (*0-226-53854-0*) U Ch Pr.

Preachers Do the Craziest Things! Edwin Purviance & Mable Purviance. 150p. (Orig.). 1993. pap. text 3.95 (*0-9620694-3-4*) E & M Purviance.

Preacher's Edge. Jerry L. Schmalenberger. LC 96-7934. 1996. 16.25 (*0-7880-0767-X*) CSS OH.

Preacher's Friend. W. G. Heslop. pap. 5.99 (*0-88019-161-9*) Schmul Pub Co.

Preacher's Girl: The Life & Crimes of Blanche Taylor Moore. Jim Schutze. 392p. 1993. mass mkt. 5.50 (*0-380-76185-8*, Avon Bks) Morrow Avon.

Preacher's Homiletic Commentary, 31. Preacher's Homiletic Commentary Staff. 19256p. 1990. 795.00 (*0-8010-6962-9*) Baker Bks.

Preacher's Kid. C. Robert Haywood. 110p. 1986. pap. 5.00 (*0-939391-04-X*) B Woodley Pr.

***Preacher's Kid: A Journey from Pious Fundamentalism to Pragmatic Humanism.** Charles P. McGinty. (Illus.). 484p. 1999. pap. 19.95 (*0-934426-89-9*) NAPSAC Reprods.

Preachers' Kids Are People Too. Arthur C. Theimer. LC 90-90355. (Illus.). 142p. 1990. pap. 7.90 (*0-9627082-0-8*) Insprtnl Pubs.

Preacher's Notebook. Neal E. Lake. 1994. pap. 5.95 (*1-55673-594-4*, 7993) CSS OH.

Preachers of Righteousness. pap. 7.99 (*0-944802-14-1*) M Barclay Pubns.

Preachers of the City: The Expansion of the Dominican Order in Castile 1217-1348. Francisco G. Serrano. (Iberian Studies: No. 2). 250p. (Orig.). 1996. pap. text 49.95 (*1-889431-02-8*) Univ Pr South.

Preachers of the Italian Ghetto. Ed. by David B. Ruderman. (C). 1992. 45.00 (*0-520-07735-0*, Pub. by U CA Pr) Cal Prin Full Svc.

***Preacher's Outline & Serman Bible Vol. 6: Numbers.** LC 96-75921. 443p. 1999. 34.95 (*1-57407-117-3*) Ldrship Minist Wrldwide.

***Preacher's Outline & Sermon Bible: Classic NIV, 3 vols.** Incl. Vol. 1. Preacher's Outline & Sermon Bible: Classic NIV. LC 00-133113. 1794p. 2000. (*1-57407-143-2*); Vol. 2. Preacher's Outline & Sermon Bible: Classic NIV. LC 00-133113. 1336p. 2000. (*1-57407-144-0*); Vol. 3. Preacher's Outline & Sermon Bible: Classic NIV. LC 00-133113. 1499p. 2000. (*1-57407-145-9*); LC 00-133113. 4629p. 2000. write for info. (*1-57407-142-4*) Ldrship Minist Wrldwide.

Preacher's Outline & Sermon Bible: Classic NIV see Preacher's Outline & Sermon Bible: Classic NIV

Preacher's Outline & Sermon Bible: Romans, Vol. 7. (KOR.). 1994. 32.95 (*0-945863-86-1*) Ldrship Minist Wrldwide.

***Preacher's Outline & Sermon Bible: What Men & Women of the Old Testament Teach...** LC 96-75921. 53p. 1999. pap. 4.95 (*1-57407-140-8*) Ldrship Minist Wrldwide.

***Preacher's Outline & Sermon Bible Vol. 6: Numbers.** LC 96-75921. 443p. 1999. pap. 29.95 (*1-57407-118-1*) Ldrship Minist Wrldwide.

***Preacher's Outline & Sermon Bible Vol. 7: Deutoronomy.** 450p. 2000. pap. 29.95 (*1-57407-146-7*); ring bd. 34.95 (*1-57407-147-5*) Ldrship Minist Wrldwide.

Preacher's Outline & Sermon Bible - New Testament Set, 14 vols. 2nd ed. Incl. Acts. 2nd ed. 407p. 1996. ring bd. 32.95 (*1-57407-031-2*); I & II Corinthians. 2nd ed. 368p. 1996. ring bd. 32.95 (*1-57407-033-9*); I & II Peter, I, II & III John, Jude. 2nd ed. 412p. 1996. ring bd. 32.95 (*1-57407-037-1*); I & II Thessalonians, I & II Timothy, Titus, Philemon. 2nd ed. 390p. 1996. ring bd. 32.95 (*1-57407-035-5*); Galatians, Ephesians, Philippians, Colossians. 2nd ed. 452p. 1996. ring bd. 32.95 (*1-57407-034-7*); Hebrews & James. 2nd ed. 317p. 1996. ring bd. 32.95 (*1-57407-036-3*); John. 2nd ed. 457p. 1996. ring bd. 32.95 (*1-57407-030-4*); Luke. 2nd ed. 565p. 1996. ring bd. 32.95 (*1-57407-029-0*); Mark. 2nd ed. 374p. 1996. ring bd. 32.95 (*1-57407-028-2*); Master Subject Index. 2nd ed. 537p. 1995. 32.95 (*1-57407-039-8*); Matthew. 2nd ed. 366p. 1996. ring bd. 32.95 (*1-57407-026-6*); Matthew 2. 392p. 1996. ring bd. 32.95 (*1-57407-027-4*); Revelation. 2nd ed. 326p. 1996. ring bd. 32.95 (*1-57407-038-X*); Romans. 2nd ed. 338p. 1996. ring bd. 32.95 (*1-57407-032-0*); 5700p. Set ring bd. 489.30 (*1-57407-040-1*) Ldrship Minist Wrldwide.

***Preacher's Outline & Sermon Bible, NT, Calssic, KJV Vol. 2: Acts - Colossians.** LC 98-68032. 1425p. 1999. 99.95 (*1-57407-072-X*) Ldrship Minist Wrldwide.

***Preacher's Outline & Sermon Bible, NT, Classic, KJV Vol. 1: Matthew - John.** LC 98-68032. 1915p. 1999. 99.95 (*1-57407-071-1*) Ldrship Minist Wrldwide.

***Preacher's Outline & Sermon Bible, NT, Classic, KJV Vol. 1: Matthew - John, Tabbed Version.** LC 98-68032. 1915p. 1999. write for info. (*1-57407-096-7*) Ldrship Minist Wrldwide.

***Preacher's Outline & Sermon Bible, NT, Classic, KJV Vol. 2: Acts - Colossians, Tabbed Version.** LC 98-68032. 1425p. 1999. write for info. (*1-57407-097-5*) Ldrship Minist Wrldwide.

***Preacher's Outline & Sermon Bible, NT, Classic, KJV Vol. 3: Thessalonians - Revelation, Master Index.** LC 98-68032. 1540p. 1999. 99.95 (*1-57407-073-8*) Ldrship Minist Wrldwide.

***Preacher's Outline & Sermon Bible, NT, Classic, KJV Vol. 3: Thessalonians - Revelation, Master Index, Tabbed Version.** LC 98-68032. 1540p. 1999. write for info. (*1-57407-098-3*) Ldrship Minist Wrldwide.

***Preacher's Outline & Sermon Bible, NT, Classic, KJV Vols. 1-3: Matthew-Revelation, Master Index.** LC 98-68032. 4880p. 1999. 289.95 (*1-57407-070-3*); 309.95 (*1-57407-095-9*) Ldrship Minist Wrldwide.

***Preacher's Outline & Sermon Bible, NT, NIV: Matthew, Vol. 1.** LC 98-67967. 394p. 1999. pap. 32.95 (*1-57407-076-2*); ring bd. 34.95 (*1-57407-126-2*) Ldrship Minist Wrldwide.

***Preacher's Outline & Sermon Bible, NT, NIV: Matthew, Vol. 2.** LC 98-67967. 334p. 1999. pap. 32.95 (*1-57407-077-0*); ring bd. 34.95 (*1-57407-127-0*) Ldrship Minist Wrldwide.

***Preacher's Outline & Sermon Bible, NT, NIV: New Testament & Master Index, 14 vols., Set.** LC 98-67967. 5168p. 1999. pap. 369.88 (*1-57407-075-4*); ring bd. 479.50 (*1-57407-125-4*) Ldrship Minist Wrldwide.

***Preacher's Outline & Sermon Bible, NT, NIV Vol. 3: Mark.** LC 98-67967. 356p. 1999. pap. 32.95 (*1-57407-078-9*); ring bd. 34.95 (*1-57407-128-9*) Ldrship Minist Wrldwide.

***Preacher's Outline & Sermon Bible, NT, NIV Vol. 4: Luke.** LC 98-67967. 520p. 1999. pap. 32.95 (*1-57407-079-7*); ring bd. 34.95 (*1-57407-129-7*) Ldrship Minist Wrldwide.

***Preacher's Outline & Sermon Bible, NT, NIV Vol. 5: John.** LC 98-67967. 420p. 1999. pap. 32.95 (*1-57407-080-0*); ring bd. 34.95 (*1-57407-130-0*) Ldrship Minist Wrldwide.

***Preacher's Outline & Sermon Bible, NT, NIV Vol. 6: Acts.** LC 98-67967. 382p. 1999. pap. 32.95 (*1-57407-081-9*); ring bd. 34.95 (*1-57407-131-9*) Ldrship Minist Wrldwide.

***Preacher's Outline & Sermon Bible, NT, NIV Vol. 7: Romans.** LC 98-67967. 314p. 1999. pap. 32.95 (*1-57407-082-7*); ring bd. 34.95 (*1-57407-132-7*) Ldrship Minist Wrldwide.

***Preacher's Outline & Sermon Bible, NT, NIV Vol. 8: 1 & 2 Corinthians.** LC 98-67967. 358p. 1999. pap. 32.95 (*1-57407-083-5*); ring bd. 32.95 (*1-57407-133-5*) Ldrship Minist Wrldwide.

***Preacher's Outline & Sermon Bible, NT, NIV Vol. 9: Galatians, Ephesians, Philippians, Colossians.** LC 98-67967. 434p. 1999. pap. 32.95 (*1-57407-084-3*); ring bd. 32.95 (*1-57407-134-3*) Ldrship Minist Wrldwide.

***Preacher's Outline & Sermon Bible, NT, NIV Vol. 10: 1 & 2 Thessalonians, 1 & 2 Timothy, Titus, Philemon.** LC 98-67967. 372p. 1999. pap. 32.95 (*1-57407-085-1*); ring bd. 32.95 (*1-57407-135-1*) Ldrship Minist Wrldwide.

***Preacher's Outline & Sermon Bible, NT, NIV Vol. 11: Hebrews, James.** LC 98-67967. 320p. 1999. pap. 32.95 (*1-57407-086-X*); ring bd. 32.95 (*1-57407-136-X*) Ldrship Minist Wrldwide.

***Preacher's Outline & Sermon Bible, NT, NIV Vol. 12: 1 & 2 Peter, 1, 2 & 3 John, Jude.** LC 98-67967. 396p. 1999. pap. 32.95 (*1-57407-087-8*); ring bd. 32.95 (*1-57407-137-8*) Ldrship Minist Wrldwide.

***Preacher's Outline & Sermon Bible, NT, NIV Vol. 13: Revelation.** LC 98-67967. 318p. 1999. pap. 32.95 (*1-57407-088-6*); ring bd. 32.95 (*1-57407-138-6*) Ldrship Minist Wrldwide.

***Preacher's Outline & Sermon Bible, NT, NIV Vol. 14: Master Outline & Subject Index.** LC 98-67967. 250p. 1999. pap. 32.95 (*1-57407-089-4*); ring bd. 32.95 (*1-57407-139-4*) Ldrship Minist Wrldwide.

***Preacher's Outline & Sermon Bible, OT, KJV Vol. 5: Leviticus.** LC 96-75921. 400p. 1999. ring bd. 34.95 (*1-57407-109-2*); im. lthr. 29.95 (*1-57407-110-6*) Ldrship Minist Wrldwide.

Preachers, Poets, & the Early English Lyric. Siegfried Wenzel. LC 85-43322. 285p. reprint ed. pap. 88.40 (*0-608-08023-3*, 206798800001) Bks Demand.

An Asterisk (*) at the beginning of an entry indicates that the title is appearing for the first time.

Preacher's Portrait in the New Testament. John R. Stott. 1988. pap. 8.00 (*0-8028-1191-4*) Eerdmans.

Preachers Provoke Not Your Children to Wrath. Joseph L. Hadley, 2nd. 48p. (Orig.). (C). 1996. pap. 4.50 (*0-9649715-0-X*) J L Hadley.

Preachers, Rebels, & Traders: Connecticut 1818 to 1865 see Series in Connecticut History

Preacher's Son. Marc Adams. 224p. 1996. 22.95 (*1-889829-00-5*) Window Books.

Preacher's Wife & Other Selected Poems. Rosemary F. Jackson. LC 90-81648. (Illus.). 48p. (Orig.). 1990. pap. 5.95 (*0-940975-22-X*) Just Us Bks.

***Preacher's Wife Sings.** Frederick Leroy Davison, II. 350p. 2000. pap. 13.95 (*0-9628544-3-3*) Blk Thoroughbred.

Preachers with Power. Douglas Kelly. 198p. 1993. 23.99 (*0-85151-628-9*) Banner of Truth.

***Preachers Wives Tell All.** Mattie Mullins. 2000. pap. 13.95 (*1-891874-08-X*) Recover Comns.

***Preachers' Wives Tell All: Lively Tales & Tasty Recipes from Country Parsonage Kitchens.** Mattie Mullins. (Illus.). 2000. pap. 13.95 (*1-891874-04-7*) Recover Comns.

Preaching. Fred B. Craddock. 1990. pap. 14.95 (*0-687-33648-1*) Abingdon.

Preaching: The Art & the Craft. Walter J. Burghardt. 256p. 1987. pap. 14.95 (*0-8091-2906-X*) Paulist Pr.

***Preaching: The Secret to Parish Revival.** Richard Hart. LC 00-131183. 112p. 2000. pap. 9.95 (*1-58595-021-1*) Twenty-Third.

Preaching - Chinese Edition. G. Campbell Morgan. Tr. by John J. Liu. (CHI.). 78p. 1997. pap. 5.00 (*1-56582-031-2*) Christ Renew Min.

Preaching about Death: Eighteen Sermons Dealing with the Experience of Death from the Christian Perspective. Ed. by Alton M. Motter. LC 74-26336. 94p. reprint ed. pap. 30.00 (*0-608-16838-6*, 202686200052) Bks Demand.

Preaching about the Mass. Gabe Huck. (Illus.). 104p. (Orig.). 1992. pap. 10.00 (*0-929650-47-6*, MASS) Liturgy Tr Pubns.

***Preaching & Culture Identity: Proclaiming the Gospel in Africa.** John W. Kurewa. LC 99-44306. 2000. write for info. (*0-687-09031-8*) Abingdon.

***Preaching & Intimacy.** Charles B. Bugg. LC 99-14807. 160p. 1999. pap. 15.00 (*1-57312-263-7*) Smyth & Helwys.

Preaching & Pastoral Care. Arthur L. Teikmanis. LC 64-23551. 144p. reprint ed. pap. 44.70 (*0-608-16840-8*, 202686300052) Bks Demand.

Preaching & Politics in Late Medieval England. Alan Fletcher. 320p. 1998. boxed set 55.00 (*1-85182-377-8*, Pub. by Four Cts Pr) Intl Spec Bk.

Preaching & Practical Theology: An African American Perspective. Olin P. Moyd. LC 94-9198. 1994. 9.95 (*0-910683-23-9*) Townsnd-Pr.

Preaching & Preachers. 325p. 1972. 22.99 (*0-310-27870-8*, 10573) Zondervan.

Preaching & Teaching with Imagination: The Quest for Biblical Ministry. Warren W. Wiersbe. LC 94-1710. 400p. (gr. 12). 1997. pap. 19.99 (*0-8010-5757-4*) Baker Bks.

Preaching & the Challenge of Pluralism. Joseph M. Webb. LC 98-17316. 184p. 1998. pap. 19.99 (*0-8272-2952-6*) Chalice Pr.

Preaching & the Literary Forms of the Bible. Thomas G. Long. LC 88-45243. 144p. 1988. pap. text 15.00 (*0-8006-2313-4*, 1-2313, Fortress Pr) Augsburg Fortress.

Preaching & Worship in the Small Church. William H. Willimon & Robert L. Wilson. LC 79-24529. (Creative Leadership Ser.). (Orig.). 1980. pap. 12.95 (*0-687-33820-4*) Abingdon.

Preaching Apocalyptic Texts. Larry P. Jones & Jerry L. Sumney. LC 99-38562. (Preaching Classic Texts Ser.). 1999. pap. 15.99 (*0-8272-2954-2*) Chalice Pr.

Preaching As a Theological Task: World, Gospel, Scripture. David G. Buttrick. Ed. by Thomas G. Long & Edward Farley. LC 96-8619. 216p. (Orig.). 1996. pap. 26.95 (*0-664-25617-1*) Westminster John Knox.

Preaching As Local Theology & Folk Art. Leonora T. Tisdale. LC 96-48011. (Fortress Resources for Preaching Ser.). 176p. 1997. pap. 17.00 (*0-8006-2773-3*, 1-2773, Fortress Pr) Augsburg Fortress.

Preaching As the Art of Sacred Conversation. Ed. by Roger Alling & David J. Schlafer. 144p. 1997. pap. 10.95 (*0-8192-1699-2*) Morehouse Pub.

Preaching As Weeping, Confession, & Resistance: Radical Responses to Radical Evil. Christine M. Smith. 224p. (Orig.). 1992. pap. 22.95 (*0-664-25216-8*) Westminster John Knox.

Preaching Basics: A Model & a Method. Edward Foley. 1998. pap. 12.00 (*1-56854-170-8*, PREACH) Liturgy Tr Pubns.

Preaching Better: A Practical Guide for Homilists. Kenneth Untener. LC 98-48870. 160p. 1999. 10.95 (*0-8091-3849-2*) Paulist Pr.

Preaching Biblically. Ed. by Don M. Wardlaw. LC 83-1276. 174p. (Orig.). (C). 1983. pap. 18.95 (*0-664-24478-5*) Westminster John Knox.

Preaching Christ. Alger Fitch. 178p. (Orig.). 1992. pap. text 9.99 (*0-89900-416-4*) College Pr Pub.

Preaching Christ from the Old Testament: A Contemporary Hermeneutical Method. Sidney Greidanus. LC 99-23521. 383p. 1999. pap. 22.00 (*0-8028-4449-9*) Eerdmans.

***Preaching Creation: Throughout the Church Year.** Jennifer M. Phillips. LC 99-49302. 250p. 2000. pap. 16.95 (*1-56101-174-6*) Cowley Pubns.

Preaching Doctrine. Robert G. Hughes & Robert Kysar. LC 97-23757. (Fortress Resources for Preaching Ser.). 144p. 1997. pap. text 15.00 (*0-8006-2965-5*, 1-2965, Fortress Pr) Augsburg Fortress.

Preaching Eyes for Listening Ears: Sermons & Commentary for Preachers & Students of Preaching. J. Will Ormond & Lucy A. Rose. LC 98-48038. 184p. 1999. pap. 15.95 (*0-7880-1320-3*) CSS OH.

***Preaching 1 Corinthians 13.** Susan K. Hedahl & Richard P. Carlson. (Preaching Classic Texts Ser.). 2000. pap. 17.99 (*0-8272-2969-0*) Chalice Pr.

Preaching for Black Self-Esteem. Henry H. Mitchell & Emil M. Thomas. LC 94-12500. 192p. (Orig.). 1994. pap. 15.95 (*0-687-33843-3*) Abingdon.

***Preaching for God's Glory.** Alistair Begg. LC 99-36911. (Today's Issues Ser.). 48p. 1999. pap. 4.99 (*1-58134-123-7*) Crossway Bks.

Preaching for Recovery in a Strife-Torn Church. Jerrien Gunnink. 128p. 1989. pap. 7.99 (*0-310-31121-7*) Zondervan.

Preaching for the Church. R. R. Caemmerer. 353p. 1976. pap. 19.00 (*0-570-03735-2*, 12-2639) Concordia.

Preaching for the Church Today: The Skills, Prayer, & Art of Sermon Preparation. Paul V. Marshall. 224p. 1990. 21.95 (*0-89869-187-7*) Church Pub Inc.

***Preaching from a Pulpit of Bones: We Need Morality but Not Traditional Morality.** Bob Avakian. LC 83-22294. 90p. 1999. pap. 8.00 (*0-916650-49-9*, Pub. by Banner Pr Intl) Liberation Distributors.

Preaching from Camelot to Covenant. William K. McElvaney. LC 89-14948. 144p. 1989. pap. 10.95 (*0-687-33842-5*) Abingdon.

Preaching from Hebrews. James E. Massey. 288p. 1988. pap. 12.95 (*0-310-37181-3*, 12408P) Zondervan.

Preaching from Second Corinthians 3-5. Reuben R. Welch. 112p. 1988. pap. 7.99 (*0-8341-1253-1*) Beacon Hill.

Preaching from the Minor Prophets: Texts & Sermon Suggestions. Elizabeth Achtemeier. LC 97-38554. 155p. (Orig.). 1997. pap. 14.00 (*0-8028-4370-0*) Eerdmans.

Preaching from the Old Testament. Elizabeth Achtemeier. 200p. (Orig.). 1989. pap. 22.95 (*0-664-25042-4*) Westminster John Knox.

Preaching from the Pew. Patricia G. Brown. LC 97-47075. 176p. 1997. pap. 12.95 (*0-664-50019-6*) Geneva Press.

Preaching from the Prophets see Profetas Del Antiguo Testamento (Preaching from the Prophets)

Preaching from the Prophets. James Ward & Christine Ward. 144p. (Orig.). 1995. pap. 12.95 (*0-687-00235-4*) Abingdon.

Preaching from the Psalms see Psalms of Joy & Faith

Preaching from the Types & Metaphors of the Bible. Benjamin Keach. LC 78-165059. (Kregel Reprint Library). 1040p. 1975. lib. bdg. 49.99 (*0-8254-3008-9*, Kregel Class) Kregel.

Preaching Grace: Possibilities for Growing Your Preaching & Touching People's Lives. Kennon L. Callahan. LC 98-51232. 192p. 1999. 22.00 (*0-7879-4295-2*) Jossey-Bass.

Preaching: Hands at Work see Predicacion: Manos a la Obra

Preaching Hard Texts of the Old Testament. Elizabeth Achtemeier. LC 98-20141. 192p. 1998. pap. 14.95 (*1-56563-333-4*) Hendrickson MA.

Preaching in a Revolutionary Age. Garfield B. Oxnam. LC 75-142687. (Essay Index Reprint Ser.). 1977. reprint ed. 20.95 (*0-8369-2421-5*) Ayer.

Preaching in a Tavern & 129 Other Surprising Stories from Brethren Life. Kenneth J. Morse. LC 96-51491. 1997. pap. 14.95 (*0-87178-005-4*) Brethren.

***Preaching in Revival: Preaching & a Theology of Awakening.** Philip W. Keevil. LC 99-38758. 192p. 1999. 49.00 (*0-7618-1493-0*); pap. 27.50 (*0-7618-1494-9*) U Pr of Amer.

***Preaching in the Context of Worship.** Ed. by David M. Greenhaw & Ronald J. Allen. 160p. 2000. pap. 16.99 (*0-8272-2956-9*) Chalice Pr.

***Preaching in the Gospel of Luke: Proclaiming God's Royal Rule.** Keith F. Nickle. 352p. 2000. pap. 21.95 (*0-664-50120-6*, Pub. by Westminster John Knox) Presbyterian Pub.

Preaching in the New Creation: The Promise of New Testament Apocalyptic Texts. David Jacobsen. LC 99-30509. 172p. 1999. pap. 20.95 (*0-664-25845-X*) Westminster John Knox.

Preaching in the Spirit: A Preacher Looks for Something That Human Energy Cannot Provide. 2nd ed. Dennis F. Kinlaw. LC 98-72658. 128p. 1998. reprint ed. pap. 12.50 (*0-916035-82-4*, Ausbury Press) Evangel Indiana.

Preaching in Two Voices: Sermons on the Women in Jesus' Life. William D. Watley & Suzan D. Cook. 128p. 1992. pap. 12.00 (*0-8170-1173-0*) Judson.

Preaching Jesus: New Directions for Homiletics in Hans Frei's Post-Liberal Theology. Charles L. Campbell. LC 96-53633. 272p. 1997. pap. 28.00 (*0-8028-4156-2*) Eerdmans.

***Preaching Job.** John C. Holbert. (Preaching Classic Texts Ser.). 1999. pap. 18.99 (*0-8272-2959-3*) Chalice Pr.

Preaching Justice: Ethnic & Cultural Perspectives. Ed. by Christine M. Smith. LC 98-26012. 176p. 1998. pap. 14.95 (*0-8298-1291-1*) Pilgrim OH.

***Preaching Justice: The Ethical Vocation of Word & Sacrament Ministry.** James S. Childs, Jr. LC 99-87137. 2000. pap. 13.00 (*1-56338-313-6*) TPI PA.

Preaching Law & Gospel. Herman G. Stuempfle. 106p. 1991. reprint ed. pap. 12.00 (*0-9623642-2-3*) Sigler Pr.

Preaching Liberation. James H. Harris. LC 95-43458. (Fortress Resources for Preaching Ser.). 144p. 1995. pap. 15.00 (*0-8006-2841-1*, 1-2841) Augsburg Fortress.

Preaching Life. Barbara B. Taylor. LC 92-34743. 174p. 1993. pap. 10.95 (*1-56101-074-X*) Cowley Pubns.

***Preaching Like Paul: Homiletical Wisdom for Today.** James W. Thompson. 170p. 2000. pap. 19.95 (*0-664-22294-3*) Westminster John Knox.

***Preaching Luke - Acts.** Ronald J. Allen. 2000. pap. 16.99 (*0-8272-2965-8*) Chalice Pr.

Preaching Luke's Gospel: A Narrative Approach. Richard A. Jensen. LC 97-11701. 234p. (Orig.). 1997. pap. 22.95 (*0-7880-1110-3*) CSS OH.

Preaching Machine: The Biography of Bishop Paul A. Bowers. Holly Broach-Sowels. Ed. by Jean E. Daniel. (Illus.). 240p. (Orig.). 1994. pap. 14.95 (*0-9637441-1-9*) Kehori.

Preaching Mark. Robert S. Reid. LC 99-37930. 1999. pap. 19.99 (*0-8272-2958-5*) Chalice Pr.

Preaching Mark's Gospel. Richard A. Jensen. 1997. cd-rom 17.25 (*0-7880-0836-6*) CSS OH.

Preaching Mark's Gospel: A Narrative Approach. Richard A. Jensen. LC 96-4053. (Orig.). 1996. pap. 17.25 (*0-7880-0833-1*) CSS OH.

Preaching Mary's Praises - Homilies on the Mother of the Lord. David Q. Liptak. 105p. 1992. 3.95 (*1-56036-013-5*, 38608) AMI Pr.

Preaching Matthew's Gospel: A Narrative Approach. Richard A. Jensen. 1998. pap. 17.95 (*0-7880-1224-X*) CSS OH.

Preaching Matthew's Gospel: A Narrative Approach. Richard A. Jensen. LC 98-5618. 234p. 1998. pap. 17.95 (*0-7880-1221-5*) CSS OH.

***Preaching Ministry: Twenty-One Sermons Preached by Harry Emerson Fosdick.** Ed. & Intro. by David Pultz. 400p. 2000. pap. 25.00 (*0-9606818-1-7*) First Presbyterian Church in City.

Preaching Moment. 2nd ed. Charles Bartow. 128p. (C). 1995. pap. text 19.95 (*0-7872-1252-0*) Kendall-Hunt.

Preaching of Islam. T. W. Arnold. 19.50 (*1-56744-185-8*) Kazi Pubns.

Preaching of Islam. T. W. Arnold. 480p. 1986. 300.00 (*1-85077-132-4*, Pub. by Darf Pubs Ltd) St Mut.

Preaching of Islam: A History of Propagation of the Muslim Faith. Thomas W. Arnold. LC 72-180319. (Mid-East Studies). reprint ed. 47.50 (*0-404-56214-0*) AMS Pr.

Preaching of Islam: A History of the Propogation of the Muslim Faith. T. W. Arnold. 1990. reprint ed. 15.00 (*81-85395-60-8*, Pub. by Low Price) S Asia.

Preaching of the Crusades to the Holy Land, 1095-1270. Penny J. Cole. LC 89-63251. (Medieval Academy Bks.: No. 98). xiv, 281p. 1991. 35.00 (*0-915651-03-3*) Medieval Acad.

Preaching Old Testament: Proclamation & Narrative in the Hebrew Bible. John C. Holbert. 1991. pap. 12.95 (*0-687-33870-0*) Abingdon.

Preaching on Death: An Ecumenical Resource. Ed. by Virginia Sloyan et al. 1997. pap. 10.95 (*0-918208-77-7*) Liturgical Conf.

Preaching on the Words of Jesus. Clovis G. Chappell. (Chappell Sermon Library). 712p. 1997. pap. 29.99 (*0-8010-5750-7*) Baker Bks.

***Preaching Peace in Renaissance Italy: Bernardino of Siena & His Audience.** Cynthia Polecritti. LC 99-36513. 2000. 61.95 (*0-8132-0960-9*) Cath U Pr.

***Preaching Pity: Dickens, Gaskell & Sentimentalism in Victorian Culture.** Mary Lenard. LC 97-32896. (Studies in Nineteenth-Century British Literature: Vol. 11). viii, 157p. (C). 1999. text 43.95 (*0-8204-3903-7*) P Lang Pubng.

Preaching, Planning & Plumbing: Discovering God's Call to Service & Joy. Steve Clapp et al. (Illus.). 128p. 1999. pap. 12.00 (*1-893270-02-5*, Chrstn Commnty) LifeQuest IN.

Preaching Priest. Date not set. pap. 6.99 (*1-871676-08-8*, Pub. by Christian Focus) Spring Arbor Dist.

Preaching Proverbs: Wisdom for the Pulpit. Alyce M. McKenzie. LC 96-17775. 160p. (Orig.). 1996. pap. 17.95 (*0-664-25653-8*) Westminster John Knox.

Preaching That Connects: Using the Techniques of Journalists to Add Impact to Your Sermons. Mark Galli. 176p. 1994. pap. 14.99 (*0-310-38621-7*) Zondervan.

Preaching That Matters: The Bible & Our Lives. Stephen Farris. LC 97-41406. 184p. (Orig.). 1998. pap. 19.95 (*0-664-25759-3*) Westminster John Knox.

Preaching the Burden & the Joy. Harry B. Adams. LC 96-1791. 168p. (Orig.). 1996. pap. 16.99 (*0-8272-2951-8*) Chalice Pr.

***Preaching the Cross.** Darrel A. Rhodes. 1998. pap. 9.45 (*0-9678509-1-6*) D A Rhodes.

Preaching the Cross. Darrel A. Rhodes. Ed. by Douglas A. Studor. 230p. 1999. pap. 9.45 (*0-7392-0182-4*, PO3149) Morris Pubng.

Preaching the Crusades: Mendicant Friars & the Cross in the Thirteenth Century. Christoph T. Maier. LC 93-32162. (Cambridge Studies in Medieval Life & Thought: No. 28). 210p. (C). 1994. text 54.95 (*0-521-45246-5*) Cambridge U Pr.

Preaching the Crusades: Mendicant Friars & the Cross in the Thirteenth Century. Christoph T. Maier. (Cambridge Studies in Medieval Life & Thought: No. 28). 212p. (C). 1998. reprint ed. pap. text 19.95 (*0-521-63873-9*) Cambridge U Pr.

Preaching the Epistles. Raymond F. Collins. LC 95-44476. 160p. (Orig.). 1996. pap. 9.95 (*0-8091-3625-2*) Paulist Pr.

***Preaching the Funeral Homily: Proclaiming the Gospel of Heavenly Hope.** R. C. Sonefeld. LC 99-88468. 192p. 2000. pap. 20.95 (*0-89390-480-5*) Resource Pubns.

Preaching the Good News. George E. Sweazey. 368p. 1976. 27.00 (*0-13-694802-2*) P-H.

Preaching the Gospel. Ed. by Henry J. Young & William H. Borders. LC 75-36449. 95p. (Orig.). reprint ed. pap. 30.00 (*0-608-16810-6*, 202682800052) Bks Demand.

Preaching the Gospel: A Theological Perspective & a Personal Method. Richard P. Belcher. 120p. (C). 1995. pap. 7.95 (*1-883265-10-X*) Richbarry Pr.

Preaching the Gospel Anew Series 1: Saint Clement Maria Hofbauer. Josef Heinzmann. Tr. by Bernard J. McGrade from GER. LC 97-53212. 224p. 1998. reprint ed. pap. 14.95 (*0-7648-0164-3*) Liguori Pubns.

Preaching the Gospel from the Gospels. rev. ed. George R. Beasley-Murray. 282p. 1996. pap. 16.95 (*1-56563-166-8*) Hendrickson MA.

***Preaching the Gospel of Luke: Proclaiming God's Royal Rule.** Keith Fullerton Nickle. LC 99-53854. 296p. 2000. pap. text 21.95 (*0-664-22239-0*) Westminster John Knox.

Preaching the Hard Sayings of Jesus. John T. Carroll & James R. Carroll. LC 96-15771. 174p. 1996. pap. 14.95 (*1-56563-230-3*) Hendrickson MA.

Preaching the Just Word. Walter J. Burghardt. LC 96-15779. 224p. 1998. 27.50 (*0-300-06768-2*); pap. 14.95 (*0-300-07721-1*) Yale U Pr.

Preaching the Lectionary: The Word of God for the Church Today. 2nd rev. ed. Reginald H. Fuller. 650p. 1984. pap. 19.95 (*0-8146-1351-9*) Liturgical Pr.

Preaching the Miracles. Dallas A. Brauninger. LC 96-46487. (Series II: Vol. 3). 162p. 1997. pap. 16.75 (*0-7880-1020-4*) CSS OH.

Preaching the Miracles. Dallas A. Brauninger. 1998. pap. 13.50 (*0-7880-1204-5*) CSS OH.

Preaching the Miracles, Vol. II, Pt. B. Dallas A. Brauninger. LC 96-5303. (Series II). 1996. pap. 13.50 (*0-7880-0829-3*) CSS OH.

Preaching the Miracles: Series II, Cycle A. Dallas A. Brauninger. LC 98-2528. 168p. 1998. pap. 13.50 (*0-7880-1201-0*) CSS OH.

***Preaching the Miracles: Series III, Cycle B.** Harold H. Lentz. LC 99-36619. 132p. 1999. pap. 12.00 (*0-7880-1358-0*) CSS OH.

Preaching the New & the Now. David Buttrick. LC 98-6848. 176p. 1998. pap. 15.00 (*0-664-25789-5*) Westminster John Knox.

***Preaching the New Lectionary, Year C.** Dianne Bergant & Richard N. Fragomeni. 456p. 2000. pap. 29.95 (*0-8146-2474-X*) Liturgical Pr.

Preaching the New Lectionary, Year B Edition. Dianne Bergant & Richard N. Fragomeni. LC 99-16138. 440p. (C). 1999. pap. 29.95 (*0-8146-2473-1*) Liturgical Pr.

Preaching the New Millennium. John Killinger. LC 98-39715. 160p. 1999. pap. 15.00 (*0-687-08737-6*) Abingdon.

Preaching the New Testament. Archibald M. Hunter. LC 81-19482. 156p. reprint ed. pap. 48.40 (*0-608-14498-3*, 202532800043) Bks Demand.

Preaching the Parables. William E. Keeney. (Series II). 1995. pap. 15.25 (*0-7880-0541-3*) CSS OH.

***Preaching the Parables.** William E. Keeney. (Series II). 1998. mac hd 17.75 (*0-7880-0544-8*) CSS OH.

Preaching the Parables, Cycle C. William E. Keeney. LC 96-46513. (Series II, Cycle C Ser.). 268p. 1997. pap., wbk. ed. 25.25 (*0-7880-1017-4*) CSS OH.

Preaching the Parables, Vol. II, Pt. A. William E. Keeney. LC 96-5305. (Series II). 1996. pap. 10.95 (*0-7880-0825-0*) CSS OH.

***Preaching the Parables: Applications for Contemporary Life.** William E. Keeney. (Series II). 1998. cd-rom 17.75 (*0-7880-0542-1*) CSS OH.

Preaching the Practice. Richard Thompson. LC 95-77351. (Illus.). (Orig.). 1995. pap. 8.95 (*0-9646915-0-7*) Heavenly Host.

Preaching the Presence of God: A Homiletic from an Asian American Perspective. Eunjoo M. Kim. LC 99-28021. 160p. 1999. pap. 16.00 (*0-8170-1303-2*) Judson.

Preaching the Revised Common Lectionary: Year A - after Pentecost 1. Marion L. Soards et al. 192p. (Orig.). 1992. pap. 12.95 (*0-687-33872-7*) Abingdon.

Preaching the Revised Common Lectionary: Year A - after Pentecost 2. Marion L. Soards et al. 196p. (Orig.). 1992. pap. 12.95 (*0-687-33871-9*) Abingdon.

Preaching the Revised Common Lectionary: Year B - Advent, Christmas & Epiphany. Marion L. Soards et al. LC 92-36840. 1993. pap. 12.95 (*0-687-33802-6*) Abingdon.

Preaching the Revised Common Lectionary: Year B - after Pentecost 1. Marion L. Soards et al. LC 92-36840. 192p. (Orig.). 1993. pap. 12.95 (*0-687-33877-8*) Abingdon.

Preaching the Revised Common Lectionary: Year B - after Pentecost 2. Marion L. Soards et al. LC 92-36840. 192p. (Orig.). 1993. pap. 12.95 (*0-687-33876-X*) Abingdon.

Preaching the Revised Common Lectionary: Year B - Lent & Easter. Marion L. Soards et al. LC 92-36840. 1993. pap. 12.95 (*0-687-33803-4*) Abingdon.

Preaching the Revised Common Lectionary: Year C - Advent, Christmas & Epiphany. Marion L. Soards & Thomas Dozeman. LC 93-30550. (Orig.). 1994. pap. 12.95 (*0-687-33804-2*) Abingdon.

Preaching the Revised Common Lectionary: Year C - after Pentcost 2. Marion L. Soards et al. LC 93-30550. 192p. (Orig.). 1994. pap. 12.95 (*0-687-33807-7*) Abingdon.

Preaching the Revised Common Lectionary: Year C - after Pentecost 1. Marion L. Soards et al. LC 93-30550. 192p. (Orig.). 1994. pap. 12.95 (*0-687-33806-9*) Abingdon.

Preaching the Revised Common Lectionary: Year C - Lent & Easter. Marion L. Soards et al. LC 93-30550. 202p. (Orig.). 1994. pap. 12.95 (*0-687-33805-0*) Abingdon.

Preaching the Revised Common Lectionary Year A Vol. I: Year A - Advent, Christmas & Epiphany. Marion L. Soards et al. 192p. (Orig.). 1992. pap. 12.95 (*0-687-33800-X*) Abingdon.

An Asterisk (*) at the beginning of an entry indicates that the title is appearing for the first time.

Preaching the Revised Common Lectionary Year A Vol. II: Year A - Lent & Easter. Marion L. Soards et al. 192p. (Orig.). 1992. pap. 12.95 (*0-687-33801-8*) Abingdon.

Preaching the Rites of Christian Initiation. Jan M. Joncas. LC 94-34932. (Forum Essays Ser.). 127p. (Orig.). 1994. pap. 6.00 (*0-929650-79-4*, P&I) Liturgy Tr Pubns.

Preaching the Topical Sermon. Ronald J. Allen. 176p. (Orig.). 1992. pap. 17.95 (*0-664-25306-7*) Westminster John Knox.

Preaching the Tradition: Homily & Hermeneutics after the Exile. Rex Mason. 334p. (C). 1990. text 75.00 (*0-521-38304-8*) Cambridge U Pr.

***Preaching the Wedding Sermon.** Susan K. Hedahl. LC 99-50581. 128p. 2000. pap. 14.99 (*0-8272-2960-7*) Chalice Pr.

***Preaching the Whole Bible as Christian Scripture: The Application of Biblical Theology to Expository Preaching.** Graeme Goldsworthy. 280p. 2000. pap. 20.00 (*0-8028-4730-7*) Eerdmans.

Preaching the Word of God. Anthony M. Coniaris. LC 83-18416. 137p. 1983. pap. 6.95 (*0-916586-65-0*, Pub. by Holy Cross Orthodox) BookWorld.

Preaching Through a Storm: Confirming the Power of Preaching in the Tempest of Church Conflict. H. Beecher Hicks, Jr. 224p. 1987. mass mkt. 14.99 (*0-310-20091-1*) Zondervan.

Preaching Through the Apocalypse: Sermons from Revelation. Ed. by Joseph R. Jeter, Jr. & Cornish R. Rogers. 168p. (Orig.). 1992. pap. 15.99 (*0-8272-2944-5*) Chalice Pr.

Preaching Through the Bible, 14. Joseph Parker. 11300p. 1978. reprint ed. 295.00 (*0-8010-7032-5*) Baker Bks.

Preaching Through the Christian Year: Year A - A Comprehensive Commentary on the Lectionary. Fred B. Craddock et al. LC 92-25860. 576p. 1992. pap. 30.00 (*1-56338-054-4*) TPI PA.

Preaching Through the Christian Year: Year B - A Comprehensive Commentary on the Lectionary. Fred B. Craddock et al. LC 92-25860. 544p. (Orig.). (C). 1993. pap. 30.00 (*1-56338-068-4*) TPI PA.

Preaching Through the Christian Year: Year C - A Comprehensive Commentary on the Lectionary. Fred B. Craddock et al. LC 92-25860. 544p. (Orig.). (C). 1994. pap. 30.00 (*1-56338-100-1*) TPI PA.

Preaching Through the Year of Mark: Sermons That Work VIII. Ed. by Roger Alling & David J. Schlafer. LC 99-28155. 144p. 1997. pap. 9.95 (*0-8192-1761-1*, 2504) Morehouse Pub.

Preaching Thru Bibl-1s. Michael Eaton. 1996. pap. 7.99 (*1-85240-172-9*) SOV5.

Preaching Thru the Bible. Sovereign World Ltd. Staff. 1996. pap. text 7.99 (*1-85240-173-7*) SOV5.

Preaching to a Church in Crisis: A Homiletic for the Last Days of the Mainline Church. John Killinger. LC 94-38058. 124p. (Orig.). 1995. pap. 12.75 (*0-7880-0308-9*) CSS OH.

Preaching to a TV Generation: Preaching for an Electronic Age. Michael Rogness. LC 93-47208. 1994. pap. 11.50 (*1-55673-838-2*) CSS OH.

***Preaching to America.** Lee Roberson. 213p. 1999. pap. write for info. (*0-87398-667-9*) Sword of the Lord.

***Preaching to Head & Heart.** Thomas R. Swears. LC 99-49219. 160p. 2000. pap. 15.00 (*0-687-06830-4*) Abingdon.

Preaching to Programmed People: Effective Communication in a Media-Weary World. Timothy A. Turner. 160p. 1995. pap. 9.99 (*0-8254-3849-7*, 95-012) Kregel.

Preaching to Strangers: Evangelism in Today's World. William H. Willimon & Stanley Hauerwas. 112p. (Orig.). 1992. pap. 13.95 (*0-664-25105-6*) Westminster John Knox.

***Preaching to the Black Middle Class: Words of Challenge, Words of Hope.** Marvin A. McMickle. LC 99-37472. 176p. 2000. pap. 16.00 (*0-8170-1328-8*) Judson.

Preaching to the Nations: Origins of Mission in the Early Church. GRYS ALAN LE. 1999. pap. text 28.95 (*0-281-05148-8*) Society Prom Christ Know.

Preaching to the Spirits in Prison. W. Kelly. pap. 4.95 (*0-88172-105-0*) Believers Bkshelf.

Preaching Values of a Church Covenant. Eric A. Mayes, Jr. Ed. by Robert Brown. xii, 188p. (Orig.). 1991. pap. write for info. (*1-890025-01-1*) B E A M Oklhma City.

Preaching Vedanta. Swamiji Iraianban. LC 97-914272. 1997. 30.00 (*81-7017-350-7*, Pub. by Abhinav Pubns) S Asia.

Preaching Verse by Verse. Ronald J. Allen & Gilbert L. Bartholomew. LC 99-47265. 160p. 1999. pap. 14.95 (*0-664-25804-2*) Westminster John Knox.

Preaching While the Church Is under Reconstruction: The Visionary Role of Preachers in a Fragmented World. Thomas H. Troeger. LC 98-48163. 176p. 1999. pap. 17.00 (*0-687-08549-7*) Abingdon.

Preaching with a Cupped Ear: Hans-Georg Gadamer's Philosophical Hermeneutics As Postmodern Wor(l)d. Jeffrey F. Bullock. LC 97-27265. (Berkeley Insights in Linguistics & Semiotics Ser.: Vol. 34). X, 204p. (C). 1999. text 46.95 (*0-8204-3898-7*) P Lang Pubng.

Preaching with Freshness: Avoiding Burnout & Renewing Enthusiasm for Biblical Preaching. Bruce Mawhinney. LC 96-52007. 264p. 1997. pap. 12.99 (*0-8254-3198-0*) Kregel.

***Preaching with Passion.** Alex D. Montoya. 2000. pap. 10.99 (*0-8254-3346-0*) Kregel.

Preaching with Power. Edward Fudge. pap. 2.50 (*0-686-12680-7*) E Fudge.

Preaching with Power: Sermons by Black Preachers. Ed. by Joe D. Aldred. 160p. 1998. pap. 16.50 (*0-304-70439-3*) Continuum.

Preaching with Purpose: The Urgent Task of Homiletics. Jay Edward Adams. (Jay Adams Library). 176p. 1986. pap. 14.99 (*0-310-51091-0*, 12121P) Zondervan.

Preaching with Spiritual Passion: How to Sustain the Fire. David L. Goetz. 176p. 1998. text 16.99 (*1-55661-970-7*) Bethany Hse.

Preaching Workbook. David Day. LC 99-229396. 168p. 1998. pap. 15.95 (*1-901443-15-9*) Intl Pubs Mktg.

Preachments. Elbert Hubbard. (Elbert Hubbard's Selected Writings: Vol. 4). 470p. 1998. reprint ed. pap. 33.00 (*0-7661-0385-4*) Kessinger Pub.

Preachments: Poems from Hollywood. Mark Dunster. 11p. 1999. pap. 5.00 (*0-89642-736-6*) Linden Pubs.

Preacquisition Assessment of Commercial & Industrial Property. Pollution Engineering Staff. 96p. 1994. 24.95 (*0-934165-30-0*, 65309) Gulf Pub.

Preacquisition Assessments: Recommended Management Procedures for Consulting Engineering Firms. Ed. by P. H. Collin et al. 288p. 25.00 (*0-614-05191-6*, GC10895MPPRP) ASFE.

Preadamite Theory & the Marriage of Science & Religion. David N. Livingstone. LC 92-76986. (Transactions Ser.: Vol. 82, Pt. 3). 89p. (C). 1992. pap. 16.00 (*0-87169-823-4*, T821-LID) Am Philos.

Preadamites Vol. 1: The Existence of Men Before Adam. Alexander Winchell. Ed. by Al I. Obaba. (Illus.). 208p. 1880. pap. text 27.00 (*0-916157-89-X*) African Islam Miss Pubns.

Preadamites Vol. 2: The Existence of Men Before Adam. Alexander Winchell. Ed. by Al I. Obaba. (Illus.). 176p. 1880. pap. text 27.00 (*0-916157-90-3*) African Islam Miss Pubns.

Preadamites Vol. 3: The Existence of Men Before Adam. Alexander Winchell. Ed. by Al I. Obaba. (Illus.). 154p. 1880. pap. text 27.00 (*0-916157-91-1*) African Islam Miss Pubns.

Preadamites Vol. 4: The Existence of Man Before Adam. Alexander Winchell. Ed. by Al I. Obaba. (Illus.). 172p. 1880. pap. text 27.00 (*0-916157-92-X*) African Islam Miss Pubns.

Preadmissions Policy & Procedures. Olga Cotera. 1993. 70.00 (*1-879575-32-9*) Acad Med Sys.

Preadolescent: A Handbook of Middle School Classroom Strategies. Mary Prentice & Edna Yancey. LC 98-150722. 92 p. 1997. write for info. (*0-8251-3267-3*) J W Walch.

Preah Khan Conservation Project, Angkor Vol. 2: Report VII, Field Campaign IV. J. Sanday et al. Ed. by J. Calame. (Illus.). 1997. pap. 15.00 (*0-9627931-9-1*) World Monuments.

Preah Khan Conservation Project, Historic City of Angkor Report Vol. 5: Field Campaign II. World Monuments Fund Staff. (Illus.). 292p. 1994. pap. 20.00 (*1-890879-02-9*) World Monuments.

Preah Khan Conservation Project, Historic City of Angkor Report Vol. 6: Field Campaign III. Ed. by World Monuments Fund Staff. (Illus.). 209p. 1995. pap. 20.00 (*1-890879-03-7*) World Monuments.

Preakness & the Preakness Reformed Church, Passaic County: A History, 1695-1902, with Genealogical Notes, the Records of the Church & Tombstone Inscriptions. George W. Labaw. (Illus.). 344p. 1997. reprint ed. lib. bdg. 39.50 (*0-8328-6075-1*) Higginson Bk Co.

***Prealgbera: Project Problem Manual.** Carson. 2000. pap. 8.00 (*0-201-70404-8*) Addison-Wesley.

Prealgebra. (C). 1994. pap. text 21.00 (*0-201-56688-5*) Addison-Wesley.

Prealgebra. (C). 1996. text. write for info. (*0-201-42992-6*) Addison-Wesley.

***Prealgebra.** (C). 1998. VHS 133.00 (*0-321-03144-X*) Addison-Wesley.

***Prealgebra.** (C). 2000. text. write for info. (*0-201-65553-5*) Addison-Wesley.

***Prealgebra.** 288p. (C). 1999. 25.20 (*0-321-02990-9*) Addson-Wesley Educ.

Prealgebra, 2 vols. (C). 1995. pap., teacher ed. 11.96 (*0-395-72390-6*) HM.

Prealgebra. (C). 1995. pap. text 68.36 (*0-395-76564-1*) HM.

***Prealgebra.** (C). 1999. pap. text 69.00 (*0-321-05665-5*, Celebration) Addson-Wesley Educ.

***Prealgebra.** (C). 1999. pap. text 25.00 (*0-321-03146-6*) Addson-Wesley Educ.

Prealgebra. 1p. (C). 1999. pap. text 88.00 (*0-321-03148-2*, Celebration); pap. text 25.00 (*0-321-03145-8*, Celebration) Addson-Wesley Educ.

***Prealgebra.** 1p. (C). 1999. pap. text 88.00 (*0-321-03147-4*, Celebration) Addson-Wesley Educ.

Prealgebra. Aufmann. (C). 1993. pap. text 58.76 (*0-395-66524-8*) HM.

Prealgebra. Aufmann. (C). 1993. pap., teacher ed., suppl. ed. 7.96 (*0-395-66526-4*) HM.

Prealgebra. Aufmann. (C). 1994. pap. text, student ed. 22.36 (*0-395-69291-1*) HM.

Prealgebra, 2 vols. Bach. (C). Date not set. pap., teacher ed., suppl. ed. 58.76 (*0-395-71707-8*) HM.

Prealgebra. Bach. (C). 1991. pap. text, student ed. 11.96 (*0-395-57080-8*) HM.

Prealgebra, 2 vols. Bach. (C). 1994. pap., teacher ed., suppl. ed. 11.96 (*0-395-72391-4*) HM.

Prealgebra. Joshua Berebom & Umesh Nagarkatte. 670p. (C). 1991. pap. text 71.50 (*0-15-571043-5*) SCP.

Prealgebra. Berenbom. (C). 1990. pap. text, student ed. 24.50 (*0-15-571044-3*) Harcourt Coll Pubs.

Prealgebra. Berenbom. (C). 1991. pap. text, teacher ed. 11.75 (*0-15-571045-1*) Harcourt Coll Pubs.

Prealgebra. Marvin L. Bittinger & David J. Ellenbogen. (Illus.). 640p. (C). 1991. pap. text 63.00 (*0-201-50843-5*) Addison-Wesley.

Prealgebra. Blair & Tobey. (C). 1998. pap. text, student ed. write for info. (*0-13-020669-5*) P-H.

Prealgebra. Blair & Tobey. LC 99-10558. 704p. 1999. pap. text 78.00 (*0-13-260936-3*, Pub. by P-H) S&S Trade.

Prealgebra. Diana Hestwood. LC 97-16486. 682p. (C). 1998. pap. text 75.00 (*0-321-01607-6*) Addison-Wesley.

***Prealgebra.** Hutchinson. 1999. text 16.50 (*0-07-031772-0*, McGrw-H College) McGrw-H Hghr Educ.

Prealgebra. Jones Staff. (Mathematics Ser.). 1998. mass mkt., lab manual ed. 12.00 (*0-534-36260-5*) Brooks-Cole.

Prealgebra. Charles P. McKeague. (Math). 462p. (C). 1987. mass mkt. 34.50 (*0-534-07596-7*) PWS Pubs.

Prealgebra. Thompson. (C). 1998. text 47.00 (*0-03-096691-4*) Harcourt Coll Pubs.

Prealgebra. Lawrence A. Trivieri. (C). 1993. pap. text, student ed. 20.50 (*0-07-065227-9*) McGraw.

Prealgebra. Alan S. Tussy & R. David Gustafson. (Mathematics Ser.). 608p. (C). 1997. mass mkt. 75.95 (*0-534-34326-0*) Brooks-Cole.

Prealgebra. Alan S. Tussy & R. David Gustafson. (Mathematics Ser.). (C). 1997. student ed. 16.75 (*0-534-34386-4*); mass mkt., teacher ed. 20.75 (*0-534-34387-2*) Brooks-Cole.

Prealgebra. James Van Dyke et al. 448p. (C). 1990. pap. text. write for info. (*0-03-014832-4*) SCP.

Prealgebra. D. Franklin Wright. 544p. (C). 1993. pap. text 59.16 (*0-669-16807-6*); teacher ed. 2.66 (*0-669-16809-2*); teacher ed. 20.36 (*0-669-32911-8*); student ed. write for info. incl. VHS (*0-669-32976-2*); student ed. 22.36 (*0-669-32909-6*); student ed. 22.36 (*0-669-32910-X*); 2.66 (*0-669-32908-8*); VHS 400.00 (*0-669-32977-0*) HM Trade Div.

Prealgebra. Katherine Yoshiwara. (C). 1997. text, teacher ed. write for info. (*0-534-95452-9*) Brooks-Cole.

Prealgebra. Katherine Yoshiwara. LC 96-44238. (Mathematics Ser.). 752p. (C). 1997. mass mkt. 75.95 (*0-534-95448-0*) Brooks-Cole.

Prealgebra. Katherine Yoshiwara. (Mathematics Ser.). (C). 1997. mass mkt., student ed., lab manual ed. 21.75 (*0-534-95451-0*) Brooks-Cole.

Prealgebra. Katherine Yoshiwara. LC 95-23679. 1995. pap. 28.95 (*0-534-95016-7*) PWS Pubs.

Prealgebra. annot. ed. Alan S. Tussy & R. David Gustafson. (C). 1997. mass mkt., teacher ed. 44.00 (*0-534-34327-9*) Brooks-Cole.

Prealgebra. annot. ed. D. Franklin Wright. 544p. (C). 1993. teacher ed. 60.36 (*0-669-32907-X*) HM Trade Div.

Prealgebra. rev. ed. CMSP Projects. (Illus.). 101p. (YA). reprint ed. pap. text. write for info. (*0-942851-00-5*) CMSP Projects.

Prealgebra. 2nd ed. 96p. (C). 1995. text 24.00 (*0-201-85531-3*); pap. text 25.20 (*0-201-85527-5*) Addison-Wesley.

***Prealgebra.** 2nd ed. (C). 2001. text. write for info. (*0-321-06460-7*) Addson-Wesley Educ.

Prealgebra. 2nd ed. (Prentice Hall College Titles Ser.). 1997. write for info. (*0-13-258112-4*) P-H.

Prealgebra, 2 vols. 2nd ed. Bach. (C). 1995. pap. text, student ed. 22.36 (*0-395-72389-2*) HM.

Prealgebra. 2nd ed. Marvin L. Bittinger & David Ellenbogen. 672p. (C). 1995. pap. text 72.00 (*0-201-55753-3*) Addison-Wesley.

Prealgebra. 2nd ed. Martin. 1997. pap. text, student ed. 29.33 (*0-13-258229-5*) P-H.

***Prealgebra.** 2nd ed. Martin-Gay. 2000. 71.00 (*0-13-026179-3*) P-H.

Prealgebra. 2nd ed. K. Elayn Martin-Gay. LC 97-3525. 710p. (C). 1997. pap. text 78.00 (*0-13-242470-3*) P-H.

Prealgebra. 2nd ed. McKeague. (Mathematics Ser.). 1992. teacher ed. 45.00 (*0-534-14470-5*) Brooks-Cole.

Prealgebra. 2nd ed. Charles P. McKeague. (Math). 550p. (C). 1991. mass mkt. 47.25 (*0-534-14466-7*) PWS Pubs.

Prealgebra. 2nd ed. Van Dyke. (C). 1993. pap. text, teacher ed. 25.25 (*0-03-072972-6*) Harcourt Coll Pubs.

***Prealgebra.** 3rd ed. (C). 1999. text 26.00 (*0-201-64609-9*) Addison-Wesley.

***Prealgebra.** 3rd ed. (C). 1999. text. write for info. (*0-201-64604-8*) Addison-Wesley.

***Prealgebra.** 3rd ed. 720p. (C). 1999. text 71.00 (*0-201-64602-1*) Addison-Wesley.

***Prealgebra.** 3rd ed. (C). 1999. write for info. (*0-201-70412-9*) Addison-Wesley.

***Prealgebra.** 3rd ed. (C). 1999. write for info. (*0-201-70321-1*); write for info. (*0-201-70327-0*) Addison-Wesley.

***Prealgebra.** 3rd ed. (C). 1999. text 6.67 (*0-201-70056-5*) Addison-Wesley.

***Prealgebra.** 3rd ed. (C). 2000. text 25.00 (*0-201-64806-7*); text 29.00 (*0-201-66192-6*); text 67.00 (*0-201-64607-2*); text 25.46 (*0-201-64603-X*); text 133.00 (*0-201-64807-5*); text 21.00 (*0-201-34026-7*); cd-rom 34.00 (*0-201-70066-2*) Addison-Wesley.

***Prealgebra.** 3rd ed. (C). 2001. text. write for info. (*0-13-026461-X*); text 29.33 (*0-13-026462-8*); text. write for info. (*0-13-026450-4*); text 29.33 (*0-13-026459-8*) P-H.

Prealgebra. 3rd ed. Marvin Bittinger. LC 99-26893. 693p. (C). 1999. pap. text 75.00 (*0-201-34024-0*) Addison-Wesley.

***Prealgebra.** 3rd ed. K. Elayn Martin-Gay. LC 00-35951. 800p. 2000. pap. 72.00 (*0-13-026037-1*) P-H.

Prealgebra. 3rd ed. McKeague. (Mathematics Ser.). 1995. teacher ed. 18.25 (*0-534-95274-7*) Brooks-Cole.

Prealgebra. 3rd ed. Charles P. McKeague. 1995. mass mkt. 71.95 (*0-534-94764-6*) PWS Pubs.

Prealgebra. 3rd ed. Van Dyke. (C). 1997. pap. text 21.00 (*0-03-019942-5*) Harcourt.

Prealgebra. 3rd ed. Van Dyke. (C). 1998. pap. text, teacher ed. 34.50 (*0-03-019952-2*) Harcourt.

Prealgebra. 3rd ed. Van Dyke. (C). 1998. text 26.75 (*0-03-024564-8*) Harcourt Coll Pubs.

Prealgebra. 4th ed. (C). 1996. write for info. (*0-8087-7062-4*) Pearson Custom.

***Prealgebra.** 4th ed. McKeague. (Mathematics Ser.). 2000. text 47.00 (*0-534-37893-5*) Brooks-Cole.

Prealgebra. 6th ed. (C). 1995. text 147.00 (*0-201-54454-7*) Addison-Wesley.

Prealgebra: A Process Education Approach. Carol Atnip & Richard Benner. (Illus.). 316p. (C). 1997. pap. text 24.00 (*1-878437-60-7*) Pac Crest Soft.

Prealgebra: A Transition from Arithmetic to Algebra. Dwight M. Steedley. (Illus.). 767p. (C). 1992. pap. text 119.00 (*1-878907-73-5*) TechBooks.

Prealgebra: A Worktext, 2 Vols. 2nd ed. Frank Wright. (C). 1996. pap. text, teacher ed. 13.17 (*0-669-41818-8*) HM Trade Div.

Prealgebra: A Worktext: Complete Solutions Manual. 2nd ed. Frank Wright. (C). 1996. pap. text 18.76 (*0-669-41817-X*) HM Trade Div.

Prealgebra: A Worktext: Student Solutions Manual, 2 Vols. 2nd ed. Frank Wright. (C). 1996. pap. text 20.36 (*0-669-41819-6*) HM Trade Div.

Prealgebra: An Integrated Approach. Lawrence A. Trivieri. LC 93-10359. (C). 1994. text 61.25 (*0-07-065225-2*) McGraw.

Prealgebra Custom Version. 3rd ed. Marvin L. Bittinger. 752p. (C). 1999. pap. 69.00 (*0-201-66059-8*) Addison-Wesley.

Prealgebra: Mathematics for a Variable World, 2 vols. 2nd ed. Daniel J. Bach & Patricia J. Leitner. 620p. (C). 1995. pap. text 58.76 (*0-395-71106-1*) HM.

Prealgebra: Student Solutions Manual. Diana L. Hestwood. 272p. (C). 1999. pap. text, student ed. 22.00 (*0-321-02282-3*) Addson-Wesley Educ.

Prealgebra: Student Solutions Manual. 2nd ed. Marvin L. Bittinger. 192p. (C). 1995. pap. text, student ed. 21.00 (*0-201-85525-9*) Addison-Wesley.

Prealgebra: Student's Solution Manual. Beer. 272p. (C). 1997. student ed. 21.00 (*0-321-01274-7*) Addison-Wesley.

***Prealgebra Algebra.** BEER & PEAKE. 540p. 1999. pap. text 72.00 (*0-201-59768-3*) Addison-Wesley.

Prealgebra & Basic Math: Video Workbook. 2nd ed. Charles P. McKeague. (Mathematics Ser.). 1992. pap., wbk. ed. 9.50 (*0-534-14455-1*) PWS Pubs.

Prealgebra College Preparatory Mathematics: College Preparatory Mathematics. J. Louis Nanney & John L. Cable. (Illus.). 431p. (C). 1989. text 48.75 (*0-697-06428-X*) Quant Syst.

Prealgebra for College Students. John R. Kennedy. (Mathematics Ser.). 1992. pap., student ed. 15.95 (*0-534-93058-1*) PWS Pubs.

Prealgebra for College Students: A Problem Solving Approach. Robert Shloming. 360p. (C). 1990. pap. text 28.00 (*0-15-571103-2*) Harcourt Coll Pubs.

Prealgebra for College Students: A Problem Solving Approach. Robert Shloming. (C). 1990. teacher ed. write for info. (*0-15-571102-4*); teacher ed. write for info. (*0-318-67034-8*); VHS, disk. write for info. (*0-318-67035-6*); disk. write for info. (*0-318-67036-4*) SCP.

Prealgebra for Problem Solvers. Loyd V. Wilcox. 624p. (C). 1991. text 60.95 (*0-534-12750-9*) Brooks-Cole.

Prealgebra for Problem Solvers: Lectures. Loyd V. Wilcox. (Mathematics Ser.). 1990. pap., teacher ed. 22.95 (*0-534-12752-5*) Brooks-Cole.

***Prealgebra Mathematics.** 96p. (C). 2000. 9.50 (*0-536-01392-6*) Pearson Custom.

***Prealgebra Royalty Transfer.** 3rd ed. (C). 2000. pap. text. write for info. (*0-201-64724-9*) S&S Trade.

Prealgebra Student Solutions Manual. Marvin L. Bittinger. (C). 1994. pap. text 24.00 (*0-201-50845-1*) Addison-Wesley.

***Prealgebra 2001.** 3rd ed. 2000. write for info. (*0-13-027994-3*) P-H.

Preamble to the U. S. Constitution. Douglas M. Rife. Ed. by Judy Mitchell. (Illus.). 32p. (J). (gr. 4-8). 1998. pap., teacher ed. 5.95 (*1-57310-129-X*) Teachng & Lrning Co.

Preambles to Pension & Benefits Regulations, 1999. rev. ed. Contrib. by In-House Professionals Staff. 1426p. 1999. pap. text 49.00 (*0-7811-0211-1*) Res Inst Am.

Preambles to Pension & Benefits Regulations, 1993. rev. ed. RIA In-House Professional Staff. 1400p. 1993. pap. text 49.00 (*0-7811-0070-4*) Res Inst Am.

Preambles to Pension & Benefits Regulations, 1994 Edution. rev. ed. RIA In-House Professional Staff. 1504p. 1994. pap. 49.00 (*0-7811-0088-7*) Res Inst Am.

Preambles to Pension & Benefits Regulations, 1995. RIA In-House Professional Staff. 1570p. 1995. pap. text 49.00 (*0-7811-0104-2*) Res Inst Am.

Preambles to Pension & Benefits Regulations, 1996. rev. ed. RIA In-House Professional Staff. 1728p. 1996. pap. 49.00 (*0-7811-0135-2*) Res Inst Am.

Preambles to Pension & Benefits Regulations, 1997. rev. ed. 1880p. 1997. pap. text 49.00 (*0-7811-0159-X*) Res Inst Am.

Preambles to Pension & Benefits Regulations, 1998 Edition. rev. ed. 1300p. 1998. pap. text 49.00 (*0-7811-0178-6*) Res Inst Am.

***Preambles to Pension & Benefits Regulations, 2000.** rev. ed. In-House Professionals Staff. 1656p. 2000. pap. 49.00 (*0-7811-0232-4*) Res Inst Am.

Preambulo a la Magia: Guia Instructiva. Amber K. LC 99-26133. (SPA., Illus.). 288p. 1999. pap. 7.95 (*1-56718-019-1*, K-019-1) Llewellyn Pubns.

Preanesthetic Assessment, Vol. 4. Ed. by Elizabeth Frost. 366p. 1994. 29.95 (*0-9641623-0-X*) McMahon Grp.

Prearranged Gulf War. Ali Towfik. 88p. (Orig.). 1991. pap. 8.95 (*0-9630696-0-8*) A A Towfik.

Prebatholithic Stratigraphy of Peninsular California. Ed. by R. G. Gastil & R. H. Miller. (Special Papers: No. 279). 1993. pap. 32.50 (*0-8137-2279-9*) Geol Soc.

Prebiological Self Organization of Matter: The Eighth College Park Colloquium on Chemical Evolution. Ed. by Cyril Ponnamperuma & Frederick Eirich. LC 90-3640. (Illus.). 305p. 1990. 50.00 *(0-937194-18-2)* A Deepak Pub.

Prebiotic Chemistry in Space: Proceedings of Symposium B1.4 of COSPAR Scientific Commission B & Symposium F3.3 of COSPAR Scientific Commission F Which Were Held During the 30th COSPAR Scientific Assembly, Hamburg, Germany, 11-21 July, 1994. Ed. by A. C. Levasseur-Regourd & F. Raulin. (Advances in Space Research Ser.: Vol. 16). 120p. 1995. pap. 97.75 *(0-08-042622-0,* Pergamon Pr) Elsevier.

Preble County, Ohio Common Pleas Court Records, 1810-185. Anita Short & Ruth Bowers. 142p. 1995. pap. 16.00 *(0-8063-4603-5)* Clearfield Co.

Preble County, Ohio, 1850 Census. Rose Shilt. 1974. 14.00 *(0-935057-02-1)* OH Genealogical.

Preble County, Ohio Marriage Records, 1808-1840, 2 vols. in 1. Anita Short & Ruth Bowers. 148p. 1994. reprint ed. pap. 17.50 *(0-8063-4895-X)* Clearfield Co.

Precalc . . . Including Trigonometry. 2nd ed. Bob Miller. LC 97-43437. (Bob Miller's Calc for the Clueless Ser.). (Illus.). 176p. (C). 1997. pap. text, student ed. 10.95 *(0-07-043407-7,* Schaums Outlne) McGraw-Hill Prof.

Precalc High School. 2nd ed. Cohen. (Math). 1987. mass mkt. 51.75 *(0-314-26211-3)* West Pub.

***Precalculus.** (C). 2000. text. write for info. *(0-321-05763-5)* Addison-Wesley.

***Precalculus.** (C). 2000. text. write for info. *(0-321-07594-3)*; text. write for info. *(0-321-07595-1)*; text. write for info. *(0-321-07596-X)*; text. write for info. *(0-321-07597-8)*; text. write for info. *(0-321-07699-0)*; text. write for info. *(0-321-07700-8)*; text. write for info. *(0-321-07701-6)*; text. write for info. *(0-321-07702-4)* Addison-Wesley.

Precalculus. Andersen. (C). 2000. text. write for info. *(0-03-024964-3)*; pap. text 29.50 *(0-03-022228-1)* Harcourt Coll Pubs.

Precalculus, 2 vols. Aufmann. (C). Date not set. text, teacher ed., suppl. ed. 72.36 *(0-395-63826-7)* HM.

Precalculus, 2 vols. Aufmann. (C). 1993. pap., student ed. 13.16 *(0-395-63829-1)* HM.

Precalculus, 2 vols. Aufmann. (C). 1993. pap. 9.16 *(0-395-63830-5)* HM.

***Precalculus.** Ziegler Barnett. 708p. 1999. student ed. 25.63 *(0-07-228398-X)* McGraw.

Precalculus. Ziegler Barnett. LC 99-49637. 1056p. 1999. 77.81 *(0-07-005717-6)* McGraw.

Precalculus. Phillip W. Bean et al. LC 92-27803. 672p. 1993. text 68.95 *(0-534-93160-X)* PWS Pubs.

Precalculus. Dennis Bila & Donald Ross. 480p. (gr. 12). 1986. 18.36 *(0-935115-00-5)* Instruct Tech.

Precalculus. Dennis Carrie. (C). 1990. pap. text 71.96 *(0-395-44464-0)*; pap. text 3.96 *(0-395-53219-1)* HM.

Precalculus. Dennis Carrie. (C). 1990. pap. 2.76 *(0-395-44465-9)* HM.

Precalculus. Dennis Carrie. (C). 1990. pap. 5.16 *(0-395-52649-3)* HM.

Precalculus. Collingwood. (C). 1998. text 40.00 *(0-03-024754-3)* Harcourt Coll Pubs.

Precalculus. Collingwood. (C). 1999. pap. text 29.50 *(0-03-023512-X,* Pub. by Harcourt Coll Pubs); pap. text 19.50 *(0-03-023513-8)* Harcourt Coll Pubs.

Precalculus. David E. Dobbs & John C. Peterson. 720p. (C). 1992. text 56.25 *(0-697-16235-4,* WCB McGr Hill) McGrw-H Hghr Educ.

Precalculus. David E. Dobbs & John C. Peterson. 720p. (C). 1993. text, student ed. 21.88 *(0-697-16289-3,* WCB McGr Hill) McGrw-H Hghr Educ.

Precalculus. Driscoll. 504p. 1997. pap. 54.69 *(0-07-017867-4)* McGraw.

Precalculus. Dugopolski. 944p. (C). 1995. text 55.00 *(0-201-85964-5)* Addison-Wesley.

Precalculus. Dwyer. 2000. mass mkt. 74.95 *(0-534-35287-1)* Brooks-Cole.

***Precalculus.** Dwyer. (Mathematics Ser.). (C). 2000. text 12.00 *(0-534-37903-6)* Brooks-Cole.

Precalculus. Dwyer. 2000. mass mkt., student ed. 30.95 *(0-534-35289-8)* Brooks-Cole.

Precalculus. Elich & Cannon. (C). 1989. pap. text, student ed. 25.00 *(0-673-38447-0)* Addson-Wesley Educ.

Precalculus. J. Douglas Faires. (Mathematics Ser.). 1997. mass mkt., student ed. 16.50 *(0-534-34583-2)* Wadsworth Pub.

Precalculus. J. Douglas Faires & James DeFranza. LC 96-29911. (Mathematics Ser.). 460p. (C). 1997. mass mkt. 48.50 *(0-534-25236-2)* Brooks-Cole.

Precalculus. Murray Gechtman. 704p. (C). 1991. text 62.50 *(0-697-11773-1,* WCB McGr Hill) McGrw-H Hghr Educ.

Precalculus. Hirsch Goodman. (Mathematics Ser.). 2000. pap. text, student ed. 19.00 *(0-534-37182-5)* Brooks-Cole.

Precalculus. Grossman. (C). 1990. pap. text, teacher ed., suppl. ed. 40.50 *(0-03-007122-4,* Pub. by Harcourt Coll Pubs) Harcourt.

Precalculus. Bodh R. Gulati & Helen G. Bass. 650p. (C). 1987. text 53.44 *(0-697-06763-7,* WCB McGr Hill) McGrw-H Hghr Educ.

Precalculus. Jerome E. Kaufmann. (Math). 640p. (C). 1988. mass mkt. 39.25 *(0-534-92007-1)* PWS Pubs.

Precalculus. Roland E. Larson & Robert P. Hostetler. 826p. (C). 1993. teacher ed. 22.36 *(0-669-28313-4)*; 2.66 *(0-669-28314-2)* HM Trade Div.

Precalculus. Charles S. Rees. LC 96-45922. (C). 1997. mass mkt. 88.95 *(0-314-06770-1)* West Pub.

Precalculus. Steven Roman. 672p. (C). 1987. text 81.00 *(0-15-571052-4)*; teacher ed. write for info. *(0-15-571055-9)* SCP.

Precalculus. Stockton. (C). 1992. text 49.50 *(0-07-061599-3)* McGraw.

Precalculus. Viglino. (Mathematics Ser.). 1997. mass mkt., student ed. 13.50 *(0-534-35534-X)* Brooks-Cole.

Precalculus. Wells. 1998. pap. text, student ed. 29.33 *(0-13-263732-4)* P-H.

Precalculus. annot. ed. Roland E. Larson & Robert P. Hostetler. 826p. (C). 1993. text, teacher ed. 53.56 *(0-669-33236-4)* HM Trade Div.

***Precalculus.** 2nd ed. 256p. (C). 1998. pap. text 25.00 *(0-201-38392-6)* Addison-Wesley.

***Precalculus.** 2nd ed. (C). 1998. 25.00 *(0-201-38386-1)* Addison-Wesley.

Precalculus. 2nd ed. 336p. (C). 1998. text 25.00 *(0-201-38393-4)* S&S Trade.

Precalculus, 2 vols. 2nd ed. Aufmann. (C). 1993. text 72.36 *(0-395-63825-9)* HM.

Precalculus, 2 vols. 2nd ed. Aufmann. (C). 1993. pap. text, student ed. 21.96 *(0-395-63828-3)* HM.

Precalculus. 2nd ed. Lawrence O. Cannon & Joseph Elich. LC 93-15109. 192p. (C). 1997. pap. text 23.50 *(0-673-46729-5)* Addison-Wesley.

Precalculus. 2nd ed. Lawrence O. Cannon & Joseph Elich. LC 93-15109. (C). 1994. text 61.00 *(0-673-46728-7)* HarpC.

Precalculus. 2nd ed. Dennis T. Christy. 672p. (C). 1992. text 17.50 *(0-697-16431-4,* WCB McGr Hill) McGrw-H Hghr Educ.

Precalculus. 2nd ed. Dennis T. Christy. 672p. (C). 1992. text 56.25 *(0-697-12345-6,* WCB McGr Hill) McGrw-H Hghr Educ.

Precalculus. 2nd ed. Dennis T. Christy. 672p. (C). 1992. text, student ed. 22.50 *(0-697-12349-9,* WCB McGr Hill) McGrw-H Hghr Educ.

Precalculus. 2nd ed. Cohen. Date not set. pap. text, student ed. 21.95 *(0-314-60651-3)* West Pub.

Precalculus. 2nd ed. David C. Cohen. (Illus.). 725p. (C). 1987. pap. text, teacher ed. 13.00 *(0-314-34724-0)* West Pub.

Precalculus. 2nd ed. Mark Dugopolski. 976p. (C). 1998. 91.00 *(0-201-34713-X)* Addison-Wesley.

Precalculus. 2nd ed. Defranza Faires. LC 99-33033. (Mathematics Ser.). 1999. pap. text 60.95 *(0-534-37115-9)* Brooks-Cole.

***Precalculus.** 2nd ed. Defranza Faires. (Mathematics Ser.). 1999. pap. 20.00 *(0-534-37353-4)* Brooks-Cole.

Precalculus. 2nd ed. Jerome E. Kaufmann. (Math). 640p. (C). 1991. mass mkt. 55.00 *(0-534-92474-3)* PWS Pubs.

Precalculus. 2nd ed. Roland E. Larson. 736p. (C). 1990. text 72.36 *(0-669-16277-9)*; pap. text, student ed. 22.36 *(0-669-17345-2)*; teacher ed. 2.00 *(0-685-67669-2)*; student ed. 10.50 *(0-685-58267-1)*; trans. 84.36 *(0-669-17346-0)* HM Trade Div.

Precalculus. 3rd ed. Barnett. 1993. teacher ed. 26.87 *(0-07-004963-7)* McGraw.

Precalculus. 3rd ed. Roland E. Larson & Robert P. Hostetler. 826p. (C). 1993. text 72.36 *(0-669-28310-X)*; pap. text, student ed. 22.36 *(0-669-28312-6)* HM Trade Div.

Precalculus. 4th ed. Cohen. Date not set. pap. text, teacher ed. write for info. *(0-314-02298-8)* West Pub.

Precalculus. 4th ed. Cohen. 1993. mass mkt., student ed. 18.75 *(0-314-02299-6)* West Pub.

Precalculus. 4th ed. Roland E. Larson & Robert P. Hostetler. 826p. (C). 1993. pap. text 21.56 *(0-669-21885-5)* HM Trade Div.

Precalculus. 4th ed. Sullivan. 1996. pap. text. write for info. *(0-13-237207-X)* Allyn.

Precalculus. 5th ed. (C). 1999. 485.00 *(0-13-022274-7)* P-H.

Precalculus. 5th ed. M. A. Munem. 1989. text 51.95 *(0-87901-418-0)* Worth.

Precalculus. 5th ed. Sullivan. LC 98-30905. 1073p. 1998. 92.00 *(0-13-095402-0)* P-H.

Precalculus. 5th ed. Sullivan. 1998. pap. text, student ed. 26.67 *(0-13-934266-4)* P-H.

Precalculus. 5th ed. James P. Yizze & M. A. Munem. 1989. pap. text, student ed. 12.95 *(0-87901-419-9)* Worth.

Precalculus. 6th ed. M. A. Munem. LC 96-61159. 864p. 1996. text 53.20 *(1-57259-157-9)* Worth.

Precalculus. 6th ed. M. A. Munem. 1997. pap. text, student ed. 12.80 *(1-57259-239-7)* Worth.

Precalculus. 6th ed. Munem & Yizze. 1997. student ed. 61.00 *(1-57259-471-3)* W H Freeman.

Precalculus. 7th ed. Earl W. Swokowski. (Mathematics Ser.). 1994. mass mkt., student ed. 19.75 *(0-534-93703-9)* PWS Pubs.

Precalculus, Testbank. 3rd ed. Hungerford. (C). 1992. pap. text, teacher ed., suppl. ed. 24.50 *(0-03-052859-3,* Pub. by Harcourt Coll Pubs) Harcourt.

Precalculus: A Functional Approach. Lawrence Runyan & Holly Runyan. 1991. text. write for info. *(0-07-909943-2)* McGraw.

Precalculus: A Graphing Approach. Roland E. Larson et al. 826p. (C). 1993. text 72.36 *(0-669-28500-5)*; text, teacher ed. 2.66 *(0-669-33232-1)*; pap. text, student ed. 22.36 *(0-669-28501-3)*; write for info. *(0-318-70106-5)* HM Trade Div.

Precalculus: A Graphing Approach. 4th ed. Franklin Demana. 992p. (C). 1996. student ed. 81.00 *(0-201-87012-6)* Addison-Wesley.

Precalculus: A Problem Oriented Approach. 5th ed. Cohen. (Mathematics Ser.). 1996. student ed. 25.00 *(0-314-20385-0)* Brooks-Cole.

Precalculus: A Problems-Oriented Approach. 5th ed. David Cohen. LC 95-47495. 750p. (C). 1996. 88.95 *(0-314-06921-6)* West Pub.

Precalculus: A Quantitative Reasoning Approach. 2nd ed. Myers. 466p. (C). 1998. per. 69.95 *(0-7872-5252-2,* 41525201) Kendall-Hunt.

***Precalculus: A Quantitative Reasoning Approach.** 2nd ed. Leon E. Myers et al. 466p. (C). 1999. per. 69.95 *(0-7872-6281-1,* 41628102) Kendall-Hunt.

Precalculus: A Student Study Manual. Steven Roman. 672p. (C). 1987. text, student ed. 24.50 *(0-15-571054-0)* SCP.

Precalculus: A View of the World Around Us. Dave Wells & Lynn Tilson. LC 97-36136. 727p. (C). 1998. 92.00 *(0-02-425451-7)* P-H.

PreCalculus: An Intuitive Approach-Michigan Technological University Customized Edition. MTU Staff & Andrew Hugine. 644p. (C). 1995. per. 46.14 *(0-7872-1451-5)* Kendall-Hunt.

Precalculus: Concepts in Context Lab Book. 2nd ed. Marsha Davis & Judy Flagg Moran. LC 97-43190. 1998. mass mkt. 34.95 *(0-534-35232-4)* Brooks-Cole.

***Precalculus: Contexts & Concepts.** 2nd ed. Moran et al. (Mathematics Ser.). (C). 2000. text 12.00 *(0-534-37822-6)* Brooks-Cole.

***Precalculus: Function & Graphs.** 9th ed. Swokowski & Cole. (Mathematics Ser.). 2001. text 12.00 *(0-534-37896-X)* Brooks-Cole.

Precalculus: Functions & Graphs. (C). 1993. 27.00 *(0-201-52908-4)* Addison-Wesley.

Precalculus: Functions & Graphs. Frank Demana & Bert K. Waits. (Illus.). 718p. (C). 1990. text 36.76 *(0-201-52780-4)*; pap. text, student ed. 21.50 *(0-201-52783-9)* Addison-Wesley.

Precalculus: Functions & Graphs. Bernard Kolman & Arnold L. Shapiro. 565p. (C). 1990. 6.50 *(0-15-571066-4)* SCP.

Precalculus: Functions & Graphs. 2nd ed. Franklin Demana. 192p. (C). 1993. pap. text 26.00 *(0-201-56734-2)* Addison-Wesley.

Precalculus: Functions & Graphs. 2nd ed. Franklin D. Demana et al. (Illus.). 784p. (C). 1992. text 65.00 *(0-201-56731-8)* Addison-Wesley.

Precalculus: Functions & Graphs. 2nd ed. Bernard Kolman & Arnold L. Shapiro. 565p. (C). 1990. text 84.00 *(0-15-571063-X)* SCP.

Precalculus: Functions & Graphs. 2nd ed. Bernard Kolman & Arnold L. Shapiro. 565p. (C). 1990. pap. text 34.00 *(0-15-571064-8)* SCP.

Precalculus: Functions & Graphs. 3rd ed. 128p. (C). 1996. text 18.00 *(0-201-44094-6)* Addison-Wesley.

Precalculus: Functions & Graphs. 3rd ed. Raymond A. Barnett & Michael R. Ziegler. LC 92-15631. (C). 1993. text 61.74 *(0-07-004961-0)* McGraw.

Precalculus: Functions & Graphs. 3rd ed. Raymond A. Barnett & Michael R. Ziegler. LC 92-15631. (C). 1993. pap. text, teacher ed. 26.74 *(0-07-005007-4)* McGraw.

***Precalculus: Functions & Graphs.** 4th ed. (C). 2000. pap. 26.40 *(0-201-69975-3)*; text 25.29 *(0-201-69973-7)*; text. write for info. *(0-201-61136-8)*; text 86.00 *(0-201-69977-X)*; text 25.29 *(0-201-70049-2)* Addison-Wesley.

***Precalculus: Functions & Graphs.** 4th ed. (C). 2000. text 19.80 *(0-201-69976-1)*; cd-rom 49.97 *(0-201-69972-9)* Addison-Wesley.

Precalculus: Functions & Graphs. 4th ed. Raymond A. Barnett et al. LC 98-18537. 1016p. 1998. 74.06 *(0-07-006341-9)* McGraw.

Precalculus: Functions & Graphs. 4th ed. James P. Yizze & M. A. Munem. (Illus.). (C). 1985. text 34.95 *(0-87901-258-7)* Worth.

Precalculus: Functions & Graphs. 4th ed. James P. Yizze & M. A. Munem. (Illus.). (C). 1985. pap. text 8.95 *(0-87901-259-5)* Worth.

***Precalculus: Functions & Graphs.** 5th ed. (C). 2000. pap. 78.67 *(0-201-69974-5)* Addison-Wesley.

***Precalculus: Functions & Graphs.** 5th ed. (C). 2000. pap. 29.38 *(0-07-242737-X)* McGrw-H Hghr Educ.

PreCalculus: Functions & Graphs. 5th ed. Earl W. Swokowski. (Math). (C). 1986. mass mkt. 38.25 *(0-87150-060-4,* 33L4350) PWS Pubs.

***Precalculus: Functions & Graphs.** 6th ed. Mustafa Munem & J. Yizze. 716p. (C). 1999. text 80.95 *(0-7872-6044-4,* 41604401) Kendall-Hunt.

Precalculus: Functions & Graphs. 6th ed. Earl W. Swokowski. 672p. (C). 1990. text 50.95 *(0-534-92086-1)* PWS Pubs.

Precalculus: Functions & Graphs. 7th ed. Swokowski. (Mathematics Ser.). 1994. teacher ed. 25.50 *(0-534-93704-7)* Brooks-Cole.

Precalculus: Functions & Graphs. 7th ed. Earl W. Swokowski & Jeffery A. Cole. LC 93-28896. (Math). 1993. mass mkt. 56.50 *(0-534-93702-0)* PWS Pubs.

Precalculus: Functions & Graphs. 8th ed. Swokowski. LC 97-45594. 1997. mass mkt. 81.95 *(0-534-35263-4)* Brooks-Cole.

Precalculus: Functions & Graphs. 8th ed. Swokowski. 1998. mass mkt. 20.00 *(0-534-35264-2)* Brooks-Cole.

***Precalculus: Functions & Graphs.** 9th ed. Swokowski & Cole. (Mathematics Ser.). 2001. text 15.00 *(0-534-37897-8)* Brooks-Cole.

***Precalculus: Functions & Graphs.** 9th ed. Swokowski/Cole. 2001. pap. 58.00 *(0-534-37757-2)* Thomson Learn.

Precalculus: Functions & Graphs - Instructor's Solution Manual. 6th ed. M. Munem & James Yizze. 1997. teacher ed. write for info. *(1-57259-240-0)* Worth.

Precalculus: Functions & Graphs: A Graphing Approach. Roland E. Larson et al. 750p. (C). 1994. text 72.36 *(0-669-35206-3)* HM Trade Div.

Precalculus: Functions & Graphs, Calculator Enhancement for Precalculus. 3rd ed. Carolyn L. Meitler. 1993. pap. text. write for info. *(0-07-041367-3)* McGraw.

Precalculus: Functions & Graphs with Lab Manual. 2nd ed. Frank Demana. (C). 1993. 66.00 *(0-201-52910-6)* Addison-Wesley.

Precalculus: Functions Graphs. 3rd ed. 368p. (C). 1996. text 24.00 *(0-201-42338-3)* Addison-Wesley.

***Precalculus: Graphing & Data Analysis.** 2nd ed. Michael Sullivan. LC 00-39994. (Illus.). 2001. write for info. *(0-13-026927-1)* P-H.

***Precalculus: Graphing Approach.** 5th ed. 2000. teacher ed. 78.67 *(0-201-70318-1)* Addison-Wesley.

Precalculus: Graphs & Models. 400p. (C). 1996. text 24.00 *(0-201-49808-1)* Addison-Wesley.

Precalculus: Graphs & Models. (C). 1997. text. write for info. *(0-201-30428-7)* Addison-Wesley.

Precalculus: Graphs & Models. (C). 1997. text 267.00 *(0-201-87352-4)*; pap. text 67.00 *(0-201-87353-2)*; pap. text 67.00 *(0-201-87354-0)* Addison-Wesley.

Precalculus: Graphs & Models. (C). 1997. text 145.00 *(0-201-32233-1)* Addison-Wesley.

Precalculus: Graphs & Models. (C). 1997. pap. text 8.40 *(0-201-34569-2)* Addison-Wesley.

Precalculus: Graphs & Models. Marvin L. Bittinger. Ed. by Karen Guardino. LC 96-8880. 832p. (C). 1996. 95.00 *(0-201-69442-5)* Addison-Wesley.

***Precalculus: Graphs & Models.** 2nd ed. (C). 2000. text. write for info. *(0-201-61674-2)* Addison-Wesley.

Precalculus: Making Connections. Runyan. 752p. 1998. pap. text 44.00 *(0-13-095674-0)* P-H.

Precalculus: Math for Calculus. 3rd ed. James Stewart & Lothar Redlin. (Mathematics Ser.). 1998. pap., student ed. 26.95 *(0-534-34507-7)* Course Tech.

***Precalculus: Math for Calculus.** 3rd ed. Stewart et al. (Mathematics Ser.). 1999. text 92.95 *(0-534-37610-X)* Brooks-Cole.

Precalculus: Mathematics for Calculus. 3rd ed. James Stewart et al. LC 97-28428. (Mathematics Ser.). 800p. (C). 1997. mass mkt. 56.00 *(0-534-34504-2)* Brooks-Cole.

Precalculus: Mathematics for Calculus. 3rd ed. James Stewart et al. (C). 1998. pap., teacher ed. 21.50 *(0-534-34505-0)*; mass mkt., student ed. 18.00 *(0-534-34506-9)* Brooks-Cole.

Precalculus: OmniTest Mac Version & Functions & Graphs. 3rd ed. Franklin D. Demana. (C). 1996. 67.00 incl. disk *(0-201-44090-3)* Addison-Wesley.

Precalculus: Preliminary Edition. Esty. 1996. pap. text, student ed. 29.33 *(0-13-264425-8)* P-H.

Precalculus: Problem Solving with Technology. 2nd alternate ed. Lawrence O. Cannon & Joseph Elich. (C). 1996. teacher ed. write for info. *(0-673-97334-4)* Addson-Wesley Educ.

***Precalculus: Solutions Manual.** 4th ed. Raymond Barnett et al. (C). 1998. student ed. 29.38 *(0-07-365582-1)* McGrw-H Hghr Educ.

Precalculus: Student's Solutions Manual. 2nd alternate ed. Lawrence O. Cannon & Joseph Elich. (C). 1996. pap. text, student ed. 12.00 *(0-673-99971-8)* Addson-Wesley Educ.

Precalculus: Study Functions & Applications - Student Solutions Manual. Swanson. (C). 2000. pap. text, student ed. write for info. *(0-03-022224-9)* Harcourt Coll Pubs.

Precalculus: Teacher's Solution Manual. 2nd ed. Mark Dugopolski. (C). 1999. text, teacher ed. write for info. *(0-201-34714-8)* Addison-Wesley.

Precalculus: The Graphing Workbook, 2 vols. 2nd ed. Richard N. Aufmann et al. (C). 1993. pap. text 13.16 *(0-395-65941-8)* HM.

Precalculus: A Graphing Approach. Hall. (Math). 2000. pap. 39.00 *(0-534-93870-1)* Brooks-Cole.

Precalculus, a Problems-Oriented Approach. 4th ed. David C. Cohen. Ed. by Marshall. LC 92-41652. 725p. (C). 1993. text 62.50 *(0-314-01255-9)* West Pub.

Precalculus Algebra & Trigonometry. 2nd ed. Manoug Manougian. LC 86-34332. 1987. 34.50 *(0-931541-07-7)* Mancorp Pub.

Precalculus & Discrete Mathematics. University of Chicago School Mathematic Project St. 1992. text 43.99 *(0-673-33366-3)*; text, teacher ed. 55.40 *(0-673-33367-1)* Addison-Wesley Educ.

Precalculus & Its Applications. Larry J. Goldstein. 640p. (C). 1994. text 58.13 *(0-697-21655-1,* WCB McGr Hill) McGrw-H Hghr Educ.

Precalculus & Its Applications. Larry J. Goldstein. 640p. (C). 1994. text 17.50 *(0-697-21660-8,* WCB McGr Hill) McGrw-H Hghr Educ.

Precalculus & Its Applications: Instructor's Edition. Larry Goldstein. (Illus.). 704p. Date not set. text, teacher ed. write for info. *(1-891304-11-9)* Mobius Communs.

Precalculus & Its Applications: Instructor's Solutions Manual. Larry Goldstein. 458p. Date not set. pap. text, teacher ed. write for info. *(1-891304-14-3)* Mobius Communs.

Precalculus & Its Applications: Student Edition. Larry Goldstein. 656p. (C). Date not set. text, student ed. 44.50 *(1-891304-10-0)* Mobius Communs.

Precalculus & Its Applications: Student Solutions Manual. Larry Goldstein. (Illus.). 234p. (C). Date not set. pap. text, student ed. 15.00 *(1-891304-12-7)* Mobius Communs.

Precalculus Component. Frank Demana & Bert K. Waits. (Illus.). 718p. (C). 1990. text 38.25 *(0-201-52781-2)* Addison-Wesley.

Precalculus Concepts in Context. Judith Moran et al. LC 95-35595. (Mathematics Ser.). 1997. mass mkt. 93.95 *(0-534-19789-2)* PWS Pubs.

Precalculus Concepts Preliminary: Preliminary Edition. Warren Esty. 576p. (C). 1996. pap. text 47.00 *(0-13-261694-7)* P-H.

Precalculus Enhanced with Graphing Utilities. 2nd ed. Ed. by Prentice-Hall Staff. (C). 1999. text. write for info. *(0-13-022503-7)* P-H.

Precalculus Enhanced with Graphing Utilities. 2nd ed. Ed. by Prentice-Hall Staff. (C). 1999. text. write for info. *(0-13-022504-5)*; text. write for info. *(0-13-022505-3)* P-H.

P

An Asterisk (*) at the beginning of an entry indicates that the title is appearing for the first time.

***Precalculus Enhanced with Graphing Utilities.** 2nd ed. Michael J. Sullivan & Michael J. Sullivan, III. LC 99-52615. (Illus.). 1006p. 2000. 92.00 (*0-13-020692-X*) P-H.

Precalculus Experiments with the Casio Graphic Calculator. Lawrence G. Gilligan. 154p. (C). 1991. pap. text 25.96 (*0-669-27644-8*) HM Trade Div.

Precalculus Experiments with the TI-81 Graphic Calculator. Lawrence G. Gilligan. 170p. (C). 1991. pap. text 25.96 (*0-669-27746-0*) HM Trade Div.

Precalculus Explorations Using the TI-82. Deborah J. Cochener. (Mathematics Ser.). 336p. (C). 1996. mass mkt. 26.95 (*0-534-34227-2*) Brooks-Cole.

Precalculus Functions & Graph Value Edition. 2nd ed. Demana. (C). 1996. text 40.00 (*0-201-40196-7*) Addison-Wesley.

Precalculus Functions & Graph Value Edition. 3rd ed. Demana. (C). 1996. student ed. 90.00 (*0-201-85751-0*) Addison-Wesley.

***Precalculus Functions & Graphs.** (C). 2000. text. write for info. (*0-321-05764-3*) Addison-Wesley.

Precalculus Functions & Graphs. A. Robert Marshall. (C). 1991. text 53.75 (*0-201-19095-8*) Addison-Wesley.

Precalculus, Functions & Graphs. 3rd ed. Franklin Demana et al. LC 96-11383. 848p. (C). 1996. 86.00 (*0-201-82297-0*) Addison-Wesley.

Precalculus, Functions & Graphs. 4th ed. Franklin Demana. 1056p. (C). 1996. teacher ed. 72.00 (*0-201-87011-8*) Addison-Wesley.

Precalculus: Functions & Graphs: A Graphing Approach. Roland E. Larson et al. teacher ed. 1.99 (*0-669-35207-1*) Free Pr.

Precalculus Funtions Graphs. 5th ed. Ziegler Bylee Barnett. (Barnett, Ziegler & Byleen's Precalculus Ser.). 2000. 58.00 (*0-07-236871-3*) McGraw.

Precalculus in Context: Concepts & Project for Real World. 2nd ed. Moran & Davis. (Mathematics Ser.). 2000. pap. 45.00 (*0-534-36240-0*) Brooks-Cole.

***Precalculus in Context: Concepts & Project for the Real World.** 2nd ed. Moran et al. (Mathematics Ser.). (C). 2000. text 15.00 (*0-534-37902-8*) Brooks-Cole.

Precalculus in Context: Functioning in the Real World. Marsha Davis et al. (C). 1992. mass mkt. 22.25 (*0-534-19788-4*) PWS Pubs.

Precalculus Investigations: A Preliminary Edition. Gary M Simundza. 336p. 1998. pap. text, lab manual ed. 22.00 (*0-13-010954-1*) P-H.

Precalculus Investigations Using Derive. David M. Mathews. LC 93-33006. 144p. (C). 1997. 28.00 (*0-673-99097-4*) Addson-Wesley Educ.

Precalculus Investigations Using Maple V. David M. Mathews. (C). 1997. 26.73 (*0-673-99410-4*) Addson-Wesley Educ.

Precalculus Learning Activites. Gloria Child. (C). 1997. pap. text. write for info. (*0-201-54852-6*) Addison-Wesley.

Precalculus Math: A Functional Approach. 4th ed. Smith & Simonds. (Mathematics Ser.). 1990. student ed. 17.00 (*0-534-11923-9*) Brooks-Cole.

Precalculus Math: Graphing Approach Teachers Ed. 3rd ed. (C). 1995. pap. text. write for info. (*0-201-59097-2*) Addison-Wesley.

Precalculus Math Solutions Manual. 5th ed. Laurel Technical Services Staff. 1995. pap. text, student ed. 28.00 (*0-13-159626-8*) P-H.

Precalculus Math-A Functional Approach. Smith. (Math). 1979. 22.25 (*0-8185-0269-X*) Brooks-Cole.

Precalculus Math: A Functional Approach. 3rd ed. Karl J. Smith. LC 85-14678. (Math). 550p. (C). 1986. mass mkt. 40.50 (*0-534-05232-0*) Brooks-Cole.

Precalculus Math for Electronics Technology. Eric Hiob. (C). 1997. pap. text. write for info. (*0-201-89297-9*) Addison-Wesley.

Precalculus Math, High School Version with Graphing Calculator & Computer Graphing. 2nd ed. Franklin Demana. (C). 1992. 68.00 (*0-201-56855-1*) Addison-Wesley.

Precalculus Mathematics. Vivian S. Groza & Susanne Shelley. LC 76-158479. 1972. text 22.95 (*0-03-077670-8*) Irvington.

Precalculus Mathematics. 2nd ed. Harley Flanders & Justin J. Price. 416p. (C). 1981. pap. text, teacher ed. 19.75 (*0-03-058251-2*) SCP.

Precalculus Mathematics. 3rd ed. Thomas W. Hungerford & Richard Mercer. 548p. (C). 1992. teacher ed. write for info. (*0-03-054967-1*) SCP.

Precalculus Mathematics. 4th ed. Max A. Sobel & Norbert Lerner. 848p. (C). 1991. text 85.00 (*0-13-683756-5*) P-H.

Precalculus Mathematics. 5th ed. Norbert Lerner & Max A. Sobel. LC 94-11433. 778p. (C). 1995. 90.00 (*0-13-112095-6*) P-H.

Precalculus Mathematics: A Graphing Approach. 2nd ed. Ed. by Franklin D. Demana et al. (Illus.). 736p. (C). 1992. text 60.00 (*0-201-52626-3*) Addison-Wesley.

Precalculus Mathematics: A Graphing Approach. 3rd annot. ed. Franklin D. Demana et al. LC 92-44754. 1994. teacher ed. 88.00 (*0-201-52905-X*) Addison-Wesley.

Precalculus Mathematics: A Study of Functions. George W. Polites. (Illus.). 511p. (C). 1991. reprint ed. 83.00 (*1-878907-32-8*) TechBooks.

Precalculus Mathematics: Graphing Approach. 2nd ed. (C). 1995. text 16.67 (*0-201-55861-0*) Addison-Wesley.

Precalculus Mathematics Vol. II: A Graphing Approach. Frank Demana & Bert K. Waits. (Illus.). 786p. (C). 1988. pap. text 10.75 (*0-201-19288-8*) Addison-Wesley.

Precalculus Mathematics - A Graphing Approach: High School Version. 3rd ed. Franklin D. Demana et al. (Illus.). 800p. 1993. 87.00 (*0-201-52900-9*) Addison-Wesley.

Precalculus Mathematics in a Nutshell. 119p. (YA). (gr. 10 up). 1987. pap. 14.95 (*0-939765-13-6*, GK109) Janson Pubns.

Precalculus Notebook. Stockton. (C). 1994. pap. text 16.00 (*0-07-061600-0*) McGraw.

Precalculus... Notebook. 2nd ed. Jonathan Lewin. 314p. (C). 1999. per. 51.95 (*0-7872-5798-2*, 41579802) Kendall-Hunt.

Precalculus Plus. Ferguson. Date not set. pap. text, teacher ed. write for info. (*0-314-03278-9*) West Pub.

Precalculus Recover of College Algebra & Trigonometry. Lial. (C). 1997. text 84.00 (*0-321-00968-1*) Addson-Wesley Educ.

***Precalculus Through Modeling & Visualization.** Rockswold. LC 99-35868. 936p. (C). 1999. 91.00 (*0-321-05777-5*) Addson-Wesley Educ.

Precalculus: Understanding Functions a Graphing Approach. 2nd ed. Goodman & Hirsch. LC 99-54169. (Math Ser.). 896p. 2000. pap. text 83.95 (*0-534-37176-0*) Brooks-Cole.

Precalculus Using the TI Calculator. Denny Burzynski et al. (C). 1995. text 65.95 (*0-534-18864-8*) PWS Pubs.

Precalculus w/Applications. Grossman. (C). 1992. text 81.50 (*0-03-097032-6*) Harcourt Coll Pubs.

Precalculus Whetstone. Runyan. 1999. pap. text, student ed. 10.00 (*0-13-934282-6*) P-H.

Precalculus with Applications. Grossman. (C). 1990. pap. text, teacher ed. 34.00 (*0-03-007118-6*) Harcourt Coll Pubs.

Precalculus with Applications. Lacey. (C). 1990. pap. text, teacher ed., suppl. ed. 40.50 (*0-03-032727-X*, Pub. by Harcourt Coll Pubs) Harcourt.

Precalculus with Applications. Philip H. Mahler et al. 608p. (C). 1995. text 30.00 (*0-697-11656-5*, WCB McGr Hill) McGrw-H Hghr Educ.

Precalculus with Applications. Schaufele. (C). 1998. text, student ed. write for info. (*0-321-01612-2*) Addson-Wesley Educ.

Precalculus with Applications. Terry H. Wesner et al. 256p. 1995. pap., student ed. write for info. (*0-697-16781-X*, WCB McGr Hill) McGrw-H Hghr Educ.

Precalculus with Graphing. Sullivan. 1996. pap. text, student ed. 29.33 (*0-13-238700-X*) P-H.

Precalculus with Graphing Calculators. Joan E. Girard & Michael Sullivan. 704p. (C). 1996. text 85.00 (*0-02-343742-1*, Macmillan Coll) P-H.

Precalculus with Graphing Technology. David E. Stevens. LC 96-31151. 1996. mass mkt. 92.95 (*0-314-09974-3*) West Pub.

Precalculus with Graphing Utilities. Sullivan. 1996. pap. text. write for info. (*0-13-238692-5*) Allyn.

Precalculus with Graphs & Problem Solving. 5th ed. Smith & White. (Mathematics Ser.). 1993. pap., student ed. 22.95 (*0-534-16784-5*) Brooks-Cole.

Precalculus with Limits: A Graphing Approach. Roland E. Larson et al. 932p. (C). 1994. text 72.36 (*0-669-35251-9*) HM Trade Div.

Precalculus with Scientific Notebook. Jonathan Lewin. 310p. (C). 1997. per. 41.95 (*0-7872-3935-6*) Kendall-Hunt.

Precalculus with Unit Circle Trigonometry. 3rd ed. Cohen. (Mathematics Ser.). 1998. student ed. 21.00 (*0-534-35277-4*) Brooks-Cole.

***Precalculus with Unit-Circle Trigonometry.** 3rd ed. David Cohen. LC 97-27630. 1998. mass mkt. 86.95 (*0-534-35275-8*) Brooks-Cole.

Precalculus W/unit-circle Trigonometry. 2nd ed. David C. Cohen. Ed. by Marshall. LC 93-2612. (Math). 725p. (C). 1994. mass mkt. 53.50 (*0-314-01254-0*) West Pub.

PRECALCULUS 3RD EDITION. 3rd ed. Thomas W. Hungerford & Richard Mercer. 548p. (C). 1992. text 84.00 (*0-03-046929-5*) SCP.

Precalcus. Crabtree. 34.21 (*0-673-23434-7*, Scott Frsmn) Addson-Wesley Educ.

Precalulus. Michael Sullivan. LC 97-23427. 1100p. (C). 1997. 92.00 (*0-13-778499-6*) P-H.

Precambrian: Conterminous U. S. Ed. by John C. Reed, Jr. et al. LC 92-30479. (DNAG, Geology of North America Ser.: Vol. C2). 1993. 49.25 (*0-8137-5218-3*) Geol Soc.

Precambrian & Paleozoic Geology & Ore Deposits in the Midcontinental Region. Ed. by Hagni. (IGC Field Trip Guidebooks Ser.). 72p. 1989. 21.00 (*0-87590-588-9*, T147) Am Geophysical.

Precambrian Continental Crust & Its Economic Resources: Developments in Precambrian Geology, No. 13. Ed. by S. M. Naqvi. 690p. 1990. 201.25 (*0-444-88310-X*) Elsevier.

Precambrian Crustal Evolution in the North Atlantic Region. Ed. by T. S. Brewer. (Geological Society Special Publication Ser.: No. 112). (Illus.). 376p. 1996. 115.00 (*1-897799-62-4*, 245, Pub. by Geol Soc Pub Hse) AAPG.

Precambrian Crustal Evolution of China. Ed. by X. Ma & J. Bai. LC 98-4244. (Illus.). 336p. 1998. 159.00 (*3-540-61710-8*) Spr-Verlag.

Precambrian Empirical Metallogeny: Precambrian Lithologic Associations & Metallic Ores. P. Laznicka. (Developments in Economic Geology Ser.: Vol. 29). 1640p. 1993. 408.25 (*0-444-89953-7*) Elsevier.

Precambrian Geology: Proceedings of the 27th International Geological Congress, Vol. 5. International Geological Congress Staff. 362p. 1984. lib. bdg. 113.00 (*90-6764-014-X*) Coronet Bks.

Precambrian Geology: The Dynamic Evolution of the Continental Crust. Alan M. Goodwin. (Academic Press Geology Ser.). 666p. 1991. text 255.00 (*0-12-289870-2*) Acad Pr.

Precambrian Geology & Metamorphic Petrology see Proceedings of the 30th International Geological Congress

Precambrian Geology of North Snowy Block, Beartooth Mountains, Montana. Rolland R. Reid & William J. McMannis. LC 74-28529. (Geological Society of America, Special Paper: No. 157). 188p. reprint ed. pap. 58.30 (*0-608-13544-5*, 202547000044) Bks Demand.

Precambrian Geology of the U. S. S. R. Ed. by D. V. Rundqvist & F. P. Mitrofanov. LC 92-8594. 528p. 1993. 218.00 (*0-444-89380-6*) Elsevier.

Precambrian in Younger Fold Belts: European Variscides, the Carpathians & Balkans. fac. ed. Ed. by Vladimir Zoubek et al. LC 86-15974. (Illus.). 897p. 1988. pap. 200.00 (*0-7837-7659-4*, 204741200007) Bks Demand.

Precambrian Ore Deposits of the East European & Siberian Cratons. D. V. Rundkvist & Con Gillen. LC 97-38578. (Developments in Economic Geology Ser.). 1997. write for info. (*0-444-82657-2*) Elsevier.

Precambrian Rocks & Mineralization, Southern Wyoming Province. Ed. by George Snyder. (IGC Field Trip Guidebooks Ser.). 56p. 1989. 28.00 (*0-87590-613-3*, T332) Am Geophysical.

Precambrian Symposium: The Relationship of Mineralization to Precambrian Stratigraphy in Certain Mining Areas of Ontario & Quebec. Geological Association of Canada Staff. LC 68-43. (Geological Association of Canada. Special Paper: No. 3). 144p. reprint ed. pap. 44.70 (*0-608-17217-0*, 202783800056) Bks Demand.

Precambrian Tectonics Illustrated: Final Report. International Union of Geological Sciences, Commission on Tectonics, Subcommittee on Precambrian Structural Type Regions. Ed. by A. Kroener & R. Greiling. (Illus.). viii, 419p. 1984. pap. 111.00 (*3-510-65118-9*, Pub. by E Schweizerbartsche) Balogh.

Precambrian Tungsten & Copper-Zinc Skarn Deposits of South-Central Colorado. E. William Heinrich. (Resource Ser.: No. 21). (Illus.). 115p. (Orig.). 1981. pap. 3.00 (*1-884216-32-3*) Colo Geol Survey.

Precancer: Biology, Importance & Possible Prevention. Ed. by J. Ponten. (Cancer Surveys Ser.: No. 32). (Illus.). 238p. (C). 1998. text 93.00 (*0-87969-540-4*) Cold Spring Harbor.

Precancerous Lesions of the Gastrointestinal Tract. Ed. by Paul Sherlock et al. LC 82-24011. 344p. 1983. reprint ed. pap. 106.70 (*0-608-00430-8*, 206114500007) Bks Demand.

Precarious: The Art & Poetry of Cecilia Vicuna. Catherine M. de Zegher & Cecilia Vicona. Tr. by Esther Allen from SPA. LC 97-61784. (Wesleyan Poetry Ser.). (Illus.). 250p. 1997. 30.00 (*0-8195-6324-2*, Wesleyan Univ Pr) U Pr of New Eng.

Precarious Balance. 108p. 1998. pap. 25.00 (*3-928762-76-1*, Pub. by Richter Verlag) Dist Art Pubs.

Precarious Balance: Hong Kong Between China & Britain, 1842-1992. Ed. by Ming K. Chan. 248p. 1994. pap. 52.50 (*962-209-333-7*, Pub. by HK Univ Pr) Intl Spec Bk.

Precarious Balance: Hong Kong Between China & Britain, 1842-1992. Ed. by Ming K. Chan. LC 93-32290. (Hong Kong Becoming China: the Transition to 1997 Ser.). 235p. (gr. 13). 1994. 81.95 (*1-56324-380-6*, East Gate Bk); pap. 36.95 (*1-56324-381-4*, East Gate Bk) M E Sharpe.

Precarious Balance Vol. I: Democratic Consolidation & Economic Reform in Eastern Europe & Latin America. Ed. by Joan Nelson. LC 94-20970. 1994. pap. 19.95 (*1-55815-322-5*) ICS Pr.

Precarious Balance Vol. II: Democratic Consolidation & Economic Reform in Eastern Europe & Latin America. Ed. by Joan Nelson. 1994. pap. 19.95 (*1-55815-323-3*) ICS Pr.

Precarious Balances: The Middle Ages of the Next Millennium. Charles S. Goodwin. LC 98-56005. 540p. 1999. pap. 46.50 (*0-7618-1351-9*) U Pr of Amer.

Precarious Belonging: Presbyterians & the Conflict in Ireland. John Dunlop. 144p. 1996. pap. 16.95 (*0-85640-559-0*, Pub. by Blackstaff Pr) Dufour.

Precarious Dependencies: Gender, Class & Domestic Service in Bolivia. Lesley Gill. LC 94-5948. 1994. 55.50 (*0-231-09646-1*) Col U Pr.

Precarious Dependencies: Gender, Class & Domestic Service in Bolivia. Lesley Gill. LC 94-5948. 1994. pap. 19.00 (*0-231-09647-X*) Col U Pr.

Precarious Jobs in Labour Market Regulation: The Growth of Atypical Employment in Western Europe. Ed. by Gerry Rodgers & Janine Rodgers. x, 301p. (Orig.). 1989. pap. 22.50 (*92-9014-453-X*); pap. 31.50 (*92-9014-452-1*) Intl Labour Office.

Precarious Life of James Mario Matra: Voyager with Cook, American Loyalist, Servant of Empire. Alan Frost. (The Miegunyah Press Ser.: No. 2). 256p. 1996. 49.95 (*0-522-84667-X*, Pub. by Melbourne Univ Pr) Paul & Co Pubs.

Precarious Organisation: Sociological Explorations of the Church's Mission & Structure. Mady A. Thung. (Religion & Society Ser.: No. 5). 1976. text 32.35 (*90-279-7652-X*) Mouton.

Precarious Pond. Kambiz Azordegan. (Tootee's Magical Stories Ser.: Vol. 1). (Illus.). 40p. (J). 1998. 9.95 (*1-890571-25-3*) Parrot Prod.

Precarious Truce: Anglo-Soviet Relations, 1924-27. Gabriel Gorodetsky. LC 76-2279. (Soviet & East European Studies). 303p. reprint ed. pap. 86.40 (*0-608-17514-5*, 2030598) Bks Demand.

***Precarious Values: Organizations, Politics & Labour Market Policy in Ontario.** Thomas R. Klassen. (School of Policy Studies). 230p. 2000. pap. 24.95 (*0-88911-883-3*) Queens U Study Econ.

***Precarious Values: Organizations, Politics & Labour Market Policy in Ontario.** Thomas R. Klassen. 230p. 2000. text 55.00 (*0-88911-885-X*, Pub. by Queens U Inst Intergov) CUP Services.

Precarious Vision. Peter L. Berger. LC 76-1981. 238p. 1976. reprint ed. lib. bdg. 69.50 (*0-8371-8657-9*, BEPV, Greenwood Pr) Greenwood.

***Precast.** (Ironworking Lev 3 Ser.). 2000. teacher ed., ring bd. 12.00 (*0-13-031262-2*) P-H.

Precast & Prestressed Concrete for Justice Facilities. 56p. 1985. pap. 40.00 (*0-318-19722-7*, MK-6-85) P-PCI.

Precast Concrete: Handling & Erection. Joseph J. Waddell. LC 72-88703. (ACI Monograph Ser.: No. 8). (Illus.). 149p. reprint ed. pap. 46.20 (*0-608-18487-X*, 203300800082) Bks Demand.

Precast Concrete in Efficient Passive Solar Designs. (PCI Journal Reprints Ser.). 36p. 1983. pap. 20.00 (*0-318-19799-5*, JR288) P-PCI.

Precast Concrete Piles. 44p. 1985. 29.00 (*0-7277-0217-3*, Pub. by T Telford) RCH.

Precast Concrete Production. J. G. Richardson. 1977. pap. 50.00 (*0-7210-0912-3*, Pub. by C & CA) Scholium Intl.

Precast Concrete Raft Units. John W. Bull. 180p. 1991. mass mkt. 157.95 (*0-442-30296-7*, Osprey Bks) Chapman & Hall.

Precast Piling Practice. Bengt B. Broms. 132p. 1981. 25.00 (*0-7277-0121-5*, Pub. by T Telford) RCH.

Precast, Prestressed Box Beams: A State-of-the-Art Report. (PCI Journal Reprints Ser.). 25p. 1985. pap. 12.00 (*0-318-19740-5*, JR71) P-PCI.

Precast Prestressed Clinker Storage Silo Saves Time & Money. (PCI Journal Reprints Ser.). 20p. 1976. pap. 12.00 (*0-686-40089-5*, JR168) P-PCI.

Precast Prestressed Concrete Bridges for Low Volume Roads. 16p. 1985. pap. 12.00 (*0-318-19725-1*, JR-206) P-PCI.

Precast Prestressed Concrete Industry Code of Standard Practice for Precast Concrete. 19p. 1978. pap. 14.00 (*0-686-39952-8*, JR-195) P-PCI.

Precast Prestressed Concrete Short Span Bridges: Spans to 100 Feet. 2nd ed. 40p. 1985. pap. 15.00 (*0-937040-16-9*, SSB-1-85) P-PCI.

Precast Prestressed Hollow Core Floors. 38p. 1988. 47.00 (*0-7277-1375-2*) Am Soc Civil Eng.

Precast Prestressed "Space Mountain" Highlights Walt Disney World. (PCI Journal Reprints Ser.). 16p. 1975. pap. 12.00 (*0-686-40085-2*, JR165) P-PCI.

Precast Prestressed System Provides Solutions for Stadium Expansion. (PCI Journal Reprints Ser.). 16p. 1980. pap. 12.00 (*0-686-40124-7*, JR216) P-PCI.

Precast Prestressed Wall System Used for Water Storage Reservoir. (PCI Journal Reprints Ser.). 12p. 1985. pap. 12.00 (*0-318-19762-6*, JR229) P-PCI.

Precast Trapezoidal Girders Spliced with Post-Tensioning for Highway Underpass. Prestressed Concrete Institute Staff. (PCI Journal Reprints Ser.). 4p. 1980. pap. 8.00 (*0-318-19863-0*, JR219) P-PCI.

Precaution. James Fenimore Cooper. (Works of James Fenimore Cooper). 1990. reprint ed. lib. bdg. 79.00 (*0-7812-2369-5*) Rprt Serv.

Precaution. James Fenimore Cooper. LC 06-29686. reprint ed. 11.00 (*0-403-00101-3*) Scholarly.

Precaution, 2 vols., Set. James Fenimore Cooper. LC 73-1898. (BCL Ser.: No. I). reprint ed. 47.50 (*0-404-01707-X*) AMS Pr.

Precautionary Approach to Fisheries Pt. 2: Scientific Papers. (Fisheries Technical Papers: No. 350/2). 215p. 1996. pap. 26.00 (*92-5-103843-0*, F38430, Pub. by FAO) Bernan Associates.

Precautionary Labels for Chemical Containers. Neal Langerman. 176p. 1994. lib. bdg. 75.00 (*0-87371-917-4*, L917) Lewis Pubs.

Precautionary Legal Duties & Principles of Modern International Environmental Law: The Precautionary Principle: International Environmental Law Between Exploitation & Protection. Harald Hohmann. LC 94-17152. (International Environmental Law & Policy Ser.). 400p. (C). 1994. lib. bdg. 142.00 (*1-85333-911-3*, Pub. by Graham & Trotman) Kluwer Academic.

Precautionary Principle & International Law: The Challenge of Implementation. Ed. by David Freestone & Ellen Hey. (International Environmental Law & Policy Ser.: Vol. 31). 1995. 128.00 (*90-411-0143-8*) Kluwer Law Intl.

Precautions Against Death: Literature. Maria Jacobs. 1995. pap. 9.95 (*0-88962-209-4*) Mosaic.

Precautions in the Management of Patients Who Have Received Therapeutic Amounts of Radionuclides. LC 76-125343. (Report Ser.: No. 37). 66p. 1970. pap. text 25.00 (*0-913392-19-7*) NCRP Pubns.

Precedence: Poems. Rae Armantrout. 48p. 1985. pap. 5.00 (*0-930901-24-X*) Burning Deck.

Precedence & Arrow Networking Techniques for Construction. Robert B. Harris. LC 78-5786. 448p. 1978. text 103.95 (*0-471-04123-8*) Wiley.

Precedence Diagram: Successful Schedule in a Team Environment. Carl Pritchard. (Project Management Nuts & Bolts Ser.: Vol. 3). 1999. pap. write for info. (*1-890367-20-6*) ESI Int.

Precedence in England & Wales. George D. Squibb. 1981. 64.00 (*0-19-825389-3*) OUP.

Precedence Networks for Project Planning & Control. P. J. Burman. 1980. pap. text 20.00 (*0-9606344-0-1*) Blitz Pub Co.

Precedent & Law. Julius Stone. 312p. 1985. boxed set 76.00 (*0-409-49304-X*, Austral, MICHIE) LEXIS Pub.

Precedent for Peace: Ancient China's Strategy & a Plan for the Prevention of World War. Joseph A. Arminio. LC 96-77902. (Illus.). 400p. 1996. per. write for info. (*0-9644991-0-X*) Intrepid Pr.

Precedent in English Law. 4th ed. Sir Rupert Cross & J. W. Harris. (Clarendon Law Ser.). 256p. 1991. 75.00 (*0-19-876162-7*); pap. text 28.00 (*0-19-876163-5*) OUP.

Precedent in Law. Ed. by Laurence Goldstein. 296p. 1991. reprint ed. pap. 29.00 (*0-19-825724-4*) OUP.

P

An Asterisk (*) at the beginning of an entry indicates that the title is appearing for the first time.

Precedent in the Indian Legal System. A. Lakshminath. (C). 1989. 125.00 (*0-89771-768-6*, Pub. by Eastern Book); 125.00 (*0-89771-759-7*, Pub. by Eastern Book) St Mut.

Precedent in the Indian Legal System. A. Lakshminath. (C). 1990. text 125.00 (*0-89771-485-7*) St Mut.

Precedent in the World Court: Some Aspects. Mohamed Shahbuddeen. (Hersch Lauterpacht Memorial Lectures: No. 13). 265p. (C). 1996. text 74.95 (*0-521-56310-0*) Cambridge U Pr.

Precedent Inflation. Susan W. Brenner. 376p. (C). 1991. text 44.95 (*0-88738-440-4*) Transaction Pubs.

Precedents in Architecture. 2nd ed. Roger H. Clark & Michael Pause. (Architecture Ser.). 274p. 1996. 54.95 (*0-471-28703-2*, VNR) Wiley.

Precedents in Architecture. 2nd ed. Roger H. Clark & Michael Pause. (Architecture Ser.). (Illus.). 274p. 1996. text 44.95 (*0-442-02051-1*, VNR) Wiley.

Precedents, Statutes, & Analysis of Legal Concepts: Interpretation. Ed. by Scott Brewer & Robert Nozick. LC 98-5170. (Philosophy of Legal Reasoning Ser.: No. 2). 400p. 1998. reprint ed. text 75.00 (*0-8153-2656-4*) Garland.

Precept & Example. (C). 1995. 18.00 (*0-8087-2463-0*) Pearson Custom.

***Precepting Medical Students in the Office.** Paul M. Paulman. 2000. pap. 19.95 (*0-8018-6366-X*) Johns Hopkins.

Preceptor Education Project: Instructor's Manual. 1992. teacher ed. 100.00 (*0-614-23627-4*) Soc Tchrs Fam Med.

Preceptor Education Project Workbook. 1992. student ed. 20.00 (*0-614-23628-2*) Soc Tchrs Fam Med.

Preceptor for Piano-Forte, the Organ or Harpsichord. fac. ed. (Monuments of Music & Music Literature in Facsimile Ser., Series I: Vol. 16). 1967. lib. bdg. 37.50 (*0-8450-2016-1*) Broude.

***Preceptor Program.** Crowe. (Illus.). 128p. (C). 2000. pap. text, teacher ed. 62.50 (*0-7637-1222-1*) JB Pubns.

***Preceptor Program.** Tom Crowe. (Illus.). 128p. (C). 2000. pap. text, teacher ed. 31.25 (*0-7637-1226-4*) JB Pubns.

***Preceptor Program Intern Manual.** Tom Crowe. (Illus.). 96p. (C). 2000. pap. text 25.00 (*0-7637-1227-2*) JB Pubns.

Preceptors As Teachers: A Guide to Clinical Teaching. Neal A. Whitman & Thomas L. Schwenk. 30p. (Orig.). (C). 1995. reprint ed. pap. text 10.00 (*0-940193-04-3*) Univ UT Sch Med.

Preceptrol. 24p. 1992. pap. text. write for info. (*0-930009-45-2*) ATCC.

Precepts & Doctrines of Men. Duane Radcliffe & Marcus Ross. LC 97-91301. 1998. pap. 18.95 (*0-533-12622-3*) Vantage.

***Precepts for Living, 1998-1999 Vol. I: The UMI Annual Sunday School Lesson Commentary.** Okechukwu Ogbonnaya. (Illus.). 470p. 1998. text 13.50 (*0-940955-46-6*, 11-1998) Urban Ministries.

***Precepts for Living, 1999-2000 Vol. II: The UMI Annual Sunday School Lesson Commentary.** Okechukwu Ogbonnaya. 560p. 1999. text 13.50 (*0-940955-57-1*, 11-1999) Urban Ministries.

Precepts for Practice. Malcolm C. Fry. (Way of Life Ser.). 1971. teacher ed. 6.95 (*0-89265-005-2*); pap. 6.95 (*0-89265-004-4*) Randall Hse.

Precepts for the Young. Ann R. Colton. LC 68-335. 66p. (J). (gr. 1-8). 1959. pap. 2.50 (*0-917187-15-6*) A R Colton Fnd.

Precepts of the Church. (Saint Joseph Picture Bks.). (Illus.). 1987. pap. 1.25 (*0-89942-395-7*, 395-00) Catholic Bk Pub.

Prechelonian: A Literary & Fine Art Magazine. unabridged ed. Derek Pollard et al. 30p. 1999. mass mkt. 5.00 (*0-9665407-4-3*) Bl Nght Pr.

Prechter's Perspective. Robert R. Prechter, Jr. Ed. by Peter Kendall. LC 95-72498. 267p. 1996. pap. 19.00 (*0-932750-40-0*) New Classics Lib.

Precieuses et Autres Indociles. Carlo Francois & Georgette Falleur. LC 87-61484. (FRE.). 147p. 1987. lib. bdg. 21.95 (*0-917786-55-6*) Summa Pubns.

Precieuses Ridicules. Moliere. (FRE.). 1965. pap. 7.95 (*0-8288-9944-4*, F40042) Fr & Eur.

Precinct Command. Christopher Newman. 1993. mass mkt. 5.99 (*0-449-14795-9*, GM) Fawcett.

Precinct Kali & the Gertrude Spicer Story: Poems. James Bertolino. 116p. 1981. pap. 4.00 (*0-89823-034-9*) New Rivers Pr.

Precinct-Level Voting Returns for Major Races in the 1972 Primary Election in South Dakota. Alan L. Clem. 1972. 5.00 (*1-55614-082-7*) U of SD Gov Res Bur.

Precinct-Level Voting Returns for Major Races in the 1974 Primary Election in South Dakota. Alan L. Clem. 1975. 5.00 (*1-55614-083-5*) U of SD Gov Res Bur.

***Precinct Manual, 2000.** Robert P. Joyce. (C). 2000. pap. write for info. (*1-56011-369-3*) Institute Government.

Precinct Returns for Major Elections in South Dakota, 1968. Alan L. Clem. 1969. 5.00 (*1-55614-084-3*) U of SD Gov Res Bur.

Precinct Returns for Major Elections in South Dakota, 1972. Alan L. Clem. 1973. 5.00 (*1-55614-085-1*) U of SD Gov Res Bur.

Precinct Returns for the Nineteen Seventy-Six General Election in South Dakota. Alan L. Clem. 5.00 (*1-55614-087-8*) U of SD Gov Res Bur.

Precinct Voting. Alan L. Clem. 1964. write for info. (*1-55614-088-6*) U of SD Gov Res Bur.

***Precio de la Uncion.** Juan J. Churruarin. (SPA.). 1999. pap. text 6.99 (*0-8297-0913-4*) Vida Pubs.

Precio de un Marido. Diana Hamilton. (Harlequin Bianca Ser.: Vol. 155).Tr. of A Husband's Price. (SPA.). 156p. 1999. per. 3.50 (*0-373-33505-9*, 1-33505-8) Harlequin Bks.

***Precio del Paraiso.** Miguel Leguineche. (SPA.). 1998. pap. 9.95 (*84-8326-005-0*) E Martinez Roca.

Precio Del Placer. Alan L. Clem. 1975. 1.00 (*1-55614-086-X*) U of SD Gov Res Bur.

Precio del Placer. Harold Robbins. (SPA.). 256p. 1992. pap. 3.95 (*1-56780-155-2*) La Costa Pr.

Precios de Cuenta: Principios, Metodologia y Estudios de Casa. Ed. by Elio Londero. 438p. 1992. 21.50 (*0-940602-53-9*) IADB.

Precious Amber. Kathleen Drymon. 1996. mass mkt. 4.99 (*0-8217-5328-2*, Zebra Kensgtn) Kensgtn Pub Corp.

Precious & Fashion Jewelry Markets: Past Performance, Current Trends & Opportunities for Growth. 718p. 1997. 1095.00 (*0-317-55194-9*) Busn Trend.

Precious & Few. Don Breithaupt. LC 96-24779. (Illus.). 176p. 1996. pap. 9.95 (*0-312-14704-X*) St Martin.

Precious & Semi-Precious Stones. Michael Weinstein. 1977. 250.00 (*0-8490-2465-X*) Gordon Pr.

Precious Angels: A True Story of Two Slain Children & a Mother Convicted of Murder, 1 vol. Barbara Davis. LC 99-187309. 1999. mass mkt. 6.99 (*0-451-40853-5*, Onyx) NAL.

Precious Are God's Plans. Lea Fowler. 1986. 6.95 (*0-89137-440-X*) Quality Pubns.

Precious Are His Sheep. Lea Fowler. 1992. pap. 6.35 (*0-89137-463-9*) Quality Pubns.

Precious Bane. Meryl Friedman & Mary Webb. 96p. 1998. pap. 5.60 (*0-87129-799-X*, P84) Dramatic Pub.

Precious Bane. Mary Webb. lib. bdg. 25.95 (*0-8488-2079-7*) Amereon Ltd.

Precious Bane. large type ed. Mary Webb. 1988. 27.99 (*0-7089-8508-4*, Charnwood) Ulverscroft.

Precious Bane. Mary Webb. LC 80-50272. (Illus.). 320p. 1980. reprint ed. pap. 14.00 (*0-268-01538-4*) U of Notre Dame Pr.

***Precious Bane, Set.** unabridged ed. Mary Webb. (YA). (gr. 10 up). 1998. 41.95 incl. audio (*1-55685-568-0*) Audio Bk Con.

Precious Bane: Collins & the Miltonic Legacy. Paul S. Sherwin. LC 77-542. 147p. reprint ed. pap. 45.60 (*0-8357-7762-6*, 203612000002) Bks Demand.

Precious Blood. Pat Graversen. 256p. 1993. mass mkt. 4.50 (*0-8217-4293-0*, Zebra Kensgtn) Kensgtn Pub Corp.

Precious Blood. Bill O'Sullivan. LC 91-47500. 202p. 1992. 18.95 (*0-939149-67-2*) Soho Press.

Precious Blood. Frederick W. Faber. LC 78-66300. 1979. reprint ed. pap. 13.50 (*0-89555-075-X*) TAN Bks Pubs.

Precious Blood & the Angels see St. Michael & the Angels

Precious Blood of Christ. 19p. 1979. pap. 0.75 (*1-57593-986-X*, 18-019-001) Living Stream Ministry.

Precious Blood of Jesus. John E. Doonan. 37p. 1998. 5.00 (*1-893437-00-0*) Amazing Grace Pubg.

Precious Blood of Jesus. Kenneth E. Hagin. 32p. 1984. pap. 1.00 (*0-89276-263-2*) Faith Lib Pubns.

Precious Cargo: The Scots Behind the China Trade. Susan Leiper. 112p. 1997. pap. 22.50 (*0-948636-90-4*, 904, Pub. by Natl Mus Scotland) A Schwartz & Co.

Precious Creatures A-Z. Stuart A. Kallen. Ed. by Julie Berg. LC 93-19060. (Target Earth Ser.). (J). 1993. pap. 7.49 (*1-56239-417-7*) ABDO Pub Co.

Precious Creatures A-Z. Stuart A. Kallen. Ed. by Julie Berg. LC 93-19060. (Target Earth Ser.). (Illus.). 64p. (J). (ps-7). 1993. lib. bdg. 15.98 (*1-56239-202-6*) ABDO Pub Co.

Precious Damsels see Seventeenth Century French Drama

***Precious Days & Practical Love: Caring for Your Aging Parent.** James Taylor. 224p. 1999. pap. 15.95 (*1-896836-34-8*, Pub. by NStone Publ) ACCESS Pubs Network.

Precious Dead. F. Keith Wahle. (Illus.). 1973. 4.00 (*0-685-67931-4*) Windless Orchard.

Precious December Days. unabridged ed. Lea Fowler. 82p. 1996. pap. 6.50 (*0-89137-470-1*, 74701) Quality Pubns.

Precious Dust: The Saga of the Western Gold Rushes. Paula M. Marks. LC 97-50203. (Illus.). 448p. 1998. pap. 17.95 (*0-8032-8247-8*, Bison Books) U of Nebr Pr.

Precious Family Memories of Elvis: A Personal Scrapbook. Edie Hand et al. 64p. (Orig.). 1997. pap. 7.95 (*0-9657008-0-1*) Hand N Hand.

Precious Garland. Gampopa. 72p. 1996. pap. 10.00 (*0-614-22194-3*, Pub. by Rang Jung Yshe) Bookpeople.

Precious Gem in the Tabernacle. 9th ed. B. R. Hicks. (Illus.). 367p. 1961. reprint ed. 17.95 (*1-58363-067-8*, JM-3306) Christ Gospel.

Precious GEMs: Groundwater Education Strategies That Work. 80p. pap. text 40.00 (*0-7881-1596-0*) DIANE Pub.

Precious Gift. Tr. by Raja A. Ahmad et al. Orig. Title: Tuhft al-Nafis. (Illus.). 1982. 55.00 (*0-19-582507-1*) OUP.

Precious Gift. Ellen B. Jackson. (J). 1998. 16.00 (*0-671-89725-X*) S&S Bks Yung.

Precious Gift: A Navajo Creation Myth. Ellen B. Jackson. (Illus.). 40p. (J). (ps-3). 1996. mass mkt. 16.00 (*0-689-80480-6*) Atheneum Yung Read.

Precious Gift: Under the Mistletoe. Jayne Addison. (Romance Ser.). 1993. per. 2.75 (*0-373-08980-5*, 5-08980-0) Silhouette.

***Precious Gold, Precious Jade.** Sharon Heisel. LC 98-27876. 208p. (J). 2000. 16.95 (*0-8234-1432-9*) Holiday.

***Precious Greenstone, Precious Feather: In Chalchihuitl in Quetzalli: Mesoamerican Studies in Honor of Doris Heyden.** Ed. by Eloise Quinones Keber. 180p. 2000. pap. 40.00 (*0-911437-84-3*) Labyrinthos.

***Precious Heart.** Doris Johnson. 2000. mass mkt. 5.99 (*1-58314-083-2*) BET Bks.

***Precious Heritage: The Status of Biodiversity in the United States.** Ed. by Bruce A. Stein et al. LC 99-30213. (Illus.). 416p. 2000. 45.00 (*0-19-512519-3*) OUP.

***Precious in His Sight.** 1999. 7.95 (*1-57734-586-X*, 01114417) Covenant Comms.

Precious in His Sight: A Guide to Child Advocacy. 2nd rev. ed. Diana Garland. LC 96-204387. 210p. 1996. pap. text 10.95 (*1-56309-187-9*, N967117, New Hope) Womans Mission Union.

Precious in His Sight: Childhood & Children in the Bible. Roy B. Zuck. LC 96-25788. 288p. (gr. 10). 1996. pap. 19.99 (*0-8010-5715-9*) Baker Bks.

Precious in His Sight: Prayers of the Children of the World. Photos by David Dobson. LC 98-109801. (Illus.). 112p. 1997. 14.99 (*0-8499-5334-0*) Word Pub.

Precious in the Father's Sight. abr. ed. Catherine Marshall. (Pocket Devotion Ser.). (Illus.). 384p. 1997. 9.99 (*0-8007-7158-3*, Day by Day with) Revell.

Precious in the Sight of God. Lea Fowler. 1983. pap. 6.90 (*0-89137-428-0*) Quality Pubns.

***Precious Inheritance.** Emily Dalton. 2000. per. 4.25 (*0-373-16823-3*) Harlequin Bks.

Precious Irony: The Theatre of Jean Giraudoux. Paul A. Mankin. LC 78-165146. (Studies in French Literature: No. 19). 195p. (Orig.). 1971. pap. text 40.00 (*90-279-1918-6*) Mouton.

Precious Jewel Person: Reflections on the Spirituality of Everyday Life. Barbara R. Garrison. LC 90-62136. 144p. (Orig.). 1990. pap. 8.95 (*0-914070-99-1*, 118) ACTA Pubns.

Precious Jewels of Tibet: A Journey to the Roof of the World. Jane Bay. LC 98-12269. 208p. 1998. pap. 14.95 (*1-57416-004-4*) Clear Light.

Precious Life. Illus. by Rosalyn White. LC 88-33455. (Jataka Tales Ser.). 32p. (Orig.). (J). (ps-3). 1989. pap. 7.95 (*0-89800-185-4*) Dharma Pub.

Precious Little One, 1. Erika MacArthur. 1998. 20.00 (*1-58134-001-X*) Crossway Bks.

Precious Little Spice Box & Other Stories. Gershon Kranzler. (Illus.). 110p. (YA). 1988. 11.00 (*0-8266-0347-5*, Merkos LInyonei Chinuch) Kehot Pubn Soc.

***Precious Lives.** large type ed. Margaret Forster. LC 99-14890. 307p. 1999. 22.95 (*0-7862-1984-X*) Mac Lib Ref.

Precious Lives Painful Choices: A Prenatal Decision-Making Guide. 3rd ed. Sherokee Ilse. 88p. (Orig.). 1995. reprint ed. pap. 9.95 (*0-9609456-9-5*) Wntergrn.

Precious Lord. Arnold Sevier. 1.25 (*0-687-06178-4*) Abingdon.

Precious Lord! How to Play Black Gospel, Bk. 1. 2nd ed. Robert L. Jefferson. 119p. 1995. 24.95 (*1-880549-04-2*) Pensacola Pubns.

Precious Lord! How to Play Soul Gospel, Tape 1. Robert L. Jefferson. 125p. 1992. audio 9.95 (*1-880549-02-6*) Pensacola Pubns.

Precious Love. Vella Munn. 288p. 1995. mass mkt. 4.99 (*0-8217-0124-X*, Zebra Kensgtn) Kensgtn Pub Corp.

Precious Love. large type ed. Vella Munn. (Black Satin Romance Ser.). 353p. 1996. 27.99 (*1-86110-014-0*) Ulverscroft.

Precious Memories. Gladys Allende. 160p. 1997. pap. 13.00 (*0-8059-4217-3*) Dorrance.

Precious Memories. Deborah Cole & Daniel Demoss. Ed. by Charles E. Norris. 135p. (Orig.). 1995. pap. 10.95 (*0-9647602-0-7*) Heartworks.

Precious Memories. Hazel S. Cotton. 90p. (Orig.). 1996. pap. write for info. (*1-57502-255-9*, P0937) Morris Pubng.

Precious Memories. Friedman. 1996. text 14.95 (*1-56799-407-5*) M Friedman Pub Grp Inc.

Precious Memories. James P. Massey. Ed. by David B. Reyner & Carole J. Massey-Reyner. LC 96-94328. (Collective Works of James P. Massey Ser.: Vol. IV). 105p. (Orig.). 1996. pap. 14.95 (*0-9650514-3-9*) Massey-Reyner.

Precious Memories. 2nd ed. Josephine Fitzgerald. LC 93-86523. (Illus.). 160p. (Orig.). 1994. reprint ed. pap. 7.95 (*0-910487-28-6*) Royalty Pub.

Precious Memories. 3rd ed. Josephine Fitzgerald. 160p. (Orig.). 1997. pap. 7.95 (*0-910487-42-1*) Royalty Pub.

Precious Memories, Vol. 1. rev. ed. Deborah Cole & Daniel Demoss. Ed. by Charles E. Norris. 140p. (Orig.). 1995. reprint ed. pap. 10.95 (*0-9647602-1-5*) Heartworks.

Precious Memories: Girl/Boy. David Roper. 1987. pap. 2.75 (*0-89137-443-4*) Quality Pubns.

Precious Memories: The Life of a Minister. William W. Cutlip. Ed. by Beverly H. Erickson. LC 95-60695. (Illus.). 300p. 1996. write for info. (*1-885527-03-9*) Feather Fables.

Precious Memories of a Black Socialite: A Narrative of the Life & Times of Constance Houston Thompson. Naomi W. Lede. LC 91-65957. 300p. (Orig.). 1991. 24.95 (*0-9630007-0-5*) Lede Consult.

Precious Memories of a Black Socialite: Narrative on the Life & Times of Constance Houston Thompson. 300p. 1991. 24.95 (*0-614-30078-9*) NAAMAC.

Precious Metal Databook. Ed. by Richard Serjeantson. 250p. (Orig.). 1989. pap. text 144.00 (*0-947671-24-2*) Metal Bulletin.

***Precious Metal Jewelry in Japan: A Strategic Entry Report, 1998.** Compiled by Icon Group International Staff. (Country Industry Report). (Illus.). 155p. 1999. ring bd. 1550.00 incl. audio compact disk (*0-7418-0503-0*) Icon Grp.

Precious Metals: Minerals & Health. Ed. by Laura Pawlak & Marjorie Freedman. 108p. 1998. pap. 10.00 (*1-893549-05-4*) Biomed Genl.

Precious Metals: Mining, Extraction, & Processing: Proceedings of an International Symposium Held at the AIME Annual Meeting, Los Angeles, CA, February 27-29, 1984. International Symposium on Precious Metals Staff. Ed. by Val Kudryk et al. LC 83-63270. 633p. reprint ed. pap. 196.30 (*0-8357-2515-4*, 205239500013) Bks Demand.

Precious Metals & Commerce. Om Prakash. (Collected Studies: No. CS 443). 312p. 1994. 101.95 (*0-86078-434-7*, Pub. by Variorum) Ashgate Pub Co.

Precious Metals, Coinage & Changes of Monetary Structures in Latin America, Europe & Asia: Late Middle Ages - Early Modern Times. Ed. by E. Van Cauwenberghe. (Studies in Social & Economic History: No. 2). 222p. (Orig.). 1989. pap. 47.50 (*90-6186-335-X*, Pub. by Leuven Univ) Coronet Bks.

Precious Metals, '89: Proceedings of an. fac. ed. Minerals, Metals & Materials Society Staff. LC 88-62441. (Illus.). 533p. 1988. pap. 165.30 (*0-7837-8606-9*, 205253700008) Bks Demand.

Precious Metals (Gold, Silver & Platinum) Industry & Trade Summary. Deborah McNay. (Illus.). 45p. (Orig.). (C). 1995. pap. text 30.00 (*0-7881-2103-0*) DIANE Pub.

Precious Metals Guide to Trading. Anthony George Gero. 1985. 12.00 (*0-8184-0371-3*) Carol Pub Group.

Precious Metals Processing & Mineral Waste & the Environment see Proceedings of the XIX International Mineral Processing Congress

Precious Metals Trade Guide - Adventure in Noble Metals: A to Z Reference Source. James W. Bushnell. Ed. by Lieselotte Bushnell. (Illus.). 248p. (Orig.). (C). 1993. per. 22.50 (*0-9632771-0-3*) Trident Pubns.

Precious Mom: Living for God. 1997. pap. text 9.99 (*1-55976-182-2*) CEF Press.

Precious Moments. (J). pap. 2.99 (*0-307-05539-6*, 05539, Goldn Books) Gldn Bks Pub Co.

Precious Moments. Golden Books Staff. (Super Coloring Book Ser.). 70p. (J). 1995. pap. text 2.29 (*0-307-03216-7*, 03216, Goldn Books) Gldn Bks Pub Co.

Precious Moments: Book of Prayers. Regina Press Staff. 1992. 15.95 (*0-88271-276-4*) Regina Pr.

***Precious Moments: Jonah & the whale.** LC 99-89383. 2000. text. write for info. (*0-8010-4419-7*) Baker Bks.

Precious Moments: Little Blessings. Stephen R. Covey. (Super Shape Bks.). (Illus.). 24p. (J). (ps-3). 1996. pap. text 3.29 (*0-307-10001-4*, 10001, Goldn Books) Gldn Bks Pub Co.

Precious Moments: Little Prayers. Alan Benjamin. LC 97-70653. (Naptime Tales Bks.). (Illus.). 16p. (J). (ps). 1997. bds. 3.99 (*0-307-12829-6*, 12829, Goldn Books) Gldn Bks Pub Co.

Precious Moments: Little Thank-Yous. Alan Benjamin. LC 97-70280. (Naptime Tales Bks.). (Illus.). 16p. (J). (ps). 1997. bds. 3.99 (*0-307-12831-8*, 12831, Goldn Books) Gldn Bks Pub Co.

Precious Moments: My First Book of Prayers. Regina Press Staff. (J). 1992. 6.95 (*0-88271-277-2*) Regina Pr.

Precious Moments: My First Holy Communion - Girls. Victor Hoagland. 1992. 15.92 (*0-88271-279-9*); pap. 12.95 (*0-88271-281-0*) Regina Pr.

Precious Moments: Remembrance of My First Holy Communion - Boys. Victor Hoagland. 1992. 15.95 (*0-88271-278-0*); pap. 12.95 (*0-88271-280-2*) Regina Pr.

Precious Moments: Very Shy Angel. Joanne De Jonge. LC 97-24113. (Precious Moments for Children Ser.). (Illus.). 128p. (J). (gr. 2 up). 1998. 14.99 (*0-8010-4295-X*) Baker Bks.

Precious Moments Catholic Ed. My First Book of Prayers. Regina Press Staff. (Precious Moments Ser.). (J). 1991. 8.95 (*0-88271-275-6*) Regina Pr.

Precious Moments Activity Art Tablet. Dalmatian Press Staff. (Precious Moments Ser.). (Illus.). (J). 1998. pap. 2.29 (*1-57759-057-0*) Dalmatian Pr.

Precious Moments Activity Fun Tablet. Dalmatian Press Staff. (Precious Moments Ser.). (J). 1998. pap. 2.29 (*1-57759-058-9*) Dalmatian Pr.

***Precious Moments Addition & Subtraction.** Dalmatian Press Staff. (Precious Moments Workbooks Ser.). (Illus.). (J). 2000. pap. 2.99 (*1-57759-290-5*) Dalmatian Pr.

Precious Moments Baby Bible. (Illus.). 1108p. (ps-k). 1999. 19.99 (*0-7852-0040-1*) Nelson.

***Precious Moments Baby Bible for Catholics.** NelsonWord Staff. (Illus.). (J). 1999. 19.99 (*0-7852-0083-5*) Nelson.

Precious Moments Baby Record Book: Catholic Ed. Date not set. 17.95 (*0-88271-289-6*, 1940) Regina Pr.

Precious Moments Bible. 1999. 24.99 (*0-7852-0048-7*); 24.99 (*0-7852-0049-5*); 24.99 (*0-7852-0050-9*) Nelson.

***Precious Moments Bible.** 2000. 24.99 (*0-7852-5507-9*) W1CL.

***Precious Moments Bible.** Nelson Word Publishing Group Staff. (Illus.). 1104p. (ps-3). 2000. 24.99 (*0-7852-0453-9*); 24.99 (*0-7852-0485-7*) W1CL.

***Precious Moments Bible for Catholics.** 1999. 24.99 (*0-7852-0052-5*); pap. 24.99 (*0-7852-0053-3*) Nelson.

***Precious Moments Bible for Catholics.** Catholic PM Staff. 1999. pap. text 24.99 (*0-7852-0054-1*) Word Pub.

Precious Moments Bible Promises. 2nd rev. ed. Illus. by Sam Butcher. LC 97-27093. 32p. (J). (ps-2). 1997. 10.99 (*0-8499-1463-9*) Tommy Nelson.

***Precious Moments Bible Stories.** Samuel J. Butcher. LC 00-29737. (Illus.). (J). 2000. write for info. (*0-8010-4447-2*) Baker Bks.

Precious Moments Bible Stories: Old Testament. Samuel J. Butcher. LC BS551.2.P75 1999. (Precious Moments for Children Ser.). (Illus.). 32p. (J). (ps-2). 1999. 9.99 (*0-8010-4427-8*) Baker Bks.

Precious Moments Boxed Set: The Four Seasons, 4 bks. (J). 1999. bds. 19.95 (*1-57145-362-8*, Silver Dolph) Advantage Pubs.

Precious Moments Boy's Communion Remembrance Gift Book. deluxe gif. ed. (J). Date not set. write for info. (*0-88271-294-2*, 1900/290) Regina Pr.

P

Precious Moments Caring Angels. Helen Steiner Rice. LC 94-17006. (Illus.). 64p. (gr. 11). 1994. 11.99 (0-8007-7139-7) Revell.

Precious Moments Christmas. 2nd rev. ed. Illus. by Sam Butcher. LC 97-22769. 32p. (J). (ps-2). 1997. 10.99 (0-8499-1517-1) Tommy Nelson.

Precious Moments Christmas Angels. Helen Steiner Rice. LC 94-17018. (Illus.). 64p. (gr. 11). 1994. 11.99 (0-8007-7140-0) Revell.

***Precious Moments Christmas Play.** Joanne De Jonge. LC 99-29927. (Illus.). 32p. (J). (gr. k-4). 1999. 9.99 (0-8010-4424-3) Baker Bks.

***Precious Moments Easter.** Joanne De Jonge. LC BT481.D385 1998. (Precious Moments for Children Ser.). 32p. (J). 2000. 9.99 (0-8010-4418-9) Baker Bks.

Precious Moments Gift of Love. 2nd rev. ed. Illus. by Sam Butcher. LC 97-22774. 32p. (J). (ps-2). 1997. 10.99 (0-8499-1523-6) Tommy Nelson.

Precious Moments Girl's Communion Remembrance Gift Book. deluxe gif. ed. (J). Date not set. write for info. (0-88271-295-0, 1900/292) Regina Pr.

Precious Moments in Plastic Canvas, Bk. 10. Leisure Arts Staff. (Illus.). 96p. 1997. pap. 16.95 (1-57486-051-8, 1763) Leisure AR.

Precious Moments Iron-on Transfers. Leisure Arts Staff. (Illus.). 170p. 1996. pap. 16.95 (1-57486-011-9, 1649) Leisure AR.

Precious Moments Iron-On Transfers, Book 2. 169p. 1996. pap. 16.95 (1-57486-015-1) Leisure AR.

Precious Moments Last Forever. Laura C. Martin. LC 94-27040. (Illus.). 304p. 1994. 17.98 (1-55859-859-6) Abbeville Pr.

Precious Moments Last Forever. Laura C. Martin. (Illus.). 304p. 1997. 17.98 (0-89660-083-1, Artabras) Abbeville Pr.

***Precious Moments Lowercase Alphabet.** Dalmatian Press Staff. (Precious Moments Ser.). (Illus.). (J). (ps-3). 1999. pap., wbk. ed. 2.99 (1-57759-208-5) Dalmatian Pr.

***Precious Moments Lowercase Colors & Shapes.** Dalmatian Press Staff. (Precious Moments Ser.). (Illus.). (J). (ps-3). 1999. pap., wbk. ed. 2.99 (1-57759-207-7) Dalmatian Pr.

Precious Moments My First Book of Prayers: Catholic Edition - Boy. gif. ed. (J). Date not set. 12.95 (0-88271-518-6, 1900/190) Regina Pr.

Precious Moments My First Book of Prayers: Catholic Edition - Girl. gif. ed. (J). Date not set. 12.95 (0-88271-519-4, 1900/192) Regina Pr.

Precious Moments My First Book of Prayers: Catholic Edition Baptismal Remembrance Edition Girl's Edition. (J). 12.95 (0-614-24936-8); 12.95 (0-614-24963-5) Regina Pr.

Precious Moments My First Book of Prayers: Gift Edition - Boy. deluxe gif. ed. (J). Date not set. 12.95 (0-88271-516-X, 1903/190) Regina Pr.

Precious Moments My First Book of Prayers: Gift Edition - Girl. deluxe gif. ed. (J). Date not set. 12.95 (0-88271-517-8, 1903/192) Regina Pr.

Precious Moments My Guardian Angel. Regina Staff. (J). (ps-3). 9.95 (0-88271-288-8) Regina Pr.

Precious Moments 1999 Value Guide. CheckerBee Publishing Staff. (Illus.). 287p. 1999. pap. 19.95 (1-888914-44-0) CheckerBee.

Precious Moments Nursery Rhymes. Sam Butcher. LC PZ8.3.P88935 1999. (Precious Moments Ser.). (Illus.). 32p. (J). (ps-3). 1999. 9.99 (0-8010-4426-X) Baker Bks.

Precious Moments of Celebration. Helen Steiner Rice. LC 93-6575. (Illus.). 64p. (gr. 11). 1993. 11.99 (0-8007-1691-4) Revell.

Precious Moments Pocket Prayerbook. Date not set. 1.50 (0-88271-290-X, 1990) Regina Pr.

Precious Moments Prayers for Boys & Girls. Regina Staff. (J). (ps-3). bds. 3.95 (0-88271-291-8) Regina Pr.

Precious Moments, Prayers for Boys & Girls. 2nd rev. ed. Illus. by Sam Butcher. LC 97-27093. 32p. (J). (ps-2). 1997. 10.99 (0-8499-1476-0) Tommy Nelson.

***Precious Moments Reading Readiness.** Dalmatian Press Staff. (Precious Moments Workbooks Ser.). (Illus.). (J). 2000. pap. 2.99 (1-57759-288-3) Dalmatian Pr.

***Precious Moments Seasons, Vol. 4.** C. E. F. Press Publishing Staff. (Illus.). 1999. pap. text 19.95 (1-55976-190-3) CEF Press.

Precious Moments Small Hands Bible. 1999. 19.99 (0-7852-0042-8) Nelson.

Precious Moments Small Hands Bible. 1999. 19.99 (0-7852-0043-6) Tommy Nelson.

***Precious Moments Small Hands Bible.** Thomas Nelson Publishing Staff. (J). 1999. 16.97 (0-7852-0044-4) Nelson.

***Precious Moments Small Hands Bible: Supersaver Edition.** Nelson Word Publishing Staff. 1999. 16.97 (0-7852-0045-2) Nelson.

Precious Moments Spring Value Guide, 1998. Joe T. Nguyen et al. (Illus.). 240p. 1998. pap. 19.95 (1-888914-11-4) CheckerBee.

Precious Moments Stories from the Bible. Sheri D. Haan. LC 78-97507. (Precious Moments for Children Ser.). (Illus.). 286p. (J). (gr. 1-6). 1992. 16.99 (0-8010-4311-5) Baker Bks.

Precious Moments Stories from the Bible. Sheri D. Haan. LC 78-97507. (Precious Moments for Children Ser.). (Illus.). 288p. (J). (gr. k-7). 1995. pap. 12.99 (0-8010-4085-X) Baker Bks.

Precious Moments Storybook Collection: Stories That Celebrate Everyday Joys. V. Gilbert Beers. (Illus.). 416p. (J). 1997. 19.99 (0-88486-182-1, Inspirational Pr) Arrowood Pr.

***Precious Moments Storybook Treasury.** Illus. by Samuel J. Butcher. (Precious Moments for Children Ser.). 384p. (J). (gr. k-7). 2000. text 24.99 (0-8010-4458-8, Precious Moment) Baker Bks.

Precious Moments Through-the-Day Stories. Gilbert V. Beers. LC 90-1265. (Precious Moments for Children Ser.). (Illus.). 256p. (J). (gr. k-7). 1991. pap. 12.99 (0-8010-4099-X) Baker Bks.

***Precious Moments Transition Math.** Dalmatian Press Staff. (Precious Moments Workbooks Ser.). (Illus.). (J). 2000. pap. 2.99 (1-57759-289-1) Dalmatian Pr.

Precious Moments Twelve Days of Christmas. LC 98-37895. (Precious Moments for Children Ser.). (Illus.). 32p. (J). (ps-2). 1998. 9.99 (0-8010-4410-3) Baker Bks.

***Precious Moments 2000.** 3rd ed. CheckerBee Publishing Staff. (Illus.). 240p. 2000. pap. 19.95 (1-888914-84-X) CheckerBee.

Precious Mother, Precious Crown: The Life & Mission of Elizabeth Taylor Watkins. F. Calvin Parker. 336p. 1997. pap. 16.95 (1-57087-343-7) Prof Pr NC.

Precious Nonsense: The Gettysburg Address, Ben Jonson's Epitaphs on His Children, & Twelfth Night. Stephen Booth. LC 97-27979. 216p. 1998. 35.00 (0-520-21288-6, Pub. by U CA Pr) Cal Prin Full Svc.

***Precious Passion.** Elizabeth Doyle. 1999. mass mkt. 4.99 (0-8217-6446-2) Kensgtn Pub Corp.

Precious Pearl. Abd al-Rahman al-Jami. Tr. by Nicholas L. Heer from ARA. LC 78-12607. 237p. (C). 1992. pap. text 18.95 (0-7914-1490-6) State U NY Pr.

Precious Pearl: A Translation from the Arabic. Jane I. Smith. LC 79-140. (Harvard University Center for the Study of World Religions: Vol. 1). 128p. 1979. reprint ed. pap. 39.70 (0-608-08856-0, 206949500004) Bks Demand.

Precious Pearl: Al-Durra Al-Fakhira. Ed. by Page Smith. LC 79-140. (Studies in World Religions: No. 1). 120p. (C). 1979. pap. 9.95 (0-89130-305-7) Harvard U Wrld Relig.

Precious Pearl: The Lives of Saints Barlaam & Joasaph, Notes & Comments By Augoustinos Kantiotes, Bishop of Florida, Greece. St. John Damascene. Tr. & Intro. by Asterios Gerostergios. LC 97-70030. (Illus.). 438p. 1997. pap. 22.95 (1-884729-23-1) Inst Byzantine.

Precious Place: A Naturalist Explores New Jersey. Don Freiday. Ed. by Nicholas DiGiovanni. (Illus.). 176p. 1998. pap. 9.95 (0-9662789-0-9) Hunterdon Cnty.

***Precious Poetry.** large type ed. Dianne Webb. 59p. 2000. pap. 12.95 (0-9700847-0-6) Sanctified Pub.

Precious Present. Spencer Johnson. 80p. 1984. 19.95 (0-385-46805-9) Doubleday.

Precious Promises. Illus. by Ginger Oakes. 32p. 1987. pap. 4.95 (0-929510-01-1) Lewis & Stanley.

***Precious Promises New Testament.** Precious Promises Staff. 1999. pap. 8.99 (0-89957-970-1) AMG Pubs.

***Precious Promises New Testament.** Precious Promises Staff. 1999. pap. 1.89 (0-89957-969-8) AMG Pubs.

Precious R. Thyme: A Spicy Tail. 128p. 1997. pap. 10.00 (0-9662163-0-X) J S Risley.

Precious Rascal. Larry Incollingo. 1991. pap. 9.50 (0-9619795-3-4) Reunion Bks.

Precious Records: Women in China's Long Eighteenth Century. Susan Mann. LC 96-25757. 1997. write for info. (0-8047-2743-0); pap. 19.95 (0-8047-2744-9) Stanford U Pr.

Precious Remedies Against Satan's Devices. Thomas Brooks. 253p. 1984. reprint ed. pap. 7.50 (0-85151-002-7) Banner of Truth.

Precious Sense of Place: The Early Years of Chico State. W. H. Hutchinson & Clarence F. McIntosh. (Illus.). 116p. 1991. 32.50 (0-9628519-0-6) Frnds of Meriam Lib.

***Precious Solitude: Finding Peace & Serenity in a Hectic World.** Ruth Fishel. LC 99-15772. 256p. 1999. pap. 10.95 (1-58062-209-7) Adams Media.

Precious Spring. large type ed. Myrna Diffey. (Linford Romance Library). 304p. 1997. pap. 16.99 (0-7089-5184-8) Ulverscroft.

Precious Stone That Heal. N. N. Saha. 249p. (C). 1980. pap. 16.95 (0-317-07703-1, Pub. by Allied Pubs) Asia Bk Corp.

Precious Stones. William Russell. LC 94-506. (From This Earth Discovery Library). 24p. (J). (gr. k-4). 1994. lib. bdg. 10.95 (0-86593-361-8) Rourke Corp.

Precious Stones: For Curative Wear, Other Remedial Uses & Likewise the Nobler Metals. William t. Fernie. 492p. 1997. reprint ed. pap. 29.95 (0-7661-0112-6) Kessinger Pub.

Precious Stones Vol. 1: A Popular Account of Their Characters, Occurrence & Applications. Max Bauer. Tr. by L. J. Spencer. (Illus.). (C). 1968. pap. 10.95 (0-486-21910-0) Dover.

Precious Stones Vol. 2: A Popular Account of Their Characters, Occurrence & Applications. Max Bauer. Tr. by L. J. Spencer. (Illus.). (C). 1968. pap. 12.95 (0-486-21911-9) Dover.

Precious Stones & Gems. Edwin M. Streeter. 1977. 79.95 (0-8490-2466-8) Gordon Pr.

Precious Stones for Curative Wear & Other Remedial Uses. William T. Fernie. 1973. 69.95 (0-8490-0886-7) Gordon Pr.

Precious Stones That Heal. N. N. Saha. 252p. 1980. 16.95 (0-318-36379-8) Asia Bk Corp.

Precious Things of God. Octavius Winslow. 424p. 1993. 29.95 (1-877611-61-1) Soli Deo Gloria.

Precious Things of the Lasting Hills see Children of the Hills

Precious Thoughts from the Heart: Inspirational Prayer Poems. Ruth H. Calkin. 1994. 10.99 (0-88486-101-5) Arrowood Pr.

Precious Time: Children Living with Muscular Dystrophy see Don't Turn Away

Precious to Precocious: The Humor of Parenting Birth Through Age 12. limited ed. Janis Y. Chun. Ed. by Bill Stone. LC 97-92822. (Illus.). 128p. 1998. pap. 12.95 (0-9663551-0-5) JYC Co.

Precious Training: The New Method to Achieve Optimum Muscularity. John Little & Peter Sisco. 241p. 1995. 14.95 (1-886691-18-5) Power Factor.

Precious Treasures. Willie H. Halbert. (WeWrite Bks.: No. 2). 200p. 1998. pap. 14.95 (1-57635-023-1) WeWrite.

***Precious Truth, Plain & Simple.** Benjamin O. Powell, Sr. 112p. 2000. 15.95 (1-56167-586-5) Am Literary Pr.

Precious Truths Revived & Defended Through J. N. Darby Vol. 2: Defense of Truth, 1845-1850. R. A. Huebner. 332p. 1994. pap. text 14.00 (0-9640037-0-8) Pres Truth.

Precious Truths Revived & Defended Through J. N. Darby Vol. 3: Defense of Truth. R. A. Huebner. 120p. 1995. pap. text 10.00 (0-9640037-4-0) Pres Truth.

Precious Truths Revived & Recovered Through J. N. Darby, 1826-1845, Vol. 1. Roy A. Huelner. 254p. 1991. pap. text 12.00 (1-888749-08-3) Pres Truth.

Precious Umbrella. Roberto Valenza. (Illus.). 45p. 1996. pap. 7.50 (1-878888-20-X) Nine Muses Books.

***Precious Unborn Human Persons.** Gregory Koukl. 51p. 1999. 4.00 (0-9673584-0-X) Stand to Reason.

***Precious Vessels: 2000 Years of Chinese Pottery.** Eldon Worrall. Ed. by Margaret Warhurst. 107p. 2000. pap. 20.00 (0-7881-9429-1) DIANE Pub.

Precious Volumes: An Introduction to Chinese Sectarian Scriptures from the 16th & 17th Centuries, Vol.49. Daniel Overmeyer. LC 99-19188. (Harvard-Yenching Institute Monograph Ser.). 1999. 55.00 (0-674-69838-X) HUP.

***Precipice.** John Donoghue. LC 99-71363. 63p. 2000. pap. 13.95 (1-884800-28-9, Pub. by Four Way Bks) SPD-Small Pr Dist.

Precipice. Ivan A. Goncharov. Tr. by Laury Magnus & Boris Jakim from RUS. 1994. 39.95 (0-87501-096-2) Ardis Pubs.

Precipice. Dan Pollock. Ed. by Toby Stein. 459p. 1997. 29.95 (0-9658653-0-4) Coun Logistics Mgt.

Precipice. Tom Savage. 416p. 1995. mass mkt. 6.99 (0-451-18333-9, Onyx) NAL.

Precipice. Ivan A. Goncharov. Tr. by M. Bryant from RUS. LC 73-21714. vii, 320p. 1975. reprint ed. 40.00 (0-86527-295-6) Fertig.

Precipice. Elia W. Peattie. (Prairie State Bks.). 272p. 1989. reprint ed. 14.95 (0-252-06093-8) U of Ill Pr.

Precipitating Lead Chromate on a Small Scale. H. Anthony Neidig & James N. Spencer. (Modular Laboratory Program in Chemistry Ser.). 12p. (C). 1992. pap. text 1.50 (0-87540-420-0, STOI 420-0) Chem Educ Res.

Precipitation: Basic Principles. J. Garfield & O. Sohnel. (Illus.). 400p. 1993. text 190.00 (0-7506-1107-3) Buttrwrth-Heinemann.

Precipitation Chemistry, Vol. 2. Ed. by J. P. Hales, Jr. 200p. 1982. pap. 35.00 (0-08-028782-4, Pergamon Pr) Elsevier.

Precipitation Enhancement: A Scientific Challenge. Ed. by Roscoe R. Braham, Jr. (Meteorological Monograph: Vol. 21, No. 43). (Illus.). 171p. 1986. 50.00 (0-933876-65-3) Am Meteorological.

Precipitation from Iron-Based Alloys: Preceedings of a Symposium, Cleveland Ohio, October 21, 1963. Ed. by Gilbert R. Speich & John B. Clark. LC 65-18397. (Metallurgical Society Conference Ser.: Vol. 28). 420p. reprint ed. pap. 130.20 (0-608-11244-5, 200151600079) Bks Demand.

Precipitation Hardening. J. Martin & W. Hume-Rothery. LC 67-31505. (Selected Readings in Metallurgy Ser.). 1968. reprint ed. 113.00 (0-08-203608-X, Pub. by Pergamon Repr) Franklin.

Precipitation Hardening. 2nd ed. J. W. Martin. LC 98-33489. 240p. 2000. text 80.00 (0-7506-3885-0) Buttrwrth-Heinemann.

Precipitation Processes in Solids: Proceedings of a Symposium Sponsored by the TMS-AIME Heat Treatment Committee at the 1976 TMS Fall Meeting at Niagara Falls, New York, September 20-21. Ed. by K. C. Russell & H. I. Aaronson. LC 78-66760. 324p. reprint ed. pap. 100.50 (0-608-11267-4, 202276900029) Bks Demand.

Precipitation Scavenging & Atmosphere-Surface Exchange, 3 vols., Set. Ed. by Stephen E. Schwartz & W. G. Slinn. 2200p. 1992. 420.00 (1-56032-263-2) Hemisp Pub.

Precipitation Scavenging (1970) Proceedings. Ed. by Rudolph J. Engelmann & W. G. Slinn. LC 70-609397. (AEC Symposium Ser.). 513p. 1970. pap. 20.75 (0-685-01482-7, CONF-700601) DOE.

Precipitation Scavenging (1974) Proceedings. Ed. by Richard W. Semonin & Robert W. Beadle. LC 76-53788. (ERDA Symposium Ser.). 855p. 1977. pap. 29.50 (0-87079-309-8, CONF-741003); fiche 9.00 (0-87079-310-1, CONF-741003) DOE.

Precipitation-Strengthened, Weldable Low-Carbon Structural Steels for Line Pipe Applications. E. E. Fletcher & A. R. Elsea. 162p. 1975. pap. 8.00 (0-318-12670-2, L32076) Am Gas Assn.

Precis: A Primer. rev. ed. Mary Dykstra. LC 87-17617. 280p. 1988. reprint ed. pap. 23.50 (0-8108-2060-9) Scarecrow.

Precis: An Update in Obstetrics & Gynecology. American College of Obstetrics & Gynecology. 1978. text 27.50 (0-07-001134-6) McGraw.

Precis: An Update in Obstetrics & Gynecology. 2nd ed. American College of Obstetricians & Gynecologists. LC 99-15357. 1999. write for info. (0-915473-51-8) Am Coll Obstetric.

Precis de Bibliotheconomie. 5th rev. ed. Brigitte Richter. (FRE.). ix, 298p. 1992. lib. bdg. 32.50 (3-598-11077-4) K G Saur Verlag.

Precis de Cadres Militaires: German-French, French-German. deluxe ed. Miguel A. Del Arco Torres. (SPA.). 768p. 1984. 150.00 (0-7859-6052-X, 8470162594) Fr & Eur.

Precis de Climatologie. Charles Peguy. (FRE., Illus.). 468p. 1970. 150.00 (0-686-54865-5, 2225615233) Fr & Eur.

Precis de Decomposition. E. M. Cioran. (FRE.). 1978. pap. 18.95 (0-7859-2749-2) Fr & Eur.

Precis de Grammaire Francaise. Maurice Grevisse. 291p. 1990. 29.95 (0-8288-7474-3) Fr & Eur.

Precis de Grammaire Francaise. 29th ed. Maurice Grevisse. (FRE.). 292p. 1990. lib. bdg. 29.95 (0-8288-3320-6, F134898) Fr & Eur.

Precis de Protistology. P. De Puytorac et al. (FRE., Illus.). 581p. 1987. pap. text 112.50 (0-317-68057-9) Lubrecht & Cramer.

Precis de Semantique Francaise. S. Ullman. 350p. 1952. 10.95 (0-8288-7430-1) Fr & Eur.

Precis de Terminologie Medicale. 4th ed. J. Chevalier. 280p. 1983. 35.00 (0-8288-1795-2, M6070) Fr & Eur.

Precis, Gynecology: An Update in Obstetrics & Gynecology. American College of Obstetricians & Gynecologists. LC 97-52566. 1998. pap. write for info. (0-915473-41-0) American College of Emergency Physicians.

Precis, Obstetrics: An Update in Obstetrics & Gynecology. American College of Obstetricians & Gynecologists. LC 97-52567. 1998. pap. write for info. (0-915473-40-2) American College of Emergency Physicians.

Precis of Mathematical Logic. J. M. Bochenski. Tr. by Otto Bird from FRE. (Snthese Library: No.1). 110p. 1960. text 113.00 (90-277-0073-7, D Reidel) Kluwer Academic.

Precis of Postal Service Manual. Jack Rudman. (General Aptitude & Abilities Ser.: No. CS-22). pap. 19.95 (0-8373-6722-0, CS-22) Nat Learn.

Precis of Procedure. 5th ed. Ed. by House of Collectibles Staff. LC 97-181288. (FRE & ENG., Illus.). 147p. 1996. pap. 21.95 (0-660-60028-5, Pub. by Canadian Govt Pub) Accents Pubns.

***Precis of the Lectures on Architecture: With, Graphic Portion of the Lectures on Architecture.** Jean-Nicolas-Louis Durand. LC 99-57591. (Illus.). 352p. 2000. 55.00 (0-89236-580-3, Getty Res Inst) J P Getty Trust.

Precis, Oncology: An Update in Obstetrics & Gynceology. American College of Obstetricians & Gynecologists. LC 97-51748. 1998. pap. write for info. (0-915473-42-9, A2841) American College of Emergency Physicians.

Precis Ou Abrege des Voyages, Travaux, et Recherches de C. S. Rafine. C. Boewe et al. (Verhandelingen der Koninklijke Nederlandse Akademie van Wetenschappen, Afd. Natuurkunde Ser.: No. 86). 114p. 1987. pap. 48.75 (0-444-85663-3) Elsevier.

Precis Pratique de Psychiatrie. 2nd ed. R. Duguay. (FRE.). 756p. 1984. 125.00 (0-8288-1802-9, M15382) Fr & Eur.

Precis Pratique de Traduction Medicale see Practical Manual of Medical Translation English-French

Precis, Primary & Preventive Care: An Update in Obstetrics & Gynecology. American College of Obstetricians & Gynecologists. Ed. by Leo J. Dunn. LC 97-52069. 230p. 1998. pap. 45.00 (0-915473-39-9) American College of Emergency Physicians.

Precis, Reproductive Endocrinology: An Update in Obstetrics & Gynecology. American College of Obstetricians & Gynecologists. LC 97-51260. 1998. 39.00 (0-915473-43-7) Am Coll Obstetric.

Precise Formulas for Over-Pin Measurements of Helical Forms. E. C. Varnum & S. J. Johnson. (Technical Papers: Vol. P239.03). (Illus.). 11p. 1957. pap. text 30.00 (1-55589-300-7) AGMA.

Precise Intrigues. Mary Angeline. LC 94-1789. 72p. (Orig.). 1994. pap. 12.00 (0-942996-22-4) Post Apollo Pr.

Precise Numerical Methods Using C++ - KSO. Oliver Aberth. LC 98-117803. (Illus.). 238p. 1998. text, boxed set 59.95 incl. cd-rom (0-12-041750-2) Acad Pr.

Precise Progressed Charts. Mohan Koparkar. 110p. 1976. pap. 5.95 (0-918922-03-8) Mohan Ents.

***Precise Stellar Radial Velocities: IAU Colloquium 170.** Ed. by J. B. Hearnshaw & C. D. Scarfe. (Conference Series Proceedings: Vol. 185). 431p. 1999. text 52.00 (1-58381-011-0) Astron Soc Pacific.

Precise Technique for Accurate Checking of Gear Dimensions. W. S. Tandler. (Technical Papers: Vol. P239.02). (Illus.). 10p. 1954. pap. text 30.00 (1-55589-299-X) AGMA.

Precise Tone Plan for End Offices. Thomas B. Norling. (ABC Pocket Guide for the Field Ser.). (Illus.). 40p. 1996. pap. 7.95 (1-56016-033-0) ABC TeleTraining.

Precisely Complete, 6 vols. Ed. by Richard Kostelanetz & Stephen Scobie. 1000p. 1985. pap. 32.00 (0-932360-63-7) Archae Edns.

Precisely the Point Being Made. Norman Fischer. LC 92-37856. 72p. 1993. 10.00 (1-882022-14-9) O Bks.

Precision: A New Approach to Communication. Michael McMaster & John Grinder. LC 93-28602. 304p. 1994. pap. 15.95 (1-55552-049-9) Grinder Delozier.

Precision Agriculture, 2 vols. 1999. 220.00 (1-85996-236-X) Bios Sci.

Precision Agriculture. P. C. Robert. Ed. by R. H. Rust & W. E. Larson. LC 96-80281. 1222p. 1996. 42.00 (0-89118-132-6) Am Soc Agron.

***Precision Agriculture & Biological Quality.** Ed. by George E. Meyer & James A. DeShazer. LC 99-208071. 400p. 1999. pap. text 89.00 (0-8194-3155-9) SPIE.

Precision Agriculture & Biological Quality, Vol. 3543. Ed. by George E. Meyer & James A. DeShazer. 176p. 1999. 89.00 (0-8194-3005-6) SPIE.

P

Precision Agriculture in the 21st Century: Geospatial & Information Technologies in Crop Management. National Research Council (U. S.) Staff. LC 97-45268. 1997. 39.95 (*0-309-05893-7*) Natl Acad Sci.

Precision Agriculture in the 21st CEntury: Geospatial & Information Technologies in Crop Management. Committee on Assessing Crop Yield, National Resear. 260p. 1997. 39.95 (*0-309-05643-8*, Joseph Henry Pr) Natl Acad Pr.

Precision & Design in Accountancy. Frank S. Bray. Ed. by Richard P. Brief. LC 80-1473. (Dimensions of Accounting Theory & Practice Ser.). 1980. reprint ed. lib. bdg. 18.95 (*0-405-13503-3*) Ayer.

Precision & Soul: Essays & Addresses. Robert Musil. Ed. & Tr. by Burton Pike & David S. Luft. xxviii, 329p. 1994. pap. 17.95 (*0-226-55409-0*) U Ch Pr.

Precision & Soul: Essays & Addresses. Robert Musil. Ed. & Tr. by Burton Pike & David S. Luft. LC 90-10828. 330p. 1996. 35.95 (*0-226-55408-2*) U Ch Pr.

***Precision Attachments: A Link to Successful Restorative Treatment.** Gareth Jenkins. 144p. 1999. 68.00 (*1-85097-038-6*) Quint Pub Co.

Precision Bridge. Jannersten. 11.95 (*0-910791-43-0*, 3516) Devyn Pr.

Precision Conducting: The Seven Disciplines of the Masterful Conductor. Timothy W. Sharp. (Illus.). 144p. (Orig.). 1996. pap. 12.95 (*1-889411-01-9*, K1010) Tempo Music.

Precision Editing. Ed. by Gassaway. (C). 1999. pap. text, wbk. ed. write for info. (*0-321-01091-4*) Addson-Wesley Educ.

***Precision Farming Guide for Agriculturists.** Ed. by Deere & Company Staff. 70p. 1999. pap., teacher ed. 20.95 (*0-86691-263-0*, FP401T); pap., student ed. 15.95 (*0-86691-264-9*, FP401W) Deere & Co.

Precision Farming Guide for Agriculturists: The Nuts & Bolts Guide to "Getting up to Speed" Fast & Effectively with This Exciting New Management Tool. Mark Morgan & Dan Ess. Ed. by Stephen L. Rawlins et al. (Agricultural Primer Ser.). (Illus.). 124p. 1997. pap. text 25.95 (*0-86691-245-2*, FP401NC) Deere & Co.

Precision Fixed Prosthodontics: Clinical & Laboratory Aspects. M. Martignoni & Schonenberger. Tr. by Pittwood & Rutter from ITA.Tr. of Precisione e Contorno nella Ricostruzione Protesica. (Illus.). 579p. 1990. text 188.00 (*0-86715-214-1*) Quint Pub Co.

Precision Frequency Control, 2 vols. Gerber. 1985. 283.00 (*0-12-280603-4*) Acad Pr.

Precision Frequency Control Vol. 1: Acoustic Resonators & Filters. Ed. by Eduard A. Gerber & Arthur Ballato. 1985. text 142.00 (*0-12-280601-8*) Acad Pr.

Precision Frequency Control Vol. 2: Oscillators & Standards. Ed. by Eduard A. Gerber & Arthur Ballato. 1985. text 142.00 (*0-12-280602-6*) Acad Pr.

Precision-Guided Logistics: Flexible Support for the Force-Projection Army's High-Technology Weapons. Marc L. Robbins & D. W. McIver. LC 94-30295. 1994. pap. 15.00 (*0-8330-1574-5*, MR-437-A) Rand Corp.

Precision Handcutting of Dovetails: With a Sequence to the Author's Fifty Years a Planemaker & User. Cecil E. Pierce. (Illus.). 56p. 1995. 18.00 (*0-9628001-4-7*) Monmouth Pr.

Precision Heart Rate Training. Ed. by Edmund R. Burke. LC 97-44079. (Illus.). 224p. 1998. pap. 15.95 (*0-88011-770-2*, PBUR0770) Human Kinetics.

Precision in Questioning. Dennis Matthies. (Illus.). 430p. (C). 1996. spiral bd. 35.00 (*1-887981-03-9*) Stanford Bookstore.

Precision Journalism: A Reporter's Introduction to Social Science Methods. 2nd ed. Philip Meyer. LC 79-2172. (Illus.). 444p. reprint ed. pap. 137.70 (*0-8357-6688-8*, 205686800094) Bks Demand.

Precision Kill. Don Pendelton. LC 96-2389. (Superbolan Ser.: Vol. 46). 349p. 1996. per. 4.99 (*0-373-61446-2*, 1-61446-0, Wrldwide Lib) Harlequin Bks.

Precision, Language & Logic. F. H. George. 224p. 1977. 106.00 (*0-08-019650-0*, Pub. by Pergamon Repr) Franklin.

Precision Machine Design. Alexander H. Slocum. LC 91-23689. (Illus.). 750p. 1998. reprint ed. 95.00 (*0-87263-492-2*, 2597) SME.

Precision Machining: Technology & Machine Development & Improvement. Ed. by M. Jouaneh & S. S. Rangwala. (PED Ser.: Vol. 58). 220p. 1992. 57.50 (*0-7918-1067-4*, G00711) ASME.

Precision Makers: History of the Instruments Industry in Britain & France 1870 - 1939. Mari E. Williams. LC 94-104909. (Comparative & International Business: Modern Histories Ser.). 240p. (C). 1993. pap. 77.95 (*0-415-03732-8*) Thomson Learn.

Precision Management: How to Build & Manage the Winning Organization. 2nd ed. Richard Lynch. 230p. (Orig.). 1988. reprint ed. pap. 10.00 (*0-933445-00-8*) Abbott Pr WA.

Precision Manufacturing Costing. E. Ralph Sims. (Cost Engineering Ser.: Vol. 23). (Illus.). 352p. 1995. text 110.00 (*0-8247-9083-9*) Dekker.

Precision Measurement in the Metal Working Industry. rev. ed. IBM Education Department Staff. (Illus.). (C). 1978. pap. 34.95 (*0-8156-2194-9*) Syracuse U Pr.

Precision Measuring Tools. William Knapp. 26p. (YA). (gr. 10 up). 1991. pap., wbk. ed. 7.00 (*0-8064-1329-8*, G11) Bergwall.

Precision Mechanical Measuring. Tel-A-Train, Inc. Staff. 1989. student ed. 17.50 (*1-56355-048-2*) Tel-A-Train.

Precision Metalforming Process Handbook. H. E. Theis. LC 99-14995. (Illus.). 672p. 1999. text 225.00 (*0-8247-9317-X*) Dekker.

***Precision Motion Control.** Kok Kiong Tan. LC 00-39473. (Advances in Industrial Control Ser.). 2001. write for info. (*1-85233-328-6*) Spr-Verlag.

Precision Photometry: Astrophysics of the Galaxy. Ed. by A. G. Davis Philip et al. 300p. 1991. 32.00 (*0-933485-13-1*) L Davis Pr.

Precision Plastic Optics for Optical Storage, Displays, Imaging & Communications. Ed. by Werner F. Frank. LC 98-122574. (Proceedings Ser.). 248p. 1997. 69.00 (*0-8194-2557-5*) SPIE.

***Precision Play: The Executioner.** Don Pendleton. 2000. per. 4.50 (*0-373-64257-1*) Harlequin Bks.

Precision Pool: Your Guide to Mastering Key Skills,Shots & Strategies. Gerry D. Kanov & Shari J. Stauch. LC 98-44031. (Illus.). 256p. 1999. pap. 18.95 (*0-88011-897-0*, PKAN0897) Human Kinetics.

Precision Power: The First Half Century of Bodine Electric Company. Howard F. Bennett. LC 75-41747. (Companies & Men: Business Enterprises in America Ser.). (Illus.). 1976. reprint ed. 37.95 (*0-405-08064-6*) Ayer.

***Precision Press Brake.** (Illus.). 350p. (C). 1999. pap. text 65.00 (*1-929513-03-8*, A5) Advnce Sht Metl.

Precision Process Technology: Perspectives for Pollution Prevention. Ed. by M. P. Weijnen & A. A. Drinkenburg. LC 92-46139. 732p. (C). 1993. text 402.50 (*0-7923-2150-2*) Kluwer Academic.

Precision Putting. James A. Frank. LC 98-27032. (Golf Drills & Strategy Ser.). (Illus.). 168p. 1998. pap. 16.95 (*0-88011-822-9*, PFRA0822) Human Kinetics.

Precision Radiotherapy Planning. James M. Slater. (Oncologic Ser.: Vol. 19). 1984. pap. 120.00 (*0-08-027470-6*, Pergamon Pr) Elsevier.

Precision Sensors, Actuators, & Systems. Ed. by H. S. Tzou & T. Fukuda. LC 92-32458. (Solid Mechanics & Its Applications Ser.: Vol. 17). 1992. text 279.50 (*0-7923-2015-8*) Kluwer Academic.

Precision Sheet Metal Blueprint Reading. Richard S. Budzik. LC 75-86373. 1969. 5.50 (*0-672-20687-0*, Bobbs); teacher ed. 5.00 (*0-672-20689-7*, Bobbs); student ed. 4.55 (*0-672-20688-9*, Bobbs) Macmillan.

Precision Sheet Metal Blueprint Reading: Instructor Guide. 3rd ed. Richard S. Budzik. LC 75-86373. (Illus.). 127p. 1988. teacher ed. 29.95 (*0-912914-13-0*) Practical Pubns.

Precision Sheet Metal Blueprint Reading: Student Workbook. 3rd ed. Richard S. Budzik. LC 75-86373. (Illus.). 127p. 1988. student ed. 24.95 (*0-912914-12-2*) Practical Pubns.

Precision Sheet Metal Blueprint Reading: Textbook. 3rd ed. Richard S. Budzik. LC 75-86373. (Illus.). 127p. text 24.95 (*0-912914-40-8*) Practical Pubns.

Precision Sheet Metal Mathematics. Richard S. Budzik. LC 71-83129. 1969. 9.70 (*0-672-97591-2*, Bobbs); teacher ed. 6.67 (*0-672-97593-9*, Bobbs); student ed. 4.80 (*0-672-97592-0*, Bobbs) Macmillan.

Precision Sheet Metal Mathematics. Richard S. Budzik. (Precision Sheet Metal Series). (Illus.). 349p. 1988. pap. text 24.95 (*0-912914-49-1*) Practical Pubns.

Precision Sheet Metal Mathematics: Instructor Guide. 2nd ed. Richard S. Budzik. LC 71-83129. (Illus.). 349p. 1988. teacher ed. 29.95 (*0-912914-16-5*) Practical Pubns.

Precision Sheet Metal Mathematics: Student Workbook. 2nd ed. Richard S. Budzik. LC 71-83129. (Illus.). 349p. 1988. student ed. 24.95 (*0-912914-15-7*) Practical Pubns.

Precision Sheet Metal Shop Practice. Richard S. Budzik. LC 78-97566. 1969. 4.55 (*0-672-97594-7*, Bobbs); teacher ed. 6.67 (*0-672-97596-3*, Bobbs); student ed. 4.80 (*0-672-97595-5*, Bobbs) Macmillan.

Precision Sheet Metal Shop Practice: Instructor Guide. Richard S. Budzik. LC 78-97566. (Illus.). 96p. 1969. teacher ed. 29.95 (*0-912914-19-X*) Practical Pubns.

Precision Sheet Metal Shop Practice: Student Workbook. Richard S. Budzik. LC 78-97566. (Illus.). 96p. 1969. student ed. 24.95 (*0-912914-18-1*) Practical Pubns.

Precision Sheet Metal Shop Practice: Textbook. Richard S. Budzik. LC 78-97566. (Illus.). 96p. 1969. 24.95 (*0-912914-17-3*) Practical Pubns.

Precision Sheet Metal Shop Theory. Richard S. Budzik. LC 79-77586. 1969. teacher ed. 5.00 (*0-672-20681-1*, Bobbs); pap. 9.20 (*0-672-20679-X*, Bobbs); student ed. 4.80 (*0-672-20680-3*, Bobbs) Macmillan.

Precision Sheet Metal Shop Theory: Instructor Guide. 2nd ed. Richard S. Budzik. LC 79-77566. (Illus.). 450p. 1988. teacher ed. 29.95 (*0-912914-10-6*) Practical Pubns.

Precision Sheet Metal Shop Theory: Student Workbook. 2nd ed. Richard S. Budzik. LC 79-77566. (Illus.). 450p. 1988. student ed. 24.95 (*0-912914-09-2*) Practical Pubns.

Precision Sheet Metal Shop Theory: Textbook. 2nd ed. Richard S. Budzik. LC 79-77566. (Illus.). 450p. 1988. 24.95 (*0-912914-25-4*) Practical Pubns.

Precision Shooting - The Trapshooter's Bible. James Russell. (Illus.). 220p. 1998. pap. 34.95 (*0-916367-10-X*, PS) James Russell.

Precision Spark Injection (PSI) System. Roy E. McAlister. 1986. pap. 4.95 (*0-685-24740-6*) Research Analysts.

***Precision Spectroscopy, Diode Lasers, & Optical Frequency Measur.** Ed. by Leo Hollberg. (Illus.). 420p. (C). 2000. reprint ed. pap. text 35.00 (*0-7881-8614-0*) DIANE Pub.

Precision Spectroscopy Diode Lasers & Optical Frequency Measurement Technology: Selected Publications of the Optical Frequency Measurement Group of the Time & Frequency Division. Leo Hollberg. 284p. 1998. per. 22.00 (*0-16-056693-2*) USGPO.

Precision Summary. C. C. Wei. 10p. (Orig.). 1.00 (*0-87643-040-X*) M Lisa Precision.

Precision Tests of the Standard Electroweak Model. Paul Langacker. 1032p. 1995. text 162.00 (*981-02-1284-4*) World Scientific Pub.

Precision Tests of the Standard Model at High Energy Colliders. Ed. by F. Del Aguila et al. 516p. (C). 1991. text 115.00 (*981-02-0685-2*) World Scientific Pub.

Precision Therapy: A Professional Manual of Fast & Effective Hypnoanalysis Techniques. Duncan McColl. 224p. 1995. pap. text 81.95 (*1-85398-069-2*, Pub. by Ashgrove Pr) Words Distrib.

Precision Therapy: A Professional Manual of Fast & Effective Hypnoanalysis Techniques. Duncan McColl. 270p. 1998. pap. 25.00 (*1-899836-18-7*, Pub. by Crown Hse) LPC Group.

Precision Time & GPS. Allan. text 125.00 (*0-471-38179-9*, Wiley Heyden) Wiley.

Precision Time Measures: Their Construction & Repair. C. T. Higginbotham. (Illus.). 343p. 27.50 (*0-930163-65-6*) Arlington Bk.

Precision Training - The Science of Strength. John Little & Peter Sisco. 1995. 9.95 (*1-886691-19-3*) Power Factor.

Precision Type Font Reference Guide Version 5.0: Complete Front Software Resource for Electronic Publishing. Jeff Level et al. 653p. 2000. pap. 39.95 (*0-88179-182-2*, Pub. by Hartley & Marks) Andrews & McMeel.

Precision Type Font Reference Guide 5.0: The Complete Font Software Resource for Electronic Publishing. Jeff Level et al. (Illus.). 704p. (Orig.). 1996. pap. 39.95 (*0-9646252-0-2*) Precision Type.

Precision Valley: The Machine Tool Companies of Springfield, Vermont. Wayne G. Broehl, Jr. LC 75-41748. (Companies & Men: Business Enterprises in America Ser.). (Illus.). 1976. reprint ed. 31.95 (*0-405-08065-4*) Ayer.

Precision Wedge & Bunker Shots. James FitzGerald & David Gould. LC 97-49862. (Precision Golf Ser.). (Illus.). 136p. 1998. pap. 16.95 (*0-88011-727-3*, PFIT0727) Human Kinetics.

Precision Woods & Long Iron Shots. Daniel McDonald & Richard A. Goodman. LC 97-47390. (Precision Golf Ser.). (Illus.). 144p. 1998. pap. text 16.95 (*0-88011-766-4*, PMCD0766) Human Kinetics.

Precision Writing. Antony Oldknow. 188p. 1998. pap. text 18.00 (*1-881604-26-8*) Scopcraeft.

Precisione e Contorno nella Ricostruzione Protesica see Precision Fixed Prosthodontics: Clinical & Laboratory Aspects

Precision's One Club Complete. Katherine Wei & Judi Radin. 169p. (Orig.). 1981. pap. 7.95 (*0-87643-042-6*) M Lisa Precision.

Precision's One Club Complete. Kathie Wei & Judi Radin. 169p. (Orig.). 1981. 7.95 (*0-685-08329-2*) Barclay Bridge.

Preclassic Maya Pottery at Cuello, Belize. Laura J. Kosakowsky. LC 87-16249. (Anthropological Papers: No. 47). 101p. 1987. 30.95 (*0-8165-1017-2*) U of Ariz Pr.

Preclassical Monetary Theories. Thomas Guggenheim. 200p. 1992. 54.00 (*0-86187-958-9*, Pub. by P P Pubs) Cassell & Continuum.

Preclinical & Clinical Development of New Vaccines: Symposium, Institut Pasteur, Paris, May, 1997, Vol.95. Ed. by Stanley A. Plotkin et al. (Developments in Biological Standardization Ser.: Vol. 95). (Illus.). xii, 284p. 1998. pap. 235.00 (*3-8055-6734-0*) S Karger.

Preclinical & Clinical Modulation of Anticancer Drugs. Kenneth D. Tew. (Pharmacology & Toxicology Ser.). 384p. 1993. lib. bdg. 129.00 (*0-8493-7291-7*, RC271) CRC Pr.

Preclinical & Clinical Strategies for the Treatment of Neurodegenerative, Cerebrovascular & Mental Disorders: Workshop, Tokyo, October/November 1994. Ed. by T. K. Shibuya. (International Academy for Biomedical & Drug Research Ser.: Vol. 11). (Illus.). xiv, 302p. 1996. 291.50 (*3-8055-6244-6*) S Karger.

Preclinical Drug Disposition: A Laboratory Handbook. Francis L. Tse & James M. Jaffe. (Drugs & the Pharmaceutical Sciences Ser.: Vol. 46). (Illus.). 184p. 1991. text 130.00 (*0-8247-8500-2*) Dekker.

Preclinical Hyperthermia. Ed. by W. Hinkelbein et al. (Recent Results in Cancer Research Ser.). (Illus.). 295p. 1988. 120.00 (*0-387-18487-2*) Spr-Verlag.

Preclinical Sciences. 3rd ed. Matthew T. Wood & E. Jeff Burkes, Jr. (Dental Assisting Manuals Ser.: No. 3). ix, 92p. (C). 1980. pap. text 17.95 (*0-8078-1377-X*) U of NC Pr.

Precoat Filtration. 2nd ed. (AWWA Manual of Water Supply Practices Ser.: No. M30). (Illus.). 56p. 1995. pap. 55.00 (*0-89867-787-4*, 30030) Am Water Wks Assn.

Precocious Parrot Caper. Georgette Livingston. LC 96-96401. (Jennifer Gray Veterinarian Mystery Ser.: Bk. 6). 192p. 1996. 18.95 (*0-8034-9213-8*, Avalon Bks) Bouregy.

Precognition. Cass Hook. (Illus.). 86p. (Orig.). 1986. pap. 10.00 (*0-918855-02-0*) Aldin Pub.

Precollege Science & Mathematics Teachers: Monitoring Supply, Demand, & Quality. National Research Council Staff. 266p. 1990. pap. text 25.00 (*0-309-04197-X*) Natl Acad Pr.

Precolonial African Intergroup Relations in Kaura & Pengana Polities of Central Nigerian Highlands 1800-1900. John Gareh Nengel. LC 98-33249. (European University Studies: Vol. 814). (Illus.). 260p. 1999. pap. 45.95 (*0-8204-3231-8*) P Lang Pubng.

Precolonial Black Africa. Cheikh Anta Diop. Tr. by Harold J. Salemson from FRE. LC 86-22804. 240p. (C). 1987. pap. 13.95 (*1-55652-088-3*, Lawrence Hill) Chicago Review.

***Precolonial India in Practices: Society, Region & Identity in Medieval Andhra.** Cynthia Talbot. LC 99-49890. (Illus.). 368p. 2000. text. write for info. (*0-19-513661-6*) OUP.

Precolumbian Architecture in the Eastern United States. William N. Morgan. LC 98-29504. (Ripley P. Bullen Ser.). (Illus.). xiv, 272 p. (Orig.). 1999. pap. 19.95 (*0-8130-1659-2*) U Press Fla.

Precolumbian Art: From the Collection of Paul L. & Alice C. Baker. Jane Stevenson Day. (Illus.). 90p. 1996. pap. 20.00 (*0-911611-05-3*) Tucson Mus Art.

Precolumbian Art Rockefeller. Kelly. 1981. 15.00 (*0-671-43735-6*) Simon & Schuster.

Precolumbian Child. Max Shein. Tr. by Marina Castaneda from SPA. LC 91-78398.Tr. of El/Nino Precolombino. (Illus.). 152p. (Orig.). 1992. pap. 16.50 (*0-911437-18-5*) Labyrinthos.

Precolumbian Jade: New Geological & Cultural Interpretations. Ed. by Frederick W. Lange. LC 92-34099. (Illus.). 416p. (C). 1993. text 45.00 (*0-87480-393-4*) U of Utah Pr.

***Preconceived Notions.** Robyn Williams. LC 99-73775. 308p. 1999. pap. 12.95 (*1-930097-01-8*) Lushena Bks.

Preconceived Notions. Robyn Williams. 350p. 1995. 24.95 (*1-879360-37-3*) Noble Pr.

Preconcentration Techniques for Trace Elements. Zeev B. Alfassi. 480p. 1991. lib. bdg. 239.00 (*0-8493-5213-4*, QD139) CRC Pr.

Preconceptional Health Care: A Practical Guide. 2nd ed. Robert C. Cefalo & Merry K. Moos. LC 94-10569. (Illus.). 276p. (C). (gr. 13). 1994. pap. text 50.95 (*0-8151-1638-1*, 24064) Mosby Inc.

Preconceptional Health Promotion. Merry K. Moos & Margaret C. Freda. Ed. by Karla Damus. LC 94-37837. 1994. write for info. (*0-86525-061-8*) March of Dimes.

Preconditioned Conjugate Gradient Methods: Proceedings of a Conference Held in Nijmegen, The Netherlands, June 19-21, 1989. Ed. by O. Axelsson & L. Y. Kolotilina. (Lecture Notes in Mathematics Ser.: Vol. 1457). v, 196p. 1991. 41.95 (*0-387-53515-2*) Spr-Verlag.

Preconditioning Iterative Methods. Ed. by David J. Evans. LC 93-35717. 488p. 1994. text 134.00 (*2-88124-956-6*) Gordon & Breach.

Preconditioning Methods: Theory & Application. Ed. by David J. Evans. (Topics in Computer Mathematics Ser.: Vol. 1). xii, 556p. 1983. text 312.00 (*0-677-16320-7*) Gordon & Breach.

Preconditions of Revolution in Early Modern Europe. Ed. by Robert Forster & Jack P. Greene. LC 76-122010. (Johns Hopkins Symposia in Comparative History Ser.). 224p. reprint ed. pap. 69.50 (*0-608-14338-3*, 201982000014) Bks Demand.

Preconditions of Socialism. Eduard Bernstein. Ed. & Tr. by Henry Tudor. LC 92-23175. (Cambridge Texts in the History of Political Thought Ser.). 265p. (C). 1993. text 59.95 (*0-521-39121-0*); pap. text 19.95 (*0-521-39808-8*) Cambridge U Pr.

***Preconfigured Client Made Easy 4.5B.** SAP Labs, Inc. Staff. (R-Three Made Easy Guidebks.). (Illus.). 718p. 1999. pap. 88.00 (*1-893570-32-0*) SAP Labs.

***Preconfigured Client Made Easy 4.0B.** rev. ed. SAP Labs, Inc. Staff. (R-Three Made Easy Guidebks.). 320p. 1999. pap. 71.00 (*1-893570-31-2*) SAP Labs.

Preconscious Stimulation in Dreams, Associations & Images: Classical Studies. Otto Potzl et al. (Psychological Issues Monographs: No. 7, Vol. 2, No. 3). 156p. (Orig.). 1961. 27.50 (*0-8236-4260-7*) Intl Univs Pr.

Precontractual Liability: Reports to the XIIIth International Congress of Comparative Law, Montreal, Canada, 18-24 August 1990. Ewoud H. Hondius. 400p. 1991. pap. 108.00 (*90-6544-516-1*) Kluwer Law Intl.

Precontrol. S. Caola. 1997. text. write for info. (*0-442-01237-3*, VNR) Wiley.

Precultural Primate Behavior see Primatology: Proceedings of the International Congress of Primatology, 4th, Portland, 1972

Precurseurs de la Photographie au Senegal, 1950. Mama Casset. (Illus.). 96p. 1996. pap. 96.00 (*2-909571-07-6*, 610603, Pub. by Revue Noire) Dist Art Pubs.

Precursor. C. J. Cherryh. 416p. 1999. 23.95 (*0-88677-836-0*, Pub. by DAW Bks) Penguin Putnam.

***Precursor.** C. J. Cherryh. 2000. mass mkt. 6.99 (*0-88677-910-3*, Pub. by DAW Bks) Penguin Putnam.

Precursor. Ahmad Nawaz. LC 98-70760. xiv, 64p. 1998. pap. 10.00 (*1-58225-013-8*) Ananta Prakashani.

***Precursor.** Ahmad Nawaz. LC 00-131438. 64p. 2000. pap. 10.00 (*1-58225-213-0*) Ananta Prakashani.

Precursor & Essential Chemicals in Illicit Drug Production: Approaches to Enforcement. large type ed. James R. Sevick. (Illus.). 68p. (Orig.). (C). 1994. pap. text 25.00 (*0-7881-0789-5*) DIANE Pub.

***Precursor-Derived Ceramics: Synthesis, Structure & High-Temperature Mechanical Properties.** Fritz Aldinger et al. 314p. 1999. 180.00 (*3-527-29814-2*) Wiley.

Precursors & Causes in Development & Psychopathology. Ed. by Dale F. Hay & Adrian Angold. LC 92-49875. (Studies in Child Psychiatry). 334p. 1993. 219.95 (*0-471-92211-0*, Wiley Heyden) Wiley.

Precursors & Chemicals Frequently Used in the Illicit Manufacture of Narcotic Drugs & Psychotropic Substances. pap. 15.00 (*92-1-148093-0*) UN.

Precursors & Chemicals Frequently Used in the Illicit Manufacture of Narcotic Drugs & Psychotropic Substances. 100p. 18.00 (*92-1-148108-2*) UN.

***Precursors & Chemicals Frequently Used in the Illicit Manufacture of Narcotic Drugs & Psychotropic Substances.** International Narcotics Control Board Staff. 90p. 1998. pap. 18.00 (*92-1-148105-8*) UN.

Precursors & Chemicals Frequently Used in the Illicit Manufacture of Narcotic Drugs & Psychotropic Substances. Ed. by Barry Leonard. (Illus.). 89p. (C). 1998. pap. text 25.00 (*0-7881-7394-4*) DIANE Pub.

An Asterisk (*) at the beginning of an entry indicates that the title is appearing for the first time.

Precursors & Chemicals Frequently Used in the Illicit MAnufacture of Narcotic Drugs & Psychotropic Substances: Chemicals Frequently Used in the Illicit Manufacture of Narcotic Drugs. International Narcotics Board Staff. 100p. pap. 18.00 (*92-1-148097-3*) UN.

Precursors for Advanced Materials. 1992. 2650.00 (*0-89336-941-1*, GB-126) BCC.

Precursors of Gastric Cancer. Ed. by Si-Chun Ming. LC 83-27025. 334p. 1984. 85.00 (*0-275-91444-5*, C1444, Praeger Pubs) Greenwood.

Precursors of Modern Management: An Original Anthology. Ed. by Alfred D. Chandler, Jr. LC 79-7527. (History of Management Thought & Practice Ser.). 1980. lib. bdg. 31.95 (*0-405-12311-6*) Ayer.

Precursors of Prostatic Adenocarcinoma: Recent Findings & New Concepts. Ed. by R. Montironi & C. C. Schulman. (Journal: European Urology: Vol. 30, No. 2, 1996). (Illus.). iv, 148p. 1996. reprint ed. 77.50 (*3-8055-6367-1*) S Karger.

Precursors to Potential Severe Core Damage Accidents: 1982-1983 Status Report. J. A. Forester. 556p. 1997. per. 49.00 (*0-16-062840-7*) USGPO.

***Precursors to Potential Severe Core Damage Accidents: 1996, A Status Report.** R. J. Belles. 296p. 1998. per. 24.00 (*0-16-062880-6*) USGPO.

***Precursors to Potential Severe Core Damage Accidents: 1997 a Status Report.** R. J. Belles. 208p. 1998. per. 17.00 (*0-16-062978-0*) USGPO.

Precursory Physical Science: The Science You Need Before Taking Science in School. Thomas A. Boyle. LC 96-90843. (Illus.). xii, 168p. (Orig.). (C). 1997. pap. 17.95 (*0-9655241-2-4*) Technical Directions.

Precvicme Si Pravopis, Vol. 6. Ryzkova et al. (SLO.). 80p. 1996. write for info. (*80-08-01761-9*, Pub. by Slov Pegagog Naklad) IBD Ltd.

Precvicme Si Pravopis, Vol. 7. Ryzkova et al. (SLO.). 80p. 1996. write for info. (*80-08-01770-8*, Pub. by Slov Pegagog Naklad) IBD Ltd.

Precvicme Si Pravopis, Vol. 8. Ryzkova et al. (SLO.). 96p. 1996. write for info. (*80-08-01771-6*, Pub. by Slov Pegagog Naklad) IBD Ltd.

Predacious Arthropods: Agriculture's First Line of Defense. Willard H. Whitcomb. 350p. 1994. lib. bdg. 59.95 (*1-57444-177-9*) CRC Pr.

Predacious Midges of the World: Diptera: Ceratopogonidae: Tribe Ceratopogoninil. Willis W. Wirth & William L. Grogan, Jr. (Flora & Fauna Handbook Ser.: No. 4). (Illus.). xv, 160p. (Orig.). 1988. lib. bdg. 49.00 (*0-916846-43-1*) Sandhill Crane.

Predannaia Revolutsiia - Chto Takoe SSSR I Kuda on Idet: (Russian Original of The Revolution Betrayed - What Is the USSR & Where Is It Going) Leon Trotsky. LC 93-77085.Tr. of Revolution Betrayed -- What is the USSR & Where is it Going. (RUS.). 1993. pap. 10.00 (*1-883468-00-0*) Iskra Res.

Predation & Competition Between Rainbow Trout in Crane Prairie Reservoir, Oregon. Terry Shrader & Barron Moody. 36p. 1998. reprint ed. pap. 4.60 (*0-89904-868-4*, Cascade Geog Soc) Crumb Elbow Pub.

Predation & Defense Amongst Reptiles. J. L. Cloudsley-Thompson. LC 95-159289. (Illus.). 138p. 1994. pap. 19.95 (*1-872688-03-9*, Pub. by R&A Pub Ltd) Serpents Tale.

Predation & Freshwater Communities. Thomas M. Zaret. LC 80-5399. (Illus.). 201p. reprint ed. pap. 62.40 (*0-8357-8282-4*, 203393200087) Bks Demand.

Predation in Vertebrate Communities: The Bialowieza Primeval Forest As a Case Study. B. Jedrzejewska & W. Jedrzejewski. LC 98-2772. (Ecological Studies). (Illus.). 500p. 1998. 189.00 (*3-540-64138-6*) Spr-Verlag.

Predator. K. A. Applegate. LC 49-117690. (Animorphs Ser.: No. 5). 152p. (J). (gr. 4-7). 1996. pap. 4.99 (*0-590-62981-6*) Scholastic Inc.

Predator. K. A. Applegate. (Animorphs Ser.: No. 5). (J). (gr. 3-7). 1996. 9.09 (*0-606-10127-6*, Pub. by Turtleback) Demco.

Predator! Bruce Brooks. (Knowing Nature Ser.). 80p. (J). (gr. 5 up). 1991. bds. 13.95 (*0-374-36111-8*) FS&G.

Predator! Bruce Brooks. 80p. (J). (gr. 10 up). 1994. 8.95 (*0-374-36112-6*) FS&G.

Predator. Kathryn M. Griffith. 352p. 1993. mass mkt. 4.50 (*0-8217-4402-X*, Zebra Kensgtn) Kensgtn Pub Corp.

Predator. Jesse Jones. 256p. (Orig.). 1992. mass mkt. 3.95 (*0-87067-380-7*) Holloway.

Predator: Big Game. Sandy Schofield. 240p. 1999. mass mkt. 5.50 (*0-553-57733-6*) Bantam.

Predator: Big Game. unabridged ed. John Arcudi et al. Ed. by Diana Schutz. (Predator Ser.). (Illus.). 96p. (YA). (gr. 7 up). 1996. pap. 20.95 (*1-56971-166-6*) Dark Horse Comics.

Predator: Cold War. Nathan Archer. 272p. 1997. mass mkt. 4.99 (*0-553-57493-0*, Spectra) Bantam.

Predator: Cold War Collection. Mark Verheiden & Ron Randall. (Illus.). 112p. 1993. pap. 13.95 (*1-878574-79-5*) Dark Horse Comics.

Predator: Concrete Jungle. Nathan Archer. 320p. 1995. mass mkt. 4.99 (*0-553-56557-5*, Spectra) Bantam.

Predator: Hell & Hot Water. Mark Schultz. (Illus.). 1998. pap. text 9.95 (*1-56971-271-9*) Dark Horse Comics.

Predator: Kindred. Scott Tolson. 1998. pap. text 14.95 (*1-56971-270-0*) Dark Horse Comics.

Predator Bk. 1: Race War. Andrew H. Vachss & Randy Stradley. LC 97-213189. (Illus.). 144p. 1995. pap. 17.95 (*1-56971-112-7*) Dark Horse Comics.

Predator Vol. 1: Concrete Jungle. 3rd ed. Mark Verheiden et al. Ed. by Randy Stradley & Jerry Prosser. (Predator Ser.). (Illus.). 112p. 1996. pap. 14.95 (*1-56971-165-8*) Dark Horse Comics.

Predator ACTD: A Case Study for Transition Planning to the Formal Acquisition Process. Michael R. Thirtle et al. LC 97-31084. xxix, 86p. 1997. pap. 15.00 (*0-8330-2541-4*, MR-899) Rand Corp.

***Predator & Prey: Vampire.** Carl Bowen. 2000. pap. 6.50 (*1-56504-969-1*) White Wolf.

Predator Calling with Gerry Blair. Gerry Blair. LC 95-77319. (Illus.). 208p. 1995. pap. 14.95 (*0-87341-359-8*, PCG01) Krause Pubns.

Predator in the House. Gay Brewer. 40p. (Orig.). 1996. pap. 9.00 (*0-9628478-7-9*) North Star OH.

Predator-Prey Model: Do We Live in a Volterra World? M. Peschel & W. Mende. (Illus.). 260p. 1986. 53.95 (*0-387-81848-0*) Spr-Verlag.

Predator-Prey Relations. Helms. 1997. 1.50 (*0-7167-9347-4*) W H Freeman.

Predator-Prey Relationships: Perspectives & Approaches from the Study of Lower Vertebrates. Ed. by Martin E. Feder & George V. Lauder. LC 85-24709. (Illus.). x, 198p. 1986. pap. text 11.95 (*0-226-23946-2*) U Ch Pr.

Predator-Prey Relationships: Perspectives & Approaches from the Study of Lower Vertebrates. Ed. by Martin E. Feder & George V. Lauder. LC 85-24709. (Illus.). x, 198p. 1986. lib. bdg. 31.50 (*0-226-23945-4*) U Ch Pr.

Predator Training: The Inner Beast of San Soo. Greg Jones. (Illus.). 164p. 1993. pap. 20.00 (*0-87364-724-6*) Paladin Pr.

Predator vs. Judge Dredd. John Wagner & Enrique Alcatena. (Illus.). 80p. 1999. pap. 9.95 (*1-56971-345-6*) Dark Horse Comics.

Predator vs. Magnus Robot Fighter, Bk. 1. Jim Shooter & John Ostrander. (Illus.). 64p. 1994. pap. 7.95 (*1-56971-040-6*) Dark Horse Comics.

Predators. (Funpax Ser.). (J). 1997. pap. text 2.95 (*0-7894-2114-3*) DK Pub Inc.

Predators. Daina Graziunas & Jim Starlin. Orig. Title: Thinning the Predators. 432p. 1997. mass mkt. 6.99 (*0-446-60400-3*, Pub. by Warner Bks) Little.

Predators. Harold Robbins. 407p. 1999. mass mkt. 6.99 (*0-8125-7178-9*, Pub. by Forge NYC) St Martin.

Predators. Harold Robbins. LC 98-5553. 348p. 1998. text 24.95 (*0-312-85294-0*) St Martin.

***Predators: By Land, Sea & Air.** 76p. 1999. write for info. (*1-893698-04-1*) SeaWorld Inc.

Predators & Predation: The Struggle for Life in the Animal World. Ed. by Pierre Pfeffer. LC 88-3880. (Illus.). 429p. reprint ed. pap. 133.00 (*0-7837-5349-7*, 204509200005) Bks Demand.

***Predators & Prey.** Michael Chinery. LC 00-20390. (Secrets of the Rainforest Ser.). (Illus.). 32p. (J). (gr. k-8). 2000. lib. bdg. 19.96 (*0-7787-0217-0*) Crabtree Pub Co.

***Predators & Prey.** Michael Chinery. (Secrets of the Rain Forest Ser.). (Illus.). 32p. (J). (gr. 3-8). 2000. pap. 7.95 (*0-7787-0227-8*) Crabtree Pub Co.

Predators & Who's for Dinner? Discovery Communications Staff & Carolyn B. Mitchell. LC 97-42899. (Animal Planet Ser.). (J). 1998. lib. bdg. 13.99 (*0-517-80005-5*) C Potter.

***Predators at Risk in the Pacific Northwest.** Dan A. Nelson. (Illus.). 144p. 2000. pap. 14.95 (*0-89886-733-9*) Mountaineers.

Predators' Ball: The Inside Story of Drexel Burnham & the Rise of the Junk Bond Raiders. Connie Bruck. 384p. 1989. pap. 13.95 (*0-14-012090-4*, Penguin Bks) Viking Penguin.

Predators in Our Pulpits. W. Phillip Keller. 192p. (Orig.). 1998. text 12.99 (*1-55661-018-1*) Bethany Hse.

Predators in the Rain Forest. Saviour Pirotta. (Deep in the Rain Forest Ser.). (Illus.). 32p. (J). (gr. 2-5). 1998. pap. 5.95 (*0-8172-8113-4*) Raintree Steck-V.

Predators in the Rain Forest. Saviour Pirotta. LC 98-4588. (Deep in the Rain Forest Ser.). (J). 1999. 22.83 (*0-8172-5132-4*) Raintree Steck-V.

Predator's Waltz. Jay Brandon. Ed. by Dana Isaacson. 304p. 1992. reprint ed. mass mkt. 4.99 (*0-671-70889-9*) PB.

Predatory Behavior among Wild Chimpanzees. Geza Teleki. LC 70-124442. (Illus.). 232p. 1975. 40.00 (*0-8387-7747-3*) Bucknell U Pr.

Predatory Cladocera (Onychopoda: Podonidae, Polyphemidae, Cercopagidae) & Leptodorida of the World) Onychoponda: Podonidae, Polyphemidae, Ceropagidae & Leptodorida of the World. I. K. Rivier. (Guides to the Identification of the Microinvertebrates of the Continental Waters of the World Ser.: Vol. 13). (Illus.). 214p. 1998. pap. 70.00 (*90-73348-85-4*, Pub. by Backhuys Pubs) Balogh.

Predatory Female. Lawrence Shannon. 171p. (Orig.). 1986. pap. 8.95 (*0-9615938-0-6*) Banner Bks.

Predatory Globalization: A Critique. Richard Falk. 224p. 1999. 59.95 (*0-7456-0935-X*, Pub. by Polity Pr); pap. 26.95 (*0-7456-0936-8*, Pub. by Polity Pr) Blackwell Pubs.

Predatory Heteroptera: Their Ecology & Use in Biological Control. M. Coll & J. R. Ruberson. (Thomas Say Publications in Entomology). 1997. pap. 35.00 (*0-938522-62-0*, ESATSP12) Entomol Soc.

Predatory Mammals in Britain. R. M. Stuttard. (C). 1986. 35.00 (*0-7855-3759-7*) St Mut.

Predatory Marketing. C. Britt Beemer & Robert L. Shook. LC 97-43240. 304p. 1998. pap. 14.00 (*0-7679-0189-4*) Broadway BDD.

Predatory Pricing. LC 96-83850. 78p. 1996. pap. 30.00 (*1-57073-305-8*, 503-0276, ABA Antitrust) Amer Bar Assn.

Predatory Pricing in a Market Economy. Roland H. Koller, II. LC 77-14781. (Dissertations in American Economic History Ser.). 1978. 41.95 (*0-405-11043-X*) Ayer.

Predatory Society: Deception in the American Marketplace. Paul Blumberg. 272p. 1990. reprint ed. pap. text 19.95 (*0-19-506654-5*) OUP.

Predecessors, et Cetera. Amy Clampitt. (Poets on Poetry Ser.). 184p. (C). 1991. pap. 13.95 (*0-472-06457-6*, 06457); text 39.50 (*0-472-09457-2*, 09457) U of Mich Pr.

***Predecessors Intellectual Lineages in American Studies.** Ed. by Rob Kroes. 300p. 2000. 50.00 (*90-5383-662-4*, Pub. by VU Univ Pr) Paul & Co Pubs.

Predecisional Process in Educational Administration: A Philosophical Analysis. Ellis A. Joseph. LC 74-17065. iv, 105p. 1975. 12.95 (*0-88280-017-5*); pap. 12.95 (*0-88280-018-3*) ETC Pubns.

Predestinacion. Loraine Boettner. (SPA.). 373p. 12.00 (*1-55883-064-2*, 6709-1510C) Libros Desafio.

Predestination. Gordon H. Clark. LC 87-16815. 224p. (Orig.). 1987. pap. 9.99 (*0-87552-169-X*) P & R Pubng.

***Predestination.** Reginald Garrigou-Lagrange. Tr. by Dom Bede Rose. LC 98-61398. Orig. Title: La Predestination des Saints et la Grace. 382p. 1999. reprint ed. pap. 15.00 (*0-89555-634-0*, 1574) TAN Bks Pubs.

Predestination: Bible Study - PBT. John A. Moldstad, Jr. 1998. 37.99 (*0-8100-0798-3*, 22N0906) Northwest Pub.

Predestination: Chosen in Christ. John A. Moldstad, Jr. LC 97-66994. (People's Bible Teachings Ser.). 125 p. 1997. 8.99 (*0-8100-0752-5*) Northwest Pub.

Predestination: Its Meaning, Blessing, Evidence, Implications. George P. Fletcher. pap. 0.99 (*0-87377-038-2*) GAM Pubns.

Predestination & Free Will. David Basinger & Randall Basinger. LC 85-23887. 180p. (Orig.). 1986. pap. 13.99 (*0-87784-567-0*, 567) InterVarsity.

Predestination, God's Foreknowledge, & Future Contingents. 2nd ed. William of Ockham. Tr. by Norman Kretzmann & Marilyn M. Adams from LAT. LC 82-23317. (HPC Classics Ser.). 146p. (C). 1983. 27.95 (*0-915144-14-X*); pap. text 9.95 (*0-915144-13-1*) Hackett Pub.

Predestination, Grace & Free Will. M. John Farrelly. 317p. 1994. reprint ed. 45.00 (*1-56518-060-7*) Coun Res Values.

Predestination, Policy & Polemic: Conflict & Consensus in the English Church from the Reformation to the Civil War. P. O. White. 350p. (C). 1993. text 69.95 (*0-521-39433-3*) Cambridge U Pr.

***Predestined & Designed for Purpose.** Tijuana Stamper. 112p. 2000. pap. text 9.95 (*1-889668-18-4*) S & D.

Predestined Love. Dick Sutphen. 264p. 1996. pap. text 14.95 (*0-87554-596-3*, B940) Valley Sun.

Prediabetes. Ed. by R. A. Camerini-Davalos & H. S. Cole. (Illus.). 418p. 1989. 110.00 (*0-306-43105-X*, Plenum Trade) Perseus Pubng.

Prediabetes - Are We Ready to Intervene? Ed. by Z. Laron & M. Karp. (Pediatric & Adolescent Endocrinology Ser.: Vol. 23). (Illus.). x, 192p. 1993. 213.25 (*3-8055-5665-9*) S Karger.

Predicacion: Manos a la Obra. Luis Palau.Tr. of Preaching: Hands at Work. (SPA.). 142p. 1995. 7.99 (*0-7899-0106-4*, 498629) Editorial Unilit.

***Predicacion: Puente Entre dos Mundos.** John Stott. Ed. by Alejandro Pimentel. Tr. by Anabella Rivas.Tr. of I Believe in Preaching. (SPA.). 2000. 22.00 (*1-55883-118-5*) Libros Desafio.

Predicacion Biblica - Biblical Preaching: Desarrollo de Mensajes Expositivos. Compilado. pap. write for info. (*0-7899-0233-8*) Editorial Unilit.

Predicament of Culture: Twentieth-Century Ethnography, Literature, & Art. James Clifford. LC 87-24173. (Illus.). 384p. 1988. 42.50 (*0-674-69842-8*); pap. 22.00 (*0-674-69843-6*) HUP.

Predicament of Democratic Man. Edmond N. Cahn. LC 78-16399. 194p. 1979. reprint ed. lib. bdg. 55.00 (*0-313-20597-3*, CAPR, Greenwood Pr) Greenwood.

Predicaments. Louis E. Shipman. LC 71-142276. (Short Story Index Reprint Ser.). (Illus.). 1977. 17.95 (*0-8369-3760-0*) Ayer.

Predicaments: Moral Difficulty in Everyday Life. Robert A. Stebbins. LC 93-2207. 164p. (Orig.). (C). 1993. pap. text 21.50 (*0-8191-9213-9*); lib. bdg. 48.50 (*0-8191-9212-0*) U Pr of Amer.

Predicaments of Love. J. Miriam Benn. 304p. (C). 59.95 (*0-7453-0528-8*); pap. 24.95 (*0-7453-0529-6*, Pub. by Pluto GBR) Stylus Pub VA.

Predicaments, or Music & the Future: An Essay in Constructive Criticism. Cecil Gray. LC 79-103652. (Select Bibliographies Reprint Ser.). 1977. 26.95 (*0-8369-5152-2*) Ayer.

Predicate Calculus & Program Semantics. E. W. Dijkstra & C. S. Scholten. (Texts & Monographs in Computer Science). 224p. 1989. 71.95 (*0-387-96957-8*) Spr-Verlag.

Predicate Formation in the Verbal System of Modern Hebrew. J. Junger. (Functional Grammar Ser.). vi, 182p. 1988. pap. 42.35 (*90-6765-368-3*) Mouton.

Predicate Logic: Predicate Logic. Richard L. Epstein. (The Semantic Foundations of Logic Ser.). (Illus.). 432p. 1994. text 75.00 (*0-19-508760-7*) OUP.

Predicate Nominals: A Partial Surface Syntax of Russian. Johanna Nichols. LC 80-16745. (University of California Publications in Social Welfare: No. 97). 415p. reprint ed. pap. 128.70 (*0-608-18190-0*, 203291800081) Bks Demand.

Predicate Structure in a Functional Grammar of Hungarian. Casper De Groot. (Functional Grammar Ser.). 248p. (Orig.). (C). 1989. pap. 53.60 (*90-6765-435-3*) Mouton.

Predicate-Transformation Semantics with Recursion & Unbounded Choice. Wim H. Hesselink. (Cambridge Tracts in Theoretical Computer Science Ser.: No. 27). (Illus.). 235p. (C). 1992. text 49.95 (*0-521-40436-3*) Cambridge U Pr.

Predicate Transformer Semantics. Ernest G. Manes. (Cambridge Tracts in Theoretical Computer Science Ser.: No. 33). 233p. (C). 1992. text 49.95 (*0-521-42036-9*) Cambridge U Pr.

Predicates & Temporal Arguments. Theodore B. Fernald. LC 98-45488. (Illus.). 176p. 2000. text 39.95 (*0-19-511435-3*) OUP.

Predicates & Terms in Functional Grammar. Ed. by A. M. Bolkestein et al. (Functional Grammar Ser.: No. 2). 304p. 1985. pap. 65.40 (*90-6765-104-4*) Mouton.

***Predicates & Their Subjects.** Susan D. Rothstein. LC 00-34898. (Studies in Linguistics & Philosophy). 2000. write for info. (*0-7923-6409-0*) Kluwer Academic.

Predication: A Study of Its Development. Carol Wall. LC 74-76119. (Janua Linguarum, Ser. Minor: No. 201). 1974. pap. 61.55 (*90-279-2665-4*) Mouton.

Predication in Caribbean English Creoles. Donald Winford. LC 92-34478. (Creole Language Library: No. 10). viii, 419p. 1993. 85.00 (*1-55619-164-2*) J Benjamins Pubng Co.

Predication Theory: A Case-Study for Indexing Theory. Donna J. Napoli. (Cambridge Studies in Linguistics: No. 50). (Illus.). 384p. 1989. text 95.00 (*0-521-35298-3*); pap. text 35.95 (*0-521-36820-0*) Cambridge U Pr.

***Predicative Forms in Natural Language & in Lexical Knowledge Bases.** Patrick Saint-Dizier. (Text, Speech, & Language Technology Ser.). 11p. 1999. write for info. (*0-7923-5499-0*) Kluwer Academic.

Prediciones Hasta el Ano 2000. Domingo Fernandez.Tr. of Predictions to the Year 2000. (SPA.). 200p. 1975. pap. 4.99 (*1-56063-264-X*, 497690) Editorial Unilit.

Predict & Applications Development Guide. Kim Canavan. 1994. 55.00 (*1-878960-21-0*) WH&O Intl.

Predict Prevent Hospital Decline. James J. Unland. 1993. text 40.00 (*0-7602-0119-6*, Irwn Prfssnl) McGraw-Hill Prof.

Predict Your Own Future with Solarhythm see Sun Cycles: The New Way to Discover Your Future

Predictability & Nonlinear Modeling in Natural Sciences & Economics. Ed. by J. Grasman & G. Van Straten. LC 94-21243. 1994. text 361.00 (*0-7923-2943-0*) Kluwer Academic.

Predictability, Correlation, & Contiguity. Ed. by Peter Harzem & Michael D. Zeiler. LC 80-40843. (Advances in Analysis of Behaviour Ser.: No. 2). (Illus.). 431p. reprint ed. pap. 133.70 (*0-608-17649-4*, 203050700069) Bks Demand.

Predictability of Complex Dynamical Systems. Yurii A. Kravtsov & James B. Kadtke. LC 96-31944. (Springer Series in Synergetics). (Illus.). 248p. 1996. 69.50 (*3-540-61287-4*) Spr-Verlag.

Predictability of Corporate Failure. R. A. Van Frederikslust. 1978. lib. bdg. 77.50 (*90-207-0736-1*) Kluwer Academic.

Predictability of Fluid Motions: AIP Conference Proccedings, La Jolla Institute, 1983, No. 106. Ed. by Greg Holloway & Bruce J. West. LC 83-73641. 60p. 1984. lib. bdg. 48.25 (*0-88318-305-6*) Am Inst Physics.

Predictability of Informal Conversation. Christine Cheepen. 224p. 1992. 49.00 (*0-86187-707-1*) St Martin.

Predictability, Stability & Chaos in N-Body Dynamical Systems. A. E. Roy. (NATO ASI Ser.: Vol. 272). (Illus.). 616p. (C). 1991. text 155.00 (*0-306-44034-2*, Plenum Trade) Perseus Pubng.

Predictable Failure of Educational Reform: Can We Change Course Before It's Too Late? Seymour B. Sarason. LC 90-40656. (Education-Higher Education Ser.). 205p. 1993. reprint ed. pap. text 19.00 (*1-55542-623-9*) Jossey-Bass.

***Predictable Secure Pension for Life: Defined Benefit Pensions.** 20p. 2000. per. 1.25 (*0-16-050223-3*, Pension Benefit) USGPO.

Predictably Dependable Computing Systems. Ed. by European Communities Staff et al. (ESPRIT Basic Research Ser.). 608p. 1995. 112.00 (*3-540-59334-9*) Spr-Verlag.

Predicted & Measured Behavior of Five Spread Footings on Sand: Proceedings of a Prediction Symposium Sponsored by the Federal Highway Administration at the Occasion of the Settlement of the '94 ASCE Conference at Texas A&M University, June 16-18, 1994. Ed. by Jean-Louis Briaud & Robert Gibbens. LC 94-19960. (Geotechnical Special Publications: No. 41). 260p. 1994. 32.00 (*0-7844-0025-3*) Am Soc Civil Eng.

Predicted & Observed Axial Behavior of Piles: Results of a Pile Prediction Symposium. Ed. by Richard J. Finno. 396p. 1989. pap. text 34.00 (*0-87262-721-7*, 721) Am Soc Civil Eng.

Predicted Log Contests. (Learning Guides Ser.). (Illus.). 64p. Date not set. pap. text 5.79 (*1-891148-11-7*) US Power.

Predicting. Group Diagram Staff. (Collins Gem Ser.). 1991. pap. 8.00 (*0-00-458996-3*) Collins.

Predicting Adult Stature for Individuals. Ed. by Alex F. Roche. (Monographs in Pediatrics: Vol. 3). 1975. 42.75 (*3-8055-1843-9*) S Karger.

Predicting & Designing for Natural & Man-Made Hazards. Compiled by American Society of Civil Engineers Staff. 297p. 1979. pap. 6.00 (*0-87262-187-1*) Am Soc Civil Eng.

Predicting Breeding Values with Applications in Forest Tree Improvement. Timothy L. White & Gary R. Hodge. (Forestry Sciences Ser.). (C). 1989. text 209.50 (*0-7923-0460-8*) Kluwer Academic.

Predicting CO2 Corrosion in the Oil & Gas Industry. Ed. by B. Kermani. (European Federation of Corrosion Publications Ser.: No. 13). 182p. 1994. 100.00 (*0-901716-58-8*, Pub. by Inst Materials) Ashgate Pub Co.

Predicting Criminality: Forecasting Behavior on Parole. Ferris F. Laune. LC 73-10851. 163p. 1974. reprint ed. lib. bdg. 22.50 (*0-8371-7041-9*, LAPC, Greenwood Pr) Greenwood.

Predicting Crop Phenology. Ed. by Thomas Hodges. 248p. 1990. lib. bdg. 210.00 (*0-8493-6745-X*, SB112) CRC Pr.

P

An Asterisk (*) at the beginning of an entry indicates that the title is appearing for the first time.

Predicting Duff Consumption from Prescribed Burns on Conifer Clearcuts in Western Oregon & Western Washington. Susan N. Little et al. (Illus.). 38p. 1998. reprint ed. pap. 8.40 (*0-89904-934-6*, Ecosystems Resrch) Crumb Elbow Pub.

Predicting Ecosystem Risk, Vol. XX. John Cairns, Jr. et al. (Advances in Modern Environmental Toxicology Ser.: Vol. 20). (Illus.). 345p. (Orig.). 1992. 65.00 (*0-911131-27-2*) Specialist Journals.

Predicting Events with Astrology. Celeste Teal. LC 99-22609. (Illus.). 288p. 1999. pap. 14.95 (*1-56718-704-8*, K704) Llewellyn Pubns.

Predicting First Grade Reading Achievement: A Study in Reading Readiness. Erby C. Deputy. LC 77-176705. (Columbia University. Teachers College. Contributions to Education Ser.: No. 426). reprint ed. 37.50 (*0-404-55426-1*) AMS Pr.

Predicting from Data. Hirsch & Coxford. (Mathematics Replacement Units Ser.). 1995. student ed. 8.63 (*0-02-824208-4*) Glencoe.

Predicting from Data: Teacher's Edition. Hirsch & Coxford. (Mathematics Replacement Units Ser.). 1995. teacher ed. 14.86 (*0-02-824209-2*) Glencoe.

Predicting Health Behaviour: Research & Practice with Social Cognition Models. Ed. by Mark Connor & Paul Norman. LC 95-14732. 240p. 1995. pap. 34.95 (*0-335-19320-X*) OpUniv Pr.

Predicting Intercity Freight Flows. Patrick T. Harker. (Topics in Transportation Ser.). 270p. 1987. lib. bdg. 102.00 (*90-6764-064-6*, Pub. by VSP) Coronet Bks.

Predicting Love, Marriage, Sex & Money: Predictive Astrology. Timothy E. Curley. 182p. 1995. pap. text 12.95 (*0-937533-18-1*) TEC Pubns.

Predicting Military Innovation. Jeffrey A. Isaacson et al. LC 99-184241. (Illus.). 72p. 1999. pap. 6.00 (*0-8330-2675-5*, DB-242-A) Rand Corp.

Predicting N Fertilizer Needs for Corn in Humid Regions: Proceedings of Soil Science Society of America Symposium on the Same Title, Denver, Nov. 1991. B. R. Bock & K. R. Kelley. (Bulletin Y-226 Ser.). 1992. write for info. (*0-87077-007-1*) TVA.

Predicting Outcomes. rev. ed. Rev. by Beth Bridgman. (Horizons Concepts Ser.: Level 1). (Illus.). 24p. (J). (gr. 4-9). 1998. pap. 5.95 (*1-58086-045-1*, Usborne) EDC.

Predicting Outcomes. rev. ed. Rev. by Beth Bridgman. (Horizons Concepts Ser.: Level 2). (Illus.). 24p. (J). (gr. 4-9). 1998. pap. 5.95 (*1-58086-055-9*, Usborne) EDC.

Predicting Outcomes in United States-Japan Trade Negotiations. Norio Naka. LC 95-24916. 296p. 1996. 65.00 (*1-56720-005-2*) Greenwood.

Predicting Photosynthesis for Ecosystem Models, 2 vols., Vol. 1. John D. Hesketh & J. W. Jones. 288p. 1980. 119.00 (*0-8493-5335-1*, QK882, CRC Reprint) Franklin.

Predicting Photosynthesis for Ecosystem Models, 2 vols., Vol. 2. John D. Hesketh & J. W. Jones. 304p. 1980. 119.00 (*0-8493-5336-X*, CRC Reprint) Franklin.

Predicting Seniors' Use of Cyberspace. rev. ed. Janet Dixon. LC 96-36709. (Studies on the Elderly in America). (Illus.). 144p. 1996. text 51.00 (*0-8153-2628-9*) Garland.

Predicting Social Maladjustment. J. Sarnecki & S. Sollenhag. 158p. (Orig.). 1985. pap. text 29.50 (*91-38-08877-0*, Pub. by Almqvist Wiksell) Coronet Bks.

Predicting Soil Erosion by Water: A Guide to Conservation Planning with the Revised Universal Soil Loss Equation (rusle) K. G. Renard. 404p. 1997. boxed set 47.00 (*0-16-060813-9*, Agriculture Dept) USGPO.

Predicting Stop-&-Go Traffic Noise Levels. (NCHRP Report: No. 311). 97p. 1989. 11.00 (*0-309-04608-4*, NR311) Transport Res Bd.

Predicting Success in Higher-Level Positions: A Guide to the System for Testing & Evaluation of Potential. Melany E. Baehr. LC 91-22017. 296p. 1992. 65.00 (*0-89930-626-8*, BTS, Quorum Bks) Greenwood.

Predicting Successful Hospital Mergers & Acquisitions: A Financial & Marketing Analytical Tool. David P. Angrisani & Robert L. Goldman. LC 96-24638. (Illus.). 132p. (C). 1997. 49.95 (*0-7890-0057-1*); pap. 22.95 (*0-7890-0182-9*) Haworth Pr.

P

Predicting the Behavior of the Educational System. Thomas F. Green et al. LC 97-61631. (Illus.). 220p. (C). 1997. pap. 24.95 (*0-9658339-2-5*) Educ Intl Pr.

Predicting the Behavior of the Educational System. Thomas F. Green et al. LC 80-12183. (Illus.). 222p. 1980. reprint ed. pap. 68.90 (*0-608-06972-8*, 206718000009) Bks Demand.

Predicting the Future. Ed. by Leo Howe & Alan Wain. (Darwin College Lectures). (Illus.). 201p. (C). 1993. 36.95 (*0-521-41323-0*) Cambridge U Pr.

Predicting the Future. Abr. by Sarah Zehavi. (Illus.). 240p. 1999. pap. 14.95 (*965-494-093-0*) Astrolog Pub.

Predicting the Future: AI Approaches to Time-Series Problems: Papers from the AAAI Workshop. Ed. by Andrea Danyluk. (Technical Reports: Vol. WS-98-07). (Illus.). 92p. 1998. spiral bd. 25.00 (*1-57735-060-X*) AAAI Pr.

Predicting the Future: An Introduction to the Theory of Forecasting. Nicholas Rescher. LC 97-1986. 315p. (C). 1997. text 65.50 (*0-7914-3553-9*); pap. text 21.95 (*0-7914-3554-7*) State U NY Pr.

Predicting the Future: From Jules Verne to Bill Gates. John Malone. LC 97-21360. 194p. 1997. 19.95 (*0-87131-830-X*) M Evans.

Predicting the Future, the Future of Social & Personal Care: The Role of Social Services Organisations in the Public Private & Voluntary Sectors. Daphne Statham. 1990. pap. 50.00 (*1-899942-11-4*, Pub. by Natl Inst Soc Work) St Mut.

Predicting the Future with Astrology: A Step-by-Step Guide. Sasha Fenton. LC 96-51973. 240p. 1997. pap. 10.95 (*0-8069-9697-8*) Sterling.

Predicting the Future with the Wonderful Wizard of Oz. Nancy Polette. (Illus.). 48p. 1998. pap. 7.95 (*1-880505-27-4*, GGA2005) Pieces of Lrning.

Predicting the Next Great Quake. David Nabhan. (Illus.). 68p. (Orig.). 1996. pap. 6.95 (*0-9654681-0-0*) Red Lion Pub.

*__Predicting the Past: An Exploration of Myth, Science & Prehistory.__ Roger W. Wescott. Ed. by Dwardu Cardona. (Osiris Ser.: Vol. III). (Illus.). 320p. 2000. 38.00 (*0-917994-16-7*) Kronos Pr.

Predicting the Performance of Multistage Separation Process. F. Khoury. 256p. 1995. 125.00 (*0-88415-641-9*, 5641) Gulf Pub.

*__Predicting the Performance of Multistage Separation Processes.__ 2nd ed. Fouad M. Khoury. LC 99-15552. 488p. 1999. boxed set 99.95 (*0-8493-1495-X*) CRC Pr.

*__Predicting the Performance of Multistage Separation Processes.__ 2nd ed. Fouad M. Khoury. (C). 1999. ring bd. write for info. (*0-8493-0349-4*) CRC Pr.

Predicting the Properties of Mixtures: Mixture Rules in Science & Engineering. Lawrence E. Nielsen. LC 77-16705. 108p. reprint ed. pap. 33.50 (*0-8357-3501-X*, 203455700090) Bks Demand.

Predicting the Quality of Teaching: The Predictive Value of Certain Traits for Effectiveness in Teaching. Arthur L. Odenweller. LC 72-177130. (Columbia University. Teachers College. Contributions to Education Ser.: No. 676). reprint ed. 37.50 (*0-404-55676-0*) AMS Pr.

Predicting Tillage Effects on Soil Physical Properties & Processes. Ed. by P. W. Unger et al. (ASA Special Publications: No. 44). 198p. (C). 1982. pap. 7.00 (*0-89118-069-9*) Am Soc Agron.

Predicting Violent Behavior: An Assessment of Clinical Techniques. John Monahan. LC 81-851. (Sage Library of Social Research: No. 114). 183p. reprint ed. pap. 56.80 (*0-8357-8499-1*, 203477500091) Bks Demand.

Predicting Water Contamination from Metal Mines & Mining Waste. Kathleen S. Smith et al. (Illus.). 112p. (Orig.). (C). 1995. pap. text 40.00 (*0-7881-2007-7*) DIANE Pub.

Predicting Your Future. Diagram Group Staff. 128p. 1985. pap. 10.00 (*0-345-33579-1*) Ballantine Pub Grp.

*__Prediction: Science, Decision Making & the Future of Nature.__ Ed. by Daniel Sarewitz et al. LC 00-8179. 400p. 2000. pap. 29.50 (*1-55963-776-5*) Island Pr.

Prediction & Classification. Ed. by Don M. Gottfredson & Michael H. Tonry. LC 80-642217. (Studies in Crime & Justice: Vol. 9). 432p. (C). 1987. lib. bdg. 33.00 (*0-226-80803-3*) U Ch Pr.

Prediction & Classification: Criminal Justice Decision Making. Ed. by Don M. Gottfredson & Michael H. Tonry. LC 80-642217. (Studies in Crime & Justice: A Review of Research Ser.: Vol. 9). 440p. 1988. pap. text 18.00 (*0-226-80809-2*) U Ch Pr.

Prediction & Estimation in Arma Models. Helgi Tomasson. 118p. (Orig.). 1986. pap. text 32.50 (*91-22-00798-9*) Coronet Bks.

Prediction & Improved Estimation in Linear Models. John Bibby & Helge Toutenburg. LC 76-7533. 202p. reprint ed. pap. 62.70 (*0-8357-3394-7*, 203965100013) Bks Demand.

Prediction & Optimal Decision: Philosophical Issues of a Science Values. Charles W. Chruchman. LC 82-6264. (International Management Ser.). 394p. 1982. reprint ed. lib. bdg. 79.50 (*0-313-23418-3*, CHUP, Greenwood Pr) Greenwood.

Prediction & Perception of Natural Hazards: Proceedings Symposium, 22-26 October 1990, Perugia, Italy. Ed. by Jaromir Nemec et al. LC 93-4585. (Advances in Natural & Technological Hazards Research Ser.: Vol. 2). 216p. (C). 1993. lib. bdg. 100.00 (*0-7923-2355-6*) Kluwer Academic.

Prediction & Performance in Geotechnical Engineering: Proceedings of an International Symposium on Prediction & Performance in Geotechnical Engineering, Calgary, 17-19 June 1987. Ed. by R. C. Joshi & F. J. Griffiths. 464p. (C). 1987. text 201.00 (*90-6191-707-7*, Pub. by A A Balkema) Ashgate Pub Co.

Prediction & Performance in Rock Mechanics & Rock Engineering: Proceedings/Comptes-Rendus/ Sitzungsberichte/SPE/ISRM International Conference, EUROCK '96, Turin, 2-5.09.1996, 3 vols. Ed. by Giovanni Barla. (Illus.). 1000p. (C). 1996. 362.00 (*90-5410-843-6*, Pub. by A A Balkema) Ashgate Pub Co.

*__Prediction & Prevention of Reading Failure.__ Ed. by Nathlie A. Badian. (C). 2000. Price not set. (*0-912752-57-2*) York Pr.

Prediction & Regulation by Linear Least-Square Methods. 2nd rev. ed. Peter Whittle. LC 83-6881. 205p. reprint ed. pap. 63.60 (*0-7837-2905-7*, 205754900006) Bks Demand.

Prediction & Regulation of Air Pollution: Revised & Updated Version of the Russian Edition. M. E. Berlyand. (Atmospheric Sciences Library). 320p. 1991. lib. bdg. 141.50 (*0-7923-1000-4*) Kluwer Academic.

Prediction au XIIIe Siecle en France & Italie: Etudes & Documents. Louis-Jacques Bataillon. (Collected Studies: No. CS 402). (ENG, FRE & ITA.). 352p. 1993. 119.95 (*0-86078-375-8*, Pub. by Variorum) Ashgate Pub Co.

Prediction de Meredith. Regan Forest. (Rouge Passion Ser.). (FRE.). 1997. pap. 3.50 (*0-373-37436-4*, 1-37436-2) Harlequin Bks.

Prediction in Astrology: A Master Volume of Technique & Practice. Noel Tyl. LC 91-32897. (New World Astrology Ser.). (Illus.). 360p. (Orig.). 1991. pap. 17.95 (*0-87542-814-2*) Llewellyn Pubns.

Prediction in Criminology. Ed. by David P. Farrington & Roger Tarling. LC 84-16447. (SUNY Series in Critical Issues in Criminal Justice). 278p. (C). 1985. text 67.50 (*0-88706-004-8*); pap. text 24.95 (*0-88706-003-X*) State U NY Pr.

Prediction in Psychotherapy Research: A Method for the Transformation of Clinical Judgments into Testable Hypotheses. Helen D. Sargent et al. LC 68-18496. (Psychological Issues Monographs: No. 21, Vol. 6, No. 1). 154p. (Orig.). 1968. 27.50 (*0-8236-4285-2*) Intl Univs Pr.

Prediction Methods for Organo-Metallic Compounds: Supplements. K. H. Myers & R. P. Danner. (Design Institute for Physical Property Data Ser.). 186p. 1991. spiral bd. 45.00 (*0-8169-0560-6*) Am Inst Chem Eng.

Prediction of Achievement & Creativity. Raymond B. Cattell & H. J. Butcher. LC 67-18662. 1968. 39.50 (*0-672-60641-0*); pap. text 14.95 (*0-89197-900-X*) Irvington.

Prediction of Bypass Transition with Differential Reynolds Stress Models. K. J. Westin & R. A. Henkes. (Series 01 - Aerodynamics: No. 10). (Illus.). 74p. 1998. pap. 18.95 (*90-407-1573-4*, Pub. by Delft U Pr) Coronet Bks.

Prediction of Concrete Durability. Ed. by J. Glanville & A. M. Neville. LC 97-198693. (Illus.). 208p. (C). 1997. 95.00 (*0-419-21170-5*, E & FN Spon) Routledge.

Prediction of Creep, Shrinkage, & Temperature Effects in Concrete Structures. 47p. 1992. 40.95 (*0-685-62957-0*, 209R-92BOW6) ACI.

Prediction of Criminal Behaviour: Statistical Approaches. Thomas Gabor. 121p. 1986. text 35.00 (*0-8020-5691-1*) U of Toronto Pr.

Prediction of Effects Caused by a Cable Fire Experiment Within the HDR Facility Final Comparison Report 8-93. H. Karwat. 180p. 1994. pap. 25.00 (*92-826-8180-7*, Pub. by Comm Europ Commun) Bernan Associates.

Prediction of GAC Performance Using Rapid Small-Scale Column Tests. 212p. 1989. pap. 32.00 (*0-89867-480-8*, 90549) Am Water Wks Assn.

Prediction of Gear Noise from Design Data. Irving Laskin. (Technical Papers: Vol. P299.03). (Illus.). 19p. (Orig.). 1968. pap. text 30.00 incl. audio compact disk (*1-55589-382-1*) AGMA.

Prediction of Growth in Uneven-Aged Timber Stands on the Basis of Diameter Distributions. Jesse H. Buell. LC SD0555.B9. (Duke University, School of Forestry Bulletin Ser.: No. 11). (Illus.). 70p. reprint ed. pap. 30.00 (*0-7837-6049-3*, 204586200008) Bks Demand.

Prediction of Interannual Climate Variations. NATO Advanced Research Workshop on Prediction of I. Ed. by J. Shukla. LC 93-18453. (ASI Series 1, Global Environmental Change: Vol. 6). 1993. 174.95 (*0-387-54591-3*) Spr-Verlag.

Prediction of Ionospheric Conditions. G. S. Ivanov-Kholodny & A. V. Mikhailov. 1986. text 144.00 (*90-277-2143-2*) Kluwer Academic.

Prediction of Neuroleptic Treatment Outcome in Schizophrenia: Concepts & Methods. Ed. by W. Gaebel & A. G. Awad. LC 95-10013. (Illus.). 224p. 1994. pap. 59.00 (*0-387-82602-5*) Spr-Verlag.

Prediction of Organizational Behavior. N. Frederiksen et al. LC 72-188309. 344p. (C). 1973. 157.00 (*0-08-016967-8*, Pub. by Pergamon Repr) Franklin.

Prediction of Percutaneous Penetration: Methods, Measurement, Modelling. R. C. Scott et al. 450p. (C). 1990. 350.00 (*1-85271-117-5*, Pub. by IBC Tech Srvs) St Mut.

Prediction of Performance in Clinical Psychology. Everett L. Kelly & Donald W. Fiske. LC 69-10113. (Illus.). 1969. reprint ed. lib. bdg. 79.50 (*0-8371-0914-0*, KECP, Greenwood Pr) Greenwood.

Prediction of Polymer Properties. Jozef Bicerano. LC 92-44567. (Plastics Engineering Ser.: Vol. 27). (Illus.). 427p. reprint ed. pap. 132.40 (*0-608-08914-1*, 206954900005) Bks Demand.

Prediction of Polymer Properties. 2nd ed. Jozef Bicerano. LC 96-25977. (Plastics Engineering Ser.: Vol. 38). (Illus.). 552p. 1996. text 180.00 (*0-8247-9781-7*) Dekker.

Prediction of Protein Structure & the Principles of Protein Conformation. G. D. Fasman. (Illus.). 776p. (C). 1989. text 125.00 (*0-306-43131-9*, Kluwer Plenum) Kluwer Academic.

Prediction of Reservoir Quality Through Chemical Modeling. Ed. by Indu D. Meshri & Peter J. Ortoleva. (AAPG Memoir Ser.: No. 49). (Illus.). 175p. 1990. 15.00 (*0-89181-327-6*, 563) AAPG.

Prediction of Response in Radiation Therapy, Pts. 1 & 2: Proceedings of the Third International Conference on Dose, Time & Fractionation Held at the University of Wisconsin, Madison, Wisconsin, September 14-17, 1988, Pt. 1. Ed. by Bhudatt R. Paliwal et al. (American Association of Physicists in Medicine Symposium Ser.: No. 7). 770p. 1989. 60.00 (*0-685-72476-X*, Pub. by Am Inst Physics) Med Physics Pub.

Prediction of Response in Radiation Therapy, Pts. 1 & 2: Proceedings of the Third International Conference on Dose, Time & Fractionation Held at the University of Wisconsin, Madison, Wisconsin, September 14-17, 1988, Pt. 2. Ed. by Bhudatt R. Paliwal et al. 770p. 1989. text. write for info. (*0-318-68430-6*, Pub. by Am Inst Physics) Med Physics Pub.

Prediction of Solar Radiation in Areas with a Specific Microclimate. Ed. by R. Dogiaux. 120p. (C). 1994. text 85.50 (*0-7923-2596-6*) Kluwer Academic.

Prediction of Solar Radiation on Inclined Surfaces. Ed. by J. K. Page. 1986. text 209.50 (*90-277-2260-9*) Kluwer Academic.

Prediction of Success in Professional Courses for Teachers. Laura B. Krieger. LC 71-176942. (Columbia University. Teachers College. Contributions to Education Ser.: No. 420). reprint ed. 37.50 (*0-404-55420-2*) AMS Pr.

Prediction of Suicide. Ed. by Aaron T. Beck et al. LC 86-71588. 256p. 1987. reprint ed. pap. 19.95 (*0-914783-16-5*) Charles.

Prediction of Temperature Gradients in Large Buildings. K. E. Moreton-Smith. 1992. pap. 60.00 (*0-86022-330-2*, Pub. by Build Servs Info Assn) St Mut.

Prediction of the Deformation Properties of Polymeric & Composite Materials. A. Ya. Goldman. Ed. & Tr. by M. Shelef & R. A. Dickie. LC 93-42915. (ACS Professional Reference Bk.). 349p. 1994. 78.00 (*0-8412-2504-4*, Pub. by Am Chemical) OUP.

Prediction of the Peak Temperature on the Surface of Thermoplastic Gear Teeth. R. Gauvin et al. (Technical Papers: Vol. P149.03). (Illus.). 28p. 1983. pap. text 30.00 (*1-55589-082-2*) AGMA.

Prediction of Transport & Other Physical Properties of Fluids. S. Bretsznajder. 424p. 1971. 191.00 (*0-08-013412-2*, Pub. by Pergamon Repr) Franklin.

Prediction of Turbulent Reacting Flows in Practical Systems: Presented at the Fluids Engineering Conference, Boulder, Colorado, June 22-24, 1981. Fluids Engineering Conference Staff. Ed. by Thomas Morel. LC 80-71113. (Illus.). 44p. reprint ed. pap. 30.00 (*0-8357-2897-8*, 203913300011) Bks Demand.

Prediction of Wind & Current Loads on VLCCs. OCIMF Staff. (C). 1977. 400.00 (*0-7855-4682-0*, Pub. by Witherby & Co) St Mut.

Prediction of Wind & Current Loads on VLCCS. OCIMF Staff. 1993. 240.00 (*1-85609-042-6*, Pub. by Witherby & Co) St Mut.

Prediction of Wind Loads on Large Liquefied Gas Carriers. OCIMF Staff & SIGTTO Staff. (C). 1985. 600.00 (*0-900886-97-8*, Pub. by Witherby & Co) St Mut.

Prediction 1. Alexander Marr. LC 82-71346. 152p. 1981. 14.00 (*0-86690-032-2*, M2581-014) Am Fed Astrologers.

Prediction or Premonition - Coincidence Be Damned. Lorna Middleton. 94p. (C). 1989. text 50.00 (*0-946270-80-5*, Pub. by Pentland Pr) St Mut.

Prediction Recidivism Using Survival Models. P. C. Schmidt & A. D. Witte. (Research in Criminology Ser.). (Illus.). 160p. 1988. 87.95 (*0-387-96596-3*) Spr-Verlag.

*__Prediction Techniques Regarding Romance.__ 49p. 1998. spiral bd. 8.00 (*0-86690-490-5*) Am Fed Astrologers.

Prediction Theory for Finite Populations. H. Bolfarine & S. Zacks. Ed. by J. O. Berger et al. (Series in Statistics). 224p. (C). 1992. 72.95 (*0-387-97785-6*) Spr-Verlag.

Prediction vs. Performance in Geotechnical Engineering: Proceedings of the Symposium, Bangkok, November-December 1992. Ed. by A. S. Balasubramaniam et al. (Illus.). 450p. (C). 1994. text 136.00 (*90-5410-355-8*, Pub. by A A Balkema) Ashgate Pub Co.

Predictions: Society's Telltale Signature Reveals the Past & Forecasts the Future. Theodore Modis. 288p. 1992. 21.00 (*0-671-75917-5*) S&S Trade.

*__Predictions: Thirty Great Minds Predict the Future.__ Ed. by Sian Griffiths. (Popular Science Ser.). 352p. 2000. 16.95 (*0-19-286210-3*) OUP.

Predictions for a New Millennium. Noel Tyl. LC 96-24922. (Illus.). 304p. (Orig.). 1999. pap. 14.95 (*1-56718-737-4*) Llewellyn Pubns.

Predictions for the Next Millennium: Thoughts on the 1,000 Years Ahead from Celebrities of Today. David Kristof & Todd W. Nickerson. LC 98-7513. 288p. 1998. 18.95 (*0-8362-6916-0*) Andrews & McMeel.

Predictions of Hamilton & de Tocqueville. James B. Bryce. LC 78-63775. (Johns Hopkins University. Studies in the Social Sciences. Thirtieth Ser. 1912: 9). reprint ed. 11.50 (*0-404-61041-2*) AMS Pr.

Predictions of Public Opinion from the Mass Media: Computer Content Analysis & Mathematical Modeling, 12. David P. Fan. LC 88-5683. (Contributions to the Study of Mass Media & Communications Ser.: No. 12). 220p. 1988. 57.95 (*0-313-26296-9*, FNP/) Greenwood.

Predictions of Wind & Current Loads on VLCC's. OCIMF Staff. 1977. 360.00 (*0-7855-1776-6*, Pub. by Witherby & Co) St Mut.

Predictions of Wind Loads on Large Liquified Gas Carrers. OCIMF Staff & SSIGTTO Staff. 1987. 540.00 (*0-7855-1777-4*, Pub. by Witherby & Co) St Mut.

Predictions to the Year 2000 see Predicciones Hasta el Ano 2000

Predictive Astrology. Ernest Grant & Catherine Grant. LC 88-70467. (Grant Textbook Ser.: Vol. 4). 238p. 1988. 23.00 (*0-86690-344-5*, G2812-014) Am Fed Astrologers.

*__Predictive Astrology: An Insight.__ Dinesh S. Mathur. LC 99-932617. 435p. 1999. pap. 100.00 (*81-208-1627-7*, Pub. by Motilal Bnarsidass) St Mut.

Predictive Astrology: The Eagle & the Lark. Bernadette Brady. LC 98-42896. Orig. Title: The Eagle & the Lark: A Textbook of Predictive Astrology. (Illus.). 388p. 1999. reprint ed. pap. 19.95 (*1-57863-112-2*) Weiser.

Predictive Astrology of the Hindus. G. K. Ojha. (Illus.). 347p. 1990. 19.95 (*0-318-36380-1*) Asia Bk Corp.

Predictive Behavior: An Experimental Study. Gunnar Brennscheidt. LC 93-33121. (Lecture Notes in Economics & Mathematical Systems Ser.: Vol. 403). 1993. 55.95 (*0-387-57311-9*) Spr-Verlag.

Predictive Control with Constraints. Jan Maclejonski. 256p. (C). 2000. 84.95 (*0-201-39823-0*) Addison-Wesley.

Predictive Corrosion & Failure Control in the Petrochemical Industry. Peter F. Timmins. 220p. 1996. 154.00 (*0-87170-581-8*, 6487) ASM.

An Asterisk (*) at the beginning of an entry indicates that the title is appearing for the first time.

Predictive Data Mining. Sholom M. Weiss & Nitin Indurkhya. LC 97-30682. 225p. 1997. 39.95 (*1-55860-403-0*) Morgan Kaufmann.

Predictive Data Mining, Incl. Web Site Access. Sholom W. Weiss & Nitin Indurkhya. 225p. (C). 1997. 59.95 (*1-55860-478-2*) Morgan Kaufmann.

Predictive Dialing Fundamentals: An Overview of Predictive Dialing Technologies, Their Applications & Usage Today. Aleksander Szlam & Ken Thatcher. (Illus.). 153p. 1996. pap. 24.95 (*0-936648-80-5*) Telecom Bks.

***Predictive Formulae for Weld Distortion: A Critical Review.** G. Verhaeghe. 96p. 1999. 135.00 (*1-85573-444-3*) Am Educ Systs.

Predictive High Resolution Sequence Stratigraphy. K. O. Sandvik et al. LC 99-183873. 450p. 1998. write for info. (*0-444-82780-3*) Elsevier.

Predictive Limnology: Methods for Predictive Modeling. L. Hakanson & R. H. Peters. (Illus.). xi, 464p. 1995. 199.00 (*90-5103-104-1*, Pub. by SPB Acad Pub) Balogh.

Predictive Methods for Assessing Corrosion Damage to BWR Piping & PWR Steam Generators. LC 81-85852. (Illus.). 393p. 1982. 10.00 (*0-915567-52-0*) NACE Intl.

Predictive Methods for the Energy Conserving Design of Buildings. Henry J. Cowan. (Illus.). 128p. 1983. text 37.00 (*0-08-029838-9*, Pergamon Pr) Elsevier.

Predictive Modular Neural Networks: Applications to Time Series. Vassilios Petridis & Athansios Kehagias. LC 98-38777. (International Series in Engineering & Computer Science). 1998. 125.00 (*0-7923-8290-0*) Kluwer Academic.

Predictive Planetary Periods. Barbara Cameron. LC 82-73122. 158p. 1984. 17.00 (*0-86690-235-X*, C2645-014) Am Fed Astrologers.

Predictive Process Control of Crowded Particulate Suspensions: Applied to Ceramic Manufacturing. James E. Funk. LC 93-32257. 824p. (C). 1993. lib. bdg. 259.50 (*0-7923-9409-7*) Kluwer Academic.

Predictive Prophecy. George P. Fletcher. pap. 0.15 (*0-87377-091-9*) GAM Pubns.

Predictive Techniques in Annual Harmonics. Charles Hannan & Lois Hannan. LC 85-71463. 99p. 1986. 13.00 (*0-86690-296-1*, H2347-014) Am Fed Astrologers.

Predictive Toxicology of Chemicals: Experiences & Impacts of AI Tools: Papers from the AAAI Spring Symposium. Ed. by Giuseppina C. Gini & Alan B. Katritzky. (Technical Reports: Vol. SS-99-01). (Illus.). 152p. 1998. spiral bd. 25.00 (*1-57735-073-1*) AAAI Pr.

Predictors. Thomas A. Bass. 1998. write for info. (*0-201-62473-7*) Addison-Wesley.

***Predictors.** Thomas A. Bass. LC 98-41820. 336p. 1999. 25.00 (*0-8050-5756-0*) H Holt & Co.

Predictors: How a Band of Maverick Physicists Used Chaos Theory to Trade Their Way to a Fortune on Wall Street. Thomas A. Bass. 320p. 2000. pap. 15.00 (*0-8050-5757-9*, Owl) H Holt & Co.

Predictors of Moral Reasoning: How the School Helps Children to Develop Appropriate Values. Pertti V. Yli-Luoma. (International Association for the Evaluation of Education Achievement Monograph Ser.: No. 14). (Illus.). 173p. (Orig.). 1990. pap. 41.00 (*91-22-01334-2*) Coronet Bks.

Predictors of Relapse in Schizophrenia. Ed. by Jeffrey A. Lieberman & John M. Kane. LC 86-10900. (Clinical Insights Ser.). 167p. reprint ed. pap. 51.80 (*0-8357-7847-9*, 203622300002) Bks Demand.

Predictors of Treatment Response in Mood Disorders. Ed. by Paul J. Goodnick. (Clinical Practice Ser.: No. 34). 224p. 1995. text 32.00 (*0-88048-494-2*, 8494) Am Psychiatric.

Predigten see Luthers Werke in Auswahl

Predigten des Hl. Bernhard in Altfranzosischer Ubertragung. Bernard De Clarivaux. xx, 442p. 1979. reprint ed. write for info. (*3-487-06877-X*) G Olms Pubs.

Predique por un Ano, No. 1. Roger Campbell. (SPA.). 224p. 1996. pap. 8.99 (*0-8254-1114-9*, Edit Portavoz) Kregel.

Predique por un Ano: 104 Boxquejos de Sermones, Vol. 2. Roger F. Campbell. (SPA.). 224p. 1997. pap. 8.99 (*0-8254-1115-7*, Edit Portavoz) Kregel.

Predique por un Ano (Preach for a Year), Vol. 3. Roger Campbell. (SPA.). 224p. 1998. pap. 8.99 (*0-8254-1116-5*, Edit Portavoz) Kregel.

Predique por un Ano (Preach for a Year), Vol. 4. Roger Campbell. (SPA.). 224p. 1999. pap. 8.99 (*0-8254-1117-3*, Edit Portavoz) Kregel.

Predoctoral Astrophysics School: 5th: 1992: Berlin, Germany: Star Formation & Techniques in Infrared & mm-Wave Astronomy: Lectures Held at the Predoctoral Astrophysics School V, Organized by the European Astrophysics Doctoral Network (EADN) in Berlin, Germany, 21 Sept.-20 Oct. 1992. Thomas P. Ray. Ed. by S. Beckwith. LC 94-25872. 1994. 72.95 (*0-387-58196-0*) Spr-Verlag.

Predominantly Fish: New Interpretations for Cooking Fish & Shellfish. Nancy Longo. LC 87-82252. (Illus.). 128p. 1987. pap. 9.95 (*0-9619112-0-4*) Fissurelle.

Predstavlenie I Drugie Rasskazy. Sergei Dovlatov. LC 87-60054. 100p. (Orig.). 1987. pap. 8.50 (*0-89830-111-4*) Russica Pubs.

Predstavujeme Vam Svepomocne Vzajemne Poradenstvi (SVP) see Introduction to Co-Counseling

Predynastic Egypt. Barbara Adams. (Shire Egyptology Ser.). (Illus.). 76p. 1988. pap. text 12.00 (*0-85263-938-4*, Pub. by Shire Pubns) Lubrecht & Cramer.

Preemie Parents' Companion: The Essential Guide to Caring for Your Premature Baby in the Hospital, at Home & Through the First Years. Susan L. Madden. LC 99-25790. (Illus.). 336p. 2000. pap. 14.95 (*1-55832-135-7*) Harvard Common Pr.

Preemie Parents' Companion: The Essential Guide to Caring for Your Premature Baby in the Hospital, at Home & Through the First Years. Susan L. Madden. LC 99-25790. (Illus.). 336p. 2000. 27.95 (*1-55832-134-9*) Harvard Common Pr.

***Preemies: A Companion Guide for Parents of Premature Babies.** Dana Wechsler Linden et al. 2000. pap. write for info. (*0-671-02413-2*, PB Trade Paper) PB.

***Preemies: The Essential Guide for Parents of Premature Babies.** Dana Wechsler Linden et al. (Illus.). 576p. 2000. 24.95 (*0-671-03491-X*) PB.

***Preeminent Person of Christ: Hebrews 1-10.** Charles R. Swindoll. 1998. pap., student ed. 5.95 (*1-57972-196-6*) Insight Living.

Preemployment Honesty Testing: Current Research & Future Directions. Ed. by John W. Jones. LC 90-45145. 280p. 1991. 65.00 (*0-89930-620-9*, JPE, Quorum Bks) Greenwood.

Preemployment Integrity Testing: How to Ace the Test & Land the Job. Charles Clifton. 112p. 1993. pap. 12.00 (*0-87364-725-4*) Paladin Pr.

Preemployment Process: Avoiding Impermissible Inquiries & the Effect of the Americans with Disabilities Act. Janet L. Horton. (Monograph Ser.). 40p. 1993. text 18.00 (*1-56534-081-7*) Ed Law Assn.

Preempting the Holocaust. Lawrence L. Langer. LC 98-60967. (Illus.). 232p. 1998. 27.50 (*0-300-07357-7*) Yale U Pr.

***Preempting the Holocaust.** Lawrence L. Langer. (Illus.). 232p. 2000. pap. 12.95 (*0-300-08268-1*) Yale U Pr.

Preemptive Defense: Allied Air Power Versus Hitler's V-weapons, 1943-1945. Adam L. Gruen. 43p. 1998. pap. 2.50 (*0-16-049671-3*) USGPO.

Preempts from A to Z. Ron Andersen & Sabine Zenkel. 300p. 1993. pap. text 14.95 (*0-9637533-0-4*) Magnus Bks.

Preempts from A to Z. 2nd rev. ed. Ron Andersen & Sabine Zenkel. Ed. by Henry Francis. 328p. 1996. pap. 15.95 (*0-9637533-3-9*) Magnus Bks.

***Prefab Kid: A Postwar Childhood in Kent.** large type unabridged ed. Gregory Holyoake. 2000. 25.95 (*0-7531-5719-5*, 157195, Pub. by ISIS Lrg Prnt) ISIS Pub.

Prefabricated Bridge Elements & Systems. (National Cooperative Highway Research Program Report Ser.: No. 119). 75p. 1985. 8.80 (*0-309-04002-7*) Transport Res Bd.

Prefabricated Construction in Turkey: A Strategic Entry Report, 1996. Compiled by Icon Group International Staff. (Illus.). 144p. 1999. ring bd. 1440.00 incl. audio compact disk (*0-7418-0717-3*) Icon Grp.

Prefabricated Housing in Argentina: A Strategic Entry Report, 1997. Compiled by Icon Group International Staff. (Illus.). 135p. 1999. ring bd. 1350.00 incl. audio compact disk (*0-7418-0131-0*) Icon Grp.

Prefabricated Housing in Costa Rica: A Strategic Entry Report, 1995. Compiled by Icon Group International Staff. (Illus.). 141p. 1999. ring bd. 1410.00 incl. audio compact disk (*0-7418-0718-1*) Icon Grp.

Prefabricated Thin-Walled Concrete Units. 33p. 1984. 26.00 (*0-7277-0213-0*, Pub. by T Telford) RCH.

Prefabricated Vertical Drains & Pavement Drainage Systems. (Research Record Ser.: No. 1159). 67p. 1988. 10.50 (*0-309-04668-8*) Transport Res Bd.

***Prefabrication & Preassembly: Applying the Techniques to Building Engineering Services.** D. G. Wilson et al. 153p. 1998. pap. 340.00 (*0-86022-505-4*, Pub. by Build Servs Info Assn) St Mut.

Prefabrication with Concrete. A. S. Bruggeling & G. F. Huyghe. (Illus.). 397p. (C). 1991. text 155.00 (*90-6191-183-4*, Pub. by A A Balkema) Ashgate Pub Co.

Prefabs: The History of the U. K. Temporary Housing Programme. Brenda Vale. LC 95-194398. (Studies in History, Planning & the Environment). (Illus.). 200p. (C). 1995. 85.00 (*0-419-18800-2*, E & FN Spon) Routledge.

Preface a la Vie d'Ecrivain. Gustave Flaubert. (FRE.). 297p. 1990. 45.00 (*0-7859-1071-9*, 2020122987) Fr & Eur.

Preface Marketing Management. 8th ed. Peter. LC 99-10058. 336p. 1999. pap. 48.75 (*0-07-366151-1*) McGraw.

Preface Milton. 2nd ed. Lois Potter. (Preface Bks.). 184p. (C). 1986. pap. text 30.94 (*0-582-35479-X*, 72231) Longman.

Preface to a Neo-Firthian Linguistics. William M. Christie, Jr. LC 80-21016. (Edward Sapir Monographs in Language, Culture & Cognition: No. 7). viii, 70p. (Orig.). (C). 1980. pap. 18.00 (*0-933104-11-1*) Jupiter Pr.

Preface to Ambedkarism. R. C. Prasad. (C). 1993. 21.00 (*81-208-1088-0*, Pub. by Motilal Bnarsidass) S Asia.

Preface to American Political Theory. Donald S. Lutz. LC 92-11700. (American Political Thought Ser.). xii, 188p. 1992. 27.50 (*0-7006-0545-2*); pap. 12.95 (*0-7006-0546-0*) U Pr of KS.

Preface to Banking. 2nd rev. ed. David H. Friedman. 72p. (C). 1991. pap. text 27.00 (*0-685-59017-8*) Am Bankers.

Preface to Chaos: War in the Making. C. Hartley Grattan. 1973. 59.95 (*0-8490-0887-5*) Gordon Pr.

Preface to Democratic Theory. Robert A. Dahl. LC 56-6642. (Walgreen Foundation Lectures). 160p. 1963. pap. text 7.95 (*0-226-13426-1*, P115) U Ch Pr.

Preface to Donne. rev. ed. James Winny. LC 80-40184. (Preface Bks.). (Illus.). 208p. reprint ed. pap. 64.50 (*0-608-08063-2*, 206902800002) Bks Demand.

Preface to Economic Democracy. Robert A. Dahl. LC 84-8483. (Quantum Bks.: No. 28). 1985. pap. 15.95 (*0-520-05877-1*, Pub. by U CA Pr) Cal Prin Full Svc.

Preface to Ezra Pound: Peter Wilson. Peter Wilson. LC 96-21679. (Preface Bks.). (C). 1997. text 54.38 (*0-582-25868-5*, Pub. by Addison-Wesley); pap. text 20.63 (*0-582-25867-7*, Pub. by Addison-Wesley) Longman.

Preface to Fiction: A Discussion of Great Modern Novels. Robert M. Lovett. LC 68-16948. (Essay Index Reprint Ser.). 1977. 17.95 (*0-8369-0625-X*) Ayer.

Preface to Greene. Cedric Watts. (C). 1997. pap. text 20.00 (*0-582-25049-8*) Longman.

Preface to Greene. Cedric T. Watts. LC 96-1729. (Preface Bks.). (C). 1997. text 48.75 (*0-582-25020-X*, Pub. by Addison-Wesley) Longman.

Preface to Greene. Cedric T. Watts. LC PR6013.R44Z925 1997. 1997. pap. write for info. (*0-582-25019-6*) Longman.

Preface to Hopkins. 2nd ed. Graham Storey. (C). 1995. pap. text 26.66 (*0-582-08845-3*) Addison-Wesley.

Preface to Law: The Professional Milieu. Thomas Holton. LC 83-81896. 254p. 1983. reprint ed. lib. bdg. 27.50 (*0-89941-284-X*, 302240) W S Hein.

Preface to Leibniz' Novissima Sinice. Gottfried Wilhelm Leibniz. Tr. by Donald F. Lach. LC 57-14876. 116p. reprint ed. pap. 36.00 (*0-608-30401-8*, 200116800065) Bks Demand.

Preface to Literacy: An Inquiry into Pedagogy, Practice & Progress. Myron C. Tuman. LC 85-29010. (Illus.). 208p. reprint ed. pap. 64.50 (*0-608-09249-5*, 205275300005) Bks Demand.

Preface to Mark: Notes on the Gospel in Its Literary & Cultural Settings. Christopher Bryan. 232p. 1997. reprint ed. pap. text 18.95 (*0-19-511567-8*) OUP.

Preface to Marketing Management. 6th ed. J. Paul Peter & James H. Donnelly, Jr. LC 93-19853. (Marketing Ser.). 368p. (C). 1993. text 37.50 (*0-256-12251-2*, Irwn McGrw-H) McGrw-H Hghr Educ.

Preface to Marketing Management. 7th ed. J. Paul Peter & James H. Donnelly, Jr. LC 95-51535. (Series in Marketing). 368p. (C). 1997. text 37.50 (*0-256-20281-8*, Irwn McGrw-H) McGrw-H Hghr Educ.

***Preface to Marlowe.** Stevie Simkin. LC 99-53716. (Preface Bks.). 280p. 2000. pap. 22.95 (*0-582-31298-1*) Addison-Wesley.

Preface to Metaphysics: Seven Lectures on Being. Jacques Maritain. LC 74-157346. (Select Bibliographies Reprint Ser.). 1979. reprint ed. 20.95 (*0-8369-5807-1*) Ayer.

Preface to Modern Nigeria: The "Sierra Leonians" in Yoruba, 1830-1890. LC 65-24184. 416p. reprint ed. pap. 129.00 (*0-608-11592-4*, 200497300048) Bks Demand.

Preface to Modernism. Art Berman. LC 93-36653. 360p. 1994. text 39.95 (*0-252-02103-7*); pap. text 15.95 (*0-252-06391-0*) U of Ill Pr.

Preface to Morality. John Wilson. LC 87-11574. (C). 1987. pap. text 16.00 (*0-389-20750-0*, N8308) B&N Imports.

Preface to Morals. Walter Lippman. LC 82-2035. (Social Science Classics Ser.). 375p. 1982. reprint ed. pap. 21.95 (*0-87855-907-8*) Transaction Pubs.

Preface to Oscar Wilde. Anne Varty. LC 97-27984. (Preface Bks.). (C). 1998. 60.00 (*0-582-23483-2*) Longman.

Preface to Paradise Lost. C. S. Lewis. 154p. 1961. text 14.95 (*0-19-500345-4*) OUP.

Preface to Peasantry: A Tale of Two Black Belt Counties. Arthur F. Raper. LC 72-137183. (Poverty U. S. A. Historical Record Ser.). 1971. reprint ed. 33.95 (*0-405-03121-1*) Ayer.

Preface to Philosophy. 3rd ed. Mark B. Woodhouse. 153p. (C). 1984. pap. write for info. (*0-534-01503-4*) Wadsworth Pub.

Preface to Philosophy. 4th ed. Mark B. Woodhouse. 160p. (C). 1989. mass mkt. 16.95 (*0-534-12012-1*) Wadsworth Pub.

Preface to Philosophy. 5th ed. Mark B. Woodhouse. 174p. (C). 1993. 19.50 (*0-534-20556-9*) Wadsworth Pub.

***Preface to Philosophy.** 6th ed. Woodhouse. LC 99-16351. (Philosophy Ser.). 1999. pap. 29.95 (*0-534-52830-9*) Wadsworth Pub.

Preface to Philsophy. Woodhouse. (Philosophy Ser.). 1975. pap. 5.00 (*0-8221-0164-5*) Wadsworth Pub.

Preface to Plato. Eric A. Havelock. 344p. 1982. pap. 19.50 (*0-674-69906-8*) HUP.

Preface to Plato. Eric A. Havelock. LC 62-13859. (History of the Greek Mind Ser.: Vol. 1). 341p. reprint ed. pap. 105.80 (*0-608-10086-2*, 200600100055) Bks Demand.

Preface to Pope. 2nd ed. I. R. Gordon. LC 93-10076. (Preface Bks.). (C). 1994. pap. text 23.50 (*0-582-08927-1*, 79865) Longman.

Preface to Public Administration. 2nd rev. ed. Richard J. Stillman, II. LC 98-25493. 282p. 1999. pap. 24.95 (*1-57420-065-8*) Chatelaine.

Preface to Romans: Notes on the Epistle in Its Literary & Cultural Setting. Christopher Bryant. LC 99-10412. 336p. 2000. text 60.00 (*0-19-513023-5*) OUP.

Preface to Samuel Johnson. Thomas Woodman. LC 92-46734. (Preface Bks.). 1994. write for info. (*0-582-08666-3*) Longman.

Preface to Sartre. Dominick LaCapra. LC 78-58022. 256p. 1978. pap. text 14.95 (*0-8014-9448-6*) Cornell U Pr.

Preface to Social Economics: Essays on Economic Theory & Social Problems. John M. Clark. LC 67-28453. (Reprints of Economic Classics Ser.). (Illus.). xxi, 435p. 1967. reprint ed. 49.50 (*0-678-00333-5*) Kelley.

Preface to the Aeneis of Virgil, Translated into Blank Verse. Joseph Trapp. LC 92-2401. (Augustan Reprints Ser.: Nos. 214-215). 1982. reprint ed. 21.50 (*0-404-70214-7*, PA6826) AMS Pr.

Preface to the Brontes. Felicia Gordon. Date not set. pap. text. write for info. (*0-582-35464-1*, Pub. by Addison-Wesley) Longman.

Preface to the Essays of Michel de Montaigne by His Adoptive Daughter, Marie le Jars de Gournay. Ed. by Richard Hillman & Colette Quesnel. LC 98-8719. (Medieval & Renaissance Texts & Studies: No. 193). 120p. 1998. 18.00 (*0-86698-235-3*, MR193) MRTS.

Preface to the Info Age. Paul Starr. Date not set. write for info. (*0-465-06189-3*); pap. write for info. (*0-465-06190-7*) Basic.

***Preface to the Information Age.** Starr. 2000. 27.00 (*0-465-08193-2*, Pub. by Basic); pap. 15.00 (*0-465-08194-0*, Pub. by Basic) HarpC.

Preface to the Information Age. Paul Starr. 1998. write for info. (*0-201-48407-2*, Health Sci) Addison-Wesley.

Preface to the 'Nibelungenlied' Theodore M. Andersson. LC 86-28064. viii, 307p. 1987. 45.00 (*0-8047-1362-6*) Stanford U Pr.

Preface to the Past. James Branch Cabell. (American Biography Ser.). 309p. 1991. reprint ed. lib. bdg. 79.00 (*0-7812-8056-7*) Rprt Serv.

Preface to the Presidency: Selected Speeches of Bill Clinton, 1974-1992. Bill Clinton. Ed. & Intro. by Stephen A. Smith. LC 96-22577. 1996. pap. 30.00 (*1-55728-441-5*) U of Ark Pr.

Preface to the Presidency: Selected Speeches of Bill Clinton, 1974-1992. Bill Clinton. Ed. & Intro. by Stephen A. Smith. LC 96-22577. 1996. 48.00 (*1-55728-440-7*) U of Ark Pr.

Preface to the Study of Paul. Stephen Westerholm. LC 96-49741. 140p. 1997. pap. 13.00 (*0-8028-4258-5*) Eerdmans.

Preface to Theology. W. Clark Gilpin. LC 96-10871. (Illus.). 248p. 1996. pap. text 15.95 (*0-226-29400-5*); lib. bdg. 38.00 (*0-226-29399-8*) U Ch Pr.

Preface to Thomistic Metaphysics: A Contribution to the Neo-Thomist Debate on the Start of Metaphysics. John F. Knasas. LC 90-35984. (American University Studies: Philosophy: Ser. V, Vol. 106). 205p. (C). 1991. text 54.95 (*0-8204-1421-2*) P Lang Pubng.

Preface to Urban Economics. Wilbur Thompson. LC 68-4313. 431p. reprint ed. pap. 133.70 (*0-608-12067-7*, 202414800035) Bks Demand.

Preface to Wilfred Owen. John Purkis. 1999. 62.95 (*0-582-27651-9*); pap. text 29.81 (*0-582-27652-7*) Addison-Wesley.

Preface to Wills, Trusts & Administration. 2nd ed. Paul G. Haskell. LC 94-7713. (University Casebook Ser.). 396p. 1994. text 30.50 (*1-56662-148-8*) Foundation Pr.

Preface Yeates Edition. 2nd rev. ed. Edward Malins. LC 93-39017. (Preface Bks.). 280p. (C). 1994. pap. text 33.25 (*0-582-09093-8*, Pub. by Addison-Wesley) Longman.

Prefaces: Light Reading for Certain Classes As the Occasion May Require, by Nicolaus Notabene. Soren Kierkegaard. Tr. by William McDonald. 120p. 1989. 39.95 (*0-8130-0930-8*); pap. text 13.95 (*0-8130-0918-9*) U Press Fla.

Prefaces: Poems from Hollywood. Mark Dunster. 17p. (Orig.). (YA). (gr. 9-12). 1997. pap. 5.00 (*0-89642-350-6*) Linden Pubs.

Prefaces: Writing Sampler. Soren Kierkegaard. Tr. by Todd W. Nichol from DAN. LC 97-8631. (Kierkegaard's Writings). 208p. 1997. text 39.50 (*0-691-04827-4*, Pub. by Princeton U Pr) Cal Prin Full Svc.

Prefaces & Essays. George E. Saintsbury. LC 72-99722. (Essay Index Reprint Ser.). 1977. 27.95 (*0-8369-1377-9*) Ayer.

Prefaces & Essays on Poetry. William Wordsworth. (Green Integer Bks.: No. 31). 100p. 1999. pap. text 10.95 (*1-892295-18-0*, Pub. by Green Integer) Consort Bk Sales.

Prefaces by Bernard Shaw. George Bernard Shaw. 1988. reprint ed. lib. bdg. 140.00 (*0-7812-0349-X*) Rprt Serv.

Prefaces by Bernard Shaw. George Bernard Shaw. LC 71-145294. 1971. reprint ed. 89.00 (*0-403-00785-2*) Scholarly.

Prefaces of Henry James: Framing the Modern Reader. John H. Pearson. LC 96-31044. 1997. 28.50 (*0-271-01659-0*) Pa St U Pr.

***Prefaces to Canon Law Books in Latin Christianity: Selected Translations, 500-1245.** Robert Somerville & Bruce C. Brasington. LC 97-36931. 256p. 1998. 32.00 (*0-300-07146-9*) Yale U Pr.

Prefaces to Contemporaries, 1882-1920. William Dean Howells. LC 57-6416. 224p. 1978. reprint ed. 50.00 (*0-8201-1238-0*) Schol Facsimiles.

Prefaces to Renaissance Literature. Douglas Busch. LC 65-13837. 126p. 1965. reprint ed. pap. 39.10 (*0-7837-4455-2*, 205798500012) Bks Demand.

Prefaces to Shakespeare. Harley Granville-Barker. 1972. 42.50 (*0-7134-2070-7*) D & C Pub.

Prefaces to Terence's Comedies & Plautus's Comedies, Amphitryon, Epidicus, & Rudens. Lawrence Echard. LC 92-24822. (Augustan Reprints Ser.: No. 129). 1968. reprint ed. 14.50 (*0-404-70129-9*, PA6768) AMS Pr.

Prefaces to the Diaphora: Rhetorics, Allegory, & the Interpretation of Postmodernity. Peter Carravetta. LC 89-70239. (Illus.). 368p. 1991. 39.95 (*1-55753-004-1*) Purdue U Pr.

Prefaces to the Experience of Literature. Lionel Trilling. LC 79-1850. 352p. 1979. 12.95 (*0-15-173915-3*); pap. 8.95 (*0-685-02105-X*) Harcourt.

Prefaces to the Waverley Novels. Sir Walter Scott. Ed. by Mark A. Weinstein. LC 78-2710. 287p. reprint ed. pap. 89.00 (*0-8357-2949-4*, 203920500011) Bks Demand.

Prefaces Without Books: Prefaces & Introductions to Thirty Books. Christopher Morley. Ed. by Herman Abromson. LC 76-14891. (Illus.). 1970. 15.00 (*0-87959-062-9*) U of Tex H Ransom Ctr.

Prefacing the Waverley Prefaces: A Reading of Sir Walter Scott's Prefaces to the Waverley Novels. Patricia S. Gaston. LC 90-15741. (American University Studies: English Language & Literature: Ser. IV, Vol. 130). 181p. (C). 1992. text 35.95 (*0-8204-1611-8*) P Lang Pubng.

***Prefailure Deformation Characteristics of Geomaterials: Proceedings of the Second International Symposium, IS Torino '99, Italy, 28-30 September 1999, 2 vols.** Ed. by M. Jamiolkowski et al. (Illus.). 1400p. 1999. 140.00 (*90-5809-075-2*, Pub. by A A Balkema) Ashgate Pub Co.

Prefatory Epistles of Jacques Lefevre d'Etaples & Related Texts. Eugene F. Rice, Jr. LC 71-123577. 480p. (C). 1972. text 90.50 (*0-231-03163-7*) Col U Pr.

Prefatory Lyrics. Lyle Glazier. (Morning Coffee Chapbook Ser.). 16p. (Orig.). 1991. pap. 20.00 (*0-918273-66-8*) Coffee Hse.

Preference Laws for Syllable Structure & the Explanation of Sound Change: With Special Reference to German, Germanic, Italian, & Latin. Theo Vennemann. 96p. (C). 1988. pap. text 9.85 (*0-89925-411-X*) Mouton.

Preference Modelling. M. Roubens & P. Vincke. (Lecture Notes in Economics & Mathematical Systems Ser.: Vol. 250). (Illus.). viii, 94p. 1985. 29.50 (*0-387-15685-2*) Spr-Verlag.

Preference, Production & Capital: Selected Papers. Hirofumi Uzawa. (Illus.). 384p. 1989. text 85.00 (*0-521-36174-5*) Cambridge U Pr.

Preference Reversals. Paul Slovic. (Working Papers on Risk & Rationality). 1988. 2.50 (*0-318-33319-8*, RR2) IPPP.

Preferences. Ed. by Christoph Fehige & Ulla Wessels. (Perspectives in Analytical Philosophy Ser.: No. 19). (Illus.). 600p. 1998. 80.00 (*3-11-015910-4*); pap. text 36.00 (*3-11-015007-7*) De Gruyter.

Preferences. Julien Gracq. (FRE.). 256p. 1989. reprint ed. pap. 36.95 (*0-7859-4595-4*) Fr & Eur.

***Preferences & Decisions under Incomplete Knowledge.** J. A. Fodor et al. LC 00-31364. (Studies in Fuzziness & Soft Computing). 2000. write for info. (*3-7908-1303-6*, Pub. by Physica-Verlag) Spr-Verlag.

Preferences & Democracy: Villa Colombella Papers. Ed. by Albert Brenton et al. LC 92-42163. (International Studies in Economics & Econometrics: Vol. 28). 416p. 1993. lib. bdg. 169.50 (*0-7923-9321-X*) Kluwer Academic.

Preferences, Institutions, & Rational Choice. Ed. by Keith Dowding & Desmond King. (Illus.). 304p. 1995. text 55.00 (*0-19-827895-0*) OUP.

Preferential Flow: Proceedings National Symposium, December 1991. LC 91-77316. 408p. 1991. pap. 56.75 (*0-929355-23-7*, P1291) Am Soc Ag Eng.

Preferential Option: A Christian & Neoliberal Strategy for Latin America's Poor. Amy L. Sherman. LC 92-17172. 240p. 1992. reprint ed. pap. 74.40 (*0-7837-6569-X*, 204613400011) Bks Demand.

Preferential Policies in Malaysia. Amita Shastri. (Pew Case Studies in International Affairs). 50p. (C). 1993. pap. text 3.50 (*1-56927-458-4*) Geo U Inst Dplmcy.

***Preferential Trading Arrangement in South Asia: Nepalese Perspective.** K. Shyam Shrestha. 1999. pap. 22.00 (*0-7855-7620-7*) St Mut.

Preferential Treatment in Public Employment & Equality of Opportunity. S. S. Gupta. 242p. 1979. 125.00 (*0-7855-1362-0*) St Mut.

Preferential Treatment of the Actual Settler in the Primary Disposition of the Vacant Lands in the United States to 1841. Henry W. Tatter. Ed. by Stuart Bruchey. LC 78-53568. (Development of Public Land Law in the U. S. Ser.). 1979. lib. bdg. 35.95 (*0-405-11367-6*) Ayer.

Preferred Collection. Cathy D. Johnson. 54p. 1999. pap. 10.95 (*0-9654480-1-0*) Gam-Jam Pub.

Preferred Freedoms. Gillman. 1997. 24.95 (*0-226-29388-2*) U Ch Pr.

Preferred Futures for the United Nations. Ed. by Saul H. Mendlovitz & Burns H. Weston. LC 95-31316. 528p. 1996. 75.00 (*1-57105-008-6*) Transnatl Pubs.

Preferred Futuring: Envision the Future You Want & Unleash the Energy to Get There. Lawrence L. Lippitt. LC 98-35916. 292p. 1998. pap. 24.95 (*1-57675-041-8*) Berrett-Koehler.

Preferred Lies & Other Tales: Skimming the Cream of a Life in Sports. Jack Whitaker. LC 98-21895. 288p. (YA). 1998. 24.00 (*0-684-84272-6*) S&S Trade.

Preferred Metric Units for General Use by the Federal Government: Federal Standard 376B. 40p. (Orig.). (C). 1994. pap. text 25.00 (*0-7881-1325-9*) DIANE Pub.

Preferred Orientation in Deformed Materials. Ed. by Hans R. Wenk. 1985. text 149.00 (*0-12-744020-8*) Acad Pr.

Preferred Player's Guide to Tennessee Golf Directory, 1999. pap. 20.00 (*1-893304-03-5*, Pub. by Golf Dir Inc) Booksource.

Preferred Provider Organizations: Planning, Structure & Operation. Dale H. Cowan. 320p. 1984. 87.00 (*0-89443-593-0*) Aspen Pub.

Preferred Provider's Handbook: Building a Successful Private Therapy Practice in the Managed Care Marketplace. William L. Poynter. LC 93-38869. 184p. 1994. pap. text 23.95 (*0-87630-708-X*, 708X) Brunner-Mazel.

Preferred Resources. 2nd ed. California Design Publications Staff. (Illus.). 144p. 1989. pap. 19.95 (*0-929374-02-9*) CA Design Pubns.

Preferred Wisdom of Elementary Schools. 52p. 4.00 (*0-318-17474-X*) Mid St Coll & Schl.

Preferring Christ: A Devotional Commentary on the Rule of St. Benedict. Norvene Vest. (Illus.). 186p. 1990. pap. 17.95 (*0-940147-14-9*) Source Bks CA.

Preferring Justice: Rationality, Self-Transformation & the Sense of Justice. Eric M. Cave. LC 98-119238. 200p. (C). 1997. text 69.00 (*0-8133-2808-X*, Pub. by Westview) HarpC.

Prefiguracion Como Recurso: Estilistico En Amalia. Hector P. Marquez. (SPA.). 14p. (Orig.). 1989. pap. 3.00 (*0-89729-552-8*) Ediciones.

Prefiguration et Structure Romanesque dans A la Recherche du Temps Perdu. Marcel Muller. LC 78-73096. (French Forum Monographs: No. 14). (Illus.). 95p. (Orig.). 1979. pap. 9.95 (*0-917058-13-5*) French Forum.

Prefigurations in Meistergesang. Clarence W. Friedman. LC 75-140020. (Catholic University of America. Studies in Romance Languages & Literatures: No. 18). reprint ed. 37.50 (*0-404-50238-5*) AMS Pr.

Prefixes & Other Word-Initial Elements of English. Laurence Urdang & Alexander Humez. LC 83-20662. 533p. 1998. reprint ed. 49.95 (*0-930454-10-3*) Verbatim Bks.

Prefixes & Suffixes. (Home Workbooks Ser.). (Illus.). 64p. (Orig.). (J). (gr. 2-3). 1995. pap., wbk. ed. 2.49 (*0-88724-330-4*, CD-6827) Carson-Dellos.

Prefixes & Suffixes. Carlos F. Navarro. Ed. by Judith Navarro. (Start Smart Ser.). 80p. 1990. student ed. 7.50 (*0-685-35594-2*) Start Smart Bks.

Prefixes, Bases, Suffixes. rev. ed. Contrib. by Beth Bridgman. (Horizons Grammar Ser.). (Illus.). 24p. (J). (gr. 4-9). 1998. pap. 5.95 (*1-58086-066-4*, Usborne) EDC.

Prefixes, Suffixes & Base Words. 2nd rev. ed. James Scott. 40p. (YA). (gr. 7-12). 1996. pap., wbk. ed. 2.50 (*1-58049-364-5*, MW41A) Prestwick Hse.

Preflight. Against the Clock, Inc. Staff. LC 98-23213. 1998. pap. text. write for info. (*0-13-095825-5*) P-H.

***Preflight: An Introduction to File Analysis & Repair.** Against the Clock, Inc. Staff. 384p. 1998. pap. text 33.33 (*0-13-020558-3*, Prentice Hall) P-H.

Preformulating the News: An Analysis of the Metapragmatics of Press Releases. Geert Jacobs. LC 99-22395. (Pragmatics & Beyond NS Ser.: Vol. 60). xviii, 428p. 1999. 89.00 (*1-55619-823-X*) J Benjamins Pubng Co.

Prefrontal Cortex. Diamond. 220p. 1997. pap. text 15.00 (*0-226-14477-1*) U Ch Pr.

Prefrontal Cortex: Anatomy, Physiology, & Neuropsychology of the Frontal Lobe. 3rd ed. Joaquin M. Fuster. (Illus.). 320p. 1997. text 83.00 (*0-397-51849-8*) Lppncott W & W.

Prefrontal Cortex: Executive & Cognitive Functions. Ed. by A. C. Roberts et al. LC 97-51746. (Illus.). 256p. 1998. text 95.00 (*0-19-852442-0*); pap. text 45.00 (*0-19-852441-2*) OUP.

Prefrontal Cortex: Its Structure, Function & Pathology: Proceedings of the 16th International Summer School of Brain Research, Amsterdam, The Netherlands, 28 Aug.-1 Sept., 1989. Ed. by H. B. Uylings et al. (Progress in Brain Research Ser.: No. 85). 574p. 1991. 297.75 (*0-444-81124-9*) Elsevier.

Pregancy Project: Encounters with Reproductive Therapy. Karen Propp. LC 99-6058. (Emerging Writers in Creative Nonfiction Ser.). 175p. 1999. 24.95 (*0-8207-0302-8*) Duquesne.

Preghiere a Maria see Prayers to Mary

Pregnancy. Cathie Cush. LC 93-25155. (Teen Hotline Ser.). (Illus.). 80p. (J). (gr. 6-7). 1993. lib. bdg. 25.68 (*0-8114-3530-X*) Raintree Steck-V.

Pregnancy. Bruce Goldberg. 1989. 12.00 incl. audio (*1-885577-38-9*) B Goldberg.

Pregnancy. Silver et al. (Psychoanalytic Inquiry Book Ser.: Vol. 8, No. 2). 1995. pap. 20.00 (*0-88163-962-1*) Analytic Pr.

Pregnancy. rev. ed. Gordon Bourne. (Illus.). 575p. (Orig.). 1996. pap. 24.00 (*0-330-33912-5*, Pub. by Pan) Trans-Atl Phila.

Pregnancy: A Time for Caring. Ed. by John Gallagher. (Illus.). 150p. (Orig.). 1988. 6.95 (*0-317-90484-1*) St Marys Hospt.

Pregnancy: Private Decisions, Public Debates. Kathlyn Gay. LC 93-29456. 112p. (YA). (gr. 7-12). 1994. lib. bdg. 24.00 (*0-531-11167-9*) Watts.

Pregnancy: The Complete Guide from Planning to Birth. Heather Welford. Ed. by Reader's Digest Editors. LC 97-38730. (Illus.). 224p. 1998. 19.95 (*0-7621-0040-0*, Pub. by RD Assn) Penguin Putnam.

Pregnancy: The Inside Story. Joan Raphael-Leff. LC 95-32293. 1995. 40.00 (*1-56821-579-7*) Aronson.

Pregnancy: The Miracle Journey. Jessica L. Kelly. LC 98-45340. 128p. (YA). 1999. pap. 12.95 (*0-8361-9088-2*) Herald Pr.

Pregnancy - The Time to Develop the Child's Awareness. Eunice J. Bernard. 15p. (Orig.). 1997. pap. text 5.00 (*0-9629950-8-8*) Ashbrook Pub.

Pregnancy after a Loss: A Guide to Pregnancy after a Miscarriage, Stillbirth or Infant Death. Carol C. Lanham. 1999. pap. 14.95 (*0-425-17047-0*) Berkley Pub.

Pregnancy after Loss. Task Force of Parents. Ed. by Joann O'Leary. (SPA.). (Orig.). 1997. pap. 2.85 (*1-891633-04-X*) Abbott NW Hosp.

Pregnancy after Loss. Task Force of Parents. Ed. by Joann O'Leary. (Illus.). (Orig.). 1991. reprint ed. pap. 2.85 (*1-891633-02-3*) Abbott NW Hosp.

Pregnancy after Loss: Your Next Baby. 2nd ed. Task Force of Parents. Ed. by Katie Campbell & Joann O'Leary. 64p. (Orig.). 1998. pap. 5.95 (*1-891633-06-6*) Abbott NW Hosp.

Pregnancy after Thirty-Five. Carole S. McCauley. 224p. 1987. pap. 3.95 (*0-317-59883-X*) PB.

***Pregnancy & a Proposal: (The Daddy Club)** Mindy Neff. (American Romance Ser.: No. 809). 2000. per. 4.25 (*0-373-16809-8*, 1-16809-5, Harlequin) Harlequin Bks.

Pregnancy & Abortion Counselling. Joanna Brien & Ida Fairbairn. LC 96-6101. 216p. (C). 1996. 75.00 (*0-415-12278-3*); pap. 24.99 (*0-415-12010-1*) Routledge.

Pregnancy & Abortion in Adolescence: Proceedings of the WHO Expert Committee, Geneva, 1974. WHO Staff. (Technical Reports: No. 583). 1975. pap. text 6.00 (*92-4-120583-0*, 1100583) World Health.

***Pregnancy & Birth.** Dianne R. Hales. LC 99-51569. (21st Century Health & Wellness Ser.). (Illus.). 128p. 1999. 24.95 (*0-7910-5527-2*) Chelsea Hse.

Pregnancy & Birth: Your Questions Answered. Christopher C. Lees et al. LC 96-33518. 240p. 1997. 19.95 (*0-7894-1470-8*) DK Pub Inc.

Pregnancy & Birth Sourcebook. Ed. by Heather Aldred. LC 97-36154. (Health Reference Ser.: Vol. 31). 1997. lib. bdg. 78.00 (*0-7808-0216-0*) Omnigraphics Inc.

Pregnancy & Childbir Rev. rev. ed. Tracy Hotchner. LC 96-23748. 672p. 1997. pap. 12.50 (*0-380-78039-9*, Avon Bks) Morrow Avon.

Pregnancy & Childbirth. Jan De Vries. 144p. 1996. pap. 10.95 (*1-85158-657-1*, Pub. by Mainstream Pubng) Trafalgar.

Pregnancy & Childbirth: The Basic Illustrated Guide. Margaret Martin. LC 96-37277. (Illus.). 128p. (Orig.). 1997. pap. 9.95 (*1-55561-114-1*) Fisher Bks.

Pregnancy & Childbirth: The Complete Guide for a New Life. Tracy Hotchner. 832p. (Orig.). 1990. pap. 11.00 (*0-380-75946-2*, Avon Bks) Morrow Avon.

Pregnancy & Childcare Issues in the Workplace. Gerard P. Panaro. 1987. pap. 39.95 (*0-88057-775-4*) Exec Ent Pubns.

Pregnancy & Diabetes: An Annotated Bibliography. 54p. 1996. reprint ed. pap. text 30.00 (*0-7881-2760-8*) DIANE Pub.

***Pregnancy & Infertility.** (Ultrasound & Women's Health Ser.: Pt. I). 1998. write for info. (*1-930047-46-0*, 981) Am Inst Ultrasound.

***Pregnancy & Infertility.** (Ultrasound & Women's Health Ser.: Vol. I). 1998. pap. write for info. (*1-930047-50-9*, 98 I-P) Am Inst Ultrasound.

Pregnancy & Parenthood. Compiled by National Childbirth Trust Staff & Anne Loader. (Illus.). 1980. 16.95 (*0-19-217684-6*); pap. 8.95 (*0-19-286006-2*) OUP.

Pregnancy & Parenting. Phyllis N. Stern. (Health Care for Women International Publication). 201p. 1988. 32.95 (*0-89116-846-X*) Hemisp Pub.

Pregnancy & Parenting Program. Kathy M. Johnson. (Illus.). 423p. 1987. teacher ed. 250.00 (*0-9616488-2-1*) Alef Bet Comns.

Pregnancy & Prayer. Janet Alampi. (Illus.). 80p. (Orig.). 1995. pap. 3.95 (*0-8198-5892-7*) Pauline Bks.

Pregnancy & Renal Disorders. Ed. by Graeme R. Catto. (New Clinical Applications Nephrology Ser.). (C). 1988. text 95.50 (*0-7462-0057-9*) Kluwer Academic.

Pregnancy & Work. Jean G. Fitzpatrick. 256p. 1984. pap. 7.95 (*0-380-88666-9*, Avon Bks) Morrow Avon.

Pregnancy & Your Baby's First Year. Lawrence Kutner. (Parent & Child Ser.). 224p. 1994. pap. 10.00 (*0-380-71352-7*, Avon Bks) Morrow Avon.

Pregnancy at Work. Burrows. 54.95 (*1-85521-030-4*) Ashgate Pub Co.

Pregnancy, Autoimmunity, & Connective Tissue Disorders. Ed. by J. S. Scott & H. A. Bird. (Illus.). 360p. 1990. 82.00 (*0-19-261775-3*) OUP.

Pregnancy Bedrest: A Guide for the Pregnant Woman & Her Family. Susan H. Johnston. 88p. 1995. pap. 14.95 (*0-8050-1350-4*, Owl) H Holt & Co.

Pregnancy, Birth & Family Planning. Alan F. Guttmacher & Irwin H. Kaiser. 1973. mass mkt. 6.99 (*0-451-16632-9*, Sig) NAL.

Pregnancy, Birth & Parenthood. Frances K. Grossman et al. LC 80-16518. (Jossey-Bass Social & Behavioral Science Ser.). 326p. reprint ed. pap. 101.10 (*0-8357-4979-7*, 203791200009) Bks Demand.

Pregnancy, Birth & the Early Months. 2nd ed. Richard I. Feinbloom. 1992. pap. 15.00 (*0-201-58149-3*) Addison-Wesley.

Pregnancy, Birth, & the Early Months. 3rd ed. Richard Feinbloom. Date not set. pap. write for info. (*0-201-36099-3*) Addison-Wesley.

***Pregnancy, Birth & the Early Months: The Thinking Woman's Guide.** 3rd ed. Richard I. Feinbloom. (Illus.). 400p. 2000. reprint ed. pap. 17.00 (*0-7382-0181-2*, Pub. by Perseus Pubng) HarpC.

Pregnancy Bk Today W. 2nd ed. Harold I. Shapiro. LC 92-53284. 544p. 1993. pap. 19.00 (*0-06-273030-4*, Harper Ref) HarpC.

Pregnancy Book. Linda H. Holt et al. LC 96-48905. (Illus.). 448p. 1997. pap. 21.95 (*0-316-77914-8*, Back Bay) Little.

Pregnancy Book for Today's Woman: An Obstetrician Answers All Your Questions about Pregnancy & Childbirth & Some You May Not Have Considered. Howard I. Shapiro. LC 80-7916. (Illus.). 448p. 1983. pap. 12.95 (*0-318-36208-2*, CN1059, Perennial) HarperTrade.

Pregnancy-Care & Physiology: Index of Modern Authors & Subjects with Guide for Rapid Research. rev. ed. Scott W. Towers. 1994. 47.50 (*0-7883-0188-8*); pap. 44.50 (*0-7883-0189-6*) ABBE Pubs Assn.

Pregnancy, Childbirth & the Newborn. rev. ed. Penny Simkin et al. (Illus.). 330p. 1991. 12.00 (*0-671-74182-9*) S&S Trade.

Pregnancy, Childbirth & the Newborn: The Complete Guide. rev. ed. Penny Simkin et al. LC 91-29224. 311p. 1991. pap. 12.00 (*0-88166-177-5*) Meadowbrook.

Pregnancy, Children, & the Vegan Diet. Michael Klaper. Ed. by Cynthia Klaper. 109p. 1988. pap. 9.95 (*0-9614248-2-6*) Gentle World.

***Pregnancy Clause.** Elizabeth Sinclair. (American Romance Ser.: Vol. 827). 2000. mass mkt. 4.25 (*0-373-16827-6*) Harlequin Bks.

Pregnancy Cookbook. Hope Ricciotti & Vincent Connelly. LC 95-6383. (Illus.). 336p. 1996. pap. 15.95 (*0-393-31386-7*) Norton.

Pregnancy Counseling for Success: A Guide to Effective Counseling. Bethany Productions Staff. 80p. (Orig.). 1990. pap. 16.95 (*1-879058-02-2*) Bethany Prods.

***Pregnancy Day by Day.** Sheila Kitzinger & Vicky Bailey. (Illus.). 128p. 2001. 19.95 (*0-375-70945-2*) Knopf.

Pregnancy, Diabetes & Birth: A Management Guide. 2nd ed. Dorothy R. Hollingsworth et al. (Illus.). 328p. 1992. 75.00 (*0-683-04103-7*) Lppncott W & W.

Pregnancy Diary. Tracy Hotchner. (Illus.). 240p. 1992. pap. 12.50 (*0-380-76543-8*, Avon Bks) Morrow Avon.

Pregnancy Diary: A Christian Mother's Reflections. Mary Arnold. LC 95-79887. 156p. (Orig.). 1996. pap. 9.95 (*0-89870-564-9*) Ignatius Pr.

Pregnancy Diet. Eileen Behan. 336p. 1998. pap. 14.00 (*0-671-74794-0*, PB Trade Paper) PB.

Pregnancy Diet: A Healthy Weight Control Program for Pregnant Women. Eileen Behan. LC 98-53461. 288p. 1999. pap. 12.00 (*0-671-00393-3*) S&S Trade.

Pregnancy Exclusions in State Living Will & Medical Proxy Statutes. Kathleen D. Stoll. (Law & Pregnancy Ser.). (C). 1992. pap. 8.00 (*1-877966-14-2*) Ctr Women Policy.

***Pregnancy Exercise Book: A Step-by-Step Program for Achieving Optimal Fitness Throughout the Trimesters.** Judy Di Fiori. LC 99-39669. (Illus.). 96p. 2000. pap. 19.95 (*0-06-273734-1*, HarpRes) HarpInfo.

Pregnancy Fitness. Fitness Magazine Staff & Ginny Graves. LC 98-50550. 208p. 1999. pap. 16.00 (*0-609-80159-7*, Crown) Crown.

Pregnancy for Dummies. Joanne Stone et al. LC 99-62376. (For Dummies Ser.). (Illus.). 408p. 1999. pap. 19.99 (*0-7645-5074-8*) IDG Bks.

***Pregnancy for Dummies: Stone,&Joanne.** abr. ed. Joanne Stone & Mary Murray. 1999. audio 12.00 (*0-694-52182-5*) HarperAudio.

Pregnancy for Older Women: Assessing the Medical Risks. Phyllis K. Mansfield. LC 86-9440. 230p. 1986. 59.95 (*0-275-92184-0*, C2184, Praeger Pubs) Greenwood.

Pregnancy in a High-Tech Age: Paradoxes of Choice. Robin Gregg. 232p. (C). 1995. pap. text 18.50 (*0-8147-3075-2*) NYU Pr.

Pregnancy in a High-Tech Age: Paradoxes of Choice. Robin Gregg. 232p. (C). 1995. text 45.00 (*0-8147-3067-1*) NYU Pr.

Pregnancy in the Executive Suite. Valerie Lee. LC 87-61045. 224p. (C). 1988. 19.95 (*0-944315-00-3*) Success Pubns.

***Pregnancy Journal.** Broadman & Holman Publishing Staff. 1999. 11.99 (*0-8054-0590-9*) Broadman.

Pregnancy Journal. James Dalley & Tamara Dalley. 136p. 1994. 18.95 (*0-9642259-0-5*) Castle Peak.

Pregnancy Journal. Tamara Dalley. 136p. 1994. 15.95 (*0-9642259-2-1*) Castle Peak.

Pregnancy Journal: A Day-To-Day Guide to a Happy & Healthy Pregnancy. A. Christine Harris. LC 95-12870. 176p. 1996. spiral bd. 18.95 (*0-8118-1156-5*) Chronicle Bks.

***Pregnancy Loss & Perinatal Death: Debating the Issues.** Nancy Kohner. 224p. 2000. pap. 24.99 (*0-415-17058-3*) Routledge.

Pregnancy-Mayo Clinic Co. Mayo Foundation for Medical Education & Research. LC 94-7264. (Illus.). 750p. 1994. 33.00 (*0-688-11761-9*, Wm Morrow) Morrow Avon.

Pregnancy Metabolism, Diabetes & the Fetus. Symposium on Pregnancy Metabolism, Diabetes, & the. LC 78-32046. (Ciba Foundation Symposium: New Ser.: No. 63). 334p. reprint ed. pap. 103.60 (*0-608-16206-X*, 201464800093) Bks Demand.

Pregnancy Myths: An Obstetrician Demystifies Pregnancy from Conception to Birth. Michael D. Benson. LC 98-28523. 352p. 1998. pap. 14.95 (*1-56924-695-5*) Marlowe & Co.

Pregnancy Myths: What Not to Expect When You're Expecting. Michael Benson. 156p. 1995. pap. 9.95 (*1-56924-822-2*) Marlowe & Co.

Pregnancy Nutrition: Good Health for You & Your Baby. American Dietetic Association Staff. 96p. 1998. pap. 8.95 (*0-471-34697-7*) Wiley.

Pregnancy Prescription: The Success-Oriented Approach to Overcoming Infertility. Hugh D. Melnick & Nancy Intrator. LC 97-94304. (Illus.). 184p. (Orig.). 1998. pap. 17.95 (*0-9660419-0-9*, JO) Josara Pub.

Pregnancy Proteins in Animals: Proceedings of the International Meeting, Copenhagen, Denmark, April 22-24, 1985. Ed. by Jann Hau. (Illus.). xi, 536p. 1986. lib. bdg. 215.40 (*3-11-010520-9*) De Gruyter.

Pregnancy Pure & Simple: Everything Expectant Parents Need to Know. Tracy Hotchner. LC 94-34817. 352p. (Orig.). 1995. pap. 12.50 (*0-380-77434-8*, Avon Bks) Morrow Avon.

Pregnancy, Sex Hormones, & the Liver: Proceedings of the 89th Falk Symposium, Held in Santiago, Chile, 10-11 November 1995. Ed. by H. B. Reyes et al. LC 96-17382. 1996. text 147.00 (*0-7923-8704-X*) Kluwer Academic.

Pregnancy Sickness: Using Your Body's Natural Defenses to Protect Your Baby-to-Be. Margie Profet. 1997. pap. 11.00 (*0-614-28115-6*) Addison-Wesley.

Pregnancy Sourcebook. 2nd ed. M. Sara Rosenthal. 288p. 1997. pap. 15.00 (*1-56565-804-3*, Anodyne) Lowell Hse.

Pregnancy Sourcebook. 3rd ed. M. Sara Rosenthal. (Illus.). 336p. 1999. pap. 17.95 (*0-7373-0105-8*, 01058W) NTC Contemp Pub Co.

Pregnancy Sourcebook: Everything You Need to Know. M. Sara Rosenthal. 288p. 1995. pap. 16.00 (*1-56565-345-9*) Lowell Hse.

P

An Asterisk (*) at the beginning of an entry indicates that the title is appearing for the first time.

***Pregnancy the Natural Way.** Sarah Brewer. 2000. pap. 13.95 (*0-285-63511-5*) Souvenir Pr Ltd.

***Pregnancy Tips for Moms-to-Be.** Karen N. Salt. (Illus.). 144p. 2000. pap. 10.95 (*1-55561-234-2*) Fisher Bks.

Pregnancy to Parenthood: Your Personal Step-by-Step Journey Through the Childbirth Experience. Ginny Brinkley et al. LC 97-46507. (Illus.). 336p. 1999. pap. 12.95 (*0-89529-635-7*, Avery) Penguin Putnam.

Pregnancy Week-by-Week. Amanda Roberts. LC 97-177472. (Illus.). 96p. 1997. pap. 18.00 (*0-06-273483-0*, Perennial) HarperTrade.

***Pregnancy Week-by-Week: Everything You Need to Know about Yourself & Your Developing Baby.** Ed. by Jane MacDougall & Madeleine Jennings. (Illus.). 96p. 2000. reprint ed. pap. 17.00 (*0-7881-9247-7*) DIANE Pub.

***Pregnancy Weight Management.** Theresa Francis-Cheung. 256p. 2000. pap. 12.95 (*1-58062-333-6*) Adams Media.

Pregnancy, Women, Teenagers, Their Infants & Alcohol Tobacco & Other Drugs: A Resource Guide. 1995. lib. bdg. 251.95 (*0-8490-6798-7*) Gordon Pr.

Pregnancy Workbook. Ellen K. Anderson. (Illus.). 96p. (Orig.). 1983. pap. 8.95 (*0-939374-01-3*) Homefront Graphics.

Pregnancy Workout. (Great Shapes Ser.). Date not set. pap. write for info. (*0-614-14297-0*) Personal Fitness Pub.

Pregnant? Adoption Is an Option. (YA). pap., teacher ed. 2.50 (*1-885356-18-8*); pap., wbk. ed. 2.50 (*1-885356-17-X*) Morning Glory.

Pregnant? Adoption Is an Option. Jeanne W. Lindsay. (Illus.). 192p. 1996. pap. 11.95 (*1-885356-08-0*, 56080) Morning Glory.

Pregnant Adolescent: Problems of Premature Parenthood. Frank G. Bolton. LC 79-27082. (Sage Library of Social Research: No. 100). 247p. reprint ed. pap. 76.60 (*0-8357-4769-7*, 203770600009) Bks Demand.

Pregnant & Chic. Lynn Sutherland & Audrey Brooks. LC 86-40642. (Illus.). 192p. 1989. pap. 8.95 (*0-89480-302-6*, 1302) Workman Pub.

***Pregnant & Practically Married: The Bridal Circle.** Andrea Edwards. (Special Edition Ser.: No. 1283). 1999. per. 4.25 (*0-373-24283-2*, 1-24283-2) Silhouette.

Pregnant & Single: Help for the Tough Choices. Linda Roggow & Carolyn Owens. LC 98-21074. 152p. (YA). 1998. pap. 9.99 (*0-8361-9092-0*) Herald Pr.

Pregnant Angels Can't Fly. Bob Wayman. LC 99-93244. 200p. 1999. pap. 10.95 (*0-9644021-2-2*) Peaceful Express.

Pregnant Bears & Crawdad Eyes: Excursions & Encounters in Animal Worlds. Paul D. Schullery. LC 91-11164. (Illus.). 186p. 1991. pap. 12.95 (*0-89886-292-2*) Mountaineers.

Pregnant by Mistake: The Stories of Seventeen Women. rev. ed. Katrina Maxtone-Graham. LC 87-28353. 440p. 1990. reprint ed. 21.95 (*0-943362-01-6*); reprint ed. pap. 12.95 (*0-943362-02-4*) Remi Bks.

Pregnant Fathers: Entering Parenthood Together. rev. ed. Jack Heinowitz. Ed. by Ellen Kleiner. (Illus.). 200p. 1995. pap. 14.95 (*0-9641024-0-4*) Parents As Ptnrs.

Pregnant Feelings: Developing Trust in Birth. Rahima Baldwin & Terra Palmarini. LC 85-62305. (Illus.). 208p. (Orig.). 1995. pap. 17.95 (*0-89087-423-9*) Celestial Arts.

Pregnant Husband's Handbook. Jeff Justice. Ed. by Diane Pfeifer. (Illus.). 96p. (Orig.). 1989. pap. 5.95 (*0-9618306-8-9*) Strawberry GA.

Pregnant Lady Cooking. B. Carlson. (Illus.). 160p. 1994. spiral bd. 5.95 (*1-57166-008-9*) Hearts N Tummies.

Pregnant Man. 2nd ed. Deirdre Barrett. 256p. 1999. pap. 13.00 (*0-8129-2906-3*, Times Bks) Crown Pub Group.

Pregnant Man, Vol. 3. 4th rev. ed. Roberto Zapperi. ix, 246p. 1991. text 93.00 (*3-7186-5033-9*) Gordon & Breach.

Pregnant Man: Cases from a Hypnotherapist's Couch. Deirdre Barrett. LC 97-46345. 256p. 1998. 23.00 (*0-8129-2905-5*, Times Bks) Crown Pub Group.

Pregnant Men: Practice, Theory, & Law. Ruth Colker. LC 94-3922. 1994. 29.95 (*0-253-31371-6*) Ind U Pr.

Pregnant Nudes. Catherine Steinmann. (Illus.). 60p. 1994. pap. text 30.00 (*0-9640297-0-7*) C Steinmann.

Pregnant Pause or: Love's Labor Lost. Georges Feydeau. Tr. by Norman R. Shapiro from FRE. (Tour de Farce Ser.: Vol. 1). 96p. 1987. pap. 6.95 (*0-936839-58-9*) Applause Theatre Bk Pubs.

Pregnant Pauses. Joyce Armour. 256p. 1995. mass mkt. 4.99 (*0-7860-0137-2*) Kensgtn Pub Corp.

***Pregnant Pauses.** Brenda Buttner. 2000. 22.00 (*0-8129-3257-9*, Times Bks) Random.

***Pregnant Pictures.** Sandra Matthews & Laura Wexler. LC 99-53026. (Illus.). 2000. 35.00 (*0-415-92120-1*) Routledge.

Pregnant Pictures. Sandra Matthews & Laura Wexler. LC 99-53026. (Illus.). 288p. (C). (gr. 13). 2000. 85.00 (*0-415-90449-8*) Routledge.

Pregnant, Pissed & Perplexed: A Pregnancy Prevention Guide for Curious Teens & Concerned Parents. Melody Fleming. Ed. by Patricia A. Hartman. (Illus.). 64p. (Orig.). (YA). (gr. 6-10). 1999. pap. 7.95 (*0-9668887-0-7*) Creat Conns.

Pregnant Poems. Anne F. Walker. 64p. 1994. pap. write for info. (*0-88753-237-3*) Black Moss.

***Pregnant Princess: (Royally Wed)** Anne M. Winston. (Desire Ser.: No. 1268). 2000. mass mkt. 3.75 (*0-373-76268-2*, 1-76268-1) Harlequin Bks.

Pregnant, Substance-Using Women: A Treatment Improvement Protocol. 98p. (Orig.). 1993. pap. text 45.00 (*1-57979-153-0*) DIANE Pub.

Pregnant, Substance-Using Women: A Treatment Improvement Protocol. (Illus.). 92p. (Orig.). (C). 1994. pap. text 40.00 (*0-7881-1165-5*) DIANE Pub.

Pregnant, Substance-Using Women: Treatment Improvement. 1995. lib. bdg. 251.95 (*0-8490-6822-3*) Gordon Pr.

Pregnant Vegetarian. Gail S. Brewer. 1999. pap. 7.95 (*0-14-008150-X*, Penguin Bks) Viking Penguin.

***Pregnant Virgin.** Anne Eames. (Desire Ser.). 2000. per. 3.99 (*0-373-76283-6*) Silhouette.

Pregnant Virgin. Marion Woodman. 208p. 1995. pap. 18.00 (*0-919123-20-1*, Pub. by Inner City Bks) BookWorld.

Pregnant Virgin: A Process of Psychological Transformation. deluxe ed. Marion Woodman. (Illus.). 208p. 1985. 22.00 (*0-919123-41-4*, Pub. by Inner City Bks) BookWorld.

Pregnant with His Child. Carla Cassidy. 1997. per. 3.25 (*0-373-19259-2*, 1-19259-0) Silhouette.

Pregnant Woman's Comfort Book: A Self-Nurturing Guide to Your Emotional Well-Being During Pregnancy & Early Motherhood. Jennifer Louden. LC 94-47638. 240p. 1995. pap. 16.00 (*0-06-251165-3*, Pub. by Harper SF) HarpC.

Pregnant Woman's Comfort Guide: Safe, Quick, & Easy Relief from the Discomforts of Pregnancy & Postpartum. Sherry L. Jimenez. LC 91-33379. (Illus.). 192p. (Orig.). pap. 10.95 (*0-89529-490-7*, Avery) Penguin Putnam.

Pregnant Woman's Guide to Farting. Herbert I. Kavet. (Illus.). 96p. (Orig.). 1996. pap. 5.95 (*1-889647-04-7*) Boston Am.

Pregnant Women on Drugs: Combating Stereotypes & Stigma. Sheigla Murphy & Marsha Rosenbaum. LC 98-20130. 192p. (C). 1999. text 49.00 (*0-8135-2602-7*); pap. text 19.00 (*0-8135-2603-5*) Rutgers U Pr.

Pregnenolone. Victoria Dolby. (Good Health Guides Ser.). 1998. pap. 3.95 (*0-87983-885-X*, 3885XK, Keats Publng) NTC Contemp Pub Co.

Pregnenolone: The Ultimate Hormone Precursor. Rita Elkins. (The Woodland Health Ser.). 1997. pap. text 3.95 (*1-885670-49-4*) Woodland UT.

***Prego! An Invitation to Italian.** Graziana Lazzarino. LC 00-23140. 2000. write for info. (*0-07-365513-9*) McGraw.

Prego! An Invitation to Italian. 4th ed. Graziana Lazzarino et al. LC 94-42536. 544p. (C). 1995. 68.13 (*0-07-037722-7*) McGraw.

***Prego! An Invitation to Italian.** 5th ed. Graziana Lazzarino et al. (ITA & ENG.). (C). 2000. pap., student ed. 66.56 (*0-07-234221-8*) McGrw-H Hghr Educ.

Prego! An Invitation to Italian. Graziana Lazzarino. 1990. student ed. write for info. (*0-07-909486-4*) McGraw.

Prego! An Invitation to Italian. 3rd ed. Graziana Lazzarino. (C). 1990. text 63.75 (*0-07-557426-8*) McGraw.

Prego! An Invitation to Italian. 3rd ed. Graziana Lazzarino. 1990. write for info. (*0-07-540866-X*) McGraw.

Prego! An Invitation to Italian. 4th ed. Mara M. Jacobsen et al. 1995. pap. text. write for info. (*0-07-037727-8*) McGraw.

Prego! An Invitation to Italian. 4th ed. Mara M. Jacobsen et al. (C). 1995. pap., wbk. ed. 28.13 (*0-07-037724-3*) McGraw.

Prego! An Invitation to Italian. 4th ed. Mara M. Jacobsen et al. (C). 1995. pap., lab manual ed. 25.31 (*0-07-037725-1*) McGraw.

Prego! An Invitation to Italian. 4th ed. Mara M. Jacobsen et al. (C). 1995. audio 34.38 (*0-07-911937-9*) McGraw.

Prego! An Invitation to Italian. 4th ed. Mara M. Jacobsen et al. 1995. write for info. incl. audio (*0-07-911936-0*) McGraw.

Prego! An Invitation to Italian. 4th ed. Mara M. Jacobsen et al. 1995. write for info. incl. VHS (*0-07-911939-5*) McGraw.

Pregones. Alma F. Ada. (Cuentos con Alma Ser.).Tr. of Merchants. (SPA., Illus.). 24p. (J). (gr. 3-4). 1993. 16.95 (*1-56492-110-7*) Laredo.

Pregroups & Bass-Serre Theory. Frank S. Rimlinger. LC 86-32112. (Memoirs of the American Mathematical Society Ser.: No. 361). 73p. 1987. pap. 16.00 (*0-8218-2421-X*, MEMO/65/361C) Am Math.

Pregunta de Maria Rosa. Ann P. Wright. Orig. Title: The Question of Mary Rose. (SPA.). 128p. 1980. mass mkt. 3.99 (*0-8254-1888-7*, Edit Portavoz) Kregel.

Preguntale a Nostradamus Por Tus Suenos. Nostradamus. 1997. pap. text 14.98 (*968-855-234-8*) J H Surovek.

Preguntale a Paulo Coelho. Paulo Coelho. 1997. pap. text 14.50 (*968-855-226-7*) J H Surovek.

Preguntas Mas Communes en Torno a "Un Curso de Milagros" Gloria Wapnick & Kenneth Wapnick. LC 96-47996. (SPA.). 152p. 1997. pap. 8.00 (*0-933291-28-0*) Foun Miracles.

Preguntas Mujeres Hacen en Privado. Norman Wright.Tr. of Questions Women Ask in Private. (SPA.). 11.99 (*1-56063-478-2*, 498568) Edit Carisma.

Preguntas Practicas y Dificiles Contestadas. R. A. Torrey. Orig. Title: Practical & Perplexing Questions Answered. (SPA.). 128p. 1980. mass mkt. 4.99 (*0-8254-1722-8*, Edit Portavoz) Kregel.

Preguntas Que Hacen, Padres Sobre la Disciplina. James C. Dobson. (Serie Enfoque a la Familia - Focus on the Family Ser.).Tr. of Questions Parents Ask about Discipline. (SPA.). 39p. 1991. pap. 1.99 (*1-56063-188-0*, 497407) Editorial Unilit.

Preguntas Que las Mujeres Hacen en Privado. Wright.Tr. of Questions Women Ask in Private. (SPA.). 1995. write for info. (*0-614-27114-2*) Editorial Unilit.

Preguntas Que las Mujeres Hacen en Privado - Questions Women Ask in Private. Wright. (SPA.). 1995. write for info. (*0-614-24396-3*) Editorial Unilit.

Preguntas Serias, Capciosas Y. Rafael Escandon. (SPA., Illus.). 199p. 1997. pap. text 15.98 (*968-13-2821-3*) Edit Diana.

Preharvest Field Sprouting in Cereals. Ed. by N. F. Derera. LC 87-32553. 192p. 1989. 110.00 (*0-8493-6848-0*, SB189, CRC Reprint) Franklin.

***Preheating.** (Welding Lev 2 Ser.). 2000. teacher ed., ring bd. 16.00 (*0-13-019284-8*) P-H.

Prehensile-Tailed Skinks. John Coborn. (Illus.). 64p. 1996. pap. 9.95 (*0-7938-0279-2*, RE127) TFH Pubns.

Prehispanic Chiefdoms in the Valle de la Plata Vol. 1: The Environmental Context of Human Habitation. Ed. by Robert D. Drennan et al. (University of Pittsburgh Memoirs in Latin American Archaeology Ser.: No. 2). (ENG & SPA., Illus.). 1989. pap. 15.00 (*1-877812-01-3*, M002) UPLAAP.

Prehispanic Chiefdoms in the Valle de la Plata Vol. 2: Ceramics - Chronology & Craft Production. Ed. by Robert D. Drennan et al. (University of Pittsburgh Memoirs in Latin American Archaeology Ser.: No. 5). (ENG & SPA.). xxvi, 188p. 1993. pap. 19.00 (*1-877812-07-2*, M005) UPLAAP.

Prehispanic Domestic Units in Western Mesoamerica: Studies of the Household, Compound, & Residence. Ed. by Robert S. Santley & Kenneth G. Hirth. 320p. 1992. boxed set 115.95 (*0-8493-8898-8*, F1219) CRC Pr.

Prehispanic Settlement Dynamics in Central Oaxaca, Mexico: A View from the Miahuatlan Valley. Charles W. Markmam. (Vanderbilt University Publications in Anthropology: No. 26). (Illus.). 185p. 1981. pap. 11.85 (*0-935462-17-1*) VUPA.

Prehispanic Settlement Patterns in the Lower Santa Valley, Peru: A Regional Perspective on The Origins & Development of Complex North Coast Society. David J. Wilson. LC 87-62622. (Series in Archaeological Inquiry). (Illus.). 528p. (C). 1988. text 67.00 (*0-87474-984-0*) Smithsonian.

Prehispanic Source Materials for the Study of Philippine History. enl. rev. ed. William H. Scott. (Illus.). xviii, 196p. (Orig.). 1984. pap. 16.50 (*971-10-0226-4*, Pub. by New Day Pub) Cellar.

Prehistoria Sudamericana: Nuevas Perspectivas. Ed. by Betty J. Meggers. LC 91-66122. (POR & SPA., Illus.). 381p. (Orig.). 1992. pap. 20.00 (*0-9602822-6-2*) Taraxacum.

Prehistoria Temprana de la Peninsula de Santa Elena, Ecuador: Cultura de las Vegas. Karen E. Stothert. (SPA., Illus.). 274p. 1990. pap. 20.00 (*1-877812-49-8*, UC012) UPLAAP.

Prehistoria y Arqueologia. Jose L. Lorenzo. 436p. 1991. pap. 8.00 (*968-6487-43-3*, IN050) UPLAAP.

Prehistoric: Openings in History. J. Jamieson. (C). 1989. 45.00 (*0-7855-6713-5*, Pub. by S Thornes Pubs) St Mut.

Prehistoric Adaptation to a Desert Spring Environment: Archaeological Investigations of Surprise Spring, San Bernardino County, California. Jeffrey H. Altschul. (Statistical Research Technical Ser.: No. 27). (Illus.). 189p. 1990. per. 13.50 (*1-879442-25-6*) Stats Res.

Prehistoric Agricultural Strategies in the Southwest. Ed. by Suzanne Fish & Paul R. Fish. (Anthropological Research Papers: No. 33). (Illus.). vii, 386p. 1984. pap. 25.00 (*0-685-73909-0*) AZ Univ ARP.

Prehistoric Alaska. L. J. Campbell Staff. Ed. by Penny Rennick. LC 72-92087. (Alaska Geographic Ser.: Vol. 21, No. 4). (Illus.). 112p. 1994. pap. 19.95 (*1-56661-024-9*) Alaska Geog Soc.

Prehistoric America, 5 vols., Set. Stephen D. Peet. LC 74-7993. 1905. 295.00 (*0-404-11930-1*) AMS Pr.

Prehistoric Anatolia: The Neolithic Transformation & the Early Chalcolithic Period. Jak Yakar. (Monograph Series of the Sonia & Marco Nadler Institute of Archaeology: Vol. 9). x, 361p. 1991. text 60.00 (*965-440-000-6*, Pub. by Friends Archeol Inst) Eisenbrauns.

Prehistoric Anatolia Suppl. No. 1: The Neolithic Transformation & the Early Chalcolithic Period. Jak Yakar. (Monograph Series of the Sonia & Marco Nadler Institute of Archaeology: Vol. 9a). viii, 84p. 1994. text 20.00 (*965-440-003-0*, Pub. by Friends Archeol Inst) Eisenbrauns.

Prehistoric & Historic Archaeology of Gujarat. Hasmuklal B. Sankalia. (C). 1987. 44.00 (*81-215-0049-4*, Pub. by M Manoharial) Coronet Bks.

Prehistoric & Primitive Hunter-Gatherers of South India. S. Bhaskar. 1990. 38.50 (*81-7141-107-X*) S Asia.

Prehistoric & Romano-British Settlement in the Solway Plain, Cumbria. Robert H. Bewley. (Oxbow Monographs in Archaeology: No. 36). (Illus.). 110p. 1994. pap. 32.00 (*0-946897-66-2*, Pub. by Oxbow Bks) David Brown.

Prehistoric Animals. (First Facts About Ser.). 24p. (Orig.). (J). (gr. 3-7). pap. write for info. (*1-882210-19-0*) Action Pub.

Prehistoric Animals. David Eastman. (YA). (gr. 1-5). 1997. pap. 29.95 incl. audio (*0-8167-4205-7*) Troll Communs.

Prehistoric Animals. Gail Gibbons. (Illus.). 32p. (J). (ps-3). 1988. pap. 6.95 (*0-8234-1261-X*) Holiday.

Prehistoric Animals. Gail Gibbons. LC 88-4661. (Illus.). 32p. (J). (gr. k-3). 1988. lib. bdg. 16.95 (*0-8234-0707-1*) Holiday.

Prehistoric Animals. Peter Zallinger. (Pictureback Ser.). (Illus.). 32p. (J). (ps-3). 1981. pap. 3.25 (*0-394-83737-1*, Pub. by Random Bks Yng Read) Random.

Prehistoric Animals: A Collection of U.S. Postage Stamps. Greg Varner. (Illus.). 32p. (YA). (gr. 5 up). 1996. 12.95 (*0-9644038-7-0*) Design Ed.

Prehistoric Archaeology along the Zagros Flanks. Ed. by Robert J. Braidwood et al. LC 81-85896. (Oriental Institute Publications: No. 105). (Illus.). ix, 695p. 1983. 130.00 (*0-918986-36-2*) Orient Inst.

Prehistoric Archaeology of Heritage Square. T. Kathleen Henderson. LC 95-73140. (Pueblo Grande Museum Anthropological Papers: No. 3). 316p. (Orig.). 1995. pap. text 30.00 (*1-882572-15-7*) Pueblo Grande Mus.

Prehistoric Archaeology of Heritage Square. limited ed. T. Kathleen Henderson. LC 95-73140. (Pueblo Grande Museum Anthropological Papers: No. 3). 316p. (Orig.). 1995. write for info. (*1-882572-16-5*) Pueblo Grande Mus.

Prehistoric Archaeology of Norfolk Island. Jim Specht. (Pacific Anthropological Records Ser.: No. 34). (Illus.). 76p. 1984. 6.00 (*0-910240-95-7*) Bishop Mus.

Prehistoric Archaeology of Northwest Africa. Frederick R. Wulsin. (HU PMP Ser.: Vol. 19, Pt. 1). (Illus.). 1941. 25.00 (*0-527-01247-5*) Periodicals Srv.

Prehistoric Archaeology Within Chimariko Territory, Northwest California. Janet P. Eidsness. (Illus.). 352p. 1985. reprint ed. pap. text 36.88 (*1-55567-039-3*) Coyote Press.

Prehistoric Architecture in Micronesia. William N. Morgan. (Illus.). 180p. 1988. 60.00 (*0-292-76506-1*) U of Tex Pr.

Prehistoric Arizona. Ernest E. Snyder. LC 87-25217. (Illus.). 120p. (Orig.). 1987. pap. 5.00 (*0-914846-32-9*) Golden West Pub.

Prehistoric Art. Susie Hodge. LC 97-20677. (Art in History Ser.). 32p. (J). (gr. 3-6). 1998. 13.95 (*1-57572-553-3*) Heinemann Lib.

Prehistoric Art & Civilization. Denis Vialou. LC 98-22778. (Discoveries Ser.). (Illus.). 160p. 1998. pap. 12.95 (*0-8109-2849-3*, Pub. by Abrams) Time Warner.

Prehistoric Art in Europe. 2nd ed. Nancy K. Sandars. (Pelican History of Art Ser.). (Illus.). 508p. (Orig.). (C). 1985. reprint ed. pap. 26.50 (*0-300-05286-3*) Yale U Pr.

Prehistoric Astronomy & Ritual. Aubrey Burl. (Archaeology Ser.: No. 32). (Illus.). 32p. 1983. pap. 10.50 (*0-85263-621-0*, Pub. by Shire Pubns) Parkwest Pubns.

Prehistoric Astronomy in the Southwest. rev. ed. J. McKim Malville & Claudia Putnam. LC 93-17712. (Illus.). 112p. 1993. pap. 9.95 (*1-55566-116-5*) Johnson Bks.

Prehistoric Axes, Celts Bannerstones & Other Large Tools in Virginia & Various States. W. Jack Hranicky. LC 96-208116. (Special Publications: No. 34). (Illus.). 110p. 1994. pap. text 19.00 (*1-884626-27-0*) Archeolog Soc.

Prehistoric Biological Relationships in the Great Lakes Region. Richard G. Wilkinson. LC 70-637305. (University of Michigan, Museum of Anthropology Memoirs Ser.: No. 43). 169p. 1971. reprint ed. pap. 52.40 (*0-608-01422-2*, 206218500002) Bks Demand.

Prehistoric Birds. Spizzirri Publishing Co. Staff. Ed. by Linda Spizzirri. (Illus.). 32p. (J). (gr. 1-8). pap. 4.98 incl. audio (*0-86545-023-4*) Spizzirri.

Prehistoric Britain. Timothy Darvill. (Illus.). 223p. (C). 1997. pap. 29.99 (*0-415-15135-X*) Routledge.

Prehistoric Britain. Barbara Green. LC 70-373345. 48 p. 1968. write for info. (*0-7188-0781-2*, Lutterworth-Parkwest) Parkwest Pubns.

Prehistoric Britain Activity Book. Museum Press British. 1999. pap. text 5.95 (*0-7141-1394-8*) Brimax Bks.

Prehistoric Britain from the Air. Janet Bord & Colin Bord. (Illus.). 160p. 1998. 29.95 (*1-57076-102-7*) Trafalgar.

Prehistoric Britain from the Air: A Study of Space, Time & Society. Timothy Darvill. (Air Surveys Ser.). (Illus.). 305p. (C). 1996. text 59.95 (*0-521-55132-3*) Cambridge U Pr.

Prehistoric Bugs: Trapped in Amber. Laurie Steding. (Illus.). 16p. (J). (gr. 2-7). 1998. pap., boxed set 8.95 (*0-8167-4817-9*) Troll Communs.

Prehistoric Burial Places in Maine. C. C. Willoughby. (Harvard University Peabody Museum of Archaeology & Ethnology Papers). 1974. reprint ed. pap. 25.00 (*0-527-01188-6*) Periodicals Srv.

***Prehistoric Burials Of Kashmir** A. K. Sharma. LC 98-901923. x, 126 p. 1998. write for info. (*81-7320-036-X*) S Asia.

Prehistoric Cambridgeshire. Alison Taylor. (Cambridge Town, Gown & County Ser.: Vol. 9). (Illus.). 1977. pap. 5.95 (*0-900891-05-X*) Oleander Pr.

Prehistoric Cannibalism at Mancos 5MTUMR-2346. Tim D. White. (Illus.). 492p. 1992. text 79.50 (*0-691-09467-5*, Pub. by Princeton U Pr) Cal Prin Full Svc.

***Prehistoric Ceramics of the Puerco Valley.** (Illus.). 210p. 1998. pap. 21.95 (*0-89734-122-8*) Mus Northern Ariz.

Prehistoric Coal Mining in the Jeddito Valley, Arizona. John T. Hack. (Harvard University Peabody Museum of Archaeology & Ethnology Papers). 1974. reprint ed. pap. 25.00 (*0-527-01289-0*) Periodicals Srv.

Prehistoric Coloring Book. Denver Museum of Natural History Staff. (Illus.). 32p. 1998. pap. text 4.95 (*1-57098-216-3*) Roberts Rinehart.

Prehistoric Communities of the British Isles. Vere G. Childe. LC 72-82207. (Illus.). 1980. reprint ed. 29.95 (*0-405-08358-0*, Pub. by Blom Pubns) Ayer.

Prehistoric Cordage: Identification of Impressions on Pottery. William M. Hurley. LC 79-63677. (Manuals on Archeology Ser.: No. 3). (Illus.). xii, 154p. 1979. 18.00 (*0-9602822-0-3*) Taraxacum.

Prehistoric Cultural Change at Kitselas Canyon, No. 138. Gary Coupland. (Mercury Ser.: ASC No. 138). (Illus.). 400p. 1996. pap. 24.95 (*0-660-10781-3*, Pub. by CN Mus Civilization) U of Wash Pr.

Prehistoric Cultural Ecology & Evolution: Insights from Southern Jordan. D. O. Henry. (Interdisciplinary Contributions to Archaeology Ser.). (Illus.). 492p. (C). 1995. 62.50 (*0-306-45048-8*, Kluwer Plenum) Kluwer Academic.

***Prehistoric Cultural Resources Evaluation & Impact Mitigation Program for the Silver Creek Valley Country Club, San Jose, California.** fac. ed. Randy S. Wiberg et al. (Illus.). 514p. 1999. reprint ed. pap. text 53.13 (*1-55567-871-8*) Coyote Press.

Prehistoric Cultures of Eastern Pennsylvania. Jay Custer. (Illus.). 425p. 1995. 29.95 (*0-89271-062-4*) Pa Hist & Mus.

Prehistoric Cultures of the Delmarva Peninsula: An Archaeological Study. Jay F. Custer. LC 86-40619. (Illus.). 448p. 1989. 57.50 (*0-87413-320-3*) U Delaware Pr.

An Asterisk (*) at the beginning of an entry indicates that the title is appearing for the first time.

Prehistoric Cultures of the Southwest: Anasazi. Rose Houk. Ed. by Randolph Jorgen & Ronald J. Foreman. LC 91-67394. (Illus.). 16p. (Orig.). 1991. pap. 3.95 (*1-877856-04-5*) SW Pks Mnmts.

Prehistoric Cultures of the Southwest: Hohokam. Rose Houk. Ed. by Randolph Jorgen & Ronald J. Foreman. LC 91-67392. (Illus.). 16p. (Orig.). 1992. pap. 3.95 (*1-877856-10-X*) SW Pks Mnmts.

Prehistoric Cultures of the Southwest: Mogollon. Rose Houk. Ed. by Randolph Jorgen & Ronald J. Foreman. LC 91-67391. (Illus.). 16p. (Orig.). 1992. pap. 3.95 (*1-877856-11-8*) SW Pks Mnmts.

Prehistoric Cultures of the Southwest: Salado. Rose Houk. Ed. by Randolph Jorgen & Ronald J. Foreman. LC 91-67390. (Illus.). 16p. (Orig.). 1992. pap. 3.95 (*1-877856-12-6*) SW Pks Mnmts.

Prehistoric Cultures of the Southwest: Sinagua. Rose Houk. Ed. by Randolph Jorgen & Ronald J. Foreman. LC 91-67393. (Illus.). 16p. (Orig.). 1992. pap. 3.95 (*1-877856-09-6*) SW Pks Mnmts.

Prehistoric Cypriot Skulls: A Medico-Anthropological, Archaeological & Micro-Analytical Investigation. Peter M. Fischer. (Studies in Mediterranean Archaeology: Vol. LXXV). (Illus.). 93p. (Orig.). 1986. pap. 52.50 (*91-86098-34-9*, Pub. by P Astroms) Coronet Bks.

Prehistoric Dinosaurs. (Dinosaur Coloring & Activity Bks.). (Illus.). 32p. (J). (gr. 1-3). 1997. pap. write for info. (*1-56144-451-0*, Honey Bear Bks) Modern Pub NYC.

Prehistoric Ecology at Patarata 52, Veracruz, Mexico: Adaption to the Mangrove Swamp. Barbara L. Stark. (Vanderbilt University Publications in Anthropology: No. 18). (Illus.). 259p. 1977. pap. 12.85 (*0-935462-07-4*) VUPA.

Prehistoric Europe. Timothy C. Champion et al. 1984. text 125.00 (*0-12-167550-5*); pap. text 55.00 (*0-12-167552-1*) Acad Pr.

Prehistoric Europe: An Illustrated History. Ed. by Barry Cunliffe. (Illus.). 544p. 1998. reprint ed. pap. 24.95 (*0-19-288063-2*) OUP.

Prehistoric Exchange & Sociopolitical Development in the Plateau Southwest. Amy A. Douglass. LC 90-49134. (Evolution of North American Indians Ser.). 396p. 1990. reprint ed. text 10.00 (*0-8240-2500-8*) Garland.

Prehistoric Exchange Systems in North America. T. G. Baugh & J. E. Ericson. (Interdisciplinary Contributions to Archaeology Ser.). (Illus.). 476p. (C). 1994. 64.50 (*0-306-44756-8*, Plenum Trade) Perseus Pubng.

Prehistoric Exploration & Colonisation of the Pacific. Geoffrey Irwin. (Illus.). 248p. (C). 1994. pap. text 21.95 (*0-521-47651-8*) Cambridge U Pr.

Prehistoric Farmers of the Washita River Valley: Settlement & Subsistence Patterns During Plains Village Period. Robert L. Brooks et al. (Archeological Resource Survey Report: No. 23). (Illus.). 172p. (C). 1985. pap. text 6.00 (*1-881346-16-1*) Univ OK Archeol.

Prehistoric Fish: Educational Coloring Book. Ed. by Linda Spizzirri. (Illus.). 32p. (J). (gr. 1-8). 1981. pap. 1.99 (*0-86545-021-8*) Spizzirri.

Prehistoric Fisheries of the California Bight. Roy A. Salls. 787p. (C). 1988. pap. text 81.25 (*1-55567-412-7*) Coyote Press.

Prehistoric Flint Mines. Robin Holgate. 1989. pap. 10.50 (*0-7478-0141-X*, Pub. by Shire Pubns) St Mut.

Prehistoric Food Production in North America. Ed. by Richard I. Ford. LC 85-622818. (University of Michigan, Museum of Anthropology Memoirs Ser.: Vol. 75). (Illus.). 428p. 1985. reprint ed. pap. 132.70 (*0-608-05679-0*, 206619500007) Bks Demand.

Prehistoric Fortified Village Site at Canandaigua, Ontario County, New York, No. 3. William A. Ritchie. (Rochester Museum of Arts & Sciences of Research Records Ser.). 80p. (C). 1936. pap. text 9.06 (*1-55567-828-9*) Coyote Press.

Prehistoric Game Monitoring on the Banks of Mill Creek: Data Recovery at CA-TIV-2804 Prado Basin, Riverside County, California. Donn R. Grenda. (Statistical Research Technical Ser.: No. 52). (Illus.). 127p. (Orig.). 1995. per. 17.50 (*1-879442-45-0*) Stats Res.

Prehistoric Gold in Europe - Mines, Metallurgy & Manufacture: Proceedings of the NATO Advanced Research Workshop, Seeon, Germany, September 27-October 1, 1993. Ed. by Giulio Morteani. LC 94-23902. (NATO ASI Ser.: Series E, Applied Sciences: Vol. 280). 632p. (C). 1994. text 378.00 (*0-7923-3255-5*) Kluwer Academic.

Prehistoric Great Lakes: An Illustrated History for Children. John Mitchell. (Illus.). 48p. (J). (gr. 2-7). 1999. 16.95 (*0-9621466-3-3*) Suttons Bay Pubns.

***Prehistoric Guiana.** Denis Williams. (Illus.). 450p. (C). 2000. pap. text 34.95 (*0-9639749-4-7*) Boise St U Dept Anthrop.

Prehistoric Henges. Aubrey Burl. (Archaeology Ser.: No. 66). (Illus.). 64p. 1989. pap. 10.50 (*0-7478-0123-1*, Pub. by Shire Pubns) Parkwest Pubns.

Prehistoric Households at Turkey Creek Pueblo, Arizona. Julie C. Lowell. LC 90-48539. (Anthropological Papers: No. 54). (Illus.). 95p. (Orig.). 1991. pap. 24.95 (*0-8165-1238-8*) U of Ariz Pr.

Prehistoric Houses in Britain. Malcolm Reid. (Archaeology Ser.: No. 70). (Illus.). 72p. 1989. pap. 10.50 (*0-7478-0218-1*, Pub. by Shire Pubns) Parkwest Pubns.

Prehistoric Human Bone: Archaeology at the Molecular Level. Ed. by Joseph B. Lambert & Gisela Grupe. LC 93-21141. 1993. 174.95 (*0-387-55393-2*) Spr-Verlag.

Prehistoric Hunter-Gatherer Fishing Strategies. Ed. by Mark G. Pleu. (Illus.). (Orig.). 1996. pap. 18.50 (*0-9639749-1-2*) Boise St U Dept Anthrop.

Prehistoric Hunters of the High Plains. 2nd ed. George C. Frison. (New World Archaeological Record Ser.). (Illus.). 532p. 1991. text 77.00 (*0-12-268561-X*) Acad Pr.

***Prehistoric Iberia: Genetics, Anthropology & Linguistics.** Antonio Arnaiz-Villena et al. LC 00-22850. 2000. write for info. (*0-306-46364-4*, Kluwer Plenum) Kluwer Academic.

Prehistoric Implements. Warren K. Moorehead et al. LC 76-43785. (Illus.). reprint ed. 115.00 (*0-404-15641-X*) AMS Pr.

Prehistoric India to 1000 B.C. Stuart Piggott. LC 83-45838. reprint ed. 28.00 (*0-404-20203-9*) AMS Pr.

Prehistoric Indian Rock Paintings. Erwin Neumayer. (Illus.). 1984. 54.00 (*0-19-561387-2*) OUP.

Prehistoric Indian Tools, Points & Arrowheads. Gary W. Henschel. Ed. by Rosalie Henschel & Denise Krebs. LC 96-77544. (Illus.). 102p. (Orig.). 1996. pap. 11.95 (*0-9653477-0-2*) Henschels Ind Mus.

Prehistoric Indians of the Southeast: Archaeology of Alabama & the Middle South. John A. Walthall. LC 79-13722. 304p. 1990. pap. text 19.95 (*0-8173-0552-1*) U of Ala Pr.

Prehistoric Investigations in Iraqi Kurdistan. Robert J. Braidwood & Bruce Howe. LC 60-8969. (Illus.). 1960. pap. text 17.00 (*0-226-62404-8*, SAOC31) U Ch Pr.

Prehistoric Island. (J). 1995. pap. 4.99 (*0-553-54229-X*) BDD Bks Young Read.

Prehistoric Japan: New Perspectives on Insular East Asia. Keiji Imamura. (Illus.). 320p. 1996. text 49.00 (*0-8248-1853-9*); pap. text 24.95 (*0-8248-1852-0*) UH Pr.

Prehistoric Journey: A History of Life on Earth. Kirk R. Johnson & Richard K. Stucky. LC 95-69271. (Illus.). 144p. 1995. 39.95 (*1-57098-056-X*) Roberts Rinehart.

Prehistoric Journey: A History of Life on Earth. Richard K. Stucky & Kirk R. Johnson. LC 95-69271. (Illus.). 144p. 1995. pap. 19.95 (*1-57098-045-4*) Roberts Rinehart.

Prehistoric Land Use & Settlement of the Middle Little Colorado River Valley: The Survey of the Homolovi Ruins State Park. Richard C. Lange. (Archaeological Ser.: No. 189). (Illus.). 197p. 1998. 17.95 (*1-889747-67-X*) Ariz St Mus.

Prehistoric Land Use in the Santa Lucia Mountains: An Overview of the Esselen & Their Settlement Strategy. Joan E. Brandoff-Kerr. (Illus.). xi, 142p. 1982. reprint ed. pap. text 16.88 (*1-55567-036-9*) Coyote Press.

Prehistoric Landscape & Iron Age Enclosed Settlement at Mingies Ditch, Hardwick-with-Yelford, Oxfordshire. T. G. Allen & M. A. Robinson. (Windrush Valley Ser.: Vol. 2). (Illus.). 250p. 1993. pap. 50.00 (*0-947816-82-8*, Pub. by Oxford Univ Comm Arch) David Brown.

Prehistoric Library, 6 bks. & 6 cass., Set. 39.95 incl. audio (*0-86545-088-9*) Spizzirri.

Prehistoric Life. Dougal Dixon. (Spotlights Ser.). (J). (gr. 3-5). 1996. 9.95 (*0-614-15688-2*) OUP.

Prehistoric Life. Dougal Dixon. (Spotlights Ser.). (Illus.). 46p. (J). (gr. 3-5). 1996. 11.95 (*0-19-521237-1*) OUP.

Prehistoric Life. Dennis Graham et al. (BrainBooster Ser.). (Illus.). 32p. (J). (gr. 3 up). 1989. 6.95 (*0-88679-571-0*) Educ Insights.

Prehistoric Life. Norman King. 256p. 1995. pap., per. 44.95 (*0-7872-1244-X*) Kendall-Hunt.

***Prehistoric Life.** William Lindsay. (Eyewitness Books). (Illus.). (J). (gr. 4-7). 2000. 19.99 (*0-7894-6601-5*) DK Pub Inc.

***Prehistoric Life.** William Lindsay. (Eyewitness Books). (J). (gr. 4-7). 2000. 15.95 (*0-7894-5868-3*) DK Pub Inc.

Prehistoric Life. William Lindsay. LC 93-32076. (Eyewitness Books). (Illus.). (J). (gr. 5 up). 1994. lib. bdg. 20.99 (*0-679-96001-5*, Pub. by Knopf Bks Yng Read) Random.

Prehistoric Life. Steve Parker. LC 92-54452. (See & Explore Library). (Illus.). 64p. (J). (gr. 3-7). 1993. 12.95 (*1-56458-238-8*) DK Pub Inc.

Prehistoric Life. Ed. by Scholastic, Inc. Staff. (Discovery Box Ser.). (Illus.). 32p. (J). (gr. 1-5). 1997. 11.95 (*0-590-92678-0*) Scholastic Inc.

Prehistoric Life: The Rise of the Vertebrates. David Norman. (Illus.). 248p. (J). 1994. 30.00 (*0-671-79940-1*) P-H.

Prehistoric Life on the Mississippi Flood-Plain: Stone Tool Use, Settlement Organization, & Subsistence Practices at the Labras Lake Site, Illinois. Richard W. Yerkes. LC 86-19137. (Prehistoric Archeology & Ecology Ser.). (Illus.). xxii, 304p. 1986. pap. text 12.00 (*0-226-95151-0*) U Ch Pr.

Prehistoric Life on the Mississippi Flood-Plain: Stone Tool Use, Settlement Organization, & Subsistence Practices at the Labras Lake Site, Illinois. Richard W. Yerkes. LC 86-19137. (Prehistoric Archeology & Ecology Ser.). (Illus.). xxii, 304p. 1987. lib. bdg. 30.00 (*0-226-95150-2*) U Ch Pr.

Prehistoric Life on the Olympic Peninsula: The First Inhabitants of a Great American Wilderness. Eric O. Bergland & Jerry Marr. (Illus.). 88p. (Orig.). 1988. pap. text 8.95 (*0-685-34733-8*) NW Interpretive.

***Prehistoric Lifeways in the Great Basin Wetlands: Bioarchaeological Reconstruction & Interpretation.** Ed. by Brian E. Hemphill & Clark Spencer Larsen. LC 99-43317. (Illus.). 448p. 1999. 45.00 (*0-87480-603-8*) U of Utah Pr.

Prehistoric Lithic Industry at Dover, Tennessee. Richard M. Gramly. LC 92-30494. (Monographs in Archaeology). (Illus.). 138p. (Orig.). (C). 1992. pap. 21.95 (*0-9615462-7-1*) Persimmon NY.

Prehistoric London. E. O. Gordon. LC 84-72709. (Illus.). 176p. 1985. reprint ed. pap. 7.00 (*0-934666-16-4*) Artisan Pubs.

Prehistoric Lowland Maya Community & Social Organization: A Case Study at Dzibilchaltun, Yucatan, Mexico. Edward B. Kurjack. (Publications: No. 38). (Illus.). 105p. 1974. 25.00 (*0-939238-43-8*) Tulane MARI.

Prehistoric Lowland Maya Environment & Subsistence Economy. Ed. by Mary D. Pohl. LC 84-62626. (Peabody Museum Papers: Vol. 77). (Illus.). 209p. 1985. reprint ed. pap. 25.00 (*0-87365-203-7*) Peabody Harvard.

Prehistoric Macedonia: An Archaeological Reconnaisance of Greek Macedonia (West of the Struma) in the Neolithic, Bronze & Early Iron Ages. W. A. Heurtley. LC 77-86430. reprint ed. 46.00 (*0-404-16646-6*) AMS Pr.

Prehistoric Mammals. 6.95 (*0-8431-6431-X*, Price Stern) Peng Put Young Read.

Prehistoric Mammals. Anne McCord. (Picture History Ser.). (Illus.). 32p. (J). (gr. 3-7). 1985. pap. 6.95 (*0-86020-128-7*, Usborne) EDC.

Prehistoric Mammals. Querida L. Pearce. 48p. 1989. 1.95 (*0-8125-9493-2*, Pub. by Tor Bks) St Martin.

Prehistoric Mammals. Rita Warner. (Doodle Art Travel Packs Ser.). (Illus.). 4p. (J). (ps-3). 1996. boxed set 8.95 (*0-8431-6557-X*, TP-17, Price Stern) Peng Put Young Read.

Prehistoric Mammals: An Educational Coloring Book. Ed. by Linda Spizzirri. (Illus.). 32p. (J). (gr. 1-8). 1981. pap. 1.99 (*0-86545-022-6*) Spizzirri.

Prehistoric Mammals Coloring Book. Jan Sovak. (Illus.). (J). (gr. k-3). 1991. pap. 2.95 (*0-486-26673-7*) Dover.

Prehistoric Man. Anthony Harvey. LC 73-154921. 75 p. 1972. write for info. (*0-600-33461-9*) P HM.

Prehistoric Man in the New World. Ed. by Jesse D. Jennings & Edward Norbeck. LC 63-18852. 1971. pap. 5.45 (*0-226-39739-4*, P432) U Ch Pr.

Prehistoric Man in the New World. Rice University Staff. Ed. by Jesse D. Jennings & Edward Norbeck. LC 63-18852. (Rice University Semicentennial Publications). (Illus.). 643p. reprint ed. pap. 199.40 (*0-608-09418-8*, 205421800004) Bks Demand.

Prehistoric Man of the Santa Barbara Coast. fac. ed. David B. Rogers. (Santa Barbara Museum of Natural History Ser.). (Illus.). 547p. (C). 1929. reprint ed. pap. text 56.25 (*1-55567-802-5*) Coyote Press.

Prehistoric Man of the Santa Barbara Coast. David B. Rogers. LC 76-43812. reprint ed. 74.50 (*0-404-15667-3*) AMS Pr.

Prehistoric Maori Fortifications in the North Island of New Zealand: New Zealand Archaeological Association Monographs : No.6. Aileen Fox. (New Zealand Archaeological Association Monographs: No. 6). (Illus.). 1976. text 15.95 (*0-582-71746-9*) Longman.

Prehistoric Maritime Adaptations of the Circumpolar Zone. Ed. by William Fitzhugh. (World Anthropology Ser.). (Illus.). x, 406p. 1975. 62.35 (*90-279-7639-2*) Mouton.

Prehistoric Maya Settlement Patterns at Becan Campeche, Mexico. Prentice M. Thomas, Jr. (Publications: No. 45). (Illus.). xiv, 116p. 1981. 25.00 (*0-939238-50-0*) Tulane MARI.

Prehistoric Mesoamerica. rev. ed. Richard E. Adams. LC 90-50679. (Illus.). 480p. 1996. pap. 18.95 (*0-8061-2834-8*) U of Okla Pr.

Prehistoric Migrations in Europe. V. Gordon Childe. 1976. lib. bdg. 69.95 (*0-8490-2467-6*) Gordon Pr.

Prehistoric Mining & Allied Industries. R. Shephers. (Studies in Archaeology). 1981. text 130.00 (*0-12-639480-6*) Acad Pr.

Prehistoric Native American Adoptations along the Central California Coast of San Mateo & Santa Cruz Counties. Mark G. Hylkema. (Illus.). 520p. (C). 1991. pap. text 52.50 (*1-55567-830-0*) Coyote Press.

Prehistoric New Mexico: Background for Survey. David E. Stuart et al. LC 88-20450. (Illus.). 459p. 1981. reprint ed. pap. 27.50 (*0-8263-1066-4*) U of NM Pr.

Prehistoric Occupation of Chavin de Huantar, Peru. Richard L. Burger. LC 83-1389. (University of California Publications in Anthropdogy: No. 14). 421p. reprint ed. pap. 130.60 (*0-7837-7473-7*, 204919500010) Bks Demand.

Prehistoric Occupation of Voigt Mesa, Arizona: The 1983 TEP Springerville Project. Katharina J. Schreiber & Alan P. Sullivan, 3rd. (Archaeological Ser.: No. 166). (Illus.). 113p. 1984. pap. 8.95 (*1-889747-39-4*) Ariz St Mus.

Prehistoric Occupation Patterns in Southwest Wyoming & Cultural Relationships with the Great Basin & Plains Culture Areas. Floyd W. Sharrock. (Utah Anthropological Papers: No. 77). reprint ed. 24.00 (*0-404-60677-6*) AMS Pr.

Prehistoric Ocean Discovery Kit: An Explorer's Kit. Warren Allmon. (Illus.). 64p. (J). (gr. 4-7). 1996. 18.95 (*1-56138-593-X*) Running Pr.

Prehistoric Origami: Dinosaurs & Other Creatures. John Montroll. LC 88-84160. (Illus.). 120p. (Orig.). 1989. pap. text 9.95 (*1-877656-01-1*) Antroll Pub.

Prehistoric Origami Dinosaurs & Other Creatures. John Montroll. 143p. 1990. pap. 9.95 (*0-486-26588-9*) Dover.

Prehistoric Panhandle Farmers: The Roy Smith Site. Mary A. Holmes & Claudette M. Gilbert. Ed. by Lois Albert. (Prehistoric People of Oklahoma Ser.: No. 3). (Illus.). 13p. 1979. pap. text 2.00 (*1-881346-26-9*) Univ OK Archeol.

***Prehistoric Peoples: Discover the Long-Ago World of the First Humans.** Lorenz Books Staff. (Exploring History Ser.). (Illus.). 64p. (J). (gr. 3-7). 2000. 12.95 (*0-7548-0442-9*, Lorenz Bks) Anness Pub.

Prehistoric Peoples of Minnesota. rev. ed. Elden Johnson. LC 87-32663. (Illus.). 35p. 1988. pap. 3.95 (*0-87351-223-5*) Minn Hist.

Prehistoric Peoples of North America see Junior Library of American Indians

Prehistoric Peoples of Scotland. Ed. by Stuart Piggott. LC 80-27371. (Studies in Ancient History & Archaeology). (Illus.). 165p. 1981. reprint ed. lib. bdg. 59.50 (*0-313-22916-3*, PIPR, Greenwood Pr) Greenwood.

Prehistoric Peoples of South Florida. William E. McGoun. LC 92-40833. 152p. 1993. pap. text 19.95 (*0-8173-0686-2*) U of Ala Pr.

Prehistoric Peoples of Southern Illinois. James S. Penny, Jr. (Illus.). ix, 70p. (Orig.). 1986. pap. 3.50 (*0-88104-062-2*) Center Archaeol.

Prehistoric Period in South Africa. J. P. Johnson. 1977. lib. bdg. 59.95 (*0-8490-2468-4*) Gordon Pr.

Prehistoric Pinkerton. Steven Kellogg. (Picture Puffin Ser.). 1991. 11.19 (*0-606-12486-1*, Pub. by Turtleback) Demco.

Prehistoric Plies: A Structural & Comparative Analysis of Cordage, Netting, Basketry, & Fabric from Ozark Bluff Shelters. Sandra C. Scholtz. (Illus.). 193p. 1975. pap. 6.00 (*1-56349-013-7*, RS09) AR Archaeol.

Prehistoric Political Dynamics: A Case Study From the American Southwest. Kent G. Lightfoot. LC 83-25079. 193p. 1984. 30.00 (*0-87580-097-1*) N Ill U Pr.

Prehistoric Pottery for the Archaeologist. 2nd rev. ed. Alex Gibson & Ann Woods. (Illus.). 320p. 1997. pap. 49.50 (*0-7185-1954-X*) Bks Intl VA.

Prehistoric Pottery in the Collection from el Acebuchal: Site Near Carmona, Province of Sevilla. A. W. Frothingham. (Illus.). 1953. pap. 1.00 (*0-87535-075-5*) Hispanic Soc.

Prehistoric Pueblo Settlement Patterns: The Arroyo Hondo, New Mexico, Site Survey. D. Bruce Dickson. LC 79-21542. (Arroyo Hondo Archaeological Ser.: Vol. 2). (Illus.). 150p. 1983. pap. 14.95 (*0-933452-02-0*) Schol Am Res.

Prehistoric Pueblo World, A. D., 1150-1350. Ed. by Michael A. Adler. LC 95-32452. (Illus.). 278p. 1996. 47.50 (*0-8165-1468-2*) U of Ariz Pr.

***Prehistoric Pueblo World, A. D. 1150-1350.** Michael A. Adler. (Illus.). 2000. pap. text 24.95 (*0-8165-2048-8*) U of Ariz Pr.

Prehistoric Religion in Greece. J. V. Leuven. (Illus.). 280p. 1987. lib. bdg. 84.00 (*0-317-54494-2*, Pub. by AM Hakkert) Coronet Bks.

Prehistoric Reptiles of the Sea & Air: Text Editions. Joseph Gabriele. (Illus.). 32p. (J). (gr. 1-3). 1985. pap. 1.95 (*0-911211-58-6*) Penny Lane Pubns.

Prehistoric Ritual & Religion. Ed. by Alex Gibson & Derek Simpson. LC GN803.P75 1998. (Illus.). 256p. 1998. 39.95 (*0-7509-1597-8*, Pub. by Sutton Pub Ltd) Intl Pubs Mktg.

Prehistoric Ritual & Religion. Ed. by Alex Gibson & Derek Simpson. LC GN803.P75 1998. (Illus.). 566p. 1998. pap. 19.95 (*0-7509-1598-6*, Pub. by Sutton Pub Ltd) Intl Pubs Mktg.

Prehistoric Rock Art of the Cross Timbers Management Unit, East Central Oklahoma: An Introductory Study. Charles D. Neel & Kenneth Sampson. (Archeological Resource Survey Report: No. 27). (Illus.). 130p. (C). 1986. pap. text 8.50 (*1-881346-18-8*) Univ OK Archeol.

Prehistoric Rock Pictures in Europe & Africa. Leo Frobenius & Douglas C. Fox. LC 74-169302. (Museum of Modern Art Publications in Reprint). (Illus.). 80p. 1972. reprint ed. 20.95 (*0-405-01561-5*) Ayer.

Prehistoric Sandals NE Arizona: The Earl H. Morris & Ann Axtell Morris Research. Kelley Hays-Gilpin et al. LC 97-33785. (Anthropological Papers of the University of Arizona). 168p. 1998. pap. 15.95 (*0-8165-1801-7*) U of Ariz Pr.

Prehistoric Sea Life. Spizzirri Publishing Co. Staff. Ed. by Linda Spizzirri. (Illus.). 32p. (J). (gr. 1-8). pap. 4.98 incl. audio (*0-86545-020-X*) Spizzirri.

Prehistoric Sequence in the Middle Pecos Valley, New Mexico, with a Contribution on Palynology, by Paul S. Martin. Arthur J. Jelinek. LC 68-7817. (University of Michigan, Museum of Anthropology, Anthropological Papers: No. 31). (Illus.). 196p. reprint ed. pap. 60.80 (*0-8357-8627-7*, 203505000091) Bks Demand.

Prehistoric Settlement along the Eastern Margin of Rogers Dry Lake, Western Mojave Desert, California. Brian F. Byrd et al. (Brian F. Mooney Associates Anthropological Technical Ser.). (Illus.). 195p. 1994. pap. text 20.00 (*0-9639458-1-5*) B Mooney Assocs.

Prehistoric Settlement & Physical Environment in the Mesa Verde Area. Joyce Herold. (Utah Anthropological Papers: No. 53). reprint ed. 38.00 (*0-404-60653-9*) AMS Pr.

Prehistoric Settlement & Subsistence in the Upper South Umpqua River Drainage, Southwestern Oregon. Rick Minor. (Illus.). 140p. 1989. write for info. (*0-318-64857-1*) NW Herit Pr.

Prehistoric Settlement & Trade Models in the Santa Clara Valley, California. Judith C. Bergthold. x, 328p. (C). 1985. reprint ed. pap. text 35.63 (*1-55567-017-2*) Coyote Press.

Prehistoric Settlement of the Pacific. Ed. by Ward H. Goodenough. LC 96-84050. (Transactions Ser.: Vol. 86, Pt. 5). 201p. (Orig.). 1996. pap. 20.00 (*0-87169-865-X*, T85-gow) Am Philos.

Prehistoric Settlement Patterns & Cultures in Susiana, Southwestern Iran: The Analysis of the F. G. L. Gremliza Survey Collection. Abbas Alizadeh. (Technical Reports Ser.: No. 24). xiv, 176p. (Orig.). 1992. pap. 15.00 (*0-915703-29-7*) U Mich Mus Anthro.

Prehistoric Settlement Patterns in Clay County, Mississippi. John T. Sparks. (Mississippi Department of Archives & History Archaeological Reports). (Illus.). 65p. (Orig.). 1987. pap. 5.00 (*0-938896-52-0*) Mississippi Archives.

An Asterisk (*) at the beginning of an entry indicates that the title is appearing for the first time.

Prehistoric Settlement Patterns in the Libyan Desert. James J. Hester & Philip M. Hobler. (Nubian Ser.: No. 4). reprint ed. 44.00 (*0-404-60692-X*, UAP NO. 92) AMS Pr.

Prehistoric Settlement Patterns in the New World, Twenty-three. Gordon R. Wiley. LC 81-13233. (Viking Fund Publications in Anthropology: No. 23). 202p. 1982. reprint ed. lib. bdg. 65.00 (*0-313-23223-7*, WIPE, Greenwood Pr) Greenwood.

Prehistoric Settlement Patterns in the Southern Valley of Mexico: The Chalco-Xochimilco Region. Jeffrey R. Parsons et al. (Memoirs Ser.: No. 14). (Orig.). 1982. pap. 16.00 (*0-932206-88-3*) U Mich Mus Anthro.

Prehistoric Settlement Patterns in the Texcoco Region, Mexico. Jeffrey R. Parsons. (Memoirs Ser.: No. 3). (Illus.). 1971. pap. 4.00 (*0-932206-65-4*) U Mich Mus Anthro.

Prehistoric Settlement Patterns in the Viru Valley, Peru. Gordon R. Willey. (Bureau of American Ethnology Bulletins Ser.). 453p. 1995. lib. bdg. 109.00 (*0-7812-4155-3*) Rprt Serv.

Prehistoric Settlement-Subsistence Relationships in the Fishing River Drainage, Western Missouri. Terrell L. Martin. Ed. by Robert T. Bray. (Missouri Archaeologist Ser.: Vol. 37). (Illus.). 170p. (Orig.). 1976. pap. 6.00 (*0-943414-54-7*) MO Arch Soc.

Prehistoric Sharks & Modern-Day Sharks. Marianne Johnston. LC 98-3879. (Prehistoric Animals & Their Modern-Day Relatives Ser.). 24p. (J). 1999. 13.45 (*0-8239-5206-1*, PowerKids) Rosen Group.

Prehistoric Sites in the Prado Basin California: Regional Context & Significance Evaluation. S. K. Goldberg & J. E. Arnold. (Illus.). 144p. (C). 1988. reprint ed. pap. text 15.63 (*1-55567-450-X*) Coyote Press.

Prehistoric Social, Political, & Economic Development in the Area of the Tehuacan Valley: Some Results of the Palo Blanco Project. Ed. by Robert D. Drennan. (Technical Reports Ser.: No. 11). (Illus.). (Orig.). 1979. pap. 3.00 (*0-932206-82-4*) U Mich Mus Anthro.

Prehistoric Southern Ozark Marginality: A Myth Exposed. James A. Brown. Ed. by W. Raymond Wood. LC 83-63187. (Special Publications: No. 6). (Illus.). 85p. (Orig.). 1984. pap. 5.00 (*0-943414-18-0*) MO Arch Soc.

Prehistoric Southwesterners from Basketmaker to Pueblo. Charles A. Amsden. xiv, 163p. 1976. reprint ed. pap. 5.00 (*0-916561-57-7*) Southwest Mus.

Prehistoric Southwesterners from Basketmaker to Pueblo. Charles A. Amsden & Alfred V. Kidder. LC 76-43642. reprint ed. 39.50 (*0-404-15477-8*) AMS Pr.

Prehistoric Sticker Book. Deni Bown. (Ultimate Sticker Books Ser.). (Illus.). 20p. (J). (gr. 2 up). 1994. pap. 6.95 (*1-56458-561-1*) DK Pub Inc.

Prehistoric Stone Circles, 9. Aubrey Burl. (Archaeology Ser.: No. 98). (Illus.). 52p. 1999. pap. 10.50 (*0-85263-962-7*, Pub. by Shire Pubns) Parkwest Pubns.

Prehistoric Stone Implements of Northeastern Arizona. R. B. Woodbury. (HU PMP Ser.: Vol. 34). (Illus.). 1954. 38.00 (*0-527-01286-6*) Periodicals Srv.

Prehistoric Stone Technology on Northern Black Mesa, Arizona. William J. Parry & Andrew L. Christenson. LC 87-72676. (Center for Archaeological Investigations Occasional Paper Ser.: No. 12). (Illus.). xx, 312p. (Orig.). 1988. pap. 23.00 (*0-88104-052-5*) Center Archaeol.

Prehistoric Subsistence & Population Change along the Lower Agua Fria River, Arizona: A Model Simulation. Donald E. Dove. (Anthropological Research Papers: No. 32). (Illus.). viii, 139p. 1984. pap. 15.00 (*0-685-73908-2*) AZ Univ ARP.

Prehistoric Tewa Economy: Modeling Subsistence Production on the Pajarito Plateau. Nicholas Trierweiler. LC 90-21626. (Evolution of North American Indians Ser.). 316p. 1991. reprint ed. text 10.00 (*0-8240-7063-1*) Garland.

Prehistoric Textiles: The Development of Cloth in the Neolithic & Bronze Ages with Special Reference to the Aegean. E. J. Barber. (Illus.). 416p. 1991. text 95.00 (*0-691-03597-0*, Pub. by Princeton U Pr); pap. text 35.00 (*0-691-00224-X*, Pub. by Princeton U Pr) Cal Prin Full Svc.

Prehistoric Thailand: From Early Settlement to Sukothai. Charles Higham & Rachanee Thosarat. LC 98-837131. (Illus.). 200p. 1998. pap. 30.00 (*974-8225-30-5*, Pub. by River Books) Weatherhill.

Prehistoric Thessaly. Alan J. Wace. LC 75-41286. reprint ed. 72.50 (*0-404-14734-8*) AMS Pr.

Prehistoric Times. Jane Chisolm. (Illus.). 24p. (J). (gr. 2-4). 1985. pap. text 4.50 (*0-86020-623-8*) EDC.

Prehistoric to Western Zhou see Chinese Archaeological Abstracts

Prehistoric Tuberculosis in the Americas. Ed. by Jane E. Buikstra. LC 80-28660. (Scientific Papers Ser.: No. 5). (Illus.). 194p. (Orig.). 1981. pap. 7.25 (*0-942118-10-3*) Ctr Amer Arche.

Prehistoric Use of a Marginal Environment: Continuity & Change in Occupation of the Volcanic Tablelands, Mono & Inyo Counties, California. Mark E. Basgall & Mark A. Giambastiani. (Center for Archaeological Research at Davis Ser.). (Illus.). 351p. (Orig.). 1995. pap. 22.50 (*1-883019-13-3*) U CA Dept Anthrop.

Prehistoric Villages, Castles & Towers of Southwestern Colorado. Ed. by Jesse W. Fewkes. (Bureau of American Ethnology Bulletins Ser.). 79p. 1995. lib. bdg. 79.00 (*0-7812-4070-0*) Rprt Serv.

Prehistoric Villages, Castles & Towers of Southwestern Colorado. Jesse W. Fewkes. reprint ed. 59.00 (*0-403-03690-9*) Scholarly.

Prehistoric Warfare in the American Southwest. Steven A. LeBlanc. LC 98-42327. 1999. 34.95 (*0-87480-581-3*) U of Utah Pr.

Prehistoric Warfare on the Great Plains: Skeletal Analysis of the Crow Creek Massacre Victims. P. Willey. LC 90-48882. (Evolution of North American Indians Ser.). 240p. 1990. text 10.00 (*0-8240-7167-0*) Garland.

***Prehistoric World.** Fiona Chandler et al. (World History Ser.). (Illus.). 96p. (YA). (gr. 3 up). 2000. 21.95 (*0-7460-2758-3*, Usborne) EDC.

Prehistoric Zoobooks, 10 bks., Set. Wildlife Education, Ltd. Staff. (Illus.). 1989. pap. 24.95 (*0-937934-43-7*) Wildlife Educ.

Prehistories of the Future: The Primitivist Project & the Culture of Modernism. Ed. by Elazar Barkan & Ronald Bush. LC 94-28152. (Cultural Sitings Ser.). (Illus.). 472p. 1995. 55.00 (*0-8047-2390-7*); pap. 18.95 (*0-8047-2486-5*) Stanford U Pr.

***Prehistory.** Roberto De Carvalho. (Art & Civilization Ser.). (Illus.). 40p. (J). (gr. 3-7). 2000. 16.95 (*0-87226-615-X*, 6615XB, P Bedrick Books) NTC Contemp Pub Co.

Prehistory: An Introduction. Derek A. Roe. LC 70-81799. (Illus.). 288p. reprint ed. pap. 89.30 (*0-608-18296-6*, 203154600075) Bks Demand.

Prehistory: Study of Early Cultures in Europe & the Mediterranean Basin. 2nd ed. Miles C. Burkitt. LC 73-169752. (Select Bibliographies Reprint Ser.). 1977. reprint ed. 42.95 (*0-8369-5972-8*) Ayer.

Prehistory: The World of Early Man. Ed. by Jean Guilaine. Tr. by Stephen M. Bunson. LC 90-22931. 192p. 1991. reprint ed. pap. 59.60 (*0-608-02864-9*, 206392800007) Bks Demand.

Prehistory & History of Ceramic Kilns. Ed. by Prudence M. Rice. (Ceramics & Civilization Ser.: Vol. VII). 262p. 1997. 95.00 (*1-57498-026-2*, CC07) Am Ceramic.

Prehistory & History of Glassmaking Technology. Ed. by Patrick McCray & W. David Kingery. (Ceramics & Civilization Ser.: Vol. 8). (Illus.). 360p. 1998. 95.00 (*1-57498-041-6*, CC08) Am Ceramic.

Prehistory & Management of Cultural Resources in the Red Mountain Area. M. C. Hall & J. P. Barker. Ed. by H. W. Lawton. (Illus.). 208p. (C). 1981. reprint ed. pap. text 21.88 (*1-55567-400-3*) Coyote Press.

Prehistory & Paleoecology of Guadalupe Ruin, New Mexico. Lonnie C. Pippin. (Anthropological Papers: No. 112). (Illus.). 272p. (Orig.). 1987. pap. text 25.00 (*0-87480-281-4*) U of Utah Pr.

Prehistory & Paleoenvironments in the Central Negev, Israel Vol. I, Pt. 1: The Avdat-Aqev Area. Ed. by Anthony E. Marks. LC 75-40116. (Institute for the Study of Earth & Man: Reports of Investigations Ser.: No. 1). (Illus.). 392p. 1976. pap. 27.50 (*0-87074-153-5*) SMU Press.

Prehistory & Paleoenvironments in the Central Negev, Israel Vol. II, Pt. 2: The Avdat-Aqev Area & the Har Harif. Ed. by Anthony E. Marks. LC 75-40116. (Institute for the Study of Earth & Man: Reports of Investigations Ser.: No. 2). (Illus.). x, 368p. 1977. pap. 25.00 (*0-89643-000-6*) SMU Press.

Prehistory & Paleoenvironments in the Central Negev, Israel Vol. III, Pt. 3: The Advat-Aqev Area. Ed. by Anthony E. Marks. LC 75-40116. (Institute for the Study of Earth & Man: Reports of Investigations Ser.: No. 3). (Illus.). xvi, 368p. 1983. pap. 35.00 (*0-89643-113-4*) SMU Press.

Prehistory & Protohistory to Eleven Hundred B.C. Ed. by George A. Christopoulos & John C. Bastias. Tr. by Philip Sherrard. LC 75-18610. (History of the Hellenic World Ser.: Vol. 1). (Illus.). 420p. 1975. 56.50 (*0-271-01199-8*) Pa St U Pr.

Prehistory, History, & Historiography of Language, Speech, & Linguistic Theory: Papers in Honor of Oswald Szemerenyi I. Ed. by Bela Brogyanyi. LC 92-8921. (Current Issues in Linguistic Theory Ser.: No. 64). x, 414p. 1992. 124.00 (*1-55619-064-6*) J Benjamins Pubng Co.

Prehistory in Haiti: A Study in Method. Irving Rouse. LC 64-21834. (Yale University Publications in Anthropology Reprints Ser.: No. 21). 202p. 1964. pap. 20.00 (*0-87536-504-3*) HRAFP.

Prehistory in Northeastern Arabia: The Problem of Interregional Interaction. Abdullah H. Masry. LC 95-35863. (Illus.). 280p. (C). 1996. 212.50 (*0-7103-0536-2*, Pub. by Kegan Paul Intl) Col U Pr.

Prehistory in Peril: The Worst & Best in Durango Archaeology. Florence C. Lister. LC 96-53288. (Illus.). 320p. 1997. 45.00 (*0-87081-443-5*) Univ Pr Colo.

Prehistory in Peril: The Worst & Best in Durango Archaeology. Florence C. Lister. LC 96-53288. (Illus.). 320p. 1997. pap. 24.95 (*0-87081-448-6*) Univ Pr Colo.

Prehistory in the Pacific Islands. John E. Terrell. 320p. 1988. pap. text 42.95 (*0-521-36956-8*) Cambridge U Pr.

Prehistory of Agriculture: New Experimental & Ethnographic Approaches. Ed. by Patricia C. Anderson. LC 98-31101. (Monograph Ser.: No. 40). (Illus.). 1999. pap. text 50.00 (*0-917956-93-1*) UCLA Arch.

Prehistory of Arid North Africa: Essays in Honor of Fred Wendorf. Ed. by Angela E. Close. LC 86-31510. (Illus.). 374p. 1987. 39.95 (*0-87074-222-1*); pap. 19.95 (*0-87074-223-X*) SMU Press.

Prehistory of Australia. John Mulvaney & Johan Kamminga. LC 99-21564. (Illus.). 512p. 1999. pap. 27.95 (*1-56098-804-5*) Smithsonian.

Prehistory of Aviation. Berthold Laufer. LC 28-30680. (Field Museum of Natural History, Publication 184, Anthropological Ser.: Vol. 18, No. 1). 120p. 1928. reprint ed. pap. 37.20 (*0-608-02114-8*, 206276300004) Bks Demand.

Prehistory of Central Anatolia I: The Neolithic Period. Ian A. Todd. (Studies in Mediterranean Archaeology: Vol. LX). (Illus.). 203p. (Orig.). 1980. pap. 57.50 (*91-85058-87-4*) P Astroms.

Prehistory of Colorado & Adjacent Areas. Tammy Stone. LC 98-31020. (Illus.). 214p. 1999. pap. 17.50 (*0-87480-578-3*) U of Utah Pr.

Prehistory of Dickson Mounds: The Dickson Excavation. rev. ed. Alan D. Harn. (Reports of Investigations: No. 35). (Illus.). 146p. 1991. pap. 6.00 (*0-89792-085-6*) Ill St Museum.

Prehistory of Eastern Zambia. D. W. Phillipson. (Illus.). 230p. 1977. pap. 28.50 (*1-872566-03-0*, Pub. by Brit Inst Estrn Africa) David Brown.

Prehistory of Egypt. Beatrix Midant-Reynes. Tr. by Ian Shaw. LC 99-33594. 320p. 1999. 64.95 (*0-631-20169-6*); pap. 29.95 (*0-631-21787-8*) Blackwell Pubs.

Prehistory of Fishtrap, Kentucky. R. C. Dunnell. LC 72-90078. (Publications in Anthropology: No. 75). 1972. pap. 7.00 (*0-913516-08-2*) Yale U Anthro.

Prehistory of Japan. Gerard J. Groot. Ed. by Bertram S. Kraus. LC 79-37884. (Select Bibliographies Reprint Ser.). 1977. reprint ed. 39.95 (*0-8369-6721-6*) Ayer.

Prehistory of Kern County. fac. ed. Robert A. Schiffman & Alan P. Garfinkel. (Bakersfield College Publications in Archaeology: No. 1). 262p. 1981. reprint ed. pap. text 27.50 (*1-55567-552-2*) Coyote Press.

Prehistory of Languages. Mary R. Haas. LC 76-75689. (Janua Linguarum, Ser. Minor: No. 57). 1978. pap. text 20.00 (*90-279-0681-5*) Mouton.

Prehistory of Metallurgy in the British Isles. Ronald F. Tylecote. (Illus.). 260p. 1990. pap. 20.00 (*0-901462-96-9*, Pub. by Inst Materials) Ashgate Pub Co.

Prehistory of Missouri. Michael J. O'Brien & W. Raymond Wood. LC 97-20654. (Illus.). 488p. 1998. pap. 39.95 (*0-8262-1131-3*) U of Mo Pr.

Prehistory of North America. 3rd ed. Jesse D. Jennings. LC 88-13308. 365p. (C). 1989. text 53.95 (*0-87484-865-2*, 865) Mayfield Pub.

Prehistory of North Carolina: An Archaeological Symposium. David S. Phelps et al. Ed. by Mark A. Mathis & Jeffrey J. Crow. (Illus.). xvi, 206p. 1993. reprint ed. pap. 12.00 (*0-86526-225-X*) NC Archives.

Prehistory of Northern North America As Seen from the Yukon. Frederica De Laguna. LC 76-43687. (Society for American Archaeology Memoirs Ser.: No. 3). reprint ed. 65.00 (*0-404-15520-0*) AMS Pr.

Prehistory of Photography: Original Anthology. Ed. by Robert A. Sobieszek. LC 76-23040. (Sources of Modern Photography Ser.). (Illus.). 1979. lib. bdg. 18.95 (*0-405-09661-5*) Ayer.

Prehistory of Polynesia. Jesse D. Jennings. LC 79-1055. (Illus.). 407p. reprint ed. pap. 126.20 (*0-7837-4158-8*, 205900600012) Bks Demand.

Prehistory of Salts Cave, Kentucky. Patty J. Watson. (Reports of Investigations: No. 16). (Illus.). 86p. 1992. pap. 6.00 (*0-89792-037-6*) Ill St Museum.

Prehistory of Sardinia, 2300-500 B. C. Gary S. Webster. (MMA Ser.: Vol. 5). 224p. 1996. 75.00 (*1-85075-508-6*, Pub. by Sheffield Acad) CUP Services.

Prehistory of Sex: Four Million Years of Human Sexual Culture. Timothy Taylor. 368p. 1997. pap. 15.95 (*0-553-37527-X*) Bantam.

Prehistory of the Americas. 2nd ed. Stuart J. Fiedel. (Illus.). 422p. (C). 1992. text 65.00 (*0-521-41532-2*); pap. text 24.95 (*0-521-42544-1*) Cambridge U Pr.

Prehistory of the Americas: Colloquium 34: Colloquium 35. Thomas R. Hester et al. LC 98-205545. (Colloquia Ser.). (ENG, ITA & SPA.). 148p. 1996. write for info. (*88-86712-31-6*) MAC.

Prehistory of the Ayacucho Basin, Peru: Nonceramic Artifacts, Vol. III. Richard S. MacNeish et al. (Illus.). 360p. 1980. text 57.50 (*0-472-02707-7*, 02707) U of Mich Pr.

Prehistory of the Ayacucho Basin, Peru Vol. II: Excavations & Chronology. Richard S. MacNeish et al. LC 80-13960. (Illus.). 296p. (C). 1981. text 57.50 (*0-472-04907-0*, 04907) U of Mich Pr.

Prehistory of the Borderlands: Recent Research in the Archaeology of Northern Mexico & the Southern Southwest. Ed. by John Carpenter et al. LC 97-70874. (Archaeological Ser.: No. 186). 175p. 1997. pap. 14.95 (*1-889747-51-3*) Ariz St Mus.

Prehistory of the Burnt Bluff Area. James E. Fitting. LC 74-626974. (Anthropological Papers: Vol. 34). (Illus.). 146p. 1968. reprint ed. pap. 45.30 (*0-7837-9216-6*, 204996700004) Bks Demand.

Prehistory of the Central Maine Coast. Bruce J. Bourque. LC 90-24498. (Evolution of North American Indians Ser.). (Illus.). 328p. 1992. text 10.00 (*0-8240-2049-9*) Garland.

Prehistory of the Central Mississippi Valley. Ed. by Charles H. McNutt. LC 95-21893. (Illus.). 344p. (Orig.). (C). 1996. pap. text 34.95 (*0-8173-0807-5*) U of Ala Pr.

Prehistory of the Chickamauga Basin in Tennessee, 2 vols., Set, Vol. 1. Thomas R. Lewis & Madeline D. Lewis. (Illus.). 320p. (C). 1995. lib. bdg. 50.00 (*0-87049-861-4*) U of Tenn Pr.

Prehistory of the Chickamauga Basin in Tennessee, 2 vols., Set, Vol. 1. Thomas M. Lewis & Madeline D. Lewis. (Illus.). 320p. (C). 1995. pap. text 25.00 (*0-87049-863-0*) U of Tenn Pr.

Prehistory of the Chickamauga Basin in Tennessee, 2 vols., Set, Vol. 2. Thomas M. Lewis & Madeline D. Lewis. (Illus.). 432p. (C). 1995. pap. text 25.00 (*0-87049-864-9*); lib. bdg. 50.00 (*0-87049-862-2*) U of Tenn Pr.

Prehistory of the Eastern Highlands of New Guinea. Virginia D. Watson & J. David Cole. LC 76-49166. (Anthropological Studies in the Eastern Highlands of New Guinea: No. 3). (Illus.). 243p. 1978. 40.00 (*0-295-95541-4*) U of Wash Pr.

Prehistory of the Far East: Homes of Vanished Peoples. Luther S. Cressman. LC 75-30153. (Illus.). 269p. reprint ed. pap. 83.40 (*0-8357-6849-X*, 203554400095) Bks Demand.

PreHistory of the Far Side: A Tenth Anniversary Exhibit. Gary Larson. (Illus.). 288p. 1989. pap. 12.95 (*0-8362-1851-5*) Andrews & McMeel.

Prehistory of the Far Side: A Tenth Anniversary Exhibit. Gary Larson. (Illus.). 288p. 1989. 19.95 (*0-8362-1861-2*) Andrews & McMeel.

Prehistory of the Gathright Dam Area, Virginia, No. M2. Howard A. MacCord, Sr. 75p. 1975. pap. 15.00 (*1-884626-19-X*) Archeolog Soc.

Prehistory of the Indo-Malaysian Archipelago. Peter S. Bellwood. 1986. text 125.00 (*0-12-085370-1*) Acad Pr.

Prehistory of the Indo-Malaysian Archipelago. rev. ed. Peter S. Bellwood. LC 96-44400. (Illus.). 400p. 1997. text 58.00 (*0-8248-1883-0*); pap. text 32.95 (*0-8248-1907-1*) UH Pr.

Prehistory of the Levant: A Reader. Ed. by J. L. Phillips & O. Bar-Yosef. (Illus.). 490p. (C). 1999. write for info. (*0-306-46077-7*, Kluwer Plenum) Kluwer Academic.

Prehistory of the Levant: A Reader. Ed. by J. L. Phillips & O. Bar-Yosef. (Illus.). 490p. (C). 1999. pap. write for info. (*0-306-46078-5*, Plenum Trade) Perseus Pubng.

Prehistory of the Mind: The Cognitive Origins of Art, Religion & Science. Steve Mithen. LC 96-60367. (Illus.). 288p. 1999. pap. 17.95 (*0-500-28100-9*, Pub. by Thames Hudson) Norton.

Prehistory of the Mind: The Cognitive Origins of Art, Religion, & Science. Steven Mithen. LC 96-60367. (Illus.). 304p. 1996. 27.50 (*0-500-05081-3*, Pub. by Thames Hudson) Norton.

Prehistory of the Netherlands. Ed. by P. W. Van den Broeke et al. (C). Date not set. 92.50 (*90-5356-160-9*, Pub. by Amsterdam U Pr) U of Mich Pr.

Prehistory of the Nile Valley. Anthony J. Arkell. LC 76-361917. (Handbuch Der Orientalistik Ser.). ix, 55 p. 1975. 36.00 (*90-04-04397-7*) Brill Academic Pubs.

Prehistory of the Nile Valley. Fred Wendorf et al. LC 75-13097. (Studies in Archeology). xxiv, 404 p. 1976. write for info. (*0-12-743950-1*) Acad Pr.

Prehistory of the Northwest Coast. R. G. Matson & Gary Coupland. (Illus.). 364p. 1994. text 75.00 (*0-12-480260-5*) Acad Pr.

Prehistory of the Oregon Coast: The Effects of Excavation Strategies & Assemblage Size on Archaeological Inquiry. R. Lee Lyman. (Illus.). 391p. (C). 1991. text 74.95 (*0-12-460415-3*) Acad Pr.

***Prehistory of the Rustler Hills: Granado Cave.** Donny L. Hamilton & John R. Bratten. LC 00-8892. (Texas Archaeology & Ethnohistory Ser.). (Illus.). 352p. 2001. pap. 55.00 (*0-292-73141-8*) U of Tex Pr.

Prehistory of the St. Johns Area, East-Central Arizona: The TEP St. Johns Project. Deborah A. Westfall. (Archaeological Ser.: No. 153). (Illus.). 459p. 1981. pap. 19.95 (*1-889747-30-0*) Ariz St Mus.

Prehistory of Uganda Protectorate. Terence P. O'Brien. LC 76-44772. reprint ed. 34.50 (*0-404-15874-9*) AMS Pr.

Prehistory of Utah & the Eastern Great Basin: A Review, 1968-1976. Jesse D. Jennings. (Anthropological Papers: No. 98). (Illus.). 1978. pap. 24.95 (*0-87480-121-4*) U of Utah Pr.

Prehistory of Wadi Kubbaniya: Stratigraphy, Paleoeconomy, & Environments & Late Paleolithic Archaeology, 2 vols. Fred Wendorf & Romuald Schild. Ed. by Angela E. Close. LC 86-1964. (Illus.). 882p. 1989. text 65.00 (*0-87074-290-6*) SMU Press.

Prehistory of Western Siberia. Valeriui Chernetsov & W. Moszynska. LC 73-79092. (Arctic Institute of North America-Anthropology of the North; Translation from Russian Sources Ser.: No. 9). (Illus.). 407p. reprint ed. pap. 126.20 (*0-7837-1174-3*, 204170200022) Bks Demand.

Prehistory-Renaissance see Creative Ways to Teach World History

Prehistory to Egypt. Gloria Verges & Oriol Verges. (Journey Through History Ser.). (ENG & SPA., Illus.). 32p. (J). (gr. 2-4). 1988. pap. 6.95 (*0-8120-3390-6*); pap. 6.95 (*0-8120-3391-4*) Barron.

Prehistory to Politics: John Mulvaney, the Humanities & the Public Intellectual. Tim Bonyhady & Tom Griffiths. LC 97-205478. (Illus.). 284p. 1997. pap. 29.95 (*0-522-84748-X*, Pub. by Melbourne Univ Pr) Paul & Co Pubs.

Prehistory to the Peace of Utrecht see Western Civilization

Prehl'ad Biologie 1, 2 (A Survey of Bioiloyg 1, 2), Vol. 1. (SLO.). 320p. 1997. write for info. (*80-08-00990-X*, Pub. by Slov Pegagog Naklad) IBD Ltd.

Prehl'ad Biologie 1, 2 (A Survey of Bioiloyg 1, 2), Vol. 2. (SLO.). 320p. 1997. write for info. (*80-08-01002-9*, Pub. by Slov Pegagog Naklad) IBD Ltd.

Prehl'ad Chemie 1, 2 (A Survey of Chemistry 1, 2), Vol. 2. P. Silny & P. Zahradnik. (SLO.). 290p. 1997. pap. write for info. (*80-08-01005-3*, Pub. by Slov Pegagog Naklad) IBD Ltd.

Prehl'ad Matematika 1, 2 (A Survey of Mathematics 1, 2), Vol. 2. V. Burjan et al. (SLO.). 240p. 1997. pap. write for info. (*80-08-02490-9*, Pub. by Slov Pegagog Naklad) IBD Ltd.

Prehl'ad Stredoskolskej Fyziky. Zamecnik. (SLO.). 232p. 1996. write for info. (*80-08-00404-5*, Pub. by Slov Pegagog Naklad) IBD Ltd.

Prehn: Journal of a Genealogist, with Ancestral Wills, Includes Anderson, Bass, Elder, Gaddy, Griggs, Ingersoll, Kelsey, Lewis, Westall, Wright Families. Alyene E. Prehn. (Illus.). 864p. 1994. reprint ed. pap. 115.00 (*0-8328-4099-8*); reprint ed. lib. bdg. 125.00 (*0-8328-4098-X*) Higginson Bk Co.

P

Prehospital Care: Administrative & Clinical Management. Ed. by Victoria L. Cleary et al. 369p. 1987. 85.00 (*0-87189-616-8*, 89616) Aspen Pub.

Prehospital Care Administration: Issues, Readings, Cases. Joseph J. Fitch. (C). (gr. 13). 1995. text 46.95 (*0-8151-3391-X*, 25879) Mosby Inc.

Prehospital Care for the EMT-Intermediate: Assessment & Intervention. Stephen Le Fevers & Loren Marshall. 288p. 1983. pap. 18.95 (*0-317-58949-0*) P-H.

Prehospital Care of Pediatric Emergencies. James S. Seidel & Deborah P. Henderson. (Nursing-Health Science Ser.). 109p. (C). 1987. pap. text 35.00 (*0-86720-680-2*) Jones & Bartlett.

Prehospital Care of Pediatric Emergencies. 2nd ed. James S. Seidel & Deborah P. Henderson. LC 96-32245. 1996. pap. 36.25 (*0-86720-505-9*) Jones & Bartlett.

Prehospital Documentation: A Systematic Approach. Armando S. Bevelacqua. 144p. 1992. pap. text 22.00 (*0-89303-948-9*) P-H.

Prehospital Drug Therapy. Sheryl M. Gonsoulin & William Raynovich. LC 93-120. (Illus.). 336p. (gr. 13). 1993. pap. text 35.95 (*0-8016-1969-6*, 01969) Mosby Inc.

Prehospital Drug Therapy 2. 2nd ed. Sheryl M. Gonsoulin et al. 416p. 2000. pap. text 30.95 (*0-8151-2965-3*, 31834) Mosby Inc.

Prehospital Emergency Care. 5th ed. Hafen. pap. text, teacher ed. 60.00 (*0-89303-768-0*) Appleton & Lange.

Prehospital Emergency Care. 5th ed. Brent Q. Hafen & Keith J. Karren. LC 99-23560. 896p. 1995. pap. 46.00 (*0-89303-763-X*) P-H.

Prehospital Emergency Care. 5th ed. Brent Q. Hafen & Keith J. Karren. (C). 1996. pap. text, teacher ed. 15.00 (*0-89303-771-0*) P-H.

Prehospital Emergency Care. 6th ed. Hafen & Karren. 1999. pap. text, teacher ed. 45.00 (*0-8359-5739-X*) Globe Fearon.

Prehospital Emergency Care. 6th ed. Keith J. Karren & Brent Q. Hafen. 1999. 38.00 (*0-8359-5331-9*) P-H.

Prehospital Emergency Care. 6th ed. Mistovich & Hafen. 1999. pap. 54.00 (*0-8359-5705-5*) Pearson Custom.

Prehospital Emergency Care: A Guide for Paramedics. 3rd ed. Jean T. Abbott & Marilyn J. Gifford. LC 95-49532. (Clinical Handbook Ser.). (Illus.). 382p. 1996. pap. text 23.95 (*1-85070-636-0*) Prthnon Pub.

Prehospital Emergency Care & Crisis Intervention. 4th ed. Brent A. Hafen & Keith J. Karren. 752p. 1993. reprint ed. pap. text 57.00 (*0-89303-978-0*) P-H.

Prehospital Emergency Care Secrets: Questions You Will Be Asked--At the Scene, in the ER, on Oral Exams. Peter T. Pons & V. Markovchick. LC 97-51462. (Secrets Ser.). 1998. 34.00 (*1-56053-250-5*) Hanley & Belfus.

Prehospital Emergency Medicine: Challenges & Options in Emergency Services. 2nd ed. Ed. by John Schou. 448p. 1997. text 49.00 (*90-5702-003-3*, Harwood Acad Pubs) Gordon & Breach.

Prehospital Emergency Pharmacology. Bryan E. Bledsoe et al. LC 83-15893. 336p. pap. text 19.95 (*0-89303-765-6*) P-H.

Prehospital Emergency Pharmacology. 2nd ed. Bryan E. Bledsoe. (Illus.). 304p. 1988. pap. text 31.00 (*0-89303-797-4*) P-H.

Prehospital Emergency Pharmacology. 4th ed. Bryan E. Bledsoe et al. LC 95-24665. 432p. 1995. 49.00 (*0-8359-6065-X*) P-H.

Prehospital Medicine: The Art of on-Line Medical Command. Ed. by Paul M. Paris & Ronald N. Roth. (Illus.). 288p. (C). (gr. 13). 1996. pap. text 50.95 (*0-8151-6849-7*, 24810) Mosby Inc.

Prehospital Medicine: The Principles & Practice of Immediate Care. I. Greaves & K. M. Porter. (Arnold Publications). (Illus.). 832p. 1999. text 239.50 (*0-340-67656-6*) OUP.

Prehospital Medicine & the Law. (C). Date not set. 42.67 (*0-13-021220-2*) P-H.

Prehospital Nursing: A Collaborative Approach. Renee S. Holleran. (Illus.). 394p. (C). (gr. 13). 1994. text 59.95 (*0-8016-7894-3*, 07894) Mosby Inc.

Prehospital Pediatric Emergencies. Martin R. Eichelberger et al. 1991. pap. 22.00 (*0-89303-802-4*, 740801) P-H.

***Prehospital Providers' Guide to Medication.** Alan J. Azzara. LC 99-21429. (Illus.). 255p. 1998. pap. write for info. (*0-7216-1136-2*, W B Saunders Co) Harcrt Hlth Sci Grp.

Prehospital Trauma Life Support. 4th ed. National Association of Emergency Medical Technici. LC 98-27270. (Illus.). 384p. (gr. 13). 1998. pap. text 36.95 (*0-8151-4569-1*, 30219) Mosby Inc.

***Prehospital Trauma Life Support.** 4th ed. National Association of Emergency Technicians Staff. 1998. teacher ed. write for info. (*0-323-00300-1*) Mosby Inc.

12-Lead ECG in Acute Myocardial Infarction. Tim Phalen. (Illus.). 252p. (C). (gr. 13). 1995. pap. text 29.00 (*0-8151-6752-0*, 25863) Mosby Inc.

Prehysterical Pogo (in Pandemonia) Walt Kelly. (Pogo Collector's Edition Ser.). 176p. 1995. 19.95 (*1-886460-02-7*) Sunday Comics.

Preimplantation Diagnosis of Genetic Disease: A New Technique in Assisted Reproduction. Ed. by Yuri Verlinsky & Anver Kuliev. 166p. 1992. 135.00 (*0-471-58824-5*, Wiley-Liss) Wiley.

Preimplantation Diagnosis of Human Genetic Disease. Ed. by Robert G. Edwards. (Illus.). 352p. (C). 1993. text 110.00 (*0-521-40425-8*) Cambridge U Pr.

Preimplantation Embryo Development. Ed. by Barry D. Bavister. LC 92-49441. 352p. 1993. 129.00 (*0-387-97934-4*); write for info. (*3-540-97934-4*) Spr-Verlag.

Preimplantation Genetic Disorders. Harper. text 134.95 (*0-471-98500-7*) Wiley.

Preimplantation Genetics. Ed. by Yuri Verlinsky & Anver Kuliev. (Illus.). 336p. (C). 1991. text 126.00 (*0-306-43937-9*, Kluwer Plenum) Kluwer Academic.

Preise und Produktion. Friedrich A. Hayek. (International Carl Menger Library). (GER.). 124p. 1976. reprint ed. pap. 39.00 (*3-88405-026-5*) Philosophia Pr.

Prejudice. Addelston. 2002. write for info. (*0-07-000505-2*) McGraw.

Prejudice. Thomas F. Pettigrew et al. (Dimensions in Ethnicity Ser.). 128p. 1982. pap. 13.50 (*0-674-70063-5*) HUP.

Prejudice see Kadima Kesher Series

Prejudice: Index of Modern Information with Bibliography. Ward J. Nugent. LC 88-47787. 150p. (Orig.). 1988. 47.50 (*0-88164-902-3*); pap. 44.50 (*0-88164-903-1*) ABBE Pubs Assn.

Prejudice: Its Social Psychology. Rupert Brown. (Illus.). 272p. (C). 1995. pap. 28.95 (*0-631-18315-9*) Blackwell Pubs.

Prejudice: Stories About Hate, Ignorance, Revelation & Transformation. Ed. by Daphne Muse. 212p. (J). 1998. pap. 7.95 (*0-7868-1310-5*, Pub. by Hyperion) Time Warner.

Prejudice: The Target's Perspective. Ed. by Janet K. Swim & Charles Stangor. LC 97-80793. (Illus.). 332p. 1998. text 69.95 (*0-12-679130-9*) Morgan Kaufmann.

***Prejudice Across America.** James Waller. LC 00-35195. 300p. 2000. pap. 18.00 (*1-57806-313-2*); lib. bdg. 45.00 (*1-57806-269-1*) U Pr of Miss.

Prejudice Against Nature. Michael J. Cohen. (Illus.). 1983. pap. 10.00 (*0-89166-016-X*) Cobblesmith.

Prejudice & Dignity: An Introduction to Community-Based Rehabilitation. 241p. 1993. 20.00 (*92-1-126032-9*) UN.

Prejudice & Discrimination: Can We Eliminate Them. 2nd ed. F. Holmes. 1977. pap. 11.84 (*0-13-695320-4*) P-H.

***Prejudice & Discrimination: Stereotypes.** Nancy Brekke & Sergio Guglielmi. 2000. pap. text, write for info. (*1-57259-717-8*) Worth.

Prejudice & Property. U. S. Department of Justice Staff et al. LC 75-90725. 104p. 1970. reprint ed. lib. bdg. 65.00 (*0-8371-2221-X*, PRPR, Greenwood Pr) Greenwood.

Prejudice & Racism. James M. Jones. 196p. (C). 1972. pap. text 36.50 (*0-07-554806-2*) McGraw.

Prejudice & Racism. 2nd ed. James M. Jones. LC 96-34940. (Mcgraw-Hill Series in Social Psychology). 592p. (C). 1996. pap. 52.50 (*0-07-033117-0*) McGraw.

***Prejudice & the Old Politics: The Presidential Election of 1928.** Allan J. Lichtman. 400p. 2000. pap. 26.95 (*0-7391-0126-9*) Lxngtn Bks.

Prejudice & the Old Politics: The Presidential Election of 1928. Allan J. Lichtman. LC 78-26813. 380p. reprint ed. pap. 117.80 (*0-7837-0302-3*, 204062400018) Bks Demand.

Prejudice & Tolerance in Ireland. Michael MacGreil. LC 79-49275. 600p. 1980. 75.00 (*0-275-90515-2*, C0515, Praeger Pubs) Greenwood.

Prejudice & Your Child. Kenneth B. Clark. LC 85-17862. 327p. 1988. reprint ed. pap. 19.95 (*0-8195-6155-X*, Wesleyan Univ Pr) U Pr of New Eng.

Prejudice Book. David A. Shiman. (J). (gr. 3-6). 1981. 19.95 (*0-686-74872-7*) ADL.

Prejudice in Discourse: An Analysis of Ethnic Prejudice in Cognition & Conversation. Teun A. Van Dijk. LC 84-24189. (Pragmatics & Beyond Ser.: Vol. V:3). x, 170p. 1985. pap. 58.00 (*0-915027-43-7*) J Benjamins Pubng Co.

Prejudice or Productivity: Ethnicity, Language & Discrimination in Labor Markets. M. D. R. Evans. (Social Inequality Ser.). 150p. (C). 2000. pap. 28.50 (*0-8133-8738-8*) Westview.

Prejudice, Polemic or Progress? Ed. by James Lynch et al. (Cultural Diversity & the Schools Ser.: Vol. 2). 500p. 1992. 110.00 (*1-85000-991-0*, Falmer Pr) Taylor & Francis.

Prejudice, Politics, & the American Dilemma. Ed. by Paul M. Sniderman et al. LC 93-22210. 352p. 1993. 47.50 (*0-8047-2132-7*) Stanford U Pr.

Prejudice, Politics, & the American Dilemma. Ed. by Paul M. Sniderman. 3488p. (C). 1995. pap. 16.95 (*0-8047-2482-2*) Stanford U Pr.

Prejudiced Witness. large type ed. Dilys A. Gater. 1990. 27.99 (*0-7089-2317-8*) Ulverscroft.

Prejudices: A Philosophical Dictionary. Robert A. Nisbet. 336p. 1982. pap. text 9.95 (*0-674-70066-X*) HUP.

Prejudices: A Selection. H. L. Mencken. Ed. & Intro. by James T. Farrell. LC 95-42524. (Maryland Paperback Bookshelf Ser.). 280p. (C). 1996. reprint ed. pap. 15.95 (*0-8018-5341-9*) Johns Hopkins.

Prejudices: First Series. H. L. Mencken. 285p. 1998. reprint ed. 25.00 (*0-936128-89-5*) De Young Pr.

Prejudices about Bias. Baruch Fischoff. (Working Papers on Risk & Rationality). 1988. 2.50 (*0-317-01533-8*, RR1) IPPP.

Prejudices & Antipathies: A Tract on the LC Subject Heads Concerning People. Sanford Berman. LC 92-50944. 229p. 1993. pap. 24.95 (*0-89950-828-6*) McFarland & Co.

Prejudicial Error. Bill Blum. 368p. 1996. mass mkt. 5.99 (*0-451-18309-6*, Sig) NAL.

Prejuicio Racial en Puerto Rico. Tomas Blanco. LC 85-80186. (Obras Completas de Tomas Blanco Ser.). (SPA.). 145p. 1985. pap. 7.50 (*0-940238-79-9*) Ediciones Huracan.

Prejuicio Racial en Puerto Rico: Racial Prejudice in Puerto Rico, Spanish Text. Tomas Blanco. LC 74-14222. (Puerto Rican Experience Ser.). (Illus.). 90p. 1975. reprint ed. 13.95 (*0-405-06212-5*) Ayer.

Prelate As Pastor: The Episcopate of James I. Kenneth Fincham. (Illus.). 378p. 1990. text 98.00 (*0-19-822921-6*) OUP.

Prelature's Reaction: The Official Response from Opus Dei to "Parents' Guide to Opus Dei" annot. ed. J. J. Garvey. 64p. (Orig.). pap. write for info. (*0-9628502-2-5*) Sicut Dixit Pr.

Preleukemic Syndrome: Hemopoietic Dysplasia. Ed. by Grover C. Bagby. LC 84-14975. 256p. 1985. 147.00 (*0-8493-5084-0*, RC642, CRC Reprint) Franklin.

Prelevements en Biologie Medicale. C. Perez. 82p. 1991. pap. 45.00 (*2-906077-17-8*) Elsevier.

Preliminaries, & Other Stories. Cornelia A. Comer. LC 78-128726. (Short Story Index Reprint Ser.). 1977. 17.95 (*0-8369-3617-5*) Ayer.

Preliminaries of the Revolution, 1763-1775. George E. Howard. LC 71-110349. reprint ed. 51.50 (*0-404-03355-5*) AMS Pr.

Preliminaries of the Revolution, 1763-1775. George E. Howard. (BCL1 - U. S. History Ser.). 359p. 1991. reprint ed. lib. bdg. 89.00 (*0-7812-6098-1*) Rprt Serv.

Preliminaries to Linguistic Phonetics. Peter Ladefoged. 128p. 1980. pap. text 15.95 (*0-226-46787-2*) U Ch Pr.

Preliminary, Bk. 1. Yoon-Il Auh. (Auh School of Violin Ser.). 60p. (J). (gr. 1-8). 1983. student ed. 14.00 (*1-882858-00-X*) Yoon-il Auh.

Preliminary, Bk. 2. Yoon-Il Auh. (Auh School of Violin Ser.). 60p. (J). (gr. 1-8). 1983. student ed. 14.00 (*1-882858-01-8*) Yoon-il Auh.

Preliminary, Bk. 3. Yoon-Il Auh. (Auh School of Violin Ser.). 45p. (J). (gr. 1-8). 1983. student ed. 14.00 (*1-882858-02-6*) Yoon-il Auh.

Preliminary Advance, Bk. 1. Yoon-Il Auh. (Auh School of Violin Ser.). 50p. (J). (gr. 1-8). 1983. student ed. 14.00 (*1-882858-17-4*) Yoon-il Auh.

Preliminary Agaric Flora of East Africa. David N. Pegler. (Kew Bulletin Additional Ser.: Vol. VI). (Illus.). 615p. 1977. pap. 60.00 (*0-11-241101-0*, Pub. by Royal Botnic Grdns) Balogh.

Preliminary Analysis of the October 1, 1965, Coup in Indonesia. Benedict R. Anderson & Ruth T. McVey. LC 71-30341. (Cornell University, Modern Indonesia Project, Monograph Ser.: No. 52). 174p. reprint ed. pap. 54.00 (*0-8357-3667-9*, 203639300003) Bks Demand.

Preliminary Analysis of the October 1, 1965, Coup in Indonesia (Prepared in Jan. 1966), No. 52. 4th ed. Benedict R. Anderson & Ruth T. McVey. (Modern Indonesia Project Ser.). 174p. (C). 1991. reprint ed. pap. 10.75 (*0-87763-008-9*) Cornell Mod Indo.

Preliminary Analysis of the Public Costs of Environmental Protection: 1981-2000. (Illus.). 65p. (Orig.). (C). 1993. pap. text 25.00 (*1-56806-444-6*) DIANE Pub.

Preliminary & Interim Report on the Hebrew Old Testament Text Project Vol. 1: Pentateuch. Ed. by UBS Committee. xxxii, 317p. 1973. pap. 18.99 (*0-8267-0008-X*, 102683) Untd Bible Soc.

Preliminary & Interim Report on the Hebrew Old Testament Text Project Vol. 2: Historical Books. Ed. by UBS Committee. xxxiv, 556p. 1976. pap. 24.99 (*0-8267-0009-8*, 102684) Untd Bible Soc.

Preliminary & Interim Report on the Hebrew Old Testament Text Project Vol. 3: Poetical Books. Ed. by UBS Committee. xxxiii, 620p. 1977. pap. 26.99 (*0-8267-0010-1*, 102685) Untd Bible Soc.

Preliminary & Interim Report on the Hebrew Old Testament Text Project Vol. 4: Prophetical Books I. Ed. by UBS Committee. xxxiii, 355p. 1979. pap. 12.99 (*0-8267-0011-X*, 102686) Untd Bible Soc.

Preliminary & Interim Report on the Hebrew Old Testament Text Project Vol. 5: Prophetical Books II. Ed. by UBS Committee. xxxiii, 443p. 1980. pap. 16.99 (*0-8267-0012-8*, 102702) Untd Bible Soc.

Preliminary & Partial Bibliography of Miscellaneous Research Materials on Laos: With Special Reference to the Mekong Development Scheme Plus Selected Items on Cambodia, Thailand, & Vietnam. Joel M. Halpern & James A. Hafner. 113p. 1990. reprint ed. pap. 15.00 (*0-923135-16-2*) Dalley Bk Service.

Preliminary Annotated Bibliography Related to State Government Reform. Corey Cook. 16p. 1994. pap. write for info. (*1-58703-028-4*) CA St Libry.

Preliminary Announcement. Incl. English Influence on the French Vocabulary. Englishing of French Words. Robert Bridges. Ed. by Steele Commager. 1979. lib. bdg. Few Practical Suggestions. Robert Bridges. Ed. by Steele Commager. 1979. lib. bdg. Language of Anatomy. Robert Bridges. Ed. by Steele Commager. 1979. lib. bdg. On English Homophones. Robert Bridges. Ed. by Steele Commager. 1979. lib. bdg. On Grammatical Inversion. Robert Bridges. Ed. by Steele Commager. 1979. lib. bdg. On Hyphens & Shall & Will, Should & Would. Robert Bridges. Ed. by Steele Commager. 1979. lib. bdg. Pronunciation of English Words. Robert Bridges. Ed. by Steele Commager. 1979. lib. bdg. What Is Pure French? Robert Bridges. Ed. by Steele Commager. 1979. lib. bdg. (Society for Pure English Ser.: Vol. 1). 1979. Set lib. bdg. 46.00 (*0-8240-3665-4*) Garland.

Preliminary Appraisal of the Risk from Benzene with A High Octane Unleaded Petrol: Technical Note. LC 96-134936. 1995. write for info. (*0-478-00179-7*) Manaaki Whenua.

Preliminary Approaches to Language Development. Kim Plunkett. (Illus.). 154p. (C). 1985. pap. 15.95 (*87-7288-001-5*, Pub. by Aarhus Univ Pr) David Brown.

Preliminary Assessment of Archeological Resources Within the Grand Staircase-Escalante National Monument, Utah. David B. Madsen. LC 97-150128. (Circular of the Utah Geological Survey Ser.: Vol. 95). (Illus.). 23p. 1997. pap. 3.00 (*1-55791-605-5*, C-95) Utah Geological Survey.

Preliminary Assessment of Energy & Mineral Resources Within the Grand Staircase-Escalante National Monument. Ed. by M. Lee Allison. LC QE168.A322. (Circular of the Utah Geological Survey Ser.: Vol. 93). (Illus.). 36p. 1997. pap. 4.00 (*1-55791-601-2*, C-93) Utah Geological Survey.

Preliminary Assessment of Paleontological Resources Within the Grand Staircase-Escalante National Monument, Utah. David D. Gillette & Martha C. Hayden. LC QE169.A322. (Circular of the Utah Geological Survey Ser.: Vol. 96). (Illus.). 34p. 1997. pap. 4.00 (*1-55791-606-3*, C-96) Utah Geological Survey.

Preliminary Bibliography of Modern Criminal Law & Criminology. John H. Wigmore. (Gary Library of Law, Northwestern University Law School Bulletin Ser.: No. 1). xii, 128p. 1981. reprint ed. 32.00 (*0-8377-1311-0*, Rothman) W S Hein.

Preliminary Bibliography of Rice-Fish Culture. R. M. Temprosa & Ziad H. Shehadeh. 20p. 1983. pap. text 4.50 (*0-89955-389-3*, Pub. by ICLARM) Intl Spec Bk.

Preliminary Bibliography of the Geology & Mineral Deposits of Nicaragua. H. A. Pierce. 34p. (Orig.). (C). 1993. pap. text 25.00 (*1-56806-360-1*) DIANE Pub.

Preliminary Calculus for Engineers. 94th ed. Carr. (C). 1994. pap. text 19.50 (*0-03-011647-3*) Harcourt.

Preliminary Checklist of Indonesian Imprints, 1945-1949: With Cornell University Holdings. John M. Echols. LC 66-212. (Cornell University. Modern Indonesia Project. Bibliography Ser.: No. 39). 192p. reprint ed. pap. 59.60 (*0-8357-3666-0*, 203639200003) Bks Demand.

Preliminary Consideration of Aboriginal Australian Decorative Art. Daniel S. Davidson. LC 38-6677. (American Philosophical Society, Philadelphia. Memoirs Ser.: Vol. 9). 163p. reprint ed. pap. 50.60 (*0-608-11231-3*, 200035800025) Bks Demand.

***Preliminary Design of an Experimental World-Circling Spaceship.** LC 98-51758. 321p. 1998. reprint ed. pap. text 25.00 (*0-8330-2672-0*, SM-11827) Rand Corp.

Preliminary Design of Boats & Ships. Cyrus Hamlin. LC 88-38779. (Illus.). 314p. 1990. 34.95 (*0-87033-391-7*) Cornell Maritime.

Preliminary Design of Modern Bridges for Architects & Engineers. Melaragno. LC 98-25608. (Illus.). 552p. 1998. text 195.00 (*0-8247-0184-4*) Dekker.

Preliminary Discourse on the Study of Natural Philosophy. John F. Herschel. xxviii, 400p. (C). 1997. pap. text 17.95 (*0-226-32777-9*) U Ch Pr.

Preliminary Discourse to the Encyclopedia of Diderot. Jean Le Rond D'Alembert. Tr. by Richard N. Schwab. 224p. 1995. pap. text 10.95 (*0-226-13476-8*) U Ch Pr.

***Preliminary Edition Introduction to Algebra: Models, Concepts & Skills.** Robertson, Jr. & Storla. 1999. pap. 37.95 (*0-534-36894-8*) Thomson Learn.

Preliminary Edition of the Unpublished Dead Sea Scrolls: The Hebrew & Aramaic Texts from Cave Four - A Concordance of Fascicles 1-3, 7H94, Vol. 4. Ed. by Ben Z. Wacholder & Martin G. Abegg. (ARC & HEB., Illus.). 419p. 1996. 89.95 (*1-880317-45-1*) Biblical Arch Soc.

Preliminary Edition of the Unpublished Dead Sea Scrolls: The Hebrew & Aramaic Texts from Cave Four: Fascicle One. Ben Z. Wacholder & Martin G. Abegg. LC 91-73446. (ARA & HEB.). 118p. (C). 1991. text 25.00 (*0-9613089-9-0*, 7H91) Biblical Arch Soc.

Preliminary Edition of the Unpublished Dead Sea Scrolls: The Hebrew & Aramaic Texts from Cave Four: Fascicle One. Ben Z. Wacholder & Martin G. Abegg. LC 91-73446. (ARA & HEB.). 309p. (C). 1992. text 67.50 (*1-880317-04-4*, 7H92) Biblical Arch Soc.

Preliminary Edition of the Unpublished Dead Sea Scrolls Fascicle 3: The Hebrew & Aramaic Texts from Cave Four. Ben Z. Wacholder & Martin G. Abegg. LC 91-73446. 442p. (Orig.). (C). 1995. text 89.95 (*1-880317-39-7*, 7H93) Biblical Arch Soc.

Preliminary English Skills. A. Heaton. 1997. pap. write for info. (*0-582-01843-9*) Addison-Wesley.

Preliminary Essay on the Oppression of the Exiled Sons of Africa. Thomas Branagan. LC 70-82177. (Anti-Slavery Crusade in America Ser.). 1970. reprint ed. 15.95 (*0-405-00616-0*) Ayer.

Preliminary Estimates from the Drug Abuse Warning Network, 1995. Linda McCaig. 75p. 1998. pap. text 30.00 (*0-7881-4034-5*) DIANE Pub.

Preliminary Evaluation Findings for Ice Ban. Highway Innovative Technology Evaluation Center (H. LC 98-3501. (Technical Evaluation Report Ser.). 1998. 40.00 (*0-7844-0340-6*) Am Soc Civil Eng.

Preliminary Evaluation of Quantitative Clinical Laboratory Methods. (Tentative Guideline Ser.: Vol. 9). 1993. 85.00 (*1-56238-022-2*, EP10-T2) NCCLS.

Preliminary Evaluation of the B2000 Nonlinear Shell Element Q8N.SM. C. Wohlever. (Series 05 - Aerospace Structures & Computational Mechanics: No. 03). (Illus.). 38p. 1998. pap. 14.95 (*90-407-1585-8*, Pub. by Delft U Pr) Coronet Bks.

Preliminary Evidence Regarding the Transfer Function Relationship of Quarterly Earnings for Closely-Related Industries. Clarence E. Fries. LC 85-24596. (McQueen Accounting Monographs: Vol. 2). xvi, 128p. (Orig.). (C). 1985. pap. text 10.00 (*0-935951-01-6*) U AR Acc Dept.

Preliminary Excavation Reports: Bab ed-Dhra, Sardis, Meiron, Tell el-Hesi, Carthage (Punic) David N. Freedman. LC 77-13341. (Annuals of the American Schools of Oriental Research Ser.: Vol. 43). 190p. 1978. 65.00 (*0-89757-043-X*, Pub. by Sheffield Acad) CUP Services.

An Asterisk (*) at the beginning of an entry indicates that the title is appearing for the first time.

Preliminary Guide to Pre-Nineteen Hundred & Four County Records in the Virginia State Library & Archives. Compiled by Suzanne S. Ray et al. xxv, 331p. 1994. reprint ed. pap. 12.00 (*0-88490-179-3*) Library of VA.

Preliminary Guide to Pre-Nineteen Hundred Four Municipal Records in the Archives Branch, Virginia State Library & Archives. Ed. by J. Christian Kolbe. xxv, 61p. (Orig.). 1987. pap. 7.95 (*0-88490-144-0*) Library of VA.

Preliminary Handlist of Books to Which Dr. Samuel Johnson Subscribed. Donald D. Eddy & J. D. Fleeman. 34p. 1993. pap. 10.00 (*1-883631-01-7*) Biblgraph Soc.

Preliminary Index of Shah-Nameh Illustrations. Compiled by Jill Norgren & Edward Davis. 1969. pap. text 5.00 (*0-932098-02-9*) UM Ctr MENAS.

Preliminary Inventory of Spanish Colonial Resources Associated with National Park Service Units & National Historic Landmarks 1987. Ed. by Richard R. Henderson. LC 89-4682. (Illus.). 503p. (C). 1989. pap. text 16.00 (*0-911697-03-9*) US ICOMOS.

Preliminary Investigation of Electrode-Position of Dispersion-Hardening Copper Refractory Oxide Alloys. U. S. Metals Refining Company Staff. 50p. 1966. 7.50 (*0-317-34540-0*, 31) Intl Copper.

Preliminary List of Early Alaska Imprints, Eighteen Sixty-Nine Through Nineteen Thirteen. Charles H. Parr. LC 76-623405. (Elmer E. Rasmuson Library Occasional Papers: No. 3). 66p. 1974. pap. 2.00 (*0-937592-04-8*) U Alaska Rasmuson Lib.

***Preliminary Memorandum of the President of the United States Concerning Referral of the Office of the Independent Counsel & Initial Response of the President, Communication, September 28, 1998.** 65p. 1998. pap. 4.25 (*0-16-063305-2*) USGPO.

Preliminary Noise Enquiry - A Form for Purchasers. EEMUA Editors. (C). 1988. 125.00 (*0-85931-039-6*, Pub. by EEMUA) St Mut.

Preliminary Objections. Ciobanu. 1976. pap. text 121.50 (*90-247-1774-4*, Pub. by M Nijhoff) Kluwer Academic.

***Preliminary Overview of the Economies of Latin America & the Caribbean.** 110p. 1998. 15.00 (*92-1-121233-2*) UN.

Preliminary Overview of the Economy of Latin America & the Caribbean. 72p. 25.00 (*92-1-121204-9*); 25.00 (*92-1-121216-2*) UN.

***Preliminary Phenomena Identification & Ranking Tables for Simplified Boiling Water Reactor Loss of Coolant Accident Scenarios.** P. G. Kroeger. 162p. 1998. per. 14.00 (*0-16-062910-1*) USGPO.

Preliminary Phenomena Identification & Ranking Tables (PIRT) for SBWR Start-up Stability. U. S. Rohatgi. 92p. 1997. pap. 8.50 (*0-16-062819-9*) USGPO.

Preliminary Piano Work for the Student of Music, Set. Irena Bubniuk. (Illus.). (J). (gr. k up). 1992. student ed. 75.00 (*1-882596-00-5*) BML.

Preliminary Piano Work for the Student of Music, Vol. 1. Irena Bubniuk. (Illus.). 159p. (J). (gr. k up). 1992. student ed. write for info. (*1-882596-01-3*); student ed., spiral bd. write for info. (*1-882596-02-1*) BML.

Preliminary Poly Ore Flora of East Africa. Inger Johansen & Leif Ryvarden. (Illus.). 636p. 1980. pap. text 55.00 (*0-945345-14-3*) Lubrecht & Cramer.

Preliminary Report: Education of the Royal Commission on Bilingualism & Biculturalism, 3 vols. Royal Commission on Bilingualism & Biculturalism. Ed. by Francesco Cordasco. LC 77-17707. (Bilingual-Bicultural Education in the U. S. Ser.). 1978. reprint ed. lib. bdg. 70.95 (*0-405-11109-6*) Ayer.

Preliminary Report: Marmes Rockshelter Archaeological Site, Southern Columbia Plateau. fac. ed. David G. Rice. (Washington Archaeological Laboratory of Anthropology Ser.). (Illus.). 205p. (C). 1969. reprint ed. pap. text 21.88 (*1-55567-506-9*) Coyote Press.

Preliminary Report - An Emergency Guide for Collectors of Roseville Art Pottery: The Real - the Repaired - the Damaged - the Fake. James S. Jenkins, Jr. 36p. (Orig.). 1997. pap. 9.95 (*0-9658617-0-8*) Clinic Pharm.

Preliminary Report Concerning Explorations & Surveys Principally in Nevada & Arizona. George M. Wheeler. LC 70-137389. (Select Bibliographies Reprint Ser.). 1977. 23.95 (*0-8369-5590-0*) Ayer.

Preliminary Report of the Committee on General Welfare in the Matter of a Request of the Conference of Organized Labor Relative to Educational Facilities. Meeting of June 26, 1917. New York City Board of Alderman, Committee on Gene. LC 73-11924. (Metropolitan America Ser.). 350p. 1974. reprint ed. 28.95 (*0-405-05407-6*) Ayer.

Preliminary Report of the Inland Waterways Commission Message from the President of the United States. United States Inland Waterways Commission. LC 72-2844. (Use & Abuse of America's Natural Resources Ser.). 714p. 1972. reprint ed. 57.95 (*0-405-04529-8*) Ayer.

Preliminary Report on a Visit to the Navaho National Monument, Arizona. Jesse W. Fewkes. (Bureau of American Ethnology Bulletins Ser.). 99p. 1995. lib. bdg. 69.00 (*0-7812-4050-6*) Rprt Serv.

Preliminary Report on the Mill Creek Area of Andrew County, Missouri. Francis L. Stubbs. Ed. by Carl H. Chapman. (Missouri Archaeologist Ser.: Vol. 12, No. 1). (Illus.). 43p. (Orig.). 1950. pap. 1.50 (*0-943414-29-6*) MO Arch Soc.

Preliminary Reports of ASOR-Sponsored Excavations, 1980-84. Ed. by Walter E. Rast & Marion Zeiger. (BASOR Supplements Ser.: Vol. 26). (Illus.). 177p. (C). 1990. pap. 15.00 (*0-89757-326-9*, Pub. by Am Sch Orient Res) David Brown.

Preliminary Reports of ASOR-Sponsored Excavations, 1981-83. Ed. by Walter E. Rast & Marion Zeiger. LC 85-12851. (BASOR Supplements Ser.: No. 23). (Illus.). 135p. 1985. pap. 15.00 (*0-89757-323-4*, Pub. by Am Sch Orient Res) David Brown.

Preliminary Reports of ASOR-Sponsored Excavations, 1982-85. Ed. by Walter E. Rast & Marion Zeiger. (BASOR Supplements Ser.: Vol. 25). (Illus.). 222p. (C). 1988. pap. 15.00 (*0-8018-3697-2*, Pub. by Am Sch Orient Res) David Brown.

Preliminary Reports of ASOR-Sponsored Excavations, 1982-89. Ed. by Walter E. Rast & Marion Zeiger. (BASOR Supplements Ser.: Vol. 27). (Illus.). 154p. 1991. pap. 15.00 (*0-89757-327-7*, Pub. by Am Sch Orient Res) David Brown.

Preliminary Reports on Precast Trapezoidal Box Girders, Spliced 1 Girders. (PCI Journal Reprints Ser.). 36p. 1977. pap. 14.00 (*0-686-40028-3*, JR96) P-PCI.

Preliminary Results from the 1997 National Household Survey on Drug Abuse. 129p. pap. text 30.00 (*0-7881-8224-2*) DIANE Pub.

Preliminary Results of the Rand Study of Class Action Litigation. Deborah Hensler et al. (Illus.). 32p. 1997. pap. 6.00 (*0-8330-2507-4*, DB-220-ICJ) Rand Corp.

Preliminary SAT/National Merit Scholarship Qualifying Test (PSAT/NMSQT) (Admission Test Ser.: Vol. ATS-122). 1997. 39.95 (*0-8373-5872-8*); pap. 23.95 (*0-8373-5822-1*) Nat Learn.

***Preliminary Sketch: The Galbraiths from Gigha, Scotland, to America.** Albert L. Hester. (Illus.). 76p. 1999. pap. 29.95 (*0-9673027-4-9*) Green Berry Pr.

Preliminary Sketch of the Yaqui Language. fac. ed. J. Alden Mason. (University of California Publications in American Archaeology & Ethnology: Vol. 20: 12). 20p. (C). 1923. reprint ed. pap. text 2.50 (*1-55567-248-5*) Coyote Press.

Preliminary Stray-Current Tests HVDC Power Transmission: The Dallas-Los Angeles. Ebasco Services Inc. 500p. 1969. 10.00 (*0-318-12671-0*, L19720) Am Gas Assn.

Preliminary Study in Black & White. William H. Taylor. LC 97-90483. 70p. (Orig.). 1997. pap. 7.00 (*1-57502-505-1*, P01504) Morris Pubng.

Preliminary Study of the Homeless in Omaha-Douglas County. Jeffrey S. Luke. 43p. (Orig.). 1986. pap. 3.50 (*1-55719-020-8*) U NE CPAR.

Preliminary Study of the Prehistoric Ruins of Nakum, Guatemala. Alfred M. Tozzer. (HU PMM Ser.). 1974. reprint ed. 29.00 (*0-527-01167-3*) Periodicals Srv.

Preliminary Study of the Pueblo of Taos, New Mexico. Merton L. Miller. LC 74-7992. reprint ed. 31.50 (*0-404-11879-8*) AMS Pr.

Preliminary Study of the Ruins of Coba, Quintana Roo, Mexico. John E. Thompson et al. LC 77-11526. (Carnegie Institution of Washington. Publications: No. 424). reprint ed. 33.00 (*0-404-16285-1*) AMS Pr.

Preliminary Study of the Ruins of Xcaret, Quintana Roo, Mexico, with Notes on Other Archaeological Remains on the Central East Coast of the Yucatan Peninsula. E. Wyllys Andrews, IV & Anthony P. Andrews. (Publications: No. 40). (Illus.). xii, 117p. 1975. 25.00 (*0-939238-45-4*) Tulane MARI.

Preliminary Suggestions see Monitoring the Outcome of Social Services

Preliminary Surface Load Capacity Evaluation of Precision, Integrally Forged Spiral Bevel Gears. Raymond J. Drago. (Technical Papers: Vol. P219.09). (Illus.). 11p. 1977. pap. text 30.00 (*1-55589-254-X*) AGMA.

Preliminary Survey in East Arabia. T. G. Bibby. (Jutland Archaeological Society Publications: No. 12). (Illus.). 67p. (C). 1967. pap. 9.95 (*87-00-91091-0*, Pub. by Aarhus Univ Pr) David Brown.

Preliminary Survey of the Fontenelle Reservoir, Wyoming. David S. Dibble & C. Day Kent. (Upper Colorado Ser.: No. 7). reprint ed. 18.00 (*0-404-60658-X*) AMS Pr.

Preliminary Survey of the Vocabulary of White Alabamians. Virginia O. Foscue. (Publications of the American Dialect Society: No. 56). (Illus.). 46p. 1971. pap. 4.75 (*0-8173-0656-0*) U of Ala Pr.

Preliminary Taxonomic Review of the South American Bearded Saki Monkeys Genus Chiropotes (Cebidae, Platyrrhini) With the Description of a New Subspecies. Philip Hershkovitz. LC 85-80318. (Field Museum of Natural History, Publication 1363, Zoological Ser.: No. 27). 51p. 1985. reprint ed. pap. 30.00 (*0-608-03792-3*, 206465200009) Bks Demand.

Preliminary Testing & Evaluation of the Grobin Davis Archeological Site 34Mc-253, McCurtain County, OK. Don G. Wyckoff & Linda R. Fisher. (Archeological Resource Survey Report: No. 22). (Illus.). 110p. (C). 1985. pap. text 4.00 (*1-881346-15-3*) Univ OK Archeol.

Preliminary Treatise on Evidence at Common Law. James B. Thayer. 636p. 1969. reprint ed. text 75.00 (*0-8377-2625-5*, Rothman) W S Hein.

Preliminary Treatment for Wastewater Facilities. Leo A. Ebel et al. LC 94-24482. (Manual of Practice Ser.). 1994. 95.00 (*1-881369-96-X*) Water Environ.

Preliminary Union List of Materials on Chinese Law: With a List of Chinese Studies & Translations of Foreign Law. Harvard University, Law School Library Staff. (Studies in Chinese Law: No. 6). 927p. 1967. text 40.00 (*0-674-70070-8*) HUP.

Preliminary Version Algorithms. 3rd ed. Robert Sedgewick. LC 97-23418. 720p. (C). 1997. pap. text 44.95 (*0-201-31452-5*) Addison-Wesley.

Preliminary Working Papers: Chapters 14-18. 4th ed. (C). 1998. Price not set. (*0-13-084791-7*) S&S Trade.

Prelinguistic Communication in Infancy. Alan Ziajka. LC 81-379. 178p. 1981. 45.00 (*0-275-90747-3*, C0747, Praeger Pubs) Greenwood.

***Prellidio & Passacaglia: For Seven-String Bass Viol.** Martha Bishop. (Contemporary Instrumental Ser.: Vol. 10). 6p. 1999. pap. 5.00 (*1-56571-173-4*, CI010) PRB Prods.

Prelude. Raynor Carroll. 4p. 1996. pap. 3.95 (*1-891188-13-5*) Batterie Music.

Prelude. Jon Cook et al. Ed. by Nigel Wood. LC 92-32420. (Theory in Practice Ser.). 1993. pap. 25.00 (*0-335-09624-7*) OpUniv Pr.

Prelude. Stephen Waghsel. LC 93-81197. (Illus.). 100p. (Orig.). 1994. pap. 8.95 (*1-879629-03-8*) Galaxy Pub CO.

Prelude. Ed. by Nigel Wood. (Theory in Practice Ser.). 176p. 1993. pap. 29.95 (*0-335-09626-3*) OpUniv Pr.

Prelude. William Wordsworth. LC 93-17408. (Revolution & Romanticism Ser.). 398p. 1994. reprint ed. 75.00 (*1-85477-135-3*) Continuum.

Prelude: Or Growth of a Poet's Mind. William Wordsworth. 368p. 1970. pap. text 17.95 (*0-19-281074-X*) OUP.

Prelude: Seventeen Ninety-Nine, Eighteen Hundred & Five, Eighteen Fifty. William Wordsworth. Ed. by Jonathan Wordsworth et al. (Critical Editions Ser.). 684p. (C). 1979. pap. text 20.25 (*0-393-09071-X*) Norton.

Prelude: The Four Texts. William Wordsworth. Ed. & Compiled by Jonathan Wordsworth. 704p. 1996. pap. 19.95 (*0-14-043369-4*) Viking Penguin.

***Prelude a "l'Apres-MIDI d'Un Faune"/Trois Nocturnes.** Claude Debussy. (Miniature Scores Ser.). 1999. pap. 4.95 (*0-486-40865-5*) Dover.

Prelude & Fugue in C Major: Bach Flute Choir. McGinty. 1990. 10.00 (*0-685-32130-4*, 77193) Hansen Ed Mus.

Prelude & Selected Poems & Sonnets. William Wordsworth. 480p. (C). 1954. pap. text 32.50 (*0-03-007800-8*, Pub. by Harcourt Coll Pubs) Harcourt.

Prelude & Three Fugues for Five Viols. Johann Sebastian Bach. Ed. by Peter Ballinger. (Viol Consort Ser.: No. 7). i, 50p. 1991. pap. text 12.00 (*1-56571-027-4*) PRB Prods.

Prelude, 1870-1900. Time-Life Books Editors. LC 98-54213. (Our American Century Ser.). (Illus.). 192p. 2000. 29.95 (*0-7835-5512-1*) Time-Life.

Prelude, 1870-1900 see This Fabulous Century

Prelude in C# Minor Op3 No2. Rachmaninov. 12p. 1997. per. 4.95 (*0-7935-8319-5*) H Leonard.

Prelude in F Major. Catherine Rollin. 4p. Date not set. pap. 2.50 (*0-7390-0725-4*, 19707) Alfred Pub.

Prelude No. 24 & Fugue No. 8 for Three Viols. Johann Sebastian Bach. Ed. by Peter Ballinder. (Viol Consort Ser.: No. 3). i, 17p. 1990. pap. text 8.00 (*1-56571-024-X*) PRB Prods.

Prelude, 1798-1799. William Wordsworth. Ed. by Stephen M. Parrish. (Cornell Wordsworth Ser.). (Illus.). 324p. 1977. text 70.00 (*0-8014-0854-7*) Cornell U Pr.

Prelude to a Kiss. 1990. pap. 6.95 (*0-88145-067-7*) Broadway Play.

***Prelude to a Kiss & Other Plays.** Craig Lucas. 300p. 2000. pap. 16.95 (*1-55936-193-X*) Theatre Comm.

Prelude to Appeasement: East European Central Diplomacy in the Early 1930's. Lisanne Radice. (East European Monographs: No. 80). 218p. 1981. text 55.00 (*0-914710-74-5*, Pub. by East Eur Monographs) Col U Pr.

Prelude to Armaggedon. 100p. (Orig.). 2000. pap. text 10.00 (*1-882821-15-7*) DPK Pubns.

Prelude to Ascension. Janet McClure. 850p. 1996. pap. 29.95 (*0-929385-54-3*) Light Tech Pubng.

Prelude to Balfour Declaration see Letters & Papers of Chaim Weizmann

***Prelude to Biblical Folklore: Underdogs & Tricksters.** Susan Niditch. LC 99-52086. 2000. pap. 15.00 (*0-252-06883-1*) U of Ill Pr.

Prelude to Black Saturday: A Play for Good Friday. C. Alton Robertson. 24p. (Orig.). 1997. pap. 5.25 (*0-7880-0732-7*) CSS OH.

Prelude to Bolshevism. Alexander Kerensky. LC 72-740. (World History Ser.: No. 48). 1972. reprint ed. lib. bdg. 75.00 (*0-8383-1422-8*) M S G Haskell Hse.

Prelude to Calculus. Ruud. (Mathematics Ser.). 1990. student ed. 15.75 (*0-534-10291-3*) Brooks-Cole.

Prelude to Calculus. 3rd ed. Warren L. Ruud. (Mathematics Ser.). 1999. text 63.95 (*0-534-94848-0*) PWS Pubs.

Prelude to Chemistry: An Outline of Alchemy, Its Literature & Relationships. John Read. LC 79-8622. (Illus.). reprint ed. 48.00 (*0-404-18488-X*) AMS Pr.

Prelude to Chemistry: An Outline of Alchemy, its Literature & Relationships. John Read. 328p. 1992. reprint ed. pap. 24.95 (*1-56459-015-1*) Kessinger Pub.

Prelude to Civil War: The Nullification Controversy in South Carolina, 1816-1836. William W. Freehling. (Illus.). 416p. 1992. pap. 16.95 (*0-19-507681-8*) OUP.

Prelude to Conquest, 1561-1595 see History of Micronesia: A Collection of Source Documents

Prelude to Design: A Workbook to Elicit the Information Needed to Design Your New Home. Joseph H. Wythe. 32p. 1997. 6.50 (*0-9661909-2-0*) Unicorn ID.

Prelude to Empire. John A. Brinkman. (Occasional Publications of the Babylonian Fund: No. 7). xii, 159p. 1984. 25.00 (*0-934718-62-8*) U Museum Pubns.

***Prelude to Empire: Plassey Revolution of 1757.** Sushil Chaudhury. 2000. 27.50 (*81-7304-301-9*, Pub. by Manohar) S Asia.

Prelude to Empire: Portugal Overseas before Henry the Navigator. Bailey W. Diffie. LC 60-14301. (Bison Book Original Ser.: No. BB108). (Illus.). 141p. reprint ed. pap. 43.80 (*0-7837-4660-1*, 204438400002) Bks Demand.

Prelude to Fame. Nellie McCaslin. LC 93-14390. 24p. (Orig.). 1993. pap. 5.00 (*0-88734-433-X*) Players Pr.

Prelude to Foundation. Isaac Asimov. 448p. 1989. mass mkt. 6.99 (*0-553-27839-8*) Bantam.

Prelude to Galileo: Essays on Medieval & Sixteenth-Century Sources of Galileo's Thought. William A. Wallace. (Boston Studies in the Philosophy of Science Ser.: No. 62). 375p. 1981. lib. bdg. 112.00 (*90-277-1215-8*) Kluwer Academic.

Prelude to Gettysburg: Encounter at Hanover. Historical Publications of Hanover Chamber of Comm. LC 88-20786. (Civil War Classics Ser.). (Illus.). 274p. 1994. pap. 14.95 (*0-942597-70-2*, Burd St Pr) White Mane Pub.

Prelude to Glory Vol. 1: Our Sacred Honor. Ron Carter. xv, 605p. 1998. 19.95 (*1-57008-431-9*) Bookcraft Inc.

Prelude to Happiness. large type ed. Angela Petron. (Linford Romance Library). 288p. 1989. pap. 16.99 (*0-7089-6649-7*, Linford) Ulverscroft.

Prelude to Heidelberg: The Artists Camp at Box Hill. (VCP Ser.). 1991. 126.00 (*0-949580-10-4*, Pub. by Deakin Univ) St Mut.

Prelude to Independence: The Newspaper War on Britain, 1764-1776. Arthur Meier Schlesinger, Sr. LC 80-22830. 349p. (C). 1980. reprint ed. pap. text 22.50 (*0-930350-13-8*) NE U Pr.

Prelude to Infamy. Gordon Brooke-Shepherd. 1962. 12.95 (*0-8392-1086-8*) Astor-Honor.

Prelude to Israel's Past: Background & Beginnings of Israelite History & Identity. Niels P. Lemche. Tr. by E. F. Maniscalco from GER. Orig. Title: Die Vorgeschichte Israels. 248p. 1998. 24.95 (*1-56563-343-1*) Hendrickson MA.

Prelude to Leadership: The European Diary of John F. Kennedy, Summer 1945. John F. Kennedy. Ed. by Deirdre Henderson. (Illus.). 152p. 1995. 24.95 (*0-89526-459-5*) Regnery Pub.

Prelude to Leadership: The European Diary of John F. Kennedy, Summer 1945. John F. Kennedy. Ed. by Deirdre Henderson. (Illus.). 256p. 1997. pap. 12.95 (*0-89526-431-5*) Regnery Pub.

Prelude to Literacy: A Preschool Child's Encounter with Picture & Story. Maureen Crago & Hugh Crago. LC 82-19235. (Illus.). 320p. 1983. 20.95 (*0-8093-1077-5*) S Ill U Pr.

Prelude to Mathematics. W. W. Sawyer. (Popular Science Ser.). 224p. 1982. reprint ed. pap. 5.95 (*0-486-24401-6*) Dover.

Prelude to Neural Networks: Adaptive & Learning Systems. Jerry Mendel. 1993. text 41.25 (*0-685-70703-2*) P-H.

Prelude to Nuremberg: Allied War Crimes Policy & the Question of Punishment. Arieh J. Kochavi. LC 97-47745. 328p. 1998. 34.95 (*0-8078-2433-X*) U of NC Pr.

Prelude to Partition: The Indian Muslims & the Imperia; System of Control, 1920-32. David Page. 1982. 29.95 (*0-19-561303-1*) OUP.

***Prelude to Passion: Journey to Love.** Maureen McCarthy. (Illus.). 84p. 1999. pap. 7.95 (*1-879007-36-3*) St Bedes Pubns.

***Prelude to Patterns in Computer Science Using Java.** Ed C. Epp. (C). 2000. pap. write for info. (*1-887902-55-4*) Franklin Beedle.

Prelude to Performance Assessments in the Arts, K-12. California Department of Education Staff. (Illus.). 68p. 1994. pap. 8.50 (*0-8011-1119-6*) Calif Education.

Prelude to Physics. Clifford E. Swartz. LC 82-16037. 202p. 1983. pap. 61.95 (*0-471-06028-3*) Wiley.

Prelude to Pleasure: A Bilingual Edition of Vispera del Gozo. Pedro Salinas. Tr. by Noel Valis. LC 92-54549. (ENG & SPA.). 104p. (C). 1993. 24.50 (*0-8387-5242-X*) Bucknell U Pr.

Prelude to Point Four: American Technical Missions Overseas 1838 to 1938. Merle E. Curti & Kendall Birr. LC 78-4874. 284p. 1978. reprint ed. lib. bdg. 65.00 (*0-313-20397-0*, CUPP, Greenwood Pr) Greenwood.

***Prelude to Political Economy: A Study of the Social & Political Foundations of Economics.** Kaushik Basu. 336p. 2000. text 39.95 (*0-19-829671-1*) OUP.

Prelude to Power: The Parisian Radical Press, 1789-1791. Jack R. Censer. LC 76-7968. 206p. reprint ed. pap. 63.90 (*0-608-14684-6*, 202584100046) Bks Demand.

Prelude to Protectorate in Morocco: Precolonial Protest & Resistance, 1860-1912. Edmund Burke. LC 75-43228. (Illus.). 328p. 1996. lib. bdg. 30.00 (*0-226-08075-7*) U Ch Pr.

Prelude to Protectorate in Morocco: Precolonial Protest & Resistance, 1860-1912. Edmund Burke. LC 75-43228. (Studies in Imperialism Ser.). 328p. Date not set. reprint ed. pap. 101.70 (*0-608-20619-9*, 205458700003) Bks Demand.

Prelude to Purgatory: Thomas Hutchinson in Provincial Massachusetts Politics. Malcolm Freiberg. (Outstanding Studies in Early American History). 357p. 1990. reprint ed. 25.00 (*0-8240-6180-2*) Garland.

Prelude to Quebec's Quiet Revolution: Liberalism vs. Neo-Nationalism, 1945-60. Michael D. Behiels. 400p. 1985. 60.00 (*0-7735-0423-0*, Pub. by McG-Queens Univ Pr); pap. 22.95 (*0-7735-0424-9*, Pub. by McG-Queens Univ Pr) CUP Services.

***Prelude to Rebellion.** Jan Strnad et al. (Star Wars Ser.). (Illus.). 144p. (J). (gr. 7-12). 2000. pap. text 14.95 (*1-56971-448-7*) Dark Horse Comics.

Prelude to Restoration in Ireland: The End of the Commonwealth, 1659-1660. Aidan Clarke. LC 98-36968. (Illus.). 280p. (C). 1999. text 59.95 (*0-521-65061-5*) Cambridge U Pr.

Prelude to Revolution. Richard Baum. 1975. text 52.50 (*0-231-03900-X*) Col U Pr.

Prelude to Revolution: The Petrograd Bolsheviks & the July, 1917, Uprising. Alexander Rabinowitch. LC 68-10278. 315p. reprint ed. 97.70 (*0-8357-9236-6*, 205522400011) Bks Demand.

P

An Asterisk (*) at the beginning of an entry indicates that the title is appearing for the first time.

Prelude to Revolution: The Petrograd Bolsheviks & the July 1917 Uprising. Alexander Rabinowitch. LC 91-8422. (Illus.). 314p. 1991. reprint ed. 36.95 (*0-253-34768-8*); reprint ed. pap. 6.95 (*0-253-20661-8*, MB-661) Ind U Pr.

Prelude to Solidarity: Poland & the Politics of the Gierek Regime. Keith J. Lepak. 320p. 1988. text 61.50 (*0-231-06608-2*) Col U Pr.

Prelude to Space. Arthur C. Clarke. 192p. 1986. mass mkt. 5.99 (*0-345-34102-3*, Del Rey) Ballantine Pub Grp.

Prelude to Strategic Planning: Making Your Organization & Community Fit for Success. American Hospital Association Staff. (Illus.). 52p. (Orig.). 1989. pap. 35.00 (*0-87258-521-2*, 184206) Am Hospital.

Prelude to Synchronous Harmonics. limited ed. I. B. Iverson. (Illus.). v, 29p. 1976. pap. 20.00 (*1-883401-11-9*) ITAM.

Prelude to the Civil War: The Nullification Controversy in South Carolina 1816-1836. William W. Freehling. 1995. 25.25 (*0-8446-6869-9*) Peter Smith.

Prelude to the Cold War: The Tsarist, Soviet, & U. S. Armies in the Two World Wars. Jonathan R. Adelman. LC 88-2048. 287p. 1988. lib. bdg. 50.00 (*1-55587-123-2*) L Rienner.

Prelude to the Dawn. Allen Richardson & Owen Richardson. 256p. 1997. pap. 12.95 (*1-890828-04-1*, 04-1, Pub. by Camden Ct) Origin Bk Sales.

***Prelude to the Easter Rising.** Reinhard R. Doerries. 288p. 2000. 59.50 (*0-7165-2640-9*, Pub. by Irish Acad Pr); 26.50 (*0-7165-2707-3*, Pub. by Irish Acad Pr) Intl Spec Bk.

***Prelude to the Easter Rising: Sir Roger Casement in Imperial Germany (New Directions in Irish History)** Reinhard R. Doerries. LC 99-39128. (Case Studies in Intelligence). (Illus.). 256p. 2000. 59.50 (*0-7146-5003-X*, Pub. by F Cass Pubs); pap. 26.50 (*0-7146-8070-2*, Pub. by F Cass Pubs) Intl Spec Bk.

Prelude to the Presidency: The Political Character & Legislative Leadership Style of Governor Jimmy Carter, 40. Gary M. Fink. LC 79-7725. (Contributions in Political Science Ser.: No. 40). (Illus.). 225p. 1980. 59.95 (*0-313-22055-7*, FPP/) Greenwood.

Prelude to the Reformation: A Study of English Church Life from the Age of Wycliffe to the Breach with Rome. Richard S. Arrowsmith. LC 83-45573. reprint ed. 57.50 (*0-404-19891-0*) AMS Pr.

***Prelude to the Welfare State.** Price Van Meter Fishback & Shawn E. Kantor. LC 99-38648. (NBER Series on Long-Term Factors in Economic Development). 2000. 37.50 (*0-226-25163-2*) U Ch Pr.

Prelude to Trade Wars: American Tariff Policy, 1890-1922, 152. Edward S. Kaplan & Thomas W. Ryley. LC 93-28032. (Contributions in Economics & Economic History Ser.: No. 152). 160p. 1994. 57.95 (*0-313-29061-X*, Greenwood Pr) Greenwood.

***Prelude to Tragedy: Vietnam, 1960-1965.** Ed. by Harvey Neese & John O'Donnell. (Illus.). 344p. 2000. 32.95 (*1-55750-491-1*) Naval Inst Pr.

Prelude to Victory of the Ten Hour Movement, 1844. LC 72-2536. (British Labour Struggles Before 1850 Ser.). 1974. 20.95 (*0-405-04429-1*) Ayer.

***Prelude to War.** (Illus.). 216p. 2000. 29.95 (*0-7835-5713-2*) Time-Life.

Prelude to War. Christopher Nicole. 256p. 1999. 26.00 (*0-7278-5416-X*, Pub. by Severn Hse) Chivers N Amer.

***Prelude to War.** 35th ed. Norma Jean Lutz. LC 99-27054. (American Adventure Ser.: No. 35). (Illus.). (J). (gr. 3-7). 1998. pap. 3.97 (*1-57748-410-X*) Barbour Pub.

Prelude to War: A Sourcebook on the Civil War. C. Carter Smith. (American Albums from the Collections of the Library of Congress). 1993. 14.15 (*0-606-08036-8*) Turtleback.

Prelude to War: A Sourcebook on the Civil War. Ed. by Carter Smith. LC 92-16545. (American Albums from the Collections of the Library of Congress). (Illus.). 96p. (J). (gr. 5-8). 1993. lib. bdg. 25.90 (*1-56294-261-1*) Millbrook Pr.

Prelude to War: A Sourcebook on the Civil War. Ed. by Carter Smith. (American Albums from the Collections of the Library of Congress). (Illus.). 96p. (J). (gr. 5-8). 1995. pap. 8.95 (*1-56294-878-4*) Millbrook Pr.

Prelude to Yorktown: The Southern Campaign of Nathanael Greene, 1780-1781. M. F. Treacy. LC 63-21081. 272p. reprint ed. pap. 84.40 (*0-8357-3857-4*, 203659000004) Bks Demand.

Preludes. Frederic Chopin. Ed. by Ignacy J. Paderewski. 76p. 1999. pap. 9.95 (*0-934009-14-7*, 410-41330) Presser Co.

Preludes Bk. 1: The Autograph Score, Book 1. Claude Debussy. 48p. 1988. pap. 8.95 (*0-486-25549-2*) Dover.

***Preludes & Impromptus.** Frederic Chopin. 1998. pap. 7.98 (*963-8303-81-6*) Konemann.

Preludes & Other Symphonic Poems in Full Score. Franz Liszt. 320p. 1994. pap. 13.95 (*0-486-28322-4*) Dover.

Preludes for Piano, Bk. 1. Catherine Rollin. 16p. 1989. pap. 5.50 (*0-7390-0898-6*, 3609) Alfred Pub.

Preludes for Piano, Set, Bks. 1 & 2. Claude Debussy. 160p. 1991. per. 14.95 (*0-7935-0435-X*, 50480346) H Leonard.

Preludes for Piano & Audio Cassette. Harold Zabrack. 1979. pap. 17.95 (*0-934286-10-8*) Kenyon.

Preludes for Worship: Organ, Vol. 3. Gordon Young. 1997. pap. 9.95 (*0-634-00362-3*) H Leonard.

***Preludes for Worship: Organ, Vol. 2.** Gordon Young. 1998. pap. 9.95 (*0-634-00361-5*) H Leonard.

Preludes I. Alexander Skrjabin. 80p. 1998. pap. 7.95 (*963-8303-62-X*) Konemann.

Preludes II. Alexander Skrjabin. 84p. 1998. pap. 7.95 (*963-8303-74-3*) Konemann.

Preludes, Opus 28. Frederic Chopin. Ed. by Thomas Higgins. (C). 1974. pap. text 15.50 (*0-393-09699-8*) Norton.

Preludes to Genetics. Ed. by Gloria Robinson. 1979. 25.00 (*0-87291-127-6*) Coronado Pr.

Preludes to My Autobiography. J. L. Moreno. 8.00 (*0-685-52594-5*) Beacon Hse.

Preludes to Victory: The Battle of Ormoc Bay in WWII. William L. Griggs. LC 97-94215. (Illus.). vii, 288p. 1997. pap. 20.00 (*0-9659837-0-6*) W L Griggs.

***Preludes, Toccatas & Ciacconas for Organ (Pedaliter)** Dieterich Buxtehude. Ed. by Michael Belotti. (Collected Works: No. 15, Pt. 1). (Illus.). 341p. 1998. lib. bdg. 200.00 (*0-8450-7515-2*, Broud Trust) Broude.

Preludio al Armagedon. Arthur E. Bloomfield.Tr. of Before the Last Battle. 192p. 1977. 8.99 (*0-88113-003-6*) Caribe Betania.

Prema Vahini (Writings on Divine Love) Sathya Sai Baba. 1987. pap. 1.50 (*1-57836-067-6*, BA-309) Sathya Sai Bk Ctr.

Premachining Planning & Tool Presetting. Ed. by Robert R. Runck. LC 67-28208. (American Society of Tool & Manufacturing Engineers Manufacturing Data Ser.). 82p. 1967. reprint ed. pap. 30.00 (*0-608-09975-9*, 201600500097) Bks Demand.

Premadasa of Sri Lanka: A Political Biography. Bradman Weerakoon. 175p. (C). 1992. text 16.00 (*0-7069-5983-3*, Pub. by Vikas) S Asia.

Premalignancy & Early Cancer: In General Surgery. J. W. Fielding & W. L. Allum. (Illus.). 212p. 1996. text 115.00 (*0-19-263028-8*) OUP.

Premanufacture Notification: Chemistry Assistance for Submitters. Stephen C. Devito & Carol A. Farris. LC 97-1034. 138p. 1997. 59.95 (*0-471-19151-5*) Wiley.

Premarital & Marital Contracts: A Lawyer's Guide to Drafting & Negotiating Enforceable Marital & Cohabitation Agreements. LC 93-71397. 228p. 1993. pap. 54.95 (*0-89707-882-9*, 513-0051) Amer Bar Assn.

Premarital & Remarital Counseling: The Professional's Handbook. Robert F. Stahmann & William J. Heibert. LC 96-49300. 1997. pap. 25.95 (*0-7879-0845-2*) Jossey-Bass.

Premarital Counseling: A Manual for Clergy & Counselors. John L. Mitman. 128p. (Orig.). 1984. 8.95 (*0-86683-879-1*, 7874) Harper SF.

Premarital Counseling Handbook see Manual de Asesoramiento Permarital

Premarital Counseling Handbook. Norman Wright. 271p. 22.99 (*0-8024-6382-7*, 256) Moody.

***Premarital Discussion: Aligning Expectations for Marital Success.** Robert J. Weingartner. 2000. pap. 7.95 (*0-533-13317-3*) Vantage.

***Premarital Guidance.** Charles W. Taylor. LC 98-43461. (Creative Pastoral Care & Counseling Ser.). 112p. 1999. pap. 16.00 (*0-8006-2712-1*, 1-2712, Fortress Pr) Augsburg Fortress.

Premarital Guide for Couples & Their Counselors. David A. Thompson. 8p. 1979. pap. 7.99 (*0-87123-465-3*) Bethany Hse.

Premarital Intercourse & Interpersonal Relationships: A Research Study of Interpersonal Relationships Based on Case Histories of 668 Premarital Intercourse Experiences Reported by 200 College Level Males. Lester A. Kirkendall. LC 83-22576. 302p. 1984. reprint ed. lib. bdg. 65.00 (*0-313-24293-3*, KIPR) Greenwood.

***Premarital Prediction of Marital Quality or Breakup: Research, Theory & Practice.** Thomas Holman. LC 00-22849. (Longitudinal Research in the Social & Behavioral Sciences Ser.). 2000. write for info. (*0-306-46326-1*, Kluwer Plenum) Kluwer Academic.

Premarital Sexuality: Attitudes, Relationships, Behavior. John DeLamater & Patricia MacCorquodale. LC 78-65019. 293p. reprint ed. pap. 90.90 (*0-608-20423-4*, 207167600002) Bks Demand.

Premarric. Susan Howatch. 1984. mass mkt. 6.99 (*0-449-20622-X*, Crest) Fawcett.

Premature Baby Book: A Parents Guide to Coping & Caring in the First Years. Helen Harrison & Ann Kositsky. (Illus.). 320p. 1983. pap. 19.95 (*0-312-63649-0*) St Martin.

***Premature Baby Book: A Parent's Guide to Coping & Caring in the First Years.** rev. ed. Helen Harrison & Ann Kositsky. (Illus.). 273p. 2000. reprint ed. pap. 20.00 (*0-7881-9361-9*) DIANE Pub.

Premature Death in the New Independent States. Ed. by Jose L. Bobadilla et al. LC 97-67217. 408p. (Orig.). 1997. pap. 59.00 (*0-309-05734-5*, Joseph Henry Pr) Natl Acad Pr.

Premature in Context. Max Sugar. 141p. 1982. text 20.00 (*0-88331-183-6*) R B Luce.

Premature Infant: Nursing Assessment & Management. Lyn E. Vargo et al. LC 98-42498. 1998. write for info. (*0-86525-082-0*) March of Dimes.

Premature Infants & Their Families: Developmental Interventions. M. Virginia Wyly. (Education). (Illus.). 276p. (Orig.). (C). 1995. pap. text 45.00 (*1-879105-87-X*, 0350) Thomson Learn.

Premature Menopause Book: When the "Change of Life" Comes Too Early. Kathryn Petras. LC 99-94866. 416p. 1999. pap. 14.00 (*0-380-80541-3*, Avon Bks) Morrow Avon.

Premature Reformation: Wycliffite Texts & Lollard History. Anne Hudson. 560p. 1988. text 110.00 (*0-19-822762-0*) OUP.

Premature Subdivision of Land in Colorado: A Survey with Commentary. Michael M. Shultz & Jeffrey B. Gray. LC HD0259.S38. (Lincoln Institute of Land Policy Monograph: No. 86-10). 104p. reprint ed. pap. 32.30 (*0-7837-5759-X*, 204542100006) Bks Demand.

Premature Vascular Disease in Homocystinaemia. Ed. by S. Coccheri. (Journal: Haemostasis: Vol. 19, Suppl. 1, 1989). (Illus.). iv, 50p. 1989. pap. 77.50 (*3-8055-4998-9*) S Karger.

Prematurely Saved. John Garvey. 128p. 1986. pap. 8.95 (*0-87243-150-9*) Templegate.

Prematurely Yours: The Baby Book Designed Exclusively for the Premature Infant. 3rd ed. Kim Bryant & Becky Meloan. (Illus.). 40p. (J). Date not set. reprint ed. 21.95 (*0-9614786-0-8*) Premature Yours.

Prematurely Yours, Jessica. Kellie S. Makinson. 144p. 2000. pap. 15.95 (*1-58244-021-2*) Rutledge Bks.

Premchand: A Western Appraisal. S. A. Schulz. 1983. 4.50 (*0-8364-1023-8*, Pub. by Allied Pubs) S Asia.

PreMed: Who Makes It & Why. Mary Ann Maguire. LC 98-48715. 6. 176p. 1999. 44.00 (*0-8077-3833-6*) Tchrs Coll.

PreMed: Who Makes It & Why. Mary Ann Maguire. LC 98-48715. 1999. pap. text 21.95 (*0-8077-3832-8*) Tchrs Coll.

***Premeditated Mercy: A Spirituality of Reconciliation.** Joe Nassal. LC 99-53862. 2000. 12.95 (*0-939516-49-7*) Forest Peace.

Premeditated Murder. Slobodan Selenic. Tr. by Jelena Petrovic from CRO. 272p. 1997. 24.00 (*1-86046-133-6*) Harvill Press.

Premeditation. Francis Iles. (FRE.). 1973. pap. 10.95 (*0-7859-2314-4*, 2070364216) Fr & Eur.

Premenstrual Dysphorias: Myths & Realities. Ed. by Judith H. Gold & Sally K. Severino. 262p. 1994. text 19.95 (*0-88048-666-X*, 8666) Am Psychiatric.

Premenstrual Dysphorias: Myths & Realities. Judith H. Gold. Ed. by Sally K. Severino. LC 93-47479. (Illus.). 282p. 1994. reprint ed. pap. 87.50 (*0-608-06665-6*, 206686200009) Bks Demand.

Premenstrual Solution: How to Tame the Shrew in You. Jo Ann C. Friedrich. 168p. 1987. pap. 14.95 (*0-9617317-0-2*) Bright Bks CA.

***Premenstrual Syndrome.** Susan R. Gregson. LC 99-55030. (Perspectives on Physical Health Ser.). 64p. (YA). (gr. 7-12). 2000. lib. bdg. 22.60 (*0-7368-0421-8*, LifeMatters Bks) Capstone Pr.

Premenstrual Syndrome. Keye. 1988. pap. text 55.00 (*0-7216-2560-6*, Grune & Strat) Harcrt Hlth Sci Grp.

Premenstrual Syndrome: A Clinician's Guide. Sally K. Severino & Margaret L. Moline. (Illus.). 340p. 1997. reprint ed. text 15.00 (*0-7881-5054-5*) DIANE Pub.

Premenstrual Syndrome: A Guide for Young Women. 3rd rev. ed. Gilda Berger. LC 91-34647. (Illus.). 96p. (YA). (gr. 7-12). 1991. pap. 7.95 (*0-89793-088-6*) Hunter Hse.

Premenstrual Syndrome: A Nutritional Approach. Louise Tenney. (Today's Health Ser.: No. 3). pap. 3.95 (*0-913923-30-3*) Woodland UT.

Premenstrual Syndrome: A Self Help Guide. Wendy V. Rappoport. (Illus.). 96p. (Orig.). 1984. pap. 4.95 (*0-936320-19-2*) Compact Books.

Premenstrual Syndrome: Current Findings & Future Directions. Ed. by Howard J. Osofsky & Susan J. Blumenthal. LC 85-6100. (Progress in Psychiatry Ser.). (Illus.). 111p. 1985. reprint ed. pap. 34.50 (*0-608-06671-0*, 206686800009) Bks Demand.

Premenstrual Syndrome: Ethical & Legal Implications in a Biomedical Perspective. Ed. by Benson E. Ginsburg & Bonnie F. Carter. LC 86-30562. 452p. 1987. 79.50 (*0-306-42498-3*, Plenum Trade) Perseus Pubng.

Premenstrual Syndrome: How You Can Benefit from Diet, Vitamins. Michael T. Murray. LC 97-5744. (Getting Well Naturally Ser.). 176p. 1997. pap., per. 11.00 (*0-7615-0820-1*) Prima Pub.

Premenstrual Syndrome: Index of Modern Information. Jacob L. Liehaus. LC 88-47618. 150p. 1990. 47.50 (*1-55914-138-7*); pap. 44.50 (*1-55914-139-5*) ABBE Pubs Assn.

Premenstrual Tension: A Multidisciplinary Approach. Ed. by Charles M. Debrovner. LC 81-6659. 111p. 1982. 30.95 (*0-89885-019-3*, Kluwer Acad Hman Sci) Kluwer Academic.

Premerger Notification Practice Manual. LC 91-72111. 282p. 1991. 89.00 (*0-89707-696-6*, 503-0209) Amer Bar Assn.

Premerger Notification Program of the U. S. Federal Trade Commission: A Complete Handbook. (Illus.). 75p. (Orig.). (C). 1994. pap. text 30.00 (*0-7881-1175-2*) DIANE Pub.

Premices Philosophiques. Pierre Duhem. Ed. by Stanley L. Jaki. (Brill's Studies in Intellectual History: Vol. 3). 260p. 1987. 71.00 (*90-04-08117-8*) Brill Academic Pubs.

Premier Amour. Samuel Beckett. pap. 8.95 (*0-685-37200-6*, F86100) Fr & Eur.

Premier Amour. Samuel Beckett. (FRE.). 298p. 1970. 14.95 (*0-7859-4776-0*) Fr & Eur.

***Premier Autoportrait de Rembrandt 1628: Etude sur la Formation de Jeune Rembrandt.** Judith K. Portier-Theisz. xii, 165p. (C). 1999. pap. text 29.95 (*3-906763-42-0*) P Lang Pubng.

Premier Beer: A Guide to America's Best Bottled Microbrews. Elaine Louie. LC 96-21554. 192p. 1996. per. 14.00 (*0-671-53676-1*) PB.

Premier Book of Major Poets. Anita Dore. LC 96-96611. 1996. pap. 11.00 (*0-449-91186-1*) Fawcett.

Premier Book of Major Poets: An Anthology. Anita Dore. (Fawcett Premier Bks.). 1970. 16.10 (*0-606-03893-0*, Pub. by Turtleback) Demco.

Premier Cours de Linguistique Generale (1907): (Saussure's First Course of Lecture on General Linguistics, 1907): D'Apres les Cahiers D'Albert Riedlinger: (From the Notebooks of Albert Riedlinger see Saussures 1st, 2nd & 3rd Course of Lectures on General Linguistics

Premier Dictionnaire de Pigeon Voyageur a l'Usage des Colombophiles et de Tous Ceux Qui S'Interessent Au Sport Colombophile. Guy Brasseur. (FRE.). 526p. 1991. 145.00 (*0-7859-8178-0*, 2876710870) Fr & Eur.

Premier Eastern Asia Conference on Insurance Taxation. Date not set. ring bd. write for info. (*1-56423-045-7*) Ntl Ctr Tax Ed.

Premier Enquete de Maigret. Georges Simenon. (FRE.). pap. 3.95 (*0-685-11513-5*) Fr & Eur.

Premier et le Secont Livre de Fauvel. Paul Helmer. (Musicological Studies Ser.: Vol. 70, Pt. 1). (ENG & FRE.). 378p. 1997. 112.00 (*1-896926-08-8*) Inst Mediaeval Mus.

Premier Fascicule des Melanges see Maitres Musiciens de la Renaissance Francaise

Premier Fascicule des 150 Psaumes see Maitres Musiciens de la Renaissance Francaise

Premier Homme. Albert Camus. 331p. 1994. 49.95 (*0-7859-9876-4*) Fr & Eur.

Premier Homme. Albert Camus. (FRE.). 1995. pap. 29.95 (*2-07-073827-2*) Schoenhof.

Premier Hotels of Great Britain & Ireland. 59th ed. Alistair Hankey. 1998. pap. text 17.95 (*1-56554-342-4*) Pelican.

***Premier ICD-9-CM Code Book, 1999-2000.** St. Anthony's Publishing Staff. (C). 1999. pap. 72.00 (*1-56329-667-5*) Thomson Learn.

Premier Livre de Chanson a Deux Parties (Paris, 1758) Ed. by Jane A. Bernstein. LC 92-753535. (Sixteenth Century Chanson Ser.: Vol. 15). 264p. 1992. text 94.00 (*0-8240-3114-8*) Garland.

Premier Livre des Amours de Pierre de Ronsard, (I-XIX) see Monuments de la Musique Francaise au Temps de la Renaissance

Premier livre des Amours de Pierre de Ronsard, (XX-XXXV) see Monuments de la Musique Francaise au Temps de la Renaissance

Premier livre des Octonaires de la vanite du Monde see Monuments de la Musique Francaise au Temps de la Renaissance

Premier Planete a Droite en Sortant par la Voie Lactee. Pierre Daninos. (FRE.). 1975. 15.95 (*0-8288-9170-2*, M3360) Fr & Eur.

Premier See: A History of the Archdiocese of Baltimore, 1789-1989. Thomas W. Spalding. (Maryland Paperback Bookshelf Ser.). (Illus.). 624p. 1995. reprint ed. pap. 18.95 (*0-8018-5215-3*) Johns Hopkins.

Premier Selections. Silhouette Staff. 1982. pap. 1.75 (*0-373-30787-X*) Silhouette.

Premier Voyage de Monsieur Patapoum - Mr. Patapoum's First Trip. Gilles Tibo & Francois Vaillancourt. (Picture Bks.). (FRE., Illus.). 32p. (J). 1996. pap. 6.95 (*1-55037-329-3*, Pub. by Les Editions); lib. bdg. 15.95 (*1-55037-326-9*, Pub. by Les Editions) Firefly Bks Ltd.

Premier Voyage du Sieur de la Courbe Fait a la Coste d'Afrique en 1685. P. Cultru. (B. E. Ser.: No. 164). (FRE.). 1913. 45.00 (*0-8115-3079-5*) Periodicals Srv.

***Premier Wedding Planner: Spring/Summer 2000.** rev. ed. B. J. Seaburn. (Illus.). 88p. 2000. pap. write for info. (*0-9700391-0-7*) Premier Wed Plan.

***Premier Wrestling Ringside No. 6: Hardcore.** Ed. by Michael Benson. 2000. pap. 3.99 (*0-88013-015-6*, Pub. by Starlog Grp Inc) Kable News Co Inc.

Premiere Education Sentimentale. Gustave Flaubert. 1963. 14.95 (*0-686-55987-8*) Fr & Eur.

Premiere Enquete de Maigret, Les Fantomes du Chapelier, Mon Ami Maigret, Les Quatres Jours du Pauvre Homme, Maigret Chez le Cororner, Un Nouveau dans la Ville, La Neige Etait Sale, Le Fond de la Bouteille. Georges Simenon. (FRE.). 49.95 (*0-7859-0478-6*, 2258021421) Fr & Eur.

***Premiere Events: Library Programs That Inspire Elementary Patrons.** Patricia Potter Wilson. 180p. 2001. 35.00 (*1-56308-795-2*) Libs Unl.

***Premiere 5.1 for Macintosh & Windows: Visual QuickStart Guide.** Anthony Bolante. 352p. (C). 1999. pap. text 19.99 (*0-201-35475-6*) Peachpit Pr.

Premiere Formation d'une Chaine de Postes entre le Fleuve Saint-Laurent et le Golfe du Mexique (1683-1724) see Decouvertes et Establissements des francais dans l'ouest et dans le sud de l'Amerique septentrional: 1614-1754

***Premiere Generation Ink: Winter 2000.** Ed. by Sachin Pandya et al. 46p. 2000. pap. 4.00 (*1-930254-04-0*) Premiere Gen.

Premiere Internationale en Espagne. M. Nettlau. (FRE., Illus.). 683p. 1969. lib. bdg. 296.00 (*90-277-0103-2*) Kluwer Academic.

***Premiere Parent Los Angeles: The Survival Guide for Parents of Toddlers & Preschoolers.** Lisa Precious. 2000. pap. 14.95 (*0-658-00401-8*, Natl Textbk Co) NTC Contemp Pub Co.

Premiere Planete a Droite en Sortant par la Voie Lactee. Pierre Daninos. (FRE.). 1975. pap. 3.95 (*0-686-55572-4*) Fr & Eur.

***Premiere to Go.** Dennis Chominsky. 350p. 2000. pap. text 34.99 (*0-13-027739-8*, Prentice Hall) P-H.

Premiere with a Passion. 2nd ed. Michael Feerer. 416p. 1995. pap. text 34.95 (*1-56609-165-9*) Peachpit Pr.

Premieres Etapes du Machinisme see Histoire Generale des Techniques

Premieres of the Year. Jacob T. Grein. LC 77-93162. 275p. 1972. reprint ed. 24.95 (*0-405-08581-8*, Pub. by Blom Pubns) Ayer.

Premieres Poesies, 1829-1835. Alfred Musset. Ed. by Maurice Allem. (FRE.). 338p. 1958. 29.95 (*0-8288-9649-6*, F69060) Fr & Eur.

Premieres Poesies. Poesies Nouvelles. Alfred De Musset. (Poesie Ser.). (FRE.). 1976. pap. 13.95 (*2-07-032155-X*) Schoenhof.

Premieres Salves de la Troisieme Guerre Mondiale: La Guerre Contre l'Irak (Opening Guns of World War III: Washington's Assault on Iraq) Jack Barnes. (Illus.). 333p. (Orig.). (C). 1991. pap. 13.00 (*0-87348-647-1*) Pathfinder NY.

Premiers Echanges. 2nd ed. Ariew. (College French Ser.). (FRE.). (C). 1993. student ed., suppl. ed. 13.95 incl. audio (*0-8384-4433-4*) Heinle & Heinle.

Premiers Echanges. 2nd ed. Ariew. (College French Ser.). (C). 1993. mass mkt., suppl. ed. 36.95 (*0-8384-4439-3*) Heinle & Heinle.

P

An Asterisk (*) at the beginning of an entry indicates that the title is appearing for the first time.

Premiers Echanges. 2nd ed. Ariew. (College French Ser.). (C). 1993. mass mkt., suppl. ed. 28.95 (*0-8384-4437-7*) Heinle & Heinle.

Premiers Echanges. 2nd ed. Ariew. (College French Ser.). (FRE.). (C). 1993. suppl. ed., lab manual ed. 28.95 incl. audio (*0-8384-4434-2*) Heinle & Heinle.

Premiers Echanges. 2nd ed. Ariew. (College French Ser.). (FRE.). (C). 1993. mass mkt., suppl. ed. 21.95 (*0-8384-4438-5*) Heinle & Heinle.

Premiers Exchanges. 2nd ed. Robert Ariew & Anne Nerenz. LC 92-40946. (C). 1993. 60.95 (*0-8384-4443-1*) Heinle & Heinle.

Premiers Exchanges. 2nd ed. Robert Ariew & Anne Nerenz. LC 92-40946. (C). 1993. mass mkt., student ed. 36.95 (*0-8384-4432-6*) Heinle & Heinle.

Premiers Lundis. (Bibliotheque de la Pleiade Ser.). write for info. Schoenhof.

Premiers of Queensland: Revised Edition of Queensland Political Portraits 1859-1952. rev. ed. Denis Murphy et al. 1990. pap. 34.95 (*0-7022-2249-6*, Pub. by Univ Queensland Pr) Intl Spec Bk.

Premiers of Western Australia, 1890-1982. G. S. Reid & M. R. Oliver. (Illus.). viii, 122p. 1983. 16.95 (*0-85564-214-9*, Pub. by Univ of West Aust Pr) Intl Spec Bk.

Premiers Pas see Basic French

Premiers Poemes. Ruth P. Weinreb. (gr. 8-10). 1982. pap. text 11.96 (*0-88334-156-5*, 76123); audio 31.96 (*0-8013-0147-5*, 75810) Longman.

Premiers Poemes: Anthologie avec Exercices de Vocabulaire, de Grammaire et de Prononciation. Ruth P. Weinreb. (FRE.). 115p. (C). 1998. pap. 19.95 (*0-8442-1282-2*, VF1282-2) NTC Contemp Pub Co.

Premio. M. Vasquez Montalban. 1998. pap. 9.95 (*84-08-02239-3*) Planeta.

Premio. Maria Puncel. (Illus.). 32p. (Orig.). (J). (gr. 3-5). pap. text 7.50 (*1-56492-107-7*) Laredo.

Premio Nobel: Once Grandes Escritores del Mundo Hispanico. Compiled by Barbara Mujica. LC 96-44386. (SPA.). 368p. 1997. pap. 24.95 (*0-87840-642-5*) Georgetown U Pr.

Premise & the Promise: Free Trade in the Americas. Ed. by Sylvia Saborio. (U. S. Third World Policy Perspectives Ser.: No. 18). 280p. (C). 1992. 32.95 (*1-56000-060-0*); pap. 17.95 (*1-56000-619-6*) Transaction Pubs.

Premises: Essays on Philosophy & Literature from Kant to Celan. Werner Hamacher. Tr. by Peter Fenves. 416p. 1996. 54.00 (*0-674-70073-2*) HUP.

***Premises: Essays On Philosophy & Literature from Kant to Celan.** Werner Hamacher. 1999. pap. text 19.95 (*0-8047-3620-0*) Stanford U Pr.

Premises: Invested Spaces in Visual Arts & Architecture from France, 1958-98. Benjamin H. D. Buchloh. (Illus.). 500p. 1998. 85.00 (*0-8109-6915-7*, Pub. by Abrams) Time Warner.

Premises & Conclusions: Symbolic Logic for Legal Analysis. Howard Pospesel & Robert E. Rodes. LC 96-33572. 387p. (C). 1996. 67.00 (*0-13-262635-7*) P-H.

Premises & Process of Maldevelopment. Ed. by Franklin Vivekananda. 204p. (Orig.). 1989. pap. 68.50 (*91-86702-03-3*) Coronet Bks.

Premises Cabling. Mike Gilmore & M. Daly. (Illus.). 192p. 1999. 130.00 (*0-7506-0901-X*, Newnes) Buttrwrth-Heinemann.

***Premises Cabling.** 2nd ed. Donald Sterling. (Electrical Trades Ser.). (C). 2000. pap. 48.95 (*0-7668-1735-0*) Delmar.

***Premises Cabling.** 2nd ed. Donald J. Sterling & Les Baxter. LC 00-24067. 2000. pap. text. write for info. (*0-7668-1736-9*) Delmar.

Premises Liability. James L. Branton & Jim D. Lovett. (Trial Lawyer's Ser.: Vols. 3 & 3A). (Illus.). 1986. ring bd. 185.00 (*1-878337-11-4*) Knowles Pub Inc.

Premises Liability: Law & Practice, 4 vols. Norman J. Landau et al. 1987. 590.00 (*0-8205-1568-X*) Bender.

***Premises Liability for Owners & Occupiers of Real Property: A Legal Research Guide.** David H. Estes. LC 99-57717. (Legal Research Guides Ser.). 2000. write for info. (*1-57588-620-0*) W S Hein.

Premises Liability Service, 12 vols. LC 91-76946. 1992. ring bd. 500.00 (*0-685-59902-7*) West Group.

Premises of Political Economy: Being a Re-Examination of Certain Fundamental Principles of Economic Science. Simon . Patten. LC 68-30540. (Reprints of Economic Classics Ser.). 244p. 1968. reprint ed. 39.50 (*0-678-00446-3*) Kelley.

Premises Security: A Guide for Attorneys & Security Professionals. William F. Blake. LC 98-34862. 128p. 1998. pap. 34.95 (*0-7506-7030-4*) Buttrwrth-Heinemann.

Premises Security & Liability: A Comprehensive Guide from the Experts, Vols. 1 & 2. Steven C. Kaufer & Jurg W. Mattman. Ed. by Jean Chaney. (Illus.). 900p. 1997. ring bd. 237.00 (*0-9637790-6-0*) Inter-Act Assocs.

Premises Wiring for High-Performance Buildings. Donald J. Sterling, Jr. (Electrical Trades Ser.). 208p. 1995. mass mkt. 50.95 (*0-8273-7244-2*) Delmar.

Premises Wiring Systems (U. S.) Market Intelligence Staff. 350p. 1992. 3300.00 (*1-56753-906-8*, A2479) Frost & Sullivan.

Premium Adult Desserts. Ed. by Peter Allen. 250p. 1988. 1295.00 (*0-941285-18-9*) FIND-SVP.

***Premium & Incentive, 1999.** Salesman's Guide Staff. 1110p. 1999. pap. 259.95 (*0-87228-123-X*, Salesmn Gde) Douglas Pubns.

Premium & Incentive 1998. Salesman's Guide Staff. 1008p. 1998. pap. 269.95 (*0-87228-111-6*, Salesmn Gde) Douglas Pubns.

Premium Auditing Applications, Vols. 1 & 2. 4th ed. Everett D. Randall. LC 97-77730. 673p. 1997. pap. text 41.00 (*0-89462-119-X*, 9202) IIA.

***Premium Beer Drinker's Guide: The World's Strongest, Boldest & Most Unusual Beers.** Stephen Beaumont. (Illus.). 224p. 2000. pap. 24.95 (*1-55209-510-X*) Firefly Bks Ltd.

Premium Calculation in Insurance. Ed. by F. De Vylder et al. 1984. text 256.50 (*90-277-1732-X*) Kluwer Academic.

Premium Calculation in Insurance. F. De Vylder et al. (C). 1984. 690.00 (*0-7855-4060-1*, Pub. by Witherby & Co) St Mut.

Premium Incentives with Herbal Books: A Samphlet. Ed. by A. Doyle. (Illus.). 52p. (Orig.). 1997. pap. 29.95 (*1-890928-09-7*) Frieda Carrol.

Premium Incentives with Story Books: Story Samphlet. Ed. by A. Doyle. (Illus.). 50p. (Orig.). 1997. pap. text 29.95 (*1-890928-06-2*) Frieda Carrol.

Premium Insert Sports Cards. Sports Collectors Digest Editors. LC 95-60366. (Illus.). 384p. 1995. pap. 16.95 (*0-87341-355-5*, PSC01) Krause Pubns.

Premium Manuscript Book. 64p. 1985. pap. 4.95 (*0-87166-970-6*, 93963) Mel Bay.

Premium Polymeric Raw Materials & Their Biomedical Applications. 176p. 1992. 2650.00 (*0-89336-901-2*, P-211) BCC.

Premium Spiral Manuscript Book. 84p. 1984. spiral bd. 5.95 (*0-87166-641-3*, 93964) Mel Bay.

Premiums, Gifts & Competitions & Other Promotions: Regulation & Self-Regulation in 42 Countries. J. J. Boddewyn. 160p. 1988. 60.00 (*0-317-02008-0*) Intl Advertising Assn.

Premlata & the Festival of Lights. Rumer Godden. LC 96-2756. (Illus.). 64p. (J). (gr. 2 up). 1997. 15.00 (*0-688-15136-1*, Grenwillow Bks) HarpC Child Bks.

***Premlata & the Festival of Lights.** Rumer Godden. 1999. 9.70 (*0-606-15861-8*, Pub. by Turtleback) Demco.

Premlata & the Festival of Lights. Sandra Hirshkowith. LC 98-7215. (Chapter Bks.). (Illus.). 96p. (J). (gr. 2-5). 1999. pap. 4.25 (*0-06-442091-4*, HarpTrophy) HarpC Child Bks.

***Premo: A Framework for Multimedia Middleware: Specification, Rationale & Java Binding.** David J. Duke et al. LC 99-52205. (Lecture Notes in Computer Science Ser.: Vol. 1591). xii, 254p. 1999. pap. 42.00 (*3-540-66720-2*) Spr-Verlag.

***Premodern Chinese Economy: Structural Equilibrium & Capitalist Sterility.** Gang Deng. LC 98-25901. 5p. 1999. write for info. (*0-415-16239-4*) Routledge.

Premodern Japan: A Historical Survey. Mikiso Hane. 258p. (C). 1990. pap. 25.00 (*0-8133-8065-0*, Pub. by Westview) HarpC.

Premodern Sexualities. Louise Fradenburg. LC 95-30227. 288p. (C). 1996. pap. 20.99 (*0-415-91258-X*) Routledge.

Premodern Sexualities. Ed. by Louise Fradenburg & Carla Freccero. 50p. 1995. pap. text 10.00 (*2-88449-182-1*) Gordon & Breach.

Premodern Sexualities. Ed. by Louise Fradenburg & Carla Freccero. LC 95-30227. 288p. (C). (gr. 13). 1996. 65.00 (*0-415-91257-1*) Routledge.

Premonitions: The Kaya Anthology of New Asian American Poetry. Ed. by Walter K. Lew. LC 94-75916. (Illus.). 616p. 1995. 44.95 (*1-885030-13-4*); pap. 22.95 (*1-885030-14-2*) Kaya Prod.

***Premonitions in Retrospect: Strong-Cuevas.** Donald Kuspit. 22p. 1999. pap. 10.00 (*0-9665644-1-3*) Grnds for Sclpture.

Premonitions of an Uneasy Guest. Carolyne Wright. 69p. (Orig.). (C). 1983. pap. 5.95 (*0-910075-01-8*); pap. text 5.95 (*0-910075-02-6*) Hardin-Simmons.

Premonitions of Confirmed Suspicions. Rajiv S. Kairon. 81p. write for info. (*0-9638110-0-2*) Renaiss Pubng.

Premonitions, Visitations & Dreams of the Bereaved. Erin Linn. Ed. by Jo Saulisbury. (Orig.). 1991. pap. 6.95 (*0-9614636-4-3*) Pub Mark.

***Premonstratensian Order in Late Medieval England.** Joseph A. Gribbin. (Studies in the History of Medieval Religion). (Illus.). 258p. 2000. 75.00 (*0-85115-799-8*) Boydell & Brewer.

Premye Pa, Ansanm Haitian Creole. Fequiere Vilsaint. 32p. Date not set. wbk. ed. 3.95 (*1-881839-66-4*) Educa Vision.

Prenatal & Obstetric Care in Los Angeles County, 1990. Toni Richards et al. LC 93-20333. 1993. pap. text 9.00 (*0-8330-1343-2*, MR-182-NHF) Rand Corp.

Prenatal & Perinatal Biology & Medicine, 2 vols., Vol. 2. Norman Kretchmer et al. Incl. Vol. 1. Physiology & Growth. x, 350p. 1987. text 195.00 (*3-7186-0344-6*); Vol. 2. Disorders, Diagnosis & Therapy. x, 364p. 1987. text 195.00 (*3-7186-0345-4*); 1987. Set text 252.00 (*3-7186-0359-4*) Gordon & Breach.

Prenatal & Perinatal Factors in the Development of Childhood Reading Disorders. A. A. Kawi. (SRCD M Ser.: Vol. 24, No. 4). 1959. 25.00 (*0-527-01580-6*) Periodicals Srv.

Prenatal & Perinatal Infections. (EURO Reports & Studies: No. 93). 147p. 1985. pap. text 12.00 (*92-890-1259-5*, 1330093) World Health.

Prenatal & Perinatal Psychology & Medicine. Ed. by P. G. Fedor-Freybergh & M. L. Vogel. (Illus.). 699p. 1987. 68.00 (*1-85070-181-4*) Prthnon Pub.

Prenatal Care. Miriam Stoppard. LC 97-48451. (Healthcare Ser.). 1998. pap. 7.95 (*0-7894-3097-5*) DK Pub Inc.

Prenatal Care: Effectiveness & Implementation. Ed. by Marie C. McCormick & Joanna E. Siegel. (Illus.). 300p. (C). 1999. pap. 67.95 (*0-521-66196-X*) Cambridge U Pr.

Prenatal Care: Reaching Mothers, Reaching Infants. Institute of Medicine Staff. 264p. 1988. pap. text 27.95 (*0-309-03892-8*) Natl Acad Pr.

Prenatal Care for Hispanic Women: Opportunities for Improvement. Helen M. Wallace et al. (Illus.). 130p. (Orig.). 1994. pap. 19.95 (*0-89914-046-7*) Third Party Pub.

Prenatal Care in the United States, 1980-94. Caroline T. Lewis. 23p. 1996. pap. 3.00 (*0-16-061446-5*) USGPO.

Prenatal Care in the United States, 1980-94. National Center For Health Statistics Staff. LC 96-9472. (Vital & Health Statistics Ser.: Series 21, No. 54). 1996. write for info. (*0-8406-0518-8*) Natl Ctr Health Stats.

Prenatal Cocaine Exposures. Ed. by Richard J. Konkol & George D. Olsen. LC 95-48362. 208p. 1996. boxed set 134.95 (*0-8493-9465-1*) CRC Pr.

Prenatal Culture: How to Create the Perfect Baby. R. S. Clymer. (Illus.). 144p. 1950. 4.95 (*0-916285-56-1*) Humanitarian.

Prenatal Diagnosis. Curry. text. write for info. (*0-7216-6813-5*, W B Saunders Co) Harcrt Hlth Sci Grp.

Prenatal Diagnosis: Past, Present, & Future: Report of an International Workshop Held at Val David, Quebec, November 4-8, 1979. Ed. by John L. Hamerton & Nancy E. Simpson. LC RG0628.. (Prenatal Diagnosis, December 1980, Special Issue Ser.). 67p. reprint ed. pap. 30.00 (*0-608-15398-2*, 202926900059) Bks Demand.

Prenatal Diagnosis: The Human Side. J. Chapple. Ed. by L. Abramsky. 240p. 1994. 39.99 (*1-56593-286-2*, 0610) Singular Publishing.

Prenatal Diagnosis & Reproductive Genetics. Jeffrey A. Kuller & Robert C. Cefalo. (Illus.). 320p. (C). (gr. 13). 1995. text 45.95 (*0-8151-5209-4*, 24021) Mosby Inc.

Prenatal Diagnosis & Screening. Ed. by M. A. Ferguson-Smith et al. (Illus.). 785p. 1992. text 210.00 (*0-443-04379-5*) Church.

Prenatal Diagnosis & Selective Abortion. Harry Harris. LC 75-3847. 101p. 1975. 22.50 (*0-674-70080-5*) HUP.

Prenatal Diagnosis in Europe Proceedings of an EUCROMC Workshop, Paris, May 1996. Ed. by Nico J. Leschot & Lars O. Vejerslev. (European Journal of Human Genetics Ser.: Vol. 5, Suppl. 1, 1997). (Illus.). iv, 90p. 1997. pap. text 36.50 (*3-8055-6506-2*) S Karger.

Prenatal Diagnosis in Obstetric Practice. 2nd ed. Ed. by M. J. Whittle & J. M. Connor. LC 94-26804. 360p. 1995. 125.00 (*0-632-03838-1*) Blackwell Sci.

Prenatal Diagnosis of Congenital Anomalies. Roberto Romero et al. (Illus.). 466p. (C). 1997. pap. text 135.00 (*0-8385-7921-3*, A7921-8, Apple Lange Med) McGraw.

Prenatal Diagnosis of Foetal Malformations & Diseases: Teaching Atlas of Amniofoetography. Lothar Abet et al. 88p. 1991. 65.00 (*3-05-500611-9*, Pub. by Akademie Verlag) Wiley.

Prenatal Diagnosis of Heritable Skin Diseases. Ed. by Tobias Gedde-Dahl & K. D. Wuepper. (Current Problems in Dermatology Ser.: Vol. 16). (Illus.). viii, 216p. 1987. 189.75 (*3-8055-4397-2*) S Karger.

Prenatal Diagnosis of Thalassemia & the Hemoglobinopathies. Ed. by Dimitris Loukopoulos. 272p. 1988. 151.00 (*0-8493-5972-4*, RJ416, CRC Reprint) Franklin.

Prenatal Drug Exposure: Kinetics & Dynamics. 1992. lib. bdg. 88.00 (*0-8490-5496-6*) Gordon Pr.

Prenatal Exposure to Drugs - Alcohol: Characteristics & Educational Implications of Fetal Alcohol Syndrome & Cocaine - Polydrug Effects. Jeanette M. Soby. LC 93-23234. (Illus.). 138p. 1994. pap. 23.95 (*0-398-06436-9*) C C Thomas.

Prenatal Exposure to Drugs - Alcohol: Characteristics & Educational Implications of Fetal Alcohol Syndrome & Cocaine - Polydrug Effects. Jeanette M. Soby. LC 93-23234. (Illus.). 138p. (C). 1994. text 37.95 (*0-398-05891-1*) C C Thomas.

Prenatal Exposure to Toxicants: Developmental Consequences. Ed. by Herbert L. Needleman & David Bellinger. LC 93-34394. (Series in Environmental Toxicology). 352p. 1994. 90.00 (*0-8018-4704-4*) Johns Hopkins.

Prenatal Exposures in Schizophrenia. Ed. by Ezra S. Susser et al. LC 97-41045. (Progress in Psychiatry Ser.). 1999. text 38.00 (*0-88048-499-3*, 8499) Am Psychiatric.

***Prenatal Growth Reduction & Postnatal Endocrinopathies.** Inge Francois. (Acta Biomedica Lovaniensia Ser.: Vol. 197). (Illus.). 131p. 1999. pap. 46.50 (*90-6186-962-5*, Pub. by Leuven Univ) Coronet Bks.

Prenatal Life: Biological & Clinical Perspectives, Proceedings. Symposium on the Physiology & Pathology of Human R. Ed. by Harold C. Mack. LC 73-91873. 249p. reprint ed. pap. 77.20 (*0-608-17025-9*, 202760900055) Bks Demand.

Prenatal Origin of Genius. Raymond Bernard. 75p. 1996. reprint ed. spiral bd. 12.00 (*0-7873-1215-0*) Hlth Research.

Prenatal Person: Frank Lake's Maternal-Fetal Distress Syndrome. Stephen M. Maret. LC 97-3170. 224p. (C). 1997. 39.00 (*0-7618-0768-3*) U Pr of Amer.

Prenatal Screening for Major Fetal Disorders Vol. II: Screening for Down Syndrome. James E. Haddow et al. (Illus.). 296p. 1998. ring bd. 90.00 (*0-9653655-4-9*) Fnd Blood Res.

Prenatal Screening, Policies, & Values: The Example of Neural Tube Defects. Elena O. Nightingale. 1993. pap. 10.95 (*0-674-87125-1*) HUP.

Prenatal Screening, Policies, & Values: The Example of Neural Tube Defects. Ed. by Elena O. Nightingale & Susan B. Meister. (Illus.). 160p. 1987. pap. 10.95 (*0-674-70075-9*) HUP.

Prenatal Testing: A Sociological Perspective. Aliza Kolker & B. Meredith Burke. LC 93-43731. 248p. 1994. 59.95 (*0-89789-337-9*, Bergin & Garvey) Greenwood.

Prenatal Testing: A Sociological Perspective with new Afterword. Aliza Meredith Kolker & B. Burke. LC 93-43731. 280p. 1998. pap. 22.95 (*0-89789-633-5*, Bergin & Garvey) Greenwood.

***Prenatal Testing & Disability Rights.** Ed. by Erik Parens & Adrienne Asch. LC 00-26361. (Hastings Center Studies in Ethics). 352p. 2000. pap. 23.95 (*0-87840-804-5*); text 65.00 (*0-87840-803-7*) Georgetown U Pr.

Prenatal Yoga & Natural Birth. rev. ed. Jeannine Parvati Baker. (Illus.). 64p. 1986. reprint ed. pap. 9.95 (*0-938190-89-X*) North Atlantic.

Prenatal Yoga & Natural Birth. 2nd expanded ed. Jeannine P. Baker. LC 74-19553. (Illus.). 1986. reprint ed. pap. text 10.00 (*0-913512-52-4*) Freestone Pub Co.

PreNatally Exposed Kids. Danni Odom-Winn & Dianne E. Dunagan. Ed. by J. Lynne Dodson & Rosalie Dow. LC 91-77184. (Illus.). 120p. (Orig.). 1991. pap. 14.95 (*0-7925-1867-5*, B302) Ed Activities.

Prenda Estilo Sastre. Singer. (SPA., Illus.). 128p. 17.95 (*0-86573-274-4*) Creat Pub Intl.

Prenegotiation Planning Book. William F. Morrison. LC 91-32393. 272p. (C). 1992. reprint ed. lib. bdg. 33.50 (*0-89464-671-0*) Krieger.

Prenn Drifting. Jozsef Lengyel. 293p. 1966. 19.95 (*0-8464-0747-7*) Beekman Pubs.

Prensa: The Republic of Paper. Jaime C. Cardenal. LC 88-24295. (Focus on Issues Ser.: No. 5). (Illus.). 206p. (Orig.). (C). 1989. 22.95 (*0-932088-24-4*); pap. text 9.95 (*0-932088-25-2*) Freedom Hse.

Prentice Alvin, 3. Orson Scott Card. (Tales of Alvin Maker Ser.). 1989. 11.09 (*0-606-11761-X*, Pub. by Turtleback) Demco.

Prentice Alvin, Vol. 3. Orson Scott Card. (Tales of Alvin Maker Ser.: Bk. III). 1989. mass mkt. 4.95 (*0-8125-0212-4*, Pub. by Tor Bks) St Martin.

Prentice Hall Accounting Faculty Directory, 1992. James R. Hasselback. pap. text. write for info. (*0-318-68775-5*) P-H.

***Prentice Hall Algebra: Tools California Sample Pack 1998c.** (gr. 8-9). 1999. write for info. (*0-13-051965-0*) P-H.

***Prentice Hall Anthology of Science Fiction & Fantasy.** Garyn G. Roberts & Prentice-Hall Publishing Staff. LC 00-26411. 1000p. 2000. pap. 44.00 (*0-13-021280-6*) P-H.

***Prentice Hall Anthology Women's Literature.** Deborah H. Holdstein. LC 99-39922. 1085p. 1999. pap. 49.00 (*0-13-081974-3*) P-H.

Prentice-Hall Author's Guide. 5th ed. 128p. 1975. pap. text 41.00 (*0-13-695015-9*) P-H.

Prentice Hall Business Appointment Book 1999. Ed. by Prentice-Hall Staff. (C). 1999. 29.95 (*0-13-022045-0*) P-H.

Prentice Hall Case Series for Management Information Systems. Elam. (C). 1997. 3.42 (*0-13-207598-9*) P-H.

***Prentice Hall Cat Hospital Travel & Tourism 2000.** 1999. write for info. (*0-13-021905-3*) P-H.

***Prentice Hall Catalog Agriculture 2000 1/e.** 1999. write for info. (*0-13-021906-1*) P-H.

***Prentice Hall Catalog Construction.** 1999. write for info. (*0-13-021898-7*, Prentice Hall) P-H.

***Prentice Hall Catalog Criminal Justice 2000.** 1999. write for info. (*0-13-021904-5*, Prentice Hall) P-H.

Prentice Hall Catalog for Focus on Application 2000. (C). 2000. pap. text. write for info. (*0-13-026316-8*) S&S Trade.

***Prentice Hall Catalog Techers Math.** 1999. write for info. (*0-13-021901-0*, Prentice Hall) P-H.

Prentice Hall Complete Business Etiquette Handbook. Barbara Pachter. 350p. (C). 1994. text 29.95 (*0-13-156951-1*) P-H.

Prentice Hall Credit & Collection Answer Book. Lynn Tylczak. LC 92-40626. 352p. (C). 1993. text 69.95 (*0-13-117300-6*) P-H.

Prentice-Hall Dictionary of Nutrition & Health. Kenneth Anderson & Lois Harmo. LC 84-11590. 257p. 1985. 21.95 (*0-13-695610-6*); pap. 9.95 (*0-13-695602-5*) P-H.

***Prentice Hall Dictionary of Real Estate: A Complete Reference.** Barbara Cox et al. 2000. pap. text. write for info. (*0-13-020832-9*) P-H.

***Prentice Hall Dictionary of Real Estate: A Handy Reference Pocket Edition.** Barbara Cox et al. (Illus.). 256p. 2000. pap. text 16.00 (*0-13-020835-3*) P-H.

Prentice Hall Directory of On-Line Social Studies Resources: 1,000 of the Most Valuable Social Studies Web Sites, Electronic Mailing Lists & Newsgroups. Ronald L. Partin. LC 97-30121. 249p. (C). 1997. pap. text 32.95 (*0-13-679887-X*) P-H.

Prentice Hall Directory of Online Education Resources. Vicki S. Bigham & George D. Bigham. LC 98-15621. (Illus.). 450p. (C). 1998. pap. text 34.95 incl. cd-rom (*0-13-618588-6*) P-H.

Prentice Hall Encyclopedia Marketing & Advertising. Alexander Hiam & Dillman Laura. (C). 1992. 59.95 (*0-13-718644-4*) P-H.

Prentice Hall Encyclopedia of Model Business Plans. Wilbur Cross. LC 98-15279. 450p. 1998. pap. text 24.95 (*0-7352-0024-6*) PH Pr.

Prentice Hall Encyclopedia of World Proverbs. Ed. by Wolfgang Mieder. 582p. 1996. reprint ed. 12.98 (*1-56731-126-1*, MJF Bks) Fine Comms.

Prentice Hall English Developmental Diagnostic Tests. 56p. (C). 1997. write for info. (*0-13-621657-9*, Macmillan Coll) P-H.

Prentice Hall Enviromental Technology. Ed. by Neal K. Ostler. LC 95-30512. (Prentice Hall Environmental Technology Ser.: Vol. 1). 334p. 1995. 70.00 (*0-02-389532-2*, Macmillan Coll) P-H.

Prentice Hall Enviromental Technology. Neal K. Ostler. (Environmental Technology Ser.: Vol. 2). 220p. (C). 1995. 70.00 (*0-02-389542-X*, Macmillan Coll) P-H.

Prentice Hall Enviromental Technology. Neal K. Ostler. (Environmental Technology Ser.: Vol. 3). 256p. (C). 1996. 70.00 (*0-02-389551-9*, Macmillan Coll) P-H.

P

Prentice Hall Enviromental Technology. Neil K. Ostler & Patrick Holley. LC 96-48897. (Prentice Hall Technology Ser.: Vol. 4). 272p. 1997. 68.00 (*0-02-389534-9*, Macmillan Coll) P-H.

Prentice Hall Eviromental Technology Service. Neal K. Ostler & John T. Nielsen. LC 97-22365. (Prentice Hall's Environmental Technology Ser.: Vol. 5). 356p. 1997. 63.00 (*0-02-389545-4*) P-H.

Prentice Hall Federal Tax Course. Prentice-Hall Staff. Ed. by Alan Rubin. 1981. student ed. 21.00 (*0-685-03902-1*); pap., student ed. 7.95 (*0-685-03903-X*) P-H.

Prentice-Hall Federal Tax Course, 1983. Dale D. Bandy. (Illus.). 368p. (C). 1982. pap. text, student ed. 9.95 (*0-13-312637-4*) P-H.

Prentice-Hall Federal Tax Course, 1986. Ed. by Alan Rubin. 1440p. (C). 1985. text, student ed. 34.95 (*0-13-312794-X*) P-H.

Prentice-Hall Federal Tax Course, 1984: Student Guide. Dale D. Bandy. (Illus.). 368p. (C). 1983. pap. 10.95 (*0-13-312736-2*) P-H.

Prentice-Hall Federal Tax Course, 1986: Student Guide. Dale D. Bandy. (Illus.). 352p. (C). 1985. 11.95 (*0-13-312802-4*) P-H.

Prentice Hall Federal Tax Handbook see Federal Tax Handbook, 1992

Prentice Hall Federal Tax Treaties, 2 vols., Set. Prentice-Hall Staff. ring bd. write for info. (*0-318-57895-6*) P-H.

***Prentice Hall Federal Taxation 2000: Comprhn.** (C). 2000. write for info. (*0-13-026021-5*); write for info. (*0-13-026023-1*); write for info. (*0-13-026024-X*); write for info. (*0-13-026025-8*); write for info. (*0-13-026026-6*); write for info. (*0-13-026027-4*); write for info. (*0-13-026028-2*); 20.00 (*0-13-026029-0*) S&S Trade.

***Prentice Hall Federal Taxation 2000: Comprhn.** (C). 2000. write for info. (*0-13-026020-7*) S&S Trade.

Prentice Hall Federal Taxation 2000: Comprhn. Cramer. 1456p. (C). 1999. pap. text 90.00 (*0-13-020357-2*) P-H.

***Prentice Hall Federal Taxation 2001: Individual.** 1104p. (C). 2000. 86.67 (*0-13-026017-7*) S&S Trade.

***Prentice Hall Finance & Accounting Internet Guide: A Guided Tour of the Information Superhighway.** Brenda J. Mizgorski. LC 99-10588. (Illus.). 432p. 1999. pap. 49.95 (*0-13-095285-0*) P-H.

Prentice Hall Guide for College Writers. Stephen Reid. LC 88-25341. Date not set. write for info. (*0-13-150160-7*) P-H.

Prentice Hall Guide for College Writers. 5th ed. Stephen Reid. LC 99-24814. 736p. 1999. write for info. (*0-13-022547-9*) P-H.

***Prentice Hall Guide for College Writers: Brief Edition.** 5th ed. Ed. by Prentice-Hall Staff. LC 99-24814. 634p. (C). 1999. pap. text 42.00 (*0-13-021029-3*) P-H.

Prentice Hall Guide for College Writers: Customized. 316p. (C). 1995. text 37.40 (*0-536-58894-5*) Pearson Custom.

Prentice Hall Guide for College Writers: Full Edition with Handbook. 5th ed. Stephen Reid. 701p. 1999. pap. 47.00 (*0-13-021028-5*) P-H.

Prentice Hall Guide to Research Writing. 2nd ed. W. Dean Memering. 384p. (C). 1989. pap. text 20.60 (*0-13-774480-3*) P-H.

Prentice Hall Handbook for Writers. 10th ed. Glenn H. Leggett et al. LC 87-25927. Date not set. write for info. (*0-13-695728-5*) P-H.

Prentice-Hall Handbook for Writers. 12th ed. Melinda G. Kramer et al. LC 94-32494. 736p. 1994. pap. text 29.40 (*0-13-149618-2*) P-H.

Prentice-Hall Handbook for Writers. 12th ed. Melinda G. Kramer et al. LC 94-32494. 1995. text 30.60 (*0-13-037425-3*) P-H.

Prentice Hall Handbook for Writers Basic Workbook. 12th ed. T. Beery. 1994. pap. text, wbk. ed. 26.60 (*0-13-149154-7*) P-H.

Prentice Hall Health Catalog 2000. (C). 2000. pap. text. write for info. (*0-13-025680-3*) P-H.

Prentice Hall Illustrated Dictionary of Computing. 2nd ed. Jonah Nader. LC 94-47617. 650p. (C). 1995. pap. text 24.95 (*0-13-205725-5*) P-H.

Prentice Hall Inheritance Taxes. Prentice-Hall Staff. (Illus.). write for info. (*0-318-58375-5*) P-H.

***Prentice Hall Literature Timeless Voices Timeless Themes: Mini Anthology Short Drama/teleplay.** 5th ed. (gr. 7). 1999. write for info. (*0-13-437206-9*, Prentice Hall) P-H.

***Prentice Hall Literaturey Author: Timeless Voices Timeless Themes Novel, Anthology.** 5th ed. (gr. 10). 1999. write for info. (*0-13-050403-3*) P-H.

Prentice Hall Miracle Sales Guide. 4th ed. (C). 1993. 59.95 (*0-13-068743-X*, Macmillan Coll) P-H.

Prentice-Hall 1985 Federal Tax Course. 1985th ed. Dale D. Bandy. (Illus.). 368p. (C). 1984. 11.95 (*0-13-312778-8*) P-H.

Prentice-Hall, 1987. Dale D. Bandy. (Illus.). 352p. (C). 1986. student ed. 11.95 (*0-317-46064-1*) P-H.

Prentice Hall, 1998-1999 Marketing Faculty Directory. (C). 1999. text. write for info. (*0-13-020666-0*) P-H.

***Prentice Hall Office Administrator's Deskbook.** Mary Ann De Vries. LC 00-41667. 2000. write for info. (*0-13-022683-1*) P-H.

***Prentice Hall Pilot Materials.** 542p. (C). 1998. 20.00 (*0-13-095960-X*) P-H.

Prentice Hall Pocket Guide for Writers. Anthony C. Winkler & Jo R. McCuen. LC 94-34485. 144p. 1995. pap. text 16.60 (*0-13-309717-X*) P-H.

Prentice Hall Pract Problms for Individuals. Prentice-Hall Staff. 1996. pap. text 6.67 (*0-13-239401-4*) P-H.

Prentice Hall Prep Series for the Toefl Test: Listening Skills Builder. Linford Lougheed. (C). 1994. pap., student ed. 48.00 (*0-13-187790-9*) P-H.

Prentice Hall PTR/Sunsoft Press Graphic Java. David Geary & Alan McClellan. 1996. 39.95 incl. cd-rom (*0-614-20319-8*) P-H.

Prentice Hall Reader. 4th ed. Compiled by George Miller, II. LC 94-32237. 593p. 1994. pap. text 33.00 (*0-13-079302-7*) P-H.

Prentice Hall Reader. 5th ed. George Miller, II. LC 97-40656. 628p. 1997. pap. text 37.00 (*0-13-627902-3*) P-H.

***Prentice Hall Reader.** 6th ed. George Miller. LC 00-31347. 656p. 2000. pap. 35.33 (*0-13-022563-0*) P-H.

Prentice Hall Real Estate Appraisal Deskbook. Frank J. Blankenship. 320p. 1986. 39.95 (*0-13-696378-1*) P-H.

Prentice Hall Real Estate Investors Encyclopedia. Frank J Blakenship. 1990. pap. 24.95 (*0-685-32931-3*) P-H.

***Prentice Hall Reference Guide to Grammar & Usage.** 4th ed. Muriel Harris. LC 99-19691. 404p. 1999. spiral bd. 32.20 (*0-13-021022-6*) P-H.

Prentice Hall Reference Guide to Grammar & Usage with exercises. 2nd ed. Muriel Harris. LC 93-34200. 448p. 1993. spiral bd. 25.20 (*0-13-225624-X*) P-H.

Prentice Hall Reference Guide to Grammar & Usage, Without Exercises. 2nd ed. Muriel Harris. 336p. (C). 1993. spiral bd. 24.20 (*0-13-399817-7*) P-H.

Prentice Hall Regent Prep Series for the Toefl Test. Lin Lougheed. (Regents Prep Series for the TOEFL Test). (Illus.). 80p. 1995. pap. text 15.80 (*0-13-100645-2*) P-H.

Prentice Hall Regents Practice TOEIC Test. Steven A. Stupak. (C). 1994. pap. 27.25 incl. digital audio (*0-13-148693-4*) P-H.

Prentice Hall Regents Prep Book for the TOEIC Test. Steven A. Stupak. (C). 1994. pap. 75.25 incl. digital audio (*0-13-157330-6*) P-H.

Prentice Hall Regents Prep Book for the TOEIC Test. 2nd ed. Steven A. Stupak. LC 94-25985. 304p. (C). 1994. pap. text 28.20 (*0-13-125816-8*) P-H.

Prentice Hall Regents Prep Series for the Toefl Test: Vocabulary Reading Skills Builder. Linford Lougheed. (Regents Prep Series for the TOEFL Test). (Illus.). 80p. 1994. pap. text 15.80 (*0-13-100660-6*) P-H.

Prentice Hall Regents Prep Series for the TOEFL Test: 4 Practice Tests. Linford Lougheed. (C). 1994. pap. 50.25 (*0-13-187717-8*) P-H.

Prentice Hall Regents Preparation TOEFL: Grammar. Lin Lougheed. (Regents Prep Series for the TOEFL Test). (Illus.). 112p. 1994. pap. text 15.80 (*0-13-100637-1*, PH Regents) P-H.

Prentice Hall Small Business Model Letter Book. Wilbur Cross. 370p. (C). 1992. text 39.95 (*0-13-718602-9*, Busn) P-H.

Prentice Hall Small Business Survival Guide: A Blueprint for Success. Richard M. Turitz & Michael Cross. LC 93-6514. (C). 1993. pap. text 16.95 (*0-13-045329-3*) P-H.

Prentice Hall 1040 Handbook, 1990: For Filing 1989 Individual Income Tax Returns. Prentice-Hall Staff. 1989. pap. 49.50 (*0-13-903634-2*) P-H.

Prentice Hall Writer's Style Guide, Borders Press Edition. 304p. (C). 1998. pap. text 5.98 (*0-13-020878-7*) P-H.

Prentice-Hall's Corporation Library. write for info. (*0-318-63275-6*) P-H.

Prentice Hall's Daily Sales Planner, 1988. Herbert F. Holtje. 432p. 1987. text 32.50 (*0-13-695686-6*, Busn) P-H.

Prentice-Hall's Explanation of the Tax Reform Act of 1986: As Passed by the House of Representatives (September 25, 1986) & Sent to the Senate. PH Editorial Staff. LC 86-222025. 1986. 12.00 (*0-13-695123-6*) P-H.

Prentice Hall's Federal Taxation. John L. Kramer. 1999. 91.75 (*0-13-080940-3*) P-H.

Prentice Hall's 97 Individual Federal Tax Guide. Thomas R. Pope. 1104p. 1996. 72.00 (*0-13-239484-7*) P-H.

***Prentice Hall's Federal Taxation 1999.** Kenneth E. Anderson. 1999. 87.50 (*0-13-022582-7*) P-H.

Prentice Hall's Federal Taxation 2000: Comprehensive. Kramer. 1664p. (C). 1999. text 90.00 (*0-13-020292-4*) P-H.

***Prentice Hall's Federal Taxation, 2000: Corporations, Partnerships, Estates & Trus.** John L. Kramer & Thomas R. Pope. 1040p. 1999. text 91.00 (*0-13-020283-5*, Prentice Hall) P-H.

***Prentice Hall's Federal Taxation, 2000: Corporations, Partnerships, Estates & Trusts.** Kramer & Pope. (C). 1999. ring bd. 86.67 (*0-13-020284-3*) P-H.

***Prentice Hall's Federal Taxation 2000: Individuals.** (C). 1999. pap. text 79.33 (*0-13-020276-2*) P-H.

***Prentice Hall's Federal Taxation 2001: Comprehensive.** Thomas R. Pope et al. 1664p. 2000. 92.00 (*0-13-026019-3*, Prentice Hall) P-H.

***Prentice Hall's Federal Taxation 2001: Corporations, Partnerships, Estates, & Trusts.** Kenneth E. Anderson et al. 1040p. 2000. 89.33 (*0-13-026047-9*, Prentice Hall) P-H.

Prentice Hall's Get a Grip on Finance & Accounting. Corporate Classrooms Staff. LC 98-12786. 192p. (C). 1998. pap. text 69.95 (*0-13-616483-8*) P-H.

Prentice Hall's Get a Grip on Grammar. Corporate Classrooms Staff. 160p. (C). 1992. ring bd. 69.95 (*0-13-012428-1*, Pub. by P-H) S&S Trade.

Prentice Hall's Get a Grip on Grammar: Language Skills for Today's Business World. Corporate Classrooms Staff. LC 92-22769. 1992. 99.95 (*0-685-60782-8*) P-H.

Prentice Hall's Get a Grip on Writing: Critical Skills for Success in Today's Business World. Corporate Classrooms Staff. 192p. (C). 1996. text 69.95 (*0-13-232414-8*) P-H.

Prentice Hall's Guide to Sales & Use Taxes. Prentice-Hall Staff. 720p. 1988. 37.95 (*0-13-705881-0*, Busn) P-H.

Prentice Hall's Illustrated Dictionary of Computing. Jonar Nader. LC 92-19637. 544p. (C). 1992. pap. text 24.95 (*0-13-719998-8*) P-H.

Prentice Hall's Illustrated Dictionary of Computing. 3rd ed. Jonar C. Nader. LC 98-4713. (Illus.). 792p. (C). 1998. pap. 34.95 incl. cd-rom (*0-13-095104-8*) P-H.

Prentice Hall's IRS Practice & Procedure Handbook. 280p. write for info. (*0-318-62940-2*) P-H.

***Prentice Hall's One-Day MBA in Finance & Accounting.** Mike Muckian. 2000. pap. 20.00 (*0-7352-0148-X*) PH Pr.

Prentice Hall's Social Security Deskbook, 1988. Prentice-Hall Staff. Ed. by Marvin Hillman. 450p. 1988. pap. 30.00 (*0-13-703035-5*, Busn) P-H.

Prentice Hall's Worker's Compensation Handbook. Jay E. Grenig. 512p. 1989. pap. 47.59 (*0-13-703910-7*, Busn) P-H.

Prentice. History & Genealogy of the Prentice, Prentis & Prentiss Families in New England from 1631 to 1883 (Based on the 1883 Edition by C. J. F. Binney, Which Is Included) Linus J. Dewald. 551p. 1997. pap. 79.50 (*0-8328-9493-1*); lib. bdg. 89.50 (*0-8328-9492-3*) Higginson Bk Co.

***Prenups for Lovers: A Romantic Guide to Premarital Agreements.** LC 00-43370. (Illus.). 2001. write for info. (*0-375-75535-7*) Villard Books.

Prenuptial Agreement. Kasey Michaels. (Romance Ser.). 1992. pap. 2.69 (*0-373-08898-1*, 5-08898-4) Silhouette.

Prenuptial Agreement. Doris Rangel. 1998. per. 4.25 (*0-373-24224-7*, 1-24224-7, Mira Bks) Harlequin Bks.

Prenuptial Agreement. large type ed. Kasey Michaels. 215p. 1993. reprint ed. lib. bdg. 13.95 (*1-56054-614-X*) Thorndike Pr.

Prenuptial Agreement: Halakhic & Pastoral Considerations. Ed. by Kenneth Auman & Basil Herring. LC 95-48948. 94p. 1996. pap. 20.00 (*1-56821-917-2*) Aronson.

Prenuptial Agreements. 1995. 99.00 incl. audio PA Bar Inst.

PreNuptial Bliss: What Every Woman Should Know Before Planning a Wedding. Yvonne D. McClendon. LC 98-91273. 112p. 1998. pap. 10.99 (*0-9663013-0-7*) McSterling Pubg.

Preobrazhenie Mira. M. Gor'kii. 398p. 1980. 39.00 (*0-7855-0893-7*) St Mut.

Preobrazhenije Gospodnje. Ed. by Moscow Synod Staff.Tr. of Transfiguration of the Lord. 128p. pap. 6.00 (*0-317-29169-6*) Holy Trinity.

Preoccupations: Selected Prose, 1968-1978. Seamus Heaney. 224p. 1981. pap. 12.00 (*0-374-51650-2*) FS&G.

Preocular Tear Film: In Health, Disease, & Contact Lens Wear. Ed. & Pref. by Frank J. Holly. 1986. 150.00 (*0-9616938-0-0*) Dry Eye Inst.

Preodolevaia Grantisy. Vladimir Ashkenazi & Jasper Parrot. Tr. by Igor Efimov & Marina Yefimov. (RUS., Illus.). 240p. (Orig.). 1989. pap. 12.50 (*1-55779-008-6*) Hermitage Pubs.

Preoedipal Origin & Psychoanalytic Therapy of Sexual Perversions. Charles W. Socarides. 1988. 80.00 (*0-8236-4287-9*) Intl Univs Pr.

Preons: Models of Leptons, Quarks & Gauge Bosons as Composite Particles. I. D'Souza & C. S. Kalman. 100p. 1992. text 36.00 (*981-02-1019-1*) World Scientific Pub.

Preoperative & Postoperative Dermatologic Surgical Care. Ed. by Hubert T. Greenway, Jr. & Terry L. Barrett. LC 94-22504. (Illus.). 224p. 1995. 69.50 (*0-89640-261-4*) Igaku-Shoin.

Preoperative Cardiac Assessment: A Society of Cardiovascular Anesthesiologists Mono. Dennis T. Mangano. (Illus.). 200p. 1990. text 38.00 (*0-397-51089-6*) Lppncott W & W.

Preoperative Events: Their Effects on Behavior Following Brain Damage. J. Schulkin. 368p. 1989. 79.95 (*0-8058-0021-2*); pap. 39.95 (*0-8058-0535-4*) L Erlbaum Assocs.

Preoperative (Neoadjuvant) Chemotherapy. Ed. by J. Ragaz et al. (Recent Results in Cancer Research Ser.: Vol. 103). (Illus.). 196p. 1986. 76.00 (*0-387-16129-5*) Spr-Verlag.

Preoperative Preparation & Intraoperative Monitoring. LC 96-53605. (Atlas of Anesthesia Ser.). 1997. text 135.00 (*0-443-07902-1*) Church.

PREP for Effective Family Living. Don Dinkmeyer, Sr. et al. (YA). (gr. 7 up). 1985. 134.95 (*0-88671-225-4*, 6400) Am Guidance.

PREP for Effective Family Living: Student Handbook. Don Dinkmeyer, Sr. et al. (PREP Ser.). 1985. teacher ed. 42.95 (*0-88671-229-7*, 6401); student ed. 6.95 (*0-88671-228-9*, 6405); pap. 14.95 (*0-88671-226-2*, 6403); text 24.95 (*0-88671-227-0*, 6402) Am Guidance.

Prep for TASP with Rinehart's Handbook. 4th ed. Carter. (C). 1995. pap. text 6.00 (*0-15-503606-8*, Pub. by Harcourt Coll Pubs) Harcourt.

Prep Guide: Texas Real Estate Sales Licensing Exams. 4th ed. Leslie K. Purvis. Ed. by Lynn Purvis. (Illus.). 220p. 1999. pap. text 29.95 (*0-9638207-2-9*) Purvis Real Est.

Prep Pak for FLMI 351. Michael F. Gibson et al. (FLMI Insurance Education Program Ser.). 211p. 1998. spiral bd. 24.00 (*1-57974-050-2*) Life Office.

Prep Pak for FLMI 301: Insurance Administration. Barbara F. Brown et al. (FLMI Insurance Education Program Ser.). 227p. 1997. spiral bd. 24.00 (*0-939921-95-2*) Life Office.

Prep Pak for FLMI 310. Jo Ann Appleton et al. (FLMI Insurance Education Program Ser.). 247p. 1998. spiral bd. 24.00 (*1-57974-052-9*) Life Office.

Prep Pak for FLMI 320. 2nd rev. ed. Jo Ann Appleton et al. (FLMI Insurance Education Program Ser.). 211p. spiral bd. 24.00 (*1-57974-009-X*, Pub. by Life Office) PBD Inc.

Prep Pak for FLMI 371. Sean S. Gilley et al. (FLMI Insurance Education Program Ser.). 205p. spiral bd., wbk. ed. 24.00 (*0-939921-84-7*, Pub. by Life Office) PBD Inc.

Prep Pak for FLMI 361. Robert MacGrogan et al. Ed. by Gene Stone. (FLMI Insurance Education Program Ser.). 281p. spiral bd., wbk. ed. 24.00 (*0-939921-88-X*, Pub. by Life Office) PBD Inc.

Prep Pak for FLMI 330. Kim Martin et al. (FLMI Insurance Education Program Ser.). 201p. spiral bd., wbk. ed. 24.00 (*0-939921-92-8*, Pub. by Life Office) PBD Inc.

Prep Pak for FLMI 280. Beth Burnett-Balga et al. (FLMI Insurance Education Program Ser.). 259p. 1999. spiral bd. 24.00 (*1-57974-030-8*) PBD Inc.

***Prep Pak for FLMI 290.** rev. ed. Ernest L. Martin et al. (FLMI Insurance Education Progam Ser.). (C). 2000. spiral bd. 24.00 (*1-57974-082-0*, Pub. by Life Office) PBD Inc.

Prep School Hockey Guide. 7th rev. ed. Ed. by Thomas E. Keegan. (Illus.). 184p. 1996. pap. 22.95 (*1-880941-09-0*) Athletic Guide.

Prep School Hockey Guide. 8th ed. Tom Keegan. (Illus.). 200p. 1998. reprint ed. pap. 25.95 (*1-880941-15-5*) Athletic Guide.

***Prep School Hockey Guide.** 9th rev. ed. Ed. by Tom Keegan. 240p. 1999. pap. 19.95 (*1-880941-31-7*, Pub. by Athletic Guide) ACCESS Pubs Network.

***Prep School Hockey Guide 2000.** 10th ed. Thomas E. Keegan. 280p. 1999. pap. 24.95 (*1-880941-37-6*, Pub. by Athletic Guide) ACCESS Pubs Network.

***Prepack 2 Joy of Sex Box Set 98: A Gourmet Guide to Lovemaking for the Nineties.** Alex Comfort. 1998. per., boxed set 40.00 (*0-671-71782-0*) PB.

Prepage Tempates for Adobe Pagemaker: Start Your Next Project with Most of the Work Already Done! Chuck Green. (Illus.). 128p. 1998. pap. 99.00 (*0-9669587-0-5*) Logic Arts.

Prepaid Legal Services State Regulation Summaries. 6th ed. 125p. 1991. 47.50 (*0-685-56620-X*) Am Prepaid.

Prepaint Specialties & Surface Tolerant Coatings. Ernest W. Flick. LC 91-8702. (Illus.). 614p. 1991. 129.00 (*0-8155-1273-2*) Noyes.

Prepalatial Cemeteries at Mochlos & Gournia & the House Tombs of Bronze Age Crete. Jeffrey S. Soles. LC 91-22767. (Hesperia Supplement Ser.: No. 24). (Illus.). 320p. 1992. pap. 35.00 (*0-87661-524-8*) Am Sch Athens.

Preparacion Para la Translacion (Preparation for Translation) rev. ed. Milton G. Crane. LC 93-61527. (SPA.). 272p. 1995. per. 8.95 (*0-945383-66-5*) Teach Servs.

Preparadas... Listas... Ya! Jeannine Atkins. Tr. by Esther Sarfatti. LC 98-7777. (SPA., Illus.). 32p. (YA). (ps up). 1998. 15.95 (*1-880000-77-6*); pap. 6.95 (*1-880000-78-4*) Lee & Low Bks.

Preparados en Cristo. Warren W. Wiersbe. Ed. by Gary Hilliker. (New Testament Ser.). (SPA.). 166p. 1992. 7.95 (*1-879892-09-X*) Editorial Bautista.

***Preparando el Matrimonio en el Camino de Dios (Preparing for Marriage God's Way)** Wayne A. Mack. 163p. 1999. pap. 14.99 (*1-56322-066-0*) Hensley Pub.

Preparandose para el Alumbramiento. D. Evans. (Serie Guia de Bolsillo - Pocket Guides Ser.).Tr. of Preparing for Childbirth. (SPA.). 1991. pap. 2.79 (*1-56063-070-1*, 498062) Editorial Unilit.

Preparandose Para el Exito. 2nd ed. Emilio Santarita. (SPA.). 146p. (C). 1995. text 20.80 (*0-536-59046-X*) Pearson Custom.

Preparandose Para la Lectura. 2nd ed. Ruth Bowdoin. (Bowdoin Method I Ser.). Orig. Title: Getting Ready for Reading. (Illus.). 36p. 1991. reprint ed. pap. write for info. (*1-55997-067-7*) Websters Intl.

Preparandose Para Triunfar. Emilio S. Rita. (SPA.). (C). 1991. pap. text 41.00 (*0-536-57965-2*) Pearson Custom.

***Preparation: Dramas for Lent.** Alice Bass. LC 99-38521. (Intermission Scripts Ser.). 80p. 1999. 13.00 (*0-570-05391-9*) Concordia.

Preparation: For Better Reading. 3rd ed. Adams. (C). 1988. pap. text, teacher ed. 27.50 (*0-03-013323-8*) Harcourt Coll Pubs.

Preparation & Analysis of Protein Crystals. Alexander McPherson. LC 88-32577. 384p. (C). 1989. reprint ed. lib. bdg. 59.00 (*0-89464-355-X*) Krieger.

Preparation & Assay of Enzymes see Methods in Enzymology

Preparation & Assay of Substrates see Methods in Enzymology

Preparation & Crystal Growth of Materials with Layered Structures. Ed. by Ronald M. Lieth. (Physics & Chemistry of Materials with Layered Structures Ser.: Vol. I). 200p. 1977. text 176.50 (*90-277-0638-7*) Kluwer Academic.

Preparation & Presentation of Expert Testimony in Child Abuse Litigation: A Guide for Expert Witnesses & Attorneys. Paul Stern. LC 96-45811. (Interpersonal Violence: the Practice Ser.). 202p. 1997. pap. 21.50 (*0-7619-0013-6*) Sage.

Preparation & Presentation of the Show Dog: The Complete Handling Guide. 3rd ed. Jeff Brucker & Betty Brucker. LC 95-44723. (Illus.). 96p. 1995. reprint ed. pap. 12.95 (*0-931866-80-4*) Alpine Pubns.

Preparation & Properties of Solid State Materials: Aspects of Crystal Growth, Vol. 1. Ed. by Robert A. Lefever. LC 78-155744. (Illus.). 292p. reprint ed. pap. 90.60 (*0-608-30578-2*, 201785600009) Bks Demand.

Preparation & Pursuance of Civil Litigation. Leon Rock. LC 76-24398. (Illus.). ix, 753p. 1983. 37.50 (*0-317-00679-7*) Natl Ctr PT.

Preparation & Revision for DRCOG. Janice Rymer et al. (Illus.). 258p. 1990. pap. text 43.00 (*0-443-04248-9*) Church.

Preparation & Revision for the Diploma of the Royal College of Obstetricians & Gynaecologists. 2nd ed. Janice Rymer. LC 97-18740. 1998. write for info. (*0-443-05097-X*) Church.

An Asterisk (*) at the beginning of an entry indicates that the title is appearing for the first time.

***Preparation & Revision for the MRCPCH, Pt. 1.** R. Skinner et al. (Illus.). 400p. 1998. pap. write for info. (*0-443-06139-4*) Church.

***Preparation & Revision for the MRCS & AFRCS Examinations.** 2nd ed. W. E. Thomas. (Illus.). 220p. 1998. pap. write for info. (*0-443-05046-5*) Church.

Preparation & Testing of Reagent Water in the Clinical Laboratory. 3rd ed. National Committee for Clinical Laboratory Standar. (Approved Guideline Ser.: Vol. 8). 1991. 75.00 (*1-56238-127-X*, C3-A2) NCCLS.

Preparation & Testing of Reagent Water in the Clinical Laboratory: Approved Guideline (1997) 3rd ed. 1997. 75.00 (*1-56238-336-1*, C3-A-3) NCCLS.

Preparation & Trial of Medical Malpractice Cases. Richard E. Shandell. 400p. 1985. reprint ed. ring bd. 90.00 (*0-318-21439-3*, 00564) NY Law Pub.

Preparation & Use of Checklists. (Fossil Power Plant Startup Training Ser.). (Illus.). 59p. 1983. spiral bd. 21.50 (*0-87683-360-1*) GP Courseware.

***Preparation & Use of the Historic Structure Report.** 16p. 1998. pap. 2.00 (*0-16-061690-5*) USGPO.

Preparation & Work of Alabama High School Teachers. Henry C. Pannell. LC 77-177142. (Columbia University. Teachers College. Contributions to Education Ser.: No. 551). reprint ed. 37.50 (*0-404-55551-9*) AMS Pr.

***Preparation, Collaboration & Emphasis on the Family in School Counseling for the New Millennium.** Gwendolyn M. Duhon & Tony Manson. LC 99-58572. (Studies in Education: Vol. 48). 300p. 2000. text 89.95 (*0-7734-7847-7*) E Mellen.

Preparation Course for the TOEFL Test Vol. A: Skills & Strategies. 2nd ed. Deborah Phillips. LC 95-31469. 432p. 1995. pap. text, student ed. 25.36 (*0-201-84676-4*) Addison-Wesley.

Preparation Course for the TOEFL Test Vol. B: Practice Tests. 2nd ed. Deborah Phillips. LC 95-31469. 1995. pap. text, student ed. 19.85 (*0-201-84961-5*) Longman.

Preparation du Bois les Pates Mechaniques. Claude Cossette. (FRE., Illus.). 242p. 1991. pap. text (*2-9801486-5-2*) CA66.

***Preparation for a Revolution: The Young Turks, 1902-1908.** M. Sukru Hanioglu. LC 99-35526. (Studies in Middle Eastern History). 560p. 2000. text 75.00 (*0-19-513463-X*) OUP.

Preparation for a 25,000 Dollar U. S. Postal Job. Kenneth J. Cross. LC 91-90315. 140p. (Orig.). 1991. spiral bd. 14.95 (*0-9629673-3-5*) Letterman Pubs.

Preparation for Adulthood: Standards for Good Practice in Residential Care. 36p. 1997. spiral bd. 21.00 (*1-874579-95-4*, Pub. by Natl Childrens Bur) Paul & Co Pubs.

Preparation for Aging: Proceedings of the Seventeenth International Congress of IAUTA Held in Jyvaskyla, Finland, August 12-14, 1994. Ed. by Eino Heikkinen et al. (Illus.). 306p. 1995. 95.00 (*0-306-45068-2*, Kluwer Plenum) Kluwer Academic.

Preparation for Algebra. J. Louis Nanney & John L. Cable. (Illus.). 530p. (C). 1992. text 50.00 (*0-697-12801-6*) Quant Syst.

Preparation for Apprenticeship Through CETA, Vol. I. Kenneth W. Tolo. 130p. 1980. pap. 4.95 (*0-89940-800-1*) LBJ Sch Pub Aff.

Preparation for Birth: The Complete Guide to the Lamaze Method. Beverly Savage & Diana Simkin. 224p. (Orig.). 1987. pap. 14.00 (*0-345-31230-9*, Ballantine) Ballantine Pub Grp.

Preparation for Board Certification & Licensing Examinations in Psychology: The Professional, Legal & Ethical Components. Robert G. Meyer. 184p. 1992. 29.00 (*0-9634417-0-1*) Monkestee Pr.

Preparation for Calculus. Claudia Pinter-Lucke & Barbara Shabell. 196p. (C). 1996. pap. text, per. 23.95 (*0-7872-2699-8*) Kendall-Hunt.

Preparation for Citizenship. Delores D. De Valdez et al. 1997. pap., student ed. 10.56 (*0-8114-7987-0*) Raintree Steck-V.

Preparation for Civil Service. Leonard S. Bennett et al. 1980. pap. 4.95 (*0-87738-019-8*) Youth Ed.

Preparation for Coast Guard License: Preparation for Examinations of up to 100 Ton Vessels. (Learning Guides Ser.). (Illus.). 50p. Date not set. pap. text 5.79 (*1-891148-12-5*) US Power.

Preparation for Confirmation: According to the Baltimore Catechism. Baltimo. 26p. (J). (gr. 5-12). 1996. pap. 3.45 (*0-935952-34-9*) Angelus Pr.

Preparation for Credentialing in Radiography. 9th ed. Mary A. Sherer. LC 92-13350. (Illus.). 255p. 1992. pap. text 26.00 (*0-7216-3282-3*, W B Saunders Co) Harcrt Hlth Sci Grp.

Preparation for Death. abr. ed. Alphonsus Liguori. LC 82-50596. 146p. 1991. reprint ed. pap. 8.00 (*0-89555-174-8*) TAN Bks Pubs.

Preparation for Death: Prayers & Consolations for the Final Journey. Saint Alphonsus Liguori. Ed. by Norman J. Muckerman. LC 98-17295. 128p. 1998. pap. 8.95 (*0-7648-0223-2*) Liguori Pubns.

Preparation for Discipleship: A Handbook for New Christians (Lutheran Christians & Their Beliefs) Jerry Schmalenberger. LC 97-28497. 110p. 1998. pap. 10.95 (*0-7880-1181-2*) CSS OH.

Preparation for Eighth-Grade Math TAAS Test. Margaret Dominguez. Ed. & Illus. by Monica Dominguez. 53p. (J). (gr. 8). 1996. spiral bd. 19.95 (*1-889684-00-7*) Texas Testing.

Preparation for End-of-Year Algebra 1 Test. Margaret Dominguez & Marissa Dominguez. (Illus.). 74p. (YA). (gr. 9-12). 1994. spiral bd. 19.95 (*0-9650840-2-7*) Texas Testing.

Preparation for Examinations Nuclear Medicine Technology. Ann M. Steves. LC 97-5945. 1997. pap. text 25.00 (*0-932004-49-0*) Soc Nuclear Med.

Preparation for Licensing & Board Certification Examinations in Psychology: The Professional, Legal, & Ethical Components. 2nd ed. Robert G. Meyer. LC 94-23369. (Continuing Education in Psychiatry & Psychology Ser.: No. 4). 224p. 1995. pap. 24.95 (*0-87630-767-5*, 7675) Brunner-Mazel.

Preparation for Life? Vocationalism & the Equal Opportunities Challenge. Sue Heath. LC 97-74445. (Illus.). 232p. 1997. text 69.95 (*1-85972-647-X*, Pub. by Ashgate Pub) Ashgate Pub Co.

Preparation for Life in the 21st Century: Actualizing the Opportunity of a Lifetime. Gerald D. Kessel. Ed. by Jane E. Wulff. 45p. 1990. pap. 6.95 (*0-9615232-3-9*) Human Cult Consort.

Preparation for NCLEX-RN: Saunders Nursing Review & Practice Tests. 4th ed. Dee A. Gillies. 416p. 1987. pap. text 36.00 (*0-7216-1454-X*, W B Saunders Co) Harcrt Hlth Sci Grp.

Preparation for Nuclear Disaster. Wayne LeBaron. 387p. 1998. 38.00 (*1-56072-557-5*) Nova Sci Pubs.

Preparation for Ordination. Herman Hersey. 1981. pap. 1.95 (*0-89265-069-9*) Randall Hse.

Preparation for Parenting: A Biblical Perspective: A Study in the Philosophy, Psychology & Practice of Nurturing a Newborn. Gary Ezzo & Anne M. Ezzo. 202p. 1991. student ed. 12.00 (*1-883035-09-0*) Grow Families.

Preparation for Pentecost. James A. Stewart. 1966. pap. 2.49 (*1-56632-035-6*) Revival Lit.

Preparation for Seventh-Grade Math TAAS Test. Margaret Dominguez. Ed. & Illus. by Monica Dominguez. 53p. (J). (gr. 7). 1996. spiral bd. 19.95 (*1-889684-01-5*) Texas Testing.

Preparation for TAAS Mathematics Test (Exit Level) Margaret Dominguez & Marissa Dominguez. (Illus.). 60p. (YA). (gr. 9-12). 1994. spiral bd. 19.95 (*0-9650840-1-9*) Texas Testing.

Preparation for the CLEP: College-Level Examination Program. 5th ed. 1995. pap. 12.00 (*0-671-89923-6*, Arco) Macmillan Gen Ref.

Preparation for the DCH. N. J. Gilbertson & S. Walker. (Illus.). 256p. (Orig.). 1993. pap. text 39.95 (*0-443-04375-2*) Church.

Preparation for the Final Crisis. Fernando Chaij. LC 66-29118. 1966. pap. 9.99 (*0-8163-0939-6*, 16510-0) Pacific Pr Pub Assn.

Preparation for the Final Crisis Study Work Book. Brenda D. Hill. 196p. 1997. pap. 9.99 (*0-8163-1564-7*) Pacific Pr Pub Assn.

Preparation for the GRE: Graduate Records Examinations, Bklet. 2. Mauricio Waintrub et al. 60p. 1997. pap. 10.00 (*1-884083-93-5*) Maval Pub.

Preparation for the GRE: Graduate Records Examinations, Bklet. 3. Mauricio Waintrub et al. 60p. 1997. pap. 10.00 (*1-884083-94-3*) Maval Pub.

Preparation for the GRE: Graduate Records Examinations, Bklet. 4. Mauricio Waintrub et al. 60p. 1997. pap. 10.00 (*1-884083-91-9*) Maval Pub.

Preparation for the GRE Test: Graduate Records Examinations, Vol. 1. Mauricio Waintrub et al. (Illus.). 70p. (Orig.). 1997. pap. text 10.00 (*1-884083-92-7*) Maval Pub.

Preparation for the Hereafter. Muhammad Imram. 155p. (Orig.). 1987. pap. 5.50 (*1-56744-357-5*) Kazi Pubns.

Preparation for the Landing. Ruth E. Norman. (Illus.). 493p. 1987. 22.00 (*0-935097-07-4*) Unarius Acad Sci.

Preparation for the Law School Admission Test: LSAT. Edward C. Gruber & Gary R. Gruber. (Exam Preparation Ser.). 1982. pap. 8.95 (*0-685-03403-8*, Arco) Macmillan Gen Ref.

Preparation for the MCAT: The Medical College Admission Test, Bklet. B. Northwestern Learning Center Staff. 80p. 1997. pap. 15,00 (*1-884083-97-8*) Maval Pub.

Preparation for the MCAT Test: The Medical College Admission Test, Booklet A. Johan Eptekar & Northwestern Learning Center Staff. (Illus.). 100p. 1997. pap. text 15.00 (*1-884083-95-1*) Maval Pub.

Preparation for the S. A. T. Mathematics Examination. 2nd ed. Daniel J. Svenconis. 254p. (Orig.). (gr. 10-12). 1978. pap. 12.95 (*0-930124-02-2*) Transemantics.

Preparation for the S. A. T. Verbal Examination. 2nd ed. Daniel J. Svenconis. 400p. (Orig.). (gr. 10-12). 1981. pap. 12.95 (*0-930124-03-0*) Transemantics.

Preparation for the SAT. 12th ed. 1995. pap. 29.95 incl. disk (*0-671-89964-3*) PB.

Preparation for the SAT. 12th ed. Deptula. 1995. pap. 12.00 (*0-671-89962-7*) PB.

Preparation for the SAT & PSAT. 12th ed. Ed. by Edward J. Deptula. 640p. 1995. 12.95 (*0-02-860323-0*, Arco) Macmillan Gen Ref.

Preparation for the SAT & PSAT. 12th ed. Ed. by Edward J. Deptula. 640p. 1995. 22.95 incl. disk (*0-02-860324-9*, Arco) Macmillan Gen Ref.

Preparation for the Study of Medicine: Proceedings. Conference on the Optimal Preparation for the Stud. Ed. by Robert G. Page & Mary H. Littlemeyer. LC 69-19280. 295p. reprint ed. pap. 91.50 (*0-608-12087-1*, 202412300035) Bks Demand.

Preparation for the Toddler Years: The Next Step. Gary Ezzo & Anne M. Ezzo. (Illus.). 118p. 1994. student ed. 25.00 (*1-883035-19-8*) Grow Families.

Preparation for the TOEFL. 7th ed. Grace Y. Qiu Zhong & Patricia N. Sullivan. 416p. 1995. 12.95 (*0-02-860563-2*, Arco) Macmillan Gen Ref.

Preparation for the TOEFL. 7th ed. Grace Y. Qiu Zhong & Patricia N. Sullivan. 416p. 1995. 29.95 incl. audio (*0-02-860564-0*, Arco) Macmillan Gen Ref.

Preparation for the TOEFL: Test of English As a Foreign Language. 8th ed. Grace Y. Zhong & Patricia N. Sullivan. 448p. 1997. 12.95 (*0-02-861785-1*, Arco) Macmillan Gen Ref.

Preparation for the TOEFL: Test of English As a Foreign Language. 8th ed. Grace Y. Zhong & Patricia N. Sullivan. 448p. 1997. pap. 29.95 incl. audio (*0-02-861784-3*, Arco) Macmillan Gen Ref.

Preparation for the TOEFL: Test of English As a Foreign Language, Bklet. 2. George Luder. 60p. (Orig.). 1996. pap. 15.00 incl. audio (*1-884083-33-1*) Maval Pub.

Preparation for the TOEFL: Test of English As a Foreign Language, Bklet. 3. George Luder. 60p. (Orig.). 1996. pap. 15.00 incl. audio (*1-884083-35-8*) Maval Pub.

Preparation for the TOEFL: The Ultimate TOEFL Study Program. 7th ed. Patricia N. Sullivan & Grace Y. Zhong. LC 97-162356. 424p. 1996. pap. 34.95 incl. cd-rom (*0-02-861268-X*, Arco) Macmillan Gen Ref.

Preparation for the United States Medical Licensing Examinations, Bk. 6. Mauricio W. Waintrub & Medical Education Board Staff. 160p. (C). 1995. pap. 25.00 (*1-884083-56-0*) Maval Pub.

Preparation for the United States Medical Licensing Examinations, Step 1, Bk. F. Medical Education Board. (USMLE Ser.). (Illus.). 150p. (C). 1997. 18.00 (*1-884083-08-0*) Maval Pub.

Preparation for the United States Medical Licensing Examinations, Step 1, Bklt. C. Mauricio L. Waintrub & Medical Education Board Staff. 76p. (C). 1998. lib. bdg., student ed. 15.00 (*1-884708-15-3*) Maval Pub.

Preparation for the United States Medical Licensing Examinations, Step 1, Bklt. C. Hobart Walling et al. (USMLE Ser.). (Illus.). 27p. (C). 1998. student ed. 18.00 (*1-884083-21-8*) Maval Pub.

Preparation for the United States Medical Licensing Examinations, Step 1, Bklt. D/E. 4th ed. Mauricio L. Waintrub et al. (USMLE Ser.). (Illus.). 76p. (C). 1998. pap. text 15.00 (*1-884083-16-1*) Maval Pub.

Preparation for the United States Medical Licensing Examinations, Step 1, Bklt. A. 4th ed. Valentin Waintrub & Maria Luder. Ed. by Mauricio L. Waintrub & Maval Medical Education Staff. (USMLE Ser.). (Illus.). 76p. (C). 1998. pap. text 15.00 (*1-884083-13-7*) Maval Pub.

Preparation for the United States Medical Licensing Examinations, Step 1, Bklt. B. 4th ed. Mauricio L. Waintrub et al. (USMLE Ser.). (Illus.). 76p. (C). 1998. pap. text, student ed. 15.00 (*1-884083-14-5*) Maval Pub.

Preparation for the United States Medical Licensing Examinations, Step 2, Bklt. 2. 3rd ed. Mauricio W. Waintrub & Medical Education Board Staff. 76p. (C). 1995. pap. 15.00 (*1-884083-58-7*) Maval Pub.

Preparation for the United States Medical Licensing Examinations, Step 2, Bklt. 3. 3rd ed. Mauricio W. Waintrub & Medical Education Board Staff. 76p. (C). 1995. pap. 15.00 (*1-884083-59-5*) Maval Pub.

Preparation for the United States Medical Licensing Examinations, Step 2, Bklt. 4/5. 3rd ed. Mauricio W. Waintrub & Medical Education Board Staff. 60p. (C). 1995. pap. 15.00 (*1-884083-60-9*) Maval Pub.

Preparation for the United States Medical Licensing Examinations, Step 3, Bklet. C. 3rd ed. Mauricio L. Waintrub & Medical Education Board Staff. 76p. (C). 1995. lib. bdg. 15.00 (*1-884083-81-1*) Maval Pub.

Preparation for the United States Medical Licensing Examinations, Step 3, Bklt. C. 3rd ed. Mauricio L. Waintrub & Medical Education Board. 76p. (C). 1995. lib. bdg. 15.00 (*1-884083-83-8*) Maval Pub.

Preparation for the United States Medical Licensing Examinations, Step 3, Bklt. A. 3rd ed. Mauricio L. Waintrub & Medical Education Board. 76p. (C). 1995. lib. bdg. 15.00 (*1-884083-80-3*) Maval Pub.

Preparation for the United States Medical Licensing Examinations: English Test 1, Booklet 1. 2nd ed. Mauricio W. Waintrub. 44p. (C). 1997. pap. 15.00 incl. audio (*1-884083-28-5*) Maval Pub.

Preparation for the United States Medical Licensing Examinations: English Test 2, Booklet 2. 2nd ed. Mauricio W. Waintrub. 44p. (C). 1997. pap. 15.00 incl. audio (*1-884083-29-3*) Maval Pub.

Preparation for the United States Medical Licensing Examinations: English Test 3, Bklet. 3. 2nd ed. Mauricio L. Waintrub. 44p. (C). 1997. pap. 15.00 incl. audio (*1-884083-30-7*) Maval Pub.

Preparation for the USMLE: Step 1 Booklet C, Booklet C. 4th ed. Mauricio L. Waintrub et al. (USMLE Ser.). 76p. (C). 1998. pap. text 15.00 (*1-884083-15-3*) Maval Pub.

Preparation for Total Consecration. 1958. pap. 3.00 (*0-910984-10-7*) Montfort Pubns.

Preparation for Translation, Ver. 3. rev. ed. Milton G. Crane. LC 88-50091. 229p. 1992. pap. 7.95 (*0-945383-33-9*, 945-5818) Teach Servs.

Preparation for Work. Elliott Medrich. 22p. 1997. pap. 4.00 (*0-16-048970-9*) USGPO.

Preparation Guide for the ASE Compressed Natural Gas Vehicle Test. Texas State Technical College Staff. Ed. by Robert W. Gentry. LC 95-49556. 112p. 1996. pap. 22.95 (*0-8273-7791-6*) Delmar.

Preparation Guide for the ASE Parts Specialist Test P-2. Texas State Technical College, EDIT Department Sta & Norris Martin. Ed. by Robert W. Gentry. LC 95-40817. (Automotive Technology Ser.). 112p. 1995. mass mkt., student ed. 21.95 (*0-8273-7552-2*) Delmar.

Preparation Guide to Form 990, 990-T & 990-PF. Michael J. Tucker. 464p. 1995. pap. text 65.00 (*0-7811-0110-7*) Res Inst Am.

Preparation of a Product Liability Case. Scott Baldwin et al. 1054p. 1981. 80.00 (*0-316-07925-1*, Aspen Law & Bus) Aspen Pub.

Preparation of a Product Liability Case. 2nd ed. Scott Baldwin & Frances E. McGovern. 1066p. boxed set 125.00 (*0-316-07973-1*, 79731) Aspen Law.

Preparation of a Product Liability Case. 2nd ed. Scott Baldwin et al. 1072p. 1992. 125.00 (*0-316-07962-6*, Aspen Law & Bus) Aspen Pub.

Preparation of a Product Liability Case, 1. 3rd ed. Scott Baldwin et al. LC 98-20960. 1066p. 1998. ring bd. 145.00 (*0-7355-0145-9*) Panel Pubs.

Preparation of Alkenes: A Practical Approach. Ed. by Johnathan M. Williams. (The Practical Approach in Chemistry Ser.). (Illus.). 268p. 1996. spiral bd. 55.00 (*0-19-855794-9*) OUP.

Preparation of Alkenes: A Practical Approach. Ed. by Johnathan M. Williams. (The Practical Approach in Chemistry Ser.). (Illus.). 268p. (C). 1996. text 115.00 (*0-19-855795-7*) OUP.

Preparation of Aluminum Hydroxides & Aluminas. Taicho Sato. (Illus.). 1997. 79.95 (*0-937557-12-9*) Litarvan Lit.

Preparation of Annual Disclosure Documents under the New Proxy Rules, 1993, 2 vols. (Corporate Law & Practice Course Handbook, 1985-86 Ser.). 1248p. 1993. 90.00 (*0-685-65503-2*, B4-7029) PLI.

Preparation of Annual Disclosure Documents, 1990. (Corporate Law & Practice Course Handbook, 1985-86 Ser.). 878p. 1990. 17.50 (*0-685-69477-1*) PLI.

Preparation of Annual Disclosure Documents, 1995, 2 vols., Set. (Corporate Law & Practice Course Handbook, 1994-95 Ser.). 1416p. 1995. pap. 149.00 (*0-685-56892-X*, B4-7079) PLI.

Preparation of Annual Disclosure Documents, 1996, 2 vols., Set. (Corporate Law & Practice Course Handbook, 1985-86 Ser.). Date not set. pap. 149.00 (*0-614-17201-2*, B4-7118) PLI.

Preparation of Biological Specimens for Scanning Electron Microscopy. Judith A. Murphy. Ed. by Godfried M. Roomans. (Illus.). 352p. (Orig.). (C). 1984. pap. text 32.00 (*0-931288-33-9*) Scanning Microscopy.

Preparation of Calibration Procedures: RP-3. Product Design Special Committee Staff. (NCSL Recommended Practices Ser.). 1990. 15.00 (*0-614-18742-7*) Natl Conf Stds Labs.

Preparation of Catalysts No. 5: Scientific Basis for the Preparation of Heterogeneous Catalysts: Proceedings of the 5th International Symposium, Louvain-la-Neuve, Sept. 3-6, 1990. Ed. by G. Poncelet et al. (Studies in Surface Science & Catalysis: No. 63). 748p. 1991. 305.00 (*0-444-88616-8*) Elsevier.

Preparation of Catalysts VII. Ed. by B. Delman et al. 1006p. 1998. 431.00 (*0-444-50031-6*, Excerpta Medica) Elsevier.

Preparation of Catalysts VI: Scientific Bases for the Preparation of Catalysts. Ed. by J. A. Martens et al. (Studies in Surface Science & Catalysis: Vol. 91). 1204p. 1995. 389.50 (*0-444-82078-7*) Elsevier.

Preparation of Dispersions in Liquids. Ed. by H. N. Stein. (Surfactant Science Ser.: Vol. 58). (Illus.). 264p. 1995. text 145.00 (*0-8247-9674-8*) Dekker.

Preparation of Esters. Conrad L. Stanitski. (Modular Laboratory Program in Chemistry Ser.). 12p. (C). 1995. pap. text 1.50 (*0-87540-470-7*, SYNT 470-7) Chem Educ Res.

***Preparation of Fire Hazard analyses for Nuclear Power Plants.** International Atomic Energy Agency. (Safety Report Ser.). 64p. 1998. pap. 30.00 (*92-0-102798-2*, Pub. by IAEA) Bernan Associates.

Preparation of Foreign Language Teachers see Culture, Literature, & Articulation

Preparation of Formula for Infants: Guidelines for Health Care Facilities. American Dietetic Association Staff et al. LC 91-26127. 1991. pap. 10.95 (*0-88091-089-5*, 0164) Am Dietetic Assn.

Preparation of Inexpensive Teaching Materials. 3rd ed. Leonard J. Espinosa & John E. Morlan. 1988. pap. 18.99 (*0-8224-5606-0*) Fearon Teacher Aids.

Preparation of Nucleoside Phosphorothioates, Phosphorodithioates & Related Compounds, Vol. 11. Otto Dahl. (Sulfur Reports). 209p. 1991. pap. text 338.00 (*3-7186-5236-6*, Harwood Acad Pubs) Gordon & Breach.

Preparation of Professional Evaluators: Issues, Perspectives, & Programs. Ed. by James W. Altschuld & Molly Engle. LC 85-644749. (New Directions for Evaluation Ser.: No. PE 62). 97p. (Orig.). 1994. pap. 22.00 (*0-7879-9968-7*) Jossey-Bass.

Preparation of Programs for An Electronic Digital Computer: With Special Reference to the Edsac & the Use of A Library of Subroutines M. V. Wilkes et al. LC 82-50766. (Charles Babbage Institute Reprint Series for the History of Computing). xxxi, 167p. 1982. write for info. (*0-938228-03-X*) Tomash Pubs.

Preparation of Scientific Papers for Written or Oral Presentation. (National Information Standards Ser.). 1979. reprint ed. 12.00 (*0-88738-985-6*, Z39.16) Transaction Pubs.

***Preparation of Solid Catalysis.** Ed. by Gerhardx Ertl et al. 622p. 1999. 210.00 (*3-527-29826-6*) Wiley.

Preparation of Specifications: RP-5. Calibration Interval Committee. (RP Ser.: No. 5). (Illus.). 6p. 1980. reprint ed. 15.00 (*1-58464-013-8*) Natl Conf Stds Labs.

Preparation of Strontium Iodate Monohydrate. M. Royer et al. Ed. by H. Anthony Neidig. (Modular Laboratory Program in Chemistry Ser.). 12p. (C). 1988. pap. text 1.50 (*0-87540-347-6*, SYNT 347-6) Chem Educ Res.

Preparation of Teachers of Brain-Injured Children. William M. Cruickshank et al. LC 68-31430. (Syracuse University: Special Education & Rehabilitation Monograph Ser.: No. 8). (Illus.). 223p. reprint ed. pap. 69.20 (*0-8357-3988-0*, 203668600005) Bks Demand.

***Preparation of Teachers of Students with Emotional/Behavioral Disorders.** Lyndal M. Bullock et al. 122p. 1998. pap. 19.95 (*0-86586-321-0*) Coun Exc Child.

Preparation of the Case. David B. Baum. (Art of Advocacy Ser.). 1981. 160.00 (*0-8205-1038-6*) Bender.

Preparation of the Fiduciary Income Tax Return, 1989. (Tax Law & Estate Planning Ser.). 673p. 1989. 17.50 (*0-317-99794-7*, D4-5208) PLI.

P

Preparation of Thin Films. Ed. by Joy George. (Illus.). 392p. 1992. text 185.00 (*0-8247-8196-1*) Dekker.

Preparation Techniques for the Failure Analysis of Integrated Circuits. Friedrich Beck. LC 97-11255. (Wiley Series in Quality & Reliability Engineering). 190p. 1998. 115.00 (*0-471-97401-3*) Wiley.

Preparation to Care: A Foundation NVQ Text for Health Care Assistants. Ed. by Aileen Richardson. (Illus.). 246p. 1995. pap. write for info. (*0-7020-1793-0*, Pub. by W B Saunders) Saunders.

Preparation to Deathe: A Boke As Devout As Eloquent. Desiderius Erasmus. LC 74-28852. (English Experience Ser.: No. 733). 1975. reprint ed. 20.00 (*90-221-0733-7*) Walter J Johnson.

Preparations for Flight & Other Swedish Stories. Ed. by Robin Fulton. 176p. (Orig.). 1990. pap. 19.95 (*0-948259-66-3*) Dufour.

Preparations for the November 12, 1995 Elections to the Milli Mejlis & Constitutional Referendum in the Republic of Azerbzijan: Initial Recommendations & Conclusions, September, 1995. Linda V. Edgeworth & Scott B. Lansell. ii, 50p. 1996. pap. text 7.00 (*1-879720-06-X*) Intl Fndt Elect.

Preparative Acetylenic Chemistry. 2nd ed. L. Brandsma. (Studies in Organic Chemistry: No. 34). x,322p. 1988. 210.50 (*0-444-42960-3*) Elsevier.

Preparative & Production Scale Chromatography. Ed. by G. Ganetsos & P. E. Barker. LC 92-24391. (Chromatographic Science Ser.: Vol. 61). (Illus.). 816p. 1992. text 250.00 (*0-8247-8738-2*) Dekker.

Preparative Centrifugation: A Practical Approach. David Rickwood. (Practical Approach Ser.: Vol. 113). (Illus.). 420p. 1993. pap. 55.00 (*0-19-963211-1*) OUP.

Preparative Centrifugation: A Practical Approach. Ed. by David Rickwood. (Practical Approach Ser.: Vol. 113). (Illus.). 420p. 1993. 95.00 (*0-19-963208-1*) OUP.

Preparative Chromatography Techniques. K. Hostettmann et al. (Illus.). 150p. 1986. 83.00 (*0-387-16165-1*) Spr-Verlag.

Preparative Chromatography Techniques: Applications in Natural Product Isolation. 2nd enl. rev. ed. K. Hostettmann et al. LC 98-116711. (Illus.). 200p. 1997. 129.00 (*3-540-62459-7*) Spr-Verlag.

Preparative Gel Chromatography on Sephadex Lh-20. Hans Henke. Tr. by Anthony J. Rackstraw. 1998. 130.00 (*3-527-29706-5*) Wiley.

Preparative Liquid Chromatography. B. A. Bidingmeyer. (Journal of Chromatography Library: Vol. 38). xiv,342p. 1987. 201.50 (*0-444-42832-1*) Elsevier.

Preparative Liquid Chromatography. Brian A. Bidlingmeyer. (Journal of Chromatography Library: Vol. 38). 1988. 193.75 (*0-318-32589-6*) Elsevier.

Preparative Polar Organometallic Chemistry, Vol. 1. L. Brandsma & H. D. Verkruijsse. 240p. 1987. 69.95 (*0-387-16916-4*) Spr-Verlag.

Preparative Polar Organometallic Chemistry, Vol. 2. L. Brandsma. (Illus.). xii, 227p. 1991. 69.95 (*0-387-52749-4*) Spr-Verlag.

Preparative-Scale Chromatography. Eli Grushka. (Chromatographic Science Ser.: Vol. 46). (Illus.). 344p. 1988. text 170.00 (*0-8247-8061-2*) Dekker.

Preparative to Mariage: Whereunto Is Annexed a Treatise of the Lords Supper, & Another of Usurie. Henry Smith. LC 74-28885. (English Experience Ser.: No. 762). 1975. reprint ed. 25.00 (*90-221-0762-0*) Walter J Johnson.

Preparativos para la Crucifixion-bL-Alumno. Gary Teja. (SPA.). 1990. pap. 1.00 (*1-55955-044-9*) CRC Wrld Lit.

Preparativos para la Crucifixion-bL-Maestro. Gary Teja. (SPA.). 1990. pap. 1.00 (*1-55955-045-7*) CRC Wrld Lit.

Preparativos para la Crucifixion-C-Alumno. Gary Teja. (SPA.). 1990. pap. 1.00 (*1-55955-040-6*) CRC Wrld Lit.

Preparativos para la Crucifixion-C-Maestro. Gary Teja. (SPA.). 1990. pap. 1.00 (*1-55955-041-4*) CRC Wrld Lit.

Preparativos para la Crucifixion-Db-Alumno. Gary Teja. (SPA.). 1990. pap. 1.00 (*1-55955-042-2*) CRC Wrld Lit.

Preparativos para la Crucifixion-Db-Maestro. Gary Teja. (SPA.). 1990. pap. 1.00 (*1-55955-043-0*) CRC Wrld Lit.

Preparator's Guide to Biology. Mccourt. 1988. 12.18 (*0-07-553862-8*) McGraw.

Preparatory Chemistry: Instructor's Solutions Manual. Ed. by Timberlake. (C). 1999. pap. text. write for info. (*0-321-40088-7*) Addison-Wesley.

Preparatory Chemistry Lab Studies. Rebecca Williams. 136p. (C). 1998. pap. text 27.95 (*0-7872-4749-9*, 41474902) Kendall-Hunt.

Preparatory Draft for the Revised Penal Code of Japan 1961. Ed. by B. J. George. (American Series of Foreign Penal Codes: Vol. 8). xiv, 104p. 1964. 20.00 (*0-8377-0028-0*, Rothman) W S Hein.

Preparatory Exercise for Piano, Op. 16. Schmitt. Ed. by Robert Biederman. (Carl Fischer Music Library: No. 15). 1935. pap. 5.00 (*0-8258-0096-X*, L15) Fischer Inc NY.

Preparatory Exercises in Double-Stopping Violin Opus 9. Otakar Sevcik. 24p. 1986. pap. 7.95 (*0-7935-4800-4*) H Leonard.

Preparatory Exercises in Score Reading. Reginald O. Morris & Howard Ferguson. 116p. 1968. 21.95 (*0-19-321475-X*) OUP.

Preparatory Exercises Opus 16: Piano. Abraham Schmitt. 32p. 1986. pap. 3.95 (*0-7935-2557-8*) H Leonard.

Preparatory Guide to Microbiology. Stukus. (C). 1996. pap. text 26.75 (*0-03-018553-X*) Harcourt.

Preparatory Method for Saxophone: Classical Technique, Vol. 1. George Wolfe. 41p. (C). 1986. pap. text 15.00 (*0-939103-01-X*) Roncorp.

Preparatory States & Processes. Ed. by Sylvan Kornblum & Jean Requin. 400p. 1984. text 79.95 (*0-89859-325-5*) L Erlbaum Assocs.

Prepare! A Weekly Worship Planbook for Pastors & Musicians, 1998-1999. David L. Bone & Mary J. Scifres. Orig. Title: Music & Worship Planner. 144p. 1998. pap. 16.95 (*0-687-18999-3*) Abingdon.

***Prepare! A Weekly Worship Planbook for Pastors & Musicians, 1999-2000.** David L. Bone & Mary J. Scifres. 1999. 17.00 (*0-687-07401-0*) Abingdon.

Prepare & Enjoy Creative Dental Retirement. Armen Z. Mesrobian. LC 92-81607. (Illus.). 195p. 1992. spiral bd. 29.95 (*0-9632735-0-7*) EPS Excel Pub.

Prepare & Enjoy Creative Retirement. Armen Z. Mesrobian. LC 93-90246. (Illus.). 202p. (Orig.). 1993. pap. 17.95 (*0-9632735-1-5*) EPS Excel Pub.

Prepare Child to Read & Write. University of Southern Florida Staff. 96p. 1995. pap., per. 8.95 (*0-7872-1248-2*) Kendall-Hunt.

Prepare Curriculum: Teaching Prosocial Competencies. 2nd rev. ed. Arnold P. Goldstein. 910p. 1999. pap. text 39.95 (*0-87822-419-X*) Res Press.

Prepare for Battle! Basic Training in Spiritual Warfare. Neal Pirolo & Yvonne Pirolo. 250p. (Orig.). 1997. pap. 8.95 (*1-880185-06-7*) Emmaus Rd Intl.

Prepare for College. Marjorie Eberts & Margaret Gisler. LC 98-8250. (Here's How Ser.). 256p. 1998. pap. 12.95 (*0-8442-6630-2*, 66302) NTC Contemp Pub Co.

Prepare for Eldercare Pt. 1: An Assessment Manual for Medical Groups, 2 vols. Mary A. Krill. 44p. (Orig.). (C). 1990. pap. 24.00 (*0-933948-27-1*, 2551) Ctr Res Ambulatory.

Prepare for Eldercare Pt. 2: A Community Resource Manual for Medical Groups, 2 vols. Oscar Kurren & Lynette Kurren. 33p. (Orig.). (C). 1990. pap. 24.00 (*0-933948-28-X*, 2551) Ctr Res Ambulatory.

Prepare for Saints: Gertrude Stein, Virgil Thomson & the Mainstreaming of American Modernism. Steven Watson. LC 98-17496. (Illus.). 512p. 1999. 35.00 (*0-679-44139-5*) Random.

***Prepare for Saints: Gertrude Stein, Virgil Thomson & the Mainstreaming of American Modernism.** Steven Watson. LC 99-87188. (Illus.). 371p. 2000. pap. 19.95 (*0-520-22353-5*, Pub. by U CA Pr) Cal Prin Full Svc.

Prepare for Surgery, Heal Faster: A Guide of Mind-Body Techniques. Peggy Huddleston. 276p. 1996. pap. 14.95 (*0-9645757-4-4*) Angel River Pr.

Prepare for the Great Tribulation. 11th ed. John Leary. 1998. pap. text 3.95 (*1-57918-096-5*) Queenship Pub.

Prepare for the Great Tribulation, Vol. 9. John Leary. 1998. pap. 3.95 (*1-57918-073-6*) Queenship Pub.

***Prepare for the Great Tribulation & Era of Peace, Vol. XIV.** John Leary. (Illus.). 108p. 1999. pap. 3.95 (*1-57918-115-5*, 3474) Queenship Pub.

***Prepare for The Great Tribulation & The Era Of Peace, 13.** Queenship Publishing Company Staff & John Leary. 1999. pap. text 3.95 (*1-57918-113-9*) Queenship Pub.

Prepare for the Great Tribulation & the Era of Peace, Vol. I. John Leary. LC 96-68181. 244p. (Orig.). 1996. pap. text 7.95 (*1-882972-69-4*, 3461) Queenship Pub.

Prepare for the Great Tribulation & the Era of Peace, Vol. II. John Leary. LC 96-68181. 348p. (Orig.). 1996. pap. 8.95 (*1-882972-77-5*, 3462) Queenship Pub.

Prepare for the Great Tribulation & the Era of Peace, Vol. III. 2nd ed. John Leary. LC 96-68181. 371p. (Orig.). 1996. pap. 8.95 (*1-882972-72-4*, 3463) Queenship Pub.

Prepare for the Great Tribulation & the Era of Peace, Vol. IV. John Leary. LC 96-68181. (Illus.). 89p. (Orig.). 1996. pap. 3.95 (*1-882972-91-0*, 3464) Queenship Pub.

Prepare for the Great Tribulation & the Era of Peace, Vol. V. John Leary. LC 96-68181. (Illus.). (Orig.). 1997. pap. text 2.95 (*1-882972-97-X*, 3465) Queenship Pub.

Prepare for the Great Tribulation & the Era of Peace, Vol. VI. John Leary. LC 97-68596. (Illus.). 94p. (Orig.). 1997. pap. 2.95 (*1-57918-002-7*, 3466) Queenship Pub.

Prepare for the Great Tribulation & the Era of Peace, Vol. VII. John Leary. (Illus.). 122p. (Orig.). 1997. pap. 2.95 (*1-57918-010-8*, 3467) Queenship Pub.

Prepare for the Great Tribulation & the Era of Peace, Vol. VIII. John Leary. LC 97-68596. (Illus.). 100p. (Orig.). 1997. pap. 3.95 (*1-57918-053-1*, 3468) Queenship Pub.

Prepare for the Great Tribulation & the Era of Peace, Vol. IX. John Leary. LC 95-73237. (Illus.). 152p. (Orig.). 1998. pap. 3.95 (*1-57918-066-3*, 3469) Queenship Pub.

***Prepare for the Great Tribulation & the Era of Peace, Vol. 15.** John Leary. LC 95-73237. (Illus.). 114p. (Orig.). 2000. pap. 3.95 (*1-57918-122-8*) Queenship Pub.

***Prepare for the Great Tribulation & the Era of Peace, Vol. 16.** John Leary. LC 95-73237. (Prepare for the Great Tribulation Ser.). (Illus.). 119p. (Orig.). 2000. pap. text 3.95 (*1-57918-126-0*) Queenship Pub.

Prepare for the Job Search Module, Connections: School & Work Transitions - Work Skills-Job Search Skills. National Center for Research in Vocational Educati. 1987. write for info. (*0-318-67183-2*, SP100CB02) Ctr Educ Trng Employ.

Prepare for the Texas Real Estate Exam. 6th ed. Johnnie L. Rosenauer et al. LC 97-21407. 232p. (C). 1997. pap. text 20.40 (*0-13-636416-0*) P-H.

Prepare for the Winds of Change II. 3rd rev. ed. Nita Johnson. Ed. by Ricci Wilson & Edwina Fitzgerald. 192p. 1991. pap. 9.95 (*0-9656528-0-7*) Eagles Nest NE.

Prepare for War see Preparemonos para la Guerra

Prepare for War. Rebecca Brown. LC 97-36659. 336p. 1992. pap. 12.99 (*0-88368-324-5*) Whitaker Hse.

***Prepare Him Room: Advent for Busy Christians.** Mary E. Latela. LC 98-75662. 64p. 1999. pap. 5.95 (*0-7648-0397-2*) Liguori Pubns.

Prepare My People. Vincent M. Walsh. 100p. (Orig.). (YA). 1986. pap. text 5.00 (*0-943374-13-8*) Key of David.

Prepare the Bait: Workbook 3. Robert D. Noble. (Reach Out Ser.). 64p. (Orig.). 1987. 10.00 (*0-944687-08-3*) Gather Family Inst.

***Prepare the Way.** Morningstar. 1998. audio 10.99 (*7-5124-0169-8*) Destiny Image.

Prepare the Way: Daily Meditations for Advent & Lent. R. Mark Liebenow. LC 99-41004. 144p. 1999. pap. 15.95 (*0-8298-1351-9*) Pilgrim OH.

***Prepare the Way: Songs from the Heart of David Worship & Warfare.** Heart of David. 1998. pap. 15.99 (*7-5124-0162-0*) Morningstar Pr.

Prepare the Way: Twelve Spiritual Signposts for the New Millennium. Robert Stearns. LC 99-26043. 228p. 1999. pap. 12.99 (*0-88419-630-5*) Creation House.

Prepare the Way of the Lord: Reflections on the Advent Season. Richard E. Gribble. LC 96-10672. 106p. (Orig.). 1996. pap. 10.50 (*0-7880-0850-1*) CSS OH.

Prepare to Be Healed: Gaining Emotional & Spiritual Independence. Milly Day & Richard N. Holzapfel. LC 95-76714. 1995. 11.95 (*0-88494-988-5*) Bookcraft Inc.

Prepare to Prosper. Joyce Meyer. 64p. 1997. pap. text 1.50 (*0-89274-996-2*) Harrison Hse.

Prepare to Win. John P. Troup. 300p. (Orig.). (C). 1991. pap. text 20.00 (*1-879160-01-3*) US Swimming Pr.

Prepare to Win. Carroll Smith. (Carroll Smith's "to Win" Ser.: Vol. 1). (Illus.). 174p. (Orig.). (YA). 1975. reprint ed. pap. 19.95 (*0-9651600-1-7*) C Smith Cnslting.

***Prepare Today-Survive Tomorrow!** rev. ed. Joe Harold. LC 83-82241. 182p. 1999. 14.98 (*0-88290-661-5*) Horizon Utah.

Prepare with Honor: A Guide for Future Missionaries. Randy L. Bott. LC 95-35451. (Orig.). (YA). (gr. 7-12). 1995. pap. 10.95 (*0-87579-954-X*) Deseret Bk.

Prepare Ye: For a New Advent of God's Love in Our World. John Carr & Adrienne Carr. 1991. pap., teacher ed. 7.00 (*0-8358-0628-6*) Upper Room Bks.

Prepare Ye Participants Notebook: For a New Advent of God's Love in Our World. John Carr & Adrienne Carr. 1991. pap., student ed. 5.00 (*0-8358-0629-4*) Upper Room Bks.

Prepare Ye, Prepare Ye. 1994. 15.00 (*0-941227-04-9*) Cosmic Pr Chico.

Prepare Year for New Advent. Carr. 1991. pap. 6.95 (*0-687-60010-3*); pap. 4.95 (*0-687-60011-1*) Abingdon.

Prepare Your Church for the Future. Carl F. George. LC 91-3827. (Illus.). 240p. 1990. pap. 10.99 (*0-8007-5365-8*) Revell.

***Prepare Your Curriculum Vitae.** Acy L. Jackson. LC 98-8248. (Here's How Ser.). 192p. 1998. pap. 15.95 (*0-8442-6631-0*, 66310) NTC Contemp Pub Co.

***Prepare Your Image for a Professional Promotion.** deluxe ed. Isha Eefa. 50p. (C). 1999. 12.00 (*1-929300-06-9*) Just Friends Prod.

Prepare Your Own Last Will & Testament - Without a Lawyer see Prepare Your Own Will: The National Will Kit

Prepare Your Own Will: The National Will Kit. 4th ed. Daniel Sitarz. LC 94-1325. (Legal Self-Help Ser.). Orig. Title: Prepare Your Own Last Will & Testament - Without a Lawyer. 246p. 1994. pap. 15.95 (*0-935755-12-8*) Nova Pub IL.

Prepare Your Own Will: The National Will Kit. 4th ed. Daniel Sitarz. LC 94-1325. (Legal Self-Help Ser.). Orig. Title: Prepare Your Own Last Will & Testament - Without a Lawyer. 246p. 1996. pap. 27.95 incl. disk (*0-935755-24-1*) Nova Pub IL.

***Prepare Your Own Will: The National Will Kit.** 5th rev. ed. Daniel Sitarz. (Legal Self-Help Ser.). Orig. Title: Prepare Your Own Last Will & Testament - Without a Lawyer. 2000. per. 27.95 incl. audio compact disk (*0-935755-73-X*) Nova Pub IL.

***Prepare Your Own Will: The National Will Kit.** 5th rev. expanded ed. Daniel Sitarz. (Legal Self-Help Ser.). Orig. Title: Prepare Your Own Last Will & Testament - Without a Lawyer. 2000. pap. 17.95 (*0-935755-72-1*) Nova Pub IL.

***Prepare Your Taxes in a Weekend.** Diane Tinney. 1999. pap. 19.99 (*0-7615-2304-9*) Random.

Prepare Your Taxes with Turbo Tax in a Weekend. Diane Tinney. LC 98-68115. (In a Weekend Ser.). 350p. 1998. pap. 19.99 (*0-7615-1965-3*) Prima Pub.

Prepared Childbirth - The Family Way. 6th rev. ed. Debby Amis & Jeanne Green. 1998. 5.00 (*0-9662875-0-9*) Family Way Pubns.

Prepared for Battle: A Guide for the Christian Journey. Charles E. Cravey. (Illus.). 48p. (Orig.). 1988. pap. 4.95 (*0-938645-01-3*) In His Steps.

Prepared for Life? How to Measure Cross-Curricular Competencies. Jules L. Peschar & Siteske Waslander. LC 97-181101. 196p. (Orig.). 1997. pap. 20.00 (*92-64-05259-3*, 96-97-01-3, Pub. by Org for Econ) OECD.

Prepared for Us to Walk In. All Saints' Church Members & Morton S. Jaffe. (Illus.). xvii, 168p. (Orig.). 1986. lib. bdg. 25.00 (*0-9617365-0-X*) M S Jaffe.

Prepared Frozen Foods. Ed. by Peter Allen. 232p. 1987. pap. 1250.00 (*0-941285-05-7*) FIND-SVP.

Prepared Takeout Foods. 300p. 1988. pap. 1295.00 (*0-941285-24-3*) FIND-SVP.

Prepared Tests. 4th ed. Barker. (C). 1995. pap. text, teacher ed. 37.50 (*0-03-010264-2*, Pub. by Harcourt Coll Pubs) Harcourt.

Prepared Tests & Printed. 4th ed. Barker. (C). 1995. pap. text 35.50 (*0-03-010269-3*, Pub. by Harcourt Coll Pubs) Harcourt.

Prepared Tests Statistics. Anthony A. Salvia. (C). 1994. pap. text. write for info. (*0-03-053208-6*) Harcourt Coll Pubs.

Prepared to Answer. 2nd ed. Gordon Ferguson. 232p. 1998. pap. 12.99 (*1-57782-070-3*) Discipleshp.

Prepared to Answer Workbook. Gordon Ferguson. 31p. 1995. pap., wbk. ed. 3.99 (*1-884553-62-1*) Discipleshp.

Prepared to Endure: Nine Essentials for Missionary Success. Harold E. Amstutz. 150p. (Orig.). 1987. pap. text 8.95 (*1-888796-05-7*) ABWE Pubng.

Preparedness & Response in Radiation Accidents. 1986. lib. bdg. 175.00 (*0-8490-3500-7*) Gordon Pr.

Preparedness for Epidemics & Bioterrorism: Hearing Before a Subcommittee of the Committee on Appropriations, United States Senate, One Hundred Fifth Congress, Second Session, Special Hearing. USGPO Staff. LC 98-214957. (S. Hrg. Ser.). iii, 61 p. 1998. write for info. (*0-16-057529-X*) USGPO.

Preparemonos Para la Adolescencia. James Dobson.Tr. of Preparing for Adolescence. 192p. 1981. 8.99 (*0-88113-253-5*) Caribe Betania.

Preparemonos para la Guerra. Rebecca Brown. LC 97-44282.Tr. of Prepare for War. (SPA.). 328p. 1992. pap. 11.99 (*0-88368-321-0*) Whitaker Hse.

Preparen a Mi Pueblo. Vincent M. Walsh. 122p. 1986. pap. 5.00 (*0-943374-18-9*) Key of David.

Preparense para el Matrimonio. Jerry D. Hardin & Dianne C. Slone.Tr. of Getting Ready for Marriage. (SPA.). 272p. 1996. 10.99 (*0-88113-139-3*, B001-1393) Caribe Betania.

Preparer & Reussir le TOEFL. Suzette Marko-Geenen & Carleen Caillat. (FRE.). 158p. 1993. pap. 49.95 (*0-7859-1003-4*, 2708115367) Fr & Eur.

Preparese Para Evangelizar - Un Programa de Evangelizacion Personal: Training for Evangelism - A Program for Personal Evangelism. Richard Sisson et al. Tr. by David Powell & Esteban Ditmore. (SPA.). 224p. (Orig.). 1984. pap. 10.99 (*0-311-13839-X*) Casa Bautista.

Preparing a Business Plan. 83p. 1994. 24.95 (*0-644-32566-6*, Pub. by Aust Gov Pub) Accents Pubns.

Preparing a Business Plan for a Small-Scale Recycling Related Venture. Michael Lewis. 8p. 1994. 6.00 (*0-614-18037-6*) Inst Local Self Re.

Preparing a Commercial Credit Information Policy. 2nd ed. Ed. by Joan H. Behr. LC 89-13522. 156p. 1989. 64.00 (*0-936742-70-4*, 32091) Robt Morris Assocs.

Preparing a Drug Information Response: Module 3. Kimberly A. Galt et al. (Clincial Skills Program Drug Information Ser.). (C). 1995. 50.00 (*1-879907-55-0*) Am Soc Hlth-Syst.

***Preparing a Nation's Teachers: Models for English & Foreign Language Programs.** Ed. by Phyllis Franklin et al. LC 99-22216. xiv, 422p. 1999. pap. 22.00 (*0-87352-374-1*) Modern Lang.

Preparing a Successful Business Plan. 3rd ed. Rodger Touchie. 152p. 1998. 15.95 (*1-55180-177-9*) Self-Counsel Pr.

Preparing a Winning Business Plan. Keith W. Schilit. 1990. text 55.00 (*0-13-701301-9*) P-H.

***Preparing a Winning Business Plan: How to Plan to Succeed & Secure Financial Banking.** 3rd ed. Matthew Record. (Business & Management Ser.). (Illus.). 160p. 2000. pap. 19.95 (*1-85703-542-9*, Pub. by How To Bks) Trans-Atl Phila.

Preparing Adolescents for Life After Foster Care: The Central Role of Foster Parents. Ed. by Anthony N. Maluccio et al. 1990. pap. 24.95 (*0-87868-433-6*, 3526) Child Welfare.

Preparing Adolescents for the Twenty-First Century: Challenges Facing Europe & the United States. Ed. by Ruby Takanishi & David A. Hamburg. (Illus.). 266p. (C). 1997. text 39.95 (*0-521-57065-4*) Cambridge U Pr.

***Preparing Africa for the Twenty-First Century: Strategies for Peaceful Coexistence & Sustainable Development.** John M. Mbaku. LC 99-72656. 357p. 1999. 78.95 (*0-7546-1085-3*) Ashgate Pub Co.

***Preparing Americans for Retirement: The Roadblock to Increased Savings: Congressional Hearing.** Ed. by Charles E. Grassley. (Illus.). 125p. (C). 1999. reprint ed. pap. text 25.00 (*0-7881-8451-2*) DIANE Pub.

***Preparing America's Foreign Policy for the Twenty-First Century.** David L. Boren. LC 98-43713. 1999. 24.95 (*0-8061-3123-3*) U of Okla Pr.

***Preparing America's Foreign Policy for the Twenty-First Century.** Ed. by David L. Boren & Edward J. Perkins. 448p. 2000. pap. 19.95 (*0-8061-3271-X*) U of Okla Pr.

Preparing America's Teachers. Ed. by Donald R. Cruickshank. LC 96-68562. 150p. 1996. pap. 11.50 (*0-87367-486-3*) Phi Delta Kappa.

Preparing & Conducting Administrative Hearings. 61p. 1983. pap. 5.75 (*0-317-03748-X*, 36,181) NCLS Inc.

Preparing & Cooking Alabama's Wild Game. Mike Bolton. (Illus.). 160p. (Orig.). 1992. pap. 10.00 (*1-878561-07-3*) Seacoast AL.

***Preparing & Delivering Effective Technical Presentations.** 2nd ed. David L. Adamy. 297p. 2000. write for info. (*1-58053-017-6*) Artech Hse.

Preparing & Directing a Teacher Institute. Cheryl Mason. 32p. 1993. pap. text 6.50 (*0-87355-116-8*) Natl Sci Tchrs.

Preparing & Evaluating Liturgy. Bernadette Gasslein. (Preparing for Liturgy Ser.). 48p. 1997. pap. 3.95 (*0-8146-2444-8*) Liturgical Pr.

Preparing & Handling Industrial Tribunals. R. Pettinger. 1996. pap. 129.00 (*1-85953-070-2*, Pub. by Tech Comm) St Mut.

Preparing & Handling Industrial Tribunals. Richard Pettinger. (Financial Times Management Briefings Ser.). 1997. pap. 94.50 (*0-273-63191-8*, Pub. by F T P-H) Trans-Atl Phila.

Preparing & Producing Business Documents. Learning Business Staff. 1997. 32.95 (*0-7506-3158-9*) Buttrwrth-Heinemann.

Preparing & Protecting the Saints in the Last Days: Words from the Prophets to Inspire & Warn. Compiled by Arlene K. Butler. 1997. pap. 19.95 (*0-9660284-1-4*) Nelson Bk.

P

An Asterisk (*) at the beginning of an entry indicates that the title is appearing for the first time.

Preparing & Proving Survey Research in Trademark Litigation. Robert C. Sorensen. 78p. 1990. pap. 30.00 (*0-614-29591-2*) Intl Trademark.

Preparing & Studying Oxygen & Some of Its Compounds. Grover W. Everett, Jr. (Modular Laboratory Program in Chemistry Ser.). 11p. (C). 1992. pap. text 1.50 (*0-87540-413-8*, REAC 413-8) Chem Educ Res.

Preparing & Trying the Medical Malpractice Case. 1996. 68.00 incl. audio PA Bar Inst.

Preparing & Using Individualized Learning Packages for Ungraded, Continuous Progress Education. Philip G. Kapfer & Glen F. Ovard. LC 73-125877. 272p. 1971. pap. 39.95 (*0-87778-015-3*) Educ Tech Pubns.

Preparing & Using Speech-Language Pathology Assistants. Ann Horton & Thomas Longhurst. LC 98-176658. 1997. 38.00 incl. audio (*1-58041-006-5*, 0112078) Am Speech Lang Hearing.

Preparing & Winning Medical Negligence: 1990 Supplement, Vol. 2. Cyril H. Wecht. 1992. write for info. (*0-87473-724-9*, 66054-10, MICHIE) LEXIS Pub.

Preparing & Winning Medical Negligence Cases, 3 vols., Set. 2nd ed. Stanley E. Preiser et al. 1989. 240.00 (*1-55834-132-3*, MICHIE) LEXIS Pub.

***Preparing Children for Court: A Practitioner's Guide.** Lynn M. Copen. LC 00-8184. (Interpersonal Violence Ser.). 2000. pap. write for info. (*0-7619-2182-6*) Sage.

Preparing Children for School & Life. 112p. 1988. pap. 5.05 (*0-7399-0215-6*, 2352) Rod & Staff.

Preparing Citizens: Linking Authentic Assessment & Instruction in Civic/Law-Related Education. Barbara Miller & Laurel R. Singleton. (Illus.). 246p. (Orig.). 1997. pap. 18.95 (*0-89994-389-6*, 389-6) Soc Sci Ed.

Preparing Convicts for Law-Abiding Lives: The Pioneering Penology of Richard A. McGee. Daniel Glaser. LC 95-8938. (SUNY Series in New Directions in Crime & Justice Studies). 224p. (C). 1995. pap. text 19.95 (*0-7914-2696-3*) State U NY Pr.

***Preparing Counselors: Creating Constructivist & Developmental Programs.** Garrett McAuliffe & Karen Eriksen. Ed. by Association for Counselor Education & Supervision Staff. LC 00-25186. (Illus.). 2000. write for info. (*1-57864-100-4*) Donning Co.

Preparing Customer Correspondence. Larry Mikulecky. 1990. mass mkt. 9.00 (*0-13-852278-2*) P-H.

Preparing Dairy Cattle for Show. Shelly Mayer. LC 95-167817. (Illus.). 48p. (C). 1995. pap. text 4.00 (*0-932147-25-9*) Hoard & Sons Co.

Preparing Design Office Brochures: A Handbook. 2nd ed. David Travers. (Illus.). 1982. pap. 12.95 (*0-931228-08-5*) Arts & Arch.

Preparing Educational Leaders: A Review of Recent Literature. Robin H. Farquhar & Phillip K. Piele. 64p. (Orig.). (C). 1972. pap. text 1.25 (*1-55996-112-0*, W111) Univ Council Educ Admin.

Preparing Educators of Adults. Stanley M. Grabowski et al. LC 81-48552. (Jossey-Bass Series in Higher Education). 186p. reprint ed. pap. 57.70 (*0-8357-4942-8*, 203787200009) Bks Demand.

Preparing Effective Outdoor Pursuit Leaders (People) Simon Priest. 122p. 1987. pap. write for info. (*0-943272-18-1*) Inst Recreation Res.

Preparing Estate Tax Returns. Leo J. Cushing et al. LC 96-80039. 780p. 1997. ring bd. 95.00 (*1-57589-053-4*, 97-08.06-BK) Mass CLE.

Preparing Faculty for the New Conceptions of Scholarship. Ed. by Laurie Richlin. LC 85-644763. (New Directions for Teaching & Learning Ser.: No. TL 54). 113p. 1993. pap. 22.00 (*1-55542-726-X*) Jossey-Bass.

Preparing Fiduciary Income Tax Returns. Jeremiah W. Doyle, IV. LC 96-80039. 600p. 1997. ring bd. 95.00 (*1-57589-064-X*) Mass CLE.

Preparing Files for Output. Robin B. McAllister. (C). 1997. pap. 12.95 (*0-8273-7925-0*) Delmar.

***Preparing Fish & Wild Game.** (Illus.). 2000. 29.95 (*0-86573-125-X*) Creat Pub Intl.

Preparing for a Career in Medicine. Kent Shih. LC 98-67821. 142p. 1998. write for info. (*0-9666809-0-1*) Christ Med & Dental Soc.

Preparing for a DCAA Audit. 118p. 1992. ring bd. 93.50 (*1-56726-003-9*) Mgmt Concepts.

Preparing for a Deposition in a Business Case. Jeffrey A. Jannuzzo. text 320.00 (*0-8205-2471-9*) Bender.

Preparing for a Global Community: Achieving an International Perspective in Higher Education. Sarah M. Pickert. Ed. by Jonathan D. Fife. LC 92-85442. (ASHE-ERIC Higher Education Reports: No. 92-2). 94p. 1992. 24.00 (*1-878380-15-X*) GWU Grad Schl E&HD.

Preparing for a Home Economics Career. G. Polly Jacoby. Ed. by Ruth P. Hughes. (Careers in Home Economics Ser.). 1978. text 26.32 (*0-07-032240-6*) McGraw.

Preparing for a New Calculus: Conference Proceedings. Ed. by Anita Solow. 250p. 1994. pap. text 34.95 (*0-88385-092-3*, NTE-36) Math Assn.

Preparing for a Show. Jane Holderness-Roddam. (Threshold Picture Guides Ser.). (Illus.). 24p. (J). (gr. 3 up). 1989. pap. 12.00 (*0-901366-09-9*) Half Halt Pr.

Preparing for Accreditation: A Handbook for Academic Librarians. Sara Lou Whildin & Patricia A. Sacks. LC 93-19712. 84p. 1993. pap. text 18.00 (*0-8389-0621-4*) ALA.

Preparing for Adolescence see Preparemonos Para la Adolescencia

Preparing for Adolescence. James Dobson. 160p. 1984. mass mkt. 3.95 (*0-553-26445-1*) Bantam.

***Preparing for Adolescence.** James Dobson. 186p. 1999. pap. 9.99 (*0-8307-2499-0*); pap. 9.99 (*0-8307-2497-4*, Regal Bks) Gospel Lght.

Preparing for Adolescence. James Dobson. 1992. pap. 5.99 (*0-8423-5037-3*) Tyndale Hse.

Preparing for Adolescence: Family Guide. James Dobson. 1999. pap. text 14.99 (*0-8307-2501-6*) Gospel Lght.

Preparing for Algebra. Martha Haehl. LC 97-42050. 430p. (C). 1997. pap. text 42.00 (*0-13-608878-3*) P-H.

Preparing for an Uncertain Climate, 2 vols., Set. 1995. lib. bdg. 975.99 (*0-8490-7407-X*) Gordon Pr.

Preparing for & Conducting a Winning Deposition. Ronald J. Cohen & Paula M. Demore. 265p. 1995. pap. 185.00 incl. audio (*0-943380-99-5*) PEG MN.

Preparing for & Trying a Civil Lawsuit. Neil A. Goldberg & Gregory P. Joseph. LC 87-62967. 450p. 1987. 60.00 (*0-942954-17-3*) NYS Bar.

Preparing for Baptism. Elsje Chun. (Illus.). 28p. (Orig.). 1995. pap. 2.95 (*1-57665-015-4*) Muggli Graphics.

Preparing for Baptism. Sandy Halverson. 48p. (J). (gr. 1-3). 1983. pap. 6.98 (*0-88290-233-4*) Horizon Utah.

***Preparing for Baptism & Nurturing Your Child's Spirituality: Parent Guide.** Kathy Coffey. (Baptism & Beyond Ser.: Vol. 2). (Illus.). 160p. 2000. pap. 10.95 (*1-889108-72-3*) Liv Good News.

Preparing for Battle: A Spiritual Warfare Workbook. Mark Bubeck. 1999. pap. 12.99 (*0-8024-9082-4*) Moody.

Preparing for Birth with Yoga: Exercises for Pregnancy & Childbirth. Janet Balaskas. (Home Library of Alternative Medicine). (Illus.). 192p. 1994. pap. 18.95 (*1-85230-431-6*, Pub. by Element MA) Penguin Putnam.

Preparing for California's Earthquakes: Local Government & Seismic Safety. Alan J. Wyner & Dean E. Mann. LC 85-9714. 132p. (Orig.). reprint ed. pap. 41.00 (*0-608-20132-4*, 207140400011) Bks Demand.

Preparing for Career Success. Jerry Ryan & Roberta Ryan. LC 95-37416. 1995. pap. 48.00 (*0-314-04883-9*) West Pub.

***Preparing for Cash Management Certification: A Self-Study Guide.** Kenneth L. Parkinson. 200p. 2000. pap. 75.00 (*0-9633680-3-6*) Treasury Info.

Preparing for Catastrophe on a Budget. Illus. by Janette Fowles. viii, 131p. 1998. pap. 10.95 (*0-9663428-0-1*) Blue For Bks.

Preparing for Childbirth see Preparandose para el Alumbramiento

Preparing for Childbirth: Relaxing for Labor, Learning for Life. Betty Parsons. LC 97-7177. (Illus.). 144p. 1997. pap. 9.95 (*1-55561-128-1*) Fisher Bks.

Preparing for Christian Marriage: Couples. Joan A. Hunt & Richard A. Hunt. LC 81-1770. 96p. 1982. pap. 12.95 (*0-687-33919-7*, 1048) Abingdon.

Preparing for Christian Ministry: An Evangelical Approach. Ed. by David P. Gushee & Walter C. Jackson. LC 96-8799. 350p. (gr. 12). 1996. pap. 19.99 (*0-8010-9034-2*, Bridgept Bks) Baker Bks.

Preparing for Christ's Return. Charles Stanley. (In Touch Study Ser.). 120p. 1999. pap. 7.99 (*0-7852-7291-7*) Nelson.

Preparing for Citizenship: Teaching Youth to Live Democratically. Ralph Mosher, Jr. & Robert A. Kenny. LC 94-6379. 216p. 1994. pap. 19.95 (*0-275-95096-4*, Praeger Pubs) Greenwood.

Preparing for Citizenship: Teaching Youth to Live Democratically. Ralph Mosher et al. LC 94-6379. 216p. 1994. 59.95 (*0-275-94606-1*, Praeger Pubs) Greenwood.

Preparing for Client Change in Rational Emotive Behavior Therapy. Dryden. 149p. 1994. pap. 32.95 (*1-56593-511-X*, 1180) Singular Publishing.

Preparing for Climate Change: Proceedings, Second North American Conference, 1988. (Illus.). 696p. (Orig.). (C). 1993. pap. text 70.00 (*1-56806-482-9*) DIANE Pub.

Preparing for College Writing: Grammar & Composition. 2nd ed. 308p. (C). 1999. pap. text, student ed. 18.70 (*0-536-02521-5*) S&S Trade.

Preparing for Confession. Joseph L. Letendre. 1987. pap. 2.95 (*0-937032-52-2*) Light&Life Pub Co MN.

Preparing for Construction in the 21st Century. Luh-Maan Chang. LC 91-24956. 816p. 1991. pap. text 9.00 (*0-87262-801-9*) Am Soc Civil Eng.

Preparing for Contact: A Metamorphosis of Consciousness. Lyssa Royal & Keith Priest. 192p. (Orig.). 1994. pap. 12.95 (*0-9631320-2-4*) Royal Priest.

Preparing for Council Tax Benefit: A Study of Local Authorities. N. Smith & C. Wright. (DSS Research Report Ser.). 1993. write for info. (*0-11-762061-0*, Pub. by Statnry Office) Bernan Associates.

Preparing for Crises in the Schools: A Manual for Building School Crises Response Teams. Stephen E. Brock et al. 200p. 1996. 64.95 (*0-471-16212-4*) Wiley.

***Preparing for Crises in the Schools: A Manual for Building School Crises Response Teams.** 2nd ed. Stephen E. Brock et al. 320p. 2001. 45.00 (*0-471-38423-2*) Wiley.

Preparing for Crises in the Schools: Manual for Building School Crisis Response Teams. Stephen E. Brock et al. LC 95-4474. 1995. write for info. (*0-88422-156-3*) Clinical Psych.

Preparing for Drought: A Guidebook for Developing Countries. Donald A. Wilhite. (Illus.). 78p. (Orig.). (C). 1994. pap. text 30.00 (*0-7881-0267-2*) DIANE Pub.

***Preparing for Educational Administration Using Case Analysis.** Karen L. Hanson. LC 99-86443. 160p. 2000. pap. 25.00 (*0-13-023024-3*) P-H.

Preparing for el Nino: Hearing Before the Subcommittee on Energy & Environment of the Committee on Science, U.S. House of Representatives, One Hundred Fifth Congress, First Session, September 11, 1997. United States Government. LC 98-142268. vi, 203 p. 1997. write for info. (*0-16-056044-6*) USGPO.

Preparing for Electronic Commerce in Asia. Douglas Bullis. LC 98-7576. 288p. 1999. 69.50 (*1-56720-206-3*, Quorum Bks) Greenwood.

Preparing for END Board Exams: Study Tools & Survival Tips. ASET Task Force Staff. (Illus.). iv, 236p. 1996. per. 57.00 incl. VHS (*1-57797-021-7*); per. 28.00 (*1-57797-022-5*) ASET.

Preparing for FDA Pre-Approval Inspections. Ed. by Martin D. Hynes, III. LC 98-27750. (Drugs & the Pharmaceutical Sciences Ser.). (Illus.). 304p. 1998. text 165.00 (*0-8247-0218-2*, 0218-2) Dekker.

Preparing for Financial Prosperity: Through the Application of Biblical Principles, 1. large type ed. Ann M. Sweeney. 240p. 1999. pap. 14.95 (*1-881524-49-3*) Milligan Bks.

Preparing for Fire Service Assessment Centers. Patrick T. Maher & Richard S. Michelson. 115p. 1992. 21.95 (*0-941943-04-6*, 35597) Fire Pubns.

***Preparing for Future Multilateral Trade Negotiations: Issues & Research Needs from a Development Perspective.** 250p. 1999. 28.00 (*92-1-112456-5*) UN.

Preparing for General Physics: Math Skill Drills & Other Useful Help: Calculus Version. Arnold D. Pickar. LC 92-41812. 188p. (C). 1993. pap. text 19.80 (*0-201-53802-4*) Addison-Wesley.

Preparing for Global Change Vol. 9: A Midwestern Perspective. E. Carmichael et al. (Illus.). 302p. 1994. 100.00 (*90-5103-102-5*, Pub. by SPB Acad Pub) Balogh.

Preparing for Graduate Study in Psychology: 101 Questions & Answers. William Buskist & Thomas R. Sherburne. LC 96-185889. 128p. (C). 1995. pap. text 16.00 (*0-205-19858-9*) Allyn.

Preparing for Grief. Dorothy Childers. 80p. (Orig.). 1994. pap. 13.95 (*0-9640973-0-3*) D Childers.

Preparing for High School Equivalency Tests. Nicholas S. Vazzana. 1979. 39.95 (*0-89507-001-4*); student ed. 5.50 (*0-685-49938-3*) Multi Dimen.

Preparing for High Technology: CAD-CAM Programs. Robert E. Abram et al. 79p. 1983. 6.50 (*0-318-22175-6*, RD234) Ctr Educ Trng Employ.

Preparing for High Technology: Model Programs in the U. S. A. Charles R. Doty. 100p. 1985. 8.00 (*0-318-20416-9*, RD258) Ctr Educ Trng Employ.

Preparing for High Technology: Robotics Programs. William L. Ashley et al. 57p. 1983. 5.75 (*0-318-22176-4*, RD233) Ctr Educ Trng Employ.

Preparing for High Technology: Successful Co-Op Strategies. Stephen J. Franchak & O. Michael Smith. 124p. 10.50 (*0-318-22177-2*, RD263) Ctr Educ Trng Employ.

Preparing for High Technology: Thirty Steps to Implementation. Robert E. Abram et al. 49p. 1983. 6.50 (*0-318-22178-0*, RD232) Ctr Educ Trng Employ.

Preparing for High Technology Bk. I: Programs That Work. Robert E. Abram et al. 55p. 1982. 4.95 (*0-318-22172-1*, RD229) Ctr Educ Trng Employ.

Preparing for High Technology Bk. II: Strategies for Change. Constance Faddis et al. 43p. 1982. 4.25 (*0-318-22173-X*, RD230) Ctr Educ Trng Employ.

Preparing for High Technology Bk. III: A Guide for Community Colleges. James P. Long & Catharine P. Warmbrod. 15p. 1982. 2.75 (*0-318-22174-8*, RD231) Ctr Educ Trng Employ.

Preparing for His Glory. Mark Brazee. 120p. 1993. pap. 7.00 (*0-934445-02-8*) Eternal Word.

Preparing for Incarnations: Poems. Louis Daniel Brodsky. LC 99-24793. 1999. spiral bd. 9.95 (*1-56809-057-9*) Time Being Bks.

***Preparing for Incarnations: Poems.** 2nd rev. expanded ed. Louis D. Brodsky. LC 99-35469. 1999. spiral bd. 9.95 (*1-56809-058-7*) Time Being Bks.

Preparing for Independence: Counseling Issues with the Maltreated Adolescent. Barbara Jaklitsch & Marty Beyer. 64p. 1990. 5.00 (*1-878848-06-2*, 128) Natl Res Ctr.

***Preparing for iNet+ Certification.** Paul Nelson & Susan D. Lanier-Graham. Ed. by Jamie Tillman & Kevin C. Dietz. (Illus.). (YA). 2000. pap. write for info. (*0-7423-0471-X*) ComputerPREP.

Preparing for Instrumentation Technician Evaluation: Self-Study System. Donald A. Coggan. LC 90-24340. 307p. reprint ed. pap. 95.20 (*0-7837-5144-3*, 204487200004) Bks Demand.

Preparing for Interviews. Shelley Burt. 89p. (Orig.). 1993. pap. 27.50 (*0-273-60133-4*, Pub. by Pitman Pub) Trans-Atl Phila.

Preparing for JCAHO Survey: Hospital-Based Home Care Services. 46p. 1998. pap. text 20.00 (*0-916499-67-7*) Care Educ Grp.

Preparing for Jesus: Meditations on the Coming of Christ, Advent, Christmas & the Kingdom. Walter Wangerin. LC 99-35510. 192p. 2000. 15.99 (*0-310-20644-8*) Zondervan.

Preparing for Korean Unifications: Scenarios & Implications. Jonathan D. Pollack & Chung Min Lee. LC 99-13282. 1999. pap. 15.00 (*0-8330-2721-2*) Rand Corp.

Preparing for Leadership: A Young Adult's Guide to Leadership Skills in a Global Age. Robert B. Woyach. LC 92-45076. 240p. 1993. 39.95 (*0-313-28602-7*, WPQ, Greenwood Pr); 15.95 (*0-313-29053-9*, WPQPB, Greenwood Pr) Greenwood.

Preparing for Liturgy: A Theology & Spirituality. Austin Fleming. LC 97-14057. 135p. 1997. pap. 12.00 (*1-56854-040-X*, PREPAR) Liturgy Tr Pubns.

Preparing for Marriage. Center for Learning Network Staff. 116p. 1993. teacher ed., spiral bd. 15.95 (*1-56077-276-X*) Ctr Learning.

Preparing for Marriage: A Guide for Christian Couples. Ed. by Donald J. Luther. 72p. 1992. pap. 8.99 (*0-8066-2569-4*, 9-2569) Augsburg Fortress.

Preparing for Marriage Couples Pack. Dennis Rainey. 1997. pap. 16.99 (*0-8307-2157-6*) Gospel Lght.

Preparing for Marriage God's Way. Wayne A. Mack. 153p. pap. 12.99 (*1-56322-019-9*) Hensley Pub.

Preparing for Medical Practice Made Ridiculously Simple. Daniel Lichtstein. 70p. 1998. pap. text 12.95 (*0-940780-38-0*) MedMaster.

Preparing for My Baptism. Val Bagley. (J). 1996. pap. 2.95 (*1-55503-564-7*, 01111299) Covenant Comms.

Preparing for Parenthood. Grace H. Ketterman. (Framing Better Families Ser.: Vol. 2). 104p. (Orig.). 1996. pap. 8.99 (*0-8341-1619-7*) Beacon Hill.

Preparing for Peace: Conflict Transformation Across Cultures. John P. Lederach. 1996. pap. text 17.95 (*0-8156-2725-4*) Syracuse U Pr.

***Preparing for Peace: Military Identity, Value Orientations & Professional Military Education.** Volker Franke. LC 99-34123. 216p. 1999. 62.95 (*0-275-96338-1*) Greenwood.

Preparing for Performance: Driving. Meredith Hodges. (Training Mules & Donkeys: A Logical Approach to Longears Ser.: Vol. 3). spiral bd., wbk. ed. 39.95 incl. VHS Willman Prodns.

Preparing for Performance: Ground Work. Meredith Hodges. (Training Mules & Donkeys: A Logical Approach to Longears Ser.: Vol. 2). spiral bd., wbk. ed. 39.95 incl. VHS Willman Prodns.

Preparing for Power: America's Elite Boarding Schools. Peter W. Cookson, Jr. & Caroline H. Persell. LC 85-47559. 272p. 1987. pap. 17.50 (*0-465-06269-5*, Pub. by Basic) HarpC.

Preparing for Promotion & Tenure Review: A Faculty Guide. Robert M. Diamond. 80p. (C). 1995. pap. text 9.50 (*1-882982-07-X*) Anker Pub.

Preparing for PSI Real Estate Examination: A Guide for Success. 2nd ed. Van Reken. 1997. pap. 18.97 (*0-13-780586-1*) P-H.

Preparing for Retirement: The Employer's Guide. Joanna Walker. 160p. (C). 1992. 80.00 (*0-86242-068-7*, Pub. by Age Concern Eng) St Mut.

Preparing for Science in the Twenty-First Century. Ed. by Donald C. Harrison et al. 192p. (Orig.). 1991. pap. 19.95 (*1-879694-00-X*) AAH Ctrs.

***Preparing for SEC Inspections & Examinations.** Lori A. Richards et al. LC 98-207506. (Corporate Law & Practice Course Handbook Ser.). 576p. 1998. write for info. (*0-87224-493-8*) PLI.

Preparing for Secondary School Teaching. 5th ed. 174p. (C). 1990. 25.80 (*0-536-57718-8*) Pearson Custom.

Preparing for Spiritual Direction. Jean LaPlace. 192p. 1975. pap. 4.95 (*0-8199-0550-X*, Frncscn Herld) Franciscan Pr.

Preparing for Standardization, Certification & Quality Control. Kenneth S. Stephens. 298p. 1979. text 19.00 (*92-833-1049-7*) Productivity Inc.

Preparing for Standardized Reasons. Lynda G. Vern. (C). 1995. pap. text 11.50 (*0-15-503244-5*, Pub. by Harcourt Coll Pubs) Harcourt.

Preparing for Supervision. 37p. 1989. teacher ed. 33.00 (*0-685-63177-X*, 628603); teacher ed. 21.00 (*0-685-63178-8*, 628603); pap., student ed. 18.00 (*0-685-63176-1*, 628604); pap., student ed. 29.00 (*0-89982-338-6*, 628604) Am Bankers.

Preparing for Surgery: A Mind-Body Approach to Enhance Healing & Recovery. William W. Deardorff & John Reeves. LC 96-71159. 232p. (Orig.). 1997. pap. 17.95 (*1-57224-071-7*) New Harbinger.

Preparing for Tantra: The Mountain of Blessings. Tsongkapa. Tr. by Khen Rinpoche et al. (Classics of Middle Asia Ser.). 1995. write for info. (*0-918753-11-2*) Mahayana.

Preparing for TASP. 5th ed. Ed. by Prentice-Hall Staff. 40p. (C). 1998. text 6.67 (*0-13-081640-X*) P-H.

Preparing for Terrorism: An Emergency Services Guide. George Buck. LC 97-24209. 288p. 1997. mass mkt. 55.95 (*0-8273-8397-5*) Delmar.

Preparing for the ACSM Health/Fitness Instructor Certification Examination. Larry D. Isaacs & Roberta Pohlman. LC 97-21454. (Illus.). 280p. 1997. pap. text 22.00 (*0-87322-732-8*, BISA0732) Human Kinetics.

Preparing for the Anesthesia Orals: Board Stiff. Christopher J. Gallagher & David A. Lubarsky. (Illus.). 199p. 1989. pap. text 47.50 (*0-7506-9240-5*) Buttrwrth-Heinemann.

Preparing for the Architect Registration Examination. NCARB Staff. (Illus.). 148p. 1997. pap. text 85.00 incl. vdisk (*0-941575-28-4*) NCARB.

Preparing for the ASI Real Estate Exam: A Guide to Successful Test Taking. Van Reken. 231p. (C). 1997. pap. text 20.00 (*0-13-777202-5*) P-H.

Preparing for the Athletic Trainers' Certification Examination. Lorin Cartwright. LC 94-29306. 264p. (Orig.). 1994. pap. text 26.00 (*0-87322-504-X*, BCAR0504) Human Kinetics.

Preparing for the Baby Boomers' Retirement: The Role of Employment : Forum Before the Special Committee on Aging, United States Senate, One Hundred Fifth Congress, First Session, Washington, DC, July 25, 1997. United States Government. LC 98-139085. (S. Hrg. Ser.). iii, 154 p. 1997. write for info. (*0-16-055901-4*) USGPO.

Preparing for the "Big One" Saving Lives Through Earthquake Mitigation in Los Angeles, California. (Illus.). 52p. (Orig.). (C). 1995. pap. text 20.00 (*0-7881-1997-4*) DIANE Pub.

***Preparing for the California Notary Public Exam.** Notary Association National Notary Association. 1999. pap. text 18.00 (*1-891133-14-4*) Natl Notary.

Preparing for the CLAST. Barbara Sloan & Carolyn C. West. 74p. 1997. pap. text 6.95 (*0-312-17855-7*) St Martin.

Preparing for the CLAST. 5th ed. Ed. by Prentice-Hall Staff. 48p. (C). 1999. text 6.67 (*0-13-081649-3*) P-H.

Preparing for the CLAST with "The Bedford Guide for College Writers" 1996. pap. text, student ed. 6.95 (*0-312-11989-5*) St Martin.

P

An Asterisk (*) at the beginning of an entry indicates that the title is appearing for the first time.

Preparing for the CLAST with "The Bedford Reader" 1997. 12.66 (*0-312-13294-8*) St Martin.

Preparing for the Coming Depression & the Death of the American Economy: Managing Your Finances & Your Life & Outwitting the Machinations of Big Banks, Big Government, Big Business & Big Law. 1992. lib. bdg. 88.95 (*0-8490-5368-4*) Gordon Pr.

Preparing for the Coming Revival: How to Lead a Successful Fasting & Prayer Gathering. Bill Bright. 48p. 1995. pap., teacher ed. 3.99 (*1-56399-075-X*) NewLife Pubns.

***Preparing for the CRM Examination: A Guideline.** 9th ed. 144p. 1999. 35.00 (*0-933887-90-6*) ARMA Intl.

Preparing for the Drug (Free) Years: A Family Activity Book. 2nd ed. Developmental Research & Programs, Inc. Staff & Roberts, Fitzmahan & Associates Staff. 142p. (Orig.). 1988. pap. text 16.95 (*0-935529-03-9*) Comprehen Health Educ.

Preparing for the Engineer-in-Training Examination. 3rd ed. Irving J. Levinson. LC 82-18251. 242p. 1992. 29.50 (*0-910554-85-4*) Engineering.

Preparing for the English 104 Equivalency Exam. Balester & Gibson. 44p. (C). 1998. pap. 6.95 (*0-7872-4898-3*) Kendall-Hunt.

Preparing for the FCC General Radiotelephone Operator Exam. Fred Monaco. 336p. (C). 1991. pap. text 38.20 (*0-675-21313-4*, Merrill Coll) P-H.

***Preparing for the Future: A Vision of West Africa in the Year 2020.** Ed. by Jean-Marie Cour & Serge Snrech. (West Africa Long-Term Perspective Study Ser.). 156p. 1998. pap. 27.00 (*92-64-15407-8*, 44 98 01 1 P, Pub. by Org for Econ) OECD.

Preparing for the Future: An Essay on the Rights of Future Generations. John Ahrens. (Studies in Social Philosophy & Policy: No. 2). 44p. (Orig.). 1983. pap. 18.95 (*0-912051-00-0*) Transaction Pubs.

Preparing for the GED Essay Test. Richard Alden. 140p. (C). 1990. pap. text 17.07 (*1-56226-017-0*) CAT Pub.

Preparing for the Greatest Two Years of Your Life. Mark A. Dennison. pap. 3.95 (*0-89036-128-2*) Liahona Pub Trust.

Preparing for the Interview. Brian Jud. Ed. by Charles Lipka. 20p. (Orig.). (C). 1995. pap., student ed. 1.45 (*1-880218-17-8*) Mktg Dir Inc.

Preparing for the Loss of Your Pet: The Complete Guide to Helping Your Family Accept the Inevitable. Myrna Milani. LC 98-38778. 356p. 1998. per. 15.95 (*0-7615-1648-4*) Prima Pub.

Preparing for the Next War: American Plans for Postwar Defense, 1941-45. Michael S. Sherry. LC 76-27853. Vol. 114. (Illus.). 260p. 1977. 42.50 (*0-300-02031-7*) Yale U Pr.

Preparing for the Post-Petroleum Era: What Policy Analysts & Administrators Need to Know about Alternative Fuel Vehicles. Steve McCrea. 12p. 1995. pap. text 5.00 (*1-57074-249-9*) Greyden Pr.

***Preparing for the Project Management Professional (PMP) Certification Exam.** Micael W. Newell. 2000. pap. 27.95 (*0-8144-7088-2*) AMACOM.

Preparing for the Retirement of the Baby Boom Generation: Hearing Before the Special Committee on Aging, United States Senate, 105th Congress, 2nd Session, Baton Rouge, LA, February 18, 1998. USGPO Staff. LC 98-175935. iii, 75 p. 1998. pap. write for info. (*0-16-056573-1*) USGPO.

Preparing for the Science RCT. Lorraine Godlewski et al. (WPCO's Science Ser.). (Illus.). (Orig.). (J). 1987. student ed. 3.45 (*0-937323-08-X*) United Pub Co.

Preparing for the Sixth Epoch. Rudolf Steiner. Orig. Title: How Anthroposophic Groups Prepare for the Sixth Epoch. 22p. 1976. pap. 3.95 (*0-910142-72-6*) Anthroposophic.

Preparing for the Spring. Phyllis R. Weprin. 48p. (Orig.). 1992. pap. 6.00 (*0-9623552-3-2*, Border Pr) Ed Arcas.

Preparing for the State Exam: Situational Problems for Cosmetology. (STANDARD TEXTS OF COSMETOLOGY). 129p. 1991. pap., teacher ed. 16.95 (*1-56253-019-4*) Thomson Learn.

Preparing for the Twenty-First Century. Paul M. Kennedy. 1994. pap. 15.00 (*0-679-74705-2*) Villard Books.

Preparing for the 21st Century: An Appraisal of U. S. Intelligence. Harold Brown & Warren B. Rudman. (Illus.). 200p. (Orig.). (C). 1996. pap. text 35.00 (*0-7881-3179-6*) DIANE Pub.

Preparing for the Twenty-First Century: Proceeding of the Mountain Plains Library Association Academic Library Section Research Fourm. Ed. & Intro. by V. Sue Hatfield. 104p. (Orig.). 1986. pap. 7.50 (*0-934068-03-8*) Memorial Union.

Preparing for the Twenty-First Century: Public Education Reform in Texas. Catherine Clark et al. (Policy Research Project Report: No. 107). 107p. 1994. pap. 10.50 (*0-89940-715-3*) LBJ Sch Pub Aff.

Preparing for the 21st Century: Value Added Marketing for Value Added Products. (Illus.). 186p. 1997. pap. 40.00 (*0-935018-92-1*, 7279) Forest Prod.

Preparing for the 2000 Census: Interim Report II. National Research Council Staff. LC 97-214302. 104p. (C). 1997. pap. text 21.25 (*0-309-05880-5*) Natl Acad Pr.

Preparing for the Urban Future: Global Pressures & Local Forces. Ed. by Michael A. Cohen et al. (Woodrow Wilson Center Press Ser.). 448p. (C). 1996. text 55.00 (*0-943875-78-1*); pap. text 19.95 (*0-943875-79-X*) Johns Hopkins.

***Preparing for the Voluntary Protection Programs: Building Your Star.** Margaret Richardson. LC 99-10454. 182p. 1999. pap. 59.95 (*0-471-32405-1*) Wiley.

Preparing for the Workplace: Charting a Course for Federal Postsecondary Training Policy. National Research Council Staff. Ed. by Janet S. Hansen. LC 93-37934. 224p. (C). 1993. text 34.95 (*0-309-04935-0*) Natl Acad Pr.

***Preparing for the Year 2000: Financial Institutions, Customers, Telecommunications & Power Industries: Hearing Before the Committee on Banking & Financial Services, U. S. House of Representatives, 105th Congress, 2nd Session, September 17, 1998.** USGPO Staff. LC 99-179843. iv, 295p. 1998. pap. write for info. (*0-16-057766-7*) USGPO.

Preparing for Tomorrow . . . Today! Designing a Personalized Plan to Prevent Your Child's Alcohol-Drug Abuse. J. Stuart Rahrer. LC 97-69513. (New Parent Awareness Ser.: No. 2). (Illus.). 88p. (Orig.). 1997. pap. 14.95 (*1-890897-01-9*) Pharos Consult.

***Preparing for Trial - Action Guide - Spring 1999.** Maureen E. McClain & Jeffrey D. Polsky. Ed. by Linda A. Compton. 88p. 1999. ring bd. 58.00 (*0-7626-0330-5*, CP-11135) Cont Ed Bar-CA.

Preparing for Trial in Federal Court. 2nd ed. Phillip J. Kolczynski. 319p. 1996. ring bd. 99.00 (*0-938065-91-2*) James Pub Santa Ana.

Preparing for Weltpolitik: German Sea Power Before the Tirpitz Era. Lawrence Sondhaus. LC 96-52043. (Illus.). 344p. 1997. 39.95 (*1-55750-745-7*) Naval Inst Pr.

Preparing for Winter. Gail Saunders-Smith. (J). 1998. 53.00 (*0-516-29780-5*) Childrens.

Preparing for Winter Series, 4 bks. Gail Saunders-Smith. Incl. Animals in the Fall. LC 97-29804. (Illus.). 24p. (J). 1997. lib. bdg. 13.25 (*1-56065-588-7*, Pebble Bks); Fall Harvest. LC 97-29800. 24p. (J). 1998. lib. bdg. 13.25 (*1-56065-587-9*, Pebble Bks); Warm Clothes. LC 97-29802. (Illus.). 24p. (J). 1997. lib. bdg. 13.25 (*1-56065-589-5*, Pebble Bks); 53.00 (*1-56065-678-6*, Pebble Bks) Capstone Pr.

Preparing for Work: Setting Your Objectives, Education & Training Options, Skills for Success. rev. ed. JIST Works, Inc. Staff & Northern Virginia Community College Staff. (Career Emphasis Ser.). 57p. 1990. pap. text 5.95 (*0-942784-11-1*, CE13) JIST Works.

Preparing for Worship: Sundays & Feast Days, Cycle A. Daniel Donovan. 224p. (Orig.). 1995. pap. 11.95 (*0-8091-3571-X*) Paulist Pr.

Preparing for Worship: Sundays & Feast Days, Cycle B. Daniel Donovan. LC 93-13704. 224p. (Orig.). 1993. pap. 11.95 (*0-8091-3424-1*) Paulist Pr.

Preparing for Worship: Sundays & Feast Days, Cycle C. Daniel Donovan. 176p. 1994. pap. 11.95 (*0-8091-3507-8*) Paulist Pr.

***Preparing for Year-End & 2001.** 17th rev. ed. Brent Gow. 350p. 2000. ring bd. 375.00 (*1-930471-08-4*, 10199) American Payroll.

Preparing for Your Baby's Dedication: A Guide for Parents. Kay Kuzma. LC 97-105779. 64p. 1998. pap. 9.99 (*0-8280-1074-9*) Review & Herald.

Preparing for Your Deposition: A Comprehensive Guide to the Deposition Process for Physicians & Other Professionals. 2nd rev. ed. Raymond M. Fish et al. Ed. by Gregg Rogers. LC 94-9088. 160p. (C). 1995. 29.95 (*1-878487-19-1*, 5588M) Practice Mgmt Info.

Preparing for Your Interview: Getting the Job You Want. Diane Berk. Ed. by Elaine Brett. LC 89-82098. (Fifty-Minute Ser.). 62p. (Orig.). 1990. pap. 10.95 (*1-56052-033-7*) Crisp Pubns.

Preparing for Your Marriage. William J. McRae. 211p. (Orig.). 1980. pap. 10.99 (*0-310-42761-4*, 9366P) Zondervan.

Preparing for Your Mission. Ed J. Pinegar. 109p. (YA). (gr. 12 up). 1992. pap. 7.95 (*0-87579-646-X*) Deseret Bk.

Preparing for Your Mission. Ed J. Pinegar & Patricia Pinegar. pap. 14.95 (*1-55517-347-0*) CFI Dist.

Preparing for Your New Baby. 1991. write for info. (*1-55513-663-X*, Victor Bks) Chariot Victor.

Preparing for Y2K: A Checklist for Families, Communities & Businesses. Lisa R. Brown. 16p. 1999. pap. write for info. (*1-889482-09-9*) Nat Congress CED.

Preparing for Y2K & Beyond: A Comprehensive Resource Guide. 4th rev. ed. Roderick Cameron. LC 99-70207. 256p. (Orig.). 1999. pap. 19.95 (*0-9644958-1-3*) One Wrld Press.

Preparing Foster Youths for Adult Living: Proceedings of an Invitational Research Conference. Ed. by Edmund V. Mech & Joan R. Rycraft. LC 95-185119. 1995. pap. text 7.50 (*0-87868-593-6*) Child Welfare.

Preparing Graduate Students to Teach: A Guide to Programs That Improve Undergraduate Education & Develop Tomorrow's Faculty. Ed. by Leo Lambert & Stacey L. Tice. 150p. 1993. pap. 22.00 (*1-56377-029-6*, TI9201) Am Assn Higher Ed.

Preparing Helping Professionals to Meet Community Needs: Generalizing from the Rural Experience. Ed. by Shirley J. Jones & Joan L. Zlotnik. LC 97-53247. 1998. pap. text 8.00 (*0-87293-059-9*) Coun Soc Wk Ed.

Preparing Humanists for Work: A National Study of Undergraduate Internships in the Humanities. 99p. 1985. 13.00 (*0-937883-03-4*) NSEE.

Preparing India for the Global Information Infrastructure: Engineering the Global Information Highway. Ed. by Carol A. Charles et al. (GIIC - International Communications Report Ser.). 91p. (C). 1997. pap. 20.00 (*0-89206-375-0*) CSIS.

Preparing Instructional Objectives. 2nd rev. ed. Robert F. Mager. LC 83-60503. 1984. pap. 17.95 (*1-56103-341-3*) Ctr Effect Perf.

Preparing Instructional Objectives: A Critical Tool in the Development of Effective Instruction see Mager Six-Pack

Preparing Instructional Text: Document Design Using Desktop Publishing. Earl R. Misanchuk. LC 91-32872. (Illus.). 327p. (Orig.). 1992. pap. 39.95 (*0-87778-241-5*) Educ Tech Pubns.

Preparing International Proposals. Robert R. Bartlett. LC 97-217878. 256p. 1997. 68.00 (*0-7277-2582-3*, 2582, Pub. by T Telford) RCH.

Preparing Isopentyl Acetate by the Fischer Esterification. Ronald J. Wikholm. Ed. by J. Jeffers. (Modular Laboratory Program in Chemistry Ser.). 16p. (C). 1998. pap. text 1.75 (*0-87540-713-7*, SYNT 713) Chem Educ Res.

***Preparing IT Systems for Economic & Monetary Union (EMU)** Trevor Smith. (Management Briefings Ser.). (Illus.). 81p. 1998. pap. 142.50 (*0-273-63386-4*, Pub. by Pitman Pbg) Trans-Atl Phila.

Preparing Liturgy for Children, Children for Liturgy: Leader's Manual. Gabe Huck et al. 147p. 1989. pap. 12.00 (*0-929650-10-7*, HYMLDR) Liturgy Tr Pubns.

Preparing Loan Proposals. 2nd ed. John C. Wisdom. LC 96-42470. 752p. 1997. 150.00 incl. disk (*0-471-16452-6*) Wiley.

Preparing Loan Proposals, 1998 Supplement. 2nd ed. John C. Wisdom. 33p. 1998. pap. 55.00 (*0-471-28357-6*) Wiley.

Preparing Matrimonial Agreements. Stanley Plesent. (Basic Practice Skills Ser.). 237p. 1989. text 15.00 (*0-87224-001-0*, Q1-3003) PLI.

Preparing Middle-Level Educators: Practicing What We Preach. Ed. by Toni Sills-Briegel et al. LC 99-32545. (Source Books on Education: Vol. 56). 488p. 1999. 60.00 (*0-8153-3166-5*, SS1473) Garland.

Preparing Migration Data for Population Projections. (Population Studies: No. 127). 46p. pap. 12.50 (*92-1-151243-3*, E.92.XIII.6) UN.

Preparing Mixtures for Diesel & SI Engines. 1997. pap. 69.00 (*0-7680-0074-2*) Soc Auto Engineers.

Preparing Morning & Evening Prayer. James Richards. (Preparing for Liturgy Ser.). 48p. 1997. pap. 3.95 (*0-8146-2516-9*) Liturgical Pr.

Preparing Music for Celebration. Heather Reid. LC 96-6577. (Preparing for Liturgy Ser.). 1997. pap. 3.95 (*0-8146-2480-4*) Liturgical Pr.

Preparing National Regulations for Water Resources Mgnt: Principles & Practice. Stefano Burci. (Legislative Studies: 52). 400p. 1994. 43.00 (*92-5-103462-1*, F34621, Pub. by FAO) Bernan Associates.

Preparing New Teachers: Operating Successful Field Experience Programs. Gloria A. Slick. (Illus.). 152p. 1995. pap. 21.95 (*0-8039-6209-6*) Corwin Pr.

Preparing New Teachers: Operating Successful Field Experience Programs. Ed. by Gloria A. Slick. LC 95-6658. (Illus.). 152p. 1995. 49.95 (*0-8039-6208-8*) Corwin Pr.

Preparing Nursing Research for the 21st Century: Evolution, Methodologies, Challenges. Faye G. Abdellah & Eugene Levine. LC 94-6045. 288p. 1994. 39.95 (*0-8261-8440-5*) Springer Pub.

Preparing Organizations to Manage the Future: An International Overview. Contrib. by FMAC Staff. LC 97-177898. 100p. 1997. pap. 20.00 (*1-887464-24-7*) Intl Fed Accts.

Preparing Orthopedic Disability Cases 5th ed. Mikel A. Rothenberg. LC 98-51350. 1998. boxed set 150.00 (*1-56706-983-5*) Aspen Law.

Preparing Participants for Intergenerational Interaction: Training from Success. Melissa O. Hawkins et al. LC 98-31395. 1998. write for info. (*0-7890-0367-8*) Haworth Pr.

Preparing Perfect Pianists. Kristeen Polhamus. (Illus.). 75p. 1996. text 9.99 (*0-9659959-2-5*) K Polhamus.

Preparing Personnel to Work with Infants & Young Children & Their Families: A Team Approach. Diane D. Bricker & Anne Widerstrom. LC 95-39289. 1996. 45.00 (*1-55766-237-1*) P H Brookes.

Preparing Practitioners to Work with Infants, Toddlers & Their Families: Issues & Recommendations for Educators & Trainers. Emily Fenichel et al. (Orig.). 1990. pap. 5.00 (*0-943657-23-7*) ZERO TO THREE.

Preparing Practitioners to Work with Infants, Toddlers & Their Families: Issues & Recommendations for Parents, 4 vols. Emily Fenichel et al. (Orig.). 1990. pap. 5.00 (*0-943657-24-5*) ZERO TO THREE.

Preparing Practitioners to Work with Infants, Toddlers & Their Families: Issues & Recommendations for Policymakers, 4 vols. Emily Fenichel et al. (Orig.). 1990. pap. 5.00 (*0-943657-22-9*) ZERO TO THREE.

Preparing Practitioners to Work with Infants, Toddlers & Their Families: Issues & Recommendations for the Professions, 4 vols. Emily Fenichel et al. (Orig.). 1990. pap. 5.00 (*0-943657-21-0*) ZERO TO THREE.

Preparing Preschoolers: An Easy-to-Use Nursery School Program with Lesson Plans & Teaching Aids for Parents & Professionals. Suzan W. Allen & Karen H. Talbot. LC 80-83029. 150p. (Orig.). 1981. pap. 15.98 (*0-88290-160-5*, 2047) Horizon Utah.

Preparing Presenting Expert Testimony in Child Abuse Litigation: A Guide for Expert Witnesses & Attorneys. Paul Stern. LC 96-45811. (Interpersonal Violence: the Practice Ser.). 202p. 1997. 51.00 (*0-7619-0012-8*) Sage.

Preparing Psychologists for the Twenty-First Century: Proceedings of the National Conference on Graduate Education in Psychology. Ed. by Leonard Bickman & Henry Ellis. 256p. 1990. text 69.95 (*0-8058-0574-5*) L Erlbaum Assocs.

Preparing Public Writing. 4th ed. Dave Bird. 160p. (C). 1998. pap. text 29.95 (*1-56226-411-7*) CAT Pub.

Preparing School Leaders for Educational Improvement. Ed. by Kenneth A. Leithwood et al. (Educational Management Ser.). 224p. 1987. 45.00 (*0-7099-4123-4*, Pub. by C Helm) Routldge.

Preparing Scientific Illustrations: A Guide to Better Posters, Presentations, & Publications. 2nd ed. Mary H. Briscoe. LC 95-34366. (Illus.). 204p. 1996. 29.95 (*0-387-94581-4*) Spr-Verlag.

Preparing Staff to Serve Patrons with Disabilities: A-How-to-Do-It Manual for Librarians. Courtney Deines-Jones & Connie Van Fleet. (A How-to-do-it Manual Ser.: Vol. 57). (Illus.). 160p. (Orig.). 1995. pap. 45.00 (*1-55570-234-1*) Neal-Schuman.

Preparing Students for CLAS (California Learning Assessment Systems) Reading & Writing-Elementary. Michael Ormsby. 213p. 1994. pap. text 18.95 (*0-9643281-0-0*) Catalysts for Lrning.

Preparing Students for the 21st Century. Donna Uchida. 74p. 1996. 14.95 (*0-87652-193-6*, 021-0528) Am Assn Sch Admin.

Preparing Students for the World of Work. Tracey H. DeBruyn. LC 88-93071. 70p. 1989. ring bd. 49.95 (*0-914607-26-X*) Master Tchr.

Preparing Students to Raise Achievement Scores: Grades 1-2. Leland Graham & Darriel Ledbetter. (Illus.). 96p. (Orig.). 1996. pap. text 10.95 (*0-86530-331-2*, IP 301-5) Incentive Pubns.

Preparing Students to Raise Achievement Scores: Grades 3-4. Leland Graham & Darriel Ledbetter. (Illus.). 96p. (Orig.). 1996. pap. text 10.95 (*0-86530-332-0*, IP 301-6) Incentive Pubns.

Preparing Students to Raise Achievement Scores: Grades 5-6. Leland Graham & Darriel Ledbetter. (Illus.). 96p. (Orig.). 1996. pap. text 10.95 (*0-86530-333-9*, IP 301-7) Incentive Pubns.

Preparing Students to Raise Achievement Scores: Grades 7-8. Leland Graham & Darriel Ledbetter. (Illus.). 96p. (Orig.). 1996. pap. text 10.95 (*0-86530-341-X*, IP 301-9) Incentive Pubns.

Preparing Sunday Without the Eucharist. Andrew Britz & Zita Maier. LC 96-52680. (Preparing for Liturgy Ser.). 1997. pap. 3.95 (*0-8146-2479-0*) Liturgical Pr.

Preparing Teachers As Professionals: The Role of Educational Studies & Other Liberal Disciplines. Landon E. Beyer et al. 168p. (C). 1989. pap. text 17.95 (*0-8077-2988-4*) Tchrs Coll.

Preparing Teachers for Cultural Diversity. James King et al. LC 96-37523. 304p. (C). 1997. text 50.00 (*0-8077-3606-6*); pap. text 23.95 (*0-8077-3605-8*) Tchrs Coll.

***Preparing Teachers for Diverse Student Populations & for Equity.** Edwina B. Vold et al. 164p. (C). 1999. per. 41.95 (*0-7872-6474-1*, 41647401) Kendall-Hunt.

Preparing Teachers for Inclusive Education: Case Pedagogies & Curricula for Teacher Educators. Ed. by Suzanne E. Wade. LC 99-37806. 176p. 1999. pap. write for info. (*0-8058-2509-6*) L Erlbaum Assocs.

Preparing Teachers for Japan's Classrooms. Edward R. Beauchamp. LC 96-67186. (Fastback Ser.: No. 394). 44p. (Orig.). 1996. pap. 3.00 (*0-87367-594-0*) Phi Delta Kappa.

***Preparing Teachers for National Board Certification: A Facilitator's Guide.** Kathleen Anderson Steeves & Barbara Cole Browne. 182p. 2000. pap. text 40.00 (*1-57230-542-8*, C0542) Guilford Pubns.

Preparing Teachers for Urban Schools: Lessons from Thirty Years of School Reform. Lois Weiner. LC 93-4540. 192p. 1993. pap. 18.95 (*0-8077-3250-8*); text 43.00 (*0-8077-3251-6*) Tchrs Coll.

Preparing Teachers of Art. Ed. by Michael Day. 154p. 1997. pap. text 22.00 (*1-890160-01-6*, 271) Natl Art Ed.

Preparing Teachers to Teach Global Perspectives: A Handbook for Teacher Educators. Merry M. Merryfield et al. LC 97-4905. (Illus.). 288p. 1996. 69.95 (*0-8039-6518-4*); pap. 32.95 (*0-8039-6519-2*) Corwin Pr.

Preparing Teens for the World of Work: A School to Work Transition Guide. Dianne Schilling et al. (Illus.). 170p. (Orig.). (YA). (gr. 7-12). 1995. pap. text 24.95 (*1-56499-027-3*, IP9027) Innerchoice Pub.

Preparing Tetraamminecopper (II) Sulfate Monohydrate. Philip J. Squattrito. Ed. by H. Anthony Neidig. (Modular Laboratory Program in Chemistry Ser.). 12p. (C). 1993. pap. text 1.50 (*0-87540-432-4*, SYNT 432-4) Chem Educ Res.

Preparing the Assembly to Celebrate. Kim Aldi. (Preparing for Liturgy Ser.). 48p. 1997. pap. 3.95 (*0-8146-2500-2*) Liturgical Pr.

Preparing the Best Will for You: A Clear Language Explanation for Illinois Residents. Robert S. Hunter. (Klear-E-Lex Ser.). 144p. (Orig.). 1994. pap. 14.95 (*1-884177-12-3*) Justice IL.

Preparing the Children: Information & Ideas for Families Facing Terminal Illness & Death. Kathy Nussbaum. (Illus.). iv, 65p. 1998. pap. 8.95 (*0-9665496-0-0*) Gifts Hope Trst.

Preparing the Consolidated Return, 1992. Joseph R. Oliver. 360p. 1992. 54.95 (*0-7811-0004-6*, Maxwell Macmillan) Macmillan.

Preparing the Economic Element of the Comprehensive Plan: A Handbook for Florida's Local Governments & Economic Development Agencies. Robert W. Hopkins et al. (BEBR Monographs: Issue No. 6). 140p. (Orig.). 1989. pap. 12.00 (*0-930885-08-2*) Bur Econ & Bus Res.

Preparing the 1120 Return, 1992. Joseph R. Oliver. 580p. 1992. 54.95 (*0-7811-0002-X*, Maxwell Macmillan) Macmillan.

Preparing the 1120 Return, 1993. rev. ed. Joseph R. Oliver. LC 88-60292. (Professional Tax Advisor's Guide Ser.). (Illus.). 1992. pap. text 56.00 (*0-7811-0060-7*) Res Inst Am.

P

An Asterisk (*) at the beginning of an entry indicates that the title is appearing for the first time.

Preparing the Environment for Worship. David McNorgan. (Preparing for Liturgy Ser.). 48p. 1997. pap. 3.95 (*0-8146-2443-X*) Liturgical Pr.

Preparing the Eucharistic Table. Barry Glendinning. LC 96-52679. (Preparing for Liturgy Ser.). 48p. (Orig.). 1997. pap. 3.95 (*0-8146-2482-0*) Liturgical Pr.

Preparing the General Intercessions. Michael Kwatera. 64p. (Orig.). 1996. pap. 5.95 (*0-8146-2362-X*, Litturg Pr Bks) Liturgical Pr.

Preparing the Heart, Vol. I. Thomas B. Warren. (You Can Understand the Bible Ser.). 1994. pap. text 4.50 (*0-934916-14-4*) Natl Christian Pr.

***Preparing the Information Professional: An Agenda for the Future, 93.** Sajjad ur Rehman. LC 99-462056. (Contributions in Librarianship & Information Science Ser.: Vol. 93). 192p. 2000. 57.50 (*0-313-30673-7*, GM0673, Greenwood Pr) Greenwood.

Preparing the Initiation Rites with Adults & Children of Catechetical Age. Bill Corcoran. (Preparing for Liturgy Ser.). 48p. (Orig.). 1997. pap. 3.95 (*0-8146-2498-7*) Liturgical Pr.

Preparing the Liturgical Year Vol. 1: Sunday & the Paschal Triduum. Corbin Eddy. (Preparing for Liturgy Ser.). 1997. pap. 3.95 (*0-8146-2487-1*) Liturgical Pr.

Preparing the Liturgical Year Vol. 2: Lent - Easter & Advent - Christmas. Corbin Eddy. (Preparing for Liturgy Ser.). 1997. pap. 3.95 (*0-8146-2488-X*) Liturgical Pr.

Preparing the Marketing Plan. David Parmelee. (AMA Marketing Toolbox Ser.). (Illus.). 160p. 1995. pap. 19.95 (*0-8442-3579-2*) NTC Contemp Pub Co.

***Preparing the Marketing Plan: AMA Marketing Toolbox.** David Parmerlee. LC 99-52068. (American Marketing Association Marketing Toolbox Ser.). 176p. 2000. pap. 24.95 (*0-658-00134-5*, 001345, NTC Business Bks) NTC Contemp Pub Co.

Preparing the Pharmacy for a Joint Commission Survey. 3rd ed. Charles P. Coe. LC 97-132864. 185p. 1996. pap. 40.50 (*1-879907-70-4*) Am Soc Hlth-Syst.

Preparing the Pharmacy for a Joint Commission Survey. 4th rev. ed. Charles P. Coe. 336p. 1998. pap. 69.00 (*1-879907-86-0*) Am Soc Hlth-Syst.

***Preparing the Portfolio for an Assessment of Prior Learning.** Roslyn Snow. 61p. 1999. pap. text 25.00 (*0-9679093-0-9*, WebSpeed) Easy Guides.

Preparing the Professoriate of Tomorrow to Teach: Selected Readings in TA Training. Nyquist (CIDR) Staff. 480p. (C). 1990. per. 52.95 (*0-8403-6374-5*) Kendall-Hunt.

Preparing the Project Management: A Guide for the New Architectural or Engineering Project Manager in Private Practice. David J. Williams. LC 96-17832. 100p. 1996. 26.00 (*0-7844-0175-6*) Am Soc Civil Eng.

Preparing the Table of the Word. Norman Bonneau. (Preparing for Liturgy Ser.). 48p. (Orig.). 1997. pap. 3.95 (*0-8146-2499-5*) Liturgical Pr.

Preparing the 1040 Return, 1992. Franklyn E. Lee & Lawrence B. Berkowitz. 650p. 1992. 54.95 (*0-7811-0001-1*, Maxwell Macmillan) Macmillan.

Preparing the 1040 Return, 1993. rev. ed. Franklyn E. Lee & Lawrence B. Berkowitz. LC 78-71966. (Professional Tax Advisor's Guide Ser.). (Illus.). 650p. 1992. pap. text 56.00 (*0-7811-0058-5*) Res Inst Am.

Preparing the 1065 Return, 1992. Alvin A. Clay, III. 425p. 1992. 54.95 (*0-7811-0003-8*, Maxwell Macmillan) Macmillan.

Preparing the 1065 Return, 1993. rev. ed. Alvin A. Clay, III & James E. Maule. (Professional Tax Advisor's Guide Ser.). (Illus.). 384p. 1992. pap. text 56.00 (*0-7811-0059-3*) Res Inst Am.

Preparing the U. S. Air Force for Military Operations Other Than War. Alan Vick. LC 97-3058. 1997. pap. 15.00 (*0-8330-2492-2*, MR-842-AF) Rand Corp.

Preparing the Way: Beginning Listening. J. Huizenga. 1987. audio 24.95 (*0-8013-0117-3*, 75781) Longman.

Preparing the Way: Preliminary Studies of the Texas Catholic Historical Society. Paul J. Foik & Carlos E. Castaneda. Ed. by Jesus F. De La Teja. Tr. by Gabriel Tous. (Studies in Southwestern Catholic History). (Illus.). xvi, 240p. 1997. pap. 17.95 (*0-9660966-0-6*) TX Cath Hist.

Preparing the Winning Bid. M. T. Lyons & A. Johnson. 352p. 1992. 60.00 (*0-85314-377-3*, Pub. by Tolley Pubng) St Mut.

Preparing Theses & Other Typed Manuscripts. Roy O. Billett. (Quality Paperback Ser.: No. 63). (Orig.). 1968. reprint ed. pap. 11.00 (*0-8226-0063-3*) Littlefield.

Preparing to Be Happy. Alan Broughton. LC 87-71456. (Poetry Ser.). 1988. pap. 11.95 (*0-88748-061-6*) Carnegie-Mellon.

Preparing to Be Happy. Alan Broughton. LC 87-71456. (Poetry Ser.). 1988. 20.95 (*0-88748-060-8*) Carnegie-Mellon.

***Preparing to Be President: The Memos of Richard E. Neustadt.** Ed. by Charles O. Jones. 250p. 2000. 25.00 (*0-8447-4139-6*, Pub. by Am Enterprise) Pub Resources Inc.

***Preparing to Care: Induction & Development for Residential Social Workers.** Predencia Gabbidon & Barry Goldson. LC 99-495113. 312p. 1999. ring bd. 65.00 (*1-900990-31-8*, Pub. by Natl Childrens Bur) Paul & Co Pubs.

Preparing to Celebrate in Schools. Margaret Bick. LC 96-52681. (Preparing for Liturgy Ser.). 48p. (Orig.). 1997. pap. 3.95 (*0-8146-2481-2*) Liturgical Pr.

Preparing to Celebrate with Youth. Marilyn Sweet. 48p. 1997. pap. 3.95 (*0-8146-2515-0*) Liturgical Pr.

Preparing to Enter Medical School. Shailer A. Peterson. 1980. text 14.95 (*0-13-697342-6*, Spectrum IN) Macmillan Gen Ref.

***Preparing to Export & Identifying Potential Foreign Markets, 2000.** annuals John R. Jagoe. Ed. by Agnes Brown. (Illus.). 90p. 2000. pap. 50.00 (*0-943677-38-6*) Export USA.

Preparing to Hear the Gospel: A Proposal for Natural Theology. Ned Wisnefske. LC 98-27764. 160p. 1998. 49.00 (*0-7618-1234-2*); pap. 27.50 (*0-7618-1235-0*) U Pr of Amer.

Preparing to Integrate Students with Behavioral Disorders. Robert A. Gable et al. 36p. 1991. pap. text 9.00 (*0-86586-199-4*, P340) Coun Exc Child.

Preparing to Manage: Frameworks for Tenant Management Work Programmes & Complete. HMSO Staff. (Right to Manage Ser.). 72p. 1994. pap. 17.00 (*0-11-752985-0*, HM29850, Pub. by Statnry Office) Bernan Associates.

Preparing to Marry Again. Dick Dunn. LC 98-88823. 96p. 1999. pap. 14.95 (*0-88177-276-3*, DR276, Pub. by Discipleship Res) P B D Inc.

***Preparing to Parent Teenagers.** Paul Scott-Evans. 178p. 1999. reprint ed. pap. 12.99 (*1-898938-69-5*, Pub. by Alpha GBR) OM Literature.

Preparing to Preach. barry Glendinning. (Preparing for Liturgy Ser.). 48p. 1997. pap. 3.95 (*0-8146-2508-8*) Liturgical Pr.

***Preparing to Preach.** Ed. by Bill D. Whittaker. LC 99-64289. 224p. 1999. pap. 18.95 (*1-57736-150-4*) Providence Hse.

Preparing to Receive Holy Communion. Tom Avramis. 1986. pap. 2.95 (*0-937032-43-3*) Light&Life Pub Co MN.

Preparing to Receive Jesus. Daughters of St. Paul Staff. 1978. 2.75 (*0-8198-0548-3*); pap., teacher ed. 7.50 (*0-8198-0549-1*); student ed. 1.95 (*0-8198-0550-5*) Pauline Bks.

Preparing to Receive the Baptism of the Holy Spirit. Richard A. Heckman. 57p. (Orig.). 1992. pap., student ed. 8.00 (*0-9633924-0-9*) Lighthse NJ.

Preparing to Serve: Training for Cross-Cultural Mission. David Harley. (World Evangelical Fellowship Ser.: No. 3). 156p. (Orig.). (C). 1995. pap. text 7.95 (*0-87808-260-3*, WCL260-3) William Carey Lib.

Preparing to Serve As a God Parent. William S. Chiganos. 1986. pap. 1.95 (*0-937032-44-1*) Light&Life Pub Co MN.

Preparing to Serve at the Table. John C. Hibbard. (Preparing for Liturgy Ser.). 48p. 1997. pap. 3.95 (*0-8146-2507-X*) Liturgical Pr.

Preparing to Sit for the PT Licensure Examination. Patricia R. Evans. LC 99-22839. 161p. 1999. pap. 25.00 (*0-8036-0251-0*) Davis Co.

Preparing to Study. Ed. by Michael Richardson et al. 72p. 1979. pap. 33.95 (*0-335-00255-2*) OpUniv Pr.

Preparing to Survive the New Age/New World Order. R. Maurice Smith. (Illus.). 325p. (Orig.). 1995. pap. 29.95 (*0-9650735-0-5*) Preparedness.

Preparing to Teach Music in Today's Schools: The Best of MEJ. Ed. by Russell L. Robinson. LC 94-234103. (Illus.). 72p. reprint ed. pap. 30.00 (*0-608-20275-4*, 207153400012) Bks Demand.

Preparing to Teach Writing. James D. Williams. LC 95-53223. 368p. 1996. pap. 24.95 (*0-8058-2276-3*) L Erlbaum Assocs.

Preparing to Teach Writing: Research, Theory, & Practice. 2nd ed. James D. Williams. LC 97-28118. 369p. 1998. pap. 24.95 (*0-8058-2266-6*) L Erlbaum Assocs.

Preparing Tomorrow's Teachers: Integrating Alcohol & Other Drug Prevention into Preservice Training Proceedings. Ed. by Brian Buford et al. (Illus.). 59p. (C). 1996. reprint ed. pap. text 20.00 (*0-7881-2803-5*) DIANE Pub.

Preparing Tomorrow's Teachers: The Field Experience. Ed. by D. John McIntyre & David M. Byrd. LC 97-11181. (Teacher Education Yearbook Ser.: Vol. 4). 309p. reprint ed. pap. 95.80 (*0-608-09125-1*, 206975700006) Bks Demand.

Preparing Tris (2, 4-Pentanedionato) Iron (III), an Iron Coordination Complex. George S. Patterson. Ed. by H. Anthony Neidig. (Modular Laboratory Program in Chemistry Ser.). 8p. (C). 1993. pap. text 1.50 (*0-87540-431-6*, SYNT 431-6) Chem Educ Res.

Preparing U. S. Trademark Applications: Avoiding Common Mistakes. Elizabeth H. Wang. 120p. 1996. pap. 65.00 (*0-939190-20-6*) Intl Trademark.

***Preparing Visual Aids for Presentations.** 2nd ed. Dan Cavanaugh. 24p. 1999. pap. text 3.00 (*0-205-30482-6*) Allyn.

Preparing Web Graphics. Lynda Weinman. LC 97-6924. 256p. 1997. pap. text 39.99 (*1-56205-686-7*) New Riders Pub.

Preparing Written Assignments. (Study Skills for Adults Ser.). 1997. pap., student ed. 4.20 (*0-8114-2527-4*) Raintree Steck-V.

Preparing Written Material. Jack Rudman. (General Aptitude & Abilities Ser.: No. CS-37). pap. 23.95 (*0-8373-6737-9*, CS-37) Nat Learn.

Preparing Young Children for Christmas. Oden. (J). 1994. pap. 1.00 (*0-687-33915-4*) Abingdon.

Preparing Your Body to Fly, Vol. 1. Millicent Linden. 1977. pap. 7.00 (*0-912628-05-7*) M Linden NY.

Preparing Your Business Budget with SYMPHONY. Dennis P. Curtin & William R. Osgood. (Illus.). 160p. 1985. pap. 34.95 (*0-13-698804-0*) P-H.

Preparing Your Business for Sale: Sell Your Business for the Most Money! Russell L. Brown. LC 98-92392. (Illus.). 304p. 1998. 29.95 (*0-9657400-1-3*, Busn Bk Pr); 49.95 (*0-9657400-2-1*, Busn Bk Pr) RDS Assocs.

Preparing Your Business for the Global Economy. Business Week Staff. LC 97-7418. (Illus.). 120p. 1997. pap. 14.95 (*0-07-009438-1*) McGraw.

Preparing Your Business Plan with LOTUS 1-2-3. William R. Osgood & Dennis P. Curtin. (Illus.). 176p. 1984. pap. 34.95 (*0-13-698424-X*); disk. write for info. (*0-318-58084-5*) P-H.

Preparing Your Business Plan with MULTIPLAN. William R. Osgood & Dennis P. Curtin. 44.95 (*0-685-09440-5*) P-H.

Preparing Your Business Plan with Symphony. William R. Osgood. LC 84-18158. 1986. 19.95 (*0-13-698978-0*) P-H.

Preparing Your Business Plan with SYMPHONY. William R. Osgood & Dennis P. Curtin. 27.95 (*0-685-09442-1*) P-H.

Preparing Your Campus for a Networked Future. Mark Luker. LC 99-48099. 8p. 1999. pap. text 16.95 (*0-7879-4734-2*) Jossey-Bass.

Preparing Your Child for College: A Resource Book for Parents. 49p. (Orig.). 1993. pap. text 15.00 (*0-7881-0014-9*) DIANE Pub.

Preparing Your Child for College: A Resource Book for Parents. Elizabeth Eisner. 55p. 1995. pap. 4.50 (*0-16-048111-2*) USGPO.

Preparing Your Child for College: A Resource Book for Parents. Elizabeth Eisner et al. (Illus.). 57p. 1998. pap. text 15.00 (*0-7881-7223-9*) DIANE Pub.

Preparing Your Child for Dating. LC 98-14679. 144p. 1998. pap. 10.99 (*0-310-20136-5*) Zondervan.

Preparing Your Child for Surgery: What a Family Can Do. Barbara Riley. 20p. 1998. pap. 5.95 (*0-9666043-0-X*) Team Surgery.

Preparing Your Company for QS-9000: A Guide for the Automotive Industry. 2nd ed. Richard Clements et al. LC 95-13759. 89p. 1996. pap. 24.00 (*0-87389-344-1*, H0928) ASQ Qual Pr.

Preparing Your Company for Terrorist Attack. James E. Lukaszewski. 5p. 1998. pap. 20.00 (*1-883291-24-0*) Lukaszewski.

***Preparing Your Enterprise for Windows 2000.** Karen Ellington. 368p. 2000. pap. 49.95 (*1-930713-02-9*) Gearhead Pr CA.

Preparing Your Family Business for Strategic Change, Vol. 9. Craig E. Aronoff & John L. Ward. (Family Business Leadership Ser.). (Illus.). 70p. 1997. pap. 14.95 (*0-9651011-9-3*) Busn Owner Res.

***Preparing Your Family Records & Finances for an Emergency.** Sandrajeanne Bushell. (Illus.). 234p. 1999. 25.00 (*1-58499-004-X*, 170) Full Spectrums.

Preparing your Manuscript. rev. ed. Elizabeth Preston. LC 93-43417. 114p. 1994. pap. 12.00 (*0-87116-172-9*) Writer.

Preparing Your Research Paper. J. Harris Nierman. (Illus.). 23p. (Orig.). (gr. 10 up). 1979. pap. 1.95 (*0-935770-00-3*) Creative Res & Educ.

Preparing Your Schools for the 21st Century: ASCD 1999 Yearbook. Ed. by David D. Marsh. 228p. (Orig.). 1999. pap. 20.95 (*0-87120-335-9*, 199000) ASCD.

Preparing Your Teenager for Sexuality. Dawson McAllister & Tim Altman. Ed. by Wayne Peterson. (Illus.). 1988. pap. 6.95 (*0-923417-00-1*) Shepherd Minst.

Preparing Yourself for Mass. Romano Guardini. LC 96-40445. Orig. Title: Meditations Before Mass. 216p. 1997. reprint ed. pap. 15.95 (*0-918477-50-6*) Sophia Inst Pr.

Preparing Youth for the Information Age: A Federal Role for the 21st Century. Patricia W. McNeil. 51p. (Orig.). 1996. pap. text 5.00 (*1-887031-55-3*) Am Youth Policy.

***Preparing Youth for the 21st Century: The Transition from Education to the Labour Market: Proceedings of the Washington D. C. Conference, 23-24 February 1999.** OECD Staff. (OECD Proceedings Ser.). 504p. 1999. pap. 60.00 (*92-64-17076-6*, 91 1999 03 1 P, Pub. by Org for Econ) OECD.

Preparitive Carobohydrate Chemistry. Ed. by Stephen Hanessian. LC 96-39338. (Illus.). 664p. 1997. text 150.00 (*0-8247-9802-3*) Dekker.

Preparticipation Physical Evaluation. 2nd ed. American Academy Of Family Physicians Staff & Preparticipation Physical Evaluation Task Force. LC 96-27879. 1996. text 29.95 (*0-07-001627-5*) McGraw.

Prepayment Mortgage Yield Table for Monthly Payment Mortgages. 7th ed. Financial Publishing Company Staff. 960p. 1999. pap. 40.00 (*0-87600-435-4*) Finan Pub.

Prepoetice of William Carlos Williams: Kora in Hell. Roy Miki. LC 83-15551. (Studies in Modern Literature: No. 32). (Illus.). 223p. reprint ed. pap. 69.20 (*0-8357-1476-4*, 207056300001) Bks Demand.

Preponderance Espagnole 1559-1660. Henri Hauser. (Nouvelle Introduction Par Pierre Chaunu Reeditions Ser.: No. 11). 1973. pap. 60.00 (*3-10-800064-0*) Mouton.

Preponderance of Power: National Security, the Truman Administration, & the Cold War. Melvyn P. Leffler. (Nuclear Age Ser.). (Illus.). 711p. 1992. 69.50 (*0-8047-1924-1*) Stanford U Pr.

Preponderance of Power: National Security, the Truman Administration, & the Cold War. Melvyn P. Leffler. (Illus.). 711p. (C). 1993. pap. 24.95 (*0-8047-2218-8*) Stanford U Pr.

Preporation for Confession & the Receiving of the Holy Mysteries see Prigotovlenije k Ispovjedi i Blagogvejnomy Prithashcheniju Svjatikh Khristvikh Tajin

Preposition Practice. L. L. Keane. 64p. 1991. pap. text 13.51 (*0-8013-0760-0*, 78790) Longman.

Preposition Stranding: From Syntactic to Functional Analyses. Ken-Ichi Takami. LC 92-17274. (Topics in English Linguistics Ser.: Vol. 7). xii, 304p. (C). 1992. lib. bdg. 98.50 (*3-11-013376-8*, 107-92) Mouton.

Prepositional Analysis Within the Framework of Role & Reference Grammar. Julia Jolly. LC 89-12358. (American University Studies: Linguistics: Ser. XIII, Vol. 14). (Illus.). XII, 142p. (C). 1991. text 31.95 (*0-8204-0998-7*) P Lang Pubng.

Prepositional Phrases & Prepositional Verbs: A Study in Grammatical Function. T. Vestergaard. (Janua Linguarum, Series Minor: No. 161). 1977. 48.50 (*90-279-7616-3*) Mouton.

Prepositions: An Analytical Bibliography. Claude Guimier. (Library & Information Sources in Linguistics: No. 8). viii, 244p. 1981. 52.00 (*90-272-3734-4*) J Benjamins Pubng Co.

Prepositions & Complement Clauses: A Syntactic & Semantic Study of Verbs Governing Prepositions & Complement Clauses in Present-Day English. Juhani Rudanko. LC 95-22230. (SUNY Series in Linguistics). 211p. (C). 1996. text 59.50 (*0-7914-2873-7*); pap. text 19.95 (*0-7914-2874-5*) State U NY Pr.

Prepositions & Conjunctions. rev. ed. Contrib. by Beth Bridgman. (Horizons Grammar Ser.). (Illus.). 24p. (J). (gr. 4-9). 1998. pap. 5.95 (*1-58086-063-X*, Usborne) EDC.

Prepositions & Particles in English: A Discourse-Functional Account. Elizabeth M. O'Dowd. LC 98-18309. 232p. 1998. text 65.00 (*0-19-511102-8*) OUP.

Prepositions, Conjunctions & Interjections. S. Harold Collins. (Straight Forward English Ser.). (Illus.). 32p. (Orig.). (J). (gr. 4-8). 1992. pap. 3.95 (*0-931993-43-1*, GP-043) Garlic Pr OR.

Prepositions Illustrated. Gloria Wahlen. (Illus.). 296p. 1995. pap. text 17.95 (*0-472-08289-2*, 08289) U of Mich Pr.

***Prepositions + the Collected Critical Essays Vol. II: The Wesleyan Centenial Edition of the Complete Critical Writings of Louis Zukofsky.** rev. expanded ed. Louis Zukofsky & Mark Scroggins. LC 00-35169. 2000. pap. 16.95 (*0-8195-6428-1*, Wesleyan Univ Pr) U Pr of New Eng.

Preposterous Puzzle. Rolf Heimann. 48p. 1991. mass mkt. 6.95 (*0-385-25300-1*) Doubleday.

Preposterous Rhinoceros: or Alvin's Beastly Birthday. Robert Bender. LC 93-14200. (J). 1995. 14.95 (*0-8050-2806-4*) H Holt & Co.

Preposterous Violence: Fables of Aggression in Modern Culture. James B. Twitchell. (Illus.). 350p. 1989. text 30.00 (*0-19-505887-9*) OUP.

Preppie Murder Trial. Bryna Taubman. 1988. pap. 3.95 (*0-318-32998-0*) St Martin.

Prepping Your Preschooler: A Sourcebook for Helping Your Child Succeed in School. Patsy Lord & Margaret Sebern. (Illus.). 1987. 16.95 (*0-07-038755-9*) McGraw.

Preppy Chef. rev. ed. Karen B. Riggs. LC 82-960707. (Illus.). 229p. 1982. reprint ed. 7.00 (*0-9655657-0-X*) Riggs.

Prepregnancy Care: A Manual for Practice. Ed. by Geoffrey V.P. Chamberlain & Judith Lumley. LC 85-13983. (Wiley-Medical Publication). 289p. reprint ed. pap. 89.60 (*0-7837-3234-1*, 204325300007) Bks Demand.

PrePress Awards, 1992-1993. LC 93-85039. 264p. 1993. pap. 11.95 (*0-9636327-0-1*) PrePress Pub.

Prepress Specialists' Ratios see 1996 PIA Ratios

Preprimer Cooking: or Cooking Techniques for the Blind, 2 vols., Set. large type rev. ed. S. Jones. 304p. (YA). (gr. 9 up). 1973. 80.00 (*0-317-01923-6*, J-21820-00) Am Printing Hse.

Preprint Proposals for Revision of the 1990 Edition of the National Electrical Safety Code for the 1993 Edition. Institute of Electrical & Electronics Engineers, I. (Illus.). 176p. 1991. pap. 35.00 (*1-55937-101-3*, SH14076) IEEE Standards.

Preprints of Papers for the Physics & Chemistry of the Silver Halide Crystal: An International Colloquium at the University of Montreal. Society of Photographic Scientists & Engineers Sta. LC 72-170666. 334p. reprint ed. pap. 103.60 (*0-608-14981-0*, 202569900046) Bks Demand.

Preproduction Planning for Video Taped Television: Grassroots Handbook. Virginia Brookbush. LC 87-61787. 51p. 1990. 10.00 (*0-9619120-0-6*) Cmnt TV Agcy.

PrepTest XVIII 1992, Vol. XVIII. 1995. pap. 8.00 (*0-942639-48-0*) Law Schl Admission.

PrepTest XI 1994. 1994. pap. 8.00 (*0-942639-44-8*) Law Schl Admission.

PrepTest XV 1995, No. XV. 1995. pap. 8.00 (*0-942639-49-9*) Law Schl Admission.

PrepTest XIV 1995, No. XIV. 1995. pap. 8.00 (*0-942639-47-2*) Law Schl Admission.

PrepTest XIX 1996, No. XIX. 1996. pap. 8.00 (*0-942639-53-7*) Law Schl Admission.

PrepTest XVII 1995, No. XVII. 1996. pap. 8.00 (*0-942639-51-0*) Law Schl Admission.

PrepTest XVI 1995, No. XVI. 1995. pap. 8.00 (*0-942639-50-2*) Law Schl Admission.

PrepTest XIII 1994, No. XIII. 1995. pap. 8.00 (*0-942639-46-4*) Law Schl Admission.

PrepTest XII 1994. 1994. pap. 8.00 (*0-942639-45-6*) Law Schl Admission.

PrepTest XXIV. 1998. pap. 8.00 (*0-942639-58-8*) Law Schl Admission.

PrepTest XX 1996, No. XX. 1996. pap. 8.00 (*0-942639-54-5*) Law Schl Admission.

PrepTest XXI 1996, No. XXI. 1997. pap. 8.00 (*0-942639-55-3*) Law Schl Admission.

PrepTest XXIII. 1997. pap. 8.00 (*0-942639-57-X*) Law Schl Admission.

PrepTest XXII. 1997. pap. 8.00 (*0-942639-56-1*) Law Schl Admission.

Prepublishing Handbook: What You Should Know Before You Publish Your First Book. Patricia J. Bell. LC 92-72686. 130p. (Orig.). 1992. pap. 12.00 (*0-9618227-2-4*) Cats-paw MN.

P

Prequalification Education, Assessment of Professional Competence & Experience Requirements of Professional Accountants: International Education Guideline. rev. ed. 28p. 1996. pap. 10.00 (*1-887464-17-4*) Intl Fed Accts.

Preraphaelite Diaries & Letters. Ed. by William M. Rossetti. LC 70-148293. reprint ed. 52.50 (*0-404-08898-8*) AMS Pr.

***Prereading Activities for Content Area Reading & Learning.** 3rd ed. John E. Readence et al. (Orig.). 2000. pap., teacher ed. 15.95 (*0-87207-261-4*, 261) Intl Reading.

Prerequisites for Community Wellbeing. Brown et al. 1972. pap. 1.50 (*0-910420-20-3*) Comm Serv OH.

Prerequisites for Peace. Norman M. Thomas. LC 78-13967. 189p. 1979. reprint ed. lib. bdg. 35.00 (*0-313-20732-1*, THPP, Greenwood Pr) Greenwood.

Prerequisites for Peace in the Middle East. LC 96-100969. 258p. pap. 19.95 (*92-1-100544-2*, E.95.I.6) UN.

Prerequisites for Winning Government R&D Contracts. rev. ed. Robert Guyton et al. LC 81-52984. (Project-Contract Acquisition & Management Ser.). 170p. 1983. pap. 28.00 (*0-912426-08-X*) Univ Tech.

Preretirement Planning: Individual, Institutional, & Social Perspectives. Carl I. Brahce. 49p. 1983. 4.95 (*0-318-17789-7*, IN264) Ctr Educ Trng Employ.

Prerogativa Regis: Tertia Lectura Roberti Constable De Lyncolnis Inne. Robert Constable. Ed. by Samuel E. Thorne. 1949. 79.50 (*0-685-69876-9*) Elliots Bks.

***Prerogative Court of Canterbury Wills & Other Probate Records.** Miriam Scott. 94p. 1999. pap. 9.95 (*1-873162-23-5*, Pub. by PRO Pubns) Midpt Trade.

Prerogative of Parliaments in England: Proved in a Dialogue. Walter Raleigh. LC 74-80207. (English Experience Ser.: No. 686). 68p. 1974. reprint ed. 15.00 (*90-221-0686-1*) Walter J Johnson.

Prerogatives: Contemporary Plays by Women. Blizzard Publishing Staff. LC 98-232149. 256p. 1998. pap. 24.95 (*0-921368-69-0*) Blizzard Publ.

Preromanticism. Marshall Brown. LC 90-21043. (Illus.). 516p. 1991. 55.00 (*0-8047-1561-0*) Stanford U Pr.

Preromanticism. Marshall Brown. (Illus.). 516p. (C). 1993. pap. 19.95 (*0-8047-2211-0*) Stanford U Pr.

Pres: The Story of Lester Young. Luc Delannoy. Tr. by Elena B. Odio from FRE. LC 92-22003. (Illus.). 280p. 1993. pap. 18.00 (*1-55728-264-1*); text 30.00 (*1-55728-263-3*) U of Ark Pr.

***Presage of Passage: Sculpture for a New Century.** Herman Du Toit et al. (Illus.). 61p. 1999. pap. 15.00 (*0-8425-2456-8*, BYU Press) Brigham.

Presagio/Omen. Ed. by Colombian Cultural Concil Staff. (Poesia Ser.: Vol. 3). 81p. 1996. pap. 7.00 (*88-911106-0-4*) Colombian Cultural.

Presbyopia: A Marketing Guide for Vision Professionals. Vision Council of America Staff. 128p. 1996. pap. text, per. 24.95 (*0-7872-1691-7*) Kendall-Hunt.

Presbyopia Research: From Molecular Biology to Visual Adaptation. G. Obrecht & L. W. Stark. (Illus.). 318p. (C). 1990. text 85.00 (*0-306-43659-0*, Kluwer Plenum) Kluwer Academic.

Presbyterian Bibliography. Compiled by Harold B. Prince. LC 83-10116. (American Theological Library Association Monograph: No. 8). 466p. 1983. pap. 41.50 (*0-8108-1639-3*) Scarecrow.

Presbyterian Church (U. S. A.) Foundation: A Bicentennial History, 1799-1999. Douglas Brackenridge. LC 98-41835. (Illus.). 200p. 1999. 25.95 (*0-664-50043-9*) Geneva Press.

Presbyterian Churches & the Federal Union, 1861-1869. Lewis G. Vander-Velde. LC 32-30007. (Historical Studies: No. 33). 590p. 1932. 35.00 (*0-674-70151-8*) HUP.

Presbyterian Churches in Alabama 1811-1936: Sketches of Churches, Outposts, & Preaching Points in the Synod of Alabama, Pt. I: Abbeville-Butler, & Megargel. James W. Marshall. Ed. by Kenneth J. Foreman, Jr. (Illus.). 519p. (Orig.). 1985. 29.95 (*0-935883-01-0*); 69.95 incl. disk (*0-935883-02-9*); pap. 14.95 (*0-935883-00-2*) Cooling Spring.

Presbyterian Conflict. Edwin H. Rian. 242p. 1992. reprint ed. pap. 11.95 (*0-934688-67-2*) Comm Hist Orthodox.

Presbyterian Conflict & Resolution on the Missouri Frontier. Joseph H. Hall. LC 87-24674. (Studies in American Religion: Vol. 26). (Illus.). 232p. 1988. lib. bdg. 89.95 (*0-88946-670-X*) E Mellen.

Presbyterian Controversy: Fundamentalists, Modernists & Moderates. Bradley J. Longfield. (Religion in America Ser.). (Illus.). 352p. 1993. reprint ed. pap. text 19.95 (*0-19-508674-0*) OUP.

Presbyterian Creeds: A Guide to the Book of Confessions. J. Rogers. 1991. pap. 17.95 (*0-664-25496-9*) Westminster John Knox.

Presbyterian Elder. rev. ed. Paul S. Wright. Ed. by W. Ben Lane. LC 92-13900. 1992. pap. 10.95 (*0-664-25427-6*) Westminster John Knox.

Presbyterian Hymnal Companion. LindaJo McKim. LC 92-17830. 368p. (Orig.). 1993. pap. 25.95 (*0-664-25180-3*) Westminster John Knox.

Presbyterian in the South, Vol. 1. Ernest T. Thompson. LC 63-19121. (Presbyterian Society Publication Ser.: Vol. 13). 629p. reprint ed. pap. 195.00 (*0-608-09976-7*, 202729500001) Bks Demand.

Presbyterian in the South, Vol. 2. Ernest T. Thompson. LC 63-19121. (Presbyterian Society Publication Ser.). 528p. reprint ed. pap. 163.70 (*0-608-09977-5*, 202729500002) Bks Demand.

Presbyterian in the South, Vol. 3. Ernest T. Thompson. LC 63-19121. (Presbyterian Society Publication Ser.). 636p. reprint ed. pap. 197.20 (*0-608-09978-3*, 202729500003) Bks Demand.

Presbyterian Mission Work in New Mexico: Memoirs of Alice Blake. Alice A. Blake. Ed. by Beryl C. Roper. Tr. by Jimmy Ning. (Illus.). 1997. pap. 24.95 (*1-885812-03-5*) Aquamarine.

Presbyterian Missionary Attitudes Toward American Indians, 1837-1893. Michael C. Coleman. LC 85-7496. (Illus.). 222p. 1985. text 32.00 (*0-87805-278-X*) U Pr of Miss.

Presbyterian Missions & Cultural Interaction in the Far Southwest, 1850-1950. Mark T. Banker. (Illus.). 248p. (C). 1992. text 36.95 (*0-252-01929-6*) U of Ill Pr.

Presbyterian Odyssey, 1908-1996. Pamela Salmon. (Illus.). 140p. 1996. write for info. (*0-614-12983-4*) Salmon Communs.

Presbyterian Parochial Schools, 1846-1870. Lewis J. Sherrill. LC 74-89234. (American Education: Its Men, Institutions, & Ideas. Series 1). 1970. reprint ed. 14.95 (*0-405-01471-6*) Ayer.

Presbyterian Patchwork. Ed. by Robert Chase & Linda Chase. 128p. (Orig.). 1989. text 39.95 (*0-9622902-0-3*); pap. text 19.95 (*0-9622902-1-1*) CCM Inc.

Presbyterian Pluralism: Competition in a Protestant House. William J. Weston. LC 96-51236. 208p. (C). 1997. text 30.00 (*0-87049-982-3*) U of Tenn Pr.

Presbyterian Polity for Church Members. 2nd rev. ed. Joan S. Gray & Joyce C. Tucker. LC 86-2797. 216p. (Orig.). 1991. pap. 17.95 (*0-664-25144-7*) Westminster John Knox.

Presbyterian Polity for Church Officers. 3rd rev. ed. Joan S. Gray & Joyce C. Tucker. LC 98-42258. 212p. 1998. pap. 16.95 (*0-664-50018-8*) Geneva Press.

Presbyterian Predicament: Six Perspectives. Ed. by Milton J. Coalter, Jr. et al. (Presbyterian Presence Ser.). 168p. (Orig.). 1990. pap. 19.95 (*0-664-25097-1*) Westminster John Knox.

Presbyterian Reformers in Central Africa: A Documentary Account of the American Presbyterian Congo Mission & the Human Rights Struggle in the Congo, 1890-1918. Ed. by Robert Benedetto. Tr. by Winifred K. Vass. LC 96-46461. 580p. 1996. 156.00 (*90-04-10239-6*) Brill Academic Pubs.

Presbyterian Source: Bible Words That Shape a Faith. Louis B. Weeks. 96p. (Orig.). 1990. pap. 13.95 (*0-664-25100-5*) Westminster John Knox.

Presbyterian Women: Glimpses of a Goodly Heritage--Challenges for a Godly Future. Judy Theriault. (Illus.). 100p. (Orig.). Date not set. pap. write for info. (*0-9652533-1-7*) Presby Ctr Mission.

Presbyterian Women in America: Two Centuries of a Quest for Status, 46. Lois A. Boyd & R. Douglas Brackenridge. LC 95-50519. (Contributions to the Study of Religion Ser.: Vol. 46). 216p. 1996. 57.95 (*0-313-29841-6*, Greenwood Pr) Greenwood.

Presbyterianism: A Restatement in Question & Answer Form. Carl G. Howie. 44p. 1989. pap. write for info. (*1-889711-02-0*) Cathedral Direct.

Presbyterianism's Unique Gift: Ordained Lay Elders. Harry S. Hassall. LC 98-68172. (Illus.). 144p. 1999. pap. 14.95 (*1-57736-134-2*) Providence Hse.

Presbyterians. Randall Balmer & John R. Fitzmier. LC 92-17840. (Religious Traditions in American Culture Ser.). 152p. 1994. pap. 18.95 (*0-275-94847-1*, Praeger Pubs) Greenwood.

***Presbyterians: A Spiritual Journey.** John Knox Westminster Staff. LC 00-26165. (Illus.). 240p. 2000. 49.95 (*0-664-50116-8*) Westminster John Knox.

Presbyterians: Denominations in America, 5. Randall H. Balmer & John R. Fitzmier. LC 92-17840. 288p. 1993. lib. bdg. 69.50 (*0-313-26084-2*, BPD, Greenwood Pr) Greenwood.

Presbyterians - People of the Middle Way: For Adult Inquirers & New Members. Harry S. Hassall. LC 96-69314. (Illus.). 64p. (Orig.). 1996. pap., teacher ed. 8.95 (*1-881576-89-2*); pap., student ed. 12.95 (*1-881576-88-4*) Providence Hse.

Presbyterians Awake: An Expatriate Looks Across the Border. Ed. by Alexander Johnston. 128p. (C). 1988. pap. text 35.00 (*0-7152-0625-7*) St Mut.

Presbyterians in World Mission: A Handbook for Congregations. 2nd rev. ed. G. Thompson Brown. (Illus.). 160p. 1995. pap. 11.95 (*1-885121-11-3*) CTS Press.

Presbyterians of Cane Hill, Arkansas. David B. Ellis. 64p. (Orig.). 1991. 10.00 (*0-938041-06-1*) Arc Pr AR.

Presbyterians, Their History & Beliefs. Walter L. Lingle & John W. Kuykendall. LC 77-15750. 1958. reprint ed. pap. 14.95 (*0-8042-0985-5*) Westminster John Knox.

Presbyteries & Profits: Calvinism & the Development of Capitalism in Scotland, 1560 - 1707. Gordon Marshall. 416p. 1992. pap. 28.00 (*0-7486-0333-6*, Pub. by Edinburgh U Pr) Col U Pr.

Preschool. (More Giant Basic Skills Workbooks Ser.). (Illus.). 320p. (J). (ps-1). 1997. pap. write for info. (*1-56144-982-2*, Honey Bear Bks) Modern Pub NYC.

***Preschool.** Broadman & Holman Publishers Staff. (Learning Activities from the Bible Ser.). (Illus.). (J). 2000. pap. 15.99 (*0-8054-0982-3*) Broadman.

Preschool. Penny Nye. (Illus.). 16p. (J). (ps). 1997. pap. 12.00 (*1-890703-08-7*) Penny Laine.

Preschool. Gene Sines. (J). 1997. write for info. (*0-676-53966-1*, Bullseye Bks) Random Bks Yng Read.

Preschool: Appropriate Practices. 2nd ed. Janice J. Beaty. (C). 1995. pap. text 42.00 (*0-15-502633-X*, Pub. by Harcourt Coll Pubs) Harcourt.

***Preschool: Bible Coloring & Crafts Pages.** Warner Press Staff. (Illus.). (J). 1999. pap. 3.95 (*0-87162-863-5*) Warner Pr.

Preschool AAC Checklist. Judy M. Henderson. (Illus.). 116p. 1994. spiral bd. 19.00 (*1-884135-00-5*) Mayer-Johnson.

Preschool Activities. (Be Smart Bks.). (Illus.). 24p. (J). (ps). 1986. 3.98 (*0-86734-064-9*, FS-3056) Schaffer Pubns.

Preschool Alphabet. American Education Publishing Staff. (Beginners Bible Ser.). (J). 1997. pap. text 2.25 (*1-56189-469-9*) Amer Educ Pub.

Preschool Alphabet. Score Kaplan Staff. 2000. pap. 4.95 (*0-684-85242-X*) Kaplan.

Preschool Alphabet Interactive Workbook with CD-ROM, Vol. 8203. School Zone Publishing Interactive Staff. Vol. 8203. (Illus.). 80p. (J). (ps-4). 1998. pap., wbk. ed. 14.99 incl. cd-rom (*0-88743-553-X*, 08203) Sch Zone Pub Co.

Preschool & Early Childhood Treatment Directions. Ed. by Maribeth Gettinger et al. (Advances in School Psychology Ser.). 264p. 1992. text 59.95 (*0-8058-0757-8*) L Erlbaum Assocs.

Preschool & Kindergarten Behavior Scales. Kenneth W. Merrell. LC 94-12893. 60p. 1994. 19.95 (*0-88422-152-0*) Clinical Psych.

Preschool & Kindergarten Skills. (Home Workbooks Ser.). (Illus.). 64p. (Orig.). (J). (ps-k). 1995. pap., wbk. ed. 2.49 (*0-88724-308-8*, CD6805) Carson-Dellos.

***Preschool & Kindergarten Skills: Fun Early Learning Activities.** Jo Ellen Moore. Ed. by Marilyn Evans. (Learn on the Go Practice Bks.). (Illus.). 64p. (J). (ps-k). 1998. pap., wbk. ed. 2.25 (*1-58610-004-1*, Learn on the Go) Learn Horizon.

Preschool & Your Child. Diana Townsend-Butterworth. 96p. (Orig.). 1995. pap. 7.95 (*0-8027-7472-5*) Walker & Co.

Preschool Art: It's the Process, Not the Product. MaryAnn F. Kohl. LC 94-15714. (Illus.). 260p. (Orig.). (J). 1994. pap. text 19.95 (*0-87659-168-3*) Gryphon Hse.

Preschool Arts & Crafts. Grace Jasmine. LC 96-61506. (Creative Kids Ser.). 160p. (J). (ps up). 1997. pap. 14.95 (*1-57690-097-5*) Tchr Create Mat.

***Preschool Associate Credential Manual.** ACSI Staff. 30p. 2000. 18.00 (*1-58331-046-0*) Assn Christ Sch.

Preschool Can You Find Picture Book. Tony Tallarico. (Tuffy Search Bks.). (Illus.). 12p. (J). (ps-1). 1991. bds. 3.95 (*0-448-48800-0*, Tuffy) Putnam Pub Group.

Preschool Child: Assessment, Diagnosis, & Treatment. Paul V. Trad. LC 88-20731. 672p. 1989. 199.95 (*0-471-61757-1*) Wiley.

Preschool Children with Inadequate Communication: Developmental Language Disorder, Autism, Mental Deficiency. Ed. by Isabelle Rapin. (Clinics in Developmental Medicine Ser.: No. 139). (Illus.). 256p. (C). 1996. 69.95 (*1-898683-07-7*, Pub. by Mc Keith Pr) Cambridge U Pr.

Preschool Children with Special Disabilities. Janet Lerner et al. LC 97-33961. 400p. 1998. 57.00 (*0-205-26735-1*) P-H.

Preschool Children with Special Health Care Needs. Mary T. Urbano. (Illus.). 240p. (Orig.). (C). 1992. pap. 34.95 (*1-879105-41-1*, 0225) Thomson Learn.

Preschool Church: Church School Lesson for Three to Five Year Olds. Eve Parker. LC 96-6866. (Orig.). 1996. pap. 10.95 (*0-7880-0848-X*) CSS OH.

Preschool Coloring Book. Jo Neal. (Word of the Week Ser.). (Illus.). 40p. (J). (ps up). 1997. pap. 4.00 (*1-57074-359-2*) Greyden Pr.

Preschool Colors & Shapes. American Education Publishing Staff. (Beginners Bible Ser.). (J). 1997. pap. text 2.25 (*1-56189-468-0*) Amer Educ Pub.

Preschool Connections. Sarah Felsteiner & Annalisa Suid. (Illus.). 352p. 1994. pap. 24.95 (*1-878279-72-6*) Monday Morning Bks.

Preschool Craft-Play: More Than 100 Just-for-Fun, Easy-to-Make, Interactive Crafts Your Children Will Play with Again & Again! LC 95-45599. 1996. 16.99 (*1-55945-610-8*) Group Pub.

***Preschool Daycare Guidebook for Metropolitan Boston.** Mary Ann Keenan. (Illus.). 277p. 1999. pap. 16.95 (*0-9664502-0-5*) Child Concern.

Preschool Director's Survival Guide: 135 Forms, Checklists & Letters for Day-to-Day Management. Rebecca Graff. 224p. (C). 1990. pap. text 29.95 (*0-87628-619-8*) P-H.

Preschool Education. Bhoodev Singh. xix, 249p. 1997. 36.00 (*81-7024-896-5*, Pub. by APH Pubng) Nataraj Bks.

Preschool Education in America: The Culture of Young Children from the Colonial Era to the Present. Barbara Beatty. 270p. 1997. pap. 18.00 (*0-300-07273-2*) Yale U Pr.

Preschool Education Programs for Children with Autism. Ed. by Sandra L. Harris & Jan S. Handleman. LC 93-9577. 252p. 1994. pap. 31.00 (*0-89079-587-8*, 6665) PRO-ED.

***Preschool Education Programs for Children with Autism.** 2nd ed. Sandra L. Harris & Jan S. Handleman. LC 99-86984. 2000. pap. write for info. (*0-89079-850-8*) PRO-ED.

Preschool for Parents: What Every Parent Needs to Know about Preschool. Diane T. Dodge & Toni S. Bickart. LC 98-17216. 192p. 1998. pap. 12.95 (*1-57071-172-0*) Sourcebks.

Preschool Games. Grace Jasmine. 1997. pap. text 24.95 (*1-57690-008-8*) Tchr Create Mat.

Preschool Games & Activities. Sandra Taetzsch & Lyn Taetzsch. (J). (ps-k). 1974. pap. 7.99 (*0-8224-5605-2*) Fearon Teacher Aids.

Preschool in the Suzuki Spirit. Susan Grilli. (Illus.). 216p. 1987. pap. 14.95 (*0-15-673830-9*) Harcourt.

Preschool in Three Cultures: Japan, China & the United States. Joseph T. Tobin et al. (Illus.). 240p. (C). 1991. reprint ed. pap. 17.00 (*0-300-04812-2*) Yale U Pr.

***Preschool Inclusion.** Claire C. Cavallaro & Michele Haney. LC 99-11264. 320p. 1999. 45.00 (*1-55766-419-6*) P H Brookes.

Preschool Interactive Learning Center. School Zone Publishing Staff. 1997. pap. text 34.99 incl. cd-rom (*0-88743-511-4*, 08901) Sch Zone Pub Co.

Preschool Interactive Workbook with CD-ROM, Vol. 8208. School Zone Publishing Interactive Staff. Vol. 8208. (Illus.). 80p. (J). (ps-4). 1998. pap., wbk. ed. 22.99 incl. cd-rom (*0-88743-558-0*, 08208) Sch Zone Pub Co.

Preschool Issues in Autism. Ed. by Eric Schopler et al. LC 93-20597. (Current Issues in Autism Ser.). (Illus.). 294p. (C). 1993. 54.00 (*0-306-44440-2*, Plenum Trade) Perseus Pubng.

Preschool Learning Activities. Stan Wonderley. (Illus.). 200p. 1996. pap. 19.95 (*0-933025-43-2*) Blue Bird Pub.

Preschool Lessons about Jesus. Maria Mccrea. Date not set. pap. text 8.95 (*0-86653-767-8*) Good Apple.

Preschool Mazes Interactive Workbook with CD-ROM, Vol. 8204. School Zone Publishing Interactive Staff. Vol. 8204. (Illus.). 80p. (J). (ps-4). 1998. pap., wbk. ed. 14.99 incl. cd-rom (*0-88743-554-8*, 08204) Sch Zone Pub Co.

Preschool Numbers. American Education Publishing Staff. (Beginners Bible Ser.). (J). 1997. pap. text 2.25 (*1-56189-470-2*) Amer Educ Pub.

Preschool Numbers. Score Kaplan Staff. 2000. pap. 4.95 (*0-684-85241-1*) Kaplan.

***Preschool Play & Learn: 150 Games & Learning Activities for Children Ages Three to Six.** Penny Warner. 168p. 2000. pap. 10.00 (*0-671-31821-7*) S&S Trade.

Preschool Plus: Preschool Curriculum. Donna R. Fisher. 81p. (C). 1998. pap. text 16.50 (*1-57896-040-1*, 2554) Hewitt Res Fnd.

Preschool Praise. 100p. (J). 1987. ring bd. 7.99 (*0-8341-9083-4*, MB-586) Lillenas.

Preschool Programs for the Disadvantaged: Five Experimental Approaches to Early Childhood Education: Proceedings. Hyman Blumberg Symposium on Research in Early Chil. Ed. by Julian C. Stanley. LC 72-170019. 215p. reprint ed. pap. 66.70 (*0-608-06130-1*, 206646300008) Bks Demand.

Preschool Puppet Board Books. Incl. Airplanes. 2.50 Farm Animals. 2.50 Pandas. 2.50 Puppies. Illus. by Tadasu Izawa. 1973. 2.50 (Puppet Board Bks.). 7p. (J). (ps-2). 1973. write for info. (*0-318-52381-7*, G & D) Peng Put Young Read.

Preschool Puppet Plays. Connie Matricardi. (Illus.). 36p. (Orig.). (J). (gr. k). 1993. pap. 9.95 (*1-884555-00-4*) P Depke Bks.

Preschool Readiness Book. M. Quint. (J). 1993. pap. 19.50 (*1-58095-988-1*) Alpha AZ.

Preschool Readiness Guidebook. deluxe ed. Stewart Burgess. (Illus.). 176p. Date not set. write for info. (*1-929651-14-7*) Brllnt Begnngs.

Preschool Readiness Kit 4. deluxe ed. (Illus.). 4p. Date not set. write for info. (*1-929651-12-0*) Brllnt Begnngs.

Preschool Report. Directors of Participating Schools Staff. Ed. by Kyra Faison-Gardner. ii, 36p. (Orig.). 1996. pap. 5.50 (*0-9652127-0-X*) Fmly First Res.

Preschool Resource Guide: Educating & Entertaining Children Aged Two Through Five. H. Friedes. (Illus.). 258p. (C). 1993. pap. 17.50 (*0-306-44473-9*, Plen Insight) Perseus Pubng.

Preschool Shapes & Colors. Score Kaplan Staff. 2000. pap. 4.95 (*0-684-85243-8*) Kaplan.

Preschool Skills. (Kelley Wingate Ser.). (Illus.). 130p. (J). 1995. pap. text 10.95 (*0-88724-420-3*, CD-3702) Carson-Dellos.

Preschool Skills. Kathleen A. Cole. (Illus.). 64p. (YA). 1993. pap. 3.49 (*0-307-03667-7*, 03667) Gldn Bks Pub Co.

Preschool Teacher Messages. Judi S. Estes. 64p. 8.99 (*0-86653-918-2*, FE0918) Fearon Teacher Aids.

Preschool Teacher Training Video Series. pap., teacher ed. 149.00 incl. VHS (*1-55945-148-3*) Group Pub.

Preschool Teacher's Daily Plan Book. Sherrill Flora. 32p. 1985. 3.25 (*0-513-01792-5*) Denison.

Preschool Teachers Month by Month Activities Program. Lorraine Clancy. 304p. 1991. pap. text 27.95 (*0-87628-632-5*) Ctr Appl Res.

Preschool Theme Calendar. Elizabeth McKinnon. LC 98-61488. (Theme Calendar Ser.). (Illus.). 48p. 1999. pap. 6.95 (*1-57029-243-4*, 00191) Totline Pubns.

Preschool to the Rescue. Judy Sierra. LC 99-6475. (Illus.). (J). 2001. write for info. (*0-15-202035-7*, Harcourt Child Bks) Harcourt.

***Preschool Toys in Taiwan: A Strategic Entry Report, 1997.** Compiled by Icon Group International Staff. (Illus.). 115p. 1999. ring bd. 1150.00 incl. audio compact disk (*0-7418-0935-4*) Icon Grp.

Preschool Years: Family Strategies That Work - from Experts & Parents. Ellen Galinsky & Judy David. 528p. 1991. pap. 14.00 (*0-345-36597-6*) Ballantine Pub Grp.

Preschooler & the Library. Ann D. Carlson. LC 91-18073. (Illus.). 172p. 1991. 28.00 (*0-8108-2457-4*) Scarecrow.

Preschoolers - Questions & Answers: Psychoanalytic Consultations with Parents, Teachers, & Caregivers. Erna Furman. 150p. 1995. 32.50 (*0-8236-4255-0*) Intl Univs Pr.

Preschoolers & Substance Abuse: Strategies for Prevention & Intervention. Pedro J. Lecca & Thomas D. Watts. LC 91-35921. 112p. 1993. pap. 14.95 (*1-56024-235-3*); lib. bdg. 39.95 (*1-56024-234-5*) Haworth Pr.

Preschoolers As Authors: Literacy Learning in the Social World of the Classroom. Deborah Rowe. Ed. by Judith Green. LC 93-1672. (Language & Social Processes Ser.). 288p. (C). 1993. text 57.50 (*1-881303-71-3*); pap. text 23.95 (*1-881303-72-1*) Hampton Pr NJ.

PreSchooler's Bible. Retold by V. Gilbert Beers. LC 94-211236. (Illus.). 432p. (J). (ps-k). 1994. 17.99 (*1-56476-317-X*, 6-3317, Victor Bks) Chariot Victor.

Preschooler's Bible Paint with Water. V. Gilbert Beers. (Preschoolers Bible Ser.). (J). 1995. pap. 2.99 (*1-56476-531-8*, 6-3531, Victor Bks) Chariot Victor.

__Preschooler's Bible Sticker Book.__ V. Gilbert Beers. (Preschoolers Bible Ser.). (J). 1995. pap. 2.99 (_1-56476-530-X_, 6-3530, Victor Bks) Chariot Victor.

__Preschooler's Busy Book: 365 Creative Games & Activities to Keep Your 2- to 6-Year-Old Busy.__ Trish Kuffner. (Illus.). 384p. (J). (ps-1). 1998. pap. 9.95 (_0-671-31633-8_, Pub. by Meadowbrook) S&S Trade.

__Preschooler's Busy Book: 365 Creative Games & Activities to Occupy Your 3 to 6 Year-Old.__ Trish Kuffner. LC 98-29639. 384p. (J). 1998. 9.00 (_0-88166-351-4_) Meadowbrook.

__Preschoolers Can Read.__ Francis H. Wise. Ed. by Joyce M. Wise. (Illus.). 48p. (Orig.). 1987. pap. write for info. (_0-915766-66-3_) Wise Pub.

__Preschooler's Family Story.__ V. Gilbert Beers. (Preschoolers Bible Ser.). 256p. (J). 1995. 16.99 (_1-56476-492-3_, 6-3492, Victor Bks) Chariot Victor.

__Preschoolers Sing & Say: Songs & Rhymes for Church Learning Times.__ rev. ed. (Illus.). 104p. (Orig.). 1996. spiral bd. 6.25 (_0-87227-195-1_, RBP5049) Reg Baptist.

__Preschoolers with Special Needs: Children-at-Risk or Who Have Disabilities: Instructor's Manual with Tests.__ Janet Lerner et al. (C). 1998. text, teacher ed. write for info. (_0-205-26736-X_, T6736-7) Allyn.

*__Prescott Fur-Ever.__ Raymond W. Whitaker. 93p. 2000. 27.50 (_0-7404-0162-9_); pap. 17.50 (_0-7404-0163-7_) Higginson Bk Co.

*__Prescott Fur-Ever.__ Raymond W. Whitaker. (Illus.). 96p. 2000. 27.50 (_0-8328-1785-6_); pap. 17.50 (_0-8328-1786-4_) Higginson Bk Co.

__Prescott Has Everything.__ Milly Singletary. (Illus.). 52p. (Orig.). 1992. pap. 3.95 (_0-941244-11-3_) Singletary Pubns.

__Prescott Macroeconomics Theory & Policy Study Guide with Brochure.__ 1992. write for info. (_0-201-55330-9_) Addison-Wesley.

__Prescott Means . . .__ Ed. by Barbara L. Warren. (Illus.). 64p. (Orig.). 1989. pap. 9.95 (_0-924956-03-8_) Imagine Rainbows.

__Prescott Memorial: A Genealogical Memoir of the Prescott Family in America.__ W. Prescott. (Illus.). 667p. 1989. reprint ed. pap. 100.00 (_0-8328-0991-8_); reprint ed. lib. bdg. 108.00 (_0-8328-0990-X_) Higginson Bk Co.

__Prescott Peninsula Wanderings.__ J. Apple Henry. 346p. (Orig.). 1985. pap. 6.95 (_0-931691-18-4_) Spring St Pr.

__Prescott Proposals.__ Howard Lindsey & Russel Crouse. 1954. pap. 5.25 (_0-8222-0909-8_) Dramatists Play.

__Prescott Street Reader: Poetry & Prose.__ Ed. by Vi Gale. 171p. (Orig.). (C). 1995. pap. 20.00 (_0-915986-26-4_) Prescott St Pr.

*__Prescott Years.__ Raymond W. Whitaker. (Illus.). 128p. 2000. 29.50 (_0-7404-0174-2_); pap. 19.50 (_0-7404-0175-0_) Higginson Bk Co.

__Prescott's Unique Mountain Club.__ Ruby Schmieder. (Illus.). (Orig.). 1993. pap. text 18.00 (_0-9626013-8-1_) Cordell Expeditions.

__Prescribed Burning for Bushland Management: The South Texas Example.__ W. T. Hamilton & Charles J. Scifres. LC 92-19152. (Illus.). 264p. 1993. 40.00 (_0-89096-539-0_); pap. 19.50 (_0-89096-512-9_) Tex A&M Univ Pr.

__Prescribed Burning In California Wildlands Vegetation Management.__ Harold Biswell. 295p. 1999. pap. 18.95 (_0-520-21945-7_, Pub. by U CA Pr) Cal Prin Full Svc.

__Prescribed Drugs & the Alternative Practitioner: The Essential Guide.__ Stephen Gascoigne. 1992. pap. 39.95 (_1-85398-022-6_, Pub. by Ashgrove Pr) Words Distrib.

__Prescribed Prayer Made Simple.__ T. W. Arnold. 770p. 1996. pap. 10.50 (_0-614-21473-4_, 978) Kazi Pubns.

__Prescribed Usage.__ Roger Brown. Date not set. 19.95 (_0-465-06271-7_, Pub. by Basic); pap. 18.00 (_0-465-06270-9_) Basic.

__Prescriber.__ Clarke. 31.95 (_0-8464-4495-X_) Beekman Pubs.

__Prescriber.__ John Henrik Clarke. 109p. 1972. 21.00 (_0-85032-088-7_, Pub. by C W Daniel) Natl Bk Netwk.

__Prescriber.__ 11th ed. John Henrik Clarke. 382p. (C). 1972. pap. 31.95 (_0-8464-1041-9_) Beekman Pubs.

__Prescriber's Guide to Hormone Replacement Therapy.__ Ed. by M. I. Whitehead. LC 98-10869. (Illus.). 220p. 1998. 110.00 (_1-85070-974-2_) Prthnon Pub.

__Prescribing for the Elderly.__ Peter P. Lamy. LC 78-55289. 714p. reprint ed. pap. 200.00 (_0-8357-7865-7_, 203628200002) Bks Demand.

__Prescribing Hemodialysis: A Guide to Urea Modeling, No. 29.__ D. A. Depner. (Developments in Nephrology Ser.). (C). 1990. text 152.00 (_0-7923-0833-6_) Kluwer Academic.

__Prescribing in General Practice.__ Ed. by Conrad M. Harris. 1995. write for info. (_1-85775-042-X_, Radcliffe Med Pr) Scovill Paterson.

*__Prescribing in Pregnancy.__ 3rd ed. Ed. by Peter Rubin. 198p. 2002. pap. text 35.95 (_0-7279-1449-9_) BMJ Pub.

__Prescribing in Primary Care.__ Ed. by Colin P. Bradley. (Oxford General Practice Ser.: No. 42). (Illus.). 228p. 1998. pap. text 52.95 (_0-19-262687-6_) OUP.

__Prescribing Narcotics: Physician Implementation of Pain Management Guidelines.__ Patricia D. Salvato et al. (Illus.). 1998. pap. 169.95 (_0-9665067-1-5_) Prefer Pub Co.

__Prescribing Our Future: Ethical Challenges in Genetic Counseling.__ Ed. by Dianne M. Bartels et al. LC 92-21469. 208p. 1993. pap. text 23.95 (_0-202-30453-1_); lib. bdg. 47.95 (_0-202-30452-3_) Aldine de Gruyter.

__Prescribing, Recording & Reporting Photon Beam Therapy.__ International Commission on Radiation Units & Measurements Staff. LC 99-13573. (ICRU Reports: Vol. 50). 1999. 60.00 (_0-913394-61-0_) Intl Comm Rad Meas.

__Prescribing, Recording & Reporting Photon Beam Therapy.__ Ed. by W. Roger Ney. LC 93-3633. (ICRU Reports: No. 50). 18p. (Orig.). 1993. pap. text 60.00 (_0-913394-48-3_) Intl Comm Rad Meas.

__Prescribing the Curvature of a Riemannian Manifold.__ J. L. Kazdan. LC 84-28274. (CBMS Regional Conference Series in Mathematics: No. 57). 55p. 1985. reprint ed. pap. 19.00 (_0-8218-0707-2_, CBMS/57) Am Math.

__Prescribing the Life of the Mind: An Essay on the Purpose of the University, the Aims of Liberal Education, the Competence of Citizens, & the Cultivation of Practical Reason.__ Charles W. Anderson. LC 92-45196. 192p. (C). 1993. 22.95 (_0-299-13830-5_) U of Wis Pr.

__Prescribing the Life of the Mind: An Essay on the Purpose of the University, the Aims of Liberal Education, the Competence of Citizens, & the Cultivation of Practical Reason.__ Charles W. Anderson. LC 92-45196. 190p. (C). 1996. pap. 12.95 (_0-299-13834-8_) U of Wis Pr.

__Prescribing the Price of Pharmaceuticals.__ W. Duncan Reekie. (Choice in Welfare Ser.: No. 26). 120p. 1995. pap. 34.50 (_0-255-36363-X_, Pub. by Inst Economic Affairs) Coronet Bks.

*__Prescription: Medicine: The Goodness of Planned Death.__ Jack Kevorkian. 268p. 1999. reprint ed. text 29.00 (_0-7881-6302-7_) DIANE Pub.

*__Prescription - Baby.__ Jule McBride. (Maitland Maternity Ser.). 2000. mass mkt. 4.50 (_0-373-65066-3_, 1650662) Harlequin Bks.

__Prescription Alternatives.__ Earl L. Mindell & Virginia Hopkins. LC 99-16218. 348p. 1999. pap. 19.95 (_0-87983-989-9_, 39899K, Keats Publng) NTC Contemp Pub Co.

__Prescription & Election in Elementary-School Teacher-Training Curricula in State Teachers Colleges.__ Edward C. Class. LC 74-176652. (Columbia University. Teachers College. Contributions to Education Ser.: No. 480). reprint ed. 37.50 (_0-404-55480-6_) AMS Pr.

__Prescription & Nonprescription Medications for Children: What Parents Need to Know/An Alphabet.__ Max Van Gilder. LC 99-200316. 1997. per. 5.99 (_0-671-51069-X_) PB.

__Prescription & Over-the-Counter Dermatology Markets: An Analysis of U. S. Worldwide Revenues, 1995-2000.__ Feedback Research Services Staff. 127p. 1996. spiral bd. 495.00 (_1-889713-00-7_) Feedback Rsch.

__Prescription Dermatology Pharmaceuticals Market.__ Frost & Sullivan Staff. 386p. 1996. spiral bd. 2895.00 (_0-7889-0584-8_, 5352-45) Frost & Sullivan.

__Prescription Drug Abuse see Drug Abuse Prevention Library: The Risks of Drug Use__

__Prescription Drug Abuse: The Hidden Epidemic; A Guide to Coping & Understanding.__ Rod Colvin. 196p. (Orig.). 1995. pap. 14.95 (_1-886039-22-4_) Addicus Bks.

__Prescription Drug Abuse & Dependence: How Prescription Drug Abuse Contributes to the Drug Abuse Epidemic.__ Daniel P. Greenfield. Ed. by Ralph Slovenko. LC 94-30116. (American Series Behavioral Science & Law: No. 1088). (Illus.). 184p. (C). 1994. text 45.95 (_0-398-05931-4_) C C Thomas.

__Prescription Drug Abuse & Dependence: How Prescription Drug Abuse Contributes to the Drug Abuse Epidemic.__ Daniel P. Greenfield. Ed. by Ralph Slovenko. LC 94-30116. (American Series Behavioral Science & Law: No. 1088). (Illus.). 184p. (C). 1994. pap. 31.95 (_0-398-05954-3_) C C Thomas.

__Prescription Drug Market: International Perspectives & Challenges for the Future.__ Ed. by Christine Huttin & Nick Bosanquet. LC 92-16413. (Advanced Series in Management: Vol. 17). 308p. 1995. 101.25 (_0-444-89559-0_, North Holland) Elsevier.

__Prescription Drug Prices: Price Gouging by Pharmaceutical Companies?__ (Illus.). 70p. (Orig.). (C). 1993. pap. text 30.00 (_1-56806-217-6_) DIANE Pub.

__Prescription Drugs.__ Consumer Guide Editors. 1997. mass mkt. 7.99 (_0-451-19240-0_, Sig) NAL.

__Prescription Drugs.__ Consumer Guide Editors. (Illus.). 384p. 1993. pap. 9.95 (_1-56173-452-7_, 4005200) Pubns Intl Ltd.

__Prescription Drugs.__ Robert M. Youngson. 1994. pap. 10.00 (_0-00-470535-1_) Collins.

__Prescription Drugs.__ rev. ed. Consumer Guide Editors. (Illus.). 1024p. 1995. mass mkt. 8.99 (_0-451-18364-9_, Sig) NAL.

__Prescription Drugs: An Indispensable Guide for People over 50.__ Brian S. Katcher. 400p. 1989. mass mkt. 4.95 (_0-380-70670-9_, Avon Bks) Morrow Avon.

__Prescription Drugs: Companies Typically Charge More in the U.S. Than in the U.K.__ 52p. pap. text 40.00 (_0-7881-1589-8_) DIANE Pub.

__Prescription Drugs: Spending Controls in Four European Countries.__ Jonathan Ratner. (Illus.). 100p. (Orig.). (C). 1994. pap. text 35.00 (_0-7881-1172-8_) DIANE Pub.

__Prescription Drugs & Medicaid: Automated Review Systems Can Help Promote Safety, Save Money.__ (Illus.). 31p. (Orig.). (C). 1996. pap. text 25.00 (_0-7881-3468-X_) DIANE Pub.

__Prescription Drugs & Their Side Effects.__ 7th ed. Edward L. Stern. 224p. 1993. pap. 9.95 (_0-399-51805-3_, Perigee Bks) Berkley Pub.

__Prescription Drugs for People over 50.__ Center for the Study of Pharmacy & Therapeutics for the Elderly Staff et al. LC 98-119623. 576p. 1997. write for info. (_0-7853-2465-8_) Pubns Intl Ltd.

__Prescription Drugs in Short Supply: Case Histories.__ Michael A. Schwartz. LC 79-24783. (Drugs & the Pharmaceutical Sciences Ser.: No. 8). 140p. reprint ed. pap. 43.40 (_0-7837-0870-X_, 204117800019) Bks Demand.

__Prescription Drugs over 40.__ Consumer Guide Editors. 1997. mass mkt. 6.99 (_0-451-19273-7_, Sig) NAL.

__Prescription Filled.__ James R. Lincoln. LC 81-51752. (Illus.). 202p. 1981. 12.50 (_0-88492-039-9_) W S Sullwold.

*__Prescription for a Healthy Church.__ Jolene L. Roehlkepartain. 2000. pap. 17.99 (_0-7644-2215-4_) Group Pub.

__Prescription for a Long & Happy Life - Age-Old Wisdom for the New Age.__ Dov Peretz Elkins. LC 93-77902. 185p. 1993. 20.00 (_0-918834-14-7_) Growth Assoc.

__Prescription for a Long Life.__ Morton Walker & Mitchel Kurk. 1997. write for info. (_0-614-25222-9_) Penguin Putnam.

*__Prescription for A Miracle: A Daily Devotional for Divine Health.__ Mark Brazee. 1999. pap. text 19.99 (_1-57794-209-4_) Harrison Hse.

*__Prescription for A Miracle: A Daily Devotional for Divine Health.__ Mark Brazee. 1999. pap. text 15.99 (_1-57794-208-6_) Harrison Hse.

*__Prescription for a Stroke Free.__ David O. Wiebers. 2000. 25.00 (_0-06-019823-0_); pap. 15.00 (_0-06-095782-4_) HarpC.

*__Prescription for Addiction? The Arizona & California Medical Drug Use Initiatives : Congressional Hearing.__ Ed. by Orrin G. Hatch. (Illus.). 133p. 2000. pap. text 30.00 (_0-7567-0063-9_) DIANE Pub.

__Prescription for Adventure: Bush Pilot Doctor.__ 2nd rev. ed. Naomi Gaede-Penner & Elmer E. Gaede. (Illus.). 247p. 1994. reprint ed. pap. 15.95 (_0-9637030-0-5_) Change Pts.

__Prescription for Advertising: A Common Sense Guide for Understanding the Complex & Confusing World of Advertising.__ unabridged ed. Edmond A. Bruneau. 176p. 1986. pap. 29.95 incl. audio (_0-9616683-2-6_); pap. 19.95 incl. audio (_0-9616683-3-4_) Boston Bks.

__Prescription for Advertising: A Common Sense Guide for Understanding the Complex & Confusing World of Advertising.__ unabridged ed. Edmond A. Bruneau. 176p. 1986. 37.95 incl. audio (_0-9616683-1-8_) Boston Bks.

__Prescription for Anger: Coping with Angry Feelings & Angry People.__ Gary D. Hankins. LC 88-19896. 1988. pap. 14.95 (_0-943367-01-8_) Princess Pub.

__Prescription for Anger: Coping with Angry Feelings & Angry People.__ Gary D. Hankins. 400p. 1993. mass mkt. 6.50 (_0-446-36392-8_, Pub. by Warner Bks) Little.

__Prescription for Anxiety.__ Leslie D. Weatherhead. (C). 1990. pap. 35.00 (_0-85305-264-6_, Pub. by Arthur James) St Mut.

__Prescription for Cooking: Designer Diets for the Healing Force Within.__ rev. ed. Phyllis Balch & James F. Balch, Jr. 306p. (Orig.). 1987. reprint ed. pap. text 14.95 (_0-685-55184-9_) P A B Bks.

__Prescription for Cooking & Dietary Wellness.__ James F. Balch & Phyllis Balch. 317p. 1993. pap. 16.95 (_0-942023-02-1_) P A B Bks.

__Prescription for Dietary Wellness: Using Food to Heal.__ Phyllis Balch & James Balch. 330p. Date not set. pap. 16.95 (_0-89529-868-6_, Avery) Penguin Putnam.

__Prescription for Disaster: The Hidden Dangers in Your Medicine Cabinet.__ Thomas J. Moore. 1999. mass mkt. 5.99 (_0-440-23484-0_) Dell.

__Prescription for Disaster: The Hidden Dangers in Your Medicine Cabinet.__ Thomas J. Moore. LC 97-47081. 272p. 1998. 25.00 (_0-684-82998-3_) S&S Trade.

__Prescription for Extinction: Endangered Species & Patented Oriental Medicines in Trade.__ Andrea L. Gaski & Kurt A. Johnson. LC 95-230919. 314p. 1994. pap. 30.00 (_1-85850-031-1_) World Wildlife Fund.

__Prescription for Failure: Race Relations in the Age of Social Science.__ Byron M. Roth. LC 93-42745. (Studies in Social Philosophy & Policy: No. 18). 370p. (C). 1994. 49.95 (_1-56000-161-5_); pap. 24.95 (_1-56000-739-7_) Transaction Pubs.

*__Prescription for Greed.__ Willis J. Hurst & Philip Hurst. LC 00-35664. 192p. (C). 2000. 24.95 (_1-929490-04-6_) Beil.

__Prescription for Growth.__ Tate Holt. 1996. pap. text 18.95 (_1-882180-72-0_) Griffin CA.

__Prescription for Health Care.__ John R. Krismer. 324p. (Orig.). 1996. pap. 17.95 (_1-57502-113-7_) Morris Pubng.

__Prescription for Health Care Policy.__ Walter M. Cadette. (Public Policy Brief Highlights Ser.: Vol. 30A). 8p. 1997. pap. write for info. (_0-941276-25-2_) J Levy.

__Prescription for Health Care Policy: The Case for Retargeting Tax Subsidies to Health Care.__ Walter M. Cadette. (Public Policy Briefs Ser.: Vol. 30). (Illus.). 40p. (Orig.). 1997. pap. text 3.00 (_0-941276-23-6_) J Levy.

*__Prescription for Herbal Healing.__ Robert Rister & Phyllis Balch. 2001. pap. 23.95 (_1-58333-094-1_, Avery) Penguin Putnam.

__Prescription for Herbal Healing: A Practical A-Z Reference to Drug-Free Remedies Using Herbs & Herbal Preparations.__ Robert Rister. 480p. 1999. pap. 19.95 (_0-89529-869-4_, Avery) Penguin Putnam.

__Prescription for Joy Daybreak.__ Zondervan Gifts. LC 98-100418. 1997. 5.99 (_0-310-97374-0_) Zondervan.

__Prescription for Justice.__ Victor Wartofsky. 1987. 14.95 (_0-8184-0423-X_) Carol Pub Group.

__Prescription for Life.__ Joe Lacy. LC 98-107142. 160p. 1997. 5.99 (_0-310-97375-9_) Zondervan.

__Prescription for Life.__ Alfred Leonard. 124p. (Orig.). 1997. pap. write for info. (_0-9653271-0-8_) J Witty.

__Prescription for Life: The Jason Winters Story, a Cancer Survivor.__ John Perkins. 290p. (Orig.). 1997. pap. 16.95 (_1-57901-016-4_) Intl Promotions.

__Prescription for Long Life: Essential Remedies for Longevity.__ Mitchell Kurk & Morton Walker. LC 97-35936. 224p. Date not set. pap. 12.95 (_0-89529-790-6_, Avery) Penguin Putnam.

__Prescription for Love.__ large type ed. Anne Ladley. 235p. 1992. reprint ed. lib. bdg. 13.95 (_1-56054-478-3_) Thorndike Pr.

__Prescription for Mayhem: Drug Legalization.__ B. Steven Mohnarke. LC 97-210213. 220p. 1997. 28.95 (_0-9639422-3-9_) Striking Impress.

__Prescription for Melissa.__ large type ed. Alice Dwyer-Joyce. 263p. 1980. 27.99 (_0-7089-0437-8_) Ulverscroft.

__Prescription for Murder.__ Susan Kirby. (You-Solve-It Mysteries Ser.: No. 9). 224p. 1994. mass mkt. 3.50 (_0-8217-4791-6_, Zebra Kensgtn) Kensgtn Pub Corp.

__Prescription for Murder: The Victorian Serial Killings of Dr. Thomas Neill Cream.__ Angus McLaren. 234p. 1995. pap. 12.95 (_0-226-56068-6_) U Ch Pr.

__Prescription for Murder: The Victorian Serial Killings of Dr. Thomas Neill Cream.__ Angus McLaren. LC 92-20219. (Chicago Series on Sexuality, History, & Society). (Illus.). 234p. (C). 1998. 22.50 (_0-226-56067-8_) U Ch Pr.

__Prescription for Nutrition.__ 1992. lib. bdg. 75.00 (_0-8490-5293-9_) Gordon Pr.

*__Prescription for Nutritional Healing: A Practical A-to-Z Reference to Drug-Free Remedies Using Vitamins, Minerals, Herbs & Food Supplements.__ 3rd ed. Phyllis A. Balch & James F. Balch. 704p. 2000. pap. 22.95 (_1-58333-077-1_, Avery); spiral bd. 27.95 (_1-58333-083-6_, Avery) Penguin Putnam.

__Prescription for Nutritional Healing: A Practical A-Z Reference to Drug-Free Remedies Using Vitamins, Minerals, Herbs & Food Supplements.__ James F. Balch & Phyllis A. Balch. LC 90-452. (Illus.). 340p. 1990. pap. 16.95 (_0-89529-429-X_, Avery) Penguin Putnam.

__Prescription for Nutritional Healing: A Practical A-Z Reference to Drug-Free Remedies Using Vitamins, Minerals, Herbs & Food Supplements.__ 2nd ed. James F. Balch & Phyllis A. Balch. 1999. 29.95 (_0-13-025447-9_) P-H.

__Prescription for Nutritional Healing: A Practical A-Z Reference to Drug-Free Remedies Using Vitamins, Minerals, Herbs & Food Supplements.__ 2nd ed. James F. Balch & Phyllis A. Balch. LC 97-157317. (Illus.). 608p. 1996. pap. 19.95 (_0-89529-727-2_, Avery) Penguin Putnam.

__Prescription for Nutritional Healing: A-to-Z Guide to Supplements : A Handy Resource to Today's Most Effective Nutritional Supplements.__ James F. Balch & Phyllis A. Balch. LC 98-156431. 256p. 1997. mass mkt. 6.95 (_0-89529-816-3_, Avery) Penguin Putnam.

__Prescription for Profit: How Doctors Defraud Medicaid.__ Paul Jesilow et al. 1993. 38.00 (_0-520-07614-1_, Pub. by U CA Pr) Cal Prin Full Svc.

__Prescription for Profitable Pigs: A Guide to Herd Level Pork Production.__ Intro. by Ann Henderson. LC 94-173655. 170p. (C). 1994. 35.00 (_1-883274-01-X_) Watt Pub.

__Prescription for Profits: How the Pharmaceutical Industry Bankrolled the Unholy Marriage between Science & State.__ Linda Marsa. LC 96-48440. 1997. 24.50 (_0-684-80002-0_, Scribners Ref) Mac Lib Ref.

__Prescription for Progress: The Uruguay Round in the New Global Economy: Version of July 7, 1994.__ Program Committee for the Comittee for Economic De. LC 94-34588. 1994. 10.00 (_0-87186-118-6_) Comm Econ Dev.

__Prescription for Prosperity: Four Paths to Economic Renewal.__ National Issues Forum Institute Staff. 32p. 1992. 3.25 (_0-8403-7438-0_) Kendall-Hunt.

__Prescription for Prosperity: Four Paths to Economic Renewal.__ Public Agenda Foundation Staff. 45p. (C). 1992. 12.19 (_0-07-051082-2_) McGraw.

__Prescription for Reading: Teach Them Phonics.__ Ernest H. Christman. LC 83-70696. (Illus.). 290p. (Orig.). 1984. reprint ed. 22.95 (_0-912329-01-7_); reprint ed. pap. 15.95 (_0-912329-00-9_) Tutorial Press.

*__Prescription for Spiritual Impotency.__ Josephine Irena Sotomayer. 1999. text 24.95 (_1-889227-02-1_) Sotomayers.

__Prescription for Success: The Life & Values of Ewing Marion Kauffman.__ Anne H. Morgan. LC 95-23169. 438p. 1995. 22.95 (_0-8362-0466-2_) Andrews & McMeel.

__Prescription for Success: The Rexall Showcase Story & What It Means to You.__ James W. Robinson. LC 98-56030. 256p. 1999. pap. 15.00 (_0-7615-1981-5_, Frum) Prima Pub.

__Prescription for Terror.__ Sandra Levy Ceren. LC 99-94664. 240p. 1999. pap. 11.95 (_0-9669861-0-5_) Andrw Scott.

__Prescription for the Boards: A Student-to-Student Guide.__ Radhika S. Breaden et al. LC 95-45312. 512p. 1995. pap. text 29.95 (_0-316-10626-7_) Lppncott W & W.

__Prescription for the Doctor.__ large type ed. Irene Samson. (Dales Large Print Ser.). 191p. 1996. pap. 18.99 (_1-85389-688-8_, Dales) Ulverscroft.

__Prescription for the Future: How the Technology Revolution Is Changing the Pulse of Global Health.__ Gwendolyn B. Moore et al. 200p. 1996. 24.95 (_1-888232-10-2_) Knowldge Exchange.

__Prescription Medicide: The Goodness of Planned Death.__ Jack Kevorkian. LC 89-92751. (Illus.). 268p. 1991. 28.95 (_0-87975-677-2_); pap. 17.95 (_0-87975-872-4_) Prometheus Bks.

__Prescription Medicines in United Kingdom: A Strategic Entry Report, 1997.__ Compiled by Icon Group International Staff. (Illus.). 98p. 1999. ring bd. 980.00 incl. audio compact disk (_0-7418-0813-7_) Icon Grp.

__Prescription Methods for ICF Systems.__ 1998. write for info. (_0-89312-197-5_) Portland Cement.

__Prescription Narcotics: The Addictive Painkillers.__ Michael Bunsey & Paul Sanberg. (Encyclopedia of Psychoactive Drugs Ser.: No. 1). (Illus.). 124p. (YA). (gr. 7 up). 1986. lib. bdg. 19.95 (_0-87754-770-X_) Chelsea Hse.

__Prescription Pads.__ Travell. 1992. pap. text 23.95 (_0-683-17536-X_) Lppncott W & W.

__Prescription Privileges for Psychologist: A Critical Appraisal.__ Ed. by Steven C. Hayes & Elaine M. Heiby. LC 98-39199. 282p. (C). 1998. 34.95 (_1-878978-30-6_) Context Pr.

__Prescription Writing.__ A. Mukherji. (C). 1989. 40.00 (_0-89771-356-7_, Pub. by Current Dist) St Mut.

P

An Asterisk (*) at the beginning of an entry indicates that the title is appearing for the first time.

Prescriptions: The Dissemination of Medical Authority, 27. Ed. by Gayle L. Ormiston & Raphael Sassower. LC 89-17183. (Contributions in Medical Studies: No. 27). 200p. 1990. 55.00 (*0-313-26625-5*, OPR/, Greenwood Pr) Greenwood.

Prescriptions & Policies: The Social Well-Being of African Americans in the 1990's. Ed. by Dionne J. Jones. 164p. (C). 1990. pap. 21.95 (*0-88738-883-3*) Transaction Pubs.

***Prescriptions for a Healthy House: A Practical Guide for Architects, Builders, & Homeowners.** Paula Baker et al. (Illus.). 250p. 1998. pap. 29.95 (*0-9702107-0-1*) Baker Laporte.

Prescriptions for a Healthy House: A Practical Guide for Architects, Builders & Homeowners. Paula Baker et al. LC 97-42428. 280p. 1997. pap. 29.95 (*1-56690-355-6*, InWord Pr) High Mtn.

Prescriptions for Child Mental Health. Goldstein. (C). 1978. 52.95 (*0-205-14356-3*, H4356); pap. 25.95 (*0-205-14355-5*, H4355) Allyn.

Prescriptions for Children with Learning & Adjustment Problems: A Consultant's Desk Reference. 3rd ed. Ralph F. Blanco & David F. Bogacki. 264p. 1988. 43.95 (*0-398-05390-1*); pap. 29.95 (*0-398-06022-3*) C C Thomas.

Prescriptions for Good Eating. Cline et al. 304p. (Orig.). 1984. pap. 11.95 (*0-9613679-0-3*) Greenville County Med.

Prescriptions for Good Taste. Walgreen Drug Stores Historical Foundation Staff. 464p. 1995. 19.95 (*0-9648458-0-6*) Walgrn Drug.

Prescriptions for Happiness. Ken Keyes, Jr. LC 80-84855. (Illus.). 144p. 1981. pap. 7.95 (*0-915972-02-6*) Love Line Bks.

Prescriptions for Healthy Farm Animals. John B. Herrick. Ed. by Kelly Lessiter & Frank D. Lessiter. LC 90-92107. (Illus.). 434p. (Orig.). (C). 1991. pap. 8.95 (*0-944079-01-6*) Lessiter Pubns.

Prescriptions for Independence: Working with Older People Who Are Visually Impaired. Nora Griffin-Shirley & Gerda Groff. 87p. 1993. pap. 29.95 (*0-89128-244-0*) Am Foun Blind.

Prescriptions for Life with Cancer. Eric Fairbank. 1996. pap. text 7.95 (*0-85572-269-X*, Pub. by Hill Content Pubng) Seven Hills Bk.

Prescriptions for Living: Inspirational Lessons for a Joyful, Loving Life. Bernie Siegel. LC 98-39059. 240p. 1998. 23.00 (*0-06-019196-1*) HarpC.

Prescriptions for Living: Inspirational Lessons for a Joyful, Loving Life. Bernie Siegel. 256p. 1999. pap. 12.95 (*0-06-092936-7*) HarpC.

***Prescriptions for Living: Siegel,&Bernie, Set.** Bernie S. Siegel. 1998. audio 18.00 (*0-694-52035-7*) HarperAudio.

Prescriptions for Parenting. Carolyn A. Meeks. 1990. mass mkt. 9.99 (*0-446-39148-4*, Pub. by Warner Bks) Little.

Prescriptions for Saving China: Selected Writings of Sun Yat-sen. Yat-sen Sun. Ed. by Julie Wei et al. (Publication Ser.: No. 420). 372p. (C). 1994. 42.95 (*0-8179-9281-2*); pap. 26.95 (*0-8179-9282-0*) Hoover Inst Pr.

Prescriptions for Survival Index. Ed. by Bibliotheca Press Staff. LC 82-70345. 102p. 1982. ring bd. 25.95 (*0-939476-43-6*) Prosperity & Profits.

Prescriptions for Survival with Workpages. Frieda Carrol. LC 78-72312. 148p. 1981. ring bd. 26.95 (*0-9605246-1-4*) Prosperity & Profits.

Prescriptions for Working Statisticians. A. Madansky. (Texts in Statistics Ser.). (Illus.). 350p. 1988. 53.95 (*0-387-96627-7*) Spr-Verlag.

Prescriptions from God's Word. Contrib. by Tim McPherson. 28p. 1997. 1.35 (*0-89827-185-1*) Wesleyan Pub Hse.

Prescriptions That Count: Preventative Medication for Church Problems. Charles F. Scheide, Sr. 280p. (Orig.). 1996. pap. 8.50 (*1-57502-105-6*) Morris Pubng.

***Prescriptive Method for Residential Cold-Formed Steel Framing.** Nader R. Elhajj et al. (Illus.). 81p. 2000. reprint ed. pap. text 20.00 (*0-7881-4330-1*) DIANE Pub.

***Prescriptive Psychotherapy: A Practical Guide to Systematic Treatment Selection.** Larry E. Beutler & T. Mark Harwood. LC 99-42912. 208p. 2000. 29.95 (*0-19-513669-1*) OUP.

Prescriptive Seating for Wheeled Mobility: Theory, Application, & Terminology, Vol. I. Diane E. Ward. LC 93-78396. (Illus.). 214p. (C). 1994. pap. text 29.95 (*0-9614029-1-1*) HealthWealth.

Prescriptive Seating for Wheeled Mobility Vol. II: Human Assessment. Diane E. Ward. 250p. (C). 2000. pap. text. write for info. (*0-9614029-2-X*) HealthWealth.

Prescriptives. Joyan Saunders. (Illus.). 23p. 1984. pap. 10.00 (*0-939784-08-4*) CEPA Gall.

Preseances. Francois Mauriac. pap. 9.95 (*0-685-34300-6*) Fr & Eur.

Preseances: Galigai. Francois Mauriac. (FRE.). 1990. pap. 18.95 (*0-7859-3422-7*) Fr & Eur.

***Presenca Portuguesa Na California.** Eduardo Mayone Dias. Ed. by Peregrinacao Publications Staff. (Documentos Ser.). (POR.). 128p. 2000. boxed set 13.95 (*1-889358-23-1*, 24) Peregrinacao.

Presence see Who Is This Ghost Called Holy?: The Ministry of the Holy Spirit

Presence. Naosherwan Anzar. 90p. (Orig.). 1992. pap. 9.95 (*0-9613907-2-7*) Beloved Bks.

Presence. T. Davis Bunn. 352p. (Orig.). 1990. pap. 9.99 (*1-55661-137-4*) Bethany Hse.

***Presence.** T. Davis Bunn. 352p. (Orig.). 1999. pap. 10.99 (*0-7642-2301-1*) Bethany Hse.

Presence. William Flygare. 120p. 1982. 12.50 (*0-933704-14-3*) Dawn Pr.

Presence. Bruce Meyer. LC 98-55995. 60p. 1999. pap. 10.95 (*1-885266-75-8*, Pub. by Story Line) Consort Bk Sales.

***Presence.** John Saul. 1998. mass mkt. 7.99 (*0-449-00241-1*, Crest) Fawcett.

***Presence.** Christopher Torockio. 212p. 1999. pap. 12.95 (*1-879934-63-9*) St Andrews NC.

Presence. deluxe limited ed. Photos by Shirley C. Burden. (Illus.). 96p. 1981. 250.00 (*0-89381-076-2*) Aperture.

Presence. large type ed. John Saul. LC 97-44301. 580p. 1997. 26.95 (*0-7838-8361-7*, G K Hall & Co) Mac Lib Ref.

Presence. George E. Failing. 32p. 1982. reprint ed. pap. 1.00 (*0-937296-04-X*, 221-A) Presence Inc.

Presence, Bk. 4. John Saul. LC 97-14756. 338p. 1997. 25.00 (*0-449-91055-5*, Columbine) Fawcett.

Presence: Poems, 1984-87. Kathleen Raine. 80p. 1987. 14.95 (*0-940262-20-7*, Lindisfarne) Anthroposophic.

Presence & Absence of God. Ed. by Christopher F. Mooney. LC 68-8748. (Cardinal Bea Lectures). 190p. reprint ed. pap. 58.90 (*0-7837-0458-5*, 204078100018) Bks Demand.

Presence & Coincidence: The Transformation of Transcendental into Ontological Phenomenology. Christopher E. Macann. 152p. (C). 1991. lib. bdg. 102.00 (*0-7923-0923-5*, Pub. by Kluwer Academic) Kluwer Academic.

Presence & Desire: Essays on Gender, Sexuality, Performance. Jill Dolan. (Critical Perspectives on Women & Gender Ser.). 232p. (C). 1994. pap. text 17.95 (*0-472-06530-0*, 06530) U of Mich Pr.

Presence & Function of Scripture in Galatians 1 & 2. Roy E. Ciampa. (Wissenshaftliche Untersuchungen zum Neuen Testament Ser.: No. 102). 461p. 1998. pap. 95.00 (*3-16-146895-3*, Pub. by JCB Mohr) Coronet Bks.

Presence & Power. Robert W. Dell. (Covenant Bible Studies). 40p. (Orig.). 1991. pap. 4.95 (*0-87178-720-2*, 8202) Brethren.

Presence & Power: Releasing the Holy Spirit. Harold E. Bauman. LC 88-34747. 128p. (Orig.). 1989. pap. 8.99 (*0-8361-3493-1*) Herald Pr.

Presence & Pre-Expressivity 1. Ralph Yarrow. 88p. 1998. pap. text 14.00 (*90-5702-174-9*, Harwood Acad Pubs) Gordon & Breach.

Presence & Pre-Expressivity 2, Vol. 2. Ed. by Robert Yarrow. 88p. 1998. pap. text 14.00 (*90-5702-175-7*, Harwood Acad Pubs) Gordon & Breach.

Presence & Presentation: Women in the Chinese Literati Tradition. LC 98-26386. 307p. 1999. text 59.95 (*0-312-21054-X*) St Martin.

Presence & Resistance: Postmodernism & Cultural Politics in Contemporary American Performance. Philip Auslander. (Theater: Theory-Text-Performance Ser.). 216p. 1994. pap. text 17.95 (*0-472-08278-7*, 08278) U of Mich Pr.

Presence & Thought: An Essay on the Religious Philosophy of Gregory of Nyssa. Hans U. Von Balthasar. LC 94-79302. 194p. (Orig.). pap. 17.95 (*0-89870-521-5*) Ignatius Pr.

Presence at a Distance: The Educator-Learner Relationship in Distance Education. Jane S. Munro. (Research Monograph: No. 16). 1998. pap. text. write for info. (*1-877780-21-9*) ACSDE.

Presence at the Center: The Twelve Steps & the Journey Deep Within. James Jennings. 76p. pap. 8.00 (*1-56838-001-1*) Hazelden.

Presence in the Flesh: The Body in Medicine. Katharine G. Young. LC 96-39721. (Illus.). 224p. 1997. 29.00 (*0-674-70181-X*) HUP.

Presence in the Parlor, Vol. 5. Ed Okonowicz. (Spirits Between the Bays Ser.). (Illus.). (Orig.). 1997. pap. 9.95 (*0-9643244-7-4*) Myst & Lace.

***Presence in the Promise: First Lesson Sermons for Advent/Christmas/Epiphany, Cycle C.** Harry N. Huxhold. LC 00-35793. 142p. 2000. pap. 12.95 (*0-7880-1713-6*); disk 12.95 (*0-7880-1714-4*) CSS OH.

Presence Is in Exile, Too: Collected Stories. Hanan Ayalti. LC 96-52864. (Illus.). 256p. 1998. 25.00 (*1-881320-22-7*, Black Belt) Black Belt Communs.

***Presence Lingers: Face to Face with Nature in the Southern Appalachians.** Earle P. Barron. 114p. 1999. pap. 9.00 (*0-7392-0465-3*, 3777) Morris Pubng.

Presence of Absence: New Installations. Nina Felshin. LC 88-80869. (Illus.). 60p. 1988. pap. 15.00 (*0-916365-26-3*) Ind Curators.

Presence of Absence: On Prayers & an Epiphany. Doris Grumbach. LC 97-52256. 126p. 1998. 18.00 (*0-8070-7084-X*) Beacon Pr.

Presence of Absence: On Prayers & an Epiphany. Doris Grumbach. LC 97-52256. 144p. 1999. pap. 13.00 (*0-8070-7093-9*) Beacon Pr.

Presence of Absence: On Prayers & an Epiphany. large type ed. Doris Grumbach. LC 98-42254. 1999. 30.00 (*0-7838-0390-7*, G K Hall Lrg Type) Mac Lib Ref.

Presence of Angels. Judyth Hill. 72p. 1995. pap. 12.00 (*0-9644196-1-0*) Sherman Asher Pub.

Presence of Camoes: Influences on the Literature of England, America, & Southern Africa. George Monteiro. LC 95-46725. (Studies in Romance Languages: No. 40). (Illus.). 200p. (C). 1996. text 24.95 (*0-8131-1952-9*) U Pr of Ky.

Presence of Care: The History of St. Luke's Hospital. Edward T. Matheny, Jr. Ed. by Frederic J. Hron. (Illus.). 456p. 1997. 24.95 (*0-9657425-0-4*) St Lukes Hosp.

Presence of Caring in Nursing. Ed. by Delores A. Gaut. 292p. (C). 1992. pap. text 12.95 (*0-88737-547-2*) Natl League Nurse.

Presence of Faulkner in the Writings of Garcia Marquez. Harley D. Oberhelman. (Graduate Studies: No. 22). (Illus.). 43p. 1980. pap. 7.00 (*0-89672-080-2*) Tex Tech Univ Pr.

Presence of Feeling in Thought. Ed. by Bernard Den Ouden & Marcia Moen. LC 91-3822. (Revisioning Philosophy Ser.: Vol. 7). 243p. 1992. 44.95 (*0-8204-1503-0*) P Lang Pubng.

Presence of God, 4 vols. Marie-Agnes Gaudrat. (What Is God Like? Ser.). (Illus.). 10p. (J). 1992. bds. 4.95 (*0-8146-2135-X*) Liturgical Pr.

Presence of God & Prayer see Presencia de Dios y la Oracion

Presence of God in the Christian Life: John Wesley & the Means of Grace. Henry H. Knight, III. (Pietist & Wesleyan Studies: No. 3). 270p. 1992. 41.00 (*0-8108-2589-9*) Scarecrow.

Presence of Grace. James F. Powers. LC 77-85694. (Short Story Index Reprint Ser.). 1977. 19.95 (*0-8369-3037-1*) Ayer.

Presence of Mind. Fred W. Hunter. (WWL Mystery Ser.). 1998. per. 4.99 (*0-373-26282-5*, 1-26282-3, Wrldwide Lib) Harlequin Bks.

Presence of Mind. Fred W. Hunter. LC 93-22962. 1994. 19.95 (*0-8027-3245-3*) Walker & Co.

Presence of Mind. Daniel D. Hutto. LC 99-22516. (Advances in Consciousness Research Ser.: Vol. 17). xiv, 252p. 1999. pap. 34.95 (*1-55619-433-1*) J Benjamins Pubng.

Presence of Mind. Anthea Fraser. 1994. reprint ed. lib. bdg. 20.00 (*0-7278-4704-X*) Severn Hse.

Presence of Mind: Education & the Politics of Deception. Pepi Leistyna. LC 98-34588. (Edge). 224p. (C). 1999. pap. 21.00 (*0-8133-3476-4*, Pub. by Westview); text 69.00 (*0-8133-3475-6*, Pub. by Westview) HarpC.

Presence of Mind: Literary & Philosophical Roots of a Wise Psychotherapy. Stephen Schoen. 312p. 1993. 28.50 (*0-939266-19-9*) Gestalt Journal.

Presence of Mind: Museums & the Spirit of Learning. Ed. by Bonnie Pitman. LC 98-53146. 250p. 1999. pap. 40.00 (*0-931201-58-6*) Am Assn Mus.

Presence of Mind: Writing & the Domain Beyond the Cognitive. Ed. by Alice Brand & Richard Graves. LC 93-42727. (Illus.). 246p. (C). 1994. pap. text 25.00 (*0-86709-336-6*, 0336, Pub. by Boynton Cook Pubs) Heinemann.

Presence of Montaigne in the Lettres Persanes. John M. Bomer. LC 88-62882. (ENG & FRE.). 193p. 1989. lib. bdg. 26.95 (*0-917786-68-8*) Summa Pubns.

Presence of Myth. Leszek Kolakowski. Tr. by Adam Czerniawski. 150p. 1989. 25.00 (*0-226-45041-4*) U Ch Pr.

Presence of Other Worlds: The Psychological - Spiritual Findings of Emanuel Swedenborg. Wilson Van Dusen. 256p. 1994. pap. 11.95 (*0-87785-247-2*) Swedenborg.

Presence of Others. Andrea A. Lunsford. 1996. pap. text 21.00 (*0-312-14830-5*) St Martin.

Presence of Others. Angela A. Lunsford. 1994. pap. text, teacher ed. 45.00 (*0-312-09571-6*) St Martin.

Presence of Others. 2nd ed. Andrea A. Lunsford. LC 95-73172. 668p. 1996. pap. text 35.95 (*0-312-13295-6*) St Martin.

***Presence of Others.** 3rd ed. Andrea Lunsford. 1999. pap. text 35.95 (*0-312-20172-9*) St Martin.

Presence of Pauline Thought in the Works of Dante. Giuseppe C. DiScipio. LC 94-40269. 366p. 1995. text 99.95 (*0-7734-9000-0*) E Mellen.

Presence of Persons: Essays on the Literature & Thought of the Nineteenth Century. William Myers. LC 98-23626. (Nineteenth Century Ser.). 256p. 1998. text 78.95 (*1-84014-645-1*, PR453.M94, Pub. by Ashgate Pub) Ashgate Pub Co.

Presence of Pessoa: English, American, & Southern African Literary Responses. George Monteiro. LC 97-40435. (Studies in Romance Languages). (Illus.). 164p. (C). 1998. 24.95 (*0-8131-2053-5*) U Pr of Ky.

Presence of Self. Robert S. Perinbanayagam. LC 99-35069. 304p. 1999. 67.00 (*0-8476-9384-8*) Rowman.

Presence of Self. Robert S. Perinbanayagam. LC 99-35069. 304p. 2000. pap. 27.95 (*0-8476-9385-6*) Rowman.

Presence of Stoicism in Medieval Thought. Gerard Verbeke. LC 82-4134. 109p. reprint ed. pap. 33.80 (*0-7837-4634-2*, 204435800002) Bks Demand.

Presence of the Actor. Joseph Chaikin. LC 91-22915. 176p. 1991. reprint ed. pap. 10.95 (*1-55936-030-5*) Theatre Comm.

Presence of the Dead on the Spiritual Path. Rudolf Steiner. Tr. by Christian Von Arnim from GER.Tr. of Wie Erwirbt Man Sich Verstandnisfur Die Geistige Welt?. 124p. 1990. 24.95 (*0-88010-282-9*); pap. 12.95 (*0-88010-283-7*) Anthroposophic.

Presence of the Future. George E. Ladd. 384p. pap. 16.00 (*0-8028-1531-6*) Eerdmans.

Presence of the Kingdom. Jacques Ellul. Tr. by Olive Wyon from FRE. 192p. 1989. reprint ed. pap. 17.95 (*0-939443-14-7*) Helmers Howard Pub.

Presence of the Light. Annabel Chaplin. LC 94-68112. 100p. (Orig.). 1994. pap. 9.95 (*0-87516-676-8*) DeVorss.

Presence of the Nude in Drawing. Thomas W. Sokolowski. Ed. by Judy Steinberg. (Illus.). 20p. (Orig.). (C). 1994. pap. text. write for info. (*1-883592-07-0*) Perm Mission.

Presence of the Past. Marilyn Turkovich. (Passages to India Ser.). (C). 1989. spiral bd. 20.00 (*1-56709-006-0*) Indep Broadcast.

Presence of the Past: Chronicles, Politics & Culture in Sinhala Life. Steven Kemper. LC 91-55059. (Wilder House Series in Politics, History, & Culture). 272p. 1992. text 37.50 (*0-8014-2395-3*) Cornell U Pr.

Presence of the Past: Essays on the State & the Constitution. Sheldon S. Wolin. LC 89-2672. (Series in Constitutional Thought). 256p. 1989. text 40.00 (*0-8018-3803-7*) Johns Hopkins.

Presence of the Past: Essays on the State & the Constitution. Sheldon S. Wolin. LC 89-2672. (Series in Constitutional Thought). 256p. 1990. reprint ed. pap. text 15.95 (*0-8018-4116-X*) Johns Hopkins.

Presence of the Past: John Dewey & Alfred Schutz on the Genesis & Organization of Experience. Rodman B. Webb. LC 76-25461. (University of Florida Monographs: Social Sciences: No. 57). 143p. reprint ed. pap. 44.40 (*0-7837-5084-6*, 204478200004) Bks Demand.

Presence of the Past: Male Violence in the Family. Jan Horsfall. 172p. pap. 19.95 (*0-04-442326-8*, Pub. by Allen & Unwin Pty) Paul & Co Pubs.

Presence of the Past: Morphic Resonance & the Habits of Nature. Rupert Sheldrake. LC 94-44868. (Illus.). 416p. 1995. pap. 16.95 (*0-89281-537-X*, Park St Pr) Inner Tradit.

Presence of the Past: Morphic Resonance & the Habits of Nature. Rupert Sheldrake. 1989. pap. 8.95 (*0-318-41763-4*) Vin Bks.

***Presence of the Past: Popular Uses of History in American Life.** Roy Rosenzweig. 2000. pap. text 18.50 (*0-231-11149-5*) Col U Pr.

Presence of the Past: Popular Uses of History in American Life. Roy Rosenzweig & David P. Thelen. LC 97-47535. 320p. 1998. 27.50 (*0-231-11148-7*) Col U Pr.

Presence of the Past: T. S. Eliot's Victorian Inheritance. David N. Tobin. Ed. by A. Walton Litz. LC 83-5733. (Studies in Modern Literature: No. 8). 192p. reprint ed. 59.60 (*0-8357-1413-6*, 207034300085) Bks Demand.

Presence of the Past in a Spanish Village. Ruth Behar. (Illus.). 426p. 1991. pap. text 21.95 (*0-691-02866-4*, Pub. by Princeton U Pr) Cal Prin Full Svc.

Presence of the Past in Modern American Drama. Patricia R. Schroeder. LC 87-46427. 152p. 1989. 32.50 (*0-8386-3332-3*) Fairleigh Dickinson.

***Presence of the Past in Politics: '1956' after 1956 in Hungary.** Heino Nyyssonen. 311p. 1999. pap. 27.50 (*951-39-0547-0*, Pub. by SoPhi Academic) Intl Spec Bk.

Presence of the Past, the Pastness of the Present: History, Time, & Paradigm in Rabbinic Judaism. Jacob Neusner. 1995. 42.00 (*1-883053-22-6*) CDL Pr.

Presence of the Present: Topics of the Day in the Victorian Novel. Richard D. Altick. LC 90-34806. (Studies in Victorian Life & Literature). 854p. 1991. text 65.00 (*0-8142-0518-6*) Ohio St U Pr.

Presence of Things Past. John Taylor. 133p. 1992. pap. 15.95 (*0-934257-69-8*) Story Line.

Presence of Things Unseen: Giant Talk. Chezia Thompson-Cager. (Illus.). 140p. 1996. pap. text 11.95 (*0-944624-32-4*) Maisonneuve Pr.

Presence of Thought: Introspective Accounts of Reading & Writing. Marilyn Sternglass. Ed. by Roy O. Freedle. LC 88-16636. (Advances in Discourse Processes Ser.: Vol. 34). 224p. 1988. pap. 42.50 (*0-89391-568-8*); text 78.50 (*0-89391-516-5*) Ablx Pub.

Presence of Whales: Contemporary Writings on the Whale. Ed. by Frank Stewart. LC 95-2745. 320p. (Orig.). 1995. pap. 15.95 (*0-88240-464-4*, Alaska NW Bks) Gr Arts Ctr Pub.

Presence Unanime: Poemes. Robert Yergeau. LC PQ3919.2.Y47. (Collection l'Astrolabe: Vol. 4). (FRE.). 65p. 1981. reprint ed. pap. 30.00 (*0-608-02176-8*, 206284500004) Bks Demand.

***Presences: A Bishop's Life in the City.** Paul Moore. LC 99-33821. (Illus.). 344p. 1999. pap. 16.95 (*1-56101-168-1*) Cowley Pubns.

Presences: A Bishop's Life in the City. Paul Moore. (Illus.). 344p. 1997. text 28.00 (*0-374-17567-5*) FS&G.

Presences Contemporaines: Auteurs Francais du XXe Siecle. G. Brodin. 9.95 (*0-685-37147-6*) Fr & Eur.

Presences of Mind: The Collected Books of Jack Sharpless. Jack Sharpless. Ed. & Intro. by Ronald Johnson. LC 89-85706. 128p. (Orig.). 1989. pap. 12.50 (*0-917788-39-7*) Gnomon Pr.

Presences of Nature: British Landscapes, 1780-1830. Louis Hawes. 214p. 1982. pap. 18.95 (*0-300-02931-4*) Yale Ctr Brit Art.

Presencia de Dios y la Oracion. S. Fernandez.Tr. of Presence of God & Prayer. (SPA.). 3.99 (*1-56063-948-2*, 493034) Editorial Unilit.

Presencia de la Cultura de San Agustin en la Depresion Calida del Valle del Rio Magdalena Garzon-Huila. Hector Llanos. (SPA., Illus.). 100p. (Orig.). (C). 1993. pap. 9.50 (*1-877812-35-8*, BR035, Pub. by Banco de la Repub) UPLAAP.

Presencia de un Pueblo see Colombia, Sangil, Gods, Gold, Sex & Violence: Presence of a People, Reminiscence of the City of Sangil

Presencia Espanola en los Estados Unidos. 3rd ed. Carlos M. Fernandez-Shaw. LC E 184.S75F47. (SPA.). 384p. 1992. reprint ed. pap. 119.10 (*0-608-02862-2*, 206392600007) Bks Demand.

Presencia Hispano en Los Estados Unidos Desde 1492 Hasta el Presente. Carlos Fernandez-Shaw. (SPA.). 400p. 1991. 45.00 (*0-8160-2314-X*) Facts on File.

Presencia Militar de Estados Unidos en Puerto Rico, 1898-1918. Maria E. Estades. LC 88-80565. 245p. 1988. pap. 8.50 (*0-940238-58-6*) Ediciones Huracan.

Presencia y Ausencia de Maria en la Poesia Cubana. Julio M. Gomez. (SPA.). 50p. (Orig.). 1989. pap. 6.00 (*0-917049-21-7*) Saeta.

Presencias y Encuentros: Investigaciones Arqueologicas de Salvamento. Direccion de Salvamento Arqueologico Staff. (SPA., Illus.). 394p. 1995. pap. 23.00 (*968-29-5222-0*, IN97, Pub. by Dir Gen Pubicaiones) UPLAAP.

Presenilins & Alzheimer's Disease. Ed. by S. G. Youkin et al. LC 97-52014. (Research & Perspectives in Alzheimer's Disease Ser.). (Illus.). xiv, 100p. 1998. 99.00 (*3-540-63997-7*) Spr-Verlag.

Present see Gift

Present. Alfred Dewitt Corn. LC 96-51671. 112p. 1997. 22.00 (*1-887178-31-7*, Pub. by Counterpt DC) HarpC.

P

An Asterisk (*) at the beginning of an entry indicates that the title is appearing for the first time.

Present. Alfred Dewitt Corn. 112p. 1998. pap. 13.50 (*1-887178-69-4*, Pub. by Counterpt DC) HarpC.

Present. Barbara Emberley. 1991. 14.95 (*0-316-88878-8*) Little.

***Present.** Johanna Lindsey. LC 98-35230. (Malory Holiday Novel Ser.). (Illus.). 352p. 1999. mass mkt. 6.99 (*0-380-80438-7*, Avon Bks) Morrow Avon.

Present. Johanna Lindsey. LC 98-48909. (Wheeler Large Print Book Ser.). 189 p. 1998. write for info. (*1-56895-592-8*) Wheeler Pub.

Present: A Malory Holiday Novel. Johanna Lindsey. LC 98-35230. (Malory Novels Ser.). 192p. 1998. 16.00 (*0-380-97725-7*, Avon Bks) Morrow Avon.

Present a Positive Image Module, Connections: School & Work Transitions - Work Skills-Work Maturity Skills. National Center for Research in Vocational Educati. 1987. write for info. (*0-318-67184-0*, SP100CB07) Ctr Educ Trng Employ.

Present Age. Soren Kierkegaard. Ed. & Tr. by Alexander Dru. 112p. 1962. pap. 12.00 (*0-06-130094-2*, TB94, Torch) HarpC.

Present Age & Inner Life: A Sequel to Spiritual Intercourse. Andrew J. Davis. 281p. 1996. reprint ed. spiral bd. 21.00 (*0-7873-0244-9*) Hlth Research.

Present & Future Aspects in Endocrinology: Thirteenth International Symposium on Endocrinology & Development, Rome, October 1994. Ed. by A. Attansio & S. Bernasconi. (Journal Ser.: Vol. 43, No. 4, 1995). (Illus.). 60p. 1995. pap. 47.00 (*3-8055-6139-3*) S Karger.

Present & Future Automotive Fuels: Performance & Exhaust Clarification. Ed. by Osamu Hirao & Richard K. Pefley. LC 87-6234. 570p. 1988. 210.00 (*0-471-80259-X*) Wiley.

Present & Future Military Uses of Outer Space: International Law, Politics & the Practice of States. 137p. (Orig.). (C). 1994. pap. text 40.00 (*0-941375-90-0*) DIANE Pub.

Present & Future of High-Energy Physics: Proceedings of the 5th Nishinomiya-Yukawa Memorial Symposium on Theoretical Physics, Nishinomiya City, Japan, October 25-26, 1990. Ed. by K. Aoki & M. Kobayashi. (Proceedings in Physics Ser.: Vol. 65). (Illus.). ix, 233p. 1992. 97.95 (*0-387-55283-9*) Spr-Verlag.

Present & Future of Prevention: Essays in Honor of George W. Albee. Marc Kessler et al. (Primary Prevention of Psychopathology Ser.: Vol. 15). 288p. (C). 1992. text 56.00 (*0-8039-4590-6*) Sage.

Present & Future of the Cosmic Microwave Background: Proceedings of the Workshop Held in Santander, Spain, June-July 1993. Ed. by J. L. Sanz et al. LC 94-285. (Lecture Notes in Physics Ser.: Vol. 429). (Illus.). viii, 233p. 1994. 65.95 (*0-387-57755-6*) Spr-Verlag.

Present & Future Role of Monoclonal Antibodies in the Management of Cancer: 24th Annual San Francisco Cancer Symposium, San Francisco, Calif., February 1989. Ed. by J. M. Vaeth & J. L. Meyer. (Frontiers of Radiation Therapy & Oncology Ser.: Vol. 24). (Illus.). x, 266p. 1990. 221.00 (*3-8055-5029-4*) S Karger.

Present & Futures: Architecture in Cities. Jean Nouvel. 1997. 52.00 (*84-89698-01-5*, Pub. by Actar) Dist Art Pubs.

Present & Past: Essays for Teachers in the History of Education. Clinton B. Allison. (Counterpoints Ser.: Vol. 6). 232p. (C). 1995. pap. text 29.95 (*0-8204-1780-7*) P Lang Pubng.

Present & Projected Airframe Control Gearing Requirements. R. W. Weber. (Technical Papers: Vol. P990.08). (Illus.). 25p. 1956. pap. text 30.00 (*1-55589-460-7*) AGMA.

Present & the Past: A Study of Anamnesis. Richard J. Ginn. (Princeton Theological Monographs: No. 20). (Orig.). 1989. pap. 12.00 (*1-55635-004-X*) Pickwick.

Present Appearances: Aspects of Poetic Structure in Rimbaud's "Illuminations" Nathaniel Wing. LC 74-7380. (Romance Monographs: No. 9). 1974. pap. 19.00 (*84-399-2424-0*) Romance.

Present As History: Essays & Reviews of Capitalism & Socialism. Paul M. Sweezy. LC 53-12728. 384p. reprint ed. pap. 119.10 (*0-8357-9443-1*, 201644600004) Bks Demand.

Present at Sinai: The Giving of the Law Commentaries Selected by S. Y. Agnon. Tr. by Michael Swirsky from HEB. 400p. 1994. 40.00 (*0-8276-0503-X*) JPS Phila.

Present at the Creation: My Years in the State Department. Dean Acheson. (Illus.). 848p. 1987. 29.95 (*0-393-07448-X*); pap. 19.95 (*0-393-30412-4*) Norton.

Present at the Creation: The Fortieth Anniversary of the Marshall Plan. Archie C. Epps & Armand Cleese. 1989. text 29.95 (*0-88730-405-2*, HarpBusn) HarpInfo.

Present Concerns. C. S. Lewis. Ed. by Walter Hooper. 112p. 1987. pap. 10.00 (*0-15-673840-6*, Harvest Bks) Harcourt.

Present Crisis. Gopi Krishna. (Illus.). 198p. (Orig.). 1981. pap. 3.95 (*0-941136-01-9*, Pub. by Kieffer Assocs) Kundalini Research.

Present Danger. Susan Andersen. 288p. 1993. mass mkt. 4.50 (*0-8217-4067-9*, Zebra Kensgtn) Kensgtn Pub Corp.

Present Danger. Norman Podhoretz. 1980. pap. 3.95 (*0-671-41328-7*, Touchstone) S&S Trade Pap.

Present Dangers: Crisis & Opportunity in American Foreign & Defense Policy. Paul Wolfowitz et al. Ed. by Robert Kagan & William Kristol. 200p. 2000. 22.95 (*1-893554-13-9*) Encounter Bks.

***Present Dangers: Crisis & Opportunity in American Foreign & Defense Policy.** 2nd ed. Paul Wolfowitz et al. Ed. by Robert Kagan & William Kristol. 230p. 2000. reprint ed. pap. 15.95 (*1-893554-16-3*) Encounter Bks.

Present-Day Concepts in the Treatment of Chronic Renal Failure: Dialysis & Transplantation. Ed. by J. E. Traeger et al. (Contributions to Nephrology Ser.: Vol. 71). (Illus.). viii, 184p. 1989. 29.75 (*3-8055-4946-6*) S Karger.

Present-Day Law Schools in the United States & Canada. Alfred Z. Reed. LC 75-22836. (America in Two Centuries Ser.). 1976. reprint ed. 51.95 (*0-405-07707-6*) Ayer.

Present-Day Law Schools in the United States & Canada. Alfred Z. Reed. LC 87-80146. (Historical Writings in Law & Jurisprudence Ser.: No. 12). xv, 508p. 1987. reprint ed. lib. bdg. 47.50 (*0-89941-546-6*, 305100) W S Hein.

Present-Day Ministry of Jesus Christ. 2nd ed. Kenneth E. Hagin. 1969. pap. 2.95 (*0-89276-014-1*) Faith Lib Pubns.

Present-Day Political Organization of China. H. S. Brunnert & V. V. Hagelstrom. 288p. 1998. text 60.00 (*0-7007-1018-3*, Pub. by Curzon Pr Ltd) UH Pr.

Present Day Problems: A Collection of Addresses Delivered on Various Occasions. William H. Taft. LC 67-26788. (Essay Index Reprint Ser.). 1977. 21.95 (*0-8369-0922-4*) Ayer.

Present Day Rock Garden. Sampson Clay. LC 76-1833. (Illus.). 1976. reprint ed. 25.00 (*0-913728-09-8*) Theophrastus.

Present Day Spanish. 2nd ed. J. R. Scarr. 1976. pap. text 6.30 (*0-08-020716-2*, Pergamon Pr) Elsevier.

Present Day Truths. Dick Iverson. 237p. 1998. pap. 12.99 (*0-914936-88-3*) City Bible Pub.

Present Discontents: American Politics in the Very Late Twentieth Century. Byron E. Shafer et al. LC 96-45775. (Illus.). 192p. (C). 1997. pap. text 21.95 (*1-56643-050-X*, Chatham House Pub) Seven Bridges.

Present Fears. Elisabeth R. Taylor. 1997. pap. text 18.95 (*0-900850-04-3*, Pub. by Arcadia Bks) Dufour.

Present Fears. Elisabeth R. Taylor. LC 97-147067. 160p. 1997. pap. 18.95 (*1-900850-04-4*) Dufour.

Present for Alice. Fiona Pragoff. LC 99-202892. 20p. (J). 1999. 12.95 (*0-385-32625-4*) BDD Bks Young Read.

Present for Daddy, Bk. N. Jessica Schulte. LC 96-68719. 24p. (ps-1). 1996. 3.25 (*0-689-80824-0*) S&S Childrens.

Present for Grandfather. Illus. by Daniel M. Duffy. LC 98-6219. (Adventures of Benny & Watch: No. 2). 32p. (J). (gr. 1-3). 1998. pap. 3.95 (*0-8075-6625-X*) A Whitman.

Present for Grandfather. Created by Gertrude Chandler Warner. (Adventures of Benny & Watch: No. 2). (J). (gr. 1-3). 1998. 9.40 (*0-606-13216-3*) Turtleback.

Present for Mama Bear. Bonnie Staenberg. LC 98-29848. (Hello Reader! Ser.). (Illus.). 32p. (J). (gr. 1-3). 1999. 3.99 (*0-590-28154-2*) Scholastic Inc.

Present for Mr. Lincoln: The Story of Savannah from Secession to Sherman. Alexander A. Lawrence. 1997. reprint ed. 25.00 (*1-891495-00-3*) Oglethorpe Pr.

Present for Prince Paul. Ann Love. (Illus.). (J). 1995. 13.99 (*0-85953-943-1*) Childs Play.

Present for Rose. Cooper Edens. (Illus.). 32p. (J). (ps up). 1993. text 15.95 (*0-912365-89-7*) Sasquatch Bks.

Present for Santa. James Lee Burke. 256p. 1989. pap. 3.95 (*0-380-70483-8*, Avon Bks) Morrow Avon.

Present for Santa. James Lee Burke. 304p. 1986. 16.95 (*0-685-14542-5*) St Martin.

Present Formal Classroom Instruction. (EUITS Ser.: No. D-1). 110p. 1991. spiral bd. 69.50 (*0-87683-507-8*) GP Courseware.

Present from Pinocchio. Claire Jones & Bob Varga. 35p. (J). (gr. k-5). 1995. mass mkt. 4.00 (*1-58193-172-7*) Brown Bag Prods.

Present from the Past. Annabel Dilke. 240p. 1994. 23.95 (*0-233-98800-9*, Pub. by Andre Deutsch) Trafalgar.

Present from the Past. Janet Golio & Mike Golio. Ed. by David Anderson & Andrea Tronslin. LC 95-186651. (Environmental Adventure Ser.). 159p. (J). (gr. 4-6). 1995. pap. 8.95 (*0-9641330-5-9*) Portunus Pubng.

Present History of West Bengal: Essays in Political Criticism. Partha Chatterjee. LC 96-912037. (Illus.). 238p. 1997. text 26.00 (*0-19-563945-6*) OUP.

***Present History of West Bengal: Essays in Political Criticism.** Partha Chatterjee. (Illus.). 240p. 1999. pap. 10.95 (*0-19-564767-X*) OUP.

Present Hope: Philosophy, Architecture, Judaism. Andrew Benjamin. LC 97-205268. 192p. (C). 1997. 80.00 (*0-415-13385-8*); pap. 22.99 (*0-415-13386-6*) Routledge.

Present Imperfect: Imagining Utopia. National Textbook Company Staff. LC 98-43950. 1998. 21.19 (*0-8442-0513-3*); 17.44 (*0-8442-1127-3*) NTC Contemp Pub Co.

Present Imperfect: Imagining Utopia. National Textbook Company Staff. LC 98-43950. 1998. 17.44 (*0-8442-0514-1*) NTC Contemp Pub Co.

Present in Spirit. Joseph M. Sackett. LC 97-93265. 369p. 1997. pap. 16.95 (*0-9648966-5-6*) Live Oak AL.

Present Is a Dangerous Place to Live. Keorapetse Kgositsile. 35p. 1993. reprint ed. pap. 8.00 (*0-88378-057-7*) Third World.

Present Is Past: Some Uses of Tradition in Native Societies. Marie Mauze. LC 96-51052. 250p. 1997. write for info. (*0-7618-0684-9*); pap. write for info. (*0-7618-0685-7*) U Pr of Amer.

Present It: New Ideas for Stylish Garnishes. Deborah Gray. (Illus.). 80p. 1999. pap. 14.00 (*0-7624-0502-3*) Running Pr.

Present Knowledge in Nutrition. 6th ed. Ed. by Myrtle L. Brown et al. LC 90-82033. (Illus.). 532p. (C). 1990. pap. text 40.00 (*0-944398-05-1*) ILSI.

Present Knowledge in Nutrition. 7th ed. Ed. by Ekhard E. Ziegler & Lloyd J. Filer, Jr. LC 96-77097. (Illus.). 684p. 1996. pap. 50.00 (*0-944398-72-3*, 398723) ILSI.

***Present Lasts a Long Time: Essays in Cultural Politics.** Francis Mulhern. LC 98-42849. (Clitical Conditions Ser.: 7). 280p. 1998. pap. 30.00 (*0-268-03861-9*, Pub. by U of Notre Dame Pr) Chicago Distribution Ctr.

***Present Law & Analysis Relating to Individual Effective Marginal Tax Rates: Scheduled for a Public Hearing by the House Committee on Ways & Means on February 4, 1998.** United States Congress House Committee on Ways & Means & United States Congress Joint Committee on Taxation. LC 98-139733. 120p. 1998. 7.00 (*0-16-056106-X*) USGPO.

***Present Moment.** Marjorie Macgoye. 2000. 30.00 (*1-55861-254-8*); pap. 11.95 (*1-55861-248-3*) Feminist Pr.

***Present Moment: A Daybook of Clarity & Intuition.** Penney Peirce. LC 99-88335. 416p. 2000. pap. 14.95 (*0-8092-2475-5*, 247550, Contemporary Bks) NTC Contemp Pub Co.

Present Moment in World History: A Judeo-Catholic Analysis of the Rise & Fall of the Cold War. Thomas J. Kuna-Jacob. 44p. 1992. ring bd. 4.14 (*1-878030-01-9*) Assn World Peace.

Present Moment Wonderful Moment: Mindfulness Verses for Daily Living. Thich Nhat Hanh. Tr. by Annabel Laity from VIE. LC 90-37062. (Illus.). 75p. 1990. per. 7.00 (*0-938077-21-X*) Parallax Pr.

Present Moments. Stephen Miller. LC 99-11113. 1999. pap. 4.97 (*1-56955-055-7*) Servant.

***Present of Things Past.** Theodore Draper. 2000. pap. 24.95 (*0-7658-0713-0*) Transaction Pubs.

Present Opposition Between Art & Theory. Stephen L. Albaugh. 175p. (C). 1989. text. write for info. (*0-318-65314-1*) Iowa Inst Philos.

Present Passe, Passe Present. Eugene Ionesco. 274p. 1968. 29.95 (*0-8288-7464-6*) Fr & Eur.

Present Passe, Passe Present. Eugene Ionesco. (Idees Ser.). (FRE.). 1976. pap. 8.95 (*2-07-035343-5*) Schoenhof.

Present Past: Modernity & the Memory Crisis. Richard Terdiman. LC 93-1183. 400p. 1993. text 52.50 (*0-8014-2897-1*); pap. text 19.95 (*0-8014-8132-5*) Cornell U Pr.

Present Past, Past Present: A Personal Memoir. Eugene Ionesco. LC 97-11706. 196p. 1998. pap. 13.95 (*0-306-80803-X*) Da Capo.

Present Perfect: The Essential Guide to Gift Giving. Sherri L. Athay & Lawrence D. Athay. Ed. by Kristen V. Black. (Illus.). (Orig.). 1996. pap. 12.95 (*0-9650617-0-1*) Mobius UT.

Present Perfect: Unforgettable Gifts for Every Occasion. 2nd rev. ed. Sherri Athay & Lawrence Athay. (Illus.). 1998. pap. 15.00 (*0-9650617-4-4*) Mobius UT.

Present Peril. Cornelius R. Stam. 153p. 1986. pap. 7.50 (*1-893874-22-2*) Berean Bibl Soc.

Present Philosophical Tendencies. Ralph B. Perry. LC 68-21328. 383p. 1968. reprint ed. lib. bdg. 69.50 (*0-8371-0191-3*, PEPT, Greenwood Pr) Greenwood.

Present Poets. Jenni Calder. (Illus.). 64p. 1998. pap. 6.95 (*1-901663-14-0*, 3140, Pub. by Natl Mus Scotland) A Schwartz & Co.

Present Practice of Musick Vindicated. fac. ed. Matthew Locke. (Monuments of Music & Music Literature in Facsimile Ser., Series II: Vol. 16). (Illus.). 1974. lib. bdg. 37.50 (*0-8450-2216-4*) Broude.

PRESENT SFR(3.5 DSK&DOC)-COMP. 3rd ed. Steven C. Lawlor. LC 93-72826. 266p. (C). 1994. pap. 102.00 incl. disk (*0-03-098201-4*) Dryden Pr.

Present Sfwr(ibm 3.5)liv W/computers 4e+ 4th ed. Goldberg. (C). 1994. 3.5 hd 25.00 (*0-03-097770-3*) Harcourt.

Present Situation & Perspectives of Library Services in Latin America: Conference Proceedings of the 9th Annual Conference of the IASL. Ed. by Nelson R. Trujillo. Tr. by Roger Salvador & Lesley Johnson. 268p. 1980. pap. 25.00 (*0-9617248-9-7*) IASL.

Present Situation of Multidrug-Resistant Tuberculosis & the Possibility of MDR-TB Treatment by New Quinolones: Proceedings of a Satellite Symposium for the 14th Asia Pacific Congress on Diseases of the Chest, Bali, June 1996. Ed. by Mangunnegoro Hadiarto. (Journal Ser.: Vol. 42, Supplement 3, 1996). (Illus.). iv, 36p. 1996. pap. 21.75 (*3-8055-6406-6*) S Karger.

Present State & Future Prospect of the Liquid Crystal-Related Market. Ed. by Jack Bernstein. 1998. 945.00 (*1-884730-17-5*, Interlingua) JB & Me.

Present State of Australia. Robert Dawson. (Discovery of the Pacific & Australia Ser.). (Illus.). 488p. 1998. reprint ed. pap. 240.00 (*1-85297-003-0*, Pub. by Archival Facs) St Mut.

Present State of Consumer Theory. 2nd ed. Timothy P. Roth. LC 89-34175. 220p. (Orig.). (C). 1989. pap. text 22.50 (*0-8191-7506-4*) U Pr of Amer.

Present State of Consumer Theory: The Implications for Social Welfare Theory. 3rd ed. Timothy P. Roth. LC 97-40090. 236p. (C). 1998. pap. text 31.00 (*0-7618-0944-9*) U Pr of Amer.

Present State of England in Regard to Agriculture, Trade & Finance. 2nd ed. Joseph Lowe. LC 66-21682. (Reprints of Economic Classics Ser.). xxviii, 524p. 1967. reprint ed. 65.00 (*0-678-00320-3*) Kelley.

Present State of French Studies: A Collection of Research Reviews. Charles B. Osburn. LC 78-149990. 995p. 1971. 68.50 (*0-8108-0373-9*) Scarecrow.

Present State of Haiti: Santo Domingo-with Remarks on Its Agriculture, Commerce, Laws, Religion, Finance & Population. James Franklin. LC 79-109325. 411p. 1970. reprint ed. lib. bdg. 59.50 (*0-8371-3591-5*, FRH&, Greenwood Pr) Greenwood.

Present State of Haiti (Saint Domingo) James Franklin. 412p. 1972. reprint ed. 47.50 (*0-7146-2707-0*, Pub. by F Cass Pubs) Intl Spec Bk.

Present State of Leptospirosis Diagnosis & Control. Ed. by W. A. Ellis & T. W. Little. (Current Topics in Veterinary Medicine & Animal Science Ser.). 1986. text 145.50 (*0-89838-777-9*) Kluwer Academic.

Present State of Music in France & Italy. fac. ed. Charles Burney. (Monuments of Music & Music Literature in Facsimile Ser., Series II: Vol. 70). 1969. lib. bdg. 50.00 (*0-8450-2270-9*) Broude.

Present State of Music in France & Italy. 2nd ed. Charles Burney. LC 74-24263. 1976. reprint ed. 55.00 (*0-404-12875-0*) AMS Pr.

Present State of Music in Germany, The Netherlands & United Provinces. fac. ed. Charles Burney. (Monuments of Music & Music Literature in Facsimile Ser., Series II: Vol. 117). 1969. lib. bdg. 125.00 (*0-8450-2317-9*) Broude.

Present State of New England. Cotton Mather. LC 68-24989. (American History & Americana Ser.: No. 47). 1969. reprint ed. lib. bdg. 75.00 (*0-8383-0214-9*) M S G Haskell Hse.

Present State of New England. Cotton Mather. (BCL1 - U. S. History Ser.). 52p. 1991. reprint ed. lib. bdg. 59.00 (*0-7812-6099-X*) Rprt Serv.

Present State of New England. Cotton Mather. (Notable American Authors Ser.). 1999. reprint ed. lib. bdg. 125.00 (*0-7812-3953-2*) Rprt Serv.

Present State of Physics: Proceedings of the American Advancement of Science, New York, 1949. American Association for the Advancement of Science Staff. Ed. by Frederick S. Brackett. LC 75-99617. (Essay Index Reprint Ser.). 1977. 30.95 (*0-8369-1542-9*) Ayer.

Present State of Scholarship in Historical & Contemporary Rhetoric. rev. ed. Ed. by Winifred B. Horner. LC 82-20002. 272p. (C). 1990. text 22.50 (*0-8262-0763-4*) U of Mo Pr.

Present State of the European Settlements on the Mississippi: With a Geographical Description of That River Illustrated by Plans & Draughts. Philip M. Pittman. LC 73-2821. (Floridiana Facsimile & Reprint Ser.). (Illus.). 156p. 1973. reprint ed. 16.95 (*0-8130-0368-7*) U Press Fla.

Present State of the Greek & Armenian Churches. Paul Rycaut. LC 75-13321. reprint ed. 45.00 (*0-404-05476-5*) AMS Pr.

Present State of the Greek Church in Russia. Platon. LC 75-131031. reprint ed. 49.50 (*0-404-05059-X*) AMS Pr.

Present State of the Ottoman Empire. Paul Rycaut. LC 76-135845. (Eastern Europe Collection). 1971. reprint ed. 17.95 (*0-405-02787-7*) Ayer.

Present State of Thoracic Surgery. Ed. by J. A. Dyde & R. E. Smih. 300p. 1981. pap. 59.00 (*0-8464-1218-7*) Beekman Pubs.

Present State of Virginia. Hugh Jones. (Notable American Authors Ser.). 1992. reprint ed. lib. bdg. 75.00 (*0-7812-3510-3*) Rprt Serv.

Present Status & Future Tasks of Telecommunications Policy in Korea. unabridged ed. Yun-Sik Shin. LC 95-197759. 9p. (Orig.). 1995. pap. text. write for info. (*1-879716-21-6*, I-95-1) Ctr Info Policy.

Present Status & Research Needs in Energy Recovery from Wastes: Proceedings of the 1976 Conference Presented at Hueston Woods State Park, Oxford, Ohio, September 19-24, 1976. American Society of Mechanical Engineers Staff. Ed. by Richard A. Matula. LC 77-151398. (Illus.). 452p. reprint ed. pap. 140.20 (*0-8357-2876-5*, 203911200011) Bks Demand.

Present Status of Non-Toxic Concepts in Cancer. Ed. by K. F. Klippel & E. Macher. (Illus.). xii, 288p. 1987. pap. 61.75 (*3-8055-4437-5*) S Karger.

Present Status of the Philosophy of Law & of Rights. William E. Hocking. viii, 97p. 1986. reprint ed. 30.00 (*0-8377-2234-9*, Rothman) W S Hein.

Present Status of the Quantum Theory of Light: Proceedings of a Symposium in Honour of Jean-Pierre Vigier. Ed. by Stanley Jeffers. LC 96-49519. (Fundamental Theories of Physics Ser.). 572p. (C). 1996. text 291.00 (*0-7923-4337-9*) Kluwer Academic.

Present System of Trade & Payment Versus Full Employment & Welfare State. Eprime Eshag. LC 76-1515. 42p. 1966. 10.00 (*0-678-06278-1*) Kelley.

Present Tense. Stephen Ratcliffe. 104p. (Orig.). 1995. pap. 12.00 (*0-935724-71-0*) Figures.

Present Tense. C. G. Shepard. (Illus.). 53p. 1997. pap. 9.00 (*0-9639055-1-1*) C G R Pubng.

Present Tense: Rock & Roll & Culture. Ed. by Anthony DeCurtis. LC 92-1651. (Illus.). 332p. 1992. pap. 17.95 (*0-8223-1265-4*); text 49.95 (*0-8223-1261-1*) Duke.

Present Tense: Round Two of the Great Game, Vol. 2. Dave Duncan. 432p. (Orig.). 1997. mass mkt. 5.99 (*0-380-78130-1*) Morrow Avon.

Present Tense: The United States since 1945, 2 vols. 2nd ed. Michael Schaller et al. LC 95-76985. 576p. (C). 1995. pap. text 33.56 (*0-395-74534-9*) HM.

Present Tense: Writing & Art by Young Women. Ed. by Micki Reaman et al. LC 96-24820. (Illus.). 176p. (Orig.). (C). 1997. 26.95 (*0-934971-54-4*); pap. 14.95 (*0-934971-53-6*) Calyx Bks.

Present Tense & Personal Effects: A Pair of Comedies. John McNamara. 1986. pap. 5.25 (*0-8222-0910-1*) Dramatists Play.

Present-Tense Forms, Apple, Unit 3 see Grammar Lab

Present-Tense Verbs, IBM, Unit 3 see Grammar Lab

Present Theology & Participatory. Ross. 1996. pap. 3.90 (*0-86153-177-9*) St Mut.

Present to the Newborn. Emily H. Slingluff. Orig. Title: A Primer for Positive Parenting. 111p. (Orig.). 1987. reprint ed. pap. 7.95 (*0-9619456-0-5*) E H Slingluff.

Present Truth in the Real World: Can Adventists Keep & Share Their Faith in a Secular Society? Jon Paulien. LC 92-32316. 1993. pap. 10.99 (*0-8163-1127-7*) Pacific Pr Pub Assn.

P

An Asterisk (*) at the beginning of an entry indicates that the title is appearing for the first time.

Present Value Applications for Accountants & Financial Planners. G. Eddy Birrer & Jean L. Carrica. LC 89-10218. 148p. 1990. 55.00 (0-89930-307-2, BPI/, Greenwood Pr) Greenwood.

Present Value Approach for the Determination of the Accounting Income & Wealth of the Firm. Evangelina Vives-Amengual. 154p. 1974. pap. 4.00 (0-8477-2621-5) U of PR Pr.

Present Value Models & Investment Analysis. Lindon J. Robison & Peter J. Barry. 690p. (C). 1996. text 49.00 (0-945704-00-3) Genesis Comns.

Present Value Models & Investment Analysis. Lindon J. Robison & Peter J. Barry. (Illus.). 661p. (C). 1998. text 49.00 (0-87013-488-4) Mich St U Pr.

Present Value of Debt Settlements. 5p. 1979. pap. 40.00 (0-939050-37-4) Credit Res NYS.

Present Your Sale. John Nemec. LC 87-90713. 50p. (Orig.). 1987. pap. 2.95 (0-9618998-1-6) Nemec Pub.

Present Yourself! Captivate Your Audience with Great Presentation Skills. Michael J. Gelb. Ed. by Bradley L. Winch. LC 88-80768. (Right Brain - Whole Brain Learning Ser.). (Illus.). 128p. (Orig.). 1988. pap. 12.95 (0-915190-51-6, JP9051-6) Jalmar Pr.

Presentacion Breve de Lo Que es el Recobro Del Senor. Witness Lee.Tr. of BRIEF PRESENTATION OF THE LORD'S RECOVERY. (SPA.). 59p. 1991. pap. 3.75 (0-87083-570-X, 08-032-002) Living Stream Ministry.

Presentacion del Evangelio del Senor Jesucristo. 2nd ed. Earl Blackburn.Tr. of Presentation of the Gospel of Our Lord Jesus Christ. (SPA., Illus.). 32p. 1983. reprint ed. pap. 0.99 (1-56632-093-3) Revival Lit.

***Presentating to Win: A Guide for Finance & Business Professionals.** Khalid Aziz. 270p. 2001. pap. 19.95 (1-86076-167-4, Pub. by Oak Tr) Midpt Trade.

Presentation. Gary A. Borger. (Illus.). 320p. 1995. 34.95 (0-9628392-5-6) Tomorrow Riv Pr.

Presentation. David Gilgrist & Rex Davies. LC 96-901. 250p. 1996. 51.95 (0-566-07717-5, Pub. by Gower) Ashgate Pub Co.

Presentation. deluxe limited ed. Gary A. Borger. (Illus.). 320p. 1995. 250.00 (0-9628392-6-4) Tomorrow Riv Pr.

Presentation & Analysis of Financial Management Information. James A. Hyatt. Ed. by Deirdre McDonald. 176p. 1989. 16.95 (0-915164-50-7) NACUBO.

Presentation & Settlement of Contractors'Claims. 2nd ed. Trickey. (Civil Engineering Ser.). 1998. pap. 74.00 (0-419-20500-4) Thomson Learn.

Presentation Critique d'Hortense Felxner. Marguerite Yourcenar. (FRE.). 124p. 1970. 13.95 (0-7859-0453-0, 2070269957) Fr & Eur.

Presentation des Haidoucs (les Recits d'Adrien Zograffi) Panait Istrati. (FRE.). 1983. pap. 10.95 (0-7859-2470-1, 2070374475) Fr & Eur.

Presentation Graphics: Applications for Reinforcement. Jaehne. (DF - Computer Applications Ser.). 1998. 24.95 (0-538-71453-0) S-W Pub.

Presentation Graphics for Engineering, Science & Business. Peter H. Milne. (Illus.). 256p. (Orig.). 1991. 49.95 (0-412-32050-9, E & FN Spon); pap. write for info. (0-412-32060-6, E & FN Spon) Routledge.

Presentation Graphics for Engineering, Science & Business. Peter H. Milne. (Illus.). 208p. (Orig.). (C). 1991. pap. 37.99 (0-419-15840-5, E & FN Spon) Routledge.

***Presentation Management Systems: Earth Science.** 9th ed. 1999. text. write for info. (0-13-011646-7) P-H.

Presentation Manager. 2nd ed. (C). 2000. Price not set. (0-13-012682-9) P-H.

Presentation Manager. 3rd ed. (C). 2000. Price not set. (0-13-021479-5) P-H.

Presentation Manager. 4th ed. (C). 1999. text. write for info. (0-13-011325-5) P-H.

Presentation Manager. 6th ed. (C). 1998. write for info. (0-13-081910-7); text. write for info. (0-13-082170-5) P-H.

Presentation Manager. 6th ed. Ed. by Prentice-Hall Staff. (C). 1999. (0-13-935040-3) P-H.

***Presentation Manager.** 6th ed. Ed. by Prentice-Hall Staff. (C). 1999. text. write for info. (0-13-013860-6) P-H.

Presentation Manager. 9th ed. (C). 1999. text. write for info. (0-13-082180-2) P-H.

Presentation Mgr Social Psych. 6th ed. Myers. 1998. 15.00 (0-07-290223-X) McGraw.

Presentation of Clinical Data. Bert Spilker & John Schoenfelder. 576p. 1989. text 102.00 (0-88167-566-0, 2035) Lppncott W & W.

Presentation of Data in Science. Linda Reynolds & Doig Simmonds. 223p. 1981. lib. bdg. 104.50 (90-247-2398-1) Kluwer Academic.

Presentation of Data in Science. Linda Reynolds & Doig Simmonds. 223p. 1982. pap. text 73.00 (90-247-3054-6) Kluwer Academic.

Presentation of Evidence to Juries. Ed. by Robert M. Krivoshey. LC 93-31984. (Readings in Trial Advocacy & the Social Sciences Ser.: Vol. 3). 552p. 1993. text 20.00 (0-8153-1421-3) Garland.

Presentation of Maat: Ritual & Legitimacy in Ancient Egypt. Emily Teeter. LC 97-65427. (Studies in Ancient Oriental Civilization: No. 57). (Illus.). l, 166p. 1997. pap. text 40.00 (1-885923-05-8) Orient Inst.

Presentation of Perfection. Mark Eckart. 203p. (Orig.). 1994. pap. 12.99 (0-88019-315-8) Schmul Pub Co.

Presentation of Self in Everyday Life. Erving Goffman. LC 59-9138. 272p. 1959. pap. 11.95 (0-385-09402-7, Anchor NY) Doubleday.

***Presentation of Self in Everyday Life.** Erving Goffman. 1999. 24.00 (0-8446-7017-0) Peter Smith.

Presentation of the Gospel of Our Lord Jesus Christ see Presentacion del Evangelio del Senor Jesucristo

Presentation of the Gospel of the Lord Jesus Christ. Earl Blackburn. pap. 0.99 (1-56632-005-4) Revival Lit.

Presentation of Time in the Elizabethan Drama. Mable Buland. 354p. (C). 1966. reprint ed. lib. bdg. 75.00 (0-8383-0517-2) M S G Haskell Hse.

Presentation Perfect: How to Excel at Business Presentations, Meetings & Public Speaking. Alastair Grant. 96p. 1998. pap. 12.95 (1-85835-493-5, Indust Soc) Stylus Pub VA.

Presentation Power! Steve Mandel. 85p. 1995. pap. 149.00 incl. audio, VHS (1-56052-370-0) Crisp Pubns.

Presentation Power! Steve Mandel. 1995. pap. 24.95 incl. audio (1-56052-371-9) Crisp Pubns.

Presentation Power Tools for Fine Artists. Renee Phillips. 100p. 1998. pap. 18.95 (0-9646358-5-2) Manhattan Arts Intl.

Presentation Primer: Getting Your Point Across. Robert B. Nelson & Jennifer Wallick. LC 93-29855. 168p. 1993. 19.95 (1-55623-846-0, Irwn Prfssnl) McGraw-Hill Prof.

Presentation Rate, Retention Interval, & Encoding in Short-Term Recognition Memory for Homonyms, Synonyms, & Identical Words. Harvey G. Shulman. LC 70-135077. 125p. 1969. 22.00 (0-403-04540-1) Scholarly.

Presentation Reference Bible. 1995. boxed set, lthr. 130.00 (0-521-50911-4, Pub. by Cambdge U Bibles) Baker Bks.

***Presentation Skills.** Suzy Siddons. 96p. 2000. pap. 17.95 (0-8464-5133-6) Beekman Pubs.

Presentation Skills. Suzy Sliddons. 1998. pap. 22.00 (0-85292-743-6, Pub. by IPM Hse) St Mut.

Presentation Skills: Trainer's Guide. Phil Lowe. LC 94-13299. (McGraw-Hill One-Day Workshop Ser.). 156p. 1994. 110.00 (0-07-038852-0) McGraw.

Presentation Skills Training: 30 High-Involvement Training Designs. Wendy Denham & Elizabeth Sansom. 330p. 1997. pap. 89.95 (0-07-016393-6) McGraw.

***Presentation Skills Using Powerpoint 2000.** TBD. (New Perspectives Ser.). (C). 2000. text 24.50 (0-619-01978-6) Course Tech.

***Presentation Skills Workshop: Helping People Create & Deliver Great Presentations.** Sherron Bienvenu. LC 99-48052. (Trainer's Workshop Ser.: Vol. 2). 300p. 1999. pap. 35.00 (0-8144-0518-5) AMACOM.

Presentation Strategies in Architecture. Edward T. White. (Illus.). 110p. 1977. pap. 12.00 (1-928643-08-6) Archit Media.

***Presentational Speaking.** (C). 1998. wbk. ed. write for info. (0-8087-9991-6) Pearson Custom.

Presentational Speaking. Gerri Smith. 128p. (C). 1995. pap., per. 14.95 (0-7872-1597-X) Kendall-Hunt.

Presentational Speaking & Persuasion Pak. 2nd ed. George McLemore et al. 144p. (C). 1996. 48.24 (0-7872-2619-X) Kendall-Hunt.

Presentations: A Collection of Culinary Favorites. Friends of Lied Staff. 224p. 1993. 19.95 (0-9636502-0-3) Frnds of Lied.

***Presentations: The Right Way to Make Effective Presentations.** J. Stuart Williams. 128p. 2000. pap. 6.95 (0-7160-2062-9, Pub. by Elliot RW Bks) Midpt Trade.

Presentations for Decision Makers. 3rd ed. Marya W. Holcombe & Judith K. Stein. (Business Technology Ser.). 336p. 1996. 54.95 (0-471-28765-2, VNR) Wiley.

Presentations for Decision Makers. 3rd rev. ed. Marya W. Holcombe & Judith K. Stein. (Industrial Engineering Ser.). (Illus.). 250p. 1996. text 41.95 (0-442-02272-7, VNR) Wiley.

Presentations for Profit II: State of the Art in Tabletop Architecture. Martin B. Shellenberger. Ed. by Ira Brichtn. (Illus.). 80p. (Orig.). 1989. pap. 1.00 (0-685-74080-3) Syracuse China.

Presentations from the Third European Workshop on Ecological Psychology: A Special Issue of "Ecological Psychology", Vol. 7, No. 4, 1995. Guski & Heine. 1996. pap. 20.00 (0-8058-9916-2) L Erlbaum Assocs.

Presentations Kit: Ten Steps for Selling Your Ideas. 2nd ed. Claudyne Wilder. 288p. 1994. pap. 17.95 (0-471-31089-1) Wiley.

Presentations Kit: Ten Steps for Selling Your Ideas. 2nd rev. ed. Claudyne Wilder. 266p. 1994. 74.95 (0-471-31092-1) Wiley.

Presentations of Groups. D. L. Johnson. LC 96-36823. (London Mathematical Society Student Texts Ser.: No. 15). 228p. 1997. pap. text 28.95 (0-521-58542-2) Cambridge U Pr.

Presentations Plus: David Peoples' Proven Techniques. 2nd rev. ed. David A. Peoples. LC 92-57. 304p. 1992. 49.95 (0-471-55926-1) Wiley.

Presentations Plus: David Peoples' Proven Techniques. 2nd rev. ed. David A. Peoples. LC 92-57. (Illus.). 304p. 1992. pap. 18.95 (0-471-55956-3) Wiley.

Presentations That Get Results: 14 Reasons Yours May Not. Marian K. Woodall. LC 97-4729. (Illus.). 150p. 1997. 14.95 (0-941159-97-3) Prof Busn Comns.

Presentations That Work, Vol. 1. Carole M. Mablekos. (Engineers Guide to Business Ser.). (Illus.). 1991. 19.95 (0-7803-0305-9, EG101) Inst Electrical.

***Presente! U. S. Latino Catholics from Colonial Origins to the Present.** Ed. by Timothy M. Matovina et al. (American Catholic Identities Ser.). 288p. 2000. 50.00 (1-57075-347-4) Orbis Bks.

***Presente! U. S. Latino Catholics from Colonial Origins to the Present.** Ed. by Timothy M. Matovina et al. (American Catholic Identities Ser.). (Illus.). 288p. 2000. pap. 30.00 (1-57075-328-8) Orbis Bks.

Presented in Leather. (Orig.). 1997. mass mkt. 6.95 (1-56333-576-X) Masquerade.

Presenter's EZ Graphics Kit: A Guide for the Artistically Challenged. Lori Backer & Michele Deck. (Illus.). 240p. (gr. 13). 1996. spiral bd. 37.95 (0-8151-1378-1, 29944) Mosby Inc.

Presenter's Fieldbook: A Practical Guide of Tips, Treasures & Treats. Robert Garmston. LC 98-108251. (Illus.). 225p. 1997. pap. 29.95 (0-926842-65-X) CG Pubs Inc.

Presenter's Journal: A Tool for Making Presentations Memorable. (Illus.). 100p. 1999. 39.95 (0-9667050-0-9) Varga IL.

Presenter's Survival Kit: It's a Jungle Out There. Lori Backer. LC 95-171568. 432p. (C). (gr. 13). 1994. spiral bd. 28.95 (0-8151-0373-5, 26258) Mosby Inc.

Presenting . . . Sister NoBlues. Hattie Gossett. LC 88-30146. 144p. (Orig.). 1988. pap. 8.95 (0-932379-49-4); lib. bdg. 18.95 (0-932379-50-8) Firebrand Bks.

Presenting a Case for a Building & Energy Management System. G. J. Levermore. 1989. pap. 320.00 (0-86022-241-1, Pub. by Build Servs Info Assn) St Mut.

Presenting a Yielded Will, Vol. 2. Warren Hunter. Ed. by Richard Phillips. 96p. (Orig.). 1997. pap. 6.00 (1-889816-06-X) Sword Ministries.

Presenting Across Cultures. (Management Booklets Ser.). Date not set. write for info. (1-882390-89-X) Princeton Trng.

Presenting Active X. Warren Ernst. LC 96-68942. 336p. 1996. pap. text 29.99 incl. audio compact disk (1-57521-156-4) Sams.

Presenting & Training with Magic: 50 Simple Magic Tricks You Can Use to Energize Any Audience. Ed Rose. LC 97-41426. (Illus.). 184p. 1997. pap. 24.95 (0-07-054040-3) McGraw.

Presenting & Training with Magic: 50 Simple Magic Tricks You Can Use to Energize Any Audience. Ed Rose. LC 97-41426. (Illus.). 288p. 1997. 34.95 (0-07-054041-1) McGraw.

Presenting Archaeology to the Public: Digging for Truths. Ed. by John H. Jameson, Jr. LC 96-45776. (Illus.). 288p. 1997. 65.00 (0-7619-8908-0); pap. 24.95 (0-7619-8909-9) AltaMira Pr.

Presenting Arms: Museum Representation of British Military History, 1660-1900. Ed. by Peter Thwaites. (Museum Studies). (Illus.). 208p. 1996. 85.00 (0-7185-1534-X) Bks Intl VA.

***Presenting Australia: The Making of a Nation.** Bruce Elder. 2000. 39.95 (1-86436-527-7, Pub. by New Holland) BHB Intl.

Presenting Avi. Cathryn M. Mercier & Susan P. Bloom. LC 96-53878. (Twayne's United States Young Adult Authors Ser.). 206p. (gr. 6 up). 1997. 24.95 (0-8057-4569-6, Twyne) Mac Lib Ref.

Presenting Barbara Wersba. Elizabeth A. Poe. LC 97-44279. 180p. (YA). (gr. 10 up). 1998. 24.95 Mac Lib Ref.

Presenting Benchmarking Results: A Librarian's Guide. Holly J. Muir. 44p. 1994. pap. text 33.00 (1-884935-16-8) Lib Benchmarking.

Presenting Chris Crutcher. large type ed. Terry Davis. LC 97-14505. 144p. (gr. 6 up). 1997. 24.95 (0-8057-8223-0, Twyne) Mac Lib Ref.

Presenting Cynthia Voigt. Suzanne Reid. (Young Adult Authors Ser.). 1995. 28.00 (0-8057-8219-2, Twyne) Mac Lib Ref.

***Presenting ESL Units to New Immigrant Students: Sample Lesson Plans & Activities.** Trung Hieu Nguyen. LC 99-41131. 1999. pap. write for info. (0-9662708-2-7) Nghia Sinh.

Presenting Evidence in Court: It's the Way You Do It That Counts. Meridith B. Cox. (Risk Management Ser.). (Illus.). (C). 1999. pap. text 25.00 (0-912665-27-0) BusinessWatch.

Presenting Facts & Figures. (Longman Business English Skills Ser.). 1992. pap. text. write for info. (0-582-09307-4, Pub. by Addison-Wesley) Longman.

Presenting Figures. 2nd ed. (Open Learning Super Ser.). 1991. pap. text 26.00 (0-08-041617-9, Pergamon Pr) Elsevier.

Presenting Financing Proposals to Banks. 2nd ed. Christopher A. Bloomfield. 135p. 1991. pap. 57.00 (0-406-00282-7, U.K., MICHIE) LEXIS Pub.

Presenting Gary Paulsen. Gary M. Salvner. 1996. 28.00 (0-8057-4150-X, Hall Reference) Macmillan.

Presenting Harry Mazer. large type ed. Arthea Reed. 1996. 28.00 (0-8057-4512-2, Twyne) Mac Lib Ref.

Presenting Harvard Graphics 3.0 for Windows. Susan Lehner & Linda M. Sourek. (DF - Computer Applications Ser.). 320p. 1995. mass mkt. 32.95 (0-7895-0179-1) Course Tech.

Presenting Information & Data Level 3 Workbook. Learning Business Staff. 1997. wbk. ed. 26.95 (0-7506-3153-8) Buttrwrth-Heinemann.

Presenting Java. John December. 224p. 1995. pap. 25.00 (1-57521-039-8) Sams.

Presenting JavaBeans. Michael Morrison. LC 96-72398. 352p. 1997. 35.00 (1-57521-287-0) Sams.

Presenting Judy Blume. Maryann N. Weidt. (Twayne's United States Authors Ser.: No. YA 555). 168p. (YA). (gr. 9-12). 1989. 28.00 (0-8057-8208-7, Twyne) Mac Lib Ref.

Presenting Kathry Lasky. JoAnne Brown. LC 98-35177. 173p. 1998. 28.00 (0-8057-1677-7, Twyne) Mac Lib Ref.

Presenting Laurence Yep. Dianne Johnson-Feelings. LC 95-10307. (Twayne's United States Young Adult Authors Ser.). 1995. 28.00 (0-8057-8201-X, Twyne) Mac Lib Ref.

Presenting Lois Duncan. Cosette N. Kies. (Twayne's Young Adult Authors Ser.: No. 635). 139p. 1994. 28.00 (0-8057-8221-4, Twyne) Mac Lib Ref.

Presenting Lynn Hall. Susan Stan. 1996. 28.00 (0-8057-8218-4, Twyne) Mac Lib Ref.

Presenting M. E. Kerr. Alleen P. Nilsen. (Twayne's Young Adult Authors Ser.: No. 527). 136p. 1986. 20.95 (0-8057-8202-8, Twyne) Mac Lib Ref.

Presenting M. E. Kerr. rev. ed. Ed. by Alleen P. Nilsen. LC 96-39134. (Young Adult Authors Ser.). 173p. (YA). (gr. 8 up). 1997. 24.95 (0-8057-9248-1, Twyne) Mac Lib Ref.

Presenting Madeleine L'Engle. Donald R. Hettinga. LC 93-9188. (Twayne's United States Young Adult Authors Ser.). 192p. 1993. 28.00 (0-8057-8222-2, Twyne) Mac Lib Ref.

Presenting Magic Cap: A Guide to General Magic's Revolutionary Communicator Software. Barbara Knaster. LC 93-46018. 272p. 1994. pap. 16.95 (0-201-40740-X) Addison-Wesley.

***Presenting Mildred Taylor.** Chris Crowe. LC 99-25527. (United States Authors Ser.). 150p. (YA). 1999. 28.00 (0-8057-1687-4, Twyne) Mac Lib Ref.

Presenting MMX Programming. 1997. 35.00 (0-672-31198-4) Macmillan.

Presenting Nature: The Historic Landscape Design of the National Park Service, 1916 To 1942. Linda Flint McClelland. 326p. 1995. per. 27.00 (0-16-045136-1) USGPO.

Presenting Nature: The Historic Landscape Design of the National Park Service, 1916 to 1942. Linda F. McClelland. (Illus.). 314p. 1997. reprint ed. pap. text 45.00 (0-7881-4716-1) DIANE Pub.

Presenting Nature: The Historic Landscape Design of the National Park Service, 1916-1942. 1997. lib. bdg. 252.99 (0-8490-6203-9) Gordon Pr.

Presenting Norma Klein. Allene S. Phy. (United States Authors Ser.). 176p. 1988. 20.95 (0-8057-8205-2, TUSAS 538, Twyne) Mac Lib Ref.

Presenting NT 5.0. Clayton Johnson. 1997. 35.00 (0-672-31161-5) Sams.

Presenting Numbers Clearly in Judicial & Other Public Hearings: Trainer Guide. Margaret M. Whilden. (Illus.). 103p. (Orig.). 1983. pap. 8.00 (0-941077-07-1, 35,969) NCLS Inc.

Presenting Ouida Sebestyen. Virginia Monseau. (Twayne's Young Adult Authors Ser.). 152p. 1994. 28.00 (0-8057-8224-9, Twyne) Mac Lib Ref.

Presenting Past: The Core of Psychodynamic Counselling & Therapy. 2nd ed. Michael Jacobs. LC 98-18440. 1998. 85.00 (0-335-20197-0); pap. 29.95 (0-335-20196-2) OpUniv Pr.

Presenting Paul Zindel. Jack J. Forman. (United States Authors Ser.). 168p. 1988. 20.95 (0-8057-8206-0, TUSAS 540, Twyne) Mac Lib Ref.

Presenting Paula Danziger. Kathleen Krull. (Young Adult Authors Ser.). (YA). 1995. 28.00 (0-8057-4153-4, Twyne) Mac Lib Ref.

Presenting Performances. rev. ed. Thomas Wolf. LC 91-32210. (Illus.). 280p. 1991. pap. 16.95 (0-915400-98-7, ACA Bks) Am for the Arts.

Presenting Phyllis Reynolds Naylor. Thomas Stover. LC 96-36022. 187p. (YA). (gr. 8 up). 1997. 20.95 (0-8057-7805-5, Twyne) Mac Lib Ref.

Presenting Poetry: Composition, Publication, Reception. Ed. by Howard Erskine-Hill & Richard A. McCabe. (Illus.). 280p. (C). 1995. text 64.95 (0-521-47360-8) Cambridge U Pr.

Presenting Reader's Theater: Plays & Poems to Read Aloud. Caroline Feller Bauer. (Illus.). 254p. 1987. 45.00 (0-8242-0748-3) Wilson.

Presenting Richard Peck. Donald R. Gallo. LC 89-32346. (Twayne's United States Authors Ser.: No. 554). 176p. (YA). (gr. 8 up). 1989. 20.95 (0-8057-8209-5, Twyne) Mac Lib Ref.

Presenting Robert Cormier. rev. ed. Patricia J. Campbell. (Twayne's United States Authors Ser.: No. 496). 142p. (C). 1989. 28.00 (0-8057-8212-5, Twyne) Mac Lib Ref.

Presenting Robert Lipsyte. Michael Cart. (Young Adult Authors Ser.). (YA). 1995. 28.00 (0-8057-4151-8, Twyne) Mac Lib Ref.

Presenting Rosa Guy. Jerrie Norris. (United States Authors Ser.: No. 543). 112p. 1988. 20.95 (0-8057-8207-9, TUSAS 543, Twyne) Mac Lib Ref.

Presenting S. E. Hinton. Jay Daly. (Twayne's United States Authors Ser.: No. 528). 160p. (C). 1989. 28.00 (0-8057-8211-7, Twyne) Mac Lib Ref.

Presenting Science with Impact: Presentation Skills for Scientists, Medical Researchers & Health Care Professionals. Cindy Todoroff. LC 96-931842. (Illus.). 112p. 1997. pap. 16.95 (1-895579-87-2) TRI.

Presenting Signs & Symptoms in the Emergency Department Evaluation & Treatment. Glenn C. Hamilton. (Illus.). 840p. 1993. 99.00 (0-683-03869-9) Lppncott W & W.

Presenting South Africa. Peter Joyce. LC 99-158908. 1999. 49.95 (1-86872-146-9) Stikk Co.

Presenting Statistics: A Manager's Guide to the Persuasive Use of Statistics. Lawrence P. Witzling. LC 89-31521. 241p. 1989. pap. 28.95 (0-471-80307-3) Wiley.

Presenting Sue Ellen Bridgers. Ted Hipple. (Twayne's United States Authors Ser.: No. 563). 144p. (C). 1990. 20.95 (0-8057-8213-3, Twyne) Mac Lib Ref.

Presenting Tanya, the Ugly Duckling. Patricia L. Gauch. LC 98-22266. (Illus.). 32p. (J). (ps-3). 1999. 15.95 (0-399-23200-1, Philomel) Peng Put Young Read.

Presenting Technical Ideas: A Guide to Audience Communication. W. A. Mambert. LC 67-28335. (Wiley Series on Human Communication). (Illus.). 229p. reprint ed. pap. 71.00 (0-608-11433-2, 205517500011) Bks Demand.

Presenting the Catholic Faith: A Modern Catechism for Inquirers. Frank P. DiSiano. 144p. (Orig.). 1987. pap. 7.95 (0-8091-2841-1) Paulist Pr.

Presenting the Fly: A Practical Guide to the Most Important Element of Fly Fishing. Bernard Kreh. LC 98-25828. (Illus.). 352p. 1999. 40.00 (1-55821-788-6) Lyons Pr.

Presenting the Gattegno Prisms & Cubes. David Wheeler. 1974. pap. 1.25 (0-87825-029-8) Ed Solutions.

Presenting the Holy Spirit. Fuchsia Pickett. (Orig.). 1997. 15.99 (0-88419-518-X) Creation House.

Presenting the Library Service. Roger Stoakley. LC 82-147198. (Outlines of Modern Librarianship Ser.). 110p. reprint ed. pap. 34.10 (*0-7837-5323-3*, 204506200005) Bks Demand.

Presenting the Past: Essays on History & the Public. Ed. by Susan P. Benson et al. (Critical Perspectives on the Past Ser.). (Illus.). 448p. 1986. pap. 22.95 (*0-87722-413-7*) Temple U Pr.

Presenting the Past: Psychoanalysis & Sociology of Misremembering. Jeffrey Prager. LC 97-49904. 240p. 1999. text 31.00 (*0-674-56641-6*) HUP.

***Presenting the Past: Psychoanalysis & the Sociology of Misremembering.** Jeffrey Prager. 272p. 2000. pap. 16.95 (*0-674-00419-1*) HUP.

Presenting the Thirty-Fifth Infantry Division in World War II. (Divisional Ser.). (Illus.). 244p. 1988. reprint ed. 49.95 (*0-89839-112-1*) Battery Pr.

Presenting the Tournament of Roses. Bob Kelly. (Illus.). 32p. (Orig.). 1989. pap. write for info. (*0-318-65908-5*) Kelly Comns.

Presenting Unexpected Outcomes: A Childbirth Educator's Guide. Sherokee Ilse. 44p. 1999. pap. 9.50 (*0-9609456-8-7*) Wintergrn.

Presenting Ursula Le Guin. Suzanne E. Reed. LC 96-38622. 1997. 28.00 (*0-8057-4609-9*, Twyne) Mac Lib Ref.

Presenting Walter Dean Myers. Rudine S. Bishop. (Twayne's United States Young Adult Authors Ser.: No. 565). 136p. (C). 1990. 28.00 (*0-8057-8214-1*, Twyne) Mac Lib Ref.

Presenting William Sleator. James Davis & Hazel Davis. (Twayne's Young Adult Authors Ser.: No. 594). 130p. 1991. 21.95 (*0-8057-8215-X*, 594, Twyne) Mac Lib Ref.

Presenting with Pizzazz! Terrific Tips for Topnotch Trainers! Sharon L. Bowman. LC 97-92966. (Illus.). 107p. (Orig.). 1997. pap. 14.95 (*0-9656851-0-1*) Bowperson Pub.

***Presenting Women Philosophers.** Ed. by Cecile T. Tougas & Sara Ebenreck. LC 99-53448. (New Academy Ser.). 280p. 2000. pap. 24.95 (*1-56639-761-8*) Temple U Pr.

***Presenting Women Philosophers.** Ed. by Cecile T. Tougas & Sara Ebenreck. LC 99-55717. (New Academy Ser.). 280p. (C). 2000. 79.50 (*1-56639-760-X*) Temple U Pr.

Presenting XML. Richard Light. LC 97-67511. 448p. 1997. pap. 24.99 (*1-57521-334-6*) Sams.

***Presenting Young Adult Fantasy.** Macrae. LC 98-12896. 464p. 1998. 26.95 (*0-8057-8220-6*, Twyne) Mac Lib Ref.

Presenting Young Adult Horror Fiction. Cosette Kies. (Twayne's Young Adult Authors Ser.: No. 595). 160p. (C). 1992. 28.00 (*0-8057-8217-6*, Twyne) Mac Lib Ref.

Presenting Young Adult Science Fiction. Antczak. 1998. 22.95 (*0-8057-4152-6*, Twyne) Mac Lib Ref.

Presenting Young Adult Science Fiction. Reid. LC 98-35178. 1998. 28.00 (*0-8057-1653-X*, Twyne) Mac Lib Ref.

Presenting Your Findings: A Practical Guide for Creating Tables. Adelheid A. M. Nicol & Penny Pexman. LC 99-24966. 157p. 1999. pap. 14.95 (*1-55798-593-6*, 431-621A) Am Psychol.

Presenting Zibby Oneal. Susan P. Bloom & Cathyrn M. Mercier. (Twayne's Young Adult Authors Ser.: No. 585). 128p. (C). 1991. 20.95 (*0-8057-8216-8*, Twyne) Mac Lib Ref.

Presenting Zionist Case at Paris & San Remo Conferences see Letters & Papers of Chaim Weizmann

Presently a Beast. Gay Brewer. 67p. (Orig.). 1996. pap. 8.95 (*0-9647127-4-1*) Coreopsis Bks.

Presentment Concerning the Enforcement of the City of New York of the Laws Against Gambling by the Grand Jury for the Additional Extraordinary Special & Trial Term. New York, Kings Country, Grand Jury Staff. LC 73-3844. (Criminal Justice in America Ser.). 1974. reprint ed. 19.95 (*0-405-06148-X*) Ayer.

Presents. Irene Newington. LC 95-60782. (Fun to Do Ser.). (Illus.). 32p. (J). (gr. 2 up). 1995. lib. bdg. 15.95 (*1-887238-05-0*) Fitzgerald.

Presents: A Gift Record Book. Text by Miren Lopategui. (Illus.). 142p. 1991. 14.95 (*0-948751-03-7*) Interlink Pub.

Presents for Joe. Judith Settle. 24p. (J). (gr. 3-6). 1994. pap. write for info. (*0-9636489-1-8*) Celest Pr.

***Presents for Santa.** Harriet Ziefert. LC 99-50872. (Illus.). 32p. (ps-2). 2000. 13.89 (*0-670-88390-5*, Viking Child) Peng Put Young Read.

***Presents for Santa.** Harriet Ziefert. LC 99-50872. (Illus.). 32p. (J). (ps-2). 2000. pap. 3.99 (*0-14-038186-4*, PuffinBks) Peng Put Young Read.

Presents of Mind: Haiku. Jim Kacian. (Illus.). 124p. 1996. pap. 14.95 (*0-9638551-8-2*) Katsura Pr.

Preservation Activities in Bulgaria: The State of Affairs & Possibilities for Cooperation. Sonja Jordan. 12p. 1995. pap. 10.00 (*1-887334-36-X*) Coun Lib & Info.

Preservation Activities in Canada: A Unifying Theme in a Decentralised Country. Karen Turko. LC 96-151449. 16p. 1996. pap. 10.00 (*1-887334-47-5*) Coun Lib & Info.

Preservation & Access Technology: A Structured Glossary of Technical Terms. M. Stuart Lynn. 68p. 1990. pap. 5.00 (*1-887334-03-3*) Coun Lib & Info.

Preservation & Archives in Vietnam. Judith Henchy. LC 98-160193. 22p. 1998. pap. 10.00 (*1-887334-56-4*) Coun Lib & Info.

Preservation & Conservation in Small Libraries. Macia D. Lowry. (LAMA Small Libraries Publications: No. 5). 16p. 1989. pap. text 8.00 (*0-8389-5718-8*) ALA.

Preservation & Conservation of Sci-Tech Materials. Ed. by Ellis Mount. LC 86-33540. (Science & Technology Libraries: Vol. 7, No. 3). 171p. 1987. text 5.95 (*0-86656-650-3*) Haworth Pr.

Preservation & Maintenance of Living Fungi. D. Smith & H. S. Onions. 51p. (Orig.). 1983. pap. text 21.00 (*0-85198-524-6*) Lubrecht & Cramer.

Preservation & Maintenance of Living Fungi. 2nd ed. Ed. by D. Smith & A. H. Onions. (IMI Technical Handbks.: No. 2). (Illus.). 136p. (Orig.). 1994. spiral bd. 45.00 (*0-85198-902-0*) OUP.

***Preservation & Protection of America's Cultural Resources: A Legal Research Guide.** Jenny Hodgkins. LC 99-57713. (Legal Research Guide Ser.: Vol. 36). xi, 52p. 2000. 43.00 (*1-57588-618-9*, 323640) W S Hein.

Preservation & Repair of Historic Clay Tile Roofs. Anne E. Grimmer. 16p. 1993. pap. 1.25 (*0-16-061657-3*) USGPO.

Preservation & Repair of Historic Log Buildings. Bruce D. Bomberger. 16p. 1992. pap. 1.00 (*0-16-061647-6*) USGPO.

Preservation & Repair of Historic Stained & Leaded Glass. Neal A. Vogel. 16p. 1993. pap. 1.50 (*0-16-061661-1*) USGPO.

Preservation & the Management of Library Collections. John Feather. 144p. 1996. 65.00 (*1-85604-190-5*, LAP1905, Pub. by Library Association) Bernan Associates.

Preservation & Transmission of Anglo-Saxon Culture: Selected Papers from the 1991 Meeting of the International Society of Anglo-Saxonists. Paul E. Szarmach et al. LC 97-34096. (Studies in Medieval Culture). 1997. pap. 20.00 (*1-879288-91-5*); text 50.00 (*1-879288-90-7*) Medieval Inst.

Preservation & Valuation of Biological Resources. Ed. by Gordon H. Orians et al. LC 90-12118. 304p. 1990. 40.00 (*0-295-97004-9*) U of Wash Pr.

Preservation Briefs: Recognizing & Resolving Common Preservation Problems, 1-14. 1987. pap. 16.00 (*0-16-003548-1*) USGPO.

Preservation Briefs: Recognizing & Resolving Common Preservation Problems, 15-23. 1991. pap. 14.00 (*0-16-034862-5*) USGPO.

Preservation Challenges in a Changing Political Climate: A Report from Russia. Galina Kislovskaya. LC 98-165439. 19p. (Orig.). 1996. pap. 10.00 (*1-887334-51-3*) Coun Lib & Info.

Preservation Directory: A Guide to Programs, Organizations, & Agencies in New York State. rev. ed. New York State Preservation League Staff. (Illus.). 232p. 1989. pap. 15.00 (*0-942000-06-4*) Pres League NYS.

Preservation Education. 7th ed. Compiled by Christopher D. Coleman. 69p. 1995. spiral bd. 8.50 (*0-8389-7767-7*) ALA.

Preservation Education Institute Final Report. Deanna B. Marcum. 13p. 1990. pap. 10.00 (*1-887334-02-5*) Coun Lib & Info.

Preservation for Profit: Ten Case Studies in Commercial Rehabilitation. Cornelia B. Gilder. (Illus.). 27p. (Orig.). 1980. pap. 3.00 (*0-942000-02-1*) Pres League NYS.

Preservation Guide: Saving the Past & the Present for the Future. Barbara Sagraves. LC 95-38059. (Illus.). 48p. 1995. pap. 6.95 (*0-916489-59-0*, 240) Ancestry.

Preservation Guide No. 1: Family Papers. Susan Cole. LC 84-106237. (Illus.). ii, 14p. 1983. pap. 3.95 (*0-917860-16-0*) Historic New Orleans.

Preservation Guide No. 2: Photographs. John H. Lawrence. LC 84-106237. (Illus.). ii, 14p. 1983. pap. 3.95 (*0-917860-17-9*) Historic New Orleans.

Preservation Guide No. 3: Paintings. Priscilla O'Reilly. LC 84-106237. (Illus.). ii, 14p. 1986. pap. 3.95 (*0-917860-22-5*) Historic New Orleans.

Preservation Guide No. 4: Furniture. Maureen A. Donnelly. LC 84-106237. (Illus.). ii, 14p. (Orig.). 1987. pap. 3.95 (*0-917860-24-1*) Historic New Orleans.

Preservation Guide No. 5: Books. Pamela D. Arceneaux & Jessica Travis. LC 84-106237. (Illus.). ii, 14p. (Orig.). 1989. pap. 3.95 (*0-917860-27-6*) Historic New Orleans.

Preservation Guide No. 6: Matting & Framing. Alan Balicki. LC 84-106237. (Illus.). ii, 14p. (Orig.). 1989. pap. 3.95 (*0-917860-28-4*) Historic New Orleans.

Preservation Guide No. 7: Silver. Maureen Donnelly. LC 84-106237. (Illus.). ii, 14p. 1994. pap. 3.95 (*0-917860-34-9*) Historic New Orleans.

***Preservation Hall.** William Carter. 1999. pap. text. write for info. (*1-871478-01-4*) Cass Hill.

Preservation Hall. William Carter. LC 81-70962. (Illus.). 315p. (C). 1998. pap. 24.95 (*0-304-70517-9*) Continuum.

Preservation Management: Policies & Practices in British Libraries. John Feather et al. LC 95-36428. 192p. 1996. 74.95 (*0-566-07622-5*, Pub. by Gower) Ashgate Pub Co.

Preservation Microfilming: A Guide for Librarians & Archivists. Ed. by Nancy E. Gwinn. LC 87-10020. 238p. reprint ed. pap. 73.80 (*0-7837-5967-3*, 204576800007) Bks Demand.

Preservation Microfilming: A Guide for Librarians & Archivists. 2nd ed. Ed. by Lisa L. Fox. LC 95-4741. (Illus.). 394p. 1995. 80.00 (*0-8389-0653-2*, 0653-2-2045) ALA.

Preservation of Chinese Traditional Books in Cultural Institutions in Taiwan. Edward Martinique. LC 98-26409. (Illus.). 168p. 1998. text. write for info. (*0-7734-8290-3*) E Mellen.

Preservation of Food by Ionizing Radiation, Vol. I. Ed. by Edward S. Josephson & Martin S. Peterson. 400p. 1983. 217.00 (*0-8493-5323-8*, TP371, CRC Reprint) Franklin.

Preservation of Food by Ionizing Radiation, Vol. II. Ed. by Edward S. Josephson & Martin S. Peterson. 360p. 1983. 198.00 (*0-8493-5324-6*, CRC Reprint) Franklin.

Preservation of Food by Ionizing Radiation, Vol. III. Ed. by Edward S. Josephson & Martin S. Peterson. 296p. 1983. 162.00 (*0-8493-5325-4*, CRC Reprint) Franklin.

Preservation of Food by Irradiation. Don Robbins. 128p. (C). 1991. 320.00 (*1-85271-149-3*, Pub. by IBC Tech Srvs) St Mut.

Preservation of Foods with Pulsed Electric Fields. Gustavo V. Barbosa-Canovas. LC 99-60092. (Food Science & Technology International Ser.). 197p. 1999. 89.95 (*0-12-078149-2*) Acad Pr.

Preservation of Fruits & Vegetables Foods Products. S. D. Holdsworth. (Science in Horticulture Ser.). (Illus.). 171p. (Orig.). (C). 1984. pap. text 30.00 (*0-333-32292-4*) Scholium Intl.

Preservation of Historical Records. National Research Council Staff. 108p. 1986. text 17.95 (*0-309-03681-X*) Natl Acad Pr.

Preservation of Library & Archival Materials. 66p. 1991. pap. 31.00 (*0-913359-60-2*) APPA VA.

Preservation of Library & Archival Materials: A Manual. Ed. by Sherelyn Ogden. LC 92-61755. (Illus.). 155p. 1992. write for info. (*0-9634685-0-2*) NE Document.

Preservation of Library & Archival Materials: A Manual. expanded rev. ed. Ed. by Sherelyn Ogden. LC 94-67348. 250p. 1996. spiral bd. 54.50 (*0-9634685-1-0*) Am Assn Mus.

***Preservation of Library & Archival Materials: A Manual.** 3rd rev. exp. ed. Ed. by Sherelyn Ogden. 400p. 1999. 75.69 (*0-9634685-2-9*) NE Document.

Preservation of Library Materials: Austrian National Library, Vienna, Austria; April 7-10, 1986, Set. Peter Sparks et al. (IFLA Publications: Vols. 40-41). 314p. 1987. lib. bdg. 68.00 (*3-598-21770-6*) K G Saur Verlag.

Preservation of Library Materials: Proceedings of a Seminar Sponsored by the Library Binding Institute & the Princeton-Trenton Chapter of Special Libraries Association Held at Rutgers University, July 20-21, 1979. Ed. by Joyce R. Russell. LC 80-20706. (Illus.). 104p. reprint ed. pap. 32.30 (*0-8357-7538-0*, 203626100001) Bks Demand.

***Preservation of Microforms in an Active Environment - Guidelines: ANSI/AIIM TR13-1998.** Association for Information & Image Management Staff. 30p. 1998. 33.00 (*0-89258-342-8*, TR13) Assn Inform & Image Mgmt.

Preservation of Near-Earth Space for Future Generations. Ed. by John A. Simpson. LC 93-11837. (Illus.). 258p. (C). 1994. text 95.00 (*0-521-44508-6*) Cambridge U Pr.

Preservation of New Technology: A Report of the Technology Assessment Advisory Committee. Michael Lesk. 19p. 1992. pap. 5.00 (*1-887334-19-X*) Coun Lib & Info.

Preservation of Open Space in the New Jersey Pinelands. D. Berry et al. (Discussion Papers: No. 73). 1974. pap. 10.00 (*1-55869-098-0*) Regional Sci Res Inst.

Preservation of Paper & Textiles of Historic & Artistic Value. Ed. by W. Williams. (C). 1991. text 350.00 (*0-89771-677-9*, Pub. by Intl Bk Distr) St Mut.

Preservation of Paper & Textiles of Historic & Artistic Value: A Symposium Sponsored by the Cellulose, Paper, & Textile Division at the 172nd Meeting of the American Chemical Society, San Francisco, CA, Aug. 30-31, 1976. Ed. by John C. Williams. LC 77-13137. (Advances in Chemistry Ser.: No. 164). (Illus.). 414p. 1977. reprint ed. pap. 128.40 (*0-608-06820-9*, 206701700009) Bks Demand.

Preservation of Paper & Textiles of Historic & Artistic Value II. Ed. by John C. Williams. LC 81-46. (ACS Advances in Chemistry Ser.: No. 193). 1981. 49.95 (*0-8412-0553-1*) Am Chemical.

Preservation of Paper & Textiles of Historic & Artistic Value II: Based on a Symposium. Ed. by John C. Williams. LC 81-46. (Advances in Chemistry Ser.: No. 193). (Illus.). 366p. 1981. reprint ed. pap. 113.50 (*0-608-04358-3*, 206513900001) Bks Demand.

Preservation of Species: The Value of Biological Diversity. Ed. by Bryan G. Norton. 1986. 45.00 (*0-317-05211-X*); pap. 16.95 (*0-317-05212-8*) IPPP.

Preservation of Species: The Value of Biological Diversity. Ed. by Bryan G. Norton. LC 85-42696. 272p. 1986. text 45.00 (*0-691-08389-4*) IPPP.

Preservation of Species: The Value of Biological Diversity. Ed. by Bryan G. Norton. LC 85-42696. 318p. 1986. reprint ed. pap. 98.60 (*0-608-04591-8*, 206536100003) Bks Demand.

Preservation of the Self in the Oldest Years: With Implications for Practice. 2nd ed. Sheldon S. Tobin. LC 98-31378. 256p. 1999. 41.95 (*0-8261-7581-3*) Springer Pub.

Preservation of the Village: New Mexico's Hispanics & the New Deal. rev. ed. Suzanne Forrest. LC 98-22906. (New Mexico Land Grant Ser.). (Illus.). 271p. 1989. pap. 19.95 (*0-8263-1973-4*) U of NM Pr.

Preservation of Timber in the Tropics. Ed. by W. P. Findlay. (Forestry Sciences Ser.). 1985. text 184.00 (*90-247-3112-7*) Kluwer Academic.

Preservation Planning: Guidelines for Writing a Long-Range Plan. Sherelyn Ogden. (Professional Practice Ser.). 150p. 1998. spiral bd. 41.50 (*0-931201-45-4*) Am Assn Mus.

Preservation Planning Program: An Assisted Self-Study Manual for Libraries. 3rd rev. ed. Jan Oldham-Merrill & Jutta Reed-Scott. 138p. 1993. pap. 45.00 (*0-918006-69-4*) ARL.

Preservation Planning Program Resource Guides: Collection Maintenance & Improvement. Sherry Byrne. 195p. 1993. pap. 15.00 (*0-918006-62-7*) ARL.

Preservation Planning Program Resource Guides: Collections Conservation. Robert DeCandido. 134p. 1993. pap. 15.00 (*0-918006-67-8*) ARL.

Preservation Planning Program Resource Guides: Disaster Preparedness. Constance Brooks. 184p. 1993. pap. 15.00 (*0-918006-65-1*) ARL.

Preservation Planning Program Resource Guides: Managing a Library Binding Program. Jan Merrill-Oldham. 159p. 1993. pap. 15.00 (*0-918006-68-6*) ARL.

Preservation Planning Program Resource Guides: Options for Replacing & Reformatting Deteriorated Materials. Jennifer S. Banks. 51p. 1993. pap. 15.00 (*0-918006-63-5*) ARL.

Preservation Planning Program Resource Guides: Organizing Preservation Activities. Michele Cloonan. 98p. 1993. pap. 15.00 (*0-918006-66-X*) ARL.

Preservation Planning Program Resource Guides: Staff Training & User Awareness in Preservation Management. Wesley Boomgaarden. 89p. 1993. pap. 15.00 (*0-918006-64-3*) ARL.

Preservation Priorities in Latin America: A Report from the Sixtieth IFLA Meeting Havana, Cuba. Dan Hazen. 7p. 1995. pap. 10.00 (*1-887334-41-6*) Coun Lib & Info.

Preservation Program Models: A Study Project & Report. Jan Merrill-Oldham et al. 54p. 1991. pap. 45.00 (*0-918006-20-1*) ARL.

Preservation Resource Guide for Public Works Managers. Larry N. Sypolt. LC 97-45628. (Illus.). 100p. 1998. pap. write for info. (*1-885907-05-2*) WV U Inst Hist of Tech.

Preservation Sourcebook Vol. 1: Mid-Atlantic Edition, 1998. Ed. by Julie Taylor. (Illus.). 220p. 1997. pap. 24.95 (*0-9660570-0-7*) Preserv Pubns.

Preservation Yellow Pages: The Complete Information Source for Homeowners, Communities & Professionals. rev. ed. National Trust for Historic Preservation Staff. LC 97-7456. (Illus.). 277p. 1997. pap. 24.95 (*0-471-19183-3*) Wiley.

Preservationist Manifesto: Progressive & Conservative Politics Were Invented Two Hundred Years Ago, at a Time When Modernization & Progress Were Sweeping Away Privilege & Challenging the Status Quo. They Are Irrelevant Now That Modernization & Progress Are the Status Quo. Charles Siegel. LC 95-92602. 160p. 1996. pap. 12.95 (*0-9648397-4-1*) Northbrae Bks.

Preservations. Clyde Kessler. LC 89-6175. (Illus.). 40p. (Orig.). 1989. pap. 5.00 (*0-926487-00-0*) Rowan Mtn Pr.

Preservative-Free & Self-Preserving Cosmetic & Drug Products: Principles & Practices. Ed. by Jon J. Kabara & Donald S. Orth. LC 96-47675. (Cosmetic Science & Technology Ser.: Vol. 16). (Illus.). 284p. 1997. text 150.00 (*0-8247-9366-8*) Dekker.

Preservative, or Triacle, Agaynst the Poyson of Pelagius. William Turner. LC 78-171795. (English Experience Ser.: No. 418). 208p. 1971. reprint ed. 20.00 (*90-221-0418-4*) Walter J Johnson.

Preservative Treatments for Leather Covered Cameras. 1988. 4.95 (*0-89816-026-X*) Embee Pr.

Preservatives for Cosmetics. David C. Steinberg. (Ingredient Resource Ser.). (Illus.). 47p. 1996. pap. 69.00 (*0-931710-54-5*) Allured Publishing Corp.

Preserve & Create: Essays in Marxist Literary Criticism. Gaylord C. LeRoy & Ursula Beitz. LC 72-75793. (AIMS Monogram Ser.: No. 4). iv, 276p. 1973. write for info. (*0-391-00233-3*) Humanities.

***Preserve & Protect.** large type ed. Allen Drury. LC 99-48201. 690p. 1999. 34.95 (*1-56000-471-1*) Transaction Pubs.

Preserve Them, O Lord: A Guide for Couples Preparing for Marriage in the Orthodox Church. John Mack. (Illus.). 1996. wbk. ed. 11.95 (*1-888212-01-2*) Conciliar Pr.

Preserve Your Love for Science: Life of William Hammond, American Neurologist. Bonnie E. Blustein. (History of Medicine Ser.). (Illus.). 301p. (C). 1991. text 74.95 (*0-521-39262-4*) Cambridge U Pr.

***Preserved: 50 Treasures from American Film Archives.** Scott Simmon & Martin Miller Marks. LC 00-31855. 2000. write for info. (*0-615-11556-X*) Natl Film Preserv.

Preserved Evidence, 2 vols., Set. Jehoshua Eibeshitz & Anna Eibeshitz. (Illus.). 700p. 1996. 49.95 (*0-932351-56-5*) B P Marketing.

Preserved in Glass. large type ed. Margaret Sonnenberg. 1990. 27.99 (*0-7089-2260-0*) Ulverscroft.

Preserved Steam Locomotives of Britain Colin Dennis Garratt. LC 82-197732. 160 p. 1982. 4.95 (*0-7137-0917-0*) Blandford Pr.

Preserved Steam Traction. Eric H. Sawford. LC 86-135995. 160p. 1985. 11.95 (*0-85059-739-0*) Haynes Manuals.

***Preserver.** (Star Trek Ser.). 2000. per. 23.95 (*0-7434-1119-6*) S&S Trade.

Preservers Journal: Putting down What You Put Up. Diane Dunas. 96p. 1996. per. 9.95 (*0-914667-17-3*) Culinary Arts Ltd.

Preservice Art Education: Issues & Practice. Ed. by Lynn Galbraith. 188p. (Orig.). 1995. pap. text 22.00 (*0-937652-86-5*, 232) Natl Art Ed.

Preservice Challenge: Discipline-Based Art Education & Recent Reports on Higher Education. LC 88-13164. (Illus.). 240p. 1988. pap. 10.00 (*0-89236-144-1*, Pub. by J P Getty Trust) OUP.

Preserving. Oded Schwartz. LC 96-10833. 192p. 1996. 29.95 (*0-7894-1053-2*) DK Pub Inc.

Preserving a Good Political Order & a Democratic Republic: Reflections from Philosophy, Great Thinkers, Popes & America's Founding Era. Stephen M. Krason. LC 98-10403. (Studies in Social & Political Theory: Vol. 19). 232p. 1998. text 89.95 (*0-7734-8487-6*) E Mellen.

Preserving Abandoned Railroad Rights-of-Way for Public Use: A Legal Manual. Charles H. Montange. 178p. (Orig.). (C). 1989. pap. text 42.50 (*0-925794-00-7*) Rails Trails.

Preserving Access to Justice: The Impact on State Courts of the "Proposed Long Range Plan for Federal Courts" Roscoe Pound Foundation Staff. Ed. by James Rooks & Barbara Wolfson. (Papers of the Roscoe Pound Foundation). 82p. (Orig.). (C). 1996. pap. 35.00 (*0-933067-17-8*) Roscoe Pound Inst.

P

An Asterisk (*) at the beginning of an entry indicates that the title is appearing for the first time.

Preserving Agricultural Land: An International Annotated Bibliography. Thaddeus C. Trzyna et al. LC 81-21629. (Environmental Studies: No. 7). 100p. (Orig.). 1984. pap. 25.00 (*0-912102-59-4*) Cal Inst Public.

Preserving Alaskan Style. Lavon Barve. (ENG.). 127p. 1992. pap. text 8.00 (*1-57833-056-4*) Todd Commns.

***Preserving America[0012]s Future Today: Congressional Hearing.** Ed. by Rick Santorum. 63p. 2000. reprint ed. pap. text 20.00 (*0-7881-8496-2*) DIANE Pub.

Preserving America's Past. Ed. by Donald J. Crump. LC 81-48076. (Special Publications Series 17: No. 4). 200p. 1983. 12.95 (*0-87044-415-8*); lib. bdg. 12.95 (*0-87044-420-4*) Natl Geog.

Preserving America's Performing Arts. Ed. by Barbara Cohen-Stratyner & Brigitte Kueppers. LC 85-20975. (Illus.). 170p. (Orig.). 1986. pap. 25.00 (*0-932610-05-6*) Theatre Lib.

***Preserving & Strengthening Small Towns & Rural Communities.** Iris B. Carlton-LaNey et al. LC 99-33081. 401p. 1999. 36.95 (*0-87101-310-X*, NASW Pr) Natl Assn Soc Wkrs.

Preserving Archives & Manuscripts. Mary L. Ritzenthaler. (Archival Fundamentals Ser.). 228p. 1993. 27.00 (*0-931828-94-5*) Soc Am Archivists.

Preserving Capital & Making It Grow. John Train. LC 93-73844. 274p. (C). 1993. reprint ed. pap. 18.00 (*0-87034-112-X*) Fraser Pub Co.

Preserving Charleston's Past, Shaping Its Future: The Life & Times of Susan Pringle Frost. Sidney R. Bland. LC 98-40218. 192p. 1999. pap. 16.95 (*1-57003-290-4*) U of SC Pr.

Preserving Charleston's Past, Shaping Its Future: The Life & Times of Susan Pringle Frost, 105. Sidney R. Bland. LC 94-17309. (Contributions in American Studies: No. 105). 256p. 1994. 55.00 (*0-313-29294-9*, Greenwood Pr) Greenwood.

Preserving Childhood for Children in Shelters. Ed. by Thelma Harnes et al. LC 97-18708. 1998. pap. 16.95 (*0-87868-612-6*) Child Welfare.

***Preserving Cultural Landscapes in America** Arnold R. Alanen & Robert Melnick. LC 99-38598. (Center Books on Contemporary Landscape Design Ser.). 2000. 22.50 (*0-8018-6264-7*) Johns Hopkins.

Preserving Different Pasts: The American National Monuments. Hal Rothman. (Illus.). 304p. 1989. text 29.95 (*0-252-01548-7*) U of Ill Pr.

Preserving Digital Information. Gregory S. Hunter. (How-to-Do-It Manuals for Librarians Ser.: Vol. 93). 200p. 1999. pap. 59.95 (*1-55570-353-4*) Neal-Schuman.

Preserving Digital Information, Report of the Task Force on Archiving of Digital Information: Report of the Task Force on Archiving of Digital Information. Donald Waters & John Garrett. LC 96-177538. 59p. 1996. pap. 15.00 (*1-887334-50-5*) Coun Lib & Info.

***Preserving Dignity for People in Your Care.** Suzanne A. Rymer. (Illus.). 79p. 2000. pap. 29.95 (*1-888343-32-X*) Hartman Pub.

Preserving Disorder. David Widgery. 256p. 1989. text 32.95 (*0-7453-0347-1*) Routledge.

Preserving Ecological Systems: The Agenda for Long-Term Research & Development. Ed. by Sidney Draggan et al. 327p. 1987. 45.95 (*0-275-92337-1*, C2337, Praeger Pubs) Greenwood.

Preserving Eden: The Nature Conservancy. Noel Grove. (Illus.). 192p. 1992. 39.95 (*0-8109-3663-1*, Pub. by Abrams) Time Warner.

Preserving Families: Evaluation Resources for Practitioners & Policymakers. Ed. by Ying-Ying Yuan. (Focus Editions Ser.: Vol. 117). 176p. (C). 1990. text 59.95 (*0-8039-3685-0*); pap. text 26.00 (*0-8039-3686-9*) Sage.

Preserving Family Lands, Bk. I. 3rd rev. ed. Small. (Illus.). 110p. 1998. pap. 14.95 (*0-9624557-4-1*) Landowner.

Preserving Family Lands, Bk. II. LC 96-95381. (Illus.). 110p. 1997. reprint ed. pap. 14.95 (*0-9624557-3-3*) Landowner.

Preserving Family Memories: A Guide to Creating Oral Histories. Marc A. Seligman. 32p. 1997. pap. 9.95 (*0-9653409-2-9*) Tapestry Bks.

Preserving Family Wealth & Peace of Mind: Estate Planning: Caring for & Communicating to Your Family Though the Legacies You Leave. Loren Dunton & Kim C. Banta. 225p. 1994. text 27.50 (*1-55738-832-6*, Irwn Prfssnl) McGraw-Hill Prof.

Preserving Family Wealth Using Tax Magic. Richard W. Duff. 400p. (Orig.). 1995. pap. 16.95 (*0-425-14432-1*) Berkley Pub.

Preserving Family Wealth Using Tax Magic: Strategies Worth Millions! Richard W. Duff. LC 93-92696. (Illus.). 288p. 1992. 36.95 (*1-882703-07-3*) RWD Ent.

Preserving Field Records: Archival Techniques for Archaeologists & Anthropologists. Mary A. Kenworthy et al. (Illus.). x, 102p. 1985. pap. 9.95 (*0-934718-72-5*) U Museum Pubns.

***Preserving for All Seasons.** Anne Gardon. (Illus.). 176p. 1999. pap. 24.95 (*1-55209-322-0*) Firefly Bks Ltd.

Preserving Fruits. Deni Bown. LC 97-46921. (One Hundred One Essential Tips Ser.). (Illus.). 72p. 1998. pap. 4.95 (*0-7894-2779-6*) DK Pub Inc.

Preserving Fruits & Vegetables: Making the Most of Seasonal Abundance. Carol W. Costenbader. LC 95-42379. (Well Stocked Pantry Ser.). (Illus.). 96p. 1996. 16.95 (*0-88266-852-8*, 852-8, Storey Pub) Storey Bks.

Preserving Geoscience Imagery: Proceedings, Geoscience Information Society Meeting, Cincinnati, 1992. Ed. by L. S. Zipp. (Proceedings Ser.: Vol. 23). 1993. 45.00 (*0-934485-21-6*) Geosci Info.

Preserving Geoscience Imagery: Proceedings of the 27th Meeting of the Geoscience Information Society, October 26-29, 1992, Cincinnati, OH. Geoscience Information Society, Meeting (27th: 1992: Cincinnati, OH) Staff. Ed. by Louise S. Zipp. LC QE0048.85.G4. (Geoscience Information Society Ser.: Vol. 23). (Illus.). 139p. reprint ed. pap. 43.10 (*0-608-08901-X*, 206953600023) Bks Demand.

Preserving Grace: Protestants, Catholics, & Natural Law. Ed. by Michael Cromartie. LC 96-48112. 201p. (Orig.). 1997. pap. 20.00 (*0-8028-4306-9*) Eerdmans.

Preserving Historic Building Materials: Wood, Paint, Masonry, Concrete, 20th Century Materials. 1994. lib. bdg. 350.00 (*0-8490-8424-5*) Gordon Pr.

Preserving Historic Ceramic Tile Floors. Anne E. Grimmer. 16p. 1997. pap. 1.50 (*0-16-061679-4*) USGPO.

Preserving Historic New England: Preservation, Progressivism & the Remaking of Memory. James M. Lindgren. (Illus.). 256p. 1995. 45.00 (*0-19-509363-1*) OUP.

Preserving HUD-Assisted Housing for Use by Low-Income Tenants: An Advocate's Guide. National Housing Law Project Staff & Sara E. Johnson. 484p. (Orig.). 1985. pap. 25.00 (*0-941077-05-5*, 38,900) NCLS Inc.

Preserving Intellectual Freedom: Fighting Censorship in Our Schools. Ed. & Intro. by Jean E. Brown. LC 94-19860. 252p. 1994. 19.95 (*0-8141-3671-0*) NCTE.

Preserving Jewishness in Your Family: After Intermarriage Has Occurred. Alan Silverstein. LC 95-8310. 272p. 1996. pap. 25.00 (*1-56821-543-6*) Aronson.

Preserving Knowledge: The Case for Alkaline Paper. Association of Research Libraries Staff. 130p. 1990. 18.00 (*0-918006-18-X*) ARL.

Preserving Lemons. Gregory W. Wilson. 1997. pap. 9.95 (*0-9510523-8-1*, Pub. by Staples) Intl Spec Bk.

Preserving Library Materials: A Manual. 2nd ed. Susan G. Swartzburg. LC 94-18868. (Illus.). 514p. 1995. text 62.50 (*0-8108-2855-3*) Scarecrow.

Preserving Library Materials: A Manual. 2nd abr. ed. Susan G. Swartzburg. LC 94-18868. 328p. 1995. pap. 31.00 (*0-8108-2980-0*) Scarecrow.

Preserving Natural Conditions: Science & the Perception of Nature in Yellowstone National Park. Contrib. by James Pritchard. LC 98-51144. (Illus.). 1999. text 45.00 (*0-8032-3722-7*) U of Nebr Pr.

Preserving Nature in the National Parks: A History. Richard W. Sellars. LC 97-16154. (Illus.). 364p. 1997. write for info. (*0-300-06931-6*) Yale U Pr.

Preserving Nature in the National Parks: A History. Richard West Sellars. (Illus.). 416p. 1999. pap. text 14.95 (*0-300-07578-2*) Yale U Pr.

Preserving Our Ideals: Papers from the 1993 Principals Academy. Ed. by Regina Haney & Frank X. Savage. LC 94-188981. 137p. 1994. pap. 8.00 (*1-55833-133-6*) Natl Cath Educ.

Preserving Our Italian Heritage. 1991. pap. 14.95 (*0-9629303-0-X*) Sons Italy FL.

Preserving Our Italian Heritage: A Cookbook. Ed. by Rose M. Boniello. 222p. 1998. text 15.00 (*0-7881-5748-5*) DIANE Pub.

Preserving Paradise: Why Regulation Won't Work. David L. Callies. LC 93-28244. (C). 1994. pap. 16.95 (*0-8248-1576-9*) UH Pr.

Preserving Perishables with Vacuum Packing. Myron Ort. 130p. (Orig.). 1981. pap. text. write for info. (*0-941446-00-X*) Tethys Pr.

Preserving Porches: Two Experts Tell You How to Restore Your Porch to Its Original Beauty. Renee Kahn & Ellen Meagher. (Illus.). 112p. (Orig.). 1995. pap. 19.95 (*0-8050-1209-5*, Owl) H Holt & Co.

Preserving Public Lands for the Future: The Politics of Intergenerational Goods. William R. Lowry. Ed. by Barry Rabe & John Tierney. LC 98-13259. (American Governance & Public Policy Ser.). 320p. 1998. 60.00 (*0-87840-701-4*); pap. 24.95 (*0-87840-702-2*) Georgetown U Pr.

Preserving Rural Australia: Issues & Solutions. Ed. by Alistar Robertson & Robyn Watts. 168p. (Orig.). pap. 39.95 (*0-643-06388-9*, Pub. by CSIRO) Accents Pubns.

Preserving Scientific Data on Our Physical Universe: A New Strategy for Archiving the Nation's Scientific Information Resources. National Research Council Staff. LC 94-68991. 80p. 1995. pap. text 25.00 (*0-309-05186-X*) Natl Acad Pr.

***Preserving Self in South Seas.** Jonathan Lamb. 1999. pap. text 18.00 (*0-226-46849-6*); lib. bdg. 45.00 (*0-226-46848-8*) U Ch Pr.

Preserving Strength While Meeting Challenges: Summary Report of a Workshop on Actions for the Mathematical Sciences. National Research Council Staff. LC 97-216317. 92p. (C). 1997. pap. text 15.00 (*0-309-05883-X*) Natl Acad Pr.

Preserving Summer's Bounty: A Quick & Easy Guide to Freezing, Canning, Preserving, & Drying What You Grow. Susan McClure. 384p. 1998. pap. 14.95 (*0-87596-979-8*) Rodale Pr Inc.

Preserving Summer's Bounty: A Quick & Easy Guide to Freezing, Canning, Preserving & Drying What You Grow. Ed. by Susan A. McClure. (Illus.). 372p. 1995. text 26.95 (*0-87596-648-9*) Rodale Pr Inc.

Preserving Texas' Natural Heritage, No. 31. Keith Arnold. (Policy Research Project Report Ser.). 40p. 1978. pap. 3.00 (*0-89940-627-0*) LBJ Sch Pub Aff.

***Preserving Textiles: A Guide for the Nonspecialist.** Harold F. Mailand & Dorothy Stites Alig. LC 99-16496. 96p. 1999. pap. 15.00 (*0-936260-71-8*) Ind Mus Art.

Preserving the Astronomical Windows. Ed. by Syuzo Isobe & Tomohiro Hirayama. LC 98-71191. (Conference Series Proceedings: Vol. 139). 243p. 1998. 52.00 (*1-886733-59-7*) Astron Soc Pacific.

Preserving the Built Heritage: Tools for Implementation. J. Mark Schuster. LC 97-5520. 241p. 1997. pap. 25.00 (*0-87451-831-8*); text 50.00 (*0-87451-813-X*) U Pr of New Eng.

Preserving the Chesapeake Bay. Gerald L. Baliles. LC 95-62287. (Illus.). 64p. 1996. 14.95 (*1-884549-02-0*) VA Mus Natl Hist.

***Preserving the Chesapeake Bay: Lessons in the Political Reality of Natural Resource Stewardship.** Gerald L. Baliles. (Illus.). 60p. 2000. reprint ed. text 25.00 (*0-7881-9097-0*) DIANE Pub.

Preserving the Cultural Legacy: Black Adoption Placement & Research Center. Marjorie Beggs. 28p. (Orig.). 1992. pap. 5.00 (*0-936434-62-7*, Pub. by Zellerbach Fam Fund) Intl Spec Bk.

Preserving the Dead. E. Myers & A. J. Dodge. 1997. reprint ed. pap. 9.95 (*0-917914-24-4*) Lindsay Pubns.

Preserving the Deterrent: A Missile Defence for Europe. Michael Ruhle. (C). 1990. 35.00 (*0-907967-78-7*, Pub. by Inst Euro Def & Strat) St Mut.

Preserving the Family Farm: Women, Community & the Foundations of Agribusiness in the Midwest, 1900-1940. Mary C. Neth. (Revisiting Rural America Ser.). 272p. 1995. text 39.95 (*0-8018-4898-9*) Johns Hopkins.

Preserving the Game: Gambling, Mining, Hunting & Conservation in the Vanishing West. J. R. Jones. Ed. by Tom Trusky. (Hemingway Western Studies). (Illus.). 180p. (Orig.). 1989. pap. 14.95 (*0-932129-06-4*) Heming W Studies.

Preserving the Global Environment: The Challenge of Shared Leadership. Ed. by Jessica T. Mathews. 384p. (C). 1990. pap. text 15.50 (*0-393-96093-5*) Norton.

Preserving the Glory Days: Ghost Towns & Mining Camps of Nye County, Nevada. rev. ed. Shawn Hall. LC 98-24318. Orig. Title: Guide to the Ghost Towns & Mining Camps of Nye County. (Illus.). 296p. 1998. pap. 21.95 (*0-87417-317-5*) U of Nev Pr.

Preserving the Higher Education Legacy: A California with California Leaders. John Immerwahr. 23p. (Orig.). 1995. pap. write for info. (*1-889483-20-6*) Public Agenda.

Preserving the Hunger: An Isaac Rosenfeld Reader. Ed. & Intro. by Mark Shechner. LC 87-27929. 464p. 1988. pap. 19.95 (*0-8143-1880-0*) Wayne St U Pr.

Preserving the Hunger: An Isaac Rosenfeld Reader. Isaac Rosenfeld. Ed. & Intro. by Mark Schechner. LC 87-27929. 464p. reprint ed. pap. 143.90 (*0-608-10600-3*, 2071221) Bks Demand.

Preserving the Illustrated Text: Report of the Joint Task Force on Text & Image. Commission on Preservation & Access Staff. 31p. 1992. pap. 10.00 (*1-887334-15-7*) Coun Lib & Info.

Preserving the Independence of the Judiciary: Report of the 1993 Forum for State Court Judges. Roscoe Pound Foundation Staff. Ed. by Barbara Wolfson. LC 94-67264. 67p. 1994. pap. 35.00 (*0-933067-16-X*) Roscoe Pound Inst.

Preserving the Intellectual Heritage: A Report of the Bellagio Conference. Commission on Preservation & Access Staff. 36p. 1993. pap. 10.00 (*1-887334-28-9*) Coun Lib & Info.

Preserving the Legacy. Priscilla G. Watkins. (Illus.). 56p. 1998. pap. 20.00 (*0-9636398-2-X*) St Croix Lndmrks.

***Preserving the Legacy: Concepts in Support of Sustainability.** Ed. by Allen G. Noble & Frank J. Costa. LC 98-45368. 256p. 1999. 60.00 (*0-7391-0015-7*) Lxngtn Bks.

Preserving the Legacy of a Small Business Family: Estate Planning & Business Succession. Tim Bachmeyer & William A. Snyder. 225p. 1998. pap. 24.95 (*0-9660538-0-X*) Est Busn Comns.

Preserving the Monarchy: The Comte de Vergennes, 1774-1787. Munro Price. 268p. (C). 1995. text 59.95 (*0-521-46566-4*) Cambridge U Pr.

Preserving the Old Dominion: Historic Preservation & Virginia Traditionalism. James M. Lindgren. LC 92-46301. (Illus.). 400p. 1993. text 42.50 (*0-8139-1450-7*) U Pr of Va.

Preserving the Past: The Rise of Heritage in Modern Britain. Ed. by Michael Hunter. (Illus.). 224p. 1996. 44.95 (*0-7509-0951-X*, Pub. by Sutton Pub Ltd) Intl Pubs Mktg.

Preserving the Person: A Look at the Human Sciences. C. Stephen Evans. 175p. 1994. reprint ed. pap. 19.95 (*1-57383-026-7*) Regent College.

Preserving the Preserved Word of the Authorized King James Version. 2nd ed. O. Talmadge Spence. 61p. 2000. pap. 3.50 (*1-882542-24-X*) Fndtns NC.

Preserving the Press: How Daily Newspapers Mobilized to Keep Their Readers. Leo Bogart. 1991. text 61.00 (*0-231-07262-7*) Col U Pr.

Preserving the Vital Base: America's Semiconductor Materials & Equipment Industry. (Illus.). 31p. (Orig.). (C). 1993. pap. text 20.00 (*1-56806-631-7*) DIANE Pub.

***Preserving the Whole: A Two-Track Approach to Rescuing Social Science Data & Meta Data.** Ann Green et al. (Illus.). 45p. 1999. pap. 15.00 (*1-887334-68-8*) Coun Lib & Info.

Preserving the Word: The Library Association Conference Proceedings, Harrogate, 1986. Library Association, Conference Staff. Ed. by R. E. Palmer. LC 87-16523. 159p. reprint ed. pap. 49.30 (*0-7837-5316-0*, 204505500005) Bks Demand.

Preserving Today. Jeanne Lesem. LC 96-29834. 288p. 1997. pap. 15.95 (*0-8050-4881-2*) H Holt & Co.

Preserving Valves Through Reading Children's Literature. Althea S. Southwick. 76p. (Orig.). 1987. pap. 6.95 (*0-9614058-3-X*) Southco.

Preserving Washington's Wild Lands: A Guide to the Nature Conservancy's Preserves in Washington. Nature Conservancy of Washington Staff. LC 92-85124. 96p. (Orig.). 1992. pap. 14.95 (*0-89886-350-3*) Mountaineers.

Preserving Wildlife: An International Perspective. Mark Michael. LC 99-38312. 275p. 1999. pap. 21.95 (*1-57392-727-9*, Humanity Bks) Prometheus Bks.

Preserving World's Cities. Tung A. Max. 2001. 40.00 (*0-517-70148-0*) Random.

Preserving Your American Heritage: A Guide to Family & Local History. 2nd rev. ed. Norman E. Wright. LC 80-27934. (Illus.). viii, 285p. (C). 1981. pap. text 11.95 (*0-8425-1863-0*, Friends of the Library) Brigham.

Preserving Your Family Heritage. Nancy E. Carlberg. LC 87-162874. 100p. (Orig.). 1987. pap. 5.00 (*0-944878-04-0*) Carlberg Pr.

Preserving Your Family Treasures. 2nd rev. ed. Michael Trinkley & Debi Hacker. LC 98-33884. (Illus.). 1998. pap. 7.50 (*1-58317-001-4*) Chicora Found.

Preshipment Inspection Services. Patrick Low. LC 94-49060. (World Bank Discussion Papers: No. 278). 176p. 1995. pap. 22.00 (*0-8213-3185-X*, 13185) World Bank.

Preshistoric Life. David Unwin. (Mysteries of...Ser.). (Illus.). 40p. (J). (gr. 4-6). 1996. lib. bdg. 22.90 (*0-7613-0535-1*, Copper Beech Bks) Millbrook Pr.

Presidencialismo en Mexico y los E. U. Alicia Hernandez. (SPA.). pap. 10.99 (*968-16-4526-X*, Pub. by Fondo) Continental Bk.

Presidencialismo Mexicano (The Mexican Presidentialism) Eliseo M. Berrueto. (SPA.). 299p. 1996. pap. 14.99 (*968-16-4967-2*, Pub. by Fondo) Continental Bk.

Presidencies of Grover Cleveland. Richard E. Welch, Jr. LC 88-268. (American Presidency Ser.). xviii, 246p. 1988. 29.95 (*0-7006-0355-7*) U Pr of KS.

Presidencies of James A. Garfield & Chester A. Arthur. Justus D. Doenecke. LC 80-18957. (American Presidency Ser.). xiv, 230p. 1981. 29.95 (*0-7006-0208-9*) U Pr of KS.

Presidencies of William Henry Harrison & John Tyler. Norma L. Peterson. LC 89-5341. (American Presidency Ser.). xiv, 330p. 1989. 29.95 (*0-7006-0400-6*) U Pr of KS.

Presidencies of Zachary Taylor & Millard Fillmore. Elbert B. Smith. LC 88-5722. (American Presidency Ser.). xii, 308p. 1988. 29.95 (*0-7006-0362-X*) U Pr of KS.

Presidency. Richard B. Bernstein & Jerome Agel. LC 88-21026. (Into the Third Century Ser.). (YA). (gr. 7 up). 1989. 12.95 (*0-8027-6829-6*); lib. bdg. 13.85 (*0-8027-6831-8*) Walker & Co.

Presidency. Carl Green & William Sanford. (American Government Ser.). (Illus.). 96p. (YA). (gr. 7 up). 1990. lib. bdg. 18.95 (*0-86593-084-8*) Rourke Corp.

Presidency. Richard M. Pious. LC 95-12298. 464p. (C). 1995. pap. text 44.00 (*0-02-395792-1*, Macmillan Coll) P-H.

Presidency. Patricia R. Quiri. LC 97-48964. (True Bks.). (J). 1998. 21.00 (*0-516-20674-5*) Childrens.

Presidency. Patricia R. Quiri. (True Bks.). (Illus.). 48p. (J). (gr. 3-5). 1999. pap. text 6.95 (*0-516-26438-9*) Childrens.

***Presidency.** Ed. by Arthur Meier Schlesinger, Jr. (Illus.). 64p. (YA). (gr. 3 up). 2000. 17.95 (*0-7910-5533-7*) Chelsea Hse.

***Presidency.** Ed. by Steadwell Books Publishing Staff. (American Government Today Ser.). (Illus.). (YA). 2000. 22.83 (*0-7398-1786-8*) Raintree Steck-V.

Presidency. Shirley Anne Warshaw. (C). 2000. pap. 30.00 (*0-205-26815-3*, Macmillan Coll) P-H.

Presidency, Incl. Test Bank. Richard M. Pious. (C). 1997. pap., teacher ed. write for info. (*0-205-26702-5*, T6702-9) Allyn.

Presidency: Crisis & Regeneration. Herman Finer. 1993. pap. text 2.95 (*0-226-24970-0*, P588) U Ch Pr.

Presidency: Crisis & Regeneration - An Essay in Possibilities. Herman Finer. LC 60-14230. 386p. reprint ed. pap. 119.70 (*0-608-09435-8*, 205423500004) Bks Demand.

Presidency A to Z **see CQ's New A to Z Collection**

Presidency A to Z: A Ready Reference Encyclopedia. rev. ed. Ed. by Michael Nelson. LC 94-17668. (Encyclopedia of American Government Ser.: Vol. 2). 574p. (YA). (gr. 11). 1994. text 145.00 (*1-56802-056-2*) Congr Quarterly.

Presidency & a World in Change. Ed. by Kenneth W. Thompson. (World in Change Ser.: Vol. I). 110p. (C). 1991. pap. text 17.00 (*0-8191-8453-5*); lib. bdg. 41.50 (*0-8191-8452-7*) U Pr of Amer.

Presidency & Arms Control Vol. IV: Process, Procedures, & Problems. Ed. by Kenneth Thompson. (W. Alton Jones Foundation Series on the Presidency & Arms Control). 208p. 1997. 48.50 (*0-7618-0727-6*); pap. 26.50 (*0-7618-0728-4*) U Pr of Amer.

Presidency & Black Civil Rights: Eisenhower to Nixon. Allan Wolk. LC 70-135029. 276p. 1975. 38.50 (*0-8386-7805-X*) Fairleigh Dickinson.

Presidency & Domestic Policies of Jimmy Carter, 327. Ed. by Herbert D. Rosenbaum & Alexej Ugrinsky. LC 93-9321. (Contributions in Political Science Ser.: No. 327). 876p. 1993. 110.00 (*0-313-28845-3*, GM8845, Greenwood Pr) Greenwood.

***Presidency & Domestic Policy: Comparing Leadership Styles, F. D. R. to Clinton.** William W. Lammers & Michael A. Genovese. LC 99-88686. 2000. 28.95 (*1-56802-124-0*) CQ Pr.

***Presidency & Domestic Policy: Comparing Leadership Styles, FDR to Clinton.** William W. Lammers. 330p. 2000. 38.95 (*1-56802-125-9*) CQ Pr.

Presidency & Education, Vol. 1. Ed. by Kenneth W. Thompson. 196p. (C). 1990. pap. text 24.00 (*0-8191-7811-X*); lib. bdg. 44.00 (*0-8191-7810-1*) U Pr of Amer.

P

Presidency & Governance in Poland: Yesterday & Today. Ed. by Kenneth W. Thompson. LC 97-27416. (World in Change: Vol. X). 164p. (C). 1997. 38.00 (*0-7618-0870-1*); pap. 18.50 (*0-7618-0871-X*) U Pr of Amer.

Presidency & Information Policy. Harold C. Relyea et al. 216p. (Orig.). 1981. 10.00 (*0-938204-03-3*); pap. 8.00 (*0-938204-04-1*) Ctr Study Presidency.

Presidency & Legislation: The Growth of Central Clearance. Richard E. Neustadt. (Reprint Series in Social Sciences). (C). 1993. reprint ed. pap. text 5.00 (*0-8290-3230-4*, PS-216) Irvington.

Presidency & National Security Policy, Vol. V. R. Gordon Hoxie et al. 502p. 1984. 21.00 (*0-938204-05-X*); pap. 13.00 (*0-938204-06-8*) Ctr Study Presidency.

Presidency & Public Policy: The Four Arenas of Presidential Power. Robert J. Spitzer. LC 81-19802. (Illus.). 205p. 1983. pap. 63.60 (*0-7837-8406-6*, 205921700009) Bks Demand.

Presidency & Science Advising. Ed. by Kenneth W. Thompson. (Tenth Anniversary Series of the White Burkett Miller Center of Public Affairs). 94p. (Orig.). 1986. pap. text 14.00 (*0-8191-5312-5*, Pub. by White Miller Center); lib. bdg. 32.00 (*0-8191-5311-7*, Pub. by White Miller Center) U Pr of Amer.

Presidency & Science Advising, Vol. II. Ed. by Kenneth W. Thompson. LC 86-4132. 88p. (Orig.). (C). 1987. pap. text 13.50 (*0-8191-6345-7*) U Pr of Amer.

Presidency & Science Advising, Vol. II. Ed. by Kenneth W. Thompson. LC 86-4132. 88p. (Orig.). (C). 1987. lib. bdg. 29.50 (*0-8191-6344-9*, Pub. by White Miller Center) U Pr of Amer.

Presidency & Science Advising, Vol. III. Ed. by Kenneth W. Thompson. LC 87-8206. 142p. (Orig.). 1987. pap. text 16.50 (*0-8191-6459-3*) U Pr of Amer.

Presidency & Science Advising, Vol. III. Ed. by Kenneth W. Thompson. LC 87-8206. 142p. (Orig.). 1987. lib. bdg. 39.00 (*0-8191-6458-5*, Pub. by White Miller Center) U Pr of Amer.

Presidency & Science Advising, Vol. IV. Kenneth W. Thompson. LC 87-8206. 90p. (Orig.). (C). 1988. pap. 13.50 (*0-8191-6671-5*) U Pr of Amer.

Presidency & Science Advising, Vol. V. Ed. by Kenneth W. Thompson. LC 86-4132. 124p. (Orig.). (C). 1988. pap. text 15.00 (*0-8191-6958-7*, Pub. by White Miller Center); lib. bdg. 33.00 (*0-8191-6957-9*, Pub. by White Miller Center) U Pr of Amer.

Presidency & Science Advising, Vol. VI. Ed. by Kenneth W. Thompson. LC 86-4132. 158p. (Orig.). (C). 1988. lib. bdg. 38.00 (*0-8191-7133-6*, Pub. by White Miller Center) U Pr of Amer.

Presidency & Science Advising, Vol. VII. Ed. by Kenneth W. Thompson. 160p. (Orig.). (C). 1990. pap. text 22.00 (*0-8191-7819-5*); lib. bdg. 41.50 (*0-8191-7818-7*) U Pr of Amer.

Presidency & Science Advising, Vol. VIII. Ed. by Kenneth W. Thompson. (Presidency & Science Advising Ser.). 122p. (Orig.). (C). 1991. pap. text 19.00 (*0-8191-8321-0*); lib. bdg. 45.00 (*0-8191-8320-2*) U Pr of Amer.

Presidency & Science Advising, Vol. IX: Congress, Governance, & Science, Vol. IX. Ed. by Kenneth W. Thompson. 175p. (Orig.). 1994. pap. text 24.50 (*0-8191-8712-7*); lib. bdg. 49.00 (*0-8191-8711-9*) U Pr of Amer.

Presidency & the Congress: A Shifting Balance of Power? William S. Livingston et al. 450p. 1979. pap. 7.00 (*0-89940-407-3*) LBJ Sch Pub Aff.

***Presidency & the Middle Kingdom: China, the United States & Executive Leadership.** Michael P. Riccards. 256p. 2000. 60.00 (*0-7391-0129-3*) Lxngtn Bks.

Presidency & the Persian Gulf War. Ed. by Marcia L. Whicker et al. LC 92-38778. (Praeger Series in Presidential Studies). 296p. 1993. 55.00 (*0-275-94469-7*, C4469, Praeger Pubs) Greenwood.

Presidency & the Political System. 5th ed. Michael Nelson. LC 97-40586. 607p. (YA). 1997. text 41.95 (*1-56802-305-7*) Congr Quarterly.

Presidency & the Political System. 5th ed. Michael Nelson. LC 97-40586. 607p. (YA). 1997. pap. text 30.95 (*1-56802-304-9*) Congr Quarterly.

***Presidency & the Political System.** 6th ed. Michael Nelson. LC 99-54451. 600p. 2000. pap. 35.95 (*1-56802-496-7*) CQ Pr.

***Presidency & the Political System.** 6th ed. Michael Nelson. 2000. 45.95 (*1-56802-497-5*) CQ Pr.

Presidency & the Politics of Racial Inequality: Nation-Keeping from 1831 to 1965. Russell Riley. LC 98-37018. (Power, Conflict, & Democracy Ser.). 480p. 1999. lib. bdg. 49.50 (*0-231-10722-6*) Col U Pr.

***Presidency & the Politics of Racial Inequality: Nation-Keeping from 1831 to 1965.** Russell Riley. LC 98-37018. (Power, Conflict, & Democracy Ser.). 480p. 1999. pap. 22.50 (*0-231-10723-4*) Col U Pr.

Presidency & the Press. Hoyt H. Purvis. (Symposia Ser.). 120p. 1976. pap. 3.00 (*0-89940-405-7*) LBJ Sch Pub Aff.

Presidency & the Quality of American Life. Louis W. Keonig. 1971. 1.00 (*1-55614-089-4*) U of SD Gov Res Bur.

Presidency & the Rhetoric of Foreign Crisis. Denise M. Bostdorff. LC 93-21561. 315p. 1993. text 34.95 (*0-87249-968-5*) U of SC Pr.

Presidency Banks & the Indian Economy, 1876-1914. Amiya K. Bagchi. 312p. 1990. 12.95 (*0-19-562412-2*) OUP.

Presidency in a Separated System. Charles O. Jones. 338p. (C). 1994. 42.95 (*0-8157-4710-1*); pap. text 18.95 (*0-8157-4709-8*) Brookings.

Presidency in an Age of Limits, 326. Michael A. Genovese. LC 92-45085. (Contributions in Political Science Ser.: No. 326). 224p. 1993. 57.95 (*0-313-27476-2*, GUP, Greenwood Pr) Greenwood.

Presidency in the Courts. Glendon A. Schubert. LC 72-8122. (American Constitutional & Legal History Ser). 408p. 1973. reprint ed. lib. bdg. 42.50 (*0-306-70529-X*) Da Capo.

Presidency in Transition. Ed. by James P. Pfiffner. 550p. (Orig.). (C). 1989. 30.00 (*0-938204-00-9*) Ctr Study Presidency.

Presidency of Abraham Lincoln. Phillip S. Paludan. LC 93-46830. (American Presidency Ser.). 408p. (Orig.). (C). 1994. 29.95 (*0-7006-0671-8*) U Pr of KS.

Presidency of Abraham Lincoln. Phillip S. Paludan. LC 93-46830. 388p. (Orig.). (C). 1995. pap. 15.95 (*0-7006-0745-5*) U Pr of KS.

Presidency of Andrew Jackson. Donald B. Cole. LC 92-43377. (American Presidency Ser.). 352p. 1999. 29.95 (*0-7006-0600-9*); pap. 15.95 (*0-7006-0961-X*) U Pr of KS.

Presidency of Andrew Johnson. Albert Castel. LC 79-11050. (American Presidency Ser.). x, 262p. 1979. 29.95 (*0-7006-0190-2*) U Pr of KS.

Presidency of Benjamin Harrison. Homer E. Socolofsky & Allan Spetter. LC 86-32592. (American Presidency Ser.). xii, 268p. 1987. 29.95 (*0-7006-0320-4*) U Pr of KS.

Presidency of Calvin Coolidge. Robert H. Ferrell. LC 97-51128. (American Presidency Ser.). (Illus.). 272p. 1998. 29.95 (*0-7006-0892-3*) U Pr of KS.

Presidency of Dwight D. Eisenhower. rev. ed. Chester J. Pach, Jr. & Elmo Richardson. LC 90-45952. (American Presidency Ser.). xiv, 290p. 1991. 29.95 (*0-7006-0436-7*); pap. 15.95 (*0-7006-0437-5*) U Pr of KS.

***Presidency of Franklin Delano Roosevelt.** George McJimsey. LC 99-55956. (Illus.). 376p. 2000. text 34.95 (*0-7006-1012-X*) U Pr of KS.

Presidency of Franklin Pierce. Larry Gara. LC 91-8367. (American Presidency Ser.). xiv, 218p. 1991. 29.95 (*0-7006-0494-4*) U Pr of KS.

Presidency of George Bush. John Robert Greene. LC 99-35836. (American Presidency Ser.). (Illus.). 248p. 2000. 35.00 (*0-7006-0993-8*) U Pr of KS.

Presidency of George Washington. Forrest McDonald. LC 73-11344. (American Presidency Ser.). xiv, 210p. 1974. 29.95 (*0-7006-0110-4*); pap. 12.95 (*0-7006-0359-X*) U Pr of KS.

Presidency of Gerald R. Ford. John R. Greene. LC 94-20037. (American Presidency Ser.). 282p. 1995. 29.95 (*0-7006-0638-6*); pap. 15.95 (*0-7006-0639-4*) U Pr of KS.

Presidency of Harry S. Truman. Donald R. McCoy. LC 84-3624. (American Presidency Ser.). xii, 356p. 1984. 29.95 (*0-7006-0252-6*); pap. 15.95 (*0-7006-0255-0*) U Pr of KS.

Presidency of Herbert C. Hoover. Martin L. Fausold. LC 84-17252. (American Presidency Ser.). xii, 292p. 1985. 29.95 (*0-7006-0259-3*); pap. 15.95 (*0-7006-0358-1*) U Pr of KS.

Presidency of James Buchanan. Elbert B. Smith. LC 74-31220. (American Presidency Ser.). xvi, 228p. 1975. 29.95 (*0-7006-0132-5*) U Pr of KS.

Presidency of James Earl Carter, Jr. Burton I. Kaufman. LC 92-18134. (American Presidency Ser.). 260p. 1993. 29.95 (*0-7006-0572-X*); pap. 15.95 (*0-7006-0573-8*) U Pr of KS.

Presidency of James K. Polk. Paul H. Bergeron. LC 87-2174. (American Presidency Ser.). xvi, 312p. 1987. 29.95 (*0-7006-0319-0*) U Pr of KS.

Presidency of James Madison. Robert A. Rutland. LC 89-70419. (American Presidency Ser.). xiv, 234p. 1990. 29.95 (*0-7006-0465-0*) U Pr of KS.

Presidency of James Monroe. Noble E. Cunningham, Jr. LC 95-34157. (American Presidency Ser.). 256p. (C). 1996. 29.95 (*0-7006-0728-5*) U Pr of KS.

Presidency of John Adams. Ralph A. Brown. LC 75-5526. (American Presidency Ser.). xii, 248p. 1975. 29.95 (*0-7006-0134-1*) U Pr of KS.

Presidency of John F. Kennedy. James N. Giglio. LC 91-16841. (American Presidency Ser.). x, 334p. 1991. pap. 15.95 (*0-7006-0520-7*) U Pr of KS.

Presidency of John F. Kennedy. James N. Giglio. LC 91-16841. (American Presidency Ser.). x, 334p. 1991. 29.95 (*0-7006-0515-0*) U Pr of KS.

Presidency of John Quincy Adams. Mary W. Hargreaves. LC 85-11147. (American Presidency Ser.). xvi, 400p. 1985. 29.95 (*0-7006-0272-0*) U Pr of KS.

Presidency of Lyndon B. Johnson. Vaughn D. Bornet. LC 83-12560. (American Presidency Ser.). xvi, 416p. 1984. 29.95 (*0-7006-0237-2*); pap. 17.95 (*0-7006-0242-9*) U Pr of KS.

Presidency of Martin Van Buren. Major L. Wilson. LC 83-17871. (American Presidency Ser.). xiv, 258p. 1984. 29.95 (*0-7006-0238-0*) U Pr of KS.

Presidency of Richard Nixon. Melvin Small. LC 99-13148. (American Presidency Ser.). (Illus.). 368p. 1999. 29.95 (*0-7006-0973-3*) U Pr of KS.

Presidency of Rutherford B. Hayes. Ari Hoogenboom. LC 88-5709. (American Presidency Ser.). x, 278p. 1988. 29.95 (*0-7006-0338-7*) U Pr of KS.

Presidency of Rutherford B. Hayes, 3. Kenneth E. Davison. LC 79-176289. (Contributions in American Studies: No. 3). 266p. 1972. 69.50 (*0-8371-6275-0*, DPH/, Greenwood Pr) Greenwood.

Presidency of the Continental Congress, 1774-89: A Study in American Institutional History. Jennings B. Sanders. 1990. 16.50 (*0-8446-0889-0*) Peter Smith.

Presidency of the European Commission under Jacques Delors: The Politics of Shared Leadership. Ken Endo. LC 98-17302. (St. Antony's Ser.). 1999. text 69.95 (*0-312-21597-5*) St Martin.

Presidency of the 1970's. R. Gordon Hoxie. LC 73-75234. 196p. 1973. 11.00 (*0-317-39575-0*) Ctr Study Presidency.

Presidency of the United States. David Health. (J). 1998. 19.00 (*0-516-21388-1*) Childrens.

Presidency of the United States. David Heath. LC 98-7105. (American Civics Ser.). (J). 1999. write for info. (*0-7368-0002-6*, Cpstone High Low) Capstone Pr.

Presidency of the United States. Karen Judson. LC 95-13476. (American Government in Action Ser.). (Illus.). 128p. (YA). (gr. 6 up). 1996. lib. bdg. 20.95 (*0-89490-585-6*) Enslow Pubs.

Presidency of Theodore Roosevelt. Lewis L. Gould. LC 90-11184. (American Presidency Ser.). xii, 355p. 1991. 29.95 (*0-7006-0435-9*); pap. 15.95 (*0-7006-0565-7*) U Pr of KS.

Presidency of Thomas Jefferson. Forrest McDonald. LC 76-803. (American Presidency Ser.). xii, 204p. 1976. 29.95 (*0-7006-0147-3*); pap. 12.95 (*0-7006-0330-1*) U Pr of KS.

Presidency of Warren G. Harding. Eugene P. Trani & David L. Wilson. LC 76-26110. (American Presidency Ser.). xii, 232p. 1977. 29.95 (*0-7006-0152-X*) U Pr of KS.

Presidency of William Howard Taft. Paolo E. Coletta. LC 97-50019. (American Presidency Ser.). xii, 308p. 1973. 29.95 (*0-7006-0096-5*) U Pr of KS.

Presidency of William McKinley. Lewis L. Gould. LC 80-16022. (American Presidency Ser.). xiv, 294p. 1981. 29.95 (*0-7006-0206-2*) U Pr of KS.

Presidency of Woodrow Wilson. Leon H. Canfield. LC 66-24796. (Illus.). 299p. 1975. 39.50 (*0-8386-6744-9*) Fairleigh Dickinson.

Presidency of Woodrow Wilson. Kendrick A. Clements. LC 91-30591. (American Presidency Ser.). xvi, 304p. 1992. 29.95 (*0-7006-0523-1*); pap. 15.95 (*0-7006-0524-X*) U Pr of KS.

Presidency Reagan. David Mervin. 1990. text 48.50 (*0-582-03487-6*, Pub. by Addison-Wesley) Longman.

***Presidency Then & Now.** Ed. by Phillip G. Henderson. LC 99-38796. 352p. 2000. text 70.00 (*0-8476-9738-X*) Rowman.

***Presidency Then & Now.** Phillip G. Henderson. LC 99-38796. 352p. 2000. pap. 24.95 (*0-8476-9739-8*) Rowman.

President. Toni Goffe. LC 92-259. (J). 1992. 5.99 (*0-85953-787-0*); pap. 3.99 (*0-85953-788-9*) Childs Play.

President. Rufus Goodwin. 1996. 65.00 (*0-614-19992-1*) Urban Pr.

President. Parker Hudson. 504p. 1998. pap. 12.99 (*1-57673-457-9*) Multnomah Pubs.

***President.** Barbara L. Ray. Ed. by OluFemi Alexander. (Divine Weight Loss Formula Ser.). (Illus.). 15p. 1999. spiral bd. write for info. (*0-9673712-0-1*) B Ray.

President. Miguel Angel Asturias. Tr. by Frances Partridge from SPA. Orig. Title: El Senor Presidente. 288p. (C). 1997. reprint ed. pap. text 11.95 (*0-88133-951-2*) Waveland Pr.

President: America's Leader. Mary Oates-Johnson. 48p. (gr. 1-4). 1996. pap. text 5.95 (*0-8114-5580-7*) Raintree Steck-V.

President: Office & Powers. rev. ed. Edward S. Corwin. Ed. by Randall W. Bland et al. 600p. (C). 1984. pap. text 35.00 (*0-8147-1391-2*) NYU Pr.

President: Preacher, Teacher, Salesman-Selected Presidential Speeches, 1933-1983. Ed. by Thomas T. Lyons. LC 84-51315. (Illus.). 206p. (Orig.). (C). 1985. pap. text 11.95 (*0-960814-4-8*) World Eagle.

President & Civil Rights Policy: Leadership & Change, 231. Steven A. Shull. LC 88-24705. (Contributions in Political Science Ser.: No. 231). 270p. 1989. 57.95 (*0-313-26583-6*, SVR, Greenwood Pr) Greenwood.

President & Congress. Rowland Egger & Joseph P. Harris. LC 88-2329. (Foundations of American Government & Political Science Ser.). 136p. 1963. reprint ed. lib. bdg. 57.50 (*0-313-24217-8*, EGPC, Greenwood Pr) Greenwood.

President & Congress: Collaboration & Combat in National Policymaking. Lance T. Leloup & Steven A. Shull. LC 98-13341. 278p. 1998. pap. text 39.06 (*0-205-26534-0*) Allyn.

President & Congress: Executive Hegemony at the Crossroads of American Government. Robert Spitzer. LC 92-14781. 320p. 1992. 59.95 (*1-56639-016-8*) Temple U Pr.

President & Congress: Executive Hegemony at the Crossroads of American Government. Robert J. Spitzer. 336p. (C). 1993. pap. 30.31 (*0-07-060351-0*) McGraw.

***President & Congress in Post-Authoritarian Chile: Institutional Constraints to Democratic Consolidation.** Peter Siavelis. LC 98-54921. 1999. write for info. (*0-271-01947-6*) Pa St U Pr.

President & Congress in Post-Authoritarian Chile: Institutional Constraints to Democratic Consolidation. Peter Siavelis. LC 98-54921. 1999. 19.00 (*0-271-01948-4*) Pa St U Pr.

President & Foreign Affairs: Evaluation, Performance & Power. Ryan J. Barilleaux. LC 84-26282. 224p. 1985. 49.95 (*0-275-90057-6*, C0057, Praeger Pubs) Greenwood.

President & Fund Raising. Ed. by James L. Fisher & Gary H. Quehl. LC 96-32499. (American Council on Education/Oryx Press Series on Higher Education). 252p. reprint ed. pap. 78.20 (*0-608-20854-X*, 207195300003) Bks Demand.

***President & His Inner Circle: Leadership Style & the Advisory Process in Foreign Policy Making.** Thomas Preston. 256p. 2001. text 49.50 (*0-231-11620-9*); pap. text 21.00 (*0-231-11621-7*) Col U Pr.

President & I: Richard Nixon's Rabbi Reveals His Role in the Saga That Tramatized the Nation. Baruch Korff. 1995. 25.00 (*0-9645841-0-7*) Ktav.

President & Parliament: A Short History of the French Presidency. Leslie Derfler. LC 82-16133. 296p. 1983. reprint ed. pap. 91.80 (*0-608-04487-3*, 206523200001) Bks Demand.

President & Power in Nigeria: The Life of Shehu Shagari. David Williams. (Illus.). 302p. 1982. text 35.00 (*0-7146-3182-5*, Pub. by F Cass Pubs) Intl Spec Bk.

President & Protest: Hoover, MacArthur, & the Bonus March. 2nd ed. Donald J. Lisio. xviii, 246p. 1994. reprint ed. 32.00 (*0-8232-1571-7*) Fordham.

President & Protest: Hoover, MacArthur, & the Bonus March. 2nd ed. Donald J. Lisio. LC 94-19465. xviii, 246p. 1994. reprint ed. pap. 17.95 (*0-8232-1572-5*) Fordham.

President & the Executive Director in Girl Scouting. rev. ed. Girl Scouts of the U. S. A. Staff. 32p. 1984. reprint ed. pap. 7.50 (*0-88441-452-3*, 26-173) Girl Scouts USA.

President & the Indian Constitution. Valmiki Chaudhary. 379p. 1985. 32.95 (*0-318-36598-7*) Asia Bk Corp.

President & the Parties: The Transformation of the American Party System since the New Deal. Sidney M. Milkis. LC 92-42965. 424p. (C). 1993. pap. text 24.95 (*0-19-508425-X*) OUP.

President & the Public Philosophy. Kenneth W. Thompson. LC 80-26165. (Miller Center Series on the American Presidency). x, 214p. 1981. text 32.50 (*0-8071-0795-6*) La State U Pr.

President As Interpreter-in-Chief. Mary E. Stuckey. LC 91-13427. (Chatham House Studies in Political Thinking). 192p. (C). 1991. pap. text 19.95 (*0-934540-92-6*, Chatham House Pub) Seven Bridges.

President As Leader: Appealing to the Better Angels of Our Nature. Erwin C. Hargrove. LC 98-10515. (Illus.). 240p. 1998. 29.95 (*0-7006-0900-8*) U Pr of KS.

***President As Leader: Appealing to the Better Angels of Our Nature.** Erwin C. Hargrove. LC 98-10515. (Illus.). 240p. 1999. reprint ed. pap. 15.95 (*0-7006-0996-2*) U Pr of KS.

President As Party Leader. James W. Davis. LC 91-35809. (Contributions in Political Science Ser.: No. 295). 240p. 1992. pap. 18.95 (*0-275-94112-4*, B4112, Greenwood Pr) Greenwood.

President As Party Leader, 295. James W. Davis. LC 91-34997. (Contributions in Political Science Ser.: No. 295). 248p. 1992. 57.95 (*0-313-28007-X*, DVP/, Greenwood Pr) Greenwood.

President As Prisoner: A Structural Critique of the Carter & Reagan Years. William F. Grover. LC 89-11518. (SUNY Series on the Presidency). 232p. (C). 1989. text 22.50 (*0-7914-0090-5*) State U NY Pr.

President As Statesman: Woodrow Wilson & the Constitution. Daniel D. Stid. LC 97-50019. (American Political Thought Ser.). 244p. 1998. 35.00 (*0-7006-0884-2*) U Pr of KS.

President Bait. Debby Head & Libby Pollett. (Curiosity Bait Ser.). 1998. pap. 32.00 (*1-885775-13-X*) BBY Pubns.

President Castello Branco: Brazilian Reformer. John W. Dulles. LC 79-5281. (Illus.). 568p. 1981. 39.95 (*0-89096-092-5*) Tex A&M Univ Pr.

President Citizen. Michael Twinn. (J). 1996. lib. bdg. 11.95 (*0-85953-844-3*) Childs Play.

***President Clinton & Vice President Gore: A Healthy Environment For The 21st Century.** 56p. 2000. pap. 7.00 (*0-16-050352-3*) USGPO.

President Clinton Visits Hyde Park: Story & Coloring Book. Trip Sinnott. (Illus.). 52p. (Orig.). (J). (gr. k-5). 1993. pap. 4.95 (*1-883551-00-5*) Attic Studio Pub.

President Clinton Will Continue the New World Order. Dennis L. Cuddy. 70p. (Orig.). 1994. pap. 2.95 (*1-879366-87-8*) Hearthstone OK.

President Clinton's Economic Plan. Gary Robbins & Aldona Robbins. (Illus.). 23p. 1993. pap. text 4.00 (*1-56808-008-5*, BG 125) Natl Ctr Pol.

President Clinton's Haiti Dilemma. Curtis H. Martin. (Pew Case Studies in International Affairs). 50p. (C). 1997. pap. text 3.50 (*1-56927-375-8*) Geo U Inst Dplmcy.

President Clinton's Proposed Fiscal Policy Changes: Impacts on California. Joseph Fitz. 33p. 1993. pap. write for info. (*1-58703-011-X*, CRB-93-005) CA St Libry.

President, Congress & Legislation. Lawrence H. Chamberlain. LC 72-181927. (Columbia University. Studies in the Social Sciences: No. 523). reprint ed. 32.50 (*0-404-51523-1*) AMS Pr.

President Dr. Shankar Dayal Sharma: Patriot, Scholar, Statesman. K. L. Chanchreek & Saroj Prasad. 231p. 1992. 25.00 (*81-7249-014-3*, Pub. by H K Pubs & Dist) Nataraj Bks.

President Dwight D. Eisenhower's Office Files, 1953-1961. Robert Lester et al. LC 91-43074. (Research Collections in American Politics Ser.). 64p. 1990. write for info. (*1-55655-166-5*) U Pubns Amer.

President Eisenhower's Meetings with Legislative Leaders, 1953-1961: Microfilmed from the Holdings of the Dwight D. Eisenhower Library. Robert Lester & Dwight D. Eisenhower Library. LC 90-28587. (Research Collections in American Politics Ser.). 2p. 1986. write for info. (*0-89093-980-2*) U Pubns Amer.

President Express. Lin Oliver. 1999. 14.95 (*1-56799-867-4*) M Friedman Pub Grp Inc.

***President Express** Lin Oliver. LC 98-85456. (Great Railway Adventures Ser.). 1998. write for info. (*1-890647-54-3*) Lrning Curve.

President Franklin D. Roosevelt's Office Files, 1933-1945. Robert Lester et al. LC 92-25443. (Research Collections in American Politics Ser.). 1990. write for info. (*1-55655-265-3*) U Pubns Amer.

P

President Grant Reconsidered. Frank J. Scaturro. LC 99-36093. (Illus.). 137p. 1999. pap. 16.95 (*1-56833-132-0*, Pub. by Madison Bks UPA) Natl Bk Netwk.

President Harry S. Truman's Office Files, 1945-1953. Gary Hoag et al. LC 90-956100. (Research Collections in American Politics Ser.). 1989. write for info. (*1-55655-153-3*) U Pubns Amer.

President Has Been Shot: Confusion, Disability & the 25th Amendment. Herbert L. Abrams. 424p. 1994. pap. 17.95 (*0-8047-2325-7*) Stanford U Pr.

President Has Been Shot! True Stories of the Attacks on Ten U. S. Presidents. Rebecca C. Jones. 100p. (J). (gr. 3 up). 1998. pap. 7.99 (*0-14-038505-3*, PuffinBks) Peng Put Young Read.

***President Has Been Shot! True Stories of the Attacks on Ten U. S. Presidents.** Rebecca C. Jones. (J). 1998. 13.09 (*0-606-13720-3*, Pub. by Turtleback) Demco.

President Has Been Shot: True Stories of the Attacks on Ten U.S. Presidents. Rebecca C. Jones. (Illus.). 144p. (J). (gr. 3-8). 1996. 15.99 (*0-525-45333-4*, Dutton Child) Peng Put Young Read.

President in the Legislative Arena. Jon R. Bond & Richard Fleisher. (Illus.). 272p. 1990. pap. text 19.95 (*0-226-06410-7*) U Ch Pr.

President in the Legislative Arena. Jon R. Bond & Richard Fleisher. (Illus.). 272p. 1998. lib. bdg. 56.50 (*0-226-06409-3*) U Ch Pr.

President in the Twentieth Century, Vol. I: The Ascendant President: From William McKinley to Lyndon B. Johnson. Ed. by Louis Filler. 418p. (C). 1983. pap. text 28.95 (*0-89198-128-4*); lib. bdg. 42.95 (*0-89198-127-6*) Ozer.

President in the Twentieth Century, Vol. 2: The Presidency in Crisis - From Lyndon B. Johnson to Ronald W. Reagan. Ed. by Louis Filler. 352p. (C). 1990. lib. bdg. 42.95 (*0-89198-140-3*) Ozer.

President Is at Camp David. W. Dale Nelson. LC 94-37083. (Illus.). 260p. 1995. 29.95 (*0-8156-0318-5*) Syracuse U Pr.

***President Is at Camp David.** W. Dale Nelson. (Illus.). 344p. 2000. pap. 18.95 (*0-8156-0628-1*) Syracuse U Pr.

President Is Born. Fannie Hurst. 492p. Date not set. 30.95 (*0-8488-2338-9*) Amereon Ltd.

President is Dead. Virginia T. Gross. 1999. pap. 3.99 (*0-14-037618-6*) Viking Penguin.

President James Buchanan: A President. Philip S. Klein. Ed. by Katherine E. Speirs. (Signature Ser.). (Illus.). 506p. 1995. reprint ed. 35.00 (*0-945707-11-8*) Amer Political.

President John F. Kennedy's Office Files, 1961-1963. Paul Kesaris et al. LC 89-20157. (Research Collections in American Politics Ser.). 103 p. 1989. write for info. (*1-55655-089-8*) U Pubns Amer.

President John Fitzgerald Kennedy's Grand & Global Alliance: World Order for the New Century. John F. Kennedy. Ed. by Joseph A. Bagnall. 122p. (C). 1992. pap. text 21.00 (*0-8191-8594-9*); lib. bdg. 41.00 (*0-8191-8593-0*) U Pr of Amer.

President John Smith: The Story of a Peaceful Revolution. Frederick U. Adams. LC 72-154428. (Utopian Literature Ser.). (Illus.). 1976. reprint ed. 25.95 (*0-405-03511-X*) Ayer.

President Johnson's War on Poverty: Rhetoric & History. David Zarefsky. LC 84-24098. 304p. 1986. text 34.95 (*0-8173-0266-2*) U of Ala Pr.

President Kennedy. Richard Reeves. (Illus.). 480p. 1993. 30.00 (*0-671-64879-9*) S&S Trade.

President Kennedy: Profile of Power. Richard Reeves. (Illus.). 800p. 1994. per. 15.00 (*0-671-89289-4*) S&S Trade Pap.

President Kennedy & the Press, 1961-1963. Paul Kesaris. LC 86-890141. (The Presidential Documents Ser.). 20 p. 1981. write for info. (*0-89093-358-8*) U Pubns Amer.

President Kennedy's Policy Toward the Arab States & Israel. Mordechai Gazit. 134p. (Orig.). 1983. pap. text 12.95 (*0-8156-7051-6*, Pub. by Shiloah Ctr Mid East & African Studies) Syracuse U Pr.

President Kennedy's Policy Toward the Arab States & Israel: Analysis & Documents. Mordechai Gazit. LC 83-208921. (Shiloah Center for Middle Eastern & African Studies, Tel Aviv University). 133p. 1983. reprint ed. pap. 41.30 (*0-608-07606-6*, 205992100010) Bks Demand.

President Lincoln's Attitude Toward Slavery & Emancipation. Henry W. Wilbur. 1914. 30.00 (*0-8196-0267-1*) Biblo.

President Lincoln's Third Largest City: Brooklyn & the Civil War. E. A. Livingston. 187p. (Orig.). 1993. pap. 13.95 (*0-9638981-0-8*) E A Livingston.

President Masaryk. Cecil J. Street. LC 74-119945. (Select Bibliographies Reprint Ser.). 1977. 21.95 (*0-8369-5388-6*) Ayer.

President Masaryk Tells His Story. Karel Capek. LC 71-135797. (Eastern Europe Collection). 1979. reprint ed. 28.95 (*0-405-02739-7*) Ayer.

President Needs Help: Proceedings of a Conference Held on January 15, 1987. Ed. by Frederick C. Mosher. (Miller Center Tenth Anniversary Commemorative Publication, 1975-1985). 98p. (Orig.). (C). 1988. lib. bdg. 29.50 (*0-8191-6780-0*, Pub. by White Miller Center) U Pr of Amer.

President of a Small College. Peter Sammartino. 162p. 1982. 9.95 (*0-8453-4757-8*, Cornwall Bks) Assoc Univ Prs.

***President of the Underground Railroad: A Story about Levi Coffin.** Gwenyth Swain. LC 00-8579. (Creative Minds Biography Ser.). (Illus.). 2001. lib. bdg. write for info. (*1-57505-551-1*, Carolrhoda) Lerner Pub.

***President Reagan: The Role of a Lifetime.** Lou Cannon. LC 99-88017. 992p. 2000. pap. 18.00 (*1-891620-91-6*, Pub. by PublicAffairs NY) HarpC.

President Reagan & the World, 376. Ed. by Eric J. Schmertz et al. LC 96-5791. (Contributions in Political Science Ser.: No. 376). 552p. 1997. 85.00 (*0-313-30115-8*, Greenwood Pr) Greenwood.

President Roosevelt & the Origins of the 1939 War. David L. Hoggan. 1983. lib. bdg. 250.00 (*0-87700-469-2*) Revisionist Pr.

President Roosevelt's Campaign to Incite War in Europe: The Secret Documents. 1983. lib. bdg. 250.00 (*0-87700-468-4*) Revisionist Pr.

President, the Bureaucracy & World Regions in Arms Control. Ed. by Kenneth W. Thompson. (W. Alton Jones Foundation Series on the Presidency & Arms Control: Vol. V). (Illus.). 166p. 1998. 46.00 (*0-7618-1082-X*); pap. 24.50 (*0-7618-1083-8*) U Pr of Amer.

President, the Congress, & Foreign Policy: A Joint Project of the Association of Former Members of Congress & the Atlantic Council of the United States. Kenneth Rush et al. LC 86-1634. 1986. 52.00 (*0-8191-5283-8*) U Pr of Amer.

President, the Congress & the Making of Foreign Policy. Ed. by Paul E. Peterson. LC 94-11855. 312p. 1994. pap. 18.95 (*0-8061-2685-X*) U of Okla Pr.

President, the Public & the Parties. 2nd ed. LC 96-30004. 184p. (YA). 1997. text 29.95 (*1-56802-313-8*) Congr Quarterly.

President Thomas Woodrow Wilson, Portrait Psychologique. Sigmund Freud. Ed. by W. C. Bullitt. (FRE.). 1990. pap. 29.95 (*0-7859-3042-6*) Fr & Eur.

President Travels by Train: Politics & Pullmans. Bob Withers. LC 95-61264. (Illus.). 436p. 1997. 39.95 (*1-883089-17-4*) TLC VA.

President Truman & the Atomic Bomb. Michael O'Neal. LC 90-35611. (Great Mysteries Ser.). (Illus.). 112p. (J). (gr. 5-8). 1990. lib. bdg. 22.45 (*0-89908-079-0*) Greenhaven.

President Truman's Committee on Civil Rights. William E. Juhnke. LC 86-893394. (Black Studies Research Sources). 10p. 1984. write for info. (*0-89093-657-9*) U Pubns Amer.

President Trump: A Play about Love, Not a Messy Divorce. Joseph Ben-Po. Ed. by Glory Fontaine. (Illus.). 88p. (Orig.). 1990. pap. 15.95 (*0-9625878-0-X*) White Hse NY.

President Washington's Indian War: The Struggle for the Old Northwest, 1790-1795. Wiley Sword. LC 85-40481. 1993. pap. 18.95 (*0-8061-2488-1*) U of Okla Pr.

President who Pardoned a Turkey & Other Wacky Tales of American History Allan Zullo. LC 99-159823. 63p. 1996. write for info. (*0-8167-4059-3*) Troll Communs.

President Witherspoon. Varnum L. Collins. LC 78-83416. (Religion in America, Ser. 1). 1980. reprint ed. 33.95 (*0-405-00242-4*) Ayer.

President Wore Spats: A Biography of Glenn Frank. Lawrence H. Larsen. LC 65-63009. (Illus.). 198p. 1965. 4.50 (*0-87020-056-9*) State Hist Soc Wis.

President Zachary Taylor & Senator Hannibal Hamlin: Union or Death. Edward L. Jones. (Illus.). 30p. (Orig.). (C). 1991. pap. 8.00 (*0-9602458-8-X*) Ed-Lynne Jones.

Presidential Wives: An Anecdotal History. 2nd ed. Paul Boller, Jr. 576p. 1998. 30.00 (*0-19-512702-1*) OUP.

Presidential Wives: An Anecdotal History. 2nd ed. Paul Boller, Jr. LC 98-3480. 576p. 1999. pap. 14.95 (*0-19-512142-2*) OUP.

Presidential Accountability: New & Recurring Problems, 254. John M. Orman. LC 89-26058. (Contributions in Political Science Ser.: No. 254). 184p. 1990. 49.95 (*0-313-27314-6*, OPA/, Greenwood Pr) Greenwood.

Presidential Addresses: American Society for Horticultural Science. Compiled by Jules Janick. LC 93-42679. 1994. pap. 25.00 (*0-931682-40-1*) Purdue U Pubns.

***Presidential Addresses of the American Philosophical Association, 1911-1920.** Richard T. Hull & American Philisophical Association Staff. LC 98-50254. (American Philosophical Association Centennial Ser.). 1p. 1999. write for info. (*0-7923-5558-X*) Kluwer Academic.

***Presidential Addresses of the American Philosophical Association, 1921-1930.** Richard T. Hull & American Philosophical Association Staff. LC 99-51549. (American Philosophical Association Centennial Ser.). 1999. write for info. (*0-7923-6042-7*) Kluwer Academic.

Presidential Addresses of the Paleontological Society: Original Anthology. Ed. by Thomas J. Schopf & Stephen Jay Gould. LC 79-8358. (History of Paleontology Ser.). (Illus.). 1980. lib. bdg. 75.95 (*0-405-12753-7*) Ayer.

***Presidential Administration Profiles.** Ed. by Kellie S. Sisung. LC 99-39017. 687p. 1998. 85.00 (*0-7876-2796-8*) Gale.

Presidential Advisory Commissions: Truman to Nixon. Thomas R. Wolanin. LC 74-27317. 311p. reprint ed. pap. 96.50 (*0-8357-6793-0*, 203547000095) Bks Demand.

Presidential Advisory Committee on Gulf War Veterans' Illnesses: Final Report. Ed. by Joyce C. Laslof et al. (Illus.). 174p. (Orig.). 1997. pap. text 40.00 (*0-7881-4271-2*) DIANE Pub.

Presidential Advisory Committee on Gulf War Veterans' Illnesses: Interim Report. 60p. (Orig.). 1996. pap. text 30.00 (*0-7881-3279-2*) DIANE Pub.

Presidential Advisory Committee on Gulf War Veterans' Illnesses: Interim Report. (Orig.). 1997. lib. bdg. 250.95 (*0-8490-7646-3*) Gordon Pr.

Presidential Advisory Committee on Gulf War Veterans' Illnesses: Special Report. Government Printing Office Staff. LC 97-220693. 75p. 1997. pap. 7.50 (*0-16-049285-8*) USGPO.

Presidential Advisory System. Ed. by Thomas E. Cronin & Sanford D. Greenberg. LC 69-18487. 395p. reprint ed. pap. 122.50 (*0-7837-8664-6*, 204906400011) Bks Demand.

Presidential Also-Rans & Running Mates, 1788 Through 1996. 2nd ed. Ed. by Leslie H. Southwick. LC 97-34099. (Illus.). 848p. 1998. boxed set 99.50 (*0-7864-0310-1*) McFarland & Co.

Presidential Ambition: Gaining Power At Any Cost. Richard Shenkman. LC 99-42198. 384p. 2000. pap. 14.00 (*0-06-093054-3*) HarpC.

Presidential Ambition: How the Presidents Gained Power, Kept Power, & Got Things Done. Richard Shenkman. LC 98-27045. 400p. 1999. 26.00 (*0-06-018373-X*) HarpC.

Presidential & Executive Office Financial Accountability Act of 1997 & Special Government Employee Act of 1997: Hearing Before the Subcommittee on Government Management, Information & Technology of the Committee on Government Reform & Oversight, House of Representatives, One Hundred Fifth Congress, First Session, May 1, 1997. United States Government. LC 98-139029. iii, 102 p. 1997. write for info. (*0-16-055826-3*) USGPO.

Presidential & First Lady Jingo. Gary Grimm & Phoebe Wear. 32p. (J). (gr. k-6). 1995. 12.00 (*1-56490-011-8*) G Grimm Assocs.

Presidential Anecdotes. rev. ed. Paul F. Boller, Jr. 472p. 1996. pap. 14.95 (*0-19-509731-9*) OUP.

Presidential Anecdotes. rev. ed. Paul F. Boller, Jr. 472p. 1996. text 30.00 (*0-19-510715-2*) OUP.

Presidential Approval: A Sourcebook. George C. Edwards, III & Alec M. Gallup. LC 90-4160. 150p. 1990. text 36.00 (*0-8018-4085-6*) Johns Hopkins.

Presidential Archives. John Griffiths. 384p. 1996. 23.00 (*0-7867-0316-4*) Carroll & Graf.

***Presidential Assasins.** Patricia D. Netzley. (History Makers Ser.). (Illus.). 144p. (YA). (gr. 6-9). 2000. lib. bdg. 23.70 (*1-56006-623-7*) Lucent Bks.

Presidential Assessment. John W. Nason. 86p. 1980. 18.00 (*0-318-17382-4*) Assn Gov Bds.

Presidential Ballots, 1836-1892. W. Dean Burnham. LC 75-22806. (America in Two Centuries Ser.). 1976. reprint ed. 78.95 (*0-405-07678-9*) Ayer.

Presidential Blips: Dips, Flips, Lip, Pips, Quips, Rips, Slips, Tips & Zips. B.S. McReynolds. LC 98-231375. 1998. pap. 19.95 (*0-9667203-6-9*) BS Bk Pubg.

Presidential Branch. John Hart. (Government & Politics Ser.). 250p. 1987. text 52.00 (*0-08-030939-9*, Pergamon Pr); pap. text 19.95 (*0-08-030938-0*, Pergamon Pr) Elsevier.

Presidential Branch: From Washington to Clinton. 2nd ed. John Hart. LC 94-29016. 300p. (C). 1995. pap. text 22.95 (*1-56643-010-0*, Chatham House Pub) Seven Bridges.

Presidential Campaign. Thomas R. Raber. (American Politics Ser.). (Illus.). 88p. (J). (gr. 4-8). 1988. lib. bdg. 9.50 (*0-8225-1750-7*, Lerner Publctns) Lerner Pub.

Presidential Campaign. 3rd ed. Stephen Hess. LC 87-27858. 134p. 1988. 28.95 (*0-8157-3600-2*); pap. 10.95 (*0-8157-3599-5*) Brookings.

Presidential Campaign Discourse: Strategic Communication Problems. Ed. by Kathleen E. Kendall. LC 95-14650. (SUNY Series, Human Communication Processes). 319p. (C). 1995. text 59.50 (*0-7914-2681-5*); pap. text 19.95 (*0-7914-2682-3*) State U NY Pr.

Presidential Campaign Film: A Critical History. Joanne Morreale. LC 93-20129. (Praeger Series in Political Communication). 224p. 1993. 65.00 (*0-275-93882-4*, C3882, Praeger Pubs) Greenwood.

Presidential Campaign Film: A Critical History. Joanne Morreale. LC 93-20129. 224p. 1996. pap. 21.95 (*0-275-95580-X*, Praeger Pubs) Greenwood.

Presidential Campaign Funds. Louise Overacker. LC 76-29407. reprint ed. 29.50 (*0-404-15341-0*) AMS Pr.

Presidential Campaign Illustrated Envelopes & Letter Paper 1840-1872. James W. Milgram. 1994. 42.50 (*0-9614018-2-6*) D G Phillips.

Presidential Campaign, 1976: A Selection of Campaign Speeches. Eckhard Breitinger. 183p. 1978. 38.00 (*3-261-02605-7*) P Lang Pubng.

Presidential Campaign of Eighteen Sixty. Emerson D. Fite. (History - United States Ser.). 356p. 1992. reprint ed. lib. bdg. 89.00 (*0-7812-6151-1*) Rprt Serv.

Presidential Campaign of Eighteen Thirty-Two. Samuel R. Gammon, Jr. LC 78-96952. (Law, Politics & History Ser.). 1969. reprint ed. lib. bdg. 25.00 (*0-306-71830-8*) Da Capo.

Presidential Campaign of Eighteen Thirty-Two. Samuel R. Gammon, Jr. LC 76-13176. ix, 180p. 1972. reprint ed. 9.00 (*0-403-00603-1*) Scholarly.

Presidential Campaigns. rev. ed. Paul F. Boller, Jr. 480p. 1996. pap. 15.95 (*0-19-509730-0*) OUP.

Presidential Cars & Transportation. William D. Siuru & Andrea Stewart. LC 95-76860. (Illus.). 160p. 1995. 19.95 (*0-87341-341-5*, PCT01) Krause Pubns.

Presidential Certification of Narcotics Producing & Transit Countries. Ed. by Barbara Larkin. 49p. (C). 1999. pap. text 20.00 (*0-7881-7842-3*) DIANE Pub.

Presidential Character: Predicting Performance in the White House. 4th ed. James D. Barber. 544p. (C). 1992. pap. text 18.00 (*0-13-718123-X*) P-H.

Presidential Clemency Board: Report to the President. xxxiii, 409p. 1990. 45.00 (*1-57588-350-3*, 305380) W S Hein.

Presidential Commissions. Carl Marcy. LC 72-8109. (Studies in American History & Government). 156p. 1973. reprint ed. lib. bdg. 25.00 (*0-306-70532-X*) Da Capo.

Presidential Committees & White House Conferences. Ed. by Michal R. Belknap. LC 91-3628. (Civil Rights, White House & Justice Dept. Ser.: Vol. 2). 304p. 1991. text 28.00 (*0-8240-3368-X*) Garland.

Presidential Communication: Description & Analysis. Robert E. Denton, Jr. & Dan F. Hahn. LC 86-9294. 356p. 1986. pap. 21.95 (*0-275-92176-X*, B2176, Praeger Pubs) Greenwood.

Presidential Communication: Description & Analysis. Robert E. Denton, Jr. & Dan F. Hahn. LC 86-9294. 356p. 1986. 59.95 (*0-275-92175-1*, C2175, Praeger Pubs) Greenwood.

Presidential-Congressional Political Dictionary. Jeffrey M. Elliot & Sheikh R. Ali. LC 84-6316. (Clio Dictionaries in Political Science Ser.: No. 9). 365p. (C). 1984. pap. text 20.50 (*0-87436-358-6*); lib. bdg. 49.00 (*0-87436-357-8*) ABC-CLIO.

Presidential-Congressional Relations: Policy & Time Approaches. Steven A. Shull. (Illus.). 192p. (C). pap. text 19.95 (*0-472-08704-5*, 08704) U of Mich Pr.

Presidential-Congressional Relations: Policy & Time Approaches. Steven A. Shull. LC 97-4778. 192p. (C). 1997. text 44.50 (*0-472-10832-8*, 10832) U of Mich Pr.

Presidential Conspiracy. Walter E. Adams. LC 93-78842. 400p. (Orig.). 1993. pap. text 11.95 (*0-937408-89-1*) GMI Pubns Inc.

Presidential Contest. 5th ed. Joseph A. Pika & Richard A. Watson. LC 95-25241. 218p. (YA). (gr. 11). 1995. pap. text 20.95 (*0-87187-837-2*) Congr Quarterly.

Presidential Conventions. Christopher E. Henry. LC 95-45288. (First Bks.). (Illus.). 64p. (J). (gr. 4-7). 1996. lib. bdg. 22.00 (*0-531-20219-4*) Watts.

Presidential Crisis Rhetoric & the Press in the Post-Cold War World. Jim A. Kuypers. LC 97-5588. (Praeger Series in Political Communication). 264p. 1997. 57.95 (*0-275-95721-7*, Praeger Pubs) Greenwood.

Presidential Deal: A Novel. Les Standiford. LC 97-31642. 304p. 1998. 24.00 (*0-06-018655-0*) HarpC.

Presidential Deal: A Novel. Les Standiford. 432p. 1999. mass mkt. 6.50 (*0-06-109553-2*, Harp PBks) HarpC.

***Presidential Debates: Forty Years of High-Risk TV.** Alan Schroeder. LC 00-35831. 2000. 24.95 (*0-231-11400-1*) Col U Pr.

Presidential Debates: Media, Electoral & Policy Perspective. Robert G. Meadow & Marilyn Jackson-Beeck. Ed. by George F. Bishop et al. LC 78-70323. 324p. 1978. 69.50 (*0-275-90285-4*, C0285, Praeger Pubs) Greenwood.

Presidential Debates: The Challenge of Creating an Informed Electorate. Kathleen H. Jamieson & David S. Birdsell. (Illus.). 276p. 1990. reprint ed. pap. text 22.00 (*0-19-506660-X*) OUP.

Presidential Decision Making Adrift: The Carter Administration & the Mariel Boatlift. David W. Engstrom. LC 96-42305. 256p. 1997. 66.00 (*0-8476-8413-X*); pap. 25.95 (*0-8476-8414-8*) Rowman.

Presidential Decisionmaking in Foreign Policy: The Effective Use of Information & Advice. Alexander L. George. (Special Studies in International Relations). 268p. 1980. text 39.00 (*0-89158-380-7*) Westview.

***Presidential Decisionmaking in Foreign Policy: The Effective Use of Information & Advice.** 2nd ed. Alexander L. George & Eric K. Stern. 320p. 1999. pap. text 17.95 (*0-8133-1940-4*) Westview.

***Presidential Decisions for War: Korea, Vietnam & the Persian Gulf.** Gary R. Hess. LC 00-8957. (American Moment Ser.). 2001. pap. write for info. (*0-8018-6516-6*) Johns Hopkins.

Presidential Defiance of 'Unconstitutional' Laws: Reviving the Royal Prerogative, 86. Christopher N. May. LC 98-11095. (Contributions in Legal Studies: Vol. 86). 232p. 1998. 59.95 (*0-313-30064-X*, GM0064, Greenwood Pr) Greenwood.

***Presidential Determination Regarding Certification of the Thirty-Two Major Illicit Narcotics Producing & Transit Countries.** Ed. by Newt Gingrich. 45p. (C). 1999. reprint ed. pap. text 20.00 (*0-7881-3186-9*) DIANE Pub.

Presidential Diaries of Henry Morgenthau, Jr., 1938-1945. Henry Morgenthau et al. LC 86-892370. (The Presidential Documents Ser.). 2 p. 1982. write for info. (*0-89093-350-2*) U Pubns Amer.

Presidential Difference. Fred I. Greenstein. 1996. 25.00 (*0-02-874038-6*) Free Pr.

Presidential Difference: Leadership Style from FDR to Clinton. Fred I. Greenstein. LC 99-59290. 288p. 2000. 25.00 (*0-684-82733-6*) Free Pr.

Presidential Dilemma: Leadership in the American System. Michael A. Genovese. LC 94-42724. 160p. (C). 1997. pap. text 33.53 (*0-673-99278-0*) Addson-Wesley Educ.

Presidential Disrespect: From Thomas Paine to Rush Limbaugh. Marcus G. Raskin. (Illus.). 240p. 1996. 19.95 (*1-55972-374-2*, Birch Ln Pr) Carol Pub Group.

***Presidential Documents.** Fred L. Israel & J. F. Watts. LC 99-20927. 368p. 1999. 75.00 (*0-415-92037-X*) Routledge.

Presidential Economics: The Making of Economic Policy from Roosevelt to Clinton. 2nd rev. ed. Herbert Stein. LC 88-3498. (Illus.). 450p. (C). 1988. pap. 12.75 (*0-8447-3656-2*) Am Enterprise.

Presidential Economics: The Making of Economic Policy from Roosevelt to Clinton. 3rd rev. ed. Herbert Stein. (AEI Studies: No. 473). (Illus.). 100p. 1994. pap. 19.75 (*0-8447-3851-4*) Am Enterprise.

Presidential Election & Transition, 1980-1981. Ed. by Paul T. David & David H. Everson. LC 82-19145. 304p. 1983. 31.95 (*0-8093-1109-7*) S Ill U Pr.

Presidential Election Game. Steven J. Brams. LC 78-5815. 1978. 17.00 (*0-300-02254-9*); pap. 17.00 (*0-300-02296-4*) Yale U Pr.

P

An Asterisk (*) at the beginning of an entry indicates that the title is appearing for the first time.

Presidential Election of 1896. Stanley L. Jones. LC 64-12725. (Illus.). 456p. 1964. reprint ed. pap. 141.40 (*0-608-02733-2*, 206339800004) Bks Demand.

Presidential Election of Eighteen Twenty-Eight. Florence Weston. LC 73-16252. (Perspectives in American History Ser.: No. 22). 217p. 1974. reprint ed. lib. bdg. 35.00 (*0-87991-334-7*) Porcupine Pr.

Presidential Election of 1996: Clinton's Incumbency & Television. E. D. Dover. LC 98-4946. 216p. 1998. 57.95 (*0-275-96259-8*, Praeger Pubs) Greenwood.

Presidential Election Show: Campaign '84 & Beyond on the Nightly News. Keith Blume. LC 85-13472. 363p. 1985. 39.95 (*0-89789-080-9*, Bergin & Garvey) Greenwood.

Presidential Election, 1996 Vol. 1: States of Counties, Nov. 5, 1996 General Election, 3 vols. Clark H. Bensen. (Election Reports). (Illus.). 640p. 1997. lib. bdg. 112.00 (*1-57708-911-1*, ERA-999-96Z) Polidata.

Presidential Election, 1996 Vol. 2: Districts of the 105th Congress, Nov. 5, 1999 General Election, 3 vols. Clark H. Bensen. (Election Reports: Vol. 4). 500p. 1997. lib. bdg. 100.00 (*1-57708-913-8*, ERC-999-96Z) Polidata.

Presidential Election, 1996 Vol. 3: Statistical Areas & Markets, Nov. 5, 1996 General Election, 3 vols. Clark H. Bensen. (Election Reports: Vol. 5). 500p. 1997. lib. bdg. 115.00 (*1-57708-915-4*, ERE-999-96Z) Polidata.

Presidential Elections. Dean Cantu. LC 97-78307. (Perspectives on History Ser.: Pt. III). (Illus.). 66p. 1998. pap. 6.95 (*1-57960-023-9*) Disc Enter Ltd.

Presidential Elections. Miles Harvey. LC 95-1560. (Cornerstones to Freedom Ser.). (Illus.). 32p. (J). (gr. 4-7). 1995. lib. bdg. 19.50 (*0-516-06629-3*) Childrens.

Presidential Elections. Christopher E. Henry. LC 95-43857. (First Bks.). (Illus.). 64p. (J). (gr. 4-7). 1996. lib. bdg. 22.00 (*0-531-20222-4*) Watts.

Presidential Elections. Miles Harney. LC 95-1560. (Cornerstones to Freedom Ser.). (Illus.). 32p. (J). (gr. 4-7). 1996. reprint ed. pap. 5.95 (*0-516-46629-1*) Childrens.

Presidential Elections. 6th ed. Nelson W. Polsby & Aaron B. Wildavsky. 400p. (C). 1984. pap. 57.00 (*0-02-396260-7*, Pub. by P-H) S&S Trade.

***Presidential Elections: A Complete Resource with Historical Information, Reproducible Activities & Creative Ideas.** Julia Hargrove. Ed. by Judy Mitchell. 32p. (J). (gr. 4-8). 1999. 6.95 (*1-57310-205-9*) Teachng & Lrning Co.

***Presidential Elections: And Other Cool Facts.** Sylvan A. Sobel. (Educational Ser.). 48p. 2000. pap. 6.95 (*0-7641-1438-7*) Barron.

Presidential Elections: Contemporary Strategies of American Electoral Politics. 7th ed. Nelson W. Polsby & Aaron B. Wildavsky. 350p. 1988. pap. 14.95 (*0-02-925262-8*) Free Pr.

Presidential Elections: Law, Practice, & Procedure, 1989. Lok Sabha. (C). 1989. 50.00 (*0-685-36474-7*) St Mut.

Presidential Elections: Strategies & Structures in American Politics. 9th ed. Nelson W. Polsby & Aaron Wildavsky. LC 95-32493. (Illus.). 368p. (C). 1996. pap. text 29.95 (*1-56643-029-1*, Chatham House Pub) Seven Bridges.

Presidential Elections: Strategies & Structures of American Politics. 10th ed. Nelson W. Polsby & Aaron Wildavsky. (Illus.). 416p. 1999. pap. text 29.95 (*1-889119-26-1*, Chatham House Pub) Seven Bridges.

Presidential Elections & American Politics: Voters, Candidates & Campaigns since 1952. 5th ed. Herbert B. Asher. 394p. (C). 1991. pap. text 43.00 (*0-534-16926-0*) Harcourt.

Presidential Elections from Abraham Lincoln to Franklin D. Roosevelt. Cortez A. Ewing. LC 70-142857. (Illus.). 226p. (C). 1972. reprint ed. lib. bdg. 35.00 (*0-8371-5956-3*, EWPE, Greenwood Pr) Greenwood.

Presidential Elections in Maryland. John T. Willis. LC 83-83257. (Illus.). 375p. 1984. 38.50 (*0-912338-45-8*); fiche 12.50 (*0-912338-46-6*) Lomond.

Presidential Elections in the Television Age, 1960-1992. E. D. Dover. LC 93-42803. 250p. 1994. 52.95 (*0-275-94840-4*, Praeger Pubs) Greenwood.

Presidential Elections in the United States: A Statistical History, 1860-1992. Russell O. Wright. LC 94-47546. 199p. 1995. lib. bdg. 29.95 (*0-89950-770-0*) McFarland & Co.

Presidential Elections, 1789-1996. Congressional Quarterly, Inc. Staff. LC 97-19084. 280p. (YA). 1997. text 37.95 (*1-56802-065-1*) Congr Quarterly.

Presidential Executive Orders: Numbered Series (1862-1938); List & Index, 2 vols. 1981. 120.00 (*0-89453-263-4*) Scholarly Res Inc.

Presidential Fact Book. Joseph N. Kane. 1998. pap. 17.95 (*0-375-70244-X*) Random Ref & Info.

Presidential Follies: Those Who Would Be President & Those Who Should Think Again! Bradley S. O'Leary & Ralph Z. Hallow. Ed. by Ann O. Weems. 250p. 1995. text 19.95 (*1-887161-00-7*, Boru Bks); pap. text 7.95 (*1-887161-07-4*, Boru Bks) Boru Pubng.

Presidential Forum: Citizens with Mental Retardation & Community Integration. 250p. 1988. write for info. (*1-55672-036-X*) US HHS.

Presidential Forum: Citizens with Mental Retardation & Community Integration (Forum Proceedings) (Illus.). 289p. (C). 1996. reprint ed. pap. text 35.00 (*0-7881-3268-7*) DIANE Pub.

Presidential Frontiers: Underexplored Issues in White House Politics. Ed. by Ryan J. Barilleaux. LC 97-43955. (Praeger Series in Presidential Studies). 256p. 1998. 59.95 (*0-275-96107-9*, Praeger Pubs) Greenwood.

Presidential Game: The Origins of American Presidential Politics. Richard P. McCormick. 288p. 1984. pap. text 21.95 (*0-19-503455-4*) OUP.

Presidential Government in Gaullist France: A Study of Executive-Legislative Relations, 1958-1974. William G. Andrews. LC 82-222528. 304p. (C). 1983. text 24.50 (*0-87395-604-4*) State U NY Pr.

***Presidential Greatness.** Marc Landy & Sidney M. Milkis. LC JK511.L357 2000. 288p. 2000. text 34.95 (*0-7006-1005-7*) U Pr of KS.

Presidential Greatness: The Image & the Man from George Washington to the Present. Thomas A. Bailey. LC 66-19996. reprint ed. 30.00 (*0-89197-356-7*); reprint ed. pap. text 14.95 (*0-89197-642-6*) Irvington.

Presidential Impeachment. John R. Labovitz. LC 77-76300. 268p. 1978. 45.00 (*0-300-02213-1*) Yale U Pr.

Presidential Inaugurations: Planning for More Than Pomp & Circumstances. Joy W. Viola. 121p. 1993. pap. 32.00 (*0-89964-294-2*, 28501) Coun Adv & Supp Ed.

Presidential Indiscretions: The Unofficial, Unexpurgated Guide to Naughty Behavior Kept Under Wraps (or Under the Covers) by the White House! Gregory Leland. LC 98-53045. 256p. 1999. pap. 9.95 (*0-440-50792-8*, Dell Trade Pbks) Dell.

Presidential Influence & Environmental Policy, 307. Robert A. Shanley. LC 92-15584. (Contributions in Political Science Ser.: No. 307). 200p. 1992. 52.95 (*0-313-25883-X*, SYA, Greenwood Pr) Greenwood.

Presidential Influence & the Administrative State. Richard W. Waterman. LC 88-33960. 270p. 1989. text 39.00 (*0-87049-609-3*) U of Tenn Pr.

***Presidential Initiative for Increasing Seat Belt Use Nationwide: Recommendations from the Secretary of Transportation.** Government Printing Office Staff. 24p. 1999. pap. 3.75 (*0-16-049978-X*) USGPO.

Presidential Initiative: Operation Kiddie Care: Food & Nutrition Service, Child & Adult Food Care Program, National Report on Program Abuss. 102p. pap. text. write for info. (*0-7881-8897-6*) DIANE Pub.

Presidential Institutions & Democratic Politics: Comparing Regional & National Contexts. Ed. by Kurt Von Mettenheim. LC 96-21694. 248p. 1997. text 45.00 (*0-8018-5313-3*); pap. text 15.95 (*0-8018-5314-1*) Johns Hopkins.

Presidential Landmarks. David Kruh & Louis Kruh. (Illus.). 480p. 1999. reprint ed. text 25.00 (*0-7881-6175-X*) DIANE Pub.

Presidential Leadership. 4th ed. Wayne. 526p. 1997. pap. 34.95 (*0-312-14498-9*) St Martin.

Presidential Leadership. 5th ed. Edwards. 1998. pap. 39.95 (*0-312-16739-3*) St Martin.

Presidential Leadership: From Eisenhower to Clinton. Lance Blakesley. LC 94-45059. 1995. pap. text 31.95 (*0-8304-1308-1*) Thomson Learn.

Presidential Leadership: Making a Difference. James L. Fisher & James V. Koch. LC 95-26661. 440p. 1996. boxed set 34.95 (*1-57356-020-0*) Oryx Pr.

Presidential Leadership & Civil Rights Policy, 356. Ed. by James W. Riddlesperger & Donald W. Jackson. LC 95-5268. (Contributions in Political Science Ser.: Vol. 356). 208p. 1995. 57.95 (*0-313-29624-3*, Greenwood Pr) Greenwood.

Presidential Leadership of Public Opinion. Elmer E. Cornwell, Jr. LC 78-11946. (Illus.). 370p. 1979. reprint ed. lib. bdg. 38.50 (*0-313-21076-4*, COPL, Greenwood Pr) Greenwood.

Presidential Libraries & Collections. Fritz Veit. LC 86-25732. (Illus.). 169p. 1987. lib. bdg. 52.95 (*0-313-24996-2*, VPL, Greenwood Pr) Greenwood.

Presidential Libraries & Museums. 2nd ed. Pat Hyland. LC 95-17795. 174p. (YA). (gr. 11). 1995. text 44.95 (*0-87187-960-3*) Congr Quarterly.

Presidential Lies: Illustrated History of White House Golf. Shepherd Campbell. LC 96-161800. (Illus.). 288p. 1996. 23.95 (*0-02-861258-2*) Macmillan.

Presidential Lies: The Illustrated History of White House Golf. Shepherd Campbell. (Illus.). 288p. 1998. pap. text 14.95 (*0-02-862356-8*) Macmillan.

Presidential Lightning Rods: The Politics of Blame Avoidance. Richard J. Ellis. LC 94-12007. (Studies in Government & Public Policy). 330p. 1994. 29.95 (*0-7006-0636-X*) U Pr of KS.

Presidential Machismo: Executive Authority, Military Intervention, & Foreign Relations. Alexander DeConde. LC 99-30588. 380p. 1999. text 40.00 (*1-55553-403-1*) NE U Pr.

Presidential Management of Science & Technology: The Johnson Presidency. W. Henry Lambright. (Administrative History of the Johnson Presidency Ser.). 238p. 1985. text 25.00 (*0-292-76494-4*) U of Tex Pr.

Presidential Medal of Freedom: Winners & Their Achievements. Bruce Wetterau. LC 96-24499. 546p. (C). 1996. text 41.40 (*1-56802-128-3*) Congr Quarterly.

Presidential Medal of Freedom Winners. Carmen Bredeson. LC 96-1743. (Collective Biographies Ser.). (Illus.). 104p. (YA). (gr. 6 up). 1996. lib. bdg. 20.95 (*0-89490-705-0*) Enslow Pubs.

Presidential Mystery. Dandi Daley Mackall. LC 98-30769. (Cinnamon Lake Mysteries Ser.). 80p. (J). (gr. 1-4). 1999. pap. 4.99 (*0-570-05354-4*, 12-3405GJ) Concordia.

Presidential Nation. Joseph A. Califano, Jr. 1975. pap. text 3.95 (*0-393-09135-X*) Norton.

Presidential Nominating Process: Broadening & Narrowing the Debate. Ed. by Kenneth W. Thompson. LC 83-6790. (George Gund Lectures: Vol. II). 124p. (C). 1984. pap. text 15.00 (*0-8191-3567-4*) U Pr of Amer.

Presidential Nominating Process: Change & Continuity in the 1980's. Ed. by Kenneth W. Thompson. (George Gund Lectures: Vol. IV). 144p. (Orig.). 1986. pap. text 15.00 (*0-8191-4964-0*) U Pr of Amer.

Presidential Nominating Process: Change & Continuity in the 1980's. Ed. by Kenneth W. Thompson. (George Gund Lectures: Vol. IV). 144p. (Orig.). 1986. lib. bdg. 44.00 (*0-8191-4963-2*, Pub. by White Miller Center) U Pr of Amer.

Presidential Nominating Process: Constitutional, Economic & Political Issues. Ed. by Kenneth W. Thompson. LC 83-6790. (George Gund Lectures: Vol. III). 120p. (Orig.). 1984. pap. text 14.00 (*0-8191-4152-6*); lib. bdg. 41.50 (*0-8191-4151-8*) U Pr of Amer.

Presidential Nominations in a Reform Age. Thomas R. Marshall. LC 81-1684. 211p. 1981. 45.00 (*0-275-90677-9*, C0677, Praeger Pubs) Greenwood.

Presidential Odyssey of John Glenn. Richard F. Fenno, Jr. 302p. 1990. pap. 21.95 (*0-87187-567-5*) Congr Quarterly.

Presidential Personality & Performance. Alexander L. George & Juliette L. George. LC 97-32849. 304p. (C). 1998. pap. text 29.00 (*0-8133-2591-9*, Pub. by Westview) HarpC.

Presidential Perspectives on Space Exploration: Guiding Metaphors from Eisenhower to Bush. Linda T. Krug. LC 91-8299. 160p. 1991. 47.95 (*0-275-93612-0*, C3612, Praeger Pubs) Greenwood.

Presidential Pets - Postcards. Niall Kelly. (Illus.). 108p. 1991. 10.95 (*1-55859-302-0*) Abbeville Pr.

***Presidential Places: A Guide to the Historic Sites of U. S. Presidents.** Gary Ferris. LC 98-50395. (Illus.). 256p. 1999. pap. 15.95 (*0-89587-176-9*) Blair.

Presidential Policy Making. Ed. by Norman Thomas et al. (Orig.). 1984. pap. 15.00 (*0-918592-71-2*) Pol Studies.

Presidential Policy Making: An End-of-Century Assessment. Ed. by Steven A. Shull. LC 98-8233. 330p. (C). (gr. 13). 1999. pap. text 27.95 (*0-7656-0260-1*) M E Sharpe.

Presidential Policymaking: An End-of-Century Assessment. Ed. by Steven A. Shull. LC 98-8233. 330p. (C). 1999. text 70.95 (*0-7656-0259-8*) M E Sharpe.

Presidential Politics in Louisiana, 1952, Vol. 1. L. V. Howard & D. R. Deener. LC 55-1667. 1954. 11.00 (*0-930598-00-8*) Tulane Stud Pol.

Presidential Politics in South Dakota. Alan L. Clem. 1967. 1.00 (*1-55614-090-8*) U of SD Gov Res Bur.

Presidential Popularity & the Economy. Kristen R. Monroe. LC 83-13943. 289p. 1984. 55.00 (*0-275-91231-0*, C1231, Praeger Pubs) Greenwood.

***Presidential Power.** Robert Y. Shapiro et al. LC 00-20655. (Power, Conflict & Democracy Ser.). 2000. 24.50 (*0-231-10933-4*) Col U Pr.

Presidential Power: Case Studies in the Use of the Opinions of the Attorney General. Martin S. Sheffer. 148p. (Orig.). (C). 1991. pap. text 18.00 (*0-8191-8378-4*); lib. bdg. 39.00 (*0-8191-8377-6*) U Pr of Amer.

***Presidential Power: Forging the Presidency for the Twenty-first Century.** Ed. by Robert Y. Shapiro et al. 544p. 2000. text 49.50 (*0-231-10932-6*) Col U Pr.

Presidential Power & Accountability: Toward a New Constitution. Charles M. Hardin. LC 73-92022. x, 258p. 1993. pap. text 3.95 (*0-226-31624-6*) U Ch Pr.

Presidential Power & Accountability: Toward a New Constitution. Charles M. Hardin. LC 73-92022. x, 258p. 1994. lib. bdg. 21.00 (*0-226-31623-8*) U Ch Pr.

Presidential Power & Management Techniques: The Carter & Reagan Administrations in Historical Perspective, 175. James G. Benze, Jr. LC 87-233. (Contributions in Political Science Ser.: No. 175). 171p. 1987. 49.95 (*0-313-25601-2*, BZP/) Greenwood.

Presidential Power & the Constitution: Essays. Edward S. Corwin. Ed. by Richard Loss. LC 75-38000. 185p. 1976. text 52.50 (*0-8014-0982-9*) Cornell U Pr.

Presidential Power & the Modern Presidents: The Politics of Leadership from Roosevelt to Reagan. Richard E. Neustadt. 1989. 22.95 (*0-02-922975-8*) Free Pr.

Presidential Power & the Modern Presidents: The Politics of Leadership from Roosevelt to Reagan. Richard E. Neustadt. 1991. pap. 19.95 (*0-02-922796-8*) Free Pr.

***Presidential Power in 5th Republic France.** David Bell. 224p. 2000. 65.00 (*1-85973-371-9*, Pub. by Berg Pubs); pap. 19.50 (*1-85973-376-X*, Pub. by Berg Pubs) NYU Pr.

***Presidential Power In Russia.** Eugene Huskey. LC 99-20508. (New Russian Political System Ser.). (Illus.). 312p. 1999. text 64.95 (*1-56324-536-1*) M E Sharpe.

***Presidential Power in Russia.** Eugene Huskey. (The New Russian Political System Ser.). (Illus.). 312p. 1999. pap. text 24.95 (*1-56324-537-X*) M E Sharpe.

Presidential Powers. Michael E. Gerhardt. LC 99-73159. vi, 378p. 1999. 24.95 (*0-9671825-2-2*) Impact Press.

Presidential Premonitions. unabridged ed. Stephan R. Hutchinson. (Icon Cowboy Ser.: Bk. 1). 300p. 1998. pap. 6.95 (*0-9663394-0-1*) Earl Wayne.

Presidential Press Conference: Its History & Role in the American Political System. Blaire A. French. LC 81-40883. 54p. (Orig.). 1982. pap. text 11.50 (*0-8191-2064-2*) U Pr of Amer.

Presidential Press Conferences: A Critical Approach. Carolyn D. Smith. LC 90-30026. (Praeger Series in Political Communication). 280p. 1990. 65.00 (*0-275-93574-4*, C3574, Praeger Pubs); pap. 22.95 (*0-275-93575-2*, B3575, Praeger Pubs) Greenwood.

Presidential Primaries: Road to the White House, 41. James W. Davis. LC 79-54062. (Contributions in Political Science Ser.: No. 41). 395p. 1980. 69.50 (*0-313-22057-3*, DPP/, Greenwood Pr) Greenwood.

Presidential Primaries & Caucuses, 1992: A Handbook of Election Statistics. Alice V. McGillivray. LC 92-33506. 294p. (YA). 1993. text 142.00 (*0-87187-890-9*) Congr Quarterly.

Presidential Primaries & Nominations. William Crotty & John S. Jackson, III. LC 84-17662. 251p. 1985. pap. 9.95 (*0-87187-260-9*) Congr Quarterly.

Presidential Primaries & the Dynamics of Public Choice. Larry M. Bartels. LC 87-38187. (Illus.). 397p. reprint ed. pap. 123.10 (*0-608-06384-3*, 206674500008) Bks Demand.

Presidential Primary. Louise Overacker. LC 73-19168. (Politics & People Ser.). (Illus.). 318p. 1974. reprint ed. 26.95 (*0-405-05890-X*) Ayer.

Presidential Problems. Grover Cleveland. LC 78-152978. (Select Bibliographies Reprint Ser.). 1977. reprint ed. 23.95 (*0-8369-5730-X*) Ayer.

Presidential Public Funding Program. (Illus.). 80p. (Orig.). (C). 1994. pap. text 30.00 (*0-7881-0606-6*) DIANE Pub.

Presidential Pulse of Congressional Elections. 2nd ed. James E. Campbell. LC 97-18724. 312p. 1997. pap. 24.95 (*0-8131-0926-4*) U Pr of Ky.

Presidential Puzzlers. Jeanne Cheyney. 1998. pap. text 12.95 (*0-673-58654-5*) Addison-Wesley.

Presidential Recordings, 3 vol. set. Timothy Naftali. 150.00 (*0-393-04954-X*) Norton.

***Presidential Redwork: A Stitch in Time.** Michael Buckingham. Ed. by Helen Squire & Bonnie K. Browning. (Illus.). 80p. 2000. pap. 16.95 (*1-57432-744-5*, Am Quilters Soc) Collector Bks.

Presidential Republic: Executive Representation & Deliberative Democracy. Gary L. Gregg, II. LC 96-33214. 256p. 1996. 60.50 (*0-8476-8377-X*); pap. 24.95 (*0-8476-8378-8*) Rowman.

Presidential Responsiveness & Public Policy-Making: The Public & the Policies That Presidents Choose. Jeffrey E. Cohen. LC 97-4690. 304p. (C). 1997. text 54.50 (*0-472-10812-3*, 10812) U of Mich Pr.

***Presidential Responsiveness & Public Policy-Making: The Public & the Policies That Presidents Choose.** Jeffrey E. Cohen. 304p. (C). 1999. pap. text 19.95 (*0-472-08630-8*, 08630) U of Mich Pr.

Presidential Roast. Julie A. Waterman. 5p. 1985. 1.25 (*0-943334-10-1*) Carmonelle Pubns.

Presidential Scandals. Jeffrey Schultz. LC 99-43953. 300p. 1999. 99.00 (*1-56802-414-2*) Congr Quarterly.

Presidential Search. John W. Nason. 92p. 1982. 18.00 (*0-318-17380-8*) Assn Gov Bds.

Presidential Secrecy & Deception: Beyond the Power to Persuade, 43. John M. Orman. LC 79-8410. (Contributions in Political Science Ser.: No. 43). (Illus.). 239p. 1980. 59.95 (*0-313-22036-0*, OPS/, Greenwood Pr) Greenwood.

Presidential Seizure in Labor Disputes. John L. Blackman. LC 67-20871. (Wertheim Publications in Industrial Relations). 367p. reprint ed. pap. 113.80 (*0-7837-4449-8*, 205797900012) Bks Demand.

Presidential Selection. LC 82-71080. 150p. 1982. pap. 5.00 (*0-686-47958-0*, 357-0006) Amer Bar Assn.

Presidential Selection. Ed. by Alexander Heard & Michael Nelson. LC 87-9164. x, 413p. (C). 1987. text 59.95 (*0-8223-0750-2*); pap. text 24.95 (*0-8223-0785-5*) Duke.

Presidential Selection: Theory & Development. James W. Ceaser. LC 78-70282. 392p. 1979. pap. text 19.95 (*0-691-02188-0*, Pub. by Princeton U Pr) Cal Prin Full Svc.

Presidential Sex: From the Founding Fathers to Bill Clinton. Wesley Hagood. 288p. 1995. 19.95 (*1-55972-308-4*, Birch Ln Pr) Carol Pub Group.

Presidential Sex: From the Founding Fathers to Bill Clinton. Wesley Hagood. (Illus.). 288p. 1996. pap. text 14.95 (*0-8065-1816-2*, Citadel Pr) Carol Pub Group.

Presidential Sex: From the Founding Fathers to Bill Clinton. rev. ed. Wesley O. Hagood. LC 98-16179. (Illus.). 288p. 1998. pap. 18.95 (*0-8065-2007-8*) Carol Pub Group.

Presidential Sins. Darrell Jenkins. LC 98-88477. 325p. 1998. 25.00 (*0-7388-0169-0*); pap. 15.00 (*0-7388-0170-4*) Xlibris Corp.

Presidential Sites: A Directory of Places Associated with Presidents of the United States. William G. Clotworthy. LC 98-11173. (Illus.). 357p. (Orig.). 1998. pap. 18.95 (*0-939923-64-5*) M & W Pub Co.

Presidential Succession, 18. Ruth C. Silva. LC 68-54437. (Illus.). 213p. 1968. reprint ed. lib. bdg. 59.50 (*0-8371-0229-4*, SIPS, Greenwood Pr) Greenwood.

Presidential Succession of 1910. Francisco I. Madero. Tr. by Thomas Davis from SPA. (American University Studies: Ser. IX, Vol. 89). XXII, 307p. (C). 1990. text 51.50 (*0-8204-1250-3*) P Lang Pubng.

Presidential System: A Better Alternative. J. B. Mehta. (Illus.). 79p. 1979. 7.95 (*0-318-36606-1*) Asia Bk Corp.

Presidential System: The Indian Debate. A. G. Noorani. 136p. (C). 1989. 25.00 (*0-8039-9610-1*) Sage.

Presidential Temperament: The Unfolding of Character in Forty Presidents of the United States. David West Keirsey & Ray Choiniere. Ed. by Stephen E. Montgomery. 610p. (Orig.). 1992. pap. 19.95 (*0-9606954-6-X*) Prometheus Nemesis.

***Presidential Transitions: From Politics to Practice.** John P. Burke. 430p. 2000. 65.00 (*1-55587-916-0*) L Rienner.

Presidential Transitions: The Reagan to Bush Experience, Vol. 8. Ed. by David Clinton. 199p. (C). 1992. pap. text 24.50 (*0-8191-8710-0*, Pub. by White Miller Center); lib. bdg. 51.00 (*0-8191-8709-7*, Pub. by White Miller Center) U Pr of Amer.

Presidential Trivia. 1998. pap. 14.95 (*0-910119-56-2*) SOCO Pubns.

Presidential Trivia. Ernie Couch. LC 96-2523. 192p. 1996. pap. text 6.95 (*1-55853-412-1*) Rutledge Hill Pr.

Presidential Veto. Robert J. Spitzer. LC 88-2119. (SUNY Series in Leadership Studies). 181p. (C). 1988. pap. text 21.95 (*0-88706-803-0*) State U NY Pr.

Presidential Veto. Robert J. Spitzer. LC 88-2119. (SUNY Series in Leadership Studies). 181p. (C). 1988. text 64.50 (*0-88706-802-2*) State U NY Pr.

P

An Asterisk (*) at the beginning of an entry indicates that the title is appearing for the first time.

Presidential Vetoes & Public Policy. Richard A. Watson. LC 93-15887. (Studies in Government & Public Policy). 232p. 1993. 25.00 (*0-7006-0620-3*) U Pr of KS.

Presidential War Power. Louis Fisher. LC 94-39353. 264p. 1995. 29.95 (*0-7006-0690-4*); pap. 14.95 (*0-7006-0691-2*) U Pr of KS.

Presidential Wit & Wisdom: Maxims, Mottos, Soundbites, Speeches & Asides: Memorable Quotes from America's Presidents. Jess M. Brallier & Sally C. Chabert. LC 95-23184. 336p. 1996. pap. 12.95 (*0-14-023904-9*, Penguin Bks) Viking Penguin.

Presidential Wives. Paul F. Boller, Jr. 544p. 1989. reprint ed. pap. 12.95 (*0-19-505976-X*) OUP.

Presidential Yacht Potomac. Walter W. Jaffee. LC 97-77617. (Illus.). 224p. 1998. 40.00 (*1-889901-06-7*) Glencannon Pr.

Presidentialism: New Recipes for Nigeria's Political System. William J. Oyaide et al. LC 88-114523. 133p. 1987. write for info. (*978-30055-0-2*) Adelekan Pub Co.

Presidentialism & Democracy in Latin America. Ed. by Scott Mainwaring & Matthew S. Shugart. LC 96-26086. (Cambridge Studies in Comparative Politics). 502p. 1997. text 74.95 (*0-521-57266-5*); pap. text 29.95 (*0-521-57614-8*) Cambridge U Pr.

Presidents. (High Q Ser.). (Illus.). 60p. (J). (gr. 2-4). 1998. pap. 2.99 (*0-7681-0069-0*, McClanahan Book) Learn Horizon.

***Presidents.** (Fandex Family Field Guides Ser.). 1998. pap. 9.95 (*0-7611-1203-0*) Workman Pub.

Presidents. Jerry Aten. (Illus.). 176p. (J). (gr. 4 up). 1985. student ed. 13.95 (*0-86653-281-1*, GA 627) Good Apple.

***Presidents.** James G. Barber. LC 99-43281. (Eyewitness Books). (Illus.). 64p. (J). (gr. 4-7). 2000. 15.95 (*0-7894-5243-X*, D K Ink) DK Pub Inc.

***Presidents.** Cathryn Long. (Crossword America Ser.). (Illus.). 64p. (J). (gr. 3-6). 2000. pap. 5.95 (*0-7373-0364-6*, 03646W, Pub. by Lowell Hse Juvenile) NTC Contemp Pub Co.

***Presidents.** Martin W. Sandler. (J). 2001. pap. write for info. (*0-06-446263-3*, HarpTrophy) HarpC Child Bks.

Presidents. rev. ed. Jerry G. Aten. 176p. teacher ed. 14.99 (*0-86653-780-5*, GA1472) Good Apple.

Presidents: A Library of Congress Book. Martin W. Sandler. LC 93-49403. (Library of Congress Bk.). 96p. (YA). (gr. 4-7). 1995. 24.95 (*0-06-024534-4*) HarpC.

Presidents: A Reference History. 2nd ed. Ed. by Henry F. Graff. (Illus.). 811p. 1997. pap. 39.95 (*0-684-80551-0*) Macmillan.

***Presidents: A Reference History.** 2nd ed. Ed. by Henry F. Graff. (Illus.). 815p. 1999. reprint ed. pap. text 40.00 (*0-7881-6394-9*) DIANE Pub.

Presidents: A Reference History. 2nd rev. ed. Ed. by Henry F. Graff. 1996. 125.00 (*0-684-80471-9*, Hall Reference) Macmillan.

Presidents: George Washington to Bill Clinton. Walter A. Hazen. (Illus.). 160p. 1995. pap. text 13.95 (*1-58037-032-2*, Pub. by M Twain Media) Carson-Dellos.

Presidents above Party: The First American Presidency, 1789-1829. Ralph Ketcham. LC 83-12517. (Institute of Early American History & Culture Ser.). xiv, 269p. 1987. pap. 19.95 (*0-8078-4179-X*) U of NC Pr.

President's Agenda: Domestic Policy Choice from Kennedy to Clinton. 3rd ed. Paul Charles Light. LC 98-34586. 1999. pap. 16.95 (*0-8018-6066-0*) Johns Hopkins.

***President's Agenda: Domestic Policy Choice from Kennedy to Clinton.** 3rd ed. Paul Charles Light. LC 98-34586. 1999. 49.95 (*0-8018-6065-2*) Johns Hopkins.

President's Agenda: Domestic Policy Choice from Kennedy to Reagan. rev. ed. Paul Charles Light. LC 91-3779. 304p. 1991. pap. text 15.95 (*0-8018-4279-4*) Johns Hopkins.

President's Agenda: Domestic Policy Choice from Kennedy to Reagan. 2nd rev. ed. Paul Charles Light. LC 91-3779. 304p. 1991. text 49.95 (*0-8018-4278-6*) Johns Hopkins.

Presidents Almanac. Paula N. Kessler. 1996. 13.05 (*0-606-09765-1*, Pub. by Turtleback) Demco.

President's Almanac. rev. ed. Paula N. Kessler & Justin Segal. LC 98-23339. (History Ser.). (Illus.). 112p. (J). (gr. 3-6). 1998. pap. 8.95 (*1-56565-978-3*, 09783W, Pub. by Lowell Hse Juvenile) NTC Contemp Pub Co.

Presidents & Arms Control. Ed. by Kenneth W. Thompson. LC 94-92. (W. Alton Jones Foundation Series on the Presidency & Arms Control: Vol. 1). 228p. 1994. pap. 26.00 (*0-8191-9463-8*); lib. bdg. 54.50 (*0-8191-9462-X*) U Pr of Amer.

Presidents & Arms Control Vol. II. Ed. by Kenneth W. Thompson. (W. Alton Jones Foundation Series on the Presidency & Arms Control). 174p. (C). 1994. pap. text 24.50 (*0-8191-9710-6*, Pub. by White Miller Center); lib. bdg. 54.00 (*0-8191-9709-2*, Pub. by White Miller Center) U Pr of Amer.

Presidents & Assemblies: Constitutional Design & Electoral Dynamics. Matthew S. Shugart & John M. Carey. (Illus.). 330p. (C). 1992. text 69.95 (*0-521-41962-X*); pap. text 21.95 (*0-521-42990-0*) Cambridge U Pr.

Presidents & Civil Disorder, 42. Bennett M. Rich. LC 79-26839. (Institute for Government Research of the Brookings Institution, Studies in Administration Ser.: No. 42). 235p. 1980. reprint ed. lib. bdg. 65.00 (*0-313-22299-1*, RIPD) Greenwood.

Presidents & First Ladies of the United States. Doranne Jacobson. 1998. pap. text 12.98 (*1-880908-36-0*) Todtri Prods.

Presidents & Foreign Policy: Countdown to Ten Controversial Decisions. Edward R. Drachman & Alan Shank. LC 96-47514. (SUNY Series on the Presidency). 390p. (C). 1997. text 59.50 (*0-7914-3339-0*); pap. text 23.95 (*0-7914-3340-4*) State U NY Pr.

Presidents & Foreign Policy Making: From FDR to Reagan. Cecil V. Crabb & Kevin V. Mulcahy. LC 86-7508. (Political Traditions in Foreign Policy Ser.). 375p. 1986. pap. 106.90 (*0-7837-8530-5*, 2049339) Bks Demand.

***Presidents & Prime Ministers: Conviction Politics in the Anglo-American Tradition.** Patricia L. Sykes. LC 99-89938. 456p. 2000. text 45.00 (*0-7006-1017-0*) U Pr of KS.

Presidents & Protesters: Political Rhetoric in the 1960's. Theodore O. Windt, Jr. LC 90-35831. (Studies in Rhetoric & Communication). 336p. 1990. text 39.95 (*0-8173-0506-8*); pap. text 19.95 (*0-8173-0588-2*) U of Ala Pr.

Presidents & the Negro. Romeo B. Garrett. (YA). 1990. 24.45 (*0-87498-013-5*) Assoc Pubs DC.

Presidents & the Press: The Nixon Legacy. Joseph C. Spear. 367p. 1986. pap. text 10.95 (*0-262-69100-0*) MIT Pr.

Presidents & the Press: The Nixon Legacy. Joseph C. Spear. LC 83-26304. 420p. 1984. 25.00 (*0-262-19228-4*) MIT Pr.

Presidents & Their Pets. Vera F. Rollo. LC 93-86023. 120p. 1993. 19.50 (*0-917882-29-6*) MD Hist Pr.

Presidents & Their Pets. Vera F. Rollo. LC 93-86023. (Illus.). 120p. 1993. pap. 14.25 (*0-917882-36-9*) MD Hist Pr.

Presidents & Their Wives. 6th rev. ed. 82p. 1997. pap. text 3.50 (*0-9656315-2-4*) Coffman Pubns.

Presidents As Candidates: Inside the White House for the Presidential Campaign. Kathryn D. Tenpas. Ed. by Steven A. Shull. LC 97-18440. (Politics & Policy in American Institutions Ser.: Vol. 1). 230p. 1997. text 54.00 (*0-8153-2506-1*, SS1132) Garland.

President's Astrologer. Barbara Shafferman. LC 98-42517. (Illus.). 400p. 1999. 12.95 (*1-56718-674-2*, K674) Llewellyn Pubns.

Presidents at Play. George A. Sullivan. LC 94-15002. (J). 1995. lib. bdg. 16.85 (*0-8027-8334-1*) Walker & Co.

Presidents at Play. George A. Sullivan. LC 94-15002. (Illus.). 176p. (J). 1995. 15.95 (*0-8027-8333-3*) Walker & Co.

Presidents' Birthplaces, Homes & Burial Sites: A Pictorial Guide. annuals rev. ed. Rachel M. Kochmann. (Illus.). 162p. 1999. pap. text 14.95 (*0-9616666-1-7*) Osage Pub.

***President's Bodyguard.** John Miles. 2000. pap. 11.95 (*1-891929-59-3*) Four Seasons.

Presidents by Accident. Edmund Lindop. LC 91-17056. (Non-Fiction Ser.). (Illus.). 160p. (YA). (gr. 9-12). 1991. lib. bdg. 24.00 (*0-531-11059-1*) Watts.

President's Cabinet & How It Grew. Nancy Winslow Parker. LC 89-70851. (Illus.). 40p. (J). (gr. 3-5). 1991. 14.95 (*0-06-021617-4*) HarpC Child Bks.

President's Call: Executive Leadership from FDR to George Bush. Judith E. Michaels. LC 97-4562. (Policy & Institutional Studies). 348p. 1997. pap. 22.00 (*0-8229-5628-4*); text 50.00 (*0-8229-3977-0*) U of Pittsburgh Pr.

President's Cancer Panel Meeting: Evaluating the National Cancer Program: Transcript of Proceedings, September 22, 1993. 281p. (Orig.). (C). 1995. pap. text 50.00 (*0-7881-1951-6*) DIANE Pub.

President's Car. Nancy Winslow Parker. LC 79-7898. (Illus.). 64p. (J). (gr. 3-5). 1981. 11.95 (*0-690-03963-8*); lib. bdg. 11.89 (*0-690-03964-6*) HarpC Child Bks.

President's Commission for the Study of Ethical Problems in Medicine & Biomedical & Behavioral Research, 16 vols. in 6 bks., Set. Ed. by President's Commission for the Study of Ethical Pr. LC 97-80015. 1997. reprint ed. 595.00 (*1-57588-391-0*, 311430) W S Hein.

Presidents Confront Reality: From Edifice Complex to University Without Walls. Lyman A. Glenny et al. LC 75-24014. (Carnegie Council Ser.). 271p. reprint ed. pap. 84.10 (*0-608-14793-1*, 202565400045) Bks Demand.

President's Crime Commission Report, 1967: Its Impact 25 Years Later. Ed. by John A. Conley. LC 93-79360. (ACJS - Anderson Monographs). 160p. (C). 1993. pap. 19.95 (*0-87084-126-2*) Anderson Pub Co.

President's Daughter. Nan Britton. 1977. 30.95 (*0-8369-7132-9*, 7966) Ayer.

President's Daughter. Annette Broadrick. 1999. per. 4.25 (*0-373-24226-3*, Harlequin) Harlequin Bks.

President's Daughter. William W. Brown. (X Press Black Classics Ser.). 178p. 1996. pap. 9.95 (*1-874509-25-5*, Pub. by X Pr) LPC InBook.

President's Daughter. Jack Higgins. 304p. 1998. mass mkt. 6.99 (*0-425-16341-5*) Berkley Pub.

President's Daughter. Jack Higgins. LC 96-48654. 320p. 1997. 23.95 (*0-399-14239-8*, G P Putnam) Peng Put Young Read.

President's Daughter. Ellen E. White. 304p. 1984. pap. 2.95 (*0-380-88740-1*, Avon Bks) Morrow Avon.

President's Daughter. Ellen E. White. 256p. (J). (gr. 7-9). 1994. pap. 3.25 (*0-590-47799-4*) Scholastic Inc.

President's Daughter. large type ed. Jack Higgins. LC 97-34580. (Large Print Book Ser.). 1997. 26.95 (*1-56895-495-6*) Wheeler Pub.

President's Day. Mir Tamim Ansary. LC 98-14380. (Holiday Histories Ser.). 32p. (J). 1999. 19.92 (*1-57572-875-3*) Heinemann Lib.

***Presidents' Day.** Helen Frost. LC 99-49613. (National Holidays Ser.). (Illus.). 24p. (J). (ps-2). 2000. lib. bdg. 13.25 (*0-7368-0545-1*, Pebble Bks) Capstone Pr.

Presidents Day. Dianne M. MacMillan. LC 96-27290. (Best Holiday Bks.). (Illus.). 48p. (J). (gr. 1-4). 1997. lib. bdg. 18.95 (*0-89490-820-0*) Enslow Pubs.

Presidents Day. Lynda Sorensen. LC 94-3354. (Holidays Ser.). (J). 1994. lib. bdg. 14.60 (*1-57103-073-5*) Rourke Pr.

Presidents Day. Jack Winder. Ed. by Alton Jordan. (Holiday Set). (Illus.). (J). (gr. k-3). 1984. 7.95 (*0-89868-028-X*, Read Res); pap. 3.95 (*0-89868-061-1*, Read Res) ARO Pub.

President's Day: Let's Meet George Washington & Abraham Lincoln. Barbara DeRubertis. (Holidays & Heroes Ser.). (Illus.). (Orig.). (J). (gr. 1-5). 1991. pap. 4.95 (*0-7915-1918-X*) Kane Pr.

President's Day: Let's Meet George Washington & Abraham Lincoln. Barbara DeRubertis. (Holidays & Heroes Ser.). (Illus.). 32p. (Orig.). (J). (gr. 1-5). 1996. pap. 7.95 incl. audio (*1-57565-014-2*) Kane Pr.

President's Day Activities. Teacher Created Materials Staff. (Holiday Activities Ser.). 32p. (J). (gr. k-8). 1997. pap. 2.95 (*1-55734-789-1*) Tchr Create Mat.

Presidents' Day & Martin Luther King, Jr. Day: A Thematic Unit. Mary E. Sterling. (Thematic Units Ser.). (Illus.). 80p. (Orig.). (J). (gr. 1-3). 1992. student ed. 9.95 (*1-55734-262-8*) Tchr Create Mat.

***President's Doctor: An Insider's View of Three First Families.** Milton F. Heller, Jr. LC 99-93823. 2000. 22.95 (*0-533-13159-6*) Vantage.

Presidents, Elections, & Democracy. 1992. pap. 16.95 (*0-614-04161-9*) Acad Poli Sci.

Presidents, First Ladies, & Vice Presidents: White House Biographies, 1789-1997. Daniel C. Diller & Stephen L. Robertson. LC 96-37389. 180p. (YA). (gr. 11). 1996. pap. text 29.95 (*1-56802-311-1*) Congr Quarterly.

President's Fiscal Year 1998 Budget. LC 98-107333. iii, 94 p. 1997. write for info. (*0-16-055397-0*) USGPO.

President's Fiscal Year 1998 Budget: Hearing Before the Committee on Ways & Means, House of Representatives, & Congress, First Session, February 11 & 12, 1997. LC 98-211669. iii, 232p. 1998. write for info. (*0-16-057252-5*) USGPO.

President's Fiscal Year 1999 Budget Request for the U.s. Coast Guard: Hearing Before the Subcommittee on Coast Guard & Maritime Transportation of the Committee on Transportation & Infrastructure, House of Representatives, One Hundred Fifth Congress, Second Session, March 4, 1998. United States. LC 98-206975. iv, 598p. 1998. write for info. (*0-16-057259-2*) USGPO.

President's Foreign Assistance Budget Request for Fiscal Year 1999: Hearing Before the Committee on International Relations, House of Representatives, One Hundred Fifth Congress, Second Session, March 5, 1998. United States. LC 98-190324. iii, 90p. 1998. write for info. (*0-16-057008-5*) USGPO.

President's Guide to People: Power Strategies. H. William Koch, Jr. 1982. 89.50 (*0-13-697557-7*) Exec Reports.

President's Health Security Plan: Health Care That's Always There. White House Domestic Policy Co. Staff. 1993. pap. 8.00 (*0-8129-2356-1*, Times Bks) Crown Pub Group.

President's House: A History, 2 vols. William Seale. (Illus.). 1226p. 1986. 39.95 (*0-8109-1490-5*, Pub. by Abrams) Time Warner.

President's House: A History, 2 vols. William Seale. (Illus.). 1304p. 1986. 39.95 (*0-912308-28-1*) White House Hist.

President's House: A History, 2 vols. William Seale. (Illus.). 1304p. 1986. 200.00 (*0-912308-29-X*) White House Hist.

Presidents in a Time of Change. Ed. by Carter Smith. (American Albums from the Collections of the Library of Congress). (Illus.). 96p. (J). (gr. 5-8). 1993. pap. 8.95 (*1-56294-877-6*) Millbrook Pr.

Presidents in a Time of Change: A Sourcebook on the U. S. Presidency. Ed. by Carter Smith. LC 93-15092. (American Albums from the Collections of the Library of Congress). (Illus.). 96p. (J). (gr. 5-8). 1993. lib. bdg. 25.90 (*1-56294-362-6*) Millbrook Pr.

Presidents in a Time of Change: A Sourcebook on the U.S. Presidency. C. Carter Smith. (American Albums from the Collections of the Library of Congress). 1993. 14.15 (*0-606-08037-6*) Turtleback.

Presidents I've Known & Two Near Presidents. Charles W. Thompson. LC 71-93383. (Essay Index Reprint Ser.). 1977. 26.95 (*0-8369-1728-6*) Ayer.

President's Journey: Issues & Ideals in the Community College. Cathryn L. Addy. 164p. (C). 1995. text 30.95 (*1-882982-04-5*) Anker Pub.

President's Lady. Irving Stone. LC 96-32822. 288p. 1996. pap. 14.95 (*1-55853-431-8*) Rutledge Hill Pr.

Presidents' Last Years: George Washington to Lyndon B. Johnson. Homer F. Cunningham. LC 88-35089. 349p. 1989. lib. bdg. 37.50 (*0-89950-408-6*) McFarland & Co.

Presidents Leadership Manual. 81p. 2.00 (*0-318-15189-8*, 111-833) Natl Assoc Realtors.

President's Letter Book. John R. Taylor & Elise D. Bigger. 288p. 1986. 39.95 (*0-13-700493-1*) P-H.

President's Line-Item Veto Action on Fiscal Year 1998 Defense & Military Construction Appropriation Bills. USGPO Staff. LC 98-160875. iii, 107p. 1998. pap. write for info. (*0-16-056212-0*) USGPO.

President's List of Articles Which May Be Designated or Modified As Eligible Articles for Purposes of the U. S. Generalized System of Preferences. Richard Witherspoon et al. (Illus.). 228p. (Orig.). (C). 1994. pap. text 20.00 (*0-7881-1433-6*) DIANE Pub.

President's Little Instruction Book. Honor Books Staff. (In the Midst of Greatness Ser.). 160p. 1996. per. 5.99 (*1-57757-008-1*) Trade Life.

President's Man. large type ed. Elliot Conway. (Dales Large Print Ser.). 224p. 1996. pap. 18.99 (*1-85389-645-4*, Dales) Ulverscroft.

President's Man: Leo Crowley & Franklin Roosevelt in Peace & War. Stuart L. Weiss. LC 95-14363. 311p. (C). 1996. 39.95 (*0-8093-1996-9*) S Ill U Pr.

Presidents, Management, & Regulation. Edward P. Fuchs. (Illus.). 176p. (C). 1988. pap. text 22.05 (*0-13-698813-X*) P-H.

President's Medals. N. MacNeil. LC 76-49563. (Illus.). 1977. lib. bdg. 15.00 (*0-517-52918-1*) S J Durst.

President's Mediation Commission, 1917-1918. Martin P. Schipper & Melvyn Dubofsky. LC 86-893396. (Research Collections on Labor Studies). 3 p. 1985. write for info. (*0-89093-712-5*) U Pubns Amer.

President's Murderer. Ed. by Tricia Hedge. (Illus.). 48p. 1991. pap. text 5.95 (*0-19-422677-8*) OUP.

President's National Urban Policy Report. (Illus.). 100p. (Orig.). (C). 1993. pap. text 25.00 (*0-7881-0131-5*) DIANE Pub.

Presidents of a Divided Nation: A Sourcebook on the U.S. Presidency. C. Carter Smith. (American Albums from the Collections of the Library of Congress). 1993. 14.15 (*0-606-08038-4*) Turtleback.

Presidents of a Growing Country: A Sourcebook on the U. S. Presidency. Ed. by Carter Smith. (American Albums from the Collections of the Library of Congress). (Illus.). 96p. (J). (gr. 5-8). 1993. pap. 8.95 (*1-56294-875-X*); lib. bdg. 25.90 (*1-56294-358-8*) Millbrook Pr.

Presidents of a Growing Country: A Sourcebook on the U.S. Presidency. C. Carter Smith. (American Albums from the Collections of the Library of Congress). 1993. 14.15 (*0-606-08039-2*, Pub. by Turtleback) Demco.

Presidents of a World Power: A Sourcebook on the U. S. Presidency. Ed. by Carter Smith. LC 93-15091. (American Albums from the Collections of the Library of Congress). (Illus.). 96p. (J). (gr. 5-8). 1993. lib. bdg. 25.90 (*1-56294-361-8*) Millbrook Pr.

Presidents of a World Power: A Sourcebook on the U.S. Presidency. C. Carter Smith. (American Albums from the Collections of the Library of Congress). 1993. 14.15 (*0-606-08040-6*) Turtleback.

Presidents of a Young Republic: A Sourcebook on the U. S. Presidency. Ed. by Carter Smith. (American Albums from the Collections of the Library of Congress). (Illus.). 96p. (J). (gr. 5-8). 1993. pap. 8.95 (*1-56294-873-3*); lib. bdg. 25.90 (*1-56294-359-6*) Millbrook Pr.

Presidents of a Young Republic: A Sourcebook on the U.S. Presidency. C. Carter Smith. (American Albums from the Collections of the Library of Congress). 1993. 14.15 (*0-606-08041-4*) Turtleback.

Presidents of Central America, Mexico, Cuba, & Hispaniola: Conversations & Correspondence. Robert J. Alexander. LC 95-6323. 280p. 1995. 65.00 (*0-275-95278-9*, Praeger Pubs) Greenwood.

Presidents of the Church. Pref. by Leonard J. Arrington. LC 85-31117. 460p. 1993. reprint ed. pap. 11.95 (*0-87579-683-4*) Deseret Bk.

Presidents of the LDS Church Coloring Book. Illus. by Bob Brower. (Coloring Bks.). 50p. (Orig.). (J). (gr. 2-6). 1993. pap. 5.95 (*0-910523-21-5*) Grandin Bk Co.

Presidents of the United States. Walt Hazen & Marilyn Evans. (People & Places Ser.). (Illus.). 32p. (J). (gr. 4-6). Date not set. pap., wbk. ed. 2.50 (*1-58610-134-X*) Learn Horizon.

Presidents of the United States. John T. Marck. (Illus.). 45p. (Orig.). 1997. pap. text 19.95 (*1-884604-00-5*) Creative Impress.

Presidents of the United States. Lloyd Ultan. Ed. by Gary D. Hermalyn. (Bicentennial of U. S. Constitution Ser.). (Illus.). (C). 1989. text 20.00 (*0-941980-24-3*) Bronx County.

Presidents of the United States: Portraits & Biographies. August Dietz, Sr. 1988. pap. 2.50 (*0-87517-014-5*) Dietz.

Presidents of the United States: The First Twenty Years. Ed. by Marilyn K. Parr. LC 92-18145. 1992. 5.50 (*0-8444-0698-8*) Lib Congress.

Presidents of the United States: Their Written Measure. 1997. lib. bdg. 251.95 (*0-8490-6148-2*) Gordon Pr.

Presidents of the United States: Their Written Measure. James Sayler. (Illus.). 216p. pap. 19.00 (*0-8444-0902-2*) Lib Congress.

Presidents of the United States: Their Written Measure, a Bibliography. James Sayler. 226p. 1996. pap. text 20.00 (*0-16-048592-4*, Library of Cong) USGPO.

Presidents of the United States Fact Cards. Toucan Valley Staff. (Fact Cards Ser.). (Illus.). 84p. (YA). (gr. 5-8). 1998. ring bd. 34.00 (*1-884925-56-1*) Toucan Valley.

Presidents of the United States of America. Hugh Sidey. 96p. 1996. 5.50 (*0-912308-57-5*) White House Hist.

Presidents of the United States of America. 13th ed. Frank Freidel. (Illus.). 91p. 1998. pap. text 25.00 (*0-7881-7027-9*) DIANE Pub.

Presidents of the United States of America. 14th ed. Hugh Sidey. 96p. 1996. pap. 4.50 (*0-912308-56-7*) White House Hist.

Presidents of the University of Chicago: A Centennial View. Richard L. Popp. LC 92-28533. (Illus.). 57p. (C). 1992. pap. 7.00 (*0-943056-18-7*) Univ Chi Lib.

Presidents of U. S. A. Nicholas Best. (Illus.). 96p. 1996. 8.95 (*0-8212-2256-2*, Pub. by Bulfinch Pr) Little.

Presidents on the Net. Gary M. Garfield. 1998. pap. 12.95 (*0-673-36403-8*) Addison-Wesley.

***Presidents, Parties & the State: A Party System Perspective on Democratic Regulatory Choice, 1884-1936.** Scott C. James. (Illus.). 320p. (C). 2000. text 59.95 (*0-521-66277-X*) Cambridge U Pr.

President's Partner: The First Lady in the Twentieth Century, 105. Myra G. Gutin. LC 89-1926. (Contributions in Women's Studies: No. 105). 205p. 1989. 49.95 (*0-313-25335-8*, GFL, Greenwood Pr) Greenwood.

An Asterisk (*) at the beginning of an entry indicates that the title is appearing for the first time.

Presidents, Pitchers, & Passers. John A. Hurst. LC 87-2291. (And so the Story Goes...Ser.: No. 2). 80p. (Orig.). 1987. pap. 7.95 (*0-89196-133-X*, 31698) Quality Bks IL.

Presidents, Politics, & Policy. Erwin C. Hargrove & Michael Nelson. LC 84-47959. 304p. reprint ed. pap. 94.30 (*0-7837-1108-5*, 204163800021) Bks Demand.

Presidents, Prime Ministers & Governors of the English-Speaking Caribbean & Puerto Rico: Conversations & Correspondence. Robert J. Alexander. LC 96-33194. 304p. 1997. 69.50 (*0-275-95803-5*, Praeger Pubs) Greenwood.

Presidents, Prime Ministers & the Press. Ed. by Kenneth W. Thompson. (White House Press on the Presidency Ser.: Vol.6). 98p. (Orig.). (C). 1986. pap. text 14.00 (*0-8191-5438-5*, Pub. by White Miller Center) U Pr of Amer.

Presidents, Professors & Trustees: The Evolution of American Academic Government. William H. Cowley. Ed. by Donald T. Williams, Jr. LC 79-92461. (Jossey-Bass Series in Higher Education). 280p. reprint ed. pap. 86.80 (*0-8357-4937-1*, 203786700009) Bks Demand.

Presidents, Public Opinion & Power. Terry L. Deibel. LC 87-80536. (Headline Ser.: No. 280). (Orig.). 1986. pap. 5.95 (*0-87124-112-9*) Foreign Policy.

President's Quality Award Program Self-Assessment Process for Federal, State & Local Government. Jerry Arcaro. LC 97-206857. (Illus.). 260p. 1997. lib. bdg. 125.00 (*1-57444-167-1*) St Lucie Pr.

***President's Request for Fast Track Trade Negotiating Authority: Hearing Before the Committee on Commerce, Science & Transportation, United States Senate, 105th Congress, 1st Session, September 30, 1997.** USGPO Staff. LC 99-179856. iii, 79 p. 1998. write for info. (*0-16-057861-2*) USGPO.

President's Rule in India. Shriman Maheshwari. 1977. 12.50 (*0-88386-985-3*) S Asia.

President's Rule in Indian States. S. C. Arora. 1990. 32.50 (*81-7099-234-6*, Pub. by Mittal Pubs Dist) S Asia.

President's Salary: A Study in Constitutional Declension, 1789-1990. James F. Vivian. LC 93-8543. (Distinguished Studies in American Legal & Constitutional History). 184p. 1993. text 10.00 (*0-8153-1249-0*) Garland.

President's Scientists: Reminiscences of a White House Science Advisor. D. Allan Bromley. LC 94-10424. Vol. 47. (Illus.). 232p. 1994. 37.00 (*0-300-06006-8*) Yale U Pr.

Presidents' Secret Wars: CIA & Pentagon Covert Operations from World War II Through the Persian Gulf. rev. ed. John Prados. 576p. 1996. pap. 17.95 (*1-56663-108-4*, EL134, Pub. by I R Dee) Natl Bk Netwk.

President's Son. Krandall Kraus. 320p. (Orig.). 1996. pap. 6.95 (*1-55583-603-8*) Alyson Pubns.

Presidents' Sons: The Prestige of Name in a Democracy. Joseph J. Perling. LC 70-148226. (Biography Index Reprint Ser.). 1977. 29.95 (*0-8369-8073-5*) Ayer.

Presidents Speak: The Inaugural Addresses of the American Presidents, from Washinton to Clinton. Davis N. Lott. 434p. 1995. 35.00 (*0-8050-3305-X*) H Holt & Co.

Presidents Sticker Book. (Illus.). 64p. (Orig.). (J). (gr. 1-5). 1997. pap. 6.95 (*1-56293-940-8*, McClanahan Book) Learn Horizon.

President's Task Force on the Value of the Information Professional: Final Report, Preliminary Study, Special Libraries Association, 78th Annual Conference, Anaheim, CA. rev. ed. Special Libraries Association Staff. LC 88-215263. (Illus.). 64p. reprint ed. pap. 30.00 (*0-608-08052-7*, 206901700002) Bks Demand.

***Presidents, the First Ladies & the Other Ladies.** Ron Puckett. Ed. by Pamela Brooks. (Illus.). 64p. 1999. pap. 9.95 (*1-929940-00-9*) Hert Pub Kentucky.

Presidents vs. Congress: Conflict & Compromise. Edmund Lindop. LC 93-30784. (Democracy in Action Ser.). (Illus.). 128p. (YA). (gr. 9-12). 1994. lib. bdg. 24.00 (*0-531-11165-2*) Watts.

President's War Powers. 1984. pap. 12.95 (*0-614-04173-2*) Acad Poli Sci.

***Presidents Who Shaped the Nation.** Beth Button. Ed. by Kathy Rogers. (Famous Faces Ser.). (Illus.). 8p. 2000. 6.95 (*1-56472-275-9*) Edupress Inc.

***Presidents' Wives: Reassessing the Office of First Lady.** Robert P. Watson. LC 99-27842. 361p. 2000. 55.00 (*1-55587-860-1*); pap. 19.95 (*1-55587-948-9*) L Rienner.

Presidents' Wives: The Lives of 44 American Women of Strength. Carole C. Waldrup. LC 89-42572. (Illus.). 391p. 1989. lib. bdg. 35.00 (*0-89950-393-4*) McFarland & Co.

Presiding & Leading: How to Be a President. Vernon Reed. 113p. 1994. 23.95 (*0-9641116-0-8*) Woodflower Pr.

Presiding Ideas in Wordsworth's Poetry. Melvin M. Rader. LC 68-8341. 94p. (C). 1968. reprint ed. 40.00 (*0-87752-090-9*) Gordian.

Presiding over a Divided World: Changing U. N. Roles, 1945-1993. Adam Roberts & Benedict Kingsbury. LC 94-4467. (International Peace Academy Occasional Paper Ser.). 95p. 1994. pap. text 9.95 (*1-55587-519-X*) L Rienner.

Presidio: Bastion of the Spanish Borderlands. Max L. Moorhead. LC 74-15908. (Illus.). 304p. 1991. pap. 15.95 (*0-8061-2317-6*) U of Okla Pr.

Presidio: From Army Post to National Park. Lisa Benton. LC 97-51930. (Illus.). 288p. 1998. text 29.95 (*1-55553-335-3*) NE U Pr.

Presidio & Militia on the Northern Frontier of New Spain: A Documentary History - 1570-1700, Vol. I. Ed. by Thomas H. Naylor & Charles W. Polzer. LC 86-13283. 756p. 1986. 72.00 (*0-8165-0903-4*) U of Ariz Pr.

Presidio & Militia on the Northern Frontier of New Spain: A Documentary History, 1700-1765, Vol. 2, Pt. 2. Ed. by Diana Hadley et al. 575p. 1997. text 65.00 (*0-8165-1693-6*) U of Ariz Pr.

Presidio & Militia on the Northern Frontier of New Spain Vol. II, Pt. I: A Documentary History: The Californias & Sinaloa-Sonora, 1700-1765. Ed. by Charles W. Polzer & Thomas E. Sheridan. (Illus.). 470p. 1997. 65.00 (*0-8165-1692-8*) U of Ariz Pr.

Presidio de San Francisco: A History under Spain & Mexico, 1776. John P. Langellier & Daniel B. Rosen. (Frontier Military Ser.: Vol. XIX). (Illus.). 200p. 1996. 35.50 (*0-87062-239-0*) A H Clark.

Presidio Gateways: Views of a National Landmark at San Francisco's Golden Gate. Delphine Hirasuna. LC 94-19708. 1994. 29.95 (*0-8118-0874-2*) Chronicle Bks.

Presley Family & Friends Cookbook. Donna P. Early & Edie Hand. Ed. by Jim Clark & Ken Beck. LC 98-21681. (Illus.). 288p. 1998. pap. 16.95 (*1-888952-75-X*) Cumberland Hse.

Presleyana: The Elvis Presely Price Guide. 3rd ed. 224p. 1992. pap. 24.95 (*0-932117-17-1*) Osborne Enterps.

Presleyana: The Elvis Presely Price Guide. 4th ed. 342p. 1997. pap. 25.00 (*0-932117-26-0*) Osborne Enterps.

Preso sin nombre, celda sin numero see Prisoner Without a Name, Cell Without a Number

Presocratic Philosophers. Jonathan Barnes. (Arguments of the Philosophers Ser.). 358p. (C). 1983. pap. 32.99 (*0-415-05079-0*) Routledge.

Presocratic Philosophers. rev. ed. Jonathan Barnes. (Arguments of the Philosophers Ser.). 680p. 1982. pap. 27.50 (*0-7100-9200-8*, Routledge Thoemms) Routledge.

Presocratic Philosophers: A Critical History with a Selections of Texts. 2nd ed. Malcolm Schofield et al. LC 82-23505. 520p. 1984. pap. text 34.95 (*0-521-27455-9*) Cambridge U Pr.

Presocratic Philosophers: An Annotated Bibliography. Luis E. Navia. LC 93-16207. 752p. 1993. text 120.00 (*0-8240-9776-9*, SS704) Garland.

Presocratic Reflexivity: The Construction of Philosophical Discourse c. 600-450 B. C. Barry Sandywell. LC 95-16091. (Logological Investigations Ser.: Vol. 3). 536p. (C). (gr. 13). 1996. 125.00 (*0-415-10170-0*) Routledge.

Presocratic Tradition from Parmenides to Democritus see History of Greek Philosophy

Presocratics. Edward Hussey. 184p. 1995. 34.95 (*0-87220-277-1*); pap. 10.95 (*0-87220-276-3*) Hackett Pub.

Presocratics. Philip Wheelwright. 352p. (Orig.). (C). 1966. pap. text 23.60 (*0-02-426640-X*, Macmillan Coll) P-H.

Presocratics see Studies in Greek Philosophy

Presocratics: The Main Fragments. M. R. Wright. (Bristol Greek Texts Ser.). 214p. 1985. 22.95 (*0-86292-079-5*, Pub. by Brist Class Pr) Focus Pub-R Pullins.

Presocratics after Heidegger. Ed. by David C. Jacobs. LC 98-47345. (SUNY Series in Contemporary Continental Philosophy). 320p. (C). 1999. text 73.50 (*0-7914-4199-7*); pap. text 24.95 (*0-7914-4200-4*) State U NY Pr.

Presocratics Reader: Selected Fragments & Testimonia. Ed. by Patricia Curd. Tr. by Richard D. McKirahan, Jr. LC 95-39291. 144p. 1996. pap. text 8.95 (*0-87220-326-3*); lib. bdg. 32.95 (*0-87220-327-1*) Hackett Pub.

Presowing Irradiation of Plant Seeds. N. M. Berezina & D. A. Kaushanski. (C). 1989. 37.50 (*81-7087-041-0*, Pub. by Oxford IBH) S Asia.

Presowing Irradiation of Plant Seeds. 2nd enl. rev. ed. N. M. Berezina & D. A. Kaushankii. Tr. by A. K. Dhote. (Russian Translation Ser.: No. 70). (Illus.). 294p. (C). 1989. text 110.00 (*90-6191-946-0*, Pub. by A A Balkema) Ashgate Pub Co.

Prespective, Libel, & the Ten Rules of 90's Journalism: Medicine, Music, Stand-up Comedy, Janitor Work, & the Systematic Dismantling of Individual Liberties by an Irresponsible Press. Harold Bays. LC 95-78352. (Orig.). 1995. 29.95 (*0-9647944-0-3*); pap. 19.95 (*0-9647944-1-1*) Blue Shoes Pubng.

Presque Isle. Daniel Morris. (Illus.). 102p. (Orig.). 1988. pap. write for info. (*0-318-62978-X*) Osage Pr.

Presque Isle, Caribou, & New Sweden. Jackie Graves et al. LC 95-166511. (Images of America Ser.). 128p. 1994. pap. 14.99 (*0-7524-0082-7*) Arcadia Publng.

Presque Isle Register, 1904 (Town History & Directory) Compiled by Mitchell & Pittingill. 130p. 1997. reprint ed. pap. 21.50 (*0-8328-5899-4*) Higginson Bk Co.

Presqu'ile: Avec: La Route, Le Roi Cophetua. Julien Gracq. (FRE.). 256p. 1991. reprint ed. pap. write for info. (*0-7859-4596-2*) Fr & Eur.

Press: A Neglected Factor in the Economic History of the Twentieth Century. Harold Adams Innis. LC 76-29440. 1977. reprint ed. write for info. (*0-404-15310-0*) AMS Pr.

Press: Free & Responsible? Hoyt H. Purvis. (Symposia Ser.). 114p. 1982. pap. 6.00 (*0-89940-411-1*) LBJ Sch Pub Aff.

Press & Abortion, 1838-1988. Marvin N. Olasky. (Communication Ser.). 208p. (C). 1988. pap. text 27.50 (*0-8058-0485-4*) L Erlbaum Assocs.

***Press & America: An Interpretive History of the Mass Media.** 9th ed. Michael C. Emery et al. LC 99-44295. 698p. 1999. 64.00 (*0-205-29557-6*) Allyn.

Press & American Politics: The New Mediator. 2nd ed. Richard Davis. LC 95-16059. 432p. 1995. pap. text 41.00 (*0-13-185943-9*) P-H.

***Press & American Politics: The New Mediator.** 3rd ed. Richard Davis. LC 99-86445. 368p. 2000. pap. text 36.00 (*0-13-026404-0*) P-H.

Press & Apartheid: Repression & Propaganda in South Africa. William A. Hachten & C. Anthony Giffard. Ed. by Harva Hachten. LC 84-40150. 352p. 1984. reprint ed. pap. 109.20 (*0-608-01935-6*, 206259000003) Bks Demand.

Press & China Policy: The Illusion of Sino-American Relations, 1950-1984. Tsan-Kuo Chang. LC 92-38944. (Communication & Information Science Ser.). 288p. 1993. pap. 39.50 (*1-56750-014-5*); text 73.25 (*0-89391-887-3*) Ablx Pub.

Press & Communications of the Empire see British Empire

Press & Foreign Policy. Bernard C. Cohen. LC 83-12989. 288p. 1993. reprint ed. pap. 14.95 (*0-87772-346-X*) UCB IGS.

Press & Media Access to the Criminal Courtroom. Warren Freedman. LC 88-4039. 139p. 1988. 65.00 (*0-89930-328-5*, FPB/, Quorum Bks) Greenwood.

Press & People, 1790-1850: Opinion in Three English Cities. Donald Read. (Modern Revivals in Economic & Social History Ser.). 225p. (C). 1993. text 56.95 (*0-7512-0245-2*, Pub. by Gregg Revivals) Ashgate Pub Co.

Press & Poetry of Modern Persia. Edward G. Browne. (Illus.). xi, 357p. 1983. reprint ed. 35.00 (*0-933770-39-1*) Kalimat.

Press & Political Dissent. Mark Hollingsworth. LC 87-100403. viii, 367 p. 1986. 6.95 (*0-7453-0139-8*) Pluto GBR.

Press & Politics: Britain & France, 1620-1800. Bob Harris. LC 96-4540. (Historical Connections Ser.). 144p. (C). 1996. pap. 16.99 (*0-415-12273-2*) Routledge.

***Press & Politics in Africa.** Ed. by Ritchard Tamba M'Bayo et al. LC 00-36435. (African Studies: Vol. 53). 2000. pap. 99.95 (*0-7734-7684-9*) E Mellen.

Press & Politics in Israel: The Jerusalem Post from 1932 to the Present, 44. Erwin Frenkel. LC 93-7709. (Contributions to the Study of Mass Media & Communications Ser.: No. 44). 208p. 1993. 59.95 (*0-313-28957-3*, GM8957, Greenwood Pr) Greenwood.

Press & Public: Who Reads What, When, Where, & Why in American Newspapers. 2nd ed. Leo Bogart. 384p. 1989. 89.95 (*0-8058-0431-5*) L Erlbaum Assocs.

Press & Public: Who Reads What, Where, & Why in American Newspapers. 2nd ed. Leo Bogart. LC 80-18357. 384p. 1981. pap. 39.95 (*0-8058-0432-3*) L Erlbaum Assocs.

Press & Society. R. D. Parikh. 154p. 1965. 9.95 (*0-318-37280-0*) Asia Bk Corp.

Press & Society: From Caxton to Northcliffe. Geoffrey A. Cranfield. LC 77-21904. (Themes in British Social History). 250p. reprint ed. pap. 77.50 (*0-8357-3502-8*, 203448800090) Bks Demand.

Press & Speech Freedoms in America, 1619-1995: A Chronology. Compiled by Louis E. Ingelhart. LC 96-41287. 384p. 1997. lib. bdg. 75.00 (*0-313-30174-3*, Greenwood Pr) Greenwood.

Press & Speech Freedoms in the World, from Antiquity until 1998: A Chronology. Louis E. Ingelhart. LC 98-21823. 320p. 1998. lib. bdg. 69.50 (*0-313-30851-9*, Greenwood Pr) Greenwood.

Press & the Bush Presidency. Mark J. Rozell. LC 96-10429. (Presidential Studies). 200p. 1996. 57.95 (*0-275-95653-9*, Praeger Pubs) Greenwood.

Press & the Cold War. exp. ed. James Aronson. 352p. 1990. 33.00 (*0-85345-805-7*, Pub. by Monthly Rev); pap. 16.00 (*0-85345-806-5*, Pub. by Monthly Rev) NYU Pr.

Press & the Constitution, 1931-1947. J. Edward Gerald. 1990. 16.50 (*0-8446-0641-3*) Peter Smith.

Press & the Decline of Democracy: The Democratic Socialist Response in Public Policy, 4. Robert G. Picard. LC 85-5585. (Contributions to the Study of Mass Media & Communications Ser.: No. 4). (Illus.). 176p. 1985. 49.95 (*0-313-24915-6*, PPD/) Greenwood.

Press & the Ford Presidency. Mark J. Rozell. LC 92-8700. 264p. (C). 1992. text 49.50 (*0-472-10350-4*, 10350) U of Mich Pr.

Press & the Modern Presidency: Myths & Mindsets from Kennedy to Clinton. Louis W. Liebovich. LC 97-23010. 256p. 1998. 59.95 (*0-275-95926-0*, Praeger Pubs) Greenwood.

Press & the Origins of the Cold War, 1944-1947. Louis W. Liebovich. LC 87-38478. 181p. 1988. 55.00 (*0-275-92999-X*, C2999, Praeger Pubs) Greenwood.

Press & the Rebirth of Iberian Democracy, 99. Ed. by Kenneth Maxwell. LC 82-24201. (Contributions in Political Science Ser.: No. 99). (Illus.). 198p. 1983. 57.95 (*0-313-23100-1*, MPI/, Greenwood Pr) Greenwood.

Press & the State: Sociohistorical & Contemporary Interpretations. Walter M. Brasch & Dana R. Ulloth. LC 86-15855. 826p. (Orig.). (C). 1987. lib. bdg. 84.00 (*0-8191-5502-0*) U Pr of Amer.

Press & the Suburbs: The Daily Newspapers of New Jersey. David Sachsman & Warren Sloat. LC 85-5934. 151p. (Orig.). 1985. pap. text 1.00 (*0-88285-108-X*) Ctr Urban Pol Res.

Press & Working Class Consciousness in Developing Societies. Manu Bhaskar. 130p. 1988. 10.00 (*81-212-0246-9*, Pub. by Gian Publng Hse) S Asia.

Press & World Affairs. Robert W. Desmond. LC 72-4665. (International Propaganda & Communications Ser.). (Illus.). 449p. 1972. reprint ed. 27.95 (*0-405-04746-0*) Ayer.

Press As Public Educator. Lutton Staff. 1997. pap. 29.95 (*1-86020-536-4*, Pub. by U of Luton Pr) Bks Intl VA.

Press Beyond Calcutta-North & East. Katherine S. Diehl. (Printers & Printing in the East Indies to 1850 Ser.: Vol. VI). write for info. (*0-89241-395-6*) Caratzas.

Press Box & City Room. Peter L. Simpson & George H. Gurley. LC 87-72141. 120p. 1988. 10.95 (*0-933532-62-8*) BkMk.

Press Brake Technology: A Guide to Precision Sheet Metal Bending. Steve D. Benson. LC 96-70755. (Illus.). 212p. 1997. 48.00 (*0-87263-483-3*, 2545) SME.

Press Censorship in Elizabethan England. Cyndia S. Clegg. 312p. (C). 1997. text 64.95 (*0-521-57312-2*) Cambridge U Pr.

Press Concentration & Monopoly: New Perspectives on Newspaper Ownership & Operation. Ed. by Robert G. Picard et al. LC 87-33328. (Communication & Information Science Ser.). 256p. 1988. text 73.25 (*0-89391-464-9*) Ablx Pub.

Press Control Around the World. Jane L. Curry. LC 82-9837. 283p. 1982. 39.95 (*0-275-90775-9*, C0775, Praeger Pubs) Greenwood.

Press Corps of Old Shanghai. Malcolm Rosholt. (Illus.). 36p. (Orig.). 1994. pap. write for info. (*0-910417-10-5*) Rosholt Hse.

Press Corpse. Ron Nessen. (Knight & Day Ser.). 224p. 1997. mass mkt. 5.99 (*0-8125-6793-5*, Pub. by Forge NYC) St Martin.

Press Council: A Self Regulatory Mechanism for the Indian Press. N. K. Trikha. (C). 1987. 26.00 (*81-7039-121-1*, Pub. by Somaiya) S Asia.

Press During the Hungarian Revolution. Dominic G. Kosary. 374p. 1987. text 79.50 (*0-88033-091-0*, Pub. by East Eur Monographs) Col U Pr.

Press Enter & Hawksbill Station. John Varley & Robert Silverberg. 1990. pap. 3.50 (*0-8125-5948-7*, Pub. by Tor Bks) St Martin.

Press, Film, Radio, 5 vols. UNESCO Staff. LC 72-4683. (International Propaganda & Communications Ser.). 2114p. 1972. reprint ed. 39.95 (*0-405-04773-8*) Ayer.

Press, Film, Radio, 5 vols., Set. UNESCO Staff. LC 72-4683. (International Propaganda & Communications Ser.). 2114p. 1972. reprint ed. 116.95 (*0-405-04767-3*) Ayer.

Press, Film, Radio, 5 vols., Vol. 1. UNESCO Staff. LC 72-4683. (International Propaganda & Communications Ser.). 2114p. 1972. reprint ed. 39.95 (*0-405-04772-X*) Ayer.

Press, Film, Radio, 5 vols., Vol. 5. UNESCO Staff. LC 72-4683. (International Propaganda & Communications Ser.). 2114p. 1972. reprint ed. 39.95 (*0-405-04774-6*) Ayer.

Press for Success: Secrets for Precise & Speedy Quiltmaking. Myrna Giesbrecht. LC 95-26023. (Joy of Quilting Ser.). (Illus.). 52p. (Orig.). 1996. pap. 12.95 (*1-56477-136-9*, B253) Martingale & Co.

Press Freedom & Communication in Africa. Festus Eribo. LC 97-13289. 1997. pap. text 21.95 (*0-86543-551-0*) Africa World.

Press Freedom & Communication in Africa. Festus Eribo & William Jong-Ebot. LC 97-13289. 1997. 79.95 (*0-86543-550-2*) Africa World.

Press Freedom & Development: A Research Guide & Selected Bibliography, 11. Clement E. Asante. LC 97-21983. (Bibliographies & Indexes in Mass Media & Communications Ser.: 11). 232p. 1997. lib. bdg. 75.00 (*0-313-29994-3*, Greenwood Pr) Greenwood.

***Press Freedom & Global Politics.** Douglas A. Van Belle. LC 99-43102. 184p. 2000. 59.95 (*0-275-96790-5*, Praeger Pubs) Greenwood.

Press Freedom in Africa. Gunilla L. Faringer. LC 90-24509. 160p. 1991. 47.95 (*0-275-93771-2*, C3771, Praeger Pubs) Greenwood.

Press Freedoms: A Descriptive Calender of Concepts, Interpretations, Events & Court Actions, from 4000 BC to the Present. Louis E. Ingelhart. LC 86-31834. 449p. 1987. lib. bdg. 85.00 (*0-313-25636-5*, IPF/, Greenwood Pr) Greenwood.

Press Gallery: Congress & the Washington Correspondents. Donald A. Ritchie. LC 90-43676. (Illus.). 288p. 1991. 42.00 (*0-674-70375-8*, RITPRE) HUP.

Press Gallery: Congress & the Washington Correspondents. Donald A. Ritchie. (Illus.). 312p. 1992. pap. 18.00 (*0-674-70376-6*) HUP.

Press Gang: Newspapers & Politics, 1865-1878. Mark W. Summers. LC 93-36489. (Illus.). xvi, 406p. (C). 1994. pap. 19.95 (*0-8078-4446-2*); text 55.00 (*0-8078-2140-3*) U of NC Pr.

Press Ideas. Dock. 679p. 1996. pap. 38.95 (*0-312-13319-7*) St Martin.

Press Ideas/Online. Dock. 1997. pap. text 28.60 (*0-312-18788-2*) St Martin.

Press in Authoritarian Countries see International Press Institute Surveys

Press in Colonial Queensland: A Social & Political History, 1845-1875. Denis Cryle. (Illus.). 350p. (Orig.). 1989. pap. text 29.95 (*0-7022-2181-3*, Pub. by Univ Queensland Pr) Intl Spec Bk.

Press in English Society from the Seventeenth to the Nineteenth Centuries. Ed. by Michael Harris & Alan J. Lee. LC 85-45535. (Illus.). 264p. 1986. 44.50 (*0-8386-3272-6*) Fairleigh Dickinson.

Press in Ghana: Problems & Prospects. Clement E. Asante. 230p. (C). 1995. lib. bdg. 42.50 (*0-7618-0167-7*) U Pr of Amer.

Press in India. R. C. Sarkar. 320p. 1984. 32.95 (*0-318-37287-8*) Asia Bk Corp.

Press in India: A New History. G. N. Raghaven. (C). 1994. 28.50 (*81-212-0482-8*, Pub. by Gian Publng Hse) S Asia.

Press in New Order Indonesia. David T. Hill. LC 97-102049. (Asia Papers: No. 4). pap. 18.95 (*1-875560-53-X*, Pub. by Univ of West Aust Pr) Intl Spec Bk.

P

Press in Nigeria: An Annotated Bibliography, 12. Compiled by Chris W. Ogbondah. LC 90-3676. (African Special Bibliographic Ser.: No. 12). 144p. 1990. lib. bdg. 47.95 (*0-313-26521-6*, OPN/, Greenwood Pr) Greenwood.

Press in Perspective. Ed. by Ralph D. Casey. LC 63-16657. 235p. reprint ed. pap. 72.90 (*0-608-14446-0*, 205187600013) Bks Demand.

Press in South Africa. Keyan Tomaselli et al. (Studies on the South African Media). 264p. (C). 1990. 35.00 (*0-941702-24-3*); pap. 19.95 (*0-620-10575-5*) Lake View Pr.

Press in Tamil Nadu & the Struggle for Freedom, 1917-1937. A. Ganesan. (C). 1988. 19.00 (*81-7099-082-3*, Pub. by Mittal Pubs Dist) S Asia.

Press in the French Revolution. Ed. by W. Gilchrist & W. J. Murray. LC 77-150256. 1971. 67.50 (*0-89197-596-9*) Irvington.

Press in Times of Crisis. Ed. by Lloyd E. Chiasson, Jr. LC 95-2903. 272p. 1995. pap. 24.95 (*0-275-95340-8*, Praeger Pubs) Greenwood.

Press in Times of Crisis: An Historical Analysis, 48. Ed. by Lloyd E. Chiasson, Jr. LC 95-2903. (Contributions to the Study of Mass Media & Communications Ser.: No. 48). 272p. 1995. 65.00 (*0-313-29364-3*, Greenwood Pr) Greenwood.

Press Law & Press Freedom for High School Publications: Court Cases & Related Decisions Discussing Free Expression Guarantees & Limitations for High School Students & Journalists, 6. Louis E. Ingelhart. LC 85-24807. (Contributions to the Study of Mass Media & Communications Ser.: No. 6). 178p. 1986. 49.95 (*0-313-25154-1*, IPL/) Greenwood.

Press Law in South Korea. Kyulto Youm. LC 96-341. 456p. 1996. text 41.95 (*0-8138-2327-7*) Iowa St U Pr.

Press Manning. 129.95 (*0-614-25564-3*, 00IR19020) Print Indus Am.

Press Mess. Page McBrier. (Treehouse Times Ser.: No. 6). 128p. (Orig.). (J). (gr. 4-5). 1990. pap. 2.95 (*0-380-75900-4*, Avon Bks) Morrow Avon.

Press of Ideas. 2nd ed. Dock. 2000. pap. text 31.95 (*0-312-20182-6*) St Martin.

Press of Latin America: A Tentative & Selected Bibliography in Spanish & Portuguese. Mary A. Gardner. LC 72-619723. (Guides & Bibliographies Ser.: No. 4). 44p. reprint ed. pap. 30.00 (*0-608-16495-X*, 202733000055) Bks Demand.

Press of the Young Republic, 1783-1833, 2. Carol S. Humphrey. LC 96-7140. (History of American Journalism Ser.). 200p. 1996. 59.95 (*0-313-28406-7*, Greenwood Pr) Greenwood.

Press On! An Overview of Printing - Binding. Maria E. den Boer. (Author's Assistant Ser.: Vol. 8). (Illus.). 10p. 1999. 3.95 (*1-928929-07-9*) Blue Thunder.

Press On! Further Adventures in the Good Life. large type ed. Chuck Yeager & Charles Leerhsen. (General Ser.). 350p. 1989. lib. bdg. 18.95 (*0-8161-4751-5*, G K Hall Lrg Type) Mac Lib Ref.

Press On: I'll Meet You at the Gate. Jo Ann Fox. (Illus.). 480p. (Orig.). 1987. pap. 20.95 (*0-944039-03-0*) Van Winkle Pr.

Press on Trial: Crimes & Trials As Media Events. Ed. by Lloyd Chiasson, Jr. LC 96-53030. (Contributions to the Study of Media & Communications Ser.). 248p. 1997. pap. 23.95 (*0-275-95936-8*, Praeger Pubs) Greenwood.

Press on Trial: Crimes & Trials As Media Events, 51. Ed. by Lloyd Chiasson, Jr. LC 96-53030. (Contributions to the Study of Media & Communications Ser.: Vol. 51). 248p. 1997. 59.95 (*0-313-30022-4*, Greenwood Pr) Greenwood.

Press 1 for More Options: Poems by Lynn M. Skapyak. Lynn M. Skapyak. 30p. 1997. pap. 4.95 (*1-891232-01-0*, Closet Bks) R Crane Pub.

Press Operator. Jack Rudman. (Career Examination Ser.: C-3190). 1994. pap. 27.95 (*0-8373-3190-0*) Nat Learn.

Press Pass, the Journalist's Tale. Sidney L. James. 478p. 1994. pap. 12.80 (*0-89412-230-4*) Aegean Park Pr.

Press, Politics, & Perserverance: Everett C. Johnson & The Press of Kells. Robert C. Barnes & Judith M. Pfeiffer. LC 98-31420. (Illus.). 320p. 1998. write for info. (*1-884718-82-5*) Oak Knoll.

Press, Politics, & Power: Egypt's Heikal & Al-Ahram. Munir K. Nassar. LC 79-11924. 183p. 1979. reprint ed. pap. 56.80 (*0-608-00075-2*, 206083800006) Bks Demand.

***Press, Politics & Society: Uttar Pradesh, 1885-1914.** Kirti Narain. LC 98-905069. 1998. 20.00 (*81-7304-223-3*, Pub. by Manohar) S Asia.

Press, Politics & Votes for women, 1910, 1918. Ragnhild Nessheim. 384p. 1997. pap. 45.00 (*82-00-12695-1*) Scandnvan Univ Pr.

Press, Presidents, & Crises. Brigitte L. Nacos. 288p. 1990. text 44.00 (*0-231-07064-0*) Col U Pr.

Press Restrictions in Albania. MN. Advocates for Human Rights Staff. 23p. (Orig.). 1995. pap. 7.50 (*0-929293-29-0*) MN Advocates.

Press, the Rosenbergs & the Cold War. John F. Neville. LC 94-22655. 224p. 1995. 57.95 (*0-275-94995-8*, Praeger Pubs) Greenwood.

Press Time. 3rd ed. Julian Adams & Kenneth Stratton. 1975. text 21.80 (*0-13-699041-X*) P-H.

Press Tool Making. 1982. 50.00 (*0-7855-2882-2*) St Mut.

Press Tools & Presswork. John A. Waller. 454p. (C). 1985. 295.00 (*0-86108-168-4*, Pub. by Fuel Metallurgical Jrnl) St Mut.

Press Tools & Presswork. 3rd ed. Ed. by John A. Waller. (C). 1989. 395.00 (*0-7855-6858-1*, Pub. by Fuel Metallurgical Jrnl) St Mut.

Press Toward the Mark: History of the United Lutheran Synod of New York & New England, 1830-1930. Robert F. Scholz. LC 95-11378. (ATLA Monographs: No. 37). (Illus.). 470p. 1995. 52.00 (*0-8108-3026-4*) Scarecrow.

Press under Siege: Censorship in Indonesia. Article 19 (Organization) Staff. LC 95-126155. ii, 31 p. 1994. write for info. (*1-870798-62-7*) Article Nineteen.

Press vs. the Government. D. R. Mankekar. 187p. 1978. 14.95 (*0-318-37288-6*) Asia Bk Corp.

Pressburg under Siege. Moshe Safer. 96p. (C). 1991. 8.95 (*1-56062-078-1*); pap. 6.95 (*1-56062-079-X*) CIS Comm.

Presse de la Liberte: Journee d'etudes Organisee par le Groupe de Travail IFLA sur les Journaux, Paris le 24 aout 1989. Ed. by Carol Henry. (IFLA Publications: Vol. 58). iv, 122p. 1991. 48.00 (*3-598-21786-2*) K G Saur Verlag.

Presse et le Mouvement National Chez les Musulmans De Russie Avant 1920 see Mouvements Nationaux Chez les Musulmans de Russie

Pressearchiv Zur Geschichte Deutschlands Sowie Zur Internationalen Politik Von, 1949-1960: Index. Compiled by Erdmunte Horn-Sauder & Michael Peschke. xvi, 252p. 1996. pap. write for info. (*3-598-33853-8*) K G Saur Verlag.

Pressed Against Divinity: W. B. Yeats's Feminine Masks. Janis T. Haswell. LC 96-43942. 192p. 1997. lib. bdg. 32.00 (*0-87580-222-2*) N Ill U Pr.

Pressed down but Looking Up. Joy Haney. 1993. pap. 8.95 (*1-880969-03-3*) Schl Prophet.

Pressed down but Not Forgotten: Depression. H. Curtis Lyon & John Juern. LC 93-84289. 112p. 1993. 11.99 (*0-8100-0490-9*, 15N2001) Northwest Pub.

Pressed Flint Glass. Raymond Notley. (Album Ser.: No. 162). (Illus.). 32p. 1999. pap. 5.25 (*0-85263-782-9*, Pub. by Shire Pubns) Parkwest Pubns.

Pressed Flower Crafting. Judy Neave. (Illus.). 32p. (Orig.). 1994. pap. 8.95 (*1-884555-03-9*) P Depke Bks.

Pressed Flower Pictures. Raymond Foster. (Illus.). 96p. 1995. write for info. (*1-85391-482-7*, Pub. by Merehurst Ltd) Sterling.

Pressed Flowercraft. Lorenz. 1999. 12.95 (*1-85967-904-8*, Lorenz Bks) Anness Pub.

Pressed Flowers. Pamela Le Bailly. (Illus.). 76p. 1996. 18.95 (*1-870586-14-X*, D Porteous-Parkwest) Parkwest Pubns.

***Pressed Flowers.** Pamela Le Bailly. (Illus.). 1999. pap. 15.95 (*1-870586-37-9*, D Porteous-Parkwest) Parkwest Pubns.

Pressed Flowers: A Creative Guide. Cathy Bussi. 72p. (C). 1988. 75.00 (*1-85368-010-9*, Pub. by New5 Holland) St Mut.

Pressed Glass Toothpick Holders Identification & Values. Neila Bredehoft et al. LC 99-462674. 208p. 1999. 24.95 (*1-57432-127-7*) Collector Bks.

Pressed Melodeon. Ben Howard. 192p. (Orig.). 1996. pap. 12.95 (*1-885266-24-3*) Story Line.

***Pressed Plant: The Art of Botanical Specimens, Nature Prints & Sun Prints.** Andrea DiNoto & David Winter. LC 99-16501. (Illus.). 160p. 1999. text 29.95 (*1-55670-936-6*) STC Pubns.

Presser. Jack Rudman. (Career Examination Ser.: C-1397). 1994. pap. 27.95 (*0-8373-1397-X*) Nat Learn.

Presses: Presses, Feeds, Guards, Brake Monitors. Society of Manufacturing Engineers Staff. LC 84-52742. (Productivity Equipment Ser.). (Illus.). 694p. reprint ed. pap. 200.00 (*0-8357-6472-9*, 203584300097) Bks Demand.

Pressing Business: An Organizational Manual for Independent Publishers. Volunteer Lawyers for the Arts Staff & Barbara S. Taylor. LC 85-8876. 59p. 1984. 9.95 (*0-917103-01-7*) Vol Lawyers Arts.

Pressing Ceramics with Air Release. Reid Harvey. (Illus.). 28p. 1996. reprint ed. pap. 9.95 (*1-889250-00-7*) Gentle Br.

Pressing for Peace: Can Aid Induce Reform? Nicole Ball. LC 92-31498. (Policy Essay Ser.: No. 6). 96p. (C). 1992. pap. 13.95 (*1-56517-006-7*) Overseas Dev Council.

***Pressing Forward with the Book of Mormon.** John W. Welch et al. LC 99-36849. 1999. pap. write for info. (*0-934893-42-X*, F A R M S) Brigham.

Pressing Ideas. Dock. 1996. pap. text, teacher ed. 5.00 (*0-312-13318-9*) St Martin.

Pressing In: It's Worth It All. Gloria Copeland. 29p. 1992. pap. 1.00 (*0-88114-842-3*) K Copeland Pubns.

Pressing into the Kingdom: Jonathan Edwards on Seeking Salvation. Jonathan Edwards. Ed. by Don Kistler. 350p. 1998. 26.95 (*1-57358-087-2*) Soli Deo Gloria.

Pressing Issues of Inequality & American Indian Communities. Ed. by Elizabeth A. Segal & Keith M. Kilty. LC 98-38650. 98p. 1998. 29.95 (*0-7890-0663-4*) Haworth Pr.

***Pressing on with Joy: Fulfilling Your Destiny Through Transformation.** Paul Crum. 173p. 1999. pap. 10.00 (*1-929595-03-4*) Hrvst Pubns.

Pressing Point Massage: Applications for Internal Healing. Wang Jin Huai & Andrew Nugent-Head. 84p. pap. 13.50 (*1-888179-55-4*) Assn For Tradit.

Pressing Problems for Toady's World. Mason Scott et al. (Illus.). 220p. 1990. pap. 9.50 (*0-933704-83-6*) Dawn Pr.

Pressing Problems in Law: Criminal Justice & Human Rights. Ed. by Peter B. H. Birks. 176p. 1995. pap. text 42.00 (*0-19-826042-3*) OUP.

Pressing Problems in Law Vol. 2: What are Law Schools for? Ed. by Peter B. H. Birks. LC 97-111444. 138p. 1996. pap. text 55.00 (*0-19-826293-0*) OUP.

***Pressing Problems in Modern Organizations (That Keep Us Up at Night) Transforming Agendas for Research & Practice.** Robert E. Quinn et al. LC 99-32844. (Illus.). 290p. 1999. 34.95 (*0-8144-7052-1*) AMACOM.

Pressing Tasks of China's Economic Transition. Chi Fulin. 296p. 1996. pap. 14.95 (*7-119-01967-8*, Pub. by Foreign Lang) China Bks.

***Pressing the Point: Parallel Expressions in the Graphic Arts of the Chicano & Puerto Rican Movement.** Yasmin Ramirez & Henry Estrada. (ENG & SPA., Illus.). 56p. 1999. pap. write for info. (*1-882454-09-X*) El Museo Barrio.

Pressing Toward the Mark. Richard Booker. 72p. (Orig.). 1994. wbk. ed. 9.95 (*0-9615302-8-6*) Sounds of Trumpet Inc.

Pressing Toward the Mark: Essays Commemorating Fifty Years of the Orthodox Presbyterian Church (1936-1986) Ed. by Charles G. Dennison & Richard C. Gamble. 489p. 1986. pap. 11.95 (*0-934688-36-2*) Comm Hist Orthodox.

Pressland's Great Book of Tin Toys. David Pressland. (Illus.). 335p. 1995. 250.00 (*1-872727-31-X*) Pincushion Pr.

Pressroom Manager's Guidebook. 3rd ed. Frank Drazan. (Illus.). 112p. 1989. pap. 20.00 (*0-318-21788-0*) F Drazan.

Pressroom Manager's Training Guide. 165p. spiral bd. 100.00 (*0-318-23319-3*) F Drazan.

Presstime in Paradise: The Life & Times of The Honolulu Advertiser, 1856-1995. George Chaplin. LC 97-35954. (Illus.). 480p. 1998. text 42.00 (*0-8248-1963-2*, Latitude Twenty); pap. text 29.95 (*0-8248-2032-0*, Latitude Twenty) UH Pr.

Pressure. Ron Marson. (Task Cards Ser.: No. 16). (Illus.). 80p. 1992. teacher ed. 14.50 (*0-941008-86-X*) Tops Learning.

Pressure at Work. Tanya Arroba & Kim James. 208p. 1989. pap. 11.95 (*0-07-084931-5*) McGraw.

Pressure Boys: The Inside Story of Lobbying in America. Kenneth G. Crawford. LC 73-19139. (Politics & People Ser.). 320p. 1974. reprint ed. 23.95 (*0-405-05864-0*) Ayer.

Pressure Buildup & Flow Tests in Wells. C. S. Matthews & D. G. Russell. 163p. 1967. 47.00 (*0-89520-200-X*, FEMONO001) Soc Petrol Engineers.

Pressure Cooker: Thermal Properties of Matter. Malcolm K. Smith & John W. McWane. (Physics of Technology Ser.). 82p. 1975. 17.00 (*0-07-001730-1*, PT-5) Am Assn Physics.

***Pressure Cooker Cookbook.** Ed. by Better Homes & Gardens. LC 95-75621. (Better Homes & Gardens Ser.). (Illus.). 96p. 2000. 12.95 (*0-696-21215-3*) Meredith Bks.

Pressure Cooker Cookbook. Toula Patsoulis. 208p. (Orig.). 1994. pap. 12.00 (*1-55788-189-8*, HP Books) Berkley Pub.

Pressure Cookers, UL 136. 6th ed. (C). 1995. pap. text 175.00 (*1-55989-901-8*) Underwrtrs Labs.

***Pressure Cooking for Everyone.** Rick Rodgers & Arlene Ward. LC 99-53959. 2001. pap. 19.95 (*0-8118-2525-6*) Chronicle Bks.

Pressure Cooking the Easy Way: Home-Cooked Flavors for Today's Easy-to-Use Pressure Cookers. Maureen B. Keane & Daniella Chace. LC 97-40598. 208p. 1997. per. 12.00 (*0-7615-1285-3*) Prima Pub.

Pressure Cooking the Meatless Way: Over 125 Delicious & Nutritious Recipes for Today's Busy Cooks. Daniella B. Chace & Maureen B. Keane. 216p. 1996. per. 14.95 (*0-7615-0032-4*) Prima Pub.

Pressure Effects on Materials Processing & Design. Ed. by Kozo Ishizaki et al. (Symposium Proceedings Ser.: Vol. 251). 343p. 1992. text 30.00 (*1-55899-145-X*) Materials Res.

Pressure for the Poor: The Poverty Lobby & Policy Making. Paul Whiteley & Stephen Winyard. 250p. 1987. lib. bdg. 67.50 (*0-416-36370-9*) Routledge.

Pressure Games for Golf: Games to Play on the Practice Tee to Deal with Pressure on the Course. George Haughton. (Illus.). 122p. (Orig.). 1988. pap. 9.95 (*0-945151-00-4*) Pk One Thous.

Pressure Garments: A Manual on Their Design & Fabrication. Joanne Pratt & Gil West. LC 94-33550. (Illus.). 160p. 1995. pap. text 50.00 (*0-7506-2064-1*) Buttrwrth-Heinemann.

Pressure Gauge Handbook. Ed. by Philip W. Harland. LC 85-13054. (Mechanical Engineering Ser.: Vol. 40). (Illus.). 312p. 1985. reprint ed. pap. 96.80 (*0-608-08005-5*, 206797000012) Bks Demand.

Pressure Gauges. EEMUA Staff. 1972. 75.00 (*0-7855-3009-6*, Pub. by EEMUA) St Mut.

Pressure Groups. Central Office of Info. LC 95-189767. (Aspects of Britain Ser.). (Illus.). 84p. 1997. pap. 12.00 (*0-11-701849-X*, HM1849X, Pub. by Statnry Office) Bernan Associates.

Pressure Groups. Ed. by Jeremy J. Richardson. LC 92-42267. (Readings in Politics & Government Ser.). (Illus.). 282p. 1993. pap. text 18.95 (*0-19-878052-4*) OUP.

Pressure Groups among "Small Businessmen" Roger S. Pepper. Ed. by Stuart Bruchey & Vincent P. Carosso. LC 78-18973. (Small Business Enterprise in America Ser.). 1979. lib. bdg. 15.95 (*0-405-11476-1*) Ayer.

Pressure Groups & British Politics. Grant Staff. LC 99-23758. 2000. text 55.00 (*0-312-22648-9*) St Martin.

Pressure Groups & Government in Great Britain. Geoffrey Alderman. LC 83-733. 172p. reprint ed. pap. 53.40 (*0-7837-1592-7*, 204188400024) Bks Demand.

Pressure on Education. John Brynin. 240p. 1993. 66.95 (*1-85628-339-9*, Pub. by Avebry) Ashgate Pub Co.

Pressure on the Public. Ed. by Mitchell Kane. (Illus.). 88p. (Orig.). 1992. pap. 20.00 (*1-881616-04-5*) Dist Art Pubs.

Pressure Pipe & Couplings, Glass Fiber-Reinforced, for Underground Fire Service, UL 1713. 2nd ed. (C). 1995. pap. text 95.00 (*1-55989-802-X*) Underwrtrs Labs.

Pressure Play. Matt Christopher. (Illus.). 168p. (J). (gr. 3-7). 1995. pap. 3.95 (*0-316-14121-6*) Little.

Pressure Play. Matt Christopher. 1993. 9.30 (*0-606-08042-2*) Turtleback.

Pressure Point. large type ed. Basil Copper. (Linford Mystery Library). 1991. pap. 16.99 (*0-7089-7085-0*) Ulverscroft.

***Pressure-Point Fighting: A Guide to the Secret Heart of Asian Martial Arts.** Rick Clark. (Illus.). 196p. 2000. pap. 19.95 (*0-8048-3217-X*) Tuttle Pubng.

Pressure Point Karate Made Easy: A Guide to the Dillman Pressure Point Method for Beginners & Younger Martial Artists. George A. Dillman & Chris Thomas. LC 97-68274. (Illus.). 144p. (YA). (gr. 7 up). 1999. pap. 14.95 (*1-889267-02-3*, Pub. by G Dillman Karate) Assoc Pubs Grp.

Pressure Point Therapy: The Complete Do-It-Yourself. Michael Pinkus. LC 94-94008. (At Home Treatment Manual Ser.). (Illus.). 58p. (Orig.). 1994. pap. 29.90 (*0-9640393-0-3*) Alternat Hlth.

Pressure Point Therapy System: The Complete Book, Video & Chart Pack. Michael Pinkus. (Illus.). 65p. 1995. pap. 79.90 incl. VHS (*0-9640393-3-8*) Alternat Hlth.

Pressure Points. Peggy Overstein. 1999. write for info. (*0-679-45288-5*) McKay.

Pressure Points. unabridged ed. Terri Warden. 20p. 1995. pap. 5.00 (*1-929326-46-7*) Hal Bar Pubg.

Pressure Points: Stress. Dave Carlson. (Inter Acta Ser.). (Illus.). 6p. (C). 1994. teacher ed., ring bd. 1.25 (*1-885702-95-7*, 741-060t, Inter Acta); student ed., ring bd. 3.25 (*1-885702-94-9*, 741-060s, Inter Acta) WSN Pr.

Pressure, Power & Policy: Policy Networks & State Autonomy in Britain & the United States. Martin J. Smith. (Political Science Ser.). 272p. (C). 1993. pap. 22.95 (*0-8229-5522-9*) U of Pittsburgh Pr.

Pressure Regulating Valves for LP-Gas, UL 144. 7th ed. (C). 1999. pap. text 135.00 (*1-55989-597-7*) Underwrtrs Labs.

Pressure Safety Design Practices for Refinery & Chemical Operations. Nicholas P. Cheremisinoff. LC 97-46603. (Illus.). 384p. 1998. 145.00 (*0-8155-1414-X*) Noyes.

Pressure Sensitive: Popular Musicians under Stress. Geoff Wills & Cary L. Cooper. (Communications in Society Ser.). 160p. (C). 1988. text 42.75 (*0-8039-8141-4*); pap. text 16.95 (*0-8039-8142-2*) Sage.

Pressure-Sensitive Adhesives & Applications. Istran Benedek & Luc J. Heymans. LC 96-31582. (Illus.). 616p. 1996. text 195.00 (*0-8247-9765-5*) Dekker.

Pressure Sensors. Richard K. Miller & Terri C. Walker. LC 88-84054. (Survey on Technology & Markets Ser.: No. 48). 50p. 1989. pap. text 200.00 (*1-55865-106-3*) Future Tech Surveys.

Pressure Sensors: Selection & Application. Ed. by Duane Tandeske. (Mechanical Engineering Ser.: Vol. 72). (Illus.). 312p. 1990. text 155.00 (*0-8247-8365-4*) Dekker.

Pressure Sore Prevention. Dickson Weir-Hughes et al. (Illus.). 118p. (Orig.). 1996. pap. 24.95 (*1-56593-818-6*, 1608) Singular Publishing.

Pressure Sores. Jenny Phillips. LC 97-17573. (Access to Clinical Education Ser.). 1997. text 65.00 (*0-443-05532-7*) Church.

Pressure Sores. Betty Garee. LC 87-71477. 32p. (Orig.). 1987. reprint ed. pap. 3.50 (*0-915708-20-5*) Cheever Pub.

Pressure Surge in Pipe & Duct Systems. J. A. Swaffield & Adrian P. Boldy. 358p. 1993. 109.95 (*0-291-39796-4*) Ashgate Pub Co.

Pressure Swing Absorption. Douglas M. Ruthven et al. LC 93-33965. 1993. 95.00 (*1-56081-517-5*, Wiley-VCH) Wiley.

Pressure Swing Adsorption. D. M. Ruthven & S. Farooq. 376p. 1993. 165.00 (*0-471-18818-2*, Wiley-VCH) Wiley.

***Pressure Tennis.** Paul Wardlaw. LC 99-59765. (Illus.). 216p. 2000. pap. 17.95 (*0-7360-0156-5*) Human Kinetics.

Pressure Ulcer in Adults. 1995. lib. bdg. 251.95 (*0-8490-6778-2*) Gordon Pr.

Pressure Ulcer Treatment 15: Reference for Clinicians. Nancy Bergstrom. 27p. 1994. pap. 32.00 (*0-16-061538-0*) USGPO.

***Pressure Ulcers: Guidelines for Prevention & Management.** 3rd ed. JoAnn Maklebust & Mary Sieggreen. LC 00-44625. P. ;p. 2000. write for info. (*1-58255-035-2*) Springhouse Corp.

Pressure Ulcers: Guidelines for Prevention & Nursing Management. 2nd ed. JoAnn Maklebust & Mary Sieggreen. 320p. 1995. pap. 34.95 (*0-87434-836-6*) Springhouse Corp.

Pressure Ulcers: Principles & Techniques of Management. Ed. by Mark B. Constantian. 320p. 1980. text 50.00 (*0-316-15330-3*, Little Brwn Med Div) Lppncott W & W.

Pressure Ulcers in Adults: Prediction & Prevention. (Illus.). 73p. (Orig.). (C). 1994. pap. text 20.00 (*0-7881-0469-1*) DIANE Pub.

Pressure Ulcers in Adults: Prediction & Prevention, Quick Reference Guide for Clinicians. 1993. pap. write for info. (*0-16-042255-8*) USGPO.

Pressure Ulcers in Adults No. 3: Prediction & Prevention, Clinical Practice Guidelines. 75p. 1993. pap. 3.75 (*0-16-042253-1*) USGPO.

Pressure under Grace. William Greenway. LC 82-1284. 45p. 1982. pap. 5.95 (*0-932576-10-9*) Breitenbush Bks.

Pressure Vessel Analysis. David Burgreen. 363p. 1979. 48.00 (*0-916877-05-1*) Arcturus Pubs.

Pressure Vessel & Piping Codes & Standards, 1998: Proceedings, ASME/JSME Joint Pressure Vessels & Piping Conference (1998, San Diego, CA) Ed. by Bernard Lubin. LC 98-207927. 360. 536p. 1998. pap. 140.00 (*0-7918-1865-9*) ASME.

P

An Asterisk (*) at the beginning of an entry indicates that the title is appearing for the first time.

Pressure Vessel & Piping Technology. J. S. Cheung & L. S. Ong. 528p. 1993. text 121.00 (*981-02-1435-9*) World Scientific Pub.

Pressure Vessel & Piping, 1972 Computer Programs Verification: An Aid to Developers & Users. Ed. by I. S. Tuba & W. B. Wright. LC 72-94235. (Illus.). 199p. reprint ed. pap. 61.70 (*0-608-30485-9*, 201690600005) Bks Demand.

Pressure Vessel Design: Concepts & Principles. Ed. by Spence & A. S. Tooth. LC 92-31293. (Illus.). 512p. (C). 1994. 160.00 (*0-419-19080-5*, E & FN Spon) Routledge.

Pressure Vessel Design: 36 Miscellaneous Computer Programs. B. Fred Forman & Technical Research Service, Inc. Staff. 495.00 (*0-914458-13-2*) Pressure Vessel.

Pressure Vessel Design Handbook. 2nd ed. Henry H. Bednar. LC 90-5043. 446p. (C). 1990. 62.50 (*0-89464-503-X*) Krieger.

Pressure Vessel Design Manual. 2nd ed. Dennis R. Moss. LC 97-24025. 1997. 115.00 (*0-88415-647-8*, 5647) Gulf Pub.

Pressure Vessel Design Manual: Illustrated Procedures for Solving Every Major Pressure Vessel Design Problem. Dennis R. Moss. LC 87-360. (Illus.). 236p. 1987. 89.00 (*0-87201-719-2*, 1719) Gulf Pub.

Pressure Vessel Handbook. 10th ed. Eugene F. Megyesy. 490p. 1995. 118.00 (*0-914458-18-3*) Pressure Vessel.

***Pressure Vessel Handbook.** 11th ed. Eugene F. Megyesy. LC 98-91427. (Illus.). 1998. write for info. (*0-914458-19-1*) Pressure Vessel.

Pressure Vessel Integrity - 1993. Ed. by W. E. Pennell. (PVP Ser.: Vol. 250). 304p. 1993. 60.00 (*0-7918-0977-3*, H00809) ASME.

Pressure Vessel Technology: Proceedings of the International Conference, 6th, Beijing, People's Republic of China, 11-15 September 1988, 2 vols. Ed. by Cengdian Liu & R. W. Nichols. (Illus.). 1750p. 1989. 789.00 (*0-08-035896-9*, Pub. by Pergamon Repr); 260.00 (*0-08-035897-7*, Pub. by Pergamon Repr) Franklin.

Pressure Vessels: A Workbook for Engineers. American Society of Mechanical Engineers Staff. Ed. by E. J. Hicks. LC 81-111549. 58p. reprint ed. pap. 30.00 (*0-608-14291-3*, 201737200007) Bks Demand.

Pressure Vessels: The ASME Code Simplified. 7th ed. Robert Chuse & Bryce E. Carson, Sr. LC 92-17243. 323p. 1992. 69.95 (*0-07-010939-7*) McGraw.

Pressure Vessels Analysis for Design: Proceedings of the Conference in Honour of Emeritus Professor Sidney Gill, held at UMIST, Manchester, U. K., April 1981. Ed. by W. C. Johnson. (Illus.). 80p. 1983. pap. 21.00 (*0-08-029349-2*, Pergamon Pr) Elsevier.

Pressure Vessels & Piping: Design & Analysis - A Decade of Progress, 4 vols. Incl. Vol. 1. Analysis. 780p. 35.00 Vol. 2. Components & Structural Dynamics. Ed. by G. J. Bohm & R. L. Cloud. 812p. 1972. 35.00 1972. write for info. (*0-318-50921-0*, G00019) ASME.

Pressure Vessels & Piping: Design & Analysis - A Decade of Progress, 4 vols. Ed. by G. J. Bohm et al. 1972. write for info. (*0-685-00843-6*, G00020) ASME.

Pressure Vessels & Piping: Design & Analysis - A Decade of Progress: Quality Assurance - Applications - Components, Vol. 4. Ed. by H. H. Waite. 1976. text 50.00 (*0-685-72346-1*, G00101) ASME.

Pressure Vessels & Piping: Design Technology, 1982-A Decade of Progress. Ed. by S. Y. Zamrik & D. Dietrich. 647p. 1982. 85.00 (*0-685-06278-3*, G00213) ASME.

Pressure Vessels & Piping: Verification & Qualification of Inelastic Analysis Computer Programs, Proceedings of the National Congress on Pressure Vessels & Piping, 2nd, San Francisco, 1975. National Congress on Pressure Vessels & Piping Staff. Ed. by J. M. Corum & W. B. Wright. LC 75-8090. (Illus.). 117p. reprint ed. pap. 36.30 (*0-608-30361-5*, 201681300005) Bks Demand.

Pressure Vessels & Piping Codes & Standards: Proceedings ASME Pressure Vessels & Piping Conference (1997, Orlando, FL) Ed. by Thomas C. Esselman et al. LC 97-73340. (PVP Ser.: Vol. 353). 407p. 1997. pap. 130.00 (*0-7918-1570-6*) ASME.

Pressure Vessels & Piping Computer Program Evaluation & Qualification: Presented at the Energy Technology Conference, Houston TX, Sept. 18-23, 1977. Energy Technology Conference Staff. Ed. by D. E. Dietrich. LC 77-82203. 127p. reprint ed. pap. 39.40 (*0-608-16902-1*, 205630600056) Bks Demand.

Pressure Vessels & Piping Design Analysis & Severe Accidents. Ed. by A. A. Dermenjian. 213p. 1996. pap. text 100.00 (*0-7918-1778-4*, TS283) ASME Pr.

Pressure Vessels, Pumps, Valves, Pipe Supports & Components: Proceedings of the Pressure Vessels & Piping Conference, Minneapolis, MN, 1994. Ed. by L. I. Ezekoye. LC 94-71663. (PVP Ser.: Vol. 282). 157p. 1994. pap. 50.00 (*0-7918-1355-X*) ASME.

Pressure Vessels under External Pressure: Statics & Dynamics. C. T. Ross. 250p. 1990. mass mkt. 153.95 (*1-85166-433-5*) Elsevier.

Pressure Without Sanctions: The Influence of World Jewry on Israeli Policy. Charles S. Liebman. LC 75-18242. 304p. (C). 1976. 39.50 (*0-8386-1791-3*) Fairleigh Dickinson.

***Pressured Cook: Over 75 One-Pot Meals In Minutes, Made In Today's 100Safe Pressure Cookers.** Lorna Sass. LC 98-38885. (Illus.). 272p. 1999. 20.45 (*0-688-15828-5*, Wm Morrow) Morrow Avon.

Pressuremeter. Jean-Louis Briaud. (Illus.), 336p. (C). 1992. text 128.00 (*90-6191-125-7*, Pub. by A A Balkema) Ashgate Pub Co.

Pressuremeter & Foundation Engineering. F. Baguelin et al. (Rock & Soil Mechanics Ser.). (Illus.). (C). 1978. 60.00 (*0-87849-019-1*, Pub. by Trans T Pub) Enfield Pubs NH.

Pressuremeter & Its Marine Applications: Second International Symposium, STP 950. Ed. by Jean-Louis Briaud & M. E. Audibert. LC 86-3337. (Special Technical Publication Ser.). (Illus.). 505p. 1986. text 64.00 (*0-8031-0454-5*, STP950) ASTM.

Pressuremeter & Its New Avenues: Proceedings of the 4th International Symposium, 17-19 May 1995, Sherbrooke, Quebec, Canada. Ed. by Gerard Ballivy. (Illus.). 502p. (C). 1995. text 149.00 (*90-5410-545-3*, Pub. by A A Balkema) Ashgate Pub Co.

Pressuremeters in Geotechnical Design. B. G. Clarke. LC 94-71805. 364p. 1994. 164.95 (*0-7514-0041-6*, Pub. by B Acad & Prof) Routldge.

Pressures of Life. Longman Imprint Bks. Staff. Date not set. pap. text. write for info. (*0-582-23329-1*, Pub. by Addison-Wesley) Longman.

Pressures of the Hand: Expressionist Impulses in Recent American Art. Carter Ratcliff. (Illus.). 36p. 1984. pap. 12.50 (*0-942746-05-8*) SUNYP R Gibson.

Pressures on American Monetary Policy. Thomas M. Havrilesky. LC 92-31889. (C). 1992. lib. bdg. 125.00 (*0-7923-9300-7*) Kluwer Academic.

Pressures on American Monetary Policy. 2nd ed. Ed. by Thomas M. Havrilesky. LC 95-1081. 400p. (C). 1995. lib. bdg. 133.00 (*0-7923-9561-1*) Kluwer Academic.

Pressurization Characteristics, PE Communication Cable. 1965. 30.00 (*0-614-18679-X*, P-47-434) Insulated Cable.

Pressurized Enclosures: RP12.4. ISA Staff. (Hazardous Locations Ser.). 1996. 40.00 (*1-55617-594-9*, RP12.4) ISA.

Pressurized-Water Reactor Internals Aging Degradation Study: Phase 1. 1994. lib. bdg. 250.00 (*0-8490-8556-X*) Gordon Pr.

Presswise. LC 98-45542. 192p. (C). 1998. pap. text 33.33 (*0-13-095823-9*, Pub. by P-H) S&S Trade.

***Presswise: Digital Imposition & Student CD Package.** Ellenn Behoriam. 304p. (C). 1999. pap. text 33.33 (*0-13-020815-9*) P-H.

Pressworking: Stampings & Dies. Ed. by Karl A. Keyes. LC 80-53009. (Manufacturing Update Ser.). (Illus.). 265p. reprint ed. pap. 82.20 (*0-7837-6273-9*, 204598800010) Bks Demand.

Pressworking Aids for Designers & Diemakers. Daniel B. Dallas. LC 77-90988. (Manufacturing Data Ser.). 275p. 1978. 42.00 (*0-87263-042-0*) SME.

Pressworking of Metals. 1996. lib. bdg. 350.95 (*0-8490-8335-4*) Gordon Pr.

Prestamo en el Espanol de los Estados Unidos. Eva Mendieta. (Studies in Ethnolinguistics: Vol. 1). (SPA.). 192p. (C). 1999. text 44.95 (*0-8204-4036-1*, 40361) P Lang Pubng.

Prestekragen, Vol. 101. Ed. & Tr. by Janne Lillestol. (Listen & Learn Language Audio Ser.: Vol. LL0399).Tr. of Daisy. (ENG & NOR., Illus.). 28p. 1999. pap. 15.95 incl. audio (*1-892623-06-4*) Intl Book.

Prestekragen, Vol. 101. unabridged ed. Ed. & Tr. by Janne Lillestol. (Listen & Learn Language Audio Ser.: Vol. LL0399).Tr. of Daisy. (ENG & NOR., Illus.). 28p. 1999. pap. 15.95 incl. audio (*1-892623-07-2*) Intl Book.

Prestel Art Game. 1998. 39.95 (*3-7913-1945-0*) Prabhupada Inst.

***Prestel Dictionary of Twentieth-Century Art & Artists.** Wieland Schmied & Frank Whitford. (Illus.). 2000. 75.00 (*3-7913-2325-3*, Pub. by Prestel) te Neues.

***Prestel Postcard Book.** Ed. by Prestel Art Press Staff. (Illus.). 1999. pap. 8.95 (*3-7913-2232-X*); pap. 8.95 (*3-7913-2233-8*) Prestel Pub NY.

Prester John. John Buchan. LC 75-131650. (Illus.). 1970. 65.00 (*0-403-00537-X*) Scholarly.

Prester John. John Buchan. 1988. reprint ed. lib. bdg. 49.00 (*0-7812-0160-8*) Rprt Serv.

Prester John, the Mongols, & the Ten Lost Tribes. Ed. by Bernard Hamilton & Charles F. Beckingham. LC 96-17094. 336p. 1996. 86.95 (*0-86078-553-X*, Pub. by Variorum) Ashgate Pub Co.

Prestige. Christopher Priest. 1999. 36.00 (*0-671-71924-6*) S&S Trade.

Prestige. Christopher Priest. LC 97-19381. 416p. 1997. pap. 14.95 (*0-312-85886-8*) St Martin.

Prestige & Association in an Urban Community: An Analysis of an Urban Stratification System. Edward O. Laumann. LC 66-29709. (Orig.). 1966. pap. 4.95 (*0-672-60620-8*, Bobbs) Macmillan.

***Prestige, Authority & Power in Late Medieval Manuscripts & Texts.** Felicity Riddy. LC 99-58712. (York Manuscripts Conference Ser.: No. 0955-9663). (Illus.). 192p. 2000. 75.00 (*0-9529734-6-4*) Boydell & Brewer.

Prestige, Class & Mobility. Kaare Svalastoga. Ed. by Lewis A. Coser & Walter W. Powell. LC 79-7024. (Perennial Works in Sociology). (Illus.). 1980. reprint ed. lib. bdg. 41.95 (*0-405-12123-7*) Ayer.

Prestige Label: A Discography, 3. Compiled by Michel Ruppli. LC 79-8294. (Discographies Ser.: No. 3). 390p. 1980. lib. bdg. 95.00 (*0-313-22019-0*, RPL/, Greenwood Pr) Greenwood.

Prestige of Schiller in England, 1788-1859. Frederic Ewen. reprint ed. 29.50 (*0-404-02364-9*) AMS Pr.

Prestige Posters, Vol. 4. Jack Rennert. (Illus.). 1987. 40.00 (*1-929530-12-9*) Pstr Auctns Intl.

Prestige, Profit & Pleasure: The Market for Modern Art in New York in the 1940s & 1950s. A. Diedre Robson. LC 94-40929. (Garland Publications in the Fine Arts). (Illus.). 392p. 1995. text 83.00 (*0-8153-1364-0*) Garland.

Prestigious Watches. Sophie A. Terrisse. LC 96-96942. (Illus.). 200p. 1997. 49.95 (*0-8478-1991-4*, Pub. by Rizzoli Intl) St Martin.

Presto Change-O. Audrey Wood. (GRE.). (J). 1989. pap. 3.99 (*0-85953-817-6*) Childs Play.

Presto Change-O. Audrey Wood. (J). 1996. lib. bdg. 11.95 (*0-85953-832-X*) Childs Play.

Presto Change-o. Audrey Wood. LC 90-46912. 32p. (J). 1989. 7.99 (*0-85953-181-3*); pap. 3.99 (*0-85953-322-0*) Childs Play.

Presto Change-O & Tooth Fairy. Audrey Wood. (J). 12.85 (*0-85953-374-3*) Childs Play.

Presto Scherzo Book: Ensemble Energy. P. Keveren. 40p. 1994. pap. 10.95 (*0-7935-3826-2*, 00290476) H Leonard.

Preston: Descendants of Roger Preston. C. H. Preston. (Illus.). 355p. 1991. reprint ed. pap. 56.00 (*0-8328-2081-4*); reprint ed. lib. bdg. 66.00 (*0-8328-2080-6*) Higginson Bk Co.

Preston Catalogue. Intro. by Mark Rees. (Illus.). 224p. 1991. reprint ed. pap. 19.95 (*0-9618088-9-6*) Astragal Pr.

Preston County. Charles A. Thomas. (Images of America Ser.). 1998. pap. 16.99 (*0-7524-0930-1*) Arcadia Publng.

Preston Falls. David Gates. LC 97-36890. 338p. 1998. 25.00 (*0-679-43667-7*) Knopf.

Preston Falls. David Gates. (Vintage Contemporaries Ser.). 338p. 1999. pap. 13.00 (*0-679-75643-4*) Random.

Preston Genealogy: Tracing the History of the Family from about 1040. Ed. by L. A. Wilson & W. B. Preston. (Illus.). 376p. 1989. reprint ed. pap. 56.00 (*0-8328-0993-4*); reprint ed. lib. bdg. 64.00 (*0-8328-0992-6*) Higginson Bk Co.

Preston Jones. Mark Busby. LC 82-74092. (Western Writers Ser.: No. 58). (Illus.). 52p. (Orig.). 1983. pap. 4.95 (*0-88430-032-3*) Boise St U W Writ Ser.

Preston Manning & the Reform Party. Murray Dobbin. 298p. 1992. mass mkt. 6.95 (*0-88780-161-7*, Pub. by Formac Publ Co) Formac Dist Ltd.

Preston Morton Collection of American Art. Ed. by Katherine H. Mead. LC 81-52029. (Illus.). 272p. (Orig.). 1981. pap. 12.00 (*0-89951-043-4*) Santa Barb Mus Art.

***Preston Smith: The People's Governor.** Wanda Evans. (Illus.). 196p. 1999. pap. 14.95 (*1-887150-21-8*) Millennia Bks.

Preston Sturges. write for info. (*0-8386-3102-9*) Fairleigh Dickinson.

Preston Sturges's Vision of America: Critical Analyses of Fourteen Films. Jay Rozgonyi. LC 94-24196. (Illus.). 207p. 1995. lib. bdg. 34.50 (*0-89950-985-1*) McFarland & Co.

Preston's Goal! Colin McNaughton. LC 97-39947. (Illus.). 32p. (J). (gr. 1-3). 1998. 15.00 (*0-15-201816-6*) Harcourt.

Preston's Masonry. William Preston. 410p. 1997. reprint ed. pap. 29.95 (*0-7661-0064-2*) Kessinger Pub.

Prestons of Smithfield & Greenfield in Virginia. John F. Dorman & James R. Bentley. LC 80-2841. (Filson Club, Second Publications Ser.: No. 3). (Illus.). 441p. 1982. 28.75 (*0-9601072-1-5*) Filson Club.

Preston's Practice. large type ed. (Mills & Boon Large Print Ser.). 288p. 1997. 23.99 (*0-263-15331-2*, Pub. by Mills & Boon) Ulverscroft.

Prestressed Bodies. Iesan. 1989. pap. text. write for info. (*0-582-03761-1*, Pub. by Addison-Wesley) Longman.

Prestressed Concrete. 1990. text 121.95 (*0-13-739103-X*, Macmillan Coll) P-H.

Prestressed Concrete. I. I. Graduck. x, 140p. 1970. text 189.00 (*0-677-61730-5*) Gordon & Breach.

Prestressed Concrete: A Fundamental Approach. 2nd ed. Edward G. Nawy. LC 95-13788. (C). 1995. text 100.00 (*0-13-123480-3*) P-H.

***Prestressed Concrete: A Fundamental Approach.** 3rd ed. Edward G. Nawy. LC 99-38322. 939p. 1999. 105.00 (*0-13-020593-1*) P-H.

Prestressed Concrete: Analysis & Design. Antoine E. Naaman. (Illus.). 736p. (C). 1982. text 73.00 (*0-07-045761-1*) McGraw.

***Prestressed Concrete: Fundamental Approach.** 3rd ed. (C). 2000. write for info. (*0-13-025992-6*) S&S Trade.

Prestressed Concrete Analysis & Design. Antoine E. Naaman. (C). 1983. pap. text, teacher ed. 27.50 (*0-07-045762-X*) McGraw.

Prestressed Concrete Bridges. Christian Menn. (Illus.). 512p. 1990. text 180.00 (*0-8176-2414-7*) Birkhauser.

Prestressed Concrete Buildings. Menn. 535p. 1990. 198.00 (*3-7643-2414-7*) Birkhauser.

Prestressed Concrete Channel Slabs for Short Span Bridges see Standards for Selected Prestressed Units

Prestressed Concrete Column Behavior. 208p. 1988. 30.00 (*0-937040-29-0*, R&D3) P-PCI.

Prestressed Concrete Design. M. K. Hurst. 350p. (gr. 13). 1989. text 69.95 (*0-412-28960-1*) Chapman & Hall.

Prestressed Concrete Design. 2nd rev. ed. Ed. by M. K. Hurst. LC 98-166632. (Illus.). 280p. (C). (gr. 13). 1998. 49.99 (*0-419-21800-9*, D5595, E & FN Spon) Routledge.

Prestressed Concrete Design by Computer. R. Hulse & W. H. Mosley. (Illus.). 148p. (C). 1987. text 90.00 (*0-333-44549-X*); pap. text 30.00 (*0-333-44550-3*) Scholium Intl.

Prestressed Concrete Designer's Handbook. 3rd ed. P. W. Abeles & B. K. Bardhan-Roy. LC 98-206515. xxii, 556 p. 1981. write for info. (*0-7210-1232-9*) C & CA.

Prestressed Concrete for Buildings. (PCI Journal Reprints Ser.). 48p. 1976. pap. 16.00 (*0-685-06894-3*, JR177) P-PCI.

Prestressed Concrete Pedestrian Bridges. 28p. 1985. pap. 14.00 (*0-318-19726-X*, JR-199) P-PCI.

Prestressed Concrete Piles. (PCI Journal Reprints Ser.). 29p. 1985. pap. 14.00 (*0-318-19739-1*, JR67) P-PCI.

Prestressed Concrete Piling Interaction Diagrams. (PCI Journal Reprints Ser.). 56p. 1985. pap. 31.00 (*0-318-19764-2*, JR187A) P-PCI.

Prestressed Concrete Poles: State-of-the-Art. 52p. 1984. pap. 22.00 (*0-318-19813-4*, JR302) P-PCI.

Prestressed Concrete Saves Energy. (PCI Journal Reprints Ser.). 2p. 1980. pap. 8.00 (*0-686-40127-1*, JR221) P-PCI.

Prestressed Concrete Technology. Gy. Fogarasi. 317p. (C). 1986. 150.00 (*963-05-4206-4*, Pub. by Akade Kiado) St Mut.

Prestressed Steel Bridges. M. S. Troitsky. 386p. (gr. 13). 1990. text 72.95 (*0-442-31922-3*) Chapman & Hall.

Prestressing the CN Tower. (PCI Journal Reprints Ser.). 32p. 1985. pap. 14.00 (*0-318-19757-X*, JR174) P-PCI.

Presumed Dead. Hugh Holton. 320p. 1995. 4.99 (*0-8125-4813-2*, Pub. by Forge NYC) St Martin.

Presumed Guilty. Tess Gerritsen. 1997. per. 5.50 (*1-55166-299-X*, Mira Bks) Harlequin Bks.

Presumed Guilty. Junius Podrug. LC 97-16925. 384p. 1997. text 24.95 (*0-312-86242-3*) St Martin.

Presumed Guilty. Junius Podrug. 1998. mass mkt. 6.99 (*0-8125-5507-4*, Pub. by Tor Bks) St Martin.

Presumed Guilty: An Investigation into the JonBenet Ramsey Case, the Media & the Culture of Pornography, 1. Stephen Singular. 256p. 1999. 19.95 (*1-893224-00-7*, New Millenn Pr) New Millenn Enter.

***Presumed Guilty: Brian Mulroney, the Airbus Affair & the Government of Canada.** William Kaplan. (Illus.). 384p. 2000. pap. 14.99 (*0-7710-4593-X*) McCland & Stewart.

Presumed Guilty: The Tim Wilkes Story. Ben Greer. Ed. by Charles L. Wyrick, Jr. LC 94-36249. 136p. 1995. 18.95 (*0-941711-29-3*) Wyrick & Co.

Presumed Guilty: The Tragedy of the Rodney King Affair. Stacey C. Koon & Robert Deitz. LC 92-29422. 274p. 1992. 19.95 (*0-89526-507-9*) Regnery Pub.

Presumed Guilty: When Innocent People Are Wrongly Convicted. Martin D. Yant. LC 90-26301. (Illus.). 231p. (C). 1991. 27.95 (*0-87975-643-8*) Prometheus Bks.

Presumed Ignorant! Over 400 Cases of Legal Looniness, Daffy Defendants, & Bloopers from the Bench! Leland H. Gregory. LC 97-44905. 224p. 1998. pap. 9.95 (*0-440-50789-8*) Dell.

Presumed Innocence. Jean Crutchfield. LC 99-224701. (Illus.). 80p. 1998. pap. 25.00 (*0-295-97718-3*) U of Wash Pr.

Presumed Innocent. Scott Turow. 431p. 1987. 30.00 (*0-374-23713-1*) FS&G.

***Presumed Innocent.** Scott Turow. LC 99-35536. 1999. write for info. (*0-7621-0254-3*) RD Assn.

Presumed Innocent. Scott Turow. 1991. mass mkt. 71.40 (*0-446-11431-6*) Warner Bks.

Presumed Innocent. abr. ed. Scott Turow. 1988. 17.00 incl. audio (*0-671-65218-4*, Audioworks) PB.

Presumed Innocent. Scott Turow. 432p. 1989. reprint ed. mass mkt. 7.99 (*0-446-35986-6*, Pub. by Warner Bks) Little.

***Presumed Innocent.** Scott Turow. 2000. reprint ed. pap. write for info. (*0-446-67644-6*) Warner Bks.

Presumed Innocent, Vol. 1. Tracy Voigt et al. 1982. write for info. (*0-318-56592-7*) T Voigt.

Presumee Dangereuse. Janice Kaiser. (Rouge Passion Ser.: No. 482). (FRE.). 1998. mass mkt. 3.50 (*0-373-37482-8*, 1-37482-6) Harlequin Bks.

Presumpscot River Watch Guide to the Presumpscot River: Its History, Ecology, & Recreational Uses. Amy MacDonald et al. 80p. (Orig.). 1994. pap. 9.99 (*0-9639872-0-8*) Presumpscot River.

Presumption: An Entertainment: A Sequel to Pride & Prejudice. Julia Barrett, pseud & Jane Austen. LC 93-5778. 240p. 1993. 19.95 (*0-87131-736-2*) M Evans.

Presumption: An Entertainment: A Sequel to Pride & Prejudice. large type ed. Julia Barrett, pseud. LC 93-43082. 409p. 1994. lib. bdg. 21.95 (*0-7862-0153-3*) Thorndike Pr.

Presumption: An Entertainment: A Sequel to Pride & Prejudice. Julia Barrett, pseud & Jane Austen. LC 95-4686. 238p. 1995. reprint ed. pap. 11.95 (*0-226-03813-0*) U Ch Pr.

Presumption of Guilt. Terri Blackstock. LC 97-254. (Sun Coast Chronicles Ser.: Vol. 4). 352p. 1997. pap. 9.99 (*0-310-20018-0*) Zondervan.

Presumption of Guilt. Lelia Kelly. 224p. 1998. 22.95 (*1-57566-249-3*, Knsington) Kensgtn Pub Corp.

Presumption of Guilt. Lelia Kelly. 352p. 1998. mass mkt. 5.99 (*0-7860-0584-X*, Pinncle Kensgtn) Kensgtn Pub Corp.

Presumption of Guilt. large type ed. Jeffrey Ashford. (Dales Mystery Ser.). 1993. pap. 13.95 (*1-85389-345-5*, Dales) Ulverscroft.

Presumption of Guilt, Vol. 4. Terri Blackstock. LC 99-21873. (Sun Coast Chronicles Ser.). 1999. 24.95 (*0-7862-1959-9*, G K Hall & Co) Mac Lib Ref.

***Presumption of Innocence.** P. J. Schwikkard. 215p. 2000. pap. 41.50 (*0-7021-5144-0*, 18664, Pub. by Juta & Co) Gaunt.

Presumptions in the Law: A Suggestion. Otis H. Fisk. 81p. 1996. 20.00 (*1-57588-351-1*, 310580) W S Hein.

Presumptions in the Law: A Suggestion. Otis H. Fisk. LC 96-78127. iv, 81p. 1997. reprint ed. 28.00 (*1-57588-176-4*, 310580) W S Hein.

Presumptive Engagement: Australia's Asia-Pacific Security Policy in the 1990s. Desmond Ball & Pauline Kerr. LC 96-176162. 200p. 1997. pap. text 24.95 (*1-86373-977-7*, Pub. by Allen & Unwin Pty) Paul & Co Pubs.

Presumptive Income Taxation: Proceedings of a Seminar Held in New Delhi, in 1997 During the 51st Congress of the International Fiscal Association. International Fiscal Association Staff. LC 98-34312. (IFA Congress Seminar Ser.). 1998. pap. 36.00 (*90-411-1045-3*) Kluwer Law Intl.

***Presumptive Meanings: The Theory of Generalized Conversational Implicature.** Stephen C. Levinson. LC 99-46140. (Language, Speech & Communication Ser.). 1999. text 85.00 (*0-262-12218-9*) MIT Pr.

An Asterisk (*) at the beginning of an entry indicates that the title is appearing for the first time.

Presumptive Meanings: The Theory of Generalized Conversational Implicature. Stephen C. Levinson. LC 99-46140. (Illus.). 450p. 1999. pap. 35.00 (*0-262-62130-4*) MIT Pr.

***Presumptuous Dreamers: A Sociological History of the Life & Times of Abigail Scott Duniway, 1834-1871.** Helen K. Smith & Harriet L. Smith. LC 74-79460. (Western Americana Bks.: Vol. 3). (Illus.). (Orig.). 2000. pap. 30.00 (*0-913626-39-2*) S S S Pub Co.

Presumptuous Dreamers: A Sociological History of the Life & Times of Abigail Scott Duniway, 1834-1871, Vol. 1. Helen K. Smith. LC 74-79460. (Western Americana Bks.). (Orig.). 1974. 30.00 (*0-913626-11-2*); pap. 30.00 (*0-913626-12-0*) S S S Pub Co.

Presumptuous Dreamers: A Sociological History of the Life & Times of Abigail Scott Duniway, 1872-1876, Vol. 2. Helen K. Smith. LC 74-79460. (Western Americana Bks.). (Orig.). 1983. pap. 30.00 (*0-913626-27-9*) S S S Pub Co.

Presupposition. David E. Cooper. (Janua Linguarum, Ser. Minor: No. 203). 130p. 1974. pap. text 33.85 (*90-279-3152-6*) Mouton.

Presupposition & Anaphora. Krahmer. LC 98-26092. (Lecture Notes Ser.: No. 89). 250p. (C). 1998. 64.95 (*1-57586-147-X*); pap. 22.95 (*1-57586-146-1*) CSLI.

Presuppositional Analysis of Specific Indefinites: Common Grounds As Structured Information States. Jae Yeom, II. LC 98-17121. (Outstanding Dissertations in Linguistics Ser.). 258p. 1998. 65.00 (*0-8153-3175-4*) Garland.

Presuppositions & Implicatures of the Founding Fathers. Abdul K. Bangura. LC 97-142650. 194p. (Orig.). (C). 1996. pap. text 14.95 (*0-943025-84-2*) Cummngs & Hath.

Presuppositions & Non-Truth-Conditional Semantics. Deidre Wilson. (Modern Revivals in Philosophy Ser.). 175p. 1992. 51.95 (*0-7512-0021-2*, Pub. by Gregg Revivals) Ashgate Pub Co.

***Presuppositions & Pronouns.** Bart Geurts. LC 99-54254. (Current Research in the Semantics/Pragmatics Interface Ser.). (Illus.). 234p. 1999. write for info. (*0-08-043592-0*) Elsevier.

Presuppositions of Critical History Bound with Aphorisms: 1874/1930 Editions. Francis H. Bradley. (Key Texts Ser.). 132p. 1996. reprint ed. pap. 19.95 (*1-85506-214-3*) Bks Intl VA.

Presuppositions of India's Philosophies. Karl H. Potter. (C). 1991. reprint ed. 24.00 (*81-208-0779-0*, Pub. by Motilal Bnarsidass) S Asia.

Presupuesto Publico y Fiscalizacion Glossary German & Spanish, Europa-Glossar der Rechts und Verwaltungssprache, No. 28. Langenscheidt Staff. (GER & SPA.). 183p. pap. 22.50 (*0-7859-7565-9*, 346849078X) Fr & Eur.

Presupuesto y Control: Pautas de Reforma para America Latina. Humberto Petrei. (SPA.). 494p. 1997. pap. text 24.95 (*1-886938-28-8*) IADB.

Presurgical Evaluation of Epileptics. Ed. by H. G. Wieser & C. E. Elger. (Illus.). 415p. 1987. 206.00 (*0-387-16344-1*) Spr-Verlag.

Presurgical Psychological Screening in Chronic Pain Syndromes: A Guide for the Behavioral Health Practitioner. Andrew R. Block. LC 96-18082. 150p. 1996. 49.95 (*0-8058-2407-3*); pap. 24.50 (*0-8058-2408-1*) L Erlbaum Assocs.

Presurvey Questionnaire, 1992-93. rev. ed. 49p. 1991. student ed. write for info. (*0-932915-07-8*) Accredit Assn Ambulatory.

Presynadtic Receptors: Proceedings of the Satellite Symposium, Paris, July 22-23 1978, 7th International Congress of Pharmacology. S. Z. Langer et al. (Illus.). 340p. 1979. 81.00 (*0-08-023190-X*, Pergamon Pr) Elsevier.

Presynaptic Inhibition & Neural Control. Ed. by Pablo et al. LC 97-2286. (Illus.). 466p. 1997. text 85.00 (*0-19-510516-8*) OUP.

Presynaptic Receptors & Neuronal Transporters: Proceedings of the Official Satellite Symposium to the IUPHAR 1990 Congress Held in Rouen, France, 26-29 June 1990. Ed. by S. Z. Langer et al. (Advances in the Biosciences Ser.: No. 82). (Illus.). 372p. 1992. 181.50 (*0-08-041165-7*, Pergamon Pr) Elsevier.

Presynaptic Receptors in the Mammalian Brain. Ed. by Thomas V. Dunwiddie & David M. Lovinger. (Illus.). 272p. 1993. 109.00 (*0-8176-3651-X*) Birkhauser.

Pretani. Robert C. Wallace. 572p. 1996. pap. 12.00 (*0-9634992-5-4*) Pretani.

Preteen Ministry: Between a Rock & a Hard Place. Ed Robinson & Kathryn L. Mowry. 95p. (Orig.). 1993. pap. 7.99 (*0-8341-1409-7*) Beacon Hill.

Preteen Power: A Treasury of Solid Gold Advice for Those Just Entering Their Teens. Eric Chester. 193p. (YA). (gr. 6 up). 1997. pap. text 11.95 (*0-9651447-3-9*) ChesPress.

Preteen's First Book about Love, Sex & AIDS. Michelle Harrison. 100p. 1995. 16.95 (*0-88048-698-8*, 8698) Am Psychiatric.

Pretend Family Relationships: Testimonies of Lesbian & Gay Parents. Turan Ali. (Sexual Politics Ser.). 192p. 1996. pap. 17.95 (*0-304-33150-3*) Continuum.

Pretend Indians: Images of Native Americans in the Movies. Ed. by Gretchen M. Bataille & Charles L. Silet. LC 79-27432. 232p. reprint ed. pap. 72.00 (*0-608-18795-X*, 203031700068) Bks Demand.

Pretend Passport & Currency. Virginia McLean. (Illus.). 8p. 1997. teacher ed., ring bd. 5.50 (*1-885870-03-5*) Redbird.

Pretend Play Among Three-Year-Olds. Mira Stambak & Hermine Sinclair. 144p. 1993. text 39.95 (*0-8058-1243-1*) L Erlbaum Assocs.

Pretend Play As Improvisation: Conversation in the Preschool Classroom. R. Keith Sawyer. 240p. (C). 1996. text 39.95 (*0-8058-2119-8*) L Erlbaum Assocs.

Pretend Soup & Other Real Recipes: A Cookbook for Preschoolers & Up. Mollie Katzen & Ann Henderson. LC 93-48579. (Illus.). 96p. (J). (ps-3). 1994. 16.95 (*1-883672-06-6*) Tricycle Pr.

Pretend the World Is Funny & Forever: A Psychological Analysis of Comedians, Clowns, & Actors. Seymour Fisher & Rhoda L. Fisher. LC 80-7777. 288p. 1981. text 49.95 (*0-89859-073-6*) L Erlbaum Assocs.

Pretend Time. Chuck Murphy. (Razzle Dazzle Bks.). (Illus.). 12p. (J). (ps-1). 1998. 4.99 (*0-689-82055-0*) S&S Childrens.

Pretend You Don't See Her. Mary Higgins Clark. LC 97-150693. 320p. 1997. 25.00 (*0-684-81039-5*) S&S Trade.

Pretend You Don't See Her. Mary Higgins Clark. 1998. per. 7.99 (*0-671-86715-6*) S&S Trade.

Pretend You Don't See Her. Mary Higgins Clark. 1998. 13.09 (*0-606-13721-1*, Pub. by Turtleback) Demco.

Pretend You Don't See Her. large type ed. Mary Higgins Clark. 1997. 25.00 (*0-684-83416-2*) S&S Trade.

Pretend You're a Cat. Jean Marzollo. (Picture Puffin Ser.). (J). 1997. 10.19 (*0-606-11762-8*, Pub. by Turtleback) Demco.

Pretend You're Dead, Okay? Date not set. pap. 12.00 (*0-9679135-1-9*) Novella Club Pubs.

Pretendent na Prestol see Pretender to the Throne: The Further Adventures of Private Ivan Chonkin

Pretender. K. A. Applegate. (Animorphs Ser.: No. 23). 154p. (J). (gr. 3-7). 1998. pap. 4.99 (*0-590-76256-7*, Pub. by Scholastic Inc) Penguin Putnam.

Pretender: Science Fiction. Piers Anthony & Frances Hall. LC 79-317. (Illus.). 159p. 1979. pap. 19.00 (*0-89370-230-7*) Millefleurs.

Pretender to the Throne: The Further Adventures of Private Ivan Chonkin. Vladimir Voinovich. Tr. by Richard Lourie from RUS. LC 94-48940. (European Classics Ser.).Tr. of Pretendent na Prestol. 358p. 1995. pap. 15.95 (*0-8101-1244-2*) Northwestern U Pr.

Pretenders. Gwen Davis. 1987. mass mkt. 4.95 (*0-446-34563-6*, Pub. by Warner Bks) Little.

Pretenders. Joan Wolf. 352p. 1999. mass mkt. 6.50 (*0-446-60535-2*, Pub. by Warner Bks) Little.

***Pretenders: Gifted People Who Have Difficulty Learning.** Barbara P. Guyer. LC 96-80002. (Illus.). 191p. 2000. 24.50 (*0-9653744-1-6*, Pub. by High Tide Pr) IPG Chicago.

***Pretenders: Gifted People Who Have Difficulty Learning.** Barbara P. Guyer. LC 96-80002. (Illus.). 191p. 2000. reprint ed. pap. 17.95 (*1-892696-06-1*, Pub. by High Tide Pr) IPG Chicago.

Pretenders & Popular Monarchism in Early Modern Russia: The False Tsars of the Time of Troubles. Maureen Perrie. (Illus.). 287p. (C). 1995. text 64.95 (*0-521-47274-1*) Cambridge U Pr.

***Pretender's Games.** Louise Clark. 320p. 1999. mass mkt. 4.99 (*0-8439-4514-1*, Leisure Bks) Dorchester Pub Co.

Pretending & Meaning: Toward a Pragmatic Theory of Fictional Discourse, 57. Richard Henry. LC 95-48367. (Contributions in Philosophy Ser.: Vol. 57). 144p. 1996. 57.95 (*0-313-29889-0*, Greenwood Pr) Greenwood.

Pretending at Home: Early Development in a Sociocultural Context. Wendy L. Haight & Peggy J. Miller. LC 92-22784. (SUNY Series, Children's Play in Society). 150p. (C). 1993. text 59.50 (*0-7914-1471-X*); pap. text 19.95 (*0-7914-1472-8*) State U NY Pr.

Pretending Dreams - The Ladies. 2nd rev. ed. Charles R. Beam. LC 97-91245. (Illus.). 72p. 1997. 14.95 (*0-9653985-7-9*) StarSide Pr.

Pretending Dreams - The Men. Charles R. Beam. LC 97-91246. (Illus.). 73p. 1997. 14.95 (*0-9653985-2-8*) StarSide Pr.

Pretending the Bed Is a Raft. Nanci Kincaid. 256p. 1998. pap. 11.95 (*0-385-33293-9*) Dell.

Pretending the Bed Is a Raft: Stories. Nanci Kincaid. LC 97-15475. 252p. 1997. 17.95 (*1-56512-177-5*, 72177) Algonquin Bks.

***Pretending to Be Normal: Living with Asperger's Syndrome.** Liane Holliday Willie. 1999. pap. 17.95 (*1-85302-749-9*) Jessica Kingsley.

Pretending to Communicate. Ed. by Herman Parret. LC 93-46021. 1993. 136.95 (*3-11-011832-7*) De Gruyter.

Pretending to Communicate. Ed. by Herman Parret. (Foundations of Communication & Cognition Ser.). xv, 304p. (C). 1993. lib. bdg. 118.70 (*3-11-011732-0*) Mouton.

Pretends to Be Free: Runaway Slave Advertisements from Colonial & Revolutionary New York & New Jersey. Graham R. Hodges & Alan E. Brown. LC 93-37771. (Illus.). 940106p. 1994. text 62.00 (*0-8153-1531-7*, H1811) Garland.

Pretense. Lori Wick. LC 98-19833. 700p. 1998. pap. 12.99 (*1-56507-945-0*) Harvest Hse.

Pretense . . . of Innocence. Atticus King. LC 95-74970. 256p. (Orig.). 1996. pap. 12.95 (*1-56184-081-5*) New Falcon Pubns.

Pretense of Glory: The Life of General Nathaniel P. Banks. James G. Hollandsworth, Jr. LC 98-24709. (Illus.). 360p. 1998. 34.95 (*0-8071-2293-9*) La State U Pr.

Preterm Labor. M. G. Elder et al. LC 97-18582. 1997. text. write for info. (*0-443-05857-1*) Church.

Preterm Labor: Prevention & Nursing Management. Margaret Comerford Freda & Ellen T. Patterson. Ed. by Karla Damus. 1994. write for info. (*0-86525-062-6*) March of Dimes.

Preterm Prelabour Amniorrhexis. S. G. Carroll et al. LC 95-15963. (Frontiers in Fetal Medicine Ser.). (Illus.). 176p. 1995. 65.00 (*1-85070-692-1*) Prthnon Pub.

Preternatural. Margaret W. Bonanno. 23.95 (*0-614-26957-1*) Tor Bks.

Preternatural, Vol. 1. Margaret W. Bonanno. 1997. mass mkt. 5.99 (*0-8125-6764-1*, Pub. by Tor Bks) St Martin.

***Preternatural Too: Gyre.** Margaret Wander Bonanno. LC 99-89847. 320p. 2000. 23.95 (*0-312-86671-2*, Pub. by Tor Bks) St Martin.

***Pretest Analyses of the Steel Containment Vessel Model.** V. I. Porter. 158p. 1999. per. 14.00 (*0-16-062990-X*) USGPO.

Pretest & Review for Acupuncture Examination. Sidong Chen. Ed. by Elizabeth Jones. (Illus.). 275p. (C). 1995. pap. text 109.00 (*0-9645339-0-1*) Dr Chens.

Pretest, EMT-Intermediate. Richard E. Westfal. LC 98-36143. 1998. pap. 29.95 (*0-07-069636-5*) McGraw.

***Pretest for EMT Paramedics.** Westfal. LC 00-28748. (Illus.). 170p. 2000. pap. 29.95 (*0-07-134156-0*) McGraw.

***Pretest Prediction Analysis & Posttest Correlation of the Sizewell-B 1: Ten Scale Prestressed Concrete Containment Model Test.** R. A. Dameron. 204p. 1998. per. 17.00 (*0-16-062941-1*) USGPO.

Pretest Step 1 Simulated Exam. 7th ed. Ed. by John R. Thornborough. (Pretest Simulated Exam Ser.). 80p. 1991. text 30.00 (*0-07-911008-8*) McGraw-Hill HPD.

Pretest Step 2 Simulated Exam. Ed. by John R. Thornborough. (Pretest Simulated Exam Ser.). (Illus.). 176p. 1992. text 30.00 (*0-07-064521-3*) McGraw-Hill HPD.

***Pretext, Vol. 45.** Rae Armantrout. 2000. pap. 9.95 (*1-892295-39-3*) Green Integer.

Pretext Book. E. Roy Slade & James R. Gotz. 60p. (Orig.). 1992. pap. 29.95 (*0-918487-50-1*) Thomas Investigative.

Pretexta. Federico Campbell. (SPA.). pap. 10.99 (*968-16-4855-2*, Pub. by Fondo) Continental Bk.

Pretextes et Nouveaux Pretextes. Andre Gide. 12.95 (*0-685-34153-4*) Fr & Eur.

Pretexts of Authority: The Rhetoric of Authorship in the Renaissance Preface. Kevin Dunn. LC 93-6279. xvi, 198p. 1994. 35.00 (*0-8047-2284-6*) Stanford U Pr.

Pretre. Pierre Teilhard De Chardin. pap. 4.95 (*0-685-36600-6*) Fr & Eur.

Pretre Marie. Jules Barbey d'Aurevilly. (FRE.). 1980. pap. 16.95 (*0-7859-1913-9*, 2070371832) Fr & Eur.

Pretreat Conference Proceedings, 1990. Products Finishing Staff. 347p. 1990. pap. 45.00 (*1-56990-076-0*) Hanser-Gardner.

Pretreat Conference Proceedings, 1993. Products Finishing Staff. 360p. 1993. pap. 45.00 (*1-56990-077-9*) Hanser-Gardner.

Pretreatment & Reclamation of Dusts, Sludges & Scales in Steel Plants. (McMaster University Symposia Ser.). 298p. 1993. pap. 50.00 (*0-614-13093-X*, PC96/067) Iron & Steel.

Pretreatment Facility Inspection. 3rd rev. ed. Kenneth D. Kerri. (Illus.). 910p. (C). 1996. pap. text 33.00 (*1-884701-24-8*) CA St U Ofc Water.

Pretreatment for Separation. Ed. by K. J. Ives et al. 150p. 1998. pap. 159.00 (*0-08-043386-3*) Elsevier.

Pretreatment of Condenser Tubing for Enhanced Corrosion Resistance. 54p. 1982. write for info. (*0-318-61816-8*, 284C) Intl Copper.

Pretreatment of Industrial Wastes. Water Pollution Control Federation Staff. 159p. 1981. pap. 20.00 (*0-318-40176-2*, MFD3PA) Water Environ.

Pretreatment of Industrial Wastewaters. Andreadakis & Christoulas. (Water Science & Technology Ser.: No. 29). 354p. 1994. pap. 210.50 (*0-08-042542-9*, Pergamon Pr) Elsevier.

Pretreatment of Industrial Wastewaters II: Selected Proceedings of the 2nd IAWQ International Conference on Pretreatment of Industrial Wastewaters, Held in Athens, Greece, 16-18 October, 1996. Ed. by A. Andreadakis. 402p. 1997. pap. 255.00 (*0-08-043371-5*, Pergamon Pr) Elsevier.

Pretres anciens, pretres nouveau selon le nouveau testament see Old Testament Priests & the New Priest

Pretrial. 3rd ed. Thomas A. Mauet. 448p. 1995. 31.00 (*0-316-55108-2*, Aspen Law & Bus) Aspen Pub.

Pretrial. 4th ed. Thomas A. Mauet. 1999. pap. text 38.95 (*0-7355-0052-5*) Panel Pubs.

Pretrial Advocacy: Planning, Analysis, & Strategy. Marilyn J. Berger et al. 752p. 1988. teacher ed. write for info. (*0-316-09164-2*, 91642) Aspen Law.

Pretrial Advocacy: Planning, Analysis & Strategy. Marilyn J. Berger et al. 752p. 1988. pap. text 50.00 (*0-316-09162-6*, Aspen Law & Bus) Aspen Pub.

Pretrial Discovery: Strategy & Tactics. Edward A. Imwinkelried & Theodore Blumoff. 1990. 130.00 (*0-318-42413-4*) West Group.

Pretrial Discovery: Strategy & Tactics. annuals Edward A. Imwinkelried & Theodore Blumoff. 1990. suppl. ed. write for info. (*0-318-65005-3*) West Group.

Pretrial Discovery & the Adversary System. William A. Glaser. LC 68-54410. 300p. 1968. 34.95 (*0-87154-305-2*) Russell Sage.

Pretrial Discovery, Development - Professional Judgment: 1993 Edition. Blumoff et al. 1993. 25.00 (*1-55834-062-9*, 10636-10, MICHIE) LEXIS Pub.

Pretrial Hearings & Criminal Motion Practice. 327p. 1994. pap. 30.00 (*0-614-26663-7*, 1037); pap. 92.00 incl. audio (*0-614-26664-5*, 20371) NYS Bar.

Pretrial Litigation: Law Policy & Practice. 2nd ed. Lawrence Dessem. LC 95-25323. (Paralegal). 625p. (C). 1996. pap. text 38.50 (*0-314-06775-2*) West Pub.

Pretrial Litigation in a Nutshell. Dessem. LC 97-225463. (Paralegal Ser.). (C). 1998. pap. 15.00 (*0-314-22438-6*) West Pub.

Pretrial Litigation in a Nutshell. Lawrence Dessem. LC 92-16019. (Nutshell Ser.). 382p. (C). 1992. pap. text 17.00 (*0-314-00844-6*) West Pub.

Pretrial Motions in Criminal Prosecutions. James A. Adams & Daniel D. Blinka. 764p. 1994. 95.00 (*1-55834-190-0*, MICHIE) LEXIS Pub.

Pretrial Motions in Criminal Prosecutions. 2nd ed. Daniel D. Blinka & James A. Adams. LC 98-87879. 886p. 1998. 110.00 (*0-327-00497-5*, 6003511) LEXIS Pub.

Pretrial Problems of the Prosecutor see Roles & Functions of the Prosecutor

Pretrial Release & Detention & Pretrial Services. Ed. by Daniel B. Ryan. 80p. (Orig.). (C). 1993. pap. text 30.00 (*1-56806-350-4*) DIANE Pub.

Prettiest Feathers. John Philpin & Patricia Sierra. 336p. 1997. mass mkt. 5.50 (*0-553-57555-4*) Bantam.

***Prettiest Love Letters in the World: Letters Between Lucrezia Borgia & Pietro Bembo, 1503-1519.** Ed. by Hugh Shankland. (Illus.). 2000. reprint ed. pap. 16.95 (*1-56792-163-9*) Godine.

***Pretty & Practical Salmon Flies.** Dick Talleur. LC 99-72514. (Illus.). 224p. 1999. 65.00 (*0-9638388-1-4*) Abenaki Pubs.

Pretty As a Picture: A Guide to Manners, Poise & Style. Maria P. Everding. 138p. (Orig.). (J). (gr. 4-7). 1986. pap. 19.95 (*0-9617665-0-6*) GME Pub Co.

Pretty As a Picture: Fabric Frames. Pam Aulson. (Illus.). 24p. 1981. pap. 3.00 (*0-9601896-4-5*) Patch As Patch.

Pretty Babies. Julia Grice. 320p. 1995. mass mkt. 5.99 (*0-8125-1935-3*, Pub. by Forge NYC) St Martin.

Pretty Baby see Maybe . . . Maybe Not Again!

***Pretty Baby.** Susan Branch. 2000. pap. 4.95 (*0-7683-2187-5*) CEDCO Pub.

Pretty Baby. Sherry Keene-Osborne. 1998. mass mkt. 5.99 (*0-345-41761-5*) Ballantine Pub Grp.

Pretty Ballerina. John Wessel. LC 97-47758. 240p. 1998. 23.50 (*0-684-81464-1*) S&S Trade.

Pretty Ballerinas, Vol. 1. Sylvia Walker. 1999. pap. 4.99 (*0-448-42075-9*, G & D) Peng Put Young Read.

Pretty Boy. Roy Shaw. 256p. 1999. 26.00 (*1-85782-361-3*, Pub. by Blake Publng) Seven Hills Bk.

Pretty Boy: The Life & Times of Charles Arthur Floyd. Michael Wallis. (Illus.). 396p. 1994. pap. 14.95 (*0-312-11046-4*) St Martin.

Pretty Boy Dead: A Novel. rev. ed. Joseph Hansen. 208p. 1984. reprint ed. pap. 8.95 (*0-917342-48-8*) Gay Sunshine.

Pretty Boy Floyd. Sue Hamilton. Ed. by John Hamilton. LC 89-84923. (America's Most Wanted Ser.). (Illus.). 32p. (J). (gr. 4). 1989. lib. bdg. 11.96 (*0-939179-63-6*) ABDO Pub Co.

Pretty Boy Floyd. Larry McMurtry. 1995. mass mkt. 6.99 (*0-671-89167-7*) PB.

Pretty Boy Floyd. large type ed. Larry McMurtry & Diana Ossana. LC 96-54511. 653p. 1997. 24.95 (*0-7862-1045-1*) Thorndike Pr.

Pretty Boy Floyd: A Novel. Larry McMurtry & Diana Ossana. 352p. 1994. 24.00 (*0-671-89165-0*) S&S Trade.

Pretty Brown Face. Andrea Pinkney. LC 96-75235. (Illus.). 16p. (J). (ps). 1997. pap. 4.95 (*0-15-200643-5*, Red Wagon Bks) Harcourt.

Pretty Bubbles in the Air: America in 1919. William D. Miller. 248p. 1991. text 29.95 (*0-252-01823-0*) U of Ill Pr.

Pretty Faire Eats: Dr. Ray's Recipe Book of Pretty Faire Eats. Ray Calhoun. 288p. 1991. pap. 11.95 (*0-9630855-0-6*) Pretty Faire.

Pretty Gifts That Say I Love You: Over 35 Projects with Step-by-Step Instructions. Juliet Bawden. (Illus.). 112p. 1998. 24.95 (*1-85028-408-3*, Pub. by Collins & Br) Trafalgar.

Pretty Girl Is Like a Melody & Other Favorite Song Hits, 1918-1919. David A. Jasen. 1997. pap. 12.95 (*0-486-29421-8*) Dover.

Pretty Good Ain't Good Enough: The Dilemma of Education in the United States. Richard Diggs & Eleanor Clancey. (Orig.). 1991. pap. 9.95 (*0-937157-10-4*) Progressive Pubns.

***Pretty Good for a Girl: A Memoir.** Leslie Haywood. LC 98-18532. 240p. (YA). 1998. 23.50 (*0-684-85070-2*) Free Pr.

Pretty Good Jim's Journal Treasury: The Definitive Collection of Every Published Cartoon. Scott Dikkers. 320p. 1999. pap. 14.95 (*0-7407-0007-3*) Andrews & McMeel.

***Pretty Good Joke Book.** Ed. by Prairie Home Collection Staff. 2000. pap. 11.95 (*1-56511-368-3*, Pub. by HighBridge) Penguin Putnam.

Pretty Good Magic. Cathy East Dubowski. LC 87-4784. (Step into Reading Ser.: A Step 2 Book). (Illus.). 48p. (J). (ps-3). 1987. pap. 3.99 (*0-394-89068-X*, Pub. by Random Bks Yng Read) Random.

Pretty Good Magic. Cathy East Dubowski. (Step into Reading Ser.: A Step 2 Book). (J). (gr. 1-3). 1987. 9.19 (*0-606-12487-X*, Pub. by Turtleback) Demco.

Pretty Good Privacy 5.5.5. Source Code Update. Ed. by Philip R. Zimmermann et al. 512p. 1998. spiral bd. 24.00 (*1-891064-07-X*) Warthman Assocs.

Pretty Good Privacy 5.5.5. Platform - Independent Source Code. Ed. by Philip R. Zimmermann et al. 2968p. 1998. spiral bd. write for info. (*1-891064-08-8*) Warthman Assocs.

Pretty Good Privacy 5.5.5. Windows - Specific Source Code. Ed. by Philip R. Zimmermann et al. 2201p. 1998. spiral bd. write for info. (*1-891064-09-6*) Warthman Assocs.

Pretty Good Privacy 5.5.5. Macintosh - Specific Source Code. Ed. by Philip R. Zimmermann et al. 2247p. 1998. spiral bd. write for info. (*1-891064-10-X*) Warthman Assocs.

Pretty Good Privacy 5.0: Macintosh Specific Source Code, Vol. 1. 2nd ed. Ed. by Philip R. Zimmermann & Mark H. Weaver. 459p. 1997. pap., spiral bd. write for info. (*1-891064-00-2*) Warthman Assocs.

An Asterisk (*) at the beginning of an entry indicates that the title is appearing for the first time.

Pretty Good Privacy 5.0: Platform Independent Source Code, Vol. 1. 2nd ed. Ed. by Philip R. Zimmermann & Mark H. Weaver. 504p. 1997. pap., spiral bd. write for info. (*0-9649654-8-8*) Warthman Assocs.

Pretty Good Privacy 5.0: Unix Specific Source Code, Vol. 1. 2nd ed. Ed. by Philip R. Zimmermann & Mark H. Weaver. 380p. 1997. pap., spiral bd. write for info. (*1-891064-01-0*) Warthman Assocs.

Pretty Good Privacy 5.0: Windows 95/NT Specific Source Code, Vol. 1. 2nd ed. Ed. by Philip R. Zimmermann & Mark H. Weaver. 348p. 1997. pap., spiral bd. write for info. (*0-9649654-9-6*) Warthman Assocs.

Pretty Good Privacy 5.0 Macintosh Specific Source Code, Vol. 1. Ed. by Philip R. Zimmermann & Mark H. Weaver. 2092p. (Orig.). 1997. pap. write for info. (*0-9649654-7-X*) Warthman Assocs.

Pretty Good Privacy 5.0 Platform Independent Source Code, Vol. 1. Ed. by Philip R. Zimmermann & Mark H. Weaver. 2326p. (Orig.). 1997. pap. write for info. (*0-9649654-5-3*) Warthman Assocs.

Pretty Good Privacy 5.0 Windows 95/NT Specific Source Code, Vol. 1. Ed. by Philip R. Zimmermann & Mark H. Weaver. 1395p. (Orig.). 1997. pap. write for info. (*0-9649654-6-1*) Warthman Assocs.

Pretty Good Privacy 5.5 Macintosh - Specific Source Code, 5 vols. Ed. by Philip R. Zimmermann et al. 2216p. 1997. spiral bd. write for info. (*1-891064-05-3*) Warthman Assocs.

Pretty Good Privacy 5.5 Platform - Independent Source Code, 6 vols. Ed. by Philip R. Zimmermann et al. 2958p. 1997. spiral bd. write for info. (*1-891064-03-7*) Warthman Assocs.

Pretty Good Privacy 5.5 Windows - Specific Source Code, 5 vols. Ed. by Philip R. Zimmermann et al. 2104p. 1997. spiral bd. write for info. (*1-891064-04-5*) Warthman Assocs.

Pretty Good Privacy 5.0 Unix Specific Source Code Update. Ed. by Philip R. Zimmermann & Mark H. Weaver. 185p. 1997. spiral bd. 20.00 (*1-891064-06-1*) Warthman Assocs.

Pretty Good Privacy PGP Mail 4.5: Quick Guide. (Illus.). 38p. (Orig.). 1997. pap. write for info. (*0-9649654-3-7*) Warthman Assocs.

Pretty Good Privacy PGP Mail 4.5: Reference Manual. (Illus.). 216p. (Orig.). 1997. pap. write for info. (*0-9649654-4-5*) Warthman Assocs.

Pretty Good Privacy 3.0 Pre-Alpha Source Guide: Preliminary Release 1. Ed. by Philip R. Zimmermann. (Orig.). 1996. pap. write for info. (*0-9649654-1-0*) Warthman Assocs.

Pretty Good Privacy 3.0 Pre-Alpha Source Code Update: Preliminary Release 1.1. Ed. by Philip R. Zimmermann. LC 96-61896. 320p. (Orig.). 1996. pap. write for info. (*0-9649654-2-9*) Warthman Assocs.

Pretty Good, Really Cheap Paperback Logic Book. O. A. Robinson. 1998. pap. 6.50 (*0-934135-03-7*) Klare Ltd.

Pretty Hairstyle. Judy Katschke. (Illus.). 12p. (J). (gr. k-3). 1999. bds. 11.99 (*1-57584-335-8*, Pub. by Rdrs Digest) S&S Trade.

Pretty Happy! Peter Johnson. 96p. (Orig.). 1997. pap. 12.00 (*1-877727-75-X*) White Pine.

Pretty in Pink: The Golden Age of Teenage Movies. Jon Bernstein. LC 96-44748. (Illus.). 224p. 1997. pap. 14.95 (*0-312-15194-2*) St Martin.

Pretty in Punk: Girls' Gender Resistance in a Boys' Subculture. Lauraine Leblanc. LC 98-51532. (Illus.). 288p. (C). 1999. text 50.00 (*0-8135-2650-7*); pap. text 20.00 (*0-8135-2651-5*) Rutgers U Pr.

Pretty Kitty Journal: A Record Keeper for Your Pet. H D R Campbell. (Illus.). 160p. 1999. text 15.95 (*1-55670-951-X*) Stewart Tabori & Chang.

Pretty Lady. Marian Babson. 128p. 1992. mass mkt. 4.50 (*0-446-36212-3*, Pub. by Warner Bks) Little.

Pretty Lady. large type ed. Marian Babson. LC 92-35899. (General Ser.). 221p. 1993. lib. bdg. 15.95 (*0-8161-5256-X*, G K Hall Lrg Type) Mac Lib Ref.

Pretty Lady. Arnold Bennett. LC 74-17298. (Collected Works of Arnold Bennett: Vol. 67). 1977. reprint ed. 25.95 (*0-518-19148-6*) Ayer.

Pretty Lady. Arnold Bennett. LC 72-144876. 1971. reprint ed. 18.00 (*0-403-00863-8*) Scholarly.

Pretty Lady of Saratoga see Treasured Horses Collection

Pretty Maids All in a Row. large type ed. Rose Meadows. (Linford Romance Library). 368p. 1997. pap. 16.99 (*0-7089-7985-8*, Linford) Ulverscroft.

Pretty Maids in a Row. Marilyn Campbell. 416p. (Orig.). 1995. mass mkt. 5.99 (*0-451-40571-4*, Onyx) NAL.

Pretty Mrs. Gaston & Other Stories. John E. Cooke. LC 74-94713. (Short Story Index Reprint Ser.). 1977. 20.95 (*0-8369-3092-4*) Ayer.

Pretty Ones. Dorothy Eden. 1994. reprint ed. lib. bdg. 18.00 (*0-7278-4711-2*) Severn Hse.

Pretty Perfect Plant. Thomas-Cochran. (What a Wonderful World Intro Ser.). 1993. pap. text. write for info. (*0-582-91086-2*, Pub. by Addison-Wesley) Longman.

Pretty Pictures: Production Design & the History Film. C. S. Tashiro. LC 97-4762. (Illus.). 246p. (C). 1998. 35.00 (*0-292-78156-3*, TASPRE); pap. 18.95 (*0-292-78150-4*, TASPRP) U of Tex Pr.

Pretty Pillows: 40 Inspiring Projects to Grace Your Home. Susie Johns. (Illus.). 128p. 1997. pap. 19.95 (*0-8019-8938-8*) Krause Pubns.

Pretty Pink Shroud. E. X. Ferrars. 1992. reprint ed. lib. bdg. 19.00 (*0-7278-4273-0*) Severn Hse.

Pretty Plate. Jedediah V. Huntington. (Notable American Authors Ser.). 1992. reprint ed. lib. bdg. 75.00 (*0-7812-3290-2*) Rprt Serv.

Pretty Please. Diane Hoh. (Nightmare Hall Ser.: No. 7). 176p. (YA). (gr. 7-9). 1994. pap. 3.50 (*0-590-47690-4*) Scholastic Inc.

Pretty Poison: The Tuesday Weld Story. Floyd Conner. LC 95-22145. 256p. 1995. 22.00 (*1-56980-015-4*) Barricade Bks.

Pretty Polly. large type ed. Marion Chesney. LC 97-43616. 204p. 1998. 21.95 (*0-7838-8389-7*, G K Hall & Co) Mac Lib Ref.

***Pretty Primitives: Just for You.** Karen Stone. (Illus.). 44p. 1999. pap. 10.95 (*1-57377-086-8*, 19884-2310) Easl Pubns.

Pretty Red Wing: Historic River Town. Patricia C. Johnston. LC 83-80138. (Illus.). 96p. (Orig.). 1984. 12.95 (*0-942934-27-X*) Johnston Pub.

Pretty Ribbons. Donigan Cumming. (Illus.). 132p. 1996. 45.00 (*3-905514-82-6*, Pub. by Edit Stemmle) Dist Art Pubs.

Pretty-Shield. Frank B. Linderman. (Native American Voices Ser.). (Illus.). 256p. 1993. reprint ed. 24.95 (*0-7835-1758-0*) Time-Life.

Pretty-Shield: Medicine Woman of the Crows. Frank B. Linderman. LC 72-3273. (Illus.). 256p. 1974. reprint ed. pap. 9.95 (*0-8032-5791-0*, Bison Books) U of Nebr Pr.

Pretty Story. Francis Hopkinson. LC 73-76925. (American Fiction Reprint Ser.). 1977. 12.95 (*0-8369-7004-7*) Ayer.

Pretty Valentine Vol. 7: Pasitos English Language Development Books. Darlyne F. Schott. (Pasitos Hacia la Lectura Ser.). 19p. (J). (gr. k-1). 1990. pap. text 11.50 (*1-56537-066-X*) D F Schott Educ.

Pretty Village. McLoughlin Bros. Staff. pap. 5.95 (*0-486-23938-1*) Dover.

Pretty Witty Nell: An Account of Nell Gwyn & Her Environment. Clifford Bax. LC 76-83871. (Illus.). 306p. 1972. reprint ed. 24.95 (*0-405-08243-6*, Pub. by Blom Pubns) Ayer.

Pretty Woman. (P-V-G (Piano-Vocal-Guitar) Ser.). (Illus.). 80p. (Orig.). 1990. per. 14.95 (*0-7935-0067-2*, 00490371) H Leonard.

Pretzel. Margret Rey. LC 96-9669. (Illus.). 32p. (J). 1997. pap. 4.95 (*0-395-83733-2*) HM.

Pretzel. Margret Rey. LC 96-9669. (Illus.). 32p. (J). 1997. 15.00 (*0-395-83737-5*) HM.

Pretzel. Margret Rey. LC 44-9584. (Trophy Picture Bk.). (Illus.). 32p. (J). (ps-3). 1984. pap. 3.95 (*0-06-443051-0*, HarpTrophy) HarpC Child Bks.

Pretzel & Pop's Closetful of Stories. Jerry Smath. (Illus.). 64p. (J). (gr. 1-3). 1991. 4.95 (*0-671-72232-8*, Silver Pr NJ); lib. bdg. 7.95 (*0-671-72231-X*, Silver Pr NJ) Silver Burdett Pr.

Pretzel As a Strategic Weapon: A Humor Anthology. Michael Bloom. 32p. 1997. pap. 7.00 (*0-8059-4131-2*) Dorrance.

Pretzel Book. Phyllis R. Emert. LC 84-167042. (Illus.). 160p. 1984. pap. 4.95 (*0-912661-01-1*) Woodsong Graph.

Pretzel Logic: A Novel. Lisa A. Rogak. 256p. 1999. pap. 15.00 (*0-9652502-4-5*) Williams Hill.

Pretzel of Peculiar Proportion. Amy Adams. (J). (gr. 3-7). 1996. pap. 10.00 (*1-888166-50-9*) Shining Lght.

Preusser the Landscapes of Ice. 1976. pap. text 206.50 (*90-6193-028-6*) Kluwer Academic.

Preussische BGB-Entwurf von 1842. Bettina Kern. (Rechtshistorische Reihe Ser.: Band 176). (GER.). 265p. 1998. pap. 48.95 (*3-631-33011-1*) P Lang Pubng.

Prev. Alcohol. Boyd. (JRA Ser.: Vol. 4, No. 2). 1994. 20.00 (*0-8058-9972-3*) L Erlbaum Assocs.

Prevail: A Handbook for the Overcomer. Kelley H. Varner. 292p. 1982. pap. 10.99 (*0-938612-06-9*) Destiny Image.

***Prevailing in a Well-Armed World: Devising Competitive Strategies Against Weapons Proliferation.** Ed. by Henry D. Sokolski. (Illus.). 180p. 2000. pap. write for info. (*1-58487-013-3*) SSI US Army.

Prevailing over Time: Ethnic Adjustment on the Kansas Prairies, 1875-1925. D. Aidan McQuillan. LC 89-28957. xx, 292p. 1990. text 50.00 (*0-8032-3143-1*) U of Nebr Pr.

Prevailing Prayer. Charles G. Finney. LC 65-25846. (Charles G. Finney Memorial Library). 64p. 1975. pap. 6.99 (*0-8254-2603-0*) Kregel.

Prevailing Prayer. Francis Frangipane. 1995. pap. text 2.50 (*1-886296-01-4*) Arrow Publications.

Prevailing Prayer. Dwight Lyman Moody. 1997. pap. 8.99 (*1-898787-93-X*) Emerald House Group Inc.

Prevailing Prayer. Dwight Lyman Moody. (Classics Ser.). mass mkt. 4.99 (*0-8024-6731-8*, 394) Moody.

Prevailing Prayer. Dwight Lyman Moody. 1997. pap. text 6.95 (*1-888445-01-7*) Sonstar Pubns.

Prevailing Prayer to Peace see Oracion Que Prevalece

Prevailing Prayer to Peace. 2nd ed. Kenneth E. Hagin. 1973. pap. 5.95 (*0-89276-071-0*) Faith Lib Pubns.

Prevailing Through Prayer. Sarah Bowling. 1998. pap. 1.00 (*1-56441-177-X*) M Hickey Min.

Prevailing Trade Winds: Weather & Climate in Hawai'i. Ed. by Marie Sanderson. LC 93-21595. (Illus.). 156p. 1993. pap. text 19.00 (*0-8248-1491-6*) UH Pr.

Prevailing Types of Philosophy: Can They Logically Reach Reality? James McCosh. LC 75-3262. reprint ed. 35.00 (*0-404-59248-1*) AMS Pr.

Prevailing Voices: Stories of Triumph & Survival. Ed. by Maxine Alexander et al. (Southern Exposure Ser.). (Illus.). (Orig.). (C). 1982. pap. 3.00 (*0-943810-70-1*) Inst Southern Studies.

Prevailing Wage Legislation: The Davis-Bacon Act, State "Little Davis-Bacon" Acts, the Walsh-Healey Act, & the Service Contract Act. Armand J. Thieblot, Jr. LC 85-81948. (Labor Relations & Public Policy Ser.: Vol. 27). 279p. 1986. pap. 27.50 (*0-89546-055-6*) U PA Ctr Hum Res.

Prevalance of Child Sexual Abuse in Britain: A Feasible Study for Large-Scale. Deborah Ghate & Liz Spencer. LC 96-183948. 150p. 1995. pap. text 40.00 (*0-11-321783-8*, HM17838, Pub. by Statnry Office) Bernan Associates.

Prevalence & Characteristics of Persons with Hearing Trouble: United States, 1990-91. LC 93-4737. (Vital & Health Statistics Ser. 10: Data from the National Health Interview Survey: No. 188). 1993. write for info. (*0-8406-0483-1*) Natl Ctr Health Stats.

Prevalence of Back Pain in Great Britain in 1996: A Report on Research for the Department of Health Using the ONS Omnibus Survey. Tricia Dodd. (Omnibus Survey Publications Report: No. OS 8). 15p. 1997. 26.00 (*0-11-620968-2*, Pub. by Statnry Office) Balogh.

Prevalence of Deceit. F. G. Bailey. LC 90-42148. 168p. 1991. 35.00 (*0-8014-2542-5*); pap. text 12.95 (*0-8014-9773-6*) Cornell U Pr.

Prevalence of Drug Use in the D. C. Metropolitan Area Institutionalized Population 1991. (Illus.). 353p. (Orig.). (C). 1995. pap. text 50.00 (*0-7881-2577-X*) DIANE Pub.

Prevalence of Humbug & Other Essays. Max Black. LC 82-22211. 188p. (Orig.). (C). 1983. pap. text 15.95 (*0-8014-9321-8*) Cornell U Pr.

Prevalence of Psychiatric Morbidity among Adults Living in Institutions Report 4: OPCS Surveys of Psychiatric Morbidity in Great Britain. Howard Meltzer. x, 101p. 1995. 32.00 (*0-11-691661-3*, Pub. by Statnry Office) Balogh.

Prevalence of Psychiatric Morbidity among Adults Living in Private Households Report 1: OPCS Surveys of Psychiatric Morbidity in Great Britain. Howard Meltzer. xii, 174p. 1995. 35.00 (*0-11-691627-3*, HM16273, Pub. by Statnry Office) Balogh.

Prevalence of Selected Chronic Conditions: Medical Statistics. 1994. lib. bdg. 250.95 (*0-8490-5700-0*) Gordon Pr.

Prevalence of Selected Chronic Conditions: United States, 1986-88. U. S. Dept. of Health & Human Services Staff et al. LC 92-38011. No. 182. 1992. write for info. (*0-8406-0472-6*) Natl Ctr Health Stats.

Prevalence of Selected Chronic Conditions: United States, 1990-1992. John G. Collins. LC 96-50061. (Vital & Health Statistics Ser.: Series 10, No. 194). 1996. write for info. (*0-8406-0522-6*) Natl Ctr Health Stats.

Prevalence of Selected Chronic Conditions: United States, 1990-92. John Gary Collins. 94p. 1997. per. 12.00 (*0-16-061455-4*) USGPO.

***Prevalence of Substance Use among Racial & Ethnic Subgroups in the United States, 1991-1993.** Robert A. Johnson & Cindy Larison. Ed. by Dean R. Gerstein. (Illus.). 190p. 1999. pap. text 35.00 (*0-7881-8170-X*) DIANE Pub.

Prevalence, Predictablity, & Policy Implications of Recidivism. Stephen P. Klein et al. LC 86-216517. (Illus.). 71p. 1986. pap. text 7.50 (*0-8330-0762-9*, R-3413-BJS) Rand Corp.

Prevalent Single Chip Packages for Integrated Circuit Packages. David Kellerman. LC 98-120748. 132p. 1997. 2950.00 (*1-56965-247-3*, GB-195) BCC.

Prevencao de Infeccoes para Servicos de Planejamento Familiar: Um Manual de Reforencia para Solucao de Problemas. Linda Tietjen et al. (POR., Illus.). 252p. 1993. pap. text 15.00 (*0-929817-67-2*) JHPIEGO.

Prevencion de Infecciones para los Programas de Planificacion Familiar: Un Manual de Referencia para Solucionar Problemas. Linda Tietjen et al. (SPA., Illus.). 258p. 1992. pap. text 15.00 (*0-929817-69-9*) JHPIEGO.

Prevencion de la Deficiencia de Hierro: La Experiencia de Chile. Vivian Beyda et al. Ed. by Catherine E. Adams et al. Tr. by Eva Hertrampf. (SPA., Illus.). 64p. (Orig.). 1986. pap. text 3.50 (*0-318-35293-1*) ILSI.

Prevent Cancer Now. 2nd ed. Micheal Colgan. (Illus.). 140p. 1992. pap. text 9.95 (*0-9624840-3-2*, C I Pubns CA) Colgan Inst.

***Prevent Cancer Now! Arm Yourself with Powerful Weapons Against Cancer.** M. Colgan. 2000. pap. text 12.95 (*1-896817-07-6*) ApPubng.

Prevent Cancer Now: Your Guide to Self Protection, 2nd Edition. Michael Colgan. (Illus.). 140p. 1992. 19.50 (*0-9624840-2-4*) Colgan Inst.

Prevent Complications Due to Impaired Mobility. Donna D. Laken. 1995. pap. 3.95 (*0-915708-43-4*, 3164) Cheever Pub.

Prevent Gas on Stomach. Max. (Illus.). 50p. 1997. pap. 40.00 (*0-922070-89-X*) M Tecton Pub.

Prevent Hemorrhoids/How To. Max. 50p. 1997. pap. 32.00 (*0-922070-36-9*) M Tecton Pub.

Prevent, Repent, Reform, Revenge: Adolescents' Aims of Sanctions for Crimes & Misdeeds, 30. Ann C. Divers-Stamnes & R. Murray Thomas. LC 95-16145. (Contributions in Psychology Ser.: Vol. 30). 240p. 1995. 59.95 (*0-313-29730-4*, Greenwood Pr) Greenwood.

Prevent the Common Cold: It's Ridiculous to Catch a Cold in This Modern Age. Max. 50p. 1997. pap. 40.00 (*0-922070-34-2*) M Tecton Pub.

Prevent Tooth Decay. Max. 50p. 1997. pap. 40.00 (*0-922070-42-3*) M Tecton Pub.

***Prevent War: A New Strategy for America.** Jack Kidd. 200p. 2000. pap. 12.95 (*0-9675786-0-4*, Pub. by Three Pres) ACCESS Pubs Network.

Preventable Disasters: Why Governments Fail. Frederick L. Shiels. 256p. 1990. 47.50 (*0-8476-7623-4*) Rowman.

Preventative Agencies & Methods. Charles R. Henderson. (Russell Sage Foundation Reprint Ser.). reprint ed. lib. bdg. 47.00 (*0-697-00204-7*) Irvington.

Preventative Health Care in Companion Animals. Ed. by Caroline Jevring & Thomas E. Catanzaro. (Illus.). 255p. 1998. pap. write for info. (*0-7020-2393-0*) W B Saunders.

***Preventative Management of Children with Congenital Anomalies & Syndromes.** Golder N. Wilson & W. Carl Cooley. (Illus.). 300p. (C). 2000. pap. text 64.95 (*0-521-77673-2*) Cambridge U Pr.

Preventative Medicine & Public Health. 2nd ed. (National Medical Ser.). 1992. 26.00 (*0-685-75185-6*) Lppncott W & W.

Preventing a Crisis: AIDS & Family Planning Work. rev. ed. Gill Gordon & Tony Klouda. (Illus.). 200p. 1989. reprint ed. pap. text 12.00 (*0-333-51721-0*) Scholium Intl.

Preventing Abuse & Neglect: A Guide for Care Givers. Jetta Fuzy. (Illus.). 53p. 1998. pap. 29.95 (*1-888343-19-2*) Hartman Pub.

Preventing Academic Failure: A Multisensory Curriculum for Teaching, Reading, Spelling & Handwriting in the Elementary Classroom. 10th rev. ed. Phyllis Bertin & Eileen Perlman. 234p. 1980. spiral bd. 42.00 (*0-9636471-0-5*) Monroe Assocs.

Preventing Accidents. 96p. 1997. pap. text 34.95 (*0-7506-3706-4*) Buttrwrth-Heinemann.

Preventing Accidents & Illness at Work. Steve Morris & Graham Willcocks. 300p. 1995. pap. 47.50 (*0-273-61687-0*, Pub. by Pitman Pub) Trans-Atl Phila.

Preventing Adolescent Drug Abuse: From Theory to Practice. 1992. lib. bdg. 88.00 (*0-8490-8819-4*) Gordon Pr.

Preventing Adolescent Drug Abuse: Intervention Strategies. 1986. lib. bdg. 175.00 (*0-8490-3519-8*) Gordon Pr.

Preventing Adolescent Pregnancy: Model Programs & Evaluations. Ed. by Brent C. Miller et al. (Focus Editions Ser.: Vol. 140). (Illus.). 304p. 1992. 59.95 (*0-8039-4390-3*) Sage.

Preventing Adolescent Pregnancy: Model Programs & Evaluations. Ed. by Brent C. Miller et al. LC 91-45070. (Sage Focus Editions Ser.: No. 140). (Illus.). 304p. reprint ed. pap. 94.30 (*0-608-09625-3*, 205278300007) Bks Demand.

Preventing Adolescent Pregnancy: Model Programs & Evaluations, No. 140. Ed. by Brent C. Miller et al. (Focus Editions Ser.: Vol. 140). (Illus.). 304p. 1992. pap. 26.00 (*0-8039-4391-1*) Sage.

Preventing Adolescent Relapse, a Guide for Parents, Teachers, & Counselors. Tammy L. Bell. 225p. 1990. pap. text 14.00 (*0-8309-0571-5*) Herald Pub Hse.

***Preventing Adverse Events in Behavioral Health Care: A Systems Approach to Sentinel Events.** Joint Commission on Accreditation of Healthcare Organizations. (Illus.). 250p. 1999. pap. 45.00 (*0-86688-640-0*, BHSE-50) Joint Comm Hlthcare.

Preventing Adverse Medication Reactions. Bonnie Walker. (Injury Prevention for the Elderly Ser.). 1996. write for info. incl. VHS (*0-8342-0832-6*, 20832) Aspen Pub.

Preventing AIDS: A Guide to Effective Education for the Prevention of HIV Infection. Nicholas Freudenberg. 236p. 1989. 28.50 (*0-87553-166-0*) Am Pub Health.

Preventing AIDS.. A Practical Guide for Everyone. Joseph F. Benza, Jr. & Ralph D. Zumwalde. 85p. (Orig.). 1987. 18.95 (*0-9617818-0-7*); pap. text 9.95 (*0-317-55082-9*) Jalsco Inc.

Preventing AIDS: A Programmatic Perspective. Ed. by Ronald O. Valdiserri. LC 88-36573. 350p. (C). 1989. text 38.00 (*0-8135-1433-9*); pap. text 17.00 (*0-8135-1434-7*) Rutgers U Pr.

Preventing AIDS: A Sourcebook for Behavioral Interventions. Seth C. Kalichman. LC 97-39257. 275p. 1998. write for info. (*0-8058-2490-1*); pap. write for info. (*0-8058-2491-X*) L Erlbaum Assocs.

Preventing AIDS: Theories & Methods of Behavioral Interventions. Ed. by R. J. DiClemente & J. L. Peterson. (AIDS Prevention & Mental Health Ser.). (Illus.). 356p. (C). 1994. text 59.00 (*0-306-44606-5*, Kluwer Plenum) Kluwer Academic.

Preventing AIDS among Industrial Workers in India: Special Reference to the Third World Countries. R. M. Kalra. LC 98-917866. 108 p. 1999. write for info. (*81-259-0275-9*) S Asia.

Preventing AIDS in Drug Users & Their Sexual Partners. James L. Sorensen et al. LC 91-24707. (Substance Abuse Ser.). 220p. 1991. lib. bdg. 28.95 (*0-89862-173-9*) Guilford Pubns.

Preventing Alcohol Abuse: Alcohol, Culture, & Control. David J. Hanson. LC 94-37889. 160p. 1995. 55.00 (*0-275-94926-5*, Praeger Pubs) Greenwood.

Preventing Alcohol & Tobacco Problems: Manipulating Consumption: Information, Law & Voluntary Controls, Vol. 2. Ed. by Christine Godfrey & David Robinson. (Illus.). 226p. 1990. text 77.95 (*0-566-05702-6*, Pub. by Avebry) Ashgate Pub Co.

Preventing Alcohol & Tobacco Problems: The Addiction Market: Consumption, Production & Policy Development, Vol. 1. Ed. by Alan Maynard & Philip Tether. (Illus.). 270p. 1990. text 77.95 (*0-566-05701-8*, Pub. by Avebry) Ashgate Pub Co.

Preventing Alcohol-Related Problems on Campus: Impaired Driving: A Guide for Program Coordinators. William De Jong. (Illus.). 58p. (C). 1997. pap. text 20.00 (*0-7881-4731-5*) DIANE Pub.

Preventing Alcohol-Related Problems on Campus: Impaired Driving, a Guide for Program Coordinators. William DeJong. 72p. 1995. pap. 4.25 (*0-16-048439-1*) USGPO.

Preventing Alcohol/Drug Problems in Inner-City Communities: Model. Addie J. Key. 35p. (C). 1997. reprint ed. pap. text 15.00 (*0-7881-3063-3*) DIANE Pub.

Preventing & Controlling Cancer in North America: A Cross-Cultural Perspective. Diane Weiner. LC 99-19202. 264p. 1999. 69.50 (*0-275-96180-X*, Praeger Pubs) Greenwood.

Preventing & Controlling Discipline Problems. Ted Kowalski. (C). 1994. pap. text. write for info. (*0-8013-1356-2*) Longman.

Preventing & Controlling Drug Abuse. M. Gossop & m. Grant. 138p. 1990. 24.00 (*92-4-156134-3*) World Health.

P

Preventing & Controlling Iron Deficiency Anaemia through Primary Health Care: A Guide for Health Administrators & Programme Managers. E. DeMaeyer & P. Dallman. 58p. 1989. 11.00 (*92-4-154249-7*) World Health.

***Preventing & Detecting Managed Care Fraud.** Carolyn McElroy. Ed. by Nina Youngstrom. 100p. 1998. pap. 93.00 (*0-929156-36-6*) Atlantic Info Services Inc.

Preventing & Handling Product Liability. Randall L. Goodden. LC 95-33240. (Illus.). 312p. 1995. text 69.75 (*0-8247-9681-0*) Dekker.

Preventing & Handling Trouble in Closely Held Corporations. Robert C. Clark. 1989. write for info. (*1-55917-556-7*, 9321); audio 115.00 (*1-55917-555-9*) Natl Prac Inst.

Preventing & Managing Communicable Diseases. 146p. 1996. pap. 15.00 (*0-16-042681-2*) USGPO.

Preventing & Managing Conflict in Schools. Neil Katz & John W. Lawyer. Ed. by Jerry J. Herman & Janice L. Herman. LC 94-21624. (Road Maps to Success Ser.). 80p. 1994. pap. 14.95 (*0-8039-6146-4*) Corwin Pr.

Preventing & Managing Riots & Disturbances Correspondence Course, Bk. I, 152p.; Bk. II, 136p.; Test, 16p. Dennis H. Sherman. (Orig.). 1996. pap. 70.00 (*1-56991-012-X*) Am Correctional.

Preventing & Mitigating AIDS in Sub-Saharan Africa: Research & Data Priorities for the Social & Behavioral Science. National Research Council Staff. Ed. by Barney Cohen & James Trussell. LC 96-11347. 368p. (Orig.). 1996. pap. text 39.00 (*0-309-05480-X*) Natl Acad Pr.

***Preventing & Reversing Arthritis Naturally: The Untold Story.** Raquel Martin & Karen J. Romano. 208p. 2000. pap. 14.95 (*0-89281-891-3*, Heal Arts VT) Inner Tradit.

Preventing & Reversing Osteoporosis: Every Woman's Essential Guide. Alan Gaby. LC 92-42618. 320p. 1993. 19.95 (*1-55958-298-7*) Prima Pub.

Preventing & Reversing Osteoporosis: Every Woman's Essential Guide. Alan Gaby. 320p. 1995. pap. 14.95 (*0-7615-0022-7*) Prima Pub.

Preventing & Treating Carpal Tunnel Syndrome. Roger Williams. LC 95-135684. (Illus.). 32p. 1994. pap. text 6.00 (*1-56900-012-3*) Am Occup Therapy.

Preventing Antisocial Behavior: Interventions from Birth Through Adolescence. Ed. by Joan McCord & Richard E. Tremblay. LC 92-1444. 391p. 1992. lib. bdg. 49.00 (*0-89862-882-2*) Guilford Pubns.

Preventing Automobile Injury: New Findings from Evaluation Research. Ed. by John D. Graham. LC 88-14636. 308p. (C). 1988. 59.95 (*0-86569-185-1*, Auburn Hse) Greenwood.

Preventing Bank Crises: Lessons from Recent Global Bank Failures. Ed. by Gerard Caprio et al. (EDI Development Studies). 392p. 1998. pap. 40.00 (*0-8213-4202-9*, 14202) World Bank.

Preventing Banking Sector Distress & Crises in Latin America: Proceedings of a Conference Held in Washington, D. C., April 15-16, 1996. Suman K. Bery. (Discussion Papers: No. 360). 118p. 1997. pap. 22.00 (*0-8213-3893-5*, 13893) World Bank.

Preventing Breast Cancer: The Politics of an Epidemic. Cathy Read. 264p. 1995. pap. text 13.00 (*0-04-440909-5*) NYU Pr.

Preventing Breast Cancer: The Story of a Major, Proven, Preventable Cause of This Disease. 2nd ed. John W. Gofman. LC 96-2453. (Illus.). 422p. (Orig.). 1996. pap. 17.00 (*0-932682-96-0*) Comm Nuclear Respon.

Preventing Burns & Scalds. Walker. (Injury Prevention for the Elderly Ser.). 1996. write for info. incl. VHS (*0-8342-0826-1*, 20826) Aspen Pub.

Preventing CAN Deaths: An International Study of Deaths Due to Child Abuse & Neglect. Cyril Greenland. 250p. 1987. lib. bdg. 57.50 (*0-422-61210-3*) Routledge.

Preventing Cancers. Ed. by Tom Heller et al. 208p. 1992. 123.00 (*0-335-19004-9*); pap. 37.95 (*0-335-19003-0*) OpUniv Pr.

Preventing Car Accidents: Tips on How to Drive Safely see Lam The Nao Lai Xe Duoc An Tuan: Tinh Thuong Va Hanh Phuc

Preventing Car Theft & Crime in Car Parks. S. Geason & P. Wilson. 46p. 1990. pap. 12.00 (*0-642-14939-9*, Pub. by Aust Inst Criminology) Advent Bks Div.

Preventing Caregiver Burnout. James R. Sherman. Ed. by Merlene T. Sherman & Christopher J. Sherman. (Illus.). 80p. (Orig.). 1994. pap. 9.95 (*0-935538-16-X*) Pathway Bks.

Preventing Chaos in a Crisis: Strategies for Prevention, Control, & Damage Limitation. Patrick Lagadec. LC 92-33415. 356p. 1993. 29.95 (*0-07-707774-1*) McGraw.

Preventing Child Abuse: A Guide for Churches. Beth Swagman. LC 97-32483. 156p. 1997. pap. 8.45 (*1-56212-328-9*, 1700-5010) CRC Pubns.

Preventing Child Abuse & Neglect Through Parent Education. N. Dickon Reppucci. LC 97-9036. 1997. pap. text 25.95 (*1-55766-289-4*) P H Brookes.

Preventing Child Abuse What You Can Do. Al Sarno. 48p. 1998. pap. 8.00 (*0-8059-4369-2*) Dorrance.

Preventing Child Maltreatment Through Social Support: A Critical Analysis. Ross A. Thompson. LC 95-7702. 224p. (C). 1995. 45.00 (*0-8039-5594-4*); pap. 21.00 (*0-8039-5595-2*) Sage.

Preventing Child Sexual Abuse: A Curriculum for Children Ages Five Through Eight. Kathryn G. Reid. LC 94-3395. (Illus.). 160p. (Orig.). 1994. pap. 11.95 (*0-8298-1016-1*) Pilgrim OH.

Preventing Child Sexual Abuse: A Curriculum for Children Ages Nine Through Twelve. Kathryn G. Reid & Marie M. Fortune. LC 89-33084. (Illus.). 128p. (Orig.). (YA). 1989. pap. 9.95 (*0-8298-0810-8*) Pilgrim OH.

Preventing Child Sexual Abuse: Research Inconclusive about Effectiveness of Child Education Programs. (Illus.). 21p. (Orig.). (C). 1996. pap. text 25.00 (*0-7881-3457-4*) DIANE Pub.

Preventing Child Sexual Abuse: Sharing the Responsibility. Sandy K. Wurtele & Cindy L. Miller-Perrin. LC 92-3600. (Child, Youth, & Family Services Ser.: Vol. 2). (Illus.). xiv, 285p. 1992. pap. text 15.00 (*0-8032-9750-5*, Bison Books) U of Nebr Pr.

Preventing Childhood Disorders, Substance Abuse, & Delinquency. Ed. by Ray D. Peters & Robert J. McMahon. LC 96-4477. (Banff International Behavioral Science Ser.: Vol. 3). (Illus.). 344p. 1996. 54.00 (*0-7619-0014-4*); pap. 24.95 (*0-7619-0015-2*) Sage.

Preventing Childhood Eating Problems. 3rd ed. Jane R. Hirschmann & Lela Zaphiropoulos. LC 89-91514. 176p. 1993. pap. 10.95 (*0-936077-25-5*) Gurze Bks.

Preventing Childhood Injuries: A Guide for Parents. Modena Wilson. Ed. by Frank A. Oski. (Pediatrics Ser.). (Illus.). 32p. 1997. pap. 2.95 (*1-885274-30-0*) Health InfoNet Inc.

Preventing Choking & Aspiration. Walker. (Injury Prevention for the Elderly Ser.). 1996. write for info. incl. VHS (*0-8342-0824-5*, 20824) Aspen Pub.

Preventing Clash of Civilation. Herzog. LC 99-21773. 6p. 1999. text 45.00 (*0-312-22444-3*) St Martin.

Preventing Classroom Discipline Problems. 3rd ed. Howard Seeman. LC 93-61710. 385p. 1994. text 39.95 (*1-56676-093-3*) Rowman.

***Preventing Classroom Discipline Problems.** 3rd ed. Howard Seeman. 498p. 1999. 165.00 (*0-8108-3753-6*) Scarecrow.

***Preventing Classroom Discipline Problems.** 3rd ed. Howard Seeman. 498p. 1999. 129.95 incl. VHS (*1-56676-876-4*) Scarecrow.

***Preventing Classroom Discipline Problems: A Classroom Management Handbook.** 3rd ed. Howard Seeman. LC 99-64546. 496p. 1999. text 49.95 (*1-56676-834-9*, Pub. by Scarecrow) Rowman.

Preventing Computer Injury: The HAND Book with KeyMoves Software. Stephanie Brown. 100p. 1993. pap. 49.95 incl. 3.5 hd (*1-884388-01-9*) Ergonome.

Preventing Conflict in Central Asia: The Ferghana Valley. Nancy Lubin et al. LC 99-30898. 120p. 1998. pap. 11.95 (*0-87078-414-5*) Century Foundation.

Preventing Conflict in the Post-Communist World: Mobilizing International & Regional Organizations. Ed. by Abram Chayes & Antonia H. Chayes. 605p. 1996. pap. 24.95 (*0-8157-1385-1*) Brookings.

Preventing Coronary Artery Disease: Cardioprotective Therapeutics in Practice. 2nd ed. Martin J. Kendall & Richard C. Horton. 176p. 1998. write for info. (*1-85317-508-0*) Martin Dunitz.

Preventing Coronary Artery Disease: Cardioprotective Therapeutics in the 1990s. Martin J. Kendall & Richard C. Horton. 1994. 39.95 (*1-85317-175-1*, M Dunitz) Scovill Paterson.

Preventing Coronary Heart Disease: The Role of Antioxidants, Vegetables & Fruit. TSO Staff. 86p. 1997. pap. 45.00 (*0-11-322001-4*, HM20014, Pub. by Statnry Office) Bernan Associates.

***Preventing Corporate Embezzlement.** Paul Shaw & Jack Bologna. LC 99-89139. (Illus.). 2000. pap. 34.95 (*0-7506-7254-4*) Buttrwrth-Heinemann.

***Preventing Crime.** Farrington et al. 340p. 2000. 75.00 (*0-8133-9780-4*, Pub. by Westview) HarpC.

Preventing Crime. Ed. by James A. Cramer. LC 78-8400. (Sage Criminal Justice System Annuals Ser.: No. 10). 255p. reprint ed. pap. 79.10 (*0-8357-8451-7*, 203471500091) Bks Demand.

Preventing Crime: What Works, What Doesn't, What's Promising. Lawrence W. Sherman et al. (Illus.). 510p. (Orig.). (C). 1997. pap. text 50.00 (*0-7881-4625-4*) DIANE Pub.

Preventing Crime & Promoting Responsibility. (Illus.). 108p. 1995. pap. text 25.00 (*1-57979-255-3*) DIANE Pub.

Preventing Crime & Promoting Responsibility: 50 Programs That Help Communities Help Their Youth. 1997. lib. bdg. 250.95 (*0-8490-8237-4*) Gordon Pr.

***Preventing Crime & Promoting Responsibility: 50 Programs That Help Communities Help Their Youth.** Frwd. by Al Gore. (Illus.). 96p. (C). 2000. reprint ed. pap. text 20.00 (*0-7881-8630-2*) DIANE Pub.

Preventing Crime in America & Japan: A Comparative Study. Robert Y. Thornton & Katsuya Endo. LC 91-3511. 240p. (gr. 13). 1992. text 70.95 (*0-87332-788-8*) M E Sharpe.

Preventing Crime in America & Japan: A Comparative Study. Robert Y. Thornton & Katsuya Endo. LC 91-3511. 240p. (gr. 13). 1992. pap. text 34.95 (*0-87332-789-6*) M E Sharpe.

Preventing Crime on Public Transport. Patricia W. Easteal. 75p. 1991. pap. 18.00 (*0-642-16609-9*, Pub. by Aust Inst Criminology) Advent Bks Div.

Preventing Crime Package. Richard K. Riegelman. 1988. 350.00 (*0-316-74522-7*, Aspen Law & Bus) Aspen Pub.

Preventing Dance Injuries: An Interdisciplinary Perspective. Ed. by Ruth Solomon et al. (Illus.). 351p. 1990. pap. text 30.00 (*0-88314-425-5*) Princeton Bk Co.

Preventing Deadly Conflict. Ed. by David A. Hamburg & Cyrus R. Vance. (Illus.). 257p. (C). 1998. pap. text 40.00 (*0-7881-7090-2*) DIANE Pub.

Preventing Deadly Conflict: Final Report. Carnegie Commission on Preventing Deadly Conflict. LC 98-29056. 257p. 1998. pap. write for info. (*1-885039-01-8*) Carnegie Corp.

Preventing Deaths & Injuries from Excavation Cave-Ins. 1995. lib. bdg. 250.75 (*0-8490-7509-2*) Gordon Pr.

Preventing Derailment: What to Do Before It's Too Late. Michael M. Lombardo & Robert W. Eichinger. (Technical Reports: No. 138G). 62p. 1989. pap. 25.00 (*0-912879-36-X*) Ctr Creat Leader.

Preventing Diabetes. Cheta. LC 99-14783. 198p. 1999. 64.95 (*0-471-99914-8*) Wiley.

Preventing Disability in the Elderly: Report on a WHO Working Group. (Euro Reports & Studies Ser.: No. 65). 55p. 1982. pap. text 4.00 (*92-890-1231-5*) World Health.

Preventing Disease: Beyond the Rhetoric. Ed. by R. B. Goldbloom & R. S. Lawrence. (Frontiers of Primary Care Ser.). (Illus.). xxx, 478p. 1991. 69.00 (*0-387-97063-0*) Spr-Verlag.

Preventing Displacement in FmHA [RHS] Rural Rental Housing: A Guide for Public Agencies & Private Nonprofit Organizations on Prepayment. Housing Assistance Council Staff. 153p. 1994. 7.00 (*1-58064-044-3*) Housing Assist.

Preventing Drop-Outs. Richard Diggs. LC 96-70272. 160p. (Orig.). 1996. pap. 19.95 (*0-937157-14-7*) Progressive Pubns.

Preventing Drug Abuse: What Do We Know? National Research Council Staff. Ed. by Dean R. Gerstein & Lawrence W. Green. 176p. 1993. text 32.95 (*0-309-04627-0*) Natl Acad Pr.

Preventing Drug & Alcohol Problems in Inner-City Communities. 1993. lib. bdg. 256.99 (*0-8490-8502-0*) Gordon Pr.

Preventing Drug Use among Youth Through Community Outreach: The Military's Pilot Programs. Jonathan P. Caulkins et al. LC 94-24075. 1994. pap. text 13.00 (*0-8330-1618-0*, MR-536-OSD) Rand Corp.

Preventing Drunk Driving. Ed. by Elsie R. Shore & Joseph R. Ferrari. LC 98-12120. 107p. 1998. 29.95 (*0-7890-0511-5*) Haworth Pr.

Preventing Early School Failure. Robert E. Slavin. (C). 1993. pap. text 35.95 (*0-205-15684-3*) Allyn.

Preventing Early School Failure: Research, Policy, & Practice. Ed. by Robert E. Slavin et al. LC 93-16546. 256p. (C). 1993. pap. text 54.50 (*0-205-13991-4*, Longwood Div) Allyn.

Preventing Eating Disorders: A Handbook of Interventions & Special Challenges. Niva Piran et al. LC 99-21923. 347p. 1999. 54.95 (*0-87630-968-6*) Brunner-Mazel.

Preventing Elder Abuse. Walker. (Injury Prevention for the Elderly Ser.). 1996. write for info. incl. VHS (*0-8342-0827-X*, 20827) Aspen Pub.

Preventing Elderly Suicide: Overcoming Personal Despair, Professional Indifference, & Social Bias. Joseph Richman. LC 92-35995. (Death & Suicide Ser.: Vol. 11). 176p. 1993. 29.95 (*0-8261-7480-9*) Springer Pub.

Preventing Employment Lawsuits. James G. Frierson. LC 94-15327. 600p. 1994. text 65.00 (*0-87179-848-4*) BNA Books.

Preventing Falls. Walker. (Injury Prevention for the Elderly Ser.). 1996. write for info. incl. VHS (*0-8342-0823-7*, 20823) Aspen Pub.

***Preventing Falls: A Defensive Approach.** J. Thomas Hutton. LC 99-40082. 145p. 2000. pap. 18.95 (*1-57392-761-9*); pap. 34.95 (*1-57392-763-5*); pap. 21.95 incl. VHS (*1-57392-762-7*) Prometheus Bks.

***Preventing Falls in the Elderly.** Kathlene Benson. (Illus.). 77p. 2000. pap. 29.95 (*1-888343-28-1*) Hartman Pub.

Preventing Family Violence. Kevin Browne & Martin Herbert. LC 96-28875. (Series in Family Psychology). 402p. 1997. 119.95 (*0-471-92771-6*) Wiley.

Preventing Family Violence. Kevin Browne & Martin Herbert. LC 96-28875. (Series in Family Psychology). 250p. 1999. pap. text 35.00 (*0-471-94140-9*) Wiley.

Preventing Famine: Policies & Prospects for Africa. Donald Curtis et al. 250p. 1988. text 59.95 (*0-415-00711-9*) Routledge.

Preventing Fatalities of Workers Who Contact Electrical Energy. 1995. lib. bdg. 250.75 (*0-8490-7510-6*) Gordon Pr.

***Preventing Financial Chaos: An International Guide to Legal Rules & Operational Procedures for Handling Insolvent Banks.** John W. Head & Robert Lee Ramsey. LC 00-30205. 2000. write for info. (*90-411-8848-7*) Kluwer Law Intl.

Preventing Food Crises in the Sahel: Ten Years of Network Experience in Action. Johny Egg & Jean-Jacques Gabas. LC 98-100533. 204p. 1997. pap. 18.00 (*92-64-15406-X*, 44-97-01-1, Pub. by Org for Econ) OECD.

Preventing Foodborne Illness. Walker. (Injury Prevention for the Elderly Ser.). 1996. write for info. incl. VHS (*0-8342-0829-6*, 20829) Aspen Pub.

Preventing Gang- & Drug-Related Witness Intimidation. (Illus.). 164p. 1996. pap. text 45.00 (*1-57979-233-2*) DIANE Pub.

Preventing Gang & Drug Related Witness Intimidation. Peter Finn & Kerry M. Healy. (Illus.). 152p. (C). 1998. pap. text 30.00 (*0-7881-4292-5*) DIANE Pub.

Preventing Gang Violence in Your School. Mark Sanders. 1995. pap. 4.50 (*1-56246-112-5*, 3174, HazeldenJohnson Inst) Hazelden.

Preventing Graffiti & Vandalism. S. Geason & P. Wilson. 83p. 1990. pap. 15.00 (*0-642-14936-4*, Pub. by Aust Inst Criminology) Advent Bks Div.

***Preventing Heart Disease: What Every Woman Should Know.** Rita Baron-Faust. 280p. 2000. text 20.00 (*0-7881-9141-1*) DIANE Pub.

Preventing Heat Stress & Human Heat Strain: Recognition, Evaluation, & Control. Roger L. Wabeke. LC 98-18177. 1998. write for info. (*1-885581-16-5*) ASSE.

Preventing Heterosexism & Homophobia. Esther D. Rothblum & Lynne A. Bond. LC 96-4511. (Primary Prevention of Psychopathology Ser.: Vol. 17). 360p. 1996. 55.00 (*0-7619-0022-5*); pap. 24.95 (*0-7619-0023-3*) Sage.

Preventing HIV in Developing Countries: Biomedical & Behavioral Approaches. Ed. by L. Gibney et al. LC 98-44310. (AIDS Prevention & Mental Health Ser.). (Illus.). 424p. (C). 1999. text 75.00 (*0-306-45961-2*, Kluwer Plenum) Kluwer Academic.

Preventing HIV Transmission: The Role of Sterile Needles & Bleach. Institute of Medicine Staff. Ed. by Jacques Normand et al. LC 95-35458. 352p. 1995. 37.95 (*0-309-05296-3*) Natl Acad Pr.

Preventing Hyperthermia, Hypothermia & Drowning. Walker. (Injury Prevention for the Elderly Ser.). 1996. write for info. incl. VHS (*0-8342-0833-4*, 20833) Aspen Pub.

Preventing Illness among People with Coronary Heart Disease. Ed. by John D. Piette et al. LC 96-27430. (Journal of Prevention & Intervention in the Community: Vol. 13, Nos. 1/2). 200p. (C). 1996. 34.95 (*0-7890-0006-7*) Haworth Pr.

***Preventing Industrial Pollution at Its Source: The Final Report of the Michigan Source Reduction Initiative.** 76p. 1999. pap. text 10.50 (*0-9674974-0-X*) Meridan.

Preventing Industrial Toxic Hazards: A Guide for Communities. 2nd rev. ed. Marian Wise & Lauren Kenworthy. LC 92-41873. 208p. 1993. pap., student ed. 25.00 (*0-918780-60-8*) INFORM NY.

Preventing Injury & Death of Firefighters. 1995. lib. bdg. 251.99 (*0-8490-6679-4*) Gordon Pr.

Preventing Internal Theft: A Bar Owner's Guide. 2nd ed. Robert Plotkin. 1998. pap. 19.95 (*0-945562-24-1*) PSD Pub.

Preventing Interpersonal Violence among Youth: An Introduction to School, Community, & Mass Media Strategies. William DeJong. (Illus.). 70p. 1995. pap. text 20.00 (*0-7881-2520-6*) DIANE Pub.

Preventing Job Burnout. 75p. 6.95 (*0-318-41636-0*, 227) Am Bartenders.

Preventing Job Burnout: Transforming Work Pressures into Productivity. rev. ed. Beverly A. Potter. Ed. by Janis Paris. LC 95-78810. (Fifty-Minute Ser.). (Illus.). 104p. (Orig.). 1995. pap. 10.95 (*1-56052-357-3*) Crisp Pubns.

Preventing Juvenile Crime. Ed. by Sandra McKillop & J. Vernon. (Australian Institute Conference Proceedings Ser.: Vol. 9). 203p. 1991. pap. 25.00 (*0-642-16637-4*, Pub. by Aust Inst Criminology) Advent Bks Div.

Preventing Law Enforcement Stress: The Organization's Role. (Illus.). 232p. (Orig.). (C). 1994. pap. text 40.00 (*0-7881-0667-8*) DIANE Pub.

Preventing Lead Poisoning in Young Children. (Illus.). 107p. (Orig.). (C). 1993. pap. text 30.00 (*0-7881-0076-9*) DIANE Pub.

Preventing Legal Malpractice. 2nd ed. Jeffrie M. Smith. (C). 1996. pap. 18.50 (*0-314-20138-6*) West Pub.

Preventing Legal Malpractice. 3rd ed. Jeffrey M. Smith & Ronald E. Mallen. 264p. 1989. text. write for info. (*0-314-66223-5*) West Pub.

Preventing Legal Malpractice: California Case Studies on Legal Malpractice. Stephen M. Blumberg & Willis S. Baughman. 200p. (Orig.). (C). 1989. pap. write for info. (*0-318-64461-4*) Lawyers Mutual Insur.

Preventing Legal Malpractice in the Specialties: Commercial-Transactional, Vol. 4. 200p. (C). text 15.00 (*0-9621808-4-X*) Lawyers Mutual Insur.

Preventing Legal Malpractice in the Specialties: Family Law, Vol. 1. 200p. (C). text 15.00 (*0-9621808-1-5*) Lawyers Mutual Insur.

Preventing Legal Malpractice in the Specialties: Litigation, Vol. 2. 200p. (C). text 15.00 (*0-9621808-2-3*) Lawyers Mutual Insur.

Preventing Legal Malpractice in the Specialties: Probate-Estate Planning, Vol. 3. 200p. (C). text 15.00 (*0-9621808-3-1*) Lawyers Mutual Insur.

Preventing Legal Malpractice in the Specialties: Real Property, Vol. 5. 200p. (C). text 15.00 (*0-9621808-5-8*) Lawyers Mutual Insur.

Preventing Legal Malpractice in the Specialties Series, 5 vols., Set. (C). text. write for info. (*0-9621808-6-6*) Lawyers Mutual Insur.

Preventing Low Birthweight. Institute of Medicine Staff. 296p. 1985. pap. text 27.95 (*0-309-03530-9*) Natl Acad Pr.

Preventing Low Birthweight: Summary. Institute of Medicine Staff. 41p. (C). 1985. pap. text 5.00 (*0-309-03535-X*) Natl Acad Pr.

Preventing Major Chemical & Related Process Accidents. Ed. by B. F. Street et al. (European Federation of Chemical Engineering Ser.). (Illus.). 400p. 1988. 137.00 (*0-89116-065-5*) Hemisp Pub.

Preventing Maladjustment from Infancy Through Adolescence. Annette U. Rickel & La Rue Allen. (Developmental Clinical Psychology & Psychiatry Ser.: Vol. 11). 160p. 1987. text 42.00 (*0-8039-2868-8*); pap. text 18.95 (*0-8039-2869-6*) Sage.

Preventing Malnutrition. Walker. (Injury Prevention for the Elderly Ser.). 1996. write for info. incl. VHS (*0-8342-0830-X*, 20830) Aspen Pub.

Preventing Malpractice: The Co-Active Solution. T. L. Leaman & J. W. Saxton. (Illus.). 254p. (C). 1993. text 39.50 (*0-306-44441-0*, Kluwer Plenum) Kluwer Academic.

***Preventing, Managing & Resolving Intrastate Ethnic Conflict: An Evaluation of Theory & Evidence.** David Carment & Frank Harvey. LC 99-86108. (Praeger Studies on Ethnic & National Identities in Politics). 224p. 2000. 49.00 (*0-275-96979-7*, C6979, Praeger Pubs) Greenwood.

An Asterisk (*) at the beginning of an entry indicates that the title is appearing for the first time.

Preventing Mass Transit Crime. Ed. by Ronald V. Clarke. (Crime Prevention Studies: Vol. 6). 225p. 1996. 47.50 (*0-9606960-8-3*, Criminal Justice) Willow Tree NY.

Preventing Mass Violence Toward a Doctrine of Sovereign Responsibility. John D. Steinbruner. (New Ser.: No. 17). 1998. pap. 15.00 (*0-86682-104-X*) Ctr Intl Relations.

Preventing Maternal Deaths. E. Royston & S. Armstrong. 233p. 1989. 40.00 (*92-4-156128-9*) World Health.

Preventing Medical Malpractice Suits: A Handbook for Doctors & Those Who Work with Them. James E. Schutte. (Illus.). 230p. 1995. text 39.00 (*0-88937-135-0*) Hogrefe & Huber Pubs.

Preventing Mental Illness. Jennifer Newton. 272p. 1988. text 65.00 (*0-7102-0930-4*, Routledge Thoemms) Routledge.

Preventing Mental Illness: Mental Health Promotion in Primary Care. Rachel Jenkins et al. LC 97-16272. 518p. 1998. 159.95 (*0-471-97562-1*) Wiley.

Preventing Mental Illness in Practice. Jennifer Newton. 240p. (C). 1997. pap. 24.99 (*0-415-11993-6*, C0607) Routledge.

Preventing Misbehavior in Children. 2nd ed. Dewey J. Moore. LC 96-8763. 158p. 1996. text 36.95 (*0-398-06671-X*); pap. text 23.95 (*0-398-06672-8*) C C Thomas.

Preventing Miscarriage: The Good News. Jonathan Scher & Carol Dix. LC 89-45063. (Illus.). 256p. 1991. reprint ed. pap. 13.00 (*0-06-092056-4*, Perennial) HarperTrade.

Preventing Misdiagnosis of Women: A Guide to Physical Disorders That Have Psychiatric Symptoms. Elizabeth A. Klonoff & Hope Landrine. LC 96-25183. (Women's Mental Health & Development Ser.: Vol. 1). 190p. 1996. 28.00 (*0-7619-0046-2*) Sage.

Preventing Misdiagnosis of Women: A Guide to Recognizing Physiological Disorders That Have Psychiatric Symptoms. Elizabeth A. Klonoff & Hope Landrine. LC 96-25183. (Women's Mental Health & Development Ser.: Vol. 1). 190p. 1996. pap. 12.99 (*0-7619-0047-0*) Sage.

Preventing Missing Children. Gerald S. Arenberg et al. 128p. (Orig.). 1984. pap. 6.95 (*0-936320-21-4*) Compact Books.

Preventing Missing Children: A Parental Guide to Child Security. Gerald S. Arenberg et al. 128p. 1987. pap. 3.95 (*0-380-70429-3*, Avon Bks) Morrow Avon.

Preventing Nuclear Genocide: Essays on Peace & War. George H. Hampsch. (American University Studies: Philosophy: Ser. V, Vol. 50). XIV, 170p. 1988. 28.40 (*0-8204-0616-3*) P Lang Pubng.

Preventing Nuclear Proliferation in South Asia. Devin T. Hagerty & Asia Society Staff. LC 96-201704. viii, 39p. 1995. write for info. (*0-87848-512-0*) Asia Soc.

Preventing Nuclear Theft: Guidelines for Industry & Government. Ed. by Robert B. Leachman & Philip Althoff. LC 72-76452. (Special Studies in U. S. Economic, Social & Political Issues). 1972. 52.50 (*0-275-28618-5*) Irvington.

Preventing Nuclear War: A Realistic Approach. Ed. by Barry M. Blechman. LC 84-43115. (Illus.). 197p. reprint ed. pap. 61.10 (*0-608-09329-7*, 205407500002) Bks Demand.

Preventing Obsolescence Through Retraining: Contexts, Policies, & Programs. Jeanne P. Gordus et al. 64p. 1987. 7.00 (*0-318-35272-9*, IN 322) Ctr Educ Trng Employ.

Preventing Occupational Disease & Injury. Ed. by James L. Weeks et al. 750p. 1991. 28.50 (*0-87553-172-5*) Am Pub Health.

Preventing Occupational Fatalities in Confined Spaces. 1995. lib. bdg. 250.95 (*0-8490-7502-5*) Gordon Pr.

Preventing Occupational Hearing Loss: Practical Guide. John R. Franks. 105p. 1996. per. 9.00 (*0-16-061559-3*) USGPO.

Preventing Organic Dust Toxic Syndrome. 1995. lib. bdg. 251.75 (*0-8490-6678-6*) Gordon Pr.

***Preventing Osteoporosis with Ipriflavone: Discover the Proven, Safe Alternative to Estrogen Replacement Therapy.** Andrea Girman & Carol A. Pooley. 2000. pap. 14.95 (*0-7615-2222-0*) Prima Pub.

Preventing Pain & Injury from Your Computer. Francis T. Robinson & Roger D. Dennis. LC 93-93633. (Illus.). 50p. (Orig.). 1993. pap. write for info. (*0-9638697-0-1*) R&D Pubng.

Preventing Patient Falls. Janice M. Morse. 200p. 1996. 46.00 (*0-7619-0592-8*); pap. 21.95 (*0-7619-0593-6*) Sage.

Preventing Physical & Emotional Abuse of Children. David A. Wolfe. LC 91-24679. (Treatment Manuals for Practitioners Ser.). 168p. 1991. pap. text 21.00 (*0-89862-219-0*); lib. bdg. 49.95 (*0-89862-208-5*) Guilford Pubns.

Preventing Plagiarism & Cheating: An Instructor's Guide. Gary K. Clabaugh & Edward G. Rozycki. 1999. pap., teacher ed. 6.95 (*1-929463-01-4*) NewFound.

Preventing Pregnancy, Protecting Health: A New Look at Birth Control Choices in the United States. Susan Harlap et al. 128p. 1991. pap. 10.00 (*0-939253-21-6*) Guttmacher Inst.

Preventing Prejudice: A Guide for Counselors & Educators. Joseph G. Ponterotto & Paul B. Pedersen. (Multicultural Aspects of Counseling Ser.: Vol. 2). (Illus.). 238p. 1993. 42.00 (*0-8039-5284-8*); pap. 18.95 (*0-8039-5285-6*) Sage.

Preventing Prenatal Harm: Should the State Intervene? Deborah R. Mathieu. LC 95-36923. (Clinical Medical Ethics Ser.). 208p. 1996. pap. 19.95 (*0-87840-600-X*) Georgetown U Pr.

Preventing Prenatal Harm: Should the State Intervene? Deborah R. Mathieu. 168p. 1991. lib. bdg. 88.00 (*0-7923-0984-7*, Pub. by Kluwer Academic) Kluwer Academic.

Preventing Pressure Ulcers: A Patient's Guide. 1994. lib. bdg. 250.00 (*0-8490-8407-5*) Gordon Pr.

Preventing Pressure Ulcers: A Patient's Guide. 11p. 1993. pap. write for info. (*0-16-042254-X*) USGPO.

Preventing Problem Use of Alcohol. Walker. (Injury Prevention for the Elderly Ser.). 1996. write for info. incl. VHS (*0-8342-0825-3*, 20825) Aspen Pub.

Preventing Prostate Cancer: Screening Versus Chemoprevention Pros & Cons Based on New Views of Its Biology, Early Events & Clinical Behaviour. Ed. by Roderick T. Oliver et al. LC 95-175636. (Cancer Surveys Ser.: Vol. 23). (Illus.). 351p. reprint ed. pap. 108.90 (*0-608-09129-4*, 206976100006) Bks Demand.

Preventing Racism at the Workplace: A Report on 16 European Countries. 196p. 1996. pap. 30.00 (*92-827-7105-9*, SY95-96-576-ENC, Pub. by Comm Europ Commun) Bernan Associates.

Preventing Random Cracking in Concrete Flatwork. 1999. 8.95 (*0-924659-31-9*, 1601) Hanley.

Preventing Reactive Hypoglycemia: The Great Dilemma. Fred D. Hofeldt. 144p. 1983. 18.50 (*0-87527-214-2*) Green.

Preventing Reading Difficulties in Young Children. National Research Council Staff. Ed. by Catherine E. Snow et al. LC 98-9031. 350p. (C). 1998. text 35.95 (*0-309-06418-X*) Natl Acad Pr.

Preventing Reading Failure: A Practical Approach. Richard C. Culyer, III & Gail B. Culyer. LC 87-17424. 802p. 1987. lib. bdg. 75.00 (*0-8191-6496-8*) U Pr of Amer.

Preventing Reading Failure: An Examination of the Myths of Reading Instruction. Patrick Groff. 230p. 1987. pap. 19.95 (*0-89420-252-9*, 341150) Natl Book.

Preventing Relapse in Addictions. Emil Chiauzzi. (Practitioner Guidebook Ser.). 176p. (C). 1991. pap. text 41.00 (*0-205-14303-2*, H4303, Longwood Div) Allyn.

Preventing Residential Burglary: Toward More Effective Community Programs. J. R. Gillham. (Illus.). ii, 169p. 1991. 63.95 (*0-387-97610-8*) Spr-Verlag.

Preventing Retail Crime. S. Geason & P. Wilson. 88p. 1992. pap. 18.00 (*0-642-17047-9*, Pub. by Aust Inst Criminology) Advent Bks Div.

***Preventing school dropouts: Comprehensive Preparation for Students & Practitioners.** 2nd ed. Celeste Roseberry-McKibbin & M. N. Hegde. LC 99-24479. 1999. write for info. (*0-89079-824-9*) PRO-ED.

Preventing School Dropouts: Tactics for At-Risk, Remedial, & Mildly Handicapped Adolescents. Thomas C. Lovitt. LC 90-27493. 509p. 1991. pap. text 38.00 (*0-89079-454-5*, 1998) PRO-ED.

Preventing School Injuries: A Comprehensive Guide for School Administrators, Teachers & Staff. Marc Posner. LC 99-15070. 2000. write for info. (*0-8135-2749-X*); text 34.00 (*0-8135-2748-1*) Rutgers U Pr.

***Preventing School Problems - Promoting School Success: Strategies & Programs That Work.** Ed. by Kathleen M. Minke & George G. Bear. 425p. 2000. pap. text, wbk. ed. 65.00 (*0-932955-89-4*, N0016) Natl Assn Schl Psych.

***Preventing School Violence: Resource Guide to Safe Schools.** Jo Gulledge et al. LC 00-36220. 2000. pap. write for info. (*0-8342-1833-X*) Aspen Pub.

Preventing Self Destruction: A Manual for School Crisis Response Teams. William Steele. 1992. pap. 19.95 (*1-55691-064-9*, 649) Learning Pubns.

Preventing Sexual Abuse: Curriculum Guides for K-6, 7-12, & Special Populations. 2nd ed. Carol A. Plummer. LC 83-82306. (Illus.). 192p. 1997. pap. text 23.95 (*1-55691-114-9*, 149) Learning Pubns.

Preventing Sexual Harassment. (Illus.). 9p. 1998. write for info. (*0-945100-86-8*) Parlay Intl.

Preventing Sexual Harassment: A Training Manual for the Workplace. rev. ed. Virginia A. Lathan. 50p. 1997. spiral bd. 16.95 (*0-9636195-4-3*) Curry-Co Pubns.

Preventing Sexual Harassment: An Employer's Guide. 1994. per. 30.50 (*1-56726-023-3*) Mgmt Concepts.

Preventing Sexual Harassment in Schools. Miriam McLaughlin & Sandra Peyser. LC 98-35040. (Issues in Focus Ser.). 1999. 19.95 (*0-89490-962-2*) Enslow Pubs.

Preventing Sexual Harassment in the Workplace. Professional Resources, Inc. Staff. 300p. 1994. ring bd. 125.00 (*0-87425-979-7*) HRD Press.

Preventing Sexual Harassment On-Campus: Policies & Practices for Higher Education. Ben T. Allen. 60p. 1995. 18.00 (*1-878240-40-4*) Coll & U Personnel.

Preventing Shoplifting Without Getting Sued: Practical Advice for Retail Executives. Michael Craig Budden. LC 98-6020. 176p. 1999. 55.00 (*1-56720-119-9*, Quorum Bks) Greenwood.

***Preventing Sibling Rivalry: Six Strategies to Build a Jealousy-Free Home.** Sybil Hart. 2001. 24.00 (*0-684-87178-5*) Free Pr.

Preventing Social & Health Problems Through Life Skills Training. Ed. by Lewayne D. Gilchrist & Steven P. Schinke. (Center for Social Welfare Research Monograph: No. 3). 96p. (Orig.). 1985. pap. text 9.00 (*0-935035-00-1*) U WA Ctr Pol Rsch.

Preventing Stress, Improving Productivity: European Case Studies in the Workplace. Cary L. Cooper & Michiel Kompier. LC 98-35612. 10p. 1999. write for info. (*0-415-16556-3*); pap. write for info. (*0-415-16557-1*) Routledge.

Preventing Students from Dropping Out. Alexander W. Astin. LC 74-28915. (Jossey-Bass Series in Higher Education). 222p. reprint ed. pap. 68.90 (*0-8357-4803-0*, 203774000009) Bks Demand.

Preventing Substance Abuse: A Comprehensive Program for Catholic Education. Frank McCorry. 111p. 1990. pap. 6.00 (*1-55833-040-2*) Natl Cath Educ.

Preventing Substance Abuse: Intervention That Works. Michael J. Stoil & Gary Hill. LC 96-44747. (Illus.). 194p. 1996. pap. 28.00 (*0-306-45455-6*, Kluwer Plenum) Kluwer Academic.

Preventing Substance Abuse: Interventions That Work. Michael J. Stoil & Gary Hill. LC 96-44747. (Illus.). 214p. (C). 1996. 47.00 (*0-306-45454-8*, Kluwer Plenum) Kluwer Academic.

Preventing Substance Abuse among Children & Adolescents: Family-Centered Approaches, Reference Guide. Prakash L. Grover. (DHHS Publication Ser.: Vol. 3223-FY98). (Illus.). 308p. 1998. pap. 25.00 (*0-16-049679-9*) USGPO.

Preventing Substance Abuse in the Workplace: A Corporate Handbook. Richard J. Largent. (Illus.). v, 189p. (Orig.). 1996. pap. text 49.95 (*0-9656503-0-8*) Target Investigations.

Preventing Suicide & Depression. Walker. (Injury Prevention for the Elderly Ser.). 1996. write for info. incl. VHS (*0-8342-0831-8*, 20831) Aspen Pub.

Preventing Teen Pregnancy: Coordinating Community Efforts. Ed. by Christopher Shays. (Illus.). 150p. 1999. reprint ed. pap. text 30.00 (*0-7881-8060-6*) DIANE Pub.

Preventing Teenage Pregnancy. Susan Foster. LC 86-4486. 132p. 1986. 12.95 (*0-934842-46-9*) CSPA.

Preventing Teenage Pregnancy: What Educators Need to Know. 49p. (Orig.). 1994. pap. text 20.00 (*1-56806-162-5*) DIANE Pub.

Preventing Teenage Suicide. Bill Steele. 1983. pap. text 5.00 (*0-87879-815-3*, Ann Arbor Div) Acad Therapy.

Preventing Teenage Suicide: The Living Alternative Handbook. Polly Joan. LC 84-27872. (Illus.). 153p. 1985. 30.95 (*0-89885-247-1*, Kluwer Acad Hman Sci); pap. 18.95 (*0-89885-349-4*, Kluwer Acad Hman Sci) Kluwer Academic.

Preventing Teenage Violence: An Empirically Paradigm for Schools & Families. John S. Wodarski & Lois A. Wodarski. LC 97-38766. (Series on Social Work). (Illus.). 160p. 1998. 32.95 (*0-8261-1188-2*) Springer Pub.

Preventing the Misuse of Evaluation. Ed. by Carla J. Stevens & Micah Dial. LC 85-644749. (New Directions for Evaluation Ser.: No. PE 64). 110p. (Orig.). 1994. pap. 22.00 (*0-7879-9993-8*) Jossey-Bass.

Preventing the Transmission of the Human Immunodeficiency Virus (HIV) Hearing Before the Subcommittee on Health & Environment of the Committee on Commerce, House of Representatives, 105th Congress, Second Session, February 5, 1998. LC 98-168056. iii, 124p. 1998. write for info. (*0-16-056488-3*) USGPO.

***Preventing the Use of Weapons of Mass Destruction.** Ed. by Eric Herring. 200p. 2000. 57.50 (*0-7146-5044-7*, Pub. by F Cass Pubs); pap. 24.50 (*0-7146-8097-4*, Pub. by F Cass Pubs) Intl Spec Bk.

Preventing TMJ & OS6's Injuries in Dental Practice. Reda A. Abdel-Fattah. 352p. 1993. 207.00 (*0-8493-4725-4*) CRC Pr.

Preventing Tobacco Use Among Young People. 1997. lib. bdg. 255.99 (*0-8490-6231-4*) Gordon Pr.

Preventing Tobacco Use Among Young People: A Report of the Surgeon General, 2 vols. (Illus.). 326p. 1994. pap. text 60.00 (*1-57979-061-5*) DIANE Pub.

Preventing Tobacco Use Among Young People: A Report of the Surgeon General. M. Jocelyn Elders. (Illus.). 314p. (Orig.). (C). 1994. pap. text 50.00 (*0-7881-0569-8*) DIANE Pub.

Preventing Tobacco Use Among Young People: Report of the Surgeon General. 323p. 1994. per. 22.00 (*0-16-061388-4*) USGPO.

Preventing Torture: A Study of the European Convention for the Prevention of Torture & Inhuman or Degrading Treatment or Punishment. Malcolm Evans & Rod Morgan. 512p. 1999. text 99.00 (*0-19-826257-4*) OUP.

Preventing Unknown Barriers from Creeping into Your Treatment. Mary-Kim Arnold. (Orig.). 1995. pap. 39.95 (*1-884937-32-2*) Manisses Communs.

Preventing Violence: Program Ideas & Examples. Ed. by Jean O'Neil. 80p. 1992. pap. 11.95 (*0-934513-45-7*, M21A) Natl Crime DC.

Preventing Violence: Why Families Are Important, What They Can Do. Richard A. Panzer. (Illus.). 88p. 1999. pap. 7.95 (*1-888933-12-7*) Ctr Educ Media.

Preventing Violence Against Women: Not Just a Women's Issue. Mary J. Marvin. Ed. by Jean O'Neil. (Special Focus Ser.). 100p. (Orig.). 1995. reprint ed. pap. 16.95 (*0-934513-09-0*, M38) Natl Crime DC.

Preventing Violence Against Women & Children. Ronald B. Taylor. LC 97-160856. 64p. (Orig.). 1997. pap. write for info. (*1-887748-07-5*) Milbank Memorial.

Preventing Violence in America. Ed. by Robert L. Hampton et al. LC 95-34981. (Issues in Children's & Families' Lives Ser.: Vol. 4). 344p. 1995. 52.00 (*0-7619-0040-3*); pap. 25.50 (*0-7619-0041-1*) Sage.

***Preventing Violence in Our Schools.** Gerry Dunne. (Illus.). 144p. (YA). (gr. 4-12). 1999. pap. text 21.95 (*1-880396-65-3*) Jalmar Pr.

Preventing Violence in the Workplace. Charles E. Labig. LC 95-117. 224p. 1995. 24.95 (*0-8144-0287-9*) AMACOM.

Preventing Violent Conflicts: A Strategy for Preventive Diplomacy. Michael Lund. LC 96-4786. 1996. pap. text 14.95 (*1-878379-52-6*) US Inst Peace.

***Preventing War: The United Nations & Macedonia.** Abiodun Williams. 224p. 2000. 69.00 (*0-7425-0907-9*); pap. 28.95 (*0-7425-0908-7*) Rowman.

Preventing War in the Nuclear Age. Dietrich Fischer. (Illus.). 248p. (C). 1984. 57.50 (*0-8476-7342-1*); pap. 24.95 (*0-8476-7343-X*) Rowman.

Preventing Waste at the Source. Norman J. Crampton. LC 98-29657. 220p. 1998. lib. bdg. 49.95 (*1-56670-317-4*) Lewis Pubs.

Preventing Workplace Theft: They're Stealing from You. Lynn Tylczak & Thomas Sheets. Ed. by Kay Keppler. LC 94-72275. (Fifty-Minute Ser.). (Illus.). 62p. (Orig.). 1994. pap. 10.95 (*1-56052-272-0*) Crisp Pubns.

Preventing Workplace Violence. (Illus.). 96p. 1997. write for info. (*0-945100-60-4*) Parlay Intl.

Preventing Workplace Violence: A Guide for Employers & Practitioners. Mark Braverman. LC 98-40177. (Advanced Topics in Organizational Behavior Ser.). 168p. 1999. 36.50 (*0-7619-0614-2*) Sage.

Preventing Workplace Violence: A Guide for Employers & Practitioners. Mark Braverman. (Advanced Topics in Organizational Behavior Ser.). 1999. pap. write for info. (*0-7619-0615-0*) Sage.

Preventing Workplace Violence: Positive Management Strategies. Marianne Minor. Ed. by Carol Henry. LC 93-73145. (Fifty-Minute Ser.). (Illus.). 85p. (Orig.). 1994. pap. 10.95 (*1-56052-258-5*) Crisp Pubns.

***Preventing Youth Hate Crime: A Manual for Schools & Communities.** Government Printing Office Staff. 24p. 1998. pap. 2.50 (*0-16-049734-5*) USGPO.

Preventing Youth Suicide. Sandra McKillop. (Australian Institute Conference Proceedings Ser.: Vol. 13). 1992. pap. 30.00 (*0-642-17512-8*, Pub. by Aust Inst Criminology) Advent Bks Div.

Preventing Youth Suicide: A Handbook for Educators & Human Service Professionals. Alan W. McEvoy & Marcia McEvoy. 1994. pap. 22.95 (*1-55691-056-8*, 568) Learning Pubns.

***Preventing Youth Violence: A Guide for Parents, Teachers & Counselors.** Raymond B. Flannery, Jr. LC 98-49543. 160p. 1999. 19.95 (*0-8264-1148-7*) Continuum.

Preventing Youth Violence & Aggression & Promoting Safety in Schools. Sean Mulhern et al. 20p. (C). 1994. pap. text 9.00 (*1-57337-028-2*) WI Dept Pub Instruct.

Prevention. Consumer Guide Editors. LC 96-208567. 1996. mass mkt. 5.99 (*0-451-18810-1*, Sig) NAL.

Prevention: Basic & Clinical Aspects. Ed. by G. Nikiforuk. (Understanding Dental Caries (Ltd. Vol.) Ser.: Vol. 2). (Illus.). xiv, 290p. 1985. 50.50 (*3-8055-3905-3*) S Karger.

Prevention: The Critical Need. Jack Pransky. (Illus.). 384p. (Orig.). 1991. pap. 24.95 (*0-943741-02-5*) NEHRI Pubns.

Prevention: The Michigan Experience. Ed. by Betty Tableman & Robert Hess. LC 85-8071. (Prevention in Human Services Ser.: Vol. 3, No. 4). 121p. 1985. text 29.95 (*0-86656-458-6*) Haworth Pr.

Prevention: Toward a Multidisciplinary Approach. Leonard A. Jason et al. LC 87-19806. (Prevention in Human Services Ser.: Vol. 5, Issue 2, 1987). 309p. 1987. 59.95 (*0-86656-675-9*) Haworth Pr.

Prevention Across the Life Span: Healthy People for the Twenty-First Century. Ed. by Ruth N. Knollmueller. 120p. (C). 1994. pap. text 14.95 (*1-55810-091-1*, CH-27) Am Nurses Pub.

Prevention Action Plan for Alcohol-Related Problems. Ed. by Andrew M. Mecca. (Illus.). 90p. (Orig.). (C). 1994. pap. text 30.00 (*0-7881-1430-1*) DIANE Pub.

Prevention & Care of Athletic Injuries. 3rd ed. James M. Booher. 202p. 1995. pap. 18.95 (*0-945483-40-6*) E Bowers Pub.

Prevention & Care of Pressure Sores. Jetta Fuzy. (Illus.). 68p. 1997. pap. 29.95 (*1-888343-05-2*) Hartman Pub.

Prevention & Collection of Problem Loans. Dennis McCuistion. 1988. per. 42.50 (*1-55520-041-9*, Irwn Prfssnl) McGraw-Hill Prof.

Prevention & Control of Accidental Releases of Hazardous Gases. Vasilis M. Fthenakis. (Industrial Health & Safety Ser.). 532p. 1993. 120.00 (*0-471-28408-4*, VNR) Wiley.

Prevention & Control of Accidental Releases of Hazardous Gases. Ed. by Vasilis M. Fthenakis. LC 92-38460. 544p. 1993. text 98.95 (*0-442-00489-3*, VNR) Wiley.

Prevention & Control of Cardiovascular Diseases. (EMRO Technical Publications, Eastern Mediterranean Ser.: Vol. 22). 65p. (Orig.). 1995. pap. 5.00 (*92-9021-205-5*, 1450022) World Health.

Prevention & Control of Juvenile Delinquency. 2nd ed. Richard J. Lundman. (Illus.). 304p. (C). 1993. pap. text 21.95 (*0-19-506407-0*) OUP.

Prevention & Control of Nosocomial Infections. 2nd ed. Richard P. Wenzel. LC 92-18119. (Illus.). 1072p. 1992. 115.00 (*0-683-08921-8*) Lppncott W & W.

Prevention & Control of Nosocomial Infections. 3rd ed. Richard P. Wenzel. LC 96-17731. 1200p. 1997. 120.00 (*0-683-08916-1*) Lppncott W & W.

Prevention & Control of Pain in Children. (Illus.). 116p. 1997. pap. 29.00 (*0-614-31251-5*, Pub. by BMJ Pub) Login Brothers Bk Co.

Prevention & Control of Water-Caused Problems in Building Potable Water Systems (TPC 7) LC 80-85055. (TPC Publications: No. 7). (Illus.). 58p. 1995. pap. 32.00 (*1-877914-86-X*) NACE Intl.

Prevention & Control of Wildlife Damage. rev. ed. Ed. by Robert M. Timm. (Illus.). 640p. 1983. ring bd. 26.00 (*0-9613015-0-3*) Coop Ext Serv Univ Nebraska.

Prevention & Control of Wildlife Damage: A Handbook for People Who Deal with Wildlife Damage Problems. rev. ed. Ed. by Scott E. Hygnstrom et al. (Illus.). 650p. (C). 1997. pap. text 75.00 (*0-7881-3705-0*) DIANE Pub.

Prevention & Control of Yellow Fever in Africa. 99p. 1986. pap. text 17.00 (*92-4-156091-6*, 1150242) World Health.

P

*Prevention & Cure: The London School of Hygiene & Tropical Medicine, a 20th Century Quest. Lise Wilkinson & Anne Hardy. LC 99-22748. (Illus.). 350p. 1999. 110.00 (0-7103-0624-5, Pub. by Kegan Paul Intl) Col U Pr.

Prevention & Detection of Cancer: Proceedings of the Third International Symposium on Detection & Prevention of Cancer, New York, April 26 to May 1, 1976, 4 vols., Pt. 1, Vol. 1. International Symposium on Detection & Prevention. Ed. by Herbert E. Nieburgs. LC 77-87546. (Illus.). 1215p. reprint ed. pap. 200.00 (0-7837-0847-5, 204115900001) Bks Demand.

Prevention & Detection of Cancer: Proceedings of the Third International Symposium on Detection & Prevention of Cancer, New York, April 26 to May 1, 1976, 4 vols., Pt. 1, Vol. 2. International Symposium on Detection & Prevention. Ed. by Herbert E. Nieburgs. LC 77-87546. (Illus.). 1231p. reprint ed. pap. 200.00 (0-7837-0848-3, 204115900002) Bks Demand.

Prevention & Detection of Cancer: Proceedings of the Third International Symposium on Detection & Prevention of Cancer, New York, April 26 to May 1, 1976, 4 vols., Pt. 2, Vol. 1. International Symposium on Detection & Prevention. Ed. by Herbert E. Nieburgs. LC 77-87546. (Illus.). 1323p. reprint ed. pap. 200.00 (0-7837-0849-1, 204115900003) Bks Demand.

Prevention & Detection of Cancer: Proceedings of the Third International Symposium on Detection & Prevention of Cancer, New York, April 26 to May 1, 1976, 4 vols., Pt. 2, Vol. 2. International Symposium on Detection & Prevention. Ed. by Herbert E. Nieburgs. LC 77-87546. (Illus.). 1183p. reprint ed. pap. 200.00 (0-7837-0850-5, 204115900004) Bks Demand.

Prevention & Detection of Cracks in Ferrous P - M Parts: Preprint of a Seminar Held at the 1988 International Powder Metallurgy Conference, Orlando, Florida, June 10, 1988. Metal Powder Industries Federation Staff. LC TN0695.P84. 128p. reprint ed. pap. 39.70 (0-7837-1742-3, 205727500024) Bks Demand.

Prevention & Detection of Crime, Criminal Offenses see Tennessee Code Annotated 1999 Supplement

Prevention & Detection of Gynecologic & Breast Cancer. Istvan Nyirjesy. 150p. 1994. pap. text. write for info. (0-9642179-0-2) Intl Fnd Gynecol.

Prevention & Early Detection of Colorectal Cancer. Ed. by Graeme P. Young et al. (Illus.). 399p. 1996. text 94.50 (0-7020-2018-4, Pub. by W B Saunders) Saunders.

Prevention & Early Intervention: Individual Differences As Risk Factors for the Mental Health of Children - A Festschrift for Stella Chess & Alexander Thomas. Ed. by William B. Carey & Sean C. McDevitt. LC 93-25940. 328p. 1994. text 47.95 (0-87630-723-3) Brunner-Mazel.

*Prevention & Early Intervention with Children in Need. Michael Little & Kevin Mount. (Dartington Social Research Ser.). 166p. 1999. text 52.95 (0-7546-2074-3, Pub. by Ashgate Pub) Ashgate Pub Co.

*Prevention & First-Aid Treatment of Childhood Injuries. Ed. by William H. Brady. (Illus.). 228p. 1999. reprint ed. pap. text 20.00 (0-7881-6421-X) DIANE Pub.

Prevention & Health: Directions for Policy & Practice. Ed. by Alfred Katz et al. LC 87-17634. (Prevention in Human Services Ser.: Vol. 5, No. 1). 136p. 1987. text 39.95 (0-86656-668-6) Haworth Pr.

Prevention & Management of Laparoendoscopic Surgical Complications. Society of Laparoendoscopic Surgeons Inc. LC 98-61024. (Illus.). 1999. text 145.00 (0-9663768-0-3) Soc Laparo Surg.

Prevention & Noninvasive Therapy of Atherosclerosis. Alexander Leaf & Peter C. Weber. LC 90-8445. (Atherosclerosis Reviews Ser.: No. 21). (Illus.). 220p. 1990. reprint ed. pap. 68.20 (0-608-00603-3, 206119000007) Bks Demand.

Prevention & School Transitions. Ed. by Karen E. Danner & Karen S. Kurasaki. LC 93-33337. (Prevention in Human Services Ser.). (Illus.). 222p. 1994. lib. bdg. 39.95 (1-56024-576-X) Haworth Pr.

Prevention & Screening in Office Practice. Andrew K. Diehl. (Contemporary Management in Internal Medicine Ser.: Vol. 1, No. 4). (Illus.). 169p. 1991. text 36.00 (0-443-08826-8) Church.

Prevention & Screening in Office Practice. Ed. by Andrew K. Diehl. LC 92-34537. (Contemporary Management in Internal Medicine Ser.: Vol. 1, No. 5). (Illus.). 185p. reprint ed. pap. 57.40 (0-7837-6236-4, 204595000010) Bks Demand.

Prevention & Social Medicine. 12th ed. Ed. by P. Park. (C). 1989. 110.00 (0-7855-4677-4, Pub. by Current Dist) St Mut.

Prevention & Societal Impact of Drug & Alcohol Abuse. Ed. by Robert T. Ammerman et al. 432p. 1999. 89.95 (0-8058-3157-6); pap. 39.95 (0-8058-3158-4) L Erlbaum Assocs.

Prevention & Treatment of Alcohol Problems: Research Opportunities. Institute of Medicine Staff. 354p. (C). 1989. pap. text 30.00 (0-309-04182-1) Natl Acad Pr.

Prevention & Treatment of Cancer. Robert Bell. 88p. 1996. reprint ed. spiral bd. 10.00 (0-7873-0089-6) Hlth Research.

Prevention & Treatment of Cancer. Robert Bell. 88p. 1996. reprint ed. pap. 8.95 (1-56459-890-X) Kessinger Pub.

Prevention & Treatment of Complications of Diabetes: A Guide for Primary Care Practitioners. Frwd. by Charles M. Clark, Jr. 93p. (Orig.). (C). 1992. pap. text 20.00 (1-56806-015-7) DIANE Pub.

Prevention & Treatment of Contraceptive Failure. Ed. by S. Shan Ratnam & Uta Landy. LC 86-25318. 256p. 1986. 69.50 (0-306-42477-0, Plenum Trade) Perseus Pubng.

Prevention & Treatment of Diabetic Late Complications. Ed. by C. E. Mogensen & E. Standl. x, 226p. (C). 1989. pap. 69.25 (3-11-012297-9) De Gruyter.

Prevention & Treatment of Diabetic Nephropathy. Harry Keen & M. Legrain. 400p. 1983. text 164.00 (0-85200-744-2) Kluwer Academic.

Prevention & Treatment of Osteoporosis. Ed. by Lawrence B. Riggs. LC 92-48734. (Illus.). 50p. 1993. 19.90 (0-88937-098-2) Hogrefe & Huber Pubs.

Prevention & Treatment of Severe Behavior Problems: Methods & Models in Developmental Disabilities. Nirbhay N. Singh. (Special Education Ser.). 320p. (C). 1996. 59.95 (0-534-34418-6) Brooks-Cole.

Prevention des Infections Guide Pratique a l'Itention des Programmes de Planification Familiale: Manuel de Reference pour la Resolution de Problemes. Linda Tietjen et al. (FRE., Illus.). 254p. 1992. pap. text 15.00 (0-929817-66-4) JHPIEGO.

Prevention, Detection & Diagnosis of Cancer. Susan L. Groenwald. 1991. pap. 24.95 (0-86720-301-3) Jones & Bartlett.

Prevention Education: A Guide to Research. William J. Derivan & Natalie A. Silverstein. LC 89-39996. (Bibliographies in Contemporary Education Ser.: Vol. 9). 302p. 1990. reprint ed. text 44.00 (0-8240-3716-2, SS524) Garland.

Prevention Effectiveness: A Guide to Decision Analysis & Economic Evaluation, Vol.2. Ed. by Anne C. Haddix et al. (Illus.). 248p. (C). 1996. text 36.00 (0-19-510063-8) OUP.

Prevention Funding Information Bulletin: A Compendium of State, Federal & Private Funding Sources for Prevention & Children's Programs. 63p. (Orig.). (C). 1993. pap. text 20.00 (0-7881-0178-1) DIANE Pub.

Prevention, Health, & British Politics. Michael P. Mills. 200p. 1993. 61.95 (1-85628-190-6, Pub. by Avebry) Ashgate Pub Co.

Prevention "How-To Dictionary of Healing Remedies & Techniques" Prevention Magazine Editors. 1996. mass mkt. 7.99 (0-425-15191-3) Berkley Pub.

Prevention How-To Dictionary of Healing Remedies & Techniques. Prevention Medicine Editors. 1996. pap. 7.99 (0-425-15475-0) Berkley Pub.

Prevention How-To Dictionary of Healing Remedies & Techniques: From Acupressure & Aspirin to Yoga & Yogurt -- Over 350 Curative Options. Prevention Magazine Staff. 500p. 1994. 9.98 (1-56731-033-8, MJF Bks) Fine Comms.

Prevention in Child Welfare: States' Response to Federal Mandate. Krishna Samantrai. LC 92-32111. (Children of Poverty Ser.). 152p. 1993. text 20.00 (0-8153-1126-5) Garland.

Prevention in Childhood & Youth of Adult Cardiovascular Diseases - Time for Action: Report of a WHO Expert Committee. (Technical Reports: No. 792). (CHI, ENG, FRE, RUS & SPA.). 105p. 1990. pap. text 12.00 (92-4-120792-2, 1100792) World Health.

Prevention in Clinical Practice. D. H. Becker & L. B. Gardner. LC 88-12568. (Illus.). 468p. (C). 1988. text 85.00 (0-306-42624-2, Kluwer Plenum) Kluwer Academic.

Prevention in Community Mental Health Centers. Robert E. Hess & John Morgan. LC 90-4418. (Prevention in Human Services Ser.). 171p. 1990. text 4.95 (0-86656-999-5) Haworth Pr.

Prevention in Community Mental Health Practice. Jeffery J. Haugaard & N. Dickon Reppucci. 1991. pap. 27.95 (0-914797-70-0) Brookline Bks.

Prevention in Mental Health. Ed. by Henri Parens & Selma Kramer. LC 93-19429. 232p. 1993. pap. 27.50 (1-56821-027-2) Aronson.

Prevention in Mental Health: Research, Policy & Practice. Ed. by Richard H. Price et al. LC 80-14676. (Sage Annual Reviews of Community Mental Health Ser.: No. 1). 320p. reprint ed. pap. 99.20 (0-8357-4846-4, 203777700009) Bks Demand.

Prevention in Nephrology. Ed. by Marc E. De Broe. (Developments in Nephrology Ser.). 120p. 1991. text 102.00 (0-7923-0951-0) Kluwer Academic.

Prevention Magazine's Nutrition Advisor. Prevention Magazine Editors & Mark Bricklin. 596p. 1995. reprint ed. 12.98 (1-56731-039-7, MJF Bks) Fine Comms.

Prevention Magazine's Quick & Healthy Low-Fat Cooking: Light Ways with Poultry. Ed. by Prevention Magazine Health Editors. (Prevention Magazine's Quick & Healthy Low-Fat Cooking Ser.). (Illus.). 127p. 1995. pap. 15.95 (0-87596-245-9) Rodale Pr Inc.

Prevention Magazine's Quick & Healthy Low-Fat Cooking: Pastas & Sauces. Ed. by Prevention Magazine Health Book Editors. 128p. 1995. pap. 15.95 (0-87596-236-X) Rodale Pr Inc.

Prevention Material for Intervention in Drug, Alcohol & Tobacco Abuse: Resource Guide. 1995. lib. bdg. 250.75 (0-8490-6800-2) Gordon Pr.

Prevention Methods & Programmes for Oral Diseases: Report of a WHO Expert Committee, 1984. WHO Staff. (Technical Report Ser.: No. 713). 46p. 1984. 5.00 (92-4-120713-2) World Health.

Prevention of a Biological & Toxin Arms Race & the Responsibility of Scientists. Ed. by Erhard Geissler & Robert H. Haynes. 517p. 1991. 68.00 (3-05-501286-0, Pub. by Akademie Verlag) Wiley.

Prevention of Alcohol Abuse. Ed. by Peter M. Miller & Ted D. Nirenberg. 536p. 1984. 100.00 (0-306-41328-0, Plenum Trade) Perseus Pubng.

Prevention of an Arms Race in Outer Space: A Guide to the Discussions in the Conference on Disarmament. 203p. 36.00 (92-9045-056-8, E.GV.91.0.17) UN.

Prevention of Atherosclerosis & Hypertension Beginning in Youth. Lloyd J. Filer et al. (Illus.). 270p. 1994. text 48.50 (0-8121-1641-0) Lppncott W & W.

Prevention of Blindness: Proceedings of the WHO Scientific Group, Geneva, 1972. WHO Staff. (Technical Reports: No. 518). 1973. pap. text 3.00 (92-4-120518-0, 1100518) World Health.

Prevention of Cancer. (Technical Report Ser.: No. 276). 53p. 1964. pap. text 3.00 (92-4-120276-9) World Health.

Prevention of Cardiovascular Disease in Primary Care: An Evidence-Based Approach. Ed. by Andrew Neil et al. (General Practice Ser.). (Illus.). 352p. 1996. pap. text 59.50 (0-19-262397-4) OUP.

Prevention of Chemical Accidents: The Health Dimension. World Health Organization Staff. (Illus.). 168p. 1989. 60.95 (0-89116-946-6) Hemisp Pub.

*Prevention of Child Sexual Abuse in Ireland: The Development & Evaluation of the Stay Safe Programme. Deirdre MacIntyre & Alan Carr. LC 00-34864. (Studies in Health & Human Services). 2000. write for info. (0-7734-7715-2) E Mellen.

Prevention of Childhood Blindness. vii, 51p. 1992. pap. text 15.00 (92-4-156151-3, 1150378) World Health.

Prevention of Clinical Parasitology. Tsieh Sun. 1989. 56.00 (0-938607-23-5) Field & Wood Inc Medical.

Prevention of Contact Dermatitis. Ed. by Howard I. Maibach et al. LC 96-20543. (Current Problems in Dermatology Ser.: Vol. 25, 1996). (Illus.). x, 226p. 1996. text 240.00 (3-8055-6311-6) S Karger.

Prevention of Coronary Heart Disease. (Technical Report Ser.: No. 678). 53p. 1982. pap. text 5.00 (92-4-120678-0) World Health.

Prevention of Coronary Heart Disease. Ed. by Ira S. Ockene & Judith Ockene. LC 92-10336. 1992. 85.00 (0-316-62214-1, Little Brwn Med Div) Lppncott W & W.

Prevention of Corrosion. pap. 24.95 (0-8464-5186-7) Beekman Pubs.

Prevention of Corrosion & Scaling in Water Supply Systems. L. Legrand & P. Leroy. (Ellis Horwood Series in Water & Waste Water Management). 1990. text 92.00 (0-470-21647-6) P-H.

Prevention of Corruption Act & Accomplice. S. Seithi & A. Anand. (C). 1990. 235.00 (0-89771-168-8) St Mut.

Prevention of Crime: Social & Situational Strategies. Dennis P. Rosenbaum & Arthur J. Lurigio. LC 98-14883. (Criminal Justice Ser.). (C). 1998. 35.95 (0-534-50760-3) Wadsworth Pub.

Prevention of Delinquent Behavior. Ed. by John D. Burchard & Sara N. Burchard. LC 86-26095. (Primary Prevention of Psychopathology Ser.: No. 10). 376p. 1987. reprint ed. pap. 116.60 (0-608-01457-5, 205950100001) Bks Demand.

Prevention of Dental Disease. 2nd ed. John J. Murray. (Illus.). 520p. 1989. 95.00 (0-19-261807-5) OUP.

Prevention of Dental Disease. 2nd ed. John J. Murray. (Illus.). 528p. 1989. pap. 49.95 (0-19-261806-7) OUP.

Prevention of Depression: Research & Practice. Ricardo F. Munoz et al. LC 92-49536. (Series in Psychiatry & Neuroscience). (Illus.). 360p. 1993. text 65.00 (0-8018-4496-7) Johns Hopkins.

Prevention of Diabetes Mellitus: Report of a WHO Study Group. LC 95-103034. (Technical Reports: No. 844). (CHI, ENG, FRE & SPA.). viii, 100p. 1994. pap. text 15.00 (92-4-120844-9, 1100844) World Health.

Prevention of Disabilities in Patients with Leprosy: A Practical Guide. H. Srinivasan. (ENG, FRE & SPA.). viii, 140p. 1993. pap. text 29.00 (92-4-154456-2, 1150401) World Health.

Prevention of Discolorations in Hardwood & Softwood Logs & Lumber. (Illus.). 96p. 1997. pap. 40.00 (0-935018-94-8, 7283) Forest Prod.

Prevention of Drug Dependence - Evaluation of the European Drug Prevention Week: 1994 Technical Report. 182p. 1996. pap. 25.00 (92-827-6158-4, CE91-95-584-ENC, Pub. by Comm Europ Commun) Bernan Associates.

Prevention of Eating Disorders. Walter Vandereycken & Greta Noordenbos. LC 98-4537. 1998. text 50.00 (0-8147-8798-3); pap. text 18.50 (0-8147-8799-1) NYU Pr.

Prevention of Eye Disease. Ed. by Mitchell H. Friedlaender. 208p. 1988. 156.00 (0-913113-17-4) M Liebert.

Prevention of Falls & Hip Fractures in the Elderly. Ed. by David F. Apple, Jr. & Wilson C. Hayes. 148p. 1994. pap. 45.00 (0-89203-101-8) Amer Acad Ortho Surg.

Prevention of Fires & Explosions in Dryers: A User Guide. 2nd ed. Ed. by John Abbott. 138p. 1990. 40.00 (0-85295-257-0, 9CH24) Gulf Pub.

Prevention of Food Adulteration Act. A. P. Mathur. 838p. 1983. 320.00 (0-7855-1289-6) St Mut.

Prevention of Food Adulteration Act. 9th rev. ed. Rev. by G. C. Mathur. (C). 1989. 225.00 (0-7855-5108-5) St Mut.

Prevention of Food Adulteration Act 1954 with Central & State Rules & Notification. D. J. De. (C). 1988. 180.00 (0-7855-3701-5) St Mut.

Prevention of Food Adulteration Act, 1954. A. P. Mathur. (C). 1990. 125.00 (0-7855-5338-X) St Mut.

Prevention of Food Adulteration Act with Central & State Rules & Notifications. D. J. De. (C). 1989. 180.00 (0-7855-4796-7) St Mut.

Prevention of Food Adulteration Act, 1989, with Supplement. 9th ed. A. P. Mathur. (C). 1990. text 225.00 (0-7855-6596-5) St Mut.

Prevention of Food Adulteration Act, 1989, with Supplement. 9th rev. ed. Rev. by A. P. Mathur. (C). 1990. 225.00 (0-7855-5557-9) St Mut.

Prevention of Food Poisoning. 3rd ed. Jill Trickett. 137p. 1999. pap. 29.50 (0-7487-1522-3, Pub. by S Thornes Pubs) Trans-Atl Phila.

Prevention of Football Injuries: Protecting the Health of the Student Athlete. O. Charles Olson. LC 70-157472. 136p. reprint ed. 42.20 (0-8357-9413-X, 201456900094) Bks Demand.

Prevention of Genocide. Leo Kuper. LC 85-40465. 296p. reprint ed. pap. 91.80 (0-7837-2791-7, 204318300006) Bks Demand.

Prevention of Geographical Proliferation of Nuclear Weapons: Nuclear-Weapon-Free Zones & Zones of Peace in the Southern Hemisphere. (UNDIR Research Papers: No.4). 57p. 1989. 15.00 (92-9045-034-7, E.GV.89.0.8) UN.

Prevention of Head Injuries in Skiing. S. Oh. (Illus.). viii, 164p. 1985. pap. 42.75 (3-8055-3978-9) S Karger.

Prevention of Infant Mortality & Morbidity. Ed. by Frank Falkner. (Child Health & Development Ser.: Vol. 4). (Illus.). viii, 176p. 1985. 77.50 (3-8055-3989-4) S Karger.

*Prevention of Ischemic Stroke. Ed. by Cesare Fieschi & Marc Fisher. 290p. 1999. 99.95 (1-85317-738-5, Pub. by Martin Dunitz) Blackwell Sci.

Prevention of Liver Cancer: Report of a WHO Meeting, 1983. (Technical Report Ser.: No. 691). 30p. 1983. pap. text 3.00 (92-4-120691-8, 1100691) World Health.

Prevention of Mental Disorders, Alcohol, & Other Drug Use in Children & Adolescents. Ed. by David Shaffer et al. 478p. (Orig.). (C). 1996. reprint ed. pap. text 45.00 (0-7881-2970-8) DIANE Pub.

Prevention of Mental Illness in Primary Care. 371p. 1996. pap. text 52.95 (0-521-57648-2) Cambridge U Pr.

Prevention of Mental Illness in Primary Care. Ed. by Tony Kendrick et al. LC 95-38679. (Illus.). 371p. (C). 1996. text 150.00 (0-521-47057-9) Cambridge U Pr.

Prevention of Mental Retardation & Other Developmental Disabilities. Ed. by Michael K. McCormack. LC 80-24771. (Pediatric Habilitation Ser.: No. 1). (Illus.). 680p. reprint ed. pap. 200.00 (0-7837-0831-9, 204114500019) Bks Demand.

Prevention of Micronutrient Deficiencies: Tools for Policymakers & Public Health Workers. Ed. by Institute of Medicine Committee et al. LC 98-133582. 207p. 1998. pap. 30.00 (0-309-06029-X) Natl Acad Pr.

Prevention of Myocardial Infraction. Ed. by Joann E. Manson et al. (Illus.). 584p. 1996. text 65.00 (0-19-508582-5) OUP.

Prevention of Nuclear War: Soviet Scientists' Viewpoints. A. N. Kaliadin et al. 91p. 1983. text 15.00 (92-1-157038-7, E.83.XV.RR/31) UN.

Prevention of Nuclear War: U. N. Perspective. 1984. 20.00 (0-89946-184-0, E 84.XV.RR/30H) UN.

Prevention of Nuclear War: U. S. Approach. 1985. 20.00 (0-89946-206-5, E 85.XV.RR/32H) UN.

Prevention of Obstruction of Coronary & Vital Arteries. William Dock. LC 79-50185. 200p. (C). 1983. 42.50 (0-87527-202-9) Green.

Prevention of Occupational Cancer. Ed. by Charles R. Shaw. 256p. 1981. 145.00 (0-8493-5625-3, RC628, CRC Reprint) Franklin.

Prevention of Occupational Cancer International Symposium: Proceedings of the International Symposium on the Prevention of Occupational Cancer, Helsinki, April 21-24. International Agency for Research on Cancer Staff. (Occupational Safety & Health Ser.: No. 46). viii, 658p. (Orig.). 1982. pap. 42.75 (92-2-002907-3) Intl Labour Office.

Prevention of Occupationally-Acquired Blood-Borne Infections. Ed. by C. H. Collins & D. A. Kennedy. (A CAB International Publication). 320p. 1998. text 100.00 (0-85199-167-X) OUP.

*Prevention of Oil Pollution from Ships: Instructions for the Guidance of Surveyors. Maritime & Coastguard Agency Staff. 82p. 1999. ring bd. 50.00 (0-11-552111-9, Pub. by Statnry Office) Balogh.

Prevention of Oil Spillages Through Cargo Pumproom Sea Valves. ICS Staff & OCIMF Staff. (C). 1976. 60.00 (0-7855-3334-6, Pub. by Witherby & Co) St Mut.

Prevention of Oil Spillages Through Cargo Pumproom Sea Valves. ICS Staff & OCIMF Staff. (C). 1991. 170.00 (1-85609-019-1, Pub. by Witherby & Co) St Mut.

Prevention of Oral Disease. 3rd ed. Ed. by John J. Murray. (Illus.). 294p. 1996. pap. text 59.95 (0-19-262457-1) OUP.

Prevention of Oral Diseases. WHO Staff. (WHO Offset Publications: No. 103). 88p. 1987. 14.00 (92-4-170103-X) World Health.

Prevention of Perinatal Mortality & Morbidity. Frank Falkner. (Child Health & Development Ser.: Vol. 3). (Illus.). vi, 182p. 1984. 64.50 (3-8055-3854-5) S Karger.

Prevention of Perinatal Mortality & Morbidity: Proceedings of the WHO Expert Committee, Geneva, 1970. WHO Staff. (Technical Reports: No. 457). 60p. 1970. pap. text 6.00 (92-4-120457-5, 1100457) World Health.

Prevention of Perinatal Mortality & Morbidity: Proceedings of the WHO Seminar, Tours, 1969. WHO Staff. (Public Health Papers: No. 42). 97p. 1972. pap. text 5.40 (92-4-130042-6, 1110042) World Health.

Prevention of Perioperative Infections. H. Schoenfeld. (Antibiotics & Chemotherapy Ser.: Vol. 33). (Illus.). viii, 208p. 1985. 129.75 (3-8055-3936-3) S Karger.

*Prevention of Pollution by Garbage from Ships & the Provision & Use of Port Waste Reception Facilities: Instructions for the Guidance of Surveyors. Maritime & Coastguard Agency Staff. 22p. 1999. ring bd. 30.00 (0-11-552107-0, Pub. by Statnry Office) Balogh.

Prevention of Post-Harvest Food Losses: Fruits, Vegetables & Root Crops, a Training Manual. (Training Ser.: No. 17-2). 157p. 1989. 25.00 (92-5-102766-8, F7668, Pub. by FAO) Bernan Associates.

Prevention of Premature Staining of New Buildings. Ed. by Phil Parnham. (Illus.). 72p. (C). 1996. pap. 45.00 (0-419-17130-4, E & FN Spon) Routledge.

Prevention of Pressure Sores: Engineering & Clinical Aspects. Ed. by J. G. Webster. (Biomedical Engineering Ser.). (Illus.). 250p. 1991. 116.00 (0-7503-0099-X) IOP Pub.

P

An Asterisk (*) at the beginning of an entry indicates that the title is appearing for the first time.

Prevention of Progressive Chronic Renal Failure. Ed. by A. Meguid El Nahas et al. LC 92-48906. (Oxford Clinical Nephrology Ser.). (Illus.). 352p. 1993. text 65.00 (*0-19-262237-4*) OUP.

Prevention of Progressive Uremia, 2 Vols. Eli Friedman. 1989. 65.00 (*0-938607-07-3*) Field & Wood Inc Medical.

Prevention of Progressive Uremia, 2 Vols. Eli Friedman. 1990. 125.00 (*0-938607-28-6*) Field & Wood Inc Medical.

Prevention of Progressive Uremia, Vol. 2. Eli Friedman. 1989. 75.00 (*0-938607-15-4*) Field & Wood Inc Medical.

Prevention of Progressive Uremia, Vol. 3. Friedman. Date not set. write for info. (*0-938607-41-3*) Field & Wood Inc Medical.

Prevention of Reflective Cracking in Pavements. Ed. by A. Vanelstraete & L. Francken. LC 98-174558. (Rilem Report Ser.: No. 18). (Illus.). 152p. (C). (gr. 13). 1998. 90.00 (*0-419-22950-7*, D5596, E & FN Spon) Routledge.

Prevention of Repeated Crime. John B. Waite. (Michigan Legal Publications). xi, 221p. 1971. 42.00 (*1-57588-352-X*, 301850) W S Hein.

Prevention of Respiratory Diseases. Ed. by Albert Hirsch et al. (Lung Biology in Health & Disease Ser.: Vol. 68). (Illus.). 728p. 1993. text 245.00 (*0-8247-8850-8*) Dekker.

Prevention of Rh Sensitization: Proceedings of the WHO Scientific Group, Geneva, 1970. WHO Staff. (Technical Reports: No. 468). 1971. pap. text 5.00 (*92-4-120468-0*, 1100468) World Health.

Prevention of Rheumatic Fever. (Technical Report Ser.: No. 126). 27p. 1957. pap. text 3.00 (*92-4-120126-6*) World Health.

Prevention of Sexual Transmission of Human Immunodeficiency Virus. (WHO AIDS Ser.: No. 6). (ARA, ENG, FRE & SPA.). iii, 27p. 1990. pap. text 8.00 (*92-4-121006-0*, 1870006) World Health.

Prevention of Sexually Transmitted Diseases. Stanberry. (Illus.). 424p. 1999. 112.50 (*0-12-663330-4*) Acad Pr.

Prevention of Spillages Through Cargo Pumproom Sea Valves. ICS Staff & OCIMF Staff. (C). 1976. 75.00 (*0-7855-3918-2*, Pub. by Witherby & Co) St Mut.

Prevention of Spillages Through Cargo Sea Valves. ICS Staff & OCIMF Staff. 1976. 45.00 (*0-7855-1779-0*, Pub. by Witherby & Co) St Mut.

Prevention of Spina Bifida & Other Neural Tube Defects. Ed. by John Dobbing. 1983. text 99.00 (*0-12-218860-8*) Acad Pr.

Prevention of Sports Injuries: A Biomechanical Approach. Carole J. Zebas & Mike Chapman. 200p. 1990. pap. 24.95 (*0-945483-01-5*) E Bowers Pub.

Prevention of Stroke. Ed. by J. W. Norris & Vladimir C. Hachinski. (Illus.). 280p. 1991. 159.00 (*0-387-97442-3*) Spr-Verlag.

Prevention of Structural Failures: The Role of NDT, Fracture Mechanics & Failure Analysis: Proceedings of Two Annual Forums, 19-22 June, 1977 & 14-16 June 1976, Tarpon Springs, Florida. American Society for Metals Staff. LC 78-15388. (Materials-Metalworking Technology Ser.). (Illus.). 360p. reprint ed. pap. 111.60 (*0-608-10738-7*, 201948900013) Bks Demand.

Prevention of Suicide. (Public Health Papers: No. 35). 84p. 1968. pap. text 4.00 (*92-4-130035-3*, 1110035) World Health.

Prevention of Suicide: Guidelines for the Forumlation & Implementation of National Strategies. LC 96-172589. 39p. pap. 5.00 (*92-1-130178-5*) UN.

Prevention of Tachyarrhythmias with Cardiac Pacing. Ed. by J. Claude Daubert et al. LC 96-46589. (Illus.). 224p. 1996. 39.50 (*0-87993-651-7*) Futura Pub.

Prevention of Terroristic Crimes. (Criminology Ser.). 1992. lib. bdg. 83.95 (*0-8490-8753-8*) Gordon Pr.

Prevention of the Arms Race in Outer Space. 26p. 1986. pap. 4.00 (*92-9045-012-6*, GV.E.86.O.2) UN.

Prevention of the Re-Introduction of Malaria: Report of a WHO Meeting, 1967. (Technical Report Ser.: No. 375). 32p. 1967. pap. text 3.00 (*92-4-120374-9*, 1100374) World Health.

Prevention of Thermal Cracking in Concrete at Early Ages: State of the Art Report. R. Springenschmid & Rilem Technical Committee 119. LC 98-36759. (Rilem Report Ser.). 1999. write for info. (*0-419-22310-X*, E & FN Spon) Routledge.

Prevention of Thromboembolism in Spinal Cord Injury. unabridged ed. Consortium for Spinal Cord Medicine Staff. (Clinical Practice Guidelines Ser.). 18p. (Orig.). 1997. pap. write for info. (*0-614-30208-0*) Paralyzed Vets.

Prevention of Traffic Accidents in Childhood: Report on a WHO Study. J. P. Deschamps. (EURO Reports & Studies: No. 26). 54p. 1981. pap. text 4.00 (*92-9020-165-7*, 1330026) World Health.

Prevention of Type One Diabetes & Autoimmune Thyroid Disease. Ed. by Shigenobu Nagataki et al. (Current Clinical Practice Ser.: Vol. 49). 158p. 1988. 65.75 (*0-685-20122-8*) Elsevier.

Prevention of Venous Thromboembolism. Ed. by Samuel Z. Goldhaber. LC 92-49981. (Fundamental & Clinical Cardiology Ser.: Vol. 12). (Illus.). 632p. 1992. text 140.00 (*0-8247-8757-9*) Dekker.

Prevention of Water Pollution by Agriculture & Related Activities. 362p. 1993. 41.00 (*92-5-103380-3*, F33803, Pub. by FAO) Bernan Associates.

Prevention of Wind Loads on Large Liquified Gas Carriers. OCIMF Staff & SIGGTO Staff. (C). 1985. 600.00 (*0-7855-3919-0*, Pub. by Witherby & Co) St Mut.

Prevention of Youth Violence: A Framework for Community Action. Mary A. Fenley et al. (Illus.). 96p. (Orig.). 1994. pap. text 25.00 (*0-7881-0613-9*) DIANE Pub.

Prevention of Youth Violence: A Resource Guide for Youth Development & Family Life Professionals & Volunteers. Heidi L. Haugen. 80p. 1998. pap. 26.00 (*1-57753-222-8*, 301PYV) Corn Coop Ext.

Prevention or Pork? A Hard Headed Look at Youth-Oriented Anti-Crime Programs. Richard A. Mendel. 33p. 1995. pap. text. write for info. (*1-887031-50-2*) Am Youth Policy.

Prevention Pain-Relief System: A Total Program for Relieving Any Pain in Your Body. Prevention Magazine Editors. 752p. 1994. mass mkt. 6.99 (*0-553-56491-9*) Bantam.

Prevention Planning in Mental Health. Ed. by Jared A. Hermalin & Jonathan A. Morell. LC 86-3874. (Sage Studies in Community Mental Health: No. 9). 261p. 1987. reprint ed. pap. 81.00 (*0-608-01458-3*, 205950200001) Bks Demand.

Prevention Plus III: Assessing Alcohol & Other Drug Prevention Programs at the School & Community Level: A Four-Step Guide to Useful Program Assessment. Jean A. Linney & Abraham Wandersman. (Illus.). 461p. (Orig.). (C). 1993. pap. text 50.00 (*0-7881-0085-8*) DIANE Pub.

Prevention Plus II: Tools for Creating & Sustaining Drug-Free Communities. (Illus.). 541p. (Orig.). (C). 1994. pap. text 50.00 (*0-7881-0295-8*) DIANE Pub.

Prevention Practice. Rothman. 1992. text 78.95 (*0-7216-3261-0*, W B Saunders Co) Harcrt Hlth Sci Grp.

Prevention Practice in Substance Abuse. Ed. by Carl G. Leukefeld et al. LC 95-13748. (Drugs & Society Ser.: Vol. 8, No. 3 & 4). 141p. 1995. 39.95 (*1-56024-734-7*) Haworth Pr.

Prevention Primer: An Encyclopedia of Alcohol, Tobacco, & Other Drug Prevention Terms. 134p. (Orig.). 1995. pap. text 25.00 (*0-7881-2136-7*) DIANE Pub.

Prevention Programs for Youth: A Guide to Outcomes Evaluation, Best Practices, & Successful Funding. Ed. by Karienne Stovell. 150p. 1998. pap. 69.95 (*1-884937-52-7*) Manisses Communs.

Prevention Research: Determining Drug Abuse among Children & Adolescents. 1986. lib. bdg. 175.00 (*0-8490-3498-1*) Gordon Pr.

Prevention Strategies for Mental Health. Ed. by Eugene Aronowitz. LC 82-24133. 1982. pap. 9.95 (*0-88202-139-7*, Prodist) Watson Pub Intl.

Prevention 2000 - A Public-Private Partnership. Ed. by Andrew M. Mecca. (Illus.). 126p. 1994. reprint ed. pap. text 30.00 (*0-7881-1429-8*) DIANE Pub.

Preventions & Treatments of Alcohol & Drug Abuse: A Socio-Epidemiological Sourcebook. Brenda Forster & Jeffrey C. Salloway. LC 91-22618. (Interdisciplinary Studies in Alcohol & Drug Use & Abuse: Vol. 7). 596p. 1991. lib. bdg. 119.95 (*0-7734-9714-5*) E Mellen.

***Prevention's Best.** Ed. by Prevention Health Books Editors. 288p. 2000. 5.99 (*0-312-97503-1*, St Martins Paperbacks) St Martin.

***Prevention's Best: Vitamin Cures.** Ed. by Prevention Health Books Staff. 560p. 2000. mass mkt. 6.99 (*0-312-97476-0*, St Martins Paperbacks) St Martin.

***Prevention's Complete Book of Walking: Everything You Need to Know to Walk Your Way to Better Health.** Maggie Spilner. (Illus.). 272p. 2000. pap. 14.95 (*1-57954-236-0*) Rodale Pr Inc.

Prevention's Cooking for Good Health: Easy Recipes for Low-Fat Living. Ed. by Jean Rogers. (Illus.). 384p. 1994. 27.95 (*0-87596-210-6*) Rodale Pr Inc.

Prevention's Fight Fat: The Best New Ways to Cut Fat--from Your Plate & Your Waist. Mark Bricklin & Gale Maleskey. LC 96-27692. 1997. pap. 9.95 (*0-87596-420-6*) Rodale Pr Inc.

Prevention's Food & Nutrition. Prevention Magazine Editors. 1996. mass mkt. 7.99 (*0-425-15520-X*) Berkley Pub.

Prevention's Freezer Cookbook: Great Dishes You Can Cook & Freeze. Ed. by Sharon Sanders, pseud. 1998. pap. 14.95 (*0-87596-468-0*) Rodale Pr Inc.

Prevention's Guide to High-Speed Healing. Rodale Press Editors. 1995. reprint ed. 12.98 (*1-56731-072-9*, MJF Bks) Fine Comms.

Prevention's Healing with Vitamins. Prevention Magazine Health Book Editors. 512p. 1996. text 27.95 (*0-87596-292-0*) Rodale Pr Inc.

Prevention's Healing with Vitamins: The Ultimate Guide to Using Nature's Powerhouse Nutrients for Preventing & Curing Disease. Prevention Health Books Editors. LC 98-19052. 593 p. 1998. 29.95 (*1-57954-064-3*) Rodale Pr Inc.

Prevention's Health Guaranteed Cookbook: Custom-Tailored Eating Plans for Men, Women, & Dieters That Deliver the Maximum in Vitamins & Minerals, the Minimum in Fat, & the Ultimate in Taste. David Joachim & Prevention Magazine Health Books Editors. LC 97-27739. 464p. 1998. text 29.95 (*0-87596-537-7*) Rodale Pr Inc.

Prevention's Healthy Heart Cookbook: Over 200 Truly Satisfying Recipes. Prevention Health Books Editors. LC 99-30421. (Illus.). 416p. 1999. text 29.95 (*0-87596-503-2*) Rodale Pr Inc.

Prevention's Healthy Weeknight Meals. David Joachim. LC 96-35996. (Illus.). 320p. 1996. 25.95 (*0-87596-369-2*) Rodale Pr Inc.

Prevention's Healthy Weeknight Meals in Minutes. Ed. by David Joachim. LC 96-35997. (Illus.). 320p. 1996. pap. 15.95 (*0-87596-370-6*) Rodale Pr Inc.

Prevention's Low-Fat Italian Favorites. Ed. by Jean Rogers. LC 95-24995. (Illus.). 320p. 1996. pap. 15.95 (*0-87596-306-4*) Rodale Pr Inc.

Prevention's New Foods for Healing. Prevention Health Books Editors & Selene Yeager. 624p. 2000. pap. 16.95 (*1-57954-095-3*) Rodale Pr Inc.

***Prevention's Quick & Healthy Family Favorites Cookbook: Over 215 Delicious Recipes.** Prevention Magazine Health Books Staff. LC 00-36915. (Illus.). 2000. write for info. (*1-57954-310-3*) Rodale Pr Inc.

Prevention's Quick & Healthy Low-Fat Cooking: Featuring All-American Food. Ed. by Jean Rogers. LC 94-39507. (Illus.). 320p. 1995. pap. 15.95 (*0-87596-237-8*) Rodale Pr Inc.

Prevention's Quick & Healthy Low-Fat Cooking: Featuring All-American Food. Ed. by Jean Rogers. LC 94-39507. (Illus.). 320p. 1995. text 25.95 (*0-87596-235-1*) Rodale Pr Inc.

Prevention's Quick & Healthy Low-Fat Cooking: Featuring Healthy Cuisines from the Mediterranean. Ed. by Jean Rogers. LC 93-35544. (Illus.). 320p. 1994. pap. 15.95 (*0-87596-193-2*) Rodale Pr Inc.

Prevention's Quick & Healthy Low-Fat Cooking: Featuring Healthy Cuisines from the Mediterranean. Ed. by Jean Rogers. LC 93-35544. (Illus.). 320p. 1994. text 25.95 (*0-87596-192-4*) Rodale Pr Inc.

Prevention's Quick & Healthy Low-Fat Cooking: Featuring Pasta & Other Italian Favorites. Ed. by Jean Rogers. LC 95-24994. (Illus.). 320p. 1996. text 25.95 (*0-87596-305-6*) Rodale Pr Inc.

Prevention's Quick & Healthy Low-Fat Cooking: From Entertaining to Everyday. Ed. by Jean Rogers. 272p. 1993. 25.95 (*0-87596-174-6*) Rodale Pr Inc.

Prevention's Quick & Healthy Low-Fat Cooking: From Entertaining to Everyday. Ed. by Jean Rogers. (Illus.). 272p. 1993. pap. 15.95 (*0-87596-175-4*) Rodale Pr Inc.

Prevention's Super Foods Cookbook: Two Hundred Fifty Delicious Recipes Using Nature's Healthiest Foods. Prevention Magazine Editors. LC 92-37485. (Illus.). 320p. 1993. 24.95 (*0-87596-167-3*) St Martin.

Prevention's Symptom Solver for Dogs & Cats: From Arfs & Arthritis to Whimpers & Worms, an Owner's Cure Finder. Ed. by Matthew Hoffman. LC 98-39964. 512p. 1999. text 29.95 (*0-87596-523-7*) Rodale Pr Inc.

***Prevention's Symptom Solver for Dogs & Cats: From Arfs & Arthritis to Whimpers & Worms, an Owner's Cure Finder.** Matthew Hoffman. 480p. 2000. reprint ed. pap. 14.95 (*0-425-17439-5*) Berkley Pub.

***Prevention's the Healthy Cook: The Ultimate Illustrated Kitchen Guide to Great Low-Fat Foods.** Ed. by David Joachim & Matthew Hoffman. (Illus.). 608p. 2000. pap. 18.95 (*1-57954-243-3*) Rodale Pr Inc.

Prevention's the Healthy Cook: The Ultimate Kitchen Guide to Great Low-Fat Food. Matthew Hoffman et al. LC 96-27695. 1997. text 27.95 (*0-87596-310-2*) Rodale Pr Inc.

Prevention's Your Perfect Weight: Diet-Free Weight Loss Method Developed by the World's Leading Health Magazine. Mark Bricklin & Linda Konner. LC 94-5318. 1995. text 27.95 (*0-87596-229-7*) Rodale Pr Inc.

Prevention's Your Perfect Weight: Diet-Free Weight Loss Method Developed by the World's Leading Health Magazine. Mark Bricklin & Linda Konner. LC 94-5318. 1997. pap. 14.95 (*0-87596-452-4*) Rodale Pr Inc.

Preventive Action: Cases & Strategies. Ed. by Barnett R. Rubin. LC 97-41268. 247p. 1997. pap. 11.95 (*0-87078-412-9*) Century Foundation.

Preventive & Community Medicine. 2nd ed. Ed. by Duncan W. Clark & Brian Macmahon. 1981. 65.00 (*0-316-14596-3*, Little Brwn Med Div) Lppncott W & W.

***Preventive Approaches to Couples Therapy.** Rony Berger. LC 99-14074. 1999. text 39.95 (*0-87630-876-0*) Brunner-Mazel.

Preventive Cardiology. Ed. by Eugene I. Chazov et al. (Soviet Medical Reviews Supplement, Cardiology Ser.: No. 1). xviii, 680p. 1987. text 436.00 (*3-7186-0338-1*) Gordon & Breach.

Preventive Cardiology. Ed. by Eugene I. Chazov & Raphael G. Oganov. LC 89-15394. 320p. 1989. 45.00 (*0-8236-4293-3*) Intl Univs Pr.

Preventive Cardiology. Nathan D. Wong et al. LC 99-34769. (Illus.). 480p. 1999. 65.00 (*0-07-071856-3*) McGraw-Hill HPD.

Preventive Cardiology: A Guide for Clinical Practice. Ed. by Killian Robinson. LC 98-6277. (Illus.). 432p. 1998. 69.00 (*0-87993-692-4*) Futura Pub.

Preventive Cardiology: An Introduction. Ed. by H. S. Wasir. (Illus.). xxx, 409p. (C). 1992. 40.00 (*0-7069-5891-8*, Pub. by Vikas) S Asia.

***Preventive Cardiology: Insights into the Prevention & Treatment of Coronary Artery Disease.** Ed. by Joanne Micale Foody & Eugene Braunwald. (Contemporary Cardiology Ser.). 420p. 2000. 99.50 (*0-89603-811-4*) Humana.

Preventive Cardiology Vol. 2, Pt. B: Metabolism of Ischemic Myocardium, Vol. 2. E. I. Chazov et al. Ed. by V. N. Smirnov. (Soviet Medical Reviews Supplement Ser.). xii, 304p. 1989. pap. text 437.00 (*3-7186-4925-X*) Gordon & Breach.

Preventive Care for Elderly People. David C. Kennie. 335p. (C). 1993. text 95.00 (*0-521-43044-5*); pap. text 32.95 (*0-521-43629-X*) Cambridge U Pr.

Preventive Care Sourcebook, 1997-1998: 1997 Edition. Aspen Reference Group Staff. 288p. 1997. pap. 89.00 (*0-8342-0880-6*, 20880) Aspen Pub.

Preventive Care Sourcebook, 1998-99. Aspen Reference Group Staff. 200p. 1998. pap. 89.00 (*0-8342-1056-8*, 10568) Aspen Pub.

Preventive Defense: A New Security Strategy for America. Ashton B. Carter. LC 98-51245. 1999. 24.95 (*0-8157-1308-8*) Brookings.

Preventive Defense: An American Security Strategy for the 21st Century Ashton B. Carter & William J. Perry. LC 98-51245. 1998. write for info. (*0-8157-1307-X*) Brookings.

Preventive Detention: A Comparative & International Law Perspective. Ed. by Stanislaw Frankowski & Dinah Shelton. (International Studies in Human Rights). 320p. (C). 1992. lib. bdg. 124.50 (*0-7923-1465-4*) Kluwer Academic.

Preventive Detention after Schall V. Martin. LC 85-72727. 55p. 1986. pap. 6.50 (*0-89707-198-0*, 509-0022-01) Amer Bar Assn.

Preventive Detention & Security Law: A Comparative Survey. Ed. by Andrew J. Harding & John Hatchard. LC 93-26604. (International Studies in Human Rights: Vol. 31). 353p. (C). 1993. lib. bdg. 117.00 (*0-7923-2432-3*) Kluwer Academic.

Preventive Diet for Heart & Overweight: Transition to Vegetarian Diet. Edmond B. Szekely. (Illus.). 48p. 1977. pap. 3.50 (*0-89564-040-6*) IBS Intl.

***Preventive Diplomacy: Stopping Wars Before They Start.** 2nd ed. Ed. by Kevin M. Cahill. 384p. 2000. 80.00 (*0-415-92284-4*); pap. 24.99 (*0-415-92285-2*) Routledge.

Preventive Discipline: A Roadmap for Good Behavior from Toddler to Teen, Vol. I. Janice S. Barnhart. LC 96-94978. (Illus.). 148p. (Orig.). 1997. pap. 9.95 (*0-9654940-0-4*) J S Barnhart.

Preventive Family Therapy: Patterns of Change in the Family, Bk. 6. Rose A. Parvin. LC 95-35697. 288p. 1995. write for info. (*1-885917-05-8*) Univrsl Pubng.

Preventive Health Care. Robert S. Chang. LC 80-24183. 1981. 35.00 (*0-8161-2165-6*) Mac Lib Ref.

Preventive Health Care for Children: Experience from Selected Foreign Countries. (Illus.). 37p. (Orig.). (C). 1994. pap. text 30.00 (*0-7881-0198-6*) DIANE Pub.

Preventive Health Care for Young Children: Findings from a 10-Country Study & Directions for United States Policy. C. Arden Miller & Bret C. Williams. LC 91-61824. 80p. (Orig.). 1991. pap. 9.50 (*0-943657-16-4*) ZERO TO THREE.

***Preventive Home Maintenance Manual.** Dan Baldwin. (Illus.). 171p. 2000. pap. 24.95 (*0-9701918-0-4*) Baldwin & Assocs.

Preventive Law. Louis M. Brown. LC 72-97326. 346p. 1970. reprint ed. lib. bdg. 75.00 (*0-8371-3077-8*, BRPL, Greenwood Pr) Greenwood.

Preventive Law: Materials on a Non Adversarial Legal Process. Robert M. Hardaway. 656p. 1997. 54.95 (*0-87084-353-2*) Anderson Pub Co.

Preventive Law: Strategies for Avoidance of Litigation in Public Schools. Harold L. Hawkins. Ed. by Frederick C. Wendel & Edgar Kelley. LC 89-114380. (UCEA Monographs). (Illus.). 47p. (Orig.). (C). 1986. pap. text 4.25 (*0-922971-10-2*, MS1-PL) Univ Council Educ Admin.

Preventive Law in Corporate Practice. Michael Goldblatt. Vol. C3. text 82.00 (*0-8205-2415-8*) Bender.

Preventive Law Reporter, 1982-1992, 12 vols., Set. 1982. 660.00 (*0-8377-9223-1*, Rothman) W S Hein.

Preventive Maintenance. Joseph D. Patton, Jr. LC 82-48557. (Illus.). 208p. 1983. reprint ed. pap. 64.50 (*0-7837-9043-0*, 204979400003) Bks Demand.

Preventive Maintenance. 2nd ed. Joseph D. Patton, Jr. LC 94-47619. 200p. 1995. pap. 56.00 (*1-55617-533-7*) ISA.

Preventive Maintenance. 4th rev. ed. Ed. by Deere & Company Staff. (Fundamentals of Machine Operation Ser.). 240p. 1991. 240.95 incl. sl. (*0-614-24204-5*, FMO16204S) Deere & Co.

Preventive Maintenance. 5th rev. ed. Ed. by Deere & Company Staff. (Fundamentals of Machine Operation Ser.). (Illus.). 276p. 1992. pap. text 31.95 (*0-86691-171-5*, FMO16105NC); pap. text, teacher ed. 33.95 incl. trans. (*0-86691-064-6*, FMO16503T); pap. text, student ed. 16.95 (*0-86691-065-4*, FMO16603W) Deere & Co.

Preventive Maintenance & Troubleshooting Control Circuits No. 612: Video Booklet/Workbook. L. A. Bryan & E. A. Bryan. Ed. by L. B. Thompson. (Illus.). 40p. 1995. pap. 32.00 (*0-944107-14-1*, 612) Indust Text.

Preventive Maintenance Inspection Guidelines: Dry-Van Trailers. Ed. by Maintenance Council Staff. 1996. pap. 49.95 (*0-88711-327-3*) Am Trucking Assns.

Preventive Maintenance Inspection (P. M. I.) Guidelines: Class 7 & 8 Diesel-Powered Tractors with Air Brakes. 1996. pap. text 59.95 (*0-88711-297-8*) Am Trucking Assns.

Preventive Maintenance of Electrical Equipment. 2nd ed. Charles I. Hubert. 1969. text 41.94 (*0-07-030839-X*) McGraw.

Preventive Maintenance Supervisor. Jack Rudman. (Career Examination Ser.: C-3499). 1994. pap. 29.95 (*0-8373-3499-3*) Nat Learn.

Preventive Management. Ed. by Henry B. Elkind. LC 70-142621. (Essay Index Reprint Ser.). 1977. 20.95 (*0-8369-2044-9*) Ayer.

Preventive Measures: Building Risk Assessment & Crisis Early Warning Systems. Ed. by John L. Davies & Ted R. Gurr. LC 98-28589. (Illus.). 304p. 1998. 65.00 (*0-8476-8873-9*); pap. 24.95 (*0-8476-8874-7*) Rowman.

Preventive Medicine: Natural Options for Keeping Well. Time-Life Books Editors. LC 96-43447. (Illus.). 144p. (gr. 11). 1997. pap. 16.95 (*0-7835-4916-4*) Time-Life.

Preventive Medicine & Public Health. 2nd ed. B. Cassens. (National Medical Series for Independent Study). (Illus.). 497p. 1992. 26.00 (*0-683-06262-X*) Lppncott W & W.

Preventive Medicine & Public Health: PreTest Self-Assessment & Review. 8th ed. Ed. by Sylvie Ratelle. LC 97-22240. (Pretest Clinical Science Ser.). (Illus.). 200p. 1997. pap. text 18.95 (*0-07-052534-X*) McGraw-Hill HPD.

P

An Asterisk (*) at the beginning of an entry indicates that the title is appearing for the first time.

Preventive Medicine in the United States, 1900-1975, Trends & Interpretations. George Rosen. LC 75-35978. (Illus.). 128p. 1976. pap. text 6.95 (*0-685-63141-9*, Sci Hist); lib. bdg. 15.00 (*0-88202-103-6*, Sci Hist) Watson Pub Intl.

Preventive Medicine in the United States 1900-1990: Trends & Interpretations. Bonnie Bullough & George Rosen. LC 92-20428. 1992. 15.95 (*0-88135-180-6*, Sci Hist); pap. 11.95 (*0-88135-177-6*, Sci Hist) Watson Pub Intl.

***Preventive Negotiation: Avoiding Conflict Escalation.** I. William Zartman. LC 99-87905. 352p. 2000. 69.00 (*0-8476-9894-7*); pap. 28.95 (*0-8476-9895-5*) Rowman.

Preventive Nutrition: The Comprehensive Guide for the Health Professionals. Ed. by Adrianne Bendich & Richard J. Deckelbaum. LC 96-37937. (Nutrition & Health Ser.). (Illus.). 616p. 1997. 99.50 (*0-89603-351-1*) Humana.

Preventive Obstacle, or Conjugal Onanism. L. F. Bergeret. Tr. by P. De Marmon from FRE. LC 73-20616. (Sex, Marriage & Society Ser.). 192p. 1974. reprint ed. 20.95 (*0-405-05794-6*) Ayer.

Preventive Parenting with Love, Encouragement, & Limits: The Preschool Years. Thomas J. Dishion & Scot Patterson. (Illus.). xiv, 130p. (Orig.). 1995. pap. 10.95 (*0-916154-13-0*) Castalia Pub.

Preventive Psychiatry: Early Intervention & Situational Crisis Management. Ed. by Samuel C. Klagsbrun et al. LC 88-663414. 272p. 1989. text 38.95 (*0-914783-28-9*); pap. text 23.95 (*0-914783-29-7*) Charles.

Preventive Remedial Associative Model (PRAM) Modelo Asociativo Remedial Preventivo (MARP) Eneida B. Guernica. Ed. by Charles C. Humphries. (Illus.). 294p. 1997. pap. text 37.50 (*0-9675885-0-2*, Trade Litho Inc) IKE Pubns Inc.

Preventive Services for School-Age Children. Ed. by O. Jeanneret. (Journal: Pediatrician: Vol. 15, No. 3, 1988). (Illus.). 68p. 1988. pap. 35.00 (*3-8055-4824-9*) S Karger.

Preventive Services in the Clinical Setting: What Works & What It Costs. 1994. lib. bdg. 250.95 (*0-8490-5823-6*) Gordon Pr.

Preventive Strategies for Living in a Chemical World: A Symposium in Honor of Irving J. Selikoff. Ed. by Eula Bingham & David Rall. LC 97-39041. (Annals of the New York Academy of Sciences Ser.: No. 837). 588p. 1998. 110.00 (*1-57331-074-3*); pap. 110.00 (*1-57331-075-1*) NY Acad Sci.

Preventive Strategies on Suicide. Ed. by Rene F. Diekstra. (Advances in Suicidology Ser.: Vol. 2). xii, 369p. 1995. pap. 83.00 (*90-04-10339-2*) Brill Academic Pubs.

Preventive Stress Management in Organizations. 2nd ed. James C. Quick et al. LC 97-12689. (Illus.). 368p. 1997. text 39.95 (*1-55798-432-8*, 431-7920) Am Psychol.

Preventive Therapy in Asthma. Ed. by John Morley. (Perspectives in Asthma Ser.: Vol. 5). (Illus.). 300p. (C). 1991. text 83.00 (*0-12-506448-9*) Acad Pr.

Preventive Treatment of Neglected Children with Special Papers by Leading Authorities. Hastings H. Hart. LC 70-137169. (Poverty U. S. A. Historical Record Ser.). 1974. reprint ed. 29.95 (*0-405-03107-6*) Ayer.

Preventive Work with Families: The Role of Mainstream Services. Ruth Sinclair et al. LC 98-130876. 64p. 1997. pap. 17.00 (*1-900990-08-3*, Pub. by Natl Childrens Bur) Paul & Co Pubs.

Preventv Treatmnt Athers. D. H. Blankenhorn. (C). 1984. text 39.95 (*0-201-10638-8*, Health Sci) Addison-Wesley.

***Preverbs of Tell: News Torqued from Undertime.** George Quasha. 150p. 2001. pap. 14.95 (*1-58177-070-7*) Barrytown Ltd.

Prevert. Bergens. (Classiques du XXe Siecle Ser.). pap. 9.95 (*0-685-37054-2*, F119340) Fr & Eur.

Preview Chapter & Contents Principles of Patent Law. F. Scott Kieff et al. LC 98-21245. (University Casebook Ser.). 198p. 1998. pap. write for info. (*1-56662-619-6*) Foundation Pr.

Preview for the Spacecraft Landing on Earth 2001 A. D. Ruth E. Norman. (Illus.). 139p. 1987. pap. 10.00 (*0-935097-06-6*) Unarius Acad Sci.

Preview II: An Introduction to Applications Software. Jeffery I. Mock. 1987. write for info. (*0-8053-2335-X*) Benjamin-Cummings.

Preview of an Analytical Guide to Helicopter Transmission Design. C. P. Hardersen & R. B. Bossler. (Technical Papers). 1972. pap. text 30.00 (*1-55589-199-3*) AGMA.

Preview of Asking about Life. Tobin. (C). 1997. pap. text 37.50 (*0-03-025182-6*, Pub. by Harcourt Coll Pubs) Harcourt.

Preview of General Chemistry. Harvey F. Carroll. LC 88-5735. 432p. 1989. pap. 64.95 (*0-471-86002-6*) Wiley.

Preview of President Clinton's Historic Visit to Africa. United States Government Printing Office Staff. LC 98-213486. iii, 28 p. 1998. write for info. (*0-16-057237-1*) USGPO.

Preview of the Allergy Diet Guide & Cookbook. Nicolette M. Dumke. 52p. (Orig.). 1995. pap. 6.95 (*1-887624-03-1*) Adapt Bks.

Preview of the Danciger Peruvian Collection. Ed. by Edward M. Davis & William W. Newcomb. LC 60-63787. (Illus.). 1960. pap. 5.00 (*0-87959-023-8*) U of Tex H Ransom Ctr.

Preview of the Dream. Zack Rogow. 64p. (Orig.). 1985. pap. 6.00 (*0-940584-10-7*) Gull Bks.

Preview to Algebra. Eleanor S. Young. 1996. 39.90 (*4-00-019678-2*) Tichenor Pub.

Preview 2 Apple Lab Manuel. Jeffery I. Mock. 1987. pap. text 11.95 (*0-8053-2407-0*) Benjamin-Cummings.

Preview 2 Lab Manuel (Without Disk) Jeffery I. Mock. 1987. pap. text 11.95 (*0-8053-2405-4*) Benjamin-Cummings.

Preview 2001+ Popular Culture Studies in the Future. Ed. by Ray B. Browne & Marshall W. Fishwick. LC 95-46247. 222p. 1996. 35.95 (*0-87972-689-X*); pap. 15.95 (*0-87972-690-3*) Bowling Green Univ Popular Press.

***Preview 2001 Silverthorn Human Physiology.** 2nd ed. 2000. write for info. (*0-13-019310-0*) P-H.

Previews & Premises. Alvin Toffler. 230p. write for info. (*0-920057-36-5*); pap. write for info. (*0-920057-37-3*) Black Rose.

Previews & Premises. Alvin Toffler. LC 82-62941. 230p. 1983. reprint ed. pap. 7.50 (*0-89608-210-5*) South End Pr.

Previews of Coming Attractions. Ronald J. Lavin. 1991. pap. 8.25 (*1-55673-317-8*, 9138) CSS OH.

Previous Convictions: A Journey Through the 1950s. Nora Sayre. (Illus.). 464p. (C). 1995. 37.95 (*0-8135-2231-5*) Rutgers U Pr.

Prevision of History: A Study of Daniel & Revelation. Elizabeth Williams. 336p. 1974. pap. 7.95 (*1-882449-18-5*) Messenger Pub.

Prevocational English: Text 1. 128p. 1994. pap. 11.95 (*0-8325-0672-9*, Natl Textbk Co) NTC Contemp Pub Co.

Prevocational English: Text 1. 85th ed. 128p. 1994. student ed. 7.95 (*0-8325-0673-7*, Natl Textbk Co) NTC Contemp Pub Co.

Prevocational English: Text 1. 88th ed. 128p. 1994. teacher ed. 6.60 (*0-8325-0671-0*, Natl Textbk Co) NTC Contemp Pub Co.

Prevocational English: Text 2. 128p. 1986. text 11.95 (*0-8325-0674-5*, Natl Textbk Co) NTC Contemp Pub Co.

Prevocational English: Text 2. 86th ed. 128p. 1994. student ed. 7.95 (*0-8325-0675-3*, Natl Textbk Co) NTC Contemp Pub Co.

***Prevost: Manon Lescaut.** Abbe Prevost. Ed. by Patrick Byrne. (Modern Language Ser.). (FRE.). 216p. 1999. pap. text 20.95 (*1-85399-517-7*, Pub. by Brist Class Pr) Focus Pub-R Pullins.

Prevost Romancier. Jean Sgard. 40.25 (*0-685-34053-8*) Fr & Eur.

Prevost's Mentors: The Master-Pupil Relationship in the Major Novels of the Abbe Prevost. James P. Gilroy. 1990. 39.95 (*0-916379-69-8*) Scripta.

Prexies. unabridged ed. Roland Rustad. Ed. by Leonard Piszkiewicz. (Illus.). 343p. 1994. pap. 30.00 (*0-930412-23-0*) Bureau Issues.

Prey. Dan Durk. LC 98-66732. 400p. 1998. pap. 7.99 (*0-88100-101-5*) Natl Writ Pr.

Prey. Kenneth M. Goddard. 416p. 1993. mass mkt. 5.99 (*0-8125-1198-0*, Pub. by Tor Bks) St Martin.

Prey. William W. Johnstone. 352p. 1996. mass mkt. 5.99 (*0-7860-0312-X*, Pinncle Kensgtn) Kensgtn Pub Corp.

Prey. Masterton. 2000. text 23.95 (*0-312-85103-0*) St Martin.

***Prey.** Graham Masterton. 352p. 1999. mass mkt. 4.99 (*0-8439-4633-4*, Leisure Bks) Dorchester Pub Co.

Prey: Designing & Tying New Imitations of Fresh & Saltwater Forage Foods. Carl Richards. (Illus.). 144p. 1995. 24.95 (*1-55821-332-5*) Lyons Pr.

Prey: Exclusive Strategy Guide. Gamewizards Press Staff. 1999. pap. text 19.95 (*1-56893-925-6*) GT Interactive Software.

Prey: Prima's Unauthorized Game Secrets. Prima Publishing Staff. 244p. 1998. per. 19.99 (*0-7615-1417-1*) Prima Pub.

***Prey Dancing.** Jonathan Gash. 288p. 1999. pap. 5.99 (*0-14-028016-2*, Penguin Bks) Viking Penguin.

***Prey Dancing.** Jonathan Gash. LC 98-46990. (Dr. Clare Burtonall Mysteries Ser.). 1999. 23.95 (*1-56895-626-6*) Wheeler Pub.

Prey for Survival. S. Bradley Stoner. LC 89-40414. (Illus.). 221p. (Orig.). 1989. pap. 10.95 (*0-923568-03-4*) Wilderness Adventure Bks.

Prey into Hunter: The Politics of Religious Experience. Maurice Bloch. (Lewis Henry Morgan Lectures). 131p. (C). 1991. text 54.95 (*0-521-41154-8*); pap. text 17.95 (*0-521-42312-0*) Cambridge U Pr.

Prey, Messiah. Jamie Rhodes. 150p. 1998. pap. 9.95 (*0-9661752-0-4*) Twnty-Fifth Dynasty.

Prey of the Falcon. large type ed. Robert Charles. (Linford Mystery Library). 368p. 1996. pap. 16.99 (*0-7089-7872-X*, Linford) Ulverscroft.

***Prey to All.** Natasha Cooper. 2000. 23.95 (*0-312-26636-7*) St Martin.

Prey to Murder. large type ed. Ann Cleeves. 1992. 27.99 (*0-7089-2386-0*) Ulverscroft.

Prez: Homage to Lester Young. Jamie Reid. 1993. pap. text 9.95 (*0-88982-129-1*, Pub. by Oolichan Bks) Genl Dist Srvs.

PRI Idea: 500 Foundation Charitable Loans & Investments. 65p. 1997. 75.00 (*0-87954-758-8*, PRIX) Foundation Ctr.

Prial. Mark Dunster. 32p. (Orig.). 1995. pap. 6.00 (*0-89642-270-4*) Linden Pubs.

Priam's Lens. Jack L. Chalker. 1999. 6.99 (*0-345-40294-4*) Ballantine Pub Grp.

Priapea: Poems for a Phallic God. Tr. by W. H. Parker. 240p. 1988. 27.00 (*0-7099-4099-8*, Pub. by C Helm) Routldge.

Priapea - Concordantiae In Corpus Priapeorum et In Pervigilium Veneris. Ed. by Hermann Morgenroth & Dietmar Najock. (Alpha-Omega, Reihe A Ser.: Bd. LIX). (LAT.). 181p. 1983. 52.50 (*3-487-07328-5*) G Olms Pubs.

Priapus Poems: Erotic Epigrams from Ancient Rome. Tr. by Richard W. Hooper from LAT. LC 98-19725. 160p. 1999. pap. 14.95 (*0-252-06752-5*) U of Ill Pr.

Priapus Poems: Erotic Epigrams from Ancient Rome. Richard W. Hooper. LC 98-19725. 160p. 1999. 35.00 (*0-252-02443-5*) U of Ill Pr.

Priapusa, Manicure & Fardeuse: or the Reine des Ribauds in the Land of the Queen of Love. David March. (Illus.). 32p. (Orig.). 1988. pap. 100.00 (*0-9615493-1-9*) D March.

Pribilof Islands: A Guide to St. Paul, Alaska. Susan H. Johnson. (Illus.). 1978. pap. 5.10 (*0-9601948-1-9*) Tanadgusix Corp.

Priblizhennye Metody Vychisleniia Kontinualnykh Integralov see Functional Integrals: Approximate Evaluations & Applications

PRICAI '98: Topics in Artificial Intelligence: Proceedings of the 5th Pacific Rim International Conference on Artificial Singapore, November 22-27, 1998. Ed. by Hiroshi Motoda & Hing- Yan Lee. LC 98-48078. xix, 646p. 1998. pap. 95.00 (*3-540-65271-X*) Spr-Verlag.

PRICAI '96: Topics in Artificial Intelligence: 4th Pacific Rim International Conference on Artificial Intelligence, Cairns, Australia, August 26-30, 1996 Proceedings, Vol. 111. Ed. by N. Y. Foo & Randy Goebel. LC 96-32234. (Lecture Notes in Artificial Intelligence). 658p. 1996. 100.00 (*3-540-61532-6*) Spr-Verlag.

Price. Nyla Chantry. LC 98-91402. 1998. pap. 13.95 (*0-533-12662-2*) Vantage.

Price. Arthur Miller. 1969. pap. 5.25 (*0-8222-0911-X*) Dramatists Play.

Price. Arthur Miller. (Plays Ser.). 128p. 1985. pap. 8.95 (*0-14-048194-X*, Penguin Bks) Viking Penguin.

***Price.** limited ed. Arthur Miller. 1999. 375.00 (*0-910457-42-5*) Arion Pr.

***Price: A Novel.** Jim Kraus & Terri Kraus. LC 99-56687. (Circle of Destiny Ser.). 2000. pap. 10.99 (*0-8423-1835-6*) Tyndale Hse.

Price - Ratio: A Program for the HP 17BII & HP 19BII Financial Calculators. 46p. 1991. pap. 14.95 incl. disk (*0-916785-09-2*) E Cane Sem.

Price above Rubies. Yakin Boaz. (Illus.). 160p. (Orig.). 1999. pap. 14.00 (*0-571-19644-6*) Faber & Faber.

Price & Discount Schedule Analysis: A Guide for Purchasing, Marketing, Materials, & Financial Managers. Paul J. Kuzdrall & Robert R. Britney. LC 90-20710. 280p. 1991. 72.95 (*0-89930-366-8*, KZP/, Quorum Bks) Greenwood.

Price & Identification Guide to Pin-Up Artists: Alberto Varga's & George Petty. 4th rev. ed. Denis C. Jackson. (Illus.). 52p. (Orig.). 1997. pap. 7.95 (*1-888687-05-3*) Illust Collectors.

Price & Power: A Twentieth-Century Reinterpretation of Interconnected Phenomena. B. Csikos-Nagy & P. S. Bela-Elek. 166p. 1995. pap. 69.00 (*963-05-6802-0*, Pub. by Akade Kiado) St Mut.

***Price & Power of Revival.** 38p. 1998. reprint ed. pap. text 3.00 (*0-942889-10-X*) Christ Life Pubns.

Price & Price Policies. Walton Hamilton et al. LC 73-2510. (Big Business; Economic Power in a Free Society Ser.). 1973. reprint ed. 40.95 (*0-405-05091-7*) Ayer.

***Price & Privilege of Growing Old.** W. Gunther Plaut. LC 99-33766. (Illus.). 152p. 2000. 22.95 (*0-88123-080-4*, Pub. by Central Conf); pap. 14.95 (*0-88123-081-2*, Pub. by Central Conf) Natl Bk Netwk.

Price & Quantity Trends in the Foreign Trade of the United States. Robert E. Lipsey. (Studies in International Economic Relations: No. 2). 505p. 1963. reprint ed. 131.30 (*0-87014-154-6*) Natl Bur Econ Res.

Price & Related Controls in the United States. Seymour E. Harris. LC 76-10831. 393p. 1976. reprint ed. lib. bdg. 49.50 (*0-306-70828-0*) Da Capo.

***Price-Anderson Act, Crossing the Bridge to the Next Century: Report to Congress.** P. Bailey. 178p. 1998. per. 15.00 (*0-16-062957-8*) USGPO.

Price Behaviour in Illegal Markets. Susan Pozo. 116p. 1996. text 58.95 (*1-85972-349-7*, Pub. by Avebry) Ashgate Pub Co.

Price below Rubies: Jewish Women As Rebels & Radicals. Naomi Shepherd. 352p. 1993. 27.95 (*0-674-70410-X*) HUP.

Price below Rubies: Jewish Women As Rebels & Radicals. Naomi Shepherd. (Illus.). 352p. 1994. pap. 15.95 (*0-674-70411-8*, SHEPRX) HUP.

Price Beyond Rubies: A Novel of the Civil War. Louise M. Barry. (Illus.). 492p. 1996. pap. 25.95 (*0-89745-201-1*) Sunflower U Pr.

Price Caps & Incentive Regulation in Telecommunications. Ed. by Michael A. Einhorn. 256p. (C). 1991. lib. bdg. 91.00 (*0-7923-9113-6*) Kluwer Academic.

***Price Changes in the Gasoline Market: Are Midwestern Gasoline Prices Downward Sticky?** 59p. 1999. pap. 7.00 (*0-16-063560-8*) USGPO.

Price Competition & Price Convergence. European Commission. (Single Market Review: Vol. 1). 259p. 1997. 30.00 (*92-827-8801-6*, Pub. by Comm Europ Commun) Bernan Associates.

Price Competition & Price Convergence, Vol. V-1. Pate Kogan. (Single Market Review Ser.). 1998. 80.00 (*0-7494-2334-X*) Kogan Page Ltd.

Price Competitiveness in World Trade. Irving B. Kravis & Robert E. Lipsey. (Studies in International Economic Relations: No. 6). 765p. 1971. text 160.00 (*0-87014-227-5*) Natl Bur Econ Res.

Price Control under Fair Trade Legislation. Ewald T. Grether. LC 75-39245. (Getting & Spending: The Consumer's Dilemma Ser.). (Illus.). 1976. reprint ed. 42.95 (*0-405-08019-0*) Ayer.

Price Controls. Ed. by Hugh Rockoff. (International Library of Macroeconomic & Financial History: Vol. 6). 404p. 1992. 170.00 (*1-85278-431-8*) E Elgar.

Price Controls & the Economics of Institutions in China. Jean-Jacques Laffont & Claudia Senik-Leygonie. LC 99-172753. (Development Centre Studies). 100p. 1997. pap. 19.00 (*92-64-15473-6*, Pub. by Org for Econ) OECD.

Price Crawford's Official Las Vegas Bartender's Guide. C. Price Crawford. 58p. 1996. pap. 6.95 (*0-9659986-0-6*) T Zimmerman.

Price Data & European Economic History: England, 1300-1600. Clyde G. Reed. Ed. by Stuart Bruchey. LC 80-2826. (Dissertations in European Economic History Ser.: No. 2). (Illus.). 1981. lib. bdg. 17.95 (*0-405-14010-X*) Ayer.

Price Determination in Oligopolistic & Monopolistic Situations. Wilford J. Eiteman. LC 60-63554. (Michigan Business Studies: No. 33). 52p. reprint ed. pap. 30.00 (*0-608-13521-6*, 202209500024) Bks Demand.

Price Discrimination in Selling Gas & Electricity. Ralph K. Davidson. LC 78-64222. (Johns Hopkins University. Studies in the Social Sciences. Thirtieth Ser. 1912: 1). 192p. 1982. reprint ed. 36.50 (*0-404-61325-X*) AMS Pr.

Price Effects in Input-Output Relations: A Theoretical & Empirical Study for the Netherlands 1949-1967. Paul M. De Boer. (Lecture Notes in Economics & Mathematical Systems Ser.: Vol. 201). (Illus.). 140p. 1982. 29.00 (*0-387-11550-1*) Spr-Verlag.

***Price Expectations in Goods & Financial Markets: New Developments in Theory & Empirical Research.** Francis Gardes & Georges Prat. LC 99-87208. 2000. write for info. (*1-84064-322-6*) E Elgar.

Price Family & Related Lines Vol. 2: Of Beaufort, Martin, Pitt & Washington Counties, North Carolina. 2nd rev. ed. Jennifer M. Sheppard. Ed. by Margaret A. Johnson. LC 97-72340. (Illus.). 203p. 1997. pap. text 41.00 (*1-878916-05-X*) Modlins Ancestral.

Price Family & Related Lines of Beaufort, Martin, Pitt & Washington Counties, North Carolina Vol. 1, Vol. 1. rev. ed. Jennifer M. Sheppard. Ed. by Margaret A. Johnson. LC 94-77058. (Illus.). 158p. 1994. pap. 38.00 (*1-878916-04-1*) Modlins Ancestral.

Price Fixing in New Zealand. William B. Sutch. LC 68-58626. (Columbia University. Studies in Social Sciences: No. 371). reprint ed. 21.00 (*0-404-51371-9*) AMS Pr.

Price Flexibility & Employment, No. 8--8. Oscar R. Lange. LC 78-6631. (Cowles Commission for Research in Economics, Monograph Ser.: No. 8). (Illus.). 114p. 1978. reprint ed. lib. bdg. 35.00 (*0-313-20480-2*, LAPF, Greenwood Pr) Greenwood.

Price for a People. Tom Wells. 165p. 1992. pap. 6.99 (*0-85151-623-8*) Banner of Truth.

***Price for an Education.** Michael Skinner. 504p. 2000. pap. 25.95 (*0-595-09309-4*, Writers Club Pr) iUniversecom.

Price for Everything. Mary Steepshanks. 256p. 1996. 21.95 (*0-312-14394-X*) St Martin.

Price for Everything: Rosamunde Pilcher's Bookshelf, Vol. 1. Mary Sheepshanks. 1998. mass mkt. 5.99 (*0-312-96478-1*) St Martin.

Price-Forecasting Techniques & Their Application to Minerals & Metals in the Global Economy. 80p. 1984. pap. 9.50 (*92-1-106191-1*, E.84.11.C.3) UN.

Price Formation in Natural Gas Fields, No. 14--14. Paul W. MacAvoy. LC 76-43984. (Yale Studies in Economics: No. 14). 281p. 1977. reprint ed. lib. bdg. 49.50 (*0-8371-8981-0*, MAPF, Greenwood Pr) Greenwood.

Price. Golden Wedding of Benjamin & Jane Price, with Brief Family Record. 48p. 1996. reprint ed. pap. 10.00 (*0-8328-5348-8*); reprint ed. lib. bdg. 20.00 (*0-8328-5347-X*) Higginson Bk Co.

Price Guide - Collectors' Compendium of Roseville Pottery, Vols. 1 & 2. Randall B. Monsen. 12p. 1997. pap. 5.00 (*0-9636102-7-9*) Monsen & Baer.

Price Guide & Bibliographic Checklist for Children's & Illustrated Books 1880-1960. E. Lee Baumgarten. LC 95-96231. 382p. 1995. 95.00 (*0-9647285-0-8*); pap. 68.00 (*0-9647285-1-6*) E L Baumgarten.

Price Guide & Bibliography to Children's & Illustrated Books. Edward S. Postal. (Illus.). 295p. (Orig.). 1995. pap. 59.95 (*0-9644800-1-8*) M & P Pr.

Price Guide & Introduction to Movie Posters & Movie Memorabilia. 2nd ed. James S. Dietz. 175p. 1985. pap. 11.95 (*0-910041-02-4*) Baja Pr.

Price Guide for Bicentennial Two Dollar Bill Cancellations. Andrew J. Vero. (Illus.). 1980. pap. 14.95 (*0-939368-04-8*) B-TwoC.

Price Guide for Composition Dolls. 2nd ed. 1975. 4.00 (*0-686-51212-X*) R Shoemaker.

Price Guide for Composition Dolls. 3rd ed. 1981. 6.50 (*0-686-69470-8*) R Shoemaker.

Price Guide for Madame Alexander Dolls. 3rd ed. 1981. 7.50 (*0-686-69471-6*) R Shoemaker.

Price Guide for Madame Alexander Dolls. 4th ed. 1983. 8.00 (*0-686-84006-2*) R Shoemaker.

Price Guide for Volumes One, Two, Three & Four of the Glass Industry in Sandwich. Raymond E. Barlow & Joan E. Kaiser. 40p. 1993. pap. 15.00 (*0-88740-554-1*) Schiffer.

Price Guide of United States, Canada & United Nations, 1989 Edition, Vol. I. rev. ed. Ed. by Lewis Kaufman. 240p. 1989. pap. 6.95 (*0-936937-16-5*) Brookman Stamp.

Price Guide of United States Stamps, 1989 Edition. rev. ed. Ed. by Lewis Kaufman. 144p. 1989. pap. 4.95 (*0-936937-17-3*) Brookman Stamp.

Price Guide to Antique & Classic Cameras, 1997-1998. 10th ed. James M. McKeown & Joan C. McKeown. (Illus.). 640p. 1996. pap. 69.95 (*0-931838-28-2*) Centennial Photo Serv.

Price Guide to Antique & Classic Cameras 1997-1998. 10th ed. James M. McKeown & Joan C. McKeown. (Illus.). 640p. 1996. 79.95 (*0-931838-29-0*) Centennial Photo Serv.

Price Guide to Antique Clocks. Robert Swedberg & Harriet Swedberg. LC 98-84444. (Illus.). 320p. 1998. pap. 27.95 (*0-87069-760-9*, WCLOC) Krause Pubns.

P

An Asterisk (*) at the beginning of an entry indicates that the title is appearing for the first time.

Price Guide to Antique Silver. 2nd ed. P. Waldron. (Illus.). 368p. 1992. 69.50 (*1-85149-165-1*) Antique Collect.

***Price Guide to Antique Tools.** 2nd rev. ed. Herbert P. Kean. (Illus.). 160p. 1998. pap. 17.95 (*1-879335-80-8*) Astragal Pr.

Price Guide to Big Little Books, Etc. (Illus.). 104p. (Orig.). 1995. pap. 19.95 (*0-89538-041-2*) L-W Inc.

Price Guide to Black & White Pot Lids. 2nd ed. Ronald Dale. (Price Guide Ser.). (Illus.). 480p. 1987. pap. 19.50 (*1-85149-008-6*) Antique Collect.

Price Guide to Collectible Pin-Back Buttons 1896-1986. Ted Hake & Russ King. LC 86-80807. (Illus.). 336p. 1991. pap. 19.95 (*0-87069-604-1*, Wllce-Homestd) Krause Pubns.

Price Guide to Cookbooks & Recipe Leaflets. Linda Dickinson. 1995. pap. 9.95 (*0-89145-426-8*, 2080) Collector Bks.

Price Guide to Flea Market Treasures. 4th ed. Harry L. Rinker. LC 97-198430. (Illus.). 356p. 1997. pap. 19.95 (*0-87069-748-X*, Wllce-Homestd) Krause Pubns.

Price Guide to Holt-Howard Collectibles & Other Related Ceramicwares of the 50s & 60s. Walter Dworkin. LC 97-80622. (Illus.). 160p. 1998. pap. 24.95 (*0-87341-517-5*, HHCK) Krause Pubns.

Price Guide to Jewellery. Michael Poynder. (Illus.). 385p. 1999. 69.50 (*1-85149-309-3*) Antique Collect.

Price Guide to Jewellery, 3000 B. C.-1950 A. D. Michael Poynder. (Price Guide Ser.). (Illus.). 388p. 1980. 69.50 (*0-902028-50-2*) Antique Collect.

***Price Guide to Limited Edition Collectibles 2001.** 6th rev. ed. Mary L. Sieber. LC 95-77317. (Illus.). 944p. 2000. pap. 19.95 (*0-87341-929-4*, LEP06) Krause Pubns.

Price Guide to Majolica. L-W Book Sales (Firm). LC 97-120017. (Illus.). 1997. write for info. (*0-89538-080-3*) L-W Inc.

Price Guide to Medieval Coins in the Christian J. Thomsen Collection, Vol. 1. Alex G. Malloy. 1993. 9.50 (*0-915018-46-2*) Attic Bks.

Price Guide to Metal Toys. G. Gardiner & A. Morris. (Price Guide Ser.). (Illus.). 216p. 1986. pap. 39.50 (*1-85149-016-7*) Antique Collect.

Price Guide to Miniature Lamps. Marjorie Hulsebus. LC 97-81444. 112p. 1998. pap. 14.95 (*0-7643-0542-5*) Schiffer.

Price Guide to Nineteenth & Twentieth Century British Pottery. 2nd ed. David Battie & Michael Turner. (Price Guide Ser.). (Illus.). 244p. 1987. 49.50 (*1-85149-109-0*) Antique Collect.

Price Guide to Packers Memorabilia. John Carpentier. LC 97-80607. (Illus.). 304p. 1998. pap. 17.95 (*0-87341-572-8*, GBMEM) Krause Pubns.

Price Guide to Pepsi Cans. Paul Bates. (Illus.). 83p. (Orig.). 1992. pap. 5.00 (*1-56046-131-4*) Interact Pubs.

Price Guide to Pocket Knives, 1890-1970. rev. ed. Jacob N. Jarrett. (Illus.). 264p. (Orig.). 1995. reprint ed. pap. 14.95 (*0-89538-024-2*) L-W Inc.

Price Guide to Pot-Lids. A. Ball. (Price Guide Ser.). (Illus.). 320p. 1980. 59.50 (*0-902028-56-1*) Antique Collect.

Price Guide to Red Wing Potters & Their Wares. rev. ed. Gary T. Tefft & Bonnie J. Tefft. 1997. pap. 2.00 (*0-9606730-9-1*) Locust Ent.

Price Guide to the Decorated Tumbler. Hazel M. Weatherman. (Illus.). 128p. 1983. pap. 4.00 (*0-913074-19-5*) Glassbooks MO.

Price Guide to the Non-Sports Cards, 1930-1960, No. 2. C. Benjamin. (Sport Americana Ser.). 448p. 1993. pap. 14.95 (*0-937424-66-8*) Edgewater.

Price Guide to Victorian, Edwardian & 1920s Furniture (1860-1930) John Andrews & Antique Collectors Club Staff. LC 82-234219. 217p. 1980. write for info. (*0-902028-89-8*) Antique Collect.

Price Guide to Vintage Coca-Cola Collectibles, 1896-1965. Deborah Goldstein-Hill. LC 98-87356. (Illus.). 208p. 1999. per. 21.95 (*0-87341-723-2*) Krause Pubns.

Price Index. S. N. Afriat. LC 77-2134. 203p. reprint ed. pap. 57.90 (*0-608-12285-8*, 2024409) Bks Demand.

Price Inflation in the Soviet Machine-Building & Metal Working Sector. Fyodor I. Kushnirsky. 106p. (Orig.). 1983. pap. text 75.00 (*1-55831-025-8*) Delphic Associates.

Price Is Not Greater Than God's Grace. Oretha Hagin. 1991. pap. 5.95 (*0-89276-952-1*) Faith Lib Pubns.

Price Is Right: Discipleship Requirements. Gary Purdy & Eric Swanson. (Inter Acta Ser.). (Illus.). 4p. (C). 1994. student ed., ring bd. 3.25 (*1-57334-000-6*, 741-050s, Inter Acta) WSN Pr.

Price Is Right: Discipleship Requirements. rev. ed. Gary Purdy & Eric Swanson. (Inter Acta Ser.). (Illus.). 6p. (C). 1995. teacher ed., ring bd. 1.25 (*1-57334-007-3*, 741-050t, Inter Acta) WSN Pr.

Price It Right for Profit: Tax Assessment Approach to Real Estate Values. John R. Hough. LC 97-93085. 150p. (Orig.). 1997. pap. 34.95 (*0-614-30248-X*) Hough Co.

Price It Right for Profit: Tax Assessment Approach to Real Estate Values. John R. Hough. LC 97-93085. (Illus.). 120p. (Orig.). 1997. pap. 34.95 (*0-9657297-0-2*) Hough Co.

Price Level Changes & Financial Statements: Case Studies of Four Companies. Ralph C. Jones. 179p. 1955. 6.00 (*0-86539-003-7*) Am Accounting.

Price Level Measurement. Ed. by W. E. Diewert. (Contributions to Economic Analysis Ser.: No. 196). viii,378p. 1991. 128.50 (*0-444-88108-5*, North Holland) Elsevier.

Price Level Regulation for Diversified Public Utilities. Jordan J. Hillman. (C). 1989. lib. bdg. 72.50 (*0-7923-9028-8*) Kluwer Academic.

Price List of General Photographic Apparatus & Materials. Kodak Staff. Ed. by Peter C. Bunnell & Robert A. Sobieszek. LC 78-19590. (Sources of Modern Photography Ser.). (Illus.). 1979. reprint ed. lib. bdg. 30.95 (*0-405-09662-3*) Ayer.

Price Making in a Democracy. Edwin G. Nourse. LC 75-39262. (Getting & Spending: The Consumer's Dilemma Ser.). 1976. reprint ed. 46.95 (*0-405-08035-2*) Ayer.

Price Management. H. Simon. 320p. 1989. 138.50 (*0-444-87327-9*, North Holland) Elsevier.

Price Measurements & Their Uses. Ed. by Murray F. Foss et al. LC 93-6874. (National Bureau of Economic Research Studies in Income & Wealth). (Illus.). 408p. 1993. lib. bdg. 62.00 (*0-226-25730-4*) U Ch Pr.

Price of a Bride. 1999. 21.95 (*0-263-15928-0*) Chivers N Amer.

Price of a Bride. Michelle Reid. (Presents Ser.: No. 2033). 1999. per. 3.75 (*0-373-12033-8*, 1-12033-6, Harlequin) Harlequin Bks.

Price of a Child. Lorene Cary. 1996. pap. 13.00 (*0-679-74467-3*) Random.

Price of a Constitution: The Origin of Japan's Postwar Politics. Tetsuya Kataoka. 288p. 1991. pap. 36.95 (*0-8448-1714-7*, Crane Russak) Taylor & Francis.

Price of a Dream: The Story of the Grameen Bank & the Idea That Is Helping the Poor to Change Their Lives. David Bornstein. LC 97-22604. 370p. (gr. 2). 1997. pap. 15.95 (*0-226-06644-4*) U Ch Pr.

***Price of a Gift: A Lakota Healer's Story.** Gerald Mohatt & Joseph Eagle Elk. LC 99-47755. (Illus.). 2000. text 29.95 (*0-8032-3204-7*) U of Nebr Pr.

Price of a Horse. Ralph Cotton. 1996. mass mkt. 5.99 (*0-312-95793-9*, Pub. by Tor Bks) St Martin.

Price of a Princess. N. Tranter. (Illus.). (J). 1995. mass mkt. 11.95 (*0-340-60994-X*, Pub. by Hodder & Stought Ltd) Trafalgar.

Price of a Princess. large type ed. Nigel Tranter. 528p. 1996. 27.99 (*0-7089-3455-2*) Ulverscroft.

Price of a Rumour. David M. Deif. 165p. Date not set. 15.95 (*0-7541-0035-9*) Communs Plus.

Price of a Wife. Helen Brooks. 1997. per. 3.50 (*0-373-11914-3*, 1-11914-8) Harlequin Bks.

Price of a Wife. large type ed. Helen Brooks. (Mills & Boon Large Print Ser.). 288p. 1997. 23.99 (*0-263-15120-4*, Pub. by Mills & Boon) Ulverscroft.

Price of Achievement: Coming Out in the Reagan Days. W. Scott Thompson. LC 96-176700. 1995. 21.95 (*0-304-33301-8*, Pub. by Cassell) LPC InBook.

Price of Admiralty: The Evolution of Naval Warfare. John Keegan. 320p. 1990. pap. 14.95 (*0-14-009650-7*, Penguin Bks) Viking Penguin.

Price of Admission. Sam Eisenstein. (New American Fiction Ser.: No. 25). 250p. (Orig.). 1991. pap. 12.95 (*1-55713-121-X*) Sun & Moon CA.

Price of Admission: Campaign Spending in the 1990 Elections. Larry Makinson. (Illus.). 160p. 1992. pap. text 19.95 (*0-939715-16-3*) Ctr Politics.

Price of Admission: Campaign Spending in the 1994 Elections. Larry Makinson. 250p. 1995. pap. 19.95 (*0-939715-25-2*) Ctr Politics.

Price of Admission: Rethinking How Americans Pay for College. Thomas J. Kane. LC 99-6357. 1999. 36.95 (*0-8157-5014-5*); pap. 15.95 (*0-8157-5013-7*) Brookings.

Price of Adventure: Mountain Rescue Stories from Four Continents. Hamish MacInnes. (Illus.). 200p. 1988. 15.95 (*0-89886-174-8*) Mountaineers.

Price of American Foreign Policy: Congress, the Executive & Foreign Affairs Funding. William I. Bacchus. LC 96-49106. 1997. 55.00 (*0-271-01692-2*); pap. 18.95 (*0-271-01693-0*) Pa St U Pr.

Price of an Orphan. Patricia Carlon. LC 99-30787. 208p. 1999. 22.00 (*1-56947-173-8*) Soho Press.

***Price of an Orphan.** Patricia Carlon. 272p. 2000. pap. 12.00 (*1-56947-195-9*) Soho Press.

Price of Ashes. Richard Barnard & Sam Hertogs. LC 95-75128. 625p. 1995. 21.95 (*0-9644751-1-1*); pap. write for info. (*0-9644751-0-3*) L Hubbard Pub.

Price of Ashes. Richard Barnard & Sam Hertogs. Ed. by Barbara Field. (Jacob's Star Trilogy Ser.: Vol. 1). ix, 502p. 1999. pap. 7.50 (*0-9644751-3-8*) L Hubbard Pub.

Price of Blood. Chuck Logan. 496p. 1998. mass mkt. 6.99 (*0-06-109622-9*, Harp PBks) HarpC.

Price of Blood & Honor. Elizabeth Willey. 480p. 1996. 25.95 (*0-312-85784-5*) Tor Bks.

Price of Blood & Honor. Elizabeth Willey. 1997. mass mkt. 5.99 (*0-8125-5049-8*, Pub. by Tor Bks) St Martin.

Price of Command: A Biography of General Guy Simonds. Dominick Graham. (Illus.). 336p. 1993. 29.95 (*0-7737-2692-6*) Genl Dist Srvs.

Price of Command: Nate Lawton's War of 1812. Ronald Wanttaja. Ed. by Myrna Kemnitz. (Illus.). 330p. (J). 1998. pap. 9.99 (*0-88092-286-9*, 2869) Royal Fireworks.

***Price of Death: The Funeral Industry in Contemporary Japan.** Hikaru Suzuki. 2000. 35.00 (*0-8047-3561-1*) Stanford U Pr.

Price of Disobedience. Michael Howard. Ed. by Rozella Heyns. 52p. (Orig.). 1996. pap. 5.00 (*1-888529-04-0*) Out of Africa Pub.

Price of Doing Business in Mexico. Bobby Byrd. LC 98-27011. 131p. 1998. pap. 12.95 (*0-938317-40-7*) Cinco Puntos.

***Price of Doubt.** Nathan Nicholas. LC 00-27028. (International Library of Philosophy). 2000. write for info. (*0-415-23415-8*) Routledge.

Price of Eggs. Anne Panning. LC 92-817. 160p. (Orig.). 1992. pap. 11.95 (*0-918273-95-1*) Coffee Hse.

Price of Energy. Greenpeace Staff & Deutsches Institut fur Wirtschaftsforschung Staff. LC 96-44643. (DIW Ser.). (Illus.). 192p. 1997. text 72.95 (*1-85521-931-X*, Pub. by Dartmth Pub) Ashgate Pub Co.

Price of Everything. Andrew Motion. 128p. (Orig.). 1995. pap. 11.95 (*0-571-16900-7*) Faber & Faber.

Price of Exit. Tom Marshall. 1998. mass mkt. 6.99 (*0-8041-1715-2*) Ivy Books.

Price of Experience: Power, Money, Image & Murder in Los Angeles. Randall Sullivan. 720p. 1996. 27.50 (*0-87113-512-4*, Atlntc Mnthly) Grove-Atltic.

Price of Failure. Jeffrey Ashford. LC 97-49345. 195p. 1997. text 20.95 (*0-312-18156-6*) St Martin.

Price of Failure. large type ed. Jeffrey Ashford. LC 97-36721. 278p. 1998. 18.95 (*0-7838-8111-8*, G K Hall Lrg Type) Mac Lib Ref.

Price of Fear. Randall Boyll. Ed. by Scott Shannon. (Darkman Ser.: No. 2). 224p. (Orig.). 1994. mass mkt. 5.50 (*0-671-79434-5*) PB.

Price of Federalism. Paul E. Peterson. (Twentieth Century Bks.). 239p. (C). 1995. pap. 16.95 (*0-8157-7023-5*) Brookings.

Price of Federalism. Paul E. Peterson. LC 95-13773. (Twentieth Century Bks.). 239p. (C). 1995. 38.95 (*0-8157-7024-3*) Brookings.

Price of Folly: British Blunders in the War of American Independence 1775-1783. William Seymour. (Illus.). 284p. 1995. 26.95 (*1-85753-018-7*, Pub. by Brasseys) Brasseys.

Price of Free Land. Treva A. Strait. LC 78-24287. (Illus.). (J). (gr. 4-6). 1979. 12.95 (*0-397-31836-7*); lib. bdg. 12.89 (*0-397-31883-9*) HarpC Child Bks.

Price of Free Speech. William Nygaard. 84p. (C). 1996. pap. 9.00 (*82-00-22749-9*, Pub. by Scand Univ Pr) IBD Ltd.

Price of Freedom. Brian Campbell & Janice Sellers. 1999. 25.00 (*0-671-04003-0*) S&S Trade.

Price of Freedom: A History of East Central Europe from the Middle Ages to the Present. Piotr S. Wandycz. LC 93-16894. (Illus.). 352p. (C). (gr. 13). 1993. pap. 25.99 (*0-415-07627-7*, B2469) Routledge.

Price of Freedom: A Wing Commander Novel. William R. Forstchen & Ben Ohlander. 352p. 1996. per. 5.99 (*0-671-87751-8*) Baen Bks.

***Price of Freedom: Slavery & Freedom in Baltimore & Early National Maryland.** T. Stephen Whitman. LC 99-45752. 256p. 2000. pap. 19.99 (*0-415-92608-4*) Routledge.

Price of Freedom: Slavery & Manumission in Baltimore & Early National Maryland. T. Stephen Whitman. LC 96-27386. 256p. 1997. text 35.95 (*0-8131-2004-7*) U Pr of Ky.

Price of Freedom: The Criminal Threat in Russia, Eastern Europe & the Baltic Region. Christopher J. Ulrich. (Illus.). 30p. (Orig.). 1994. pap. text 35.00 (*1-57979-086-0*) DIANE Pub.

Price of Freedom: The Criminal Threat in Russia, Eastern Europe & the Baltic Region. Christopher J. Ulrich. (Illus.). 30p. (Orig.). (C). 1994. pap. text 30.00 (*0-7881-1377-1*) DIANE Pub.

Price of Freedom: Young Indochinese Refugees in Australia. Ed. by Jerzy Krupinski & G. Burrows. 500p. 1986. text 54.00 (*0-08-029884-2*) Elsevier.

***Price of Freedom Vol. I: Slavery & the Civil War.** Ed. by Martin H. Greenburg & Edna Greene Medford. 600p. 2000. pap. 18.95 (*1-58182-085-2*, Cumberland Hearthside) Cumberland Hse.

***Price of Freedom Vol. II: Slavery & the Civil War.** Ed. by Martin H. Greenburg & Edna Greene Medford. 480p. 2000. pap. 16.95 (*1-58182-091-7*, Cumberland Hearthside) Cumberland Hse.

Price of Glory: Verdun, 1916. Alistair Horne. (Illus.). 400p. 1994. pap. 14.95 (*0-14-017041-3*, Penguin Bks) Viking Penguin.

Price of Greatness: Resolving the Creativity & Madness Controversy. Arnold M. Ludwig. LC 94-44905. 310p. 1995. lib. bdg. 38.95 (*0-89862-839-3*) Guilford Pubns.

Price of Greatness: Resolving the Creativity & Madness Controversy. Arnold M. Ludwig. LC 94-44905. 310p. 1996. pap. text 18.95 (*1-57230-117-1*) Guilford Pubns.

***Price of Guilt.** Margaret Yorke. LC 99-88102. 336p. 2000. text 24.95 (*0-312-25332-X*, Minotaur) St Martin.

Price of Health. Ed. by George J. Agich & Charles E. Begley. 312p. (C). 1986. text 126.50 (*90-277-2285-4*, D Reidel) Kluwer Academic.

Price of Health: Australian Governments & Medical Politics, 1910-1960. James A. Gillespie. (Studies in Australian History). (Illus.). 376p. (C). 1991. text 69.95 (*0-521-38183-5*) Cambridge U Pr.

Price of Honor. David H. Hackworth. LC 99-31098. 512p. 1999. 25.95 (*0-385-49164-6*) Doubleday.

Price of Honor: Muslim Women Lift the Veil of Silence on the Islamic World. Jan Goodwin. LC 95-5272. 1995. pap. 14.95 (*0-452-27430-3*, Plume) Dutton Plume.

Price of Honor: The World War One Letters of Naval Aviator Kenneth Macleish. Ed. by Geoffrey L. Rossano. LC 90-45844. (Illus.). 320p. 1991. 32.95 (*0-87021-584-1*) Naval Inst Pr.

***Price of Honor: Wilders of Wyatt County.** Janis Reams Hudson. (Special Edition Ser.: Bk. 1332). 2000. per. 4.50 (*0-373-24332-4*, 1-24332-8) Silhouette.

Price of Innocence. James Kass. LC 98-88533. 187p. 1999. pap. 11.95 (*1-56315-128-6*) SterlingHse.

Price of Innocence. Susan Sizemore. LC 98-94810. 371p. 1999. mass mkt. 5.99 (*0-380-80418-2*, Avon Bks) Morrow Avon.

Price of Justice, No. AJ3. Howard Levenson. 87p. (C). 1981. pap. 30.00 (*0-900137-17-7*, Pub. by NCCL) St Mut.

Price of Land in Shelby. Laurie Alberts. LC 96-24556. (Hardscrabble Bks.). 330p. 1996. pap. 14.95 (*0-87451-844-X*); text 30.00 (*0-87451-782-6*) U Pr of New Eng.

Price of Liberty. Alan Barth. LC 74-176486. (Civil Liberties in American History Ser.). 1972. reprint ed. lib. bdg. 29.50 (*0-306-70416-1*) Da Capo.

Price of Liberty. Wayne Whipple. (Illus.). 180p. (YA). 1997. reprint ed. 15.00 (*1-889128-29-5*) Mantle Ministries.

Price of Liberty: Perspectives on Civil Liberties by Member of the A.C.L.U. Ed. by Alan Reitman. (C). 1969. pap. 2.00 (*0-393-00505-4*) Norton.

Price of Liberty: The Public Debt of the American Revolution. William G. Anderson. LC 82-17420. (Illus.). 192p. reprint ed. pap. 59.60 (*0-7837-1769-5*, 204196600001) Bks Demand.

Price of Life: The Future of American Health Care. Robert H. Blank. LC 96-3465. 352p. 1997. 31.00 (*0-231-10294-1*) Col U Pr.

Price of Love. Beverly Clark. (Indigo Love Stories Ser.). 239p. 1999. pap. 8.95 (*1-885478-61-5*, Pub. by Genesis Press) BookWorld.

Price of Love. Created by Francine Pascal. (Sweet Valley University Ser.: No. 43). 240p. (YA). (gr. 7 up). 1998. mass mkt. 3.99 (*0-553-57031-5*) BDD Bks Young Read.

Price of Love. Arnold Bennett. LC 74-17050. (Collected Works of Arnold Bennett: Vol. 68). 1977. reprint ed. 39.95 (*0-518-19149-4*) Ayer.

***Price of Love.** unabridged ed. Joe Sharp & Edie Tinstman. (Illus.). 119p. 1998. pap. 15.00 (*1-929326-25-4*, 0050) Hal Bar Pubg.

Price of Missing Life. Simon Schrock. LC 92-80704. 128p. 1992. pap. 6.95 (*0-89221-221-7*) New Leaf.

Price of Murder. John D. MacDonald. 1976. 19.95 (*0-8488-0569-0*) Amereon Ltd.

Price of Nationhood: American Revolution in Charles County. Jean B. Lee. (C). 1996. pap. text. write for info. (*0-393-96847-2*) Norton.

Price of Nationhood: The American Revolution in Charles County. Jean B. Lee. LC 93-42536. 1994. write for info. (*0-393-36958-7*) Norton.

Price of Nationhood: The American Revolution in Charles County. Jean B. Lee. 1994. 29.95 (*0-393-03658-8*) Norton.

Price of Neglect. A. W. Tozer. LC 90-86216. 154p. 1991. pap. 9.99 (*0-87509-447-3*) Chr Pubns.

Price of Pain. Bob Snyder. 132p. 1993. pap. 5.95 (*1-883624-00-2*) Hope Hurt Minist.

Price of Paradise, Vol. II. Ed. by Randall W. Roth. 320p. 1993. pap. 14.95 (*1-56647-042-0*) Mutual Pub HI.

Price of Paradise: Lucky We Live Hawaii? Ed. by Randall Roth. 268p. 1992. pap. 14.95 (*1-56647-016-1*) Mutual Pub HI.

Price of Paradise: The Magazine Career of F. Scott Fitzgerald. Stephen W. Potts. LC 93-344. (Milford Ser.: Popular Writers of Today: Vol. 58). 136p. 1993. pap. 19.00 (*0-89370-287-0*) Millefleurs.

Price of Passion. Evelyn Palfrey. LC 97-93486. 350p. 1997. pap. 14.95 (*0-9654190-1-0*) Moon Child.

***Price of Passion.** Evelyn Palfrey. 384p. 2000. pap. 12.95 (*0-671-04220-3*, PB Trade Paper) PB.

Price of Passion: An Erotic Journey. Jess Wells. LC 99-47445. 120p. 1999. lib. bdg. 22.95 (*1-56341-113-X*) Firebrand Bks.

***Price of Passion: An Erotic Journey.** Jess Wells. LC 99-47445. 120p. 1999. pap. 10.95 (*1-56341-112-1*) Firebrand Bks.

Price of Patriotism: Indiana County, Pennsylvania & the Civil War. W. Wayne Smith. LC 97-49400. 124p. 1997. 24.95 (*1-57249-099-3*, Burd St Pr) White Mane Pub.

Price of Peace. Cahal B. Daly. 251p. 1991. 24.00 (*0-85640-471-3*, Pub. by Blackstaff Pr) Dufour.

Price of Peace. Cahal B. Daly. 251p. 1991. pap. 12.95 (*0-85640-472-1*) Dufour.

Price of Peace. Mary Miller. (Illus.). 304p. 1975. 10.15 (*0-7399-0134-6*, 2355) Rod & Staff.

***Price of Peace.** Mike Moscoe. 2000. mass mkt. 5.99 (*0-441-00695-7*) Ace Bks.

Price of Peace: Emergency Economic Intervention & U. S. Foreign Policy. David J. Rothkopf. LC 98-17009. 114p. 1998. pap. 10.95 (*0-87003-150-3*) Carnegie Endow.

Price of Peace: Incentives & International Conflict Prevention. Ed. by David Cortright. LC 97-22989. (Carnegie Commission on Preventing Deadly Conflict Ser.). (Illus.). 320p. 1997. 68.50 (*0-8476-8556-X*); pap. 26.95 (*0-8476-8557-8*) Rowman.

Price of Pity: Poetry, History & Myth in the Great War. Martin Stephen. 256p. 1996. text 32.95 (*0-85052-450-4*, Pub. by Leo Cooper) Trans-Atl Phila.

***Price of Power.** James W. Huston. 528p. 2000. mass mkt. 6.99 (*0-380-73160-6*, Avon Bks) Morrow Avon.

Price of Power. W. W. Baldwin. LC 76-990. (FDR & the Era of the New Deal Ser.). 361p. 1976. reprint ed. lib. bdg. 39.50 (*0-306-70803-5*) Da Capo.

Price of Power: A Novel. James W. Huston. LC 99-18566. 448p. 1999. 25.00 (*0-688-15918-4*, Wm Morrow) Morrow Avon.

Price of Power: America since Nineteen Forty-Five. Herbert Agar. LC 57-8575. (Chicago History of American Civilization Ser.). xii, 211p. 1957. pap. text 10.95 (*0-226-00937-8*, CHAC1) U Ch Pr.

Price of Power: America since Nineteen Forty Five. Herbert Agar. LC 57-8575. (Chicago History of American Civilization Ser.). 212p. reprint ed. pap. 65.80 (*0-608-10910-X*, 202001800016) Bks Demand.

Price of Redemption: The Spiritual Economy of Puritan New England. Mark A. Peterson. LC 97-33712. 360p. 1997. 45.00 (*0-8047-2912-3*) Stanford U Pr.

Price of Reindeer. John Elsberg. (WEP Poetry Ser.: No. 2). 1979. pap. 2.00 (*0-917976-05-3*, White Ewe Pr) Thunder Baas Pr.

Price of Salt. Claire Morgan, pseud. 276p. 1991. pap. 12.95 (*1-56280-003-5*) Naiad Pr.

Price of Salt. Claire Morgan, pseud. LC 75-12340. (Homosexuality Ser.). 1979. reprint ed. 19.95 (*0-405-07384-4*) Ayer.

An Asterisk (*) at the beginning of an entry indicates that the title is appearing for the first time.

Price of Silence. Judy Baer. LC 93-74538. (Live from Brentwood High Ser.: No. 2). 16p. (YA). (gr. 7-10). 1994. mass mkt. 4.99 (*1-55661-387-3*) Bethany Hse.

Price of Sparrows. Jim Meals. Date not set. pap. 15.95 (*0-934468-50-8*) Gaslight.

Price of Spiritual Power. Roberts Liardon. 48p. 1996. pap. 3.99 (*1-880089-68-8*, Pub. by Albury Pub) Appalach Bk Dist.

Price of Spiritual Power. Roberts Liardon. 47p. 1987. pap. 2.95 (*0-88144-090-6*) Christian Pub.

Price of Success: An Autobiography. J. B. Phillips. LC 84-23472. 222p. (Orig.). 1985. pap. 8.99 (*0-87788-659-8*, H Shaw Pubs) Waterbrook Pr.

***Price of Surrender.** 1999. per. 4.50 (*0-373-80671-X*) S&S Trade.

Price of Taming a River: The Decline of Puget Sound's Duwamish/Green Waterway. Mike Sato. LC 97-12101. (Illus.). 112p. (Orig.). 1997. pap. 12.95 (*0-89886-490-9*) Mountaineers.

Price of Tea in China. E. Shaskan Bumas. LC 94-18665. (Associated Writing Programs Awards for Short Fiction Ser.). 216p. (C). 1995. 22.95 (*0-87023-930-9*) U of Mass Pr.

Price of the Past: Russia's Struggle with the Legacy of a Militarized Economy. Clifford G. Gaddy. 250p. 1998. pap. 18.95 (*0-8157-3015-2*); text 42.95 (*0-8157-3016-0*) Brookings.

Price of the Ride. Thomas Farber. Ed. by Donald S. Ellis. (Illus.). 80p. (Orig.). 1996. pap. 5.95 (*0-88739-103-6*) Creat Arts Bk.

Price of the Stars. Debra Doyle & James D. MacDonald. (MageWorlds Ser.: No. 1). 448p. (Orig.). 1992. mass mkt. 4.99 (*0-8125-1704-0*, Pub. by Tor Bks) St Martin.

Price of the Ticket: Collected Nonfiction, 1948-1985. James Baldwin. 704p. 1985. text 35.00 (*0-312-64306-3*) St Martin.

Price of Victory. Vincent S. Green. 240p. 1992. 19.95 (*0-8027-1200-2*) Walker & Co.

Price of War: Urbanization in Vietnam, 1954-1985. Nigel J. Thrift & Dean Forbes. (Illus.). 224p. 1986. text 49.95 (*0-04-301210-8*) Routledge.

***Price of Water: Trends in OECD Countries.** OECD Staff. 176p. 1999. pap. 29.00 (*92-64-17079-0*, 97 1999 06 1, Pub. by Org for Econ) OECD.

Price of Wealth: Economics & Institutions in the Middle East. Kiren A. Chaudhry. LC 97-1536. (Cornell Studies in Political Economy). 344p. 1996. text 45.00 (*0-8014-3164-6*); pap. text 19.95 (*0-8014-8430-8*) Cornell U Pr.

Price of Wisdom. Shannah Jay. LC 97-221105. (Chronicles of Tenebrak Ser.). 539p. 1996. write for info. (*0-330-35789-1*) Pan.

Price of Wisdom: The Heroic Struggle to Become a Person. James M. McMahon. LC 95-46021. 192p. (Orig.). 1996. pap. 14.95 (*0-8245-1553-6*) Crossroad NY.

Price on Contemporary Estate Planning. John R. Price. 1360p. 1992. boxed set 145.00 (*0-316-71859-9*, Aspen Law & Bus) Aspen Pub.

Price Policies & Economic Growth. Ed. by Antonio Jorge & Jorge Salazar-Carrillo. LC 96-20689. 272p. 1997. 69.50 (*0-275-95322-X*, Praeger Pubs) Greenwood.

Price Policy. Ed. by Malcolm S. Adiseshiah. (C). 1987. 26.00 (*81-7062-027-9*, Pub. by Ashish Pub Hse) S Asia.

Price, Policy & Production Coffee & Uganda. Todd Titterud. 85p. 1986. pap. 2.00 (*0-941934-58-6*) Indiana Africa.

Price Portfolio: Forty-Six Reprints of Medical Papers of Dr. Weston A. Price. 1978. 35.00 (*0-916764-04-4*) Price-Pottenger.

Price, Quality & Trust: Inter-Firm Relations in Britain & Japan. Mari Sako. (Studies in Management: No. 18). (Illus.). 284p. (C). 1992. text 64.95 (*0-521-41386-9*) Cambridge U Pr.

Price-Quality Interactions in Business Cycles. Frederick C. Mills. LC 75-19728. (National Bureau of Economic Research Ser.). (Illus.). 1975. reprint ed. 19.95 (*0-405-07606-1*) Ayer.

Price-Quantity Interactions in Business Cycles. Frederick C. Mills. (Twenty-Fifth Anniversary Ser.: No. 2). 152p. 1946. reprint ed. 41.10 (*0-87014-114-7*) Natl Bur Econ Res.

Price Reform & Fertilizer Use in Smallholder Agriculture in Tanzania. Florens Turuka. 288p. 1995. pap. text 24.95 (*3-8258-2563-9*) Transaction Pubs.

Price Research in the Steel & Petroleum Industries. (Conference on Price Research Ser.: No. 3). 187p. 1939. reprint ed. 48.70 (*0-87014-189-9*) Natl Bur Econ Res.

Price Rigidity: Causes & Macroeconomic Implications. Torben M. Andersen. (Illus.). 194p. 1995. text 38.00 (*0-19-828760-7*) OUP.

Price She Paid see Collected Works of David G. Phillips

Price She Paid. David C. Phillips. (Collected Works of David G. Phillips). 1988. reprint ed. lib. bdg. 59.00 (*0-7812-1343-6*) Rprt Serv.

Price Spiral Method. B. J. Howard. 1989. 50.00 (*0-930233-32-8*) Windsor.

Price Stabilization on World Agricultural Markets: An Application to the World Market for Sugar. Bernd Lucke. LC 92-31169. (Lecture Notes in Economics & Mathematical Systems Ser.: Vol. 393). 1992. 58.95 (*0-387-56099-8*) Spr-Verlag.

Price Statistics of the Federal Government. Report of the Price Statistics Review Committee. (General Ser.: No. 73). 518p. 1961. reprint ed. 134.70 (*0-87014-072-8*) Natl Bur Econ Res.

Price Theory. Milton Friedman. LC 76-1397. 367p. 1976. lib. bdg. 49.95 (*0-202-06074-8*) Aldine de Gruyter.

Price Theory. 3rd ed. Date not set. pap. text, teacher ed. write for info. (*0-314-05407-3*) West Pub.

Price Theory. 3rd ed. Steven E. Landsburg. 1995. pap., student ed. 19.00 (*0-314-04899-5*) West Pub.

Price Theory: Microeconomic Analysis of Markets. John O. Ifediora. 406p. (C). 1994. pap. 61.00 (*0-536-58566-0*) Pearson Custom.

Price Theory & Applications. Peter B. Pashigian. (C). 1994. text 87.25 (*0-07-048741-3*) McGraw.

Price Theory & Applications. 2nd ed. B. Peter Pashigian. LC 97-1282. 784p. 1997. 83.44 (*0-07-048778-2*) McGraw.

Price Theory & Applications. 3rd ed. Steven E. Landsburg. LC 94-32600. 832p. (C). 1995. pap. 65.75 (*0-314-04059-5*) West Pub.

Price Theory & Applications. 4th ed. Landsburg. LC 98-4436. (Intermediate Microeconomics Ser.). 1998. pap. 93.95 (*0-538-88206-9*) S-W Pub.

***Price Theory & Applications.** 5th ed. Landsburgs & University of Rochester Staff. (SWC-General Business Ser.). (C). 2001. pap. 65.00 (*0-324-05979-5*); text, student ed. 25.95 (*0-324-05990-6*) Sth-Wstrn College.

Price Theory & Applications. 5th ed. Sproul. (C). 1991. pap. text, student ed. 20.00 (*0-13-714833-X*) P-H.

Price Theory & Applications. 6th ed. Jack Hirshleifer & David A. Hirshleifer. LC 97-29938. 591p. 1997. 98.00 (*0-13-190778-6*) P-H.

Price Theory & Its Applications. Ed. by Bernard Saffran & F. M. Scherer. LC 97-47487. (International Library of Critical Writings in Economics Ser.). 680p. 1998. 255.00 (*1-85898-610-9*) E Elgar.

Price Theory & Its Uses. 5th ed. Donald S. Watson & Malcolm Getz. 552p. (C). 1991. reprint ed. pap. text 51.25 (*0-8191-8073-4*) U Pr of Amer.

Price Theory Applications Sg. 2nd ed. Pashigian. 1997. pap. 23.44 (*0-07-048781-2*) McGraw.

Price Trends of Royal Tribute Commodities in Nueva Galicia. Woodrow Borah. 1992. pap. 42.50 (*0-520-09769-6*, Pub. by U CA Pr) Cal Prin Full Svc.

Price-Value Relationships at Restaurants. 77p. 1991. pap. 75.00 (*0-614-31112-8*, CS073) Natl Restaurant Assn.

Price Wars: The Independent Retailer's Guide to Winning the Battle for the Customer. Thomas J. Winninger. (Illus.). 240p. 1995. 24.95 (*0-7615-0164-9*) Prima Pub.

Price Was High. F. Scott Fitzgerald. Ed. by Matthew J. Bruccoli. 784p. 1996. 14.98 (*1-56731-106-7*, MJF Bks) Fine Comms.

Price Watch, 1981. H. M. Weatherman. (Illus.). 152p. 1981. pap. 6.00 (*0-913074-16-0*) Weatherman.

Price Waterhouse A-Z of Vat. Ed. by Price Waterhouse Staff. 160p. 1990. lib. bdg. 45.00 (*1-85333-308-5*, Pub. by Graham & Trotman) Kluwer Academic.

Price, Waterhouse & Company in America: A History of a Public Accounting Firm. C. W. DeMond. Ed. by Richard P. Brief. LC 80-1485. (Dimensions of a Accounting Firm Ser.). 1980. reprint ed. lib. bdg. 44.95 (*0-405-13515-7*) Ayer.

***Price Waterhouse coopers Regulatory Handbook Series: Pricewaterhousecoopers.** (Illus.). 1213p. 2000. pap. 299.99 (*0-7656-0649-6*) M E Sharpe.

Price Waterhouse Guide to Activity-Based Costing for Financial Institutions. Julie Mabberley. 240p. 1996. 75.00 (*0-7863-0143-0*, Irwn McGrw-H) McGrw-H Hghr Educ.

Price Waterhouse Guide to TIN Compliance: Interest, Divident, Backup Withholding & Related IRS Reporting Issues, 1996-1997 Edition. 7th ed. Price Waterhouse Staff. LC 96-34764. 288p. 1996. pap. 75.00 (*0-7863-1105-3*, Irwn Prfssnl) McGraw-Hill Prof.

Price Waterhouse Investment Tax Advisor. Price Waterhouse Staff. 1990. pap. 5.50 (*0-13-717463-2*) P-H.

Price Waterhouse Personal Financial Adviser. Price Waterhouse LLP Staff. 320p. 1995. text 15.00 (*0-7863-0461-8*, Irwn Prfssnl) McGraw-Hill Prof.

Price Waterhouse Personal Financial Adviser: Special Edition. Price Waterhouse Staff. 1996. text 25.00 (*0-7863-1141-X*, Irwn Prfssnl) McGraw-Hill Prof.

Price Waterhouse Personal Tax Adviser, 1994-1995. Price Waterhouse Staff. 1994. text 2.17 (*0-7863-0434-0*, Irwn Prfssnl) McGraw-Hill Prof.

Price Waterhouse Retirement Advisor. Price Waterhouse Staff. 1990. pap. 5.50 (*0-13-717471-3*) P-H.

Price Waterhouse Reversal Provisions of the Civil Rights Act of 1990: Jeopardizing Affirmative Action to Punish Motives Without Consequences. Robert E. Williams. 10p. 1990. pap. 10.00 (*0-614-06161-X*, 2031-PP-4040) EPF.

Price Waterhouse Tax Strategy '97. Price Waterhouse Staff. (Illus.). 288p. 1996. mass mkt. 16.95 (*0-385-25615-9*) Doubleday.

Price We Pay the Case Against Racist Speech, Hate Propaganda, & Pornography. Laura Lederer. 384p. 1995. 30.00 (*0-8090-7883-X*); pap. 15.00 (*0-8090-1577-3*) Hill & Wang.

Price You Pay. Barbara Summers. LC 93-36960. 304p. 1993. 19.95 (*1-56743-047-3*, Amistad) HarperTrade.

***Price You Pay.** Ellen Winters. 232p. 2000. 19.95 (*0-87074-456-9*) SMU Press.

Price You Pay: The Hidden Cost of Women's Relationship to Money. Margaret Randall. LC 95-50497. 223p. (C). 1996. 65.00 (*0-415-91203-2*); pap. 17.99 (*0-415-91204-0*) Routledge.

Priceless. Mary L. Baxter. 368p. (Orig.). 1995. mass mkt. 5.99 (*0-446-36495-9*, Pub. by Warner Bks) Little.

Priceless. Christina Dodd. 384p. 1992. mass mkt. 5.99 (*0-06-104153-X*, Harp PBks) HarpC.

Priceless. Christina Dodd. 384p. 1998. mass mkt. 3.99 (*0-06-108563-4*) HarpC.

Priceless. Donna Schaff. 384p. 1998. mass mkt. 5.99 (*0-440-22586-8*) Doubleday.

Priceless. Mariah Stewart. (Orig.). 1999. per. 6.50 (*0-671-02625-9*) PB.

Priceless. Deborah L. Tolentino & Eduardo D. Tolentino. (Illus.). 115p. 1995. write for info. (*0-9650212-0-3*) Tolentino.

Priceless Acquisition. Cathleen Clare. 256p. 1997. mass mkt. 4.99 (*0-8217-5790-3*, Zebra Kensgtn) Kensgtn Pub Corp.

Priceless Gift of Christmas. Helen Steiner Rice. 1990. 14.95 (*0-89952-060-X*) Littlebrook.

Priceless Gifts: Celebrating the Holidays with Joseph & Emma Smith. Gracia N. Jones. Ed. by Susan Roylance. 96p. (Orig.). pap. 4.50 (*0-685-30412-4*) Roylance Pub.

Priceless Gifts: Celebrating the Holidays with Joseph & Emma Smith. Gracia N. Jones. LC 99-168039. 92p. 1998. 11.95 (*1-57734-342-5*, 0113631) Covenant Comms.

Priceless Gifts: Simple Ways to Make a Difference in the Lives of Others. Alan Gibson. LC 95-45563. 180p. 1996. 12.99 (*0-7852-7735-8*, J Thoma Bks) Nelson.

Priceless Guide to the Antique Business. Patrick L. Campbell. (Illus.). 128p. (Orig.). 1994. pap. 5.95 (*0-89538-066-8*) L-W Inc.

Priceless Ingredient. Eugene E. Whitworth. 50p. 1989. 2.50 (*0-944155-05-7*) Grt Western Univ.

Priceless Jewel. Sangharakshita. 240p. (Orig.). 1996. pap. 12.95 (*0-904766-58-6*) Windhorse Pubns.

Priceless Knowledge? Natural Science in Economic Perspective. Nicholas Rescher. LC 96-18508. 198p. 1996. 55.50 (*0-8476-8244-7*); pap. 23.95 (*0-8476-8245-5*) Rowman.

***Priceless Markets.** Philip T. Hoffman. 1999. 50.00 (*0-226-34801-6*) U Ch Pr.

Priceless Privilege. Lucy Conley. (Illus.). 242p. 1981. 9.25 (*0-7399-0146-X*, 2360) Rod & Staff.

Priceless Souls. Desmond Tarrant. LC 93-37372. 192p. 1996. 16.95 (*0-913720-85-2*) Beil.

Priceless Spirit: A History of the Sisters of the Holy Cross, 1841-1893. M. Georgia Costin. LC 93-23642. (C). 1994. text 29.00 (*0-268-03804-X*) U of Notre Dame Pr.

Priceless Treasures. Ed. by Melisa Mitchell. 1997. 69.95 (*1-57553-576-9*) Watermrk Pr.

Priceless II. Eduardo D. Tolentino & Deborah L. Tolentino. 112p. (Orig.). 1996. pap. 12.00 (*0-9650212-1-1*) Tolentino.

***Priceless Weddings for under $5,000.** Kathleen Kennedy. 256p. 2000. pap. 14.00 (*0-609-80460-X*, Three Riv Pr) Crown Pub Group.

Prices & Choices: Microeconomic Vignettes. 2nd ed. David Hemenway. LC 87-17437. 336p. (C). 1987. text 27.50 (*0-88730-242-4*, HarpBusn) HarpInfo.

Prices & Choices: Microeconomic Vignettes. 3rd ed. David Hemenway. 292p. (C). 1993. lib. bdg. 57.00 (*0-8191-8946-4*) U Pr of Amer.

Prices & Choices: Microeconomic Vignettes. 3rd ed. David Hemenway. 292p. (C). 1994. pap. text 27.50 (*0-8191-8947-2*) U Pr of Amer.

Prices & Economic Fluctuations in India, 1861-1947. A. K. Ghosh. 1983. text 22.00 (*0-685-14092-X*) Coronet Bks.

Prices & Financial Statistics in the ESCWA Region. 166p. 28.00 (*92-1-128137-7*, B.94.II.L.1) UN.

Prices & Financial Statistics in the ESCWA Region. 170p. 1990. 39.00 (*92-1-128117-2*, 90.II.L.7) UN.

Prices & Financial Statistics in the ESCWA Region, No. 13. Economic & Social Commission for Western Asia Staf. 192p. 42.00 (*92-1-128155-5*, HG151) UN.

Prices & Markets in Ghana. Harold Alderman & Gerald Shively. (Working Papers). (C). 1991. pap. text 7.00 (*1-56401-110-0*) Cornell Food.

Prices & Price Controls. Intro. by Hans F. Sennholz. (Freeman Classics Ser.). 169p. (Orig.). 1992. pap. 9.95 (*0-910614-82-2*) Foun Econ Ed.

Prices & Production. A. Ritschl. (Contributions to Economics Ser.). (Illus.). v, 132p. 1989. 27.90 (*0-387-50916-X*) Spr-Verlag.

Prices & Quantities: A Macroeconomic Analysis. Arthur M. Okun. LC 80-70076. 367p. 1981. pap. 18.95 (*0-8157-6479-0*) Brookings.

Prices, Competition & Equilibrium. Ed. by Richard E. Quandt & Maurice H. Peston. LC 86-3549. 352p. 1986. 72.50 (*0-389-20626-1*, N8184) B&N Imports.

Prices, Cycles, & Growth. Hukukane Nikaido. (Studies in Dynamical Economic Science). (Illus.). 305p. (C). 1996. 42.00 (*0-262-14059-4*) MIT Pr.

Prices, Food, & Wages in Scotland, 1550-1780. A. J. Gibson & T. C. Smout. LC 93-41395. (Illus.). 414p. (C). 1995. text 80.00 (*0-521-34656-8*) Cambridge U Pr.

Prices, Growth & Cycles: Essays in Honor of Andras Brody. Ed. by Andras Simonovits & Albert E. Steenge. 288p. 1997. text 75.00 (*0-312-15970-6*) St Martin.

Prices in a War Economy: Some Aspects of the Present Price Structure of the United States. Frederick C. Mills. (Occasional Papers: No. 12). 104p. 1943. reprint ed. 27.10 (*0-87014-327-1*) Natl Bur Econ Res.

Prices in Financial Markets. Michael U. Dothan. (Illus.). 360p. (C). 1990. text 57.95 (*0-19-505312-5*) OUP.

Prices in Recession & Recovery: A Survey of Recent Changes. Frederick C. Mills. (General Ser.: No. 31). 601p. 1936. reprint ed. 156.30 (*0-87014-030-2*) Natl Bur Econ Res.

***Prices, Markets & the Pharmaceutical Revolution.** John E. Calfee. 87p. 2000. pap. 9.95 (*0-8447-7147-3*, Pub. by Am Enterprise) Pub Resources Inc.

Prices of Agricultural Products & Selected Inputs in Europe & North America, 1986-1987. 176p. 1988. pap. 25.00 (*92-1-116423-0*, 88.II.E.19) UN.

Prices of Agricultural Products & Selected Inputs in Europe & North America, 1987-88, No. 38. 1989. 30.00 (*92-1-116447-8*) UN.

Prices of Agricultural Products & Selected Inputs in Europe & North America, 1988-1989. 155p. 1989. 36.00 (*92-1-116470-2*, 90.II.E.5) UN.

Prices of Agricultural Products & Selected Inputs in Europe & North America, 1989/90. 155p. 1991. 38.00 (*92-1-116506-7*, 91.II.E.19) UN.

Prices of Agricultural Products & Selected Inputs in Europe & North America, 1992/93. annuals (Annual ECE/FAO Price Review Ser.: No. 43). 202p. 36.00 (*92-1-116599-7*) UN.

Prices of Agricultural Products & Selected Inputs in Europe & North America, 1993/94. FAO/ECE Agriculture & Timber Division of the Econo. (Annual ECE/FAO Price Review Ser.: No. 44). 212p. 36.00 (*92-1-116633-0*, HD9018) UN.

Prices, Productivity, & Investment: Assessing Financial Strategies in Higher Education. Edward P. St. John. Ed. & Frwd. by Jonathan D. Fife. (ASHE-ERIC Higher Education Reports: No. 94-3). 137p. (Orig.). (C). 1995. pap. 24.00 (*1-878380-59-1*) GWU Grad Schl E&HD.

Prices, Products, & People: Analyzing Agricultural Markets in Developing Countries. Ed. by Gregory J. Scott. LC 95-21262. 495p. 1995. pap. 39.95 (*1-55587-609-9*) L Rienner.

Prices, Profits & Rhythms of Accumulation. Gilbert Abraham-Frois et al. Tr. by Sonia Ben Ouagrham. LC 94-42383. 299p. (C). 1997. text 59.95 (*0-521-39532-1*) Cambridge U Pr.

Prices, Quantities, & Expectations: Keynes & Macroeconomics in the Fifty Years since the Publication of the General Theory. Ed. by P. J. Sinclair. (Oxford Economic Papers Special Issue). (Illus.). 572p. 1987. pap. 32.50 (*0-19-828589-2*) OUP.

Prices Realized on Rare Imprinted American Wooden Planes. Emil S. Pollak & Martyl Pollak. (Illus.). 152p. 1993. pap. 16.95 (*1-879335-36-0*) Astragal Pr.

Prices, Wages & Business Cycles: A Dynamic Theory. Burton H. Klein. (Illus.). 256p. 1984. 72.00 (*0-08-030126-6*, Pergamon Pr) Elsevier.

PricewaterhouseCoopers: The WetFeet.com Insider Guide. 2000th ed. WetFeet.com Staff. (Insider Guides Ser.). 63p. 1999. per. 25.00 (*1-58207-047-4*) WetFeet.

PricewaterhouseCoopers Regulatory Handbook Series, Set. PricewaterhouseCoopers Staff. (PricewaterhouseCoopers Regulatory Handbook Ser.). 1213p. (gr. 13). 1998. pap. text 329.95 (*0-7656-0379-9*, Sharpe Prof) M E Sharpe.

***Prichina Pechali - The Reason of Sadness.** Boris Kushner. LC 99-70832. (RUS., Illus.). 216p. 1999. pap. 14.00 (*1-885563-18-3*) VIA Press MD.

Pricing: Concepts & Practices for Effective Marketing. Andre Gabor. 300p. 1987. text 78.95 (*0-566-02703-8*, Pub. by Gower) Ashgate Pub Co.

Pricing: Hints on How-to-Do-It! Barbara Massie. 72p. 1995. lib. bdg. 9.95 (*1-884053-07-6*) Magnolia AR.

Pricing: Making Profitable Decisions. 2nd ed. Kent B. Monroe. 1990. text 63.50 (*0-07-042782-8*) McGraw.

Pricing & Bidding: Handbook & Workbook. D. Miles et al. (Improve Your Construction Business Ser.: Vol. 1). 112p. 1994. pap. 24.75 (*92-2-109160-0*) Intl Labour Office.

Pricing & Bidding Handbook. C. A. Andersson et al. LC 94-223507. (Improve Your Construction Business Ser.: No. 1). 1996. 13.50 (*92-2-108738-7*) Intl Labour Office.

Pricing & Capacity Determination in International Air Transport. Peter P. Haanappel. 1984. pap. text 66.00 (*90-6544-154-9*) Kluwer Law Intl.

***Pricing & Cost Accounting: A Handbook for Goverment Contractors.** Darrell J. Oyer. 250p. 1999. 125.00 (*1-56726-089-6*) Mgmt Concepts.

Pricing & Cost Recovery in Long Distance Transport. Ed. by D. N. Starkie. 1982. lib. bdg. 126.50 (*90-247-2683-2*) Kluwer Academic.

Pricing & Costs of Monographs & Serials: National & International Issues. Ed. by Sul H. Lee. LC 86-33653. (Journal of Library Administration Supplement: No. 1). 109p. 1987. text 39.95 (*0-86656-620-1*) Haworth Pr.

Pricing & Growth: A Neo-Ricardian Approach. Stanley Bober. LC 91-6972. 168p. (C). (gr. 13). 1992. text 61.95 (*0-87332-856-6*); pap. text 32.95 (*0-87332-857-4*) M E Sharpe.

***Pricing & Hedging of Derivative Securities.** Lars Nielsen. (Illus.). 460p. 1999. text 55.00 (*0-19-877619-5*) OUP.

Pricing & Hedging Swaps. Paul Miron & Philip Swannell. 240p. 1991. 245.00 (*1-85564-052-X*, Pub. by Euromoney) Am Educ Systs.

Pricing & Inflation in India. Pulapre Balakrishnan. (Illus.). 290p. 1992. text 29.95 (*0-19-562833-0*) OUP.

Pricing & Investment Strategies for Guaranteed Equity-Linked Life Insurance. Eduardo S. Schwartz & J. David Cummins. LC 78-62409. (S. S. Huebner Foundation Monographs: No. 7). (Illus.). 123p. (C). 1979. pap. 15.00 (*0-918930-07-3*) Huebner Foun Insur.

Pricing & Managing Exotic & Hybrid Options. Vineer Bhansali. LC 97-32770. (Irwin Library of Investment & Finance). 300p. 1998. 70.00 (*0-07-006669-8*) McGraw-Hill Prof.

Pricing & Markets: U. S. & Japanese Responses to Currency Fluctuations. Julia Lowell & Loren Yager. LC 94-16352. 1994. pap. text 13.00 (*0-8330-1540-0*, MR-438-CAPP) Rand Corp.

Pricing & Planning in the U. S. Natural Gas Industry: An Econometric & Programming Study. Anthony G. Lawrence. Ed. by Stuart Bruchey. LC 78-22693. (Energy in the American Economy Ser.). (Illus.). 1979. lib. bdg. 19.95 (*0-405-11996-8*) Ayer.

Pricing & Price Regulation: An Economic Theory for Public Enterprises & Public Utilities. 3rd ed. Dieter Bos. LC 94-36208. (Advanced Textbooks in Economics Ser.: Vol. 34). 470p. 1994. 76.50 (*0-444-88478-5*, North Holland) Elsevier.

Pricing & Rate Forecasting Using Broadcast Yield Management. Shane Fox. 137p. 1992. pap. 39.95 (*0-89324-150-4*, 3555) Natl Assn Broadcasters.

P

An Asterisk (*) at the beginning of an entry indicates that the title is appearing for the first time.

Pricing & Regulatory Innovations under Increasing Competition. Michael A. Crew. LC 96-36206. (Topics in Regulatory Economics & Policy Ser.). 216p. (C). 1996. lib. bdg. 91.00 (*0-7923-9810-6*) Kluwer Academic.

Pricing Behavior in Philippine Corn Markets: Implications for Market Efficiency. Meyra S. Mendoza & Mark W. Rosegrant. LC 95-8312. (International Food Policy Research Institute Research Report Ser.: Vol. 101). 1995. write for info. (*0-89629-104-9*) Intl Food Policy.

Pricing Convertible Bonds. Kevin B. Connolly. LC 98-19146. 268p. 1998. 79.95 incl. disk (*0-471-97872-8*) Wiley.

Pricing Decision: Economic Theory & Business Practice. Neil Dorward. 200p. (C). 1987. pap. 50.00 (*0-06-318369-2*, Pub. by P Chapman) St Mut.

***Pricing Derivative Securities.** T. Wake Epps. LC 00-33564. 600p. 2000. 84.00 (*981-02-4298-0*) World Scientific Pub.

Pricing Financial Instruments: The Finite Difference Method. Domingo Tavella & Curt Randall. (Series in Financial Engineering). 256p. 2000. text 79.95 (*0-471-19760-2*) Wiley.

Pricing for Profit. Joe Butts. 46p. 1995. pap. 19.50 (*0-934420-19-X*) Studio Pr NE.

Pricing for Profit. Paisley College Staff. (Marketing for Manufacturing Managers Ser.). 1989. 105.00 (*0-08-037126-4*) Elsevier.

Pricing for Profit see Marketing for Manufacturing Managers

Pricing for Profits. Allan H. Smith & Judy Smith. 175p. 1988. pap. 8.00 (*0-931113-26-1*) Success Publ.

Pricing for Profits: Estimating Costs & Setting Prices for Textile Screen Printers. 2nd ed. Mark Goodridge. 68p. 1995. pap. 9.95 (*0-944094-01-5*) ST Pubns.

Pricing for Results. fac. ed. John Winkler. LC 83-20630. (Illus.). 217p. 1984. reprint ed. pap. 67.30 (*0-7837-8140-7*, 204794800008) Bks Demand.

Pricing for Value: A Professional's Guide 1998. 98th ed. Ronald J. Baker. (C). 1998. pap. 79.00 (*0-15-606291-7*, Pub. by Harcourt Coll Pubs) Harcourt.

Pricing for Welfare. Geeta Gouri. (C). 1988. 7.50 (*81-204-0322-3*, Pub. by Oxford IBH) S Asia.

Pricing Foreign Exchange Options: Incorporating Purchasing Power Parity. Michael T. Cheung & David W. Yeung. 96p. 1992. pap. 22.50 (*962-209-322-1*, Pub. by HK Univ Pr) Coronet Bks.

Pricing Foreign Exchange Options: Incorporating Purchasing Power Parity. 2nd ed. Michael TowCheung & David W. Yeung. 104p. 1998. pap. 19.95 (*962-209-454-6*, Pub. by HK Univ Pr) Coronet Bks.

Pricing Guide for Desktop Services. 4th ed. Robert C. Brenner. Ed. by Dawn M. Essman. (Illus.). 382p. (YA). (gr. 12). 1995. pap. 34.95 (*0-929535-15-4*) Brenner Info Group.

***Pricing Guide for Web Services.** 2nd rev. ed. Robert C. Brenner. Ed. by Jenny Hanson. (Illus.). 320p. 2000. pap. 32.95 (*1-930199-03-1*) Brenner Info Group.

Pricing, Hedging, & Trading Exotic Options: Understand the Intricacies of Exotic Options & How to Use Them to Maximum Advantage. Israel Nelken. LC 99-34153. (Illus.). 256p. 1999. 60.00 (*0-07-047236-X*, Irwn Prfssnl) McGraw-Hill Prof.

Pricing in Big Business: A Case Approach. Abraham D. Kaplan et al. LC 79-28354. (Illus.). 344p. 1980. reprint ed. lib. bdg. 35.00 (*0-313-22291-6*, KAPI, Greenwood Pr) Greenwood.

Pricing in Business. D. C. Hague. (University of Manchester Centre for Business Research Ser.). 1973. pap. 22.95 (*0-8464-0752-3*) Beekman Pubs.

***Pricing in Competitive Electricity Markets.** Ahmad Faruqui & Kelly Eakin. LC 00-35709. 2000. write for info. (*0-7923-7839-3*) Kluwer Academic.

***Pricing in Theory & Practice.** Bjarke Fog. LC 98-106648. 1999. 26.00 (*87-16-13229-7*) Mksgaard.

Pricing Life: Why It's Time for Health Care Rationing. Peter A. Ubel. LC 99-20664. (Basic Bioethics Ser.). (Illus.). 264p. 1999. 25.00 (*0-262-21016-9*) MIT Pr.

Pricing of Military Procurements. John P. Miller. (Yale Studies in National Policy: No. 2). 1949. 89.50 (*0-685-69842-4*) Elliots Bks.

Pricing of Shares with Different Voting Power & the Theory of Oceanic Games. Kristian Rydqvist. Ed. by Stockholm School of Economics Staff. 178p. (Orig.). 1986. pap. text 65.00 (*91-7258-211-1*) Coronet Bks.

***Pricing Options & Derivative Securities: An Engineering Approach.** Marlo Avellaneda. 268p. 1999. 59.95 (*0-8493-0383-4*, Chap & Hall CRC) CRC Pr.

Pricing Options with Futures-Style Margining: A Genetic Adaptive Neural Network Approach, 1. A Jay White. LC 99-41196. 120p. 1999. 40.00 (*0-8153-3392-7*) Garland.

Pricing Photography: The Complete Guide to Assignment & Stock Prices. 2nd rev. ed. Michal Heron & David MacTavish. LC 96-79668. 152p. (Orig.). 1997. pap. 24.95 (*1-880559-68-4*) Allworth Pr.

Pricing Policies & Procedures. Nessim Hanna & H. Robert Dodge. LC 94-12862. (C). 1995. text 62.50 (*0-8147-3517-7*) NYU Pr.

Pricing Policies of Financial Intermediaries. J. Dermine. (Studies in Contemporary Economics: Vol. 5). 174p. 1984. pap. 29.00 (*0-387-13080-2*) Spr-Verlag.

Pricing Postal Services in a Competitive Environment. (Illus.). 104p. (Orig.). (C). 1993. pap. text 30.00 (*1-56806-291-5*) DIANE Pub.

Pricing Power & the Public Interest: A Study Based on Steel. Gardiner C. Means. LC 75-39260. (Getting & Spending: The Consumer's Dilemma Ser.). (Illus.). 1976. reprint ed. 31.95 (*0-405-08033-6*) Ayer.

Pricing Strategies. Alfred R. Oxenfeldt. LC 74-78207. 267p. reprint ed. pap. 82.80 (*0-608-13027-3*, 202352700033) Bks Demand.

Pricing Strategy: An Interdisciplinary Approach. Morris Engelson. 222p. 1995. 50.00 (*0-9642870-6-4*) Joint Mgnt Strategy.

***Pricing Systems, Indexes & Price Behavior.** Nancy D. Ruggles & Richard Ruggles. LC 99-17051. 528p. 1999. 115.00 (*1-85898-993-0*) E Elgar.

***Pricing Tables - California.** 6th ed. Robert C. Brenner. Ed. by Jenny Hanson. 127p. 1999. ring bd. 49.95 (*0-929535-20-0*, 200) Brenner Info Group.

***Pricing Tables - Canada.** 6th ed. Robert C. Brenner. Ed. by Jenny Hanson. 183p. 1999. ring bd. 49.95 (*0-929535-11-1*, 111) Brenner Info Group.

***Pricing Tables - Mid Atlantic Region.** 6th ed. Robert C. Brenner. Ed. by Jenny Hanson. 1999. pap. 49.95 (*1-930199-01-5*) Brenner Info Group.

***Pricing Tables - Mountain States.** Robert C. Brenner. Ed. by Jenny Hanson. 2000. pap. 49.95 (*1-930199-07-4*) Brenner Info Group.

***Pricing Tables - New England.** 6th ed. Robert C. Brenner. Ed. by Jenny Hanson. 2000. pap. 49.95 (*1-930199-06-6*) Brenner Info Group.

***Pricing Tables - North Central.** 6th ed. Robert C. Brenner. Ed. by Jenny Hanson. 146p. 2000. pap. 49.95 (*1-930199-05-8*) Brenner Info Group.

***Pricing Tables - Pacific Region.** 6th ed. Robert C. Brenner. Ed. by Jenny Hanson. 2000. 49.95 (*1-930199-08-2*) Brenner Info Group.

***Pricing Tables - South Atlantic.** 6th ed. Robert C. Brenner. Ed. by Jenny Hanson. 136p. 2000. pap. 49.95 (*1-930199-04-X*) Brenner Info Group.

Pricing Tables - South Central. Robert C. Brenner & Marisa Harker. 1996. pap. 49.95 (*1-930199-09-0*) Brenner Info Group.

***Pricing the Planet: Economic Analysis for Sustainable Development.** Peter H. May. 2000. pap. text 20.00 (*0-231-10175-9*) Col U Pr.

Pricing the Planet: Economic Analysis for Sustainable Development. Peter H. May & Ronaldo S. DaMotta. (Illus.). 220p. 1996. 45.00 (*0-231-10174-0*) Col U Pr.

Pricing the Priceless Child: The Changing Social Value of Children. Viviana A. Zelizer. LC 93-39140. 296p. 1994. pap. text 15.95 (*0-691-03459-1*, Pub. by Princeton U Pr) Cal Prin Full Svc.

Pricing Theory in Post-Keynesian Economics: A Realist Approach. Paul Downward. LC 98-6257. (New Directions in Modern Economics Ser.). 240p. 1999. 90.00 (*1-85898-791-1*) E Elgar.

Pricing, Valuation & Systems: Essays in Neoinstitutional Economics. Marc R. Tool. 256p. 1995. 95.00 (*1-85278-976-X*) E Elgar.

Pricing Without Fear: A Sewing Entrepreneurs Guide. Barbara W. Sykes. (Illus.). 208p. 1999. pap. 16.95 (*0-9632857-6-9*) Collins Pubns.

***Pricing Your Products for Export & Budgeting for Export, 2000.** annuals John R. Jagoe. Ed. by Agnes Brown. (Illus.). 50p. 2000. pap. 40.00 (*0-943677-39-4*) Export USA.

***Pricipes de l'Interpretation de l'Ecriture dans l'Eglise Ancienne.** Michael Fiedrowicz. (Traditio Christiana Ser.: Vol. 10). xli, 203p. 1998. 70.95 (*3-906760-72-3*, Pub. by P Lang) P Lang Pubng.

Pricipia Discordia: Or, How I Found the Goddess, & What I Did to Her When I Found Her. 2nd ed. (Illus.). 100p. 1980. pap. text 10.00 (*1-55950-040-9*) Loompanics.

***Priciples of Financial Asset Pricing: A Discrete Time Maringale Approach.** Takeaki Kariya. 250p. 2000. 59.95 (*3-540-65314-7*) Spr-Verlag.

***Prick Up Your Ears: The Biography of Joe Orton.** John Lahr. (Illus.). 320p. 2000. pap. 16.95 (*0-520-22666-6*) U CA Pr.

Pricke of Conscience (Stimulus Conscientiae) A Northumbrian Poem. Rolle Richard of Hampole. LC 74-178551. reprint ed. 42.50 (*0-404-56666-9*) AMS Pr.

Prickle Says I'm Sorry. Lisa Wilkinson. Ed. by Laura Ring. LC 98-61300. (Happy Day Books). (Illus.). 24p. (J). (ps-2). 1999. pap. 1.99 (*0-7847-0893-2*, 04266) Standard Pub.

Prickly & Poisonous: The Deadly Defenses of Nature's Strangest Animals & Plants. Anita Ganeri. (Weird & Wonderful! Ser.). 45p. (J). 1999. pap. text 7.99 (*0-7681-0185-9*, McClanahan Book) Learn Horizon.

Prickly & Smooth. Rod Theodorou & Carole Telford. (Animal Opposites Ser.). (Illus.). (J). 1998. (*1-57572-064-7*) Heinemann Lib.

Prickly & Soft Animals see Animal Opposites

Prickly Hedgehog. Mark Ezra. LC 94-48116. (Illus.). 32p. (J). (ps-3). 1995. 14.95 (*1-56656-189-2*, Crocodile Bks) Interlink Pub.

***Prickly Pear.** Ronda Thompson. 320p. 1999. mass mkt. 4.99 (*0-8439-4624-5*, Leisure Bks) Dorchester Pub Co.

Prickly Pete, Cody Coyote & That Bowlegged Horse. Jacqueline Joyce. Tr. by DelMar Communication Int'l. Staff. (SPA., Illus.). 36p. (Orig.). (J). (ps-4). 1998. pap. 7.95 (*0-9652211-9-9*, 11138); pap. 7.95 (*0-9652211-8-0*, 11137) Bear Path.

Prickly Pete, Cody Coyote & That Bowlegged Horse-Ghost Rider. Jacqueline Joyce. (Illus.). 36p. (J). (ps-4). 1998. pap. 7.95 (*0-614-31261-2*, 11153) Bear Path.

Prickly Pete, Cody Coyote & That Bowlegged Horse-Ghost Rider. Jacqueline Joyce. Tr. by DelMar Communication International Staff. (SPA., Illus.). 36p. (J). (ps-4). 1998. pap. 7.95 (*0-614-31262-0*, 11154) Bear Path.

Prickly Problem. Ragnhild Scamell. LC 96-39751. (Illus.). 32p. (YA). 1998. 16.00 (*0-689-81382-1*) S&S Bks Yung.

***Pricksongs & Descants.** Robert Coover. 1999. pap. 12.95 (*0-8050-6169-X*) St Martin.

***Pricksongs & Descants: Fictions.** Robert Coover. LC 99-51707. 256p. 2000. reprint ed. pap. 12.00 (*0-8021-3667-2*, Grove) Grove-Atltic.

Pricky, a Pet Porcupine. E. Greenleaf. LC 65-22311. (Illus.). 48p. (J). (gr. 2-5). 1968. lib. bdg. 10.95 (*0-87783-031-2*) Oddo.

Pricky, a Pet Porcupine. deluxe ed. E. Greenleaf. LC 65-22311. (Illus.). 48p. (J). (gr. 2-5). 1968. pap. 3.94 (*0-87783-158-0*) Oddo.

Pride. Mel B. 24p. (Orig.). 1985. pap. 2.00 (*0-89486-267-7*, 1397B) Hazelden.

***Pride.** Philip Boast. 1999. pap. 11.00 (*0-7472-3629-1*, Pub. by Headline Bk Pub) Trafalgar.

Pride. large type ed. Judith A. Saxton. 512p. 1983. 27.99 (*0-7089-0963-9*) Ulverscroft.

Pride: A Novel. Lorene Cary. 336p. 1999. pap. 12.95 (*0-385-48183-7*, Anchor NY) Doubleday.

Pride: A Novel. William Wharton. LC 95-25698. 288p. 1996. pap. 12.95 (*1-55704-259-4*, Pub. by Newmarket) Norton.

Pride: The Charley Pride Story. Charley Pride. 1995. pap. 10.00 (*0-688-14232-X*, Quil) HarperTrade.

Pride According to Gregory the Great: A Study of the Moralia. Matthew Baasten. LC 86-18057. (Studies in the Bible & Early Christianity: Vol. 7). 216p. 1986. lib. bdg. 89.95 (*0-88946-606-8*) E Mellen.

Pride Against Prejudice: The Biography of Larry Doby. Joseph T. Moore. LC 87-32874. 206p. 1988. pap. 12.95 (*0-275-92984-1*, B2984, Praeger Pubs) Greenwood.

Pride Against Prejudice: The Biography of Larry Doby, 113. Joseph T. Moore. LC 87-17743. (Contributions in Afro-American & African Studies: No. 113). 206p. 1988. 55.00 (*0-313-25995-X*, MPJ/, Greenwood Pr) Greenwood.

Pride Against Prejudice: Work in the Lives of Older Blacks & Young Puerto Ricans. Dean W. Morse. LC 78-65534. (Conservation of Human Resources Ser.: No. 9). 254p. 1981. text 38.50 (*0-916672-67-0*) Rowman.

Pride & a Daily Marathon. Jonathan Cole. LC 95-13650. 214p. 1995. pap. text 15.00 (*0-262-53136-4*, Bradford Bks) MIT Pr.

Pride & Joi. Gay G. Gunn. (Indigo Love Stories Ser.). 202p. 1998. 15.95 (*1-885478-34-8*, Pub. by Genesis Press) BookWorld.

***Pride & Joi.** unabridged ed. Gay C. Gunn. 202p. 1999. pap. 8.95 (*1-885478-77-1*, Pub. by Genesis Press) BookWorld.

***Pride & Joy, Vol. 1.** Cathie Linz. LC 98-15557. 1998. pap. text 23.95 (*0-7862-1494-5*) Mac Lib Ref.

Pride & Joy: African American Baby Celebrations. Janice Robinson. 1999. pap. write for info. (*0-446-67412-5*) Warner Bks.

Pride & Joy: The Lives & Passions of Women Without Children. Terri Casey. LC 98-7952. 224p. 1998. pap. 14.95 (*1-885223-82-X*) Beyond Words Pub.

Pride & Joy of Working Cattle. Ray Ludwig & Ivy Morrison. Ed. by Edgar C. Alward & Sally Bannish. (Illus.). 68p. (Orig.). 1995. pap. 24.50 (*1-880836-09-2*) Pine Isl Pr.

Pride & Passion: An Exhilarating Half Century of Cricket in Pakistan. Omar Noman. LC 98-931026. (The Jubilee Ser.). (Illus.). 438p. 1999. 26.00 (*0-19-577801-6*) OUP.

Pride & Predator. Sally S. Wright. 336p. 1999. mass mkt. 5.99 (*0-345-42589-8*) Ballantine Pub Grp.

Pride & Predator. Sally S. Wright. LC 97-15561. (Ben Reese Mystery Ser.: Vol. 2). 300p. 1997. pap. 9.99 (*1-57673-084-0*, Multnomah Bks) Multnomah Pubs.

Pride & Predator. large type ed. Sally S. Wright. LC 98-55245. 1999. 23.95 (*0-7862-1801-0*) Thorndike Pr.

***Pride & Prejudice.** 1999. 9.95 (*1-56137-766-X*) Novel Units.

***Pride & Prejudice.** (YA). 1999. 11.95 (*1-56137-767-8*) Novel Units.

Pride & Prejudice. Jane Austen. LC 95-69125. 352p. 1998. mass mkt. 4.95 (*0-451-52588-4*) Addson-Wesley Educ.

Pride & Prejudice. Jane Austen. (YA). Date not set. lib. bdg. 25.95 (*0-8488-0420-1*) Amereon Ltd.

Pride & Prejudice. Jane Austen. 304p. (YA). (gr. 9-12). 1983. mass mkt. 4.95 (*0-553-21310-5*, Bantam Classics) Bantam.

Pride & Prejudice. Jane Austen. 1991. mass mkt. 4.95 (*0-553-54088-2*) Bantam.

***Pride & Prejudice.** Jane Austen. LC 99-25620. (Classic Novels). 392p. 1999. pap. text 8.95 (*0-7641-1147-7*) Barron.

Pride & Prejudice. Jane Austen. Ed. by Walter Kendrick. (Mcdonald Classics Ser.). 410p. (YA). 1980. 19.95 (*0-8464-1071-0*) Beekman Pubs.

Pride & Prejudice. Jane Austen. (YA). 1988. lib. bdg. 19.95 (*0-89966-243-9*) Buccaneer Bks.

Pride & Prejudice. Jane Austen. Ed. by Richard Bain. LC 97-190825. (Literature Ser.). 384p. (C). 1996. pap. 11.95 (*0-521-57654-7*) Cambridge U Pr.

Pride & Prejudice. Jane Austen. 107p. 1942. pap. 5.50 (*0-87129-686-1*, P36) Dramatic Pub.

Pride & Prejudice. Jane Austen. 327p. 1991. write for info. (*1-85715-001-5*) Everymns Lib.

Pride & Prejudice, 001. Jane Austen. Ed. by Mark Schorer. LC 56-13877. (YA). (gr. 9 up). 1956. pap. 13.96 (*0-395-05101-0*, RivEd) HM.

Pride & Prejudice. Jane Austen. (YA). 1997. pap. 8.25 (*0-03-051487-8*) Holt R&W.

Pride & Prejudice. Jane Austen. (Cloth Bound Pocket Ser.). 240p. 1998. 7.95 (*3-89508-207-4*) Konemann.

Pride & Prejudice. Jane Austen. Ed. by Richard Adams. (Study Texts Ser.). (YA). 1983. pap. text 5.95 (*0-582-33086-6*, 72039) Longman.

Pride & Prejudice. Jane Austen. 368p. 1991. 17.00 (*0-679-40542-9*) Modern Lib NY.

***Pride & Prejudice.** Jane Austen. (Classics Ser.). 2000. pap. 7.95 (*0-679-78326-1*) Modern Lib NY.

Pride & Prejudice. Jane Austen. (C). pap. text. write for info. (*0-393-99771-5*) Norton.

Pride & Prejudice. Jane Austen. Ed. by Tricia Hedge. (Illus.). 112p. 1995. pap. text 5.95 (*0-19-422710-3*) OUP.

Pride & Prejudice. Jane Austen. Ed. by James Kinsley. (Oxford World's Classics Ser.). 390p. 1998. pap. 6.95 (*0-19-283355-3*) OUP.

Pride & Prejudice. Jane Austen. LC 99-462506. (Oxford World's Classics Hardcovers Ser.). 366p. 1999. 12.50 (*0-19-210026-2*) OUP.

Pride & Prejudice. Jane Austen. 144p. 1996. pap. 20.00 (*81-209-0025-1*, Pub. by Pitambar Pub) St Mut.

Pride & Prejudice. Jane Austen. (Short Classics Learning Files Ser.). (J). (gr. 4 up). 1988. 22.00 (*0-8172-2188-3*) Raintree Steck-V.

Pride & Prejudice. Jane Austen. (J). 1998. pap. 6.95 (*0-8114-6836-4*) Raintree Steck-V.

Pride & Prejudice. Jane Austen. (Illus.). 304p. 1995. 13.00 (*0-679-60168-6*) Random.

***Pride & Prejudice.** Jane Austen. LC 92-50183. (Literary Classics Ser.). 368p. 1999. 8.98 (*0-7624-0550-3*) Running Pr.

Pride & Prejudice. Jane Austen. Ed. by Andrew Worrall. (Thornes Classic Novels Ser.). (Illus.). 376p. 1997. pap. 19.95 (*0-7487-2977-1*, Pub. by S Thornes Pubs) Trans-Atl Phila.

Pride & Prejudice. Jane Austen. (J). 1996. pap. 2.25 (*0-590-08576-X*) Scholastic Inc.

***Pride & Prejudice.** Jane Austen. 416p. (YA). (gr. 7-12). 2000. pap. 4.99 (*0-439-10135-2*) Scholastic Inc.

Pride & Prejudice. Jane Austen. 384p. 1994. pap. 2.50 (*0-8125-2336-9*, Pub. by Tor Bks) St Martin.

***Pride & Prejudice.** Jane Austen. (Signature Classics Ser.). (Illus.). 352p. 1999. 24.95 (*1-58279-032-9*) Trident Pr Intl.

Pride & Prejudice. Jane Austen. (J). 1997. pap. 2.95 (*0-89375-611-3*) Troll Communs.

Pride & Prejudice. Jane Austen. 1950. 10.05 (*0-606-01933-2*, Pub. by Turtleback) Demco.

Pride & Prejudice. Jane Austen. Ed. by Pamela Norris. 384p. 1993. pap. 3.95 (*0-460-87212-5*, Everyman's Classic Lib) Tuttle Pubng.

Pride & Prejudice. Jane Austen. LC 97-140981. (Penguin Classics Ser.). 336p. 1996. pap. 7.95 (*0-14-043426-7*, Penguin Classics) Viking Penguin.

Pride & Prejudice. Jane Austen. (Classics Library). 265p. 1997. pap. 3.95 (*1-85326-000-2*, 0002WW, Pub. by Wrdsworth Edits) NTC Contemp Pub Co.

***Pride & Prejudice.** Jane Austen & Michael Kerrigan. (Literature Made Easy Ser.). (Illus.). 96p. (YA). 1999. pap. 4.95 (*0-7641-0834-4*) Barron.

***Pride & Prejudice.** Ed. by Cliffs Notes Staff. LC 00-38058. (Cliffs Notes Ser.). 96p. 2000. pap. 4.99 (*0-7645-8607-6*) IDG Bks.

***Pride & Prejudice, 5 vols.** Steck-Vaughn Company Staff. (Illus.). (J). 2000. pap. 26.95 (*0-8114-6972-7*) Raintree Steck-V.

Pride & Prejudice. abr. ed. Jane Austen. (Puffin Classics Ser.). (Illus.). 384p. (YA). (gr. 5 up). 1995. pap. 4.99 (*0-14-037337-3*, PuffinBks) Peng Put Young Read.

Pride & Prejudice. abr. large type ed. Jane Austen. (Great Illustrated Classics Ser.: Vol. 52). (Illus.). 240p. (gr. 3-7). 1996. 9.95 (*0-86611-871-3*) Playmore Inc.

***Pride & Prejudice.** deluxe ed. Jane Austen. (Signature Classics Ser.). (Illus.). 352p. 1999. 29.95 (*1-58279-044-2*) Trident Pr Intl.

Pride & Prejudice. large type ed. Jane Austen. (Large Print Heritage Ser.). 560p. 1997. lib. bdg. 36.95 (*1-58118-009-8*, 21967) LRS.

Pride & Prejudice. large type ed. Jane Austen. 480p. 1998. lib. bdg. 24.00 (*0-939495-50-3*) North Bks.

Pride & Prejudice. large type ed. Jane Austen. 532p. (YA). 1984. 27.99 (*0-7089-8228-X*, Charnwood) Ulverscroft.

***Pride And Prejudice.** large type ed. Jane Austen. 480p. 1999. pap. 20.00 (*0-06-093325-9*) HarpC.

Pride & Prejudice. Jane Austen. 355p. 1998. reprint ed. lib. bdg. 24.00 (*1-58287-058-6*) North Bks.

Pride & Prejudice. unabridged ed. Jane Austen. (Classics Ser.). (YA). (gr. 10 up). 1962. mass mkt. 4.95 (*0-8049-0001-9*, CL-1) Airmont.

Pride & Prejudice. unabridged ed. Jane Austen. (Thrift Editions Ser.). 272p. 1995. pap. 2.00 (*0-486-28473-5*) Dover.

Pride & Prejudice. 2nd ed. Jane Austen. (Illus.). 126p. 1993. pap. text 5.95 (*0-19-585472-1*) OUP.

Pride & Prejudice. 3rd ed. Jane Austen. (Norton Critical Editions Ser.). (C). pap. text. write for info. (*0-393-97604-1*) Norton.

Pride & Prejudice, Vol. II. 3rd ed. Jane Austen. Ed. by R. W. Chapman. (Illus.). 430p. (YA). 1988. reprint ed. 20.00 (*0-19-254702-X*) OUP.

Pride & Prejudice: A Study in Artistic Economy. Kenneth L. Moler. (Twayne's Masterwork Studies: No. 21). 144p. 1988. 25.95 (*0-8057-7983-3*, Twyne); pap. 18.00 (*0-8057-8032-7*, Twyne) Mac Lib Ref.

Pride & Prejudice: A Unit Plan. Mary B. Collins. 174p. 1994. teacher ed., ring bd. 26.95 (*1-58337-115-X*) Teachers Pet Pubns.

Pride & Prejudice: An Authoritative Text, Backgrounds, Reviews, & Essays in Criticism. 2nd ed. Jane Austen. Ed. by Donald J. Gray. LC 92-32426. (Critical Editions Ser.). (C). 1993. pap. text 12.50 (*0-393-96294-6*) Norton.

Pride & Prejudice: Hatians in the U. S. Nancy Foner & Alex Stepick. LC 97-228211. 134p. 1997. pap. 20.00 (*0-205-16817-5*) Allyn.

Pride & Prejudice: Penguin Readers Level 5. Jane Austen. 80p. 1998. pap. 7.00 (*0-14-081507-4*) Viking Penguin.

P

***Pride & Prejudice: Reproducible Teaching Unit.** James Scott. 69p. 1999. teacher ed., ring bd. 29.50 (*1-58049-146-4*, TU112) Prestwick Hse.

Pride & Prejudice: School Desegregation & Urban Renewal in Norfolk, 1950-1959. Forrest R. White. LC 92-7491. 352p. 1992. 59.95 (*0-275-94274-0*, C4274, Praeger Pubs) Greenwood.

Pride & Prejudice (Austen) Ed. by Ruth Goode. LC 84-18437. (Barron's Book Notes Ser.). 104p. (C). 1984. pap. 3.95 (*0-8120-3437-6*) Barron.

Pride & Prejudice Notes. Eric Peterson. (Cliffs Notes Ser.). 56p. 1959. pap. 4.95 (*0-8220-1084-4*, Cliff) IDG Bks.

Pride & Prejudice Readalong. Jane Austen. (Illustrated Classics Collection 5). 64p. 1994. pap. 14.95 incl. audio (*0-7854-0801-0*, 40573) Am Guidance.

Pride & Prodigies: Studies in the Monsters of the Beowulf-Manuscript. Andy Orchard. 360p. (C). 1995. 75.00 (*0-85991-456-9*, DS Brewer) Boydell & Brewer.

Pride & Promise: A Centennial History of East Stroudsburg University. Lawrence Squeri et al. LC 93-3736. 1993. write for info. (*0-89865-864-0*) Donning Co.

Pride & Promise: The Harlem Renaissance. Intro. by Kathryn Cryan-Hicks. LC 93-72240. (Perspectives on History Ser.). (Illus.). 52p. (YA). (gr. 5-12). 1994. pap. 6.95 (*1-878668-30-7*) Disc Enter Ltd.

***Pride & Promises.** B. J. James. 2000. mass mkt. 4.50 (*0-373-82231-6*, 1-82231-1) Harlequin Bks.

Pride & Promises. B. J. James. (Desire Ser.). 1993. mass mkt. 2.99 (*0-373-05789-X*, 5-05789-8) Silhouette.

Pride & Prosperity: The 80s. Time-Life Books Editors. LC 98-51346. (Our American Century Ser.). (Illus.). 192p. (J). (gr. 7). 1999. 29.95 (*0-7835-5510-5*) Time-Life.

***Pride & Protest: The Novel in Indiana.** Jeanette Vanausdall. LC 99-23984. (Illus.). xviii,169p. 1999. 27.95 (*0-87195-134-7*) Ind Hist Soc.

Pride & Protest (Postcard Book) A Celebration. (Postcard Book). 64p. 1994. pap. 7.95 (*0-304-32966-5*, Pub. by Cassell) LPC InBook.

Pride & Prudence: or The Married Sisters. Timothy S. Arthur. (Works of Timothy Shay Arthur). 1989. reprint ed. lib. bdg. 79.00 (*0-7812-1800-4*) Rprt Serv.

Pride & Solace: The Functions & Limits of Political Theory. Norman Jacobson. 190p. (C). 1986. pap. 8.95 (*0-416-42470-8*, 9788) Routledge.

Pride & Solidarity: A History of the Plumbers & Pipefitters of Columbus, Ohio, 1889-1989. Richard Schneirov. LC 92-47486. (Illus.). 208p. (Orig.). 1993. text 35.00 (*0-87546-306-1*); pap. text 14.95 (*0-87546-307-X*) OUP.

Pride & Splendor. Jean Pedrick. LC 75-23818. 72p. 1976. pap. 3.95 (*0-914086-10-3*) Alice James Bks.

Pride & the Passion: A Determined People Forge a New Destiny in South Africa. Jack Cavanaugh. (African Covenant Ser.: No. 1). pap. 10.99 (*0-8024-0862-1*, 257) Moody.

***Pride & Tradition: More Memories of Northeast Minneapolis.** Genny Zak Kieley. LC 99-68391. 287p. 2000. pap. 19.95 (*0-931714-85-0*, Pub. by Nodin Pr) Bookmen Inc.

Pride Cemetery. M. Edward Burtt. (Illus.). i, 16p. (Orig.). 1994. pap. write for info. (*1-888913-11-8*) M E Burtt.

Pride in Britain's High Tech Progress. Emrys Pride. 72p. (C). 1989. 59.00 (*0-905928-47-4*, Pub. by D Brown & Sons Ltd) St Mut.

Pride in the Jungle: Community & Everyday Life in Back of the Yards Chicago. Thomas J. Jablonsky. LC 92-12969. (Creating the North American Landscape Ser.). (Illus.). 216p. 1993. text 39.95 (*0-8018-4335-9*) Johns Hopkins.

Pride in the Past, Faith in the Future: A History of Michigan Livestock Exchange, 1922-1997 Carl E. Kramer & Michigan Livestock Exchange Staff. LC 96-79693. vii, 223p. 1997. write for info. (*0-9655940-0-9*) Michigan Livestock.

Pride Method: Mind over Matter in Combat Shooting. 64p. (Orig.). 1986. pap. 4.95 (*0-932373-03-8*) Potshot Pr.

Pride O' the Hilltop. Doris H. Masi. 140p. (J). 1992. per. 12.00 (*0-9628208-6-5*) Canal Side Pubs.

Pride of African Tales. Donna L. Washington. LC 94-18697. (Illus.). 80p. (J). (gr. 3-7). 1998. 16.95 (*0-06-024929-3*); lib. bdg. 16.89 (*0-06-024932-3*) HarpC Child Bks.

Pride of America, Vol. 1. Kelly Herman. (Illus.). 104p. 1985. 9.95 (*0-9613201-0-9*); 8.95 (*0-9613201-2-5*) Hal Herman Promo.

Pride of Baltimore: The Story of the Baltimore Clippers. Thomas C. Gillmer. 226p. 1994. pap. 15.95 (*0-07-023711-5*) McGraw.

Pride of Chanur. C. J. Cherryh. (Chanur Ser.: Bk. 1). 224p. 1982. mass mkt. 5.99 (*0-88677-292-3*, Pub. by DAW Bks) Penguin Putnam.

Pride of Chanur. rev. ed. C. J. Cherryh. (Chanur Ser.: Bk. 1). 225p. 1987. 17.00 (*0-932096-45-X*) Phantasia Pr.

Pride of Hannah Wade. Janet Dailey. 1994. mass mkt. 5.99 (*0-671-87510-8*) PB.

Pride of Havana: A History of Cuban Baseball. Roberto Gonzalez Echevarria. LC 98-20779. (Illus.). 512p. 1999. 35.00 (*0-19-506991-9*) OUP.

Pride of Heroes: Candid Celebrations. Jean Ackermann. v, 22p. (Orig.). (J). (gr. 8-12). 1984. pap. 6.00 (*0-9614506-0-6*) Box Four Twenty-Four.

Pride of Jared Mackade. Nora Roberts. Vol. 1000. 1995. per. 3.75 (*0-373-24000-7*, 1-24000-1) Silhouette.

Pride of Kin. Callie C. Wilson & Ellen W. Rienstra. LC 84-40555. (Wardlaw Book Ser.). 104p. 1985. 14.95 (*0-89096-226-X*) Tex A&M Univ Pr.

Pride of Lions. Suzanne Barclay. 1998. per. 4.99 (*0-373-29043-8*, 1-29043-6, Mira Bks) Harlequin Bks.

Pride of Lions. Marsha Canham. 416p. 1997. mass mkt. 5.99 (*0-440-22457-8*, Dell Trade Pbks) Dell.

Pride of Lions. Joolz et al. 64p. 1995. pap. 14.95 (*1-85224-294-9*, Pub. by Bloodaxe Bks) Dufour.

Pride of Lions. Morgan Llywelyn. 352p. 1996. 23.95 (*0-312-85700-4*) Forge NYC.

Pride of Lions. Morgan Llywelyn. 1997. mass mkt. 6.99 (*0-8125-3650-9*, Pub. by Tor Bks) St Martin.

Pride of Lions: Joshua Chamberlain & Other Maine Civil War Heroes. William Lemke. (Illus.). 256p. (Orig.). 1997. pap. 16.95 (*0-924771-95-X*, Covered Brdge Pr) Douglas Charles Ltd.

Pride of Lions: The Story of the House of Atreus. Norma Johnston. LC 99-60444. (Greek Mythology Trilogy Ser.). 200p. (YA). (gr. 9 up). 1999. reprint ed. pap. 16.00 (*1-892323-73-7*, Pierce Harris Pr) Vivisphere.

Pride of Men: Ironworking in 19th Century West Central Africa. Colleen E. Kriger. LC 98-30625. 288p. 1999. 24.95 (*0-325-00106-5*); 59.95 (*0-325-00107-3*) Greenwood.

Pride of Our People. large type ed. David C. Gross. 204p. 1991. pap. 12.95 (*0-8027-2648-8*) Walker & Co.

Pride of Palaces: Lenox Summer Cottages, 1883-1933. Ed. by Donald T. Oakes & Walter H. Scott. LC 81-82277. Orig. Title: The Summer Cottages of Edwin Hale Lincoln. (Illus.). 84p. (Orig.). 1981. pap. 15.00 (*0-685-04621-4*, Lenox Lib Assn) SnO Pubns.

Pride of Palomar. Peter B. Kyne. Ed. by Roger Daniels. LC 78-54820. (Asian Experience in North America Ser.). 1979. reprint ed. lib. bdg. 28.95 (*0-405-11276-9*) Ayer.

Pride of Place. Judith Glover. 1996. mass mkt. 13.95 (*0-340-66598-X*, Pub. by Hodder & Stought Ltd) Trafalgar.

Pride of Place: Early American Views from the Collection of Leonard L. Milberg '53. Compiled by Dale Roylance & Nancy Finlay. (Illus.). 66p. 1983. pap. 10.00 (*0-87811-029-1*) Princeton Lib.

Pride of Princes. Jennifer Roberson. (Chronicles of the Cheysuli Ser.: Bk. 5). 464p. (Orig.). 1988. pap. 6.99 (*0-88677-261-3*, Pub. by DAW Bks) Penguin Putnam.

Pride of Princesses: Princess Tales from Around the World. Shirley Climo. LC 98-41740. (Trophy Chapter Bk.). (Illus.). 112p. (J). (gr. 2-5). 1999. pap. 4.25 (*0-06-442102-3*) HarpC Child Bks.

Pride of Puerto Rico: The Life of Roberto Clemente. Paul R. Walker. LC 87-35138. 144p. (J). (gr. 3-7). 1988. 14.00 (*0-15-200562-5*, Gulliver Bks) Harcourt.

Pride of Puerto Rico: The Life of Roberto Clemente. Paul R. Walker. LC 90-45521. 144p. (J). (gr. 3-7). 1991. pap. 6.00 (*0-15-263420-7*, Gulliver Bks) Harcourt.

Pride of Quincys. LC 77-6104. (Picture Bks.). 50p. 1969. pap. 4.00 (*0-934909-13-X*) Mass Hist Soc.

Pride of Rockets, Bk. 8. Steven Kroll. (Hit & Run Gang Ser.: No. 8). 80p. (Orig.). (J). (gr. 2). 1994. pap. 3.50 (*0-380-77369-4*, Avon Bks) Morrow Avon.

Pride of Seattle: The First 300 Boeing B-17FS. Steve Birdsall. LC 98-201480. (Illus.). 64p. 1998. pap. 9.95 (*0-89747-389-2*, 6074) Squad Sig Pubns.

Pride of Small Nations: The Caucasus & Post-Soviet Disorder. Suzanne Goldenberg. (Politics in Contemporary Asia Ser.). (Illus.). 240p. (C). 1994. text 25.00 (*1-85649-238-9*, Pub. by Zed Books) St Martin.

Pride of Springfield. Mary Lou Kellar. LC 98-142920. 224p. (Orig.). 1997. pap. 9.95 (*0-89114-275-4*) Baptist Pub Hse.

Pride of St. Charles Avenue. Carole Halson. 1993. mass mkt. 3.39 (*0-373-09800-6*, 5-09800-9) Silhouette.

Pride of St. Louis: A Cooperstown Gallery. Bill Borst. (Illus.). 96p. (Orig.). 1984. pap. 6.95 (*0-9612260-0-5*) Krank Pr.

Pride of the Confederate Artillery: The Washington Artillery in the Army of Tennessee. Nathaniel C. Hughes, Jr. (Illus.). 344p. 1997. 29.95 (*0-8071-2187-8*) La State U Pr.

Pride of the Courtneys. large type ed. Margaret Dickinson. (Magna Large Print Ser.). 262p. 1997. 27.99 (*0-7505-0786-1*) Ulverscroft.

Pride of the Green Mountains. Carin Greenberg Baker. (Treasured Horses Ser.). (J). (gr. 3-9). 1998. pap. text 3.99 (*0-590-31654-0*) Scholastic Inc.

Pride of the Green Mountains see Treasured Horses Collection

Pride of the Green Mountains, 3. Carin Greenberg Baker. (Treasured Horses Ser.). (J). 1998. 9.09 (*0-606-13863-3*, Pub. by Turtleback) Demco.

Pride of the Indian Wardrobe: Northern Athapaskan Footwear. Judy Thompson. 198p. 1990. text 49.50 (*0-8020-3457-8*); pap. text 25.00 (*0-8020-3458-6*) U of Toronto Pr.

Pride of the Mountain Man. William W. Johnstone. 288p. 1998. mass mkt. 4.99 (*0-8217-6057-2*, Zebra Kensgtn) Kensgtn Pub Corp.

Pride of the Promised Land: Illustrated History of Cleveland Co. (OK) Bonnie S. Speer. (Illus.). 188p. 1988. lib. bdg. 29.95 (*0-943087-02-3*) Reliance Pr.

Pride of the River: The Forceful Story. Coughlan & Carnegie. (Illus.). (YA). 1990. pap. 30.00 (*0-86439-046-7*, Pub. by Boolarong Pubns) St Mut.

***Pride of the Rockies: The Life of Colorado's Premiere Irish Patron, John Kernan Mullen.** William J. Convery. (Illus.). 256p. 2000. 22.50 (*0-87081-591-1*) U of Okla Pr.

Pride of the Southwest: Outstanding Athletes of the Southwest Conference. Val Belfiglio. (Illus.). 144p. (J). (gr. 6-7). 1992. 14.95 (*0-89015-822-3*) Sunbelt Media.

Pride of the Terrys: Family Saga. Marguerite Steen. LC 77-18754. (Illus.). 412p. 1978. reprint ed. lib. bdg. 85.00 (*0-313-20221-4*, STPT, Greenwood Pr) Greenwood.

Pride of Tyson. Max Brand. 320p. 1996. reprint ed. mass mkt. 4.50 (*0-8439-4113-8*) Dorchester Pub Co.

***Pride of Walworth.** Mary Jane Staples. 2000. pap. 8.95 (*0-552-14291-3*, Pub. by Transworld Publishers Ltd) Trafalgar.

Pride of Walworth. large type ed. Mary Jane Staples. (Magna Large Print Ser.). 502p. 1996. 27.99 (*0-7505-0990-2*, Pub. by Mgna Lrg Print) Ulverscroft.

Pride of Women: An Illustrated Book of Days. (Archives & Special Collections on Women in Medicine Ser.). (Illus.). 110p. (Orig.). 1987. 10.00 (*0-944542-02-6*) Med Coll PA ASCWM.

***Pride Piper.** Flora Joy. (Illus.). 48p. (J). 1999. 7.00 (*1-884624-10-3*) Storytelling Wrld Pr.

Pride, Prejudice, & Politics: Roosevelt Versus Recovery, 1933-1938. Gary D. Best. LC 90-38841. 288p. 1990. 65.00 (*0-275-93524-8*, C3524, Praeger Pubs) Greenwood.

Pride Wealth of Nations. Greenfeld. 1997. 24.95 (*0-02-912664-9*) Free Pr.

Pride Without Prejudice: The Life of John O. Pastore. Ruth S. Morgenthau. (Illus.). 201p. 1989. 30.00 (*0-932840-05-1*) RI Hist Soc.

Prideful Soul's Guide to Humility. Thomas A. Jones & Mike Fontenot. 1998. pap. 10.99 (*1-57782-057-6*) Discipleshp.

***Prides: The Lions of Mormei.** Chris Harvey & Pieter W. Kat. LC 99-38644. (Illus.). 144p. 2000. 34.95 (*1-56098-838-X*) Smithsonian.

Pride's Challenge. Joanna Campbell. (Thoroughbred Ser.). (J). 1994. 8.60 (*0-606-08296-4*, Pub. by Turtleback) Demco.

Prides Crossing. Tina Howe. LC 98-14964. 112p. 1998. pap. 10.95 (*1-55936-153-0*) Theatre Comm.

Pride's Last Race. Joanna Campbell. (Thoroughbred Ser.). (J). 1994. 9.09 (*0-606-08288-3*, Pub. by Turtleback) Demco.

Priere. (FRE.). 1989. 3.95 (*0-86508-376-2*) BCM Pubn.

Priere aux Etoiles. Marcel Pagnol. (FRE.). 386p. 1978. 39.95 (*0-7859-4775-2*) Fr & Eur.

Priere de l'Absent. Tahar Ben Jelloun. 1982. pap. 14.95 (*0-7859-3375-1*) Fr & Eur.

Prieres en Ancien Francais. Keith V. Sinclair. LC 78-137. 208p. (C). 1978. lib. bdg. 36.00 (*0-208-01741-0*, Archon Bks) Shoe String.

Prieres et Meditations see Prayers & Meditations

Prierias: The Life & Works of Silvestro Mazzolini Da Prierio, 1456-1527. Michael Tavuzzi. LC 96-54041. viii, 189p. 1997. text 39.95 (*0-8223-1976-4*) Duke.

Priest. Joseph Caruso. 1978. 20.95 (*0-405-10821-4*) Ayer.

Priest. Michael P. Harding. 153p. 1986. 19.95 (*0-85640-366-0*) Dufour.

Priest. William L. Sullivan. 1978. 24.95 (*0-405-10861-3*, 11859) Ayer.

Priest. Ellen G. Traylor. LC 98-8854. 370 p. 1998. pap. 12.99 (*0-8499-4099-0*) Word Pub.

Priest: A Gothic Romance. Thomas M. Disch. 1995. 24.00 (*0-679-42880-1*) Knopf.

***Priest & Bishop.** Raymond E. Brown. 88p. 1999. pap. 12.00 (*1-57910-277-8*) Wipf & Stock.

Priest & Parish in Eighteenth-Century France: A Social & Political Study of the Cures in a Diocese of Dauphine, 1750-1791. Timothy Tackett. LC 76-29801. (Illus.). 365p. 1977. reprint ed. pap. 113.20 (*0-608-06608-7*, 206680500009) Bks Demand.

Priest & Parish in Vienna, 1780 to 1880. William D. Bowman. LC 99-22629. (Studies in Central European Histories). 1999. write for info. (*0-391-04094-4*) Humanities.

Priest & Partisan - A South African Journey: The Story of Father Michael Lapsley. Michael Worsnip. LC 96-184932. (Illus.). 168p. (Orig.). 1996. pap. 14.95 (*1-875284-96-6*) Ocean Pr NJ.

Priest & Stress. 26p. 1982. pap. 3.95 (*1-55586-832-0*) US Catholic.

Priest & the King: An Eyewitness Account of the Iranian Revolution. Harney. 224p. 2000. pap. 19.95 (*1-86064-374-4*, Pub. by I B T) St Martin.

Priest & the Protestant Woman: The Trail of Rev. Thomas Maguire, P. P., December 1827. Proinnsios O'Duigneain. (Maynooth Studies in Local History). 64p. 1997. pap. 9.95 (*0-7165-2639-5*, Pub. by Irish Acad Pr) Intl Spec Bk.

Priest Fainted: A Novel. Catherine T. Davidson. LC 97-36726. 1998. 23.00 (*0-8050-5539-8*) H Holt & Co.

Priest Fainted: A Novel. Catherine T. Davidson. 272p. 1999. pap. 12.00 (*0-8050-6109-6*, Pub. by H Holt & Co) VHPS.

Priest Family: Collection of Data, Original, Contributed & Selected, Concerning Various Branches of the Priest Family. G. E. Foster. (Illus.). 549p. 1991. reprint ed. pap. 69.00 (*0-8328-1830-5*); reprint ed. lib. bdg. 79.00 (*0-8328-1829-1*) Higginson Bk Co.

Priest for All Seasons: Masculine & Celibate. Conrad W. Baars. LC 72-87091. (Synthesis Ser.). 1972. pap. 1.00 (*0-8199-0375-2*, Frncscn Herld) Franciscan Pr.

Priest Forever. Karl Rahner. 1998. pap. 4.95 (*0-87193-115-X*) Dimension Bks.

Priest Forever: One Woman's Controversial Ordination in the Episcopal Church. Carter Heyward. 160p. 1999. reprint ed. pap. 15.95 (*0-8298-1315-2*) Pilgrim OH.

Priest Forever: The Life of Eugene Hamilton. Benedict J. Groeschel. LC 97-75379. (Illus.). 208p. (Orig.). 1998. pap. 9.95 (*0-87973-944-4*) Our Sunday Visitor.

Priest Forever & No More. John P. Epan. Ed. by Barbara Truncellito. 90p. 1998. 12.95 (*0-9631101-3-6*) Fragile Twilight.

Priest from the Heart. Mary R. Joyce. (Illus.). 96p. (YA). (gr. 4-12). 1999. pap. text 9.95 (*0-9615722-3-X*) LifeCom.

Priest in Changing Times: Memories & Opinions of Michael O'Carroll. LC 98-145453. 193 p. 1998. write for info. (*1-85607-229-0*) Intl Scholars.

Priest-Kings of Gor see Gor Promotion

Priest-Kings of Gor. John Norman. (Gor Ser.). 1996. mass mkt. 6.95 (*1-56333-488-7*) Masquerade.

Priest Konrad's "Song of Roland" Tr. & Intro. by J. W. Thomas. (GERM Ser.). (Illus.). viii, 117p. 1994. 55.00 (*1-57113-011-X*) Camden Hse.

Priest of a New Covenant. Wayne C. Gwilliam. 123p. (Orig.). 1992. pap. 7.95 (*0-9631477-1-4*) Reach Out NY.

Priest of Consciousness: Essays on Conrad Aiken. Ed. by Ted R. Spivey. (Georgia State Literary Studies: No. 6). 1988. 55.00 (*0-404-63206-8*) AMS Pr.

Priest of Music: The Life of Dimitri Mitropoulos. William R. Trotter. LC 94-23928. (Illus.). 532p. 1995. 29.95 (*0-931340-81-0*, Amadeus Pr) Timber.

Priest of the World's Destiny: John Paul the Second. Michael Parker. Ed. by Faith Publishing Company Staff. LC 95-60847. 192p. 1995. pap. 9.00 (*1-880033-19-4*) Queenship Pub.

Priest, Parish & Renewal: Concepts for Pastoral Effectiveness. Emilianos Timiadis. Ed. by George K. Duvall. 239p. (Orig.). (C). 1994. pap. 14.95 (*0-917651-91-X*, Pub. by Holy Cross Orthodox) BookWorld.

Priest, The Man of God: Dignity & Duties. St. Joseph Cafasso. 1979. pap. 13.50 (*0-89555-164-0*, 0112) TAN Bks Pubs.

Priest, the Pastor & the Rabbi: A Collection of Religious Humor. Sam Warren. (Illus.). 250p. 1998. pap. 14.95 (*0-945949-10-3*) Warren Comns.

Priest, the Woman, & the Confessional. Charles Chiniquy. 144p. 1979. pap. 6.95 (*0-937958-03-4*) Chick Pubns.

Priest to the World & Other Prose Works. Cesar T. Mella. 77p. (Orig.). 1984. pap. 7.50 (*971-10-0180-2*, Pub. by New Day Pub) Cellar.

Priest to Turn To: Biblical & Pastoral Reflections on the Priesthood. William F. Maestri. LC 88-31418. 256p. (Orig.). 1989. pap. 12.95 (*0-8189-0546-8*) Alba.

Priest with Dirty Clothes. R. C. Sproul. LC 97-14038. (Illus.). 48p. (J). (gr. 1-5). 1997. 14.99 (*0-8499-1455-8*) Tommy Nelson.

Priester und Tempel Im Hellenistischen Agypten: Ein Beitrag Zur Kulturgeschichte Des Hellenismus, 2 vols. Walter G. Otto. LC 75-10645. (Ancient Religion & Mythology Ser.). (GER.). 1976. reprint ed. 68.95 (*0-405-07278-3*) Ayer.

Priestermutter: Expertinnen in Kirche und Theologie. Barbara Korber-Hubschmann. Ed. by Ottmar Fuchs. (Bamberger Theologische Studien Ser.: Bd. 5). (GER.). 224p. 1997. 41.95 (*3-631-31874-X*) P Lang Pubng.

Priesterschrift und die Vorexilische Zeit: Yehezkel Kaufmanns Vernachlassigter Beitrag Zur Geschichte der Biblischen Religion. Thomas M. Krapf. (Orbis Biblicus et Orientalis Ser.: Vol. 119). (GER.). 351p. 1992. text 74.25 (*3-7278-0815-2*, Pub. by Presses Univ Fribourg) Eisenbrauns.

Priesterschrift von Numeri 1, 1 bis 10, 10: Literarkritisch und traditionsgeschichtlich untersucht. Diether Kellermann. (Beiheft zur Zeitschrift fuer die Alttestamentliche Wissenschaft Ser.: No. 120). 168p. (C). 1970. 70.80 (*3-11-006439-1*) De Gruyter.

Priestertum: Zur Nachkonziliaren Amtstheologie im Deutschen Sprachraum. Josef Hernoga. (Europaische Hochschulschriften Ser.: Reihe 23, Bd. 603). (GER., Illus.). 458p. 1997. 76.95 (*3-631-30657-1*) P Lang Pubng.

Priesthood. Witness Lee. 202p. 1980. per. 8.25 (*0-87083-033-3*, 14-005-001) Living Stream Ministry.

Priesthood. Spencer W. Kimball et al. LC 81-5394. 170p. 1989. reprint ed. pap. 6.95 (*0-87579-211-1*) Deseret Bk.

Priesthood. Wilhelm Stockums. 242p. 1988. reprint ed. pap. 13.50 (*0-89555-170-5*) TAN Bks Pubs.

Priesthood: A Re-Examination of the R. C. Theology. Patrick J. Dunn. LC 90-37005. 244p. (Orig.). 1990. pap. 12.95 (*0-8189-0581-6*) Alba.

Priesthood: For Others Sake. Alan D. Tyree. Ed. by Paul M. Edwards. LC 95-44711. (Faith Exploration Ser.). (Orig.). 1996. pap. text 10.00 (*0-8309-0721-1*) Herald Pub Hse.

Priesthood: Sanctifying the Saints. A. Harold Goodman. pap. 10.95 (*1-55517-101-X*) CFI Dist.

Priesthood: The Hard Questions. Ed. by Gerald P. Gleeson. 1993. pap. 9.95 (*0-85574-245-3*, Pub. by E J Dwyer) Morehouse Pub.

Priesthood Vol. VIII, No. 3: The Challenges of Pastoral Leadership in the Church of the Third Millennium. Ed. by Bernard F. Stratman. (Illus.). 71p. 1997. pap. 6.00 (*0-9653675-6-8*) NFPC.

Priesthood & Church Organization: Selections from the Encyclopedia of Mormonism. Ed. by Daniel H. Ludlow. LC 95-7691. (Orig.). 1995. pap. 18.95 (*0-87579-926-4*) Deseret Bk.

Priesthood & Cult in Ancient Israel. Ed. by Gary A. Anderson & Saul M. Olyan. (Journal for the Study of the Old Testament Supplement Ser.: No. 125). 217p. (C). 1991. 60.00 (*1-85075-322-9*, Pub. by Sheffield Acad) CUP Services.

Priesthood Blessings: A Hidden Treasure & a Crowning Privilege. Donald E. Goff. LC 97-68855. 240p. 1997. pap. 12.95 (*1-57636-042-3*, Pub. by SunRise Pbl) Origin Bk Sales.

Priesthood Imperiled: A Critical Examination of Ministry in the Catholic Church. Bernhard Haring. LC 96-10631. 192p. 1996. 20.00 (*0-89243-920-3*, Liguori Triumph) Liguori Pubns.

Priesthood in One Modern World: A Reader. Ed. by Karen S. Smith. LC 98-51555. (Church Book Ser.). 112p. 1999. pap. 11.95 (*1-58051-055-8*) Sheed & Ward WI.

***Priesthood in the Middle Years: A Commitment to Priestly Wellness & Presbyteral Vitality.** Ed. by Bernard F. Stratman & Paulette Graham. 31p. 1999. pap. text 5.00 (*1-893060-07-1*) NFPC.

Priesthood Is Changing. Kelley Varner. 238p. (Orig.). 1991. pap. 10.99 (*1-56043-033-8*) Destiny Image.

An Asterisk (*) at the beginning of an entry indicates that the title is appearing for the first time.

Priesthood of All Believers. Ed. by Walter B. Shurden. LC 93-14909. (Proclaiming the Baptist Vision Ser.: Vol. 1). 176p. 1993. pap. 14.00 (*1-880837-19-6*) Smyth & Helwys.

Priesthood of Industry: The Rise of the Professional Accountant in British Management. Derek Matthews et al. LC 97-33637. (Illus.). 372p. 1998. text 78.00 (*0-19-828960-X*) OUP.

Priesthood of the Believer: Christ Calls Believers to be Worshipping Priests unto God. Judson Cornwall & Sam Sasser. LC 98-74675. 194p. 1998. pap. 9.99 (*0-88270-765-5*, Bridge) Bridge-Logos.

Priesthood, Old & New. Edward Laity. 1980. 4.50 (*0-86544-012-3*) Salv Army Suppl South.

Priesthood Today: An Appraisal. Thomas P. Rausch. LC 92-747. 160p. 1992. pap. 9.95 (*0-8091-3326-1*) Paulist Pr.

***Priesthood 2000: Developmental & Human Resource Perspectives.** Ed. by Bernard F. Stratman & Paulette Graham. 47p. 1999. pap. text 7.00 (*1-893060-05-5*) NFPC.

Priesthoods & Apostasies of Pierce Connally: A Study of Victorian Conversion & Anticatholicism. D. G. Paz. LC 86-2487. (Studies in American Religion: Vol. 18). 418p. 1986. lib. bdg. 109.95 (*0-88946-662-9*) E Mellen.

Priestley Judith Cook. LC 98-145693. 314p. 1997. write for info. (*0-7475-3036-X*, Pub. by Blmsbury Pub) AMACOM.

Priestley in America: Seventeen Hundred Ninety-Four to Eighteen Four. Edgar F. Smith. Ed. by I. Bernard Cohen. LC 79-8408. (Three Centuries of Science in America Ser.). 1980. reprint ed. lib. bdg. 18.95 (*0-405-12557-7*) Ayer.

Priestly Celibacy Today. Thomas McGovern. 176p. 1997. pap. 30.00 (*1-85182-352-2*, Pub. by Four Cts Pr) Intl Spec Bk.

Priestly Celibacy Today. Thomas McGovern. 248p. 1998. pap. 12.95 (*1-890177-07-5*) Midwest Theol.

Priestly Fictions: Popular Irish Novelists of The Early 20th Century. Catherine Candy. LC 96-140065. 240p. 1997. pap. 19.95 (*0-86327-334-3*, Pub. by Wolfhound Press) Irish Amer Bk.

Priestly Heart. James A. Griffin. LC 83-26611. 149p. (Orig.). 1984. pap. 6.95 (*0-8189-0460-7*) Alba.

Priestly Kingdom: Social Ethics As Gospel. John H. Yoder. LC 84-40358. 208p. (C). 1986. text 16.00 (*0-268-01627-5*) U of Notre Dame Pr.

Priestly Office: A Theological Reflection. Avery Dulles. LC 97-5289. 96p. (Orig.). 1997. pap. 7.95 (*0-8091-3716-X*) Paulist Pr.

Priestly Tribe: The Supreme Court's Image in the American Mind. Barbara A. Perry. LC 99-13438. 184p. 1999. 59.95 (*0-275-96598-8*, C6598, Praeger Pubs); pap. 17.95 (*0-275-96599-6*, C6598, Praeger Pubs) Greenwood.

Priests & Kings see Corridors of Time: New Haven & London, 1927-1956

***Priests & People in Pre-Famine Ireland, 1780-1845.** 2nd ed. S. J. Connolly. 256p. 2000. pap. 29.95 (*1-85182-557-6*, Pub. by Four Cts Pr) Intl Spec Bk.

Priests & Power: The Case of the Dente Shrine in Nineteenth-Century Ghana. Donna J. Maier. LC 82-48582. (Illus.). 271p. reprint ed. pap. 84.10 (*0-7837-3717-3*, 205789500009) Bks Demand.

Priests & Prelates of Armagh in the Age of Reformation, 1518-1558. Henry A. Jefferies. LC 98-110384. 212p. 1997. boxed set 49.50 (*1-85182-336-0*, Pub. by Four Cts Pr) Intl Spec Bk.

Priests & Programmers: Colonialism, Ecology & the Technologies of Power in the Balinese State. J. Stephen Lansing. (Illus.). 200p. 1991. text 39.50 (*0-691-09466-7*, Pub. by Princeton U Pr); pap. text 16.95 (*0-691-02863-X*, Pub. by Princeton U Pr) Cal Prin Full Svc.

Priests As Physicians of Souls in Marsilius of Padua's Defensor Pacis. Stephen F. Torraco. LC 91-44968. 512p. 1992. lib. bdg. 119.95 (*0-7734-9965-2*) E Mellen.

Priest's Diary. Sigbjorn Obstfelder. Tr. & Intro. by James McFarlane. LC 87-63149. (Series B: No. 1). 75p. (Orig.). 1987. pap. 9.95 (*1-870041-01-1*, Pub. by Norvik Pr) Dufour.

***Priests for the Third Millennium.** Timothy M. Dolan. LC 00-130467. 336p. 2000. 24.95 (*0-87973-319-5*) Our Sunday Visitor.

Priest's Handbook. 2nd expanded rev. ed. Karl Pruter. LC 96-25022. (St. Willibrord Studies in Philosophy & Religion: No. 4). 62p. 1996. 23.00 (*0-912134-28-3*, 35008104); pap. 13.00 (*0-912134-29-1*, 35008104) Millefleurs.

Priest's Handbook: The Ceremonies of the Church. 3rd ed. Dennis Michno. LC 98-17918. 304p. 1998. 34.00 (*0-8192-1768-9*) Morehouse Pub.

***Priests of Ancient Egypt.** Serge Sauneron & David Lorton. LC 99-88140. 2000. write for info. (*0-8014-3685-0*) Cornell U Pr.

Priests of Culture: A Study of Matthew Arnold & Henry James. Douglas W. Sterner. LC 98-33745. (Sociocriticism Ser.: Vol. 9). (Illus.). XIV, 282p. 1999. text 54.95 (*0-8204-4181-3*, 41813) P Lang Pubng.

Priests of God. Robert R. Leichtman. (From Heaven to Earth Ser.). 1997. pap. 13.95 (*0-89804-084-1*) Ariel GA.

Priests of the Future: Formation & Communion. M. Mulvey. 1991. pap. 7.95 (*0-911782-84-2*) New City.

Priests of the Most High God. Donald E. Goff. LC 96-70165. 192p. 1996. pap. 12.95 (*1-57636-022-9*, Pub. by SunRise Pbl) Origin Bk Sales.

Priests, Politics & Society in Post-Famine Ireland. John O'Shea. 368p. 1997. 27.95 (*0-905473-71-X*, Pub. by Wolfhound Press) Irish Amer Bk.

Priest's Progress: The Journey of Frances Norbert Blanchet from the Atlantic Ocean to the Pacific in Three Parishes. Harriet D. Munnick. LC 89-62677. (Illus.). 100p. 1989. 15.00 (*0-8323-0474-3*) Binford Mort.

Priests, Prophets & Scribes: Essays on the Formation & Heritage of Second Temple Judaism in Honour of Joseph Blenkinsopp. Philip R. Davies. Ed. by Eugene Ulrich et al. (Journal for the Study of the Old Testament Supplement Ser.: No. 149). (Illus.). 274p. 1992. 75.00 (*1-85075-375-X*, Pub. by Sheffield Acad) CUP Services.

Priests, Prophets, Diviners, Sages: A Socio-Historical Study of Religious Specialists in Ancient Israel. Lester L. Grabbe. LC 95-32747. 280p. (Orig.). (C). 1995. pap. 20.00 (*1-56338-132-X*) TPI PA.

Priest's Secret. Rosenberg. 1996. 20.00 (*1-883402-53-0*) S&S Trade.

Priest's Service Book. E. Constantinides. (ENG & GRE.). 1997. 20.00 (*0-9623833-0-9*) E Constantinides.

Priest's Spell. Jon Pickens. (AD&D Accessory Ser.). 1999. 24.95 (*0-7869-1359-2*, Pub. by TSR Inc) Random.

***Priest's Spell Compendium, Vol. 2.** TSR Inc. Staff. 288p. 1999. pap. text 24.95 (*0-7869-1421-1*) TSR Inc.

***Priest's Spell Compendium, Vol. 3.** Jon Pickens. (AD & D Accessory Ser.). 288p. 2000. pap. 24.95 (*0-7869-1611-7*) TSR Inc.

Priest's Story. large type ed. John Attenborough. 288p. 1986. 27.99 (*0-7089-1398-9*) Ulverscroft.

Priests Telling It Like It Is! Compiled by Dagmar Kolata. 224p. 1989. pap. 30.00 (*1-85390-108-3*, Pub. by Veritas Pubns) St Mut.

Priest's Temple. Bruce R. Cordell. 1999. 18.95 (*0-7869-1442-4*) TSR Inc.

Prietita & the Ghost Woman (Prietita y la Llorona) Gloria Anzaldua. (Illus.). 32p. (J). (gr. 2-4). 1996. 19.90 (*0-516-20000-3*) Childrens.

Prietita & the Ghost Woman (Prietita y la Llorona) Gloria Anzaldua. LC 95-37573. (ENG & SPA., Illus.). (YA). (ps-3). 1996. 15.95 (*0-89239-136-7*) Childrens Book Pr.

Prig Tales. M. G. Lord. 192p. (Orig.). 1990. mass mkt. 6.95 (*0-380-76004-5*, Avon Bks) Morrow Avon.

Prigotovlenije k Ispovjedi i Blagogvejnomy Prithashcheniju Svijatikh Khristvikh Tajin. Archpriest Michael Bogoslovsky.Tr. of Preporation for Confession & the Receiving of the Holy Mysteries. 169p. reprint ed. pap. 8.00 (*0-317-29105-X*) Holy Trinity.

Prikhodiat Veka I Ukhodiat Veka: The Ages Arrive & Go. Roman Bar-Or. LC 90-47354. (RUS.). 128p. (Orig.). 1991. pap. 8.00 (*1-55779-037-X*) Hermitage Pubs.

Prikladnye zadachi fil'tratsii i upravleniia see Filtering & Control

Priklady Z Matematiky Pre Osemrocne Gymnazia (Mathematical Problems for the Gymnasiums) L. Hrdina & M. Maxian. (SLO.). 216p. 1997. pap. write for info. (*80-08-02466-6*, Pub. by Slov Pegagog Naklad) IBD Ltd.

Prim & Improper. Liz Ireland. (Historical Ser.). 1998. per. 4.99 (*0-373-29010-1*, 1-29010-5) Harlequin Bks.

Prim & Improper. large type ed. Debra Carroll. (Black Satin Romance Ser.). 343p. 1997. 27.99 (*1-86110-023-X*) Ulverscroft.

***Prim, Proper... Pregnant.** Alice Sharpe. (Silhouette Romance Ser.: No. 1425). 2000. per. 3.50 (*0-373-19425-0*, 1-19425-7) Harlequin Bks.

Prim Rose. Millie Criswell. 352p. (Orig.). 1996. reprint ed. mass mkt. 5.99 (*0-446-60323-6*, Pub. by Warner Bks) Little.

Prima Della Rivoluzione. Michael A. Bernstein. LC 83-83108. (Poets Ser.). 65p. 1984. 25.00 (*0-915032-41-4*); pap. 11.95 (*0-915032-16-3*) Natl Poet Foun.

Prima Diner. 2nd ed. Ed. by Mildred M. Petrie. (Illus.). 172p. (Orig.). 1984. 7.95 (*0-9605844-0-4*, TX 727-394) Sarasota Opera.

Prima Donna: Her History & Surroundings from the 17th to the 19th Century, 2 vols., Set. H. Sutherland Edwards. LC 77-17875. (Music Reprint Ser.). 1978. reprint ed. lib. bdg. 75.00 (*0-306-77536-0*) Da Capo.

Prima Donna's Album: Piano 42 Celebrated Arias from Famous Operas. 304p. 1986. otabind 17.95 (*0-7935-1005-8*, 50325550) H Leonard.

Prima Facie: A Guide to Value Debate. 2nd ed. Stephen Wood & John Midgley. 304p. 1991. per. 31.95 (*0-8403-7015-6*) Kendall-Hunt.

Prima Facie, 1989-90: An Anthology of New American Plays. 240p. 1990. pap. 15.00 (*0-936947-54-3*) Denver Ctr Performing Arts.

Prima Facie, 1987: An Anthology of New American Plays. 1987. pap. 12.00 (*0-936947-52-7*) Denver Ctr Performing Arts.

Prima Facie, 1991: An Anthology of New American Plays. 1991. pap. 12.00 (*0-936947-55-1*) Denver Ctr Performing Arts.

Prima Guide to Better Business Letters: One Hundred One Effective, Ready to Go Business Letters. Michael Fitzgerald. LC 94-14156. 256p. 1994. pap. 19.95 (*1-55958-448-3*) Prima Pub.

Prima Hurt Book. Prima Publishing Staff. 1997. pap. write for info. (*0-7615-9988-6*); pap. write for info. (*0-7615-9989-4*) Prima Pub.

Prima Posters, Vol. 19. Jack Rennert. (Illus.). 1994. 40.00 (*1-929530-00-5*) Pstr Auctns Intl.

Prima Vera: Springtime. Rose T. Manes. Ed. by Gwen Costa. LC 90-21706. 1991. pap. 13.95 (*0-87949-330-5*) Ashley Bks.

Primacy & Conciliarity: Studies in the Primacy of the See of Constantinople & the Synodal Structure of the Orthodox Church. Lewis J. Patsavos. 57p. 1995. pap. 3.95 (*1-885652-02-X*, Pub. by Holy Cross Orthodox) BookWorld.

Primacy of Caring: Stress & Coping in Health & Illness. Patricia E. Benner & Judith Wrubel. 406p. (C). 1989. pap. text 52.00 (*0-201-12002-X*) Addison-Wesley.

Primacy of Faith. Richard Kroner. LC 77-27184. (Gifford Lectures: 1939-40). reprint ed. 34.50 (*0-404-60497-8*) AMS Pr.

Primacy of Movement. Maxine Sheets-Johnstone. LC 99-10250. (Advances in Consciousness Research Ser.: Vol. 14). xxxiv, 584p. 1999. pap. 79.00 (*1-55619-194-4*) J Benjamins Pubng Co.

Primacy of Perception & Other Essays on Phenomenological Psychology, the Philosophy of Art, History & Politics. Maurice Merleau-Ponty. Ed. by James M. Edie. Tr. by William Cobb et al. (Studies in Phenomenology & Existential Philosophy). 228p. 1964. 29.95 (*0-8101-0165-3*); pap. 15.95 (*0-8101-0164-5*) Northwestern U Pr.

Primacy of Persons & the Language of Culture: Essays. William H. Poteat. Ed. by James W. Stines. LC 93-14356. 360p. 1993. text 49.95 (*0-8262-0919-X*) U of Mo Pr.

Primacy of Peter: Essays in Ecclesiology & the Early Church. Nicholas Afanasieff et al. LC 92-6455. 182p. (Orig.). 1995. pap. text 11.95 (*0-88141-125-6*) St Vladimirs.

Primacy of Practical Reason: An Essay on Nicholas Resher's Philosophy. Michele Marsonet. 284p. (Orig.). (C). 1995. pap. text 32.50 (*0-7618-0120-0*); lib. bdg. 58.00 (*0-7618-0119-7*) U Pr of Amer.

Primacy of Rome: Views from the Christian East. Michael A. Fahey. 144p. 2000. pap. text 18.95 (*0-8245-1795-4*, Pub. by Crossroad NY) Natl Bk Netwk.

Primacy of Structure: Psychotherapy of Underlying Character Pathology. Althea J. Horner. LC 90-41165. 328p. 1991. 55.00 (*0-87668-748-6*) Aronson.

Primacy of the Individual in Psychoanalysis in Groups. Alexander Wolf et al. LC 90-14537. 304p. 1993. 50.00 (*0-87668-548-3*) Aronson.

Primacy of the Political. R. Sundara Rajan. 224p. 1992. text 18.95 (*0-19-562729-6*) OUP.

Primacy of Touch: The Drawings of Peter Milton. Peter Milton. LC 93-17551. (Illus.). 131p. 1993. 45.00 (*1-55595-075-2*) Hudson Hills.

Primadonna. Francis M. Crawford. (Works of Francis Marion Crawford). 1990. reprint ed. lib. bdg. 79.00 (*0-7812-2559-0*) Rprt Serv.

Primae Lineae Physiologiae. Albrecht V. Haller. (GER.). 1997. reprint ed. 138.00 (*3-487-05261-X*) G Olms Pubs.

Primaere Bau der Angiospermenwurzel. Hermann Von Guttenberg. (Handbuch der Pflanzenanatomie Encyclopedia of Plant Anatomy - Traite d' Anatomie Vegetale Ser.: Band VIII, Teil 5). (GER., Illus.). viii, 472p. 1968. 85.00 (*3-443-14001-7*, Pub. by Gebruder Borntraeger) Balogh.

Primal: From the Cradle to the Grave. Clive Barker et al. (Primal Ser.). (Illus.). 64p. 1992. pap. 9.95 (*1-878574-30-2*) Dark Horse Comics.

Primal Awareness: A True Story of Survival, Transformation, & Awakening with the Raramuri Shamans of Mexico. Don T. Jacobs. LC 98-21280. (Illus.). 320p. 1998. pap. 16.95 (*0-89281-669-4*) Inner Tradit.

Primal Destiny. Konrad Noble. Ed. by Judith Tomak et al. LC 96-68531. 525p. 1999. 42.50 (*0-9654156-0-0*, 101) Nobless Oblige.

Primal Digital Soup. John Clippinger. (C). 1998. write for info. (*0-201-40656-X*) Addison-Wesley.

Primal-Dual Interior-Point Methods. Stephen J. Wright. LC 96-42071. (Miscellaneous Bks.: Vol. 54). xx, 289p. 1996. pap. 39.50 (*0-89871-382-X*, OT54) Soc Indus-Appl Math.

Primal Fear. William Diehl. 1993. mass mkt. 6.99 (*0-345-38391-5*) Ballantine Pub Grp.

Primal Fear. William Diehl. 1994. mass mkt. 6.99 (*0-345-38877-1*) Ballantine Pub Grp.

Primal Fear. William Diehl. 1998. pap. 6.99 (*0-345-91452-X*) Ballantine Pub Grp.

Primal Fire. Alex Duarte. LC 98-231646. 197p. 1997. pap. text 15.00 (*1-891036-10-6*) Nutri Tapes.

***Primal Forces.** Michelle Gilders et al. LC 00-37181. 2000. pap. 50.00 (*1-55868-522-7*) Gr Arts Ctr Pub.

Primal Instinct. John Newland. 432p. 1994. mass mkt. 4.50 (*0-8217-4651-0*, Zebra Kensgtn) Kensgtn Pub Corp.

Primal Instinct. Robert W. Walker. (Orig.). 1994. mass mkt. 6.99 (*0-515-11949-0*, Jove) Berkley Pub.

Primal Legacy: Thinking for the 21st Century. Joseph Costa. (Illus.). 309p. 1995. lib. bdg. 24.95 (*1-883333-25-3*) Better Lfe Bks.

Primal Love. abr. ed. Douglas M. Gillette. 1995. 16.95 incl. audio (*1-882071-54-9*) B&B Audio.

Primal Mind: Vision & Reality in Indian America. Jamake Highwater. 254p. 1999. reprint ed. 29.95 (*0-7351-0127-2*) Replica Bks.

Primal Mothering in a Modern World. 2nd ed. Hygeia Halfmoon. Ed. by Stephen Arlin & David Wolfe. 188p. 1998. pap. 14.95 (*0-9653533-4-6*) Maul Bros.

Primal Myths: Creating the World. Barbara C. Sproul. 1979. pap. 8.95 (*0-06-067500-4*) HarpC.

Primal Myths: Creation Myths Around the World. 60th ed. Barbara C. Sproul. LC 78-4429. 384p. 1979. reprint ed. pap. 18.00 (*0-06-067501-2*, Pub. by Harper SF) HarpC.

Primal Order. Peter Adkison et al. 236p. 1992. pap. 20.00 (*1-880992-00-0*) Wizards Coast.

Primal Power in Man: The Kundalini Shakti. Swami Narayanananda. 155p. 1996. reprint ed. spiral bd. 15.00 (*0-7873-0631-2*) Hlth Research.

Primal Rage: The Avatars. John Vornholt. 1997. mass mkt. 5.99 (*1-57297-230-0*) Blvd Books.

Primal Religion & the Bible: William Robertson Smith & His Heritage. Gillian M. Bediako. LC 97-205426. (JSOT Supplement Ser.: No. 246). 402p. 1997. 90.75 (*1-85075-672-4*, Pub. by Sheffield Acad) CUP Services.

Primal Scenes. Richard Geha. 1999. 24.50 (*0-88739-178-8*) Creat Arts.

Primal Scenes. Richard Geha. LC 97-78454. 300p. 1998. 24.50 (*0-88739-210-5*); pap. 16.50 (*0-88739-174-5*) Creat Arts Bk.

Primal Scenes: Literature, Philosophy, Psychoanalysis. Ned Lukacher. LC 85-25513. 368p. (C). 1986. 45.00 (*0-8014-1886-0*); pap. text 17.95 (*0-8014-9486-9*) Cornell U Pr.

***Primal Scenes of Communication: Communication Theory, Social Movements & Consumer Society.** Ian Angus. LC 99-54268. (C). 2000. pap. text 19.95 (*0-7914-4666-2*) State U NY Pr.

***Primal Scenes of Communication: Communication Theory, Social Movements & Consumer Society.** Ian Angus. LC 99-54268. (C). 2000. text 59.50 (*0-7914-4665-4*) State U NY Pr.

Primal Scream: An Illustrated Biography. Stuart Coles. (Illus.). 73p. (YA). 1998. pap. 14.95 (*0-7119-6807-1*, OP48047) Omnibus NY.

Primal Scream: Scream If You Want, Live If You Can. Michael Slade. 432p. 1998. mass mkt. 6.99 (*0-451-19566-3*, Sig) NAL.

Primal Screamer. Nick Blinko. (Illus.). 128p. (Orig.). 1995. pap. 12.95 (*0-9525744-0-3*, Pub. by Spare Change) AK Pr Dist.

Primal Slayer: 11 Songs of Aggressive Perfection. 86p. Date not set. pap. 19.95 (*0-89524-969-3*, Pub. by Cherry Lane) H Leonard.

Primal Spirituality of the Vedas: Its Renewal & Renaissance. R. Balasubramanian. LC 96-902382. (C). 1996. 23.00 (*81-215-0721-9*, Pub. by M Manoharial) Coronet Bks.

Primal Vision. Gottfried Benn. Ed. by E. B. Ashton. LC 58-13434. 1971. reprint ed. pap. 8.95 (*0-8112-0008-6*, NDP322, Pub. by New Directions) Norton.

Primal Vision: Selected Writings. Gottfried Benn. Ed. by E. B. Ashton. Tr. by Michael Hamburger & Christopher Middleton from GER. 292p. 1985. reprint ed. pap. 18.00 (*0-7145-2529-4*) M Boyars Pubs.

Primal Wound: A Transpersonal View of Trauma, Addiction, & Growth. John Firman & Ann Gila. LC 96-43767. (SUNY Series in the Philosophy of Psychology). (Illus.). 284p. (C). 1997. text 59.50 (*0-7914-3293-9*); pap. text 21.95 (*0-7914-3294-7*) State U NY Pr.

Primal Wound: Understanding the Adopted Child. Nancy N. Verrier. 252p. (Orig.). 1993. pap. 15.00 (0-9636480-0-4) Verrier Pub.

THE PRIMAL WOUND: UNDERSTANDING THE ADOPTED CHILD, by Nancy Verrier, is a challenging & courageous work. A book which adoptees call their "bible," it is a must read for anyone connected with adoption: adoptees, birth parents, adoptive parents, therapists, educators & attorneys. Dr. Thomas Verny, author of THE SECRET LIFE OF THE UNBORN CHILD, calls it "the best psychodynamic study of adoptees ever undertaken...tremendously helpful to those who really want to understand their psychological process." In its application of information about perinatal psychology, attachment, bonding, & loss, THE PRIMAL WOUND clarifies the effects of separation from the birthmother on adopted children. In addition, it gives adoptees, whose pain has long been unacknowledged or misunderstood, validation for their feelings, as well as explanations for their behavior. As one adoptee said, "Only one thing has caused me more pain & damage than the existence of the primal wound: the world's insistence that it does not exist." The existence of the primal wound & suggestions for healing that wound are intelligently & compassionately set forth in this book, which is fast becoming the quintessential work about the complex & life-long process of adoption. The insight the author brings to the experience of abandonment & loss will contribute not only to the healing of those connected with adoption, but will bring understanding & encouragement to anyone who has ever felt abandoned. To order Contact: Nancy Verrier, publisher, P.O. Box 208, Lafayette, CA 94549, 925-284-5813, Fax 925-284-4248. Bookstores receive a 40
discount when ordering directly from publisher. Also available from Baker & Taylor & Ingram. (PA)
Publisher Paid Annotation.

Primality & Cryptography. Evangelos Kranakis. LC 85-29485. 252p. 1986. 175.00 (*0-471-90934-3*) Wiley.

Primality Testing & Abelian Varieties over Finite Fields. L. M. Adleman & M. D. Huang. (Lecture Notes in Mathematics Ser.: Vol. 1512). 142p. 1992. 29.95 (*0-387-55308-8*) Spr-Verlag.

P

Primariamente Fisica - Primarily Physics: Investigaciones del Sonido, la Luz y la Energia Termica. rev. ed. Evalyn Hoover et al. Ed. by Judith A. Hillen. Tr. by Iso Sands. (ENG & SPA., Illus.). 155p. (J). (gr. k-3). 1994. 16.95 (1-881431-47-9, 1404) AIMS Educ Fnd.

Primariamente Plantas - Primarily Plants. Evalyn Hoover & Sheryl Mercier. (ENG & SPA.). 149p. (J). (gr. k-3). 1992. 16.95 (1-881431-32-0, 1405) AIMS Educ Fnd.

Primarily Bears: A Collection of Elementary Activities. Maureen Allen et al. (J). (gr. k-6). 1987. 16.95 (1-881431-15-0, 1207) AIMS Educ Fnd.

Primarily Earth. Evalyn Hoover & Sheryl Mercier. Ed. by Betty Cordel. (Illus.). 147p. (Orig.). (J). (gr. k-3). 1996. pap., teacher ed., wbk. ed. 16.95 (1-881431-63-0, 1109) AIMS Educ Fnd.

Primarily Physics: Investigations in Sound, Light, & Heat Energy. rev. ed. Evalyn Hoover & Sheryl Mercier. (Illus.). (J). (gr. k-3). 1994. 16.95 (1-881431-46-0, 1104) AIMS Educ Fnd.

Primarily Plants. Evalyn Hoover & Sheryl Mercier. (Illus.). (J). (gr. k-3). 1990. 16.95 (1-881431-24-X, 1105) AIMS Educ Fnd.

Primarily Portfolios. Veronica Terrill & Linda Karges-Bone. 96p. teacher ed. 10.99 (0-86653-853-4, GA1534) Good Apple.

Primarily Puppets see Easy-to-Make Puppets

Primarily Speaking Vol. 2: Organizations. J. Lewis. 1990. pap. 7.95 (0-88494-751-3) Bookcraft Inc.

Primarily Speaking Vol. 3: Reverence/Articles of One Faith. Lewis. 1989. pap. 7.95 (0-88494-718-1) Bookcraft Inc.

Primary Abilities at Mental Age Six. C. E. Meyers et al. (SRCD M Ser.: Vol. 27, No. 1). 1962. pap. 25.00 (0-527-01592-X) Periodicals Srv.

Primary Acoustic Nuclei. Rafael Lorente De No. LC 81-968. 189p. 1981. reprint ed. pap. 58.60 (0-608-00388-3, 206110200007) Bks Demand.

Primary Acts in Radiation Chemical Processes: A Portion of Proceedings of the 1st All-Union Conference on Radiation Chemistry, Moscow, 1957 in English Translation. Consultants Bureau Staff. LC QD0601.. 34p. reprint ed. pap. 30.00 (0-608-30046-2, 202068800018) Bks Demand.

Primary Aeronautical Language Manual. Aviation Language School, Inc. Staff. 201p. 1994. pap. text. write for info. (0-941456-00-5) Aviation Lang Sch.

Primary Afferent Neuron: A Survey of Recent Morpho-Functional Aspects. Ed. by W. Zenker & W. L. Neuhuber. LC 89-70967. (Illus.). 270p. 1990. 85.00 (0-306-43480-6, Plenum Trade) Perseus Pubng.

Primary Alaska. Jane Niedergall. (Teaching Alaska Ser.: Vol. 2). (Illus.). 60p. (J). (ps-3). Date not set. pap., teacher ed. 7.95 (1-878051-17-2, CP061) Circumpolar Pr.

Primary Alphabet Soup: A Curriculum for Your First Week of School. Kathy Gritzmacher. Ed. by Ron Marson. (Master Teacher Ser.). (Illus.). 80p. 1988. teacher ed. 15.00 (0-941008-64-9) Tops Learning.

Primary Anatomy. John V. Basmajian. (Illus.). 404p. (C). 1998. pap. text 19.80 (0-87563-806-6) Stipes.

Primary & Emergency Dental Care: A Practitioner's Guide. Keith H. Figures & David J. Lamb. LC 96-115807. 176p. 1995. pap. text 45.00 (0-7236-1013-4) Buttrwrth-Heinemann.

Primary & Secondary Brain Stem Lesions. G. Csecsei et al. (Illus.). 150p. 1987. 131.00 (0-387-82025-6) Spr-Verlag.

Primary & Secondary Eating Disorders: A Psychoneuroendocrine & Metabolic Approach. Ed. by E. Ferrari et al. (Advances in the Biosciences Ser.: Vol. 90). 532p. 1994. 174.00 (0-08-042192-X, Pergamon Pr) Elsevier.

Primary & Secondary Lead Processing. Jaeck. (Proceedings of the Metallurgical Society of Canada Ser.). 1989. 65.00 (0-08-037293-7, Pergamon Pr) Elsevier.

Primary & Secondary Metabolism of Plant Cell Cultures. Ed. by K. H. Neumann et al. LC 85-17257. (Proceedings in Life Sciences Ser.). (Illus.). 400p. 1985. 167.95 (0-387-15797-2) Spr-Verlag.

Primary & Secondary Metabolism of Plant Cell Cultures II. Ed. by W. G. Kurz. (Illus.). 328p. 1989. 142.95 (0-387-50861-9) Spr-Verlag.

Primary & Secondary Metabolism of Plants & Plant Cell Cultures III: Proceedings of the Workshop Primary & Secondary Metabolism of Plants & Plant Cell Culture III, Leiden, Netherlands, 4-7 April. Ed. by J. Schripsema & R. Verpoorte. LC 94-44744. 288p. (C). 1995. text 161.50 (0-7923-3363-2) Kluwer Academic.

Primary & Secondary Prevention of Malignant Melanoma. Ed. by R. M. Mackie. (Pigment Cell Ser.: Vol. 11, 1996). (Illus.). viii, 130p. 1996. 158.25 (3-8055-6273-X) S Karger.

***Primary & Secondary Preventive Nutrition.** Ed. by Adrianne Bendich & Richard J. Deckelbaum. (Nutrition & Health Ser.). (Illus.). 500p. 2000. 99.50 (0-89603-758-4) Humana.

Primary & Team Health Care Education. Ed. by Troy L. Thompson & Richard L. Byny. LC 83-2156. 245p. 1983. 65.00 (0-275-91416-X, C1416, Praeger Pubs) Greenwood.

Primary Arts Education: Contemporary Issues. Ed. by David Holt. LC 97-147781. 192p. 1996. pap. 27.95 (0-7507-0595-7, Falmer Pr) Taylor & Francis.

Primary Batteries: Turning Chemicals into Electricity. 1996. lib. bdg. 251.95 (0-8490-8299-4) Gordon Pr.

Primary Bible Stories, Vol. 1. large type ed. write for info. (0-318-68661-9, 5600) LBW.

Primary Biliary Cirrhosis: From Pathogenesis to Clinical Treatment. Ed. by Keith D. Lindor et al. 192p. 1998. 86.00 (0-7923-8740-6) Kluwer Academic.

***Primary Bilingual Literature Collection.** Raintree Steck-Vaughn Publishers Staff. 2000. 86.95 (0-8172-6189-3) Raintree Steck-V.

Primary Bone Cancer: The Multidiscipline Disease: Proceedings of the Annual West Coast Cancer Symposium, 10th, San Francisco, CA, September 1974. Annual West Coast Cancer Symposium Staff. Ed. by J. M. Vaeth. (Frontiers of Radiation Therapy & Oncology Ser.: Vol. 10). viii, 243p. 1975. 82.75 (3-8055-2185-5) S Karger.

Primary Brain Tumors. Ed. by William S. Fields. (Illus.). 295p. 1989. 55.00 (0-387-97055-X) Spr-Verlag.

Primary Cardiology. Lee Goldman & Eugene Braunwald. Ed. by Richard Zorab. LC 97-50317. (Illus.). 496p. 1998. text 60.00 (0-7216-6402-4, W B Saunders Co) Harcrt Hlth Sci Grp.

Primary Cardiology: International Edition. Goldman. (C). 1998. text 50.00 (0-8089-2060-X, Grune & Strat) Harcrt Hlth Sci Grp.

Primary Care. John Noble. 1987. 142.00 (0-316-61150-6, Little Brwn Med Div) Lppncott W & W.

Primary Care. Joanne K. Singleton & Robert V. Digregorio. LC 98-42214. 1200p. 1998. text 59.95 (0-7817-1041-3) Lppncott W & W.

Primary Care: A Collaborative Approach. Ed. by Terry Mahan Buttaro et al. LC 99-26596. (Illus.). 1450p. 1999. text 84.95 (0-8151-3823-7, 31844) Mosby Inc.

Primary Care: America's Health in a New Era. Institute of Medicine Staff. Ed. by Molla S. Donaldson et al. 416p. 1996. text 42.95 (0-309-05399-4) Natl Acad Pr.

Primary Care: Balancing Health Needs, Services, & Technology. Barbara Starfield. (Illus.). 448p. 1998. pap. text 27.50 (0-19-512543-6) OUP.

Primary Care: Balancing Health Needs, Services & Technology. Barbara Starfield. (Illus.). 448p. 1998. text 49.95 (0-19-512542-8) OUP.

***Primary Care: The Art & Science of Advanced Practice Nursing.** Lynn M. Dunphy & Jill E. Winland-Brown. 2000. text 99.00 (0-8036-0589-7) Davis Co.

Primary Care: Understanding Health Need & Demand. Anne Rogers & Heather Elliott. LC 97-14955. (National Primary Care Research & Development Centre Ser.). 1997. write for info. (1-85775-237-6, Radcliffe Med Pr) Scovill Paterson.

***Primary Care Across the Life Span.** Denise Robinson & Pamela Kidd. LC 99-37349. (Illus.). 1300p. 1999. write for info. (0-323-00148-3) Mosby Inc.

Primary Care & Home Care Scenarios, 1990-2005: Scenario Report Commissioned by the Steering Committee on Future Health Scenarios. E. Schade. LC 94-2258. 1994. pap. text 106.00 (0-7923-2658-X) Kluwer Academic.

Primary Care Annotated Bibliography & Reference List, 2 vols. Joyce J. Fitzpatrick. LC 97-205908. 570p. 1996. pap. 39.95 (1-55810-130-6, Am Acad Nursing); pap. 39.95 (1-55810-131-4, Am Acad Nursing) Am Nurses Pub.

Primary Care Cardiology. Glenn N. Levine. LC 99-42866. 205p. 2000. 19.95 (0-683-30688-X) Lppncott W & W.

Primary Care Cardiology: A Board Review for Internists & Family Practitioners. George J. Taylor. LC 94-15573. (Illus.). 256p. 1994. pap. 49.95 (0-86542-358-X) Blackwell Sci.

Primary Care Challenge. Robinson. (C). 1999. pap. text. write for info. (0-443-05634-X) Church.

Primary Care Consultant. Shelia A. Dunn. LC 97-42363. (Illus.). 704p. (C). (gr. 13). 1998. text 49.95 (0-8151-2950-5, 29682) Mosby Inc.

Primary Care Dermatology, 2 vols. Kenneth A. Arndt et al. Ed. by Judy Fletcher. LC 96-44227. (Illus.). 352p. 1997. pap. text 49.95 (0-7216-6096-7, W B Saunders Co) Harcrt Hlth Sci Grp.

Primary Care for Older Americans: A Primer. Tim M. Henderson & Linda R. Lipson. 75p. 1997. 20.00 (1-55516-706-3, 6715) Natl Conf State Legis.

***Primary Care for Older People: A Guide to Action in the 21st Century.** Steve Iliffe. (Oxford General Practice Ser.: Vol. 43). (Illus.). 288p. 2001. pap. text 59.95 (0-19-262951-4) OUP.

Primary Care for Physician Assistants. Ed. by Rodney L. Moser. LC 97-50437. (Illus.). 641p. 1998. text 65.00 (0-07-043491-3) McGraw-Hill HPD.

Primary Care for Physician Assistants: Companion Handbook. Ed. by Rick Dehn. LC 98-22423. (Illus.). 608p. 1999. pap. text 32.00 (0-07-016151-8) McGraw-Hill HPD.

Primary Care for Physician Assistants: PreTest Self-Assessment & Review. Rodney L. Moser. (Illus.). 207p. 1998. pap. 34.00 (0-07-052406-8) McGraw-Hill HPD.

Primary Care for the Obstetrician & Gynecologist. Thomas E. Nolan. LC 95-46498. (Illus.). 349p. 1996. pap. 59.95 (0-471-12279-3) Wiley.

Primary Care for the Obstetrician & Gynecologist. Ed. by Yvonne S. Thornton. LC 96-31525. (Illus.). 288p. 1996. pap. 69.50 (0-89640-324-6) Igaku-Shoin.

Primary Care for the Older Adult. Mary Burke. (Illus.). 550p. 1999. text 54.95 (0-8151-8916-8, 31744) Mosby Inc.

Primary Care for Women. Phyllis Leppert. LC 96-30176. 1,048p. 1996. text 79.00 (0-397-51523-5) Lppncott W & W.

Primary Care Geriatrics: A Case-Based Approach. 3rd ed. Ed. by Richard J. Ham & Philip D. Sloane. LC 96-12932. (Illus.). 640p. (C). (gr. 13). 1996. pap. text 64.95 (0-8151-4188-2, 25866) Mosby Inc.

Primary Care Geriatrics: A Case-Based Learning Program. Richard J. Ham. 352p. 1988. reprint ed. pap. 54.95 (0-318-39849-4) Mosby Inc.

***Primary Care Hiv Aids Site.** Appleton. 1999. text 2500.00 (0-8385-8144-7) Appleton & Lange.

Primary Care in Gynecology. Frank W. Ling et al. LC 95-42303. (Illus.). 512p. 1996. 75.00 (0-683-05057-5) Lppncott W & W.

Primary Care in Obstetrics & Gynecology: A Handbook for Clinicians. Roger P. Smith & Joseph S. Sanfilippo. LC 96-29795. 680p. 1997. pap. 40.00 (0-387-94739-6) Spr-Verlag.

Primary Care Making Connection: Making Connections. P. Boaden. LC 97-13905. (State of Health Ser.). 1997. 98.00 (0-335-19749-3); pap. 31.95 (0-335-19748-5) OpUniv Pr.

Primary Care Management: Cases & Discussions. Goutham Rao. LC 98-25307. 1998. 56.00 (0-7619-1204-5); pap. 29.95 (0-7619-1205-3) Sage.

Primary Care Medicine. Allan H. Goroll et al. 1997. 99.00 (0-397-58410-5) Lppncott W & W.

Primary Care Medicine: Office Evaluation & Management of the Adult Patient. 2nd ed. Allan H. Goroll et al. LC 65-8816. (Illus.). 1024p. 1987. text 57.50 (0-397-50717-8, Lippnctt) Lppncott W & W.

Primary Care Medicine: Office Evaluation & Management of the Adult Patient. 3rd ed. Allan H. Goroll. 1,200p. 1994. text 63.95 (0-397-51130-2) Lppncott W & W.

Primary Care Medicine: Office Evaluation & Management of the Adult Patient. 4th ed. Allan H. Goroll et al. text 69.95 (0-7817-1248-3) Lppncott W & W.

Primary Care Medicine for Psychiatrists: A Practitioner's Guide. Ed. by John R. Hubbard & Delmar Short. LC 97-23366. (Illus.). 372p. (C). 1997. spiral bd. 45.00 (0-306-45533-1, Kluwer Plenum) Kluwer Academic.

Primary Care Meets Mental Health "Tools for the 21st Century" Ed. by Joel D. Haber & Grant E. Mitchell. 1997. 97.50 (1-887452-12-5) Manisses Communs.

***Primary Care of Adolescent Girls.** Ed. by Susan M. Coupey. LC 99-47482. (Illus.). 376p. 1999. 36.00 (1-56053-369-2, Pub. by Hanley & Belfus) Mosby Inc.

Primary Care of Children. 3rd ed. Jackson. LC 99-48131. 1999. text 69.95 (0-323-00883-6) Mosby Inc.

Primary Care of Hand Injuries. William L. Newmeyer. LC 78-31444. 310p. reprint ed. pap. 96.10 (0-8357-3248-7, 205714400012) Bks Demand.

***Primary Care of Landmine Injuries in Africa.** Ian Maddocks et al. (Illus.). 72p. 2000. pap. 10.00 (1-893368-03-3) Intl Phys PONW.

Primary Care of Native American Patients: Diagnosis, Therapy & Epidemiology. James M. Galloway et al. LC 98-29285. (Illus.). 408p. 1998. pap. text 49.00 (0-7506-9989-2) Buttrwrth-Heinemann.

Primary Care of Neurological Disorders. Ed. by A. John Popp. 468p. 75.00 (1-879284-57-X) Am Assn Neuro.

Primary Care of the Anterior Segment. 2nd ed. Louis J. Catania. (Illus.). 552p. (C). 1996. pap. text 129.95 (0-8385-7911-6, A7911-9, Apple Lange Med) McGraw.

Primary Care of the Cataract Patient. Cynthia A. Murrill et al. (Illus.). 267p. (C). 1994. pap. text 110.00 (0-8385-7899-3, A7899-6, Apple Lange Med) McGraw.

Primary Care of the Child with a Chronic Condition. 2nd ed. Ed. by Patricia L. Jackson & Judith A. Vessey. (Illus.). 816p. (C). (gr. 13). 1996. text 54.00 (0-8151-4851-8, 27883) Mosby Inc.

Primary Care of the Glaucomas. Thomas L. Lewis & Murray Fingeret. (Illus.). 410p. (C). 1993. pap. text 110.00 (0-8385-7998-1, A7998-6, Apple Lange Med) McGraw.

Primary Care of the Glaucomas. 2nd ed. Composed by Fingeret. (C). 1999. pap. text 125.00 (0-8385-8158-7) Appleton & Lange.

Primary Care of the Newborn. 2nd ed. Beryl J. Rosenstein & Henry M. Seidel. (Illus.). 664p. (C). (gr. 13). 1996. pap. text 32.95 (0-8151-8681-9, 28972) Mosby Inc.

Primary Care of the Posterior Segment. 2nd ed. Larry L. Alexander. (Illus.). 525p. (C). 1998. pap. text 125.00 (0-8385-7970-1, A7970-5, Apple Lange Med) McGraw.

Primary Care of Women. Karen J. Carlson & Stephanie A. Eisenstat. (Illus.). 608p. (C). (gr. 13). 1995. text 79.95 (0-8016-7677-0, 07677) Mosby Inc.

Primary Care of Women. Dawn P. Lemcke. (Illus.). 624p. (C). 1996. pap. text 39.95 (0-8385-9813-7, A9813-5, Apple Lange Med) McGraw.

Primary Care of Women & Children with HIV Infection: A Multidisciplinary Approach. Ed. by Patricia Kelly. LC 94-34337. (Series in Oncology & HIV-Related Illnesses). 1995. pap. 40.00 (0-86720-709-4) Jones & Bartlett.

Primary Care Oncology. Kathryn L. Boyer et al. Ed. by Shirley Kuhn. LC 98-5822. (Illus.). 416p. (C). 1998. pap. text 45.00 (0-7216-7316-3, W B Saunders Co) Harcrt Hlth Sci Grp.

Primary Care Optometry. 3rd ed. Theodore Grosvenor. 656p. 1996. text 87.50 (0-7506-9733-4) Buttrwrth-Heinemann.

Primary Care Orthopaedics. Royce C. Lewis, Jr. (Illus.). 328p. 1987. text 54.95 (0-443-08356-8) Church.

Primary Care Orthopaedics in Chiropractic. Steven Brier. (Illus.). 494p. (C). (gr. 13). 1999. text 59.00 (0-8016-6381-4, 06381) Mosby Inc.

Primary Care Orthopedics. Victoria R. Masear. (Illus.). 336p. 1995. text 60.00 (0-7216-5436-3, W B Saunders Co) Harcrt Hlth Sci Grp.

***Primary Care Orthopedics.** Scott W. Shiffer & William McDaniel. (Illus.). 170p. 2000. pap. 29.95 (0-8290-5214-3) Ardent Media.

Primary Care Patient Education Manual. annuals Aspen Reference Group Staff. LC 98-45294. 500p. 1999. 149.00 (0-8342-1015-0, S498) Aspen Pub.

Primary Care Pediatric Otolaryngology. Patrick S. Pasquariello, Jr. et al. 244p. 1995. text 35.00 (1-887064-00-1) J M Ryan.

Primary Care Pediatrics. Carol Green-Hernandez & Joanne K. Singleton. 1000p. text 64.95 (0-7817-2008-7) Lppncott W & W.

Primary Care Physicians: Financing Their Graduate Medical Education in Ambulatory Settings. Institute of Medicine Staff. 274p. 1989. pap. text 33.00 (0-309-04134-1) Natl Acad Pr.

Primary Care Podiatry. Ed. by Jeffrey M. Robbins. LC 93-17926. 1994. text 69.00 (0-7216-4363-9, W B Saunders Co) Harcrt Hlth Sci Grp.

***Primary Care Provider's Guide to Reimbursement & Quality Audits.** Carolyn Buppert. 2000. 89.00 (0-8342-1744-9) Aspen Pub.

Primary Care Psychiatry. Knesper. LC 96-43966. 350p. 1997. pap. text 41.00 (0-7216-6509-8, W B Saunders Co) Harcrt Hlth Sci Grp.

Primary Care Psychiatry & Behavioral Medicine: Brief Office Treatment & Management Pathways. Ed. by Robert E. Feinstein & Anne A. Brewer. LC 98-42017. 528p. 1998. 59.95 (0-8261-1224-2) Springer Pub.

Primary Care Radiology. (Illus.). 315p. Date not set. pap. text. write for info. (0-7216-8333-9, W B Saunders Co) Harcrt Hlth Sci Grp.

Primary Care Research: Encounter Records & the Denominator Problem. S. J. Kilpatrick, Jr. & Russell Boyle. LC 83-24744. 156p. 1984. 45.00 (0-275-91439-9, C1439, Praeger Pubs) Greenwood.

Primary Care Research: Traditional & Innovative Approaches. Ed. by Peter G. Norton et al. LC 90-21954. (Research Methods for Primary Care Ser.: No. 1). (Illus.). 253p. 1991. pap. 78.50 (0-608-05070-9, 206562500005) Bks Demand.

Primary Care Research: Traditional & Innovative Approaches. Ed. by Peter G. Norton et al. (Research Methods for Primary Care Ser.: Vol. 1). (Illus.). 272p. (C). 1990. text 58.00 (0-8039-3870-5); pap. text 26.00 (0-8039-3871-3) Sage.

Primary Care Secrets. 2nd rev. ed. Jeanette Mladenovic. LC 98-42098. (Secrets Ser.). (Illus.). 500p. 1998. text 38.00 (1-56053-305-6) Hanley & Belfus.

Primary Care Urology: A Practitioner's Guide. Larry I. Lipshultz & Isaac Kleinman. 1996. mass mkt. 43.95 (0-7234-2482-9, Pub. by Martin Dunitz) Mosby Inc.

Primary Care Women No. 2. 2nd ed. Carlson. 2001. pap. text. write for info. (0-323-01065-2) Mosby Inc.

Primary Cats. 2nd ed. Marsha Heatwole. LC 97-67648. (Illus.). 14p. (J). (ps-5). 1997. 7.95 (0-9642712-2-2) Creative Art Pr.

Primary Central Business in the San Francisco Bay Area: Spatial & Structural Shifts, 1981-1988. 1991. 25.00 (0-317-05657-3, P91003PRO) Assn Bay Area.

Primary Cereal Processing: A Comprehensive Sourcebook. Ed. by Bernard Godon & Claude Willm. LC 93-17543. 1993. 145.00 (1-56081-609-0, Wiley-VCH) Wiley.

Primary Cereal Processing: A Comprehensive Sourcebook. Ed. by Bernard Godon & Claude Willm. 544p. 1994. 225.00 (0-471-18579-5) Wiley.

Primary Child Care Bk. 2: Book Two: a Guide for the Community Teacher, Manager & Teacher. Maurice H. King et al. (Illus.). 204p. 1980. pap. text 14.95 (0-19-264230-8) OUP.

Primary Christmas Concerts. Carol Ogilvy & Trudy Tinkham. 112p. (J). (gr. k-3). 1989. 12.99 (0-86653-485-7, GA1091) Good Apple.

Primary Colors. Alexander Theroux. LC 93-29692. 1995. 17.95 (0-8050-3105-7) H Holt & Co.

Primary Colors. Alexander Theroux. 1995. pap. write for info. (0-446-67197-5) Warner Bks.

Primary Colors: A Novel of Politics. Anonymous. 1998. mass mkt. 6.99 (0-446-78840-6) Warner Bks.

Primary Colors: A Novel of Politics. Anonymous. 528p. 1996. reprint ed. mass mkt. 6.99 (0-446-60427-5, Pub. by Warner Bks) Little.

Primary Commodities: Market Developments & Outlook. International Monetary Fund Staff. LC 86-15401. (International Monetary Fund, Occasional Paper: No. 45). 82p. reprint ed. pap. 30.00 (0-608-18029-7, 202908900058) Bks Demand.

Primary Commodities: Market Developments & Outlook, May, 1988. International Monetary Fund Staff. LC 88-15625. (World Economic & Financial Surveys Ser.). 105p. reprint ed. pap. 32.60 (0-608-18437-3, 203262100080) Bks Demand.

Primary Commodities in International Trade. John W. Rowe. LC 65-18930. 236p. (Orig.). reprint ed. pap. 67.30 (0-608-11103-1, 2022467) Bks Demand.

Primary Commodity Control. C. P. Brown. (Illus.). 1977. pap. text 18.50 (0-19-580304-3) OUP.

Primary Commodity Exports & Economic Development: Theory, Evidence & a Study of Malaysia. John T. Thoburn. LC 76-26337. 338p. reprint ed. pap. 104.80 (0-608-12448-6, 202520600042) Bks Demand.

Primary Commodity Markets & Models: An International Bibliography. Walter C. Labys. 298p. 1987. text 96.95 (0-566-05324-1, Pub. by Avebry) Ashgate Pub Co.

Primary Commodity Prices: Economic Models & Policy. Ed. by L. Alan Winters & David Sapsford. (Illus.). 326p. (C). 1991. text 69.95 (0-521-38550-4) Cambridge U Pr.

Primary Core National Curriculum: Policy into Practice. 2nd ed. Ed. by David Coulby & Stephen Ward. (Education Ser.). (Illus.). 160p. 1996. pap. 29.95 (0-304-33804-4) Continuum.

Primary Cosmic Radiation. Ed. by D. V. Skobel'tsyn. Tr. by Julian B. Barbour from RUS. LC 75-22281. (Proceedings of the P. N. Lebedev Physics Institute Ser.: No. 64). 115p. 1975. reprint ed. pap. 35.70 (0-608-05524-7, 206599200006) Bks Demand.

Primary Crullers: A Robotman Book. Jim Meddick. LC 97-71633. (Illus.). 128 p. (Orig.). 1997. pap. 9.95 (0-8362-3662-9) Andrews & McMeel.

Primary Crushing Plant Design. F. W. McQuiston & Roberts Shoemaker. LC 77-94869. (Illus.). 297p. reprint ed. pap. 92.10 (*0-608-18319-9*, 203159100075) Bks Demand.

Primary Curriculum: Learning from International Perspectives. Janet R. Moyles & Linda Hargreaves. LC 97-17424. 240p. (C). 1998. pap. 22.99 (*0-415-15832-X*) Routledge.

Primary Degenerative Dementias Other Than Alzheimer's Disease. Arthur W. Clark. LC 97-38212. 400p. 1998. pap. write for info. (*0-89089-713-1*) Carolina Acad Pr.

Primary Dermatologic Care. Bonnie J. Hooper & Mitchel P. Goldman. LC 98-29425. 368p. 1998. pap. text 49.95 (*1-55664-412-4*) Mosby Inc.

Primary Design & Technology: A Process for Learning. Ron Ritchie. 192p. 1995. pap. text 23.00 (*1-85346-340-X*, Pub. by David Fulton) Taylor & Francis.

Primary Design Technology in Practice. Bentley. Date not set. pap. text. write for info. (*0-582-05700-0*, Pub. by Addison-Wesley) Longman.

Primary Dictionary, No. 1. Amy Brown et al. 96p. 1987. mass mkt. 3.99 (*0-515-09093-X*, Jove) Berkley Pub.

Primary Dictionary, No. 4. Amy Brown et al. 432p. 1987. mass mkt. 4.99 (*0-515-09096-4*, Jove) Berkley Pub.

Primary Directions Made Easy. A. Sepharial. 80p. 1991. pap. 10.00 (*0-89540-183-5*, SB-183, Sun Bks) Sun Pub.

Primary Domino Thinking: Creating the Life You Want. Anthony S. Dallmann-Jones. (Source Book of the Primary Domino Thinking Ser.). 154p. (Orig.). 1997. pap. 12.95 (*1-881952-40-1*) Wolf Creek WI.

Primary Ecology Series, 5 bks. Bobbie Kalman & Janine Schaub. Incl. I Am a Part of Nature. LC 93-30695. (Illus.). 32p. (J). (gr. k-8). 1992. lib. bdg. 19.16 (*0-86505-552-1*); (J). lib. bdg. write for info. (*0-86505-577-7*) Crabtree Pub Co.

Primary Education: Goals, Processes & Practices. Clare Madott Kosnik. 29.95 (*0-921252-83-8*) LEGAS.

Primary Education: Structure & Context. Philip Gammage. 112p. (C). 1986. 50.00 (*0-06-318345-5*, Pub. by P Chapman) St Mut.

Primary Education from Plowden to the Nineties. N. Thomas. 1990. 75.00 (*1-85000-708-X*, Falmer Pr); pap. 34.95 (*1-85000-709-8*, Falmer Pr) Taylor & Francis.

Primary Education in India. LC 96-48041. (Development in Practice Ser.). 320p. 1997. 30.00 (*0-8213-3840-4*, 13840) World Bank.

Primary Education Thinking Skills. Dodie Merritt et al. (Illus.). 208p. (Orig.). 1997. pap., teacher ed. 18.95 (*1-880505-24-X*, CLC0199) Pieces of Lrning.

Primary Education Thinking Skills 2. Jody Nichols et al. (Illus.). 208p. 1998. pap. 18.95 (*1-880505-37-1*, CLC0221) Pieces of Lrning.

Primary Elections in the South. Cortez A. Ewing. LC 80-12616. (Illus.). xii, 112p. 1980. reprint ed. lib. bdg. 65.00 (*0-313-22452-8*, EWPR, Greenwood Pr) Greenwood.

Primary English Class: A Play in Two Acts. Israel Horovitz. 1976. pap. 5.25 (*0-8222-0913-6*) Dramatists Play.

Primary Eye Care Manual. (PAHO Scientific Publication Ser.). 63p. 1985. pap. text 15.00 (*92-75-11490-0*) World Health.

Primary Eyecare in Systemic Disease. Ed. by Esther S. Marks et al. LC 94-10704. 706p. (C). 1995. pap. text 115.00 (*0-8385-7997-3*, A7997-8, Apple Lange Med) McGraw.

Primary Guitar Method, Bk. 2. D. Bennett. (Easy Play Ser.). 48p. 1986. pap. 4.95 (*0-7935-2851-8*, 50394080) H Leonard.

Primary Guitar Method, Bk. 3. D. Bennett. (Easy Play Ser.). 1986. pap. 4.95 (*0-7935-2852-6*, 50394090) H Leonard.

Primary Guitar Method Bk. 1: Basic Class or Individual Instruction. D. Bennett. (Easy Play Ser.). 48p. 1986. pap. 4.95 (*0-7935-2850-X*, 50394070) H Leonard.

Primary Guitar Method Bk. 4: Basic Class or Individual Instruction. D. Bennett. (Easy Play Ser.). 1986. pap. 4.95 (*0-7935-2853-4*, 50394100) H Leonard.

Primary Guitar Method Bk. 5: Basic Class or Individual Instruction. D. Bennett. (Easy Play Ser.). 1986. pap. 4.95 (*0-7935-2854-2*, 50394110) H Leonard.

Primary Head: Roles, Responsibilities & Reflections. Peter Morimore & Jo Mortimore. 144p. 1991. pap. 27.00 (*1-85396-140-X*, Pub. by P Chapman) Taylor & Francis.

Primary Headache Disorders. Alan M. Rapoport & Fred D. Sheftell. Ed. by Bill Schmitt. 176p. 1996. text 41.00 (*0-7216-4051-6*, W B Saunders Co) Harcrt Hlth Sci Grp.

Primary Headship in 1990s. Craig. 1989. pap. text. write for info. (*0-582-04007-8*, Pub. by Addison-Wesley) Longman.

Primary Headteacher: The Pleasure, Pain & Principles of Leadership in the Primary School. David W. Clegg & Shirley Billington. LC 97-19357. 128p. 1998. 85.00 (*0-335-19645-4*) OpUniv Pr.

Primary Health Care: Report of the International Conference on Primary Health Care, 1978. 1978. text. write for info. (*92-4-180001-1*) World Health.

Primary Health Care: The African Experience. Ed. by Raymond W. Carlaw & William B. Ward. LC 80-54741. (Case Studies in Community Health Education: Vol. 2). 472p. 1988. pap. 19.95 (*0-89914-025-4*) Third Party Pub.

Primary Health Care: The Chinese Experience. WHO Staff. 103p. 1983. 14.00 (*92-4-156077-0*) World Health.

Primary Health Care - From Theory to Action: Report on a WHO Symposium. (Euro Reports & Studies Ser.: No. 69). 29p. 1982. pap. text 4.00 (*92-890-1235-8*) World Health.

Primary Health Care & Local Health Systems in the Caribbean. 206p. 1989. text 25.00 (*92-75-12022-6*) World Health.

Primary Health Care & Psychiatric Epidemiology. Brian Cooper & Robin Eastwood. 320p. (C). 1992. text 110.00 (*0-415-07073-2*, A6619) Routledge.

Primary Health Care & the Private Sector. Maureen Devlin. LC 98-198177. (National Primary Care Research & Development Centre Ser.). 79 p. 1998. write for info. (*1-85775-244-9*) Scovill Paterson.

Primary Health Care Buildings. Gordon Staff. (Briefing & Design Guides Ser.). (Illus.). 128p. 1997. pap. text. write for info. (*0-419-20130-0*, E & FN Spon) Routledge.

Primary Health Care in Industrialized Countries. (EURO Reports & Studies: No. 95). 60p. 1985. pap. text 6.30 (*92-890-1261-7*, 1330095) World Health.

Primary Health Care in Omaha Nebraska: A Case Study of Nine Primary Health Care Centers. Stella G. Limson. (Illus.). 50p. (Orig.). 1986. pap. 3.50 (*1-55719-025-9*) U NE CPAR.

Primary Health Care in the Kingdom of Lesotho: The Nurses' Perspective. Ed. by Faye A. Gary & Jacquelyn K. Warren. (Illus.). 315p. (C). 1991. write for info. (*0-9629485-2-7*) Gary & Warren.

Primary Health Care in Undergraduate Medical Education: Summaries in French, German & Russian. 1984. pap. text 9.00 (*92-890-1027-4*) World Health.

Primary Health Care in Urban Communities. Ed. by Beverly J. McElmurry et al. 1997. 25.95 (*0-88737-734-3*, 14-7343, NLN Pr) Natl League Nurse.

Primary Health Care of the Young. Jane Fox. (Illus.). 1024p. 1981. text 51.95 (*0-07-021741-6*) McGraw.

Primary Health Care Pioneer: The Selected Works of Dr. Cicely D. Williams. Ed. by Naomi Baumslag. 1986. 12.00 (*0-87553-140-7*) Am Pub Health.

Primary Health Care Provision in Nepal. Shailendra Sigdel. 1998. pap. 47.00 (*0-7855-7480-8*, Pub. by Ratna Pustak Bhandar) St Mut.

Primary Health Care Reviews: Guidelines & Methods. A. El Bindari-Hammad & D. L. Smith. (ENG & FRE.). xiv, 226p. 1992. pap. text 40.00 (*92-4-154437-6*, 1150374) World Health.

***Primary Health Care Sciences: A Reader.** Jane Sims. 1999. pap. text 46.95 (*1-86156-103-2*) Whurr Pub.

Primary Health Education. Young. 1987. pap. text. write for info. (*0-582-77924-3*, Pub. by Addison-Wesley) Longman.

Primary Health Worker: Superseded by the Community Health Worker. (Nonserial Publication). 346p. 1980. pap. text 12.00 (*92-4-154144-X*, 1150134) World Health.

Primary Healthcare Centers. Martin Valins. (C). 1993. 89.95 (*0-582-09383-X*, Pub. by Addison-Wesley) Longman.

Primary Healthcare of Children. Ed. by Jane A. Fox. LC 97-187475. (Illus.). 1120p. (C). (gr. 13). 1997. text 72.00 (*0-8151-3310-3*, 28202) Mosby Inc.

Primary Help! Book: Book of Mormon. Susan Taylor Brown & Glorianne Muggli. (Help! Bks.). (Illus.). 100p. (Orig.). 1995. pap. 7.95 (*1-57665-009-X*) Muggli Graphics.

Primary Help! Book: New Testament. Susan Taylor Brown & Glorianne Muggli. (Help! Bks.). (Illus.). 80p. (Orig.). 1994. pap. 6.95 (*1-57665-006-5*) Muggli Graphics.

***Primary Hematology.** Ed. by Ayalew Tefferi. 450p. 2000. 99.50 (*0-89603-664-2*) Humana.

***Primary Hematopoietic Cells.** Manfred R. Koller et al. LC 99-31925. (Human Cell Culture Ser.). 342p. 1999. write for info. (*0-7923-5821-X*) Kluwer Academic.

Primary Homotopy Theory. Joseph Neisendorfer. LC 80-12109. (Memoirs of the American Mathematical Society Ser.: No. 25/232). 67p. 1983. reprint ed. pap. 16.00 (*0-8218-2232-2*, MEMO/25/232) Am Math.

Primary Hyperparathyroidism: Report Presented at the 93rd French Surgical Congress, Paris, September 1991. Ed. by J. Barbier & J. F. Henry. 168p. 1993. 96.95 (*0-387-59578-3*) Spr-Verlag.

***Primary Idea Book.** Glorianne Muggli. (Illus.). 64p. 1999. pap. 7.95 (*1-57665-056-1*) Muggli Graphics.

Primary Inversion. Catherine Asaaro. 1996. mass mkt. 5.99 (*0-8125-5023-4*, Pub. by Tor Bks) St Martin.

Primary Justice. William Bernhardt. 1992. mass mkt. 5.99 (*0-345-37479-7*) Ballantine Pub Grp.

***Primary Justice.** William Bernhardt. LC 98-42592. 1998. 20.95 (*0-7862-1659-X*) Five Star.

Primary Language Arts: Grades 1-3. Avaril Wedemeyer & Joyce Cejka. 1978. pap. 6.95 (*0-89108-082-1*, 7809) Love Pub Co.

Primary Language Book. 2nd ed. Peter Dougill & Richard Knott. LC 92-33218. 1993. 31.95 (*0-335-19021-9*) OpUniv Pr.

Primary Language Leader's Book: A Handbook for English Curriculum Leaders at Key Stages 1 & 2. Robin Peel & Mary Bell. 160p. 1994. pap. 27.50 (*1-85346-249-7*, Pub. by David Fulton) Taylor & Francis.

Primary Language Lessons. Emma Serl. LC 96-76987. (Illus.). 148p. (J). (gr. 2-4). 1997. 14.95 (*0-9652735-1-2*) Lost Classics.

Primary Language of Poetry in the 1740's & 1840's. Josephine Miles. LC 83-45454. reprint ed. 27.50 (*0-404-20177-6*) AMS Pr.

Primary Language of Poetry in the 1640's, Vol. 19, No. 1. Josephine Miles. LC 78-11614. (Univ. of California Publications in English: Vol. 19, No. 1). (Illus.). 160p. 1979. reprint ed. lib. bdg. 38.50 (*0-313-20661-9*, MIPP, Greenwood Pr) Greenwood.

Primary Language Record: Handbook for Teachers. Myra Barrs et al. 64p. 1989. pap. text 30.00 (*0-435-08521-2*, 08521) Heinemann.

Primary Law Appendix For Employment In Oregon. Lexis Law Publishing Staff. 1300p. 1998. write for info. (*0-327-06641-5*) LEXIS Pub.

Primary Law Appendix for Employment in Texas. Lexis Law Publishing Staff. 1300p. write for info. (*0-327-06656-3*) LEXIS Pub.

Primary Lessons in Christian Living & Healing (1918) Annie R. Militz. 180p. 1998. reprint ed. pap. 19.95 (*0-7661-0307-2*) Kessinger Pub.

Primary Liver Cancer. Ed. by Z. Tang & M. Wu. (Illus.). 520p. 1989. 368.00 (*0-387-50228-9*) Spr-Verlag.

Primary Liver Cancer: Etiology & Progression Factors. Christian Brechot. 320p. 1994. lib. bdg. 195.00 (*0-8493-4913-3*) CRC Pr.

Primary Liver Cancer in Japan. Ed. by T. Tobe. (Illus.). 466p. 1993. 331.00 (*0-387-70089-7*) Spr-Verlag.

Primary Low Vision Care. Rodney W. Nowakowski. LC 94-8438. 300p. (C). 1995. pap. text 75.00 (*0-8385-7980-9*, A7980-4, Apple Lange Med) McGraw.

Primary Management of Musculoskeletal Trauma. David Seligson & Kurt Voos. LC 96-42532. 256p. 1996. pap. text 37.00 (*0-397-51389-5*) Lppncott W & W.

Primary Market for Municipal Debt: Bidding Rules & Cost of Long Term Borrowing. G. O. Bierwag. Ed. by Edward I. Altman & Ingo I. Walter. LC 80-82480. (Contemporary Studies in Economic & Financial Analysis: Vol. 29). 272p. 1981. 78.50 (*0-89232-167-9*) Jai Pr.

Primary Math Puzzlers. Ann R. Fisher. (Illus.). 112p. (J). (gr. 1-4). 1994. 11.99 (*0-86653-812-7*, GA1504) Good Apple.

Primary Medical Practice: A Psychiatric Evaluation. Lucy M. Zabarenko et al. LC 67-26018. (Illus.). 272p. 1968. 11.75 (*0-87527-090-5*) Green.

***Primary Medical Therapy for Breast Cancer: Clinical & Biologicalaspects.** A. Howell & M. Dowsett. LC 99-42956. (European School of Oncology Scientific Updates Ser.). 133p. 1999. 91.50 (*0-444-50327-7*) Elsevier.

Primary Mental Health Care. James Behrman. 161p. (Orig.). 1992. pap. 12.95 (*0-929240-48-0*) EMIS.

Primary Modalities of Visual Expression. Robert Sowers. 1990. 45.00 (*0-520-06632-4*, Pub. by U CA Pr) Cal Prin Full Svc.

Primary Neurologic Care. Petit. 2000. text 49.95 (*0-8151-5304-X*, 29742) Mosby Inc.

Primary Nursing: Nursing in the Burford & Oxford Nursing Development Units. Ed. by Alan Pearson. 160p. 1988. pap. text 25.00 (*0-7099-4066-1*, Pub. by C Helm) Routldge.

Primary Nursing Practice. Gloria Caliandro & Barbara L. Judkins. 663p. (C). 1988. text 50.00 (*0-673-39731-9*) Lppncott W & W.

Primary Objective: Neuro-Linguistic Psychology & Guerilla Warfare. William D. Horton. 208p. 1998. pap. 12.50 (*1-57353-116-2*) Eschaton Prods.

Primary 1 see Math Mini-Tests

Primary Orthopedic Care. Christy Crowther. LC 99-36528. (Illus.). 450p. (C). (gr. 13). 1999. pap. text 54.95 (*0-8151-1376-5*, 29560) Mosby Inc.

Primary Orthopedics. Brinker. LC 97-43313. (Illus.). xiii, 390p. 1999. pap. text 35.00 (*0-7216-6698-1*, W B Saunders Co) Harcrt Hlth Sci Grp.

Primary Ousia: An Essay on Aristotle's Metaphysics Z & H. Michael J. Loux. LC 90-25775. 288p. 1991. text 49.95 (*0-8014-2598-0*) Cornell U Pr.

Primary Partners: Achievement Days. Mary Ross & Jennette Guymon. (J). (gr. 3-6). 1996. pap. 9.95 (*1-55503-989-8*, 01112406) Covenant Comms.

Primary Partners: Ages 4 to 7 (CTR A): A-Z Activities to Make Learning Fun! Mary H. Ross. (Illus.). 96p. 1996. pap., teacher ed. 8.95 (*1-55503-905-7*, 01112228) Covenant Comms.

Primary Partners: Ages 4 to 7 (CTR B) Mary Ross & Jennette Guymon. 1996. pap., teacher ed. 8.95 (*1-57734-034-5*, 01112562) Covenant Comms.

***Primary Partners: Ages 8 to 11 (Book of Mormon)** Ross & Guymon-King. 1999. pap. 9.95 (*1-57734-519-3*, 01114484) Covenant Comms.

Primary Partners: Ages 8 to 11 (D & C) Mary Ross & Jennette Guymon. (J). (gr. 3-6). 1996. pap. 8.95 (*1-57734-065-5*, 01112759) Covenant Comms.

Primary Partners: Ages 8 to 11 (New Testament) Ross. pap., teacher ed. 9.95 (*1-57734-344-1*, 01113658) Covenant Comms.

Primary Partners: Ages 8 to 11 (Old Testament) Mary Ross & Jennette Guymon. (J). (gr. 3-6). 1998. pap. 8.95 (*1-57734-264-X*, 01113291) Covenant Comms.

Primary Partners: Nursery-Age 3: A-Z Activities to Make Learning Fun. Mary H. Ross & Jennette Guymon. (J). (ps-3). 1996. pap. 8.95 (*1-55503-809-3*, 01111914) Covenant Comms.

***Primary Partners: Sharing Time: Faith in the Lord Jesus Christ.** Mary H. Ross. LC 99-192544. 123 p. 1998. pap. 2.97 (*1-57734-338-7*, 01113690) Covenant Comms.

Primary Partners Vol. 2: Nursery-Age 3. Mary Ross & Jennette Guymon. (J). (ps-3). Date not set. pap. 8.95 (*1-57734-185-6*, 01113208) Covenant Comms.

***Primary Partners Sharing Time: I Will Make & Keep My Baptismal Covenant.** Ross. 1999. pap. 9.95 (*1-57734-515-0*, 01114158) Covenant Comms.

***Primary Partners Singing Fun: I Will Make & Keep My Baptismal Covenant.** Ross. 1999. pap. 9.95 (*1-57734-551-7*, 01114433) Covenant Comms.

Primary Passages Plus: Favorite Songs & Hymns Arranged for Newcomers to the Piano. Vicky L. Hammond & Judy N. Dalby. (Primary Passages Ser.). (Illus.). 32p. (Orig.). (J). 1989. pap. 5.95 (*0-9624262-3-7*) Hammond Dalby Music.

Primary Pastoral Care. Journal of Pastoral Care Editorial Committee Staff. Ed. by Orlo Strunk, Jr. LC 90-40554. 100p. 1990. pap. 6.95 (*0-929670-01-9*) JPCP.

Primary Pediatric Care. 3rd ed. Robert A. Hoekelman. (Illus.). 1936p. (C). (gr. 13). 1996. text 99.95 (*0-8151-4547-0*, 24922) Mosby Inc.

Primary Pediatric Care Companion. Robert A. Hoekelman. (Illus.). 320p. (C). (gr. 13). 1996. text 27.95 (*0-8151-4485-7*, 27884) Mosby Inc.

Primary Pediatric Care Package. Robert A. Hoekelman. 1996. write for info. (*0-8151-2396-5*) Mosby Inc.

***Primary Perceptions.** unabridged ed. Eva S. Jungermann. LC 00-131260. (Illus.). 64p. 2000. pap. 14.95 (*0-927015-23-4*) Bridgewood Pr.

Primary Photoexcitations in Conjugated Polymers: Molecular Exciton vs. Semiconductor Band Model. 350p. 1997. lib. bdg. 67.00 (*981-02-2880-5*) World Scientific Pub.

Primary Physical Education Handbook. abr. ed. Jim Hall. 1999. pap. text 14.95 (*0-7136-5088-5*) A & C Blk.

Primary Praise. Compiled by Ken Bible. 60p. 1990. 7.99 (*0-8341-9306-X*, MB-620) Lillenas.

Primary Prevention & Cancer. Ed. by Willy J. Eylenbosch et al. (Recent Results in Cancer Research Ser.). (Illus.). 144p. 1991. 69.00 (*0-387-53704-X*) Spr-Verlag.

Primary Prevention & Promotion in the Schools. Ed. by Lynne A. Bond & Bruce E. Compas. (Primary Prevention of Psychopathology Ser.: Vol. 12). 440p. (C). 1989. text 49.95 (*0-8039-3526-9*) Sage.

Primary Prevention & Promotion in the Schools. Ed. by Lynne A. Bond & Bruce E. Compas. LC 89-10130. (Primary Prevention of Psychopathology Ser.: Vol. 12). 452p. 1989. reprint ed. pap. 140.20 (*0-608-03007-4*, 206345700006) Bks Demand.

Primary Prevention for Children & Families. Ed. by Mary Frank. LC 81-17858. (Journal of Children in Contemporary Society: Vol. 14, Nos. 2-3). 119p. 1982. text 39.95 (*0-86656-107-2*) Haworth Pr.

Primary Prevention of AIDS. Ed. by Vickie M. Mays et al. (Primary Prevention of Psychopathology Ser.: Vol. 13). (Illus.). 400p. (C). 1989. 49.95 (*0-8039-3600-1*) Sage.

Primary Prevention of Child Abuse. Christopher Cloke. pap. text 32.00 (*0-471-97775-6*) Wiley.

Primary Prevention of Coronary Heart Disease. (Euro Reports & Studies Ser.: No. 97). 96p. 1985. pap. text 10.00 (*92-890-1264-1*) World Health.

Primary Prevention of Essential Hypertension. (Technical Report Ser.: No. 686). 40p. 1983. pap. text 4.00 (*92-4-120686-1*) World Health.

Primary Prevention of Psychiatric Disorders. Charles A. Roberts et al. Ed. by F. C. R. Chalke & John J. Day. LC 77-364638. (Clarence M. Hincks Memorial Lectures). viii, 168 p. 1968. write for info. (*0-8020-3205-2*) U of Toronto Pr.

Primary Prevention of Rheumatic Diseases. R. D. Wigley. (Illus.). 370p. 1994. text 85.00 (*1-85070-366-3*) Prthnon Pub.

Primary Prevention Practices. Martin Bloom. (Issues in Children's & Families' Lives Ser.: Vol. 5). (Illus.). 512p. 1996. 58.00 (*0-8039-7151-6*); pap. 27.95 (*0-8039-7152-4*) Sage.

Primary Prevention Works. Ed. by George W. Albee & Thomas P. Gullotta. (Issues in Children's & Families' Lives Ser.: Vol. 6). 454p. 1996. 59.95 (*0-7619-0467-0*); pap. 27.95 (*0-7619-0468-9*) Sage.

Primary Preventive Dentistry. 4th rev. ed. Ed. by Norman O. Harris & Arden G. Christen. LC 94-19930. (C). 1994. reprint ed. pap. text 57.95 (*0-8385-8000-9*, A8000-0) Appleton & Lange.

Primary Preventive Dentistry. 5th ed. Norman O. Harris & Franklin Garcia-Godoy. LC 98-37950. 1998. boxed set 52.95 (*0-8385-8129-3*) Appleton & Lange.

Primary Problem Solving in Math. Jack A. Coffland & Gilbert J. Cuevas. (Illus.). 200p. (Orig.). (J). (gr. k-3). 1992. pap. 13.95 (*0-673-38745-3*, GoodYrBooks) Addson-Wesley Educ.

Primary Processing see Resource Recovery from Municipal Solid Wastes

Primary Processing in Photobiology. Ed. by T. Kobayashi. (Proceedings in Physics Ser.: Vol. 20). (Illus.). 260p. 1987. 70.95 (*0-387-18068-0*) Spr-Verlag.

Primary Productivity & Biogeochemical Cycles in the Sea. P. G. Falkowski & A. D. Woodhead. (Environmental Science Research Ser.: Vol. 43). (Illus.). 560p. (C). 1992. text 145.00 (*0-306-44192-6*, Kluwer Plenum) Kluwer Academic.

Primary Productivity of Japanese Forests: Productivity of Terrestrial Communities. Ed. by T. Shidel & T. Kira. LC 78-320793. (JIBP Synthesis Ser.: No. 16). 299p. 1977. reprint ed. pap. 92.70 (*0-608-01550-4*, 206195900001) Bks Demand.

Primary Productivity of the Biosphere. Ed. by Helmut Lieth & R. H. Whittaker. LC 74-26627. (Ecological Studies: Vol. 14). (Illus.). 350p. 1975. 175.00 (*0-387-07083-4*) Spr-Verlag.

Primary Program K: Course Code 181-1. Tricia Jordan. Ed. by Bonnie Schroeder. (Illus.). 58p. (Orig.). 1989. teacher ed. 24.95 (*0-917531-60-4*) CES Compu-Tech.

Primary Program K: Course code 181-1. Tricia Jordan. Ed. by Bonnie Schroeder. (Illus.). 58p. (Orig.). (gr. k). 1989. student ed. 5.95 (*0-917531-35-3*) CES Compu-Tech.

Primary Program K: Course Code 181-2. Tricia Jordan. Ed. by Bonnie Schroeder. (Illus.). 56p. (Orig.). 1989. 9.95 (*0-917531-36-1*); teacher ed. 24.95 (*0-917531-61-2*) CES Compu-Tech.

Primary Program K, Pt. 1: Lab Pack. Tricia Jordan. Ed. by Bonnie Schroeder. (Illus.). teacher ed., student ed. 299.95 incl. disk (*1-56177-004-3*, L181-1); disk 15.95 (*1-56177-000-0*, D181-1A); disk 15.95 (*1-56177-002-7*, D181-2A) CES Compu-Tech.

Primary Program K, Pt. 2: Lab Pak. Tricia Jordan. Ed. by Bonnie Schroeder. (Illus.). teacher ed., student ed. 299.95 incl. disk (*1-56177-005-1*, L181-2); disk 15.95 (*1-56177-001-9*, D181-1B); disk 15.95 (*1-56177-003-5*, D181-2B) CES Compu-Tech.

P

Primary Program 1: Course Code 101-1. Tricia Jordan. Ed. by Bonnie Schroeder. (Illus.). 88p. 1989. teacher ed. 24.95 (*0-917531-37-X*) CES Compu-Tech.

Primary Program 1: Course Code 101-2. Tricia Jordan. Ed. by Bonnie Schroeder. (Illus.). 41p. 1989. teacher ed. 24.95 (*0-917531-63-9*) CES Compu-Tech.

Primary Program 2: Course Code 191-1. Irene Danziger et al. Ed. by Cathy Doheny & Bonnie Schroeder. (Illus.). 90p. 1989. teacher ed. 24.95 (*0-917531-64-7*) CES Compu-Tech.

Primary Program 2: Course Code 191-1. Irene Danziger et al. Ed. by Cathy Doheny & Bonnie Schroeder. (Illus.). 54p. 1989. reprint ed. student ed. 5.95 (*0-917531-39-6*) CES Compu-Tech.

Primary Program 2: Course Code 191-2. Irene Danziger et al. (Illus.). 120p. 1986. teacher ed. 24.95 (*0-917531-65-5*) CES Compu-Tech.

Primary Program 2: Course Code 191-2. Irene Danziger et al. Ed. by Cathy Doheny & Bonnie Schroeder. (Illus.). 46p. 1989. student ed. 5.95 (*0-917531-40-X*) CES Compu-Tech.

Primary Program 2: Course Code 391-1. Jeanne Black et al. Ed. by Catherine Doheny & Bonnie Schroeder. (Illus.). 85p. 1989. pap., student ed. 5.95 (*0-917531-83-3*) CES Compu-Tech.

Primary Program 2: Course Code 391-2. Jeanne Black et al. Ed. by Cathy Doheny & Bonnie Schroeder. (Illus.). 95p. (gr. 2). 1989. pap., student ed. 5.95 (*0-917531-84-1*) CES Compu-Tech.

Primary Program 2 Pt. 2: Lab Pack. Irene Danziger et al. Ed. by Cathy Doheny & Bonnie Schroeder. (Illus.). teacher ed., student ed. 299.95 incl. disk (*1-56177-017-5*, L191-2) CES Compu-Tech.

Primary Program 1, Pt. 1: Lab Pack. Tricia Jordan. Ed. by Bonnie Schroeder. (Illus.). teacher ed., student ed. 299.95 incl. disk (*1-56177-010-8*, L101-1); teacher ed. 15.95 incl. disk (*1-56177-006-X*, D101-1A); write for info. (*1-56177-007-8*, D101-1B) CES Compu-Tech.

Primary Program 1, Pt. 2: Lab Pack. Tricia Jordan. Ed. by Bonnie Schroeder. teacher ed., student ed. 299.95 incl. disk (*1-56177-011-6*, L101-2); disk 15.95 (*1-56177-008-6*, D101-2A); disk 15.95 (*1-56177-009-4*, D101-2B) CES Compu-Tech.

Primary Program 2, Pt. 1: Lab Pack. Irene Danziger et al. Ed. by Bonnie Schroeder. (Illus.). teacher ed., student ed. 299.95 incl. disk (*1-56177-016-7*, L191-1); disk 15.95 (*1-56177-012-4*, D191-1A); disk 15.95 (*1-56177-013-2*, D191-1B) CES Compu-Tech.

Primary Pulmonary Hypertension. Ed. by Lewis J. Rubin & Stuart Rich. LC 96-36758. (Lung Biology in Health & Disease Ser.: Vol. 99). (Illus.). 384p. 1996. text 170.00 (*0-8247-9505-9*) Dekker.

Primary Pulmonary Hypertension: Proceedings of the WHO Expert Committee, Geneva, Oct. 15-17, 1973. WHO Staff. Ed. by S. Hatano & T. Strasser. 1975. pap. text 9.00 (*92-4-156044-4*, 1150131) World Health.

Primary Purpose see Primera Prioridad

Primary Purpose: Making It Hard to Go to Hell from Your City. Ted Haggard. LC 94-73850. 1995. pap. 12.99 (*0-88419-381-0*) Creation House.

Primary Puzzlers. Ann R. Fisher. 144p. teacher ed. 13.99 (*0-86653-720-1*, GA1438) Good Apple.

Primary RE Coordinator's Handbook. Derek Bastide. 159p. 1997. pap. 23.95 (*0-7507-0613-9*, Falmer Pr) Taylor & Francis.

Primary Readings in Philosophy for Understanding Theology. Ed. by Diogenes Allen & Eric O. Springsted. 336p. (Orig.). 1997. pap. 24.95 (*0-664-25208-7*) Westminster John Knox.

Primary Recitations: Short Bright Selections for Children of Seven Years. Ed. by Amos M. Kellogg. LC 70-160906. (Granger Index Reprint Ser.). 1977. reprint ed. 17.95 (*0-8369-6270-2*) Ayer.

Primary Reference Preparations Used to Standardize Calibration of Immunochemical Assays for Serum Prostate Specific Antigen (PSA) Approved Guideline (1996) Contrib. by Robert M. Nakamura. 1996. 75.00 (*1-56238-263-2*, I/LA19-A) NCCLS.

Primary Reference Preparations Used to Standardize Calibration of Immunochemical Assys for Serum Prostate Specific Antigen (PSA) Approved Guideline (1997) 1997. 75.00 (*1-56238-323-X*, I/LA19-A) NCCLS.

Primary Rheumatology. Harris. LC 99-17269. (C). 1999. text. write for info. (*0-7216-7172-1*, W B Saunders Co) Harcrt Hlth Sci Grp.

Primary Rhinoplasty. John B. Tebbetts. LC 98-20961. (Illus.). 368p. (C). (gr. 13). 1998. text 275.00 (*0-8151-8892-7*, 28888) Mosby Inc.

Primary Route Network. 188p. 1986. 50.00 (*0-7277-0356-0*, Pub. by T Telford) RCH.

Primary Safety Controls for Gas- & Oil-Fired Appliances, UL 372. 5th ed. (C). 1994. pap. text 330.00 (*1-55989-524-1*) Underwrtrs Labs.

Primary Salt-Effect in Aqueous Solutions see Progress in Reaction Kinetics

Primary School & Equal Opportunities: International Perspectives on Gender Issues. Ed. by Gaby Weiner. (Council of Europe Ser.). 128p. 1990. pap. text 29.95 (*0-304-31792-6*) Continuum.

Primary School Geography. Ed. by Bill Marsden & Jo Hughes. LC 94-233197. 176p. 1994. pap. 29.00 (*1-85346-281-0*, Pub. by David Fulton) Taylor & Francis.

Primary School Kit on the United Nations. 72p. 11.95 (*92-1-100587-6*) UN.

Primary School Management & Leadership Towards 2000. Ed. by Eric Spear. 336p. 1995. pap. 47.50 (*0-582-22925-1*, Pub. by Addison-Wesley) Trans-Atl Phila.

Primary School Package. 19.95 (*92-1-100620-1*) UN.

Primary School People: Getting to Know Your Colleagues. Ed. by Jean Mills & Richard W. Mills. LC 94-20730. 1995. write for info. (*0-415-11396-2*) Routledge.

***Primary School Student Achievement in Environmental Education.** B. D. Pande & U. Karki. 1998. pap. 25.00 (*0-7855-7619-3*) St Mut.

Primary School Teacher. Ed. by Sara Delamont. (Contemporary Analysis in Education Ser.). 225p. 1987. 69.95 (*1-85000-281-9*, Falmer Pr) Taylor & Francis.

Primary Schooling in Victoria. John Ainley. (C). 1990. pap. 55.00 (*0-86431-064-1*, Pub. by Aust Council Educ Res) St Mut.

Primary Schools & Special Needs: Policy, Planning & Provision. 2nd ed. Sheila Wolfendale. 224p. 1992. pap. text 33.95 (*0-304-32426-4*) Continuum.

Primary Schools & the Future: Celebration, Challenges, & Choices. P. Whitaker. LC 96-24014. 1997. pap. 27.95 (*0-335-19423-0*) OpUniv Pr.

Primary Science: Making it Work. Chris Ollerenshaw & Ron Ritchie. (Primary Curriculum Ser.). 192p. 1993. pap. 32.00 (*1-85346-199-7*, Pub. by David Fulton) Taylor & Francis.

Primary Science: Symbol Or Substance? Philip Morrison & Phylis Morrison. 20p. (Orig.). (C). 1984. pap. 3.00 (*0-317-45086-7*) City Coll Wk.

Primary Science: The Challenge of the Nineteen Nineties. Ed. by Lynn D. Newton. LC 92-31457. 144p. 1992. 29.95 (*1-85359-176-9*, Pub. by Multilingual Matters) Taylor & Francis.

Primary Science . . . Taking the Plunge: How to Teach Primary Science More Effectively. Ed. by Wynne Harlen. 168p. (Orig.). (C). 1985. pap. text 22.00 (*0-435-57350-0*, 57350) Heinemann.

Primary Science - Making It Work. 2nd ed. Chris Ollerenshaw & Ron Ritchie. LC 97-196074. (Primary Curriculum Ser.). 240p. 1997. pap. 32.00 (*1-85346-439-2*, Pub. by David Fulton) Taylor & Francis.

Primary Science & Technology: Practical Alternatives. Di Bentley & Mike Watts. LC 93-10657. 224p. 1994. 103.95 (*0-335-19029-4*); pap. 31.95 (*0-335-19028-6*) OpUniv Pr.

Primary Sclerosing Cholangitis. R. W. Chapman et al. Ed. by M. P. Manns. 144p. 1998. 108.00 (*0-7923-8745-7*) Kluwer Academic.

Primary Scriptural Passages: Book of Mormon Songs for Early Piano. Vicky L. Hammond & Judy N. Dalby. (Primary Passages Ser.). (Illus.). 32p. (Orig.). (J). 1996. pap. 7.95 (*0-9624262-5-3*) Hammond Dalby Music.

***Primary Securities Markets: Cross Country Findings.** Anthony Aylward & Jack Glen. LC 99-23806. (IFC Discussion Paper Ser.: No. 39). 48p. 1999. pap. 22.00 (*0-8213-4522-2*, 14522) World Bank.

Primary Sedimentary Structures & Their Hydrodynamic Interpretation: A Symposium. Ed. by Gerard V. Middleton. LC 76-219474. (Society of Economic Paleontologists & Mineralogists, Special Publication Ser.: No. 12). 272p. reprint ed. pap. 84.40 (*0-608-12955-0*, 202473800038) Bks Demand.

Primary Social Studies. Morrisey. 1991. pap. text. write for info. (*0-582-07515-7*, Pub. by Addison-Wesley) Longman.

***Primary Song Visual Aids, 3 vols.** Incl. Bk. 1. (Illus.). 100p. (J). 1999. pap. 8.95 (*1-57665-057-X*); Bk. 2. (Illus.). 100p. (J). 1999. pap. 8.95 (*1-57665-058-8*); Bk. 3. (Illus.). 100p. (J). 1999. pap. 8.95 (*1-57665-059-6*); (Illus.). (J). 1999. Set pap. 23.95 (*1-57665-063-4*) Muggli Graphics.

Primary Source: Tropical Forests & Our Future. 2nd ed. Norman Myers. (Illus.). 448p. 1992. pap. 12.95 (*0-393-30828-6*) Norton.

Primary Source Readings: World History. Jackson J. Spielvogel. (Social Studies Ser.). 1998. mass mkt. 10.75 (*0-314-14095-6*) S-W Pub.

Primary Sources: Selected Writings on Color from Aristotle to Albers. Patricia Sloane. 1991. 16.95 (*0-07-157590-1*) McGraw.

Primary Sources: Selected Writings on Color from Aristotle to Albers. Ed. by Patricia Sloane. 320p. 1990. pap. 16.95 (*0-8306-3481-9*, 3481) McGraw-Hill Prof.

Primary Sources for Victorian Studies. Lionel Madden & Richard Storey. (C). 1977. 30.00 (*0-85033-252-4*) St Mut.

Primary Sources in African-American History. Finkenbine. LC 97-104190. 128p. (C). 1996. pap. text 16.88 (*0-673-99202-0*) Addson-Wesley Educ.

***Primary Sources in Economics: Economics in Our Times.** 2nd ed. Arnold. 2000. pap. 11.95 (*0-538-43088-5*) Sth-Wstrn College.

Primary Sources in European Diplomacy, 1914-1945: A Bibliography of Published Memoirs & Diaries, 6. Compiled by Frederic M. Messick. LC 87-186. (Bibliographies & Indexes in World History Ser.: No. 6). 243p. 1987. lib. bdg. 69.50 (*0-313-24555-X*, MEU) Greenwood.

***Primary Sources of Liturgical Theology: A Reader.** Dwight W. Vogel. 344p. 2000. pap. 39.95 (*0-8146-6178-5*) Liturgical Pr.

Primary Sources of the Civil War: An Activity Book for Teachers: Featuring Documents from the National Archives & Records Administration. Jean West & National Archives & Records Administration Staff. 224p. (Orig.). 1996. teacher ed., ring bd. 28.95 (*0-942389-21-2*) Cobblestone Pub Co.

Primary Speech: A Psychology of Prayer. Barry Ulanov & Ann B. Ulanov. LC 81-85328. 192p. 1982. 19.95 (*0-8042-1134-5*) Westminster John Knox.

Primary Structure of Fabrics: An Illustrated Classification. 2nd ed. Irene Emery. 1994. reprint ed. 69.00 (*0-500-01623-2*) Thames Hudson.

Primary Structure of the Stem. Evert. 1998. 1.50 (*0-7167-9371-7*) W H Freeman.

Primary Structure of Transfer RNA. Tat'kilana Venkstern. Ed. by James T. Madison. LC 79-186259. 313p. reprint ed. pap. 97.10 (*0-608-14550-5*, 202471700038) Bks Demand.

Primary Succession on Land. Ed. by J. Miles & D. W. Walton. LC 92-35652. 309p. 1993. 65.00 (*0-632-03547-1*) Blackwell Sci.

Primary Synopsis of Universology & Alwato: The New Scientific Universal Language. Stephen P. Andrews. Ed. by Madeleine B. Stern. (C). 1971. 20.00 (*0-87730-007-0*) M & S Pr.

***Primary Target, Vol. 1.** Joe Weber. 384p. 1999. mass mkt. 6.99 (*0-425-17255-4*) Berkley Pub.

Primary Teacher Education: High Status? High Standards? Ed. by Colin Richards. LC 99-160750. 232p. 1998. 85.00 (*0-7507-0846-8*, Falmer Pr) Taylor & Francis.

Primary Teacher's Book of Instant Word Games. Judie L. Strouf. (Illus.). 252p. (C). 1996. pap. text, teacher ed. 27.50 (*0-87628-596-5*); spiral bd. 27.95 (*0-87628-635-X*) P-H.

Primary Teacher's Guide to the New National Curriculum. Ed. by Kate Ashcroft & David Palacio. LC 95-9165. 1995. 85.00 (*0-7507-0467-5*, Falmer Pr); pap. 27.95 (*0-7507-0468-3*, Falmer Pr) Taylor & Francis.

Primary Teacher's Pet. Linda Schwartz. (Teacher Time-Savers Ser.). (Illus.). 192p. (J). (gr. 1-3). 1984. pap. 15.95 (*0-88160-110-1*, LW 131) Learning Wks.

Primary Teaching & the Negotiation of Power. Sylvia Warham. 144p. 1993. pap. 29.00 (*1-85396-228-7*, Pub. by P Chapman) Taylor & Francis.

Primary Teaching Skills. Edward C. Wragg. 208p. (C). 1993. pap. 18.99 (*0-415-08352-4*, B0178) Routledge.

Primary Teaching Skills. Edward C. Wragg. LC 93-15546. 224p. (C). (gr. 13). 1993. 75.00 (*0-415-08351-6*, B0174) Routledge.

Primary Themes Clip Art, Vol. 2344. Barbara Maio & Sue Lewis. (Illus.). 56p. 1998. pap. 18.98 (*1-57471-369-8*) Creat Teach Pr.

Primary 3 see Math Mini-Tests

Primary Treatment at Wastewater Treatment Plants. Glenn M. Tillman. (Operator's Guide Ser.). 100p. 1991. lib. bdg. 75.00 (*0-87371-428-8*, L428) Lewis Pubs.

Primary Triangle. Elizabeth Fivaz-Depeur et al. 224p. 2000. 42.00 (*0-465-09582-8*, Pub. by Basic) HarpC.

Primary Trouble: An Anthology of Contemporary American Poetry. Ed. by Leonard Schwartz et al. 498p. (Orig.). 1996. pap. 24.95 (*1-883689-28-7*); lib. bdg. 45.95 (*1-883689-29-5*) Talisman Hse.

Primary Tumors of the Brain & Spinal Cord. S. Clifford Schold, Jr. et al. LC 96-45076. 181p. 1996. text 55.00 (*0-7506-9060-7*) Buttrwrth-Heinemann.

Primary 2 see Math Mini-Tests

Primary Understanding. Kieran Egan. (Critical Social Thought Ser.). 256p. 1988. text 27.50 (*0-415-90003-4*) Routledge.

***Primary Veterinary Anatomy.** Ranajit Kumar Ghosh. 350p. 1999. pap. (*81-86793-34-8*) Current Bks Intl.

Primary Wreck-Diving Guide. Gary Gentile. LC 94-158241. (Illus.). 160p. 1993. pap. 20.00 (*0-9621453-9-4*) GGP.

Primary Writer's Workshop: Developing Process Writing Skills. Carol Kieczykowski. 80p. (J). (gr. k-2). 1996. 10.99 (*1-56417-863-3*, FE7863) Fearon Teacher Aids.

Primary Writing. D. Huby. LC 97-40295. 166p. 1998. 79.95 (*0-335-19814-7*); pap. 23.95 (*0-335-19813-9*) OpUniv Pr.

Primaryplots: A Book Talk Guide for Use with Readers Ages 4-8. Rebecca L. Thomas. 392p. 1989. 41.00 (*0-8352-2514-3*) Bowker.

Primaryplots 2: A Book Talk Guide for Use with Readers. Rebecca L. Thomas. 431p. (J). (ps-3). 1993. 42.00 (*0-8352-3411-8*) Bowker.

Resident Evil 2: Unauthorized Game Secrets. Ward Kip. LC 96-71682. 160p. 1998. per. 12.99 (*0-7615-1027-3*) Prima Pub.

***Prima's Guide to Seagate Crystal Reports, No. 8.** Bridge Builder Company Staff. 2000. pap. 39.99 (*0-7615-2483-5*) Prima Pub.

Prima's Official Guide to Crystal Reports 7. Karen A. Mayer. LC 98-66121. 456p. 1999. pap. 29.99 (*0-7615-1656-5*) Prima Pub.

***Primasia Guide to the Companies of Hong Kong.** Edinburgh Financial Publishing Staff. (Illus.). 336p. 1999. pap. 45.00 (*962-7982-54-7*, Pub. by EFP Intl) Am Educ Systs.

Primate Adaptation & Evolution. John G. Fleagle. 486p. 1988. text 55.00 (*0-12-260340-0*) Acad Pr.

Primate Adaptation & Evolution. 2nd ed. John G. Fleagle. LC 98-87186. (Illus.). 596p. (C). 1998. text 59.95 (*0-12-260341-9*) Acad Pr.

***Primate Anatomy: An Introduction.** 2nd ed. Friderun Ankel-Simons. LC 99-62861. (Illus.). 510p. 1999. 49.95 (*0-12-058670-3*) Acad Pr.

Primate Atherosclerosis. G. A. Gresham. Ed. by David Kritchevsky et al. (Monographs on Atherosclerosis: Vol. 7). 1976. 42.75 (*3-8055-2270-3*) S Karger.

Primate Behavior. Sarah Lindsay. 112p. 1997. 20.00 (*0-8021-1619-1*, Grove) Grove-Atltic.

Primate Behavior. Sarah Lindsay. 112p. 1998. reprint ed. pap. 11.00 (*0-8021-3557-9*, Grove) Grove-Atltic.

Primate Behavior: An Exercise Workbook. J. D. Paterson. (Illus.). 105p. (C). 1992. pap. text 12.95 (*0-88133-618-1*) Waveland Pr.

Primate Behavior & Social Ecology. (Illus.). 200p. 1984. pap. 27.50 (*0-412-23220-0*, 6894) Chapman & Hall.

Primate Behavioral Ecology. Karen B. Strier. LC 99-38879. 392p. 1999. pap. text 37.00 (*0-205-20019-2*) Allyn.

Primate Behaviour: Information, Social Knowledge, & the Evolution of Culture. Duane Quiatt & Vernon Reynolds. (Studies in Biological Anthropology: No. 12). (Illus.). 330p. (C). 1995. pap. text 26.95 (*0-521-49832-5*) Cambridge U Pr.

Primate Brain. Ed. by C. R. Noback & W. Montagna. LC 73-95612. (Advances in Primatology Ser.: Vol. 1). 334p. reprint ed. pap. 103.60 (*0-608-12430-3*, 205569200030) Bks Demand.

Primate Brain Evolution: Methods & Concepts. Ed. by Este Armstrong & Dean Falk. LC 81-21150. 346p. (C). 1982. 79.50 (*0-306-40914-3*, Plenum Trade) Perseus Pubng.

Primate Cognition. Michael Tomasello & Josep Call. LC 96-41424. (Illus.). 528p. 1997. pap. 35.00 (*0-19-510624-5*); text 70.00 (*0-19-510623-7*) OUP.

Primate Communities. Ed. by J. G. Fleagle et al. LC 98-54414. (Illus.). 352p. (C). 1999. 74.95 (*0-521-62044-9*); pap. 29.95 (*0-521-62967-5*) Cambridge U Pr.

Primate Conservation: The Role of Zoological Parks. Ed. by Janette Wallis. LC 97-72389. (Special Topics in Primatology Ser.). (Illus.). ix, 250p. (Orig.). 1997. pap. 25.00 (*0-9658301-0-1*) Am Soc Primatologists.

***Primate Conservation Biology.** Guy Cowlishaw. 1999. pap. text 27.00 (*0-226-11637-9*); lib. bdg. 70.00 (*0-226-11636-0*) U Ch Pr.

***Primate Diversity.** Dean Falk. LC 99-36427. 2000. per. 44.50 (*0-393-97428-6*) Norton.

***Primate Ecology & Social Structure.** 2nd ed. 218p. (C). 2000. 39.00 (*0-536-60265-4*) Pearson Custom.

***Primate Encounters: Models of Science, Gender & Society.** Shirley C. Strum & Linda Marie Fedigan. LC 99-87519. 2000. pap. write for info. (*0-226-77755-3*) U Ch Pr.

***Primate Encounters: Models of Science, Gender & Society.** Shirley Strum & Linda Marie Fedigan. LC 99-87519. 1999. 35.00 (*0-226-77754-5*) U Ch Pr.

Primate Evolution. Glenn Conroy. (Illus.). 492p. (C). 1990. pap. text 55.75 (*0-393-95649-0*) Norton.

Primate Evolution. Ed. by James G. Else & Phyllis C. Lee. (Selected Proceedings of the Tenth Congress of the International Primatological Society Ser.: No. 1). (Illus.). 340p. 1986. pap. text 38.95 (*0-521-31011-3*) Cambridge U Pr.

Primate Evolution & Human Origins. Ed. by Russell L. Ciochon & John G. Fleagle. (Evolutionary Foundations of Human Behavior Ser.). (Illus.). 406p. 1987. reprint ed. pap. text 36.95 (*0-202-01175-5*) Aldine de Gruyter.

Primate Functional Morphology & Evolution. Ed. by Russell H. Tuttle. (World Anthropology Ser.). (Illus.). xvi, 584p. 1975. 73.10 (*90-279-7689-9*) Mouton.

Primate Laterality: Current Behavioral Evidence of Primate Asymmetrics. Ed. by J. P. Ward & W. D. Hopkins. (Recent Research in Psychology Ser.). (Illus.). xii, 356p. 1993. 72.95 (*0-387-97961-1*) Spr-Verlag.

Primate Laterality: Current Behavioral Evidence of Primate Asymmetrics. Ed. by Jeanette P. Ward & William D. Hopkins. LC 92-484856. (Recent Research in Psychology Ser.). 1993. 68.95 (*0-387-97962-X*) Spr-Verlag.

Primate Locomotion Recent Advances: Proceedings of a Symposium Held in Davis, California, March 27-28, 1995. Ed. by Elizabeth Strasser et al. LC 98-38702. (Illus.). 492p. (C). 1998. text 110.00 (*0-306-46022-X*, Kluwer Plenum) Kluwer Academic.

***Primate Males: Causes & Consequences of Variation in Group Composition.** Ed. by Peter M. Kappeler. (Illus.). 350p. (C). 2000. text 85.00 (*0-521-65119-0*); pap. text 37.95 (*0-521-65846-2*) Cambridge U Pr.

Primate Model for the Study of Colitis & Colonic Carcinoma: The Cotton Top Tamarin (Saguinus Oedipus) Neal K. Clapp. 352p. 1993. lib. bdg. 225.00 (*0-8493-5363-7*, RC862) CRC Pr.

Primate Morphophysiology, Locomotor Analyses & Human Bipedalism. Shireo Kondeo. LC 85-173489. xv, 303 p. 1985. 69.50 (*0-86008-370-5*, Pub. by U of Tokyo) Col U Pr.

Primate Nervous System Pt. II. F. E. Bloom et al. (Handbook of Chemical Neuroanatomy Ser.: Vol. 14). 1998. write for info. (*0-444-82912-1*) Elsevier.

Primate Nervous System Pt. II, Pt. 1. Ed. by F. E. Bloom. LC 97-3750. (Handbook of Chemical Neuroanatomy Ser.: 14). 552p. 1997. 264.50 (*0-444-82558-4*) Elsevier.

***Primate Nervous System, Part III.** Ed. by F. E. Bloom et al. 1999. write for info. (*0-444-50043-X*, Excerpta Medica) Elsevier.

Primate Origins & Evolution: A Phylogenetic Reconstruction. R. D. Martin. (Illus.). 832p. 1990. text 95.00 (*0-691-08565-X*, Pub. by Princeton U Pr) Cal Prin Full Svc.

Primate Ovary. Ed. by Richard L. Stouffer. LC 88-2545. (Serono Symposia U. S. A. Ser.). (Illus.). 288p. 1988. 75.00 (*0-306-42824-5*, Plenum Trade) Perseus Pubng.

Primate Paradigms: Sex Roles & Social Bonds. Linda M. Fedigan. (Illus.). 424p. 1992. pap. text 22.00 (*0-226-23948-9*) U Ch Pr.

Primate Phylogeny. Ed. by E. E. Grine et al. 146p. (Orig.). 1988. pap. text 34.00 (*0-12-303960-6*) Acad Pr.

Primate Politics. Ed. by Roger D. Maaster & Glendon A. Schubertt. LC 90-9611. 224p. (C). 1991. 42.00 (*0-8093-1611-0*) S Ill U Pr.

Primate Politics. Ed. by Roger D. Masters & Glendon A. Schubert. LC 93-45842. 1994. pap. 32.00 (*0-8191-9386-0*) U Pr of Amer.

Primate Postcranial Remains from the Oligocene of Egypt. G. C. Conroy. (Contributions to Primatology Ser.: Vol.8). 140p. 1976. 55.00 (*3-8055-2333-5*) S Karger.

Primate Reader. Russell L. Ciochon & Richard Nisbett. LC 97-26732. 246p. 1997. pap. text 32.80 (*0-13-613845-4*) P-H.

P

An Asterisk (*) at the beginning of an entry indicates that the title is appearing for the first time.

Primate Reproductive Behavior see Primatology: Proceedings of the International Congress of Primatology, 4th, Portland, 1972

Primate Retina & Choroid: Atlas of Its Fine Structure in Man & Monkey. W. Krebs & I. Krebs. (Illus.). 160p. 1991. 91.95 (0-387-97432-6) Spr-Verlag.

Primate Sexuality: Comparative Studies of the Prosimians, Monkeys, Apes, & Human Beings. Alan Dixson. LC 98-18400. (Illus.). 560p. 1999. pap. text 60.00 (0-19-850182-X) OUP.

Primate Social Conflict. Ed. by William A. Mason & Sally P. Mendoza. LC 91-39372. 419p. (C). 1993. pap. text 21.95 (0-7914-1242-3) State U NY Pr.

Primate Social Conflict. Ed. by William A. Mason & Sally P. Mendoza. LC 91-39372. 419p. (C). 1993. text 64.50 (0-7914-1241-5) State U NY Pr.

Primate Societies. Ed. by Richard W. Wrangham et al. LC 86-7091. (Illus.). 580p. (C). 1987. pap. text 34.95 (0-226-76716-7) U Ch Pr.

Primate Societies. Ed. by Richard W. Wrangham et al. LC 86-7091. (Illus.). 608p. (C). 1998. lib. bdg. 70.00 (0-226-76715-9) U Ch Pr.

Primate Societies: Group Techniques of Ecological Adaptations. Hans Kummer. LC 78-140010. (Worlds of Man Ser.). (C). 1971. pap. text 12.95 (0-88295-613-2) Harlan Davidson.

Primate Sociobiology. J. Patrick Gray. LC 85-60629. (Monographs). 376p. (Orig.). 1985. pap. 25.00 (0-87536-344-X) HRAFP.

Primate Visions: Gender, Race & Nature in the World of Modern Science. Donna Jeanne Haraway. (Illus.). 544p. 1989. 35.00 (0-415-90114-6, A3153) Routledge.

Primate Visions: Gender, Race & Nature in the World of Modern Science. Donna Jeanne Haraway. (Illus.). 486p. (gr. 13). 1990. pap. 23.99 (0-415-90294-0) Routledge.

Primates. Dave Beaty. (Nature Books Ser.). (Illus.). 32p. (J). (gr. 2-6). 1992. lib. bdg. 22.79 (0-89565-851-8) Childs World.

Primates. Ed. by Kurt Benirschke. (Illus.). 1120p. 1986. 142.00 (0-387-96270-0) Spr-Verlag.

Primates. Maria A. Julivert. (Fascinating World Of...Ser.). (Illus.). 32p. (J). (gr. 2-6). 1996. lib. bdg. 14.95 (1-56674-201-3) Forest Hse.

Primates: A Higher Intelligence see Secrets of the Animal World New Releases

Primates: An Educational Coloring Book. Spizzirri Publishing Co. Staff. Ed. by Linda Spizzirri. (Illus.). 32p. (J). (gr. 1-8). 1981. pap. 1.99 (0-86545-030-7) Spizzirri.

Primates: From Howler Monkeys to Humans. Erin Pembrey Swan. (Animals in Order Ser.). (Illus.). 48p. (J). (gr. 3-5). 1999. pap. text 6.95 (0-531-15921-3) Watts.

Primates: From Howler Monkeys to Humans. Erin P. Swan. LC 97-29567. (Animals in Order Ser.). (J). 1998. 23.00 (0-531-11487-2) Watts.

Primates: Lemurs, Monkeys & You. Ian Tattersall. LC 94-15072. (Beyond Museum Walls Ser.). (Illus.). 72p. (J). (gr. 4-6). 1995. lib. bdg. 23.90 (1-56294-520-3) Millbrook Pr.

Primates & Their Relatives in Phylogenetic Perspective. R. D. MacPhee. (Advances in Primatology Ser.). (Illus.). 398p. (C). 1993. text 95.00 (0-306-44422-4, Kluwer Plenum) Kluwer Academic.

Primate's Dream: Literature, Race & Ethnicity in America. James W. Tuttleton. LC 98-50376. 320p. 1999. 27.50 (1-56663-234-X, Pub. by I R Dee) Natl Bk Netwk.

Primates in Nature. Alison F. Richard. LC 84-18802. (Illus.). 588p. (C). 1985. pap. text 38.95 (0-7167-1647-X) W H Freeman.

Primates in the Classroom: An Evolutionary Perspective on Children's Education. J. Gary Bernhard. LC 87-19153. 216p. (Orig.). (C). 1988. pap. text 16.95 (0-87023-610-5) U of Mass Pr.

Primates in the Zoo. Roland Smith. LC 91-46968. (New Zoo Ser.). (Illus.). 64p. (J). (gr. 3-6). 1992. lib. bdg. 21.90 (1-56294-210-7, Copper Beech Bks) Millbrook Pr.

Primates of South Asia: Ecology, Sociobiology, & Behavior. Mithan L. Roonwal & S. M. Mohnot. LC 76-28309. (Illus.). 442p. reprint ed. pap. 137.10 (0-7837-4184-7, 205903400012) Bks Demand.

Primates of the Americas: Strategies for Conservation & Sustained Use in Biomedical Research: Proceedings of the First Ordinary Meeting, Regional Primatology Committee for the Americas (CORP-1), Battelle Seattle Conference Center, October 29-31, 1990. Ed. by Primo Arambulo, III et al. LC 93-16987. 336p. 1993. pap. 34.95 (0-935470-73-5) Battelle.

Primates of the World. Rod Preston-Mafham. 192p. 1999. pap. text 19.95 (0-7137-2791-8) Blandford Pr.

Primates of the World. Rod Preston-Mafham & Ken Preston-Mafham. (Of the World Ser.). (Illus.). 192p. 1992. lib. bdg. 29.95 (0-8160-2745-5) Facts on File.

Primates of the World: Distribution, Abundance & Conservation. Jaclyn H. Wolfheim. xiv, 832p. 1983. text 267.00 (3-7186-0190-7) Gordon & Breach.

Primates of the World: Distribution, Abundance & Conservation. Jaclyn H. Wolfheim. LC 82-13464. (Illus.). 854p. 1983. 57.50 (0-295-95899-5) U of Wash Pr.

Primatology: Proceedings of the International Congress of Primatology, 4th, Portland, 1972, 4 vols, Set. Incl. Vol 1. Precultural Primate Behavior. Ed. by E. W. Menzel. 200p. 1973. 100.00 (3-8055-1494-8); Vol 2. Primate Reproductive Behavior. Ed. by C. H. Phoenix. 200p. 1973. 50.50 (3-8055-1495-6); Vol 3. Craniofacial Biology of Primates. Ed. by M. R. Zingesel. 180p. 1973. 100.00 (3-8055-1496-4); Vol. 4. Nonhuman Primates & Human Diseases. Ed. by W. P. McNulty, Jr. 180p. 1973. 59.25 (3-8055-1497-2); 1974. 278.50 (3-8055-1498-0) S Karger.

Primatology: Proceedings of the International Congress, 3rd, Zurich, 1970, 3 vols., Set. Incl. Vol. 1. Taxonomy, Anatomy, Reproduction. Ed. by J. Biegert & W. Leutenegger. (Illus.). xvi, 278p. 1971. 82.75 (3-8055-1244-9); Vol. 2. Neurobiology, Immunology, Cytology. Ed. by J. Biegert & W. Leutenegger. (Illus.). x, 245p. 1971. 78.50 (3-8055-1245-7); Vol. 3. Behavior. Ed. by H. Kummer. (Illus.). x, 191p. 1971. 61.00 (3-8055-1246-5); 1971. 221.75 (3-8055-1247-3) S Karger.

Primatology in China. Ed. by N. G. Jablonski et al. (Journal: Folia Primatologica: Vol. 60, No. 1-2, 1993). (Illus.). 132p. 1993. pap. 87.00 (3-8055-5825-2) S Karger.

Primatology Today: Proceedings of the 13th Congress of the International Primatological Society, Nagoya & Kyoto, Japan, 18-24 July, 1990. Ed. by A. Ehara et al. xxvi, 732p. 1991. text 265.50 (0-444-81177-X, Excerpta Medica) Elsevier.

Primavera. Asun Balzola. (Cuatro Estaciones Ser.). (SPA.). 1986. 12.15 (0-606-02306-2, Pub. by Turtleback) Demco.

***Primavera.** Karen Bryant-Mole. (Picture This! Ser.).Tr. of Spring. (SPA., Illus.). 24p. 1999. lib. bdg. 12.95 (1-57572-910-5) Heinemann Lib.

Primavera. Stevie Davies. pap. 11.95 (0-7043-4299-5, Pub. by Womens Press) Trafalgar.

Primavera. Ron Hirschi. 1999. pap. 14.99 (0-525-65229-9) NAL.

Primavera. J. M. Parramon et al. (Four Seasons Ser.). (SPA., Illus.). 32p. (J). (ps). 1986. pap. 6.95 (0-8120-3648-4) Barron.

Primavera. Lynn M. Stone. (Mientras la Tierra Gira Ser.).Tr. of Spring. 24p. (J). (gr. k-4). 1994. lib. bdg. 17.27 (1-55916-060-8) Rourke Bk Co.

Primavera, Vol. X. Ed. by Lisa Grayson et al. LC 76-674540. (Illus.). 80p. 1986. pap. 5.00 (0-916980-09-X) Primavera.

Primavera, Vol. XI-XII. Ed. by Lisa Grayson et al. LC 76-647540. (Illus.). 108p. 1988. pap. 6.00 (0-685-34868-7) Primavera.

Primavera, Vol. XIII. Ed. by Lisa Grayson et al. LC 76-647540. (Illus.). 76p. 1989. pap. 6.00 (0-685-34869-5) Primavera.

Primavera, Vols. VI & VII. Harriet Susskind et al. Ed. by Janet R. Heller et al. LC 76-647540. (Illus.). 120p. (Orig.). (C). 1981. pap. 5.00 (0-916980-06-5) Primavera.

Primavera: Poems. deluxe ed. David Miller. (Burning Deck Poetry Chapbooks Ser.). 1979. pap. 15.00 (0-930900-63-4) Burning Deck.

Primavera: Spring. Ron Hirschi. (SPA.). 1999. pap. 4.99 (0-14-055787-3) NAL.

Primavera V. Felicia Cotich et al. Ed. by Janet R. Heller et al. LC 76-647540. (Illus.). (C). 1979. pap. 4.00 (0-916980-05-7) Primavera.

Primavera IV. Lisel Mueller et al. Ed. by Janet R. Heller et al. LC 76-647540. (Illus.). (C). 1978. pap. 4.00 (0-916980-04-9) Primavera.

Primavera II. Ed. by Janet R. Heller et al. LC 76-647540. (Illus.). (Orig.). (C). 1976. pap. 4.00 (0-916980-02-2) Primavera.

Primavera of Sandro Botticelli: A Neoplatonic Interpretation. Joanne Snow-Smith. LC 92-216. (New Connections: Studies in Interdisciplinarity: Vol. 5). (Illus.). XX, 297p. (C). 1993. text 40.95 (0-8204-1736-X) P Lang Pubng.

Primavera I: Women Writers & Artists Anthology. Ed. by Janet R. Heller. (Illus.). 90p. (C). 1975. pap. 4.00 (0-916980-00-6) Primavera.

Primavera III. Ed. by Janet R. Heller et al. LC 76-647540. (Illus.). (C). 1977. pap. 4.00 (0-916980-03-0) Primavera.

Prime: International Bonds & Certificates of Deposit. Terence Prime. 380p. 1990. boxed set 160.00 (0-406-11460-9, MICHIE) LEXIS Pub.

Prime: Notes - Genealogical, Biographical & Bibliographical - of the Prime Family. E. D. Prime. 118p. 1992. reprint ed. pap. 19.50 (0-8328-2709-6); reprint ed. lib. bdg. 29.50 (0-8328-2708-8) Higginson Bk Co.

***Prime: Poems from Hollywood.** Mark Dunster. 11p. 1999. pap. 5.00 (0-89642-827-3) Linden Pubs.

Prime: The Autobiography of an Octogenarian, with the Genealogy of His Ancestors & Sketches of Their History. Daniel N. Prime. 293p. 1992. reprint ed. pap. 44.00 (0-8328-2397-X); reprint ed. lib. bdg. 54.00 (0-8328-2396-1) Higginson Bk Co.

Prime Bank Instrument Frauds II: Fraud of the Century. rev. ed. ICC Commercial Crime Bureau Staff. 60p. (C). 1996. pap. 49.95 (92-842-1213-8, 559) ICC Pub.

Prime Bank Instruments Legitimate Investment: Opportunities or Financial Scam of the 90s. 247p. 1995. pap. 45.00 (1-888870-04-4) Inst Intl Bnking.

Prime Candidate. Gordon Cotler. 1996. mass mkt. 5.99 (0-312-96072-7) St Martin.

Prime Cash: First Steps in Treasury Management. 2nd ed. Kuhlmann et al. (C). 1993. pap. text 14.25 (0-07-035220-8) McGraw.

Prime Chaos: Adventures in Chaos Magic. Phil Hine. LC 98-862439. (Illus.). 240p. 1998. pap. 14.95 (1-56184-137-4) New Falcon Pubns.

***Prime Contract Awards by Region & State, Fiscal Years 1997, 1996 & 1995.** 88p. 1998. pap. 7.50 (0-16-061136-9) USGPO.

***Prime Contract Awards by Service Category & Federal Supply Classification, Fiscal Years 1997, 1996, 1995 & 1994.** 85p. 1998. pap. 7.00 (0-16-061131-8) USGPO.

***Prime Contract Awards by State, Fiscal Year 1997.** 45p. 1998. pap. 4.00 (0-16-061130-X) USGPO.

***Prime Contract Awards, Size Distribution, Fiscal Year 1997.** 20p. 1998. pap. 2.25 (0-16-061133-4) USGPO.

Prime Cut. Diane Mott Davidson. LC 98-47822. 1998. 26.95 (1-56895-588-X) Wheeler Pub.

Prime Cut. Diane Mott Davidson. 336p. 2000. reprint ed. mass mkt. 6.50 (0-553-57467-1) Bantam.

Prime Cut: Livestock Raising & Meatpacking in the United States, 1607-1983. Jimmy M. Skaggs. LC 85-40742. (Illus.). 280p. 1986. 29.95 (0-89096-249-9) Tex A&M Univ Pr.

Prime Cut: Livestock Raising & Meatpacking in the United States, 1607-1983. Jimmy M. Skaggs. (Illus.). 263p. 1999. reprint ed. text 28.00 (0-7881-6274-8) DIANE Pub.

***Prime Cuts: Sumptuous, Succulent, Sizeable - The Last Word in Steak.** Sonia Stevenson. (Illus.). 160p. 2000. pap. 24.95 (0-8092-2441-0, 244100, Contemporary Bks) NTC Contemp Pub Co.

Prime Cuts Acoustic Rock Guitar EZ: Easy Tab Deluxe. Ed. by Colgan Bryan. (Prime Cuts Ser.). 128p. (Orig.). 1997. pap. 16.95 (1-57623-905-5, 0026B) Wrner Bros.

Prime Cuts Alternative Rock Gtr. Easy Tab Deluxe. Ed. by Colgan Bryan. (Prime Cuts Ser.). 128p. (Orig.). 1997. pap. 16.95 (1-57623-906-3, 0027B) Wrner Bros.

Prime Cuts Classic Rock Guitar: Easy Tab Deluxe. Colgan Bryan. (Prime Cuts Ser.). 128p. (Orig.). 1997. pap. 16.95 (1-57623-904-7, 0025B) Wrner Bros.

Prime Decision: Your Guide for Success. Bert Warren. LC 92-71210. 215p. (Orig.). 1992. pap. 38.00 (1-880571-00-5) Decision Pt.

***Prime Directive.** Judith Reeves-Stevens. 1999. pap. 12.98 (0-671-04465-6) PB.

Prime Directive. Judith Reeves-Stevens & Garfield Reeves-Stevens. Ed. by Dave Stern. (Star Trek Ser.). 416p. 1991. reprint ed. mass mkt. 5.99 (0-671-74466-6) PB.

Prime Easy Piano Classics. Charles Bateman. 80p. (Orig.). 1996. pap. 11.95 (1-56922-103-0, 07-2039) Creat Cncpts.

***Prime Evil.** Diana G. Gallagher. (Buffy the Vampire Slayer Ser.: Vol. 10). 352p. (YA). (gr. 7-12). 2000. per. 5.99 (0-671-03930-X) PB.

Prime Evil. Nora Roberts. 256p. 1995. mass mkt. 5.99 (0-553-56437-4, Fanfare) Bantam.

Prime Evil. Billene Spellins. LC 97-92444. 252p. 1997. pap. 14.95 (0-9659785-0-8) Picturesque.

Prime Farmland Restoration. Russell Boulding. Ed. by Pamela Mavrolas & Chuck Sheketoff. (Your Rights in the Coalfields Ser.). 1984. pap. 3.00 (0-943724-06-6) Illinois South.

Prime Fitness & Health. Ed. by Neil Feinman. (Illus.). 132p. (Orig.). 1995. pap. 2.95 (0-945797-23-0) Weider Health.

Prime Highway. Richard L. Francis. (Illus.). 123p. (YA). (gr. 7-12). 1997. pap. 10.95 (0-89278-001-0) Carolina Biological.

Prime Ideals in Skew & Q-Skew Polynomial Rings. K. R. Goodearl & E. S. Letzter. LC 94-4145. (Memoirs of the American Mathematical Society Ser.: Vol. 521). 106p. 1994. pap. 32.00 (0-8218-2583-6, MEMO/109/521) Am Math.

Prime Life Guide to Personal Success: A Planning Guide for the 40-Plus Generation. Marion E. Haynes. LC 95-70884. 230p. (Orig.). 1995. pap. 12.95 (1-56052-377-8) Crisp Pubns.

Prime Minister. Anthony Trollope. Ed. by Jennifer Uglow. (Palliser Novels Ser.). (Illus.). 864p. 1991. 21.00 (0-19-520899-4) OUP.

Prime Minister. Anthony Trollope. Ed. & Intro. by David Skilton. LC 96-163835. 736p. 1996. pap. 11.95 (0-14-043349-X, Penguin Classics) Viking Penguin.

Prime Minister. Anthony Trollope. Ed. by Jennifer Uglow. (Oxford World's Classics Ser.). (Illus.). 864p. 2000. reprint ed. pap. 10.95 (0-19-283532-7) OUP.

Prime Minister: (trollope 1991) Skilton. 1991. 45.00 (1-870587-15-4) Ashgate Pub Co.

Prime Minister, Cabinet, & Core Executive. Ed. by R. A. Rhodes & Patrick Dunleavy. LC 94-49141. 1995. text 65.00 (0-312-12616-6) St Martin.

Prime Minister Cabinet Today. Foster. LC 97-18845. (Politics Today Ser.). 1998. 69.95 (0-7190-3950-9) Manchester Univ Pr.

Prime Minister Cabinet Today. Foster. LC 97-18845. 1998. pap. 24.95 (0-7190-3951-7) St Martin.

Prime Minister H. D. Deve Gowda: The Gain & the Pain: A Biographical Study. Attar Chand. (C). 1997. 60.00 (81-212-0558-1, Pub. by Gian Publng Hse) S Asia.

***Prime Minister Nehru to Vajpayee.** S. Thakur. 1998. pap. 163.00 (81-86982-72-8, Pub. by Business Pubns) St Mut.

Prime Minister P. V. Naraimha Rao: The Scholar & the Statesman. (C). 1991. text 30.00 (81-212-0398-8, Pub. by Gian Publng Hse) S Asia.

Prime Ministers: From Walpole to Macmillan. (Illus.). 1994. pap. 13.50 (0-905702-22-0) Intl Spec Bk.

Prime Ministers of Australia. LC 94-151802. 82p. 1994. 17.95 (0-644-29669-0, Pub. by Aust Gov Pub) Accents Pubns.

Prime Ministers of Britain. Charles C. Mersey. LC 74-86772. (Essay Index Reprint Ser.). 1977. 36.95 (0-8369-1422-8) Ayer.

Prime Ministers of Canada. Gordon Donaldson. 352p. 1994. pap. 19.95 (0-385-25454-7) Doubleday.

Prime Mover. Bill Coffin. Ed. by Myrna Kemnitz. (Illus.). 465p. (Orig.). (YA). (gr. 7 up). 1996. pap. 10.00 (0-88092-349-0) Royal Fireworks.

Prime Mover, Opus III: The String Model Universe Where Strings Are Everything. 2nd ed. Rocky McCollum. (Illus.). 500p. 1988. reprint ed. pap. 10.00 (0-317-91063-9) KIVA Pub.

Prime Mover, Opus III: The String Model Universe, Where Strings Are Everything. 3rd ed. Rocky McCollum. (Illus.). 500p. (C). 1988. reprint ed. pap. 10.00 (0-317-91116-3) KIVA Pub.

***Prime Movers: Define Your Business or Have Someone Define It Against You.** Ramirez. 350p. 2000. 34.95 (0-471-89944-5, Wiley Heyden) Wiley.

Prime Movers: Engines, Motors, Turbines, Pumps, Blowers & Generators. Ed. by Water Pollution Control Federation Staff. LC 84-51933. (Manual of Practice Ser.: No. OM-5). (Illus.). 181p. (Orig.). (C). 1984. pap. text 50.00 (0-943244-56-0, MOM5) Water Environ.

Prime Movers: Role of the Individual in History. Madhu Limaye. xii, 448p. 1986. text 45.00 (81-7027-087-1, Pub. by Radiant Pubs) S Asia.

Prime Movers: The Makers of Modern Dance in America. 2nd ed. Joseph H. Mazo. (Illus.). 384p. 1999. pap. 21.95 (0-87127-211-3) Princeton Bk Co.

***Prime Movers: Traits of the Great Wealth Creators.** Edwin A. Locke. LC 99-89272. 228p. 2000. 27.95 (0-8144-0570-3) AMACOM.

Prime Movers Vol. IV, Module III, Vol. I. Multimedia Development Services Staff. (Plant Fundamentals Ser.). (Illus.). (Orig.). 1995. teacher ed. 49.95 (1-57431-054-2); student ed. 30.00 (1-57431-014-3) Tech Trng Systs.

Prime Number: Seventeen Stories from Illinois Short Fiction. Ed. by Ann L. Weir. LC 88-10076. 352p. 1988. 12.95 (0-252-06032-6); text 24.95 (0-252-01572-X) U of Ill Pr.

Prime Numbers & Computer Methods for Factorization. Hans Riesel. (Progress in Mathematics Ser.: No. 57). 1987. 62.50 (0-8176-3291-3) Birkhauser.

Prime Numbers & Computer Methods for Factorization. 2nd ed. Hans Riesel. LC 94-27688. xvi, 464p. 1994. 69.50 (0-8176-3743-5) Birkhauser.

***Prime Numbers & Their Distribution.** Gerald Tenenbaum & Michel Mendaes France. LC 00-20740. 2000. pap. write for info. (0-8218-1647-0) Am Math.

Prime of Life. Simone de Beauvoir. (Illus.). 479p. 1994. pap. 14.95 (1-56924-956-3) Marlowe & Co.

Prime of Miss Jean Brodie. Muriel Spark. 1998. 31.95 (1-56849-698-2) Buccaneer Bks.

Prime of Miss Jean Brodie. Muriel Spark. 2000. write for info. (0-06-099587-4) HarpC.

Prime of Miss Jean Brodie: Perennial Classics Edition. Muriel Spark. LC 98-51439. 160p. 1999. pap. 13.00 (0-06-093173-6) HarpC.

Prime of Yiddish. David Passow. LC 96-1786. 128 1p. 1995. 16.95 (965-229-152-8, Pub. by Gefen Pub Hse) Gefen Bks.

Prime of Your Life. Joe Michaels et al. LC 80-21205. 366p. reprint ed. pap. 113.50 (0-608-12288-2, 202515900042) Bks Demand.

Prime of Your Life: A Guide for Fifty & Beyond. Woodrow Michael Kroll & Don Hawkins. LC 99-20767. 263p. 1999. pap. 11.99 (0-8007-5704-1) Revell.

Prime Period Lengths. Samuel Yates. 525p. 1975. pap. 10.00 (0-9608652-1-7) S Yates.

Prime Rib & Apple. Jill Briscoe. 1976. pap. 6.95 (0-310-21811-X, 9257P) Zondervan.

Prime Rib or Potted Meat? Thoughts on Getting More Out of Life. W. Jones Loflin. 239p. 1998. pap. 12.95 (0-9662361-0-6) HOPE Inc.

Prime Sources of California & Nevada Local History: 151 Rare & Important City, County & State Directories, 1850-1906. Richard Quebedeaux. LC 91-74139. (Illus.). 238p. 1992. 65.00 (0-87062-213-7) A H Clark.

Prime Suspect. Maggie Price. 1997. per. 3.99 (0-373-07816-1, 1-07816-1) Silhouette.

Prime Target. Don Pendleton. (Executioner Ser.: No. 201). 1995. per. 3.50 (0-373-64201-6) Harlequin Bks.

Prime Target: Security Measures for the Executive at Home & Abroad. Bruce L. Danto. LC 90-33084. 256p. 1990. pap. 20.95 (0-914783-39-4); text 34.95 (0-914783-38-6) Charles.

Prime Targets. Donald S. Vogel. Ed. by Peggy Goad & Billie Anastasi. (Adventure Cases of Joe & Heather Ser.: No. 4). 280p. 1996. write for info. (1-879154-11-0) Vlly Hse Gllry.

***Prime Time.** Catherine Anderson. 1998. pap. 18.15 (1-57232-621-2) Seymour Pubns.

Prime Time. Joan Collins. 1989. mass mkt. 5.99 (0-671-67962-7) PB.

Prime Time. Barbara Cummings & Jo-Ann Power. 384p. 1992. mass mkt. 4.99 (1-55817-667-5, Pinncle Kensgtn) Kensgtn Pub Corp.

Prime Time. Douglas Dean. Ed. by Harry Bernstein. 360p. (Orig.). 1988. pap. 5.95 (0-939477-02-5) Micro Pro Litera Pr.

Prime Time. Sandra Brown. 240p. 1995. reprint ed. mass mkt. 6.99 (0-446-36429-0, Pub. by Warner Bks) Little.

Prime Time: A Comprehensive Drug Education Program, Level I, Grs. k-3. Dianne Schilling et al. (Illus.). 215p. 1991. ring bd. 95.00 (0-9625486-5-0, IP4865) Innerchoice Pub.

Prime Time: A Comprehensive Drug Education Program, Level II. Dianne Schilling et al. (Illus.). 250p. 1991. ring bd. 95.00 (0-9625486-6-9, IP4866) Innerchoice Pub.

Prime Time: A Comprehensive Drug Education Program, Level III. Dianne Schilling et al. (Illus.). 200p. 1991. ring bd. 95.00 (0-9625486-7-7, IP4867) Innerchoice Pub.

Prime Time: A Comprehensive Drug Education Program, Level IV. Dianne Schilling et al. (Illus.). 250p. 1991. ring bd. 95.00 (0-9625486-8-5) Innerchoice Pub.

Prime Time: A Daily Guide to Spending Time with God. David B. Earley. Ed. by Cindy G. Spear. 111p. 1996. ring bd. 21.95 (1-57052-063-1) Chrch Grwth VA.

Prime Time: Factors & Multiples. Glenda Lappan et al. Ed. by Catherine Anderson & Stacey Miceli. (Connected Mathematics Ser.). (Illus.). (Orig.). 1995. student ed. 5.95 (1-57232-146-6, DS21441) Seymour Pubns.

An Asterisk (*) at the beginning of an entry indicates that the title is appearing for the first time.

Prime Time: Factors & Multiples. Glenda Lappan et al. Ed. by Catherine Anderson et al. (Connected Mathematics Ser.). (Illus.). (Orig.). 1995. teacher ed. 16.50 (*1-57232-147-4*, DS21442) Seymour Pubns.

Prime Time: Factors & Multiples. rev. ed. Glenda Lappan et al. Ed. by Catherine Anderson et al. (Connected Mathematics Ser.). (Illus.). 70p. (Orig.). (YA). (gr. 6 up). 1997. pap. text, student ed. 5.95 (*1-57232-620-4*, 45815) Seymour Pubns.

Prime Time: How Baby-Boomers Will Revolutionize Retirement & Transform America. Photos by Alex Harris & Thomas Roma. LC 99-26333. (Illus.). 304p. 2000. 25.00 (*1-891620-17-7*, Pub. by PublicAffairs NY) HarpC.

Prime Time: How TV Portrays American Culture. S. Robert Lichter et al. 336p. 1993. 22.95 (*0-89526-491-9*) Regnery Pub.

Prime Time: The Lobels' Guide to Great Grilled Meats. Leon Lobel et al. (Illus.). 224p. 1999. 25.00 (*0-02-862333-9*, Pub. by Macmillan) S&S Trade.

Prime Time: The Middle Aged in Twentieth-Century Britain. John Benson. LC 97-20597. 1997. text. write for info. (*0-582-25658-5*, Pub. by Addison-Wesley) Longman.

Prime Time: The Middle Aged in Twentieth-Century Britain. John Benson. LC 97-20597. (C). 1998. pap. text 20.63 (*0-582-25657-7*, Pub. by Addison-Wesley) Longman.

Prime Time: Three Hundred Sixty-Five Devotions for Seniors. H. Robert Cowles. LC 91-73585. 366p. 1991. kivar 10.99 (*0-87509-468-6*) Chr Pubns.

Prime Time Activism: Media Strategies for Grassroots Organizing. Charlotte Ryan. 295p. 1991. 30.00 (*0-89608-402-7*) South End Pr.

Prime Time Aerobics. Leslie Johnson & Charlene Schade. Orig. Title: Rhythmic Aerobex. (Illus.). 98p. 1985. 17.95 incl. audio (*0-9610234-0-6*) Exer Fun.

Prime Time & Misdemeanors: Investigating the 1950s TV Quiz Scandal - A D.A.'s Account. Joseph Stone & Tim Yohn. LC 91-19782. (Illus.). 370p. 1992. 35.00 (*0-8135-1753-2*) Rutgers U Pr.

Prime Time & Misdemeanors: Investigating the 1950's T.V. Quiz Scandal - A D.A.'s Account. Joseph Stone & Tim Yohn. (Illus.). 350p. (C). 1994. reprint ed. pap. 14.95 (*0-8135-2100-9*) Rutgers U Pr.

Prime Time Computing: A Seniors Guide to Home Computing. Mark Mathosian. (Illus.). 164p. 1993. lib. bdg. 14.95 (*0-9631924-1-8*) Inkwell Pubs.

Prime-Time Crime. Franklin W. Dixon. Ed. by Anne Greenberg. (Hardy Boys Mystery Stories Ser.: No. 109). 160p. (Orig.). (J). (gr. 4-7). 1991. pap. 3.99 (*0-671-69278-X*, Minstrel Bks) PB.

Prime Time Crime. William Gleason. 87p. 1977. pap. 5.50 (*0-87129-983-6*) Dramatic Pub.

Prime Time English. Michael A. Rost. (YA). 1994. pap. text, teacher ed. 18.95 (*0-582-09224-8*) Longman.

Prime Time English, Vol. 1. Michael Rost. 1998. pap. text. write for info. (*0-201-49138-9*) Addison-Wesley.

Prime Time English, Vol. 2. Michael Rost. 1998. pap. text. write for info. (*0-201-49139-7*) Addison-Wesley.

Prime Time English, Vol. 3. Michael Rost. 1998. pap. text, student ed. write for info. (*0-201-49140-0*) Addison-Wesley.

Prime Time English, Vol. 4. Michael Rost. 1998. pap. text, student ed. write for info. (*0-201-49141-9*) Addison-Wesley.

Prime Time English Workbook. Michael Rost. 1996. pap. text, wbk. ed. 7.35 (*0-582-25974-6*, Pub. by Addison-Wesley) Longman.

Prime-Time Families: Television Culture in Post-War America. Ella Taylor. (Illus.). 208p. 1991. pap. 15.95 (*0-520-07418-1*, Pub. by U CA Pr) Cal Prin Full Svc.

Prime-Time Feminism: Television, Media Culture, & the Women's Movement since 1970. Bonnie J. Dow. (Feminist Cultural Studies, the Media, & Political Culture). 272p. 1996. pap. text 17.50 (*0-8122-1554-0*) U of Pa Pr.

Prime-Time Feminism: Television, Media Culture, & the Women's Movement Since 1970. Bonnie J. Dow. (Feminist Cultural Studies, the Media, & Political Culture). 296p. 1996. text 39.95 (*0-8122-3315-8*) U of Pa Pr.

Prime Time Freeware for UNIX, Issue 4-1. Ed. by Rich Morin. (Orig.). (C). 1997. pap. 60.00 (*1-881957-03-9*) PT Freeware.

Prime-Time Hits: Television's Most Popular Network Programs. Susan Sackett. (Illus.). 368p. 1993. pap. 19.95 (*0-8230-8392-6*, Billboard Bks) Watsn-Guptill.

Prime Time Law: Fictional Television As Legal Narrative. Ed. by Robert M. Jarvis & Paul R. Joseph. LC 98-85333. 336p. 1998. 32.50 (*0-89089-805-7*); pap. 17.50 (*0-89089-808-1*) Carolina Acad Pr.

Prime Time Law Enforcement: Crime Show Viewing & Attitudes Toward the Criminal Justice System. James M. Carlson. LC 85-9420. 238p. 1985. 38.95 (*0-275-90070-3*, C0070, Praeger Pubs) Greenwood.

Prime Time Life Skills. Jerry Aten. (Illus.). 64p. (J). (gr. 2-5). 1983. student ed. 8.99 (*0-86653-126-2*, GA 487) Good Apple.

Prime Time Maps. Jerry Aten. (Illus.). 64p. (J). (gr. 2-5). 1983. student ed. 8.99 (*0-86653-108-4*, GA 470) Good Apple.

Prime Time Math Skills. Jerry Aten. (Illus.). 64p. (J). (gr. 2-5). 1984. student ed. 7.99 (*0-86653-155-6*, GA 524) Good Apple.

Prime Time Network Serials: Episode Guides, Casts & Credits for 37 Continuing Television Dramas, 1964-1993. Bruce B. Morris. LC 96-31166. (Illus.). 847p. 1997. lib. bdg. 95.00 (*0-7864-0164-8*) McFarland & Co.

Prime Time Pitcher, 59. Matt Christopher. (Matt Christopher Sports Classics Ser.). 1998. 9.05 (*0-606-13722-X*, Pub. by Turtleback) Demco.

Prime Time Pitcher: Can Koby Handle the Spotlight? Matt Christopher. LC 97-46394. 160p. (J). (gr. 3-7). 1998. 15.95 (*0-316-14215-8*) Little.

Prime Time Pitcher: Can Koby Handle the Spotlight? Matt Christopher. LC 97-46394. (Illus.). 160p. (J). (gr. 3-7). 1998. pap. 3.95 (*0-316-14213-1*) Little.

Prime-Time Preaching: Planning Services on Sensitive Subjects. Eldon Weisheit. LC 97-7487. 1997. 12.99 (*0-570-04977-6*, 12-3327) Concordia.

Prime Time, Prime Movers: From I Love Lucy to L. A. Law--America's Greatest TV Shows & the People Who Created Them. David Marc & Robert J. Thompson. (Television Ser.). (Illus.). 350p. 1995. pap. 17.95 (*0-8156-0311-8*) Syracuse U Pr.

Prime Time, Prime Movers: The Inside Story of the Inside People Who Made American Television. David Marc & Robert J. Thompson. (Illus.). 304p. 1992. 22.95 (*0-316-54589-9*) Little.

Prime-Time Principles for Success. Dale E. Galloway. Orig. Title: Confidence Without Conceit. 187p. 1984. pap. 8.95 (*1-885605-04-8*) Scott-Twnty-Twnty.

Prime Time Reading Skills. Jerry Aten. (Illus.). 64p. (J). (gr. 2-5). 1984. student ed. 8.99 (*0-86653-185-8*, GA 525) Good Apple.

Prime-Time Religion: An Encyclopedia of Religious Broadcasting. Ed. by Phillip Lucas et al. LC 96-39495. (Illus.). 432p. 1997. boxed set 64.95 (*0-89774-902-2*) Oryx Pr.

Prime-Time Society: An Anthropological Analysis of Television & Culture. Conrad P. Kottak. 247p. (C). 1989. 20.00 (*0-534-12498-4*) Wadsworth Pub.

Prime-Time Style: The Ultimate T. V. Guide to Fashions Hits & Misses. Valerie Frankel & Ellen Tien. LC 96-36378. (Illus.). 176p. 1996. pap. 12.00 (*0-399-52261-1*, Perigee Bks) Berkley Pub.

Prime-Time Television: Content & Control. 2nd ed. Muriel B. Cantor & Joel M. Cantor. (CommText Ser.: Vol. 3). 160p. (C). 1991. text 42.00 (*0-8039-3169-7*); pap. text 18.95 (*0-8039-3170-0*) Sage.

Prime-Time Television: Content & Control. 2nd ed. Muriel G. Canto & Joel M. Cantor. LC 91-30889. (Sage Commtext Ser.: No. 3). 143p. 1992. reprint ed. pap. 44.40 (*0-608-04303-6*, 206508200012) Bks Demand.

Prime Time Together . . . with Kids. Donna Erickson. LC 89-6956. (Illus.). 128p. (Orig.). 1989. kivar 14.99 (*0-8066-2430-2*, 9-2430) Augsburg Fortress.

Prime Times. Madolyn Jamieson. LC 94-78041. (Illus.). 136p. (Orig.). 1994. pap. write for info. (*0-9642741-0-8*) M Jamieson.

Prime Times: A Handbook for Excellence in Infant & Toddler Programs. Jim Greenman & Anne Stonehouse. LC 96-28321. 229p. (Orig.). 1996. pap. 29.95 (*1-884834-15-9*, 1229) Redleaf Pr.

Prime Witness. Steve Martini. 416p. 1994. mass mkt. 7.99 (*0-515-11264-X*, Jove) Berkley Pub.

Prime Witness. large type ed. Steve Martini. LC 93-34152. 590p. 1993. 23.95 (*0-8161-5869-X*, G K Hall Lrg Type) Mac Lib Ref.

Primer see McGuffey's Revised Eclectic Readers

Primer. Peter Cook. LC 98-116516. 1p. 1995. pap. 30.00 (*1-85490-388-8*, Pub. by Wiley) Wiley.

Primer. Mark Dunster. 10p. (Orig.). (YA). (gr. 9-12). 1996. pap. 5.00 (*0-89642-320-4*) Linden Pubs.

Primer. John Martone. 56p. (Orig.). 1994. pap. 5.00 (*1-57141-008-2*) Runaway Spoon.

Primer: A Tool for Developing Early Reading Materials. David Weber et al. LC 94-65077. (Occassional Publications in Academic Computing: No. 18). 280p. (Orig.). 1994. pap. 26.00 (*0-88312-678-8*) S I L Intl.

Primer: Preservation for the Property Owner. Ed. by Diana S. Waite & Frederick D. Cawley. (Illus.). 35p. (Orig.). 1978. pap. 3.00 (*0-942000-01-3*) Pres League NYS.

Primer: The Art of Native American Beadwork. Z. Susanne Aikman. (Illus.). 64p. 1980. reprint ed. pap. 6.95 (*0-9629155-0-5*) Morning Flower.

Primer Ano de la Vida del Nino (The First Year of Life) Rene Spitz. (SPA.). 294p. 1969. pap. 12.99 (*968-16-0181-5*, Pub. by Fondo) Continental Bk.

Primer Ano de Vida del Nino. Alina Vinas. 1999. 19.95 (*84-08-00164-7*) Planeta Edit.

Primer Conference on Environmental Science: UCLA, 20-22 August 1991. Ed. by A. Y. Wong. 400p. 1997. text 109.00 (*981-02-0972-X*) World Scientific Pub.

Primer Dia de Escuela. Kim Jackson. (J). 1996. pap. 3.95 (*0-8167-3064-4*) Troll Communs.

Primer Drug Action. 8th ed. Julien. 2000. pap. 24.00 (*0-7167-3365-X*) W H Freeman.

Primer for American History. David M. Laushey. LC 95-77375. (Illus.). 240p. (Orig.). (C). 1995. pap. text 24.00 (*0-15-502081-1*, Pub. by Harcourt Coll Pubs) Harcourt.

Primer for Angry Christians. Steve Clapp & Sue I. Mauck. (Illus.). 138p. (Orig.). 1981. pap. 6.00 (*0-914527-09-6*) C-Four Res.

Primer for Beginning Psychotherapy. William N. Goldstein. LC 97-25327. (Basic Principles into Practice Ser.). 101p. 1997. pap. write for info. (*0-87630-859-0*) Brunner-Mazel.

Primer for Beginning Rural Housing Developers. Housing Assistance Council Staff. 32p. 1995. 5.00 (*1-58064-033-8*) Housing Assist.

Primer for Blacks. Gwendolyn Brooks. 16p. 1991. 4.00 (*0-88378-056-9*) Third World.

Primer for Board of Review Members. 4th ed. Charles Press. LC 87-620000. 65p. 1987. 5.00 (*0-941872-53-X*) MSU Dept Res Dev.

Primer for Buford. Wilma E. McDaniel. 1990. 15.00 (*0-914610-88-0*); pap. 9.00 (*0-914610-87-2*) Hanging Loose.

Primer for Calculus. Leonard I. Holder. (Math). 1978. student ed. 8.75 (*0-534-00590-X*) Brooks-Cole.

Primer For Calculus. 3rd ed. Leonard I. Holder. (Math). 630p. (C). 1984. mass mkt. 32.00 (*0-534-02692-3*) PWS Pubs.

Primer For Calculus. 4th ed. Leonard I. Holder. (Math). 565p. (C). 1986. mass mkt. 38.75 (*0-534-06750-6*) PWS Pubs.

Primer For Calculus. 5th ed. Leonard I. Holder. (Math). 570p. (C). 1989. mass mkt. 47.50 (*0-534-11760-0*) PWS Pubs.

Primer for Calculus. 6th ed. Leonard I. Holder. (C). 1992. mass mkt. 59.75 (*0-534-17748-4*) PWS Pubs.

Primer for Child Psychotherapists. Diana Siskind. LC RJ504.S543 1999. 9216p. 1999. 40.00 (*0-7657-0233-9*) Aronson.

Primer for Choreographers. Lois Ellfeldt. (Illus.). 113p. (C). 1988. reprint ed. pap. text 13.95 (*0-88133-350-6*) Waveland Pr.

Primer for Clients (Humor) Elton Dunbar. 1972. pap. 2.00 (*0-911214-47-X*) Rational Isl.

Primer for Corporate America on Civil Rights for the Disabled. Patricia A. Morrissey. LC 91-25397. 139p. (Orig.). 1991. pap. 12.95 (*0-934753-49-0*) LRP Pubns.

Primer for Critics. George Boas. LC 68-55100. (Illus.). 153p. 1968. reprint ed. lib. bdg. 55.00 (*0-8371-0318-5*, BOPC, Greenwood Pr) Greenwood.

Primer for Daily Life. Susan Willis. (Studies in Culture & Communication). (Illus.). 224p. (C). (gr. 13). 1991. 75.00 (*0-415-04180-5*, A5340) Routledge.

Primer for Dance, Bk. I. Ann H. Guest. (Illus.). 24p. (J). (ps). 1958. pap. text 6.95 (*0-932582-64-8*) Dance Notation.

Primer for Dance, Bk. II. Ann H. Guest. (Illus.). 32p. (J). (ps). 1957. pap. text 6.95 (*0-932582-65-6*) Dance Notation.

***Primer for Disaster Recovery Planning in an IT Environment.** Ed. by Charlotte Hiatt. LC 99-50147. (Illus.). 250p. (C). 2000. pap. 64.95 (*1-878289-81-0*) Idea Group Pub.

Primer for Diversity in Middle & Secondary School Classrooms. Joan Rasool. LC 99-56808. (Education). 2000. pap. 52.95 (*0-534-50847-2*) Wadsworth Pub.

Primer for Environmental Literacy. Frank B. Golley. LC 97-34440. (Environmental Studies). (Illus.). 272p. 1998. 37.50 (*0-300-07315-1*); pap. 18.00 (*0-300-07049-7*) Yale U Pr.

Primer for Finite Elements in Elastic Structures. W. F. Carroll. LC 98-13435. (Illus.). 512p. 1998. 85.00 (*0-471-28345-2*) Wiley.

Primer for Graphic Arts Profitability: A Money-Making Formula. Gary W. Millet & Ralph G. Rosenberg. 96p. (Orig.). 1992. pap. 14.95 (*1-881637-04-2*) Millet Grp.

***Primer for Health Care Ethics.** 2nd ed. Ed. by Kevin D. O'Rourke. LC 00-25273. 240p. 2000. pap. text 21.95 (*0-87840-802-9*) Georgetown U Pr.

Primer for Health Care Ethics: Essays for a Pluralistic Society. Patrick Norris et al. LC 94-11005. 255p. 1994. pap. 19.95 (*0-87840-562-3*) Georgetown U Pr.

Primer for Health Care, Health Education & All Disciplines Amidst Change. Ed. by Joseph S. DiPietro. LC 99-21013. (Studies in Health & Human Services: Vol. 33). 156p. 1999. 69.95 (*0-7734-7958-9*) E Mellen.

***Primer for Heart Disease: For Patients & Their Families.** Joe R. Wise. LC 00-102173. (Illus.). 112p. 2000. pap. 9.95 (*1-890437-28-X*) Western Reflections.

Primer for Homeokinetics: A Physical Foundation for Complex Systems. Arthur S. Iberall & Harry Soodak. 1998. pap. 9.00 (*0-9638799-1-X*) Cri-de-Coeur.

Primer for Impairment Evaluations. Gabriel E. Sella. 397p. (C). 1995. pap. text 120.00 (*1-884325-10-6*) G E Sella.

Primer for Local Historical Societies. 2nd expanded rev. ed. Dorothy W. Creigh. LC 91-14071. (American Association for State & Local History Book Ser.). (Illus.). 132p. 1991. reprint ed. pap. 19.95 (*0-942063-12-0*) AltaMira Pr.

Primer for Local Officials & Citizens: Local Land Use Law & Practice in New York. John R. Nolon. 80p. 1998. pap. 16.95 (*0-9668221-2-9*) Pace Univ Land Use.

Primer for Modern Mathematics. Bernard W. Banks. 144p. (C). 1993. text 23.13 (*0-697-21494-X*, WCB McGr Hill) McGrw-H Hghr Educ.

Primer for Movement Description Using Effort/Shape. 2nd ev. ed. Cecily Dell. LC 78-111086. 123p. 1970. pap. text 17.95 (*0-932582-03-6*) Dance Notation.

Primer for Natal Chart. Katie Holiday. 118p. 1980. 15.00 (*0-86690-114-0*, H1188-014) Am Fed Astrologers.

Primer for New Corporate Lawyers: What Business Lawyers Do. Clifford R. Ennico. 1990. pap. 39.95 (*0-87632-731-5*) West Group.

Primer for Novice Investors. C. H. Winecoff. (Illus.). 20p. 1996. write for info. (*0-9655789-0-9*) Airycott Pr.

Primer for PHIGS: C Programmers' Edition. Frank R. Hopgood et al. LC 92-14806. (Wiley Professional Computing Ser.). (Illus.). 312p. 1992. reprint ed. pap. 96.80 (*0-608-05283-3*, 206582100001) Bks Demand.

Primer for Policy Analysis. Edith Stokey & Richard Zeckhauser. (Illus.). (C). 1978. pap. 31.25 (*0-393-09098-1*) Norton.

Primer for Positive Parenting see Present to the Newborn

Primer for Prevention. Paul Terry et al. 1991. student ed. write for info. (*1-884153-05-4*) Prk Nicollet.

Primer for Psychiatric Nurses. Ed. by Ed Lister & A. Silva. 159p. (Orig.). (C). 1990. pap. text 24.95 (*0-9627287-9-9*) Cnslts Psych Nursing.

Primer for Research on the Freshman Year Experience. Dorothy S. Fidler. 25p. (Orig.). 1992. pap. 10.00 (*1-889271-19-5*) Nat Res Ctr.

Primer for Soft Modeling. R. Frank Falk & Nancy B. Miller. LC 92-14749. (Illus.). 99p. (Orig.). (C). 1992. pap. text 13.99 (*0-9622628-4-6*) U Akron Pr.

Primer for Stuttering Therapy. Howard D. Schwartz. LC 98-23833. 226p. (C). 1998. pap. text 76.00 (*0-205-27556-7*) Allyn.

Primer for Teachers & Leaders see Pedagogia Ilustrada: Principios Generales

Primer for the Beginning Teacher. Francis A. Filardo. 136p. 1998. pap. 14.99 (*0-7392-0026-7*, PO2911) Morris Pubng.

Primer for the Catechism of the Catholic Church. 2nd ed. John-Peter Pham. 112p. Date not set. reprint ed. pap. 4.95 (*1-890177-01-6*) Midwest Theol.

Primer for the Catholic Choir Member. Lawrence J. Johnson. 56p. 1996. pap. 1.95 (*1-56929-064-4*, Pastoral Press) OR Catholic.

Primer for the Monte Carlo Method. Ilya Sobol. LC 93-50716. 128p. 1994. per. 73.95 (*0-8493-8673-X*) CRC Pr.

Primer for the Nuclear Age. Ed. by Graham T. Allison et al. (Occasional Papers: No. 6). 152p. (C). 1990. pap. text 21.00 (*0-8191-7701-6*); lib. bdg. 40.00 (*0-8191-7700-8*) U Pr of Amer.

Primer for Those Who Would Govern. Hermann Oberth. 320p. 1986. pap. 20.00 (*0-914301-06-3*) West-Art.

Primer for Today's Substance Abuse Counselors. Rostyslaw Roback. 152p. 1991. 23.95 (*0-669-26935-2*) Lxngtn Bks.

Primer for Treating Substance Abusers. Jerome D. Levin. LC 98-6397. 1998. 30.00 (*0-7657-0078-6*) Aronson.

Primer for University Presidents: Managing the Modern University. Peter T. Flawn. 224p. 1990. 24.95 (*0-292-76522-3*) U of Tex Pr.

Primer for Using Video in the Classroom. (Sense Making in Science Ser.). 42p. 1996. pap. text 5.00 (*0-435-07130-0*, 07130) Heinemann.

Primer for Working with Child Abuse & Neglect. Vernon R. Wiehe. (Interpersonal Violence: the Practice Ser.: Vol. 15). 208p. 1996. 48.00 (*0-7619-0348-8*); pap. 21.50 (*0-7619-0349-6*) Sage.

Primer for Writing Teachers: Theories, Theorists, Issues, Problems. 2nd ed. David Foster. LC 92-7941. 252p. (Orig.). (C). 1992. pap. text 27.50 (*0-86709-302-1*, 0302, Pub. by Boynton Cook Pubs) Heinemann.

Primer Garcia Marquez: Un Estudio de Su Periodismo de 1948-1955. Robert L. Sims. 220p. 1991. 48.00 (*0-916379-84-1*) Scripta.

Primer Halloween de Clifford. Norman Bridwell. Tr. by Teresa Mlawer from ENG. (Clifford, the Big Red Dog Ser.).Tr. of Clifford's First Halloween. (SPA.). 32p. (J). (gr. k-2). 1995. pap. 2.50 (*0-590-50928-4*) Scholastic Inc.

Primer Halloween de Clifford. Norman Bridwell. (Clifford, the Big Red Dog Ser.).Tr. of Clifford's First Halloween. (SPA.). (J). (gr. k-2). 1995. 7.70 (*0-606-07475-9*, Pub. by Turtleback) Demco.

Primer in Data Reduction: An Introductory Statistics Textbook. A. S. Ehrenberg. 324p. 1982. reprint ed. pap. 89.95 (*0-471-10135-4*) Wiley.

Primer in Ethics. 2nd ed. James F. Smurl. LC 85-51229. 65p. (C). 1989. text 32.00 (*1-55605-077-1*); text 28.00 (*0-932269-44-3*) Wyndham Hall.

Primer in Eu Macroeconomics. Manfred Gartner. 300p. 1997. pap. text 35.00 (*0-13-268897-2*) P-H.

Primer in Fluid Mechanics. William B. Brower, Jr. LC 98-34265. 1998. 69.95 (*0-8493-9368-X*, HE9368) CRC Pr.

Primer in Organizational Behavior: With Lewicki Experience in Management of Organizational Behavior. 3rd ed. James L. Bowditch & Roy J. Lewicki. 912p. 1993. text 39.50 (*0-471-04296-X*) Wiley.

Primer in Particle Physics, Alpha, Beta, Gamma...Z. L. B. Okun. xii, 114p. 1987. text 52.00 (*3-7186-0374-8*); pap. text 24.00 (*3-7186-0405-1*) Gordon & Breach.

Primer in Petri Net Design. W. Reisig. Ed. by S. S. Muchnick & Peter Schnupp. (Compass International Ser.). (Illus.). xiv, 120p. 1992. 51.95 (*0-387-52044-9*) Spr-Verlag.

Primer in Phenomenological Psychology. Ernest Keen. LC 81-40901. (Illus.). 192p. 1982. reprint ed. pap. text 16.50 (*0-8191-2262-9*) U Pr of Amer.

Primer in Political Economy. Larry P. Arnn. (Occasional Paper of the Study of Statesmanship & Political Philosophy: No. 1). 18p. (C). 1982. pap. text 2.00 (*0-930783-07-7*) Claremont Inst.

Primer in Preventive Cardiology. T. A. Pearson et al. (Illus.). 290p. (C). 1994. pap. write for info. (*0-87493-006-5*) Am Heart.

Primer in Private Security. Mahesh Nalla & Graeme Newman. LC 89-26994. (Special Edge Supplementary Text Ser.). 170p. 1990. pap. text 22.50 (*0-911577-18-1*, Criminal Justice) Willow Tree NY.

Primer in Probability. 2nd rev. ed. Kathleen Subrahmaniam. LC 96-108. (Statistics: Textbooks & Monographs: Vol. 111). (Illus.). 336p. 1990. text 65.00 (*0-8247-8348-4*) Dekker.

Primer in Radical Criminology: Special Edge Supplementary Texts. 2nd rev. ed. Michael J. Lynch & W. Byron Groves. LC 89-24402. 150p. 1989. pap. text 19.90 (*0-911577-15-7*, Criminal Justice) Willow Tree NY.

Primer in Sociology of Law. 2nd rev. ed. Dragan Milovanovic. LC 94-26536. (Illus.). 214p. (C). 1994. pap. text 27.50 (*0-911577-27-0*, Criminal Justice) Willow Tree NY.

Primer in Soviet Government. Larry P. Arnn et al. (Claremont Paper: No. 10). 58p. (Orig.). 1987. pap. text 3.00 (*0-317-61646-3*) Claremont Inst.

Primer in the Politics of Criminal Justice. Nancy E. Marion. 120p. (C). 1995. pap. text 21.50 (*0-911577-32-7*, Criminal Justice) Willow Tree NY.

An Asterisk (*) at the beginning of an entry indicates that the title is appearing for the first time.

Primer in the Psychology of Crime. S. Glora Shoham & Mark Seis. LC 93-37012. 200p. (C). 1993. pap. 19.90 (*0-911577-17-3*, Criminal Justice) Willow Tree NY.

Primer in the Sociology of Crime. S. Giora Shoham & John Hoffman. LC 91-14531. (Special Edge Supplementary Text Ser.). 200p. (C). 1991. pap. text 19.90 (*0-911577-19-X*, Criminal Justice) Willow Tree NY.

Primer in Theory Construction. Paul D. Reynolds. 194p. (Orig.). (C). 1971. pap. text 34.00 (*0-02-399600-5*, Macmillan Coll) P-H.

***Primer Libro de la Misa.** (SPA.). 96p. 1999. pap. 4.95 (*0-89942-823-1*, 809-S/67W) Catholic Bk Pub.

***Primer Libro de la Misa (First Mass Book)** (SPA.). 96p. (J). (gr. 2-6). 1999. pap. 4.95 (*0-89942-825-8*, 809-S/67B) Catholic Bk Pub.

Primer Mechanism Organic. Peter Sykes. LC 95-5706. (C). 1995. pap. text 26.50 (*0-582-26644-0*, Pub. by Addison-Wesley) Longman.

Primer of Abstract Mathematics. Robert M. Ash. LC 98-85593. (Classroom Resource Materials Ser.). 191p. 1998. pap. text 27.95 (*0-88385-708-1*) Math Assn.

Primer of Adlerian Psychology: The Analytic-Behavioral-Cognitive Psychology of Alfred Adler. Harold H. Mosak & Michael P. Maniacci. LC 99-25738. 1999. 27.95 (*1-58391-003-4*) Brunner-Mazel.

Primer of Algebraic D-Modules. S. C. Coutinho. (London Mathematical Society Student Texts Ser.: No. 33). 219p. (C). 1995. text 69.95 (*0-521-55119-6*); pap. text 25.95 (*0-521-55908-1*) Cambridge U Pr.

Primer of Applied Radiation Physics. F A Smith. 1999. pap. text 46.00 (*981-02-3713-8*) World Scientific Pub.

Primer of Applied Regression & Analysis of Variance. Stanton A. Glantz & Brian K. Slinker. 320p. 1990. text 69.00 (*0-07-023407-8*) McGraw-Hill HPD.

***Primer of Applied Regression & Analysis of Variance.** 2nd ed. Stanton A. Glantz & Bryan K. Slinker. LC 00-27760. 2000. write for info. (*0-07-136086-7*) McGraw-Hill HPD.

Primer of Behavioral Pharmacology. Peter L. Carlton. LC 83-9083. (Illus.). 301p. (C). 1983. pap. text 17.60 (*0-7167-1451-5*) W H Freeman.

Primer of Biblical Greek. N. Clayton Cros. LC 99-34385. 256p. 1999. pap. 18.00 (*0-8028-4628-9*) Eerdmans.

Primer of Biomechanics. George L. Lucas et al. LC 97-48865. 240p. 1998. pap. 45.00 (*0-387-98456-9*) Spr-Verlag.

Primer of Biostatistics. 3rd ed. Stanton A. Glantz. (Illus.). 416p. 1992. text 29.00 (*0-07-023511-2*); pap. text 68.00 incl. disk (*0-07-864124-1*); pap. text 68.00 incl. mac hd (*0-07-864126-8*); disk 57.00 (*0-07-864120-9*); mac hd 57.00 (*0-07-864115-2*) McGraw-Hill HPD.

Primer of Biostatistics. 4th ed. Stanton A. Glantz. LC 96-26907. (Illus.). 416p. 1996. text 32.00 (*0-07-024268-2*) McGraw-Hill HPD.

Primer of Biostatistics: The Program, Incl. MAC Software. 4th ed. Stanton A. Glantz. (Illus.). 416p. 1997. pap. text 69.00 (*0-07-864184-5*) McGraw-Hill HPD.

Primer of Biostatistics: The Program, Incl. Windows Software. 4th ed. Stanton A. Glantz. (Illus.). 416p. 1996. pap. text 69.00 incl. disk (*0-07-864182-9*) McGraw-Hill HPD.

Primer of Biostatistics: The Program, Macintosh Software. Stanton A. Glantz. 1997. disk 59.00 (*0-07-864216-7*) McGraw-Hill HPD.

Primer of Biostatistics: The Program, Windows Software. 4th ed. Stanton A. Glantz. 1996. disk 59.00 (*0-07-864219-1*) McGraw-Hill HPD.

Primer of Brain Tumors. 7th ed. American Brain Tumors Association Staff. (Illus.). 132p. 1998. pap. write for info. (*0-944093-52-3*) Am Brain Tumor.

Primer of Brief Psychotherapy. John F. Cooper. 160p. (C). 1995. 23.00 (*0-393-70189-1*) Norton.

Primer of Cardiac Diagnosis: The Physical & Technical Study of the Cardiac Patient. Aldo A. Luisada & Gurmukh S. Sainani. LC 68-20943. (Illus.). 262p. 1968. 12.75 (*0-87527-049-2*) Green.

Primer of Cardiology. 4th ed. George E. Burch. LC 78-135690. 366p. reprint ed. pap. 104.40 (*0-608-17756-3*, 2056503); reprint ed. pap. 113.50 (*0-608-09979-1*, 201452800090) Bks Demand.

Primer of Chemical Pathology. 408p. 1997. 22.00 (*981-02-2571-7*); 22.00 (*981-02-2585-7*) World Scientific Pub.

Primer of Chemical Pathology. E. S. Koay & R. N. Walmsley. 360p. 1997. text 48.00 (*981-02-2449-4*, QBcQm-UTB2921) World Scientific Pub.

Primer of Chess. Jose Capablanca. 160p. 1995. pap. 15.95 (*1-85744-165-6*, Pub. by Cadgn Bks) Macmillan.

Primer of Chess. Jose R. Capablanca. LC 35-3374. (Illus.). 288p. 1977. pap. 12.00 (*0-15-673900-3*, Harvest Bks) Harcourt.

Primer of Child Psychology. 2nd ed. Paul L. Adams. 1982. 19.00 (*0-316-03726-5*, Little Brwn Med Div) Lppncott W & W.

***Primer of Christianity: For Pew Sitters & Other People.** Sally Campbell. LC 99-95092. 150p. 1999. pap. 10.00 (*0-9673650-0-7*) Springs.

Primer of Christianity & Ethics. Douglas Young. Ed. by Constance Hunting. 200p. (Orig.). (YA). (gr. 9-12). 1985. pap. 12.95 (*0-913006-34-3*) Puckerbrush.

Primer of Clinical Intersubjectivity. Joseph M. Natterson & Raymond J. Friedman. LC 94-43799. 184p. 1995. pap. 35.00 (*1-56821-446-4*) Aronson.

Primer of Clinical Radiology. 2nd ed. Thomas T. Thompson. 1980. 19.95 (*0-316-84184-6*, Little Brwn Med Div) Lppncott W & W.

Primer of Conservation Biology. Richard B. Primack. LC 95-13972. (Illus.). 246p. (C). 1995. pap. text 31.95 (*0-87893-730-7*) Sinauer Assocs.

***Primer of Conservation Biology.** 2nd ed. Richard B. Primack. LC 00-29693. 2000. pap. write for info. (*0-87893-732-3*) Sinauer Assocs.

Primer of Cooking & Housekeeping. Elizabeth Cooper. (Illus.). 192p. 1979. 10.95 (*0-89496-023-7*); pap. 9.95 (*0-89496-015-6*) Ross Bks.

Primer of Dermatopathology. 2nd ed. Antoinette F. Hood. 496p. 1993. pap. text 97.00 (*0-316-37233-1*) Lppncott W & W.

***Primer of Developmental Psychology.** Gertrude Blanck. 2000. 40.00 (*0-7657-0286-X*) Aronson.

Primer of Diagnostic Imaging. 2nd ed. Jack Wittenberg & H. Weissleder. (Illus.). 992p. (C). (gr. 13). 1996. pap. text 89.95 (*0-8151-9478-1*, 29192) Mosby Inc.

Primer of Diffusion Problems. Richard Ghez. LC 87-37284. 264p. 1988. pap. 99.95 (*0-471-84692-9*) Wiley.

Primer of Discrete Mathematics. Daniel T. Finkbeiner & Wendell D. Lindstrom. LC 86-18349. (Mathematics Ser.). (Illus.). 363p. (C). 1986. text 29.60 (*0-7167-1815-4*) W H Freeman.

Primer of Drug Action. 6th ed. Robert Julien. (C). 1991. text 21.60 (*0-7167-2260-7*) W H Freeman.

Primer of Drug Action. 6th ed. Robert M. Julien. (C). 1991. pap. text 15.20 (*0-7167-2261-5*) W H Freeman.

Primer of Drug Action. 8th ed. Julien. 1997. student ed. 5.00 (*0-7167-3138-X*) W H Freeman.

Primer of Ecclesiastical Latin. John F. Collins. LC 84-22957. 451p. (C). 1985. pap. 17.95 (*0-8132-0667-7*) Cath U Pr.

Primer of Ecological Theory. Jonathan Roughgarden. LC 97-5917. 456p. 1997. pap. text 58.00 (*0-13-442062-4*) P-H.

Primer of Ecology. 2nd ed. Nicholas J. Gotelli. LC 98-3508. (Illus.). (C). 1998. pap. 27.95 (*0-87893-274-7*) Sinauer Assocs.

Primer of Educational Policy Research & Analysis. Yeakey. (C). 1995. pap. text. write for info. (*0-8013-0299-4*) Addison-Wesley.

Primer of Educational Policy Research & Analysis. Yeakey. (C). 1994. write for info. (*0-8013-0298-6*) Longman.

Primer of Educational Research. W. Newton Suter. 317p. 1997. pap. text 49.00 (*0-205-27014-X*) P-H.

Primer of Epidemiology. 4th ed. Gary D. Friedman. LC 93-47357. 336p. 1994. pap. text 27.00 (*0-07-022454-4*) McGraw-Hill HPD.

Primer of Ethics see Ethics: An Early American Handbook

Primer of Exemplary Strategies, Basics: Bridging Vocational & Academic Skills - The Bridger's Guide. National Center for Research in Vocational Educati. 1987. 11.95 (*0-317-03906-7*, SP300AB) Ctr Educ Trng Employ.

Primer of Experimental Psychology. Werner. (C). 1992. text 21.00 (*0-07-069547-4*) McGraw.

***Primer of Freudian Psychology.** Calvin S. Hall. LC 98-34780. 144p. 1999. pap. 13.95 (*0-452-01183-3*, Plume) Dutton Plume.

Primer of Freudian Psychology: Twenty-Fifth Anniversary Edition. Calvin S. Hall. 1955. mass mkt. 6.99 (*0-451-62625-7*, ME2253, Ment) NAL.

Primer of Genetic Analysis: A Problems Approach. 2nd ed. James N. Thompson et al. (Illus.). 284p. (C). 1996. text 64.95 (*0-521-47312-8*) Cambridge U Pr.

Primer of Genetic Analysis: A Problems Approach. 2nd ed. James N. Thompson, Jr. et al. (Illus.). 287p. (C). 1996. pap. text 24.95 (*0-521-47891-X*) Cambridge U Pr.

Primer of Greek Grammar. Evelyn Abbott & E. D. Mansfield. 1990. reprint ed. pap. text 14.95 (*0-89341-626-6*, Longwood Academic) Hollowbrook.

Primer of Greek Grammar: Accidence & Syntax. Evelyn Abbott & Edwin D. Mansfield. 230p. (C). 1977. reprint ed. pap. text 20.95 (*0-7156-1258-1*, Pub. by G Duckworth) Focus Pub-R Pullins.

Primer of Greenhouse Effect Gases. Donald L. Wuebbles & Jae Edmonds. (Illus.). 320p. 1991. lib. bdg. 89.95 (*0-87371-222-6*, L222) Lewis Pubs.

Primer of Group Psychotherapy. Ray Naar. LC 81-4244. 215p. 1982. 35.95 (*0-89885-027-4*, Kluwer Acad Hman Sci); pap. 22.95 (*0-89885-289-7*, Kluwer Acad Hman Sci) Kluwer Academic.

Primer of Gynecologic Oncology. Robert C. Wallach. LC 93-80457. (Illus.). 175p. 1995. pap. 11.95 (*1-880906-11-2*) Prthnon Pub.

Primer of Happenings & Time Space Art. Al Hansen. LC 65-26157. (Illus.). 1965. 45.00 (*0-89366-057-4*) Ultramarine Pub.

Primer of Higher Space (1939) Claude Bragdon. 84p. 1998. reprint ed. pap. 12.95 (*0-7661-0468-0*) Kessinger Pub.

Primer of Hinduism. D. S. Sarma. 1987. pap. 2.95 (*81-7120-444-9*, Pub. by Ramakrishna Math) Vedanta Pr.

Primer of Human Behavioral Pharmacology. Alan D. Poling. (Applied Clinical Psychology Ser.). (Illus.). 262p. (C). 1986. 65.00 (*0-306-42186-0*, Plenum Trade) Perseus Pubng.

Primer of Immunology. Lyndon E. Mansfield. 1991. 25.00 (*0-07-039919-0*) McGraw.

Primer of Infinitesimal Analysis. J. L. Bell. LC 97-41877. (Illus.). 136p. (C). 1998. text 29.95 (*0-521-62401-0*) Cambridge U Pr.

Primer of Intraoperative Neurophysiologic Monitoring. Garfield B. Russell & Lawrence D. Rodichok. LC 95-12875. 331p. 1995. text 69.95 (*0-7506-9553-6*) Buttrwrth-Heinemann.

Primer of Invertebrate Learning: The Behavioral Perspective. Charles I. Abramson. LC 94-4300. 273p. 1994. pap. 19.95 (*1-55798-228-7*) Am Psychol.

Primer of Irish Metrics. Kuno Meyer. LC 78-72640. (Celtic Language & Literature Ser.: Goidelic & Brythonic). 88p. 1984. reprint ed. 27.50 (*0-404-17569-4*) AMS Pr.

Primer of Islam, Vol. 1. Abdur-Rahman Shad. (J). 1992. pap. 4.50 (*1-56744-192-0*) Kazi Pubns.

Primer of Italian Fascism. Ed. by Jeffrey T. Schnapp. Tr. by Olivia Sears et al. LC 99-32168. 416p. 1999. pap. 25.00 (*0-8032-9268-6*); text 60.00 (*0-8032-4279-4*) U of Nebr Pr.

Primer of Jungian Psychology. Calvin S. Hall. LC 98-34779. 144p. 1999. pap. 13.95 (*0-452-01186-8*, Plume) Dutton Plume.

Primer of Jungian Psychology. Calvin S. Hall & Vernon J. Nordby. 144p. 1973. mass mkt. 6.99 (*0-451-62578-1*, ME2233, Ment) NAL.

Primer of Kleinian Therapy. Irving Solomon. LC 94-36578. 240p. 1995. pap. text 45.00 (*1-56821-391-3*) Aronson.

Primer of Labor Relations. 25th ed. Linda G. Kahn. 220p. 1994. trans. 45.00 (*0-87179-806-9*) BNA Books.

Primer of Lebesgue Integration. Ed. by Herbert S. Bear. LC 94-42043. (Illus.). 163p. 1995. text 21.00 (*0-12-083970-9*) Acad Pr.

Primer of Libertarian Education. Joel Spring. 1998. pap. 17.99 (*1-55164-116-X*, Pub. by Black Rose) Consort Bk Sales.

Primer of Libertarian Education. Joel Spring. 157p. 1998. 46.99 (*1-55164-117-8*, Pub. by Black Rose) Consort Bk Sales.

Primer of Libertarian Education. Joel H. Spring. 157p. 1975. 38.99 (*0-919618-62-6*, Pub. by Black Rose) Consort Bk Sales.

Primer of LISREL. B. M. Byrne. (Illus.). 225p. 1989. 72.95 (*0-387-96972-1*) Spr-Verlag.

Primer of Magnetic Resonance Imaging. J. W. Hennel et al. LC 99-158922. 100p. 1997. pap. text 18.00 (*1-86094-060-9*) World Scientific Pub.

Primer of Malayalam Literature. T. K. Menon. (C). 1990. text 15.00 (*81-206-0603-5*, Pub. by Asian Educ Servs) S Asia.

Primer of Mathematical Writing: Being a Disquisition on Having Your Ideas Recorded, Typeset, Published, Read & Appreciated. Steven George Krantz. LC 96-45732. 223p. 1996. pap. 19.00 (*0-8218-0635-1*, PMW) Am Math.

Primer of Medical RadioBiology. 2nd ed. E. L. Travis. 320p. (gr. 13). 1989. pap. text 41.95 (*0-8151-8837-4*, 20123) Mosby Inc.

Primer of Medieval Latin: An Anthology of Prose & Poetry. Charles H. Beeson. LC 86-8301. 390p. (C). 1986. reprint ed. pap. 14.95 (*0-8132-0635-9*) Cath U Pr.

Primer of Misbehavior: An Introduction to Abnormal Psychology. George R. Wesley. (Quality Paperback Ser.: No. 262). 203p. 1975. reprint ed. pap. 3.95 (*0-8226-0262-8*) Littlefield.

Primer of Modern Analysis. 2nd ed. K. T. Smith. (Undergraduate Texts in Mathematics Ser.). 512p. 1997. 54.95 (*0-387-90797-1*) Spr-Verlag.

Primer of Modern Standard Hindi. Michael C. Shapiro. (C). 1989. 23.00 (*81-208-0475-9*, Pub. by Motilal Bnarsidass) S Asia.

Primer of Modern Virtue Ethics. Steven M. Duncan. 124p. (Orig.). (C). 1995. pap. text 17.50 (*0-8191-9875-7*) U Pr of Amer.

Primer of Navigation. Ed. by George W. Mixter & Herrold Headley. 632p. 1995. 35.00 (*0-393-03508-5*) Norton.

Primer of Newspaper Chinese. rev. ed. Yu-Ju Chih. 1982. 14.95 (*0-88710-056-2*) Yale Far Eastern Pubns.

Primer of Newspaper Chinese. rev. ed. Yu-Ju Chih. 1982. audio 8.95 (*0-88710-057-0*) Yale Far Eastern Pubns.

Primer of Noninvasive Vascular Technology. Terrence D. Case. LC 94-21978. 336p. 1994. pap. text 49.00 (*0-316-13035-4*) Lppncott W & W.

Primer of Nonlinear Analysis. Antonio Ambrosetti & Giovanni Prodi. (Studies in Advanced Mathematics: No. 34). (Illus.). 179p. (C). 1995. pap. text 25.95 (*0-521-48573-8*) Cambridge U Pr.

Primer of North American Indian Pottery & Restoration Terms. (Illus.). 24p. (Orig.). 1997. pap. 8.00 (*0-9660406-0-0*) Darrel Wilson.

Primer of Nursing Research. Mary R. Castles. (Illus.). 208p. 1987. pap. text 29.00 (*0-7216-1713-1*, W B Saunders Co) Harcrt Hlth Sci Grp.

Primer of Nursing Research. Mary R. Castles. 1987. pap. text, teacher ed. write for info. (*0-03-013054-9*) SCP.

Primer of Nursing Research. Divina Grossman. (C). 1999. pap. text. write for info. (*0-8053-3240-5*) Benjamin-Cummings.

Primer of Offshore Operations. 3rd ed. Ron Baker. Ed. by Kathy Bork. Tr. by Jonell Clardy. (Illus.). 132p. 1997. pap. text 35.00 (*0-88698-178-6*, 1.10030) PETEX.

Primer of Oil & Gas Measurement. S. T. Horton. Ed. by Kathy Bork. (Illus.). 184p. 1993. pap. text 30.00 (*0-88698-160-3*, 8.20010) PETEX.

Primer of Oil & Gas Measurement Workbook. S. T. Horton. (Illus.). 62p. 1994. ring bd., wbk. ed. 20.00 (*0-88698-173-5*, 8.20016) PETEX.

Primer of Oilwell Drilling. 5th rev. ed. Ron Baker. Ed. by Kathy Bork. LC 92-46408. (Illus.). 151p. 1996. pap. text 25.00 (*0-88698-159-X*, 2.00050) PETEX.

Primer of Oilwell Drilling Workbook. Ron Baker. (Illus.). 60p. 1994. ring bd., wbk. ed. 20.00 (*0-88698-174-3*, 2.00056) PETEX.

Primer of Oilwell Service, Workover, & Completion. Kate Van Dyke. Ed. by Kathryn Roberts. LC 96-9918. Orig. Title: A Primer of Oilwell Service & Workover. (Illus.). 172p. (Orig.). 1996. pap. text 25.00 (*0-88698-175-1*, 3.60110) PETEX.

Primer of Orthopaedic Biomechanics. George V. Cochran. LC 81-38485. (Illus.). 429p. reprint ed. pap. 133.00 (*0-8357-6411-7*, 203577200096) Bks Demand.

Primer of Palliative Care. Porter Storey. 57p. (Orig.). 1994. pap. 4.95 (*1-889296-00-7*) Am Acad Hospice.

Primer of Palliative Care. 2nd ed. Porter Storey. 57p. (Orig.). 1996. pap. text. write for info. (*1-889296-11-2*) Am Acad Hospice.

Primer of Pancreatitis. P. G. Lankisch et al. LC 97-28507. (Illus.). vi, 68p. pap. write for info. (*3-540-63259-X*) Spr-Verlag.

Primer of Pelvicology, Pt. 1. F. H. Barclay. 31p. 1985. reprint ed. spiral bd. 10.00 (*0-7873-1154-5*) Hlth Research.

Primer of Peripheral Vascular Diseases. Travis Winsor & Chester Hyman. LC 65-24808. 348p. reprint ed. pap. 107.90 (*0-608-14009-0*, 205544800022) Bks Demand.

Primer of Playwriting. 2nd ed. Kenneth Macgowen. LC 80-39768. 199p. 1981. reprint ed. lib. bdg. 67.50 (*0-313-22896-5*, MACP, Greenwood Pr) Greenwood.

Primer of Population Biology. Edward O. Wilson & William H. Bossert. LC 73-155365. (Illus.). 192p. (Orig.). (C). 1971. pap. text 19.95 (*0-87893-926-1*) Sinauer Assocs.

Primer of Population Dynamics. Krishnan Namboodiri. (Plenum Series on Demographic Methods & Population Analysis). (Illus.). 349p. (C). 1996. text 59.00 (*0-306-45338-X*, Kluwer Plenum) Kluwer Academic.

***Primer of Population Genetics.** 3rd rev. ed. Daniel L. Hartl. LC 99-45796. (Illus.). 200p. (C). 1999. pap. text 29.95 (*0-87893-304-2*) Sinauer Assocs.

Primer of Practical Logic see Practical Logic

Primer of Prayer. Bartholomew J. O'Brien. Ed. by Faith Publishing Company Staff. LC 91-71541. 124p. 1991. pap. 4.50 (*0-9625975-8-9*) Queenship Pub.

Primer of Prayer Gesture. Kay Irwin. 43p. 1977. pap. 3.00 (*0-941500-21-7*) Sharing Co.

Primer of Probability Logic. Adams. LC 97-20385. (Lecture Notes Ser.: No. 68). 450p. (C). 1998. 70.00 (*1-57586-067-8*); pap. 24.95 (*1-57586-066-X*) CSLI.

Primer of Projective Techniques of Psychological Assessment. Ed. by James C. Crumbaugh. LC 87-92178. 1989. 20.00 (*0-87212-215-8*) Libra.

Primer of Psychotherapy. Robert J. Langs. LC 86-22869. 256p. (C), 1993. reprint ed. pap. text 29.50 (*0-89876-197-2*) Gardner Pr.

***Primer of Public Personnel Administration: Human Resource Development.** Syoum Gebregziabher. LC 00-20801. 2000. pap. write for info. (*0-86543-856-0*) Africa World.

Primer of Quantum Chemistry. Frank C. Goodrich. LC 80-11938. 244p. 1982. reprint ed. lib. bdg. 24.00 (*0-89874-149-1*) Krieger.

Primer of Quantum Mechanics. rev. ed. Marvin Chester. LC 91-44779. 328p. (C). 1992. reprint ed. 54.50 (*0-89464-701-6*) Krieger.

Primer of Real Analytic Functions. Steven George Krantz & Harold R. Parks. LC 92-19718. (Basler Lehrbucher: Vol. 4). x, 184p. 1992. 49.50 (*3-7643-2768-5*, Pub. by Birkhauser); 58.50 (*0-8176-2768-5*) Birkhauser.

Primer of Real Functions. 4th rev. ed. Ralph P. Boas, Jr. LC 96-77785. (Carus Mathematical Monograph: No. 13). 314p. (C). 1996. text 43.95 (*0-88385-029-X*, CAM-13R) Math Assn.

Primer of Reliability Theory. Doris L. Grosh. 232p. 1989. pap. text, teacher ed. 6.25 (*0-471-62024-6*) Wiley.

Primer of Roman Law. W. H. Kelke. LC 93-79702. 170p. 1994. reprint ed. 55.00 (*1-56169-060-0*) Gaunt.

Primer of Rotational Physics. Myrna M. Milani & Brian R. Smith. LC 84-13518. (Rational Physics Ser.). (Illus.). (Orig.). 1985. 15.00 (*0-943290-02-3*); pap. 10.00 (*0-943290-01-5*) Fainshaw Pr.

Primer of Sectional Anatomy with MRI & CT Correlation. 2nd ed. Charles P. Barrett et al. (Illus.). 160p. 1994. pap. 25.00 (*0-683-00472-7*) Lppncott W & W.

Primer of Sidereal Astrology. Fagan & Firebrace. 171p. 1992. 10.00 (*0-86690-389-5*) Am Fed Astrologers.

Primer of Soto Zen: A Translation of Dogen's Shobogenzo Zuimonki. Tr. by Reiho Masumaga from JPN. LC 76-126044. 128p. (C). 1975. pap. text 8.00 (*0-8248-0357-4*) EW Ctr HI.

Primer of Stagecraft. Henning Nelms. 1941. pap. 5.95 (*0-8222-0914-4*) Dramatists Play.

Primer of Structured Program Design. Gary L. Richardson et al. 1980. pap. 15.00 (*0-89433-110-8*) Petrocelli.

Primer of Supportive Psychotherapy. Henry Pinsker. LC 97-41400. 312p. 1997. 49.95 (*0-88163-274-0*) Analytic Pr.

Primer of Tennyson. W. MacNelle Dixon. LC 70-130255. (Studies in Tennyson: No. 27). 1971. reprint ed. lib. bdg. 75.00 (*0-8383-1147-4*) M S G Haskell Hse.

Primer of the Helicopter War. Charles Holley & Mike Sloniker. LC 98-135301. (Illus.). 212p. 1997. 24.99 (*0-944372-11-2*) Nissi Pubns.

Primer of the North American Fur Trade. James A. Crutchfield. 1986. 9.50 (*0-913150-52-5*) Pioneer Pr.

Primer of the Novel: For Readers & Writers. David Madden. LC 79-21881. 466p. 1980. lib. bdg. 29.00 (*0-8108-1265-7*) Scarecrow.

Primer of the Sanskrit Language. A. F. Stenzler. Tr. by Renate Sohnen. (C). 1995. reprint ed. 22.00 (*0-7286-0193-1*, Pub. by Sch Orient & African Stud) S Asia.

Primer of Towing. 2nd rev. ed. George H. Reid. LC 92-13816. (Illus.). 256p. 1992. pap. text 17.00 (*0-87033-430-1*) Cornell Maritime.

Primer of Vectorcardiography. Travis Winsor. LC 76-146035. (Illus.). 319p. reprint ed. 98.90 (*0-8357-9415-6*, 201458800092) Bks Demand.

Primer of Veterinary Anatomic. Dunstan. 1993. write for info. (*0-397-51102-7*) Lppncott W & W.

Primer of Visual Literacy. Donis A. Dondis. (Illus.). 206p. 1973. pap. text 13.50 (*0-262-54029-0*) MIT Pr.

Primer of Water, Electrolyte & Acid-Base Syndromes. 7th ed. Emanuel Goldberger. LC 85-19909. 426p. reprint ed. pap. 132.10 (*0-7837-2709-7*, 204308800006) Bks Demand.

P

An Asterisk (*) at the beginning of an entry indicates that the title is appearing for the first time.

Primer of Water, Electrolyte, & Acid-Base Syndromes. 8th ed. Jeffrey M. Brensilver & Emanuel Goldberger. LC 95-11650. (Illus.). 416p. (C). 1996. pap. text 32.50 (*0-8036-0054-2*) OUP.

Primer of Wordsworth. Laurie Magnus. LC 72-3170. (Studies in Wordsworth: No. 29). 1972. reprint ed. lib. bdg. 75.00 (*0-8383-1519-4*) M S G Haskell Hse.

Primer on Adlerian Psychology: Behavior Management Techniques for Children at Home & in School. Alex L. Chew. Ed. by Nancy Brand. (Illus.). 1997. pap. 16.95 (*0-89334-271-8*, Humanics Pub); lib. bdg. 26.95 (*0-89334-272-6*) Humanics Ltd.

Primer on American Labor Law. 3rd ed. William B. Gould, IV. (Illus.). 357p. 1993. pap. text 21.00 (*0-262-57099-8*) MIT Pr.

Primer on Amputations & Artificial Limbs. George Murdoch & A. Bennett Wilson, Jr. LC 97-22982. (Illus.). 314p. 1997. text 63.95 (*0-398-06800-3*); pap. text 49.95 (*0-398-06801-1*) C C Thomas.

Primer on Business Finance. Ed. by Frank De Felice. LC 73-20489. 1974. 37.75 (*0-8422-5132-4*) Irvington.

Primer on Cerebrovascular Diseases. Ed. by K. M. Welch et al. LC 96-49201. (Illus.). 823p. 1997. text 159.00 (*0-12-743170-5*); pap. text 87.00 (*0-12-743171-3*) Morgan Kaufmann.

Primer on Composite Materials Analysis. 2nd rev. ed. John C. Halpin. LC 91-66928. 200p. 1992. pap. text 49.95 (*0-87762-754-1*) Technomic.

Primer on Computer System Interoperability. William A. Linton, Jr. (Orig.). pap. 19.95 (*0-939547-00-7*) SMC.

Primer on Connective Tissue Biochemistry. Maxwell Schubert & David Hamerman. LC 68-25209. 330p. reprint ed. pap. 102.30 (*0-608-14007-4*, 205544300022) Bks Demand.

Primer on Corticosteroid-Induced Osteoporosis. Jonathan D. Adachi & George Ioannidis. 54p. pap. text 29.95 (*0-7817-2443-0*) Lppncott W & W.

Primer on Crime & Delinquency. Robert M. Bohm. LC 96-21953. (Contemporary Issues in Crime & Justice Ser.). 180p. 1996. 32.95 (*0-534-50711-5*) Wadsworth Pub.

***Primer on Death & Dying for Medical Students.** rev. ed. Richard M. Blacher et al. 60p. 2000. reprint ed. 8.95 (*0-930194-91-8*) Ctr Thanatology.

Primer on Decision Making: How Decisions Happen. James G. March. LC 94-4414. 1994. 35.00 (*0-02-920035-0*) Free Pr.

Primer on Determinism. John Earman. 292p. 1986. lib. bdg. 126.00 (*90-277-2240-4*, D Reidel) Kluwer Academic.

Primer on Determinism. John Earman. 287p. 1986. pap. text 39.00 (*90-277-2241-2*, D Reidel) Kluwer Academic.

Primer on Dispensationalism. John H. Gerstner. 1982. pap. 2.99 (*0-87552-273-4*) P & R Pubng.

Primer on Divine Revelation: Scripture & Tradition. Dwight P. Campbell. 78p. 1998. pap. 4.95 (*1-890177-06-7*) Midwest Theol.

Primer on Environmental Policy Design. R. W. Hahn. Ed. by Jacques Lesourne & H. Sonenschein. (Fundamentals of Pure & Applied Economics Ser.: Vol. 34). xii, 140p. 1989. pap. text 102.00 (*3-7186-4897-0*) Gordon & Breach.

Primer on Equal Employment Opportunity. 6th ed. Nancy Sedmak & Chrissie Vidas. LC 94-20546. 220p. 1994. pap. text 45.00 (*0-87179-842-5*) BNA Books.

Primer on ERISA. 4th ed. Barbara J. Coleman. LC 92-35173. 214p. 1993. text 45.00 (*0-87179-781-X*, 0781) BNA Books.

Primer on ERISA Fiduciary Duties. Dana J. Domone. LC 94-23864. 350p. 1994. trans. 45.00 (*0-87179-809-3*) BNA Books.

***Primer on Ethics.** Freeman. LC 99-41890. (Counseling). 1999. pap. 30.95 (*0-534-36638-4*) Brooks-Cole.

Primer on Ethics. Tibor R. Machan. LC 96-6502. 1997. 19.95 (*0-8061-2946-8*) U of Okla Pr.

Primer on EXSYS for DOS. Luvai Montiwalla. LC 94-145. 128p. (C). 1995. per. 25.95 (*0-256-16336-7*, Irwn Prfssnl) McGraw-Hill Prof.

Primer on Fiber Optic Sensors. 1996. 45.00 (*0-614-18481-9*, 135P01) Info Gatekeepers.

Primer on FLSA & Other Wage & Hour Laws. 3rd ed. Joseph E. Kalet. LC 90-18155. 270p. 1994. pap. text 45.00 (*0-87179-833-6*) BNA Books.

Primer on Foreign Exchange. Jon G. Taylor & F. John Mathis. LC 85-10561. (Illus.). 112p. (Orig.). 1985. pap. text 31.00 (*0-936742-23-2*) Robt Morris Assocs.

Primer on Free Will. John H. Gerstner. 1982. pap. 2.99 (*0-87552-272-6*) P & R Pubng.

Primer on Gas Integrated Resource Planning. 318p. 1993. 25.00 (*0-317-05947-5*) NARUC.

Primer on German Enlightenment: With a Translation of Karl Leonhard Reinhold's the Fundamental Concepts & Principles of Ethics. Sabine Roehr. LC 94-44811. 304p. 1995. text 39.95 (*0-8262-0997-1*) U of Mo Pr.

Primer on Highway Finance. Grant M. Davis & William A. Cummingham. 206p. (Orig.). (C). 1994. pap. text 29.50 (*0-8191-9362-3*); lib. bdg. 52.00 (*0-8191-9361-5*) U Pr of Amer.

Primer on Indicator Development & Application: Measuring Quality in Healthcare. Joint Commission on Accreditation of Healthcare Organizations. (Illus.). 124p. 1990. pap. 45.00 (*0-86688-213-8*, RD-300) Joint Comm Hlthcare.

Primer on Individual Employee Rights. 2nd ed. Alfred G. Feliu. LC 96-10893. 1996. pap. 45.00 (*1-57018-026-1*) BNA Books.

Primer on Industrial Environmental Impact. Michael R. Greenberg et al. 280p. 1978. boxed set 29.95 (*0-88285-050-4*) Transaction Pubs.

Primer on Integral Equations of the First Kind. G. Milton Wing. LC 91-38059. (Miscellaneous Bks.: No. 27). xiv, 135p. 1991. pap. 38.00 (*0-89871-263-7*) Soc Indus-Appl Math.

Primer on Integrating Psychotherapies for Children & Adolescents. Sebastiano Santostefano. LC 97-29509. 352p. 1998. pap. 50.00 (*0-7657-0109-X*) Aronson.

Primer on Intellectual property Law & Patent Litigation: Understanding & Defending Your Clients Patents, Trademarks & Copyrights. Edward F. O'Connor. LC 96-78634. 175p. 1997. pap. 49.95 (*1-57073-412-7*) Amer Bar Assn.

Primer on ISDN. (Satellites in an ISDN World Ser.). 1996. 50.00 (*0-614-18395-2*, 126P70) Info Gatekeepers.

Primer on Kidney Diseases. 2nd ed. Greenberg. (C). 1998. 49.95 (*0-12-299095-1*) Acad Pr.

Primer on Kidney Diseases. 2nd ed. Ed. by Arthur Greenberg. LC 98-106530. (Illus.). 542p. 1997. pap. text 57.95 (*0-12-299090-0*) Morgan Kaufmann.

Primer on Law for DREs & Youth Ministers. Mary A. Shaughnessy. 64p. (Orig.). 1992. pap. 5.00 (*1-55833-115-8*) Natl Cath Educ.

Primer on Licensing. 2nd ed. Jack Revoyr. 264p. 1996. 37.95 (*0-9627106-4-4*); pap. 15.95 (*0-9627106-5-2*) Kent Communs.

Primer on Limb Prosthetics. A. Bennett Wilson, Jr. (Illus.). 164p. 1998. text 38.95 (*0-398-06900-X*); pap. text 25.95 (*0-398-06897-6*) C C Thomas.

Primer on Linear Programming. Neebe. 56p. (C). 1991. pap. text 10.00 (*0-536-58006-5*) Pearson Custom.

Primer on Managed Competition. John C. Goodman & Gerald L. Musgrave. 53p. (Orig.). 1994. pap. text 10.00 (*1-56808-017-4*, 183) Natl Ctr Pol.

Primer on Measurement: An Introductory Guide to Measurement Issues. 146p. 1993. pap. 32.95 (*0-912452-92-7*, P-98) Am Phys Therapy Assn.

Primer on Medical Malpractice. Harry Rein. 400p. 1988. student ed. 100.00 (*1-55917-569-9*, 132B) Natl Prac Inst.

Primer on Natural Hazard Management in Integrated Regional Development Planning. 65.00 (*0-8270-3008-8*) OAS.

Primer on Non-Cognitive Psychotherapy: The Way Forward. L. Russell Hoover. 64p. 1996. pap. 8.95 (*0-614-96388-5*) Audio Lrn.

Primer on Nuclear Effects on Fiber Optic Transmission Systems. (Fiber Optics User's Manual & Design Ser.: Vol. XVI). 1987. 75.00 (*0-614-18472-X*, 152U16) Info Gatekeepers.

Primer on Nuclear Non-Proliferation. Gary Gardner. (Illus.). 110p. pap. write for info. (*0-9633859-3-3*) Ctr Nonproliferation.

Primer on Occupational Safety & Health. Fred Blosser. LC 91-43769. 374p. 1992. trans. 55.00 (*0-87179-741-0*, 0741) BNA Books.

Primer on Organizational Behavior. 4th ed. James L. Bowditch & Anthony F. Buono. LC 96-26881. (Wiley Series in Management). 416p. 1996. pap. 48.95 (*0-471-16006-7*) Wiley.

Primer on Personal Money Management for Midlife & Older Women. (Illus.). 86p. (Orig.). 1993. pap. text 20.00 (*1-56806-941-3*) DIANE Pub.

Primer on Pneumatic Valves & Controls. Robert B. Goodman. LC 96-13242. (Illus.). 108p. (C). 1997. 24.50 (*0-89464-965-5*) Krieger.

Primer on Prayer. W. T. Purkiser. (Christian Living Ser.). 48p. (Orig.). 1987. pap. 3.50 (*0-8341-1191-8*) Beacon Hill.

***Primer on Quality in the Analytical Laboratory.** John Kenkel. LC 99-43691. 96p. (C). 1999. per. 39.95 (*1-56670-516-9*) Lewis Pubs.

Primer on Racism. Roberto Villegas, Jr. 42p. (C). 1996. pap. 4.95 (*0-930962-13-3*) Villegas Pub.

Primer on Radical Christianity. Gene W. Marshall. LC 85-71566. 231p. 1985. pap. 10.00 (*0-9611552-1-3*) Realistic Living.

Primer on Rational-Emotive Therapy. Windy Dryden & Raymond DiGiuseppe. LC 89-69838. 108p. (Orig.). 1990. pap. text 11.95 (*0-87822-319-3*, 4420) Res Press.

***Primer on Regression Artifacts.** Donald T. Campbell & David A. Kenny. LC 99-23003. (Methodology in the Social Sciences Ser.). 202p. 1999. lib. bdg. 32.00 (*1-57230-482-0*, CO482) Guilford Pubns.

Primer on Roman Catholicism. John H. Gerstner. 42p. 1995. pap. 3.00 (*1-57358-013-9*) Soli Deo Gloria.

Primer on School Budgeting. Robert N. Kratz et al. LC 98-60467. 160p. 1998. pap. text 29.95 (*1-56676-639-7*) Scarecrow.

Primer on School Law: A Guide for Board Members in Catholic Schools. Mary A. Shaughnessey. 48p. (Orig.). 1988. pap. 6.00 (*1-55833-000-3*) Natl Cath Educ.

***Primer on Securities Arbitration Law for Investors, Brokers & Attorneys.** Franklin D. Ormsten. LC 99-93322. 115p. 1999. pap. 49.99 (*0-9673982-0-7*) Cadrey Pubg.

Primer on Securitization. Ed. by Leon T. Kendall & Michael J. Fishman. LC 95-53328. (Illus.). 199p. (C). 1996. 29.00 (*0-262-11211-6*) MIT Pr.

***Primer on Securitization.** Ed. by Leon Kendall & Michael J. Fishman. (Illus.). 199p. (C). 2000. reprint ed. pap. 18.95 (*0-262-61163-5*) MIT Pr.

Primer on Sediment-Trace Element Chemistry. 2nd ed. Arthur J. Horowitz. 144p. 1991. lib. bdg. 79.95 (*0-87371-499-7*, L499) Lewis Pubs.

Primer on Sexual Harassment. Barbara Lindemann & David D. Kadue. LC 92-25748. 319p. 1992. trans. 45.00 (*0-87179-764-X*, 0764) BNA Books.

***Primer on Simplified Statistics - For the Health Care Professional.** Paula S. Swain et al. Ed. & Illus. by Stephanie Yalesky. 67p. 1998. pap., wbk. ed. 35.00 (*0-9673662-0-8*, P55001) Swain.

Primer on Single-Subject Design for Clinical Social Workers. Tony Tripodi. LC 94-19703. 153p. (C). 1994. lib. bdg. 31.95 (*0-87101-238-3*, 2383) Natl Assn Soc Wkrs.

Primer on Soft Tissue Injuries. Harry Rein. 272p. 1988. student ed. 25.00 (*1-55917-566-4*, 131B) Natl Prac Inst.

Primer on Spectral Theory. B. Aupetit. Ed. by J. H. Ewing et al. (Universitext Ser.). (Illus.). 208p. 1990. 48.95 (*0-387-97390-7*) Spr-Verlag.

Primer on Success in the Private Investigative Profession: A Business & Investigative Manual for Establishing a Successful Investigative Agency & Working the Most In-Demand Types of Cases! Irv Baggett. (Illus.). 65p. (C). 1996. pap. text 25.00 (*0-918487-89-7*) Thomas Investigative.

Primer on Sustainable Building. Dianna L. Barnett & William D. Browning. (Illus.). 138p. (Orig.). 1995. pap. 16.95 (*1-881071-05-7*) Rocky Mtn Inst.

Primer on Technology Licensing. Gregory J. Battersby. 200p. 1996. 34.95 (*1-888206-06-3*) Kent Communs.

Primer on the Analysis & Presentation of Legal Argument. Bradley G. Clary. 106p. (C). 1992. pap. 14.50 (*0-314-00742-3*) West Pub.

Primer on the Autonomic Nervous System. Ed. by David Robertson et al. (Illus.). 343p. 1996. text 79.95 (*0-12-589760-X*); pap. text 47.00 (*0-12-589761-8*) Acad Pr.

Primer on the Complexities of Traumatic Memory of Childhood Sexual Abuse: A Psychological Approach. Fay H. Knopp & Anna Benson. Ed. by Euan Bear. 320p. (C). 1997. text 20.00 (*1-884444-20-2*) Safer Soc.

Primer on the Federal Price Discrimination Laws: A General Review of the Robinson-Patman Act for Business Managers. 24p. 1992. pap. 4.00 (*0-89707-754-7*, 503-0222, ABA Antitrust) Amer Bar Assn.

Primer on the Language Theory of St. Augustine: The Literal Level. Daniel J. Voiku. LC 97-4375. 125p. 1997. write for info. (*0-7734-2230-7*) E Mellen.

Primer on the Law of Information Exchange: A General Review of the Law of Benchmarking & Information Exchange for Business Managers. LC 95-80579. 24p. 1995. pap. 5.00 (*1-57073-241-8*, 503-0270, ABA Antitrust) Amer Bar Assn.

Primer on the Metabolic Bone Diseases & Disorders of Mineral Metabolism. 3rd ed. Murray J. Favus et al. LC 96-1618. 512p. 1996. pap. text 44.00 (*0-397-51763-7*) Lppncott W & W.

Primer on the Metabolic Bone Diseases & Disorders of Mineral Metabolism. 4th ed. Murray J. Favus et al. 500p. pap. text 49.50 (*0-7817-2038-9*) Lppncott W & W.

Primer on the Rheumatic Diseases. 10th ed. Ed. by H. Ralph Schumacher, Jr. et al. LC 93-31510. 1993. 25.00 (*0-912423-07-2*) Arthritis Found.

Primer on the Rheumatic Diseases. 11th ed. John H. Klippel et al. Ed. by Arthritis Foundation Staff. LC 97-25311. 528p. 1998. pap. 39.95 (*0-912423-16-1*) Longstreet.

Primer on the Taguchi Method. Ranjit Roy. LC 89-14736. (Illus.). 247p. 1990. 58.00 (*0-87263-468-X*) SME.

Primer on Thematic Instruction for Developing Speaking & Writing Skills. Charles Haynes & Terrill Jennings. (Orig.). (J). (gr. 1-12). 1992. pap. text 20.00 (*0-9624119-1-4*) Landmark Found.

Primer on Theory & Operation of Linear Accelerators in Radiation Therapy. 2nd ed. C. J. Karmark & Robert J. Morton. LC 96-24382. 1997. pap. text 26.95 (*0-944838-66-9*) Med Physics Pub.

Primer on Thermography. Harry Rein. 275p. 1988. 85.00 (*1-55917-563-X*, 133B) Natl Prac Inst.

Primer on Transplantation. Douglas J. Norman et al. LC 97-50158. (Illus.). xxii, 586p. 1997. text 120.00 (*0-9660150-0-2*) ASTP.

Primer on Workers' Compensation. 2nd ed. Jeffrey V. Nackley. 200p. 1989. trans. 45.00 (*0-87179-596-5*, 0596) BNA Books.

Primer on Working with Resistance. Martha Stark. LC 93-32471. 280p. 1994. pap. 45.00 (*1-56821-093-0*) Aronson.

Primer Otono de Clifford. Norman Bridwell. (Clifford, the Big Red Dog Ser.).Tr. of Clifford's First Autumn. (SPA.). (J). (ps-3). 1997. pap. text 2.99 (*0-590-37332-3*) Scholastic Inc.

Primer Otono de Clifford. Norman Bridwell. (Clifford, the Big Red Dog Ser.).Tr. of Clifford's First Autumn. (SPA.). (J). (gr. k-2). 1997. 8.19 (*0-606-11295-2*, Pub. by Turtleback) Demco.

Primer Paseo de Spot. Eric Hill. Orig. Title: Spot's First Walk. (SPA., Illus.). 32p. (J). (ps-2). 1983. 12.95 (*0-399-21019-9*, G P Putnam) Peng Put Young Read.

Primer Periodo de Enrique Jardel Poncela, 1927-1936: Valoracion del Humorismo de un Iconoclasta Espanol. Paul W. Seaver, Jr. LC 92-11670. 248p. 1992. lib. bdg. 89.95 (*0-7734-9886-9*) E Mellen.

Primer Puesto. Jamie Suzanne. Tr. by Conchita Peraire del Molino. (Sweet Valley Twins Ser.: No. 8).Tr. of First Place. (J). (gr. 3-7). 1989. 12.05 (*0-606-10458-5*, Pub. by Turtleback) Demco.

1 Samuel, 2 Samuel & 1 Cronras. Ed. by Daniel Carro et al. (Comentario Biblico Mundo Hispano Ser.: Vol. 5).Tr. of Samuel & I Chronicles. (SPA.). 440p. 1997. pap. text 13.50 (*0-311-03105-6*, Edit Mundo) Casa Bautista.

Primer San Valentin de Clifford. Norman Bridwell. LC 49-242900. (Clifford, the Big Red Dog Ser.).Tr. of Clifford's First Valentine's Day. (SPA.). 32p. (J). (gr. k-2). 1997. pap. text 2.99 (*0-590-97469-6*) Scholastic Inc.

Primer San Valentin de Clifford. Norman Bridwell. (Clifford, the Big Red Dog Ser.).Tr. of Clifford's First Valentine's Day. (SPA.). (J). (gr. k-2). 1996. 8.19 (*0-606-10799-1*, Pub. by Turtleback) Demco.

Primer Set Forth by the Kinges Maiestie & His Clergie (1545) LC 74-5335. 175p. 1974. reprint ed. 50.00 (*0-8201-1129-5*) Schol Facsimiles.

Primer Simposio sobre Ecologia Islena-First Symposium on Island Ecological Systems: Papers of the Symposium Held at Inter American University, Oct. 28, 1983. Intro. by Herminio L. Lugo. (ENG & SPA.). 160p. (Orig.). (C). 1984. pap. text 5.95 (*0-913480-62-2*) Inter Am U Pr.

Primer Taller Latinoamericano, Preguntas y Demostraciones. Harvey Jackins. Tr. by Francisco Lopez-Bustos. (SPA.). 1993. pap. 5.00 (*0-913937-70-3*) Rational Isl.

Primer to California Politic. Lawrence G. Brewster. LC 95-73317. 304p. 1996. pap. text 24.95 (*0-312-13699-4*) St Martin.

Primer to California Politics. Lawrence & Leonard. pap. text. write for info. (*0-312-13677-3*) St Martin.

Primer to International Trade. Russell D. Roberts. (C). 1994. pap. 10.60 (*0-13-101650-4*, Macmillan Coll) P-H.

Primer to Postmodernism. Stanley J. Grenz. 211p. (Orig.). (C). 1996. pap. 14.00 (*0-8028-0864-6*) Eerdmans.

Primer to Postmodernity. Joseph P. Natoli. LC 97-7779. 224p. 1997. text 57.95 (*1-57718-060-7*); pap. text 21.95 (*1-57718-061-5*) Blackwell Pubs.

Primer to Real Estate Income Tax Law. George M. Yeiter & James M. Trippon. 224p. (C). 1992. pap. 39.95 (*1-882347-00-5*) Am Inst Real Est.

Primer Trueno (First Thunder) Una Aventura de Descubrimiento. MSI Staff. Tr. by Ambala Ishaya. pap. 12.95 (*0-931783-23-2*) SFA Pubns.

Primera & Segunda Tesalonicenses. Charles Erdman. (SPA.). 101p. 1993. pap. 5.95 (*0-939125-28-5*) CRC Wrld Lit.

***Primera Comunion.** Francine M. O'Connor. (SPA., Illus.). 32p. 1998. pap. 1.95 (*0-7648-0193-7*, Libros Liguori) Liguori Pubns.

Primera Comunion. Sadlier Team Staff & Thomas H. Groome. (Programa Sacramental Bilingue de Sadlier Ser.). (ENG & SPA., Illus.). 118p. (J). (gr. 1-3). 1997. pap. text 7.80 (*0-8215-1277-3*) Sadlier.

Primera Comunion de Su Hijo. Una Publicacion Pastoral Redentorista Staff. (SPA., Illus.). 16p. (Orig.). 1997. pap. 2.95 (*0-7648-0049-3*) Liguori Pubns.

Primera Comunion, Guia para el Catequista. Sadlier Team Staff. (Programa Sacramental Bilingue de Sadlier Ser.). (ENG & SPA., Illus.). 160p. (J). (gr. 1-3). 1997. pap. 14.55 (*0-8215-1287-0*) Sadlier.

Primera Confesion de Su Hijo. Una Publicacion Pastoral Redentorista Staff. (SPA., Illus.). 16p. (Orig.). 1998. pap. 2.95 (*0-7648-0187-2*) Liguori Pubns.

Primera Epistola a los Corintios. Ernesto Trenchard. (SPA.). 344p. 1970. pap. 9.99 (*0-8254-1727-9*, Edit Portavoz) Kregel.

Primera Epistola de Pablo a los Corentios. Charles Erdman. (SPA.). 194p. 1993. pap. 6.95 (*0-939125-22-6*) CRC Wrld Lit.

Primera Memoria. Ana M. Matute. (SPA.). pap. 17.95 (*84-233-0726-3*, Pub. by Destino) Continental Bk.

Primera Memoria. 8th ed. Ana Matute Ausejo. (SPA.). 248p. 1991. pap. 12.95 (*0-7859-4990-9*) Fr & Eur.

Primera Navidad de Clifford. Norman Bridwell. (Clifford, the Big Red Dog Ser.).Tr. of Clifford's First Christmas. (SPA.). (J). (gr. k-2). 1994. 8.19 (*0-606-06516-4*, Pub. by Turtleback) Demco.

Primera Navidad (Historias Biblicas) A. M. De Graaf.Tr. of First Christmas. (SPA.). (J). 3.49 (*0-7899-0526-4*) Editorial Unilit.

Primera Pascua de Resurreccion. Penny Frank & Tony Morris. (Serie Historias de la Biblia - Children's Bible Story Books Ser.).Tr. of First Easter. (SPA.). 24p. (J). 1986. 1.50 (*0-8423-6309-2*, 490348) Editorial Unilit.

***Primera Penitencia.** Francine M. O'Connor. (SPA., Illus.). 1998. pap. 1.95 (*0-7648-0195-3*, Libros Liguori) Liguori Pubns.

Primera Prioridad. T. Haggard.Tr. of Primary Purpose. (SPA.). pap. 6.99 (*958-9354-17-3*, 550054) Editorial Unilit.

Primera Reconciliacion. Sadlier Team Staff & Thomas H. Groome. (Programa Sacramental Bilingue de Sadlier Ser.). (ENG & SPA., Illus.). 110p. (J). (gr. 1-3). 1997. pap. text 7.80 (*0-8215-1276-5*) Sadlier.

Primera Reconciliacion, Guia para el Catequista. Sadlier Team Staff. (Programa Sacramental Bilingue de Sadlier Ser.). (ENG & SPA., Illus.). 152p. (J). (gr. 1-3). 1997. pap. 14.55 (*0-8215-1286-2*) Sadlier.

Primera Tesalonicenses, Filipenses, Filemon, Segunda Tesalonicenses, Colosenses, Efesios. Ivan Havener. LC 95-18228. 124p. 1995. pap. 4.95 (*0-8146-2351-4*) Liturgical Pr.

Primera y Segunda Pedro. Louis A. Barbieri. (Comentario Biblico Portavoz Ser.). Orig. Title: First & Second Peter, (Everyman's Bible Commentary). (SPA.). 144p. 1981. pap. 6.99 (*0-8254-1051-7*, Edit Portavoz) Kregel.

Primera y Segunda Tesalonicenses. Charles C. Ryrie. (Comentario Biblico Portavoz Ser.). Orig. Title: First & Second Thessalonians. (SPA.). 104p. 1981. pap. 6.99 (*0-8254-1634-5*, Edit Portavoz) Kregel.

Primera y Segunda Timoteo. D. Edmond Hiebert. (Comentario Biblico Portavoz Ser.). Orig. Title: First & Second Timothy (Everyman's Bible Commentary). (SPA.). 256p. 1988. pap. 7.99 (*0-8254-1316-8*, Edit Portavoz) Kregel.

Primeras Ciudades Cubanas y Sus Antecedentes Urbanisticos. Guillermo De Zendegui. LC 97-60444. (Coleccion Arte Ser.). (SPA., Illus.). 87p. 1997. pap. 16.00 (*0-89729-836-5*, 836-5) Ediciones.

***Primeras Palabras en Ingles.** Usborne Books Staff. (SPA., Illus.). 48p. (ps-3). 2000. 20.95 (*1-58086-233-0*) EDC.

P

An Asterisk (*) at the beginning of an entry indicates that the title is appearing for the first time.

***Primeras Palabras en Ingles (Everyday Words in English)** (Everyday Words Ser.). (SPA., Illus.). 48p. (ps-3). 2000. 12.95 (*0-7460-3675-2*, Pub. by Usbrne Pbng UK) EDC.

Primeras Sociedades Jerarquicas. Griselda Sarmiento. 135p. 1992. pap. 11.00 (*968-29-3775-2*, IN022) UPLAAP.

Primero Dios: Alcoholics Anonymous & the Hispanic Community. Kenneth G. Davis. LC 93-29626. 1994. 29.50 (*0-945636-50-4*) Susquehanna U Pr.

Primero Dios: Hispanic Liturgical Resource. Arturo P. Rodriguez & Mark Francis. 160p. 1997. pap. 18.00 (*1-56854-142-2*, CUSTOM) Liturgy Tr Pubns.

Primero... el Reino - First the Kingdom. Ed. by Thomas A. Jones & Sheila Jones. (SPA.). 132p. 1994. pap. 7.99 (*1-884553-40-0*) Discipleshp.

Primero y Segundo de Cronicas. John N. Sailhamer. (SPA.). 112p. 1996. pap. 6.99 (*0-8254-1649-3*, Edit Portavoz) Kregel.

Primero y Segundo de Reyes. Richard McNeely. (Comentario Biblico Portavoz Ser.). Orig. Title: First & Second Kings (Everyman's Bible Commentary). (SPA.). 160p. 1993. pap. 6.99 (*0-8254-1476-8*, Edit Portavoz) Kregel.

Primero y Segundo de Samuel. J. Carl Laney. (Comentario Biblico Portavoz Ser.). (SPA.). 144p. 1996. pap. 6.99 (*0-8254-1423-7*, Edit Portavoz) Kregel.

Primeros Anfibios see First Amphibians

Primeros Anfibios. Chelsea House Publishing Staff et al. Ed. by Isidro Sanchez. (SPA., Illus.). 32p. (YA). (gr. 3 up). 1996. lib. bdg. 15.95 (*0-7910-4031-3*) Chelsea Hse.

Primeros Auxilios para un Matrimonio: Herido. 32p. 1986. pap. text. write for info. (*1-884794-03-3*) Eden Pubng.

Primeros Auxilios y RCP. 92p. Date not set. 25.00 (*0-614-11244-3*) Inter-Am Safety.

Primeros Auxilios y RCP. National Safety Council Staff. (Emergency Care Ser.). 96p. (C). 1994. pap. text 12.50 (*0-86720-847-3*) Jones & Bartlett.

Primeros Encuentros - First Encounters. Sabine R. Ulibarri. LC 81-71732. (ENG & SPA.). ii, 87p. 1982. pap. 9.00 (*0-916950-27-1*) Biling Rev-Pr.

Primeros Lectores Ciencias: Alimentos, 2 vols. Ann Burckhardt. 1999. pap. text 28.00 (*0-7368-0144-8*, Cpstone High Low) Capstone Pr.

Primeros Memoriales. Fray Bernardino de Sahagun. LC 96-45377. (Civilization of the American Indian Ser.: Vol. 200, Pt. 1). 192p. 1993. pap. 170.00 (*0-8061-1688-9*) U of Okla Pr.

Primeros Memoriales, Vol. 200. Fray Bernardino de Sahagun. Tr. by Thelma D. Sullivan. LC 96-45377. (Civilization of the American Indian Ser.: Vol. 200, Pt. II). (Illus.). 352p. 1997. 75.00 (*0-8061-2909-3*) U of Okla Pr.

Primeros Nueve Meses. (Serie Enfoque a la Familia - Focus on the Family Ser.).Tr. of First Nine Months. (SPA.). 15p. 1994. pap. 1.79 (*1-56063-256-9*, 497437) Editorial Unilit.

Primeros Pasos: Comenzando con Jesus. Gordon Staff et al.Tr. of First Steps in the Way. (SPA.). 87p. 2001. 2.99 (*1-56063-416-2*, 550010) Editorial Unilit.

Primeros Pasos: Una Bibliografia Para Empezar A Investigar la Historia De Puerto Rico. rev. ed. Maria de los A. Castro et al. (SPA.). 204p. (C). 1994. pap. text 8.50 (*0-929157-29-X*) Ediciones Huracan.

***Primeros Pasos Ayudas Visales, Vol. PP-02.** Tr. & Prod. by Life Publishers International Staff. (Vida Nueva Ser.). (SPA., Illus.). 28p. 2001. pap. write for info. (*0-7361-0170-5*) Life Pubs Intl.

***Primeros Pasos II Ayudas Visuales Vol. PP2-04: March to August 2000.** (SPA., Illus.). 28p. 1999. pap. write for info. (*0-7361-0106-3*) Life Pubs Intl.

Primeros Pasos II Ayudas Visuales Sep 98 a Feb 99, No. PP2-03. Life Publishers International Staff. (SPA., Illus.). 28p. (J). (ps-k). 1999. pap. write for info. (*0-7361-0058-X*) Life Pubs Intl.

***Primeros Pasos II Maestro Vol. 9: March to August 2000, Teachers Manual.** (SPA., Illus.). 112p. 1999. pap., teacher ed. write for info. (*0-7361-0107-1*) Life Pubs Intl.

Primeros Pasos II Maestro, Sept 99. Life Publishers International Staff. (SPA., Illus.). 112p. 1999. pap., teacher ed. write for info. (*0-7361-0059-8*) Life Pubs Intl.

***Primeros Pasos II Trabajo Manual: June to August 2000.** (SPA., Illus.). 16p. (J). (ps-k). 1999. pap. write for info. (*0-7361-0105-5*) Life Pubs Intl.

***Primeros Pasos II Trabajo Manual: March to May 2000.** (SPA.). 16p. (J). (ps-k). 1999. pap. write for info. (*0-7361-0104-7*) Life Pubs Intl.

Primeros Pasos II Trabajo Manual, Dec. 1999-Feb. 2000. Life Publishers International Staff. (SPA., Illus.). 16p. (J). (ps-k). 1999. pap. write for info. (*0-7361-0057-1*) Life Pubs Intl.

Primeros Pasos II Trabajo Manual, Sept. 99-Nov. 99. Life Publishers International Staff. (SPA., Illus.). 16p. (J). (ps). 1999. pap. write for info. (*0-7361-0056-3*) Life Pubs Intl.

***Primeros Pasos Maestro, Vol. 10, No. 3.** Tr. & Prod. by Life Publishers International Staff. (Vida Nueva Ser.). (SPA., Illus.). 112p. 2001. pap., teacher ed. write for info. (*0-7361-0169-1*) Life Pubs Intl.

***Primeros Pasos Manual.** Tr. & Prod. by Life Publishers International Staff. (Vida Nueva Ser.). (SPA., Illus.). 16p. (J). (ps). 2001. pap., student ed. write for info. (*0-7361-0171-3*) Life Pubs Intl.

***Primeros Pasos Manual 2.** Tr. & Prod. by Life Publishers International Staff. (Vida Nueva Ser.). (SPA., Illus.). 16p. (J). (ps). 2001. pap., student ed. write for info. (*0-7361-0172-1*) Life Pubs Intl.

Primeros Pasos I Ayudas Visuales, Sep. 1999-Feb. 2000, No. PP1-03. Life Publishers International Staff. (SPA., Illus.). 28p. (J). 1999. pap. write for info. (*0-7361-0054-7*) Life Pubs Intl.

Primeros Pasos I Trabajo Manual, Dec 1999-Feb 2000. Life Publishers International Staff. (SPA., Illus.). 16p. (J). 1999. pap. write for info. (*0-7361-0053-9*) Life Pubs Intl.

***Primeros Pasos I Ayudas Visuales, Vol. 10.** Prod. by Life Publishers International Staff. (SPA., Illus.). 28p. 2000. pap., teacher ed. write for info. (*0-7361-0129-2*) Life Pubs Intl.

***Primeros Pasos I Ayudas Visuales Vol. PP1-04: March to August 2000.** (SPA., Illus.). 28p. 1999. pap. write for info. (*0-7361-0102-0*) Life Pubs Intl.

Primeros Pasos I Maestro, Vol. 9 Tomo. Life Publishers International Staff. (SPA., Illus.). 112p. 1999. pap., teacher ed. write for info. (*0-7361-0055-5*) Life Pubs Intl.

***Primeros Pasos I Maestro, Vol. 10.** Prod. by Life Publishers International Staff. (SPA., Illus.). 112p. 2000. pap., teacher ed. write for info. (*0-7361-0128-4*) Life Pubs Intl.

***Primeros Pasos I Maestro Vol. 9: March to August 2000.** (SPA.). 112p. 1999. pap., teacher ed. write for info. (*0-7361-0103-9*) Life Pubs Intl.

***Primeros Pasos I Trabajo Manual: June to August 2000.** (SPA.). 16p. (J). 1999. pap. write for info. (*0-7361-0101-2*) Life Pubs Intl.

***Primeros Pasos I Trabajo Manual: March to May 2000.** (SPA., Illus.). 16p. (J). 1999. pap. write for info. (*0-7361-0100-4*) Life Pubs Intl.

***Primeros Pasos I Trabajo Manual, Dec. 2000 to Feb. 2001, Vol. 10.** Prod. by Life Publishers International Staff. (SPA., Illus.). 16p. 2000. pap., student ed. write for info. (*0-7361-0131-4*) Life Pubs Intl.

***Primeros Pasos I Trabajo Manual, Sept. to Nov. 2000, Vol. 10.** Prod. by Life Publishers International Staff. (SPA., Illus.). 16p. 2000. pap., student ed. write for info. (*0-7361-0130-6*) Life Pubs Intl.

***Primers for Prudery: Sexual Advice to Victorian America** Ronald G. Walters. LC 99-41166. 2000. pap. 15.95 (*0-8018-6348-1*) Johns Hopkins.

***Primes: A Computational Perspective.** Richard Crandall. 2000. 49.95 (*0-387-94777-9*) Spr-Verlag.

Primes & Programming: Computers & Number Theory. P. J. Giblin. (Illus.). 251p. (C). 1993. pap. text 24.95 (*0-521-40988-8*) Cambridge U Pr.

Primes & Their Neighbors: Ten Tales of Middle Georgia. Richard M. Johnston. LC 77-101285. (Short Story Index Reprint Ser.). 1977. 21.95 (*0-8369-3222-6*) Ayer.

Primes Associated to an Ideal. S. McAdam. LC 89-27624. (Contemporary Mathematics Ser.: Vol. 102). 167p. 1989. pap. 37.00 (*0-8218-5108-X*, CONM/102) Am Math.

Primes of the Form x2 + ny2: Fermat, Class Field Theory & Complex Multiplication. David A. Cox. LC 89-5555. (Pure & Applied Mathematics Ser.). 351p. 1997. pap. 59.95 (*0-471-19079-9*, Wiley-Interscience) Wiley.

Prime's Work-at-Home Directory. (Illus.). 32p. 1998. pap. 3.00 (*1-893128-03-2*, W1998) Prime Pub.

Prime's Work-at-Home Directory: Work at Home. rev. ed. Ed. by B. Becker. (Illus.). 32p. 1999. pap. 3.95 (*1-893128-04-0*) Prime Pub.

Primetime! Strategies for Life-Long Learning in Mathematics & Science in the Middle & High School Grades. Hal Hemmrich et al. LC 94-30528. 76p. 1994. pap. text 15.00 (*0-435-08363-5*, 08363) Heinemann.

***Primetime Blues: African Americans on Network Television.** Donald Bogle. (Illus.). 512p. 2000. 27.00 (*0-374-23720-4*) FS&G.

Primetime Pregnancy: Proven programs for staying in Shape Before & After Your Baby is Born. Cynthia Tivers & Kathy Kaehler. LC 97-29942. (Illus.). 160p. 1997. pap. 16.95 (*0-8092-3072-0*, 307200, Contemporary Bks) NTC Contemp Pub Co.

Primetime Presidency of Ronald Reagan: The Era of the Television Presidency. Robert E. Denton, Jr. LC 88-5910. 128p. 1988. 47.95 (*0-275-92603-6*, C2603, Praeger Pubs) Greenwood.

Primeval Creatures of the Animal World. Marco Ferrari. (Illus.). 144p. 1997. 24.98 (*0-7651-9274-8*) Smithmark.

Primeval Forest. Albert Schweitzer. LC 98-6946. (Albert Schweitzer Library). 240p. 1998. pap. 15.95 (*0-8018-5958-1*) Johns Hopkins.

Primeval Forest: Including on the Edge of the Primeval Forest; And, More from the Primeval Forest. Albert Schweitzer & Albert Schweitzer Institute for the Humanities Sta. LC 98-6946. (Albert Schweitzer Library). 1998. pap. write for info. (*0-8018-6034-2*) Johns Hopkins.

***Primeval Revelation in Myths & in Genesis: A Dynamic Subject Much Neglected by Theologians.** Anthony Zimmerman. LC 99-40929. 216p. 1999. pap. 31.50 (*0-7618-1487-6*) U Pr of Amer.

Primi Saggi di Logismografia Presentati, All' XI Congresso Degli Scienziati Italiani in Roma. Giuseppe Cerboni. Ed. by Richard P. Brief. LC 80-1477. (Dimensions of Accounting Theory & Practice Ser.). (ITA.). 1980. reprint ed. lib. bdg. 17.95 (*0-405-13507-6*) Ayer.

Primii Pasi in Esperanto. Ionel Onet. (RUM.). 68p. 1993. pap. text 5.00 (*1-882251-03-2*) Eldonejo Bero.

Priming the Anabolic Environment: A Practical, Scientific Guide to the Art & Science of Building Muscle. William D. Brink. (Illus.). viii, 120p. 1996. pap. 14.95 (*1-55210-003-0*, Pub. by MuscleMag Intl) BookWorld.

Priming the German Economy: American Occupational Policies, 1945-1948. John H. Backer. LC 70-142289. 222p. reprint ed. pap. 68.90 (*0-608-13867-3*, 202375800033) Bks Demand.

Primis Reader in Sociology. Hugh Lena. 1992. pap. text. write for info. (*0-07-037581-X*) McGraw.

Primitiae Monographiae Rosarum: Materiaux Pour Servir a L'Histoire Des Roses, 6 pts. in 1 vol. F. Crepin. 1972. reprint ed. 60.00 (*3-7682-0759-5*) Lubrecht & Cramer.

Primitive American Armor: Including Armor, Shields, & Other Defensive Devices. Walter Hough. (Illus.). reprint ed. 19.95 (*0-8488-0033-8*, J M C & Co) Amereon Ltd.

Primitive & Ancient Legal Institutions. Albert Kocourek & John H. Wigmore. LC 93-78308. xii, 704p. 1993. reprint ed. 75.00 (*0-89941-842-2*, 307870) W S Hein.

Primitive & Ancient Medicine see Mellen History of Medicine

Primitive & Folk Jewelry. Martin Gerlach. (Illus.). 219p. 1971. pap. 13.95 (*0-486-22747-2*) Dover.

Primitive Art. Franz Boas. (Illus.). 378p. 1955. pap. 9.95 (*0-486-20025-6*) Dover.

Primitive Art. Franz Boas. (Illus.). 1962. 23.50 (*0-8446-1695-8*) Peter Smith.

Primitive Art in Civilized Places. Sally Price. LC 89-4932. (Illus.). xii, 160p. 1991. pap. 13.95 (*0-226-68064-9*) U Ch Pr.

Primitive Art in Civilized Places. Sally Price. (Illus.). 208p. 1993. 19.95 (*0-226-68063-0*) U Ch Pr.

Primitive Arts & Crafts. Roderick U. Sayce. (Illus.). 1963. reprint ed. 30.00 (*0-8196-0124-1*) Biblo.

Primitive Baptists of the Wiregrass South: 1815 to the Present. John Gordon Crowley, Jr. LC 98-39624. (Illus.). 320p. 1999. 49.95 (*0-8130-1640-1*) U Press Fla.

Primitive Behavior. William I. Thomas. (Reprint Series in Sociology). (Illus.). reprint ed. lib. bdg. 52.50 (*0-697-00220-9*) Irvington.

Primitive Beliefs in the North-East of Scotland. Joseph M. McPherson. Ed. by Richard M. Dorson. LC 77-70605. (International Folklore Ser.). 1977. reprint ed. lib. bdg. 26.95 (*0-405-10109-0*) Ayer.

Primitive Beliefs (1921) H. M. Tichener. 65p. 1998. reprint ed. pap. 7.95 (*0-7661-0621-7*) Kessinger Pub.

***Primitive Benchmark: A Short Treatise on a General Theory of Sailing with the Limits for Sailboat Speed.** unabridged ed. Jerry N. Selness. LC 99-95091. (Illus.). 240p. 1999. pap. 19.95 (*0-9671566-0-2*) Windward Enterp.

Primitive Capital Accumulation in Sudan. Abbas Abdelkarim. 1992. text 42.50 (*0-7146-3324-0*, Pub. by F Cass Pubs) Intl Spec Bk.

Primitive Christianity & Its Non-Jewish Sources. D. D. Clemen. 1977. lib. bdg. 59.95 (*0-8490-2472-2*) Gordon Pr.

Primitive Church. Maurice Goguel & H. C. Snape. 610p. 1964: 100.00 (*0-614-00155-2*) Elliots Bks.

Primitive Church. D. I. Lanslots. LC 79-67862. 295p. 1980. reprint ed. pap. 10.00 (*0-89555-134-9*) TAN Bks Pubs.

Primitive Church: Studies in the Origin of the Christian Ministry. Burnett H. Streeter. 1977. lib. bdg. 59.95 (*0-8490-2473-0*) Gordon Pr.

Primitive Church in the Modern World. Ed. by Richard T. Hughes. LC 95-5366. 264p. (C). 1995. text 23.95 (*0-252-02194-0*) U of Ill Pr.

Primitive Civilizations or Outlines of the History of Ownership in Archaic Communities, 2 vols. E. J. Simcox. 1977. lib. bdg. 200.00 (*0-8490-2474-9*) Gordon Pr.

Primitive Classification. Emile Durkheim & Marcel Mauss. Tr. by Rodney Needham. LC 63-9737. 113p. 1967. pap. text 13.00 (*0-226-17334-8*, P273) U Ch Pr.

***Primitive Clothing of the Native Americans: Patterns & Ideas for Making Authentic Primitive Clothing, Making Modern Buckskin Clothing & a Section on Tanning Buckskins & Furs.** Evard H. Gibby. Ed. by Monte Smith. 136p. 2000. pap. 15.95 (*0-943604-61-3*, BOO/45) Eagles View.

Primitive Conceptions of Death & the Nether World in the Old Testament. Nicholas J. Tromp. (Biblica et Orientalia Ser.: Vol. 21). 1969. pap. 21.50 (*88-7653-321-4*) Loyola Pr.

Primitive Culture, 2 vols. E. Tylor. 1973. lib. bdg. 600.00 (*0-87968-091-1*) Gordon Pr.

Primitive Culture in Italy. Herbert J. Rose. LC 73-168503. (Select Bibliographies Reprint Ser.). 1977. reprint ed. 27.95 (*0-8369-5948-5*) Ayer.

Primitive Drinking: A Study of the Uses & Functions of Alcohol in Preliterate Societies. Chandler Washburne. 1961. 25.95 (*0-8084-0253-6*) NCUP.

Primitive Edge of Experience see Limita Primitiva a Experientei

Primitive Edge of Experience. Thomas H. Ogden. LC 89-6878. 256p. 1989. 40.00 (*0-87668-982-9*) Aronson.

Primitive Edge of Experience. Thomas H. Ogden. LC 89-6878. 256p. 1993. pap. 40.00 (*0-87668-290-5*) Aronson.

Primitive Family in Its Origin & Development. Carl N. Starcke. Ed. by Rodney Needham. LC 75-12232. 336p. 1980. pap. text 14.00 (*0-226-77133-4*, Midway Reprint) U Ch Pr.

Primitive Ghost Moths. Ebbe S. Nielsen & Niels P. Kristensen. (Monographs on Australian Lepidoptera: Vol. 1). (Illus.). 230p. (C). 1989. text 70.00 (*0-643-04999-1*, Pub. by CSIRO) Accents Pubns.

Primitive History of Hamilton County, Indiana. Augustus F. Shirts. 370p. 1993. reprint ed. lib. bdg. 39.50 (*0-8328-2938-2*) Higginson Bk Co.

Primitive Hyde Park. N. H. Hannan. 51p. (Orig.). 1991. pap. 10.00 (*0-913553-12-3*) Albert Hse Pub.

Primitive Internalized Object Relations: A Clinical Study of Schizophrenic, Borderline, & Narcissistic Patients. Vamik D. Volkan. LC 75-18608. 304p. 1976. 52.50 (*0-8236-4995-4*) Intl Univs Pr.

Primitive Law. A. S. Diamond. x, 451p. 1998. reprint ed. 135.00 (*1-56169-410-X*, 15576) Gaunt.

Primitive Love & Love-Stories. Henry T. Finck. 1976. lib. bdg. 75.00 (*0-8490-2476-5*) Gordon Pr.

Primitive Man in Ohio. Warren K. Moorehead. (Ohio History, Prehistoric Indians, Archaeology Ser.). (Illus.). 276p. (C). 1991. reprint ed. pap. 31.80 (*1-56651-017-1*); reprint ed. lib. bdg. 48.90 (*1-56651-018-X*) A W McGraw.

Primitive Man in Ohio. Warren K. Moorehead. LC 76-43787. reprint ed. 41.50 (*0-404-15642-8*) AMS Pr.

Primitive Marriage & European Law: A South African Investigation. D. W. Shropshire. 186p. 1970. reprint ed. 35.00 (*0-7146-1913-2*, Pub. by F Cass Pubs) Intl Spec Bk.

Primitive Mental States Vol. 1: Across the Lifespan, Vol. I. Ed. by Shelley Alhanati & Katina Kostoulas. LC 10-901949. 296p. 1997. 52.00 (*1-56821-685-8*) Aronson.

Primitive Mental States & the Rorschach Test. Ed. by Howard D. Lerner & Paul M. Lerner. 1988. 80.00 (*0-8236-4295-X*) Intl Univs Pr.

Primitive Mentality. Lucien Levy-Bruhl. Tr. by Lilian A. Clare. LC 75-41174. 1976. reprint ed. 69.50 (*0-404-14568-X*) AMS Pr.

Primitive Methodist Connexion: Its Background & Early History. Julia S. Werner. LC 84-40161. (Illus.). 352p. 1984. text 35.00 (*0-299-09910-5*) U of Wis Pr.

Primitive Methodist Connexion: Its Background & Early History. Julia S. Werner. LC 84-40161. 269p. 1984. reprint ed. pap. 83.40 (*0-608-07463-2*, 206769000009) Bks Demand.

Primitive Mind & Modern Civilization. Charles R. Aldrich. LC 79-98401. reprint ed. 27.50 (*0-404-00309-5*) AMS Pr.

Primitive Music. Richard Wallaschek. LC 72-125062. (Music Ser.). 1970. reprint ed. lib. bdg. 39.50 (*0-306-70028-X*) Da Capo.

Primitive Nervous Systems. Thomas L. Lentz. LC 68-27760. 160p. reprint ed. pap. 49.60 (*0-8357-8283-2*, 203379900087) Bks Demand.

Primitive Ordeal & Modern Law. H. Goitein. xvii, 302p. 1980. reprint ed. 42.50 (*0-8377-0612-2*, Rothman) W S Hein.

***Primitive Outdoor Skills: More Wilderness Techniques from Woodsmoke Journal.** rev. ed. Ed. by Richard L. Jamison. LC 84-82234. 144p. 1999. 17.98 (*0-88290-666-6*) Horizon Utah.

Primitive Painters in America, 1750-1950: An Anthology. Jean Lipman & Alice Winchester. LC 70-179732. (Biography Index Reprint Ser.). 1980. reprint ed. 16.95 (*0-8369-8100-6*) Ayer.

Primitive Passions: Men, Women & the Quest for Ecstacy. Marianna Torgovnick. LC 98-25005. 1998. pap. 16.00 (*0-226-80837-8*) U Ch Pr.

Primitive Passions: Men, Women & the Quest for Ecstasy. Marianna Torgovnick. LC 96-25552. 272p. 1997. 26.00 (*0-679-43086-5*) McKay.

Primitive Passions: Visuality, Sexuality, Ethnograhy & Contemporary Chinese Cinema. Rey Chow. LC 94-27796. (Film & Culture Ser.). 253p. 1995. 57.50 (*0-231-07682-7*); pap. 19.00 (*0-231-07683-5*) Col U Pr.

Primitive Paternity: The Myth of Supernatural Birth in Relation to the Family, Vols. I-II. Edwin S. Hartland. (Folk-Lore Society, London Monographs: Vols. 65 & 67). 1974. reprint ed. pap. 60.00 (*0-8115-0530-8*) Periodicals Srv.

Primitive Paternity: The Myth of Supernatural Birth in Relation to the History of the Family, 2 vols. Edwin S. Hartland. LC 70-173100. 654p. 1972. reprint ed. 33.95 (*0-405-08602-4*) Ayer.

Primitive People. Francine Prose. 250p. 1992. 20.00 (*0-374-23722-0*) FS&G.

***Primitive Peoples Without Salt: A Perspective for Industrialized Societies** William J. Oliver. LC 97-92346. 290 p. 1998. write for info. (*0-9658325-0-3*) W J Oliver.

Primitive Piety Revived. Henry C. Fish. 1992. 17.99 (*0-87377-970-3*) GAM Pubns.

Primitive Pleasure see Placer Primitivo: Boots in the Bedroom!

Primitive Poems of a Psychotic Poet: Yes, Some of Us Are Completely Crazy! Janet S. Wade. LC 98-90134. (Illus.). 50p. 1998. 12.00 (*0-9663340-0-0*) J S Wade.

Primitive Polluters: Semang Impact on the Malaysian Tropical Rain Forest Ecosystem. A. Terry Rambo. (Anthropological Papers Ser.: No. 76). (Illus.). 104p. (Orig.). 1985. pap. 8.00 (*0-915703-04-1*) U Mich Mus Anthro.

Primitive Property. Emile De Laveleye. Tr. by G. R. Marriott from FRE. xlvii, 356p. 1985. reprint ed. 48.00 (*0-8377-0817-6*, Rothman) W S Hein.

Primitive Pursuit: Stories Afield of Muzzleloader Hunting. Peter R. Schoonmaker. (Illus.). 166p. (Orig.). 1992. reprint ed. pap. 6.95 (*1-881399-05-2*) Beaver Pond P&P.

***Primitive Renaissance: Rethinking German Expressionism.** David Pan. (Modern German Culture & Literature Ser.). 2001. text 49.95 (*0-8032-3727-8*) U of Nebr Pr.

Primitive Revolutionaries of China: A Study of Secret Societies in the Late Nineteenth Century. Fei-Ling Davis. LC 76-45585. 262p. reprint ed. pap. 74.70 (*0-8357-3503-6*, 2034637) Bks Demand.

Primitive Soluble Permutation Groups of Degree Less Than 256. Mark W. Short. Ed. by A. Dold et al. LC 92-13513. (Lecture Notes in Mathematics Ser.: Vol. 1519). x, 145p. 1992. 34.00 (*0-387-55501-3*) Spr-Verlag.

Primitive Survivals in Modern Thought. Chapman Cohen. LC 74-169207. (Atheist Viewpoint Ser.). 142p. 1976. reprint ed. 16.95 (*0-405-03807-0*) Ayer.

Primitive Technology: A Book of Earth Skills. Ed. by David Wescott. LC 98-54428. (Illus.). 232p. 1999. pap. 24.95 (*0-87905-911-7*) Gibbs Smith Pub.

P

Primitive Theology: The Collected Primers of John H. Gerstner. John H. Gerstner. Ed. by Don Kistler. LC 97-104321. 483p. 1996. 29.95 (*1-57358-045-7*) Soli Deo Gloria.

Primitive Trade: Its Psychology & Economics. Elizabeth E. Hoyt. LC 68-30529. (Reprints of Economic Classics Ser.). 191p. 1968. reprint ed. 37.50 (*0-678-00409-9*) Kelley.

Primitive Traditional History: The Primitive History & Chronology of India, Southeastern & Southwestern Asia, Egypt, & Europe, 2 vols. J. F. Hewitt. 1977. lib. bdg. 200.00 (*0-8490-2477-3*) Gordon Pr.

Primitive Traits in Religious Revivals. Frederick M. Davenport. LC 72-163669. reprint ed. 34.50 (*0-404-01929-3*) AMS Pr.

Primitive Traits in Religious Revivals: A Study in Mental & Social Evolution. F. M. Davenport. 1977. lib. bdg. 59.95 (*0-8490-2478-1*) Gordon Pr.

Primitive Wilderness Living & Survival Skills. John McPherson & Geri McPherson. (Illus.). 408p. 1993. pap. 24.95 (*0-89745-997-0*) Sunflower U Pr.

Primitive Wilderness Living & Survival Skills: Naked into the Wilderness. John McPherson. Ed. by Geri McPherson. (Illus.). 408p. 1993. reprint ed. pap. 24.95 (*0-9678777-7-6*) Prairie Wolf.

Primitive Wilderness Living & Survival Skills 2: Applied & Advanced. John McPherson & Geri McPherson. (Illus.). 296p. 1996. pap. 24.95 (*0-89745-984-9*) Sunflower U Pr.

Primitive World & Its Transformations. Robert Redfield. 198p. 1957. pap. text 11.95 (*0-8014-9028-6*) Cornell U Pr.

Primitive Worlds: People Lost in Time. Ed. by National Geographic Society Staff. LC 73-830. (Special Publications Series 8: No. 2). 1973. 8.95 (*0-87044-127-2*) Natl Geog.

Primitives: Our American Heritage, Second Series, Vol. 2. 2nd ed. Kathryn McNerney. (Illus.). 160p. 1996. pap. 14.95 (*0-89145-331-8*, 1759) Collector Bks.

Primitives & the Supernatural. Lucien Levy-Bruhl. LC 73-4358. (Studies in Comparative Literature: No. 35). 1972. reprint ed. lib. bdg. 75.00 (*0-8383-1589-5*) M S G Haskell Hse.

Primitives in the Wilderness: Deep Ecology & the Missing Human Subject. Peter C. Van Wyck. LC 97-3612. 186p. (C). 1997. text 53.50 (*0-7914-3433-8*); pap. text 17.95 (*0-7914-3434-6*) State U NY Pr.

Primitives, Patriarchy, & the Picaresque in Vicente Blasco Ibanez's "Canas y Barro" Christopher Anderson. xi, 186p. 1995. 65.00 (*1-882528-16-6*) Scripta.

Primitivism & Decadence. Yvor Winters. 1972. 250.00 (*0-87968-051-2*) Gordon Pr.

Primitivism & Decadence. Yvor Winters. LC 70-92994. (Studies in Comparative Literature: No. 35). 1969. reprint ed. lib. bdg. 75.00 (*0-8383-1213-6*) M S G Haskell Hse.

Primitivism & Decadence: Study of American Experimental Poetry. Yvor Winters. (BCL1-PS American Literature Ser.). 146p. 1993. reprint ed. lib. bdg. 69.00 (*0-7812-6587-8*) Rprt Serv.

***Primitivism & Identity in Latin America: Essays on Art, Literature & Culture.** Ed. by Erik Camayd-Freixas & Jose Eduardo Gonzalez. LC 00-8340. (Illus.). 285p. 2000. 50.00 (*0-8165-2045-3*) U of Ariz Pr.

Primitivism & Modern Art. Colin Rhodes. LC 94-60286. (World of Art Ser.). (Illus.). 216p. (Orig.). 1995. pap. 14.95 (*0-500-20276-1*, Pub. by Thames Hudson) Norton.

Primitivism & Related Ideas in Antiquity. Arthur Oncken Lovejoy et al. LC 96-47993. 496p. 1997. reprint ed. pap. text 19.95 (*0-8018-5611-6*) Johns Hopkins.

Primitivism & Related Ideas in the Middle Ages. George Boas. LC 96-29536. 240p. 1997. reprint ed. pap. text 16.95 (*0-8018-5610-8*) Johns Hopkins.

Primitivism & the Idea of Progress in English Popular Literature of the Eighteenth Century. Lois Whitney. (BCL1-PR English Literature Ser.). 343p. 1992. reprint ed. lib. bdg. 89.00 (*0-7812-7046-4*) Rprt Serv.

Primitivism, Cubism, Abstraction: The Early Twentieth Century. Gill Perry et al. LC 92-50988. (Illus.). 280p. (C). 1993. 60.00 (*0-300-05515-3*); pap. 30.00 (*0-300-05516-1*) Yale U Pr.

Primitivism in Modern Art. Robert Goldwater. (Illus.). 352p. 1986. pap. 18.50 (*0-674-70490-8*) Belknap Pr.

Primitivism in Modern Art: A Research Guide. Miriam Deutch. (Art-Architect Reference Ser.). 300p. Date not set. text 45.00 (*0-8153-1942-8*) Garland.

Primitivism in 20th Century Art: Affinity of the Tribal & the Modern. William S. Rubin. (Illus.). 706p. 1990. 125.00 (*0-8109-6067-2*, Pub. by Abrams) Time Warner.

Primitivism in 20th Century Art: Affinity of the Tribal & the Modern, 2 vols. Ed. by William S. Rubin. (Illus.). 706p. 1990. pap. 65.00 (*0-8109-6068-0*, Pub. by Abrams) Time Warner.

Primitivism in Twentieth Century Art: Affinity of the Tribal & the Modern. Ed. by William S. Rubin. (Illus.). 706p. 1984. 125.00 (*0-87070-518-0*, 0-8109-6067-2, Pub. by Mus of Modern Art); pap. 65.00 (*0-87070-534-2*, 0-8109-6068-0, Pub. by Mus of Modern Art) Abrams.

"Primitivism" in 20th Century Art: Affinity of the Tribal & the Modern, 2 vols. Rubin. 1995. pap. text. write for info. (*0-8109-6134-2*) Abrams.

Primitivism, Radicalism, & the Lamb's War: The Baptist-Quaker Conflict in Seventeenth-Century England. T. L. Underwood. LC 96-5508. (The Oxford Studies in Historical Theology). (Illus.). 200p. 1997. text 49.95 (*0-19-510833-7*) OUP.

Primitivist-Modernism: Black Culture & the Origins of Transatlantic Modernism. Sieglinde Lemke. LC 97-1352. (W. E. B. Dubois Institute Ser.). (Illus.). 192p. 1998. text 45.00 (*0-19-510403-X*) OUP.

Primitivist Piety: The Ecclesiology of the Early Plymouth Brethren. James Callahan. LC 96-614. 312p. 1996. 48.00 (*0-8108-3126-0*) Scarecrow.

***Primmy's Daughter.** large type ed. Rowena Summers. 448p. 1999. 31.99 (*0-7505-1374-8*, Pub. by Mgna Lrg Print) Ulverscroft.

***Primo: The Story of Man Mountain Carnera, World Heavyweight Champion.** Frederic Mullally. 210p. 1999. pap. 13.95 (*1-86105-242-1*) Robson.

Primo de Rivera & Abd-El-Krim: The Struggle in Spanish Morocco, 1923-1927. Shannon E. Fleming. LC 91-2976. (Modern European History Outstanding Studies & Dissertations). 462p. 1991. text 25.00 (*0-8240-2548-2*) Garland.

***Primo Levi.** Ian Thomson. 2000. 20.00 (*0-09-178531-6*) Random House.

Primo Levi: Bridges of Knowledge. Mirna Cicioni. Ed. by John E. Flower. (New Directions in European Writing Ser.). 224p. 1995. 49.50 (*1-85973-058-2*); pap. 19.50 (*1-85973-063-9*) Berg Pubs.

Primo Levi: Tragedy of an Optimist. Myriam Anissimov. Tr. by Steve Cox. LC 97-9904. 452p. 1999. 35.00 (*0-87951-806-5*, Pub. by Overlook Pr) Penguin Putnam.

***Primo Levi: Tragedy of an Optimist.** Myriam Anissimov. (Illus.). 604p. 2000. pap. 18.95 (*1-58567-020-0*, Pub. by Overlook Pr) Penguin Putnam.

Primo Libro de Canzoni Francese a Due Voci. Ed. by Albert Seay. (Transcriptions Ser.: No. 1). iv, 40p. 1979. 4.00 (*0-933894-02-3*) Colo Coll Music.

Primo Libro de Madrigali a Quatro Voci (Venice, 1542) Bk. 1: Madrigals. Domenico M. Ferrabosco. Ed. by Jessie A. Owens. LC 94-41447. (Sixteenth-Century Madrigal Ser.: Vol. 11). (ITA.). 223p. 1995. text 99.00 (*0-8240-5511-X*) Garland.

Primo libro de' madrigali italiani et canzoni francese a due voci. Ihan Gero. (Masters & Monuments of the Renaissance Ser.: Vol. 1). (FRE & ITA., Illus.). xliv, 213p. 1980. pap. 75.00 (*0-8450-7301-X*) Broude.

Primo Libro de Madrigali Italiani et Canzoni Francese a Due Voci Bk. 4: Madrigals, Voices. Taglia Pietro. Ed. by Jessie A. Owens. LC 95-3164. (Sixteenth-Century Madrigal Ser.: Vol. 27). (ITA.). 138p. 1995. text 83.00 (*0-8240-5529-2*) Garland.

Primo Plant: Growing Marijuana Outdoors. Carolyn Garcia. (Illus.). 100p. 1998. pap. text 14.95 (*0-932551-27-0*) Quick Am Pub.

Primo Vino. Rose B. Green. 4.95 (*0-8453-1660-5*, Cornwall Bks) Assoc Univ Prs.

Primordial Bond: Exploring Connections Between Man & Nature Through the Humanities & Sciences. Stephen H. Schneider & Lynne Morton. LC 80-20376. (Illus.). 336p. 1981. 15.95 (*0-306-40519-9*, Plenum Trade) Perseus Pubng.

Primordial Breath Vol. I: An Ancient Chinese Way of Prolonging Life Through Breath Control. Tr. by Jane Lu Huang & Michael Wurmbrand from CHI. 170p. (C). 1987. 22.50 (*0-944558-00-3*) Original Bks.

Primordial Breath Vol. II: An Ancient Chinese Way of Prolonging Life Through Breath Control. Tr. by Jane Huang from CHI. 288p. 1990. 36.50 (*0-944558-01-1*) Original Bks.

Primordial Challenge: Ethnicity in the Contemporary World, 154. Ed. by John F. Stack, Jr. LC 85-30219. (Contributions in Political Science Ser.: No. 154). (Illus.). 242p. 1986. 59.95 (*0-313-24759-5*, STK/, Greenwood Pr) Greenwood.

Primordial Characters. Rodney Needham. LC 78-17230. 104p. reprint ed. pap. 32.30 (*0-7837-5314-4*, 204471200004) Bks Demand.

Primordial Field. Charles Leach. 24p. 1996. reprint ed. spiral bd. 10.50 (*0-7873-0540-5*) Hlth Research.

Primordial Germ Cells in the Chordates: Embryogenesis & Phylogenesis. Pieter D. Niewkoop & Lien A. Sutasurya. LC 78-18101. (Developmental & Cell Biology Ser.: No. 7). 199p. reprint ed. pap. 56.80 (*0-608-15759-7*, 2031700) Bks Demand.

Primordial Image: African, Afro-American & Caribbean Mythopoetic Text. Ikenna Dieke. LC 90-6299. (American University Studies: Comparative Literature: Ser. III, Vol. 37). XIV, 434p. (C). 1993. text 6.95 (*0-8204-1320-8*) P Lang Pubng.

Primordial Immunity: Foundations for the Verterbrate Immune System. Ed. by Gregory Beck. LC 94-4703. (Annals Ser.). 1994. pap. 100.00 (*0-89766-840-5*) NY Acad Sci.

Primordial Lure. Emma L. Moffatt. 20p. (Orig.). 1994. pap. write for info. (*1-885206-06-2*, Iliad Pr) Cader Pubng.

Primordial Nuclei & Their Galactic Evolution: Proceedings of an Issi Workshop, 6-10 May 1997, Bern, Switzerland. Nikos Prantzos et al. LC 98-23730. (Space Sciences Series of Issi). 325p. 1998. write for info. (*0-7923-5114-2*) Kluwer Academic.

Primordial Nucleosynthesis. Ed. by W. J. Thompson et al. 132p. (C). 1990. text 74.00 (*981-02-0149-4*) World Scientific Pub.

Primordial Nucleosynthesis & Evolution of the Early Universe. Ed. by Kazuo Sato & Jean Audouze. (C). 1991. text 234.00 (*0-7923-1193-0*) Kluwer Academic.

Primordial Truth & Postmodern Theology. David R. Griffin & Huston Smith. LC 89-4388. (SUNY Series in Constructive Postmodern Thought). 216p. (C). 1989. text 19.50 (*0-7914-0198-7*) State U NY Pr.

Primordial VRM System & Evolution of Vertebrate Immunity. J. Stewart. (Molecular Biology Intelligence Unit Ser.). 1994. 99.00 (*1-57059-119-9*) Landes Bioscience.

Primorskiy Kray: Economy, Industry, Government, Business. 2nd rev. ed. Russian Information & Business Center, Inc. Staff. (Russian Regional Business Directories Ser.). (Illus.). 200p. 1997. pap. 99.00 (*1-57751-377-0*) Intl Business Pubns.

***Primorskiy Kray Regional Investment & Business Guide.** Global Investment & Business Center, Inc. Staff. (Russian Regional Investment & Business Guides Ser.: Vol. 60). (Illus.). 350p. 1999. pap. 99.00 (*0-7397-0827-9*) Intl Business Pubns.

***Primorskiy Kray Regional Investment & Business Guide.** Contrib. by Global Investment & Business Center, Inc. Staff. (Russian Regional Investment & Business Guides Ser.: Vol. 56). (Illus.). 350p. 2000. pap. 99.95 (*0-7397-3008-8*) Intl Business Pubns.

Primos - Cousins. Virginia Hamilton. (SPA.). (J). (gr. 5-8). pap. 8.95 (*84-204-4747-1*) Santillana.

Primos - Cousins. Virginia Hamilton. 1993. 14.05 (*0-606-10491-7*, Pub. by Turtleback) Demco.

Primrose. Deborah Camp. 384p. (Orig.). 1988. pap. 3.95 (*0-380-75435-5*, Avon Bks) Morrow Avon.

Primrose Convention. Jo Bannister. LC 97-51169. 272p. 1998. text 22.95 (*0-312-18157-4*) St Martin.

Primrose Convention. large type ed. Jo Bannister. LC 97-52115. 263p. 1998. pap. write for info. (*0-7540-3253-1*) Chivers N Amer.

Primrose Convention. large type ed. Jo Bannister. 1998. 22.95 (*0-7862-1383-3*) Thorndike Pr.

Primrose for Sarah. large type ed. Carol Marsh. 288p. 1989. 27.99 (*0-7089-2042-X*) Ulverscroft.

***Primrose Hill.** Helen L. Falconer. 224p. 2001. 23.95 (*0-89255-255-7*, Pub. by Persea Bks) Norton.

Primrose McConnell's the Agricultural Notebook. 19th ed. Ed. by R. J. Soffe. LC 94-41071. 1995. pap. 55.00 (*0-632-03643-5*) Blackwell Sci.

Primrose Path. Carol Matas. LC 95-225985. 152p. (J). (gr. 7-12). 1997. pap. 7.95 (*0-921368-55-0*) Genl Dist Srvs.

Primrose Path. Barbara Metzger. 1997. mass mkt. 4.50 (*0-449-22509-7*, Crest) Fawcett.

***Primrose Path.** Barbara Metzger. LC 98-50509. 341 p. 1999. 27.95 (*0-7862-1764-2*) Thorndike Pr.

***Primrose Path: His First Novel.** Bram Stoker. 128p. 1999. 29.95 (*1-874287-21-X*, Pub. by Desert Island Bks) Firebird Dist.

Primrose Way. Jackie F. Koller. LC 92-5322. (Great Episodes Ser.). 352p. (YA). (gr. 7 up). 1992. 15.95 (*0-15-256745-3*, Gulliver Bks) Harcourt.

Primrose Way. Jackie F. Koller. LC 91-44681. (Great Episodes Ser.). 352p. (YA). (gr. 7 up). 1995. pap. 6.00 (*0-15-200372-X*, Gulliver Bks) Harcourt.

Primrose Way. Jackie French Koller. 1995. 11.35 (*0-606-08043-0*) Turtleback.

Primulas. Andrew Mikoljksi. (The New Plant Library). (Illus.). 64p. 1998. 9.95 (*1-85967-595-6*, Lorenz Bks) Anness Pub.

Primulas: The Complete Guide. Mary A. Robinson. (Illus.). 272p. 1994. pap. 22.95 (*1-85223-811-9*, Pub. by Cro1wood) Trafalgar.

Primulas of the British Isles. John Richards. (Natural History Ser.: No. 38). (Illus.). 24p. 1989. pap. 5.25 (*0-7478-0020-0*, Pub. by Shire Pubns) Parkwest Pubns.

Primum Non Nocere Today. 2nd ed. Ed. by G. Roberto Burgio & John D. Lantos. LC 98-47922. (International Congress Ser.). 190p. 1998. 161.00 (*0-444-82923-7*, Excerpta Medica) Elsevier.

Primum Non Nocere Today - a Symposium on Pediatric Bioethics: Proceedings of the International Symposium on Pediatric Bioethics, Pavia, 26-28 May 1994. Ed. by G. Roberto Burgio et al. LC 94-40670. (International Congress Ser.: Vol. 1071). 186p. 1994. 158.50 (*0-444-81920-7*) Elsevier.

Primum Scriptum Sententiarum see Questions on an Ethics of Divine Commands

***Primus Three.** Lin Y. Cawthra. Ed. by Seth E. Cawthra. LC 99-93091. (Space Voyagers Ser.: Vol. 1). 288p. 1999. pap. 7.99 (*1-893906-00-0*) Maze Pubg.

Prin Bio Lm Kilgore Cb. 4th ed. Tietjen. (C). 1997. lab manual ed. 33.75 (*0-201-30470-8*) Addison-Wesley.

Prin.-Clin. Applications. Sean Longacre. 176p. 1994. pap. text, per. 20.95 (*0-7872-0073-5*) Kendall-Hunt.

Prin Fin & Mangrial Acct Looseleaf Text. 5th ed. Warren & Reeve. (SWC-Accounting). Date not set. teacher ed., spiral bd. 63.25 (*0-538-86621-7*) S-W Pub.

Prin Fin/mang Acct. Carl S. Warren & Philip E. Fess. LC 85-61429. (Thomson Executive Press). 1986. mass mkt. 44.50 (*0-538-01202-1*, A20) S-W Pub.

Prin Types Spch Ndsu CB. Bruce E. Gronbeck. (C). 1997. pap. text 42.19 (*0-201-33842-4*) Addison-Wesley.

Princ. Behavior: Pronunciation Guide. Beatty. 1995. 2.25 (*0-697-29199-5*, WCB McGr Hill) McGrw-H Hghr Educ.

Princ. Microbiology. 2nd ed. Atlas Staff. 416p. 1997. pap. 30.63 (*0-8151-8451-4*) McGraw.

Princ. Microbiology. 2nd ed. Atlas Staff. 1997. 290.31 (*0-8151-1306-4*) Mosby Inc.

Princ Of Descriptive Inorganic Chemistry. Gary Wulfsberg. LC 86-23285. (Chemistry). (Illus.). 461p. (C). 1987. ring bd. 38.00 (*0-534-07494-4*) Brooks-Cole.

***Princ of Ferm Tech 2ed.** P.F. Stanbury. 2000. pap. text 64.95 (*0-7506-4501-6*) Buttrwrth-Heinemann.

Princ. Organic Biol. & SSG Student Manual. 2nd ed. Caret. 1997. 57.74 (*0-07-561226-7*) McGraw.

Prince. (Penguin Readers Level 2). 1995. write for info. (*0-201-43903-4*) Addison-Wesley.

Prince. Bruce Brooks. LC 97-40265. (Wolfbay Wings Ser.: No. 5). (Illus.). 144p. (J). (gr. 3-7). 1998. pap. 4.50 (*0-06-440600-8*) HarpC.

Prince. Bruce Brooks. LC 97-40265. (Wolfbay Wings Ser.: No. 5). (Illus.). 144p. (J). (gr. 4-7). 1998. lib. bdg. 14.89 (*0-06-027542-1*) HarpC.

Prince. Bruce Brooks. (Wolfbay Wings Ser.: No. 5). (J). (gr. 4-7). 1998. 9.60 (*0-606-13925-7*, Pub. by Turtleback) Demco.

Prince. Geoff Brown. (Complete Guides to the Music Of...Ser.). (Illus.). 136p. (Orig.). (C). 1995. pap. 8.95 (*0-7119-4979-4*, OP 47773) Omnibus NY.

Prince. Jean Giraudoux. 9.95 (*0-686-54009-3*) Fr & Eur.

Prince. Niccolo Machiavelli. (C). 1997. pap. text 10.00 (*0-321-02595-4*) Addson-Wesley Educ.

Prince. Niccolo Machiavelli. 1998. pap. text 2.00 (*0-451-62755-5*) Addson-Wesley Educ.

Prince. Niccolo Machiavelli. (Airmont Classics Ser.). (YA). (gr. 11 up). 1965. mass mkt. 2.95 (*0-8049-0056-6*, CL-56) Airmont.

Prince. Niccolo Machiavelli. 17.95 (*0-89190-547-2*) Amereon Ltd.

Prince. Niccolo Machiavelli. 1994. lib. bdg. 18.95 (*1-56849-500-5*) Buccaneer Bks.

Prince. Niccolo Machiavelli. Ed. by Russell Price & Quentin Skinner. (Cambridge Texts in the History of Political Thought Ser.). 192p. 1988. pap. text 8.95 (*0-521-34993-1*) Cambridge U Pr.

Prince. Niccolo Machiavelli. Ed. by Russell Price & Quentin Skinner. (Cambridge Texts in the History of Political Thought Ser.). 192p. 1989. text 29.95 (*0-521-34240-6*) Cambridge U Pr.

Prince. Niccolo Machiavelli. Tr. by David Wootton from ITA. LC 94-44698. (HPC Classics Ser.). 128p. (C). 1995. pap. text 3.95 (*0-87220-316-6*); lib. bdg. 24.95 (*0-87220-317-4*) Hackett Pub.

Prince. Niccolo Machiavelli. Ed. & Tr. by Thomas G. Bergin. (Crofts Classics). 96p. 1947. pap. text 4.95 (*0-88295-053-3*) Harlan Davidson.

Prince. Niccolo Machiavelli. Tr. & Intro. by Paul Sonnino. LC 95-17621. 144p. (C). 1995. pap. 9.95 (*0-391-03940-7*) Humanities.

Prince. Niccolo Machiavelli. Ed. by James Atkinson. LC 75-15946. (Library of Liberal Arts: Vol. 172). 448p. 1976. pap. write for info. (*0-672-61244-5*) Macmillan.

Prince. Niccolo Machiavelli. 1992. 16.00 (*0-679-41044-9*) McKay.

Prince. Niccolo Machiavelli. LC 99-21656. 1999. mass mkt. 3.95 (*0-451-52746-1*, Sig Classics) NAL.

Prince. Niccolo Machiavelli. 1999. audio. write for info. (*0-14-086109-2*) NAL.

Prince. Niccolo Machiavelli. Ed. & Tr. by Peter Bondanella. Tr. by Mark Musa. (Oxford World's Classics Ser.). 126p. 1998. pap. 4.95 (*0-19-283397-9*) OUP.

Prince. Niccolo Machiavelli. Tr. by H. H. Thompson. LC 86-70377. (Great Books in Philosophy). 92p. 1986. pap. 4.95 (*0-87975-344-7*) Prometheus Bks.

Prince. Niccolo Machiavelli. 1995. pap. 11.95 (*1-57392-423-7*) Prometheus Bks.

Prince. Niccolo Machiavelli. (Bantam Classics Ser.). 1985. 9.05 (*0-606-02466-2*, Pub. by Turtleback) Demco.

Prince. Niccolo Machiavelli. Tr. & Intro. by George Bull. (Penguin Classics Ser.). 96p. (YA). (gr. 9 up). 1961. pap. 5.95 (*0-14-044107-7*) Viking Penguin.

Prince. Niccolo Machiavelli. Tr. by George Bull. LC 99-228739. (Penguin Classics Ser.). 107p. 1999. pap. 5.95 (*0-14-044752-0*) Viking Penguin.

Prince. Niccolo Machiavelli. (Classics of World Literature Ser.). 1998. pap. 5.95 (*1-85326-775-9*, 7759WW, Pub. by Wrdsworth Edits) NTC Contemp Pub Co.

Prince. Niccolo Machiavelli. (FRE.). 192p. 1986. pap. 10.95 (*0-7859-4477-X*, 204016653X) Fr & Eur.

Prince. Niccolo Machiavelli et al. Tr. by Angelo Codevilla. LC 96-50047. (Rethinking the Western Tradition Ser.). 192p. 1997. 25.00 (*0-300-06402-0*); pap. 11.00 (*0-300-06403-9*) Yale U Pr.

Prince. Mayer. LC 94-77863. (Magic Days Ser.). (Illus.). 32p. (J). (ps-3). 1995. pap. text 4.69 (*0-307-16665-1*, 16665, Goldn Books) Gldn Bks Pub Co.

Prince. Ib Michael. Tr. by Barbara Haveland from DAN. LC 99-32515. 352p. 1999. text 25.00 (*0-374-23723-9*) FS&G.

***Prince.** John Rossant. 2000. write for info. (*0-688-16457-9*, Wm Morrow) Morrow Avon.

Prince. Margery Van Susteren. (Illus.). 48p. (J). 1991. pap. 7.95 (*0-922510-05-9*) Lucky Bks.

Prince. Niccolo Machiavelli. Tr. by Edward Dacres. LC 73-172705. (Tudor Translations, First Ser.). reprint ed. write for info. (*0-318-50527-4*) AMS Pr.

Prince. Niccolo Machiavelli. Tr. by Hill Thompson from ITA. 186p. 1988. reprint ed. 19.95 (*0-88280-115-5*); reprint ed. pap. 15.95 (*0-88280-116-3*) ETC Pubns.

Prince. Niccolo Machiavelli. Tr. by Leo P. De Alvarez from ITA. (Illus.). 168p. (C). 1989. reprint ed. pap. text 7.95 (*0-88133-444-8*) Waveland Pr.

Prince. unabridged ed. Niccolo Machiavelli. 80p. 1992. reprint ed. pap. text 1.00 (*0-486-27274-5*) Dover.

Prince. unabridged ed. Niccolo Machiavelli. Tr. by George Bull. (Classics on Cassette Ser.). 1994. 24.00 incl. audio (*0-453-00893-3*, Pub. by Penguin-HghBrdg) Penguin Putnam.

Prince. 2nd ed. Niccolo Machiavelli. Ed. & Tr. by Robert M. Adams. LC 91-32538. (Critical Editions Ser.). 288p. (C). 1992. pap. text 9.25 (*0-393-96220-2*) Norton.

Prince. 2nd ed. Niccolo Machiavelli. Tr. by Harvey C. Mansfield. LC 98-5772. 152p. 1998. 24.00 (*0-226-50043-8*); pap. text 8.00 (*0-226-50044-6*) U Ch Pr.

Prince: A Historical Critique. Victor A. Rudowski. (MWS Ser.: No. 82). 180p. (C). 1992. per. 13.95 (*0-8057-8555-8*, Twyne) Mac Lib Ref.

Prince: A Historical Critique. Victor A. Rudowski. (MWS Ser.: No. 82). 180p. (C). 1992. 23.95 (*0-8057-8079-3*, Twyne) Mac Lib Ref.

Prince: A New Translation. Niccolo Machiavelli. Tr. by Harvey C. Mansfield, Jr. from ITA. LC 85-2536. xxviii, 144p. 1999. pap. text 8.00 (*0-226-50038-1*) U Ch Pr.

Prince: Alter Ego. Dwayne McDuffie. Ed. by Margaret Clark. 32p. 1991. pap. 2.00 (*1-56389-058-5*, Piranha Pr) DC Comics.

Prince: And Selected Discourses. Niccolo Machiavelli. Ed. by Daniel Donno. 160p. (YA). (gr. 9-12). 1984. mass mkt. 3.95 (*0-553-21278-8*, Bantam Classics) Bantam.

An Asterisk (*) at the beginning of an entry indicates that the title is appearing for the first time.

***Prince: Reproducible Teaching Unit.** James Scott. 46p. 1999. teacher ed., ring bd. 29.50 (*1-58049-185-5*, TU127) Prestwick Hse.
***Prince: The Persnickety Pony That Didn't Like Grown-Ups.** Heather Grovet. Ed. by Jerry D. Thomas. (Julius & Friends Ser.: Vol. 8). (Illus.). 95p. (J). (gr. k-4). 2000. pap. 6.99 (*0-8163-1787-9*) Pacific Pr Pub Assn.
***Prince: Wordsworth Classics of World Literature.** Niccolo Machiavelli. Tr. by C. E. Detmold. 143p. 2000. reprint ed. pap. text 15.00 (*0-7881-9159-4*) DIANE Pub.
Prince No. 2: A Practical Guide. Colin Bentley. LC 97-168234. 350p. 1997. pap. text 44.95 (*0-7506-3240-2*) Buttrwrth-Heinemann.
Prince - Come. Ed. by Carol Cuellar. 60p. (Orig.). (C). 1995. pap. text 16.95 (*0-89724-470-2*, VF2173) Wrner Bros.
Prince - Sign o' the Times. Carol Cuellar. 112p. (Orig.). (C). 1987. pap. text 16.95 (*0-7692-0538-0*, VF1393) Wrner Bros.
Prince - The Gold Experience. Ed. by Carol Cuellar. 92p. (Orig.). (C). 1996. pap. text 19.95 (*0-7692-0478-3*, PF9552) Wrner Bros.
Prince - The Hits, No. 1. 200p. 1994. pap. 26.95 (*0-89724-118-5*, VF2088) Wrner Bros.
***Prince Albert: The Life & Lies of Al Gore.** David N. Bossie & Floyd G. Brown. 192p. 2000. 9.95 (*0-936783-28-1*, Pub. by Merril Pr) Midpt Trade.
Prince Albert & the University: The Prince Albert Sesquicentennial Lecture. Owen Chadwick. LC 97-42161. (Illus.). 32p. 1998. pap. text 8.95 (*0-521-63756-2*) Cambridge U Pr.
Prince Albert Studies Vol. 13: Local Self-Government. Ed. by Saur, K. G., Staff. 164p. 1996. 55.00 (*3-598-21413-8*) K G Saur Verlag.
Prince Albert Studies (Prinz-Albert-Studien) Vol. 14: Banking Systems in Modern History (Das Kreditwesen in der Neuzeit) Ed. by Franz Bosbach & Hans Pohl. 160p. 1997. write for info. (*3-598-21414-6*) K G Saur Verlag.
Prince Albert Wind. Wilma E. McDaniel. 1994. 10.95 (*0-9636829-1-1*); pap. 7.95 (*0-9636829-2-X*) Mother Road.
Prince among Men. Kate Moore. 384p. 1997. mass mkt. 5.99 (*0-380-78458-0*, Avon Bks) Morrow Avon.
Prince among Slaves. Terry Alford. (Illus.). 304p. 1986. pap. 14.95 (*0-19-504223-9*) OUP.
Prince Amos. Gary Paulsen. (Culpepper Adventures Ser.). (J). (gr. 3-5). 1994. 8.70 (*0-606-05979-2*, Pub. by Turtleback) Demco.
Prince & His Lady. Mollie Gillen. 314p. 1970. mass mkt. 5.95 (*0-88780-139-0*, Pub. by Formac Publ Co) Formac Dist Ltd.
Prince & Letters. Vittorio Alfieri. Tr. by Beatrice Corrigan & Julius A. Molinaro. LC 75-185707. (Illus.). 214p. reprint ed. pap. 66.40 (*0-608-10985-1*, 201944400011) Bks Demand.
Prince & Mr. Jones. Samuel Spewack. 1961. pap. 5.25 (*0-8222-0915-2*) Dramatists Play.
Prince & Other Discourses. Niccolo Machiavelli et al. Tr. by Luigi Ricci. (Modern Library College Editions). 540p. (C). 1950. pap. 6.25 (*0-07-553577-7*, T25) McGraw.
***Prince & Other Dogs.** Libby Hall. (Illus.). 128p. 2000. 12.95 (*1-58234-097-8*) Bloomsbury Pubg.
Prince & Other Political Writings. Niccolo Machiavelli. Ed. by Stephen Milner. 288p. 1995. 5.50 (*0-460-87629-5*, Everyman's Classic Lib) Tuttle Pubng.
Prince & Other Works. Niccolo Machiavelli. Ed. & Tr. by Alan H. Gilbert. (University Classics Ser.). 332p. 1964. pap. 12.95 (*0-87532-101-1*) Hendricks House.
Prince & Plays. Henry Gregor. Tr. by Harvey I. Dunkle. LC 95-4996. (Studies in Austrian Literature, Culture, & Thought). 366p. 1996. 34.50 (*0-929497-82-1*); pap. 24.50 (*1-57241-033-7*) Ariadne CA.
Prince & Princess of Wales: A Royal Colouring Album. Peggy Howe. (Illus.). 24p. 1982. pap. 4.95 (*0-912027-00-2*) Howe & Assoc.
Prince & the Bogus Bride. Jennifer Drew. (Yours Truly Ser.). 1998. per. 3.50 (*0-373-52060-3*, 1-52060-0) Silhouette.
Prince & the Cave. Frances Thomas. 56p. (J). (gr. 4). 1992. pap. 7.95 (*0-8464-4878-5*) Beekman Pubs.
Prince & the Cave. Frances Thomas. (YA). 1992. pap. 50.00 (*0-86383-768-9*, Pub. by Gomer Pr) St Mut.
Prince & the Goosegirl. Henrietta Bredin. LC 92-260. (Illus.). 32p. (J). 1992. 5.99 (*0-85953-146-5*) Childs Play.
Prince & the King - Healing the Father-Son Wound: A Guided Journey of Initiation. Michael Gurian. 1993. pap. 15.95 (*0-87477-742-9*, Tarcher Putnam) Putnam Pub Group.
Prince & the Law, 1200-1600: Sovereignty & Rights in the Western Legal Tradition. Kenneth Pennington. LC 92-40544. 1993. 55.00 (*0-520-07995-7*, Pub. by U CA Pr) Cal Prin Full Svc.
Prince & the Li Hing Mui: Hawaii's Princess & the Pea. Sandi Takayama. (Illus.). 24p. (J). (ps-2). 1998. 9.95 (*1-57306-077-1*) Bess Pr.
Prince & the New Power Generation. Ed. by Carol Cuellar. 92p. (Orig.). (C). 1993. pap. text 18.95 (*0-7692-0922-X*, VF1905) Wrner Bros.
Prince & the New Power Generation - Diamonds & Pearls. Ed. by Carol Cuellar. 84p. (Orig.). (C). 1991. pap. text 17.95 (*0-7692-0510-0*, VF1748) Wrner Bros.
Prince & the Pauper. (J). 9.95 (*1-56156-311-0*) Kidsbks.
Prince & the Pauper. (Illus.). 78p. 1995. pap. text 5.95 (*0-19-586304-6*) OUP.
Prince & the Pauper. Jane Gerver. LC 98-41049. (Step into Classics Ser.). 95p. (J). (gr. 3-5). 1999. pap. 3.99 (*0-679-89213-3*, Pub. by Random Bks Yng Read) Random.
Prince & the Pauper. Aurand Harris. (J). (gr. 1-6). 1995. 6.00 (*0-87602-337-5*) Anchorage.
Prince & the Pauper. Mark Twain, pseud. (Airmont Classics Ser.). (J). (gr. 5 up). 1964. mass mkt. 2.50 (*0-8049-0032-9*, CL-32) Airmont.
Prince & the Pauper. Mark Twain, pseud. (Illustrated Classics Collection: No. 4). 64p. 1994. pap. 4.95 (*0-7854-0751-0*, 40506) Am Guidance.
Prince & the Pauper. Mark Twain, pseud. 19.95 (*0-8488-0849-5*) Amereon Ltd.
Prince & the Pauper. Mark Twain, pseud. (Andre Deutsch Classics). 240p. (J). (gr. 5-8). 1996. 9.95 (*0-233-99080-1*, Pub. by Andre Deutsch) Trafalgar.
Prince & the Pauper. Mark Twain, pseud. (Bantam Classics Ser.). 240p. (J). (gr. 4-12). 1983. mass mkt. 3.95 (*0-553-21256-7*) Bantam.
***Prince & the Pauper.** Mark Twain, pseud. 176p. 2000. pap. 2.00 (*0-486-41110-9*) Dover.
Prince & the Pauper. Mark Twain, pseud. 223p. (J). (gr. 6). 1964. mass mkt. 3.95 (*0-451-52193-5*, Sig Classics) NAL.
Prince & the Pauper. Mark Twain, pseud. Ed. by Lucy Rollin. (World's Classics Ser.). (Illus.). 274p. (C). 1996. pap. 7.95 (*0-19-282401-5*) OUP.
Prince & the Pauper. Mark Twain, pseud. Ed. by Lucy Rollin. (Illus.). 280p. 2000. pap. 7.95 (*0-19-283960-8*) OUP.
Prince & the Pauper. Mark Twain, pseud. Ed. by John N. Fago. (Now Age Illustrated IV Ser.). (Illus.). (gr. 4-12). 1978. student ed. 1.25 (*0-88301-341-X*); pap. text 2.95 (*0-88301-317-7*) Pendulum Pr.
Prince & the Pauper. Mark Twain, pseud. Ed. by Malvina Vogel. (Great Illustrated Classics Ser.: Vol. 22). (Illus.). 240p. (J). (gr. 3-6). 1992. 9.95 (*0-86611-973-6*) Playmore Inc.
Prince & the Pauper. Mark Twain, pseud. 256p. (YA). 1992. mass mkt. 2.50 (*0-8125-0477-1*, Pub. by Tor Bks) St Martin.
Prince & the Pauper. Mark Twain, pseud. LC 89-33892. (Illustrated Classics Ser.). (Illus.). 48p. (J). (gr. 3-6). 1990. lib. bdg. 19.95 (*0-8167-1873-3*) Troll Communs.
Prince & the Pauper. Mark Twain, pseud. Ed. by Raymond James. LC 89-33892. (Illustrated Classics Ser.). (Illus.). 48p. (J). (gr. 3-6). 1996. pap. 5.95 (*0-8167-1874-1*) Troll Communs.
Prince & the Pauper. Mark Twain, pseud. Ed. by Victor Fischer et al. (Iowa-California Edition of the Works of Mark Twain: No. 6). (Illus.). 533p. 1979. 45.00 (*0-520-03622-0*, Pub. by U CA Pr) Cal Prin Full Svc.
Prince & the Pauper. Mark Twain, pseud. LC 83-47882. (Mark Twain Library: No. 5). (Illus.). 324p. (C). 1983. 45.00 (*0-520-05088-6*, Pub. by U CA Pr) Cal Prin Full Svc.
Prince & the Pauper. Mark Twain, pseud. LC 83-47882. (Mark Twain Library: No. 5). (Illus.). 324p. (C). 1984. pap. 14.95 (*0-520-05108-4*, Pub. by U CA Pr) Cal Prin Full Svc.
Prince & the Pauper. Mark Twain, pseud. LC 97-13726. 199p. 1997. pap. 8.95 (*0-14-043669-3*) Viking Penguin.
Prince & the Pauper. Mark Twain, pseud. (Children's Library). 1998. pap. 3.95 (*1-85326-147-5*, 1475WW, Pub. by Wrdsworth Edits) NTC Contemp Pub Co.
Prince & the Pauper. ed. Mark Twain, pseud. 1.43 (*1-929120-66-4*) Electric Umb OR.
Prince & the Pauper. abr. ed. Mark Twain, pseud. (Illus.). 288p. (YA). (gr. 5 up). 1996. pap. 4.99 (*0-14-036749-7*, PuffinBks) Peng Put Young Read.
Prince & the Pauper. abr. ed. Mark Twain, pseud et al. LC 96-9804. (Children's Thrift Editions Ser.). (Illus.). 107p. (J). 1997. reprint ed. pap. text 1.00 (*0-486-29383-1*) Dover.
Prince & the Pauper. deluxe ed. Marianna Mayer. Ed. by Diane Arico. LC 98-36176. (Illus.). 48p. (J). (gr. 2-4). 1999. 17.99 (*0-8037-2099-8*, Dial Yng Read) Peng Put Young Read.
***Prince & the Pauper.** large type ed. Mark Twain, pseud. (Large Print Heritage Ser.). 360p. 2000. lib. bdg. 33.95 (*1-58118-068-3*, 23662) LRS.
***Prince & the Pauper.** large type ed. Mark Twain, pseud. 317p. 2000. 26.95 (*0-7838-9061-3*) Mac Lib Ref.
Prince & the Pauper. Mark Twain, pseud. 1982. reprint ed. lib. bdg. 20.95 (*0-89966-380-X*) Buccaneer Bks.
Prince & the Pauper. Mark Twain, pseud. (Works of Mark Twain). 1988. reprint ed. lib. bdg. 79.00 (*0-7812-1120-4*) Rprt Serv.
Prince & the Pauper: A Tale for Young People of All Ages. Mark Twain, pseud. (J). 1964. 9.05 (*0-606-01271-0*, Pub. by Turtleback) Demco.
Prince & the Pauper: A Tale for Young People of All Ages (1881) Ed. by Shelley F. Fishkin. (Oxford Mark Twain). (Illus.). 496p. 1997. text 22.00 (*0-19-511406-X*) OUP.
Prince & the Pauper - Musical. Lewis Hardee. 80p. 1995. 5.50 (*0-87129-467-2*, P74) Dramatic Pub.
Prince & the Pauper - Straight. Mark Twain, pseud & Anne C. Martens. 1970. 3.75 (*0-87129-417-6*, P37) Dramatic Pub.
Prince & the Pauper by Mark Twain: Curriculum Unit. Center for Learning Network Staff & Mark Twain. (Novel - Drama Ser.). 54p. (YA). (gr. 8-12). 1996. teacher ed., spiral bd. 18.95 (*1-56077-493-2*) Ctr Learning.
Prince & the Pauper Notes. L. David Allen. (Cliffs Notes Ser.). 80p. (Orig.). (C). 1980. pap. text 4.95 (*0-8220-1096-8*, Cliff) IDG Bks.
Prince & the Pauper Readalong. Mark Twain, pseud. (Illustrated Classics Collection: No. 4). 64p. 1994. pap. 14.95 incl. audio (*0-7854-0767-7*, 40508) Am Guidance.
Prince & the Pilgrim. Mary Stewart. LC 96-90776. 308p. 1997. mass mkt. 6.50 (*0-449-22443-0*) Fawcett.
Prince & the Pilgrim. large type ed. Mary Stewart. (Romance Ser.). 402p. 1996. 26.95 (*0-7862-0586-5*) Thorndike Pr.
***Prince & the Pole Star.** Kosha Ely. (Illus.). 32p. (J). (gr. 1-6). 2000. 14.95 (*1-887089-29-2*, Pub. by Torchlght Pub) Natl Bk Netwk.
Prince & the Pooch. Caroline Leavitt. LC 97-72877. (Adventures of Wishbone Ser.: Vol. 3). (Illus.). 128p. (J). (gr. 3-7). 1997. mass mkt. 3.99 (*1-57064-196-X*, Big Red) Lyrick Pub.
Prince & the Pooch. Caroline Leavitt. (Adventures of Wishbone Ser.). (Illus.). (J). 1997. 10.34 (*0-606-18272-1*) Turtleback.
Prince & the Pooch see Adventures of Wishbone
Prince & the Poor Boy. Mark Twain, pseud. Date not set. pap. text. write for info. (*0-17-557043-4*) Addison-Wesley.
Prince & the Pretender: Two Views of the '45. A. J. Youngston. 280p. 1996. pap. 52.00 (*1-873644-62-0*, Pub. by Mercat Pr Bks) St Mut.
Prince & the Professor: A Dialogue on the Place of the Monarchy in the 21st Century L. L. Blake. LC 96-162612. 126p. 1995. pap. write for info. (*0-85683-165-4*, Pub. by Shepheard-Walwyn Pubs) Paul & Co Pubs.
Prince & the Prophet: The Rise of Naseem Hamed. Nick Pitt. LC 98-54243. (Illus.). 256p. 1999. pap. 16.00 (*1-56858-130-0*) FWEW.
Prince & the Prosecutor. Peter J. Heck. LC 96-6549. 336p. 1997. pap. 21.95 (*0-425-15970-1*, Prime Crime) Berkley Pub.
Prince & the Prosecutor. Peter J. Heck. (Mark Twain Ser.: No. 3). 336p. 1998. pap. 5.99 (*0-425-16567-1*, Prime Crime) Berkley Pub.
Prince & the Revolution - Parade. Ed. by Carol Cuellar. 64p. (Orig.). (C). 1986. pap. text 12.95 (*0-7692-0505-4*, VF1308) Wrner Bros.
Prince & the Revolution - Purple Rain. Ed. by Carol Cuellar. 72p. (Orig.). (C). 1984. pap. text 16.95 (*0-7692-0552-6*, VF1179) Wrner Bros.
Prince & the Scholar. S. J. Revich. LC 92-70596. 128p. 1992. 12.95 (*1-56062-111-7*); pap. 9.95 (*1-56062-112-5*) CIS Comm.
Prince & the Showgirl. Joann Ross. (Men at Work Ser.: Vol. 27). 1998. mass mkt. 4.50 (*0-373-81039-3*, 1-81039-9) Harlequin Bks.
Prince & the Three Beggars. R. Edward Miller. 33p. (Orig.). (YA). (gr. 12). 1975. pap. 2.00 (*0-945818-04-1*) Peniel Pubns.
Prince & Utopia: Curriculum Unit. Center for Learning Network Staff et al. (Novel Ser.). 93p. (YA). 1994. spiral bd. 18.95 (*1-56077-308-1*) Ctr Learning.
Prince Borghese's Trail: 10,000 Miles over Two Continents, Four Deserts & the Roof of the World in the Peking to Paris Motor Challenge. Genevieve Obert. LC 99-34574. (Illus.). 308p. 1999. 23.95 (*1-57178-085-8*, Pub. by Coun Oak Bks) SPD-Small Pr Dist.
Prince Caspian. C. S. Lewis. LC 99-57458. (Chronicles of Narnia Ser.: Bk. 2). (J). (gr. 4-8). 1950. 30.00 (*0-7862-2234-4*) Mac Lib Ref.
Prince Caspian. C. S. Lewis. (Chronicles of Narnia Ser.: Bk. 2). 224p. (J). (gr. 4-8). 1970. pap. 3.95 (*0-02-044240-8*) Macmillan.
Prince Caspian. C. S. Lewis. (Chronicles of Narnia Ser.: Bk. 2). (J). (gr. 4-8). 1994. 12.05 (*0-606-06680-2*, Pub. by Turtleback); 10.05 (*0-606-06681-0*, Pub. by Turtleback) Demco.
***Prince Caspian.** C. S. Lewis. (Chronicles of Narnia Ser.: Bk. 2). (J). (gr. 4-8). 1998. lib. bdg. 18.95 (*1-56723-072-5*) Yestermorrow.
Prince Caspian. C. S. Lewis. LC 85-18999. (Chronicles of Narnia Ser.: Bk. 2). (Illus.). 192p. (J). (gr. 4-8). 1986. reprint ed. pap. 7.95 (*0-02-044430-3*) Macmillan.
***Prince Caspian: Full-Color Collector's Edition.** C. S. Lewis. LC 93-11514. (Chronicles of Narnia Ser.: Bk. 2). (Illus.). 240p. (J). (gr. 4-7). 2000. mass mkt. 7.95 (*0-06-440944-9*, HarpTrophy) HarpC Child Bks.
Prince Caspian: The Return to Narnia. C. S. Lewis. LC 93-11514. (Chronicles of Narnia Ser.: Bk. 2). (Illus.). 240p. (J). (gr. 4-7). 1994. 16.95 (*0-06-023483-0*); pap. 6.95 (*0-06-440500-1*, HarpTrophy); pap. 4.95 (*0-06-447105-5*, Harper Keypoint); lib. bdg. 16.89 (*0-06-023484-9*) HarpC Child Bks.
Prince Caspian Audio. abr. ed. C. S. Lewis. (Chronicles of Narnia Ser.). (J). (gr. 4-7). 1989. audio 11.95 (*0-89845-090-X*, CPN 1603) HarperAudio.
Prince Charles. Joan Veon. 1997. pap. text 11.95 (*1-57558-021-7*) Hearthstone OK.
Prince Charles & the Architect. 1990. 19.95 (*0-312-04525-5*) St Martin.
Prince Charles Edward. Andrew Lang. LC 01-25240. reprint ed. 105.00 (*0-404-03855-7*) AMS Pr.
***Prince Charming.** Gaelen Foley. 400p. 2000. mass mkt. 6.50 (*0-449-00635-2*) Ivy Books.
Prince Charming. Julie Garwood. Ed. by Linda Marrow. 560p. 1995. per. 6.99 (*0-671-87096-3*, Pocket Star Bks) PB.
***Prince Charming.** Julie Garwood. 1999. pap. 9.98 (*0-671-04426-5*) PB.
***Prince Charming.** Robin Wells. 400p. 1999. mass mkt. 5.99 (*0-505-52344-2*, Love Spell) Dorchester Pub Co.
***Prince Charming: The John F. Kennedy Jr. Story, Vol. 1.** Wendy Leigh. 1999. mass mkt. 6.99 (*0-451-40921-3*, Sig) NAL.
***Prince Charming: The John F. Kennedy, Jr. Story.** Wendy Leigh. 368p. 2000. pap. 9.95 (*0-451-20080-2*, Sig) NAL.
Prince Charming Isn't Coming: How Women Get Smart about Money. Barbara Stanny. LC 97-12681. (Illus.). 240p. (ps-5). 1999. pap. 12.95 (*0-14-026693-3*) Viking Penguin.
Prince Charming Lives! Finding the Love of Your Life. Phyllis B. Light. LC 93-6409. 240p. 1994. pap. 12.95 (*0-931892-78-3*) Lght Unltd.
Prince Charming, M. D. Prescription: Marriage. Susan Mallery. 1998. per. 4.25 (*0-373-24209-3*, 1-24209-8) Silhouette.
Prince Charming's Child: Man of the Month. Jennifer Greene. (Desire Ser.: Bk. 1225). 1999. per. 3.75 (*0-373-76225-9*, 1-76225-1) Silhouette.
Prince Charming's Return: Fabulous Fathers. Myrna MacKenzie. 1999. per. 3.50 (*0-373-19361-0*, 1-19361-4) Silhouette.
Prince Cinders. Babette Cole. (CHI & ENG.). (J). write for info. (*1-85430-308-2*, 93437, Pub. by MAGI1 UK); write for info. (*1-85430-309-0*, 93438, Pub. by MAGI1 UK) Midpt Trade.
Prince Cinders. Babette Cole. (BEN.). (J). 1995. write for info. (*1-85430-306-6*, Pub. by MAGI1 UK); write for info. (*1-85430-307-4*, Pub. by MAGI1 UK) Midpt Trade.
Prince Cinders. Babette Cole. (Illus.). 32p. (J). (ps-3). 1997. pap. 5.99 (*0-698-11554-6*, PapStar) Peng Put Young Read.
***PRINCE Companion: Project & Team Manager.** David E. Marsh. 212p. 1998. 70.00 (*0-11-702296-9*, Pub. by Statnry Office) Balogh.
***PRINCE Companion: Project Assurance Function.** David E. Marsh. 200p. 1998. 70.00 (*0-11-702297-7*, Pub. by Statnry Office) Balogh.
***PRINCE Companion: Project Board Member.** David E. Marsh. 203p. 1998. 70.00 (*0-11-702295-0*, Pub. by Statnry Office) Balogh.
Prince Conor. Maura Seger. (Intimate Moments Ser.). 1993. per. 3.50 (*0-373-07520-0*, 5-07520-5) Silhouette.
Prince Duekalion. Bayard Taylor. (Notable American Authors). 1999. reprint ed. lib. bdg. 125.00 (*0-7812-8995-5*) Rprt Serv.
Prince Edward County Marriages, 1754-1810. Catherine L. Knorr. 108p. 1982. reprint ed. 15.00 (*0-89308-263-5*, VA 21) Southern Hist Pr.
Prince Edward County, Virginia Deed Book 1 (1754-1759) T.L.C. Genealogy Staff. LC 90-71429. 71p. (Orig.). 1990. pap., spiral bd. 10.00 (*1-57445-001-8*) TLC Genealogy.
Prince Edward County, Virginia Deed Book 2 (1759-1765) T.L.C. Genealogy Staff. LC 90-71429. 74p. (Orig.). 1990. pap., spiral bd. 10.00 (*1-57445-002-6*) TLC Genealogy.
Prince Edward County, Virginia Wills, 1754-1776. T.L.C. Genealogy Staff. LC 91-66082. 91p. (Orig.). 1991. pap., spiral bd. 14.00 (*1-57445-003-4*) TLC Genealogy.
***Prince Edward Island.** (Canada in the Twenty First Century Ser.). (Illus.). (J). 2000. 18.95 (*0-7910-6069-1*) Chelsea Hse.
Prince Edward Island. Harry Beckett. LC 97-1421. (Journey Across Canada Ser.). 24p. (J). (gr. 3-5). 1997. lib. bdg. 18.60 (*1-55916-200-7*) Rourke Bk Co.
Prince Edward Island. Kumari Campbell. LC 95-4221. (Hello Canada Ser.). (Illus.). 76p. (J). 1996. lib. bdg. 19.95 (*0-8225-2762-6*, Lerner Publctns) Lerner Pub.
***Prince Edward Island.** Kumari Campell. (Hello Canada Ser.). 1999. pap. 7.95 (*1-55041-267-1*) Fitzhenry & W Ltd.
Prince Edward Island. 2nd ed. Ed. by Laurie Brinklow. 200p. 1998. pap. 16.95 (*0-88780-438-1*, Pub. by J Lorimer) Formac Dist Ltd.
Prince Edward Island: A Color Guidebook. Laurie Brinklow. (Illus.). 200p. 1995. pap. 16.95 (*0-88780-318-0*, Pub. by Formac Publ Co) Formac Dist Ltd.
Prince Edward Island Sayings. T. K. Pratt. LC 98-209478. (Illus.). 152p. 1998. text 29.95 (*0-8020-0920-4*) U of Toronto Pr.
Prince Elmo. Elmo E. Cunningham. LC 99-70101. 112p. 1999. pap. 11.95 (*1-57197-163-7*) Pentland Pr.
Prince Eugene & the Cinder Queen. Mickey Wright. 25p. (Orig.). (YA). (gr. 6-12). 1991. pap. 3.00 (*1-57514-156-6*, 1124) Encore Perform Pub.
Prince Eugene at War, 1809. Robert M. Epstein. LC 84-81744. (Napoleon's Commanders Ser.). (Illus.). 160p. 1984. 24.95 (*0-913037-05-2*) Empire Games Pr.
Prince Exile. Lisa K. Laurel. (Horizon Ser.: No. 483). (FRE.). 1998. mass mkt. 3.50 (*0-373-39483-7*, 1-39483-2) Harlequin Bks.
Prince Friedrich of Homburg. Heinrich Von Kleist. Tr. by Diana L. S. Peters & Frederick G. Peters from GER. LC 78-6670. 1978. pap. 8.95 (*0-8112-0694-7*, NDP462, Pub. by New Directions) Norton.
Prince George: Rivers, Railways. Bev Christensen. 1989. 29.95 (*0-89781-266-2*, 5314) Am Historical Pr.
Prince George County, Virginia, Vol. 6. Lindsay O. Duvall. (Virginia Colonial Abstracts, Series II). 80p. 1978. reprint ed. pap. 17.50 (*0-89308-067-5*) Southern Hist Pr.
Prince George's Co. MD Marriages & Deaths in Nineteenth Century Newspapers, Vol. 1 A-J. Shirley V. Baltz & George E. Baltz. (Illus.). 331p. (Orig.). 1995. pap. 25.00 (*0-7884-0626-4*) Heritage Bk.
Prince George's County & the Beltway Street Guide & Directory: 1999 Edition. Thomas Bros. Maps Staff. (Illus.). 280p. 1998. pap. 14.95 (*1-58174-039-5*) Thomas Bros Maps.
Prince George's County Land Records, 1696-1702, Vol. A. Ed. by Shirley L. Wilcox. 98p. 1992. reprint ed. 10.00 (*0-916805-00-X*) Prince Georges County Gen Soc.
***Prince George's County, Maryland.** Prince George's County Historical Trust Staff et al. (Images of America Ser.). (Illus.). 128p. 1999. pap. 18.99 (*0-7385-0265-0*) Arcadia Publng.
Prince George's County, Maryland Vol. 2: Marriages & Deaths in Nineteenth Century Newspapers, K-Z. Shirley V. Baltz & George E. Baltz. 291p. (Orig.). 1995. pap. 25.00 (*0-7884-0282-X*) Heritage Bk.
Prince George's County, Maryland, Land Records, 1739-1743. T.L.C. Genealogy Staff. 228p. (Orig.). 1997. pap., spiral bd. 20.00 (*1-57445-026-3*) TLC Genealogy.

P

Prince George's County, Maryland, Land Records, 1746-1749. 214p. 1998. spiral bd. 25.00 (*1-57445-049-2*) TLC Genealogy.

***Prince George's County Street Guide & Directory: 2000 Edition.** (Illus.). 176p. 2000. pap. 10.95 (*1-58174-144-8*) Thomas Bros Maps.

Prince Habib's Iceberg. Edward Hyams. LC 74-14539. 288p. (J). 1975. write for info. (*0-393-08704-2*) Norton.

***Prince Hagen.** Upton Sinclair. (Collected Works of Upton Sinclair). 249p. 1999. reprint ed. lib. bdg. 98.00 (*1-58201-830-8*) Classic Bks.

Prince Hagen: A Phantasy. Upton Sinclair. Ed. by R. Reginald & Douglas Melville. LC 77-84267. (Lost Race & Adult Fantasy Ser.). 1978. reprint ed. lib. bdg. 23.95 (*0-405-11008-1*) Ayer.

Prince Hal. Mark Dunster. 18p. (Orig.). 1995. pap. 4.00 (*0-89642-274-7*) Linden Pubs.

Prince Hall: Social Reformer. Arthur Diamond. Ed. by Nathan I. Huggins. (Black Americans of Achievement Ser.). (Illus.). 124p. (YA). (gr. 5 up). 1992. lib. bdg. 19.95 (*1-55546-588-9*) Chelsea Hse.

Prince Hall & His Followers. George W. Crawford. LC 74-144591. reprint ed. 32.50 (*0-404-00145-9*) AMS Pr.

Prince Hall Masonic Quiz Book. Joseph A. Walkes. xix, 153p. 1993. pap. 12.00 (*0-88053-085-5*, M315) Macoy Pub.

***Prince Harry.** Wendy Brody. (Illus.). (Orig.). 2000. mass mkt. 5.99 (*0-7860-1145-9*, Pinncle Kensgtn) Kensgtn Pub Corp.

Prince Henry: The Navigator. Edward G. Bourne. (Works of Edward Gaylord Bourne). 1989. reprint ed. lib. bdg. 79.00 (*0-7812-2008-4*) Rprt Serv.

Prince Henry of Prussia, Brother of Frederick the Great. Chester V. Easum. LC 75-113061. (Illus.). 403p. 1971. reprint ed. lib. bdg. 35.00 (*0-8371-4697-6*, EAPH, Greenwood Pr) Greenwood.

Prince Henry Sinclair. Frederick J. Pohl. LC E109. (Illus.). 232p. 1998. pap. text 14.95 (*1-55109-122-4*) Nimbus Publ.

***Prince Henry "the Navigator" A Life.** P. E. Russell. LC 99-49569. (Illus.). 464p. 2000. 35.00 (*0-300-08233-9*) Yale U Pr.

Prince in Camelot. Courtway Jones. 1995. mass mkt. 5.99 (*0-671-73408-3*) PB.

Prince in Prison: The Previous Lubavitcher Rebbe's Account of His Incarceration in Stalinist Russia in 1927. Tr. by Uri Kaploun. LC 98-224392. 144p. 1997. 15.00 (*1-881400-27-1*) S I E.

Prince in the Tower: Perceptions of la Vida es Sueno. Ed. by Frederick A. De Armas. LC 92-54454. (C). 1993. 39.50 (*0-8387-5252-7*) Bucknell U Pr.

Prince in Waiting see Sword of the Spirits Trilogy

Prince in Waiting. John Christopher. (J). (gr. 5-9). 1984. 18.25 (*0-8446-6157-0*) Peter Smith.

Prince in Waiting. John Christopher. 1990. reprint ed. lib. bdg. 25.95 (*0-89966-668-X*) Buccaneer Bks.

Prince in Waiting. 2nd ed. John Christopher. (Sword of the Spirits Trilogy Ser.). (J). 1989. 9.05 (*0-606-02269-4*, Pub. by Turtleback) Demco.

Prince in Waiting. 2nd ed. John Christopher. (Sword of the Spirits Trilogy Ser.). (Illus.). 192p. (YA). (gr. 5-9). 1989. reprint ed. mass mkt. 3.95 (*0-02-042573-2*) Macmillan.

Prince Ishmael. Marianne Hauser. (Sun & Moon Classics Ser.: No. 4). 316p. 1989. pap. 11.95 (*1-55713-039-6*) Sun & Moon CA.

Prince Ito. Kengi Hamada. LC 79-65475. (Studies in Japanese History & Civilization). 240p. 1979. reprint ed. lib. bdg. 72.50 (*0-313-26996-3*, U6996, Greenwood Pr) Greenwood.

Prince Ivan & the Firebird. Illus. & Retold by Laszlo Gal. 1991. pap. 14.99 (*0-7710-3300-1*) McCland & Stewart.

Prince Ivan & the Firebird. Bernard Lodge. (Illus.). 32p. (J). (gr. k-5). 1996. pap. 6.95 (*1-879085-63-1*, Whispering Coyote) Charlesbridge Pub.

Prince Ivan & the Firebird: A Russian Folk Tale. Bernard Lodge. 1996. 12.15 (*0-606-08848-2*, Pub. by Turtleback) Demco.

Prince Jamil & Fair Leila. (J). (gr. 1-6). 1990. 9.95 (*0-86685-487-8*) Intl Bk Ctr.

Prince Joe. Suzanne Brockmann. (Intimate Moments Ser.). 1996. per. 3.99 (*0-373-07720-3*, 1-07720-5) Silhouette.

***Prince Joe.** large type ed. Suzanne Brockmann. 1999. 21.95 (*0-373-59598-0*) S&S Trade.

Prince John Magruder: His Life & Campaigns. Paul D. Casdorph. LC 96-16598. (Illus.). 400p. 1996. 30.00 (*0-471-15941-7*) Wiley.

Prince Leapinhigh. P. J. Meltabarger. 26p. (J). (ps). 1996. 12.95 (*1-56763-173-8*); pap. text 3.95 (*1-56763-172-X*) Ozark Pub.

Prince Leopold: The Untold Story of Queen Victoria's Youngest Son. Charlotte Zeepvat. (Illus.). 224p. 1998. 35.95 (*0-7509-1308-8*, Pub. by Sutton Pub Ltd) Intl Pubs Mktg.

Prince Leopold: The Untold Story of Queen Victoria's Youngest Son. Charlotte Zeepvat. 2000. pap. text 17.95 (*0-7509-2292-3*) Sutton Pub Ltd.

Prince Lichnowsky & the Great War. Harry F. Young. LC 75-11448. 295p. reprint ed. pap. 91.50 (*0-608-15800-3*, 203105700073) Bks Demand.

Prince Lost to Time. Ann Dukthas. 1996. mass mkt. 5.99 (*0-312-95843-9*) St Martin.

Prince (Machiavelli) Tessa Krailing. (Barron's Book Notes Ser.). (C). 1985. pap. 2.95 (*0-8120-3536-4*) Barron.

Prince Madoc: Founder of Clark County Indiana. Dana Olson. (Illus.). 128p. 1987. pap. 10.00 (*0-9677903-0-1*) Olson Enter.

Prince Mammoth Pumpkin: A Parable. James Adams. LC 97-36879. (Illus.). 48p. 1998. 14.95 (*0-8091-0492-X*) Paulist Pr.

Prince Marko: The Hero of South Slavic Epics. Tatyana Popovic. (Illus.). 280p. 1988. 45.00 (*0-8156-2444-1*) Syracuse U Pr.

Prince Michael & the Dragon (A True Story) John C. Orndorff. LC 99-65997. (Illus.). vi, 87p. (J). (gr. 5-8). 1998. pap. 5.95 (*1-893213-00-5*) Amulet.

Prince Michael Vorontsov: Viceroy to the Tsar. Anthony L. Rhinelander. 304p. (C). 1990. text 65.00 (*0-7735-0747-7*, Pub. by McG-Queens Univ Pr) CUP Services.

Prince Nautilus. Laura Krauss Melmed. LC 93-37432. (Illus.). (J). 1994. 16.00 (*0-688-04566-9*) Lothrop.

Prince Notes. Luisa Vergani. (Cliffs Notes Ser.). 80p. 1967. pap. 4.95 (*0-8220-1093-3*, Cliff) IDG Bks.

Prince of a Fellow. Shelby Hearon. LC 91-5178. (Texas Tradition Ser.: No. 18). 206p. 1992. reprint ed. 14.95 (*0-87565-099-6*) Tex Christian.

Prince of Abissinia: A Tale, 1759, 2 vols. in 1. Samuel Johnson. LC 74-17303. (Novel in England, 1700-1775 Ser.). 159p. 1974. lib. bdg. 61.00 (*0-8240-1150-3*) Garland.

Prince of Akko. R. Sackville. (Tamar Bks.). 1992. 16.99 (*0-89906-148-6*); pap. 13.99 (*0-89906-149-4*) Mesorah Pubns.

Prince of Annwn: The First Branch of the Mabinogion. Evangeline Walton. 192p. 1992. pap. 8.95 (*0-02-026471-2*) Macmillan.

***Prince of Butterflies.** Bruce Coville. LC 99-50811. (Illus.). (J). 2002. write for info. (*0-15-201454-3*, Harcourt Child Bks) Harcourt.

Prince of Chaos. Roger Zelazny. 256p. 1992. mass mkt. 5.99 (*0-380-75502-5*, Avon Bks) Morrow Avon.

Prince of Darkness. LC 99-201798. 1999. pap. text 10.95 (*1-874509-64-6*) XPr.

Prince of Darkness. P. C. Doherty. (WWL Mystery Ser.). 1995. per. 3.99 (*0-373-26164-0*, 1-26164-3) Harlequin Bks.

Prince of Darkness. Jeffrey. pap. 13.95 (*0-921714-04-1*, Pub. by Fon3tier Res) Spring Arbor Dist.

Prince of Darkness. Grant R. Jeffrey. 368p. 1995. mass mkt. 6.99 (*0-553-56223-1*) Bantam.

Prince of Darkness. Barbara Michaels, pseud. 240p. 1988. mass mkt. 6.99 (*0-425-10853-8*) Berkley Pub.

Prince of Darkness. Joan O'Grady. 1993. pap. 12.95 (*1-85230-056-6*, Pub. by Element MA) Penguin Putnam.

Prince of Darkness. Kate Proctor. LC 96-259. 186p. 1995. per. 3.25 (*0-373-11767-1*, 1-11767-0) Harlequin Bks.

Prince of Darkness. large type ed. P. C. Doherty. 400p. 1996. 27.99 (*0-7089-3482-X*) Ulverscroft.

Prince of Darkness: Radical Evil & the Power of Good in History. Jeffrey B. Russell. LC 88-47744. (Illus.). 304p. 1992. pap. 14.95 (*0-8014-8056-6*) Cornell U Pr.

Prince of Delights. Renee Roszel. (Romance Ser.: No. 198). 1992. per. 2.89 (*0-373-03198-X*, 1-03198-8) Harlequin Bks.

Prince of Delights. Renee Roszel. (Family Continuity Program Ser.: No. 38). 1999. mass mkt. 4.50 (*0-373-82186-7*, 1-82186-7) Harlequin Bks.

Prince of Demons. Mickey Z. Reichert. LC 96-228053. (Renshai Chronicles Ser.: Vol. 2). 688p. 1996. pap. 22.95 (*0-88677-715-1*, Pub. by DAW Bks) Penguin Putnam.

Prince of Demons Vol. 2: The Renshai Chronicles, Vol. 2. Mickey Z. Reichert. 704p. 1997. mass mkt. 6.99 (*0-88677-759-3*, Pub. by DAW Bks) Penguin Putnam.

Prince of Dogs. Kate Elliott. LC 98-150410. 532p. 1998. pap. 23.95 (*0-88677-770-4*, Pub. by DAW Bks) Penguin Putnam.

Prince of Dogs. Kate Elliott. (Crown of Stars Ser.: Vol. 2). 627p. 1999. pap. 6.99 (*0-88677-816-6*, Pub. by DAW Bks) Penguin Putnam.

Prince of Dreams. Lisa Kleypas. (Orig.). 1995. mass mkt. 5.99 (*0-380-77355-4*, Avon Bks) Morrow Avon.

Prince of Dreams. Susan Krinard. 448p. 1995. mass mkt. 5.99 (*0-553-56776-4*) Bantam.

***Prince of Egypt.** 585p. 1999. pap. 9.95 (*1-57560-157-5*, Pub. by Cherry Lane) H Leonard.

Prince of Egypt. Cherry Lane Music Staff. 1999. pap. text 14.95 (*1-57560-156-7*, Pub. by Cherry Lane); pap. text 16.95 (*1-57560-155-9*, Pub. by Cherry Lane) H Leonard.

Prince of Egypt. Charles Solomon. LC 98-34121. (Illus.). 192p. 1998. 45.00 (*0-8109-4369-7*, Pub. by Abrams) Time Warner.

Prince of Egypt. Jane Yolen. LC 99-190532. (Illus.). 80p. (J). (ps-4). 1998. 8.99 (*0-525-46050-0*, PuffinBks) Peng Put Young Read.

Prince of Egypt: A New Vision in Animation. Charles Solomon. 1998. 60.00 (*0-670-88213-5*) Viking Penguin.

Prince of Egypt: Classic Edition. Jane Yolen. (Prince of Egypt Ser.). (J). 1998. 8.99 (*0-8499-5894-6*) Tommy Nelson.

Prince of Egypt: Coloring Art Book. (Illus.). 64p. (YA). 5.99 (*0-14-056473-X*) Peng Put Young Read.

Prince of Egypt: Read Along Story book & Tape. Andre Mika. (Illus.). 32p. 1998. pap. text 8.99 (*0-14-088862-4*, PuffinBks) Peng Put Young Read.

Prince of Egypt: The Movie Scrapbook. Tommi Lewis. LC 99-190555. (Illus.). 64p. 1998. pap. 8.99 (*0-14-056474-8*, PuffinBks) Peng Put Young Read.

Prince of Egypt: The Novel. Lynne Reid Banks. 128p. 1998. pap. 4.99 (*0-14-130217-8*, PuffinBks) Peng Put Young Read.

***Prince of Egypt Family Passover Haggadah.** Michel Schwartz. 1999. 12.99 (*1-879016-25-7*) UOJC Amer.

Prince of Fire: An Anthology of Contemporary Serbian Short Stories. Ed. by Radmilla Gorup & Nadezda Obradovic. LC 97-45345. (Pitt Series in Russian & East European Studies). 335p. 1998. pap. 19.95 (*0-8229-5661-6*); text 50.00 (*0-8229-4058-2*) U of Pittsburgh Pr.

Prince of Forgers. Tr. by Joseph Rosenblum from FRE. LC 98-14515. (Illus.). 200p. 1998. 39.95 (*1-884718-51-5*, 50317) Oak Knoll.

Prince of Frogs see Principe de las Ranas

Prince of Garden Hills. Vance Wampler. 218p. 1988. 19.50 (*0-935632-68-9*) Wolfe Pub Co.

Prince of Georgia, & Other Tales. Julian Ralph. LC 74-142274. (Short Story Index Reprint Ser.). 1977. 19.95 (*0-8369-3758-9*) Ayer.

Prince of Graustark. George B. McCutcheon. 1976. 23.95 (*0-8488-0289-6*) Amereon Ltd.

Prince of Gravas: A Story of the Past. Alfred C. Fleckenstein. Ed. by R. Reginald & Douglas Melville. LC 77-84233. (Lost Race & Adult Fantasy Ser.). (Illus.). 1978. reprint ed. lib. bdg. 26.95 (*0-405-10976-8*) Ayer.

Prince of Havoc: Twilight of the Clans, Vol. VII. Michael A. Stackpole. (Battletech Ser.). 287p. 1998. mass mkt. 5.99 (*0-451-45706-4*, ROC) NAL.

***Prince of Hearts.** Katy Cooper. (Historical Ser.). 2000. mass mkt. 4.99 (*0-373-29125-6*, 1-29125-1) Harlequin Bks.

Prince of Her Dreams see Principe de Sus Suenos

Prince of Homburg. Heinrich Von Kleist. Tr. & Intro. by Bernard Sahlins. Intro. by Nicholas Rudall. (Plays for Performance Ser.). 104p. 1990. pap. 7.95 (*0-929587-44-8*, Pub. by I R Dee); lib. bdg. 15.95 (*0-929587-47-2*, Pub. by I R Dee) Natl Bk Netwk.

Prince of Humbugs: The Life of P. T. Barnum. Cathy Andronik. LC 93-36724. (Illus.). 160p. (J). (gr. 5-9). 1994. 15.95 (*0-689-31796-4*) Macmillan.

Prince of India; or Why Constantinople Fell. Lewis Wallace. (Notable American Authors Ser.). 1999. reprint ed. lib. bdg. 125.00 (*0-7812-9867-9*) Rprt Serv.

Prince of Kisses. Colleen Shannon. 400p. (Orig.). 1997. mass mkt. 5.99 (*0-505-52200-4*, Love Spell) Dorchester Pub Co.

Prince of Lies. Robyn Donald. LC 96-283. 187p. 1995. per. 3.25 (*0-373-11783-3*, 1-11783-7) Harlequin Bks.

Prince of Lost Kingdom. unabridged ed. Alph A. Adams. LC 97-68759. 250p. 1997. pap. 11.95 (*0-9662823-0-2*) Gemini Pub Hse.

Prince of Magic. Anne Stuart. 352p. 1998. mass mkt. 5.99 (*0-8217-6053-X*, Zebra Kensgtn) Kensgtn Pub Corp.

Prince of Martyrs: A Brief Account of Imam Husayn. A. Q. Faizi. 74p. 1977. pap. 4.00 (*0-85398-073-X*) G Ronald Pub.

Prince of Mercenaries. Jerry Pournelle. 352p. (Orig.). 1989. mass mkt. 5.99 (*0-671-69811-7*) Baen Bks.

Prince of Midnight. Laura Kinsale. 1990. mass mkt. 4.95 (*0-380-76130-0*, Avon Bks) Morrow Avon.

Prince of Midnight. large type ed. Laura Kinsale. LC 91-2804. 683p. 1991. reprint ed. lib. bdg. 20.95 (*1-56054-168-7*) Thorndike Pr.

Prince of Midnight. Laura Kinsale. 416p. 1991. reprint ed. 22.00 (*0-7278-4214-5*) Severn Hse.

Prince of Mount Kinabalu. F. I. Rejab. (Illus.). 40p. (J). 1995. 9.95 (*983-9808-26-5*, Pub. by Delta Edits) Weatherhill.

Prince of Our Disorder: The Life of T. E. Lawrence. John E. Mack. LC 98-141432. 609p. 1999. pap. text 19.50 (*0-674-70494-0*) HUP.

Prince of Peace. Robert A. Allen. 60p. 1995. pap. 4.00 (*1-57514-140-X*, 1076) Encore Perform Pub.

Prince of Peace. James Carroll. 544p. 1998. pap. 13.00 (*0-395-92619-X*) HM.

Prince of Peace & His Love: Is the Sweetest Story Ever Told. Josephine C. Trust. (Illus.). 160p. 1940. reprint ed. 6.00 (*1-892203-15-4*, 15, Superet Pr) Mother Trust.

***Prince of Perfect.** Sharyn Cannon. Ed. by Noreen Wise. (Lemonade Collection). (Illus.). 48p. (YA). (ps up). 2000. pap. 5.95 (*1-58584-212-5*) Huckleberry CT.

Prince of Persia: The Official Strategy Guide. Rusel DeMaria. LC 93-9695. (Illus.). 272p. (Orig.). 1993. pap. 19.95 (*1-55958-373-8*) Prima Pub.

Prince of Persia 3D: Prima's Official Strategy Guide. Prima Publishing Staff. 244p. 1998. per. 19.99 (*0-7615-1729-4*) Prima Pub.

Prince of Players: Edwin Booth. Eleanor Ruggles. 27.95 (*0-89190-565-0*) Amereon Ltd.

Prince of Pleasure: The Prince of Wales & the Making of the Regency. Saul David. LC 98-46754. (Illus.). 496p. 1999. 30.00 (*0-87113-739-9*) Grove-Atltic.

***Prince of Pleasure: The Prince of Wales & the Making of the Regency.** Saul David. 496p. 2000. pap. 15.00 (*0-8021-3703-2*, Pub. by Grove-Atltic) Publishers Group.

Prince of Publishers: A Study of the Work & Career of Jacob Tonson. Harry M. Geduld. LC 68-64121. (Indiana University Humanities Ser.: No. 66). 260p. reprint ed. pap. 80.60 (*0-608-11157-0*, 200574200059) Bks Demand.

Prince of Shadows. Susan Krinard. 384p. 1996. mass mkt. 5.99 (*0-553-56777-2*) Bantam.

Prince of Silence. S. Adel. 272p. 1999. pap. 7.50 (*1-892614-12-X*, BWP-PS) Briarwood VA.

Prince of Sparta. Jerry Pournelle & S. M. Stirling. 416p. (Orig.). 1993. per. 4.99 (*0-671-72158-5*) Baen Bks.

Prince of Stars in the Cavern of Time. Ian Dennis. 430p. 1989. 22.50 (*0-87951-298-9*, Pub. by Overlook Pr) Penguin Putnam.

Prince of Sunset. Steve White. 400p. 1998. per. 5.99 (*0-671-87869-7*) Baen Bks.

Prince of Swords. Anne Stuart. 270p. 1997. lib. bdg. 21.95 (*0-7862-1116-4*) Five Star.

Prince of Swords. Anne Stuart. 384p. 1996. mass mkt. 5.99 (*0-8217-5397-5*, Zebra Kensgtn) Kensgtn Pub Corp.

Prince of Tarn. Hazel J. Hutchins. (Illus.). 144p. (J). (gr. 3-7). 1997. pap. 5.95 (*1-55037-438-9*, Pub. by Annick) Firefly Bks Ltd.

Prince of Tarn. Hazel J. Hutchins. (Illus.). 144p. (J). (gr. 4-6). 1997. 14.95 (*1-55037-439-7*, Pub. by Annick) Firefly Bks Ltd.

***Prince of Tennessee: How Al Gore Met His Fate.** David Maraniss. 224p. 2000. 21.50 (*0-7432-0411-5*) S&S Trade.

Prince of the Blood. Raymond E. Feist. 400p. 1990. mass mkt. 6.99 (*0-553-28524-6*, Spectra) Bantam.

Prince of the Captivity. John Buchan. 236p. 1996. pap. 16.95 (*1-873631-68-5*, Pub. by B&W Pub) Firebird Dist.

Prince of the City: The True Story of a Cop Who Knew Too Much. Robert Daley. 400p. 1994. mass mkt. 5.99 (*0-446-36569-6*, Pub. by Warner Bks) Little.

***Prince of the Clouds.** Gianni Riotta. Tr. by Stephen Sartarelli from ITA. LC 99-55335. 288p. 2000. 24.00 (*0-374-23725-5*) FS&G.

Prince of the Fairway: The Tiger Woods Story. LC 97-24122. (Young Adult Ser.). 112p. (YA). (gr. 7-12). 1997. lib. bdg. 18.50 (*1-888105-22-4*) Avisson Pr.

Prince of the Ghetto. Maurice Samuel. LC 87-8191. (Brown Classics in Judaica Ser.). 306p. 1987. reprint ed. pap. text 29.00 (*0-8191-5784-8*) U Pr of Amer.

Prince of the House of David. F. Ingraham. Orig. Title: Three Years in the Holy City. 340p. 1994. reprint ed. 35.95 (*0-89841-003-7*) Zoe Pubns.

Prince of the People: The Life & Times of a Brazilian Free Man of Colour. Eduardo Silva. 288p. (C). (gr. 13). 1993. 35.00 (*0-86091-417-8*, B2485, Pub. by Verso) Norton.

Prince of the Pond: Otherwise Known as De Fawg Pin. Donna Jo Napoli. LC 91-40340. (Illus.). 112p. (J). (gr. 2-5). 1992. 15.99 (*0-525-44976-0*, Dutton Child) Peng Put Young Read.

Prince of the Pond: Otherwise Known as De Fawg Pin. Donna Jo Napoli. (Illus.). 160p. (J). (gr. 3-7). 1994. pap. 4.99 (*0-14-037151-6*, PuffinBks) Peng Put Young Read.

Prince of the Pond: Otherwise Known as De Fawg Pin. Donna Jo Napoli. 1994. 9.60 (*0-606-07071-0*, Pub. by Turtleback) Demco.

Prince of the Quotidian. Paul Muldoon. LC 94-60895. 40p. 1994. pap. 5.95 (*0-916390-63-2*) Wake Forest.

Prince of the Ring: The Naseem Hamed Story. Gavin Evans. (Illus.). 280p. 1997. 28.95 (*1-86105-021-6*, Robson-Parkwest) Parkwest Pubns.

Prince of the Stable: A Hungarian Legend. Christopher Keane. LC 96-9612. (Legends of the World Ser.). (Illus.). 32p. (J). (gr. 2-5). 1998. pap. 4.95 (*0-8167-4022-4*) Troll Communs.

Prince of the Stable: A Hungarian Legend. Christopher Keane. (Legends of the World Ser.). 1996. 10.15 (*0-606-09766-X*, Pub. by Turtleback) Demco.

Prince of Thieves. Saranne Dawson. 368p. 1998. mass mkt. 5.50 (*0-505-52288-8*, Love Spell) Dorchester Pub Co.

Prince of Tides. Pat Conroy. 672p. 1987. mass mkt. 7.99 (*0-553-26888-0*) Bantam.

Prince of Tides, 001. Pat Conroy. 576p. 1986. 30.00 (*0-395-35300-9*) HM.

Prince of Tides. Pat Conroy. LC 86-10689. 1991. 12.60 (*0-606-03895-7*, Pub. by Turtleback) Demco.

Prince of Tides, Set. abr. ed. Pat Conroy. 1987. audio 16.99 (*0-553-45096-4*, 391403) BDD Aud Pub.

Prince of Tides: Movie Selections. Ed. by Carol Cuellar. 32p. (Orig.). (C). 1992. pap. text 14.95 (*0-7692-0488-0*, P0941SMX) Wrner Bros.

Prince of Time. Rebecca York. (Promo Ser.). 1999. per. 4.50 (*0-373-21952-0*, 1-21952-6) Harlequin Bks.

Prince of Time: 43 Light Street. Rebecca York. 1995. per. 3.50 (*0-373-22338-2*) Harlequin Bks.

Prince of Wales. Jonathan Dimbleby. 640p. 1994. 32.95 (*0-385-25472-5*) Doubleday.

Prince of Wales: A Biography. large type ed. Jonathan Dimbleby. LC 95-2629. 894p. 1995. lib. bdg. 26.95 (*0-7862-0426-5*) Thorndike Pr.

Prince of Wales & Stories. Jonathan Mallalieu. 272p. 1993. pap. (*1-897580-11-8*) Phoenix Hse.

Prince of Wales Own, the Scinde Horse: A Regimental History. Ed. by Picton Publishing (Chippenham) Ltd. Staff. (C). 1987. 150.00 (*0-7855-5332-0*, Pub. by Picton) St Mut.

Prince of Wales Prize in Urban Design, 1990: The Urban Public Spaces of Barcelona 1981-1987. Henry N. Cobb et al. (Illus.). 47p. 1991. 10.00 (*0-614-14661-5*) Harvard Univ Graduate Schl of.

Prince of West End Avenue. Alan Isler. 256p. 1995. pap. 12.95 (*0-14-024514-6*, Penguin Bks) Viking Penguin.

Prince of West End Avenue: A Novel. Alan Isler. LC 93-35927. 246p. 1994. 19.95 (*1-882593-04-9*) Bridge Wrks.

Prince of Whales. R. L. Fisher. 160p. (YA). 1988. pap. 2.95 (*0-8125-6637-8*, Pub. by Tor Bks) St Martin.

Prince of Whales. R. L. Fisher. (Illus.). 160p. (J). (gr. 3 up). 1987. reprint ed. pap. 2.50 (*0-8125-6635-1*, Pub. by Tor Bks) St Martin.

Prince of Wolves. Susan Krinard. 480p. 1994. mass mkt. 5.99 (*0-553-56775-6*) Bantam.

Prince Ombra. Roderick MacLeish. 320p. 1994. pap. 12.95 (*0-312-89024-9*) Orb NYC.

Prince, People, & Confession: The Second Reformation in Brandenburg. Bodo Nischan. LC 93-49639. (Illus.). 384p. (C). 1994. text 51.95 (*0-8122-3242-9*) U of Pa Pr.

Prince Peter & the Teddy Bear. David McKee. LC 96-62032. (Illus.). 32p. (J). (ps-1). 1997. 15.00 (*0-374-36123-1*) FS&G.

***Prince Peter Kropotkin: His Thoughts & Works.** Ed. by Subrata Mukherjee & Sushila Ramaswamy. 1998. 78.00 (*81-7100-765-1*) Deep & Deep Pubns.

Prince Philip. large type ed. John Parker. (Non-Fiction Ser.). 528p. 1992. 27.99 (*0-7089-8642-0*) Ulverscroft.

Prince Poloka of Uli Loko. Becky Daniel. (Illus.). 48p. (J). (gr. 3-5). 1994. 9.95 (*0-9642050-0-9*) Great Creations.

Prince Rabbit see Creative Short Stories

Prince Rabbit. A. A. Milne, pseud. 40p. 1983. pap. 3.50 (*0-87129-776-0*, P56) Dramatic Pub.

Prince Raynor. Henry Kuttner. Ed. by Gary Lovisi. (Illus.). 80p. 1987. 5.95 (*0-936071-06-0*) Gryphon Pubns.

Prince Regent's Silver Bell. Gladys McGorian. 256p. 1987. 16.95 (*0-8027-0954-0*) Walker & Co.

An Asterisk (*) at the beginning of an entry indicates that the title is appearing for the first time.

Prince Rupert: Admiral & General-at-Sea. Frank Kitson. (Illus.). 304p. 1998. 40.00 (*0-09-475800-X*, Pub. by Constable & Co) Trafalgar.

Prince Rupert: Portrait of a Soldier. Frank Kitson. (Illus.). 302p. 1998. pap. 22.95 (*0-09-475500-0*, Pub. by Constable & Co) Trafalgar.

Prince, Showgirl & Me. Colin Clark. 1996. pap. 13.95 (*0-00-638710-1*, Pub. by HarpC) Trafalgar.

Prince Siddhartha: Coloring Book. Jonathan Landaw. (Illus.). 48p. (J). 1996. pap. 6.95 (*0-86171-121-1*) Wisdom MA.

Prince Siddhartha: The Story of Buddha. rev. ed. Jonathan Landaw. (Illus.). 144p. (J). (gr. 1-8). 1996. pap. 18.95 (*0-86171-016-9*) Wisdom MA.

Prince Skippy's Quest. Gwen Hoelscher. (Illus.). 64p. (Orig.). (J). (gr. 6 up). 1986. pap. 7.95 (*0-9617597-0-4*) Wright Monday Pr.

Prince, Suivi de l'Antiprince. Niccolo Machiavelli. (FRE.). 1996. pap. 7.95 (*2-87714-327-9*, Pub. by Bookking Intl) Distribks Inc.

Prince Tandi of Cumba: or The New Menoza. J. M. Lenz. Ed. & Tr. by David Hill & Michael Butler from GER. (Contemporary Theatre Studies: Vol. 9). 127p. 1996. text 36.00 (*3-7186-5595-0*, ECU43, Harwood Acad Pubs); pap. text 18.00 (*3-7186-5603-5*, ECU14, Harwood Acad Pubs) Gordon & Breach.

Prince the First Decade: DanceMusicSexRomance. Per Nilsen. 224p. 1999. pap. 18.95 (*0-946719-23-3*, Pub. by Helter Skelter) Interlink Pub.

Prince, the Lady & the Tower. Muriel Jensen. (Fairy Tale Ser.). 1997. per. 3.75 (*0-373-16669-9*, 1-116669-3) Harlequin Bks.

***Prince, the Show Girl & Me: Six Months on the Set with Marilyn & Olivier.** Colin Clark. (Illus.). 219p. 2000. reprint ed. 21.00 (*0-7881-9380-5*) DIANE Pub.

Prince Travestil l'Ile des Esclaves: Le Triomphe de l'Amour. Pierre Carlet de Chamblain de Marivaux. (FRE.). 1989. pap. 10.95 (*0-7859-2996-7*) Fr & Eur.

Prince Valiant. Martin Delrio. LC 96-95128. 246p. (gr. 4-7). 1998. mass mkt. 5.99 (*0-380-79405-5*, Avon Bks) Morrow Avon.

***Prince Valiant.** Martin Delrio. 1999. mass mkt. 3.99 (*0-380-79404-7*, Avon Bks) Morrow Avon.

Prince Valiant: Arn Triumphant, Vol. 38. Hal Foster. (Illus.). 48p. 2000. pap. 16.95 (*1-56097-370-6*) Fantagraph Bks.

Prince Valiant: Tillicum's Counsel, Vol. 33. Hal Foster. (Illus.). 48p. 1997. pap. 16.95 (*1-56097-311-0*) Fantagraph Bks.

Prince Valiant: 1967-1968, Vol. 36. Hal Foster. 1999. pap. 16.95 (*1-56097-348-X*) Fantagraph Bks.

Prince Valiant: 1968-1969, Vol. 37. Hal Foster. 1999. pap. text 16.95 (*1-56097-352-8*) Fantagraph Bks.

Prince Valiant Vol. 8: "Prince of Thule" Harold Foster. (Illus.). 48p. 1990. 14.95 (*1-56097-011-1*) Fantagraph Bks.

Prince Valiant Vol. 9: "Queen of the Misty Isles" Harold Foster. (Illus.). 48p. 1990. 14.95 (*1-56097-012-X*) Fantagraph Bks.

Prince Valiant Vol. 10: "Aleta" Harold Foster. (Illus.). 48p. 1990. 14.95 (*1-56097-033-2*) Fantagraph Bks.

Prince Valiant Vol. 11: Intrigues at Camelot. Hal Foster. (Illus.). 48p. (Orig.). 1991. pap. 14.95 (*1-56097-046-4*) Fantagraph Bks.

Prince Valiant Vol. 12: The New World. Hal Foster. (Illus.). 48p. (Orig.). 1991. pap. 16.95 (*1-56097-047-2*) Fantagraph Bks.

Prince Valiant Vol. 13: "The Sun Goddess" Hal Foster. (Illus.). 48p. (Orig.). 1991. pap. 16.95 (*1-56097-059-6*) Fantagraph Bks.

Prince Valiant Vol. 14: "Sword & Sorcery" Hal Foster. (Illus.). 48p. (Orig.). 1992. pap. 16.95 (*1-56097-060-X*) Fantagraph Bks.

Prince Valiant Vol. 15: Young Geoffrey. Hal Foster. 48p. 1992. pap. 16.95 (*1-56097-065-0*) Fantagraph Bks.

Prince Valiant Vol. 16: Love & War. Hal Foster. (Illus.). 48p. 1992. pap. 16.95 (*1-56097-073-1*) Fantagraph Bks.

Prince Valiant Vol. 17: Return from Rome. Hal Foster. (Illus.). 48p. 1993. per. 16.95 (*1-56097-089-8*) Fantagraph Bks.

Prince Valiant Vol. 18: The Stolen River. Hal Foster. (Illus.). 48p. (Orig.). 1993. pap. 16.95 (*1-56097-109-6*, Pub. by Fantagraph Bks) Seven Hills Bk.

Prince Valiant Vol. 19: Duel in Ireland. Hal Foster. (Illus.). 48p. 1993. pap. 16.95 (*1-56097-122-3*) Fantagraph Bks.

Prince Valiant Vol. 20: The Pilgrimage. Hal Foster. (Illus.). 48p. (Orig.). 1993. pap. 16.95 (*1-56097-123-1*) Fantagraph Bks.

Prince Valiant Vol. 21: Prisoner of the Khan. Hal Foster. (Illus.). 48p. (Orig.). 1994. pap. 16.95 (*1-56097-124-X*) Fantagraph Bks.

Prince Valiant Vol. 22: Homeward Bound. Hal Foster. 48p. 1994. pap. 16.95 (*1-56097-142-8*) Fantagraph Bks.

Prince Valiant Vol. 23: The Kings of Cornwall. Hal Foster. (Illus.). 48p. (Orig.). 1995. pap. 16.95 (*1-56097-158-4*) Fantagraph Bks.

Prince Valiant Vol. 24: The Red Stallion. Hal Foster. 48p. 1995. pap. 16.95 (*1-56097-167-3*) Fantagraph Bks.

Prince Valiant Vol. 25: The Curse. Hal Foster. 48p. 1995. pap. 16.95 (*1-56097-195-9*) Fantagraph Bks.

Prince Valiant Vol. 26: Lithway's Law. Hal Foster. 48p. 1984. pap. 16.95 (*1-56097-197-5*) Fantagraph Bks.

Prince Valiant Vol. 27: The Eternal Quest. Hal Foster. 48p. 1985. pap. 16.95 (*0-930193-03-2*) Fantagraph Bks.

Prince Valiant Vol. 28: The Savage Girl. Hal Foster. 48p. 1985. pap. 16.95 (*0-930193-12-1*, Pub. by Fantagraph Bks) Seven Hills Bk.

Prince Valiant Vol. 29: Monastery of the Demons. Hal Foster. (Illus.). 48p. (Orig.). 1986. pap. 16.95 (*0-930193-08-3*) Fantagraph Bks.

Prince Valiant Vol. 34: Murdred's Revenge. Hal Foster. (Illus.). 48p. 1998. pap. 16.95 (*1-56097-312-9*) Fantagraph Bks.

Prince Valiant Vol. 35: Doppleganger, 40, 35. Hal Foster. (Illus.). 48p. 1998. pap. 16.95 (*1-56097-332-3*) Fantagraph Bks.

Prince Valiant - An American Epic, Vol. 1. Hal Foster. LC 82-17919. (Complete Prince Valiant Ser.: Bk. 1). 56p. 1982. 150.00 (*0-936414-04-9*) Manuscript Pr.

Prince Valiant - An American Epic, Vol. 2. Hal Foster. Ed. by Rick Norwood. (Complete Prince Valiant Ser.: Bk. 2). (Illus.). 60p. 1984. pap. 100.00 (*0-936414-05-7*) Manuscript Pr.

Prince Valiant - An American Epic: 1939, Vol. 3. Hal Foster. Ed. by Rick Norwood. (Complete Prince Valiant Ser.: Bk. 3). (Illus.). 60p. (Orig.). 1993. pap. 150.00 (*0-936414-08-1*) Manuscript Pr.

Prince Valiant - An American Epic: 1939, 3 vols., Vols. 1-3. limited ed. Hal Foster. Ed. by Rick Norwood. (Complete Prince Valiant Ser.). (Illus.). 172p. (Orig.). 1993. 850.00 (*0-936414-09-X*) Manuscript Pr.

Prince Valiant Coloring Book: Authorized Edition. deluxe limited ed. Intro. by John Dandola. (Illus.). 52p. 1990. reprint ed. pap. 6.95 (*1-878452-00-2*, Tory Corner) Quincannon.

Prince Vijaya Pala of Ceylon, 1634-1654. P. E. Pieris. 1995. 8.50 (*0-614-18150-X*, Pub. by Asian Educ Servs) S Asia.

Prince Wen Hui's Cook. Bob Flaws & Honora L. Wolfe. 208p. (Orig.). 1995. pap. text 14.00 (*0-912111-05-4*) Paradigm Publns.

Prince Who Became a Beggar see Tales of Heaven & Earth

Prince Who Became a Cuckoo: A Tale of Liberation. Lo-dro of Drepung. Tr. by Geshe Wangyal. (Bhaisajaguru Ser.). 1982. pap. 12.95 (*0-87830-574-2*, Thtre Arts Bks) Routledge.

Prince Who Turned into a Rooster: One Hundred Tales from Hasidic Tradition. Tzvi M. Rabinowicz. LC 93-31396. 280p. 1994. pap. 30.00 (*0-87668-685-4*) Aronson.

Prince Who Wouldn't Shut Up: Adapted from a Scandinavian Folktale. Papa Joe. (Step into a Story Book Ser.). 21p. 1996. pap. 3.50 (*1-889238-10-4*) Papa Joes.

Prince Who Wrote a Letter. Ann Love. LC 92-27587. (Illus.). 32p. (J). 1992. 13.99 (*0-85953-398-0*, Pub. by Childs Play); pap. 6.99 (*0-85953-399-9*, Pub. by Childs Play) Random House.

Prince Who Wrote a Letter. Ann Love. (J). 1996. lib. bdg. 15.95 (*0-85953-888-5*) Childs Play.

Prince Who Wrote a Letter. Ann Love. (FRE., Illus.). 32p. (J). (gr. k-3). 1996. pap. 6.99 (*0-85953-459-6*) Childs Play.

Prince Who Wrote a Letter. Ann Love. (Children's Stories Published in Other Lands Ser.). (Illus.). 32p. (J). (gr. k-3). 1996. lib. bdg. 16.95 (*1-56674-212-9*) Forest Hse.

Prince William. Tamara L. Britton. LC 98-38113. (J). 1999. 13.98 (*1-57765-324-6*) ABDO Pub Co.

Prince William. Valerie Garner. (Illus.). 95p. 1998. pap. 12.95 (*1-56649-049-9*) Welcome Rain.

Prince William. Paul Joseph. LC 98-38113. (Young Profiles Ser.). 1999. pap. text 5.95 (*1-57765-336-X*) ABDO Pub Co.

***Prince William.** Kristin McCracken. (High Interest Bks.). (Illus.). (J). 2000. 19.00 (*0-516-23325-4*) Childrens.

***Prince William.** Kristin McCracken. LC 00-24227. (High Interest Bks.). (Illus.). 48p. (J). (gr. 4-7). 2000. pap. write for info. (*0-516-23525-7*) Childrens.

***Prince William.** Contrib. by Miniature Book Collection Staff & Smithmark Staff. LC 99-189484. (Pocket Romeos Ser.). (Illus.). 48p. (gr. 5 up). 1998. 4.98 (*0-7651-0942-5*) Smithmark.

Prince William. Catherine Murphy. LC 98-85422. (Little Bks.). (Illus.). 80p. 1998. 4.95 (*0-8362-7133-5*) Andrews & McMeel.

Prince William. Gloria Rand. LC 91-25180. (J). (ps-3). 1995. pap. 5.95 (*0-8050-3384-X*) H Holt & Co.

Prince William. Gloria Rand. LC 91-25180. (Illus.). 32p. (J). (gr. 1-3). 1995. 14.95 (*0-8050-1841-7*, Bks Young Read) H Holt & Co.

Prince William. Scott. Date not set. pap. 6.99 (*0-689-82691-5*) S&S Childrens.

***Prince William: A Birthday Scrapbook.** M. E. Crane. Orig. Title: Prince William Bio, Prince William Comes of Age. (J). (gr. 4-6). 2000. per. 6.99 (*0-689-83532-9*) Aladdin.

Prince William: A Journey to the Throne. Ed. by Brock Wylan. (Illus.). 36p. (J). (gr. 3-11). 1998. mass mkt. 8.95 (*0-9664074-0-7*) Centrl Pk Pubng.

Prince William: Prince of Hearts. Lisa Degnen. LC 98-86955. 96p. 1998. mass mkt. 9.99 (*0-446-67539-3*, Pub. by Warner Bks) Little.

Prince William: The Boy Who Will Be King. Randi Reisfeld. LC 99-195322. (Illus.). (YA). (gr. 5 up). 1997. per. 4.99 (*0-671-88785-8*, Archway) PB.

Prince William: The Boy Who Will Be King. rev. ed. Randi Reisfeld. (J). 1998. pap. 4.99 (*0-671-02358-6*, Archway) PB.

Prince William: The Story So Far. Michael Johnstone. 48p. 1999. 5.95 (*0-7894-4668-5*) DK Pub Inc.

Prince William B. The Philosophical Conceptions of William Blake. Norman Nathan. LC 75-331669. (Studies in English Literature ; V. 100). 164 p. 1975. write for info. (*90-279-3071-6*) Mouton.

Prince William B. The Philosophical Conceptions of William Blake. Norman Nathan. (Studies in English Literature: No. 100). 164p. 1975. pap. text 35.40 (*90-279-3117-8*) Mouton.

Prince William Bio, Prince William Comes of Age see Prince William: A Birthday Scrapbook

Prince William, Born to Be King, 1 vol. Richard Buskin. 1998. mass mkt. 6.99 (*0-451-19927-8*) NAL.

Prince William County Street Guide & Directory: 1999 Edition. Thomas Bros. Maps Staff. (Illus.). 96p. 1998. pap. 9.95 (*1-58174-097-2*) Thomas Bros Maps.

Prince William Sound. Alaska Geographic Society Staff. Ed. by Penny Rennick. LC 72-92087. (Alaska Geographic Ser.: Vol. 20-1). (Illus.). 112p. 1993. pap. 19.95 (*1-56661-008-7*) Alaska Geog Soc.

Prince William Sound Environmental Reader. Ed. by Nancy Lethcoe & Lisa Nurnberger. (Illus.). 118p. (J). 1989. pap. 12.00 incl. audio (*0-9613146-9-9*) Prince W Sound.

Prince William Sound, West, AK. Ed. by Trails Illustrated Staff. 1995. 8.99 (*1-56695-017-1*) Trails Illustrated.

Prince William, the Boy Who Will Be King: An Unauthorized Biography. Randi Reisfeld. LC 49-252540. (J). 1997. 10.09 (*0-606-11763-6*, Pub. by Turtleback) Demco.

Prince William, the Story of Its People & Its Places. Writers Program, Virginia Staff. LC 73-3657. (American Guide Ser.). 1941. reprint ed. 10.50 (*0-404-57957-4*) AMS Pr.

Prince with Many Castles & Other Stories. Sarah Churchill. LC 68-93638. (Illus.). 5-60 p. (J). 1967. write for info. (*0-09-084550-1*, Pub. by Arrow Bks) Trafalgar.

Prince Zaleski. Matthew P. Shiel. reprint ed. lib. bdg. 21.95 (*0-89190-486-7*, Rivercity Pr) Amereon Ltd.

Prince Zaleski. Matthew P. Shiel. LC 75-32782. (Literature of Mystery & Detection Ser.). 1976. reprint ed. 17.95 (*0-405-07898-6*) Ayer.

Prince Zaleski & Cummings King Monk. Matthew P. Shiel. LC 76-17993. 1977. 12.95 (*0-87054-007-6*, Mycroft & Moran) Arkham.

***Princely Courts of Europe 1500-1750.** John Adamson. 352p. 1999. 60.00 (*0-297-83653-6*) Weidenfeld & Nicolson.

Princely Gifts & Papal Treasures: The Franciscan Mission to China & Its Influence on the Art of the West, 1250-1350. Lauren Arnold. (Illus.). 175p. 1999. 49.95 (*0-9670628-0-2*) Desiderata Pr.

Princely Press: Machiavelli on American Journalism. John C. Merrill. LC 98-10555. 160p. (C). 1998. 52.00 (*0-7618-1035-8*); pap. 29.50 (*0-7618-1036-6*) U Pr of Amer.

Princely Profits of Party Plan. 12th ed. Dean F. Du Vall. 84p. 1980. pap. 10.00 (*0-931232-08-2*) Du Vall Financial.

Princely Sailor: Mountbatten of Burma. Ian McGeoch. LC 96-42448. (Illus.). 288p. 1996. 29.95 (*1-85753-161-2*, Pub. by Brasseys) Brasseys.

Princes. Sonya Hartnett. LC 97-60742. (Illus.). 137p. (J). (gr. 10 up). 1998. 14.99 (*0-670-87821-9*) Viking Penguin.

Princes & Peasants: Smallpox in History. Donald R. Hopkins. LC 83-6472. (Illus.). 384p. 1983. 25.00 (*0-226-35176-9*) U Ch Pr.

Princes & Peasants: Smallpox in History. Donald R. Hopkins. LC 83-6472. (Illus.). xx, 380p. 1985. pap. 12.95 (*0-226-35177-7*) U Ch Pr.

Princes & Propaganda: Electoral Saxon Art of the Reformation. Carl C. Christensen. (Sixteenth Century Essays & Studies: Vol. 20). (Illus.). 149p. 1992. text 40.00 (*0-940474-21-2*, SCJP) Truman St Univ.

Princes as Patrons: The Art Collections of the Princes of Wales from the Renaissance to the Present. Mark Evans. LC 98-204636. (Illus.). 112p. 1999. 45.00 (*1-85894-054-0*, Pub. by Merrell Holberton) U of Wash Pr.

Prince's Baby. Lisa K. Laurel. 1997. per. 3.25 (*0-373-19263-0*, 1-19263-2) Silhouette.

Prince's Bride. Lisa K. Laurel. 1997. per. 3.25 (*0-373-19251-7*, 1-19251-7) Silhouette.

***Prince's Bride, Vol. 16.** Tracy Cozzens. (Zebra Bouquet Ser.). 1999. mass mkt. 3.99 (*0-8217-6351-2*, Zebra Kensgtn) Kensgtn Pub Corp.

***Prince's Bride-to-Be.** Valerie Parv. (Romance Ser.). 2000. mass mkt. 3.50 (*0-373-19465-X*, 1-19465-3) Silhouette.

Princes et Principautes Russes, XE-XVIIE Siecles. Wladimir Vodoff. (Collected Studies: No. CS304). (FRE.). 348p. (C). 1989. reprint ed. text 124.95 (*0-86078-252-2*, Pub. by Variorum) Ashgate Pub Co.

Prince's Heir. Sally Carleen. (Romance Ser.: No. 1397). 1999. per. 3.50 (*0-373-19397-1*, 1-19397-8) Silhouette.

Princes in the Tower. Alison Weir. 304p. 1995. pap. 12.50 (*0-345-39178-0*) Ballantine Pub Grp.

Princes Ne Sont Pas Tous Charmants. Sylvie Desrosiers. (Novels in the Roman Jeunesse Ser.). (FRE.). 96p. (J). (gr. 4-7). 1995. pap. 8.95 (*2-89021-233-5*, Pub. by La Courte Ech) Firefly Bks Ltd.

Princes of India in the Endgame of Empire, 1917-1947. Ian Copland. (Cambridge Studies in Indian History & Society: No. 2). 316p. 1997. text 59.95 (*0-521-57179-0*) Cambridge U Pr.

***Princes of Ireland, Planters of Maryland: A Carroll Saga, 1500-1782.** Ronald Hoffman. LC 99-52475. (Illus.). 480p. 2000. 39.95 (*0-8078-2556-5*) U of NC Pr.

Princes of Naranja: An Essay in Anthrohistorical Method. Paul Friedrich & Dennis Tedlock. LC 86-16075. 325p. 1987. text 29.95 (*0-292-76432-4*) U of Tex Pr.

Princes of Naranja: An Essay in Anthrohistorical Method. Paul Friedrich. LC 86-16075. (Illus.). 325p. reprint ed. pap. 100.80 (*0-608-20111-1*, 207138300011) Bks Demand.

Princes of Orange: The Stadholders in the Dutch Republic. Herbert H. Rowen. (Studies in Early Modern History). (Illus.). 264p. (C). 1990. pap. text 19.95 (*0-521-39653-0*) Cambridge U Pr.

Princes of the Trenches: Narrating the German Experience of the First World War. Ann Linder. (GERM Ser.). x, 206p. 1997. 55.00 (*1-57113-075-6*) Camden Hse.

***Princes of Victorian Bohemia.** D. W. Wynfield. (Illus.). 2000. 49.95 (*3-7913-2301-6*, Pub. by Prestel) te Neues.

Princes, Pastors & People: The Church & Religion in England, 1529-1689. Susan Doran & Christopher Durston. (Illus.). 224p. (C). 1991. pap. 18.99 (*0-415-05964-X*, A5674) Routledge.

Princes, Peasants, & Other Polish Selves: Ethnicity in American Literature. Thomas S. Gladsky. LC 91-42671. 328p. (C). 1992. lib. bdg. 35.00 (*0-87023-775-6*) U of Mass Pr.

Princes, Politics & Religion, 1547-1589. N. M. Sutherland. 240p. (C). 1984. 55.00 (*0-907628-44-3*) Hambledon Press.

Princes, Potentates, & Plain People: The Saga of the Germans from Russia. Reuben Goertz. (Prairie Plains Ser.). (Illus.). 250p. (Orig.). 1994. pap. 13.95 (*0-931170-58-3*) Ctr Western Studies.

Princes, Soldiers, & Rogues: The Politic Malcontent of Renaissance Drama. James R. Keller. LC 92-41529. (American University Studies: English Language & Literature: Ser. IV, Vol. 153). 192p. (C). 1993. text 37.95 (*0-8204-1972-9*) P Lang Pubng.

Prince's Tale & Other Collected Writings. E. M. Forster. LC 98-215815. 280p. 1998. 45.00 (*0-233-99168-9*, Pub. by Andre Deutsch) Trafalgar.

Princes to Act: Royal Audience & Royal Performance, 1578-1792. Matthew H. Wikander. LC 92-351. 368p. 1993. text 52.00 (*0-8018-4428-2*) Johns Hopkins.

Princesa & Friskie. Diana F. Johnson. Tr. by Carlos E. Castillo. LC 97-91811. (ENG & SPA., Illus.). 32p. (Orig.). (J). (ps-6). 1997. pap. 9.95 (*0-9657928-0-3*) Interkids.

Princesa Pirata. Suzanne Simms.Tr. of Pirate Princess. (SPA.). 1996. per. 3.50 (*0-373-35131-3*) Harlequin Bks.

Princesa Vestida con una Bolsa de Papel. Robert Munsch.Tr. of Paperbag Princess. (SPA., Illus.). 32p. (YA). (ps up). 1991. pap. 5.95 (*1-55037-098-7*, Pub. by Annick) Firefly Bks Ltd.

Princesa y el Pintor. Jane Johnson.Tr. of Princess & the Painter. (SPA.). (J). (gr. 3-5). 1996. pap. text 15.95 (*1-56014-618-4*) Santillana.

Princesa y el Pirata (The Princess & the Pirate) Alfredo G. Cerda. (SPA.). 32p. (J). (gr. 1-3). 1991. 12.99 (*968-16-3654-6*, Pub. by Fondo) Continental Bk.

Princesa y el Sapo: Grade 3 Best Loved Tales Series 700. (Spanish Well Loved Tales Ser.: No. 700-2).Tr. of Princess & the Toad. (SPA.). (J). (gr. 3). 1990. boxed set 3.50 (*0-7214-1410-9*, Ladybrd) Penguin Putnam.

Princesa y el Vagabundo. Nancy Martin. (Deseo Ser.).Tr. of Princess & the Pauper. (SPA.). 1996. per. 3.50 (*0-373-35167-4*, 1-35167-5) Harlequin Bks.

Princeship of Wales. Jan Morris. Ed. by Meic Stephens. (Changing Wales Ser.). 32p. 1995. pap. 11.95 (*0-8464-4717-7*) Beekman Pubs.

Princesita. (Spanish Children's Classics Ser.: No. 800-2).Tr. of Little Princess. (SPA.). (J). 1990. boxed set 3.50 (*0-7214-1396-X*, Ladybrd) Penguin Putnam.

Princess. Alan Brown. 1990. 17.95 (*1-55972-017-4*, Birch Ln Pr) Carol Pub Group.

Princess. Claire Delacroix. (Bride Quest Ser.: Vol. 1). 416p. 1998. mass mkt. 5.99 (*0-440-22603-1*) Dell.

Princess. Jude Deveraux. 1991. per. 6.99 (*0-671-74380-5*) PB.

Princess. Gaelen Foley. 1999. mass mkt. 5.50 (*0-449-00246-2*) Fawcett.

Princess. Susan L. Roth. LC 92-55042. (Illus.). 32p. (J). (ps-3). 1993. 13.95 (*1-56282-465-1*, Pub. by Hyprn Child) Little.

Princess. large type ed. Ann Morrow. 541p. 1992. 27.99 (*0-7505-0398-X*, Pub. by Mgna Lrg Print) Ulverscroft.

***Princess.** rev. ed. Ivan Bulloch. (I Wish I Were Ser.). (Illus.). (J). 2000. 9.95 (*1-58728-033-7*); pap. 4.95 (*1-58728-037-X*) Two Can Pub.

***Princess: A Novel.** Lori Wick. LC 98-47195. 294p. 1999. pap. 10.99 (*0-7369-0034-9*) Harvest Hse.

***Princess: A Novel.** large type ed. Lori Wick. LC 00-24256. (Christian Fiction Ser.). 448p. 2000. 26.95 (*0-7862-2526-2*) Thorndike Pr.

***Princess A Precious Gift to Unlock & Treasure.** Maureen Rissik. 1999. pap. text 9.95 (*0-7624-0539-2*) Running Pr.

Princess: A True Story of Life Behind the Veil in Saudi Arabia. Jean P. Sasson. (Illus.). 283p. 1993. mass mkt. 6.99 (*0-380-71918-5*, Avon Bks) Morrow Avon.

Princess: A True Story of Life Behind the Veil in Saudi Arabia. large type ed. Jean P. Sasson. LC 92-45238. (General Ser.). 383p. 1993. reprint ed. lib. bdg. 18.95 (*1-56054-667-0*) Thorndike Pr.

Princess: Based on Hans Christian Andersen's "The Princess & the Pea" Anne Wilsdorf. LC 92-20636. Orig. Title: Prindsessen paa aerten. (Illus.). 32p. (J). (ps up). 1993. lib. bdg. 13.93 (*0-688-11542-X*, Grenwillow Bks) HarpC Child Bks.

Princess: Collection #1. Golden Books Staff. 32p. 1999. pap. text 3.99 (*0-307-22500-3*) Gldn Bks Pub Co.

Princess: Collection #2. Golden Books Staff. 32p. 1999. pap. text 3.99 (*0-307-22501-1*) Gldn Bks Pub Co.

Princess Alexandra. 2nd large type ed. Paul James. 335p. 1993. 24.95 (*1-85695-100-6*, Pub. by ISIS Lrg Prnt) Transaction Pubs.

Princess Alopecia. Yaacov Peterseil. (Illus.). 32p. (J). (gr. k-3). 1999. 14.95 (*0-943706-26-2*) Pitspopany.

***Princess Alopecia.** Yaacov Peterseil. (Illus.). 32p. (J). (gr. k-3). 1999. pap. 8.95 (*0-943706-25-4*) Pitspopany.

Princess & Ballet. Donna R. Davis. (Illus.). 52p. (Orig.). (J). (gr. k-5). 1996. pap. 5.95 (*0-9644890-5-8*) Spirit Bks.

Princess & Curdie. George MacDonald. (Illus.). (YA). (gr. 5 up). 1996. pap. 4.99 (*0-14-036762-4*, Viking) Viking Penguin.

Princess & Curdie. George MacDonald. (J). 1997. pap. 1.95 (*0-8167-0473-2*) Troll Communs.

Princess & Curdie. large type ed. George MacDonald. 274p. 1997. reprint ed. lib. bdg. 22.00 (*0-939495-22-8*) North Bks.

P

An Asterisk (*) at the beginning of an entry indicates that the title is appearing for the first time.

Princess & Curdie. George MacDonald. 306p. (J). 1989. reprint ed. lib. bdg. 26.95 (0-89966-591-8) Buccaneer Bks.

Princess & Curdie. George MacDonald. 177p. 1998. reprint ed. lib. bdg. 22.00 (1-58287-059-4) North Bks.

Princess & Curdie: With Colour Plates. George MacDonald. (George MacDonald Original Works Ser.: Series III). (Illus.). 320p. (YA). (gr. 5 up). 1997. reprint ed. 26.00 (1-881084-15-9) Johannesen.

Princess & Frog, Set. (Illus.). 12.95 incl. audio (0-86685-634-X) Intl Bk Ctr.

Princess & Froggie. Harve Zemach & Kaethe Zemach. (Illus.). 48p. (J). (ps-3). 1992. reprint ed. pap. 4.95 (0-374-46011-6, Sunburst Bks) FS&G.

Princess & Goblin. George MacDonald. (Illus.). (YA). (gr. 5 up). 1997. pap. 3.99 (0-14-036746-2, Viking) Viking Penguin.

***Princess & Her Garden: A Fable of Awakening & Arrival.** Patricia R. Adson. LC 99-60298. (Illus.). 64p. 2000. 16.95 (1-883477-34-4) Lone Oak MN.

***Princess & Other Stories.** Anton Chekhov. Tr. by Ronald Hingley. (Oxford World's Classics Ser.). 272p. 1999. pap. 7.95 (0-19-283788-5) OUP.

Princess & the Admiral. Charlotte Pomerantz. LC 91-32614. (Illus.). 48p. (YA). (gr. 3 up). 1992. pap. 8.95 (1-55861-061-8) Feminist Pr.

Princess & the Admiral. Charlotte Pomerantz. LC 91-32614. (Illus.). 48p. (gr. 4-7). 1992. 17.95 (1-55861-060-X) Feminist Pr.

Princess & the Baby: Exodus 1:8-2:10. Janice Kramer. (Arch Bks.: Set 6). (Illus.). 24p. 1970. 1.99 (0-570-06043-5, 59-1158) Concordia.

Princess & the Barbarian. Betina M. Krahn. 416p. (Orig.). 1993. mass mkt. 4.99 (0-380-76772-4, Avon Bks) Morrow Avon.

Princess & the Beggar. Harry Chinchinian. LC 98-65251. (Heather & Hally Brown Ser.). (Illus.). 152p. (J). (gr. 4-9). 1998. 16.95 (0-9653535-8-3) Plum Tree.

Princess & the Beggar: A Korean Folktale. Anne S. O'Brien. LC 92-11988. (Illus.). 32p. (J). (gr. k-4). 1993. 14.95 (0-590-46092-7) Scholastic Inc.

Princess & the Cowboy: Virgin Bride. Martha Shields. (Romance Ser.: No. 1403). 1999. per. 3.50 (0-373-19403-X, 1-19403-4) Silhouette.

Princess & the Dragon. Audrey Wood. (ITA.). (J). 1989. pap. 3.99 (0-85953-571-1) Childs Play.

Princess & the Dragon. Audrey Wood. LC 90-49098. (Illus.). 32p. (J). (ps-2). 1989. 7.99 (0-85953-150-3); pap. 3.99 (0-85953-013-2) Childs Play.

Princess & the Dragon. Audrey Wood. (J). 1996. lib. bdg. 11.95 (0-85953-897-4) Childs Play.

Princess & the Duchess. Josephine Fairley. 1989. 17.95 (0-318-42517-3) St Martin.

***Princess & the Fisherman.** (Illus.). 40p. (YA). 1998. pap. 7.99 (0-9676090-0-3) L Palmer.

Princess & the Frog. (Ladybird Stories Ser.). (ARA., Illus.). (J). (gr. 4-6). 1987. 4.95 incl. audio (0-86685-217-4, LDL137C) Intl Bk Ctr.

Princess & the Frog. Lisa Bingham. (Fairy Tale Ser.). 1997. per. 3.75 (0-373-16692-3, 1-16692-5) Harlequin Bks.

Princess & the Frog. Will Eisner. (Illus.). 32p. (J). (gr. k-4). 1999. 15.95 (1-56163-244-9) NBM.

Princess & the Frog. Amanda Vesey. (Illus.). 32p. (J). (ps-3). 1985. 14.95 (0-316-90036-2, 900362, Joy St Bks) Little.

Princess & the Frog: Story Pak. Retold by K. Hollenbeck. (Graphic Learning Literature Program Series: Folk Tales). (ENG & SPA., Illus.). (J). 1992. 45.00 (0-87746-233-X) Graphic Learning.

Princess & the Goblin. MacDonald. LC 99-21546. (Illus.). 192p. (J). 1999. pap. text 2.50 (0-486-40787-X) Dover.

Princess & the Goblin. George MacDonald. (Airmont Classics Ser.). (J). (gr. 3 up). 1967. mass mkt. 1.50 (0-8049-0156-2, CL-156) Airmont.

Princess & the Goblin. George MacDonald. (J). 1997. pap. 2.95 (0-8167-0472-4) Troll Communs.

Princess & the Goblin. George MacDonald. (Puffin Classics). 1997. 9.09 (0-606-12489-6, Pub. by Turtleback) Demco.

Princess & the Goblin. George MacDonald. 160p. (J). 1998. 24.95 (1-85149-701-3) Antique Collect.

Princess & the Goblin. George MacDonald. LC 93-11264. (Everyman's Library of Children's Classics). (J). (gr. 2 up). 1993. 12.95 (0-679-42810-0) Everymns Lib.

Princess & the Goblin. George MacDonald. LC 86-2532. (Books of Wonder). (Illus.). 208p. (J). (ps up). 1986. 22.95 (0-688-06604-6, Wm Morrow) Morrow Avon.

***Princess & the Goblin.** Barbara McClintock. 40p. (J). (ps-3). 2002. 14.95 (0-06-028228-2) HarpC Child Bks.

Princess & the Goblin. R. McClintock. 40p. (J). (ps-3). 2000. pap. 4.95 (0-06-443538-5) HarpC Child Bks.

Princess & the Goblin. Ed. by Zondervan Publishing Staff. 1996. pap. 13.99 (0-7208-2384-6) Zondervan.

Princess & the Goblin. large type ed. George MacDonald. 260p. 1998. lib. bdg. 22.00 (0-939495-24-4) North Bks.

Princess & the Goblin. George MacDonald. (J). 1989. reprint ed. lib. bdg. 26.95 (0-89966-598-5) Buccaneer Bks.

Princess & the Goblin. George MacDonald. 154p. 1998. reprint ed. lib. bdg. 22.00 (1-58287-060-8) North Bks.

Princess & the Goblin: A Two-Act Play for Children's Theatre. R. Eugene Jackson. 48p. (J). (gr. 3 up). 1983. pap. 3.50 (0-88680-207-5) I E Clark.

Princess & the Goblin: With Colour Plates. George MacDonald. (George MacDonald Original Works Ser.: Series III). (Illus.). 308p. (YA). (gr. 5 up). 1997. reprint ed. 26.00 (1-881084-14-0) Johannesen.

Princess & the God. Doris Orgel. 128p. (YA). (gr. 9 up). 1997. mass mkt. 4.50 (0-440-22691-0) BDD Bks Young Read.

Princess & the God. Doris Orgel. LC 95-33527. 128p. (YA). (gr. 6 up). 1996. lib. bdg. 16.99 (0-531-08866-9) Orchard Bks Watts.

Princess & the God. Doris Orgel. 1997. 9.60 (0-606-13723-8, Pub. by Turtleback) Demco.

***Princess & the Kiss: A Story of God's Gift of Purity.** Warner Press Staff. 2000. 9.95 (0-87162-868-6) Warner Pr.

Princess & the Lord of Night. Emma Bull. LC 93-19151. (Illus.). 32p. (J). (ps-5). 1994. 14.95 (0-15-263543-2, Harcourt Child Bks) Harcourt.

Princess & the P. I. Donna Sterling. (Temptation Ser.: Vol. 694). 1998. per. 3.75 (0-373-25794-5, 1-25794-8) Harlequin Bks.

Princess & the P. O. W. 2nd ed. Richard W. Britt. (Illus.). 283p. 1988. pap. 11.95 (1-881809-25-0) Gabriel TX.

Princess & the Package. Michael Levine. LC 98-26672. 304p. 1998. 24.95 (1-58063-028-6) Renaissance.

***Princess & the Package,** abr. ed. Michael Levine. 1998. pap. 16.95 incl. audio (1-55927-511-1) Audio Renaissance.

Princess & the Painter see Princesa y el Pintor

Princess & the Painter. Jane Johnson. LC 93-39987. 32p. (J). (ps-3). 1994. 15.00 (0-374-36118-5) FS&G.

Princess & the Pauper see Princesa y el Vagabundo

Princess & the Pauper. Tracy Hughes. 1994. per. 3.50 (0-373-70594-8) Harlequin Bks.

Princess & the Pauper: An Erotic Fairy Tale. Gwen Davis. 288p. 1989. 17.95 (0-316-17499-8) Little.

Princess & the Pea. Hans Christian Andersen. LC 81-13395.Tr. of Prindsessen Paa Aerten. (Illus.). 32p. (J). (gr. k-3). 1982. lib. bdg. 15.95 (0-8234-0442-0) Holiday.

Princess & the Pea. Hans Christian Andersen. LC 81-13395.Tr. of Prindsessen Paa Aerten. (Illus.). 32p. (J). (gr. k-3). 1989. pap. 6.95 (0-8234-0753-5) Holiday.

Princess & the Pea. Hans Christian Andersen. (Ladybird Stories Ser.).Tr. of Prindsessen Paa Aerten. (ARA., Illus.). 52p. (J). (gr. 4-6). 1989. 4.95 (0-86685-218-2, LDL163); audio 12.95 (0-86685-633-1) Intl Bk Ctr.

Princess & the Pea. Hans Christian Andersen. LC 85-7199.Tr. of Prindsessen Paa Aerten. (Illus.). 32p. (J). (gr. k-3). 1985. 15.95 (1-55858-034-4, Pub. by North-South Bks NYC) Chronicle Bks.

Princess & the Pea. Hans Christian Andersen. LC 85-7199.Tr. of Prindsessen Paa Aerten. (Illus.). 32p. (J). (gr. k-3). 1995. pap. 6.95 (1-55858-381-5, Pub. by North-South Bks NYC) Chronicle Bks.

Princess & the Pea. Hans Christian Andersen. (Fairy Tale Fun Ser.).Tr. of Prindsessen Paa Aerten. (J). 3.95 (0-7214-5433-X, Ladybrd) Penguin Putnam.

Princess & the Pea. Hans Christian Andersen. (Story Activity Bks.: No. S909-5).Tr. of Prindsessen Paa Aerten. (J). 1991. pap. 1.95 (0-7214-5282-5, Ladybrd) Penguin Putnam.

Princess & the Pea. Hans Christian Andersen.Tr. of Prindsessen Paa Aerten. 1995. 12.15 (0-606-08849-0, Pub. by Turtleback) Demco.

Princess & the Pea. Hans Christian Andersen. (Fairy Tale Pop-ups Ser.). (Illus.). 16p. (J). 1994. 3.95 (0-7214-9421-8, Ladybrd) Penguin Putnam.

Princess & the Pea. Illus. by Emily Bolam. (Easy-to-Read Classics Ser.). 32p. (J). (ps-3). 1996. 13.99 (0-670-86054-9, Viking Child) Peng Put Young Read.

Princess & the Pea. Houghton Mifflin Company Staff. (Literature Experience 1991 Ser.). (J). (gr. 1). 1990. pap. 8.72 (0-395-55141-2) HM.

Princess & the Pea. Houghton Mifflin Company Staff. (Literature Experience 1993 Ser.). (J). (gr. 1). 1992. pap. 8.72 (0-395-61766-9) HM.

Princess & the Pea. Paul Lavrakas. (J). 1993. pap. 6.00 (0-87602-321-9) Anchorage.

Princess & the Pea. Illus. & Adapted by Janet Stevens. (J). (ps-3). 24.95 incl. audio (0-87499-353-9); pap. 15.95 incl. audio (0-87499-352-0) Live Oak Media.

Princess & the Pea. Sucie Stevenson. LC 90-3212. 1992. 10.19 (0-606-06682-9, Pub. by Turtleback) Demco.

Princess & the Pea. Mike Thaler. LC 95-73254. (Happily Ever Laughter Ser.). 1997. pap. 2.99 (0-590-89825-6, Cartwheel) Scholastic Inc.

Princess & the Pea. Harriet Ziefert. 1999. pap. 3.99 (0-14-055546-3) NAL.

Princess & the Pea. Harriet Ziefert. (Easy-to-Read Bks.: Level 2). (Illus.). 32p. (J). (gr. k-3). 1996. pap. 3.99 (0-14-038083-3, PuffinBks) Peng Put Young Read.

Princess & the Pea. Harriet Ziefert. (Puffin Easy-to-Read Ser.). 1996. 9.19 (0-606-09767-8, Pub. by Turtleback) Demco.

Princess & the Pea, 4 bks., Set. Illus. & Adapted by Janet Stevens. (J). (ps-3). pap. 37.95 incl. audio (0-87499-354-7) Live Oak Media.

Princess & the Pea: A Fairy Tale. Hans Christian Andersen. LC 98-35941. (Little Pebbles Ser.). (Illus.). 32p. (J). (ps-1). 1999. 6.95 (0-7892-0515-7, Abbeville Kids) Abbeville Pr.

Princess & the Pea & Inchelina. (Once upon a Time Children's Classics Retold in ASL Ser.: Vol. 5). 32p. (J). (ps-5). VHS 24.95 (0-915035-43-X, 4505) Dawn Sign.

***Princess & the Pea, No TV & Other Plays.** Ric Averill. 75p. 1999. pap. 5.60 (0-87129-926-7, P90) Dramatic Pub.

Princess & the Peacocks: Or, the Story of the Room. Linda Merrill & Sarah Ridley. LC 92-72019. (Illus.). 32p. (J). (gr. k-4). 1993. lib. bdg. 14.89 (1-56282-328-0, Pub. by Hyprn Child) Little.

Princess & the Peacocks: or The Story of the Room. Linda Merrill & Sarah Ridley. LC 92-72019. (Illus.). 32p. (J). (gr. k-4). 1993. 14.95 (1-56282-327-2, Pub. by Hyprn Child) Little.

Princess & the Pee-Pee. Wanda Wargo. (Illus.). (J). 1997. 10.95 (0-614-28719-7, Dove Audio) NewStar Media.

Princess & the Philosopher: Letters of Elisabeth of the Palatine to Rene Descartes. Andrea Nye. 208p. 1999. pap. 18.95 (0-8476-9265-5) Rowman.

Princess & the Philosopher: Letters of Elisabeth of the Palatine to Rene Descartes. Andrea Nye. LC 98-44821. 208p. 1999. text 57.95 (0-8476-9264-7) Rowman.

Princess & the Pig. Heather Amery. (Castle Tales Ser.). (Illus.). 16p. (J). (ps-3). 1996. pap. 4.50 (0-7460-2510-6, Usborne) EDC.

Princess & the Playboy. Valerie Parv. (Romance Ser.: No. 416). 1999. mass mkt. 3.50 (0-373-17416-0, 1-17416-8) Harlequin Bks.

Princess & the Potty. Wendy C. Lewison. LC 93-7853. (Illus.). 32p. (J). (ps-k). 1998. per. 5.99 (0-689-82253-7) Aladdin.

Princess & the Potty. Wendy C. Lewison. LC 93-7853. (Illus.). 40p. (J). (ps up). 1994. pap. 15.00 (0-671-87284-2) S&S Bks Yung.

Princess & the Rose. Burnett R. Toskey. (Illus.). 112p. 1995. pap. 14.95 (0-9647821-0-3) B R Toskey.

Princess & the Sea-Bear: And Other Tsimshian Stories. Joan Skogan. (Illus.). 48p. (Orig.). (J). (gr. 4-8). 1990. pap. write for info. (0-919591-54-X) Polstar Bk.

Princess & the Swineherd. Madge Miller. (J). 1946. 6.00 (0-87602-181-X) Anchorage.

Princess & the Toad see Princesa y el Sapo: Grade 3 Best Loved Tales Series 700

Princess Ann & Some of Her Branches: Ashley Families from Robeson County, N. C., Alabama & Texas. Wiley R. Taylor & Linda A. Rhodes. LC 98-51159. 1999. write for info. (0-939710-20-X) Meridional Pubns.

Princess Anne: A Biography. large type ed. Nicholas Courtney. (Illus.). 256p. 1987. 17.95 (0-7089-8409-6, Charnwood) Ulverscroft.

Princess Anne County Loose Paper, 1700-89 (Vol. I of "Virginia Antiquary") Ed. by John H. Creecy. 221p. 1997. reprint ed. lib. bdg. 37.50 (0-8328-6519-2) Higginson Bk Co.

Princesss Anne County Loose Paper, 1700-89, Vol. 1. Ed. by John H. Creecy. 221p. 1997. reprint ed. pap. 27.50 (0-8328-6520-6) Higginson Bk Co.

Princess Anne County, Virginia, Land & Probate Records Abstracted from Deed Books One to Eighteen 1691-1783. Anne E. Maling. 243p. (Orig.). 1995. pap. text 19.00 (0-7884-0175-0) Heritage Bk.

Princess Anne County, Virginia, Land & Probate Records Abstracted from Deed Books 1-7. Anne E. Maling. 118p. (Orig.). 1992. pap. 14.50 (1-55613-620-X) Heritage Bk.

Princess Anne County, Virginia Marriage Bonds, 1822-1850. Carolyn L. Barkley. 277p. 1997. pap. 19.00 (1-888265-15-9) Willow Bend.

Princess Anne County, Virginia, Wills, 1783-1871. Anne E. Maling. 255p. (Orig.). 1994. pap. 22.50 (1-55613-966-7) Heritage Bk.

Princess Anne County, Virginia, 1749-1821, Marriages Of, Vol. 1. Elizabeth B. Wingo. 158p. 1961. pap. 18.50 (0-89308-404-2, BVA 83) Southern Hist Pr.

Princess Annie. Linda Lael Miller. Ed. by Linda Marrow. 480p. 1994. mass mkt. 5.99 (0-671-79793-X, Pocket Star Bks) PB.

Princess Bella & the Red Velvet Hat. T. Davis Bunn. 32p. 1998. text 14.99 (0-7642-2097-7) Bethany Hse.

Princess Bernice Pauahi Bishop. rev. ed. Julie S. Williams. (Kamehameha Intermediate Reading Program Ser.). (Illus.). 103p. (J). (gr. 3-7). 1998. pap. 9.95 (0-87336-057-5) Kamehameha Schools.

***Princess Bride.** William Goldman. 1999. 24.95 (0-345-91612-3); mass mkt. write for info. (0-345-43462-5) Ballantine Pub Grp.

Princess Bride. Diana Palmer. 1998. mass mkt. 3.50 (0-373-19282-7, 1-19282-2) Silhouette.

Princess Bride: S. Morgenstern's Classic Tale of True Love & High Adventure. William Goldman. 1976. 29.95 (0-8488-0696-4) Amereon Ltd.

Princess Bride: S. Morgenstern's Classic Tale of True Love & High Adventure. William Goldman. 283p. 1987. mass mkt. 6.99 (0-345-34803-6, Del Rey) Ballantine Pub Grp.

Princess Bride: S. Morgenstern's Classic Tale of True Love & High Adventure. William Goldman. 1974. 11.09 (0-606-03428-5, Pub. by Turtleback) Demco.

Princess Bride: S. Morgenstern's Classic Tale of True Love & High Adventure. William Goldman. 290p. 1991. reprint ed. lib. bdg. 35.95 (0-89966-809-7) Buccaneer Bks.

***Princess Bride: S. Morgenstern's Classic Tale of True Love & High Adventure.** 25th abr. annot. ed. William Goldman. LC 98-39556. 399p. 1998. 24.00 (0-345-43014-X) Ballantine Pub Grp.

Princess Caroline. Jill C. Wheeler. LC 92-16676. (Leading Ladies Ser.). (J). 1992. lib. bdg. 13.98 (1-56239-117-8) ABDO Pub Co.

Princess Casamassima. Henry James. 640p. 1991. 20.00 (0-679-40672-7) Everymns Lib.

Princess Casamassima. Henry James. Ed. & Intro. by Derek S. Brewer. 608p. 1987. pap. 12.95 (0-14-043254-X, Penguin Classics) Viking Penguin.

Princess Casamassima see Works of Henry James Jr.: Collected Works

Princess Casamassima. Henry James. LC 70-158784. (Novels & Tales of Henry James Ser.: Vol. 5). 430p. 1977. reprint ed. lib. bdg. 37.50 (0-678-02805-2) Kelley.

Princess Catherine. 2nd ed. Catherine Caradja. Ed. by Dorothy Britt. (Illus.). 212p. 1991. pap. 15.00 (1-881809-26-9) Gabriel TX.

***Princess Chamomile Gets Her Way.** Hiawyn Oram. (Illus.). 32p. (J). (ps-4). 1999. 15.99 (0-525-46148-5, Dutton Child) Peng Put Young Read.

***Princess Chamomile's Garden.** Hiawyn Oram. LC 99-87242. (Illus.). 32p. (J). (ps-4). 2000. 16.95 (0-525-46387-9, Dutton Child) Peng Put Young Read.

Princess Charming. Jane Heller. LC 96-79084. 304p. 1997. 22.00 (1-57566-148-9, Knsington) Kensgtn Pub Corp.

Princess Charming. Jane Heller. 352p. 1998. pap. 5.99 (1-57566-261-2) Kensgtn Pub Corp.

Princess Charming. large type ed. Jane Heller. LC 97-36060. 1997. lib. bdg. 24.95 (1-57490-102-8, Beeler LP Bks) T T Beeler.

Princess Club. Adapted by C. Archer. LC 96-26806. (Christy Fiction Ser.: No. 7). 128p. (J). (gr. 5-9). 1996. pap. text 4.99 (0-8499-3958-5) Tommy Nelson.

Princess Collection: Stories from the Films. Ann Braybrooks. LC 94-80012. (Disney Press Miniature Classics Ser.). (Illus.). 96p. (J). 1996. 5.95 (0-7868-3076-X, Pub. by Disney Pr) Time Warner.

***Princess Collection Disney Press.** (Illus.). 32p. (J). 1999. 12.99 (0-7868-3269-X, Pub. by Disney Pr) Time Warner.

Princess Collection Two: A Dream Come True for Every Little Princess. Walt Disney Records. (J). 1998. 16.98 incl. audio compact disk (0-7634-0450-0) W Disney Records.

Princess Daisy. Judith Krantz. 512p. 1984. mass mkt. 7.50 (0-553-25609-2) Bantam.

Princess Daisy Finds a Friend. Kirsten Hall. (Illus.). 24p. (J). (ps-1). 1999. 12.95 (0-8118-2361-X) Chronicle Bks.

Princess dans un Sac (The Paper Bag Princess) Robert Munsch. (FRE., Illus.). 32p. (J). 1996. pap. 4.95 (1-55037-344-7, Pub. by Annick) Firefly Bks Ltd.

***Princess Diana.** Walter G. Oleksy. LC 99-53455. 144p. (YA). (gr. 4-12). 2000. 18.96 (1-56006-579-6) Lucent Bks.

Princess Diana. Jill C. Wheeler. LC 98-8410. (Women of the World Ser.). (J). 2002. lib. bdg. 21.35 (1-57765-314-9) ABDO Pub Co.

Princess Diana: Glitter, Glamous, & A Lot of Hard Work. Nancy E. Krulik. (J). (gr. 4-7). 1993. pap. 2.95 (0-590-46282-2) Scholastic Inc.

Princess Diana: Royal Ambassador. Renora Licata. 1993. 13.15 (0-606-12596-5, Pub. by Turtleback) Demco.

***Princess Diana: Royal Ambassador.** rev. ed. Renora Licata. LC 92-42255. (Library of Famous Women). (Illus.). 64p. (J). (gr. 4-7). 1998. lib. bdg. 17.95 (1-56711-013-4) Blackbirch.

Princess Diana: The Book of Love. Celestial Arts Publishing Co. Staff. 1997. pap. 6.95 (0-89087-866-8) Celestial Arts.

Princess Diana: The Palace Years. Martin James. LC 98-170531. (Gold Collectors Ser.). 96 p. 1997. write for info. (1-878667-32-7) H & S Media.

Princess Diana - Forever in Our Hearts: A Scrapbook of Memories. 439th ed. Kimberly Weinberger. (Illus.). 48p. (gr. 1-4). 1998. pap. 5.99 (0-439-04529-0) Scholastic Inc.

Princess Diana, 1961-1997. rev. ed. Richard Buskin. (Illus.). 224p. 1997. mass mkt. 5.99 (0-451-19711-9, Sig) NAL.

Princess Diana, the House of Windsor & Palm Beach: America's Fascination with "The Touch of Royalty" H. J. Roberts. LC 98-158451. (Illus.). 120p. 1998. pap. 24.95 (1-884243-06-1) Sunshine Sentinel.

***Princess Diana's Death.** Shaykh Nazim Al-Naqshbandi. 64p. (C). 2000. pap. 9.50 (1-898863-14-8, Pub. by Zero Prods) Kazi Pubns.

***Princess Diaries.** Meg Cabot. LC 99-46479. (Illus.). 240p. (J). (gr. 7 up). 2000. 14.95 (0-380-97848-2, Avon Bks) Morrow Avon.

***Princess Diaries.** Meg Cabot. LC 99-46479. 224p. (J). (gr. 7 up). 2000. 14.89 (0-06-029210-5) Morrow Avon.

Princess Dinosaur. Jill Kastner. (J). 2001. 15.95 (0-688-17045-5, Grenwillow Bks); lib. bdg. 15.89 (0-688-17046-3, Grenwillow Bks) HarpC Child Bks.

Princess, Dragon & Baker. Tedi T. Wixom. (Illus.). 40p. (J). (ps-8). 1994. pap. 6.95 (1-885227-33-7) TNT Bks.

Princess for a Day. Maryann Cocca-Leffler. LC 98-11365. (All Aboard Reading Ser.: Level 1). (Illus.). 32p. (J). (ps-1). 1998. lib. bdg. 13.89 (0-448-41605-0, G & D); mass mkt. 3.99 (0-448-41604-2, G & D) Peng Put Young Read.

***Princess Freak.** Nancy Agabian. 161p. 2000. pap. 10.00 (1-892184-07-9) Beyond Baroque.

***Princess from St. Petersburg: The Life of Princess Catherine Radzwill.** Leda Farrant. (Illus.). 400p. 2000. 32.50 (1-85776-404-8, Pub. by Book Guild Ltd) Trans-Atl Phila.

Princess Frownsalot. John Bianchi. (Illus.). 24p. (J). (ps-8). 1987. pap. 4.95 (0-921285-04-3, Pub. by Bungalo Books); lib. bdg. 16.95 (0-921285-06-X, Pub. by Bungalo Books) Firefly Bks Ltd.

Princess Furball. Charlotte S. Huck. LC 88-18780. (Illus.). 40p. (J). (ps up). 1989. lib. bdg. 15.93 (0-688-07838-9, Grenwillow Bks) HarpC Child Bks.

Princess Furball. Charlotte S. Huck. (J). 1994. 11.15 (0-606-05980-6, Pub. by Turtleback) Demco.

Princess Furball. Charlotte S. Huck. LC 93-11729. (Illus.). 40p. (J). (ps-3). 1994. reprint ed. mass mkt. 5.95 (0-688-13107-7, Wm Morrow) Morrow Avon.

Princess Gets Engaged. Tracy Sinclair. 1997. per. 3.99 (0-373-24133-X, 1-24133-0) Silhouette.

Princess Grace. Sarah Bradford. (Illus.). 242p. 1998. text 12.00 (0-7881-5300-5) DIANE Pub.

Princess Hoppy: or The Tale of Labrador. Jacques Roubaud. Tr. by Bernard Hoepffner from FRE. LC 93-18995. (Illus.). 133p. (Orig.). 1993. pap. 9.95 (1-56478-032-5) Dalkey Arch.

Princess in Berlin. Arthur R. Solmssen. (Illus.). 374p. 1980. 25.00 (0-316-80369-3) Hastings Bks.

Princess in Calico. Illus. by Lester Miller. (Still Waters Ser.). 92p. 1989. pap. 4.65 (0-7399-0141-9, 2362) Rod & Staff.

Princess in Denim. Jenna McKnight. (American Romance Ser.). 1998. per. 3.99 (0-373-16719-9, 1-16719-6) Harlequin Bks.

An Asterisk (*) at the beginning of an entry indicates that the title is appearing for the first time.

Princess in Peril: Xena, Warrior Princess. Kerry Milliron. LC 96-7299. (Random House Pictureback Ser.). (J). (ps-3). 1996. pap. 3.25 (0-679-88259-6) Random.

Princess in the Forest. Sibylle Von Olfers. (J). 14.95 (0-86315-189-2, 1784, Pub. by R Steiner Pr) Anthroposophic.

Princess in the Pigpen. Jane R. Thomas. LC 89-856. 128p. (J). (gr. 3-7). 1989. 15.00 (0-395-51587-4, Clarion Bks) HM.

Princess in the Pigpen. Jane R. Thomas. 1995. pap. 9075.00 (0-15-305231-7) Harcourt Schl Pubs.

Princess in the Pigpen. Jane R. Thomas. 144p. (J). (gr. 3-7). 1993. pap. 3.50 (0-380-71194-X, Avon Bks) Morrow Avon.

*__Princess in Waiting.__ large type ed. Judith Saxton. 352p. 1998. 29.99 (0-7505-1296-2) Mgna Lrg Print.

Princess Jessica Rescues a Prince. Jennifer Brooks. Ed. by Chas Ridley. LC 93-92628. (Illus.). 40p. (J). (ps-2). 1994. 15.95 (0-9636335-0-3) Nadja Pub.

Princess Josie's Pets. Maryann MacDonald. LC 96-27186. (Hyperion Chapters Ser.). (Illus.). 64p. (J). (gr. 1-3). 1997. lib. bdg. 14.49 (0-7868-2263-5, Pub. by Hyprn Ppbks) Little.

Princess Josie's Pets. Maryann MacDonald. LC 96-27186. (Hyperion Chapters Ser.). (Illus.). 64p. (J). (gr. 1-3). 1998. pap. 3.95 (0-7868-1134-X, Pub. by Hyprn Ppbks) Little.

Princess Josie's Pets. Maryann MacDonald. (Hyperion Chapters Ser.). 1998. 9.05 (0-606-13724-6, Pub. by Turtleback) Demco.

*__Princess June: A Novel.__ Veronica Lee. LC 00-8261. 288p. 2001. pap. 14.95 (1-56474-346-2) Fithian Pr.

*__Princess Justina Albertina.__ Ellen Davidson. Ed. by Noreen Wise. (Book-a-Day Collection). (Illus.). 32p. (YA). (ps up). 2000. pap. 5.95 (1-58584-366-0) Huckleberry CT.

Princess K'iulani: Hope of a Nation, Heart of a People. Sharon Linnea. LC 97-14260. (Illus.). 224p. (YA). (gr. 5 up). 1999. 18.00 (0-8028-5145-2, Eerdmans Bks); pap. 10.00 (0-8028-5088-X, Eerdmans Bks) Eerdmans.

Princess Lily. Judith Fine & Barbara Bazilian. LC 98-14727. (Illus.). 32p. (J). (gr. 1-5). 1998. 6.95 (1-58089-010-5, Whispering Coyote) Charlesbridge Pub.

Princess Lily. Judith Fine & Barbara Bazilian. (Illus.). 32p. (J). (gr. 1-5). 1998. 15.95 (1-58089-006-7, Whispering Coyote) Charlesbridge Pub.

Princess' Lover. E. Clough. LC 92-82950. 640p. 1993. 14.95 (1-877978-49-3, FLF Pr) FL Lit Foundation.

Princess Lulu Goes to Camp. Kathryn Cristaldi. LC 96-30742. (All Aboard Reading Ser.: Level 2). (Illus.). 48p. (J). (gr. 1-3). 1997. pap. 3.95 (0-448-41125-3, G & D) Peng Put Young Read.

Princess Lulu Goes to Camp. Kathryn Cristaldi. LC 96-30742. (All Aboard Reading Ser.). 1997. 9.15 (0-606-11764-4, Pub. by Turtleback) Demco.

Princess Malah. J. H. Hill. 1990. 15.00 (0-87498-035-6) Assoc Pubs DC.

Princess Malah. John H. Hill. LC 70-144637. reprint ed. 37.50 (0-404-00171-8) AMS Pr.

Princess Mandisa. Wanda Hoosier. (J). 1998. 10.95 (0-533-12787-4) Vantage.

Princess Megan. Trisha Magraw. (Magic Attic Club Ser.). (Illus.). 72p. (J). (gr. 2-6). 1995. 12.95 (1-57513-004-1); pap. 5.95 (1-57513-005-X) Magic Attic.

Princess Megan. Trisha Magraw. (Magic Attic Club Ser.). (J). (gr. 2-6). 1995. 11.15 (0-606-08590-4, Pub. by Turtleback) Demco.

Princess Mononoke: The Art & Making of Japan's Most Popular Film of All Time. LC 98-51766. (Illus.). 224p. 1999. pap. 19.95 (0-7868-8385-5, Pub. by Hyperion) Little.

Princess Mononoke: The Art & Making of Japan's Most Popular Film of All Time. Hyperion Staff. 223p. 1999. text 39.95 (0-7868-6609-8, Pub. by Hyperion) Time Warner.

Princess Nada & the City of Ice. Robert J. Resetar & Mary K. Schulte. LC 97-37475. (New Tales of the Arabian Nights Ser.: Vol. 1). (Illus.). 32p. (J). (gr. k-5). 1997. 16.95 (1-880090-55-4) Galde Pr.

*__Princess Naughty & the Voodoo Cadillac.__ Fred Willard. LC 00-105060. 320p. 2000. 22.00 (1-56352-622-0) Longstreet.

Princess Navina Visits Malvolia. Nef. (Illus.). 64p. (Orig.). 1990. pap. 9.95 (0-915728-09-5) Lytton Pub.

Princess Navina Visits Mandaat. James L. Payne. (Illus.). 56p. 1994. pap. 9.95 (0-915728-10-9) Lytton Pub.

Princess Navina Visits Nueva Malvolia. Count Nef. (Illus.). 52p. (Orig.). 1999. pap. 9.95 (0-915728-14-1) Lytton Pub.

Princess Nevermore. Dian Curtis Regan. LC 94-30020. 240p. (YA). (gr. 4-7). 1995. 14.95 (0-590-45758-6, Scholastic Hardcover) Scholastic Inc.

Princess Nevermore. Dian Curtis Regan. LC 94-30020. 240p. (J). (gr. 5-9). 1997. mass mkt. 4.50 (0-590-45759-4) Scholastic Inc.

Princess Nevermore. Dian Curtis Regan. LC 94-30020. (Point Fantasy Ser.). 1995. 9.60 (0-606-11765-2, Pub. by Turtleback) Demco.

*__Princess Nobody: A Tale of Fairyland.__ Richard Doyle & Andrew Lang. (Illus.). 64p. (J). 2000. pap. 9.95 (0-486-41020-X) Dover.

Princess of Celle. Jean Plaidy, pseud. 27.95 (0-8488-0608-5) Amereon Ltd.

Princess of Celle. large type ed. Jean Plaidy, pseud. (Shadows of the Crown Ser.). 1974. 27.99 (0-85456-594-9) Ulverscroft.

Princess of Cleves. Madame De Lafayette. Ed. by John Lyons. (Critical Editions Ser.). (C). 1993. pap. text 12.50 (0-393-96333-0) Norton.

Princess of Cleves. Marie J. Lafayette. LC 77-22941. 210p. 1977. reprint ed. lib. bdg. 38.50 (0-8371-9729-5, LAFPC, Greenwood Pr) Greenwood.

Princess of Cleves: Novel. Madame De Lafayette. Tr. & Intro. by Nancy Mitford. LC 88-12472. (Classics Ser.: Vol. 660). 240p. 1988. pap. 12.95 (0-8112-1070-7, NDP660, Pub. by New Directions) Norton.

Princess of Coldwater Flat. Natalie Bishop. (Special Edition Ser.). 1994. per. 3.50 (0-373-09882-0, 5-09882-7) Silhouette.

*__Princess of Dhagabad.__ Anna Kashina. (Spirits of the Ancient Sands Ser.: Bk. I). 288p. 2000. 25.00 (1-928746-07-1) Herodias.

Princess of Fire. Drake. LC 97-50360. 1998. 24.95 (0-7862-1386-8) Thorndike Pr.

Princess of Fire. Shannon Drake. 512p. 1994. mass mkt. 5.99 (0-8217-4796-7, Zebra Kensgtn) Kensgtn Pub Corp.

Princess of Fire - Tomorrow the Glory. Shannon Drake. 1994. mass mkt. 5.99 (0-8217-8890-6, Zebra Kensgtn) Kensgtn Pub Corp.

Princess of Hollywood. Pleasant Gehman. LC 97-130530. (Illus.). 152p. 1996. pap. 12.00 (1-884615-10-4) Incommcdo San Diego.

Princess of Mars. Edgar Rice Burroughs. 159p. Date not set. 18.95 (0-8488-2221-8) Amereon Ltd.

Princess of Mars. Edgar Rice Burroughs. 160p. 1985. mass mkt. 4.99 (0-345-33138-9, Del Rey) Ballantine Pub Grp.

Princess of Mars. abr. ed. Edgar Rice Burroughs. (Mars Ser.). (YA). (gr. 8-12). 1995. 16.95 incl. audio (1-882071-51-4, 393368, Pub. by B&B Audio) Lndmrk Audiobks.

Princess of Peachburg. Anne C. Wallace. LC 94-43769. 64p. 1995. pap. 14.95 (0-7734-2732-5, Mellen Poetry Pr) E Mellen.

Princess of Power. Gabrielle Charbonnet. (Disney Girls Ser.). (J). (gr. 2-5). 1999. pap. text 3.99 (0-7868-4274-1, Pub. by Disney Pr) Time Warner.

Princess of 72nd Street. Elaine Kraf. LC 79-12784. 1979. 9.95 (0-8112-0749-8, Pub. by New Directions) Norton.

*__Princess of 72nd Street.__ Elaine Kraf. LC 00-20979. 117p. 2000. reprint ed. pap. 10.95 (1-56478-235-2, Pub. by Dalkey Arch) Chicago Distribution Ctr.

Princess of Spadina. Ramabai Espinet. (Illus.). 32p. (J). 1993. per. write for info. (0-920813-66-6) Sister Vis Pr.

Princess of the Night Rides. John D. Holt. LC 76-12962. 1977. 4.95 (0-914916-21-1); pap. 2.50 (0-914916-22-X) Ku Paa.

Princess of the Press: The Story of Ida B. Wells-Barnett. Angela S. Medearis. LC 97-8520. (Rainbow Biography Ser.). (Illus.). 48p. (J). (gr. 2-5). 1997. 14.99 (0-525-67493-4, Dutton Child) Peng Put Young Read.

Princess on Parade. Carolyn Keene. (Nancy Drew Notebooks: No. 21). (Illus.). (J). (gr. 2-4). 1981. pap. 1.50 (0-671-00815-3) PB.

Princess on Parade. Carolyn Keene. (Nancy Drew Notebooks: No. 21). (J). (gr. 2-4). 1997. 9.09 (0-606-12998-7, Pub. by Turtleback) Demco.

Princess Patty in Peace on Earth. rev. ed. Betsy A. Bradford. (Illus.). 56p. (J). (gr. k-4). 1995. 16.95 (0-9633846-3-5) Scope Pub.

Princess Penelope's Parrot. Helen Lester. LC 95-53266. (Illus.). 32p. (J). (ps-3). 1996. 14.95 (0-395-78320-8) HM.

Princess Pickle Head. Loch A. Dreizler. LC 88-80123. (Illus.). 42p. (Orig.). (J). (ps-4). 1988. pap. 2.95 (0-9620053-0-4) LAD Redondo Beach.

Princess Plays. Colleen Neuman. 96p. (YA). 1996. pap. 5.00 (0-87440-030-9) Bakers Plays.

Princess Pocahontas & the Blue Spots. Monique Mojica. 86p. pap. 9.95 (0-88961-165-3, Pub. by Womens Pr) LPC InBook.

Princess Pooh. Kathleen M. Muldoon. Ed. by Judith Mathews. LC 88-33978. (Illus.). 32p. (J). (gr. 2-5). 1989. lib. bdg. 14.95 (0-8075-6627-6) A Whitman.

*__Princess Portia's Enchanted Journey.__ Valerie L. Woods. Ed. by Janell W. Agyeman. (Illus.). 33p. (J). (gr. 1-7). 2000. write for info. (0-615-11490-3) Valikus.

Princess Pourquoi. Margaret P. Sherwood. LC 73-178461. (Short Story Index Reprint Ser.). 1977. reprint ed. 20.95 (0-8369-4062-8) Ayer.

Princess Primrose & the Pea. Pamela Duncun Edwards. (Illus.). 32p. (J). 2001. 13.99 (0-7868-0471-8, Pub. by Hyprn Child); lib. bdg. 14.49 (0-7868-2413-1, Pub. by Hyprn Child) Little.

Princess Priscilla. Stacey Apeitos. (Illus.). 32p. 1998. pap. 6.95 (0-207-18198-5) HarpC.

*__Princess Promila.__ Contrib. by Krishna Kumar. 1998. pap. 5.50 (81-250-1402-0, Pub. by Orient Longman Ltd) S Asia.

Princess Prunella & the Purple Peanut. Margaret Atwood. LC 95-21059. (Illus.). 32p. (J). (ps-3). 1995. 13.95 (0-7611-0166-7, 10166) Workman Pub.

Princess Sarah & the King. David L. Grams. (Illus.). 56p. (J). 1999. 20.00 (0-9663002-0-3) Court Jester.

Princess Scargo & the Birthday Pumpkin: The Native American Legend. Eric Metaxas. LC 95-36728. (Illus.). 48p. (J). (ps-3). 1996. pap. 19.95 incl. audio (0-689-80231-5) Aladdin.

Princess September & the Nightingale. W. Somerset Maugham. LC 98-9230. (The Iona & Peter Opie Library of Children's Literature). (Illus.). 48p. (YA). (gr. k-6). 1998. 16.95 (0-19-512480-4) OUP.

Princess Shayna's Invisible Visible Gift. Sheila N. Glazov. Ed. by Janet Potter. (Illus.). 128p. 1997. pap. 18.95 (0-9655619-9-2) Peridot Prods.

Princess Sister. Copeland. 2000. text 24.95 (0-312-19948-1) St Martin.

Princess Smartypants. Babette Cole. (ENG & SPA.). (J). write for info. (1-85430-297-3, 93436, Pub. by MAGI1 UK) Midpt Trade.

Princess Smartypants. Babette Cole. (J). 1996. write for info. (1-85430-296-5, Pub. by MAGI1 UK); write for info. (1-85430-298-1, Pub. by MAGI1 UK); write for info. (1-85430-299-X, Pub. by MAGI1 UK) Midpt Trade.

Princess Smartypants. Babette Cole. (BEN., Illus.). 32p. (J). 1996. write for info. (1-85430-295-7, Pub. by MAGI1 UK) Midpt Trade.

Princess Smartypants. Babette Cole. LC 86-12381. (Illus.). 32p. (J). (ps-3). 1997. pap. 5.99 (0-698-11555-4, PapStar) Peng Put Young Read.

Princess Sonora & the Long Sleep. Gail Carson Levine. LC 98-53740. (Princess Tales Ser.). (Illus.). 107p. (J). (gr. 2-7). 1999. 8.95 (0-06-028064-6) HarpC Child Bks.

Princess Sonora & the Long Sleep. Gail Carson Levine. LC 98-53470. (Princess Tales Ser.). (Illus.). 112p. (J). (gr. 2-7). 1999. lib. bdg. 8.89 (0-06-028065-4) HarpC Child Bks.

*__Princess Stories.__ McCaughrean. (J). 2000. pap. 22.95 (0-385-40783-1, Pub. by Transworld Publishers Ltd) Trafalgar.

Princess Sultana Daughters. large type ed. Ernest Haycox & Sasson. 398p. 1995. lib. bdg. 19.95 (0-7862-0201-7) Thorndike Pr.

*__Princess Sultana's Circle.__ Jean Sasson. LC 99-96954. 256p. 2000. 24.95 (0-9676737-1-2, Pub. by Windsor Brooke) Allnce Hse.

Princess Sultana's Daughters. Jean P. Sasson. 400p. 1995. mass mkt. 6.99 (0-440-21850-0) Dell.

Princess Sultana's Daughters. large type ed. Jean P. Sasson. 1995. pap. 18.95 (0-614-32384-3) Thorndike Pr.

Princess Takamatsu Symposia, Vol. 22. Ed. by Curtis C. Harris. 1993. 94.00 (0-8493-7749-8, RC268) CRC Pr.

Princess Tappintoe. P. J. Meltabarger. 21p. (J). (ps). 1996. 12.95 (1-56763-175-4); pap. text 3.95 (1-56763-174-6) Ozark Pub.

Princess Test. Gail Carson Levine. LC 98-27960. (Princess Tales Ser.). (Illus.). 96p. (J). (gr. 2-7). 1999. 9.95 (0-06-028062-X) HarpC Child Bks.

Princess Test. Gail Carson Levine. LC 98-27960. (Princess Tales Ser.). (Illus.). 96p. (J). (gr. 2-7). 1999. lib. bdg. 8.89 (0-06-028063-8) HarpC Child Bks.

Princess, the Dragon & Scaredy Cats. Audrey Wood. (J). 12.85 (0-85953-375-1) Childs Play.

Princess, the Lucky Horse. large type ed. William O. Beazley. (White Horse Ser.). (Illus.). 47p. (J). (gr. k-5). 1994. reprint ed. spiral bd. 7.95 (1-884758-07-X) W O Beazley.

Princess Thora. Burland Harris. Ed. by R. Reginald & Douglas Melville. LC 77-92408. (Lost Race & Adult Fantasy Ser.). (Illus.). 1978. reprint ed. lib. bdg. 34.95 (0-405-10961-X) Ayer.

Princess Who Believed in Fairy Tales. Marcia Grad. LC 94-61729. 202p. 1995. pap. 10.00 (0-87980-436-X) Wilshire.

Princess Who Changed the World. Nicholas Davies. 1998. 27.95 (1-85782-204-8, Pub. by Blake Publng) Seven Hills Bk.

Princess Who Changed the World. Nicholas Davies. 256p. 1998. mass mkt. 7.99 (1-85782-380-X) Blake Publng.

Princess Who Could Never Be: The Untold Story of Mary Vetsera. Irene Colvin. LC 94-68856. (Illus.). 320p. (Orig.). 1995. pap. 12.99 (0-9628093-0-6) NuDawn Pub.

Princess Who Danced with Cranes. Annette LeBox. (J). 1998. pap. 5.95 (0-929005-87-2, Pub. by Sec Story Pr) LPC InBook.

Princess Who Danced with Cranes. Annette LeBox. (Illus.). (J). 1998. 13.95 (0-929005-88-0, Pub. by Sec Story Pr) LPC InBook.

Princess Who Lost Her Hair: An Akamba Legend. Illus. by Charles Reasoner. LC 92-13273. 32p. (J). (gr. 2-5). 1992. pap. 4.95 (0-8167-2816-X) Troll Communs.

Princess Who Lost Her Hair: An Akamba Legend. Illus. by Charles Reasoner. LC 92-13273. 32p. (J). (gr. 2-5). 1997. lib. bdg. 18.60 (0-8167-2815-1) Troll Communs.

Princess Who Overcame Evil. Illus. by Julia Witwer. 32p. (J). (gr. k-6). Date not set. pap. 7.95 (0-89800-294-X) Dharma Pub.

Princess Who Wanted to Be Poor. Juwairiah J. Simpson. Ed. by American Trust Publications. (Illus.). 52p. (J). (gr. 5-9). 1987. pap. 4.75 (0-89259-104-8) Am Trust Pubns.

Princess Who Was Afraid of the Dark. Karla Andersdatter. 1988. 8.00 (0-935430-09-1) In Between.

*__Princess with the Golden Hair: Letters of Elizabeth Waugh to Edmund Wilson, 1933-1942.__ Elizabeth Dey Jenkinson Waugh et al. LC 00-25744. (Illus.). 184p. 2000. 35.00 (0-8386-3855-4) Fairleigh Dickinson.

*__Princess Within: The Restoring of a Woman's Soul.__ Serita Jakes. 1999. 19.99 (1-57778-101-5) Albury Pub.

Princessa: Machiavelli for Women. Harriet Rubin. 208p. 1998. pap. 9.95 (0-440-50832-0, Dell Trade Pbks) Dell.

*__Princesse Aux Petit Pois.__ Hans Christian Andersen. 1999. pap. 11.95 (2-09-202112-5) Distribks Inc.

Princesse dans un Sac. Robert Munsch. (Annikins Ser.). (FRE., Illus.). (J). 1996. 0.99 (1-55037-391-9, Pub. by Annick) Firefly Bks Ltd.

Princesse de Cleves. Marie-Madeleine De La Fayette. 1958. write for info. (0-318-63581-X) Fr & Eur.

Princesse de Cleves. Marie-Madeleine De La Fayette. (Folio Ser.: No. 778). 1958. pap. 9.95 (2-07-036778-9) Schoenhof.

Princesse de Cleves. unabridged ed. Marie-Madeleine De La Fayette. (FRE.). pap. 7.95 (2-87714-160-8, Pub. by Bookking Intl) Distribks Inc.

Princesse de Cleves. 8th ed. Madame De Lafayette. Tr. & Intro. by Robin Buss. 192p. 1992. pap. 10.95 (0-14-044587-0, Penguin Classics) Viking Penguin.

Princesse de Cleves: The Princesse de Montpensier; The Comtesse de Tende. Madame De Lafayette. (Oxford World Classics Ser.). 274p. 1999. pap. 8.95 (0-19-283726-5) OUP.

Princesse Isabelle. Maurice Maeterlinck. (FRE.). 196p. 1967. reprint ed. pap. 11.95 (0-7859-4687-X) Fr & Eur.

Princesse Qui Voulait Choisir Son Prince. Bertrand Gauthier. (FRE., Illus.). 24p. pap. (2-89021-270-X) La Courte Ech.

*__Princesses: Coloring, Paint with Water, Activities.__ Ed. by Golden Books Publishing Company. (Illus.). (J). 2000. pap. text 3.99 (0-307-25402-X, Goldn Books) Gldn Bks Pub Co.

*__Princesses: Pull-Out Posters & Game Cards Book.__ (Illus.). 32p. (J). (gr. 1-4). 2000. 7.99 (0-7364-1067-8) Mouse Works.

*__Princesses Games & Spinner Activities & Crafts.__ (Illus.). 32p. (J). (ps-3). 2000. pap. text. write for info. (0-307-30157-5) Gldn Bks Pub Co.

*__Princess's Proposal.__ Valerie Parv. (Silhouette Romance Ser.: Vol. 1471). 2000. mass mkt. 3.50 (0-373-19471-4, 1-19471-1) Harlequin Bks.

Princess's White Knight: Royally Wed. Carla Cassidy. (Romance Ser.: Vol. 1415). 1999. per. 3.50 (0-373-19415-3, 1-19415-8) Silhouette.

Princeton. Robert Gambee. (Illus.). 1987. 39.00 (0-393-02423-7) Norton.

Princeton. Richard D. Smith. (Images of America Ser.). 1997. pap. 16.99 (0-7524-0586-1) Arcadia Publng.

Princeton: A Picture Postcard History of Princeton. William K. Evans. LC 92-24805. (Illus.). 136p. (Orig.). 1993. pap. 18.95 (0-930256-18-2, Vestal Pr) Madison Bks UPA.

Princeton Alumni Collections: Works on Paper. Princeton University Art Museum Staff. LC 81-80640. (Illus.). 264p. 1981. text 44.50 (0-691-03977-1, Pub. by Princeton U Pr) Cal Prin Full Svc.

Princeton & the Republic, 1768-1822: The Search for a Christian Enlightenment in the Era of Samuel Stanhope Smith. Mark A. Noll. LC 88-39309. 356p. 1989. reprint ed. pap. 110.40 (0-608-02942-4, 206400800008) Bks Demand.

Princeton Atlas of Fault-Related Rocks. Arthur W. Snoke et al. LC 97-19775. 629p. 1998. text 100.00 (0-691-01220-2, Pub. by Princeton U Pr) Cal Prin Full Svc.

Princeton Companion. Alexander Leitch. LC 78-51178. 576p. 1978. text 55.00 (0-691-04654-9, Pub. by Princeton U Pr) Cal Prin Full Svc.

Princeton Companion to Classical Japanese Literature. Earl Miner et al. LC 83-24475. (Illus.). 560p. 1986. pap. text 24.95 (0-691-00825-6, Pub. by Princeton U Pr) Cal Prin Full Svc.

Princeton Encyclopedia of Classical Sites. Ed. by Richard Stillwell. LC 75-30210. 1067p. reprint ed. pap. 200.00 (0-8357-7559-3, 205232300097) Bks Demand.

Princeton Encyclopedia of Poetry & Poetics. 3rd ed. Ed. by Alex Preminger & T. V. Brogan. 143p. 1993. pap. text 35.00 (0-691-02123-6, Pub. by Princeton U Pr) Cal Prin Full Svc.

Princeton Field Guide to the Birds of Australia. Ken Simpson & Nicolas Day. LC 95-43361. 408p. (C). 1996. 39.50 (0-691-02575-4, Pub. by Princeton U Pr) Cal Prin Full Svc.

Princeton Guide to Advanced Physics. Alan C. Tribble. 375p. 1996. text 59.50 (0-691-02670-X, Pub. by Princeton U Pr); pap. text 19.95 (0-691-02662-9, Pub. by Princeton U Pr) Cal Prin Full Svc.

Princeton Guide to the Birds & Mammals of Coastal Patagonia. Graham Harris. LC 97-43118. 251p. 1998. 65.00 (0-691-05831-8, Pub. by Princeton U Pr) Cal Prin Full Svc.

Princeton Guide to the Birds of the West Indies. Herbert A. Raffaele. LC 97-41790. 512p. 1998. 49.50 (0-691-08736-9, Pub. by Princeton U Pr) Cal Prin Full Svc.

Princeton Handbook of Multicultural Poetries. Ed. by T. Brogan. 352p. 1996. text 49.50 (0-691-01089-7, Pub. by Princeton U Pr) Cal Prin Full Svc.

Princeton Handbook of Multicultural Poetries. Ed. by T. V. Brogan. LC 95-30610. 352p. (C). 1996. pap. text 18.95 (0-691-00168-5, Pub. by Princeton U Pr) Cal Prin Full Svc.

Princeton-in-Asia: A Century of Service Reminiscences & Reflections, 1898-1998. Melanie Kirkpatrick. LC 98-86289. 64p. 1998. 25.00 (0-9665577-1-9) Princeton-in-Asia.

Princeton in the Nation's Service: Religious Ideals & Educational Practice, 1868-1928. P. C. Kemeny. (Religion in America Ser.). 368p. 1998. text 45.00 (0-19-512071-X) OUP.

Princeton Law School - Civil Procedures. Sam Hamadeh. 400p. 1995. pap. 23.00 (0-679-76459-3) Villard Books.

Princeton Lectures on Biophysics. William Bialek. 424p. 1993. text 109.00 (981-02-1325-5); pap. text 48.00 (981-02-1326-3) World Scientific Pub.

Princeton Manuscripts: A Guide to Modern Manuscripts in the Princeton University Library. Princeton University Staff. (Library Reference Ser.). 2000p. 1989. 290.00 (0-8161-0469-7, G K Hall & Co) Mac Lib Ref.

Princeton Physics, 30 bks. (Science Library). 1990. pap. 263.50 (0-691-02436-7, Pub. by Princeton U Pr) Cal Prin Full Svc.

Princeton Problems in Physics with Solutions. Nathan Newbury et al. 336p. 1991. pap. text 19.95 (0-691-02449-9, Pub. by Princeton U Pr) Cal Prin Full Svc.

Princeton Raphael Symposium: Science in the Service of Art History. Ed. by John Shearman & Marcia B. Hall. (Illus.). 264p. 1990. text 95.00 (0-691-04079-6, Pub. by Princeton U Pr) Cal Prin Full Svc.

Princeton Readings in Political Thought: Essential Texts since Plato. Ed. by Mitchell Cohen & Nicole Fermon. LC 95-23990. 600p. 1996. pap. text 19.95 (0-691-03689-6, Pub. by Princeton U Pr) Cal Prin Full Svc.

P

Princeton Review: GRE. Adam Robinson. 1989. pap. 10.95 (*0-394-75684-3*) Random.

Princeton Review: GRE Subject, Vol. 6. Princeton Review Publishing Staff. Date not set. pap. write for info. (*0-679-76935-8*) McKay.

Princeton Review: Inside the GRE. Princeton Review Publishing Staff. 144p. 1996. 36.95 incl. cd-rom (*1-884536-57-3*) Villard Books.

Princeton Review: Inside the SAT. Princeton Review Publishing Staff. 1996. 34.95 incl. cd-rom (*1-884536-56-5*) Villard Books.

Princeton Review: LSAT-GRE Analytic Workout. Karen Lurie. 1996. pap. 16.00 (*0-679-77358-4*) Villard Books.

Princeton Review: Prelaw School Companion. Ron Coleman. LC 97-189221. 1996. pap. 15.00 (*0-679-77372-X*) Villard Books.

Princeton Review: The Student Access Guide to College Admissions. Adam Robinson. 176p. 1993. pap. 12.00 (*0-679-74590-4*) Villard Books.

Princeton Review: Word Smart. Adam Robinson & Julian Fleisher. 1993. 25.00 incl. audio (*0-517-59355-6*) Liv Lang.

Princeton Review: Word Smart 2. Adam Robinson. 1994. 25.00 incl. audio (*0-517-59761-6*) Liv Lang.

Princeton Review - Word Smart: Building an Educated Vocabulary. Adam Robinson & John Katzman. LC 87-40580. (Illus.). 256p. 1988. 10.00 (*0-394-75686-X*) Villard Books.

***Princeton Review America's Top Internships 2001.** 8th ed. Princeton Publishing Staff. 416p. 2000. pap. 21.00 (*0-375-75637-X*, Pub. by PRP NY) Random.

Princeton Review Archaeology Smart Junior, Vol. 3. Karen Laubenstein & Ronald Roy. LC 97-27238. (Smart Juniors Ser.: No. 3). (YA). 1997. pap. 10.00 (*0-679-77537-4*) Random.

***Princeton Review Best Distance Learning.** 2nd ed. Princeton Publishing Staff. 336p. 2000. pap. 21.00 (*0-375-75636-1*, Pub. by PRP NY) Random.

Princeton Review Cracking the Biology Achievement, 1994. Theodore Silver. 1993. pap. 14.00 (*0-679-74962-4*) Villard Books.

Princeton Review Cracking the System - The SAT. John Katzman & Adam Robinson. LC 85-51739. (Illus.). 288p. 1986. pap. 9.95 (*0-394-74342-3*) Villard Books.

Princeton Review Gourman Guide to Graduate Schools. Jack Gourman. (Princeton Review Ser.). 320p. 1997. pap. 21.95 (*0-679-78374-1*) Random.

Princeton Review Gourman Undergraduate Guide. 10th ed. Jack Gourman. (Princeton Review Ser.). 320p. 1997. pap. 21.95 (*0-679-77780-6*) Random.

Princeton Review Grammar Smart: An Audio Guide to Perfect Useage. Julian Fleisher. 1993. audio 14.00 (*0-517-59545-1*) Liv Lang.

Princeton Review GRE Computer Diagnostics 95: IBM Version. Ed. by Princeton Review Publishing Staff. 1995. pap. text 15.25 incl. 3.5 hd (*1-884536-11-5*) Villard Books.

***Princeton Review Internship Bible 2001.** Princeton Publishing Staff. 672p. 2000. pap. 25.00 (*0-375-75638-8*, Pub. by PRP NY) Random.

Princeton Review Law School Course Summary, Vol. 3. Princeton Review Publishing Staff. Date not set. pap. write for info. (*0-679-76918-8*) McKay.

Princeton Review Law School Course Summary, Vol. 4. Princeton Review Publishing Staff. 1998. pap. 20.00 (*0-679-76930-7*) McKay.

Princeton Review Law School Course Summary, Vol. 7. Princeton Review Publishing Staff. Date not set. pap. write for info. (*0-679-76933-1*) McKay.

Princeton Review Law School Course Summary No. 6, Vol. 6. Princeton Review Publishing Staff. Date not set. pap. write for info. (*0-679-76932-3*) McKay.

Princeton Review SAT: Math. Questron Staff. 1986. pap. 4.95 (*0-394-88624-0*) Random.

***Princeton Review SAT Math Workout.** 2nd ed. Princeton Review Publishing Staff. 256p. 2000. pap. 16.00 (*0-375-76177-2*, Pub. by PRP NY) Random.

***Princeton Review SAT Verbal Workout.** 2nd ed. Princeton Review Publishing Staff. 240p. 2000. pap. 16.00 (*0-375-76176-4*, Pub. by PRP NY) Random.

Princeton Review Science Smart, Jr. Princeton Review Publishing Staff. LC 97-193671. 1996. pap. 12.00 (*0-679-76906-4*) McKay.

Princeton Review Student Guide to Finance. Princeton Review Publishing Staff. Date not set. pap. write for info. (*0-679-76937-4*) McKay.

Princeton Science Library, Set. 1988. pap. 288.50 (*0-691-02420-0*, Pub. by Princeton U Pr) Cal Prin Full Svc.

Princeton Stories. Jesse L. Williams. LC 73-101292. (Short Story Index Reprint Ser.). 1977. 21.95 (*0-8369-3229-3*) Ayer.

Princeton Theological Seminary: A Narrative History, 1812-1992. William K. Selden. LC 92-35559. (C). 1992. write for info. (*0-9634444-0-9*) W K Selden.

***Princeton University: The Campus Guide.** Raymond Rhinehart. LC 99-29961. (Illus.). 188p. 2000. pap. 21.95 (*1-56898-209-7*) Princeton Arch.

Princeton University: The First 250 Years. Don Oberdorfer. Ed. by J. T. Miller. LC 95-20342. (Illus.). 250p. 1995. text 69.50 (*0-691-01122-2*, Pub. by Princeton U Pr) Cal Prin Full Svc.

Princeton Verse Between Two Wars. Ed. by Allen Tate. LC 76-80380. (Granger Index Reprint Ser.). 1977. 18.95 (*0-8369-6065-3*) Ayer.

Princeton, 1746-1896. Thomas J. Wertenbaker. LC 96-220746. 453p. 1946. pap. text 18.95 (*0-691-02612-2*, Pub. by Princeton U Pr) Cal Prin Full Svc.

Princeton, 1746-1896. Thomas J. Wertenbaker. LC LD4609.W4. 446p. reprint ed. pap. 138.30 (*0-7837-0242-6*, 20405510017) Bks Demand.

Princetonians Vol. 5: A Biographical Dictionary, 1791-1794. Princetonians Staff et al. LC 81-47074. 641p. 1991. reprint ed. pap. 198.80 (*0-608-07126-9*, 206735200005) Bks Demand.

Princetonians, 1748-1768: A Biographical Dictionary. James McLachlan. LC 76-4063. 735p. 1976. reprint ed. pap. 200.00 (*0-608-03334-0*, 206404600008) Bks Demand.

Princetonians, 1784-1790: A Biographical Dictionary. Ruth L. Woodward & Wesley F. Craven. (Illus.). 624p. 1991. text 70.00 (*0-691-04771-5*, Pub. by Princeton U Pr) Cal Prin Full Svc.

Princetonians, 1791-1794: A Biographical Dictionary. J. Jefferson Looney & Ruth L. Woodward. (Illus.). 586p. 1991. text 75.00 (*0-691-04772-3*, Pub. by Princeton U Pr) Cal Prin Full Svc.

Princeton/Masters Handbook of Outstanding Resumes & Letters. Bob Gerberg. Ed. by Princeton/Masters Press Staff. (Easier Way Ser.). (Illus.). 186p. 1995. pap. 9.95 (*1-882885-05-8*) Prince-Mstrs.

Princeton's Athletic Training Lab Manual. Arnheim. 1999. 22.66 (*0-8151-2383-3*) McGraw.

Principados y Potestades. Bob Gordon.Tr. of Principalities & Powers. (SPA.). 95p. 1995. pap. write for info. (*0-614-27115-0*) Editorial Unilit.

Principados y Potestades. T. Marshall.Tr. of Principalities & Powers. (SPA.). 3.50 (*1-56063-430-8*, 550014) Editorial Unilit.

Principados y Potestades - Principalities & Powers. Bob Gordon. (SPA.). 95p. 1995. write for info. (*0-614-24397-1*) Editorial Unilit.

Principal. John T. Seyfarth. LC 98-33526. 354p. 1998. 64.00 (*0-13-436528-3*) P-H.

Principal: Creative Leadership for Effective Schools. 3rd ed. Gerald C. Ubben & Larry W. Hughes. LC 95-53714. 368p. 1996. 80.33 (*0-205-19865-1*) Allyn.

***Principal: Creative Leadership for Effective Schools.** 4th ed. Gerald C. Ubben et al. LC 00-42143. 2001. write for info. (*0-205-32211-5*) Allyn.

Principal, Academic High School. Jack Rudman. (Teachers License Examination Ser.: S-5). 1994. pap. 49.95 (*0-8373-8105-3*) Nat Learn.

Principal Account-Audit Clerk. Jack Rudman. (Career Examination Ser.: C-2008). 1994. pap. 27.95 (*0-8373-2008-9*) Nat Learn.

Principal Account Clerk. Jack Rudman. (Career Examination Ser.: C-655). 1994. pap. 27.95 (*0-8373-0655-8*) Nat Learn.

Principal Accountant. Jack Rudman. (Career Examination Ser.: C-654). 1994. pap. 34.95 (*0-8373-0654-X*) Nat Learn.

Principal Actuarial Clerk. Jack Rudman. (Career Examination Ser.: C-2424). 1994. pap. 29.95 (*0-8373-2424-6*) Nat Learn.

Principal Actuary. Jack Rudman. (Career Examination Ser.: C-610). 1994. pap. 49.95 (*0-8373-0610-8*) Nat Learn.

Principal Addiction Specialist. Jack Rudman. (Career Examination Ser.: C-1398). 1994. pap. 34.95 (*0-8373-1398-8*) Nat Learn.

Principal Administrative Analyst. Jack Rudman. (Career Examination Ser.: C-2710). 1994. pap. 39.95 (*0-8373-2710-5*) Nat Learn.

Principal Administrative Associate. Jack Rudman. (Career Examination Ser.: C-2394). 1994. pap. 29.95 (*0-8373-2394-0*) Nat Learn.

Principal Administrative Services Clerk. Jack Rudman. (Career Examination Ser.: C-2871). 1994. pap. 29.95 (*0-8373-2871-3*) Nat Learn.

Principal Admitting Clerk. Jack Rudman. (Career Examination Ser.: C-656). 1994. pap. 27.95 (*0-8373-0656-6*) Nat Learn.

Principal Affirmative Action Officer. Jack Rudman. (Career Examination Ser.: C-2689). 1994. pap. 34.95 (*0-8373-2689-3*) Nat Learn.

Principal Alcoholism Rehabilitaion Counselor. Jack Rudman. (Career Examination Ser.: C-2796). 1994. pap. 34.95 (*0-8373-2796-2*) Nat Learn.

Principal & Subsidiary Dialect Areas in the North-Central States; English Loan Words in the Low German Dialect of Westphalia, Missouri. Albert H. Marckwardt & W. A. Willibrand. (Publications of the American Dialect Society: No. 27). 32p. 1957. pap. 5.50 (*0-8173-0627-7*) U of Ala Pr.

Principal As Chief Executive Officer. Ed. by Andrew E. Dubin. 224p. 1991. pap. 29.95 (*1-85000-806-X*, Falmer Pr) Taylor & Francis.

Principal As Curriculum Leader: Shaping What Is Taught & Tested. Allan A. Glatthorn. LC 97-4585. (Illus.). 168p. 1997. 55.95 (*0-8039-6427-7*, 2319); pap. 24.95 (*0-8039-6428-5*) Corwin Pr.

***Principal as Curriculum Leader: Shaping What Is Taught & Tested.** 2nd ed. Allan A. Glatthorn. LC 00-8950. 2000. pap. write for info. (*0-7619-7557-8*) AltaMira Pr.

Principal As Educational Leader, Vol. 1. 2nd ed. Ed. by Maria Ciriello. (Formation & Development for Catholic School Leaders Ser.). 480p. 1998. pap. 29.95 (*1-57455-077-2*) US Catholic.

Principal as Leader. 2nd ed. Larry W. Hughes. LC 98-13640. 346p. 1998. 57.00 (*0-13-629585-1*) P-H.

Principal as School Manager. William L. Sharp & James K. Walter. LC 94-60442. 185p. 1994. text 34.95 (*1-56676-127-1*) Scarecrow.

Principal as Staff Developer. Richard DuFour. Ed. by Dennis Sparks. 105p. (Orig.). 1991. pap. 21.95 (*1-879639-01-7*) Natl Educ Serv.

Principal as Steward. John R. McCall. LC 96-3417. 250p. 1997. 35.95 (*1-883001-32-3*) Eye On Educ.

Principal Attorney. Jack Rudman. (Career Examination Ser.: C-1913). 1994. pap. 44.95 (*0-8373-1913-7*) Nat Learn.

Principal Audit Clerk. Jack Rudman. (Career Examination Ser.: C-657). 1994. pap. 27.95 (*0-8373-0657-4*) Nat Learn.

Principal Auditor. Jack Rudman. (Career Examination Ser.: C-2405). 1994. pap. 39.95 (*0-8373-2405-X*) Nat Learn.

Principal Bank Examiner. Jack Rudman. (Career Examination Ser.: C-658). 1994. pap. 34.95 (*0-8373-0658-2*) Nat Learn.

Principal Bookkeeper. Jack Rudman. (Career Examination Ser.: C-1756). 1994. reprint ed. pap. 29.95 (*0-8373-1756-8*) Nat Learn.

Principal Budget Analyst. Jack Rudman. (Career Examination Ser.: C-2416). 1994. pap. 39.95 (*0-8373-2416-5*) Nat Learn.

Principal Budget Examiner. Jack Rudman. (Career Examination Ser.: C-1637). 1994. reprint ed. pap. 39.95 (*0-8373-1637-5*) Nat Learn.

Principal Budget Officer. Jack Rudman. (Career Examination Ser.: C-2685). 1994. pap. 39.95 (*0-8373-2685-0*) Nat Learn.

Principal Building Inspector. Jack Rudman. (Career Examination Ser.: C-2853). 1994. pap. 34.95 (*0-8373-2853-5*) Nat Learn.

Principal Buyer. Jack Rudman. (Career Examination Ser.: C-3419). 1994. pap. 29.95 (*0-8373-3419-5*) Nat Learn.

Principal Cashier. Jack Rudman. (Career Examination Ser.: C-1974). 1994. pap. 23.95 (*0-8373-1974-9*) Nat Learn.

***Principal Cause of Death.** Richard L. Baldwin. (Louis Searing & Margaret McMillan Mystery Ser.). 264p. 1999. pap. 12.95 (*0-9660685-2-1*) Buttonwood.

Principal Cause of Death. Mark R. Zubro. (Tom & Scott Ser.). 192p. 1993. pap. 11.95 (*0-312-09896-0*, Stonewall Inn) St Martin.

Principal Characteristics of Sausages of the World Listed by Country of Origin. Donald M. Kinsman. 134p. (Orig.). 1983. pap. text 14.95 (*0-89641-122-2*) American Pr.

Principal Chemist. Jack Rudman. (Career Examination Ser.: C-2403). 1994. pap. 34.95 (*0-8373-2403-3*) Nat Learn.

Principal Children's Counselor. Jack Rudman. (Career Examination Ser.: C-1602). 1994. pap. 34.95 (*0-8373-1602-2*) Nat Learn.

Principal Civil Engineer. Jack Rudman. (Career Examination Ser.: C-318). 1994. pap. 34.95 (*0-8373-0318-4*) Nat Learn.

Principal Clerk. Jack Rudman. (Career Examination Ser.: C-611). 1994. pap. 23.95 (*0-8373-0611-6*) Nat Learn.

Principal Clerk (Personnel) Jack Rudman. (Career Examination Ser.: C-1399). 1994. pap. 27.95 (*0-8373-1399-6*) Nat Learn.

Principal Clerk-Stenographer. Jack Rudman. (Career Examination Ser.: C-3327). 1994. pap. 23.95 (*0-8373-3327-X*) Nat Learn.

Principal Clerk Surrogate. Jack Rudman. (Career Examination Ser.: C-2129). 1994. reprint ed. pap. 29.95 (*0-8373-2129-8*) Nat Learn.

Principal Commissary Clerk. Jack Rudman. (Career Examination Ser.: C-2049). 1994. pap. 27.95 (*0-8373-2049-6*) Nat Learn.

Principal Communication Systems. 2nd ed. Manela. 1986. student ed. 34.68 (*0-07-062956-0*) McGraw.

Principal Communications Technician. Jack Rudman. (Career Examination Ser.: C-2413). 1994. pap. 34.95 (*0-8373-2413-0*) Nat Learn.

Principal Component Analysis. I. T. Jolliffe. (Series in Statistics). (Illus.). 290p. 1986. 72.95 (*0-387-96269-7*) Spr-Verlag.

Principal Component Neural Networks: Theory & Applications. Kostas Diamantaras. LC 95-242. (Adaptive & Learning Systems for Signal Processing, Communications & Control Ser.). 272p. 1996. 84.95 (*0-471-05436-4*) Wiley.

Principal Components: Manual. D. L. Massart & P. J. Lewi. 1994. write for info. (*0-444-81653-4*) Elsevier.

Principal Components Analysis, No. 69. George H. Dunteman. (Quantitative Applications in the Social Sciences Ser.: Vol. 69). 96p. (C). 1989. pap. text 10.95 (*0-8039-3104-2*) Sage.

Principal, Comprehensive High School. Jack Rudman. (Teachers License Examination Ser.: S-11). 1994. pap. 49.95 (*0-8373-8111-8*) Nat Learn.

Principal Computer Programmer. Jack Rudman. (Career Examination Ser.: C-1626). 1994. pap. 34.95 (*0-8373-1626-X*) Nat Learn.

Principal Construction Inspector. Jack Rudman. (Career Examination Ser.: C-1400). 1994. pap. 34.95 (*0-8373-1400-3*) Nat Learn.

Principal Consumer Affairs Inspector. Jack Rudman. (Career Examination Ser.: C-1658). 1994. reprint ed. pap. 29.95 (*0-8373-1658-8*) Nat Learn.

Principal Consumer Affairs Investigator. Jack Rudman. (Career Examination Ser.: C-2377). 1994. pap. 29.95 (*0-8373-2377-0*) Nat Learn.

Principal Contributions of Henry Walter Bates to a Knowledge of the Butterflies & Longicorn Beetles of the Amazon Valley: Original Anthology. Ed. by Earle G. Linsley & Keir B. Sterling. LC 77-81106. (Biologists & Their World Ser.). (Illus.). 1978. lib. bdg. 72.95 (*0-405-10690-4*) Ayer.

Principal Court Clerk. Jack Rudman. (Career Examination Ser.: C-2588). 1994. pap. 29.95 (*0-8373-2588-9*) Nat Learn.

Principal Currents for a Pair of Unitary Operators. Joel D. Pincus & Shaojie Zhou. LC 94-4146. (Memoirs of the American Mathematical Society Ser.: No. 522). 103p. 1994. pap. 32.00 (*0-8218-2609-3*, MEMO/109/522) Am Math.

Principal Custodial Foreman. Jack Rudman. (Career Examination Ser.: C-2560). 1994. pap. 29.95 (*0-8373-2560-9*) Nat Learn.

Principal Data Entry Machine Operator. Jack Rudman. (Career Examination Ser.: C-2866). 1994. pap. 29.95 (*0-8373-2866-7*) Nat Learn.

Principal Data Processing Control Clerk. Jack Rudman. (Career Examination Ser.: C-2485). 1994. pap. 29.95 (*0-8373-2485-8*) Nat Learn.

Principal Data Processing Equipment Operator. Jack Rudman. (Career Examination Ser.: C-2303). 1994. reprint ed. pap. 29.95 (*0-8373-2303-7*) Nat Learn.

Principal Developmental Specialist. Jack Rudman. (Career Examination Ser.: C-925). 1994. pap. 34.95 (*0-8373-0925-5*) Nat Learn.

Principal Diseases of Marine Fish & Shellfish, Vol. 1. 2nd ed. Ed. by Carl J. Sindermann. 521p. 1990. text 126.00 (*0-12-645851-0*) Acad Pr.

Principal Diseases of Marine Fish & Shellfish: Diseases of Marine Shellfish, Vol. 2. 2nd ed. Carl J. Sindermann. 516p. 1990. text 126.00 (*0-12-645852-9*) Acad Pr.

Principal Drafting Technician. Jack Rudman. (Career Examination Ser.: C-2680). 1994. pap. 29.95 (*0-8373-2680-X*) Nat Learn.

Principal Draftsman. Jack Rudman. (Career Examination Ser.: C-1576). 1994. pap. 29.95 (*0-8373-1576-X*) Nat Learn.

Principal Drug & Alcohol Counselor. Jack Rudman. (Career Examination Ser.: C-2743). 1994. pap. 34.95 (*0-8373-2743-1*) Nat Learn.

Principal Ecclesiastical Judgments Delivered in the Court of Arches 1867 to 1875. Robert Phillimore. xiii, 420p. 1981. reprint ed. 46.00 (*0-8377-2504-6*, Rothman) W S Hein.

Principal Editorial Clerk. Jack Rudman. (Career Examination Ser.: C-2566). 1994. pap. 29.95 (*0-8373-2566-8*) Nat Learn.

***Principal Election Engineer Mateirals Devices.** 2nd ed. Safa Kasap. 2001. text 64.00 (*0-07-239342-4*) McGraw.

Principal, Elementary School. Jack Rudman. (Teachers License Examination Ser.: S-3). 1994. pap. 49.95 (*0-8373-8103-7*) Nat Learn.

Principal Emergency Response & Preparedness Requirements in Osha Standards & Guidance for Safety & Health Programs. 52p. 1994. pap. 4.00 (*0-16-061780-4*) USGPO.

Principal Employment Security Clerk. Jack Rudman. (Career Examination Ser.: C-2352). 1994. pap. 29.95 (*0-8373-2352-5*) Nat Learn.

Principal Engineering Aide. Jack Rudman. (Career Examination Ser.: C-1561). 1994. pap. 29.95 (*0-8373-1561-1*) Nat Learn.

Principal Engineering Inspector. Jack Rudman. (Career Examination Ser.: C-911). 1994. pap. 39.95 (*0-8373-0911-5*) Nat Learn.

Principal Engineering Technician. Jack Rudman. (Career Examination Ser.: C-1425). 1994. pap. 29.95 (*0-8373-1425-9*) Nat Learn.

Principal Engineering Technician (Drafting) Jack Rudman. (Career Examination Ser.: C-1954). 1994. pap. 29.95 (*0-8373-1954-4*) Nat Learn.

Principal Engineering Technician (Environmental Quality) Jack Rudman. (Career Examination Ser.: C-3239). 1994. pap. 34.95 (*0-8373-3239-7*) Nat Learn.

Principal Environmental Analyst. Jack Rudman. (Career Examination Ser.: C-2661). 1994. pap. 39.95 (*0-8373-2661-3*) Nat Learn.

Principal Environmental Planner. Jack Rudman. (Career Examination Ser.: C-2664). 1994. pap. 39.95 (*0-8373-2664-8*) Nat Learn.

Principal Evidence Technician. Jack Rudman. (Career Examination Ser.: C-2750). 1994. pap. 34.95 (*0-8373-2750-4*) Nat Learn.

Principal Examiner of Municipal Affairs. Jack Rudman. (Career Examination Ser.: C-2727). 1994. pap. 44.95 (*0-8373-2727-X*) Nat Learn.

Principal Executive Officer. Jack Rudman. (Career Examination Ser.: C-2827). 1994. pap. 39.95 (*0-8373-2827-6*) Nat Learn.

Principal Family & Estate Collections Pt. 1: Families A-K. Royal Commission on Historical Manuscripts Staff. 1996. pap. 60.00 (*0-11-440265-5*) Statnry Office.

Principal Family & Estate Collections Pt. 2: Families L-Z. Royal Commission on Historical Manuscripts Staff. 1999. pap. 75.00 (*0-11-440276-0*, Pub. by Statnry Office) Balogh.

Principal Farm Products see Report of the Federal Trade Commission on Agricultural Income Inquiry

Principal Field Accountant. Jack Rudman. (Career Examination Ser.: C-1570). 1994. pap. 34.95 (*0-8373-1570-0*) Nat Learn.

Principal File Clerk. Jack Rudman. (Career Examination Ser.: C-659). 1994. pap. 23.95 (*0-8373-0659-0*) Nat Learn.

Principal Financial Analyst. Jack Rudman. (Career Examination Ser.: C-2644). 1994. pap. 44.95 (*0-8373-2644-3*) Nat Learn.

Principal Forestry Technician. Jack Rudman. (Career Examination Ser.: C-2716). 1994. pap. 29.95 (*0-8373-2716-4*) Nat Learn.

Principal from the Black Lagoon. Mike Thaler. LC 94-158718. 32p. (J). (ps-3). 1993. pap. 2.99 (*0-590-45782-9*) Scholastic Inc.

Principal from the Black Lagoon. Mike Thaler. (J). 1993. 8.19 (*0-606-02847-1*, Pub. by Turtleback) Demco.

Principal Gold Producing District of Alaska. A. H. Koschmann & M. H. Bergendahl. Ed. by Mary Carson. (Principal Gold Producing Ser.). (Illus.). 25p. 1993. reprint ed. pap. 5.95 (*0-941620-51-4*) Carson Ent.

Principal Gold Producing District of Arizona. A. H. Koschmann & M. H. Bergendahl. Ed. by Mary Carson. (Principal Gold Producing Ser.). (Illus.). 22p. 1993. reprint ed. pap. 5.95 (*0-941620-52-2*) Carson Ent.

An Asterisk (*) at the beginning of an entry indicates that the title is appearing for the first time.

Principal Gold Producing District of Montana. A. H. Koschmann & M. H. Bergendahl. Ed. by Mary Carson. (Principal Gold Producing Ser.). (Illus.). 32p. 1993. reprint ed. pap. 5.95 (*0-941620-55-7*) Carson Ent.
Principal Gold Producing District of Nevada. A. H. Koschmann & M. H. Bergendahl. Ed. by Mary Carson. (Principal Gold Producing Ser.). (Illus.). 30p. 1993. reprint ed. pap. 5.95 (*0-941620-54-9*) Carson Ent.
Principal Gold Producing District of New Mexico. A. H. Koschmann & M. H. Bergendahl. Ed. by Mary Carson. (Principal Gold Producing Ser.). (Illus.). 12p. 1993. reprint ed. pap. 5.95 (*0-941620-58-1*) Carson Ent.
Principal Gold Producing District of Oregon. A. H. Koschmann & M. H. Bergendahl. Ed. by Mary Carson. (Principal Gold Producing Ser.). (Illus.). 16p. 1993. reprint ed. pap. 5.95 (*0-941620-50-6*) Carson Ent.
Principal Gold Producing District of Washington. A. H. Koschmann & M. H. Bergendahl. Ed. by Mary Carson. (Principal Gold Producing Ser.). (Illus.). 8p. 1993. reprint ed. pap. 5.95 (*0-86142-056-X*) Carson Ent.
Principal Gold Producing Districts of Colorado. A. H. Koschmann & M. H. Bergendahl. Ed. by Mary Carson. (Principal Gold Producing Ser.). (Illus.). 32p. 1993. reprint ed. pap. 5.95 (*0-941620-46-8*) Carson Ent.
Principal Gold Producing Districts of Michigan, South Dakota & Wyoming. A. H. Koschmann & M. H. Bergendahl. Ed. by Mary Carson. (Principal Gold Producing Ser.). (Illus.). 10p. (Orig.). 1993. reprint ed. pap. 5.95 (*0-941620-57-3*) Carson Ent.
Principal Grants Analyst. Jack Rudman. (Career Examination Ser.: C-2835). 1994. pap. 39.95 (*0-8373-2835-7*) Nat Learn.
Principal Grounds & Maxims with an Analysis of the Laws of England. 3rd ed. William Noy. xxvii, 219p. 1980. reprint ed. 37.00 (*0-8377-0906-7*, Rothman) W S Hein.
Principal Groundskeeper. Jack Rudman. (Career Examination Ser.: C-1573). 1994. pap. 29.95 (*0-8373-1573-5*) Nat Learn.
Principal Home Economist. Jack Rudman. (Career Examination Ser.: C-1627). 1994. pap. 34.95 (*0-8373-1627-8*) Nat Learn.
Principal Hospital Care Investigator. Jack Rudman. (Career Examination Ser.: C-612). 1994. pap. 34.95 (*0-8373-0612-4*) Nat Learn.
Principal Housing Inspector. Jack Rudman. (Career Examination Ser.: C-1426). 1994. reprint ed. pap. 34.95 (*0-8373-1426-7*) Nat Learn.
Principal Human Resources Specialist. Jack Rudman. (Career Examination Ser.: C-974). 1994. pap. 34.95 (*0-8373-0974-3*) Nat Learn.
Principal Illustrator. Jack Rudman. (Career Examination Ser.: C-1713). 1994. pap. 34.95 (*0-8373-1713-4*) Nat Learn.
Principal in Metropolitan Schools. Ed. by Donald A. Erickson & Theodore L. Reller. LC 78-62641. (Contemporary Educational Issues Ser.). 347p. 1978. 35.00 (*0-8211-0417-9*) McCutchan.
Principal Infectious Diseases of Childhood. Nelles Silverthorne et al. LC 66-6101. 146p. reprint ed. pap. 45.30 (*0-608-13471-6*, 201441100095) Bks Demand.
Principal Instruction. 3rd ed. Walter W. Wager. (C). 1990. student ed. 23.50 (*0-03-033982-0*, Pub. by Harcourt Coll Pubs) Harcourt.
Principal Insurance Examiner. Jack Rudman. (Career Examination Ser.: C-2696). 1994. pap. 34.95 (*0-8373-2696-6*) Nat Learn.
Principal International Businesses: The World Marketing Directory. Dun & Bradstreet Staff. 3336p. 1995. 595.00 (*1-56203-461-8*) Dun & Bradstreet.
Principal Investigation. B. B. Jordan. 320p. 1997. mass mkt. 5.99 (*0-425-16090-4*, Prime Crime) Berkley Pub.
Principal Investigator. Jack Rudman. (Career Examination Ser.: C-1791). 1994. pap. 34.95 (*0-8373-1791-6*) Nat Learn.
Principal, Junior High School. Jack Rudman. (Teachers License Examination Ser.: S-4). 1994. pap. 49.95 (*0-8373-8104-5*) Nat Learn.
Principal Juvenile Counselor. Jack Rudman. (Career Examination Ser.: C-422). 1994. pap. 34.95 (*0-8373-0422-9*) Nat Learn.
Principal Key Punch Operator. Jack Rudman. (Career Examination Ser.: C-2103). 1994. pap. 27.95 (*0-8373-2103-4*) Nat Learn.
Principal Labor-Management Practices Adjustor. Jack Rudman. (Career Examination Ser.: C-613). 1994. pap. 44.95 (*0-8373-0613-2*) Nat Learn.
Principal Labor Relations Analyst. Jack Rudman. (Career Examination Ser.: C-2231). 1994. pap. 44.95 (*0-8373-2231-6*) Nat Learn.
Principal Labor Specialist. Jack Rudman. (Career Examination Ser.: C-2670). 1994. pap. 39.95 (*0-8373-2670-2*) Nat Learn.
Principal Laboratory Animal Caretaker. Jack Rudman. (Career Examination Ser.: Vol. C-3794). 1997. pap. 29.95 (*0-8373-3794-1*) Nat Learn.
Principal Laboratory Technician. Jack Rudman. (Career Examination Ser.: C-3014). 1994. pap. 34.95 (*0-8373-3014-9*) Nat Learn.
Principal Land Management Specialist. Jack Rudman. (Career Examination Ser.: C-2620). 1994. pap. 39.95 (*0-8373-2620-6*) Nat Learn.
Principal Librarian. Jack Rudman. (Career Examination Ser.: C-2915). 1994. pap. 29.95 (*0-8373-2915-9*) Nat Learn.
Principal Library Clerk. Jack Rudman. (Career Examination Ser.: C-1932). 1994. pap. 27.95 (*0-8373-1932-3*) Nat Learn.
Principal Mail & Supply Clerk. Jack Rudman. (Career Examination Ser.: C-975). 1994. pap. 27.95 (*0-8373-0975-1*) Nat Learn.
Principal Management Analyst. Jack Rudman. (Career Examination Ser.: C-1737). 1994. pap. 39.95 (*0-8373-1737-1*) Nat Learn.
Principal Management Technician. Jack Rudman. (Career Examination Ser.: C-2753). 1994. pap. 34.95 (*0-8373-2753-9*) Nat Learn.
Principal Manpower Development Specialist. Jack Rudman. (Career Examination Ser.: C-2819). 1994. pap. 39.95 (*0-8373-2819-5*) Nat Learn.
Principal Manuscript Collections in the National Library of Australia. 3rd ed. LC 94-150589. 99p. 1992. write for info. (*0-642-10547-2*, Pub. by Aust Gov Pub) Accents Pubns.
Principal Mechanical Engineer. Jack Rudman. (Career Examination Ser.: C-3249). 1994. pap. 39.95 (*0-8373-3249-4*) Nat Learn.
Principal Methods Analyst. Jack Rudman. (Career Examination Ser.: C-1738). 1994. pap. 39.95 (*0-8373-1738-X*) Nat Learn.
Principal Motor Vehicle License Examiner. Jack Rudman. (Career Examination Ser.: Vol. C-3799). 1997. pap. 34.95 (*0-8373-3799-2*) Nat Learn.
Principal Museum Curator. Jack Rudman. (Career Examination Ser.: C-2375). 1994. pap. 34.95 (*0-8373-2375-4*) Nat Learn.
Principal Navigations, Voyages, Traffiques & Discoveries of the English Nation, 12 vols. Richard Hakluyt. LC 76-181901. reprint ed. write for info. (*0-404-03030-0*) AMS Pr.
Principal Occupational Analyst. Jack Rudman. (Career Examination Ser.: C-2535). 1994. pap. 34.95 (*0-8373-2535-8*) Nat Learn.
Principal of Land Management & Soil Conservation. S. S. Negi. (C). 1991. 170.00 (*81-7136-016-5*, Pub. by Periodical Expert) St Mut.
Principal of Macroeconomics. 2nd ed. Ed. by Hammer. 366p. 1999. pap. text 36.00 (*0-536-02652-1*) P-H.
***Principal of Microecnomics.** 2nd ed. Ed. by Silberberg. 504p. 1999. pap. text 42.00 (*0-536-02620-3*) P-H.
Principal of the Thing: The Journal of a High School Principal. Ed Boykin. 435p. (Orig.). (C). 1990. pap. 24.95 (*0-9625988-0-1*) Crooked Hacienda Pr.
Principal Office Assistant. Jack Rudman. (Career Examination Ser.: C-2595). 1994. pap. 23.95 (*0-8373-2595-1*) Nat Learn.
Principal Office Stenographer. Jack Rudman. (Career Examination Ser.: C-3377). 1994. pap. 23.95 (*0-8373-3377-6*) Nat Learn.
Principal Office Typist. Jack Rudman. (Career Examination Ser.: C-3375). 1994. pap. 23.95 (*0-8373-3375-X*) Nat Learn.
Principal Park Supervisor. Jack Rudman. (Career Examination Ser.: C-2355). 1994. pap. 29.95 (*0-8373-2355-X*) Nat Learn.
Principal Personnel Administrator. Jack Rudman. (Career Examination Ser.: C-2411). 1994. pap. 44.95 (*0-8373-2411-4*) Nat Learn.
Principal Personnel Analyst. Jack Rudman. (Career Examination Ser.: C-2346). 1994. pap. 39.95 (*0-8373-2346-0*) Nat Learn.
Principal Personnel Clerk. Jack Rudman. (Career Examination Ser.: C-2944). 1994. pap. 27.95 (*0-8373-2944-2*) Nat Learn.
Principal Personnel Examiner. Jack Rudman. (Career Examination Ser.: C-1915). 1994. pap. 39.95 (*0-8373-1915-3*) Nat Learn.
Principal Photography: Interviews with Feature Film Cinematographers. Vincent LoBrutto. LC 98-46797. 264p. 1999. 65.00 (*0-275-94954-0*, Praeger Pubs); pap. 22.95 (*0-275-94955-9*, Praeger Pubs) Greenwood.
Principal Planner. Jack Rudman. (Career Examination Ser.: C-1764). 1994. reprint ed. pap. 34.95 (*0-8373-1764-9*) Nat Learn.
Principal Planner (Education) Jack Rudman. (Career Examination Ser.: C-1669). 1994. pap. 39.95 (*0-8373-1669-3*) Nat Learn.
Principal Planner (Manpower) Jack Rudman. (Career Examination Ser.: C-1599). 1994. pap. 39.95 (*0-8373-1599-9*) Nat Learn.
Principal Portfolio. Genevieve Brown & Beverly J. Irby. LC 97-4757. (Illus.). 72p. 1997. 51.95 (*0-8039-6541-9*); pap. 22.95 (*0-8039-6542-7*) Corwin Pr.
Principal Portfolio. Genevieve Brown & Beverly J. Irby. 72p. 1997. wbk. ed. 39.95 (*2-8106-6541-9*); pap., wbk. ed. 19.95 (*2-8106-6542-7*) NEA.
Principal Probation Officer. Jack Rudman. (Career Examination Ser.: C-1427). 1994. pap. 29.95 (*0-8373-1427-5*) Nat Learn.
Principal Products of Portugal: Prose Pieces. Donald Hall. LC 94-33667. 288p. 1996. pap. 14.00 (*0-8070-6203-0*) Beacon Pr.
Principal Program Evaluation Specialist. Jack Rudman. (Career Examination Ser.: C-2701). 1994. pap. 39.95 (*0-8373-2701-6*) Nat Learn.
Principal Program Examiner. Jack Rudman. (Career Examination Ser.: C-2756). 1994. pap. 39.95 (*0-8373-2756-3*) Nat Learn.
Principal Program Research Analyst. Jack Rudman. (Career Examination Ser.: C-2218). 1994. reprint ed. pap. 39.95 (*0-8373-2218-9*) Nat Learn.
Principal Program Specialist. Jack Rudman. (Career Examination Ser.: C-2863). 1994. pap. 39.95 (*0-8373-2863-2*) Nat Learn.
Principal Program Specialist (Correction) Jack Rudman. (Career Examination Ser.: C-2259). 1994. reprint ed. pap. 39.95 (*0-8373-2259-6*) Nat Learn.
Principal Programmer Analyst. Jack Rudman. (Career Examination Ser.: C-3739). 1994. pap. 34.95 (*0-8373-3739-9*) Nat Learn.
Principal Public Health Engineer. Jack Rudman. (Career Examination Ser.: C-3099). 1994. pap. 39.95 (*0-8373-3099-8*) Nat Learn.
Principal Public Health Nutritionist. Jack Rudman. (Career Examination Ser.: C-1566). 1994. pap. 34.95 (*0-8373-1566-2*) Nat Learn.
Principal Public Health Representative. Jack Rudman. (Career Examination Ser.: C-3025). 1994. pap. 34.95 (*0-8373-3025-4*) Nat Learn.
Principal Public Health Sanitarian. Jack Rudman. (Career Examination Ser.: C-3347). 1994. pap. 34.95 (*0-8373-3347-4*) Nat Learn.
Principal Purchase Inspector. Jack Rudman. (Career Examination Ser.: C-1747). 1994. reprint ed. pap. 34.95 (*0-8373-1747-9*) Nat Learn.
Principal Purchasing Agent. Jack Rudman. (Career Examination Ser.: C-912). 1994. pap. 29.95 (*0-8373-0912-3*) Nat Learn.
Principal Quantitative Analyst. Jack Rudman. (Career Examination Ser.: C-1715). 1994. pap. 39.95 (*0-8373-1715-0*) Nat Learn.
Principal Real Estate Manager. Jack Rudman. (Career Examination Ser.: C-1628). 1994. pap. 34.95 (*0-8373-1628-6*) Nat Learn.
Principal Records Center Assistant. Jack Rudman. (Career Examination Ser.: C-1914). 1994. pap. 29.95 (*0-8373-1914-5*) Nat Learn.
Principal Rent Examiner. Jack Rudman. (Career Examination Ser.: C-2093). 1994. reprint ed. pap. 34.95 (*0-8373-2093-3*) Nat Learn.
Principal Research Analyst. Jack Rudman. (Career Examination Ser.: C-2353). 1994. pap. 39.95 (*0-8373-2353-3*) Nat Learn.
Principal Right-Of-Way Aide. Jack Rudman. (Career Examination Ser.: C-2737). 1994. pap. 29.95 (*0-8373-2737-7*) Nat Learn.
Principal Safety Coordinator. Jack Rudman. (Career Examination Ser.: C-2669). 1994. pap. 39.95 (*0-8373-2669-9*) Nat Learn.
Principal Sanitary Engineer. Jack Rudman. (Career Examination Ser.: C-1819). 1994. pap. 39.95 (*0-8373-1819-X*) Nat Learn.
Principal Senior Citizens' Program Coordinator. Jack Rudman. (Career Examination Ser.: C-2799). 1994. pap. 34.95 (*0-8373-2799-7*) Nat Learn.
Principal, Six Hundred School. Jack Rudman. (Teachers License Examination Ser.: S-7). 1994. pap. 49.95 (*0-8373-8107-X*) Nat Learn.
Principal Social Welfare Examiner. Jack Rudman. (Career Examination Ser.: C-2495). 1994. pap. 29.95 (*0-8373-2495-5*) Nat Learn.
Principal Solutions of Ordinary Differential Equations in the Complex Domain. Walter Strodt. LC 52-42839. (Memoirs Ser.: No. 1/26). 107p. 1972. reprint ed. pap. 19.00 (*0-8218-1226-2*, MEMO/1/26) Am Math.
Principal Special Investigator. Jack Rudman. (Career Examination Ser.: C-1590). 1994. pap. 34.95 (*0-8373-1590-5*) Nat Learn.
Principal Special Officer. Jack Rudman. (Career Examination Ser.: C-3420). 1994. pap. 29.95 (*0-8373-3420-9*) Nat Learn.
Principal Staff Development Specialist. Jack Rudman. (Career Examimation Ser.: C-2703). 1994. pap. 39.95 (*0-8373-2703-2*) Nat Learn.
Principal Stationary Engineer. Jack Rudman. (Career Examination Ser.: C-1719). 1994. pap. 39.95 (*0-8373-1719-3*) Nat Learn.
Principal Statistician. Jack Rudman. (Career Examination Ser.: C-976). 1994. pap. 39.95 (*0-8373-0976-X*) Nat Learn.
Principal Statistics Clerk. Jack Rudman. (Career Examination Ser.: C-977). 1994. pap. 27.95 (*0-8373-0977-8*) Nat Learn.
Principal Stenographer. Jack Rudman. (Career Examination Ser.: C-614). 1994. pap. 23.95 (*0-8373-0614-0*) Nat Learn.
Principal Stenographer (Law) Jack Rudman. (Career Examination Ser.: C-3294). 1994. pap. 27.95 (*0-8373-3294-X*) Nat Learn.
Principal Storekeeper. Jack Rudman. (Career Examination Ser.: C-3013). 1994. pap. 29.95 (*0-8373-3013-0*) Nat Learn.
Principal Stores Clerk. Jack Rudman. (Career Examination Ser.: C-978). 1994. pap. 27.95 (*0-8373-0978-6*) Nat Learn.
Principal Succession: Establishing Leadership in Schools. Ann W. Hart. LC 91-45300. (SUNY Series, Educational Leadership). 349p. (C). 1992. pap. text 24.95 (*0-7914-1292-X*) State U NY Pr.
Principal Succession: Establishing Leadership in Schools. Ann W. Hart. LC 91-45300. (SUNY Series, Educational Leadership). 349p. (C). 1993. text 64.50 (*0-7914-1291-1*) State U NY Pr.
Principal Suspect: The True Story of Dr. Jay Smith & the Main Line Murders. William C. Costopoulos. LC 96-5989. (Illus.). 312p. 1996. 22.00 (*0-940159-36-8*) Camino Bks.
Principal Symbols of World Religions. Swami Harshananda. 56p. 1988. pap. 4.50 (*0-89540-178-9*, SB-178) Sun Pub.
Principal Systems Analyst. Jack Rudman. (Career Examination Ser.: C-2388). 1994. pap. 39.95 (*0-8373-2388-6*) Nat Learn.
Principal Tax Compliance Agent. Jack Rudman. (Career Examination Ser.: C-2954). 1994. pap. 34.95 (*0-8373-2954-X*) Nat Learn.
Principal Teachings of Buddhism. Tsongkapa. Tr. by Geshe L. Tharchin & Michael Roach. 216p. pap. 6.95 (*0-918753-09-0*) Mahayana.
Principal Telephone Operator. Jack Rudman. (Career Examination Ser.: C-2493). 1994. pap. 27.95 (*0-8373-2493-9*) Nat Learn.
Principal Threats Facing Communities & Local Emergency Management Coordinators. (Illus.). 128p. (Orig.). (C). 1993. pap. text 35.00 (*1-56806-719-4*) DIANE Pub.
Principal Typist. Jack Rudman. (Career Examination Ser.: C-615). 1994. pap. 23.95 (*0-8373-0615-9*) Nat Learn.
Principal Unemployment Insurance Hearing Representative. Jack Rudman. (Career Examination Ser.: C-2730). 1994. pap. 34.95 (*0-8373-2730-X*) Nat Learn.
Principal Unemployment Insurance Investigator. Jack Rudman. (Career Examination Ser.: C-2831). 1994. pap. 34.95 (*0-8373-2831-4*) Nat Learn.
Principal Upanisads. Ed. & Intro. by Sarvepalli Radhakrishnan. LC 91-47550. (Humanities Paperback Library). 960p. (C). 1992. pap. 32.50 (*0-391-03479-0*) Humanities.
Principal Upanishads. Sarvepalli Radhakrishnan. 958p. (C). 1995. pap. 12.00 (*81-7223-124-5*, Pub. by Harper SF) HarpC.
Principal, Vocational High School. Jack Rudman. (Teachers License Examination Ser.: S-6). 1994. pap. 49.95 (*0-8373-8106-1*) Nat Learn.
Principal Water Plant Supervisor. Jack Rudman. (Career Examination Ser.: C-2960). 1994. pap. 34.95 (*0-8373-2960-4*) Nat Learn.
Principal Workers' Compensation Review Analyst. Jack Rudman. (Career Examination Ser.: C-310). 1994. pap. 34.95 (*0-8373-0310-9*) Nat Learn.
Principal Workmen's Compensation Examiner. Jack Rudman. (Career Examination Ser.: C-1548). 1994. pap. 34.95 (*0-8373-1548-4*) Nat Learn.
Principal Works of George Bancroft. George Bancroft. 1989. reprint ed. lib. bdg. 65.00 (*0-685-27842-5*) Rprt Serv.
Principal Works of Simon Stevin Vol. 1: General Introduction - Mechanism. Ed. by E. J. Dijksterhuis. v, 617p. 1955. text 211.00 (*90-265-0070-X*) Swets.
Principal Works of Simon Stevin Vol. 3: Astronomy & Navigation. Ed. by A. Pannekoek & E. Croone. v, 632p. 1961. text 211.00 (*90-265-0073-4*) Swets.
Principal Works of Simon Stevin Vol. 4: Art of War. Ed. by W. H. Schukking. v, 525p. 1965. text 211.00 (*90-265-0074-2*) Swets.
Principal Works of Simon Stevin Vol. 5: Engineering-Music-Civic Life. R. J. Forbes et al. xi, 609p. 1966. text 211.00 (*90-265-0075-0*) Swets.
Principal Works of Simon Stevin Vols. 2A & B: Mathematics. Ed. by Dirk J. Struik. v, 455p. 1958. 211.00 (*90-265-0071-8*) Swets.
Principal Writings on Religion including Dialogues Concerning Natural Religion & The Natural History of Religion. David Hume & J. C. A. Gaskin. (Oxford World's Classics). 256p. 1999. pap. 8.95 (*0-19-283876-8*) OUP.
Principal X-Ray Technician. Jack Rudman. (Career Examination Ser.: C-979). 1994. pap. 29.95 (*0-8373-0979-4*) Nat Learn.
Principal, Youth & Adult Center. Jack Rudman. (Teachers License Examination Ser.: S-8). 1994. pap. 49.95 (*0-8373-8108-8*) Nat Learn.
Principal Zoning Inspector. Jack Rudman. (Career Examination Ser.: C-2854). 1994. pap. 34.95 (*0-8373-2854-3*) Nat Learn.
Principali Problematiche del Dialogus de Oratoribus. Domenico Bo. (Spudasmata Ser.: Bd. 51). (GER.). 462p. 1993. 75.00 (*3-487-09687-0*) G Olms Pubs.
Principalities & Powers see Principados y Potestades
Principalities & Powers in the New Testament. Heinrich Schlier. LC 79-8119. reprint ed. 32.50 (*0-404-18432-4*) AMS Pr.
Principality: A Novel. Dennis F. Holt. LC 99-207865. 288p. 1998. pap. 18.00 (*1-892031-25-6*) Cornelius Hse.
Principality of Monaco. Casa Bonechi. 128p. pap. text 14.95 (*88-7009-418-9*, Pub. by Bonechi) Eiron.
Principality of Sorrows. Keith Bunin. 68p. 1997. pap. 5.60 (*0-87129-767-1*, P82) Dramatic Pub.
Principalization of Plastic Surgery. D. Ralph Millard, Jr. 1986. 235.00 (*0-316-57153-9*, Little Brwn Med Div) Lppncott W & W.
Principally Speaking. Ronald F. Dameron. LC 97-91405. (Illus.). 168p. 1998. pap. 10.95 (*0-9662148-0-3*) Walnut Vista.
Principalmente Imanes - Mostly Magnets. Evelyn Hoover. (ENG & SPA.). (J). (gr. 2-8). 1994. 16.95 (*1-881431-36-3*, 1435) AIMS Educ Fnd.
Principal's Administrative Manual. rev. ed. Nochem Kaplan. Ed. by Yaakov Fruchter. 1991. 38.00 (*0-914131-97-4*) Torah Umesorah.
Principals & Agents: The Structure Of Business. Harvard Business School Press Staff. 250p. 1991. pap. 1516.00 (*0-07-103308-4*) McGraw.
Principals & Agents: The Structure of Business. John W. Pratt & Richard J. Zeckhauser. 250p. 1991. pap. 16.95 (*0-87584-256-9*) Harvard Busn.
***Principals & Practices in Pain Management.** Carol A. Warfield. 2000. 125.00 (*0-07-135209-0*) McGraw.
Principal's Book of Lists. Robert D. Ramsey. LC 96-28871. 402p. (C). 1996. pap. text 34.95 (*0-13-447749-9*) P-H.
Principals' Classroom Observation Handbook: Classroom Observation & Visitation Handbook. Donald R. Wilson. 48p. 1998. pap. text 12.95 (*0-939136-21-X*) School Admin.
Principal's Companion: A Workbook for Future School Leaders. 2nd ed. John D. Bowser & Ross Sherman. LC 96-14343. 174p. 1996. pap. text 26.50 (*0-7618-0339-4*); lib. bdg. 49.50 (*0-7618-0338-6*) U Pr of Amer.
Principal's Companion: Strategies & Hints to Make the Job Easier. Pam Robbins & Harvey B. Alvy. (Illus.). 304p. 1995. pap. 32.95 (*0-8039-6197-9*) Corwin Pr.

P

Principal's Companion: Strategies & Hints to Make the Job Easier. Pam Robbins & Harvey B. Alvy. 304p. 1995. 65.95 (*2-8106-6196-0*); pap. 29.95 (*2-8106-6197-9*) NEA.

Principal's Companion: Strategies & Hints to Make the Job Easier. Pamela Robbins & Harvey B. Alvy. Ed. by Susan Gingell. LC 95-7976. (Illus.). 304p. 1995. 69.95 (*0-8039-6196-0*) Corwin Pr.

Principal's Decision: A Teaching Monograph on Corporal Punishment. Ronald T. Hyman & Charles H. Rathbone. (Monograph Ser.: No. 48A). 34p. 1993. text 15.00 (*1-56534-079-5*) Ed Law Assn.

Principal's Edge. Jack McCall. LC 94-4121. (Illus.). 250p. 1994. 35.95 (*1-883001-08-0*) Eye On Educ.

Principals for Our Changing Schools: The Knowledge & Skill Base. Illus. by Beth M. Conny. 590p. (C). 1998. pap. text 39.95 (*1-56676-303-7*) Scarecrow.

Principal's Guide for Implementing the Regents Action Plan: A Practical Handbook for School Administrators. 2nd ed. John D. Thyen & Michael DeCristofaro. 450p. (C). 1988. ring bd. 85.00 (*0-9617117-1-X*) Educators Lib.

Principal's Guide for Implementing the Regents Action Plan in New York State. 3rd rev. ed. John D. Thyen & Michael DeCristofaro. LC 88-83678. 450p. 1991. ring bd. 95.00 (*0-9617117-3-6*) Educators Lib.

Principal's Guide to Attention Deficit Hyperactivity Disorder. Elaine K. McEwan. 240p. 1997. 65.95 (*0-8039-6531-1*); pap. 29.95 (*0-8039-6532-X*) Corwin Pr.

Principal's Guide to Creating a Building Climate for Inclusion. Teresa VanDover. LC 95-75069. 203p. 1995. ring bd. 49.95 (*0-914607-36-7*) Master Tchr.

Principal's Guide to High School Journalism. Benedict. 2.00 (*0-318-19221-7*) Quill & Scroll.

Principal's Guide to Improving Reading Instruction. Robert L. Hillerich. 300p. 1983. 39.95 (*0-205-07820-6*, H78207) Allyn.

Principal's Guide to Raising Reading Achievement. Elaine K. McEwan. LC 98-8874. 120p. 1998. 55.95 (*0-8039-6627-X*); pap. 24.95 (*0-8039-6628-8*) Corwin Pr.

Principal's Guide to the Educational Rights of Handicapped Students. T. Page Johnson. LC 86-149951. 68p. reprint ed. pap. 30.00 (*0-7837-0590-5*, 204093600019) Bks Demand.

Principal's Guide to Winning Grants. David G. Bauer. (Education Ser.). 144p. 1998. pap. 24.95 (*0-7879-4494-7*) Jossey-Bass.

Principal's Handbook: Newsletter Extravaganza: Guidance, Resources & Samples for Use in Production of School Newsletters. ACSA Elementary Education Committee. 166p. 1998. ring bd. 45.00 (*0-943397-46-4*, 167) Assn Calif Sch Admin.

Principal's Handbook: Proven Practical Strategies, Solutions & Samples for Use in the Day-to-Day Management of Your School. ACSA Elementary Education Committee. (Illus.). 450p. (J). (gr. k-8). 1996. ring bd. 95.00 (*0-943397-39-1*, 163) Assn Calif Sch Admin.

***Principals in Operations Management.** 3rd ed. Heizer & Render. LC 98-24981. 682p. 1998. pap. text 84.00 (*0-13-095808-5*) P-H.

Principals in Transition: Tips for Surviving Succession. Barbara L. Brock & Marilyn L. Grady. LC 95-7973. (RTS Ser.). 64p. 1995. pap. 14.95 (*0-8039-6238-X*, 7694) Corwin Pr.

***Principal's Kid, Vol. 2.** Joan Weir. 176p. (J). (gr. 2-6). 2000. pap. 5.95 (*1-896095-98-4*, Pub. by Polstar Bk) Orca Bk Pubs.

Principal's Legal Handbook. rev. ed. Ed. by William E. Camp et al. 320p. 1993. text 35.00 (*1-56534-056-6*) Ed Law Assn.

Principals' Lending Library - Math. 1990. pap. text 137.75 (*0-201-28661-0*) Addison-Wesley.

Principals' Lending Library - Reading. 1990. pap. text 114.75 (*0-201-28663-7*) Addison-Wesley.

Principals Lending Library ESL. 1990. 101.40 (*0-201-52808-8*) Addison-Wesley.

Principal's New Clothes. Stephanie Calmenson. (Illus.). (J). (ps-3). 1989. pap. 13.95 (*0-590-41822-X*) Scholastic Inc.

Principal's New Clothes. Stephanie Calmenson. LC 88-30314. (Illus.). 40p. (J). (ps-3). 1991. pap. 4.95 (*0-590-44778-5*, Blue Ribbon Bks) Scholastic Inc.

Principal's New Clothes. Stephanie Calmenson. 1991. 10.15 (*0-606-12490-X*, Pub. by Turtleback) Demco.

Principals of Business for Owner Operators: A Management & Study Text for Going into the Trucking Business. Lewis J. Grill. (Part of the Owner Operator Mgt Training Series). (Illus.). 70p. (C). 1995. pap. text 13.95 (*1-881912-10-8*) Atlantic Pac Res.

Principals of Dynamic Schools: Taking Charge of Change. Ellen B. Goldring & Sharon F. Rallis. LC 93-15409. 200p. 1993. 55.95 (*0-8039-6067-0*); pap. 24.95 (*0-8039-6068-9*) Corwin Pr.

***Principals of Dynamic Schools: Taking Charge of Change.** 2nd ed. Sharon F. Rallis & Ellen B. Goldring. LC 99-50782. (One-Off Ser.). 212p. 2000. pap. 24.95 (*0-7619-7610-8*); lib. bdg. 55.95 (*0-7619-7609-4*) Corwin Pr.

Principals of Electrodynamics. Melvin Schwartz. (Illus.). 352p. 1987. reprint ed. pap. text 10.95 (*0-486-65493-1*) Dover.

Principals of Financial & Managerial Accounting. 2nd ed. James D. Edwards et al. 576p. (C). 1993. text, student ed. 27.50 (*0-256-13001-9*, Irwn McGrw-H) McGrw-H Hghr Educ.

Principals of Financial & Manual Accounting: Chapters 14-28. 3rd ed. Philip E. Fess. (AB - Accounting Principles Ser.). (C). 1992. mass mkt. 36.50 (*0-538-83656-3*) S-W Pub.

Principals of Medical Biology Vol. 12: Reproductive Endocrinology & Biology. E. Edward Bittar & Neville Bittar. LC 98-18709. 1998. 128.50 (*1-55938-817-X*) Jai Pr.

***Principals of Neural Ensemble & Distributed Coding in the Central Nervous System.** Ed. by M. A. Nicolelis. (Progress in Brain Research Ser.). 2000. write for info. (*0-444-50110-X*, Excerpta Medica) Elsevier.

***Principals of Neutral Science.** 4th rev. ed. Eric R. Kandel et al. (Illus.). 1414p. 2000. pap. 85.00 (*0-8385-7701-6*, Apple Lange Med) McGraw.

Principals of Pharmacology: Basic Concepts & Clinical Applications. Ed. by Paul L. Munson et al. LC 94-41659. 1800p. (gr. 13). 1994. text 92.00 (*0-412-04701-2*) Chapman & Hall.

Principals of Photography in FPS. M. Eugene Tardy. (American Academy of Facial Plastic & Reconstructive Surgery Monograph: Vol. 11). (Illus.). 96p. 1992. pap. text 79.00 (*0-86577-148-0*) Thieme Med Pubs.

Principals of Physical Chemistry. Kuhn. LC 98-48542. 998p. (C). 1999. 120.00 (*0-471-95902-2*) Wiley.

Principals' Principles: A Pocket Assistant for Administrators. Sandra M. Evans & David H. Feser. (Illus.). 168p. 1997. 15.95 (*1-888793-06-6*) Tchrs Little Secrets.

Principal's Story: Two-Year Effort to Turn Around Edison Elementary School in San Francisco. Ken Romines. Ed. by Marjorie Beggs. LC 96-70005. 112p. 1997. pap. 12.95 (*0-936434-98-8*) SF Study Ctr.

Principalship. James M. Lipham et al. 335p. (C). 1985. text 32.95 (*0-582-28581-X*, 71607) Longman.

Principalship. Marsha Speck. LC 98-26326. 240p. 1998. pap. text 38.00 (*0-13-440686-9*) P-H.

Principalship. Ed. by Jeffrey S. Kaiser. 312p. (C). 1991. reprint ed. text 39.95 (*1-878016-01-6*) Stylex Pub.

Principalship. 5th ed. Thelbert L. Drake. LC 98-17494. 482p. 1998. 76.00 (*0-13-263260-8*) P-H.

Principalship: A Reflective Practice Perspective. 3rd ed. Thomas J. Sergiovanni. LC 94-26379. 384p. 1994. 80.33 (*0-205-15585-5*) Allyn.

***Principalship: A Reflective Practice Perspective.** 4th ed. Thomas J. Sergiovanni. 384p. 2000. 81.00 (*0-205-32185-2*) Allyn.

Principalship: A Social Leadership Approach. Ann W. Hart & Paul V. Bredeson. LC 95-16628. 336p. (C). 1995. 57.19 (*0-07-026913-0*) McGraw.

Principalship: Dimensions in Instructional Leadership. 2nd ed. Lawrence F. Rossow & Linda Sue Warner. LC 98-53521. 300p. 1999. pap. 30.00 (*0-89089-908-8*) Carolina Acad Pr.

Principalship: New Perspectives. Paul B. Jacobson et al. 512p. (C). 1973. 37.00 (*0-13-700856-2*) P-H.

Principate. Lewis Roman. 1973. 20.00 (*0-88866-574-1*) Edgar Kent.

Principe. Niccolo Machiavelli. 1999. 14.95 (*88-17-12037-5*) CE27.

Principe. Nicolas Maquiavelo. (Biblioteca De Cultura Basica Ser.). 621p. 1991. 11.50 (*0-8477-0727-X*) U of PR Pr.

***Principe by Nicole Machiavelli, Vol. 4.** Niccolo Machiavelli. Ed. by Maurizio Falyhera & Cristina Giocometti. (ITA.). 1999. 19.95 incl. audio (*1-58214-106-1*) Mltilingl Bks.

Principe (Commentado por Napolean Bonaparte) Nicolas Maquiavelo. Tr. by Eli L. Jungl. (Nueva Austral Ser.: Vol. 215). (SPA.). 1991. pap. text 24.95 (*84-239-7215-1*) Elliots Bks.

Principe de las Ranas. Vivi Escriva.Tr. of Prince of Frogs. (SPA., Illus.). 32p. (J). (gr. k-6). Date not set. 17.50 (*1-56492-218-9*) Laredo.

Principe de las Ranas: El Rabo de Gato. Clarita Kohen. (Laredo Children's Bilingual Library). (SPA., Illus.). 16p. (J). (gr. k-3). 1993. lib. bdg. 7.50 (*1-56492-102-6*) Laredo.

***Principe de Sus Suenos.** Robyn Donald. (Bianca Ser.).Tr. of Prince of Her Dreams. (SPA.). 2000. mass mkt. 3.50 (*0-373-33563-6*, 1-33563-7) Harlequin Bks.

Principe d'Existence. Serge Valdinoci. 178p. (C). 1989. lib. bdg. 142.00 (*0-7923-0125-0*, Pub. by Kluwer Academic) Kluwer Academic.

Principe du Phenix: Le Reve Comme Processus de Transformation Selon la Psychologie de C. G. Jung. Rene Caya & Henriette Montcalm. (FRE.). 1994. 22.95 (*2-920083-85-6*) Edns Roseau.

***Principe Encantado.** Jennifer Greene. Vol. 209.Tr. of Charming Prince. (SPA.). 2000. per. 3.50 (*0-373-35339-1*, 1-35339-0) Harlequin Bks.

Principe Feliz: Children's Classics. (Spanish Children's Classics Ser.: No. 800-7). (SPA.). (J). 1990. boxed set 3.50 (*0-7214-1400-1*, Ladybrd) Penguin Putnam.

Principe Que Ha de Venir. Robert Anderson.Tr. of Coming Prince. (SPA.). 288p. 1980. pap. 8.99 (*0-8254-1021-5*, Edit Portavoz) Kregel.

Principe Que Todo Lo Aprendio en los Libros. Jacinto Benavente. (Clasicos Ser.). (SPA.). 72p. 1996. pap. write for info. (*0-929441-39-7*) Pubns Puertorriquenas.

Principe Que Todo Lo Aprendio en los Libros. 6th ed. Jacinto Benavente. 80p. 1983. pap. 8.95 (*0-7859-5208-X*) Fr & Eur.

Principe y Mecenas: Alfonso V En Los "Dichos y Hechos" De A. Beccadelli. Nadia Patrone. (Currents in Comparative Romance Languages & Literatures Ser.: Vol. 17). (SPA.). XII, 106p. (C). 1995. text 36.95 (*0-8204-2150-2*) P Lang Pubng.

Principes de la Philosophie, Vol. 1. 3rd ed. Rene Descartes. (FRE.). 158p. 1989. 13.95 (*0-7859-1194-4*, 2711601870) Fr & Eur.

Principes de la Philosophie, Vol. 1. 5th ed. Julien Gracq. (FRE.). 256p. 1989. 19.95 (*0-7859-1197-9*, 2714302963) Fr & Eur.

Principes de Phonetique Francaise a l' Usage des Etudiants Anglo-Americains. Pierre Delattre. (FRE.). 1951. pap. 4.95 (*0-910408-01-7*) Coll Store.

Principes de Tout Gouvernement, 2 vols., Set. Claude F. D'Auxiron. (Economistes Francais du XVIIIe Siecle Ser.). 1990. reprint ed. pap. 68.00 (*3-601-00145-4*) Periodicals Srv.

Principes d'Economique Politique, 2 vols., Vol. 2. 2nd ed. A. Marshall. 1156p. 1971. pap. text 123.00 (*0-677-50535-3*) Gordon & Breach.

***Principes des Assurances de Personnes et des Rentes.** 2nd rev. ed. Harriett E. Jones & Doni L. Long. Ed. by Vivian F. Heeden. (FLMI Insurance Education Program Ser.). (FRE., Illus.). 500p. 2000. pap. text 88.00 (*1-57974-048-0*) Life Office.

Principes des Mathematiques. Louis Couturat. viii, 310p. 1979. reprint ed. 55.00 (*3-487-00847-5*) G Olms Pubs.

Principes des Techniques d'Analyse see Analytical Techniques for Foods & Agricultural Products

Principes du Droit Naturel. Jean-Jaques Burlamaqui. xxiv, 473p. 1984. reprint ed. 95.00 (*3-487-07400-1*) G Olms Pubs.

Principes et Observations Oeconomiques, 2 vols., Set. Francois Veron de Forbonnais. (Economistes Francais du XVIIIe Siecle Ser.). 1990. reprint ed. pap. 68.00 (*3-601-00147-0*) Periodicals Srv.

Principes Fondamentaux de la Vie Chretienne. James A. Berg. Ed. by Hautz Bernard.Tr. of Basics for Believers. (FRE.). 1987. pap. 1.95 (*0-89084-393-7*, 031948) Bob Jones Univ.

Principi di Ingegneria dei Giacimenti Petroliferi see Principles of Petroleum Reservoir Engineering

Principia, 2 vols. in 1, Set. Sir Isaac Newton. Tr. by Andrew Motte. LC 95-6733. (Great Minds Ser.). 465p. 1995. pap. 14.95 (*0-87975-980-1*) Prometheus Bks.

Principia: Mathematical Principles of Natural Philosophy. Sir Isaac Newton. Tr. by I. Bernard Cohen & Anne Whitman from LAT. LC 99-10278. 1025p. 1999. 75.00 (*0-520-08816-6*, Pub. by U CA Pr) Cal Prin Full Svc.

***Principia: Mathematical Principles of Natural Philosophy.** Sir Isaac Newton. Tr. by I. Bernard Cohen & Anne Whitman from LAT. LC 99-10278. 1025p. 1999. pap. 35.00 (*0-520-08817-4*, Pub. by U CA Pr) Cal Prin Full Svc.

Principia: Or the First Principles of Natural Things, Set, Vols. I & II. Emanuel Swedenborg. Tr. & Intro. by Augustus Clissold. (Illus.). 1988. reprint ed. 26.00 (*0-915221-20-9*) Swedenborg Sci Assn.

Principia: Or the First Principles of Natural Things, Vol. 1. Emanuel Swedenborg. Tr. & Intro. by Augustus Clissold. (Illus.). 380p. 1988. reprint ed. 14.00 (*0-915221-37-3*) Swedenborg Sci Assn.

Principia: Or the First Principles of Natural Things, Vol. 2. Emanuel Swedenborg. Tr. & Intro. by Augustus Clissold. (Illus.). 413p. 1988. reprint ed. 14.00 (*0-915221-38-1*) Swedenborg Sci Assn.

Principia Discordia. Intro. by Omar K. Ravenhurst. (Illus.). 120p. 1991. reprint ed. pap. 9.95 (*0-9626534-2-X*) IllumiNet Pr.

Principia Discordia: or How I Found Goddess & What I Did to Her When I Found Her. Macalypse The Younger. 1976. lib. bdg. 250.00 (*0-685-75085-X*) Revisionist Pr.

Principia Economica. George Bernard. (C). 1989. lib. bdg. 182.50 (*0-7923-0186-2*) Kluwer Academic.

Principia Ethica. G. E. Moore. LC 88-61329. (Great Books in Philosophy). 253p. (C). 1988. pap. 8.95 (*0-87975-498-2*) Prometheus Bks.

Principia Ethica: With the Preface to the Second Edition & Other Papers. rev. ed. G. E. Moore. Ed. by Thomas Baldwin. LC 93-6493. 351p. (C). 1993. text 59.95 (*0-521-44378-4*); pap. text 21.95 (*0-521-44848-4*) Cambridge U Pr.

Principia Ideologica: A Treatise on Combatting Human Malignance. Stephen Edward Seadler. 550p. 1999. pap. 40.00 (*0-9669865-0-4*) ID Ctr.

Principia Mathematica, 3 vols., Set. Alfred North Whitehead & Bertrand Russell. 1994p. 1927. text 595.00 (*0-521-06791-X*) Cambridge U Pr.

Principia Mathematica to *56. Alfred North Whitehead & Bertrand Russell. LC 97-223757. (Mathematical Library). 456p. 1997. pap. text 49.95 (*0-521-62606-4*) Cambridge U Pr.

Principia or Basis of Social Science: A Survey from the Moral & Theological, Yet Liberal & Progressive Standpoint. Robert J. Wright. LC 73-14190. (Perspectives in Social Inquiry Ser.). 528p. 1974. reprint ed. 36.95 (*0-405-05533-1*) Ayer.

Principia Politica. Valadez. (SPA.). 320p. 2000. 60.00 (*0-8133-9114-8*) Westview.

***Principia Practica: The Logic of Practice.** Arnold A. Johanson. LC 99-49178. 360p. 1999. 57.50 (*0-7618-1530-9*) U Pr of Amer.

Principio de Peter. Laurence J. Peter. 1998. pap. 6.50 (*84-01-45124-8*) Lectorum Pubns.

Principio del Fin. John Hagee.Tr. of Beginning of the End. 1989. pap. 10.99 (*0-88113-436-8*) Caribe Betania.

***Principio Desastroso.** 2000. per. 3.50 (*0-373-35332-4*) S&S Trade.

Principios Basicos para la Ensenanza de la Biologia. rev. ed. (Serie de Biologia: No. 4). (SPA.). 1976. pap. 1.25 (*0-8270-1385-X*) OAS.

Principios Basicos para la Rehabilitacion de la Fauna Silvestre - IAB. Jan White. Ed. by Louise Shimmel. Tr. by Maria Del Pilar de Restrepo from ENG. (SPA., Illus.). 350p. Date not set. pap. 30.00 (*1-884196-08-X*) IWRC.

Principios de Construccion de Pavimentos de Mezcla Asfaltica de Caliente see Principles of Construction of Hot-Mix Asphalt Pavements: Spanish Edition

Principios De Contabilidad Tomo I V50. Fess. (C). 1997. 22.66 (*0-673-19252-0*) Addison-Wesley.

Principios de Economia. James Killoran et al. (SPA., Illus.). 202p. (YA). (gr. 11-12). 1995. pap. text 13.95 (*1-882422-18-X*) Jarrett Pub.

Principios de Interpretacion Biblica. Otis Pinkston. (TEE Ser.). (SPA.). 126p. 1989. 5.95 (*1-879892-22-7*) Editorial Bautista.

Principios de Interpretacion Biblica. rev. ed. Louis Berkhof. (SPA.). 175p. 1990. pap. 8.50 (*0-939125-04-8*) CRC Wrld Lit.

Principios de la Ensenanza Cristiana. W. V. Gritter. (SPA.). 1990. pap. 7.95 (*1-55955-097-X*, 6761-1510C) Libros Desafio.

Principios de Manejo de Materials: Principles of Materials Management. J. R. Arnold & Lloyd Clive. (SPA.). (Orig.). 1996. pap., teacher ed. 400.00 (*0-614-24998-8*); pap., student ed. 30.00 (*0-614-24999-6*) Am Prod & Inventory.

Principios de Telecomunicaciones. 2nd ed. J. J. O'Reilly. (SPA.). 192p. (C). 1994. pap. text 12.66 (*0-201-62563-6*) Addison-Wesley.

Principios del Diseno Escenografico. Rafael Cruz Emeric. (SPA.). 262p. 1979. pap. 8.00 (*0-8477-3190-1*) U of PR Pr.

***Principios del Seguro de Vida, Salud y Rentas Vitalicias.** Harriet E. Jones & Dani L. Long. Ed. by Ines Vallenilla. Tr. by Traductoras Asociadas Traductoras from ENG. (PFSL Insurance Education Program Ser.: Vol. 1). (SPA.). 556p. (C). 1998. pap. text. write for info. (*1-57974-016-2*, Pub. by Life Office) PBD Inc.

Principios Fundamentales de Evaluacion para Educadores. 4th ed. Harris F. Bunker. 156p. 1976. 4.00 (*0-8477-2730-0*); pap. 3.00 (*0-8477-2702-5*) U of PR Pr.

Principios Generales de Microbiologia: Serie de Biologia No. 7. 2nd ed. OAS General Secretariat, Department of Scientific Research Staff. (Serie de Biologia: No. 7). 143p. (C). 1980. text 3.50 (*0-8270-1097-4*) OAS.

Principios y Fines del "Quijote" Eduardo Urbina. 1990. 45.00 (*0-916379-79-5*) Scripta.

Principios y Metodos Estadisticos para Comercio y Economia, Tomo I. Ramon J. Garcia. (SPA.). (C). 1997. pap. 23.33 (*0-673-19279-2*) HEPC Inc.

Principios y Practicas de la Educacion Cristiana. Robert W. Pazmino.Tr. of Principles & Practices of Christian Education. (SPA.). 180p. 1995. 11.99 (*0-89922-436-9*, C96-4369) Caribe Betania.

Principito. Antoine de Saint-Exupery. LC 73-5511.Tr. of Le Petit Prince. (SPA., Illus.). 128p. 1973. reprint ed. pap. 6.00 (*0-15-628450-2*, Harvest Bks) Harcourt.

Principito - The Little Prince. Antoine de Saint-Exupery. (ENG & SPA., Illus.). 85p. (J). (gr. 4 up). 1985. pap. 6.95 (*0-8442-7622-7*, Natl Textbk Co) NTC Contemp Pub Co.

Principius de la Economia del Movimiento. (SPA.). 1978. 5.00 (*0-940876-10-8*) City Hope.

Principle & Interest: Thomas Jefferson & the Problem of Debt. Herbert E. Sloan. LC 94-16400. 392p. 1995. text 50.00 (*0-19-505878-X*) OUP.

Principle & Practicality: Essays in Neo-Confucianism & Practical Learning. Ed. by William T. Debary & Irene Bloom. LC 78-11530. (Neo-Confucian Series & Studies in Oriental Culture). 1979. pap. text 31.50 (*0-231-04613-8*) Col U Pr.

Principle & Practice in Applied Linguistics: Studies in Honour of H. G. Widdowson. Guy Cook. (Illus.). 442p. 1995. pap. text 23.95 (*0-19-442148-1*) OUP.

Principle & Practice of Mahayana Buddhism: An Interpretation of Professor Suzuki's Translation of Ashvaghosa's Awakening of Faith. Asvaghosa. Ed. by Dwight Goodard. LC 78-72373. reprint ed. 27.50 (*0-404-17223-7*) AMS Pr.

Principle & Practice of Nurse Anesthesia. 2nd ed. Wynne R. Waugaman. (Illus.). 912p. (C). 1992. pap. text 105.00 (*0-8385-7962-0*, A7962-2) Appleton & Lange.

Principle Aspects of Clinical Nutrition. Ed. by J. C. Somogyi. (Bibliotheca Nutritio et Dieta Ser.: No. 35). (Illus.). viii, 132p. 1985. 98.50 (*3-8055-3950-9*) S Karger.

Principle B VP Ellipsis & Interpretation in Child Grammar. Rosalind Thornton & Kenneth Wexler. LC 98-51296. (Current Studies in Linguistics). 1999. write for info. (*0-262-70069-7*) MIT Pr.

Principle B, VP Ellipsis & Interpretation in Child Grammar. Rosalind Thornton & Kenneth Wexler. LC 98-51296. (Current Studies in Linguistics: No. 31). (Illus.). 261p. 1999. 35.00 (*0-262-20119-4*) MIT Pr.

Principle-Based Parsing: Computation & Psycholinguistics. Ed. by Robert C. Berwick. 416p. (C). 1991. lib. bdg. 133.00 (*0-7923-1173-6*) Kluwer Academic.

Principle-Based Parsing: Computation & Psycholinguistics. Robert C. Berwick. (Studies in Linguistics & Philosophy). 418p. (C). 1992. pap. text 61.50 (*0-7923-1637-1*) Kluwer Academic.

***Principle by Nicole Machiavelli, Vol. 4.** Niccolo Machiavelli. Ed. by Maurizio Falyhera & Cristina Giocometti. (ITA.). 1999. 29.95 incl. audio compact disk (*1-58214-107-X*) Mltilingl Bks.

Principle-Centered Church: Resources for Training Church Leaders. Stan Toler. 96p. 1999. 124.99 (*0-8341-1742-8*) Nazarene.

Principle-Centered Leadership. Stephen R. Covey. 336p. 1991. 24.50 (*0-671-74910-2*) Summit Bks.

Principle-Centered Leadership: Strategies for Personal & Professional Effectiveness. Stephen R. Covey. 336p. 1992. per. 14.00 (*0-671-79280-6*) S&S Trade.

Principle Hotel Catering Law. Pannett. (C). 1984. pap. write for info. (*0-03-910481-8*) Harcourt Coll Pubs.

Principle Microbiology. Atlas Staff. 1995. (*0-8151-0315-8*) Mosby Inc.

Principle Money Banking. 8th ed. Paul D. Warner. 336p. (C). 1997. pap., student ed. 24.00 (*0-465-06369-1*) Addson-Wesley Educ.

P

An Asterisk (*) at the beginning of an entry indicates that the title is appearing for the first time.

Principle of Authority in Relation to Certainty, Sanctity & Society: An Essay in the Philosophy of Experimental Religion. Peter T. Forsyth. 485p. 1996. pap. 30.00 (*1-57910-019-8*) Wipf & Stock.

Principle of Autologous, Allogenic & Cyropreserved Venous Transplantation. Ed. by Kevin G. Brockbank. LC 95-19008. (Medical Intelligence Unit Ser.). 110p. 1995. text 79.00 (*1-57059-221-7*) Landes Bioscience.

***Principle of Biology.** 5th ed. (C). 1998. 20.00 (*0-8087-1762-6*) Pearson Custom.

Principle of Biology. 9th ed. (C). 1997. student ed. write for info. (*0-8087-9942-8*) Pearson Custom.

Principle of Biology 1. (C). 1996. write for info. (*0-8087-2127-5*) Pearson Custom.

Principle of Creation. Ed. by Chung H. Kwak. (Home Study Course). 60p. (C). 1980. pap. 4.00 (*0-685-42757-9*) HSA Pubns.

Principle of Dynamics. 2nd ed. Wendy M. Greenfield. 576p. 1987. 105.00 (*0-13-709981-9*) P-H.

Principle of Ecology. (C). 1995. write for info. (*0-8087-2241-7*) Pearson Custom.

***Principle of Equality in European Taxation.** 2nd ed. Gerard T. Meussen. LC 99-16460. (Eucotax Series on European Taxation). 1999. 135.00 (*90-411-9693-5*) Kluwer Law Intl.

Principle of Fairness & Political Obligation. George Klosko. Ed. by James P. Sterba. (Studies in Social & Political Philosophy). 256p. (C). 1991. 62.50 (*0-8476-7718-4*) Rowman.

Principle of Federation. Pierre-Joseph Proudhon. Tr. & Intro. by Richard Vernon. LC 79-4192. 136p. reprint ed. pap. 42.20 (*0-8357-3504-4*, 203403500089) Bks Demand.

Principle of General Relativity & Einstein's Theory of Gravitation. Leigh Page. (Connecticut Academy of Arts & Sciences Ser., Trans.: Vol. 23). 1920. pap. 49.50 (*0-685-22830-4*) Elliots Bks.

Principle of Hope, 3 vols. Ernst Bloch. Tr. by Neville Plaice. 1995. pap. text 65.00 (*0-262-52204-7*) MIT Pr.

Principle of Hope, Vol. 1. Ernst Bloch. Tr. by Neville Plaice et al. Vol. 1. 488p. 1995. pap. text 24.00 (*0-262-52199-7*) MIT Pr.

Principle of Integrated Solid Waste Management. H. Lanier Hickman. Ed. by William C. Anderson. (Illus.). 640p. 1999. text 99.95 (*1-883767-26-1*) Am Acad Environ.

Principle of Interchange & Other Stories. P. V. LeForge. LC 89-92412. 179p. (Orig.). 1990. pap. 7.95 (*0-9624878-0-5*) Paperback Rack Bks.

Principle of Legality in International Human Rights Institutions: Selected Legal Opinions, Vol. RAWA 3. Ed. by B. G. Ramcharan. LC 97-12116. (Raoul Wallenberg Institute Human Rights Guides Ser.). 1997. 225.00 (*90-411-0299-X*) Kluwer Law Intl.

Principle of Macroeconomics. Gerry F. Welch. (C). 1998. pap. text, student ed. 11.00 (*0-03-008864-X*) Harcourt.

Principle of Mercy: Taking the Crucified People from Their Cross. Jon Sobrino. Ed. by Robert R. Barr et al. LC 94-18075. 210p. 1994. reprint ed. pap. 18.00 (*0-88344-986-2*) Orbis Bks.

Principle of Non-Resistance As Held by the Mennonite Church. John Horsch. LC 74-147672. (Library of War & Peace; Relig. & Ethical Positions on War). 1974. lib. bdg. 46.00 (*0-8240-0430-2*) Garland.

Principle of Peace. Evelyn C. Coning & William H. Coning. Orig. Title: The Principle of Peace & Its Abuse. 128p. 1999. pap. 14.95 (*0-9670986-0-2*) Principle of Peace.

Principle of Peace & Its Abuse see Principle of Peace

Principle of Practice for the Acute Care Nurse Practioner. Logan. LC 98-26249. 1999. pap. text 115.00 (*0-8385-8125-0*, Medical Exam) Appleton & Lange.

Principle of Proportionality in European Law: A Comparative Study. rev. ed. Nicholas Emiliou. 1995. pap. 107.00 (*90-411-0866-1*) Kluwer Law Intl.

Principle of Proportionality in the Laws of Europe. Ed. by Evelyn Ellis. LC 99-488451. 224p. 1999. 45.00 (*1-84113-007-9*, Pub. by Hart Pub) Intl Spec Bk.

Principle of Protestantism. Philip Schaff. (Notable American Authors Ser.). 1999. reprint ed. lib. bdg. 125.00 (*0-7812-8861-4*) Rprt Serv.

Principle of Protestantism: Chambersburg, PA, 1845. Philip Schaff. Ed. by Bruce Kuklick. (American Religious Thought of the 18th & 19th Centuries Ser.). 343p. 1987. lib. bdg. 50.00 (*0-685-17911-7*) Garland.

Principle of Protestantism: What Is Church History? Philip Schaff. LC 87-11896. (American Religious Thought of the 18th & 19th Centuries Ser.). 215p. 1987. write for info. (*0-8240-6971-4*) Garland.

Principle of Reason. Martin Heidegger. Tr. by Reginald Lilly. LC 90-25454. (Studies in Continental Thought). 178p. 1992. 35.00 (*0-253-32724-5*) Ind U Pr.

Principle of Reason. Martin Heidegger. 1996. pap. text 13.95 (*0-253-21066-6*) Ind U Pr.

Principle of Relativity. Albert Einstein et al. 216p. (C). 1952. pap. 7.95 (*0-486-60081-5*) Dover.

Principle of Relativity in the Light of the Philosophy of Science. Paul Carus. LC 75-3109. reprint ed. 32.50 (*0-404-59105-1*) AMS Pr.

Principle of Reserve in the Writings of John Henry, Cardinal Newman. Robin Selby. (Oxford Theological Monographs). (C). 1975. 29.95 (*0-19-826711-8*) OUP.

Principle of Self-Determination in International Law. W. B. Ofuatey-Kodjoe. 250p. 1977. text 26.50 (*0-8290-1569-8*) Irvington.

Principle of Sovereignty over Natural Resources. G. Elian. 250p. 1979. lib. bdg. 98.50 (*90-286-0049-3*) Kluwer Academic.

Principle of Spiritual Economy. Rudolf Steiner. Tr. by Peter Mollenhauer.Tr. of Das/Prinzip der Spirituellen Okonomie im Zusammenhang mit Wiederverkorperungsfragen. 220p. 1986. 20.00 (*0-88010-163-6*) Anthroposophic.

Principle of Spiritual Economy: In Connection with Questions of Reincarnation. Rudolf Steiner. Tr. by Peter Mollenhauer.Tr. of Das/Prinzip der Spirituellen Okonomie im Zusammenhang mit Wiederverkorperungsfragen. 220p. 1986. pap. 12.95 (*0-88010-162-8*) Anthroposophic.

Principle of Stellar Structure, 2 vols., Vol. 2. Ed. by J. P. Cox. LC 68-26755. (Illus.). L, 1328p. (C). 1968. text 1063.00 (*0-677-01950-5*) Gordon & Breach.

Principle of Sufficient Reason in Some Scholastic Systems 1750-1900. John E. Gurr. LC 59-8093. 206p. 1959. reprint ed. pap. 63.90 (*0-608-04197-1*, 206493200011) Bks Demand.

Principle of the Nazarite. 18p. 1979. pap. 0.75 (*1-57593-987-8*, 19-029-001) Living Stream Ministry.

Principle of the Personality of Law in the Germanic Kingdoms of Western Europe from the Fifth to the Eleventh Century. Simeon L. Guterman. (American University Studies: History: Ser. IX, Vol. 44). X, 355p. 1990. 55.95 (*0-8204-0731-3*) P Lang Pubng.

Principle or Pragmatism: Interest Groups, PACs, & Campaign Contributions in 1984. Michael W. Rubinoff. write for info. (*0-318-61041-8*) Free Congr Res.

Principle, Praxis, & the Politics of Educational Reform in Meiji Japan. Mark E. Lincicome. LC 94-35279. (Illus.). 304p. (C). 1995. text 45.00 (*0-8248-1620-X*) UH Pr.

Principle Remote Sensing. P. J. Currin. (Illus.). 296p. (C). 1996. pap. 78.00 (*0-582-30097-5*) Longman.

Principle Study Guide to Fundamental Accounts. 14th ed. Larson. 1996. 84.00 (*0-256-23714-X*) McGraw.

Principle Works of Elizabeth Whitfield Bellamy, Set. Elizabeth W. Bellamy. 1989. reprint ed. lib. bdg. 63.00 (*0-685-27268-0*) Rprt Serv.

Principle Works of Herbert Baxter Adams, Set. Herbert B. Adams. 1989. reprint ed. lib. bdg. 63.00 (*0-685-27424-1*) Rprt Serv.

Principled Bargaining. James G. Matkin. LC 86-156970. 11 p. 1986. write for info. (*0-88886-128-1*) Que8ens U Indus Relat.

Principled Diplomacy: Security & Rights in U. S. Foreign Policy, 313. Cathal J. Nolan. LC 92-30006. (Contributions in Political Science Ser.: No. 313). 312p. 1993. 65.00 (*0-313-28006-1*, NPD/, Greenwood Pr) Greenwood.

Principled Dressage. 256p. 1999. 29.95 (*0-87605-317-7*) Howell Bks.

***Principled Headship: A Headteacher's Guide to the Galaxy.** Terry Mahony. 1999. pap. 14.95 (*1-899836-40-3*, Pub. by Crown Hse) LPC Group.

Principled Leadership & Business Diplomacy: Values-Based Strategies for Management Development. Manuel London. LC 99-27821. 192p. 1999. 59.95 (*1-56720-347-7*, Quorum Bks) Greenwood.

Principled Policing: Protecting the Public with Integrity. John Alderson. 185p. 1998. pap. 39.00 (*1-872870-71-6*, Pub. by Waterside Pr) Gaunt.

Principled Positions: Postmodernism & the Rediscovery of Value. Ed. by Judith Squires. 240p. (C). 1993. pap. 19.50 (*0-85315-780-4*, Pub. by Lawrence & Wishart) NYU Pr.

Principled Practice: A Comprehensive Guide to the Non-Clinical Aspects of Dentistry. Cheryl A. Matschek. LC 94-47411. 1995. write for info. (*0-943367-05-0*) Princess Pub.

***Principled World Politics: The Challenge of Normative International Relations at the Millennium.** Richard A. Falk. Ed. by Paul K. Wapner & Lester E. Ruiz. LC 99-53985. 352p. 2000. pap. 26.95 (*0-7425-0065-9*) Rowman.

***Principled World Politics: The Challenge of Normative International Relations at the Millennium.** Ed. by Paul Wapner & Lester Edwin J. Ruiz. 352p. 2000. 75.00 (*0-7425-0064-0*) Rowman.

Principles, 1. 5th ed. Weygandt. 354p. (C). 1998. pap. text, teacher ed. 50.00 (*0-471-19455-7*) Wiley.

Principles, Vol. 4, Chapters 1-14. Solomon. Date not set. pap. text, teacher ed. write for info. (*0-314-01874-3*) West Pub.

Principles: Practice of Mechanical Ventilation. John J. Marini & Sue A. Ravenscraft. (Illus.). 544p. 1994. write for info. (*0-683-05556-9*) Lppncott W & W.

Principles: Solutions, 1. 5th ed. Weygandt. 752p. (C). 1998. pap. text 75.00 (*0-471-19451-4*) Wiley.

***Principles: The Gay Man's Guide Getting & Keeping.** Orland Outland. 2000. pap. text 12.00 (*1-57566-626-X*, Knsington) Kensgtn Pub Corp.

Principles: The Gay Man's Guide to Getting & Keeping Mr. Right. Orland Outland. 112p. 1998. pap. 6.99 (*1-57566-281-7*) Kensgtn Pub Corp.

Principles Vol. II: Working Papers, 2. 5th ed. Weygandt. 576p. 1998. pap. 36.95 (*0-471-19442-5*) Wiley.

Principles Ai Using Common Lisp. Harrison. 2001. text. write for info. (*0-13-720491-4*) P-H.

Principles Aimed at Promoting the Distribution & Broadcasting of Audiovisual Works Originating in Countries or Regions with a Low Audiovisual Output or a Limited Geographic or Linguistic Coverage on the European Television Markets (Recommendation & Explan, No. R(93)5. 1995. 12.00 (*92-871-2721-2*, Pub. by Council of Europe) Manhattan Pub Co.

Principles American Journalism. Don Ranly. 336p. (C). 1996. pap. text, per. 48.95 (*0-7872-0748-9*) Kendall-Hunt.

Principles & a Philosophy for Vocational Education. Melvin D. Miller. 250p. 1985. 17.00 (*0-318-17790-0*, SN48) Ctr Educ Trng Employ.

Principles & Algorithms of Relational Database Systems. Georges Gardarin. (C). 1989. text. write for info. (*0-201-50370-0*) Addison-Wesley.

Principles & Analysis of AlGaAs/GaAs Heterojuntion Bipolar Transistors. Juin J. Liou. LC 95-53772. 227p. 1996. 85.00 (*0-89006-587-X*) Artech Hse.

Principles & Application of Collective Dose in Radiation Protection. Intro. by Charles B. Meinhold. LC 95-26030. (NCRP Reports: No. 121). 106p. (Orig.). 1995. pap. 25.00 (*0-929600-46-0*) NCRP Pubns.

Principles & Applications in Assessment Counseling. Susan C. Whiston. LC 99-16349. (Counseling Ser.). 412p. 1999. mass mkt. 67.95 (*0-534-34849-1*) Brooks-Cole.

Principles & Applications of Aquatic Chemistry. Francios M. Morel & Janet G. Hering. LC 92-18608. 608p. 1993. 79.95 (*0-471-54896-0*) Wiley.

Principles & Applications of Biomedical Magnetic Resonance Imaging. Ed. by Felix W. Wehrli et al. LC 87-29566. 601p. 1988. 115.00 (*0-89573-349-8*, Wiley-VCH) Wiley.

Principles & Applications of Cardiorespiratory Equipment. Ed. by David Eubanks & Roger C. Bone. LC 93-30441. (Illus.). 394p. (C). (gr. 13). 1994. text 56.00 (*0-8016-7448-4*, 01534) Mosby Inc.

Principles & Applications of Chemical Defects. R. J. Tilley. (Read Ser.). 320p. (C). 1998. pap. 57.50 (*0-7487-3978-5*) St Mut.

Principles & Applications of Chemistry. 6th ed. Dale Alexander. 304p. (C). 1994. pap. text, spiral bd. 28.95 (*0-7872-0038-7*) Kendall-Hunt.

Principles & Applications of Density Functional Theory. Ed. by L. J. Sham & L. Schluter. 500p. (C). 1997. text 99.00 (*9971-5-0675-0*); pap. text 48.00 (*9971-5-0699-8*) World Scientific Pub.

Principles & Applications of Digital Devices. Richard A. Gilbert & J. A. Llewellyn. LC TK7868.D5G54. (Instructional Resource Package Ser.). (Illus.). 187p. reprint ed. pap., student ed. 58.00 (*0-7837-8780-4*, 204952500012) Bks Demand.

Principles & Applications of Digital Devices: Instructor's Guide. Richard A. Gilbert & J. A. Llewellyn. LC TK7868.D5G54. (Instructional Resource Package Ser.). 78p. reprint ed. pap. 30.00 (*0-7837-5137-0*, 204486500004) Bks Demand.

Principles & Applications of Direct Digital Controls. Ivan Stepnich. LC 88-30251. 1989. 11.95 (*0-912524-47-2*) Busn News.

Principles & Applications of Economic Geography: Economy, Policy, Environment. Dean M. Hanink. LC 96-34962. 512p. 1996. text 90.95 (*0-471-10933-9*) Wiley.

Principles & Applications of Electrical Engineering. 2nd ed. Giorgio Rizzoni. LC 95-18650. 944p. (C). 1995. text 76.50 (*0-256-17770-8*, Irwn Prfssnl) McGraw-Hill Prof.

Principles & Applications of Electrical Engineering. 2nd ed. Bahman Saminy. 296p. (C). 1996. text, student ed. 10.00 (*0-256-22498-6*, Irwn McGrw-H) McGrw-H Hghr Educ.

***Principles & Applications of Electrical Engineering.** 3rd ed. Giorgio Rizzoni. LC 99-25420. 976p. 2000. 119.27 incl. audio compact disk (*0-256-26116-4*, Irwn McGrw-H) McGrw-H Hghr Educ.

Principles & Applications of Electrochemistry. D. R. Crow. (Illus.). 260p. 1988. pap. text 27.95 (*0-412-30270-5*) Chapman & Hall.

Principles & Applications of Geochemistry: A Comprehensive Textbook for Geology Students. 2nd ed. Gunter Faure. LC 97-44563. 625p. 1997. 96.00 (*0-02-336450-5*) P-H.

Principles & Applications of GSM. Vijay K. Garg. LC 98-36519. 512p. 1998. 69.99 (*0-13-949124-4*) P-H.

Principles & Applications of Imaging Radar: Manual of Remote Sensing, Vol.2. 3rd ed. Ed. by Floyd M. Henderson & Anthony J. Lewis. LC 98-7865. 896p. 1998. 198.00 (*0-471-29406-3*) Wiley.

Principles & Applications of Imaging Radar Manual of Remote Sensing Series. 3rd ed. F. M. Henderson & A. J. Lewis. 800p. 1996. 390.00 (*1-57083-038-X*, Pub. by R-I-C-S Bks) St Mut.

Principles & Applications of Information Science for Library Professionals. Ed. by John N. Olsgaard. LC 88-36876. 152p. reprint ed. pap. 47.20 (*0-7837-5922-3*, 204572100007) Bks Demand.

Principles & Applications of Inorganic, Organic, & Biological Chemistry. 2nd ed. Robert L. Caret et al. LC 96-83936. 736p. (C). 1996. text 83.68 (*0-697-25003-2*, WCB McGr Hill) McGrw-H Hghr Educ.

Principles & Applications of Inorganic Organizations. Caret. 1992. pap. 11.25 (*0-697-17024-1*) McGraw.

Principles & Applications of Intraocular Gas. Marc M. Whitacre. LC 97-21509. (Illus.). 400p. 1997. text 89.95 (*0-7506-9713-X*) Buttrwrth-Heinemann.

Principles & Applications of Liquid Penetrant Testing: A Classroom Training Text. Bernie Boisvert. (Illus.). 156p. (C). 1994. pap. 53.50 (*0-931403-49-9*, 2004) Am Soc Nondestructive.

Principles & Applications of Millimeter-Wave Radar. Nicholas C. Currie & Charles E. Brown. 874p. 1987. text. write for info. (*0-89006-202-1*) Artech Hse.

Principles & Applications of Nonlinear Optical Materials. Ed. by R. W. Munn & C. N. Ironside. 1993. 101.00 (*0-8493-7109-0*, QC446) CRC Pr.

Principles & Applications of Nonlinear Optical Materials. Ed. by Routledge Chapman Hall, Inc Staff. text 210.50 (*0-7514-0085-8*) B Acad & Prof.

Principles & Applications of Optical Communications. Max M. Liu. (C). 1993. text 44.95 (*0-256-16541-6*, Irwn McGrw-H) McGrw-H Hghr Educ.

Principles & Applications of Optical Communications. Max Ming-Kang Liu. LC 95-25240. 1004p. (C). 1996. text 71.50 (*0-256-16415-0*, TK5103, Irwn McGrw-H) McGrw-H Hghr Educ.

Principles & Applications of Organic & Biological Chemistry. Robert L. Caret et al. 576p. (C). 1993. text, student ed. 23.12 (*0-697-14871-8*, WCB McGr Hill) McGrw-H Hghr Educ.

Principles & Applications of Organic & Biological Chemistry. Robert L. Caret et al. (C). 1995. text, student ed. write for info. (*0-697-29619-9*, WCB McGr Hill) McGrw-H Hghr Educ.

Principles & Applications of Organic & Biological Chemistry. 2nd ed. Robert L. Caret & Joseph J. Topping. 528p. (C). 1997. per. write for info. (*0-07-114294-0*, WCB McGr Hill) McGrw-H Hghr Educ.

Principles & Applications of Organic & Biological Chemistry. 2nd ed. Robert L. Caret et al. LC 96-83906. 560p. (C). 1996. text 46.50 (*0-697-25002-4*, WCB McGr Hill) McGrw-H Hghr Educ.

Principles & Applications of Organic & Biological Chemistry: (With Solutions Manual) 2nd ed. Robert L. Caret et al. 240p. (C). 1996. text, student ed. 24.37 (*0-697-37661-3*, WCB McGr Hill) McGrw-H Hghr Educ.

Principles & Applications of Organotransition Metal Chemistry. 2nd ed. James P. Collman et al. (Illus.). 989p. (C). 1987. text 65.00 (*0-935702-51-2*) Univ Sci Bks.

Principles & Applications of Permanent GPS Arrays. C. D. De Jong. (Illus.). 116p. 1997. pap. 39.50 (*90-407-1492-4*, Pub. by Delft U Pr) Coronet Bks.

Principles & Applications of Polarization Division Interferometry. Ed. by Prasad L. Polavarapu. LC 97-17447. 214p. 1997. 135.00 (*0-471-97420-X*) Wiley.

Principles & Applications of Polarography & Other Electroanalytical Processes. George W. Milner. LC 57-3248. 757p. reprint ed. pap. 200.00 (*0-608-10815-4*, 200494700048) Bks Demand.

Principles & Applications of Quinoproteins. Victor Davidson. LC 92-26045. (Illus.). 472p. 1992. text 199.00 (*0-8247-8764-1*) Dekker.

Principles & Applications of Resonance Ionisation Spectroscopy. G. S. Hurst & M. G. Payne. (Illus.). 440p. 1988. 200.00 (*0-85274-460-9*) IOP Pub.

Principles & Applications of Soil Geography. Ed. by Edwin M. Bridges & D. A. Davidson. LC 80-41509. (Illus.). 309p. reprint ed. pap. 95.80 (*0-8357-2983-4*, 203924600011) Bks Demand.

Principles & Applications of Soil Microbiology: Principles & Applications. David Sylvia et al. LC 97-12659. 550p. 1997. 110.00 (*0-13-459991-8*) P-H.

Principles & Applications of Stereochemistry. M. North. 192p. 1998. pap. text 42.50 (*0-7487-3994-7*) St Mut.

Principles & Applications of Superconducting Quantum Interference Devices. Antonio Barone. 500p. 1992. text 109.00 (*981-02-0911-8*) World Scientific Pub.

Principles & Applications of Tribology. Bharat Bhushan. LC 98-41591. 1020p. 1999. 150.00 (*0-471-59407-5*) Wiley.

Principles & Applications of Tribology. D. F. Moore. (C). 1975. 181.00 (*0-08-017902-9*, Pub. by Pergamon Repr) Franklin.

Principles & Applications of Visualization in Science & Engineering. Adam Drobot. (C). 1996. text. write for info. (*0-201-56740-7*) Addison-Wesley.

Principles & Art of Cure by Homeopathy. Roberts. 1996. 25.95 (*1-869975-19-7*, Pub. by C W Daniel) Natl Bk Netwk.

Principles & Art of Cure by Homoeopathy. 1942. 14.95 (*0-85032-049-6*) Formur Intl.

Principles & Art of Cure by Homoeopathy. Herbert A. Roberts. 286p. (C). 1942. pap. 38.95 (*0-8464-1042-7*) Beekman Pubs.

Principles & Clinical Applications of MRI Technology. Luann Culbreth & Carolyn Kaut. Ed. by Andrew Allen & Lisa Biello. LC 97-134. (Illus.). 480p. 1998. text 65.00 (*0-7216-6632-9*, W B Saunders Co) Harcrt Hlth Sci Grp.

Principles & Concepts for Active Solar Systems. Ed. by Solar Energy Research Institute Staff. (Science Information Research Center Ser.). 295p. 1988. 78.95 (*0-89116-855-9*) Hemisp Pub.

Principles & Design of Mechanical Face Seals. Alan O. Lebeck. LC 90-24783. 800p. 1991. 250.00 (*0-471-51533-7*) Wiley.

Principles & Development of Jewish Law. Mendell Lewittes. LC 87-11778. 298p. (Orig.). pap. 12.95 (*0-8197-0506-3*) Bloch.

Principles & Digest of Law of Evidence. M. Monir. (C). 1988. 550.00 (*0-7855-3683-3*) St Mut.

Principles & Digest of the Arbitration Law. S. B. Malik & R. K. Mehra. (C). 1990. 120.00 (*0-89771-249-8*) St Mut.

Principles & Digest of the Law of Evidence, 2 vols., Set. M. Monir. Ed. by Deoki Nandan. (C). 1990. 325.00 (*0-89771-178-5*) St Mut.

Principles & Dynamics of Local Skin Flaps. 4th rev. ed. Terence M. Davidson et al. LC 98-3832. (Self-Instructional Package Ser.). (Illus.). 110p. 1998. pap. text 25.00 (*1-56772-062-5*) AAO-HNS.

Principles & Elements of Art & Design. Michael DeSiano. 1992. pap. 9.99 (*0-685-24556-X*) Trillium Pr.

Principles & Elements of Thought Construction, Artificial Intelligence & Cognitive Robotics. Charles M. Bowling. LC 87-73448. (Illus.). 152p. (C). 1987. 29.95 (*0-945541-00-7*) CSY Pub Inc.

Principles & General Procedures for Handling Emergency & Accidental Exposure of Workers. ICRP Staff. (International Commission on Radiological Protection Ser.: Vol. 28). 22p. 1978. 15.00 (*0-08-022636-1*, Pergamon Pr) Elsevier.

Principles & Guidelines in Software User Interface Design. Deborah J. Mayhew. 544p. (C). 1991. text 60.80 (*0-13-721929-6*) P-H.

P

Principles & Issues in Nutrition. Yiu H. Hui. LC 84-27051. (Nursing-Health Science Ser.). 700p. (C). 1985. pap., teacher ed. 10.00 (*0-534-04375-5*) Jones & Bartlett.

Principles & Law of Sales Tax. S. D. Singh. 1200p. 1973. 225.00 (*0-7855-1700-6*) St Mut.

Principles & Management of Adrenal Cancer. Ed. by Nasser Javadpour. 195p. 1987. 110.00 (*0-387-16210-0*) Spr-Verlag.

Principles & Management of Lipid Disorders: A Primary Care Approach. Albert Oberman et al. (Illus.). 368p. 1992. 49.00 (*0-683-06623-4*) Lppncott W & W.

Principles & Methodology see Assessment of Logging Costs from Forest Inventories in the Tropics

Principles & Methods. S. Mandelbrojt. LC 75-170339. (Dirichlet Ser.). 166p. 1971. text 139.00 (*90-277-0214-4*) Kluwer Academic.

Principles & Methods for Evaluating the Toxicity of Chemicals. (Environmental Health Criteria Ser.: No. 6). 272p. 1978. text 45.00 (*92-4-154066-4*, 1160006) World Health.

Principles & Methods for the Assessment of Nephrotoxicity Associated with Exposure to Chemicals. (Environmental Health Criteria Ser.: No. 119). (ENG, FRE & SPA.). 266p. 1991. pap. text 46.00 (*92-4-157119-5*, 1160119) World Health.

Principles & Methods for the Assessment of Neurotoxicity Associated with Exposure to Chemicals. (Environmental Health Criteria Ser.: No. 60). 180p. 1986. pap. 26.00 (*92-4-154260-8*) World Health.

Principles & Methods in Historical Phonology: From Proto-Algonkian to Arapaho. Marc Picard. 208p. 1994. 65.00 (*0-7735-1171-7*, Pub. by McG-Queens Univ Pr) CUP Services.

***Principles & Methods in Supramolecular Chemistry.** Hans-Jorg Schneider. LC 99-24125. (Illus.). 362p. 2000. 180.00 (*0-471-97370-X*) Wiley.

Principles & Methods in Supramolecular Chemistry. Hans-Jorg Schneider & Anatoly Yatsimirski. LC 99-24125. 362p. 2000. pap. 75.00 (*0-471-97253-3*) Wiley.

***Principles & Methods of Adapted Physical Education & Recreation.** 9th ed. David Auxter et al. LC 00-37990. 2000. write for info. (*0-07-232926-2*) McGraw.

Principles & Methods of Contemporary Structural Linguistics. Yuri D. Apresjan. Tr. by Dina B. Crockett from DUT. LC 72-94441. (Janua Linguarum, Ser. Minor: No. 144). (Illus.). 349p. (Orig.). 1973. pap. text 65.40 (*90-279-2386-8*) Mouton.

Principles & Methods of Extended Period Forecasting in the United States. Robert P. Harnack. (Monograph Ser.: No. 1-86). 42p. (C). 1986. pap. text 8.00 (*1-883563-00-3*) Natl Weather.

Principles & Methods of Musical Criticism. M. D. Calvocoressi. LC 79-9864. (Music Reprint Ser.). 1979. reprint ed. 29.50 (*0-306-79557-4*) Da Capo.

Principles & Methods of Plant Breeding. S. Borojevic. (Developments in Crop Science Ser.: Vol. 17). 364p. 1990. 154.50 (*0-444-98832-7*, DIC 17) Elsevier.

Principles & Methods of Scheduling Reservations. 2nd ed. David W. Howell. (Illus.). 296p. (Orig.). 1983. pap. text 23.95 (*0-935920-56-0*, Ntl Pubs Blck) P-H.

Principles & Methods of Scheduling Reservations. 3rd ed. David W. Howell. 352p. (Orig.). 1991. pap. text 76.00 (*0-13-726464-X*) P-H.

Principles & Methods of Social Psychology. 4th ed. Edwin P. Hollander. (Illus.). (C). 1981. teacher ed. write for info. (*0-318-54885-2*) OUP.

Principles & Methods of Social Psychology. 4th ed. Edwin P. Hollander. (Illus.). 574p. (C). 1981. text 38.95 (*0-19-502822-8*) OUP.

Principles & Methods of Sterilization in Health Sciences. 2nd ed. John J. Perkins. (Illus.). 580p. 1983. 55.95 (*0-398-01478-7*) C C Thomas.

Principles & Methods of Temperature Measurement. Thomas D. McGee. LC 87-22926. 608p. 1988. 175.00 (*0-471-62767-4*) Wiley.

Principles & Methods of Toxicology. 2nd ed. Andrew W. Hayes. LC 85-42509. (Illus.). 943p. reprint ed. pap. 200.00 (*0-7837-7128-2*, 204695700004) Bks Demand.

Principles & Models of Biological Transport. M. H. Friedman. (Illus.). 280p. 1986. 140.00 (*0-387-16370-0*) Spr-Verlag.

Principles & Parameters: An Introduction to Syntactic Theory. Peter W. Culicover. LC 96-22237. (Oxford Textbooks in Linguistics). (Illus.). 460p. (C). 1997. pap. text 31.95 (*0-19-870014-8*) OUP.

Principles & Parameters in Comparative Grammar. Ed. by Robert Freidin. (Current Studies in Linguistics). 507p. 1991. 58.00 (*0-262-06140-6*) MIT Pr.

Principles & Persons: An Ethical Interpretation of Existentialism. Frederick A. Olafson. LC 67-16038. 276p. reprint ed. pap. 85.60 (*0-7837-6426-X*, 204642400012) Bks Demand.

Principles & Perspective in Drug Bioavailability. J. Blanchard et al. 1978. 85.25 (*3-8055-2440-4*) S Karger.

Principles & Perspectives of Photothermal & Photoacoustic Phenomena. Ed. by Andreas Mandelis. 1991. 110.00 (*0-444-01641-4*) P-H.

Principles & Positioning for MRI. Noyes. (Allied Health Ser.). (C). 2001. pap. 49.95 (*0-7668-1204-9*) Delmar.

Principles & Positioning for MRI-Exam Review. Noyes. (Allied Health Ser.). (C). 2001. pap. 24.95 (*0-7668-1205-7*) Delmar.

Principles & Positioning For Ultrasound. Noyes. (C). 2002. pap. 45.00 (*0-7668-1304-5*) Delmar.

Principles & Practice for Nursing Research. Laura A. Talbot. 752p. (C). 1995. text, teacher ed. write for info. (*0-8151-8925-7*) Mosby Inc.

***Principles & Practice in American Politics.** Samuel Kernell & Steven S. Smith. LC 00-24984. 2000. pap. write for info. (*1-56802-576-9*) CQ Pr.

Principles & Practice in Art. Page Clement. Date not set. pap. text. write for info. (*0-05-005082-6*) Addison-Wesley.

Principles & Practice in Business & Management Research. V. J. Wass & P. E. Wells. 324p. 1994. 77.95 (*1-85521-438-5*, Pub. by Dartmth Pub) Ashgate Pub Co.

Principles & Practice in Business & Management Research. P. E. Wells & V. J. Wass. LC 94-19808. (Illus.). 336p. 1994. pap. 34.95 (*1-85521-450-4*, Pub. by Dartmth Pub) Ashgate Pub Co.

Principles & Practice in Second Language Acquisition. Krashen. 304p. (C). 1988. 26.50 (*0-13-710047-7*, Macmillan Coll) P-H.

Principles & Practice of Accident Insurance. W. A. Dinsdale. 268p. 1975. 80.00 (*0-948691-06-9*, Pub. by Witherby & Co) St Mut.

Principles & Practice of Accountancy, Vol. 1. N. D. Kapoor & Bharat Bhushan. 512p. 1997. pap. 81.00 (*81-209-0180-0*, Pub. by Pitambar Pub) St Mut.

Principles & Practice of Accountancy, Vol. 2. N. D. Kapoor & Bharat Bhushan. 572p. 1997. pap. 91.75 (*81-209-0660-8*, Pub. by Pitambar Pub) St Mut.

Principles & Practice of Acute Cardiac Care. Ed. by Dipanker S. Das Gupta. LC 83-12340. (Illus.). 511p. 1984. reprint ed. pap. 158.50 (*0-8357-7671-9*, 205699900001) Bks Demand.

Principles & Practice of Addictions in Psychitry. Ed. by Norman S. Miller. LC 95-20662. (Illus.). 589p. 1997. 73.00 (*0-7216-5211-5*, W B Saunders Co) Harcrt Hlth Sci Grp.

Principles & Practice of Adult Health Nursing. Patricia G. Beare & Judith L. Myers. 50p. 1990. 75.00 (*0-8016-0389-7*) Mosby Inc.

Principles & Practice of Adult Health Nursing. 2nd ed. Patricia G. Beare. 2328p. (C). (gr. 13). 1993. text, teacher ed. 38.00 (*0-8151-0423-5*, 24199) Mosby Inc.

Principles & Practice of Adult Health Nursing. 3rd ed. Ed. by Patricia G. Beare & Judith L. Myers. LC 97-35022. (Illus.). 1920p. (C). (gr. 13). 1997. text 67.00 (*0-8151-1006-5*, 29567) Mosby Inc.

Principles & Practice of Adult Health Nursing: Learning Guide. 3rd ed. Patricia G. Beare & Judith L. Myers. 168p. (C). (gr. 13). 1997. pap. text 14.95 (*0-8151-1012-X*, 29579) Mosby Inc.

Principles & Practice of Adult Health Nursing: With Study Guide. 3rd ed. Patricia G. Beare & Myers. (Illus.). 2048p. (C). (gr. 13). 1997. text, student ed. 74.00 (*0-8151-1032-4*, 29577) Mosby Inc.

Principles & Practice of Ambulatory Pediatrics. S. Rajkumar & C. Toback. (Illus.). 856p. (C). 1988. text 210.00 (*0-306-42500-9*, Kluwer Plenum) Kluwer Academic.

Principles & Practice of Anesthesiology. 2nd ed. John H. Tinker. Ed. by David E. Longnecker. LC 97-24668. (Illus.). 2720p. (C). (gr. 13). 1997. text 225.00 (*0-8151-5479-8*, 29082) Mosby Inc.

Principles & Practice of Auditing. R. P. Maheshwari & B. Singh. 624p. 1988. 70.00 (*81-209-0002-2*, Pub. by Pitambar Pub) St Mut.

Principles & Practice of Auditing. 7th ed. G. Puttick & S. D. Van Esch. LC 99-215274. 1997. pap. write for info. (*0-7021-3772-3*, Pub. by Juta & Co) Intl Spec Bk.

Principles & Practice of Automatic Process Control. 2nd ed. Carlos A. Smith & Armando B. Corripio. LC 96-46446. 784p. 1997. text 106.95 (*0-471-57588-7*) Wiley.

***Principles & Practice of Behavioral Assessment.** Stephen N. Haynes & William H. O'Brien. LC 99-46705. (Applied Clinical Psychology Ser.). 348p. 1999. 59.95 (*0-306-46221-4*) Kluwer Academic.

***Principles & Practice of Bioanalysis.** Richard F. Venn. 2000. pap. 47.95 (*0-7484-0843-6*) Tay Francis Ltd.

Principles & Practice of Biologic Therapy of Cancer. 3rd ed. Steven A. Rosenberg. 1056p. text 145.00 (*0-7817-2272-1*) Lppncott W & W.

***Principles & Practice of Biological Mass Spectrometry.** Chhabil Dass. 573p. (C). 2000. 94.95 (*0-471-33053-1*) Wiley.

Principles & Practice of Brachytherapy. Ed. by Subir Nag. LC 96-46939. (Illus.). 752p. 1997. 160.00 (*0-87993-654-1*) Futura Pub.

Principles & Practice of Burn Management. Settle. 1996. text 178.00 (*0-443-04476-7*, S3611) Church.

Principles & Practice of Cardiopulmonary Physical Therapy. 3rd ed. Donna L. Frownfelter & Dean. (Illus.). 864p. (C). (gr. 13). 1996. text 66.00 (*0-8151-3340-5*, 24124) Mosby Inc.

Principles & Practice of Cardiopulmonary Physical Therapy: Clinical Case. 3rd ed. Dean & Donna L. Frownfelter. (Illus.). 256p. (C). (gr. 13). 1996. pap. text, student ed. 19.95 (*0-8151-2243-8*, 24873) Mosby Inc.

Principles & Practice of Cardiovascular Imaging. Gerald M. Pohost. 1990. 135.00 (*0-316-71247-7*, Little Brwn Med Div) Lppncott W & W.

Principles & Practice of Cardiovascular Medicine. Ed. by James T. Willerson & Jay N. Cohn. (Illus.). 1976p. 1994. text 135.00 (*0-443-08781-4*) Church.

Principles & Practice of Child Psychiatry. 2nd ed. Stella Chess & Mahin Hassibi. (Illus.). 550p. (C). 1986. text 78.00 (*0-306-42167-4*, Kluwer Plenum) Kluwer Academic.

Principles & Practice of Chromatography. B. Ravindranath. 1989. text 79.95 (*0-470-21328-0*) P-H.

Principles & Practice of Civil Engineering. 3rd ed. Merle Potter. 1998. 69.95 (*1-881018-25-3*) Grt Lks Pr.

***Principles & Practice of Civil Engineering.** 4th ed. Merle C. Potter. 2000. 79.95 (*1-881018-47-4*) Grt Lks Pr.

Principles & Practice of Civil Engineering: Solutions Manual. Great Lakes Press Staff. 1998. pap. text 22.95 (*1-881018-21-0*) Grt Lks Pr.

Principles & Practice of Clinical Anaerobic Bacteriology. Paul Engelkirk et al. (Illus.). 450p. 1992. pap. text 49.95 (*0-89863-160-2*) Star Pub CA.

Complete textbook & laboratory bench reference manual for anaerobic bacteria. Anaerobic bacteria are important in many different types of infections yet are widely overlooked-- particularly when found in a mixed culture-- as they usually are. Authors Paul Engelkirk, Ph.D., Janet Duben-Engelkirk, Ed.D, University of Texas, Houston Medical Center & V. R. Dowell, Jr. Ph.D., Centers for Disease Control, Atlanta Georgia, provide a comprehensive explanation of these important bacteria. Chapters include: Introduction, Classification, Endogenous Anaerobes, Anaerobe-Associated Diseases, Specimen Quality, Specimen Processing Processing Anaerobic Isolates, Presumptive Identifications, Definitive Identifications, Susceptibility Testing, Quality Assurance, Cost Containment, Veterinary Anaerobic Bacteriology, Future Directions. Extensive appendices: Equipment, Services & Supplies, Commercial Sources, Published evaluations of minisystems for anaerobe identification, Laboratory procedures, Compendium of clinically encountered anaerobes, additional reading, answers to self-assessment exercises. Each chapter includes a list of definitions for important terms, self-assessment exercises, & case presentations (where appropriate). A valuable resource for clinical laboratory professionals: clinical microbiologists, MLTs, CLSs, veterinary laboratory technicians, veterinarians, & physicians. See also: Summanen et al, WADSWORTH ANAEROBIC BACTERIOLOGY MANUAL, 5th ed. 1992 & Finegold et al, CLINICAL GUIDE TO ANAEROBIC INFECTIONS, 1992.

Publisher Paid Annotation.

Principles & Practice of Clinical Bacteriology. Ed. by A. M. Emmerson et al. LC 95-39525. 818p. 1997. 333.95 (*0-471-93617-0*) Wiley.

Principles & Practice of Clinical Gynecology. 2nd ed. Ed. by Nathan G. Kase et al. LC 89-22137. (Illus.). 1096p. reprint ed. pap. 200.00 (*0-7837-6244-5*, 204595700010) Bks Demand.

Principles & Practice of Clinical Mycology. C. C. Kibbler et al. 288p. 1996. 216.50 (*0-471-96104-3*, Wiley-Interscience) Wiley.

Principles & Practice of Clinical Psychopharmacotherapy. Philip G. Janicak et al. (Illus.). 608p. 1993. 80.00 (*0-683-04373-0*) Lppncott W & W.

Principles & Practice of Clinical Virology. 4th ed. Arie J. Zuckerman et al. LC 98-50139. 800p. 1999. text 325.00 (*0-471-97340-8*) Wiley.

Principles & Practice of Constraint Programming. Ed. by A. Borning. (Lecture Notes in Computer Science Ser.: Vol. 874). 361p. 1994. 55.95 (*3-540-58601-6*) Spr-Verlag.

Principles & Practice of Constraint Programming. Ed. by Vijay Saraswat & Pascal Van Hentenryck. (Illus.). 500p. 1995. 55.00 (*0-262-19361-2*) MIT Pr.

Principles & Practice of Constraint Programming: Proceedings of the Second International Workshop, PPCR '94, Rosario, Orcas Island, WA, U. S. A., May 2-4, 1994. Workshop on the Principles of Constraint Programmi. Ed. by Alan Borning. LC 94-25166. (Lecture Notes in Computer Science Ser.). 1994. write for info. (*0-387-58601-6*) Spr-Verlag.

Principles & Practice of Constraint Programming - CP '95: First International Conference, Cassis, France, September 19-22, 1995, Proceedings, Vol. XIII. Ed. by Ugo Montanari et al. (Lecture Notes in Computer Science Ser.: Vol. 976). 651p. 1995. 100.00 (*3-540-60299-2*) Spr-Verlag.

Principles & Practice of Constraint Programming - CP97: 3rd International Conference, CP97, Linz, Austria, October 29-November 1, 1997, Vol. 133. Ed. by Gert Smolka. LC 97-43398. (Lecture Notes in Computer Science Ser.: Vol. 1330). xii, 563p. 1997. pap. 79.00 (*3-540-63753-2*) Spr-Verlag.

***Principles & Practice of Constraint Programming - CP'99: Proceedings of the 5th International Conference, CP'99, Alexandria, VA, U. S. A., October 11-14, 1999.** rev. ed. Ed. by Joxan Jaffar. LC 99-51668. (Lecture Notes in Computer Science Ser.: Vol. 1713). xii, 492p. 1999. pap. 79.00 (*3-540-66626-5*) Spr-Verlag.

Principles & Practice of Constraint Programming-CP '96: Second International Conference, CP 96, Cambridge, MA, U. S. A., August 1996: Proceedings. Ed. by Eugene C. Freuder. LC 96-27445. (Lecture Notes in Computer Science Ser.: Vol. 1118). 574p. 1996. pap. 87.00 (*3-540-61551-2*) Spr-Verlag.

Principles & Practice of Constraint Programming, CP98: 4th International Conference, CP98, Pisa, Italy, October 26-30, 1998, Proceedings. Ed. by M. Maher et al. LC 98-44829. (Lecture Notes in Computer Science Ser.: Vol. 1520). 482p. 1998. pap. 69.00 (*3-540-65224-8*) Spr-Verlag.

***Principles & Practice of Consumer Credit Risk.** Anthea Wynn & Helen McNab. 266p. 2000. pap. 80.00 (*0-85297-519-8*, Pub. by Chartered Bank) St Mut.

Principles & Practice of Critical Care. Ed. by Christopher G. Garrard et al. LC 96-31346. (Illus.). 880p. 1997. 295.00 (*0-632-03283-9*) Blackwell Sci.

Principles & Practice of Criticism: Hamlet, the Merry Wives, Othello. Allan H. Gilbert. LC 59-9050. (Illus.). 171p. reprint ed. pap. 53.10 (*0-7837-3797-1*, 204361700010) Bks Demand.

Principles & Practice of Database Systems. S. M. Deem. (Computer Science Ser.). (Illus.). 404p. (Orig.). (C). 1985. pap. text 35.00 (*0-333-37100-3*) Scholium Intl.

Principles & Practice of Day Surgery Nursing. Sarah Penn & Tony Davenport. LC 96-34126. (Illus.). 244p. (Orig.). 1996. pap. text 34.95 (*0-632-03973-6*) Blackwell Sci.

***Principles & Practice of Declarative Programming: International Conference, PPDP '99, Paris, France, September 29-October 1, 1999, Proceedings.** Gopalan Nadathur. Ed. by G. Goos et al. LC 99-47356. (Lecture Notes in Computer Science Ser.: Vol. 1702). x, 434p. 1999. pap. 69.00 (*3-540-66540-4*) Spr-Verlag.

Principles & Practice of Dentofacial Orthopaedics. Hugo Stockfisch.Tr. of Rationelle Kieferorthop Adie. (Illus.). 527p. 1995. text 98.00 (*1-85097-029-7*) Quint Pub Co.

Principles & Practice of Dermatology. 2nd ed. Ed. by W. Mitchell Sams & Peter J. Lynch. LC 95-38678. 1996. text 160.00 (*0-443-08988-4*) Church.

Principles & Practice of Diagnostic Immunology. D. E. Normansell. 149p. 1994. 89.95 (*0-471-18566-3*, Wiley-VCH) Wiley.

Principles & Practice of Diagnostic Immunology. David E. Normansell. LC 94-3583. (Analytical Techniques in Clinical Chemistry & Laboratory Medicine Ser.). 1994. 60.00 (*1-56081-534-5*, Wiley-VCH) Wiley.

Principles & Practice of Dialysis. Ed. by William L. Henrich. LC 93-14146. (Illus.). 496p. 1994. 129.00 (*0-683-03973-3*) Lppncott W & W.

Principles & Practice of Dialysis. 2nd ed. William L. Henrich. LC 98-10017. 601p. 1998. 99.00 (*0-683-30241-8*) Lppncott W & W.

Principles & Practice of Disinfection, Preservation & Sterilisation. 3rd ed. A. D. Russell et al. LC 98-14781. (Illus.). 826p. 1999. 185.00 (*0-632-04194-3*) Blackwell Sci.

Principles & Practice of Disinfection, Preservation & Sterilization. 2nd ed. Ed. by A. D. Russell et al. (Illus.). 656p. 1992. 165.00 (*0-632-02625-1*) Blackwell Sci.

Principles & Practice of Echocardiography. 2nd ed. Arthur E. Weyman. LC 90-13578. (Illus.). 1335p. 1993. text 175.00 (*0-8121-1207-5*) Lppncott W & W.

Principles & Practice of Electrical Engineering: The Most Effective PE Exam Review. Merle Potter et al. 600p. 1997. 69.95 (*1-881018-13-X*); teacher ed. 19.95 (*1-881018-71-7*) Grt Lks Pr.

Principles & Practice of Electrical Epilation. 2nd ed. Sheila Godfrey. 192p. 1996. pap. text 36.95 (*0-7506-2924-X*, RL115) Buttrwrth-Heinemann.

Principles & Practice of Electrotherapy. Joseph Kahn. LC 87-5135. (Illus.). 208p. 1987. reprint ed. pap. 64.50 (*0-8357-3067-0*, 203932300012) Bks Demand.

Principles & Practice of Electrotherapy. 2nd ed. Joseph Kahn. (Illus.). 170p. 1991. pap. text 36.00 (*0-443-08730-X*) Church.

Principles & Practice of Electrotherapy. 2nd fac. ed. Joseph Kahn. LC 90-2340. (Illus.). 178p. 1991. pap. 55.20 (*0-7837-7555-5*, 204730800007) Bks Demand.

Principles & Practice of Electrotherapy. 3rd ed. Joseph Kahn. (Illus.). 1994. pap. text 54.00 (*0-443-08919-1*) Church.

***Principles & Practice of Electrotherapy.** 4th ed. Joseph Kahn. (Illus.). 220p. 1999. pap. text. write for info. (*0-443-06553-5*, W B Saunders Co) Harcrt Hlth Sci Grp.

Principles & Practice of Emergency Medicine. 4th ed. George R. Schwartz et al. LC 98-3827. (Illus.). 1936p. 1998. 179.00 (*0-683-07646-9*) Lppncott W & W.

Principles & Practice of Emergency Medicine, 2 vols., Set. 3rd ed. C. Gene Cayten et al. Ed. by Thom Mayer & Mary A. Mangelsen. (Illus.). 1992. text 199.00 (*0-8121-1373-X*) Lppncott W & W.

Principles & Practice of Endocrinology & Metabolism. 2nd ed. Ed. by Kenneth L. Becker & John P. Bilezikian. LC 94-42416. 2,208p. 1995. text 194.00 (*0-397-51404-2*) Lppncott W & W.

Principles & Practice of Endocrinology & Metabolism. 3rd ed. Kenneth L. Becker et al. 2208p. text 199.00 (*0-7817-1750-7*) Lppncott W & W.

***Principles & Practice of Engineering (PE) Sample Problems & Solutions in Electrical Engineering.** National Council of Examines Staff. 1998. pap. 41.75 (*0-7803-4596-7*) Inst Electrical.

Principles & Practice of Environmental Medicine. Ed. by A. B. Tarcher. (Illus.). 648p. (C). 1992. text 114.00 (*0-306-42893-8*, Kluwer Plenum) Kluwer Academic.

Principles & Practice of Family Medicine: An Asian-Pacific Perspective of Primary Health Care. Ed. by John Fry & Nat Yuen. 1994. 45.00 (*1-85775-045-4*, Radcliffe Med Pr) Scovill Paterson.

Principles & Practice of Forensic Psychiatry. Ed. by Richard Rosner. LC 93-20238. (An Arnold Publication). (Illus.). 656p. 1999. text 145.00 (*0-442-01118-0*) OUP.

Principles & Practice of Gastroenterology & Hepatology. 2nd ed. Ed. by Gary Gitnick et al. (Illus.). 1162p. (C). 1994. pap. text 150.00 (*0-8385-8064-5*, A8064-6, Apple Lange Med) McGraw.

Principles & Practice of General Surgery: Essentials of Practice. Gordon J. Ritchie et al. (Illus.). 1200p. (C). 1994. text 162.00 (*0-397-51114-0*, Lippnctt) Lppncott W & W.

Principles & Practice of Genitourinary Oncology. Derek Raghavan. LC 96-8893. 1104p. 1996. text 158.00 (*0-397-51458-1*) Lppncott W & W.

Principles & Practice of Geriatric Medicine, 2 Vols. 3rd ed. Ed. by M. S. Pathy & Emeritus. LC 96-37118. 1688p. 1998. 595.00 (*0-471-96348-8*) Wiley.

An Asterisk (*) at the beginning of an entry indicates that the title is appearing for the first time.

Principles & Practice of Geriatric Psychiatry. John R. Copeland et al. LC 92-48920. 1084p. 1994. 575.00 (*0-471-92654-X*, Wiley-Interscience) Wiley.

Principles & Practice of Geriatric Surgery. Ed. by Ronnie A. Rosenthal et al. (Illus.). 848p. 2000. 195.00 (*0-387-98393-7*) Spr-Verlag.

Principles & Practice of Gynecologic Laser Surgery. Joseph H. Bellina & Gaetano Bandieramonte. LC 84-3434. 308p. 1984. 75.00 (*0-306-41543-7*, Plenum Trade) Perseus Pubng.

Principles & Practice of Gynecologic Oncology. 2nd ed. William J. Hoskins. LC 96-2751. 1056p. 1996. text 195.00 (*0-397-51563-4*) Lppncott W & W.

Principles & Practice of Gynecologic Oncology. 3rd ed. William J. Hoskins et al. 1200p. text 199.00 (*0-7817-1978-X*) Lppncott W & W.

Principles & Practice of Hemodialysis. Total Renal Care, Inc., Educ. Dept. Staff. 214p. 1982. ring bd. 95.00 (*1-56488-000-1*) Dialyrn.

Principles & Practice of Heterogeneous Catalysis. J. M. Thomas & J. W. Thomas. LC 96-18014. 676p. 1996. 165.00 (*3-527-29288-8*, Wiley-VCH); pap. 79.95 (*3-527-29239-X*, Wiley-VCH) Wiley.

Principles & Practice of Hormone Therapy in Gynaecology & Obstetrics. Joachim Ufer. (C). 1969. 49.25 (*3-11-000614-6*) De Gruyter.

Principles & Practice of Immunoassay. 2nd ed. Ed. by Christopher P. Price & David J. Newman. 650p. 1997. 140.00 (*1-56159-175-0*) Groves Dictionaries.

Principles & Practice of Immunotoxicology. K. Miller et al. (Illus.). 392p. 1991. 195.00 (*0-632-02563-8*) Blackwell Sci.

Principles & Practice of Impedance. 2nd ed. Rufus P. Turner & Stan Gibilisco. (Illus.). 224p. 1987. 21.95 (*0-8306-0725-0*) McGraw-Hill Prof.

Principles & Practice of Indigenous Church Planting. Charles D. Brock. 96p. 1981. pap. 6.00 (*1-885504-45-4*) Church Gwth.

Principles & Practice of Infectious Diseases. 2nd ed. Ed. by Gerald L. Mandell et al. LC 84-13076. (Illus.). 1800p. 1988. pap. 200.00 (*0-8357-6554-7*, 203591900097) Bks Demand.

Principles & Practice of Infectious Diseases. 3rd ed. Ed. by Gerald L. Mandell et al. (Illus.). 2340p. 1990. text 225.00 (*0-443-08686-9*) Church.

Principles & Practice of Infectious Diseases, 2 vols. 4th ed. Ed. by Gerald L. Mandell et al. 1994. text 295.00 (*0-443-08935-3*) Church.

Principles & Practice of Infectious Diseases, Vol. 1. 3rd ed. Ed. by Gerald L. Mandell et al. LC 89-15734. (Illus.). 1304p. reprint ed. pap. 200.00 (*0-7837-8713-8*, 204956100001) Bks Demand.

Principles & Practice of Infectious Diseases, Vol. 2. 3rd ed. Ed. by Gerald L. Mandell et al. LC 89-15734. (Illus.). 1307p. reprint ed. pap. 200.00 (*0-7837-8737-5*, 204956100002) Bks Demand.

Principles & Practice of Infectious Diseases: Antimicrobial Therapy, 1992. Gerald L. Mandell et al. LC 91-36236. 184p. reprint ed. pap. 57.10 (*0-7837-6255-0*, 204596700010) Bks Demand.

Principles & Practice of Infectious Diseases: Antimicrobial Therapy, 1993-1994. Gerald L. Mandell et al. LC 93-194225. 191p. 1993. reprint ed. pap. 59.30 (*0-7837-9616-1*, 206037300005) Bks Demand.

Principles & Practice of Infectious Diseases: Antimicrobial Therapy 1996/1997. G. L. Mandell et al. 200p. 1996. pap. write for info. (*0-443-07844-0*) Church.

Principles & Practice of Infectious Diseases: Handbook of Antimicrobial Therapy. Gerald L. Mandell et al. 166p. (Orig.). 1992. 19.95 (*0-443-08818-7*) Church.

Principles & Practice of Insurance. Mark S. Dacey. 110p. (C). 1989. pap. 95.00 (*0-948691-83-2*, Pub. by Witherby & Co) St Mut.

Principles & Practice of Intensive Care Monitoring. Ed. by Martin Tobin. LC 97-42653. (Illus.). 1200p. 1997. text 145.00 (*0-07-065094-2*) McGraw-Hill HPD.

Principles & Practice of Interruption Insurance. G. J. Hickmott. 934p. (C). 1982. 350.00 (*0-900886-56-0*, Pub. by Witherby & Co) St Mut.

Principles & Practice of Interventional Cardiology. M. Sue Apple. LC 99-38188. 380p. 1998. pap. text 42.95 (*0-7817-1020-0*) Lppncott W & W.

Principles & Practice of Laser-Doppler Anemometry. 2nd ed. F. Durst et al. 1981. text 177.00 (*0-12-225260-8*) Acad Pr.

Principles & Practice of Laser Technology. Hrand M. Muncheryan. (Illus.). 294p. 1983. 15.95 (*0-8306-0129-5*) McGraw-Hill Prof.

Principles & Practice of Leadhing: 25th Annual Hydrometallurgy Meeting. W. C. Cooper & D. B. Dreisinger. (Illus.). 398p. 1995. 226.50 (*0-444-82255-0*) Elsevier.

Principles & Practice of Management. W. Haynes. (C). 1989. 90.00 (*0-89771-434-2*, Pub. by Current Dist) St Mut.

Principles & Practice of Managing Soilborne Plant Pathogens. Ed. by Robert Hall. LC 96-79341. (Illus.). 342p. (C). 1997. text 49.00 (*0-89054-223-6*) Am Phytopathol Soc.

Principles & Practice of Marketing. J. Frain. 514p. (Orig.). (C). 1987. 150.00 (*0-7855-5659-1*, Pub. by Inst Pur & Supply) St Mut.

Principles & Practice of Marketing. J. Frain. 514p. (Orig.). (C). 1989. 135.00 (*0-7855-4625-1*, Pub. by Inst Pur & Supply) St Mut.

Principles & Practice of Marketing. David Jobber. 1995. write for info. (*0-07-707935-3*) McGraw.

Principles & Practice of Maternal Nutrition. B. Luke & Louis G. Keith. (Illus.). 161p. 1992. 39.00 (*1-85070-324-8*) Prthnon Pub.

Principles & Practice of Mathematics. Ed. by W. Meyer. (Textbooks in Mathematical Sciences Ser.). 686p. 1996. 64.95 (*0-387-94612-8*) Spr-Verlag.

Principles & Practice of Mechanical Engineering: The Most Effective PE Exam Review. 3rd ed. Merle C. Potter. 586p. 1999. 74.95 (*1-881018-42-3*) Grt Lks Pr.

Principles & Practice of Mechanical Ventilation. Ed. by Martin J. Tobin. LC 93-37105. 1300p. 1994. text 155.00 (*0-07-064943-X*) McGraw-Hill HPD.

Principles & Practice of Medical Intensive Care. Ed. by Richard W. Carlson & Michael A. Geheb. (Illus.). 1824p. 1993. text 220.00 (*0-7216-3396-X*, W B Saunders Co) Harcrt Hlth Sci Grp.

Principles & Practice of Medical Laboratory Science Vol. 1: Basic Histotechnology. Ed. by A. S. Leong. (Illus.). 172p. 1996. pap. write for info. (*0-443-05369-3*) Church.

Principles & Practice of Medical Laboratory Science Vol. 2: Medical Microbiology, Virology & Molecular Technology. Ed. by A. S. Leong. (Illus.). 252p. 1997. pap. write for info. (*0-443-05982-9*) Church.

Principles & Practice of Medical Therapy in Pregnancy. 2nd ed. Norbert Gleicher et al. (Illus.). 1362p. (C). 1991. pap. text 140.00 (*0-8385-7979-5*, A7979-6) Appleton & Lange.

Principles & Practice of Medical Therapy in Pregnancy. 3rd ed. Louis Buttino, Jr. 200p. 1998. pap., student ed. 55.00 (*0-8385-6296-5*, Apple Lange Med) McGraw.

Principles & Practice of Medical Therapy in Pregnancy. 3rd ed. Norbert Gleicher. LC 97-46683. 1600p. (C). 1998. 150.00 (*0-8385-7677-X*, A-7677-6, Apple Lange Med) McGraw.

Principles & Practice of Medicine. 23rd ed. John D. Stobo. LC 96-23756. 1064p. (C). 1996. pap. text 49.95 (*0-8385-7963-9*, A7963-0, Apple Lange Med) McGraw.

Principles & Practice of Medicine. 24th ed. Composed by Stobo. (Illus.). 1200p. (C). 1999. pap. text 41.95 (*0-8385-8128-5*) Appleton & Lange.

Principles & Practice of Modern Chromatography. K. Robards et al. (Illus.). 495p. 1994. 59.00 (*0-12-589570-4*) Acad Pr.

*__Principles & Practice of Modern Management.__ Tony Dawson. 406p. 2000. 32.95 (*1-872807-97-6*, Pub. by Tudor Business Pubg Ltd) Intl Spec Bk.

Principles & Practice of Movement Disorders. Ed. by S. Fahn et al. (Illus.). 600p. 1998. text. write for info. (*0-443-07941-2*) Church.

Principles & Practice of Multi-Frequency Telegraphy. Ed. by J. D. Ralphs. (Telecommunications Ser.: No. 11). 206p. 1985. boxed set 109.00 (*0-86341-022-7*, TE011) INSPEC Inc.

Principles & Practice of Naturopathy. Ernest W. Cordingley. 25p. 1996. reprint ed. spiral bd. 8.50 (*0-7873-0200-7*) Hlth Research.

Principles & Practice of Navigation. A. Frost. (C). 1987. text 45.00 (*0-85174-542-3*, Pub. by Brown Son & Ferguson) Sheridan.

Principles & Practice of Nuclear Medicine. 2nd ed. Early & Sodee. (Illus.). 896p. (gr. 13). 1994. text 99.00 (*0-8016-2577-7*, 02577) Mosby Inc.

*__Principles & Practice of Nurse Education.__ 3rd ed. F. M. Quinn. 496p. 1999. pap. (*0-7487-3170-9*) S Thornes Pubs.

Principles & Practice of Nurse Education. 3rd ed. Francis M. Quinn. (Illus.). 496p. 1994. pap. text 47.50 (*1-56593-295-1*, 0619) Singular Publishing.

*__Principles & Practice of Nurse Education.__ 4th ed. F. M. Quinn. (Illus.). 656p. 2000. pap. 42.50 (*0-7487-3895-9*, Pub. by S Thornes Pubs) Intl Spec Bk.

Principles & Practice of Nursing Research. Laura A. Talbot. (Illus.). 752p. (C). (gr. 13). 1994. text 46.00 (*0-8016-6450-0*, 06450) Mosby Inc.

Principles & Practice of Obstetric Anaesthesia & Analgesia. A. Holdcroft & T. Thomas. LC 99-21230. (Illus.). 466p. 2000. 125.00 (*0-86542-828-X*) Blackwell Sci.

Principles & Practice of Obstetric Analgesia & Anesthesia. 2nd ed. John J. Bonica & John S. McDonald. (Illus.). 1344p. 1994. text 175.00 (*0-683-00930-3*) Lppncott W & W.

*__Principles & Practice of Obstetrics.__ V. Padubidri. (Illus.). 400p. 2000. text 39.95 (*0-19-564951-6*) OUP.

Principles & Practice of Ophthalmic Plastic & Reconstructive Surgery, 2 vols., Set. Stephen Bosniak. LC 95-12616. (Illus.). 1152p. 1995. text 375.00 (*0-7216-3559-8*, W B Saunders Co) Harcrt Hlth Sci Grp.

Principles & Practice of Ophthalmology, 6 vols., Set. Ed. by Daniel M. Albert & Frederick A. Jakobiec. (Illus.). 1993. text 825.00 (*0-7216-6592-6*, W B Saunders Co) Harcrt Hlth Sci Grp.

Principles & Practice of Ophthalmology: Basic Sciences, Vol. 1. Ed. by Daniel M. Albert & Frederick A. Jokobiec. LC 93-12658. (Illus.). 1435p. 1993. text 195.00 (*0-7216-3416-8*, W B Saunders Co) Harcrt Hlth Sci Grp.

Principles & Practice of Ophthalmology: Clinical Practice, 5 vols., Set. Ed. by Daniel M. Albert & Frederick A. Jakobiec. LC 93-7247. (Illus.). 1993. text 695.00 (*0-7216-3418-4*, W B Saunders Co) Harcrt Hlth Sci Grp.

Principles & Practice of Oral Medicine. 2nd ed. Stephen T. Sonis et al. (Illus.). 512p. 1994. text. write for info. (*0-7216-8449-1*, W B Saunders Co) Harcrt Hlth Sci Grp.

Principles & Practice of Ornamental & Complex Turning. John J. Holtzapffel. (Illus.). 656p. 1990. reprint ed. pap. 17.95 (*0-486-26567-6*) Dover.

Principles & Practice of Orthodontics. 2nd ed. J. R. Mills. LC 87-10291. (Dental Ser.). (Illus.). 294p. 1987. pap. text 69.00 (*0-443-03608-X*) Church.

Principles & Practice of Orthopaedic Sports Medicine. William E. Garrett, Jr. et al. 796p. text 145.00 (*0-7817-2578-X*) Lppncott W & W.

Principles & Practice of Pain Management. Ed. by Carol A. Warfield. LC 92-20392. (Illus.). 608p. 1992. text 85.00 (*0-07-068291-7*) McGraw-Hill HPD.

Principles & Practice of Past Life Therapy, Vol. 1. 3rd ed. Ruth E. Norman & Charles Spaegel. (Illus.). 414p. 1991. 20.00 (*0-932642-79-9*) Unarius Acad Sci.

Principles & Practice of Pediatric Infectious Diseases. Sarah S Long et al. LC 96-19019. 1996. text 225.00 (*0-443-08943-4*) Church.

Principles & Practice of Pediatric Neurosurgery. A. Leland Albright et al. LC 98-29770. (Illus.). 1472p. 1999. 239.00 (*0-86577-799-3*) Thieme Med Pubs.

Principles & Practice of Pediatric Neurosurgery. Leland A. Albright et al. LC 98-29770. 1999. 239.00 (*3-13-114691-5*) Thieme Med Pubs.

Principles & Practice of Pediatric Oncology. 3rd ed. Philip A. Pizzo & David G. Poplack. LC 96-41637. 1200p. 1996. text 205.00 (*0-397-51561-8*) Lppncott W & W.

Principles & Practice of Pediatric Optometry. David Rosenbloom & Meredith W. Morgan. (Illus.). 496p. 1990. text 73.00 (*0-397-50917-0*) Lppncott W & W.

Principles & Practice of Pediatrics. Frank A. Oski et al. (Illus.). 2155p. 1989. text 99.50 (*0-397-50707-0*) Lppncott W & W.

Principles & Practice of Pediatrics. 2nd ed. Frank A. Oski. 2,400p. (C). 1993. text 99.50 (*0-397-51221-X*) Lppncott W & W.

Principles & Practice of Perfumery & Cosmetics: The Scientific Background. George Howard & W. E. Arnould-Taylor. 144p. (Orig.). 1987. pap. 32.50 (*0-85950-576-6*, Pub. by S Thornes Pubs) Trans-Atl Phila.

Principles & Practice of Pharmacology for Anaesthetists. 3rd ed. T. N. Calvey & N. E. Williams. LC 96-20973. (Illus.). 608p. 1997. 165.00 (*0-632-04156-0*) Blackwell Sci.

*__Principles & Practice of Phycology.__ Mills. (C). 1999. text 72.00 (*0-443-06016-9*, Pub. by Harcourt Coll Pubs) Harcourt.

Principles & Practice of Physical Therapy. 3rd ed. W. E. Arnould-Taylor. (Illus.). 224p. 1991. pap. 29.50 (*0-7487-1250-X*, Pub. by S Thornes Pubs) Trans-Atl Phila.

Principles & Practice of Physiologic Acupuncture. George A. Ulett. 232p. 1982. 42.50 (*0-87527-309-2*) Green.

Principles & Practice of Plant Conservation. David R. Given. LC 93-5240. (Illus.). 292p. 1994. 39.95 (*0-88192-249-8*) Timber.

Principles & Practice of Plant Hormone Analysis, Vol. 1. Ed. by Laurent Rivier & Alan Crozier. (Biological Techniques Ser.). 1987. text 104.00 (*0-12-198375-7*) Acad Pr.

Principles & Practice of Plant Hormone Analysis, Vol. 2. Ed. by Laurent Rivier & Alan Crozier. (Biological Techniques Ser.). 1987. text 104.00 (*0-12-198376-5*) Acad Pr.

Principles & Practice of Planting Trees & Shrubs. Gary W. Watson & E. B. Himelick. (Illus.). 200p. (C). 1997. pap. text 40.00 (*1-881956-18-0*) Int Soc Arboricult.

*__Principles & Practice of Podiatric Medicine.__ 2nd ed. L. A. Levy & V. J. Hetherington. (Illus.). 854p. 1998. text. write for info. (*0-443-07940-4*) Church.

Principles & Practice of Podiatry. Frank Weinstein. LC 66-23237. (Illus.). 521p. reprint ed. pap. 161.60 (*0-608-30518-9*, 205544700022) Bks Demand.

Principles & Practice of Political Compromise: A Case Study of the United States Senate. Barry J. Seltser. LC 84-14838. (Studies in American Religion: Vol. 12). 320p. 1984. lib. bdg. 99.95 (*0-88946-657-2*) E Mellen.

Principles & Practice of Psychopharmacotherapy. 2nd ed. Philip G. Janicak et al. LC 97-13497. 719p. 1997. 95.00 (*0-683-30266-3*) Lppncott W & W.

Principles & Practice of Public Administration in Nigeria. Augustus Adebayo. LC 80-41173. 207p. reprint ed. pap. 64.20 (*0-608-18416-0*, 203049200069) Bks Demand.

Principles & Practice of Public Health Surveillance. 380p. (Orig.). (C). 1993. pap. text 65.00 (*1-56806-516-7*) DIANE Pub.

Principles & Practice of Public Health Surveillance. Ed. by Steven M. Teutsch & R. Elliott Churchill. (Illus.). 288p. 1994. text 52.50 (*0-19-508021-1*) OUP.

Principles & Practice of Pulmonary Rehabilitation. Ed. by Richard Casaburi & Thomas L. Petty. LC 92-13386. (Illus.). 528p. 1993. text 92.00 (*0-7216-3304-8*, W B Saunders Co) Harcrt Hlth Sci Grp.

Principles & Practice of Radiation Oncology. 3rd ed. Ed. by Carlos A. Perez & Luther Brady. (Illus.). 2000p. 1997. text 225.00 (*0-397-58416-4*) Lppncott W & W.

Principles & Practice of Radiation Oncology. 3rd ed. Carlos A. Perez & Luther W. Brady. 2368p. 1997. 325.00 (*0-7817-1691-8*) Lppncott W & W.

Principles & Practice of Radiation Therapy: Physics, Simulation, & Treatment Planning. 2nd ed. Charles M. Washington & Dennis T. Leaver. (Illus.). 320p. (C). (gr. 13). 1996. text 61.00 (*0-8151-9136-7*, 24803) Mosby Inc.

Principles & Practice of Radiation Therapy: Practical Applications, 3. 3rd ed. Charles M. Washington & Dennis T. Leaver. (Illus.). 384p. (C). (gr. 13). 1996. text 59.00 (*0-8151-9137-5*, 24804) Mosby Inc.

Principles & Practice of Radiation Therapy: Practical Applications, Vol. 3. Charles M. Washington & Dennis T. Leaver. 1997. teacher ed. write for info. (*0-8151-9253-3*) Mosby Inc.

Principles & Practice of Radiation Therapy Physics, Simulation & Treatment Planning, Vol. 2. Charles M. Washington & Dennis T. Leaver. (Illus.). 1997. teacher ed. write for info. (*0-8151-9252-5*) Mosby Inc.

Principles & Practice of Radiation Therapy Technology. Charles M. Washington & Dennis T. Leaver. (Illus.). 1996. teacher ed. write for info. (*0-8151-9251-7*) Mosby Inc.

Principles & Practice of Radiotherapy Treatment Planning. Euan Thomson et al. (Illus.). 300p. 2000. pap. text 49.50 (*1-900151-89-8*) OUP.

Principles & Practice of Rational-Emotive Therapy. Ruth A. Wessler & Richard L. Wessler. LC 80-8319. (Jossey-Bass Social & Behavioral Science Ser.). 296p. reprint ed. pap. 91.80 (*0-7837-2527-2*, 204268600006) Bks Demand.

Principles & Practice of Refractive Surgery. Richard E. Elander et al. Ed. by Richard Lampert. LC 96-17646. 640p. 1997. text 236.00 (*0-7216-6552-7*, W B Saunders Co) Harcrt Hlth Sci Grp.

Principles & Practice of Regional Anesthesia. J. A. Wildsmith & Edward N. Armitage. (Illus.). 288p. 1987. 85.00 (*0-443-03128-2*) Church.

Principles & Practice of Regional Anesthesia. 2nd ed. Ed. by J. A. Wildsmith & Edward N. Armitage. LC 92-49107. (Illus.). 272p. 1993. text 122.00 (*0-443-04475-9*) Church.

Principles & Practice of Relapse Prevention. Ed. by Peter H. Wilson. LC 92-1558. 383p. 1992. lib. bdg. 45.00 (*0-89862-891-1*) Guilford Pubns.

Principles & Practice of Renal Nursing. Paul Challinor & John Sedgewick. (Illus.). 1998. pap. 59.50 (*0-7487-3331-0*, Pub. by S Thornes Pubs) Trans-Atl Phila.

Principles & Practice of Research: Strategy for Surgical Investigators. Ed. by H. Troidl et al. (Illus.). 385p. 1986. 78.00 (*0-387-16340-9*) Spr-Verlag.

Principles & Practice of Respiratory Therapy. 2nd ed. Ed. by Jimmy A. Young & Dan Crocker. LC 75-16023. (Illus.). 793p. reprint ed. pap. 200.00 (*0-8357-7637-9*, 205696000096) Bks Demand.

*__Principles & Practice of Sedation.__ J. G. Whitwam & M. R. Vinik. LC 97-46160. (Illus.). 300p. 1998. 99.95 (*0-86542-678-3*) Blackwell Sci.

Principles & Practice of Sedation. 2nd rev. ed. J. G. Whitwam. 1998. 99.95 (*0-632-05219-8*) Blackwell Sci.

*__Principles & Practice of Sex Therapy.__ 3rd ed. Sandra R. Leiblum. (Illus.). 518p. 2000. 50.00 (*1-57230-574-6*) Guilford Pubns.

Principles & Practice of Sex Therapy: Update for the 1990s. 2nd ed. Ed. by Sandra R. Leiblum & Raymond C. Rosen. LC 89-7458. 413p. 1989. lib. bdg. 46.95 (*0-89862-389-8*) Guilford Pubns.

Principles & Practice of Skin Excisions. Borut I. Jemec & Gregor B. Jemec. 308p. 1995. 262.50 (*0-444-82341-7*) Elsevier.

Principles & Practice of Sleep Medicine. 2nd ed. Ed. by Meir H. Kryger et al. LC 92-48200. (Illus.). 1008p. 1993. text 140.00 (*0-7216-4217-9*, W B Saunders Co) Harcrt Hlth Sci Grp.

Principles & Practice of Sleep Medicine in the Child. Richard Ferber & Meir H. Kryger. (Illus.). 320p. 1995. text 52.00 (*0-7216-4761-8*, W B Saunders Co) Harcrt Hlth Sci Grp.

Principles & Practice of Slurry Flow. C. A. Shool. (Chemical Engineering Ser.). 336p. 1991. text 89.95 (*0-7506-9110-7*) Buttrwrth-Heinemann.

Principles & Practice of Soil Science: The Soil as a Natural Resource. 3rd ed. R. E. White. LC 97-7175. (Illus.). 1997. pap. 49.95 (*0-86542-960-X*) Blackwell Sci.

Principles & Practice of Spectroscopic Calibration. Howard Mark. LC 91-15260. (Chemical Analysis: A Series of Monographs on Analytical Chemistry & Its Applications: No. 1075). 192p. 1991. 115.00 (*0-471-54614-3*) Wiley.

Principles & Practice of Sport Management. Lisa P. Masteralexis et al. LC 98-12301. 522p. 1998. 49.00 (*0-8342-1021-5*, 10215) Aspen Pub.

Principles & Practice of Stress Management. Ed. by Robert L. Woolfolk & Paul M. Lehrer. LC 83-5689. 512p. reprint ed. pap. 158.80 (*0-7837-1208-1*, 204174000023) Bks Demand.

Principles & Practice of Structural Equation Modeling. Rex B. Kline. LC 97-46642. (Methodology in the Social Sciences Ser.). 354p. 1998. pap. text 37.00 (*1-57230-337-9*, C0337); lib. bdg. 55.00 (*1-57230-336-0*, C0336) Guilford Pubns.

Principles & Practice of Supportive Oncology. Ann Berger et al. LC 97-41365. 800p. 1997. text 85.00 (*0-397-51559-6*) Lppncott W & W.

Principles & Practice of Surgery. 2nd ed. Ed. by A. P. Forrest et al. (Illus.). 729p. 1990. text 49.95 (*0-443-03909-7*) Church.

Principles & Practice of Surgery. 2nd ed. Ed. by A. P. Forrest et al. LC 89-20967. (Illus.). 739p. 1991. reprint ed. pap. 200.00 (*0-7837-9750-8*, 206047800005) Bks Demand.

Principles & Practice of Surgery for the Colon, Rectum, & Anus. 2nd ed. Philip H. Gordon & Santhat Nivatvongs. LC 98-35898. 1398p. 1998. 235.00 (*1-57626-017-8*) Quality Med Pub.

Principles & Practice of Surgical & Cytopathology. 3rd ed. Steven G. Silverberg et al. LC 97-2455. 1997. text 460.00 (*0-443-07541-7*) Church.

Principles & Practice of Surgical Laparoscopy. Ed. by Simon Paterson-Brown & James Garden. (Illus.). 619p. 1994. pap. text 76.00 (*0-7020-1712-4*, W B Saunders Co) Harcrt Hlth Sci Grp.

Principles & Practice of Surgical Pathology, Vol. 1. Ed. by Steven G. Silverberg. LC 81-21891. 863p. reprint ed. pap. 200.00 (*0-8357-6569-5*, 203594400001) Bks Demand.

Principles & Practice of Surgical Pathology, Vol. 2. Ed. by Steven G. Silverberg. LC 81-21891. 944p. reprint ed. pap. 200.00 (*0-8357-6570-9*, 203594400002) Bks Demand.

P

An Asterisk (*) at the beginning of an entry indicates that the title is appearing for the first time.

Principles & Practice of Surveying, 2 vols. Charles B. Breed & George L. Hosmer. Incl. Vol. 1. Principles & Pratice of Surveying. 11th ed. 728p. 1977. text 106.95 (0-471-02979-3); Vol. 2. Higher Surveying. 8th ed. 543p. 1962. text 102.95 (0-471-10164-8); write for info. (0-318-56436-X) Wiley.

***Principles & Practice of 3-D Radiation Treatment: Symposium on 3-D Radiation Treatment: Technological Innovations & Clinical Results, Munich, March 1999.** Ed. by H. J. Feldmann et al. (Frontiers of Radiation Therapy & Oncology Ser.: Vol. 34). (Illus.). x, 250p. 2000. 217.50 (3-8055-6947-5) S Karger.

Principles & Practice of Travel. Zuckerman. text. write for info. (0-471-49079-2) Wiley.

Principles & Practice of Veterinary Technology. James Pratt. LC 97-14020. (Illus.). 730p. (gr. 13). 1997. text 56.00 (0-8151-7308-3, 27767) Mosby Inc.

***Principles & Practice of Veterinary Technology.** Paul W. Pratt. (Illus.). 1998. teacher ed. write for info. (0-323-00051-7) Mosby Inc.

Principles & Practice of X-Ray Spectrometric Analysis. 2nd ed. E. P. Bertin. LC 74-28043. (Illus.). 1080p. (C). 1975. text 175.00 (0-306-30809-6, Kluwer Plenum) Kluwer Academic.

Principles & Practice of Yoga. R. K. Garde. (Illus.). 131p. 1975. 7.95 (0-318-36398-4) Asia Bk Corp.

***Principles & Practices.** Prophet Andromeda. Ed. by Sherry Knecht. (Pathways Through Consciousness Ser.: Vol. 4). (Illus.). 129p. (Orig.). 1999. pap. text 69.95 (1-929589-07-7) Branching Leaf.

***Principles & Practices, 4 vols., No. 4.** 2nd rev. ed. Andromeda Knecht. (Pathways Through Consciousness Ser.). (Illus.). 139p. 1999. pap. text 69.95 (1-929589-20-4) Branching Leaf.

Principles & Practices for Baptist Churches. Edward T. Hiscox. LC 80-8083. 608p. 1985. reprint ed. pap. 20.99 (0-8254-2860-2, Kregel Class) Kregel.

Principles & Practices for Diesel Contaminated Soils, Vol. 1. Ed. by Paul T. Kostecki et al. (Illus.). 240p. 1994. text 49.95 (1-884940-01-3) Amherst Sci Pubs.

Principles & Practices for Diesel Contaminated Soils, Vol. 2. Ed. by Paul T. Kostecki et al. (Illus.). 157p. 1993. text 39.95 (1-884940-17-X) Amherst Sci Pubs.

Principles & Practices for Diesel Contaminated Soils, Vol. 4. Ed. by Paul T. Kostecki et al. (Illus.). 198p. 1995. text 49.95 (1-884940-03-X) Amherst Sci Pubs.

Principles & Practices for Diesel Contaminated Soils, Vol. 5. Ed. by Paul T. Kostecki et al. (Illus.). 197p. 1996. text 49.95 (1-884940-06-4) Amherst Sci Pubs.

Principles & Practices for Diesel Contaminated Soils, Vol. 6. Ed. by Paul T. Kostecki et al. (Illus.). 120p. 1997. text 49.95 (1-884940-15-3) Amherst Sci Pubs.

Principles & Practices for Diesel Contaminated Soils, Vol. 7. Ed. by Christopher P. Barkan et al. 120p. 1998. text 49.95 (1-884940-21-8) Amherst Sci Pubs.

Principles & Practices for the Safe Processing of Foods. H. J. Heinz Company Staff. 472p. 1993. pap. 81.00 (1-85573-362-5, Pub. by Woodhead Pubng) Am Educ Systs.

Principles & Practices for the Safe Processing of Foods. Contrib. by D. A. Shapton & N. F. Shapton. (Illus.). 467p. 1994. pap. text 44.95 (0-7506-1775-6) Buttrwrth-Heinemann.

Principles & Practices in Air Transport Regulation. Henri Wassenbergh. 268p. 1993. pap. 45.00 (2-908537-09-5, Pub. by Inst Air Transport) Bks Intl VA.

***Principles & Practices in Arithmetic Teaching: Innovative Approaches for the Primary Classroom.** Julia Anghileri. LC 00-23299. 2000. pap. write for info. (0-335-20634-4, Pub. by OpUniv Pr) Taylor & Francis.

Principles & Practices in Cardio Pulmonary Phy. 2nd ed. 1996. text 75.00 (0-8151-3313-8, 28997) Mosby Inc.

Principles & Practices in Classroom Evaluation. Fred O. Brooks. 152p. (C). 1990. pap. 30.60 (0-536-57728-5) Pearson Custom.

***Principles & Practices in Plant Ecology: Allelochemical Interactions.** Ed. by Inderjit et al. LC 98-44681. 10p. 1999. lib. bdg. 129.95 (0-8493-2116-6) CRC Pr.

Principles & Practices in Socialcum-Community Forestry Pub. V. N. Prasadd. 118p. (C). 1985. 110.00 (81-7089-032-2, Pub. by Intl Bk Distr) St Mut.

Principles & Practices of Animal Taxonomy. V. C. Kapoor. (Illus.). 247p. 1998. pap. 45.00 (1-57808-024-X) Science Pubs.

Principles & Practices of Chiropractic Techniques. 2nd ed. Scott Haldeman. (Illus.). 641p. (C). 1993. pap. text 95.00 (0-8385-6360-0, A6360-0, Apple Lange Med) McGraw.

Principles & Practices of Cholera Control. J. De Araoz et al. (Public Health Papers: No. 40). 139p. 1970. pap. text 13.00 (92-4-130040-X, 1110040) World Health.

Principles & Practices of Christian Education see Principios y Practicas de la Educacion Cristiana

Principles & Practices of Contemporary Acupuncture. Sung J. Liao et al. LC 94-21951. (Illus.). 472p. 1994. text 69.75 (0-8247-9291-2) Dekker.

Principles & Practices of Disability Management in Industry. Ed. by Donald E. Shrey & Michael Lacerte. 680p. 1995. boxed set 114.95 (1-878205-63-3) St Lucie Pr.

Principles & Practices of Dryland Farming. K. G. Brengle. LC 80-70691. 190p. reprint ed. pap. 58.90 (0-8357-5507-X, 203512200093) Bks Demand.

Principles & Practices of Electron Microscopy. 2nd ed. Ian M. Watt. LC 95-37567. (Illus.). 472p. (C). 1997. text 135.00 (0-521-43456-4); pap. text 47.95 (0-521-43591-9) Cambridge U Pr.

Principles & Practices of Grading, Drainage & Road Alignment: An Ecological Approach. Richard Untermann. (Illus.). 1978. text 63.80 (0-87909-641-1) P-H.

Principles & Practices of Heavy Construction. 3rd ed. (C). 1999. write for info. (0-13-701947-5, Macmillan Coll) P-H.

Principles & Practices of Heavy Construction. 4th ed. Ronald C. Smith & Cameron K. Andres. 464p. 1993. text 86.67 (0-13-717646-5, Pub. by P-H) S&S Trade.

***Principles & Practices of Heavy Construction.** 4th ed. Ronald C. Smith & Cameron K. Andres. 2000. pap. text 66.67 (0-13-029181-1, Prentice Hall) P-H.

Principles & Practices of Isokinetics in Sports Medicine & Rehabilitation. Kai-Ming Chan et al. (Illus.). 232p. 1996. write for info. (962-356-016-8) Lppncott W & W.

Principles & Practices of Isokinetics in Sports Medicine & Rehabilitation. Kai-Ming Chan et al. (CHI., Illus.). 500p. 1997. write for info. (962-356-027-3) Lppncott W & W.

Principles & Practices of Organizational Performance Excellence. 2nd ed. Thomas J. Cartin. LC 98-42726. 250p. 1997. 33.00 (0-87389-428-6, H0995) ASQ Qual Pr.

Principles & Practices of Performance Assessment. Michael B. Kane et al. LC 97-45967. 350p. 1998. write for info. (0-8058-2970-9); pap. write for info. (0-8058-2971-7) L Erlbaum Assocs.

Principles & Practices of Plant Science. Peter D. Walton. (Illus.). 448p. 1988. text 34.00 (0-8359-5788-8) P-H.

Principles & Practices of Psychology Nursing I. Laraia. (C). text. write for info. (981-4033-14-6) Harcourt Coll Pubs.

Principles & Practices of Range Management. R. B. Lal. (C). 1989. text 125.00 (0-89771-578-0, Pub. by Intl Bk Distr) St Mut.

Principles & Practices of Range Management. R. B. Lal. 120p. 1990. pap. 175.00 (81-7089-129-9, Pub. by Intl Bk Distr) St Mut.

Principles & Practices of Real Estate Mathematics: Self-Teaching with Step by Step Examples. John R. Jonisch. (Illus.). 1977. pap. text 11.95 (0-914256-06-8) Real Estate Pub.

Principles & Practices of Rehabilitation. Henry H. Kessler. Ed. by William R. Phillips & Janet Rosenberg. LC 79-6909. (Physically Handicapped in Society Ser.). (Illus.). 1980. reprint ed. lib. bdg. 44.95 (0-405-13119-4) Ayer.

Principles & Practices of Residential Construction. Joseph D. Falcone. (Illus.). 448p. 1987. text 49.00 (0-13-702002-3) P-H.

Principles & Practices of Rice Production. Surajit K. De Datta. LC 86-21370. 640p. 1987. reprint ed. lib. bdg. 72.50 (0-89874-994-8) Krieger.

Principles & Practices of Secondary Education. 2nd ed. Vernon E. Anderson & William T. Gruhn. LC 62-11648. 523p. reprint ed. 162.20 (0-8357-9958-1, 201246300081) Bks Demand.

Principles & Practices of Ship Stability: Including Supplement-Guide Lines to the Safe Handling of Roll on-Roll off Vessels. Ed. by L. G. Taylor. (C). 1987. 120.00 (0-85174-488-5); suppl. ed. 30.00 (0-7855-6053-X) St Mut.

Principles & Practices of Sleep Medicine. 3rd ed. Meir H. Kryger et al. LC 99-31929. 1225p. 1999. text. write for info. (0-7216-7670-7, W B Saunders Co) Harcrt Hlth Sci Grp.

Principles & Practices of Solvent Extraction. Ed. by Jan Rydberg & Claude Musikas. (Illus.). 576p. 1992. text 225.00 (0-8247-8668-8) Dekker.

Principles & Practices of Stress Management. 2nd ed. Ed. by Paul M. Lehrer & Robert L. Woolfolk. LC 92-49253. 621p. 1993. pap. text 39.95 (0-89862-162-3) Guilford Pubns.

Principles & Practices of Student Health, 3 vols. Ed. by Helen M. Wallace et al. Incl. Vol. 1: Foundations. (Illus.). 228p. (Orig.). 1992. pap. text 19.95 (0-89914-035-1); Vol. 2: School Health. (Illus.). 320p. (Orig.). 1992. pap. text 19.95 (0-89914-036-X); Vol. 3: College Health. (Illus.). 452p. (Orig.). 1992. pap. text 19.95 (0-89914-037-8); 39.95 (0-89914-034-3) Third Party Pub.

Principles & Practices of Surgery. 3rd ed. Forrest. 1995. text 55.00 (0-443-04860-6, W B Saunders Co) Harcrt Hlth Sci Grp.

Principles & Practices of Teaching Reading. 9th ed. Arthur W. Heilman et al. LC 97-606. 589p. 1997. 72.00 (0-13-267857-8, Merrill Coll) P-H.

Principles & Practices of the College-Based Radiography Program. Gary Lauer. Ed. by Alvin F. Gardner. (Allied Health Professions Monograph). 294p. (C). 1984. 37.50 (0-87527-310-6) Green.

Principles & Practices of the Restored Gospel. Victor L. Ludlow. LC 92-29955. ix, 656p. 1992. 21.95 (0-87579-649-4) Deseret Bk.

Principles & Practices of TQM. Thomas J. Cartin. 241p. (Orig.). 1993. pap. 28.00 (0-87389-153-8, H0691) ASQ Qual Pr.

Principles & Practices of Winemaking. Vernon L. Singleton & Roger B. Boulton. 604p. 1996. 155.00 (0-8342-1270-6) Aspen Pub.

Principles & Pratice of Surveying see Principles & Practice of Surveying

Principles & Prediction: The Analysis of Natural Language. Papers in Honor of Gerald Sanders. Ed. by Mushira Eid & Gregory K. Iverson. LC 93-6529. (Current Issues in Linguistic Theory Ser.: No. 98). xix, 382p. 1993. 85.00 (1-55619-550-8) J Benjamins Pubng Co.

Principles & Prevention of Corrosion. 2nd ed. Denny A. Jones. LC 95-21163. 572p. 1995. 105.00 (0-13-359993-0) P-H.

Principles & Privilege: Two Women's Lives on a Georgia Plantation. Frances A. Kemble & Frances A. Leigh. 648p. (C). 1995. text 44.50 (0-472-09522-6, 09522, Ann Arbor Bks); pap. text 19.95 (0-472-06522-X, 06522, Ann Arbor Bks) U of Mich Pr.

Principles & Problems of Electrical Machines. Douglas Griffiths. LC 94-4676. (C). 1994. pap. text 74.00 (0-13-249798-0) P-H Intl.

Principles & Procedures for General Chemistry Laboratory. Louis Trudell. 1994. spiral bd. 28.65 (0-88252-169-1) Paladin Hse.

Principles & Procedures in Anesthesiology. Ed. by Philip L. Liu. LC 91-42092. (Illus.). 446p. 1992. reprint ed. pap. 138.30 (0-608-07263-X, 206749100009) Bks Demand.

Principles & Procedures of Plant Protection. 3rd rev. ed. S. B. Chattopadhyay. (C). 1991. 18.00 (81-204-0013-5, Pub. by Oxford IBH) S Asia.

Principles & Procedures of Statistics: A Biometrical Approach. 3rd ed. Robert G. Steel et al. LC 96-6766. (McGraw-Hill Series in Probability & Statistics). (Illus.). 672p. (C). 1996. 82.19 (0-07-061028-2) McGraw.

Principles & Processes for Evaluating Endocrine Disruption in Wildlife. Ed. by Ronald J. Kendall et al. LC 97-31743. (Illus.). 491p. 1998. 98.00 (1-880611-17-1, SETAC Pr) SETAC.

Principles & Proofs: Aristotle's Theory of Demonstrative Science. Richard D. McKirahan, Jr. 356p. 1992. text 52.50 (0-691-07363-5, Pub. by Princeton U Pr) Cal Prin Full Svc.

Principles & Purposes of Vedanta. 8th ed. Swami Paramananda. 1937. pap. 1.95 (0-911564-30-6) Vedanta Ctr.

Principles & Recommendations for Early Childhood Assessments. Ed. by Ken Nelson. (Illus.). 40p. 1998. pap. text 15.00 (0-7881-7361-8) DIANE Pub.

***Principles & Standards for School Mathematics.** National Council of Teachers of Mathematics Staff. LC 00-32109. 2000. write for info. (0-87353-480-8) NCTM.

Principles & Success Strategies for Everyday Living. Ralph H. Palmen. (Orig.). 1986. pap. 6.95 (0-9617213-0-8) Palmen Inst.

Principles & Techniques for an Integrated Chemistry Laboratory. rev. ed. David A. Aikens et al. (Illus.). 420p. (C). 1984. reprint ed. pap. text 28.95 (0-88133-102-3) Waveland Pr.

Principles & Techniques for the Beauty Specialists. 3rd ed. Ann Gallant et al. (Illus.). 328p. 1993. 39.50 (0-7487-1550-9, Pub. by S Thornes Pubs) Trans-Atl Phila.

Principles & Techniques in Combinatorics. C. C. Chen & K. M. Koh. 312p. 1992. text 44.00 (981-02-1114-7); pap. text 21.00 (981-02-1139-2) World Scientific Pub.

Principles & Techniques of Applied Mathematics. Bernard Friedman. ix, 315p. 1990. pap. 9.95 (0-486-66444-9) Dover.

Principles & Techniques of Appraisal Review. 3rd ed. Robert Whelan et al. LC 86-51460. 457p. 1989. reprint ed. text 29.50 (0-685-47318-X, 302) Todd Pub.

Principles & Techniques of Cutaneous Surgery. Ed. by Gary P. Lask & Ronald L. Moy. 637p. 1995. text 179.00 (0-07-036471-0) McGraw-Hill HPD.

Principles & Techniques of Electromagnetic Compatibility. Christos Christopoulos. LC 94-26751. (Electronic Mail Ser.), 336p. 1995. boxed set 119.95 (0-8493-7892-3) CRC Pr.

Principles & Techniques of Electron Microscopy. 3rd ed. M. A. Hayat. 1989. 71.00 (0-8493-7111-2) CRC Pr.

Principles & Techniques of Electron Microscopy: Biological Applications. 4th ed. M. A. Hayat. LC 99-35134. (Illus.). 700p. (C). 2000. 100.00 (0-521-63287-0) Cambridge U Pr.

Principles & Techniques of Horse Training & Management. S. P. Webb et al. 94p. (C). 1986. pap. text 12.95 (0-89641-162-1) American Pr.

Principles & Techniques of Nerve Regeneration: Alzheimer's Disease & the Dementias: Based on the Readings of Edgar Cayce. David McMillin. LC 97-4120. (Edgar Cayce Health Ser.). 164p. 1997. pap. 14.95 (0-87604-381-3, 496) ARE Pr.

Principles & Techniques of Patient Care. 2nd ed. Frank M. Pierson. Ed. by Shirley Kuhn. LC 98-5492. (Illus.). 384p. (C). 1998. pap. text 39.95 (0-7216-7524-7, W B Saunders Co) Harcrt Hlth Sci Grp.

Principles & Techniques of Practical Biochemistry. 4th ed. Ed. by Keith M. Wilson & John M. Walker. LC 93-6823. (Illus.). 616p. (C). 1994. text 100.00 (0-521-41769-4); pap. text 38.95 (0-521-42809-2) Cambridge U Pr.

Principles & Techniques of Practical Biochemistry. 5th ed. Ed. by Keith Wilson & John M. Walker. (Illus.). 512p. (C). 2000. 110.00 (0-521-65104-2); pap. 39.95 (0-521-65873-X) Cambridge U Pr.

Principles & Techniques of Spine Surgery. Howard S. An. LC 97-5525. (Illus.). 1452p. 1997. 150.00 (0-683-30260-4) Lppncott W & W.

Principles & Techniques of Vibrations. Leonard Meirovitch. 694p. (C). 1996. 105.00 (0-02-380141-7, Macmillan Coll) P-H.

Principles & Treatment of Lipoprotein Disorders. Ed. by F. Gotthard Schettler & Andreas J. Habenicht. LC 93-6449. (Handbook of Experimental Pharmacology Ser.: Vol. 109). 1994. 449.95 (0-387-57121-3) Spr-Verlag.

Principles & Trends in Business Education. Louis C. Nanassy et al. LC 76-57995. 1977. text. write for info. (0-672-97092-9) Macmillan.

Principles & Types of Speech. 14th ed. Gronbeck. 464p. (C). 1999. pap. text Price not set. (0-321-05557-8) Addson-Wesley Educ.

***Principles & Types of Speech Communication.** 14th ed. 224p. (C). 1999. text 26.00 (0-321-06324-4) Addison-Wesley.

***Principles & Types of Speech Communication.** 14th ed. 344p. (C). 1999. text. write for info. (0-321-06325-2); text 67.00 (0-321-07526-9) Addison-Wesley.

***Principles & Types of Speech Communication.** 14th ed. (C). 1999. write for info. (0-321-07542-0); text 34.00 (0-321-07527-7); cd-rom 67.00 (0-321-06326-0); cd-rom 71.00 (0-321-07524-2) Addison-Wesley.

***Principles & Types of Speech Communication.** 14th ed. (C). 2000. write for info. (0-321-06330-9); text. write for info. (0-321-06327-9) Addson-Wesley Educ.

Principles & Types of Speech Communication. 14th ed. Bruce E. Gronbeck. 434p. (C). 1999. 52.00 (0-321-04425-8) Addson-Wesley Educ.

Principles & Values in School & Society. James J. Jelinek. LC 74-156779. 1978. 15.00 (0-931702-28-3) Far Western Phil.

Principles Behavioral Neurosciences. 3rd ed. Beatty. 2000. pap. text, student ed. 14.30 (0-697-36165-9) McGraw.

Principles Economics. 6th ed. Paul Gregory & Roy J. Ruffin. LC 96-16568. (Economics Ser.). (C). 1997. 96.00 (0-673-99488-0) Addson-Wesley Educ.

Principles Education & Psychology Measurement. 4th ed. Sax. (Education Ser.). 1996. 19.00 (0-534-25750-X) Wadsworth Pub.

Principles, Elements & Types of Persuasion. James Benjamin. LC 96-76311. 352p. (C). 1996. pap. text 49.00 (0-15-502355-1) Harcourt Coll Pubs.

Principles Food Science & Technology: Integrated Approach. Torres. (Food Science & Technology Ser.). 1999. text 69.95 (0-412-15571-0) Chapman & Hall.

Principles for a Catholic Morality: Revised Edition. rev. ed. Timothy E. O'Connell. LC 89-45553. 324p. 1990. pap. 18.00 (0-06-254865-4) HarpC.

Principles for a Free Society: Reconciling Individual Liberty with the Common Good. Richard A. Epstein. LC 98-86404. 384p. 1998. text 30.00 (0-7382-0041-7) Perseus Pubng.

***Principles for Care of Patients at the End of Life: An Emerging Consensus among the Specialities of Medicine.** Christine K. Cassel & Kathleen M. Foley. 32p. 1999. pap. write for info. (1-887748-34-2) Milbank Memorial.

***Principles for Determining the Air Force Active/Reserve Mix.** Albert A. Robbert et al. LC 99-42520. (Illus.). 1999. pap. 15.00 (0-8330-2762-X, MR-1091-AF) Rand Corp.

Principles for Educational Reform in the United States. United States Catholic Conference Staff. 12p. (Orig.). 1995. pap. 0.75 (1-57455-071-3) US Catholic.

Principles for Electric Power Policy. Technology Futures, Inc. Staff et al. LC 84-4692. (Illus.). 448p. 1984. 75.00 (0-89930-095-2, FRK/, Quorum Bks) Greenwood.

Principles for Evaluating Chemical Effects on the Aged Population. (Environmental Health Criteria Ser.: No. 144). (ENG, FRE & SPA.). 159p. 1993. pap. text 30.00 (92-4-157144-6, 1160144) World Health.

Principles for Evaluating Epidemiologic Data in Regulatory Risk Assessment. Ed. by William Kelly. LC 96-88998. 115p. (Orig.). 1996. pap. write for info. (0-9654148-0-9) Fed Focus.

Principles for Evaluating Health Risks from Chemicals During Infancy & Early Childhood: The Need for a Special Approach. (Environmental Health Criteria Ser.: No. 59). 73p. 1986. pap. text 15.00 (92-4-154259-4, 1160059) World Health.

Principles for Evaluating Health Risks to Progeny Associated with Exposure to Chemicals During Pregnancy. (Environmental Health Criteria Ser.: No. 30). 177p. 1984. pap. text 26.00 (92-4-154090-7, 1160030) World Health.

Principles for Federal Managers of Community-Bases Program. 96p. 1997. pap. write for info. (1-57744-051-X) Nat Acad Public Admin.

Principles for Health Care Reform. Debra L. Miller. (CSIS Panel Reports). 34p. (Orig.). (C). 1994. pap. 10.95 (0-89206-269-X) CSIS.

Principles for Interactive Multimedia. Williams. (C). 2000. 44.00 (0-205-27134-0) Allyn.

Principles for Intervention for Protection of the Public in a Radiological Emergency. ICRP Staff. (International Commission on Radiological Protection Ser.: Vol. 63). 40p. 1993. 65.00 (0-08-042204-7, Pergamon Pr) Elsevier.

Principles for Living on the Edge. Douglas R. Pittman. ix, 131p. 1997. 25.00 (1-890225-00-2) Quantum Hse Pubg.

Principles for Living on the Edge. Douglas R. Pittman. LC 97-65265. ix, 146p. 1997. pap. 14.95 (1-890225-02-9) Quantum Hse Pubg.

Principles for Management Health Care Professionals. Toot. 1998. text. write for info. (0-7216-3259-9, W B Saunders Co) Harcrt Hlth Sci Grp.

***Principles for Maternal & Child Health Services (in Minnesota)** Ed. by Mary J. O'Brien. 92p. (C). 2000. reprint ed. pap. text 25.00 (0-7881-8715-5) DIANE Pub.

Principles for Nurse Staffing with Annotated Bibliography. American Nurses Association Staff. LC 99-19077. 56p. 1999. pap. 19.95 (1-55810-144-6, 9902AB) Am Nurses Pub.

Principles for Oral Narrative Research. Axel Olrik. Tr. by Kirsten Wolf & Jody Jensen. LC 88-46034. (Folklore Studies in Translation). 240p. 1992. text 31.95 (0-253-34175-2) Ind U Pr.

Principles for Pre-Clinical Testing of Drug Safety: Report of a WHO Scientific Group, 1966. (Technical Report Ser.: 22p. 1966. pap. 3.00 (92-4-120341-2, 1100341) World Health.

P

An Asterisk (*) at the beginning of an entry indicates that the title is appearing for the first time.

Principles for the Safety Assessment of Food Additives & Contaminants in Food. (Environmental Health Criteria Ser.: No. 70). (RUS.). 174p. 1987. pap. text 23.00 (*92-4-154270-5*, 1160070) World Health.

Principles for the Selection of Doses in Chronic Rodent Bioassays. Ed. by Jeffery A. Foran. 200p. 1997. pap. write for info. (*0-944398-71-5*, 398715) ILSI.

Principles for the Testing & Evaluation of Drugs for Carcinogenicity: Proceedings of the WHO Scientific Group, Geneva, 1968. WHO Staff. (Technical Reports: No. 426). 1969. pap. text 3.00 (*92-4-120426-5*, 1100426) World Health.

Principles for the Testing of Drugs for Teratogenicity: Report of a WHO Scientific Group, 1967. (Technical Report Ser.: No. 350). 18p. 1967. pap. text 3.00 (*92-4-120364-1*, 1100364) World Health.

Principles for the Toxicological Assessment of Pesticide Residues in Food. (Environmental Health Criteria Ser.: No. 104). (CHI, ENG & RUS.). 117p. 1990. pap. text 24.00 (*92-4-157104-7*, 1160104) World Health.

***Principles Genetics.** (C). 1998. 61.00 (*0-8053-4490-X*) Addison-Wesley.

Principles Genetics. Robert J. Brooker. LC 98-34247. 761p. (C). 1998. 92.00 (*0-8053-9175-4*) Benjamin-Cummings.

Principles, Guidelines & Guarantees for the Protection of Persons Detained on Grounds of Mental Ill-Health or Suffering from Mental Disorder. 38p. 1986. mass mkt. 7.00 (*92-1-154056-9*, E.85.XIV.9) UN.

Principles Human Resource Management. Goss. 1993. pap. write for info. (*1-86152-388-2*, Pub. by ITBP) Thomson Learn.

Principles in Chemistry, 3 vols. Zumdahl. (C). Date not set. pap. 11.96 (*0-395-83563-1*) HM.

Principles in General Pharmacology. Ronald J. Tallarida et al. (Pharmacologic Science Ser.). (Illus.). 250p. 1988. 103.00 (*0-387-96602-1*) Spr-Verlag.

***Principles in Practicing Ophthalmology, Vol. 6.** 2nd ed. Albert. LC 99-29496. (C). 1999. text 950.00 (*0-7216-7500-X*, W B Saunders Co) Harcrt Hlth Sci Grp.

Principles in Weed Management. 2nd ed. R. J. Aldrich & R. J. Kremer. LC 96-28049. (Illus.). 1997. 64.95 (*0-8138-2023-5*) Iowa St U Pr.

Principles into Practice in Early Childhood Education. Geva Blenkin. LC 97-221357. 1997. pap. text 26.95 (*1-85396-306-2*, Pub. by P Chapman) P H Brookes.

Principles Macroeconomics. Gordon Staff. (C). pap. text, teacher ed. 23.75 (*0-03-002579-6*); pap. text, student ed. 11.50 (*0-03-002582-6*) Harcourt Coll Pubs.

Principles Macroeconomics. 6th ed. Roy J. Ruffin & Paul R. Gregory. LC 96-17800. (C). 1997. pap. text 70.00 (*0-673-99491-0*) Addson-Wesley Educ.

***Principles Managerial Finance.** 9th ed. 672p. (C). 1999. pap. text 25.20 (*0-321-05068-1*, Celebration) Addson-Wesley Educ.

Principles Marketing. (C). Date not set. pap. text 0.00 (*0-321-01418-9*) HEPC Inc.

Principles Marketing. Randall. 1993. pap. write for info. (*1-86152-344-0*, Pub. by ITBP) Thomson Learn.

Principles, Mechanisms & Biological Consequences of Induction. Ed. by Klaus Ruckpaul & Horst Rein. (Frontiers in Biotransformation Ser.: Vol. 2). 352p. 1991. 90.00 (*0-85066-799-2*, Pub. by Tay Francis Ltd) Taylor & Francis.

Principles Microeconomics. Gordon Staff. (C). Date not set. pap. text, student ed. 11.50 (*0-03-002437-4*) Harcourt Coll Pubs.

Principles Microeconomics. 6th ed. Roy J. Ruffin & Paul R. Gregory. LC 96-15001. (C). 1997. pap. text 70.00 (*0-673-99493-7*) Addson-Wesley Educ.

Principles Modern Chemistry. 2nd ed. Oxtoby. (C). 1991. pap. text, teacher ed. 28.00 (*0-03-053502-6*) Harcourt Coll Pubs.

***Principles Money Banking Financial Markets.** 10th ed. (C). 2000. pap. text 67.00 (*0-321-06474-7*, Celebration) Addson-Wesley Educ.

Principles of a New International Economic Order: A Study of International Law in the Making. Jerzy Makarczyk. (C). 1988. lib. bdg. 150.50 (*90-247-3746-X*) Kluwer Academic.

Principles of a Sound State School Finance System. Education Partners Project of the Foundation for S. LC 97-170650. 24p. 1996. pap. 20.00 (*1-55516-598-2*, 3132) Natl Conf State Legis.

Principles of Abilities & Human Learning. Michael J. Howe. (Principles of Psychology Ser.). 1998. pap. 17.95 (*0-86377-533-0*, Pub. by Psychol Pr) Taylor & Francis.

Principles of Abilities & Human Learning. Michael J.A. Howe. (Principles of Psychology Ser.). 1998. 37.50 (*0-86377-532-2*, Pub. by Psychol Pr) Taylor & Francis.

Principles of Abrasive Processing. Milton C. Shaw. (Advanced Manufacturing Ser.: No. 13). (Illus.). 592p. 1996. text 180.00 (*0-19-859021-0*) OUP.

Principles of Abrasive Water Jet Machining. A. W. Momber & R. Kovacevic. LC 98-4667. (Illus.). xxvi, 398p. 1998. 99.00 (*3-540-76239-6*) Spr-Verlag.

Principles of Acarology. G. O. Evans. (Illus.). 584p. 1992. text 160.00 (*0-85198-822-9*) OUP.

Principles of Accounting. 1990. write for info. (*0-318-66710-X*) HM.

Principles of Accounting. (C). 1987. 18.66 (*0-13-708645-8*, Macmillan Coll); 18.66 (*0-13-708652-0*, Macmillan Coll) P-H.

Principles of Accounting. Ed. by John Cerepak. (C). 1999. write for info. (*0-13-709239-3*, Macmillan Coll) P-H.

Principles of Accounting. John G. Helmkamp. 483p. 1983. pap. text 596.50 (*0-471-86295-9*) Wiley.

Principles of Accounting. John G. Helmkamp et al. LC 82-20124. 1150p. (C). 1984. pap. text 20.50 (*0-471-87859-6*) Wiley.

Principles of Accounting. John G. Helmkamp et al. 1986. 98.50 (*0-471-00902-4*) Wiley.

Principles of Accounting. Herzlinger. (AB - Accounting Principles Ser.). 1998. pap., student ed. 17.95 (*0-538-81906-5*); pap., student ed. 15.95 (*0-538-81907-3*) S-W Pub.

Principles of Accounting, 001. Belverd E. Needles, Jr. et al. LC 80-80503. (Illus.). 1008p. (C). 1980. text 27.95 (*0-395-29527-0*) HM.

Principles of Accounting. William A. Paton & Russell A. Stevenson. Ed. by Richard P. Brief. LC 77-87284. (Contemporary Accounting Thought Ser.). 1978. reprint ed. lib. bdg. 59.95 (*0-405-10912-1*) Ayer.

Principles of Accounting. William A. Paton & Russell A. Stevenson. LC 75-18479. (History of Accounting Ser.). 1978. reprint ed. 18.95 (*0-405-07561-8*) Ayer.

***Principles of Accounting.** 2nd ed. Chasteen. 1999. pap. text 7.78 (*0-07-010954-0*); pap. text, wbk. ed. 7.78 (*0-07-010955-9*) McGraw.

Principles of Accounting. 2nd ed. John G. Helmkamp et al. LC 85-26357. 1264p. 1986. text 50.95 (*0-471-82018-0*); pap. text 17.50 (*0-471-83462-9*) Wiley.

Principles of Accounting. 2nd ed. John G. Helmkamp et al. 190p. 1986. pap. text 17.95 (*0-471-83463-7*) Wiley.

Principles of Accounting. 2nd ed. John G. Helmkamp et al. 542p. 1986. pap. text 20.50 (*0-471-84014-9*) Wiley.

Principles of Accounting. 2nd ed. John G. Helmkamp et al. 460p. 1986. pap. text 20.50 (*0-471-84016-5*) Wiley.

Principles of Accounting. 2nd ed. John G. Helmkamp et al. 72p. 1986. pap. text 17.50 (*0-471-84805-0*) Wiley.

Principles of Accounting. 2nd ed. John G. Helmkamp et al. 200p. 1986. pap. text 18.95 (*0-471-84806-9*) Wiley.

Principles of Accounting. 2nd ed. Morgenstein. (C). 1997. pap. text 50.00 (*0-15-504508-3*) Harcourt Coll Pubs.

Principles of Accounting. 2nd ed. Rufus Wixon & Robert G. Cox. LC 69-14676. 839p. reprint ed. pap. 200.00 (*0-8357-9959-X*, 205514100008) Bks Demand.

Principles of Accounting. 3rd ed. John G. Helmkamp et al. 2010p. 1989. text 54.00 (*0-471-51760-7*) Wiley.

Principles of Accounting, 3 vols. 3rd ed. Belverd E. Needles, Jr. et al. 1058p. (C). 1987. pap. 15.16 (*0-395-43144-1*); text 47.16 (*0-685-18701-2*); 17.56 (*0-685-18702-0*) HM.

Principles of Accounting, 4 vols. 4th ed. (C). 1990. pap. text 9.56 (*0-395-52959-X*); pap. text 9.56 (*0-395-52966-2*); 9.56 (*0-395-52873-9*) HM.

Principles of Accounting, 4 vols. 4th ed. (C). 1990. 19.96 (*0-395-53508-5*) HM.

Principles of Accounting, 4 vols. 4th ed. (C). 1990. pap. text 9.56 (*0-395-52967-0*) HM.

Principles of Accounting, 4 vols. 4th ed. Belverd E. Needles, Jr. et al. (C). 1990. pap. 5.96 (*0-395-53274-4*); text 32.06 (*0-395-43350-9*) HM.

Principles of Accounting, 4 vols. 4th ed. Belverd E. Needles, Jr. et al. (C). 1990. pap. text 3.96 (*0-395-52758-9*) HM.

Principles of Accounting, 4 vols. 4th ed. Belverd E. Needles, Jr. et al. (C). 1990. pap. 21.96 (*0-395-52961-1*) HM.

Principles of Accounting, 4 vols. 4th ed. Belverd E. Needles, Jr. et al. (C). 1990. pap. 21.96 (*0-395-52963-8*) HM.

Principles of Accounting, 4 vols. 4th ed. Belverd E. Needles, Jr. et al. (C). 1990. pap. 21.96 (*0-395-52962-X*); pap., student ed. 19.16 (*0-395-52960-3*); text 58.36 (*0-395-53506-9*) HM.

Principles of Accounting, 4 vols. 4th ed. Belverd E. Needles, Jr. et al. (C). 1990. text 58.36 (*0-395-53507-7*) HM.

Principles of Accounting. 5th ed. A. Douglas Hillman & Richard F. Kochanek. 1371p. (C). 1989. teacher ed. 5.60 (*0-15-571180-6*); write for info. (*0-318-67136-0*) Harcourt Coll Pubs.

Principles of Accounting. 5th ed. Paul H. Walgenbach et al. 1160p. (C). 1990. student ed. 16.00 (*0-15-571394-9*) Dryden Pr.

Principles of Accounting, 6 vols. 6th ed. Belverd E. Needles, Jr. et al. 1344p. (C). 1995. text 80.76 (*0-395-72219-5*) HM.

Principles of Accounting. 7th ed. Hanson. (C). 1996. text. write for info. (*0-03-009849-1*); pap. text, teacher ed. write for info. (*0-03-010277-4*); pap. text, student ed. write for info. (*0-03-009854-8*) Harcourt Coll Pubs.

Principles of Accounting 7th ed. Belverd E. Needles. LC 98-72069. 1229 p. 1999. text 69.57 (*0-395-92758-7*) HM.

Principles of Accounting, 1. 6th ed. Ernest I. Hanson et al. 814p. (C). 1993. teacher ed. 14.75 (*0-03-097433-X*) Dryden Pr.

Principles of Accounting, No. 2. 7th ed. Hanson. 1996. pap. text, student ed. write for info. (*0-03-009857-2*) Harcourt Coll Pubs.

Principles of Accounting, 2 vols., Set. 5th ed. A. Douglas Hillman & Richard F. Kochanek. 1371p. (C). 1989. teacher ed. 5.85 (*0-15-571179-2*) Harcourt Coll Pubs.

Principles of Accounting, Vol. 1. 2nd rev. ed. Terry L. Campbell. 333p. (C). 1989. pap. text 14.50 (*0-15-601651-6*) Harcourt Coll Pubs.

Principles of Accounting, 6 vols., Vol. I. 6th ed. Belverd E. Needles, Jr. et al. (C). 1995. text, teacher ed. 11.96 (*0-395-75278-7*) HM.

Principles of Accounting, 6 vols., Vol. II. 6th ed. Belverd E. Needles, Jr. et al. (C). 1995. text, teacher ed. 11.96 (*0-395-75279-5*) HM.

Principles of Accounting: Raising Issues & Providing Solutions. 7th ed. Hillman et al. 1997. 74.95 (*0-87393-525-X*) Dame Pubns.

Principles of Accounting: Raising Issues & Providing Solutions (Study Guide), Vol. 1. 7th ed. Hillman et al. 1997. pap., student ed. 23.95 (*0-87393-526-8*) Dame Pubns.

Principles of Accounting: Raising Issues & Providing Solutions (Study Guide), Vol. II. Hillman et al. 1997. pap., student ed. 23.95 (*0-87393-595-0*) Dame Pubns.

Principles of Accounting: Raising Issues & Providing Solutions (Working Papers), Vol. 1. 7th ed. Hillman et al. 1997. pap., student ed. 25.95 (*0-87393-527-6*) Dame Pubns.

Principles of Accounting: Raising Issues & Providing Solutions (Working Papers), Vol. 2. 7th ed. Hillman et al. 1997. pap., student ed. 25.95 (*0-87393-528-4*) Dame Pubns.

Principles of Accounting - Working Papers 1-2. Herzlinger. (AB - Accounting Principles Ser.). 1998. pap. 17.95 (*0-538-81905-7*) S-W Pub.

Principles of Accounting & Finance. Peter Sneyd. LC 93-44753. 256p. (C). 1994. pap. 21.95 (*0-415-07932-2*) Thomson Learn.

Principles of Accounting & General Ledger Software 3. 5 Set. 4th ed. Jerry J. Weygandt et al. 1280p. 1995. pap. text 125.90 (*0-471-15414-8*) Wiley.

***Principles of Accounting 1 - Faculty Guide.** 230p. (C). 2000. pap. write for info. (*1-58313-118-3*) Univ Access.

***Principles of Accounting I - Student Guide.** 210p. (C). 2000. pap., student ed. write for info. (*1-58313-117-5*) Univ Access.

Principles of Accounting II. Mary A. Emery. (College Outline Ser.). 277p. (C). 1987. pap. text 10.95 (*0-15-600029-6*) Harcourt Coll Pubs.

Principles of Active Network Synthesis & Design. Gobind Daryanani. 512p. 1976. text 106.95 (*0-471-19545-6*) Wiley.

Principles of Acupuncture. A. Hicks. 1998. pap. 11.00 (*0-7225-3409-4*) Genl Dist Srvs.

Principles of Adaptation for Film & Television. Ben Brady. LC 93-8798. 240p. (Orig.). 1994. pap. 14.95 (*0-292-70807-6*); text 30.00 (*0-292-70804-1*) U of Tex Pr.

***Principles of Adaptive Behavior.** LC 99-73324. 126p. 1999. 24.95 (*0-8187-0326-1*) Harlo Press.

Principles of Adaptive Optics. 2nd ed. Robert K. Tyson. LC 97-35786. (Illus.). 345p. 1997. text 95.00 (*0-12-705902-4*) Morgan Kaufmann.

Principles of Addiction Medicine. 2nd ed. Ed. by Allan W. Graham & Terry K. Schultz. (Illus.). 1338p. 1998. 155.00 (*1-880425-04-1*) Am Soc Addict Med.

Principles of Addiction Medicine: ASAM Review Course Syllabus. Ed. by Norman Miller et al. 1000p. 1994. 140.00 (*1-880425-02-5*) Am Soc Addict Med.

Principles of Administration Applied to Nursing Service. H. A. Goddard. (Monographs: No. 41). 1958. pap. text 12.00 (*92-4-140041-2*, 1140041) World Health.

Principles of Administrative Law. David Stott & Alexandra Felix. 380p. 1997. pap. 34.50 (*1-85941-370-6*, Pub. by Cavendish Pubng) Gaunt.

Principles of Administrative Law in Sri Lanka. Sunil F. Coorey. LC 99-933001. lxvi, 750p. 1998. pap. 125.00 (*955-96262-0-5*, Pub. by Simmonds & Hill Pubng) Gaunt.

Principles of Administrative Procedure in EC Law. Jans Peter Nehl. LC 98-198357. 220p. 1998. 45.00 (*1-84113-008-7*, Pub. by Hart Pub) Intl Spec Bk.

Principles of Adsorption & Adsorption Processes. Douglas M. Ruthven. LC 83-16904. 464p. 1984. 175.00 (*0-471-86606-7*) Wiley.

Principles of Adsportion Chromatography: The Separation of Nonionic Organic Compounds. Lloyd R. Snyder. LC 68-17426. (Chromatographic Science Ser.: Vol. 3). (Illus.). 429p. reprint ed. pap. 133.00 (*0-608-30574-X*, 201785800009) Bks Demand.

Principles of Advanced Mathematical Physics, Vol. 1. R. D. Richtmyer. (Texts & Monographs in Physics). (Illus.). 1985. 75.95 (*0-387-08873-3*) Spr-Verlag.

Principles of Advanced Mathematical Physics, Vol. II. R. D. Richtmyer. (Texts & Monographs in Physics). (Illus.). 350p. 1986. 79.95 (*0-387-10772-X*) Spr-Verlag.

Principles of Advertising: A Global Perspective. Monle Lee & Carla Johnson. LC 99-15065. (Illus.). 355p. 1999. lib. bdg. 69.95 (*0-7890-0615-4*) Haworth Pr.

Principles of Aeration in Aquaculture. B. J. Watten et al. (Developments in Aquaculture & Fisheries Science Ser.). Date not set. write for info. (*0-444-88742-3*) Elsevier.

Principles of Aeroelasticity. 2nd ed. Raymond L. Bisplinghoff & Holt Ashley. LC 74-20442. (Illus.). 527p. (C). 1975. reprint ed. 12.95 (*0-486-61349-6*) Dover.

Principles of Agribusiness Management. 2nd rev. ed. James G. Beierlein et al. (Illus.). 328p. (C). 1995. text 36.95 (*0-88133-844-3*) Waveland Pr.

Principles of Agricultural Economics: Markets & Prices in Less Developed Countries. David Caman & Trevor Young. (Wye Studies in Agricultural & Rural Development). (Illus.). 336p. 1989. pap. text 33.95 (*0-521-33664-3*) Cambridge U Pr.

Principles of Agricultural Research Management. David R. MacKenzie. LC 95-45495. 342p. (C). 1995. pap. text 42.00 (*0-7618-0198-7*); lib. bdg. 59.00 (*0-7618-0197-9*) U Pr of Amer.

Principles of Aikido: The Only Introduction You'll Ever Need. Paul Wildish. (Illus.). 160p. 1999. pap. 11.00 (*0-7225-3588-0*) Thorsons PA.

Principles of Air Conditioning. 4th ed. V. Paul Lang. LC 86-32988. 384p. (C). 1987. pap. 46.95 (*0-8273-2759-5*) Delmar.

Principles of Air Conditioning. 4th ed. V. Paul Lang. LC 86-32988. 384p. (C). 1987. teacher ed. 14.95 (*0-8273-2760-9*) Delmar.

Principles of Air Conditioning. 5th ed. Lang. 28p. 1995. teacher ed. 13.95 (*0-8273-6592-6*) Delmar.

Principles of Air Conditioning. 5th ed. V. Paul Lang. LC 94-44734. 1995. mass mkt. 79.95 (*0-8273-6591-8*) Delmar.

Principles of Air Pollution Meteorology. T. J. Lyons & W. D. Scott. 1990. 49.95 (*0-8493-7106-6*, QC) CRC Pr.

Principles of Air Quality Management. Roger D. Griffin. 400p. 1994. lib. bdg. 75.00 (*0-87371-315-X*, L315) Lewis Pubs.

Principles of Airway Management. 2nd ed. Brendan T. Finucane & Albert H. Santora. LC 95-32783. (Illus.). 368p. (C). (gr. 13). 1995. pap. text 39.95 (*0-8151-3337-5*, 24020) Mosby Inc.

Principles of Algebraic Geometry. Phillip Griffiths & Joseph Harris. LC 78-6993. (Pure & Applied Mathematics: A Wiley-Interscience Series of Texts, Monographs & Tracts). 832p. 1978. 235.00 (*0-471-32792-1*, Wiley-Interscience) Wiley.

Principles of Algebraic Geometry. Phillip Griffiths & Joseph Harris. (Classics Library). 832p. 1994. pap. 72.50 (*0-471-05059-8*) Wiley.

Principles of Ambulatory Medicine see Handbook of Ambulatory Medicine

Principles of Ambulatory Medicine. 3rd ed. L. Randol Barker et al. 1487p. 1990. 109.00 (*0-683-00437-9*) Lppncott W & W.

Principles of Ambulatory Medicine. 4th ed. Ed. by L. Randol Barker et al. LC 93-46869. (Illus.). 1584p. 1995. 115.00 (*0-683-00438-7*) Lppncott W & W.

Principles of Ambulatory Medicine. 5th ed. L. Randol Barker et al. LC 97-40570. 1600p. 1998. 109.00 (*0-683-30352-X*) Lppncott W & W.

Principles of American Government: A PSI Handbook. Theodore T. Hindson et al. 111p. 1978. pap. text 9.95 (*0-89641-006-4*) American Pr.

Principles of American Journalism: Introduction. Don Ranly. 322p. (C). 1990. 58.00 (*0-536-57827-3*) Pearson Custom.

Principles of American Prosperity. Leighton A. Wilkie & Richard S. Rimanoczy. LC 75-5394. 256p. 1975. 10.00 (*0-8159-6512-5*) Devin.

Principles of Amino Acid Nutrition for Ruminants. Ed. by John Malcolm Asplund. 224p. 1994. lib. bdg. 169.00 (*0-8493-4910-9*, SF98) CRC Pr.

***Principles of Analytical Chemistry: A Textbook.** Miguel Valcarcel Cases. LC 00-33829. 2000. write for info. (*3-540-64007-X*) Spr-Verlag.

Principles of Analytical Electron Microscopy. D. C. Joy et al. (Illus.). 464p. (C). 1986. text 65.00 (*0-306-42387-1*, Kluwer Plenum) Kluwer Academic.

Principles of Analytical System Dynamics. Richard A. Layton. LC 97-45237. (Mechanical Engineering Ser.). (Illus.). 158p. 1998. text 49.00 (*0-387-98405-4*) Spr-Verlag.

***Principles of Anatomy & Physiology.** Gerald J. Tortora. 1200p. 1999. text 108.95 (*0-471-36692-7*, Wiley-Liss) Wiley.

Principles of Anatomy & Physiology. 7th ed. Tortora. (C). 1995. 65.50 (*0-06-046702-9*) HarpC.

Principles of Anatomy & Physiology. 7th ed. Gerard J. Tortora & Sandra R. Grabowski. LC 92-18562. (C). 1993. pap. 91.88 (*0-06-501714-5*) Addson-Wesley Educ.

Principles of Anatomy & Physiology. 8th ed. Langley. Date not set. pap., teacher ed. write for info. (*0-673-55777-4*) Addson-Wesley Educ.

Principles of Anatomy & Physiology. 8th ed. Kathleen S. Prezbindowski & Gerald J. Tortora. LC 95-40981. 1152p. (C). 1996. pap. text, student ed., suppl. ed. 25.31 (*0-673-99356-6*) Addson-Wesley Educ.

Principles of Anatomy & Physiology. 8th ed. Gerard J. Tortora. 1996. 106.95 (*0-471-37280-3*) Wiley.

Principles of Anatomy & Physiology. 8th ed. Gerard J. Tortora. (C). 1996. 88.13 (*0-321-40297-9*) Addson-Wesley Educ.

Principles of Anatomy & Physiology. 8th ed. Gerard J. Tortora & Sandra R. Garbowski. LC 92-18562. 1152p. (C). 1996. text 88.13 (*0-673-99354-X*) Addson-Wesley Educ.

Principles of Anatomy & Physiology 9th ed. Gerard J. Tortora. LC 99-31201. (C). 2000. text 88.13 (*0-321-02035-9*) Addson-Wesley Educ.

Principles of Anatomy & Physiology: Cat Lab Manual. 5th ed. George A. Wistreich & Patricia J. Donnelly. LC 95-49973. 704p. (C). 1997. pap. text, lab manual ed. 65.00 (*0-673-99939-4*) Addson-Wesley Educ.

Principles of Anatomy & Physiology: Concept Maps. 7th ed. Tortora & Grabowski. (Illus.). (C). 1992. pap. 13.50 (*0-06-501550-9*) Addson-Wesley Educ.

Principles of Anatomy & Physiology: Concept Maps. 8th ed. Smith. (C). 1996. text, suppl. ed. 41.25 (*0-673-99357-4*) Addson-Wesley Educ.

***Principles of Anatomy & Physiology: Illustrated Notebook.** 9th ed. Gerard J. Tortora & Sandra Reynolds Grabowski. 631p. 1999. pap. 17.95 (*0-471-37468-7*) Wiley.

Principles of Anatomy & Physiology: Learning Guide. 7th ed. Gerard J. Tortora & Sandra R. Grabowski. (C). 1993. pap. 28.13 (*0-06-501197-X*) Addson-Wesley Educ.

Principles of Anatomy & Physiology: Practice Test. 8th ed. Tortora. 1996. pap., student ed. 28.95 (*0-471-36590-4*) Wiley.

***Principles of Anatomy & Physiology with Atlas of Human Skeleton.** 8th ed. Gerard Tortora. 1998. 88.13 (*0-321-03733-2*) Addison-Wesley.

Principles of Anesthesiology: General & Regional Anesthesia. 3rd ed. Vincent J. Collins. LC 91-7038. (Illus.). 850p. 1992. 198.50 (*0-8121-1322-5*) Lppncott W & W.

Principles of Anesthetic Techniques & Anesthetic Emergencies. Kevin K. Tremper. LC 97-28243. (Atlas of Anesthesia Ser.). 1998. text 135.00 (*0-443-07903-X*) Church.

Principles of Angiosperm Taxonomy. P. H. Davis & V. H. Heywood. 578p. (C). 1991. reprint ed. 57.50 (*81-7019-383-4*, 203836) Krieger.

Principles of Animal Cognition. William A. Roberts. LC 97-5653. 480p. 1997. 59.38 (*0-07-053138-2*) McGraw.

Principles of Animal Communication. Jack W. Bradbury & Sandra L. Vehrencamp. LC 97-44014. (Illus.). 780p. (C). 1998. text 69.95 (*0-87893-100-7*) Sinauer Assocs.

P

Principles of Animal Design: The Optimization & Symmorphosis Debate. Ed. by Ewald F. Weibel et al. LC 97-13547. (Illus.). 314p. (C). 1998. text 85.00 (*0-521-58370-5*); pap. text 33.95 (*0-521-58667-4*) Cambridge U Pr.

Principles of Animal Extrapolation. Edward J. Calabrese. 616p. 1991. lib. bdg. 119.00 (*0-87371-410-5*, L410) Lewis Pubs.

Principles of Animal Taxonomy. George G. Simpson. LC 60-13939. (Columbia Biological Ser.: No. 20). (Illus.). 1961. text 61.50 (*0-231-02427-4*) Col U Pr.

Principles of Anthropology & Sociology in Their Relations to Criminal Procedure. Maurice Parmelee. viii, 410p. 1980. reprint ed. 45.00 (*0-8377-1004-9*, Rothman) W S Hein.

Principles of Antineoplastic Drug Development & Pharmacology. Ed. by Richard L. Schilsky et al. (Basic & Clinical Oncology Ser.: Vol. 9). (Illus.). 760p. 1996. text 195.00 (*0-8247-9314-5*) Dekker.

Principles of Antitrust Law. Stephen F. Ross. (University Textbook Ser.). 542p. 1992. text 34.95 (*1-56662-003-1*) Foundation Pr.

Principles of Applied Biomedical Instrumentation. 3rd ed. Leslie A. Geddes & L. E. Baker. LC 88-27915. 992p. 1989. 185.00 (*0-471-60899-8*) Wiley.

Principles of Applied Clinical Chemistry: Chemical Background & Medical Applications, 2 vols. Ed. by Samuel Natelson & Ethan A. Natelson. Incl. Erythrocyte Chemical Composition, Normal & Aberrant Metabolism. LC 75-4798. 584p. 1978. 79.50 (*0-306-35232-X*, Kluwer Plenum); Maintenance of Fluid & Electrolyte Balance. LC 75-4798. 394p. 1975. 55.00 (*0-306-35231-1*, Kluwer Plenum); LC 75-4798. (Illus.). write for info. (*0-318-55335-X*, Plenum Trade) Perseus Pubng.

Principles of Applied Geophysics. D. S. Parasnis. 450p. 1986. text 75.00 (*0-412-28320-4*, 9937) Chapman & Hall.

Principles of Applied Geophysics. 5th ed. D. S. Parasnis. 1997. pap. text 74.95 (*0-412-64080-5*) Chapman & Hall.

***Principles of Applied Mathematics: Transformation & Approximation.** James P. Keener. 624p. 2000. text 60.00 (*0-7382-0129-4*, Pub. by Perseus Pubng) HarpC.

Principles of Applied Mathematics: Transformation & Approximation. James P. Kenner. (C). 1995. pap. 58.00 (*0-201-48363-7*) Addison-Wesley.

***Principles of Applied Mechanics.** 156p. (C). 1999. text 7.50 (*0-536-60418-5*) Pearson Custom.

Principles of Applied Reservoir Simulation Instructor's Guide. John R. Franchi. 1997. teacher ed. 20.00 (*0-88415-118-2*, 5118) Gulf Pub.

Principles of Applied Statistics. Michael C. Fleming & Joseph G. Nellis. LC 93-48403. (Series in the Principles of Management). 352p. (C). 1994. mass mkt. 27.95 (*0-415-07379-0*) Routledge.

***Principles of Applied Statistics.** 2nd ed. Fleming & Nellis. 2000. pap. write for info. (*1-86152-586-9*) Thomson Learn.

Principles of Applied Statistics & Information Management. Michael C. Fleming & Joseph G. Nellis. (Illus.). 352p. 1994. pap. 32.95 (*1-86152-234-7*) Thomson Learn.

Principles of Aquaculture. Robert R. Stickney. 520p. 1994. 140.00 (*0-471-57856-8*) Wiley.

Principles of Aquatic Chemistry. Francois M. Morel. LC 83-6840. (Wiley-Interscience Publications). 456p. reprint ed. pap. 141.40 (*0-7837-2404-7*, 204008900006) Bks Demand.

Principles of Archaeological Stratigraphy. 2nd ed. Ed. by Edward C. Harris. 200p. 1989. text 59.95 (*0-12-326651-3*) Acad Pr.

Principles of Architectural Drafting: A Sourcebook of Techniques & Graphic Standards. Hugh C. Browning. (Illus.). 256p. 1996. pap. text 35.00 (*0-8230-4288-X*) Watsn-Guptill.

Principles of Arithmeticke. Bernard Salignacus. Tr. by William Bedwell. LC 70-26250. (English Experience Ser.: No. 130). 134p. 1969. reprint ed. 25.00 (*90-221-0130-4*) Walter J Johnson.

Principles of Art. Robin George Collingwood. 360p. 1958. pap. text 14.95 (*0-19-500209-1*) OUP.

Principles of Art History: The Problem of the Development of Style in Later Art. Heinrich Wolfflin. (Illus.). 253p. pap. 7.95 (*0-486-20276-3*) Dover.

Principles of Art History Writing. David Carrier. (Illus.). 264p. 1991. 35.00 (*0-271-00711-7*); pap. 18.95 (*0-271-00945-4*) Pa St U Pr.

Principles of Art Therapies. D. Brown. 1998. pap. 11.00 (*0-7225-3495-7*) Thorsons PA.

Principles of Arterial Blood Gases. Vincent C. Madama. (Respiratory Care Ser.). 1994. teacher ed. 12.00 (*0-8273-5560-2*) Delmar.

Principles of Arterial Blood Gases. Vincent C. Madama. (Respiratory Care Ser.). 1997. pap. 46.95 (*0-8273-5559-9*) Delmar.

Principles of Artificial Intelligence. Nils J. Nilsson. LC 86-2815. (Illus.). 476p. 1980. reprint ed. text 58.95 (*0-934613-10-9*) Morgan Kaufmann.

Principles of Artificial Neural Networks. 250p. 1997. text 27.00 (*981-02-2516-4*) World Scientific Pub.

Principles of Assessment. Kathleen M. Bailey. LC 97-30858. (Teaching Methods Ser.). 256p. (J). 1997. mass mkt. 22.95 (*0-8384-6688-5*) Wadsworth Pub.

Principles of Assisted Human Reproduction. Robert G. Edwards & Steven A. Brody. LC 94-25781. 1995. text 131.00 (*0-7216-3626-8*, W B Saunders Co) Harcrt Hlth Sci Grp.

Principles of Association Management. 3rd ed. Henry Ernstthal & Bob Jones, Jr. 131p. 1996. pap. text 43.95 (*0-88034-112-2*) Am Soc Assn Execs.

Principles of Astrological Geomancy. Franz Hartmann. 136p. 1996. reprint ed. spiral bd. 14.00 (*0-7873-0382-8*) Hlth Research.

Principles of Astrological Geomancy: The Art of Divining by Punctuation According to Cornelius Agrippa & Others. Franz Hartmann. 136p. 1993. reprint ed. pap. 12.95 (*1-56459-397-5*) Kessinger Pub.

Principles of Asymmetric Synthesis. R. E. Gawley & Aube. LC 97-122813. (Tetrahedron Organic Chemistry Ser.: Vol. 14). 372p. 1996. pap. 48.00 (*0-08-041875-9*, Pergamon Pr) Elsevier.

Principles of Asymmetric Synthesis. R. E. Gawley & J. Aube. LC 97-122813. (Tetrahedron Organic Chemistry Ser.: Vol. 14). 372p. 1996. 115.00 (*0-08-041876-7*, Pergamon Pr) Elsevier.

Principles of Athletic Training. 10th ed. Daniel D. Arnheim. 1999. 10.31 (*0-07-236104-2*) McGraw.

Principles of Athletics Training. 10th ed. Daniel D. Arnheim & William E. Prentice. LC 99-20214. (Illus.). 864p. 1999. 54.50 (*0-07-109255-2*) McGraw-Hill HPD.

Principles of Atmospheric Chemistry & Physics. Richard E. Goody. (Illus.). 336p. (C). 1995. text 62.95 (*0-19-509362-3*) OUP.

Principles of Atomic Orbitals. Greenwood. 1989. 10.00 (*0-85404-028-5*) CRC Pr.

Principles of Auditing. 2nd ed. Ray Whittington. 1997. pap. text, teacher ed. write for info. (*0-256-16781-8*) McGraw.

Principles of Auditing. 11th ed. Kurt J. Pany & O. Ray Whittington. 216p. (C). 1994. text, student ed. 28.12 (*0-256-13371-9*, Irwn McGrw-H) McGrw-H Hghr Educ.

Principles of Auditing. 11th enl. ed. O. Ray Whittington. LC 94-20940. (Series in Undergraduate Accounting). 752p. (C). 1994. text 75.40 (*0-256-13370-0*, Irwn McGrw-H) McGrw-H Hghr Educ.

Principles of Auditing. 12th ed. O. Ray Whittington & Kurt Pany. LC 97-19641. 768p. (C). 1997. 75.40 (*0-256-16779-6*, Irwn McGrw-H) McGrw-H Hghr Educ.

Principles of Auditing. 12th ed. Ray Whittington. 1997. pap., student ed. 30.63 (*0-256-16780-X*) McGraw.

Principles of Auditing. 13th ed. Whittington. 832p. 2000. 90.31 (*0-07-232726-X*) McGraw.

Principles of Auditing: With Audit Practice Case. 11th ed. Kurt J. Pany et al. 752p. (C). 1996. text 97.20 (*0-256-24127-9*, Irwn McGrw-H) McGrw-H Hghr Educ.

Principles of Aural Rehabilitation. Mark Ross. LC 78-183116. (Studies in Communicative Disorders). (C). 1972. pap. write for info. (*0-672-61283-6*, Bobbs) Macmillan.

Principles of Australian Administrative Law. 6th ed. S. D. Hotop. xxxv, 516p. 1985. pap. 59.00 (*0-455-20576-0*, Pub. by LawBk Co) Gaunt.

Principles of Auto Body Repairing & Repainting. 4th ed. Andre G. Deroche & N. N. Hildebrand. (Illus.). 752p. (C). 1986. text 43.00 (*0-13-708173-1*) P-H.

Principles of Auto Body Repairing & Repainting. 6th ed. A. G. Deroche. LC 95-18952. 664p. 1995. 92.00 (*0-13-440033-X*) P-H.

Principles of Automated Drafting. Daniel L. Ryan. (Mechanical Engineering Ser.: Vol. 28). (Illus.). 336p. 1984. text 99.75 (*0-8247-7175-3*) Dekker.

Principles of Automated Theorem Proving. David A. Duffy. LC 91-9103. (Wiley Professional Computing Ser.). 261p. 1991. reprint ed. pap. 81.00 (*0-608-05262-0*, 206580000001) Bks Demand.

Principles of Avionics Databusses. Ed. by Avionics Communications Inc. Staff. 260p. 1993. pap. 89.00 (*1-885544-00-6*) Avionics Comm.

***Principles of Ayurveda.** Anne Green. 2000. pap. 11.00 (*0-7225-3745-X*, Pub. by Thorsons PA) HarpC.

Principles of Ayurvedic Therapeutics. Atmakuri V. Kumar. LC 95-904683. (C). 1995. 36.00 (*81-7030-463-6*, Pub. by Sri Satguru Pubns) S Asia.

***Principles of Bach Flower Remedies: The Only Introduction You'll Ever Need.** Stefan Ball. 2000. pap. 11.00 (*0-7225-3919-3*) Thorsons PA.

***Principles of Bacterial Pathogenesis.** Eduardo Groisman. 512p. 2000. text 79.95 (*0-12-304220-8*) Acad Pr.

Principles of Baha'i Administration. 116p. 1964. 8.00 (*0-900125-13-6*) Bahai.

Principles of Bank Accounting & Reporting. James D. Edwards & Cynthia D. Heagy. (Illus.). 493p. (C). 1991. text 51.00 (*0-89982-371-8*) Am Bankers.

Principles of Banking. 4th rev. ed. Eric N. Compton. Ed. by Hunter V. Moss. (Illus.). 400p. (C). 1991. text 45.00 (*0-89982-368-8*) Am Bankers.

Principles of Banking Law. Ross Cranston. LC 96-40367. (Illus.). 568p. 1997. text 120.00 (*0-19-876484-7*) OUP.

Principles of Banking Law. Ross Cranston. (Illus.). 568p. 1997. pap. text 47.00 (*0-19-876483-9*) OUP.

Principles of Banking, 1998. Francis et al. LC 98-160068. (Illus.). 290p. (C). 1998. write for info. (*0-89982-063-8*) Am Bankers.

Principles of Behavior Analysis. (C). 1997. 24.00 (*0-06-500367-5*) Addson-Wesley Educ.

Principles of Behavior Change: Understanding Behavior Modification Techniques. Edward P. Sarafino. LC 95-49741. 608p. 1996. pap. 80.95 (*0-471-10954-1*) Wiley.

Principles of Behavior Neuroscience: Student Study Art Notebook. Beatty. 1995. 15.74 (*0-697-29192-8*, WCB McGr Hill) McGrw-H Hghr Educ.

Principles of Behavior Therapy. G. Terence Wilson & K. Daniel O'Leary. (Social Learning Theory Ser.). (Illus.). 1980. text 24.95 (*0-13-701102-4*) P-H.

Principles of Behavioral Analysis. Lyle Grant & Annabel Evans. 500p. (C). 1997. 86.00 (*0-06-500366-7*) Addson-Wesley Educ.

***Principles of Behavioral & Cognitive Neurology.** 2nd ed. Ed. by M. Marsel Mesulam. LC 99-15581. (Illus.). 570p. 2000. text 79.95 (*0-19-513475-3*) OUP.

Principles of Behavioral Neuroscience. Beatty. 1995. 78.75 (*0-697-22876-2*, WCB McGr Hill) McGrw-H Hghr Educ.

Principles of Behavioral Neuroscience. Jackson Beatty. LC 93-74861. 576p. (C). 1994. text 55.50 (*0-697-12741-9*) Brown & Benchmark.

Principles of Behavioral Neuroscience. Jackson Beatty. LC 93-74861. 224p. (C). 1995. text, student ed. 23.12 (*0-697-12743-5*) Brown & Benchmark.

Principles of Behavioural Analysis. 3rd ed. Julian Leslie. 340p. 1996. text 38.00 (*3-7186-5901-8*, Harwood Acad Pubs); pap. text 15.00 (*3-7186-5902-6*, Harwood Acad Pubs) Gordon & Breach.

Principles of Benthic Marine Paleo-Ecology. Arthur J. Boucot. LC 79-8535. 1981. text 107.00 (*0-12-118980-5*) Acad Pr.

Principles of Bible Interpretation, Vol. 3. Roger E. Dickson. 143p. (Orig.). 1996. pap. 7.95 (*1-56794-126-5*, C-2448) Star Bible.

Principles of Biblical Hermeneutics. J. Edwin Hartill. 123p. 1960. 24.99 (*0-310-25900-2*, 9774) Zondervan.

Principles of Bibliographical Description. Fredson Bowers. LC 94-4383. 536p. 1995. pap. 29.95 (*1-884718-00-0*) Oak Knoll.

Principles of Bicycle Retailing. 2nd ed. Randy W. Kirk. Ed. by Herb Wetenkamp. (Illus.). 104p. 1987. pap. 19.95 (*0-924272-00-7*) Info Net Pub.

Principles of Bicycle Retailing, No. III. 3rd rev. ed. Randy W. Kirk. (Illus.). 220p. 1992. pap. 19.95 (*0-924272-05-8*) Info Net Pub.

Principles of Bioc. Student Study Art Notebook. Zubay et al. 1995. 17.00 (*0-697-26476-9*, WCB McGr Hill) McGrw-H Hghr Educ.

Principles of Biochemical Toxicology. John A. Timbrell. 240p. 1982. pap. text 21.00 (*0-685-10493-1*) Taylor & Francis.

Principles of Biochemical Toxicology. 2nd ed. John A. Timbrell. 416p. 1991. 110.00 (*0-85066-829-8*, Pub. by Tay Francis Ltd); pap. 42.00 (*0-85066-832-8*, Pub. by Tay Francis Ltd) Taylor & Francis.

Principles of Biochemical Toxicology. 3rd ed. John Timbrell. LC 99-31712. 420p. 1998. text 90.00 (*0-7484-0737-5*, Pub. by Tay Francis Ltd); pap. text 44.95 (*0-7484-0736-7*, Pub. by Tay Francis Ltd) Taylor & Francis.

Principles of Biochemistry. Zubay. 1995. 147.50 (*0-697-22871-1*, WCB McGr Hill) McGrw-H Hghr Educ.

Principles of Biochemistry. Zubay. 1996. teacher ed. 10.62 (*0-697-14276-0*, WCB McGr Hill) McGrw-H Hghr Educ.

Principles of Biochemistry. Geoffrey L. Zubay et al. (C). 1995. text, student ed. write for info. (*0-697-27016-5*, WCB McGr Hill) McGrw-H Hghr Educ.

Principles of Biochemistry, 3 vols. Geoffrey L. Zubay et al. 320p. (C). 1995. text, student ed. 20.00 (*0-697-22870-3*, WCB McGr Hill) McGrw-H Hghr Educ.

Principles of Biochemistry. 2nd ed. H. Robert Horton et al. 801p. 1996. 100.00 (*0-13-439167-5*) P-H.

Principles of Biochemistry. 2nd ed. Albert L. Lehninger et al. (Illus.). 1013p. (C). 1984. teacher ed. 19.95 (*0-87901-178-5*) Worth.

***Principles of Biochemistry.** 3rd ed. Lehninger. 2000. pap. text, student ed. write for info. (*1-57259-167-6*) St Martin.

Principles of Biochemistry. 3rd ed. Lehninger. LC 99-49137. 2000. pap. text. write for info. (*1-57259-153-6*) W H Freeman.

Principles of Biochemistry, 3 vols., Set. Geoffrey L. Zubay et al. LC 94-70034. (Illus.). 1030p. (C). 1995. text 80.47 (*0-697-14275-2*, WCB McGr Hill) McGrw-H Hghr Educ.

Principles of Biochemistry: Solutions Manual. 2nd ed. 1993. write for info. (*0-87901-729-5*) Worth.

Principles of Biochemistry: Study Guide. Marcy Osgood & Karen Ocorr. 1993. pap., student ed. write for info. (*1-57259-100-5*) Worth.

Principles of Biochemistry: Test Index File. Zubay et al. 1995. 14.68 (*0-697-28109-4*, WCB McGr Hill) McGrw-H Hghr Educ.

Principles of Biochemistry Vol. 1: Energy, Proteins & Catalysis, Vol. 1. Geoffrey L. Zubay et al. 352p. (C). 1994. text 25.00 (*0-697-24169-6*, WCB McGr Hill) McGrw-H Hghr Educ.

Principles of Biochemistry Vol. 2: Metabolism, Vol. 2. Geoffrey L. Zubay et al. 528p. (C). 1994. text 31.00 (*0-697-24170-X*, WCB McGr Hill) McGrw-H Hghr Educ.

Principles of Biochemistry Vol. 3: Molecular Genetics, Vol. 3. Geoffrey L. Zubay et al. 368p. (C). 1994. text 26.00 (*0-697-24171-8*, WCB McGr Hill) McGrw-H Hghr Educ.

Principles of Biochemistry. 2nd ed. Albert L. Lehninger et al. (Illus.). 1075p. (C). 1993. text 67.80 (*0-87901-711-2*) Worth.

Principles of Biodegradation. D. Focht. (Illus.). 448p. (C). (gr. 13). 1997. text 59.00 (*0-412-04191-X*) Chapman & Hall.

***Principles of Biodegration.** Ed. by Lawrence Wachett. 400p. 2000. text 59.95 (*1-55581-179-5*) ASM Pr.

Principles of Bioinorganic Chemistry. Stephen J. Lippard & Jeremy Berg. LC 91-67871. (Illus.). 411p. (C). 1994. text 56.00 (*0-935702-72-5*) Univ Sci Bks.

Principles of Bioinstrumentation. Richard A. Normann. LC 88-5893. 576p. 1988. text 99.95 (*0-471-60514-X*) Wiley.

Principles of Biological Autonomy. Francisco J. Varela. (North Holland Series in General Systems Research: Vol. 2). 336p. 1979. 76.00 (*0-444-00321-5*) P-H.

Principles of Biological Systems & Neural Network Analysis. Chi-Sang Poon. (C). 1995. text. write for info. (*0-201-57890-5*) Addison-Wesley.

Principles of Biology. Gallagher. (C). 1994. pap. text, lab manual ed. 7.25 (*0-07-022808-6*) McGraw.

Principles of Biology. Thomas Graham. 192p. (C). 1995. pap. text, spiral bd. 32.95 (*0-7872-0495-1*, 41049501) Kendall-Hunt.

Principles of Biology. Rehm. 188p. 1998. pap. text 14.40 (*0-536-01432-9*) Pearson Custom.

Principles of Biology. Allen J. Scism. 1996. pap. text, student ed. 28.33 (*0-13-449091-6*) P-H.

Principles of Biology. Raghunat Virkar & H. Bruce Reid. 176p. (C). 1997. pap. text, spiral bd., lab manual ed. 12.50 (*0-7872-3410-9*) Kendall-Hunt.

***Principles of Biology.** 2nd ed. (C). 1999. 12.00 (*0-8087-9641-0*) Pearson Custom.

***Principles of Biology.** 2nd ed. 144p. (C). 2000. lab manual ed. 19.00 (*0-536-60812-1*) Pearson Custom.

Principles of Biology 3rd ed. 198p. (C). 1999. pap. text, lab manual ed. 12.70 (*0-536-02517-7*) Pearson Custom.

Principles of Biology. 6th ed. Roger R. Ragonese & Joseph Dipierro. 508p. (C). 1995. pap. text, spiral bd. 45.95 (*0-7872-0619-9*) Kendall-Hunt.

Principles of Biology: Laboratory Investigations. 3rd ed. Virginia G. Latta et al. 218p. 1991. pap. text, teacher ed. 26.95 (*0-88725-150-1*) Hunter Textbks.

Principles of Biology: Laboratory Investigations & Lecture Supplements. 2nd ed. John W. Thornton. 160p. (C). 1996. spiral bd. 20.95 (*0-8403-8901-9*) Kendall-Hunt.

Principles of Biology: Laboratory Manual. Janine Caira. (C). 1993. student ed. 20.52 (*1-56870-077-6*) RonJon Pub.

Principles of Biology 1. (C). 1997. 10.00 (*0-8087-3089-4*) Pearson Custom.

***Principles of Biology 2.** 3rd ed. (C). 1998. lab manual ed. 18.80 (*0-8087-9635-6*) Pearson Custom.

Principles of Biomedical Ethics. 4th ed. Thomas L. Beauchamp & James F. Childress. LC 93-24390. 560p. (C). 1994. pap. text 29.95 (*0-19-508537-X*) OUP.

Principles of Biomedical Instrumentation & Measurement. Richard Aston. 576p. (C). 1990. 82.60 (*0-675-20943-9*, Merrill Coll) P-H.

Principles of Biopsy: A Self-Instructional Guide, Bk. 8. 3rd rev. ed. Thomas H. Morton, Jr. et al. (Illus.). 94p. 1983. pap. 14.95 (*0-89939-081-1*) Stoma Pr.

Principles of Biopsychology. Simon Green. Ed. by Michael W. Eysenck et al. (Principles of Psychology Ser.). 224p. 1994. 29.95 (*0-86377-281-1*) L Erlbaum Assocs.

Principles of Biostatistics. Pagano. (Statistics Ser.). 1993. pap., teacher ed. 26.25 (*0-534-14066-1*) Brooks-Cole.

Principles of Biostatistics. Marcello Pagano & Kimberlee Gauvreau. LC 92-32841. 524p. 1993. text 52.95 (*0-534-14064-5*) Wadsworth Pub.

Principles of Biostatistics. 2nd ed. Robert R. Pagano et al. (Statistics Ser.). 525p. (C). 2000. pap. 77.95 (*0-534-22902-6*) Wadsworth Pub.

Principles of Biostatistics with Disk. Robert R. Pagano. (Statistics Ser.). 1994. mass mkt. 55.50 (*0-534-14069-6*) Wadsworth Pub.

Principles of Black Political Economy. Lloyd Hogan. 224p. (Orig.). 22.50 (*0-7102-0177-X*, Routledge Thoemms); pap. 9.95 (*0-7102-0241-5*, Routledge Thoemms) Routledge.

***Principles of Black Political Economy.** Lloyd Hogan. 200p. (Orig.). 1999. pap. 19.81 (*1-55212-253-0*, 99-0022) Tra3fford.

Principles of Bone Biology. Ed. by John P. Bilezikian et al. LC 96-32323. (Illus.). 1398p. 1996. text 165.00 (*0-12-098650-7*) Acad Pr.

Principles of Botany. B. D. Davis. (Illus.). 78p. (C). 1998. 18.00 (*1-887052-06-2*) SOS Pubns NJ.

Principles of Botany. Uno. 2001. 47.00 (*0-07-228592-3*) McGraw.

Principles of Brain Functioning: A Synergetic Approach to Brain Activity, Behavior, & Cognition. Hermann Haken. (Series in Synergetics: Vol. 67). 424p. 1995. 69.95 (*3-540-58967-8*) Spr-Verlag.

Principles of Brain Stimulation. John S. Yeomans. (Illus.). 192p. 1990. text 45.00 (*0-19-506138-1*) OUP.

***Principles of Brazilian Soccer.** Thadeu Goncalves. (Illus.). 287p. 1999. pap. 16.95 (*1-890946-06-0*) Reedswain.

***Principles of Breathwork: The Only Introduction You'll Ever Need.** Swami Ambikananda. (Illus.). 160p. 1999. pap. 11.00 (*0-7225-3830-8*) Thorsons PA.

Principles of Brewing Science: A Study of Serious Brewing Issues. 2nd rev. ed. George Fix. LC 99-36534. (Illus.). 200p. 2000. pap. 29.95 (*0-937381-74-8*, Pub. by Brewers Pubns) Natl Bk Netwk.

Principles of Budgetary & Financial Policy. Willem H. Buiter. 474p. 1990. 52.50 (*0-262-02303-2*) MIT Pr.

Principles of Building Construction. Madan Mehta. LC 96-33105. 362p. 1996. 49.60 (*0-13-205881-2*) P-H.

Principles of Business Communication. D. A. Jameson et al. 1984. pap. 6.80 (*0-87563-256-4*) Stipes.

Principles of Business Communication. 5th ed. Cullinan. (C). 1993. pap. text, teacher ed. 5.50 (*0-03-096875-5*) Harcourt Coll Pubs.

***Principles of Business Law.** Brenda Barrett. 2000. pap. write for info. (*1-86152-575-3*) Thomson Learn.

Principles of Business Law. 2nd ed. David Kelly & Ann Holmes. (Principles of Law Ser.). liii, 456p. 1997. pap. 32.50 (*1-85941-371-4*, Pub. by Cavendish Pubng) Gaunt.

Principles of Business Law. 3rd ed. Mark E. Roszkowski. (C). 1997. pap. text 31.00 (*0-673-52219-9*) Addson-Wesley Educ.

Principles of Business Organization. C. C. O'Catroux. 89p. 1995. pap. write for info. (*0-9675578-0-1*) Baavi House.

Principles of Business Studies, Vol. 1. R. P. Maheshwari. 448p. 1997. pap. 61.50 (*81-209-0188-6*, Pub. by Pitambar Pub) St Mut.

Principles of Business Studies, Vol. 2. R. P. Maheshwari. 256p. 1997. pap. 40.00 (*81-209-0189-4*, Pub. by Pitambar Pub) St Mut.

An Asterisk (*) at the beginning of an entry indicates that the title is appearing for the first time.

Principles of Cad Cam Cae Systems. Kunwoo Lee. 608p. (C). 1998. text Price not set. (*0-201-38043-9*) Addison-Wesley.

Principles of CAD/CAM/CAE. Kunwoo Lee. LC 98-18040. 640p. (C). 1999. 97.00 (*0-201-38036-6*, Prentice Hall) P-H.

Principles of California Real Estate. 8th rev. ed. Kathryn J. Haupt. 486p. (Orig.). 1996. pap. text 36.25 (*1-887051-02-3*) Rockwell WA.

Principles of California Real Estate Workbook. Megan Dorsey & David L. Rockwell. 265p. (Orig.). 1996. pap. text, wbk. ed. 27.45 (*1-887051-03-1*) Rockwell WA.

Principles of Cancer Biotherapy. Ed. by Robert K. Oldham. LC 86-42899. 512p. 1987. reprint ed. pap. 158.80 (*0-608-00356-5*, 206107300007) Bks Demand.

Principles of Cancer Biotherapy. 2nd rev. ed. Ed. by Robert K. Oldham. 696p. 1991. text 185.00 (*0-8247-8504-5*) Dekker.

Principles of Cancer Biotherapy. 3rd ed. Ed. by Robert K. Oldham. LC 97-2588. 892p. 1997. lib. bdg. 380.00 (*0-7923-3507-4*) Kluwer Academic.

Principles of Canon Law. Hubert S. Box. LC 86-3163. 82p. 1986. reprint ed. lib. bdg. 35.00 (*0-313-25204-1*, BPRC, Greenwood Pr) Greenwood.

Principles of Cardiac Diagnosis & Treatment: A Surgeon's Guide. 2nd ed. D. N. Ross et al. (Illus.). ix, 269p. 1991. 129.00 (*0-387-17494-X*) Spr-Verlag.

Principles of Cardiac Toxicology. Steven I. Baskin. (Illus.). 576p. 1991. lib. bdg. 159.00 (*0-8493-8809-0*, RC682) CRC Pr.

Principles of Cardiac Toxicology. Ed. by Steven I. Baskin. 500p. 1990. 62.50 (*0-936923-48-2*) Telford Pr.

***Principles of Cardiovascular Neural Regulation in Health.** Alberto Malliani. 240p. 2000. 160.00 (*0-7923-7775-3*) Kluwer Academic.

Principles of Caribbean Geography. London & Senior. 1992. pap. text. write for info. (*0-582-03989-4*, Pub. by Addison-Wesley) Longman.

Principles of Cartesian Philosophy: With Metaphysical Thoughts & Lodewijk Meyer's Inaugural Dissertation. Baruch Spinoza. Tr. by Samuel Shirley. LC 97-51491. (Classics Ser.). 192p. (C). 1998. pap. text 14.95 (*0-87220-400-6*); lib. bdg. 34.95 (*0-87220-401-4*) Hackett Pub.

Principles of Cartography. Erwin J. Raisz. (Geography Ser.). (C). 1962. text 33.00 (*0-07-051151-9*) McGraw.

Principles of CASE Tool Integration. Alan W. Brown et al. (Illus.). 288p. 1994. text 65.00 (*0-19-509478-6*) OUP.

Principles of Catalyst Development. J. T. Richardson. (Fundamental & Applied Catalysis Ser.). (Illus.). 304p. (C). 1989. text 75.00 (*0-306-43162-9*, Kluwer Plenum) Kluwer Academic.

Principles of Catholic Social Teaching. David A. Boileau. LC 97-45330. (Studies in Philosophy). 1998. 25.00 (*0-87462-638-2*) Marquette.

Principles of Catholic Theology: A Synthesis of Dogma & Morals. Edward Gratsch et al. LC 80-26272. 401p. (Orig.). 1981. pap. 12.95 (*0-8189-0407-0*) Alba.

Principles of Catholic Theology: Building Stones for Fundamental Theology. Joseph C. Ratzinger. Tr. by Mary F. McCarthy from GER. LC 86-83133.Tr. of Theologische Prinzipienlehre. 398p. (Orig.). 1986. 31.95 (*0-89870-133-3*) Ignatius Pr.

***Principles of Cattle Production.** C. J. C. Phillips. (CABI Publishing Ser.). 2000. write for info. (*0-85199-438-5*) OUP.

Principles of Cell Adhesion. Peter D. Richardson. 400p. 1994. 157.95 (*0-8493-4559-6*) CRC Pr.

Principles of Cell & Molecular Biology. 2nd ed. Lewis J. Kleinsmith & Valerie M. Kish. LC 94-22311. 810p. (C). 1997. 104.00 (*0-06-500404-3*) Addson-Wesley Educ.

Principles of Cell Growth & Division. Cooper. 384p. 1999. 69.95 (*0-12-188010-9*) Acad Pr.

Principles of Cellular & Molecular Immunology. Jonathan M. Austyn & Kathryn J. Wood. (Illus.). 746p. 1994. pap. text 59.50 (*0-19-854195-3*) OUP.

Principles of Cellular, Molecular & Developmental Neuroscience. O. Steward. (Illus.). 280p. 1989. 58.00 (*0-387-96803-2*) Spr-Verlag.

Principles of Ceramics Processing. 2nd ed. James S. Reed. 688p. 1995. 89.95 (*0-471-59721-X*) Wiley.

Principles of Cereal Science & Technology. 2nd ed. R. Carl Hoseney. LC 93-74154. (Illus.). 378p. (C). 1994. pap. 99.00 (*0-913250-79-1*, BEF3135) Am Assn Cereal Chem.

Principles of Chemical & Biological Sensors. Ed. by Dermot Diamond. LC 97-31765. (Chemical Analysis). 368p. 1998. 98.95 (*0-471-54619-4*, Wiley-Interscience) Wiley.

Principles of Chemical Equilibrium. 4th ed. K. G. Denbigh. (Illus.). 516p. 1981. pap. text 47.95 (*0-521-28150-4*) Cambridge U Pr.

Principles of Chemical Kinetics. James House. LC 95-83493. 256p. (C). 1996. text. write for info. (*0-697-32881-3*, WCB McGr Hill) McGrw-H Hghr Educ.

Principles of Chemical Nomenclature: A Guide to IUPAC Recommendations. G. J. Leigh et al. LC 97-28587. (Illus.). 128p. 1998. pap. 28.95 (*0-86542-685-6*) Blackwell Sci.

Principles of Chemical Reaction Engineering & Plant Design see Ullmann's Encyclopedia of Industrial Chemistry

Principles of Chemical Reactor Analysis & Design: New Tools for Industrial Chemical Reactor Operations. Uzi Mann. 450p. 1999. 89.00 (*0-9673761-0-6*) Plains.

Principles of Chemical Sensors. J. Janata. (Illus.). 332p. (C). 1989. text 55.00 (*0-306-43183-1*, Kluwer Plenum) Kluwer Academic.

Principles of Chemical Vapor Deposition: Thermal Plasma Deposition of Electronic Materials. Srinivasan Sivaram. (Electrical Engineering Ser.). (Illus.). 456p. 1995. text 64.95 (*0-442-01079-6*, VNR) Wiley.

***Principles of Chemistry.** M. Munowitz. LC 98-26497. 1000p. 1999. 104.25 (*0-393-97288-7*) Norton.

Principles of Chemistry. Michael Munowitz. (C). pap. text. write for info. (*0-393-97550-9*); pap. text, student ed. write for info. (*0-393-97365-4*) Norton.

Principles of Chemistry. C. Stuart Patterson et al. LC 66-28993. (Illus.). (C). 1967. 40.00 (*0-89197-530-6*) Irvington.

Principles of Chemistry. W. W. Norton & Company Staff. 2000. pap., lab manual ed. write for info. (*0-393-97360-3*) Norton.

***Principles of Chemistry.** 3rd ed. 224p. (C). 2000. 15.40 (*0-536-61044-4*) Pearson Custom.

Principles of Chemistry: Lab Manual, Chemistry 113 Spring, 1998. 5th ed. Terrence Swift. 116p. (C). 1998. spiral bd., lab manual ed. 25.95 (*0-7872-4754-5*) Kendall-Hunt.

Principles of Chemistry: Lab Manual Chemistry 133 Fall 1998. 6th ed. Terrence J. Swift. 118p. (C). 1998. spiral bd., lab manual ed. 25.95 (*0-7872-5315-4*) Kendall-Hunt.

Principles of Chemistry: Laboratory Manual. 5th ed. Terrence Swift. 116p. (C). 1997. spiral bd. 23.95 (*0-7872-4159-8*) Kendall-Hunt.

Principles of Chemistry in Biology: A Teaching Companion. Elizabeth C. Thiel. LC 98-28645. (An American Chemical Society Publication). (Illus.). 250p. 1998. text 45.00 (*0-8412-3506-6*, Pub. by Am Chemical) OUP.

Principles of Chemistry with Other Treatises. Emanuel Swedenborg. Tr. & Intro. by Charles E. Strutt. (Illus.). 253p. 1976. reprint ed. 14.95 (*0-915221-22-5*) Swedenborg Sci Assn.

Principles of Chemoprevention. Ed. by Paul Kleihues et al. (IARC Scientific Publications: No. 139). (Illus.). 370p. 1997. pap. text 89.50 (*92-832-2139-7*) OUP.

Principles of Chest Roentgenology: A Programmed Text. Benjamin Felson et al. LC 65-23091. (Illus.). 1965. text 49.00 (*0-7216-3605-5*, W B Saunders Co) Harcrt Hlth Sci Grp.

Principles of Child Development. Bornstein. 2001. write for info. (*0-07-006550-0*); teacher ed. write for info. (*0-07-006555-1*) McGraw.

Principles of Child Neurology. Ed. by Bruce O. Berg. (Illus.). 1500p. 1996. text 135.00 (*0-07-005193-3*) McGraw-Hill HPD.

Principles of Children's Services in Public Libraries. Mae Benne. LC 90-47427. 332p. 1991. 45.00 (*0-8389-0555-2*) ALA.

Principles of Chinese Bible Translation As Expressed in Five Selected Versions of the New Testament & Exemplified by Mathew 5.1 & Coloosians 1. Thor Strandenaes. 166p. (Orig.). 1987. pap. 44.00 (*91-22-00993-0*) Coronet Bks.

Principles of Chinese Medicine: Health, Nutrition, Fitness. Angela Hicks. 160p. 1996. pap. 11.00 (*0-7225-3215-6*) Harper SF.

Principles of Chinese Painting. 2nd rev. ed. George Rowley. LC ND1040.R6. (Princeton Monographs in Art & Archaeology: Vol. 24). (Illus.). 105p. 1959. reprint ed. pap. 32.60 (*0-608-07636-8*, 205995200010) Bks Demand.

Principles of Christian Art. Percy Gardner. 1977. lib. bdg. 59.95 (*0-8490-2479-X*) Gordon Pr.

Principles of Christian Morality. Joseph C. Ratzinger et al. Tr. by Graham Harrison from GER. LC 85-82176. Orig. Title: Prinzipien Chrislicher Moral. (Illus.). 104p. (Orig.). 1986. pap. 7.95 (*0-89870-086-8*) Ignatius Pr.

Principles of Christian Religion. Thomas Becon. LC 76-57355. (English Experience Ser.: No. 774). 1977. reprint ed. lib. bdg. 25.00 (*90-221-0774-4*) Walter J Johnson.

Principles of Christian Theology. John MacQuarrie. 1985. 24.00 (*0-684-14777-7*) S&S Trade.

Principles of Christian Theology. 2nd ed. John Macquarrie. LC 76-23182. 544p. (C). 1977. pap. text 36.00 (*0-02-374510-X*, Macmillan Coll) P-H.

Principles of Church Life. Bill Scheidler. 115p. 1977. pap. 12.99 (*0-914936-23-9*) City Bible Pub.

Principles of Circular Accelerators & Storage Rings. Philip J. Bryant & Kjell Johnsen. (Illus.). 383p. (C). 1993. text 110.00 (*0-521-35578-8*) Cambridge U Pr.

Principles of City Land Values. Richard M. Hurd. LC 78-112551. (Rise of Urban America Ser.). (Illus.). 1974. reprint ed. 17.95 (*0-405-02458-4*) Ayer.

Principles of Civil Procedure. Neil Andrews. 1994. 104.00 (*0-421-48710-0*, Pub. by Sweet & Maxwll) Gaunt.

Principles of Civil Procedure in the Magistrates' Courts. C. F. Eckard. 373p. 1990. pap. 44.00 (*0-7021-2281-5*, Pub. by Juta & Co) Gaunt.

***Principles of Classroom Management.** 3rd ed. James Levin & James F. Nolan. LC 99-12693. 246p. (C). 1999. pap. text 36.00 (*0-205-28862-6*, Longwood Div) Allyn.

Principles of Clinical Anatomy. Lawrence H. Mathers, Jr. et al. (Illus.). 816p. (C). (gr. 13). 1995. text 57.00 (*0-8016-6356-3*, 06356) Mosby Inc.

Principles of Clinical Cytogenetics. Steven L. Gersen & Martha B. Keagle. LC 98-21743. (Illus.). 568p. 1999. 79.50 (*0-89603-553-0*) Humana.

Principles of Clinical Electromyography: Case Studies. Shin J. Oh. LC 98-10426. 352p. 1998. pap. 50.00 (*0-683-18106-8*) Lppncott W & W.

Principles of Clinical Immunohematology. Paul Weisz-Carrington. LC 85-20297. (Illus.). 530p. reprint ed. pap. 164.30 (*0-608-17814-4*, 203230200080) Bks Demand.

Principles of Clinical Medicine. Ed. by D. G. Williams & P. John Rees. (Illus.). 960p. 1995. pap. text 34.95 (*0-340-56300-1*, Pub. by E A) OUP.

Principles of Clinical Neuropsychology. Zillmer. (Psychology Ser.). 2000. mass mkt. 49.95 (*0-534-34144-6*) Brooks-Cole.

Principles of Clinical Practice: An Introductory Textbook. Ed. by Mark B. Mengel. (Illus.). 432p. (C). 1991. text 45.00 (*0-306-43847-X*, Kluwer Plenum) Kluwer Academic.

Principles of Clinical Toxicology. 2nd fac. ed. Thomas A. Gossel & Douglas Bricker. LC 87-45470. (Illus.). 427p. pap. 132.40 (*0-7837-7177-0*, 204712200005) Bks Demand.

Principles of CMOS VLSI: A Systems Perspective. Neil H. Weste & Karman Eshraghian. LC 84-16738. 1985. text 52.75 (*0-201-08222-5*) Addison-Wesley.

Principles of CMOS VLSI Design: A Systems Perspective. 2nd ed. Neil H. Weste & Karman Eshragian. (Illus.). 608p. (C). 1993. 69.00 (*0-201-53376-6*) Addison-Wesley.

Principles of Coaching Football. Mike Bobo & Spike Dykes. LC 97-29510. 287p. 1997. pap. text 29.00 (*0-205-26253-8*) P-H.

***Principles of Cognition, Language & Action: Essays on the Foundations for a Science of Psychology.** Nini Pratorius. LC 00-27387. 2000. write for info. (*0-7923-6230-6*, Kluwer Plenum) Kluwer Academic.

***Principles of Cognition, Language & Action - Essays on the Foundations for a Science of Psychology.** N. Praetorius & R. J. Enbody. 500p. 2000. pap. 55.00 (*0-7923-6231-4*) Kluwer Academic.

Principles of Colloid & Surface Chemistry. 3rd ed. Paul C. Hiemenez & Raj Rajagopalan. LC 97-4015. (Undergraduate Chemistry Ser.). (Illus.). 672p. 1997. text 65.00 (*0-8247-9397-8*) Dekker.

Principles of Colonic Irrigation: The Only Introduction You'll Ever Need. Jillie Collings. 160p. 1996. pap. 11.00 (*0-7225-3029-3*) Harper SF.

Principles of Color. rev. ed. Faber Birren. LC 88-61471. (Illus.). 96p. 1987. pap. 14.95 (*0-88740-103-1*) Schiffer.

Principles of Color Design. 2nd rev. ed. Wucius Wong. LC 96-8346. (Design & Graphic Design Ser.). (Illus.). 224p. 1997. pap. 29.95 (*0-442-02067-8*, VNR) Wiley.

Principles of Color Design: Designing with Electronic Color. 2nd ed. Wucius Wong. 224p. 1996. pap. 34.95 (*0-471-28708-3*, VNR) Wiley.

Principles of Color Proofing: A Manual on the Measurement & Control of Tone & Color Reproduction. Michael H. Bruno. 395p. 65.00 (*0-614-25601-1*, 00DC44105) Print Indus Am.

***Principles of Color Reproduction.** 2nd rev. ed. John A. Yule & Gary Field. (Illus.). 500p. (C). 2000. 75.00 (*0-88362-222-X*) GATFPress.

Principles of Color Reproduction, Applied to Photomechanical Reproduction, Color Photography, & the Ink, Paper, & Other Related Industries. John A. Yule. LC 66-26764. (Wiley Series on Photographic Science & Technology & the Graphic Arts). 447p. reprint ed. pap. 138.60 (*0-608-16428-3*, 205615300051) Bks Demand.

Principles of Colour Healing. Ambika Wauters & Gerry Thompson. 1998. pap. 11.00 (*0-7225-3340-3*) Thorsons PA.

Principles of Command & Control. Ed. by Jon L. Boyes & Stephen J. Andriole. LC 87-3574. (AFCEA Signal Magazine C3I Ser.: Vol. VI). (Illus.). 500p. 1987. 21.95 (*0-916159-12-4*) AFCEA Intl Pr.

Principles of Commerce & Commercial Law: Explained in a Course of Lectures. George Stephen. v, 269p. 1991. reprint ed. 39.00 (*0-8377-2645-X*, Rothman) W S Hein.

Principles of Communication Engineering. John M. Wozencraft & Irwin M. Jacobs. (Illus.). (C). 1990. reprint ed. text 61.95 (*0-88133-554-1*) Waveland Pr.

Principles of Communication Systems. 2nd ed. Herbert Taub & Donald L. Schilling. (Electrical Engineering Ser.). 736p. (C). 1986. 101.56 (*0-07-062955-2*) McGraw.

Principles of Communications: Systems, Modulation & Noise. 4th ed. Tranter & Rodger E. Ziemer. 816p. 1994. text 103.95 (*0-471-12496-6*) Wiley.

Principles of Communications Satellites. Gary D. Gordon & Walter L. Morgan. LC 92-29459. 568p. 1993. 99.00 (*0-471-55796-X*, Pub. by Interscience) Wiley.

***Principles of Community Health Promotion.** Marlene Tape & Regina Galer-Unti. (Illus.). 480p. (C). 1999. pap. text 53.75 (*0-7637-1077-6*) JB Pubns.

Principles of Community Property. 2nd ed. William Q. De Funiak & Michael J. Vaughn. LC 72-101099. 575p. reprint ed. pap. 178.30 (*0-608-13694-8*, 205534700017) Bks Demand.

Principles of Community Psychology: Perspectives & Trends. 2nd ed. Murray Levine & David V. Perkins. (Illus.). 512p. (C). 1996. text 54.95 (*0-19-509844-7*) OUP.

Principles of Company Law. Simon Goulding. 338p. 1996. pap. 32.50 (*1-874241-83-X*, Pub. by Cavendish Pubng) Gaunt.

Principles of Comparative Anatomy of Invertebrates, 2 vols. V. N. Beklemishev. Ed. by Z. Kabata. Tr. by J. M. McLennan. LC 70-97749. 1970. lib. bdg. 72.00 (*0-226-04175-1*) U Ch Pr.

Principles of Comparative Psychology. Greenberg. (C). 2000. 64.00 (*0-205-28014-5*, Macmillan Coll) P-H.

Principles of Composite Material Mechanics. Ronald F. Gibson. (C). 1993. pap. text 35.00 (*0-07-023452-3*) McGraw.

Principles of Composite Material Mechanics. Ronald F. Gibson. LC 93-22119. (Series in Mechanical Engineering-Series in Aeronautical & Aerospace Engineering). 425p. (C). 1994. 84.38 (*0-07-023451-5*) McGraw.

Principles of Composition in Hindu Sculpture: Cave Temple Period. Alice Boner. (Illus.). 290p. 1992. 115.00 (*0-7103-0443-9*, A6782) Routledge.

Principles of Composition in Near Eastern Glyptic of the Later Second Millennium BC. Donald M. Matthews. (Orbis Biblicus et Orientalis Ser.: Vol. 8). 176p. 1990. text 58.25 (*3-7278-0698-2*, Pub. by Presses Univ Fribourg) Eisenbrauns.

***Principles of Computer Architecture.** 2000. write for info. (*0-13-028686-9*) P-H.

***Principles of Computer Architecture.** Miles Murdocca. LC 99-46113. 640p. (C). 1999. 95.00 (*0-201-43664-7*) Addison-Wesley.

Principles of Computer Architecture. Miles J. Murdocca. 656p. (C). 1996. text. write for info. (*0-8053-5460-3*) Benjamin-Cummings.

Principles of Computer Automated Fabrication. Jerome L. Johnson. (Illus.). 169p. 1994. 95.00 (*0-9618005-3-4*) Palatino Pr.

Principles of Computer Hardware. 3rd ed. Alan Clements. (Illus.). 816p. (C). 2000. text 82.00 (*0-19-856454-6*) OUP.

Principles of Computer Networking. D. Russell. (Cambridge Computer Science Texts Ser.). 513p. (C). 1990. pap. text 44.95 (*0-521-33992-8*) Cambridge U Pr.

Principles of Computer Organisation: A First Course Using the 68000 Processor. P. Leng & C. Charlton. 288p. (C). 1990. 47.81 (*0-07-707217-0*) McGraw.

Principles of Computer Science. V. B. Aggarwal et al. 620p. 1990. pap. 120.00 (*81-209-0713-2*, Pub. by Pitambar Pub) St Mut.

Principles of Computer Science. Ulrich W. Eschholz. (Orig.). (C). 1995. pap. 24.10 (*1-56870-189-6*) RonJon Pub.

Principles of Concurrent & Distributed Programming. 2nd ed. M. Ben-Ari. 350p. 1990. pap. 64.00 (*0-13-711821-X*) P-H.

Principles of Condensed Matter Physics. P. M. Chaikin & T. C. Lubensky. LC 93-44244. (Illus.). 719p. (C). 1995. text 59.95 (*0-521-43224-3*) Cambridge U Pr.

***Principles of Condensed Matter Physics.** P. M. Chaikin & T. C. Lubensky. (Illus.). 720p. 2000. pap. write for info. (*0-521-79450-1*) Cambridge U Pr.

Principles of Conduct: Aspects of Biblical Ethics. John Murray. 280p. 1957. pap. 15.00 (*0-8028-1144-2*) Eerdmans.

Principles of Configuration Management. 1985. 26.00 (*0-934321-08-6*, 503-1) Adv Appl Consul.

Principles of Conflict of Laws. 3rd ed. Abla J. Mayss. LC 99-168454. (Principles of Law Ser.). xiiii, 464 p. 1998. pap. 32.57 (*1-85941-460-5*, Pub. by Cavendish Pubng) Gaunt.

Principles of Conservation Biology. 2nd ed. Gary K. Meffe & C. Ronald Carroll. LC 97-8018. (Illus.). 673p. (C). 1997. text 69.95 (*0-87893-521-5*) Sinauer Assocs.

Principles of Constructing Linguistic Models. P. N. Denisov. LC 72-88205. (Janua Linguarum, Ser. Minor: No. 91). 173p. (Orig.). 1973. pap. text 52.35 (*90-279-2376-0*) Mouton.

Principles of Construction. 2nd ed. Greeno. 1995. pap. text. write for info. (*0-582-23086-1*, Pub. by Addison-Wesley) Longman.

Principles of Construction Law. Michael P. O'Reilly. xxiii, 300p. (C). 1993. 71.95 (*0-582-21585-4*, 15740) Gaunt.

Principles of Construction Management. 3rd ed. Roy Pilcher. (International Series in Civil Engineering). (C). 1992. text 59.74 (*0-07-707236-7*) McGraw.

Principles of Construction of Hot-Mix Asphalt Pavements. 300p. 1983. 18.00 (*0-318-17743-9*, MS-22) Asphalt Inst.

Principles of Construction of Hot-Mix Asphalt Pavements: Spanish Edition. Tr. of Principios de Construccion de Pavimentos de Mezcla Asfaltica de Caliente. (SPA., Illus.). 300p. (Orig.). 1995. pap. 18.00 (*0-614-23295-3*, MS22) Asphalt Inst.

Principles of Contaminant Hydrogeology. Christopher M. Palmer et al. 232p. 1991. lib. bdg. 59.95 (*0-87371-280-3*, L280) Lewis Pubs.

Principles of Contaminant Hydrogeology. Christopher M. Palmer. LC 96-4967. 256p. 1996. reprint ed. lib. bdg. 75.00 (*1-56670-169-4*, L1169) Lewis Pubs.

Principles of Contaminant Transport in Soils. R. N. Yong et al. LC 92-31963. (Developments in Geotechnical Engineering Ser.: Vol. 73). 328p. 1992. 182.25 (*0-444-88293-6*) Elsevier.

Principles of Continuous Learning, Vol. II. Saito. (C). 1996. pap. text 38.25 (*0-07-057939-3*) McGraw.

Principles of Continuous System Simulation. Wolfgang K. Giloi. (Illus.). 1976. pap. 34.00 (*3-519-02336-9*) Adlers Foreign Bks.

Principles of Continuum Mechanics. Mysore N. Narasimhan. 584p. 1992. 139.00 (*0-471-54000-5*) Wiley.

Principles of Contract at Law & in Equity: A Treatise on the General Principles Concerning the Validity of Agreements in the Law of England & America. Frederick Pollock. cliv, 985p. 1988. reprint ed. 95.00 (*0-8377-2516-X*, Rothman) W S Hein.

Principles of Contract Law. Steven J. Burton. LC 95-3030. (American Casebook Ser.). 699p. (C). 1995. 57.50 (*0-314-04972-X*) West Pub.

Principles of Contract Law. 3rd ed. Richard Stone. (Principles of Law Ser.). xlvii, 377p. 1997. pap. 32.50 (*1-85941-372-2*, Pub. by Cavendish Pubng) Gaunt.

Principles of Control Engineering. write for info. (*0-340-62541-4*, Pub. by E A) Routldge.

Principles of Convective Heat Transfer. Massoud Kaviany. LC 94-1483. 1994. 79.95 (*0-387-94271-8*) Spr-Verlag.

Principles of Corporate Communication. Cees Van Riel. 256p. (C). 1995. pap. 47.00 (*0-13-150996-9*, Macmillan Coll) P-H.

Principles of Corporate Finance. Dye. 1998. pap. text 19.35 (*0-13-679911-6*) P-H.

P

An Asterisk (*) at the beginning of an entry indicates that the title is appearing for the first time.

Principles of Corporate Finance. Levy. (FN - Financial Management Ser.). 1998. pap. 19.95 (*0-538-85438-3*) S-W Pub.

Principles of Corporate Finance. Levy & Perry. LC 97-36159. (AB - Accounting Principles Ser.). (C). 1997. mass mkt. 98.95 (*0-538-84741-7*) S-W Pub.

Principles of Corporate Finance. 2nd ed. Levy. (SWC-Finance Ser.). 2001. pap. text 57.00 (*0-324-02394-4*) Sth-Wstrn College.

Principles of Corporate Finance. 5th ed. Richard A. Brealey & Stewart C. Myers. LC 96-76441. (Illus.). 664p. (C). 1996. text 99.75 (*0-07-007417-8*) McGraw.

Principles of Corporate Finance. 5th ed. Richard A. Brealey & Stewart C. Myers. (C). 1996. pap. text, student ed. 29.38 (*0-07-007477-1*) McGraw.

Principles of Corporate Finance. 6th ed. Brealey. 1999. 70.25 (*0-07-290999-4*) McGraw.

***Principles of Corporate Finance.** 6th ed. Richard A. Brealey. 1999. pap., student ed. 89.69 (*0-07-235236-1*) McGraw.

***Principles of Corporate Finance: Solutions Manual.** 6th ed. Richard Brealey & Stewart C. Myers. 384p. (C). 1999. pap. 20.63 (*0-07-234659-0*) McGrw-H Hghr Educ.

Principles of Corporate Governance: Analysis & Recommendations, 2 vols. American Law Institute Staff. Ed. by Mike Greenwald. LC 93-31619. liv, 477p. 1994. text 135.00 (*0-314-02630-4*, 5463) Am Law Inst.

Principles of Corporate Governance: Analysis & Recommendations, 2 vols., Vol. 1. American Law Institute Staff. Ed. by Mike Greenwald. LC 93-31619. liv, 432p. 1994. text 135.00 (*0-314-02629-0*, 5463) West Pub.

Principles of Corporate Renewal. Harlan D. Platt. LC 97-38129. (Illus.). 440p. (C). 1998. text 57.50 (*0-472-10838-7*, 10838) U of Mich Pr.

Principles of Cosmology & Gravitation. M. Berry. (Illus.). 192p. 1989. pap. 27.00 (*0-85274-037-9*) IOP Pub.

Principles of Cost Accounting. 9th ed. Schmiedicke et al. (C). 1991. pap., student ed. 24.25 (*0-538-81293-1*) Thomson Learn.

Principles of Cost Accounting. 10th ed. Nagy. (AB - Accounting Principles Ser.). (C). 1995. pap. 49.95 (*0-538-84403-5*) S-W Pub.

Principles of Cost Accounting. 10th ed. Vanderbeck. 1995. pap. 21.75 (*0-538-85099-X*) S-W Pub.

Principles of Cost Accounting. 11th ed. Vander Beck. LC 98-8478. 1998. pap. 62.95 (*0-538-87342-6*) S-W Pub.

Principles of Cost Accounting. 11th ed. Vander Beck. (SWC-Accounting). 1998. pap., student ed. 24.95 (*0-538-87343-4*) S-W Pub.

Principles of Cost Accounting: Practice Set. 9th ed. Robert E. Schmiedicke et al. (C). 1991. pap. 21.75 (*0-538-81292-3*) Thomson Learn.

Principles of Cost Accounting, Study Guide & Working Papers. 10th ed. Nagy. (AB - Accounting Principles Ser.). (C). 1995. pap. 27.95 (*0-538-84404-3*) S-W Pub.

Principles of Cost-Benefit Analysis for Developing Countries. Caroline Dinwiddy & Francis Teal. 302p. (C). 1996. text 64.95 (*0-521-47358-6*); pap. text 20.95 (*0-521-47916-9*) Cambridge U Pr.

Principles of Course Design for Language Teaching. Janice Yalden. (New Directions in Language Teaching Ser.). 222p. 1987. text 54.95 (*0-521-30989-1*); pap. text 20.95 (*0-521-31221-3*) Cambridge U Pr.

***Principles of CPT Coding.** American Medical Association Staff. (Coding Ser.). (Illus.). 325p. 1999. pap. 49.95 (*0-89970-996-6*) AMA.

Principles of Credit Evaluation see Installment Credit Series

Principles of Criminal Evidence. Adrian A. Zuckerman. (Clarendon Law Ser.). 408p. 1989. 90.00 (*0-19-876103-1*); pap. text 35.00 (*0-19-876234-8*) OUP.

Principles of Criminal Law. (C). 1995. 24.00 (*0-8013-0837-2*) Longman.

Principles of Criminal Law. J. M. Burchell & J. R. Milton. 1991. pap. 45.00 (*0-7021-2639-X*, Pub. by Juta & Co) Gaunt.

Principles of Criminal Law. Harvey Wallace. (C). 1995. pap. text. write for info. (*0-8013-1480-1*) Addison-Wesley.

Principles of Criminal Law. Harvey Wallace & Cliff Roberson. LC 95-9387. 416p. (C). 1996. pap. text 46.88 (*0-8013-0836-4*) Longman.

***Principles of Criminal Law.** 2nd ed. Harvey Wallace & Clifford Roberson. 432p. 2000. pap. 48.00 (*0-8013-1919-6*) Longman.

Principles of Criminal Law. 2nd ed. O. P. Srivastava. (C). 1990. reprint ed. 75.00 (*0-7855-4717-7*) St Mut.

***Principles of Criminal Law.** 3rd ed. Andrew Ashworth. LC 99-32728. 568p. 1999. write for info. (*0-19-876557-6*) OUP.

Principles of Criminal Law. 3rd ed. Duncan Bloy & Philip Parry. (Principles of Law Ser.). xxxix, 410p. 1997. pap. 29.00 (*1-85941-373-0*, Pub. by Cavendish Pubng) Gaunt.

Principles of Criminal Law in New South Wales. J. Oxley-Oxland. 1985. pap. 54.00 (*0-409-49135-7*, AT, MICHIE) LEXIS Pub.

Principles of Criminal Law (with Model Questions & Suggested Readings) O. P. Srivastava. 186p. 1985. 36.00 (*0-7855-1720-0*) St Mut.

Principles of Criminology. 11th ed. Edwin H. Sutherland et al. LC 91-75943. 704p. 1992. pap. text 39.95 (*0-930390-69-5*); lib. bdg. 65.95 (*0-930390-70-9*) Gen Hall.

Principles of Criminology: Crime & Investigation. R. Deb. (C). 1990. 110.00 (*0-89771-160-2*) St Mut.

Principles of Critical Care. Jesse B. Hall et al. (Illus.). 2432p. 1992. text 155.00 (*0-07-071589-0*) McGraw-Hill HPD.

Principles of Critical Care. Janet K. Ihde et al. (Illus.). 456p. 1987. pap. text 45.00 (*0-7216-1802-2*, W B Saunders Co) Harcrt Hlth Sci Grp.

Principles of Critical Care. Farokh E. Udwadia. (Illus.). 696p. 1996. text 62.50 (*0-19-563728-3*) OUP.

***Principles of Critical Care.** Farokh Erach Udwadia. LC 99-934732. (Illus.). 1999. write for info. (*0-19-564893-5*) OUP.

Principles of Critical Care. 2nd ed. Jesse B. Hall et al. LC 97-45852. (Illus.). 1800p. 1998. text 175.00 (*0-07-025934-8*) McGraw-Hill HPD.

Principles of Critical Care, 1. Jesse B. Hall. write for info. (*0-07-025874-0*) McGraw.

Principles of Critical Care, 2. Jesse B. Hall. write for info. (*0-07-025875-9*) McGraw.

Principles of Critical Care: Companion Handbook. Ed. by Jesse B. Hall et al. LC 92-48941. (Companion Handbook Ser.). (Illus.). 608p. 1993. pap. text 32.00 (*0-07-025828-7*) McGraw-Hill HPD.

Principles of Critical Care: Companion Handbook. 2nd ed. Ed. by Jesse B. Hall et al. (Illus.). 650p. 1998. pap. text 32.00 (*0-07-026029-X*) McGraw-Hill HPD.

Principles of Critical Care: PreTest Self-Assessment & Review. 2nd ed. Jesse B. Hall et al. (Pretest Specialty Level Ser.). (Illus.). 256p. 1997. pap. text 45.00 (*0-07-052294-4*) McGraw-Hill HPD.

***Principles of Crop Improvement.** 2nd ed. Ed. by N. W. Simmonds & J. Smartt. LC 99-59354. (Illus.). 320p. 2000. text 104.95 (*0-632-04191-9*, Pub. by Blckwell Science) Iowa St U Pr.

Principles of Crystal Chemistry. E. Cartmell. 1989. 22.00 (*0-85404-017-X*) CRC Pr.

Principles of Crystal Chemistry. E. Cartnell. 1971. pap. 10.00 (*0-85404-018-8*) CRC Pr.

Principles of Cultivar Development: Theory & Technique. Walter R. Fehr. (Illus.). 536p. (C). 1987. reprint ed. 31.90 (*0-9635989-0-2*) W & E Fehr.

Principles of Dairy Farming. Diamond Farm Book Publishers Staff. (Illus.). 1991. 38.95 (*0-85236-147-5*) Farming Pr.

Principles of Data Conversion System Design. Behzad Razavi. LC 94-26694. 272p. 1994. 79.95 (*0-7803-1093-4*, PC4465) Inst Electrical.

Principles of Data Fusion Automation. Richard T. Antony. LC 95-15178. 470p. 1995. 105.00 (*0-89006-760-0*) Artech Hse.

***Principles of Data Mining.** David J. Hand et al. (Adaptive Computation & Machine Learning Ser.). 425p. 2000. 50.00 (*0-262-08290-X*) MIT Pr.

Principles of Data Mining & Knowledge Discovery: Proceedings of the First European Symposium, PKDD '97, Trondheim, Norway, June 24-27, 1997, Vol. 126. J. Komorowski & Jan M. Zytkow. LC 97-18149. (Lecture Notes in Artificial Intelligence Ser.). ix, 397p. 1997. pap. write for info. (*3-540-63223-9*) Spr-Verlag.

Principles of Data Mining & Knowledge Discovery: Second European Symposium, PKDD'98, Nantes, France, September 23-26, 1998, Proceedings, Vol. 101. Jan Zytkow & Mohamed Quafafou. Ed. by G. Goos et al. LC 98-41489. (Lecture Notes in Computer Science Ser.: Vol. 1510). xi, 481p. 1998. pap. 69.00 (*3-540-65068-7*) Spr-Verlag.

***Principles of Data Mining & Knowledge Discovery: 3rd European Conference, PKDD'99, Prague, Czech Republic, September 15-18, 1999, Proceedings.** Ed. by Jan M. Zytkow et al. LC 99-47028. (Lecture Notes in Computer Science Ser.: Vol. 1704). xiv, 593p. 1999. pap. 91.00 (*3-540-66490-4*) Spr-Verlag.

Principles of Data Processing & Essentials of Basic Programming Supplement. 2nd ed. Ralph Janaro & Ralph M. Stair. (C). 1984. 29.00 (*0-256-05007-4*, Irwin McGrw-H) McGrw-H Hghr Educ.

Principles of Data Security. Ernst L. Leiss. LC 82-22272. (Foundations of Computer Science Ser.). (Illus.). 238p. (C). 1982. 71.00 (*0-306-41098-2*, Plenum Trade) Perseus Pubng.

Principles of Database Query Processing for Advanced Applications. Clement Yu & Weiyi Meng. LC 97-38044. 600p. (C). 1997. text 69.95 (*1-55860-434-0*) Morgan Kaufmann.

Principles of DC-AC Circuits. Colin D. Simpson. LC 95-18399. 1995. write for info. (*0-614-07803-2*) P-H.

Principles of DC & AC Circuits. Angerbauer. (Electronics Technology Ser.). 1990. lab manual ed. 26.95 (*0-8273-3846-5*) Delmar.

Principles of Deductive Logic. John T. Kearns. LC 86-23035. 471p. (C). 1987. text 59.50 (*0-88706-478-7*); pap. text 24.95 (*0-88706-479-5*) State U NY Pr.

Principles of Delict. J. M. Burchell. 292p. 1993. pap. 29.50 (*0-7021-2941-0*, Pub. by Juta & Co) Gaunt.

Principles of Dental Imaging. Olaf E. Langland & Robert P. Langlais. LC 97-2361. (Illus.). 467p. 1997. pap. 42.00 (*0-683-18241-2*) Lppncott W & W.

***Principles of Dental Suturing: The Complete Guide to Surgical Closure.** Lee M. Silverstein. Ed. by Allison Loperfido. (Illus.). 80p. 2000. pap. text 45.00 (*0-9673009-0-8*) Montage Media Corp.

Principles of Dental Treatment Planning. Robert B. Morris. LC 82-15370. 252p. reprint ed. pap. 78.20 (*0-7837-2731-3*, 204311100006) Bks Demand.

Principles of Depreciation. Earl A. Saliers. Ed. by Richard P. Brief. LC 80-1576. (Dimensions of Accounting Theory & Practice Ser.). 1980. reprint ed. lib. bdg. 23.95 (*0-405-13542-4*) Ayer.

Principles of Dermatology. 2nd ed. Donald P. Lookingbill & James G. Marks, Jr. LC 92-48750. (Illus.). 384p. 1993. pap. text 55.00 (*0-7216-4290-X*, W B Saunders Co) Harcrt Hlth Sci Grp.

Principles of Dermatology. 3rd ed. Donald P. Lookingbill & James G. Marks. 335p. Date not set. pap. text. write for info. (*0-7216-7971-4*, W B Saunders Co) Harcrt Hlth Sci Grp.

Principles of Descriptive Inorganic Chemistry. Gary Wulfsberg. LC 90-72042. (Illus.). 461p. (C). 1990. reprint ed. text 58.50 (*0-935702-66-0*) Univ Sci Bks.

***Principles of Design.** Jill A. Rinner. (Scrapbooking Made Easy Ser.). 1998. pap. 3.95 (*1-891520-25-3*) Red Pt Publ.

Principles of Design. Nam P. Suh. (Oxford Series on Advanced Manufacturing: No. 6). (Illus.). 418p. 1990. text 88.00 (*0-19-504345-6*) OUP.

Principles of Design & Operation of the Brain: Proceedings of a Study Week Organized by the Pontifical Academy of Sciences Casina Pius IV, Vatican City. Ed. by John C. Eccles & O. Creutzfeldt. (Experimental Brain Research Ser.: Vol. 21). 600p. 1991. 115.00 (*0-387-53416-4*) Spr-Verlag.

Principles of Desirable Society. Chin-Fu Woo. LC 97-90375. 219p. 1997. 18.95 (*0-533-12372-0*) Vantage.

Principles of Development. Lewis Wolpert et al. LC 97-31108. (Illus.). 504p. (C). 1997. text 77.95 (*0-19-850263-X*) OUP.

Principles of Development of Model Health Care Programmes. (EURO Reports & Studies: No. 96). 41p. 1985. pap. text 6.00 (*92-890-1262-5*, 1330096) World Health.

Principles of Developmental Sexology. John Money. LC 56-7503. 324p. (C). 1997. 59.50 (*0-8264-1026-X*) Continuum.

Principles of Diagnostic Techniques in Plant Pathology. R. T. Fox. (Illus.). 228p. 1993. pap. text 45.00 (*0-85198-740-0*) OUP.

Principles of Dialogue. Studies & Research Unit of Wamy Staff. (ARA.). 79p. (YA). pap. write for info. (*1-882837-00-2*) W A M Y Intl.

Principles of Dielectrics. B. K. Scaife. (Monographs on the Physics & Chemistry of Materials: Vol. 45). (Illus.). 448p. 1998. pap. text 59.00 (*0-19-856557-7*) OUP.

Principles of Differential & Integral Equations. 2nd ed. Constantin Corduneanu. LC 77-2962. 1977. text 19.95 (*0-8284-0295-7*) Chelsea Pub.

Principles of Digital & Analog Communication. Jerry D. Gibson. (Illus.). 592p. (C). 1992. teacher ed. write for info. (*0-318-69332-1*) Macmillan.

Principles of Digital & Analog Communication. 2nd ed. Jerry D. Gibson. (Illus.). 576p. (C). 1992. 66.00 (*0-02-341860-5*, Macmillan Coll) P-H.

Principles of Digital Audio. 3rd ed. K. Pohlmann. LC 95-17259. (Illus.). 640p. 1995. pap. 44.95 (*0-07-050469-5*) McGraw.

Principles of Digital Audio & Video. Arch Luther. LC 97-12550. (Communications Engineering Ser.). 408p. 1997. 79.00 (*0-89006-892-5*) Artech Hse.

Principles of Digital Design. Daniel D. Gajski. 447p. 1996. 100.00 (*0-13-301144-5*) P-H.

Principles of Digital Document Processing: 4th International Workshop, PODDP '98, Saint-Malo, France, March 29-30, 1998: Proceedings, Vol. 148. Ethan V. Munson et al. LC 98-41918. (Lecture Notes in Computer Science Ser.). 1998. pap. 37.00 (*3-540-65086-5*) Spr-Verlag.

Principles of Digital Image Synthesis, 2 vols. Andrew S. Glassner. LC 94-36565. 1600p. 1995. text 98.95 (*1-55860-276-3*) Morgan Kaufmann.

Principles of Digital Transmission with Wireless Applications. S. Benedetto & E. Biglieri. LC 98-46066. (Series in Telecommunications). (Illus.). (C). 1999. write for info. (*0-306-45753-9*, Plenum Trade) Perseus Pubng.

Principles of Direct & Database Marketing. Alan Tapp. 336p. 2000. pap. write for info. (*0-273-62717-1*) F T P H.

Principles of Direct Current Resistivity Prospecting. Geza Kunetz. Ed. by H. Braekken & R. Van Nostrand. (Geoexploration Monographs: No. 1). (Illus.). xvi, 103p. 1966. 17.00 (*3-443-13001-1*, Pub. by Gebruder Borntraeger) Balogh.

Principles of Discipleship. Charles G. Finney. Ed. by Louis G. Parkhurst. LC 87-34108. 24p. (Orig.). 1988. pap. 8.99 (*0-87123-860-8*) Bethany Hse.

Principles of Discrete-Time Speech Processing. Thomas F. Quatieri. (C). 1999. 65.00 (*0-13-242942-X*, Macmillan Coll) P-H.

Principles of Distributed Database Systems. 2nd ed. M. Tamer Ozsu & Patrick Valduriez. LC 98-11901. 666p. (C). 1999. 76.00 (*0-13-659707-6*) P-H.

Principles of Distributed Systems. Vijay K. Garg. LC 95-45498. 272p. (C). 1996. text 119.50 (*0-7923-9668-5*) Kluwer Academic.

Principles of Document Processing: 3rd International Workshop, PODP '96, Palo Alto, California, U. S. A., September 23, 1996. Selected Papers. Ed. by C. Nicholas et al. (Lecture Notes in Computer Science Ser.: Vol. 1293). xi, 195p. 1997. pap. 43.00 (*3-540-63620-X*) Spr-Verlag.

Principles of Doppler & Color Doppler Imaging. 2nd ed. R. Haerten & M. Muck-Weymann. 50p. 1994. pap. 89.95 (*3-8009-4212-7*) Wiley.

***Principles of Dreams: The Only Introduction You'll Ever Need.** Soozi Holbeche. (Principles Ser.). 192p. 1998. pap. 11.00 (*0-7225-3548-1*, Pub. by Thorsons MD) Natl Bk Netwk.

***Principles of Dressage.** Albrecht. 2000. 19.95 (*0-85131-569-0*, Pub. by J A Allen) Trafalgar.

Principles of Drilling Fluid Control. 12th ed. (Illus.). 232p. (C). 1969. reprint ed. pap. text 17.00 (*0-88698-118-2*, 2.70120) PETEX.

Principles of Drug Action. 3rd ed. Ed. by William B. Pratt & Palmer Taylor. (Illus.). 834p. 1990. text 83.00 (*0-443-08676-1*) Church.

***Principles of Drug Addiction Treatment: A Research--Based Guide.** Pref. by Alan I. Leshner. 54p. 2000. pap. text 20.00 (*0-7567-0065-5*) DIANE Pub.

Principles of Drug Development in Transplantation & Autoimmunity. Ronald Lieberman & Asoke Mukherjee. LC 95-37929. (Medical Intelligence Unit Ser.). 874p. 1996. 130.00 (*1-57059-283-7*) Landes Bioscience.

Principles of Drug Information & Scientific Literature Evaluation. Frank J. Ascione et al. LC 93-41705. 236p. (C). 1994. pap. text 30.00 (*0-914768-52-2*, T169) Am Pharm Assn.

Principles of Druidry: The Only Introduction You'll Ever Need. Emma R. Orr. (Illus.). 160p. 1999. pap. 11.00 (*0-7225-3674-7*) Thorsons PA.

Principles of Dynamic Programming Pt. 1: Basic Analytical & Computational Methods. Robert Edward Larson & Casti. (Control & Systems Theory Ser.: Vol. 7). 344p. 1978. text 100.00 (*0-8247-6589-3*) Dekker.

Principles of Dynamic Programming Pt.2: Advanced Theory & Applications. Robert E. Larson & John L. Casti. (Control & Systems Theory Ser.: Vol. 7). 512p. 1982. text 140.00 (*0-8247-6590-7*) Dekker.

Principles of Dynamics. 2nd ed. Donald T. Greenwood. (Illus.). 544p. (C). 1988. text 48.95 (*0-317-60135-0*) P-H.

Principles of Ecology. Ed. by Botkin. (C). Date not set. text. write for info. (*0-321-01478-2*) Addson-Wesley Educ.

Principles of Ecology. John C. Williams. 117p. (C). 1997. pap. text 19.95 (*1-885827-05-9*) NatureGraphics.

Principles of Ecology. 2nd ed. (C). 1990. write for info. (*0-8087-9227-X*) Pearson Custom.

Principles of Ecology in Plant Production. Ed. by T. R. Sinclair & F. P. Gardner. (A CAB International Publication). (Illus.). 200p. 1998. pap. text 28.00 (*0-85199-220-X*) OUP.

Principles of Economcis. Frank. 2000. student ed. 17.25 (*0-07-228966-X*) McGraw.

Principles of Econometrics. Henri Theil. (Illus.). 768p. (C). 1971. text 109.95 (*0-471-85845-5*) Wiley.

Principles of Economic Growth. Thorvaldur Gylfason. LC 98-56187. (Illus.). 200p. 1999. pap. text 35.00 (*0-19-877614-4*) OUP.

Principles of Economic Growth. Thorvaldur Gylfason. LC 98-56187. (Illus.). 200p. 1999. text 70.00 (*0-19-877613-6*) OUP.

Principles of Economics. Lawrence A. Boland. LC 91-31008. 256p. (C). (gr. 13). 1992. 90.00 (*0-415-06433-3*) Routledge.

Principles of Economics. William S. Brown. LC 94-16366. 1104p. (C). 1994. mass mkt. 97.95 (*0-314-04229-6*) West Pub.

***Principles of Economics.** Buckles. 2002. pap. text. write for info. (*1-57259-974-X*) Worth.

Principles of Economics. Vincent Byrne & James L. Gilbertie. 548p. (C). 1996. pap. text 47.75 (*1-56226-319-6*) CAT Pub.

Principles of Economics. Michael Fabritius & James L. Gilbertie. 584p. (C). 1995. pap. text 41.88 (*1-56226-218-1*) CAT Pub.

Principles of Economics. Frank. 2000. 67.50 (*0-07-228962-7*) McGraw.

Principles of Economics. Gordon Staff. (C). Date not set. pap. text, student ed. 13.50 (*0-03-002447-1*) Harcourt Coll Pubs.

Principles of Economics. Gordon Staff. (C). Date not set. text 39.00 (*0-03-002422-6*) Harcourt Coll Pubs.

Principles of Economics. Gottheil. (HB - Economics Ser.). 1996. pap. 64.95 (*0-538-86290-4*) S-W Pub.

Principles of Economics. Fred Gottheil. LC 95-8566. (C). 1995. pap. 59.50 (*0-538-84020-X*) S-W Pub.

Principles of Economics. J. Vernon Henderson & William Poole. LC 90-84759. 1235p. (C). 1991. text 76.36 (*0-669-14491-6*); pap. text 54.36 (*0-669-14492-4*); pap. text 54.36 (*0-669-14493-2*); teacher ed. 2.66 (*0-669-14495-9*); student ed. 26.36 (*0-669-14494-0*); student ed. 19.96 (*0-669-26923-9*); student ed. 19.96 (*0-669-26924-7*); trans. 93.56 (*0-669-27949-8*); trans. 93.56 (*0-669-14496-7*) HM Trade Div.

Principles of Economics. Hess. Date not set. pap. text, teacher ed. write for info. (*0-314-02061-6*); pap. text, student ed. 20.00 (*0-314-01897-2*) West Pub.

Principles of Economics. James R. Kearl. 1000p. (C). 1993. text 76.36 (*0-669-28961-2*); pap. text 54.36 (*0-669-28962-0*); pap. text 54.36 (*0-669-28963-9*); teacher ed. 2.66 (*0-669-28965-5*); 25.96 (*0-669-28964-7*); 25.16 (*0-669-33455-3*); 2.66 (*0-669-28966-3*); trans. write for info. (*0-318-70090-5*) HM Trade Div.

Principles of Economics. Shirley E. Kress. LC 90-4041. (Illus.). 354p. (C). 1990. pap. text 47.50 (*0-9625354-0-0*) Intercept Econ.

Principles of Economics. Linda Low & Mun-Heng Toh. LC 95-32430. 1995. write for info. (*0-201-42080-5*) Addison-Wesley.

Principles of Economics. Linda Low & Toh Mun Heng. LC 96-25486. 1997. write for info. (*0-201-42089-9*) Addison-Wesley.

Principles of Economics. Mankiw. (C). 1998. pap. text 157.50 (*0-03-024777-2*, Pub. by Harcourt Coll Pubs) Harcourt.

Principles of Economics. Gregory Mankiw. LC 96-71397. 688p. (C). 1997. text 85.00 (*0-03-098238-3*, Pub. by Harcourt Coll Pubs) Harcourt.

Principles of Economics. Alfred Marshall. LC 97-3368. 343p. 1997. pap. 11.95 (*1-57392-140-8*) Prometheus Bks.

Principles of Economics. Carl Menger. 328p. 1994. pap. 17.95 (*0-910884-27-7*) Libertarian Press.

Principles of Economics. Jack Rudman. (Dantes Subject Standardized Tests Ser.: DANTES-32). 1994. pap. 23.95 (*0-8373-6632-1*) Nat Learn.

P

An Asterisk (*) at the beginning of an entry indicates that the title is appearing for the first time.

Principles of Economics. Jack Rudman. (DANTES Ser.: No. 32). 1994. 39.95 (*0-8373-6532-5*) Nat Learn.

Principles of Economics. Ed. by Salvatore. (C). 1998. pap. text, student ed. write for info. (*0-321-01045-0*) Addson-Wesley Educ.

Principles of Economics. Ed. by Salvatore. (C). 2000. text. write for info. (*0-321-01041-8*) Addson-Wesley Educ.

Principles of Economics. Ed. by Snower. (C). 1999. text Price not set. (*0-321-01422-7*) Addison-Wesley.

Principles of Economics. Richard W. Tresch. Date not set. pap. text, teacher ed. write for info. (*0-314-03408-0*) West Pub.

Principles of Economics. Gerry F. Welch. (C). 1998. pap. text 16.75 (*0-03-008862-3*); pap. text, teacher ed. 23.75 (*0-03-008867-4*) Harcourt Coll Pubs.

Principles of Economics. 2nd ed. Gottheil. LC 98-7445. (Miscellaneous/Catalogs Ser.). 1998. pap. 92.95 (*0-538-86818-X*) S-W Pub.

Principles of Economics. 2nd ed. Martin L. Primack et al. 964p. (C). 1998. pap. text 56.25 (*1-56226-392-7*) CAT Pub.

Principles of Economics. 2nd ed. James F. Ragan, Jr. & Lloyd B. Thomas, Jr. LC 92-81302. 1584p. (C). 1993. text, student ed. 100.50 (*0-03-096632-9*) Dryden Pr.

Principles of Economics. 2nd aut. ed. William Walter Brown et al. (C). 1997. pap. text 37.00 (*0-201-34308-8*) Addison-Wesley.

Principles of Economics. 3rd ed. (C). 1996. 129.00 (*0-201-49804-9*) Addison-Wesley.

Principles Of Economics. 3rd ed. (C). 1996. 129.00 (*0-201-49802-2*) Addison-Wesley.

Principles Of Economics. 3rd ed. Ryan C. Amacher & Holley H. Ulbrich. (Thomson Executive Press). 1985. mass mkt. 35.25 (*0-538-08671-8*, H67) S-W Pub.

Principles of Economics. 3rd ed. Amacher & Ulbrich. (Thomson Executive Press Ser.). 1986. 13.25 (*0-538-27169-8*); mass mkt., student ed. 12.50 (*0-538-08691-2*) S-W Pub.

*__Principles of Economics.__ 3rd ed. Gottheil. (SWC-Economics Ser.). 2001. pap. 63.75 (*0-324-05591-9*) Sth-Wstrn College.

Principles of Economics. 4th ed. William Feipal & James L. Gilbertie. 554p. (C). 1994. pap. text 53.45 (*1-56226-204-1*) CAT Pub.

Principles of Economics. 4th ed. Paul Gregory & Roy J. Ruffin. (C). 1990. pap. text 34.00 (*0-673-46021-5*, Scott Frsmn); pap. text 34.00 (*0-673-46022-3*, Scott Frsmn) Addison-Wesley Educ.

Principles of Economics. 4th ed. Paul Gregory & Roy J. Ruffin. (C). 1999. text 50.33 (*0-673-46020-7*, Scott Frsmn) Addison-Wesley Educ.

Principles of Economics. 4th ed. Willis L. Peterson. (C). 1979. student ed., per. 5.95 (*0-256-02338-7*, Irwn McGrw-H) McGrw-H Hghr Educ.

Principles of Economics. 5th ed. Karl E. Case & Ray C. Fair. LC 98-23823. 959p. (C). 1998. 92.00 (*0-13-095710-0*) P-H.

Principles of Economics. 5th ed. Sonny Festejo & James L. Gilbertie. 548p. (C). 1996. pap. text 48.95 (*1-56226-315-3*) CAT Pub.

Principles of Economics. 5th ed. Roy J. Ruffin & Paul R. Gregory. LC 92-23589. (C). 1992. text 68.12 (*0-673-46590-X*) Addison-Wesley Educ.

Principles of Economics. 5th ed. Roy J. Ruffin & Paul R. Gregory. (C). 1993. pap. text, student ed. 23.12 (*0-673-46591-8*); disk 118.00 (*0-673-53880-X*) Addison-Wesley Educ.

*__Principles of Economics.__ 7th ed. Roy J. Ruffin & Paul R. Gregory. 2001. 90.00 (*0-321-07730-X*) Addison-Wesley.

Principles of Economics. 8th ed. Alfred Marshall. (Illus.). xxxii, 731p. 1982. reprint ed. pap. 28.95 (*0-87991-051-8*) Porcupine Pr.

*__Principles of Economics.__ 9th ed. Richard G. Lipsey & K. Alec Chrystal. LC 98-48332. 1999. write for info. (*0-19-877589-X*); write for info. (*0-19-877588-1*) OUP.

Principles of Economics: An Analytical Approach. Peter N. Hess & Clark G. Ross. Ed. by Fenton. LC 92-41850. 688p. (C). 1993. text 59.75 (*0-314-01259-1*) West Pub.

Principles of Economics: Macro. 7th ed. Willis L. Peterson. (C). 1988. pap. text 33.95 (*0-256-06795-3*, Irwn McGrw-H); student ed. 15.95 (*0-256-07054-7*, Irwn McGrw-H) McGrw-H Hghr Educ.

Principles of Economics: Macro. 9th ed. Willis L. Peterson. (Illus.). 359p. (C). 1994. pap. text 24.95 (*1-885079-25-7*) Willis Peterson.

Principles of Economics: Macro. 9th ed. Willis L. Peterson. (Illus.). 120p. (C). 1994. teacher ed. write for info. (*1-885079-75-3*) Willis Peterson.

Principles of Economics: Macro. 10th ed. Willis Peterson. 430p. (C). 1997. text 44.95 (*1-885079-26-5*) Willis Peterson.

Principles of Economics: Macro Ready Notes. 2nd ed. Gottheil. (Swc-Economics Ser.). 1998. pap. 9.00 (*0-538-86836-8*) S-W Pub.

Principles of Economics: Macroeconomics. David E. Emery. LC 86-7653. (College Outline Ser.). 347p. (C). 1987. pap. text 12.25 (*0-15-601586-2*) Harcourt Coll Pubs.

Principles of Economics: Micro. 7th ed. Willis L. Peterson. (C). 1988. student ed. 15.95 (*0-256-07055-5*, Irwn McGrw-H) McGrw-H Hghr Educ.

Principles of Economics: Micro. 9th ed. Willis L. Peterson. (Illus.). 303p. (C). 1994. pap. text 24.95 (*1-885079-00-1*) Willis Peterson.

Principles of Economics: Micro. 9th ed. Willis L. Peterson. (Illus.). 120p. 1994. teacher ed. write for info. (*1-885079-50-8*) Willis Peterson.

Principles of Economics: Micro. 10th ed. Willis Peterson. 440p. (C). 1997. text 44.95 (*1-885079-01-X*) Willis Peterson.

Principles of Economics: Micro Ready Notes. 2nd ed. Gottheil. (Swc-Economics Ser.). 1998. 9.00 (*0-538-86835-X*) S-W Pub.

Principles of Economics: Microeconomics. E. David Emery. (College Outline Ser.). 319p. (C). 1984. pap. text 13.25 (*0-15-600053-9*) Harcourt Coll Pubs.

Principles of Economics: Some Lies My Teachers Told Me. Lawrence A. Boland. LC 95-21630. 256p. (Orig.). (C). 1995. pap. 29.99 (*0-415-13208-8*) Routledge.

Principles of Economics: Study Guide. 4th ed. James L. Gilbertie. 168p. (C). 1993. pap. text 16.19 (*1-56226-163-0*) CAT Pub.

Principles of Economics: Test Bank. James L. Gilbertie. 158p. 1995. pap. text. write for info. (*1-56226-245-9*) CAT Pub.

Principles of Economics: The Big 10 Way. Axelrod. LC 99-17542. (Midterms & Finals Ser.). (Illus.). 340p. 1999. pap. 16.95 (*0-07-007006-7*) McGraw.

Principles of Economics: Theory & Practice. Maxwell. (Illus.). 704p. 1989. 12.95 (*0-8016-2423-1*) Mosby Inc.

Principles of Economics for Today & Tomorrow. Stamos & Riddel. pap. 63.95 (*0-538-87177-6*) S-W Pub.

Principles Of Economics Macro. 3rd ed. Ryan C. Amacher & Holley H. Ulbrich. (Thomson Executive Press). 1986. mass mkt. 24.50 (*0-538-08690-4*, H69) S-W Pub.

Principles of Economics, Macro: Personal Learning Aid. 4th ed. Lloyd G. Reynolds & Nicholas Michas. (Plaid Ser.). 1983. pap. 13.00 (*0-87094-430-4*, Irwn Prfssnl) McGraw-Hill Prof.

Principles Of Economics Micro. 3rd ed. Ryan C. Amacher & Holley H. Ulbrich. (Thomson Executive Press). 1986. mass mkt. 24.50 (*0-538-08681-5*, H68) S-W Pub.

Principles of Economics (with CD-ROM) 5th ed. (C). 1998. text, teacher ed. write for info. incl. cd-rom (*0-13-020418-8*) P-H.

Principles of Ecotoxicology. C. H. Walker et al. 321p. 1996. 99.95 (*0-7484-0220-9*); pap. 39.95 (*0-7484-0221-7*) Taylor & Francis.

*__Principles of Ecotoxicology.__ 2nd ed. C. H. Walker. LC 00-37777. 2000. pap. write for info. (*0-7484-0940-8*) Taylor & Francis.

Principles of Editing: A Comprehensive Guide for Students & Journalists. Daryl F. Frazell & George Tuck. LC 95-25047. 318p. (C). 1995. pap. 54.06 (*0-07-021926-5*) McGraw.

Principles of Editing: A Comprehensive Guide for Students & Journalists. Daryl L. Frazell & George Tuck. 1996. pap. text, wbk. ed. write for info. (*0-07-841181-5*) McGraw.

Principles of Editing: A Comprehensive Guide for Students & Journalists, Exercises in Line Editing & Headline Writing. Daryl L. Frazell & George Tuck. (C). 1996. pap. text, student ed. 26.88 (*0-07-021945-1*) McGraw.

Principles of Education. S. Venkateswaran. 25.00 (*0-7069-7050-0*, Pub. by Vikas) S Asia.

Principles of Education & Guidance. 2nd ed. Joseph I. Schneersohn. Tr. by Y. Eliezer Danziger from HEB. LC 90-19400. 46p. 1990. reprint ed. pap. 6.00 (*0-8266-0427-7*) Kehot Pubn Soc.

Principles of Education Management. Ed. by Tony Bush & John West-Burnham. 288p. 1994. pap. 57.50 (*0-582-23904-4*, Pub. by Addison-Wesley) Trans-Atl Phila.

Principles of Educational & Psychological Measurement & Evaluation. 2nd ed. Gilbert Sax. 688p. (C). 1980. pap. write for info. (*0-534-00832-1*) Wadsworth Pub.

Principles of Educational & Psychological Measurement & Evaluation. 3rd ed. Gilbert Sax. 678p. (C). 1989. pap. 46.00 (*0-534-09978-5*) Wadsworth Pub.

Principles of Educational & Psychological Measurement & Evaluation: Measurement & Evaluation. 4th ed. Gilbert Sax. (Education Ser.). (C). 1996. 85.95 (*0-534-25749-6*) Wadsworth Pub.

Principles of Educational Psychology Measurement & Evaluation. 3rd ed. Sax. (Education Ser.). 1989. mass mkt., student ed. 16.00 (*0-534-09979-3*) Wadsworth Pub.

Principles of Effective Insurance Agents. Didactic Systems Staff. (Simulation Game Ser.). 1973. pap. 26.25 (*0-685-77372-8*) Didactic Syst.

Principles of Effective Salesmanship. J. S. Schiff et al. (Simulation Game Ser.). 1971. pap. 26.25 (*0-89401-075-1*) Didactic Syst.

Principles of Efficient Information Management. 2nd rev. ed. August-Wilhelm Scheer. Orig. Title: Computer, a Challenge for Business Administration. (Illus.). x, 305p. 1991. 59.00 (*0-387-54106-3*) Spr-Verlag.

Principles of Egyptian Art. Henrich Schafer. 498p. 1986. pap. 55.00 (*0-900416-51-3*, Pub. by Aris & Phillips) David Brown.

Principles of Eidetics: Outline of a Theory. A. Arduini. xii, 251p. 1991. 99.00 (*0-387-54506-9*) Spr-Verlag.

Principles of Electoral Reform. Michael Dummett. LC 96-40027. 208p. 1997. text 65.00 (*0-19-829247-3*); pap. text 24.95 (*0-19-829246-5*) OUP.

*__Principles of Electric Circuits.__ 6th ed. David Buchla. 1999. 37.33 (*0-13-021958-4*) P-H.

*__Principles of Electric Circuits.__ 6th ed. Thomas L. Floyd. LC 99-36382. 927p. 1999. text 96.00 incl. audio compact disk (*0-13-095997-9*) P-H.

Principles of Electric Circuits: Electron-Flow Version. 5th ed. Ed. by Prentice-Hall Staff. LC 99-36154. 925p. (C). 1999. 96.00 incl. cd-rom (*0-13-095998-7*) P-H.

Principles of Electric Machines & Power Electronics. 2nd ed. P. C. Sen. LC 96-47305. 640p. 1996. text 99.95 (*0-471-02295-0*) Wiley.

Principles of Electrical Circuits. Burns. (West Engineering Ser.). 1987. pap., student ed. 16.95 (*0-534-93868-X*); text 60.50 (*0-534-93812-4*); trans. 92.95 (*0-534-93869-8*) PWS Pubs.

Principles of Electrical Engineering. Peyton Z. Peebles, Jr. & Tayeb A. Giuma. (C). 1991. text 64.50 (*0-07-049252-2*) McGraw.

*__Principles of Electrical Engineering Materials & Devices.__ S. O. Kasap. LC 99-32138. (Illus.). 2000. write for info. (*0-07-235644-8*) McGrw-H Hghr Educ.

Principles of Electrical Materials & Devices. Safa Kasap. LC 96-47581. 704p. (C). 1996. text 62.00 (*0-256-16173-9*, Irwn McGrw-H) McGrw-H Hghr Educ.

Principles of Electroanalytical Methods. Tom Riley & Colin Tomlinson. Ed. by Arthur M. James. LC 86-23397. (Analytical Chemistry by Open Learning Ser.). (Illus.). 273p. reprint ed. pap. 84.70 (*0-608-00194-5*, 206097700006) Bks Demand.

Principles of Electrochemistry. 2nd ed. Jiri Koryta et al. LC 92-24345. 502p. 1993. pap. 94.95 (*0-471-93838-6*) Wiley.

Principles of Electrodynamics & Relativity see Encyclopedia of Physics

Principles of Electromagnetic Compatibility. 2nd ed. Bernhard E. Keiser. LC 79-12032. (Illus.). 343p. reprint ed. pap. 106.40 (*0-8357-5583-5*, 203521400093) Bks Demand.

Principles of Electromagnetic Compatibility. 3rd ed. B. J. Keiser. 383p. 1987. 47.00 (*0-89006-206-4*) Artech Hse.

Principles of Electromagnetic Theory. A. H. Kovetz. (Illus.). 238p. (C). 1990. pap. text 30.95 (*0-521-39997-1*) Cambridge U Pr.

Principles of Electromagnetic Theory & Relativity. Marie A. Tonnelat. Tr. by Arthur J. Knodel from FRE. 475p. 1966. text 211.50 (*90-277-0107-5*) Kluwer Academic.

Principles of Electron Optics, 3 vols., Set. Ed. by P. W. Hawkes & Erich Kasper. (Illus.). 1899p. 1996. pap. 120.00 (*0-12-333340-7*) Acad Pr.

Principles of Electron Optics, Vol. 1. Ed. by P. W. Hawkes & Erich Kasper. (Illus.). 1996. pap. text 40.00 (*0-12-333341-5*) Acad Pr.

Principles of Electron Optics, Vol. 1. Ed. by Peter W. Hawkes & E. Kaspar. 623p. 1989. text 126.00 (*0-12-333351-2*) Acad Pr.

Principles of Electron Optics, Vol. 2. Ed. by P. W. Hawkes & Erich Kasper. (Illus.). 1996. pap. text 40.00 (*0-12-333342-3*) Acad Pr.

Principles of Electron Optics, Vol. 2. Peter W. Hawkes & E. Kaspar. 559p. 1989. text 126.00 (*0-12-333352-0*) Acad Pr.

Principles of Electron Optics, Vol. 3. Ed. by P. W. Hawkes & Erich Kasper. (Illus.). 1996. pap. text 40.00 (*0-12-333343-1*) Acad Pr.

Principles of Electron Optics Vol. 3: Wave Optics. Ed. by P. W. Hawkes & Erich Kasper. (Illus.). 752p. 1994. text 128.00 (*0-12-333354-7*) Acad Pr.

Principles of Electron Tubes: Understanding & Designing Simple Circuits. Herbert J. Reich. (Illus.). 379p. 1995. reprint ed. pap. text 34.95 (*1-882580-07-9*) Audio Amateur.

Principles of Electronic Circuits. 2nd ed. Stanley G. Burns & Paul R. Bond. LC 96-173342. (West Engineering Ser.). 1000p. (C). 1996. mass mkt. 109.95 (*0-534-95494-4*) PWS Pubs.

Principles of Electronic Communication Systems. Jack Rudman. (Dantes Subject Standardized Tests Ser.: DANTES-44). 1994. pap. 23.95 (*0-8373-6644-5*) Nat Learn.

Principles of Electronic Controls & Devices: Printed Test Bank. David E. LaLond & John A. Ross. 182p. 1994. pap. 32.50 (*0-8273-6385-0*) Delmar.

Principles of Electronic Devices. William D. Stanley. 912p. (C). 1994. text 72.00 (*0-02-415560-8*, Macmillan Coll) P-H.

Principles of Electronic Devices & Circuits: Computerized Testmaker & Testbank for DOS Compatible Computers. David E. LaLond & John A. Ross. 1994. 49.95 (*0-8273-6510-1*) Delmar.

Principles of Electronic Devices & Circuits: Transparencies. John A. Ross & David E. Lalond. 1994. pap. 69.95 (*0-8273-6421-0*) Delmar.

Principles of Electronic Devices & Circuits - Ross & LaLond: Flashcards. Larry Parker. 128p. 1994. 19.95 (*0-8273-6420-2*) Delmar.

Principles of Electronic Instrumentation. 3rd ed. Diefenderf. (C). 1994. pap. text, lab manual ed. 40.50 (*0-03-097263-9*) Harcourt Coll Pubs.

Principles of Electronic Instrumentation. 3rd ed. Diefenderf. (C). 1994. pap. text, teacher ed. 33.75 (*0-03-097262-0*) Harcourt Coll Pubs.

Principles of Electronic Instrumentation. 3rd ed. A. James Diefenderfer & Brian E. Holton. LC 93-8672. (Golden Sunburst Ser.). (C). 1994. text 93.00 (*0-03-074709-0*, Pub. by SCP) Harcourt.

Principles of Electronic Instrumentation & Measurement. Howard M. Berlin & Frank C. Getz, Jr. 512p. (C). 1990. pap. text, lab manual ed. 25.80 (*0-675-20450-X*, Merrill Coll) P-H.

Principles of Electronic Packaging. Donald P. Seraphim et al. 962p. (C). 1989. 105.31 (*0-07-056306-3*) McGraw.

Principles of Electronic Warfare. Robert J. Schlesinger et al. LC 61-15515. (Illus.). 1979. reprint ed. pap. 22.95 (*0-932146-01-5*) Peninsula CA.

Principles of Electronics. Colin D. Simpson. LC 95-18400. 760p. (C). 1995. 70.60 (*0-13-034406-0*) P-H.

Principles of Electronics, Pt. 1. Ian B. Thomas. (C). 1991. text 32.50 (*0-07-064246-X*) McGraw.

Principles of Electronics: Analog & Digital. Lloyd R. Fortney. (Illus.). 656p. (C). 1995. text 97.00 (*0-15-571630-1*); 2.65 (*0-15-571631-X*) OUP.

Principles of Electronics: Custom Pub, Pt. 2. 2nd ed. Ian B. Thomas. (C). 1994. pap. text 39.25 (*0-07-064391-1*) McGraw.

Principles of Electronics Analog & Digital. Lloyd R. Fortney. 656p. (C). 1987. text. write for info. (*0-318-69072-1*) SCP.

Principles of Electronics Ceramics. Larry L. Hench & Jon West. LC 89-30955. 576p. 1990. 175.00 (*0-471-61821-7*) Wiley.

Principles of Electronics Ceramics. Larry L. Hench & Jon West. 101p. 1990. pap., teacher ed. 49.95 (*0-471-52943-5*) Wiley.

Principles of Electrosurgery: Practical Overview of R. F. Electrosurgical Generators. Ronald L. Bussiere. (Illus.). 33p. 1997. 45.00 (*0-9661128-0-6*) Tektran.

*__Principles of Element Design.__ 3rd ed. Peter Rich. 168p. 1999. pap. text 32.95 (*0-7506-3113-9*) Buttrwrth-Heinemann.

Principles of Elementary Algebra with Applications. 2nd ed. Harry L. Nustad & Terry H. Wesner. 640p. (C). 1991. text 50.00 (*0-697-01351-0*, WCB McGr Hill); text, student ed. 18.75 (*0-697-11083-4*, WCB McGr Hill) McGrw-H Hghr Educ.

Principles of Elocution. Alexander M. Bell. (Works of Alexander Melville Bell). xvi, 240p. 1885. reprint ed. lib. bdg. 39.00 (*0-932051-80-4*) Rprt Serv.

Principles of Emendation in Shakespeare. Walter W. Greg. (BCL1-PR English Literature Ser.). 72p. 1992. reprint ed. lib. bdg. 59.00 (*0-7812-7307-2*) Rprt Serv.

Principles of Emendation in Shakespeare. Walter W. Greg. 1971. reprint ed. 10.00 (*0-403-00613-9*) Scholarly.

Principles of Emergency Medical Dispatch. 2nd ed. Jeff J. Clawson & Kate B. Dernocoeur. Ed. by Gordon W. Cottle & Robert L. Martin. (Illus.). ix, 250p. (C). 1997. 44.99 (*0-9658890-0-9*); pap. 36.99 (*0-9658890-1-7*) Medical Priority.

*__Principles of Emergency Medical Dispatch.__ 3rd ed. Jeff J. Clawson et al. Ed. by Bob Sinclair. (Illus.). 450p. 2000. write for info. (*0-9658890-2-5*) Medical Priority.

Principles of Emergent Realism: Philosophical Essays of Roy Wood Sellars. Ed. by W. Preston Warren. LC 70-96993. (Illus.). 380p. 1970. 14.00 (*0-87527-083-2*) Green.

Principles of Emerging Telecommunication Systems. Rolf Stadler. 1999. 69.95 (*0-8493-1878-5*) CRC Pr.

Principles of Empirical, or Inductive Logic see Principles of Inductive Logic

Principles of Employment Law. 3rd ed. Michael Jefferson. (Principles of Law Ser.). lxxiii, 458p. 1997. pap. 34.50 (*1-85941-374-9*, Pub. by Cavendish Pubng) Gaunt.

Principles of EMS Systems. 2nd ed. American College of Emergency Physicians Staff. 1994. 95.00 (*0-07-000213-4*) McGraw.

Principles of Endocrine Pharmacology. John A. Thomas & Edward J. Keenan. LC 85-28251. (Illus.). 310p. (C). 1986. pap. text 47.00 (*0-306-42143-7*, Kluwer Plenum) Kluwer Academic.

Principles of Endodontics. Mumford & Jedynakiewicz. 1988. pap. text 54.00 (*1-85097-006-8*, 1569) Quint Pub Co.

Principles of Endosurgery. Kevin R. Loughlin et al. (Illus.). 352p. 1995. pap. 59.95 (*0-86542-264-8*) Blackwell Sci.

Principles of Energetics. K. S. Spiegler. (Illus.). 175p. 1983. 69.95 (*0-387-12441-1*) Spr-Verlag.

Principles of Energy Conversion. 2nd ed. Culp. 1991. student ed. 27.50 (*0-07-014929-1*) McGraw.

Principles of Energy Conversion. 2nd ed. Archie W. Culp. (Mechanical Engineering Ser.). 576p. (C). 1990. 92.50 (*0-07-014902-X*) McGraw.

Principles of Engineering Design. V. Hubka. (Illus.). 130p. 1989. pap. 33.10 (*0-387-50126-6*) Spr-Verlag.

Principles of Engineering Drawing. L. Gary Lamit & Kathleen L. Kitto. Ed. by Conty. LC 93-33033. 700p. (C). 1994. pap. text 43.25 (*0-314-02805-6*) West Pub.

Principles of Engineering Drawing. Louis G. Lamit. Date not set. pap. text, student ed. write for info. (*0-314-03409-9*) West Pub.

Principles of Engineering Economic Analysis. 4th ed. John H. White et al. LC 97-20876. 512p. 1997. text 106.95 (*0-471-11027-2*) Wiley.

Principles of Engineering Economics. 7th ed. Eugene Grant. 227p. 1982. pap. text 14.00 (*0-471-08439-5*) Wiley.

Principles of Engineering Economy. 3rd ed. Eugene L. Grant et al. 230p. 1990. pap. text, teacher ed. 10.00 (*0-471-51813-1*) Wiley.

Principles of Engineering Economy. 8th ed. Eugene L. Grant et al. LC 89-33571. 608p. 1990. text 102.95 (*0-471-63526-X*) Wiley.

Principles of Engineering Geology. Robert B. Johnson & Jerome V. DeGraff. LC 88-5510. 512p. 1988. text 97.95 (*0-471-03436-3*) Wiley.

Principles of Engineering Graphics. 2nd ed. Frederick E. Giesecke et al. LC 93-16447. 929p. (C). 1993. pap. text 90.67 (*0-02-342820-1*, Macmillan Coll) P-H.

Principles of Engineering Instrumentation. write for info. (*0-340-64569-5*, Pub. by E A) Routldge.

Principles of Engineering Instrumentation. Douglas Ramsay. 216p. 1996. pap. text 44.95 (*0-470-23616-7*) Halsted Pr.

Principles of Engineering Manufacture. 3rd ed. write for info. (*0-340-63195-3*, Pub. by E A) Routldge.

Principles of Engineering Manufacturing. 3rd ed. Vic Chiles et al. 637p. 1996. pap. text 59.95 (*0-470-23558-6*) Halsted Pr.

Principles of Engineering Materials. C. Barrett et al. (C). 1973. text 63.75 (*0-13-709394-2*) P-H.

Principles of Engineering Mechanics. 2nd ed. write for info. (*0-340-56831-3*, Pub. by E A) Routldge.

Principles of Engineering Mechanics Vol. 1: Kinematics: The Geometry of Motion. M. F. Beatty. (Mathematical Concepts & Methods in Science & Engineering Ser.: Vol. 32). (Illus.). 414p. (C). 1986. 110.00 (*0-306-42131-3*, Plenum Trade) Perseus Pubng.

Principles of Engineering Organization. 2nd ed. Stephen Wearne. 166p. 1993. 5.00 (*0-7277-1656-5*) Am Soc Civil Eng.

P

An Asterisk (*) at the beginning of an entry indicates that the title is appearing for the first time.

Principles of English Etymology. Walter W. Skeat. 25.95 (*0-405-18884-6*) Ayer.

Principles of English Grammar. Peter Bullions. LC 82-10418. (American Linguistics Ser.). 264p. 1983. 50.00 (*0-8201-1386-7*) Schol Facsimiles.

Principles of English Metre. Egerton Smith. LC 79-109849. 326p. 1971. reprint ed. lib. bdg. 65.00 (*0-8371-4340-3*, SMEM, Greenwood Pr) Greenwood.

Principles of English Prosody, Pt. 1. Lascelles Abercrombie. LC 75-41000. (BCL Ser.: No. II). reprint ed. 24.50 (*0-404-14735-6*) AMS Pr.

Principles of English Stress. Luigi Burzio. LC 93-43093. (Studies in Linguistics: No. 72). 387p. (C). 1995. text 64.95 (*0-521-44513-2*) Cambridge U Pr.

Principles of Enhanced Heat Transfer. Ralph L. Webb. LC 93-4513. 556p. 1994. 140.00 (*0-471-57778-2*) Wiley.

Principles of Environmental & Resource Economics: A Guide for Students & Decision-Makers. Ed. by Henk Folmer et al. LC 95-4051. 512p. 1995. 150.00 (*1-85898-224-3*) E Elgar.

Principles of Environmental & Resource Economics: A Guide for Students & Decision-Makers. Ed. by Henk Folmer et al. (New Horizons in Environmental Economics Ser.). (Illus.). 512p. 1996. pap. 40.00 (*1-85898-298-7*) E Elgar.

***Principles of Environmental & Resource Economics: A Guide for Students & Decision-Makers.** 2nd ed. Henk Folmer & H. Landis Gabel. LC 99-86198. (New Horizons in Environmental Economics Ser.). 816p. 2000. text 180.00 (*1-85898-944-2*) E Elgar.

Principles of Environmental Conservation with Many Figures & Plates. H. S. Singh. 250p. 1989. pap. 175.00 (*81-7089-101-9*, Pub. by Intl Bk Distr) St Mut.

***Principles of Environmental Economics: Economics, Ecology & Environmental Policy.** Ahmed M. Hussen. LC 99-17809. 1999. write for info. (*0-415-19570-5*) Routledge.

Principles of Environmental Economics: Economics, Ecology & Environmental Policy. Ahmed M. Hussen. LC 99-17809. 1999. pap. 27.99 (*0-415-19571-3*) Routledge.

Principles of Environmental Health & Safety Management. Arthur Andersen & Co. Staff & Pilko Associates Staff. Ed. by Gordon A. West & Ronald W. Michaud. 335p. 1995. pap. text 69.00 (*0-86587-478-6*) Gov Insts.

Principles of Environmental Health Science. Douglas Crawford-Brown. 350p. 1998. 49.95 (*0-8342-0656-0*) Aspen Pub.

Principles of Environmental Law. 2nd ed. Susan Wolf & Anna White. (Principles of Law Ser.). lix, 497p. 1997. pap. 38.00 (*1-85941-376-5*, Pub. by Cavendish Pubng) Gaunt.

Principles of Environmental Management: The Greening of Business. 2nd ed. Rogene A. Buchholz. LC 97-32583. 448p. (C). 1998. pap. text 57.00 (*0-13-684895-8*) P-H.

Principles of Environmental Medicine. Descotes. pap. text 45.00 (*0-471-97786-1*) Wiley.

Principles of Environmental Physics. 2nd ed. J. L. Monteith & M. H. Unsworth. (Illus.). 228p. 1990. pap. text 39.95 (*0-7131-2931-X*, Pub. by E A) Routldge.

Principles of Environmental Sampling. Ed. by Lawrence H. Keith. LC 87-22975. (Illus.). xxiv, 480p. 1988. 69.95 (*0-8412-1173-6*); pap. 39.95 (*0-8412-1437-9*) Am Chemical.

Principles of Environmental Sampling. Ed. by Lawrence H. Keith. LC 87-22975. (ACS Professional Reference Book Ser.). (Illus.). 485p. 1988. reprint ed. pap. 150.40 (*0-608-04154-8*, 206488700011) Bks Demand.

Principles of Environmental Sampling. 2nd ed. Ed. by Lawrence H. Keith. LC 96-9386. (Professional Reference Book Ser.). (Illus.). 880p. 1996. text 104.95 (*0-8412-3152-4*, Pub. by Am Chemical) OUP.

Principles of Environmental Science & Technology. 2nd rev. ed. S. E. Jorgensen & I. G. Johnson. (Studies in Environmental Science: No. 33). 628p. 1989. 186.00 (*0-444-43024-5*) Elsevier.

Principles of Environmental Toxicology. Sigmund F. Zakrzewski. LC 91-29942. (Illus.). 270p. 1991. 64.95 (*0-8412-2125-1*); pap. 44.95 (*0-8412-2170-7*) Am Chemical.

Principles of Environmental Toxicology. Sigmund F. Zakrzewski. LC 91-29942. (ACS Professional Reference Book Ser.). (Illus.). 288p. 1991. reprint ed. pap. 89.30 (*0-608-04155-6*, 206488800011) Bks Demand.

Principles of Environmental Toxicology, Vol. 190. 2nd ed. Sigmund F. Zakrzewski. LC 96-52362. (ACS Monographs). 352p. 1997. text 85.00 (*0-8412-3380-2*, Pub. by Am Chemical) OUP.

Principles of Enzymology for Technological Applications. Biotol. (BIOTOL Ser.). 300p. 1993. pap. text 66.95 (*0-7506-0689-4*) Buttrwrth-Heinemann.

Principles of Enzymology for the Food Sciences. 2nd expanded rev. ed. Ed. by John R. Whitaker. (Food Science & Technology Ser.: Vol. 61). (Illus.). 648p. 1993. text 225.00 (*0-8247-9148-7*) Dekker.

Principles of Epistemology in Islamic Philosophy: Knowledge by Presence. Mehdi H. Yazdi. 232p. 1996. pap. 59.95 (*0-614-21236-7*, 980) Kazi Pubns.

Principles of Epistemology in Islamic Philosophy: Knowledge by Presence. Mehdi H. Yazdi. LC 91-1999. (SUNY Series in Islam). 240p. (C). 1992. text 24.50 (*0-7914-0947-3*) State U NY Pr.

Principles of Equine Osteosynthesis. G. E. Fackelman. (Illus.). 380p. 1999. 199.00 incl. cd-rom (*0-86577-826-4*) Thieme Med Pubs.

Principles of Equitable Remedies. 4th ed. I. C. Spry. lxix, 693p. 1990. 105.50 (*0-455-20977-4*, Pub. by LawBk Co) Gaunt.

Principles of Equity. Ed. by Patrick Parkinson. LC 97-146623. 1000p. 1996. pap. 100.00 (*0-455-21395-X*, Pub. by LawBk Co) Gaunt.

***Principles of Esoteric Healing.** Dion Fortune. Ed. by Gareth Knight. (Illus.). 166p. 2000. pap. 12.95 (*1-928754-03-1*) Sun Chalice.

Principles of Esthetic Integration. Claude R. Rufenacht. (Illus.). 300p. 128.00 (*0-86715-369-5*) Quint Pub Co.

Principles of Ethics. Borden P. Bowne. LC 75-3073. (Philosophy in America Ser.). reprint ed. 49.50 (*0-404-59074-8*) AMS Pr.

Principles of Ethics, 2 vols. Herbert Spencer. LC 77-1274. 550p. 1980. reprint ed. pap. 12.50 (*0-913966-34-7*) Liberty Fund.

Principles of Ethics, 2 vols., Set. Herbert Spencer. LC 77-71453. 1978. reprint ed. 20.00 (*0-913966-33-9*) Liberty Fund.

Principles of European Community Law: Commentary & Materials. Simon Bronitt et al. 500p. 1995. 95.00 (*0-455-21309-7*, Pub. by LawBk Co) Gaunt.

***Principles of European Contract Law.** Ole Lando et al. LC 99-51943. 1999. 195.00 (*90-411-1305-3*) Kluwer Law Intl.

Principles of European Contract Law: Prepared by the Commission on European Contract Law, Chairman, Ole Lando. Ed. by Ole Lando & Hugh Beale. LC 94-21316. 1995. lib. bdg. 136.00 (*0-7923-2957-0*) Kluwer Academic.

***Principles of European Trust Law.** Ed. by David J. Hayton. (Law of Business & Finance Ser.: Vol. 1). 236p. 1999. 60.00 (*90-411-9726-5*) Kluwer Law Intl.

Principles of Everyday Behavior Analysis. Miller. (Psychology Ser.). 1975. 14.75 (*0-8185-0141-3*) Brooks-Cole.

Principles of Everyday Behavior Analysis. 2nd ed. L. Keith Miller. LC 79-27797. 512p. (C). 1980. pap. 30.75 (*0-8185-0373-4*) Brooks-Cole.

Principles of Everyday Behavior Analysis. 3rd ed. L. Keith MIller. LC 96-2625. (Psychology Ser.). 4448p. (C). 1996. mass mkt. 60.95 (*0-534-16146-4*) Brooks-Cole.

Principles of Everyday Behavior Analysis. 3rd ed. L. Keith Miller. (C). 1997. pap. text, teacher ed. write for info. (*0-534-34313-9*) Brooks-Cole.

Principles of Evidence. P. J. Schwikkard et al. LC 97-162756. 500p. 1997. pap. 45.00 (*0-7021-3897-5*, Pub. by Juta & Co) Gaunt.

Principles of Evidence. Irving Younger & Michael Goldsmith. LC 84-61800. 1984. 38.50 (*1-55917-572-9*, 322B) Natl Prac Inst.

Principles of Evidence. 3rd ed. Irving Younger et al. LC 97-161798. 976p. 1997. 57.95 (*0-87084-733-3*) Anderson Pub Co.

***Principles of Evidence.** 4th ed. Irving Younger et al. 978p. (C). 2000. text 57.95 (*1-58360-755-2*) Anderson Pub Co.

Principles of Evidence: 1987 Supplement. 181p. 1988. student ed. 14.95 (*1-55917-575-3*, 322S) Natl Prac Inst.

Principles of Evidence & Proof. 3rd ed. David W. Louisell et al. 1977. text 35.00 (*0-88277-424-7*) Foundation Pr.

Principles of Excellence in Community Service Vols. 1 & 2: A Message to America's Business Leaders & a Plan to A. C. T. (Illus.). 1992. pap. write for info. (*1-58534-002-2*) Points of Light.

Principles of Exchange & Power: Integrating the Theory of Social Institutions & the Theory of Value. Nikolaus Horster. LC 97-45112. (European University Studies: Series 20, Vol. 549). (Illus.). 197p. (C). 1997. pap. text 37.95 (*0-8204-3551-1*) P Lang Pubng.

Principles of Exercise Biochemistry. Ed. by J. R. Poortmans. (Medicine & Sport Science Ser.: Vol. 27). (Illus.). viii, 260p. 1988. 195.00 (*3-8055-4790-0*) S Karger.

Principles of Exercise Biochemistry. 2nd rev. ed. Ed. by J. R. Poortmans. (Medicine & Sport Science Ser.: Vol. 38). (Illus.). viii, 304p. 1993. 135.75 (*3-8055-5778-7*) S Karger.

***Principles of Exercise Prescription.** Mark R. Bookhout & Philip E. Greenman. (Illus.). 368p. 2000. 49.50 (*0-7506-9885-3*) Buttrwrth-Heinemann.

Principles of Exercise Testing & Interpretation. 2nd ed. Karlman Wasserman et al. (Illus.). 489p. 1994. text 59.50 (*0-8121-1634-8*) Lppncott W & W.

***Principles of Exercise Testing & Interpretation.** 3rd ed. Karlman Wasserman. LC 98-43362. 1999. 62.00 (*0-683-30646-4*) Lppncott W & W.

Principles of Experimental Biology. 3rd ed. University of Maryland (Presson) Staff. 104p. (C). 1997. spiral bd., lab manual ed. 28.50 (*0-7872-4272-1*) Kendall-Hunt.

Principles of Experimental Design for Art Conservation Research. Terry F. Reedy & Chandra L. Reedy. (Illus.). 114p. 1992. pap. 15.00 (*0-89236-243-X*, Getty Conservation Inst) J P Getty Trust.

Principles of Experimental Design for the Life Sciences. Murray R. Selwyn. LC 96-321. 176p. 1996. boxed set 59.95 (*0-8493-9461-9*) CRC Pr.

Principles of Experimental Phonetics. Ed. by Norman J. Lass. (Illus.). 600p. (C). (gr. 13). 1995. text 69.00 (*0-8016-7975-3*, 07975) Mosby Inc.

Principles of Experimental Psychology: Instructor's Course Planner. Levin. 1994. 14.68 (*0-697-12795-8*) McGraw.

Principles of Expert Systems. Ed. by Amar Gupta & Bandreddi E. Prasad. LC 87-26294. (Illus.). 464p. 1988. text 59.95 (*0-87942-220-3*, PC02287) Inst Electrical.

Principles of Expository Preaching. Merrill F. Unger. 1973. reprint ed. pap. 7.95 (*0-310-33411-X*) Zondervan.

Principles of Exposure Measurement in Epidemiology. Bruce Armstrong et al. (Monographs in Epidemiology & Biostatistics: No. 21). (Illus.). 360p. 1994. reprint ed. pap. text 59.95 (*0-19-262020-7*) OUP.

Principles of Expression in Pianoforte Playing. Adolph Christiani. LC 74-1348. (Music Reprint Ser.). 303p. 1974. reprint ed. lib. bdg. 35.00 (*0-306-70623-7*) Da Capo.

Principles of External Auditing. Brenda Porter. LC 96-23713. 396p. 1997. pap. 75.00 (*0-471-96212-0*) Wiley.

Principles of Extractive Metallurgy. Terkel Rosenqvist. (Illus.). 528p. (C). 1991. reprint ed. text 129.00 (*1-878907-13-1*) TechBooks.

Principles of Extrication. IFSTA Committee. Ed. by Gene P. Carlson & Michael A. Wieder. LC 89-82640. (Illus.). 365p. 1990. pap. text 35.00 (*0-87939-086-7*) IFSTA.

Principles of Extrication: Davis Study Guide. 69p. Date not set. pap. text 14.95 (*0-614-31234-5*, S600) Davis Pub Co.

Principles of Facial Reconstruction. Wayne Larrabee, Jr. (Illus.). 272p. 1995. text 104.00 (*0-7817-0150-3*) Lppncott W & W.

Principles of Faith. Avaneda D. Hobbs. (Illus.). 150p. (Orig.). 1996. pap. 14.95 (*1-878898-10-8*) CAP Pub.

Principles of Faith (Rosh Amanah) Isaac Abravanel. Ed. & Tr. by Menachem M. Kellner from HEB. (Littman Library of Jewish Civilization). 272p. 1985. 26.00 (*0-19-710045-7*) OUP.

Principles of Farm Irrigation System Design. Larry G. James. LC 92-29458. 560p. (C). 1993. reprint ed. lib. bdg. 81.95 (*0-89464-802-0*) Krieger.

Principles of Federal Appropriations Law, 3 vols., Set. (Orig.). 1996. lib. bdg. 999.95 (*0-8490-6014-1*) Gordon Pr.

Principles of Federal Appropriations Law, Vol. 3. 2nd ed. (Illus.). 1616p. (Orig.). (C). 1994. pap. text 95.00 (*0-7881-1251-1*) DIANE Pub.

Principles of Federal Appropriations Law: The Red Book, 6 vols. 1997. lib. bdg. 1899.95 (*0-8490-7682-X*) Gordon Pr.

Principles of Federal Pollution Control Law. Mark Sagoff. 1986. 2.50 (*0-318-33308-2*) IPPP.

Principles of Feedback Control Vol. 1: Feedback System Design. George A. Biernson. LC 87-30539. 497p. 1988. 172.00 (*0-471-82167-5*) Wiley.

Principles of Feedback Control Vol. 2: Advanced Control Topics, Vol. 2, Advanced Control Topics. George A. Biernson. 637p. 1988. 192.00 (*0-471-50120-4*) Wiley.

***Principles of Feng Shui, Bk. 1.** 3rd ed. Larry Sang & Helen Luk. 197p. 1999. pap. 18.75 (*0-9644583-0-6*) Am Feng Shui Inst.

Principles of Feng Shui: An Illustrated Guide to Chinese Geomancy. Sherman Tai. (Illus.). 140p. (C). 1998. pap. 14.95 (*981-3068-93-0*, Pub. by Asiapac) China Bks.

Principles of Fermentation Technology. 2nd ed. A. Whitaker & P. F. Stanbury. 348p. 1995. pap. text 64.95 (*0-08-036131-5*, Prgamon Press) Buttrwrth-Heinemann.

Principles of Field Crop Production. 3rd ed. John Holmes Martin. 1030p. (C). 1976. 135.00 (*0-02-376720-0*, Macmillan Coll) P-H.

***Principles of Field Crop Production.** 4th ed. (C). 2001. text. write for info. (*0-13-025967-5*) P-H.

Principles of Finance. Besley. (C). 1999. pap. text, student ed. 22.50 (*0-03-025263-6*, Pub. by Harcourt Coll Pubs) Harcourt.

Principles of Finance. Besley. (C). 1999. pap. text 38.00 (*0-03-025258-X*, Pub. by Harcourt Coll Pubs) Harcourt.

Principles of Finance. Scott Besley. 816p. (C). 1999. text 89.00 (*0-03-025253-9*, Pub. by Harcourt Coll Pubs) Harcourt.

Principles of Finance. Jack Rudman. (Dantes Subject Standardized Tests (DANTES) Ser.: Vol. 46). 43.95 (*0-8373-6546-5*) Nat Learn.

Principles of Finance. Jack Rudman. (Dantes Subject Standardized Tests Ser.: DANTES-46). 1994. pap. 23.95 (*0-8373-6646-1*) Nat Learn.

Principles of Finance. 2nd ed. Robert W. Kolb & Ricardo J. Rodriguez. 817p. (C). 1992. teacher ed. 2.66 (*0-669-27386-4*); trans. 16.00 (*0-669-21761-1*) HM Trade Div.

Principles of Finance & Management Accounting. 5th ed. James M. Reeve & Carl S. Warren. (AB - Accounting Principles Ser.). 1996. pap., student ed. 23.95 (*0-538-85310-7*) S-W Pub.

Principles of Finance & Management Accounting. 5th ed. James M. Reeve & Carl S. Warren. (Accounting Principles Ser.). 1996. pap., student ed. 22.95 (*0-538-85311-5*) S-W Pub.

Principles of Financial Accounting. 256p. (C). 1988. pap. 150.00 (*0-13-710385-9*) P-H.

Principles of Financial Accounting. Jack Rudman. (Dantes Subject Standardized Tests (DANTES) Ser.: Vol. 47). 43.95 (*0-8373-6547-3*) Nat Learn.

Principles of Financial Accounting. Jack Rudman. (Dantes Subject Standardized Tests Ser.: DANTES-47). 1994. pap. 23.95 (*0-8373-6647-X*) Nat Learn.

***Principles of Financial Accounting.** 5th ed. Jerry J. Weygandt et al. LC 98-25285. 980p. 1998. pap. 81.95 (*0-471-19437-9*) Wiley.

Principles of Financial Accounting, 6 vols. 6th ed. Belverd E. Needles. (C). 1995. pap. text 60.36 (*0-395-74566-7*) HM.

Principles of Financial Accounting. 7th ed. Belverd E. Needles. LC 98-72070. 884 p. 1999. text 49.47 (*0-395-92629-7*) HM.

Principles of Financial Accounting Chapters 1-19, General Ledger Windows & Working Papers 4th ed. Jerry J. Weygandt et al. 1412p. 1996. pap. text 157.85 (*0-471-16908-0*) Wiley.

Principles of Financial Accounting, Chapters 1-19 & Overture: An Interactive Guide to Mastering Accounting Principles. 4th ed. Jerry J. Weygandt et al. 836p. 1996. pap. 121.95 incl. disk (*0-471-17373-8*) Wiley.

Principles of Financial Accounting Chapters 1-19 & Working Papers I, Chapters 1-13 to Accompany Accounting Principles & Overture: An Interactive Guide to Mastering Accounting Principles. 4th ed. Jerry J. Weygandt et al. 1394p. 1996. pap. 153.90 (*0-471-17372-X*) Wiley.

Principles of Financial & Management Accounting: A Corporate Approach. Charles T. Horngren et al. LC 93-31194. 1504p. 1993. 105.00 (*0-13-037748-1*) P-H.

Principles of Financial & Managerial Accounting. Hanson. (C). 1996. text. write for info. (*0-03-010514-5*) Harcourt Coll Pubs.

Principles of Financial & Managerial Accounting. Hubbard & Lawrence. 1999. student ed. 18.95 (*0-87393-803-8*) Dame Pubns.

Principles of Financial & Managerial Accounting. Belverd E. Needles, Jr. et al. LC 87-80110. 950p. (C). 1988. 15.96 (*0-685-73859-0*); trans. 159.96 (*0-685-73860-4*) HM.

Principles of Financial & Managerial Accounting. 2nd ed. Roger H. Hermanson et al. LC 92-31865. 1344p. (C). 1993. text 72.00 (*0-256-13000-0*, Irwn McGrw-H) McGrw-H Hghr Educ.

Principles of Financial & Managerial Accounting. 4th ed. Philip E. Fess & Carl S. Warren. (C). 1993. mass mkt. 51.75 (*0-538-83336-X*, AB60DA) S-W Pub.

Principles of Financial & Managerial Accounting, Vol. 1. 6th ed. Hubbard & Lawrence. 1998. 42.95 (*0-87393-776-7*) Dame Pubns.

Principles of Financial & Managerial Accounting, Vol. 2. 6th ed. Hubbard & Lawrence. 1999. 42.95 (*0-87393-802-X*) Dame Pubns.

Principles of Financial & Managerial Accounting Vol. I: Student Solutions Manual. 6th ed. Hubbard & Lawrence. 1998. pap., student ed. 21.95 (*0-87393-779-1*) Dame Pubns.

Principles of Financial & Managerial Accounting Vol. I: Working Papers. 6th ed. Hubbard & Lawrence. 1998. pap. 18.95 (*0-87393-778-3*) Dame Pubns.

Principles of Financial & Managerial Accounting Vol. II: Student Solutions Manual. 6th ed. Hubbard & Lawrence. 1999. pap., student ed. 21.95 (*0-87393-805-4*) Dame Pubns.

Principles of Financial & Managerial Accounting Vol. II: Working Papers. 6th ed. Hubbard & Lawrence. 1999. pap. 18.95 (*0-87393-804-6*) Dame Pubns.

***Principles of Financial Derivatives: U. S. & International Taxation.** Steven D. Conlon & Vincent M. Aquilino. LC 99-62057. 1999. write for info. (*0-7913-3770-7*) Warren Gorham & Lamont.

***Principles of Financial Economics.** Stephen F. LeRoy & Jan Werner. (Illus.). 300p. 2001. write for info. (*0-521-58434-5*); pap. write for info. (*0-521-58605-4*) Cambridge U Pr.

Principles of Financial Management. (C). 1998. text. write for info. (*0-13-096825-0*) P-H.

Principles of Financial Management. Douglas R. Emery et al. LC 97-22392. 785p. 1997. 92.00 (*0-13-433541-4*) P-H.

***Principles of Financial Manager 50/50.** Kimmel. 1999. text 102.95 (*0-471-35891-6*) Wiley.

Principles of Fire Behavior. James G. Quintiere. LC 97-11199. (Career Education Ser.). 288p. (C). 1997. mass mkt. 55.95 (*0-8273-7732-0*) Delmar.

Principles of Fire Phenomena. Quintiere. (Career Education Ser.). 1997. teacher ed. 18.95 (*0-8273-7733-9*) Delmar.

Principles of Fire Protection. Percy Bugbee & A. E. Cote. 1988. text 67.00 (*0-87765-345-3*, ST-1) Natl Fire Prot.

Principles of Fire Protection Chemistry & Physics. 3rd ed. Raymond Friedman. LC 76-26781. (C). 1998. pap. text 67.00 (*0-87765-440-9*, PFPC98) Natl Fire Prot.

Principles of Fish & Wildlife Ecology. Lawrence D. Burton. (Agriculture Ser.). 1995. pap., teacher ed. 12.00 (*0-8273-6066-5*) Delmar.

Principles of Fish Nutrition. Werner Steffens. 1990. text 123.00 (*0-470-21559-3*) P-H.

Principles of Fishery Science. 2nd ed. W. Harry Everhart & William D. Youngs. (Illus.). 343p. 1981. text 45.00 (*0-8014-1334-6*) Cornell U Pr.

Principles of Flat Pattern Design. Nora M. McDonald & Ruth E. Weibel. (Illus.). 320p. 1988. pap. text. write for info. (*0-318-62257-2*) P-H.

Principles of Fluid Mechanics. Jhon. (C). 1999. text 85.00 (*0-13-970716-6*) P-H.

Principles of Fluid Mechanics. Wen-Hsiung Li & Sau-Hai Lam. 1964. write for info. (*0-201-04240-1*) Addison-Wesley.

Principles of Fluorescence Spectroscopy. J. R. Lakowicz. LC 85-28251. (Illus.). 510p. (C). 1983. text 59.50 (*0-306-41285-3*, Kluwer Plenum) Kluwer Academic.

Principles of Fluorescence Spectroscopy. 2nd ed. J. R. Lakowicz. LC 99-30047. (Illus.). 725p. (C). 1999. text. write for info. (*0-306-46093-9*, Kluwer Plenum) Kluwer Academic.

Principles of Fluoroscopic Image Intensification & Television Systems: Workbook & Laboratory Manual. Robert J. Parelli. (Illus.). 240p. 1996. lib. bdg. 39.95 (*1-57444-082-9*) St Lucie Pr.

Principles of Foam Fire Fighting. Michael A. Wieder. LC 96-85269. (Illus.). 296p. 1996. pap. text 35.00 (*0-87939-128-6*, 35921) IFSTA.

Principles of Foam Fire Fighting: Study Guide for First Edition. Pam Griffith. Ed. by Susan Walker & Barbara Adams. (Illus.). 174p. 1996. pap. 17.00 (*0-87939-134-0*, 36001) IFSTA.

Principles of Foam Firefighting: Davis Study Guide. 90p. Date not set. pap. text 14.95 (*0-614-31242-6*, S921) Davis Pub Co.

Principles of Food Analysis for Filth, Decomposition & Foreign Matter. 2nd ed. Ed. by J. Richard Gorman. (FDA Technical Bulletin Ser.: No. 1). (Illus.). 286p. 1985. pap. 48.00 (*0-935584-33-1*) AOAC Intl.

P

Principles of Food & Agriculture. Colin Spedding. 49.95 (*0-8464-4397-X*) Beekman Pubs.

***Principles of Food & Beverage Labor Cost: Set of Text & Workbook.** 5th ed. Dittmer. 1999. 63.95 (*0-471-35979-3*) Wiley.

Principles of Food, Beverage & Lab. 4th ed. Dittmerp. (Hospitality, Travel & Tourism Ser.). 1989. teacher ed. 20.95 (*0-442-23433-3*, VNR) Wiley.

Principles of Food, Beverage & Labor Cost. 5th ed. Dittmer. (C). 1994. pap. text, wbk. ed. 22.95 (*0-442-01827-4*, VNR) Wiley.

Principles of Food, Beverage & Labor Cost Controls. 5th ed. Paul R. Dittmer. 562p. 1993. text 48.95 (*0-442-01601-8*, VNR) Wiley.

***Principles of Food, Beverage, & Labor Cost Controls.** 6th ed. Paul R. Dittmer & Gerald G. Griffin. LC 98-31455. 592p. 1999. 54.95 (*0-471-29325-3*) Wiley.

***Principles of Food, Beverage & Labor Cost Controls: For Hotels & Restaurants.** Paul R. Dittmer & Gerald G. Griffin. 1999. wbk. ed. 76.50 (*0-471-37844-5*) Wiley.

Principles of Food, Beverage & Labor Cost Controls for Hotels & Restaurants. 5th ed. Paul R. Dittmer & Gerald G. Griffin. 576p. 1993. text 49.95 (*0-471-28577-3*, VNR) Wiley.

Principles of Food Preparation: A Laboratory Manual. 2nd ed. Jeanne H. Freeland-Graves. 377p. (C). 1987. pap., lab manual ed. 58.00 (*0-02-339350-5*, Macmillan Coll) P-H.

Principles of Food Preservation. Ed. by V. Kyzlink. (Developments in Food Science Ser.: No. 22). 590p. 1990. 331.00 (*0-444-98844-0*) Elsevier.

Principles of Food Processing. Richard W. Hartel & Dennis R. Heldman. 288p. 1997. 62.00 (*0-8342-1269-2*) Aspen Pub.

Principles of Food Sanitation. Norman G. Marriott. 1989. text 59.95 (*0-442-31807-3*) Chapman & Hall.

Principles of Food Sanitation. 3rd ed. Norman G. Marriott. 1993. text 59.95 (*0-442-01201-2*) Chapman & Hall.

Principles of Food Sanitation. 4th ed. Norman G. Marriott. LC 98-43373. 450p. 1999. 63.00 (*0-8342-1232-3*) Aspen Pub.

Principles of Food Science: Physical Methods of Food Preservation, Pt. 2. Owen R. Fennema. (Food Science & Technology Ser.: Vol. 4). (Illus.). 485p. 1975. text 150.00 (*0-8247-6322-X*) Dekker.

Principles of Food Science Pt. 1: Food Chemistry. Owen R. Fennema. LC 75-29694. (Food Science Ser.: No. 4). (Illus.). 808p. reprint ed. pap. 200.00 (*0-7837-0807-6*, 204112200019) Bks Demand.

Principles of Forensic Medicine. 3rd enl. rev. ed. William A. Guy. LC 75-23715. (Illus.). reprint ed. 54.00 (*0-404-13268-5*) AMS Pr.

Principles of Forensic Toxicology. Barry Levine. 363p. 1998. pap. 49.00 (*1-890883-07-7*, 202024) Am Assn Clinical Chem.

Principles of Forest & Environmental Economics. rev. ed. Douglas B. Rideout & Hayley Hesseln. LC 97-69028. (Illus.). 285p. 1997. pap. text 42.50 (*0-9659183-0-0*) Res & Environ Mgmt.

Principles of Forest Entomology. Douglas C. Allen. LC 84-8509. (Illus.). 224p. 1984. student ed. 18.95 (*0-8156-2318-6*) Syracuse U Pr.

Principles of Forest Pathology. F. H. Tainter & F. A. Baker. LC 95-17500. 832p. 1996. 125.00 (*0-471-12952-6*) Wiley.

Principles of Form & Design. Wucius Wong. 352p. 1993. pap. 24.95 (*0-442-01405-8*, VNR); pap. 34.95 (*0-471-28552-8*, VNR) Wiley.

Principles of Foundation Engineering. 2nd ed. Braja M. Das. 624p. (C). 1990. text 69.95 (*0-534-92171-X*) PWS Pubs.

Principles of Foundation Engineering. 3rd ed. Braja M. Das. LC 94-48565. (Engineering Ser.). 1995. 70.00 (*0-534-20646-8*) PWS Pubs.

Principles of Foundation Engineering. 4th ed. Braja M. Das. LC 98-36450. 1998. 94.95 (*0-534-95403-0*) PWS Pubs.

Principles of Free-Electron Lasers. H. P. Freund & T. M. Antonsen. (Illus.). 480p. (C). (gr. 13). text 104.95 (*0-412-45790-3*, Chap & Hall NY) Chapman & Hall.

Principles of Free Radical Chemistry. Cadogan. 1989. 9.00 (*0-85186-829-0*) CRC Pr.

Principles of Free Trade: Illustrated in a Series of Short & Familiar Essays. 2nd ed. Condy Raguet. LC 68-56569. (Reprints of Economic Classics Ser.). xix, 439p. 1969. reprint ed. 49.50 (*0-678-00529-X*) Kelley.

Principles of French Law. John Bell. 578p. 1998. pap. text (*0-19-876395-6*) OUP.

Principles of French Law. John Bell et al. LC 98-12331. 578p. 1998. text 95.00 (*0-19-876394-8*) OUP.

Principles of Functional Management. R. P. Maheshwari. 284p. 1997. pap. 55.00 (*81-209-0448-6*, Pub. by Pitambar Pub) St Mut.

***Principles of Fusion Energy: An Introduction to Fusion Energy for Students of Science & Engineering.** A. A. Harms et al. 300p. 2000. 56.00 (*981-02-4335-9*) World Scientific Pub.

Principles of Gardening. Hugh Johnson. LC 97-117443. 1997. 40.00 (*0-684-83524-X*) S&S Trade.

Principles of Gas-Solid Flows. Liang-Shih Fan & Chao Zhu. LC 96-41141. (Series in Chemical Engineering). (Illus.). 576p. (C). 1998. text 90.00 (*0-521-58148-6*) Cambridge U Pr.

Principles of General Grammar. S. Silvestre De Sacy & Antoine Isaac. LC 90-43612. 168p. 1990. reprint ed. 50.00 (*0-8201-1444-8*) Schol Facsimiles.

Principles of General Thermodynamics. George N. Hatsopoulos & Joseph H. Keenan. LC 80-25946. 830p. 1981. reprint ed. 83.00 (*0-89874-303-6*) Krieger.

Principles of Genetic Counseling. Edmond A. Murphy & Gary A. Chase. LC 75-16020. 409p. reprint ed. pap. 126.80 (*0-608-12350-1*, 202426700036) Bks Demand.

Principles of Genetic Epistemology see Jean Piaget

Principles of Genetic Toxicology. 2nd ed. D. Brusick. LC 87-17169. (Illus.). 302p. (C). 1987. text 54.50 (*0-306-42532-7*, Kluwer Plenum) Kluwer Academic.

Principles of Genetics. D. Peter Snustad et al. LC 96-39102. 848p. 1997. text 96.95 (*0-471-31196-0*) Wiley.

Principles of Genetics. Robert H. Tamarin. (C). 1981. pap. 27.00 (*0-87150-756-0*) Wadsworth Pub.

Principles of Genetics. 2nd ed. James W. Fristrom. 795p. (C). 1989. pap. text 77.95 (*0-7167-2083-3*) W H Freeman.

***Principles of Genetics.** 2nd ed. Snustad. 470p. 1999. pap., student ed., wbk. ed. 34.95 (*0-471-35878-9*) Wiley.

Principles of Genetics. 2nd ed. D. Peter Snustad & Michael J. Simmons. LC 99-15482. 896p. 1999. text 96.95 (*0-471-29800-X*) Wiley.

Principles of Genetics. 4th ed. Robert H. Tamarin. 624p. (C). 1992. text. write for info. (*0-697-16658-9*) Brown & Benchmark.

Principles of Genetics. 5th ed. Tamarin. 1996. teacher ed. 14.37 (*0-697-21890-2*, WCB McGr Hill) McGrw-H Hghr Educ.

Principles of Genetics. 5th ed. Robert H. Tamarin & Ken Zwicker. 152p. (C). 1996. text, student ed. 21.25 (*0-697-21891-0*, WCB McGr Hill) McGrw-H Hghr Educ.

Principles of Genetics. 5th ed. Robert H. Tamerin. 688p. (C). 1995. text. write for info. (*0-697-21889-9*, WCB McGr Hill) McGrw-H Hghr Educ.

Principles of Genetics. 6th ed. Robert Tamarin. LC 98-18181. 1998. pap. text 59.25 (*0-697-35462-8*) McGraw.

Principles of Genetics. 7th ed. Robert H. Tamarin. 2001. 62.00 (*0-07-233419-3*); student ed. 22.50 (*0-07-233420-7*) McGraw.

Principles of Genetics. 7th ed. Eldon J. Gardner & D. Peter Snustad. LC 83-21798. (Illus.). 664p. 1984. reprint ed. pap. 200.00 (*0-7837-3488-3*, 205782100008) Bks Demand.

Principles of Genetics. 8th ed. Eldon J. Gardner et al. LC 90-48758. 736p. 1991. text 89.95 (*0-471-50487-4*) Wiley.

Principles of Genetics. 8th ed. Eldon J. Gardner et al. 151p. 1991. pap. text, teacher ed. 21.50 (*0-471-53519-2*) Wiley.

Principles of Genetics. 8th ed. Eldon J. Gardner et al. 140p. 1991. pap. text 429.00 (*0-471-53521-4*) Wiley.

Principles of Genetics/How Scientists Think. 4th ed. Robert H. Tamarin et al. (C). 1995. text. write for info. (*0-697-34039-2*, WCB McGr Hill) McGrw-H Hghr Educ.

Principles of Genitourinary Radiology Vol. 2: Nervous System & Sensory Organs. 2nd rev. ed. Z. L. Barbaric. (Flexibook Ser.). (Illus.). 520p. 1994. 99.00 (*0-86577-493-5*) Thieme Med Pubs.

Principles of Genome Analysis: A Guide to Mapping & Sequencing DNA from Different Organisms. S. B. Primrose. LC 95-6173. 1995. pap. 32.95 (*0-86542-946-4*) Blackwell Sci.

***Principles of Genome Analysis: A Guide to Mapping & Sequencing DNA from Different Organisms.** 2nd ed. S. B. Primrose. LC 97-36818. (Illus.). 1998. pap. 47.95 (*0-632-04983-9*) Blackwell Sci.

Principles of Geoarchaeology: A North American Perspective. Michael R. Waters. LC 92-13120. (Illus.). 398p. (Orig.). 1993. text 41.00 (*0-8165-0989-1*) U of Ariz Pr.

Principles of Geoarchaeology: A North American Perspective. Michael R. Waters. LC 92-13120. (Illus.). 424p. (Orig.). 1997. reprint ed. pap. 24.95 (*0-8165-1770-3*) U of Ariz Pr.

Principles of Geochemistry. Giulio Ottonello. LC 96-23987. 1997. 95.00 (*0-231-09984-3*) Col U Pr.

***Principles of Geochemistry.** Giulio Ottonello. (Illus.). 2000. pap. text 40.00 (*0-231-09985-1*) Col U Pr.

Principles of Geodynamics. 3rd rev. ed. Adrian E. Scheidegger. (Illus.). 380p. 1982. 129.00 (*0-387-11323-1*) Spr-Verlag.

Principles of Geographical Information Systems. 2nd ed. Peter A. Burrough & Rachel A. McDonnell. (Spatial Information Systems Ser.). (Illus.). 346p. (C). 1998. text 104.00 (*0-19-823366-3*); pap. text 49.95 (*0-19-823365-5*) OUP.

Principles of Geology. Charles Lyell. Ed. & Intro. by James A. Secord. LC 98-165644. xlvii, 472p. 1998. pap. 15.95 (*0-14-043528-X*) Viking Penguin.

Principles of Geology, 4 vols. 11th unabridged ed. Charles Lyell. (Classic Reprint Ser.). (Illus.). 1323p. 1997. reprint ed. 120.00 (*0-936128-60-7*) De Young Pr.

Principles of Geology, 3 vols., Set. Charles Lyell. (Illus.). 1970. reprint ed. text 100.00 (*3-7682-0685-8*) Lubrecht & Cramer.

Principles of Geology, Vol. 1. Charles Lyell. LC 90-11008. (Illus.). 586p. 1990. pap. text 22.00 (*0-226-49794-1*) U Ch Pr.

Principles of Geology, Vol. 1. Charles Lyell. LC 90-11008. (Illus.). 576p. 1995. lib. bdg. 48.00 (*0-226-49793-3*) U Ch Pr.

Principles of Geology, Vol. 3. Charles Lyell. LC 90-11008. (Illus.). 620p. 1991. pap. text 21.00 (*0-226-49799-2*) U Ch Pr.

Principles of Geology, Vol. 3. Charles Lyell. LC 90-11008. (Illus.). 620p. 1991. lib. bdg. 46.00 (*0-226-49798-4*) U Ch Pr.

Principles of Geology, Vol. 2: An Inquiry How Far the Former Changes of the Earth's Surface Are Referable to Causes Now in Operation, Vol. 2. Charles Lyell. (Illus.). 352p. 1991. lib. bdg. 42.00 (*0-226-49796-8*) U Ch Pr.

Principles of Geology, Vol. 2: An Inquiry How Far the Former Changes of the Earth's Surface Are Referable to Causes Now in Operation, Vol. 2. Charles Lyell. (Illus.). 352p. 1991. pap. text 19.50 (*0-226-49797-6*) U Ch Pr.

Principles of Geometrie Gathered out of G. Henischius by F. Cooke. Georg Henisch. LC 71-25788. (English Experience Ser.: No. 321). 88p. 1971. reprint ed. 20.00 (*90-221-0321-8*) Walter J Johnson.

Principles of Geophysics. Norman H. Sleep & Kazuya Fujita. LC 96-38995. (Illus.). 1997. boxed set 76.95 (*0-86542-076-9*) Blackwell Sci.

Principles of Geotechnical Engineering. 2nd ed. Braja M. Das. 606p. (C). 1990. text 69.95 (*0-534-92130-2*) PWS Pubs.

Principles of Geotechnical Engineering. 3rd ed. Braja M. Das. LC 93-5738. 1993. mass mkt. 69.50 (*0-534-93375-0*) PWS Pubs.

Principles of Geotechnical Engineering. 4th ed. Braja M. Das. LC 97-28512. (C). 1997. mass mkt. 102.95 (*0-534-95179-1*) PWS Pubs.

Principles of Geriatric Medicine & Gerontology. 4th ed. Ed. by William R. Hazzard et al. LC 98-3613. (Illus.). 1560p. 1999. text 140.00 (*0-07-027502-5*) McGraw-Hill HPD.

Principles of Gestalt Family Therapy. Walter Kempler. LC 74-26006. 1973. pap. 10.00 (*0-9600808-1-3*) Kempler Inst.

***Principles of Global Security.** John D. Steinbruner. LC 99-50913. 272p. 2000. pap. 18.95 (*0-8157-8095-8*) Brookings.

***Principles of Global Security.** John D. Steinbruner. LC 99-50913. 272p. 2000. 44.95 (*0-8157-8096-6*) Brookings.

Principles of Good Policing: Avoiding Violence Between Police & Citizens. 1995. lib. bdg. 252.75 (*0-8490-6712-X*) Gordon Pr.

Principles of Good Policing: Avoiding Violence Between Police & Citizens. 1996. lib. bdg. 252.95 (*0-8490-6907-6*) Gordon Pr.

Principles of Governance & Administration in Higher Education. Paul Westmeyer. (Illus.). 250p. 1990. pap. 37.95 (*0-398-06493-8*) C C Thomas.

Principles of Governance & Administration in Higher Education. Paul Westmeyer. (Illus.). 250p. (C). 1990. text 54.95 (*0-398-05696-X*) C C Thomas.

Principles of Government: A Treatise on Free Institutions. Nathaniel Chipman. LC 76-99478. (American Constitutional & Legal History Ser). 1970. reprint ed. 39.50 (*0-306-71851-0*) Da Capo.

***Principles of Government: A Treatise on Free Institutions, Including the Constitution.** fac. ed. Nathaniel Chipman. LC 99-48863. 2000. write for info. (*1-58477-046-5*) Lawbk Exchange.

Principles of Government Purchasing. Arthur G. Thomas. (Brookings Institution Reprint Ser.). reprint ed. lib. bdg. 32.50 (*0-697-00173-3*) Irvington.

Principles of Grace. rev. ed. Bobby W. Austin. 175p. 1995. pap. write for info. (*0-9639640-3-8*) Grace Vision.

Principles of Grammar & Learning. William D. O'Grady. LC 86-11402. 248p. (C). 1987. 33.00 (*0-226-62074-3*) U Ch Pr.

Principles of Grammar Theory. W. G. Admoni. Ed. by Theo Harden & Harald Weydt. LC 95-39815. X, 109p. 1995. pap. 29.95 (*0-8204-2911-2*, 68704) P Lang Pubng.

Principles of Grammar Theory. Wladimir G. Admoni. Ed. by Theo Harden & Harald Weydt. x, 109p. 1995. pap. 29.95 (*3-631-49183-2*) P Lang Pubng.

Principles of Greek Art. Percy Gardner. 352p. 1914. pap. 24.00 (*0-8196-2088-2*) Biblo.

Principles of Groundwater Engineering. William Clarence Walton. 568p. 1990. lib. bdg. 95.00 (*0-87371-283-8*, L283) Lewis Pubs.

Principles of Groundwater Hydrology Environmental Application. Robert Haag. Date not set. 59.95 (*0-87371-988-3*) Lewis Pubs.

Principles of Group Solidarity. Michael Hechter. LC 87-5074. (California Series on Social Choice & Political Economy: Vol. 11). 288p. 1987. pap. 16.95 (*0-520-06462-3*, Pub. by U CA Pr) Cal Prin Full Svc.

Principles of Growth & Processing of Semiconductors. Subhash Mahajan & K. S. Sreeharsha. LC 98-3385. 528p. 1998. 91.56 (*0-07-039605-1*) McGraw.

Principles of Guidance. Jack Rudman. (Dantes Subject Standardized Tests Ser.: DANTES-33). 1994. pap. 23.95 (*0-8373-6633-X*) Nat Learn.

Principles of Guidance. Jack Rudman. (DANTES Ser.: No. 33). 1994. 39.95 (*0-8373-6533-3*) Nat Learn.

Principles of Gynaecological Surgery. Ed. by S. L. Stanton. (Illus.). 320p. 1987. 49.50 (*0-387-17485-0*) Spr-Verlag.

Principles of Hand Surgery. Ed. by F. D. Burke et al. (Illus.). 392p. 1989. text 75.00 (*0-443-03466-4*) Church.

Principles of Hand Surgery. F. D. Burke et al. LC 88-35268. (Illus.). 382p. 1990. reprint ed. pap. 118.50 (*0-7837-9747-8*, 206047500005) Bks Demand.

Principles of Harmonic Analysis. Walter Piston. 1933. pap. 19.95 (*0-911318-05-4*) E C Schirmer.

Principles of Harmonic Substitution. Dom Minasi. Ed. by Thomas Gambino. 48p. (Orig.). 1979. pap., student ed. 11.95 (*0-936519-02-9*) Sunrise Artistries.

Principles of Harmony & Contrast of Colors & Their Applications to the Arts. M. E. Chevreul. LC 87-60121. 256p. 1987. 49.50 (*0-88740-090-6*) Schiffer.

Principles of Hazardous Materials Management. Roger D. Griffin. (Illus.). 220p. 1988. lib. bdg. 75.00 (*0-87371-145-9*, L145) Lewis Pubs.

Principles of Health & Disability Insurance Selling. 3rd rev. ed. 180p. 1992. pap. text 24.95 (*0-7931-0585-4*, 5403-043A) Dearborn.

Principles of Health & Hygiene in the Workplace. Timothy J. Key & Michael A. Mueller. Date not set. 69.95 (*1-56670-229-1*) Lewis Pubs.

Principles of Health & Safety in Agriculture. James A. Dosman & Cockcroft. 456p. 1989. lib. bdg. 129.00 (*0-8493-0160-2*, RC965) CRC Pr.

Principles of Health Care Ethics. Ann Lloyd. Ed. by Raanan Gillon. LC 92-23746. 1152p. 1994. 477.50 (*0-471-93033-4*) Wiley.

***Principles of Health Economics for Developing Countries.** The World Bank Staff. LC 99-40975. (A World Bank Publication). 305p. 1999. 30.00 (*0-8213-4571-0*, 14571, Pub. by World Bank) OUP.

Principles of Health Maintenance. Paul R. Schnurrenberger. Ed. by Robert S. Sharman. LC 82-18067. 291p. 1983. 65.00 (*0-275-91413-5*, C1413, Praeger Pubs) Greenwood.

Principles of Health Planning in the U. S. S. R. G. A. Popov. (Public Health Papers: No. 43). 1971. pap. text 9.00 (*92-4-130043-4*, 1110043) World Health.

Principles of Hearing Aid Audiology. M. Tate. 304p. 1994. 52.50 (*1-56593-296-X*, 0705) Singular Publishing.

Principles of Heat Transfer. 5th ed. Kreith. (West Engineering Ser.). 1994. text 59.00 (*0-534-93830-2*) PWS Pubs.

Principles of Heat Transfer in Porous Media, Vol. XXII. 2nd ed. Massoud Kaviany. Ed. by F. F. Ling. (Mechanical Engineering Ser.). (Illus.). 708p. 1995. 79.95 (*0-387-94550-4*) Spr-Verlag.

Principles of Heat Transmission. 5th rev. ed. Frank Kreith. (General Engineering Ser.). 1996. mass mkt. 105.95 (*0-534-95420-0*) Wadsworth Pub.

Principles of Heat Treatment of Steel. George Krauss. LC 80-16118. (Illus.). 301p. reprint ed. pap. 93.40 (*0-7837-1856-X*, 204205700001) Bks Demand.

Principles of Heating, Ventilation & Air-Conditioning. H. Sauer et al. Ed. by Robert Parsons. (Illus.). 254p. (C). 1998. text 66.00 (*1-883413-56-7*, 90380) Am Heat Ref & Air Eng.

***Principles of Helicopter Aerodynamics.** J. Gordon Leishman. (Aerospace Ser.: Vol. 12). (Illus.). 560p. 2000. text 95.00 (*0-521-66060-2*) Cambridge U Pr.

Principles of Helicopter Flight. Jean-Pierre Harrison. (Illus.). 1462p. 1993. pap. 19.95 (*0-9638491-0-7*) Pilot Trning.

Principles of Helicopter Flight: #ASA-PHF. Walter J. Wagtendonk. LC 95-52965. (Illus.). 288p. 1996. pap. 24.95 (*1-56027-217-1*, ASA-PHF) ASA Inc.

Principles of Hematology. Peter J. Haen. LC 94-70283. 472p. (C). 1995. text. write for info. (*0-697-13301-X*, WCB McGr Hill) McGrw-H Hghr Educ.

Principles of Highway Engineering & Traffic Analysis. 2nd ed. Fred L. Mannering & Walter P. Kilareski. LC 97-3077. 352p. 1997. pap. 64.95 (*0-471-13085-0*) Wiley.

Principles of Hindu Law. M. Mulla. (C). 1990. 100.00 (*0-89771-144-0*) St Mut.

Principles of Historical Linguistics. Hans H. Hock. (Trends in Linguistics, Studies & Monographs: No. 34). (Illus.). xiv, 706p. 1986. lib. bdg. 204.65 (*0-89925-220-6*) Mouton.

Principles of Historical Linguistics. 2nd rev. ed. Hans H. Hock. (Trends in Linguistics, Studies & Monographs: No. 34). (Illus.). xiv, 706p. 1991. pap. 34.95 (*3-11-012962-0*) Mouton.

Principles of History: And Other Writings in Philosophy of History. R. G. Collingwood. Ed. by Williams H. Dray & W. Dussen. LC 98-49637. (Illus.). 382p. 1999. text 75.00 (*0-19-823703-0*) OUP.

Principles of Holistic Therapy with Herbal Essences. 2nd ed. Dietrich Gumbel. Tr. by Ritva Abao from GER. (Illus.). 268p. 1993. pap. text 25.00 (*2-8043-4002-3*, Pub. by K F Haug Pubs) Medicina Bio.

Principles of Holography. 2nd ed. Howard M. Smith. LC 75-5631. 293p. reprint ed. pap. 90.90 (*0-608-16189-6*, 205615500052) Bks Demand.

Principles of Home Canning. (Illus.). 40p. (Orig.). 1996. pap. text 15.00 (*0-7881-3333-0*) DIANE Pub.

***Principles of Home Decoration.** Candace Wheeler. (Illus.). 2000. pap. 14.95 (*1-55709-497-7*) Applewood.

Principles of Homeopathic Philosophy. Margaret Roy. LC 93-14982. 150p. 1993. pap. text. write for info. (*0-344-30482-5*) Church.

Principles of Hope, Vol. 2. Ernst Bloch et al. Tr. by Neville Plaice et al. (Studies in Contemporary German Social Thought). 488p. 1995. pap. text 24.00 (*0-262-52200-4*) MIT Pr.

Principles of Hope, Vol. 3. Ernst Bloch. Tr. by Neville Plaice et al. 504p. 1995. pap. text 24.00 (*0-262-52201-2*) MIT Pr.

Principles of Horseshoeing II: An Illustrated Textbook of Farrier Science & Craftsmanship. Doug Butler. (Illus.). 567p. 1985. text 79.95 (*0-916992-02-0*) Btler Pub.

Principles of Horticulture. 2nd ed. C. R. Adams et al. (Illus.). 204p. 1993. pap. 44.95 (*0-7506-1722-5*) Buttrwrth-Heinemann.

Principles of Hospitality Law. Michael Boella & Alan Pannett. 416p. 1998. pap. 32.95 (*0-304-70472-5*) Continuum.

Principles of Hospitality Law. Alan Pannett & Michael Boella. 400p. 1996. pap. 37.95 (*0-304-33575-4*); text 90.00 (*0-304-33574-6*) Continuum.

Principles of Host-Plant Resistance to Insect Pests. N. C. Panda. LC 78-59169. (Illus.). 406p. 1980. text 59.00 (*0-916672-93-X*) Rowman.

Principles of Hotel & Catering Law. 3rd ed. Alan Pannett. LC 92-34125. 384p. 1992. text 100.00 (*0-304-32609-7*) Continuum.

Principles of Hotel Front Office Operations: A Study Guide. Sue Baker et al. LC 93-3152. (Hotel & Catering Ser.). 304p. 1994. pap. 35.00 (*0-304-32729-8*) Continuum.

***Principles of Human Anatomy.** 8th ed. Gerard J. Tortora. LC 98-7560. (C). 1999. text 88.13 (*0-321-00037-4*) Addison-Wesley.

P

***Principles of Human Anatomy.** 8th ed. Gerard J. Tortora. (Illus.). 944p. 1999. text 106.95 (*0-471-36729-X*) Wiley.

***Principles of Human Anatomy Applications to Health Learning Guide.** 8th ed. Gerald J. Tortora. 1999. pap. text 31.95 (*0-471-36760-5*) Wiley.

Principles of Human Anatomy: Lab Manual for Human Cadavers. 2nd ed. Victor P. Eroschenko. (C). 1995. teacher ed. write for info. (*0-673-55986-6*) Addson-Wesley Educ.

Principles of Human-Centered Aviation Automation. Charles E. Billings. (Human Factors in Transportation Ser.). 376p. (C). 1996. 69.95 (*0-8058-2126-0*); pap. 45.00 (*0-8058-2127-9*) L Erlbaum Assocs.

***Principles of Human Commiunication.** 5th ed. Robert Smith. 448p. 2000. per. 40.95 (*0-7872-6874-7*) Kendall-Hunt.

Principles of Human Communication. 2nd ed. Robbin Crabtree & Blain Goss. 62p. (C). 1996. pap. text, student ed., spiral bd. 15.95 (*0-7872-2724-2*, 41272401) Kendall-Hunt.

Principles of Human Communication Text: A Workbook. 4th ed. Robert E. Smith. 448p. (C). 1995. pap. text, per., wbk. ed. 29.95 (*0-8403-9518-3*) Kendall-Hunt.

Principles of Human Ecology. 396p. (C). 1996. text 56.00 (*0-536-59267-5*) Pearson Custom.

Principles of Human Evolution. Roger Lewin. LC 97-21774. (Illus.). 224p. (C). 1997. pap. text 51.95 (*0-86542-542-6*) Blackwell Sci.

Principles of Human Knowledge see Empiricists

Principles of Human Knowledge & Three Dialogues. George Berkeley. Ed. by Howard Robinson. (Oxford World's Classics Ser.). 278p. 1999. pap. 9.95 (*0-19-283549-1*) OUP.

Principles of Human Knowledge & Three Dialogues Between Hylas & Philonius. George Berkeley. Ed. & Intro. by Roger Woolhouse. 224p. 1988. pap. 10.95 (*0-14-043293-0*, Penguin Classics) Viking Penguin.

Principles of Human Knowledge & Three Dialogues Between Hylas & Philonous. George Berkeley. 1990. 16.50 (*0-8446-5833-2*) Peter Smith.

Principles of Human Nutrition. Martin Eastwood. 576p. 1997. pap. 55.00 (*0-8342-1290-0*) Aspen Pub.

Principles of Human Resource Development. Jerry W. Gilley. 1989. 40.00 (*0-201-09013-9*) Addison-Wesley.

Principles of Human Resource Management. David Goss. LC 94-184294. 256p. (C). 1993. pap. 24.95 (*0-415-09188-8*) Thomson Learn.

Principles of Humane Experimental Technique. W. M. Russell & R. L. Burch. 238p. 1992. pap. 100.00 (*0-900767-78-2*, Pub. by Univs Fed Animal Welfare) St Mut.

Principles of HVAC Solutions Manual. H. Saures et al. Ed. by Robert Parsons. 1998p. (C). 1998. pap. text 48.00 (*1-883413-58-3*, 90382) Am Heat Ref & Air Eng.

***Principles of Hydrogeology.** 2nd ed. Paul F. Hudak. LC 99-40090. 216p. 1999. boxed set (*1-56670-500-2*) Lewis Pubs.

Principles of Hydrology. Viessman. (C). 2000. text. write for info. (*0-673-99337-X*) Addison-Wesley.

Principles of Hydrometallurgical Extraction & Reclamation. Eric Jakson. 1986. text 51.95 (*0-470-20314-5*) P-H.

Principles of Hypnotherapy see Medical Hypnosis

Principles of Ideal-Fluid Aerodynamics. K. Karamcheti. LC 79-26876. 654p. 1980. reprint ed. lib. bdg. 69.50 (*0-89874-113-0*) Krieger.

Principles of Igneous Petrology. S. Maaloe. (Illus.). 415p. 1985. 167.95 (*0-387-13520-0*) Spr-Verlag.

Principles of Imaging. Thompson. (C). 1994. teacher ed. 21.00 (*0-7216-3429-X*) Harcourt.

Principles of Imaging Science & Protection. Michael A. Thompson et al. LC 93-12638. 1994. text 59.00 (*0-7216-3428-1*, W B Saunders Co) Harcrt Hlth Sci Grp.

Principles of Imaging Science & Protection, Solutions to the Exercises. Ed. by Michael A. Thompson et al. (Illus.). 531p. 1994. write for info. (*0-7216-3430-3*, W B Saunders Co) Harcrt Hlth Sci Grp.

Principles of Imaging Science & Protection, Vol. 2. Ed. by Michael A. Thompson et al. (Illus.). 1994. 485.00 (*0-7216-4221-7*, W B Saunders Co) Harcrt Hlth Sci Grp.

Principles of Immunological Diagnosis in Medicine. Ed. by Felix Milgrom et al. LC 80-20724. (Illus.). 536p. reprint ed. pap. 166.20 (*0-8357-7650-6*, 205697600096) Bks Demand.

Principles of Immunology & Immunodiagnostics. Ralph M. Aloisi. LC 87-31150. 248p. reprint ed. pap. 76.90 (*0-7837-2689-9*, 204306700006) Bks Demand.

Principles of Immunopharmacology. Ed. by F. P. Nijkamp & M. J. Parnham. LC 99-10441. 450p. 1999. pap. 95.00 (*3-7643-5780-0*) Birkhauser.

Principles of Immunopharmacology. Franciscus P. Nijkamp & Michael J. Parnham. LC 99-10441. 1999. pap. write for info. (*0-8176-5780-0*) Birkhauser.

Principles of Induction Melting. 96p. 1977. pap. 52.00 (*0-317-59859-7*, TE7705) Am Foundrymen.

Principles of Inductive Logic. 2nd ed. John Venn. LC 72-119162. Orig. Title: The Principles of Empirical, or Inductive Logic. 624p. 1973. lib. bdg. 29.50 (*0-8284-0265-5*) Chelsea Pub.

Principles of Industrial Facility Planning. Howard A. Stafford. LC 80-26737. (Illus.). 289p. 1980. pap. 11.95 (*0-910436-08-8*) Conway Data.

Principles of Industrial Welding. Enrico P. Bongio. 1978. text 6.50 (*0-686-24289-0*); text 5.85 (*0-686-26120-8*) Lincoln Arc Weld.

Principles of Infertility Nursing. Catherine H. Garner. 187p. 1991. lib. bdg. 69.95 (*0-8493-4652-5*, RC889, CRC Reprint) Franklin.

Principles of Information Ethics. Richard J. Severson. LC 96-52983. 172p. (C). (gr. 13). 1997. text 60.95 (*1-56324-957-X*) M E Sharpe.

Principles of Information Ethics. Richard J. Severson. LC 96-52983. (Illus.). 172p. (C). (gr. 13). 1997. pap. text 21.95 (*1-56324-958-8*) M E Sharpe.

Principles of Information Processing. Donald D. Spencer. 250p. (C). 1985. suppl. ed. write for info. (*0-318-58997-4*, Merrill Pub Co) Macmillan.

Principles of Information Retrieval. Manfred Kochen. LC 74-1204. (Information Sciences Ser.). (Illus.). 222p. reprint ed. pap. 68.90 (*0-7837-3452-2*, 205777800008) Bks Demand.

Principles of Information Systems. John Ward. LC 94-46391. (Series in the Principles of Management). 256p. (C). 1995. pap. 16.99 (*0-415-07267-0*) Thomson Learn.

Principles of Information Systems. 4th ed. Stair & Reynolds. LC 98-47464. (C). 1999. pap. 65.95 (*0-7600-1079-X*) Course Tech.

Principles of Information Systems: A Managerial Approach. R. M. Stair. (Illus.). 800p. (C). 1992. pap. 53.95 (*0-87835-789-0*) Course Tech.

Principles of Information Systems: A Managerial Approach. 2nd ed. Ralph M. Stair. 720p. (C). 1996. mass mkt. 49.95 (*0-87709-825-5*) Course Tech.

Principles of Information Systems: A Managerial Approach. 2nd annot. ed. Ralph M. Stair. 1995. mass mkt., teacher ed. write for info. (*0-87709-826-3*) Course Tech.

Principles of Information Systems: A Managerial Approach. 3rd ed. Ralph M. Stair & George W. Reynolds. LC 97-16525. (C). 1997. pap. 44.50 (*0-7600-4954-8*) Course Tech.

Principles of Information Systems: A Managerial Approach, Course Test Manager. 2nd ed. Ralph M. Stair. (C). 1996. pap. write for info. (*0-7600-4943-2*) Course Tech.

Principles of Information Systems: A Managerial Approach, Net Test IV. 2nd ed. Ralph M. Stair. (C). 1996. pap. write for info. (*0-7895-0058-2*) Course Tech.

Principles of Information Systems: A Managerial Approach, Solutions Manual. 2nd ed. Ralph M. Stair. 1995. mass mkt. write for info. (*0-87709-827-1*) Course Tech.

Principles of Information Systems: A Managerial Approach, Test Item File. 2nd ed. Ralph M. Stair. 1995. mass mkt. write for info. (*0-87709-828-X*) Course Tech.

Principles of Information Systems for Management. 4th ed. Niv Anitav et al. 704p. (C). 1994. text 69.25 (*0-697-12421-5*) Bus & Educ Tech.

Principles of Insect Morphology. R. E. Snodgrass. (Comstock Bk.). (Illus.). 768p. 1993. pap. text 29.95 (*0-8014-8125-2*) Cornell U Pr.

Principles of Insect Parasitism Analyzed from New Perspectives: Practical Implications for Regulating Insect Populations by Biological Means. 1994. lib. bdg. 275.95 (*0-8490-6440-6*) Gordon Pr.

Principles of Insect Pathology. Drion G. Boucias & Jacquelyn C. Pendland. LC 98-45713. 568p. 1998. 250.00 (*0-412-03591-X*) Kluwer Academic.

Principles of Instructional Analysis. 5th ed. Skoog. (C). 1997. text 7.50 (*0-03-020917-X*) Harcourt Coll Pubs.

Principles of Instructional Design. (Instructor Training Ser.). (Illus.). 340p. 1983. 59.50 (*0-685-48115-8*); teacher ed. 75.00 (*0-685-48116-6*) GP Courseware.

Principles of Instructional Design. 4th ed. Robert M. Gagne. (C). 1992. text 66.50 (*0-03-034757-2*) Holt R&W.

Principles of Instructional Design. 4th ed. Robert M. Gagne et al. 384p. (C). 1992. text. write for info. (*0-318-69121-3*) Harcourt Coll Pubs.

***Principles of Instructional Design.** 5th ed. Gagne & Walter W. Wager. 2002. pap. 50.00 (*0-534-58284-2*) Wadsworth Pub.

Principles of Instrumental Analysis. 5th ed. Skoog. LC 97-67376. (Illus.). 960p. (C). 1997. text 122.50 (*0-03-002078-6*, Pub. by SCP) Harcourt.

Principles of Instrumental Logic: John Dewey's Lectures in Ethics & Political Ethics, 1895-1896. John Dewey. Ed. by Donald F. Koch. LC 97-48994. (Illus.). 272p. 1998. 39.95 (*0-8093-2173-4*) S Ill U Pr.

Principles of Instrumented Spinal Surgery. Harms. (Illus.). 208p. 1999. 149.00 (*0-86577-744-6*) Thieme Med Pubs.

Principles of Insurance: Life, Health & Annuities. 2nd rev. ed. Harriet E. Jones & Dani L. Long. LC 99-73129. (FLMI Insurance Education Program Ser.). 491p. pap. text 44.95 (*1-57974-029-4*, Pub. by Life Office) PBD Inc.

Principles of Insurance Law. Emeric Fischer & Swisher. 333p. (C). 1986. teacher ed. write for info. (*0-8205-0187-5*) Bender.

Principles of Insurance Law. 2nd ed. Emeric Fischer & Peter N. Swisher. LC 94-25036. (Cases & Materials Ser.). 944p. (C). 1994. 56.00 (*0-8205-0188-3*) Bender.

Principles of Insurance Law in Australia & New Zealand. D. S. Kelly & M. L. Ball. 650p. 1991. pap. 102.00 (*0-409-49577-8*, NZ, MICHIE); boxed set 154.00 (*0-409-49576-X*, NZ, MICHIE) LEXIS Pub.

Principles of Integral Science of Religion. Georg Schmid. (Religion & Reason Ser.). 1979. text 66.95 (*90-279-7864-6*) Mouton.

***Principles of Integrated Maritime Surveillance Systems.** A. Nejat Ince. LC 99-47097. (International Series in Engineering & Science). 1999. write for info. (*0-7923-8672-8*) Kluwer Academic.

Principles of Integrative Environmental Physiology. G. Edgar Folk, Jr. et al. LC 97-43186. (Illus.). 820p. (C). 1997. pap. 59.95 (*1-57292-108-0*) Austin & Winfield.

Principles of Integrative Environmental Physiology. G. Edgar Folk, Jr. et al. LC 97-43186. (Illus.). 820p. (C). 1998. 72.95 (*1-57292-109-9*) Austin & Winfield.

Principles of Intensive Psychotherapy. Frieda Fromm-Reichmann. LC 50-9782. 263p. 1960. pap. text 12.95 (*0-226-26599-4*, P49) U Ch Pr.

Principles of Interactive Design. abr. rev. ed. Lisa J. Graham. LC 98-3357. 225p. (C). 1998. pap. 49.95 (*0-8273-8557-9*) Delmar.

Principles of Intermediate Algebra with Applications. 2nd ed. Harry L. Nustad & Terry H. Wesner. 736p. (C). 1991. text 51.25 (*0-697-01338-3*, WCB McGr Hill) McGrw-H Hghr Educ.

Principles of Intermediate Algebra with Applications. 2nd ed. Harry L. Nustad et al. 304p. (C). 1991. text, student ed. 18.75 (*0-697-11084-2*, WCB McGr Hill) McGrw-H Hghr Educ.

Principles of Intermediate Swimming. Joel A. Bloom. (Illus.). 111p. 1978. spiral bd. 9.95 (*0-89641-002-1*); per. 9.95 (*0-89641-010-2*) American Pr.

Principles of Internal Control. Alan Trenerry. 264p. 1998. pap. 45.00 (*0-86840-401-2*) Intl Spec Bk.

Principles of International Development Law: Progressive Development of the Principles of International Law Relating to the New International Economic Order. 2nd rev. ed. Milan Bulajic. LC 92-31349. (C). 1993. lib. bdg. 200.00 (*0-7923-1971-0*) Kluwer Academic.

Principles of International Environmental Law, 3 vols. Ed. by Philippe Sands et al. (Studies in International Law). 1994. text 430.00 (*0-7190-4438-3*, Pub. by Manchester Univ Pr) St Martin.

Principles of International Environmental Law I: Frameworks, Standards, & Implementation. Philippe Sands. LC 94-10229. (Studies in International Law). 1995. text 160.00 (*0-7190-3483-3*, Pub. by Manchester Univ Pr); text 59.95 (*0-7190-3484-1*, Pub. by Manchester Univ Pr) St Martin.

Principles of International Finance. Daniel R. Kane. 256p. 1987. pap. text 16.95 (*0-7099-3134-4*, Pub. by C Helm); lib. bdg. 59.50 (*0-7099-1584-5*, Pub. by C Helm) Routldge.

Principles of International Law. T. J. Lawrence. xxi, 645p. 1987. reprint ed. 65.00 (*0-8377-2405-8*, Rothman) W S Hein.

Principles of International Law. 4th rev. ed. T. J. Lawrence. xxi, 745p. 1999. reprint ed. 192.50 (*1-56169-500-9*) Gaunt.

Principles of International Market Research. L. W. J. Groves. LC 94-15840. (Principles of Export Guidebooks Ser.). 250p. (C). 1994. pap. text 43.95 (*0-631-19355-3*) Blackwell Pubs.

Principles of International Marketing. Julia Spencer. (Principles of Export Guidebooks Ser.). 250p. (C). 1994. pap. 43.95 (*0-631-19251-4*) Blackwell Pubs.

Principles of International Physical Distribution. Jim Sherlock. LC 94-15834. (Principles of Export Guidebooks Ser.). 250p. (C). 1994. pap. text 43.95 (*0-631-19169-0*) Blackwell Pubs.

***Principles of International Politics: People's Power, Preferences & Perceptions.** Bruce Bueno de Mesquita. LC 99-47472. 588p. 1999. pap. 48.95 (*1-56802-423-1*) CQ Pr.

Principles of International Strategy. David Faulkner & Susan Segal-Horn. 224p. 1999. pap. 19.99 (*1-86152-015-8*) Thomson Learn.

Principles of International Tax: A Multinational Perspective. Adrian Ogley. 1993. 95.00 (*0-9520442-0-X*, Pub. by Interfisc Pub) Intl Info Srvcs Inc.

Principles of International Trade & Payments. Peter D. Briggs. Ed. by Michael Z. Brooke. LC 94-15853. (Principles of Export Guidebooks Ser.). 256p. (C). 1994. pap. text 43.95 (*0-631-19163-1*) Blackwell Pubs.

***Principles of International Trade Law.** Indira Carr. 519p. 1999. pap. 42.00 (*1-85941-383-8*, Pub. by Cavendish Pubng) Gaunt.

***Principles of Internet Marketing.** Ward Hanson. LC 99-36514. (SB - Marketing Education Ser.). 467p. 1999. pap. 69.95 (*0-538-87573-9*) S-W Pub.

Principles of Interpretation. Edward G. Ballard. LC 83-4281. (Series in Continental Thought : Vol. 5). 261p. 1983. text 36.95 (*0-8214-0688-4*); pap. text 19.95 (*0-8214-0689-2*) Ohio U Pr.

Principles of Interpretation: Mastering Clear & Concise... 45.00 (*1-56821-798-6*) Aronson.

Principles of Inventory & Materials Management. 3rd ed. Richard J. Tersine. 554p. 1987. 45.50 (*0-444-01162-5*) P-H.

Principles of Inventory & Materials Management. 4th ed. Richard J. Tersine. LC 93-1583. 608p. (C). 1993. 60.80 (*0-13-457888-0*) P-H.

Principles of Investigation. John P. Kenney & Harry W. More, Jr. (Criminal Justice Ser.). (Illus.). 448p. 1979. teacher ed. write for info. (*0-8299-0592-8*) West Pub.

Principles of Investigation. 2nd ed. Kenney. (Criminal Justice Ser.). 1994. mass mkt. 20.00 (*0-314-03967-8*) West Pub.

Principles of Investigation. 2nd ed. Simon & Schuster Staff. LC 93-44444. 550p. (C). 1994. 49.50 (*0-314-02874-9*) West Pub.

Principles of Investment. Aaron M. Sakolski. LC 75-2665. (Wall Street & the Security Market Ser.). 1975. reprint ed. 42.95 (*0-405-06989-8*) Ayer.

Principles of Islamic Education. K. Ahmed. 1992. 3.00 (*1-56744-193-9*) Kazi Pubns.

Principles of Islamic Faith: Al-Aqidah Al-Wasitiyah. 2nd rev. ed. Sheikh A. Taimiyah. Ed. by Fadel Abdallah & Akram Safadi. Tr. by Assad N. Busool from ARA. (Aqa'id & Figh Ser.). 50p. 1994. mass mkt. 4.00 (*1-56316-056-0*) Iqra Intl Ed Fdtn.

Principles of Islamic Jurisprudence. Mohammad H. Kamali. 420p. 1996. 59.50 (*0-614-21206-5*, 982); pap. 22.95 (*0-614-21205-7*, 982) Kazi Pubns.

Principles of Islamic Jurisprudence. Mohammad H. Kamali. 417p. (C). 1996. reprint ed. 67.95 (*0-946621-23-3*, Pub. by Islamic Texts); reprint ed. pap. 32.50 (*0-946621-24-1*, Pub. by Islamic Texts) Intl Spec Bk.

***Principles of Islamic Jurisprudence.** rev. ed. Mohammad H. Kamali. 2000. pap. 29.50 (*0-946621-82-9*) Islamic Texts.

Principles of Islamic Jurisprudence, Vol. I. Ahmad Hasan. 412p. 1993. pap. 22.50 (*1-56744-484-9*) Kazi Pubns.

Principles of Isotope Geology. 2nd ed. Gunter Faure. LC 86-9147. 608p. 1986. text 93.95 (*0-471-86412-9*) Wiley.

Principles of Japanese Discourse: A Handbook. Senko K. Maynard. LC 97-3091. 318p. (C). 1998. text 64.95 (*0-521-59095-7*); pap. text 25.95 (*0-521-59909-1*) Cambridge U Pr.

Principles of Jewish Law. Ed. by Menachem Elon. LC BM0521.E43. (Hebrew University of Jerusalem, Institute for Research in Jewish Law Publication Ser.: No. 6). 443p. reprint ed. pap. 137.40 (*0-8357-3506-0*, 205229700089) Bks Demand.

Principles of Jewish Law. Ed. by Menachem Elon. (Institute for Research in Jewish Law Publication Ser.: No. 6). 866p. 1995. reprint ed. 72.50 (*0-7065-1415-7*, Pub. by Coronet Bks) Coronet Bks.

***Principles of Jewish Spirituality: The Only Introduction You'll Ever Need.** Cheryl Isaacson. LC 99-491024. (Illus.). 160p. 1999. pap. 11.00 (*0-7225-3731-X*) Thorsons PA.

Principles of Joint Replacement Surgery. Clement B. Sledge & Myron B. Spector. 1993. text 125.00 (*0-07-058173-8*) McGraw.

Principles of Judicial Administration. W. F. Willoughby. xxii, 662p. 1981. reprint ed. 65.00 (*0-8377-1312-9*, Rothman) W S Hein.

Principles of Judicial Proof: As Given by Logic, Psychology & General Experience & Illustrated in Judicial Trials. Compiled by John H. Wigmore. (Illus.). xvi, 1179p. 1988. reprint ed. 95.00 (*0-8377-2745-6*, Rothman) W S Hein.

***Principles of Jungian Spirituality: The Only Introduction You'll Ever Need.** Vivianne Crowley. LC 99-204414. (Illus.). 160p. 1998. pap. 11.00 (*0-7225-3578-3*, Pub. by Thorsons MD) Natl Bk Netwk.

Principles of Justice in Taxation. Stephen F. Weston. LC 68-56695. (Columbia University. Studies in Social Sciences: No. 45). 1968. reprint ed. 49.50 (*0-404-51045-0*) AMS Pr.

Principles of Kinesic Interview & Interrogation. Contrib. by Stan B. Walters. (Practical Aspects of Criminal Investigation Ser.). 272p. 1995. boxed set 69.95 (*0-8493-8153-3*, 8153) CRC Pr.

Principles of Knitting: Methods & Techniques of Hand Knitting. June H. Hiatt. (Illus.). 448p. 1989. 35.00 (*0-671-55233-3*) S&S Trade.

Principles of Knowledge Representation. Ed. by Gerhard Brewka. LC 96-23338. (Studies in Logic, Language & Information). 334p. (C). 1996. pap. text 25.95 (*1-57586-056-2*) Cambridge U Pr.

Principles of Labor Legislation. 4th ed. John R. Commons & John B. Andrews. LC 66-22620. (Reprints of Economic Classics Ser.). xviii, 606p. 1967. reprint ed. 57.50 (*0-678-00207-X*) Kelley.

Principles of Laboratory Animal Science: A Contribution to the Humane Use & Care of Animals & to the Quality of Experimental Results. Ed. by L. F. Van Zutphen et al. LC 93-7467. 404p. 1993. 221.00 (*0-444-81270-9*) Elsevier.

Principles of Lake Sedimentology. Lars Hakanson & Mats Jansson. (Illus.). 320p. 1983. 172.95 (*0-387-12645-7*) Spr-Verlag.

Principles of Language Learning & Teaching. 3rd ed. H. Douglas Brown. LC 93-26090. 352p. (C). 1993. pap. text 34.60 (*0-13-191966-0*) P-H.

***Principles of Language Learning & Teaching.** 4th ed. H. Douglas Brown. LC 99-58205. 2000. write for info. (*0-13-017816-0*) P-H.

Principles of Laparoscopic Surgery: Basic & Advanced Techniques. Ed. by Maurice E. Arregui. LC 94-22505. 1995. write for info. (*3-540-94236-X*) Spr-Verlag.

Principles of Laparoscopic Surgery: Basic & Advanced Techniques. Ed. by Maurice E. Arregui et al. LC 94-22505. (Illus.). 1032p. 1995. 215.00 (*0-387-94236-X*) Spr-Verlag.

Principles of Laryngeal Videostroboscopy. Joseph C. Stemple & Leslie E. Glaze. 1997. 110.00 incl. VHS (*1-58041-016-2*, 0112090) Am Speech Lang Hearing.

Principles of Laser Dynamics. Y. I. Khanin. 420p. 1995. 191.50 (*0-444-89696-1*) Elsevier.

Principles of Laser Inferometry. 448p. 1995. 230.00 (*0-8493-7542-8*) CRC Pr.

Principles of Lasers. 3rd ed. Orazio Svelto. Tr. by David C. Hanna from ITA. (Illus.). 508p. 1989. 45.00 (*0-306-42967-5*, Plenum Trade) Perseus Pubng.

***Principles of Lasers.** 4th ed. Orazio Svelto. Tr. by David C. Hanna from ITA. LC 98-5077. (Illus.). 440p. (C). 1998. 59.50 (*0-306-45748-2*, Plenum Trade) Perseus Pubng.

Principles of Law. Michael D. Bayles. 388p. 1989. pap. text 65.50 (*90-277-2413-X*, D Reidel) Kluwer Academic.

Principles of Law: A Normative Analysis. Michael D. Bayles. LC 87-4542. (Law & Philosophy Library). 388p. 1987. lib. bdg. 159.50 (*90-277-2412-1*, D Reidel) Kluwer Academic.

Principles of Law for Managers. Ed. by Anne Ruff. LC 94-37890. (Series in the Principles of Management). 304p. (C). 1996. pap. 16.99 (*0-415-07378-2*, B4298) Thomson Learn.

Principles of Law of Contract. Praful R. Desai. (C). 1988. 80.00 (*0-7855-3720-1*) St Mut.

Principles of Law of Contract. 4th ed. A. J. Kerr. 723p. 1989. boxed set 140.00 (*0-409-03746-X*, SA, MICHIE) LEXIS Pub.

P

Principles of Law of Crimes. Shamsul Huda. 505p. 1982. 225.00 (*0-7855-7562-6*) St Mut.
Principles of Law of Tort. P. S. Pillai. 1986. 70.00 (*0-7855-1476-7*) St Mut.
Principles of Law Office Management: Concepts & Applications. Eileen P. Rosenberg. Ed. by Hannan. LC 93-9794. (Paralegal). 510p. (C). 1993. text 43.25 (*0-314-01359-8*) West Pub.
Principles of Law Office Managment. Eileen Popkoski Rosenberg. (Paralegal Ser.). (C). 1993. 15.25 (*0-314-02910-9*) Thomson Learn.
Principles of Law Relating to International Trade. Nicholas Kouladis. Ed. by Michael Z. Brooke. LC 94-15835. (Principles of Export Guidebooks Ser.). 256p. (C). 1994. pap. text 43.95 (*0-631-19356-1*) Blackwell Pubs.
Principles of Law Relating to MRTP. Ed. by S. Krishnamurthi. (C). 1990. 125.00 (*0-89771-226-9*) St Mut.
Principles of Learning & Behavior. 2nd ed. Domjan. (Psychology Ser.). 1986. text, teacher ed. write for info. (*0-534-05209-6*) Brooks-Cole.
Principles of Learning & Behavior. 3rd ed. Michael Domjan & Barbara Burkhard-Ebin. LC 92-10828. 448p. (C). 1992. mass mkt. 52.25 (*0-534-18912-1*) Brooks-Cole.
Principles of Learning & Behavior. 4th ed. Domjan. LC 97-21562. (Psychology Ser.). 435p. 1997. pap. 71.95 (*0-534-34670-7*) Brooks-Cole.
Principles of Legislation: The Uses of Political Authority. Michael D. Bayles. LC 78-3220. 237p. reprint ed. pap. 73.50 (*0-608-16056-3*, 203318600084) Bks Demand.
Principles of Letter-Writing: A Bilingual Text of Justi Lipsii Epistolica Institutio. Justus Lipsius. Ed. & Tr. by R. V. Young & M. Thomas Hester from LAT. LC 93-41720. (Library of Renaissance Humanism: Vol. 3). (ENG & LAT.). 136p. (C). 1995. 34.95 (*0-8093-1958-6*) S Ill U Pr.
Principles of Life & Morality. Roland T. Satrom. LC 92-93862. 96p. 1996. pap. write for info. (*0-9620837-1-2*) R T Satrom.
Principles of Light & Color. Edwin B. Babbitt. 1980. pap. text 9.95 (*0-8065-0748-9*, Citadel Pr) Carol Pub Group.
Principles of Light & Color. Edwin D. Babbitt. (Illus.). 576p. 1992. pap. 55.00 (*0-89540-060-X*, SB-060) Sun Pub.
Principles of Light & Color (1878) Edwin D. Babbitt. 290p. 1998. reprint ed. pap. 24.95 (*0-7661-0537-7*) Kessinger Pub.
Principles of Lightwave Communications. G. H. Einarsson. LC 95-930. 368p. 1996. pap. 89.95 (*0-471-95298-2*) Wiley.
Principles of Lightwave Communications. G. H. Einarsson. LC 95-930. 368p. 1996. 195.00 (*0-471-95297-4*) Wiley.
Principles of Linear Systems. Philip E. Sarachik. (Illus.). 291p. (C). 1997. text 85.00 (*0-521-57057-3*); pap. text 37.95 (*0-521-57606-7*) Cambridge U Pr.
***Principles of Linguistic Change Vol. 2: Social Factors.** William Labov. (Language in Society Ser.: Vol. 29). (Illus.). 400p. 2000. text 74.95 (*0-631-17915-1*); pap. text 34.95 (*0-631-17916-X*) Blackwell Pubs.
Principles of Linguistic Philosophy. Labov. 1994. 36.95 (*0-631-17914-3*) Blackwell Pubs.
Principles of Literary Criticism. Lascelles Abercrombie. LC 78-21288. 160p. 1979. reprint ed. lib. bdg. 49.75 (*0-313-20025-4*, ABPL, Greenwood Pr) Greenwood.
Principles of Logic & Logic Programming. Anil Nerode & G. Metakides. LC 96-12490. (Studies in Computer Science & Artificial Intelligence: No. 13). 344p. 1996. 149.50 (*0-444-81644-5*, North Holland) Elsevier.
Principles of Long-Term Health Care Administration. Peter J. Buttaro. LC 99-14786. 300p. 1999. pap. text 99.00 (*0-8342-1371-0*) Aspen Pub.
Principles of Lotus 1-2-3. 4th ed. Solomon. Date not set. pap. text 10.25 (*0-314-02205-8*) West Pub.
Principles of Lubrication. Alastair Cameron. LC 67-70366. 625p. reprint ed. pap. 193.80 (*0-608-18645-7*, 205594300040) Bks Demand.
Principles of Lutheran Theology. Carl E. Braaten. LC 82-16542. 160p. 1983. pap. 16.00 (*0-8006-1689-8*, 1-1689, Fortress Pr) Augsburg Fortress.
Principles of Machine Design. Samuel J. Berard. LC 55-6078. 546p. reprint ed. pap. 169.30 (*0-608-11699-8*, 201244700081) Bks Demand.
Principles of Machine Design for Engineering & Industrial Technology. Robert H. Nickolaisen. (C). 2000. write for info. (*0-13-720632-1*, Macmillan Coll) P-H.
Principles of Machine Dynamics. fac. ed. George Raczkowski. LC 78-72995. (Illus.). 111p. pap. 34.50 (*0-7837-7413-3*, 204720800006) Bks Demand.
Principles of Machine Operation & Maintenance. 2nd ed. Jeffrey. (Mechanical Technology Ser.). 1992. pap. 35.75 (*0-17-008705-0*) Thomson Learn.
Principles of Machine Tools. Ed. by S. Sen & B. Bhattacharyya. (C). 1989. 140.00 (*0-89771-379-6*, Pub. by Current Dist) St Mut.
***Principles of Macro Brief.** 2nd ed. Mankiw. (C). 2000. pap. text. write for info. (*0-03-028336-1*, Pub. by Harcourt Coll Pubs) Harcourt.
Principles of Macroeconometric Modeling. Lawrence Robert Klein et al. LC 98-56164. (Advanced Textbooks in Economics Ser.). 366p. 1999. 99.00 (*0-444-81878-2*, North Holland) Elsevier.
Principles of Macroeconomics. 392p. (C). 1997. text 32.00 (*0-536-00305-X*) S&S Trade.
Principles of Macroeconomics. Bernanke. 2000. 41.00 (*0-07-228967-8*); student ed. 12.74 (*0-07-228968-6*) McGraw.
Principles Of Macroeconomics. William S. Brown. LC 94-16368. (SWC-Economics). 688p. (C). 1995. mass mkt. 72.95 (*0-314-04230-X*) West Pub.
Principles of Macroeconomics. Gordon Staff. (C). Date not set. pap. text 26.50 (*0-03-002512-5*) Harcourt Coll Pubs.
Principles of Macroeconomics. Gottheil. (HB - Economics Ser.). 1996. text 47.95 (*0-538-86274-2*) S-W Pub.
Principles of Macroeconomics. Fred Gottheil. LC 95-8988. (C). 1995. pap. 43.75 (*0-538-84044-7*) S-W Pub.
Principles of Macroeconomics. Mankiw. 1997. pap. text 82.00 (*0-03-025233-4*) Harcourt.
Principles of Macroeconomics. Mankiw. (C). 1997. pap. text. write for info. (*0-03-024779-9*) Harcourt Coll Pubs.
Principles of Macroeconomics. N. Gregory Mankiw. (C). 1997. pap. text 60.50 (*0-03-024501-X*, Pub. by Harcourt Coll Pubs) Harcourt.
Principles of Macroeconomics. Martin L. Primack et al. 358p. (C). 1994. pap. text 42.75 (*1-56226-175-4*) CAT Pub.
Principles of Macroeconomics. Ed. by Salvatore. (C). 1998. pap. text, student ed. write for info. (*0-321-01044-2*) Addson-Wesley Educ.
Principles of Macroeconomics. Snower. (C). 1999. text Price not set. (*0-321-01423-5*) Addison-Wesley.
***Principles of Macroeconomics.** David St. Clair. 458p. 1999. pap. text 46.95 (*1-56226-428-1*) CAT Pub.
Principles of Macroeconomics. John B. Taylor. LC 94-47577. (C). 1995. pap. text 53.16 (*0-395-66031-9*) HM.
Principles of Macroeconomics. Richard W. Tresch. Ed. by Fenton. LC 93-36015. (SWC-Economics). 500p. (C). 1994. 47.25 (*0-314-02847-1*) West Pub.
***Principles of Macroeconomics.** Michael G. Vogt. (Illus.). 141p. 2000. pap. 20.95 (*0-9671766-4-6*) Huron Valley.
Principles of Macroeconomics. Gerry F. Welch. (C). 1998. pap. text 25.00 (*0-03-008863-1*) Harcourt Coll Pubs.
Principles of Macroeconomics. 2nd ed. Stephanie Owings & James L. Gilbertie. 308p. (C). 1996. pap. text 39.95 (*1-56226-342-0*) CAT Pub.
Principles of Macroeconomics. 2nd ed. Bob A Rabboh & Ronald J. Bartson. 552p. (C). 1991. text 65.00 (*0-536-58029-4*) Pearson Custom.
Principles of Macroeconomics. 2nd ed. Joseph E. Stiglitz. LC 95-21272. (C). 1997. pap. text 45.00 (*0-393-96838-3*) Norton.
Principles Of Macroeconomics. 3rd ed. Bob A. Rabboh & Ronald J. Bartson. (C). 1991. text 56.00 (*0-536-58105-3*) Pearson Custom.
Principles of Macroeconomics. 4th ed. Ronald J. Bartson & Bob Rabboh. LC 96-144247. 508p. (C). 1996. pap. text 48.00 (*0-536-59284-5*, HB172) Pearson Custom.
Principles of Macroeconomics. 4th ed. Case. 1995. text, teacher ed. write for info. (*0-13-440926-4*) Allyn.
Principles of Macroeconomics. 4th ed. Karl E. Case & Ray C. Fair. LC 95-39055. 588p. 1995. pap. text 63.00 (*0-13-440843-8*) P-H.
Principles of Macroeconomics. 5th ed. (C). 1998. text, teacher ed. write for info. incl. cd-rom (*0-13-020417-X*) P-H.
***Principles of Macroeconomics.** 5th ed. Case. 1999. 32.00 (*0-13-020498-6*) P-H.
Principles of Macroeconomics. 5th ed. Karl E. Case. LC 98-23825. 575p. 1998. pap. text 66.60 (*0-13-095733-X*) P-H.
Principles of Macroeconomics. 5th ed. Karl E. Case & Ray C. Fair. 1998. pap. text, student ed. write for info. (*0-13-095735-6*) P-H.
Principles of Macroeconomics. 5th ed. Mohammad Zaheer. 196p. (C). 1990. 29.80 (*0-536-57837-0*) Pearson Custom.
***Principles of Macroeconomics.** 6th ed. James Gilbertie. 446p. (C). 1998. pap. text 48.50 (*1-56226-421-4*) CAT Pub.
Principles of Macroeconomics. 7th ed. Edwin Mansfield. (Illus.). (C). 1992. pap. text 58.50 (*0-393-96173-7*) Norton.
Principles of Macroeconomics. 7th ed. Edwin Mansfield. (C). 1993. pap. text, student ed. 42.00 (*0-393-96524-4*) Norton.
Principles of Macroeconomics. 7th ed. Mohammad Zaheer. 198p. (C). 1995. text 29.40 (*0-536-59050-8*) Pearson Custom.
Principles of Macroeconomics: An Analytical Approach. Peter N. Hess & Clark G. Ross. Ed. by Fenton. LC 93-9211. 400p. (C). 1993. pap. text 42.75 (*0-314-01258-3*) West Pub.
Principles of Macroeconomics: Outline & Notes. David A. Denslow & Carol Badger-Dole. 208p. (C). 1993. spiral bd. 20.95 (*0-8403-9034-3*) Kendall-Hunt.
Principles of Macroeconomics: Reading Issues & Cases. 4th ed. Edwin Mansfield. (C). 1983. pap. text 8.50 (*0-393-95340-8*) Norton.
Principles of Macroeconomics: Study Guide. 7th ed. Edwin Mansfield. (Illus.). (C). 1992. pap. 21.00 (*0-393-96174-5*) Norton.
Principles of Macroeconomics - Beta Version. Mankiw. (C). 1997. pap. text 14.00 (*0-03-020643-X*) Harcourt Coll Pubs.
Principles of Macroeconomics & Study Guide Pkg. 6th ed. Ruffin. (C). 1997. 65.95 (*0-321-80119-9*) Addison-Wesley.
Principles of Macroeconomics & the Canadian Economy. 2nd ed. Joseph E. Stiglitz & Robin W. Boadway. LC 97-16541. xxviii, 489p. 1997. pap. write for info. (*0-393-97054-X*) Norton.
Principles of Macroeconomics Study Guide for Principals of Macroeconomics. 2nd ed. Stiglitz. 1997. pap. text 16.00 (*0-393-96841-3*) Norton.
Principles of Magnesium Technology. E. F. Emley. 1966. 448.00 (*0-08-010673-0*, Pub. by Pergamon Repr) Franklin.
Principles of Magnetic Resonance. 3rd ed. Charles P. Slichter. 1996. pap. text 49.00 (*3-540-60663-7*) Spr-Verlag.
Principles of Magnetic Resonance. 3rd enl. ed. Charles P. Slichter. Ed. by H. J. Queisser et al. (Solid-State Sciences Ser.: Vol. 1). (Illus.). xi, 655p. 1996. reprint ed. 59.00 (*0-387-50157-6*) Spr-Verlag.
Principles of Magnetic Resonance. 3rd enl. rev. ed. Charles P. Slichter. (Series in Solid-State Sciences: Vol. 1). (Illus.). xii, 655p. 1996. 59.00 (*3-540-50157-6*) Spr-Verlag.
Principles of Magnetic Resonance Imaging. Barry R. Friedman et al. (Illus.). 192p. 1988. text 40.00 (*0-07-041604-4*) McGraw-Hill HPD.
Principles of Magnetic Resonance Imaging. Robert J. Parelli. (Illus.). 28p. (Orig.). 1997. pap., wbk. ed. 15.00 (*1-880359-12-X*) Par Rad.
***Principles of Magnetic Resonance Imaging: A Signal Processing Perspective** Zhi-Peng Lang et al. LC 99-27706. (Series in Biomedical Engineering). 1999. 89.95 (*0-7803-4723-4*) IEEE Standards.
***Principles of Magnetic Resonance Imaging: A Signal Processing Perspective.** Zi-Pei Liang. 1999. 90.00 (*0-8194-3516-3*) SPIE.
Principles of Magnetic Resonance Imaging: Student Workbook. Ritenour. (gr. 13). 1985. spiral bd. 13.95 (*0-8016-4532-8*, 04532) Mosby Inc.
Principles of Magneto-Telluric Prospecting. Gottfried Porstendorfer. Ed. by G. Kunetz & D. S. Parasnis. (Geoexploration Monographs: No. 5). (Illus.). viii, 118p. 1975. 38.00 (*3-443-13007-0*, Pub. by Gebruder Borntraeger) Balogh.
Principles of Magnetoplasma Dynamics. L. C. Woods. (Illus.). 544p. 1987. 140.00 (*0-19-856220-9*) OUP.
Principles of Malaysian Revenue Law, 3 vols. N. Subramaniam. 1989. pap. 154.00 (*9971-70-066-2*, MICHIE) LEXIS Pub.
Principles of Malaysian Revenue Law, 3 vols., Vol. 1. N. Subramaniam. 1989. pap. 64.00 (*9971-70-063-8*, MICHIE) LEXIS Pub.
Principles of Malaysian Revenue Law, 3 vols., Vol. 2. N. Subramaniam. 1989. pap. 70.00 (*9971-70-064-6*, MICHIE) LEXIS Pub.
Principles of Malaysian Revenue Law, 3 vols., Vol. 3. N. Subramaniam. 1989. pap. 64.00 (*9971-70-065-4*, MICHIE) LEXIS Pub.
Principles of Management. Leap. (C). 1996. text. write for info. (*0-03-096375-3*) Harcourt Coll Pubs.
Principles of Management. Tony Morden. LC 96-23917. 1996. pap. write for info. (*0-07-709123-X*) McGraw.
Principles of Management: Modular Text. 4th ed. 266p. (C). 1997. pap. 23.00 (*0-536-00549-4*) Pearson Custom.
Principles of Management for Quality Projects. Michael Carruthers. (ITBP Textbooks Ser.). 1999. pap. 19.99 (*1-86152-522-2*) Thomson Learn.
Principles of Management (Human Resources) Jack Rudman. (ACT Proficiency Examination Program (PEP) Ser.: Vol. 18). 43.95 (*0-8373-5568-0*) Nat Learn.
Principles of Management (Human Resources) Jack Rudman. (ACT Proficiency Examination Program Ser.: PEP-18). 1994. pap. 23.95 (*0-8373-5518-4*) Nat Learn.
Principles of Management in Export. James Conlan. Ed. by Michael Z. Brooke. LC 94-15839. (Principles of Export Guidebooks Ser.). 256p. (C). 1994. pap. text 43.95 (*0-631-19194-1*) Blackwell Pubs.
Principles of Management of Health Laboratories. L. Houang & M. M. El-Nageh. (WHO Regional Publications: No. 3). x, 120p. 1993. pap. text 10.00 (*92-9021-180-6*, 1440003) World Health.
Principles of Management Science. David Windle et al. 430p. 1996. pap. 26.95 (*0-412-62540-7*) Chapman & Hall.
Principles of Managerial Finance. Gitman. 688p. 1999. pap. 65.95 (*0-201-61431-6*) Addison-Wesley.
Principles of Managerial Finance. Lawrence Gitman. 1999. pap. text, student ed. 29.95 (*0-201-61432-4*) Addison-Wesley.
Principles of Managerial Finance. Lawrence J. Gitman. (C). 1998. pap. text, student ed. 24.38 (*0-321-02028-6*) Addison-Wesley.
***Principles of Managerial Finance.** 2nd ed. 576p. (C). 2000. pap. text 25.20 (*0-321-06084-9*, Celebration) Addson-Wesley Educ.
***Principles of Managerial Finance.** 2nd ed. Lawrence J. Gitman. (C). 1999. pap. text 67.00 (*0-321-06085-7*, Celebration) Addson-Wesley Educ.
***Principles of Managerial Finance.** 2nd ed. Lawrence J. Gitman. 544p. (C). 2000. pap. text 27.40 (*0-321-06083-0*, Celebration) Addson-Wesley Educ.
Principles of Managerial Finance. 7th ed. Lawrence J. Gitman. 488p. (C). 1997. pap., student ed. 30.00 (*0-06-501980-6*) Addson-Wesley Educ.
Principles of Managerial Finance. 7th ed. Lawrence J. Gitman. LC 93-39412. (C). 1994. text 7.20 (*0-06-502347-1*) HarpC.
Principles of Managerial Finance. 8th ed. Lawrence J. Gitman. LC 96-30358. (C). 1997. pap. text 78.00 (*0-673-98062-6*) Longman.
***Principles of Managerial Finance.** 9th ed. 752p. (C). 1999. text 26.00 (*0-321-05067-3*); text 67.00 (*0-321-05750-3*) Addison-Wesley.
***Principles of Managerial Finance.** 9th ed. (C). 1999. write for info. (*0-321-07856-X*); write for info. (*0-321-07857-8*); write for info. (*0-321-07859-4*); write for info. (*0-321-07860-8*) Addison-Wesley.
***Principles of Managerial Finance.** 9th ed. (C). 2000. text. write for info. (*0-321-07665-6*); text. write for info. (*0-321-05749-X*) Addison-Wesley.
***Principles of Managerial Finance.** 9th ed. (C). 2000. text. write for info. (*0-321-07878-0*) Addson-Wesley Educ.
Principles of Managerial Finance. 9th ed. Lawrence J. Gitman. LC 99-25883. 936p. (C). 1999. 97.00 incl. cd-rom (*0-321-04308-1*) Addson-Wesley Educ.
Principles of Managerial Finance. 9th ed. Lawrence J. Gitman. 736p. (C). 1999. pap. text 28.00 (*0-321-05066-5*) Addson-Wesley Educ.
Principles of Managerial Finance: Brief Edition. Lawrence J. Gitman. LC 97-40201. 688p. (C). 1997. text 61.00 (*0-321-03069-9*) Addison-Wesley.
Principles of Managerial Finance: Brief Edition. Lawrence J. Gitman. (C). 1998. pap. text. write for info. (*0-321-02817-1*) Addison-Wesley.
Principles of Managerial Finance: Brief Edition. Lawrence J. Gitman. 688p. (C). 1998. text. write for info. (*0-321-03228-4*) Addson-Wesley Educ.
***Principles of Managerial Finance: Brief Edition.** 2nd ed. (C). 1999. write for info. (*0-321-07853-5*); write for info. (*0-321-07855-1*) Addison-Wesley.
Principles of Managerial Finance: Student Lecture Notes. 7th ed. Ed. by Liesz. 448p. (C). 1997. pap. text 18.00 (*0-06-502329-3*) Addison-Wesley.
Principles of Managerial Finance: The Brief Edition. 2nd ed. Lawrence J. Gitman. 544p. (C). 1999. pap. text 23.60 (*0-321-06082-2*) Addson-Wesley Educ.
Principles of Managerial Finance: The Brief Edition. 5th ed. Lawrence J. Gitman. (C). 1998. pap. text. write for info. (*0-321-02030-8*) Addison-Wesley.
***Principles of Managerial Finance: Webcases Generic Subscription.** 9th ed. Michael Seiler. 2000. pap. write for info. (*0-321-07858-6*) Addson-Wesley Educ.
***Principles of Managerial Finance Brief Edition.** Gitman. 1998. 67.00 (*0-321-02027-8*) Addison-Wesley.
***Principles of Managerial Finance Brief Edition.** Gitman. 1998. (*0-321-02026-X*) S&S Trade.
Principles of Managerial Finance 8e+kmt Software-DOS. 8th ed. Gitman. 1997. 76.00 (*0-673-98542-3*) Addison-Wesley.
Principles of Manual Medicine. Philip E. Greenman. (Illus.). 364p. 1989. text 62.00 (*0-683-03556-8*) Lppncott W & W.
Principles of Manual Medicine. 2nd ed. Philip E. Greenman. (Illus.). 584p. 1996. 65.00 (*0-683-03558-4*) Lppncott W & W.
Principles of Marine Insurance. 7th ed. H. A. Turner. Ed. by E. V. Alexander. (C). 1986. 195.00 (*0-7855-4059-8*, Pub. by Witherby & Co) St Mut.
Principles of Marketing. Frances Brassington & Stephen Pettitt. (Illus.). xviii, 1086p. 1997. pap. 72.50 (*0-273-60513-5*, Pub. by Pitman Pub) Trans-Atl Phila.
Principles of Marketing. Robin Peterson. (College Outline Ser.). 285p. (C). 1989. pap. text 14.50 (*0-15-601641-9*) Harcourt Coll Pubs.
Principles of Marketing. Geoffrey Randall. LC 92-45846. (Series in the Principles of Management). 256p. (C). 1993. pap. 21.95 (*0-415-07266-2*) Thomson Learn.
Principles of Marketing. Jack Rudman. (ACT Proficiency Examination Program (PEP) Ser.: Vol. 21). 43.95 (*0-8373-5571-0*) Nat Learn.
Principles of Marketing. Jack Rudman. (ACT Proficiency Examination Program Ser.: PEP-21). 1994. pap. 23.95 (*0-8373-5521-4*) Nat Learn.
Principles of Marketing. Ken Wainwright. (Principles of Export Guidebooks Ser.). 256p. (C). 1994. pap. text 43.95 (*0-631-19164-X*) Blackwell Pubs.
Principles of Marketing. Fred E. Clark. Ed. by Henry Assael. LC 78-255. (Century of Marketing Ser.). 1979. reprint ed. lib. bdg. 51.95 (*0-405-11158-4*) Ayer.
Principles of Marketing 2nd ed. (C). 1991. text, suppl. ed. 26.80 (*0-536-57937-7*) Pearson Custom.
***Principles Of Marketing.** 2nd ed. 1120p. 2000. write for info. (*0-273-64444-0*) F T P H.
Principles of Marketing. 2nd ed. Hair & Charles W. Lamb. (SB - Marketing Education Ser.). 1994. pap., student ed. 18.00 (*0-538-82984-2*) S-W Pub.
Principles of Marketing. 2nd ed. Carl McDaniel, Jr. et al. (C). 1994. mass mkt. 54.75 (*0-538-82982-6*, SB61BA) S-W Pub.
Principles of Marketing. 2nd ed. Palmer. (SB - Marketing Education Ser.). 1990. 5.95 (*0-538-60439-5*); mass mkt. 38.95 (*0-538-60437-9*) S-W Pub.
Principles of Marketing. 3rd ed. Joel R. Evans. 1995. pap. text, student ed. 14.80 (*0-02-334719-8*, Macmillan Coll) P-H.
Principles of Marketing. 3rd ed. Joel R. Evans & Barry Berman. LC 94-8845. 700p. (C). 1994. text 84.00 (*0-02-334701-5*, Macmillan Coll) P-H.
Principles of Marketing. 4th ed. Cooper. (C). 1995. pap. text, student ed. 22.95 (*0-673-46556-X*) Addson-Wesley Educ.
Principles of Marketing. 4th ed. Jay Diamond & Gerald Pintel. 496p. (C). 1990. text 55.60 (*0-13-714668-X*) P-H.
Principles of Marketing. 7th ed. Kotler. (Orig.). 1995. text, teacher ed. write for info. incl. VHS (*0-13-436817-7*) Allyn.
Principles of Marketing. 8th ed. Philip Kotler & Gary Armstrong. LC 98-3761. (Series in Marketing). 720p. 1998. 92.00 (*0-13-957002-0*) P-H.
***Principles of Marketing.** 8th ed. Thomas J. Paczkowski. (Illus.). 1999. pap. 25.00 (*0-13-099816-8*) P-H.
***Principles of Marketing.** 9th ed. Philip Kotler & Gary Armstrong. LC 00-27875. 716p. 2000. 88.00 (*0-13-026312-5*) P-H.
Principles of Marketing: An Interactive Approach. Wardlow. 1997. 38.95 (*0-538-84187-7*) Sth-Wstrn College.
Principles of Marketing - Marketing Plan Project. 2nd ed. Hair & Charles W. Lamb. (SB - Marketing Education Ser.). (C). 1994. 15.75 (*0-538-83467-6*) S-W Pub.
Principles of Marketing & Careers in Marketing. 2nd ed. (C). 1994. 94.60 (*0-13-205899-5*) P-H.
Principles of Mas Alla de la Lectura, 2. Gallego. pap. text. write for info. (*0-471-29759-3*) Wiley.
Principles of Mass Spectrometry & Negative Ions. Charles E. Melton. LC 72-134445. 327p. reprint ed. pap. 101.40 (*0-608-17004-6*, 202711100054) Bks Demand.

P

Principles of Materials Science & Engineering. 2nd ed. W. F. Smith. (C). 1990. text 77.74 (*0-07-059169-5*) McGraw.

Principles of Materials Science & Engineering. 2nd ed. W. F. Smith. 1990. trans. write for info. (*0-07-074433-5*) McGraw.

Principles of Materials Science & Engineering. 3rd ed. William F. Smith. LC 94-48015. (Materials Science & Engineering Ser.). (C). 1995. text 74.25 (*0-07-059241-1*) McGraw.

Principles of Materials Selection for Engineering Design. P. L. Mangonon. LC 97-39039. 824p. 1998. 105.00 (*0-13-242595-5*) P-H.

Principles of Mathematical Analysis. 3rd ed. Walter Rudin. (International Series in Pure & Applied Mathematics). 325p. (C). 1976. 90.94 (*0-07-054235-X*) McGraw.

Principles of Mathematical Geology. Andrei B. Vistelius. (Diverse Ser.). 500p. (C). 1992. text 374.00 (*0-7923-0076-9*) Kluwer Academic.

***Principles of Mathematical Logic** David Hilbert et al. LC 99-15531. 1999. write for info. (*0-8218-2024-9*) Am Math.

Principles of Mathematical Modeling. Clive L. Dym & Elizabeth Ivey. LC 79-65441. (Computer Science & Applied Mathematics Ser.). 261p. 1980. text 71.00 (*0-12-226550-5*) Acad Pr.

Principles of Mathematical Problem Solving. Martin J. Erickson. LC 98-8331. 252p. 1998. 73.33 (*0-13-096445-X*) P-H.

Principles of Mathematics. Bertrand Russell. (Illus.). 576p. 1996. reprint ed. pap. 17.95 (*0-393-31404-9*, Norton Paperbks) Norton.

Principles of Mathematics. 2nd ed. Sweney & Cook. 592p. (C). 1997. spiral bd. 41.95 (*0-7872-3736-1*) Kendall-Hunt.

Principles of Mathematics Revisited. Jaakko Hintikka. 300p. (C). 1996. text 69.95 (*0-521-49692-6*) Cambridge U Pr.

Principles of Mathematics Revisited. Jaakko Hintikka. 304p. (C). 1998. pap. text 18.95 (*0-521-62498-3*) Cambridge U Pr.

Principles of Measuring Currents. G. Bohnecke. 28p. 1955. write for info. (*0-318-61387-5*) Intl Assoc Phys Sci Ocean.

Principles of Meat Science. 3rd ed. Harold B. Hedrick et al. 368p. 1995. pap. 50.95 (*0-8403-8470-X*) Kendall-Hunt.

Principles of Mechanical Constraint Design. Douglass L. Blanding. (C). 1999. ring bd. 39.95 (*0-201-37966-X*) Addison-Wesley.

Principles of Mechanics & Biomechanics. F. Bell. (Illus.). 250p. (Orig.). 1998. pap. 41.50 (*1-56593-047-9*, 0295) Singular Publishing.

Principles of Mechanics & Biomechanics. Frank Bell. (Illus.). 224p. 1998. pap. 42.50 (*0-7487-3332-9*, Pub. by S Thornes Pubs) Trans-Atl Phila.

Principles of Media Development. Walter Hanclosky. (Illus.). 224p. 1995. pap. 32.95 (*0-86729-335-7*, Focal) Buttrwrth-Heinemann.

Principles of Medical Biochemistry. Gerhard Meisenberg & William H. Simmons. LC 98-2505. (Illus.). 768p. (C). (gr. 13). 1998. pap. text 38.95 (*0-8151-4410-5*, 30897) Mosby Inc.

Principles of Medical Biology, 2 vols., Vol. 1. Ed. by E. Edward Bittar & Neville Bittar. 616p. 1994. 257.00 (*1-55938-779-3*) Jai Pr.

Principles of Medical Biology: Membranes & Cell Signaling, 7 part 2. Ed. by E. Edward Bittar & Neville Bittar. 1997. 257.00 (*0-614-16885-6*) Jai Pr.

Principles of Medical Biology Vol. 1A: Bioethics. Ed. by E. Edward Bittar & Neville Bittar. LC 94-15763. 208p. 1994. 128.50 (*1-55938-801-3*) Jai Pr.

Principles of Medical Biology Vol. 1B: Evolutionary Biology. Ed. by E. Edward Bittar & Neville Bittar. LC 94-11633. 392p. 1994. 128.50 (*1-55938-802-1*) Jai Pr.

Principles of Medical Biology Vol. 2: Cellular Organelles. Ed. by E. Edward Bittar & Neville Bittar. LC 95-16568. 304p. 1995. 128.50 (*1-55938-803-X*) Jai Pr.

Principles of Medical Biology Vol. 3: Cellular Organelles & the Extracellular Matrix. Ed. by E. Edward Bittar & Neville Bittar. LC 95-24345. (Principles of Medical Biology Ser.). 304p. 1995. 128.50 (*1-55938-804-8*) Jai Pr.

Principles of Medical Biology Vol. 4, Pt. I: Cell Chemistry & Physiology. Ed. by E. Edward Bittar & Neville Bittar. 400p. 1995. 128.50 (*1-55938-805-6*) Jai Pr.

Principles of Medical Biology Vol. 4, Pt. II: Cell Chemistry & Physiology. Ed. by E. Edward Bittar & Neville Bittar. 416p. 1996. 128.50 (*1-55938-806-4*) Jai Pr.

Principles of Medical Biology Vol. 4, Pt. III: Cell Chemistry & Physiology. Ed. by E. Edward Bittar & Neville Bittar. 360p. 1996. 128.50 (*1-55938-807-2*) Jai Pr.

Principles of Medical Biology Vol. 4, Pt. IV: Cell Chemistry & Physiology. Ed. by E. Edward Bittar & Neville Bittar. 572p. 1996. 128.50 (*1-55938-808-0*) Jai Pr.

Principles of Medical Biology Vol. 5: Molecular & Cellular Genetics. Ed. by E. Edward Bittar & Neville Bittar. LC 96-20598. 432p. 1996. 128.50 (*1-55938-809-9*) Jai Pr.

Principles of Medical Biology Vol. 6: Immunobiology. Ed. by E. Edward Bittar & Neville Bittar. LC 96-35160. 352p. 1996. 128.50 (*1-55938-811-0*) Jai Pr.

Principles of Medical Biology Vol. 7, Pts. I & II: Membranes & Cell Signalling. Ed. by E. Edward Bittar & Neville Bittar. LC 97-5100. 680p. 1997. 257.00 (*1-55938-812-9*) Jai Pr.

Principles of Medical Biology Vol. 8A, B & C: Molecular & Cellular Pharmacology. Ed. by E. Edward Bittar & Neville Bittar. LC 97-15195. 1208p. 1997. 375.00 (*1-55938-813-7*) Jai Pr.

Principles of Medical Biology Vol. 9A & B: Microbiology. Ed. by E. Edward Bittar & Neville Bittar. LC 97-36100. 743p. 1998. 257.00 (*1-55938-814-5*) Jai Pr.

Principles of Medical Biology Vol. 10A & B: Molecular & Cellular Endocrinology. Ed. by E. Edward Bittar & Neville Bittar. LC 97-41660. 684p. 1998. 257.00 (*1-55938-815-3*) Jai Pr.

Principles of Medical Biology Vol. 11: Developmental Biology. E. Edward Bittar & Neville Bittar. LC 98-18490. 1998. 128.50 (*1-55938-816-1*) Jai Pr.

Principles of Medical Biology Vol. 13: Cell Injury, Vol. 13. E. Edward Bittar & Neville Bittar. LC 98-16467. 1998. 128.50 (*1-55938-818-8*) Jai Pr.

Principles of Medical Biology Vol. 14: Psychiatry. Ed. by E. Edward Bittar & Neville Bittar. Date not set. 128.50 (*1-55938-819-6*) Jai Pr.

Principles of Medical Ethics: With Annotations Especially Applicable to Psychiatry. American Psychiatric Association Staff. LC 95-179629. 33p. 1993. reprint ed. pap. 30.00 (*0-608-02020-6*, 206267600003) Bks Demand.

Principles of Medical Ethics Relevant to the Protection of Prisoners Against Torture. (CIOMS Nonserial Publication Ser.). 1983. pap. text 4.00 (*92-9036-015-1*) World Health.

Principles of Medical Ethics with Annotations Especially Applicable to Psychiatry: 1998 Edition. American Psychiatric Association Ethics Committee. 38p. 1998. pap. text 3.00 (*0-89042-140-4*, 2140) Am Psychiatric.

Principles of Medical Genetics. Thomas D. Gelehrter. (Illus.). 300p. 1990. pap. 38.00 (*0-683-03447-2*) Lppncott W & W.

Principles of Medical Genetics. 2nd ed. Thomas F. Gelehrter et al. (Illus.). 352p. 1997. pap. 39.95 (*0-683-03445-6*) Lppncott W & W.

Principles of Medical Imaging. K. Kirk Shung et al. (Illus.). 289p. 1992. text 73.00 (*0-12-640970-6*) Acad Pr.

***Principles of Medical Law: Second Cumulative Supplement.** Andrew Grubb. 104p. 2000. pap. text 45.00 (*0-19-829882-X*) OUP.

Principles of Medical Law: With Paperback Supplement. Ed. by Ian Kennedy & Andrew Grubb. LC 98-29926. 1032p. 1999. text 225.00 (*0-19-825808-9*) OUP.

Principles of Medical Pharmacology. Derek Waller & Andrew Renwick. (Illus.). 409p. 1994. pap. text 35.95 (*0-7020-1613-6*, Pub. by W B Saunders) Saunders.

Principles of Medical Pharmacology. 6th ed. Ed. by Harold Kalant & Walter H. Roschlau. LC 96-29399. (Illus.). 976p. 1997. text 59.95 (*0-19-510024-7*) OUP.

Principles of Medical Psychiatry. 2nd ed. Ed. by Alan Stoudemire & Barry S. Fogel. LC 92-16193. (Illus.). 1000p. 1993. text 155.00 (*0-19-506477-1*) OUP.

Principles of Medical Psychology: Being the Outlines of a Course of Lectures. Ernst F. Von Feuchtersleben. Ed. by B. G. Babington. Tr. by H. Evans Lloyd from GER. LC 75-16704. (Classics in Psychiatry Ser.). 1976. reprint ed. 34.95 (*0-405-07430-1*) Ayer.

Principles of Medical Therapy in Pregnancy. N. Gleicher. LC 84-24903. (Illus.). 1320p. (C). 1985. text 250.00 (*0-306-41845-2*, Kluwer Plenum) Kluwer Academic.

Principles of Medicinal Chemistry. 3rd ed. Ed. by William O. Foye. LC 87-21395. 950p. (C). 1988. text 60.00 (*0-8121-1098-6*) Lppncott W & W.

Principles of Medicinal Chemistry. 4th ed. Ed. by William O. Foye et al. LC 94-29481. (Illus.). 1024p. 1995. 70.00 (*0-683-03323-9*) Lppncott W & W.

Principles of Medicinal Chemistry. 4th ed. William O. Foye et al. 1,024p. 85.00 (*0-683-30621-9*) Lppncott W & W.

Principles of Medicine in Africa. 2nd ed. Ed. by E. H. Parry. (Illus.). 1985. 115.00 (*0-19-261337-5*) OUP.

Principles of Meditation. Christina Feldman. 1998. pap. 11.00 (*0-7225-3526-0*) Thorsons PA.

Principles of Meditation: Eastern Wisdom for the Western Mind. Annellen M. Simpkins & C. Alexander. (Illus.). 144p. (Orig.). 1996. pap. 16.95 (*0-8048-3074-6*) Tuttle Pubng.

Principles of Mental Hygiene. William A. White. LC 76-180596. (Medicine & Society in America Ser.). 344p. 1972. reprint ed. 25.95 (*0-405-03979-4*) Ayer.

Principles of Mental Physiology. William B. Carpenter. 763p. 160.00 (*1-85506-662-9*) Thoemmes Pr.

Principles of Mercantile Law. Avtar Singh. (C). 1992. 150.00 (*0-89771-789-9*, Pub. by Eastern Book) St Mut.

Principles of Mercantile Law. 5th ed. Avtar Singh. (C). 1993. 80.00 (*81-7012-472-7*, Pub. by Eastern Book) St Mut.

Principles of Mercantile Law: With Supplement. 4th ed. Avtar Singh. (C). 1989. 85.00 (*0-7855-5486-6*) St Mut.

Principles of Merchandising. Melvin T. Copeland. Ed. by Henry Assael. LC 78-277. (Century of Marketing Ser.). 1979. reprint ed. lib. bdg. 33.95 (*0-405-11182-7*) Ayer.

Principles of Metal Cutting. Amitabha Bhattacharyya. (C). 1989. 140.00 (*0-89771-380-X*, Pub. by Current Dist) St Mut.

Principles of Metal Manufacturing Processes. 336p. 1999. pap. 49.95 (*0-470-35241-8*) Wiley.

Principles of Metal Refining. T. Abel Engh. (Illus.). 504p. 1992. text 110.00 (*0-19-856337-X*) OUP.

Principles of Meterological Analysis. Walter J. Saucier. 454p. 1989. pap. 14.95 (*0-486-65979-8*) Dover.

Principles of Micro & Macroeconomics. Mankiw. (C). 1997. text 132.50 (*0-03-024288-6*) Harcourt.

***Principles of Micro-Economics.** unabridged ed. N. Dean Eckhoff. LC 99-91093. 372p. 2000. lib. bdg. 60.00 (*0-9669365-3-1*) Lycra Cnslt.

Principles of Microbiology. Atlas. 1995. 30.62 (*0-8151-0319-0*) McGraw.

Principles of Microbiology. Ronald M. Atlas & Lawrence C. Parks. 576p. (C). 1995. text, lab manual ed. write for info. (*0-8151-0324-7*, WCB McGr Hill) McGrw-H Hghr Educ.

Principles of Microbiology. Ronald M. Atlas & Renk. 144p. (C). 1995. text, student ed. 30.00 (*0-8151-0323-9*, WCB McGr Hill) McGrw-H Hghr Educ.

Principles of Microbiology. Frank H. Osborne. 136p. (C). 1996. spiral bd. 31.95 (*0-8403-8606-0*) Kendall-Hunt.

Principles of Microbiology. 2nd ed. 1996. 37.95 (*0-8151-0890-7*) Mosby Inc.

Principles of Microbiology. 2nd ed. Frank Osborne. 144p. (C). 1997. spiral bd. 38.95 (*0-7872-4413-9*, 41441301) Kendall-Hunt.

Principles of Microeconomics. Leigh Anderson & David A. Hennes. 1995. pap. text, student ed. 26.00 (*0-13-157703-4*) P-H.

***Principles of Microeconomics.** Bernanke. 2000. 66.50 (*0-07-021991-5*, McGrw-H College) McGrw-H Hghr Educ.

Principles of Microeconomics. Cecil Bohanon. 224p. (C). 1994. pap. text 15.50 (*1-57074-101-8*) Greyden Pr.

Principles of Microeconomics. William S. Brown. LC 94-16367. 768p. (C). 1995. mass mkt. 72.95 (*0-314-04231-8*) West Pub.

Principles of Microeconomics. Peter Curwen & Peter K. Else. 480p. (C). 1990. text 90.00 (*0-04-338151-0*) Routledge.

Principles of Microeconomics. Gordon Staff. (C). Date not set. pap. text 26.50 (*0-03-002433-1*) Harcourt Coll Pubs.

Principles of Microeconomics. Fred Gottheil. LC 95-18161. (C). 1995. pap. 43.75 (*0-538-84043-9*) S-W Pub.

Principles of Microeconomics. Gotthel. (HB - Economics Ser.). 1999. mass mkt. 47.95 (*0-538-86273-4*) S-W Pub.

Principles of Microeconomics. Mankiw. (C). 1997. pap. text. write for info. (*0-03-024778-0*) Harcourt Coll Pubs.

Principles of Microeconomics. N. Gregory Mankiw. 528p. (C). 1997. pap. text 73.00 (*0-03-024502-8*) Dryden Pr.

Principles of Microeconomics. Edwin Mansfield. (Illus.). (C). 1992. student ed. write for info. (*0-393-96179-6*) Norton.

Principles of Microeconomics. Edwin Mansfield. (Illus.). (C). 1992. pap. text, student ed. write for info. (*0-393-96178-8*) Norton.

Principles of Microeconomics. Martin L. Primack et al. 476p. (C). 1994. pap. text 42.75 (*1-56226-174-6*) CAT Pub.

Principles of Microeconomics. Ed. by Salvatore. (C). 1998. pap. text, student ed. write for info. (*0-321-01046-9*) Addson-Wesley Educ.

Principles of Microeconomics. Ed. by Salvatre. (C). 1998. text. write for info. (*0-321-01042-6*) Addson-Wesley Educ.

Principles of Microeconomics. Eugene Silberberg. LC 94-36171. 560p. 1994. pap. text 51.00 (*0-13-103714-5*) P-H.

Principles of Microeconomics. Snower. (C). 2000. text Price not set. (*0-321-01424-3*) Addison-Wesley.

Principles of Microeconomics. John B. Taylor. LC 94-48758. (C). 1995. pap. text 53.16 (*0-395-66032-7*) HM.

Principles of Microeconomics. Gerry F. Welch. (C). 1998. pap. text 25.00 (*0-03-008874-7*); pap. text, student ed. 11.00 (*0-03-008877-1*) Harcourt Coll Pubs.

Principles of Microeconomics. James F. Willis et al. 500p. (C). 1995. pap. text 37.00 (*1-56226-277-7*) CAT Pub.

Principles of MicroEconomics. 2nd ed. Mark Rush & Carol Badger-Dole. 240p. (C). 1995. pap. text, spiral bd. 23.95 (*0-7872-0343-2*) Kendall-Hunt.

Principles of Microeconomics. 2nd ed. Joseph E. Stiglitz. LC 95-22777. (C). 1997. pap. text 45.00 (*0-393-96929-0*) Norton.

Principles of Microeconomics. 3rd ed. Martin L. Primack et al. 322p. (C). 1992. pap. text 39.32 (*1-56226-106-1*) CAT Pub.

Principles of Microeconomics. 3rd ed. Bob A Rabboh & Ronald J. Bartson. (C). 1991. 56.00 (*0-536-58081-2*) Pearson Custom.

Principles of Microeconomics. 4th ed. Bob Rabboh & Ronald J. Bartson. LC 96-144242. 472p. (C). 1996. pap. text 52.00 (*0-536-59294-2*, HB172) Pearson Custom.

Principles of Microeconomics. 5th ed. Karl E. Case & Ray C. Fair. LC 98-23824. 607p. 1998. pap. text 66.60 (*0-13-095725-9*) P-H.

Principles of Microeconomics. 5th ed. Karl E. Case & Ray C. Fair. 1998. pap. text, student ed. write for info. (*0-13-095729-1*) P-H.

***Principles of Microeconomics.** 5th ed. Bob Rabboh & Ronald J. Bartson. 436p. 1999. pap. text 50.00 (*0-536-02794-3*) Pearson Custom.

***Principles of Microeconomics.** 6th ed. James Gilbertie. 456p. 1998. ring bd. 48.60 (*1-56226-422-2*) CAT Pub.

Principles of Microeconomics. 7th ed. Edwin Mansfield. (Illus.). (C). 1992. pap. text 58.50 (*0-393-96175-3*) Norton.

Principles of Microeconomics. 7th ed. Edwin Mansfield. (C). 1993. pap. text, student ed. 42.00 (*0-393-96525-2*) Norton.

Principles of Microeconomics. 7th ed. Mohammad Zaheer. 182p. (C). 1995. text 27.00 (*0-536-59051-6*) Pearson Custom.

Principles of Microeconomics: Readings, Issues & Cases. 4th ed. Edwin Mansfield. (C). 1983. pap. text 8.50 (*0-393-95331-9*) Norton.

Principles of Microeconomics: Study Guide. 2nd ed. Lawrence Martin. (C). 1997. pap., student ed. write for info. (*0-393-96932-0*) Norton.

Principles of Microeconomics: Study Guide. 7th ed. Edwin Mansfield. (Illus.). (C). 1992. pap., student ed. 21.00 (*0-393-96176-1*) Norton.

Principles of Microeconomics & the Canadian Economy. 2nd ed. Joseph E. Stiglitz & Robin W. Boadway. LC 97-14590. (Illus.). xxviii, 468p. 1997. pap. write for info. (*0-393-97053-1*) Norton.

Principles of Microelectrode Techniques. M. B. Djamgoz. 120p. 1997. pap. 16.00 (*1-86094-011-0*) World Scientific Pub.

Principles of Microeonomics. 5th ed. (C). 1999. text, teacher ed. write for info. incl. cd-rom (*0-13-020416-1*) P-H.

Principles of Microprocessors. I. L. Sayers et al. (Illus.). 362p. 1991. boxed set 94.95 (*0-8493-8605-5*, QA) CRC Pr.

Principles of Microprocessors. Ian L. Sayers. LC 90-24929. 1991. write for info. (*0-86542-135-8*) Blackwell Sci.

Principles of Microprocessors. Ian L. Sayers. 367p. 1991. per. 64.95 (*0-8493-8622-5*) CRC Pr.

Principles of Microsurgery for Lumbar Disc Disease. John A. McCulloch. 317p. 1989. text 126.00 (*0-88167-487-7*) Lppncott W & W.

Principles of Microsurgery for Lumbar Disc Disease. John McCulloch. LC 86-42896. (Illus.). 317p. reprint ed. pap. 98.30 (*0-608-09633-4*, 205440900001) Bks Demand.

Principles of Microsurgical Techniques in Infertility. Ed. by J. Victor Reyniak & Niels H. Lauersen. LC 81-3045. 310p. 1982. 65.00 (*0-306-40781-7*, Kluwer Plenum) Kluwer Academic.

Principles of Microwave Circuits. Ed. by C. G. Montgomery et al. (Electromagnetic Waves Ser.: No. 25). 502p. 1987. 99.00 (*0-86341-100-2*, EW025) INSPEC Inc.

Principles of Microwave Measurements. G. H. Bryant. (Electrical Measurement Ser.: No. 5). 373p. 1993. reprint ed. pap. 49.00 (*0-86341-296-3*, EL005z) INSPEC Inc.

Principles of Military Communication Systems. Don J. Torrieri. LC 81-67379. 310p. reprint ed. pap. 96.10 (*0-608-16255-8*, 202716000054) Bks Demand.

Principles of Mineralogy. 2nd ed. William H. Blackburn & William H. Dennen. 432p. (C). 1993. text 53.65 (*0-697-15078-X*, WCB McGr Hill) McGrw-H Hghr Educ.

Principles of Mini-Computer Operations, TI-990. Stewart Ferguson. (Illus.). 218p. 1986. pap. text 12.95 (*0-935920-26-9*, Ntl Pubs Blck) P-H.

Principles of Mining & Tunnelling by Machine. 1994. write for info. (*0-08-041689-6*, Pergamon Pr) Elsevier.

Principles of Mobile Communication. Gordon Stuber. LC 96-8122. 1996. text 96.50 (*0-7923-9732-0*) Kluwer Academic.

***Principles of Modeling & Asynchronous Distributed Simulation of Complex Systems.** Sumit Ghosh & Tony Lee. LC 99-44085. (Microelectroic Systems Ser.). 304p. 2000. write for info. (*0-7803-5398-6*) Inst Electrical.

Principles of Modelling & Rendering with 3D Studio. Stuart Mealing et al. LC 98-4539. 1998. 69.00 (*90-265-1523-5*) Swets.

Principles of Modern Chemistry. 3rd ed. Oxtoby. (C). 1995. student ed. 124.00 (*0-03-018402-9*) Harcourt.

Principles of Modern Chemistry. 3rd ed. Oxtoby. (C). 1995. pap. text, teacher ed. 28.00 (*0-03-015649-1*); trans. 261.00 (*0-03-015653-X*, Pub. by Harcourt Coll Pubs) Harcourt.

Principles of Modern Chemistry. 3rd ed. David W. Oxtoby. (C). 1995. text 107.00 (*0-03-005904-6*) Harcourt Coll Pubs.

Principles of Modern Chemistry. 4th ed. Oxtoby. (C). 1998. pap. text, teacher ed. 26.75 (*0-03-024752-7*) Harcourt Coll Pubs.

Principles of Modern Chemistry. 4th ed. Oxtoby. (C). 1998. text 138.50 incl. cd-rom (*0-03-027392-7*, Pub. by Harcourt Coll Pubs) Harcourt.

Principles of Modern Chemistry. 4th ed. David W. Oxtoby. LC 98-84384. 1008p. (C). 1998. text 124.00 (*0-03-024427-7*, Pub. by SCP) Harcourt.

Principles of Modern Chemistry: Study Guide & Student Solutions Manual to Accompany. 4th ed. Oxtoby et al. 624p. 1998. pap., student ed. 37.50 (*0-03-024751-9*) SCP.

Principles of Modern Digital Design. Richard S. Sandige. 736p. (C). 1990. 101.56 (*0-07-054857-9*) McGraw.

Principles of Modern Genetics. Gerald Elseth & Kandy Baumgardner. LC 94-23062. 744p. (C). 1995. pap. 94.95 (*0-314-04207-5*) West Pub.

Principles of Modern Immunobiology: Basic & Clinical. Byung H. Park & Robert A. Good. LC 73-13831. (Illus.). 627p. reprint ed. 194.40 (*0-8357-9416-4*, 201457300093) Bks Demand.

Principles of Modern Marketing. Stewart W. Husted et al. 756p. 1989. teacher ed. write for info. (*0-318-63871-1*, H15795); student ed. 20.00 (*0-685-44213-6*, H15779); write for info. (*0-318-63872-X*, H15886); trans. write for info. (*0-318-63873-8*, H15845) P-H.

***Principles of Modern Microbiology.** Mark Wheelis. (Illus.). 832p. (C). 2001. text 81.25 (*0-7637-1075-X*) JB Pubns.

Principles of Modern Optical Systems, Vol. 1. fac. ed. Ed. by Ivan Andonovic & Deepak Uttamchandani. LC 89-304. (Artech House Telecommunications Library). (Illus.). 624p. 1989. reprint ed. pap. 193.50 (*0-608-00943-1*, 206173500011) Bks Demand.

Principles of Modern Psychological Measurement: A Festschrift for Frederic M. Lord. Ed. by Howard Wainer & Samuel Messick. 416p. 1983. text 79.95 (*0-89859-277-1*) L Erlbaum Assocs.

Principles of Modern Radar Systems. Michel H. Carpentier. LC 88-10563. (Artech House Radar Library). 320p. reprint ed. pap. 99.20 (*0-7837-0413-5*, 204073500018) Bks Demand.

Principles of Modern Technology. Adrian C. Melissinos. (Illus.). 350p. (C). 1990. pap. text 39.95 (*0-521-38965-8*) Cambridge U Pr.

Principles of Modern Technology. Adrian C. Melissinos. (Illus.). 351p. (C). 1990. text 95.00 (*0-521-35249-5*) Cambridge U Pr.

Principles of Modified-Atmosphere & Sous Vide Product Packaging. Jeffrey M. Farber & Karen Dodds. LC 95-60888. 475p. 1995. text 69.95 (*1-56676-276-6*) Technomic.

Principles of Mohammedan Law. M. Mulla. (C). 1990. 85.00 (*0-89771-143-2*) St Mut.

***Principles of Molecular Mechanics.** Katsunosuke MacHida. 328p. 1999. 149.95 (*0-471-35727-8*) Wiley.

Principles of Molecular Medicine. Ed. by J. Larry Jameson. LC 98-17729. (Illus.). 1156p. 1998. 175.00 (*0-89603-529-8*) Humana.

Principles of Molecular Oncology. Ed. by Miguel H. Bronchud et al. LC 99-16733. 468p. 2000. 125.00 (*0-89603-581-6*) Humana.

***Principles of Molecular Regulation.** Ed. by P. Michael Conn & Anthony R. Means. 476p. 2000. 135.00 (*0-89603-630-8*) Humana.

***Principles of Molecular Rheumatology.** Ed. by George C. Tsokos. (Current Molecular Medicine Ser.: Vol. 1). 542p. 2000. 145.00 (*0-89603-773-8*) Humana.

Principles of Molecular Virology. 2nd ed. Ed. by Alan Cann. LC 96-47478. (Illus.). 328p. 1997. pap. text 29.95 (*0-12-158532-8*) Morgan Kaufmann.

Principles of Money: Banking & Financing (Study Guide) 9th ed. Lawerence S. Ritter. 320p. (C). 1997. pap. text, student ed. 28.00 (*0-673-98416-8*) Addison-Wesley.

Principles of Money & Banking: Test Master for the Macintosh. Paul D. Warner. (C). 108.50 (*0-465-06371-3*); 108.50 (*0-465-06372-1*) Basic.

***Principles of Money Banking & Finacial Markets.** 10th ed. 368p. (C). 1999. 25.20 (*0-321-06480-1*) Addison-Wesley.

***Principles of Money Banking & Finacial Markets.** 10th ed. 192p. (C). 1999. 26.00 (*0-321-06470-4*) Addison-Wesley.

Principles of Money, Banking & Finance. 7th ed. Alvarez. (C). 1990. text 17.00 (*0-465-06354-3*) Basic.

Principles of Money, Banking, & Financial Markets. 8th ed. Lawrence S. Ritter & William L. Silber. LC 93-14741. 688p. (C). 1993. pap. 66.50 (*0-465-06367-5*) Basic.

***Principles of Money, Banking & Financial Markets.** 10th ed. (C). 2000. text 67.00 (*0-321-06473-9*) Addison-Wesley.

Principles of Money, Banking & Financial Markets. 10th ed. Lawrence S. Ritter. LC 99-28472. 640p. (C). 1999. 92.00 (*0-321-02020-0*) Addson-Wesley Educ.

Principles of Monitoring for the Radiation Protection of the Public. Ed. by F. D. Sowby. (International Commission of Radiological Protection Ser.: No. 43). (Illus.). 20p. 1984. pap. 32.75 (*0-08-032335-9*, Pergamon Pr) Elsevier.

Principles of Moral & Political Science, 2 vols. Adam Ferguson. LC 71-147970. reprint ed. 85.00 (*0-404-08222-X*) AMS Pr.

Principles of Moral Philosophy: An Inquiry into the Wise & Good Government of the Moral World, 2 vols., Set. George Turnbull. (Anglistica & Americana Ser.: No. 167). 1976. reprint ed. 167.70 (*3-487-06027-2*) G Olms Pubs.

Principles of Morals & Legislation. Jeremy Bentham. LC 88-60151. (Great Books in Philosophy). 354p. (C). 1988. pap. 8.95 (*0-87975-434-6*) Prometheus Bks.

***Principles of Mortgage Origination.** Professional Resource Group Staff. (Learning System Ser.). (Illus.). xviii, 399p. 1999. ring bd. 395.00 (*1-929246-02-1*) Schl Mortg Lend.

Principles of MRI: Selected Topics. 2nd ed. Markisz. 260p. (C). 1998. pap. 45.00 (*0-8385-8152-8*, Apple Lange Med) McGraw.

Principles of Multimedia Database Systems. V.S. Subrahmanian. LC 97-44810. 442p. (C). 1998. text 54.95 (*1-55860-466-9*) Morgan Kaufmann.

***Principles of Multivariate Analysis.** 20th rev. ed. Wojtek Krzanowski. (Oxford Statistical Science Ser.: Vol. 21). 608p. 2000. pap. text 70.00 (*0-19-850708-9*) OUP.

Principles of Multivariate Analysis: A User's Perspective. W. J. Krzanowski. (Oxford Statistical Science Ser.: No. 3). (Illus.). 584p. 1990. reprint ed. pap. text 65.00 (*0-19-852230-4*) OUP.

Principles of Music & Visual Arts. Horton Presley. LC 86-1525. (Illus.). 144p. (Orig.). 1986. pap. text 14.00 (*0-8191-5258-7*) U Pr of Amer.

Principles of Musik, in Singing & Setting. Charles Butler. LC 74-25439. (English Experience Ser.: No. 284). 136p. 1971. reprint ed. 20.00 (*90-221-0284-X*) Walter J Johnson.

Principles of Natural & Politic Law. 5th ed. Jean-Jaques Burlamaqui. Tr. by Thomas Nugent. LC 70-38249. (Evolution of Capitalism Ser.). 500p. 1972. reprint ed. 38.95 (*0-405-04114-4*) Ayer.

Principles of Natural Theology. George H. Joyce. LC 79-170829. reprint ed. 42.50 (*0-404-03609-0*) AMS Pr.

Principles of Nature see Selected Writings of St. Thomas Aquinas

Principles of Nature. Elihu Palmer. LC 75-3301. reprint ed. 37.50 (*0-404-59286-4*) AMS Pr.

Principles of Nature, Her Divine Revelations, (&) a Voice to Mankind, 2 vols. 34th ed. Andrew J. Davis. 800p. 1996. reprint ed. pap. 62.50 (*0-7873-0255-4*) Hlth Research.

Principles of Naval Architecture, 3 vols., Set. Ed. by Edward V. Lewis. LC 88-60829. 1988. 180.00 (*0-685-56498-3*) Soc Naval Arch.

Principles of Naval Architecture, 3 vols., Set. rev. ed. Ed. by Edward V. Lewis. 1988. 192.00 (*0-614-06723-5*) Soc Naval Arch.

Principles of Naval Architecture Vol. I: Stability & Strength, 3 vols. Ed. by Edward V. Lewis. LC 88-60829. 320p. 1988. 90.00 (*0-939773-00-7*) Soc Naval Arch.

Principles of Naval Architecture Vol. 2: Resistance, Propulsion & Vibrations. rev. ed. 1988. 90.00 (*0-939773-01-5*) Soc Naval Arch.

Principles of Naval Architecture Vol. 3: Seakeeping & Controllability. rev. ed. 1988. 90.00 (*0-939773-02-3*) Soc Naval Arch.

Principles of Naval Weapons Systems. Ed. by David R. Frieden. LC 85-4777. (Illus.). 607p. 1985. 39.95 (*0-87021-537-X*) Naval Inst Pr.

***Principles of Naval Weapons Systems.** USNA (Pinnix) Staff. 356p. 1999. per. 24.95 (*0-7872-5635-8*) Kendall-Hunt.

Principles of Naval Weapons Systems Workbook. 96p. 1985. ring bd., wbk. ed. 9.95 (*0-87021-539-6*) Naval Inst Pr.

Principles of Network Thermodynamics. L. Peusner. xv, 255p. 1987. 19.95 (*0-938876-21-X*) Entropy Ltd.

Principles of Neural Aging. Ed. by S. U. Dani et al. LC 97-218825. 490p. 1997. 120.00 (*0-444-82329-8*) Elsevier.

Principles of Neural Development. Dale Purves & Jeff W. Lichtman. LC 84-10566. (Illus.). 433p. 1985. text 62.95 (*0-87893-744-7*) Sinauer Assocs.

Principles of Neural Model Identification, Selection & Adequacy: With Applications in Financial Econometrics. A. D. Zapranis & Apostolos-Paul Refenes. LC 98-51734. (Perspective in Neural Computing Ser.). xii, 272p. 1999. 79.95 (*1-85233-139-9*, Pub. by Spr-Verlag) Spr-Verlag.

Principles of Neural Science. 3rd ed. Ed. by Eric R. Kandel et al. 1135p. (C). 1991. text 85.00 (*0-8385-8034-3*, A8034-9, Apple Lange Med) McGraw.

Principles of Neural Science & Atlas of Neuroanesthesia. 2nd ed. Kandel. 1996. 105.00 (*0-8385-6690-1*, Apple Lange Med) McGraw.

Principles of Neuroanatomy. Jay B. Angevine, Jr. & Carl W. Cotman. (Illus.). 393p. 1981. text 29.95 (*0-19-502885-6*) OUP.

Principles of Neurocomputer Science & Engineering. Ham. 2000. 83.00 (*0-07-025966-6*) McGraw.

***Principles of Neuroepidemiology.** Tracy Batchelor & Merit E. Cudkowicz. (Illus.). 400p. 2000. text 90.00 (*0-7506-7042-8*) Buttrwrth-Heinemann.

Principles of Neurologic Rehabilitation. Ed. by Richard B. Lazar. (Illus.). 752p. 1997. text 85.00 (*0-07-036794-9*) McGraw-Hill HPD.

Principles of Neurology. 5th ed. Raymond D. Adams & Maurice Victor. LC 92-48805. (Illus.). 1402p. 1993. text 79.00 (*0-07-000341-6*) McGraw-Hill HPD.

Principles of Neurology. 6th ed. Raymond D. Adams. 1998. 135.00 (*0-07-864230-2*) McGraw.

Principles of Neurology. 6th rev. ed. Raymond D. Adams et al. (Illus.). 1440p. 1997. text 85.00 (*0-07-067439-6*) McGraw-Hill HPD.

Principles of Neurology: Companion Handbook. 6th ed. Raymond D. Adams et al. LC 98-132505. (Illus.). 512p. 1997. text 32.00 (*0-07-000514-1*) McGraw-Hill HPD.

Principles of Neuropsychological Rehabilitation. George P. Prigatano. LC RC387.5.P754 1999. (Illus.). 374p. 1999. text 49.95 (*0-19-508143-9*) OUP.

Principles of Neuropsychopharmacology. Robert S. Feldman et al. LC 96-3306. (Illus.). 909p. (C). 1996. text 82.95 (*0-87893-175-9*) Sinauer Assocs.

Principles of Neurosurgery. Ed. by Robert G. Grossman & Winifred J. Hamilton. 496p. 1991. text 185.50 (*0-88167-750-7*, 2233) Lppncott W & W.

Principles of Neurosurgery. Ed. by Setti S. Rengachary & Robert H. Wilkins. LC 93-10153. (gr. 13). 1994. 210.00 (*1-56375-022-8*) Mosby Inc.

Principles of Neurosurgery. 2nd ed. Ed. by Robert G. Grossman & Christopher M. Loftus. LC 98-27638. (Illus.). 608p. 1998. text 169.00 (*0-397-51840-4*) Lppncott W & W.

Principles of Neurotoxicology, No. 26. Louis W. Chang. LC 94-7435. (Neurological Disease & Therapy Ser.: Vol. 26). (Illus.). 824p. 1994. text 245.00 (*0-8247-8836-2*) Dekker.

Principles of New Testament Christianity. Charles E. Crouch. 1984. pap. 8.25 (*0-89137-546-5*) Quality Pubns.

Principles of Nonimpact Printing. 3rd ed. Jerome L. Johnson. LC 98-228473. (Illus.). 460p. 1998. text 195.00 (*0-9618005-4-2*) Palatino Pr.

Principles of Nonlinear Optical Spectroscopy. Shaul Mukamel. (Oxford Series on Optical & Imaging Sciences: Vol. 6). (Illus.). 576p. (C). 1999. pap. text 55.00 (*0-19-513291-2*) OUP.

Principles of Nonlinear Optics. Y. R. Shen. LC 83-23259. (Pure & Applied Optics Ser.: No. 1-349). 576p. 1984. 155.00 (*0-471-88998-9*) Wiley.

Principles of Nuclear Geology. U. Aswathanarayana. 410p. (C). 1985. text 123.00 (*90-6191-572-4*, Pub. by A A Balkema) Ashgate Pub Co.

Principles of Nuclear Magnetic Resonance in One & Two Dimensions. Richard R. Ernst et al. (International Series of Monographs on Chemistry: No. 14). (Illus.). 634p. 1990. reprint ed. pap. text 65.00 (*0-19-855647-0*) OUP.

Principles of Nuclear Magnetic Resonance Microscopy. Paul T. Callaghan. (Illus.). 510p. 1994. reprint ed. pap. text 55.00 (*0-19-853997-5*) OUP.

Principles of Nuclear Magnetism. Anatole Abragam. (The International Series of Monographs on Physics: No. 32). (Illus.). 614p. 1983. pap. text 59.00 (*0-19-852014-X*) OUP.

Principles of Nuclear Medicine. 2nd ed. Ed. by Henry N. Wagner, Jr. et al. LC 95-10051. (Illus.). 1248p. 1995. text 249.00 (*0-7216-9091-2*, W B Saunders Co) Harcrt Hlth Sci Grp.

Principles of Nucleic Acid Structure. W. Saenger. (Advanced Texts in Chemistry Ser.). (Illus.). xx, 556p. 1995. 54.95 (*0-387-90761-0*) Spr-Verlag.

Principles of Numerology: The Only Introduction You'll Ever Need. Sonia Ducie. (Illus.). 160p. 1998. pap. 11.00 (*0-7225-3580-5*, Pub. by Thorsons MD) Natl Bk Netwk.

Principles of Nursing in Process Context. 4th ed. Nancy Roper. (Illus.). 336p. (Orig.). 1988. text 30.00 (*0-443-03576-8*) Church.

Principles of Nutrition: Study Guide. Ed. by Deakin University Press Staff. (C). 1986. pap. 75.00 (*0-7300-0751-0*, SHN710, Pub. by Deakin Univ) St Mut.

Principles of Nutrition Management in Primary Health Care. (SEARO Regional Health Papers: No. 26). 43p. 1995. pap. 9.00 (*0-614-32420-3*, 1580026) World Health.

Principles of Nutritional Assessment. Ed. by Rosalind S. Gibson. (Illus.). 712p. 1990. text 67.95 (*0-19-505838-0*) OUP.

***Principles of Object: Oriented Software Development.** 2nd ed. Anten Eliens. LC 00-20005. 496p. (C). 2000. pap. 60.00 (*0-201-39856-7*) Addison-Wesley.

Principles of Object-Oriented Analysis & Design. James Martin & James J. Odell. 412p. 1992. 46.60 (*0-13-720871-5*) P-H.

Principles of Occult Healing. Ed. by Mary W. Burnett. 135p. 1981. pap. 14.00 (*0-89540-072-3*, SB-072) Sun Pub.

Principles of Occult Healing. 2nd ed. Mary W. Burnett. 135p. 1996. reprint ed. spiral bd. 12.00 (*0-7873-0133-7*) Hlth Research.

Principles of Occult Healing (1918) Mary W. Burnett. 136p. 1996. reprint ed. pap. 10.95 (*1-56459-888-8*) Kessinger Pub.

Principles of Ocean Physics. John R. Apel. (International Geophysics Ser.). 520p. 1987. text 135.00 (*0-12-058865-X*); pap. text 73.00 (*0-12-058866-8*) Acad Pr.

***Principles of Ocean Physics.** 2nd ed. Raymond S. Bradley. 1999. 79.00 (*0-12-059795-0*) Morgan Kaufmann.

Principles of Oceanography. 7th ed. M. Grant Gross. (Illus.). 240p. (C). 1995. pap. text 33.33 (*0-02-347981-7*, Macmillan Coll) P-H.

***Principles of Ocular Pharmacology.** (Illus.). 352p. 2000. pap. text 80.00 (*0-7506-4326-9*) Buttrwrth-Heinemann.

Principles of Office Management. J. P. Mahajan. 306p. 1996. pap. 50.00 (*81-209-0391-9*, Pub. by Pitambar Pub) St Mut.

Principles of Oocyte & Embryo Donation. Ed. by M. V. Sauer. LC 97-17443. (Illus.). 272p. 1998. 95.00 (*0-387-94960-7*) Spr-Verlag.

Principles of Operation Management. 6th ed. Raturi. (SWC-Management Ser.). 2000. pap. text 35.00 (*0-324-00896-1*) Thomson Learn.

Principles of Operations Management. Galloway. (Business Press-New Ser.). 256p. 1993. 23.95 (*1-86152-172-3*) Thomson Learn.

Principles of Operations Management. R. L. Galloway. LC 92-2480. (Series in the Principles of Management). 240p. (C). 1993. pap. 21.95 (*0-415-07376-6*, B0152) Routledge.

Principles of Operations Management. Mike Harrison. 192p. (Orig.). 1996. pap. 47.50 (*0-273-61450-9*, Pub. by Pitman Pub) Trans-Atl Phila.

Principles of Operations Management, Vol. 1. 2nd ed. Galloway. (ITBP Textbooks Ser.). 1998. pap. 15.99 (*1-86152-378-5*) Thomson Learn.

Principles of Ophthalmic Lenses. Mohammed Jalie. (C). 1989. 150.00 (*0-900099-20-8*, Pub. by Assn Brit Dispen Opticians) St Mut.

Principles of Optical Circuit Engineering. Mark A. Mentzer. (Optical Engineering Ser.: Vol. 26). (Illus.). 328p. 1990. text 155.00 (*0-8247-8202-6*) Dekker.

Principles of Optical Engineering. Francis T. Yu & Iam-Choon Khoo. 124p. 1990. pap. text, teacher ed. 10.00 (*0-471-60785-1*) Wiley.

Principles of Optical Fiber Measurements. Dietrich Marcuse. 1996. 64.50 (*0-614-18456-8*, B01031) Info Gatekeepers.

Principles of Optics: Electromagnetic Theory of Propagation, Interference & Diffraction of Light. 6th ed. Max Born & E. Wolf. (Illus.). 808p. 1980. pap. 65.00 (*0-08-026481-6*, Pergamon Pr) Elsevier.

Principles of Optics: Electromagnetic Theory of Propagation, Interference & Diffraction of Light. 7th ed. Max Born & Emil Wolf. (Illus.). 900p. (C). 1999. 59.95 (*0-521-64222-1*) Cambridge U Pr.

***Principles of Optimal Design: Modeling & Computation.** Panos Y. Papalambros & Douglass J. Wilde. (Illus.). 475p. 2000. pap. write for info. (*0-521-62727-3*) Cambridge U Pr.

***Principles of Optimal Design: Modeling & Computation.** 2nd ed. Panos Y. Papalambros & Douglass J. Wilde. LC 99-47982. 2000. write for info. (*0-521-62215-8*) Cambridge U Pr.

Principles of Oral & Maxillofacial Surgery, 3 vols., Set. Larry J. Peterson et al. (Illus.). 2256p. 1992. text 446.00 (*0-397-51011-X*) Lppncott W & W.

Principles of Orchestration. Nikolay Rimsky-Korsakov. 489p. 1922. pap. text 12.95 (*0-486-21266-1*) Dover.

Principles of Orchestration: General Overview: Getting the Sounds in Your Head. 2nd rev. ed. Nikolay Rimsky-Korsakov. (Rimsky-Korsakov Ser.: Vol. 1). (Illus.). 341p. (C). 1989. pap. text 34.95 (*0-939067-73-0*) Alexander Pub.

Principles of Organ Transplantation. M. Wayne Flye. (Illus.). 688p. 1989. text 205.00 (*0-7216-1323-3*, W B Saunders Co) Harcrt Hlth Sci Grp.

Principles of Organ Transplantation. 2nd ed. Flye. 2000. text. write for info. (*0-7216-6907-7*) Harcrt Hlth Sci Grp.

***Principles of Organismal Biology.** 4th ed. 420p. (C). 1999. text 26.96 (*0-536-60469-X*) Pearson Custom.

Principles of Organization in Organisms. Arthur B. Baskin. (C). 1992. pap. 40.00 (*0-201-58789-0*) Addison-Wesley.

Principles of Organization, Policy, & Management. Seth B. Goldsmith. 300p. 45.00 (*0-8342-0701-X*) Aspen Pub.

Principles of Organizational Behaviour. 3rd ed. Robin Fincham & Peter Rhodes. LC 98-50445. (Illus.). 608p. 2000. text 80.00 (*0-19-877578-4*) OUP.

***Principles of Organizational Behaviour.** 3rd ed. Robin Fincham & Peter S. Rhodes. LC 98-50445. 1999. write for info. (*0-19-877577-6*) OUP.

Principles of Organometallic Chemistry. 2nd ed. Paul Powell. (C). pap. text 58.50 (*0-412-27590-2*) Chapman & Hall.

Principles of Orthopaedic Medicine & Surgery. Sam W. Wiesel & John Delahey. (Illus.). 735p. (C). 2000. text. write for info. (*0-7216-8189-1*, W B Saunders Co) Harcrt Hlth Sci Grp.

Principles of Orthopedic Practice. 2nd ed. Ed. by Roger Dee et al. LC 96-38647. (Illus.). 1344p. 1996. text 179.00 (*0-07-016356-1*) McGraw-Hill HPD.

Principles of Osmotic Phenomena. Thain. 1989. 10.00 (*0-85404-025-0*) CRC Pr.

Principles of Outer Space Law in Hindsight. H. A. Wassenbergh. 176p. 1991. lib. bdg. 87.00 (*0-7923-1350-X*) Kluwer Academic.

***Principles of P: Framework for Successful Living.** large type ed. Annie Tyson Jett. Ed. by James Jett. (Illus.). v, 110p. 1999. pap. 9.95 (*0-9674057-0-X*) External Res.

Principles of Package Development. 2nd ed. Roger C. Griffin, Jr. et al. 390p. (C). 1993. reprint ed. lib. bdg. 59.50 (*0-89464-811-X*) Krieger.

Principles of Paint Formulation. Ed. by R. Woodbridge. (Illus.). 272p. 1991. 170.00 (*0-412-02951-0*, A6366, Chap & Hall NY) Chapman & Hall.

***Principles of Paleoclimatology.** Thomas M. Cronin. LC 98-48495. (Perspectives in Paleobiology & Earth History Ser.). 1999. 75.00 (*0-231-10954-7*) Col U Pr.

***Principles of Paleoclimatology.** Thomas M. Cronin. LC 98-48495. (Perspectives in Paleobiology & Earth H Ser.). (Illus.). 560p. 1999. pap. 32.00 (*0-231-10955-5*) Col U Pr.

Principles of Paleontology. 2nd ed. David M. Raup & Steven M. Stanley. LC 77-17443. (Illus.). 481p. (C). 1978. text 66.95 (*0-7167-0022-0*) W H Freeman.

Principles of Palmistry. Lilian Verner-Bonds. 1998. pap. 11.00 (*0-7225-3464-7*) Thorsons PA.

Principles of Parenting. William T. Weathers. 78p. (Orig.). 1993. pap. write for info. (*0-9638066-0-2*) Creat Ent SC.

Principles of Party Line Station Identification. Thomas B. Norling. (ABC Pocket Guide for the Field Ser.). (Illus.). 36p. 1982. pap. 7.95 (*1-56016-034-9*) ABC TeleTraining.

Principles of Pastoral Success. Richard S. Taylor. 160p. (Orig.). 1989. mass mkt. 9.99 (*0-310-75401-1*) Zondervan.

Principles of Patent Law. Donald S. Chisum et al. LC 98-8153. (University Casebook Ser.). 1409p. 1998. text 42.50 (*1-56662-614-5*) Foundation Pr.

Principles of Pathology see Oxford Textbook of Pathology

Principles of Patristic Exegesis: Romans 9-11 in Origen, John Chrysostom & Augustine. Peter Gorday. LC 83-20588. (Studies in the Bible & Early Christianity: Vol. 4). 430p. 1983. lib. bdg. 109.95 (*0-88946-602-5*) E Mellen.

Principles of Pattern Design. Richard M. Proctor. (Illus.). 144p. 1990. pap. 8.95 (*0-486-26349-5*) Dover.

Principles of Pavement Design. 2nd ed. E. J. Yoder & M. W. Witczak. 736p. 1975. 140.00 (*0-471-97780-2*) Wiley.

Principles of Payroll Administration. Debera J. Salam & Lucy K. Price. 500p. 1988. pap. 48.00 (*0-13-709932-0*, Busn) P-H.

Principles of Payroll Administration: The Complete Learning & Reference Guide. Debera J. Salam & Lucy K. Price. 1993. ring bd. 120.00 (*0-685-69678-2*, PROP) Warren Gorham & Lamont.

Principles of Peace. Thomas Hancock. 1972. 59.95 (*0-8490-0891-3*) Gordon Pr.

Principles of Pediatric Fluid Therapy. 2nd ed. Robert W. Winters. 1982. 22.00 (*0-316-94738-5*, Little Brwn Med Div) Lppncott W & W.

Principles of Pediatric Nursing. 2nd ed. Rosa M. Sacharin. LC 85-11685. (Illus.). 617p. (C). 1986. text 60.00 (*0-443-03301-3*) Church.

Principles of Peptide Synthesis. M. Bodanszky. (Reactivity & Structure Ser.: Vol. 16). (Illus.). 240p. 1991. 89.00 (*0-387-12395-4*) Spr-Verlag.

Principles of Peptide Synthesis. 2nd rev. ed. M. Bodanszky. (Illus.). 320p. 1993. pap. write for info. (*3-540-56431-4*) Spr-Verlag.

Principles of Peptide Synthesis. 2nd rev. ed. Miklos Bodanszky. LC 93-3332. (Illus.). 330p. 1993. 54.95 (*0-387-56431-4*) Spr-Verlag.

Principles of Performance Engineering for Telecommunication & Information Systems. M. Ghanbari et al. (Telecommunications Ser.: No. 35). 327p. 1997. 75.00 (*0-85296-883-3*) INSPEC Inc.

Principles of Perinatal-Neonatal Metabolism. Ed. by R. M. Cowett. (Illus.). xxi, 774p. 1991. 240.00 (*0-387-97499-7*) Spr-Verlag.

Principles of Perinatal-Neonatal Metabolism. 2nd ed. Ed. by Richard M. Cowett. LC 97-24816. (Illus.). 1088p. 1998. 250.00 (*0-387-94965-8*) Spr-Verlag.

Principles of Persian Calligraphy. James R. Ballantyne. 1977. lib. bdg. 59.95 (*0-8490-2480-3*) Gordon Pr.

Principles of Personal Defense. rev. ed. Jeff Cooper. 56p. 1988. pap. 14.00 (*0-87364-497-2*) Paladin Pr.

Principles of Personal Selling. 1968. teacher ed. write for info. (*0-672-96053-2*); pap. write for info. (*0-672-96052-4*) Macmillan.

P

An Asterisk (*) at the beginning of an entry indicates that the title is appearing for the first time.

Principles of Personal Selling. Harry R. Tosdal. Ed. by Henry Assael. LC 78-322. (Century of Marketing Ser.). (Illus.). 1979. reprint ed. lib. bdg. 64.95 (*0-405-11184-3*) Ayer.

Principles of Persuasion. 2nd ed. (C). 1997. write for info. (*0-8087-6769-0*) Pearson Custom.

Principles of Petroleum Contaminated Soils. Edward J. Calabrese. 672p. 1992. lib. bdg. 110.00 (*0-87371-394-X*, L394) Lewis Pubs.

Principles of Petroleum Geology. Robert C. Laudon. LC 95-24201. (Petroleum Engineering Ser.). 224p. 1995. 105.00 (*0-13-649468-4*) P-H.

Principles of Petroleum Reservoir Engineering, No. 2. G. L. Chierici. Tr. by Peter J. Westaway. LC 93-26019. 388p. 1994. 126.95 (*0-387-56742-9*) Spr-Verlag.

Principles of Petroleum Reservoir Engineering, Vol. 1. Gian Luigi Chierici. Tr. by Peter J. Westaway from ITA. LC 93-26019.Tr. of Principi di Ingegneria dei Giacimenti Petroliferi. 1994. 126.95 (*0-387-56037-8*) Spr-Verlag.

Principles of Pharmaceutical Marketing. 3rd ed. Ed. by Mickey C. Smith. LC 82-6624. (Illus.). 542p. reprint ed. pap. 168.10 (*0-8357-7660-3*, 205698700096) Bks Demand.

Principles of Pharmacoeconomics. 2nd ed. J. Lyle Bootman et al. 312p. 1996. pap. 54.75 (*0-929375-17-3*) H W Bks.

Principles of Pharmacology. Bills. 96p. 1997. text, teacher ed. 19.95 (*0-8273-8300-2*) Delmar.

Principles of Pharmacology. 2nd ed. Georgine W. Bills & Robert C. Soderberg. LC 97-22776. 400p. 1997. mass mkt. 50.95 (*0-8273-8299-5*) Delmar.

Principles of Pharmacology: A Tropical Approach. David T. Okpako. (Illus.). 590p. (C). 1991. text 170.00 (*0-521-34095-0*) Cambridge U Pr.

Principles of Pharmacology: Basic Concepts & Clinical Applications. 2nd ed. Paul L. Munson et al. (Illus.). 1808p. 1996. text 93.95 (*0-412-12231-6*) OUP.

Principles of Pharmacology for Medical Assistants. Rice. (Medical Assisting Ser.). 1989. pap., teacher ed. 14.00 (*0-8273-3093-6*) Delmar.

Principles of Pharmacology for Medical Assisting. 2nd ed. Jane Rice. LC 93-26739. 548p. (C). 1994. pap. 32.00 (*0-8273-5744-3*) Delmar.

Principles of Pharmacology for Medical Assisting. 3rd ed. Jane Rice. LC 98-21887. 560p. (C). 1998. text 45.95 (*0-7668-0325-2*) Delmar.

Principles of Pharmacology for Medical Assisting: Instructor's Guide. 2nd ed. Jane Rice. 89p. 1994. 16.00 (*0-8273-6353-2*) Delmar.

Principles of Pharmacology for Medical Assisting - IML. 3rd ed. Rice. 112p. 1998. teacher ed. 19.95 (*0-7668-0326-0*) Delmar.

Principles of Pharmacology for Respiratory Care. Georgine W. Bills & Robert C. Soderberg. LC 93-48582. 333p. 1994. pap. 34.95 (*0-8273-5274-3*) Delmar.

Principles of Pharmacology for Respiratory Care Workbook. Georgine W. Bills & Robert C. Soderberg. 111p. 1994. 17.95 (*0-8273-5275-1*) Delmar.

Principles of Pharmacy for Respiratory Care. Bills. (Respiratory Care Ser.). 1994. 15.00 (*0-8273-6360-5*) Delmar.

Principles of Phase Conjugation. B. Y. Zel'dovich et al. (Optical Sciences Ser.: Vol. 42). (Illus.). 270p. 1985. 78.00 (*0-387-13458-1*) Spr-Verlag.

Principles of Phase Diagrams in Materials Systems. Paul Gordon. LC 82-14073. 248p. 1983. reprint ed. 29.50 (*0-89874-408-3*) Krieger.

Principles of Philosophical Reasoning. Ed. by James H. Fetzer. LC 83-15985. (American Philosophical Quarterly Library of Philosophy). 304p. (C). 1984. text 60.50 (*0-8476-7158-5*) Rowman.

Principles of Philosophical Reasoning. Ed. by James H. Fetzer. LC 83-15985. 304p. 1984. pap. 29.50 (*0-8476-7341-3*) Rowman.

Principles of Philosophy. Rene Descartes. Tr. by Blair Reynolds. LC 88-26640. (Studies in the History of Philosophy: Vol. 6). 250p. 1989. lib. bdg. 89.95 (*0-88946-308-5*) E Mellen.

Principles of Phonetics. John Laver. LC 93-18183. (Textbooks in Linguistics Ser.). (Illus.). 735p. (C). 1994. pap. text 32.95 (*0-521-45655-X*) Cambridge U Pr.

P

Principles of Photochemistry. J. A. Barltrop & J. D. Coyle. LC 78-16622. 223p. reprint ed. pap. 69.20 (*0-608-12207-6*, 202479600038) Bks Demand.

Principles of Photochemistry, No. 22. Paul Suppan. 1989. 9.00 (*0-85186-769-3*) CRC Pr.

Principles of Physical & Chemical Metallurgy. Giles F. Carter. LC 79-19184. 447p. reprint ed. pap. 138.60 (*0-608-12109-6*, 202514600042) Bks Demand.

Principles of Physical Biochemistry. K. E. Van Holde & W. Curtis Johnson. LC 97-46067. 657p. (C). 1998. 90.00 (*0-13-720459-0*) P-H.

Principles of Physical Chemistry. Kuhn. LC 98-48542. 998p. 1999. pap. 50.00 (*0-471-96541-3*) Wiley.

***Principles of Physical Chemistry.** Lionel M. Raff. LC 00-41687. 2000. write for info. (*0-13-027805-X*) P-H.

Principles of Physical Chemistry. E. Kirk Roberts. (C). 1984. pap. text 51.00 (*0-205-08011-1*, H80112); teacher ed. 7.00 (*0-685-07782-9*, H80120) P-H.

Principles of Physical Cosmology. P. J. Peebles. LC 92-33370. (Physics Ser.). 736p. (C). 1993. text 79.50 (*0-691-07428-3*, Pub. by Princeton U Pr); pap. text 35.00 (*0-691-01933-9*, Pub. by Princeton U Pr) Cal Prin Full Svc.

Principles of Physical Geography: An Introduction to Natural Phenomena. Ted J. Alsop. 384p. (C). 1993. per. 38.95 (*0-8403-8777-6*) Kendall-Hunt.

Principles of Physical Medicine & Rehabilitation in the Musculoskeletal Diseases. Ed. by James C. Leek et al. 544p. 1986. text 129.00 (*0-8089-1773-0*, 792502, Grune & Strat) Harcrt Hlth Sci Grp.

Principles of Physical, Organic & Biological Chemistry: An Introduction to the Molecular Basis of Life. John R. Holum. LC 68-9249. (Illus.). 738p. reprint ed. pap. 200.00 (*0-608-30094-2*, 205514200008) Bks Demand.

Principles of Physical Security. fac. ed. Donald O. Schultz. LC 77-86192. (Illus.). 176p. 1978. reprint ed. pap. 54.60 (*0-608-00977-6*, 206183100012) Bks Demand.

Principles of Physical Sedimentology. John R. Allen. (Illus.). 400p. (C). 1985. text 60.00 (*0-04-551095-4*); pap. text 39.95 (*0-04-551096-2*) Routledge.

***Principles of Physical Sedimentology.** J. R. L. Allen. 272p. 2000. reprint ed. pap. 74.95 (*1-930665-10-5*) Blackburn Pr.

Principles of Physics. Ohanian. 1995. pap. text, teacher ed., suppl. ed. write for info. (*0-393-96586-4*) Norton.

Principles of Physics. Hans C. Ohanian. (C). 1994. pap. text 97.25 (*0-393-95773-X*) Norton.

Principles of Physics. Hans C. Ohanian. (C). 1994. pap. text. write for info. (*0-393-96336-5*) Norton.

Principles of Physics. Serway. (C). 1994. pap. text, teacher ed. 33.75 (*0-03-097743-6*) Harcourt Coll Pubs.

Principles of Physics. 2nd ed. Serway. (C). 1997. 441.50 (*0-03-020672-3*) Harcourt.

Principles of Physics. 2nd ed. Serway. LC 97-209140. (Illus.). 1056p. (C). 1997. text 69.00 (*0-03-020457-7*, Pub. by SCP) Harcourt.

Principles of Physics. 2nd ed. Raymond A. Serway. (C). 1997. pap. text, teacher ed. 20.00 (*0-03-020669-3*) Harcourt Coll Pubs.

Principles of Physics. 2nd ed. Raymond A. Serway. (C). 1997. pap. text, teacher ed. 49.50 (*0-03-020668-5*, Pub. by Harcourt Coll Pubs) Harcourt.

Principles of Physics. 3rd ed. Frank J. Blatt. 912p. 1989. teacher ed. write for info. (*0-318-63881-9*, H17866); pap., student ed. 10.67 (*0-685-44214-4*, H19391); pap., student ed. 21.00 (*0-685-22014-1*, H17858); write for info. (*0-318-63882-7*, H19540); trans. write for info. (*0-318-63883-5*, H21546) P-H.

Principles of Physics. 3rd ed. Serway. (C). 2001. text. write for info. (*0-03-027157-6*) Harcourt Coll Pubs.

Principles of Physics. 6th ed. Bueche. 1994. pap., student ed. 86.88 (*0-07-008986-8*) McGraw.

Principles of Physics. 6th ed. Saxena. 1995. student ed. 26.88 (*0-07-008949-3*) McGraw.

Principles of Physics, Vol. I. Michigan State University Staff. (C). 1993. pap. text 35.00 (*1-881592-35-9*) Hayden-McNeil.

Principles of Physics, Vol. 1. 2nd ed. Serway. LC 97-65256. 528p. (C). 1997. pap. text 62.00 (*0-03-024558-3*, Pub. by SCP) Harcourt.

Principles of Physics, Vol. I. 2nd ed. Serway. (Illus.). 312p. (C). 1997. pap. text, student ed. 19.00 (*0-03-020663-4*, Pub. by SCP) Harcourt.

Principles of Physics, Vol. II. Michigan State University, Project Physnet Staff. (C). 1993. pap. text 35.00 (*1-881592-36-7*) Hayden-McNeil.

Principles of Physics, Vol. 2. 2nd ed. Serway. 624p. (C). 1997. pap. text 60.50 (*0-03-024559-1*, Pub. by SCP) Harcourt.

Principles of Physics, Vol. 2. 2nd ed. Serway. (Illus.). 328p. (C). 1997. pap. text, student ed. 19.00 (*0-03-024628-8*, Pub. by SCP) Harcourt.

Principles of Physics: Answer Pamphlet. Ohanian. (C). 1994. pap. text 6.00 (*0-393-96394-2*) Norton.

Principles of Physics: Pocket Guide. 2nd ed. Serway. (Illus.). 376p. (C). 1997. pap. text, student ed. 17.50 (*0-03-020664-2*, Pub. by SCP) Harcourt.

Principles of Physics: Student Solution Manual. Hans O'Hanian. (C). Date not set. student ed. write for info. (*0-393-96781-6*) Norton.

Principles of Physics: Study Guide. Hans C. Ohanian. (C). 1994. pap. text 27.25 (*0-393-95780-2*) Norton.

Principles of Physiology. Ed. by Grabowski. (C). 1999. pap. text, student ed. write for info. (*0-06-502183-5*) Addison-Wesley.

Principles of Physiology. 2nd ed. Robert M. Berne & Levy. (Illus.). 816p. (C). (gr. 13). 1995. pap. text 53.00 (*0-8151-0523-1*, 24422) Mosby Inc.

***Principles of Physiology.** 3rd ed. Ed. by Robert Berne. LC 99-19992. 1999. text 54.00 (*0-323-00813-5*) Harcourt.

Principles of Pictorial Photography. John W. Gillies. LC 72-9201. (Literature of Photography Ser.). 1973. reprint ed. 23.95 (*0-405-04910-2*) Ayer.

Principles of Pig Science. Ed. by D. J. A. Cole et al. 472p. 1999. 200.00 (*1-897676-22-0*, Pub. by Nottingham Univ Pr) St Mut.

Principles of Piping Analysis. David Burgreen. 483p. 1977. 48.00 (*0-916877-04-3*) Arcturus Pubs.

Principles of Plant Pathology. E. C. Stakman & J. G. Harrar. LC 57-9298. (Illus.). 593p. reprint ed. 183.90 (*0-8357-9960-3*, 201243900081) Bks Demand.

Principles of Plasma Diagnostics. Ian H. Hutchinson. (Illus.). 380p. (C). 1990. pap. text 37.95 (*0-521-38583-0*) Cambridge U Pr.

Principles of Plasma Discharges & Materials Processing. Michael A. Lieberman & Allan J. Lichtenberg. 600p. 1994. 89.95 (*0-471-00577-0*) Wiley.

Principles of Plasma Electrodynamics. A. F. Alexandrov et al. (Electrophysics Ser.: Vol. 9). (Illus.). 510p. 1984. 102.95 (*0-387-12613-9*) Spr-Verlag.

Principles of Plasma Mechanics. 2nd ed. Bishwanath Chakraborty. LC 90-26596. 612p. 1991. text 105.00 (*0-470-21729-4*) Halsted Pr.

Principles of Plasma Spectroscopy. Hans R. Griem. LC 96-37158. (Cambridge Monographs on Plasma Physics: Vol. 2). 386p. 1997. text 100.00 (*0-521-45504-9*) Cambridge U Pr.

Principles of Playmaking. Brander Matthews. LC 79-134113. (Essay Index Reprint Ser.). 1977. 23.95 (*0-8369-1989-0*) Ayer.

Principles of Poetry: Shi No Genri, Vol. 96. Hagiwara Sakutaro. Tr. by Chester Wang from JPN. LC 99-191522. xviii, 170p. (C). 1998. pap. 11.90 (*1-885445-96-2*) Cornell East Asia Pgm.

Principles of Poetry Vol. 96: Shi No Genri. Hagiwara Sakutaro. Tr. by Chester Wang from JPN. LC 99-191522. (Illus.). 192p. (C). 1998. 18.70 (*1-885445-76-8*) Cornell East Asia Pgm.

Principles of Polargraphy. R. C. Kapoor. (C). 1991. 18.00 (*0-685-51526-5*) S Asia.

Principles of Polarity. R. C. Kapoor. (C). 1991. 24.00 (*81-224-0306-9*) S Asia.

Principles of Police Patrol. Nathan F. Iannone. 1975. text 58.71 (*0-07-031667-8*) McGraw.

Principles of Police Patrol Study Guide. Davis Publishing Company Staff. 208p. (Orig.). 1990. pap. 28.95 (*1-56325-015-2*, DS072) Davis Pub Law.

Principles of Political Economy. Charles Gide. Tr. by Ernest F. Row from FRE. LC 78-126685. reprint ed. 35.00 (*0-404-02739-3*) AMS Pr.

Principles of Political Economy. Simon Newcomb. LC 65-26372. (Reprints of Economic Classics Ser.). xvi, 548p. 1966. reprint ed. 57.50 (*0-678-00156-1*) Kelley.

Principles of Political Economy. Simon Newcomb. (Notable American Authors Ser.). 1999. reprint ed. lib. bdg. 125.00 (*0-7812-4621-0*) Rprt Serv.

Principles of Political Economy. William Roscher. LC 72-38255. (Evolution of Capitalism Ser.). 964p. 1972. reprint ed. 65.95 (*0-405-04136-5*) Ayer.

Principles of Political Economy. 2nd ed. Henry Vethake. LC 61-21698. (Reprints of Economic Classics Ser.). liv, 415p. 1971. reprint ed. 49.50 (*0-678-00301-7*) Kelley.

Principles of Political Economy, 3 Vols, Set. Henry C. Carey. LC 65-16983. (Reprints of Economic Classics Ser.). 1965. reprint ed. 125.00 (*0-678-00071-9*) Kelley.

Principles of Political Economy: And Chapters on Socialism. John Stuart Mill. Ed. & Intro. by Jonathan Riley. (Oxford World's Classics Ser.). 512p. 1999. pap. 10.95 (*0-19-283672-2*) OUP.

Principles of Political Economy: Considered with a View to Their Practical Application. 2nd ed. Thomas Robert Malthus. LC 86-10606. (Reprints of Economic Classics Ser.). liv, 460p. 1986. reprint ed. 49.50 (*0-678-00038-7*) Kelley.

Principles of Political Economy: Deduced from the Natural Laws of Social Welfare. George J. Scrope & G. J. Poulett. LC 68-58008. (Reprints of Economic Classics Ser.). xxiv, 457p. 1969. reprint ed. 49.50 (*0-678-00563-X*) Kelley.

Principles of Political Economy: Variorum Edition, 2 vols., Set. Thomas Robert Malthus. Ed. by John Pullen. 1147p. 1990. 150.00 (*0-521-24775-6*) Cambridge U Pr.

Principles of Political Economy: With Some Inquiries Respecting Their Application. 5th ed. John R. McCulloch. LC 65-19651. (Reprints of Economic Classics Ser.). xxiv, 518p. 1965. reprint ed. 49.50 (*0-678-00097-2*) Kelley.

Principles of Political Economy: With Some of Their Applications to Social Philosophy. John Stuart Mill. Ed. & Intro. by William J. Ashley. (Reprints of Economic Classics Ser.). liii, 1013p. 1987. reprint ed. 57.50 (*0-678-00073-5*); reprint ed. pap. 29.95 (*0-678-01453-1*) Kelley.

Principles of Political Economy Vol. 3: Just Economy. James E. Meade. LC 65-26549. 247p. (C). 1976. text 29.50 (*0-87395-205-7*) State U NY Pr.

Principles of Political Economy & Taxation. David Ricardo. LC 96-28486. (Great Minds Ser.). 305p. 1996. pap. 10.95 (*1-57392-109-2*) Prometheus Bks.

Principles of Political Theory & Organization. L. S. Rathore & S. A. Haqqi. (C). 1988. 60.00 (*0-7855-5447-5*) St Mut.

Principles of Politics. Arthur R. Lord. LC 70-179637. (Select Bibliographies Reprint Ser.). 1977. reprint ed. 23.95 (*0-8369-6658-9*) Ayer.

Principles of Politics & Government. 5th ed. Edwin M. Coulter. LC 92-74917. 320p. (C). 1993. text. write for info. (*0-697-12697-8*) Brown & Benchmark.

Principles of Politics & Government. 6th ed. Edwin M. Coulter. LC 96-84171. 320p. (C). 1996. text. write for info. (*0-697-23762-1*) Brown & Benchmark.

Principles of Pollination Ecology. 4th ed. Knut Faegri & L. Anders Nilsson. Date not set. 59.95 (*0-8493-9235-7*) CRC Pr.

***Principles of Pollution Abatement at the Beginning of the 21st Century.** Jorgensen. 2000. 156.00 (*0-08-043626-9*, Pergamon Pr); pap. 80.00 (*0-08-043625-0*, Pergamon Pr) Elsevier.

Principles of Polymer Chemistry. Paul J. Flory. (George Fisher Baker Non-Resident Lectureship in Chemistry at Cornell University Ser.). (Illus.). 688p. 1953. text 69.50 (*0-8014-0134-8*) Cornell U Pr.

Principles of Polymer Chemistry. A. Ravve. (Illus.). 510p. (C). 1995. text 71.00 (*0-306-44873-4*, Kluwer Plenum) Kluwer Academic.

***Principles of Polymer Chemistry.** 2nd ed. A. Ravve. LC 99-89493. (Illus.). 708p. 2000. 89.00 (*0-306-46368-7*, Kluwer Plenum) Kluwer Academic.

Principles of Polymer Composites. A. A. Berlin et al. (Polymers, Properties & Applications Ser.: Vol. 10). (Illus.). 150p. 1985. 141.95 (*0-387-15051-X*) Spr-Verlag.

Principles of Polymer Engineering. 2nd ed. N. G. McCrum et al. LC 97-12589. (Illus.). 462p. 1997. text 95.00 (*0-19-856527-5*); pap. text 44.95 (*0-19-856526-7*) OUP.

Principles of Polymer Processing. Zehev Tadmor & Costas G. Gogos. LC 78-17859. (SPE Monographs). 752p. 1979. 175.00 (*0-471-84320-2*) Wiley.

Principles of Polymer Science & Technology in Cosmetics & Personal Care. Ed. by Goddard & Gruber. LC 99-17274. (Cosmetic Science & Technology Ser.). (Illus.). 704p. 1999. text 225.00 (*0-8247-1923-9*) Dekker.

Principles of Polymer Systems. 3rd ed. Ferdinand Rodriguez. (Illus.). 612p. 1989. 66.95 (*0-89116-176-7*) Hemisp Pub.

Principles of Polymer Systems. 4th ed. Ferdinand Rodriguez. 732p. 1996. 85.00 (*1-56032-325-6*) Hemisp Pub.

Principles of Polymerization. 3rd ed. Odian. 800p. 1994. pap. text 89.95 (*0-471-01005-7*) Wiley.

Principles of Polymerization. 3rd ed. George Odian. LC 90-24785. 792p. 1991. 89.95 (*0-471-61020-8*) Wiley.

Principles of Polymerization Engineering. Joseph A. Biesenberger & Donald H. Sebastican. 768p. 1993. reprint ed. 92.00 (*0-89464-603-6*) Krieger.

Principles of Population & Development: With Illustrations from Asia & Africa. Nigel Crook. Ed. by Ian M. Timaeus. 1997. 65.00 (*0-614-31301-5*) OUP.

Principles of Population & Development: With Illustrations from Asia & Africa. Nigel Crook. Ed. by Ian M. Timligus. LC 96-28079. (Illus.). 236p. 1997. text 65.00 (*0-19-877489-3*) OUP.

Principles of Population & Development: With Illustrations from Asia & Africa. Nigel Crook. Ed. by Ian M. Timaeus. LC 96-28079. (Illus.). 236p. 1997. pap. text 32.00 (*0-19-877488-5*) OUP.

Principles of Population & Production; As They Are Affected by the Progress of Society. John Weyland. LC 68-58665. (Reprints of Economic Classics Ser.). xl, 493p. 1969. reprint ed. 57.50 (*0-678-00485-4*) Kelley.

***Principles of Population Dynamics & Their Application.** Alan A. Berryman. (Illus.). 192p. 1999. pap. 47.50 (*0-7487-4015-5*, Pub. by S Thornes Pubs) Trans-Atl Phila.

Principles of Population Genetics. 3rd ed. Daniel L. Hartl & Andrew G. Clark. LC 97-34505. 481p. (C). 1997. text 69.95 (*0-87893-306-9*) Sinauer Assocs.

Principles of Positive Leadership: Lessons for Positive Living. Mike Magee. 116p. 1995. 14.95 (*1-889793-01-9*) Spencer Bks.

Principles of Poultry Science. S. P. Rose. LC 96-48884. (CAB International Publication). 145p. 1997. pap. text 25.00 (*0-85199-122-X*) OUP.

Principles of Powder Technology. Ed. by M. J. Rhodes. LC 89-70570. 452p. 1990. 250.00 (*0-471-92422-9*) Wiley.

Principles of Power: The Great Political Crises of History. Guglielmo Ferrero. Tr. by Theodore R. Jaeckel. LC 72-4274. (World Affairs Ser.: National & International Viewpoints). 346p. 1972. reprint ed. 24.95 (*0-405-04569-7*) Ayer.

***Principles of Power: Women Superintendents & the Riddle of the Heart.** C. Cryss Brunner. LC 99-47840. (C). 2000. text 57.50 (*0-7914-4569-0*); pap. text 18.95 (*0-7914-4570-4*) State U NY Pr.

Principles of Power Electronics. John G. Kassakian et al. (Electrical Engineering Ser.). (Illus.). 740p. (C). 1991. 100.00 (*0-201-09689-7*) Addison-Wesley.

Principles of Practical Cost-Analysis. Robert Sugden & Alan L. Williams. (Illus.). 288p. 1978. pap. text 24.00 (*0-19-877041-3*) OUP.

Principles of Practical Tectonic Analysis of Cratonic Regions: With Particular Reference to Western North America. Gerald M. Friedman et al. LC 98-51416. (Illus.). xx, 372p. 1999. pap. 129.00 (*3-540-65346-5*) Spr-Verlag.

Principles of Practice of Plant Hormone Analysis, 2 vols. Rivier. 1987. 210.00 (*0-12-198374-9*) Acad Pr.

Principles of Pragmatism: A Philosophical Interpretation of Experience. Henry H. Bawden. LC 75-3034. (Philosophy in America Ser.). 1976. reprint ed. 37.50 (*0-404-59042-X*) AMS Pr.

Principles of Prayer. Billy J. Daugherty. LC 98-119430. 265p. 1997. pap. 9.99 (*1-56267-099-9*) Victory Ctr OK.

Principles of Prayer. Charles G. Finney. Ed. by Louis G. Parkhurst. LC 80-17856. 112p. (Orig.). 1980. pap. 6.99 (*0-87123-468-8*) Bethany Hse.

Principles of Precambrian Geology. Ed. by Alan M. Goodwin. (Illus.). 352p. 1996. pap. text 54.95 (*0-12-289770-6*) Acad Pr.

Principles of Precision Engineering. Hiromu Nakazawa. LC 93-43452. (Illus.). 280p. (C). 1994. text 115.00 (*0-19-856266-7*) OUP.

Principles of Premium Auditing. 3rd rev. ed. Everett D. Randall. LC 95-81903. (Associate in Premium Auditing Ser.: Vol. 2). (Illus.). 317p. (C). 1995. pap. text 41.00 (*0-89462-097-5*, 9102/9103) IIA.

Principles of Primary Wound Management: A Guide to the Fundamentals. Michael D. Mortiere. LC 96-94515. (Illus.). 96p. (Orig.). 1996. pap. text 16.00 (*0-9652878-0-7*) Clifton Pub.

Principles of Process Engineering. 4th rev. ed. S. M. Henderson et al. LC 97-74549. 353p. 1997. pap. text 52.00 (*0-929355-85-7*, M0297) Am Soc Ag Eng.

Principles of Process Research & Chemical Development in the Pharmaceutical Industry. Oljan Repic. LC 97-13904. 240p. 1997. 84.95 (*0-471-16516-6*) Wiley.

Principles of Professional Cooking: Student Manual. Educational Foundation of the National Restaurant. 71p. (Orig.). 1991. pap. write for info. (*0-915452-66-9*) Educ Found.

Principles of Professional Fundraising: Useful Foundations for Successful Practice. Joseph R. Mixer. LC 93-14551. (Nonprofit Sector-Public Administration Ser.). 277p. 1993. text 32.95 (*1-55542-590-9*) Jossey-Bass.

***Principles of Program Analysis.** F. Nielson et al. LC 99-47677. 450p. 1999. 46.00 (*3-540-65410-0*) Spr-Verlag.

Principles of Program Design. M. A. Jackson. (Automatic Programming Information Centre Studies in Data Processing). 310p. 1975. text 69.00 (*0-12-379050-6*) Acad Pr.

An Asterisk (*) at the beginning of an entry indicates that the title is appearing for the first time.

Principles of Programming Languages: Design, Evaluation & Implementation. 2nd ed. Bruce J. MacLennan. (Illus.). 592p. 1995. reprint ed. text 76.00 (*0-19-510583-4*) OUP.

Principles of Programming Languages: Design, Evaluation & Implementation. 3rd ed. Bruce J MacLenan. LC 98-27755. (Illus.). 528p. 1999. text 77.95 (*0-19-511306-3*) OUP.

Principles of Project Formulation for Irrigation & Drainage Projects. Ed. by George R. Baumli. LC 82-73505. 144p. 1982. pap. 18.00 (*0-87262-345-9*) Am Soc Civil Eng.

Principles of Project Management: Collected Handbooks from the Project Management Institute. J. Adams et al. LC 96-51592. 307p. 1997. pap. 59.95 (*1-880410-30-3*) Proj Mgmt Inst.

Principles of Protein Structure. G. E. Schulz & R. H. Schirmer. LC 78-11500. (Advanced Texts in Chemistry Ser.). (Illus.). x, 314p. 1990. 27.00 (*0-387-90386-0*) Spr-Verlag.

Principles of Protein Structure. G. E. Schulz & R. H. Schirmer. LC 78-11500. (Advanced Texts in Chemistry Ser.). (Illus.). x, 314p. 1996. 49.95 (*0-387-90334-8*) Spr-Verlag.

Principles of Protein X-Ray Crystallography. Jan Drenth. LC 93-6235. (Advanced Texts in Chemistry Ser.). (Illus.). 305p. 1995. 54.95 (*0-387-94091-X*) Spr-Verlag.

Principles of Protein X-Ray Crystallography. 2nd ed. Jan Drenth. LC 98-26970. (Advanced Texts in Chemistry Ser.). (Illus.). 336p. 1999. 64.50 (*0-387-98587-5*) Spr-Verlag.

Principles of Protocol Design. 300p. 1995. pap. 48.00 (*0-13-182155-5*) P-H.

*__Principles of Psychic Protection: The Only Introduction You'll Ever Need.__ Judy Hall. 2000. pap. 11.00 (*0-7225-3884-7*) Thorsons PA.

Principles of Psychoanalysis: Their Application to the Neuroses. Herman Nunberg. LC 55-11549. 382p. (Orig.). 1969. reprint ed. 57.50 (*0-8236-4300-X*); reprint ed. pap. 24.95 (*0-8236-8198-X*, 24300) Intl Univs Pr.

Principles of Psychoanalytic Psychotherapy: A Manual for Supportive-Expressive Treatment. Lester Luborsky. LC 83-54377. 292p. 1984. pap. 37.50 (*0-465-06328-4*, Pub. by Basic) HarpC.

Principles of Psychology. Engle. 1989. pap. text, teacher ed. 45.00 (*0-15-374801-X*); pap. text, wbk. ed. 12.25 (*0-15-374802-8*) Holt R&W.

Principles of Psychology, 2 vols. William James. 1990. 52.50 (*0-8446-2310-5*) Peter Smith.

Principles of Psychology, 2 vols. William James. 714p. 1260.00 (*1-85506-679-3*) Thoemmes Pr.

Principles of Psychology. Intro. by William James & George A. Miller. 1312p. 1983. pap. text 33.00 (*0-674-70625-0*) HUP.

Principles of Psychology. Herbert Spencer. 632p. 145.00 (*1-85506-655-6*) Thoemmes Pr.

Principles of Psychology. William James. (Notable American Authors Ser.). 1992. reprint ed. lib. bdg. 75.00 (*0-7812-3472-7*) Rprt Serv.

Principles of Psychology, 2 vols., Set. J. R. Kantor. 1926. 20.00 (*0-911188-44-4*) Principia Pr.

Principles of Psychology, 2 vols., Vol. 1. William James. 1950. pap. text 12.95 (*0-486-20381-6*) Dover.

Principles of Psychology, 2 vols., Vol. 2. William James. 1950. pap. text 12.95 (*0-486-20382-4*) Dover.

Principles of Psychology, Vol. 3. William James. Ed. by Frederick H. Burkhardt. LC 81-4194. (Works of William James Ser.). 449p. 1981. reprint ed. pap. 139.20 (*0-7837-4156-1*, 205900400003) Bks Demand.

Principles of Psychology: A Systematic Text in the Science of Behavior. Fred S. Keller & William N. Schoenfeld. (R. F. Skinner Reprint Ser.). 431p. (C). 1995. pap. text 20.00 (*0-87411-765-8*) Copley Pub.

Principles of Psychology: Tests. Engle. 1989. pap. 11.25 (*0-15-374803-6*) Holt R&W.

Principles of Psychopathology: Two Worlds - Two Minds - Two Hemispheres. John C. Cutting. LC 96-29144. (Illus.). 604p. (C). 1997. text 120.00 (*0-19-262240-4*) OUP.

Principles of Psychophysiology: A Survey of Modern Scientific Psychology, 3 vols. Leonard T. Troland. LC 68-57643. (Illus.). 1970. reprint ed. lib. bdg. 145.00 (*0-8371-9954-9*, TRPS) Greenwood.

Principles of Psychophysiology: A Survey of Modern Scientific Psychology, 3 vols., Vol. 1. Leonard T. Troland. LC 68-57643. (Illus.). 1970. reprint ed. lib. bdg. 55.00 (*0-8371-1007-6*, TRPT) Greenwood.

Principles of Psychophysiology: A Survey of Modern Scientific Psychology, 3 vols., Vol. 2. Leonard T. Troland. LC 68-57643. (Illus.). 1970. reprint ed. lib. bdg. 55.00 (*0-8371-1008-4*, TRPU) Greenwood.

Principles of Psychophysiology: A Survey of Modern Scientific Psychology, 3 vols., Vol. 3. Leonard T. Troland. LC 68-57643. (Illus.). 1970. reprint ed. lib. bdg. 55.00 (*0-8371-1009-2*, TRPV) Greenwood.

Principles of Psychophysiology: Physical, Social & Inferential Elements. Ed. by John T. Cacioppo & Louis G. Tassinary. (Illus.). 926p. (C). 1990. pap. text 47.95 (*0-521-34885-4*) Cambridge U Pr.

Principles of Psychotherapy. Pierre M. Janet. Tr. by H. M. Guthrie & Edwin R. Guthrie. (Select Bibliographies Reprint Ser.). 1977. reprint ed. 24.95 (*0-8369-5894-2*) Ayer.

*__Principles of Psychotherapy.__ 2nd ed. Irving B. Weiner. LC 97-50225. 336p. 1998. 55.00 (*0-471-19128-0*) Wiley.

Principles of Public Health Practice. Keck Scutchfield & C. William Keck. LC 96-14785. (Health Services Administration Ser.). 432p. (C). 1996. mass mkt. 84.95 (*0-8273-6271-4*) Delmar.

Principles of Public International Law. 5th ed. Ian Brownlie. LC 98-38843. 792p. 1999. text 110.00 (*0-19-876298-4*); pap. text 49.95 (*0-19-876299-2*) OUP.

*__Principles of Public Law.__ 2nd ed. Andrew Le Sueur et al. 584p. 1999. pap. 34.50 (*1-85941-381-1*, Pub. by Cavendish Pubng) Gaunt.

Principles of Public Presentation. Isa N. Engleberg. 382p. (C). 1997. 53.00 (*0-06-500738-7*) Addson-Wesley Educ.

Principles of Public Speaking. Jack Rudman. (Dantes Subject Standardized Tests (DANTES) Ser.: Vol. DANTES-59). pap. 23.95 (*0-8373-6659-3*) Nat Learn.

*__Principles of Public Speaking.__ 14th ed. (C). 2000. write for info. (*0-321-08102-1*) Addison-Wesley.

*__Principles of Public Speaking.__ 14th ed. 2000. 24.00 (*0-321-08567-1*) P-H.

Principles of Pulmonary Medicine. 3rd ed. Steven E. Weinberger. Ed. by Judy Fletcher. LC 97-4388. (Illus.). 432p. 1998. pap. text 39.00 (*0-7216-8668-0*, W B Saunders Co) Harcrt Hlth Sci Grp.

Principles of Pyrotechnics. deluxe ed. Claude-Fortune Ruggieri. Tr. by Stuart Carlton. 364p. 1995. text 114.00 (*0-9643114-0-2*) MP Assocs.

Principles of Pyrotechnics. limited ed. Claude-Fortune Ruggieri. Tr. by Stuart Carlton. 364p. 1995. text 750.00 (*0-9643114-1-0*) MP Assocs.

Principles of Pyrotechnics. 2nd rev. ed. A. A. Shidlovsky. (Illus.). 272p. 1997. pap. text 49.00 (*0-929931-13-0*) Amer Fireworks.

Principles of Qabalah: The Only Introduction You'll Ever Need. Amber Jayanti. 1999. pap. 11.00 (*0-7225-3680-1*) Thorsons PA.

Principles of Quality Assurance & Cost Containment in Health Care: A Guide for Medical Students, Residents, & Other Health Professionals. John W. Williamson et al. LC 82-48072. (Jossey-Bass Series in Higher Education). 168p. reprint ed. pap. 52.10 (*0-7837-2542-6*, 204270100006) Bks Demand.

Principles of Quality Control. Jerry Banks. LC 88-22763. 672p. 1989. text 102.95 (*0-471-63551-0*) Wiley.

Principles of Quality Costs: Principles, Implementation & Use. 2nd rev. ed. ASQ Quality Costs Committee. Ed. by Jack Campanella. (Quality Ser.). (Illus.). 140p. 1990. pap. 45.00 (*0-87389-084-1*, H0593) ASQ Qual Pr.

*__Principles of Quality Costs: Principles, Implementation & Use.__ 3rd ed. Jack Campanella. LC 98-46411. 175p. 2000. 49.50 (*0-87389-443-X*) ASQ Qual Pr.

Principles of Quantitative Chemical Analysis. Robert De Levie. LC 96-75572. (C). 1996. text 69.25 (*0-07-016362-6*) McGraw.

Principles of Quantitative Living Systems Science. J. R. Simms. LC 98-42066. (IFSR International Series on Systems Science: Vol. 13). (Illus.). 280p. (C). 1998. write for info. (*0-306-45979-5*, Plenum Trade) Perseus Pubng.

Principles of Quantum General Relativity. Eduard Prugovecki. 376p. 1995. pap. 36.00 (*981-02-2138-X*) World Scientific Pub.

Principles of Quantum General Relativity. Edward Prugovecki. LC 94-41518. 376p. 1995. text 74.00 (*981-02-2077-4*) World Scientific Pub.

Principles of Quantum Mechanics. Hans C. Ohanian. 384p. (C). 1989. text 66.00 (*0-13-712795-2*) P-H.

Principles of Quantum Mechanics. 2nd ed. R. Shankar. (Illus.). 694p. (C). 1994. text 55.00 (*0-306-44790-8*, Kluwer Plenum) Kluwer Academic.

Principles of Quantum Mechanics. 4th ed. P. A. Dirac. (International Series of Monographs on Physics). 324p. 1982. pap. text 39.95 (*0-19-852011-5*) OUP.

Principles of Quantum Mechanics: As Applied to Chemistry & Chemical Physics. Donald D. Fitts. LC 98-39486. (Illus.). 280p. (C). 1999. text 74.95 (*0-521-65124-7*); pap. text 39.95 (*0-521-65841-1*) Cambridge U Pr.

*__Principles of Quantum Scattering Theory.__ D. S. Belkic. 1999. 145.00 (*0-7503-0496-0*) IOP Pub.

Principles of Quick Kill. U. S. Army Infantry School, Ft. Benning, Ga. Staff. (Illus.). 72p. 1967. reprint ed. pap. 17.00 (*0-87364-065-9*) Paladin Pr.

Principles of R & D Management. Philip H. Francis. LC 77-24179. 240p. reprint ed. pap. 74.40 (*0-608-12911-9*, 202353400033) Bks Demand.

Principles of Radiation Oncology for Cancer of the Head & Neck. Robert M. Kellman & Chung T. Chung. (Self-Instruction Package Ser.). (Illus.). 85p. (Orig.). 1993. pap. text 25.00 (*1-56772-003-X*) AAO-HNS.

Principles of Radical Copolymerization. S. I. Kuchanov. 1996. write for info. (*0-614-17903-3*) Elsevier.

Principles of Radio Communication. Fraidoon Mazda. LC 96-213594. (Telecommunication Ser.). (Illus.). 270p. 2000. pap. text 32.95 (*0-240-51457-2*, Focal) Buttrwrth-Heinemann.

Principles of Radiographic Imaging. Richard R. Carlton & Arlene M. Adler. 1990. text 53.50 (*0-8273-3605-5*) Delmar.

Principles of Radiographic Imaging. 2nd ed. Carlton. (Radiographic Technology Ser.). 96p. 1996. teacher ed. 18.00 (*0-8273-6865-8*) Delmar.

Principles of Radiographic Imaging. 2nd ed. Carlton. (Radiographic Technology Ser.). (C). 1996. lab manual ed. 23.00 (*0-8273-6866-6*) Delmar.

*__Principles of Radiographic Imaging: An Art & a Science.__ Richard R. Carlton. (Illus.). 2000. 64.95 (*0-7668-1300-2*) Delmar.

Principles of Radiographic Imaging: An Art & a Science. 2nd ed. Richard R. Carlton. (Radiographic Technology Ser.). (Illus.). 736p. (C). 1996. mass mkt. 77.95 (*0-8273-6864-X*) Delmar.

Principles of Radiographic Imaging: Instructor's Guide. Richard R. Carlton & Arlene M. Adler. 1991. pap., teacher ed. 18.00 (*0-8273-3606-3*) Delmar.

Principles of Radiographic Imaging: Lab Manual. Richard R. Carlton et al. 1992. pap., wbk. ed., lab manual ed. 21.95 (*0-8273-3607-1*) Delmar.

Principles of Radiographic Positioning & Procedures Pocket Guide. 2nd ed. Carlton. LC 98-43726. 448p. (C). 1999. pap. 21.95 (*0-8273-6372-9*) Delmar.

Principles of Radiography for Technologists. Perry Sprawls, Jr. 384p. (C). 1990. 58.00 (*0-8342-0088-0*) Aspen Pub.

Principles of Radioisotope Methodology. 3rd ed. Grafton D. Chase & Joseph L. Rabinowitz. LC 66-19903. (C). 1967. text. write for info. (*0-8087-0308-0*) Pearson Custom.

Principles of Radiological Health. Earnest F. Gloyna & Joe O. Ledbetter. LC 69-18429. (Environmental Health Engineering Textbooks Ser.). (Illus.). 491p. reprint ed. pap. 152.30 (*0-7837-4061-1*, 204401100011) Bks Demand.

Principles of Radiological Physics. 2nd ed. Robin J. Wilks. LC 86-17526. (Illus.). 608p. (Orig.). (C). 1987. pap. text 69.00 (*0-443-03780-9*) Church.

Principles of Radiological Physics. 3rd ed. D. T. Graham. (Illus.). 667p. 1996. pap. write for info. (*0-443-04816-9*) Church.

Principles of Radiopharmacology. Ed. by H. Deckhart & Peter H. Cox. 1987. text 161.50 (*0-89838-774-4*) Kluwer Academic.

Principles of Radiopharmacology, 3 vols., Vol. 1. Ed. by Lelio G. Columbetti. 304p. 1979. 165.00 (*0-8493-5465-X*, RM858, CRC Reprint) Franklin.

Principles of Radiopharmacology, 3 vols., Vol. 2. Ed. by Lelio G. Columbetti. 288p. 1979. 158.00 (*0-8493-5466-8*, CRC Reprint) Franklin.

Principles of Radiopharmacology, 3 vols., Vol. 3. Ed. by Lelio G. Columbetti. 352p. 1979. 194.00 (*0-8493-5467-6*, CRC Reprint) Franklin.

Principles of Random Variate Generation. John Dagpunar. (Illus.). 248p. 1988. 75.00 (*0-19-852202-9*) OUP.

Principles of Reaction Kinetics. 2nd ed. Ashmore. 80p. 1989. 18.00 (*0-85404-024-2*) CRC Pr.

Principles of Reading. Anderson. (Teaching Methods Ser.). 1999. pap. 22.95 (*0-8384-6685-0*) Wadsworth Pub.

Principles of Real Analysis. 3rd ed. Charalambos D. Aliprantis & Owen Burkinshaw. LC 98-3955. (Illus.). 415p. (C). 1998. boxed set 59.95 (*0-12-050257-7*) Acad Pr.

Principles of Real Estate. 39.95 (*0-8373-6552-X*, DANTES-52) Nat Learn.

Principles of Real Estate. (Dantes Subject Standardized Tests Ser.: DANTES-52). pap. 23.95 (*0-8373-6652-6*) Nat Learn.

Principles of Real Estate Decisions. Donald R. Epley & Joseph S. Rabianski. LC 80-21354. (C). 1981. text 29.50 (*0-201-03188-4*) Addison-Wesley.

Principles of Real Estate Decisions. Donald R. Epley & Joseph S. Rabianski. 752p. 1986. pap. text. write for info. (*0-317-44720-3*) P-H.

Principles of Real Estate Decisions. 2nd ed. Donald R. Epley & Joseph Rabianski. LC 84-24551. 1986. 30.95 (*0-201-10472-5*) Addison-Wesley.

Principles of Real Estate Law. Paul G. Creteau. LC 76-52549. (Illus.). 1977. 22.00 (*0-9603372-0-2*) Castle Pub Co.

Principles of Real Estate Management. 13th ed. (Illus.). 320p. (C). 1991. 44.95 (*0-944298-59-1*) Inst Real Estate.

Principles of Real Estate Practice. unabridged ed. Stephan R. Mettling & David Cusic. (Illus.). 416p. (Orig.). 1996. pap. text 25.00 (*0-9652158-0-6*) Perfrmnce Pub.

Principles of Real-Time Sonography in Modern Obstetrics: A Handbook for the Practicing Physician. Nicola Perone. LC 83-42848. (Illus.). 173p. 1984. reprint ed. pap. 53.70 (*0-7837-9536-X*, 206028500005) Bks Demand.

Principles of Reasoning. Lilly-Marlene Russow & Martin Curd. LC 88-60527. 372p. (C). 1988. pap. text 24.00 (*0-312-17506-X*) St Martin.

Principles of Receptorology. Ed. by M. K. Agarwal. LC 83-15441. (Illus.). vii, 677p. 1983. 196.15 (*3-11-009558-0*) De Gruyter.

Principles of Reflexology: The Only Introduction You'll Ever Need. 2nd ed. Nicola M. Hall. 1996. pap. 10.00 (*0-7225-3352-7*) Thorsons PA.

Principles of Refrigeration. Jack Rudman. (Dantes Subject Standardized Tests (DANTES) Ser.: Vol. 45). 43.95 (*0-8373-6545-7*) Nat Learn.

Principles of Refrigeration. Jack Rudman. (Dantes Subject Standardized Tests Ser.: DANTES-45). 1994. pap. 23.95 (*0-8373-6645-3*) Nat Learn.

Principles of Refrigeration. 2nd ed. Roy J. Dossat. LC 78-2938. 98p. 1978. pap. text 9.00 (*0-471-03771-0*) P-H.

Principles of Refrigeration. 3rd ed. C. Thomas Olivo. (Heating, Ventilation & Air Conditioning Ser.). 1990. pap., teacher ed. 14.95 (*0-8273-3559-8*) Delmar.

Principles of Refrigeration. 3rd ed. C. Thomas Olivo & R. W. Marsh. LC 76-14089. 1990. mass mkt. 46.50 (*0-8273-3557-1*) Delmar.

Principles of Refrigeration. 4th ed. Roy J. Dossat. LC 96-18469. 512p. 1996. 92.00 (*0-13-233371-6*) P-H.

Principles of Regression Analysis. Robert L. Plackett. LC 60-50875. 184p. reprint ed. pap. 57.10 (*0-608-10285-7*, 205161300097) Bks Demand.

Principles of Reiki. Kasja K. Borang. 1998. pap. 11.00 (*0-7225-3406-X*) Genl Dist Srvs.

Principles of Reinsurance, 2 vols., Set. 2nd ed. Michael W. Elliott et al. LC 95-79605. 446p. (C). 1995. pap. text 41.00 (*0-89462-087-8*, 14102/14103) IIA.

Principles of Relief. Edward T. Devine. LC 74-137162. (Poverty U. S. A. Historical Record Ser.). 1971. reprint ed. 27.95 (*0-405-03132-7*) Ayer.

Principles of Remedies. W. Covell & K. Lupton. LC 96-150595. 320p. 1995. pap. write for info. (*0-409-30777-7*, MICHIE) LEXIS Pub.

Principles of Renal Physiology. Homer W. Smith. LC 56-6992. 247p. reprint ed. pap. 76.60 (*0-608-14425-8*, 205176100007) Bks Demand.

*__Principles of Renal Physiology.__ 4th ed. Christopher J. Lote. LC 99-52097. 1999. write for info. (*0-7923-6074-5*) Kluwer Academic.

Principles of Representative Government. Bernard Manin. (Themes in the Social Sciences Ser.). 252p. 1997. pap. text 16.95 (*0-521-45891-9*) Cambridge U Pr.

Principles of Representative Government. Bernard Manin. (Themes in the Social Sciences Ser.). 252p. 1997. text 54.95 (*0-521-45258-9*) Cambridge U Pr.

Principles of Rescue No. 1. J. Steven Kidd & John Czajkowski. 1994. teacher ed. write for info. (*0-8151-5142-X*) Mosby Inc.

Principles of Research Data Audit. Ed. by Adil E. Shamoo. viii, 182p. 1989. text 62.00 (*2-88124-378-9*); pap. text 31.00 (*2-88124-379-7*) Gordon & Breach.

*__Principles of Research Design in Social Sciences.__ Frank Bechhofer & Lindsay Paterson. LC 99-44348. 192p. (C). 2000. text. write for info. (*0-415-21442-4*) Routledge.

*__Principles of Research Design in the Social Sciences.__ Frank Bechhofer & Lindsay Paterson. LC 99-44348. 2000. pap. 24.99 (*0-415-21443-2*) Routledge.

Principles of Research in Behavioral Science. Bernard E. Whitley, Jr. LC 95-24593. 692p. (C). 1995. text 68.95 (*1-55934-249-8*, 1249) Mayfield Pub.

*__Principles of Research in Communication.__ (C). 2000. teacher ed. write for info. (*0-321-08708-9*) Addson-Wesley Educ.

Principles of Research in Psychology. James Green. (C). 1995. pap. 13.34 (*1-56870-181-0*) RonJon Pub.

Principles of Respiratory Care. Robert Kacmarek & David J. Pierson. (Illus.). 864p. 1999. write for info. (*0-07-034379-9*) McGraw-Hill HPD.

Principles of Retirement Planning. 2nd ed. Ed. by Dearborn Financial Pub. Staff. LC 97-24343. 220p. (Orig.). 1997. pap. text 34.95 (*0-7931-2591-X*, 5442-0102, R & R Newkirk) Dearborn.

*__Principles of Retirement Planning.__ 3rd ed. Dearborn Financial Publishing Staff. LC 99-23664. 240p. 1999. pap. 37.00 (*0-7931-3427-7*) Dearborn.

Principles of Revival. rev. ed. Charles G. Finney. Ed. by Louis G. Parkhurst. LC 87-18433. 224p. 1987. pap. 8.99 (*0-87123-929-9*) Bethany Hse.

Principles of RF Linear Accelerators. Thomas Wangler. LC 97-13439. (Series in Beam Physics & Accelerator Technology). 400p. 1998. 98.95 (*0-471-16814-9*, Wiley-Interscience) Wiley.

Principles of Rheology for Polymer Engineers. White. LC 88-33830. 336p. 1990. 115.00 (*0-471-85362-3*) Wiley.

Principles of Rhetoric & Their Application: A Facsimile Reproduction of the 1888 Edition. fac. ed. Adams S. Hill. LC 94-24334. (American Linguistics, 1700-1900 Ser.: Vol. 491). 348p. 1995. 50.00 (*0-8201-1491-X*) Schol Facsimiles.

Principles of Riding: The Official Instruction Handbook of the German National Equestrian Federation. 2nd rev. ed. German National Equestrian Federation Staff. (Complete Riding & Driving System Ser.). Date not set. 28.95 (*1-872082-93-9*, Pub. by Kenilworth Pr) Half Halt Pr.

Principles of Risk Assessment. Edward J. Calabrese. Date not set. 59.95 (*1-56670-016-7*) Lewis Pubs.

Principles of Risk Management & Insurance. 4th ed. George E. Rejda. (C). 1992. 25.00 (*0-673-46542-X*) Addson-Wesley Educ.

Principles of Risk Management & Insurance. 5th ed. George E. Rejda. LC 94-17221. (C). 1997. 97.00 (*0-673-99027-3*) Addson-Wesley Educ.

Principles of Risk Management & Insurance. 6th ed. Rejda. 336p. (C). 1997. text, student ed. 30.00 (*0-321-00026-9*) Addison-Wesley.

Principles of Risk Management & Insurance. 6th ed. George E. Rejda. (C). 1997. text. write for info. (*0-321-00677-1*) Addson-Wesley Educ.

Principles of Risk Management & Insurance. 6th ed. Ed. by George E. Rejda. LC 97-28269. 566p. (C). 1997. 98.00 (*0-321-01451-0*) Addson-Wesley Educ.

*__Principles of Risk Management & Insurance.__ 7th ed. (C). 2001. write for info. (*0-321-07697-4*) Addson-Wesley Educ.

*__Principles of Risk Management & Insurance.__ 7th ed. George E. Rejda. LC 00-41633. 2000. write for info. (*0-321-05065-7*) Addson-Wesley Educ.

Principles of Rock Deformation. Adolphe Nicolas. 1987. pap. text 66.00 (*90-277-2369-9*) Kluwer Academic.

*__Principles of Rock Drilling.__ U. M. Rao Karanam & B. Misra. (Illus.). 272p. (C). 1998. text 52.00 (*90-5410-788-X*, Pub. by A A Balkema) Ashgate Pub Co.

Principles of Rock Drilling & Bit Wear, Pt. 1. George B. Clark. Ed. by Jon W. Raese. LC 82-1148. (Colorado School of Mines Quarterly Ser.: Vol. 77, No. 1). (Illus.). 118p. 1982. 12.00 (*0-685-06987-7*) Colo Sch Mines.

Principles of Rock Drilling & Bit Wear, Pt. 2. rev. ed. George B. Clark. Ed. by Jon W. Raese. LC 82-1148. (Colorado School of Mines Quarterly Ser.: Vol. 77 No. 2). (Illus.). 42p. 1982. pap. text 10.00 (*0-686-79748-5*) Colo Sch Mines.

*__Principles of Roman Architecture.__ Jones Mark Wilson. LC 99-14920. (Illus.). 280p. 1999. 60.00 (*0-300-08138-3*) Yale U Pr.

Principles of Roman Law & Their Relation to Modern Law. William L. Burdick. LC 89-46051. xii, 748p. 1989. reprint ed. 125.00 (*0-912004-77-0*) Gaunt.

Principles of Rorschach Interpretation. Irving B. Weiner. LC 98-7193. (Personality & Clinical Psychology Ser.). 375p. 1998. 49.95 (*0-8058-3108-8*) L Erlbaum Assocs.

Principles of Route-to-Route Extrapolation for Risk Assessment. Ed. by T. R. Gerrity & C. J. Henry. 336p. 1990. 100.00 (*0-444-01582-5*) P-H.

Principles of Running: Practical Lessons from My First 100,000 Miles. Amby Burfoot. LC 99-17991. 1999. 15.95 (*1-57954-038-4*) Rodale Pr Inc.

P

An Asterisk (*) at the beginning of an entry indicates that the title is appearing for the first time.

Principles of Safety in Physical Education & Sport. 2nd ed. Ed. by Neil J. Dougherty, IV. (Illus.). 256p. (Orig.). 1994. pap. text 35.00 (0-88314-556-1, A5561) AAHPERD.

Principles of Salesmanship. Richard Howland. (C). 1972. text 4.50 (0-256-01261-X, Irwn Prfssnl) McGraw-Hill Prof.

Principles of Salmonid Culture. William Pennell & Bruce A. Barton. LC 96-31360. (Developments in Aquaculture & Fisheries Ser.: No. 29). 1070p. 1996. 222.25 (0-444-82152-X) Elsevier.

Principles of Salvation. Charles G. Finney. Ed. by Louis G. Parkhurst. LC 89-14961. 288p. (Orig.). 1989. pap. 9.99 (1-55661-032-7) Bethany Hse.

Principles of Sample Handling & Sampling Systems Design for Process Analysis. E. A. Houser. LC 72-85741. 118p. reprint ed. pap. 36.60 (0-608-14398-7, 201757500007) Bks Demand.

Principles of Sanctification. rev. ed. Charles G. Finney. LC 86-9664. 28p. 1986. pap. 8.99 (0-87123-859-4) Bethany Hse.

Principles of School Supply Management. Robert B. Taylor. LC 71-177722. (Columbia University. Teachers College. Contributions to Education Ser.: No. 228). reprint ed. 37.50 (0-404-55228-5) AMS Pr.

Principles of Science. Joseph M. Brown. 215p. 1991. 39.95 (0-9626768-0-2) Basic Res Pr.

Principles of Science. 2nd rev. ed. W. Stanley Jevons. 1986. reprint ed. lib. bdg. 56.95 (0-935005-47-1) Lincoln-Rembrandt.

Principles of Scientific Man, Vol. 1. McQuade. 2000. pap. text. write for info. (0-312-11595-4) St Martin.

Principles of Scientific Management. unabridged ed. Frederick W. Taylor. LC 97-31521. (Illus.). 144p. 1998. reprint ed. pap. 5.95 (0-486-29988-0) Dover.

Principles of Scientific Management. 2nd ed. Frederick W. Taylor. LC 98-16091. (EMP Classics Presents . . . Ser.). 131p. 1998. reprint ed. write for info. (0-89806-182-2, PRINCI) Eng Mgmt Pr.

Principles of Scientific Sociology. Walter L. Wallace. LC 83-11764. 557p. 1983. lib. bdg. 53.95 (0-202-30304-7) Aldine de Gruyter.

Principles of Scientific Thinking. Rom Harre. LC 78-126074. 1993. lib. bdg. 22.50 (0-226-31708-0) U Ch Pr.

Principles of Scottish Private Law, Vol. IV. 4th ed. David M. Walker. 488p. 1989. 95.00 (0-19-876218-6) OUP.

Principles of Scottish Private Law Vol. I, Bk. I: Book I: Introductory & General; Book II: International Private Law; Book III: Law of Persons. 4th ed. David M. Walker. 570p. 1988. 98.00 (0-19-876215-1) OUP.

Principles of Scottish Private Law Vol. II, Bk. IV: Law of Obligations. 4th ed. David M. Walker. (Illus.). 816p. 1988. 89.00 (0-19-876216-X) OUP.

Principles of Seating the Disabled. R. Mervyn Letts. (Illus.). 384p. 1991. lib. bdg. 139.00 (0-8493-6021-8, RD757) CRC Pr.

Principles of Secondary Processing & Casting of Liquid Steel. Ahindra Ghosh. 1991. 28.00 (81-204-0558-7, Pub. by Oxford IBH) S Asia.

Principles of Secure Communication Systems. Don J. Torrieri. LC 85-47815. (Artech House Communications & Electronic Defense Library). 465p. reprint ed. pap. 144.20 (0-7837-1337-1, 204148500002) Bks Demand.

Principles of Security. 3rd ed. Truett A. Ricks et al. LC 93-71748. (Illus.). 462p. (C). 1993. pap. 34.95 (0-87084-746-5) Anderson Pub Co.

Principles of Security Management. 2nd ed. Richard J. Healy & Timothy J. Walsh. LC 81-81449. 274p. 1983. pap. text 15.75 (0-9605954-0-6) Prof Pubns.

Principles of Sedimentary Basin Analysis. Andrew D. Miall. (Illus.). 550p. 1985. 48.50 (0-387-90941-9) Spr-Verlag.

Principles of Sedimentary Basin Analysis. 2nd ed. Andrew D. Miall. (Illus.). 424p. 1997. 74.95 (0-387-97119-X) Spr-Verlag.

***Principles of Sedimentary Basin Analysis.** 3rd enl. ed. Andrew D. Miall. LC 99-36198. (Illus.). xv, 672p. 1999. 79.95 (3-540-65790-8) Spr-Verlag.

Principles of Sedimentology & Stratigraphy. 2nd ed. Sam Boggs, Jr. (Illus.). 774p. (C). 1994. 99.00 (0-02-311792-3, Macmillan Coll) P-H.

Principles of Seduction: How to Get Another Person to Fall in Love with You. George C. Viddler. LC 90-62605. 268p. 1993. 19.95 (0-9627602-6-9) Pedestal Pr.

Principles of Seed Pathology, 2 vols. Vijendra K. Agarwal & James B. Sinclair. 352p. 1987. 279.90 (0-8493-4313-5, SB732) CRC Pr.

Principles of Seed Pathology. 2nd ed. Vijendra K. Agarwal & James B. Sinclair. 560p. (C). 1996. boxed set 99.00 (0-87371-670-1, L670) Lewis Pubs.

Principles of Seed Pathology, Vol. 1. V. K. Agarwal & J. B. Sinclair. LC 86-6147. 1987. 110.00 (0-8493-4314-3, SB732, CRC Reprint) Franklin.

Principles of Seed Pathology, Vol. II. Agarwal. 184p. 1987. 174.00 (0-8493-4315-1) CRC Pr.

Principles of Seismology. Augustin Udias. LC 98-32174. (Illus.). 475p. (C). 2000. 90.00 (0-521-62434-7); pap. 39.95 (0-521-62478-9) Cambridge U Pr.

Principles of Self-Damage. Edmund Bergler. LC 92-1423. 506p. (C). 1992. reprint ed. 70.00 (0-8236-4315-8) Intl Univs Pr.

Principles of Self Hypnosis: Pathways to the Unconscious. C. Alexander Simpkins & Annellen M. Simpkins. (Frontiers of Consciousness Ser.). 244p. 1991. 19.95 (0-8290-2415-8); 42.95 incl. audio (0-8290-2465-4) Irvington.

Principles of Self Organization: Symposium on Self-Organization, Robert Allerton Park, June, 1961. Von Foerster & G. Zopf. LC 61-16895. (International Tracts Computer Science & Technology & Their Application Ser.: Vol. 9). 1962. 247.00 (0-08-009598-4, Pub. by Pergamon Repr) Franklin.

Principles of Semantic Networks: Explorations in the Representation of Knowledge. Ed. by John F. Sowa. (Illus.). 500p. 1991. text 58.95 (1-55860-088-4) Morgan Kaufmann.

Principles of Semiotic. D. S. Clarke, Jr. 160p. 1987. 35.00 (0-7102-0981-9, Routledge Thoemms); pap. 14.95 (0-7102-1136-8, Routledge Thoemms) Routledge.

Principles of Sericulture. Hisao Aruga. (Illus.). 392p. (C). 1994. text 104.00 (90-5410-254-3, Pub. by A A Balkema) Ashgate Pub Co.

Principles of Services Marketing. Adrian Palmer. LC 94-4289. 1994. 18.95 (0-07-707746-6) McGraw.

Principles of Services Marketing & Management. Christopher H. Lovelock. LC 98-49946. 414p. (C). 1999. 93.00 (0-13-676875-X, Macmillan Coll) P-H.

Principles of Shakespearian Production with Special Reference to the Tragedies. George W. Knight. reprint ed. 69.00 (0-403-04222-4) Somerset Pub.

Principles of Shakespearian Production with Special Reference to Tragedies. George W. Knight. 1988. reprint ed. lib. bdg. 49.00 (0-7812-0031-8) Rprt Serv.

Principles of Signaling for Cell Relay & Frame Relay. Daniel Minoli & George Dobrowski. LC 94-11381. 305p. 1994. 89.00 (0-89006-708-2) Artech Hse.

Principles of Singing: A Textbook for Voice Class or Studio. 2nd ed. Kenneth E. Miller. 288p. (C). 1989. pap. text 45.00 (0-13-712712-X) P-H.

Principles of Small Business. Robert Brown & Barrow. 224p. 1997. pap. 18.99 (1-86152-189-8) Thomson Learn.

Principles of Social Evolution. Christopher R. Hallpike. LC 86-5437. (Illus.). 424p. 1987. text 85.00 (0-19-827265-0) OUP.

Principles of Social Evolution. Christopher R. Hallpike. (Illus.). 422p. 1988. reprint ed. pap. text 24.95 (0-19-827596-X) OUP.

Principles of Social Justice. David Miller. LC 99-21281. 384p. 1999. 45.00 (0-674-70628-5) HUP.

Principles of Social Order: Selected Essays of Lon L. Fuller. Ed. by Kenneth I. Winston. LC 80-68477. 313p. 1981. pap. text 22.95 (0-8223-0477-5) Duke.

Principles of Social Organization in Southern Kurdistan. Fredrik Barth. LC 77-87641. reprint ed. 37.50 (0-404-16423-4) AMS Pr.

Principles of Social Psychiatry. Dinesh K. L. Bhugra & Julian P. Leff. (Illus.). 600p. 1993. 165.00 (0-632-03336-3) Blackwell Sci.

Principles of Social Psychology. 3rd ed. Kelly G. Shaver. 656p. 1987. text 39.95 (0-89859-592-4) L Erlbaum Assocs.

Principles of Social Psychology. 3rd ed. Kelly G. Shaver. 210p. 1987. pap. text, teacher ed. write for info. (0-8058-0041-7) L Erlbaum Assocs.

Principles of Social Reconstruction. 2nd ed. Bertrand Russell. LC 97-171658. 192p. (Orig.). (C). 1997. pap. 18.99 (0-415-14349-7) Routledge.

Principles of Social Science, 3 Vols, Set. Henry C. Carey. LC 63-22257. (Reprints of Economic Classics Ser.). 1963. reprint ed. 150.00 (0-678-00013-1) Kelley.

Principles of Social Science Measurement. James L. Payne. LC 75-7177. 157p. (Orig.). (C). 1975. pap. text 9.95 (0-915728-02-8) Lytton Pub.

Principles of Social Welfare: An Introduction to Thinking about the Welfare State. Paul Spicker. 224p. (C). 1989. lib. bdg. 49.50 (0-415-00630-9) Routledge.

Principles of Social Welfare: An Introduction to Thinking about the Welfare State. Paul Spicker. LC 88-4409. 198p. reprint ed. pap. 61.40 (0-608-20386-6, 207163900002) Bks Demand.

Principles of Social Work Practice: A Generic Practice Approach. Molly R. Hancock. LC 96-28126. 261p. (C). 1997. pap. 24.95 (0-7890-0188-8) Haworth Pr.

Principles of Social Work Practice: A Generic Practice Approach. Molly R. Hancock. LC 96-28126. 261p. (C). 1997. 49.95 (0-7890-6024-8) Haworth Pr.

Principles of Software Engineering Management. Tom Gilb. Ed. by Susannah Finzi. (Illus.). 464p. (C). 1988. pap. text 44.95 (0-201-19246-2) Addison-Wesley.

Principles of Software Engineering Management. 2nd ed. Tom Gilb. (C). 1997. pap. text 43.25 (0-201-42782-6) Addison-Wesley.

Principles of Soil Chemistry. 3rd ed. Kim H. Tan. LC 97-44103. (Books in Soils, Plants & the Environment Ser.). (Illus.). 560p. 1998. text 79.75 (0-8247-0147-X) Dekker.

Principles of Soil Dynamics. Braja M. Das. 1992. 70.50 (0-534-93129-4) PWS Pubs.

Principles of Solar Engineering. Frank Kreith & Jan F. Kreider. 778p. 1978. pap. 66.95 (0-89116-678-5) Hemisp Pub.

Principles of Solar Engineering. Frank Kreith & Jan F. Kreider. 778p. 1986. write for info. (0-89116-529-0) Hemisp Pub.

***Principles of Solar Engineering.** 2nd ed. D. Yogi Goswami et al. LC 99-31349. 1999. 95.00 (1-56032-714-6) Taylor & Francis.

Principles of Soldering & Brazing. Giles Humpston & David M. Jacobson. LC 93-70224. (Illus.). 281p. 1993. 134.00 (0-87170-462-5, 6630) ASM.

Principles of Solid State. H. V. Keer. LC 92-36075. 379p. 1993. text 79.95 (0-470-22052-X) Halsted Pr.

Principles of Solidification & Materials Processing. Ed. by R. Trivedi et al. 1989. 78.50 (81-204-0448-3, Pub. by Oxford IBH) S Asia.

Principles of Solidification & Materials Processing. Ed. by R. Trivedi et al. 980p. 1990. text 333.00 (0-87849-594-0, Pub. by Trans T Pub) Enfield Pubs NH.

Principles of Solution & Solubility. Kozo Shinoda. Tr. by Paul Becher. LC 78-13385. (Undergraduate Chemistry Ser.: No. 5). (Illus.). 236p. reprint ed. pap. 73.20 (0-608-18030-0, 202901600058) Bks Demand.

Principles of Space Instrument Design. A. M. Cruise et al. LC 97-16356. (Aerospace Ser.: Vol. 9). (Illus.). 418p. (C). 1998. 110.00 (0-521-45164-7) Cambridge U Pr.

***Principles Of Speech Communication.** 14th ed. 352p. (C). 2000. pap. text 45.33 (0-321-07015-1) Addison-Wesley.

***Principles of Speech Communication: Brief Edition.** 13th ed. (C). 1998. pap. 36.00 (0-321-02511-3) Addison-Wesley.

Principles of Speech Communication: Brief Edition. 13th ed. (C). 1997. text. write for info. (0-321-00391-8) Addson-Wesley Educ.

***Principles of Speech Communication: Brief Edition.** 13th ed. (C). 1998. text. write for info. (0-321-00390-X); text. write for info. (0-321-02476-1); text. write for info. (0-321-02477-X) Addson-Wesley Educ.

Principles of Speech Communication: Brief Edition. 13th ed. Ed. by Bruce E. Gronbeck. LC 97-7433. 295p. (C). 1997. pap. text 40.06 (0-321-01004-3) Addson-Wesley Educ.

Principles of Speedwriting. (Landmark Ser.). 304p. 1977. teacher ed. write for info. (0-672-98002-9); teacher ed. write for info. (0-672-98005-3); student ed. 9.03 (0-672-98003-7); text 13.16 (0-672-98001-0); write for info. (0-672-98004-5); write for info. (0-672-98358-3); audio. write for info. (0-672-98027-4) Macmillan.

Principles of Speedwriting: College Edition. LC 76-41045. (Landmark Ser.). 1977. teacher ed. write for info. (0-672-98049-5); student ed. write for info. (0-672-98050-9); pap. text. write for info. (0-672-98048-7) Macmillan.

Principles of Speedwriting: Premier Edition. 373p. 1977. teacher ed. write for info. (0-672-98097-5); text. write for info. (0-672-98096-7); write for info. (0-672-98098-3); write for info. (0-672-98100-9); audio. write for info. (0-672-98142-4) Macmillan.

Principles of Speedwriting Shorthand. Cheryl Pullis. 1984. pap. 14.50 (0-02-679840-9) Macmillan.

Principles of Speedwriting Shorthand: Regency Edition. Joe M. Pullis & Linda Bippen. (Speedwriting Shorthand Ser.). 304p. (gr. 10-12). 1984. teacher ed. write for info. (0-672-98502-0); text. write for info. (0-672-98501-2); student ed. write for info. (0-672-98503-9) Macmillan.

Principles of Speedwriting Shorthand, Regency Professional Edition (First Course) Joe Pullis. 1987. text 27.64 (0-02-685100-8) Glencoe.

Principles of Spinal Surgery, 2 vols. Ed. by Arnold H. Menezes & Volker K. Sonntag. LC 95-30569. 1520p. 1995. text 295.00 (0-07-912043-1) McGraw-Hill HPD.

Principles of Spiritual Growth. Orig. Title: The Green Letters. 91p. 1994. pap. text 4.95 (0-942889-08-8) Christ Life Pubns.

Principles of Spiritual Science. Carl Unger. Tr. & Intro. by Alan Howard. 1976. pap. 4.95 (0-910142-69-6) Anthroposophic.

***Principles of Spiritualism: The Only Introduction You'll Ever Need.** Lynn De. (Illus.). 160p. 1999. pap. 11.00 (0-7225-3813-8) Thorsons PA.

Principles of Sport Biomechanics. 5th ed. Joe D. Bell et al. 400p. (C). 1996. pap. text 32.95 (0-89641-284-9) American Pr.

Principles of Spread Spectrum Theory & Systems. Athanassios N. Manikas. 300p. 1998. 38.00 (1-86094-043-9); pap. 20.00 (1-86094-044-7) World Scientific Pub.

***Principles of Stable Isotope Distribution.** Robert E. Criss. LC 98-24609. (Illus.). 264p. 1999. text 65.00 (0-19-511775-1) OUP.

Principles of Stage Combat. Claude D. Kezer. (Illus.). 62p. 1983. pap. 12.50 (0-88680-156-7) I E Clark.

Principles of Stage Combat Handbook. 2nd ed. Claude D. Kezer. LC 94-43588. (Illus.). 96p. (Orig.). 1995. pap. 15.00 (0-88734-650-2) Players Pr.

Principles of State: Government in Islam. Muhammad Asad. 108p. 1961. reprint ed. 18.00 (0-939660-11-3, Pub. by Dar Al-Andalus) Threshold CA.

Principles of State & Government. Muhammad Asad. 107p. (Orig.). 1980. pap. 9.95 (0-317-52457-7) New Era Publns MI.

Principles of State & Government in Islam. Muhammad Asad. 110p. 1996. 19.95 (0-614-21498-X, 985) Kazi Pubns.

Principles of State Interference. David G. Ritchie. LC 70-94282. (Select Bibliographies Reprint Ser.). 1977. 21.95 (0-8369-5060-7) Ayer.

Principles of Statistical Data Handling. Fred Davidson. LC 95-41821. 319p. 1996. pap. 23.50 (0-7619-0103-5); text 49.95 (0-7619-0102-7) Sage.

Principles of Statistical Inference from a Neo-Fisherian Perspective, Vol. 4. LC 97-10525. 550p. 1997. text 47.00 (981-02-3066-4) World Scientific Pub.

Principles of Statistical Mechanics. Richard C. Tolman. LC 79-52649. 661p. 1980. pap. text 15.95 (0-486-63896-0) Dover.

Principles of Statistical Mechanics: The Information Theory Approach. Amnon Katz. LC 67-12181. 200p. reprint ed. pap. 62.00 (0-608-30986-9, 205554900028) Bks Demand.

Principles of Statistical Radiophysics, No. 1. S. M. Rytov et al. (Illus.). 260p. 1987. 111.95 (0-387-12562-0) Spr-Verlag.

Principles of Statistical Radiophysics, No. 2. S. M. Rytov et al. (Illus.). 240p. 1988. 126.95 (0-387-16186-4) Spr-Verlag.

Principles of Statistical Radiophysics, No. 3. S. M. Rytov et al. (Illus.). 255p. 1989. 135.95 (0-387-17829-5) Spr-Verlag.

Principles of Statistical Radiophysics, No. 4. S. M. Rytov et al. (Illus.). 200p. 1989. 108.95 (0-387-17828-7) Spr-Verlag.

Principles of Statistics. M. G. Bulmer. LC 78-72991. 252p. (C). 1979. reprint ed. pap. 8.95 (0-486-63760-3) Dover.

Principles of Statistics. Paul A. Herzberg. LC 89-2542. 534p. (C). 1989. reprint ed. lib. bdg. 64.00 (0-89464-374-6) Krieger.

Principles of Statutory Interpretations. 4th ed. G. P. Singh. (C). 1989. 250.00 (0-7855-4766-5) St Mut.

Principles of Steam Generation, 20 Modules. (Illus.). 1830p. 1982. teacher ed. 325.00 (0-87683-292-3) GP Courseware.

Principles of Steam Generation, 20 Modules, Set. (Illus.). 1830p. 1982. spiral bd. 575.00 (0-87683-250-8) GP Courseware.

Principles of Stellar Evolution & Nucleosynthesis. Donald D. Clayton. LC 83-5106. (Illus.). xii, 634p. 1984. reprint ed. pap. text 26.00 (0-226-10953-4) U Ch Pr.

Principles of Sterile Product Preparation. E. Clyde Buchanan et al. (Illus.). 192p. (Orig.). (C). 1995. pap. text 50.00 (1-879907-57-7) Am Soc Hlth-Syst.

Principles of Stress Management, 1. Vera Peiffer. 1997. pap. 11.00 (0-7225-3243-1) Thorsons PA.

Principles of String Theory. L. Brink & M. Henneaux. LC 87-29815. (Centro de Estudios Cientificos de Santiago Ser.). (Illus.). 312p. (C). 1988. text 89.50 (0-306-42657-9, Kluwer Plenum) Kluwer Academic.

Principles of Structural Equilibrium: A Study of Equilibrium Conditions by Graphic, Force-Moment & Virtual Displacement. George C. Ernst et al. LC 62-7876. 170p. reprint ed. pap. 52.70 (0-608-11418-9, 200197700011) Bks Demand.

Principles of Structural Linguistics. S. K. Saumjan. Tr. by James Miller. (Janua Linguarum, Ser. Major). 359p. 1971. text 88.50 (90-279-1658-6) Mouton.

Principles of Structural Typology. Boris Uspensky. LC 68-17893. (Janua Linguarum, Series Minor). (Orig.). 1968. pap. text 36.95 (90-279-0590-8) Mouton.

Principles of Structure. Ken J. Wyatt. 140p. pap. 24.95 (0-86840-086-6, Pub. by NSW U Pr) Intl Spec Bk.

Principles of Structure. Ken J. Wyatt. (Illus.). 140p. 1998. reprint ed. pap. 25.00 (0-86840-040-8, Pub. by New South Wales Univ Pr) Intl Spec Bk.

Principles of Structures. Ariel Hanaor. LC 98-12769. 1998. pap. 34.95 (0-632-04262-1) Blackwell Sci.

Principles of Studies on Diseases of Suspected Chemical Etiology & their Prevention. WHO Staff. (Environmental Health Criteria Ser.: No. 72). 79p. 1987. 15.00 (92-4-154272-1) World Health.

Principles of Success for the Classroom Teacher of the Autistic Impaired. Bryant S. Domina. 150p. 1998. pap. text 17.50 (0-9652495-5-7) Individual Educ.

Principles of Sufism. Al-Qushayri. Tr. by B. R. Von Schlegell from ARA. LC 92-82685. 366p. 1993. text 29.95 (0-933782-21-7); pap. text 19.95 (0-933782-20-9) Mizan Pr.

Principles of Sufism. Nahid Angha. 114p. (Orig.). 1991. pap. 8.00 (0-918437-03-2) Intl Sufism.

Principles of Sufism. Nahid Angha. LC 94-29491. 128p. (Orig.). 1995. pap. 12.95 (0-87573-061-2) Jain Pub Co.

Principles of Superconductive Devices & Circuits. Ed. by O. Turner & Theodore Van Duzer. 370p. 1981. 53.50 (0-444-00411-4) P-H.

Principles of Superconductive Devices & Circuits. 2nd ed. Theodore Van Duzer & Charles W. Turner. LC 98-31979. 448p. (C). 1998. 84.00 (0-13-262742-6, Macmillan Coll) P-H.

Principles of Suretyship, 2 vols. John B. Fitzgerald et al. LC 91-73928. 524p. (C). 1991. pap. 41.00 (0-89462-066-5, 15102/15103) IIA.

Principles of Surgery. 7th ed. Ed. by Seymour I. Schwartz et al. LC 98-28061. (Illus.). 2176p. 1999. text 110.00 (0-07-054256-2); text 129.00 (0-07-912318-X) McGraw-Hill HPD.

Principles of Surgery, 1. 6th ed. Seymour I. Schwartz. Date not set. write for info. (0-07-055929-5) McGraw.

Principles of Surgery, 2. 6th ed. Seymour I. Schwartz. write for info. (0-07-055930-9) McGraw.

Principles of Surgery: Companion Handbook. 6th ed. Ed. by Seymour I. Schwartz et al. LC 93-31244. 250p. 1993. pap. 32.00 (0-07-056055-2) McGraw-Hill HPD.

Principles of Surgery: Companion Handbook. 7th ed. Ed. by Seymour I. Schwartz et al. LC 98-45752. (Illus.). 1118p. 1999. pap. text 48.00 (0-07-058085-5) McGraw-Hill HPD.

Principles of Surgery: PreTest Self-Assessment & Review. 7th ed. Ed. by Seymour I. Schwartz. (Illus.). 264p. 1999. pap. text 45.00 (0-07-057964-4) McGraw-Hill HPD.

Principles of Surgical Technique: The Art of Surgery. 2nd ed. Gary G. Wind & Norman M. Rich. LC 86-15910. (Illus.). 224p. 1987. text 42.50 (0-683-09133-6) Lppncott W & W.

Principles of Surveying. 4th ed. Charles A. Herubin. 352p. (C). 1991. text 50.00 (0-13-717695-3, 430102) P-H.

Principles of Sustainable Development. Ed. by F. Douglas Muschett. LC 97-116850. (Illus.). 192p. 1996. boxed set 64.95 (1-57444-079-9) St Lucie Pr.

Principles of Switching. Paul Fleming, Jr. LC 73-85629. (ABC of the Telephone Ser.: Vol. 10). (Illus.). 128p. (C). 1983. spiral bd. 24.95 (1-56016-061-6) ABC TeleTraining.

Principles of Symmetry, Dynamics, & Spectroscopy. William G. Harter et al. LC 92-11123. 880p. 1993. 225.00 (0-471-05020-2) Wiley.

Principles of Synastry. Henry Weingarten. 2000. reprint ed. pap. 9.95 (0-88231-100-X) ASI Pubs Inc.

Principles of Systems. Jay W. Forrester. (System Dynamics Ser.). (Illus.). 285p. 2000. pap. text 25.00 (1-883823-41-2, XPRSYS) Pegasus Comm.

P

An Asterisk (*) at the beginning of an entry indicates that the title is appearing for the first time.

Principles of Systems. Jay W. Forrester. 392p. (C). 1991. reprint ed. pap. text 25.00 (*0-915299-87-9*) Productivity Inc.
Principles of Systems & Network. Burgess. pap. text. write for info. (*0-471-82303-1*) Wiley.
Principles of Systems Programming. Robert M. Graham. 438p. 1975. text 56.50 (*0-471-32100-1*) Krieger.
Principles of Tai Chi. Paul Brecher. 1998. pap. 11.00 (*0-7225-3474-4*) Thorsons PA.
Principles of Tantra, 2 vols., Set. John Woodroffe. 1979. 40.00 (*0-89744-129-X*) Auromere.
Principles of Tax Business Investment Plans. 2nd ed. Jones Staff. 1998. 65.50 (*0-07-303594-7*) McGraw.
Principles of Tax-Deferred Exchanging. 2nd rev. ed. Jo K. Cebuhar. (Illus.). x, 298p. 1997. pap., spiral bd. 85.00 (*0-9661851-0-2*) XPr.
Principles of Taxation for Business & Investment Planning. Sally Jones & University of Virginia Staff. LC 97-17863. 648p. 1997. 77.50 (*0-256-23047-1*) McGraw-Hill Prof.
Principles of Taxation for Business & Investment Planning. Jones Staff. 304p. 1997. pap., student ed. 25.94 (*0-256-23052-8*) McGraw.
***Principles of Taxation for Business & Investment Planning.** 3rd ed. Sally Jones. 312p. (C). 1999. pap. 25.94 (*0-07-229871-5*) McGrw-H Hghr Educ.
***Principles of Taxation for Business & Investment Planning 2000.** 3rd ed. Sally Jones. 576p. (C). 1999. 83.75 (*0-07-229870-7*) McGrw-H Hghr Educ.
***Principles of Taxation for Business & Investment Planning 2001.** 4th ed. Sally Jones. 528p. 2000. 83.75 (*0-07-240824-3*) McGraw.
Principles of Technical Consulting & Project Management. Duane L. Winegardner et al. 120p. 1991. 70.00 (*0-87371-423-7*, TH371, CRC Reprint) Franklin.
Principles of Technical Drawing. 572p. (C). 1998. text 35.75 (*0-536-01494-9*) Pearson Custom.
Principles of Technical Management. William A. Cohen. LC 79-54829. 234p. reprint ed. pap. 72.60 (*0-608-12697-7*, 202351500033) Bks Demand.
Principles of Technology. Center for Occupational Research & Development Staff. 1996. pap., student ed. 4.75 (*1-55502-386-X*) Thomson Learn.
Principles of Technology: Unit 10 Energy Converters. 2nd ed. Cord. 1996. pap. 4.75 (*1-55502-381-9*) Thomson Learn.
Principles of Technology: Unit 11 Transducers. 2nd ed. Cord. 1996. pap. 4.75 (*1-55502-382-7*) Thomson Learn.
Principles of Technology: Unit 12 Radiation. 2nd ed. Cord. 1996. pap. 4.75 (*1-55502-383-5*) Thomson Learn.
Principles of Technology: Unit 13 Optical Systems. 2nd ed. Cord. 1996. pap. 4.75 (*1-55502-384-3*) Thomson Learn.
Principles of Technology: Unit 14 Time Constants. 2nd ed. Cord. 1996. pap. 4.75 (*1-55502-385-1*) Thomson Learn.
Principles Of Technology: Unit 8 Momentum. 2nd ed. Cord. 1996. pap. 4.75 (*1-55502-379-7*) Thomson Learn.
Principles of Technology: Unit 9 Wave & Vibrations. 2nd ed. Cord. 1996. pap. 4.75 (*1-55502-380-0*) Thomson Learn.
Principles of Technology: Year 1. 2nd ed. Cord. 1996. pap. 33.75 (*1-55502-913-2*) Thomson Learn.
Principles of Technology, Unit 10: Energy Convertors. Center for Occupational Research & Development Staff. (Illus.). 1985. pap. text. write for info. (*1-55502-010-0*) CORD Commns.
Principles of Technology, Unit 11: Transducers. Center for Occupational Research & Development Staff. (Illus.). 1985. pap. text. write for info. (*1-55502-011-9*) CORD Commns.
Principles of Technology, Unit 12: Radiation. Center for Occupational Research & Development Staff. (Illus.). 1985. pap. text. write for info. (*1-55502-012-7*) CORD Commns.
Principles of Technology, Unit 13: Optics & Optical Systems. Center for Occupational Research & Development Staff. (Illus.). 1985. pap. text. write for info. (*1-55502-013-5*) CORD Commns.
Principles of Technology, Unit 14: Time Constants. Center for Occupational Research & Development Staff. (Illus.). 1985. pap. text. write for info. (*1-55502-014-3*) CORD Commns.
Principles of Technology, Unit 2: Work. 2nd ed. Center for Occupational Research & Development Staff. (Illus.). 102p. 1996. pap., student ed. write for info. (*1-55502-373-8*) Thomson Learn.
Principles of Technology, Unit 3: Rate. Center for Occupational Research & Development Staff. (Illus.). 1985. pap. text. write for info. (*1-55502-003-8*) CORD Commns.
Principles of Technology, Unit 3: Rate. 2nd ed. Center for Occupational Research & Development Staff. (Illus.). 134p. 1996. pap., student ed. write for info. (*1-55502-374-6*) Thomson Learn.
Principles of Technology, Unit 4: Resistance. Center for Occupational Research & Development Staff. (Illus.). 1985. pap. text. write for info. (*1-55502-004-6*) CORD Commns.
Principles of Technology, Unit 4: Resistance. 2nd ed. Center for Occupational Research & Development Staff. (Illus.). 142p. 1996. pap., student ed. write for info. (*1-55502-375-4*) Thomson Learn.
Principles of Technology, Unit 5: Energy. Center for Occupational Research & Development Staff. (Illus.). 1985. pap. text. write for info. (*1-55502-005-4*) CORD Commns.
Principles of Technology, Unit 5: Energy. 2nd ed. Center for Occupational Research & Development Staff. (Illus.). 146p. 1996. pap., student ed. write for info. (*1-55502-376-2*) Thomson Learn.
Principles of Technology, Unit 6: Power. Center for Occupational Research & Development Staff. (Illus.). 1985. pap. text. write for info. (*1-55502-006-2*) CORD Commns.
Principles of Technology, Unit 6: Power. 2nd ed. Center for Occupational Research & Development Staff. (Illus.). 106p. 1996. pap., student ed. write for info. (*1-55502-377-0*) Thomson Learn.
Principles of Technology, Unit 7: Force Transformers. Center for Occupational Research & Development Staff. (Illus.). 1985. pap. text. write for info. (*1-55502-007-0*) CORD Commns.
Principles of Technology, Unit 7: Force Transformers. 2nd ed. Center for Occupational Research & Development Staff. (Illus.). 144p. 1996. pap., student ed. write for info. (*1-55502-378-9*) Thomson Learn.
Principles of Technology, Unit 8: Momentum. Center for Occupational Research & Development Staff. (Illus.). 1985. pap. text. write for info. (*1-55502-008-9*) CORD Commns.
Principles of Technology, Unit 9: Vibrations & Waves. Center for Occupational Research & Development Staff. (Illus.). 1985. pap. text. write for info. (*1-55502-009-7*) CORD Commns.
Principles of Test Theories. Hoi K. Suen. 256p. (C). 1990. text 69.95 (*0-8058-0197-9*) L Erlbaum Assocs.
Principles of Test Theories. Hoi K. Suen. 256p. (C). 1990. pap. 39.95 (*0-8058-0198-7*) L Erlbaum Assocs.
Principles of Testing Electronic Circuits. Samiha Mourad & Yervant Zorian. LC 99-52179. 400p. 2000. 79.95 (*0-471-31931-7*) Wiley.
Principles of Testing Soils, Rock, & Concrete. T. S. Nagaraj. LC 92-25238. 708p. 1993. 299.50 (*0-444-88911-6*) Elsevier.
Principles of Textual Criticism. James Thorpe. LC 72-179135. 209p. 1972. reprint ed. pap. 9.95 (*0-87328-055-5*) Huntington Lib.
***Principles of the Administrative Law of the United States.** Frank Johnson Goodnow. LC 99-73233. 480p. 1999. 155.00 (*1-56169-529-7*) Gaunt.
Principles of the Alexander Technique. Jeremy Chance. (Illus.). 160p. 1999. 11.00 (*0-7225-3705-0*) Thorsons PA.
Principles of the Ancient Teachings of the Masters: With ATOM Workbook & Spiritual Terminology. Darwin Gross. 309p. 1997. pap. 16.95 (*0-931689-25-2*) Be Good To Your Self.
Principles of the Christian Faith: A Biblical Study Series for Laying Foundations in Spirit Filled for Believers. 3rd rev. ed. Harold McDougal. 339p. 1997. pap. 13.99 (*1-884369-66-9*) McDougal Pubng.
Principles of the Common Law: An Elementary Work Intended for the Use of Students & the Profession. John Indermaur. Ed. by Edmund H. Bennett. LC 97-47218. xxiv, 522p. 1997. reprint ed. 75.00 (*0-8377-2275-6*, Rothman) W S Hein.
Principles of the Conflict of Laws: National & International. Kurt Lipstein. 160p. 1981. 21.50 (*90-286-0750-1*) Kluwer Academic.
Principles of the Conflict of Laws: National & International. Kurt Lipstein. 160p. 1981. pap. text 75.50 (*90-247-2544-5*) Kluwer Academic.
Principles of the Constitutional Order: The Ratification Debates. Ed. by Robert L. Utley, Jr. LC 88-20888. 198p. (Orig.). (C). 1989. pap. text 21.00 (*0-8191-7189-1*); lib. bdg. 39.50 (*0-8191-7188-3*) U Pr of Amer.
***Principles of the Customary Laws of Eritrea.** Carlo C. Rossini. LC 99-15795. 1999. write for info. (*1-56902-111-2*) Red Sea Pr.
Principles of the Distribution of Videograms Having a Violent, Brutal or Pornographic Content (Recommendation & Explanatory Memorandum), No. R(89)7. 1995. 12.00 (*92-871-2704-2*, Pub. by Council of Europe) Manhattan Pub Co.
Principles of the English Legal System. 3rd ed. Gary Slapper & David Kelly. LC 98-219314. (Principles of Law Ser.). 415p. 1997. pap. 31.00 (*1-85941-375-7*, 15532, Pub. by Cavendish Pubng) Gaunt.
Principles of the Flute, Recorder & Oboe. Jacques-Martin Hotteterre. (Music (General) Ser.). 88p. 1984. pap. 5.95 (*0-486-24606-X*) Dover.
Principles of the Gospel in Practice. Ed. by Sperry Symposium Staff. 257p. 1989. 10.95 (*0-934126-75-5*) CFI Dist.
Principles of the Heat Treatment of Plain Carbon & Low Alloy Steel. Charlie R. Brooks. 490p. 1996. 134.00 (*0-87170-538-9*, 6456) ASM.
Principles of the Human Mind. Alfred Smee. LC 80-68665. (Illus.). 96p. 1980. pap. 5.95 (*0-89708-030-0*) And Bks.
Principles of the Institutional Law of International Organizations. C. F. Amerasinghe. (Cambridge Studies in International & Comparative Law). 549p. (C). 1996. text 95.00 (*0-521-56254-6*) Cambridge U Pr.
Principles of the Jesuits: Developed in a Collection of Extracts from Their Own Authors to Which Are Prefixed a Brief Account of the Origin of the Order & a Sketch of Its Institute. Henry H. Norris. 300p. 1992. reprint ed. pap. 21.00 (*1-56459-292-8*) Kessinger Pub.
Principles of the Law. Avtar Singh. (C). 1985. 55.00 (*0-7855-5537-4*) St Mut.
Principles of the Law of Arrest, Search, Seizure, & Liability Issues. Irving J. Klein. Ed. by Marta Arias-Klein et al. LC 94-70088. (Criminal Justice & Law Ser.). 302p. (Orig.). (C). 1994. pap. text 22.00 (*0-938993-16-X*) Coral Gables Pub.
Principles of the Law of Contract. 5th ed. Alastair James Kerr. LC 98-214111. xviii, 821 p. 1998. write for info. (*0-409-03748-6*) Buttrwrth-Heinemann.
Principles of the Law of Crimes: With Supplement. Shamsul Huda. (C). 1990. 100.00 (*0-7855-5607-9*) St Mut.
Principles of the Law of Crimes with a Supplement. Shamsul Huda. 1993. 250.00 (*81-7012-517-0*, Pub. by Eastern Book) St Mut.
Principles of the Law of Evidence. Avtar Singh. (C). 1990. 55.00 (*0-89771-149-1*) St Mut.
Principles of the Law of Evidence. 7th ed. Justice McGechan. 445p. 1984. pap. 63.00 (*0-409-70174-2*, NZ, MICHIE) LEXIS Pub.
***Principles of the Law of Mortgage, Pledge & Lien.** Konrad Kritzinger. xviii, 78p. 1999. pap. 23.50 (*0-7021-4813-X*, Pub. by Juta & Co) Gaunt.
Principles of the Law of Partnership. 5th ed. Anne Webb & P. R. Webb. 310p. 1992. pap. 81.00 (*0-409-78956-9*, NZ, MICHIE) LEXIS Pub.
***Principles of the Law of Personal Property: Chattels & Choses Including Sales of Goods, Sales on Execution, Chattel Mortgages, Gifts, Lost Property, Insurance, Patents, Copyrights, Trade Marks, Limitations of Actions, Etc.** Frank Hall Childs. xv, 607p. 2000. reprint ed. 156.00 (*1-56169-585-8*) Gaunt.
Principles of the Law of Sale of Goods & Hire Purchase (Sale of Goods Act 1930, Hire Purchase Act 1972) 3rd ed. Ed. by Avtar Singh. (C). 1985. 25.00 (*0-7855-5433-5*) St Mut.
Principles of the Law of Scotland. 6th ed. George J. Bell & William Guthrie. xxxvi, 1047p. 1998. reprint ed. 220.00 (*1-56169-362-6*) Gaunt.
***Principles of the Law of Sedition: With an Appendix Giving the Law in India as It Was & as Amended.** J. Chaudhuri. vii, 48p. 1999. reprint ed. 35.00 (*1-56169-547-5*) Gaunt.
***Principles of the Law of Stoppage in Transitu, Retention & Delivery.** John Houston. xvi, 253p. 2000. reprint ed. 85.00 (*1-56169-599-8*) Gaunt.
Principles of the Law of Trusts. 2nd ed. H. A. Ford & W. A. Lee. cxv, 1096p. 1990. 135.00 (*0-455-20940-5*, Pub. by LawBk Co); pap. 105.00 (*0-455-20941-3*, Pub. by LawBk Co) Gaunt.
Principles of the Law Relating to the Discharge of Contracts. Robert Ralston. LC 97-3620. viii, 68p. 1997. reprint ed. 25.00 (*0-8377-2579-8*, Rothman) W S Hein.
Principles of the Most Ancient & Modern Philosophy. Anne Conway. 256p. 1982. text 153.00 (*90-247-2671-9*, Pub. by M Nijhoff) Kluwer Academic.
Principles of the Most Ancient & Modern Philosophy. 2nd ed. Anne Conway & Peter Loptson. LC 98-16731. (ENG & LAT.). 268p. 1998. 50.00 (*0-8201-1509-6*) Schol Facsimiles.
Principles of the New Covenant: A Study Contrasting the Old & New Covenants. Robert E. Briggs. (Illus.). 58p. (Orig.). 1997. pap. 4.59 (*0-9657749-5-3*) Eagles Nst Pubns.
Principles of the New Philosophy. 2nd rev. ed. Hugo L. Odhner. 36p. 1986. reprint ed. pap. 4.00 (*0-915221-13-6*) Swedenborg Sci Assn.
Principles of the Philosophy of the Future. Ludwig Feuerbach. Tr. by Manfred Vogel from GER. LC 86-7699. (HPC Classics Ser.). (Illus.). 112p. (C). 1986. reprint ed. pap. 7.95 (*0-915145-27-8*); reprint ed. lib. bdg. 24.95 (*0-915145-26-X*) Hackett Pub.
Principles of the Psychiatric Evaluation. Roger A. MacKinnon & Stuart C. Yudofsky. (Illus.). 325p. 1991. pap. text 39.95 (*0-397-51064-0*) Lppncott W & W.
***Principles of the Runes.** Freya Aswynn. 160p. 2000. pap. 11.00 (*0-7225-3883-9*, Pub. by Thorsons PA) HarpC.
Principles of the Sanctuary Services. Rudolph F. Rhone. LC 99-176304. 222 p. 1997. write for info. (*1-55630-826-4*) Brentwood Comm.
Principles of the Shell Process. 88p. 1976. pap. 52.00 (*0-317-59851-1*, TE7603) Am Foundrymen.
Principles of the Solid State. H. V. Keer. 1993. write for info. (*81-224-0466-9*, Pub. by Wiley Estrn) Franklin.
Principles of the Surface Treatment of Steel. Charlie R. Brooks. LC 91-67902. 290p. 1992. pap. text 49.95 (*0-87762-796-7*) Technomic.
Principles of the Theory of Heat. Ernst Mach. 1986. lib. bdg. 294.00 (*90-277-2206-4*) Kluwer Academic.
Principles of the Theory of Solids. 2nd ed. John M. Ziman. (Illus.). 448p. 1979. pap. text 44.95 (*0-521-29733-8*) Cambridge U Pr.
Principles of Thematic Design. Borden D. Dent. (Geography Ser.). (Illus.). 400p. 1985. write for info. (*0-201-11334-1*) Addison-Wesley.
Principles of Thoracic Anaesthesia see Origins of Thoracic Anaesthesia
Principles of Three-Dimensional Computer Animation: Modeling, Rendering, & Animating with 3D Graphics. rev. ed. Michael O'Rourke. LC 98-4553. (Illus.). 256p. 1998. 55.00 (*0-393-73024-7*) Norton.
Principles of Three Dimensional Imaging in Confocal Microscopes. Min Gu. LC 95-48425. 352p. 1996. write for info. (*981-02-2550-4*) World Scientific Pub.
***Principles of 3D Image Analysis & Synthesis.** Bernd Girod et al. LC 00-29626. 2000. write for info. (*0-7923-7850-4*) Kluwer Academic.
Principles of Timber Design for Architects & Builders. Don A. Halperin & G. T. Bible. 416p. 1994. 89.00 (*0-471-55768-4*) Wiley.
Principles of Tissue Engineering. Robert Lanza. LC 96-33638. (Illus.). 808p. 1996. text 139.95 (*0-12-436625-2*) Acad Pr.
***Principles of Tissue Engineering.** 2nd ed. Robert P. Lanza. LC 99-68198. 800p. 2000. 199.95 (*0-12-436630-9*) Acad Pr.
Principles of Tort Law. 3rd ed. Vivienne Harpwood. (Principles of Law Ser.). xlvii, 430p. 1997. pap. 31.00 (*1-85941-378-1*, Pub. by Cavendish Pubng) Gaunt.
Principles of Total Quality. 2nd ed. Vincent K. Omachonu et al. (Illus.). 400p. 1997. lib. bdg. 49.95 (*1-57444-094-2*) St Lucie Pr.
Principles of Toxicokinetic Studies. (Environmental Health Criteria Ser.: No. 57). 167p. 1986. pap. text 23.00 (*92-4-154257-8*, 1160057) World Health.
Principles of Toxicology. Karen Stine & Thomas M. Brown. 272p. 1996. lib. bdg. 55.00 (*0-87371-684-1*, L684) Lewis Pubs.
Principles of Toxicology. 2nd ed. Phillip L. Williams et al. 560p. 1998. 51.95 (*0-442-23738-3*, VNR) Wiley.
***Principles of Toxicology: Environmental & Industrial Applications.** 2nd ed. Phillip L. Williams et al. LC 99-42196. 624p. 2000. 89.95 (*0-471-29321-0*) Wiley.
Principles of Traffic & Network Design. 2nd ed. Howard J. Gunn. LC 73-85629. (Traffic Ser.). (Illus.). 136p. (Orig.). (C). 1986. pap. text 24.95 (*1-56016-017-9*) ABC TeleTraining.
Principles of Tragedy: A Rational Examination of the Tragic Concept in Life & Literature. Geoffrey Brereton. LC 69-12459. 1968. 19.95 (*0-87024-104-4*) U of Miami Pr.
Principles of Transaction Processing. Phillip A. Bernstein & Eric Newcomer. LC 96-47916. 364p. (Orig.). 1998. text 44.95 (*1-55860-415-4*) Morgan Kaufmann.
Principles of Transfusion Medicine. Ennio C. Rossi et al. (Illus.). 816p. 1990. 115.00 (*0-683-07385-0*) Lppncott W & W.
Principles of Transfusion Medicine. 2nd ed. Toby L. Simon. Ed. by Ennio C. Rossi. LC 95-11651. (Illus.). 992p. 1996. 139.00 (*0-683-07386-9*) Lppncott W & W.
***Principles of Transistor Circuits.** 9th ed. Mike James & S. W. Amos. 416p. 2000. pap. 39.95 (*0-7506-4427-3*, Newnes) Buttrwrth-Heinemann.
Principles of Transportation Economics. Kenneth D. Boyer. LC 97-24731. 416p. (C). 1997. 93.00 (*0-321-01103-1*) Addson-Wesley Educ.
Principles of Traveling Wave Tubes. A. S. Gilmour. LC 94-7670. (Illus.). 625p. 1994. 119.00 (*0-89006-720-1*) Artech Hse.
***Principles of Treatment in Multiple Sclerosis.** Clive Hawkins. (Illus.). 352p. 2000. pap. 75.00 (*0-7506-4270-X*) Buttrwrth-Heinemann.
***Principles of Tropical Agronomy.** S. N. Azam-ALi & G. R. Squire. (CABI Publishing Ser.). (Illus.). 304p. 2001. pap. text. write for info. (*0-85199-136-X*) OUP.
Principles of Tungsten Carbide Engineering: Including Ceramics. 2nd expanded ed. George Schneider. LC TJ1186.S35. (Illus.). 210p. 1989. reprint ed. pap. 65.10 (*0-608-02732-4*, 206339700004) Bks Demand.
Principles of Turbulent Fired Heat. F. Lebouc & E. Perthuis. (Illus.). 320p. (C). 1985. 590.00 (*2-7108-0457-3*, Pub. by Edits Technip) Enfield Pubs NH.
Principles of Two-Dimensional Design. Wucius Wong. 77p. 1972. pap. 16.95 (*0-442-29565-0*, VNR) Wiley.
Principles of Two-Dimensional Design. Wucius Wong. 104p. 1972. pap. 29.95 (*0-471-28960-4*, VNR) Wiley.
Principles of Ultraviolet Photoelectron Spectroscopy. J. Wayne Rabalais. LC 76-28413. (Wiley-Interscience Monographs in Chemical Physics). 472p. reprint ed. pap. 146.40 (*0-608-16148-9*, 205571000032) Bks Demand.
Principles of Underwater Sound. 3rd ed. Robert J. Urick. LC 96-68876. (Illus.). 448p. 1996. reprint ed. lib. bdg. 56.95 (*0-932146-62-7*) Peninsula CA.
Principles of Unemployment Law. Rohan Price. LC 97-179973. 350p. 1996. pap. 35.00 (*0-455-21433-6*, Pub. by LawBk Co) Gaunt.
Principles of Union with Christ. Charles G. Finney. Ed. by Louis G. Parkhurst. LC 84-24225. 16p. 1985. pap. 7.99 (*0-87123-447-5*) Bethany Hse.
Principles of Valuation in North Carolina Equitable Distribution Actions. rev. ed. Clarence E. Horton. (Special Ser.: No. 10). 54p. 1993. pap. 7.00 (*1-56011-254-9*) Institute Government.
Principles of Value Added Tax: A European Perspective. Adrian Ogley. 256p. 1998. 95.00 (*0-9520442-1-8*, Pub. by Interfisc Pub) Intl Info Srvcs Inc.
***Principles of Vehicle Extrication.** 2nd ed. Ed. by Carl Goodson. (Illus.). 208p. 2000. pap. write for info. (*0-87939-176-6*) IFSTA.
***Principles of Verifiable RTL Design - A Functional Coding Style Supporting Verification Processes.** Lionel Bening & Harry Foster. 272p. 2000. 98.00 (*0-7923-7788-5*) Kluwer Academic.
Principles of Verilog PLI. Swapnajit Mittra. LC 99-18028. xxviii, 372 p. 1999. write for info. (*0-7923-8477-6*) Kluwer Academic.
Principles of Veterinary Science. Keith H. Hoopes & Richard N. Thwaits. LC 96-52355. (Illus.). 300p. 1997. pap. 39.95 (*0-683-30130-6*) Lppncott W & W.
Principles of Veterinary Therapeutics. R. Einstein et al. (Illus.). 598p. 1996. 72.95 (*0-582-02963-5*, Pub. by Addison-Wesley) Longman.
Principles of Vibration. Benson H. Tongue. (Illus.). 480p. (C). 1996. text 85.00 (*0-19-510661-X*) OUP.
Principles of Vibration & Sound. Neville H. Fletcher & Thomas D. Rossing. 250p. 1994. 34.95 (*0-387-94336-6*) Spr-Verlag.
Principles of Vibration & Sound. Thomas D. Rossing & Neville H. Fletcher. LC 94-15494. (Illus.). 250p. 1994. 59.95 (*0-387-94304-8*) Spr-Verlag.
Principles of Vibrational Healing. Harvey. 1998. pap. 11.00 (*0-7225-3503-1*, 902616Q) Thorsons PA.
Principles of Victorian Decorative Design. unabridged ed. Christopher Dresser. (Illus.). 176p. 1996. reprint ed. pap. text 7.95 (*0-486-28900-1*) Dover.
Principles of Victory. Charles G. Finney. Ed. by Genevive Parkhurst. LC 81-15464. 28p. (Orig.). 1981. pap. 8.99 (*0-87123-471-8*) Bethany Hse.

P

Principles of Violin Playing & Teaching. 3rd ed. Ivan Galamian. LC 99-62988. (Illus.). 144p. 1999. 60.00 (*0-9621416-3-1*) Shar Prods.

Principles of Virology: Molecular Biology, Pathogenesis, & Control. Jane S. Flint et al. LC 99-14697. (Illus.). 700p. (C). 1999. text 89.95 (*1-55581-127-2*) ASM Pr.

Principles of Visual Anthropology. 2nd ed. Ed. by Paul Hockings. LC 95-9003. xi, 562p. (C). 1995. pap. text 31.95 (*3-11-014228-7*); lib. bdg. 61.95 (*3-11-012627-3*) Mouton.

Principles of Visual Perception. 2nd ed. Carolyn M. Bloomer. (Illus.). 192p. 1989. 29.95 (*0-8306-1704-3*) McGraw-Hill Prof.

Principles of VLSI System Planning: A Framework for Conceptual Design. Allen M. Dewey & Stephen W. Director. (C). 1990. text 108.00 (*0-7923-9102-0*) Kluwer Academic.

Principles of Voice Production. Ingo R. Titze. LC 93-13031. 354p. 1994. 82.00 (*0-13-717893-X*) P-H.

*__Principles of Voice Production.__ 2nd ed. Ingo R. Titze. (Illus.). 406p. 2000. pap. 50.00 (*0-87414-122-2*) U IA Pubns Dept.

Principles of War. Wilson. 1996. pap. 5.95 (*1-882840-05-4*) Comm Christian.

Principles of War. Ferdinand Foch. Tr. by J. De Morinni. LC 70-128436. 1970. reprint ed. 49.50 (*0-404-02439-4*) AMS Pr.

Principles of War for the Information Age. Robert R. Leonhard. LC 98-8287. 288p. 1998. 29.95 (*0-89141-647-1*, Pub. by Presidio Pr) Natl Bk Netwk.

*__Principles of War for the Information Age.__ Robert R. Leonhard. (Illus.). 304p. 2000. pap. 19.95 (*0-89141-713-3*) Presidio Pr.

Principles of Warmwater Aquaculture. Robert R. Stickney. LC 78-25642. 375p. 1979. 120.00 (*0-471-03388-X*) Wiley.

Principles of Waste Heat Recovery. Robert Goldstick & Albert Thumann. LC 85-45876. 300p. 1986. text 44.95 (*0-88173-015-7*) Fairmont Pr.

Principles of Water Law & Administration: National & International. Dante A. Caponera. (Illus.). 280p. (C). 1992. text 128.00 (*90-5410-108-3*, Pub. by A A Balkema) Ashgate Pub Co.

Principles of Water Quality. Thomas D. Waite. 1984. text 65.00 (*0-12-730860-1*) Acad Pr.

Principles of Water Quality Control. 4th ed. T.J.Y. Tebbutt. 260p. 1992. pap. 34.95 (*0-7506-2829-4*) Buttrwrth-Heinemann.

Principles of Water Quality Control. 5th ed. T. H. Tebbutt. LC 97-49852. 288p. 1998. pap. text 39.95 (*0-7506-3658-0*) Buttrwrth-Heinemann.

Principles of Water Quality Management. W. W. Eckenfelder. LC 90-5077. (Illus.). 728p. (C). 1991. reprint ed. lib. bdg. 79.50 (*0-89464-517-X*) Krieger.

Principles of Water Quality Modeling Using the Qual2E Model Seminar, Charleston, SC, April 16, 1988. Technical Association of the Pulp & Paper Industry. LC TS1080.. (TAPPI Notes Ser.). (Illus.). 229p. reprint ed. pap. 71.00 (*0-608-18424-1*, 203226900079) Bks Demand.

*__Principles of Water Rates, Fees & Charges.__ American Water Works Association Staff. LC 00-36212. (Manual of Water Supply Practices Ser.). 2000. write for info. (*1-58321-070-9*) Am Water Wks Assn.

Principles of Water Surface & Quality Modeling Control. Robert V. Thomann & John A. Mueller. 656p. (C). 1997. 75.00 (*0-06-046677-4*) Addson-Wesley Educ.

Principles of Weaving. R. Marks & A. T. Robinson. 249p. (C). 1976. pap. text 27.00 (*0-900739-79-7*, Pub. by Textile Inst) St Mut.

Principles of Weaving. T. Marks & L. Robinson. 256p. 1976. 90.00 (*0-7855-7223-6*) St Mut.

Principles of Web Design. Sklar. (Programming Ser.). (C). 2000. pap. 37.95 (*0-619-01526-8*) Course Tech.

*__Principles of Weed Science.__ 2nd ed. V. S. Rao. LC 99-39247. (Illus.). 558p. 2000. text 49.50 (*1-57808-069-X*) Science Pubs.

*__Principles of Welding: Processes, Physics, Chemistry & Metallurgy.__ Robert W. Messler, Jr. LC 98-34986. 662p. 1999. 135.00 (*0-471-25376-6*, Wiley-Interscience) Wiley.

Principles of Wet End Chemistry. William E. Scott. 1995. 52.00 (*0-89852-286-2*, 0101R241) TAPPI.

Principles of Wicca. Vivianne Crowley. 1998. pap. 11.00 (*0-7225-3451-5*) Thorsons PA.

Principles of Wildlife Management. James A. Bailey. LC 83-19766. 384p. (C). 1984. text 84.95 (*0-471-01649-7*) Wiley.

Principles of Wood Science & Technology Vol. 2: Wood Base Materials Manufacture & Properties. F. F. Kollmann et al. LC 67-29614. (Illus.). 700p. 1975. 232.95 (*0-387-06467-2*) Spr-Verlag.

Principles of Wordsworth's Poetry. Robert Marchant. (C). 1986. 110.00 (*0-9502723-3-7*, Pub. by Brynmill Pr Ltd) St Mut.

Principles of Workers Compensation Claims. 2nd ed. David Appel et al. Ed. by James R. Jones. LC 98-71633. 311p. 1998. pap. text 41.00 (*0-89462-125-4*, 3402) IIA.

Principles of Wound Management. Richard F. Edlich. (Illus.). 400p. 1988. pap. text 45.00 (*0-07-019018-6*) McGraw.

Principles of Writing for Teacher Source. Campbell. LC 98-143975. (Adult ESL Ser.). 112p. (J). 1998. mass mkt. 22.95 (*0-8384-7892-1*) Heinle & Heinle.

Principles of Yacht Design. Lars Larsson. 1995. 39.95 (*0-07-036492-3*) Intl Marine.

Principles of Yacht Design. Lars Larsson. 352p. 1999. 44.95 (*0-07-135393-3*) McGraw.

Principles of Yacht Design. Lars Larsson & Rolf E. Eliasson. (Illus.). 302p. 1994. 85.00 (*0-7136-3855-9*, Pub. by A & C Blk) Lubrecht & Cramer.

*__Principles of YMCA Child Care.__ 2nd rev. ed. YMCA of the U. S. A. Staff. LC 99-41028. (Illus.). 264p. 1999. pap. 30.00 (*0-7360-3008-5*) Human Kinetics.

*__Principles of YMCA Competitive Swimming & Diving.__ YMCA of the U. S. A. Staff. (Illus.). 152p. 2000. pap. write for info. (*0-7360-3452-8*) Human Kinetics.

Principles of YMCA Competitive Swimming & Diving. YMCA of The U.S.A. Staff. 152p. 1996. spiral bd. 25.00 (*0-88011-547-5*, Y5302, YMCA USA) Human Kinetics.

Principles of YMCA Health & Fitness. 3rd rev. ed. YMCA of the USA Staff. (Illus.). 152p. 1999. spiral bd. 22.00 (*0-7360-0186-7*, Y5437, YMCA USA) Human Kinetics.

Principles of Your Psychic Pot. David Lawson. 1998. pap. 11.00 (*1-85538-487-6*) Thorsons PA.

Principles of Zen: The Only Introduction You'll Ever Need. Martine Batchelor. 160p. 1999. pap. 11.00 (*0-7225-3672-0*) Thorsons PA.

Principles of Zerometrics, Vol. I. Dom Martin. 24p. (Orig.). 1989. pap. text 5.00 (*0-685-33290-X*) Trans Gala Pubns.

Principles of Zoology, Touching the Structure, Development, Distribution, & Natural Arrangement of the Races of Animals Living & Extinct. Louis Agassiz & Augustus Gould. LC 76-125729. (American Environmental Studies). (Illus.). 1974. reprint ed. 19.95 (*0-405-02654-4*) Ayer.

Principles on the Law of Torts: or Wrongs Independent of Contract. 2nd ed. Arthur Underhill. LC 98-5527. viii, 824p. 1998. reprint ed. 95.00 (*0-8377-2707-3*, Rothman) W S Hein.

Principles Operative Surgery. 2nd ed. Poston. 1996. pap. text 24.95 (*0-443-05019-8*, W B Saunders Co) Harcrt Hlth Sci Grp.

Principles or Expediency? Edward M. Matthews. 64p. 1989. reprint ed. pap. 3.00 (*0-935461-17-5*) St Alban Pr CA.

Principles, Origin & Establishment of the Catholic School System in the United States. J. A. Burns. LC 74-89155. (American Education: Its Men, Institutions, & Ideas. Series 1). 1975. reprint ed. 23.95 (*0-405-01393-0*) Ayer.

Principles, Processes & Systems see Mineral Metabolism: An Advanced Treatise

Principles, Promise & Power: Christian Living Counseling Finance & Career. William Thompson. LC 99-163788. 1998. pap. 9.99 (*1-56043-308-6*, Treasure Hse) Destiny Image.

Principles Relating to Copyright Law Questions in the Field of Reprography (Recommendation & Explanatory Memorandum), No. R(90)11. 1995. 12.00 (*92-871-2706-9*, Pub. by Council of Europe) Manhattan Pub Co.

*__Principles Risk Management & Insurance.__ 6th ed. (C). 1998. 141.00 (*0-321-02818-X*) Addison-Wesley.

Principles Risk Management Insurance. 6th ed. 144p. (C). 1997. text 24.00 (*0-321-00023-4*) Addson-Wesley Educ.

Principles Risk Management Insurance. 6th ed. (C). 1997. text 67.00 (*0-321-00025-0*); text 67.00 (*0-321-00024-2*) Addison-Wesley Educ.

Principles, Signals & Systems. Taylor. 1994. 21.56 (*0-07-063198-0*) McGraw.

Principles, Techniques & Applications in Microsurgery. Ed. by T. S. Chang & Peter C. Leung. 400p. 1986. text 130.00 (*9971-978-08-3*); pap. text 49.00 (*9971-978-09-1*) World Scientific Pub.

Principles to Apply & Remember. Maile. 111p. 1994. pap. 11.95 (*0-929385-59-4*) Light Tech Pubng.

Principles to Live By. Mel Rees. 96p. 1993. per. 4.95 (*0-945383-47-9*) Teach Servs.

Principles to Live By: For the Storms of Your Life. Scott Strong. 1997. pap. 14.95 (*0-7880-0935-4*, Fairway Pr) CSS OH.

Principles 5 Wrkng Pprs VI 1-1. 5th ed. Jerry J. Weygandt. 592p. 1998. pap. 36.95 (*0-471-19443-3*) Wiley.

Principles 5e Bus Pprs Pract S. 5th ed. Jerry J. Weygandt. 1998. pap. text 19.00 (*0-471-19507-3*) Wiley.

Principy Bozej Ekonomiky. 2nd ed. Vladimir Uhri. (SLO.). 78p. 1995. pap. 3.80 (*1-56983-031-2*) New Creat WI.

Principy Krestanskej Meditacie. 2nd ed. Vladimir Uhri. (SLO.). 44p. (Orig.). 1995. pap. 2.40 (*1-56983-032-0*) New Creat WI.

Princples & Practice of Endodontics. 2nd ed. Richard E. Walton & Mahmoud Torabinejad. LC 94-43383. (Illus.). 512p. 1995. text 62.95 (*0-7216-4924-6*, W B Saunders Co) Harcrt Hlth Sci Grp.

Princs of Freelectron Lasers. Chapman & Hall Staff. text 189.50 (*0-412-72540-1*) Chapman & Hall.

Prindle Genealogy, Embracing the Descendants of William Pringle, the First Settler, & Also the Ancestors & Descendants of Zalmon Prindle, 1654-1906. F. C. Prindle. 352p. 1989. reprint ed. pap. 52.75 (*0-8328-0995-0*); reprint ed. lib. bdg. 60.75 (*0-8328-0994-2*) Higginson Bk Co.

Prindle-Pringle Genealogy. Robert E. Wallace. LC 96-130074. 170p. (Orig.). 1995. pap. 27.00 (*0-7884-0347-8*) Heritage Bk.

Prindsessen Paa Aerten see Princess & the Pea

Prindsessen paa aerten see Princess: Based on Hans Christian Andersen's "The Princess & the Pea"

Prindsessen Paa Aerten see Princess & the Pea

Pringle Progression. Sheldon Wimpfen. LC 97-78335. 192p. 1998. pap. 12.95 (*1-56167-413-3*) Am Literary Pr.

Pringle's History of Gloucester: New, Indexed Edition. 2nd ed. James R. Pringle. (Illus.). 416p. 1997. reprint ed. pap. 19.95 (*0-938459-10-4*) Ten Pound Isl Bk.

Prinicples of Accounting. 6th ed. Deroche. 1995. pap. text, student ed., wbk. ed. 28.60 (*0-13-442112-4*) P-H.

Priniples of Adsorption & Reaction on Solid Surfaces. Richard I. Masel. LC 95-17776. (Chemical Engineering Ser.). 824p. 1996. 94.95 (*0-471-30392-5*, Wiley-Interscience) Wiley.

PRINS & In Situ PCR Protocols. Ed. by John R. Gosden. (Methods in Molecular Biology Ser.: Vol. 71). 180p. 1996. 64.50 (*0-89603-395-3*) Humana.

Print. (Five-Minute Art Ideas Ser.). (Illus.). 24p. (Orig.). (J). (ps up). 1995. pap. 6.95 (*1-57102-059-4*, Ideals Child) Hambleton-Hill.

Print. Ansel Adams. LC 83-950. (Ansel Adams Photography Ser.: Bk. 3). (Illus.). 210p. 1983. 40.00 (*0-8212-1526-4*, Pub. by Bulfinch Pr) Little.

Print. Ansel Adams & Robert Baker. (Illus.). 224p. 1995. pap. 22.50 (*0-8212-2187-6*, Pub. by Bulfinch Pr) Little.

Print see Communication As a Second Language

Print: Book Review Digest Author & Title Index 1985-1994. 1261p. 1995. 85.00 (*0-8242-0907-9*) Wilson.

Print: How You Can Do It Yourself! 5th ed. Jonathan Zeitlyn. LC 92-13979. 128p. (C). 44.00 (*1-85172-044-8*, Pub. by Pluto GBR); pap. 17.00 (*1-85172-049-9*, Pub. by Pluto GBR) Stylus Pub VA.

Print & Be Damaged: or How I Put My Back Out Saving Letterpress for My Grandchildren's Children. Roger B. Mason. 24p. 1994. pap. 20.00 (*0-930126-46-7*) Typographeum.

Print & Broadcast Journalism: A Critical Examination. Edd Applegate. LC 96-14725. 224p. 1996. 57.95 (*0-275-95333-5*, Praeger Pubs) Greenwood.

Print & Culture in the Renaissance: Essays on the Advent of Printing in Europe. Ed. by Sylvia S. Wagonheim & Gerald P. Tyson. LC 85-40509. (Illus.). 272p. 1986. 45.00 (*0-87413-286-X*) U Delaware Pr.

Print & Drawing Collection of the Judah L. Magnes Museum. Florence Helzel. (Illus.). 110p. 1984. pap. 15.00 (*0-943376-24-6*) Magnes Mus.

Print & Electronic. 3rd ed. Marilyn K. Moody & Jean L. Sears. (Illus.). 632p. 2000. boxed set 125.00 (*1-57356-288-2*) Oryx Pr.

Print & Electronic Publishing: Legal & Business Issues in Book & Magazine Publishing. Elizabeth A. McNamara et al. LC 98-117689. (Patents, Copyrights, Trademarks, & Literary Property Course Handbook Ser.). 736 p. 1997. 39.00 (*0-87224-329-X*) PLI.

Print & Media Resources. 5th ed. Audesirk. 280p. (C). 1998. text, teacher ed. write for info. (*0-13-081036-3*) P-H.

Print & Politics: Shibao & the Culture of Reform in Late Qing China. Joan Judge. LC 96-15405. (Studies of the East Asian Institute). 1996. write for info. (*0-8047-2741-4*) Stanford U Pr.

Print & Production Manual. Pira Staff. 1998. 200.00 (*1-85802-238-X*, Pub. by Pira Pub) Bks Intl VA.

Print & Production Manual. 5th rev. ed. Blueprint Publishing Limited Staff. 348p. 1991. 129.95 (*0-948905-48-4*) Chapman & Hall.

*__Print & Protestantism in Early Modern England.__ Ian Green. 580p. 2000. text 115.00 (*0-19-820860-X*) OUP.

Print Book. Hannah Tofts. (J). (ps-3). 1990. pap. 4.95 (*0-671-70369-2*) S&S Bks Yung.

Print Buyer's Bible Promotional & Marketing Print. 2nd ed. Michael Barnard & Robin Shobbrook. 320p. (C). 1997. ring bd. 169.95 (*0-415-15117-1*) Routledge.

Print Casebooks 9: The Best in Advertising, 1991-1992. (Illus.). 96p. 27.95 (*0-915734-70-2*) RC Pubns.

Print Casebooks 9: The Best in Annual Reports, 1991-1992. (Illus.). 96p. 27.95 (*0-915734-71-0*) RC Pubns.

Print Casebooks 9: The Best in Environmental Graphics, 1991-1992. (Illus.). 94p. 27.95 (*0-915734-72-9*) RC Pubns.

Print Casebooks 9: The Best in Exhibition Design, 1991-1992. (Illus.). 104p. 27.95 (*0-915734-73-7*) RC Pubns.

Print Casebooks 9, 1991-1992, 6 vols., Set. (Illus.). 139.00 (*0-915734-69-9*) RC Pubns.

Print Casebooks 6: 1984-85 Editions, 6 vols. Incl. Vol. 1. Best in Advertising. 1985. 19.95 (*0-915734-41-9*); Vol. 2. Best in Annual Reports. 1985. 19.95 (*0-915734-42-7*); Vol. 3. Best in Environmental Graphics. 1985. 19.95 (*0-915734-43-5*); Vol. 4. Best in Exhibition Design. 1985. 19.95 (*0-915734-44-3*); Vol. 5. Best in Packaging. 1985. 19.95 (*0-915734-45-1*); Vol. 6. Best in Covers & Designs. 1985. 19.95 (*0-915734-46-X*); 1985. 115.00 (*0-915734-40-0*) RC Pubns.

Print Club of Cleveland, 1969-1994. LC 94-1813. 1994. 24.95 (*0-940717-24-7*); pap. 19.95 (*0-940717-25-5*) Cleveland Mus Art.

Print Collecting: Selecting, Evaluating & Caring for Fine Prints. Silvie Turner. LC 96-22094. (Illus.). 192p. 1996. 30.00 (*1-55821-366-X*); pap. 20.00 (*1-55821-507-7*, 50253) Lyons Pr.

Print Collecting Today. Arthur Vershbow et al. 1969. 5.00 (*0-89073-026-1*, 131) Boston Public Lib.

Print Communications & the Electronic Media Challenge. Alan Kotok & Ralph Lyman. LC 97-6840. (Illus.). 120p. 1997. 68.00 (*1-885067-05-4*) Jelmar Pub.

Print Culture in a Diverse America. James P. Danky & Wayne A. Wiegand. LC 97-33935. (History of Communication Ser.). 336p. 1998. text 49.95 (*0-252-02398-6*); text 27.95 (*0-252-06699-5*) U of Ill Pr.

Print Culture in Renaissance Italy: The Editor & the Vernacular Text, 1470-1600. Brian Richardson. LC 93-30907. (Studies in Publishing & Printing History: No. 8). 281p. (C). 1994. text 69.95 (*0-521-42032-6*) Cambridge U Pr.

Print Estimators: The Handbook. Pira Staff. 1998. 86.00 (*0-85168-202-2*, Pub. by Pira Pub) Bks Intl VA.

Print in the Western World: An Introductory History. Linda C. Hults. LC 95-7231. (Illus.). 968p. 1996. 69.95 (*0-299-13700-7*) U of Wis Pr.

Print Index: A Guide to Reproductions, 4. Compiled by Pamela J. Parry & Kathe Chipman. LC 83-12824. (Art Reference Collection Ser.: No. 4). 310p. 1983. lib. bdg. 65.00 (*0-313-22063-8*, PPR/, Greenwood Pr) Greenwood.

Print It! One Hundred Fifty Years of the Akron Beacon Journal. Hal Fry. (Illus.). 72p. (Orig.). 1989. pap. 6.95 (*0-9621895-1-0*) Summit Cty Hist Soc.

Print Magic: The Complete Guide to Decorative Printing Techniques. Jocasta Innes & Stewart Walton. (Illus.). 192p. 1997. 29.95 (*1-85410-475-6*, Pub. by Aurum Pr) London Brdge.

Print Making. Elisabeth Harden. (Crafts for Children Ser.). (Illus.). 32p. (YA). (gr. 3 up). 1997. pap. 4.95 (*1-56010-215-2*, CC05) W Foster Pub.

Print Making Without a Press. Janet D. Erickson & Adelaide Sproul. LC 65-19672. 123p. reprint ed. pap. 38.20 (*0-608-11277-1*, 200724500063) Bks Demand.

Print Management. Pira Staff. 1998. 70.00 (*1-85802-021-2*, Pub. by Pira Pub) Bks Intl VA.

*__Print, Manuscript & Performance: The Changing Relations of Media in Early Modern England.__ Ed. by Arthur F. Marotti & Michael D. Bristol. LC 99-47596. 320p. (C). 2000. pap. text 24.95 (*0-8142-5049-1*) Ohio St U Pr.

*__Print, Manuscript & Performance: The Changing Relations of the Media in Early Modern England.__ Ed. by Arthur F. Marotti & Michael D. Bristol. LC 99-47596. 320p. (C). 2000. text 65.00 (*0-8142-0845-2*) Ohio St U Pr.

Print Market Atlas 1996 Edition (National, State & Local Print Markets) 234p. 159.00 (*0-614-25546-5*, 00BT23003) Print Indus Am.

Print Media Planning Manual: How to Prepare a Media Plan & Buy Space for Periodical Advertising. R. L. Ehler. LC 90-63642. (Print Media Advertising Ser.: Bk. 1). (Illus.). 293p. (Orig.). (C). 1991. pap. text 49.95 (*1-879299-11-9*) Richler.

Print of a Hare's Foot. Rhys Davies. LC 99-192172. 183p. 1999. pap. 17.95 (*1-85411-180-9*, Pub. by Seren Bks) Dufour.

Print of Wild Flowers. Gerry LaFemina. 32p. (Orig.). 1997. pap. text 8.00 (*1-56439-065-9*) Ridgeway.

Print Order Processing. Pira Staff. 1998. 80.00 (*0-85168-197-2*, Pub. by Pira Pub) Bks Intl VA.

Print-Out. large type ed. Basil Copper. (Dales Mystery Ser.). 246p. 1993. pap. 18.99 (*1-85389-380-3*, Dales) Ulverscroft.

Print-Out. large type ed. Basil Copper. (Linford Mystery Library). 304p. 1996. pap. 16.99 (*0-7089-7861-4*, Linford) Ulverscroft.

Print Pizzazz: Desktop Publishing for the Rest of Us. Martha Bryan & Geoffrey Bryan. (Illus.). 181p. 1997. pap. 19.95 (*0-9658513-3-8*) Gldn Dragon.

Print Politics: The Press & Radical Opposition in Early Nineteenth-Century England. Kevin Gilmartin. (Cambridge Studies in Romanticism: No. 21). (Illus.). 288p. (C). 1997. text 59.95 (*0-521-49655-1*) Cambridge U Pr.

Print, Power, & People in Seventeenth Century France. Henri-Jean Martin. Tr. by David Gerard. LC 91-39016. (Illus.). 758p. 1993. reprint ed. 90.00 (*0-8108-2477-9*) Scarecrow.

*__Print Product Assurance Services: An Introduction.__ 2nd ed. Solomon. (SWC-Accounting Ser.). 2000. pap. 5.00 (*0-324-05793-8*) Sth-Wstrn College.

*__Print Production Essentials.__ 2nd ed. Bruce Fraser & Adobe Creative Team Staff. (Essential Ser.). 120p. 2000. pap. 40.00 (*0-201-70013-1*) Adobe Pr.

Print Programming in Windows: Driving Special Printers. Jeff Potts. 432p. 1999. pap. 39.95 incl. cd-rom (*0-87930-585-1*, Pub. by C M P Books) Publishers Group.

Print Publishing for the School Market: 99-2000 Review, Trends & Forecast. Al Branch. (Illus.). 175p. 1999. 1995.00 (*0-88709-096-6*) Simba Info Inc.

Print Reading for Architecture & Construction Technology. David A. Madsen & Alan Jefferis. 72p. (C). 1994. text, teacher ed. 16.50 (*0-8273-5430-4*) Delmar.

Print Reading for Architecture & Construction Technology. David Madsen & Alan Jefferis. 415p. 1994. mass mkt. 31.75 (*0-8273-5429-0*) Delmar.

Print Reading for Construction: Residential & Commercial. Walter C. Brown. LC 96-47086. (Illus.). 276p. 1997. text 39.96 (*1-56637-355-7*) Goodheart.

Print Reading for Engineering & Manufacturing Technology. David A. Madsen. 96p. 1994. pap. text, teacher ed. 15.50 (*0-8273-5236-0*) Delmar.

Print Reading for Engineering & Manufacturing Technology. David A. Madsen. 407p. 1994. pap. 32.75 (*0-8273-5235-2*) Delmar.

Print Reading for Industry. Walter C. Brown. LC 94-17774. (Illus.). 404p. 1995. spiral bd. 38.64 (*1-56637-062-0*) Goodheart.

Print Reading for the Machine Trades. Wilfred B. Pouler. (Blueprint Reading & Drafting Ser.). 1984. teacher ed. 11.50 (*0-538-33351-0*); pap. 24.95 (*0-538-33350-2*) S-W Pub.

Print Reading for the Machine Trades. 2nd ed. Wilfred B. Pouler. LC 94-25405. (Illus.). 416p. 1995. mass mkt. 43.95 (*0-8273-6651-5*) Delmar.

Print Shop: Simple Projects. Marsha Lifter & Marian E. Adams. (Illus.). 96p. 1998. pap., teacher ed. 14.95 (*1-57690-414-8*, TCM2414) Tchr Create Mat.

*__Print Shop Deluxe for Dummies.__ Wallace Wang. (For Dummies Ser.). 392p. 2000. pap. 19.99 (*0-7645-0602-1*) IDG Bks.

Print Shop for Terrified Teachers. Marsha Lifter. (Terrified Teachers Ser.). (Illus.). 304p. pap., teacher ed. 19.95 (*1-57690-189-0*, TCM2189) Tchr Create Mat.

Print Style: Hand-Printed Patterns for Home Decoration. John Hinchcliffe & Wendy Barber. (Illus.). 160p. 1998. pap. 19.95 (*0-304-34810-4*, Pub. by Cassell) Sterling.

Print Tests of College Algebra Trigonometry. Louis Leithold. (Illus.). 702p. (C). 1989. pap. text, teacher ed. 12.95 (*0-201-15733-0*) Addison-Wesley.

*__Print the Legend: The Life & Times of John Ford.__ Scott Eyman. LC 00-33044. 2000. write for info. (*0-8018-6560-3*) Johns Hopkins.

An Asterisk (*) at the beginning of an entry indicates that the title is appearing for the first time.

Print the Legend: The Life & Times of John Ford. Scott Eyman. LC 99-37046. 656p. 1999. 40.00 (*0-684-81161-8*) S&S Trade.
Printed Bengali Character. Fiona G. Ross. 288p. (C). 1999. 55.00 (*0-7007-1135-X*, Pub. by Curzon Pr Ltd) UH Pr.
Printed Book in America. Joseph Blumenthal. LC 88-40520. (Illus.). 266p. 1989. reprint ed. pap. 29.95 (*0-87451-480-0*) U Pr of New Eng.
Printed Books, 1468-1700 in the Hispanic Society of America. Clara L. Penney. (Illus.). 614p. 1965. 15.00 (*0-87535-106-9*) Hispanic Soc.
Printed Bygones. G. Potter. 88p. 1986. pap. 25.00 (*0-7212-0742-1*, Pub. by Regency Pr GBR) St Mut.
Printed Catalogues of the Harvard College Library, 1723-1790. Ed. by William H. Bond & Hugh Amory. 738p. 1996. 75.00 (*0-9620737-3-3*, 44060) Oak Knoll.
Printed Circuit Assembly Design. Leonard Marks. (Professional Engineering Ser.). 368p. 2000. 65.00 (*0-07-041107-7*) McGraw.
Printed Circuit Assembly Design Guidelines. Phil Marcoux. 258p. (C). 1992. student ed. 395.00 (*1-884817-00-9*) PPM Assocs.
Printed Circuit Assembly Inspection, Rework, & Repair Techniques. Phil Marcoux. 115p. (C). 1993. student ed. 65.00 (*1-884817-02-5*) PPM Assocs.
Printed Circuit Assembly Manufacturing. Fred W. Kear. (Manufacturing Engineering & Materials Processing Ser.: Vol. 21). (Illus.). 384p. 1987. text 175.00 (*0-8247-7675-5*) Dekker.
Printed Circuit Board Basics. Scheiber. 1996. text 45.00 (*0-07-055175-8*) McGraw.
Printed Circuit Board Design Techniques for EMC Compliance. IEEE, Electromagnetic Compatibility Society Staff & Mark I. Montrose. LC 96-16931. 256p. 1996. write for info. (*0-7803-1131-0*) IEEE Standards.
*__Printed Circuit Board Manufacturing Equipment In Germany: A Strategic Entry Report, 1997.__ Compiled by Icon Group International Staff. (Illus.). 101p. 1999. ring bd. 1010.00 incl. audio compact disk (*0-7418-1001-8*) Icon Grp.
Printed Circuit Board Manufacturing Industry: Guide to Pollution Prevention. (Illus.). 77p. (Orig.). (C). 1994. pap. text 15.00 (*1-56806-084-X*) DIANE Pub.
Printed Circuit Board Materials Handbook. Martin W. Jawitz. LC 97-200298. 784p. 1997. 99.50 (*0-07-032488-3*) McGraw.
Printed Circuit Board Technologies. Business Communications Co., Inc. Staff. 173p. 1994. 2650.00 (*0-89336-760-5*, G-067X) BCC.
*__Printed Circuit Boards in Singapore: A Strategic Entry Report, 2000.__ Compiled by Icon Group International. (Illus.). 122p. 1999. ring bd. 1220.00 incl. audio compact disk (*0-7418-2157-5*) Icon Grp.
Printed Circuit Engineering. Clark. 1989. 44.00 (*0-07-158621-0*) McGraw.
Printed Circuit Handbook. 4th ed. Clyde F. Coombs, Jr. LC 95-25131. (Illus.). 1088p. 1995. 99.00 (*0-07-012754-9*) McGraw.
Printed Circuits Vol. 1: Engineering & Fundamentals. Clyde F. Coombs. 1990. pap. text 26.95 (*0-07-012739-5*) McGraw.
Printed Circuits Design. Gerald Ginsberg. 336p. 1991. 50.00 (*0-07-023309-8*) McGraw.
Printed Circuits Handbook. 2nd ed. Ed. by C. G. Coombes. 536p. 1979. 63.00 (*0-318-12558-7*) Am Electro Surface.
Printed Commonplace-Books & the Structuring of Renaissance Thought. Ann Moss. 358p. (C). 1996. text 85.00 (*0-19-815908-0*) OUP.
Printed Elvis: The Complete Guide to Books about the King, 75. Steven Opdyke. LC 99-11132. (Music Reference Collection: Vol. 75). 352p. 1999. lib. bdg. 49.95 (*0-313-30815-2*) Greenwood.
Printed English Pottery: History & Humour in the Reign of George III, 1760-1820. David Drakard. (Illus.). 268p. 1992. 125.00 (*0-9512140-5-5*, Pub. by J Horne) Antique Collect.
Printed Ephemera. John Lewis. (Illus.). 288p. 1990. 69.50 (*1-85149-116-3*) Antique Collect.
Printed Image & the Transformation of Popular Culture, 1790-1860. Patricia Anderson. (Illus.). 224p. 1994. pap. 18.95 (*0-19-818276-7*) OUP.
Printed in Cracow. Catherine M. Soussloff. LC 63-62002. (Illus.). 12p. 1985. 1.00 (*0-614-10423-8*) W Benton Mus.
Printed in France, Bk. 1. Nicole Yu. 1989. pap. text 10.84 (*0-582-01447-6*, 78038) Longman.
Printed in France, Bk. 2. Nicole Yu. 1989. pap. text 10.84 (*0-582-01448-4*, 78052) Longman.
Printed in Germany, Bk. 1. N. J. Morgan. 1989. pap. text 10.84 (*0-582-01450-6*, 78051) Longman.
Printed in Germany, Bk. 2. N. J. Morgan. 1989. pap. 10.84 (*0-685-32947-X*, 78050) Longman.
Printed Information of Spines, Z39.41-1997. National Information Standards Organization Staff. LC 98-37801. 24p. 1998. 40.00 (*1-880124-32-7*) NISO.
Printed Information on Spines, Z39.41-1990. National Information Standards Organization Staff. 1991. 20.00 (*0-88738-944-9*) Transaction Pubs.
Printed Maps of Lincolnshire, 1576-1900 with an Appendix on Road-Books, 1675-1900: A Carto-Bibliography with an Appendix on Road-Books, 1675-1900. R. A. Carroll. (Publications of Lincoln Record Society: Vol. 84). (Illus.). 502p. (C). 1996. 60.00 (*0-901503-57-6*) Boydell & Brewer.
Printed Maps of Utah to 1900: An Annotated Cartobibliography. Riley M. Moffat. LC 81-659. (Occasional Papers: No. 8). (Illus.). 193p. (Orig.). 1981. pap. 10.00 (*0-939112-09-4*) Western Assn Map.
Printed Matter: Bound for Glory. Baird Duncan. 1999. 45.00 (*0-688-16938-4*, Wm Morrow) Morrow Avon.
Printed Opera Scores in American Libraries, Bk. 1. Compiled by Charles H. Parsons. LC 98-36427. (Opera Reference Index Ser.: Vol. 21A). 558p. 1987. text 139.95 (*0-88946-418-9*) E Mellen.
Printed Opera Scores in American Libraries, Bk. 2. Compiled by Charles H. Parsons. LC 98-36427. (Opera Reference Index Ser.: Vol. 21B). 1998. text 199.95 (*0-88946-419-7*) E Mellen.
Printed Opera Scores in American Libraries, Bk. 3. Compiled by Charles H. Parsons. LC 98-36427. (Opera Reference Index Ser.: Vol. 21C). 1998. text 199.95 (*0-88946-695-5*) E Mellen.
Printed Poison: Pamphlet Propaganda, Faction Politics & the Public Sphere in Early Seventeenth-Century France. Jeffrey K. Sawyer. LC 89-49051. 224p. 1990. 38.00 (*0-520-06883-1*, Pub. by U CA Pr) Cal Prin Full Svc.
Printed Press & Television in the Regions of Europe. 1995. 25.00 (*92-871-2807-3*, Pub. by Council of Europe) Manhattan Pub Co.
Printed Propaganda under Louis XIV: Absolute Monarchy & Public Opinion. Joseph Klaits. LC 76-3268. 356p. reprint ed. pap. 110.40 (*0-8357-3308-4*, 203953100013) Bks Demand.
Printed Sources: A Guide to Published Genealogical Records. Kory Meyerink. LC 98-10852. (Illus.). 839p. 1998. 49.95 (*0-916489-70-1*) Ancestry.
Printed Stuff: Prints, Posters, & Ephemera by Claes Oldenburg: A Catalogue Raisonne 1958-1996. Richard H. Axsom & David Platzker. LC 96-39970. (Illus.). 454p. 1997. 125.00 (*1-55595-123-6*) Hudson Hills.
Printed Teaching Materials: A New Approach for Law Teachers. Richard Johnstone. LC 98-169290. 200p. 1996. pap. 60.00 (*1-85941-233-5*, Pub. by Cavendish Pubng) Gaunt.
Printed Test Bank & Prepared Tests to Accompany Beginning Algebra: A Text-Workbook. 5th ed. Charles P. McKeague. 392p. (C). 1998. pap. text, wbk. ed. write for info. (*0-03-022684-8*, Pub. by SCP) Harcourt.
Printed Test Bank & Prepared Tests to Accompany Intermediate Algebra: A Text Workbook. 5th ed. Charles P. McKeague. 456p. (C). 1999. pap. text, wbk. ed. write for info. (*0-03-020823-8*, Pub. by SCP) Harcourt.
Printed Test Bank Basic Statistics. Moore. 1995. pap. text 24.00 (*0-7167-2677-7*) W H Freeman.
Printed Test Bank to Accompany Digital Electronics. 3rd ed. James W. Bignell et al. 168p. 1993. pap. 25.00 (*0-8273-6099-1*) Delmar.
Printed Test Plane Trigo. Louis Leithold. (Illus.). (C). 1989. 12.95 (*0-201-17059-0*) Addison-Wesley.
Printed Testbank Abnormal Psychology Version B. Ronald Comer. (C). 1992. 16.80 (*0-7167-2453-7*) W H Freeman.
Printed Testbank Computer. George Beekman. 432p. 1994. pap. text 11.50 (*0-8053-2457-7*) Benjamin-Cummings.
Printed Testbank General Analysis. Griffiths. write for info. (*0-7167-2476-6*) W H Freeman.
Printed Tests. Frank Demana & Bert K. Waits. (Illus.). (C). 1989. student ed. 12.66 (*0-201-19576-3*) Addison-Wesley.
Printed Voice of Victorian Poetry. Eric Griffiths. 392p. 1989. 85.00 (*0-19-812989-0*) OUP.
Printed Wiring Boards & Other Interconnection Technologies for High Performance Systems. Daniel Amey. 1994. 55.00 (*0-07-001614-3*) McGraw.
Printed-Wiring Boards, UL 796. 7th ed. (C). 1993. pap. text 95.00 (*1-55989-440-7*) Underwrtrs Labs.
Printed World of Pieter Bruegel the Elder. Joseph L. Koerner & Barbara Butts. Ed. by Suzanne Tausz. (Illus.). 114p. 1995. pap. text 19.95 (*0-89178-042-4*) St Louis Art Mus.
Printemps a Rome. Emma Richmond. (Azur Ser.: No. 746). (FRE.). 1999. mass mkt. 3.50 (*0-373-34746-4*, 1-34746-7) Harlequin Bks.
Printemps Au Parking. Christiane Rochefort. (FRE.). 192p. 1971. pap. 9.95 (*0-7859-5564-X*); pap. 3.95 (*0-686-55227-X*) Fr & Eur.
Printemps et Autres Saisons. J. M. Le Clezio. (Folio Ser.: No. 2264). (FRE.). pap. 8.95 (*0-685-65407-9*) Schoenhof.
Printemps Noir. Henry Miller. (FRE.). 1975. pap. 11.95 (*0-7859-4042-1*) Fr & Eur.
Printemps Romain: Avec: Choix de Lettres de Romain Rolland a sa Mere (1889-1890) Romain Rolland. (FRE.). 360p. 1954. pap. 8.95 (*0-7859-5459-7*) Fr & Eur.
Printer. Larry McGurn. 68p. 1981. pap. 3.50 (*0-939391-00-7*) B Woodley Pr.
Printer. Jack Rudman. (Career Examination Ser.: C-616). 1994. pap. 23.95 (*0-8373-0616-7*) Nat Learn.
Printer & the Environment. Pira Staff. 1998. 35.00 (*0-85168-188-3*, Pub. by Pira Pub) Bks Intl VA.
Printer & the Pardoner: An Unrecorded Indulgence, Printed by William Caxton for the Hospital of St. Mary Rounceval, Charing Cross. Paul Needham. LC 85-18120. 101p. 1986. 35.00 (*0-8444-0508-6*) Lib Congress.
Printer in Eighteenth-Century Williamsburg. rev. ed. Colonial Williamsburg Foundation Staff. (Historic Trades Ser.). (Illus.). 34p. (Orig.). 1958. pap. 2.95 (*0-910412-20-0*) Colonial Williamsburg.
Printer of Shakespeare. Edwin W. Willoughby. LC 77-92993. (Studies in Shakespeare: No. 24). 1969. reprint ed. lib. bdg. 75.00 (*0-8383-1212-8*) M S G Haskell Hse.
Printer of Udell's: A Story of the Middle West. Harold Bell Wright. (Collected Works of Harold Bell Wright). 467p. 1999. reprint ed. lib. bdg. 98.00 (*1-58201-894-4*) Classic Bks.
Printer-Proofreader. Jack Rudman. (Career Examination Ser.: C-617). 1994. pap. 29.95 (*0-8373-0617-5*) Nat Learn.
*__Printers.__ Leonard Everett Fisher. LC 99-33361. (gr. 4-7). 1999. 21.36 (*0-7614-0929-7*) Marshall Cavendish.
Printers: A Study in American Trade Unionism. George E. Barnett. 1977. lib. bdg. 59.95 (*0-8490-2481-1*) Gordon Pr.
Printers & Men of Capital: Philadelphia Book Publishers in the New Republic. Rosalind Remer. (Early American Studies). (Illus.). 224p. 1996. text 34.95 (*0-8122-3337-9*) U of Pa Pr.
Printers & Printing. David Pottinger. LC 70-175709. (Select Bibliographies Reprint Ser.). 1977. reprint ed. 12.95 (*0-8369-6624-4*) Ayer.
Printers & Printing in Philately. John Alden. 76p. (C). 1987. 35.00 (*0-7855-2241-7*, Pub. by Picton) St Mut.
Printers & Printing in the East Indies to 1850, 9 vols., Set. Katharine S. Diehl. write for info. (*0-89241-384-0*) Caratzas.
Printers' & Publishers' Devices in England & Scotland, 1485-1640. Ronald B. McKerrow. LC Z 1008.B545. (Bibliographical Society, Illustrated Monographs: Vol. 16). (Illus.). 309p. reprint ed. pap. 95.80 (*0-608-13675-1*, 205540800020) Bks Demand.
Printers & Technology. Elizabeth Baker. LC 74-12847. (Illus.). 545p. 1974. reprint ed. lib. bdg. 79.50 (*0-8371-7763-4*, BAPT, Greenwood Pr) Greenwood.
Printer's Apprentice. Stephen Krensky. (J). 1995. 18.95 (*0-385-44631-4*) BDD Bks Young Read.
Printer's Apprentice. Stephen Krensky. (J). 1996. pap. 4.99 (*0-440-91268-7*) BDD Bks Young Read.
Printer's Apprentice. Stephen Krensky. LC 94-36721. (J). 1996. 9.09 (*0-606-11766-0*, Pub. by Turtleback) Demco.
Printer's Catch: An Artist's Guide to Pacific Coast Edible Marine Animals. 2nd ed. Christopher Dewees. LC 95-50354. (Illus.). 112p. 1996. reprint ed. pap. 22.50 (*1-883319-41-2*) Frog Ltd CA.
Printer's Composition Matrix. Richard E. Huss. (Illus.). 80p. 1985. 45.00 (*0-938768-09-3*) Oak Knoll.
Printer's Daughter: An American's Romance in Early Nineteenth Century London. Valerie Gray. 210p. 1998. 42.50 (*1-85776-203-7*, Pub. by Book Guild Ltd) Trans-Atl Phila.
Printer's Devil to Publisher: Adolph S. Ochs of the New York Times. Doris Faber. LC 96-14681. 192p. (J). 1996. pap. 8.95 (*1-883789-09-5*) Blk Dome Pr.
Printer's Dozen. Philip Gallo. (Illus.). 1992. pap. 120.00 (*0-931460-28-X*) Bieler.
Printer's Dozen: Printing Centres after London & Before 1557 - Oxford, St. Albans, Edinburgh, York, Cambridge, Tavistock, Abingdon, Canterbury, Bristol, Ipswich, Worcester, Dublin, St. Andrews, Mountgrace Priory. Sessions, William Ltd., Staff. 115p. (C). 1983. 100.00 (*0-900657-72-3*, Pub. by W Sessions) St Mut.
*__Printer's Error.__ Aaron Fogel. (Poetry Ser.). 96p. 2001. 19.95 (*1-881163-35-0*, Pub. by Miami Univ Pr); pap. 11.95 (*1-881163-36-9*, Pub. by Miami Univ Pr) Pathway Bk Serv.
Printers' First Fruits: An Exhibition of American Imprints, 1640-1742, from the Collections of the American Antiquarian Society. William S. Reese. (Illus.). 52p. 1989. pap. 15.00 (*0-944026-15-X*) Am Antiquarian.
Printers' Flowers. Paul Woodbine. (Illus.). 25p. 1988. 98.00 (*0-916258-17-3*); 110.00 (*0-916258-18-1*) Woodbine Pr.
Printers' Guide to Copyright. Pira Staff. 1998. 25.00 (*0-85168-195-6*, Pub. by Pira Pub) Bks Intl VA.
Printer's Guide to Job Descriptions, Company Structure & Growth, Vol. I. 48p. 95.00 (*0-614-25561-9*, 00HR44319) Print Indus Am.
Printer's Guide to Job Descriptions, Company Structure & Growth, Vol. II. 96p. 150.00 (*0-614-25562-7*, 00HR44320) Print Indus Am.
Printers in Appalachia: The International Printing Pressmen & Assistants' Union of North America, 1907-1967. Jack Mooney. LC 93-70235. 193p. (C). 1993. 39.95 (*0-87972-576-1*) Bowling Green Univ Popular Press.
Printers (London & South) Ed. by ICC Information Group Staff. 1987. 695.00 (*1-85036-968-2*, Pub. by ICC Info Group Ltd) St Mut.
Printers' Marks & Devices. Howard W. Winger. 1976. 20.00 (*0-940550-06-7*) Caxton Club.
Printers (Midland & North) Ed. by ICC Information Group Staff. 1987. 695.00 (*1-85036-973-9*, Pub. by ICC Info Group Ltd) St Mut.
Printers, Stationers, & Book-Binders of Westminster & London from 1476 to 1535. E. Gordon Duff. LC 78-172540. (Illus.). reprint ed. 22.00 (*0-405-08467-6*, Pub. by Blom Pubns) Ayer.
Printers, Stationers & Bookbinders of West Minster & London from 1476 to 1535. E. Gordon Duff. 256p. 1972. 20.95 (*0-405-09135-4*) Ayer.
Printers Supplies. Ed. by ICC Information Group Staff. 1987. 710.00 (*1-85036-978-X*, Pub. by ICC Info Group Ltd) St Mut.
Printers with Sales over $10,000,000 see 1996 PIA Ratios
Printers with Sales under $1,500,000 see 1996 PIA Ratios
Printing see First Step Math
Printing, 13 vols. (High Q Ser.). (Illus.). 32p. (J). (gr. k-1). 1998. pap. 2.25 (*0-7681-0027-5*, McClanahan Book) Learn Horizon.
*__Printing.__ Dalamatian Press Staff. (J). (gr. k-1). 1999. pap. text 2.99 (*1-57759-136-4*) Dalmatian Pr.
Printing. Ray Gibson. (How to Make Ser.). (Illus.). 32p. (J). (gr. 3-7). 1996. pap. 6.95 (*0-7460-2527-0*, Usborne); lib. bdg. 14.95 (*0-88110-850-2*, Usborne) EDC.
Printing. Susan N. Janes. LC 97-25658. (Arts & Crafts Skills Ser.). (Illus.). 32p. (J). (gr. 3-6). 1998. 20.00 (*0-516-20458-0*) Childrens.
Printing. Susan N. Janes. Ed. by Helaine Cohen. (Arts & Crafts Skills Ser.). (Illus.). 32p. (J). (gr. 3-5). 1998. pap. 6.95 (*0-516-26213-0*) Childrens.
*__Printing.__ Michelle Powell. LC 00-38308. (Step-by-Step Ser.). 2000. lib. bdg. write for info. (*1-57572-329-8*) Heinemann Lib.
*__Printing.__ Michelle Powell. (Step-by-Step Children's Crafts Ser.). 32p. (J). (ps-3). 2000. pap. 8.95 (*0-85532-911-4*, Pub. by Srch Pr) Midpt Trade.
Printing. Lori V. Schue. (ArtWorks for Kids Ser.: Vol. 1). (Illus.). 48p. (J). (gr. 1-6). 1995. pap. text, teacher ed. 9.95 (*1-55799-362-9*, EMC 291) Evan-Moor Edu Pubs.
Printing. Sue Stocks. LC 94-2661. (First Arts & Crafts Ser.). (Illus.). 32p. (J). (gr. 1-6). 1994. lib. bdg. 21.40 (*1-56847-210-2*) Raintree Steck-V.
Printing: Technical Dictionary Of. Ed. by Wolfgang Muller. 1020p. (C). 1981. 330.00 (*0-7855-5003-8*, Pub. by Collets) St Mut.
Printing a Book at Verona in 1622. Conor Fahy. 204p. 1993. 75.00 (*0-614-16145-2*) Oak Knoll.
Printing & Bookselling in Dublin, 1670-1800: A Bibliographical Enquiry. James W. Phillips. (Illus.). 256p. 1997. 65.00 (*0-7165-2680-8*, Pub. by Irish Acad Pr) Intl Spec Bk.
Printing & Bookselling in Dublin, 1670-1800: A Bibliographical Enquiry. James W. Phillips. LC 95-170922. (Illus.). 368p. 1998. 59.50 (*0-7165-2580-1*, Pub. by Irish Acad Pr) Intl Spec Bk.
Printing & Graphic Arts Equipment in Poland: A Strategic Entry Report, 1997. Compiled by Icon Group International Staff. (Illus.). 178p. 1999. ring bd. 1780.00 incl. audio compact disk (*0-7418-1066-2*) Icon Grp.
*__Printing & Graphic Arts Equipment in Thailand: A Strategic Entry Report, 1995.__ Compiled by Icon Group International Staff. (Illus.). 142p. 1999. ring bd. 1420.00 incl. audio compact disk (*0-7418-1628-8*) Icon Grp.
*__Printing & Graphic Arts in Mexico: A Strategic Entry Report, 1996.__ Compiled by Icon Group International Staff. (Illus.). 149p. 1999. ring bd. 1490.00 incl. audio compact disk (*0-7418-1359-9*) Icon Grp.
Printing & Graphics Equipment in Egypt: A Strategic Entry Report, 1997. Compiled by Icon Group International Staff. (Country Industry Report). (Illus.). 157p. 1999. ring bd. 1570.00 incl. audio compact disk (*0-7418-0285-6*) Icon Grp.
Printing & Publishing Evidence: Thesauri for Use in Rare Book & Special Collections Cataloging. Association of College & Research Libraries. 28p. 1986. pap. 9.00 (*0-8389-7108-3*) Assn Coll & Res Libs.
*__Printing & Publishing for the University of Cambridge: Three Hundred Years of the Press Syndicate.__ Gordon Johnson. LC 99-491007. (Illus.). 28p. (C). 2000. pap. text 7.95 (*0-521-66353-9*) Cambridge U Pr.
Printing & Publishing in the Colonial Era of the United States: A Supplement to the Book in the Americas (1988), with a Checklist of the Items in That Catalogue. Norman Fiering & Susan L. Newbury. (Illus.). 54p. 1990. pap. 10.00 (*0-916617-39-4*) J C Brown.
Printing & Publishing Your Family History. Marilyn Lind. LC 86-8100. (Illus.). 63p. (Orig.). 1986. pap. text 7.50 (*0-937463-10-8*) Linden Tree.
Printing & Society in Early America. Ed. by William L. Joyce et al. LC 83-6358. 334p. 1983. 37.50 (*0-912296-55-0*, 14220) Oak Knoll.
Printing & the Book Trade in Shakespeare's Time: A Guide to the Microfiche Collection. (Shakespeariana Ser.). 51p. (Orig.). 1991. pap. 20.00 (*0-8357-2160-4*) Univ Microfilms.
Printing & Workflow. Romano. 288p. 1998. pap. text 39.99 (*0-13-020837-X*) P-H.
Printing Arts in Texas. Al Lowman. (Illus.). 109p. 1981. 25.00 (*0-686-73811-X*, PA2-16-7528) Jenkins.
Printing, Book Collecting, & Illustrated Books: A Bibliography of Bibliographies. Theodore Besterman. LC 70-29686. 1971. write for info. (*0-87471-042-1*) Rowman.
Printing Digital Type on the Hand-Operated Flatbed Cylinder Press. Gerald Lange. 36p. 1999. pap. 20.00 (*0-931460-33-6*, Bieler Pr Monographs) Bieler.
*__Printing Equipment in Peru: A Strategic Entry Report, 1998.__ Compiled by Icon Group International Staff. (Country Industry Report). (Illus.). 137p. 1999. ring bd. 1370.00 incl. audio compact disk (*0-7418-0286-4*) Icon Grp.
Printing Estimating. Gerald A. Silver. LC 70-112001. 160p. reprint ed. pap. 49.60 (*0-608-11385-9*, 201115100074) Bks Demand.
Printing Estimating. 3rd ed. Philip K. Ruggles. 528p. 1990. text 48.95 (*0-8273-3805-8*) Delmar.
Printing Estimating. 4th ed. Philip K. Ruggles. (Graphic Communications Ser.). 800p. (C). 1996. mass mkt. 78.95 (*0-8273-6439-3*) Delmar.
Printing Estimating: Forms Book. Gerald A. Silver. LC Z 0245.S5. 78p. reprint ed. pap. 30.00 (*0-608-11543-6*, 201355800088) Bks Demand.
Printing Estimating: Policies & Procedures. Gerald A. Silver. LC 91-92965. (Illus.). 144p. (C). 1991. pap. 39.00 (*1-880472-05-8*) Edit Enter.
*__Printing Estimating Primer.__ Don Merit. (Illus.). 120p. (C). 2000. pap. text 25.00 (*0-88362-313-7*) GATFPress.
Printing Estimating Workbook. 3rd ed. Philip K. Ruggles. 48p. (C). reprint ed. pap. write for info. (*0-9638203-1-1*) Prtng Mgmt Srvs.
Printing Estimating Workbook. 4th rev. ed. Philip K. Ruggles. 64p. 1996. pap. 20.00 (*0-9638203-3-8*) Prtng Mgmt Srvs.
Printing Flaws on the Redesigned $50 Bill: Hearing before the Subcommittee on Domestic & International Monetary Policy of the Committee on Banking & Financial Services, House of Representatives, One Hundred Fifth Congress, First Session, October 1, 1997. LC 98-160113. iii, 67 p. 1997. write for info. (*0-16-056006-3*) USGPO.

P

Printing for Pleasure. John Ryder. (Illus.). 144p. 1976. reprint ed. 20.00 (*0-370-10443-9*, Pub. by Bodley Head) Oak Knoll.

Printing Fundamentals. Ed. by Alex Glassman. LC 85-50986. 340p. 1985. 68.00 (*0-89852-045-2*, 0102B045) TAPPI.

Printing Fundamentals. Ed. by Alex Glassman. LC 85-50986. reprint ed. pap. 102.30 (*0-608-17201-4*, 2027006) Bks Demand.

Printing in a Digital World. David Bergsland. (Graphic Communications Ser.). 512p. 1996. mass mkt. 55.95 (*0-8273-7280-9*) Delmar.

Printing in a Digital World - IRK. David Bergsland. 112p. 1996. 19.95 (*0-8273-7480-1*) Delmar.

Printing in Colonial Spanish America. Lawrence S. Thompson & Hensley C. Woodbridge. LC 75-8384. viii, 172p. 1976. 29.00 (*0-87875-076-2*) Whitston Pub.

Printing in Delaware, 1761-1800. Evald Rink. (Illus.). 214p. 1969. 5.00 (*0-914650-01-7*) Hagley Museum.

***Printing in Deseret: Mormons, Economy, Politics & Utah's Incunabula, 1849-1851.** Richard L. Saunders. 288p. 2000. 35.00 (*0-87480-663-1*) U of Utah Pr.

Printing In Integrated Netware Environment. Novellinc. (DF - Computer Applications Ser.). (C). 1998. pap. 80.95 (*0-538-68263-9*) S-W Pub.

Printing in Princeton, New Jersey, 1786-1876: A Bibliography. Joseph J. Felcone. (Illus.). 147p. 1992. 35.00 (*0-87811-037-2*) Princeton Lib.

Printing in Spain, 1501-1520: With a Note on the Early Editions of the "Celestina" Frederick J. Norton. LC 65-19156. (Sandars Lectures in Bibliography: 1963). 242p. reprint ed. pap. 69.00 (*0-608-11343-3*, 2022464) Bks Demand.

Printing in York from 1490's to 1976. W. K. Sessions & E. M. Sessions. 1999. 35.00 (*0-900657-37-5*, Pub. by W Sessions) St Mut.

Printing in York from 1490's to 1976. E. M. Sessions & William K. Sessions. (C). 1988. 57.00 (*0-7855-5035-6*, Pub. by W Sessions) St Mut.

Printing Industry Goldbook, 1998. Ed. by Holly Mogil. 1024p. 1998. pap. 425.00 (*1-888576-22-7*) North Am Pub Co.

Printing Industry Goldbook, 2000. Ed. by Lisa A. Denshuick. 1999. pap. 389.00 (*1-888576-62-6*) North Am Pub Co.

Printing Ink. C. Broyles. 200p. 2000. 1995.00 (*0-614-06125-3*, LE406) Lead Edge Reports.

Printing Ink & Overprint Varnish Formulations. Ernest W. Flick. 163p. 1991. 89.00 (*0-8155-1259-7*) Noyes.

Printing Ink & Overprint Varnish Formulations. 2nd ed. Ernest W. Flick. LC 99-20463. 1999. 109.00 (*0-8155-1440-9*) Noyes.

Printing Ink Formulations. Ernest W. Flick. LC 84-22636. 184p. 1985. 89.00 (*0-8155-1014-4*) Noyes.

Printing Inks. Pira Staff. 1998. 70.00 (*1-85802-027-1*, Pub. by Pira Pub) Bks Intl VA.

Printing Machines in France: A Strategic Entry Report, 1997. Compiled by Icon Group International Staff. (Illus.). 126p. 1999. ring bd. 1260.00 incl. audio compact disk (*0-7418-0880-3*) Icon Grp.

Printing Materials: Science & Tech. Pira Staff. 1999. 90.00 (*1-85802-150-2*, Pub. by Pira Pub) Bks Intl VA.

Printing of Books. Holbrook Jackson. LC 70-134100. (Essay Index Reprint Ser.). 1977. 26.95 (*0-8369-1931-9*) Ayer.

Printing of Greek in the Fifteenth Century. Robert Proctor. (Monographs: No. 8). (Illus.). 222p. 1966. reprint ed. 50.70 (*0-685-66506-2*, 05101254) G Olms Pubs.

Printing of Mathematics: Aids for Authors & Editions & Rules for Compositors & Readers at the University Press, Oxford. Theodore W. Chaundy et al. LC Z 0250.6.M3C. 119p. reprint ed. pap. 36.90 (*0-608-11126-0*, 205189600013) Bks Demand.

Printing on Specialty Items see Pocket Printer Series

Printing on Text & Cover Papers: Texture & Color. Text & Cover Paper Manufacturers of American Paper. Ed. by American Paper Institute, Inc. Staff. (Illus.). 140p. 1990. text 75.00 (*0-9625985-0-X*) Am Forest.

Printing on the Iron Handpress. Richard-Gabriel Rummonds. LC 97-26661. 1997. pap. 49.95 (*1-884718-40-X*) Oak Knoll.

Printing Paper & Inks. Charles Finley. LC 95-17854. 464p. (C). 1997. mass mkt. 54.95 (*0-8273-6441-5*) Delmar.

Printing Plant Layout & Facility Design. 2nd ed. A. John Geis. LC 97-73703. (Illus.). 120p. 1997. pap. text 65.00 (*0-88362-211-4*, 15352) GATFPress.

Printing, Politics & the People. Robert A. Gross. (James Russell Wiggins Lecture in the History of the Book in American Culture Ser.: Vol. 7). 22p. 1990. pap. 8.95 (*0-944026-20-6*) Am Antiquarian.

Printing, Politics & the People. Robert A. Gross. (James Russell Wiggins Lecture in the History of the Book in American Culture Ser.: Bk. 7). 25p. 1991. reprint ed. pap. 8.95 (*0-912296-99-2*) Am Antiquarian.

Printing Postage Stamps by Line Engraving. James H. Baxter. LC 81-50924. 1982. reprint ed. lib. bdg. 30.00 (*0-88000-129-1*) Quarterman.

Printing Power. 3rd rev. ed. Jan Z. Olsen. (Illus.). 64p. (J). (gr. 2). 1997. pap. text 4.75 (*1-891627-02-3*) Handwriting.

Printing Practice see Let's Learn Set

Printing Practice. (Home Workbooks Ser.). (Illus.). 64p. (J). (gr. k-1). 1995. pap., wbk. ed. 2.49 (*0-88724-332-0*, CD-6829) Carson-Dellos.

Printing Practice. Dona H. Rice. 32p. (J). (gr. k-2). 1997. pap. 2.95 (*1-57690-243-9*) Tchr Create Mat.

***Printing Practice Plus: Modern.** Linda Milliken. Ed. by Kathy Rogers. (Illus.). 32p. 1998. 4.95 (*1-56472-114-0*) Edupress Inc.

Printing Practice Plus/Traditional. Linda Milliken. 32p. 1998. wbk. ed. 4.95 (*1-56472-113-2*) Edupress Inc.

***Printing Press: A Breakthrough in Communication.** Richard Tames. LC 00-26084. (Point of Impact Ser.). (J). 2000. pap. write for info. (*1-57572-418-9*) Heinemann Lib.

Printing Press: Ideas into Type. Bradley Steffens. LC 90-6619. (Encyclopedia of Discovery & Invention Ser.). (Illus.). 96p. (J). (gr. 5-8). 1990. lib. bdg. 22.45 (*1-56006-205-3*) Lucent Bks.

Printing Press As an Agent of Change, 2 vols. in 1. Elizabeth L. Eisenstein. LC 77-91083. 832p. 1980. pap. text 52.95 (*0-521-29955-1*) Cambridge U Pr.

Printing Processes & Printing Inks, Carbon Black & Some Nitro Compounds: The Evaluation of Carcinogenic Risks to Humans. LC 96-209112. (IARC Monographs: No. 65). 578p. 1996. text 81.00 (*92-832-1265-7*) World Health.

Printing Production Workbook. Yoh Jinno. (Offset Printing Communication Guide System Ser.). (Illus.). 240p. 1990. 30.00 (*1-877661-06-6*); text 20.00 (*1-877661-05-8*) Jinno Intl.

Printing, Propaganda, & Martin Luther. Mark U. Edwards, Jr. LC 93-34056. 1994. 48.00 (*0-520-08462-4*, Pub. by U CA Pr) Cal Prin Full Svc.

Printing Revolution in Early Modern Europe. Elizabeth L. Eisenstein. (Canto Book Ser.). (Illus.). 314p. (C). 1993. pap. 13.95 (*0-521-44770-4*) Cambridge U Pr.

Printing Service Specialist's Handbook & Reference Guide. 850p. 200.00 (*0-614-25576-7*, 00SM44570) Print Indus Am.

Printing Teacher's Guide. 2nd ed. Jan Z. Olsen. (Illus.). 48p. 1997. pap. text, teacher ed. 4.75 (*1-891627-03-1*) Handwriting.

Printing Technology. 4th ed. Adams. (Graphic Communications Ser.). 32p. 1996. text, teacher ed. 14.00 (*0-8273-6908-5*) Delmar.

Printing Technology. 4th ed. J. Michael Adams et al. LC 95-34510. (Graphic Communications Ser.). 672p. (C). 1995. pap. 71.95 (*0-8273-6907-7*) Delmar.

Printing Technology: A Medium of Visual Communications. 3rd ed. J. Michael Adams & David D. Faux. 640p. 1987. pap. 48.95 (*0-8273-2775-7*) Delmar.

Printing Technology: A Medium of Visual Communications. 3rd ed. J. Michael Adams & David D. Faux. 640p. 1987. pap., teacher ed. 14.00 (*0-8273-2776-5*) Delmar.

***Printing the Image.** Joe Farace. LC 00-33881. (Digital Imaging Ser.). (Illus.). 2000. pap. write for info. (*1-883403-79-0*, Silver Pixel Pr) Saunders Photo.

Printing the Talmud: A History of the Individual Treatises Printed from 1700-1750. M. J. Heller. LC 98-53964. (Series in Jewish Studies). xiv, 390 p. 1999. 168.50 (*90-04-11293-6*) Brill Academic Pubs.

Printing the Written Word: The Social History of Books, c. 1450-1520. Ed. by Sandra Hindman. LC 91-55236. (Illus.). 336p. 1992. text 49.95 (*0-8014-2578-6*) Cornell U Pr.

Printing 2000. 99.00 (*0-614-25544-9*, 00BT23010) Print Indus Am.

Printing Types: An Introduction. rev. ed. Alexander S. Lawson & Dwight Agner. LC 70-136232. 160p. 1974. pap. 14.00 (*0-8070-6661-3*) Beacon Pr.

Printing Types, Their History, Forms & Use: A Study in Survivals, Vol. 1. 3rd ed. Daniel B. Updike. LC 62-5866. (Illus.). 526p. reprint ed. pap. 163.10 (*0-7837-4888-4*, 205905600001) Bks Demand.

Printing Types, Their History, Forms & Use: A Study in Survivals, Vol. 2. 3rd ed. Daniel B. Updike. LC 62-5866. (Illus.). 551p. reprint ed. pap. 170.90 (*0-7837-4889-2*, 205905600002) Bks Demand.

Printing with Peter Possum. Schaffer, Frank, Publications Staff. (Help Your Child Learn Ser.). (Illus.). 24p. (J). (gr. k-2). 1978. student ed. 3.98 (*0-86734-006-1*, FS-3007) Schaffer Pubns.

***Printing, Writers & Readers in Renaissance Italy.** Brian Richardson. LC 98-30354. (Illus.). 230p. (C). 1999. 59.95 (*0-521-57161-8*); pap. 22.95 (*0-521-57693-8*) Cambridge U Pr.

Printing 1770-1970. deluxe rev. ed. Michael Twyman. (Illus.). 285p. 1999. 95.00 (*1-884718-78-7*, 53588RB) Oak Knoll.

Printmakers: Currier & Ives; American on Stone; California on Stone. Harry T. Peters. 240.00 (*0-405-07705-X*, 93) Ayer.

Printmaker's World: Jack McLarty (1943-1996) Ed. by Barbara L. McLarty. LC 96-95351. (Illus.). 136p. (Orig.). 1997. 70.00 (*0-9644916-2-1*); pap. 35.00 (*0-9644916-3-X*) McLartys Choice.

Printmaking. (Take Five Art Ser.). (Illus.). 1997. teacher ed., student ed. 44.00 (*1-56290-171-0*, CP6093) Crystal.

Printmaking. 2nd ed. Saff. (C). 1999. pap. text 49.00 (*0-03-055358-X*) Harcourt Coll Pubs.

Printmaking: A Primary Form of Expression. Ed. by Eldon C. Cunningham. (Illus.). 264p. 1992. 39.95 (*0-87081-247-5*) Univ Pr Colo.

Printmaking: History & Process. Donald Saff & Deli Sacilotto. 158p. (C). 1978. pap. text 61.50 (*0-03-085663-9*, Pub. by Harcourt Coll Pubs) Harcourt.

Printmaking & Picture Printing: A Bibliographical Guide to Artistic & Industrial Techniques in Britain, 1750-1900. Gavin Bridson & Geoffrey Wakeman. 1984. 55.00 (*0-916271-00-5*) BkPr Ltd.

Printmaking in America: Collaborative Prints & Presses, 1960-1990. Trudy V. Hansen et al. LC 94-25246. 1995. pap. write for info. (*0-941680-15-0*) Abrams.

Printmaking in America: Collaborative Prints & Presses, 1960-1990. Trudy V. Hansen et al. LC 94-25246. (Illus.). 178p. 1995. 65.00 (*0-8109-3743-3*, Pub. by Abrams) Time Warner.

Printmaking in France, 1850-1900. Marjorie H. Beebe. 1982. 3.00 (*0-915478-48-X*) Montgomery Gallery.

Printmaking in the Service of Botany. G. D. Bridson & D. E. Wendel. (Illus.). 166p. 1986. pap. 20.00 (*0-913196-49-5*) Hunt Inst Botanical.

***Printmaking in the Sun.** Dan Welden & Pauline Muir. (Illus.). 144p. 2000. pap. 29.95 (*0-8230-4292-8*) Watsn-Guptill.

***Printout Design Made Easy 3.1H.** 236p. 1999. 45.00 (*1-893570-12-6*) SAP Labs.

***Printout Made Easy 3.0F.** 198p. 1999. 41.00 (*1-893570-11-8*) SAP Labs.

Printouts. Keith Rahmings. 36p. (Orig.). 1981. pap. 5.50 (*0-937013-06-4*) Potes Poets.

Printreading: Based on the 1999 NEC. R. T. Miller. (Illus.). 284p. 1998. pap. text 32.96 (*0-8269-1561-2*) Am Technical.

Printreading for Welders. 2nd ed. Thomas E. Proctor & Jonathan F. Gosse. LC 97-19353. (Illus.). 348p. 1997. 28.96 (*0-8269-3030-1*) Am Technical.

Prints. unabridged ed. Judy A. Sadler. (Kids Can Easy Crafts Ser.). (Illus.). 32p. (Orig.). (J). (gr. k up). 1997. pap. 5.95 (*1-55074-083-0*, Pub. by Kids Can Pr) Genl Dist Srvs.

***Prints: Art & Techniques.** Susan Lambert. (Illus.). 96p. 2000. pap. 19.95 (*1-85177-288-X*, Pub. by V&A Ent) Antique Collect.

***Prints Abound: Paris in the 1890s: From the Collections of Virginia & Ira Jackson & the National Gallery of Art.** Phillip Dennis Cate et al. LC 00-33261. (Illus.). 2000. write for info. (*0-89468-277-6*) Natl Gallery Art.

Prints & Books. William M. Ivins, Jr. LC 76-75295. (Graphic Art Ser.). 1969. reprint ed. lib. bdg. 49.50 (*0-306-71288-1*) Da Capo.

Prints & Drawings. Elizabeth Peak. (Illus.). 1982. pap. 5.00 (*0-916606-04-X*) Bowdoin Coll.

Prints & Drawings of Kathe Kollwitz. Kathe Kollwitz. Ed. by Carl Zigrosser. LC 73-76286. 72p. 1969. reprint ed. pap. 12.95 (*0-486-22177-6*) Dover.

Prints & Engraved Illustrations by & after Henry Fuseli: A Catalogue Raisonne. David H. Weinglass. LC 94-211877. (Illus.). 448p. 1994. 109.95 (*0-85967-882-2*, Pub. by Scolar Pr) Ashgate Pub Co.

Prints & Illustrated Books. Alan Wofsy. (Catalogue No. 4 Ser.). (Illus.). 1976. pap. 10.00 (*0-915346-13-3*) A Wofsy Fine Arts.

Prints & Illustrated Books Six Centuries. Antiquarian Catalogues Staff. (Illus.). 56p. 1974. 12.50 (*0-915346-21-4*) A Wofsy Fine Arts.

Prints & People: A Social History of Printed Pictures. A. Hyatt Mayor. LC 80-7817. (Illus.). 496p. 1980. pap. text 37.50 (*0-691-00326-2*, Pub. by Princeton U Pr) Cal Prin Full Svc.

Prints & Photographs: An Illustrated Guide. Bernard F. Reilly, Jr. 80p. 1995. pap. text 8.00 (*0-16-045377-1*, Library of Cong) USGPO.

Prints & Posters of Ben Shahn. Ben Shahn. (Illus.). 128p. 1982. pap. 12.95 (*0-486-24288-9*) Dover.

Prints & Posters of Ben Shahn. Ben Shahn. 1983. 25.00 (*0-8446-5944-4*) Peter Smith.

Prints & Printmakers of New York State, 1825-1940. Ed. by David Tatham. LC 86-3773. (New York State Bks.). (Illus.). 296p. 1986. 49.95 (*0-8156-0204-9*) Syracuse U Pr.

Prints & Printmakers of Texas: Proceedings of the Twentieth Annual North American Print Conference. Ed. by Ron Tyler. (Illus.). 370p. 1996. 39.95 (*0-87611-137-1*) Tex St Hist Assn.

Prints & Printmaking: An Introduction to the History & Techniques. Antony Griffiths. (Illus.). 152p. 1996. pap. 24.95 (*0-520-20714-9*, Pub. by U CA Pr) Cal Prin Full Svc.

Prints & Visual Communication. William M. Ivins, Jr. 1969. reprint ed. pap. text 18.50 (*0-262-59002-6*) MIT Pr.

Prints at the Essex Institute. Bettina A. Norton. Ed. by Anne Farnam & Bryant F. Tolles, Jr. LC 78-19448. (E.I. Museum Booklet Ser.). (Illus.). 1978. pap. 5.95 (*0-88389-069-0*, PEMP193, Essx Institute) Peabody Essex Mus.

Prints at the Smithsonian: The Origins of a National Collection. Smithsonian Institution Staff et al. LC 96-28741. 1996. write for info. (*0-929847-07-5*) Natl Mus Am.

Prints at the Smithsonian: The Origins of a National Collection. Helena E. Wright. (Illus.). 80p. (Orig.). 1996. pap. 24.95 (*1-56098-703-0*) Smithsonian.

Print's Best, No. 2: Typography. RC Pubns. Staff. (Illus.). 192p. 1996. 34.95 (*1-883915-00-7*) RC Pubns.

Print's Best, No. 4: Letterhead & Business Cards. RC Pubns. Staff. (Illus.). 192p. 1996. 34.95 (*1-883915-01-5*) RC Pubns.

Print's Best, No. 4: Logos & Symbols. 4th ed. RC Pubns. Staff. (Illus.). 192p. 1996. 34.95 (*1-883915-02-3*) RC Pubns.

Print's Best Booklets & Brochures. LC 94-67218. (Illus.). 192p. 1995. 34.95 (*0-915734-94-X*) RC Pubns.

Print's Best Corporate Publications. (Illus.). 192p. 1991. 34.95 (*0-915734-68-0*, 30355) RC Pubns.

Print's Best Illustration & Photography. Ed. by R C Publications Staff. 192p. 1994. 34.95 (*0-915734-82-6*, 30581) RC Pubns.

Print's Best Letterheads & Business Cards, No. 3. R C Publications Staff. 192p. 1994. 34.95 (*0-915734-84-2*, 30579) RC Pubns.

Print's Best Letterheads & Business Cards, 1992, No. 2. (Illus.). 192p. 1992. 34.95 (*0-915734-78-8*, 30392) RC Pubns.

***Print's Best Letterheads & Business Cards 6.** Caitlin Dover. (Illus.). 176p. 2000. 35.00 (*1-883915-10-4*) RC Pubns.

Print's Best Logos & Symbols, No. 3. R C Publications Staff. 192p. 1994. 34.95 (*0-915734-85-0*, 30580) RC Pubns.

Print's Best Logos & Symbols, 1992, No. 2. (Illus.). 192p. 1992. 34.95 (*0-915734-79-6*, 30391) RC Pubns.

***Print's Best Logos & Symbols 6.** Caitlin Dover. (Illus.). 176p. 2000. pap. 35.00 (*1-883915-09-0*) RC Pubns.

Print's Best T-Shirt Promotions. 2nd ed. (Illus.). 150p. 1995. 34.95 (*0-915734-95-8*) RC Pubns.

Print's Best T-Shirt Promotions, 1993. (Illus.). 146p. 1993. 34.95 (*0-915734-80-X*) RC Pubns.

Print's Best Typography. (Illus.). 192p. 1993. 34.95 (*0-915734-81-8*, 30498) RC Pubns.

Prints by Fairfield Porter: From the Lauris & Daniel J. Mason Collection. Joan Ludman. (Illus.). 8p. 1982. 10.00 (*0-685-70930-2*) Gal Assn NY.

Prints by Utagawa Hiroshige: The James A. Michener Collection, 2 vols., Vol. 1. Howard A. Link. (ENG & JPN., Illus.). 167p. (Orig.). (C). 1991. pap. 32.50 (*0-937426-13-X*, 6222) Honolu Arts.

Prints by Utagawa Hiroshige Vol. 2: The James A. Michener Collection, 2 vols., Set. Howard A. Link. (ENG & JPN., Illus.). 167p. (Orig.). (C). 1991. boxed set 49.95 (*0-937426-18-0*) Honolu Arts.

Prints, Drawings & Recent Accessions see Frick Collection: An Illustrated Catalogue

Prints, Drawings, Watercolors & Photographs. Barbara Morgan. LC 88-62482. (Illus.). 128p. 1988. pap. 35.00 (*0-87100-261-2*) Morgan.

Prints, 1460-1995: The Collections of the Nelson-Atkins Museum of Art. George L. McKenna. LC 96-13639. (Illus.). 358p. 1997. 74.95 (*0-942614-26-7*) Nelson-Atkins.

Prints from Kashghar: The Printing Office of the Swedish Mission in Eastern Turkestan History & Production. Gunnar Jarring. (Illus.). 140p. (Orig.). 1991. pap. 58.00 (*91-86884-04-2*) Coronet Bks.

Prints from Solo Impression, Inc., New York, New York. College of Wooster Art Museum Staff. Ed. by Thalia Gouma-Peterson. LC 94-72324. (Illus.). 52p. (C). 1994. 25.00 (*0-9604658-8-X*) Coll Wooster.

Prints from the Guggenheim Museum Collection. Linda Konheim. LC 78-59812. (Illus.). 1978. pap. 4.95 (*0-89207-015-3*) S R Guggenheim.

Prints in the Sand: The U. S. Coast Guard Beach Patrol During WWII. Eleanor Bishop. LC 89-62184. (Illus.). 92p. 1989. pap. 9.95 (*0-929521-22-6*) Pictorial Hist.

Prints, Maps & Drawings, 1677-1822. 3rd ed. (Picture Bks.). 1976. pap. 4.00 (*0-934909-61-X*) Mass Hist Soc.

Prints of a Priest: Writings by Father Elstan. Elstan Coghill. Ed. & Photos by Susan M. Orsen. LC 96-68734. (Illus.). 150p. (Orig.). 1996. pap. 16.95 (*0-9652263-0-1*) S M Orsen.

Prints of Adolf Dehn: A Catalogue Raisonne. Ed. by Thomas O'Sullivan. LC 87-7776. (Illus.). viii, 268p. 1987. 75.00 (*0-87351-203-0*) Minn Hist.

Prints of Anthony Gross: A Catalogue Raisonne. Robin Herdman. 144p. 1991. 121.95 (*0-85967-837-7*, Pub. by Scolar Pr) Ashgate Pub Co.

Prints of Barnett Newman, 1961-1969. Barnett Newman. 1997. 50.00 (*3-7757-0609-7*, Pub. by Gerd Hatje) Dist Art Pubs.

Prints of Emil Ganso. Donald E. P. Smith. LC 95-45001. (Illus.). 200p. (C). 1997. 69.50 (*0-8386-3593-8*) Fairleigh Dickinson.

Prints of J. N. Darling. Amy N. Worthen. LC 90-85789. (Illus.). 126p. 1991. pap. 19.95 (*0-8138-1995-4*) Iowa St U Pr.

Prints of Janet Fish: A Catalogue Raisonne. Linda K. Kramer & Stewart & Stewart Staff. Ed. by Carol Fuerstein. (Illus.). 61p. 1998. pap. 35.00 (*0-936598-06-9*) J Szoke Edns.

Prints of John S. DeMartelly, 1903-1979. Bill North. Ed. by Susan J. Bandes & Bonney Mayers. (Illus.). 96p. (Orig.). 1997. pap. 18.00 (*1-879147-14-9*) Kresge Art Mus.

Prints of Kathe Kollwitz. Intro. by Jack Rutberg. 20p. 1996. pap. 10.00 (*1-880566-12-5*) J Rutberg Fine Arts.

Prints of LeRoy Neiman: A Catalogue Raisonne of Serigraphs & Etchings, 1980-1990. Ed. by Maury Leibovitz & Richard Lynch. (Illus.). 212p. 1991. 150.00 (*0-685-40168-5*) Knoedler.

Prints of LeRoy Neiman: A Catalogue Raisonne of Serigraphs, Lithographs & Etchings. Ed. by Maury Leibovitz. (Illus.). 359p. 100.00 (*0-937608-00-9*) Knoedler.

Prints of Lyman Byxbe. Robert Crump & Jon Nelson. (Great Plains Art Ser.: No. 2). (Illus.). 32p. 1991. pap. text 10.00 (*0-938932-05-5*) U Nebr CFGPS.

Prints of Martin Lewis: A Catalogue Raisonne. Paul McCarron. LC 95-76596. (Illus.). 256p. 1995. 120.00 (*0-9628234-1-4*) M Hausberg.

Prints of Michael Mazur: With a Catalogue Raisonne, 1956-1999. Trudy V. Hansen et al. LC 99-54001. (Illus.). 222p. 2000. 50.00 (*1-55595-161-9*, Pub. by Hudson Hills) Natl Bk Netwk.

Prints of Michael Rothenstein. Tessa Sidey. 208p. 1993. 166.95 (*0-85967-901-2*, Pub. by Scolar Pr) Ashgate Pub Co.

Prints of New England. Ed. by Georgia B. Barnhill. (Illus.). 172p. 1991. 59.95 (*0-912296-92-5*, 39076) Oak Knoll.

Prints of Paul Jacoulet. Richard Miles. (Illus.). 140p. (C). 1982. pap. text 50.00 (*0-903697-13-0*) Pacific Asia.

Prints of Paul Jacoulet. Richard Miles. LC 82-81033. (Illus.). 140p. 1982. 75.00 (*1-877921-28-9*) Pacific Asia.

Prints of Peter Takal: Catalogue Raisonne of the Prints of Peter Takal. Compiled by Joseph Ishikawa. (Illus.). 96p. (Orig.). 1986. pap. 13.00 (*1-879147-07-6*) Kresge Art Mus.

Prints of R. B. Kitaj. Jane Kinsman. (Illus.). 200p. 1994. 121.95 (*0-85967-902-0*, Pub. by Scolar Pr) Ashgate Pub Co.

Prints of Richard Bosman, 1978-1988. Andrew Stevens. (Illus.). 1989. pap. 14.00 (*0-932900-21-6*) Elvehjem Mus.

An Asterisk (*) at the beginning of an entry indicates that the title is appearing for the first time.

***Prints of Rockwell Kent.** Dan Burne Jones. (Illus.). 2000. 150.00 (*1-55660-307-X*) A Wofsy Fine Arts.

***Prints of Roy Lichtenstein: A Catalogue Raisonne 1948-1997.** Mary Lee Corlett & Ruth E. Fine. (Illus.). 376p. 2000. 125.00 (*1-55595-196-1*, Pub. by Hudson Hills) Natl Bk Netwk.

Prints of Sam Francis: A Catalogue Raisonne, 1960-1990, 2 vols., Set. Connie W. Lembark. LC 91-58633. (Illus.). 612p. 1992. boxed set 125.00 (*1-55595-062-0*) Hudson Hills.

Prints of Samuel Chamberlain N. A. Narcissa G. Chamberlain & Jane F. Kingsland. 1984. 100.00 (*0-89073-095-4*, 300) Boston Public Lib.

Prints of Stanley William Hayter: A Complete Catalogue. Peter Black & Desiree Moorhead. (Illus.). 416p. 1992. 250.00 (*1-55921-049-4*) Moyer Bell.

Prints of the Floating World. Craig Hartley. 1997. 50.00 (*0-85331-698-8*, Pub. by Lund Humphries) Antique Collect.

Prints of the Fort Worth Circle, 1940-1960. Contrib. by Stephen Pinson. (Illus.). 45p. 1992. pap. 10.00 (*0-935213-22-8*) J S Blanton Mus.

Prints of the Remondinis: An Attempt to Reconstruct an Eighteenth-Century World of Pictures. Anton W. Boschloo. LC 98-161396. (Illus.). 450p. 1998. 75.00 (*90-5356-273-7*, Pub. by Amsterdam U Pr) U of Mich Pr.

Prints of the Twentieth Century: A History. rev. ed. Riva Castleman. LC 87-51289. (World of Art Ser.). (Illus.). 192p. 1988. pap. 14.95 (*0-500-20228-1*, Pub. by Thames Hudson) Norton.

Prints of the West: Prints from the Library of Congress. Ron Tyler. LC 93-50794. (Illus.). 208p. 1994. 39.95 (*1-55591-174-9*) Fulcrum Pub.

Prints of Theodore Roussel: A Catalogue Raisonne. Margaret D. Hausberg. LC 90-93487. (Illus.). 264p. 1991. 120.00 (*0-9628234-0-6*) M Hausberg.

***Prints U. S. A. 1999.** Contrib. by David Kiehl & Jerry A. Berger. (Illus.). 24p. 1999. 3.00 (*0-934306-25-7*) Springfield.

Printshop Handbook: A Technical Manual for Basic Intaglio, Relief, & Lithographic Processes. Beth Grabowksi. 176p. (C). 1993. text. write for info. (*0-697-14489-5*) Brown & Benchmark.

Printworld Directory of Contemporary Prints & Prices. 6th rev. ed. Selma L. Smith. (Illus.). 1200p. 1994. 249.95 (*0-943606-06-3*) Printworld.

Printworld Directory of Contemporary Prints & Prices. 7th rev. ed. Selma L. Smith. 1200p. 1996. 259.95 (*0-943606-07-1*) Printworld.

***Printworld Directory of Contemporary Prints & Prices.** 8th ed. Ed. by Selma L. Smith. 1250p. 1998. 265.00 (*0-943606-08-X*) Printworld.

Printworld Directory of Contemporary Prints & Prices, 1982. Selma L. Smith. 388p. 150.00 (*0-943606-00-4*) Printworld.

Printworld Directory of Contemporary Prints & Prices, 1983-84. Selma L. Smith. 1983. 150.00 (*0-943606-01-2*) Printworld.

Printworld Directory of Contemporary Prints & Prices, 1985-86. Selma L. Smith. 704p. 1985. 150.00 (*0-943606-02-0*) Printworld.

Printworld Directory of Contemporary Prints & Prices, 1988-89. Selma L. Smith. (Illus.). 760p. 1988. pap. 150.00 (*0-943606-03-9*) Printworld.

Printworld Directory of Contemporary Prints & Prices, 1991-92. Ed. by Selma L. Smith. 1060p. 1991. 250.00 (*0-943606-05-5*); pap. 225.00 (*0-943606-04-7*) Printworld.

Printz-Prince Family: Into the Family. Charles T. Printz. LC 94-80149. 450p. 1995. 98.00 (*0-9636320-2-7*) Nuggets Wisdom.

***Prinz Eisenbeton 2: Projects '96 To '99.** Wolf D. Prix. (Illus.). 360p. 2000. pap. 35.00 (*3-211-83323-4*) Spr-Verlag.

Prinz Louis Ferdinand. Lenk Lewald. Tr. by Linda Rogols-Siegel from GER. LC 88-13957. (Studies in German Thought & History: Vol. 6). 507p. 1989. lib. bdg. 119.95 (*0-88946-357-3*) E Mellen.

Prinzip Handlung in der Philosophie Kants. Friedrich Kaulbach. (C). 1978. 134.65 (*3-11-007219-X*) De Gruyter.

Prinzipien Chrislicher Moral see Principles of Christian Morality

Prinzipien der Ethik Emanuel Hirschs. Matthias Lobe. (Theologische Bibliothek Toepelmann Ser.: Band 68). (GER.). xi, 295p. (C). 1995. lib. bdg. 121.55 (*3-11-014429-8*) De Gruyter.

Prinzipien der Wortstellungsvariation: Eine Vergleichende Analyse. Sarah Heydenreich. (GER.). 224p. 1997. 42.95 (*3-631-31796-4*) P Lang Pubng.

Prinzipien und Praxis des Englischen Unterrichts. Rudolf Munch. (GER.). 2442p. 1972. 47.80 (*3-296-50600-4*, Pub. by Weidmann) Lubrecht & Cramer.

Prinzipien Wirtschaftlichen Handelns & Ihre Anwendung: Umrib Einer Wirtschaftsphilosophie. Wolfgang H. Muller. (Illus.). 141p. 1996. 31.95 (*3-631-30477-3*) P Lang Pubng.

Prinzipienproblem in der Philosophie des Thomas von Aquin. Wilfried Kuehn. (Bochum Studies in Philosophy: No. 1). xxxviii, 555p. 1982. 71.00 (*90-6032-227-4*, Pub. by B R Gruner) Humanities.

Prinzipienwissenschaftliche Systematik und "Politischer Impetus" Eine Untersuchung zur Padagogik Alfred Petzelts. Peter Kauder. Ed. by Wolfgang Fischer et al. (Paideia - Studien zur Systamitischen Padogogik: Bd. 14). (GER.). 171p. 1997. 39.95 (*3-631-32167-8*) P Lang Pubng.

***Prion Biology & Diseases.** Ed. by Stanley B. Prusiner. (Monographs). (Illus.). 710p. (C). 1999. 125.00 (*0-87969-547-1*) Cold Spring Harbor.

Prion Diseases. Ed. by Harry F. Baker & Rosalind M. Ridley. LC 96-3408. (Methods in Molecular Medicine Ser.: Vol. 3). (Illus.). 336p. 1996. 99.00 (*0-89603-342-2*) Humana.

Prion Diseases. Ed. by John Collinge & Mark Palmer. LC 96-30984. (Illus.). 212p. 1997. text 59.50 (*0-19-854789-7*) OUP.

Prion Diseases of Mammals & Yeast: Molecular Mechanisms & Genetic Features. Reed B. Wickner. LC 96-6593. (Medical Intelligence Unit Ser.). 71p. 1996. 99.00 (*1-57059-399-X*) Landes Bioscience.

Prions: Molecular & Cellular Biology. Ed. by David A. Harris. LC 99-206578. (Illus.). 1999. 129.99 (*1-898486-07-7*, Pub. by Horizon Sci) Intl Spec Bk.

Prions & Brain Diseases in Animals & Humans. Ed. by Douglas R. Morrison. LC 98-12133. (NATO ASI Ser.: No. 295). (Illus.). 372p. (C). 1998. text 125.00 (*0-306-45825-X*, Kluwer Plenum) Kluwer Academic.

Prions en Chantant: Devotional Songs of the Trouveres. Marcia J. Epstein. (Toronto Medieval Texts & Translations Ser.). (FRE.). 240p. 1997. pap. text 18.95 (*0-8020-7826-5*) U of Toronto Pr.

Prions (Prusiner's Particles) Index of New Information. Science & Life Consultants Association Staff. 160p. 1998. 47.50 (*0-7883-1866-7*); pap. 44.50 (*0-7883-1867-5*) ABBE Pubs Assn.

Prior Analytics. Aristotle. Ed. & Tr. by Robin Smith from GRE. LC 88-39877. (HPC Classics Ser.). 320p. (C). 1989. pap. 16.95 (*0-87220-064-7*) Hackett Pub.

Prior Analytics. Aristotle. Tr. & Intro. by Robin Smith. LC 88-39877. (HPC Classics Ser.). 320p. (C). 1989. lib. bdg. 37.95 (*0-87220-065-5*) Hackett Pub.

Prior Claim - Chinese Edition. Moody Institute of Science Staff. Tr. by CRM Staff. (CHI.). 15p. 1985. pap. 0.50 (*1-56582-067-3*) Christ Renew Min.

Prior Consent to International Direct Satellite Broadcasting. David I. Fisher. (C). 1990. lib. bdg. 99.00 (*0-7923-0692-9*) Kluwer Academic.

Prior Consultation in International Law: A Study of State Practice. Frederic L. Kirgis. LC 82-17354. (Procedural Aspects of International Law Ser.). ix, 389p. 1983. 52.00 (*0-8139-0971-6*, 306500) W S Hein.

Prior Conviction in DUI Prosecutions: A Prosecutor's Guide to Prove Out-of-State DUI - DWI Convictions. American Prosecutors Research Institute Staff. 620p. 1998. pap. write for info. (*0-327-00228-X*, 61442-10) LEXIS Pub.

Prior Convictions: Stories from the Sixties. Dave Hickey. LC 88-43253. (Southwest Life & Letters Ser.). 200p. 1989. 17.95 (*0-87074-286-8*) SMU Press.

Prior Convictions in DWI Prosecutions: A Prosecutor's Guide to Prove Out-of-State DUI/DWI Convictions. National Traffic Law Center. LC 97-71670. (Illus.). xi, 1046p. 1997. 100.00 (*1-55834-498-5*, MICHIE) LEXIS Pub.

Prior Domestic Commerical Use Act of 1995: Hearing Before the Subcommittee on Courts & Intellectual Property of the Committee on the Judiciary House of Representatives. (Illus.). 72p. 1998. pap. text 25.00 (*0-7881-4879-6*) DIANE Pub.

Prior Engagement. Elizabeth Mansfield. 240p. 1990. pap. text 4.50 (*0-515-10398-5*, Jove) Berkley Pub.

Prior Information in Linear Models. Helge Toutenburg. LC 81-14653. (Wiley Series in Probability & Mathematical Statistics). 225p. reprint ed. pap. 69.80 (*0-7837-3232-5*, 204325100007) Bks Demand.

Prior Learning Assessment. CAEL Staff. 208p. 1999. per. 24.95 (*0-7872-5589-0*, 41558901) Kendall-Hunt.

Prior to Consciousness: Talks with Sri Nisargadatta Maharaj. Nisargadatta Maharaj. Ed. by Jean Dunn. LC 89-81145. xi, 157p. 1997. reprint ed. pap. 13.95 (*0-89386-024-7*) Acorn NC.

Prior User Rights (relative To Patents) Hearing Before the Subcommittee on Intellectual Property & Judicial Administration of the Committee on the Judiciary, House of Representatives, One Hundred Third Congress, Second Session, September 13, 1994. USGPO Staff. LC 95-179038. iv, 168p. 1995. write for info. (*0-16-046811-6*) USGPO.

Prioress' Prologue & Tale. Geoffrey Chaucer. Ed. by J. Winny. LC 74-19531. (Selected Tales from Chaucer Ser.). 64p. 1975. pap. text 10.95 (*0-521-20744-4*) Cambridge U Pr.

Prioress' Tale. Margaret Frazer. 256p. 1997. mass mkt. 5.99 (*0-425-15944-2*, Prime Crime) Berkley Pub.

Prioress's Tale. Geoffrey Chaucer. Ed. by Beverly Boyd. LC 86-25064. (Variorum Edition of the Works of Geoffrey Chaucer, The Canterbury Tales Ser.: Vol. II, Pt. 20). (Illus.). 224p. 1987. 49.95 (*0-8061-2045-2*) U of Okla Pr.

Priorganize! The Working from Home Wealth Plan. Peter McGugan. (Illus.). 128p. (Orig.). 1997. pap. 12.95 (*0-614-29793-1*) Potentls Pr.

***Priori: The Great Deception.** Jay R. Kinney. 494p. 2000. pap. 18.95 (*0-9677640-1-7*) New Image Graphics.

***Priori Knowledge.** Ed. by Albert Casullo. LC 98-45963. (International Research Library of Philosophy). 560p. 1999. text 194.95 (*1-85521-983-2*, Pub. by Ashgate Pub) Ashgate Pub Co.

Prioridad Uno. Norm Lewis.Tr. of Priority One. (SPA.). 177p. 1990. pap. 4.50 (*1-56063-079-5*, 498483) Editorial Unilit.

Priorites et Strategies Pour L'Education: Une Etude de la Banque Mondiale. (Development in Practice Ser.). (FRE.). 212p. 1996. 11.95 (*0-8213-3410-7*, 13410) World Bank.

Priorites pour l'Amenagement & la Planification du Developpement des Peches Continentales dans la Region du Sahel. (FRE.). 145p. 1993. 15.00 (*92-5-203289-4*, Pub. by FAO) Bernan Associates.

Priorities. Charles E. Hummel. (Christian Basics Bible Studies). 64p. (Orig.). 1994. pap., wbk. ed. 4.99 (*0-8308-2006-X*, 2006) InterVarsity.

Priorities & Christian Ethics. Garth L. Hallett. LC 97-41080. (New Studies in Christian Ethics: Vol. 12). 240p. (C). 1998. 54.95 (*0-521-62351-0*) Cambridge U Pr.

Priorities & Strategies for Education: A World Bank Review. Development in Practice Staff. LC 95-18770. 176p. 1995. pap. 22.00 (*0-8213-3311-9*, 13311) World Bank.

Priorities & Strategies for Education: A World Work Review. (Development in Practice Ser.). (SPA.). 190p. 1996. pap. 22.00 (*0-8213-3411-5*, 13411) World Bank.

Priorities for Arts Education Research. Government Printing Office Staff. 25p. 1997. pap. 3.25 (*0-16-049264-5*) USGPO.

Priorities for Coastal Ecosystem Science. National Research Council Staff. 116p. (Orig.). (C). 1995. pap. text 29.00 (*0-309-05096-0*) Natl Acad Pr.

Priorities for Environmental Expenditures in Industry: Eastern Europe & the Former Soviet Union. Mark Ambler & John Marrow. LC 97-35148. (Report for the Environmental Action Programme for Central & Eastern Europe Ser.). 265p. 1998. pap. 22.00 (*0-8213-4086-7*, 14086) World Bank.

Priorities for Forestry & Agroforestry Policy Research: Report on an International Workshop. Ed. by Hans Gregersen et al. LC 92-11620. 1992. write for info. (*0-89629-323-8*) Intl Food Policy.

Priorities for Health Promotion & Disease Prevention. Gerald C. Hyner & Christopher L. Melby. 178p. 1987. pap. text 19.95 (*0-912855-74-6*) E Bowers Pub.

Priorities for Planning in Vocational Education: Alternatives for the 1970s. Leonard A. Lecht. LC 75-37419. 68p. 1975. 3.00 (*0-89068-006-X*) Natl Planning.

Priorities for Postsecondary Education in the South. 2.00 (*0-686-22200-8*) S Regional Ed.

***Priorities for the Conservation of Mammalian Diversity: Has the Panda Had Its Day?** Ed. by Abigail Entwistle & Nigel Dunstone. (Conservation Biology Ser.: Vol. 3). (Illus.). 421p. (C). 2000. write for info. (*0-521-77279-6*); pap. write for info. (*0-521-77536-1*) Cambridge U Pr.

***Priorities in Biopesticide Research & Development in Developing Countries.** J. Harris & D. Dent. (CABI Publishing Ser.). 90p. 2000. pap. text. write for info. (*0-85199-479-2*) OUP.

Priorities in Critical Care Nursing. Linda D. Urden et al. (Illus.). 1996. teacher ed. write for info. (*0-8151-8948-6*) Mosby Inc.

Priorities in Critical Care Nursing. 2nd rev. ed. Linda D. Urden et al. Ed. by Mary E. Lough. LC 95-20589. (Illus.). 552p. (C). (gr. 13). 1995. text 48.00 (*0-8151-8947-8*, 26419) Mosby Inc.

***Priorities in Critical Care Nursing.** 3rd ed. Stacey Urden. 1999. pap. text 54.95 (*0-323-01000-8*) Mosby Inc.

Priorities in Planning. M. Gane. 1969. 30.00 (*0-85074-007-X*) St Mut.

Priorities in Psychiatric Research. Ed. by Malcolm H. Lader. LC 80-40583. 245p. reprint ed. pap. 76.00 (*0-608-12314-5*, 202428000035) Bks Demand.

Priorities in Religious Education. Ed. by Brenda Watson. 200p. 1992. 79.95 (*0-7507-0016-5*, Falmer Pr); pap. 34.95 (*0-7507-0017-3*, Falmer Pr) Taylor & Francis.

Priorities of the British Presidency of the European Union. 40p. 1998. pap. 15.00 (*1-886607-09-5*) European Inst.

Priorities That Count Student Book, Connections: School & Work Transitions - Employer's Choice. National Center for Research in Vocational Educati. 1987. 4.00 (*0-317-03907-5*, SP100BB01) Ctr Educ Trng Employ.

Prioritization of Generic Safety Issues. 176p. 1996. ring bd. 18.00 (*0-16-062682-X*) USGPO.

***Prioritization of Generic Safety Issues.** 416p. 1998. ring bd. 32.00 (*0-16-062733-8*) USGPO.

Prioritizing Academic Programs & Services: Reallocating Resources to Achieve Strategic Balance. Robert C. Dickeson. LC 98-40254. (Higher & Adult Education Ser.). 1999. 26.95 (*0-7879-4816-0*) Jossey-Bass.

Prioritizing Instruction: The Imperative Is of the Now. Joel L. Burdin. LC 96-60905. (NCPEA Yearbook Ser.). 344p. 1996. text 49.95 (*1-56676-473-4*) Scarecrow.

***Priority.** Iselin C. Hermann. Tr. by G. Forester from DAN. 96p. 2000. 21.00 (*0-8021-1667-1*, Grove) Grove-Atltic.

Priority Areas for Threatened Birds in the Neotropics. D. C. Wege & A. J. Long. (Birdlife Conservation Ser.). (Illus.). 370p. 1995. pap. text 49.95 (*1-56098-529-1*) Smithsonian.

Priority Health Conditions: An Integrated Strategy to Evaluate the Relationship Between Illness & Exposure to Hazardous Substances. Ed. by Jeffrey A. Lybarger et al. 214p. (Orig.). (C). 1994. pap. text 50.00 (*0-7881-0530-2*) DIANE Pub.

Priority: Home! Federal Plan to Break the Cycle of Homelessness. 126p. pap. text 35.00 (*0-7881-1586-3*) DIANE Pub.

Priority Issues in Trade & Investment Liberalization: Implications for the Asia Pacific Region. Bijit Bora & Mari Pangestu. LC 98-474063. ix, 215p. 1996. write for info. (*981-00-7785-8*, Pub. by AgBe Pub) Balogh.

Priority Male: Return to Sender. Susan Kearney. (Intrigue Ser.: Vol. 478). 1998. per. 3.99 (*0-373-22478-8*, 1-22478-1) Harlequin Bks.

***Priority of Philippians.** Charles Ozanne. 36p. 2000. pap. 4.00 (*1-880573-56-3*) Bible Search Pubns.

Priority of Prudence: Virtue & Natural Law in Thomas Aquinas & the Implications for Modern Ethics. Daniel M. Nelson. 224p. 1992. text 32.50 (*0-271-00778-8*) Pa St U Pr.

Priority One see Prioridad Uno

Priority One/Faith Promise. Norm Lewis. LC 88-70157. 192p. 1988. reprint ed. pap. 7.95 (*0-87808-215-8*, WCL215-8) O M Lit.

***Priority Pasture Research & Education Needs: A Supplement to the Proceedings from Grazing in the Northeast: Assessing Current Technologies, Research Directions & Education Needs.** Ed. by Charles R. Krueger & Harry B. Pionke. 12p. 1998. pap. text, suppl. ed. 5.00 (*0-935817-41-7*, 113S) NRAES.

Priority Research for Health for All. (European Health for All Ser.: No. 3). 1988. pap. text 15.00 (*92-890-1054-1*) World Health.

Priority Setting: The Health Care Debate. Ed. by Joanna Coast et al. LC 95-42635. 294p. 1996. 98.95 (*0-471-96102-7*) Wiley.

Priority-Setting & Strategic Sourcing in the Naval Research, Development & Technology Infrastructure. Kenneth V. Saunders et al. LC 95-33014. 141p. 1995. pap. 15.00 (*0-8330-2290-3*, MR-588-NAVY/OSD) Rand Corp.

Priority Setting in Action: Purchasing Dilemmas. Frank Honigsbaum et al. LC 95-23267. 1995. text. write for info. (*1-85775-100-0*, Radcliffe Med Pr) Scovill Paterson.

***Priority-Setting in Conservation.** Biodiversity Support Program Staff. LC 99-42659. (ENG, TAR, UKR, RUS & CRE.). 1999. pap. write for info. (*1-887531-31-9*) Biodivers Supp Prog.

Priority Setting Processes for Healthcare: In Oregon, U.S.A; New Zealand; the Netherlands; Sweden; & the United Kingdom. Frank Honigsbaum. LC 94-38269. 1995. pap. 29.95 (*1-85775-033-0*, Radcliffe Med Pr) Scovill Paterson.

Priority Setting Skills see Productive Supervisor: A Program of Practical Managerial Skills

Priority Workers Visa Package. American Immigration Center Staff. (Do-it-Yourself Immigration Ser.). 52p. 1998. pap. 69.00 (*0-9663425-4-2*) Amer Immig Ctr.

Priory of St. Bernard: An Old English Tale. M. Harley. Ed. by Devendra P. Varma. LC 77-2039. (Gothic Novels III Ser.). 1977. reprint ed. lib. bdg. 51.95 (*0-405-10138-4*) Ayer.

Priscian of Caesares's "De Laude Anastasii Imperatoris" Tr. by Patricia Coyne from LAT. LC 91-20935. (Studies in Classics: Vol. 1). 248p. 1991. lib. bdg. 89.95 (*0-7734-9772-2*) E Mellen.

***Prisciani Institutionum Grammaticalium Librorum XVII et XVIII: Indices et Concordantiae.** Cirilo Garcia Roman. (Alpha-Omega Ser.: Reihe A, Bd. CXCII). (GER.). 968p. 1999. 160.00 (*3-487-10791-0*, Pub. by G Olms Verlag) Lubrecht & Cramer.

Priscians Partitiones und Ihre Stellung in der Spatantiken Schule. Manfred Gluck. (GER.). 249p. 1967. write for info. (*0-318-70617-2*) G Olms Pubs.

Priscilla. Colene Copeland. LC 81-80663. (Illus.). 212p. (Orig.). (J). (gr. 3 up). 1981. 8.95 (*0-939810-01-8*); pap. 3.95 (*0-939810-02-6*) Jordan Valley.

Priscilla Alden & the First Thanksgiving. Alice B. Boynton. 32p. (J). (ps-3). 1996. pap. text 4.95 (*0-382-39474-7*) Silver Burdett Pr.

Priscilla Alden & the First Thanksgiving. Alice Benjamin Boynton. LC 89-49539. (Let's Celebrate Ser.). 1990. 10.15 (*0-606-10288-4*, Pub. by Turtleback) Demco.

Priscilla Alden & the Story of the First Thanksgiving. Alice B. Boynton. Ed. by Bonnie Brook. (Let's Celebrate Ser.). (Illus.). 32p. (J). (gr. k-2). 1990. lib. bdg. 6.95 (*0-671-69105-8*) Silver Burdett Pr.

Priscilla Bunbury's Virginal Book: A Collection of Keyboard Music for a Young Lady of the Seventeenth Century. Ed. by Virginia Brookes. (Illus.). xi, 40p. 1993. pap. text 30.00 (*1-56571-052-5*, EK003) PRB Prods.

Priscilla Foster: The Story of a Salem Girl. Dorothy Hoobler et al. LC 96-23390. (Her Story Ser.). (Illus.). 128p. (J). (gr. 4-5). 1997. pap. 4.95 (*0-382-39641-3*); lib. bdg. 14.95 (*0-382-39640-5*) Silver Burdett Pr.

Priscilla Hauser's Book of Decorative Painting. Priscilla Hauser. LC 97-3544. (Illus.). 144p. 1997. pap. 24.99 (*0-89134-722-4*, North Lght Bks) F & W Pubns Inc.

Priscilla Hauser's Folk Art Painting for Home Decoration. Priscilla Hauser. (Illus.). 160p. 1986. pap. 19.95 (*0-13-710831-1*) P-H.

Priscilla, Queen of the Desert. 1995. 14.95 (*0-7935-4293-6*, 00313009) H Leonard.

Priscilla Scales & Other Cautionary Tales. Barbara Petrie. (C). 1990. 45.00 (*0-947333-04-5*, Pub. by Pascoe Pub) St Mut.

Priscilla Tadpole. Gwen Costello. Ed. by Mary C. Kendzia. (Illus.). 32p. (Orig.). (J). 1992. pap. 4.95 (*0-89622-527-5*) Twenty-Third.

Priscilla Twice. Judith Caseley. LC 94-12988. (Illus.). 32p. (J). (gr. k up). 1995. 15.00 (*0-688-13305-3*, Grenwillow Bks); lib. bdg. 14.93 (*0-688-13306-1*, Grenwillow Bks) HarpC Child Bks.

Priscilla's Letter: Finding the Author of the Epistle to the Hebrews. Ruth Hoppin. LC 96-52682. 264p. 1997. 74.95 (*1-57309-152-9*); pap. 54.95 (*1-57309-151-0*) Intl Scholars.

***Priscilla's Letter: Finding the Author of the Epistle to the Hebrews.** Ruth Hoppin. 176p. 2000. pap. 19.95 (*1-882897-50-1*) Lost Coast.

Priscilla's Patch. Marian F. Nelson. LC 97-69071. (Illus.). 32p. (J). (ps-2). 1997. 14.95 (*1-882792-52-1*) Proctor Pubns.

Prise: Plume Rise & Dispersion Model. B. Henderson-Sellers. 1987. ring bd. 690.00 incl. disk (*0-931215-84-6*, 1996) Computational Mech MA.

Prise De Defur & le Voyage D'Alexandre au Paradis Terrestre. L. P. Peckham. (Elliott Monographs: Vol. 35). 1974. reprint ed. 24.00 (*0-527-02638-7*) Periodicals Srv.

***Prisionero.** Jon Kregel. (SPA.). 144p. 1999. pap. 7.99 (*0-8254-1390-7*, Edit Portavoz) Kregel.

P

Prisionero de Gozo/Prisoner of Joy. Jack W. Hayford. (Serie Vida en Plenitud/Spirit Filled Ser.). 1996. pap. 7.99 (*0-89922-518-7*) Caribe Betania.

Prisionero de la Tercera Celda (Novela) - The Prisoner in Celd Third. Edwards. pap. write for info. (*0-7899-0077-7*) Editorial Unilit.

***Prism.** Austin Bay. 2000. pap. 21.00 (*0-06-095565-1*) HarpC.

Prism: The Journal of John Fish. F. R. Thomas. Ed. by Brian Browning & Joe Dionne. (Illus.). 116p. (Orig.). 1992. pap. 10.00 (*0-945950-06-3*) Canoe Pr MI.

Prism & Lens Making: A Textbook for Optical Glassworkers. 2nd ed. Frank Twyman. (Optics & Optoelectronics Ser.). (Illus.). 640p. 1988. pap. 95.00 (*0-85274-150-2*) IOP Pub.

Prism Moon. Martine Bates. (Northern Lights Young Novels Ser.). 165p. (J). (gr. 3-9). 1993. pap. 8.95 (*0-88995-095-4*, Pub. by Red Deer) Genl Dist Srvs.

Prism of Lyra: An Exploration of Human Galactic Heritage. rev. ed. Lyssa Royal & Keith Priest. 114p. 1991. reprint ed. pap. 11.95 (*0-9631320-0-8*) Royal Priest.

Prism of Night: A Biography of Anne Rice. Katherine M. Ramsland. 432p. 1994. pap. 13.95 (*0-452-27331-5*, Plume) Dutton Plume.

Prism of Science. Ed. by Edna Ullmann-Margalit. 260p. 1986. lib. bdg. 97.00 (*90-277-2160-2*, D Reidel) Kluwer Academic.

Prism of Science. Ed. by Edna Ullmann-Margalit. 260p. 1986. pap. text 62.50 (*90-277-2161-0*, D Reidel) Kluwer Academic.

Prism of Sex - Essays in the Sociology of Knowledge: Proceedings of a Symposium Sponsored by WRI of Wisconsin, Inc. Ed. by Julia A. Sherman & Evelyn T. Beck. LC 79-3969. 295p. reprint ed. pap. 91.50 (*0-608-09928-7*, 206926600003) Bks Demand.

Prism of the Self: Philosophical Essays in Honor of Maurice Natanson. Ed. by Steven G. Crowell. (Contributions to Phenomenology Ser.). 372p. (C). 1995. lib. bdg. 166.00 (*0-7923-3546-5*, Pub. by Kluwer Academic) Kluwer Academic.

Prism of Thought. Ed. by Diana Zeiger. 1997. 69.95 (*1-57553-405-3*) Watermrk Pr.

Prism of Time & Eternity: Images of Christ in American Protestant Thought, from Jonathan Edwards to Horace Bushnell. Bruce M. Stephens. LC 96-17618. (ATLA Monographs: No. 42). 224p. 1996. 42.00 (*0-8108-3172-4*) Scarecrow.

Prism on Globalization Corporate Responses to the Dollar Subramanian Rangan. LC 99-6415. 1999. 36.95 (*0-8157-7360-9*) Brookings.

Prism on Globalization: Corporate Responses to the Dollar. Subramanian Rangan. LC 99-6415. 1999. pap. text. write for info. (*0-8157-7359-5*) Brookings.

***Prism Weight Loss Program: Transforming the Whole Person.** Karen Kingsbury & Toni Vogt. 250p. 1999. 19.99 (*1-57673-578-8*, Pub. by Multnomah Pubs) GL Services.

Prism Workbook. David B. Wexler. LC 91-9530. 73p. (Orig.). 1991. pap. 12.95 (*0-393-70119-0*) Norton.

Prisma: Dokumente, Literatur, Kommunikation. Mark W. Rectanus & Renate Hiller. (GER.). 314p. (C). 1992. pap. text 31.96 (*0-669-20492-7*) HM Trade Div.

Prisma de la Razon. Armando A. Bravo. LC 89-82739. (Coleccion Espejo de Paciencia). (SPA.). 92p. (Orig.). 1990. pap. 15.00 (*0-89729-562-5*) Ediciones.

Prisma Modern English-Swedish Dictionary. B. Danielsson. (ENG & SWE.). 394p. 1980. 49.95 (*0-7859-0912-5*, M9451) Fr & Eur.

Prisma Modern Swedish-English Dictionary. T. Omarbetade. (ENG & SWE.). 394p. 1980. 24.95 (*0-8288-1678-6*, M9450) Fr & Eur.

Prisma's Abridged English-Swedish & Swedish-English Dictionary. abr. ed. Prisma Staff. LC 94-49413. (ENG & SWE.). 480p. 1995. 26.95 (*0-8166-2734-7*) U of Minn Pr.

P

Prisma's English-Swedish Dictionary. 3rd ed. Prisma Staff. LC 97-27429. (SWE.). 1997. write for info. (*0-8166-3162-X*) U of Minn Pr.

Prisma's Lilla Modern French-Swedish, Swedish-French Dictionary: Prismas Lilla Moderna Fransk-Svensk Och Svensk-Franska Ordbok. Prisma Staff. (FRE & SWE.). 585p. 1983. 75.00 (*0-8288-1680-8*, F31845) Fr & Eur.

Prisma's Unabridged Swedish-English & English-Swedish Dictionary. 3rd ed. Prisma Staff. LC 99-230157. (ENG & SWE.). 1997. 69.95 (*0-8166-3231-6*) U of Minn Pr.

Prismatic Thought: Theodor W. Adorno. Peter U. Hohendahl. LC 95-3048. (Modern German Culture & Literature Ser.). xi, 287p. 1995. pap. text 25.00 (*0-8032-7305-3*) U of Nebr Pr.

Prismatic Thought: Theodor W. Adorno. Peter U. Hohendahl. LC 95-3048. (Modern German Culture & Literature Ser.). xi, 287p. 1995. text 50.00 (*0-8032-2378-1*) U of Nebr Pr.

PRISMIND - Scientific Theory of Crystal Consciousness. L. Zachary Shatz. LC 98-96431. (Illus.). 65p. 1998. pap. 4.95 (*1-892814-10-2*) PRISMIND.

Prisms. Theodor W. Adorno. Tr. by Samuel Weber & Shierry Weber from GER. 272p. (C). 1983. pap. text 14.95 (*0-262-51025-1*) MIT Pr.

Prisms. Mark Dunster. 21p. (Orig.). (YA). (gr. 9-12). 1997. pap. 5.00 (*0-89642-341-7*) Linden Pubs.

Prisms: A Collection of Short Stories. Richard C. Baxter. LC 92-2413. 368p. 1992. 18.95 (*0-912526-57-2*) Lib Res.

Prisms: Being God's Light for Missionaries Through Prayer & Ministry. Stuart Calvert. Ed. by Susan Hansen. 96p. 1996. pap. text 7.95 (*1-56309-167-4*, N964104, New Hope) Womans Mission Union.

Prisms of the Soul: Writing from a Sisterhood. Episcopal Church Women Staff. Ed. by Marcy Darin. (Illus.). 128p. 1996. pap. 10.95 (*0-8192-1676-3*) Morehouse Pub.

Prison: Policy & Practice. Gordon J. Hawkins. LC 75-20892. (Studies in Crime & Justice). 230p. 1977. pap. text 10.00 (*0-226-32000-6*, P749) U Ch Pr.

Prison - Not Me! large type unabridged ed. Mrs. Richardson's & Mrs. Doyle's 5th Grade Class,. (WeWrite Kids! Ser.: No. 39). (Illus.). 45p. (J). (gr. 3-5). 1998. pap. 3.95 (*1-57635-021-5*) WeWrite.

Prison Administration in India. B. V. Trivedi. (C). 1987. 21.00 (*81-85024-13-8*, Pub. by Uppal Pub Hse) S Asia.

Prison & Criminological Aspects of the Control of Transmissible Diseases Including AIDS & Related Health Problems in Prison (Recommendation & Explanatory Memorandum), No. R(93)6. LC 96-147469. 1995. 12.00 (*92-871-2595-3*, Pub. by Council of Europe) Manhattan Pub Co.

Prison & Jails see Crime & Justice in American History

Prison & Plantation: Crime, Justice, & Authority in Massachusetts & South Carolina, 1767-1878. Michael S. Hindus. LC 79-19493. (Studies in Legal History). 313p. 1980. reprint ed. pap. 97.10 (*0-608-02067-2*, 206272000003) Bks Demand.

Prison & the Home: A Study of the Relationship Between Domesticity & Penality. Ann Aungles. (Institute of Criminology Monographs: No. 5). vii, 302p. 1994. pap. 33.95 (*0-86758-903-5*) Gaunt.

***Prison Architecture.** Leslie Fairweather & Sean McConville. 240p. 2000. 95.00 (*0-7506-4212-2*, Architectural Pr) Buttrwrth-Heinemann.

Prison Bars to Shining Stars: The True Story of S. T. McGinnis's Long Walk to Manhood Through Hobo Jungles, Prison Cells, & the Old-Time Religion of the 1930's. Bob Terrell. LC 96-61404. (Illus.). 128p. (Orig.). 1997. pap. 9.95 (*1-56664-100-4*) WorldComm.

Prison Bird. Lynn F. Wright. LC 91-75180. (Illus.). 24p. (J). (gr. 1-6). 1991. 13.95 (*1-881519-01-5*) WorryWart.

Prison Books & Their Authors. J. A. Langford. 1972. 59.95 (*0-8490-0892-1*) Gordon Pr.

Prison Boot Camps: Policy Considerations & Options. (State Legislative Reports: Vol. 16, No. 1). 10p. 1991. 15.00 (*1-55516-300-9*, 7302-1601) Natl Conf State Legis.

Prison Camp at Andersonville. William G. Burnett. (Civil War Ser.). (Illus.). 44p. 1995. pap. 4.95 (*0-915992-84-1*) Eastern National.

Prison Camps of the Civil War. Linda R. Wade. LC 97-37479. (The Civil War Ser.). (J). 1998. lib. bdg. 15.98 (*1-56239-822-9*) ABDO Pub Co.

Prison Chaplain: Memoirs of the Rev. John Clay with Selections from His Reports & Correspondence & a Sketch of Prison Discipline in England. Walter L. Clay. LC 69-16232. (Criminology, Law Enforcement, & Social Problems Ser.: No. 90). 1969. reprint ed. 30.00 (*0-87585-090-1*) Patterson Smith.

***Prison Chaplaincy Guidelines for Zen Buddhism: A Source Book for Prison Chaplains, Administrators & Security Personnel.** Kobutsu Malone. (EZF Monographs Ser.). (Illus.). 85p. 2000. pap. 9.95 (*0-9677775-0-X*) Engaged Zen Fndt.

Prison Conditions in Czechoslovakia: An Update. Ed. by Human Rights Watch Staff. 46p. (Orig.). 1991. pap. 5.00 (*1-56432-003-0*) Hum Rts Watch.

Prison Conditions in Egypt. Ed. by Human Rights Watch Staff. 176p. (Orig.). 1993. pap. 15.00 (*1-56432-090-1*) Hum Rts Watch.

Prison Conditions in Israel & Israeli-Occupied West Bank & Gaza Strip. Eric Goldstein. Ed. by Human Rights Watch Staff & Aryeh Neier. 88p. (Orig.). 1991. pap. 7.00 (*1-56432-011-1*) Hum Rts Watch.

Prison Conditions in Jamaica. Americas Watch Staff. LC 90-82156. (Prison Conditions Ser.). 56p. 1990. pap. 7.00 (*0-929692-57-8*, Am Watch) Hum Rts Watch.

Prison Conditions in Mexico. Americas Watch Staff. LC 90-84348. (Prison Conditions Ser.). 60p. 1991. pap. 7.00 (*0-929692-71-3*, Am Watch) Hum Rts Watch.

Prison Conditions in Poland, an Update. Helsinki Watch Staff. LC 91-70466. (Prison Conditions Ser.). 50p. 1991. pap. 7.00 (*0-929692-84-5*, Helsinki Watch) Hum Rts Watch.

Prison Conditions in Romania. Ed. by Human Rights Watch Staff. 78p. (Orig.). 1992. pap. 7.00 (*1-56432-076-6*) Hum Rts Watch.

Prison Conditions in Spain. Ed. by Human Rights Watch Staff. 44p. (Orig.). 1992. pap. 5.00 (*1-56432-061-8*) Hum Rts Watch.

Prison Conditions in the Soviet Union. Ed. by Human Rights Watch Staff. 40p. (Orig.). 1991. pap. 5.00 (*1-56432-049-9*) Hum Rts Watch.

Prison Conditions in the United Kingdom. Ed. by Human Rights Watch Staff. LC 92-14941. (Helsinki Watch Report - Prison Project). 64p. (Orig.). 1992. pap. 7.00 (*1-56432-066-9*) Hum Rts Watch.

Prison Conditions in the United States. Ed. by Human Rights Watch Staff. 120p. (Orig.). 1991. pap. 10.00 (*1-56432-046-4*) Hum Rts Watch.

Prison Conditions in Turkey. Helsinki Watch Staff. (Prison Conditions Ser.). 96p. 1989. pap. 7.00 (*0-929692-28-4*, Helsinki Watch) Hum Rts Watch.

Prison Conditions in Zaire. Human Rights Watch Helsinki Staff. LC 93-81243. 72p. 1994. pap. 7.00 (*1-56432-120-7*) Hum Rts Watch.

Prison Crisis: Critical Readings. Ed. by Robert Keller & Eduard Sbarbaro. 240p. (C). 1995. text 41.50 (*0-911577-29-7*, Criminal Justice) Willow Tree NY.

Prison Crowding: A Psychological Perspective. P. B. Paulus. (Research in Criminology Ser.). (Illus.). 105p. 1988. 96.95 (*0-387-96650-1*) Spr-Verlag.

Prison Culture: An Inside View. Ellis Finkelstein. 183p. 1993. 61.95 (*1-85628-625-8*, Pub. by Avebry) Ashgate Pub Co.

Prison Discipline in America. Francis C. Gray. LC 77-172599. (Criminology, Law Enforcement, & Social Problems Ser.: No. 189). 1973. reprint ed. 24.00 (*0-87585-189-4*) Patterson Smith.

Prison Door Is Open: What Are You Still Doing Inside? Kenneth E. Hagin, Jr. 1982. pap. 1.00 (*0-89276-710-3*) Faith Lib Pubns.

Prison Dreams. John O. Powers. 200p. mass mkt. 4.99 (*1-55197-039-2*) Picasso Publ.

Prison du Souvenir. Kathleen Korbel. (Amours d'Aujourd'Hui Ser.: Bk. 314). 1999. mass mkt. 4.99 (*0-373-38314-2*, 1-38314-0) Harlequin Bks.

Prison Epistles: Praise from Prison. Bernard Rossier. 272p. (C). 1987. 6.95 (*0-912981-18-0*) Hse BonGiovanni.

Prison et Paradis. Sidonie-Gabrielle Colette. (FRE.). 1986. pap. 31.95 (*0-8288-9151-6*, M3331) Fr & Eur.

Prison Experience: Disciplinary Institutions & Their Inmates in Early Modern Europe. Pieter C. Spierenburg. LC 90-42138. (Illus.). 350p. (C). 1991. text 45.00 (*0-8135-1639-0*) Rutgers U Pr.

Prison Expose & Muldergate: A Case Study in Changing Government-Press Relations in South Africa. Gordon Jackson. (Graduate Student Papers Competition: No. 3). 25p. (Orig.). 1980. pap. text 2.00 (*0-941934-31-4*) Indiana Africa.

Prison Guard. Jack Rudman. (Career Examination Ser.: C-618). 1984. pap. 23.95 (*0-8373-0618-3*) Nat Learn.

Prison Guards: The Culture & Perspective of an Occupational Group. G. L. Webb & David G. Morris. LC 78-72960. 1978. 5.95 (*0-933012-00-4*) Coker Pub.

Prison Guide: 1999 Edition. Andrew Goodman & Barbara Mensah. 94p. 1999. pap. 30.00 (*1-85431-976-0*, Pub. by Blackstone Pr) Gaunt.

Prison Health. K. Tomasevski. 228p. 1992. pap. 25.00 (*951-47-6436-6*, Criminal Justice) Willow Tree NY.

Prison Health Care: Guidelines for the Management of an Adequate Delivery System, 1992. National Comm. on Correctional Health Care Staff & B. Jay Anno. 350p. 1991. 55.00 (*0-929561-04-X*) NCCHC.

Prison Hostage: The Siege of the Walls Prison in Huntsville, Texas. Ronald W. Robinson. LC 97-42275. (Criminology Studies: Vol. 2). (Illus.). 164p. 1997. 79.95 (*0-7734-8564-3*) E Mellen.

Prison-House of Language: A Critical Account of Structuralism & Russian Formalism. Fredric Jameson. LC 78-173757. (Essays in Literature Ser.). 228p. 1972. pap. text 14.95 (*0-691-01316-0*, Pub. by Princeton U Pr) Cal Prin Full Svc.

Prison-House of Myth? Symptomal Readings in Virgin Land, the Madwoman in the Attic, & the Political Unconscious. Oyunn Hestetun. (Studia Anglistica Upsaliensia Ser.: No. 81). 261p. (Orig.). 1993. pap. 57.50 (*91-554-3064-3*, Pub. by Uppsala Universitet) Coronet Bks.

***Prison in America: Past, Present & Future.** (C). 2001. text. write for info. (*0-13-025993-4*) P-H.

***Prison in America: Past Present & Future.** (C). 2001. text. write for info. (*0-13-025994-2*) P-H.

***Prison Industrial Complex.** Angela Davis. 1999. cd-rom 14.98 (*1-902593-22-7*, Pub. by AK Pr) SPD-Small Pr Dist.

Prison Industrial Complex & the Global Economy. Linda Evans et al. (Illus.). 24p. 1998. pap. 1.00 (*1-889059-17-X*) Regent Pr.

Prison Journal. Luise Rinser. LC 90-200783. viii, 151p. 1987. write for info. (*0-333-44968-1*) Macmillan.

Prison Journal: An Irreverent Look at Life on the Inside. Joseph F. Timilty & Jack Thomas. LC 97-10280. (Illus.). 224p. 1997. 28.95 (*1-55553-312-4*) NE U Pr.

Prison Labor: Salvation or Slavery? Internation Perspectives. Ed. by Dirk Van Zyl Smit & Frieder Dunkel. LC 99-11976. (Onati International Series in Law & Society). 250p. 1999. 96.95 (*1-84014-797-0*, Pub. by Ashgate Pub) Ashgate Pub Co.

***Prison Labour: Salvation or Slavery? International Perspectives.** Dirk Van Zyl Smit & Frieder Duenkel. LC 99-11976. (Odnati International Series in Law & Society). 250p. 1999. 30.95 (*1-84014-799-7*, Pub. by Ashgate Pub) Ashgate Pub Co.

Prison Law. 2nd ed. Stephen Livingstone & Tim Owen. 788p. 1999. text 120.00 (*0-19-876512-6*) OUP.

Prison Law & Practice, South African. D. Van Zyl Smit. 464p. 1992. write for info. (*0-409-06074-7*, MICHIE); write for info. (*0-409-06075-5*, MICHIE) LEXIS Pub.

Prison Letters. Antonio Gramsci. 296p. 1996. 54.95 (*0-7453-1164-4*, Pub. by Pluto GBR) Stylus Pub VA.

Prison Life among the Rebels: Recollections of a Union Chaplain. Ed. by Edward D. Jervey. LC 89-39689. 112p. 1990. pap. 12.50 (*0-87338-404-0*) Kent St U Pr.

Prison Life & Reflections: Or, a Narrative of the Arrest, Trial of Work, Burr, & Thompson, 3 Pts. in 1 Vol. George Thompson. LC 79-138348. (Black Heritage Library Collection). 1977. 28.95 (*0-8369-8739-X*) Ayer.

Prison Life in America: The Crisis Today. rev. ed. Anna Kosof. LC 95-14886. 144p. (YA). (gr. 8-12). 1995. lib. bdg. 24.00 (*0-531-10984-4*) Watts.

Prison Madness: The Mental Health Crisis Behind Bars & What We Must Do about It. Terry A. Kupers & Hans Toch. LC 98-25505. 288p. 1999. 25.00 (*0-7879-4361-4*) Jossey-Bass.

Prison, Maigret Hesite, la Main. Georges Simenon. (FRE.). 896p. 1991. 49.95 (*0-7859-0489-1*, 2258033047) Fr & Eur.

Prison Maritime. Michel Mohrt. (FRE.). 1973. pap. 10.95 (*0-7859-4009-X*, 2070364089) Fr & Eur.

***Prison Masculinities.** Ed. by Donald F. Sabo et al. 296p. 2001. 79.50 (*1-56639-815-0*); pap. 24.95 (*1-56639-816-9*) Temple U Pr.

Prison Meditations on Psalms 51 & 31. Girolamo Savonarola. Ed. & Tr. by Patrick Donnelly from LAT. (Reformation Texts with Translation: Biblical Studies). (Orig.). 1994. pap. 15.00 (*0-87462-700-1*) Marquette.

Prison Memoirs of a Japanese Woman. Kaneko Fumiko. Tr. by Jean Inglis from JPN. LC 91-14196. (Foremother Legacies Ser.). 226p. (C). (gr. 13). 1991. 69.95 (*0-87332-801-9*) M E Sharpe.

Prison Memoirs of a Japanese Woman. Kaneko Fumiko. Tr. by Jean Inglis from JPN. LC 91-14196. (Foremother Legacies Ser.). 226p. (gr. 13). 1995. pap. 21.95 (*0-87332-802-7*) M E Sharpe.

***Prison Memoirs of an Anarchist.** Alexander Berkman. LC 99-15897. 260p. 1999. reprint ed. pap. 14.95 (*0-940322-34-X*, Pub. by NY Rev Bks) Midpt Trade.

Prison Methods in New York State. Philip Klein. LC 79-78000. (Columbia University. Studies in the Social Sciences: No. 205). reprint ed. 37.50 (*0-404-51205-4*) AMS Pr.

Prison Minister's Handbook: Volunteer Ministry to the Forgotten Christian. John L. Cowart. LC 95-44869. 192p. 1996. pap. 17.95 (*0-89390-338-8*) Resource Pubns.

Prison No. 5: 11 Years in Turkish Jails. Medhi Zana. Tr. by Sarah Hughes from FRE. LC 97-30282. (Human Rights & Democracy Ser.). 112p. 1997. pap. 14.95 (*1-886434-05-0*) Blue Crane Bks.

Prison Notebooks, Vol. 1. Antonio Gramsci. (Illus.). 616p. 1992. text 57.50 (*0-231-06082-3*) Col U Pr.

Prison Notebooks, Vol. 2. Antonio Gramsci. Ed. & Tr. by Joseph A. Buttigieg. (European Perspectives Ser.). 728p. 1996. 52.00 (*0-231-10592-4*) Col U Pr.

Prison Notebooks: Selections. Antonio Gramsci. Tr. by Quintin Hoare & Geoffrey N. Smith from ITA. LC 73-77646. 572p. (C). 1971. pap. 14.95 (*0-7178-0397-X*) Intl Pubs Co.

Prison Notebooks of Ricardo Flores Magon. Douglas Day. 1991. 21.95 (*0-15-174598-6*) Harcourt.

Prison of Expectations: The Family in Victorian Culture. Steven Mintz. 232p. (C). 1983. pap. text 17.50 (*0-8147-5391-4*) NYU Pr.

Prison of Life: An Autobiography. Tawfiq Al-Hakim. Tr. by Pierre A. Cachia from ARA. 160p. 1993. pap. 22.50 (*977-424-279-3*, Pub. by Am Univ Cairo Pr) Col U Pr.

Prison of Love see Jean Froissart: La Prison Amoureuse (The Prison of Love)

Prison of Souls. Mercedes Lackey & Mark Shepherd. (Bard's Tale Ser.). 368p. (Orig.). 1993. mass mkt. 5.99 (*0-671-72193-3*) Baen Bks.

Prison of Women: Testimonies of War & Resistance in Spain, 1939-1975. Tomasa Cuevas. Ed. & Tr. by Mary E. Giles from SPA. LC 97-33352. (Illus.). 256p. (C). 1998. text 65.50 (*0-7914-3857-0*); pap. text 21.95 (*0-7914-3858-9*) State U NY Pr.

Prison Officers & Their World. Kelsey Kauffman. LC 88-468. (Illus.). 320p. 1988. 44.00 (*0-674-70716-8*) HUP.

Prison on Trial: A Critical Assessment. Thomas Mathiesen. 192p. (C). 1990. text 45.00 (*0-8039-8224-0*); pap. text 17.95 (*0-8039-8225-9*) Sage.

***Prison on Wheels: From Ravensbruck to Burgau.** Eva Langley-Danos. 1999. pap. 14.95 (*3-85630-585-8*, Pub. by Daimon Pubs) Cassell & Continuum.

Prison Ordeal. G. L. Webb. LC 83-72039. (Criminal Justice Ser.). v, 232p. 1984. 12.50 (*0-933012-06-3*) Coker Pub.

Prison Organization & Inmate Subcultures. Charles W. Thomas & David M. Petersen. 1977. pap. text 4.00 (*0-672-61404-9*, Bobbs) Macmillan.

Prison Pictures from Hollywood: Plots, Critiques, Casts & Credits for 293 Theatrical & Made-for-Television Releases. James R. Parish. LC 90-53519. (Illus.). 544p. 1991. lib. bdg. 62.50 (*0-89950-563-5*) McFarland & Co.

Prison Poems. Daniel Berrigan. LC 73-76683. 124p. 1982. pap. 14.95 (*0-87775-149-8*) Unicorn Pr.

***Prison Policy in Ireland.** Paul O'Mahony. 72p. 2000. pap. 8.95 (*1-85918-243-7*, Pub. by Cork Univ) Stylus Pub VA.

Prison Population & Criminal Justice Policy in California. Franklin E. Zimring & Gordon Hawkins. LC 92-10021. 72p. (Orig.). 1992. pap. 9.95 (*0-87772-332-X*) UCB IGS.

Prison Rape Education Project: Manual/Overview for Jail/Prison Administrators & Staff. 2nd rev. ed. Stephen Donaldson. Ed. by Fay H. Knopp & Euan Bear. 70p. (Orig.). 1997. pap. 15.00 (*1-884444-38-5*) Safer Soc.

Prison Reform. Charles R. Henderson. (Russell Sage Foundation Reprint Ser.). (Illus.). reprint ed. lib. bdg. 42.00 (*0-697-00206-3*) Irvington.

Prison Reform: Together with a Discussion of the Prison of the Future by Thomas M. Osborne. Corinne Bacon. LC 70-38659. reprint ed. 37.50 (*0-404-09147-4*) AMS Pr.

Prison Reform Movement. Larry E. Sullivan. (Social Movements Past & Present Ser.). 200p. 1990. 25.95 (*0-8057-9739-4*, Twyne) Mac Lib Ref.

Prison Secrets: Things Seen, Suffered, & Recorded During Seven Years in Ludlow Street Jail. A. R. MacDonald. LC 70-90185. (Mass Violence in America Ser.). 1977. reprint ed. 17.95 (*0-405-01327-2*) Ayer.

Prison Sentences: The Prison As Site - the Prison As Subject. Russ Immarigeon et al. 80p. 1995. pap. 16.95 (*0-9649221-1-8*) Prison Sent.

Prison Service Annual Report & Accounts. Orig. Title: Report on Work of Prison Dept., 1985-86. (Illus.). 102p. 1995. pap. 35.00 (*0-10-218595-6*, HM85956, Pub. by Statnry Office) Bernan Associates.

Prison Service Annual Report & Accounts: April 1994 - March 1995. 102p. 1996. pap. 30.00 (*0-10-275296-6*, HM52966, Pub. by Statnry Office) Bernan Associates.

An Asterisk (*) at the beginning of an entry indicates that the title is appearing for the first time.

Prison Slang: Words & Expressions Depicting Life Behind Bars. William K. Bentley & James M. Corbett. LC 91-52763. 128p. 1992. lib. bdg. 28.50 (*0-89950-646-1*) McFarland & Co.
Prison Solitary. Carolyn Baxter. LC 79-54299. 1979. 2.00 (*0-912678-41-0*, Greenfld Rev Pr) Greenfld Rev Lit.
Prison Statistics - England & Wales, 1992. 166p. 1994. pap. 40.00 (*0-10-125812-7*, HM58127, Pub. by Statnry Office) Bernan Associates.
Prison Statistics - England & Wales, 1996-1997. 174p. 1997. pap. 40.00 (*0-10-137322-8*, HM86985, Pub. by Statnry Office) Bernan Associates.
Prison Suicide: An Overview & Guide to Prevention. Lindsay M. Hayes. (Illus.). 111p. (C). 1998. reprint ed. pap. text 25.00 (*0-7881-3232-6*) DIANE Pub.
Prison Systems & Correctional Laws: Europe, the United States & Japan, a Comparative Analysis. 3rd ed. Gunther Kaiser. Orig. Title: Strafvollzug Im Europeaischen Verlgeich. 250p. 1984. reprint ed. lib. bdg. 60.00 (*0-941320-12-X*) Transnatl Pubs.
Prison Systems in Central & Eastern Europe. Roy Walmsley. LC 96-218870. 513p. 1996. pap. 25.00 (*951-53-0567-5*, Pub. by Europ Inst Crime Prev & Control) Taylor & Francis.
Prison to Praise See De la Prision a la Alabanza
Prison to Praise. Merlin R. Carothers. 106p. 1970. pap. 3.95 (*0-943026-02-4*) Carothers.
Prison to Praise. unabridged ed. Merlin R. Carrothers. (Essential Christian Library Ser.). 252p. 1998. reprint ed. 9.97 (*1-57748-343-X*) Barbour Pub.
Prison to Praise: Giant Print. Merlin R. Carothers. 106p. (Orig.). 1970. pap. 5.95 (*0-943026-08-3*) Carothers.
Prison Unsought. Sherwood Smith & David Trowbridge. (Exordium Ser.: No. 3). 480p. (Orig.). 1994. mass mkt. 4.50 (*0-8125-2026-2*, Pub. by Tor Bks) St Martin.
Prison Versus Probation in California: Implications for Crime & Offender Recidivism. Joan Petersilia et al. 63p. 1986. pap. 7.50 (*0-8330-0738-6*, R-3323-NIJ) Rand Corp.
Prison Violence in America. 2nd rev. ed. Michael C. Braswell et al. LC 93-71747. 420p. (C). 1994. pap. 34.95 (*0-87084-094-0*) Anderson Pub Co.
Prison Work & Training. Frances H. Simon. LC 98-35094. 1999. write for info. (*0-415-14676-3*); pap. write for info. (*0-415-14677-1*) Routledge.
Prison Writing in 20th Century America. Ed. by H. Bruce Franklin. LC 97-42354. 368p. 1998. pap. 13.95 (*0-14-027305-0*) Viking Penguin.
***Prison Writings: My Life is My Sun Dance.** Leonard F. Peltier & Harvey Arden. (Illus.). 272p. 2000. pap. 13.95 (*0-312-26380-5*, St Martin Griffin) St Martin.
Prison Writings: My Life is My Sun Dance. 2nd ed. Leonard Peltier. Ed. by Harvey Arden. LC 99-21283. 256p. 1999. text 23.95 (*0-312-20354-3*) St Martin.
Prisoned Chickens, Poisoned Eggs: An Inside Look at the Modern Poultry Industry. Karen Davis. LC 96-45937. 176p. (Orig.). 1996. pap. 12.95 (*1-57067-032-3*) Book Pub Co.
Prisoner see Pot of Gold & Other Plays
Prisoner. Bridget Boland. 1998. pap. 5.25 (*0-8222-0916-0*) Dramatists Play.
Prisoner. Alain Carraze & Helene Oswald. (Illus.). 240p. (Orig.). 1996. pap. text 19.95 (*0-86369-557-4*, Pub. by Virgin Bks) London Brdge.
Prisoner. Newman. (J). 1995. pap. 13.95 (*0-689-31363-2*) Atheneum Yung Read.
Prisoner. Cheryl Reavis. (Historical Ser.: No. 726). 1992. per. 3.99 (*0-373-28726-7*, 1-28726-7) Harlequin Bks.
Prisoner. Nancy Rue. LC 96-38992. (Christian Heritage Ser.: Vol. 4). 192p. (J). (gr. 5-7). 1998. pap. 5.99 (*1-56179-518-6*) Focus Family.
Prisoner. Fakhar Zaman. Tr. by Khalid Hasan from PAN. LC 97-123827. 176p. 1996. 28.95 (*0-7206-1010-9*, Pub. by P Owen Ltd) Dufour.
Prisoner. 2nd ed. Paul Little. 1995. mass mkt. 5.95 (*1-56333-330-9*) Masquerade.
Prisoner: Released. unabridged ed. Brian Brookheart. 133p. 1997. pap. 10.00 (*0-9661038-0-7*) B Brookheart.
Prisoner: Shattered Visage. D. Motter & M. Askwith. Ed. by Richard Bruning & KC Carlson. (Illus.). 208p. 1990. pap. 19.95 (*0-930289-53-6*) DC Comics.
Prisoner: Shattered Visage. Dean Motter. 1991. mass mkt. 14.95 (*0-446-39245-6*, Pub. by Warner Bks) Little.
Prisoner & Yet . . . Corrie Ten Boom. 1991. pap. 9.99 (*0-87508-019-7*) Chr Lit.
Prisoner at the Bar: Sidelights on the Administration of Criminal Justice. Arthur C. Train. LC 74-3858. (Criminal Justice in America Ser.). 1974. reprint ed. 30.95 (*0-405-06174-9*) Ayer.
Prisoner Collateral Attacks. Josephine R. Potuto. LC 91-60701. 1991. 98.00 (*0-685-59842-X*) West Group.
Prisoner 1167: The Madman Who Was Jack the Ripper. James Tully. (Illus.). 416p. 1998. pap. 12.95 (*0-7867-0543-4*) Carroll & Graf.
Prisoner Exchange: The Murder of Joshua Huddy. William Lauer. (Illus.). 72p. (Orig.). 1994. pap. 6.00 (*0-941965-07-4*) Ocean Cnty Hist.
Prisoner for Peace: Aang San Suu Kyi & Burma's Struggle for Democracy. John Parenteau. LC 94-4100. (Champions of Freedom Ser.). (Illus.). 152p. (YA). (gr. 5 up). 1994. lib. bdg. 18.95 (*1-883846-05-6*) M Reynolds.
Prisoner for Polygamy: The Memoirs & Letters of Rudger Clawson at the Utah Territorial Penitentiary, 1884-87. Ed. by Stan Larson. (Illus.). 282p. (C). 1993. 29.95 (*0-252-01861-3*) U of Ill Pr.
Prisoner in the Opal. A. E. W. Mason. mass mkt. 3.95 (*0-88184-221-4*) Carroll & Graf.
Prisoner in the Third Cell. Gene Edwards. LC 92-13527. 94p. 1992. pap. 7.99 (*0-8423-5023-3*) Tyndale Hse.
Prisoner Litigation: The Paradox of the Jailhouse Lawyer. Jim Thomas. LC 87-19870. 288p. (C). 1988. text 65.00 (*0-8476-7477-0*) Rowman.
Prisoner Litigation in the United States Courts. 2nd ed. Charles R. Richey. LC 97-19989. 484p. 1997. pap. text. write for info. (*0-314-22693-1*) West Pub.
***Prisoner of Cabin 13.** John Vornholt. (Sabrina, the Teenage Witch Ser.: No. 11). 176p. (YA). (gr. 7-12). 1998. per. 4.50 (*0-671-02115-X*, Archway) PB.
Prisoner of Chillon & Don Juan Canto IX: A Facsimile of the Original Draft Manuscripts in the Beinecke Library of Yale University. fac. ed. George Gordon Byron. Ed. & Intro. by Peter Cochran. LC 94-42004. (Manuscripts of the Younger Romantics Ser.: Vol. 13). 206p. 1995. text 105.00 (*0-8153-1962-2*) Garland.
Prisoner of Chillon, 1816. George Gordon Byron. LC 93-17423. (Revolution & Romanticism Ser.). 80p. 1993. reprint ed. 35.00 (*1-85477-133-7*) Continuum.
Prisoner of Conscience. J. Guevara. LC 94-67973. 232p. (Orig.). 1994. pap. 9.95 (*0-9642792-0-7*) Seditious Pr.
Prisoner of Conscience. Susan R. Matthews. 320p. 1998. mass mkt. 3.99 (*0-380-78914-0*, Avon Bks) Morrow Avon.
Prisoner of Desire: Historical Romance. Jennifer Blake. 1994. 22.00 (*0-7278-4588-8*) Severn Hse.
Prisoner of Fear: My Long Road to Freedom from Anxiety Disease, Panic Attacks & Agoraphobia. Richard Maro. 250p. (Orig.). 1990. pap. 12.95 (*0-9628509-0-X*) Hickory Grove Pr.
Prisoner of Grace. Joyce Cary. 301p. 1976. reprint ed. lib. bdg. 23.95 (*0-88411-313-2*, Queens House) Amereon Ltd.
Prisoner of Grace. Joyce Cary. LC 85-10662. (Second Trilogy - The New Directions Classics Ser.: Bk. 1). 320p. 1985. reprint ed. pap. 7.95 (*0-8112-0964-4*, NDP606, Pub. by New Directions) Norton.
Prisoner of History: Aspasia of Miletus & Her Biographical Tradition. Madeleine M. Henry. (Illus.). 208p. 1995. text 39.95 (*0-19-508712-7*) OUP.
Prisoner of Ice: The Official Strategy Guide. John Waters. 1995. pap. text 19.95 (*0-7615-0263-7*) Prima Pub.
Prisoner of Innocence. Donna Montegna. LC 89-12775. 120p. (Orig.). 1989. pap. 8.95 (*0-9613205-7-5*) Launch Pr.
Prisoner of Joy. Jack W. Hayford. LC 94-166314. (Spirit-Filled Life Study Guide Ser.). 1994. pap. 6.99 (*0-8407-8512-7*) Nelson.
Prisoner of My Desire. Johanna Lindsey. 400p. (Orig.). 1991. mass mkt. 6.99 (*0-380-75627-7*, Avon Bks) Morrow Avon.
Prisoner of Passion. Lynne Graham. 1997. per. 3.50 (*0-373-11864-3*, 1-11864-5) Harlequin Bks.
***Prisoner of Passion.** Desiree Lindsey. 296p. 2000. pap. 14.99 (*0-9677336-1-8*) Lindsey Promo.
Prisoner of Passion. large type ed. Lynne Graham. (Harlequin Romance Ser.). 1996. 20.95 (*0-263-14664-2*) Thorndike Pr.
Prisoner of Pineapple Place. Anne M. Lindbergh. LC 87-28815. 173p. (J). (gr. 3-7). 1988. 13.95 (*0-15-263559-9*, Harcourt Child Bks) Harcourt.
Prisoner of Pineapple Place. Anne M. Lindbergh. 192p. (J). 1990. pap. 2.95 (*0-380-70765-9*, Avon Bks) Morrow Avon.
Prisoner of Portcullis Castle. P. Roxbee Cox. (Solve It Yourself Ser.). (Illus.). 48p. (YA). (gr. 7-12). 1997. pap. 7.95 (*0-7460-2697-8*, Usborne); lib. bdg. 15.95 (*0-88110-948-7*, Usborne) EDC.
Prisoner of Russia: Alexander Pushkin & the Political Uses of Nationalism. Yuri Druzhnikov. LC 98-52062. 10p. 1998. 39.95 (*1-56000-390-1*) Transaction Pubs.
Prisoner of the Devil. Michael Hardwick. 307p. 1990. mass mkt. 4.95 (*1-55817-447-8*, Pinncle Kensgtn) Kensgtn Pub Corp.
Prisoner of the Emperor: An American POW in World War II. Stanley W. Smith. Ed. by Duane A. Smith. LC 91-29101. (Illus.). 150p. reprint ed. pap. 46.50 (*0-608-20177-4*, 207143500012) Bks Demand.
Prisoner of the Fifth Moon: Doyan 1. Jerry D. Boyd. 176p. 1994. pap. text. write for info. (*0-9641152-0-4*) East KY Pubng.
Prisoner of the Horned Helmet. Frank Franzetta & James R. Silke. (Death Dealer Ser.: Vol. 1). 320p. 1990. pap. 3.95 (*0-8125-1333-9*, Pub. by Tor Bks) St Martin.
Prisoner of the Ogpu. George Kitchin. LC 70-115551. (Russia Observed Ser., No. 1). 1970. reprint ed. 19.95 (*0-405-03038-X*) Ayer.
Prisoner of the Rising Sun. William A. Berry & James Edwin Alexander. LC 92-50713. 1993. 27.95 (*0-8061-2509-8*) U of Okla Pr.
***Prisoner of the Word.** Le Huu Tri. 350p. 2000. 25.95 (*0-930773-60-8*, Pub. by Black Heron Pr) Midpt Trade.
Prisoner of Time. Caroline Cooney. 208p. (YA). 1999. mass mkt. 4.99 (*0-440-22019-X*) BDD Bks Young Read.
Prisoner of Time. Caroline B. Cooney. LC 97-24073. 208p. (YA). 1998. 15.95 (*0-385-32244-5*) Delacorte.
Prisoner of Vampires. Nancy Garden. 224p. (J). (gr. 4-7). 1993. pap. 3.95 (*0-374-46018-3*) FS&G.
Prisoner of War & Concentration Camp Money. 2nd ed. Lance K. Campbell. (Illus.). 220p. 1992. 25.00 (*0-931960-31-2*); pap. 35.00 (*0-931960-32-0*) BNR Pr.
***Prisoner of War & Peace.** Nick Mustacchia. LC 98-67436. 192p. 1999. 20.95 (*1-57197-143-2*) Pentland Pr.
Prisoner of War Der Luftwaffe. Frank Farnsley. LC 96-69082. 74p. (Orig.). 1997. pap. 11.95 (*1-57197-031-2*) Pentland Pr.
***Prisoner of Zenda.** (Penguin Ser.). (C). 2000. 7.00 (*0-582-41936-0*) Pearson Educ.
Prisoner of Zenda. Ed. by Jennifer Bassett. (Illus.). 64p. 1995. pap. text 5.95 (*0-19-422726-X*) OUP.
***Prisoner of Zenda.** Anthony Hope. Ed. by Tony Watkins. (Oxford World Classics Ser.). 208p. 2000. pap. 8.95 (*0-19-283904-7*) OUP.
Prisoner of Zenda. Anthony Hope-Hawkins. (Illustrated Classics Collection 4). 64p. 1994. pap. 4.95 (*0-7854-0752-9*, 40509) Am Guidance.
Prisoner of Zenda. Anthony Hope-Hawkins. 1976. 21.95 (*0-8488-0819-3*) Amereon Ltd.
Prisoner of Zenda. Anthony Hope-Hawkins. 1988. lib. bdg. 21.95 (*0-89966-226-9*) Buccaneer Bks.
Prisoner of Zenda. Anthony Hope-Hawkins. Ed. by John C. Fago. (Now Age Illustrated IV Ser.). (Illus.). (J). (gr. 4-12). 1978. student ed. 1.25 (*0-88301-342-8*); pap. text 2.95 (*0-88301-318-5*) Pendulum Pr.
Prisoner of Zenda. Anthony Hope-Hawkins. (J). 1997. pap. 2.95 (*0-8167-0795-2*) Troll Communs.
Prisoner of Zenda. Anthony Hope-Hawkins. 256p. 1994. 4.95 (*0-460-87534-5*, Everyman's Classic Lib) Tuttle Pubng.
Prisoner of Zenda. Rafael Sabatini & Anthony Hope. LC 99-51329. 384p. 1999. pap. 14.95 (*0-89526-309-2*, Pub. by Regnery Pub) Natl Bk Netwk.
Prisoner of Zenda. large type ed. Anthony Hope-Hawkins. Ed. & Intro. by Tony Watkins. 1995. 44.00 (*0-614-09604-9*, L-81873-00) Am Printing Hse.
Prisoner of Zenda. large type ed. Anthony Hope-Hawkins. (Mainstream Ser.). 230p. 1988. reprint ed. 18.95 (*1-85089-208-3*, Pub. by ISIS Lrg Prnt) Transaction Pubs.
Prisoner of Zenda: Masters of Literature. Anthony Hope. 1997. pap. 5.00 (*81-207-1919-0*, Pub. by Sterling Pubs) S Asia.
***Prisoner of Zenda & Rupert of Hentzau.** Anthony Hope. LC 99-33519. 400p. 2000. pap. 7.95 (*0-14-043755-X*, Penguin Classics) Viking Penguin.
Prisoner of Zenda Readalong. Anthony Hope. (Illustrated Classics Collection 4). 64p. 1994. pap. 14.95 incl. audio (*0-7854-0768-5*, 40511) Am Guidance.
Prisoner on Board the S. S. Beagle. Calvin Murry. (Prison Writing Ser.). 1983. spiral bd. 5.00 (*0-912678-53-4*, Greenfld Rev Pr) Greenfld Rev Lit.
Prisoner on the Dam. large type ed. Christopher Coram. (Dales Large Print Ser.). 256p. 1996. pap. 18.99 (*1-85389-623-3*, Dales) Ulverscroft.
Prisoner on the Run. large type ed. Christopher Coram. (Dales Large Print Ser.). 265p. 1997. pap. 18.99 (*1-85389-627-6*) Ulverscroft.
Prisoner 20-801: A French National in the Nazi Labor Camps. Aime Bonifas. Tr. by Claude R. Foster & Mildred M. Van Sice. 143p. 1987. pap. 20.00 (*1-887732-10-1*) West Chester Univ.
Prisoner Without a Name, Cell Without a Number. Jacobo Timerman. Tr. by Toby Talbot from SPA. LC 81-52261.Tr. of Preso sin nombre, celda sin numero. 164p. 1982. write for info. (*0-394-75131-0*) Vin Bks.
Prisoner Without a Name, Cell Without a Number. Jacobo Timerman. Tr. by Toby Talbot from SPA.Tr. of Preso sin nombre, celda sin numero. 1988. pap. 11.00 (*0-679-72048-0*) Vin Bks.
Prisoners. Dorothy Bryant. LC 79-55170. 178p. (Orig.). 1980. 20.00 (*0-931688-04-3*); pap. 9.95 (*0-931688-05-1*) Ata Bks.
Prisoners. Jerome Gold. 96p. 1999. pap. 12.95 (*0-930773-53-5*) Black Heron Pr.
***Prisoners.** Wayne Karlin. 172p. 2000. pap. text 15.95 (*1-880684-71-3*) Curbstone.
Prisoners. Arne Svenson. (Illus.). 160p. 1997. pap. text 24.95 (*0-922233-18-7*) Blast Bks.
Prisoners: A Novel. Wayne Karlin. LC 98-20553. 172p. 1998. 19.95 (*1-880684-56-X*) Curbstone.
Prisoners: Health & Medical Subject Analysis with Reference Bibliography. Ira T. Reece. LC 85-48088. 150p. 1987. 47.50 (*0-88164-448-X*); pap. 44.50 (*0-88164-449-8*) ABBE Pubs Assn.
Prisoners: The Civil War Letters of Ernie O'Malley. Richard English & Cormac O'Malley. (Illus.). 164p. (Orig.). 1992. pap. 15.95 (*0-685-59676-1*, Pub. by Poolbeg Pr) Dufour.
Prisoners: The Civil War Letters of Ernie O'Malley. Ernie O'Malley. Ed. by R. English & C. O'Malley. 164p. 1991. pap. 15.95 (*1-85371-140-3*, Pub. by Poolbeg Pr) Dufour.
Prisoners among Us: The Problem of Parole. David T. Stanley. LC 75-44506. 223p. reprint ed. pap. 69.20 (*0-608-17498-X*, 203000400067) Bks Demand.
***Prisoners & Luminaries.** Aaron Alexander Colton. 16p. 1999. pap. 4.00 (*1-930714-03-3*) Good SAMAR.
Prisoners & Paupers: A Study of the Abnormal Increase of Criminals & the Public Burden of Pauperism in the United States; the Causes & Remedies. Henry M. Boies. LC 72-5478. (Select Bibliographies Reprint Ser.). 1977. reprint ed. 27.95 (*0-8369-6897-2*) Ayer.
Prisoners & the Law, 4 vols., Set. Ira P. Robbins. LC 85-16678. (Civil Rights Ser.). 1985. ring bd. 450.00 (*0-87632-478-2*) West Group.
Prisoners Are People. Kenyon J. Scudder. LC 68-8072. (Illus.). 286p. 1968. reprint ed. lib. bdg. 65.00 (*0-8371-0651-6*, SCPP, Greenwood Pr) Greenwood.
Prisoners at Kota Cane, Vol. 66. Tr. by Leon Salim & Audrey R. Kahin. (Modern Indonesia Project Ser.). 112p. 1986. pap. 9.00 (*0-87763-032-1*) Cornell Mod Indo.
Prisoners at the Bar. Francis X. Busch. LC 97-81066. (Notable American Trials Ser.: Vol. 1). ix, 288p. 1998. reprint ed. 75.00 (*1-57588-424-0*, 311670) W S Hein.
Prisoners at the Bar: An Account of the Trials of the William Haywood Case, the Sacco-Vanzetti Case, the Loeb-Leopold Case, the Bruno Hauptmann Case. Francis X. Busch. LC 77-126319. (Biography Index Reprint Ser., Vol. 2). 1977. 20.95 (*0-8369-8025-5*) Ayer.
Prisoners Conference. Thomas Savile. LC 70-38222. (English Experience Ser.: No. 486). 120p. 1972. reprint ed. 15.00 (*90-221-0486-9*) Walter J Johnson.
Prisoner's Dilemma. Richard Powers. LC 96-54203. 352p. 1996. pap. 14.00 (*0-06-097708-6*) HarpC.
Prisoner's Dilemma. Richard Powers. LC 95-54203. 1996. write for info. (*0-614-95874-1*, Perennial) HarperTrade.
Prisoner's Dilemma. Richard Powers. LC 88-29039. 1989. write for info. (*0-07-050612-4*) McGraw.
Prisoner's Dilemma. Anatol Rapoport & Albert M. Chammah. LC 65-11462. (Illus.). 270p. 1965. text 42.50 (*0-472-75602-8*, 75602) U of Mich Pr.
Prisoner's Dilemma. Anatol Rapoport et al. (Illus.). 270p. 1965. pap. text 16.95 (*0-472-06165-8*, 06165, Ann Arbor Bks) U of Mich Pr.
Prisoner's Dilemma: John von Neumann, Game Theory, & the Puzzle of the Bomb. William Poundstone. LC 92-29903. 320p. 1993. pap. 15.95 (*0-385-41580-X*, Anchor NY) Doubleday.
Prisoners, Diplomats, & the Great War: A Study in the Diplomacy of Captivity, 97. Richard B. Speed. LC 89-25732. (Contributions in Military Studies Ser.: No. 97). 256p. 1990. 59.95 (*0-313-26729-4*, SEJ/, Greenwood Pr) Greenwood.
Prisoner's Duty: Great Escapes in U. S. History. Robert C. Doyle. 480p. 1999. mass mkt. 6.50 (*0-553-57973-8*) Bantam.
Prisoner's Duty: Great Escapes in U. S. Military History. Robert C. Doyle. LC 97-16453. (Illus.). 400p. 1997. 34.95 (*1-55750-180-7*) Naval Inst Pr.
Prisoner's Friend. Andrew Garve. 1997. 19.50 (*0-7451-8703-X*, Black Dagger) Chivers N Amer.
***Prisoners' Guerilla Handbook to Correspondence Programs: High School, Vocational, Paralegal & College Courses.** Jon Marc Taylor. 240p. 1999. pap. 21.95 (*1-879418-65-7*) Audenreed Pr.
Prisoners' Handbook. Mark Leech. 424p. 1995. text 55.00 (*0-19-825960-3*) OUP.
Prisoner's Hope. David Feintuch. 528p. (Orig.). 1995. reprint ed. mass mkt. 6.50 (*0-446-60098-9*, Pub. by Warner Bks) Little.
Prisoners in America: Perspectives on Our Correctional System. Ed. by Lloyd E. Ohlin. LC 73-1221. (American Assembly Guides Ser.). 224p. 1973. 6.95 (*0-13-710822-2*); pap. 2.45 (*0-13-710814-1*) Am Assembly.
***Prisoners in Paradise: American Women in the Wartime South Pacific.** Theresa Kaminski. LC 99-47059. 296p. 2000. text 34.95 (*0-7006-1003-0*) U Pr of KS.
Prisoners in Petticoats: The Women of the Yuma Territorial Prison. Elizabeth J. Klungness. (Illus.). 202p. (Orig.). 1993. pap. text 14.95 (*1-884172-15-6*) Yuma Cnty Hist.
Prisoners in Prison Societies. Ulla V. Bondeson. 356p. 1988. 44.95 (*0-88738-205-3*) Transaction Pubs.
Prisoners, 1914-1918. Robert Jackson. 240p. 1989. 35.00 (*0-415-03377-2*, A3630) Routledge.
Prisoner's Notebook: Words That Change Lives. 2nd ed. Compiled by Dorothy L. Herbert. 100p. 1995. pap. text 5.95 (*0-9640197-0-1*) Shiloh Pr.
Prisoners of a Dream: The South African Mirage. Leo Raditsa. 500p. (Orig.). 1989. pap. 25.00 (*0-927104-00-8*) Prince Grg St.
Prisoners of Aristotle. Abdulrahman M. Al-Meraie. LC 84-80999. 189p. (C). 1984. 16.95 (*0-930371-00-3*) Epistemics.
Prisoners of Belief: Exposing & Changing Beliefs That Control Your Life. Matthew McKay & Patrick Fanning. LC 90-63757. 160p. 1991. pap. 12.95 (*1-879237-04-0*) New Harbinger.
Prisoners of Childhood. Alice Miller. 128p. 1996. reprint ed. 20.00 (*0-465-06287-3*, Pub. by Basic) HarpC.
Prisoners of Culture: Representing the Vietnam POW. Elliott Gruner. LC 92-30903. (Communications, a Multi-Disciplinary Approach Ser.). (Illus.). 280p. (C). 1993. pap. 15.95 (*0-8135-1931-4*); text 37.00 (*0-8135-1930-6*) Rutgers U Pr.
Prisoners of Dunes. Isabelle Eberhardt. 128p. 1995. pap. 24.00 (*0-7206-0944-5*, Pub. by P Owen Ltd) Dufour.
Prisoners of Earth: Psychic Possession & Its Release. 2nd ed. Aloa Starr. 179p. 1993. pap. 11.95 (*0-929385-37-3*) Light Tech Pubng.
Prisoners of Elitism: The Community College's Struggle for Stature. Ed. by Billie W. Dziech & William R. Vilter. LC 85-644753. (New Directions for Community Colleges Ser.: No. CC 78). 130p. 1992. pap. 22.00 (*1-55542-750-2*) Jossey-Bass.
Prisoners of Faith: A View from Within. Nirmala Srinivasan. 220p. (C). 1989. text 22.50 (*0-8039-9604-7*) Sage.
Prisoners of Fear. Gera-Lind Kolarik. (Illus.). 272p. (Orig.). 1995. mass mkt. 5.50 (*0-380-77345-7*, Avon Bks) Morrow Avon.
Prisoners of Freedom: Contemporary Slovenian Poetry. Ed. by Ales Debeljak. LC 92-61137. 180p. (Orig.). (C). 1992. pap. 12.95 (*1-881613-00-3*) Flint Mtn-Pedernal.
***Prisoners Of Hate: The Cognitive Basis of Anger, Hostility, & Violence.** Aaron T. Beck. LC 99-22651. (Illus.). 368p. 1999. 26.00 (*0-06-019377-8*) HarpC.
Prisoners Of Hate: The Cognitive Basis of Anger, Hostility, & Violence. Andre T. Beck. 368p. 2000. pap. 14.00 (*0-06-093200-7*, Perennial) HarperTrade.
Prisoners of Hate: The Story of Israelis in Syrian Jails. Yehezkel Hameiri. 261p. 1969. 34.95 (*0-87855-189-1*) Transaction Pubs.
Prisoners of Honor: The Dreyfus Affair. David L. Lewis. LC 94-31878. 1995. pap. 12.00 (*0-8050-3766-7*) H Holt & Co.
Prisoners of Hope. Michael Calvert. (Illus.). 310p. 1996. pap. 17.95 (*0-85052-492-X*, Pub. by Leo Cooper) Trans-Atl Phila.
Prisoners of Hope. Clay Worthington Clayton. 277p. 1998. pap. 5.95 (*1-888422-00-9*) Frost Pub.
Prisoners of Hope: Exploiting the POW/MIA Myth in America. Susan K. Keating. (Illus.). 276p. 1998. reprint ed. text 23.00 (*0-7881-5179-7*) DIANE Pub.
Prisoners of Hope: Sundry Sunday Essays. Steven J. Keillor. 150p. 1996. ring bd. 13.95 (*1-57383-070-4*) Regent College.

P

An Asterisk (*) at the beginning of an entry indicates that the title is appearing for the first time.

Prisoners of Hope: The Silver Age of the Italian Jews, 1924-1974. H. Stuart Hughes. 184p. 1983. 26.95 (*0-674-70727-3*) HUP.

Prisoners of Hope: The Silver Age of the Italian Jews, 1924-1974. H. Stuart Hughes. 208p. 1996. pap. 15.50 (*0-674-70728-1*) HUP.

Prisoners of Isolation: Solitary Confinement in Canada. Michael Jackson. LC 84-163728. 342p. reprint ed. pap. 106.10 (*0-8357-6361-7*, 203571500096) Bks Demand.

Prisoners of Mahdi. Byron Farwell. 1989. pap. 8.95 (*0-393-30579-1*) Norton.

Prisoners of Myth: The Leadership of the Tennessee Valley Authority, 1930-1990. Erwin C. Hargrove. LC 94-2789. (American Politics Studies). 392p. 1994. text 49.50 (*0-691-03467-2*, Pub. by Princeton U Pr) Cal Prin Full Svc.

Prisoners of Nazis: Accounts by American POWs in World War II. Harry Spiller. LC 97-34360. 224p. 1997. pap. 30.00 (*0-7864-0348-9*) McFarland & Co.

Prisoners of Our Past: A Critical Look at Self-Defeating Attitudes Within the Black Community. James Davison. LC 92-38064. 1993. 17.95 (*1-55972-176-6*, Birch Ln Pr) Carol Pub Group.

Prisoners of Passion. Janet I. Thomas. 150p. 1994. mass mkt. 3.79 (*0-9634431-2-7*) C Y Pub Grp.

Prisoners of Peace. John Peel. Ed. by Lisa Clancy. (Star Trek: Deep Space Nine Ser.: No. 3). 128p. (J). (gr. 3-6). 1994. pap. 3.99 (*0-671-88288-0*, Minstrel Bks) PB.

Prisoners of Ritual: An Odyssey into Female Genital Circumcision in Africa. Ed. by Hanny Lightfoot-Klein. LC 89-15637. (Illus.). 306p. 1989. pap. text 14.95 (*0-918393-68-X*, Harrington Park) Haworth Pr.

Prisoners of Ritual: An Odyssey into Female Genital Circumcision in Africa. Pref. by Hanny Lightfoot-Klein. LC 89-15639. (Haworth Series on Women: No. 2). (Illus.). 306p. 1989. text 39.95 (*0-86656-877-8*) Haworth Pr.

Prisoners of Santo Tomas: A True Account of Women POWs under Japanese Control. Celia Lucas. 1996. pap. 16.95 (*0-85052-541-1*, 525411) Leo Cooper.

Prisoners of Shangri-La: Tibetan Buddhism & the West. Donald S. Lopez, Jr. LC 97-41202. 272p. 1998. 25.00 (*0-226-49310-5*) U Ch Pr.

Prisoners of Shangri-La: Tibetan Buddhism & the West. Donald S. Lopez, Jr. LC 98-11679. 284p. 1999. pap. 14.00 (*0-226-49311-3*) U Ch Pr.

***Prisoners of the American Dream: Politics & Economy in the History of the U. S. Working Class.** Mike Davis. 2000. pap. 20.00 (*1-85984-248-8*) Norton.

Prisoners of the American Dream: Politics & Economy in the History of the U. S. Working Class. Mike Davis. (Haymarket Ser.). 320p. (C). 1986. pap. 20.00 (*0-86091-840-8*, Pub. by Verso) Norton.

Prisoners of the Japanese: POWs of World War II in the Pacific. Gavan Daws. 1996. pap. 15.00 (*0-688-14370-9*, Quil) HarperTrade.

Prisoners of the Japanese in World War II: Statistical History, Personal Narratives & Memorials Concerning POWs in Camps & on Hellships, Civilian Internees, Asian Slave Laborers & Others Captured in the Pacific Theater. Van Waterford. LC 92-51097. (Illus.). 406p. 1994. lib. bdg. 49.95 (*0-89950-893-6*) McFarland & Co.

***Prisoners of the Kaiser.** Richard Van Emden. (Illus.). 2000. 29.95 (*0-85052-734-1*, Pub. by Pen & Sword Bks Ltd) Combined Pub.

***Prisoners of the Paradigm: What School Board Members, Legislators & Community Leaders Must Know to Reform American Public Education.** Alan Hafer. (Illus.). 224p. 2000. pap. write for info. (*0-9677754-4-2*) FalCo Bks.

Prisoners of the Sun. Herge. (Illus.). 62p. (J). 24.95 (*0-8288-5056-9*) Fr & Eur.

Prisoners of the Sun. Herge. LC no-na1806. (Adventures of Tintin Ser.). 62p. (J). (gr. 2 up). 1975. pap. 9.95 (*0-316-35843-6*, Joy St Bks) Little.

Prisoners of the Sun. Herge. 1986. 1.00 (*0-416-92620-7*) Routledge.

Prisoners of Time: A Simplified Cosmo-Conception. Mollie Moncrieff. 100p. 1995. write for info. (*1-888477-02-4*) Saunders & Rakauskas.

Prisoners of Time: Report of the National Education Commission on Time & Learning. 56p. 1994. pap. text 30.00 (*1-57979-219-7*) DIANE Pub.

Prisoners of Time: Schools & Programs Making Time Work for Students & Teachers. (Illus.). 56p. 1994. pap. text 30.00 (*1-57979-220-0*) DIANE Pub.

Prisoners of Time: Schools & Programs Making Time Work for Students & Teachers. Government Printing Office Staff. 62p. 1994. per. 5.00 (*0-16-045266-X*) USGPO.

Prisoners of Time: Schools & Programs Making Time Work for Students & Teachers. Ed. by John H. Jones. (Illus.). 62p. 1998. pap. text 25.00 (*0-7881-7213-1*) DIANE Pub.

Prisoners of Time: The Effect of Restricted School Schedules on Students' Learning. (Illus.). 56p. (Orig.). 1994. pap. text 25.00 (*0-7881-1216-3*) DIANE Pub.

Prisoners of Time: Time & Learning. 1997. lib. bdg. 252.99 (*0-8490-6211-X*) Gordon Pr.

Prisoners of Time: What We Know & What We Need to Know. 60p. 1994. pap. text 25.00 (*1-57979-221-9*) DIANE Pub.

Prisoners of Time: What We Know & What We Need to Know: Supplemental Report of the National Education Commission on Time & Learning. Cheryl M. Kane. (Illus.). 60p. (Orig.). (C). 1994. pap. text 25.00 (*0-7881-1499-9*) DIANE Pub.

Prisoners of Time Research: What We Know & What We Need to Know. Cheryl M. Kane. 60p. 1994. per. 5.00 (*0-16-045231-7*) USGPO.

Prisoners-of-War & Their Captors in World War II. Ed. by Bob Moore & Kent Fedorowich. (Illus.). 352p. 1996. 65.00 (*1-85973-157-0*, Pub. by Berg Pubs); pap. 22.50 (*1-85973-152-X*, Pub. by Berg Pubs) NYU Pr.

Prisoners of Welfare: Liberating America's Poor from Unemployment & Low Wages. David R. Riemer. LC 88-3926. 219p. 1988. 57.95 (*0-275-92705-9*, C2705, Praeger Pubs) Greenwood.

Prisoners on Purpose: A Peacemaker's Guide to Jails & Prisons. Nukewatch Staff. Ed. by Samuel H. Day, Jr. (Illus.). 145p. (Orig.). (C). 1989. pap. 5.00 (*0-942046-02-1*) Prog Found.

Prisoners on the Plains: The German POW Camp at Atlanta. Glenn Thompson. 300p. (C). 1993. 49.00 (*0-929115-00-7*) Gamut Pubns.

***Prisoners' Rights: The Supreme Court & Evolving Standards of Decency, 96.** John A. Fliter. LC 00-35373. (Contributions in Legal Studies: Vol. 96). 224p. 2000. 64.00 (*0-313-31475-6*) Greenwood.

Prisoners' Rights in England & the United States. A. J. Fowles. 187p. 1990. text 75.95 (*0-566-07083-9*, Pub. by Avebry) Ashgate Pub Co.

Prisoners' Self-Help Litigation Manual. 3rd ed. John Boston & Daniel E. Manville. LC 95-17299. 1088p. 1995. pap. text 32.95 (*0-379-21212-9*) Oceana.

Prisoner's Son. Jerome Gold. 194p. (Orig.). 1996. pap. 11.95 (*0-930773-37-3*); lib. bdg. 20.95 (*0-930773-36-5*) Black Heron Pr.

***Prisoner's Wife.** Asha Bandele. 240p. 2000. reprint ed. pap. 12.95 (*0-671-02148-6*, WSP) PB.

Prisoner's Wife: A Memoir. Asha Bandele. LC 99-12117. 224p. 1999. 22.50 (*0-684-85073-7*) S&S Trade.

Prisoners Without Trial: Japanese Americans in World War II. Roger Daniels. Ed. by Eric Foner. LC 92-27144. (Critical Issue Ser.). 144p. 1993. pap. 9.00 (*0-8090-1553-6*) Hill & Wang.

Prisonhouse of Psychoanalysis. Arnold Goldberg. 184p. 1990. text 29.95 (*0-88163-121-3*) Analytic Pr.

Prisonnier de Mao, 2 vols., 1. Jean Pasqualini. 1976. pap. 10.95 (*0-7859-4062-6*) Fr & Eur.

Prisonnier de Mao, 2 vols., 2. Jean Pasqualini. 1976. pap. 10.95 (*0-7859-4063-4*) Fr & Eur.

Prisonniere. Marcel Proust. (Folio Ser.: No. 785). (FRE.). 499p. 1987. pap. 12.95 (*2-07-038177-3*) Schoenhof.

Prisonniere Bk. 6: A la Recherche du Temps Perdu. Marcel Proust. (FRE.). 1989. pap. 15.95 (*0-8288-3764-3*, F119580) Fr & Eur.

Prisonniere de Sargasses. Jean Rhys. (FRE.). 1977. pap. 10.95 (*0-7859-4083-9*) Fr & Eur.

Prisonniers du Zoo. Denis Cote. (Novels in the Roman Jeunesse Ser.). (FRE.). 96p. (J). (gr. 4-7). 1988. pap. 8.95 (*2-89021-074-X*, Pub. by La Courte Ech) Firefly Bks Ltd.

Prisons. Renardo Barden. (Troubled Society Ser.: Set II). 64p. (J). 1991. lib. bdg. 17.95 (*0-86593-110-0*) Rourke Corp.

Prisons. Ann Gaines. LC 98-22353. (Crime, Justice, & Punishment Ser.). (Illus.). 100p. (YA). (gr. 8 up). 1998. lib. bdg. 19.95 (*0-7910-4315-0*) Chelsea Hse.

***Prisons.** Bryan J. Grapes. LC 99-41272. (Current Controversies Ser.). 320p. (gr. 9-12). 2000. pap. 17.45 (*0-7377-0146-3*); lib. bdg. 27.45 (*0-7377-0147-1*) Greenhaven.

Prisons. Mary Lee Settle. LC 96-2224. (Beulah Quintet Ser.: Bk. I). 1996. pap. 12.95 (*1-57003-114-2*) U of SC Pr.

***Prisons.** Michael Tonry. 300p. 1999. lib. bdg. 50.00 (*0-226-80849-1*) U Ch Pr.

Prisons: Detecting Bias. Neal Bernards & Bonnie Szumski. LC 90-45284. (Opposing Viewpoints Juniors Ser.). (Illus.). 36p. (J). (gr. 3-6). 1990. lib. bdg. 16.20 (*0-89908-604-7*) Greenhaven.

Prisons: Index of Modern Information. Helen M. Markle. LC 88-47617. 150p. 1988. 47.50 (*0-88164-862-0*); pap. 44.50 (*0-88164-863-9*) ABBE Pubs Assn.

Prisons: Inside the Big House. Andy Hjelmeland. LC 95-12723. (Pro/Con Ser.). (J). 1996. lib. bdg. 21.27 (*0-8225-2607-7*, Lerner Publctns) Lerner Pub.

***Prisons: Shut Them All Down!** Ted R. Weiland. 15p. 2000. pap. 4.00 (*0-9679392-2-4*) Mission Israel.

Prisons: The Politics of Reform. Rod Morgan. (Conflict & Change in Britain Ser.: A New Audit Ser.). (C). 1997. pap. 25.00 (*0-485-80108-6*, Pub. by Athlone Pr); text 65.00 (*0-485-80008-X*, Pub. by Athlone Pr) Humanities.

Prisons: Today & Tomorrow. Ed. by Joycelyn M. Pollock. LC 96-77254. 505p. 1997. 59.00 (*0-8342-0950-0*, 09500) Aspen Pub.

Prisons: Today's Debate. Marilyn T. Oliver. LC 96-40137. (Issues in Focus Ser.). 128p. (YA). (gr. 6 up). 1997. lib. bdg. 20.95 (*0-89490-906-1*) Enslow Pubs.

Prisons & Aids: A Public Health Opportunity. Ronald L. Braithwaite et al. LC 96-22690. (Jossey-Bass Health Ser.). 1996. 34.95 (*0-7879-0308-6*) Jossey-Bass.

Prisons & Beyond. Sanford Bates. LC 72-157324. (Select Bibliographies Reprint Ser.). 1977. reprint ed. 26.95 (*0-8369-5784-9*) Ayer.

Prisons & Corrections. Samuel J. Brakel & Bruce L. Benson. 64p. 1998. pap. 7.95 (*0-945999-60-7*, 1021) Independent Inst.

Prisons & Ideas. Milovan Djilas. 1986. 14.95 (*0-15-173087-3*) Harcourt.

Prisons & Jails. Zachary A. Kelly. LC 98-6028. (Law & Order Ser.). (J). 1998. write for info. (*0-86625-659-8*) Rourke Pub Grp.

***Prisons & Jails: A Deterrent to Crime.** rev. ed. Ed. by Abbey M. Begun. (Information Plus Reference Ser.). (Illus.). 184p. 1999. pap. text 26.95 (*1-57302-102-4*) Info Plus TX.

Prisons & Jails, Inside American Prisons. George Rush. LC 97-65246. (Illus.). 205p. (C). 1997. pap. 19.95 (*0-942728-79-3*) Copperhouse.

Prisons & Lazarettos, 2 vols. John Howard. LC 74-129312. (Criminology, Law Enforcement, & Social Problems Ser.: No. 135). (Illus.). 1973. 100.00 (*0-87585-135-5*) Patterson Smith.

Prisons & Prisoners. Constance Lytton. 1989. 10.95 (*0-86068-682-5*) Random.

Prisons & Prisoners: Historical Documents. Ed. by Sol Chaneles. LC 85-17736. (Journal of Offender Counseling, Services & Rehabilitation: Vol. 10, Nos. 1-2). 218p. 1985. text 6.95 (*0-86656-464-0*); pap. text 24.95 (*0-86656-486-1*) Haworth Pr.

Prisons & the American Conscience: A History of U. S. Federal Corrections. Paul W. Keve. (Illus.). 296p. (C). 1995. reprint ed. pap. 21.95 (*0-8093-2003-7*) S Ill U Pr.

Prisons & the Criminal Justice System. Vivian V. Gordon & Lois Smith-Owens. (Think Ser.). 160p. (YA). (gr. 7 up). 1992. pap. 9.95 (*0-8027-7370-2*); lib. bdg. 15.85 (*0-8027-8121-7*) Walker & Co.

Prisons & the Law. Robert Levy. 1995. boxed set. write for info. (*0-406-02514-2*, UK, MICHIE) LEXIS Pub.

Prisons & the Problem of Order. Richard Sparks et al. LC 96-1645. (Clarendon Studies in Criminology). (Illus.). 396p. (C). 1996. text 95.00 (*0-19-825818-6*, Clarendon Pr) OUP.

Prisons & Visions: Pierre Unik's Journey from Surrealism into Marxism. Helen Schawlow. (American University Studies: Romance Languages & Literature: Ser. II, Vol. 120). X, 209p. (C). 1989. text 37.50 (*0-8204-0942-1*) P Lang Pubng.

Prisons & Women. Blanche Hampton. 200p. 1995. pap. 17.95 (*0-86840-221-4*, Pub. by New South Wales Univ Pr) Intl Spec Bk.

Prisons Around the World: Studies in International Penology. Michael K. Carlie & Kevin I. Minor. 336p. (C). 1992. text. write for info. (*0-697-14310-4*) Brown & Benchmark.

Prisons for Profit: Public Justice, Private Interests. John Donahue. 30p. (Orig.). 1988. 10.00 (*0-944826-02-4*) Economic Policy Inst.

***Prisons Handbook.** 3rd ed. Mark Leech. LC 99-205145. 507p. 1999. pap. 80.00 (*1-872870-72-4*, Pub. by Waterside Pr) Gaunt.

***Prisons Handbook 2000.** 4th ed. Mark Leech & Deborah Cheney. 528p. 1999. pap. 95.00 (*1-872870-82-1*, Pub. by Waterside Pr) Gaunt.

***Prisons in America: A Reference Handbook.** Nicole H. Rafter & Debra L. Stanley. LC 99-35719. (Contemporary World Issues Ser.). 200p. 1999. lib. bdg. 45.00 (*1-57607-102-2*) ABC-CLIO.

Prisons in Canada. Luc Gosselin. Tr. by Penelope Williams from FRE.Tr. of Les/Penetenciers: Un Systeme a Abattre. 212p. 1982. pap. 12.99 (*0-919619-11-8*, Pub. by Black Rose) Consort Bk Sales.

Prisons in Context. Ed. by Roy D. King & Mike Maguire. (Illus.). 164p. 1994. pap. text 24.00 (*0-19-825865-8*) OUP.

Prisons in Crisis. William L. Selke. LC 92-42807. 1993. 26.95 (*0-253-35149-9*); pap. 10.95 (*0-253-20814-9*) Ind U Pr.

Prisons (Le Carceri) The Complete First & Second States. Giovanni B. Piranesi. LC 72-92762. (Illus.). 63p. 1974. reprint ed. pap. 12.95 (*0-486-21540-7*) Dover.

Prisons of Air. Moncure D. Conway. (Works of Moncure Daniel Conway). 1990. reprint ed. lib. bdg. 79.00 (*0-7812-2342-3*) Rprt Serv.

Prisons of Light: Black Holes. Kitty Ferguson. (Illus.). 214p. (C). 1986. text 27.95 (*0-521-49518-0*) Cambridge U Pr.

Prisons of Light - Black Holes. Kitty Ferguson. (Illus.). 214p. (C). 1998. reprint ed. pap. 15.95 (*0-521-62571-8*) Cambridge U Pr.

Prisons of Marguerite de Navarre. Marguerite D'Angouleme. 152p. pap. 40.00 (*0-7049-0124-2*) Pegasus Pr.

Prisons of the Mind: A True Story of a Girl - Subjected to an Arranged Polygamist Marriage at 15... Kaziah M. Hancock. (Illus.). 516p. 1987. 17.50 (*0-9619898-0-7*); pap. write for info. (*0-9619898-1-5*) Desert Blossom.

Prisons of Tomorrow. Ed. by Edwin H. Sutherland & Thorsten D. Sellin. LC 74-3815. (Criminal Justice in America Ser.). 1974. reprint ed. 26.95 (*0-405-06170-6*) Ayer.

Prisons, Peace, & Terrorism: Penal Policy in the Reduction of Political Violence in Northern Ireland, Italy, & the Spanish Basque Country, 1968-1997. Michael V. Page. LC 98-23859. 1998. text 65.00 (*0-312-21655-6*) St Martin.

Prisons That Could Not Hold. Barbara Deming. Ed. by Sky Vanderlinde. LC 94-49159. 248p. (Orig.). 1995. pap. 14.95 (*0-8203-1737-3*) U of Ga Pr.

Prisons 2000: An International Perspective on the Current State & Future of Imprisonment. Ed. by Roger Matthews & Peter Francis. 288p. 1996. text 69.95 (*0-312-16096-8*) St Martin.

Prisons under Protest. Phil Scraton et al. (Crime, Justice & Social Policy Ser.). 160p. 1991. 123.00 (*0-335-15181-7*); pap. 35.95 (*0-335-15180-9*) OpUniv Pr.

Prisons We Choose To. Doris Lessing. LC 87-45064. 96p. 1987. 10.00 (*0-06-039077-8*) HarperTrade.

Pristina Medicamenta: Ancient & Medieval Botany. Jerry Stannard. Ed. by Katherine E. Stannard & Richard Kay. LC 98-74833. (Variorum Collected Studies Ser.). 14p. 1999. text 110.95 (*0-86078-773-7*) Ashgate Pub Co.

Pristine Culture of Capitalism: Historical Essay on Old Regimes & Modern States. Ellen Meiksins-Wood. 200p. (C). 1991. pap. 18.00 (*0-86091-572-7*, Pub. by Verso) Norton.

Pristine Lessons for the E-Trader. Capra. 1999. 24.95 (*0-07-134651-1*) McGraw.

Pristine Yi King: Pure Wisdom of Ancient China. Louis T. Culling. LC 84-48090. (Inner Guide Ser.). 224p. (Orig.). 1999. pap. 7.95 (*0-87542-107-5*) Llewellyn Pubns.

Prisunic. Yves Deluc & Ruck. 4.25 (*0-88436-905-6*) EMC-Paradigm.

Pritchard Family History: The Virginia Line from Thomas, Jamestown Immigrant. Emily P. Cary. LC 99-226686. (Illus.). 432p. 1999. pap. 34.00 (*0-7884-1116-0*, C072) Heritage Bk.

Pritchard on the Law of Wills & Administration of Estates, 3 vols. 5th ed. Jack W. Robinson, Sr. & Jeff Mobley. LC 94-79590. 1994. 225.00 (*1-55834-201-X*, 66040-11, MICHIE) LEXIS Pub.

Pritchard on the Law of Wills & Administration of Estates. 5th ed. Jack W. Robinson, Sr. & Jeff Mobley. 1995. suppl. ed. 40.00 (*0-614-25256-3*, 66035-11, MICHIE) LEXIS Pub.

Pritchard on Wills & Administration of Estates Vols. 1-3: 1998 Cumulative Supplement. 5th ed. Jack W. Robinson, Sr. & Jeffrey Mobley. 120p. 1998. suppl. ed. 85.00 (*0-327-00306-5*, 66035-14) LEXIS Pub.

***Pritchard on Wills & Administration of Estates, 1999 Cumulative Supplement: Pocketpart, 3 vols.** 5th ed. Incl. Vol. 1. 1999. (*0-327-01749-X*, 66044-15); Vol. 2. 1999. (*0-327-01750-3*, 66045-15); Vol. 3. 1999. (*0-327-01751-1*, 66046-15); 250p. 1999. suppl. ed. write for info. (*0-327-01748-1*, 66035-15) LEXIS Pub.

Pritcher Mass. Gordon Rupert Dickson. 256p. 1988. pap. 3.50 (*0-8125-3540-5*, Pub. by Tor Bks) St Martin.

Pritchett Century. V. S. Pritchett. LC 97-15360. 800p. 1997. 23.00 (*0-679-60244-5*) Modern Lib NY.

Pritchett Century. V. S. Pritchett. LC 98-21226. 1999. pap. 14.95 (*0-375-75217-X*) Modern Lib NY.

Prithivinarayan Shah the Founder of Modern Nepal. Ed. by Tulasi R. Vaidya. (C). 1993. 120.00 (*0-7855-0208-4*, Pub. by Ratna Pustak Bhandar) St Mut.

Prithvinarayan Shah: The Founder of Modern Nepal. Tulsi R. Vaidya. (C). 1993. 44.00 (*81-7041-701-5*, Pub. by Anmol) S Asia.

***Pritikin Principle: The Calorie Density Solution.** Robert Pritikin. LC 99-89980. (Illus.). 224p. 2000. 24.95 (*0-7370-1616-7*) T-L Custom Pub.

Pritikin Program for Diet & Exercise. Nathan Pritikin & Patrick McGrady. 464p. 1984. mass mkt. 6.99 (*0-553-27192-X*) Bantam.

Pritikin Promise. Nathan Pritikin. 1991. mass mkt. 5.99 (*0-671-73267-6*) PB.

Pritikin Weight Loss Breakthrough: Five Easy Steps to Outsmart Your Fat Instinct. Robert Pritikin. 371p. 1999. mass mkt. 6.99 (*0-451-19572-8*, Sig) NAL.

Pritikin Weight Loss Breakthrough: 5 Easy Steps to Outsmart Your Fat Instinct. Date not set. 23.95 (*0-525-94433-8*) NAL.

Pritzker Architecture Prize: The First Twenty Years. Colin Amery et al. LC 98-41323. (Illus.). 208p. 1999. 49.50 (*0-8109-4371-9*, Pub. by Abrams) Time Warner.

Pritzker Architecture Prize: The First Twenty Years. Martha Thorne. LC 98-41323. (Illus.). 208p. 1999. pap. 29.95 (*0-8109-2910-4*, Pub. by Abrams) Art Inst Chi.

Privacy. Robinson. (Ethics & Behavior Ser.: Vol. 7, No. 3). 1997. pap. 20.00 (*0-8058-9854-9*) L Erlbaum Assocs.

Privacy. John B. Young. LC 77-12583. 358p. reprint ed. pap. 111.00 (*0-608-30069-1*, 201780300008) Bks Demand.

Privacy, Set. Ed. by Raymond I. Wacks. LC 93-9584. (International Library of Essays in Law & Legal Theory: Vol. 25). (C). 1993. lib. bdg. 250.00 (*0-8147-9218-9*) NYU Pr.

Privacy, Vol. 1. Raymond I. Wacks. (C). 1993. lib. bdg. 150.00 (*0-8147-9264-2*) NYU Pr.

Privacy, Vol. 2. Raymond I. Wacks. (C). 1993. lib. bdg. 150.00 (*0-8147-9265-0*) NYU Pr.

Privacy: A Selected Bibliography & Topical Index of Social Science Materials. Howard A. Latin. iv, 94p. 1976. pap. 17.50 (*0-8377-0805-2*, Rothman) W S Hein.

Privacy: A Vanishing Value? Ed. by William C. Bier. LC 79-56138. (Pastoral Psychology Ser.: No. 10). xii, 398p. 1980. 35.00 (*0-8232-1044-8*) Fordham.

Privacy: Cases & Materials. Richard Turkington et al. LC 91-75720. 785p. 1992. 70.00 (*0-916081-29-X*) J Marshall Pub Co.

Privacy: Individual Right vs Social Needs. Ted Gottfried. LC 93-26791. (Issue & Debate Ser.). 112p. (YA). (gr. 7 up). 1994. lib. bdg. 23.90 (*1-56294-403-7*) Millbrook Pr.

Privacy: Studies in Social & Cultural History. Barrington Moore. LC 83-23524. 342p. reprint ed. pap. 106.10 (*0-7837-0041-5*, 204010600014) Bks Demand.

Privacy: The Debate in the U. S. Strum. LC 97-74702. (C). 1997. text 21.00 (*0-15-501880-9*, Pub. by Harcourt Coll Pubs) Harcourt.

Privacy Act of 1974: Public Law 93-579. 15p. 1974. pap. 2.50 (*0-16-003302-0*) USGPO.

***Privacy & Confidentiality of Health Information.** Jill C. Dennis. LC 00-9556. 2000. 39.95 (*0-7879-5278-8*) Jossey-Bass.

Privacy & Data Protection: An International Bibliography. David H. Flaherty. LC 84-15415. (Professional Librarian Ser.). 276p. 1984. 45.00 (*0-86729-121-4*, Hall Reference) Macmillan.

***Privacy & Employment Law.** John D. R. Craig. 320p. 1999. 54.00 (*1-84113-059-1*, Pub. by Hart Pub) Intl Spec Bk.

***Privacy & Health Care.** Ed. by James M. Humber & Robert F. Almeder. (Biomedical Ethics Reviews Ser.). (Illus.). 180p. 2000. 44.50 (*0-89603-878-5*) Humana.

Privacy & Human Rights: An International & Comparative Study, with Special Reference to Developments in Information Technology. James Michael. LC 94-11932. 208p. 1994. 48.95 (*1-85521-381-8*, Pub. by Dartmth Pub) Ashgate Pub Co.

Privacy & Its Invasion. Deckle McLean. LC 95-9308. 152p. 1995. 47.95 (*0-275-95335-1*, Praeger Pubs) Greenwood.

Privacy & Loyalty: In the Law of Obligations. Ed. by Peter Birks. LC 97-23790. (SPTL Seminar Ser.). 342p. (C). 1997. text 92.00 (*0-19-876488-X*) OUP.

P

An Asterisk (*) at the beginning of an entry indicates that the title is appearing for the first time.

Privacy & Personality in the Employment Relationship. Matthew W. Finkin. 20p. 1992. 7.00 (*0-89215-178-1*) U Cal LA Indus Rel.

Privacy & Press Freedom. Raymond I. Wacks. 198p. 1995. pap. 34.00 (*1-85431-454-8*, Pub. by Blackstone Pr) Gaunt.

Privacy & Print. Cecile M. Jagodzinski. LC 98-35586. 256p. 1999. text 45.00 (*0-8139-1839-1*) U Pr of Va.

Privacy & Property. (Hume Papers on Public Policy 2.3). 96p. 1996. pap. 17.50 (*0-7486-0593-2*, Pub. by Edinburgh U Pr) Col U Pr.

Privacy & Publicity: Modern Architecture As Mass Media. Beatriz Colomina. LC 93-36205. (Illus.). 401p. 1994. 52.50 (*0-262-03214-7*) MIT Pr.

Privacy & Publicity: Modern Architecture As Mass Media. Beatriz Colomina. (Illus.). 408p. 1996. reprint ed. pap. text 25.00 (*0-262-53139-9*) MIT Pr.

Privacy & Publicity (Readings from "Communications & the Law") Ed. by Theodore R. Kupferman. vii, 262p. 1990. 45.00 (*0-88736-508-6*) W S Hein.

***Privacy & Rights to the Visual: The Internet Debate.** Jacques N. Catudal. (Philosophy & the Global Context Ser.). 1999. pap. 22.95 (*0-8476-8800-3*) Rowman.

Privacy & Social Freedom. Ferdinand D. Schoeman. (Studies in Philosophy & Public Policy). 239p. (C). 1992. text 74.95 (*0-521-41564-0*) Cambridge U Pr.

Privacy & Social Services. Terry Thomas. 160p. 1995. pap. 33.95 (*1-85742-247-3*, Pub. by Arena) Ashgate Pub Co.

Privacy & the Politics of Intimate Life. Patricia Boling. 240p. 1996. text 39.95 (*0-8014-3271-5*); pap. text 15.95 (*0-8014-8351-4*) Cornell U Pr.

Privacy & the Press: The Law, the Mass Media, & the First Amendment. Donald R. Pember. LC 79-152335. (Washington Paperback Ser.: No. 64). (Illus.). 312p. 1972. reprint ed. pap. 10.00 (*0-295-95265-2*) U of Wash Pr.

Privacy As a Constitutional Right: Sex, Drugs, & the Right to Life. Darien A. McWhirter & Jon D. Bible. LC 91-47986. 224p. 1992. 55.00 (*0-89930-638-1*, MWV, Quorum Bks) Greenwood.

Privacy, Confidentiality & Discrimination in Genetics: Task Force on Health Records & Genetic Privacy, July 22, 1997 USGPO Staff. LC 98-169378. v, 106 p. 1998. pap. write for info. (*0-16-056474-3*) USGPO.

***Privacy-Enhanced Business: Adapting to the Online Environment.** Curtis D. Frye. LC 00-32810. 2000. write for info. (*1-56720-321-3*, Quorum Bks) Greenwood.

***Privacy for Sale: How Big Brother & Others Are Selling Your Private Secrets for Profit.** Michael E. Chesbro. 184p. 1999. pap. 20.00 (*1-58160-033-X*) Paladin Pr.

Privacy in a Fishbowl. Gyeorgos C. Hatonn. 236p. (Orig.). 1995. pap. 6.00 (*1-56935-042-6*) Phoenix Source.

Privacy in America: Is Your Private Life in the Public Eye? David F. Linowes. LC 88-20645. 206p. 1989. 19.95 (*0-252-01604-1*) U of Ill Pr.

Privacy in Britain. Walter F. Pratt. LC 76-50289. 266p. 1979. 36.50 (*0-8387-2030-7*) Bucknell U Pr.

Privacy in Colonial New England. David H. Flaherty. LC 76-154804. 303p. reprint ed. pap. 94.00 (*0-7837-6209-7*, 204593300009) Bks Demand.

Privacy in Electronic Commerce: A Compendium of Essays on the Use of Information. Ed. by L. Richard Fischer. LC 97-209460. 1975. pap. 5.00 (*0-89982-055-7*) Am Bankers.

Privacy in Employment Law: 1999 Cumulative Supplement. Matthew W. Finkin. 386p. 1999. pap., suppl. ed. 135.00 (*1-57018-135-7*, 1135-PR9) BNA Books.

Privacy in Telecommunications European & an American Approach. Blanca R. Ruiz. LC 96-22773. 1997. 134.00 (*90-411-0274-4*) Kluwer Law Intl.

Privacy in the Information Age. Fred H. Cate. LC 97-21114. 248p. 1997. 39.95 (*0-8157-1316-9*); pap. 16.95 (*0-8157-1315-0*) Brookings.

Privacy in the Information Age. Harry Henderson. LC 99-21572. (Library in a Book). 272p. 1999. 39.95 (*0-8160-3870-8*) Facts on File.

Privacy in the Information Age. unabridged ed. Thomas Rilly & Robert P. Gillis. 300p. (Orig.). 1996. pap. 195.00 (*1-890299-04-9*) Gov Technology.

Privacy in the Workplace: A Guide for Human Resource Managers. Jon D. Bible & Darien A. McWhirter. LC 90-9075. 320p. 1990. 65.00 (*0-89930-473-7*, BPJ/, Quorum Bks) Greenwood.

Privacy in the Workplace: Rights, Procedures & Policies. Kurt H. Decker. LC 94-12177. 540p. 1994. ring bd. 62.50 (*0-318-72686-6*) LRP Pubns.

Privacy, Intimacy, & Isolation. Julie Inness. 176p. 1996. pap. 16.95 (*0-19-510460-9*) OUP.

Privacy, Intimacy & Isolation. Julie Inness. 176p. 1992. text 55.00 (*0-19-507148-4*) OUP.

Privacy Is Idiocy? Between Mathematics & History I. J. Fang. 1997. pap. write for info. (*0-318-72911-3*) PAIDEIA & PM.

Privacy Issues in Biomedical & Clinical Research: Privacy Issues in Biomedical & Clinical Research Proceedings of Forum on November 1, 1997, National Academy of Sciences, Washington, D. C. National Research Council. LC 99-183451. (Compass Ser.). ix, 48 p. 1998. write for info. (*0-309-06328-0*) Natl Acad Pr.

Privacy, Law & Public Policy. David M. O'Brien. LC 79-14131. (Praeger Special Studies). 262p. 1979. 67.95 (*0-275-90403-2*, C0403, Praeger Pubs) Greenwood.

Privacy 1995. Mark Nestmann. 208p. 1995. 100.00 (*3-9520851-0-3*, Pub. by W Beck Verlag) Tattered Cover.

Privacy of Storm. James C. Schaap. 193p. 1990. pap. 8.25 (*0-932914-21-7*) Dordt Coll Pr.

Privacy of the Self: Papers on Psychoanalytic Theory & Technique. M. Masud Khan. LC 73-20932. 399p. 1974. 55.00 (*0-8236-4310-7*) Intl Univs Pr.

Privacy of Wind: Poems. Perie Longo. LC 97-521. 80p. (Orig.). 1997. pap. 10.00 (*1-880284-23-5*) J Daniel.

Privacy on the Line: The Politics of Wiretapping & Encryption. Whitfield Diffie & Susan Landau. LC 97-42347. (Illus.). 352p. 1998. 30.00 (*0-262-04167-7*) MIT Pr.

Privacy on the Line: The Politics of Wiretapping & Encryption. Whitfield Diffie & Susan Landau. 360p. 1999. pap. text 15.00 (*0-262-54100-9*) MIT Pr.

Privacy I: Exploring Questions of Media Morality: A Special Issue of the "Journal of Mass Media Ethics", Vol. 9, No. 3. Ed. by Jay Black & Ralph Barney. 64p. 1995. pap. 20.00 (*0-8058-9951-0*) L Erlbaum Assocs.

Privacy One: Words Without Song. Kenneth Gaburo. (Illus.). 48p. 1977. 10.00 (*0-939044-25-0*) Lingua Pr.

***Privacy Plan: How to Keep What You Own Secret from High-Tech Snoops, Lawyers & Con Men, 1 Vol.** Robert J. Mintz & Peter S. Doft. (Illus.). 268p. 1999. 34.95 (*0-9639971-1-4*) F OBrien & Sons.

Privacy Powerpak. unabridged ed. Edward J. Leary. Ed. by Karen O'Neill. LC 97-137669. 164p. 1996. spiral bd. 35.00 (*0-9654949-0-X*) Privacy Group.

Privacy Protection. Judith W. DeCew. pap. 0.00 (*0-691-02324-7*) Princeton U Pr.

***Privacy Rights: A Reference Handbook.** Leigh Glenn. 2000. lib. bdg. 39.50 (*1-57607-133-2*) ABC-CLIO.

Privacy Rights Handbook: How to Take Control of Your Personal Information. Privacy Rights Clearinghouse Staff & Beth Givens. LC 97-16596. 336p. 1997. pap. 12.50 (*0-380-78684-2*, Avon Bks) Morrow Avon.

Privacy Rights of Employees. Linda H. McPharlin. Ed. by Marie Hagelstein. 62p. 1994. pap. text 20.00 (*0-88124-754-5*, BU-32600) Cont Ed Bar-CA.

Privacy, the Privacy Act, Security, Data Networks & Communications. Irving I. Hodell. 160p. 1998. 44.50 (*0-7883-1862-4*); pap. 39.50 (*0-7883-1863-2*) ABBE Pubs Assn.

Privacy II: Exploring Questions of Media Morality: A Special Issue of the "Journal of Mass Media Ethics", Vol. 9, No. 4, 1994. Ed. by Jay Black & Ralph Barney. 71p. 1995. pap. 20.00 (*0-8058-9950-2*) L Erlbaum Assocs.

Privacy 2: My, My, My What a Wonderful Fall. Kenneth Gaburo. (Illus.). 22p. 1976. 8.00 (*0-939044-12-9*) Lingua Pr.

Privacy 2000. Mark Nestmann. 264p. 1997. pap. 75.00 (*0-9657151-3-2*, Pub. by Asset Protection Intl) Pathway Bk Serv.

Privatangestellten in der Modernen Wirtschaftsentwicklung: White Collar Workers in Modern Economic Development. Emil Lederer. LC 74-25765. (European Sociology Ser.). 300p. 1975. reprint ed. 28.95 (*0-405-06519-1*) Ayer.

Private. Ed. by Turbaugh. 1995. 45.00 (*0-85449-099-X*, Pub. by Gay Mens Pr) LPC InBook.

Private. Lester Atwell. 500p. 1997. reprint ed. 39.95 (*0-9678035-0-0*) A & A Pubng.

Private, No. 5. Mary Ahrendt et al. (Illus.). 93p. 1990. pap. 7.00 (*1-881377-00-8*) Private Lives.

Private, No. 6. Jeffery R. Allen et al. (Illus.). 163p. 1991. pap. 7.00 (*1-881377-01-6*) Private Lives.

Private Academies of Tokugawa Japan. Richard Rubinger. LC 81-47950. (Illus.). 300p. 1982. reprint ed. pap. 93.00 (*0-608-02591-7*, 206324800004) Bks Demand.

***Private Accountant-Client Relationship in Jeopardy.** Frank M. Zaveral. 1999. pap. write for info. (*1-57655-183-0*) Independ Inst.

Private Action & the Public Good. Walter W. Powell & Elisabeth S. Clemens. LC 97-26367. 320p. 1998. 42.00 (*0-300-06449-7*) Yale U Pr.

Private Action/Public Good: Maryland's Nonprofit Sector in a Time of Change. Lester M. Salamon. LC 97-74707. 1997. pap. 60.00 (*0-9660113-0-9*) MANO.

Private Acts. Linda G. Sexton. 1992. mass mkt. 4.99 (*0-446-36328-6*, Pub. by Warner Bks) Little.

Private Acts in Public Places: A Social History of Divorce in the Formative Era of American Family Law. Richard H. Chused. LC 94-1335. 248p. (C). 1994. text 34.50 (*0-8122-3202-X*) U of Pa Pr.

Private Acts, Social Consequences: AIDS & the Politics of Public Health. Ronald Bayer. 280p. 1989. 35.00 (*0-02-901961-3*) Free Pr.

Private Acts, Social Consequences: AIDS & the Politics of Public Health. Ronald Bayer. LC 90-42039. 282p. 1991. pap. 17.95 (*0-8135-1624-2*) Rutgers U Pr.

***Private Adoption in Kentucky.** 3rd ed. Mitchell A. Charney & Mary A. Maple. (Illus.). 222p. 1998. pap. 44.00 (*1-58757-024-6*, FM031) Univ of KY.

Private Affair. C. Anderson. mass mkt. 6.95 (*0-7472-5211-4*, Pub. by Headline Bk Pub) Trafalgar.

Private Affair. Donna Hill. 384p. 1998. mass mkt. 4.99 (*0-7860-0484-3*, Pinncle Kensgtn) Kensgtn Pub Corp.

***Private Affair.** Donna Hill. (Arabesque Ser.). 2000. mass mkt. 5.99 (*1-58314-078-6*) BET Bks.

***Private Affair.** Donna Hill. (Arabesque Ser.). 2000. mass mkt. 5.99 (*1-58314-158-8*) BET Bks.

Private Affairs. Judith Michael, pseud. 1994. mass mkt. 6.99 (*0-671-89957-0*) PB.

***Private Affairs: Critical Ventures in the Culture of Social Relations.** Philip Brian Harper. LC 99-6005. 1999. pap. 16.95 (*0-8147-3594-0*) NYU Pr.

Private Affairs: Critical Ventures in the Culture of Social Relations. Phillip B. Harper. LC 99-6005. (Illus.). 200p. 1999. text 50.00 (*0-8147-3593-2*) NYU Pr.

Private Affairs of George Washington. Stephen Decatur. LC 77-86596. (American Scene Ser.). 1969. reprint ed. 45.00 (*0-306-71416-7*) Da Capo.

Private Agriculture in the Soviet Union: A Soviet Agricultural Anomaly. Stefan Hedlund. 208p. 1989. 49.95 (*0-415-03126-5*, A3443) Routledge.

Private Altars. Katherine Mosby. 384p. 1996. mass mkt. 6.99 (*0-425-15236-7*) Berkley Pub.

***Private Altars.** Katherine Mosby. 2000. 13.95 (*0-425-17126-4*) Berkley Pub.

Private Alternatives to Social Security in Other Countries. Peter J. Ferrara et al. 40p. 1995. pap. 10.00 (*1-56808-066-2*, 200) Natl Ctr Pol.

Private & Commercial: Covers All Aeronautical Knowledge Required to Pass the FAA Knowledge Exam... 2nd rev. ed. Trevor Thom. (Pilot's Manual Ser.). (Illus.). 690p. 1995. pap. 29.95 (*1-56027-304-6*, ASA-PM-2) ASA Inc.

Private & Commercial Recreation. Ed. by Arlin Epperson. LC 86-50113. 463p. 1986. 25.95 (*0-910251-12-6*) Venture Pub PA.

Private & Commerical Pilot Helicopter Practical Test Standards, FAA-8081-HD: FAA-8081-HD. rev. ed. FAA Staff. (Practical Test Standards Ser.). 1988. reprint ed. pap. 4.95 (*1-56027-370-4*, ASA-8081-HC) ASA Inc.

Private & Confidential: Letters from British Ministers in Washington to Their Foreign Secretaries in London, 1845-67. James J. Barnes & Patience P. Barnes. LC 91-50101. 480p. (C). 1993. 59.50 (*0-945636-33-4*) Susquehanna U Pr.

Private & Official Correspondence, 5 vols. Benjamin F. Butler. LC 74-39570. reprint ed. 225.00 (*0-404-01310-4*) AMS Pr.

***Private & Personal: Questions & Answers for Girls Only.** Carol Weston. LC 99-96353. 368p. (YA). (gr. 4-7). 2000. pap. 9.95 (*0-380-81025-5*, Avon Bks) Morrow Avon.

Private & Personal Reading Journal. 16p. (J). (gr. 3-7). 1989. pap. 3.50 (*0-8352-2842-8*) Bowker.

Private & Public: Individuals, Households & Body Politic in Locke & Hutcheson. Daniela Gobetti. LC 91-33774. 240p. (C). (gr. 13). 1992. 80.00 (*0-415-03174-5*) Routledge.

***Private & Public Economic Advisor: Paul W. McCracken.** Sidney L. Jones. 464p. 2000. 69.00 (*0-7618-1698-4*) U Pr of Amer.

Private & Public Ethics: Tensions Between Conscience & Institutional Responsibility. Ed. by Donald G. Jones. LC 78-78184. (Symposium Ser.: Vol. 4). 325p. 1978. lib. bdg. 99.95 (*0-88946-993-8*) E Mellen.

***Private & Public Faith.** William Stringfellow. 94p. 1999. pap. 12.00 (*1-57910-215-8*) Wipf & Stock.

Private & Public Initiatives: Working Together for Health & Education. Jacques Van Der Gaag. LC 95-222718. (Directions in Development Ser.). 76p. 1995. pap. 22.00 (*0-8213-3417-4*, 13417) World Bank.

Private & Public Prisons: Studies Comparing Operational Costs And/Or Quality of Service. (Illus.). 41p. (Orig.). (C). 1996. pap. text 25.00 (*0-7881-3602-X*) DIANE Pub.

Private & Public School Partnerships: Sharing Lessons about Decentralization. Jean Madsen. LC 96-12658. 240p. 1996. 79.95 (*0-7507-0536-1*, Falmer Pr); pap. 27.95 (*0-7507-0537-X*, Falmer Pr) Taylor & Francis.

Private & Public Social Inventions in Modern Society: Polish Philosophical Studies II. Ed. by Leon Dyczewski & John Kromkowski. LC 93-11928. (Cultural Heritage & Contemporary Change Series IVA: Vol. 2). 330p. 1994. 45.00 (*1-56518-050-X*); pap. 17.50 (*1-56518-051-8*) Coun Res Values.

Private & Untimetabled Railway Stations: Halts & Stopping Places. G. Croughton et al. 148p. (C). 1985. 75.00 (*0-85361-281-1*) St Mut.

Private Angelo. Eric Linklater. (Classics Ser.). 262p. 1995. pap. 11.95 (*0-86241-376-1*, Pub. by Canongate Books) Interlink Pub.

Private Antitrust Actions: The Structure & Process of Civil Antitrust Litigation. annuals C. Douglas Floyd et al. 1344p. 1996. boxed set 155.00 (*0-316-28653-2*, 86532) Aspen Law.

Private Antitrust Litigation: New Evidence, New Learning. Lawrence J. White. (Regulation of Economic Activity Ser.: No. 16). 448p. 1987. 55.00 (*0-262-23131-X*) MIT Pr.

Private Architecture: Masterpieces of the Twentieth Century. Susan Doubilet. LC 98-20360. (Illus.). 360p. 1998. 75.00 (*1-58093-008-5*, Pub. by Monacelli Pr) Penguin Putnam.

Private Armies & Military Intervention. David Shearer. (Adelphi Papers Ser.: No. 316). (Illus.). 88p. 1998. pap. text 28.50 (*0-19-829440-9*) OUP.

Private Assumption of Previously Public Responsibilities: The Expanding Role of Private Institutions in Public Environmental Decision-Making. American Bar Association, Standing Committee on En. LC 86-72459. 37p. 1986. pap. 15.00 (*0-89707-270-7*, 359-0015) Amer Bar Assn.

Private Assumption of Public Responsibilities: The Role of American Business in Urban Manpower Programs. Peter Kobrak. LC 72-83571. (Special Studies in U. S. Economic, Social & Political Issues). 1973. 39.50 (*0-685-02675-2*) Irvington.

Private Attorneys: Selected Attorneys' Fee Awards Against Nine Federal Agencies in 1993 & 1994. (Illus.). 32p. (Orig.). (C). 1996. pap. text 20.00 (*0-7881-3107-9*) DIANE Pub.

Private Authority & International Affairs. Ed. by A. Claire Cutler et al. LC 98-20843. (SUNY Series in Global Politics). 416p. (C). 1999. text 73.50 (*0-7914-4119-9*); pap. text 24.95 (*0-7914-4120-2*) State U NY Pr.

Private Bankers of U. S. - Canada. Ed. by S. Durst. LC 88-73214. 1989. pap. 10.00 (*0-942666-59-3*) S J Durst.

Private Banking: A Global Perspective. Lucy Weldon. (Gresham Bks.). 192p. 1997. boxed set 210.00 (*1-85573-328-5*, Pub. by Woodhead Pubng) Am Educ Systs.

Private Banking: Maximising Performance in a Competitive Market. P. Molyneux & D. Maude. 280p. 1996. 170.00 (*1-85564-448-7*, Pub. by Euromoney) Am Educ Systs.

Private Banking & Industrialization: The Case of Frankfurt Am Main, 1825-1875. Udo Heyn. Ed. by Stuart Bruchey. LC 80-2810. (Dissertations in European Economic History Ser.). (Illus.). 1981. lib. bdg. 46.95 (*0-405-13994-2*) Ayer.

Private Banking in Europe. Lyn Bicker. LC 95-40970. 200p. (C). 1996. 85.00 (*0-415-12977-X*) Routledge.

Private Banking in Europe. Cottrell & Cassis. 68.95 (*1-85928-432-9*) Ashgate Pub Co.

Private Bill Initiative for Michel Christophe Meili: Hearing Before the Subcommittee on Immigration of the Committee on the Judiciary, United States Senate, 105th Congress, 1st Session, on S. 768, a Bill for the Relief of Michel Christophe Meili, Mirjam Naomi Meili & Davide Meili, May 20, 1997. USGPO Staff. LC 98-160363. iii, 17 p. 1998. pap. write for info. (*0-16-056352-6*) USGPO.

Private Black Colleges at the Crossroads, 13. Daniel C. Thompson. LC 72-841. (Contributions in Afro-American & African Studies: No. 13). 308p. 1973. 35.00 (*0-8371-6410-9*, TBC/, Greenwood Pr) Greenwood.

Private Black Colleges in Texas, 1865-1954. Michael R. Heintze. LC 84-40565. (Southwestern Studies: No. 3). (Illus.). 228p. 1985. 32.95 (*0-89096-223-5*) Tex A&M Univ Pr.

Private Brewer's Guide: The Art of Brewing Ale & Porter. John Tuck. Ed. by Shane Weber. Orig. Title: The Private Brewer's Guide, 1822. 282p. 1995. pap. 19.95 (*0-9652166-0-8*) ZymoScribe.

Private Brewer's Guide, 1822 see Private Brewer's Guide: The Art of Brewing Ale & Porter

Private Business & Economic Reform in China. Susan Young. LC 94-32541. (Studies on Contemporary China). 190p. (C). (gr. 13). 1995. text 76.95 (*1-56324-500-0*, East Gate Bk); pap. text 35.95 (*1-56324-501-9*, East Gate Bk) M E Sharpe.

Private Business in China: Revival Between Ideology & Pragmatism. Willy Kraus. LC 91-16438. 256p. 1991. reprint ed. pap. 73.00 (*0-608-04385-0*, 2065166) Bks Demand.

Private Business in Developing Countries: Improved Prospects. Guy P. Pfeffermann. (IFC Discussion Paper Ser.: No. 1). 44p. 1988. pap. 22.00 (*0-8213-1130-1*, 11130) World Bank.

Private Capital Flows & the Environment: Lessons from Latin America. Ed. by Bradford S. Gentry. LC 98-27152. 400p. 1999. 100.00 (*1-85898-957-4*) E Elgar.

Private Capital Flows to Developing Countries: The Road to Financial Integration. LC 97-11785. (A World Bank Policy Research Report Ser.). (Illus.). 424p. 1997. pap. text 40.00 (*0-19-521116-2*, 61116, Pub. by World Bank) OUP.

Private Capital Flows to Emerging Markets after the Mexican Crisis. Ed. by Guillermo A. Calvo et al. LC 96-35399. 320p. (Orig.). 1996. pap. 18.95 (*0-88132-232-6*) Inst Intl Eco.

***Private Captain.** Marty Crisp. LC 00-25570. (Illus.). (J). 2001. write for info. (*0-399-23577-9*, Philomel) Peng Put Young Read.

Private Carriage - Facts to Consider. 1976. 1.00 (*0-686-31452-2*) Private Carrier.

Private Chapel in Ancient Egypt: A Study of the Chapels in the Workmen's Village a el Amarna with Special Reference to Deir el Medina & other Sites. Ann H. Bomann. 300p. 1990. 79.95 (*0-7103-0346-7*) Routledge.

***Private Charity & Public Inquiry: A History of the Filer & Peterson Commissions.** Eleanor L. Brilliant. LC 00-39647. (Philanthropic Studies). 2000. write for info. (*0-253-33751-8*) Ind U Pr.

Private Choices & Public Health: The AIDS Epidemic in an Economic Perspective. Tomas J. Philipson & Richard A. Posner. LC 93-17417. (Illus.). 272p. 1993. 37.95 (*0-674-70738-9*) HUP.

Private Choices, Public Consequences: A Discussion on Ethical Choices Using Gandhi's Seven Sins As Challenges & Guides. Alanson B. Houghton et al. 72p. (Orig.). 1992. pap. 2.95 (*0-88028-131-6*, 1167) Forward Movement.

Private Choices, Public Lives: Reproductive Technology & the New Ethics of Conception, Pregnancy & Family. Lynda Beck Fenwick. LC 97-28712. 368p. 1998. 27.50 (*0-525-94263-7*) NAL.

Private Choices, Social Costs, & Public Policy: An Economic Analysis of Public Health Issues. Nancy Hammerle. LC 92-3459. 248p. 1992. 57.95 (*0-275-94172-8*, C4172, Praeger Pubs) Greenwood.

Private Churches & Public Money: Church-Government Fiscal Relations, 1. Paul J. Weber & Dennis A. Gilbert. LC 80-1793. (Contributions to the Study of Religion Ser.: No. 1). (Illus.). 260p. 1981. 59.95 (*0-313-22484-6*, WCM/, Greenwood Pr) Greenwood.

Private City: Philadelphia in Three Periods of Its Growth. 2nd ed. Sam B. Warner, Jr. LC 68-21557. (Illus.). 266p. (C). 1987. 39.50 (*0-8122-8061-X*); pap. 18.95 (*0-8122-1243-6*) U of Pa Pr.

Private Civil War: Popular Thought During the Sectional Conflict. Randall C. Jimerson. LC 88-11765. (Illus.). 270p. 1994. pap. 14.95 (*0-8071-1962-8*) La State U Pr.

Private Clubs: Management & Operations. unabridged ed. (NGF Info Pacs Ser.). (Illus.). 204p. (Orig.). 1998. pap. 45.00 (*1-57701-001-9*, 99LB008) Natl Golf.

Private Collection. Sarah Fisher. (Black Lace Ser.). 1995. mass mkt. 5.95 (*0-352-32970-X*, Pub. by Virgin Bks) London Brdge.

Private Collection. Junior League of Palo Alto Staff. Ed. by Bonnie S. Mickelson. (Illus.). 120p. 1980. 15.95 (*0-9606324-0-9*) Jr League Palo Alto.

Private Collection. limited ed. Ken Haak. (Illus.). 82p. 1986. 75.00 (*0-9637815-0-2*) Rosehill Pr.

Private Collection, 2 vols., Set. Ed. by Bonnie S. Mickelson. 1994. boxed set 35.95 (*0-685-65601-2*) Pickle Point.

P

Private Collection, Vol. 2. Junior League of Palo Alto Staff. Ed. by Bonnie S. Mickelson. (Illus.). 120p. 1984. 15.95 (*0-9606324-1-7*) Jr League Palo Alto.

Private Collection of Edgar Degas. Ann Dumas & Gary Tinterow. Tr. by Mark Polizzotti from FRE. LC 97-17882. 1997. pap. 35.00 (*0-87099-799-8*) Metro Mus Art.

Private Collection of Edgar Degas. Ann Dumas et al. Tr. by Mark Polizzotti from FRE. LC 97-17882. (Illus.). 320p. 1997. 75.00 (*0-8109-6512-7*, Pub. by Abrams) Time Warner.

Private Collection of Edgar Degas. Ann Dumas et al. Tr. by Mark Polizzotti from FRE. LC 97-17882. 1997. pap. 45.00 (*0-87099-797-1*) Metro Mus Art.

Private Collection of Edgar Degas: A Summary Catalogue. Colta F. Ives et al. LC 97-31808. 1997. 60.00 (*0-87099-837-4*); pap. 45.00 (*0-87099-838-2*) Metro Mus Art.

Private Collection of Edgar Degas: A Summary Catalogue. Colta Feller Ives. (Illus.). 142p. 1998. 45.00 (*0-8109-6515-1*, Pub. by Abrams) Time Warner.

Private Collection of the Teachings of the Masters, Vol. 1. Athena Hamilton. 237p. 1998. 42.50 (*1-85776-346-7*, Pub. by Book Guild Ltd) Trans-Atl Phila.

Private Collection Set. 1993. 35.95 (*0-9606324-5-X*) Jr League Palo Alto.

Private Company Law. Mark Stamp. (Practice Notes Ser.). 115p. 1991. pap. write for info. (*0-85121-528-9*, Pub. by Cavendish Pubng) Gaunt.

Private Company Law. 3rd ed. Christopher Hugill & Mark Stamp. 1996. pap. 32.00 (*1-85941-300-5*, Pub. by Cavendish Pubng) Gaunt.

Private Company's Purchase of Own Shares. Trevor Johnson. 1997. write for info. (*0-406-01190-7*, BCPO, MICHIE) LEXIS Pub.

Private Confessions. Ingmar Bergman. LC 96-41618. 160p. 1996. 19.45 (*1-55970-364-4*, Pub. by Arcade Pub Inc) Time Warner.

Private Confessions. Ingmar Bergman. Tr. by Joan Tate from SWE. LC 96-41618. 176p. 1997. pap. 11.45 (*1-55970-395-4*, Pub. by Arcade Pub Inc) Time Warner.

Private Consciences & Public Reasons. Kent Greenawalt. (Illus.). 240p. 1995. pap. text 24.95 (*0-19-509419-0*) OUP.

Private Correspondence, 2 vols. Daniel Webster. (Notable American Authors Ser.). 1999. reprint ed. lib. bdg. 250.00 (*0-7812-9915-2*) Rprt Serv.

Private Correspondence of Henry Clay. Henry Clay. Ed. by Calvin Colton. LC 78-169756. (Select Bibliographies Reprint Ser.). 1977. reprint ed. 39.95 (*0-8369-5976-0*) Ayer.

Private Correspondence of Henry Clay. Henry Clay. (American Biography Ser.). 642p. 1991. reprint ed. lib. bdg. 109.00 (*0-7812-8073-7*) Rprt Serv.

Private Correspondence of Isaac Titsingh, 1785-1811, Vol. 1. Ed. by Frank Lequin. (Japonica Neerlandica Ser.: Vol. 4). (DUT.). xlix, 534p. 1990. 94.00 (*90-5063-052-9*, Pub. by Gieben) J Benjamins Pubng Co.

Private Correspondence of Lord Mccartney. C. C. Davies. (Camden Third Ser.). 63.00 (*0-86193-077-0*) David Brown.

Private Correspondences. Trudy Lewis. 180p. 1994. 19.95 (*0-8101-5033-6*, TriQuart) Northwestern U Pr.

Private Correspondences. Trudy Lewis. 198p. 1996. pap. 12.95 (*0-8101-5041-7*, TriQuart) Northwestern U Pr.

Private Cosmos. Philip Jose Farmer. 1993. reprint ed. lib. bdg. 18.95 (*0-89968-399-1*, Lghtyr Pr) Buccaneer Bks.

Private Cosmos, No. 3. Philip Jose Farmer. (World of Tiers Ser.). 1981. 18.00 (*0-932096-10-7*) Phantasia Pr.

Private Country Houses in the Netherlands. Heimerick Tromp. LC 97-191618. (Illus.). 304p. 1998. 75.00 (*90-400-9850-6*, Pub. by Waandrs) Consort Bk Sales.

***Private Couple Creates a Public Garden.** Frances K. Bickelhaupt. LC 98-90893. 1999. 19.95 (*0-533-12979-6*) Vantage.

***Private Cuisine: An Executive Chef's Secrets to Gourmet Cooking Made Easy.** David Daniluh. (Illus.). 1999. pap. 17.00 (*0-9673719-0-2*) D Daniluk.

Private Cures for Public Ills: The Promise of Privatization. Ed. by Lawrence W. Reed. LC 95-83090. 208p. (Orig.). 1996. pap. 10.95 (*1-57246-019-9*) Foun Econ Ed.

Private Dancer. Eva Rutland. (Romance Ser.). 1996. per. 3.25 (*0-373-03412-1*, 1-03412-3) Harlequin Bks.

Private Dancer. large type ed. Eva Rutland. (Mills & Boon Large Print Ser.). 288p. 1996. 23.99 (*0-263-14580-8*, Pub. by Mills & Boon) Ulverscroft.

Private Death of Public Discourse. Barry Sanders. LC 97-24485. 320p. 1998. 25.00 (*0-8070-0434-0*) Beacon Pr.

Private Decisions, Public Debate: Women, Reproduction & Population. Ed. by Judith Mirsky & Marty Radlett. (Illus.). 185p. 1995. pap. 14.95 (*1-870670-34-5*, Pub. by Panos Bks) Paul & Co Pubs.

Private Desires, Political Action: An Invitation to the Politics of Rational Choice. Michael Laver. 192p. 1997. 69.95 (*0-7619-5114-8*); pap. 24.95 (*0-7619-5115-6*) Sage.

Private Detective & Investigator Course. Max Dabbah. (ENG & SPA., Illus.). (Orig.). 1987. 450.00 (*0-945406-00-2*) Magnum Schl.

Private Devotions of Lancelot Andrewes. Lancelot Andrewes. Tr. & Intro. by F. E. Brightman. 1990. 25.75 (*0-8446-1534-X*) Peter Smith.

Private Diaries of Sir H. Rider Haggard, 1914-1925. D. S. Higgins. 320p. 24.95 (*0-8488-2586-1*) Amereon Ltd.

Private Diary of Dr. John Dee: And the Catalogue of His Library Manuscripts. Ed. by James O. Halliwell. 130p. (Orig.). 1992. reprint ed. pap. 16.95 (*1-56459-109-3*) Kessinger Pub.

Private Diary of Dr. John Dee & the Catalogue of His Library of Manuscripts. John Dee. Ed. by James O. Halliwell. (Camden Society, London. Publications, First Ser.: No. 19). reprint ed. 35.00 (*0-404-50119-2*) AMS Pr.

Private Die Match Stamps. Christopher West. LC 80-83685. (C. & S. Revenue Ser.). (Illus.). 288p. 1980. 44.95 (*0-9603498-2-0*) Castenholz Sons.

Private Die Proprietary Medicine Stamps. (Medical Handbook Ser.). 78p. 1969. 7.00 (*0-318-13308-3*) Am Topical Assn.

Private Diplomacy with the Soviet Union. Ed. by David D. Newsom. LC 86-28926. 166p. (Orig.). (C). 1987. pap. text 14.50 (*0-8191-5821-6*) U Pr of Amer.

Private Dispute Resolution in the Banking Industry. Patricia A. Ebener et al. LC 93-33574. 1993. pap. text 13.00 (*0-8330-1469-2*, MR-259-ICJ) Rand Corp.

Private Domain: An Autobiography. Paul Taylor. LC 99-234679. (Illus.). 324p. 1999. reprint ed. pap. 17.95 (*0-8229-5699-3*) U of Pittsburgh Pr.

Private Drinking Water Supplies: Quality, Testing & Options for Problem Waters. Karen Mancl et al. (Illus.). 60p. 1991. pap. 8.00 (*0-935817-22-0*, 47) NRAES.

Private Education & Public Policy: Studies in Choice & Public Policy. Ed. by Daniel C. Levy. LC 85-15568. 288p. 1986. text 55.00 (*0-19-503710-3*) OUP.

Private Education in Modern China. Peng Deng. LC 97-5584. 200p. 1997. 55.00 (*0-275-95639-3*, Praeger Pubs) Greenwood.

Private Elisha Stockwell, Jr. Sees the Civil War. Elisha Stockwell, Jr. Ed. by Byron R. Abernethy. LC 58-6855. (Illus.). 224p. (Orig.). 1985. pap. 13.95 (*0-8061-1921-7*) U of Okla Pr.

***Private Employment Agencies: The Impact of ILO Convention 181 (1997) & the Judgement of the European Court of Justice of 11 December 1997.** Ed. by Roger Blanpain. (Bulletin of Comparative Labour Relations Ser.: Vol. 36). 414p. 1999. pap. 138.00 (*90-411-1118-2*) Kluwer Law Intl.

Private Enemy, Public Eye: The Work of Bruce Charlesworth. Charles Hagen & Bruce Charlesworth. (New Images Book Ser.). (Illus.). 96p. 1989. 44.95 (*0-89381-337-0*) Aperture.

***Private Enforcement of Antitrust Law in the EU, Uk & USA.** Clifford Jones. LC 99-28821. 312p. 1999. text 165.00 (*0-19-826868-8*) OUP.

***Private Enterprise.** Dick Holt. LC 99-91577. 2000. 25.00 (*0-7388-0898-9*); pap. 18.00 (*0-7388-0899-7*) Xlibris Corp.

Private Enterprise. Angela M. Thirkell. LC 96-36739. 381p. 1997. pap. 13.95 (*1-55921-189-X*) Moyer Bell.

Private Enterprise & the East African Company. Ed. by Philip A. Thomas. LC 75-9431. xiv, 283p. 1969. 45.00 (*0-678-08021-6*) Kelley.

Private Enterprise & the State in Modern Nepal. Laurie Zivetz. (Illus.). 248p. 1992. 29.95 (*0-19-562872-1*) OUP.

Private Enterprise, Government & Society. Ed. by Frank Broeze. (Studies in Western Australian History: Vol. XIII). pap. 20.00 (*0-86422-206-8*, Pub. by Univ of West Aust Pr) Intl Spec Bk.

Private Enterprises & the State in Modern Nepal. Laurie Zivetz. (C). 1991. text 70.00 (*0-7855-0152-5*, Pub. by Ratna Pustak Bhandar) St Mut.

Private Enterprises in Rural China: A Study of Their Impact on Agriculture & Social Stratification. Ole Odgaard. 210p. 1992. 82.95 (*1-85628-405-0*, Pub. by Avebry) Ashgate Pub Co.

***Private Equity.** Temple. LC 99-233642. 198p. (C). 1999. 87.95 (*0-471-98396-9*) Wiley.

***Private Equity & Venture Capital: A Practical Guide for Investors & Practioners.** Rick Lake & Ronald Lake. 323p. 2000. pap. text 170.00 (*1-85564-691-9*, Pub. by Euromoney) Am Educ Systs.

***Private Equity Funds-of-Funds: State of the Market.** Ed. by Robert Pease & Steven P. Galante. 105p. 2000. pap. 495.00 (*1-893648-09-5*) Asset Alternatives.

Private Eye: Looking-Thinking by Analogy - A Guide to Developing the Interdisciplinary Mind. Kerry Ruef. (Illus.). 240p. (Orig.). 1992. pap. text 18.95 (*0-9605434-1-4*) Private Eye.

Private Eye: Observing Snow Geese. Mary Burns. LC 97-118505. (Illus.). 2244p. 1996. 29.95 (*0-7748-0575-7*) U of Wash Pr.

***Private Eye Vol. 4: Beguiled, 2 bks. in 1.** Jayne Ann Krentz & Lori Foster. (Harlequin 50th Anniversary Collection Ser.). 1999. per. 6.99 (*0-373-83412-8*, 1-83412-6) Harlequin Bks.

Private Eye Action As You Like It. unabridged ed. Joe R. Lansdale & Lewis Shiner. (Illus.). 200p. 1998. 60.00 (*1-892300-03-6*); 125.00 (*1-892300-04-4*); pap. 20.00 (*1-892300-02-8*) Crossrds Press.

Private Eye, Heart & Hip. Yates. (C). 1995. pap. text 21.95 (*0-443-05466-5*, W B Saunders Co) Harcrt Hlth Sci Grp.

Private Eye Loupe (5X) Kerry Ruef. 1992. 3.95 (*0-9605434-2-2*) Private Eye.

Private Eyeful: (Hero for Hire) Ruth J. Dale. (Temptation Ser.: No. 709). 1998. per. 3.75 (*0-373-25809-7*, 0-25809-5) Harlequin Bks.

Private Eyes. Sam Brown & Gini G. Scott. 1990. pap. 12.95 (*0-8065-1182-6*, Citadel Pr) Carol Pub Group.

Private Eyes. Steven Dietz. 1998. pap. 5.25 (*0-8222-1619-1*) Dramatists Play.

Private Eyes. Jonathan Kellerman. 1992. pap. 5.50 (*0-553-18085-1*) Bantam.

Private Eyes. Jonathan Kellerman. 560p. 1992. mass mkt. 7.50 (*0-553-29950-6*) Bantam.

Private Eyes. Madeline St. Claire. 1994. per. 2.99 (*0-373-22299-8*, 1-22299-1) Harlequin Bks.

Private Eyes: A Writer's Guide to Private Investigators. Hal Blythe et al. (Howdunit Ser.). 208p. (Orig.). 1993. pap. 15.99 (*0-89879-549-4*, Wrtrs Digest Bks) F & W Pubns Inc.

Private Eyes: One Hundred & One Knights. Robert Baker & Michael T. Nietzel. LC 85-70857. 385p. 1985. 30.95 (*0-87972-329-7*); pap. 18.95 (*0-87972-330-0*) Bowling Green Univ Popular Press.

Private Fame. Richard Burgin. (Illinois Short Fiction Ser.). 168p. 1991. 16.95 (*0-252-01843-5*) U of Ill Pr.

Private Fantasies. Janelle Denison. (Temptation Ser.). 1998. per. 3.75 (*0-373-25782-1*, 1-25782-3) Harlequin Bks.

Private Farmer: Transformation & Ligitimation in Advanced Capitalist Agriculture. Stephen Pile. (Illus.). 218p. 1990. text 66.95 (*1-85521-003-7*, Pub. by Dartmth Pub) Ashgate Pub Co.

Private File. Jerry Hurter. (Illus.). 221p. (Orig.). 1986. pap. 12.95 (*0-9615054-0-0*) J Hurter.

Private File Creation - Database Construction: A Proceeding with 5 Case Studies. Ed. by Marjorie M. Hlava. LC 85-135011. 116p. reprint ed. pap. 36.00 (*0-7837-8681-6*, 204942700011) Bks Demand.

Private Files of a Vampirologist: Case Histories & Letters. Ed. by Jeanne K. Youngson. (Illus.). 61p. (Orig.). 1997. pap. 20.00 (*1-888893-01-X*) Dracula Pr.

***Private Finance for Human Development.** Ed. by Inge Kaul & Almud Weitz. (Illus.). 288p. 2000. text 39.00 (*0-19-513470-2*); pap. text 24.95 (*0-19-513471-0*) OUP.

Private Financing for Sustainable Development. 64p. 10.00 (*92-1-126063-9*) UN.

Private Financing for Sustainable Development. (Discussion Papers: No. 9). 100p. pap. 12.00 (*92-1-126065-5*) UN.

Private Finanzpaket Hit Works Reihe Losungen. Michael Muller. (GER.). (C). 1991. text. write for info. (*0-201-55980-3*) Addison-Wesley.

Private Fire Protection & Detection. 2nd ed. IFSTA Committee. Ed. by FPP Staff. LC 94-701299. (Illus.). 222p. 1994. pap. 32.00 (*0-87939-110-3*) IFSTA.

Private Fire Protection & Detection: Davis Study Guide. 4th ed. 69p. Date not set. pap. text 14.95 (*0-614-31225-6*, S210) Davis Pub Co.

Private Fleet Directory. Transportation Technical Services Staff. 1600p. 1999. pap. text 295.00 (*1-880701-06-5*) Trans Tech Srvs.

Private Foreign Investment: Legal & Economic Realities. Seymour J. Rubin. LC 56-7594. 120p. reprint ed. pap. 37.20 (*0-608-13620-4*, 202075100018) Bks Demand.

Private Forest-Land Owners of the United States, 1994. Thomas W. Birch. (Illus.). 183p. 1998. pap. text 25.00 (*0-7881-7373-1*) DIANE Pub.

Private Forestry Policy in Western Europe. A. J. Grayson. (Illus.). 352p. 1993. text 100.00 (*0-85198-843-1*) OUP.

Private Fortunes & Company Profits in the India Trade in the 18th Century. Holden Furber & Rosane Rocher. LC 97-4074. (Variorum Collected Studies: Vol. 569). 336p. 1997. 98.95 (*0-86078-619-6*, Pub. by Ashgate Pub) Ashgate Pub Co.

***Private Foundations: Tax Law & Compliance, February 2000 Supplement.** Bruce R. Hopkins & Jody Blazek. 144p. 2000. pap. 60.00 (*0-471-36135-6*) Wiley.

Private Foundations: Tax Law Compliance. Bruce R. Hopkins & Jody Blazek. LC 97-14101. (Nonprofit Law, Finance, & Management Ser.). (Illus.). 520p. 1997. 140.00 (*0-471-16892-0*) Wiley.

Private Foundations & Public Policy: The Political Role of Philanthropy. Mary A. Colwell. LC 92-29719. (Non-profit Institutions in America Ser.). 296p. 1993. text 10.00 (*0-8153-0904-X*) Garland.

Private Franklin: The Man & His Family. Claude-Anne Lopez & Eugenia W. Herbert. (Illus.). 400p. 1985. reprint ed. pap. 9.95 (*0-393-30227-X*) Norton.

Private Freight Cars & American Railways. Louis D. Weld. LC 70-76679. (Columbia University. Studies in the Social Sciences: No. 81). reprint ed. 27.50 (*0-404-51081-7*) AMS Pr.

Private Funds, Public Purpose: Philanthropic Foundations in International Perspective. Ed. by H. K. Anheier & S. Toepler. (Nonprofit & Civil Society Studies). (Illus.). 280p. (C). 1999. 85.00 (*0-306-45946-9*, Plenum Trade); pap. 37.50 (*0-306-45947-7*, Plenum Trade) Perseus Pubng.

Private Gardens see Ancient Chinese Architecture

Private Gardens of Charleston. Louisa P. Cameron. (Illus.). 96p. 1992. 39.95 (*0-941711-14-5*) Wyrick & Co.

Private Gold Coins & Patterns of the U. S. D. Kagin. LC 79-21041. (Illus.). 1980. lib. bdg. 30.00 (*0-668-04830-1*) S J Durst.

Private Golf Facilities: The Tradition Continues. (InfoPac Ser.). (Illus.). 135p. 1999. pap. 45.00 (*1-57701-066-3*, 99LB057) Natl Golf.

Private Gollantz. large type ed. Naomi Jacob. 496p. 1985. 27.99 (*0-7089-8289-1*, Charnwood) Ulverscroft.

Private Grazing & Public Lands. Wesley Calef. Ed. by Stuart Bruchey. LC 78-56701. (Management of Public Lands in the U. S. Ser.). 1979. reprint ed. lib. bdg. 24.95 (*0-405-11321-8*) Ayer.

Private Greeting Cards. 75.00 (*4-89444-054-7*, Pub. by Pie Bks) Bks Nippan.

Private Groups & Public Life: Social Participation, Voluntary Associations & Political Involvement in Representative Democracies. Jan W. Van Deth. LC 97-6090. 264p. (C). 1997. 90.00 (*0-415-16955-0*) Routledge.

Private Health Care. Cook. 1991. pap. text. write for info. (*0-582-06775-8*, Pub. by Addison-Wesley) Longman.

Private Health Care in India: A Sociological Inquiry. Rama V. Baru. LC 98-28220. 1998. write for info. (*0-7619-9286-3*) Sage.

Private Health Insurance: Continued Erosion of Coverage Linked to Cost Pressures. Michael Gutowski et al. (Illus.). 60p. (C). 1998. pap. text 25.00 (*0-7881-4834-6*) DIANE Pub.

***Private Health Insurance: Progress & Challenges in Implementing 1996 Federal Standards.** Ed. by William J. Scanlon. (Illus.). 52p. (C). 2000. pap. text 20.00 (*0-7881-8810-0*) DIANE Pub.

Private Health Providers in Developing Countries: Serving the Public Interest? Sara Bennett et al. LC 97-6650. 1997. write for info. (*1-85649-495-0*); pap. 25.00 (*1-85649-496-9*) Humanities.

Private Health Sector Growth in Asia. William C. Newbrander & Asian Development Bank Staff. LC 96-47180. 272p. 1997. 125.00 (*0-471-97236-3*) Wiley.

***Private Hemingway Goes to War: A World War II Dairy.** Donald W. Hemingway. (Illus.). 180p. 2000. pap. (*1-55517-460-4*) CFI Dist.

Private Heroes. Francois-Marie Banier. 193p. 1999. 49.95 (*3-89322-507-2*, Pub. by Dr Cantz sche Druckerei GmbH) Dist Art Pubs.

Private High. Thomas Martin. 25p. (YA). (gr. 7 up). 1987. pap. 6.00 (*0-87602-267-0*) Anchorage.

***Private High Schools of the San Francisco Bay Area.** 2nd rev. ed. Susan Vogel. (Illus.). 250p. 1999. pap. 19.95 (*0-9648757-9-9*, Pub. by Pince Nez Pr) Sunbelt Pubns.

Private Higher Education in the United States. Manning M. Pattillo, Jr. 46p. (Orig.). (C). 1990. pap. 2.00 (*1-880647-02-8*) U GA Inst High Educ.

Private Hong Kong: Where East Meets West. Sophie Benge. LC 97-21956. (Illus.). 216p. 1997. 50.00 (*0-7892-0342-1*) Abbeville Pr.

Private Hong Kong: Where East Meets West. Sophie Benge. (Illus.). 216p. 1999. 17.98 (*0-89660-107-2*, Artabras) Abbeville Pr.

Private I. Guana: The Case of the Missing Chameleon. Nina Laden. LC 95-2828. (Illus.). 32p. (J). (gr. k-5). 1999. 14.95 (*0-8118-0940-4*); pap. 6.95 (*0-8118-2463-2*) Chronicle Bks.

Private Independent Schools, 1999: The Bunting & Lyon Blue Book. 52nd ed. Ed. by Peter G. Bunting. LC 72-122324. (Illus.). 616p. 1999. 100.00 (*0-913094-52-8*) Bunting.

***Private Independent Schools 2000.** Bunting & Lyon, Inc. Staff. 2000. 122.22 (*0-913094-53-6*) Bunting.

Private Inquiry. large type unabridged ed. Jessica Mann. 294p. 1998. 24.95 (*0-7531-5557-5*, 155575) ISIS Pub.

Private Intelligence Secrets. James L. Drake. (Illus.). 112p. (Orig.). 1988. pap. 19.95 (*0-939427-28-1*, 10030); pap. 19.95 (*0-939427-29-X*) Alpha Pubns OH.

Private Interest & Public Gain: The Dartmouth College Case, 1819. Francis N. Stites. LC 72-77574. 192p. 1972. 27.50 (*0-87023-112-X*) U of Mass Pr.

Private Interest Government Beyond Market & State. Wolfgang Streeck. Ed. by Phillipe C. Schmitter. (Studies in Neo-Corporatism). 288p. (Orig.). (C). 1986. text 49.95 (*0-8039-9722-1*); pap. text 20.95 (*0-8039-9723-X*) Sage.

Private Interest, Public Spending: Balanced-Budget Conservatism & the Fiscal Crisis. Sidney Plotkin & William E. Scheuerman. 280p. write for info. (*1-895431-99-9*); pap. 19.99 (*1-895431-98-0*, Pub. by Black Rose) Consort Bk Sales.

Private Interests, Public Policy, & American Agriculture. William P. Browne. LC 87-23131. (Studies in Government & Public Policy). xviii, 294p. (C). 1988. pap. 15.95 (*0-7006-0335-2*) U Pr of KS.

Private Interests, Public Spending: Balanced-Budget Conservatism & the Fiscal Crisis. William E. Scheuerman & Sidney Plotkin. LC 93-14852. 300p. 1994. 40.00 (*0-89608-465-5*); pap. 16.00 (*0-89608-464-7*) South End Pr.

Private International Law. William H. Rattigan. LC 96-76320. xv, 267p. 1996. reprint ed. 58.00 (*1-57588-083-0*, 310610) W S Hein.

Private International Law. Joseph A. Thomas. LC 74-31362. 174p. 1975. reprint ed. lib. bdg. 59.50 (*0-8371-7929-7*, THPI, Greenwood Pr) Greenwood.

Private International Law. 2nd ed. C. F. Forsyth. 446p. 1990. pap. 45.00 (*0-7021-2344-7*, Pub. by Juta & Co) Gaunt.

Private International Law. 3rd ed. C. F. Forsyth. LC 97-162753. 429p. 1996. pap. 55.00 (*0-7021-3581-X*, Pub. by Juta & Co) Gaunt.

Private International Law & Unclaimed Assets in Switzerland/Das Internationale Privatrecht der Nachrichten Losen Verm & Gen in der Schweiz. Daniel Girsberger. LC 98-117349. 76p. Date not set. pap. text 80.00 (*90-411-0727-4*) Kluwer Law Intl.

***Private International Law at the End of the 20th Century: Progress or Regress?: XVth International Congress of Comparative Law.** International Congress of Comparative Law Staff et al. LC 99-47000. 1999. 159.00 (*90-411-1234-0*) Kluwer Law Intl.

Private International Law in the Netherlands. R. Van Rooy & M. V. Polak. 325p. 1987. 107.00 (*90-6544-286-3*) Kluwer Law Intl.

Private International Law of Tort & Product Liability: Jurisdiction, Applicable Law & Extraterritorial Protective Measures. Peter Kaye. 144p. 1991. text 82.95 (*1-85521-194-7*, Pub. by Dartmth Pub) Ashgate Pub Co.

Private International Law Problems in Common Law Jurisdictions. Peter M. North. LC 92-18236. 1993. lib. bdg. 104.50 (*0-7923-1845-5*) Kluwer Academic.

***Private Investigaiton Trilogy: The Retail Community Connection!, 3 vols.** Bill Copeland. 1106p. 1999. 120.00 (*1-893763-36-6*) Absolutely Zero.

Private Investigating Made Easy. 2nd ed. Kelly E. Riddle. (Illus.). 127p. 1994. pap. 19.95 (*1-881825-05-1*) Hist Pubns TX.

Private Investigation: Methods & Materials. Frank J. MacHovec. 134p. 1991. pap. 23.95 (*0-398-06258-7*) C C Thomas.

P

An Asterisk (*) at the beginning of an entry indicates that the title is appearing for the first time.

Private Investigation: Methods & Materials. Frank J. MacHovec. 134p. (C). 1991. text 34.95 (*0-398-05749-4*) C C Thomas.

Private Investigative Agency Start-Up Manual. Jody Ball. 1998. spiral bd. 45.00 (*1-891247-14-X*) Thomas Investigative.

Private Investigator. Jan Goldberg. LC 98-17215. (Careers Without College Ser.). (Illus.). 48p. (J). 1998. write for info. (*0-7368-0038-7*) Capstone Pr.

Private Investigator. Jan Goldberg. (Careers Without College Ser.). (J). 1998. 19.00 (*0-516-21450-0*) Childrens.

Private Investigator. Jack Rudman. (Career Examination Ser.: C-2462). 1994. pap. 27.95 (*0-8373-2462-9*) Nat Learn.

Private Investigator: How to Be Successful. William D. Copeland. v, 220p. 1997. 40.00 (*0-9657659-9-7*) Absolutely Zero.

***Private Investigators: Undercover in Public Space.** Kathryn Walters et al. (Illus.). 96p. 1999. pap. 12.95 (*0-920159-61-3*) Banff Ctr.

Private Investigator's Basic Manual. Richard H. Akin. 208p. 1979. 37.95 (*0-398-03520-2*); pap. 24.95 (*0-398-06002-9*) C C Thomas.

Private Investigator's Book of Legal Forms & Contracts. J. Michael Ball. 80p. 1997. spiral bd. 29.95 (*0-918487-01-3*) Thomas Investigative.

Private Investigators Desk Reference. Daniel J. Benny. 40p. 1993. spiral bd. 15.00 (*1-928987-59-1*) Intl Fdtn Protect.

Private Investigator's Divorce Course. Ralph D. Thomas. 75p. 1990. pap. text 19.95 (*0-918487-33-1*) Thomas Investigative.

***Private Investigator's Guide.** John Krause. 1999. pap. 24.95 (*1-55279-021-5*) Picasso Publ.

Private Investigator's Guide for the Investigation & Location of Missing & Abducted Children. Richard Lynch. (Private Investigation Ser.). (Illus.). 90p. (C). 1996. pap. text 35.00 (*0-918487-88-9*) Thomas Investigative.

Private Investigator's Guide to the Internet. Joseph Seanor. 200p. (C). 1995. spiral bd. 35.00 (*0-918487-83-8*) Thomas Investigative.

Private Investment: The Key to International Industrial Development: a Report of the San Francisco Conference. Ed. by James Daniel & Stuart Bruchey. LC 80-606. (Multinational Corporations Ser.). 1981. reprint ed. lib. bdg. 33.95 (*0-405-13355-3*) Ayer.

Private Investments Abroad. Carol Holgren. text 170.00 (*0-8205-4177-X*) Bender.

Private Investments Abroad. Southwestern Legal Foundation Staff. 1967. write for info. (*0-8205-1662-7*) Bender.

***Private Ireland.** Simon McBride. (Illus.). 224p. 2000. text 35.00 (*0-312-26111-X*) St Martin.

Private Jessica. Created by Francine Pascal. (Sweet Valley University Ser.: No. 40). 240p. (YA). (gr. 7 up). 1998. mass mkt. 3.99 (*0-553-49224-1*) BDD Bks Young Read.

Private Journal of Aaron Burr, 2 vols., Set. Aaron Burr. LC 75-31113. reprint ed. 86.50 (*0-404-13710-5*) AMS Pr.

Private Journal of Aaron Burr, 2 vols., Set. Aaron Burr. (American Biography Ser.). 1991. reprint ed. write for info. (*0-7812-8054-0*) Rprt Serv.

Private Journal of John Glendy Sproston, U. S. N. John Sproston. (American Autobiography Ser.). 128p. 1995. reprint ed. lib. bdg. 69.00 (*0-7812-8645-X*) Rprt Serv.

***Private Journal of Judge-Advocate Larpent: Attached to the Head-Quarters of Lord Wellington During the Peninsular War from 1812 to Its Close.** Ed. by Francis Seymour Larpent. 608p. 2000. 120.00 (*1-86227-100-3*, Pub. by Spellmnt Pubs) St Mut.

Private Journal of Margaret Morris, Kept During a Portion of the Revolutionary War. Margaret Morris. Ed. by Peter Decker. LC 71-77107. (Eyewitness Accounts of the American Revolution Ser.). 1977. reprint ed. 16.95 (*0-405-01168-7*) Ayer.

Private Journals of the Long Parliament, Vol. 2. Ed. by Anne S. Young & Vernon F. Snow. 519p. 1987. 125.00 (*1-58046-013-5*) Univ Rochester Pr.

Private Journals of the Long Parliament, Vol. 3. Ed. by Anne S. Young & Vernon F. Snow. 515p. 1992. 125.00 (*1-58046-014-3*) Univ Rochester Pr.

Private Journals of the Long Parliament, Vol. 1, Vol. 1. Ed. by Anne S. Young et al. 581p. 1982. 125.00 (*1-58046-012-7*) Univ Rochester Pr.

Private Judging: Privatizing Civil Justice. Richard Chernick. LC 99-165594. 60 p. 1997. pap. write for info. (*0-937299-55-3*) Natl Legal Ctr Pub Interest.

Private Justice. Terri Blackstock. LC 98-56119. 1999. pap. text 22.95 (*0-7862-1823-1*) Mac Lib Ref.

Private Justice. Terri Blackstock. LC 97-36571. (Newpointe 911 Ser.: Bk. 1). 304p. 1998. pap. 10.99 (*0-310-21757-1*) Zondervan.

Private Keep Out! Hints for Starting Your Journal. Leslie Gebhart & Carolyn Ingram. (Illus.). 1997. pap. 12.95 (*0-9636399-7-8*) Trinehrt Pubs.

Private Label Marketing in the 1990s: The Evolution of Price Labels into Global Brands. Philip B. Fitzell. (Illus.). 328p. (C). 1993. text 45.00 (*0-9632920-1-3*) Exclusive Brands.

Private Land Use Arrangements: Real Covenants, & Equitable Servitudes. Gerald Korngold. 580p. 1990. text 95.00 (*0-07-071053-8*) Shepards.

Private Lands & Public Recreation. 34p. 1979. 1.00 (*0-318-23131-X*) Wildlife Mgmt.

Private Language? A Dip into Welsh Literature. Marion Eames. 1997. pap. 34.95 (*0-8464-4829-7*) Beekman Pubs.

Private Law among the Romans from the Pandects. John G. Phillimore. xv, 423p. 1994. reprint ed. 57.50 (*0-8377-2550-X*, Rothman) W S Hein.

***Private Law & Social Inequality in the Industrial Age: Comparing Legal Cultures in Britain, France, Germany, & the United States of America.** Willibald Steinmetz. LC 99-49287. 560p. 2000. 110.00 (*0-19-920236-2*) OUP.

Private Law in the European Union, Vol. FOIN 22. Ulrich Drobnig. LC 96-52811. (Forum Internationale Ser.). 1997. 29.00 (*90-411-0335-X*) Kluwer Law Intl.

Private Law Theory. Ed. by Jules L. Coleman. LC 93-32673. (Philosophy of Law Ser.: Vol. 5). 648p. 1994. text 105.00 (*0-8153-1401-9*) Garland.

Private Lending to Sovereign States: A Theoretical Autopsy. Daniel Cohen. (Illus.). 196p. 1991. 27.50 (*0-262-03172-8*) MIT Pr.

Private Lessons. Anne Cavaliere. (Desire Ser.: No. 693). 1992. per. 2.79 (*0-373-05693-1*, 5-05693-2) Harlequin Bks.

Private lessons. C. Mildenhall. mass mkt. 6.95 (*0-7472-5125-8*, Pub. by Headline Bk Pub) Trafalgar.

Private Lessons: Customized & Personalized Instruction Tailored to the Individual Golfer. Golf Magazine Editors. (Illus.). 144p. 1998. 24.95 (*1-57243-292-6*) Triumph Bks.

Private Lessons: Interpreting the Inner Meaning of Masonry. Phylotus. 78p. 1996. reprint ed. pap. 8.95 (*1-56459-845-4*) Kessinger Pub.

***Private Lessons: John Lyons Answers Your Questions about Care & Training.** John Lyons. Ed. by Maureen Gallatin. (John Lyons Perfect Horse Library Ser.). (Illus.). viii, 200p. 2000. 26.95 (*1-879620-63-4*) Belvoir Pubns.

Private Lessons (Blaze) Julie E. Leto. (Temptation Ser.: No. 724). 1999. per. 3.75 (*0-373-25824-0*, 1-25824-3) Harlequin Bks.

Private Lessons Interpreting the Inner Meaning of Masonry & the Bible. Phylotus. 78p. 1996. reprint ed. spiral bd. 10.00 (*0-7873-0671-1*) Hlth Research.

Private Letter Rulings. ring bd. write for info. (*0-318-57351-2*) P-H.

Private Letters of Edward Gibbon, 2 vols. Edward Gibbon. Ed. by Rowland E. Prothero. LC 71-151596. reprint ed. 125.00 (*0-404-02751-2*) AMS Pr.

Private Letters of the Marquess of Dalhousie. Ed. by J. G. Baird. (C). 1993. 14.00 (*81-85557-18-7*, Pub. by Low Price) S Asia.

Private Liberal Arts Colleges in Minnesota: Their History & Contributions. Merrill E. Jarchow. LC 73-14591. (Illus.). xvi, 345p. 1973. 17.00 (*0-87351-081-X*) Minn Hist.

Private Libraries in Renaissance England: PLRE 1-4, Vol. 1. Ed. by R. J. Fehrenbach & E. S. Leedham-Green. (Medieval & Renaissance Texts & Studies: Vol. 87). 352p. 1992. 30.00 (*0-86698-099-7*, MR87) MRTS.

Private Libraries in Renaissance England: PLRE 113-137, Vol. 5. Ed. by Robert J. Fehrenbach & Elizabeth Leedham-Green. (Medieval & Renaissance Texts & Studies: No. 189). 420p. 1998. 30.00 (*0-86698-231-0*, MR189) MRTS.

Private Libraries in Renaissance England: PLRE 5-66, Vol. 2. Ed. by R. J. Fehrenbach & E. S. Leedham-Green. (Medieval & Renaissance Texts & Studies: Vol. 105). 320p. 1993. 30.00 (*0-86698-151-9*, MR105) MRTS.

Private Libraries in Renaissance England: PLRE 67-86, Vol. 3. Ed. by R. J. Fehrenbach & E. S. Leedham-Green. (Medieval & Renaissance Texts & Studies: Vol. 117). 320p. 1994. 30.00 (*0-86698-170-5*, MR117) MRTS.

Private Libraries in Renaissance England: PLRE 87-112, Vol. 4. Ed. by R. J. Fehrenbach & E. S. Leedham-Green. (Medieval & Renaissance Texts & Studies: Vol. 148). 384p. 1995. 30.00 (*0-86698-188-8*, MR148) MRTS.

Private Lies. Warren Adler. 352p. 1992. mass mkt. 4.99 (*0-380-71307-1*, Avon Bks) Morrow Avon.

Private Lies. Robyn Amos. 288p. 1998. pap. 4.99 (*0-7860-0496-7*, Pinncle Kensgtn) Kensgtn Pub Corp.

Private Lies. Judith Arnold. (American Romance Ser.). 1994. per. 3.50 (*0-373-16524-2*, 1-16524-0) Harlequin Bks.

Private Lies: Infidelity & the Betrayal of Intimacy. Frank Pittman. 312p. 1998. reprint ed. lib. bdg. 30.00 (*0-7351-0025-X*) Replica Bks.

Private Lies, Infidelity & the Betrayal of Intimacy. Frank Pittman. 1990. pap. 14.95 (*0-393-30707-7*) Norton.

Private Life see **Works of Henry James Jr.: Collected Works**

Private Life: Poems. Lisel Mueller. LC 75-5350. 64p. 1976. pap. 11.95 (*0-8071-0171-0*) La State U Pr.

Private Life of a Country House, 1912-1939. Lesley Lewis. LC 98-112897. (Illus.). 146p. 1998. pap. 17.95 (*0-7509-1678-8*, Pub. by Sutton Pub Ltd) Intl Pubs Mktg.

Private Life of a Country House, 1912-1939. 2nd large type ed. Lesley Lewis. (Illus.). 237p. 1993. 24.95 (*1-85695-001-8*, Pub. by ISIS Lrg Prnt) Transaction Pubs.

Private Life of an Elizabethan Lady: The Diary of Lady Margaret Hoby, 1599-1605. Joanna Moody. (Illus.). 320p. 1998. 35.95 (*0-7509-1349-5*, Pub. by Sutton Pub Ltd) Intl Pubs Mktg.

Private Life of Chairman Mao. Li Zhisui & Anne F. Thurston. 1996. pap. 20.00 (*0-679-76443-7*); pap. 17.00 (*0-614-12565-0*) Random.

Private Life of Daniel Webster. Charles Lanman. (Notable American Authors Ser.). 1999. reprint ed. lib. bdg. 125.00 (*0-7812-3735-1*) Rprt Serv.

Private Life of H. P. Lovecraft. Sonia H. Davis. 38p. (Orig.). 1985. pap. 4.95 (*0-318-04178-7*) Necronomicon.

Private Life of Helen of Troy (1925) John Erskine. 310p. 1998. reprint ed. pap. 24.95 (*0-7661-0356-0*) Kessinger Pub.

Private Life of Henry James: Two Women & His Art. Lyndall Gordon. LC 98-51182. (Illus.). 500p. 1999. 32.50 (*0-393-04711-3*) Norton.

Private Life of Islam: An Algerian Diary. Ian Young. (Pimlico Ser.). (Illus.). 307p. 1993. reprint ed. pap. 16.95 (*0-7126-5037-7*, Pub. by Pimlico) Trafalgar.

Private Life of James Bond. David R. Contosta. LC 93-15237. (Illus.). 130p. 1993. 16.95 (*0-915010-38-0*) Sutter House.

Private Life of John Lennon. Photos by Frederic Seaman. (Illus.). 200p. 1996. 25.00 (*1-56025-106-9*, Thunders Mouth) Avalon NY.

***Private Life of Kim Philby: The Moscow Years.** Rufina Philby et al. (Illus.). 464p. 2000. 32.00 (*0-88064-219-X*) Fromm Intl Pub.

Private Life of Plants: A Natural History of Plant Behavior. David Attenborough. LC 95-17514. 320p. 1995. 29.95 (*0-691-00639-3*, Pub. by Princeton U Pr) Cal Prin Full Svc.

Private Life of Plants: A Natural History of Plant Behavior. large type ed. David Attenborough. LC 95-47822. 22.95 (*1-56895-291-0*, Compass) Wheeler Pub.

***Private Life of Sharks: The Truth Behind the Myth.** Michael Bright. 260p. 1999. 31.95 (*1-86105-157-3*) Robson.

***Private Life of Sharks: The Truth Behind the Myth.** Michael Bright. LC 99-56906. 2000. 17.95 (*0-8117-2875-7*) Stackpole.

Private Life of Sherlock Holmes. Michael Hardwick & Mollie Hardwick. 200p. 1993. 25.00 (*0-86025-277-9*, Pub. by I Henry Pubns) Empire Pub Srvs.

***Private Life of Sherlock Holmes.** Vincent Starrett. (Vincent Starrett Memorial Library). 2001. 24.00 (*1-55246-132-7*); pap. 12.00 (*1-55246-133-5*) Battered Silicon.

Private Life of Sherlock Holmes. Vincent Starrett. LC 78-130268. (English Literature Ser.: No. 33). 1970. reprint ed. lib. bdg. 75.00 (*0-8383-1175-X*) M S G Haskell Hse.

***Private Life of the Brain: Emotions, Consciousness & the Secret of the Self.** Susan Greenfield. LC 99-46191. 224p. 2000. text 27.95 (*0-471-18343-1*) Wiley.

Private Life of the Rabbit. R. M. Lockley. (Illus.). 1995. reprint ed. lib. bdg. 29.95 (*1-56849-614-1*) Buccaneer Bks.

Private Life of the Romans. Harold W. Johnston. (Select Bibliographies Reprint Ser.). 1977. reprint ed. 35.95 (*0-8369-9915-0*) Ayer.

Private Lily. Sally Warner. 90p. (J). (gr. k-3). 1999. pap. 3.99 (*0-375-80056-5*) Knopf.

Private Lily. Sally Warner. LC 97-52932. (J). (gr. 2-4). 1998. 15.00 (*0-679-89137-4*, Pub. by Random Bks Yng Read); lib. bdg. 16.99 (*0-679-99137-9*, Pub. by Random Bks Yng Read) Random.

Private-Line Service Markets: High-Capacity T-Services, CAPS to Grow Vigorously. Market Intelligence Staff. 287p. 1993. 1695.00 (*1-56753-908-4*) Frost & Sullivan.

Private Litigation under Section 7 of the Clayton Act: Law & Policy. 144p. 1989. pap. 20.00 (*0-89707-455-6*, 503-0077-01) Amer Bar Assn.

***Private Lives.** Bruce Bothwell. 89p. 2000. pap. 10.00 (*1-929764-05-7*) Bothwell Bks.

***Private Lives.** Tom Clancy & Martin Greenberg. (Tom Clancy's Net Force Ser.: No. 9). (YA). 2000. mass mkt. 4.99 (*0-425-17367-4*) Berkley Pub.

Private Lives: Presents Plus. Carole Mortimer. (Presents Ser.). 1993. per. 2.99 (*0-373-11583-0*, 1-11583-1) Harlequin Bks.

Private Lives - Public Spaces: Homeless Adults on the Streets of New York City. Ellen Baxter & Kim Hopper. LC 82-234971. 129p. (Orig.). 1981. pap. 7.50 (*0-88156-002-2*) Comm Serv Soc NY.

Private Lives - Public Surfaces: Grassroots Perspectives & the Legitimacy Question in Yugoslav Socialism. Alvin Magid. 500p. 1992. text 66.50 (*0-88033-211-5*, Pub. by East Eur Monographs) Col U Pr.

Private Lives & Professional Identity of Medical Students. Robert S. Broadhead. LC 82-19502. 140p. 1983. 34.95 (*0-87855-478-5*) Transaction Pubs.

Private Lives & Public Accounts. Thomas J. Cottle. LC 77-73476. 208p. 1977. 27.50 (*0-87023-240-1*) U of Mass Pr.

Private Lives & Public Affairs: The Causes Celebres of Prerevolutionary France. Sara C. Maza. (Studies on the History of Society & Culture: Vol. 18). (Illus.). 354p. 1995. pap. 17.95 (*0-520-20163-9*, Pub. by U CA Pr) Cal Prin Full Svc.

Private Lives & Public Affairs: The Causes Celebres of Prerevolutionary France. Sarah Maza. LC 93-4518. (Studies on the History of Society & Culture: No. 18). 354p. 1993. 45.00 (*0-520-08144-7*, Pub. by U CA Pr) Cal Prin Full Svc.

Private Lives & Public Policies: Confidentiality & Accessibility of Government Statistics. National Research Council, Panel on Confidentialit. Ed. by Thomas B. Jabine et al. LC 93-31312. 288p. (C). 1993. text 34.95 (*0-309-04743-9*) Natl Acad Pr.

Private Lives, Imperial Virtues: The Frieze of the Forum Transitorium in Rome. Eve D'Ambra. LC 92-11126. (Illus.). 250p. (C). 1993. text 39.50 (*0-691-04097-4*, Pub. by Princeton U Pr) Cal Prin Full Svc.

Private Lives in Public Places. Dianne M. Willcocks. 1987. 49.50 (*0-422-79150-4*, 1133, Pub. by Tavistock) Routldge.

Private Lives in the Public Sphere: The German Bildungsroman As Metafiction. Todd Kontje. 192p. 1992. 35.00 (*0-271-00823-7*) Pa St U Pr.

Private Lives of Civil War Heroes: Once Patriots. Gloria J. Shepard. 68p. 1995. pap. 5.95 (*1-887223-01-0*) Pioneer NV.

Private Lives of Civil War Heroes: The Journal. Gloria J. Shepard. (Private Lives of Civil War Heroes Ser.: Vol. I). (Illus.). 48p. (Orig.). 1995. pap. 5.95 (*1-887223-00-2*) Pioneer NV.

Private Lives of English Words. Louis G. Heller et al. LC 84-8095. xxxi, 334p. 1998. reprint ed. 34.95 (*0-930454-18-9*) Verbatim Bks.

Private Lives of Minister's Wives. Liz Greenbacker & Sherry Taylor. 1991. pap. 15.95 (*0-88282-173-3*) New Horizon NJ.

***Private Lives of Noel & Gertie.** Sheridan Morley. 365p. 1999. pap. 27.95 (*1-84002-091-1*, Pub. by Theatre Comm) Consort Bk Sales.

Private Lives of Public Servants. Kenneth Lasson. LC 77-15758. 275p. reprint ed. pap. 85.30 (*0-608-17073-9*, 205623400056) Bks Demand.

Private Lives of the Three Tenors. Marcia Lewis. (Illus.). 224p. 1996. 21.95 (*1-55972-363-7*, Birch Ln Pr) Carol Pub Group.

Private Lives of the Three Tenors: Behind the Scenes with Placido Domingo, Luciano Pavarotti, & Jose Carreras. Marcia Lewis. 1998. mass mkt. 6.99 (*1-57297-332-3*) Blvd Books.

Private Lives of the Twelve Caesars. D'Hancarville. Tr. by A. F. Niemoeller. 54p. 1983. reprint ed. 7.50 (*0-914937-03-0*) Ind Pubns.

Private Lives, Public Conflicts: Battles over Gay Rights in American Communities. James W. Button et al. LC 96-53442. 223p. 1997. pap. 14.97 (*1-56802-278-6*) Congr Quarterly.

Private Lives, Public Conflicts: Battles over Gay Rights in American Communities. James W. Button et al. LC 96-53442. 223p. (YA). (gr. 11). 1997. text 22.77 (*1-56802-279-4*) Congr Quarterly.

Private Lives, Public Policy: 100 Years of State Intervention in the Family. Jane Ursel. 402p. pap. 20.95 (*0-88961-159-9*, Pub. by Womens Pr) LPC InBook.

Private Lives, Public Power: Women, the Civil War & Reconstruction in the South. Edwards. 1999. 26.95 (*0-8057-7818-7*, Twyne); per. 15.95 (*0-8057-7817-9*, Twyne) Mac Lib Ref.

Private Man. Timothy A. McInery. 1962. 12.95 (*0-8392-1087-6*) Astor-Honor.

Private Management of Public Schools. 2nd ed. Robert Selna. 20p. 1994. pap. 5.00 (*1-58434-030-4*) NASBE.

Private Management of Public Schools: Early Experiences in Four School Districts. Fred Yohey & Sherri Doughty. (Illus.). 76p. (Orig.). (C). 1996. pap. text 25.00 (*0-7881-3651-8*) DIANE Pub.

Private Manufacture of Armaments. Philip J. Noel-Baker. 1990. 15.75 (*0-8446-4593-1*) Peter Smith.

Private Manufacture of Armaments. Philip J. Noel-Baker. LC 78-145399. 1972. reprint ed. pap. 9.95 (*0-486-22736-7*) Dover.

Private Market Financing for Developing Countries. Charles Collyns & International Monetary Fund Staff. LC 95-153399. (World Economic & Financial Surveys Ser.). vii, 81 p. 1995. write for info. (*1-55775-456-X*) Intl Monetary.

Private Market Financing for Developing Countries. Dunaway et al. (World Economic & Financial Surveys Ser.). 1995. pap. 20.00 (*1-55775-469-1*) Intl Monetary.

Private Market Financing for Developing Countries. International Monetary Fund Staff et al. (World Economic & Financial Surveys Ser.). vii, 79p. 1991. pap. 20.00 (*1-55775-195-1*) Intl Monetary.

Private Market Financing for Developing Countries. Policy Development & Review Department Staff. LC 92-38191. (World Economic & Financial Surveys Ser.). vii, 80p. 1992. pap. 20.00 (*1-55775-318-0*) Intl Monetary.

Private-Market Housing Renovation in Older Urban Areas. James T. Black et al. LC 77-80214. (ULI Research Repors: No. 26). (Illus.). 47p. reprint ed. pap. 30.00 (*0-8357-8284-0*, 203394800087) Bks Demand.

Private Markets for Public Goods: Raising the Stakes in Economic Reform. Carol Graham. LC 98-19723. 330p. 1998. pap. 19.95 (*0-8157-3229-5*); pap. 49.95 (*0-8157-3230-9*) Brookings.

Private Markets in Health & Welfare: An International Perspective. Ed. by Norman Johnson. LC 94-34789. 1995. 47.50 (*0-85496-822-9*); pap. 19.50 (*1-85973-097-3*) Berg Pubs.

Private Mary Chestnut: The Unpublished Civil War Diaries. Ed. by C. Vann Woodward & Elisabeth Muhlenfeld. LC 84-12219. 292p. 1984. pap. 17.95 (*0-19-503513-5*) OUP.

Private Matter: RU-486 & the Abortion Crisis. Lawrence Lader. LC 95-20257. (Illus.). 254p. 1995. 25.95 (*1-57392-012-6*) Prometheus Bks.

Private Matters. Amberlina Wicker. 320p. 1996. pap. 4.99 (*0-7860-0246-8*, Pinncle Kensgtn) Kensgtn Pub Corp.

Private Matters: In Defense of the Personal Life. Janna M. Smith. Ed. by Elizabeth Maguire. LC 96-38158. 346p. 1997. 22.00 (*0-201-40973-9*) Addison-Wesley.

Private Matters & Public Culture in Post-Reformation England. Lena C. Orlin. (Illus.). 328p. 1994. text 45.00 (*0-8014-2858-0*) Cornell U Pr.

Private Means - Public Ends: Private Business in Social Service Delivery. Ed. by Barry J. Carroll et al. LC 86-25251. 204p. 1986. 55.00 (*0-275-92429-7*, C2429, Praeger Pubs) Greenwood.

Private Means, Public Ends: Voluntarism vs. Coercion. Ed. & Pref. by J. Wilson Mixon, Jr. LC 96-83410. 230p. (Orig.). 1996. pap. 9.95 (*1-57246-024-5*) Foun Econ Ed.

Private Medical Practice: Getting Started & Making It Work. Debi Carey. LC 97-10674. 320p. 1997. 175.00 (*0-7863-1118-5*, Irwn Prfssnl) McGraw-Hill Prof.

Private Medicine & Public Health: Profit, Politics & Prejudice in the American Health Care Enterprise. Lawrence D. Weiss. LC 96-40916. 240p. (C). 1997. pap. 25.00 (*0-8133-3351-2*, Pub. by Westview) HarpC.

Private Melville. Philip Young. LC 92-15558. 176p. (C). 1993. 32.50 (*0-271-00857-1*) Pa St U Pr.

P

Private Memoirs & Confessions of a Justified Sinner. James Hogg. (Classics Ser.). 224p. 1995. pap. 8.95 (*0-86241-340-0*, Pub. by Canongate Books) Interlink Pub.

*__Private Memoirs & Confessions of a Justified Sinner.__ James Hogg. Ed. by John Carey. 306p. 1999. pap. 8.95 (*0-19-283590-4*) OUP.

*__Private Memoirs of a Justified Sinner.__ James Hogg. (Cloth Bound Pocket Ser.). 1999. 7.95 (*3-8290-3009-6*) Konemann.

Private Memoirs of Madame Roland. 2nd ed. Marie J. Roland De La Platiere. LC 78-37719. (Women of Letters Ser.). (Illus.). reprint ed. 47.50 (*0-404-56829-7*) AMS Pr.

Private Moments in Public Places. Phyllis Prinz & Stephanie Saia. LC 79-64330. (Illus.). 72p. 1979. pap. 16.00 (*0-932966-04-7*) Permanent Pr.

Private Money: The Path to Monetary Stability. Kevin Dowd. (IEA Hobart Paper Ser.: No. 112). 71p. 1996. pap. 19.95 (*0-255-36216-1*, Pub. by Inst Economic Affairs) Coronet Bks.

Private Money & Public Currencies: The 16th Century Challenge. Marie-Therese Boyer-Xambeu et al. Tr. by Azizeh Azodi from FRE. LC 93-45467. 247p. (C). (gr. 13). 1994. pap. text 36.95 (*1-56324-508-6*) M E Sharpe.

Private Money & Public Currencies: The 16th Century Challenge. Ghislain Deleplace et al. Tr. by Azizeh Azodi. LC 93-45467. (ENG & FRE.). 247p. (C). (gr. 13). 1994. text 85.95 (*0-87332-604-0*) M E Sharpe.

Private Morality in Greece & Rome. W. Den Boer. 1979. pap. 41.00 (*90-04-05976-8*, MNS, 57) Brill Academic Pubs.

*__Private Murphy's Law.__ Mark V. Baker. (Illus.). 96p. 1999. pap. 5.95 (*0-9679357-0-9*, Pub. by Flat Earth) Byrrd Ent Inc.

Private Mythology: Poems. May Sarton. 112p. 1996. pap. 11.00 (*0-393-31552-5*) Norton.

Private Mythology: The Manuscripts & Plays of John Whiting. Gabrielle Robinson. LC 87-47983. (Illus.). 160p. 1989. 29.50 (*0-8387-5140-7*) Bucknell U Pr.

Private Myths: Dreams & Dreaming. Anthony Stevens. LC 95-45926. 400p. 1996. 27.95 (*0-674-21638-5*) HUP.

Private Myths: Dreams & Dreaming. Anthony Stevens. 400p. 1997. pap. text 15.95 (*0-674-21639-3*) HUP.

Private Nation. N. A. Diaman. LC 97-114803. 128p. (Orig.). 1997. pap. 10.95 (*0-931906-08-3*, Persona Pr) Persona Prod.

Private Needs, Public Selves: Talk about Religion in America. John K. Roth. LC 97-4613. (Public Expressions of Religion in America Ser.). 264p. 1997. 17.95 (*0-252-06651-0*); text 29.95 (*0-252-01933-4*) U of Ill Pr.

Private Network Market & Opportunities, 1996. (China Telecom-2000 Ser.: Vol. 8). 1995. 2995.00 (*0-614-18330-8*, IGIC-08) Info Gatekeepers.

Private Networks: Growth Markets. BCC Staff. 117p. 1990. 1950.00 (*0-89336-735-4*, G126) BCC.

Private Networks Public Objectives. Ed. by E. Noam. 464p. 1996. text 140.75 (*0-444-82549-5*, North Holland) Elsevier.

Private Networks Public Objectives. Eli M. Noam & Aine Nishuilleabhain. LC 96-9496. 465p. 1996. 140.75 (*0-444-82516-9*) Elsevier.

Private New York: Remarkable Residences. Chippy Irvine. (Illus.). 204p. 1990. 50.00 (*1-55859-106-0*) Abbeville Pr.

Private Nose. Andrew Taylor. LC 92-53016. (Illus.). 96p. (J). (gr. k-4). 1993. 14.95 (*1-56402-135-1*) Candlewick Pr.

Private Nose. Andrew Taylor. 1995. 9.09 (*0-606-08850-4*, Pub. by Turtleback) Demco.

Private Notebook of Katie Roberts, Age 11. Amy Hest. LC 94-37737. (Illus.). 80p. (J). (gr. 3-6). 1995. 14.95 (*1-56402-474-1*) Candlewick Pr.

Private Notebook of Katie Roberts, Age 11. Amy Hest. LC 94-37737. (Illus.). (J). (gr. 3-6). 1996. pap. 4.99 (*1-56402-859-3*) Candlewick Pr.

Private Notebook of Katie Roberts, Age 11. Amy Hest. 1996. 9.19 (*0-606-09768-6*, Pub. by Turtleback) Demco.

Private Ombudsmen & Public Law. Rhoda James. LC 97-3353. (Socio-Legal Studies). 272p. 1997. text 77.95 (*1-85521-769-4*, Pub. by Ashgate Pub) Ashgate Pub Co.

Private Options: Tools & Concepts for Land Conservation. Montana Land Reliance Staff & Land Trust Exchange Staff. LC 82-13070. 292p. (Orig.). 1982. pap. text 29.95 (*0-933280-15-7*) Island Pr.

Private Options for Public Schools: Ways Public Schools Are Exploring Privatization. Karen Powe. (NSBA Best Practices Ser.). 77p. (Orig.). 1995. pap. 15.00 (*0-88364-197-6*, 04-115) Natl Sch Boards.

*__Private Oral Exam Guide: The Comprehensive Guide to Prepare You for the FAA Oral Exam.__ 6th ed. Michael D. Hayes. (Oral Exam Guide Ser.). 186p. 1999. pap. 9.95 (*1-56027-375-5*) ASA Inc.

Private Orations, Vol. IV: 27-40. Tr. by A. T. Murray. (Loeb Classical Library: No. 318, 346, 351). 538p. 1936. 18.95 (*0-674-99351-9*) HUP.

Private Orations, Vol. V: Nos. 41-49. Tr. by A. T. Murray. (Loeb Classical Library: No. 318, 346, 351). 432p. 1939. 18.95 (*0-674-99381-0*) HUP.

Private Orations, Vol. VI: Nos. 50-58. Demosthenes. (Loeb Classical Library: No. 318, 346, 351). 464p. 1939. 19.95 (*0-674-99386-1*) HUP.

Private Orations, Vols. IV-VI. Demosthenes. No. 318, 346, 351. write for info. (*0-318-53148-8*) HUP.

Private Orations of Themistius. Robert J. Penella. LC 99-30092. (The Transformation of the Classical Heritage Ser.: Vol. Xxix). 287p. 1999. 55.00 (*0-520-21821-3*, Pub. by U CA Pr) Cal Prin Full Svc.

*__Private Organisations in Global Politics.__ Karsten Ronit & Volker Schneider. LC 00-42469. 2000. write for info. (*0-415-20128-4*) Routledge.

Private Organizations with U. S. Connections: El Salvador. 52p. 1988. pap. 5.95 (*0-911213-15-5*) Interhemisp Res Ctr.

Private Organizations with U. S. Connections: Guatemala. 75p. 1988. pap. 5.95 (*0-911213-16-3*) Interhemisp Res Ctr.

Private Organizations with U. S. Connections: Honduras. 77p. 1988. pap. 5.95 (*0-911213-14-7*) Interhemisp Res Ctr.

Private Osborne Massachusetts 23rd Volunteers: Burnside Expedition, Roanoke Island, Second Front Against Richmond. Frank B. Marcotte. (Illus.). 312p. 1999. lib. bdg. 32.50 (*0-7864-0554-6*) McFarland & Co.

Private Ownership of Public Housing in Singapore. Tan Sook Yee. LC 98-945580. 162p. 1998. 18.90 (*981-210-114-4*, Pub. by Times Academic) Intl Spec Bk.

Private Papers of British Colonial Governors, 1782-1900. Royal Commission on Historical Manuscripts Staff. (Guides to Sources for British History Ser.: No. 5). 66p. 1986. 12.00 (*0-11-440206-X*, HM494, Pub. by Statnry Office) Balogh.

Private Papers of British Diplomats, 1782-1900. Royal Commission on Historical Manuscripts Staff. (Guides to Sources for British History Ser.: No. 4). 80p. 1985. 12.00 (*0-11-440188-8*, HM495, Pub. by Statnry Office) Balogh.

Private Papers of Henry Ryecroft. George R. Gissing. 1983. pap. 9.95 (*0-7108-0323-0*, NO, 3878) Routledge.

Private Papers of Henry Ryecroft. George R. Gissing. (BCL1-PR English Literature Ser.). 267p. 1992. reprint ed. lib. bdg. 79.00 (*0-7812-7535-0*) Rprt Serv.

Private Papers of Hore-Belisha. R. J. Minney. (Modern Revivals in Military History Ser.). 320p. 1992. 63.95 (*0-7512-0042-5*, Pub. by Gregg Revivals) Ashgate Pub Co.

Private Papers of John Vanderlyn (1775-1852), American Portrait Painter. Salvatore A. Mondello. LC 89-9380. (Studies in American History: Vol. 3). (Illus.). 250p. 1990. lib. bdg. 89.95 (*0-88946-096-5*) E Mellen.

Private Papers Relating to Laetrile. Ed. by G. Edward Griffin. LC 97-71430. 112p. (Orig.). 1997. pap. 24.50 (*0-912986-20-4*) Am Media.

Private Paris: The 30 Most Beautiful Apartments. Marie-France Boyer. (Illus.). 192p. 1988. 50.00 (*0-89659-922-1*) Abbeville Pr.

Private Parties. Jonathan Penner. LC 83-47825. (Drue Heinz Literature Prize Ser.). 197p. 1983. text 22.50 (*0-8229-3488-4*) U of Pittsburgh Pr.

Private Parties: Political Party Leadership in Washington's Mercenary Culture. (Orig.). 1992. pap. write for info. (*0-9629012-8-8*) Ctr Public Integrity.

Private Parties in European Community Law: Challenging Community Measures. Albertina Albors-Llorens. 310p. 1996. text 80.00 (*0-19-826080-6*) OUP.

Private Parts. John Simons. 1984. pap. 1.95 (*0-671-00944-3*) PB.

Private Parts. Howard Stern. LC 97-116783. 1994. pap. 7.50 (*0-671-51043-6*) PB.

Private Parts: An Owner's Guide to the Male Anatomy. 2nd expanded ed. Yosh Taguchi. (Illus.). 320p. 1996. pap. text 19.99 (*0-7710-9067-6*) McCland & Stewart.

Private Passions. Laura D. Young. LC 98-13234. 224p. 1998. pap. 11.95 (*1-56280-215-1*) Naiad Pr.

Private Passions of Bonnie Prince Charlie. Hugh Douglas. LC 99-192829. (Illus.). 320p. 1999. pap. 21.95 (*0-7509-1902-7*, Pub. by Sutton Pub Ltd) Intl Pubs Mktg.

Private Passions (Secret Fantasies) Joann Ross. LC 95-22365. 219p. 1995. per. 3.25 (*0-373-25662-0*) Harlequin Bks.

*__Private Peacemaking: USIP-Assissted Peacemaking Projects of Nonprofit Organizations.__ Ed. by David R. Smock. 54p. 2000. reprint ed. pap. text 20.00 (*0-7567-0046-9*) DIANE Pub.

Private Pension Funds: Projected Growth. Daniel M. Holland. (Occasional Papers: No. 97). 166p. 1966. reprint ed. 43.20 (*0-87014-411-1*) Natl Bur Econ Res.

Private Pension Plan Bulletin: Abstract of 1992 Form 5500 Annual Reports. Richard Hinz. 94p. 1996. pap. text 6.50 (*0-16-048523-1*) USGPO.

Private Pension Plans: Efforts to Encourage Infrastructure Investment. (Illus.). 42p. (Orig.). (C). 1996. pap. text 20.00 (*0-7881-3028-5*) DIANE Pub.

Private Pension Policies in Industrialized Countries. John A. Turner & Noriyasu Watanabe. 170p. 1995. 34.00 (*0-88099-150-X*); pap. 15.00 (*0-88099-149-6*) W E Upjohn.

*__Private Pension Systems & Policy Issues.__ OECD Staff. (Private Pensions Ser.: No. 1). 396p. 2000. pap. 78.00 (*92-64-17634-9*, 21 2000 03 1 P, Pub. by Org for Econ) OECD.

Private Pensions: Funding Rule Change Needed to Reduce PBGC's Multibillion Dollar Exposure. (Illus.). 64p. (Orig.). (C). 1995. pap. text 30.00 (*0-7881-1709-2*) DIANE Pub.

Private Pensions: Plan Features Provided by Employers That Sponsor Only Defined Contribution Plans. Ed. by Margaret T. Wrightson. (Illus.). 60p. (C). 1999. reprint ed. pap. text 20.00 (*0-7881-7709-5*) DIANE Pub.

Private Pensions & Employee Mobility: A Comprehensive Approach to Pension Policy. Izzet Sahin. LC 88-35745. 130p. 1989. 49.95 (*0-89930-302-1*, SVO/, Quorum Bks) Greenwood.

Private Pensions & Individual Saving. George Katona. LC 65-64300. (University of Michigan. Survey Research Center, Monograph Ser.: No. 40). 126p. reprint ed. pap. 39.10 (*0-608-18031-9*, 202912900058) Bks Demand.

Private Pensions & Public Policy. OECD Staff. 160p. (Orig.). 1992. pap. 35.00 (*92-64-13790-4*) OECD.

Private Pensions in OECD Countries: Canada. 64p. (Orig.). 1995. pap. 17.00 (*92-64-14333-5*) OECD.

Private Pensions in OECD Countries: The United States. OECD Staff. LC 94-183544. 100p. (Orig.). 1993. pap. 22.00 (*92-64-13802-1*) OECD.

Private Philanthropy & Public Policy: Pierre S. Du Pont & the Delaware Schools, 1890-1940. Robert J. Taggart. LC 86-40587. (Illus.). 256p. 1988. 37.50 (*0-87413-318-1*) U Delaware Pr.

Private Pieces. Tom Johnson. LC 76-14367. 1976. pap. 8.00 (*0-938690-01-9*) Two Eighteen.

Private Pilot - Airplane. Sarah Rambo. LC 82-21299. (Illus.). 194p. 1983. pap. 24.95 (*0-8138-1382-4*) Iowa St U Pr.

Private Pilot & Recreational Pilot FAA Written Exam. 8th ed. Irvin N. Gleim. (Illus.). 338p. (C). 1997. pap. 13.95 (*0-917539-52-4*) Gleim Pubns.

Private Pilot Flight Training Manual. Ralph L. Butcher. LC 93-92817. 304p. 1996. pap., per. 34.95 (*1-881688-00-3*) Skyroamers.

Private Pilot Glider Checkride Made Easy. 2nd unabridged ed. Robert Wander. (Gliding Made Easy! Ser.: Vol. 1). 80p. (Orig.). 1997. mass mkt. 13.95 (*0-614-29366-9*) Soaring Bks.

Private Pilot Groundschool Guide. Don Gladney. (Illus.). 80p. (Orig.). (C). 1989. pap. write for info. (*0-318-65363-X*) ATDI.

Private Pilot Lighter-Than-Air Practical Test Standards, 1996. Government Printing Office Staff. 73p. 1996. ring bd. 3.75 (*0-16-042672-3*) USGPO.

Private Pilot Maneuvers Manual. (Pilot Training Ser.). (Illus.). 176p. 1996. pap. text 9.95 (*0-88487-221-1*, JS314705) Jeppesen Sanderson.

Private Pilot Maneuvers Manual. LC 98-218639. 1997. write for info. (*0-88487-239-4*) Jeppesen Sanderson.

Private Pilot Manual. Jeppesen Sanderson Staff. LC 98-231846. 1997. 62.00 (*0-88487-238-6*) Jeppesen Sanderson.

Private Pilot Practical Test Prep & Flight Maneuvers. 3rd ed. Irvin N. Gleim. (Illus.). 360p. (Orig.). (C). 1997. pap. 16.95 (*0-917539-85-0*) Gleim Pubns.

Private Pilot-Practical Test Standards-ASMEL. rev. ed. Federal Aviation Administration Staff. 81p. 1987. pap. text 3.95 (*0-318-42428-2*) Flightshops.

*__Private Pilot Practical Test Standards for Glider, 1999.__ Government Printing Office Staff. 47p. 1999. ring bd. 3.50 (*0-16-049932-1*) USGPO.

Private Pilot, Rotorcraft: Practical Test Standards, 1996. Government Printing Office Staff. 91p. 1996. ring bd. 4.50 (*0-16-042664-2*) USGPO.

Private Pilot Syllabus & Logbook. Irvin N. Gleim. (Illus.). 92p. 1998. pap. 9.95 (*0-917539-86-9*) Gleim Pubns.

Private Pilot Test Guide, 1996-1998: FAA Practical & Computer-Based Airman Knowledge with Disk. D. S. Carmody. LC 95-50764. 257p. 1996. pap. 34.95 (*0-07-912308-2*) McGraw.

*__Private Pilot Test Prep: Study & Prepare for Recreational & Private... FAA Exams.__ Ed. by Charles L. Robertson. (Two Thousand Test Prep Ser.). (Illus.). 326p. 1999. pap. 14.95 (*1-56027-341-0*) ASA Inc.

Private Pilot Written Exam Study Guide, 1993-1995. Jeppesen Sanderson. 15.50 (*0-88487-170-3*) Jeppesen Sanderson.

Private Pilot's Blue Book. James Dwyer. LC 76-41837. 1977. write for info. (*0-685-81548-X*) Macmillan.

Private Place: Death in Prehistoric Greece. William Cavanagh & Christopher Mee. (Studies in Mediterranean Archaeology: Vol. CXXV). (Illus.). 262p. 1998. pap. 99.50 (*91-7081-178-4*, Pub. by P Astroms) Coronet Bks.

Private Placements, 1995. (Corporate Law & Practice Course Handbook, 1985-86 Ser.). 1002p. 1995. pap. 99.00 (*0-685-69716-9*, B4-7096) PLI.

Private Placements, 1996. (Corporate Law & Practice Course Handbook, 1985-86 Ser.). Date not set. pap. 99.00 (*0-614-17208-X*, B4-7127) PLI.

Private Placements, 1992: Current Developments in Private Financings. (Corporate Law & Practice Ser.). 601p. 1992. pap. text 70.00 (*0-685-56897-0*, B4-6998) PLI.

Private Placements of Securities. Lola Hale. Vol. S2. text 82.00 (*0-8205-2411-5*) Bender.

Private Pleasure, Public Plight: American Metropolitan Community Life in Comparative Perspective. David Popenoe. LC 84-16411. 192p. 1988. pap. 24.95 (*0-88738-766-7*) Transaction Pubs.

*__Private Pleasure, Public Plight: American Metropolitan Community Life in Comparative Perspective.__ David Popenoe. 2000. pap. 24.95 (*0-7658-0708-4*) Transaction Pubs.

Private Pleasures. Janelle Denison. (Temptation Ser.: Vol. 679). 1998. per. 3.75 (*0-373-25779-1*, 1-25779-9) Harlequin Bks.

Private Pleasures. Lawrence Sanders. LC 94-147480. 336p. (Orig.). 1994. mass mkt. 6.99 (*0-425-14031-8*) Berkley Pub.

Private Pleasures. Lawrence Sanders. (Orig.). 1994. pap. 9.98 (*0-671-04457-5*) PB.

Private Poets, Worldly Acts: Public & Private History in Contemporary American Poetry. Kevin Stein. LC 96-13263. 206p. (C). 1996. text 37.95 (*0-8214-1163-2*) Ohio U Pr.

*__Private Poets, Worldly Acts: Public & Private History in Contemporary American Poetry.__ Kevin Stein. (Illus.). 208p. 1999. reprint ed. pap. 19.95 (*0-8214-1282-5*) Ohio U Pr.

Private Police Systems: Report of the Committee on Education & Labor. U. S. Committee on Education & Labor. LC 77-154594. (Police in America Ser.). 1971. reprint ed. 19.95 (*0-405-03403-2*) Ayer.

Private Postal Boxes, Mail Addresses & Mail Forwarding Services: A How to Find or Locate Workbook. Compiled by Frieda Carrol. 250p. 1983. ring bd. 29.95 (*0-913597-11-2*) Prosperity & Profits.

Private Power & Centralization in France: The Notaires & the State. Ezra N. Suleiman. (Illus.). 368p. 1987. pap. text 19.95 (*0-691-02293-3*, Pub. by Princeton U Pr) Cal Prin Full Svc.

Private Power & Centralization in France: The Notaires & the State. Ezra N. Suleiman. LC 87-45540. 361p. 1987. reprint ed. pap. 112.00 (*0-608-02536-4*, 206318000004) Bks Demand.

Private Practice. McCue. 1991. 32.95 (*0-316-55531-2*, Little Brwn Med Div) Lppncott W & W.

Private Practice Handbook: The Tools, Tactics & Techniques for Successful Practice Development. 4th ed. Charles H. Browning & Beverley J. Browning. 310p. 1994. pap. 29.95 (*0-911663-77-0*) Duncliffs Intl.

Private Practice in Communication Disorders. Mary L. Wood. (Illus.). 390p. (C). 1991. reprint ed. pap. 45.00 (*1-879105-30-6*, A072) Thomson Learn.

Private Practice in Occupational Therapy. Ed. by Florence S. Cromwell. LC 85-5513. (Occupational Therapy in Health Care Ser.: Vol. 2, No. 2). 138p. 1985. text 39.95 (*0-86656-411-X*) Haworth Pr.

Private Practice in Occupational Therapy. Ed. by Florence S. Cromwell. LC 85-5513. (Occupational Therapy in Health Care Ser.: Vol. 2, No. 2). 138p. 1985. pap. text 19.95 (*0-86656-412-8*) Haworth Pr.

Private Practice Management in Physical Therapy. Ira M. Fiebert et al. (Illus.). 221p. 1990. pap. text 55.00 (*0-443-08618-4*) Church.

Private Practice of Behavior Therapy: A Guide for Behavioral Practitioners. S. J. Kaplan. LC 86-51165. (Applied Clinical Psychology Ser.). (Illus.). 306p. (C). 1986. 59.50 (*0-306-42193-3*, Plenum Trade) Perseus Pubng.

Private Practice, Public Payment: Canadian Medicine & the Politics of Health Insurance, 1911-1966. C. David Naylor. 320p. (C). 1986. text 65.00 (*0-7735-0557-1*, Pub. by McG-Queens Univ Pr); pap. text 27.95 (*0-7735-0568-7*, Pub. by McG-Queens Univ Pr) CUP Services.

Private Practices. Stephen White. 430p. 1994. mass mkt. 7.50 (*0-451-40431-9*, Sig) NAL.

Private Practices. Stephen White. 1999. pap. write for info. (*0-14-017328-5*, Viking) Viking Penguin.

Private Practices: Girls Reading Fiction & Constructing Identity. Meredith Rogers Cherland. LC 94-14194. (Critical Perspectives of Literacy & Education Ser.). 240p. 1994. 85.00 (*0-7484-0225-X*, Pub. by Tay Francis Ltd); pap. 29.95 (*0-7484-0226-8*, Pub. by Tay Francis Ltd) Taylor & Francis.

Private Praise. Elbert Willis. 1977. 2.00 (*0-89858-009-9*) Fill the Gap.

Private Presses. 2nd ed. Colin Franklin & John Turner. (Illus.). 400p. 1990. text 78.95 (*0-85967-835-0*, Pub. by Scolar Pr) Ashgate Pub Co.

Private Presses & Their Books. Will Ransom. 493p. 1992. 75.00 (*1-882860-05-5*) J Cummins Bksell.

Private Presses & Their Books. Will Ransom. LC 75-41221. reprint ed. 32.50 (*0-404-14732-1*) AMS Pr.

Private Pressure on Public Law: The Legal Career of Justice Thurgood Marshall, 1934-1991. Randall W. Bland. LC 92-34835. 250p. (C). 1993. reprint ed. pap. text 24.50 (*0-8191-8736-4*) U Pr of Amer.

Private Prisons & Public Accountability. Richard Harding. LC 97-2890. 160p. 1997. text 32.95 (*1-56000-327-8*) Transaction Pubs.

Private Prisons & Public Accountability. Richard Harding. LC 97-2890. 160p. 1997. pap. text 19.95 (*1-56000-993-4*) Transaction Pubs.

Private Prisons & the Public Interest. Ed. by Douglas C. McDonald. LC 90-30616. (Crime, Law & Deviance Ser.). 235p. (C). 1990. text 40.00 (*0-8135-1574-2*) Rutgers U Pr.

Private Prisons Now: Their Appeal Widens as Alternatives Narrow. Steve Schwiff & Gale Norton. 17p. 1988. pap. text 8.00 (*1-57655-117-2*) Independ Inst.

Private Prisons Public Account. P. Harding. 176p. 1997. 103.95 (*0-335-19850-3*); pap. 30.95 (*0-335-19849-X*) Taylor & Francis.

Private Profit & Public Interest: The Supreme Court & the Economy. Kermit L. Hall. LC 96-26444. (Equal Justice Under Law Ser.). 1996. write for info. (*0-926019-97-X*) Carlson Pub.

*__Private Prometheus: Private Higher Education & Development In the 21st Century, 77.__ Ed. by Philip G. Altbach. LC 99-16142. Vol. 77. 248p. 1999. 65.00 (*0-313-31248-6*) Greenwood.

Private Property: Charles Brockden Brown's Gendered Economics of Virtue. Elizabeth J. Hinds. LC 96-26808. 192p. 1997. 33.50 (*0-87413-603-2*) U Delaware Pr.

Private Property & Political Control. Intro. by Hans F. Sennholz. (Freeman Classics Ser.). 173p. (Orig.). 1992. pap. 9.95 (*0-910614-80-6*) Foun Econ Ed.

Private Property & the Constitution. Bruce A. Ackerman. LC 76-47667. 1978. pap. 20.00 (*0-300-02237-9*) Yale U Pr.

Private Property & the Constitution. Bruce A. Ackerman. LC 76-47667. 313p. reprint ed. pap. 97.10 (*0-8357-8752-4*, 203365800087) Bks Demand.

Private Property & the Endangered Species Act: Saving Habitats, Protecting Homes. Ed. by Jason F. Shogren. LC 98-9067. (Illus.). 176p. 1999. pap. 14.95 (*0-292-77737-X*) U of Tex Pr.

Private Property & the Limits of American Constitutionalism: The Madisonian Framework & Its Legacy. Jennifer Nedelsky. xiv, 357p. 1994. pap. text 15.95 (*0-226-56971-3*) U Ch Pr.

Private Property & the Limits of American Constitutionalism: The Madisonian Framework & Its Legacy. Jennifer Nedelsky. 360p. 1998. 35.95 (*0-226-56970-5*) U Ch Pr.

P

An Asterisk (*) at the beginning of an entry indicates that the title is appearing for the first time.

Private Property & the Public Interest: The Brandywine Experience. Ann L. Strong. LC 74-24390. (Johns Hopkins Studies in Urban Affairs). (Illus.): 232p. reprint ed. pap. 72.00 (*0-608-06132-8*, 20664650008) Bks Demand.

Private Property, Government Requisition & the Constitution, 1914-1927. G. R. Rubin. LC 93-48977. 276p. 1994. 60.00 (*1-85285-098-1*) Hambledon Press.

Private Prosecutions. Richard J. Stafford. (C). 1988. pap. 150.00 (*0-7219-1090-4*, Pub. by Scientific) St Mut.

Private Readings - Public Texts: Playreaders' Constructs of Theatre Audiences. Kenneth Krauss. LC 91-58945. 160p. 1993. 32.50 (*0-8386-3496-6*) Fairleigh Dickinson.

Private Readings in Public: Schooling the Literary Imagination. Dennis J. Sumara. LC 95-40651. (Counterpoints Ser.: Vol. 26). XV, 306p. (C). 1996. pap. text 29.95 (*0-8204-3028-5*) P Lang Pubng.

Private Real Estate Syndications. Michael Constas & Richard D. Harroch. LC 83-9417. 600p. 1983. ring bd. 90.00 (*0-317-03225-9*, 00581) NY Law Pub.

Private Realm of Marie-Antoinette. Marie-France Boyer. LC 95-61617. (Illus.). 112p. 1996. 19.95 (*0-500-01690-9*, Pub. by Thames Hudson) Norton.

Private Reasons. Justine Davis. (Desire Ser.). 1994. mass mkt. 2.99 (*0-373-05833-0*, 5-05833-4) Silhouette.

Private Redevelopment of the Central City: Spatial Processes of Structural Change in the City of Toronto. Larry S. Bourne. LC 66-30638. (University of Chicago, Department of Geography, Research Paper Ser.: No. 112). 215p. reprint ed. pap. 66.70 (*0-7837-0392-9*, 204071300018) Bks Demand.

Private Reflections on Love. James Kavanaugh. LC 90-62064. Orig. Title: I Wondered about Love. (Illus.). 112p. 1985. reprint ed. pap. 12.95 (*1-878995-23-5*) S J Nash Pub.

Private Regulation of American Health Care. Betty Leyerle. LC 93-42516. 240p. (gr. 13). 1994. 70.95 (*1-56324-288-5*); pap. 34.95 (*1-56324-289-3*) M E Sharpe.

Private Religious Foundations in the Byzantine Empire. John Philip Thomas. LC 87-8870. (Dumbarton Oaks Studies: Vol. 24). 322p. 1988. 22.50 (*0-88402-164-5*) Dumbarton Oaks.

Private Revenge see Venganza Privada

Private Revenge: A Nathaniel Drinkwater Novel. Richard Woodman. LC 98-46977. (Mariner's Library Fiction Classics). 256p. 1999. pap. 14.95 (*1-57409-078-X*) Sheridan.

Private Rights & Public Illusions. Tibor R. Machan. LC 93-45616. 379p. (C). 1994. 34.95 (*1-56000-176-3*); pap. 19.95 (*1-56000-749-4*) Transaction Pubs.

Private Rights, Public Wrongs: The Computer & Personal Privacy. Michael R. Rubin. Ed. by Brenda Dervin. LC 88-19345. (Communication & Information Science Ser.). 168p. 1989. text 73.25 (*0-89391-518-1*) Ablx Pub.

Private Road. Forrest Reid. LC 75-41225. reprint ed. 37.50 (*0-404-14587-6*) AMS Pr.

***Private Rod: Marital Violence, Sensation & the Law in Victorian Britain.** Marlene Tromp. LC 00-26131. (Victorian Literature & Culture Ser.). 288p. 2000. 37.50 (*0-8139-1949-5*) U Pr of Va.

Private Rome. Elizabeth H. Minchilli. LC 98-66951. (Illus.). 216p. 1998. 45.00 (*0-8478-2130-7*, Pub. by Rizzoli Intl) St Martin.

Private Rules in Career Decision Making. John D. Krumboltz. 33p. 1983. 5.75 (*0-318-22179-9*, SN38) Ctr Educ Trng Employ.

Private Scandals. Nora Roberts. 501p. 1994. mass mkt. 7.50 (*0-515-11400-6*, Jove) Berkley Pub.

Private Scandals. unabridged ed. Nora Roberts. 1993. 25.95 incl. audio (*1-56100-509-6*, Bkcassette) Brilliance.

Private School Administration. Aspen Editorial Staff. 1997. 119.00 (*0-8342-0994-2*) Aspen Pub.

Private School Administration Forms, Checklists & Guidelines. Sara N. Di Lima et al. LC 97-37187. 1998. write for info. (*0-8342-0992-6*) Aspen Pub.

Private School Guide Los Angeles County. Scott Beals. Ed. by David Hopkins. 340p. (Orig.). pap. 19.95 (*0-929950-19-4*) ME Pubns.

Private School Law in America. 9th ed. 1987. pap. 113.75 (*0-939675-53-6*) Data Res MN.

Private School Management. William J. McMillan. 1977. 7.95 (*0-918214-00-9*, 76-51885) F E Peters.

Private School Management. 2nd ed. William J. McMillan. LC 79-50904. 1979. 14.95 (*0-918214-03-3*) F E Peters.

***Private School Universe Survey, 1995-96.** Stephen P. Broughman. 96p. 1998. pap. 7.50 (*0-16-049499-0*) USGPO.

***Private School Universe Survey, 1997-98.** Stephen P. Broughman. 100p. 1999. pap. 9.00 (*0-16-050184-9*) USGPO.

Private School Vouchers: What Are the Real Choices? Nancy Kober. 64p. 1996. 10.95 (*0-87652-225-8*, 021-0586) Am Assn Sch Admin.

Private Schooling: Tradition, Change & Diversity. Ed. by Geoffrey Walford. 192p. 1991. pap. 39.00 (*1-85396-116-7*, Pub. by P Chapman) Taylor & Francis.

Private Schooling of Girls: Past & Present. Ed. by Geoffrey Walford. 208p. 1993. text 35.00 (*0-7130-0186-0*, Pub. by Woburn Pr) Intl Spec Bk.

Private Schools: Boards & Heads. William J. McMillan. LC 80-81654. 88p. (Orig.). 1980. pap. 5.95 (*0-918214-06-8*) F E Peters.

Private Schools & Public Power: A Case for Pluralism. E. Vance Randall. 240p. (C). 1994. text 34.00 (*0-8077-3344-X*) Tchrs Coll.

Private Schools in Ten Countries: Policy & Practice. Ed. by Geoffrey Walford. 240p. 1989. 55.00 (*0-415-03464-7*, A3283) Routledge.

Private Schools in the United States. 1996. lib. bdg. 251.75 (*0-8490-6044-3*) Gordon Pr.

Private Schools of Colonial Boston. Robert F. Seybolt. LC 77-89232. (American Education: Its Men, Institutions, & Ideas. Series 1). 1980. reprint ed. 11.95 (*0-405-01468-6*) Ayer.

Private Schools of the Future. William J. McMillan. LC 81-66535. 117p. (C). 1981. spiral bd. 12.95 (*0-918214-07-6*) F E Peters.

***Private Schools of the San Francisco Peninsula/Silicon Valley: Elementary & Middle.** Ellen Lussier & Susan Vogel. (Illus.). 130p. 1999. pap. 16.95 (*0-9648757-6-4*, Pub. by Pince Nez Pr) Sunbelt Pubns.

Private Science: Biotechnology & the Rise of the Molecular Sciences. Ed. by Arnold W. Thackray. LC 97-31823. (Illus.). 304p. (C). 1998. 52.50 (*0-8122-3428-6*) U of Pa Pr.

Private Science of Louis Pasteur. Gerald L. Geison. 392p. 1995. pap. text 16.95 (*0-691-01552-X*, Pub. by Princeton U Pr) Cal Prin Full Svc.

Private Science of Louis Pasteur. Gerald L. Geison. LC 94-35338. (Illus.). 378p. 1995. 49.50 (*0-691-03442-7*, Pub. by Princeton U Pr) Cal Prin Full Svc.

Private Screening. Richard North Patterson. 448p. 1986. mass mkt. 7.99 (*0-345-31139-6*) Ballantine Pub Grp.

Private Screening. Richard North Patterson. 1993. pap. 12.00 (*0-345-38572-1*) Ballantine Pub Grp.

Private Screening. Richard North Patterson. 1997. pap. 6.99 (*0-345-91284-5*) Ballantine Pub Grp.

***Private Screenings: Insiders Share a Century of Great Movie Moments.** Duane Byrge. (Illus.). 189p. 1999. reprint ed. pap. text 20.00 (*0-7881-6788-X*) DIANE Pub.

Private Screenings: Television & the Female Consumer. Ed. by Lynn Spigel & Denise Mann. LC 91-40919. (Illus.). 320p. (C). 1992. pap. 16.95 (*0-8166-2053-9*) U of Minn Pr.

Private Secondary Schools. 19th ed. Peterson's Guides Staff. 1408p. 1998. pap. text 29.95 (*1-56079-972-2*) Petersons.

Private Secondary Schools 1999-2000. 20th ed. Peterson's Guides Staff. 1435p. pap. 29.95 (*0-7689-0186-3*) Petersons.

Private Secretary. A. G. McBain. (C). 1982. pap. write for info. (*0-7219-0500-5*, Pub. by Scientific) St Mut.

Private Sector. J. Wilson Newman. (Credibility of Institutions, Policies & Leadership Ser.: Vol. 6). 140p. (Orig.). 1985. pap. 15.00 (*0-8191-4766-4*) U Pr of Amer.

Private Sector. J. Wilson Newman. (Credibility of Institutions, Policies & Leadership Ser.: Vol. 6). 140p. (Orig.). 1985. lib. bdg. 39.00 (*0-8191-4765-6*, Pub. by White Miller Center) U Pr of Amer.

Private Sector Alternatives for Preventing Reading Failure. Patrick Groff. 120p. 1989. pap. text 14.90 (*0-89420-262-6*, 341175) Natl Book.

Private Sector & ASEAN Business Opportunities: Cambodia, Lao Peoples Democratic Republic, Myanmar & Viet Nam. 158p. 25.00 (*92-1-119882-8*) UN.

Private Sector & Community Involvement in the Criminal Justice System. Ed. by D. Biles & J. Vernon. LC 95-173937. (Australian Institute Conference Proceedings Ser.: Vol. 23). 478p. 1994. pap. 45.00 (*0-642-20156-0*, Pub. by Aust Inst Criminology) Advent Bks Div.

***Private Sector & Development: Five Case Studies.** IFC Staff. (Results on the Ground Ser.: Vol. 2). 56p. 1998. 22.00 (*0-8213-3921-4*) World Bank.

Private Sector & Development: Five Case Studies. IFC Staff. LC 98-14422. (Results on the Ground Ser.: No. 2). 56p. 1998. pap. 22.00 (*0-8213-4199-5*) World Bank.

Private Sector & Development: Five Case Studies. IFC Staff. (Results on the Ground Ser.: Vol. 2). 56p. 1997. 22.00 (*0-8213-3920-6*) World Bank.

Private Sector & Development: Five Case Studies. International Finance Corporation Staff. LC 97-213. (IFC Results on the Ground Ser.). 64p. 1997. 22.00 (*0-8213-3889-7*, 13889) World Bank.

Private Sector Cleanup Expenditures & Transaction Costs at 18 Superfund Sites. Lloyd S. Dixon et al. LC 93-39916. 1993. pap. text 13.00 (*0-8330-1470-6*, MR-204-EPA/RC) Rand Corp.

Private Sector Costs of the Department of Labor's Pay Docking Policy. James S. Holt & Alan E. Simon. 7p. 1992. pap. 5.00 (*0-614-06147-4*, 2043-PP-4040) EPF.

Private Sector Development: A Guide to Donor Support. LC 96-102206. 110p. (Orig.). 1995. pap. 28.00 (*92-64-14305-X*, Pub. by Org for Econ) OECD.

Private Sector Development: Policies & Programs for the Pacific Islands. Mark Sturton et al. LC 92-40076. (Illus.). 264p. (C). 1993. pap. text 12.00 (*0-86638-155-4*) EW Ctr HI.

Private Sector Development & Enterprise Reforms in Growing Asian Economies. Seiji Naya. 119p. 1990. pap. 14.95 (*1-55815-083-8*) ICS Pr.

***Private Sector Development & Privatization in the Industrial Sector in Selected Central Asian Economies in Transition.** Economic & Social Commission for Asia & the Pacific Staff. 304p. 1998. 65.00 (*92-1-119863-1*) UN.

Private Sector Development During Transition: The Visegrad Countries. Michael S. Borish & Michel Noel. LC 96-10. (World Bank Discussion Papers: No. 318). 188p. 1996. pap. 22.00 (*0-8213-3569-3*) World Bank.

Private Sector Development in Egypt. Marcelo M. Guigale & Hamed Mobarak. LC 96-960263. 146p. 1996. 39.50 (*977-424-376-5*, Pub. by Am Univ Cairo Pr) Col U Pr.

Private Sector Development in Low-Income Countries. (Development in Practice Ser.). 188p. 1996. pap. 22.00 (*0-8213-3478-6*, 13478) World Bank.

Private Sector Development in Low-Income Countries. (Development in Practice Ser.). (FRE.). 210p. 1996. pap. 22.00 (*0-8213-3550-2*, 13550) World Bank.

Private Sector Development Organizations: A Directory. Mary McClean. 84p. (Orig.). 1987. pap. 20.00 (*0-317-04816-3*) Natl Coun Econ Dev.

Private Sector Federal Employment Discrimination. Luke Farber. LC 90-36229. (Legal Research Guide Ser.: Vol. 10). 42p. 1990. 30.00 (*0-89941-744-2*, 306360) W S Hein.

Private Sector Financial Performance Measures & Their Applicability to Government Operations. David J. Harr & James T. Godfrey. Ed. by Claire Barth. (Illus.). 112p. (Orig.). 1991. pap. 20.00 (*0-86641-200-X*, 91262) Inst Mgmt Account.

Private Sector in Water Supply: Competition & Regulation. LC 99-217583. 70p. 1999. pap. 35.00 (*0-8213-4484-6*, 14484) World Bank.

Private-Sector Involvement & Toll Road Financing in the Provision of Highways. (Research Record Ser.: No. 1107). 127p. 1987. 18.00 (*0-309-04455-3*) Transport Res Bd.

Private Sector Involvement in Health Care: Implications for Access, Cost, & Quality, Vol. 9. Ed. by Richard M. Scheffler et al. (Advances in Health Economics & Health Services Research Ser.). 265p. 1988. 73.25 (*0-89232-937-8*) Jai Pr.

Private Sector Involvement with the Vocational Community: An Analysis of Policy Options. Clyde F. Maurice. 106p. 1984. 8.75 (*0-318-22180-2*, IN281) Ctr Educ Trng Employ.

Private Sector Part Water Supply & Wastewater. 116p. 1997. pap. 22.00 (*0-8213-3682-7*, 13682) World Bank.

Private Sector Participation in Municipal Solid Waste Services in Developing Countries, Vol. 1: The Formal Sector. Sandra Cointreau-Levine. (Urban Management Program Ser.: Paper 13). 64p. 1994. pap. 22.00 (*0-8213-2825-5*, 12825) World Bank.

Private Sector Participation in Power Generation in Egypt: A Strategic Entry Report, 1998. Compiled by Icon Group International Staff. (Country Industry Report). (Illus.). 158p. 1999. ring bd. 1580.00 incl. audio compact disk (*0-7418-0473-5*) Icon Grp.

Private Sector Participation in Public Transit Systems. Chris Pattarozzi. (State Legislative Reports: Vol. 18, No. 4). 7p. 1993. 15.00 (*1-55516-298-3*, 7302-1804) Natl Conf State Legis.

Private Sector Participation in Water Supply & Sanitation in Latin America. Emanuel Idelovitch & Klas Ringskog. LC 95-13904. (Directions in Development Ser.). 64p. 1995. pap. 22.00 (*0-8213-3219-8*, 13219) World Bank.

Private-Sector Proposals. 1993. 69.00 (*0-937925-93-4*, PSP) Capitol Publns.

***Private Sector Response to Agricultural Marketing Liberlisation in Zambia: A Case Study of Eastern Province Maize Markets.** Dennis Chiwele. LC 99-165856. (Research Report Ser.). 90p. 1999. pap. write for info. (*91-7106-436-2*) Nordisk Afrikainstitutet.

Private Sector Role in Rural Outdoor Recreation in the United States: An Annotated Bibliography. Ken Cordell & Barbara Stanley-Saunders. (CPL Bibliographies Ser.: No. 106). 118p. 1983. 10.00 (*0-86602-106-X*, Sage Prdcls Pr) Sage.

Private Sector Solutions to the Latin American Debt Problem. Ed. by Robert Grosse. LC 92-14089. 192p. (C). 1992. pap. 17.95 (*1-56000-632-3*, Pub. by U Miami N-S Ctr) L Rienner.

***Private Sector Strategies for Social Sector Success: The Guide to Strategy & Planning for Public & Nonprofit Organizations.** Kevin P. Kearns. LC 00-20566. (Nonprofit & Public Management Ser.). 2000. 26.95 (*0-7879-4189-1*) Jossey-Bass.

Private Sector Task Force on Juvenile Justice. 7.00 (*0-318-20315-4*) Natl Coun Crime.

Private Sector Task Force on Juvenile Justice: Final Report. 1987. 8.65 (*0-318-23565-X*) Natl Coun Crime.

Private Sector Whistleblower Protections: Existing Law & Proposed Expansions. Daniel V. Yager & Ann E. Reesman. 133p. 1989. pap. 15.00 (*0-614-06166-0*, 2012-PP-4040) EPF.

Private Securities Litigation Reform Act of 1995 - Law & Explanation. 176p. 1996. pap. 25.00 (*0-614-26808-7*, 04887001) CCH INC.

Private Security. 1991. lib. bdg. 79.75 (*0-8490-4476-6*) Gordon Pr.

Private Security & Public Policing. Trevor Jones & Tim Newburn. LC 97-45973. (Clarendon Studies in Criminology). (Illus.). 302p. (C). 1998. text 78.00 (*0-19-826569-7*, Clarendon Pr) OUP.

Private Security & the Investigative Process. 2nd ed. Charles P. Nemeth. LC 97-49930. 360p. 1998. pap. 34.95 (*0-7506-9087-9*) Buttrwrth-Heinemann.

Private Security & the Law. 2nd ed. Charles P. Nemeth. LC 94-73242. 426p. (C). 1995. pap. 37.95 (*0-87084-599-3*) Anderson Pub Co.

Private Security in America: Private Security, Loss Prevention & Assets Protection. Clifford E. Simonsen. LC 97-52785. 430p. (C). 1998. 73.00 (*0-02-410534-1*, Macmillan Coll) P-H.

Private Security Industry: Issues & Trends. Ed. by Ira A. Lipman. (Annals Ser.: Vol. 498). 1988. 26.00 (*0-8039-3102-6*); pap. 17.00 (*0-8039-3103-4*) Sage.

Private Security Law: Case Studies. David Maxwell. 440p. 1992. 59.95 (*0-7506-9034-8*) Buttrwrth-Heinemann.

Private Security Trends, 1970-2000: The Hallcrest Report II. William C. Cunningham et al. 384p. 1990. 59.95 (*0-7506-9179-4*) Buttrwrth-Heinemann.

Private Self. Arnold H. Modell. LC 93-14974. 288p. 1993. 36.50 (*0-674-70752-4*) HUP.

Private Self. Arnold H. Modell. 264p. 1996. pap. text 18.00 (*0-674-70753-2*) HUP.

Private Self: Theory & Practice of Women's Autobiographical Writings. Ed. by Shari Benstock. LC 88-1282. vii, 319p. (C). 1988. 49.95 (*0-8078-1791-0*) U of NC Pr.

Private Service Firms in a Transitional Economy: Findings of A Survey in St. Petersburg. Martha De Melo & Gur Ofer. LC 94-4998. (Studies of Economies in Transformation: No. 11). 82p. 1994. pap. 22.00 (*0-8213-2797-6*, 12797) World Bank.

Private Seven. John Ashbery et al. Ed. by D. R. Heiniger & Ken Saunders. (Illus.). 175p. (Orig.). 1992. pap. 7.00 (*1-881377-02-4*) Private Lives.

Private Short-Term Capital Flows. Arthur B. Laffer. LC 75-159. (Business Economics & Finance Ser.: No. 5). 160p. reprint ed. pap. 49.60 (*0-7837-0651-0*, 204099000019) Bks Demand.

Private Side of American History, Vol. 1. 5th ed. Nash. (C). 1999. pap. text 31.00 (*0-15-505541-0*, Pub. by Harcourt Coll Pubs) Harcourt.

Private Side of American History: Readings in Everyday Life, Vol. 1: To 1877. 4th ed. Gary B. Nash et al. 459p. (C). 1987. pap. text 37.00 (*0-15-571960-2*, Pub. by Harcourt Coll Pubs) Harcourt.

Private Sins. Janice Kaiser. 402p. 1995. per. 4.99 (*1-55166-024-5*, 1-66024-0, Mira Bks) Harlequin Bks.

Private Sins. Diane Levitt. 1993. mass mkt. 4.99 (*1-55817-738-8*, Pinncle Kensgtn) Kensgtn Pub Corp.

Private Soldier under Washington. Charles K. Bolton. (American Revolution Ser.: Vol. 2). 96p. 1997. 10.95 (*1-58057-017-8*, PSUW001B) Digital Antiq.

Private Soldier under Washington. 3rd unabridged ed. Charles K. Bolton. (Illus.). 265p. 1997. reprint ed. pap. 15.95 (*0-87928-117-0*) Corner Hse.

***Private Soldiers & Public Heroes: An American Album of the Common Man's Civil War.** Milton Bagby. LC 98-27465. 1998. 29.95 (*1-55853-688-4*) Rutledge Hill Pr.

Private Speech: From Social Interaction to Self-Regulation. Ed. by Rafael M. Diaz & Laura E. Berk. 312p. 1992. pap. 32.50 (*0-8058-0887-6*); text 59.95 (*0-8058-0886-8*) L Erlbaum Assocs.

Private State: Stories. Charlotte Bacon. LC 97-14672. 200p. 1997. 24.95 (*1-55849-114-7*) U of Mass Pr.

Private Stories. Leslie A. Brothers & Steven S. High. 16p. 1991. 7.00 (*0-935519-13-0*) Anderson Gal.

Private T. Pigeon's Tale. deluxe ed. Jaimy Gordon. (Treacle Story Ser.: No. 5). (Illus.). 36p. 1979. 12.50 (*0-914232-19-3*) McPherson & Co.

Private Terror/Public Life: Psychosis & the Politics of Community. James M. Glass. LC 89-31059. 268p. reprint ed. pap. 83.10 (*0-608-20090-5*, 207136200011) Bks Demand.

Private Testimony & Public Policy. Phillips Ruopp. (C). 1959. pap. 4.00 (*0-87574-105-3*) Pendle Hill.

Private Theatricals: The Lives of the Victorians. Nina Auerbach. (Illus.). 144p. 1990. text 25.95 (*0-674-70755-9*) HUP.

Private Thoughts, Deadly Secrets. Lucinda Rutledge-Smalls. Ed. by Diane B. Seebass. 512p. (Orig.). 1997. pap. 10.95 (*0-9652072-6-9*) Melano Pub.

Private Timberlands: Private Timber Harvests Not Likely to Replace Declining Federal Harvests. (Illus.). 46p. (Orig.). (C). 1995. pap. text 20.00 (*0-7881-2054-9*) DIANE Pub.

Private Traders in Medieval India: British & Indian. Jagadish N. Sarkar. (C). 1991. 29.50 (*81-85421-06-4*, Pub. by Naya Prokash) S Asia.

Private Treaty. Kathleen Eagle. (Harlequin Historical Ser.). 1991. mass mkt. 3.99 (*0-373-15152-7*) Harlequin Bks.

Private Troubles & Public Issues: Social Problems in the Postmodern Era. David R. Simon & Joel H. Henderson. LC 96-76139. 560p. (C). 1996. pap. text 44.00 (*0-15-501368-8*, Pub. by Harcourt Coll Pubs) Harcourt.

Private Truths, Public Lies: The Social Consequences of Preference Falsification. Timur Kuran. LC 94-47969. (Illus.). 432p. (C). 1995. text 50.95 (*0-674-70757-5*, SHEPRX) HUP.

Private Truths, Public Lies: The Social Consequences of Preference Falsification. Timur Kuran. (Illus.). 448p. 1997. reprint ed. pap. 19.50 (*0-674-70758-3*) HUP.

***Private Tuition.** Jay Merson. 1999. pap. 9.99 (*1-897809-58-1*) Silver Moon.

Private Tuscany. Elizabeth H. Minchilli. (Illus.). 216p. 1999. 45.00 (*0-8478-2178-1*) Rizzoli Intl.

Private Universe. Andre Maurois. Tr. by Hamish Miles. LC 70-177963. (Essay Index Reprint Ser.). 1977. reprint ed. 22.95 (*0-8369-2564-5*) Ayer.

***Private Unternehmen im Transformationsland China: Individual und Privatunternehmen in China - Ihr Volkswirtschaftlicher Stellenwert und Ihre Funktionen im Entwicklungsprozea der Chinesischen Wirtschaft.** Stefanie Schmitt. (Europaische Hochschulschriften Ser.: Bd. 2531). 337p. 1999. 52.95 (*3-631-35151-8*) P Lang Pubng.

Private Use of Tax-Exempt Bonds: Controlling Public Subsidy of Private Activity. Dennis Zimmerman. LC 90-49016. (Illus.). 390p. (C). 1991. pap. text 33.00 (*0-87766-498-6*) Urban Inst.

Private Versus Public Enterprise: In Search of the Economic Rationale for Privatisation. Jacek Tittenbrun. LC 97-187764. 154p. 1997. pap. 18.95 (*1-85756-204-6*, Pub. by Janus Pubng) Paul & Co Pubs.

Private Versus Public Sector Insurance Coverage for Drug Abuse. Jeannette A. Rogowski. LC 93-12592. 1993. pap. text 13.00 (*0-8330-1345-9*, MR-166-DPRC) Rand Corp.

Private View. Anita Brookner. 256p. 1996. pap. 12.00 (*0-679-75443-1*) Random.

Private View. Audrey Slaughter. 336p. 1989. 26.95 (*0-385-26898-X*) Doubleday.

Private View: American Paintings from the Manoogian Collection. LC 93-17036. (Illus.). 168p. 1993. pap. 30.95 (*0-89467-062-X*) Yale Art Gallery.

Private Violence & Public Policy: The Needs of Battered Women & the Response of the Public. Ed. by Jan Pahl. 208p. (Orig.). 1985. pap. 13.95 (*0-7100-9992-4*, Routledge Thoemms) Routledge.

Private Virtue & Public Policy: Catholic Thought & National Life. Ed. by James Finn. 300p. 1990. 34.95 (*0-88738-306-8*) Transaction Pubs.

Private Voices: The Diaries of Elizabeth Cleghorn Gaskell & Sophia Isaac Holland. Anita C. Wilson & J. A. Chapple. LC 96-27994. 128p. 1996. text 39.95 (*0-312-16408-4*) St Martin.

Private Voices, Public Lives: Women Speak on the Literary Life. Ed. by Nancy O. Nelson. LC 94-48327. 345p. (Orig.). 1995. pap. 18.95 (*0-929398-88-2*) UNTX Pr.

Private Voluntary Organizations in Egypt: Islamic Development, Private Initiative & State Control. Denis J. Sullivan. LC 94-1608. 216p. 1994. 49.95 (*0-8130-1290-2*) U Press Fla.

Private Wants & Public Needs. rev. ed. Ed. by Edmund S. Phelps. (Problems of Modern Economy Ser.). (Orig.). (C). 1965. pap. text 4.95 (*0-393-09496-0*) Norton.

Private War: An American Code Officer in the Belgian Congo. limited ed. Robert Laxalt. LC 98-11581. 96p. 1998. 25.00 (*0-87417-323-X*) U of Nev Pr.

***Private War: An American Code Officer in the Belgian Congo.** limited ed. Robert Laxalt. LC 98-11581. x, 103p. 1998. pap. 14.00 (*0-87417-324-8*) U of Nev Pr.

Private War: The Letters & Diaries of Madge Preston, 1862-1867. Ed. by Virginia W. Beachamp. 374p. 1991. reprint ed. pap. 17.95 (*0-8135-1728-1*) Rutgers U Pr.

Private War of Mrs. Packard: The Dramatic Story of a Nineteenth-Century Feminist. Barbara Sapinsley. Ed. by Philip Turner. (Kodansha Globe Ser.). (Illus.). 240p. 1995. pap. 14.00 (*1-56836-106-8*, Kodansha Globe) Kodansha.

***Private Ward.** large type ed. Sonia Deane. 352p. 1999. pap. 20.99 (*1-85389-896-1*, Dales) Ulverscroft.

***Private Warriors.** Ken Silverstein. 224p. 2000. 25.00 (*1-85984-756-0*, Pub. by Verso) Norton.

***Private Wars.** 304p. 2000. 39.95 (*0-19-550799-1*) OUP.

Private Washington: Residences in the Nation's Capital. Jan Cigliano. LC 98-26054. (Illus.). 176p. 1998. 50.00 (*0-8478-2024-6*, Pub. by Rizzoli Intl) St Martin.

Private Water Systems Handbook. 4th ed. Midwest Plan Service Engineers Staff. LC 79-19040. (Illus.). 72p. 1979. pap. 7.00 (*0-89373-045-9*, MWPS-14) MidWest Plan Serv.

Private Wealth & Public Education. John E. Coons et al. LC 73-102667. (Illus.). 548p. reprint ed. pap. 169.90 (*0-7837-4101-4*, 205792400011) Bks Demand.

Private Wealth & Public Life: Foundation Philanthropy & the Reshaping of American Social Policy from the Progressive Era. Judith Sealander. LC 96-41649. (Illus.). 344p. 1997. text 39.95 (*0-8018-5460-1*) Johns Hopkins.

***Private Woman in Public Spaces: Barbara Jordan's Speeches on Ethics, Public Religion, 1974-1995.** Barbara Ann Holmes. (African American Religious Thought & Life Ser.). 162p. 2000. pap. 17.00 (*1-56338-302-0*, Pub. by TPI PA) Morehouse Pub.

Private Women, Public Meals: Social Conflict in the Synoptic Tradition. Kathleen Corley. LC 93-5702. 240p. 1993. 19.95 (*1-56563-003-3*) Hendrickson MA.

Private Woods. Sandra C. Moore. 288p. 1988. 18.95 (*0-15-174710-5*); 18.95 (*0-685-22051-6*) Harcourt.

Private World: Selections from the Diario Intimo & Selected Letters, 1890-1935. Miguel de Unamuno. Tr. by Anthony Kerrigan & Martin Nozick. LC 83-43054. (Selected Works of Miguel de Unamuno: Vol. 2). 391p. 1984. reprint ed. pap. 121.30 (*0-608-02901-7*, 206396500008) Bks Demand.

***Private World of Daphne du Maurier.** Martin Shallcross. 216p. 1999. pap. 13.95 (*1-86105-177-8*) Robson.

Private World of Daphne Du Maurier. large type ed. Martyn Shallcross. 185p. 1992. 21.95 (*1-85089-347-0*, Pub. by ISIS Lrg Prnt) Transaction Pubs.

***Private World of Family Business, Vol. 1.** Graham Connolly & Christopher Jay. 270p. (Orig.). 1999. pap. 29.95 (*0-7299-0339-7*) Pitman Pubng.

Private World of Jean Giono. Walter D. Redfern. LC 67-20396. 217p. reprint ed. pap. 67.30 (*0-8357-9115-7*, 201792400010) Bks Demand.

Private World of Katharine Hepburn. John Bryson. 176p. 1992. pap. 24.95 (*0-316-11333-6*) Little.

Private World of Katharine Hepburn. Photos by John Byrson. (Illus.). 1996. 39.95 (*0-316-11332-8*) Little.

Private World of Tasha Tudor. Tasha Tudor. 144p. (gr. 8). 1992. 37.95 (*0-316-11292-5*) Little.

Private World of the Duke & Duchess of Windsor. Hugo Vickers. LC 97-146152. (Illus.). 240p. 1996. 67.50 (*0-7892-0226-3*) Abbeville Pr.

Private World of the Hermitage: Lifestyles of the Rich & Old in an Elite Retirement Home. Mary M. Free. LC 94-27545. 184p. 1995. 55.00 (*0-89789-414-6*, Bergin & Garvey) Greenwood.

Private Worlds of Dying Children. Myra Bluebond-Langner. LC 77-85529. 298p. 1978. pap. text 15.95 (*0-691-02820-6*, Pub. by Princeton U Pr) Cal Prin Full Svc.

Private Worlds of Marcel Duchamp: Desire, Liberation, & the Self in Modern Culture. Jerrold Seigel. LC 94-49723. (Illus.). 307p. 1995. 40.00 (*0-520-20038-1*, Pub. by U CA Pr) Cal Prin Full Svc.

Private Worlds of Marcel Duchamp: Desire, Liberation, & the Self in Modern Culture. Jerrold Seigel. LC 94-49723. (Illus.). 1997. pap. 19.95 (*0-520-20903-6*, Pub. by U CA Pr) Cal Prin Full Svc.

Private Yankee Doodle. Joseph P. Martin. LC 67-29036. (Eyewitness Accounts of the American Revolution Ser.). 1980. reprint ed. 29.95 (*0-405-01137-7*) Ayer.

Private Yankee Doodle. Joseph P. Martin. Ed. by George F. Scheer. 305p. 1979. reprint ed. pap. 2.25 (*0-915992-10-8*) Eastern National.

Private Zone. 1988. mass mkt. 3.50 (*0-446-73725-9*, Pub. by Warner Bks) Little.

Privateer. R. C. Andersen. Ed. by Kathy Kaiser. LC 98-96572. 192p. 1999. 19.95 (*0-9666946-0-0*) Spring Pubg.

***Privateer.** James Doohan & S. M. Stirling. 320p. 2000. mass mkt. 6.99 (*0-671-31949-3*) Baen Bks.

Privateer: Volume 2 of the Flight Engineer. James Doohan & S. M. Stirling. LC 99-38132. 264p. 1999. pap. 21.00 (*0-671-57832-4*) Baen Bks.

Privateer Playtesters' Guide. Beth Loubet et al. (Illus.). 96p. (Orig.). 1994. pap. 14.95 (*0-929373-16-2*) Origin Syst.

Privateer 3: Prima's Official Strategy Guide. David Ladyman. 244p. 2000. pap. 19.99 (*0-7615-1586-0*) Prima Pub.

Privateer 2: The Darkening: Origin's Strategy Guide. Prima Development Staff. LC 96-70912. 288p. 1996. pap., per. 19.99 (*0-7615-0934-8*) Prima Pub.

Privateering & Colonisation in the Reign of Elizabeth I. Ed. by Joyce Youings. (Illus.). 128p. 1985. pap. text 13.95 (*0-85989-252-2*, Pub. by Univ Exeter Pr) Northwestern U Pr.

Privateering Earl: George Clifford, 3rd Earl of Cumberland, 1558-1605. Richard T. Spence. LC 95-223489. 1997. 33.95 (*0-7509-0892-0*, Pub. by Sutton Pub Ltd) Intl Pubs Mktg.

***Privateers.** Benjamin W. Bova. 400p. 2000. mass mkt. 6.99 (*0-380-79316-4*, Avon Bks) Morrow Avon.

***Privateersman.** Alexander Kent. (Classics of Nautical Fiction Ser.). 384p. 2000. reprint ed. pap. 15.95 (*0-935526-69-2*) McBooks Pr.

Privately Owned Public Space. Jerold S. Kayden. LC 00-35193. 304p. 2000. text 7.95 (*0-471-36257-3*) Wiley.

Privately Printed Papers of A. A. Girault. Gordon Gordh et al. (Memoir Ser.: No.28). 400p. 1978. 45.00 (*1-56665-026-7*) Assoc Pubs FL.

Private's Diary. Donald A. Edwards. 536p. 1994. write for info. (*0-9639706-0-7*) D A Edwards.

Private's Diary: The Battle of Germany As Seen Through the Eyes of an 18 Year Old Infantry Rifleman. Jack R. Blann. LC 97-93105. (Illus.). 196p. 1997. 24.95 (*0-9654653-0-6*) J & L Publng.

Privatisation? Ed. by Sue Hastings & Hugo Levie. 205p. 1983. 43.50 (*0-85124-393-2*, Pub. by Spkesman) Coronet Bks.

Privatisation. Ed. by Richard Parry. (Research Highlights in Social Work Ser.: Vol. 18). 128p. 1990. 37.95 (*1-85302-015-X*, Pub. by Jessica Kingsley) Taylor & Francis.

Privatisation: A Legal Perspective. 180p. 1996. 135.00 (*1-85564-510-6*, Pub. by Euromoney) Am Educ Systs.

Privatisation: A Strategic Report. Brian S. McBeth. 600p. 1996. ring bd. 765.00 (*1-85564-335-9*, Pub. by Euromoney) Am Educ Systs.

Privatisation: A Study of Housing Policy in Urban China. Xing Q. Zhang. LC 98-163512. 188p. 1998. 65.00 (*1-56072-565-6*) Nova Sci Pubs.

Privatisation: Choix Financiers et Possibilites. Amnuay Viravan. LC HD3850.A5214. (Conference Per Jacobsson Ser.: Vol. 1991). (FRE.). 38p. reprint ed. pap. 30.00 (*0-608-08744-0*, 206938300004) Bks Demand.

***Privatisation: The Asian Connection.** B. N. Ghosh. LC 99-55097. 2000. write for info. (*1-56072-760-8*) Nova Sci Pubs.

Privatisation - Focus, 1993. Ed. by Meredith M. Brown. LC 97-32. (IBA Ser.). 224p. (C). 1997. lib. bdg. 76.00 (*1-85333-096-5*, Pub. by Graham & Trotman) Kluwer Academic.

Privatisation & Deregulation in Canada & Britain. Ed. by Jeremy J. Richardson. (Illus.). 260p. 1990. text 72.95 (*1-85521-066-5*, Pub. by Dartmth Pub) Ashgate Pub Co.

Privatisation & Employment Relations: The Case of the Water Industry. Julia O. Davidson. Ed. by Tony Elger & Peter Fairbrother. LC 92-45067. (Employment & Work Relations in Context Ser.). 224p. 1993. 110.00 (*0-7201-2150-7*) Continuum.

Privatisation & Liberalisation in European Telecommunications: Comparing Britain, The Netherlands, & France. Willem Hulsink. LC 98-21492. xii, 356 p. 1998. write for info. (*0-415-18003-1*) Routledge.

Privatisation & Planning in Declining Areas. Stephen Young. 240p. 1988. 42.00 (*0-415-02333-5*) Routledge.

Privatisation & Public Enterprise: The Asia-Pacific Experience. Ed. by Geeta Gouri. (C). 1991. 38.00 (*81-204-0541-2*, Pub. by Oxford IBH) S Asia.

Privatisation & Regulation: A Review of the Issues. Ed. by Peter Jackson & Catherine Price. LC 93-50163. (Longman Economic Ser.). 1994. pap. text. write for info. (*0-582-00974-X*, Pub. by Addison-Wesley) Longman.

Privatisation & Restructuring in Central & Eastern Europe: The Role of "Bad Debts" & the Impact of Social Security see Privatisierung und Restrukturierung in Mittle und Osteuropa: Die Rolle Schlechter Schulden und der Einflu8 der sozialen Absicherung

Privatisation & Supply Chain Management: On the Effective Alignment of Purchasing & Supply after Privatisation. Andrew W. Cox et al. LC 98-38317. (Studies in Business Organization & Networks Ser.). 1999. write for info. (*0-415-17300-0*) Routledge.

Privatisation & the National Health Service: The Scope for Collaboration. Ed. by Jeffrey Chandra & Andrew Kakabadse. LC 85-16857. 120p. 1985. text 72.95 (*0-566-00813-0*, Pub. by Dartmth Pub) Ashgate Pub Co.

Privatisation & the Welfare State. Ed. by Julian Le Grand & Ray Robinson. 256p. (C). 1984. pap. text 17.95 (*0-04-336080-7*) Routledge.

***Privatisation, Competition & Regulation.** OECD Staff. 216p. 2000. pap. 55.00 (*92-64-17115-0*, 14 2000 02 1 P, Pub. by Org for Econ) OECD.

***Privatisation Competition & Regulation in the United Kingdon-Case Studies.** G. Ganesh. (Illus.). 380p. 1999. 42.00 (*81-7099-716-X*, Pub. by Mittal Pubns) Nataraj Bks.

Privatisation In Britain: Results & Implications. Marinov. 59.95 (*1-84014-358-4*) Ashgate Pub Co.

Privatisation in Central & Eastern Europe. 2nd ed. Ed. by Stephen Denyer. 1995. pap. write for info. (*0-406-05049-X*, BPCE2, MICHIE) LEXIS Pub.

***Privatisation in Developing Countries.** Paul Cook & C. H. Kirkpatrick. LC 00-34797. (International Library of Critical Writings in Economics). 2000. write for info. (*1-85898-358-4*) E Elgar.

Privatisation in Pakistan: An Evaluation. Sartaj Aziz. LC 95-930676. 76p. (Orig.). 1996. pap. 14.00 (*92-64-15310-1*, 41-96-13-1) OECD.

Privatisation in Previously Centrally Planned Economies: The Case of Azerbaijan. Lale L. Wiesner. (European University Studies, Series 5: Vol. 2093). (Illus.). xxvi, 380p. 1997. pap. 63.95 (*3-631-31625-9*) P Lang Pubng.

Privatisation in Previously Centrally Planned Economies: The Case of Azerbaijan. Lale L. Wiesner. (European University Studies, Series 5: Vol. 2093). (Illus.). XXVI, 380p. 1997. pap. 63.95 (*0-8204-3270-9*) P Lang Pubng.

Privatisation in the European Union: Theory & Policy Perspectives. David Parker. LC 97-30751. 256p. (C). 1998. 85.00 (*0-415-15469-3*) Routledge.

Privatisation in the Third World. R. Mandal. (C). 1994. 22.50 (*0-7069-7318-6*, Pub. by Vikas) S Asia.

Privatisation in the U. K. V. V. Ramanadham. 256p. (C). 1988. lib. bdg. 69.50 (*0-415-00150-1*) Routledge.

Privatisation of Belfast International Airport: Report by the Comptroller & Auditor General for Northern Ireland. Northern Ireland. Comptroller and Auditor General & Great Britain. Northern Ireland Audit Office. LC 98-122786. (Illus.). 1997. write for info. (*0-10-257598-3*) Statnry Office.

Privatisation of Crime Control. Council of Europe Staff. (Collected Studies in Criminological Research: Vol. XXVII). 1990. 25.00 (*92-871-1737-3*, Pub. by Council of Europe) Manhattan Pub Co.

Privatisation of Japanese National Railways: Railway Management, Market & Policy. Mitsuhide Imashiro & Tatsujiro Ishikawa. LC 98-5775. 220p. 1999. 90.00 (*0-485-11452-6*, Pub. by Athlone Pr) Transaction Pubs.

Privatisation of Public Enterprises: A Constitutional Anatomy. Satish Chandra & Mala Chandra. LC 97-914133. xx, 138 p. 1997. write for info. (*81-7100-988-3*) Deep & Deep Pubns.

Privatisation of Public Undertakings & Activities (Recommendation & Explanatory Memorandum), No. R(93)7. LC 97-102946. 1994. 12.00 (*92-871-2534-1*, Pub. by Council of Europe) Manhattan Pub Co.

Privatisation of Utilities & Infrastructure: Methods & Constraints. LC 98-108678. 112p. 1997. pap. 15.00 (*92-64-15417-5*, 14-97-02-1, Pub. by Org for Econ) OECD.

Privatisation, Politics & Economic Performance in Hungary. Zoltan Antal-Mokos. LC 97-15775. 248p. (C). 1998. text 59.95 (*0-521-59339-5*) Cambridge U Pr.

Privatisations & Public Procurement in the European Union: Generale Bank Lectures, 1996-1997. Ed. by Filip Abraham et al. LC 99-198884. (Leuven Law Ser.: No. 11). (Illus.). 141p. 1998. pap. 45.00 (*90-6186-872-6*, Pub. by Leuven Univ) Coronet Bks.

Privatisierung des Basler Kunstmuseums: Eine Okonomische Analyse der Alternativen In Zusammenarbeit mit dem Wirtschaftswissenschaftlichen Zentrum (WWZ) der Universitat Basel. Andrea Attenhofer. (GER., Illus.). 181p. 1997. 31.95 (*3-906757-45-5*, Pub. by P Lang) P Lang Pubng.

***Privatisierung und Restrukturierung in Mittle und Osteuropa: Die Rolle Schlechter Schulden und der Einflu8 der sozialen Absicherung.** A. Bruggermann. (Internationale Wirtschaftspolitik (International Economic Policy): Vol. 5).Tr. of Privatisation & Restructuring in Central & Eastern Europe: The Role of "Bad Debts" & the Impact of Social Security. (GER.). 260p. 1999. text 54.00 (*90-5708-057-5*, Verlag Fakultas) Gordon & Breach.

Privatising Electricity: The Politics of Power. Roberts. 1991. pap. text 65.00 (*0-471-94761-X*) Wiley.

Privatising Electricity: The Politics of Power. Jane Roberts et al. 256p. 1991. text 55.00 (*1-85293-180-9*) St Martin.

Privatism & Urban Policy in Britain & the U. S. Timothy K. Barnekov et al. (Illus.). 288p. 1989. pap. 22.00 (*0-19-823274-8*) OUP.

Privatizacion: Opciones y Oportunidades Financieras. Amnuay Viravan. LC HD3850.A5218. (Conferencia Per Jacobsson Ser.: Vol. 1991). (FRE.). 40p. reprint ed. pap. 30.00 (*0-608-08743-2*, 206938200004) Bks Demand.

Privatizacion en Chile. Dominique Hachette & Rolf Luders. 275p. 1992. 19.95 (*1-55815-176-1*) ICS Pr.

Privatization. Ed. by John C. Goodman. 1985. pap. 6.95 (*0-943802-13-X*, 4) Natl Ctr Pol.

Privatization: A Theoretical Treatment. Dieter Bos. (Illus.). 328p. 1993. text 65.00 (*0-19-828369-5*) OUP.

Privatization: An Economic Analysis. John Vickers & George Yarrow. 1988. 47.50 (*0-262-22033-4*) MIT Pr.

Privatization: An Economic Analysis. John Vickers et al. (Regulation of Economic Activity Ser.). 454p. 1988. pap. text 27.50 (*0-262-72011-6*) MIT Pr.

Privatization: Critical Perspectives on the World Economy, 4 vols., Set. Ed. by George Yarrow & Piotr Jasinski. LC 95-38870. 1824p. (C). 1996. text, boxed set 660.00 (*0-415-12124-8*) Routledge.

Privatization: Financial Choices & Opportunities. Amnuay Viravan. LC HD3850.A5218. (Per Jacobsson Lecture Ser.: Vol. 1991). 36p. reprint ed. pap. 30.00 (*0-608-08742-4*, 206938100004) Bks Demand.

Privatization: Investing in Infrastructures Around the World. Ernst & Young. 192p. 1994. 45.00 (*0-471-59323-0*) Wiley.

Privatization: Issues & Prospects. 368p. 32.00 (*92-1-119269-2*) UN.

Privatization: Lessons Learned by State & Local Governments. John K. Needham. (Illus.). 48p. (C). 1999. pap. text 20.00 (*0-7881-7643-9*) DIANE Pub.

Privatization: Principles & Practice. David J. Donaldson & Dileep M. Wagle. LC 95-24917. 96p. 1995. pap. 24.00 (*0-8213-3447-6*, 13447) World Bank.

Privatization: Social Science Themes & Perspectives. Derek Braddon & Deborah Foster. 328p. 1996. text 84.95 (*1-85521-674-4*, Pub. by Dartmth Pub) Ashgate Pub Co.

Privatization: The Lessons of Experience. John Nellis et al. LC 92-27381. 90p. 1992. pap. 22.00 (*0-8213-2181-1*, 12181) World Bank.

Privatization: The Provision of Public Services by the Private Sector. Roger L. Kemp. LC 91-52599. 336p. 1991. lib. bdg. 47.50 (*0-89950-619-4*) McFarland & Co.

Privatization: The UK Experience & International Trends. Ed. by Robert Fraser. 175p. 1988. 35.00 (*0-582-02625-3*) St James Pr.

Privatization: Toward More Effective Government--Report of the President's Commission on Privatization. Ed. by David F. Linowes. 304p. 1988. pap. text 15.95 (*0-252-06058-X*) U of Ill Pr.

Privatization Amidst Poverty: Contemporary Challenges in Latin American Political Economy. Ed. by Jorge A. Lawton. 336p. (C). 1995. pap. 22.95 (*0-935501-95-9*, Pub. by U Miami N-S Ctr) L Rienner.

Privatization & Capital Market Development: Strategies to Promote Economic Growth. Michael P. McLindon. LC 96-21320. 200p. 1996. 55.00 (*0-275-95066-2*, Praeger Pubs) Greenwood.

Privatization & Changing Ownership in the Steel Industry. United Nations. Economic Commission for Europe. (ECE Steel Ser.). 104p. 50.00 (*92-1-116655-1*) UN.

Privatization & Competition in Telecommunications: International Developments. Daniel J. Ryan. LC 96-36358. (Privatizing Government Ser.). 232p. 1997. 65.00 (*0-275-95813-2*, Praeger Pubs) Greenwood.

Privatization & Control of State-Owned Enterprises. Ravi Ramamurti & Raymond Vernon. (EDI Development Studies). 344p. 1991. pap. 30.00 (*0-8213-1863-2*, 11863) World Bank.

***Privatization & Corporate Control in the Czech Republic.** Clemens Schutte. LC 00-27264. (Studies in Comparative Economic Systems). 352p. 2000. 100.00 (*1-84064-411-7*) E Elgar.

***Privatization & Culture: Experiences in the Arts, Heritage & Cultural Industries in Europe.** P. B. Boorsma et al. LC 98-32185. 11p. 1999. write for info. (*0-7923-8409-1*) Kluwer Academic.

Privatization & Democratization in Central & Eastern Europe & the Soviet Union: The Gender Dimension Valentine M. Moghadam. LC 92-245960. (Wider Research for Action Ser.). 73p. 1992. write for info. (*952-9520-09-3*) UN.

Privatization & Deregulation in Global Perspective. Ed. by Dennis J. Gayle & Jonathan N. Goodrich. LC 89-24317. 496p. 1990. 95.00 (*0-89930-419-2*, GPV/, Quorum Bks) Greenwood.

***Privatization & Deregulation in the Gulf Energy Sector.** LC 99-901769. xii, 156 p. 1998. write for info. (*1-86064-411-2*) I B T.

Privatization & Deregulation in the Gulf Energy Sector. Emirates Center Staff. 160p. 1999. text 55.00 (*1-86064-410-4*) St Martin.

***Privatization & Deregulation of Transport.** Bill Bradshaw & Helen Lawton Smith. LC 99-88250. 2000. write for info. (*0-312-23273-X*) St Martin.

Privatization & Development. Ed. by Steve H. Hanke. 237p. 1987. pap. 19.95 (*0-917616-85-5*) ICS Pr.

Privatization & Economic Efficiency: A Comparative Analysis of Developed & Developing Countries. Ed. by Attiat F. Ott & Keith Hartley. 288p. 1991. text 100.00 (*1-85278-414-8*) E Elgar.

Privatization & Economic Performance. Ed. by Matthew Bishop et al. LC 94-10326. (Illus.). 392p. 1994. text 65.00 (*0-19-877343-9*); pap. text 26.00 (*0-19-877344-7*) OUP.

***Privatization & Economic Performance in Central & Eastern Europe: Lessons to Be Learnt from Western Europe.** Ed. by Ivan Major. LC 99-14859. (European Association for Comparative Economic Studies Ser.). 448p. 1999. 115.00 (*1-84064-119-3*) E Elgar.

Privatization & Economic Reform in Central Europe: The Changing Business Climate. Ed. by Dennis A. Rondinelli. LC 93-27714. 304p. 1994. 67.95 (*0-89930-851-1*, Quorum Bks) Greenwood.

Privatization & Emerging Equity Markets. Ira W. Lieberman & Christopher D. Kirkness. LC 98-9379. 160p. 1998. pap. 125.00 (*0-8213-4187-1*, 14187) World Bank.

Privatization & Entrepreneurial Management, Vol. 24:3. Ed. by Van Johnston. 77p. 1996. pap. 15.00 (*0-944285-47-3*) Pol Studies.

An Asterisk (*) at the beginning of an entry indicates that the title is appearing for the first time.

Privatization & Entrepreneurship: The Managerial Challenge in Central & Eastern Europe, Incl. instr's. manual. Ed. by Arieh A. Ullmann & Alfred Lewis. LC 96-28115. (Illus.). 358p. (C). 1996. 49.95 (*1-56024-972-2*, Intl Busn Pr) Haworth Pr.

Privatization & Foreign Direct Investment in Transforming Economies. Paul J. Welfrens & Piotr Jasinski. 320p. 1994. 77.95 (*1-85521-487-3*, Pub. by Dartmth Pub) Ashgate Pub Co.

Privatization & Foreign Investments in Eastern Europe. Ed. by Iliana Zloch-Christy. LC 95-6942. 272p. 1995. 65.00 (*0-275-95212-6*, Praeger Pubs) Greenwood.

Privatization & Investment in Sub-Saharan Africa. Ed. by Rexford A. Ahene & Bernard S. Katz. LC 91-37511. 264p. 1992. 65.00 (*0-275-93374-1*, C3374, Praeger Pubs) Greenwood.

Privatization & Its Alternatives. Ed. by William T. Gormley, Jr. LC 90-13402. 342p. 1991. pap. text 20.95 (*0-299-11704-9*) U of Wis Pr.

Privatization & Labor: What Happens to Countries When Governments Divest? Sunita Kilkeri. LC 97-45621. (Technical Paper Ser.: No. 396). 60p. 1998. pap. 22.00 (*0-8213-4148-0*, 14148) World Bank.

Privatization & Liberalization in the Middle East. Ed. by Iliya Harik & Denis J. Sullivan. LC 92-5174. (Indiana Series in Arab & Islamic). 256p. 1992. 36.95 (*0-253-32697-4*); pap. 15.95 (*0-253-20748-7*, MB-748) Ind U Pr.

Privatization & Mental Health Care: A Fragile Balance. Robert A. Dorwart & Sherrie S. Epstein. LC 92-38615. 208p. 1993. 55.00 (*0-86569-002-2*, T002, Auburn Hse) Greenwood.

Privatization & Political Change in Mexico. Judith A. Teichman. LC 95-25839. (Latin American Ser.). 291p. (C). 1996. pap. 19.95 (*0-8229-5586-5*); text 45.00 (*0-8229-3928-2*) U of Pittsburgh Pr.

Privatization & Popular Capitalism. Peter Saunders & Colin Harris. LC 93-41298. 1994. pap. 33.95 (*0-335-15708-4*) OpUniv Pr.

Privatization & Public Enterprises. Richard Hemming & Ali M. Mansoor. (Occasional Paper Ser.: No. 56). vi, 22p. 1988. pap. 7.50 (*1-55775-005-X*) Intl Monetary.

Privatization & Public Hospitals: Choosing Wisely for New York City. Charles Brecher & Sheila Spiezio. LC 95-11195. 96p. (C). 1995. pap. 9.95 (*0-87078-371-8*) Century Foundation.

***Privatization & Public Policy.** Ed. by Vincent Wright & Luisa Perrotti. LC 99-88524. (International Library of Comparative Public Policy). 1088p. 2000. 395.00 (*1-85898-841-1*) E Elgar.

Privatization & Public-Private Partnerships. 2nd ed. E. S. Savas. LC 99-6053. (Illus.). 350p. (C). 1999. pap. text 34.95 (*1-56643-073-9*, Chatham House Pub) Seven Bridges.

Privatization & Regulatory Change in Europe. Ed. by Michael Moran & Tony Prosser. LC 93-30284. (Law & Political Change Ser.). 1994. 104.95 (*0-335-19073-1*); pap. 41.95 (*0-335-19072-3*) OpUniv Pr.

Privatization & Restructuring in Central & Eastern Europe: Evidence & Policy Options. Gerhard Pohl et al. LC 97-13342. (Technical Paper Ser.: No. 368). 48p. 1997. pap. 22.00 (*0-8213-3975-3*, 13975) World Bank.

Privatization & Restructuring of Electricity Provision. Daniel Czamanski. LC 98-41088. (Privatizing Government Ser.). 168p. 1999. 59.95 (*0-275-95687-3*, Praeger Pubs) Greenwood.

Privatization & Restructuring of Health Services in Singapore. Phua K. Hong. (Institute for Policy Studies Occasional Papers: No. 5). 48p. 1991. 7.00 (*981-210-002-4*, Pub. by Times Academic) Intl Spec Bk.

Privatization & Structural Adjustment in the Arab Countries. Ed. by Said El-Naggar. xii, 269p. 1989. pap. 18.50 (*1-55775-042-4*) Intl Monetary.

Privatization & the Globalization of Energy Markets. 116p. 1996. per. 15.00 (*0-16-063473-3*) USGPO.

Privatization & the Globalization of Energy Markets. Mark E. Rodekohr & Mary E. Northup. (Illus.). 108p. (C). 1997. reprint ed. pap. text 30.00 (*0-7881-4742-0*) DIANE Pub.

Privatization & the Penal System: The American Experience & the Debate in Britain. Mick Ryan & Tony Ward. 176p. 1989. 45.00 (*0-335-09916-5*); pap. 14.99 (*0-335-09915-7*) OpUniv Pr.

Privatization & the Provision of Correctional Services: Context & Consequences. G. Larry Mays. Ed. by Tara Gray. LC 95-81802. (ACJS - Anderson Monographs). 175p. (C). 1996. pap. 22.95 (*0-87084-552-7*) Anderson Pub Co.

Privatization & the Rebirth of Capital Markets in Hungary. C. Edward Fletcher. LC 94-45043. 225p. 1995. lib. bdg. 39.95 (*0-89950-995-9*) McFarland & Co.

Privatization & the Welfare State. Ed. by Sheila B. Kamerman & Alfred J. Kahn. LC 88-39316. (Studies from the Project on the Federal Social Role). 293p. 1989. reprint ed. pap. 90.90 (*0-608-07789-5*, 205985600010) Bks Demand.

Privatization & the Welfare State: Implications for Consumerism & the Workforce. Philip I. Morgan. (Illus.). 336p. 1995. text 83.95 (*1-85521-404-0*, Pub. by Dartmth Pub) Ashgate Pub Co.

Privatization at the Turn of the Century. Herbert Giersch & Egon-Sohmen-Foundation Staff. LC 97-22625. (Publications of the Egon-Sohmen-Foundation). 310p. 1997. write for info. (*3-540-63027-9*) Spr-Verlag.

Privatization Challenge: A Strategic, Legal & Institutional Analysis of International Experience. Pierre Guislain. LC 96-34223. (Regional & Sectoral Studies). 412p. 1997. pap. 40.00 (*0-8213-3736-X*, 13736) World Bank.

***Privatization, Corporate Governance & the Emergence of Markets.** Eckehard F. Rosenbaum et al. LC 99-47836. (Studies in Economic Transition Ser.). 2000. text 79.95 (*0-312-23034-6*) St Martin.

Privatization Decision: Public Ends, Private Means. John D. Donahue. LC 89-42511. 272p. 1991. pap. 18.50 (*0-465-06357-8*, Pub. by Basic) HarpC.

***Privatization, Deregulation & Economic Efficiency: A Comparative Analysis of Asia, Europe & the Americas.** Mitsuhiro Kagami & Masatsugu Tsuji. LC 99-59076. 320p. 2000. text 100.00 (*1-84064-363-3*) E Elgar.

Privatization, Deregulation & the Macroeconomy: Measurement, Modelling & Policy. Peter A. Van Bergeijk & Robert C. Haffner. LC 96-6433. 256p. 1996. 90.00 (*1-85898-347-9*) E Elgar.

Privatization, Deregulation & the Transition to Markets. Ed. by David J. Teece et al. 500p. Date not set. write for info. (*1-85898-951-5*) E Elgar.

Privatization, Enterprise Development & Economic Reform: Experiences of Developing & Transitional Economies. Ed. by Paul Cook et al. LC 97-52045. 320p. 1998. 95.00 (*1-85898-376-2*) E Elgar.

Privatization in Africa. Oliver C. White & Anita Bhatia. LC 97-22582. (Directions in Development Ser.). 176p. 1998. pap. 30.00 (*0-8213-3978-8*, 13978) World Bank.

Privatization in Central & Eastern Europe. Ed. by Saul Estrin. LC 94-9121. (Key Issues in the Realignment of Central & Eastern Europe). 331p. (C). 1995. pap. text 55.00 (*0-582-22765-8*) Longman.

Privatization in Central & Eastern Europe. Ed. by Peter Sarcevic. LC 92-15996. (European Business Law & Practice Ser.). 368p. (C). 1992. lib. bdg. 171.50 (*1-85333-713-7*, Pub. by Graham & Trotman) Kluwer Academic.

Privatization in Central & Eastern Europe: Key Issues in the Realignment of Central & Eastern Europe. Ed. by Saul Estrin. LC 94-9121. (Key Issues in the Realignment of Central & Eastern Europe). (C). 1994. text 81.75 (*0-582-22766-6*) Longman.

Privatization in Central & Eastern Europe: Perspectives & Approaches. Ed. by Demetrius S. Iatridis & June G. Hopps. LC 97-40887. 224p. 1998. 59.95 (*0-275-95132-4*, Praeger Pubs) Greenwood.

Privatization in Chile: An Economic Appraisal. Dominique Hachette & Rolf Luders. 320p. 1992. pap. 19.95 (*1-55815-208-3*) ICS Pr.

Privatization in Criminal Justice. Bruce L. Benson. 68p. 1996. pap. 7.95 (*0-945999-54-2*, 1008) Independent Inst.

***Privatization in Criminal Justice: Past, Present & Future.** David Shichor & Michael J. Gilbert. LC 00-36354. 2000. pap. write for info. (*1-58360-500-2*) Anderson Pub Co.

Privatization in Developing Countries: Its Impact on Economic Development & Democracy. Jacques V. Dinavo. LC 94-32925. 176p. 1995. 59.95 (*0-275-95007-7*, Praeger Pubs) Greenwood.

Privatization in Eastern & Central Europe. Guillermo De La Dehesa. (Occasional Paper Ser.: No. 34). 36p. 1991. pap. 10.00 (*1-56708-033-2*) Grp of Thirty.

Privatization in Eastern Europe. Ed. by Vratislav Pechota. LC 94-9413. 264p. 1994. 85.00 (*1-56425-023-7*) Juris Pubng.

Privatization in Eastern Europe: A Critical Approach. Ivan Major. (Studies of Communism in Transition). (Illus.). 176p. 1993. 85.00 (*1-85278-887-9*) E Elgar.

Privatization in Eastern Germany: A Neo-Institutional Analysis. Herbert Brucker. LC 96-39063. (German Development Institute Book Ser.: Vol. 8). 304p. (Orig.). (C). 1997. pap. text 37.50 (*0-7146-4335-1*, Pub. by F Cass Pubs) Intl Spec Bk.

Privatization in Europe: West & East Experiences. Ferdinando Targetti. 256p. 1992. reprint ed. 82.95 (*1-85521-275-7*, Pub. by Dartmth Pub) Ashgate Pub Co.

Privatization in Four European Countries: Comparative Studies in Government - Third Sector Relationships. Ralph M. Kramer et al. LC 93-24985. (Comparative Public Policy Analysis Ser.). 256p. (gr. 13). 1993. text 79.95 (*1-56324-132-3*) M E Sharpe.

Privatization in Latin America. Ed. by Manuel Sanchez & Rossana Corona. (Inter-American Development Bank Ser.). 320p. (C). 1993. pap. text 21.50 (*0-940602-67-9*) IADB.

Privatization in Latin America: New Roles for the Public & Private Sectors. Ed. by Werner Baer & Melissa H. Birch. LC 93-45487. 232p. 1994. 55.00 (*0-275-94664-9*, Praeger Pubs) Greenwood.

***Privatization in Rural Eastern Europe: The Process of Restitution & Restructuring.** Ed. by David Turnock. LC 97-35281. 448p. 1998. 100.00 (*1-85898-203-0*) E Elgar.

Privatization in Sri Lanka: The Experience During the Early Years of Implementation. 76p. (Orig.). (C). 1994. pap. text 30.00 (*0-7881-1044-6*) DIANE Pub.

Privatization in the Ancient near East & Classical World. Ed. by Michael Hudson & Baruch Levine. LC 96-69972. (Museum Bulletin Ser.: Vol. 5). 320p. 1996. pap. 25.00 (*0-87365-955-4*) Peabody Harvard.

Privatization in the Developing World. L. Gray Cowan. LC 90-7573. 160p. 1990. pap. 14.95 (*0-275-93631-7*, B3631, Praeger Pubs) Greenwood.

Privatization in the Developing World, 112. L. Gray Cowan. LC 90-32461. (Contributions in Economics & Economic History Ser.: No. 112). 160p. 1990. 59.95 (*0-313-27330-8*, CPK/, Greenwood Pr) Greenwood.

Privatization in the Transition Process: Recent Experiences in Eastern Europe. LC 96-109530. 418p. 35.00 (*92-1-112359-3*) UN.

Privatization, Liberalization & Destruction: Recreating the Market in Central & Eastern Europe. Laszlo Csaba. 320p. 1994. 77.95 (*1-85521-398-2*, Pub. by Dartmth Pub) Ashgate Pub Co.

***Privatization '98: 12th Annual Report on Privatization.** Ed. by Adrian T. Moore. (Illus.). 61p. (C). 1999. pap. text 20.00 (*0-7881-7882-2*) DIANE Pub.

Privatization of Agriculture in New Market Economies: Lessons from Bulgaria. Ed. by Andrew Schmitz. LC 94-33091. (Natural Resources Management & Policy Ser.). 456p. (C). 1994. lib. bdg. 198.00 (*0-7923-9498-4*) Kluwer Academic.

Privatization of Banco Nacional del Estado. Richard S. Weinert. (Pew Case Studies in International Affairs). 50p. (C). 1994. pap. text 3.50 (*1-56927-211-5*, GU Schl Foreign) Geo U Inst Dplmcy.

Privatization of Correctional Facilities. 69p. (Orig.). (C). 1994. pap. text 20.00 (*1-56806-147-1*) DIANE Pub.

Privatization of Eastern Europe: Is the State Withering Away? Roman Frydman & Andrzej Rapaczynski. LC 94-209085. 240p. 1994. pap. 21.95 (*1-85866-004-1*) Ctrl Europ Univ.

Privatization of Fannie Mae & Freddie Mac: Desirability & Feasibility. Harold L. Bunce & John Gardner. (Illus.). 212p. (Orig.). (C). 1997. pap. text 50.00 (*0-7881-3754-9*) DIANE Pub.

Privatization of Human Services. Jack Krauskopf. 72p. (C). 1997. pap. 9.95 (*0-87078-368-8*) Brookings.

Privatization of Human Services Vol. 1: Policy & Practice Issues. Ed. by Margaret Gibelman & Harold W. Demone, Jr. LC 97-28506. (Series on Social Work). 280p. 1998. 39.95 (*0-8261-9870-8*) Springer Pub.

Privatization of Information & Agricultural Industrialization. Ed. by Steven A. Wolf. 200p. 1997. lib. bdg. 59.95 (*1-57444-104-3*) CRC Pr.

***Privatization of Municipal Services in East Africa: A Governance Approach to Human Settlements Management.** Stella S. Moyo et al. LC 99-889629. x, 100p. 1998. write for info. (*92-1-131386-4*) UN.

Privatization of Policing: Two Views. Brian Forst. LC 99-18789. (Controversies in Public Policy Ser.). 164p. (Orig.). 1999. pap. 17.95 (*0-87840-735-9*) Georgetown U Pr.

***Privatization of Policing: Two Views.** Brian Forst & Peter K. Manning. LC 99-18789. (Controversies in Public Policy Ser.). 166p. (Orig.). 1999. 45.00 (*0-87840-734-0*) Georgetown U Pr.

Privatization of Power & Water Sectors in United Arab Emirates: A Strategic Entry Report, 1998. Compiled by Icon Group International Staff. (Country Industry Report). (Illus.). 95p. 1999. ring bd. 950.00 incl. audio compact disk (*0-7418-0474-3*) Icon Grp.

Privatization of Public Assembly Facility Management: A History & Analysis. Don Jewell. LC 97-43236. 124p. 1998. 18.50 (*1-57524-063-7*) Krieger.

***Privatization of Public Education - Charter School & Vouchers: A Bibliography.** Ed. by Joan Nordquist. (Contemporary Social Issues: Vol. 58). 72p. 2000. pap. 20.00 (*1-892068-14-1*) Ref Rsch Serv.

Privatization of Public Enterprises in Latin America. Ed. by William P. Glade. 143p. 1991. pap. 12.95 (*1-55815-128-1*) ICS Pr.

Privatization of Public Utilities. Ed. & Intro. by Leonard S. Hyman. (Illus.). 500p. 1995. pap. 119.00i (*0-910325-59-6*) Public Util.

Privatization of Public Utilities: The Case of Italy. Ed. by Mario Baldassarri et al. LC 96-46621. (Central Issues in Contemporary Economic Theory & Policy Ser.). (Illus.). 320p. 1997. text 79.95 (*0-312-17258-3*) St Martin.

Privatization of Schooling: Problems & Possibilities. Joseph Murphy. LC 96-4523. 208p. 1996. pap. 27.95 (*0-8039-6394-7*); text 61.95 (*0-8039-6393-9*) Corwin Pr.

Privatization of Services. 52p. 1988. pap. 8.50 (*0-685-30178-8*, 44,200C) NCLS Inc.

Privatization of Social Policy: Occupational Welfare & the Welfare State in America, Scandinavia & Japan. Michael Shalev. LC 96-28751. 372p. 1996. text 79.95 (*0-312-16437-8*) St Martin.

Privatization of Urban Land in Shanghai. Li Ling Hin. 190p. (Orig.). 1997. pap. 39.50 (*962-209-421-X*, Pub. by HK Univ Pr) Coronet Bks.

Privatization of WEPZA. Ed. by Richard L. Bolin. LC 97-198263. 1997. pap. 40.00 (*0-945951-18-3*) Flagstaff Inst.

***Privatization or Public Enterprise Reform? International Case Studies with Implications for Public Management, 220.** Ed. by Ali Farazmand. LC 00-33127. (Contributions in Economics & Economic History Ser.: Vol. 220). 264p. 2000. 64.00 (*0-313-30631-1*, Greenwood Pr) Greenwood.

Privatization Primer: How Government Can Deliver Better Services While Cutting Costs. John Semmens. 22p. 1988. pap. text 8.00 (*1-57655-116-4*) Independ Inst.

Privatization Process: A Worldwide Perspective. Ed. by Terry L. Anderson & Peter J. Hill. (Political Economy Forum Ser.). 284p. (C). 1996. pap. text 25.95 (*0-8476-8187-4*); lib. bdg. 66.00 (*0-8476-8186-6*) Rowman.

Privatization Process in Central Europe: CPU Privatization Reports, Vol. 1. Roman Frydman et al. (Illus.). 276p. 1993. pap. 21.95 (*1-85866-000-9*) Ctrl Europ Univ.

Privatization Process in East-Central Europe: Evolutionary Process of Czech Privatizations. Michael Mejstrik et al. LC 96-24590. (International Series in Economics & Econometrics). 352p. (C). 1996. lib. bdg. 151.50 (*0-7923-4096-5*) Kluwer Academic.

Privatization Process in Russia, Ukraine & the Baltic States. Roman Frydman. (Illus.). 292p. 1993. pap. 21.95 (*1-85866-001-7*) Ctrl Europ Univ.

Privatization Putsch. Herschel Hardin. 224p. 1989. pap. text 29.95 (*0-88645-084-5*, Pub. by Inst Res Pub) Ashgate Pub Co.

Privatization Regulation & Deregulation. 2nd ed. M. E. Beesley. 480p. (C). 1997. pap. 29.99 (*0-415-16453-2*) Routledge.

Privatization Regulation & Deregulation. 2nd ed. Michael Beesley. 480p. (C). 1997. 100.00 (*0-415-16452-4*) Routledge.

***Privatization, Restructuring & Regulation of Network Utilities.** David M. Newbery. LC 99-52764. Vol. 2. (Illus.). 475p. 2000. 47.50 (*0-262-14068-3*) MIT Pr.

Privatization Sourcebook: Reports, Surveys & Other Selected Materials of Trends, Developments, Programs, Projects & Practices of Government, Trade & Professional Societies, Foundations, & Other Public & Private Groups. Ed. by John Sherrod. 452p. 1989. 75.00 (*1-55888-803-9*) Omnigraphics Inc.

Privatization South American Style. Luigi Manzetti. LC 99-28124. 392p. 2000. text 74.00 (*0-19-829466-2*) OUP.

Privatization Strategies in Africa. Ed. by Phillip LeBel. 108p. (Orig.). 1992. pap. 9.00 (*0-944572-05-7*) MSU Ctr Econ Res Africa.

Privatization Surprises in Transition Economies: Employee Ownership in Central & Eastern Europe. Ed. by Milica Uvalic & Daniel Vaughan-Whitehead. LC 96-52677. 320p. 1997. 95.00 (*1-85898-621-4*) E Elgar.

***Privatization vs.Community: The Rise & Fall of Industrial Social Welfare in Guyana.** David P. Williams. (Illus.). 1999. 53.00 (*0-8476-8995-6*) Rowman.

Privatized Infrastructure: The Build Operate Transfer Approach. Ed. by C. Walker & A. J. Smith. 270p. 1995. 105.60 (*0-7277-2053-8*, Pub. by T Telford) RCH.

Privatizing a Province: The New Right. James M. Pitsula & Ken Rasmusse. 294p. 1990. pap. 14.95 (*0-921586-09-4*, Pub. by New Star Bks) Genl Dist Srvs.

Privatizing Africa's Infrastructure: Promise & Challenge. Michel Kerf & Warrick Smith. LC 96-34340. (Technical Papers: No. 337). 120p. 1996. pap. 22.00 (*0-8213-3744-0*) World Bank.

***Privatizing Australia: The Deals So Far, the Opportunities Ahead (Victoria)** Asia Law & Practice Staff. 250p. 1998. pap. 225.00 (*962-936-002-0*, Pub. by Asia Law & Practice) Am Educ Systs.

Privatizing Correctional Institutions. Gary W. Bowman & Paul Seidenstat. Ed. by Simon W. Hakim et al. 292p. (C). 1992. 34.95 (*1-56000-055-4*) Transaction Pubs.

Privatizing Criminal Justice. Ed. by Roger Matthews. (Contemporary Criminology Ser.). 224p. (C). 1989. text 69.95 (*0-8039-8240-2*); pap. text 18.95 (*0-8039-8241-0*) Sage.

Privatizing Eastern Europe: The Role of Markets & Ownership in the Transition. Jozef M. Van Brabant. LC 92-17923. (International Studies in Economics & Econometrics: Vol. 24). 1992. lib. bdg. 166.50 (*0-7923-1861-7*) Kluwer Academic.

Privatizing Education & Educational Choice: Concepts, Plans & Experiences. Ed. by Simon W. Hakim et al. LC 94-16456. 248p. 1994. 59.95 (*0-275-94751-3*, Praeger Pubs) Greenwood.

Privatizing Education & Educational Choice: Concepts, Plans & Experiences. Simon W. Hakim et al. LC 94-16456. 248p. 1994. pap. 23.95 (*0-275-95081-6*, Praeger Pubs) Greenwood.

Privatizing Government Information: The Effects of Policy on Access to Landsat Satellite Data. Kathleen M. Eisenbeis. LC 94-27576. (Illus.). 355p. 1995. 45.00 (*0-8108-2934-7*) Scarecrow.

Privatizing Government Services: An Economic Analysis of Contracting Out by Local Governments. Werner Z. Hirsch. (Monograph & Research Ser.: No. 54). 142p. (Orig.). 1991. pap. 11.00 (*0-89215-169-2*) U Cal LA Indus Rel.

Privatizing Health Services in Africa. Meredeth Turshen. LC 98-23537. 200p. (C). 1999. text 50.00 (*0-8135-2580-2*); pap. text 23.00 (*0-8135-2581-0*) Rutgers U Pr.

Privatizing Monopolies: Lessons from the Telecommunications & Transport Sectors in Latin America. Ed. by Ravi Ramamurti. LC 95-18040. (Illus.). 401p. (C). 1996. text 55.00 (*0-8018-5135-1*) Johns Hopkins.

Privatizing Nature: Political Struggles for the Global Commons. Michael Goldman. LC 97-34878. (Transnational Institute Ser.). 1998. write for info. (*0-7453-1310-8*, Pub. by Pluto GBR) Stylus Pub VA.

Privatizing Nature: Political Struggles for the Global Commons. Ed. by Michael Goldman. LC 97-34878. 288p. (C). 1998. text 50.00 (*0-8135-2553-5*); pap. text 20.00 (*0-8135-2554-3*) Rutgers U Pr.

Privatizing Prisons: Rhetoric & Reality. Adrian James et al. LC 97-66423. 208p. 1997. 69.95 (*0-8039-7548-1*); pap. 29.95 (*0-8039-7549-X*) Sage.

Privatizing Public Education: The Texas Experience. Ed. by Delbert A. Taebel & Christine T. Brenner. (Orig.). 1994. pap. 20.00 (*0-936440-87-2*) U TX SUPA.

Privatizing Public Enterprises: Constitutions, the State, & Regulation in Comparative Perspective. Cosmo Graham & Tony Prosser. (Government-Industry Relations Ser.: No. 6). (Illus.). 284p. 1991. text 79.00 (*0-19-827339-8*, 3193) OUP.

Privatizing Public Enterprises & Foreign Investment in Developing Countries, 1988-93. Frank Sader. LC 95-23164. (Occasional Papers: Vol. 5). 58p. 1995. pap. 22.00 (*0-8213-3362-3*, 13362) World Bank.

Privatizing Public Enterprises & Foreign Investment in Developing Countries, 1988-93. Frank Sader. (Foreign Investment Advisory Service (FIAS) Occasional Paper Ser.: No. 5). (FRE.). 64p. 1996. pap. 22.00 (*0-8213-3555-3*, 13555) World Bank.

Privatizing Public Lands. Scott Lehmann. (Environmental Ethics & Science Policy Ser.). (Illus.). 264p. 1995. text 55.00 (*0-19-508972-3*) OUP.

Privatizing Russia. Maxim Boycko et al. LC 94-25308. 175p. 1995. 25.00 (*0-262-02389-X*) MIT Pr.

Privatizing Russia. Maxim Boycko et al. (Illus.). 175p. 1997. reprint ed. pap. text 12.50 (*0-262-52228-4*) MIT Pr.

***Privatizing Social Security.** Martin Feldstein. 2000. pap. text 27.50 (*0-226-24102-5*) U Ch Pr.

P

Privatizing Social Security. Martin S. Feldstein. LC 97-43851. (National Bureau of Economic Research Project Report Ser.). (Illus.). 458p. 1998. 60.00 (*0-226-24101-7*) U Ch Pr.

Privatizing Subsidized Housing. John Weicher. LC 97-176691. 50p. 1997. pap. 9.95 (*0-8447-7095-7*) Am Enterprise.

***Privatizing the Land: Rural Political Economy in Post-Communist Societies.** Ivan Szelenyi. LC 97-35426. (Research Societies in Transition Ser.). 256p. (C). 1998. 85.00 (*0-415-18204-2*) Routledge.

***Privatizing the Police State.** Maria Los et al. LC 99-88982. 272p. 2000. text 69.95 (*0-312-23150-4*) St Martin.

Privatizing the Public Sector: How to Shrink Government. Emanuel S. Savas. LC 82-4207. (Chatham House Series on Change in American Politics). (Illus.). 176p. reprint ed. pap. 54.60 (*0-8357-4826-X*, 203776300009) Bks Demand.

Privatizing the United States Justice System: Police, Adjudication, & Correction Services from the Private Sector. Simon W. Hakim & Paul Seidenstat. Ed. by Gary W. Bowman et al. LC 91-51002. 352p. 1992. lib. bdg. 49.95 (*0-89950-704-2*) McFarland & Co.

***Privatizing Toll Roads: A Public-Private Partnership.** Wendell C. Lawther. LC 99-54744. (Privatizing Government). 232p. 2000. 67.50 (*0-275-96900-2*, C6900, Praeger Pubs) Greenwood.

Privatizing Transportation Systems. Ed. by Simon W. Hakim et al. LC 96-15320. (Privatizing Government Ser.). 352p. 1996. 79.50 (*0-275-94807-2*, Praeger Pubs) Greenwood.

Privatizition: Implications for Corporate Culture Change. Alzira Salamar. 165p. 1995. 66.95 (*1-85628-912-5*, Pub. by Avebry) Ashgate Pub Co.

Privatopia: Homeowner Associations & the Rise of Residential Private Government. Evan Mckenzie. 1996. pap. 16.00 (*0-300-06638-4*) Yale U Pr.

Privatopia: Homeowner Associations & the Rise of Residential Private Government. Evan McKenzie. LC 93-37340. 248p. 1994. 32.50 (*0-300-05876-4*) Yale U Pr.

Priviatization of Human Services Vol. 2: Case Studies in the Purchase of Services, Vol. 2. Margaret Gibelman & Harold W. Demone, Jr. (Series on Social Work). 232p. 1997. 37.95 (*0-8261-9871-6*) Springer Pub.

Priviledges & Practice of Parliaments in England. LC 74-80218. (English Experience Ser.: No. 654). 1974. reprint ed. 20.00 (*90-221-0654-3*) Walter J Johnson.

Privilege. Colin Passmore. LC 98-183521. 288p. 1998. 134.50 (*1-85811-078-5*, Pub. by CLT Prof) Gaunt.

Privilege Against Self-Incrimination: Its Origins & Development. R. H. Helmholz. LC 96-35847. 1997. 29.95 (*0-226-32660-8*) U Ch Pr.

Privilege & Democracy in America. Frederic C. Howe. Ed. by Dan C. McCurry & Richard E. Rubenstein. LC 74-30634. (American Farmers & the Rise of Agribusiness Ser.). 1975. reprint ed. 31.95 (*0-405-06803-4*) Ayer.

***Privilege & Liberty & Other Essays in Political Philosophy.** Aurel Kolnai. Ed. by Daniel J. Mahoney. LC 99-37175. (Applications in Political Theory Ser.). 208p. 1999. 65.00 (*0-7391-0076-9*); pap. 23.95 (*0-7391-0077-7*) Lxngtn Bks.

Privilege & Prerogative: New York's Provincial Elite, 1710-1776. Mary L. Lustig. LC 93-51010. (C). 1995. 39.50 (*0-8386-3554-7*) Fairleigh Dickinson.

Privilege & Profit: A Business Family in Eighteenth-Century France. Paul W. Bamford. LC 88-26127. 373p. 1988. reprint ed. pap. 115.70 (*0-608-03630-7*, 206445700009) Bks Demand.

***Privilege & the Politics of Taxation in Eighteenth-Century France: Liberte, Egalite, Fiscalite.** Michael Kwass. 376p. (C). 2000. text 69.95 (*0-521-77149-8*) Cambridge U Pr.

Privilege & the Responsibility: Working in a Nursing Home. Michael Jacobs. 150p. 1999. pap. 19.00 (*0-929442-49-0*, 2118PP) Prof Prnting & Pub.

Privilege for Which We Struggle: Woman Suffrage Leaders of Minnesota. unabridged ed. Ed. by Heidi Bauer. (Illus.). 190p. 1999. pap. 12.95 (*0-914227-10-6*, 5500) Minn Hist.

Privilege in the Medical Academy: A Feminist Examines Gender, Race & Power. Delse Wear. LC 97-11213. (Athene Ser.). 1997. 42.00 (*0-8077-6290-3*); pap. 18.95 (*0-8077-6288-1*) Tchrs Coll.

Privilege in the Soviet Union. Mervyn Matthews. (Illus.). 1978. pap. text 16.95 (*0-04-323021-0*) Routledge.

Privilege of All Believers. John Waldron. 1987. reprint ed. pap. 5.95 (*0-86544-040-9*) Salv Army Suppl South.

Privilege of Being a Physicist. Victor E. Weisskopf. LC 88-24532. (Illus.). 235p. 1989. pap. text 14.95 (*0-7167-2106-6*) W H Freeman.

Privilege of Being a Physicist. Victor F. Weisskopf. LC 88-24532. 256p. 1988. text 16.00 (*0-7167-1982-7*) W H Freeman.

Privilege of Being Catholic. Oscar Lukefahr. LC 93-79725. 208p. 1993. pap. 7.95 (*0-89243-563-1*) Liguori Pubns.

Privilege of Being Catholic Workbook. Oscar Lukefahr. 64p. (Orig.). 1993. pap., student ed. 2.95 (*0-89243-564-X*) Liguori Pubns.

Privilege of Darkness. Bert Underwood. LC 85-72808. (Illus.). 395p. (C). 1986. 13.95 (*0-935763-00-7*); pap. 5.95 (*0-935763-01-5*) Chester Hse Pubs.

Privilege of His Company: Noel Coward Remembered William Marchant. LC 73-22683. 276p. 1975. write for info. (*0-672-51973-9*, Bobbs) Macmillan.

Privilege of His Company: Nohel Coward Remembered William Marchant. LC 76-367441. 248 p. 1975. write for info. (*0-297-76937-5*, Pub. by Weidenfeld & Nicolson) Trafalgar.

Privilege of the Ordained. Michael Davies. (Illus.). 1990. reprint ed. pap. 6.00 (*0-911845-21-6*) Neumann Pr.

Privilege Parliamentaire au Canada. 2nd ed. Maingot Joseph P. (FRE.). 1997. text 65.00 (*0-7735-1720-0*, Pub. by McG-Queens Univ Pr) CUP Services.

Privilege, Persecution & Prophecy: The Catholic Church in Spain, 1875-1975. Frances Lannon. (Illus.). 276p. 1987. 75.00 (*0-19-821923-7*) OUP.

Privilege Revealed: How Invisible Preference Undermines America. Stephanie M. Wildman. 270p. (C). 1996. text 45.00 (*0-8147-9298-7*); pap. text 19.00 (*0-8147-9303-7*) NYU Pr.

Privilege to Keep & Bear Arms: The Second Amendment & Its Interpretation. Warren Freedman. LC 88-38312. 152p. 1989. 55.00 (*0-89930-411-7*, FSA/, Quorum Bks) Greenwood.

Privileged Anonymity: The Writings of Madame de Lafayette. Anne Green. (Research Monographs in French Studies). 100p. 1996. pap. 25.00 (*1-900755-00-9*) David Brown.

Privileged Characters. Morris R. Werner. LC 73-19184. (Politics & People Ser.). 518p. 1974. reprint ed. 39.95 (*0-405-05905-1*) Ayer.

Privileged Class: Senior Year at Beverly Hills High School. Michael Leahy. 320p. 1988. 17.95 (*0-316-51815-8*) Little.

Privileged Communication & the Press: The Citizen's Right to Know vs. the Law's Right to Confidential News Source Evidence, 19. Maurice Van Gerpen. LC 78-55334. (Contributions in Political Science Ser.: No. 19). 239p. 1979. 55.00 (*0-313-20523-X*, VGP/) Greenwood.

***Privileged Communications.** Patricia Frieder. 288p. 2000. mass mkt. 5.50 (*0-553-57613-5*) Bantam.

***Privileged Communications & the Delaware Corporation: Corporate & Commercial Privilege Litigation in the Delaware Courts.** John E. James. 200p. 2000. pap. text 95.00 (*0-8080-0486-7*) CCH INC.

Privileged Communications As a Branch of Legal Evidence. John F. Hageman. xxix, 328p. 1983. reprint ed. 42.50 (*0-8377-0708-0*, Rothman) W S Hein.

Privileged Conversation. Evan Hunter. 336p. 1997. mass mkt. 6.99 (*0-446-60382-1*, Pub. by Warner Bks) Little.

Privileged Conversations: Dramatic Stories for Christmas. Richard P. Olson. LC 95-51168. 136p. (Orig.). 1996. pap. 10.95 (*0-8298-1078-1*) Pilgrim OH.

Privileged Gifts: Marriage & Motherhood. Anne Dearing. 96p. 1987. pap. 3.95 (*0-310-55332-6*, 19035P) Zondervan.

Privileged Hands. Geerat J. Vermeij. 1998. pap. text 14.95 (*0-7167-3199-1*) W H Freeman.

Privileged Hands: A Scientific Life. Geerat Vermeij. LC 96-22092. (Illus.). 297p. 1996. pap. text 23.95 (*0-7167-2954-7*) W H Freeman.

***Privileged Information.** Stephen White. 383p. 1999. mass mkt. 5.99 (*0-7860-0624-2*) Kensgtn Pub Corp.

Privileged Information. Stephen White. 384p. 1992. reprint ed. mass mkt. 5.99 (*0-8217-3951-4*, Zebra Kensgtn) Kensgtn Pub Corp.

Privileged Marriage: The Autobiography of Elizabeth Pschorr. Elizabeth Pschorr. LC 94-15618. 368p. 1994. 24.95 (*0-915269-13-9*) Windgate Pr.

***Privileged Moments: Encounters with Writers.** Jeffrey Meyers. LC 00-8609. 2000. 24.95 (*0-299-16940-5*) U of Wis Pr.

Privileged Pariahdom: Homosexuality in the Novels of Dominique Fernandez. Lucille Cairns. 178p. 1996. pap. 31.95 (*3-906756-16-5*, Pub. by P Lang) P Lang Pubng.

Privileged to Kill. Steven F. Havill. LC 96-33223. 224p. 1996. text 21.95 (*0-312-15196-9*) St Martin.

Privileged Woman. Joy Haney. 1997. pap. 7.95 (*1-880969-14-9*) Schl Prophet.

Privileges of Independence: Neomercantilism & the American Revolution. John E. Crowley. LC 93-3563. (Early America: History, Context, Culture Ser.). 224p. (C). 1993. text 37.50 (*0-8018-4667-6*) Johns Hopkins.

Privileges of the University of Cambridge, 2 vols. George Dyer. reprint ed. 135.00 (*0-404-07306-9*) AMS Pr.

Privileging Gender in Early Modern England. Ed. by Jean R. Brink. (Sixteenth Century Essays & Studies: Vol. 23). 250p. 1993. 40.00 (*0-940474-24-7*, SCJP) Truman St Univ.

Privileging Quick Reference Guide. Ed. by Beverly E. Pybus. 130p. 1998. pap. text 97.00 (*1-57839-022-2*) Opus Communs.

Privileging the Past: Reconstructing History in Northwest Coast Art. Judith Ostrowitz. (Illus.). 264p. 1999. 35.00 (*0-295-97814-7*) U of Wash Pr.

Privileging the Primitive: African Ethnicity & the Rehabilitation of the West. Aidan Campbell. LC 97-607. 1997. 89.95 (*0-304-70076-2*); pap. 29.95 (*0-304-70077-0*) Continuum.

Privilegio de Ser Padrino o Madrina: Guia para los Patrocinadores del Catecumenado. Ronald J. Lewinski. Tr. by Pedro Rodriguez from ENG. (SPA.). 68p. 1990. pap. 4.50 (*0-929650-25-5*, SGSPON) Liturgy Tr Pubns.

Privilegios de la Vista, I (Privileges of the View, I) Vol. VI: Arte Moderno Universal (Universal Modern Art) 2nd ed. Octavio Paz. (SPA.). 392p. 1994. 45.99 (*968-16-3895-6*, Pub. by Fondo) Continental Bk.

Privilegios de la Vista (The Privileges of the View), Vol. 1. Octavio Paz. (Mexico en la Obra de Octavio Paz Ser.: Vol. 7). (SPA., Illus.). 220p. pap. 13.99 (*968-16-3170-6*, Pub. by Fondo) Continental Bk.

Privilegios de la Vista (The Privileges of the View) Arte de Mejico. Octavio Paz. (Mexico en la Obra de Octavio Paz Ser.: Vols. 7 & 8). (SPA., Illus.). 514p. pap. 27.99 (*968-16-2575-7*, Pub. by Fondo) Continental Bk.

Privilegios de la Vista, II (Privileges of the View, II) Arte de Mejico (Mexican Art) 2nd ed. Octavio Paz. (Complete Works of Octavio Paz: Vol. VII). (SPA.). 445p. 1994. 45.99 (*968-16-3896-4*, Pub. by Fondo) Continental Bk.

Privilegios del Cristiano. M. Ramos.Tr. of Christian Privileges. (SPA.). 2.50 (*1-56063-391-3*, 493038) Editorial Unilit.

Privitization: The Financial Implications. Ed. by Kevin Davis & Ian Harper. 192p. 1994. pap. 24.95 (*1-86373-540-2*, Pub. by Allen & Unwin Pty) Paul & Co Pubs.

***Privitization Potential of Mississippi's State Programs & Services.** Ed. by Barry Leonard. 79p. 2000. reprint ed. pap. text 20.00 (*0-7881-4486-3*) DIANE Pub.

Privitization Problems at Industry Level: Road Haulage in Central Europe. Esra Bennathan & Louis S. Thompson. LC 92-33200. (Discussion Papers: No. 182). 64p. 1992. pap. 22.00 (*0-8213-2245-1*, 12245) World Bank.

Privy Seal: His Last Venture. Ford Madox Ford. LC 90-27428. 332p. reprint ed. lib. bdg. 99.95 (*0-7734-9996-2*) E Mellen.

Prix: 1975 see Chemical Engineering

Prix Ars Electronica '96: International Compendium of the Computer Arts. H. Leopoldseder. (Illus.). 240p. 1996. pap. text 38.00 (*3-211-82863-X*) Spr-Verlag.

Prix de l'Arc de Triomphe, 1949-1964. Arthur FitzGerald. 296p. 1990. 56.00 (*0-85131-371-X*, Pub. by J A Allen) St Mut.

Prix d'Excellence. Jean-Louis Bory. (FRE.). 219p. 1988. pap. 10.95 (*0-7859-2095-1*, 2070380602) Fr & Eur.

Prix Dor. John M. Bennett & Robin Crozier. 6p. (Orig.). 1993. pap. 2.00 (*0-935350-85-3*) Luna Bisonte.

Prix Nobel En. Incl. Dec. 1972. Nobel Foundation Staff. 1974. 87.25 (*0-444-99882-9*); Standard 1973. 1975. 82.00 (*0-444-99859-4*); 1971. 87.25 (*0-444-99935-3*); 1971. 87.25 (*0-444-40931-9*); 1972. 87.25 (*0-444-99909-4*); 1977. write for info. (*0-318-56736-9*) Elsevier.

Prix Volney: Its History & Significance for the Development of Linguistic Research, 1. Ed. by Joan Leopold. LC 94-27057. (Prix Volney Essay Ser.). 1994. lib. bdg. write for info. (*0-7923-2505-2*, Pub. by Kluwer Academic) Kluwer Academic.

Priyadarsika, a Sanskrit Drama. Harshadeva. Tr. by Gushtaspshah K. Nariman et al. LC 76-180683. (Columbia University. Indo-Iranian Ser.: No. 10). reprint ed. 32.50 (*0-404-50480-9*) AMS Pr.

***Prize.** Martine Berne. 2000. mass mkt. 4.99 (*0-8217-6477-2*, Zebra Kensgtn) Kensgtn Pub Corp.

Prize. Michael Burgan. LC 97-61028. (Aesop's Fables Running Start Ser.). (Illus.). 32p. (J). (ps-2). 1997. pap. 4.95 (*1-890570-19-2*) Huckleberry CT.

Prize. Julie Garwood. Ed. by Linda Marrow. 416p. 1991. per. 6.99 (*0-671-70251-3*) PB.

Prize. Junior African Writers Staff & Carolyn B. Mitchell. (Junior African Writers Ser.). (Illus.). 80p. (J). (gr. 3 up). 1995. pap. 4.95 (*0-7910-3020-2*) Chelsea Hse.

Prize. Lorraine M. Murphy. 192p. (J). (gr. 8). 1993. pap. text 7.95 (*1-883511-02-X*) Veritas Pr CA.

Prize. large type ed. Julie Garwood. LC 91-33550. 558p. 1992. reprint ed. lib. bdg. 20.95 (*1-56054-267-5*) Thorndike Pr.

Prize. rev. ed. Flavia M. Weedn. (Illus.). 136p. 1990. reprint ed. 10.00 (*0-929632-09-5*) Applause Inc.

Prize: A Collection of Stories. Flavia Weedn & Lisa Weedn. LC 99-12114. 96p. 1999. 12.95 (*0-7683-2094-1*) CEDCO Pub.

Prize: Conflicts in Love Matters. Herbert W. Denmark. 118p. 1997. mass mkt. 6.00 (*1-891511-00-9*) H W Denmark.

Prize: The Epic Quest for Oil, Money & Power. Daniel Yergin. (Illus.). 928p. 1993. pap. 18.00 (*0-671-79932-0*, Touchstone) S&S Trade Pap.

Prize: The Epic Quest for Oil, Money & Power. Daniel Yergin. 1994. reprint ed. lib. bdg. 49.95 (*1-56849-572-2*) Buccaneer Bks.

Prize Cases Decided in the United States Supreme Court, 1789-1918, 3 vols., Set. U. S. Supreme Court Staff. LC 74-19623. reprint ed. 167.50 (*0-404-12467-4*) AMS Pr.

***Prize Cases Decided in the United States Supreme Court 1789-1918: Including Also Cases on the Instance Side in Which Questions of Prize Law Were Involved.** James Brown Scott & Carnegie Endowment for International Peace Staff. LC 00-27805. 2000. write for info. (*1-57588-636-7*) W S Hein.

Prize Code of the German Empire: As in Force July 1, 1915. Ed. by Charles H. Huberich & Richard King. xxiii, 177p. 1998. reprint ed. 65.00 (*1-56169-363-4*) Gaunt.

Prize Cup. John T. Trowbridge. (Notable American Authors). 1999. reprint ed. lib. bdg. 125.00 (*0-7812-9812-1*) Rprt Serv.

Prize Essay on the Freedom of the Will. Arthur Schopenhauer. Tr. by Gunter Zoller & Eric F. Payne from GER. LC 98-22360. (Cambridge Texts in the History of Philosophy Ser.). 144p. (C). 1999. text 49.95 (*0-521-57141-3*); pap. text 14.95 (*0-521-57766-7*) Cambridge U Pr.

Prize Essays on a Congress of Nations: For the Adjustment of International Disputes, & for the Promotion of Universal Peace Without Resort to Arms. Ed. by American Peace Society Staff. LC 98-13864. xii, 706p. 1998. reprint ed. 95.00 (*0-9631902-6-1*) Canonymous.

Prize for Princes. Rex Stout. 256p. 1994. mass mkt. 4.95 (*0-7867-0104-8*) Carroll & Graf.

Prize for Princes. Rex Stout. 312p. 1999. 26.00 (*0-7278-2277-2*, Pub. by Severn Hse) Chivers N Amer.

Prize for Sister Catherine. Kathleen Rowntree. 1998. mass mkt. 14.95 (*0-552-99732-3*) Bantam.

Prize Game: Lawful Looting on the High Seas in the Days of Fighting Sail. Donald A. Petrie. LC 99-11143. 1999. 24.95 (*1-55750-669-8*) Naval Inst Pr.

***Prize of All the Oceans: The Dramatic True Story of Commodore Anson's Voyage Round the World.** Glyn Williams. (Illus.). 288p. 2000. 27.95 (*0-670-89197-5*, Viking) Viking Penguin.

Prize of Fear. large type ed. Anne Nash. (General Ser.). 336p. (Orig.). 1993. 27.99 (*0-7089-2848-X*) Ulverscroft.

Prize of War. Linda Knight. 400p. (Orig.). 1994. pap. 7.00 (*0-9630796-2-X*) Rock Church NW.

Prize Play. Mary Chase. 1961. pap. 3.25 (*0-8222-0918-7*) Dramatists Play.

Prize Poems, 1995: Pennsylvania Poetry Society, Inc. Ed. by Ann Gasser. 68p. (Orig.). 1995. pap. 4.00 (*1-884257-08-9*) AGEE Keyboard.

Prize Poems, 1997: Winning Poems of the 1997 PPS, Inc. Contest. Ed. by Ann Gasser & Marilyn Downing. 76p. (Orig.). 1997. pap. 4.00 (*1-884257-19-4*) AGEE Keyboard.

Prize Poems, 1996: Annual of the Pennsylvania Poetry Society, Inc. Ed. by Ann Gasser & Marilyn Downing. 80p. (Orig.). 1996. pap. 4.00 (*1-884257-15-1*) AGEE Keyboard.

Prize Possession. K. Randall Ball. pap. 5.99 (*0-9651605-0-5*) Five Ball.

Prize Possession: The United States & the Panama Canal, 1903-1979. John Major. LC 92-32406. (Illus.). 454p. (C). 1993. text 57.95 (*0-521-43306-1*) Cambridge U Pr.

Prize Pulitzer: The Scandal That Rocked Palm Beach - The Real Story. Roxanne Pulitzer & Kathleen Maxa. 1988. 19.95 (*0-317-66206-6*) Villard Books.

Prize Stories 1998: The O. Henry Awards. Larry Dark. 464p. 1998. pap. 11.95 (*0-385-48958-7*) Doubleday.

***Prize Stories 1999: The O. Henry Awards.** Ed. by Larry Dark. (Prize Stories: The O. Henry Awards Ser.). 464p. 1999. pap. 11.95 (*0-385-49358-4*, Anchor NY) Doubleday.

***Prize Stories 2000: The O Henry Awards.** Ed. & Intro. by Larry Dark. (Illus.). 464p. 2000. pap. 13.00 (*0-385-49877-2*, Anchor NY) Doubleday.

Prize Stories 1919: The O. Henry Memorial Award. Contrib. by O. Henry Society of Arts & Sciences. (BCL1-PS American Literature Ser.). 1992. reprint ed. lib. bdg. 79.00 (*0-7812-6656-4*) Rprt Serv.

Prize Winners: 10 Writers for Young Readers. Penelope Yunghans. LC 95-37990. (World Writers Ser.). (Illus.). 176p. (YA). (gr. 5 up). 1996. lib. bdg. 18.95 (*1-883846-11-0*) M Reynolds.

Prize-Winning Private Eyes. Judy Delton. LC 94-40329. (Lottery Luck Ser.: Bk. 2). (Illus.). 96p. (J). (gr. 2-5). 1995. pap. 3.95 (*0-7868-1019-X*, Pub. by Hyprn Ppbks) Little.

Prize-Winning Radio Stories. LC 94-153294. 208p. 1995. pap. 13.95 (*1-85635-081-9*) Dufour.

Prize-Winning Science Fair Projects. Penny R. Durant. 144p. (J). (gr. 3-7). 1992. pap. 2.95 (*0-590-44019-5*) Scholastic Inc.

Prize-Winning Short Stories & Articles, Plus 2 Novellas. Van D. Garner. 200p. 1995. pap. 14.95 (*0-9645273-0-8*) Garner Pub.

***Prized Peonies.** John D. Thompson. LC 00-132651. 112p. 2000. pap. 10.00 (*0-615-11375-3*) Vista Pr IA.

Prized Possessions. Laurali R. Wright. 336p. 1994. pap. 7.50 (*0-7704-2543-7*) Bantam.

Prizefighters: An Intimate Look at Champions & Contenders. Arlene Schulman. LC 94-19942. 176p. 1994. 27.95 (*1-55821-309-0*) Lyons Pr.

Prizes. Erich Segal. 1996. mass mkt. 6.99 (*0-8041-1427-7*) Ivy Books.

Prizes. large type ed. Erich Segal. LC 95-17123. 1995. 26.95 (*1-56895-228-7*) Wheeler Pub.

***Prizes of War: Prize Law & the Royal Navy in the Napoleonic Wars 1793-1815.** Richard Hill. LC 99-206681. 1999. 44.95 (*0-7509-1816-0*) Bks Intl VA.

Prizewinning Literature: U. K. Literary Award Winners. Anne Strachen. LC 90-122239. 281p. 1989. reprint ed. pap. 87.20 (*0-7837-9273-5*, 206001100004) Bks Demand.

Prizzi's Money. Richard Condon. 384p. 1995. mass mkt. 5.99 (*0-7860-0167-4*) Kensgtn Pub Corp.

Prizzi's Money. large type ed. Richard Condon. LC 94-4668. 401p. 1994. lib. bdg. 23.95 (*0-7862-0226-2*) Thorndike Pr.

Prncpl Poltc Contmp Brt. M. Garnett. 200p. (C). 1996. pap. text 17.81 (*0-582-28924-6*, Pub. by Addison-Wesley) Longman.

Pro. Gordon Rupert Dickson. (Illus.). 192p. 1986. reprint ed. pap. 2.95 (*0-8125-3575-8*, Pub. by Tor Bks) St Martin.

Pro - Am Book of Music & Mythology, Vol. 1. Thomas P. Lewis. (Illus.). 892p. 1992. 59.95 (*0-912483-51-2*) Pro-Am Music.

Pro - Am Book of Music & Mythology, Vol. 2. Thomas P. Lewis. 659p. 1992. 49.95 (*0-912483-82-2*) Pro-Am Music.

Pro Active Healthful Resistance. Avi Brenholz. (Illus.). 148p. 1994. pap. 18.00 (*1-889958-00-X*) A Ben Aur.

Pro-Active Management: Fifty Business Techniques Every Manager Should Know. Neil M. Glass. 200p. 1991. pap. 29.95 (*0-89397-410-2*) Nichols Pub.

Pro-Active Para Educator. Alan M. Hofmeister. pap. 10.00 (*1-56861-052-1*) Swift Lrn Res.

Pro Am Guide to U. S. Books about Music: Annotated Subject Guide to Current & Backlist Titles. Thomas P. Lewis. (General Music Ser.: Gms-6). 211p. (Orig.). 1987. pap. 35.00 (*0-912483-03-2*) Pro-Am Music.

Pro-Am Guide to U. S. Books about Music: Annotated Subject Guide to Current & Backlist Titles, 1987 Supplement. Ed. by Thomas P. Lewis. 173p. (Orig.). 1988. pap. 23.50 (*0-912483-14-8*) Pro-Am Music.

Pro-Am Murders. Patrick Cake. LC 78-70580. (Illus.). 1979. 8.95 (*0-932864-00-7*) Proteus Calif.

An Asterisk (*) at the beginning of an entry indicates that the title is appearing for the first time.

*Pro & Con. 3rd ed. (C). 1998. pap. text 45.00 (0-201-38801-4) Addison-Wesley.

Pro & Contra Wagner/Thomas Mann. Thomas Mann. Tr. by Allan Blunden. LC 85-20819. (GER.). 240p. 1992. lib. bdg. 25.00 (0-226-50334-8) U Ch Pr.

Pro Approach: For Becoming the Complete Player. unabridged ed. Ed. & Illus. by Michael Wood. 46p. 1996. pap. text 19.95 (0-9669407-0-9, 945381209) M & W.

Pro Archia. Marcus Tullius Cicero. (Loeb Classical Library: No. 158). (ENG & LAT.). (C). 14.50 (0-674-99174-5) HUP.

Pro Audio Spectrum: The Official Book. Ivan Lok. 512p. 1993. pap. 34.95 (0-07-881979-2) McGraw.

Pro Basketball Bible: Formerly Rick Barry's Pro Basketball Scouting Report. Jordan Cohn. (Illus.). 400p. 1993. pap. 16.95 (0-9636385-0-5) Basketball Bks.

Pro Basketball Megastars, 1995. Bruce Weber. 32p. (J). (gr. 4-6). 1995. pap. 3.95 (0-590-48675-6) Scholastic Inc.

Pro Basketball Megastars, 1996. Bruce Weber. (J). 1996. pap. text 4.95 (0-590-54083-1) Scholastic Inc.

Pro Basketball Statistics: Top Players & Teams by Game, Season & Career. Martin Taragano. LC 92-51094. (Illus.). 215p. 1993. lib. bdg. 37.50 (0-89950-804-9) McFarland & Co.

***Pro Basketball Today, 29 bks.** Incl. Atlanta Hawks. Richard Rambeck. LC 96-53185. 32p. (YA). (gr. 3 up). 1997. lib. bdg. 21.30 (0-88682-865-1, Creat Educ); Boston Celtics. Michael E. Goodman. LC 96-53184. 32p. (YA). (gr. 3 up). 1997. lib. bdg. 21.30 (0-88682-867-8, Creat Educ); Charlotte Hornets. Richard Rambeck. LC 96-53183. 32p. (YA). (gr. 3 up). 1997. lib. bdg. 21.30 (0-88682-868-6, Creat Educ); Chicago Bulls. Michael E. Goodman. LC 96-53021. 32p. (YA). (gr. 3 up). 1997. lib. bdg. 21.30 (0-88682-869-4, Creat Educ); Cleveland Cavaliers. Richard Rambeck. LC 96-53022. 32p. (YA). (gr. 3 up). 1997. lib. bdg. 21.30 (0-88682-870-8, Creat Educ); Dallas Mavericks. Michael E. Goodman. LC 96-53023. 32p. (YA). (gr. 3 up). 1997. lib. bdg. 21.30 (0-88682-871-6, Creat Educ); Denver Nuggets. Michael E. Goodman. LC 96-53024. 32p. (YA). (gr. 3 up). 1997. lib. bdg. 21.30 (0-88682-872-4, Creat Educ); Detroit Pistons. Richard Rambeck. LC 96-6535. 32p. (YA). (gr. 3 up). 1997. lib. bdg. 21.30 (0-88682-873-2, Creat Educ); Golden State Warriors. Michael E. Goodman. LC 96-52964. (Illus.). 32p. (YA). (gr. 3 up). 1997. lib. bdg. 21.30 (0-88682-874-0, Creat Educ); Houston Rockets. Michael E. Goodman. LC 96-6534. 32p. (YA). (gr. 3 up). 1997. lib. bdg. 21.30 (0-88682-875-9, Creat Educ); Indiana Pacers. Richard Rambeck. LC 96-6533. 32p. (YA). (gr. 3 up). 1997. lib. bdg. 21.30 (0-88682-876-7, Creat Educ); Los Angeles Clippers. Richard Rambeck. LC 96-6532. 32p. (YA). (gr. 3 up). 1997. lib. bdg. 21.30 (0-88682-877-5, Creat Educ); Los Angeles Lakers. Michael E. Goodman. LC 96-6530. 32p. (YA). (gr. 3 up). 1997. lib. bdg. 21.30 (0-88682-878-3, Creat Educ); Miami Heat. Richard Rambeck. LC 96-6529. 32p. (YA). (gr. 3 up). 1997. lib. bdg. 21.30 (0-88682-879-1, Creat Educ); Milwaukee Bucks. Jack C. Harris. LC 96-51059. 32p. (YA). (gr. 3 up). 1997. lib. bdg. 21.30 (0-88682-880-5, Creat Educ); Minnesota Timberwolves. Richard Rambeck. LC 96-51057. 32p. (YA). (gr. 3 up). 1997. lib. bdg. 21.30 (0-88682-881-3, Creat Educ); New Jersey Nets. Jack C. Harris. LC 96-51047. 32p. (YA). (gr. 3 up). 1997. lib. bdg. 21.30 (0-88682-882-1, Creat Educ); New York Knicks. Michael E. Goodman. LC 96-51064. 32p. (YA). (gr. 3 up). 1997. lib. bdg. 21.30 (0-88682-884-8, Creat Educ); Orlando Magic. Richard Rambeck. LC 96-51066. 32p. (YA). (gr. 3 up). 1997. lib. bdg. 21.30 (0-88682-885-6, Creat Educ); Philadelphia 76ers. Michael E. Goodman. LC 96-51067. 32p. (YA). (gr. 3 up). 1997. lib. bdg. 21.30 (0-88682-886-4, Creat Educ); Phoenix Suns. Richard Rambeck. LC 96-51048. 32p. (YA). (gr. 3 up). 1997. lib. bdg. 21.30 (0-88682-887-2, Creat Educ); Portland Trail Blazers. Richard Rambeck. LC 96-6528. 32p. (YA). (gr. 3 up). 1997. lib. bdg. 21.30 (0-88682-888-0, Creat Educ); Sacramento Kings. Michael E. Goodman. LC 96-6527. 32p. (YA). (gr. 3 up). 1997. lib. bdg. 21.30 (0-88682-889-9, Creat Educ); San Antonio Spurs. Richard Rambeck. LC 96-52962. 32p. (YA). (gr. 3 up). 1997. lib. bdg. 21.30 (0-88682-890-2, Creat Educ); Toronto Raptors. John Nichols. LC 97-6651. 32p. (YA). (gr. 3 up). 1998. lib. bdg. 21.30 (0-88682-894-5, Creat Educ); Utah Jazz Story. Richard Rambeck. LC 96-52961. 32p. (YA). (gr. 3 up). 1997. lib. bdg. 21.30 (0-88682-893-7, Creat Educ); Vancouver Grizzlies. John Nichols. LC 97-6652. 32p. (YA). (gr. 3 up). 1998. lib. bdg. 21.30 (0-88682-895-3, Creat Educ); Washington Wizards. Richard Rambeck. LC 96-52960. 32p. (YA). (gr. 3 up). 1997. lib. bdg. 21.30 (0-88682-892-9, Creat Educ); 32p. (YA). (gr. 3-12). 1998. Set lib. bdg. 617.70 (0-88682-864-3, Creat Educ) Creative Co.

Pro-Boers: The Anatomy of an Anti-War Movement. Stephen E. Koss. (Studies in Imperialism). 1995. lib. bdg. 30.00 (0-226-45134-8) U Ch Pr.

Pro Bono Delivery & Support: A Directory of Statewide Models. ABA Center for Pro Bono Staff & American Bar Association Staff. LC 98-157500. vi, 102p. 1998. write for info. (1-57073-516-6) Amer Bar Assn.

Pro Bono Desk Reference. LC 90-63117. 500p. 1992. ring bd. 50.00 (0-944490-23-9) Mass CLE.

Pro Bono Publico: The Shattucks of Boston. (Picture Bks.). 1971. pap. 4.00 (0-934909-55-5) Mass Hist Soc.

Pro Book: Maximizing Competitive Performance for Pool Players. Bob Henning. LC 99-183043. (Illus.). 304p. 1997. pap. 49.95 (1-887956-23-9) Bebob Pubng.

Pro Bound . . . Do You Have What It Takes to Become a Professional Athlete? Sherri Jefferson. LC 96-94896. 144p. 1996. pap. 19.95 (0-9654656-0-8) S Jefferson.

Pro Bound . . . Do You Have What It Takes to Become a Professional Athlete? rev. ed. Sherri Jefferson. LC 96-94896. 144p. 1998. pap. 19.95 (0-9654656-6-7) S Jefferson.

Pro Caelio. Marcus Tullius Cicero. (Loeb Classical Library: No. 447). 15.50 (0-674-99492-2) HUP.

Pro-Choice? Pro-Life? The Questions, the Answers. Herbert Smith. LC 94-47656. 104p. (Orig.). 1995. pap. 5.95 (0-8198-5893-5) Pauline Bks.

Pro-Choice & Anti-Abortion: Constitutional Theory & Public Policy. James R. Bowers. LC 93-14739. 152p. 1994. 57.95 (0-275-94964-8, Praeger Pubs) Greenwood.

Pro-Choice & Anti-Abortion: Constitutional Theory & Public Policy. James R. Bowers. LC 93-14739. 160p. 1997. pap. 19.95 (0-275-95964-3, Praeger Pubs) Greenwood.

Pro-Choice Movement: Organization & Activism in the Abortion Conflict. Suzanne Staggenborg. 256p. 1994. reprint ed. pap. text 18.95 (0-19-508925-1) OUP.

Pro-Choice-Pro-Life: An Annotated, Selected Bibliography (1972-1989), 20. Ed. by Joan P. Diana. LC 91-12625. (Bibliographies & Indexes in Sociology Ser.: No. 20). 264p. 1991. lib. bdg. 59.95 (0-313-27579-3, FPJ, Greenwood Pr) Greenwood.

Pro-Choice VICTORY Handbook: Strategies for Keeping Your Abortion Rights. Craig Chilton. 208p. (Orig.). 1991. pap. 8.95 (0-9631248-0-3) Boiled Owl.

Pro-Choice vs. Pro-Life: The Abortion Debate in Canada. F. L. Morton. LC 92-34959. (Illus.). 371p. 1993. pap. 21.95 (0-8061-2522-5) U of Okla Pr.

Pro-Choice/Pro - Life Issues in the 1990s: An Annotated, Selected Bibliography, 24. Richard P. Fitzsimmons & Joan Diana. LC 96-23115. (Bibliographies & Indexes in Sociology Ser.: No. 24). 304p. 1996. lib. bdg. 65.00 (0-313-29355-4, Greenwood Pr) Greenwood.

Pro Christo et Patria: A History of Geneva College. David M. Carson. LC 97-28094. 1997. write for info. (1-57864-006-7) Donning Co.

***Pro Consumer Power! How to Create Wealth by Buying Smarter, Not Cheaper.** Bill Quain. Ed. by Steve Price. 126p. 2000. pap. 11.95 (1-891279-04-1) INTI.

Pro-Democracy Protests in China: Reports from the Provinces. Ed. by Jonathan Unger. LC 90-28984. (Contemporary China Papers - Australian National University). 256p. (C). (gr. 13). 1991. text 68.95 (0-87332-836-1, East Gate Bk) M E Sharpe.

Pro-Democracy Protests in China: Reports from the Provinces. Ed. by Jonathan Unger. LC 90-28984. (Contemporary China Papers - Australian National University Ser.). 256p. (C). (gr. 13). 1991. pap. text 35.95 (0-87332-837-X, East Gate Bk) M E Sharpe.

Pro-Drugs As Novel Drug Delivery Systems. Ed. by T. Higuchi & Valentino J. Stella. LC 75-11721. (ACS Symposium Ser.: Vol. 14). 255p. 1975. reprint ed. pap. 79.10 (0-608-03549-1, 206426800008) Bks Demand.

Pro Earth: Readings on Current Land & Water Issues in the Global Environment. 1985. pap. 6.95 (0-377-00154-6) Friendship Pr.

Pro Engine Blueprinting. Ben Watson. LC 97-38039. (Power Tech Ser.). (Illus.). 144p. 1997. pap. 16.95 (0-7603-0424-6) MBI Pubg.

Pro-Engineer: Tips & Techniques. Tim McLellan & Fred Karam. 344p. (C). 1996. pap. 59.95 (1-56690-053-0) Thomson Learn.

Pro-Engineer Exercise Book: Based on Release 15. 2nd ed. Bill Paul. LC 96-136834. 192p. 1995. pap. 44.95 (1-56690-083-2, OnWord Pr) High Mtn.

Pro Engineer Stud Collectn Modeler 2.0 Libr. (C). 1998. 0.00 (0-201-35660-0) HEPC Inc.

Pro-Engineer Tutorial (Release 20) A Click-by-Click Primer. Roger Toogood. (Illus.). 230p. 1998. pap. 49.50 (1-887503-65-X) Schroff Dev Corp.

***Pro/Engineer 2000 I.** rev. ed. Louis G. Lamit. LC 99-33302. 1999. pap. 80.95 (0-534-37038-1) Brooks-Cole.

***Pro/Engineer 2000 I.** rev. ed. Louis G. Lamit. LC 99-33302. 1999. pap. text 83.95 (0-534-37786-6) Brooks-Cole.

***Pro Engnr Studnt Collectn: Modeler Rendr Lib.** (C). 1998. 212.33 (0-201-35642-2) HEPC Inc.

***Pro Femina: A Poem.** Carolyn Kizer. (Roy Fox Memorial Chapbook Ser.: Vol. 4). 32p. 2000. pap. 8.95 (1-886157-30-8) BkMk.

Pro Football: The Halls of Fame. Herma Silverstein & Terry J. Dunnahoo. LC 93-954. (Halls of Fame Ser.). (Illus.). 48p. (J). (gr. 5-6). 1994. lib. bdg. 13.95 (0-89686-851-6, Crstwood Hse) Silver Burdett Pr.

Pro Football Brain Teasers. Dom Forker & Ted Forker. LC 96-9279. 128p. 1996. pap. 5.95 (0-8069-9452-5) Sterling.

Pro Football Chronicle. Dan Daly & Bob O'Donnell. (Illus.). 416p. (Orig.). 1990. pap. 16.95 (0-02-028300-8) Macmillan.

Pro Football Encyclopedia: The Complete & Definitive Record of Professional Football. Ed. by Tod Maher & Bob Gill. 1467p. 1997. 44.95 (0-02-861989-7) Macmillan.

***Pro Football Forecaster Vol. 8: Sports Curriculum.** Laurence A. Frame. (Illus.). 50p. 1999. pap. text 20.00 (1-884480-53-5) Spts Curriculum.

***Pro Football Guide: The Ultimate 2000 Season Reference.** Ed. by Sporting News Staff. (Illus.). 416p. 2000. pap. 15.95 (0-89204-635-X, Contemporary Bks) NTC Contemp Pub Co.

Pro Football Guide: 1998 Edition. Ed. by Craig Carter. 392p. 1998. 15.95 (0-89204-596-5) Sporting News.

Pro Football Guide: 1999 Edition. Sporting News Staff. 392p. 1999. pap. 15.95 (0-89204-613-9, 06139C) NTC Contemp Pub Co.

Pro Football Guide, 1997: A Comprehensive Review of the 1995 Season & a Sneak Peek at '96. Sporting News Staff. (Illus.). 392p. 1997. pap. 15.95 (0-89204-577-9) Sporting News.

Pro Football Guide, 1996: A Comprehensive Review of the 1995 Season & a Sneak Peek at '96. Sporting News Staff. (Illus.). 384p. 1996. pap. 14.95 (0-89204-553-1) Sporting News.

Pro Football Hall of Fame: Players, Coaches, Team Owners & League Officials, 1963-1991. Denis J. Harrington. LC 91-52636. (Illus.). 368p. 1991. lib. bdg. 35.00 (0-89950-550-3) McFarland & Co.

Pro Football Hall of Fame: The Story Behind the Dream. Barney Brantingham. (Illus.). 64p. 1989. pap. 8.95 (0-917859-27-8) Sunrise SBCA.

***Pro Football Handbook 2000.** STATS Inc., Staff. (Illus.). 2000. pap. 19.95 (1-884064-79-5) STATS.

Pro Football Megastars, 1997. Bruce Weber. 32p. (J). (gr. 3-9). 1997. pap. text 4.99 (0-590-76482-9) Scholastic Inc.

Pro Football Megastars '95. Bruce Weber. 32p. (J). (gr. 4-6). 1995. pap. 3.95 (0-590-53527-7) Scholastic Inc.

Pro Football Register: 1998 Edition. annuals Ed. by Mark Bonavita & Brendan Roberts. 904p. 1998. 15.95 (0-89204-597-3) Sporting News.

Pro Football Register: 1999 Edition. Sporting News Staff. 504p. 1999. pap. 15.95 (0-89204-614-7, 06147C) NTC Contemp Pub Co.

***Pro Football Register: 2000 Edition.** Ed. by Sporting News Staff. (Illus.). 544p. 2000. pap. 15.95 (0-89204-636-8, 06368C, Contemporary Bks) NTC Contemp Pub Co.

Pro Football Register, 1996: A Who's Who of the National Football League, from A to Z. annuals Sporting News Staff. 448p. 1996. pap. 14.95 (0-89204-554-X) Sporting News.

Pro Football Register, 1997: A Who's Who of the National Football League, from A to Z. annuals Sporting News Staff. 504p. 1997. pap. 1595.00 (0-89204-578-7) Sporting News.

Pro Football Revealed, 1995: The 100-Yard War. 2nd ed. Stats, Inc. (Illus.). 351p. 1995. pap. 15.95 (1-884064-15-9) STATS.

Pro Football Revealed, 1994: The 100-Yard War. Stats Publishing Staff. 1994. pap. 15.00 (1-884064-05-1) STATS.

Pro Football Scorebook. 3rd ed. Kenneth N. Carlson. LC 94-105968. 610p. 1993. pap. 14.50 (0-938428-12-8) Rain Belt.

Pro Football Strategy: What the Sunday Fan Should Know to be a Monday Quarterback. James E. Hopkinson. LC 81-83104. 265p. (Orig.). 1982. pap. 8.95 (0-940950-00-6) Knowledge Builders.

***Pro Football Today, 31 bks.** John Nichols & Julie Nelson. 2000. lib. bdg. 700.60 (1-58341-064-3, Creat Educ) Creative Co.

Pro Football Trivia. Bob Gill. LC 98-38538. (Illus.). x, 262 p. pap. 9.95 (1-57028-232-3, 82323H, Mstrs Pr) NTC Contemp Pub Co.

Pro Football Trivia Bowl. Steve Greenberg. 224p. 1998. mass mkt. 5.99 (0-380-79946-4, Avon Bks) Morrow Avon.

Pro Football Weekly Draft Preview, 1996. Pro Football Weekly Editors & Joel Buchsbaum. (Illus.). 184p. (Orig.). 1996. pap. 18.95 (1-888924-00-4) Pro Football.

Pro Football Weekly Draft Preview, 1998. Joel Buchsbaum & Pro Football Weekly Editors. (Illus.). 184p. (Orig.). 1998. pap. 19.95 (1-888924-01-2) Pro Football.

Pro-Football Weekly, 1995 Almanac. Richard Whittingham. 448p. (Orig.). 1995. pap. 14.95 (0-399-51958-0, Perigee Bks) Berkley Pub.

Pro Football Weekly Pro Prospects Preview, 1997-98. Joel Buchsbaum & Pro Football Weekly Editors. (Illus.). 136p. (Orig.). 1997. pap. 15.95 (1-888924-02-0) Pro Football.

Pro Game. Megan Terry. (Illus.). 12p. (Orig.). 1984. 35.00 (0-317-11926-5) I E Clark.

Pro Game: One-Act Comedy. Megan Terry. (Illus.). 12p. 1984. pap. 2.50 (0-88680-217-2) I E Clark.

Pro Golf Teaching Manual. Robert Bernier. pap. 2.95 (0-89741-008-4) Gila River.

Pro-Growth. (Illus.). 54p. (C). 1992. pap. 10.00 (0-943802-70-9, 167) Natl Ctr Pol.

Pro-Growth Budget Strategy: Vision for the 1990s. Gary Robbins & Aldona Robbins. 1990. pap. 10.00 (0-943802-57-1, 154) Natl Ctr Pol.

Pro Hea Cook Garde Mg Prof Che. CIA Staff & Sonnensc. 1997. 139.95 (0-442-01475-9, VNR) Wiley.

Pro Hockey Guide. 2nd ed. Tom Keegan. (Illus.). 200p. 1998. reprint ed. pap. 25.95 (1-880941-17-1) Athletic Guide.

Pro Hockey Trivia Compendium. Jack Lautier. (Illus.). 97p. (Orig.). 1999. pap. 7.95 (0-9650315-2-7) Glacier Publng.

Pro-Illustration: Advertising. Rotovision Staff. (Illus.). 160p. 1997. pap. 37.50 (2-88046-310-6, Rotovision) Watsn-Guptill.

Pro-Lawn Service Accounting Application. 4th ed. David H. Weaver et al. 168p. 1982. text 9.04 (0-07-069334-X) McGraw.

Pro Lege Manilia. Marcus Tullius Cicero. (Loeb Classical Library: No. 198). (ENG & LAT.). 15.50 (0-674-99218-0) HUP.

Pro-Legomena: Distribution & Reference of Infinitival Subjects. Guido J. Vanden Wyngaerd. LC 93-8610. (Linguistic Models Ser.: Vol. 19). xiv, 312p. 1994. lib. bdg. 124.65 (3-11-013836-0) Mouton.

Pro-Life Christians: Heroes for the Pre-Born. Joe Gulotta. LC 92-60212. (Illus.). 146p. (Orig.). 1992. pap. 7.50 (0-89555-460-7) TAN Bks Pubs.

Pro-Life Feminism: Different Voices. Ed. by Gail Grenier-Sweet. 234p. (Orig.). (C). 1985. pap. 13.95 (0-919225-22-5) Life Cycle Bks.

Pro-Life Precinct Power: A Workbook. Robert G. Marshall. (Illus.). 45p. (Orig.). 1990. pap. 2.00 (1-890712-15-9, LW3) Amer Life League.

Pro-Life Primer on Euthanasia. Eileen Doyle. (Illus.). 84p. (Orig.). 1993. pap. 3.00 (1-890712-09-4, IE3) Amer Life League.

Pro-Lighting: Food Shots. Rotovision S. A. Staff. (Illus.). 160p. 1995. pap. text 29.95 (0-8230-6432-8, Rotovision) Watsn-Guptill.

Pro-Lighting: Glamour Shots. Rotovision S. A. Staff. (Illus.). 160p. 1995. pap. text 29.95 (0-8230-6431-X, Rotovision) Watsn-Guptill.

Pro-Lighting: Nudes. Rotovision S. A. Staff. (Illus.). 160p. 1997. pap. text 35.00 (0-8230-6520-0, Amphoto) Watsn-Guptill.

Pro-Lighting: Portraits. Rotovision S. A. Staff. (Illus.). 160p. 1997. pap. text 35.00 (0-8230-6522-7, Amphoto) Watsn-Guptill.

Pro-Lighting: Product Shots. Rotovision S. A. Staff. (Illus.). 160p. 1995. pap. text 29.95 (0-8230-6433-6) Watsn-Guptill.

Pro-Lighting: Still Life. Rotovision S. A. Staff. (Illus.). 160p. 1997. pap. text 35.00 (0-8230-6521-9, Amphoto) Watsn-Guptill.

Pro M. Caelio Oratio. 3rd ed. Marcus Tullius Cicero. Ed. by R. G. Austin. 212p. 1988. pap. text 24.00 (0-19-814062-2) OUP.

Pro Magic: The Art of Professional Deck Construction. George Baxter. LC 98-101145. 180p. 1997. pap. 12.95 (1-55622-524-5) Wordware Pub.

Pro-Mechanica Structural Tutorial: A Click-by-Click Primer. Roger Toogood. (Illus.). 256p. 1998. pap. 49.50 (1-887503-77-3) Schroff Dev Corp.

Pro Milone. Marcus Tullius Cicero. (Loeb Classical Library: No. 252). 15.50 (0-674-99278-4) HUP.

Pro Milone, Pro Marcello, Pro Ligario, Pro Rege Deiotaro, Philip Picae, 1-14 see Orationes

Pro-Mo's Secrets for Finding Walleyes. Gary Roach et al. (Illus.). 112p. (Orig.). 1988. pap. write for info. (0-318-64036-8) Fishing Pro-Mos Inc.

Pro-Mo's Secrets to Jigging Walleyes. Gary Roach et al. (Illus.). 112p. (Orig.). 1988. pap. write for info. (0-318-64037-6) Fishing Pro-Mos Inc.

Pro-Mo's Secrets to Rigging Walleyes. Gary Roach et al. (Illus.). 112p. (Orig.). 1988. pap. write for info. (0-318-64035-X) Fishing Pro-Mos Inc.

***Pro Motocross & Off-Road Riding Techniques.** 2nd ed. Donnie Bales & Gary Semics. LC 99-87809. (Illus.). 224p. 2000. pap. 24.95 (0-7603-0831-4, Pub. by MBI Pubg) Motorbooks Intl.

Pro Mountain Biker: The Complete Manual of Pro Mountain Biking. Jeremy Evans. LC 96-232393. (Illus.). 160p. 1996. pap. 21.95 (0-7603-0206-5) MBI Pubg.

Pro Musica: Patronage, Performance & a Periodical - An Index to the Quarterlies. Ed. by Paula Elliott. LC 96-6582. (MLA Index & Bibliography Ser.). 112p. 1997. 30.00 (0-914954-52-0) Music Library Assn.

Pro Musica Antiqua: Poems. fac. ed. O. B. Hardison. LC 77-3932. 63p. 1977. reprint ed. pap. 30.00 (0-7837-7736-1, 204749200007) Bks Demand.

Pro P. Quincto, Pro Q. Roscio Comoedo, Pro A. Caecina, De Lege Agraria Contra Rullum, Pro C. Rabirio Perduellionis Reo, Pro L. Flacco, In L. Pisonem, Pro C. Rabirio Postumo see Orationes

Pro Pilot: The Official Strategy Guide. Douglas Kiang. LC 97-66922. 216p. 1998. per. 19.99 (0-7615-1114-8) Prima Pub.

***Pro Pilot 4.** Prima Staff. (Official Strategy Guides Ser.). 240p. (YA). 2000. pap. 19.95 (0-7615-2614-5) Prima Pub.

Pro Pilot 99: Prima's Official Strategy Guide. Douglas Kiang. LC 98-65451. 244p. 1998. per. 19.99 (0-7615-1575-5) Prima Pub.

***Pro Pilot 2000.** Prima. 1999. pap. 19.99 (0-7615-2612-9, Prima Games) Prima Pub.

Pro Poker Playbook: 223 Ways to Win More Money Playing Poker. John Vorhaus. LC 95-67370. 175p. (Orig.). 1995. pap. 19.95 (1-884466-12-5) Poker Plus.

Pro-Poor Aid Conditionality. John P. Lewis. LC 93-19137. (Policy Essay Ser.: No. 8). 72p. (C). 1993. pap. 13.95 (1-56517-009-1) Overseas Dev Council.

Pro-Pro Handicap Go. Yutopian Enterprises. LC 99-177672. 200 p. 1997. pap. text 20.65 (1-889554-08-1) Yutopian Ent.

Pro-Protein & Pro-Hormone Convertases: Reprint from Journal Enzyme, Vol. 45, Nos. 5 & 6, 1991. Ed. by N. G. Seidah. (Illus.). iv, 88p. 1992. 85.25 (3-8055-5705-1) S Karger.

Pro Quinctio. Marcus Tullius Cicero. (Loeb Classical Library: No. 240). (ENG & LAT.). 15.50 (0-674-99265-2) HUP.

Pro Salute Novi Mundi: A History of the Pan-American Health Organization. 290p. 1992. text 60.00 (92-75-12079-X) World Health.

Pro-Se... A Real Life Soap Opera: Sampler. Edith M. Gracey. 52p. 1994. pap. text 3.00 (0-9644673-0-5) E M Gracey.

PRO Sections 1-2399, Vol. 142. 146p. 1999. write for info. (0-327-06991-0, 57768-12) LEXIS Pub.

PRO Sections 12200-End, Vol. 146. 194p. 1999. write for info. (0-327-06995-3, 57772-12) LEXIS Pub.

PRO Sections 2400-6399, Vol. 143. 218p. 1999. write for info. (0-327-06992-9, 57769-12) LEXIS Pub.

PRO Sections 6400-9599, Vol. 144. 62p. 1999. write for info. (0-327-06993-7, 57770-12) LEXIS Pub.

PRO Sections 9600-12199, Vol. 145. 49p. 1999. write for info. (0-327-06994-5, 57771-12) LEXIS Pub.

Pro Series Soccer Scorebook. Stanley Horowitz. 1994. pap. 4.00 (0-9639660-3-0) All Spts Pubng.

Pro Sestio. Marcus Tullius Cicero. (Loeb Classical Library: No. 309). 15.50 (0-674-99341-1) HUP.

P

Pro Sex. Roscio, De Imperio, Cn. Pompei, Pro Cluentio, in Catilinam, Pro Murena, Pro Caelio see Orationes

Pro-Slavery Overthrown & the True Principles of Abolitionism Declared. Thomas R. Lounsbury. 1977. 16.95 (*0-8369-9169-9*, 9044) Ayer.

***Pro Sports: How Did They Begin?** Don L. Wulffson. (Illus.). 64p. (J). (gr. 2-5). 2000. pap. 5.95 (*1-57255-814-8*) Mondo Pubng.

Pro Sports Car Racing in America 1958-1974. Dave Friedman. LC 99-32722. (Illus.). 196p. 1999. text 39.95 (*0-7603-0618-4*, 128959AP, Pub. by MBI Pubg) Motorbooks Intl.

Pro Sports Halls of Fame. LC 96-30181. 160p. (J). 1996. lib. bdg. 285.00 (*0-7172-7651-1*) Grolier Educ.

***Pro Stock Car Racing.** William P. Mara. 1999. 19.93 (*0-516-21469-1*) Capstone Pr.

Pro Stock Drag Racing see Drag Racing

Pro Stock Drag Racing. Martin Hintz & Kate Hintz. (Drag Racing Ser.). (Illus.). 48p. (J). (gr. 3-7). 1996. 19.00 (*0-516-20240-5*) Childrens.

***Pro-Style Multiple Defense for High School Football.** Al Black. LC 99-53443. (Illus.). 128p. 2000. pap. 15.00 (*1-890450-05-7*) Harding Pr.

Pro Surfing '98: Official ASP Yearbook Summer Edition 1998. Ed. by Robert Yehling & Charles Oldham. (Illus.). 88p. 1998. pap. 4.95 (*0-9644712-4-8*) Faircount Intl.

Pro 3-4: Winning Football with a Multipurpose Defense. Mike McDaniels. 228p. (C). 1986. text 27.95 (*0-13-711433-8*) P-H.

Pro Touch/Best in Pops Bk. 1: Piano. 49p. (Orig.). 1983. pap. 10.95 (*0-7692-1019-8*, PF0187) Wrner Bros.

Pro Touch/Best in Pops Bk. 4: Intermediate/Advanced Piano. 48p. (Orig.). 1989. pap. 10.95 (*0-7692-1020-1*, PF0608) Wrner Bros.

Pro Touch/Best in Pops Bk. 5: Piano. 36p. (Orig.). 1991. pap. 9.95 (*0-7692-1021-X*, PF0756) Wrner Bros.

Pro Tullio, Pro Fonteio, Pro Sulla, Pro Archia, Pro Plancio. Pro Scauro see Orationes

Pro-Vita! Plan: For Optimal Nutrition. 2nd rev. ed. Jack Tips. LC 92-70715. (Illus.). 235p. 1992. pap. text 19.95 (*0-929167-05-8*) Apple-a-Day.

Pro Wrestling. 2nd ed. (Complete Idiot's Guide Ser.). 352p. 1900. 18.95 (*0-02-863961-8*) Macmillan Gen Ref.

***Pro Wrestling: From Carnivals to Cable TV.** Keith Elliot Greenberg. LC 99-50554. (Sports Legacy Ser.). (Illus.). 144p. 2000. lib. bdg. 23.93 (*0-8225-3332-4*, LernerSports) Lerner Pub.

***Pro Wrestling: From Carnivals to Cable TV.** Keith Elliot Greenberg. (Sports Legacy Ser.). (Illus.). 144p. (YA). (gr. 6-10). 2000. pap. 9.95 (*0-8225-9864-7*, LernerSports) Lerner Pub.

***Pro Wrestling's Greatest Tag Teams.** Matt Hunter. LC 00-21866. (Pro Wrestling Legends Ser.). (Illus.). 2000. pap. 8.95 (*0-7910-5836-0*) Chelsea Hse.

***Pro Wrestling's Greatest Wars.** Dan Ross. (Pro Wrestling Legends Ser.). 2000. 17.95 (*0-7910-5837-9*) Chelsea Hse.

***Pro Wrestling's Greatest Wars.** Dan Ross. LC 00-20732. (Pro Wrestling Legends Ser.). (Illus.). 2000. pap. 8.95 (*0-7910-5838-7*) Chelsea Hse.

Proact. David K. Kauf. (Illus.). 103p. 1980. 49.50 (*0-936804-00-9*) Kauf Pubs.

***Proactive Approaches in Psychosocial Occupational Therapy.** Rita P. Cottrell. (Illus.). 516p. 2000. pap. text 42.00 (*1-55642-455-8*) SLACK Inc.

Proactive Customer Service: Transforming Your Customer Service Department into a Profit Center. Charles D. Brennan, Jr. LC 97-21788. 208p. 1997. 22.95 (*0-8144-0372-7*) AMACOM.

Proactive Customer Service: Transforming Your Customer Service Department into a Profit Center. Charles D. Brennan. LC 97-21788. 1997. write for info. (*0-8144-7943-X*) AMACOM.

ProActive Discipline: Creating a Schoolwide Behavior Management System That Works. Joseph E. Petterle. 1994. student ed. 13.00 (*1-881805-25-5*) Copernicus Systs.

Proactive Leadership in the 21st Century Classroom, School & District. Robert L. DeBruyn. x, 360p. 1997. pap. text 24.95 (*0-914607-44-8*, 1723) Master Tchr.

P

Proactive Police Management. Thibault. (C). 1999. write for info. (*0-13-711458-3*, Macmillan Coll) P-H.

Proactive Police Management. 4th ed. Edward A. Thibault & R. Bruce McBride. LC 97-12969. 423p. 1997. 84.00 (*0-13-616665-2*) P-H.

***Proactive Police Management.** 5th ed. Edward A. Thibault et al. 480p. 2000. 73.33 (*0-13-022519-3*, Prentice Hall) P-H.

Proactive Police Management Study Guide. Robert Fischer & Ronald Moser. 64p. 1995. pap. 13.95 (*0-7872-1659-3*) Kendall-Hunt.

Proactive Police Management Study Guide: Based on the Text by Thibault, Lynch & McBride. 4th ed. Davis Publishing Company Staff. 214p. 1997. 28.95 (*1-56325-060-8*, DS100) Davis Pub Law.

Proactive Procurement: The Key to Increased Profits, Productivity, & Quality. David N. Burt. (Illus.). 288p. 1984. text 54.20 (*0-13-711465-6*) P-H.

Proactive Responses to the Assisted Suicide/Euthanasia Debate. Ed. by National Hospice Organization Ethics Committee. 96p. (Orig.). 1996. pap., per. 11.85 (*0-931207-45-2*, 713438) Natl Hospice.

***ProActive Sales Management: How to Manage More Effectively & Stay Ahead of the Game.** William Miller. 256p. 2000. 24.95 (*0-8144-0545-2*) AMACOM.

Prob. Solv. in Daily Liv. Ed. by Stephen Switzer. 1992. 4.95 (*1-55708-206-5*, McR459) McDonald Pub Co.

Probabalistic Risk & Hazard Assessment. Ed. by R. E. Melchers & M. G. Stewart. 253p. 1993. 123.00 (*90-5410-349-3*, Pub. by A A Balkema) Ashgate Pub Co.

Probabilidad E Inferencia Estadistica. rev. ed. (Serie de Matematica: No. 11). (SPA.). 1975. pap. 3.50 (*0-8270-6275-3*) OAS.

Probabilist Theism of John Stuart Mill. Harry Settanni. LC 91-19620. (American University Studies: Philosophy: Ser. V, Vol. 118). IX, 237p. 1991. 44.95 (*0-8204-1513-8*) P Lang Pubng.

***Probabilistic Accident Consequence Uncertainty Analysis: Early Health Effects Uncertainty Assessment, Appendices.** F. E. Haskin. 355p. 1998. per. 28.00 (*0-16-062908-X*) USGPO.

***Probabilistic Accident Consequence Uncertainty Analysis: Early Health Effects Uncertainty Assessment, Main Report.** F. E. Haskin. 68p. 1998. pap. 6.00 (*0-16-062907-1*) USGPO.

***Probabilistic Accident Consequence Uncertainty Analysis: Late Health Effects Uncertainty Assessment, Appendices.** M. P. Little. 232p. 1998. per. 19.00 (*0-16-062878-4*) USGPO.

***Probabilistic Accident Consequence Uncertainty Analysis: Late Health Effects Uncertainty Assessment, Main Report.** M. P. Little. 63p. 1998. pap. 5.50 (*0-16-062877-6*) USGPO.

***Probabilistic Accident Consequence Uncertainty Analysis: Uncertainty Assessment for Internal Dosimetry, Main Report.** L. H. J. Goossens. 66p. 1998. pap. 5.50 (*0-16-062913-6*) USGPO.

***Probabilistic Accident Consequence Uncertainty Analysis Appendices: Uncertainty Assessment for Deposited Material & External Dose.** L. H. J. Goossens. 407p. 1998. per. 32.00 (*0-16-062876-8*) USGPO.

***Probabilistic Accident Consequence Uncertainty Analysis Appendices: Uncertainty Assessment for Internal Dosimetry.** L. H. J. Goossens. 322p. 1998. per. 26.00 (*0-16-062914-4*) USGPO.

Probabilistic Accident Consequence Uncertainty Analysis, Food Chain Uncertainty Assessment: Appendices. J. Brown. 347p. 1997. per. 29.00 (*0-16-054678-8*) USGPO.

Probabilistic Accident Consequence Uncertainty Analysis, Food Chain Uncertainty Assessment: Main Report. J. Brown. 76p. 1997. pap. 7.00 (*0-16-054677-X*) USGPO.

***Probabilistic Accident Consequence Uncertainty Assessment: Uncertainty Assessment for Deposited Material & External Doses, Main Report.** L. H. J. Goossens. 62p. 1998. pap. 5.00 (*0-16-062875-X*) USGPO.

Probabilistic Analysis & Design of Nuclear Power Plant Structures: Presented at the Winter Annual Meeting of the American Society of Mechanical Engineers, San Francisco, California, December 10-15, 1978. Symposium on Probabilistic Analysis & Design of Nu. Ed. by C. Sundararajan. LC 78-59897. (PVP Ser.: No. 030). (Illus.). 123p. reprint ed. pap. 38.20 (*0-8357-2877-3*, 203911300011) Bks Demand.

Probabilistic Analysis of Algorithms. M. Hofri. (Texts & Monographs in Computer Science). (Illus.). 255p. 1987. 87.95 (*0-387-96578-5*) Spr-Verlag.

Probabilistic Analysis of Redundant Systems. S. K. Srinivasan & R. Subramanian. (Lecture Notes in Economics & Mathematical Systems Ser.: Vol. 175). (Illus.). 356p. 1980. pap. 33.00 (*3-540-09736-8*) Spr-Verlag.

Probabilistic Analysis of Test-Response Compaction. Slawomir Pilarski & Tiko Kameda. LC 94-27227. 112p. 1995. pap. 25.00 (*0-8186-6532-7*, BP06532) IEEE Comp Soc.

Probabilistic Analysis of the Sacco & Vanzetti Evidence. Joseph B. Kadane & David A. Schum. LC 95-42458. (Probability & Statistics Ser.). 366p. 1996. 74.95 (*0-471-14182-8*) Wiley.

Probabilistic & Convex Modelling of Acoustically Excited Structures. Isaac Elishakoff et al. LC 94-41248. (Studies in Applied Mechanics: Vol. 39). (Illus.). 304p. 1994. 168.00 (*0-444-81624-0*) Elsevier.

Probabilistic & Stochastic Methods in Analysis, with Applications: Proceedings of the NATO Advanced Study Institute, Il Ciocco, Italy, July 14-27, 1991. Ed. by J. S. Byrnes et al. LC 92-11225. (NATO Advanced Study Institutes Series C, Mathematical & Physical Sciences: Vol. 372). 712p. (C). 1992. text 374.00 (*0-7923-1804-8*) Kluwer Academic.

Probabilistic Approaches to Natural Language: Papers from the 1992 Fall Symposium. Ed. by Robert Goldman. (Technical Reports). (Illus.). 142p. (Orig.). 1993. spiral bd. 25.00 (*0-929280-42-3*) AAAI Pr.

Probabilistic Aspects of Fatigue - STP 511. 203p. 1972. 19.75 (*0-8031-0103-1*, STP511) ASTM.

Probabilistic Basis for Design Criteria in Reinforced Concrete. (Reinforced Concrete Research Council Bulletin Ser.: vol. 22). 134p. 1985. 5.00 (*0-87262-487-0*) Am Soc Civil Eng.

***Probabilistic Behavior of Harmonic Functions** Rodrigo Badnuelos & Charles N. Moore. LC 99-32643. (Progress in Mathematics Ser.). 1999. write for info. (*0-8176-6062-3*) Birkhauser.

***Probabilistic Behavior of Harmonic Functions.** R. Banuelos & C. N. Moore. (Progress in Mathematics Ser.: Vol. 175). 224p. 1999. 75.00 (*3-7643-6062-3*, Pub. by Birkhauser) Spr-Verlag.

Probabilistic Causality. Ellery T. Eells. (Studies in Probability, Induction & Decision Theory). (Illus.). 427p. (C). 1991. text 85.00 (*0-521-39244-6*) Cambridge U Pr.

Probabilistic Causality in Longitudinal Studies. Mervi Eerola. LC 94-31763. (Lecture Notes in Statistics Ser.: 92). 1994. write for info. (*3-540-94367-6*) Spr-Verlag.

Probabilistic Causality in Longitudinal Studies. Mervi Eerola. LC 94-31763. (Lecture Notes in Statistics Ser.: Vol. 92). 1994. 39.95 (*0-387-94367-6*) Spr-Verlag.

Probabilistic Characterization of Soil Properties: Bridge Between Theory & Practice. Ed. by David S. Bowles & Hon-Yim Ko. 189p. 1984. 24.00 (*0-87262-398-X*) Am Soc Civil Eng.

Probabilistic Choice Models & Information, Vol. 24. Ronald W. Hilton. LC 85-72948. (Studies in Accounting Research). 194p. 1985. 15.00 (*0-86539-083-5*) Am Accounting.

Probabilistic Combinatorics & Its Applications. Bela Bollobas. LC 91-33123. (Proceedings of Symposia in Applied Mathematics Ser.). 196p. 1991. text 43.00 (*0-8218-5500-X*, PSAPM/44) Am Math.

Probabilistic Engineering Design: Principles & Applications. James N. Siddall. (Mechanical Engineering Ser.: Vol. 23). (Illus.). 544p. 1983. text 185.00 (*0-8247-7022-6*) Dekker.

Probabilistic Expert Systems. Glenn Shafer. LC 96-18757. (CBMS-NSF Regional Conference Series in Applied Mathematics: No. 67). viii, 80p. 1996. pap. 26.50 (*0-89871-373-0*, CB67) Soc Indus-Appl Math.

Probabilistic Fracture Mechanics & Fatigue Methods: Applications for Structural Design & Maintenance - STP 798. Ed. by J. M. Bloom & J. C. Ekvall. LC 82-83518. 215p. 1983. text 36.00 (*0-8031-0242-9*, STP798) ASTM.

Probabilistic Fracture Mechanics & Reliability. Ed. by James W. Provan. 1986. text 326.50 (*90-247-3334-0*) Kluwer Academic.

Probabilistic Management of Water Resource & Hydropower Systems. M. Basson et al. 1994. 65.00 (*0-918334-89-6*) WRP.

Probabilistic Mechanics & Structural & Geotechnical Reliability: Proceedings of the Sixth Specialty Conference Sponsored by the Engineering Mechanics, Structural, & Geotechnical Engineering Divisions, American Society of Civil Engineers, Denver, Colorado, July 8-10, 1992. Ed. by Y. K. Lin. LC 92-15903. 616p. 1992. pap. text 61.00 (*0-87262-873-6*) Am Soc Civil Eng.

Probabilistic Mechanics & Structural Reliability: Proceedings of a Conference Sponsored by the Engineering Mechanics, Geotechnical, & Structural Division. Ed. by Y. K. Wen. 458p. 1984. 44.00 (*0-87262-390-4*) Am Soc Civil Eng.

Probabilistic Mechanics & Structural Reliability: Proceedings of the Seventh Specialty Conference: Worcester Polytechnic Institute, Worcester, Massachusetts, USA, August 7-9, 1996. American Society of Civil Engineers Staff et al. Ed. by Dan M. Frangopol & Mircea D. Grigoriu. LC 96-22148. 1024p. 1996. 87.00 (*0-7844-0184-5*) American Society of Geolinguistics.

Probabilistic Method. Noga Alon & Joel H. Spencer. LC 91-13119. (Interscience Series in Discrete Mathematics). 272p. 1991. 99.95 (*0-471-53588-5*) Wiley.

***Probabilistic Method.** 2nd ed. Noga Alon & Joel H. Spencer. 320p. 2000. 84.95 (*0-471-37046-0*) Wiley.

Probabilistic Methods for Algorithmic Discrete Mathematics. Ed. by M. Habib et al. (Algorithms & Combinatorics Ser.: Vol. 16). 275p. 1998. 95.00 (*3-540-64622-1*) Spr-Verlag.

Probabilistic Methods for Structural Design. Ed. by C. Guedes Soares. LC 97-26094. (Solid Mechanics & Its Applications Ser.: No. 56). x412p. 1997. text 217.50 (*0-7923-4670-X*) Kluwer Academic.

Probabilistic Methods in Applied Physics. Ed. by Paul Kree & Walter Wedig. LC 95-37506. (Lecture Notes in Physics Ser.: Vol. 451). 450p. 1995. 101.95 (*3-540-60214-3*) Spr-Verlag.

Probabilistic Methods in Combinatorial Analysis. V. N. Sachov. (Encyclopedia of Mathematics & Its Applications Ser.: No. 56). 256p. (C). 1997. text 69.95 (*0-521-45512-X*) Cambridge U Pr.

Probabilistic Methods in Differential Equations: Proceedings of the Probabilistic Conference, University of Victoria, August 1974. Probabilistic Conference Staff. (Lecture Notes in Mathematics Ser.: Vol. 451). 190p. (Orig.). 1975. 23.95 (*0-387-07153-9*) Spr-Verlag.

Probabilistic Methods in Discrete Mathematics. Ed. by V. F. Kolchin et al. (Progress in Pure & Applied Discrete Mathematics Ser.: No. 1). 476p. 1994. 255.00 (*90-6764-158-8*, Pub. by VSP) Coronet Bks.

Probabilistic Methods in Discrete Mathematics. Ed. by V. F. Kolchin et al. (Illus.). 378p. 1997. 205.00 (*90-6764-245-2*, Pub. by VSP) Coronet Bks.

Probabilistic Methods in Geotechnical Engineering: Proceedings of the Conference on Probabilistic Methods in Geotechnical Engineering Canberra - Australia - 10-12 February, 1993. Ed. by K. S. Li & S. C. Lo. (Illus.). 342p. (C). 1993. text 136.00 (*90-5410-303-5*, Pub. by A A Balkema) Ashgate Pub Co.

Probabilistic Methods in Mathematical Physics: Proceedings of the International Workshop, Certosa Di Pontignano, Siena, Italy, 6-11 May 1991. Ed. by Francesco Guerra et al. LC 92-16407. 500p. 1992. text 121.00 (*981-02-0923-1*) World Scientific Pub.

Probabilistic Methods in Quantum Field Theory & Quantum Gravity. Ed. by P. H. Damgaard et al. (NATO ASI Ser.: Vol. 224). (Illus.). 384p. (C). 1990. text 150.00 (*0-306-43602-7*, Kluwer Plenum) Kluwer Academic.

Probabilistic Methods in Structural Engineering. G. Augusti et al. (Illus.). 636p. (gr. 13). 1984. mass mkt. 193.50 (*0-412-22230-2*, NO. 6823) Chapman & Hall.

Probabilistic Methods in Structural Engineering. Ed. by M. Shinozuka & James T. Yao. LC 81-69228. 415p. 1981. pap. 5.00 (*0-87262-286-X*) Am Soc Civil Eng.

Probabilistic Methods in the Mechanics of Solids & Structures. Ed. by Sigge Eggwertz & Niels Christian Lind. (International Union of Theoretical & Applied Mechanics Symposia Ser.). (Illus.). xxiv, 610p. 1985. 135.95 (*0-387-15087-0*) Spr-Verlag.

Probabilistic Methods in the Theory of Numbers. Jonas Kubilius. LC 63-21549. (Translations of Mathematical Monographs: Vol. 11). 182p. 1964. reprint ed. pap. 42.00 (*0-8218-1561-X*, MMONO/11) Am Math.

Probabilistic Methods in the Theory of Structures. unabridged ed. Isaac Elishakoff. LC 99-22871. (Illus.). 502p. 1999. pap. text 16.95 (*0-486-40691-1*) Dover.

Probabilistic Methods of Signal & System Analysis. 2nd ed. George R. Cooper & Clare D. McGillem. 408p. (C). 1986. student ed. write for info. (*0-03-070616-5*) SCP.

Probabilistic Methods of Signal & System Analysis. 3rd ed. George R. Cooper & Clare D. McGillem. (The Oxford Series in Electrical & Computer Engineering). (Illus.). 496p. 1998. text 84.00 (*0-19-512354-9*) OUP.

Probabilistic Modelling. 2nd ed. I. Mitrani. LC 97-26099. 233p. 1998. text 64.95 (*0-521-58511-2*); pap. text 24.95 (*0-521-58530-9*) Cambridge U Pr.

Probabilistic Models for Nonlinear Partial Differential Equations, Vol. 162. C. Graham et al. LC 96-26227. (Lecture Notes in Mathematics Ser.). 301p. 1996. pap. 59.00 (*3-540-61397-8*) Spr-Verlag.

Probabilistic Models for Some Intelligence & Attainment Tests. Georg Rasch. LC 80-16546. 208p. 1980. pap. text 9.00 (*0-226-70554-4*) U Ch Pr.

Probabilistic Models for Some Intelligence & Attainment Tests. expanded ed. Georg Rasch. LC 80-16546. (Illus.). 224p. reprint ed. pap. 69.50 (*0-608-09508-7*, 205430900005) Bks Demand.

Probabilistic Models for Some Intelligence & Attainment Tests. Georg Rasch. LC 80-16546. (Illus.). 222p. (C). 1993. reprint ed. pap. text 20.00 (*0-941938-05-0*) Mesa Pr.

Probabilistic Models in Engineering Science: Random Noise, Signals & Dynamic Systems. Harold J. Larson & Bruno O. Shubert. LC 89-2828. 750p. (C). 1989. reprint ed. lib. bdg. 82.50 (*0-89464-373-8*) Krieger.

***Probabilistic Networks & Expert Systems.** R. G. Cowell et al. Ed. by M. Jordan et al. LC 99-13242. (Statistics for Engineering Information Science Ser.). (Illus.). 368p. 1999. 69.95 (*0-387-98767-3*) Spr-Verlag.

Probabilistic Number Theory No. 1: Mean-Value Theorems. P. D. Elliot. (Grundlehren der Mathematischen Wissenschaften Ser.: Vol. 239). 1979. 139.95 (*0-387-90437-9*) Spr-Verlag.

Probabilistic Number Theory No. 2: Central Limit Theorems. P. D. Eliott. (Grundlehren der Mathematischen Wissenschaften Ser.: Vol. 240). 1980. 129.95 (*0-387-90438-7*) Spr-Verlag.

Probabilistic Offshore Mechanics. Ed. by P. D. Spanos. (Progress in Engineering Ser.). 120p. 1985. pap. 46.00 (*0-931215-03-X*) Computational Mech MA.

Probabilistic Performance Models of Language. Raoul N. Smith. 1973. pap. text 18.50 (*90-279-2414-7*) Mouton.

Probabilistic Problems of Discrete Mathematics. LC 88-36875. (Proceedings of the Steklov Institute of Mathematics Ser.: No. 177). 217p. 1989. pap. 113.00 (*0-8218-3123-2*, STEKLO/177) Am Math.

Probabilistic Reasoning in Intelligent Systems: Networks of Plausible Inference. Judea Pearl. (Representation & Reasoning Ser.). 552p. (C). 1991. pap. text 64.95 (*1-55860-479-0*) Morgan Kaufmann.

Probabilistic Reasoning in Intelligent Systems: Networks of Plausible Inference. Judea Pearl. (Representation & Reasoning Ser.). 552p. (C). 1998. text 59.95 (*0-934613-73-7*) Morgan Kaufmann.

Probabilistic Reliability: An Engineering Approach. 2nd ed. Martin L. Shooman. LC 85-14727. 722p. 1990. 79.50 (*0-89874-883-6*) Krieger.

Probabilistic Reliability Engineering. Boris V. Gnedenko et al. 517p. 1995. 120.00 (*0-471-30502-2*) Wiley.

Probabilistic Risk Assessment & Management for Engineers & Scientists. 2nd ed. Hiromitsu Kumamoto & Ernest J. Henley. LC 95-36502. 616p. 1995. 89.95 (*0-7803-1004-7*, PC3533) Inst Electrical.

Probabilistic Risk Assessment of Engineering Systems. Chapman & Hall Staff. text 97.50 (*0-412-80570-7*) Chapman & Hall.

Probabilistic Safety Assessment - Insag 6. IAEA Staff. (Safety Ser.: No. 75). 175p. 1992. pap. 15.00 (*92-0-102492-4*, STI/PUB/916, Pub. by IAEA) Bernan Associates.

Probabilistic Safety Assessment & Management, 4 vols. Ed. by A. Mosleh & R. A. Bari. LC 98-37885. lviii, 2934p. 1998. 375.00 incl. cd-rom (*3-540-76262-0*) Spr-Verlag.

Probabilistic Safety Assessment & Management '96: ESREL '96--PSAM-III, 3 vols. Pietro C. Cacciabue & Ioannis A. Papazoglou. LC 96-18476. 2352p. 1996. 269.50 (*3-540-76051-2*) Spr-Verlag.

***Probabilistic Safety Assessment in the Chemical & Nuclear Industries.** Ralph R. Fullwood. LC 99-37453. 544p. 1999. 75.00 (*0-7506-7208-0*) Buttrwrth-Heinemann.

Probabilistic Similarity Networks. David Heckerman. (ACM Doctoral Dissertation Award, 1990 Ser.). 264p. 1991. 37.00 (*0-262-08206-3*) MIT Pr.

Probabilistic Structural Dynamics: Advanced Theory & Applications. C. Q. Cai & Y. K. Lin. (C). 1994. pap. text, teacher ed. 20.31 (*0-07-038039-2*) McGraw.

Probabilistic Structural Mechanics: Advances in Structural Reliability Methods. Ed. by P. D. Spanos & J. Wu. LC 94-22914. (IUTAM Symposia Ser.). 1994. 202.95 (*0-387-57709-2*) Spr-Verlag.

Probabilistic Structural Mechanics Handbook. C. Sundararajan. LC 94-18578. 1994. 44.95 (*0-442-01213-6*, Osprey Bks) Chapman & Hall.

Probabilistic Structure Dynamics: Advanced Theory & Applications. rev. ed. Y. K. Lin & G. Q. Cai. LC 94-13102. 496p. (C). 1994. 77.81 (*0-07-038038-4*) McGraw.

An Asterisk (*) at the beginning of an entry indicates that the title is appearing for the first time.

Probabilistic Techniques in Analysis. Richard Bass. LC 94-34721. (Probability & its Applications Ser.). (Illus.). 350p. 1994. 67.95 (*0-387-94387-0*) Spr-Verlag.
Probabilistic Techniques in Exposure Assessment: A Handbook for Addressing Variability & Uncertainty in Models & Inputs. A. C. Cullen & C. Frey. LC 98-44311. (Illus.). 333p. (C). 1998. 99.50 (*0-306-45956-6*, Plenum Trade); pap. 49.00 (*0-306-45957-4*, Plenum Trade) Perseus Pubng.
Probabilistic Theory of Pattern Recognition. Luc Devroye et al. LC 95-44633. (Illus.). 672p. 1997. 69.95 (*0-387-94618-7*) Spr-Verlag.
Probabilistic Theory of Structural Dynamics. Y. K. Lin. LC 75-42154. 380p. 1976. reprint ed. 41.00 (*0-88275-377-0*) Krieger.
Probabilistic Voting Theory. Peter J. Coughlin. (Illus.). 266p. (C). 1992. text 69.95 (*0-521-36052-8*) Cambridge U Pr.
Probabilities. Hudson. 1991. 67.50 (*0-697-15537-4*) McGraw.
Probabilities. Joseph C. Hudson. (C). 1992. text 72.50 incl. 3.5 hd (*0-697-15536-6*, Irwn McGrw-H) McGrw-H Hghr Educ.
Probabilities. Michael Stein. LC 94-11558. 172p. 1995. 22.00 (*1-877946-57-5*) Permanent Pr.
Probabilities & Materials: Tests, Models & Applications - Proceedings of the NATO Advanced Research Workshop on PROBAMAT, Cachan, France, November 23-25, 1993. Ed. by D. Breysse. LC 94-16935. (NATO ASI Series E: Applied Sciences: Vol. 269). 552p. (C). 1994. text 332.00 (*0-7923-2876-0*) Kluwer Academic.
Probabilities & Statistics. H. P. Li. 300p. 1993. text 95.00 (*981-02-1650-5*) World Scientific Pub.
Probabilities in the Quantum World. Daniel Danin. 270p. (C). 1983. 50.00 (*0-7855-4976-5*, Pub. by Collets) St Mut.
Probabilities on the Heisenberg Group: Limit Theorems & Brownian Motion, Vol. 163. D. Neuenschwander. LC 96-26210. (Lecture Notes in Mathematics Ser.). 139p. 1996. pap. 29.00 (*3-540-61453-2*) Spr-Verlag.
Probability. write for info. (*0-7131-2787-2*, Pub. by E A) Routldge.
Probability. 1995. 16.50 (*0-340-61426-9*, Pub. by E A) Routldge.
Probability. Leo Brieman. LC 92-1381. (Classics in Applied Mathematics Ser.: No. 7). xiii, 421p. 1992. pap. 45.00 (*0-89871-296-3*) Soc Indus-Appl Math.
Probability. Alan F. Karr. (Texts in Statistics Ser.). (Illus.). 300p. 1993. text. write for info. (*3-540-94071-5*) Spr-Verlag.
Probability. Alan F. Karr. Ed. by S. Feinberg & Ingram Olkin. LC 93-28723. (Texts in Statistics Ser.). (Illus.). 300p. 1996. 60.95 (*0-387-94071-5*) Spr-Verlag.
Probability. Charles F. Linn. LC 79-171006. (Young Math Ser.). (Illus.). 40p. (J). (gr. 1-4). 1972. lib. bdg. 10.89 (*0-690-65602-5*) HarpC Child Bks.
Probability. Ron Marson & Peg Marson. (Task Cards Ser.: No. 8). (Illus.). 64p. 1995. teacher ed. 13.00 (*0-941008-78-9*) Tops Learning.
Probability. Jim Pitman. LC 92-39051. (Texts in Statistics Ser.). 596p. 1997. 58.95 (*0-387-97974-3*) Spr-Verlag.
Probability. Spode Group Staff. 1991. pap. 13.95 (*1-871315-29-8*) Ashgate Pub Co.
Probability. 2nd ed. Albert N. Shiriaev. Tr. by Ralph P. Boas. (Graduate Texts in Mathematics Ser.: Vol. 95). 621p. 1995. 68.95 (*0-387-94549-0*) Spr-Verlag.
Probability. 2nd ed. Turner. (C). 1998. pap. text 24.00 (*0-471-32008-0*) Wiley.
Probability: A Survey of the Mathematical Theory. 2nd ed. John W. Lamperti. LC 96-9559. (Wiley Probability & Mathematics Ser.). 189p. 1996. 79.95 (*0-471-15407-5*, Wiley-Interscience) Wiley.
Probability: An Introduction. Geoffrey Grimmett. (Illus.). 210p. 1986. 45.00 (*0-19-853272-5*) OUP.
Probability: An Introduction. Geoffrey Grimmett. (Illus.). 222p. 1986. pap. text 39.95 (*0-19-853264-4*) OUP.
Probability: An Introduction. Frank Hannah. 216p. (C). 1993. 25.00 (*1-886018-03-0*) Venture Pubng.
Probability: An Introduction. Samuel Goldberg. 322p. 1987. reprint ed. pap. text 10.95 (*0-486-65252-1*) Dover.
Probability: An Introduction with Statistical Applications. John J. Kinney. LC 96-15306. 528p. 1996. text 90.95 (*0-471-12210-6*) Wiley.
Probability: Graduate Texts in Mathematics, Vol. 95. A. N. Shiryayev, Jr. Tr. by Ralph P. Boas from RUS. (Soviet Mathematics Ser.). (Illus.). 500p. 1984. 59.00 (*0-387-90898-6*) Spr-Verlag.
Probability: Methods & Measurements. Anthony O'Hagan. 300p. 1988. text 65.00 (*0-412-29530-X*) Chapman & Hall.
Probability: Methods & Measurements. Anthony O'Hagan. 300p. (gr. 13). 1988. pap. text 49.95 (*0-412-29540-7*) Chapman & Hall.
Probability: Modeling Uncertainty. Donald R. Barr & Peter W. Zehna. (Illus.). 480p. 1983. pap. text, teacher ed. 2.00 (*0-201-10799-6*) Addison-Wesley.
Probability: Proceedings. Ed. by J. L. Doob. LC 77-2017. (Proceedings of Symposia in Pure Mathematics Ser.: Vol. 31). 169p. 1977. reprint ed. pap. 45.00 (*0-8218-1431-1*, PSPUM/31) Am Math.
Probability: The Mathematics of Uncertainty. Dorian Feldman & Martin Fox. (Probability Ser.: Vol. 9). (Illus.). 424p. 1991. text 195.00 (*0-8247-8452-9*) Dekker.
Probability: The Science of Uncertainty. Bean. (Mathematics Ser.). 2002. pap. 65.00 (*0-534-36603-1*) Brooks-Cole.
Probability: Theory & Example. Richard A. Durrett. LC 90-37802. 453p. (C). 1991. text 55.75 (*0-534-13206-5*) Wadsworth Pub.
Probability: Theory & Example. 2nd ed. Richard A. Durrett. LC 90-37802. (C). 1995. pap. 110.95 (*0-534-24318-5*) Wadsworth Pub.
Probability: Theory & Examples. 2nd ed. Durrett. 1995. 36.50 (*0-534-24319-3*) Brooks-Cole.
Probability Vol. 1: The Book That Proves There Is Life in Outer Space. Amir D. Aczel. LC 98-16868. 230p. 2000. pap. 12.00 (*0-15-601080-1*, Harvest Bks) Harcourt.
Probability Activities. Robert Lovell. 308p. (YA). (gr. 9-12). 1993. pap. 19.50 (*1-55953-067-7*) Key Curr Pr.
Probability & Algorithms. National Research Council Staff. 188p. (Orig.). (C). 1992. pap. text 26.00 (*0-309-04776-5*) Natl Acad Pr.
Probability & Analysis. Ed. by G. Letta & M. Pratelli. (Lecture Notes in Mathematics Ser.: Vol. 1206). viii, 283p. 1986. 48.95 (*0-387-16787-0*) Spr-Verlag.
Probability & Banach Spaces. Ed. by J. Bastero & M. San Miguel. (Lecture Notes in Mathematics Ser.: Vol. 1221). ix, 222p. 1986. 35.30 (*0-387-17186-X*) Spr-Verlag.
Probability & Bayesian Statistics. Ed. by Reinhard Viertl. LC 87-15298. (Illus.). 522p. 1987. 125.00 (*0-306-42570-X*, Plenum Trade) Perseus Pubng.
Probability & Causality. Ed. by James H. Fetzer. 371p. (C). 1987. pap. text 70.50 (*1-55608-052-2*, D Reidel); lib. bdg. 146.00 (*90-277-2607-8*, D Reidel) Kluwer Academic.
Probability & Conditionals: Belief Revision & Rational Decision. Ed. by Ellery T. Eells & Brian Skyrms. (Cambridge Studies in Probability, Induction & Decision Theory). 217p. (C). 1994. text 69.95 (*0-521-45359-3*) Cambridge U Pr.
Probability & Economics. Omar F. Hamouda & Robin Rowley. LC 95-46826. (Frontiers of Political Economy Ser.). (Illus.). 208p. (C). 1996. 75.00 (*0-415-06712-X*) Routledge.
Probability & Evidence. Alfred Jules Ayer. 1972. text 44.00 (*0-231-03650-7*) Col U Pr.
Probability & Evidence. Alfred Jules Ayer. 1979. pap. text 20.00 (*0-231-04767-3*) Col U Pr.
Probability & Inference in the Law of Evidence: The Uses & Limits of Bayesianism. Ed. by Peter Tillers & Eric D. Green. 356p. (C). 1988. lib. bdg. 173.50 (*90-277-2689-2*, Pub. by Kluwer Academic) Kluwer Academic.
Probability & Information. A. M. Yaglom & I. M. Yaglom. 1983. lib. bdg. 256.50 (*90-277-1522-X*) Kluwer Academic.
Probability & Information: An Integrated Approach. David Applebaum. (Illus.). 225p. (C). 1996. text 74.95 (*0-521-55507-8*); pap. text 26.95 (*0-521-55528-0*) Cambridge U Pr.
Probability & Information Theory: With Applications to Radar. Philip M. Woodward. LC 80-70175. (Illus.). 138p. reprint ed. pap. 42.80 (*0-608-17724-5*, 203013300067) Bks Demand.
Probability & Its Applications for Engineers. Ed. by David H. Evans. (Quality & Reliability Ser.: Vol. 35). (Illus.). 664p. 1992. text 125.00 (*0-8247-8656-4*) Dekker.
Probability & Logical Reasoning, Vol. 2661. Ed. by Janet Bruno. (Child-Centered Math Ser.: Vol. 11). (Illus.). 80p. 1997. pap. 4.98 (*1-57471-244-6*, 2661) Creat Teach Pr.
Probability & Measure. 3rd ed. Patrick Billingsley. LC 94-28500. (Series in Probability & Mathematical Statistics). 608p. 1995. 84.95 (*0-471-00710-2*) Wiley.
***Probability & Measure Theory.** 2nd ed. Robert B. Ash & Catherine A. Doleans-Dade. 560p. 1999. 59.95 (*0-12-065202-1*) Acad Pr.
Probability & Phase Transition: Proceedings of the NATO Advanced Study Institute on Probability Theory of Spatial Disorder & Phase Transition, Cambridge, U. K., July 4-16, 1993. NATO Advanced Study Institute on Probability Theory. Ed. by Geoffrey Grimmett. LC 94-669. (NATO Advanced Study Institutes Series C, Mathematical & Physical Sciences: Vol. 420). 340p. (C). 1994. text 183.00 (*0-7923-2720-9*) Kluwer Academic.
Probability & Physical Problems. American Mathematical Society Staff. LC 77-9609. (American Mathematical Society Ser.: Vol. 11). (Illus.). 401p. reprint ed. pap. 124.40 (*0-608-09198-7*, 205270200003) Bks Demand.
Probability & Physical Problems. D. I. Blohintsev et al. (Translations Ser.: Series 1, Vol. 11). 390p. 1962. reprint ed. pap. 35.00 (*0-8218-1611-X*, TRANS1/11) Am Math.
Probability & Random Processes. 2nd ed. Geoffrey Grimmett & David Stirzaker. (Illus.). 554p. (C). 1992. pap. text 62.95 (*0-19-853665-8*) OUP.
Probability & Random Processes. 2nd ed. Alberto Leon-Garcia. 128p. (C). 1993. pap. text 18.00 (*0-201-55738-X*) Addison-Wesley.
Probability & Random Processes: A First Course with Applications. 2nd ed. A. Bruce Clarke & Ralph L. Disney. LC 84-15312. (Probability & Mathematical Statistics Ser.). 336p. 1985. text 92.95 (*0-471-08535-9*) Wiley.
Probability & Random Processes: Problems & Solutions. Geoffrey Grimmett & David Stirzaker. (Illus.). 376p. (C). 1992. pap. text 52.95 (*0-19-853448-5*) OUP.
Probability & Random Processes for Electrical Engineering. Alberto Leon-Garcia. (Electrical & Computer Engineering Ser.). (Illus.). 488p. (C). 1989. text 62.50 (*0-201-12906-X*) Addison-Wesley.
Probability & Random Processes for Electrical Engineering. Yannis Viniotis. LC 97-37609. 704p. 1997. 95.94 (*0-07-067491-4*) McGraw.
Probability & Random Processes for Electrical Engineering. 2nd ed. Alberto Leon-Garcia. (Illus.). 606p. (C). 1993. 99.00 (*0-201-50037-X*) Addison-Wesley.
Probability & Random Processes for Electrical Engineering: Instructor's Solutions Manual. 2nd ed. Albert Leon-Garcia. 1994. teacher ed. 18.00 (*0-201-55739-8*) Addison-Wesley.
Probability & Random Processes Using MATLAB: With Applications to Discrete & Continuous Time Systems. Donald G. Childers. LC 96-35875. 448p. (C). 1996. text 61.00 (*0-256-13361-1*, Irwn Prfssnl) McGraw-Hill Prof.
Probability & Random Signals with Electrical Engineering Applications. Xiao-Rong Li. LC 99-25417. 1999. 69.95 (*0-8493-0433-4*) Chapman & Hall.
Probability & Random Variables: A Beginner's Guide. David Stirzaker. LC 98-29586. (Illus.). 384p. (C). 1999. text 74.95 (*0-521-64297-3*); pap. text 29.95 (*0-521-64445-3*) Cambridge U Pr.
Probability & Related Topics in Physical Sciences. Mark Kac. LC 59-10443. (Lectures in Applied Mathematics: Vol. 1A). 266p. 1972. reprint ed. pap. 44.00 (*0-8218-0047-7*, LAM/1.1) Am Math.
Probability & Statistical Decision Theory. Ed. by F. Konecny et al. 1986. text 176.50 (*90-277-2089-4*) Kluwer Academic.
Probability & Statistical Inference. Robert Bartoszynski & Magdalena Niewiadomska-Bugaj. LC 96-4105. (Series in Probability & Statistics). 848p. 1996. 84.95 (*0-471-31073-5*) Wiley.
***Probability & Statistical Inference.** Nitis Mukhopadhyay. LC 00-22901. (Statistics). 665p. 2000. 95.00 (*0-8247-0379-0*) Dekker.
Probability & Statistical Inference. Ed. by G. C. Pflug et al. 1982. text 171.00 (*90-277-1427-4*) Kluwer Academic.
Probability & Statistical Inference. 5th ed. Robert V. Hogg & Elliot A. Tanis. LC 96-31778. 640p. 1996. 101.33 (*0-13-254608-6*) P-H.
***Probability & Statistical Inference.** 6th ed. Robert V. Hogg & Elliot A. Tanis. 750p. 2000. 96.00 (*0-13-027294-9*) P-H.
Probability & Statistical Inference Vol. 1: Probability. 2nd ed. J. G. Kalbfleisch. (Texts in Statistics Ser.). (Illus.). xiii, 343p. 1995. reprint ed. 54.95 (*0-387-96144-5*) Spr-Verlag.
Probability & Statistical Inference Vol. 2: Statistical Inference. 2nd ed. J. G. Kalbfleisch. (Texts in Statistics Ser.). (Illus.). xiii, 360p. 1985. reprint ed. 58.95 (*0-387-96183-6*) Spr-Verlag.
Probability & Statistical Inference in Ancient & Medieval Jewish Literature. Nachum L. Rabinovitch. LC 79-187394. 219p. reprint ed. pap. 67.90 (*0-608-30884-6*, 201434900091) Bks Demand.
Probability & Statistics. G. Blom. (Texts in Statistics Ser.). (Illus.). 375p. 1989. 84.95 (*0-387-96852-0*) Spr-Verlag.
Probability & Statistics. Morris H. Degroot. LC 74-19691. (Behavioral Science Quantitative Methods Ser). (Illus.). 624p. (C). 1975. text 31.25 (*0-201-01503-X*) Addison-Wesley.
Probability & Statistics. Kevin J. Hastings. Ed. by Karen Guardino. LC 96-11393. 768p. (C). 1996. 87.00 (*0-201-59278-9*) Addison-Wesley.
Probability & Statistics. Johnson. (MA - Academic Math Ser.). 1988. mass mkt. 42.95 (*0-538-60015-2*) S-W Pub.
Probability & Statistics. Johnson. (MA - Academic Math Ser.). 1988. mass mkt. 14.95 (*0-538-60016-0*) S-W Pub.
Probability & Statistics. Athanasios Papoulis. 512p. 1989. boxed set 46.00 (*0-685-27164-1*) P-H.
Probability & Statistics. Athanasios Papoulis. (C). 1989. text 54.00 (*0-13-711698-5*) P-H.
Probability & Statistics. Ronald J. Rothenberg. Ed. by Emily Thompson. (College Outline Ser.). (Illus.). 391p. (C). 1992. pap. text 14.50 (*0-15-601676-1*) Harcourt Coll Pubs.
Probability & Statistics. Murray R. Spiegel. 384p. (C). 1997. pap. 14.95 (*0-07-060220-4*) McGraw.
Probability & Statistics. 2nd ed. Carnegie-Mellon University Staff & Morris H. DeGroot. LC 84-6269. 678p. (C). 1986. 110.00 (*0-201-11366-X*); pap. text, teacher ed. 7.25 (*0-201-11367-8*) Addison-Wesley.
***Probability & Statistics.** 2nd ed. Murray R. Spiegel. LC 99-57177. (Schaum's Outlines Ser.). 408p. 2000. pap. 15.95 (*0-07-135004-7*) McGraw.
Probability & Statistics. 3rd ed. Berger. 1997. 22.00 (*0-07-303744-3*) McGraw.
Probability & Statistics. 4th ed. Devore. 1995. 41.50 (*0-534-24266-9*) Thomson Learn.
Probability & Statistics: A Self-Instructional Problem Workbook. Francis B. Taylor. (Illus.). 186p. (Orig.). 1994. pap. text, wbk. ed. 60.00 (*1-882767-13-6*) ETS.
Probability & Statistics: Special Program at the Nankai Institute of Mathematics. Z. P. Jiang et al. (Nankai Series in Pure, Applied Mathematics & Theoretical Physics). 300p. 1992. text 98.00 (*981-02-0888-X*) World Scientific Pub.
Probability & Statistics Exam File. Ed. by Thomas L. Ward. LC 84-24707. (Exam File Ser.). 346p. (C). 1985. pap. 19.50 (*0-910554-45-5*) Engineering.
***Probability & Statistics, Explorations with Maple.** Zaven A. Karian & Elliot A. Tanis. LC 99-234200. (Illus.). 1999. pap. text 22.00 (*0-13-021536-8*) P-H.
Probability & Statistics F/eng & The Sci. 2nd ed. Jay L. Devore. LC 86-20731. (Statistics). 672p. (C). 1987. pap. 48.00 (*0-534-06828-6*) Brooks-Cole.
Probability & Statistics F/eng & The Sci. 3rd ed. Jay L. Devore. (Statistics). 704p. (C). 1990. pap. 59.25 (*0-534-14352-0*) Wadsworth Pub.
Probability & Statistics For Engineers. 2nd ed. Richard L. Scheaffer & James T. McClave. (Statistics Ser.). (C). 1986. pap. 38.25 (*0-534-06486-8*, 27R7000) PWS Pubs.
Probability & Statistics For Engineers. 3rd ed. Richard L. Scheaffer & James T. McClave. (Statistics). 656p. (C). 1990. pap. 57.00 (*0-534-92184-1*) Wadsworth Pub.
Probability & Statistics for Engineering & Science. Jay L. Devore. (Statistics). 1982. 7.50 (*0-534-01985-4*) Brooks-Cole.
Probability & Statistics for Engineering & Science. Hayter. (Mathematics Ser.). 1996. pap., student ed. write for info. (*0-534-95611-4*) PWS Pubs.
Probability & Statistics for Engineering & Science. Anthony J. Hayter. (Mathematics Ser.). 1996. 101.95 (*0-534-95610-6*) PWS Pubs.
***Probability & Statistics for Engineering & Science.** 5th ed. Jay L. Devore. 2000. pap., student ed. 20.00 (*0-534-37283-X*) Brooks-Cole.
Probability & Statistics for Engineering & the Physical Sciences. Jay L. Devore. LC 81-21744. (Statistics Ser.). (Illus.). 700p. (C). 1982. pap. 36.25 (*0-8185-0514-1*) Brooks-Cole.
Probability & Statistics for Engineering & the Sciences. 4th ed. Jay L. Devore. 743p. 1994. text, mass mkt. 82.95 incl. 3.5 hd (*0-534-24264-2*) Wadsworth Pub.
Probability & Statistics for Engineers. Kennedy. (C). 2001. text. write for info. (*0-06-500061-7*) Addson-Wesley Educ.
Probability & Statistics for Engineers. 4th ed. Schaeffer & James T. McClave. (Statistics Ser.). 1994. pap., student ed. 19.95 (*0-534-20965-3*) Wadsworth Pub.
Probability & Statistics for Engineers. 4th ed. Richard L. Scheaffer & James T. McClave. LC 93-43597. 745p. 1994. pap. 110.95 (*0-534-20964-5*) Wadsworth Pub.
Probability & Statistics for Engineers. 5th ed. Irwin Miller et al. LC 93-24611. 640p. 1993. text 96.00 (*0-13-721408-1*) P-H.
Probability & Statistics for Engineers & Scientists. 4th ed. Jay L. Devore. (Statistics Ser.). 1995. pap. 22.95 (*0-534-24265-0*) Wadsworth Pub.
Probability & Statistics for Engineers & Scientists. 6th ed. Ronald Walpole. LC 97-43762. 665p. 1997. 101.33 (*0-13-840208-6*) P-H.
Probability & Statistics for Modern Engineering. 2nd ed. Lawrence L. Lapin. (Illus.). 810p. (C). 1998. reprint ed. text 69.95 (*0-88133-996-2*) Waveland Pr.
Probability & Statistics for Petroleum Resource Assessment. Robert A. Crovelli. (Illus.). 143p. (C). 1999. reprint ed. pap. text 30.00 (*0-7881-7794-X*) DIANE Pub.
Probability & Statistics for the Sciences with Computer Applications. Archie W. Earl, Sr. (Probability & Statistics Ser.). 500p. (C). 1994. pap. text 47.95 (*1-884169-15-5*) Intl Educ Improve.
Probability & Statistics for the Sciences with Computer Applications. Archie W. Earl, Sr. (Probability & Statistics Ser.). 500p. (C). 1994. lib. bdg. 62.95 (*1-884169-14-7*) Intl Educ Improve.
Probability & Statistics in Engineering & Management Science. 3rd ed. William W. Hines & Douglas C. Montgomery. 752p. 1990. text 105.95 (*0-471-60090-3*) Wiley.
Probability & Statistics in Experimental Physics. Byron P. Roe. LC 92-12653. (Illus.). 224p. 1992. write for info. (*3-540-97849-6*) Spr-Verlag.
Probability & Statistics in Experimental Physics. Byron P. Roe. LC 92-12653. (Illus.). 224p. 1997. 39.95 (*0-387-97849-6*) Spr-Verlag.
Probability & Statistics in Hydrology. Vujica Yevjevich. LC 74-168494. 310p. 1972. reprint ed. pap. 35.00 (*0-918334-00-4*, PSH) WRP.
Probability & Statistics in Psychological Research & Theory. Donald W. Stilson. LC 66-11141. (Holden-Day Series in Psychology). 519p. reprint ed. pap. 160.90 (*0-608-30618-5*, 201629500003) Bks Demand.
Probability & Statistics I. D. Dacunha-Castelle & M. Duflo. Tr. by D. McHale from FRE. (Illus.). vi, 362p. 1985. 72.95 (*0-387-96067-8*) Spr-Verlag.
Probability & Statistics II. D. Dacunha-Castelle & M. Duflo. Tr. by D. McHale from FRE. (Illus.). 400p. 1986. 71.95 (*0-387-96213-1*) Spr-Verlag.
Probability & Stats F/modern Engineers. Lapin. (Statistics). 1983. 38.25 (*0-534-01460-7*) Brooks-Cole.
Probability & Stochastic Processes. Frederick Solomon. (Illus.). 400p. (C). 1987. text 66.00 (*0-13-711961-5*) P-H.
***Probability & Stochastic Processes: A Friendly Introduction for Electrical & Computer Engineers.** Roy D. Yates & David J. Goodman. LC 98-24820. 480p. 1998. text 99.95 (*0-471-17837-3*) Wiley.
Probability & the Art of Judgment. Richard C. Jeffrey. (Studies in Probability, Induction & Decision Theory). 256p. (C). 1992. text 80.00 (*0-521-39459-7*); pap. text 22.95 (*0-521-39770-7*) Cambridge U Pr.
Probability & the Logic of Rational Belief. Henry E. Kyburg. LC 61-11615. 356p. reprint ed. pap. 110.40 (*0-608-30827-7*, 200543700054) Bks Demand.
Probability & the Measure of Achievement. George S. Ingebo. 150p. (C). 1997. pap. write for info. (*0-941938-09-3*) Mesa Pr.
Probability & Theistic Explanation. Robert Prevost. (Oxford Theological Monographs). 202p. 1990. text 75.00 (*0-19-826735-5*) OUP.
***Probability Applications in Mechanical Design.** Franklin E. Fisher & Joy R. Fisher. LC 00-37686. 2000. write for info. (*0-8247-0260-3*) Dekker.
Probability Approach to Simultaneous Equations. Ed. by Omar F. Hamouda & J. C. Rowley. (Foundations of Probability, Econometrics & Economic Games Ser.: Vol. 7). 488p. 1997. 160.00 (*1-85898-439-4*) E Elgar.
Probability Approximations Via the Poison Clumping Heuristic. D. J. Aldous. (Applied Mathematical Sciences Ser.: Vol. 77). (Illus.). xv, 269p. 1988. 69.95 (*0-387-96899-7*) Spr-Verlag.
Probability Based on Radon Measures. Tue Tjur. LC 80-40503. (Wiley Series in Probability & Mathematical Statistics). 244p. reprint ed. pap. 75.70 (*0-608-15873-9*, 203075100070) Bks Demand.
Probability Broach. L. Neil Smith. 1996. mass mkt. 6.99 (*0-8125-3875-7*, Pub. by Tor Bks) St Martin.
Probability Concepts, Dialogue & Beliefs. Ed. by Omar F. Hamouda & J. C. Rowley. (Foundations of Probability, Econometrics & Economic Games Ser.: Vol. 4). 576p. 1997. 190.00 (*1-85898-436-X*) E Elgar.

P

An Asterisk (*) at the beginning of an entry indicates that the title is appearing for the first time.

Probability Concepts in Electric Power Systems. George J. Anders. LC 89-8932. 682p. 1990. 198.50 (*0-471-50229-4*) Wiley.

Probability Concepts in Engineering Planning & Design, Vol. 1. Alfredo H. Ang & Wilson H. Tang. LC 75-5892. 424p. 1975. text 99.95 (*0-471-03200-X*) Wiley.

Probability Contributions to Statistical Mechanics. Ed. by R. L. Dobrushin. LC 91-640741. (Advances in Soviet Mathematics Ser.: Vol. 20). 289p. 1994. 100.00 (*0-8218-4120-3*, ADVSOV/20C) Am Math.

Probability Distributions in Quantum Statistical Mechanics. M. A. Kon. (Lecture Notes in Mathematics Ser.: Vol. 1148). v, 120p. 1985. 29.95 (*0-387-15690-9*) Spr-Verlag.

Probability Distributions on Banach Spaces. N. N. Vakhania et al. (C). 1987. text 272.50 (*90-277-2496-2*) Kluwer Academic.

Probability, Dynamics & Causality Essays in Honour of Richard C. Jeffrey. LC 97-165191. 1997. text 90.50 (*0-7923-4361-1*) Kluwer Academic.

***Probability, Econometrics & Truth: The Methodology of Econometrics.** Hugo Keuzenkamp. 336p. 2000. write for info. (*0-521-55359-8*) Cambridge U Pr.

***Probability Essentials.** J. Jacod & P. Protter. LC 99-54504. (Universitext Ser.). viii, 220p. 2000. pap. 36.00 (*3-540-66419-X*) Spr-Verlag.

Probability for Applications. Paul E. Pfeiffer. (Texts in Statistics Ser.). (Illus.). 695p. 1989. 89.95 (*0-387-97138-6*) Spr-Verlag.

Probability for Grades 1-2. Bonnie Tank. (Math by All Means Ser.). (Illus.). 208p. 1996. pap. text 23.95 (*0-941355-15-2*) Math Solns Pubns.

Probability for Risk Management. Matthew J. Hassett & Donald A. Stewart. LC 99-12563. (Illus.). 366p. (C). 1999. pap. text 60.00 (*1-56698-347-9*) Actex Pubns.

***Probability for Statisticians.** Galen R. Shorack. LC 99-53670. (Texts in Statistics Ser.). (Illus.). 616p. 2000. 79.95 (*0-387-98953-6*) Spr-Verlag.

***Probability Games.** Ivan Moscovich. (MindGames Ser.). (Illus.). 24p. 2000. 5.95 (*0-7611-2017-3*) Workman Pub.

Probability, Grades 3-4. Marilyn Burns. (Math by All Means Ser.). 254p. 1995. pap. text. write for info. (*0-941355-12-8*) Math Solns Pubns.

Probability in Banach Spaces, No. 6. Ed. by U. Haagerup et al. (Progress in Probability Ser.: No. 20). 292p. 1990. 69.00 (*0-8176-3494-0*) Birkhauser.

Probability in Banach Spaces, No. 7. Ernst Eberlein et al. Ed. by James Kuelbs & M. Marcus. (Progress in Probability Ser.: No. 21). 300p. 1990. 69.00 (*0-8176-3475-4*) Birkhauser.

Probability in Banach Spaces: Isoperimetry & Processes. M. Ledoux & M. Talagrand. (Ergebnisse der Mathematik und Ihrer Grenzgebiete Ser.: Vol. 23). (Illus.). 490p. 1991. 171.95 (*0-387-52013-9*) Spr-Verlag.

Probability in Banach Spaces IX. Jurgen Hoffman-Jurgensen et al. LC 94-20469. (Progress in Probability Ser.: Vol. 35). vii, 431p. 1994. 98.00 (*0-8176-3744-3*) Birkhauser.

Probability in Banach Spaces V. Ed. by A. Beck et al. (Lecture Notes in Mathematics Ser.: Vol. 1153). vi, 457p. 1985. 59.95 (*0-387-15704-2*) Spr-Verlag.

Probability in Banach Spaces, VIII Vol. 30: Proceedings of the Eighth International Conference. Ed. by Richard M. Dudley et al. LC 92-17649. xi, 510p. 1992. 109.00 (*0-8176-3657-9*) Birkhauser.

Probability in Medicine. Edmond A. Murphy. LC 78-10611. 320p. 1979. text 47.50 (*0-8018-2135-5*) Johns Hopkins.

Probability in Social Science. Samuel Goldberg. (Mathematical Modelling & Applications Ser.: Vol. 1). 144p. 1983. 29.50 (*0-8176-3089-9*); pap. 14.25 (*0-8176-3128-3*) Birkhauser.

Probability in the Sciences. Ed. by Evandro Agazzi. 280p. (C). 1988. lib. bdg. 137.50 (*90-277-2808-9*, Pub. by Kluwer Academic) Kluwer Academic.

Probability Is All We Have: Uncertainties, Delays & Environmental Policy Making. James K. Hammitt. LC 90-47223. (Environment: Problems & Solutions Ser.). 305p. 1990. text 20.00 (*0-8240-0406-X*) Garland.

Probability Measures on Groups & Related Structures, No. XI. H. Heyer. 450p. 1995. text 129.00 (*981-02-2273-4*) World Scientific Pub.

Probability Measures on Groups IX. Ed. by H. Heyer. (Lecture Notes in Mathematics Ser.: Vol. 1379). viii, 437p. 1989. 56.95 (*0-387-51401-5*) Spr-Verlag.

Probability Measures on Groups VII: Proceedings of a Conference Held in Oberwolfach, 24-30 April 1983. Ed. by H. Heyer. (Lecture Notes in Mathematics Ser.: Vol. 1064). x, 588p. 1984. 67.95 (*0-387-13341-0*) Spr-Verlag.

Probability Measures on Groups VIII. Ed. by H. Heyer. (Lecture Notes in Mathematics Ser.: Vol. 1210). x, 386p. 1986. 48.90 (*0-387-16806-0*) Spr-Verlag.

Probability Measures on Groups X. H. Heyer. (Illus.). 512p. (C). 1992. text 145.00 (*0-306-44059-8*, Kluwer Plenum) Kluwer Academic.

Probability Measures on Locally Compact Groups. H. Heyer. (Ergebnisse der Mathematik und Ihrer Grenzgebiete Ser.: Vol. 94). 1977. 126.95 (*0-387-08332-4*) Spr-Verlag.

Probability Measures on Semigroups: Convolution Products, Random Walks & Random Matrices. G. Hognas & A. Mukherjea. LC 95-9418. (University Series in Mathematics). (Illus.). 400p. (C). 1995. text 107.00 (*0-306-44964-1*, Kluwer Plenum) Kluwer Academic.

***Probability Methods for Cost Uncertainty Analysis: A Systems Engineering Perspective.** Paul R. Garvey. LC 99-51460. 401p. 1999. write for info. (*0-8247-8966-0*) Dekker.

Probability, Middle Grades Mathematics Projects. Glenda Lappan. 1986. text 18.95 (*0-201-21478-4*) Addison-Wesley.

Probability Models & Statistical Methods in Genetics. Regina C. Elandt-Johnson. LC 75-140177. (Wiley Publications in Applied Statistics). 612p. reprint ed. pap. 189.80 (*0-608-13366-3*, 205576400037) Bks Demand.

Probability Models for Data. School Mathematics Project Staff. (Mathematics Series: Ages 16-19). 112p. (C). 1990. pap. text 11.95 (*0-521-40893-8*) Cambridge U Pr.

Probability Models for Lifetime Data. Marshall. 300p. (C). 1998. text. write for info. (*0-12-473940-7*) Acad Pr.

Probability Models in Mathematical Physics: Proceedings of the Conference on Probability Models in Mathematical Physics, Colorado Springs, May 16-24, 1990. Ed. by G. J. Morrow & W. S. Yang. 252p. 1991. text 104.00 (*981-02-0394-2*) World Scientific Pub.

***Probability Moon.** Nancy Kress. 2000. pap. 23.95 (*0-312-87583-5*) St Martin.

***Probability Moon.** Nancy Kress. LC 00-27117. 320p. 2000. 23.95 (*0-312-87406-5*, Pub. by Tor Bks) St Martin.

Probability, Number Theory & Statistical Physics. Kac. 1979. 65.00 (*0-262-11067-9*) MIT Pr.

Probability of Addiction: Legal, Medical & Social Implications. David A. Peters. LC 96-46207. 166p. 1997. 69.95 (*1-57292-053-X*); pap. 49.95 (*1-57292-052-1*) Austin & Winfield.

Probability of Fire-Stopping Precipitation Events. Don J. Latham & Richard C. Rothermel. 10p. 1997. reprint ed. 7.00 (*0-89904-604-5*, Bear Meadows Resrch Grp); reprint ed. pap. 2.00 (*0-89904-605-3*, Bear Meadows Resrch Grp) Crumb Elbow Pub.

Probability of Reaching the North Pole Discussed. Daines Barrington. 96p. 1987. 12.95 (*0-87770-424-4*) Ye Galleon.

Probability of Sea Level Rise. James G. Titus & Vijay K. Narayanan. 186p. (C). 1998. reprint ed. pap. text 35.00 (*0-7881-3313-6*) DIANE Pub.

***Probability on Algebraic Structures: AMS Special Session on Probability on Algebraic Structures, March 12-13, 1999, Gainesville, Florida.** AMS Special Session on Probability on Algebraic Structures Staff et al. LC 00-34992. (Contemporary Mathematics Ser.: Vol. 261). 238p. 2000. 59.00 (*0-8218-2027-3*) Am Math.

Probability on Banach Spaces. Ed. by James Kuelbs. LC 78-10268. (Advances in Probability & Related Topics Ser.: No. 4). 535p. 1978. reprint ed. pap. 165.90 (*0-608-01284-X*, 206203000001) Bks Demand.

***Probability 1: Why There Must Be Intelligent Life in the Universe.** Amir D. Aczel. LC 98-16868. 240p. 1998. 22.00 (*0-15-100376-9*) Harcourt.

Probability Path. S. Resnick. LC 98-21749. xii, 453 p. 1999. 64.50 (*0-8176-4055-X*) Birkhauser.

Probability Problem Solver. Research & Education Association Staff & Vance Berger. LC 98-68175. 1000p. 1999. 24.95 (*0-87891-839-6*) Res & Educ.

Probability, Random Processes, & Ergodic Properties. R. M. Gray. 295p. 1990. 59.00 (*0-387-96655-2*) Spr-Verlag.

Probability, Random Processes, & Estimation Theory for Engineers. 2nd ed. Henry Stark & John W. Woods. LC 93-48679. 576p. (C). 1994. pap. 99.00 (*0-13-728791-7*) P-H.

Probability, Random Variables, & Random Signal Principles. 3rd ed. Peyton Z. Peebles. 424p. (C). 1993. 87.81 (*0-07-049273-5*) McGraw.

***Probability, Random Variables & Random Signal Principles.** 4th ed. Peyton Z. Peebles. LC 00-34881. (Series in Electrical & Computer Engineering). 448p. 2000. 85.63 (*0-07-366007-8*) McGraw.

Probability, Random Variances & Stochastic Processes. 3rd ed. Athanasios Papoulis. 624p. (C). 1991. 96.88 (*0-07-048477-5*) McGraw.

Probability, Reliability & Safety Assessment International Meeting, Pittsburgh, PA, April 2-7, 2 vols. 1380p. 1989. 140.00 (*0-89448-142-8*, 700134) Am Nuclear Soc.

Probability, Statistical Optics, & Data Analysis. B. R. Frieden. (Information Sciences Ser.: Vol. 10). (Illus.). 404p. 1982. 69.95 (*0-387-11769-5*) Spr-Verlag.

Probability, Statistical Optics & Data Testing: A Problem Solving Approach, Vol. 10. 2nd ed. B. R. Frieden. (Information Sciences Ser.). (Illus.). xx, 443p. 1991. 64.95 (*0-387-53310-9*) Spr-Verlag.

Probability, Statistics & Data Uncertainties in Nuclear Science & Technology. Donald Smith. (Monograph Ser.). 250p. 1991. 28.00 (*0-89448-036-7*, 300025) Am Nuclear Soc.

Probability, Statistics, & Decisions for Civil Engineers. Jack Benjamin & C. A. Cornell. (C). 1960. text 85.00 (*0-07-004549-6*) McGraw.

Probability, Statistics & Decisions for Civil Engineers. 2nd ed. Jack Benjamin et al. 1990. text. write for info. (*0-07-004557-7*) McGraw.

Probability, Statistics & Queueing Theory: With Computer Science Applications. 3rd ed. Arnold O. Allen. 768p. 1997. write for info. (*0-12-051052-9*) Acad Pr.

Probability, Statistics, & Queueing Theory with Computer Science Applications. 2nd ed. Arnold O. Allen. (Computer Science & Scientific Computing Ser.). 740p. 1990. text 51.00 (*0-12-051051-0*) Acad Pr.

Probability, Statistics & Reliability for Engineers. Richard H. McCuen. LC 96-41741. 528p. 1997. boxed set 84.95 (*0-8493-2690-7*) CRC Pr.

Probability, Statistics & Truth. Richard Von Mises. Tr. by Hilda Geiringer from GER. xii, 244p. 1981. reprint ed. pap. 8.95 (*0-486-24214-5*) Dover.

Probability, Stochastic Processes & Queueing Theory: The Mathematics of Computer Performance Modelling. Randolph Nelson. LC 95-4041. (Illus.). 583p. 1995. 54.95 (*0-387-94452-4*) Spr-Verlag.

***Probability Supplement.** (C). 1998. pap. text 18.00 (*0-201-47224-4*) Addison-Wesley.

Probability Theory. A. M. Arthurs. (Library of Mathematics). 88p. 1973. ring bd. 29.95 (*0-7100-4359-7*, Chap & Hall CRC) CRC Pr.

Probability Theory. Heinz Bauer. Tr. by Robert B. Burckel from GER. (De Gruyter Studies in Mathematics: Vol. 23). (GER.). xv, 523p. (C). 1995. lib. bdg. 79.95 (*3-11-013935-9*) De Gruyter.

Probability Theory. A. A. Borovkov. 488p. 1999. text 81.00 (*90-5699-046-2*, ECU104, Harwood Acad Pubs) Gordon & Breach.

Probability Theory. Vladimir Rotar. 350p. 1997. text 64.00 (*981-02-2213-0*) World Scientific Pub.

Probability Theory. 2nd ed. Y. S. Chow & H. Teicher. (Texts in Statistics Ser.). 490p. 1993. 59.95 (*0-387-96695-1*) Spr-Verlag.

Probability Theory: A Concise Course. rev. ed. Y. A. Rozanov. Tr. by Richard A. Silverman from RUS. LC 77-78592. 148p. 1977. reprint ed. pap. text 7.95 (*0-486-63544-9*) Dover.

Probability Theory: An Advanced Course. V. S. Borkar. (Universitext Ser.). 160p. 1995. 36.95 (*0-387-94558-X*) Spr-Verlag.

Probability Theory: An Analytic View. Daniel W. Stroock. 528p. (C). 1994. text 57.95 (*0-521-43123-9*) Cambridge U Pr.

Probability Theory: An Introductory Course. Ya G. Sinai. Tr. by D. Haughton from RUS. (Illus.). viii, 138p. 1997. 39.95 (*0-387-53348-6*) Spr-Verlag.

Probability Theory: Basic Concepts, Limit Theorems, Random Processes. Y. V. Prohorov & J. A. Rozanov. Tr. by K. Krickeberg & H. Urmitzer. (Grundlehren der Mathematischen Wissenschaften Ser.: Vol. 157). (Illus.). 1969. 75.00 (*0-387-04508-2*) Spr-Verlag.

Probability Theory: Collection of Problems. A. I. Dorogovtsev et al. Tr. by O. I. Klesov & V. A. Kotov from ENG. LC 97-5939. (Translations of Mathematical Monographs: Vol. 163). 347p. 1997. text 119.00 (*0-8218-0372-7*, MMONO/163) Am Math.

Probability Theory: Independence, Interchangeability, Martingales. 3rd ed. Yuan S. Chow & Henry Teicher. Ed. by G. Casella et al. LC 97-9299. (Texts in Statistics Ser.). 520p. 1997. 69.95 (*0-387-98228-0*) Spr-Verlag.

Probability Theory: Proceedings of the 1989 Singapore Probability Conference Held at the National University of Singapore, June 8-16, 1989. Ed. by Louis H. Chen et al. LC 92-14169. xiv, 208p. (C). 1992. lib. bdg. 103.95 (*3-11-012233-2*) De Gruyter.

Probability Theory: Proceedings of the 7th Conference, Romania, 1982. Ed. by Marius Iosifescu et al. 676p. 1985. lib. bdg. 142.50 (*90-6764-040-9*, Pub. by VSP) Coronet Bks.

Probability Theory: Subject Indexes from Mathematical Reviews, 1980-84, 1973-79, 1940-58. LC 86-26462. (Probability of Statistics Cumulative Index Ser.: No. 40-84). 470p. 1987. pap. 82.00 (*0-8218-0108-2*, PROBIN/40/84) Am Math.

Probability Theory, an Analytic View. rev. ed. Daniel W. Stroock. 528p. (C). 2000. pap. 34.95 (*0-521-66349-0*) Cambridge U Pr.

Probability Theory & Applications. Ed. by Janos Galambos & Imre Katai. LC 92-25135. 368p. 1992. text 226.50 (*0-7923-1922-2*) Kluwer Academic.

Probability Theory & Applications. Elton P. Hsu & S.R. Varadhan. LC 98-51767. (Las/Park City Mathematics Ser.). 13p. 1999. write for info. (*0-8218-0590-8*) Am Math.

Probability Theory & Combinatorial Optimization. J. Michael Steele. LC 96-42685. (CBMS-NSF Regional Conference Series in Applied Mathematics: No. 69). (Illus.). viii, 159p. 1996. pap. 29.00 (*0-89871-380-3*, CB0069) Soc Indus-Appl Math.

Probability Theory & Its Applications in China. Ed. by Yang Chung-Chun et al. LC 91-16143. (Contemporary Mathematics Ser.: Vol. 118). 333p. 1991. pap. 48.00 (*0-8218-5126-8*, CONM/118) Am Math.

Probability Theory & Mathematical Statistics. Ed. by I. A. Ibragimov & A. Y. Zaitsev. 320p. 1996. text 136.00 (*2-919875-14-0*) Gordon & Breach.

Probability Theory & Mathematical Statistics. Ed. by S. Watanabe & Y. V. Prokhorov. (Lecture Notes in Mathematics Ser.: Vol. 1299). viii, 589p. 1988. 78.95 (*0-387-18814-2*) Spr-Verlag.

Probability Theory & Mathematical Statistics. 3rd ed. Marek Fisz. LC 80-12455. 704p. 1980. reprint ed. lib. bdg. 69.50 (*0-89874-179-3*) Krieger.

Probability Theory & Mathematical Statistics: Proceedings of the Japan-Russia Symposium, 7th. LC 96-218863. 528p. 1996. text 76.00 (*981-02-2426-5*) World Scientific Pub.

Probability Theory & Mathematical Statistics: Proceedings of the 4th Vilnius Conference, U. S. S. R., 1985, 2 Vols., Set. Ed. by Y. V. Prohorov et al. 1298p. 1986. lib. bdg. 255.00 (*90-6764-069-7*, Pub. by VSP) Coronet Bks.

Probability Theory & Mathematical Statistics: Proceedings of the 5th International Conference, Vilnius, Lithuania, 1989, 2 vols., Set. Ed. by B. Grigelionis et al. 1264p. 1991. 555.00 (*90-6764-130-8*, Pub. by VSP) Coronet Bks.

Probability Theory & Mathematical Statistics: Proceedings of the 6th USSR-Japan Symposium. A. N. Shiryayer et al. 456p. 1992. text 128.00 (*981-02-1113-9*) World Scientific Pub.

Probability Theory & Mathematical Statistics: Proceedings of the 6th Vilnius Conference, 1989. Ed. by B. Grigelionis et al. 752p. 1994. 340.00 (*90-6764-178-2*, Pub. by VSP) Coronet Bks.

***Probability Theory & Mathematical Statistics: Proceedings of the 7th Vilnius Conference & 22nd European Meeting of Statisticians Vilnius, Lithuania, 12-18 August 1998.** Ed. by B. Grigelionis et al. 752p. 1999. 350.00 (*90-6764-313-0*, Pub. by VSP) Coronet Bks.

Probability Theory & Mathematical Statistics with Applications. Ed. by W. Grossmann et al. (C). 1988. text 237.50 (*90-277-2547-0*) Kluwer Academic.

Probability Theory & Statistical Inference: Econometric Modelling with Observational Data. Aris Spanos. (Illus.). 656p. (C). 1998. text 105.00 (*0-521-41354-0*); pap. text 34.95 (*0-521-42408-9*) Cambridge U Pr.

Probability Theory for Engineers. V. P. Chistyakov et al. Ed. by A. V. Balakrishnan. LC 85-25939. (Translations Series in Mathematics & Engineering).Tr. of Teoriia veroiatnostei. 174p. 1987. text 30.00 (*0-911575-13-8*) Optimization Soft.

Probability Theory IV: Markov Processes. Y. V. Prokhorov & A. V. Skorohod. LC 92-27610. (Encyclopedia of Mathematical Sciences Ser.: Vol. 46). 1993. write for info. (*0-387-54688-X*) Spr-Verlag.

Probability Theory, Function Theory, Mechanics. LC 90-513. (Proceedings of the Steklov Institute of Mathematics Ser.: Vol. 182). 317p. 1990. pap. 167.00 (*0-8218-3132-1*, STEKLO/182) Am Math.

Probability Theory III. 1997. 99.95 (*0-387-54687-1*) Spr-Verlag.

Probability Theory, Mathematical Statistics, & Theoretical Cybernetics see Progress in Mathematics

Probability Theory, Mathematical Statistics & Theoretical Cybernetics see Progress in Mathematics

Probability Theory of Classical Euclidean Optimization Problems: Unification Via Two-Sided Additivity, Vol. 167. J. E. Yukich. LC 98-10342. (Lecture Notes in Mathematics: Vol. 1675). x, 152p. 1998. pap. 33.00 (*3-540-63666-8*) Spr-Verlag.

Probability Theory on Vector Spaces, Vol. 4. Ed. by Stamatis Cambanis & A. Weron. viii, 424p. 1989. 56.95 (*0-387-51548-8*) Spr-Verlag.

Probability Theory on Vector Spaces III, Vol. 1080. Ed. by D. Szynal & A. Weron. v, 373p. 1984. 49.95 (*0-387-13388-7*) Spr-Verlag.

Probability Theory I. 1994. 49.95 (*0-387-90210-4*) Spr-Verlag.

Probability Theory I. 4th ed. M. Loeve. LC 76-28332. (Graduate Texts in Mathematics Ser.: Vol. 45). 1977. 49.00 (*3-540-90210-4*) Spr-Verlag.

Probability Theory, Random Processes & Mathematical Statistics. Yu A. Rozanov. (Mathematics & Its Applications Ser.: Vol. 344). 268p. (C). 1995. text 161.50 (*0-7923-3764-6*) Kluwer Academic.

Probability Theory III: Stochastic Calculus. Ed. by Y. V. Prokhorov & A. N. Shiryaev. (Encyclopaedia of Mathematical Sciences Ser.: Vol. 45). 262p. 1998. 99.95 (*3-540-54687-1*) Spr-Verlag.

Probability Theory II. M. Loeve. (Graduate Texts in Mathematics Ser.: Vol. 46). 1994. 59.95 (*0-387-90262-7*) Spr-Verlag.

Probability Theory with Applications. M. M. Rao. (Probability & Mathematical Statistics Ser.). (C). 1984. text 74.00 (*0-12-580480-6*) Acad Pr.

Probability, Time & Space in Eighteenth-Century Literature. Ed. by Paula R. Backscheider. LC 78-20850. (Studies in the Eighteenth Century: No. 3). 1979. 39.50 (*0-404-16046-8*) AMS Pr.

Probability Towards 2000. Ed. by L. Accardi & C. C. Heyde. LC 97-48856. (Lecture Notes in Statistics Ser.: Vol. 128). 366p. 1998. pap. 44.95 (*0-387-98458-5*) Spr-Verlag.

Probability Tutoring Book: Intuitive Essentials to Engineers & Scientists & Everyone Else! Carol Ash. LC 92-53183. 480p. 1996. pap. 39.95 (*0-7803-1051-9*, PP2881) Inst Electrical.

Probability Via Expectation. 3rd ed. P. Whittle. Ed. by Stephen E. Fienberg & Ingram Olkin. (Texts in Statistics Ser.). (Illus.). 336p. (C). 1992. 98.95 (*0-387-97758-9*) Spr-Verlag.

Probability Via Expectation. 3rd ed. P. Whittle. Ed. by Stephen E. Fienberg & Ingram Olkin. (Texts in Statistics Ser.). (Illus.). 336p. (C). 1995. 42.95 (*0-387-97764-3*) Spr-Verlag.

***Probability via Expectation.** 4th ed. Peter Whittle. LC 99-53569. (Texts in Statistics Ser.). 376p. 2000. 69.95 (*0-387-98955-2*) Spr-Verlag.

Probability Winter School: Proceedings of the Winter School on Probability, 4th, Karpacz, Poland, Jan., 1975. Winter School on Probability Staff et al. (Lecture Notes in Mathematics Ser.: 472). 283p. 1975. 29.95 (*0-387-07190-3*) Spr-Verlag.

Probability with Martingales. David Williams. (Illus.). 272p. (C). 1991. pap. text 32.95 (*0-521-40605-6*) Cambridge U Pr.

Probability Without Equations: Concepts for Clinicians. Bert K. Holland. LC 97-18994. (Illus.). 112p. 1997. text 45.00 (*0-8018-5759-7*); pap. text 16.95 (*0-8018-5760-0*) Johns Hopkins.

Probable & Provable. L. Jonathon Cohen. (Modern Revivals in Philosophy Ser.). 380p. 1992. 63.95 (*0-7512-0011-5*, Pub. by Gregg Revivals) Ashgate Pub Co.

Probable Cause. Ridley Pearson. 1991. mass mkt. 6.99 (*0-312-92385-6*, St Martins Paperbacks) St Martin.

Probable Cause: Between the Police Officer & the Magistrate. Philip R. Tetu. LC 94-40197. 188p. (C). 1995. text 52.95 (*0-398-05941-1*); pap. text 33.95 (*0-398-05971-3*) C C Thomas.

Probable Cause: Crime Fiction in America. LeRoy L. Panek. LC 89-81987. 167p. (C). 1990. 34.95 (*0-87972-485-4*); pap. 16.95 (*0-87972-486-2*) Bowling Green Univ Popular Press.

Probable Italian Source of Shakespeare's Julius Caesar. Alexander Boecker. reprint ed. 29.50 (*0-404-00918-2*) AMS Pr.

***Probable Origin of the American Indians, with Particular Reference to That of the Caribs.** James Kennedy. (LC History-America-E). 62p. 1999. reprint ed. lib. bdg. 69.00 (*0-7812-4343-2*) Rprt Serv.

P

An Asterisk (*) at the beginning of an entry indicates that the title is appearing for the first time.

Probable Sons. Amy Le Freuvre. LC 96-46432. (Golden Inheritance Ser.). (J). 1996. pap. 5.90 (*0-921100-81-7*) Inhtce Pubns.

*__Probable State.__ Irene Tucker. 1999. lib. bdg. 42.00 (*0-226-81533-1*) U Ch Pr.

*__Probable State: The Novel, the Contract & the Jews.__ Irene Tucker. LC 00-24251. 1999. pap. text 16.00 (*0-226-81535-8*) U Ch Pr.

Probable Tomorrows: How Science & Technology Will Transform Our Lives in the Next Twenty Years. Marvin Cetron & Owen Davies. LC 96-54503. 352p. 1997. text 24.95 (*0-312-15429-1*) St Martin.

Probable Universe: An Owner's Guide to Quantum Physics. M. Y. Han. (Illus.). 160p. 1992. 21.95 (*0-8306-4191-2*, 4257); pap. 12.95 (*0-8306-4192-0*, 4257) McGraw-Hill Prof.

*__Probable World.__ Lawrence Raab. LC 99-55293. 96p. 2000. pap. 15.95 (*0-14-058921-X*) Penguin Putnam.

Probablity & Statistics for Engineers. 4th ed. Scheaffer & McClave. (Statistics Ser.). 1994. pap., student ed. 28.50 (*0-534-20966-1*) PWS Pubs.

Probably More Than You Want to Know about the Fishes of the Pacific Coast. 2nd rev. ed. Milton Love. LC 91-90108. (Illus.). 386p. 1996. pap. 19.95 (*0-9628725-5-5*) Really Big Pr.

*__Probably Pistachio.__ Stuart J. Murphy. LC 99-27695. (MathStart Ser.). (Illus.). 40p. (J). (gr. 1 up). 2000. lib. bdg. 15.89 (*0-06-028029-8*) HarpC Child Bks.

*__Probably Pistachio.__ Stuart J. Murphy. LC 99-27695. (MathStart Ser.). 40p. (J). (gr. 1 up). 2001. pap. 4.95 (*0-06-446734-1*, HarpTrophy) HarpC Child Bks.

*__Probably Pistachio.__ Stuart J. Murphy. LC 99-27695. (MathStart Ser.). (Illus.). 40p. (J). (gr. 1 up). 2001. 15.95 (*0-06-028028-X*) HarpC Child Bks.

Probably Still Nick Swansen. Virginia Euwer Wolff. LC 88-13175. 160p. (YA). (gr. 7 up). 1995. 14.95 (*0-8050-0701-6*, Bks Young Read) H Holt & Co.

Probably Still Nick Swansen. Virginia Euwer Wolff. (YA). 1997. pap. 4.50 (*0-590-43146-3*) Scholastic Inc.

Probably Still Nick Swansen. Virginia Euwer Wolff. (Point Signature Ser.). (J). 1990. 9.60 (*0-606-11767-9*, Pub. by Turtleback) Demco.

*__Probalistic Epigenesis & Evolution.__ Gilbert Gottlieb. (Heinz Werner Lectures: Vol. XXIII). (Illus.). 97p. 2000. pap. 9.00 (*0-914206-37-0*) Clark U Pr.

Probamat - 21st Century: Probabilities & Materials: Tests, Models & Applications for the 21st Century. Ed. by George N. Frantziskonis. LC 98-9331. (NATO ASI Series. High Technology). 615p. 1998. 283.00 (*0-7923-4977-6*) Kluwer Academic.

Probate - Wills. Pat J. Gregory. 89.00 (*0-685-52376-4*, B9) Sterling TX.

Probate Administration in Michigan: A Systems Approach. 3rd ed. Harold A. Draper. LC 84-82232. 654p. 1989. ring bd. 95.00 (*0-685-45473-8*, 89-015) U MI Law CLE.

Probate Administration in Michigan: A Systems Approach. 3rd ed. Harold A. Draper. LC 84-82232. 654p. 1991. suppl. ed. 49.00 (*0-685-45474-6*, 91-030) U MI Law CLE.

Probate Administration in Michigan: A Systems Approach. 3rd ed. Harold A. Draper. LC 84-82232. 654p. 1992. suppl. ed. 55.00 (*0-685-58670-7*, 92-022) U MI Law CLE.

Probate & Administration in Singapore & Malaysia - Law & Practice. Raman. 201p. 1991. boxed set 135.00 (*0-409-99602-5*, MICHIE) LEXIS Pub.

Probate & Administration of New York Estates. Ed. by Douglas H. Evans & Cheryl E. Hader. 978p. 1995. ring bd. 105.00 (*0-614-26721-8*, 4005) NYS Bar.

Probate & Family Court Speaks. Mary C. Fitzpatrick et al. LC 92-84111. 324p. 1993. pap. text 55.00 (*0-944490-49-2*) Mass CLE.

Probate & Family Court Speaks: 2001 Edition. rev. ed. write for info. (*1-57589-188-3*) Mass CLE.

Probate & Settling an Estate Step-by-Step. James J. Jurinski. LC 97-25801. (Legal-Ease Ser.). 240p. 1997. pap. text 14.95 (*0-7641-0167-6*) Barron.

Probate Confiscation: Unjust Laws Which Govern Woman. J. W. Stow. LC 74-3977. (Women in America Ser.). 276p. 1974. reprint ed. 35.95 (*0-405-06123-4*) Ayer.

Probate Court Benchbooks, 3 vols., 1. Michigan Judicial Institute Staff & Michigan Probate Judges, Blue-Ribbon Committee Sta. LC 90-84059. 1032p. 1990. pap. 65.00 (*0-685-39000-4*, 90-031) U MI Law CLE.

Probate Court Benchbooks, 3 vols., 2. Michigan Judicial Institute Staff & Michigan Probate Judges, Blue-Ribbon Committee Sta. LC 90-84059. 1032p. 1990. pap. 65.00 (*0-685-39001-2*, 90-032) U MI Law CLE.

Probate Court Benchbooks, 3 vols., 3. Michigan Judicial Institute Staff & Michigan Probate Judges, Blue-Ribbon Committee Sta. LC 90-84059. 1032p. 1990. pap. 65.00 (*0-685-39002-0*, 90-033) U MI Law CLE.

Probate Court Records, Cook County, Illinois, 1872-1873. Ed. by Diane K. McClure. 92p. 1992. pap. 12.00 (*1-881125-13-0*) Chi Geneal Soc.

Probate Courts in Maine. 49p. 1969. 1.50 (*0-318-14442-5*) IJA NYU.

Probate, Do-it-Yourself Kit. S. J. T. Enterprises, Inc. Staff. (Illus.). 14.95 (*1-880398-03-6*, 01013) SJT Enterprises.

Probate Forms: Ontario. rev. ed. David I. Botnick. (Legal Ser.). 96p. (C). 1995. 17.95 (*1-55180-103-5*) Self-Counsel Pr.

Probate Forms for Alberta: A Step-by-Step Guide to Probating an Estate - Canadian Edition. 5th ed. Cheryl Gottselig. (Legal Ser.). 88p. 1995. 16.95 (*1-55180-044-6*) Self-Counsel Pr.

Probate Guide for Alberta: A Step-by-Step Guide to Probating an Estate. 6th ed. Cheryl Gottselig. (Legal Ser.). 128p. 1995. pap. 14.95 (*1-55180-042-X*) Self-Counsel Pr.

Probate in California. 2nd rev. ed. Milton B. Scott. LC 99-70361. 306p. 1999. pap. 34.95 (*0-9659483-1-5*) Pere Bruin.

Probate Index, Mason Co., Illinois. 53p. (Orig.). 1988. pap. text 5.00 (*1-877869-12-0*) Mason Cnty Hist Proj.

Probate Inventories of Lincoln Citizens, 1661-1714. Ed. by J. A. Johnston. (Lincoln Record Society Ser.: Vol. 80). (Illus.). 237p. 1991. 45.00 (*0-901503-53-3*) Boydell & Brewer.

Probate Jurisdictions - Where to Look for Wills. 4th ed. J. S. W. Gibson. LC 98-72247. 72p. 1998. pap. 8.50 (*0-8063-1572-5*) Genealog Pub.

Probate Law. Margaret C. Jasper. LC 97-29736. (Legal Almanac Ser.). 116p. 1997. text 22.50 (*0-379-11239-6*) Oceana.

Probate Law & Procedure. Charles A. DeGrandpre & Kathleen M. Robinson. (New Hampshire Practice Ser.: Vols. 10-12). 1130p. 1994. 210.00 (*0-88063-484-7*, MICHIE) LEXIS Pub.

Probate Law & Procedure Vol. 10, 11 & 12. 2nd ed. Charles A. DeGrandpre. 225.00 (*0-327-12471-7*) LEXIS Pub.

Probate Manual. 23rd ed. R. F. Yeldham & A. Plumb. (Waterlow Practitioner's Library). 400p. 1988. 75.00 (*0-08-033109-2*) Macmillan.

Probate Mental Health see Tennessee Code Annotated 1999 Supplement

Probate Practice & Procedure. A. K. Biggs & A. P. Rogers. 1981. 40.00 (*0-7855-7334-8*, Pub. by Fourmat Pub) St Mut.

Probate Practice & Procedure. A. K. Biggs & A. P. Rogers. 1988. 112.00 (*1-85190-040-3*, Pub. by Fourmat Pub) St Mut.

Probate Practice & Procedure. 4th ed. A. K. Biggs & A. P. Rogers. 348p. 1992. 105.00 (*1-85190-154-X*, Pub. by Tolley Pubng) St Mut.

Probate Practice & Procedure. 5th ed. A. K. Biggs & A. P. Rogers. (Lawyers Practice & Procedure Ser.). 365p. (C). 1994. 175.00 (*0-85459-891-X*, Pub. by Tolley Pubng) St Mut.

Probate Practice & Procedure. 6th ed. A. K. Biggs & A. P. Rogers. 1998. pap. write for info. (*1-86012-935-8*, Pub. by Tolley Pubng) St Mut.

Probate Procedure Notes. K. Donnelly. (Waterlow Practitioner's Library). 112p. 1988. pap. 21.95 (*0-08-036898-0*) Macmillan.

Probate; Property see Rhode Island General Laws, 1998 Cumulative Supplement

Probate Records of Lincoln County Maine. William D. Patterson. LC 90-64096. 448p. 1991. reprint ed. 39.50 (*0-929539-77-X*, 1177) Picton Pr.

*__Probate Records of Lincoln County, Maine, 1760-1800.__ William D. Patterson. 421p. 1999. pap. 36.50 (*0-8063-4934-4*) Clearfield Co.

Probate Records of Lincoln County, Maine, 1760-1800. Ed. by William D. Patterson. 421p. 1996. reprint ed. lib. bdg. 47.00 (*0-8328-5201-5*) Higginson Bk Co.

Probate Reform in New Jersey. Robert Diab. 205p. 1990. ring bd. 30.00 (*0-685-14667-7*) NJ Inst CLE.

Probate/Trusts & Fiduciaries see Burns Indiana Statutes Annotated 1999 Cumulative Supplement Set: Pocket Part

Probation: Politics, Policy & Practice. Timothy May. 176p. 1990. pap. 34.95 (*0-335-09377-9*) OpUniv Pr.

Probation: Working for Justice. David Ward & Malcolm Lacey. 250p. 1995. 75.00 (*1-871177-64-2*); pap. 32.00 (*1-871177-67-7*) Paul & Co Pubs.

Probation Across the World. Ed. by Robert Harris et al. 272p. (C). 1995. pap. 27.99 (*0-415-11517-5*, C0086) Routledge.

Probation & Criminal Justice: Essays in Honor of Herbert C. Parsons. Ed. by Sheldon Glueck. LC 74-3825. (Criminal Justice in America Ser.). 1974. reprint ed. 28.95 (*0-405-06145-5*) Ayer.

Probation & Parole. Salerno. (Criminal Justice Ser.). 2000. pap. text 42.00 (*0-534-55926-3*) Thomson Learn.

Probation & Parole. Seih. 2002. mass mkt. 42.00 (*0-534-53802-9*) Brooks-Cole.

Probation & Parole. 6th ed. Abadinsky. 1996. pap. text, teacher ed. write for info. (*0-13-253709-5*) Allyn.

*__Probation & Parole.__ 7th ed. Ed. by Prentice-Hall Staff. LC 99-19288. (Correctional Issues Ser.). (Illus.). 504p. (C). 1999. 71.00 (*0-13-021459-0*) P-H.

Probation & Parole. 7th ed. Ed. by Prentice-Hall Staff. (Correctional Issues Ser.). (C). 2000. text. write for info. (*0-13-022121-X*); text. write for info. (*0-13-022122-8*) P-H.

Probation & Parole: Theory & Practice. 4th ed. Howard Abadinsky. 448p. (C). 1990. boxed set. write for info. (*0-318-68288-5*) P-H.

Probation & Parole in America. Harry E. Allen et al. LC 85-10093. 336p. (C). 1985. 35.00 (*0-02-900440-3*) Free Pr.

Probation & Parole in the United States. Dean J. Champion. 496p. (C). 1990. text 51.80 (*0-675-20997-8*, Merrill Coll) P-H.

Probation & Social Adjustment. Jay Rumney & Joseph P. Murphy. LC 68-28593. 285p. 1968. reprint ed. lib. bdg. 75.00 (*0-8371-0208-1*, RUPS, Greenwood Pr) Greenwood.

Probation Assistant. Jack Rudman. (Career Examination Ser.: C-2577). 1994. pap. 27.95 (*0-8373-2577-3*) Nat Learn.

Probation Casework: The Convergence of Theory with Practice. Joan Luxenburg. (Illus.). 174p. (Orig.). (C). 1983. pap. text 21.00 (*0-8191-3271-3*) U Pr of Amer.

Probation Consultant. Jack Rudman. (Career Examination Ser.: C-980). 1994. pap. 29.95 (*0-8373-0980-8*) Nat Learn.

Probation Counselor. Jack Rudman. (Career Examination Ser.: C-1981). 1994. pap. 29.95 (*0-8373-1981-1*) Nat Learn.

Probation Director. Jack Rudman. (Career Examination Ser.: C-2266). 1994. reprint ed. pap. 39.95 (*0-8373-2266-9*) Nat Learn.

Probation Employment Officer. Jack Rudman. (Career Examination Ser.: C-1428). 1994. pap. 29.95 (*0-8373-1428-3*) Nat Learn.

*__Probation for Adult & Juvenile Offenders: Options for Improved Accountability.__ Marcus Nieto. 24p. 1998. pap. write for info. (*1-58703-093-4*, CRB-98-014) CA St Libry.

Probation in a Cold Climate: Assessing Suitability for Community Sentences & Putting Supervision into Effect for a Sceptical Audience. David Atkinson. LC 98-101707. (Illus.). 1997. write for info. (*0-901382-19-1*) Cambs Criminology.

Probation in Minnesota: A System in Crisis. (Illus.). 55p. (Orig.). (C). 1994. pap. text 30.00 (*0-7881-0642-2*) DIANE Pub.

Probation Investigator. Jack Rudman. (Career Examination Ser.: C-981). 1994. pap. 29.95 (*0-8373-0981-6*) Nat Learn.

Probation Officer. Jack Rudman. (Career Examination Ser.: C-619). 1994. pap. 27.95 (*0-8373-0619-1*) Nat Learn.

Probation Officer, Parole Officer. 5th ed. Hy Hammer. 192p. 1996. 15.95 (*0-02-861055-5*, Arc) IDG Bks.

Probation Officer Trainee. Jack Rudman. (Career Examination Ser.: C-1429). 1994. pap. 23.95 (*0-8373-1429-1*) Nat Learn.

Probation, Parole & Community Corrections. 3rd ed. Ed. by Robert Carter & Leslie Wilkins. LC 83-23283. 432p. (C). 1984. text 26.50 (*0-471-87461-2*) P-H.

Probation, Parole, & Community Corrections. 3rd ed. Dean J. Champion. LC 98-14535. 512p. (C). 1998. 79.67 (*0-13-693368-8*) P-H.

Probation Service & Information Technology. David Colombi. (CEDR Ser.). 225p. 1994. 72.95 (*1-85628-953-2*, Pub. by Avebry) Ashgate Pub Co.

Probation Supervisor. Jack Rudman. (Career Examination Ser.: C-2262). 1994. reprint ed. pap. 29.95 (*0-8373-2262-6*) Nat Learn.

Probation Supervisor I. Jack Rudman. (Career Examination Ser.: C-1828). 1994. pap. 29.95 (*0-8373-1828-9*) Nat Learn.

Probation Supervisor II. Jack Rudman. (Career Examination Ser.: C-1829). 1994. pap. 29.95 (*0-8373-1829-7*) Nat Learn.

Probation System - An Evaluation Study. S. P. Srivastava. 257p. (C). 1987. 150.00 (*81-85009-22-8*, Pub. by Print Hse) St Mut.

Probation, Temporary Release Schemes & Reconviction: Theory & Practice. Philip Whitehead et al. 91p. 1991. text 72.95 (*1-85628-207-4*, Pub. by Avebry) Ashgate Pub Co.

Probation Training Director. Jack Rudman. (Career Examination Ser.: C-3283). 1994. pap. 39.95 (*0-8373-3283-4*) Nat Learn.

Probative Pontificating in Ugaritic & Biblical Literature: Collected Essays of Marvin H. Pope. Ed. by Mark S. Smith. (Ugaritische-Biblisch Literatur Ser.: Vol. 10). xv, 406p. 1994. text 74.00 (*3-927120-15-4*, Pub. by UGARIT) Eisenbrauns.

Probative Value of Testimony in Private Law: General Report Presented at the XIVth International Congress of Comparative Law, 31 July-6 August 1994 (Athens) Ed. by Hossein Safai. LC 95-43274.Tr. of Valeur du Temoinage en Droit Civil: Rapport Generale Presente au XIVe Congres Internationale de Droit Compare, 31 Juillet-6 Aout 1994 (Athenes). (ENG & FRE.). 1995. 101.50 (*90-411-0861-0*) Kluwer Law Intl.

Probe. Carole Nelson Douglas. 384p. (Orig.). 1986. pap. 3.50 (*0-8125-3587-1*, Pub. by Tor Bks) St Martin.

Probe. Edward M. Lerner. 1991. mass mkt. 4.99 (*0-446-36081-3*) Warner Bks.

Probe. Margaret W. Bonanno. Ed. by Dave Stern. (Star Trek Ser.). 352p. 1993. reprint ed. mass mkt. 5.99 (*0-671-79065-X*) PB.

Probe: The Principles of Business Engineering: A Management Guide for High-Involvement Change. Daniel S. Appleton. (Illus.). 268p. (Orig.). pap. 34.95 (*0-9642954-0-7*) D Appleton.

Probe into the History of Ashura. Ibrahim Ayati.Tr. of Barasi Tarkh-i-Ashura. 234p. 1985. pap. 8.00 (*0-941724-41-7*) Islamic Seminary.

Probe into the History of Hadith. rev. ed. Murtaza Askari. Tr. by Islamic Seminary Staff & M. Fazal Haq from ARA. 181p. (C). reprint ed. pap. 7.00 (*0-941724-16-6*) Islamic Seminary.

Probe Microphone Measurements: Hearing Aid Selection & Assessment. H. Gustav Mueller et al. (Illus.). 256p. (C). 1992. pap. 65.00 (*1-879105-68-3*, 0323) Thomson Learn.

Probe Programming for CNC Machining & Turning Centers. Mike Lynch. (Illus.). 211p. 1995. pap. text. write for info. (*1-930861-11-7*) C N C Con.

Probes: A Prospectus on Processes & Resources of the Bering Sea Shelf Nineteen Seventy-Five to Nineteen Eighty-Five. write for info. (*0-914500-05-8*) U of AK Inst Marine.

Probes: Processes & Resources of the Bering Sea Shelf. Ed. by D. Hood. 300p. 1985. pap. 48.00 (*0-08-032630-7*, Pub. by PPL) Elsevier.

Probetes et Prophetes. Antonin Artaud & Louis de Gonzague-Frick. 1976. 9.95 (*0-686-53836-6*) Fr & Eur.

Probing America's Past: A Critical Examination of Major Myths & Misconceptions, 2 vols. Thomas A. Bailey. 1973. pap. text 13.50 (*0-685-42171-6*) HM Trade Div.

Probing Bioactive Mechanisms. Ed. by John H. Block et al. LC 89-17998. (Symposium Ser.: No. 413). (Illus.). 400p. 1989. text 65.00 (*0-8412-1702-5*, Pub. by Am Chemical) OUP.

Probing Deep Space. Terrance Dolan. Ed. by William H. Goetzmann. (World Explorers Ser.). (Illus.). 120p. (YA). (gr. 5 up). 1993. lib. bdg. 19.95 (*0-7910-1326-X*) Chelsea Hse.

Probing Lance. L. Martin. (Illus.). 64p. 12.95 (*0-317-65041-6*) Pleasure Trove.

*__Probing Luminous & Dark Matter.__ Ed. by Ashok Das & Thomas Ferbel. 250p. 2000. 76.00 (*981-02-4286-7*) World Scientific Pub.

Probing Our Problems. R. O. Covey. 176p. (Orig.). 1986. pap. 5.95 (*0-934942-59-5*, 3950) White Wing Pub.

*__Probing Photosynthesis: Mechanisms, Regulation & Adaptation.__ Mohammad Yunus et al. LC 99-54715. 2000. 129.00 (*0-7484-0821-5*) Taylor & Francis.

Probing Polymer Structures: Based on a Symposium Cosponsored by the Divisions of Polymer Chemistry & Analytical Chemistry at the 174th Meeting of the American Chemical Society, Chicago, IL, August 29-September 2, 1977. Ed. by Jack L. Koenig. LC 79-10008. (Advances in Chemistry Ser.: No. 174). (Illus.). 287p. 1979. reprint ed. pap. 89.00 (*0-608-06754-7*, 206695100009) Bks Demand.

Probing the Atmospheric Boundary Layer. Ed. by Donald H. Lenschou. (Illus.). 269p. 1986. 45.00 (*0-933876-63-7*) Am Meteorological.

*__Probing the Atom: Interactions of Coupled States, Fast Beams & Loose Electrons__ Mark P. Silverman. LC 99-31032. 2000. 29.95 (*0-691-00962-7*, Pub. by Princeton U Pr) Cal Prin Full Svc.

*__Probing the Depths of German Antisemitism: German Society & the Persecution of the Jews, 1933-1941.__ Ed. by David Bankier. LC 99-56222. 600p. 2000. 39.95 (*1-57181-238-5*) Berghahn Bks.

Probing the Limits of Representation: Nazism & the Final Solution. Ed. by Saul Friedlander. 416p. (C). 1992. 56.00 (*0-674-70765-6*); pap. 28.00 (*0-674-70766-4*) HUP.

Probing the Planets. Thomas-Cochran. (What a Wonderful World 2 Ser.). 1992. pap. text. write for info. (*0-582-90974-0*, Pub. by Addison-Wesley) Longman.

Probing the Proverbs. Darrel Rhodes. 276p. (Orig.). 1996. pap. write for info. (*1-57502-350-4*, PO1133) Morris Pubng.

*__Probing the Proverbs.__ Darrel A. Rhodes. 1998. pap. 10.95 (*0-9678509-0-8*) D A Rhodes.

*__Probing the Quantum Vacuum: Pertubative Effective Action Aproach in Quantum Electrodynamics & Its Applications.__ Walter Dittrich & Holger Gies. LC 00-30078. (Tracts in Modern Physics Ser.). (Illus.). 2000. write for info. (*3-540-67428-4*) Spr-Verlag.

Probing the Standard Model of Particle Interactions. Ed. by R. Gupta et al. LC 99-12055. 1716p. 1999. 388.50 (*0-444-50099-5*, North Holland) Elsevier.

Probing Understanding. Ed. by Richard White & Richard F. Gunstone. 204p. 1992. pap. 32.95 (*0-7507-0048-3*, Falmer Pr) Taylor & Francis.

Probiotics: A Critical Review. Ed. by Gerald W. Tannock. 1999. 119.99 (*1-898486-15-8*, Pub. by Horizon Sci) Intl Spec Bk.

Probiotics: Nature's Internal Healers. Natasha Trenev. LC 98-11979. 272p. pap. 12.95 (*0-89529-847-3*, Avery) Penguin Putnam.

Probiotics: The Scientific Basis. Ed. by Ray Fuller. (Illus.). 416p. (C). (gr. 13). Date not set. text 80.95 (*0-412-40850-3*, Chap & Hall NY) Chapman & Hall.

Probiotics, Other Nutritional Factors & Intestinal Microflora. Lars A. Hanson et al. LC 98-20817. (Nestle Nutrition Workshop Ser.). 1998. write for info. (*0-7817-1829-5*) Lppncott W & W.

Probiotics 2: Applications & Practical Aspects, Vol. 2. R. Fuller. LC 97-65572. 224p. 1997. write for info. (*0-412-73610-1*) Kluwer Academic.

*__Probiotics 3: Immunomodulation by the Gut Microflora & Probiotics.__ R. Fuller & G. Perdigon. 280p. 2000. 132.50 (*0-7923-6244-6*) Kluwer Academic.

Probity Jones & the Fear Not Angel. Walter Wangerin, Jr. (Illus.). 32p. (J). (gr. 1-4). 1996. 16.99 (*0-8066-2992-4*, 9-2992, Augsburg) Augsburg Fortress.

Probity Jones & the Fear Not Angel. Walter Wangerin, Jr. (Illus.). 32p. (J). (ps-3). 1997. pap. 17.99 incl. audio (*0-8066-3616-5*, 9-3616) Augsburg Fortress.

Proble: One Hundred Forty-Four Problems of the Austrian-Polish Mathematics Competition, 1978-1993. Compiled by Marcin E. Kuczma. 140p. (YA). (gr. 7-12). pap. 20.00 (*0-9640959-0-4*) Acad Distrib.

Problem: A Military Novel. F. Grant Gilmore. LC 78-76109. reprint ed. 19.95 (*0-8434-0011-0*) Ayer.

Problem Adolescents: An International View. Ed. by Stuart Harrigan & Roger Bullock. 144p. (Orig.). 1992. pap. text 19.95 (*1-871177-31-6*, Pub. by Whiting & Birch) Paul & Co Pubs.

Problem Analysis: Responding to School Complexity. Charles M. Achilles et al. LC 97-18980. 160p. 1997. 29.95 (*1-883001-36-6*) Eye On Educ.

*__Problem & Failed Institutions in the Commercial Banking Industry.__ Joseph F. Sinkey. LC 99-47153. 1999. write for info. (*1-893122-37-9*) Beard Bks.

Problem at Piha. large type ed. Freda Bream. (Mystery Library). 288p. 1995. pap. 16.99 (*0-7089-7648-4*, Linford) Ulverscroft.

Problem-Based Learning: A Collection of Articles. Ed. by Robin Fogarty. LC 97-62451. 195p. 1998. pap. 24.95 (*1-57517-047-7*, 1529) SkyLght.

Problem Based Learning: An Inquiry Approach. Barrell. 168p. 1998. pap. text 30.95 (*0-205-29410-3*, Longwood Div) Allyn.

Problem-Based Learning: And Other Curriculum Models for the Multiple Intelligences Classroom. Robin Fogarty. LC 96-77876. (Illus.). xxii, 160 p. (Orig.). 1996. pap. 30.95 (*1-57517-067-1*, 1463) SkyLght.

P

Problem-Based Learning Applied to Medical Education. Howard S. Barrows. 35.00 (*0-931369-34-7*) Southern IL Univ Sch.

Problem-Based Learning for Administrators. Edwin M. Bridges. LC 92-71619. xi, 160p. (C). 1992. pap. 10.95 (*0-86552-117-4*) U of Oreg ERIC.

Problem-Based Learning in a Health Sciences Curriculum. Ed. by Christine Alavi. LC 94-35357. 224p. (C). 1995. 80.00 (*0-415-11207-9*, C0059); pap. 27.99 (*0-415-11208-7*, C0060) Routledge.

***Problem-Based Learning in Higher Education.** Maggi Savin-Baden. LC 99-41043. 2000. pap. 32.95 (*0-335-20337-X*) Taylor & Francis.

Problem Based Methodology: Research for the Improvement of Practice. Viviane Robinson. LC 92-36833. 290p. 1993. text 68.00 (*0-08-041925-9*, Pergamon Pr) Elsevier.

Problem Based Pediatrics. David J. Field. LC 97-19288. 1997. pap. text 21.95 (*0-443-05254-9*) Church.

Problem-Based Psychiatry. Ben Green. LC 95-40795. 1996. pap. text 19.95 (*0-443-05198-4*) Church.

***Problem Based Service Learning: A Fieldguide for Making a Difference in Higher Education.** Rick Gordon et al. 142p. 2000. pap. 25.00 (*1-881245-12-8*) Antioch New Eng.

Problem Behavior Management: Educator's Resource Service. 2nd ed. Robert Algozzine. LC 92-15097. ring bd. 154.00 (*0-8342-0333-2*, S53) Aspen Pub.

Problem Behavior with People with Severe Learning Disabilities. 2nd ed. J. Clements & Ewa Zarkowska. 256p. 1994. text 42.50 (*1-56593-122-X*, 0447) Singular Publishing.

Problem Behaviors in Long-Term Care: Recognition, Diagnosis, & Treatment. Ed. by Peggy A. Szwabo & George T. Grossberg. LC 92-2232. 320p. 1992. 39.95 (*0-8261-7820-0*) Springer Pub.

Problem Book for First Year Calculus. G. W. Bluman. (Problem Books in Mathematics). (Illus.). 350p. 1984. 69.95 (*0-387-90920-6*) Spr-Verlag.

Problem Book in Phonology: A Workbook for Introductory Courses in Linguistics & in Modern Phonology. Morris Halle & George N. Clements. 96p. (Orig.). (C). 1983. pap. text 15.50 (*0-262-58059-4*) MIT Pr.

Problem Book in the Theory of Functions, 2 vols. Incl. Vol. 1. Problems in the Elementary Theory of Functions. Tr. by Lipman Bers. 1948. pap. 5.95 (*0-486-60158-7*); Vol. 2. Problems in the Advanced Theory of Functions. 2nd ed. Konrad Knopp. 138p. 1952. pap. 5.95 (*0-486-60159-5*); (C). 1948. pap. write for info. (*0-318-51772-8*) Dover.

Problem Book Molecular & Cellular Biology. 2nd ed. Wolfe Mulnix. 2002. pap. 22.00 (*0-534-37531-6*) Thomson Learn.

Problem Buster's Guide. Mike Allison. 208p. 1996. pap. 26.95 (*0-566-07761-2*, Pub. by Gower) Ashgate Pub Co.

Problem Child in School. Mary B. Sayles. LC 72-2576. (Select Bibliographies Reprint Ser.). 1977. reprint ed. 20.95 (*0-8369-6863-8*) Ayer.

Problem der Integration Utilitaristischer Argumentation in die Theologische Ethik. Ekkehard Steinhauser. (Europaische Hochschulschriften Ser.: Reihe 23, Bd. 606). (GER.). 234p. 1997. 44.95 (*3-631-32085-X*) P Lang Pubng.

Problem der Parusieverzoegerung in den Synoptischen Evangelien und in der Apostelgeschichte. 3rd ed. Erich Graesser. (Beiheft zur Zeitschrift fuer die Alttestamentliche Wissenschaft Ser.). 1977. 96.95 (*3-11-007512-1*) De Gruyter.

Problem der "Reichseinheitsidee" Nach der Teilung von Verdun (843) Ursula Penndorf. (GER.). viii, 204p. 1974. 39.80 (*3-615-00154-0*, Pub. by Weidmann) Lubrecht & Cramer.

Problem der Theodicee in der Philosophie und Literatur des 18. Jahr-Hunderts bis auf Kant und Schiller. Otto Lempp. (GER.). vi, 432p. 1976. write for info. (*3-487-05879-0*) G Olms Pubs.

Problem Doctors: A Conspiracy of Silence. Ed. by P. Lens & G. Vander Wal. LC 96-77816. 300p. (gr. 12). 1997. 76.00 (*90-5199-287-4*, 287-4) IOS Press.

P

Problem Drinkers: A National Survey. Don Cahalan. LC 73-133617. (Jossey-Bass Behavioral Science Ser.). (Illus.). 220p. reprint ed. pap. 68.20 (*0-608-15165-3*, 205216300045) Bks Demand.

Problem Drinkers: Guided Self-Change Treatment. Mark B. Sobell & Linda C. Sobell. LC 92-48479. (Treatment Manuals for Practitioners Ser.). 187p. 1993. lib. bdg. 42.00 (*0-89862-212-3*) Guilford Pubns.

Problem Drinkers: Guided Self-Change Treatment. Mark B. Sobell & Linda C. Sobell. LC 92-48479. (Treatment Manuals for Practitioners Ser.). 187p. 1996. pap. text 21.00 (*1-57230-121-X*) Guilford Pubns.

Problem Drinkers Seeking Treatment. Eileen M. Corrigan. LC 73-620006. (Monographs: No. 8). 1974. 5.00 (*0-911290-39-7*) Rutgers Ctr Alcohol.

Problem Drinking. 2nd rev. ed. Nick H. Heather & Ian Robertson. (Illus.). 368p. 1990. pap. 14.95 (*0-19-261874-1*) OUP.

Problem Drinking. 3rd ed. Nick Heather & Ian Robinson. LC 97-8715. (Illus.). 238p. 1997. pap. text 39.50 (*0-19-262861-5*) OUP.

Problem Drinking: How to Help a Friend. Charles Downs. 128p. (Orig.). 1990. pap. 7.99 (*0-87788-662-8*, H Shaw Pubs) Waterbrook Pr.

Problem Drinking Among American Men. Don Cahalan & Robin Room. 1974. 25.95 (*0-8084-0380-X*) NCUP.

Problem Drinking Among American Men. Don Cahalan & Robin Room. LC 72-619570. (Monographs: No. 7). 1974. 8.25 (*0-911290-38-9*) Rutgers Ctr Alcohol.

Problem Drinking & Alcoholism. rev. ed. Mark Worden. 1999. pap. 0.50 (*0-89230-115-5*) Do It Now.

Problem Drinking Continuum. rev. ed. Mark Worden & Gay Worden. 1999. pap. 0.50 (*0-89230-119-8*) Do It Now.

Problem Employee Management: Proactive Strategies for Human Resource Managers. Willa M. Bruce. LC 89-24330. 224p. 1990. 57.95 (*0-89930-501-6*, BJE/, Quorum Bks) Greenwood.

Problem Employees & Their Personalities: A Guide to Behaviors, Dynamics, & Intervention Strategies for Personnel Specialists. William T. Martin. LC 89-3858. 198p. 1989. 57.95 (*0-89930-417-6*, MEY, Quorum Bks) Greenwood.

Problem Exercises for General Chemistry. 3rd ed. G. Gilbert Long & Forrest C. Hentz. 460p. 1986. pap. 39.95 (*0-471-82840-8*) Wiley.

Problem Finding & Problem Solving. Alfred W. Schoennauer. LC 81-9591. 208p. (C). 1981. text 37.95 (*0-88229-590-X*) Burnham Inc.

Problem-Finding Approach to Effective Corporate Planning. Robert J. Thierauf. LC 87-5971. 234p. 1987. 62.95 (*0-89930-262-9*, TPF/, Quorum Bks) Greenwood.

Problem Finding, Problem Solving, & Creativity. Ed. by Mark A. Runco. LC 94-1974. (Creativity Research Ser.). 320p. 1994. pap. 39.50 (*1-56750-013-7*); text 73.25 (*0-89391-975-6*) Ablx Pub.

Problem Foods. Walter Last. LC 86-18130. 1987. write for info. (*0-943920-54-X*) Metamorphous Pr.

Problem Frames & Methods. Michael Jackson. (C). 1998. pap. text. write for info. (*0-201-59627-X*) Addison-Wesley.

Problem-Generating Structures in Nigeria's Rural Development. Martin Igbozurike. 139p. 1976. write for info. (*91-7106-102-9*, Pub. by Nordic Africa) Transaction Pubs.

Problem Genese Husserl. Jacques Derrida. 300p. 2000. lib. bdg. 34.95 (*0-226-14315-5*) U Ch Pr.

Problem Gun Dogs: How to Identify & Correct Their Faults. Bill Tarrant. LC 92-936. (Illus.). 192p. 1992. 18.95 (*0-8117-1374-1*) Stackpole.

Problem Horse: An Owner's Guide. Karen Bush. (Illus.). 160p. 1996. pap. 29.95 (*1-85223-916-6*) Crolwood.

Problem Horses - Tested Guide for Curing Most Common & Serious Horse Behavior Habits. Reginald S. Summerhays. 1972. pap. 5.00 (*0-87980-200-6*) Wilshire.

Problem Identification: Statistical Process Control. rev. ed. James C. Campbell. (Skill Centered Leadership Ser.). (Illus.). 32p. 1997. pap., wbk. ed. 24.95 incl. audio (*1-891161-74-1*) ClamShell Pub.

Problem in Greek Ethics. John A. Symonds. LC 71-163126. (Studies in Philosophy: No. 40). 1971. lib. bdg. 75.00 (*0-8383-1253-5*) M S G Haskell Hse.

Problem in Modern Ethics. John A. Symonds. LC 73-173185. 1972. reprint ed. 13.95 (*0-405-09019-6*, Pub. by Blom Pubns) Ayer.

Problem in Punjab: A Plea for Introspection. Vivek S. Minocha. (C). 1989. pap. 2.50 (*81-202-0240-6*, Pub. by Ajanta) S Asia.

Problem Isn't Age: Work & Older Americans. Ed. by Steven H. Sandell. LC 86-30642. 278p. 1987. 65.00 (*0-275-92371-1*, C2371, Praeger Pubs) Greenwood.

***Problem Knee.** Macricol. 224p. 1998. pap. text 60.00 (*0-7506-4044-8*) Buttrwrth-Heinemann.

Problem Knee. 2nd ed. Malcolm F. Macnicol. LC 94-45158. (Illus.). 224p. 1995. 100.00 (*0-7506-0487-5*) Buttrwrth-Heinemann.

Problem Loan Problem-Solver: Step-by-Step Strategies for Resolving Bankruptcy, Lender Liability & Other Problem Loan Situations. rev. ed. Peter S. Clarke. 1994. text 55.00 (*1-55738-736-2*, Irwn Prfssnl) McGraw-Hill Prof.

Problem Loan Strategies. John E. McKinley, III et al. LC 84-27222. (Illus.). 168p. (Orig.). 1985. pap. text 53.00 (*0-936742-20-8*) Robt Morris Assocs.

Problem Loan Strategies. rev. ed. John E. McKinley et al. 157p. (Orig.). 1998. pap. 53.00 (*1-57070-022-2*, 606601) Robt Morris Assocs.

Problem Loan Workouts, 2 vols. Gerry Blanchard et al. 230.00 (*0-685-63103-6*) West Group.

***Problem Loans: A Banker's Guide.** Keith Checkley. 200p. 1999. pap. text 200.00 (*1-85564-748-6*, Pub. by Euromoney) Am Educ Systs.

Problem Loans: A Special Collection from the Journal of Commercial Bank Lending. Ed. by Charlotte Weisman. LC 85-25874. (Illus.). 100p. 1985. pap. 45.00 (*0-936742-27-5*) Robt Morris Assocs.

Problem Management. CCTA Staff. (IT Infrastructure Library Ser.). 74p. 1990. pap. 80.00 (*0-11-330527-3*, Pub. by Statnry Office) Sftware Mgmt Network.

Problem Management: A Guide for Producers & Players. James W. Bryant. LC 89-9050. (Illus.). 352p. 1989. pap. 109.20 (*0-608-05260-4*, 206579800001) Bks Demand.

Problem Management in Endocrine Surgery. Glenn W. Geelhoed. LC 82-10850. (Illus.). 198p. reprint ed. pap. 61.40 (*0-8357-6764-7*, 203542500095) Bks Demand.

Problem of a Chinese Aesthetic. Haun Saussy. (Meridian: Crossing Aesthetics Ser.). 306p. 1995. pap. 15.95 (*0-8047-2593-4*) Stanford U Pr.

Problem of a Chinese Aesthetic. Haun Saussy. LC 92-22582. (Meridian: Crossing Aesthetics Ser.). 306p. (C). 1995. 45.00 (*0-8047-2074-6*) Stanford U Pr.

Problem of Abortion. 2nd ed. Ed. by Joel Feinberg. 201p. (C). 1984. mass mkt. 18.00 (*0-534-02890-X*) Wadsworth Pub.

Problem of Abortion. 3rd ed. Susan Dwyer & Joel Feinberg. LC 96-19686. (Philosophy Ser.). (C). 1996. 33.95 (*0-534-50514-7*) Wadsworth Pub.

Problem of Africanity in the Seventh-Day Adventist Church. Alven Makapela. LC 96-17514. (African Studies: Vol. 42). 448p. 1996. text 109.95 (*0-7734-8969-X*) E Mellen.

Problem of Age, Growth, & Death. Charles S. Minot. Ed. by Robert J. Kastenbaum. LC 78-22211. (Aging & Old Age Ser.). (Illus.). 1979. reprint ed. lib. bdg. 25.95 (*0-405-11824-4*) Ayer.

Problem of American Realism: Studies in the Cultural History of a Literary Idea. Michael D. Bell. LC 92-25231. 256p. (C). 1993. 32.95 (*0-226-04201-4*) U Ch Pr.

Problem of American Realism: Studies in the Cultural History of a Literary Idea. Michael D. Bell. x, 256p. 1995. pap. text 15.95 (*0-226-04202-2*) U Ch Pr.

Problem of Americanization in the Catholic Schools of Puerto Rico. Charles J. Beirne. 144p. (Orig.). 1974. pap. 4.00 (*0-8477-2725-4*) U of PR Pr.

Problem of Asia. Alfred Thayer Mahan. (Notable American Authors Ser.). 1999. reprint ed. lib. bdg. 125.00 (*0-7812-3922-2*) Rprt Serv.

Problem of Atlantis. Lewis Spence. 278p. 1997. reprint ed. 24.95 (*0-7661-0054-5*) Kessinger Pub.

Problem of Being Modern, or the German Pursuit of Enlightenment from Christian Wolff to the French Revolution. Thomas P. Saine. LC 97-9952. 480p. 1997. text 39.95 (*0-8143-2681-1*) Wayne St U Pr.

Problem of Bureaucratic Rationality: Tax Politics in Japan. Junko Kato. LC 94-15825. 320p. 1994. text 42.50 (*0-691-03451-6*, Pub. by Princeton U Pr) Cal Prin Full Svc.

Problem of Certainty in English Thought, 1630-1690. H. G. Van Leeuwen. (International Archives of the History of Ideas Ser.: No. 3). 174p. 1970. lib. bdg. 66.50 (*90-247-0179-1*) Kluwer Academic.

Problem of Change: A Study of North-East India. B. P. Singh. 236p. 1988. 16.95 (*0-19-562052-6*) OUP.

Problem of Change: A Study of North-East India. B. P. Singh. 244p. 1996. reprint ed. pap. 10.95 (*0-19-563969-3*) OUP.

Problem of China. Bertrand Russell. 266p. 1993. reprint ed. 72.50 (*0-85124-552-8*, Pub. by Spkesman); reprint ed. pap. 29.50 (*0-85124-553-6*, Pub. by Spkesman) Coronet Bks.

Problem of Christianity in Multi-Religious Societies of Today: The Bible in a World of Many Faiths. Tord Fornberg. LC 95-47266. (Toronto Studies in Theology: Vol. 70). 308p. 1995. 99.95 (*0-7734-8877-4*) E Mellen.

Problem of Communalism in India. Ravindra Kumar. 1990. 17.50 (*81-7099-220-6*, Pub. by Mittal Pubs Dist) S Asia.

Problem of Communication. Duane Magnani. 1989. pap. 7.95 (*1-883858-17-8*) Witness CA.

Problem of Consciousness: Essays Towards a Resolution. Colin McGinn. 216p. 1993. pap. 27.95 (*0-631-18803-7*) Blackwell Pubs.

Problem of Consciousness in Modern Poetry. Hugh Underhill. 353p. (C). 1992. text 69.95 (*0-521-41033-9*) Cambridge U Pr.

***Problem of Context: Perspectives from Social Anthropology & Elsewhere.** Ed. by R. M. Dilley. LC 99-35007. (Methodology & History in Anthropology Ser.: Vol. 4). 242p. 1999. 59.95 (*1-57181-700-X*); pap. 19.50 (*1-57181-773-5*) Berghahn Bks.

Problem of Crime. John Muncie & Eugene McLaughlin. 352p. 1996. 79.95 (*0-7619-5004-4*); pap. 29.95 (*0-7619-5005-2*) Sage.

Problem of Dark Cutting in Beef: Current Topics in Veterinary Medicine & Animal Science, No. 10. Ed. by D. E. Hood & P. V. Tarrant. xii, 504p. 1981. text 206.50 (*90-247-2522-4*) Kluwer Academic.

Problem of Democracy in Cuba: Between Vision & Reality. Carollee Bengelsdorf. 240p. 1994. pap. text 23.95 (*0-19-509014-4*) OUP.

Problem of Difference: Phenomenology & Poststructuralism. Jeffrey A. Bell. (Toronto Studies in Philosophy). 368p. 1998. text 75.00 (*0-8020-4253-8*) U of Toronto Pr.

Problem of Difference: Phenomenology & Poststructuralism. Jeffrey A. Bell. (Toronto Studies in Philosophy). 368p. 1998. pap. text 24.95 (*0-8020-8095-2*) U of Toronto Pr.

Problem of 'Edwin Drood' W. Robertson Nicoll. LC 72-1330. (Studies in Dickens: No. 52). 1972. reprint ed. lib. bdg. 75.00 (*0-8383-1442-2*) M S G Haskell Hse.

Problem of Embodiment. Richard M. Zaner. (Phaenomenologica Ser.: No. 17). 306p. 1971. lib. bdg. 71.50 (*90-247-5093-8*, Pub. by M Nijhoff) Kluwer Academic.

Problem of Embodiment in Early African American Narrative, 183. Katherine Fishburn. LC 96-50295. (Contributions in Afro-American & African Studies: Vol. 183). 216p. 1997. 55.00 (*0-313-30359-2*, Greenwood Pr) Greenwood.

Problem of Error from Plato to Kant. Leo W. Keeler. 1977. lib. bdg. 59.95 (*0-8490-2482-X*) Gordon Pr.

Problem of Etiological Narrative in the Old Testament. Burke O. Long. (Beiheft zur Zeitschrift fuer die Alttestamentliche Wissenschaft Ser.: No. 108). (C). 1968. 33.85 (*3-11-005590-2*) De Gruyter.

Problem of Evil. Ed. by Marilyn M. Adams & Robert M. Adams. (Oxford Readings in Philosophy Ser.). 238p. 1991. pap. text 19.95 (*0-19-824866-0*) OUP.

***Problem of Evil.** Eric Greenleaf. 320p. 2000. text 34.95 (*1-891944-41-X*) Zeig Tucker.

Problem of Evil. Errol E. Harris & D. Litt. LC 77-72325. (Aquinas Lectures). 1977. 15.00 (*0-87462-142-9*) Marquette.

***Problem of Evil: A Reader.** Mark J. Larrimore. LC 00-9180. 2001. write for info. (*0-631-22014-3*) Blackbirch.

***Problem of Evil: An Intercultural Exploration.** Ed. by Sandra A. Wawrytko. (Value Inquiry Book Ser.: Vol. 90). xvii, 201p. 2000. pap. 38.50 (*90-420-0479-7*) Editions Rodopi.

Problem of Evil: Selected Readings. Ed. by Michael L. Peterson. LC 91-50576. (Library of Religious Philosophy: Vol. 8). (C). 1992. pap. text 23.00 (*0-268-01515-5*) U of Notre Dame Pr.

Problem of Evil & Indian Thought. Arthur L. Herman. (C). 1993. 20.00 (*81-208-0753-7*, Pub. by Motilal Bnarsidass) S Asia.

Problem of Exchange Rates. Study Group Staff. (Report Ser.). 29p. 1982. pap. 10.00 (*1-56708-055-3*) Grp of Thirty.

Problem of Freedom: Race, Labor, & Politics in Jamaica & Britain, 1832-1938. Thomas C. Holt. LC 91-17694. (Studies in Atlantic History & Culture). (Illus.). 512p. 1992. text 65.00 (*0-8018-4216-6*); pap. text 19.95 (*0-8018-4291-3*) Johns Hopkins.

Problem of Freedom in Marxist Thought: An Analysis of the Treatment of Human Freedom by Marx, Engels, Lenin & Contemporary Soviet Philosophy. James J. O'Rourke. LC 73-86095. (Sovietica Ser.: No. 32). 240p. 1974. lib. bdg. 126.50 (*90-277-0383-3*) Kluwer Academic.

Problem of Freedom in Postmodern Education: Critical Studies in Education & Culture. Tomasz Szkudlarek. LC 92-39122. 168p. 1993. 55.00 (*0-89789-322-0*, H322, Bergin & Garvey); pap. 19.95 (*0-89789-323-9*, G323, Bergin & Garvey) Greenwood.

Problem of Genre & the Quest for Justice in Cheknov's "The Island of Sakhalin" Juras T. Ryfa. LC 98-52446. (Studies in Slavic Language & Literature Ser.: Vol. 13). 252p. 1999. text 89.95 (*0-7734-8172-9*) E Mellen.

Problem of God. Edgar S. Brightman. LC 75-3085. (Philosophy in America Ser.). reprint ed. 37.50 (*0-404-59084-5*) AMS Pr.

Problem of God: A Short Introduction. rev. ed. Peter A. Angeles. LC 73-85469. 166p. 1980. pap. 21.95 (*0-87975-216-5*) Prometheus Bks.

Problem of God: Yesterday & Today. John C. Murray. (St. Thomas More Lectures: No. 1). (Orig.). (C). 1965. pap. 12.00 (*0-300-00171-1*, Y138) Yale U Pr.

***Problem of God in Modern Thought.** Philip Clayton. 544p. 2000. 39.00 (*0-8028-3885-5*) Eerdmans.

Problem of God in Philosophy of Religion: A Critical Examination of the Category of the Absolute & the Scheme of Transcendence. Henry Dumery. Tr. by Charles Courtney. (Studies in Phenomenology & Existential Philosophy). 135p. 1964. pap. 19.95 (*0-8101-0606-X*) Northwestern U Pr.

Problem of Gossip. F. Franklyn Wise. (Christian Living Ser.). 44p. 1988. pap. 3.50 (*0-8341-1246-9*) Beacon Hill.

Problem of Grace. Mark Craver. LC 85-81601. (Lost Roads Ser.: No. 29). 64p. (Orig.). (C). 1986. pap. 6.95 (*0-918786-33-9*) Lost Roads.

Problem of Group Responsibility to Society. John H. Randall, Jr. LC 72-89760. (American Labor, from Conspiracy to Collective Bargaining Ser., No. 1). 296p. 1974. reprint ed. 19.95 (*0-405-02145-3*) Ayer.

Problem of Hell. Jonathan L. Kvanvig. LC 92-44653. 192p. (C). 1993. text 39.95 (*0-19-508487-X*) OUP.

Problem of Historical Knowledge: An Answer to Relativism. Maurice H. Mandelbaum. LC 74-152993. (Select Bibliographies Reprint Ser.). 1977. reprint ed. 24.95 (*0-8369-5745-8*) Ayer.

Problem of Incomplete Information in Relational Databases. G. Grahne. (Lecture Notes in Computer Science Ser.: Vol. 554). viii, 156p. 1991. 30.00 (*0-387-54919-6*) Spr-Verlag.

Problem of Increasing Human Energy. Nikola Tesla. (Nikola Tesla Ser.). 1991. lib. bdg. 250.00 (*0-8490-4264-X*) Gordon Pr.

Problem of Increasing Human Energy. Nikola Tesla. Ed. by Steven Elswick. (Tesla Technology Ser.: Vol. I). (Illus.). 96p. (C). 1990. reprint ed. pap. text 9.95 (*1-882137-00-0*) High Enrgy Enterprises.

Problem of Increasing Human Energy. Nikola Tesla. 37p. 1993. reprint ed. spiral bd. 12.00 (*0-7873-0861-7*) Hlth Research.

Problem of Increasing Human Energy (1900) Nikola Tesla. 50p. 1996. reprint ed. pap. 7.95 (*1-56459-844-6*) Kessinger Pub.

Problem of Increasing Human Energy, with Special Reference to Harnessing the Sun's Energy. Nikola Tesla. (Nikola Tesla Ser.). 1991. lib. bdg. 250.00 (*0-87700-975-9*) Revisionist Pr.

***Problem of Indian Education.** Rai Lajpat. 1999. 30.00 (*81-7020-450-X*, Pub. by Cosmo Pubn) S Asia.

Problem of Induction & Its Solution. Jerrold J. Katz. LC 62-18116. 139p. reprint ed. pap. 43.10 (*0-608-30658-4*, 201575800003) Bks Demand.

Problem of International Confrontations see Trilateral Commission Task Force Reports

Problem of Ireland in Tudor Foreign Policy, 1485-1603. William Palmer. 171p. (C). 1995. 60.00 (*0-85115-562-6*) Boydell & Brewer.

Problem of Japanese Trade Expansion in the Post-War Situation. Miriam S. Farley. LC 75-30106. (Institute of Pacific Relations Ser.). reprint ed. 29.50 (*0-404-59523-5*) AMS Pr.

Problem of Jesus. George D. Boardman. 32p. 1984. pap. 7.00 (*0-8170-1059-9*) Judson.

Problem of Knowledge: Philosophy, Science, & History Since Hegel. Ernst Cassirer. Tr. by William H. Woglom & Charles W. Hendel. 1969. pap. 18.00 (*0-300-01098-2*, Y211) Yale U Pr.

Problem of Language in Religious Education. John I. Obilor. LC 98-39372. (Beitrage zur Erziehungswissenschaft und Biblischen Bildung Ser.: Vol. 3). 155p. 1998. pap. text 31.95 (*0-8204-3603-8*) P Lang Pubng.

Problem of Language in Religious Education. John Iheanyichuk Obilor. 155p. 1998. 31.95 (*3-631-33473-7*) P Lang Pubng.

An Asterisk (*) at the beginning of an entry indicates that the title is appearing for the first time.

Problem of Lemuria: The Sunken Continent of the Pacific. Lewis Spence. 249p. 1992. pap. 20.00 (*0-89540-194-0*, SB-194) Sun Pub.

Problem of Lemuria: The Sunken Continent of the Pacific. Lewis Spence. 249p. 1996. reprint ed. spiral bd. 17.50 (*0-7873-0808-0*) Hlth Research.

Problem of Lemuria: The Sunken Continent of the Pacific. Lewis Spence. 250p. 1992. reprint ed. pap. 16.95 (*1-56459-125-5*) Kessinger Pub.

Problem of Life & Death. Paramananda. pap. 1.95 (*0-87481-543-6*, Pub. by Ramakrishna Math) Vedanta Pr.

Problem of Loss & Mourning: Psychoanalytic Perspectives. Ed. by David R. Dietrich & Peter Shabad. 500p. 1989. 67.50 (*0-8236-4349-2*, BN 04349) Intl Univs Pr.

Problem of Meaning: Behavioral & Cognitive Perspectives. Charlotte Mandell & Allyssa McCabe. LC 97-25320. (Advances in Psychology Ser.: Vol. 122). 1997. write for info. (*0-444-82479-0*) Elsevier.

Problem of Measure for Measure: A Historical Investigation Rosalind Miles. LC 75-35037. 349 p. 1976. 22.50 (*0-06-494824-2*) HarpC.

Problem of Mental Disorder. National Research Council Committee on Psychiatric. Ed. by Gerald N. Grob. LC 78-22580. (Historical Issues in Mental Health Ser.). 1980. reprint ed. lib. bdg. 30.95 (*0-405-11932-1*) Ayer.

Problem of Metaphysics & the Meaning of Metaphysical Explanation. Hartley B. Alexander. LC 72-38480. reprint ed. 29.50 (*0-404-00322-2*) AMS Pr.

Problem of Minority Groups. Louis Wirth. (Reprint Series in Social Sciences). (C). 1993. reprint ed. pap. text 2.30 (*0-8290-2700-9*, S-318) Irvington.

Problem of Moments. J. A. Shohat & J. D. Tamarkin. LC 51-96. (Mathematical Surveys & Monographs: No. 1). 144p. 1943. pap. 42.00 (*0-8218-1501-6*, SURV/1) Am Math.

Problem of National Security, Some Economic & Administrative Aspects: A Statement on National Policy by the Research & Policy Committee of the Committee for Economic Development. Committee for Economic Development. LC 58-13649. 86p. reprint ed. pap. 30.00 (*0-608-30720-3*, 2007033000060) Bks Demand.

Problem of Nature: Environment, Culture & European Expansion. David Arnold. LC 96-2054. (New Perspectives on the Past Ser.). 224p. 1996. 60.95 (*0-631-17732-9*) Blackwell Pubs.

Problem of Nature: Environment, Culture & European Expansion. David Arnold. LC 96-2054. (New Perspectives on the Past Ser.). (Illus.). 224p. 1996. pap. 22.95 (*0-631-19021-X*) Blackwell Pubs.

Problem of Noise in Marine Propulsion Gears. G. Wohlberg. (Technical Papers: Vol. P299.01). (Illus.). 34p. (Orig.). 1948. pap. text 30.00 incl. audio compact disk (*1-55589-381-3*) AGMA.

Problem of Order: What Unites & Divides Society. Dennis H. Wrong. 275p. (Orig.). 1994. 24.95 (*0-02-935515-X*) Free Pr.

Problem of Order: What Unites & Divides Society. Dennis H. Wrong. 368p. (Orig.). (C). 1995. pap. text 17.50 (*0-674-70777-X*) HUP.

Problem of Order in Changing Societies: Essay on Crime & Policing in Argentina & Uruguay. Ed. by Lyman L. Johnson. LC 89-36709. (Illus.). 197p. reprint ed. pap. 61.10 (*0-608-20968-6*, 2071840000002) Bks Demand.

Problem of Pain. C. S. Lewis. 144p. 1996. per. 6.00 (*0-684-82383-7*, Touchstone) S&S Trade Pap.

*__Problem of Pain.__ C. S. Lewis. 1999. pap. 7.00 (*0-8054-2049-5*) Broadman.

Problem of Participation: A Radical Critique of Contemporary Democratic Theory. Lee A. Osbun. LC 85-5308. 146p. (Orig.). 1985. lib. bdg. 41.50 (*0-8191-4640-4*) U Pr of Amer.

Problem of Perversion: The View from Self Psychology. Arnold Goldberg. LC 94-28556. 1994. 32.00 (*0-300-06030-0*) Yale U Pr.

Problem of Plateau: A Tribute to Jesse Douglas & Tibor Rado. Ed. by Themistocles M. Rassias. 400p. (C). 1992. text 130.00 (*981-02-0556-2*) World Scientific Pub.

Problem of Plumbing: And Other Stories. James M. Bellarosa. LC 89-1544. 128p. (Orig.). 1989. pap. 8.95 (*0-936784-76-8*) J Daniel.

Problem of "Poetry & Belief" in Contemporary Criticism. William J. Rooney. LC 50-2632. 175p. reprint ed. pap. 54.30 (*0-608-18715-1*, 202949400061) Bks Demand.

*__Problem of Poetry in the Romantic Period.__ Mark Storey. LC 99-48510. 2000. text 59.95 (*0-312-23044-3*) St Martin.

Problem of Polarization: An Approach Based on the Writings of G. C. Berkouwer. Charles M. Cameron. LC 92-34398. (Rutherford Studies in Contemporary Theology: Vol. 2). 616p. 1992. text 129.95 (*0-7734-1633-1*) E Mellen.

Problem of Political Obligation: A Critical Analysis of Liberal Theory. Carole Pateman. LC 78-18460. 217p. reprint ed. pap. 67.30 (*0-608-17556-0*, 203053600069) Bks Demand.

Problem of Pornography. Susan Dwyer. LC 94-18082. 264p. 1994. 28.95 (*0-534-22044-4*) Wadsworth Pub.

Problem of Pornography. 2nd ed. Dwyer. (Philosophy Ser.). (C). 1919. text 21.00 (*0-534-50978-9*) Wadsworth Pub.

Problem of Pornography: Regulation & the Right to Free Speech. Susan M. Easton. LC 93-37378. 208p. (C). (gr. 13). 1994. pap. 22.99 (*0-415-09183-7*) Routledge.

Problem of Progress. Sander Griffioen. (Lecture Ser.). 56p. (Orig.). 1987. pap. 1.75 (*0-932914-14-4*) Dordt Coll Pr.

Problem of Proof: Especially As Exemplified in Disputed Documents Trials. Albert S. Osborn. LC 75-20212. 564p. 1975. reprint ed. text 57.95 (*0-88229-300-1*) Burnham Inc.

*__Problem of Proof: Especially As Exemplified in Disputed Documents Trials.__ Albert S. Osborn. xxi, 526p. 1999. reprint ed. 165.00 (*1-56169-477-0*) Gaunt.

Problem of Pure Consciousness: Mysticism & Philosophy. Ed. by Robert K. Forman. 320p. 1997. reprint ed. pap. 21.00 (*0-19-510976-7*) OUP.

*__Problem of Race in the Twenty-First Century.__ Thomas C. Holt. 144p. 2001. 22.95 (*0-674-00443-4*) HUP.

Problem of Rationality in Science & Its Philosophy: On Popper vs. Polanyi, the Polish Conferences 1988-89. Ed. by Jozef Misiek. LC 94-17897. (Boston Studies in Philosophy of Science: Vol. 160). 280p. (C). 1995. lib. bdg. 148.50 (*0-7923-2925-2*, Pub. by Kluwer Academic) Kluwer Academic.

Problem of Rebirth. Sri Aurobindo. 1979. pap. 8.95 (*0-89744-913-4*) Auromere.

Problem of Rebirth. 3rd ed. Sri Aurobindo. 186p. 1994. pap. 4.95 (*81-7058-215-6*, Pub. by SAA) E-W Cultural Ctr.

Problem of Rebirth. 3rd ed. Sri Aurobindo. 186p. 1995. 6.95 (*81-7058-216-4*, Pub. by SAA) E-W Cultural Ctr.

Problem of Reductionism in Science. Ed. by Evandro Agazzi. (Episteme Ser.). 236p. (C). 1991. lib. bdg. 122.00 (*0-7923-1406-9*, Pub. by Kluwer Academic) Kluwer Academic.

Problem of Refugees in the Light of Contemporary International Law Issues. Ed. by Vera Gowlland-Debbas. (Nijhoff Law Specials Ser.: Vol. 12). 179p. 1995. pap. text 60.50 (*90-411-0085-7*, Pub. by M Nijhoff) Kluwer Academic.

Problem of Restoration: A Study in Comparative Political History. Robert A. Kahn. LC 68-10380. 453p. reprint ed. pap. 140.50 (*0-608-18032-7*, 202904700058) Bks Demand.

Problem of Revolution in Germany, 1789-1989. Ed. by Reinhard Rurup. (German Historical Perspectives Ser.). 256p. 2000. 65.00 (*1-85973-276-3*, Pub. by Berg Pubs) NYU Pr.

Problem of Seam Strength & Thread Durability. 15p. 1953. 7.00 (*0-318-19653-0*) Clothing Mfrs.

Problem of Self-Love in St. Augustine. Oliver O'Donovan. LC 80-5397. 229p. reprint ed. pap. 71.00 (*0-8357-8285-9*, 203384600087) Bks Demand.

Problem of Shape in the Prelude: The Conflict of Private & Public Speech. Jonathan Grandine. LC 68-54018. (LeBaron Russell Briggs Prize Honors Essays in English Ser.: 1968). 55p. (Orig.). 1968. pap. 5.30 (*0-674-70800-8*) HUP.

Problem of Slavery in the Age of Revolution, 1770-1823. David Brion Davis. LC 98-19513. 576p. 1999. pap. 24.95 (*0-19-512671-8*) OUP.

Problem of Slavery in Western Culture. David B. Davis. 528p. 1988. pap. text 17.95 (*0-19-505639-6*) OUP.

Problem of Social Responsibility from the Perspective of the Mennonite Church. J. Lawrence Burkholder. 238p. (Orig.). 1989. reprint ed. pap. text 25.00 (*0-936273-14-3*) Inst Mennonite.

Problem of Sociology: An Introduction to the Discipline. David Lee & Howard Newby. 379p. (C). 1990. pap. text 21.95 (*0-04-445641-7*) Routledge.

Problem of Solidarity: Theories & Models. Ed. by Patrick Doreian & Thomas J. Fararo. 436p. 1998. text 48.00 (*90-5700-533-6*, ECU68, Harwood Acad Pubs) Gordon & Breach.

Problem of Sovereignty in the Later Middle Ages: The Papal Monarchy with Augustinus Triumphus & the Publicists. Michael J. Wilks. (Cambridge Studies in Medieval Life & Thought: Vol. 9). 633p. reprint ed. pap. 180.00 (*0-608-30054-3*, 2013890) Bks Demand.

Problem of Space in Jewish Medieval Philosophy. Israel I. Efros. LC 77-164765. (Columbia University. Oriental Studies: No. 11). reprint ed. 34.50 (*0-404-50501-5*) AMS Pr.

Problem of Space in Jewish Medieval Philosophy. Israel I. Efros. reprint ed. pap. 7.95 (*0-89197-904-2*); reprint ed. lib. bdg. 40.50 (*0-697-00037-0*) Irvington.

Problem of Space Travel: The Rocket Motor. 1996. lib. bdg. 249.99 (*0-8490-6877-0*) Gordon Pr.

Problem of Space Travel: The Rocket Motor. 1997. lib. bdg. 250.95 (*0-8490-6196-2*) Gordon Pr.

Problem of Space Travel: The Rocket Motor. Hermann Noordung. 176p. 1995. per. 13.00 (*0-16-061847-9*) USGPO.

Problem of Style. John M. Murry. LC 80-21463. 133p. 1980. reprint ed. lib. bdg. 49.50 (*0-313-22523-0*, MUPR, Greenwood Pr) Greenwood.

Problem of Suffering. Gregory Schulz. LC 95-72524. 74p. 1997. pap. 7.99 (*0-8100-0583-2*, 12N1761) Northwest Pub.

Problem of Teaching High School Pupils How to Study. Joseph S. Butterweck. LC 75-176620. (Columbia University. Teachers College. Contributions to Education Ser.: No. 237). reprint ed. 37.50 (*0-404-55237-4*) AMS Pr.

Problem of the Beginning of Dogma in Recent Theology: Theology. Paul Schrodt. (European University Studies: Ser. 23, Vol. 103). 365p. 1978. pap. 62.00 (*3-261-02464-X*) P Lang Pubng.

Problem of the Criterion. Robert P. Amico. LC 92-37597. (Studies in Epistemology & Cognitive Theory). 188p. (C). 1995. pap. 19.95 (*0-8476-8034-7*); lib. bdg. 49.50 (*0-8476-7817-2*) Rowman.

Problem of the Criterion, 1973. Roderick M. Chisholm. LC 73-75504. (Aquinas Lectures). 1973. 15.00 (*0-87462-138-0*) Marquette.

Problem of the Day. Prabhat Rainjan Sarkar. 64p. 1968. pap. 3.95 (*0-686-95454-8*) Ananda Marga.

Problem of the Earth's Shape from Newton to Clairaut: The Rise of Mathematical Science in 18th Century Paris & the Fall of "Normal" Science. John L. Greenberg. (Illus.). 799p. (C). 1995. text 95.00 (*0-521-38541-5*) Cambridge U Pr.

Problem of the Essential Indexical: And Other Essays. John Perry. LC 92-33242. (Illus.). 352p. (C). 1993. text 65.00 (*0-19-504999-3*) OUP.

*__Problem of the Evil Editor: A Charles Dodgson/Arthur Conan Doyle Mystery.__ Roberta Rogow. 288p. 2000. 23.95 (*0-312-20903-7*) St Martin.

Problem of the Judgment: Eleven Approaches to Kafka's Story. Franz Kafka. Ed. by Angel Flores. Tr. by Malcolm Pasley. LC 76-48958. 265p. 1977. 75.00 (*0-87752-210-3*) Gordian.

Problem of the Lord's Supper: The Lord's Supper in Relationship to the Life of Jesus & the History of the Early Church. Albert Schweitzer & A. J. Mattill, Jr. LC 81-22590. xiv, 144p. 1982. 10.95 (*0-86554-025-X*, MUP-H025) Mercer Univ Pr.

Problem of the Medical Profession: A Political Primer for Patients & Doctors. B. Monahan. 1991. lib. bdg. 69.00 (*0-8490-4404-9*) Gordon Pr.

Problem of the Minimum of a Quadratic Functional. Solomon G. Minkhlin. Tr. by A. Feinstein. LC 64-24626. (Holden-Day Series in Mathematical Physics). 164p. reprint ed. pap. 50.90 (*0-608-10276-8*, 201629200003) Bks Demand.

Problem of the Missing Miss. Roberta Wogow. LC 98-5329. 272p. 1998. text 22.95 (*0-312-18553-7*) St Martin.

Problem of the Multiple Interpretation of Ricardo. Ercument G. Aksoy. Ed. by William Breit & Kenneth G. Elzinga. LC 91-13684. (Political Economy & Public Policy Ser.: Vol. 8). 314p. 1991. 78.50 (*1-55938-289-9*) Jai Pr.

Problem of the Northmen. E. N. Horsford. 1977. lib. bdg. 59.95 (*0-8490-2483-8*) Gordon Pr.

Problem of the Ohio Mounds. Cyrus Thomas. (Bureau of American Ethnology Bulletins Ser.). 99p. 1995. 79.00 (*0-7812-4008-5*) Rprt Serv.

Problem of the Ohio Mounds. Cyrus Thomas. (Illus.). 56p. 1993. reprint ed. pap. 5.40 (*1-56651-097-X*) A W McGraw.

Problem of the Ohio Mounds. Cyrus Thomas. 1988. reprint ed. lib. bdg. 49.00 (*0-7812-0117-9*) Rprt Serv.

Problem of the Ohio Mounds. Cyrus Thomas. reprint ed. 19.00 (*0-685-38431-4*) Scholarly.

Problem of the Pacific in the Twentieth Century. Nikolai N. Golovin & A. D. Bubnov. LC 79-111758. (American Imperialism: Viewpoints of United States Foreign Policy, 1898-1941 Ser.). 1970. reprint ed. 19.95 (*0-405-02023-6*) Ayer.

Problem of the Passions: Feminism, Psychoanalysis & Social Theory. Cynthia Burack. 200p. (C). 1995. pap. text 16.50 (*0-8147-1252-5*) NYU Pr.

Problem of the Phytolyma Gall Bug in the Establishment of Chlorophora. M. G. White. 1966. 60.00 (*0-7855-7182-5*) St Mut.

Problem of the Pink Post Office: Reading Level 3-4. (Stormy Night Stories Ser.). 16p. 1993. 2.50 (*0-88336-073-X*) New Readers.

Problem of the Process of Transmission in the Pentateuch. Rolf Rendtorff. (Journal for the Study of the Old Testament Supplement Ser.: Vol. 89). 214p. 1990. 43.75 (*1-85075-229-X*, Pub. by Sheffield Acad) CUP Services.

*__Problem of the Puer Aeternus.__ 3rd ed. Marie-Louise von Franz. (Studies in Jungian Psychology by Jungian Analysts: Vol. 87). 288p. 1999. pap. 20.00 (*0-919123-88-0*, Pub. by Inner City Bks) BookWorld.

Problem of the Rational Soul in the Thirteenth Century. Richard C. Dales. LC 95-19416. (Studies in Intellectual History). vii, 214p. 1995. 72.00 (*90-04-10296-5*) Brill Academic Pubs.

Problem of the Spiteful Spiritualist. Roberta Rogow. LC 99-21750. (Charles Dodgson/Arthur Conan Doyle Myste Ser.). 272p. 1999. text 23.95 (*0-312-20570-8*) St Martin.

Problem of the Text of Acts. W. A. Strange. (Society for New Testament Studies Monographs: No. 71). 272p. (C). 1992. text 65.00 (*0-521-41384-2*) Cambridge U Pr.

Problem of the Third Generation Immigrant. Marcus L. Hansen. LC 86-64029. (Augustana College Library Occasional Papers, Wallin Lecture: No. 16). 27p. 1987. pap. 2.00 (*0-910182-43-4*) Augustana Coll.

Problem of the Two Prologues to Chaucer's Legend of Good Women. John C. French. 1976. lib. bdg. 59.95 (*0-8490-2484-6*) Gordon Pr.

Problem of the Two Prologues to Chaucer's Legend of Good Women. John C. French. LC 79-168140. reprint ed. 21.50 (*0-404-02576-5*) AMS Pr.

Problem of the Unity of the Sciences: Bacon to Kant. Robert McRae. LC 62-2304. 160p. reprint ed. pap. 49.60 (*0-8357-8905-5*, 201431800095) Bks Demand.

Problem of the Week. Lyle Fisher & William Medigovich. 104p. pap. text 13.95 (*0-86651-024-9*) Seymour Pubns.

Problem of the Week Contest Manual. unabridged ed. Douglas Brumbaugh & David Rock. (Problem of the Week Ser.: Vol. 1). 46p. 1997. pap. text 10.95 (*0-9659710-1-5*) Paragon Publns.

Problem of the Wire Cage. John Dickson Carr. 1986. mass mkt. 3.95 (*0-8217-3384-2*, Zebra Kensgtn) Kensgtn Pub Corp.

Problem of Thor Bridge: The Case-Book of Sherlock Holmes. Jeremy Paul. (Illus.). 50p. (Orig.). 1991. pap. 11.00 (*0-86025-434-8*, Pub. by I Henry Pubns) Empire Pub Srvs.

Problem of Time in Nietzsche. Joan Stambaugh. Tr. by John Humphrey. LC 86-47767. 224p. 1987. 38.50 (*0-8387-5113-X*) Bucknell U Pr.

*__Problem of Trieste & the Italo-Yugoslav Border: Difference, Identity, & Sovereignty in Twentieth-Century Europe.__ Glenda Sluga. (C). 2000. pap. text 22.95 (*0-7914-4824-X*) State U NY Pr.

*__Problem of Trieste & the Italo-Yugoslav Border: Difference, Identity, & Sovereignty in Twentieth-Century Europe.__ Glenda Sluga. (C). 2001. text 68.50 (*0-7914-4823-1*) State U NY Pr.

Problem of Trust. Adam B. Seligman. LC 96-51589. 224p. 1997. text 29.95 (*0-691-01242-3*, Pub. by Princeton U Pr) Cal Prin Full Svc.

*__Problem of Trust.__ Adam B. Seligman. 2000. pap. text 16.95 (*0-691-05020-1*) Princeton U Pr.

Problem of Unbelief in the Sixteenth Century: The Religion of Rabelais. Lucien Febvre. Tr. by Beatrice Gottlieb. (Illus.). 552p. 1982. pap. 27.00 (*0-674-70826-1*) HUP.

Problem of Unemployment. Paul H. Douglas & Aaron Director. LC 75-17217. (Social Problems & Social Policy Ser.). (Illus.). 1976. reprint ed. 42.95 (*0-405-07488-3*) Ayer.

Problem of Universals. Ed. by Andrew B. Schoedinger. LC 91-10228. 488p. (C). 1991. pap. 19.95 (*0-391-03726-9*) Humanities.

Problem of Values in Educational Thought. Philip L. Smith. LC 81-23650. (Illus.). 102p. 1982. reprint ed. pap. 31.70 (*0-608-00025-6*, 206079100006) Bks Demand.

Problem of Wasteland & Forest Ecology of India. Pramod Singh. (C). 1988. 58.00 (*81-7024-216-9*, Pub. by Ashish Pub Hse) S Asia.

Problem of Weak Railroads. James M. Herring. Ed. by Stuart Bruchey. LC 80-1316. (Railroads Ser.). 1981. reprint ed. lib. bdg. 18.95 (*0-405-13788-5*) Ayer.

Problem of Wealth in the Literature of Luther's Germany. John Van Cleve. (GERM Ser.: Vol. 55). (Illus.). x, 198p. 1991. 60.00 (*0-938100-86-6*) Camden Hse.

Problem of Wineland. Halldor Hermannsson. LC 36-18884. (Islandica Ser.: Vol. 25). 1936. 25.00 (*0-527-00355-7*) Periodicals Srv.

Problem Organisms in Water: Identification & Treatment, Vol. M7. (AWWA Manual of Water Supply Practices Ser.: No. M7). (Illus.). 164p. 1995. pap. 70.00 (*0-89867-760-2*, 30007) Am Water Wks Assn.

Problem-Oriented Clinical Microbiology & Infection. H. Humphreys & W. I. Irving. (Illus.). 168p. 1996. pap. write for info. (*0-443-04914-9*) Church.

Problem-Oriented Drug Enforcement: A Community-Based Approach for Effective Policing. 75p. (Orig.). (YA). (gr. 12 up). 1994. pap. text 25.00 (*0-7881-0790-9*) DIANE Pub.

Problem-Oriented Medical Diagnosis. 4th ed. Ed. by H. Harold Friedman. (Spiral Manual Ser.). (C). 1987. spiral bd. 22.50 (*0-316-29378-4*, Little Brwn Med Div) Lppncott W & W.

Problem-Oriented Medical Diagnosis. 5th ed. H. Harold Friedman. LC 95-31027. 1991. 29.95 (*0-316-29387-3*, Little Brwn Med Div) Lppncott W & W.

Problem-Oriented Medical Diagnosis. 6th ed. H. Harold Friedman. 512p. 1995. spiral bd. 34.95 (*0-316-29448-9*) Lppncott W & W.

*__Problem-Oriented Medical Diagnosis.__ 7th ed. H. Harold Friedman. LC 00-41235. (Illus.). 2000. per. write for info. (*0-7817-2955-6*) Lppncott W & W.

Problem-Oriented Medical Record for High-Risk Obstetrics. Ed. by Curtis L. Cetrulo et al. LC 83-17712. 510p. 1984. 110.00 (*0-306-41325-6*, Plenum Trade) Perseus Pubng.

Problem-Oriented Medical Records in Correctional Health Care. 51p. 1988. 4.00 (*0-317-91129-5*) NCCHC.

Problem-Oriented Nursing Assessment. Patricia Larkin & Barbara Backer. (C). 1977. text 17.95 (*0-07-036450-8*) McGraw.

Problem-Oriented Pediatric Diagnosis. Roger M. Barkin. 320p. 1990. spiral bd. 32.00 (*0-316-08102-7*) Lppncott W & W.

Problem-Oriented Policing. Herman Goldstein & McGraw-Hill Staff. 256p. (C). 1990. pap. 30.63 (*0-07-023694-1*) McGraw.

Problem-Oriented Policing: Crime-Specific Problems, Critical Issues & Making Pop Work. Ed. by Anne Grant et al. LC 98-67704. 430p. 1998. pap. 29.00 (*1-878734-60-1*) Police Exec Res.

Problem Oriented Programming Languages. Hans J. Schneider. LC 83-16688. 161p. reprint ed. pap. 50.00 (*0-608-18450-0*, 203266600080) Bks Demand.

Problem Oriented with Pediatric Diagnosis. Roger M. Barkin. 1990. 15.95 (*0-316-08104-3*, Little Brwn Med Div) Lppncott W & W.

Problem Oriented with Pediatric Diagnosis. Roger M. Barkin. 1990. 10.95 (*0-316-08103-5*, Little Brwn Med Div) Lppncott W & W.

Problem Parade. Dale Seymour. 104p. text 13.95 (*0-86651-206-3*) Seymour Pubns.

Problem People . . . And How to Manage Them. Peter Honey. 176p. (C). 1992. pap. text 60.00 (*0-85292-495-X*, Pub. by IPM Hse) St Mut.

*__Problem People & How to Manage Them.__ Peter Honey. 208p. 2000. pap. 32.95 (*0-8464-5134-4*) Beekman Pubs.

Problem Pictures: Women & Men in Victorian Painting. Pamela G. Nunn. (Illus.). 224p. 1996. 69.95 (*1-85928-152-4*, Pub. by Scolar Pr) Ashgate Pub Co.

Problem-Play. R. Balmforth. LC 76-52915. (Studies in Drama: No. 39). 1977. lib. bdg. 75.00 (*0-8383-2129-1*) M S G Haskell Hse.

Problem Pony Book. Carolyn Henderson & Lynn Russell. 1995. pap. 45.00 (*0-85131-620-4*, Pub. by J A Allen) St Mut.

Problem Posing: Reflections & Applications. Ed. by Stephen Brown & Marion Walter. 352p. 1993. pap. 34.50 (*0-8058-1065-X*) L Erlbaum Assocs.

Problem Posing: Reflections & Applications, 2 vols., Set. Ed. by Stephen Brown & Marion Walter. 1993. 45.00 (*0-8058-1331-4*) L Erlbaum Assocs.

Problem-Projects in Acting. Katharine Kester. 1937. 5.50 (*0-573-69020-0*) French.

P

An Asterisk (*) at the beginning of an entry indicates that the title is appearing for the first time.

Problem Real Estate: How to Restructure, Refinance & Remarket Troubled Commercial Properties. Howard A. Zuckerman. 350p. 1992. 65.00 (*1-55738-405-3*, Irwin Prfssnl) McGraw-Hill Prof.

Problem Recognition in Public Policy & Business Management. Ed. by V. Subramaniam. 1986. 27.50 (*81-7024-037-9*, Pub. by Ashish Pub Hse) S Asia.

Problem Representation in Foreign Policy Decision Making. Ed. by Donald A. Sylvan & James F. Voss. LC 97-41729. (Illus.). 356p. (C). 1998. text 59.95 (*0-521-62293-X*) Cambridge U Pr.

Problem Seeking: An Architectural Programming Primer. William Pena. 202p. 1987. pap. 21.95 (*0-913962-87-2*) AIA Press.

Problem Seminar. D. J. Newman. (Problem Books in Mathematics). 113p. 1982. 46.95 (*0-387-90765-3*) Spr-Verlag.

Problem Series 3 for Technical Drawing. 10th ed. Giesecke. 1997. pap. text 40.00 (*0-13-659111-6*) P-H.

Problem Sets in Economics. Mansfield. pap. text 0.00 (*0-393-09393-X*) Norton.

Problem Shared . . . A History of the Institute of London Underwriters, 1884-1984. Christopher Hewer. (Illus.). 152p. (C). 1984. 180.00 (*0-900886-91-9*, Pub. by Witherby & Co) St Mut.

Problem Snake Management: Habu & Brown Treesnake Examples. Gordon H. Rodda. LC 98-15664. (Illus.). 520p. 1998. 47.50 (*0-8014-3507-2*, Comstock Pub) Cornell U Pr.

Problem-Solution: A Reference for Writers. Patricia Byrd & Beverly Benson. LC 93-38194. 240p. (J). 1994. mass mkt. 26.95 (*0-8384-4125-4*) Heinle & Heinle.

Problem Solutions. 4th ed. (C). 1999. pap. Price not set. (*0-13-021053-6*) P-H.

***Problem Solutions for Diode Lasers & Photonic in Tegrated Circuits.** Larry A. Coldren. 204p. 1998. pap. 27.50 (*0-471-17865-9*) Wiley.

Problem Solutions Manual for the Text Economic Evaluation & Investment Decision Methods. 9th ed. Franklin J. Stermole & John M. Stermole. LC 96-75182. 198p. 1996. pap. 17.00 (*1-878740-07-5*) Invest Eval.

Problem Solver. Gerstein. pap. text. write for info. (*0-471-37972-7*) Wiley.

Problem Solver. Reader's Digest Editors. LC 99-27221. (Reader's Digest Woodworking Ser.). 312p. 1999. 29.95 (*0-7621-0225-X*, Pub. by RD Assn) Penguin Putnam.

Problem Solver. Pattii Waldo. (Educational Game Activity Ser.). (J). (gr. 5-12). 1986. 44.00 (*0-930599-05-5*) Thinking Pubns.

Problem Solver for Finite Mathematics & Applied Calculus. Kenneth L. Wiggins. 320p. (C). 1990. 33.25 (*0-534-92439-5*) PWS Pubs.

***Problem Solver Guide for Students with ADHD: Ready-to-Use Interventions for Elementary & Secondary Students.** Harvey C. Parker. 125p. (Orig.). 2000. pap. 15.00 (*1-886941-39-4*, 0982, Pub. by Spec Pr FL) IPG Chicago.

***Problem Solvers Biographies.** Betty Lou Kratoville. 2000. pap. text 17.00 (*1-57128-147-9*) Acad Therapy.

Problem Solver's Guide to Logic. William J. Edgar. LC 82-20285. 106p. (Orig.). (C). 1983. pap. text 12.25 (*0-8191-2876-7*) U Pr of Amer.

***Problem Solvers Reproducible Workbook.** Betty Lou Kratoville. 2000. pap. text 14.00 (*1-57128-148-7*) Acad Therapy.

Problem Solver's Universal Checklist. Leon Segal. 17p. (Orig.). 1983. pap. text 5.00 (*0-9607160-0-9*) Ed Acad.

***Problem Solvg Abstraction & Design Using C++ C++ Builder 3 Std.** 2nd ed. 2000. text. write for info. (*0-201-70356-4*) P-H.

***Problem Solving.** (Overcoming Obstacles). 26p. (YA). (gr. 6-9). 1999. pap. text 11.50 (*1-929393-08-3*) Community for Ed.

***Problem Solving.** (Overcoming Obstacles). 26p. (YA). (gr. 9-12). 1999. pap. text 9.38 (*1-929393-20-2*) Community for Ed.

Problem Solving. 1991. 6.95 (*1-55708-365-7*, MCC906) McDonald Pub Co.

Problem Solving. ASP Staff. (Building Skills Ser.). (Illus.). 48p. (J). (gr. 3). 1997. pap., wbk. ed. 2.49 (*1-57768-073-1*) MG-Hill OH.

Problem Solving. ASP Staff. (Building Skills Ser.). (Illus.). 48p. (J). (gr. 4). 1997. pap., wbk. ed. 2.49 (*1-57768-074-X*) MG-Hill OH.

Problem Solving. ASP Staff. (Building Skills Ser.). (Illus.). 48p. (J). (gr. 5). 1997. pap., wbk. ed. 2.49 (*1-57768-075-8*) MG-Hill OH.

Problem Solving. ASP Staff. (Building Skills Ser.). (Illus.). 48p. (J). (gr. 6). 1997. pap., wbk. ed. 2.49 (*1-57768-076-6*) MG-Hill OH.

Problem Solving. ASP Staff. (Building Skills Ser.). (Illus.). 48p. (J). (gr. 7). 1997. pap., wbk. ed. 2.49 (*1-57768-077-4*) MG-Hill OH.

Problem Solving. ASP Staff. (Building Skills Ser.). (Illus.). 48p. (J). (gr. 8). 1997. pap., wbk. ed. 2.49 (*1-57768-078-2*) MG-Hill OH.

Problem Solving. Mary S. Charuhas. (Essential Mathematics for Life Ser.: No. 8). 1995. pap. text 7.95 (*0-02-802614-4*) Glencoe.

Problem Solving. Margot Costanzo. Ed. by Julie Macfarlane. LC 95-123406. (Legal Skills Ser.). 254p. 1995. pap. 19.00 (*1-874241-46-5*, Pub. by Cavendish Pubng) Gaunt.

Problem Solving. Peggy Hapke Lewis. 1991. 6.95 (*1-55708-368-1*, C913) McDonald Pub Co.

Problem Solving. Multimedia Development Services Staff. (Plant Fundamentals Ser.). (Illus.). (Orig.). 1995. student ed. 30.00 (*1-57431-003-8*) Tech Trng Systs.

Problem Solving. School Mathematics Project Staff. (Mathematics Series: Ages 16-19). (Illus.). 106p. (C). 1993. pap. text 11.95 (*0-521-38844-9*) Cambridge U Pr.

Problem Solving. Thobum Educational Enterprises Staff. Ed. by Jennifer Whitfield. (Thinking Skills Library). (Illus.). 104p. (Orig.). (J). (gr. 2-5). 1997. pap., teacher ed. 9.95 (*1-56784-713-7*) Newbridge Educ.

Problem Solving 2nd ed. Basista. 1999. pap. text 18.00 (*0-471-37227-7*) Wiley.

Problem Solving, Vol. 1, Module III. Multimedia Development Services Staff. (Illus.). (Orig.). 1995. teacher ed. 49.95 (*1-57431-043-7*) Tech Trng Systs.

Problem Solving: A Handbook for Senior High School Teachers. Stephen Krulik & Jesse A. Rudnick. 280p. (C). 1988. pap. text 25.95 (*0-205-11788-0*, H17882) Allyn.

Problem Solving: A Statistician's Guide. Christopher Chatfield. 300p. 1989. 79.95 (*0-412-28670-X*) Chapman & Hall.

Problem Solving: A System Approach. Joseph E. Robertshaw & Stephen J. Mecca. 1991. 3.00 (*0-89433-119-1*) Petrocelli.

Problem Solving: Concepts & Methods for Community Organizations. Ralph Brody. LC 81-7221. 240p. (C). 1982. pap. 20.95 (*0-89885-079-7*, Kluwer Acad Hman Sci) Kluwer Academic.

Problem Solving: Critical Thinking & Communication Skills. Linda Little & Ingrid Greenberg. 128p. 1991. pap. text 18.23 (*0-8013-0603-5*, 78533) Longman.

Problem Solving: Current Issues. 2nd ed. Hank Kahney. LC 92-21171. (Open Guides to Psychology Ser.). 192p. 1993. pap. 34.95 (*0-335-19080-4*) OpUniv Pr.

Problem Solving: Manager's Guide. Martine Hilton et al. (Primary Health Care Management Advancement Programme (PHC MAP) Modules Ser.). 54p. 1993. pap. text. write for info. (*1-882839-19-6*) Aga Khan Fnd.

Problem Solving: Methods, Programming, & Future Concepts. Oleg V. German & Dimitri V. Ofitserov. LC 95-43865. (Studies in Computer Science & Artificial Intelligence: Vol. 12). 434p. 1995. 187.50 (*0-444-82226-7*) Elsevier.

Problem Solving: Preliminary Edition. Kadesch. 1996. pap. text, teacher ed. write for info. (*0-13-607987-3*) Allyn.

Problem-Solving: Preventing & Solving Common Horse Problems. Marty Marten. Ed. by Gary Vorhes. (Illus.). 247p. 1998. pap. 17.95 (*0-911647-43-0*) Western Horseman.

Problem-Solving: Problem-Oriented Policing in Newport News. John E. Eck & William Spelman. LC 87-62943. 150p. (Orig.). (C). 1987. pap. 19.00 (*1-878734-06-7*) Police Exec Res.

Problem Solving: Student Book. Mario C. Grignetti. (Odyssey Ser.). (J). 1995. pap. text, student ed. 5.00 (*0-88106-144-1*, PS10) Charlesbridge Pub.

Problem Solving: Teacher Manual. Mario C. Grignetti. (Odyssey Ser.). (J). 1995. teacher ed., spiral bd. 15.00 (*0-88106-143-3*, PS20) Charlesbridge Pub.

Problem Solving: Teacher Resource Book. Mario C. Grignetti. (Odyssey Ser.). 1995. teacher ed., ring bd. 90.00 (*0-88106-403-3*, PS15) Charlesbridge Pub.

Problem Solving - Decision Making: A Workbook for Managers & Supervisors. John J. Connor. (Illus.). 100p. 1998. pap. text 19.95 (*0-945820-09-7*) Harris & Connor.

Problem Solving, Abstraction & Design Using C++ 2nd ed. Frank Friedman. 768p. (C). 1997. pap. text. write for info. (*0-201-30002-8*) Addison-Wesley.

Problem Solving, Abstraction & Design Using C++ 2nd ed. Frank L. Friedman. (C). 1997. pap. text. write for info. (*0-201-84847-3*) Addison-Wesley.

Problem Solving-Across the Disciplines. R. R. Kadesch. (Illus.). 230p. (C). 1996. pap. 22.00 (*0-13-654187-9*) P-H.

Problem Solving Activities. Jean G. DeGaetano. (Illus.). 120p. (Orig.). (J). (gr. 1-6). 1996. pap. text 26.00 (*1-886143-35-8*, G830) Grt Ideas Tching.

Problem Solving Activities in Astronomy. 2nd ed. Frederick R. Hickok. 76p. (C). spiral bd. 17.95 (*0-7872-6704-X*) Kendall-Hunt.

Problem Solving Activities with Mottik. Gillian Blundell & Noel Graham. 64p. (J). (gr. k-4). pap. 12.50 (*1-871098-21-1*, Pub. by Claire Pubns) Parkwest Pubns.

Problem Solving Analytical Biochemistry. David J. Holme. (C). 1996. pap. text 24.00 (*0-582-22710-0*) Addison-Wesley.

Problem Solving & Algebra Too. 4th rev. ed. Carla Oblas. 496p. (C). 1991. pap. text 20.00 (*0-89801-022-5*) NE Univ Pub.

Problem Solving & Comprehension. 5th ed. Arthur Whimbey & Jack Lochhead. 1991. teacher ed. write for info. (*0-89859-967-9*) L Erlbaum Assocs.

Problem Solving & Comprehension. 6th ed. Arthur Whimbey & Jack Lochhead. LC 98-33156. 400p. 1999. 17.00 (*0-8058-3274-2*) L Erlbaum Assocs.

Problem Solving & Computation for Scientists: An Introduction Using C. Steven R. Lerman. LC 92-24326. 544p. 1992. pap. 67.00 (*0-13-482126-2*, Pub. by P-H) S&S Trade.

Problem Solving & Computer Programming. Peter Grogono & S. H. Nelson. 1982. pap. text. write for info. (*0-318-56705-9*) Addison-Wesley.

Problem Solving & Decision Making. Barbara J. Braham. (YA - Adult Education Ser.). 1992. pap. 9.95 (*0-538-70555-8*) S-W Pub.

***Problem Solving & Decision Making.** (Illus.). 150p. 2000. reprint ed. spiral bd. 29.95 (*1-57431-177-8*, PSDM) Tech Trng Systs.

Problem Solving & Intelligence. Helga A. Rowe. 416p. (C). 1985. text 79.95 (*0-89859-347-6*) L Erlbaum Assocs.

Problem Solving & Intelligence. Helga A. Rowe. LC 84-18855. (Illus.). 406p. 1985. reprint ed. pap. 125.90 (*0-608-05703-7*, 206621800007) Bks Demand.

Problem Solving & Investigations. David P. Lawrence. (Graphing Calculator Connection Ser.). 102p. (YA). (gr. 6-12). 1995. spiral bd. 23.95 (*1-881641-31-7*) Pencil Point.

Problem Solving & Program Design in C. 3rd ed. Jeri R. Hanly & Elliot B. Koffman. LC 98-44233. 276p. (C). 1998. pap. text 65.00 (*0-201-35748-8*) Addison-Wesley.

Problem Solving & Program Design in Computers with Advanced Topics Supplement. Jerry Hanly. (C). 1994. pap. text 58.00 (*0-201-53099-6*) Addison-Wesley.

Problem Solving & Programing Concepts. Boeve & Sprankle. 312p. 1998. pap. text 25.75 (*0-536-01520-1*) Pearson Custom.

Problem Solving & Programming Concepts. 4th ed. Maureen Sprankle. LC 97-19415. 486p. (C). 1997. pap. 80.00 (*0-13-631805-3*) P-H.

***Problem Solving & Programming Concepts.** 5th ed. (C). 2001. write for info. (*0-13-026727-9*); write for info. (*0-13-026728-7*) Addison-Wesley.

***Problem Solving & Programming Concepts.** 5th ed. Maureen Sprankle. LC 99-59393. 512p. 2000. 77.00 (*0-13-022967-9*) P-H.

Problem Solving & Structured Programming in BASIC. Elliot B. Koffman & Frank L. Friedman. LC 78-65355. 1979. pap. text 39.75 (*0-201-03888-9*) Addison-Wesley.

Problem Solving & Structured Programming in Fortran Frank L. Friedman & Elliot B. Koffman. LC 76-45154. (Addison-Wesley Computer Science & Information Processing Ser.). xvi, 404p. 1977. write for info. (*0-201-01967-1*) Addison-Wesley.

Problem Solving & Structured Programming in FORTRAN. 2nd ed. Frank L. Friedman & Elliot B. Koffman. 1981. student ed. write for info. (*0-201-02465-9*) Addison-Wesley.

Problem Solving & Structured Programming in FORTRAN. 3rd ed. Frank L. Friedman & Elliot B. Koffman. LC 86-8055. 544p. (C). 1986. pap. text. write for info. (*0-201-11561-1*) Addison-Wesley.

Problem Solving & Structured Programming in Pascal. 2nd ed. Elliot B. Koffman. LC 84-16811. (C). 1985. teacher ed. write for info. (*0-201-11737-1*); text. write for info. (*0-201-11736-3*) Addison-Wesley.

Problem Solving & Structured Programming in WATFIV. Frank L. Friedman & Elliot B. Koffman. LC 81-20598. (Illus.). 480p. 1982. pap. text 35.50 (*0-201-10482-2*) Addison-Wesley.

Problem Solving & the Computer: A Structured Concept with PL 1 (PLC) 2nd ed. Joseph Shortt & Thomas C. Wilson. 1979. pap. text 31.25 (*0-201-06916-4*) Addison-Wesley.

***Problem Solving Appraoch Math Bridgewater State.** Billstein & Libeskind. 1998. pap. text 73.00 (*0-201-63627-1*) Addison-Wesley.

***Problem Solving Approach: Mathematics for Elementary School Teachers.** Billstein & Libeskind. 1998. pap. text 69.00 (*0-201-47228-7*) Addison-Wesley.

Problem-Solving Approach to Adjustment. George Spivack et al. LC 76-19501. (Jossey-Bass Behaviorial Science Ser.). 336p. reprint ed. pap. 104.20 (*0-608-12212-2*, 202388100034) Bks Demand.

Problem-Solving Approach to Introductory Algebra. 2nd ed. Mervin L. Keedy & Marvin L. Bittinger. LC 85-18592. (C). 1986. pap. text 34.36 (*0-201-12968-X*); student ed. 14.36 (*0-201-12970-1*); write for info. (*0-201-12971-X*); write for info. (*0-318-59420-X*) Addison-Wesley.

Problem Solving Approach to Mathematics. 6th ed. Richard Billstein. Ed. by Karen Guardino. LC 96-12195. 928p. (C). 1996. 81.00 (*0-201-84664-0*) Addison-Wesley.

Problem Solving Approach to Mathematics for Elementary School Teachers. 5th ed. Richard Billstein et al. LC 92-32185. 1992. text 40.75 (*0-201-60250-4*) Addison-Wesley.

Problem Solving Approach to Mathematics for Elementary School Teachers. 6th ed. Billstein. (C). 1996. write for info. (*0-201-59130-8*) Addison-Wesley.

Problem Solving Approach to Mathematics for Elementary School Teachers. 6th ed. Richard Brillstein. Ed. by Karen Guardino. LC 96-26205. 928p. (C). 1999. 92.00 (*0-201-56649-4*) Addison-Wesley.

Problem Solving Approach to Mathematics with Student Solutions Manual Bundle. Billstein. 1995. write for info. (*0-201-85718-9*) Addison-Wesley.

Problem-Solving Approach to Pension Funding & Valuation. 2nd ed. William H. Aitken. 405p. (C). 1996. pap. text 52.50 (*1-56698-200-6*) Actex Pubns.

Problem Solving Arts: Part One Syllabus. Norman H. Crowhurst. 1976. pap. text 12.95 (*0-89420-085-2*, 256040); audio 227.10 (*0-89420-175-1*, 256000) Natl Book.

Problem Solving Arts: Part Three Syllabus. Norman H. Crowhurst. 1978. pap. text 15.95 (*0-89420-040-2*, 256130); audio 196.20 (*0-89420-177-8*, 256090) Natl Book.

Problem Solving Arts: Part Two Syllabus. Norman H. Crowhurst. 1977. pap. text 14.95 (*0-89420-029-1*, 256082); audio 195.80 (*0-89420-176-X*, 256050) Natl Book.

Problem Solving Assessment. Avish Dworkin & Nancy Dworkin. Ed. by Betty Lou Kratoville. 219p. (Orig.). 1988. pap. text 16.50 (*0-87879-593-6*) Acad Therapy.

Problem Solving Challenges. Don Miller & Bishnu Naraine. 114p. pap. text 12.00 (*1-883547-06-7*) Tricon Pub.

***Problem Solving Comprehension: Instructor's Manual.** 6th ed. Arthur Whimby & Jack Lochhead. 38p. 1999. pap. write for info. (*0-8058-3676-4*) L Erlbaum Assocs.

Problem Solving Connections see Conexiones Resolucion de Problemas: Libro del Estudiante - Nivel Anaranjado

Problem Solving Connections see Conexiones Resolucion de Problemas: Libro del Estudiante - Nivel Azul

Problem Solving Connections see Conexiones Resolucion de Problemas: Libro del Estudiante - Nivel Marron

Problem Solving Connections see Conexiones Resolucion de Problemas: Libro del Estudiante - Nivel Oro

Problem Solving Connections see Conexiones Resolucion de Problemas: Guia del Maestro - Nivel Anaranjado

Problem Solving Connections see Conexiones Resolucion de Problemas: Guia del Maestro - Nivel Azul

Problem Solving Connections see Conexiones Resolucion de Problemas: Guia del Maestro - Nivel Marron

Problem Solving Connections see Conexiones Resolucion de Problemas: Guia del Maestro - Nivel Oro

Problem Solving Connections: Blue Level Student Book. William Driscoll & Donald W. Robb. (Illus.). (J). (gr. 4). 1992. pap. text, student ed. 5.00 (*0-88106-652-4*) Charlesbridge Pub.

Problem Solving Connections: Blue Level Teacher Manual. William Driscoll & Donald W. Robb. (Illus.). 1992. pap. text, teacher ed. 15.00 (*0-88106-653-2*) Charlesbridge Pub.

Problem Solving Connections: Gold Level Student Book. William Driscoll & Donald W. Robb. (Illus.). (J). (gr. 6). 1992. pap. text, student ed. 5.00 (*0-88106-656-7*) Charlesbridge Pub.

Problem Solving Connections: Gold Level Teacher Manual. William Driscoll & Donald W. Robb. (Illus.). 1992. pap. text, teacher ed. 15.00 (*0-88106-657-5*) Charlesbridge Pub.

Problem Solving Connections: Green Level Student Book. William Driscoll & Donald W. Robb. (Illus.). (J). (gr. 2). 1996. pap. text, student ed. 5.00 (*1-57091-027-8*) Charlesbridge Pub.

Problem Solving Connections: Green Level Teacher Manual. William Driscoll & Donald W. Robb. (Illus.). 1996. pap. text, teacher ed. 30.00 (*1-57091-028-6*) Charlesbridge Pub.

Problem Solving Connections: Orange Level Student Book. William Driscoll & Donald W. Robb. (Illus.). (J). (gr. 3). 1992. pap. text, student ed. 5.00 (*0-88106-650-8*) Charlesbridge Pub.

Problem Solving Connections: Orange Level Teacher Manual. William Driscoll & Donald W. Robb. (Illus.). 1992. pap. text, teacher ed. 15.00 (*0-88106-651-6*) Charlesbridge Pub.

Problem Solving Connections: Red Level Student Book. William Driscoll & Donald W. Robb. (Illus.). (J). (gr. 1). 1996. pap. text, student ed. 5.00 (*1-57091-025-1*) Charlesbridge Pub.

Problem Solving Connections: Red Level Teacher Manual. William Driscoll & Donald W. Robb. (Illus.). 1996. pap. text, teacher ed. 30.00 (*1-57091-026-X*) Charlesbridge Pub.

Problem Solving Connections: Tan Level Student Book. William Driscoll & Donald W. Robb. (Illus.). (J). (gr. 5). 1992. pap. text, student ed. 5.00 (*0-88106-654-0*) Charlesbridge Pub.

Problem Solving Connections: Tan Level Teacher Manual. William Driscoll & Donald W. Robb. (Illus.). 1992. pap. text, teacher ed. 15.00 (*0-88106-655-9*) Charlesbridge Pub.

Problem Solving-Decision Making for Social & Academic Success: A School-Based Approach. Maurice J. Elias & STeven E. Tobias. 128p. 1990. pap. 11.95 (*0-8106-3007-9*) NEA.

Problem Solving Design. Howell. (C). 1995. pap. text 10.25 (*0-8053-6349-1*) Benjamin-Cummings.

Problem Solving Environm. Roland Ennos. (C). 1995. pap. text 29.95 (*0-582-21874-8*, Pub. by Addison-Wesley) Longman.

Problem Solving Excel Windows 95: Version 7.0. Sherry L. Fowler. LC 97-180849. 500p. 1997. pap. 51.33 (*0-13-235151-X*) P-H.

Problem-Solving Exercises for Nutrition. 5th rev. ed. Betty A. Clamp et al. (Illus.). 1997. pap. text, spiral bd. 23.95 (*1-890871-00-1*) Holcomb Hath.

Problem-Solving Experiences in Mathematics. 2nd ed. R. Charles et al. (Grade 1 BLMs Ser.). (J). 1995. pap. write for info. (*0-201-49361-6*) Addison-Wesley.

Problem-Solving Experiences in Mathematics, Grade 1. Randall Charles et al. 1994. pap. 29.95 (*0-201-49404-3*) Addison-Wesley.

Problem-Solving Experiences in Mathematics, Grade 2. R. Charles et al. Ed. by Cathy Anderson & Mali Apple. (Problem-Solving Experiences in Mathematics Ser.). (Illus.). 224p. (Orig.). 1995. pap., teacher ed. 23.95 (*0-201-49405-1*) Supplementary Div.

Problem-Solving Experiences in Mathematics, Grade 2. 2nd ed. R. Charles et al. Ed. by Cathy Anderson & Mali Apple. (Problem-Solving Experiences in Mathematics Ser.). (Illus.). (Orig.). 1995. pap., student ed. write for info. (*0-201-49362-4*) Addison-Wesley.

Problem-Solving Experiences in Mathematics, Grade 2, BLM. 2nd ed. R. Charles et al. Ed. by Cathy Anderson & Mali Apple. (Problem-Solving Experiences in Mathematics Ser.). (Illus.). (Orig.). (J). 1995. 9.75 (*0-201-49363-2*) Supplementary Div.

Problem-Solving Experiences in Mathematics, Kindergarten. R. Charles et al. Ed. by Cathy Anderson & Mali Apple. (Problem-Solving Experiences in Mathematics Ser.). (Illus.). 200p. (Orig.). 1995. pap., teacher ed. 23.95 (*0-201-49085-4*) Supplementary Div.

Problem-Solving Experiences in Mathematics, Kindergarten, BLM. R. Charles et al. Ed. by Cathy Anderson & Mali Apple. (Problem-Solving Experiences in Mathematics Ser.). (Illus.). (Orig.). (J). (gr. k). 1995. write for info. (*0-201-49086-2*) Addison-Wesley.

Problem Solving Explorations. Don Miller. 1997. pap. 86.95 (*0-471-36659-5*) Wiley.

Problem Solving for Air Monitoring. Nesss. (Biology Ser.). 1998. pap. 34.95 (*0-442-02484-3*, VNR) Wiley.

An Asterisk (*) at the beginning of an entry indicates that the title is appearing for the first time.

Problem Solving for Entrepreneurs: A Creative New Approach to Overcoming Your Business Problems. Drysdale. 1995. pap. text 15.95 (*0-9639506-1-4*) SMD Pubng.

Problem Solving for Health Care Quality Improvement: The Basics & Beyond. Barbara Katz. (Illus.). 202p. (Orig.). 1994. pap. 29.95 (*0-9640405-0-6*) Hlth Interact.

Problem Solving for Math Today, 1987, set. Abbott. (J). (gr. 8). 1987. pap., wbk. ed. 127.95 (*0-15-350098-0*) Harcourt Schl Pubs.

Problem Solving for Oil Painters: Recognizing What's Gone Wrong & How to Make It Right. Gregg Kreutz. (Illus.). 144p. 1997. pap. text 19.95 (*0-8230-4097-6*) Watsn-Guptill.

Problem Solving for Results. Victor Newman. 158p. 1995. 61.95 (*0-566-07566-0*, Pub. by Gower) Ashgate Pub Co.

Problem Solving for Results. William Roth et al. (Illus.). 208p. (Orig.). 1996. per. 34.95 (*1-57444-018-7*) St Lucie Pr.

Problem Solving for Supervisors. (Training in a Box Ser.). 74p. 1997. ring bd. 49.00 (*1-57927-027-1*) APCO Inst.

Problem Solving for Tutorials in Anatomy. Peter H. Abrahams et al. LC 95-11349. Orig. Title: Pocket Examiner in Regional & Clinical Anatomy. 1995. reprint ed. pap. text 29.95 (*0-443-05285-9*) Church.

Problem-Solving Geography Analysis in a Changing World: Analysis in a Changing World. Norman Law & David Smith. (Illus.). 240p. (Orig.). 1993. pap. 36.50 (*0-7487-1355-7*, Pub. by S Thornes Pubs) Trans-Atl Phila.

Problem-solving Group Interaction. Bobby R. Patton & Kim Giffin. LC 73-6230. xii, 264p. 1973. 6.95 (*0-06-045059-2*, HarperHorizon) HarpC.

Problem-Solving Handbook for High School Journalism Advisers. Bruce L. Plopper. 1992. 8.50 (*0-317-04966-6*) Quill & Scroll.

Problem Solving in a Dynamic Environment. Yan Hong. 200p. 1995. text 48.00 (*981-02-2029-4*) World Scientific Pub.

Problem Solving in a Project Environment: A Consulting Process. L. Thomas King. LC 80-20063. 216p. 1981. text 32.50 (*0-471-08115-9*) Krieger.

Problem Solving in Analytical Chemistry. Karen Crawford & Alan Heaton. Ed. by Denise Rafferty & Sara Sleigh. 159p. 1999. pap. 29.00 (*1-870343-46-8*) Royal Soc Chem.

Problem Solving in Analytical Chemistry & Solutions Manual, 2 vols. T. P. Hadjiioannou & Gary D. Christian. (Illus.). 618p. 1988. pap. text 33.00 (*0-08-036967-7*, Pergamon Pr) Elsevier.

Problem Solving in Apple PASCAL. Lowell A. Carmony et al. (Computers & Math Ser.). 213p. (YA). (gr. 10-12). 1984. disk 16.80 (*0-7167-8170-0*, Computer Sci Pr) W H Freeman.

Problem Solving in Arithmetic. Leon N. Neulen. LC 70-177116. (Columbia University. Teachers College. Contributions to Education Ser.: No. 483). (C). reprint ed. 37.50 (*0-404-55483-0*) AMS Pr.

***Problem Solving in Biology.** Billeter. 152p. 1999. pap. text 13.00 (*0-536-02762-5*) Pearson Custom.

Problem Solving in Biology: A Laboratory Workbook. 3rd ed. Eugene H. Kaplan. 448p. (C). 1997. pap. text 53.00 (*0-02-362050-1*, Macmillan Coll) P-H.

Problem Solving in Blood Banking. Robert R. Harr & Deirdre DeSantis. (C). 1997. 125.00 (*0-8036-0277-4*) Davis Co.

Problem Solving in Business & Management. Hicks. 1991. pap. write for info. (*1-86152-387-4*) ITBP.

Problem Solving in Business & Management: Hard, Soft & Creative Approaches. M. J. Hicks. 352p. 1991. mass mkt. 37.95 (*0-412-37490-0*) Chapman & Hall.

Problem Solving in C Including Breadth & Laboratories. Angela B. Shiflet. LC 94-37379. 1088p. (C). 1995. mass mkt. 63.95 (*0-314-04554-6*) West Pub.

Problem Solving in C++ Including Breath & Laboratories. Angela B. Shiflet. LC 97-35205. (C). 1997. mass mkt. 67.95 (*0-534-95139-2*) PWS Pubs.

Problem Solving in Chemical Engineering in Numerical Methods. Mordechai Shacham & Michael B. Cutlip. LC 98-26056. 464p. (C). 1998. pap. text 67.00 (*0-13-862566-2*) P-H.

Problem Solving in Chemometrics. Brereton. text. write for info. (*0-471-48977-8*); pap. text. write for info. (*0-471-48978-6*) Wiley.

Problem Solving in Clinical Medicine: From Data to Diagnosis. 2nd ed. Paul Cutler. (Illus.). 550p. 1997. pap. text 35.00 (*0-683-02252-0*) Lppncott W & W.

Problem Solving in Clinical Medicine: From Data to Diagnosis. 3rd ed. Paul Cutler. 531p. 1997. 49.95 (*0-683-30377-5*); pap. 35.00 (*0-683-30167-5*) Lppncott W & W.

Problem Solving in Computational Molecular Science: Molecules in Different Environments. Ed. by S. Wilson & G. H. Diercksen. LC 97-29152. (NATO ASI Series. Series C, Mathematical & Physical Sciences). 428p. 1997. text 217.50 (*0-7923-4751-X*) Kluwer Academic.

Problem-Solving in Conservation Biology & Wildlife Management: Exercises for Class, Field & Laboratory. James P. Gibbs et al. (Illus.). 215p. 1998. pap. 19.95 (*0-632-04372-5*) Blackwell Sci.

Problem Solving in Endodontics. 3rd ed. James L. Gutmann et al. LC 97-106504. (Illus.). 384p. (C). (gr. 13). 1996. text 81.95 (*0-8151-4044-4*, 25551) Mosby Inc.

Problem Solving in Families: Research & Practice. Samuel Vuchinich. LC 98-25540. (Understanding Families Ser.). 238p. 1998. 46.00 (*0-7619-0877-3*); pap. 21.95 (*0-7619-0878-1*) Sage.

Problem Solving in General Chemistry. 2nd ed. Ronald Delorenzo. 416p. (C). 1992. text. write for info. (*0-697-16411-X*) Brown & Benchmark.

Problem Solving in General Chemistry. 5th ed. Whitten. (C). 1995. wbk. ed. 24.00 (*0-03-015698-X*) Harcourt Coll Pubs.

***Problem Solving in Geology.** 2nd ed. 2000. teacher ed., lab manual ed. write for info. (*0-13-026167-X*) P-H.

Problem Solving in Groups. 2nd ed. Mike Robson. 160p. 1993. 61.95 (*0-566-07414-1*, Pub. by Gower); pap. 29.95 (*0-566-07415-X*, Pub. by Gower) Ashgate Pub Co.

Problem Solving in Mathematics. Lane County Mathematics Project Staff. 1997. pap. text 19.95 (*0-86651-184-9*); pap. text 19.95 (*0-86651-182-2*); pap. text 19.95 (*0-86651-183-0*) Seymour Pubns.

Problem Solving in Medicine, Vol. 1. Ed. by William Rosenberg & E. Edward Bittar. Date not set. 128.50 (*0-7623-0397-2*) Jai Pr.

Problem Solving in Microeconomics. Nancy T. Gallini. (C). 1991. pap. text 14.40 (*0-7167-2174-0*) W H Freeman.

Problem Solving in Microeconomics: A Study Guide. Nancy T. Gallini. (C). 1997. student ed., suppl. ed. write for info. (*0-13-501628-2*, Macmillan Coll) P-H.

Problem Solving in Open Worlds: A Case Study in Design. Thomas R. Hinrichs. 240p. 1992. text 49.95 (*0-8058-1228-8*) L Erlbaum Assocs.

Problem Solving in Orthodontics: Goal Oriented Treatment Strategies. Charles J. Burstone & Michael R. Marcotte. (Illus.). 250p. write for info. (*0-86715-353-9*) Quint Pub Co.

Problem Solving in Physiology. Joel A. Michael. 400p. (C). 1998. pap. text 36.67 (*0-13-244104-7*) P-H.

Problem Solving in Recreation & Parks. 3rd ed. Joseph J. Bannon & James A. Busser. LC 91-68237. (Illus.). 440p. (C). 1992. text 44.95 (*0-915611-50-3*) Sagamore Pub.

Problem Solving in Science & Technology: Extending Good Classroom Practice. Ed. by Mike Wass. LC 95-107788. (Roehampton Teaching Studies). 144p. 1994. pap. 27.00 (*1-85346-270-5*, Pub. by David Fulton) Taylor & Francis.

Problem Solving in Science & Technology: Workplace, No. 2. D. Rowlands. (C). 1989. 220.00 (*0-09-172781-2*, Pub. by S Thornes Pubs) St Mut.

Problem Solving in the Early Childhood Classroom. Joan Britz & Norma Richard. 96p. 1992. pap. 10.95 (*0-8106-0360-8*) NEA.

Problem Solving in Turbo Pascal Including Breadth & Laboratories. Angela B. Shiflet & John Hinkel. 750p. (C). 1997. pap. text. write for info. (*0-314-06745-0*) West Pub.

***Problem Solving Journey: Your Guide to Making Decisions & Getting Results.** Christopher Hoenig. 2000. pap. 20.00 (*0-7382-0280-0*, Pub. by Perseus Pubng) HarpC.

***Problem Solving Made Almost Easy: A Companion to Alexander/Sadiku's Fundamentals of Electric Circuits.** Matthew N. Sadiku. 352p. (C). 2000. pap. 28.13 (*0-07-236144-1*) McGrw-H Hghr Educ.

Problem-Solving Math for Middle Grades, Vol. 2604. Robert W. Smith. Ed. by Mary P. Ferraro. (Illus.). 96p. (J). (gr. 6-8). 1998. pap. 9.98 (*1-57471-364-7*) Creat Teach Pr.

Problem Solving Method. (AT&T Quality Library). (Illus.). (Orig.). pap. 24.95 (*0-932764-51-7*) AT&T Customer Info.

Problem Solving, Modeling, & Data Analysis Labs. 2nd ed. Wendy Metzger. (C). 1997. pap. text 22.76 (*0-669-41673-8*) HM Trade Div.

Problem Solving Modern Physics. Trinklein. 1992. pap. text, wbk. ed. 15.00 (*0-03-014523-6*) Harcourt.

Problem Solving, Physical Pharmacy IV. Alfred Martin. 222p. 1993. text 19.50 (*0-8121-1642-9*) Lppncott W & W.

Problem-Solving Picture Cards: Daily Living Situations for Adults with Disabilities. Mary J. Pitti & Traci Meier. 13p. 1992. pap., student ed. 72.50 (*0-7616-7798-4*) Commun Skill.

Problem-Solving Power. Thomas B. Franklin. 1988. pap. 19.95 (*0-925053-00-7*) Octagon CA.

Problem-solving Principles for Ada Programmers: Applied Logic, Psychology & Grit. William E. Lewis. LC 82-178782. 183p. 1982. write for info. (*0-8104-5211-1*) Sams.

Problem-solving Principles for Fortran Programmers: Applied Logic, Psychology & Grit. William E. Lewis. LC 81-2070. 177 p. 1981. write for info. (*0-8104-5430-0*) Sams.

Problem-solving Principles for Pascal Programmers: Applied Logic, Psychology & Grit. William E. Lewis. LC 81-2057. 179 p. 1981. write for info. (*0-8104-5767-9*) Sams.

Problem-solving Principles for Programmers: Applied Logic, Psychology & Grit. William E. Lewis. LC 80-23834. 163p. 1980. write for info. (*0-8104-5138-7*) Sams.

Problem Solving, Reasoning & Communicating: Reasoning & Communicating, Grades K to 8. Arthur J. Baroody. LC 92-27749. (Illus.). 160p. (Orig.). (J). (gr. k-8). 1992. pap. text 16.60 (*0-02-306488-9*, Macmillan Coll) P-H.

Problem Solving Safari - Art. Barbara F. Backer. Ed. by Elizabeth S. McKinnon. (Problem Solving Safari Ser.). (Illus.). 32p. (Orig.). (J). (ps). 1997. pap. 4.95 (*1-57029-118-7*) Totline Pubns.

Problem Solving Safari - Blocks. Susan A. Miller. Ed. by Gayle Bittinger. (Problem Solving Safari Ser.). (Illus.). 32p. (Orig.). 1997. pap. 4.95 (*1-57029-119-5*, 4302) Totline Pubns.

Problem Solving Safari - Dramatic Play. Susan A. Miller. Ed. by Gayle Bittinger. (Problem Solving Safari Ser.). (Illus.). 32p. 1997. pap. 4.95 (*1-57029-120-9*, 4303) Totline Pubns.

Problem Solving Safari - Manipulatives. Barbara F. Backer. Ed. by Gayle Bittinger. (Problem Solving Safari Ser.). (Illus.). 32p. (Orig.). 1997. pap. 4.95 (*1-57029-121-7*, 4304) Totline Pubns.

Problem Solving Safari - Outdoors. Susan A. Miller. Ed. by Elizabeth S. McKinnon. (Problem Solving Safari Ser.). (Illus.). 32p. (Orig.). 1997. pap. 4.95 (*1-57029-122-5*, 4305) Totline Pubns.

Problem Solving Safari - Science. Barbara F. Backer. Ed. by Gayle Bittinger. (Problem Solving Safari Ser.). (Illus.). 32p. (Orig.). 1997. pap. 4.95 (*1-57029-123-3*, 4306) Totline Pubns.

Problem Solving Simplified: A Common Sense Approach to Solving Complex Problems. Jim Burghorn. 115p. (Orig.). 1997. pap. 39.95 (*0-9640615-1-1*) Comm Sense Pubns.

Problem-Solving Situations Vol. 1: A Teacher's Resource Book. Joel Greenberg. 150p. 1990. 15.00 (*0-931011-14-0*) Grapevine Pubns.

Problem-Solving Skills see Productive Supervisor: A Program of Practical Managerial Skills

Problem Solving Skills see Career Skills Library

Problem Solving Skills for Children. Bettie B. Youngs. 80p. (J). (gr. 4-9). 1996. pap. 10.00 (*1-880396-32-7*, JP2102-02) Jalmar Pr.

Problem Solving Skills for Children. Bettie B. Youngs. 69p. (J). (gr. k-6). 1989. pap. text 9.95 (*0-940221-01-2*) Lrng Tools.

Problem Solving Strategies. Arthur Engel. LC 97-10090. (Problem Books in Mathematics Ser.). 400p. 1997. 49.00 (*0-387-98219-1*) Spr-Verlag.

Problem Solving Strategies. 5th ed. Linda Flower. (C). 1999. pap. text 25.00 (*0-15-503965-2*) Harcourt.

Problem Solving Strategies: Crossing the River with Dogs. Ted Herr & Ken Johnson. (YA). (gr. 9-12). 1994. 24.95 (*1-55953-068-5*) Key Curr Pr.

Problem Solving Strategies: Crossing the River with Dogs - Teacher's Resource Book & Answer Key. Ted Herr & Ken Johnson. (YA). (gr. 9-12). 1994. 19.95 (*1-55953-069-3*) Key Curr Pr.

Problem Solving Strategies: Grades 3-4. Sheila Frankel & Barbara Barbour. Ed. by Mary L. Muffoletto. (Illus.). 64p. (Orig.). 1996. pap., teacher ed. 6.95 (*1-889369-01-2*, TI0004) Teaching Ink.

Problem Solving Strategies: Grades 4-5. Sheila Frankel & Barbara Barbour. Ed. by Mary L. Muffoletto. (Illus.). 64p. (Orig.). 1996. pap., teacher ed. 6.95 (*1-889369-02-0*, TI0005) Teaching Ink.

Problem Solving Strategies: Grades 5-6. Ruth Emmel & Marion Ruchelle. Ed. by Mary L. Muffoletto. (Illus.). 64p. 1996. pap., teacher ed. 6.95 (*1-889369-03-9*, TI0006) Teaching Ink.

Problem Solving Strategies: Grades 6-8. Patty Corwin & Cheryl O'Callahan. Ed. by Mary L. Muffoletto. (Illus.). 64p. 1996. pap., teacher ed. 6.95 (*1-889369-04-7*, TI0007) Teaching Ink.

Problem Solving Strategies: Parent-Teacher Guide to Improving Your Child's Test Scores. Katharyn R. McPherson. 52p. Date not set. pap. text, spiral bd. 12.95 (*0-9647611-1-4*) McPhrsn Prob.

Problem Solving Strategies: Parent/Teacher Guide to Improving Your Child's Test Scores in Math, Writing, Reading (Grades 1 - College) Katharyn R. McPherson. 53p. (J). (gr. 1-13). 1996. pap. text 15.95 (*0-9647611-0-6*) McPhrsn Prob.

Problem-Solving Strategies - Student's Manual: Molding Materials & Process Troubleshooting, Module Four, Lesson 3. (Illus.). 1997. pap., student ed. write for info. (*1-58677-036-5*) Polymer Train.

Problem Solving Strategies (Adaptable for Grades 1 - 12) Improve Test Scores in Math, Writing, Reading. 2nd ed. Katharyn R. McPherson. 40p. (Orig.). (J). (gr. 1-12). 1992. pap. 9.95 (*0-9647611-8-1*) McPhrsn Prob.

Problem-Solving Strategies for Efficient & Elegant Solutions: A Resource for the Mathematics Teacher. Alfred S. Posamentier & Stephen Krulik. LC 98-19702. 264p. 1998. 69.96 (*0-8039-6697-0*) Corwin Pr.

Problem-Solving Strategies for Efficient & Elegant Solutions: A Resource for the Mathematics Teacher. Alfred S. Posamentier & Stephen Krulik. LC 98-19702. (1-Off Ser.). (Illus.). 264p. 1998. pap. 32.95 (*0-8039-6698-9*) Corwin Pr.

Problem-Solving Strategies for the Intermediate Grades. Linda Heibel. 160p. (J). (gr. 4-8). 14.99 (*0-86653-916-6*, FE0916) Fearon Teacher Aids.

Problem-Solving Strategies for Writing. 4th ed. Linda Flower. LC 91-78229. (Illus.). 351p. (C). 1992. pap. text, teacher ed. 3.50 (*0-15-500202-3*) Harcourt Coll Pubs.

Problem-Solving Strategies for Writing. 4th ed. Linda Flower. (Illus.). 351p. (C). 1993. pap. text 36.50 (*0-15-500170-1*) Harcourt Coll Pubs.

Problem Solving, Tape, Fort177 Pk. Dolores M. Etter. 1984. disk 53.95 (*0-8053-2524-7*) Benjamin-Cummings.

Problem Solving Techniques for Teams. Dartnell Corp. Staff. LC 97-66738. (Illus.). 88p. 1997. pap., wbk. ed. 16.95 (*0-85013-291-6*) Dartnell Corp.

Problem-Solving Techniques in Childrearing. Myrna B. Shure & George Spivack. LC 77-93677. (Jossey-Bass Social & Behavioral Science Ser.). 283p. reprint ed. pap. 87.80 (*0-608-18034-3*, 205220200058) Bks Demand.

Problem Solving Techniques Pascal. Peter Grogono. 320p. (C). 1982. pap. text. write for info. (*0-318-50144-9*) Addison-Wesley.

Problem-Solving Therapy. 2nd ed. Jay Haley. LC 87-45413. (Social & Behavioral Science Ser.). 287p. 1991. pap. 22.95 (*1-55542-362-0*) Jossey-Bass.

Problem-Solving Therapy: A Social Competence Approach to Clinical Intervention. 2nd ed. Thomas J. D'Zurilla & Arthur M. Nezu. LC 98-48399. (Behavior Therapy & Behavioral Medicine Ser.). (Illus.). 256p. 1999. 42.95 (*0-8261-1266-8*) Springer Pub.

Problem-Solving Therapy: New Strategies for Effective Family Therapy. Jay Haley. LC 76-11889. (Jossey-Bass Behavioral Science Ser.). 291p. reprint ed. pap. 90.30 (*0-8357-4981-9*, 203791400009) Bks Demand.

Problem-Solving Therapy for Depression: Theory, Research & Clinical Guidelines. Arthur M. Nezu et al. LC 88-17287. (Personality Processes Ser.). 274p. 1989. 105.00 (*0-471-62885-9*) Wiley.

Problem Solving Through Business & Technical Communication. 3rd ed. Rebecca S. Daley. 228p. (C). 1994. spiral bd. 26.95 (*0-8403-9151-X*) Kendall-Hunt.

Problem Solving Through Critical Thinking. Ronald R. Edwards. (J). (gr. 4-7). 1995. pap. 8.95 (*0-201-48024-7*) Addison-Wesley.

Problem Solving Through Critical Thinking. Ronald R. Edwards & Wanda D. Cook. 48p. (J). (gr. 5-8). 1980. pap. text 8.95 (*0-938587-13-7*) Cuisenaire.

Problem-Solving Through Problems. L. C. Larson. Ed. by P. R. Halmos. (Problem Books in Mathematics). (Illus.). xi, 332p. 1997. reprint ed. 45.00 (*0-387-96171-2*) Spr-Verlag.

Problem Solving Through Recreational Mathematics. Bonnie Averbach. LC 99-52198. 480p. 2000. pap. text 14.95 (*0-486-40917-1*) Dover.

Problem Solving Using C. 2nd ed. Yuksel Uckan. LC 98-21028. 750p. 1998. 43.00 (*0-256-26377-9*, Irwn McGrw-H) McGrw-H Hghr Educ.

Problem Solving Using C: Structured Programing Techniques 2nd ed. Yuksel Uckan. LC 98-21028. xxi, 750p. 1999. write for info. incl. disk (*0-07-013765-X*) McGraw.

Problem Solving Using C: Structured Programming Techniques. Yuksel Uckan. 688p. (C). 1995. text 46.75 (*0-697-22465-1*) Bus & Educ Tech.

Problem Solving Using C: Structured Programming Techniques. 2nd ed. Yuksel Uckan. 768p. (C). 1998. pap., student ed. 58.75 (*0-07-561936-9*) McGraw.

Problem Solving Using C++ Structured & Object-Oriented Programming Techniques. Yuksel Uckan. 800p. (C). 1995. text 50.00 (*0-697-22466-X*) Bus & Educ Tech.

Problem Solving Using Graphs. Margaret B. Cozzens & Richard Porter. (Hi Map Ser.). (Illus.). 9.99 (*0-614-05321-8*, HM 5606) COMAP Inc.

Problem Solving Using IBM PC PASCAL. Keith Harrow & Jacqueline A. Jones. (Illus.). 592p. 1986. pap. text 30.00 (*0-13-721358-1*) P-H.

Problem Solving Using Miranda. Kenneth Loose. 224p. (C). 1995. spiral bd. 27.95 (*0-7872-1258-X*) Kendall-Hunt.

Problem Solving Using UCSD Pascal. 2nd ed. K. L. Bowles et al. (Illus.). 350p. 1984. 58.95 (*0-387-90822-6*) Spr-Verlag.

Problem Solving with ADA. Brian H. Mayoh. LC 81-14675. (Wiley Series in Computing). 243p. reprint ed. pap. 75.40 (*0-608-18444-6*, 203265800080) Bks Demand.

Problem Solving with BASIC. Donald D. Spencer. LC 82-17875. 160p. (YA). (gr. 8 up). 1983. pap. 3.95 (*0-89218-075-7*, NO. 1135) Camelot Pub.

Problem Solving with C. Keith Harrow & Jackie Jones. LC 97-104985. 700p. (Orig.). (C). 1996. pap. text 51.98 (*1-881991-48-2*) Scott Jones Pubng.

***Problem Solving with C++ The Object of Programming---visual C++ Edition.** 2nd ed. Walter Savitch. 845p. 1999. pap. text 82.73 (*0-201-61261-5*) Addison-Wesley.

Problem Solving with C++ The Object of Programming. 2nd ed. Walter Savitch. (C). 1999. pap. text. write for info. (*0-201-35760-7*) Addison-Wesley.

Problem Solving With C++ The Object of Programming. 2nd ed. Walter Savitch. LC 98-27261. 913p. (C). 1998. pap. text 69.00 (*0-201-35749-6*) Addison-Wesley.

Problem Solving with Computers. Greg W. Scragg. LC 96-21035. (Computer Science Ser.). 512p. (C). 1996. pap. 56.25 (*0-86720-495-8*) Jones & Bartlett.

Problem Solving with Creative Mathematics. George Bradley. 178p. 1994. pap. 36.95 (*0-534-24360-6*) Brooks-Cole.

Problem Solving with Excel 5.0. Bonnie Holloway & Donna Sarber. 304p. (C). 1995. pap. write for info. (*0-697-27778-X*) Bus & Educ Tech.

Problem Solving with FORTRAN 90: For Scientists & Engineers. David Brooks. LC 97-10929. (Undergraduate Texts in Computer Science Ser.). 640p. 1997. text 49.95 (*0-387-98229-9*) Spr-Verlag.

Problem Solving with Freudian Astrology. Greenwood. 96p. 1990. 13.00 (*0-86690-396-8*, G3164-014) Am Fed Astrologers.

***Problem Solving with Java.** (C). 1999. 80.00 (*0-201-47188-4*) Addison-Wesley.

***Problem Solving with Java.** (C). 1999. text. write for info. (*0-201-61279-8*) Addison-Wesley.

***Problem Solving With Java: Visul J++6.0 Std Ed.** 2000. text. write for info. (*0-201-70348-3*) P-H.

Problem Solving with Maps. Stuart Marson. 48p. 1992. pap. text 14.95 (*0-521-42843-2*) Cambridge U Pr.

Problem Solving with Number Patterns. David R. Duncan & Bonnie H. Litwiller. (Classroom Activities Ser.: No. 1). (Illus.). 158p. 1987. pap. text 9.50 (*0-912047-06-2*) Sch Sci Math.

Problem Solving with Pascal. George W. Best. 209p. 1992. 25.00 (*1-886018-01-4*) Venture Pubng.

Problem Solving with Polyhedra Dice. Nancy S. Janes. 72p. (J). (gr. 5-8). 1994. pap. text 9.50 (*0-938587-74-9*) Cuisenaire.

Problem Solving with Spreadsheets & Databases. Anne Mitchell & Eric King. (C). 1993. student ed. 25.00 (*1-881592-44-8*) Hayden-McNeil.

Problem Solving with Structured FORTRAN 77. Dolores M. Etter. 1984. pap. text 33.50 (*0-8053-2522-0*) Benjamin-Cummings.

Problem Solving with the Calculator. 3rd ed. Russell F. Jacobs. (Illus.). 168p. (YA). (gr. 6-12). 1990. pap. text 9.95 (*0-918272-18-1*, 100) Jacobs.

Problem Solving with the Calculator: Teacher's Guide/Answer Key. 3rd ed. Russell F. Jacobs. (Illus.). 168p. (YA). (gr. 6-12). 1990. pap. text, teacher ed. 2.50 (*0-918272-19-X*, 101) Jacobs.

Problem Solving with the CFX 9850 G-9850 GA Plus Color Graphing Calculator. unabridged ed. David Rock & Douglas Brumbaugh. 50p. 1997. pap. text 10.95 (*0-9659710-2-3*) Paragon Publns.

Problem Solving with the Computer. Edwin R. Sage. (Illus.). 244p. (Orig.). 1969. pap. 18.95 (*0-87567-030-X*) Entelek.

Problem Solving with the TI-83. Gene Olmstead. 160p. (YA). (gr. 9-12). 1997. spiral bd. 27.00 (*1-886018-11-1*) Venture Pubng.

Problem Solving with Time & Money: Basic Mathematics Skills. Thomas Camilli. Ed. by Bob DeWeese. (Illus.). 31p. (J). (gr. 4-6). 1995. pap., wbk. ed. 2.50 (*1-58610-097-1*, Learn on the Go) Learn Horizon.

Problem Solving Workbook. Tracy Zimmerman. 72p. (J). (gr. 2-6). 1995. pap. 17.95 (*1-882732-31-6*) Childswork.

Problem Solving Workbook for Mathematics Today Level 1. Abbott. 1987. pap., teacher ed. 79.75 (*0-15-350091-3*); pap., student ed. 9.00 (*0-15-350081-6*) Harcourt Schl Pubs.

Problem Solving Workbook for Mathematics Today Level 2. Abbott. 1987. pap., teacher ed. 79.75 (*0-15-350092-1*); pap., student ed. 9.00 (*0-15-350082-4*) Harcourt Schl Pubs.

Problem Solving Workbook for Mathematics Today Level 3. Abbott. 1987. pap., teacher ed. 93.75 (*0-15-350093-X*); pap., student ed. 10.50 (*0-15-350083-2*) Harcourt Schl Pubs.

Problem Solving Workbook for Mathematics Today Level 4. Abbott. 1987. pap., teacher ed. 93.75 (*0-15-350094-8*); pap., student ed. 10.50 (*0-15-350084-0*) Harcourt Schl Pubs.

Problem Solving Workbook for Mathematics Today Level 5. Abbott. 1987. pap., teacher ed. 93.75 (*0-15-350095-6*); pap., student ed. 10.50 (*0-15-350085-9*) Harcourt Schl Pubs.

Problem Solving Workbook for Mathematics Today Level 6. Abbott. 1987. pap., teacher ed. 93.75 (*0-15-350096-4*); pap., student ed. 10.50 (*0-15-350086-7*) Harcourt Schl Pubs.

Problem Solving Workbook for Mathematics Today Level 7. Abbott. 1987. pap., teacher ed. 127.75 (*0-15-350097-2*); pap., student ed. 13.00 (*0-15-350087-5*) Harcourt Schl Pubs.

Problem Solving Workbook for Mathematics Today Level 8. Abbott. 1987. pap., student ed. 13.00 (*0-15-350088-3*) Harcourt Schl Pubs.

Problem Solving Workbook to Accompany the Chemical World: Concepts & Applications. Mary L. Kotz. (C). 1994. pap. text 26.50 (*0-03-000569-8*) Harcourt Coll Pubs.

Problem Solving wth Computers: Lab Manual. Greg W. Scragg. 1997. pap. 27.50 incl. cd-rom (*0-7637-0352-4*) Jones & Bartlett.

Problem Solving Your Way to HSPT Math Mastery. Jocelyn C. Walton & Sheryl Walton. (YA). (gr. 8 up). 1997. pap. text, wbk. ed. 19.95 (*1-886292-21-3*) CEO Sftware.

Problem Solving/Decision Making. Barbara J. Braham. (YA - Adult Education Ser.). 1993. pap., wbk. ed. 5.95 (*0-538-70782-8*) S-W Pub.

Problem That Won't Go Away: Reforming U. S. Health Care Financing. Ed. by Henry J. Aaron. 298p. (C). 1995. 42.95 (*0-8157-0010-5*) Brookings.

Problem with Cameron. Clarissa Lewis. LC 95-70502. (Illus.). 24p. (J). (gr. 4-8). 1995. 12.95 (*0-9647148-0-9*) Pocket Change.

Problem with Hair: A Story for Children Who Are Learning about Cancer. Karen S. Foss. LC 96-48130. (Illus.). (J). 1996. 4.95 (*1-56123-099-5*) Centering Corp.

Problem with Immorality. Blaine M. Yorgason & Brenton Yorgason. (Gospel Power Ser.). 43p. (YA). 1990. pap. text 3.50 (*0-929985-15-X*) Jackman Pubng.

Problem with Packaged Planning. Ted Kowalski. (C). 1994. pap. text. write for info. (*0-8013-1340-6*) Longman.

Problem with Pain - A Grief Observed. C. S. Lewis. LC 99-37904. (Shepherd's Notes Ser.). 1999. pap. 5.95 (*0-8054-9353-0*) Broadman.

Problem with Penpals. Maggie McMahon. (Full House Michelle Ser.). (J). (gr. 2-4). 1998. pap. 3.99 (*0-671-01732-2*, Minstrel Bks) PB.

Problem with Prickles. Barbara Davoll. (Tales from Schroon Lake Ser.: No. 3). (Illus.). (J). 7.99 (*0-8024-1035-9*, 671) Moody.

Problem with Public Education Is Administrative. James M. Carroll. 70p. 1984. pap. 3.95 (*0-89826-012-4*) Natl Paperback.

Problem with Pulcifer. Florence P. Heide. LC 81-48606. (Illus.). 64p. (J). (gr. 3-6). 1982. lib. bdg. 12.89 (*0-397-32002-7*) HarpC Child Bks.

Problem with Space Travel: The Rocket Motor. Herman Noordung. Ed. by Ernst Stuhlinger et al. (Illus.). 149p. (C). 1995. pap. text 35.00 (*0-7881-1849-8*) DIANE Pub.

Problem with Space Travel: The Rocket Motor. Hermann Noordung. (Illus.). 176p. 1995. pap. text 50.00 (*1-57979-064-X*) DIANE Pub.

Problema con los Secretos. Karen Johnsen. Tr. by Cynthia Jones.Tr. of Trouble with Secrets. (SPA., Illus.). 32p. (J). (ps-3). 1998. pap. 5.95 (*1-884734-38-3*) Parenting Pr.

Problema de la "Americanizacion" en las Escuelas Catolicas de Puerto Rico. Charles J. Beirne. Tr. by Maria E. Estades De Camara. LC 76-10347. (SPA.). 154p. 1974. pap. 4.00 (*0-8477-2726-2*) U of PR Pr.

Problema de Liberalismo. 2nd ed. Francisco Ayala. 285p. 1963. pap. 3.50 (*0-8477-2402-6*) U of PR Pr.

Problema en America: The American Problem, Spanish Text. Jose C. Cuchi. LC 74-14227. (Puerto Rican Experience Ser.). (Illus.). 246p. 1975. reprint ed. 20.95 (*0-405-06217-6*) Ayer.

Problema Que Unicamente Dios Pudo Resolver. Henry Bast. (SPA., Illus.). 86p. 1995. mass mkt. 3.99 (*0-8254-1054-1*, Edit Portavoz) Kregel.

Problemas Administrativos del Poder Judicial en Puerto Rico. Nelida M. Amato. 272p. 1964. pap. 3.00 (*0-8477-2210-4*) U of PR Pr.

Problemas con Burbujas. Frank B. Edwards. (New Reader Ser.).Tr. of Troubles with Bubbles. (SPA., Illus.). 24p. (J). (ps-1). 1998. pap. 5.95 (*0-921285-65-5*, Pub. by Bungalo Books) Firefly Bks Ltd.

Problemas De Diseno. 96p. (C). 1996. pap. 0.00 (*0-201-65303-6*) HEPC Inc.

Problemas de Diseno para Estatica. 80p. (C). 1995. write for info. (*0-201-65394-X*) P-H Intl.

Problemas de Familia. Moises Ramos. (Serie Enriquezca a la Familia - Enriching the Family Ser.).Tr. of Family Problems: Tragedies & Opportunities. (SPA.). 1.99 (*1-56063-884-2*, 498206) Editorial Unilit.

Problemas de Familia. Moises Ramos.Tr. of Family Problems: Tragedies & Opportunities. (SPA.). 100p. 1995. pap. write for info. (*0-614-27116-9*) Editorial Unilit.

Problemas de Familia - Family Problems: Tragedies & Opportunities. Moises Ramos. (SPA.). 100p. 1995. write for info. (*0-614-24398-X*) Editorial Unilit.

Problemas de Interpretacion y Conocimiento en la Filosofia Europea. Julio R. Ayala. Ed. by Rafael A. Marrero. (SPA.). 200p. (Orig.). (C). pap. 10.00 (*0-924418-01-X*) Editorial El Coqui.

Problemas de la Cultura en Puerto Rico (Foro Auspiciado por el Ateneo Puertorriqueno En 1940) Ateneo Puertorriqueno. LC 76-10701. (SPA.). 272p. (Orig.). 1976. 8.00 (*0-8477-2430-1*) U of PR Pr.

Problemas de la Filosofia: Textos Filosoficos & Contemporaneos. Ed. by Luis O. Gomez & Roberto Torretti. Tr. by Ramon Castilla et al. 1991. reprint ed. pap. 10.00 (*0-8477-2812-9*) U of PR Pr.

Problemas de la Traduccion: Problems in Translation. Ed. by Puerto Rico. Universidad. Facultad de Humanidades. LC 77-12171. 187p. 1982. pap. 5.00 (*0-8477-3187-1*) U of PR Pr.

Problemas Filosoficos de la Ciencia. Alfred Stern. LC 76-22489. (Coleccion Mente y Palabra). (SPA.). 203p. 1976. 5.00 (*0-8477-2813-7*); pap. 4.00 (*0-8477-2814-5*) U of PR Pr.

Problemas Resueltos de la Quimica Organica. 896p. (C). 1992. 28.33 (*0-201-62933-X*) P-H Intl.

Problemas Sexuales de la Mujer. deluxe ed. Ed. by Adrianne Lange. (SPA., Illus.). 192p. 1999. pap. 5.95 (*0-939193-47-7*) Edit Concepts.

Problemas Sexuales del Hombre. deluxe ed. Ed. by Anthoni M. Lescault. (SPA., Illus.). 192p. 1999. pap. 5.95 (*0-939193-29-9*) Edit Concepts.

Problemas Sociales. Henry George. Tr. by Baldomero Argente del Castillo from ENG.Tr. of Social Problems. (SPA.). 208p. (C). 1995. pap. 8.00 (*0-911312-19-6*) Schalkenbach.

Problemas Verbales para Algebra Intermedia. Carmen Rodriguez. (SPA.). 138p. 1993. pap. write for info. (*0-929441-57-5*) Pubns Puertorriquenas.

Problemas y Mas. Alan Handel & Francis Gardella. (SPA.). 1997. pap., student ed. 7.99 (*0-8114-9591-4*); pap., student ed. 7.99 (*0-8114-9592-2*); pap., student ed. 7.99 (*0-8114-9593-0*) Raintree Steck-V.

Problemata, Forscshungen Zur Klassischen Philologie, Heft 1: Die Vorbereitung des Neuplatonismus. Willy Theiler. x, 166p. 1964. write for info. (*3-296-15710-7*) G Olms Pubs.

Problemata, Forscshungen Zur Klassischen Philologie, Heft 10: Untersuchungen Zur Altlateinischen Dichtersprache. Heinz Haffter. 153p. 1974. write for info. (*3-296-12810-7*) G Olms Pubs.

Problemata, Forscshungen Zur Klassischen Philologie, Heft 11: Die Erzahlungskunst des T. Livius. Erich Burck. xxviii, 244p. 1964. 55.00 (*3-296-10910-2*) G Olms Pubs.

Problemata, Forscshungen Zur Klassischen Philologie, Heft 6: Physis und Agathon in der Alten Stoa. Ernst Grumach. 80p. 1966. write for info. (*3-296-12800-X*) G Olms Pubs.

Problemata, Forscshungen Zur Klassischen Philologie, Heft 7: Die Typischen Szenen Bei Homer. Walter Arend. x, 162p. 1975. 50.00 (*3-296-10550-6*) G Olms Pubs.

***Problemata Physica Attributed to Aristotle: The Arabic Version of Hunain ibn Ishaq & the Hebrew Version of Moses ibn Tibbon.** Aristotle. Ed. by L. S. Filius. LC 99-17460. (ARA & ENG.). 902p. 1999. 294.50 (*90-04-11483-1*) Brill Academic Pubs.

Problematic & Conceptual Structure of Classical Indian Thought about Man, Society, & Polity. Daya Krishna. LC 96-900189. 216p. 1996. text 21.95 (*0-19-563797-6*) OUP.

Problematic Behavoir in Adolescents. Haugaard. 2000. 32.25 (*0-07-231685-3*) McGraw.

Problematic Bourgeois: Twentieth-Century Criticism on Thomas Mann's Buddenbrooks & the Magic Mountain. Hugh Ridley. (LCGERM Ser.). xiv, 194p. 1994. 55.00 (*1-879751-87-9*) Camden Hse.

Problematic Characters. Friedrich Spielhagen. Tr. by S. DeVere from GER. LC 76-28509. viii, 507p. 1977. reprint ed. 45.00 (*0-86527-296-4*) Fertig.

Problematic Communication: The Construction of Invisible Walls. C. David Mortensen. LC 93-23671. 256p. 1994. 55.00 (*0-275-94632-0*, Praeger Pubs) Greenwood.

Problematic Fictions of Poe, James & Hawthorne. Judith L. Sutherland. LC 83-16817. 143p. reprint ed. pap. 44.40 (*0-7837-3202-3*, AU0043000007) Bks Demand.

Problematic Fossil Taxa. Ed. by Antoni Hoffman & Matthew H. Nitecki. (Illus.). 277p. 1986. text 110.00 (*0-19-503992-0*) OUP.

Problematic of Self in Modern Chinese Literature: Hu Feng & Lu Ling. Kirk A. Denton. LC 97-41689. 344p. 1998. 49.50 (*0-8047-3128-4*) Stanford U Pr.

Problematic Pigmented Lesions: A Case Method Approach. Martin C. Mihm, Jr. & Paul Googe. LC 89-12216. (Illus.). 543p. 1990. text 98.00 (*0-8121-1261-X*) Lppncott W & W.

Problematic Rebel: Melville, Dostoievsky, Kafka, Camus. rev. ed. Maurice Friedman. LC 72-101360. 1970. pap. text 3.95 (*0-226-26396-7*, P358) U Ch Pr.

Problematic Science. Ed. by William R. Woodward. LC 81-21080. 384p. 1982. 44.95 (*0-275-90926-3*, C0926, Praeger Pubs) Greenwood.

Problematic Self: Approaches to Identity in Stendhal, D.H. Lawrence, & Malraux. Elizabeth B. Tenenbaum. 200p. 1978. 30.50 (*0-674-70769-9*) HUP.

Problematic Soils: Proceedings of an International Symposium, Is-Tohoku '98, Sendai, Japan, 28-30 October 1998, 2 Vol. Ed. by E. Yanagisawa et al. 1300p. 1998. 138.00 (*90-5410-997-1*, Pub. by A A Balkema) Ashgate Pub Co.

Problematicos: Los Protagonistas en el Iglesia. Haugk.Tr. of Antagonists in the Church. (SPA.). 1995. write for info. (*0-614-27117-7*) Editorial Unilit.

Problematicos: Los Protagonistas en la Iglesia. Kenneth C. Haugk.Tr. of Antagonists in the Church. (SPA.). 1990. 6.50 (*1-56063-034-5*, 490217) Editorial Unilit.

***Problematics of Moral & Legal Theory.** Richard A. Posner. LC 98-29596. 1999. 31.00 (*0-674-70771-0*) Belknap Pr.

Problematics of Second Language Classroom Research. Ed. by Jacquelyn Schachter & Susan M. Gass. (SLA Research: Theoretical & Methodological Issues Ser.). 200p. 1996. pap. 19.95 (*0-8058-1936-3*) L Erlbaum Assocs.

Problematics of Second Language Classroom Research. 805th ed. Ed. by Jacquelyn Schachter & Susan M. Gass. (SLA Research: Theoretical & Methodological Issues Ser.). 200p. 1996. text 45.00 (*0-8058-1935-5*) L Erlbaum Assocs.

Problematics of Sociology: The George Simmel Lectures, 1995. Neil J. Smelser. LC 96-34335. 138p. 1997. 19.95 (*0-520-20675-4*, Pub. by U CA Pr) Cal Prin Full Svc.

Problematics of Text & Character (Le Texte et le Personnage en Question(s)) Vol. 1. Centre d'Etudes Superieures de la Renaissance Univ. LC 95-167635. (THETA Ser.: Vol. 1). (FRE.). 286p. 1994. 42.95 (*3-906752-57-7*, Pub. by P Lang) P Lang Pubng.

Problematik Mangelnder Preistransparenz im Bargeldlosen Zahlungsverkehr & Moglichkeiten der Problemlosung. Peter Russo. (GER., Illus.). 260p. 1996. 51.95 (*3-631-30595-8*) P Lang Pubng.

Problematique de la Psychologie. Georges Thines. (Phaenomenologica Ser.: No. 29). 227p. 1969. lib. bdg. 111.50 (*90-247-0265-8*, Pub. by M Nijhoff) Kluwer Academic.

Problematizing English in India. Rama K. Agnihotri & Amrit L. Khanna. LC 97-7936. (Research in Applied Linguistics Ser.: Vol. 3). 168p. 1997. text 29.95 (*0-8039-9375-7*) Sage.

***Problembereiche interdisziplinarer Forschung, 29.** Christoph Bosshardt. 1999. 46.95 (*3-906763-29-3*, Pub. by P Lang) P Lang Pubng.

Probleme. Marcel Ayme. (Folio - Cadet Bleu Ser.: No. 198). (FRE., Illus.). 71p. (J). (ps-1). 1989. pap. 9.95 (*2-07-031198-8*) Schoenhof.

Probleme Aus der Physik. H. Vogel. LC 75-15907. (Illus.). 224p. 1975. pap. text 12.00 (*0-387-07119-9*) Spr-Verlag.

Probleme de Dieu dans la Pensee de Karl Barth. Sebastian A. Matczak. (Philosophical Questions Ser.: No. 1). 1968. pap. 30.00 (*0-912116-00-5*) Learned Pubns.

Probleme de la Sexualite Chez les Champignons: Recherches sur le Genre Coprinus. A. Quintanilha. (Illus.). 1968. reprint ed. pap. 32.00 (*3-7682-0556-8*) Lubrecht & Cramer.

Probleme de l'Alsace-Lorraine Vu par les Periodiques 1871-1914: Die Elsass-Lothringische Frage im Spiegel der Zeitschriften 1871-1914. Ed. by Michel Grunewald. (Convergences Ser.: Vol. 7). xii, 492 p. 1998. 56.95 (*3-906760-44-8*) P Lang.

Probleme der Krebsnachsorge. Ed. by A. Pfleiderer. (Beitraege Zur Onkologie, Contributions to Oncology Ser.: Band 4). (Illus.). 112p. 1980. pap. 28.75 (*3-8055-1378-X*) S Karger.

Probleme der Leistungsmessung. Susanne Bolton. (Fernstudienangebot Ser.). (GER.). 200p. 1996. 11.25 (*3-468-49670-2*) Langenscheidt.

***Probleme Der Literaturgeschichtsschreibung: Uberlegungen Zur Osterreichischen Literatur In Deutschen Literaturgeschichten, Am Beispiel Von Johann Nestroy, Adalbert Stifter Und Karl Kraus Dargestellt.** Young K. Ra. 252p. 1999. 45.95 (*3-631-34586-0*) P Lang Pubng.

Probleme der Lukrezforschung. Carl J. Classen. (Olms GW Studien: Bd. 18). (GER.). xvi, 438p. 1986. 65.00 (*3-487-07660-8*) G Olms Pubs.

***Probleme der Weltorientierung in den Dramen Reinhard Goerings.** Dagmar Fath. 1999. 48.95 (*3-631-35080-5*) P Lang Pubng.

Probleme des adnominalen Attributs in der deutschen Sprache der Gegenwart. Peter Schaeublin. LC 70-174176. (Studia Linguistica Germanica): (C). 1972. 63.10 (*3-11-003346-1*) De Gruyter.

Probleme des Fachwortschatzes im Arabischen. Mohamed Badawi. (Arabistische Texte und Studien: Bd. 11). (GER.). viii, 177p. 1997. write for info. (*3-487-10564-0*) G Olms Pubs.

Probleme des Lateinischen Konigreichs Jerusalem. Hans E. Mayer. (Collected Studies: No. CS178). (GER., Illus.). 356p. (C). 1983. reprint ed. lib. bdg. 124.95 (*0-86078-126-7*, Pub. by Variorum) Ashgate Pub Co.

Probleme des Sprachstils Als Gegenstand der Lateinischen Philologie. Wolfram Ax. (Beitrage Zur Altertumswissenschaft Ser.: Band 1). (GER.). x, 304p. 1976. 50.00 (*3-487-06004-3*) G Olms Pubs.

Probleme du Style. Remy De Gourmont. LC 78-64031. (Des Imagistes: Literature of the Imagist Movement Ser.). reprint ed. 27.00 (*0-404-17109-5*) AMS Pr.

Probleme General de la Stabilite du Mouvement. M. A. Liapounoff. (Annals of Mathematics Studies: No. 17). 1947. 28.00 (*0-527-02733-2*) Periodicals Srv.

Probleme Moral dans la Philosophie de Spinoza et dans l'Histoire du Spinozisme. Victor Delbos. xii, 570p. 1988. reprint ed. write for info. (*3-487-07999-2*) G Olms Pubs.

Probleme und Chancen der Integration Westafrikas: Analyse und Evaluierung der Integrationsansatze Westafrikas von der Vorkolonialzeit bis zur Gegenwart. Abdoulaye Diallo. (Europaische Hochschulschriften: Reihe 5: Bd. 2038). (GER., Illus.). 311p. 1996. pap. 57.95 (*3-631-31096-X*) P Lang Pubng.

Probleme Unserer Zeit. Ed. by Edmund P. Kurz & Karl H. Ruhleder. LC 72-130785. (GER.). (Orig.). (C). 1971. pap. text 9.95 (*0-89197-359-1*) Irvington.

Problemes & Methodes de la Statistique Linguistique. Ed. by P. L. Guiraud. (Synthese Library: No. 2). 145p. 1960. text 126.00 (*90-277-0025-7*, D Reidel) Kluwer Academic.

Problemes Avec et Sans . . . Problemes! 2nd ed. Florentin Smarandache. Ed. by Xiquan Publishing House Staff. Tr. by Sophie Mignie from RUM. (FRE., Illus.). 175p. (C). 1997. reprint ed. pap. 19.99 (*1-879585-16-2*) Erhus Univ Pr.

Problemes de Civilisation: Avec: Traite de Depart, Fables de ma Vie, La Medicine au 20e Siecle. Georges Duhamel. (FRE.). 232p. 1962. pap. 16.95 (*0-7859-5426-0*) Fr & Eur.

Problemes de Critique et d'Histoire Textuelle. Victor Buescu. (Avienus, Ciceron, Dioscoride, Latin, Germanicus Cesar, Tibulle, Varron de l'Atax Ser.). xviii, 237p. 1973. reprint ed. 55.00 (*3-487-04670-9*) G Olms Pubs.

Problemes de Linguistique Generale. Emile Benveniste. (Tel Ser.). (FRE.). 356p. 1966. pap. 17.95 (*2-07-029338-6*) Schoenhof.

Problemes de Linguistique Generale. Emile Benveniste. (Tel Ser.). (FRE.). 286p. 1974. pap. 15.95 (*2-07-020420-0*) Schoenhof.

Problemes de Pouvoir Populaire et de Developpement: Transition Difficile en Guinee-Bissau. Lars Rudebeck. (Research Report Ser.: No. 63). 73p. 1982. write for info. (*91-7106-208-4*, Pub. by Nordic Africa) Transaction Pubs.

Problemes et Methodes de la Classification et de la Zonation Ecologique des Eaux Courantes, Considerees Surtout du Point de Vue Faunistique. Joachim Illies & Lazare Botoseanu. (International Association of Theoretical & Applied Limnology, Communications Ser.: No. 12). (FRE., Illus.). 57p. 1963. pap. 15.00 (*3-510-52012-2*, Pub. by E Schweizerbartsche) Balogh.

Problemoids: Level IV. Bill McCandliss & Albert Watson. 1988. pap., teacher ed. 15.00 (*0-89824-188-X*); pap., student ed. 4.99 (*0-89824-189-8*) Trillium Pr.

Problemoids: Math Challenge, Grade 5. Bill McCandliss & Albert Watson. 1982. pap., student ed. 4.99 (*0-89824-033-6*) Trillium Pr.

Problemoids: Math Challenge, Grade 5. Bill McCandliss & Albert Watson. 1984. pap., teacher ed. 10.00 (*0-89824-070-0*); pap., suppl. ed. 1.00 (*0-89824-069-7*) Trillium Pr.

Problemoids: Math Challenge, Grade 5. Bill McCandliss & Albert Watson. 1986. pap., teacher ed. 15.00 (*0-89824-044-1*) Trillium Pr.

Problemoids: Math Challenge, Grade 6. Bill McCandliss & Albert Watson. 1983. pap., teacher ed. 15.00 (*0-89824-039-5*); pap., student ed. 4.99 (*0-89824-038-7*); pap., student ed., suppl. ed. 1.00 (*0-89824-071-9*) Trillium Pr.

Problemoids: Math Challenge, Grade 6, Cards. Bill McCandliss & Albert Watson. 1983. 10.00 (*0-89824-072-7*) Trillium Pr.

Problems. Carol Jeffrey. (C). 1994. pap. 35.00 (*0-85305-333-2*, Pub. by Arthur James) St Mut.

Problems. John Updike. 288p. 1985. mass mkt. 4.95 (*0-449-21103-7*, Crest) Fawcett.

Problems. 6th ed. (C). 1995. write for info. (*0-201-84849-X*) Addison-Wesley.

Problems, Bks. 1-21. Tr. by W. S. Hett. (Loeb Classical Library: No. 316). 476p. 1936. 18.95 (*0-674-99349-7*) HUP.

Problems, Bks. 22-38. Tr. by H. Rackham & W. S. Hett. (Loeb Classical Library: No. 317). 15.50 (*0-674-99350-0*) HUP.

Problems & Answers in Navigation & Piloting. 2nd ed. Elbert S. Maloney. 83p. 1985. pap. 6.95 (*0-87021-150-1*) Naval Inst Pr.

Problems & Cases for Training the Child Advocate. Bruce A. Boyer & Thomas F. Geraghty. 152p. 1994. pap. 21.95 (*1-55681-454-2*) Natl Inst Trial Ad.

Problems & Cases in Health Information Management. Susan P. Bailey. (Illus.). v, 93p. (Orig.). (C). 1997. pap. text 22.95 (*0-9657783-0-4*) Lenox Pub Co.

An Asterisk (*) at the beginning of an entry indicates that the title is appearing for the first time.

Problems & Cases in Health Information Management: Instructor Guide. Susan P. Bailey. (Illus.). v, 93p. (Orig.). (C). 1997. pap. text, teacher ed. 26.95 (*0-9657783-1-2*) Lenox Pub Co.

Problems & Cases in Interviewing, Counseling & Negotiation. 3rd ed. Anthony J. Bocchino et al. 248p. 1986. pap. 26.95 (*1-55681-071-7*, FBPCICN) Natl Inst Trial Ad.

Problems & Concepts in Developmental Neurophysiology. Ed. by Peter Kellaway & Jeffrey L. Noebels. LC 88-46069. (Johns Hopkins Series in Contemporary Medicine & Public Health). (Illus.). 312p. 1989. reprint ed. pap. 96.80 (*0-608-07339-3*, 206756700009) Bks Demand.

Problems & Conflicts Between Law & Morality in a Free Society. Ed. by James E. Wood, Jr. & Derek Davis. LC 93-72950. 280p. 1994. 24.95 (*0-929182-19-7*); pap. 10.95 (*0-929182-20-0*) Baylor U J M Dawson.

Problems & Contradictions in the Development of Ox-Cultivation in Tanzania. Finn Kjaerby. (Research Report Ser.: No. 66). 164p. 1983. write for info. (*91-7106-211-4*, Pub. by Nordic Africa) Transaction Pubs.

Problems & Controversies in Television & Radio: Basic Readings. Ed. by Harry J. Skornia & Jack W. Kitson. LC 67-20825. x, 503p. 1968. 29.95 (*0-87015-167-3*) Pacific Bks.

Problems & Emotional Difficulties of Negro Children As Studied in Selected Communities & Attributed by Parents - Children to the Fact That They Are Negro. Regina M. Goff. LC 76-476808. (Columbia University. Teachers College. Contributions to Education Ser.: No. 960). reprint ed. 37.50 (*0-404-55960-3*) AMS Pr.

Problems & Examples in Differential Equations. Ed. by Piotr Biler & Tadeusz Nadzieja. (Pure & Applied Mathematics Ser.: Vol. 164). (Illus.). 264p. 1992. text 65.00 (*0-8247-8637-8*) Dekker.

Problems & Exercises in Discrete Mathematics. G. P. Gavrilov & A. A. Sapozhenko. (Mathematics & Its Applications Ser.: Vol. 369). 436p. (C). 1996. text 217.50 (*0-7923-4036-1*) Kluwer Academic.

Problems & Exercises in Organic Chemistry. A. Agronomov et al. Tr. by Mir Publishers Staff. 400p. (C). 1975. 26.50 (*0-8464-0756-6*) Beekman Pubs.

Problems & Exercises in Physical Chemistry. E. Kiselyova et al. 512p. (C). 1987. 110.00 (*0-7855-6295-8*, Pub. by Collets) St Mut.

Problems & Failed Institutions in the Commercial Banking Industry. Joseph F. Sinkey, Jr. Ed. by Edward I. Altman & Ingo I. Walter. LC 76-5760. (Contemporary Studies in Economic & Financial Analysis: Vol. 4). 365p. 1979. 78.50 (*0-89232-005-2*) Jai Pr.

Problems & Issues in Gandhism. Ed. by V. T. Patel. 1990. reprint ed. 48.50 (*81-210-0250-8*, Pub. by Inter-India Pubns) S Asia.

Problems & Issues of Diversity in the United States. Ed. by Larry L. Naylor. LC 98-41383. 232p. 1999. 65.00 (*0-89789-615-7*, Bergin & Garvey); pap. 22.95 (*0-89789-616-5*, Bergin & Garvey) Greenwood.

Problems & Materials in Business Planning. 3rd ed. William H. Painter. LC 94-5570. (American Casebook Ser.). 1127p. 1994. 65.00 (*0-314-03451-X*) West Pub.

Problems & Materials in Civil Procedure: Polisi v. Clark & Parker & Gould - Law School Edition. Anthony J. Bocchino & David A. Sonenshein. LC 96-155305. Orig. Title: Materials for a Motion Practice Workshop. 525p. 1994. 34.95 (*1-55681-465-8*) Natl Inst Trial Ad.

Problems & Materials in Civil Procedure: Polisi v. Clark & Parker & Gould - Library of Cases. Anthony J. Bocchino & David A. Sonenshein. Orig. Title: Materials for a Motion Practice Workshop. 585p. 1997. 29.95 (*1-55681-514-X*) Natl Inst Trial Ad.

***Problems & Materials in Evidence & Trial Advocacy.** 2nd ed. Robert P. Burns & Steven Lubet. LC 99-169128. 1998. 35.95 (*1-55681-631-6*) Natl Inst Trial Ad.

Problems & Materials in Evidence & Trial Advocacy. 2nd ed. Steven Lubet & Robert P. Burns. LC 99-169128. 1998. 26.95 (*1-55681-632-4*) Natl Inst Trial Ad.

Problems & Materials in Federal Income Taxation. 4th ed. Sanford M. Guerin & Philip F. Postlewaite. LC 94-75011. 1008p. 1994. teacher ed. write for info. (*0-316-36376-6*, 63766) Aspen Law.

Problems & Materials in Federal Income Taxation. 5th ed. Sanford M. Guerin & Philip F. Postlewaite. LC 98-29928. 1998. boxed set 60.00 (*1-56706-649-6*) Aspen Law.

Problems & Materials on Commercial Law. Douglas J. Whaley. 1008p. 1986. boxed set 37.00 (*0-316-93213-2*, Aspen Law & Bus) Aspen Pub.

Problems & Materials on Commercial Law. 5th ed. Douglas J. Whaley. LC 98-55954. 956p. 1997. teacher ed. write for info. (*1-56706-502-3*, 65023) Panel Pubs.

***Problems & Materials on Commercial Law.** 6th ed. Douglas J. Whaley. LC 99-51623. 2000. boxed set 60.00 (*0-7355-1237-X*) Panel Pubs.

Problems & Materials on Commercial Paper. Robert J. Nordstrom & Albert L. Clovis. 458p. 1981. reprint ed. write for info. (*0-318-57520-5*) West Pub.

Problems & Materials on Consumer Law. Douglas J. Whaley. 704p. 1991. teacher ed. write for info. (*0-316-93235-3*, 32353) Aspen Law.

Problems & Materials on Consumer Law. Douglas J. Whaley. 704p. 1991. 50.00 (*0-316-93234-5*) Little.

Problems & Materials on Consumer Law. 2nd ed. Douglas J. Whaley. LC 97-36469. 704p. 1998. boxed set. write for info. (*1-56706-697-6*) Panel Pubs.

Problems & Materials on Debtor & Creditor Law. Douglas J. Whaley & Jeffrey W. Morris. LC 97-47212. 1998. boxed set 56.00 (*1-56706-732-8*) Aspen Law.

Problems & Materials on Decedents' Estates & Trusts. Eugene F. Scoles & Edward C. Halbach, Jr. 1056p. 1993. teacher ed. write for info. (*0-316-77650-5*, 76505) Aspen Law.

Problems & Materials on Decedents' Estates & Trusts. 5th ed. Eugene F. Scoles & Edward C. Halbach, Jr. 1056p. 1993. boxed set 56.00 (*0-316-77649-1*, 76491) Aspen Law.

***Problems & Materials on Decedents' Estates & Trusts: With Teacher's Manual.** 6th rev. ed. Eugene F. Scoles et al. 1000p. 2000. write for info. (*0-7355-1235-3*, 12353) Panel Pubs.

Problems & Materials on Payment Law. 4th ed. Douglas J. Whaley. 400p. 1995. teacher ed. write for info. (*0-316-93246-9*, 32469) Aspen Law.

***Problems & Materials on Payment Law: With Teacher's Manual.** 5th ed. Douglas J. Whaley. (Casebook Ser.). 1999. teacher ed., boxed set 48.00 (*0-7355-0244-7*, 02447) Panel Pubs.

Problems & Materials on Professional Responsibility: Problems & Materials. 6th ed. Thomas D. Morgan & Ronald D. Rotunda. (University Casebook Ser.). 598p. 1995. text 38.50 (*1-56662-254-9*) Foundation Pr.

Problems & Materials on Sale & Lease of Goods. 3rd ed. Douglas J. Whaley. LC 98-48841. 464p. 1999. boxed set 46.00 (*0-7355-0057-6*, Aspen Law & Bus) Aspen Pub.

Problems & Materials on Sales. Douglas J. Whaley & Rhonda Rivera. 384p. (C). 1983. 28.00 (*0-316-93221-3*, Aspen Law & Bus) Aspen Pub.

Problems & Materials on Secured Transactions. Douglas J. Whaley. LC 81-86024. (C). 1982. 27.00 (*0-316-93216-7*, Aspen Law & Bus) Aspen Pub.

***Problems & Materials on Secured Transactions.** 5th ed. Douglas J. Whaley. LC 99-53923. 2000. boxed set 50.00 (*0-7355-1239-6*) Panel Pubs.

Problems & Materials on the Sale & Lease of Goods. 2nd ed. Douglas J. Whaley. 432p. 1990. teacher ed. write for info. (*0-316-93229-9*, 32299) Aspen Law.

Problems & Materials on the Taxation of Small Business Enterprise: Individual, Partnership & Corporation. Philip F. Postlewaite & John H. Birkeland. LC 96-36923. (American Casebook Ser.). 592p. (C). 1996. 57.50 (*0-314-06603-9*) West Pub.

Problems & Methods in Longitudinal Research: Stability & Change, Vol. 5. Ed. by David Magnusson et al. (European Network on Longitudinal Studies on Individual Development). (Illus.). 367p. (C). 1994. pap. text 42.95 (*0-521-46732-2*) Cambridge U Pr.

Problems & Methods in the History of Medicine. Roy Porter & Andrew Wear. (Welcome Institute Series in the History of Medicine). 256p. 1987. 67.50 (*0-7099-3687-7*, Pub. by C Helm) Routldge.

Problems & Methods of Literary History. Andre Morize. LC 66-13475. 1922. 28.00 (*0-8196-0168-3*) Biblo.

Problems & Methods of Optimal Control. Ed. by Leonid D. Akulenko. LC 94-14889. (Mathematics & Its Applications Ser.: Vol. 286). 360p. (C). 1994. text 220.50 (*0-7923-2855-8*) Kluwer Academic.

Problems & Methods of Optimal Structural Design. N. V. Banichuk. LC 83-8103. (Mathematical Concepts & Methods in Science & Engineering Ser.: Vol. 26). (Illus.). 336p. 1983. 85.00 (*0-306-41284-5*, Plenum Trade) Perseus Pubng.

Problems & Other Stories. John Updike. LC 79-1480. (Illus.). 260p. 1979. 30.00 (*0-394-50705-3*) Knopf.

Problems & Parables of Law: Maimonides & Nahmanides on Reasons for the Commandments (Ta'amei Ha-Mitzvot) Josef Stern. LC 97-40713. (SUNY Series in Judaica Hermeneutics, Mysticism, & Religion). 224p. (C). 1998. text 49.50 (*0-7914-3823-6*); pap. text 16.95 (*0-7914-3824-4*) State U NY Pr.

Problems & Persons. Wilfrid P. Ward. LC 68-29254. (Essay Index Reprint Ser.). 1977. 21.95 (*0-8369-0097-9*) Ayer.

Problems & Perspectives in Religious Discourse: Advaita Vedanta Implications. John A. Grimes. LC 93-18516. 209p. 1994. text 44.50 (*0-7914-1791-3*); pap. text 14.95 (*0-7914-1792-1*) State U NY Pr.

Problems & Perspectives of Watering the Crops. B. L. Sharma. 1987. 21.00 (*81-7022-191-9*, Pub. by Concept) S Asia.

Problems & Pitfalls in Real Estate Titles. 417p. 1993. pap. 30.00 (*0-614-26714-5*, 19355); pap. 92.00 incl. audio (*0-614-26715-3*, 29355); pap. 175.00 incl. VHS (*0-614-26716-1*, 39355) NYS Bar.

Problems & Poetics of the Nonaristotelian Novel. Leonard D. Orr. LC 89-46139. 176p. 1991. 32.50 (*0-8387-5182-2*) Bucknell U Pr.

Problems & Policies of American Presidents. Ed. by Kenneth W. Thompson. (In Commemoration of the Miller Center's 20th Anniversary Ser.: Vol. 2). 520p. (Orig.). (C). 1995. pap. text 42.50 (*0-7618-0054-9*); lib. bdg. 69.00 (*0-7618-0053-0*) U Pr of Amer.

Problems & Priorities in Egyptian Archaeology. Jan Assman et al. (Studies in Egyptology). (Illus.). 350p. (C). 1987. text 79.95 (*0-7103-0190-1*, A4606) Routledge.

Problems & Procedures in Dentofacial Orthopedics, Vol. 4. Frans P. G. M. Van Der Linden. (Illus.). 382p. 1990. pap. text 70.00 (*0-86715-212-5*) Quint Pub Co.

Problems & Process: International Law & How We Use It. Rosalyn Higgins. 302p. 1995. pap. text 21.00 (*0-19-876410-3*) OUP.

Problems & Programmes Related to Alcohol & Drug Dependence in 33 Countries. J. Moser. (Offset Publications: No. 6). 1974. pap. text 20.00 (*92-4-170006-8*, 1120006) World Health.

Problems & Promises of Computer-Based Training. Ed. by Theodore M. Shlechter. LC 90-26977. 336p. (C). 1991. pap. 39.50 (*0-89391-658-7*); text 73.25 (*0-89391-657-9*) Ablx Pub.

Problems & Propositions in Analysis. G. Klambauer. (Lecture Notes in Pure & Applied Mathematics Ser.: Vol. 49). (Illus.). 472p. 1979. pap. text 175.00 (*0-8247-6887-6*) Dekker.

Problems & Prospects: Accentuating the Positive: Proceedings of the 1992 Third World Symposium. Ed. by Yawsoon Sim. 85p. (C). 1996. reprint ed. pap. text 25.00 (*0-7881-3565-1*) DIANE Pub.

Problems & Prospects: Papers on Presidential Transitions in Foreign Policy, Vol. II. Ed. by Kenneth W. Thompson. 156p. (Orig.). (C). 1986. pap. text 19.50 (*0-8191-4864-4*, Pub. by White Miller Center); lib. bdg. 42.00 (*0-8191-4863-6*, Pub. by White Miller Center) U Pr of Amer.

Problems & Prospects for Nuclear Waste Disposal Policy, 283. Ed. by Eric B. Herzik & Alvin H. Mushkatel. LC 93-4280. 176p. 1993. 57.95 (*0-313-29058-X*, Greenwood Pr) Greenwood.

Problems & Prospects for U. S. Agriculture in World Markets. Timothy Josling. LC 81-83300. (Committee on Changing International Realities Ser.). 68p. 1981. 6.00 (*0-89068-057-4*) Natl Planning.

Problems & Prospects in International Education. Ed. by David G. Scanlon & James J. Shields. LC 68-23008. 421p. reprint ed. pap. 130.60 (*0-608-18033-5*, 202606300048) Bks Demand.

Problems & Prospects in Long & Medium Range Weather Forecasting. Ed. by D. M. Burridge & E. Kallen. (Topics in Atmospheric & Oceanographic Sciences Ser.). (Illus.). 290p. 1983. pap. 34.00 (*0-387-12827-1*) Spr-Verlag.

Problems & Prospects of Cottage Industries in India. S. F. Ahmad. 1990. 33.50 (*81-7041-231-5*, Pub. by Anmol) S Asia.

Problems & Prospects of Domestic & External Financing. 1969. 4.00 (*92-1-106042-7*, 69.II.B.39/16) UN.

Problems & Prospects of Economic Integration in West Africa. Nicholas G. Plessz. LC 67-29636. (Centre for Developing-Area Studies, McGill University, Keith Callard Lectures: No. 2). 102p. reprint ed. pap. 31.70 (*0-7837-1158-1*, 204168700022) Bks Demand.

Problems & Prospects of Education in Africa see Education & Foreign Aid

***Problems & Prospects of European Education.** Jurgen Schriewer. Ed. by Swing & Francois Orivel. 296p. 2000. 65.00 (*0-275-95202-9*, Praeger Pubs) Greenwood.

Problems & Prospects of Old Testament Theology. J. Hogenhaven. (Biblical Seminar Ser.: No. 6). 136p. 1988. pap. 17.95 (*1-85075-080-7*, Pub. by Sheffield Acad) CUP Services.

Problems & Prospects of Presidential Leadership in the Nineteen Eighties, Vol. II. Ed. by James S. Young. (Problems & Prospects of the Presidency Ser.). 92p. (Orig.). (C). 1983. pap. text 13.50 (*0-8191-2908-9*, Pub. by White Miller Center); lib. bdg. 40.00 (*0-8191-2907-0*, Pub. by White Miller Center) U Pr of Amer.

Problems & Prospects of Presidential Leadership in the Nineteen Eighties, Vol. III. Ed. by James S. Young. LC 82-19981. (Problems & Prospects of the Presidency Ser.). 114p. (Orig.). (C). 1984. pap. text 13.50 (*0-8191-2910-0*) U Pr of Amer.

Problems & Prospects of Presidential Leadership in the Nineteen Eighties, Vol. III. Ed. by James S. Young. LC 82-19981. (Problems & Prospects of the Presidency Ser.). 114p. (Orig.). (C). 1984. lib. bdg. 37.00 (*0-8191-2909-7*, Pub. by White Miller Center) U Pr of Amer.

Problems & Prospects of the Organization of American States: Perceptions of the Member States' Leaders. Henry H. Han. (American University Studies: Political Science: Ser. X, Vol. 10). XXXVI, 528p. (C). 1987. text 63.50 (*0-8204-0508-6*) P Lang Pubng.

Problems & Simulations in Evidence. 2nd ed. Thomas F. Guernsey. LC 95-31448. 141p. 1996. pap. 27.95 (*0-87084-299-4*) Anderson Pub Co.

Problems & Snapshots from the World of Probability. Gunnar Blom et al. LC 93-31828. (Illus.). 240p. 1994. 43.95 (*0-387-94161-4*) Spr-Verlag.

Problems & Solutions: A Guide to Psychotherapy for the Beginning Psychotherapist. Martin D. Kantor. LC 89-72198. 216p. 1990. 55.00 (*0-275-93490-X*, C3490, Praeger Pubs) Greenwood.

Problems & Solutions for Proprietors & Partnerships Business. abr. rev. ed. Intro. by Luanna C. Blagrove. (AMERCE Business Ser.). (Illus.). 250p. 1988. 24.95 (*0-939776-12-X*) Blagrove Pubns.

Problems & Solutions for Unergraduate Analysis. R. Shakarchi. (Undergraduate Texts in Mathematics Ser.). (Illus.). 344p. 1997. pap. 24.95 (*0-387-98235-3*) Spr-Verlag.

Problems & Solutions from the Mathematical Visitor, 1877-1896. Ed. by Stanley Rabinowitz. LC 94-77754. (Classic Problems Collections: No. 1). 272p. (Orig.). (YA). (gr. 9-12). 1996. pap. 24.00 (*0-9626401-5-8*) MathPro Pr.

Problems & Solutions in Complete Denture Fabrication. D. J. Lamb. (Illus.). 168p. 1993. text 52.00 (*1-85097-021-1*) Quint Pub Co.

Problems & Solutions in Complex Analysis. R. Shakarchi. LC 99-13255. (Illus.). 256p. 1999. pap. 34.00 (*0-387-98831-9*) Spr-Verlag.

Problems & Solutions in Economic Theory. K. A. Lawler & H. A. Seddighi. 1986. 100.00 (*0-7855-1834-7*) St Mut.

***Problems & Solutions in Human Assessment - Honoring Douglas N. Jackson at Seventy.** Richard G. Goffin & Edward Helmes. 384p. 2000. 130.00 (*0-7923-7768-0*) Kluwer Academic.

Problems & Solutions in Mathematics. Ed. by Ta-Tsien Li. LC 98-22020. 500p. 1998. 86.00 (*981-02-3479-1*); pap. 48.00 (*981-02-3480-5*) World Scientific Pub.

Problems & Solutions in Organotransition Metal Chemistry. Susan Kegley & Alan R. Pinhas. (Illus.). 323p. (C). 1986. pap. text 26.50 (*0-935702-23-7*) Univ Sci Bks.

Problems & Solutions in Quantum Chemistry & Physics. Charles S. Johnson, Jr. & Lee G. Pedersen. xviii, 430p. 1987. reprint ed. pap. text 13.95 (*0-486-65236-X*) Dover.

Problems & Solutions in Radiation Protection. James E. Turner et al. 316p. 1991. text 30.00 (*0-07-105322-0*) McGraw-Hill HPD.

Problems & Solutions in Small Business Management. Forum Editors. 200p. 1994. pap. 36.75 (*0-936894-71-7*, 610064-01) Dearborn.

Problems & Solutions in Solid State Physics. S. O. Pillai. 1994. write for info. (*81-224-0658-0*, Pub. by Wiley Estrn) Franklin.

Problems & Solutions in Theoretical & Mathematical Physics. 240p. 1996. lib. bdg. 20.00 (*981-02-2943-7*); lib. bdg. 20.00 (*981-02-2944-5*) World Scientific Pub.

Problems & Solutions in Theoretical & Mathematical Physics: Introductory Problems. LC 96-210472. 240p. 1996. lib. bdg. 34.00 (*981-02-2942-9*) World Scientific Pub.

Problems & Solutions in Theoretical & Mathematical Physics: Introductory Problems, 1. LC 96-210472. 240p. 1996. lib. bdg. 34.00 (*981-02-2941-0*) World Scientific Pub.

Problems & Solutions on Atomic, Nuclear & Particle Physics. Ed. by Yung K. Lim. 550p. 1999. 86.00 (*981-02-3917-3*) World Scientific Pub.

Problems & Solutions on Atomic, Nuclear & Particle Physics. Ed. by Yung K. Lim. 550p. 1999. 42.00 (*981-02-3918-1*) World Scientific Pub.

Problems & Solutions on Electromagnetism. Ed. by Y. K. Lim. 550p. (C). 1994. text 78.00 (*981-02-0625-9*); pap. text 39.00 (*981-02-0626-7*) World Scientific Pub.

Problems & Solutions on Mechanics: Major American Universities Ph.d. Qualifying Questions & Solutions. Y. K. Lim. 768p. 1994. text 99.00 (*981-02-1295-X*); pap. text 48.00 (*981-02-1298-4*) World Scientific Pub.

Problems & Solutions on Optics: Major American Univ. PhD Qualifying Questions & Solutions. Y. K. Lim. 204p. 1991. text 59.00 (*981-02-0438-8*); pap. text 30.00 (*981-02-0439-6*) World Scientific Pub.

Problems & Solutions on Quantum Mechanics. LC 98-33843. 400p. 1997. text 58.00 (*981-02-3132-6*); text 23.00 (*981-02-3133-4*) World Scientific Pub.

Problems & Solutions on Solid State Physics, Relativity & Miscellaneous Topics. Y. K. Lim. 364p. 1994. text 99.00 (*981-02-1892-3*); pap. text 38.00 (*981-02-1893-1*) World Scientific Pub.

Problems & Solutions on Thermodynamics & Statistical Mechanics. Ed. by Y. K. Lim. 420p. (C). 1990. text 74.00 (*981-02-0055-2*); pap. text 36.00 (*981-02-0056-0*) World Scientific Pub.

Problems & Solutions (SI Units) see Chemical Engineering

***Problems & Solutions to Accompany Changes Physical Chemistry for the Chemical & Biological Sciences.** Helen Leung & Mark Marshall. (Illus.). 496p. 2000. pap. text 52.00 (*1-891389-11-4*) Univ Sci Bks.

Problems & Solutions to Accompany McQuarrie - Simon Physical Chemistry: A Molecular Approach. Heather Cox. (Illus.). 956p. (C). 1997. pap. text 52.00 (*0-935702-43-1*) Univ Sci Bks.

Problems & Solutions to Accompany Molecular Thermodynamics. Heather Cox & Carole McQuarrie. (Illus.). 528p. (C). 1999. pap. text, student ed. 52.00 (*1-891389-07-6*) Univ Sci Bks.

***Problems & solutions to Tools of Radio Astronomy.** T. Wilson & S. Huettemeister. Ed. by I. Appenzeller et al. (Astronomy & Astrophysics Library). viii, 150p. 2000. pap. text (*3-540-66802-0*) Spr-Verlag.

Problems & Statistics. 2nd ed. Strait. (C). 1989. pap. write for info. (*0-15-503515-0*) Harcourt Coll Pubs.

Problems & Strategies of Development in the Eastern Himalayas. Ranuu R. Dhamala. (C). 1993. text 21.00 (*81-212-0450-X*, Pub. by Gian Publng Hse) S Asia.

Problems & Teaching Strategies in ESL Composition. Ann Raimes. (Language in Education Ser.: No. 14). 24p. (C). 1986. pap. text 3.67 (*0-13-711987-9*) P-H.

Problems & Their Solutions in Organic Chemistry. Ivor L. Finar. LC 73-166074. 369p. reprint ed. pap. 114.40 (*0-608-10200-8*, 201005000071) Bks Demand.

Problems & Theorems in Analysis. George Polya & Gabor Szego. Tr. by Dorothee Aeppli from GER. LC 97-47108. (Classics in Mathematics Ser.). 1997. pap. 39.95 (*3-540-63686-2*) Spr-Verlag.

Problems & Theorems in Analysis. George Polya & Gabor Szego. Tr. by Dorothee Aeppli. LC 97-47108. (Classics in Mathematics Ser.: Vol. I). 400p. 1997. pap. 39.95 (*3-540-63640-4*) Spr-Verlag.

Problems & Theorems in Analysis I: Series, Integral Calculus, Theory of Functions. George Polya & G. Szegoe. (Grundlehren der Mathematischen Wissenschaften Ser.: Vol. 193). 1978. 98.00 (*0-387-05672-6*) Spr-Verlag.

Problems & Theorems in Analysis I: Series, Integral Calculus, Theory of Functions. George Polya & Gabor Szego. (Illus.). 1989. reprint ed. pap. 39.00 (*0-387-90224-4*) Spr-Verlag.

Problems & Theorems in Analysis II: Theory of Functions, Zeros, Polynomials, Determinants, Number Theory, Geometry. George Polya & Gabor Szego. Tr. by C. E. Billigheimer. (Illus.). 1990. 47.95 (*0-387-90291-0*) Spr-Verlag.

Problems & Theorems in Liner Algebra. V. V. Prasolov. LC 94-13332. (Translations of Mathematical Monographs: Vol. 134). 225p. 1994. pap. 49.00 (*0-8218-0236-4*, MMONO/134) Am Math.

P

Problems Are the Doors Through Which We Walk to Peace. Stephen R. Schwartz & Kenneth Eyer. 117p. 1987. 12.00 (*0-936415-04-5*) Riverrun Piermont.

Problems As Possibilities: Problem-Based Learning for K-12 Education. Linda Torp & Sara Sage. LC 98-8888. 101p. 1998. pap. 15.95 (*0-87120-297-2*, 198010) ASCD.

Problems Associated with Export of Nuclear Power Plants. IAEA Staff. (Proceedings Ser.). (Illus.). 484p. 1978. pap. 100.00 (*92-0-020178-4*, ISP488, Pub. by IAEA) Bernan Associates.

Problems at the North Pole. Lauren Peters. Ed. by Nancy R. Thatch. LC 90-5929. (Books for Students by Students). (Illus.). 26p. (J). (ps-2). 1990. lib. bdg. 15.95 (*0-933849-25-7*) Landmark Edns.

Problems Book: Engineering Drawing & Graphic Technology. 13th ed. Hartley Rogers. (Illus.). 256p. (C). 1986. pap., wbk. ed. 40.00 (*0-07-053491-8*) McGraw.

Problems Book for Group Theory. Nelson. (C). 1990. 33.33 (*0-205-12095-4*, Macmillan Coll) P-H.

Problems, Cases & Materials in a Professional Responsibility: Problems, Cases, & Materials. 2nd ed. Robert H. Aronson et al. LC 95-30769. (American Casebook Ser.). 525p. (C). 1995. teacher ed. 50.50 (*0-314-06468-0*) West Pub.

Problems, Cases, & Materials on Evidence. 2nd ed. Eric D. Green & Charles R. Nesson. 1168p. 1994. teacher ed. write for info. (*0-316-35146-6*, 51466) Aspen Law.

Problems Concerning Amenophis III. Hans Goedicke. iv, 111p. (Orig.). (C). 1992. pap. text 24.00 (*0-9613805-7-8*) Halgo Inc.

Problems Concerning the Origin & Early Development of the Etruscan Orientalizing Style, 2 vols., Set. (Odense Classical Studies: No. 2). 404p. (Orig.). 1971. pap. 57.50 (*87-7492-033-2*, Pub. by Odense Universitets Forlag) Coronet Bks.

Problems Faced by the Da'wah & the Da'iyah. Fathi Yakan. 239p. pap. write for info. (*1-882837-11-8*) W A M Y Intl.

Problems for Computer Solution. 2nd ed. Donald D. Spencer. LC 79-20594. 128 p. 1979. write for info. (*0-8104-5191-3*) Sams.

Problems For Gen Chem & Quan A. 4th ed. C. J. Nyman et al. LC 79-24489. 352p. 1980. pap. 40.95 (*0-471-05299-X*) Wiley.

Problems for Management Accounting I. Peter Cheng. (C). 1993. student ed. 10.00 (*1-881592-37-5*) Hayden-McNeil.

Problems for Mathematicians Young & Old, DOL-12. Paul R. Halmos. LC 91-67386. (Dolciani Mathematical Expositions Ser.). 328p. (C). 1991. pap. text 35.95 (*0-88385-320-5*, DOL-12) Math Assn.

Problems for Physics Students: With Hints & Answers. K. F. Riley. LC 82-4575. 190p. 1982. pap. text 29.95 (*0-521-27073-1*) Cambridge U Pr.

Problems for Platoon & Company. Erwin Rommel. Ed. by Bruce A. Hanesalo. Tr. by Cyril Koob from GER. (Illus.). 74p. 1994. vinyl bd. 20.00 (*1-886848-01-7*) Mil-Info.

Problems for Puzzlebusters. David L. Book. LC 92-90284. (Illus.). 358p. (YA). (gr. 7-12). 1992. 24.95 (*0-9633217-0-6*) Enigmatics.

Problems for Student Investigation. Ed. by Michael B. Jackson & John R. Ramsay. LC 92-62282. (Resources for Calculus, Vol. 4; MAA Notes Ser.: Vol. 30). 224p. 1993. pap. text 38.50 (*0-88385-086-9*, NTE-30) Math Assn.

Problems from Kant. James van Cleve. LC 98-26825. 352p. 1999. text 45.00 (*0-19-508322-9*) OUP.

Problems from Locke. John L. Mackie. (Illus.). 248p. (C). 1976. pap. text 24.00 (*0-19-875036-6*) OUP.

Problems, Functions & Semantic Roles: A Pragmatists' Analysis of Montague's Theory of Sentence Meaning. E. M. Barth & R. T. Wiche. (Foundations of Communication & Cognition Ser.). xviii, 198p. 1986. lib. bdg. 80.00 (*3-11-009861-X*) De Gruyter.

Problems, God's Presence & Prayer: Experience the Joy of a Successful Christian Life. 3rd ed. C. Michael Wells. 155p. 1999. reprint ed. pap. 8.00 (*0-9670843-1-8*) Abiding Life Min.

P

Problems Impeding Career Success: (And How to Overcome Them) Bert Warren. Ed. by Angelo Medici. 60p. (Orig.). 1993. pap. 14.00 (*1-880571-05-6*) Decision Pt.

Problems in a New Medium: Autobiographies by Three Artists. Catherine C. Fraser. LC 84-47906. (American University Studies: Germanic Languages & Literature: Ser. I, Vol. 33). 151p. (C). 1984. text 19.00 (*0-8204-0160-9*) P Lang Pubng.

Problems in Advanced Organic Chemistry. J. March. LC 70-176119. 431p. reprint ed. pap. 133.70 (*0-8357-9093-2*, 205504900008) Bks Demand.

Problems in African History: Precolonial Centuries, Vol. 1. Intro. by Robert O. Collins. (Illus.). 328p. (C). 1992. pap. text 19.95 (*1-55876-059-8*) Wiener Pubs Inc.

Problems in Algebraic Number Theory. J. Esmonde & M. Ram Murty. LC 98-30323. (Graduate Texts in Mathematics Ser.: Vol. 190). 350p. 1999. 49.95 (*0-387-98617-0*) Spr-Verlag.

Problems in American Culture. Intro. by Leslie W. Hedley. 148p. (Orig.). 1990. pap. 10.95 (*0-933515-12-X*) Exile Pr.

Problems in American Social Policy Research. Ed. by Clark C. Abt. LC 79-55772. (Illus.). 300p. 1980. text 30.00 (*0-89011-540-0*) Abt Bks.

Problems in Anaesthesia: Day Surgery. David Wilkinson. 224p. 1999. pap. text 25.00 (*0-7506-1852-3*) Buttrwrth-Heinemann.

Problems in Analysis: A Symposium in Honor of Salomon Bochner. R. C. Gunning. (Mathematical Ser.: No. 31). 366p. 1970. text 69.50 (*0-691-08076-3*, Pub. by Princeton U Pr) Cal Prin Full Svc.

Problems in Anesthesia. Robert E. Galford. 480p. 1992. text 54.95 (*0-316-30289-9*) Lppncott W & W.

Problems in Applied Educational Sociolinguistics: Readings on Language & Culture Problems of United States Ethnic Groups. Ed. by Glenn G. Gilbert & Jacob Ornstein. (Janua Linguarum, Series Minor: No. 162). 1978. pap. text 35.00 (*90-279-7726-7*) Mouton.

Problems in Applied Hydrology. E. F. Schulz. 1974. pap. 35.00 (*0-918334-07-1*) WRP.

Problems in Applied, Industrial & Engineering Mathematics. Ed. by H. K. Kuiken. 274p. (C). 1992. text 185.00 (*0-7923-1680-0*) Kluwer Academic.

Problems in Applied Mathematics: Selections from SIAM Review. Ed. by Murray Klamkin. LC 90-49670. (Miscellaneous Bks.: No. 20). xxv, 588p. 1991. pap. 48.00 (*0-89871-259-9*) Soc Indus-Appl Math.

Problems in Applied Thermodynamics. Colin Bodsworth & A. S. Appleton. LC 66-78638. 223p. reprint ed. pap. 69.20 (*0-608-30459-X*, 200363600038) Bks Demand.

Problems in Argument Analysis & Evaluation. Trudy Govier. vii, 303p. 1987. pap. 90.80 (*90-6765-341-1*) Mouton.

Problems in Biblical Theology: Essays in Honor of Rolf Knierim. Rolf P. Knierim et al. Ed. by James M. Robinson & Garth I. Moller. LC 96-25403. 1996. 49.00 (*0-8028-3803-0*) Eerdmans.

Problems in Biochemistry. Michael E. Friedman & Paul Melius. 220p. (Orig.). (C). 1984. pap. text 28.95 (*0-89892-056-6*) Contemp Pub Co of Raleigh.

Problems in Biology. Carol Knox & Katheryn Rowsey. (Illus.). 90p. (Orig.). (gr. 10-11). 1980. student ed. 13.60 (*0-88334-132-8*); 9.28 (*0-8013-0095-9*) Longman.

Problems in Calculus & Related Topics. Colin R. Jones. LC 66-3023. 200p. reprint ed. pap. 62.00 (*0-608-30059-4*, 201939600011) Bks Demand.

Problems in Cardiothoracic Anaesthesia. John Gothard. LC 98-52023. 224p. 1998. pap. text 40.00 (*0-7506-2033-1*) Buttrwrth-Heinemann.

Problems in Chemistry. 2nd ed. Henry O. Daley, Jr. & O'Malley. (Undergraduate Chemistry Ser.: Vol. 11). (Illus.). 504p. 1988. text 95.00 (*0-8247-7826-X*) Dekker.

Problems in China's Transitional Economy: Property Rights & Transitional Models. Xiaobo Hu. (EAI Occasional Paper Ser.: No. 6). 76p. 1998. pap. 25.00 (*981-02-3595-X*) World Scientific Pub.

Problems In Civil Procedure. Larry L. Teply & Ralph U. Whitten. iii, 162p. 1991. 11.95 (*0-8377-1220-3*) W S Hein.

Problems in Community Wastes Management. H. M. Ellis et al. (Public Health Papers: No. 38). 89p. 1969. pap. text 6.00 (*92-4-130038-8*, 1110038) World Health.

***Problems in Comparative Chinese Dialectology: The Classification of Miin & Hakka.** David Prager Branner. LC 99-52400. (Trends in Linguistics Ser.). 500p. 1999. write for info. (*3-11-015831-0*) Mouton.

Problems in Computing. Gabriel Goldstein. LC 70-401687. (School & College Mathematical Texts Ser.). viii, 189 p. (C). 1969. write for info. (*0-05-001488-9*) Olvr & Boyd UK.

Problems in Conducting. rev. ed. Daniel Moe. 20p. 1968. pap. 6.50 (*0-8066-0834-X*, 11-9369, Augsburg) Augsburg Fortress.

Problems in Constitutional Law: A Symposium. K. E. Vanlandingham et al. LC 70-152835. (Symposia on Law & Society Ser.). 1971. reprint ed. lib. bdg. 25.00 (*0-306-70148-0*) Da Capo.

Problems in Contemporary Jewish Theology. Ed. by Dan Cohn-Sherbok. LC 91-38782. 292p. 1992. lib. bdg. 89.95 (*0-7734-9645-9*) E Mellen.

***Problems in Contract Law.** 4th ed. Charles L. Knapp et al. LC 99-29141. 1372p. 1999. boxed set 63.00 (*0-7355-0028-2*) Panel Pubs.

Problems in Contract Law: Cases & Materials. 3rd ed. Charles L. Knapp & Nathan M. Crystal. 1360p. 1993. teacher ed. write for info. (*0-316-49933-1*, 99331) Aspen Law.

Problems in Corporate Governance. Douglas M. Branson. 90p. 1997. pap., wbk. ed. 19.95 (*1-887969-05-5*) Cathedral PA.

Problems in Criminal Procedure. Joseph D. Grano. LC 81-7577. (American Casebook Ser.). 258p. (C). 1990. reprint ed. pap. text. write for info. (*0-314-79133-7*) West Pub.

Problems in Criminal Procedure. 2nd ed. Joseph D. Grano. LC 81-7577. (American Casebook Ser.). 258p. (C). 1990. reprint ed. pap. text 17.50 (*0-314-59979-7*) West Pub.

Problems in Criminal Procedure. 3rd ed. Joseph D. Grano. (American Casebook Ser.). 245p. 1997. pap. text, teacher ed., suppl. ed. write for info. (*0-314-22746-6*) West Pub.

Problems in Criminal Procedures 3E. 3rd ed. Joseph D. Grano. LC 97-9142. (Paralegal). 193p. (C). 1997. pap. text 16.00 (*0-314-06684-5*) West Pub.

Problems in Descriptive Geometry, Vol. 2. Joseph A. Bennett. LC QA0501.B4. 61p. reprint ed. pap. 30.00 (*0-608-30416-6*, 200731900063) Bks Demand.

Problems in Developing Academic Library Collections. Jasper G. Schad & Norman E. Tanis. LC 72-1944. (Bowker Series in Problem-Centered Approaches to Librianship). 207p. reprint ed. pap. 64.20 (*0-608-11873-7*, 202305300032) Bks Demand.

Problems in Diagnosis & Management of Polycystic Kidney Disease: Proceedings of the First International Workshop on PKD. Ed. by Jared J. Grantham & Kenneth D. Gardner, Jr. (Illus.). 216p. 1985. 14.95 (*0-9614567-0-1*) PKR Foundation.

***Problems in Elementary Critical State Soil Mechanics.** S. K. Jain. (Illus.). (C). 2000. pap. write for info. (*0-9605004-6-4*) Eng Pubns.

Problems in Engineering Drawing: Series A, B, D, & E. Randolph P. Hoelscher et al. 1961. pap. 12.80 (*0-318-55875-0*) Stipes.

Problems in Engineering Drawing & Geometry: Series 13 & 16. J. S. Dobrovolny et al. 1964. pap. 12.80 (*0-318-55874-2*) Stipes.

Problems in Engineering Geometry, 1. Randolph P. Hoelscher et al. 1961. pap. 12.80 (*0-685-73446-3*) Stipes.

Problems in Engineering Geometry, 2. Randolph P. Hoelscher et al. 1961. pap. 12.80 (*0-685-73447-1*) Stipes.

Problems in Engineering Graphics. T. C. Hartley & David C. O'Bryant. (Graphics Ser.: No. 31). 1975. pap. 12.80 (*0-87563-109-6*) Stipes.

Problems in Engineering Graphics. M. H. Pleck et al. (Engineering Graphics Ser.: No. 88). (Illus.). 91p. (C). 1989. pap. text 15.80 (*0-87563-413-3*) Stipes.

Problems in Engineering Graphics, No. 87. M. H. Pleck et al. (Engineering Graphics Ser.: Vol. 87). 90p. (C). 1987. pap. text, student ed. 15.80 (*0-87563-292-0*) Stipes.

Problems in Engineering Graphics & Design. Andre M. Skaff. 208p. (C). 1994. pap. text, per. 19.95 (*0-8403-3748-5*) Kendall-Hunt.

Problems in Equilibrium Theory. Charalambos D. Aliprantis. LC 96-5034. (Illus.). 245p. 1996. text, student ed. 74.50 (*3-540-60753-6*) Spr-Verlag.

Problems in Equine Medicine. Christopher M. Brown. LC 88-27255. (Illus.). 302p. 1989. text 50.00 (*0-8121-1171-0*) Lppncott W & W.

Problems in Euclidean Space Application of Convexity: Adams Prize Essay of University of Cambridge, 1955-6. H. Eggleston & Ian N. Sneddon. LC 57-14863. (International Series of Monographs on Pure & Applied Mathematics: Vol. 5). 1957. 76.00 (*0-08-009064-8*, Pub. by Pergamon Repr) Franklin.

Problems in Evidence. Kenneth S. Broun et al. (American Casebook Ser.). 238p. 1992. reprint ed. pap. text, teacher ed. write for info. (*0-314-46936-2*) West Pub.

Problems in Evidence. 3rd ed. Kenneth S. Broun et al. (American Casebook Ser.). 238p. (C). 1988. reprint ed. pap. 25.50 (*0-314-42363-X*) West Pub.

Problems in Federal Estate & Gift Taxation. rev. ed. Richard Haight. 348p. 1999. ring bd. 35.00 (*1-879581-66-3*) Lupus Pubns.

Problems in Form & Function. Ann Borkin. Ed. by John R. Ross & George Lakoff. LC 82-11417. (Language & Being Ser.). 160p. 1985. text 73.25 (*0-89391-116-X*) Ablx Pub.

***Problems in French History.** Martyn Cornick & Ceri Crossley. LC 00-40485. 2000. write for info. (*0-312-23780-4*) St Martin.

Problems in General Chemistry. N. Glinka. 256p. 1973. 26.00 (*0-8464-1121-0*) Beekman Pubs.

Problems in General Linguistics. Emile Benveniste. (Miami Linguistics Ser.: No. 8). 317p. 1973. pap. 25.00 (*0-87024-310-1*) U of Miami Pr.

Problems in General Surgery. Ed. by Jack Pickleman. LC 81-22702. (Reviewing Surgical Topics Ser.). 382p. (C). 1982. 75.00 (*0-306-40765-5*, Kluwer Plenum) Kluwer Academic.

Problems in Geometry. M. Berger et al. (Problem Books in Mathematics). (Illus.). 184p. 1984. 59.95 (*0-387-90971-0*) Spr-Verlag.

Problems in Geometry for Architects, 2 pts., Pt. 1. W. L. Schick et al. 1975. pap. 9.80 (*0-685-73448-X*) Stipes.

Problems in Geometry for Architects, 2 pts., Pt. 2. W. L. Schick et al. 1975. pap. 9.80 (*0-685-73449-8*) Stipes.

Problems in Greek History. John P. Mahaffy. Date not set. 22.95 (*0-518-10186-X*) Ayer.

Problems in Group Theory. John D. Dixon. LC 72-76597. 176p. 1973. reprint ed. pap. 8.95 (*0-486-61574-X*) Dover.

Problems in Gynaecology. E. P. Tatford. (Problems in Practice Ser.). 1986. text 164.00 (*0-85200-278-5*) Kluwer Academic.

***Problems in Health Care Law.** 8th ed. Robert D. Miller & Rebecca C. Hutton. LC 99-47599. 2000. write for info. (*0-8342-1602-7*) Aspen Pub.

Problems in High Energy Physics & Field Theory: Proceedings of the 16th Workshop on Problems on High Energy Physics & Field Theory, 1993, Protvino. Ed. by G. L. Rcheulishvili. 247p. (Orig.). (C). 1995. pap. 30.00 (*1-57485-005-9*) Hadronic Pr Inc.

Problems in Historical Epistemology. Jerzy Kmita. 194p. (C). 1988. text 153.00 (*90-277-2199-8*, D Reidel) Kluwer Academic.

Problems in Inorganic Chemistry. B. J. Aylett & B. C. Smith. LC 66-18189. 160p. reprint ed. pap. 49.60 (*0-608-10192-3*, 200764300065) Bks Demand.

Problems in Insurance Law. James R. Devines & Nicholas P. Terry. (American Casebook Ser.). 240p. (C). 1989. pap. 25.50 (*0-314-56417-9*) West Pub.

Problems in Intellectual Freedom & Censorship. Arthur J. Anderson. LC 74-4107. (Bowker Series in Problem-Centered Approaches to Librianship). 219p. reprint ed. pap. 67.90 (*0-608-11872-9*, 202305400031) Bks Demand.

Problems in International Comparative Research in the Social Sciences. Jan Berting et al. 186p. 1979. 91.00 (*0-08-025247-8*, Pub. by Pergamon Repr) Franklin.

Problems in Intrahepatic Cholestasis: Proceedings of the International Symposium, 2nd, Florence, October 13-14, 1978. International Symposium on Intrahepatic Cholestasis Staff. Ed. by Paolo Gentilini et al. (Illus.). 1979. 101.00 (*3-8055-3009-9*) S Karger.

Problems in Labor Relations. Herman Feldman. LC 78-89732. (American Labor, from Conspiracy to Collective Bargaining Ser., No. 1). 353p. 1977. reprint ed. 23.95 (*0-405-02120-8*) Ayer.

Problems in Legal Ethics. 3rd ed. Mortimer D. Schwartz et al. (American Casebook Ser.). 402p. 1993. text 29.00 (*0-314-01125-0*) West Pub.

Problems in Legal Ethics. 4th ed. Mortimer D. Schwartz. Ed. by Richard C. Wydick & Rex R. Perschbacher. LC 97-5101. (Paralegal). 402p. (C). 1997. text 27.00 (*0-314-21148-9*) West Pub.

Problems in Lexicography. 2nd ed. Ed. by Fred W. Householder & Sol Saporta. LC 62-62699. (General Publications Ser: Vol. 21). 286p. 1975. pap. text 18.00 (*0-87750-113-0*) Res Inst Inner Asian Studies.

Problems in Literary Research: A Guide to Selected Reference Works. 4th ed. Dorothea Kehler. 232p. 1996. pap., teacher ed. 20.00 (*0-8108-3218-6*) Scarecrow.

Problems in Literary Research: A Guide to Selected Reference Works. 4th ed. Dorothea Kehler. LC 96-31247. 1996. 32.50 (*0-8108-3216-X*) Scarecrow.

Problems in Literary Research: A Guide to Selected Reference Works. 4th ed. Dorothea Kehler. LC 96-31247. 1996. pap. 20.00 (*0-8108-3217-8*) Scarecrow.

Problems in Material Science. Harish D. Merchant. x, 476p. 1972. text 489.00 (*0-677-13450-9*) Gordon & Breach.

Problems in Mathematical Analysis. Piotr Biler & Alfred Witkowski. (Pure & Applied Mathematics Ser.: Vol. 132). (Illus.). 240p. 1990. text 65.00 (*0-8247-8312-3*) Dekker.

***Problems in Mathematical Analysis I: Real Numbers, Sequences & Series.** W. J. Kaczor & M. T. Nowak. (STML Ser.). 384p. 2000. 39.00 (*0-8218-2050-8*) Am Math.

Problems in Mathematical Physics. P. N. Lebedev & I. P. Skalskaya. LC 65-14785. (International Series of Monographs on Pure & Applied Mathematics: Vol. 84). 1966. 183.00 (*0-08-011134-3*, Pub. by Pergamon Repr) Franklin.

Problems in Measuring Change: Proceedings of a Conference Sponsored by the Committee on Personality Development in Youth of the Social Science Research Council, 1962. Ed. by Chester W. Harris. LC 63-19211. 269p. reprint ed. pap. 83.40 (*0-608-11319-0*, 200497200048) Bks Demand.

Problems in Mechanical Drawing. 4th ed. A. S. Levens & A. E. Edstrom. 1974. text 23.16 (*0-07-037349-3*) McGraw.

Problems in Mechanical Drawing. 6th ed. Levens. 1985. 45.66 (*0-07-037471-6*) McGraw.

Problems in Mechanical Drawing. 6th ed. A. S. Levens & S. J. Cooper. (Illus.). 224p. (C). 1985. write for info. (*0-07-022334-3*) McGraw.

Problems in Medical Microbiology. J. Holton et al. 224p. 1995. pap. 28.95 (*0-632-03834-9*, Pub. by Blckwll Scitfc UK) Blackwell Sci.

Problems in Metallurgical Thermodynamics & Kinetics. G. S. Upadhyaya & R. K. Dube. LC 77-7376. 1977. 122.00 (*0-08-020865-7*, Pub. by Pergamon Repr) Franklin.

***Problems in Mind: Readings in Contemporary Philosophy of Mind.** Jack S. Crumley, II. LC 99-33203. ix, 614p. 1999. pap. text 49.95 (*0-7674-0750-4*) Mayfield Pub.

Problems in Modern Latin American History: A Reader. Ed. by John C. Chasteen & Joseph S. Tulchin. LC 93-17715. (Latin American Silhouettes Ser.). 348p. (C). 1993. text 45.00 (*0-8420-2327-5*, SR Bks) Scholarly Res Inc.

Problems in Modern Physics. W. Smith. 180p. 1970. pap. text 137.00 (*0-677-02855-5*) Gordon & Breach.

Problems in Molecular Orbital Theory. Thomas A. Albright & Jeremy K. Burdett. LC 92-25944. (Illus.). 296p. 1992. pap. text 27.95 (*0-19-507175-1*) OUP.

Problems in National Income Analysis & Forecasting. 3rd ed. Robert H. Scott. (C). 1986. pap. text 22.00 (*0-673-15840-3*) Addson-Wesley Educ.

Problems in National Literary Identity & the Writer As Social Critic: Selected Papers of the Fourth Annual NDEA Seminar on Foreign Area Studies, February, 1980. Ed. by Anne A. Paolucci. LC 80-83126. (CNL/World Report Ser.). 72p. 1980. pap. 4.95 (*0-918680-11-5*) Griffon House.

Problems in Optometry, Vol. 3, No. 3. Ed. by Roy G. Cole & Bruce P. Rosenthal. 1991. write for info. (*1-888504-13-7*) Lighthouse NYC.

Problems in Organic Reaction Mechanisms. Fredric M. Menger. LC 68-28060. (Appleton-century-crofts Chemistry Ser.). vii, 121p. 1969. write for info. (*0-390-62638-4*) McGraw.

Problems in Organic Reaction Mechanisms. Fredric M. Menger. LC 68-28060. (Appleton-Century-Crofts Series in Chemistry). 128p. reprint ed. pap. 39.70 (*0-608-12431-1*, 205569100030) Bks Demand.

Problems in Organizational Development in English. 4th ed. P. Algeo. (C). 1993. 81.00 (*0-15-501407-2*) Harcourt.

***Problems in Paradise.** Deborah Perlberg. (Full House Sisters Ser.: Vol. 5). 112p. (J). (gr. 4-7). 1999. per. 3.99 (*0-671-04057-X*) S&S Trade.

Problems in Pediatric Drug Therapy. 3rd rev. ed. Ed. by Louis A. Pagliaro & Ann Marie Pagliaro. LC 94-37762. 1145p. 1995. pap. 60.00 (*0-914768-53-0*, T168) Am Pharm Assn.

***Problems in Pediatric Drug Therapy.** 4th rev. ed. Ed. by Louis A. Pagliaro & Ann Marie Pagliaro. 600p. 2000. 80.00 (*1-58212-001-3*) Am Pharm Assn.

Problems in Pediatric Emergency Medicine. Ed. by Robert C. Luten. LC 88-4302. (Contemporary Issues in Emergency Medicine Ser.). (Illus.). 310p. reprint ed. pap. 96.10 (*0-7837-8708-1*, 204955600013) Bks Demand.

Problems in Personal Identity. James Baillie. 176p. 1992. pap. 16.95 (*1-55778-521-X*) Paragon Hse.

Problems in Philosophical Inquiry. Julius R. Weinberg & Keith E. Yandell. LC 73-148058. 1971. reprint ed. 49.50 (*0-03-083380-9*); reprint ed. pap. text 19.95 (*0-89197-905-0*) Irvington.

An Asterisk (*) at the beginning of an entry indicates that the title is appearing for the first time.

Problems In Philosophy. Congdon. 1996. pap. 16.00 (*0-07-217389-0*) McGraw.

Problems in Philosophy: The Limits of Inquiry. Colin McGinn. LC 93-14752. 208p. 1993. pap. 25.95 (*1-55786-475-6*) Blackwell Pubs.

Problems in Physical Organic Chemistry. Anthony R. Bulter. LC 72-617. 115p. reprint ed. pap. 35.70 (*0-608-10209-1*, 201697200005) Bks Demand.

Problems in Physics. Singh A. Kumar. 1994. write for info. (*81-224-0608-4*, Pub. by Wiley Estrn) Franklin.

Problems in Prawn Culture. 2nd ed. Kunihiko Shigeno. 103p. 1979. 71.00 (*90-6191-035-8*, Pub. by A A Balkema) Ashgate Pub Co.

Problems in Pre-Columbian Textile Classification. Ina VanStan. LC 59-9294. (Florida State University Studies: 29). (Illus.). 127p. reprint ed. pap. 39.40 (*0-608-11505-3*, 201210400080) Bks Demand.

Problems in Prehistory: North Africa & the Levant. Ed. by Fred Wendorf & Anthony E. Marks. LC 74-14722. (Southern Methodist University Contributions in Anthropology Ser.: No. 13). 468p. reprint ed. pap. 145.10 (*0-608-14766-4*, 202324600032) Bks Demand.

Problems in Prehistory: North America & the Levant. Fred Wendorf et al. LC 74-14722. (Contributions in Anthropology Ser.: No. 13). 462p. 1975. write for info. (*0-87074-146-2*) SMU Pr.

Problems in Price Theory. David De Meza & Michael Osborne. LC 80-16597. (Illus.). xiv, 302p. 1993. pap. text 13.00 (*0-226-14294-9*) U Ch Pr.

Problems in Probability Theory, Mathematical Statistics & Theory of Random Functions. A. A. Sveshnikov. Tr. by Richard A. Silverman from RUS. 481p. 1979. pap. text 12.95 (*0-486-63717-4*) Dover.

Problems in Probate Law, Including a Model Probate Code & Monographs. Lewis M. Simes & Paul E. Basye. LC 46-27562. (Michigan Legal Publications). li, 782p. 1990. pap. 45.00 (*1-57588-353-8*, 301490) W S Hein.

Problems in Professional Responsibility. 2nd ed. Andrew L. Kaufman. LC 83-82906. 883p. (C). 1984. 31.00 (*0-316-48338-9*) Little.

Problems in Professional Responsibility. 3rd ed. Andrew L. Kaufman. 828p. 1989. teacher ed. write for info. (*0-316-48386-9*, 83869) Aspen Law.

Problems in Professional Responsibility. 3rd ed. Andrew L. Kaufman. 828p. 1989. 51.00 (*0-316-48385-0*, Aspen Law & Bus) Aspen Pub.

Problems in Programming: Experience Through Practice. Andrej Vitek et al. LC 91-25548. (Wiley Professional Computing Ser.). (Illus.). 342p. 1991. reprint ed. pap. 106.10 (*0-608-05308-2*, 206584600001) Bks Demand.

Problems in Public Expenditure Analysis: Papers Presented at a Conference of Experts: Sept. 15-16 1966. Ed. by Samuel B. Chase, Jr. LC 67-30589. (Brookings Institution Studies of Government Finance). 283p. reprint ed. pap. 87.80 (*0-608-12160-6*, 202536900043) Bks Demand.

Problems in Pulmonary Medicine for the Primary Physician. Ed. by Robert H. Poe & Robert H. Israel. LC 82-8972. (Illus.). 426p. reprint ed. pap. 132.10 (*0-7837-1494-7*, 205719000023) Bks Demand.

Problems in Quantum Mechanics. F. Constantinescu & E. Magyari. 1976. 185.00 (*0-08-006826-X*, Pub. by Pergamon Repr); pap. text 194.00 (*0-08-019008-1*, Pub. by Pergamon Repr) Franklin.

Problems in Quantum Mechanics. 4th ed. I. I. Goldman & V. D. Krivchenkov. Ed. by B. T. Geilikman. Tr. by E. Marquit & E. Lepa from RUS. LC 93-287. (Illus.). 283p. 1993. reprint ed. pap. 9.95 (*0-486-67527-0*) Dover.

Problems in Quantum Mechanics with Solutions. G. L. Squires. LC 93-43931. (Illus.). 264p. (C). 1995. pap. text 27.95 (*0-521-37850-8*) Cambridge U Pr.

Problems in Quantum Physics (Recent & Future Experiments & Interpretations) Proceedings on the Summer Research Workshop. Ed. by L. Kostro. 924p. (C). 1988. text 138.00 (*9971-5-0449-9*) World Scientific Pub.

Problems in Quantum Physics II: Gdansk '89. Ed. by J. Pykacz et al. 536p. (C). 1990. text 130.00 (*981-02-0177-X*) World Scientific Pub.

Problems in Real Analysis. 2nd ed. Charalambos Aliprantis & Owen Burkinshaw. LC 99-176757. (Illus.). vii, 403 p. (C). 1998. boxed set 59.95 incl. cd-rom (*0-12-050253-4*) Acad Pr.

Problems in Real Analysis: A Workbook with Solutions. Charalambos D. Aliprantis & Owen Burkinshaw. 285p. 1990. text 52.00 (*0-12-050256-9*) Acad Pr.

Problems in Real & Complex Analysis. Bernerd R. Gelbaum. Ed. by P. R. Halmos. (Problem Books in Mathematics). (Illus.). 496p. 1992. 69.95 (*0-387-97766-X*) Spr-Verlag.

Problems in Remedies. 2nd ed. Dan B. Dobbs & Kathleen Kavanagh. (American Casebook Ser.). 218p. (C). 1993. pap. 20.50 (*0-314-02619-3*) West Pub.

Problems in Roofing Design. B. Harrison McCampbell. (Illus.). 256p. 1991. pap. text 54.95 (*0-7506-9162-X*) Buttrwrth-Heinemann.

Problems in Search of Creative Solutions. H. Allen Murphey. (Illus.). 112p. 1997. pap. 11.95 (*1-880505-52-5*, CLC0205) Pieces of Lrning.

Problems in Service Life Prediction of Building & Construction Materials. Ed. by Larry W. Masters. 1985. text 184.00 (*90-247-3181-X*) Kluwer Academic.

Problems in Small Animal Neurology. 2nd ed. Cheryl L. Chrisman. LC 90-5881. (Illus.). 526p. 1991. text 70.00 (*0-8121-1349-7*) Lppncott W & W.

Problems in Social Psychology see Revisiting Wertheimer's Seminars

***Problems in Society/Making Choices/Friendship: 13 Bible-Based Sessions.** David Cook Publishers Staff. 2000. pap. 18.99 (*0-7814-5517-0*) Cook.

Problems in Stoicism. Ed. by A. A. Long. LC 96-39649. 272p. 1996. pap. 35.00 (*0-485-12128-X*, Pub. by Athlone Pr) Humanities.

Problems in Syntax. Ed. by Liliane Tasmowski & Dominique Willems. 414p. 1984. 85.00 (*0-306-41564-X*, Plenum Trade) Perseus Pubng.

Problems in the Advanced Theory of Functions see Problem Book in the Theory of Functions

Problems in the Construction of a Theory of Natural Language. Philip Tartaglia. (Janua Linguarum, Ser. Minor: No. 124). 252p. (Orig.). 1972. pap. text 46.15 (*90-279-2186-5*) Mouton.

Problems in the Constructive Trend in Mathematics, Pt. VI. Ed. by V. p. Orevkov & Nikolai A. Sanin. LC 75-11951. (Proceedings of the Steklov Institute of Mathematics Ser.: No. 129). 272p. 1976. pap. 135.00 (*0-8218-3029-5*, STEKLO/129) Am Math.

Problems in the Constructive Trend in Mathematics Pt. V: Proceedings. Ed. by V. P. Orevkov & Nikolai A. Sanin. (Proceedings of the Steklov Institute of Mathematics Ser.: No. 113). 287p. 1972. pap. 66.00 (*0-8218-3013-9*, STEKLO/113) Am Math.

Problems in the Constructive Trend in Mathematics, IV, Vol. 93. Ed. by P. Orevkov & M. A. Sanin. 329p. 1967. 69.00 (*0-8218-1893-7*, STEKLO/93C) Am Math.

Problems in the Elementary Theory of Functions see Problem Book in the Theory of Functions

Problems in the Evolution of the Solar System see Symposia Mathematica: Proceedings

Problems in the Federal Income Taxation of Business Enterprises. 3rd ed. Norton L. Steuben & William J. Turner. 403p. 1996. pap. text, teacher ed. write for info. (*1-56662-444-4*) Foundation Pr.

Problems in the Federal Income Taxation of Business Enterprises. 3rd ed. Norton L. Steuben & William J. Turnier. (Paralegal). 337p. 1996. pap. text 16.50 (*1-56662-414-2*) Foundation Pr.

Problems in the Federal Income Taxation of Partnerships & Corporations. 2nd ed. Norton L. Steuben & William J. Turnier. 1986. pap. text 16.95 (*0-88277-314-3*) Foundation Pr.

Problems in the General Theory of Relativity & Theory of Group Representations. Ed. by N. G. Basov. Tr. by Alan Mason from RUS. LC 78-12612. (Proceedings of the P. N. Lebedev Physics Institute Ser.: No. 96). (Illus.). 193p. 1978. reprint ed. pap. 59.90 (*0-608-05552-2*, 206602000006) Bks Demand.

Problems in the History of Modern Africa. Ed. by Robert O. Collins et al. (Problems in African History Ser.: Vol. III). (Illus.). 320p. (Orig.). (C). 1997. pap. text 19.95 (*1-55876-124-1*) Wiener Pubs Inc.

Problems in the International Comparison of Economic Accounts. (Studies in Income & Wealth: No. 20). 415p. 1957. reprint ed. 107.90 (*0-87014-176-7*) Natl Bur Econ Res.

Problems in the Interpretation of Jonathan Edwards' The Nature of True Virtue. Virginia A. Peacock. LC 90-35441. (Studies in American Religion: Vol. 47). 252p. 1991. lib. bdg. 89.95 (*0-88946-643-2*) E Mellen.

Problems in the Law of Mass Communications: Programmed Instruction. 1982nd ed. David Gordon. (University Casebook Ser.). 183p. 1982. pap. text 4.75 (*0-88277-104-3*) Foundation Pr.

Problems in the Life & Writings of A. E. Housman. P. G. Naiditch. 264p. (C). 1995. 40.00 (*0-9647634-1-9*) Krown & Spellman.

Problems in the Literary Biography of Mikhail Sholokhov. Roy Medvedev. Tr. by A. D. Briggs. LC 76-14032. 235p. reprint ed. pap. 67.00 (*0-608-12059-6*, 2024491) Bks Demand.

Problems in the Neogene & Quaternary in the Carpathian Basin: Geological & Geomorphological Studies Contribution to the VIIth Congress of the Regional Committee on Mediterranean Neogene Stratigraphy, Budapest, 1985. M. Kretzoi & Marton Pecsi. No. 19. 128p. (C). 1985. 42.00 (*963-05-4228-5*) St Mut.

Problems in the Psychology of Reading. J. Q. Quantz. (Psychology Monographs General & Applied: Vol. 2). 1974. reprint ed. pap. 55.00 (*0-8115-1401-3*) Periodicals Srv.

Problems in the Study of Economic Growth. Universities-National Bureau Staff. (Conference Ser.: No. 1). 254p. 1949. reprint ed. 66.10 (*0-87014-192-9*) Natl Bur Econ Res.

Problems in the Theory of Point Explosion in Gases: Proceedings. Ed. by V. P. Korobeinikov. LC 75-45104. (Proceedings of the Steklov Institute of Mathematics Ser.: No. 119). 311p. 1975. pap. 92.00 (*0-8218-3019-8*, STEKLO/119) Am Math.

Problems in the Training of Certain Special-Class Teachers. Louis M. Schleier. LC 70-177809. (Columbia University. Teachers College. Contributions to Education Ser.: No. 475). reprint ed. 37.50 (*0-404-55475-X*) AMS Pr.

Problems in Unification & Supergravity: Conference Proceedings, La Jolla Institute, 1983. Ed. by Glennys Farrar & Frank Henyey. LC 84-71246. (AIP Conference Proceedings Ser.: No. 116). 185p. 1984. lib. bdg. 35.50 (*0-88318-315-3*) Am Inst Physics.

Problems in Written Expression: Assessment & Remediation. Sharon Bradley-Johnson & Judi L. Lesiak. LC 88-32830. (School Practitioner Ser.). 178p. 1989. pap. text 22.00 (*0-89862-233-6*); lib. bdg. 49.95 (*0-89862-354-5*) Guilford Pubns.

Problems Involving Change of Type: Proceedings of a Conference Held at the University of Stuttgart, FRG, October 11-14, 1988. Ed. by K. Kirchgassner et al. (Lecture Notes in Physics Ser.: Vol. 359). xii, 207p. 1990. 44.95 (*0-387-52595-5*) Spr-Verlag.

Problems, Issues & Concepts in Therapeutic Recreation. Ronald P. Reynolds & Gerald S. O'Morrow. 304p. (C). 1985. text 39.00 (*0-13-717430-6*) P-H.

Problems of a Changing Population: Report of the Committee on Population Problems to the National Resources Committee, May, 1938. U. S. National Resources Committee, May 1938. LC 75-38145. (Demography Ser.). (Illus.). 1976. reprint ed. 25.95 (*0-405-07998-2*) Ayer.

Problems of a Mature Economy: A Text for Students of the British Economy. Frederick V. Meyer et al. LC 79-123635. xii, 627p. 1970. write for info. (*0-333-04240-9*) Macmillan.

Problems of a Political Animal: Community, Justice, & Conflict in Aristotelian Political Thought. Bernard Yack. LC 92-23296. 1993. 55.00 (*0-520-08166-8*, Pub. by U CA Pr); pap. 16.95 (*0-520-08167-6*, Pub. by U CA Pr) Cal Prin Full Svc.

Problems of a Sociology of Knowledge. Max Ferdinand Scheler. Ed. by Kenneth Strikkers. Tr. by Manfred S. Frings from GER. (International Library of Sociology Ser.). 1980. 32.50 (*0-7100-0302-1*, Routledge Thoemms) Routledge.

Problems of Absenteeism in the Mens' & Boys' Clothing Industry. 11p. 1964. 7.00 (*0-318-19669-7*) Clothing Mfrs.

Problems of Accountancy. J. N. Dey. 1985. 69.00 (*0-7855-0748-5*, Pub. by Current Dist) St Mut.

Problems of Adrenergic Mechanisms in Blood Vessel. Ed. by W. Osswald. (Journal: Blood Vessels: Vol. 21, No. 3, 1984). (Illus.). 44p. 1984. pap. 35.00 (*3-8055-3927-4*) S Karger.

Problems of Advanced Economics. Ed. by N. Miyawaki. (Studies in Contemporary Economics: Vol. 10). vi, 319p. 1984. 45.00 (*0-387-13740-8*) Spr-Verlag.

Problems of Afforestation in India. P. Bhatnagar. (C). 1991. text 150.00 (*0-89771-554-3*, Pub. by Intl Bk Distr) St Mut.

Problems of Afforestation in India. P. Bhatnagar. 170p. 1991. pap. 250.00 (*81-7089-156-6*, Pub. by Intl Bk Distr) St Mut.

Problems of Aging: Biological & Medical Aspects. Ed. by E. V. Cowdry & Robert J. Kastenbaum. LC 78-22196. (Aging & Old Age Ser.). (Illus.). 1979. reprint ed. lib. bdg. 52.95 (*0-405-11813-9*) Ayer.

Problems of American Constitutionalism. Randall W. Bland. 424p. 2000. 59.95 (*1-57292-133-1*); pap. 34.95 (*1-57292-132-3*) Austin & Winfield.

Problems of America's Aging Population. Southern Conference on Gerontology Staff. Ed. by T. Lynn Smith. LC 72-190980. (Institute of Gerontology Ser.: No. 1). 134p. reprint ed. pap. 41.60 (*0-7837-5004-8*, 204467100004) Bks Demand.

Problems of an Empirical Sociology of Knowledge. Bjorn Eriksson. (Studia Sociologica Upsaliensia: No. 10). 171p. (Orig.). 1975. pap. 27.50 (*91-554-0258-5*) Coronet Bks.

Problems of Analysis: Philosophical Essays. Max Black. LC 74-139124. 304p. (C). 1971. reprint ed. lib. bdg. 59.75 (*0-8371-5740-4*, BLPA, Greenwood Pr) Greenwood.

Problems of Antiviral Therapy. Ed. by John S. Oxford & Charles H. Stuart-Harris. (Beecham Colloquia Ser.). 360p. 1984. text 94.00 (*0-12-674760-1*) Acad Pr.

Problems of Art. Susanne K. Langer. 1985. 15.00 (*0-684-15346-7*) S&S Trade.

Problems of Authority in the Reformation Debates. G. R. Evans. 344p. (C). 1992. text 69.95 (*0-521-41686-8*) Cambridge U Pr.

Problems of Autistic Behavior: Experimental Analysis of Autism, Vol. 1. O. Ivar Lovaas et al. 300p. text. write for info. (*0-8290-0740-7*) Irvington.

Problems of Balance of Payment & Trade. Ed. by Nasrollah S. Fatemi. LC 74-4971. 261p. 1975. 38.50 (*0-8386-1587-2*) Fairleigh Dickinson.

Problems of Balkan Security: Southeastern Europe in the 1990s. Ed. by Paul S. Shoup & George W. Hoffman. (Illus.). 298p. (C). 1990. pap. text 18.75 (*0-943875-21-8*); lib. bdg. 38.50 (*0-943875-22-6*) W Wilson Ctr Pr.

Problems of Belief. Ferdinand C. Schiller. LC 75-3349. 1976. reprint ed. 37.50 (*0-404-59348-8*) AMS Pr.

Problems of Biogeochemistry. W. I. Vernadsky. Ed. by G. Evelyn Hutchinson. Tr. by George Vernadsky. (Connecticut Academy of Arts & Sciences Ser., Trans.: Vol. 35). 1944. pap. 29.50 (*0-685-22907-6*) Elliots Bks.

Problems of Calibration of Absolute Magnitudes & Temperature of Stars: Proceedings of the International Astronomical Union, Symposium No. 54. International Astronomical Union Staff. Ed. by B. Hauck & Bengt E. Westerlund. LC 73-83562. 1973. lib. bdg. 123.50 (*90-277-0365-5*) Kluwer Academic.

Problems of Capital Formation: Concepts, Measurement, & Controlling Factors. (Studies in Income & Wealth: No. 19). 623p. 1957. reprint ed. 160.00 (*0-87014-175-9*) Natl Bur Econ Res.

Problems of Capital Formation: Concepts, Measurement, & Controlling Factors. Conference on Research in Income & Wealth. LC 75-19707. (National Bureau of Economic Research Ser.). (Illus.). 1975. reprint ed. 50.95 (*0-405-07587-1*) Ayer.

Problems of Cartesianism. Ed. by Thomas M. Lennon et al. (Studies in the History of Ideas). 272p. 1982. 65.00 (*0-7735-1000-1*, Pub. by McG-Queens Univ Pr) CUP Services.

Problems of Chemistry. W. Graham Richards. (Illus.). 112p. (C). 1986. 24.95 (*0-19-219191-8*) OUP.

Problems of Collapse & Numerical Relativity. Ed. by Daniel Bancel & Monique Signore. 1984. text 185.50 (*90-277-1816-4*) Kluwer Academic.

***Problems of Communitarian Politics: Unity & Conflict.** Elizabeth Frazer. LC 99-37974. 296p. 2000. write for info. (*0-19-829563-4*); write for info. (*0-19-829564-2*) OUP.

Problems of Complex Ores Utilization. Ed. by Fathi Habashi et al. 261p. 1995. pap. text 50.00 (*2-88449-241-0*) Gordon & Breach.

Problems of Constitutional Development: Essays in Memory of Professor Istvan Kovacs. Attila J. Racz. (FRE & GER.). 225p. 1993. pap. 90.00 (*963-05-6543-9*, Pub. by Akade Kiado) St Mut.

Problems of Cooperative Development in India, with Special Reference to West Bengal. Pranab J. Chakrabarti. 1983. text 22.00 (*0-685-14093-8*) Coronet Bks.

Problems of Coordination in Economic Activity. Ed. by James W. Friedman. LC 93-14168. (Recent Economic Thought Ser.). 256p. (C). 1993. lib. bdg. 134.00 (*0-7923-9381-3*) Kluwer Academic.

Problems of Criminal Procedural Law Connected with Information Technology (Recommendation & Explanatory Memoraundum), No. R(95)13. LC 96-194058. 1996. 12.00 (*92-871-2971-1*, Pub. by Council of Europe) Manhattan Pub Co.

Problems of Daily Living. Rene Penalba. (SPA.). 1999. pap. 7.99 (*0-8297-1977-6*) Vida Pubs.

***Problems of Death.** James D. Torr. (Opposing Viewpoints Ser.). 360p. (YA). 2000. 21.96 (*0-7377-0350-4*) Greenhaven.

***Problems of Death.** James D. Torr. LC 00-22621. (Opposing Viewpoints Ser.). 360p. (YA). 2000. pap. 13.96 (*0-7377-0349-0*) Greenhaven.

Problems of Democracy in Latin America. Ed. by Roberto Espindola. LC 96-196667. (Institute of Latin American Studies). (ENG & SPA., Illus.). 172p. 1996. pap. 69.50 (*91-85894-45-1*, Pub. by Almqvist Wiksell) Coronet Bks.

Problems of Democracy in Latin America. Lasso G. Plaza. LC 81-36. (Weil Lectures on American Citizenship). 88p. 1981. reprint ed. lib. bdg. 55.00 (*0-313-22877-9*, PLPD, Greenwood Pr) Greenwood.

Problems of Democratic Transition & Consolidation: Southern Europe, South America, & Post-Communist Europe. Juan J. Linz & Alfred Stepan. LC 95-43462. (Illus.). 616p. (C). 1996. text 55.00 (*0-8018-5157-2*); pap. text 18.95 (*0-8018-5158-0*) Johns Hopkins.

***Problems of Democratization in China.** Thomas Lumm. LC 00-42692. (East Asia Ser.). 2000. write for info. (*0-8153-3871-6*) Garland.

Problems of Diglossia in Arabic: A Comparative Study of Classical & Iraqi Arabic. Salih J. Altoma. LC 69-11663. (Middle Eastern Monographs: No. 21). 177p. (C). 1969. pap. 4.50 (*0-674-70775-3*) HUP.

Problems of Drug Dependence, 2 vols. 1993. lib. bdg. 625.95 (*0-8490-8915-8*) Gordon Pr.

Problems of Drug Dependence, 2 vols., Set. 1995. lib. bdg. 625.99 (*0-8490-6828-2*) Gordon Pr.

***Problems of Drug Dependence 1996: Proceedings of the 58th Annual Scientific Meeting.** Ed. by Louis S. Harrie. 462p. 1999. reprint ed. pap. text 45.00 (*0-7881-8130-0*) DIANE Pub.

***Problems of Drug Dependence 1998: Proceedings of the 60th Annual Scientific Meeting, The College on Problems of Drug Dependence, Inc.** Louis S. Harris. 443p. 1999. per. 38.00 (*0-16-049975-5*) USGPO.

Problems of Economic & Political Transformation in the Balkans. Ian Jeffries & Alin Teodorescu. LC 95-26834. 224p. 1996. 89.50 (*1-85567-319-3*) Bks Intl VA.

Problems of Economic Growth: Three Essays & Economic Projections for Canada, 1961-1991. O. J. Firestone. LC 66-5461. (Social Sciences Studies: Vol. 2). 204p. 1965. reprint ed. pap. 63.30 (*0-608-02198-9*, 206286800004) Bks Demand.

Problems of Economic Planning: Papers on Planning & Economics. Evan F. Durbin. LC 68-29483. (Reprints of Economic Classics Ser.). x, 214p. 1968. reprint ed. 35.00 (*0-678-06514-4*) Kelley.

Problems of Economic Transition: Regional Development in Central & Eastern Europe. Ed. by Tibor Vasko. 258p. 1992. 82.95 (*1-85628-386-0*, Pub. by Avebry) Ashgate Pub Co.

Problems of Education among Scheduled Castes. Puran Singh. (C). 1988. 21.00 (*81-7099-195-1*, Pub. by Mittal Pubs Dist) S Asia.

Problems of Elastic Stability & Vibrations. Ed. by Vadim Komkov. LC 81-12833. (Contemporary Mathematics Ser.: Vol. 4). 137p. 1981. pap. 17.00 (*0-8218-5005-9*, CONM/4) Am Math.

Problems of Elastic Stability & Vibrations. American Mathematical Society Staff. Ed. by Vadim Komkov. LC 81-12833. (Contemporary Mathematics Ser.: Vol. 4). (Illus.). 147p. reprint ed. pap. 45.60 (*0-608-09609-1*, 205276700007) Bks Demand.

Problems of Ethnomusicology. Constantin Brailoiu. Ed. by A. L. Lloyd. LC 83-15224. (Illus.). 320p. 1984. text 85.00 (*0-521-24528-1*) Cambridge U Pr.

Problems of Everyday Life. Leon Trotsky. pap. 24.95 (*0-87348-854-7*) Pathfinder NY.

Problems of Everyday Life: Creating the Foundations for a New Society in Revolutionary Russia. Leon Trotsky. Tr. by G. R. Fidler et al. LC 79-186693. 351p. 1973. reprint ed. pap. 24.95 (*0-913460-15-X*); reprint ed. lib. bdg. 65.00 (*0-913460-14-1*) Pathfinder NY.

Problems of Evolution. G. F. Gause. (Connecticut Academy of Arts & Sciences Ser., Trans.: Vol. 37). 1947. pap. 39.50 (*0-685-22905-X*) Elliots Bks.

Problems of Fertilization. Frank R. Lillie. (Genes Cells & Organisms Ser.). (Illus.). 296p. 1988. text 15.00 (*0-8240-1382-4*) Garland.

P

Problems of Financial Analysis in Institutional Lending Operations: Some Lessons from Tanzania. Kami Rwegasira. LC 92-33657. 200p. 1992. 82.95 (*1-85628-299-6*, Pub. by Avebry) Ashgate Pub Co.

***Problems of Form.** Dirk Baecker. LC 99-21522. 248p. 1999. 55.00 (*0-8047-3423-2*) Stanford U Pr.

Problems of Form. Dirk Baecker. LC 99-21522. (Writing Science Ser.). 1999. pap. text 22.95 (*0-8047-3424-0*) Stanford U Pr.

Problems of Fundamental Modern Physics. R. Cherubini & P. Dalpiaz. Ed. by B. Minetti. 608p. (C). 1990. text 161.00 (*981-02-0085-4*) World Scientific Pub.

Problems of Fundamental Modern Physics: Towards the Hadronic Physics Frontiers (Procedings of the 8th Winter School) M. Gibilisco et al. 516p. 1994. text 128.00 (*981-02-1553-3*) World Scientific Pub.

Problems of Fundamental Modern Physics II: Proceedings of the 5th Winter School on Hadronic Physics, Folgaria, Italy, February 5-10, 1990. R. Cherubini et al. 544p. (C). 1991. text 137.00 (*981-02-0295-4*) World Scientific Pub.

Problems of Gauguin's Therapist: Language, Madness & Therapy. William H. Pincus. 134p. 1994. 66.95 (*1-85628-374-7*, Pub. by Avebry) Ashgate Pub Co.

Problems of Genetics. William Bateson. LC 79-15467. 1979. 17.00 (*0-300-02435-5*); pap. 15.00 (*0-300-02436-3*, Y-350) Yale U Pr.

***Problems of Governance in South Asia.** W. A. Panandiker. 2000. 36.00 (*81-220-0559-4*, Pub. by Konark Pubs Pvt Ltd) S Asia.

Problems of Governance of Pakistan. Mushahid Hussein & Akhmal Hussein. (Governance in South Asia Ser.). 1993. text 27.50 (*0-685-63383-7*, Pub. by Konark Pubs Pvt Ltd) Advent Bks Div.

Problems of Governing Sri Lanka. Kingsley M. De Silva. (Governance in South Asia Ser.). 1993. text 40.00 (*0-685-66298-5*, Pub. by Konark Pubs Pvt Ltd) Advent Bks Div.

Problems of Hamlet. G. F. Bradby. (Studies in Shakespeare: No. 24). (C). 1970. reprint ed. pap. 75.00 (*0-8383-0006-5*) M S G Haskell Hse.

Problems of Hemispheric Defense. California University Committee on International R. LC 77-167322. (Essay Index Reprint Ser.). 1977. reprint ed. 18.95 (*0-8369-2759-1*) Ayer.

Problems of Higher Education in India. K. L. Joshi. 312p. 1977. 8.95 (*0-318-36826-9*) Asia Bk Corp.

Problems of Higher Education in India. C. M. Ramachandron. 1987. 27.50 (*0-8364-2218-X*, Pub. by Mittal Pubs Dist) S Asia.

Problems of Higher Education in India: An Annotated Bibliography of Source Material. D. Kamalavijayan. 1979. 12.50 (*0-8364-0505-6*) S Asia.

Problems of Historical Psychology. Zevedei Barbu. LC 75-28659. 222p. 1976. reprint ed. lib. bdg. 55.00 (*0-8371-8476-2*, BAHP, Greenwood Pr) Greenwood.

Problems of Home-Based Workers in India. Ed. by B. B. Patel. (C). 1989. 32.50 (*81-204-0395-9*, Pub. by Oxford IBH) S Asia.

Problems of Human Pleasure & Behavior. Michael Balint. 1973. pap. 3.95 (*0-87140-279-3*, Pub. by Liveright) Norton.

Problems of Humanity. 3rd ed. Alice A. Bailey. LC 53-2808. 1964. pap. 11.00 (*0-85330-113-1*) Lucis.

Problems of Hydrothermal Ore Deposition: The Origin, Evolution & Control of Ore-Forming Fluids. Ed. by Z. Pouba & M. Stemprok. (International Association of the Genesis of Ore Deposits (IAGOD) Symposia Ser.). (Illus.). 396p. 1970. text 44.00 (*3-510-56002-7*, Pub. by E Schweizerbartsche) Balogh.

Problems of Implementing Multiple Categorical Education Programs. Jackie Kimbrough & Paul T. Hill. LC 83-15929. 1983. pap. text 4.00 (*0-8330-0515-4*, R-2957-ED) Rand Corp.

Problems of Indenture Trustees & Bondholders, 1995. (Real Estate Law & Practice Course Handbook Ser.). 1000p. 1995. pap. 99.00 (*0-685-65550-4*, N4-4591) PLI.

Problems of Indentured Trustees & Bondholders, 1992: Defaulted Bonds & Bankruptcy. (Real Estate Law & Practice Ser.). 779p. 1992. pap. text 70.00 (*0-685-59339-8*, N4-4561) PLI.

Problems of Indian Philosophy Vol. 3: Problems of Indian Philosophy. Ed. by S. P. Dubey. LC 96-902047. (C). 1997. 26.00 (*81-85636-21-4*, Pub. by M Manoharial) S Asia.

Problems of Inference & Proof in Participant Observation. Howard S. Becker. (Reprint Series in Social Sciences). (C). 1993. reprint ed. pap. text 1.00 (*0-8290-3493-5*, S-337) Irvington.

Problems of Installation in Museums of Art. Arthur W. Melton. Ed. & Intro. by Edward S. Robinson. 276p. (C). 1996. reprint ed. pap. text 30.00 (*0-931201-25-X*) Am Assn Mus.

Problems of International Money, 1972-85. Ed. by Michael Posner. ix, 191p. 1986. pap. 8.50 (*0-939934-58-2*) Intl Monetary.

Problems of International Money, 1972-85: Papers Presented at a Seminar Organized by the IMF & the Overseas Development Institute in London in March 1985. Ed. by Michael Posner. LC 86-10480. (Illus.). 202p. reprint ed. pap. 62.70 (*0-608-18035-1*, 202908800058) Bks Demand.

Problems of Intracranial Pressure in Childhood. Ed. by Robert A. Minns. (Clinics in Developmental Medicine Ser.: Nos. 113-114). (Illus.). 458p. (C). 1991. text 95.00 (*0-521-41272-2*, Pub. by Mc Keith Pr) Cambridge U Pr.

Problems of Jurisprudence. Richard A. Posner. 504p. 1990. 38.00 (*0-674-70875-X*) HUP.

Problems of Jurisprudence. Richard A. Posner. 504p. (C). 1993. pap. 20.50 (*0-674-70876-8*) HUP.

Problems of Knowledge in Legal Scholarship. Philip Shuchman. LC 79-80252. 136p. 1979. pap. text 11.00 (*0-939328-00-3*) U CT Law Sch Found.

Problems of Land Reform Implementation in Rural Ethiopia. Mengistu Woube. (Illus.). 174p. (Orig.). 1986. pap. text 65.00 (*91-506-0482-1*) Coronet Bks.

Problems of Lasting Peace Revisited. Ed. by Thomas T. Thalken. LC 86-18496. 196p. 1986. 5.00 (*0-938469-00-2*) Hoover Lib.

Problems of Life & Death: A Humanist Perspective. Kurt Baier. LC 97-12834. (Prometheus Lecture). 239p. 1997. 29.95 (*1-57392-153-X*) Prometheus Bks.

Problems of Life & Mind, 5 vols., Set. George Henry Lewes et al. Incl. Foundations of a Creed., **2 vols.** LC 78-72805. 75.00 (*0-404-60871-X*); Physical Basis of Mind. LC 78-72805. 42.50 (*0-404-60874-4*); Study of Psychology & Mind As a Function of the Organism., **2 vols.** LC 78-72805. 62.50 (*0-404-60875-2*); LC 78-72805. (Illus.). 180.00 (*0-404-60870-1*) AMS Pr.

Problems of Literary Evaluation. Ed. by Joseph P. Strelka. LC 68-56136. (Yearbook of Comparative Criticism Ser.: Vol. 2). 1969. 30.00 (*0-271-00085-6*) Pa St U Pr.

Problems of Long-Term Imprisonment. Anthony E. Bottoms & Roy Light. (Cambridge Criminology Ser.: No. 58). 250p. 1987. text 72.95 (*0-566-05427-2*, Pub. by Avebry) Ashgate Pub Co.

Problems of Market Liberalism. Ed. by Ellen Frankel Paul et al. LC 98-3392. (Social Philosophy & Policy Ser.: No. 15:2). 314p. (C). 1998. pap. 24.95 (*0-521-64991-9*) Cambridge U Pr.

Problems of Meaning in Science Curriculum. Douglas A. Roberts & Leif Ostman. LC 97-46462. (Ways of Knowing in Science Ser.). 1998. 48.00 (*0-8077-3709-7*); pap. 23.95 (*0-8077-3708-9*) Tchrs Coll.

Problems of Mental Deficiency: Eugenics, Democracy & Social Policy in Britain c.1870-1959. Mathew Thomson. LC 97-33636. (Oxford Historical Monographs). 368p. 1998. text 95.00 (*0-19-820692-5*) OUP.

Problems of Mind & Matter. John Wisdom. 231p. reprint ed. pap. 65.90 (*0-608-12916-X*, 2024557) Bks Demand.

Problems of Mixed Mode Crack Propagation. E. E. Gdoutos. 250p. 1984. text 168.50 (*90-247-3055-4*) Kluwer Academic.

Problems of Modern Democracy. Edwin L. Godkin. (Notable American Authors Ser.). 1992. reprint ed. lib. bdg. 75.00 (*0-7812-2925-1*) Rprt Serv.

Problems of Modern Faith: Essays & Addresses. Josef Pieper. Tr. by Jan Van Heurck. 307p. 1983. 7.49 (*0-8199-0856-8*, Frncscn Herld) Franciscan Pr.

Problems of Modern Industry. Beatrice Potter Webb & Sidney Webb. LC 70-37918. (Select Bibliographies Reprint Ser.). 1977. reprint ed. 23.95 (*0-8369-6755-0*) Ayer.

Problems of Modern Living: Psychology of Adjustment. Benjamin B. Wolman. (Illus.). 217p. (Orig.). (C). 1987. pap. text 19.95 (*0-89641-145-1*) American Pr.

Problems of Modern Science: A Series of Lectures Delivered at King's College (University of London) Ed. by Arthur Dendy. LC 72-314. (Essay Index Reprint Ser.). 1977. reprint ed. 20.95 (*0-8369-2789-3*) Ayer.

Problems of Modernity. Ed. by Andrew Benjamin. 224p. 1989. 37.50 (*0-415-01066-7*) Routledge.

***Problems of Moral Philosophy.** Theodor W. Adorno. 2000. 39.50 (*0-8047-3936-6*) Stanford U Pr.

Problems of Multiphase Fluid Filtration. A. N. Konolov. LC 94-2212. 200p. 1994. text 61.00 (*981-02-1735-8*) World Scientific Pub.

Problems of Mysticism & Its Symbolism see Hidden Symbolism of Alchemy & the Occult Arts

Problems of New Testament Gospel Origins: A Glasnost Approach. James W. Deardorff. LC 92-20927. 248p. 1992. text 89.95 (*0-7734-9807-9*) E Mellen.

Problems of Nonlinear Deformation: The Continuation Method Applied to Nonlinear Problems in Solid Mechanics. E. I. Grigolyuk & V. I. Shalashilin. 272p. (C). 1991. text 185.50 (*0-7923-0947-2*) Kluwer Academic.

Problems of Nonlinear Optics. S. A. Akhmanov & R. V. Khokhlov. Ed. by R. Sen. Tr. by N. Jacobi from RUS. LC 78-131021. xiii, 294p. 1972. text 312.00 (*0-677-30400-5*) Gordon & Breach.

Problems of Normal & Genetically Abnormal Retinas. Ed. by R. M. Clayton et al. 1983. text 104.00 (*0-12-176180-0*) Acad Pr.

Problems of Old Glaciations, Pre-Pleistocene Glaciogeology in the U. S. S. R., Vol. 1. N. M. Chumakov. (Soviet Scientific Reviews Ser.). 210p. 1992. pap. text 267.00 (*3-7186-5358-3*, Harwood Acad Pubs) Gordon & Breach.

Problems of Origins & Development. 4th ed. John Algeo. (C). 1993. pap. text 37.00 (*0-15-500238-4*, Pub. by Harcourt Coll Pubs) Harcourt.

Problems of Pain & Stress: Twenty-Sixth Annual Conference of the Society for Psychosomatic Research. Ed. by Andrew Steptoe. 96p. 1984. pap. 32.00 (*0-08-031301-9*, Pergamon Pr) Elsevier.

Problems of Parent & Subsidiary Corporations under Complex Statutory Law Using a Standard of "Control" Phillip I. Blumberg & Kurt A. Strasser. 1989. write for info. (*0-318-65447-4*, Aspen Law & Bus) Aspen Pub.

Problems of Parent & Subsidiary Corporations under Statutory Law of General Application. Phillip I. Blumberg. 1168p. 1989. 155.00 (*0-316-10047-1*, Aspen Law & Bus) Aspen Pub.

Problems of Parents. Benjamin M. Spock. LC 78-13982. 308p. 1979. reprint ed. lib. bdg. 35.00 (*0-313-21000-4*, SPPPA, Greenwood Pr) Greenwood.

***Problems of Passenger Interference with Flight Crews & a Review of H. R. 3064, the Carry-On Baggage Reduction Act of 1997: Hearing Before the Subcommittee on Aviation of the Committee on Transportation & Infrastructure, House of Representatives, 105th Congress, 2nd Session, June 11, 1998.** USGPO Staff. LC 99-184821. iv, 218p. 1998. pap. write for info. (*0-16-057764-0*) USGPO.

Problems of Peace: Fifth Series. Geneva Institute of International Relations Staff. LC 71-121470. (Essay Index Reprint Ser.). 1977. 23.95 (*0-8369-1808-8*) Ayer.

Problems of Peace: First Series. Geneva Institute of International Relations Staff. LC 73-105015. (Essay Index Reprint Ser.). 1977. 26.95 (*0-8369-1468-6*) Ayer.

Problems of Peace: Lectures, Eighth Series. Geneva Institute of International Relations Staff. LC 68-22914. (Essay Index Reprint Ser.). 1977. reprint ed. 20.95 (*0-8369-0470-2*) Ayer.

Problems of Peace: Lectures, Second Series. Geneva Institute of International Relations Staff. LC 70-76899. (Essay Index Reprint Ser.). 1977. 21.95 (*0-8369-0014-6*) Ayer.

Problems of Peace: Lectures, Third Series. Geneva Institute of International Relations Staff. LC 68-57317. (Essay Index Reprint Ser.). 1977. 20.95 (*0-8369-0115-0*) Ayer.

Problems of Peace: Ninth Series. Geneva Institute of International Relations Staff. LC 70-111832. (Essay Index Reprint Ser.). 1977. 23.95 (*0-8369-1609-3*) Ayer.

Problems of Peace: Thirteenth Series. Geneva Institute of International Relations Staff. LC 68-57317. (Essay Index Reprint Ser.). 1977. 20.95 (*0-8369-0042-1*) Ayer.

Problems of Peace: Twelfth Series. Geneva Institute of International Relations Staff. LC 74-111833. (Essay Index Reprint Ser.). 1977. 20.95 (*0-8369-1610-7*) Ayer.

Problems of Petroleum Migration. Ed. by W. H. Roberts, III & Robert J. Cordell. LC 80-80879. (AAPG Studies in Geology: No. 10). (Illus.). 283p. reprint ed. pap. 87.80 (*0-7837-2597-3*, 204276100006) Bks Demand.

Problems of Philosophers: An Introduction. Patrick T. Mackenzie. LC 88-17724. 316p. (C). 1989. pap. text 24.95 (*0-87975-486-9*) Prometheus Bks.

Problems of Philosophy. Francis Reeves. 85p. (C). 1993. student ed. 16.11 (*1-56870-033-4*) RonJon Pub.

***Problems of Philosophy.** Bertrand Russell. LC 98-33214. 1999. pap. text 4.95 (*0-486-40674-1*) Dover.

Problems of Philosophy. Bertrand Russell. LC 97-2432. 192p. 1997. pap. 8.95 (*0-19-511552-X*) OUP.

Problems of Philosophy. Bertrand Russell. LC 88-61328. (Great Books in Philosophy). 163p. (C). 1988. pap. 8.95 (*0-87975-497-4*) Prometheus Bks.

Problems of Philosophy. large type ed. Bertrand Russell. LC 97-30369. 168p. 1997. text 22.95 (*1-56000-539-4*) Transaction Pubs.

Problems of Philosophy. Bertrand Russell. LC 90-81389. (HPC Classics Ser.). 168p. (C). 1990. reprint ed. pap. text 7.95 (*0-87220-098-1*); reprint ed. lib. bdg. 24.95 (*0-87220-099-X*) Hackett Pub.

***Problems of Philosophy.** 2nd ed. Bertrand Russell. LC 98-7017. 1998. pap. write for info. (*0-19-289298-3*) OUP.

Problems of Philosophy & Psychology. Jay N. Eacker. LC 75-17548. 216p. 1975. text 37.95 (*0-88229-202-1*) Burnham Inc.

Problems of Philosophy in Their Interconnection. Moritz Schlick. Ed. by Henk L. Mulder et al. 224p. (C). 1987. text 206.50 (*90-277-2465-2*, D Reidel) Kluwer Academic.

Problems Of Philosophy (the) Farrell. 1998. 18.74 (*0-07-431304-5*) McGraw.

Problems of Planning, East & West. Rudolf Bicanic. (Publications of the Institute of Social Studies: No. 15). 1967. text 22.35 (*90-279-0112-0*) Mouton.

Problems of Point Blast Theory. V. P. Korobeinikov. Tr. by J. George Adashko. (Translation Ser.). (Illus.). 400p. 1990. 129.95 (*0-88318-674-8*) Spr-Verlag.

Problems of Preschool Children. Richman. 1988. pap. text 84.44 (*0-471-91952-3*) Wiley.

Problems of Psychiatry in General Practice: Neurasthenia, Obsessive-Compulsive Disorder, Advances in Treatment of Depression, Teaching & Training of the GP. Ed. by Markus Gastpar & Paul Kielholz. LC 92-48275. (Illus.). 168p. 1993. text 21.00 (*0-88937-084-2*) Hogrefe & Huber Pubs.

Problems of Psychical Research & Theories in the Realm of the Supernormal (1921) Hereward Carrington. 314p. 1998. reprint ed. pap. 24.95 (*0-7661-0528-8*) Kessinger Pub.

Problems of Psychoanalytic Technique. Otto Fenichel. 1969. pap. 16.00 (*0-911194-00-2*) Psych Qtly.

Problems of Psychoanalytic Training, Diagnosis, & the Technique of Therapy. Anna Freud. LC 67-9514. (Writings of Anna Freud: Vol. 7). 311p. 1971. 47.50 (*0-8236-6876-2*) Intl Univs Pr.

Problems of Reducing the Exhaustive Search. Vladik Kreinovich & G. E. Mints. LC 96-27577. (American Mathematical Society Translations Ser.: vol. 178). 189p. 1996. text 79.00 (*0-8218-0386-7*, TRANS2/178) Am Math.

Problems of Reflection in the System of Education, Vol. 3. Niklas Luhmann & Karl-Eberhard Schorr. Tr. by Rebecca A. Neuwirth. 480p. 1999. 85.00 (*1-57181-735-2*) Berghahn Bks.

Problems of Refugees in Africa: Boundaries & Borders. Ebenezer Q. Blavo. (University of North London Voices in Development Management Ser.). 186p. 1999. text 65.95 (*1-84014-999-X*, Pub. by Ashgate Pub) Ashgate Pub Co.

Problems of Religion: An Introductory Survey. Durant Drake. LC 68-19268. 425p. 1968. reprint ed. lib. bdg. 79.50 (*0-8371-0062-3*, DRPR, Greenwood Pr) Greenwood.

Problems of Religious Experience. C. R. Brakenhelm. 158p. 1985. pap. 32.50 (*91-554-1657-8*) Coronet Bks.

Problems of Representation in the Teaching & Learning of Mathematics. Ed. by Claude Janvier. 248p. (C). 1987. pap. 29.95 (*0-8058-0013-1*) L Erlbaum Assocs.

Problems of Savannah Development: The Sudan Case. Ed. by Gunnar Haaland. (Bergen Studies in Social Anthropology: No. 19). 198p. (Orig.). 1985. pap. text 13.95 (*0-936508-57-4*, Pub. by Bergen Univ Dept Social Anthro) MBIPubg.

Problems of Scheduled Caste & Scheduled Tribes in India. A. N. Bharadwaj. 117p. 1979. 14.95 (*0-318-36817-X*) Asia Bk Corp.

Problems of Security & Cooperation in Europe. L. J. Acimovic. 344p. 1981. lib. bdg. 129.50 (*90-286-0190-2*) Kluwer Academic.

Problems of Seismology: Selected Papers. Yu V. Riznichenko. (Illus.). xvii, 445p. 1992. 247.95 (*0-387-54230-2*) Spr-Verlag.

Problems of Semantics: A Contribution to the Analysis of the Language of Science. Ladislav Tondl. 417p. 1981. lib. bdg. 171.00 (*90-277-0148-2*, D Reidel) Kluwer Academic.

Problems of Semantics: A Contribution to the Analysis of the Language Science. Ladislav Tondl. Tr. by David Short. (Boston Studies in the Philosophy of Science: No. 66). 417p. 1981. pap. text 89.00 (*90-277-0316-7*) Kluwer Academic.

Problems of Small Business Financing. 1979. 46.95 (*0-405-11502-4*) Ayer.

Problems of Small Business Financing. U. S. House of Representatives Select Committee on. Ed. by Stuart Bruchey & Vincent P. Carosso. LC 78-18995. (Small Business Enterprise in America Ser.). (Illus.). 1979. reprint ed. lib. bdg. 17.95 (*0-405-11499-0*) Ayer.

Problems of Socialist Orientation in Africa. Ed. by Mai Palmberg. (Seminar Proceedings Ser.: No. 12). 243p. 1978. write for info. (*91-7106-141-X*, Pub. by Nordic Africa) Transaction Pubs.

Problems of Sociology in Education. Roger Girod. (Educational Sciences Ser.). 140p. 1990. 52.50 (*1-85302-031-1*) Taylor & Francis.

Problems of Solar & Stellar Oscillations. D. Gough. 1983. text 278.00 (*90-277-1554-8*) Kluwer Academic.

Problems of Soviet Literature: Reports & Speeches at the First Soviet Writer's Congress by A. Zhdanov, Maxim Gorky, N. Bukharin, K. Radek, A. Stetsky, 1st, Moscow, 1934. Vsesoiuznyi S'ezd Pisatelei Staff. Ed. by H. G. Scott. LC 79-4361. (Illus.). 278p. 1980. reprint ed. lib. bdg. 65.00 (*0-313-20998-7*, VSPR) Greenwood.

Problems of Space Science Education & the Role of Teachers. S. C. Chakravarty et al. (Advances in Space Research Ser.: Vol. 20/7). 106p. 1997. pap. 100.50 (*0-08-043304-9*) Elsevier.

Problems of Spelling Reform see Fate of French-E in English: The Plural of Nouns Ending in-th

Problems of Stable Isotopes in Tree-Rings, Lake Sediments & Peat-Bogs As Climatic Evidence for the Holocene. Ed. by Burkhard Frenzel et al. (Palaoklimaforschung/Palaeoclimate Research & Man: Vol. 15 & 10). (Illus.). 200p. 1996. pap. 50.00 (*3-437-30817-3*, Wiley-VCH) Wiley.

Problems of Students in a Graduate School of Education. Dorothy C. Stratton. (Columbia University. Teachers College. Contributions to Education Ser.: No. 550). reprint ed. 37.50 (*0-404-55550-0*) AMS Pr.

Problems of Style: Foundations for a History of Ornament. Alois Riegl. Tr. by Evelyn Kain. (Illus.). 384p. 1993. text 57.50 (*0-691-04087-7*, Pub. by Princeton U Pr) Cal Prin Full Svc.

Problems of Style: Michel Foucault's Epistomology. Walter Privitera. Tr. by Jean Keller from GER. LC 94-10398. (SUNY Series in Social & Political Thought). 168p. (C). 1995. text 49.50 (*0-7914-2333-6*); pap. text 16.95 (*0-7914-2334-4*) State U NY Pr.

Problems of Succession in Cuba. Cuban Studies Conferences Staff. Ed. by Jaime Suchlicki. 105p. (Orig.). (C). 1985. pap. text 16.95 (*1-56000-661-7*) Transaction Pubs.

Problems of Suffering in the Religions of the World. John Bowker. LC 77-93706. 330p. 1975. pap. text 22.95 (*0-521-09903-X*) Cambridge U Pr.

Problems of Technological Plasticity. B. Druyanov & R. Nepershin. LC 94-6654. (Studies in Applied Mechanics: Vol. 38). 426p. 1994. 196.50 (*0-444-81646-1*) Elsevier.

Problems of the Baltic. William F. Reddaway. LC 75-41224. reprint ed. 27.50 (*0-404-14588-4*) AMS Pr.

Problems of the Carless. Robert E. Paaswell & Wilfred W. Recker. LC 77-13730. (Praeger Special Studies). 190p. 1978. 49.95 (*0-275-90308-7*, C0308, Praeger Pubs) Greenwood.

Problems of the City School Superintendent in the Field of Arithmetic. Clarence A. Rubado. LC 71-177217. (Columbia University. Teachers College. Contributions to Education Ser.: No. 406). reprint ed. 37.50 (*0-404-55406-7*) AMS Pr.

Problems of the Distribution of Audiovisual Works in the "Smaller" European Countries. 1992. 18.00 (*92-871-2168-0*, Pub. by Council of Europe) Manhattan Pub Co.

***Problems of the Essential Indexical: And Other Essays.** expanded rev. ed. John Perry. 300p. (C). 2000. pap. 22.95 (*1-57586-246-8*, Pub. by CSLI) Cambridge U Pr.

Problems of the Fuel System. Peter Novellino. LC 74-734385. 1974. student ed. 7.00 (*0-8064-0081-1*, 408) Bergwall.

***Problems of the Gastrointestinal Tract in Anaesthesia, the Perioperative Period & Intensive Care: International Symposium in Wurzburg, October 1-2, 1998.** Ed. by M. K. Herbert et al. LC 99-39685. (Illus.). 445p. 1999. 93.00 (*3-540-65901-3*) Spr-Verlag.

P

An Asterisk (*) at the beginning of an entry indicates that the title is appearing for the first time.

Problems of the Hegelian Dialectic: Dialectic Reconstructed as a Logic of Human Reality. Menahem Rosen. 282p. 1992. lib. bdg. 152.50 (*0-7923-2047-6*, Pub. by Kluwer Academic) Kluwer Academic.

Problems of the Innermost Self: A Psychological & Conceptanalytical Study Along with Some Parapsychological Reflections. Svante Bohman. 114p. (Orig.). 1988. pap. 28.50 (*91-22-01270-2*) Coronet Bks.

Problems of the Internal Combustion Engine. Peter Novellino. LC 75-733226. 1975. student ed. 7.00 (*0-8064-0083-8*, 409) Bergwall.

Problems of the Keimbahn. W. Hilscher. (Bibliotheca Anatomica Ser.: No. 24). (Illus.). viii, 128p. 1983. pap. 85.25 (*3-8055-3614-3*) S Karger.

Problems of the Logic of Scientific Knowledge. Ed. by P. V. Tavanec. (Synthese Library: No. 25). 441p. 1969. text 176.50 (*90-277-0087-7*, D Reidel) Kluwer Academic.

Problems of the Modern Middle East in Historical Perspective: Essays in Honour of Albert Hourani. Ed. by John Spagnolo. LC 97-146854. 320p. 1997. pap. 19.95 (*0-86372-214-8*, Pub. by Garnet-Ithaca) LPC InBook.

Problems of the New Mass see Problems with the New Mass: A Brief Overview of the Major Theological Difficulties Inherent in the Novus Ordo Missae

Problems of the Peace: Proceedings, Vol. 21. Institute of World Affairs Staff. Ed. by C. E. Martin & R. B. Von Kleinsmid. LC 71-167369. (Essay Index Reprint Ser.). 1977. reprint ed. 19.95 (*0-8369-2659-5*) Ayer.

Problems of the Presidency: A Text with Readings. Barbara Hinckley. LC 93-4900. 1993. pap. 36.00 (*0-8191-9084-5*) U Pr of Amer.

Problems of the Presidency: A Text with Readings. fac. ed. Barbara Hinckley. LC 84-23657. 464p. 1985. reprint ed. pap. 143.90 (*0-7837-8338-8*, 204912500010) Bks Demand.

Problems of the Regulation of Activity: Proceedings of the 4th Meeting of Psychologists from the Danubian Countries, Visegrad, Hungary. L. Kardos & C. S. Pleh. 733p. (C). 1980. 140.00 (*963-05-2447-3*, Pub. by Akade Kiado) St Mut.

Problems of the Roman Criminal Law, 2 vols., Set. James L. Strachan-Davidson. 1991. reprint ed. 75.00 (*0-8377-2623-9*, Rothman) W S Hein.

Problems of the Self: Philosophical Papers, 1956-1972. Bernard Williams. 274p. 1976. pap. text 23.95 (*0-521-29060-0*) Cambridge U Pr.

Problems of the Shakespeare Sonnets. John M. Robertson. LC 72-8700. (Studies in Shakespeare: No. 24). 1973. reprint ed. lib. bdg. 75.00 (*0-8383-1676-X*) M S G Haskell Hse.

Problems of the Soviet Economic Reforms. Sam Marcy. 1988. pap. 2.50 (*0-89567-091-7*) World View Forum.

Problems of the Spirit-Filled Life. William S. Deal. 1993. pap. 7.99 (*0-88019-298-4*) Schmul Pub Co.

Problems of the United States As World Trader & Banker. Hal B. Lary. (Economic Relations Ser.: No. 1). 191p. 1963. reprint ed. 49.70 (*0-87014-153-8*) Natl Bur Econ Res.

Problems of the 400 Turbo Hydramatic Transmission Explained. Peter Novellino. LC 80-730755. 1981. student ed. 7.00 (*0-8064-0139-7*, 437) Bergwall.

Problems of Theoretical Phonology. S. K. Saumjan. Tr. by Anthony L. Vanek. LC 68-17897. (Janua Linguarum, Ser.: No. 41). (Orig.). 1968. pap. text 60.00 (*90-279-0576-2*) Mouton.

Problems of Therapy see Pharmacology & the Future of Man: Proceedings of the International Congress on Pharmacology, 5th, San Francisco, 1972

Problems of To-Day. Moorfield Storey. LC 67-23269. (Essay Index Reprint Ser.). 1977. 20.95 (*0-8369-0908-9*) Ayer.

Problems of Today. Moorfield Storey. 1998. lib. bdg. 251.75 (*0-8490-9090-3*) Gordon Pr.

Problems of Transition: From Communism to Democracy. Ferenc Gazdag et al. Ed. by S. Victor Papacosma. (Occasional Papers). 1993. pap. 5.00 (*1-882160-01-0*) Kent St U L L Lemnitzer.

Problems of Two Truths in Buddhism & Vedanta. Ed. by G. M. Sprung. LC 73-83570. 1973. lib. bdg. 85.50 (*90-277-0335-3*) Kluwer Academic.

Problems of Typological & Genetic Linguistics Viewed in a Generative Framework. Henrik Birnbaum. LC 70-123298. (Janua Linguarum, Ser. Minor: No. 106). (Orig.). (C). 1970. pap. text 29.25 (*90-279-1541-5*) Mouton.

"Problems" of Verbal Inspiration. Alva J. McClain. 1968. pap. 0.75 (*0-88469-116-0*) BMH Bks.

Problems of Versions in Everyday Situations. E. C. Cuff. LC 93-27025. (Studies in Ethnomethodology & Conversation Analysis: No. 2). 148p. (Orig.). (C). 1993. pap. text 26.00 (*0-8191-9292-9*); lib. bdg. 48.00 (*0-8191-9149-3*) U Pr of Amer.

Problems of Vision: An Inquiry into the Causal Theory of Perception. Gerald Vision. (Illus.). 288p. 1997. text 45.00 (*0-19-510498-6*) OUP.

Problems of War & Peace in the Society of Nations. California University Committee on International R. LC 67-23188. (Essay Index Reprint Ser.). 1977. 19.95 (*0-8369-0270-X*) Ayer.

Problems of Women Workers in Unorganized Sectors: Brick Kilns, Quaries & Mines of Bihar & West Bengal. A. B. Saran & A. N. Sandhwar. 1990. 34.00 (*81-85119-68-6*, Pub. by Northern Bk Ctr) S Asia.

Problems of Women's Liberation: A Marxist Approach. Evelyn Reed. LC 78-143808. 131p. (Orig.). 1970. pap. 12.95 (*0-87348-167-4*); reprint ed. lib. bdg. 30.00 (*0-87348-166-6*) Pathfinder NY.

Problems of Work. L. Ron Hubbard. 160p. 1989. pap. 22.00 (*0-88404-377-0*) Bridge Pubns Inc.

Problems on Algorithms. Ian Parberry. LC 94-48519. 192p. (C). 1995. pap. 18.40 (*0-13-433558-9*) P-H.

Problems on High Energy Physics & Field Theory: Dedicated to the 140th Birth Anniversary of Henri Poincare; Proceedings of the 17th Workshop on Problems on High Energy Physics & Field Theory, Protvino, 1994. Ed. by A. P. Samokhin & G. L. Rcheulishvili. 289p. (Orig.). (C). 1995. pap. 30.00 (*1-57485-004-0*) Hadronic Pr Inc.

***Problems on Statistical Mechanics.** D. A. R. Dalvit. LC 99-16504. 296p. 1999. 110.00 (*0-7503-0520-7*); pap. text 39.00 (*0-7503-0521-5*) IOP Pub.

Problems on the Equations of Mathematical Physics. M. M. Smirnov. 102p. 1967. text 156.00 (*0-677-61310-5*) Gordon & Breach.

Problems Plus. Alan Handel & Francis Gardella. 1997. pap., student ed. 7.99 (*0-8114-9590-6*) Raintree Steck-V.

Problems Plus, Level C. Alan Handel & Francis Gardella. 1997. pap., student ed. 7.99 (*1-55743-503-0*) Raintree Steck-V.

Problems Plus, Level D. Alan Handel & Francis Gardella. 1997. pap., student ed. 7.99 (*1-55743-506-5*) Raintree Steck-V.

Problems Plus, Level B. Alan Handel & Francis Gardella. 1997. pap., student ed. 7.99 (*1-55743-500-6*) Raintree Steck-V.

Problems Plus, Level E. Alan Handel & Francis Gardella. 1997. pap., student ed. 7.99 (*1-55743-509-X*) Raintree Steck-V.

Problems Plus, Level G. Alan Handel & Francis Gardella. 1997. pap., student ed. 7.99 (*1-55743-515-4*) Raintree Steck-V.

Problems Plus Solutions in Financial Accounting. Brenda M. Mallouk. Ed. by Kelly Smythe. 124p. (C). 1991. pap. text. write for info. (*0-07-551340-4*) McG-H Ryerson.

Problems! Problems! Confessions of an Agony Aunt. Virginia Ironside. 1995. pap. 10.95 (*0-86051-839-6*, Robson-Parkwest) Parkwest Pubns.

Problems, Problems & More Problems in Accounting. Brenda M. Mallouk. Ed. by Kelly Smythe. (C). 1991. reprint ed. pap. text. write for info. (*0-07-551331-5*) McG-H Ryerson.

Problems, Problems, Problems: Grade 7-9. (Cross Training Ser.). 80p. 1997. teacher ed., ring bd. 34.95 incl. VHS (*1-57405-252-7*) CharismaLife Pub.

Problems, Programs, Processing, Results: Software Techniques for Sci-Tech Programs. Pal Quittner. LC 78-310575. 381p. 1977. write for info. (*963-05-0949-0*, Pub. by Akade Kiado) Intl Spec Bk.

Problems Related to Alcohol Consumption. (Technical Report Ser.: No. 650). 72p. 1980. pap. text 5.00 (*92-4-120650-0*) World Health.

Problems Relating to the Bill of Rights & General Welfare. 684p. 1993. reprint ed. lib. bdg. 109.00 (*0-7812-5251-2*) Rprt Serv.

Problems Solving Strategies: Grades 2-3. Karla Dencker-Koenig. Ed. by Mary L. Mufoletto. (Illus.). 64p. (Orig.). 1996. pap., teacher ed. 6.95 (*1-889369-00-4*, TI0003) Teaching Ink.

Problems Supplement for Technical Mathematics. Thomas Stark & Lawrence Pucke. 1984. pap. text 16.95 (*0-8053-9537-7*) Addison-Wesley.

***Problems Surrounding the Mortgage Origination Process: Congressional Hearing.** Ed. by Lauch Faircloth & Connie Mack. 210p. (C). 2000. reprint ed. pap. text 35.00 (*0-7881-8689-2*) DIANE Pub.

***Problems Surrounding the Mortgage Origination Process: Joint Hearings Before the Subcommittee on Financial Institutions & Regulatory Relief & the Subcommittee on Housing Opportunity & Community Development of the Committee on Banking, Housing & Urban Affairs, United States Senate, 105th Congress, 1st Session, on Examination of the Real Estate Settlement Procedures Act (RESPA) & the Truth in Lending Act (TILA) ... July 9 & 15, 1997.** USGPO Staff. LC 99-170992. (S. Hrg. Ser.). 1998. write for info. (*0-16-057526-5*) USGPO.

Problems, Tasks & Outcomes. E. Matilda Goldberg et al. 1985. 110.00 (*0-7855-0845-7*, Pub. by Natl Inst Soc Work) St Mut.

Problems Unique to the Holocaust. Ed. by Harry J. Cargas. LC 98-41612. 194p. 1999. 22.50 (*0-8131-2101-9*) U Pr of Ky.

Problems Which Perplex (Mainly Psychic) Explained by Question & Answer (1890) G. Vale Owen. 156p. 1998. reprint ed. pap. 17.95 (*0-7661-0641-1*) Kessinger Pub.

Problems with Patients: Managing Complicated Transactions. Kingsley Norton & Samuel P. Smith. (Illus.). 192p. (C). 1994. text 69.95 (*0-521-43043-7*); pap. text 27.95 (*0-521-43628-1*) Cambridge U Pr.

Problems with Protease Inhibitor Development Plans. David Barr et al. 21p. (Orig.). (C). 1995. pap. text 15.00 (*0-7881-2364-5*) DIANE Pub.

Problems with Solutions see HMO Model & Its Application

Problems with the New Mass: A Brief Overview of the Major Theological Difficulties Inherent in the Novus Ordo Missae. rev. ed. Rama P. Coomaraswamy. LC 90-71558. Orig. Title: The Problems of the New Mass. 86p. 1993. reprint ed. pap. 7.00 (*0-89555-412-7*) TAN Bks Pubs.

***Problems with the New Sacraments.** Rama P. Coomaraswamy. LC 98-61408. 224p. 1999. pap. 12.00 (*0-89555-637-5*, 1585) TAN Bks Pubs.

Problems with the Prayers of the Modern Mass. Anthony Cekada. 44p. (Orig.). 1993. pap. 4.00 (*0-89555-447-X*) TAN Bks Pubs.

Problems Workbook, Engineering Drawing & Design. 2nd ed. David A. Madsen. (Mechanical Technology Ser.). 976p. (C). 1996. text, student ed. 19.95 (*0-8273-7525-5*) Delmar.

Problems Workbook for Organic Chemistry. Paris Svoronos & Edward Sarlo. 304p. (C). 1992. spiral bd. write for info. (*0-697-14551-4*, WCB McGr Hill) McGrw-H Hghr Educ.

Probo's Amazing Trunk. David R. Collins. (Illus.). (J). (ps-2). 1987. pap. 5.10 (*0-8136-5684-2*); lib. bdg. 7.95 (*0-8136-5184-0*) Modern Curr.

Proboscidea: Evolution & Palaeoecology of Elephants & Their Relatives. Ed. by Jeheskel Shoshani & Pascal Tassy. LC 93-23726. (Illus.). 502p. 1996. text 180.00 (*0-19-854652-1*) OUP.

Proboscidean & Paleoindian Interactions. Ed. by John W. Fox et al. LC 92-11168. (Illus.). 248p. (Orig.). 1992. pap. text 28.50 (*0-918954-55-X*) Baylor Univ Pr.

Proc-StatXact for SAS Users. Cyrus R. Mehta & Nitin R. Patel. (Illus.). 509p. 1997. pap. 95.00 (*1-889592-00-5*) Cytel Software.

Procane Chronicle. Ross Thomas. 192p. 1993. mass mkt. 4.99 (*0-446-40177-3*, Pub. by Warner Bks) Little.

***Proccedings of the Symposium on Management of Western Bark Beetles with Pheromones: Research & Development (June 22-25,1992 - Kailua-Kona, Hawaii)** Ed. by Patrick J. Shea. (Illus.). 52p. (C). 2000. reprint ed. pap. text 20.00 (*0-7881-8943-3*) DIANE Pub.

***Proceedings of 1998 International Symposium on Electrical Insulating Materials: 1998 Asian International Conference on Dielectrics & Electrical Insulation: 30th Symposium on Electrical Insulating Materials: September 27-30, 1998, Holiday Inn Crowne Plaza Toyohashi, Toyohashi, Japan** International Symposium on Electrical Insulating Materials Staff et al. LC 99-171534. 837 p. 1998. pap. write for info. (*0-7803-3967-3*) IEEE Standards.

Procedes d'Art en Photographie. Robert Demacy & C. Puyo Demachy. Ed. by Robert A. Sobieszek & Peter C. Bunnell. LC 76-24673. (Sources of Modern Photography Ser.). (FRE., Illus.). 1979. reprint ed. lib. bdg. 19.95 (*0-405-09649-6*) Ayer.

Procedimentos DIU para Programas de Servicos de Planejamento Familiar: Un Manual de Referencia para la Solucion de Problemas. 2nd ed. Ed. by Noel McIntosh et al. (POR., Illus.). Date not set. pap. text 15.00 (*0-929817-37-0*) JHPIEGO.

Procedimientos de Asesoria Rapida Para Programas de Nutricion y Atencion Primaria de Salud. Susan C. Scrimshaw & Elena Hurtado. (Reference Ser.). 100p. 1989. pap. 10.95 (*0-87903-113-1*) UCLA Lat Am Ctr.

Procedings of the 1997 Total Life Cycle Conference, Pt. I, Life Cycle Management & Assessment see Proceedings of the 1997 Total Life Cycle Conference

Procedings of the 1997 Total Life Cycle Conference, Pt. II, Design for the Environment, Recycling & Environmental Act see Proceedings of the 1997 Total Life Cycle Conference

***Procedural Coding Crosswalk, 2000.** Medicode, Med-Index Division Staff. (C). 1999. 80.00 (*1-56337-309-2*) Thomson Learn.

Procedural Due Process Rights in Student Discipline. Paul Weckstein. 193p. 1990. pap. 20.00 (*0-912585-05-6*) Ctr Law & Ed.

Procedural Elements for Computer Graphics. David F. Rogers. (C). 1985. text 54.50 (*0-07-053534-5*) McGraw.

Procedural Elements for Computer Graphics. 2nd ed. David F. Rogers. LC 97-13301. 752p. 1999. 64.06 (*0-07-053548-5*) McGraw.

Procedural History of the 1940 Census of Population & Housing. Robert M. Jenkins. LC 85-40368. 160p. 1985. reprint ed. pap. 49.60 (*0-608-01958-5*, 206261300003) Bks Demand.

Procedural Justice. Michael D. Bayles. 276p. (C). 1990. lib. bdg. 148.50 (*0-7923-0567-1*, Pub. by Kluwer Academic) Kluwer Academic.

Procedural Justice. Ed. by Klaus F. Rohl & Stefan Machura. LC 97-469. (Onati International Series in Law & Society). (Illus.). 256p. 1997. pap. 32.95 (*1-85521-921-2*, Pub. by Ashgate Pub) Ashgate Pub Co.

Procedural Justice. Ed. by Klaus F. Rohl & Stefan Machura. LC 97-469. (Onati International Series in Law & Society). (Illus.). 256p. 1997. 82.95 (*1-85521-919-0*, Pub. by Dartmth Pub) Ashgate Pub Co.

Procedural Manual for Classroom Teachers: A Practical Guide for Improving Job Performance. Samuel McGee. 87p. 1992. pap. text 19.95 (*0-9700155-1-8*) Quantum Mktg.

Procedural Manual for Quality Nursing Intervention in the School. Janis Hootman. 1993. 40.00 (*1-880118-11-4*) MESD Pr.

Procedural Manual of the Codex Alimentarius Commission: Joint FAO/WHO Food Standards Programme. 7th ed. 188p. 1990. 17.00 (*92-5-102893-1*, F8931, Pub. by FAO) Bernan Associates.

Procedural Manual of the Codex Alimentarius Commission: Joint FAO/WHO Food Standards Programme. 8th ed. 203p. 1993. 19.00 (*92-5-103386-2*, Pub. by FAO) Bernan Associates.

***Procedural Natural Law.** Rodney J. Blackman. LC 99-48920. 206p. 1999. pap. text 20.00 (*0-89089-688-7*) Carolina Acad Pr.

Procedural Review: Financial. Porter. (C). 1995. pap. text 28.50 (*0-15-502836-7*) Harcourt Coll Pubs.

Procedural Skills: Instructor's Manual. Wigton. (Illus.). 148p. (C). (gr. 13). 1996. teacher ed., spiral bd. 22.95 (*0-8151-9278-9*, 25693) Mosby Inc.

Procedural Structure: Success & Influence in Congress. Terry Sullivan. LC 84-6793. 224p. 1984. 57.95 (*0-275-91279-5*, C1279, Praeger Pubs) Greenwood.

Procedural System. Kenneth C. Gass. LC 95-92732. (Illus.). 69p. (C). 1995. lib. bdg. 42.00 (*0-9634906-2-1*) Special Qual.

Procedure see Tennessee Code Annotated 1999 Supplement

Procedure. Owen M. Fiss & Judith Resnik. (University Casebook Ser.). 1877p. 1988. text 48.95 (*0-88277-626-6*) Foundation Pr.

Procedure. Ed. by Dennis Galligan. (C). 1992. lib. bdg. 150.00 (*0-8147-3048-5*) NYU Pr.

Procedure & Enforcement Mechanisms see International Criminal Law

Procedure & Evidence in the Juvenile Court: A Guidebook for Judges. (Yankee Books Travel Guide). 84p. 1962. 4.00 (*0-318-15371-8*) Natl Coun Crime.

Procedure & Metaphysics: A Study in the Philosophy of Mathematical-Physical Science in the 16-17 Century. Edward W. Strong. 301p. 1977. reprint ed. lib. bdg. 19.50 (*0-915172-28-3*) Richwood Pub.

Procedure at International Conferences: A Study of the Rules of Procedure of International Inter-Governmental Conferences. Robbie Sabel. 467p. 1997. text 110.00 (*0-521-55440-3*) Cambridge U Pr.

Procedure Before the IRS. 6th ed. James W. Quiggle & Lipman Redman. LC 84-72251. (Illus.). 269p. 1987. suppl. ed. 96.00 (*0-8318-0449-1*, B449/B533) Am Law Inst.

Procedure Before the IRS - Pocket Supplement. James W. Quiggle & Lipman Redman. 15p. 1987. pap. text 11.00 (*0-8318-0533-1*, B533) Am Law Inst.

Procedure Checklist to Accompany Caroline Bunker Rosdahl's Textbook of Basic Nursing, 7th Ed. Vicki V. Earnest & Caroline B. Rosdahl. LC 98-32440. 1999. write for info. (*0-7817-1856-2*, Lippnctt) Lppncott W & W.

Procedure Checklists for Fund Raisers. 6th ed. Barbara Kozier. (C). 2000. pap. text 17.81 (*0-8053-8346-8*) Benjamin-Cummings.

Procedure Coding for Cardiologists: The American College of Cardiology Guide to CPT-4. American College of Cardiology Staff. 100p. 1992. pap. text 55.00 (*1-882764-00-5*) Am Coll Cardiology.

***Procedure Documentation for Advanced Imaging: Mammography & Quality Management.** Erica Williams. (Illus.). 168p. 1999. 34.95 (*0-07-135398-4*) McGraw.

Procedure for Commissioning Variable Air Volume Systems. R. Clark. (C). 1988. 100.00 (*0-86022-222-5*, Pub. by Build Servs Info Assn) St Mut.

Procedure for Determining Packed Cell Volume by the Microhematocrit Method. 2nd ed. (Approved Standard Ser.: Vol. 5). 1993. 75.00 (*1-56238-038-9*, H7-A2) NCCLS.

Procedure for Setting Aside T'rumot & Ma'asrot. Shaul Reichenberg. 1991. pap. 4.95 (*1-58330-141-0*) Feldheim.

Procedure for the Determination of Fibrinogen in Plasma: Approved Guidelines (1994) Contrib. by H. James Day. 1994. 75.00 (*1-56238-221-7*, H30-A) NCCLS.

Procedure for the Estimation of Markov Transition Probabilities. Allen J. Scott. (Discussion Papers: No. 8). 1965. pap. 10.00 (*1-55869-099-9*) Regional Sci Res Inst.

Procedure Handbook: Surface Preparation & Painting of Tanks & Closed Areas. James A. Giese. (Illus.). 150p. 1981. pap. text 30.00 (*0-938477-20-X*) SSPC.

Procedure in Courts & Tribunals. John Bowers & Ian Gatt. (Practice Notes Ser.). 105p. 1990. pap. write for info. (*0-85121-526-2*, Pub. by Cavendish Pubng) Gaunt.

Procedure in the Canadian House of Commons. William F. Dawson. LC 63-3048. (Canadian Government Ser.: No. 12). 284p. reprint ed. pap. 88.10 (*0-8357-4153-2*, 203692700007) Bks Demand.

Procedure Manual for the Diagnosis of Intestinal Parasites. Donald L. Price. LC 93-7450. 288p. 1994. boxed set 78.95 (*0-8493-8654-3*, RC862) CRC Pr.

Procedure of the House of Commons, 3 vols. Joseph Redlich. Tr. by A. Ernest Steinthal. LC 77-77895. reprint ed. 165.00 (*0-404-05280-0*) AMS Pr.

Procedure of the U. N. Security Council. 3rd ed. Sydney Bailey & Sam Daws. LC KZ5038.B34 1998. (Illus.). 710p. 1998. text 165.00 (*0-19-828073-4*) OUP.

Procedure Remedies & Special Proceedings see Tennessee Code Annotated 1999 Supplement

Procedure Supplement for Fund Raisers. 6th ed. Barbara Kozier. (C). 2000. pap. text 25.31 (*0-8053-8345-X*) Benjamin-Cummings.

Procedure That Accounts for Manufacturing Errors in the Design Minimization of Transmission Error in Helical Gears. Sivakumar Sundaresan & Kosuke Ishii. (Nineteen Ninety Fall Technical Meeting Ser.: Vol. 90FTM9). (Illus.). 12p. 1990. pap. text 30.00 (*1-55589-561-1*) AGMA.

Procedure Writing: Principles & Practices. 2nd ed. Douglas Wieringa et al. LC 98-7875. 243p. 1998. 34.95 (*1-57477-052-7*) Battelle.

Procedure Writing: Principles & Practices, 2nd Ed. 2nd ed. Douglas Wieringa. 1999. pap. text 34.95 (*0-7803-5368-4*, IEEE Inst Elec) IEEE Comp Soc.

Procedures, Vol. 3. 1995. write for info. (*1-880678-89-6*) HCIA.

Procedures, Vol. 3. 1996. write for info. (*1-57372-026-7*) HCIA.

***Procedures & Documentation for Advanced Imaging.** Erica Williams. LC 99-59187. (Hazelden Chronic Illness Ser.). (Illus.). 172p. 2000. pap. text 34.95 (*0-07-135399-2*) McGraw-Hill Prof.

Procedures & Guidelines for Disaster Preparedness Planning. W. Nick Carter. viii, 195p. 1985. pap. 12.25 (*0-86638-063-9*) EW Ctr HI.

Procedures & Metaphysics: A Study in the Philosophy of Mathematic-Physical Science in the Sixteenth & Seventeenth Centuries. Edward W. Strong. vii, 301p. 1966. reprint ed. 50.70 (*0-685-66521-6*, 05101348) G Olms Pubs.

Procedures & Recommendations for the Ultrasonic Testing of Butt Welds. 2nd ed. (Illus.). 48p. 1971. pap. 49.95 (*0-85300-056-5*, 327, Pub. by Woodhead Pubng) Am Educ Systs.

P

Procedures & Systems for the Office Professional. Jolene Scriven. 1991. 35.00 (*0-02-650863-X*) Macmillan.

Procedures & Techniques in Intensive Care Medicine. Ed. by James M. Rippe & Frederick J. Curley. LC 94-29395. 336p. 1994. pap. text 65.00 (*0-316-74721-1*) Lppncott W & W.

***Procedures & Techniques in Intensive Care Medicine.** 2nd ed. Richard S. Irwin et al. LC 99-20295. 352p. 1999. pap. text 55.00 (*0-7817-2047-8*) Lppncott W & W.

Procedures for a Muslim Burial. Abdullah M. Khouj. 25p. 1992. pap. 2.00 (*1-930801-07-6*) Islamc Ctr WA.

Procedures for Administrative Support in the Automated Office. 3rd ed. Rita C. Kutie & Joan L. Rhodes. 480p. (C). 1990. pap. text 47.20 (*0-13-716457-2*) P-H.

Procedures for Conducting Probabilistic Safety Assessments of Nuclear Power Plant. International Atomic Energy Agency Staff. (Safety Ser.: Vol. 50-P-12). 68p. 1996. pap. 35.00 (*92-0-103996-4*, STI/PUB/1009, Pub. by IAEA) Bernan Associates.

Procedures for Conducting Probabilistic Safety Assessments of Nuclear Power Plants. I.A.E.A. Staff. (Safety Ser.: 50-P-8). 132p. 1995. pap. 55.00 (*92-0-102195-X*, STI/PUB/969, Pub. by IAEA) Bernan Associates.

Procedures for Consignees: An Aid to Help Reduce Freight Claim Controversy. 1995. pap. text 8.50 (*0-88711-290-0*) Am Trucking Assns.

Procedures for Investigating Intentional & Unintentional Food Additives: Report of a WHO Scientific Group, 1967. (Technical Report Ser.: No. 348). 25p. 1967. pap. text 3.00 (*92-4-120348-X*, 1100348) World Health.

Procedures for Military Executions. 1953. reprint ed. 10.00 (*1-877704-02-4*) Pioneer Pr.

Procedures for School District Reorganization. Harold D. Alford. LC 75-176509. (Columbia University. Teachers College. Contributions to Education Ser.: No. 852). reprint ed. 37.50 (*0-404-55852-6*) AMS Pr.

Procedures for Structuring & Scheduling Sports Tournaments: Elimination, Consolation, Placement, & Round Robin Design. 2nd ed. Francis M. Rokosz. (Illus.). 300p. (C). 1993. pap., spiral bd. 54.95 (*0-398-05829-6*) C C Thomas.

***Procedures for Structuring & Scheduling Sports Tournaments: Elimination, Consolation, Placement & Round-Robin Design.** 3rd ed. Francis M. Rokosz. LC 99-56507. (Illus.). 2000. spiral bd. write for info. (*0-398-07050-4*) C C Thomas.

Procedures for the Automated Office. 4th ed. Sharon Burton et al. LC 97-8716. 401p. 1997. pap. text 56.00 (*0-13-261025-6*) P-H.

***Procedures for the Automated Office.** 5th ed. Sharon Burton et al. 416p. 2000. pap. 46.67 (*0-13-025431-2*, Prentice Hall) P-H.

Procedures for the Collection of Diagnostic Blood Specimens by Skin Puncture. 3rd ed. (Approved Standard Ser.: Vol. 6). 1991. 95.00 (*1-56238-111-3*, H4-A3) NCCLS.

Procedures for the Collection of Diagnostic Blood Specimens by Venipuncture: Approved Standard. 3rd ed. (Approved Standard Ser.: Vol. 6). 1991. 95.00 (*1-56238-108-3*, H3-A3) NCCLS.

Procedures for the Electron-Beam Moire Technique. E.S. Drexler. 137p. 1998. per. 11.00 (*0-16-056694-0*) USGPO.

Procedures for the Handling & Processing of Blood Specimens: Approved Guideline, Vol. 4. National Committee for Clinical Laboratory Standar. 1990. 85.00 (*1-56238-110-5*, H18-A) NCCLS.

Procedures for the Handling & Transport of Diagnostic Specimens & Etiologic Agents: Approved Standard (1994) 3rd ed. Contrib. by Joan D. Wiseman. 1994. 75.00 (*1-56238-232-2*, H5-A3) NCCLS.

Procedures for the Modern Office see Systems & Procedures for the Modern Office: A Simulation Approach

Procedures for the Modern Office: An Applications Approach. Judith C. Simon & Lilliana H. Chaney. 1988. pap. text 28.95 (*0-471-62438-1*) P-H.

Procedures for the Modern Office, Tests. 7th ed. William R. Pasewark. (KM - Office Procedures Ser.). 1983. 2.95 (*0-538-11393-6*) S-W Pub.

Procedures for the Office Professional. 2nd ed. Patsy J. Fulton. (C). 1989. mass mkt. 13.75 (*0-538-70018-1*, KE40BA) S-W Pub.

Procedures for the Office Professional. 2nd ed. Fulton et al. (KU - Office Procedures Ser.). (C). 1989. mass mkt. 35.75 (*0-538-70017-3*) S-W Pub.

Procedures for the Office Professional. 3rd ed. Fulton. (KU - Office Procedures Ser.). (C). 1995. pap. 54.95 (*0-538-71018-7*) S-W Pub.

Procedures for the Office Professional. 4th ed. Calkins. (C). 1999. pap., wbk. ed. 16.00 (*0-538-72213-4*) Thomson Learn.

***Procedures for the Office Professional** 4th ed. Patsy Fulton-Calkins & Joanna D. Hanks. LC 99-30187. 1999. write for info. (*0-538-72211-8*) S-W Pub.

Procedures for the Primary Care Practitioner. Ed. by Marilyn W. Edmunds & Maren S. Mayhew. LC 95-40072. (Illus.). 320p. (C). (gr. 13). 1996. spiral bd. 38.95 (*0-8151-3034-1*, 27060) Mosby Inc.

Procedures for the Professional Secretary. Patsy J. Fulton & Joanna D. Hanks. 608p. (C). 1984. text. write for info. (*0-538-11950-0*, K95) S-W Pub.

Procedures for the Recovery & Identification of Parasites from the Intestinal Tract: Approved Guideline (1997) 1997. 85.00 (*1-56238-342-6*, M28-A) NCCLS.

Procedures for the Recovery & Identification of Parasites from the Intestinal Tract: Proposed Guideline (1993) Contrib. by Lynne S. Garcia. 1993. 85.00 (*1-56238-212-8*, M28-P) NCCLS.

Procedures in Applied Optics. John Strong. (Optical Engineering Ser.: Vol. 17). (Illus.). 416p. 1988. text 160.00 (*0-8247-7987-8*) Dekker.

Procedures in Diagnostic Radiology. Terence Doyle et al. (Illus.). 248p. 1989. pap. text 35.00 (*0-443-02982-2*) Church.

Procedures in Electron Microscopy. Ed. by A. J. Wilson & Anthony W. Robards. LC 99-206286. 700p. 1999. 1475.00 (*0-471-92853-4*) Wiley.

Procedures in Experimental Physics, 2 vols., Set. 1996. lib. bdg. 629.95 (*0-8490-7590-4*) Gordon Pr.

***Procedures in Field Geology.** Tom Freeman. (Illus.). 1999. spiral bd. 14.95 (*0-86542-008-4*) Blackwell Sci.

Procedures in Hepatogastroenterology. 2nd ed. G. N. Tytgat & C. J. Mulder. LC 97-2359. (Developments in Gastroenterology Ser.). 1997. text 257.50 (*0-7923-4352-2*) Kluwer Academic.

Procedures in Infants & Children. Michele Walsh-Sukys & Steven E. Krug. Ed. by Lisette Bralow. LC 96-48725. 384p. 1997. text 69.00 (*0-7216-3789-2*, W B Saunders Co) Harcrt Hlth Sci Grp.

Procedures in Marriage & Family Therapy. Gregory Brock & Charles P. Barnard. 252p. 1988. text 43.00 (*0-205-11310-9*, H13105) Allyn.

Procedures in Marriage & Family Therapy. 3rd ed. Gregory W. Brock & Charles P. Barnard. LC 98-13583. 228p. 1998. pap. text 53.00 (*0-205-28782-4*) Allyn.

Procedures in Phlebotomy. Ed. by John C. Flynn, Jr. (Illus.). 256p. 1993. pap. text 25.00 (*0-7216-4685-9*, W B Saunders Co) Harcrt Hlth Sci Grp.

Procedures in Phlebotomy. 2nd ed. John C. Flynn, Jr. Ed. by Adrianne Williams. LC 98-43926. 255p. 1998. pap. text 23.00 (*0-7216-7583-2*, W B Saunders Co) Harcrt Hlth Sci Grp.

Procedures in Plastic & Reconconstructive Surgery: How They Do It. Vistnes. 1991. 325.00 (*0-316-90437-6*, Little Brwn Med Div) Lppncott W & W.

Procedures in Practice. 3rd ed. Ed. by Nigel A. Scott. (Illus.). 296p. 1994. pap. text 26.00 (*0-7279-0823-5*, Pub. by BMJ Pub) Login Brothers Bk Co.

Procedures in Scanning Probe Microscopies, 1 vol. Colton. 672p. 1998. 550.00 (*0-471-95912-X*) Wiley.

Procedures in the Justice System. 5th ed. Gilbert B. Stucky et al. LC 97-16970. 434p. (C). 1997. 83.00 (*0-13-633520-9*) P-H.

***Procedures in the Justice System.** 6th ed. Gilbert B. Stuckey et al. LC 00-39204. 448p. 2000. 64.00 (*0-13-016584-0*, Brady Emerg Care) P-H.

Procedures in Vascular Surgery. 2nd ed. Chilton Crane & Richard Warren. LC 75-22597. 1976. 47.00 (*0-316-16014-8*, Little Brwn Med Div) Lppncott W & W.

Procedures in Women's Health. Roger P. Smith & Frank W. Ling. LC 96-39955. 452p. 1997. 69.00 (*0-683-18219-6*) Lppncott W & W.

Procedures Manual for Polymer Selection in Water Treatment Plants. 232p. 1989. pap. 35.00 (*0-89867-481-6*, 90553) Am Water Wks Assn.

Procedures Manual to Accompany Fundamentals of Nursing, Fifth edition. 5th ed. Barbara Kozier et al. LC 94-33383. (C). 1995. pap. text 27.19 (*0-8053-3503-X*) Benjamin-Cummings.

Procedures of Empirical Science. Victor F. Lenzen. LC 71-131570. (Foundations of the Unity of Science Ser.: Vol. 1, No. 5). 1993. pap. text 1.95 (*0-226-57580-2*, P404) U Ch Pr.

Procedures of Industrial Water Treatment. J. N. Tanis. 400p. 1987. 48.00 (*0-942105-44-3*) Ltan Inc.

Procedures of Power & Curriculum Change: Focault & the Quest for Possibilities in Science Education. David Blades. (Counterpoints: Studies in the Postmodern Theory of Education: Vol. 35). XIII, 290p. (C). 1997. pap. text 29.95 (*0-8204-3325-X*) P Lang Pubng.

Procedures Resource Book. Center for Healthcare Industry Performance Studies. 235p. 1995. pap. 295.00 (*1-882733-03-7*) Ctr Hlthcare IPS.

Procedures Resource Book. Susan E. White. (Illus.). 295p. 1995. pap. 350.00 (*1-882733-05-3*) Ctr Hlthcare IPS.

Procedures Supplement for Fundamentals of Nursing. Barbara Kozier & Glenora L. Erb. (C). 1984. pap. text. write for info. (*0-318-59746-2*, Health Sci) Addison-Wesley.

Procedures to Enforce Foreign. Kaye. 87.95 (*0-7546-2010-7*) Ashgate Pub Co.

Procedures to Investigate Arthropod-Borne & Rodent-Borne Illness. 93p. 1983. 12.00 (*0-318-17809-5*) IAFP.

Procedures to Investigate Foodborne Illness. 5th ed. 96p. 1999. 16.00 (*0-317-02822-7*) IAFP.

Procedures to Investigate Waterborne Illness. 2nd ed. 125p. 1996. 16.00 (*0-317-02823-5*) IAFP.

Procedures Update. Ed. by Patricia Schull. LC 96-31994. (Illus.). 768p. (Orig.). 1996. 100.00 (*0-87434-869-2*) Springhouse Corp.

Proceed with Care: Final Report of the Royal Commission on New Reproductive Technologies. Royal Commission on New Reproductive Technologies. 26p. (Orig.). 1993. pap. 16.85 (*0-660-58996-6*, Pub. by Canadian Govt Pub) Accents Pubns.

Proceed with Care: Final Report of the Royal Commission on New Reproductive Technologies. Royal Commission on New Reproductive Technologies. (Illus.). 1275p. (Orig.). 1993. pap. 67.60 (*0-660-15359-9*, Pub. by Canadian Govt Pub) Accents Pubns.

Proceed with Caution. William R. Keates. LC 97-125852. 224p. 1996. pap. text 17.95 (*0-15-900181-1*) Harcourt Legal.

Proceed with Caution. Pat Leonard. LC 92-93411. 254p. 1992. pap. 19.95 (*0-9632933-1-1*); lib. bdg. 10.00 (*0-9632933-0-3*) Leonard Pubns.

Proceed with Caution: Predicting Genetic Risks in the Recombinant DNA Era. Neil A. Holtzman. LC 88-29658. (Contemporary Medicine & Public Health Ser.). 320p. 1989. text 45.00 (*0-8018-3730-8*) Johns Hopkins.

Proceed with Caution, When Engaged by Minority Writing in the Americas. Doris Sommer. LC 98-50383. 1998. 55.00 (*0-674-53658-4*) HUP.

Proceed with Caution, When Engaged by Minority Writing in the Americas. Doris Sommer. LC 98-50383. 416p. 1999. pap. 24.95 (*0-674-53660-6*) HUP.

Proceedaings [SIC] of the Fifteenth National Radio Science Conference, NRSC '98, Cairo, Egypt, February 24-26, 1998. National Radio Science Conference Staff et al. LC 98-226158. 1998. pap. write for info. (*0-7803-4310-7*) Inst Electrical.

Proceeding from the Section on Alcohol, Drugs & Traffic Safety: 35th International Congress on Alcohol & Drug Dependence, Oslo, Norway, July 31-August 6, 1988, 2 vols., I. Ed. by Kathryn G. Stewart & Barry M. Sweedler. 425p. (Orig.). 1988. write for info. (*0-9621467-1-4*) ICADTS.

Proceeding from the Section on Alcohol, Drugs & Traffic Safety: 35th International Congress on Alcohol & Drug Dependence, Oslo, Norway, July 31-August 6, 1988, 2 vols., II. Ed. by Kathryn G. Stewart & Barry M. Sweedler. 425p. (Orig.). 1988. write for info. (*0-9621467-2-2*) ICADTS.

Proceeding from the Section on Alcohol, Drugs & Traffic Safety: 35th International Congress on Alcohol & Drug Dependence, Oslo, Norway, July 31-August 6, 1988, 2 vols., Set. Ed. by Kathryn G. Stewart & Barry M. Sweedler. 425p. (Orig.). 1988. pap. write for info. (*0-9621467-0-6*) ICADTS.

Proceeding of New York University, 49th Annual Conference on Labor, Vol. NYUP 49. Ed. by Samuel Estreicher. 1997. 215.00 (*90-411-1000-3*) Kluwer Law Intl.

Proceeding of the Fifth International Conference on High Performance Computing: December 17-20, 1998, Chennai (madras) India. International Conference on High Performance Computing Staff et al. LC 99-162567. xx, 482p. 1998. write for info. (*0-8186-9197-2*) IEEE Comp Soc.

Proceeding of the Sixth International Conference on X-Ray Optics & Microanalysis. International Conference on X-Ray Optics & Microan. Ed. by G. Shinoda et al. LC 73-167762. 926p. 1972. reprint ed. pap. 200.00 (*0-608-01552-0*, 206196100001) Bks Demand.

Proceeding of the St. Petersburg Mathematical Society, Vol. III. Ed. by O. A. Ladyzhenskaya. (Translations Ser.: Series 2, Vol. 166). 267p. 1995. text 92.00 (*0-8218-0387-5*, TRANS2/166) Am Math.

***Proceedings of the 3rd European Workshop on Periodontology: Implant Dentistry.** Ed. by Niklaus P. Lang et al. (Illus.). 613p. 1999. 68.00 (*3-87652-306-0*, Pub. by Quintessenz Verlags) Quint Pub Co.

Proceeding of the 3rd Workshop on Hadronic Mechanics: Held at the University of Patras (Greece), August 25-30, 1986, 2 vols. 90.00 (*0-911767-47-9*) Hadronic Pr Inc.

Proceeding of 3rd World Conference on Structure. Fabio Casciati. text. write for info. (*0-471-48980-8*) Wiley.

Proceeding Together: The Earliest Talks of the Lubavitcher Rebbe Rabbi Menachem M. Schneerson, No. 1. Tr. by Uri Kaploun. LC 95-237470. 208p. 1995. 17.00 (*1-881400-15-8*) S I E.

Proceeding Together: The Earliest Talks of the Lubavitcher Rebbe Rabbi Menachem M. Schneerson, No. 2. Tr. by Uri Kaploun. LC 95-237470. 224p. 1996. 17.00 (*1-881400-16-6*) S I E.

Proceeding Without Anecdotal Details of Imagery. Pat Merchant. (Orig.). 1992. pap. 16.00 (*0-913412-62-7*) Brandon Hse.

Proceedings. (Second Ser.: No. 41). 105p. (C). 1991. pap. 15.00 (*0-915974-36-3*) Am Acad Arts.

Proceedings. (Second Ser.: No. 42). 116p. 1992. pap. 15.00 (*0-915974-37-1*) Am Acad Arts.

Proceedings. (Second Ser.: No. 43). (Illus.). 106p. 1993. pap. 15.00 (*0-915974-38-X*) Am Acad Arts.

Proceedings. 84p. 15.00 (*0-318-12676-1*, M70775); pap. 10.00 (*0-318-12677-X*, M70774); pap. 10.00 (*0-318-12678-8*, M11173) Am Gas Assn.

Proceedings. (Second Ser.: No. 40). 111p. (C). 1990. pap. 15.00 (*0-915974-35-5*) Am Math.

Proceedings, 2 vols. 1250p. 1963. 10.00 (*0-318-12922-1*) Am Ornithologists.

Proceedings. (Proces-Verbeaux of General Assemblies Ser.). 220p. 1974. write for info. (*0-318-14526-X*) Intl Assoc Phys Sci Ocean.

Proceedings. Ambulatory ECG Monitoring, First National Conferen. Ed. by Nancy K. Jacobsen & Stephen R. Yarnall. (Illus.). 150p. 1976. 16.50 (*0-917054-08-3*) Med Communications.

Proceedings, 5 vols. Canadian Cancer Conference Staff. Ed. by R. W. Begg. Incl. 1st Conference, 1954. 1955. 75.00 (*0-12-149001-7*); 2nd Conference, 1956. 1957. 75.00 (*0-12-149002-5*); 3rd Conference, 1958. 1959. 75.00 (*0-12-149003-3*); 4th Conference, 1960. 1961. 75.00 (*0-12-149004-1*); 5th Conference, 1962. 1963. 75.00 (*0-12-149005-X*); write for info. (*0-318-50344-1*) Acad Pr.

Proceedings. Colloquium on the Law of Outer Space 13th, Constan. Ed. by Mortimer D. Schwartz. iii, 381p. (Orig.). 1971. pap. text 27.50 (*0-685-04973-6*) U of Cal Sch Law.

Proceedings. Colloquium on the Law of Outer Space, 15th, Vienna. Ed. by Mortimer D. Schwartz. iv, 284p. (Orig.). 1973. pap. text 27.50 (*0-685-04974-4*) U of Cal Sch Law.

Proceedings. Conference of the European Cooperation in Informat. Ed. by K. Samelson et al. (Lecture Notes in Computer Science Ser.: Vol. 44). 1976. 21.95 (*0-387-07804-5*) Spr-Verlag.

Proceedings. Ecole Ete de Probabilites de Saint-Flour, 4th, 197. Ed. by X. Fernique et al. LC 75-25522. (Lecture Notes in Mathematics Ser.: Vol. 480). 293p. 1975. 37.30 (*0-387-07396-5*) Spr-Verlag.

Proceedings Euromicro Workshop on Parallel & Distributed Processing Staff et al. LC 94-102959. xv, 559 p. 1992. pap. write for info. incl. fiche (*0-8186-3611-4*) IEEE Comp Soc.

Proceedings. International Conference on Computer Vision Staff. LC 93-77713. xiv, 742 p. 1993. write for info. (*0-8186-3871-0*) IEEE Comp Soc.

Proceedings, 3 vols. International Congress of Nephrology, 4th, Stockho. Ed. by N. Alwall et al. Incl. Vol. 1. Embryology, Ultrastructure, Physiology. 1970. 52.25 (*3-8055-0950-2*); Vol. 2. Endocrinology, Metabolic Aspects. 1970. 52.25 (*3-8055-0951-0*); Vol. 3. Clinical Nephrology Immunology. 1970. 52.25 (*3-8055-0952-9*); 1970. 100.00 (*3-8055-0953-7*) S Karger.

Proceedings. International Symposium on Software Engineering for Parallel and Distributed Systems & Bernd Kramer. LC 98-84700. 263 p. 1998. write for info. (*0-8186-8469-0*) IEEE Comp Soc.

Proceedings. International Symposium on the Judicial Settlement. Ed. by R. Bernhardt & H. Mosler. LC 74-5923. (Beitrage Zum Auslandischen Offentlichen Rechtund Volkerecht Ser.: Vol. 62). 550p. 1974. 59.00 (*0-387-06756-6*) Spr-Verlag.

Proceedings, 3 vols. Lunar & Planetary Institute, 8th, Houston, 1977. (Lunar Science Ser.: No. 8). (Illus.). 1977. 1770.00 (*0-08-022052-5*, Pub. by Pergamon Repr) Franklin.

Proceedings. Ed. by G. P. Moretti. (Series Entomologica: No. 20). 471p. 1981. lib. bdg. 230.00 (*90-6193-130-4*) Kluwer Academic.

Proceedings. Seminar on Algebraic Groups & Related Finite Group. Ed. by Armand Borel et al. LC 73-119453. (Lecture Notes in Mathematics Ser.: Vol. 131). 1986. pap. 35.95 (*0-387-04920-7*) Spr-Verlag.

Proceedings. Workshop on Advances in Experimental Pharmacology. Ed. by W. Meier-Ruge. (Gerontology Ser.: Vol. 24, Suppl. 1). (Illus.). 1977. 42.75 (*3-8055-2687-3*) S Karger.

Proceedings, 6 vols. African Bibliographic Center Staff. LC 75-77167. (Special Bibliographic Ser.). 1969. reprint ed. lib. bdg. 150.00 (*0-8371-1066-1*, SBF&, Greenwood Pr) Greenwood.

Proceedings. Asiatic Exclusion League, 1907-1913. Ed. by Gerald N. Grob. LC 76-46064. (Anti-Movements in America Ser). 1977. reprint ed. lib. bdg. 65.95 (*0-405-09939-8*) Ayer.

Proceedings. Association of American Geologists & Naturalists a. Ed. by Claude C. Albritton. LC 77-6507. (History of Geology Ser.). 1978. reprint ed. lib. bdg. 51.95 (*0-405-10430-8*) Ayer.

Proceedings, 2 pts., Set. Ed. by T. Spoerri. Incl. Pt. 1. Psychotherapy & Human Science. Ed. by Heinz K. Fierz. 1972. 31.50 (*3-8055-1475-1*); Pt. 2. Living Together: Therapeutic & Social Aspects. 1972. 31.50 (*3-8055-1478-6*); (Psychotherapy & Psychosomatics Ser.: Vol. 20, Nos. 1-4). 1972. Set pap. text 62.75 (*3-8055-1541-3*) S Karger.

Proceedings, Vol. 7, Nos. 1-2. Ed. by African Bibliographic Center Staff. (Special Bibliographic Ser.). reprint ed. lib. bdg. 25.00 (*0-8371-9916-6*, SBK&, Greenwood Pr) Greenwood.

Proceedings: Acm Siguccs User Services Conference XX, Cleveland, Ohio, Stouffer Tower City Plaza Hotel, November 8-11, 1992: Learning from the Past, Stepping Into the Future. ACM SIGUCCS User Services Conference Staff & Association for Computing Machinery Staff. LC 95-151952. viii, 276 p. 1992. pap. write for info. (*0-89791-546-1*) Assn Compu Machinery.

***Proceedings: Annual Volume.** 11th ed. Wesley Addison. 1999. pap. text 35.33 (*0-201-61130-9*) Addison-Wesley.

Proceedings: C. S. Peirce Bicentennial International Congress. Ed. by Kenneth L. Ketner. (Graduate Studies: No. 23). 400p. (Orig.). 1981. 75.00 (*0-89672-075-6*); pap. 50.00 (*0-89672-074-8*) Tex Tech Univ Pr.

Proceedings: Computer Graphics International 1998 : Hannover, Germany, June 22-26, 1998. Computer Graphics International 1998 Staff et al. LC 98-84455. xxi, 800 p. 1998. write for info. (*0-8186-8447-X*) IEEE Comp Soc.

Proceedings: Conservation, Restoration, & Management of Tortoises & Turtles - An International Conference. New York Turtle & Tortoise Society Staff & WCS Turtle Recovery Program Staff. Ed. by Jim Van Abbema. LC 97-44399. (Illus.). xxiv, 494p. (Orig.). 1997. pap. 40.00 (*0-9659050-0-4*) NY Turtle & Tortoise.

Proceedings: Corrosion-Erosion-Wear of Materials at Elevated Temperatures. Ed. by A. V. Levy. (Illus.). 700p. 1991. 10.00 (*1-877914-18-5*) NACE Intl.

Proceedings: ECOOP 'Ninety-Two, European Conference on Object-Oriented Programming, Utrecht, The Netherlands, June 29-July 3, 1992. Ed. by O. Lehrmann Madsen et al. LC 92-19991. (Lecture Notes in Computer Science Ser.: Vol. 615). x, 426p. 1992. 63.95 (*0-387-55668-0*) Spr-Verlag.

Proceedings: Electrical Electronics Insulation Conference & Electrical Manufacturing & Coil Winding Conference. IEEE (Dielectrics & Insulation Society) Staff. Ed. by IEEE (Institute of Electrical & Electronics Engine. 800p. 1995. pap. text 142.00 (*0-941783-15-4*, 95CH35847); lib. bdg. 142.00 (*0-7803-2953-8*, 95CB35847); fiche 142.00 (*0-7803-2954-6*, 95CM35847) Inst Electrical.

An Asterisk (*) at the beginning of an entry indicates that the title is appearing for the first time.

Proceedings: Eleventh International Florida Artificial Intelligence Research Symposium Conference. Ed. by Diane J. Cook. LC 98-196524. (Illus.). 485p. 1998. pap. text 50.00 (*1-57735-051-0*) AAAI Pr.

Proceedings: Eleventh Lunar & Planetary Science Conference, Houston, Texas, March 17-21, 1980, 3 vols. Compiled by Lunar & Planetary Institute Staff. (Geochimica & Cosmochimica Acta Ser.: Suppl. 14). 3000p. 1981. 265.00 (*0-08-026314-3*, Pergamon Pr) Elsevier.

Proceedings: FEBS Meeting, 11th, 9 vols., Set. Ed. by Per Schambye. (Illus.). 1978. 948.00 (*0-08-021527-0*, Pub. by Pergamon Repr) Franklin.

Proceedings: Fifth Forum on Innovative Hazardous Waste Treatment Technologies: Domestic & International. (Illus.). 198p. (Orig.). (C). 1994. pap. text 60.00 (*0-7881-0878-6*) DIANE Pub.

Proceedings: Fifth International Bat Research Conference. Ed. by D. E. Wilson & A. L. Gardner. 434p. (Orig.). 1980. pap. 16.00 (*0-89672-083-7*) Tex Tech Univ Pr.

Proceedings: Fifth International Conference on Numerical Ship Hydrodynamics, No. 5. National Research Council Staff. 744p. (C). 1990. text 50.00 (*0-309-04241-0*) Natl Acad Pr.

Proceedings: First European Congress of Mathematics, Paris, July 6-10, 1992. European Congress of Mathematics. Ed. by Anthony Joseph. LC 94-26986. (Progress in Mathematics Ser.: 121). (ENG & FRE.). xiv, 574p. 1995. 79.50 (*0-8176-2800-2*) Birkhauser.

Proceedings: Fourth International Conference on Geotextiles, Geomembrances & Related Products, Vol. 3. 363p. 1994. 60.00 (*90-6191-122-2*, Pub. by A A Balkema) Ashgate Pub Co.

Proceedings: Fourth International Congress on Metallic Corrosion. LC 64-9547. (Illus.). 822p. 1972. 10.00 (*0-915567-80-6*) NACE Intl.

Proceedings: Great Lakes Solar Greenhouse Conference II Kalamazoo, Michigan, June, 8-9, 1979. Ed. by H. Lewis Batts, Jr. & Michael Tenenbaum. (Illus.). xiiii, 137p. (Orig.). 1980. pap. 10.00 (*0-939294-02-8*, SB-416-G7-1979) Beech Leaf.

Proceedings: Great Lakes Solar Greenhouse Conference IV. Kalamazoo, Michigan, Nov. 6-7, 1981. Ed. by H. Lewis Batts, Jr. et al. 177p. 1982. pap. 10.00 (*0-939294-05-2*, SB-416-G7-1981) Beech Leaf.

Proceedings: International Coastal Congress, ICC Kiel '92 - Interdisciplinary Discussion of Coastal Research & Coastal Management Issues & Problems. Hoirst Sterr et al. LC 93-22420. (Illus.). 808p. 1993. 105.00 (*3-631-45906-8*) P Lang Pubng.

Proceedings: International Symposium on Bifonazole, Kopenhagen, June 1984. Ed. by Hamburg Rieth. (Journal: Dermatologica: Vol. 169, Suppl. 1). iv, 148p. 1985. pap. 40.00 (*3-8055-4021-3*) S Karger.

Proceedings: International Workshop on Multimedia Software Engineering. International Workshop on Multimedia Software Engineering Staff et al. LC 98-87083. 1998. write for info. (*0-8186-8925-0*) IEEE Comp Soc.

Proceedings: MDS, 1986. Ed. by Ray Canada. 611p. 1986. pap. text 35.00 (*0-933957-03-3*) Marine Tech Soc.

Proceedings: Microscopy & Microanalysis, 1995. Ed. by G. W. Bailey et al. 1096p. 1996. 225.00 (*0-614-16841-4*) Begell Hse.

Proceedings: MUMPS Users' Group Meeting. Ed. by Jeffrey Rothmeier. 1976. 20.00 (*0-918118-03-4*) M Technol.

Proceedings: MUMPS Users' Group Meeting. Ed. by Richard E. Zapolin. 1977. 20.00 (*0-918118-04-2*) M Technol.

***Proceedings: National Athletic Trainers' Association, 1999 Athletic Training.** National Athletic Trainers' Association Staff. 112p. (C). 1999. pap. text 12.00 (*1-55642-414-0*) SLACK Inc.

***Proceedings: National Athletic Trainers' Association 51st Annual Meeting.** National Athletic Trainers' Association Staff. 332p. 2000. pap. 15.00 (*0-7360-3333-5*) Human Kinetics.

Proceedings: National Conference on Bilingual Education. Dissemination Center for Bilingual-Bicultural Educ. Ed. by Francesco Cordasco. LC 77-90556. (Bilingual-Bicultural Education in the U. S. Ser.). 1978. reprint ed. lib. bdg. 34.95 (*0-405-11094-4*) Ayer.

Proceedings: Papers from the Parasession on Diachronic Syntax. Ed. by Sanford B. Steever et al. LC 76-19732. 364p. 1976. pap. 7.00 (*0-914203-05-3*) Chicago Ling.

Proceedings: Papers from the Parasession on Language & Behavior. Ed. by Carrie S. Masek et al. LC 81-82977. 274p. 1981. pap. 8.00 (*0-914203-16-9*) Chicago Ling.

Proceedings: Papers from the Parasession on Nondeclaratives. Ed. by Robinson Schneider et al. LC 82-72497. 243p. 1982. pap. 8.00 (*0-914203-18-5*) Chicago Ling.

Proceedings: Papers from the Parasession on Pronouns & Anaphora. Ed. by Jody Kreiman & Almerindo E. Ojeda. LC 80-68105. 294p. 1980. pap. 7.00 (*0-914203-14-2*) Chicago Ling.

Proceedings: Papers from the Parasession on the Interplay of Phonology, Morphology & Syntax. Ed. by John F. Richardson et al. LC 83-71958. 353p. 1983. pap. 8.00 (*0-914203-20-7*) Chicago Ling.

Proceedings: Papers from the Parasession on the Lexicon. Ed. by Donka E. Farkas et al. LC 78-56478. 364p. 1978. pap. 7.00 (*0-914203-10-X*) Chicago Ling.

Proceedings: Papers from the 13th Regional Meeting. Ed. by Beach Woodford et al. LC 77-8304. 733p. 1977. pap. 7.00 (*0-914203-07-X*) Chicago Ling.

Proceedings: Papers from the 14th Regional Meeting. Ed. by Donka E. Farkas et al. LC 78-56477. 512p. 1978. pap. 7.00 (*0-914203-09-6*) Chicago Ling.

Proceedings: Papers from the 15th Regional Meeting. Ed. by Paul R. Clyne et al. LC 76-27943. 403p. 1979. pap. 7.00 (*0-914203-11-8*) Chicago Ling.

Proceedings: Papers from the 16th Regional Meeting. Ed. by Jody Kreiman & Almerindo E. Ojeda. LC 76-27943. 378p. 1980. pap. 7.00 (*0-914203-13-4*) Chicago Ling.

Proceedings: Papers from the 17th Regional Meeting. Ed. by Roberta A. Hendrick et al. LC 76-27943. 449p. 1981. pap. 8.00 (*0-914203-15-0*) Chicago Ling.

Proceedings: Papers from the 18th Regional Meeting. Ed. by Kevin Tuite et al. LC 76-27943. 541p. 1982. pap. 8.00 (*0-914203-17-7*) Chicago Ling.

Proceedings: Papers from the 19th Regional Meeting. Ed. by Amy Chukerman et al. LC 76-27943. 407p. 1983. pap. 8.00 (*0-914203-19-3*) Chicago Ling.

Proceedings: Papers from the 20th Regional Meeting. Ed. by David Testen et al. 1984. pap. 8.00 (*0-914203-22-3*) Chicago Ling.

Proceedings: Papers from the 6th Regional Meeting. Members of the Society Staff. 588p. 1970. pap. 7.00 (*0-914203-01-0*) Chicago Ling.

Proceedings: Papers from the 8th Regional Meeting. Ed. by Paul M. Peranteau et al. 615p. 1972. pap. 7.00 (*0-914203-02-9*) Chicago Ling.

Proceedings: Poison Plant Symposium. 32p. 1977. pap. text 5.00 (*0-935336-03-6*) Horticult Research.

Proceedings: Proceedings of the Basic Environmental Problems of Man in Space II, International Symposium, 6th, Bonn, Germany, November 3-6, 1980. Basic Environmental Problems of Man in Space II, I & K. E. Klein. Ed. by J. R. Hordinsky. 250p. 1982. pap. 77.00 (*0-08-028697-6*, A140, Pergamon Pr) Elsevier.

Proceedings: Proceedings of the Women's Rights Convention, Seneca Falls & Rochester, July-Aug., 1848. Woman's Rights Convention Staff. LC 76-79180. (Women's Rights & Liberation Ser.). 1969. reprint ed. 13.95 (*0-405-00117-7*) Ayer.

Proceedings: Regional Workshop on Sustainable Agriculture. 229p. 1989. 6.00 (*0-942717-37-6*) Intl Inst Rural.

Proceedings: Second Ieee Workshop on Interactive Voice Technology for Telecommunications Applications (ivtta 94), September 26-27, 1994, Kyoto Research Park, Kyoto, Japan. IEEE, Communications Society Staff et al. LC 94-77698. viii, 164p. 1994. pap. write for info. (*0-7803-2075-1*) IEEE Standards.

Proceedings: Sixth International Congress International Association of Engineering Geology, Amsterdam, 6-10 August 1990, 6 vols., Set. Ed. by D. G. Price. (Illus.). 2500p. (C). 1990. text 899.00 (*90-6191-130-3*, Pub. by A A Balkema) Ashgate Pub Co.

Proceedings: South Dakota Assessing Officers, 2nd Annual Conference. 1960. 5.00 (*1-55614-091-6*) U of SD Gov Res Bur.

Proceedings: South Dakota Assessing Officers, 4th Annual Conference. 1962. 5.00 (*1-55614-092-4*) U of SD Gov Res Bur.

Proceedings: South Dakota Assessing Officers, 5th Annual Conference. 1963. 5.00 (*1-55614-093-2*) U of SD Gov Res Bur.

Proceedings: South Dakota Assessing Officers, 7th Annual Conference. 1965. 5.00 (*1-55614-094-0*) U of SD Gov Res Bur.

Proceedings: South Dakota Assessing Officers, 8th Annual Conference. 1966. 5.00 (*1-55614-095-9*) U of SD Gov Res Bur.

Proceedings: South Dakota Assessing Officers, 9th Annual Conference. 1967. 5.00 (*1-55614-096-7*) U of SD Gov Res Bur.

***Proceedings: Sprockets, Samples & Satellites: Moving Imaging into the Third Millennium.** Ed. by Marilyn R. Waldman. 476p. 1999. pap. 50.00 (*0-940690-44-6*) Soc Motion Pic & TV Engrs.

Proceedings: Summitville Forum, '95. Ed. by Harry H. Posey et al. (Special Publications: No. 38). (Illus.). 375p. 1995. text 95.00 (*1-884216-51-X*) Colo Geol Survey.

Proceedings: Symposium on Fire in Wilderness & Park Management. Ed. by James K. Brown et al. (Illus.). 283p. (Orig.). (C). 1996. pap. text 45.00 (*0-7881-3201-6*) DIANE Pub.

Proceedings: Symposium on Incremental Motion & Control Systems & Devices, 9th Annual. LC 73-647018. (Illus.). 1980. 50.00 (*0-931538-02-5*) Incremental Motion.

Proceedings: The First International Conference on Requirements Engineering, April 18-22, 1994, Colorado Springs, Colorado International Conference on Requirements Engineering Staff & IEEE Computer Society Staff. LC 93-80706. xii, 246 p. 1994. pap. write for info. incl. fiche (*0-8186-5481-3*) IEEE Comp Soc.

Proceedings: The Integration of Remote Sensing & Geographic Information Systems. 193p. 1991. 8.00 (*0-944426-49-2*) ASP & RS.

Proceedings: Twenty-First Annual Conference of the Association of Muslim Social Scientists, Held in East Lansing, Michigan, October 30-November, 1992. Ed. by Mona Abul-Fadl. LC 93-36577. (Issues in Contemporary Islamic Thought Ser.: No. 12). (Illus.). 589p. (Orig.). 1993. pap. 15.00 (*1-56564-145-0*) IIIT VA.

Proceedings: 13th Paul D. Converse Symposium, 1992, University of Illinois. Converse, Paul D. symposium Staff. Ed. by Devanathan Sudharsan. LC 94-46837. (Proceedings Ser.). 1995. 35.00 (*0-87757-254-2*) Am Mktg.

Proceedings: 1996 ACEEE Summer Study on Energy Efficiency in Buildings, 10 vols. Ed. by Mark P. Modera & Diana Shankle. 2032p. (Orig.). (C). 1996. pap., per. 200.00 (*0-918249-26-0*) Am Coun Energy.

Proceedings: 1997 Computer Conference : April 13-16, 1997, Austin, Texas) American Water Works Association. Computer Conference & Austin, Tex. LC 97-172018. (Illus.). 1997. write for info. (*0-89867-898-6*) Am Water Wks Assn.

Proceedings: 1998 Ieee 4th Workshop on Interactive Voice Technology for Telecommunications Applications, Ivtta '98, September 29th-30th, 1998, Torino, Italy. European Speech Communication Association Staff & IEEE, Communications Society Staff. LC 98-86195. x, 228 p. 1998. pap. write for info. (*0-7803-5029-4*) IEEE Standards.

Proceedings - Ecology & Management of Annual Rangelands. Stephen B. Monsen & Stanley G. Kitchen. (Illus.). 428p. 1997. reprint ed. 50.00 (*0-89904-602-9*, Bear Meadows Resrch Grp); reprint ed. pap. 44.00 (*0-89904-603-7*, Bear Meadows Resrch Grp) Crumb Elbow Pub.

Proceedings - Fifth International Carnahan Conference on Security Technology: Electronic Crime Countermeasures. Ed. by R. William DeVore et al. (Illus.). 255p. (Orig.). 1986. pap. 10.00 (*0-89779-066-9*, UKY BU141) OES Pubns.

Proceedings - First International Symposium on the Artificial Insemination of Poultry. M. R. Bakst & G. J. Wishart. (Illus.). 300p. (Orig.). (C). 1995. pap. text 35.00 (*0-9649811-0-6*) Poultry Sci.

Proceedings - Hair Sheep Research Symposium. Pref. by Stephan Wildeus. (Illus.). 300p. (Orig.). 1991. pap. 5.00 (*0-944524-99-0*) Univ VI Agri Exp.

Proceedings - International Workshop on Sub-Alpine Stone Pines & Their Environment: The Status of Our Knowledge. Ed. by Wyman C. Schmidt & Friedrich-Karl Holtmeier. (Illus.). 336p. 1997. reprint ed. 41.00 (*0-89904-606-1*, Bear Meadows Resrch Grp); reprint ed. pap. 35.00 (*0-89904-607-X*, Bear Meadows Resrch Grp) Crumb Elbow Pub.

Proceedings - KSO XIVth International Symposium on Medicinal Chem: Maastricht, 8-12 September 1996. Frans M. Awouters. LC 97-22116. (Pharmacochemistry Library). 1997. write for info. (*0-444-82798-6*) Elsevier.

Proceedings - 7th Equipment Management Workshop. (Transportation Research Circular Ser.: No. 346). 74p. 1989. 7.00 (*0-685-38577-9*) Transport Res Bd.

Proceedings - Symposium on Plant - Herbivore Interactions. Ed. by Frederick D. Provenza et al. (Illus.). 188p. 1997. reprint ed. 25.00 (*0-89904-665-7*, Bear Meadows Resrch Grp); reprint ed. pap. 20.00 (*0-89904-666-5*, Bear Meadows Resrch Grp) Crumb Elbow Pub.

Proceedings - 3rd International Lead-Acid Battery Seminar. Ed. by D. S. Carr & A. L. Ponikvar. (Illus.). 410p. (Orig.). 1989. pap. 50.00 (*0-932893-03-1*) Intl Lead Zinc.

Proceedings - 5th International Symposium on Spatial Data Handling, 2 vols., Set. Ed. by P. Bresnahan et al. (Illus.). 725p. (Orig.). (C). 1992. pap. text 50.00 (*0-9633532-2-5*) U SC Hum & Soc Sci.

Proceedings - 5th International Symposium on Spatial Data Handling, 2 vols., Vol. 1. Ed. by P. Bresnahan et al. (Illus.). 371p. (Orig.). (C). 1992. pap. text 25.00 (*0-9633532-0-9*) U SC Hum & Soc Sci.

Proceedings - 5th International Symposium on Spatial Data Handling, 2 vols., Vol. 2. Ed. by P. Bresnahan et al. (Illus.). 454p. (Orig.). (C). 1992. pap. text 25.00 (*0-9633532-1-7*) U SC Hum & Soc Sci.

Proceedings--Pinyon - Juniper Conference. Ed. by Richard L. Everett. 596p. 1997. reprint ed. 65.00 (*0-89904-667-3*, Ecosytems Resrch); reprint ed. pap. 61.40 (*0-89904-664-9*, Ecosytems Resrch) Crumb Elbow Pub.

Proceedings A Symposium of the Bell Museum, Univ. of Minn. Med. School see Death & Attitudes Towards Death

Proceedings & Addresses at the Freethinkers' Convention Held at Watkins, N. Y., 1878. LC 73-119051. (Civil Liberties in American History Ser.). 1970. reprint ed. lib. bdg. 49.50 (*0-306-71937-1*) Da Capo.

Proceedings & Debates of the Virginia State Convention of 1829-1830, 2 vols. in 1. LC 71-139729. (Law, Politics & History Ser.). 1971. reprint ed. lib. bdg. 95.00 (*0-306-70077-8*) Da Capo.

Proceedings & Interim Report of the National Conference on Bail & Criminal Justice, May 27-29, 1964 & May 1964-April 1965. National Conference on Bail & Criminal Justice Sta. Ed. by Robert M. Fogelson. LC 74-3839. (Criminal Justice in America Ser.). 1974. reprint ed. 33.95 (*0-405-06156-0*) Ayer.

Proceedings & Papers of the Eleventh Trumpeter Swan Society Conference. Trumpeter Swan Society Staff. Ed. by Donna Compton. (Illus.). 178p. 1990. pap. text 10.00 (*0-9619936-6-9*) Trumpeter Swan Soc.

Proceedings & Papers of the 15th Trumpeter Swan Society: A Vision for the 21st Century: Trumpeter Swans. Ed. by Donna C. Compton & Madeleine H. Linck. (Illus.). 156p. (Orig.). 1996. pap. text 15.00 (*1-888377-00-3*) Trumpeter Swan Soc.

Proceedings & Papers of the Fourteenth Trumpeter Swan Society Conference: Trumpeter Swans - An Asset or a Liability? Harvey K. Nelson. Ed. by Donna C. Compton et al. (Illus.). 170p. (Orig.). 1994. pap. text 15.00 (*0-9619936-9-3*) Trumpeter Swan Soc.

Proceedings & Papers of the Georgia Association of Historians, 1980. Ed. by Ann W. Ellis et al. 84p. (Orig.). 1981. pap. 5.00 (*0-939346-00-1*) GA Assn Hist.

Proceedings & Papers of the Georgia Association of Historians, 1981. Ed. by Ann W. Ellis et al. 138p. (Orig.). 1982. pap. 5.00 (*0-939346-01-X*) GA Assn Hist.

Proceedings & Papers of the Georgia Association of Historians, 1982. Ed. by Ann W. Ellis et al. 141p. (Orig.). 1983. pap. 5.00 (*0-939346-02-8*) GA Assn Hist.

Proceedings & Papers of the Georgia Association of Historians, 1983. Ed. by Ann W. Ellis et al. 130p. (Orig.). 1984. pap. 5.00 (*0-939346-03-6*) GA Assn Hist.

Proceedings & Papers of the Georgia Association of Historians, 1984. Ed. by Ann W. Ellis. 145p. (Orig.). 1985. pap. 5.00 (*0-939346-04-4*) GA Assn Hist.

Proceedings & Papers of the Georgia Association of Historians, 1985. Ed. by Ann W. Ellis. 125p. (Orig.). 1985. pap. 5.00 (*0-939346-05-2*) GA Assn Hist.

***Proceedings & Papers of the Sixteenth Trumpeter Swan Society Conference.** Ed. by Janissa R. Balcomb et al. (Illus.). 136p. 1999. pap. text 15.00 (*1-888377-01-1*) Trumpeter Swan Soc.

Proceedings & Papers of the Thirteenth Swan Society Conference. Ed. by Carl D. Mitchell et al. 183p. 1992. pap. 15.00 (*0-9619936-8-5*) Trumpeter Swan Soc.

Proceedings & Papers of the Twelfth Trumpeter Swan Society Conference: Restoring the Trumpeter Swan to the Upper Midwest. Ed. & Illus. by Judy V. Englund. 200p. 1991. pap. text 10.00 (*0-9619936-7-7*) Trumpeter Swan Soc.

Proceedings, April 7, 1913 to March 7, 1923 see Legislative Origins of American Foreign Policy

Proceedings Before the Justices of the Peace in the Fourteenth & Fifteenth Centuries. Theodore F. Plucknett. Ed. & Photos by Bertha Haven Putnam. (Ames Foundation Publications). clxi, 590p. 1938. 85.00 (*1-893606-11-2*) W S Hein.

Proceedings, Carnahan Conference on Security Technology, 1990. Ed. by R. William De Vore. LC 82-646157. (Electronic Crime Countermeasures Ser.). (Illus.). 65p. (Orig.). 1990. pap. 10.00 (*0-89779-076-6*) OES Pubns.

Proceedings Coal, Energy & Environment. Ed. by John S. Mead & Mara L. Hawse. (Illus.). 632p. 1994. lib. bdg. write for info. (*1-885189-02-8*) Coal Res Ctr.

Proceedings: Cooperation & Competition in Communications: Europe Japan Forum Paris Round, 1994. 210p. 1990. pap. 45.00 (*1-57588-354-6*, 308590) W S Hein.

Proceedings Cumulative Index, 1990-1994. Ed. by Karen Montalto. 660p. 1998. 150.00i (*0-89382-577-8*, PCI-ZB90) Nat Assn Insurance.

Proceedings, Curricula for the Twenty-First Century, 1992: An Interinstitutional Symposium. Ed. by Denise M. Harmening. (Illus.). 54p. (Orig.). 1993. 14.95 (*0-943903-03-3*) DH Pub PA.

Proceedings Death Valley Conference on History & Prehistory, 3rd. Ed. by James Pisarowicz. LC 91-74081. (Death Valley History Conference Ser.). (Illus.). 260p. (Orig.). (C). 1992. pap. 10.95 (*1-878900-26-9*) DVNH Assn.

Proceedings, December 3, 1923 to March 3, 1933 see Legislative Origins of American Foreign Policy

Proceedings (Eight Annual) Sara G. Goodell. (C). 1996. pap. text 11.20 (*0-201-69558-8*) Addison-Wesley.

Proceedings Eighteenth European Conference Microcirculation, ESM, Rome, September 1994 No. 14, Supplement 1, No. 14. Ed. by C. Allegra & A. Carlizza. (International Journal of Microcirculation Ser.). (Illus.). iv, 262p. 1994. pap. 77.50 (*3-8055-6035-4*) S Karger.

Proceedings Eighth Annual IEEE International Asic Conference & Exhibit. IEEE (Rochester Section) Staff. Ed. by IEEE (Institute of Electrical & Electronics Engine. 500p. 1995. pap. 118.00 (*0-7803-2707-1*, 95TH8087); fiche 118.00 (*0-7803-2708-X*, 95TM8087) Inst Electrical.

Proceedings, 8th Canadian Waste Management Conference: September 3-5, 1986, Sheraton Hotel, Halifax Comptes Rendus, 8iaeme Conference Canadienne sur la Gestion des Dechets: Le 3, 4 et 5 Septembre 1986, Hotcel Sheraton, Halifax. Canadian Waste Management Conference Staff. LC 88-148814. ix, 377p. 1986. write for info. (*0-662-54631-8*) Can7 Govern Pub.

***Proceedings 8th International Conference on Computer Communications & Networks.** IEEE (Communications Society) Staff. Ed. by IEEE (Institute of Electrical & Electronics Engineers, Inc.) Staff. 550p. 1999. pap. write for info. (*0-7803-5794-9*, 99EX370) Inst Electrical.

Proceedings, Eleventh International Conference on Vacuum Web Coating, No. 11. Ed. by Robert Bakish. (Illus.). 300p. 1998. pap. 70.00 (*0-939997-21-5*) Bakish Mat.

Proceedings ESA Annual Meeting, 1999. Ed. by Joseph M. Crowley & Mark N. Horenstein. LC 99-63141. (Illus.). 138p. (C). 1999. pap. 15.00 (*1-885540-10-8*) Laplacian Pr.

Proceedings, European Simulation Symposium, ESS, '94. Ed. by Ali R. Kaylan et al. 352p. 1994. pap. 80.00 (*1-56555-034-X*, ESS-94) Soc Computer Sim.

Proceedings, Food Animal Integrated Research, 1995: Symposium on Food Animal Research Priorities. Federation of American Societies of Food Animal Sc & Forum for Animal Agriculture Staff. 120p. 1993. pap. text 10.00 (*1-884706-00-2*) Fed Animal Sci.

Proceedings for Congress' Sections & Symposia, 20 vols. (International Geological Congress Ser.). 1970. 153.00 (*3-510-99104-4*, Pub. by E Schweizerbartsche) Balogh.

Proceedings for International Congress on Welding Research, July Thirteenth to Fourteenth, 1984, in Boston, Massachusetts. 25.00 (*0-318-18645-4*) Welding Res Coun.

Proceedings for the International Symposium on Human Identification, 1989: Data Acquisition & Statistical Analysis for DNA Typing Laboratories. 173p. pap. 30.00 (*1-882274-50-4*) Promega.

***Proceedings for the Tenth ICTCM Conference.** 10th ed. Wesley. 1998. 30.00 (*0-201-38568-6*) Addison-Wesley.

P

Proceedings Forest Products Symposium, 1989 & 1990: November 5-10, 1989, San Francisco Hilton, San Francisco, CA, November 11-16, 1990, The Palmer House, Chicago, IL. Technical Association of the Pulp & Paper Industry. Ed. by James D. Lisius. LC SD0431.F67. (TAPPI Proceedings Ser.). 202p. reprint ed. pap. 62.70 (*0-7837-2436-5*, 204258800005) Bks Demand.

Proceedings Fourth Death Valley Conference on History & Pre-History. Ed. by Jean Johnson. (Illus.). 240p. (Orig.). 1996. pap. 10.95 (*1-878900-31-5*) DVNH Assn.

Proceedings, Fourth Forum on Geology of Industrial Minerals, Austin TX, March 1968. Ed. by L. F. Brown, Jr. (Illus.). 174p. 1969. pap. 2.00 (*0-318-03314-3*) Bur Econ Geology.

Proceedings from a Conference on Problems of War & Peace in the Middle East. Ashraf Ghorbal et al. (CISA Working Papers: No. 3). 41p. (Orig.). 1976. pap. 15.00 (*0-86682-002-7*) Ctr Intl Relations.

Proceedings from AAAI Eighth National Conference on Artificial Intelligence, 1990, 2 vols., Set. AAAI Press Staff. 1174p. 1990. pap. text 65.00 (*0-262-51057-X*) MIT Pr.

Proceedings from ASPE, 1990 Annual Conference. Ed. by Carl Zanoni. 247p. 1990. pap. write for info. (*1-887706-04-6*) Am Soc Prec Engr.

Proceedings from ASPE 1998 Annual Meeting. Ed. by Dan E. Luttrell. (Illus.). 648p. 1998. pap. write for info. (*1-887706-20-8*) Am Soc Prec Engr.

Proceedings from ASPE, 1994 Annual Meeting. Ed. by Thomas G. Bifano. 473p. 1994. pap. write for info. (*1-887706-12-7*) Am Soc Prec Engr.

Proceedings from ASPE, 1995 Annual Meeting. Ed. by John Ziegert. (Illus.). 467p. 1995. pap. write for info. (*1-887706-14-3*) Am Soc Prec Engr.

***Proceedings from ASPE 1999 Annual Meeting.** Ed. by Irving F. Stowers. (Illus.). 618p. 1999. pap. write for info. (*1-887706-22-4*) Am Soc Prec Engr.

Proceedings from ASPE, 1991 Annual Conference. Ed. by Richard L. Rhorer. 233p. 1991. pap. write for info. (*1-887706-06-2*) Am Soc Prec Engr.

Proceedings from ASPE, 1996 Annual Meeting. Ed. by Robert G. Wilhelm. (Illus.). 680p. 1996. pap. write for info. (*1-887706-16-X*) Am Soc Prec Engr.

Proceedings from ASPE 1997 Annual Meeting. Ed. by Don A. Lucca. (Illus.). 536p. 1997. pap. write for info. (*1-887706-18-6*) Am Soc Prec Engr.

Proceedings from ASPE, 1993 Annual Meeting. Ed. by Robert J. Hocken & Toshimichi Moriwaki. 555p. 1993. pap. write for info. (*1-887706-10-0*) Am Soc Prec Engr.

Proceedings from ASPE, 1992 Annual Meeting. Ed. by Ronald O. Scattergood. 402p. 1992. pap. write for info. (*1-887706-08-9*) Am Soc Prec Engr.

Proceedings from ASPE Spring Conference on Sub-Surface Damage in Glass. Ed. by Robert E. Parks. 237p. 1989. pap. write for info. (*1-887706-03-8*) Am Soc Prec Engr.

Proceedings from ASPE Spring Topical Meeting on Advances in Surface Metrology. Ed. by Jay Raja & Stuart T. Smith. (Illus.). 89p. 1997. pap. write for info. (*1-887706-17-8*) Am Soc Prec Engr.

Proceedings from ASPE Spring Topical Meeting on Mechanisms & Controls for Ultraprecision Motion. Ed. by David H. Youden. 136p. 1994. pap. write for info. (*1-887706-11-9*) Am Soc Prec Engr.

Proceedings from ASPE Spring Topical Meeting on Metal Platings for Precision Finishing Operations. Ed. by Chris Evans & John Taylor. 154p. 1991. pap. write for info. (*1-887706-05-4*) Am Soc Prec Engr.

Proceedings from ASPE Spring Topical Meeting on Micrometer-Tolerance Assembly of Macroscopic Structures. Ed. by E. Clayton Teague & Alan Feinerman. 71p. 1995. pap. write for info. (*1-887706-13-5*) Am Soc Prec Engr.

***Proceedings from ASPE Spring Topical Meeting on Precision Fabrication & Replication.** Ed. by Thomas A. Dow & Alex Sohn. (Illus.). 80p. 1999. pap. write for info. (*1-887706-21-6*) Am Soc Prec Engr.

Proceedings from ASPE Spring Topical Meeting on Precision Grinding of Brittle Materials. Ed. by Thomas G. Bifano et al. (Illus.). 128p. 1996. pap. write for info. (*1-887706-15-1*) Am Soc Prec Engr.

Proceedings from ASPE Spring Topical Meeting on Precision Interferometric Metrology. Ed. by Norman Bobroff & W. Tyler Estler. 103p. 1992. pap. write for info. (*1-887706-07-0*) Am Soc Prec Engr.

Proceedings from ASPE Spring Topical Meeting on Principles of Cutting Mechanics. Ed. by Richard L. Rhorer et al. 99p. 1993. pap. write for info. (*1-887706-09-7*) Am Soc Prec Engr.

Proceedings from ASPE Spring Topical Meeting on Silicon Machining. Ed. by Daniel C. Thompson & John A. Patten. (Illus.). 132p. 1998. pap. 25.00 (*1-887706-19-4*) Am Soc Prec Engr.

Proceedings from the Annual Conference - Recent Advances in Flame Retardancy of Polymeric Materials, 1992. Business Communications Company, Inc. Staff. 1992. 275.00 (*0-89336-894-6*, DFR-92) BCC.

Proceedings from the Annual Meeting of the Association for Equine Sports Medicine, 10th. LC 92-60324. (Illus.). 48p. (Orig.). (C). 1992. pap. text 10.00 (*0-9603534-1-0*) Vet Practice.

Proceedings from the Eleventh Annual Contaminated Soils Conference, University of Massachusetts October 1996. Ed. by Paul T. Kostecki et al. (Contaminated Soils Ser.: Vol. 2). (Illus.). 734p. 1997. text 59.95 (*1-884940-10-2*) Amherst Sci Pubs.

Proceedings from the Eleventh Annual Meeting of the Association for Equine Sports Medicine. LC 93-60278. (Illus.). 96p. (Orig.). 1993. pap. text 25.00 (*0-9603534-4-5*) Vet Practice.

Proceedings from the International Conference on Potential Theory, Amersfoort, The Netherlands, August 18-24, 1991. Ed. by Emile M. Bertin. LC 94-6950. 350p. (C). 1994. lib. bdg. 172.50 (*0-7923-2741-1*) Kluwer Academic.

Proceedings from the Ninth Annual Membrane Technology-Planning Conference, 1991. Business Communications Company, Inc. Staff & Filterex, Inc. Staff. 1992. 350.00 (*0-89336-817-2*, DMC-91) BCC.

Proceedings from the Scientific Conference on Omega-3 Fatty Acids in Nutrition, Vascular Biology, & Medicine. Ed. by Henry J. Pownall & Arthur A. Spector. (Illus.). 275p. write for info. (*0-614-04637-8*); pap. text. write for info. (*0-87493-007-3*) Am Heart.

Proceedings from the Scientific Conference on Omega-3 Fatty Acids in Nutrition, Vascular Biology, & Medicine: Houston, Texas, April 17-19, 1994. LC 95-15253. 1995. write for info. (*0-614-07794-X*) Am Heart.

Proceedings from the Second International Data Acquisition Workshop on Networked Data Acquisition Systems (DAS 96) Ed. by M. Nomachi & S. Ajimura. 320p. 1997. text 68.00 (*981-02-3198-9*) World Scientific Pub.

Proceedings from the Second International Symposium on Human Identification: New Technologies, Standardization of Methods & Data Sharing for DNA Typing Laboratories. 328p. pap. 45.00 (*1-882274-51-2*) Promega.

Proceedings from the Sixth Nordic Conference on Bilingualism. Ed. by Kjell Herberts & Christer Lauren. (Multilingual Matters Ser.: No. 80). 134p. 1991. 59.00 (*1-85359-137-8*, Pub. by Multilingual Matters) Taylor & Francis.

Proceedings from the Symposia Textures in Non-Metallic Materials & Microstructure & Texture Evolution During Annealing of Deformed Materials. D. B. Knorr. 106p. 1991. pap. text 383.00 (*2-88124-802-0*) Gordon & Breach.

Proceedings from the Tenth Annual Contaminated Soils Conference, University of Massachusetts October 1995. Ed. by Paul T. Kostecki et al. LC 97-101910. (Contaminated Soils Ser.: Vol. 1). (Illus.). 734p. (C). 1996. text 59.95 (*1-884940-07-2*) Amherst Sci Pubs.

Proceedings from the Tenth Annual Membrane Technology-Planning Conference, 1992. Business Communications Company, Inc. Staff & Filterex, Inc. Staff. 1993. 350.00 (*0-89336-968-3*, DMC-92) BCC.

Proceedings from the 10th Annual Telecommunications Policy Research Conference. Telecommunications Policy Research Conference Staf. Ed. by Oscar Gandy et al. LC 83-6408. 400p. (C). 1983. text 83.50 (*0-89391-195-X*) Ablx Pub.

Proceedings from the 3rd Nordic Conference for English Studies: Application of New Techniques, Standardization of Methods, Data Sharing & Legal Issues Affecting the DNA Typing Community. 421p. pap. 60.00 (*1-882274-52-0*) Promega.

Proceedings from the Third Nordic Conference for English Studies, 2 vols., Set. Ed. by Ishrat Lindblad & Magnus Ljung. (Stokholm Studies in English: LXXIII). 806p. (Orig.). 1987. pap. text 108.00 (*91-22-00870-5*) Coronet Bks.

Proceedings from the Twelfth Meeting of the Association for Equine Sports Medicine. Ed. by Jonathan Foreman. (Illus.). 94p. (Orig.). 1994. pap. 25.00 (*0-9603534-5-3*) Vet Practice.

Proceedings from World Workplace '96: October 6-8, 1996, Salt Lake City, Utah, 2 vols. (Illus.). 954p. (Orig.). 1996. pap. 75.00 (*1-883176-18-2*, 145989) Intl Facility Mgmt Assn.

Proceedings from World Workplace '95: September 17-20, 1995, Miami Beach, Florida, 2 vols., Set. (Illus.). 984p. (Orig.). 1995. pap. 50.00 (*1-883176-13-1*, 145997) Intl Facility Mgmt Assn.

Proceedings from World Workplace '97 Vol. 1: October 5-7, 1997, Dallas, Texas. (Illus.). 418p. 1997. pap. write for info. (*1-883176-21-2*, 146013) Intl Facility Mgmt Assn.

Proceedings from World Workplace '95 Vol. 1: September 17-20, 1995, Miami Beach, Florida. (Illus.). 498p. (Orig.). 1995. pap. write for info. (*1-883176-11-5*, 145997) Intl Facility Mgmt Assn.

Proceedings from World Workplace '97 Vol. 2: October 5-7, 1997, Dallas, Texas. (Illus.). 490p. 1997. pap. write for info. (*1-883176-22-0*, 146013) Intl Facility Mgmt Assn.

Proceedings from World Workplace, Salt Lake City, Utah, October 6-8, 1996, Vol. 1. (Illus.). 572p. (Orig.). 1996. pap. write for info. (*1-883176-16-6*, 145989) Intl Facility Mgmt Assn.

Proceedings from World Workplace, Salt Lake City, Utah, October 6-8, 1996, Vol. 2. (Illus.). 382p. (Orig.). 1996. pap. write for info. (*1-883176-17-4*, 145989) Intl Facility Mgmt Assn.

Proceedings from World Workplace '95 Vol. 2: September 17-20, 1995, Miami Beach, Florida. (Illus.). 486p. (Orig.). 1995. pap. write for info. (*1-883176-12-3*, 145997) Intl Facility Mgmt Assn.

Proceedings Frontiers in Education Twenty-Fifth Annual Conference. IEEE (Education Society & Computer Society) Staff. Ed. by IEEE Staff. LC 79-640910. 1044p. 1995. pap. text 154.00 (*0-7803-3022-6*, 95CH35867); lib. bdg. 154.00 (*0-7803-3023-4*, 95CB35867); fiche 154.00 (*0-7803-3024-2*, 95CM35867); cd-rom 154.00 (*0-7803-3025-0*, 95CH35867) Inst Electrical.

Proceedings Frontiers in Education 24th Annual Conference. IEEE (Education Society) Staff. Ed. by IEEE Staff. LC 79-640910. 850p. 1994. pap. text. write for info. (*0-7803-2413-7*, 94CH35723); lib. bdg. write for info. (*0-7803-2414-5*, 94CB35723); mic. film. write for info. (*0-7803-2415-3*, 94CM35723) Inst Electrical.

Proceedings High Plains Disease Symposium. Charles M. Rush & Gerald J. Michels, Jr. (Illus.). 77p. (Orig.). 1995. pap. text 10.00 (*0-926195-01-8*, AREC 96-19) TX AES.

Proceedings, ICLOE'92: 1992 International Conference on Lasers & Optoelectronics, 16-18 October, 1992, Beijing, China. Sui-Sheng Mei et al. LC 93-83315. (Spie Proceedings Ser.). xvii, 830 p. 1993. write for info. (*0-8194-1225-2*) Routledge.

Proceedings IEEE International Conference on Robotics & Automation, 1995. IEEE (Robotics & Automation Society) Staff. LC 90-640158. 3000p. 1995. pap. text. write for info. (*0-7803-2062-X*); lib. bdg. write for info. (*0-7803-2063-8*, 95CH3479-3) Inst Electrical.

Proceedings IEEE International Conference on Robotics & Automation, 1995. IEEE Robotics & Automation Society Staff. Ed. by IEEE Staff. 3000p. 1994. pap. text. write for info. (*0-7803-1965-6*); lib. bdg. write for info. (*0-7803-1966-4*, 95CH3461-1); fiche. write for info. (*0-7803-1967-2*) Inst Electrical.

Proceedings IEEE Southeastcon '96. IEEE (Region 3) Staff. 732p. 1996. pap. 140.00 (*0-7803-3088-9*, 96CH35880); lib. bdg. 140.00 (*0-7803-3089-7*, 96CB35880); fiche 140.00 (*0-7803-3090-0*, 96CM35880) Inst Electrical.

Proceedings, Ieee Symposium on Parallel Rendering (prs '97) Phoenix, Arizona 20-21 October 1997. Parallel Rendering Symposium Staff et al. LC 98-140557. 120 p. 1997. write for info. (*0-8186-8265-5*) IEEE Comp Soc.

Proceedings in Atmospheric Electricity. Ed. by Lothar H. Ruhnke & John Latham. LC 83-10096. (Illus.). 427p. 1983. 53.00 (*0-937194-04-2*) A Deepak Pub.

Proceedings in Gastrointestinal Radiology. J. Dobranowski et al. (Illus.). 265p. 1990. 110.00 (*0-387-97113-0*) Spr-Verlag.

Proceedings in Parga & the Ionian Islands. C. P. DeBosset. (Illus.). 1976. 30.00 (*0-916710-27-0*) Obol Intl.

Proceedings in Parliament, 1614 (House of Commons) Maija Jansson. LC 86-71781. (Memoirs Ser.: Vol. 172). (Illus.). 500p. (C). 1988. 25.00 (*0-87169-172-8*, M172-JAM) Am Philos.

Proceedings in Parliament, 1626, Volume 1: House of Lords, Vol. 1. 644p. 1991. 125.00 (*1-58046-002-X*) Univ Rochester Pr.

Proceedings in Parliament, 1625, Vol. 1. Maija Jansson. 808p. 1987. 125.00 (*1-58046-001-1*) Univ Rochester Pr.

Proceedings in Parliament, 1626, Volume 2: House of Commons, Vol. 2. Ed. by Maija J. Cole & William B. Bidwell. 447p. 1992. 125.00 (*1-58046-003-8*) Univ Rochester Pr.

Proceedings in Parliament, 1626: Appendices & Indices, Vol. 3. Ed. by Maija J. Cole & William B. Bidwell. 461p. 1992. 125.00 (*1-58046-004-6*) Univ Rochester Pr.

Proceedings in Parliament, 1626: Appendices & Indices, Vol. 4. Ed. by Maija J. Cole & William B. Bidwell. 537p. 1996. 125.00 (*1-58046-005-4*) Univ Rochester Pr.

Proceedings in Parliament, 1628: Appendices & Indices, Vol. 6. Ed. by Maija J. Cole et al. 616p. 1983. 125.00 (*1-58046-011-9*) Univ Rochester Pr.

Proceedings in Parliament 1628, Volume 5: Lords Proceedings, Vol. 5. Ed. by Maija Jansson Cole et al. (Commons Debates 1628 Ser.). 737p. 1983. 125.00 (*1-58046-010-0*) Univ Rochester Pr.

***Proceedings in the Court of Impeachment in the Matter of the Impeachment of George G. Barnard, 3 vol.** LC 99-73243. 2246p. 1999. reprint ed. 490.00 (*1-56169-540-8*) Gaunt.

Proceedings in the Court of Vice-Admiralty of Virginia, 1698-1775. Ed. by George H. Reese. xiii, 121p. 1983. 12.50 (*0-88490-113-0*) Library of VA.

***Proceedings in the Opening Session of the Long Parliament.** LC 99-38740. (Proceedings in Parliament Ser.). 2000. write for info. (*1-58046-074-7*) Univ Rochester Pr.

***Proceedings in the Opening Session of the Long Parliament: House of Commons, Vol. 1:3 November-19, December 1640.** Ed. by Maija Jansson. (Proceedings in Parliament Ser.: Vol. 1524-3370). (Illus.). 738p. 2000. 125.00 (*1-58046-037-2*) Univ Rochester Pr.

Proceedings in the Parliaments of Elizabeth I, 1558-1581 Pt. I, Vol. I. Ed. by Terence Hartley. LC 81-80390. 564p. 1981. 90.00 (*0-89453-225-1*) Scholarly Res Inc.

Proceedings in the Parliaments of Elizabeth I, 1585-1589 Vol. 3. Terence Hartley. 1995. 170.00 (*0-7185-2246-X*) Bks Intl VA.

Proceedings International Conference on Engineering Education Vols. 1 & 2: Progress Through Partnerships, Vols. I & II. Ed. by Dianne Throgmorton et al. 1500p. (Orig.). 1997. lib. bdg. write for info. (*1-885189-03-6*) Coal Res Ctr.

Proceedings-International Senepol Research Symposium. Pref. by Stephan Wildeus. (Illus.). 138p. 1987. pap. 5.00 (*0-944524-00-1*) Univ VI Agri Exp.

Proceedings IWISP '96: 4-7 November 1996, Manchester, United Kingdom. LC 96-45229. 728p. 1996. 272.00 (*0-444-82587-8*) Elsevier.

Proceedings-Memoria Conference on Books in Spanish for Young Readers: First Annual. James Cummins & Martin L. Ferrer. Ed. by Isabel Schon. (ENG & SPA.). 28p. (Orig.). (C). 1991. pap. 5.00 (*0-9639354-0-2*) Ctr Bks Spanish.

Proceedings-Memoria Conference on Books in Spanish for Young Readers: Second Annual. Nathan Glazer & Jorge A. Bustamante. Ed. by Isabel Schon. (ENG & SPA.). 24p. (Orig.). (C). 1992. pap. 5.00 (*0-9639354-1-0*) Ctr Bks Spanish.

Proceedings-Memoria Conference on Books in Spanish for Young Readers: Third Annual. Stephen D. Krashen & Jose L. Portillo. Ed. by Isabel Schon. (ENG & SPA.). 27p. (Orig.). (C). 1993. pap. 5.00 (*0-9639354-2-9*) Ctr Bks Spanish.

Proceedings, Modelling & Simulation, ESM, '96. Ed. by Andras Javor et al. 1137p. 1996. 200.00 incl. cd-rom (*1-56555-097-8*, ESM-96) Soc Computer Sim.

Proceedings, 1985 International Conference on Coal Science. Ed. by Robert A. Hinde. (Illus.). 1028p. (Orig.). 1986. pap. 100.00 (*0-08-029871-0*) Elsevier.

Proceedings, 1981 Carnahan Conference on Crime Countermeasures. Ed. by R. William De Vore & J. S. Jackson. LC 79-644630. (Illus.). 200p. (Orig.). 1981. pap. 10.00 (*0-89779-046-4*, UKY BU124) OES Pubns.

Proceedings, 1986: Products & Applications Proceedings of the Technical Program from the 1986 International Conference, 2 vols. Intro. by Titanium Development Association Staff. (Orig.). 1987. pap. 75.00 (*0-935297-04-9*) Intl Titanium.

Proceedings, 1980-1998 Vol. 45: Essays on Cambridge History. unabridged ed. (Illus.). 200p. 1998. pap. 15.00 (*1-878284-46-0*) Cmbrdg Hist.

Proceedings, 1982 3rd International Symposium on Vulcanospeleology. Ed. by William R. Halliday. (Illus.). 132p. (Orig.). (C). 1993. pap. text 9.50 (*1-886168-05-9*) ABC Pubng.

Proceedings 1990: 1990 International Conference on Titanium Products & Applications, 2 vols. (Illus.). 1000p. text 150.00 (*0-935297-14-6*, 9603) Intl Titanium.

***Proceedings 1998: Curricula for the 21st Century: An Interinstitutional Symposium.** Ed. by Denise M. Harmening & Cynthia Carr Stambach. (Illus.). 1999. 14.95 (*0-943903-10-6*) DH Pub PA.

Proceedings 1995 IEEE International Symposium on Information Theory. IEEE (Information Theory Society) Staff. Ed. by Institute of Electrical & Electronics Engineers, I. LC 72-179437. 500p. 1995. pap. text 110.00 (*0-7803-2453-6*, 95CH35738); lib. bdg. 110.00 (*0-7803-2454-4*, 95CB35738); fiche 110.00 (*0-7803-2455-2*, 95CM35738) Inst Electrical.

Proceedings, 1995: Curricula for the 21st Century. Ed. by Denise M. Harmening & Cynthia C. Stambach. (Illus.). 1996. 14.95 (*0-943903-07-6*) DH Pub PA.

Proceedings, 1995 Summer Computer Simulation Conference: Summer Computer Simulation Proceedings. Ed. by Birta Oren. (Illus.). 900p. 1995. 180.00 (*1-56555-081-1*, SCSC-95) Soc Computer Sim.

Proceedings, 1995 Winter Simulation Conference. Ed. by Christos Alexopoulos et al. LC 87-654182. 1463p. 1995. 210.00 (*0-7803-3018-8*, WSC-95) Soc Computer Sim.

Proceedings, 1994: Curricula for the 21st Century: An Interinstitutional Symposium. Ed. by Denise M. Harmening. (Illus.). (Orig.). 1994. 14.95 (*0-943903-04-1*) DH Pub PA.

Proceedings 1994: 10th Anniversary International Conference on Titanium Products & Applications. (Illus.). 500p. text 150.00 (*0-935297-21-9*, 9601) Intl Titanium.

Proceedings Nineteen Ninety-Four IEEE International Symposium on Information Theory. IEEE, Information Theory Society Staff. Ed. by IEEE Staff. LC 72-179437. 525p. 1994. pap. text. write for info. (*0-7803-2015-8*); lib. bdg. write for info. (*0-7803-2016-6*, 94CH3467-8); fiche. write for info. (*0-7803-2017-4*) Inst Electrical.

Proceedings, 1994 Sugar Processing Research Conference. Ed. by Margaret A. Clarke & Beryl A. Borel. (Proceedings Sugar Processing Research Conference (since 1982) Ser.). (Illus.). 411p. (Orig.). 1994. pap. text 100.00 (*1-883326-02-8*) Sugar Process Res.

Proceedings, 1994 Summer Computer Simulation Conference. Ed. by Dale K. Pace & Abdel-Moaty Fayek. 972p. 1994. 180.00 (*1-56555-029-3*, SCSC-94) Soc Computer Sim.

Proceedings, 1994 Winter Simulation Conference. Ed. by Jeffrey D. Tew et al. 1500p. 1994. 180.00 (*0-7803-2109-X*, WSC-94) Soc Computer Sim.

Proceedings, 1990 National Symposium on Mining. Ed. by Donald H. Graves & R. William De Vore. LC 83-60966. (Illus.). (Orig.). 1990. pap. 10.00 (*0-89779-077-4*) OES Pubns.

Proceedings, 1997: 13th Annual ITA Conference & Exhibition. (Illus.). 378p. 1998. text 150.00 (*0-935297-24-3*, 9630) Intl Titanium.

Proceedings, 1996: Curricula for the 21st Century an International Symposium. unabridged ed. Ed. by Denise M. Harmening & Cynthia C. Stambach. (Illus.). (Orig.). 1997. pap. 14.95 (*0-943903-08-4*) DH Pub PA.

Proceedings, 1996: 12th Annual ITA Conference & Exhibition. (Illus.). 264p. 1997. text 150.00 (*0-935297-23-5*, 9629) Intl Titanium.

Proceedings, 1996 Summer Computer Simulation Conference. Ed. by V. Wayne Ingalls et al. 632p. 1996. 180.00 (*1-56555-098-6*, SCSC-96) Soc Computer Sim.

Proceedings, 1990 Summer Computer SImulation Conference: Calgary, Alberta, Canada. Ed. by William Y. Svrcek. 1324p. 1990. 150.00 (*0-911801-74-X*, SCSC90) Soc Computer Sim.

Proceedings, 1993: Curricula for the 21st Century: An Interinstitutional Symposium. Ed. by Denise M. Harmening. (Illus.). (Orig.). 1994. pap. 14.95 (*0-943903-05-X*) DH Pub PA.

Proceedings, 1992 Sugar Processing Research Conference. Ed. by Margaret A. Clarke & Beryl T. Borel. (Proceedings Sugar Processing Research Conference (since 1982) Ser.). (Illus.). 375p. (Orig.). 1992. pap. text 100.00 (*1-883326-00-1*) Sugar Process Res.

Proceedings, 1992 Summer Computer Simulation Conference. Ed. by Paul Luker. 1273p. 1992. 180.00 (*1-56555-014-5*, SCSC-92) Soc Computer Sim.

Proceedings, 1992 Winter Simulation Conference: Arlington, Virginia. Ed. by James W. Swain et al. LC 87-654182. 1410p. 1992. 180.00 (*0-7803-0798-4*, WSC-92) Soc Computer Sim.

An Asterisk (*) at the beginning of an entry indicates that the title is appearing for the first time.

Proceedings, 1990 Winter Simulation Conference: New Orleans, Louisiana. Ed. by Osman Balci et al. 1024p. 1990. 130.00 (*0-911801-72-3*, WSC-90) Soc Computer Sim.

Proceedings, 1975 - Space & Energy see Astronautical Research: International Astronautical Congress

Proceedings, 1972, Vol. 1. North American Rapid Excavation & Tunneling Confer. Ed. by Kenneth S. Lane & Larry A. Garfield. LC 72-86918. (Illus.). 852p. reprint ed. pap. 200.00 (*0-7837-7867-8*, 200906500072) Bks Demand.

Proceedings, 1972, Vol. 2. North American Rapid Excavation & Tunneling Confer. Ed. by Kenneth S. Lane & Larry A. Garfield. LC 72-86918. (Illus.). 830p. reprint ed. pap. 200.00 (*0-7837-7868-6*, 200906500073) Bks Demand.

Proceedings, Ninth Ieee Sp Workshop on Statistical Signal & Array Processing: September 14-16, 1998, Portland, Oregon, Usa. IEEE SP Workshop on Statistical Signal and Array Processing & Institute of Electrical and Electronics Engineers. LC 98-86103. 440 p. 1998. write for info. (*0-7803-5011-1*) IEEE Standards.

Proceedings NMLRC Symposium, '93. Ed. by Y. Paul Chugh & Donna Davin. (Illus.). 302p. 1994. lib. bdg. write for info. (*1-885189-00-1*) Coal Res Ctr.

Proceedings of a Conference on Coal Mine Subsidence in the Rocky Mountain West. Ed. by Jeffrey L. Hynes. (Special Publications: No. 31). (Illus.). 315p. (Orig.). 1986. pap. 8.00 (*1-884216-45-5*) Colo Geol Survey.

Proceedings of a Conference on Currency Substitution & Currency Boards. Ed. by Nissan Liviatan. LC 93-26386. (Discussion Papers: No. 207). 128p. 1993. pap. 22.00 (*0-8213-2521-3*, 12521) World Bank.

Proceedings of a Conference on Simulation in Business & Management, 1990. Ed. by Sal Belardo & Jay Weinroth. (Simulation Ser.: Vol. 21, No. 4). 160p. 1990. 48.00 (*0-911801-63-4*, SS21-4) Soc Computer Sim.

Proceedings of a National Conference on Preventing Alcohol & Drug Abuse in Black Communities. Preston Bright & Clarence Johnson. 257p. (C). 1997. reprint ed. pap. text 50.00 (*0-7881-4188-0*) DIANE Pub.

Proceedings of a Pressure Transducer-Packer Workshop. Ed. by V. J. Latkovich. 48p. (Orig.). (C). 1994. pap. text 30.00 (*0-7881-0804-2*) DIANE Pub.

Proceedings of a Seminar on Crop Protection for Resource-Poor Farmers. R. W. Gibson & A. Sweetmore. 167p. 1992. pap. 50.00 (*0-85954-321-8*, Pub. by Nat Res Inst) St Mut.

Proceedings of a Symposium on Geothermal Energy & Colorado. Richard H. Pearl. (Bulletin Ser.: No. 35). (Illus.). 102p. (Orig.). 1974. pap. 2.00 (*1-884216-01-3*) Colo Geol Survey.

Proceedings of a Symposium on Large Scale Digital Calculating Machinery 1948. Harvard Computation Laboratory Staff & William Aspray. (Charles Babbage Institute Reprint Series for the History of Computing: No. 8). 340p. 1985. reprint ed. 45.00 (*0-262-08152-0*) MIT Pr.

Proceedings of a Symposium on Oak Woodlands: Ecology, Management, & Urban Interface Issues. Ed. by Norman H. Pillsbury et al. (Illus.). 738p. (C). 1999. reprint ed. pap. text 75.00 (*0-7881-7674-9*) DIANE Pub.

Proceedings of a Symposium on Quality Assurance of Radiotherapy Equipment: Held at the University of Kansas, Kansas City, Missouri, June 4-5, 1982. Ed. by George Starkschall. (American Association of Physicists in Medicine Symposium Ser.: No. 3). 240p. 1983. 45.00 (*0-88318-422-2*, Pub. by Am Inst Physics) Med Physics Pub.

***Proceedings of a Tri-Lateral Workshop on Natural Hazards: Sam Jakes Inn, Merrickville, Canada, Feb. 11-14, 1995.** Ed. by David Etkin. (Illus.). 273p. (C). 1999. reprint ed. pap. text 40.00 (*0-7881-8252-8*) DIANE Pub.

Proceedings of a Workshop on Coconut Shell Carbonization/Waste Heat Recovery, Colombo, Sri Lanka, September 1989. APPC Staff et al. 69p. 1991. pap. 30.00 (*0-85954-279-3*, Pub. by Nat Res Inst) St Mut.

Proceedings of a Workshop on Optical Surveys for Quasars. Ed. by Patrick Osmer et al. LC 88-71919. (Astronomical Society of the Pacific Conference Ser.: Vol. 2). (Illus.). 394p. 1988. 34.00 (*0-937707-19-8*) Astron Soc Pacific.

Proceedings of a Workshop on Tree Resources & the Environment Held in Phy Wiang Watershed, Khon Kaen, Thailand. Man-Kwun Chan et al. 1994. pap. 25.00 (*0-85954-384-6*, Pub. by Nat Res Inst) St Mut.

Proceedings of ADVMAT-91: First International Symposium on Environmental Effects on Advanced Materials. Ed. by R. D. Kane. (Illus.). 572p. 1992. 10.00 (*1-877914-35-5*) NACE Intl.

Proceedings of Aerospace Testing Seminar, 2nd, Los Angeles, California, 17-18 March 1975. Aerospace Testing Seminar Staff. LC 62-38584. 340p. reprint ed. pap. 105.40 (*0-7837-1300-2*, 204144100020) Bks Demand.

Proceedings of an All-Union School on the Theory of Functions (Miass, July 1989) Ed. by S. B. Stechkin. (Proceedings of the Steklov Institute of Mathematics Ser.: Vol. 198). 255p. 1994. 163.00 (*0-8218-3153-4*, STEKLO/198C) Am Math.

Proceedings of an Institute on the Roles of Psychology & Psychologists in Rehabilitation Held at Princeton, New Jersey, February 3-7, 1958. Beatrice A. Wright. Ed. by Janet Rosenberg. LC 79-6929. (Physically Handicapped in Society Ser.). 1980. reprint ed. lib. bdg. 18.95 (*0-405-13136-4*) Ayer.

Proceedings of an International Symposium Jointly Organized by IAEA & WHO, Parts 27-31 October 1980. IAEA Staff. (Proceedings Ser.). (Illus.). 596p. 1981. pap. 160.00 (*92-0-010281-6*, ISP567, IAEA, Pub. by IAEA) Bernan Associates.

Proceedings of an International Symposium of the Olympic Games. William Coulson & H. Kyrieleis. (Illus.). 190p. 1992. pap. 50.00 (*0-946897-53-0*) David Brown.

Proceedings of an International Workshop on Lethal Yellowing-Like Diseases of Coconut, Elmina, Ghana, November, 1995. S. J. Eden-Green & F. Ofori. 308p. 1997. pap. 150.00 (*0-85954-488-5*, Pub. by Nat Res Inst) St Mut.

Proceedings of APPA's 80th Annual Meeting. (Illus.). 302p. 1993. pap. 35.00 (*0-913359-75-0*) APPA VA.

Proceedings of APPA's 79th Annual Meeting. (Illus.). 250p. 1992. pap. 28.00 (*0-913359-62-9*) APPA VA.

Proceedings of APPA's 77th Annual Meeting. (Illus.). 314p. 1990. pap. 20.00 (*0-913359-53-X*) APPA VA.

Proceedings of APPA's 76th Annual Meeting. (Illus.). 265p. 1989. pap. 20.00 (*0-913359-51-3*) APPA VA.

Proceedings of Biotechnology: KSEA Series in Advances in Science & Engineering. Dewey D. Ryu. Ed. by Sang S. Lee & Moon H. Han. (KSEA Series in Advances in Science & Engineering: Vol. I). (ENG & KOR., Illus.). xiv, 323p. (Orig.). 1997. pap. text 100.00 (*1-889495-00-X*) U CA Biochem.

***Proceedings of Coatings for Asia, 1999.** 301p. 1999. pap. 93.00 (*0-934010-47-1*) Fed Soc Coat Tech.

Proceedings of COMPSEC International 1996. COMPSEC International Staff. LC 99-187067. vii, 624 p. 1996. write for info. (*1-85617-332-1*, Pub. by Elsvr Adv Tech) Elsevier.

Proceedings of Computer Support For Collaborative Learning, '95. Ed. by John L. Schnase & Edward L. Cunnius. 500p. 1995. pap. 39.95 (*0-8058-2243-7*) L Erlbaum Assocs.

Proceedings of Conference LXII, 8th Joint Meeting of the U. S. Japan Conference on Natural Resources, Panel on Earthquake Prediction Technology. R. L. Wesson & Yamato Miyazaki. (Illus.). 280p. (Orig.). (C). 1995. pap. text 60.00 (*0-7881-2549-4*) DIANE Pub.

Proceedings of Conference on Aerospace Simulation III. Monte Ung. (Simulation Ser.: Vol. 19, No. 2). (Illus.). 319p. (C). 1988. 60.00 (*0-911801-28-6*, SS-19-2) Soc Computer Sim.

***Proceedings of Coral Reef Monitoring Workshop June 9-11, 1998.** James E. Maragos & Rikki Dunsmore. LC 99-17029. 1999. write for info. (*0-86638-191-0*) EW Ctr HI.

Proceedings of Corrosion/96 Research Topical Symposia: Pt. I: Life Prediction of Structures Subject to Environmental Degradation; Pt. II: Crevice Corrosion. (Illus.). 250p. (Orig.). 1996. pap. text 67.00 (*1-57590-004-1*) NACE Intl.

Proceedings of Dynamic Systems & Applications, Vol. 1. Ed. by G. S. Ladde & M. Sambandham. (Illus.). 438p. (C). 1994. 100.00 (*0-9640398-4-2*); pap. 75.00 (*0-9640398-5-0*) Dynamic Pubs.

Proceedings of Dynamic Systems & Applications, Vol. 2. Ed. by G. S. Ladde & M. Sambandham. (Illus.). 600p. (C). 1996. lib. bdg. 150.00 (*0-9640398-1-8*) Dynamic Pubs.

Proceedings of Eighth International Conference on Vacuum Web Coating. 1994. 70.00 (*0-939997-17-7*) Bakish Mat.

Proceedings of 80th Convention, IAFWA. Ed. by Kenneth J. Sabol. 419p. 1996. lib. bdg. 20.00 (*0-614-06188-1*) IAFWA.

Proceedings of Electrical Manufacturing & Coil Winding '89. (Illus.). 333p. 1989. pap. 40.00 (*0-941783-09-X*) Intl Coil Wind.

Proceedings of Electrical Manufacturing & Coil Winding '90. (Illus.). 374p. 1990. pap. 40.00 (*0-941783-10-3*) Intl Coil Wind.

Proceedings of Electrical Manufacturing & Coil Winding '91. (Illus.). 374p. 1991. pap. 50.00 (*0-941783-11-1*) Intl Coil Wind.

Proceedings of Electrical Manufacturing & Coil Winding '92. (Illus.). 448p. 1992. pap. 50.00 (*0-941783-12-X*) Intl Coil Wind.

Proceedings of European Dialysis & Transplant, Vol. 17. Date not set. 39.95 (*0-8464-4465-8*) Beekman Pubs.

Proceedings of European Dialysis & Transplant, Vol. 18. Date not set. 39.95 (*0-8464-4466-6*) Beekman Pubs.

Proceedings of European Dialysis & Transplant, Vol. 19. Date not set. 39.95 (*0-8464-4467-4*) Beekman Pubs.

Proceedings of Extended Abstracts: Symposium on Responses to Changing Multiple-Use Demands: New Directions for Water Resources Planning & Management. Symposium on Responses to Changing Multiple-Use De. Ed. by Michael J. Sale & Rita O. Wadlington. LC 94-70723. (American Water Resources Association Technical Publication Ser.: Vol. TPS-94-2). 520p. 1994. reprint ed. pap. 161.20 (*0-608-02435-X*, 206307800004) Bks Demand.

Proceedings of 5th International Colloquium, North American Session: "Future Direction in Stability Research & Design" Ed. by Diana Walsh & James M. Ricles. 428p. (Orig.). 1996. pap. 50.00 (*1-879749-62-9*) Structural Stability.

Proceedings of Fifth International Conference on Pervaporation Processes in the Chemical Industry: Heidelberg, Germany, March 11-15, 1991. 510p. 1991. 120.00 (*0-939997-10-X*) Bakish Mat.

Proceedings of Fifth International Conference on Software Reuse: June 2-5, 1998, Victoria, British Columbia, Canada. International Conference on Software Reuse Staff et al. LC 98-180619. xiii, 388 p. 1998. write for info. (*0-8186-8379-1*) IEEE Comp Soc.

Proceedings of Fifth International Conference on Vacuum Web Coating. 270p. 1992. 70.00 (*0-939997-11-8*) Bakish Mat.

Proceedings of First California Thermal Insulation International Conference, Vol. I. Sarfraz A. Siddiqui. (Illus.). 125p. 1988. write for info. (*0-9621888-0-8*) BHF TI.

Proceedings of 1st International Conference on Mechanochemistry, Set. Ed. by K. Tkacova. pap. write for info. (*1-898326-39-8*, Pub. by CISP) Balogh.

Proceedings of First International Conference on Vacuum Web Coating. 175p. 1987. 70.00 (*0-939997-03-7*) Bakish Mat.

Proceedings of 1st International Symposium on Ferroelectric Liquid Crystals. Ed. by C. Destrade. 900p. 1988. pap. text 1500.00 (*2-88124-304-5*) Gordon & Breach.

Proceedings of 4th International Conference on Applied Numerical Modeling, Dec. 27-29, 1984, Tainan, Taiwan. Ed. by Han-Min Hsia et al. (Science & Technology Ser.: Vol. 63). (Illus.). 800p. 1986. 70.00 (*0-87703-242-4*, Am Astronaut Soc) Univelt Inc.

Proceedings of Fourth International Conference on Vacuum Web Coating, 1990. 235p. 1991. 70.00 (*0-939997-09-6*) Bakish Mat.

Proceedings of Frontiers in Education 1996: 26th Annual Conference. IEEE (Education Society) Staff. Ed. by IEEE, Institute of Electrical & Electronics Engine. LC 76-640910. 1000p. 1996. pap. text 170.00 (*0-7803-3348-9*, 96CH35946); lib. bdg. 170.00 (*0-7803-3349-7*, 96CB35946); fiche 170.00 (*0-7803-3350-0*, 96CM35946) Inst Electrical.

Proceedings of G. I. N. I.'s Third International Polio & Independent Living Conference, May 10-12, 1985, St. Louis, Missouri. Ed. by G. Laurie & J. Raymond. 68p. (Orig.). 1986. pap. 4.00 (*0-931301-02-5*) Gazette Intl.

Proceedings of Govoka Geometry - Topology Conference, 1993. Ed. by Selman Akbulut et al. (Illus.). 110p. (C). Date not set. pap. 20.00 (*975-403-010-3*) Intl Pr Boston.

Proceedings of Govoka Geometry - Topology Conference, 1994. Ed. by Selman Akbulut et al. (Illus.). 88p. (C). Date not set. pap. 20.00 (*975-403-023-5*) Intl Pr Boston.

Proceedings of Govoka Geometry - Topology Conference, 1995. Ed. by Selman Akbulut et al. 139p. (C). Date not set. 25.00 (*975-403-040-5*) Intl Pr Boston.

Proceedings of Govoka Geometry - Topology Conference, 1996. Ed. by Selman Akbulut et al. (Illus.). 131p. (C). Date not set. 25.00 (*975-403-071-5*) Intl Pr Boston.

Proceedings of Graduate Congress 93. Graduate Student Senate Staff. 60p. 1993. pap. write for info. (*0-9636699-0-7*) Oreg St U GSS.

Proceedings of Hawk Migration Conference IV. Ed. by Michael Harwood. LC 86-80744. (Illus.). 393p. (Orig.). 1986. pap. 29.95 (*0-938239-01-5*) Hawk Migrat.

Proceedings of HAZMACON '90, Vol. I. 298p. 1990. 5.00 (*0-317-05688-3*, P90001HAZ) Assn Bay Area.

Proceedings of HAZMACON, '93. 750p. 1993. 64.00 (*0-317-05686-7*, P93001HAZ) Assn Bay Area.

Proceedings of HAZMACON, '92. 678p. 1992. 22.00 (*0-317-05687-5*, P92001HAZ) Assn Bay Area.

Proceedings of ICHCA Canada Container Repair Seminar. ICHCA Staff. (C). 1983. 100.00 (*0-906297-39-7*, Pub. by ICHCA) St Mut.

Proceedings of ICHCA UK Conference Cargo Handling in the High Tech Age. ICHCA Staff. (C). 1986. 300.00 (*0-7855-6172-2*, Pub. by ICHCA) St Mut.

Proceedings of ICOLD Symposium on Reservoirs in River Basin Development Held 1995, Oslo, Norway: Proceedings of the ICOLD Symposium, Oslo Norway, July 6, 1995, 2 vols., Set. Ed. by Leo Santbergen & Cees-Jan Van Westen. (Illus.). 800p. 1996. 181.00 (*90-5410-559-3*, Pub. by A A Balkema) Ashgate Pub Co.

Proceedings of Indo-United States Workshop on Electronic Ceramics & Materials: A Special Issue of the Journal Ferroelectrics. Ed. by A. S. Bhalla & E. C. Subbarao. 414p. 1990. pap. text 899.00 (*2-88124-430-0*) Gordon & Breach.

Proceedings of International Conference on Allelopathy, Vols. 1 & 2. S. S. Narwal & P. Tauro. LC 96-906254. 1994. pap. 440.00 (*81-7233-132-0*, Pub. by Scientific Pubs) St Mut.

Proceedings of International Conference on Parallel Processing, 23rd Vol. 2: Software, Vol. 2. Tai. 368p. 1994. lib. bdg. 59.95 (*0-8493-2494-7*) CRC Pr.

Proceedings of International Conference on Parallell Processing, 23rd, Vol. 1. Agrawal. 336p. 1994. 59.95 (*0-8493-2493-9*) CRC Pr.

Proceedings of International Conference on Survey Measurement & Process Quality: SMPQ, April 1-4, 1995, Bristol, United Kingdom, Contributed Papers. (Illus.). (Orig.). 1996. pap. 40.00 (*1-883276-18-7*) Amer Statist.

Proceedings of International Symposium of the Qinghai-Xizang Plateau & Mountain Meteorology,March 20-24, 1984, Beijing, China. Intro. by Xu Yigang. (Illus.). 1036p. 1986. 52.50 (*0-933876-61-0*) Am Meteorological.

Proceedings of International Symposium on Advanced Topics of Quantum Physics Held in Taiyuan, Shanxi Province of China June 12-16, 1992. Ed. by J. Q. Liang et al. 493p. 1996. 59.95 (*7-03-003507-0*, Pub. by Sci Pr) Lubrecht & Cramer.

***Proceedings of International Symposium on Computers & Communications Held in Egypt, 1999.** Contrib. by IEEE Computer Society Staff. LC 99-62956. 486p. 1999. pap. 160.00 (*0-7695-0250-4*) IEEE Comp Soc.

Proceedings of International Symposium on Heavy Flavor & Electroweak Theory: August 16-19, 1995, Beijing, China. Symposium on Heavy Flavor & Electroweak Theory Sta. Ed. by Chao-Hsi Chang & Chao-Shang Huang. LC 96-17713. 320p. 1996. write for info. (*981-02-2633-0*) World Scientific Pub.

Proceedings of International Symposium on Management & Development of Red Soils in Asia & Pacific Region Held in Nanjing, China on December 3-15, 1990. Ed. by Gong Zitong. 371p. 1996. 48.00 (*7-03-003506-2*, Pub. by Sci Pr) Lubrecht & Cramer.

Proceedings of International Symposium on the Chemical Mediators on Skin Inflammation, Sendai, August 1988. Ed. by H. Tagami & Tosio Kato. (Journal: Dermatologica: Vol. 179, Suppl. 1, 1989). (Illus.). vi, 146p. 1989. pap. 66.25 (*3-8055-5065-0*) S Karger.

Proceedings of Laser & Electron Beam in Welding, Cutting & Surface Treatment - State of the Art 1991. 322p. 1991. 70.00 (*0-939997-12-6*) Bakish Mat.

Proceedings of Logo Mathematics Education Conference. Liddy Nevile & Richard Noss. (C). 1992. pap. 70.00 (*0-86431-132-X*, Pub. by Aust Council Educ Res) St Mut.

Proceedings of Lunar & Planetary Science, Vol. 21. Ed. by Graham Ryder & Virgil L. Sharpton. (Illus.). 738p. 1991. 50.00 (*0-942862-05-8*) Lunar & Planet Inst.

Proceedings of Lunar & Planetary Science, Vol. 22. Ed. by Graham Ryder & Virgil L. Sharpton. (Illus.). 481p. (C). 1992. 50.00 (*0-685-51793-4*) Lunar & Planet Inst.

Proceedings of Monroe Conference. 1988. 49.00 (*0-685-38310-5*) Pan Am Intl Ozone.

Proceedings of National Symposium on Goat Meat Production & Marketing. 230p. (C). 1991. 25.00 (*1-880667-00-2*) Lang U Agri Res & Ext.

Proceedings of NCMEC III '95: The 3rd National Concrete & Masonry Engineering Conference, San Francisco, June 1995, Vol. I. 1128p. 1995. 90.00 (*0-89312-136-3*, SR297D) Portland Cement.

Proceedings of Neural, Parallel & Scientific Computations, Vol. 1. Ed. by S. K. Aityan et al. (Illus.). 520p. (Orig.). (C). 1995. 100.00 (*0-9640398-9-3*); pap. 75.00 (*0-9640398-8-5*) Dynamic Pubs.

Proceedings of 1988 International Symposium on Data on Aging: PHS 91-1482. (Vital & Health Statistics Ser.: Series 5: No. 6). 269p. 1991. 13.00 (*0-685-61572-3*, 017-022-01139-5) Natl Ctr Health Stats.

Proceedings of 1995 Pacific Workshop on Distributed Multimedia Systems. Ed. by Knowledge Systems Institute Staff. (Illus.). 202p. 1995. pap. 40.00 (*0-9641699-1-6*) Knowldge Systs.

Proceedings of 1996 ASME Fluids Engineering Division Summer Meeting, San Diego, California, July 7-11, 1996, Vol. 2. (FED Ser.: Vol. 237). 904p. 1996. 200.00 (*0-7918-1792-X*, H01073) ASME Pr.

Proceedings of 1996 ASME Fluids Engineering Division Summer Meeting, San Diego, California, July 7-11, 1996, Vol. 3. (FED Ser.: Vol. 238). 716p. 1996. 180.00 (*0-7918-1793-8*, H01074) ASME Pr.

Proceedings of 1996 ASME Fluids Engineering Divison Summer Meeting, San Diego, California, July 7-11, 1996, Vol. 4. (FED Ser.: Vol. 239). 672p. 1996. 180.00 (*0-7918-1794-6*, H01075) ASME Pr.

Proceedings of 1996 Japan - U. S. A. Flexible Automation Conference, Boston, Massachusetts, July 7-10, 1996, Vols. 1 & 2. LC 96-84861. 1588p. 1996. 350.00 (*0-7918-1231-6*, IX0394) ASME Pr.

Proceedings of 1992 European Simulation Symposium (Dresden) Ed. by Krug & Lehmann. 620p. 1992. pap. 100.00 (*1-56555-009-9*, ESS-92) Soc Computer Sim.

Proceedings of Ninth Ozone World Congress NY, 3 vols., Set. 1989. 125.00 (*0-685-38305-9*) Pan Am Intl Ozone.

Proceedings of Ninth Ozone World Congress NY, 3 vols., Vol. 1. 1989. 65.00 (*0-685-38306-7*) Pan Am Intl Ozone.

Proceedings of Ninth Ozone World Congress NY, 3 vols., Vol. 2. 1989. 65.00 (*0-685-38307-5*) Pan Am Intl Ozone.

Proceedings of Ninth Ozone World Congress NY, 3 vols., Vol. 3. 1989. 50.00 (*0-685-38308-3*) Pan Am Intl Ozone.

Proceedings of Ophthalmic Technologies III: 16-18 January 1992, Los Angeles, California. Jean-Marie Parel et al. LC 93-83345. xii, 374 p. 1993. write for info. (*0-8194-1104-3*) SPIE.

Proceedings of Optics & Imaging in the Information Age. 1997. pap. 75.00 (*0-89208-201-1*) Soc Imaging Sci & Tech.

Proceedings of Papers Presented at Enetwork, Held in 1993, Hague, The Netherlands. 1996. 125.00 (*0-614-18585-8*, E93NPR) Info Gatekeepers.

Proceedings of Papers Presented at ISDN Conference Held in 1981, Amsterdam, The Netherlands, Europe. 1996. 50.00 (*0-614-18522-X*, E881PR) Info Gatekeepers.

Proceedings of Papers Presented at Optical Access Networks Held in 1993, Hague, The Netherlands. 1996. 125.00 (*0-614-18586-6*, E93DPR) Info Gatekeepers.

Proceedings of Papers Presented at RUSSAT Held in 1993, St. Petersburg, Russia. 1996. 195.00 (*0-614-18581-5*, R93SAT) Info Gatekeepers.

Proceedings of Papers Presented at the European Fiber Optics & Communications Conference Held in 1991, Paris, France. 1996. 145.00 (*0-614-18575-0*, E92EPR) Info Gatekeepers.

Proceedings of Papers Presented at the Australian Conference on Optical Fiber Technology Conference Held in 1987, Australia. 1996. 100.00 (*0-614-18536-X*, ACOF87) Info Gatekeepers.

Proceedings of Papers Presented at the Australian Conference on Optical Fiber Technology Held in 1988, Australia. 1996. 100.00 (*0-614-18542-4*, ACOF88) Info Gatekeepers.

Proceedings of Papers Presented at the Australian Conference on Optical Fiber Technology Held in 1989, Australia. 1996. 100.00 (*0-614-18549-1*, ACOF89) Info Gatekeepers.

Proceedings of Papers Presented at the Australian Conference on Optical Fiber Technology Held in 1990, Sydney, Australia. 1996. 195.00 (*0-614-18565-3*, ACOF90) Info Gatekeepers.

P

Proceedings of Papers Presented at the Australian Conference on Optical Fiber Technology Held in 1991, Sydney, Australia. 1996. 125.00 (*0-614-18570-X*, ACOF91); 125.00 (*0-614-18574-2*, ACOF92) Info Gatekeepers.

Proceedings of Papers Presented at the Australian Conference on Optical Fiber Technology Held 1986, Australia. 1996. 75.00 (*0-614-18531-9*, ACOF86) Info Gatekeepers.

Proceedings of Papers Presented at the Autralian Conference on Optical Fiber Technology Held in 1984, Australia. 1996. 50.00 (*0-614-18526-2*, ACOF84) Info Gatekeepers.

Proceedings of Papers Presented at the Broadband Conference Held, 1990, Baltimore, Maryland. 1996. 125.00 (*0-614-18562-9*, F90PRC) Info Gatekeepers.

Proceedings of Papers Presented at the China Fibercom Held in 1994. 1996. 195.00 (*0-614-18591-2*, CF94PR) Info Gatekeepers.

Proceedings of Papers Presented at the European Conference on Integrated Optics Held in 1993. 1996. 195.00 (*0-614-18588-2*, ECIO93) Info Gatekeepers.

Proceedings of Papers Presented at the European Conference on Integrated Optics Held in 1995. 1996. 195.00 (*0-614-18598-X*, ECIO95) Info Gatekeepers.

Proceedings of Papers Presented at the European Conference on Optical Communications Held in 1987, Helsinki, Finland. 1996. 195.00 (*0-614-18539-4*, ECOC87) Info Gatekeepers.

Proceedings of Papers Presented at the European Conference on Optical Communications Held in 1990, Amsterdam, The Netherlands. 1996. 195.00 (*0-614-18564-5*, ECOC90) Info Gatekeepers.

Proceedings of Papers Presented at the European Conference on Optical Communications Held in 1991, Berlin. 1996. 195.00 (*0-614-18577-7*, ECOC92) Info Gatekeepers.

Proceedings of Papers Presented at the European Conference on Optical Communications Held in 1991, France. 1996. 195.00 (*0-614-18573-4*, ECOC91) Info Gatekeepers.

Proceedings of Papers Presented at the European Conference on Optical Communications Held in 1993, Switzerland. 1996. 195.00 (*0-614-18590-4*, ECOC93) Info Gatekeepers.

Proceedings of Papers Presented at the European Conference on Optical Communications Held in 1994. 1996. 195.00 (*0-614-18596-3*, ECOC94) Info Gatekeepers.

Proceedings of Papers Presented at the European Conference on Optical Communications Held 1986, Barcelona, Spain. 1996. 195.00 (*0-614-18532-7*, ECOC85) Info Gatekeepers.

Proceedings of Papers Presented at the European Fiber Optic & Communications Conference Held in 1984, Las Vegas, Nevada. 1996. 75.00 (*0-614-18525-4*, 133F10) Info Gatekeepers.

Proceedings of Papers Presented at the European Fiber Optics & Communications Conference Held in 1982, Los Angeles, CA. 1996. 75.00 (*0-614-18523-8*, 133F08) Info Gatekeepers.

Proceedings of Papers Presented at the European Fiber Optics & Communications Conference Held in 1985, Montreaux. 1996. 75.00 (*0-614-18529-7*, 133E11) Info Gatekeepers.

Proceedings of Papers Presented at the European Fiber Optics & Communications Conference Held in 1987, Basel, Switzerland. 1996. 100.00 (*0-614-18540-8*, 133E87) Info Gatekeepers.

Proceedings of Papers Presented at the European Fiber Optics & Communications Conference Held in 1988, Amsterdam, The Netherlands. 1996. 100.00 (*0-614-18545-9*, E88FPR) Info Gatekeepers.

Proceedings of Papers Presented at the European Fiber Optics & Communications Conference Held in 1989, Amsterdam, The Netherlands. 1996. 135.00 (*0-614-18552-1*, E89EPR) Info Gatekeepers.

Proceedings of Papers Presented at the European Fiber Optics & Communications Conference Held in 1990, Munich, Germany. 1996. 145.00 (*0-614-18559-9*, E90EPR) Info Gatekeepers.

Proceedings of Papers Presented at the European Fiber Optics & Communications Conference Held in 1991, London, England. 1996. 145.00 (*0-614-18571-8*, E91EPR) Info Gatekeepers.

Proceedings of Papers Presented at the European Fiber Optics & Communications Conference Held in 1993, Hague, The Netherlands. 1996. 125.00 (*0-614-18584-X*, E93EPR) Info Gatekeepers.

Proceedings of Papers Presented at the European Fiber Optics & Communications Conference Held 1986, Amsterdam. 1996. 100.00 (*0-614-18533-5*, 133E14) Info Gatekeepers.

Proceedings of Papers Presented at the European Local Area Networks Conference Held in 1989, Amsterdam, The Netherlands. 1996. 135.00 (*0-614-18554-8*, E89LPR) Info Gatekeepers.

Proceedings of Papers Presented at the European Local Area Networks Conference Held in 1991, London, England. 1996. 145.00 (*0-614-18572-6*, E91LPR) Info Gatekeepers.

Proceedings of Papers Presented at the European Military Fiber Optics & Communications Conference Held in 1988, Amsterdam, The Netherlands. 1996. 100.00 (*0-614-18546-7*, E88MPR) Info Gatekeepers.

Proceedings of Papers Presented at the European Military Fiber Optics & Communications Conference Held in 1989, Amsterdam, The Netherlands. 1996. 135.00 (*0-614-18553-X*, E89MPR) Info Gatekeepers.

Proceedings of Papers Presented at the European Military Fiber Optics & Communications Conference Held in 1990, Munich, Germany. 1996. 145.00 (*0-614-18561-0*, E90MPR) Info Gatekeepers.

Proceedings of Papers Presented at the Fiber Optics & Communications/Local Area Network Conference Held in 1988, Atlanta, Georgia. 1996. 100.00 (*0-614-18547-5*, 133F88) Info Gatekeepers.

Proceedings of Papers Presented at the Fiber Optics & Communications/Local Area Networks Conference Held in 1986, Orlando, Florida. 1996. 100.00 (*0-614-18535-1*, 133F15) Info Gatekeepers.

Proceedings of Papers Presented at the Fiber Optics & Communications/Local Area Networks Conference Held in 1987, Anaheim, California. 1996. 100.00 (*0-614-18541-6*, 133F87) Info Gatekeepers.

Proceedings of Papers Presented at the Fiber Optics for Developing Countries Conference Held in 1985, Ljubliana, Yugoslavia. 1996. 75.00 (*0-614-18530-0*, 133D13) Info Gatekeepers.

Proceedings of Papers Presented at the ICOC/European Conference on Optical Communications Held in 1985, Venice, Italy. 1996. 195.00 (*0-614-18528-9*, ECOC85) Info Gatekeepers.

Proceedings of Papers Presented at the International Plastic Optical Fiber Conference Held in 1992, Paris, France. 1996. 125.00 (*0-614-18579-3*, P92PRC) Info Gatekeepers.

Proceedings of Papers Presented at the International Plastic Optical Fiber Conference Held in 1993, Hague, The Netherlands. 1996. 125.00 (*0-614-18587-4*, P93PPR) Info Gatekeepers.

Proceedings of Papers Presented at the International Soviet Fibre Optics Conference Held in 1993, St. Petersburgh, Russia. 1996. 195.00 (*0-614-18582-3*, IS93PC) Info Gatekeepers.

Proceedings of Papers Presented at the IOOC/European Conference on Optical Communications Held in 1989, Gothenburg, Sweden. 1996. 195.00 (*0-614-18551-3*, ECOC89) Info Gatekeepers.

Proceedings of Papers Presented at the ISDN Conference Held in 1986, Basel, Switzerland. 1996. 50.00 (*0-614-18534-3*, 126E86) Info Gatekeepers.

Proceedings of Papers Presented at the ISDN Conference Held in 1987, in the U. S. 1996. 50.00 (*0-614-18537-8*, 126187) Info Gatekeepers.

Proceedings of Papers Presented at the ISDN Conference Held in 1988, U. S. 1996. 75.00 (*0-614-18543-2*, 126188) Info Gatekeepers.

Proceedings of Papers Presented at the ISDN Conference Held in 1989. 1996. 100.00 (*0-614-18550-5*, 189PRC) Info Gatekeepers.

Proceedings of Papers Presented at the ISDN Conference Held in 1989, U. S. 1996. 125.00 (*0-614-18555-6*, 190PRC) Info Gatekeepers.

Proceedings of Papers Presented at the ISDN Conference Held in 1991, U. S. 1996. 125.00 (*0-614-18569-6*, 191PRC) Info Gatekeepers.

Proceedings of Papers Presented at the ISDN Conference Held in 1993, U. S. 1996. 125.00 (*0-614-18580-7*, I92PRC) Info Gatekeepers.

Proceedings of Papers Presented at the Local Area Networks Conference Held in 1990, Munich, Germany. 1996. 145.00 (*0-614-18560-2*, E90LPR) Info Gatekeepers.

Proceedings of Papers Presented at the Low Cost FDOI Conference Held in 1992, Boston, Massachusetts. 1996. 250.00 (*0-614-18578-5*, LCEP92) Info Gatekeepers.

Proceedings of Papers Presented at the Military Fiber Optics & Communications Conference Held in 1987, Washington, D. C. 1996. 100.00 (*0-614-18538-6*, 133M87) Info Gatekeepers.

Proceedings of Papers Presented at the Military Fiber Optics & Communications Conference Held in 1988, Washington, D. C. 1996. 100.00 (*0-614-18544-0*, 133M88) Info Gatekeepers.

Proceedings of Papers Presented at the Military Fiber Optics & Communications Conference Held in 1988, West Los Angeles, California. 1996. 100.00 (*0-614-18548-3*, MW88PR) Info Gatekeepers.

Proceedings of Papers Presented at the Military Fiber Optics & Communications Conference Held in 1989, Washington, D. C. 1996. 125.00 (*0-614-18557-2*, M89PRC) Info Gatekeepers.

Proceedings of Papers Presented at the Military Fiber Optics & Communications Conference Held in 1989, West Los Angeles, California. 1996. 250.00 (*0-614-18558-0*, MW89PC) Info Gatekeepers.

Proceedings of Papers Presented at the Optical Fiber Sensors Conference Held in 1990, Sydney, Australia. 1996. 195.00 (*0-614-18566-1*, 090PRC) Info Gatekeepers.

Proceedings of Papers Presented at the Optical Fibers Sensors Conference Held in 1993, Florence, Italy. 1996. 195.00 (*0-614-18589-0*, 093PRC) Info Gatekeepers.

Proceedings of Papers Presented at the Plastic Fiber Sensors Conference Held in 1995. 1996. 125.00 (*0-614-18599-8*, P95PRC) Info Gatekeepers.

Proceedings of Papers Presented at the Plastic Optical Fiber Conference Held in 1991, San Diego, California. 1996. 125.00 (*0-614-18568-8*, P91PRC) Info Gatekeepers.

Proceedings of Papers Presented at the Plastic Optical Fiber Conference Held in 1994. 1996. 125.00 (*0-614-18595-5*, P94PRC) Info Gatekeepers.

Proceedings of Papers Presented at the Plastic Optical Fibers (POF-90) Conference Held in 1990, Boston, Massachusetts. 1996. 125.00 (*0-614-18563-7*, P90PRC) Info Gatekeepers.

Proceedings of Papers Presented at the Russian Telecom Held in 1994. 1996. 195.00 (*0-614-18597-1*, R94PRC) Info Gatekeepers.

Proceedings of Papers Presented at the Third International Meeting on Chem Sensors Held in 1990, Cleveland, Ohio. 1996. 145.00 (*0-614-18567-X*, C90PRC) Info Gatekeepers.

Proceedings of Papers Presented at the 1985 Australian Conference on Optical Fiber Technology Held in 1985, Australia. 1996. 75.00 (*0-614-18527-0*, ACOF85) Info Gatekeepers.

Proceedings of Papers Presented the the European Fiber Optics & Communications Conference Held in 1983, Atlantic City, NJ. 1996. 75.00 (*0-614-18524-6*, 133F09) Info Gatekeepers.

Proceedings of PART '97: The 4th Australasian Conference on Parallel & Real-Time Systems: Newcastle, New South Wales, Australia, 29-30 November, 1997. Ed. by N. Sharda & A. Tam. 470p. 1998. pap. 59.00 (*981-3083-62-X*, Pub. by Spr-Verlag) Spr-Verlag.

Proceedings of Prime Farmland Interactive Forum. Ed. by Charles L. Hooks et al. LC 98-33648. (Illus.). 300p. 1998. lib. bdg. write for info. (*1-885189-04-4*) Coal Res Ctr.

Proceedings of Rehabilitation Gazette's Second International Post-Polio Conference & Symposium on Living Independently with Severe Disability. Ed. by G. Laurie & J. Raymond. 74p. (Orig.). 1984. pap. 4.00 (*0-931301-01-7*) Gazette Intl.

Proceedings of ReX'96: The Third International Conference on Recrystallization & Related Phenomena. T. R. McNelley et al. (Illus.). 720p. 1997. text 125.00 (*0-9645943-6-6*, ReX'96) MIAS.

Proceedings of Second European Simulation Congress. Ed. by VanSteenkiste. 820p. 1986. pap. 80.00 (*0-911801-10-3*, EURO-86) Soc Computer Sim.

Proceedings of 2nd European Workshop on Periodontology: Chemicals in Periodontics. Ed. by Niklaus P. Lang et al. (Illus.). 428p. 1997. pap. 68.00 (*3-87652-423-7*) Quint Pub Co.

Proceedings of Second International Conference on Pervaporation Processes in the Chemical Industry. R. Bakish. (Illus.). 210p. 1987. pap. 100.00 (*0-939997-01-0*) Bakish Mat.

Proceedings of Second International Conference on Vacuum Web Coating. 218p. 1988. 70.00 (*0-939997-04-5*) Bakish Mat.

Proceedings of Second Symposium on Heavy Ion Physics & Its Applications. 300p. 1996. lib. bdg. 56.00 (*981-02-2809-0*) World Scientific Pub.

Proceedings of Seminar on Stochastic Analysis, Random Fields & Applications Held 1993, Ascona, Switzerland: Centro Stefano Francini, Ascona, 1993. Ed. by Erwin Bolthausen et al. LC 95-21846. (Progress in Probability Ser.: Vol. 36). 391p. 1995. 132.00 (*0-8176-5241-8*) Birkhauser.

Proceedings of Seventh International Conference on Pervaporation Processes in the Chemical Industry. 1995. 120.00 (*0-939997-18-5*) Bakish Mat.

Proceedings of Seventh International Conference on Vacuum Web Coating. 1993. 70.00 (*0-939997-15-0*) Bakish Mat.

Proceedings of 79th Convention, IAFWA, 1989. Ed. by Kenneth J. Sabol. 421p. 1993. lib. bdg. 20.00 (*0-614-06187-3*) IAFWA.

Proceedings of Sixth International Conference on Pervaporation Processes in the Chemical Industry. 580p. 1992. 120.00 (*0-939997-13-4*) Bakish Mat.

Proceedings of 6th International Vacuum Web Coating. 280p. 1993. 70.00 (*0-939997-14-2*) Bakish Mat.

Proceedings of Static & Dynamic Light Scattering in Medicine & Biology: 21-22 January 1993, Los Angeles, California. Ralph Nossal et al. LC 93-83352. (SPIE Proceedings Ser.). ix, 366p. 1993. write for info. (*0-8194-1111-6*) SPIE.

Proceedings of Summer Computer Simulation Conference, 1988. 994p. 1988. 100.00 (*0-911801-38-3*, SCSC-88) Soc Computer Sim.

Proceedings of Summer Computer Simulation Conference, 1989: Austin, TX, 1989. Ed. by Joe K. Clema. 942p. 1989. 120.00 (*0-911801-57-X*, SCSC-89) Soc Computer Sim.

Proceedings of Symposium on Paddy Soil Symposium on Paddy Soil Staff & Chung-Kuo Hshueh-Yhuan. LC 82-198304. ix, 864 p. 1981. write for info. (*3-540-10900-5*) Spr-Verlag.

Proceedings of TAPPI, Georgia World Congress Center, Atlanta, GA, March 2-5: Annual Meeting, 1986. Technical Association of the Pulp & Paper Industry. LC TS1080.T3. 124p. pap. 38.50 (*0-8357-5616-5*, 202917900059) Bks Demand.

***Proceedings of 10th Annual UCLA Conference.** K. Jones-Bley et al. (Journal of Indo-European Studies Monographs: Vol. 32). 289p. (C). 1999. pap. 46.00 (*0-941694-70-4*) Inst Study Man.

Proceedings of 10th International Conference on Vacuum Web Coating. Ed. by R. Bakish. (Proceedings of the Internaitonal Conferences on Vacuum Web Coating Ser.: Vol. 10). (Illus.). 325p. (Orig.). (C). 1997. pap. write for info. (*0-939997-20-7*) Bakish Mat.

Proceedings of the Academy for Jewish Philosophy. Ed. by Norbert M. Samuelson. (Studies in Judaism). 426p. (C). 1992. lib. bdg. 46.75 (*0-8191-7925-6*) U Pr of Amer.

Proceedings of the ACM SIGDOC 84, Third International Conference on Systems Documentation: Papers Presented at the Conference in Mexico City, 16-18 May 1984. International Conference on Systems Documentation (1982-1989) Staff et al. LC 87-107072. 113 p. 1985. write for info. (*0-89791-148-2*) Assn Compu Machinery.

Proceedings of the ACM Sigplan '91 Conference on Programming Language Design & Implementation, Toronto, Ontario, Canada, June 26-28, 1991 ACM SIGPLAN Conference on Programming Language Design & Implementation Staff & ACM Special Interest Group on Programming Language Staff. LC 92-221908. (Sigplan Notices Ser.). viii, 356 p. 1991. 20.00 (*0-89791-428-7*) Assn Compu Machinery.

Proceedings of the ACM Sigplan '92 Conference on Programming Language Design & Implementation, San Francisco, California, June 17-19, 1992 ACM SIGPLAN Conference on Programming Language Design & Implementation Staff & ACM Special Interest Group in Programming Languages Staff. LC 93-101671. (Sigplan Notices Ser.). viii, 352 p. 1992. write for info. (*0-89791-476-7*) Assn Compu Machinery.

Proceedings of the Adams Memorial Symposium on Algebraic Topology, Vol. 1. Ed. by Nigel Ray & Grant Walker. (London Mathematical Society Lecture Note Ser.: No. 175). (Illus.). 316p. (C). 1992. pap. text 49.95 (*0-521-42074-1*) Cambridge U Pr.

Proceedings of the Adams Memorial Symposium on Algebraic Topology, Vol. 2. Ed. by Nigel Ray & Grant Walker. (London Mathematical Society Lecture Note Ser.: No. 176). (Illus.). 329p. (C). 1992. pap. text 49.95 (*0-521-42153-5*) Cambridge U Pr.

Proceedings of the Advanced Medicine Symposia, 10th, 1974. Advanced Medicine Symposia Staff & Royal College of Physicians Staff. Ed. by J. G. Ledingham. (Illus.). 1974. pap. text 50.00 (*0-7855-7130-2*) St Mut.

Proceedings of the Advanced Medicine Symposia, 11th, 1975. Advanced Medicine Symposia Staff & Royal College of Physicians Staff. Ed. by A. F. Lant. (Illus.). 1975. pap. text 40.00 (*0-7855-7131-0*) St Mut.

Proceedings of the Advanced Medicine Symposia, 7th, 1971. Advanced Medicine Symposia Staff. Ed. by I. A. Boucher. 1971. pap. text 30.00 (*0-7855-7129-9*) St Mut.

Proceedings of the Advisory Council of the State of Virginia, April 21-June 19, 1861. Ed. by James I. Robertson, Jr. LC 76-27470. (Illus.). xxiv, 182p. 1977. 15.00 (*0-88490-007-X*) Library of VA.

Proceedings of the Aerospace Testing Seminar, 6th, Los Angeles, California, 11-13 March, 1981. Aerospace Testing Seminar Staff. LC 62-38584. 261p. reprint ed. pap. 81.00 (*0-7837-1301-0*, 204144200020) Bks Demand.

Proceedings of the Aerospace Testing Seminar, 7th, Los Angeles, California, 13-15 October 1982. Aerospace Testing Seminar Staff. LC 62-38584. 185p. reprint ed. pap. 57.40 (*0-7837-1302-9*, 204144300020) Bks Demand.

Proceedings of the American Academy of Arts & Letters. American Academy of Arts & Letters Staff. 1996. 15.00 (*0-915974-41-X*) Am Acad Arts.

Proceedings of the American Academy of Arts & Letters, Vol. 46. American Academy of Arts & Letters Staff. 1997. 15.00 (*0-915974-40-1*) Am Acad Arts.

Proceedings of the American Academy of Arts & Letters, Vol. 47. American Academy of Arts & Letters Staff. 1997. 15.00 (*0-915974-42-8*) Am Acad Arts.

Proceedings of the American Academy of Arts & Letters, Vol. 48. American Academy of Arts & Letters Staff. 1998. 15.00 (*0-915974-43-6*) Am Acad Arts.

Proceedings of the American Anti-Slavery Society at Its Third Decade. Incl. Vol. 1. American Anti-Slavery Society Staff. LC 77-97417. lib. bdg. 155.00 (*0-8371-5242-9*, AAT/, Greenwood Pr); Vol. 2. American Anti-Slavery Society Staff. LC 77-97417. lib. bdg. 155.00 (*0-8371-5243-7*, AAU/, Greenwood Pr); Vol. 3. American Anti-Slavery Society Staff. LC 77-97417. lib. bdg. 155.00 (*0-8371-5244-5*, AAV/, Greenwood Pr); Vol. 4. American Anti-Slavery Society Staff. LC 77-97417. lib. bdg. 155.00 (*0-8371-5245-3*, AAW/, Greenwood Pr); Vol. 5. American Anti-Slavery Society Staff. LC 77-97417. lib. bdg. 155.00 (*0-8371-5246-1*, AAX/, Greenwood Pr); Vol. 6. American Anti-Slavery Society Staff. LC 77-97417. lib. bdg. 155.00 (*0-8371-5247-X*, AAY/, Greenwood Pr); Vol. 7. American Anti-Slavery Society Staff. LC 77-97417. lib. bdg. 155.00 (*0-8371-5248-8*, AAZ/, Greenwood Pr); Vol. 8. American Anti-Slavery Society Staff. LC 77-97417. lib. bdg. 155.00 (*0-8371-5249-6*, AAA/, Greenwood Pr); Vol. 9. American Anti-Slavery Society Staff. LC 77-97417. lib. bdg. 155.00 (*0-8371-5250-X*, AAB/, Greenwood Pr); Vol. 10. American Anti-Slavery Society Staff. LC 77-97417. lib. bdg. 155.00 (*0-8371-5251-8*, AAC/, Greenwood Pr); Vol. 11. American Anti-Slavery Society Staff. LC 77-97417. lib. bdg. 155.00 (*0-8371-5252-6*, AAD/, Greenwood Pr); Vol. 12. American Anti-Slavery Society Staff. LC 77-97417. lib. bdg. 155.00 (*0-8371-5253-4*, AAE/, Greenwood Pr); Vol. 13. LC 77-97417. lib. bdg. 155.00 (*0-8371-5254-2*, AAF/); Vol. 14. LC 77-97417. lib. bdg. 155.00 (*0-8371-5255-0*, AAG/); Vol. 15. LC 77-97417. lib. bdg. 155.00 (*0-8371-5256-9*, AAH/); Vol. 16. LC 77-97417. lib. bdg. 155.00 (*0-8371-5257-7*, AAI/); Vol. 17. LC 77-97417. lib. bdg. 155.00 (*0-8371-5258-5*, AAJ/); Vol. 18. LC 77-97417. lib. bdg. 155.00 (*0-8371-5259-3*, AAK/); Vol. 19. LC 77-97417. lib. bdg. 155.00 (*0-8371-5260-7*, AAL/); Vol. 20. LC 77-97417. lib. bdg. 155.00 (*0-8371-5261-5*, AAM/); LC 77-97417. 22.50 (*0-8371-2725-4*, AAS&, Greenwood Pr) Greenwood.

Proceedings of the American Anti-Slavery Society at Its Third Decade. American Anti-Slavery Society Staff. LC 79-82166. (Anti-Slavery Crusade in America Ser.). 1970. reprint ed. 11.95 (*0-405-00606-3*) Ayer.

Proceedings of the American Association for the Study & Cure of Inebriates: 1870 to 1875. American Association for the Study & Cure of Inebr. Ed. by Gerald N. Grob. LC 80-1271. (Addiction in America Ser.). 1981. lib. bdg. 49.95 (*0-405-13565-3*) Ayer.

P

An Asterisk (*) at the beginning of an entry indicates that the title is appearing for the first time.

Proceedings of the American Association of University Instructors in Accounting, 3 vols. American Association of University Instructors in. Ed. by Richard P. Brief. LC 80-1468. (Dimensions of Accounting Theory & Practice Ser.). 1980. lib. bdg. 125.95 (*0-405-13498-3*) Ayer.

Proceedings of the Anasazi Symposium. Ed. by Jack Smith. LC 83-63307. 200p. 1983. pap. write for info. (*0-937062-07-3*) Mesa Verde Museum.

Proceedings of the Annual Automotive Technology Development Contractors' Coordination Meeting 1994. 674p. 1995. pap. 39.00 (*1-56091-654-0*, P289) Soc Auto Engineers.

Proceedings of the Annual Conference on Genetic Programming. Ed. by John Koza. 920p. (C). 1998. pap. text 95.00 (*1-55860-548-7*) Morgan Kaufmann.

Proceedings of the Annual Congress of the National Prison Association of the United States. National Prison Association Staff. LC 77-154586. (Police in America Ser.). 1971. reprint ed. 16.95 (*0-405-03377-X*) Ayer.

Proceedings of the Annual Conventions of the International Association of Chiefs of Police, 1893-1930, 5 vols., Set. International Association of Chiefs of Police Staf. LC 75-154599. 1971. reprint ed. 270.00 (*0-405-03398-2*) Ayer.

Proceedings of the Annual ESRI User Conference, 13th, 5 vols., Set. (Orig.). 1993. 75.00 (*1-879102-13-7*) ESR Inst.

Proceedings of the Annual ESRI User Conference, 13th, Vol. I. 608p. (Orig.). 1993. write for info. (*1-879102-10-2*) ESR Inst.

Proceedings of the Annual ESRI User Conference, 13th, Vol. I: Workshop. 486p. (Orig.). 1993. write for info. (*1-879102-15-3*) ESR Inst.

Proceedings of the Annual ESRI User Conference, 13th, Vol. II. 622p. (Orig.). 1993. write for info. (*1-879102-11-0*); write for info. (*1-879102-16-1*) ESR Inst.

Proceedings of the Annual ESRI User Conference, 13th, Vol. III. 514p. (Orig.). 1993. write for info. (*1-879102-12-9*) ESR Inst.

Proceedings of the Annual ISS Electric Furnace Conference, 1996, Vol. 54. 616p. 1996. 90.00 (*1-886362-16-5*, P-PC98/029) Iron & Steel.

Proceedings of the Annual ISS Ironmaking Conference, 1997, Vol. 56. 792p. 1997. 90.00 (*1-886362-23-8*, P-PC98/056) Iron & Steel.

Proceedings of the Annual ISS Mechanical Working & Steel Processing Conference, 1996, Vol. XXXIV. 672p. 1996. 110.00 (*1-886362-15-7*, P-PC98/039) Iron & Steel.

Proceedings of the Annual ISS Steelmaking Conference, 1997, Vol. 80. 724p. 1997. 90.00 (*1-886362-24-6*, P-PC98/051) Iron & Steel.

Proceedings of the Annual Meeting of the International Continence Society, 6th, Antwerp, Sept. 1976. Annual Meeting of the International Continence Soc. Ed. by B. Coolsaet. (Urologia Internationalis Ser.: Vol. 33, No. 1-3). 1978. pap. 64.50 (*3-8055-2898-1*) S Karger.

***Proceedings of the Appalachian Biography Symposium.** Ed. by Ralph P. Eckerlin. (Special Publications: Vol. 7). (Illus.). 258p. 1999. pap. 40.00 (*1-884549-10-1*) VA Mus Natl Hist.

Proceedings of the Applied Continuum Mechanics Symposium, Vienna, 1974. Applied Continuum Mechanics Symposium Staff. Ed. by J. L. Zeman & Franz Ziegler. LC 74-12227. (Illus.). vii, 221p. 1974. 33.00 (*0-387-81260-1*) Spr-Verlag.

***Proceedings of the Aquaculture Species Genome Mapping Workshop: May 18-19, 1997, University of Massachusetts Dartmouth, North Dartmouth, Massachusetts.** Ed. by Acacia Alcivar-Warren et al. (NRAES Ser.: Vol. 124). 85p. 1999. pap. text 12.00 (*0-935817-46-8*) NRAES.

Proceedings of the ARMA International Annual Conference, 39th (Toronto) ARMA Conference Speakers Staff. 906p. 1994. pap. 30.00 (*0-933887-50-7*, A4579) ARMA Intl.

Proceedings of the ARMA International 40th Annual Conference (Nashville) ARMA Conference Speakers Staff. 582p. 1995. pap. 30.00 (*0-933887-55-8*, A4582) ARMA Intl.

Proceedings of the Arthur Purdy Stout Society Centennial Symposium on Neoplasia. Arthur Purdy Stout Society Centennial Symposium on. Ed. by Stephen S. Sternberg. LC RD0057.. (American Journal of Surgical Pathology Ser.: Vol. 10). (Illus.). 119p. 1986. reprint ed. pap. 36.90 (*0-608-00663-7*, 206121600007) Bks Demand.

Proceedings of the Artificial Ventilation Symposium, Paris, 1969. Artificial Ventilation Symposium Staff. Ed. by A. Minkowski et al. (Biology of the Neonate Ser.: Vol. 16, No. 1-3). 1970. pap. 52.25 (*3-8055-0755-0*) S Karger.

Proceedings of the Asian Mathematical Conference, 1995. Ed. by S. Tangmanee & E. Schulz. LC 98-161665. 600p. 1997. text 98.00 (*981-02-3225-X*) World Scientific Pub.

Proceedings of the ASME Dynamic Systems & Control Division Vol. 57: International Mechanical Engineering Congress & Exposition - Proceedings of the ASME Dynamic Systems & Control Division, 2 vols., Set, Vols. 1 & 2. Ed. by T. E. Alberts. LC 95-81282. (1995 ASME International Mechanical Engineering Congress & Exposition Ser.: DSC-Vol. 57). 1120p. 1995. 350.00 (*0-7918-1746-6*, H01025) ASME.

Proceedings of the ASME Fluids Engineering Division: Proceedings of the ASME International Mechanical Engineering Congress & Exposition, 1995, San Francisco, CA. Ed. by Frederick J. Moody et al. LC 95-81062. (1995 ASME International Mechanical Engineering Congress & Exposition Ser.: FED-Vol. 234). 328p. 1995. 96.00 (*0-7918-1758-X*, H01040) ASME.

Proceedings of the ASME Heat Transfer & Fluids Engineering Divisions Vol. 321-233: Proceedings of the ASME International Mechanical Engineering Congress & Exposition, 1995, San Francisco, CA. Ed. by J. W. Hoyt et al. LC 95-81063. (1995 International Mechanical Engineering Congress & Exposition Ser.: HTD-Vol. 321/FED-Vol. 233). 760p. 1995. 190.00 (*0-7918-1755-5*, H01037) ASME.

Proceedings of the ASME Heat Transfer Division, Vol. 1. (HTD Ser.: Vol. 332). 248p. 1996. 96.00 (*0-7918-1519-6*, G01014) ASME Pr.

Proceedings of the ASME Heat Transfer Division, Vol. 2. (HTD Ser.: Vol. 333). 388p. 1996. 110.00 (*0-7918-1520-X*, G01015) ASME Pr.

Proceedings of the ASME Heat Transfer Division, Vol. 3. (HTD Ser.: Vol. 334). 384p. 1996. 110.00 (*0-7918-1521-8*, G01016) ASME Pr.

Proceedings of the ASME Heat Transfer Division Vol. 3, Ed. by M. Erol Ulucakli et al. LC 97-76718. (HTD Ser.: Vol. 353). 373p. 1997. pap. 140.00 (*0-7918-1842-X*, QC320) ASME Pr.

Proceedings of the ASME Materials Division Vol. 69: Proceedings of the ASME International Mechanical Engineering Congress & Exposition, 1995, San Francisco, CA, 2 vols., Set, Vols. 1 & 2. Ed. by N. R. Sottos et al. LC 95-81061. (1995 International Mechanical Engineering Congress & Exposition Ser.: MD-Vol. 69). 1282p. 1995. 350.00 (*0-7918-1759-8*, H01041) ASME.

Proceedings of the ASME Noise Control & Acoustics Division Vol. 21: Proceedings of the ASME International Mechanical Engineering Congress & Exposition, 1995, San Francisco, CA. Ed. by R. C. Marboe et al. LC 95-81064. (1995 International Mechanical Engineering Congress & Exposition Ser.: NCA-Vol. 21). 160p. 1995. 72.00 (*0-7918-1757-1*, H01039) ASME.

***Proceedings of the ASP-DAC'98: Asia & South Pacific Design Automation Conference 1998: February 10-13, 1998, Pacifico Yokahama, Yokohama, Japan.** Asia & South Pacific Design Automation Conference Staff & Denshi Jeoheo Tseushin Gakkai (Japan) Staff. LC 97-80907. xxxvii, 506 p. 1998. write for info. (*0-7803-4427-8*) IEEE Standards.

Proceedings of the Assembly of the Lower Counties on the Delaware, 1770-1776: The Constitutional Convention of 1776, & of the House of Assembly of the Delaware State, 1776-1781. Ed. by Claudia L. Bushman et al. LC 85-40510. 616p. 1986. 60.00 (*0-685-47145-4*) U Delaware Pr.

Proceedings of the Assembly of the Lower Counties on the Delaware 1770-1776, the Constitutional Convention of 1776 & of the House of Assembly of the Delaware State 1776-1781. Claudia L. Bushman et al. LC 86-30791. (Illus.). 1024p. 1988. 75.00 (*0-87413-309-2*) U Delaware Pr.

Proceedings of the Association of Occupational & Environmental Clinics (AOEC) Workshop on Multiple Chemical Sensitivity - Advancing the Understanding of Multiple Chemical Sensitivity. Ed. by Kathleen Rest. LC 92-64374. (Toxicology & Industrial Health Ser.: Vol. 8, No. 4). (Illus.). 1992. pap. text 65.00 (*0-911131-74-4*) Specialist Journals.

Proceedings of the Association of Orthodox Jewish Scientists: Behavioral & Social Sciences, Vol. 10. Ed. by Paul R. Bindler. 160p. (Orig.). 1989. pap. 12.50 (*0-87203-131-4*) Hermon.

Proceedings of the Asthma & Chronic Bronchitis in Children & Their Prognosis into Adult Life Symposium, 3rd, Davos, 1969. Asthma & Chronic Bronchitis in Children & Their Pr. Ed. by F. Suter & R. E. Altounyan. 1970. pap. 73.25 (*3-8055-0754-2*) S Karger.

Proceedings of the Bio-Engineering Symposium for Fish Culture. Ed. by Lochie J. Allen & Edward C. Kinney. LC 80-68383. 307p. 1981. text 28.00 (*0-913235-25-3*, 530.08) Am Fisheries Soc.

Proceedings of the Bioengineering Conference, Sunriver, Oregon, 1997. Ed. by K. B. Chandran et al. LC 93-71951. 609p. 1997. pap. 120.00 (*0-7918-1805-5*) ASME.

Proceedings of the Bioflow Small Diameter Graft Symposium. Ed. & Illus. by Silent Partners, Inc. Staff. 98p. (Orig.). 1989. pap. write for info. (*1-878353-09-8*) Silent Partners.

Proceedings of the Boston Area Colloquium in Ancient Philosophy, Vol. 3. Ed. by John J. Cleary. LC 85-26323. (Illus.). 424p. (Orig.). (C). 1988. pap. text 34.50 (*0-8191-6810-6*); lib. bdg. 58.50 (*0-8191-6809-2*) U Pr of Amer.

Proceedings of the Boston Area Colloquium in Ancient Philosophy, Vol. IV. Ed. by John J. Cleary & Daniel C. Shartin. LC 85-26323. 392p. (Orig.). (C). 1989. pap. text 33.00 (*0-8191-7336-3*) U Pr of Amer.

Proceedings of the Boston Area Colloquium in Ancient Philosophy, Vol. 5. Ed. by John J. Cleary & Daniel C. Shartin. 438p. (Orig.). (C). 1990. pap. text 38.00 (*0-8191-7809-8*); lib. bdg. 65.50 (*0-8191-7808-X*) U Pr of Amer.

Proceedings of the Boston Area Colloquium in Ancient Philosophy, Vol. VI. Ed. by John J. Cleary & Daniel C. Shartin. 518p. (Orig.). (C). 1992. pap. text 37.50 (*0-8191-8401-2*); lib. bdg. 80.00 (*0-8191-8400-4*) U Pr of Amer.

Proceedings of the Boston Area Colloquium in Ancient Philosophy, Vol. 7. Ed. by John J. Cleary. 358p. (Orig.). (C). 1992. 62.00 (*0-8191-8560-4*); pap. 29.00 (*0-8191-8561-2*) U Pr of Amer.

Proceedings of the Boston Area Colloquium in Ancient Philosophy, Vol. IX. Ed. by John J. Cleary & William Wians. 320p. (Orig.). (C). 1994. pap. 29.50 (*0-8191-9512-X*); lib. bdg. 66.00 (*0-8191-9511-1*) U Pr of Amer.

Proceedings of the Boston Area Colloquium in Ancient Philosophy, Vol. X, 1994. Ed. by John J. Cleary & William Wians. 310p. (Orig.). (C). 1995. pap. text 29.50 (*0-8191-9982-6*); lib. bdg. 66.00 (*0-8191-9981-8*) U Pr of Amer.

Proceedings of the Boston Area Colloquium in Ancient Philosophy, Vol. XI. Ed. by John Cleary & William Wians. 374p. 1996. 58.50 (*0-7618-0540-0*); pap. 38.50 (*0-7618-0541-9*) U Pr of Amer.

***Proceedings of the Boston Area Colloquium in Ancient Philosophy, Vol. XIV.** Ed. by John J. Cleary & Gary M. Gurtler. 296p. (Orig.). 1999. pap. 46.00 (*90-04-11396-7*) Brill Academic Pubs.

Proceedings of the Boston Area Colloquium in Ancient Philosophy, Vol. 8: 1993. Ed. by John J. Cleary & William Wians. 365p. (Orig.). (C). 1994. pap. text 29.50 (*0-8191-9144-2*); lib. bdg. 66.00 (*0-8191-9143-4*) U Pr of Amer.

Proceedings of the Boston Area Colloquium in Ancient Philosophy, 1996. Ed. by John J. Cleary & William C. Wians. (Illus.). 340p. 1998. pap. 29.50 (*0-7618-1000-5*) U Pr of Amer.

Proceedings of the Boston Area Colloquium in Ancient Philosophy, 1996, Vol. XII. Ed. by John J. Cleary & William C. Wians. (Illus.). 340p. 1998. 65.00 (*0-7618-0999-6*) U Pr of Amer.

***Proceedings of the Boston Area Colloquium in Ancient Philosophy 1997.** Ed. by John J. Cleary & Gary M. Gurtler. 312p. 1999. 71.00 (*90-04-11394-0*); pap. 43.00 (*90-04-11393-2*) Brill Academic Pubs.

***Proceedings of the Boston Area Colloquium in Ancient Philosophy, 1999.** Ed. by John J. Cleary & Gary M. Gurtler. (Proceedings of the Boston Area Colloquium in Ancient Philosophy Ser.). 296p. 2000. 92.00 (*90-04-11704-0*) Brill Academic Pubs.

***Proceedings of the British Academy.** 580p. 2000. 110.00 (*0-19-726209-0*) OUP.

Proceedings of the British Academy. British Academy Staff. (British Academy: Vol. 97). (Illus.). 540p. 1999. text 115.00 (*0-19-726192-2*) OUP.

Proceedings of the British Academy, Vol. XII, 1976. (Illus.). (C). 1978. 33.50 (*0-19-725976-6*) OUP.

Proceedings of the British Academy, Vol. LXIII, 1977. (Illus.). (C). 1979. 89.00 (*0-19-725983-9*) OUP.

Proceedings of the British Academy, Vol. LXIV, 1978. (Illus.). 1980. 165.00 (*0-19-725989-8*) OUP.

Proceedings of the British Academy, Vol. LXVI, 1980. (Illus.). 1982. 110.00 (*0-19-726013-6*) OUP.

Proceedings of the British Academy, Vol. LXX, 1984. 655p. 1986. 89.00 (*0-19-726037-3*) OUP.

Proceedings of the British Academy, Vol. LXXI, 1985. (Illus.). 590p. 1987. 155.00 (*0-19-726049-7*) OUP.

Proceedings of the British Academy, Vol. LXXII, 1986. (British Academy Ser.). (Illus.). 550p. 1988. 145.00 (*0-19-726064-0*) OUP.

Proceedings of the British Academy, Vol. LXXIV, 1988. (British Academy Ser.). (Illus.). 516p. 1990. 185.00 (*0-19-726083-7*) OUP.

Proceedings of the British Academy, Vol. LXXV, 1989. (British Academy Ser.). (Illus.). 438p. 1991. 165.00 (*0-19-726097-7*) OUP.

Proceedings of the British Academy, Vol. LXXVI, 1990. (British Academy Ser.). (Illus.). 572p. 1992. text 135.00 (*0-19-726107-8*) OUP.

Proceedings of the British Academy: New Developments in Archaeological Science a Joint Symposium of the Royal Society & the British Academy, February, 1991. Ed. by A. M. Pollard. (British Academy Ser.: Vol. 77). (Illus.). 260p. 1992. 49.95 (*0-19-726118-3*) OUP.

Proceedings of the British Academy: 1994 Lectures & Memoirs, Vol. 8. British Academy. (Proceedings of the British Academy Ser.). (Illus.). 528p. (C). 1996. text 115.00 (*0-19-726162-0*) OUP.

Proceedings of the British Academy: 1995 Lectures & Memoirs, Vol. 90. British Academy Staff. (Proceedings of the British Academy Ser.). (Illus.). 576p. 1997. text 135.00 (*0-19-726169-8*) OUP.

Proceedings of the British Academy: 1996 Lectures & Memoirs, Vol. 94. British Academy Staff. (Proceedings of the British Academy Ser.). (Illus.). 776p. 1998. text 140.00 (*0-19-726180-9*) OUP.

Proceedings of the British Academy, 1991 Vol. 80: Lectures & Memoirs, Vol. 80. British Academy Staff. (British Academy Ser.). (Illus.). 512p. 1993. text 95.00 (*0-19-726124-8*) OUP.

Proceedings of the California Eelgrass Symposium, Chula Vista, CA, May 27 & 28, 1988. Keith W. Merkel & Robert S. Hoffman. 78p. 1990. pap. 17.50 (*0-931950-02-3*) Sweetwater River Pr.

Proceedings of the California Household Hazardous Waste Management Conference. (Illus.). 300p. (Orig.). (C). 1997. pap. text 50.00 (*0-7881-3750-6*) DIANE Pub.

Proceedings of the Canadian Conference on Electrical & Computer Engineering, 1993. Institute of Electrical & Electronics Engineers, I. Ed. by IEEE, Inc. Staff. 475p. 1993. pap. write for info. (*0-7803-1443-3*, 93TH0590-0); fiche. write for info. (*0-7803-1444-1*) Inst Electrical.

Proceedings of the Canadian Parks Service Reconstruction Workshop: Hull, Quebec, 11-13 March 1992. Canadian Parks Service Reconstruction Workshop Staff & Canadian Parks Service Staff. LC 94-182086. 107p. 1993. write for info. (*0-662-20364-X*, Pub. by Can7 Govern Pub) Intl Spec Bk.

Proceedings of the Carnahan Conference on Security Technology, 1987. Carnahan Conference on Security Technology Staff. Ed. by R. William De Vore & John S. Jackson. LC 82-646157. (Illus.). 147p. 1987. pap. 10.00 (*0-89779-068-5*, UKY BU143) OES Pubns.

Proceedings of the Carpentier-Edwards Pericardial Prostheses Mini-Symposium. Ed. & Illus. by Silent Partners, Inc. Staff. 142p. 1994. pap. write for info. (*1-878353-30-6*) Silent Partners.

Proceedings of the Catholic University of America, Washington, D. C., Plasma Space Science Symposium, June 11-14, 1963. Catholic University of America, Washington, D. C. Ed. by C. C. Chang & S. S. Huang. (Astrophysics & Space Science Library: No.3). 377p. 1965. text 192.50 (*90-277-0112-1*) Kluwer Academic.

Proceedings of the Cedar Bog Symposium, Urbana College, Nov. 3, 1973. Cedar Bog Symposium Staff. Ed. by Charles C. King & Clara M. Frederick. (Informative Circular Ser.: No. 4). 1974. pap. text 3.00 (*0-86727-071-3*) Ohio Bio Survey.

Proceedings of the Celebration of the 250th Anniversary of the Settlement of Guilford, Connecticut, September 8th, 9th, & 10th, 1889. (Illus.). 289p. 1994. reprint ed. lib. bdg. 29.50 (*0-8328-4262-1*) Higginson Bk Co.

***Proceedings of the College of Universal Wisdom: Journal of the Research from the Ministry of Universal Wisdom, 3 vols., Set.** 2nd ed. Ed. & Illus. by George S. Riddle. 650p. 2000. 350.00 (*0-9670428-6-0*) Min Universal Wisdom.

Proceedings of the Colloquium on Global Aspects of Coral Reefs: Health, Hazards, & History. Compiled by Robert N. Ginsburg. (Illus.). 420p. (Orig.). (C). 1994. pap. 30.00 (*0-932981-79-8*) Univ Miami A R C.

Proceedings of the Commissioners of Indian Affairs. Franklin B. Hough. 1981. reprint ed. lib. bdg. 59.00 (*0-403-00389-X*) Scholarly.

Proceedings of the Committee on Jewish Law & Standards of the Conservative Movement 1927-1970, 3 vols. David Golinkin. (Proceedings of the Committee on Jewish Law & Standards Ser.). 1800p. (Orig.). 1997. pap. write for info. (*0-916219-07-0*) Rabbinical Assembly.

Proceedings of the Committee on Jewish Law & Standards of the Conservative Movement 1927-1970, Vol. 1. David Golinkin. LC 96-27531. (Proceedings of the Committee on Jewish Law & Standards Ser.). 600p. (Orig.). 1997. pap. write for info. (*0-916219-10-0*) Rabbinical Assembly.

Proceedings of the Committee on Jewish Law & Standards of the Conservative Movement 1927-1970, Vol. 2. David Golinkin. (Proceedings of the Committee on Jewish Law & Standards Ser.). 600p. (Orig.). 1997. pap. write for info. (*0-916219-11-9*) Rabbinical Assembly.

Proceedings of the Committee on Jewish Law & Standards of the Conservative Movement 1927-1970, Vol. 3. David Golinkin. (Proceedings of the Committee on Jewish Law & Standards Ser.). 600p. (Orig.). 1997. pap. write for info. (*0-916219-12-7*) Rabbinical Assembly.

Proceedings of the Committees of Safety of Cumberland & Isle of Wight Counties, Virginia, 1775-1776. Ed. by Henry R. McIlwaine. 54p. 1919. text 5.00 (*0-685-52452-3*) Library of VA.

Proceedings of the Conference Accounting & Economics: In Honour of the 500th Anniversary of the Publication of Luca Pacioli's Summa de Arithmetica, Geometria, Proportioni et Proportionalita, Siena, 18th-19th November 1992. Ed. by Martin Shubik. LC 03-15026. (New Works in Accounting History). (Illus.). 248p. 1996. reprint ed. text 77.00 (*0-8153-2243-7*) Garland.

Proceedings of the Conference Different Aspects of Differentiality. Ed. by A. Prudnikov. 220p. 1996. pap. text 58.00 (*90-5699-044-6*) Gordon & Breach.

Proceedings of the Conference in Honor of Elias M. Stein's Sixtieth Birthday. Ed. by Charles Fefferman et al. (Mathematical Ser.: No. 42). 420p. 1993. text 79.50 (*0-691-08655-9*, Pub. by Princeton U Pr) Cal Prin Full Svc.

Proceedings of the Conference, New Castle, NSW, Australia, 1-2 June 1995. Ed. by R. E. Melchers & M. G. Stewart. 220p. 1995. 85.00 (*90-5410-555-0*, Pub. by A A Balkema) Ashgate Pub Co.

Proceedings of the Conference of Dance & the Child, 1991: International. Ed. by Susan W. Stinson. 304p. (Orig.). 1992. pap. 5.00 (*0-9633149-0-4*) Dance & the Child.

Proceedings of the Conference of the American Academy of Advertising, 1990. Ed. by Patricia A. Stout. 1990. pap. 25.00 (*0-931030-13-7*) Am Acad Advert.

Proceedings of the Conference of the American Academy of Advertising, 1991. Ed. by Rebecca H. Holman. 1991. pap. 25.00 (*0-931030-14-5*) Am Acad Advert.

Proceedings of the Conference of the American Academy of Advertising, 1992. Ed. by Leonard N. Reid. 1992. pap. 25.00 (*0-931030-15-3*) Am Acad Advert.

Proceedings of the Conference of the American Academy of Advertising, 1995. Ed. by Charles S. Madden. 1995. pap. text, per. 25.00 (*0-931030-18-8*) Am Acad Advert.

Proceedings of the Conference of the American Academy of Advertising, 1996. (Orig.). (C). 1996. pap. 25.00 (*0-931030-19-6*) Am Acad Advert.

Proceedings of the Conference of the American Academy of Advertising, 1997. Ed. by Carole Macklin. 1997. pap. 25.00 (*0-931030-20-X*) Am Acad Advert.

Proceedings of the Conference of the American Academy of Advertising, 1998. Ed. by Darrel D. Muehling. 1998. pap. 25.00 (*0-931030-21-8*) Am Acad Advert.

P

Proceedings of the Conference of the American Academy of Advertising, 1999. Ed. by Marilyn Roberts. 1999. pap. 25.00 (*0-931030-22-6*) Am Acad Advert.

*****Proceedings of the Conference of the American Academy of Advertising, 2000.** Ed. by Mary Alice Shaver. 2000. pap. 25.00 (*0-931030-23-4*) Am Acad Advert.

Proceedings of the Conference of the International Organization of Citrus Virologists, 2nd. International Organization of Citrus Virologists S. Ed. by W. C. Price. LC 59-63553. (Illus.). 279p. reprint ed. pap. 86.50 (*0-7837-5019-6*, 204468700004) Bks Demand.

Proceedings of the Conference of the International Organization of Citrus Virologists, 3rd. International Organization of Citrus Virologists S. Ed. by W. C. Price. LC 59-63553. (Illus.). 335p. reprint ed. pap. 103.90 (*0-7837-5022-6*, 204469000004) Bks Demand.

Proceedings of the Conference of the International Organization of Citrus Virologists, 4th. International Organization of Citrus Virologists C. Ed. by J. F. Childs. LC 59-63553. 420p. reprint ed. pap. 130.20 (*0-7837-4959-7*, 204462500004) Bks Demand.

Proceedings of the Conference of the International Organization of Citrus Virologists, 5th. International Organization of Citrus Virologists S. Ed. by W. C. Price. LC 59-63553. (Illus.). 317p. reprint ed. pap. 98.30 (*0-7837-4944-9*, 204461000004) Bks Demand.

Proceedings of the Conference on Changes in the Biota of Lakes Erie & Ontario, March 10-11, 1980. Ed. by Roberta K. Cap & V. Ray Frederick, Jr. (Bulletin of the Buffalo Society of Natural Sciences Ser.: Vol. 25, No. 4). (Illus.). 120p. (Orig.). 1981. pap. 4.75 (*0-944032-32-X*) Buffalo SNS.

Proceedings of the Conference on Changes in the Chemistry of Lakes Erie & Ontario, November 5-6, 1970. Ed. by Robert A. Sweeney. (Bulletin of the Buffalo Society of Natural Sciences Ser.: Vol. 25, No. 2). (Illus.). 85p. (Orig.). (C). 1971. pap. 3.50 (*0-944032-30-3*) Buffalo SNS.

Proceedings of the Conference on Changes in the Physical Aspects of Lakes Erie & Ontario, November 1-2, 1973. Ed. by Robert A. Sweeney. (Bulletin of the Buffalo Society of Natural Sciences Ser.: Vol. 25, No. 3). (Illus.). 93p. (Orig.). 1975. pap. 4.00 (*0-944032-31-1*) Buffalo SNS.

Proceedings of the Conference on Complex Analysis. Ed. by Zhong Li et al. (Series in Analysis). 1994. 42.00 (*1-57146-017-9*) Intl Pr Boston.

Proceedings of the Conference on Energy Contingency Planning in Urban Areas. (Special Reports: No. 203). 103p. 1984. 13.80 (*0-309-03657-7*) Transport Res Bd.

Proceedings of the Conference on Evaluating Alternative Local Transportation Financing Techniques. (Special Reports: No. 208). 76p. 1985. 10.80 (*0-309-03819-7*) Transport Res Bd.

*****Proceedings of the Conference on Experimental Research in Computer Systems, 1996.** Ed. by Lawrence Snyder. (Illus.). 235p. (C). 1999. reprint ed. pap. text 30.00 (*0-7881-8380-X*) DIANE Pub.

Proceedings of the Conference on Groups & Geometry, 2 vols., Set. Ed. by W. Crowe et al. 350p. 1986. 60.00 (*0-911767-44-4*) Hadronic Pr Inc.

Proceedings of the Conference on Inclusion Guidelines & Accommodations for Limited English Proficient Students in the National Assessment of Educational Progress. Diane August & Edith McArthur. 51p. (C). 1998. pap. text 20.00 (*0-7881-7050-3*) DIANE Pub.

*****Proceedings of the Conference on Industrial Technologies, Toulouse 27-30 October, 1997.** Conference on Industrial Technologies Staff. LC 98-231880. 253p. 1998. write for info. (*92-828-2974-X*, Pub. by Comm Europ Commun) Bernan Associates.

Proceedings of the Conference on Integration, Topology & Geometry in Linear Spaces. Ed. by William H. Graves. LC 80-25417. (Contemporary Mathematics Ser.: Vol. 2). 269p. 1980. pap. 27.00 (*0-8218-5002-4*, CONM/2) Am Math.

Proceedings of the Conference on Language & Language Behavior. Ed. by Eric M. Zale. LC 68-28144. 1968. 42.50 (*0-89197-906-9*) Irvington.

Proceedings of the Conference on Law & Information Policy for Spatial Databases. Ed. by Harlan J. Onsrud. LC 97-156416. (Illus.). 331p. (C). 1995. pap. text 35.00 (*0-9648267-0-4*) U ME Nat Ctr Geog.

Proceedings of the Conference on Low-Level Exposure to Chemicals & Neurobiological Sensitivity. Ed. by F. Mitchell. (Toxicology & Industrial Health Ser.: Vol. 10, No. 4/5). (Illus.). 252p. 1994. 65.00 (*0-911131-32-9*) Specialist Journals.

Proceedings of the Conference on Measuring Chaos in the Human Brain, April 3-5, 1991, at the Supercomputer Computations Research Institute, Florida State University, Tallahassee, FL. Ed. by D. W. Duke et al. LC 92-23707. 250p. (C). 1991. text 89.00 (*981-02-0701-8*) World Scientific Pub.

Proceedings of the Conference on Multi-Ring Basins, Houston, Texas. Ed. by Lunar & Planetary Institute Staff. 300p. 1981. 47.00 (*0-08-028045-5*, Pergamon Pr) Elsevier.

Proceedings of the Conference on Priorities for Water Resources Allocation & Management. 176p. 1993. pap. 70.00 (*0-902500-49-X*, Pub. by Nat Res Inst) St Mut.

Proceedings of the Conference on Simulation in Health Care & Social Services. Anderson. 120p. 1992. pap. 48.00 (*1-56555-010-2*, MC92-4) Soc Computer Sim.

*****Proceedings of the Conference on Summer Undergraduate Mathematics Research Programs.** Conference on Summer Undergraduate Mathematics Research Programs Staff & Joseph A. Gallian. LC 00-29329. 2000. write for info. (*0-8218-2137-7*) Am Math.

Proceedings of the Conference on Teaching Legal & Factual Research in Private Law Libraries: Westfields International Conference Center, Chantilly, Virginia, April 26-29, 1990. Contrib. by Mead Data Central, Inc. Staff. LC 91-17748. ix, 210p. 1991. 32.50 (*0-8377-0911-3*, Rothman) W S Hein.

Proceedings of the Conference on Technology in Collegiate Mathematics: The Twilight of the... Franklin Demana. 1990. pap. text 22.75 (*0-201-50049-3*) Addison-Wesley.

Proceedings of the Conference on the Capabilities & Needs of Disabled Persons in the ESCWA Region. 535p. 1990. 60.00 (*92-1-128119-9*, 90.II.L.9) UN.

*****Proceedings of the Conference on the History & Heritage of Science Information Systems.** Ed. by Trudi Bellardo Hahn et al. LC 99-36330. 1999. pap. 39.50 (*1-57387-080-3*) Info Today Inc.

Proceedings of the Conference on Training Clinician Child Psychologists. Ed. by June M. Tuma. 175p. 1989. pap. 29.95 (*0-8058-0591-5*) L Erlbaum Assocs.

Proceedings of the Conference on Training Personnel for the Computing Machine Field, 1st: Held at Wayne University, Detroit, Michigan, June 22 & 25, 1954. Conference on Training Personnel for the Computing. Ed. by Arvid W. Jacobson. LC 55-6746. 115p. reprint ed. pap. 35.70 (*0-7837-3805-6*, 204362500010) Bks Demand.

Proceedings of the Conference on Weed Control in Rice: Jointly Sponsored by the International Rice Research Institute & the International Weed Science Society, Los Banos, Laguna, Philippines, 31 August-4 September 1981. Conference on Weed Control in Rice Staff. LC SB0608.R5C66. (Illus.). 422p. 1983. reprint ed. pap. 130.90 (*0-608-07669-4*, 206704900010) Bks Demand.

Proceedings of the Constitutional Convention of South Carolina. Constitutional Convention of South Carolina Staff. LC 68-29018. (American Negro: His History & Literature. Series 1). 1968. reprint ed. 39.95 (*0-405-01837-1*) Ayer.

Proceedings of the Convocation on the Status of the Bill of Rights after 200 Years. Ed. by Ralph M. Dreger. viii, 50p. (C). 1992. pap. text 2.00 (*0-9635887-0-2*) LA Coun Hum Relat.

Proceedings of the Cornelius Lanczos International Centenary Conference. Ed. by J. David Brown et al. LC 94-22243. (Proceedings in Applied Mathematics Ser.: No. 73). lxv, 644p. 1994. pap. 89.00 (*0-89871-339-0*) Soc Indus-Appl Math.

*****Proceedings of the Corrosion - 2000 Research Topical Symposium.** Ed. by NACE Research Committee. (Illus.). 150p. 2000. pap. 45.00 (*1-57590-090-4*, 37406) NACE Intl.

Proceedings of the Corrosion 98 Research Topical Symposia. Ed. by NACE Research Committee Staff. (Illus.). 100p. 1998. pap. 36.00 (*1-57590-046-7*, 37403) NACE Intl.

Proceedings of the Corrosion 97 Research Topical Symposia. Ed. by NACE Research Committee Staff. 1997. pap. 50.00 (*1-57590-028-9*, 37402) NACE Intl.

*****Proceedings of the Corrosion/99 Research Topical Symposium.** Ed. by NACE Research Committee. (Illus.). 150p. 1999. pap. 35.00 (*1-57590-068-8*, 37405) NACE Intl.

Proceedings of the Csoma de Koros Memorial Symposium: Held at Matrafured, Hungary, 24-30 September 1976. Ed. by Louis Ligeti. (Bibliotheca Orientalis Hungarica Ser.: Vol. 23). (FRE, GER & RUS.). 586p. (C). 1978. 153.00 (*963-05-1568-7*, Pub. by Akade Kiado) St Mut.

Proceedings of the Danish Institute at Athens, Vol. 1. Ed. by Soren Dietz. (Illus.). 226p. (C). 1995. pap. 37.00 (*87-7288-721-4*, Pub. by Aarhus Univ Pr) David Brown.

Proceedings of the Danish Institute at Athens II. Ed. by Soren Dietz & Signe Isager. (Illus.). 411p. 1998. pap. 37.00 (*87-7288-722-2*, Pub. by Aarhus Univ Pr) David Brown.

Proceedings of the Digital Systems Reliability & Nuclear Safety Workshop. 341p. pap. text 50.00 (*0-7881-4147-3*) DIANE Pub.

Proceedings of the DOE-NREL 1997 Hydrogen Program Review (May 21-23) Compiled by National Renewable Energy Laboratory Staff. (Hydrogen Fuel Information Ser.: No. VI). (Illus.). 565p. 1997. lib. bdg. 255.00 (*0-89934-331-7*, BT975) Bus Tech Bks.

Proceedings of the DOE-NREL 1998 Hydrogen Program Review, 2 vols. U.S. Dept. of Energy (National Reneivalile Energy Labortory) Staff. (Hydrogen Fuel Information Ser.: Vol. IX, Pts. A & B). (Illus.). 814p. 1998. lib. bdg. 395.00 (*0-89934-333-3*, BT-989) Bus Tech Bks.

Proceedings of the Duke University Tropical Forestry Symposium, April 21-26, 1965. Duke University Tropical Forestry Symposium Staff. LC SD0131.D85. (Duke University, School of Forestry Bulletin Ser.: No. 18). 213p. reprint ed. pap. 66.10 (*0-7837-6045-0*, 204585800008) Bks Demand.

Proceedings of the Earth Summit Workshop. Ed. by Wayne O. Deason et al. LC 93-61713. 102p. (Orig.). 1994. pap. 40.00 (*1-884575-00-5*) US Comm Irrigation.

Proceedings of the Eastern Academy of Management. Ed. by Mzamo P. Mangaliso & Joan Weiner. 1995. write for info. (*0-916958-13-2*) Eastrn Acad Mgmt.

Proceedings of the Eighteenth Annual Conference. APLIC International Staff. Ed. by Jane Vanderlin & William Barrow. LC 76-643241. 129p. (Orig.). 1986. pap. 15.00 (*0-933438-11-7*) APLIC Intl.

Proceedings of the Eighteenth Annual Conference of the Cognitive Science Society. Cognitive Science Society Staff. 904p. 1996. pap. 150.00 (*0-8058-2541-X*) L Erlbaum Assocs.

Proceedings of the 18th Annual SAS Users Group International Conference. SAS Institute, Inc. Staff. 1672p. 1993. pap. 35.95 (*1-58025-238-9*, BR56647) SAS Publ.

Proceedings of the Eighteenth Annual SAS User's Group International Conference. 1672p. (C). 1993. pap. 12.50 (*1-55544-550-0*, BR56056) SAS Publ.

Proceedings of the 18th Colloquium on the Law of Outer Space, September 21-27, 1975, Lisbon, Portugal. International Institute of Space Law of the International Astronautical Federation Staff. v, 201p. 1976. pap. 27.50 (*0-8377-0413-8*, Rothman) W S Hein.

Proceedings of the Eighteenth International Technical Conference on Coal Utilization & Fuel Systems (1993) 900p. 1994. 375.00 (*0-932066-18-6*) Coal Slurry Tech.

Proceedings of the 18th National Online Meeting Proceedings. Ed. by Martha Williams. 401p. 1997. 59.00 (*1-57387-043-9*) Info Today Inc.

Proceedings of the 18th Symposium on Naval Hydrodynamics: (Actes du Dix-Huitieme Colloque de la Societe d'Histoire Coloniale Francaise. Montreal. Mai 1992) Ed. by James Pritchard. v, 116p. 1993. text 30.00 (*1-884679-00-5*) Fr Colonial Hist.

Proceeding of the 8th Annual Control Engineer Conference: Held As Part of the Control Engineering Conference & Exposition, O'Hare Exposition Center, Rosemont, IL, May 23-25, 1989. Intro. by Byron K. Ledgerwood. (Illus.). (Orig.). 1989. pap. 105.00 (*0-914331-58-2*, Control Engrng) Cahners Busn Des Plaines.

Proceedings of the Eighth Annual International Conference on Veterinary Acupuncture. annuals Ed. by David H. Jaggar. 312p. (Orig.). 1982. pap. text 40.00 (*0-318-19685-9*) Intl Vet Acup.

Proceedings of the Eighth Annual Meeting of the French Colonial Historical Society, 1982. Ed. by E. P. Fitzgerald. (Illus.). 246p. (Orig.). 1985. pap. text 22.00 (*0-8191-4409-6*) U Pr of Amer.

Proceedings of the 8th Conference on Roofing Technology. (Illus.). 102p. 1987. 18.00 (*0-934809-03-8*) Natl Roofing Cont.

Proceedings of the 8th Conference on Fluid Machinery, 2 vols., Set. L. Kisbocskoi & A. Szabo. 962p. (C). 1987. 267.00 (*963-05-4647-7*, Pub. by Akade Kiado) St Mut.

Proceedings of the 8th Conference on Fluid Machinery, 2 vols., Set. L. Kisbocskoi & A. Szabo. 962p. (C). 1987. 625.00 (*0-569-09071-7*, Pub. by Collets) St Mut.

Proceedings of the 8th International Symposium on Molten Salts. Ed. by Robert J. Gale et al. LC 92-73568. (Proceedings Ser.: Vol. 92-16). 680p. 1992. 56.00 (*1-56677-017-3*) Electrochem Soc.

*****Proceedings of the 8th International Symposium on Transport Phenomena & Dynamics of Rotating Machinery (ISOROMAC-8), Vol. I.** Ed. by J. C. Han. (Illus.). xx, 613p. (C). 2000. 100.00 (*0-9652469-8-1*) Pac Ctr Thermal.

*****Proceedings of the 8th International Symposium on Transport Phenomena & Dynamics of Rotating Machinery (ISOROMAC-8), Vol. II.** Ed. by J. C. Han. (Illus.). xx, 620p. (C). 2000. 100.00 (*0-9652469-9-X*) Pac Ctr Thermal.

*****Proceedings of the Eighth International Conference on High-level Radioactive Work Management: Las Vegas, Nevada, May 11-14, 1998.** 888p. 1998. pap. 90.00 (*0-89448-632-2*, 700252) Am Nuclear Soc.

Proceedings of the Eighth International Conference on the Study of Shamanism & Alternate Modes of Healing, 1991, Santa Sabina Center, San Rafael, California, August 31-September 2, 1991. Ed. by Ruth-Inge Heinze. LC 92-6776. (Illus.). 354p. (C). 1992. pap. 21.75 (*0-945875-08-8*) Independent Scholars Asia Inc.

Proceedings of the Eighth International Congress of Onomastic Sciences, Amsterdam, 1963. Ed. by D. P. Blok. (Janua Linguarum, Series Major: No. 17). 1966. 176.95 (*90-279-0609-2*) Mouton.

Proceedings of the Eighth International Kant Congress, Vol. 1, Pt. 1, Sections 1-2. Ed. by Hoke Robinson. LC 94-80267. 1995. 40.00 (*0-87462-479-7*) Marquette.

Proceedings of the Eighth International Kant Congress, Vol. 1, Pt. 2, Sections 3A-3L. Ed. by Hoke Robinson. LC 94-80267. 1995. 40.00 (*0-87462-480-0*) Marquette.

Proceedings of the Eighth International Kant Congress, Vol. 1, Pt. 3, Sections 3M - 3S, 4, 5. Ed. by Hoke Robinson. LC 94-80267. 1995. 40.00 (*0-87462-481-9*) Marquette.

Proceedings of the Eighth International Kant Congress Vol. II, Vol. 2, Pt. 1, Sec. 1-9. Ed. by Hoke Robinson. LC 94-80267. 1995. pap. 40.00 (*0-87462-477-0*) Marquette.

Proceedings of the Eighth International Kant Congress Vol. II, Vol. 2, Pt. 2, Sec. 10-18. Ed. by Hoke Robinson. LC 94-80267. 1995. pap. 40.00 (*0-87462-478-9*) Marquette.

Proceedings of the Eighth International Symposium on Cyclodextrins: Budapest, Hungary, March 31-April 2, 1996. Ed. by Jozsef Szejtli. LC 96-49527. (Diverse Ser.). 708p. (C). 1996. text 357.00 (*0-7923-4029-9*) Kluwer Academic.

Proceedings of the Eighth International Symposium on Human Factors in Telecommunications, 1977, Cambridge, U. K. 430p. 1977. 95.00 (*1-56851-092-6*, 125408) Info Gatekeepers.

Proceedings of the Eighth International Symposium on Insect-Plant Relationships. Ed. by S. B. Menken. (Series Entomologica). 440p. (C). 1993. text 236.00 (*0-7923-2099-9*) Kluwer Academic.

Proceedings of the Eighth International Workshop on Critical Currents in Superconductors. 500p. 1996. lib. bdg. 89.00 (*981-02-2858-9*) World Scientific Pub.

Proceedings of the Eighth Japan - U. S. Conference on Composite Materials. Japan-U.S. Conference on Composite Materials Staff et al. LC 98-87452. 1045p. 1998. 219.95 (*1-56676-718-0*) Technomic.

Proceedings of the Eighth Midwest Artificial Intelligence & Cognitive Science Conference. Ed. by Eugene Santos, Jr. (Technical Reports). (Illus.). 112p. (Orig.). 1997. pap. text 25.00 (*1-57735-023-5*) AAAI Pr.

Proceedings of the 8th (1998) International Offshore & Polar Engineering Conference, 4 vols. Incl. Vol. I. Proceedings of the 8th (1998) International Offshore & Polar Engineering Conference. Ed. by Jin S. Chung. (Illus.). 685p. 1998. pap. 120.00 (*1-880653-35-4*); Vol. II. Proceedings of the 8th (1998) International Offshore & Polar Engineering Conference. Ed. by Jin S. Chung. (Illus.). 616p. 1998. pap. 120.00 (*1-880653-36-2*); Vol. III. Proceedings of the 8th (1998) International Offshore & Polar Engineering Conference. Ed. by Jin S. Chung. (Illus.). 729p. 1998. pap. 120.00 (*1-880653-37-0*); Vol. IV. Proceedings of the 8th (1998) International Offshore & Polar Engineering Conference. Ed. by Paul Grundy. (Illus.). 547p. 1998. pap. 120.00 (*1-880653-38-9*); 2577p. 380.00 (*1-880653-34-6*) ISOPE.

Proceedings of the 8th Quadrennial IAGOD-Symposium Held in Ottawa, Canada, August 12-18, 1990. Ed. by Yvon T. Maurice. (International Association on the Genesis of Ore Deposits (IAGOD) Symposia Ser.). (Illus.). xiii, 901p. 1993. lib. bdg. 200.00 (*3-510-65153-7*, Pub. by E Schweizerbartsche) Balogh.

Proceedings of the 8th Symposium on the Geology of the Bahamas & Other Carbonate Regions. Ed. by James L. Carew. (Illus.). 213p. (C). 1997. pap. text 25.00 (*0-935909-63-X*) Bahamian.

Proceedings of the Eighth Symposium on Thermophysical Properties, 2 vols., Vol. 1. Symposium on Thermophysical Properties Staff. Ed. by Jan V. Sengers. LC 59-1391. (Illus.). 503p. reprint ed. pap. 156.00 (*0-8357-2883-8*, 203912000001) Bks Demand.

Proceedings of the Eighth Symposium on Thermophysical Properties, 2 vols., Vol. 2. Symposium on Thermophysical Properties Staff. Ed. by Jan V. Sengers. LC 59-1391. (Illus.). 455p. reprint ed. pap. 141.10 (*0-8357-2884-6*, 203912000002) Bks Demand.

*****Proceedings of the 8th U. S. Mine Ventilation Symposium.** Ed. by Jerry C. Tien. (Illus.). 732p. 1999. pap. 95.00 (*1-887009-04-3*) Cur Univ MO.

Proceedings of the Eighth West Coast Conference on Formal Linguistics, Vol. 8. Ed. by E. Jane Fee & Katherine Hunt. 1989. pap. 22.95 (*0-937073-45-8*) CSLI.

Proceedings of the 8th (1998) International Offshore & Polar Engineering Conference **see Proceedings of the 8th (1998) International Offshore & Polar Engineering Conference**

Proceedings of the Electoral Commission & of the Two Houses of Congress in Joint Meeting Relative to the Count of Electoral Votes Cast December 6, 1876, for the Presidential Term Commencing March 4, 1877. LC 69-11322. (Law, Politics & History Ser.). 1970. reprint ed. lib. bdg. 115.00 (*0-306-71185-0*) Da Capo.

Proceedings of the Electron Microscopy Society: 1961-71 Editions. Electron Microscopy Society Staff. Ed. by Claude Arcenaux. 1980. 15.00 (*0-685-01110-0*) Claitors.

Proceedings of the Electron Microscopy Society: 1971-74 Editions. Electron Microscopy Society Staff. Ed. by Claude Arcenaux. 1980. 17.50 (*0-318-51375-7*) Claitors.

Proceedings of the Electronic Processes in the Organic Condensed Phase: A Symposium in Honor of Professor Martin Pope. N. Geacintov et al. 1990. pap. text. write for info. (*0-318-72898-2*) Gordon & Breach.

Proceedings of the 11th International Ship & Offshore Structures Congress International Ship & Offshore Structures Congress Staff et al. LC 91-24211. 1991. write for info. (*1-85166-714-8*) Elsevier.

*****Proceedings of the 11th Annual ACM-SIAM Symposium on Discrete Algorithms.** Ed. by David Shmoys et al. (Proceedings in Applied Mathematics Ser.: No. 101). xvi, 965p. 2000. pap. 117.00 (*0-89871-453-2*, PR0101) Soc Indus-Appl Math.

Proceedings of the 11th Annual Pacific Climate (PACLIM) Workshop. Ed. by Caroline M. Isaacs & Vera L. Tharp. (Illus.). 236p. (Orig.). (C). 1995. pap. text 45.00 (*0-7881-2475-7*) DIANE Pub.

*****Proceedings of the Eleventh Annual UCLA Indo-European Conference.** Ed. by Karlene Jones-Bley et al. 2000. pap. text 46.00 (*0-941694-73-9*) Inst Study Man.

Proceedings of the Eleventh Biennial University-Government-Industry Microelectronics Symposium. IEEE, Electron Devices Society Staff. Ed. by Institute of Electrical & Electronics Engineers, I. 1995. pap. text. write for info. (*0-7803-2596-6*); lib. bdg. write for info. (*0-7803-2597-4*, 95CH35779) Inst Electrical.

Proceedings of the 11th Colloquium on the Law of Outer Space, October 17-18, 1968, New York. International Institute of Space Law of the International Astronautical Federation Staff. iii, 394p. 1969. pap. 27.50 (*0-8377-0406-5*, Rothman) W S Hein.

*****Proceedings of the Eleventh Conversation in Biomolecular Stereodynamics, 2 vols.; set.** Ed. by R. H. Sarma & M. H. Sarma. (Conversation in the Discipline Biomolecular Stereodynamics Ser.). (Illus.). 407p. 2000. pap. 100.00 (*0-940030-79-9*) Adenine Pr.

*****Proceedings of the Eleventh Conversation in Biomolecular Stereodynamics, Vol. 1.** Ed. by R. H. Sarma & M. H. Sarma. (Conversation in the Discipline Biomolecular Stereodynamics Ser.). (Illus.). 2000. pap. 50.00 (*0-940030-80-2*) Adenine Pr.

*****Proceedings of the Eleventh Conversation in Biomolecular Stereodynamics, Vol. 2.** Ed. by R. H. Sarma & M. H. Sarma. (Conversation in the Discipline Biomolecular Stereodynamics Ser.). (Illus.). 2000. pap. 50.00 (*0-940030-81-0*) Adenine Pr.

An Asterisk (*) at the beginning of an entry indicates that the title is appearing for the first time.

Proceedings of the 11th Fundamental Research Symposium Vol. 3: The Fundamentals of Papermaking Materials. Pulp & Paper Fundamental Research Soceity Staff. 1998. 120.00 (*1-85802-211-8*, Pub. by Pira Internatl) Bks Intl VA.

***Proceedings of the XXI International Mineral Processing Congress.** International Mineral Processing Congress & Paolo Massacci. LC 00-32150. 2000. write for info. (*0-444-50283-1*) Elsevier.

Proceedings of the 11th International Symposium on Human Factors. 450p. 1985. pap. text 95.00 (*2-9501147-0-9*, 125411) Info Gatekeepers.

Proceedings of the 11th International Seaweed Symposium. Ed. by Carolyn J. Bird & Mark A. Ragan. (Developments in Hydrobiology Ser.). 1984. text 450.50 (*90-6193-773-6*) Kluwer Academic.

Proceedings of the 11th International Conference on Software Engineering & Knowledge Engineering, SEKE '99. Ed. by Knowledge Systems Institute Staff. (Illus.). 408p. Date not set. pap. 65.00 (*1-891706-01-2*) Knowldge Systs.

Proceedings of the 11th International Conference on Composite Materials: ICCM-11, 6 vols. 1997. 849.95 (*1-85573-350-1*) Technomic.

Proceedings of the 11th International Diatom Symposium: San Francisco, California, August 12-17, 1990. Ed. by John P. Kociolek. LC 94-70113. (Memoirs of the California Academy of Sciences Ser.: No. 17). (Illus.). 672p. 1994. 75.00 (*0-940228-34-3*) Calif Acad Sci.

Proceedings of the XI International Congress of Mathematical Physics: UNESCO, Sorbonne, Paris, July 18-23, 1994. Ed. by Daniel Iagolnitzer. (Illus.). 808p. (C). 1995. 42.00 (*1-57146-030-6*) Intl Pr Boston.

Proceedings of the 11th International Conference on Composite Materials Vol. I: Composites Applications & Designs. (ICCM-11 Ser.). 866p. 1997. pap. 170.00 (*1-85573-351-X*) Am Educ Systs.

Proceedings of the 11th International Conference on Composite Materials Vol. 2: Fatigue, Fracture & Ceramic Matrix Composites. (ICCM-11 Ser.). 892p. 1997. 170.00 (*1-85573-352-8*, Pub. by Woodhead Pubng) Am Educ Systs.

Proceedings of the 11th International Conference on Composite Materials Vol. 3: Metal Matrix Composites & Physical Properties. (ICCM-11 Ser.). 810p. 1997. 170.00 (*1-85573-353-6*, Pub. by Woodhead Pubng) Am Educ Systs.

Proceedings of the 11th International Conference on Composite Materials Vol. 4: Composite Processing & Microstructure. (ICCM-11 Ser.). 872p. 1997. 170.00 (*1-85573-354-4*, Pub. by Woodhead Pubng) Am Educ Systs.

Proceedings of the Eleventh International Conference on the Study of Shamanism & Alternate Modes of Healing, Held at the Santa Sabina Center, San Rafael, California, September 3-5, 1994. Ed. by Ruth-Inge Heinze. LC 95-43549. (Illus.). vi, 352p. (C). 1995. pap. 21.75 (*0-945875-12-6*) Independent Scholars Asia Inc.

Proceedings of the Eleventh International Congress on Hyperbaric Medicine. Ed. by Wen-Ren Li & Frederick S. Cramer. LC 95-77069. (Illus.). 306p. 1995. 49.50 (*0-941332-44-6*, B0787) Best Pub Co.

Proceedings of the 11th Meeting of the World Society for Stereotactic & Functional Neurosurgery, Ixtapa, Mexico, October 1993 Pt. II: Journal: Sterotactic & Functional Neurosurgery 1994. Ed. by Philip L. Gildenberg et al. (Journal Ser.: Vol. 63, No. 1-4, 1994). (Illus.). viii, 302p. 1995. pap. 201.75 (*3-8055-6155-5*) S Karger.

Proceedings of the Eleventh Meeting of the French Colonial Historical Society, Quebec, May, 1985. Ed. by Philip Boucher. (Illus.). 338p. (Orig.). (C). 1987. pap. 56.00 (*0-8191-5658-2*) U Pr of Amer.

Proceedings of the 11th Oil Shale Symposium. Ed. by James H. Gary. (Illus.). 389p. 1978. pap. 5.00 (*0-918062-03-9*) Colo Sch Mines.

***Proceedings of the Embedded Topical Meeting on Nuclear Applications of Accelerator Technology: Acc App99, Long Beach, California, November 14-18, 1999.** 1999. pap. 95.00 (*0-89448-643-8*, 700267) Am Nuclear Soc.

Proceedings of the Enhancement of Reforestation at Surface Coal Mines: Technical Interactive Forum. Ed. by Klmery C. Vories & Dianne Throgmorton. LC 99-38937. 1999. write for info. (*1-885189-05-2*) Coal Res Ctr.

Proceedings of the Ergonomics Society's Conference, 1983. Ed. by K. Coombes. 214p. 1983. pap. 36.00 (*0-85066-252-4*) Taylor & Francis.

Proceedings of the Ergonomics Society's Conference, 1983. Ed. by K. Coombes. 214p. 1983. pap. 36.00 (*0-8002-3087-6*) Taylor & Francis.

Proceedings of the ESA-IEJ Joint Symposium on Electrostatics. J. M. Crowley et al. 350p. 1994. pap. 9.95 (*1-885540-00-0*) Laplacian Pr.

Proceedings of the ESREF Conference. IEEE (Electron Devices Society) Staff. Ed. by IEEE (Institute of Electrical & Electronics Engine. 400p. 1996. pap. 120.00 (*0-614-14934-7*, 96TH8196) Inst Electrical.

Proceedings of the ESREF Conference. IEEE (Electron Devices Society) Staff. Ed. by IEEE Staff. 400p. 1996. fiche 120.00 (*0-7803-3369-1*, 96TH8196) Inst Electrical.

Proceedings of the Ethem T. Turkdogan Symposium: Fundamentals & Analysis of New & Emerging Steelmaking Technologies, Pittsburgh, PA, May 15-17, 1994. Ethem T. Turkdogan Symposium Staff. LC 94-75172. (Illus.). 282p. 1994. reprint ed. pap. 87.50 (*0-608-07963-4*, 206793500012) Bks Demand.

Proceedings of the European Simulation Symposium on Intelligent Process Control, 1990. 250p. 1990. pap. 80.00 (*0-911801-83-9*, ESS90-1) Soc Computer Sim.

Proceedings of the European Simulation Symposium on Intelligent Process Control, 1991. 244p. 1991. pap. 80.00 (*1-56555-000-5*, ESS91-1) Soc Computer Sim.

***Proceedings of the European Workshop on Mechanical Plaque Control.** Ed. by Niklaus P. Lang et al. 314p. 2000. pap. 42.80 (*3-87652-428-8*, Pub. by Quintessenz Verlags) Quint Pub Co.

Proceedings of the Experimental Chaos Conference, 1st: Arlington, Virginia, October 1-3, 1991. Ed. by Sandeep Vohra et al. LC 92-11997. 500p. 1992. pap. write for info. (*981-02-0899-5*); text 95.00 (*981-02-0898-7*) World Scientific Pub.

Proceedings of the Expert Group Meeting on Protection of Water Resources, Water Quality & Aquatic Ecosystems. (Water Resources Ser.: No. 74). 200p. 1995. 35.00 (*92-1-119677-9*) UN.

Proceedings of the Extreme Ultraviolet Astronomy Colloquium. Ed. by Roger F. Malina. (Illus.). 208p. 1991. 80.00 (*0-08-037303-8*, Pergamon Pr) Elsevier.

Proceedings of the Exxon Valdez Oil Spill Symposium. Ed. by Stanley D. Rice et al. LC 96-85358. (American Fisheries Society Symposium Ser.: No. 18). (Illus.). 931p. 1996. text 35.00 (*0-913235-95-4*, 540.18) Am Fisheries Soc.

Proceedings of the FAO Expert Consultation on Fish Technology in Africa, Abidjan, 1988. FAO Staff. (ENG & FRE.). 355p. 1990. suppl. ed. 45.00 (*92-5-002905-5*, F9055, Pub. by FAO) Bernan Associates.

Proceedings of the FAO-WHO Expert Committee on Nutrition, 8th. FAO-WHO Joint Committee Expert Committee on Nutrit. (Technical Reports: No. 477). 80p. 1971. pap. text 5.00 (*92-4-120477-X*, 1100477) World Health.

Proceedings of the FAO-WHO Joint Expert Committee on Brucellosis, 4th, Geneva, 1963. FAO-WHO Joint Expert Committee on Brucellosis. (Technical Reports: No. 289). 65p. 1964. pap. text 5.00 (*92-4-120289-0*, 1100289) World Health.

Proceedings of the FAO-WHO Joint Expert Committee on Brucellosis, 5th, Geneva, 1970. FAO-WHO Joint Expert Committee on Brucellosis. (Technical Reports: No. 464). 76p. 1971. pap. text 5.00 (*92-4-120464-8*, 1100464) World Health.

Proceedings of the 15th Biennial Conference. ICHCA Staff. (C). 1988. 210.00 (*0-7855-6157-9*, Pub. by ICHCA) St Mut.

Proceedings of the Fifteenth Annual Conference. Ed. by Ann Leonard. LC 76-643241. iii, 79p. (Orig.). 1983. pap. 10.00 (*0-933438-07-9*) APLIC Intl.

Proceedings of the Fifteenth Annual Conference of the Cognitive Science Society. 1126p. 1993. pap. 150.00 (*0-8058-1487-6*) L Erlbaum Assocs.

Proceedings of the Fifteenth Biennial National Waste Processing Conference. 464p. 1992. pap. 175.00 (*0-7918-0665-0*, I00328) ASME.

Proceedings of the 15th Colloquium on the Law of Outer Space, October 8-15, 1972, Vienna, Austria. International Institute of Space Law of the International Astronautical Federation Staff. iv, 284p. 1973. pap. 27.50 (*0-8377-0410-3*, Rothman) W S Hein.

***Proceedings of the 15th International Pig Veterinary Society Congress, 4 vols. & CD, Set.** Ed. by S. T. Done et al. 1999. pap. 400.00 incl. cd-rom (*1-897676-84-0*, Pub. by Nottingham Univ Pr) St Mut.

Proceedings of the 15th International Conference on Offshore Mechanics & Arctic Engineering, Florence, Italy, June 16-20, 1996 Vol. II: Safety & Reliability. 528p. 1996. 170.00 (*0-7918-1491-2*, G00986) ASME Pr.

Proceedings of the 15th International Conference on Offshore Mechanics & Arctic Engineering, Florence, Italy, June 16-20, 1996 Vol. IV: Arctic - Polar Technology. 132p. 1996. 80.00 (*0-7918-1493-9*, G00988) ASME Pr.

Proceedings of the 15th International Conference on Offshore Mechanics & Arctic Engineering, Florence, Italy, June 16-20, 1996 Vol. V: Pipeline Technology. 612p. 1996. 190.00 (*0-7918-1494-7*, G00989) ASME Pr.

Proceedings of the 15th International Conference on Offshore Mechanics & Arctic Engineering, Florence, Italy, June 16-20, 1996 Vol. VI: Subsea Technology. 112p. 1996. 72.00 (*0-7918-1495-5*, G00990) ASME Pr.

Proceedings of the Fifteenth International Technical Conference on Coal & Slurry Technologies (1990) LC 86-6147. (Illus.). 790p. 1990. 175.00 (*0-932066-15-1*) Coal Slurry Tech.

Proceedings of the 15th National Online Meeting, 1994. Ed. by Martha E. Williams. 464p. 1994. pap. 55.00 (*0-938734-84-9*) Info Today Inc.

Proceedings of the 15th Oil Shale Symposium. Ed. by James H. Gary. LC 82-4294. (Illus.). 597p. 1982. pap. 20.00 (*0-918062-50-0*) Colo Sch Mines.

Proceedings of the Fifteenth West Coast Conference on Formal Linguistics. Ed. by Brian Agbayani & Sze-Wing Tang. (Proceedings of the West Coast Conference on Formal Linguistics Ser.). (Illus.). 544p. (C). 1997. 74.95 (*1-57586-079-1*); pap. 27.95 (*1-57586-078-3*) CSLI.

Proceedings of the Fifteenth World Petroleum Congress. World Petroleum Congress Staff. LC 99-169805. 1998. text 660.00 (*0-471-97542-7*) Wiley.

Proceedings of the Fifth Annual ACM-SIAM Symposium on Discrete Algorithms. LC 93-46264. (Proceedings in Applied Mathematics Ser.: No. 70). ix, 735p. 1994. pap. 76.50 (*0-89871-329-3*) Soc Indus-Appl Math.

Proceedings of the Fifth Annual Cardiac Residents' Program on Cardiovascular Surgery. Ed. & Illus. by Silent Partners, Inc. Staff. 92p. (Orig.). 1989. pap. write for info. (*1-878353-08-X*) Silent Partners.

Proceedings of the 5th Annual Control Engineering Conference. Ed. & Intro. by Byron K. Ledgerwood. (Control Engineering Conference Ser.). 478p. 1986. 85.00 (*0-914331-55-8*, Control Engrng) Cahners Busn Des Plaines.

Proceedings of the Fifth Annual International Conference on Technology in Collegiate Mathematics. Lewis Lum. (C). 1993. pap. text 29.33 (*0-201-54304-4*) Addison-Wesley.

***Proceedings of the Fifth Annual Symposium of the Institute of Islamic & Arabic Sciences in America, 1 Rajab, 1418 A. H., November 1, 1997 C. E.** Institute of Islamic & Arabic Sciences in America Staff. LC 99-16189. 1999. write for info. (*1-56923-023-4*) Inst Islamic.

Proceedings of the 5th Conference of the Canadian Number Theory Association. Canadian Number Theory Association Staff et al. LC 98-49282. (CRM Proceedings & Lecture Notes Ser.). 1999. write for info. (*0-8218-0964-4*) Am Math.

Proceedings of the Fifth European Conference on Mathematics in Industry. Ed. by Matti Heilio. (C). 1991. text 253.00 (*0-7923-1317-8*) Kluwer Academic.

Proceedings of the Fifth Florida Artificial Intelligence Research Symposium. Ed. by Mark B. Fishman. 350p. (C). 1992. pap. text 35.00 (*0-9620173-4-5*) FL AI Research.

Proceedings of the Fifth IEEE Computer Society Workshop on Future Trends of Distributed Computing Systems, August 28-30, 1995, Cheju Island, Korea. IEEE Workshop on Future Trends of Distributed Computing Systems & IEEE Computer Society. LC 95-77936. xi, 531 p. 1995. pap. write for info. (*0-7803-3066-8*) Inst Electrical.

Proceedings of the 5th International Colloqium on Differential Equations. Ed. by D. Bainov & V. Covachev. 370p. 1995. 165.00 (*90-6764-192-8*, Pub. by VSP) Coronet Bks.

Proceedings of the 5th International Conference on Principles of Knowledge Representation & Reasoning. Ed. by Stuart Shapiro. 700p. (C). 1998. pap. text 63.00 (*1-55860-421-9*) Morgan Kaufmann.

Proceedings of the Fifth International Colloquium on Paratuberculosis, September 29-October 4, 1996: A Meeting of the International Association for Paratuberculosis, Madison, Wisconsin, U. S. A. R. J. Chiodini et al. LC 97-25264. 1997. pap. write for info. (*0-9633043-3-X*) Intl Assn Paratuber.

Proceedings of the Fifth International Conference on Adaptive Structures. Ed. by Junji Tani et al. 748p. 1995. 39.95 (*1-56676-325-8*, 763258) Technomic.

Proceedings of the Fifth International Conference on Basement Tectonics. Ed. by S. Riad & D. L. Baars. (Illus.). 350p. 1986. 37.50 (*0-317-43039-4*) Intl Basement.

Proceedings of the Fifth International Conference on Intelligent Systems for Molecular Biology. Ed. by Terry Gaasterland et al. (Technical Reports). (Illus.). 372p. (Orig.). 1997. pap. text 55.00 (*1-57735-022-7*) AAAI Pr.

Proceedings of the Fifth International Conference on the Study of Shamanism & Alternate Modes of Healing, 1988, Santa Sabina Center, San Rafael, California, September 3-5, 1988. Ed. by Ruth-Inge Heinze. LC 89-2092. (Illus.). 432p. (C). 1989. pap. 21.75 (*0-945875-02-9*) Independent Scholars Asia Inc.

Proceedings of the Fifth International Congress on Biochemistry, Moscow, August, 1961, 9 vols., Set. N. Sissakian. LC 59-8791. 1963. 1601.00 (*0-08-009851-7*, Pub. by Pergamon Repr) Franklin.

Proceedings of the 5th International Meeting on Ferroelectricity, 5 pts. I. Lefkowitz & G. Taylor. 1370p. 1981. 1238.00 (*0-685-27100-5*) Gordon & Breach.

Proceedings of the 5th International Symposium on Innovative Numerical Methods, 2 vols., Set. Ed. by R. Gruber et al. LC 89-62042. (INME Ser.). 1478p. 1989. 314.00 (*0-945824-24-6*) Computational Mech MA.

Proceedings of the Fifth International Symposium on Acoustic Emission from Composite Material (AECM-5) (Illus.). 410p. 1995. pap. 31.00 (*1-57117-012-X*, 1349) Am Soc Nondestructive.

Proceedings of the Fifth International Symposium on Protection Against Chemical & Biological Warfare Agents. (Illus.). 437p. (Orig.). (C). 1996. pap. text 50.00 (*0-7881-2996-1*) DIANE Pub.

Proceedings of the Fifth International Symposium on Protection Against Chemical & Biological Warfare Agents: Supplement. (Illus.). 330p. (Orig.). (C). 1996. pap. text 30.00 (*0-7881-2997-X*) DIANE Pub.

Proceedings of the Fifth International Symposium on Silicon-on-Insulator Technology & Devices. Ed. by Wayne E. Bailey. LC 92-81318. (Proceedings Ser.: Vol. 92-13). 452p. 1992. 55.00 (*1-56677-013-0*) Electrochem Soc.

Proceedings of the Fifth International Workshop on Compressible Turbulent Mixing. LC 96-44252. 450p. 1996. lib. bdg. 47.00 (*981-02-2910-0*) World Scientific Pub.

Proceedings of the 5th Nordic Ornithological Congress, 1985. Ed. by Mats O. Eriksson. (Acta Regiae Zoologica Ser.: No. 14). (Illus.). 228p. (Orig.). 1987. pap. 81.00 (*91-85252-40-9*, Pub. by Vetenskaps) Coronet Bks.

Proceedings of the 5th Quadrennial Symposium, Snowbird, Utah, 1978. Ed. by John D. Ridge. (International Association on the Genesis of Ore Deposits (IAGOD) Symposia Ser.). (Illus.). xii, 795p. 1980. text 58.00 (*3-510-65094-8*, Pub. by E Schweizerbartsche) Balogh.

Proceedings of the 5th Round Table with European Ombudsmen (Limassol, Cyprus 8-10 May, 1996) (Human Rights & Democracy Ser.). 1996. 25.00 (*92-871-3148-1*, Pub. by Council of Europe) Manhattan Pub Co.

Proceedings of the 5th SIAM Conference on Applied Linear Algebra. SIAM Conference on Applied Linear Algebra Staff. Ed. by John G. Lewis. LC 94-19958. (Proceedings in Applied Mathematics Ser.: No. 72). x, 578p. 1994. pap. 84.50 (*0-89871-336-6*) Soc Indus-Appl Math.

Proceedings of the Fifth SIAM Conference on Parallel Processing for Scientific Computing. Ed. by Jack Dongarra et al. LC 92-26416. (Proceedings in Applied Mathematics Ser.: No. 62). xvii, 648p. 1992. pap. 112.00 (*0-89871-303-X*) Soc Indus-Appl Math.

Proceedings of the 5th Symposium on Ferroelectric Semiconductors: A Special Issue of the Journal Ferroelectrics. V. M. Fridkin. vi, 224p. 1988. pap. text 589.00 (*2-88124-303-7*) Gordon & Breach.

Proceedings of the 5th Symposium on the Geology of the Bahamas. Ed. by Roger J. Bain. (Illus.). 247p. (Orig.). (C). 1991. pap. text 20.00 (*0-935909-37-0*) Bahamian.

Proceedings of the Fifth Symposium on the Geology of Rocky Mountain Coal, 1982. Ed. by Klaus D. Gurgel. (Bulletin of the Utah Geological Survey Ser.: No. 118). (Illus.). 319p. (Orig.). 1982. pap. 20.00 (*1-55791-085-5*, B-118) Utah Geological Survey.

Proceedings of the Fifth Symposium on the Natural History of the Bahama's June 11-14, 1993. Ed. by Lee B. Kass. (Illus.). 107p. (Orig.). (C). 1994. pap. text 15.00 (*0-935909-52-4*) Bahamian.

Proceedings of the Fifth (1995) International Offshore & Polar Engineering Conference, Set, Vols. I-IV. Ed. by Jin S. Chung et al. LC 94-73796. 2543p. (Orig.). 1995. pap. 340.00 (*1-880653-16-8*) ISOPE.

Proceedings of the Fifth (1995) International Offshore & Polar Engineering Conference, Vol. I. Ed. by Jin S. Chung et al. LC 94-73796. (Orig.). 1995. pap. 100.00 (*1-880653-17-6*) ISOPE.

Proceedings of the Fifth (1995) International Offshore & Polar Engineering Conference, Vol. II. Ed. by Jin S. Chung et al. LC 94-73796. (Orig.). 1995. pap. 100.00 (*1-880653-18-4*) ISOPE.

Proceedings of the Fifth (1995) International Offshore & Polar Engineering Conference, Vol. III. Ed. by Jin S. Chung et al. LC 94-73796. (Orig.). 1995. pap. 100.00 (*1-880653-19-2*) ISOPE.

Proceedings of the Fifth (1995) International Offshore & Polar Engineering Conference, Vol. IV. Ed. by J. F. Dos Santos et al. LC 94-73796. (Orig.). 1995. pap. 100.00 (*1-880653-20-6*) ISOPE.

Proceedings of the 50th Annual Meeting Vol. 1: January 1998 Chicago. (C). 1998. pap. write for info. (*0-913447-72-2*) Indus Relations Res.

Proceedings of the 50th Annual Meeting Vol. 2: January 1998 Chicago. 1998. pap. write for info. (*0-913447-73-0*) Indus Relations Res.

Proceedings of the 50th ASIS Annual Meeting, 1987. 1987. 40.00 (*0-938734-19-9*) Info Today Inc.

Proceedings of the 55th Annual Meeting of the American Society for Information Science (ASIS), 1992. Ed. by Debora Shaw. 375p. 1992. pap. 45.00 (*0-938734-69-5*) Info Today Inc.

Proceedings of the 51st Annual Meeting of the American Society for Information Science, 1988. 264p. 1988. pap. 40.00 (*0-938734-29-6*) Info Today Inc.

Proceedings of the 51st Annual Meeting - New York City, Jan. 1999. 1999. pap. write for info. (*0-913447-75-7*) Indus Relations Res.

Proceedings of the 52nd Annual Meeting - Boston, Jan. 2000. 2000. pap. 24.95 (*0-913447-78-1*) Indus Relations Res.

Proceedings of the 52nd Purdue Industrial Waste Conference. Ed. by James E. Alleman. (Illus.). 750p. (C). 1998. ring bd. 94.95 (*1-57504-098-0*) CRC Pr.

Proceedings of the 1st Oxford-Waterloo Research Seminar Vol. 2: Planning & Design in Britian & Canada. A Comparison of Education & Practice. G. Rich. (C). 1987. 40.00 (*0-7855-3826-7*, Pub. by Oxford Polytechnic) St Mut.

Proceedings of the First Annual ACM-SIAM Symposium on Discrete Algorithms. Ed. by D. Johnson. LC 89-26304. (Miscellaneous Bks.: No. 18). xiv, 523p. 1990. pap. 42.00 (*0-89871-251-3*) Soc Indus-Appl Math.

Proceedings of the First Annual Georgia Convocation on Professionalism: "The Practice of Law - Is There Anything More to It Than Making Money?" Ed. by Michael Goldberg. 1989. pap. text 10.00 (*1-55816-000-0*) ICLE Georgia.

Proceedings of the 1st Annual Race Horse Conference. (Illus.). 51p. (Orig.). (C). 1994. pap. text 25.00 (*0-7881-1367-4*) DIANE Pub.

Proceedings of the 1st Catalan Symposium. Ed. by Josep M. Sola-Sole. LC 92-28129. (Catalan Studies: Translations & Criticism: Vol. 6). 135p. (C). 1993. text 41.95 (*0-8204-2036-0*) P Lang Pubng.

Proceedings of the First Champlain Valley Symposium, 1981. Ed. by Bruce P. Stark. 50p. 1982. pap. 5.00 (*1-890402-04-4*) Clinton Cnty Hist.

Proceedings of the First Convention of the Industrial Workers of the World: Officially Approved, Stenographically Reported see Founding Convention of the IWW: Proceedings

Proceedings of the 1st European Congress on the History of Psychiatry & Mental Health Care. Ed. by L. Goei & J. Vijselaar. 352p. 1993. pap. 48.00 (*90-5235-036-1*, Pub. by Erasmus Pub) Balogh.

Proceedings of the 1st European Workshop on Periodontology. Ed. by Niklaus P. Lang & Thorkild Karring. (Illus.). 478p. 1997. 58.50 (*1-85097-035-1*) Quint Pub Co.

P

An Asterisk (*) at the beginning of an entry indicates that the title is appearing for the first time.

Proceedings of the 1st Florida AI Research Symposium. First Florida AI Research Symposium Staff. Ed. by Mark B. Fishman. (Illus.). (Orig.). (C). 1988. pap. text 20.00 (*0-9620173-0-2*) FL AI Research.

Proceedings of the 1st High Performance Computing, 1993. Adrian Tentner. 286p. 1993. pap. 80.00 (*1-56555-052-8*, SMC93-2) Soc Computer Sim.

Proceedings of the 1st International Rotifer Symposium. Ed. by Charles W. King. (Advances in Limnology Ser.: Vol. 8). (GER., Illus.). vi, 315p. 1977. 44.00 (*3-510-47006-0*, Pub. by E Schweizerbartsche) Balogh.

Proceedings of the 1st International Conference on Principles of Knowledge Representation & Reasoning. Ed. by James Allen et al. (Representation & Reasoning Ser.). 520p. (C). 1989. pap. text 39.95 (*1-55860-032-9*) Morgan Kaufmann.

Proceedings of the 1st International Conference on Shape Memory & Superelastic Technologies (SMST-94) Alan R. Pelton et al. 527p. (C). 1995. 100.00 (*0-9645943-0-7*) MIAS.

Proceedings of the 1st International Conference on Future Energy. Ed. by Thomas Valone. (Illus.). 250p. 1999. 40.00 (*0-9641070-3-1*) Integrity Res.

Proceedings of the 1st International Conference on Smarandache Type Notions in Number Theory: Papers. Intl. Conference on Smarandache Type Nothing in Nu. Ed. by C. Dumitrescu & V. Seleacu. LC QA0292.. (Illus.). 208p. reprint ed. pap. 64.50 (*0-608-09130-8*, 206976200006) Bks Demand.

Proceedings of the 1st International Conference on Word & Image: Word & Image Special Issue, Vol. 4, No. 1. John D. Hunt et al. 1988. pap. 45.00 (*0-85066-894-8*) Taylor & Francis.

Proceedings of the First International Clinical Symposium on the CarboMedics Prosthetic Heart Valve. Ed. & Illus. by Silent Partners, Inc. Staff. 105p. (Orig.). 1989. pap. write for info. (*1-878353-11-X*) Silent Partners.

Proceedings of the First International Colloquium on Numerical Analysis. Ed. by D. Bainov & V. Covachev. viii, 178p. 1993. 107.50 (*90-6764-152-9*) Coronet Bks.

Proceedings of the First International Conference on Adaptive Structures. Ed. by Ben K. Wada et al. LC 91-65136. 1057p. 1991. 39.95 (*0-87762-832-7*) Technomic.

Proceedings of the First International Conference on Advances in Communication & Control Systems. Ed. by N. DeClaris. LC 88-27478. 224p. 1988. pap. text 98.00 (*0-911575-47-2*) Optimization Soft.

Proceedings of the First International Conference on Difference Equations: Trinity University, San Antonio, Texas, May 25-28, 1994. Ed. by Saber N. Elaydi. LC 99-510247. 512p. 1995. text 132.00 (*2-88449-145-7*); pap. text 55.00 (*2-88449-146-5*) Gordon & Breach.

Proceedings of the First International Conference on Electronic Materials: Materials Research Society International Symposium Proceedings-ICEM. Ed. by T. Sugano et al. 246p. 1989. text 17.50 (*1-55899-044-5*) Materials Res.

Proceedings of the First International Conference on Frontiers of Physics - Looking to the 21st Century. 1000p. 1997. text 66.00 (*981-02-3119-9*) World Scientific Pub.

Proceedings of the First International Conference on Genetic Algorithms & Their Applications. Ed. by John J. Grefenstette. 240p. 1988. pap. 49.95 (*0-8058-0426-9*) L Erlbaum Assocs.

Proceedings of the First International Conference on Intelligent Materials: ICIM '92. Ed. by Toshinori Takagi et al. LC 92-6210. 525p. 1992. text 119.95 (*0-87762-984-6*) Technomic.

Proceedings of the First International Conference on Intelligent Systems for Molecular Biology. Ed. by Lawrence Hunter et al. (Illus.). 460p. (Orig.). (C). 1993. pap. text 45.00 (*0-929280-47-4*) AAAI Pr.

Proceedings of the First International Conference on Mechanochemistry, 2 vols. Ed. by K. Tkacova. Incl. Vol. 1. Proceedings of the First International Conference on Mechanochemistry. 190p. (C). 1994. pap. 83.00 (*1-898326-01-0*, Pub. by CISP); Vol. 2. Proceedings of the First International Conference on Mechanochemistry. 210p. (C). 1994. pap. 83.00 (*1-898326-02-9*, Pub. by CISP); 395p. 1994. Set pap. 149.00 Balogh.

Proceedings of the First International Conference on Mechanochemistry see Proceedings of the First International Conference on Mechanochemistry

Proceedings of the First International Conference on Multiagent Systems: June 12-14, 1995, San Francisco. Ed. by Victor Lesser & Les Gasser. (AAAI Press Ser.). (Illus.). 490p. (C). 1995. pap. text 77.00 (*0-262-62102-9*) MIT Pr.

Proceedings of the First International Conference on Veterinary Behavioural Medicine. UFAW Staff. 342p. 1997. pap. 105.00 (*0-900767-97-9*, Pub. by Univs Fed Animal Welfare) St Mut.

Proceedings of the First International Congress on Cataract Surgery, Florence, 1978. International Congress on Cataract Surgery Staff. Ed. by J. Francois et al. (Documenta Ophthalmologica Proceedings Ser.: No. 21). (Illus.). 1979. text 366.50 (*90-6193-162-2*) Kluwer Academic.

Proceedings of the First International Congress on the Hellenic Diaspora from Antiquity to Modern Times, Montreal, 17-22 April 1988, Athens, 26-30 April 1988, Vols. 1 & 2. Ed. by John M. Fossey & Jacques Morin. (McGill University Monographs in Classical Archaeology & History: No. 10.1&10.2). 839p. 1991. 264.00 (*90-5063-060-X*, Pub. by Gieben) J Benjamins Pubng Co.

Proceedings of the First International DIANA Conference on Computational Mechanics. Ed. by Ger M. Kusters & Max A. Hendricks. LC 94-32854. (Diverse Ser.). 416p. (C). 1994. text 213.00 (*0-7923-3104-4*) Kluwer Academic.

Proceedings of the 1st International Symposium on Teacher Education in Deafness, 1992. (Illus.). vi, 343p. 1993. pap. 25.00 (*1-893891-15-1*) Gallaudet U Contin Ed.

Proceedings of the 1st International Symposium on Peizoelectricity. P. M. Galletti et al. iv, 326p. 1984. pap. text 306.00 (*0-677-40485-9*) Gordon & Breach.

***Proceedings of the First International Soda Ash Conference: Utilization of Natural Resources of Sodium Carbonate into the Next Century: Meeting in Rock Springs, Wyoming, June 10-12, 1997.** International Soda Ash Conference Staff et al. LC 98-183336. (Public Information Circular Ser.). 1998. write for info. (*1-884589-14-6*) Wyoming St Geol.

Proceedings of the First International Symposium on Domain Decomposition Methods for Partial Differential Equations. Ed. by Roland Glowinski et al. LC 87-51546. (Proceedings in Applied Mathematics Ser.: No. 30). x, 431p. 1988. text 54.50 (*0-89871-220-3*) Soc Indus-Appl Math.

Proceedings of the First International Symposium on Turtles & Tortoises: Conservation & Captive Husbandry. Ed. by K. R. Beaman et al. 171p. 1991. pap. 25.00 (*1-887945-00-8*) CTTC.

Proceedings of the 1st International Workshop on Sediment Phosphorus, March 1986. Ed. by Roland Psenner & Amarasinha Gunatilaka. (Advances in Limnology Ser.: Vol. 30). (GER., Illus.). vii, 115p. 1988. pap. text 32.00 (*3-510-47028-1*, Pub. by E Schweizerbartsche) Balogh.

Proceedings of the First International Workshop on Larch, Dedham, U. S. A. 13-15 July 1992. Ed. by Ursula Martin & Jeannette M. Wing. LC 92-36174. (Workshops in Computing Ser.). 1993. 79.00 (*0-387-19804-0*) Spr-Verlag.

Proceedings of the First ISOPE Ocean Mining Symposium (1995) LC 95-77708. (Illus.). 238p. (Orig.). 1995. pap. 100.00 (*1-880653-21-4*) ISOPE.

***Proceedings of the First Lighting Research Roundtable: University of Nebraska, September 16-17, 1999.** Ed. by Kevin W. Houser. (Illus.). 82p. 2000. pap. write for info. (*0-9701152-0-2*) P Kiewit Inst.

Proceedings of the 1st National Conference & Workshop, Environmental Stress Screening of Electronic Hardware, March 1979. National Conference & Workshop Staff. LC 62-38584. 1979. pap. text 65.00 (*0-915414-59-7*) IEST.

Proceedings of the First National Scientific Meeting of the Royal College of Obstetricians & Gynaecologists, Singapore, 20-23 September 1990. Ed. by F. H. Tsakok et al. LC 92-18105. 275p. (C). 1992. text 81.00 (*981-02-0794-8*) World Scientific Pub.

Proceedings of the First Offshore Mechanics, Arctic Engineering, Deepsea Systems Symposium: Presented at Energy-Sources Technology Conference & Exhibition, New Orleans, Louisiana, March 7-10, 1982, 2 vols., Vol. 1. Offshore Mechanics, Arctic Engineering, Deepsea Sy. Ed. by Jin S. Chung et al. LC 82-70515. (Illus.). 254p. reprint ed. pap. 78.80 (*0-8357-2838-2*, 203907400001) Bks Demand.

Proceedings of the First Offshore Mechanics, Arctic Engineering, Deepsea Systems Symposium: Presented at Energy-Sources Technology Conference & Exhibition, New Orleans, Louisiana, March 7-10, 1982, 2 vols., Vol. 2. Offshore Mechanics, Arctic Engineering, Deepsea Sy. Ed. by Jin S. Chung et al. LC 82-70515. (Illus.). 300p. reprint ed. pap. 93.00 (*0-8357-2839-0*, 203907400002) Bks Demand.

Proceedings of the First SAE Aerospace Manufacturing Technology Conference. 1997. pap. 99.00 (*0-7680-0228-1*, P-313) Soc Auto Engineers.

Proceedings of the First San Salvador Conference Columbus & His World. Ed. by Donald T. Gerace. LC 87-70948. 368p. 1987. pap. text 20.00 (*0-935909-23-0*) Bahamian.

Proceedings of the 1st Seattle Symposium in Biostatistics, Vol. 123. D. Mposium Lin & Thomas R. Fleming. LC 97-13962. (Lecture Notes in Statistics Ser.). 1997. pap. 34.95 (*0-387-94992-5*) Spr-Verlag.

Proceedings of the First Sino-American Workshop on Mountain Meteorology. Ed. by Zhu Baozhen et al. (Illus.). 699p. 1983. 47.50 (*0-933876-58-0*) Am Meteorological.

Proceedings of the 1st-6th International Conferences on Principles of Knowledge Representation & Reasoning (KR) Ed. by Anthony G. Cohn et al. 672p. (C). 1998. pap. text 95.00 (*1-55860-554-1*) Morgan Kaufmann.

Proceedings of the 1st Symposium on the Botany of the Bahamas. Robert R. Smith. 165p. 1986. pap. text 10.00 (*0-935909-18-4*) Bahamian.

Proceedings of the 1st Turbomachinery Maintenance Congress. (Illus.). 360p. (Orig.). 1985. pap. 52.50 (*0-9615256-0-6*) Turbomachinery.

Proceedings of the First U. S. - Japan Conference on the Frontiers of Statistical Modeling: An Informational Approach. Ed. by H. Bozdogan. (Theory & Methodology of Time Series Analysis). 300p. (C). 1994. lib. bdg. 144.00 (*0-7923-2597-4*) Kluwer Academic.

Proceedings of the First U. S. - Japan Conference on the Frontiers of Statistical Modeling: An Informational Approach, May 24-29, 1992, Knoxville, Tennessee, 3 vols. Ed. by H. Bozdogan et al. LC 93-43469. 1994. lib. bdg. 390.00 (*0-7923-2600-8*) Kluwer Academic.

Proceedings of the First U. S. - Japan Conference on the Frontiers of Statistical Modeling, an Informational Approach, Vol. 2: Multivariate Statistical Modeling. Ed. by H. Bozdogan et al. 432p. (C). 1994. lib. bdg. 203.00 (*0-7923-2598-2*) Kluwer Academic.

Proceedings of the First U. S. - Japan Conference on the Frontiers of Statistical Modeling, an Informational Approach, Vol. 3: Engineering & Scientific Applications. Ed. by H. Bozdogan. (DIVS-Diverse Ser.). 364p. (C). 1994. lib. bdg. 173.50 (*0-7923-2599-0*) Kluwer Academic.

Proceedings of the First Workshop on Neural Networks, 1990: Academic-Industrial-NASA-Defense. Ed. by Mary L. Padgett. 516p. 1990. pap. 80.00 (*0-911801-66-9*, WNN90-1) Soc Computer Sim.

Proceedings of the 1st Yuman Languages Workshop. fac. ed. Ed. by J. E. Redden. (Southern Illinois University, University Museum Ser.: No. 7). 159p. 1976. reprint ed. pap. text 17.50 (*1-55567-493-3*) Coyote Press.

Proceedings of the First (1990) European Offshore Mechanics Symposium. Jin S. Chung et al. LC 90-84691. 575p. (Orig.). 1990. pap. 80.00 (*0-9626104-4-5*) ISOPE.

Proceedings of the First (1991) International Offshore & Polar Engineering Conference, 4 vols. Ed. by Jin S. Chung et al. LC 91-71635. 2148p. (Orig.). 1991. pap. 320.00 (*0-9626104-5-3*) ISOPE.

Proceedings of the First (1991) International Offshore & Polar Engineering Conference, Vol. I. Ed. by Jin S. Chung et al. LC 91-71635. 476p. (Orig.). 1991. pap. 100.00 (*0-9626104-6-1*) ISOPE.

Proceedings of the First (1991) International Offshore & Polar Engineering Conference, Vol. II. Ed. by Michael S. Triantafyllou et al. LC 91-71635. 597p. (Orig.). 1991. pap. 100.00 (*0-9626104-7-X*) ISOPE.

Proceedings of the First (1991) International Offshore & Polar Engineering Conference, Vol. III. Ed. by Jin S. Chung et al. LC 91-71635. 546p. (Orig.). 1991. pap. 100.00 (*0-9626104-8-8*) ISOPE.

Proceedings of the First (1991) International Offshore & Polar Engineering Conference, Vol. IV. Ed. by Charles P. Ellinas et al. LC 91-71635. 529p. (Orig.). 1991. pap. 100.00 (*0-9626104-9-6*) ISOPE.

Proceedings of the Flywheel Energy Storage Workshop (October, 1995) Contrib. by David O'Kain & Joyce Carmack. (Flywheel Energy Information Ser.: No. II). 475p. 1996. lib. bdg. 205.00 (*0-89934-328-7*, BT966) Bus Tech Bks.

Proceedings of the Formalist Criticism Symposium. Formalist Criticism Symposium Staff. Ed. by William J. Handy. LC 67-63594. (Quarterly Ser.). 1965. 10.00 (*0-87959-071-8*) U of Tex H Ransom Ctr.

Proceedings of the Fortieth Annual Convention of the American Association of Equine Practitioners, Held in Vancouver, British Columbia, December 4-7, 1994. American Association of Equine Practitioners Staff. Ed. by Rebecca P. Bakhaus. LC 79-2671. 212p. 1994. reprint ed. pap. 65.80 (*0-608-01731-0*, 206238800002) Bks Demand.

Proceedings of the Forty-Fifth Annual Ohio Transportation Engineering Conference. 264p. (Orig.). (C). 1993. pap. text 50.00 (*1-56806-981-2*) DIANE Pub.

Proceedings of the Forty-First Annual Convention of the American Association of Equine Practitioners, Held in Lexington, Kentucky, December 3-6, 1995. American Association of Equine Practitioners Staff. Ed. by Susan E. Zinninger. LC 79-2671. 298p. 1995. reprint ed. pap. 92.40 (*0-608-01732-9*, 206238900002) Bks Demand.

Proceedings of the 41st Annual Technical Meeting of the Institute of Environmental Sciences, 1995, Vols. 1 & 2. LC 96-114400. 911p. 1995. 190.00 (*1-877862-41-X*) IEST.

Proceedings of the 44th Annual Convention of the American Association of Equine Practitioners, Baltimore, MD, December 6-9, 1998, Vol. YN, 1998. American Association of Equine Practitioners Staff. LC 79-2671. (Illus.). 328p. reprint ed. pap. 101.70 (*0-608-20237-1*, 207149600044) Bks Demand.

Proceedings of the 44th Annual Rocky Mountain Mineral Law Institute. 1000p. 1998. text 130.00 (*0-929047-77-X*) Rocky Mtn Mineral Law Found.

Proceedings of the 49th Industrial Waste Conference: Purdue University, May 1994. Ed. by Ronald F. Wukasch & Cynthia S. Dalton. 880p. 1994. lib. bdg. 129.00 (*1-56670-132-5*, L1132) Lewis Pubs.

Proceedings of the 42nd Annual ISA Analysis Division Symposium, Vol. 30. 165p. 1997. 25.00 (*1-55617-624-4*) ISA.

Proceedings of the 42nd Annual ISA Analysis Division Symposium: Presented at Pontchartrain Center, New Orleans, LA, April 7-9, 1997 - Sponsored by ISA & ISA Analysis Division, Vol. 30, 1997. ISA Analysis Division Symposium Staff. LC 63-25575. (Illus.). 178p. 1997. reprint ed. pap. 55.20 (*0-608-07981-2*, 206708000030) Bks Demand.

Proceedings of the 42nd ARMA International Conference (Chicago) ARMA Conference Speakers Staff. 692p. 1997. pap. 60.00 (*0-933887-75-2*, A4585) ARMA Intl.

Proceedings of the Forty-Seventh National Conference on Fluid Power. Ed. by National Fluid Power Association Staff. 378p. 1996. pap. 60.00 (*0-942220-36-6*) Natl Fluid Power.

Proceedings of the Forty-Seventh National Conference on Fluid Power, Vol. II. Ed. by National Fluid Power Association Staff. 480p. 1996. pap. 60.00 (*0-942220-37-4*) Natl Fluid Power.

***Proceedings of the 46th Annual International Instrumentation Symposium: Aerospace Industries Division/Test Measurement Division.** 560p. 2000. pap. 80.00 (*1-55617-725-9*) ISA.

Proceedings of the Forty-Third Industrial Waste Conference, May 10, 11, 12, 1988, Purdue University. Ed. by John M. Bell. (Illus.). 880p. 1989. boxed set 149.00 (*0-87371-205-6*, L205) Lewis Pubs.

Proceedings of the 43rd International Instrumentation Symposium: Presented at Sheraton North, Orlando, FL, Sponsored by Aerospace Industries Division & Test Measurement Division of ISA, May 4-8, 1997. International Instrumentation Symposium Staff. LC 63-25575. (Illus.). 846p. 1997. reprint ed. pap. 200.00 (*0-608-08007-1*, 206797200001) Bks Demand.

***Proceedings of the Founding Convention of the Mars Society, Pt. I.** Ed. by Robert M. Zubrin & Maggie Zubrin. 404p. 1999. pap. 40.00 (*0-912183-12-8*, Am Astronaut Soc) Univelt Inc.

***Proceedings of the Founding Convention of the Mars Society, Pt. II.** Ed. by Robert M. Zubrin & Maggie Zubrin. 408p. 1999. pap. 40.00 (*0-912183-13-6*, Am Astronaut Soc) Univelt Inc.

***Proceedings of the Founding Convention of the Mars Society, Pt. III.** Ed. by Robert M. Zubrin & Maggie Zubrin. (Illus.). 400p. 1999. pap. 40.00 (*0-912183-14-4*, Am Astronaut Soc) Univelt Inc.

Proceedings of the 14th Annual Conference: APLIC International. Ed. by Carann G. Turner. LC 76-643241. 159p. (Orig.). 1982. pap. text 14.00 (*0-933438-06-0*) APLIC Intl.

Proceedings of the Fourteenth Annual Conference of the Cognitive Science Society. Cognitive Science Society Staff. 1300p. 1992. pap. 150.00 (*0-8058-1291-1*) L Erlbaum Assocs.

Proceedings of the 14th Colloquium on the Law of Outer Space, September 20-25, 1971, Brussels, Belgium. International Institute of Space Law of the International Astronautical Federation Staff. iv, 298p. 1972. pap. 27.50 (*0-8377-0409-X*, Rothman) W S Hein.

Proceedings of the 14th IEEE VLSI Test Symposium: April 28-May 1, 1996, Princeton, New Jersey. IEEE VLSI Test Symposium et al. LC 96-75502. 1996. write for info. (*0-8186-7306-0*) IEEE Comp Soc.

***Proceedings of the 14th International Diatom Symposium.** Ed. by Shigeki Mayama et al. (Illus.). 638p. 1999. 228.00 (*3-87429-401-3*, Pub. by Koeltz Sci Bks) Lubrecht & Cramer.

Proceedings of the Fourteenth International Conference on High Energy Accelerators Pts. I-V: Tsukuba, Japan, August 22-26, 1989, Set. Ed. by Y. Kimura. cxxxii, 1918p. 1990. pap. text 920.00 (*2-88124-496-3*) Gordon & Breach.

Proceedings of the Fourteenth International Conference on High Energy Accelerators, August 22-26, Tsukuba, Japan, Pts. I-V: Special Issues of the Journal Particle Accelerators. Ed. by Y. Kimura et al. cxxxii, 1918p. 1990. pap. 3066.00 (*2-88124-487-4*) Gordon & Breach.

Proceedings of the Fourteenth International Technical Conference on Coal & Slurry Technologies (1989) LC 86-6147. (Illus.). 640p. 1989. 175.00 (*0-932066-14-3*) Coal Slurry Tech.

Proceedings of the Fourteenth National Convention of the Registry of Interpreters for the Deaf: A Celebration of the Profession. 230p. (Orig.). 1996. pap., per. 16.95 (*0-916883-17-5*) RID Pubns.

Proceedings of the 14th Oil Shale Symposium. Ed. by James H. Gary. LC 81-10238. (Illus.). 433p. 1981. pap. text 15.00 (*0-918062-46-2*) Colo Sch Mines.

Proceedings of the 14th Symposium: or Neuroadiologicum: London, June, 17-23, 1990. Ed. by G. H. Du Boulay et al. (Illus.). 680p. 1991. 278.00 (*0-387-53726-0*) Spr-Verlag.

Proceedings of the Fourteenth West Coast Conference on Formal Linguistics. Ed. by Jose Camacho et al. 600p. (C). 1996. 74.95 (*1-57586-043-0*) CSLI.

***Proceedings of the 14th World Congress of IFAC, 18 vols.** Chen et al. LC 99-51730. 1999. pap. 1967.50 (*0-08-043247-6*, Pergamon Pr) Elsevier.

Proceedings of the 14th World Orchid Conference. LC 97-215427. (Illus.). xliii, 428p. 1994. pap. 240.00 (*0-11-495125-X*, Pub. by Statnry Office) Balogh.

Proceedings of the Fourteenth World Petroleum Congress, Vol. 2. 14th ed. World Petroleum Congress Staff. LC 94-42850. 1994. text 950.00 (*0-471-95036-X*) Wiley.

Proceedings of the Fourth American Water Resources Conference Held November 18-22, 1968, Commodore Hotel, New York, New York. American Water Resources Association Staff. Ed. by Philip Cohen & Martha N. Francisco. LC HD1694.A5C6. (American Water Resources Association Proceedings Ser.: No. 6). 793p. reprint ed. pap. 200.00 (*0-608-13802-9*, 201781100008) Bks Demand.

Proceedings of the Fourth Annual ACM-SIAM Symposium on Discrete Algorithms. (Proceedings in Applied Mathematics Ser.: No. 66). xiv, 506p. 1993. pap. 62.00 (*0-89871-313-7*) Soc Indus-Appl Math.

Proceedings of the 4th Annual Control Engineering Conference. Ed. by Byron K. Ledgerwood. 528p. 1985. 85.00 (*0-914331-54-X*, Control Engrng) Cahners Busn Des Plaines.

Proceedings of the Fourth Annual Fuel Cells Contractors Review Meeting (July 1992) Ed. by W. J. Huber. (Fuel Cell Information Ser.: Vol. I). 176p. 1996. lib. bdg. 155.00 (*0-89934-306-6*, BT960) Bus Tech Bks.

Proceedings of the Fourth Annual L5 Space Development Conference, Apr. 25-28, 1985, Washington, D.C. Ed. by Frank Hecker. (Science & Technology Ser.: Vol. 68). (Illus.). 268p. 1988. 50.00 (*0-87703-272-6*, Am Astronaut Soc) Univelt Inc.

***Proceedings of the Fourth Annual Symposium of the Institute of Islamic & Arabic Sciences in America, 21-22 Jumada 11, 1417 A. H., November 2-3, 1996 C. E. Islamic Studies in American Universities.** Institute of Islamic & Arabic Sciences in America Staff. LC 99-16188. 1999. write for info. (*1-56923-022-6*) Inst Islamic.

Proceedings of the Fourth Asian Symposium on Information Display. IEEE, Electron Devices Society Staff. Ed. by Institute of Electrical & Electronics

An Asterisk (*) at the beginning of an entry indicates that the title is appearing for the first time.

Engineers, I. LC 97-160219. 100p. 1997. pap. write for info. (*962-8273-01-9*, 97TH8248); fiche. write for info. (*0-7803-3750-6*, 97TM8248) Inst Electrical.

Proceedings of the Fourth Bar-Ilan Symposium on Foundations of Artificial Intelligence. Ed. by Martin Golumbic et al. 225p. 1996. pap. text 50.00 (*1-57735-011-1*) AAAI Pr.

Proceedings of the Fourth Compton Symposium. Ed. by Charles S. Dermer et al. (AIP Conference Proceedings Ser.: Vol. 410). (Illus.). 1760p. 1998. 300.00 (*1-56396-659-X*) Am Inst Physics.

Proceedings of the Fourth Compton Symposium Pt. 1: The Compton Observatory in Review. Ed. by Charles D. Dermer et al. LC 97-77179. (Conference Proceedings Ser.: Vol. 410). (Illus.). xxviii, 534p. 1997. 120.00 (*1-56396-772-3*) Am Inst Physics.

Proceedings of the Fourth Copper Mountain Conference on Multigrid Methods. Ed. by Jan Mandel & S. McCormick. LC 89-48783. (Proceedings in Applied Mathematics Ser.: No. 41). xii, 438p. 1989. pap. 44.50 (*0-89871-248-3*) Soc Indus-Appl Math.

Proceedings of the Fourth Drexel Conference on Quantum Nonintegrability. Ed. by Da-Hsuan Feng. (Series in Physics). 400p. (Orig.). (C). 1997. pap. text 42.00 (*1-57146-040-3*) Intl Pr Boston.

Proceedings of the 4th Ethylene Producers Conference: March 31-April 1, 1992, Hyatt Regency, New Orleans. LC 92-38482. 1992. 65.00 (*0-8169-0585-1*, T-89) Am Inst Chem Eng.

Proceedings of the Fourth European Conference on Mathematics in Industry. Ed. by Hansjorg Wacker & Walter Zulehner. (European Consortium for Mathematics in Industry Ser.). (C). 1991. text 248.50 (*0-7923-1036-5*) Kluwer Academic.

Proceedings of the Fourth European Winter Conference on Liquid Crystals of Low Dimensional Order & Their Applications: A Special Issue of the Journal Molecular Crystals & Liquid Crystals, 2 vols., Set. R. Blinc et al. 650p. 1984. 1101.00 (*0-685-47157-8*) Gordon & Breach.

Proceedings of the Fourth Florida Artificial Intelligence Research Symposium. Ed. by Mark B. Fishman. 350p. (Orig.). (C). 1991. pap. text 35.00 (*0-9620173-3-7*) FL AI Research.

Proceedings of the Fourth Great Lakes Symposium on VLSI. IEEE Computer Society & Circuits & Systems Society. Ed. by IEEE Staff. 280p. 1994. pap. write for info. (*0-7803-1492-1*, 94TH0603-1); fiche. write for info. (*0-8186-5611-5*, 94TH0603-1) Inst Electrical.

Proceedings of the 4th International Conference on Principles of Knowledge Representation & Reasoning. Ed. by Jon Doyle et al. LC 94-9421. (Morgan Kaufmann Series in Representation & Reasoning). 655p. (C). 1994. pap. text 59.95 (*1-55860-328-X*) Morgan Kaufmann.

Proceedings of the 4th International Hamito-Semitic Congress. Herrmann Jungraithmayr & Walter W. Mueller. LC 86-17566. (Current Issues in Linguistic Theory Ser.: Vol. 44). xiv, 609p. (C). 1987. 130.00 (*90-272-3538-4*) J Benjamins Pubng Co.

Proceedings of the 4th International Workshop on the Measurement of Microbial Activities in the Carbon Cycle in Aquatic Ecosystems. Ed. by Vera Straskrabova. (Advances in Limnology Ser.: Vol. 34). (GER., Illus.). ix, 304p. 1990. pap. text 97.00 (*3-510-47035-4*, Pub. by E Schweizerbartsche) Balogh.

Proceedings of the 4th International Symposium on Kawasaki Disease. Ed. by Masato Takahashi & Kathryn A. Taubert. (Illus.). 529p. (Orig.). (C). 1993. pap. text 40.00 (*0-87493-200-9*) Am Heart.

Proceedings of the Fourth International Clinical Symposium on the CarboMedics Prosthetic Heart Valve. Ed. & Illus. by Silent Partners, Inc. Staff. 157p. (Orig.). 1994. pap. write for info. (*1-878353-32-2*) Silent Partners.

Proceedings of the Fourth International Colloquium on Differential Equations. Ed. by D. Bainov & V. Covachev. 316p. 1994. 135.00 (*90-6764-169-3*) Coronet Bks.

Proceedings of the Fourth International Conference on Adaptive Structures. Ed. by M. Natori et al. 686p. 1994. 79.95 (*1-56676-161-1*, 761611) Technomic.

Proceedings of the Fourth International Conference on AI & Molecular Biology. Ed. by David J. States et al. (Illus.). 261p. (Orig.). 1996. pap. text 50.00 (*1-57735-002-2*) AAAI Pr.

Proceedings of the Fourth International Conference on Artificial Intelligence Planning Systems. Ed. by Reid Simmons et al. LC 99-161199. (Illus.). 244p. 1998. pap. text 50.00 (*1-57735-052-9*) AAAI Pr.

Proceedings of the Fourth International Conference on Civil & Structural Engineering Computing, 2 vols., Set. Civil Comp Editors. 1989. pap. text 245.00 (*0-948749-10-5*, Pub. by Civil-Comp) St Mut.

Proceedings of the Fourth International Conference on Coccidioidomycosis. Ed. by Einstein & Catanzaro. LC 85-60255. 532p. 1985. 40.00 (*0-9614520-0-5*) NFID.

Proceedings of the Fourth International Conference on Knowledge Discovery & Data Mining. Ed. by Rakesh Agrawal & Paul Stolorz. LC 98-210525. (Illus.). 392p. 1998. pap. text 60.00 (*1-57735-070-7*) AAAI Pr.

Proceedings of the Fourth International Conference on Myopia, Sponsored by the Myopia International Research Foundation, Inc. March 14, 15 & 16, 1990, Singapore. Ed. by Joel Weintraub. (Illus.). 438p. 1990. pap. write for info. (*1-879037-00-9*) Myopia Internatl Res Fndtn.

Proceedings of the Fourth International Conference on Pervaporation Processes in the Chemical Industry. 590p. 1990. 120.00 (*0-939997-08-8*) Bakish Mat.

Proceedings of the Fourth International Conference on Rotor Dynamics. Ed. by Ronald L. Eshleman & Neville F. Rieger. 392p. 1994. pap. text 75.00 (*0-9635450-1-9*) Vibration Inst.

Proceedings of the Fourth International Conference on Seismic Zonation: Held at Stanford University, California, August 26-29, 1991, 4 vols., Set. 2500p. 1991. 125.00 (*0-943198-31-3*) Earthquake Eng.

Proceedings of the Fourth International Conference on the Study of Shamanism & Alternate Modes of Healing, 1987, Santa Sabina Center, San Rafael, California, September 5-7, 1987. Ed. by Ruth-Inge Heinze. (Illus.). 258p. (C). 1988. pap. 21.75 (*0-945875-01-0*) Independent Scholars Asia Inc.

Proceedings of the Fourth International Conference on Unconventional Photoactive Solids: A Special Issue of the Journal Molecular Crystals & Liquid Crystals Incorporating Nonlinear Optics. G. C. Wilson. viii, 512p. 1990. pap. text 1536.00 (*2-88124-449-1*) Gordon & Breach.

Proceedings of the Fourth International Offshore & Polar Engineering Conference, 1994, 4 vols., Set. Ed. by Jin S. Chung et al. LC 93-80555. 2589p. (Orig.). 1994. pap. 340.00 (*1-880653-10-9*) ISOPE.

Proceedings of the Fourth International Offshore & Polar Engineering Conference, 1994, Vol. I. Ed. by Jin S. Chung et al. LC 93-80555. 649p. (Orig.). 1994. pap. 100.00 (*1-880653-11-7*) ISOPE.

Proceedings of the Fourth International Offshore & Polar Engineering Conference, 1994, Vol. II. Ed. by Jin S. Chung et al. LC 93-80555. 640p. (Orig.). 1994. pap. 100.00 (*1-880653-12-5*) ISOPE.

Proceedings of the Fourth International Offshore & Polar Engineering Conference, 1994, Vol. III. Ed. by Jin S. Chung et al. LC 93-80555. 606p. (Orig.). 1994. pap. 100.00 (*1-880653-13-3*) ISOPE.

Proceedings of the Fourth International Offshore & Polar Engineering Conference, 1994, Vol. IV. Ed. by Yukio Ueda et al. LC 93-80555. 694p. (Orig.). 1994. pap. 100.00 (*1-880653-14-1*) ISOPE.

Proceedings of the Fourth International Symposium on Acoustic Emission from Composite Materials (AECM-4) (Illus.). 452p. 1992. pap. 31.00 (*0-931403-44-8*, 1335) Am Soc Nondestructive.

Proceedings of the Fourth International Symposium on Domain Decomposition Methods for Partial Differential Equations. Ed. by Roland Glowinski et al. LC 91-17125. (Proceedings in Applied Mathematics Ser.: No. 51). xi, 417p. 1991. pap. 74.50 (*0-89871-278-5*) Soc Indus-Appl Math.

Proceedings of the Fourth International Symposium on Integrated Ferroelectrics. Ed. by Rudolf Panholzer. (Illus.). (Orig.). (C). 1992. pap. 55.00 (*0-9634605-0-1*) ISOI Ferroelect.

Proceedings of the Fourth IUPAC Cadmium Workshop Held at Schmallenberg-Grafschaft, FRG, September 11-13, 1988: A Special Issue of the Journal Toxicological & Environmental Chemistry. Ed. by U. Glaser. viii, 196p. 1990. pap. text 677.00 (*0-677-26030-X*) Gordon & Breach.

Proceedings of the Fourth Meeting of the World Federation for Ultrasound in Medicine & Biology. Ed. by Australian Society of Ultrasound in Medicine Staff. 500p. 1986. pap. 155.00 (*0-08-032792-3*) Elsevier.

Proceedings of the 4th National Conference: Solid Waste Management. Ed. by Todd Paddock & Ruth Patrick. LC 90-82564. (Illus.). 355p. (Orig.). 1990. pap. 15.00 (*0-910006-50-4*) Acad Nat Sci Phila.

Proceedings of the 4th Pacific Islands Conference of Leaders: Sustainable Development & Population: June 24-26, 1993, Tahiti Nui, French Polynesia. Fourth Pacific Islands Conference of Leaders Staff. Ed. by Barbara Naudain. LC 95-7704. 1995. 10.00 (*0-86638-163-5*) EW Ctr HI.

Proceedings of the Fourth Pacific Rim Conference on Children's Literature: Children's Rights in the Multimedia Age, August 24-28, 1993, Kyoto, Japan. Ed. by Miyake Okiko & Diane Biesel. LC 97-10055. 240p. 1996. 68.00 (*0-8108-3206-2*) Scarecrow.

Proceedings of the Fourth School on Non-Accelerator Particle Astophysics: ICTP, Trieste, Italy, 17-28 July 1995. Bellotti. LC 96-2908. 552p. 1996. write for info. (*981-02-2688-8*) World Scientific Pub.

Proceedings of the Fourth Symposium on Ferroelectric Semiconductors, Rostov-On-Don, U. S. S. R. A Special Issue of the Journal Ferroelectrics, 2 vols., Set. V. M. Fridkin et al. 279p. 1982. 620.00 (*0-685-47167-5*) Gordon & Breach.

Proceedings of the 4th Symposium on the Geology of the Bahamas. Ed. by John E. Mylroie. (Illus.). 381p. (Orig.). (C). 1989. pap. text 20.00 (*0-935909-31-1*) Bahamian.

Proceedings of the Fourth Symposium on the Geology of Rocky Mountain Coal, 1980. Ed. by Lorna M. Carter. (Resource Ser.: No. 10). (Illus.). 131p. (Orig.). 1980. pap. 3.00 (*1-884216-30-7*) Colo Geol Survey.

Proceedings of the Fourth Symposium on the Natural History of the Bahamas. Ed. by W. Hardy Eshbaugh. (Illus.). 123p. (Orig.). (C). 1992. pap. text 18.00 (*0-935909-41-9*) Bahamian.

***Proceedings of the 4th U. S.-Japan Workshop on Earthquake Protective Systems for Bridges.** Shigeki Unjoh. (Illus.). 349p. (C). 1999. reprint ed. pap. text 45.00 (*0-7881-7875-X*) DIANE Pub.

Proceedings of the Fourth Workshop on Future Trends of Distributed Computing Systems, September 22-24, 1993, Lisbon, Portugal. IEEE Workshop on Future Trends of Distributed Computing Systems & IEEE Computer Society. LC 94-140207. x, 485p. 1993. pap. write for info. (*0-8186-4431-1*) IEEE Comp Soc.

***Proceedings of the 4th World Conference on Detergents: Strategies for the 21st Century.** Ed. by Arno Cahn. LC 99-26240. (Illus.). 360p. 1999. text 160.00 (*1-893997-01-4*, PC131) Am Oil Chemists.

Proceedings of the Fourth World Conference on Women, Beijing, China, 1995. 218p. 1996. pap. 21.00 (*92-1-130181-5*) United Nations Fund for Population.

Proceedings of the 4th World Congress on Pain, Seattle, WA, 1984. World Congress on Pain Staff. Ed. by Howard L. Fields et al. LC 85-14307. (Advances in Pain Research & Therapy Ser.: Vol. 9). 952p. 1985. reprint ed. pap. 200.00 (*0-608-04687-6*, 206540800004) Bks Demand.

Proceedings of the French Colonial Historical Society Annual Meetings, Sixth & Seventh, 1980-1981. French Colonial Historical Society Staff. Ed. by James J. Cooke. LC 76-644752. 160p. (Orig.). 1982. pap. 56.00 (*0-8191-2333-1*) U Pr of Amer.

Proceedings of the Fuel Cell Reformer Conference. Ed. by South Coast Air Quality Management District Staff. (Fuel Cell Information Ser.: Vol. 19). (Illus.). 194p. 1999. lib. bdg. 155.00 (*0-89934-357-0*, BT 991) Bus Tech Bks.

Proceedings of the Fuel Cell '96 Review Meeting (Aug. 1996) Ed. by Morgantown Energy Technology Center Staff. (Fuel Cell Information Ser.: Vol.IX). (Illus.). 272p. 1997. lib. bdg. 145.00 (*0-89934-338-4*, BT969) Bus Tech Bks.

Proceedings of the Fuel Cells '95 Review Meeting, Aug. 1995. T. J. George. (Fuel Cell Information Ser.: Vol. VI). (Illus.). 232p. 1996. lib. bdg. 135.00 (*0-89934-310-4*, BT962) Bus Tech Bks.

Proceedings of the Fuel Cells '94 Contractors Review Meeting (Aug. 1994) Ed. by C. P. Carpenter, 2nd & M. J. Mayfield. (Fuel Cell Information Ser.: Vol. IV). (Illus.). 100p. 1996. lib. bdg. 135.00 (*0-89934-304-X*, BT959) Bus Tech Bks.

Proceedings of the Furt Fourth European Symposium on Poultry Welfare. Ed. by C. J. Savory & B. O. Hughes. 318p. 1993. pap. 100.00 (*0-900767-83-9*, Pub. by Univs Fed Animal Welfare) St Mut.

Proceedings of the General Anti-Slavery Convention, London, 1843. General Anti-Slavery Convention. Ed. by John F. Johnson. LC 71-83957. 1977. reprint ed. 27.95 (*0-8369-8525-7*) Ayer.

Proceedings of the General Assembly of I.A.U., 16th, Grenoble, 1976. International Astronomical Union Staff. Ed. by Arnost Jappel & Edith A. Muller. (Transactions of the International Astronomical Union Ser.: Vol. XVIB). 1977. lib. bdg. 165.00 (*90-277-0836-3*) Kluwer Academic.

Proceedings of the Geology & Ore Deposits of the American Cordillera Symposium Held in 1995, 3 vols., Set. Contrib. by Geological Society of Nevada Staff. (Illus.). 1996. 125.00 (*1-889824-00-3*) Geological Soc.

Proceedings of the Geology & Ore Deposits of the American Cordillera Symposium Held in 1995, Vol. 1. Contrib. by Geological Society of Nevada Staff. (Illus.). 1996. write for info. (*1-889824-01-1*) Geological Soc.

Proceedings of the Geology & Ore Deposits of the American Cordillera Symposium Held in 1995, Vol. 2. Contrib. by Geological Society of Nevada Staff. (Illus.). 1996. write for info. (*1-889824-02-X*) Geological Soc.

Proceedings of the Geology & Ore Deposits of the American Cordillera Symposium Held in 1995, Vol. 3. Contrib. by Geological Society of Nevada Staff. (Illus.). 1996. write for info. (*1-889824-03-8*) Geological Soc.

Proceedings of the Gibbs Symposium, Yale University, May 15-17, 1989. Ed. by G. Mostow & D. Caldi. LC 90-37667. 321p. 1990. text 68.00 (*0-8218-0157-0*, GIBBS) Am Math.

Proceedings of the Global Village Conference, 1st. Ed. by Edward R. Sunshine. 489p. (C). 1992. pap. text 26.00 (*0-9629051-0-0*) Barry Univ.

Proceedings of the Governor's Conference on Crime, the Criminal & Society, New York, Sept. 30-Oct. 3, 1935. Governor's Conference on Crime Staff. Ed. by Robert M. Fogeleson. LC 74-3848. (Criminal Justice in America Ser.). 1974. reprint ed. 101.95 (*0-405-06161-7*) Ayer.

Proceedings of the Governors in the White House Conference, Washington, D.C., May 13-15, 1908. Ed. by W. J. McGee & Governors in the White House Conference Staff. LC 72-2855. (Use & Abuse of America's Natural Resources Ser.). 1972. 35.95 (*0-405-04519-0*) Ayer.

Proceedings of the Great Peace Commission. (American Indian Treaty Ser.: No. 10). 10.00 (*0-317-57385-3*) Inst Dev Indian Law.

Proceedings of the Grisons in the Year 1618. LC 78-171760. (English Experience Ser.: No. 383). 94p. 1971. reprint ed. 30.00 (*90-221-0383-8*) Walter J Johnson.

***Proceedings of the Hague Peace Conferences: Translation of the Original Texts.** International Peace Conference Staff et al. LC 00-26778. 2000. write for info. (*1-57588-633-2*) W S Hein.

***Proceedings of the Hague Peace Conferences: Translations of the Official Texts.** James Brown Scott. 2000. reprint ed. 495.00 (*1-57588-631-6*) W S Hein.

Proceedings of the Harvard Celtic Colloquium, Vol. V. Ed. by Paul Jefferiss & William J. Mahon. 415p. 1985. text 15.00 (*0-934665-06-0*) Quinlin C Pubs.

Proceedings of the Harvard Celtic Colloquium, Vols. VI & VII. Ed. by Brian R. Frykenberg & Kaarina Hollo. 355p. 1986. text 15.00 (*0-934665-07-9*) Quinlin C Pubs.

Proceedings of the Harvard Celtic Colloquium XIV (1994), Vol. XIV. Ed. by Pamela Hopkins et al. (Illus.). x, 220p. 1997. reprint ed. 32.50 (*0-9642446-5-9*); reprint ed. pap. 15.00 (*0-9642446-4-0*) Celtic Studies.

Proceedings of the Harvard Celtic Colloquium XV (1995) Ed. by Kathryn Chadbourne et al. (Illus.). viii, 306p. (C). Date not set. 32.50 (*0-9642446-9-1*, PHCC15); pap. write for info. (*0-9642446-8-3*, PHCC15) Celtic Studies.

Proceedings of the Heartworm Symposium, '89. Ed. by Gilbert Otto. 1990. text 43.00 (*0-940275-01-5*) Am Heartworm Soc.

Proceedings of the Heartworm Symposium '92. Ed. by Mark D. Soll. (Illus.). 341p. 1993. write for info. (*1-878353-29-2*) Silent Partners.

Proceedings of the Heartworm Symposium '95. Ed. by Mark D. Soll. (Illus.). 360p. 1996. write for info. (*1-878353-34-9*) Silent Partners.

Proceedings of the Hohokam Conference, 1973. Ed. by Susan S. Burton & Minnabell Laughlin. (Contributions to Anthropological Studies: No. 2). 1978. 10.00 (*0-916552-13-6*) Ctr Anthrop Studies.

Proceedings of the Hyderabad Conference on Algebraic Groups. Ed. by S. Ramanan. 546p. 1991. 60.00 (*81-231-0090-6*, HCAG/1C) Am Math.

Proceedings of the I. C. R. C., 1993. 250p. (Orig.). 1993. pap. 8.90 (*0-921100-49-3*) Inhtce Pubns.

Proceedings of the IAB Conference of Bryoecology, Budapest-Vacratot, Hungary, 5-10 August 1985: Budapest-Vacratot, Hungary 5-10 August, 1985. Ed. by J. Podani et al. (Symposia Biologica Hungarica Ser.: No. 35). 901p. (C). 1987. 270.00 (*963-05-4633-7*, Pub. by Akade Kiado) St Mut.

Proceedings of the ICEM '95 - 5th International Conference on Radioactive Waste Management & Environmental Remediation: Berlin, Germany September 3-7, 1995, 2 vols., Set, Vols. 1 & 2. Ed. by S. Slate et al. 912p. 1995. 700.00 (*0-7918-1219-7*, IX0382) ASME.

Proceedings of the Icsas 91: Recent Research & Development, 3 vols., Set. Ed. by S. K. Lee & N. E. Shanmugan. (Illus.). 1381p. (C). (gr. 13). 1991. text 470.00 (*1-85166-636-2*) Elsevier Applied Sci.

Proceedings of the IEEE-ASME Joint Railroad Conference, 1993. Ed. by Denise P. Godley & K. L. Hawthorne. 164p. 1993. 50.00 (*0-685-70662-1*, I00350) ASME.

Proceedings of the IEEE International Conference on Multimedia Computing & Systems '97: June 3-6, 1997, Ottawa, Ontario, Canada. International Conference on Multimedia Computing & Systems Staff & IEEE Computer Society Staff. LC 97-71759. xix, 665 p. 1997. write for info. incl. fiche (*0-8186-7821-6*) IEEE Comp Soc.

Proceedings of the IEEE International Workshop on Robot & Human Communication, 1993. Industrial Electronics Society Staff. Ed. by Institute of Electrical & Electronics Engineers, I. LC 93-79639. 500p. 1993. pap. write for info. (*0-7803-1407-7*, 93TH0577-7); fiche. write for info. (*0-7803-1408-5*, 93TH0577-7) Inst Electrical.

Proceedings of the IEEE Signal Processing Workshop on Higher-Order Statistics, July 21-23, 1997, Banff, Alberta, Canada. IEEE Signal Procesing Workshop on Higher-Order Statics Staff & IEEE Signal Processing Society Staff. LC 97-72013. xiii, 471 p. 1997. write for info. (*0-8186-8007-5*) IEEE Comp Soc.

Proceedings of the IEEE-SP International Symposium on Time-Frequency & Time-Scale Analysis. IEEE (Signal Processing Society) Staff. Ed. by IEEE (Institute Electrical & Electronics Engrs.) S. LC 94-78758. 680p. 1994. pap. write for info. (*0-7803-2127-8*); fiche. write for info. (*0-7803-2128-6*, 94th8007) Inst Electrical.

Proceedings of the Ieee-sp International Symposium on Time-frequency & Time-scale Analysis , October 6-9, 1998, Pittsburgh, Pennsylvania, Usa. IEEE-SP International Symposium on Time-Frequency and Time-Scale Analysis & IEEE, Signal Processing Society Staff. LC 98-86762. xiv, 676 p. 1998. write for info. (*0-7803-5074-X*) IEEE Standards.

Proceedings of the IEEE Tenth Annual International Workshop on Micro Electro Mechanical Systems. IEEE, Robotics & Automation Society Staff & Institute of Electrical & Electronics Engineers, I. LC 97-145405. 600p. 1997. pap. text. write for info. (*0-7803-3744-1*, 97CH36021); lib. bdg. write for info. (*0-7803-3745-X*, 97CB36021); fiche. write for info. (*0-7803-3746-8*, 97CM36021) Inst Electrical.

Proceedings of the Ieee Third International Workshop on Systems Management : April 22-24, 1998, Newport, Rhode Island. IEEE International Workshop on Systems Management et al. LC 98-84699. 151p. 1998. write for info. (*0-8186-8478-X*) IEEE Comp Soc.

Proceedings of the IEEE 1995 Custom Integrated Circuits Conference. IEEE, Electron Devices Staff. Ed. by Institute of Electrical & Electronics Engineers, I. LC 85-653738. 1995. pap. text. write for info. (*0-7803-2584-2*); lib. bdg. write for info. (*0-7803-2585-0*, 95CH35775); fiche. write for info. (*0-7803-2586-9*) Inst Electrical.

Proceedings of the IEEE 1995 National Aerospace & Electronics Conference: NAECON 1995. IEEE, Aerospace & Electronic Systems Society Staff. Ed. by Institute of Electrical & Electronics Engineers, I. 1200p. 1995. pap. text. write for info. (*0-7803-2666-0*, 95CH35797); lib. bdg. write for info. (*0-7803-2667-9*, 95CH35797); fiche. write for info. (*0-7803-2668-7*) Inst Electrical.

Proceedings of the IEEE 1996 Custom Integrated Circuits Conference. IEEE (Electron Devices Society) Staff. LC 85-653738. 690p. 1996. pap. text 134.00 (*0-7803-3117-6*, 96CH35886); lib. bdg. 134.00 (*0-7803-3118-4*, 96CB35886); fiche 134.00 (*0-7803-3119-2*, 96CM35886) Inst Electrical.

P

Proceedings of the IEEE 1996 National Aerospace & Electronics Conference NAECON 1996. IEEE Staff. LC 79-640977. 928p. 1996. pap. text 170.00 (0-7803-3306-3, 96CH35934); lib. bdg. 170.00 (0-7803-3307-1, 96CB35934); fiche 170.00 (0-7803-3308-X, 96CM35934) Inst Electrical.

Proceedings of the IEEE 1997 Custom Integrated Circuits Conference. IEEE (Electron-Devices Society) Staff. Ed. by IEEE (Institute of Electrical & Electronics Engine. LC 85-653738. 660p. 1997. pap. text. write for info. (0-7803-3669-0, 97CH36005); lib. bdg. write for info. (0-7803-3670-4, 97CB36005); mic. film. write for info. (0-7803-3671-2, 97CM36005) Inst Electrical.

Proceedings of the IEEE 1998 International Interconnect Technology Conference, Hyatt Regency Hotel, San Francisco, CA, June 1-3, 1998. IEEE Electron Devices Society Staff & International Interconnect Technology Conference. LC 97-80205. xv, 303p. 1998. pap. write for info. (0-7803-4286-0) IEEE Standards.

Proceedings of the IEEE 22nd Annual Northeast Bioengineering Conference. IEEE, Engineering in Medicine & Biology Society St. Ed. by IEEE, Institute of Electrical & Electronics Engine. LC 88-646567. 200p. 1996. pap. text 96.00 (0-7803-3204-0, 96CH35905); lib. bdg. 96.00 (0-7803-3205-9, 96CB35905); fiche 96.00 (0-7803-3206-7, 96CM35905) Inst Electrical.

Proceedings of the IEEE/IAFE/INFORMS 1998 Conference on Computational Intelligence for Financial Engineering. IEEE/IAFE/INFORMS Conference on Computational Intelligence for Financial Engineering et al. LC 98-85264. 263 p. 1998. write for info. (0-7803-4931-8) IEEE Standards.

Proceedings of the IES/PDA Joint Conference on Cleanrooms & Microenvironments. (Illus.). 151p. 1992. pap. 100.00 (1-877862-17-7) IEST.

Proceedings of the IFAC Sixth World Congress, Boston-Cambridge, Massachusetts, U. S. A., August 24-30, 1975, Part 4. International Federation of Automatic Control, Tri. LC 62-121. 840p. reprint ed. pap. 200.00 (0-608-12435-4, 205214900042) Bks Demand.

Proceedings of the Incremental Motion & Control Systems & Devices Symposium, 7th Annual, Hyatt-Regency Hotel, O'Hare, Ill. May 24-27, 1978. Incremental Motion & Control Systems & Devices Sym. Ed. by Benjamin C. Kuo. LC 78-53485. (Illus.). 1978. 45.00 (0-931538-00-9) Incremental Motion.

Proceedings of the Industrial Computing Conference, UCS, '96 Vol. 6, Pt. 1: Presented at McCormick Place Exposition Center, Chicago, IL, October 6-11, 1996. Industrial Computing Conference Staff. LC 92-659069. (Illus.). 342p. 1996. reprint ed. pap. 106.10 (0-608-04254-4, 206500900006) Bks Demand.

Proceedings of the Industrial Power Conference, 1994. (PWR Ser.: Vol. 24). 203p. 1994. pap. 50.00 (0-7918-1206-5, I00369) ASME.

Proceedings of the Intelligent Vehicle Symposium, 1993. Industrial Electronics Society Staff. Ed. by Institute of Electrical & Electronics Engineers, I. 450p. 1993. pap. write for info. (0-7803-1370-4, 93TH0569-4); fiche. write for info. (0-7803-1371-2, 93TH0569-4) Inst Electrical.

Proceedings of the International Churchill Societies, 1987. Martin Gilbert et al. (Oral History Ser.: No. 2). (Illus.). 68p. 1989. pap. 10.00 (0-943879-02-7) Churchill Ctr.

Proceedings of the International Churchill Societies, 1988-1989. Alistair Cooke et al. (Oral History Ser.: No. 3). (Illus.). 108p. 1990. pap., per. 10.00 (0-943879-05-1) Churchill Ctr.

Proceedings of the International Churchill Societies, 1990-1991. Martin Gilbert et al. (Oral History Ser.: No. 4). (Illus.). 124p. 1993. pap., per. 10.00 (0-943879-08-6) Churchill Ctr.

Proceedings of the International Churchill Societies 1992-1993. Edmund Murray et al. (Oral History Ser.). (Illus.). 152p. (Orig.). 1995. pap. 10.00 (0-943879-09-4) Churchill Ctr.

Proceedings of the International Clay Conference, 1985. Ed. by Leonard G. Schultz et al. (Illus.). 456p. (C). 1987. text 20.00 (0-935868-29-1) Clay Minerals.

Proceedings of the International Collaborative Effort on Injury Statistics: Papers & Workshop Findings Presented at the International Symposium on Injury Statistics, May, 1994, Bethesda, Maryland. Center for Disease Control Staff et al. LC 94-45553. (Department of Health & Human Services Publications: PHS 95-1252). 1994. write for info. (0-8406-0503-X) Natl Ctr Health Stats.

Proceedings of the International Collaborative Effort on Perinatal & Infant Mortality, Vol. III. Francis C. Notzon. (Illus.). 325p. (Orig.). (C). 1994. pap. text 50.00 (0-7881-1432-8) DIANE Pub.

Proceedings of the International Conference Advances in Composite Materials. Ed. by P. Ramakrihna. (C). 1991. 74.00 (81-204-0572-2, Pub. by Oxford IBH) S Asia.

Proceedings of the International Conference of Reformed Churches, October 15-23, 1997, Seoul, Korea. International Conference of Reformed Churches Staf. LC 97-38502. 1997. pap. 8.90 (0-921100-73-6) Inhtce Pubns.

Proceedings of the International Conference of Soil Mechanics & Foundation Engineering San Francisco, 11th, 12-16 August 1985, 5 vols., Set. 3700p. 1987. text 1288.00 (90-6191-560-0, Pub. by A A Balkema) Ashgate Pub Co.

Proceedings of the International Conference on Algebra Dedicated to the Memory of A. I. Mal'cev, 3 vols., Pt. 1. Ed. by L. A. Bokut et al. LC 92-9983. (Contemporary Mathematics Ser.: Vol. 131). 712p. 1992. pap. 80.00 (0-8218-5136-5, CONM/131.1) Am Math.

Proceedings of the International Conference on Algebra Dedicated to the Memory of A. I. Mal'cev, 3 vols., Pt. 2. Ed. by L. A. Bokut et al. LC 92-9983. (Contemporary Mathematics Ser.: Vol. 131). 704p. 1992. pap. 79.00 (0-8218-5137-3, CONM/131.2) Am Math.

Proceedings of the International Conference on Algebra Dedicated to the Memory of A. I. Mal'cev, 3 vols., Pt. 3. Ed. by L. A. Bokut et al. LC 92-9983. (Contemporary Mathematics Ser.: Vol. 131). 666p. 1992. pap. 70.00 (0-8218-5138-1, CONM/131.3) Am Math.

Proceedings of the International Conference on Algebra Dedicated to the Memory of A. I. Mal'cev, 3 vols., Set. Ed. by L. A. Bokut et al. LC 92-9983. (Contemporary Mathematics Ser.: Vol. 131). 2176p. 1992. pap. 206.00 (0-8218-5134-9, CONM/131) Am Math.

Proceedings of the International Conference on Allelopathy in Sustainable Agriculture, Forestry & Environmental, Vol. 1. S. S. Narwal & P. Tauro. 1999. pap. 250.00 (81-7233-130-4, Pub. by Scientific Pubs) St Mut.

Proceedings of the International Conference on Allelopathy in Sustainable Agriculture, Forestry & Environmental, Vol. 2. S. S. Narwal & P. Tauro. 1999. pap. 255.00 (81-7233-131-2, Pub. by Scientific Pubs) St Mut.

***Proceedings of the International Conference on Chinese Language Computing.** Ed. by Shi-Kuo Chang. (Illus.). 288p. 2000. pap. 65.00 (1-891706-04-7) Knowldge Systs.

Proceedings of the International Conference on Computer Communication, 10th, New Delhi, 4-9 November 1990. Ed. by S. Ramani et al. 800p. 1991. 142.95 (0-387-53449-0) Spr-Verlag.

Proceedings of the International Conference on Control & Information 1995. Ed. by Wong W. Shing. 1997. pap. text 44.50 (962-201-701-0, Pub. by Chinese Univ) U of Mich Pr.

Proceedings of the International Conference on Defects in Insulating Crystals: A Special Issue of Crystal Lattice Defects & Amorphous Materials, Vol. 1. Ed. by F. Luty. xiv, 266p. 1979. text 218.00 (3-7186-0009-9) Gordon & Breach.

Proceedings of the International Conference on Defects in Insulating Crystals: A Special Issue of Crystal Lattice Defects & Amorphous Materials, Vol. 2. Ed. by F. Luty. x, 272p. 1980. text 279.00 (3-7186-0035-8) Gordon & Breach.

Proceedings of the International Conference on Defects in Insulating Crystals: A Special Issue of Crystal Lattice Defects & Amorphous Materials, Vol. 3. Ed. by F. Luty. vii, 256p. 1981. text 249.00 (3-7186-0066-8) Gordon & Breach.

Proceedings of the International Conference on Defects in Insulating Crystals: A Special Issue of Crystal Lattice Defects & Amorphous Materials, Vol. 4. Ed. by F. Luty. x, 232p. 1982. text 249.00 (3-7186-0119-2) Gordon & Breach.

Proceedings of the International Conference on Electromagnetic Interference & Compatibility '97, 3-5 December, 1997, Hyderabad, India. Society of Electromagnetic Compatability Engineers Staff. LC 98-201977. xxviii, 497 p. 1997. pap. write for info. (0-7803-4170-8) Inst Electrical.

Proceedings of the International Conference on Environmental Epidemiology & Exposure Analysis: I, Health Hazards from Toxic Pollutants & Biological Monitoring; II, Ethics & Law in Environmental Epidemiology. Ed. by Michael D. Lebowitz. (Journal of Exposure Analysis & Environmental Epidemiology Ser.: Vol. 1, No. 1). (Illus.). 1993. pap. text 60.00 (0-911131-71-X) Specialist Journals.

Proceedings of the International Conference on Fuel Cells (February 23-24, 1994) Compiled by South Coast Air Quality Management District Staff. (Fuel Cell Information Ser.: Vol. III). (Illus.). 320p. 1996. lib. bdg. 155.00 (0-89934-308-2, BT961) Bus Tech Bks.

Proceedings of the International Conference on Functional Analysis & Related Topics, Held April 1969, Tokyo, Japan. International Conference on Functional Analysis &. LC QA0320.. 439p. 1970. reprint ed. pap. 136.10 (0-608-01242-4, 206193000001) Bks Demand.

Proceedings of the International Conference on Gravitational Waves: Sources & Detectors. 450p. 1997. lib. bdg. 84.00 (981-02-2854-6) World Scientific Pub.

Proceedings of the International Conference on Hydrology & Water Resources, New Delhi, India, December 1993. Ed. by Vijay P. Singh. Incl. Vol. 3. Water-Quality Hydrology. LC 97-117499. 300p. (C). 1996. lib. bdg. 159.00 (0-7923-3652-6); Vol. 1. LC 97-117499. 516p. (C). 1996. lib. bdg. 263.00 (0-7923-3650-X); Subsurface-Water Hydrology. LC 97-117499. 264p. (C). 1996. lib. bdg. 145.00 (0-7923-3651-8); LC 97-117499. (Water Science & Technology Library). 1995. Set lib. bdg. 690.00 (0-7923-3654-2) Kluwer Academic.

Proceedings of the International Conference on Imaging Science, Systems, & Technology, 1997: C. I. S. S. T. '97. Ed. by Hamid R. Arabnia. 565p. (C). 1997. pap. text 80.00 (0-9648666-9-2) C S R E A.

Proceedings of the International Conference on Low Dimensional Conductors: Special Issues of the Journal Molecular Crystals & Liquid Crystals, Set. A. J. Epstein & E. M. Conwell. 2012p. 1982. 1248.00 (0-677-16405-X) Gordon & Breach.

Proceedings of the International Conference on Martensitic (ICOMAT-92) C. M. Wayman & J. Perkins. 1347p. (C). 1992. 150.00 (0-9645943-2-3) MIAS.

Proceedings of the International Conference on Martensitic Transformations (ICOMAT-79) (Illus.). 755p. 1979. text 60.00 (0-9645943-1-5) MIAS.

Proceedings of the International Conference on Multi-Agent Systems: Cite des Sciences-la Villette, Paris, France, July 3-7, 1998. International Conference on Multi-Agent Systems Staff et al. LC 98-84973. xviii, 487p. 1998. pap. write for info. (0-8186-8502-6) IEEE Comp Soc.

Proceedings of the International Conference on Noise Control Engineering Held August 13-15, 1990, in Gothenburg, Sweden, Vols. 1 & 2. Ed. by Hans Jonassen. (Inter-Noise Ser.). xliv, 1444p. 120.00 (91-7848-224-0) Noise Control.

Proceedings of the International Conference on Noise Control Engineering Held August 24-26, 1993, in Leuven, Belgium Vols. 1-3, 3 vols., Set. Ed. by Pierre Chapelle & Gerrit Vemier. (Inter-Noise Ser.). cxx, 1896p. 150.00 (90-5204-024-9) Noise Control.

Proceedings of the International Conference on Noise Control Engineering Held December 8-10, 1980, in Miami, Fl, U. S. A., 2 vols., Set. International Conference on Noise Control Engineer. Ed. by George C. Maling, Jr. LC 72-91606. (Inter-Noise Ser.). lxxii, 1194p. 50.00 (0-931784-03-4) Noise Control.

Proceedings of the International Conference on Noise Control Engineering Held July 10-12, 1995 Newport Beach, CA, U. S. A., Set, Vols. 1 & 2. Ed. by Robert J. Bernhard & Stuart Bolton. (Inter-Noise Ser.). lvi, 1450p. 150.00 (0-931784-32-8) Noise Control.

Proceedings of the International Conference on Noise Control Engineering Held July 20-22, 1992, in Toronto, Canada, Vols. 1 & 2. Ed. by Gilles A. Daigle & Michael R. Stinson. (Inter-Noise Ser.). lxiv, 1264p. 125.00 (0-931784-25-5) Noise Control.

Proceedings of the International Conference on Noise Control Engineering Held May 17-19, 1982, in San Francisco, CA, U. S. A., 2 vols., Set. International Conference on Noise Control Engineer. Ed. by J. G. Seebold. (Inter-Noise Ser.). lxviii, 864p. 55.00 (0-931784-07-7) Noise Control.

***Proceedings of the International Conference on Nuclear & Hazardous Waste management - SPECTRUM '98: Denver,Colorado, September 13-17, 1998.** 1552p. 1998. pap. 200.00 (0-89448-635-7, 700257) Am Nuclear Soc.

Proceedings of the International Conference on Nuclear Structure, Kingston, Canada, August 29-September 3, 1960. International Conference on Nuclear Structure Staf. Ed. by D. A. Bromley & E. W. Vogt. LC QC0776.I58. 1004p. reprint ed. pap. 200.00 (0-608-10081-1, 201414400095) Bks Demand.

Proceedings of the International Conference on Nuclidic Masses, McMaster University, Hamilton, September 12-16, 1960. International Conference on Nuclidic Masses Staff. Ed. by H. E. Duckworth. LC 61-4023. 552p. reprint ed. pap. 171.20 (0-608-10092-7, 201419100089) Bks Demand.

Proceedings of the International Conference on Parallel & Distributed Processing Techniques & Applications. Ed. by Hamid R. Arabnia. 900p. (Orig.). 1995. pap. text 100.00 (0-9648666-0-9) C S R E A.

Proceedings of the International Conference on Parallel & Distributed Processing Techniques & Applications, 1997: P. D. P. T. A. '97, 3 vols. Ed. by Hamid R. Arabnia. Incl. Vol. I. 617p. (Orig.). (C). 1997. pap. text 70.00 (0-9648666-5-X); Vol. II. 611p. (Orig.). (C). 1997. pap. text 70.00 (0-9648666-6-8); Vol. III. 578p. (Orig.). (C). 1997. pap. text 70.00 (0-9648666-7-6); 200.00 (0-9648666-8-4) C S R E A.

Proceedings of the International Conference on Parallel & Distributed Processing Techniques & Applications-96, 3 vols. Ed. & Intro. by Hamid R. Arabnia. Incl. Vol. III. 573p. (Orig.). 1996. pap. text 70.00 (0-9648666-3-3); Vol. II. 508p. (Orig.). (C). 1996. pap. text 70.00 (0-9648666-2-5); Vol. I. 590p. (Orig.). (C). 1996. pap. text 70.00 (0-9648666-1-7); (P. D. P. T. A. Ser.). 210.00 (0-9648666-4-1) C S R E A.

Proceedings of the International Conference on Parallel Processing, Held 1992, Vol. 1. Mudge. 320p. 1992. per. 79.95 (0-8493-0781-3) CRC Pr.

Proceedings of the International Conference on Parallel Processing, Held 1992, Vol. 2. Shin. 336p. 1992. per. 69.95 (0-8493-0782-1) CRC Pr.

Proceedings of the International Conference on Parallel Processing, Held 1992, Vol. 3. Stout. 400p. 1992. per. 69.95 (0-8493-0783-X) CRC Pr.

Proceedings of the International Conference on Parallel Processing, 1992, 3 vols., Set. Ed. by Pen-Chung Yew. 1056p. 1992. pap. 150.00 (0-8493-0780-5, QA76.5) CRC Pr.

Proceedings of the International Conference on Parallel Processing, 1993, Vol. I: Architecture. Ed. by C. Y. Chen & P. Bruce Berra. 376p. 1993. lib. bdg. 79.95 (0-8493-8984-4, QA) CRC Pr.

Proceedings of the International Conference on Parallel Processing, 1993, Vol. II: Software. Ed. by Alok N. Choudhary & P. Bruce Berra. 336p. 1993. lib. bdg. 79.95 (0-8493-8985-2, QA) CRC Pr.

Proceedings of the International Conference on Parallel Processing, 1993, Vol. III: Algorithms & Applications. Ed. by Salim Hariri & P. Bruce Berra. 352p. 1993. lib. bdg. 79.95 (0-8493-8986-0, QA) CRC Pr.

Proceedings of the International Conference on Parallel Processing, 22nd, August 16-20, 1993, Sponsored by the Pennsylvania State University, Set. LC 93-26191. 1993. pap. 150.00 (0-8493-8983-6) CRC Pr.

Proceedings of the International Conference on Parallel Processing, 23rd Vol. 3: Algebra/Applications. Chandra. 336p. 1994. 69.95 (0-8493-2495-5) CRC Pr.

Proceedings of the International Conference on Port & Ocean Engineering under Arctic Conditions, Third, 2 vols., Set. International Conference on Port & Ocean Engineeri. Ed. by D. C. Burrell & D. W. Hood. 1382p. 1976. pap. 20.00 (0-914500-17-1) U of AK Inst Marine.

Proceedings of the International Conference on Raman Emission by X-Ray Scattering. LC 97-111666. 248p. 1996. lib. bdg. 60.00 (981-02-2825-2) World Scientific Pub.

Proceedings of the International Conference on Reservoir Limnology & Water Quality, June 15 to June 20, 1987 Teil 2: Chemical Limnology, Primary Production, Plankton, Benthos & Fish Interactions. Ed. by J. F. Talling et al. (Advances in Limnology Ser.: Vol. 33, Pt. 2). (GER., Illus.). viii, 356p. 1989. pap. 109.00 (3-510-47033-8, Pub. by E Schweizerbartsche) Balogh.

Proceedings of the International Conference on Reservoir Limnology & Water Quality, June 15 to 20, 1987 Teil 1: Physical Limnology, Mathematical Models & Microbial Decomposition. Ed. by B. Henderson-Sellers et al. (Advances in Limnology Ser.: Vol. 33, Pt. 1). (GER., Illus.). xiv, 287p. 1989. pap. text 95.00 (3-510-47032-X, Pub. by E Schweizerbartsche) Balogh.

Proceedings of the International Conference on Reservoir Limnology & Water Quality, June 15 to 20, 1987 Teil 3: Key Factors of Reservoir Limnology, Eutrophication, Water Quality & Its Prediction. Ed. by O. T. Lind et al. (Advances in Limnology Ser.: Vol. 33, Pt. 3). (GER., Illus.). iv, 333p. 1990. pap. text 109.00 (3-510-47034-6, Pub. by E Schweizerbartsche) Balogh.

Proceedings of the International Conference on Reservoir Limnology & Water Quality, June 15-20, 1987, Set. Ed. by Vera Straskrabova et al. (Advances in Limnology Ser.: Vol. 33). (GER., Illus.). pap. text. write for info. (3-510-47031-1, Pub. by E Schweizerbartsche) Balogh.

Proceedings of the International Conference on Satellite Communications. IEEE (Region 8) Staff. 492p. 1994. pap. write for info. (0-7803-2514-1, 94TH8046); fiche. write for info. (0-7803-2515-X) Inst Electrical.

Proceedings of the International Conference on Secure Personal Identification: Balancing Security, Efficiency & Privacy. 121p. (Orig.). 1990. pap. 4.00 (1-881290-23-9) Ctr Immigrat.

Proceedings of the International Conference on Sentential Complementation. W. De Geest & Y. Putseys. (Linguistic Models Ser.). x, 280p. (Orig.). (C). 1984. pap. 61.55 (3-11-013113-7) Mouton.

Proceedings of the International Conference on Shamanism, 1984, Santa Sabina Center, San Rafael, California, May 11-13, 1984. Ed. by Ruth-Inge Heinze. (Illus.). 248p. (C). 1984. pap. 21.75 (0-945875-05-3) Independent Scholars Asia Inc.

Proceedings of the International Conference on Spinal Manipulation, 1992. Intro. by Deborah L. Callahan. (Annual ICSM Proceedings Ser.). (Illus.). 210p. 1992. pap. 35.00 (0-9631715-1-8) Fnd Chiro Educ Res.

Proceedings of the International Conference on the Design & Construction of Non-Conventional Structures, 2 vols., Set. Civil Comp Editors. 1987. pap. 245.00 (0-948749-07-5, Pub. by Civil-Comp) St Mut.

Proceedings of the International Conference on the Individual & the Community in the Research, Development: And Use of Biologicals. (Bulletin Supplement Ser.: No. 55). 177p. 1977. pap. text 18.00 (92-4-068552-9) World Health.

Proceedings of the International Conference on the Physics & Chemistry of Low-Dimensional Synthetic Metals: Special Issues of the Journal Molecular Crystals & Liquid Crystals, 5 vols. Ed. by C. Pecile et al. 2272p. 1985. text 2980.00 (0-677-06665-1) Gordon & Breach.

***Proceedings of the International Conference on the Physics of Nuclear Science & Technology: Long Island, New York, October 5-8, 1998.** 1837p. 1998. pap. 120.00 (0-89448-631-4, 700251) Am Nuclear Soc.

Proceedings of the International Conference on Urban Poverty: 9-13 November 1997, Florence, Italy. International Conference on Urban Poverty Staff et al. LC 98-982735. viii, 99p. 1998. write for info. (92-1-131375-9) UN.

Proceedings of the International Conference on Women & Biodiversity. Lea M. Borkenhagen & Janet N. Abramovitz. 104p. (Orig.). 1993. pap. write for info. (1-883242-00-2) Comm Women & Biodiv.

Proceedings of the International Conferences on Noise Control Engineering Held December 4, 1984, in Honolulu, Hawaii, U. S. A., 2 vols., Set. International Conference on Noise Control Engineer. Ed. by George C. Maling, Jr. (Inter-Noise Ser.). lxxv, 1426p. 65.00 (0-931784-11-5) Noise Control.

Proceedings of the International Conferences on Very Large Databases Held in Amsterdam, The Netherlands: VLDB-89. 1998. pap. text 40.00 (1-55860-101-5) Morgan Kaufmann.

Proceedings of the International Conferences on Very Large Databases Held in Barcelona, Spain: VLDB-91. 1998. pap. text 40.00 (1-55860-150-3) Morgan Kaufmann.

Proceedings of the International Conferences on Very Large Databases Held in Bombay, India: VLDB-96. 1998. pap. text 40.00 (1-55860-382-4) Morgan Kaufmann.

Proceedings of the International Conferences on Very Large Databases Held in Brisbane, Australia: VLDB-90. 730p. 1998. pap. text 40.00 (1-55860-149-X) Morgan Kaufmann.

Proceedings of the International Conferences on Very Large Databases Held in Dublin, Ireland: VLDB-93. 1998. pap. text 40.00 (1-55860-152-X) Morgan Kaufmann.

P

An Asterisk (*) at the beginning of an entry indicates that the title is appearing for the first time.

Proceedings of the International Conferences on Very Large Databases Held in Florence, Italy: VLDB-83. 1998. pap. text 40.00 (*0-934613-15-X*) Morgan Kaufmann.

Proceedings of the International Conferences on Very Large Databases Held in Kyoto, Japan: VLDB-86. 1998. pap. text 40.00 (*0-934613-18-4*) Morgan Kaufmann.

Proceedings of the International Conferences on Very Large Databases Held in Los Angeles, California: VLDB-88. 500p. 1998. pap. text 40.00 (*0-934613-75-3*) Morgan Kaufmann.

Proceedings of the International Conferences on Very Large Databases Held in Santiago, Chile: VLDB-94. VLDB Staff. 600p. 1998. pap. text 40.00 (*1-55860-153-8*) Morgan Kaufmann.

Proceedings of the International Conferences on Very Large Databases Held in Singapore: VLDB-84. 1998. pap. text 40.00 (*0-934613-16-8*) Morgan Kaufmann.

Proceedings of the International Conferences on Very Large Databases Held in Stockholm, Sweden: VLDB-85. 1998. pap. text 40.00 (*0-934613-17-6*) Morgan Kaufmann.

Proceedings of the International Conferences on Very Large Databases Held in Vancouver, B. C. VLDB-92. 1998. pap. text 40.00 (*1-55860-151-1*) Morgan Kaufmann.

Proceedings of the International Conferences on Very Large Databases Held in Zurich, Switzerland: VLDB-95. 1998. pap. text 40.00 (*1-55860-379-4*) Morgan Kaufmann.

Proceedings of the International Conferences on Very Large Databases, 1985-1996, 12 bks. pap. 390.00 (*1-55860-383-2*); pap. 180.00 (*1-55860-439-1*) Morgan Kaufmann.

Proceedings of the International Conferences, 1987: Physics & Evolution of Stars - Stellar Magnetism, Vol. 2. 269p. 1992. 95.00 (*1-885471-00-9*) Vertex Intl.

Proceedings of the International Conferences, 1987 Vol. 1: Physics & Evolution of the Stars - Magnetic Stars. 328p. 1987. 65.00 (*1-885471-01-7*) Vertex Intl.

Proceedings of the International Congress of Animal Production, 9th. International Congress of Animal Production Staff. Ed. by I. Mason. 1967. 14.70 (*0-934454-70-1*) Lubrecht & Cramer.

Proceedings of the International Congress of Historical Sciences, Fourteenth, San Francisco, 1975: Fourteenth International Congress of the Historical Sciences. International Congress of Historical Sciences Staf. 1977. 15.95 (*0-405-19039-5*, 19487) Ayer.

Proceedings of the International Congress of Linguistics, 14th: Berlin, GDR, Aug. 10-15, 1987, Vols. 1-3. Ed. by Werner Bahner et al. 2818p. 1991. 400.00 (*3-05-000654-4*, Pub. by Akademie Verlag) Wiley.

Proceedings of the International Congress of Mathematicians: Cambridge, Massachusetts, 1950 (Proceedings) Series II, 6th, 2 vols. 1969. reprint ed. 125.00 (*0-8115-1200-2*) Periodicals Srv.

Proceedings of the International Congress of Mathematicians: Cambridge, 1912 (Proceedings) Series I, 5th, 2 vols., Set. 112.00 (*0-685-70686-9*, PICM/12C) Periodicals Srv.

Proceedings of the International Congress of Mathematicians: Heidelberg, 1904 (Verhandlungen) Series I, 3rd. 64.00 (*0-685-70684-2*, PICM/4C) Periodicals Srv.

Proceedings of the International Congress of Mathematicians: Rome, 1908 (Atti) Series I, 4th, 2 vols., Set. 104.00 (*0-685-70919-1*, PICM/8C) Periodicals Srv.

Proceedings of the International Congress of Mathematicians: Vancouver, 1974, 2 vols. 1975. 53.00 (*0-685-70691-5*, PICM/74) Am Math.

Proceedings of the International Congress of Mathematicians: Zurich, 1897 (Verhandlungen) Series I, 1st. 47.00 (*0-685-70683-4*, PICM/97C) Periodicals Srv.

Proceedings of the International Congress of Mathematicians, Berkley, CA, Aug. 3-11, 1986, 2 vols. 1850p. 1988. text 226.00 (*0-8218-0110-4*, PICM/86) Am Math.

Proceedings of the International Congress of Mathematicians, Kyoto, 1990. Ed. by Ichiro Satake. LC 91-4972. 1684p. 1991. text 160.00 (*4-431-70047-1*, PICM/90) Am Math.

Proceedings of the International Congress of Mathematicians 1994, August 3-11, Zurich, Switzerland, 2 vols. Ed. by S. D. Chatterji. LC 95-43141. 717p. 1995. 275.00 (*3-7643-5153-5*) Birkhauser.

Proceedings of the International Congress of Mathematicians 1994, August 3-11, Zurich, Switzerland. Ed. by S. D. Chatterji. LC 95-43141. 1995. 275.00 (*0-8176-5153-5*) Birkhauser.

Proceedings of the International Congress of Protozoology, 5th. International Congress of Protozoology Staff. Ed. by S. H. Hutner. (Illus.). 222p. 1979. pap. text 19.00 (*0-935868-00-3*) Allen Pr.

Proceedings of the International Congress on Catalysis, 6th, 2 Vols. Royal Society of Chemistry Staff. 1989. 122.00 (*0-85186-188-1*) CRC Pr.

Proceedings of the International Congress on Pharmacognosy & Phytochemistry, Munich, 1970. International Congress on Pharmacognosy & Phytoche. Ed. by H. Wagner & L. Hoerhammer. LC 79-149122. (Illus.). 1971. 68.95 (*0-387-05316-6*) Spr-Verlag.

Proceedings of the International Control Engineering Conference, 1993. Ed. by Edward J. Kompass et al. (Orig.). 1993. pap. 50.00 (*1-883127-00-9*) Reed Exhibit.

Proceedings of the International Dextran Workshop (1984) Ed. by Margaret A. Clarke. (Workshop Ser.). (Illus.). 90p. (Orig.). 1984. pap. text 100.00 (*1-883326-06-0*) Sugar Process Res.

Proceedings of the International Francophone Meeting, Conflict Prevention--African Perspective, Ottawa, September 19 - 22, 1995. International Francophone Meeting. LC 96-196922. 257p. 1996. write for info. (*0-662-62373-8*) Can7 Govern Pub.

Proceedings of the International Gemological Symposium, 1982. International Gemological Symposium Staff. Ed. by Dianne Eash. 1982. 10.00 (*0-87311-011-0*) Gemological.

Proceedings of the International Heat Pump Absorption Conference: New Orleans, Louisiana - January 19-21, 1994. Ed. by W. Ryan et al. LC 94-74375. (AES Ser.: Vol. 31). 544p. 1994. 75.00 (*0-7918-0698-7*, I00361) ASME.

Proceedings of the International Kant Congress, 3rd, University of Rochester, 1970. International Kant Congress Staff. Ed. by L. W. Beck. LC 30-12936. (Synthese Historical Library: No. 4). 730p. 1971. text 261.50 (*90-277-0188-1*, D Reidel) Kluwer Academic.

Proceedings of the International MTDR Conference, 8th, University of Manchester, Sept. 1967, Pt. 1. S. A. Tobias & F. Koenigsberger. 1968. write for info. (*0-318-69654-1*, Pub. by Pergamon Repr) Franklin.

Proceedings of the International MTDR Conference, 8th, University of Manchester, Sept. 1967, Pt. 2. S. A. Tobias & F. Koenigsberger. 1968. write for info. (*0-318-69655-X*, Pub. by Pergamon Repr) Franklin.

Proceedings of the International MTDR Conference, 8th, University of Manchester, Sept. 1967, 2 pts., Set. S. A. Tobias & F. Koenigsberger. LC 63-19240. (Advances in Machine Tool Design & Research 1967 Ser.). 1968. 611.00 (*0-08-012629-4*, Pub. by Pergamon Repr) Franklin.

Proceedings of the International Nuclear Physics Conference, Harrogate, U.K., 25-30 August 1986, Vol. 2: Invited Papers. International Nuclear Physics Conference Staff. Ed. by J. L. Durell et al. LC 89-123176. (Institute of Physics Conference Ser.: No. 86). 623p. reprint ed. pap. 193.20 (*0-7837-3247-3*, 204326600002) Bks Demand.

Proceedings of the International Oxygen Steelmaking Congress: Linz, Austria, May 25-29, 1987. International Oxygen Steelmaking Congress Staff. LC 87-82799. 640p. 1987. reprint ed. pap. 198.40 (*0-608-00470-7*, 206128900007) Bks Demand.

Proceedings of the International Program Development in Undersea Robotics & Intelligent Control. George N. Saridis. 300p. (Orig.). 1995. pap. write for info. (*0-9646979-0-4*) USL.

Proceedings of the International School of Nuclear Physics, Erice, 2-14 Sept. 1976. Ed. by D. Wilkinson. (Progress in Particle & Nuclear Physics Ser.: Vol. 1). 1978. 98.00 (*0-08-020327-2*, Pergamon Pr) Elsevier.

Proceedings of the International Seminar on the State-of-the-Art of Hydrology & Hydrogeology in the Arid & Semi-Arid Areas of Africa, Ouagadougou, Burkina Faso: Proceedings of the Sahel Forum. 2nd ed. Ed. by G. E. Stout & M. Demissie. 990p. (Orig.). 1989. 20.00 (*0-923227-05-9*) Intl Water Resc.

Proceedings of the International Symposia on Human Factors in Telecommunications Held in 1968, Bad Wiesse, FRG: The International Symposia on Human Factors in Telecommunications, Vol. 4. 520p. 1996. 65.00 (*0-614-18600-5*, 125404) Info Gatekeepers.

Proceedings of the International Symposia on Human Factors in Telecommunications Held in 1970, London, U. K., Vol. 5. 300p. 1996. 75.00 (*0-614-18601-3*, 125405) Info Gatekeepers.

Proceedings of the International Symposia on Human Factors in Telecommunications Held in 1972, Stockholm, Sweden: The International Symposia on Human Factors in Telecommunications, Vol. 6. 545p. 1996. 85.00 (*0-614-18602-1*, 125406) Info Gatekeepers.

Proceedings of the International Symposia on Human Factors in Telecommunications Held in 1988, Netherlands: The International Symposia on Human Factors in Telecommunications, Vol. 12. 440p. 1960. 125.00 (*0-614-18603-X*, 125412) Info Gatekeepers.

Proceedings of the International Symposia on Human Factors in Telecommunications Held in 1990, Torino, Italy: The International Symposia on Human Factors in Telecommunications, Vol. 13. 696p. 1996. 195.00 (*0-614-18604-8*, 125413) Info Gatekeepers.

Proceedings of the International Symposia on Human Factors in Telecommunications Held March, 1995, in Sydney, Australia, Vol. 15. 1996. 195.00 (*0-614-18606-4*, 125415) Info Gatekeepers.

Proceedings of the International Symposia on the Human Factors in Telecommunications Held May, 1993, in Damstadt, Germany, Vol. 14. 1996. 195.00 (*0-614-18605-6*, 125414) Info Gatekeepers.

Proceedings of the International Symposium. Ed. by Francesco Degrada. (Pergolesi Studies: Vol. 1). (ENG & ITA.). 217p. 1987. lib. bdg. 54.00 (*0-918728-79-7*) Pendragon NY.

Proceedings of the International Symposium ECOS '92: On Efficiency, Costs, Optimization & Simulation of Energy Systems: Zaragoza, Spain, June 15-18, 1992. ECOS '92 (1992: Zaragoza, Spain) Staff. Ed. by Antonio Valero & Georges Tsatsaronis. LC TK1005.E26. 756p. 1992. reprint ed. pap. 200.00 (*0-608-00688-2*, 205933100010) Bks Demand.

Proceedings of the International Symposium of Nitrogen in Grapes & Wine. Ed. by Joanne M. Rantz. 323p. (C). 1991. lib. bdg. 50.00 (*0-9630711-0-6*) Am Soc Enology.

Proceedings of the International Symposium on Applications of Ferroelectrics, Switzerland, August 29 to September 1, 1988, Pts. 1-4: Special Issues of the Journal Ferroelectrics, Vols. 91-94. Ed. by P. E. Gunter. cxxviii, 1692p. 1989. pap. text 4227.00 (*2-88124-384-3*) Gordon & Breach.

Proceedings of the International Symposium on Biotechnology Applications in Aquaculture. Ed. by C. M. Kuo et al. (Asian Fisheries Society Spec. Publications: No. 10). 279p. 1995. write for info. (*971-8709-78-9*, Pub. by ICLARM) Intl Spec Bk.

Proceedings of the International Symposium on Carbonate Fuel Cell Technology, 3rd. Ed. by D. Shores et al. LC 93-70054. (Proceedings Ser.: Vol. 93-3). 512p. 1993. 50.00 (*1-56677-072-6*) Electrochem Soc.

Proceedings of the International Symposium on Chemical Vapor Deposition, 12th. Ed. by K. F. Jensen & G. W. Cullen. LC 93-70056. (Proceedings Ser.: Vol. 93-2). 440p. 1993. 63.00 (*1-56677-074-2*) Electrochem Soc.

Proceedings of the International Symposium on Clonal Selection, 1995. Ed. by Joanne M. Rantz. 1995. 25.00 (*0-9630711-2-2*) Am Soc Enology.

Proceedings of the International Symposium on Corrosion & Reliability of Electronic Materials & Devices, 2nd. Ed. by R. B. Comizzoli & J. D. Sinclair. LC 92-74540. (Proceedings Ser.: Vol. 93-1). 612p. 1993. 56.00 (*1-56677-051-3*) Electrochem Soc.

Proceedings of the International Symposium on Diamond Materials, 3rd. Ed. by J. P. Dismukes et al. LC 93-70063. (Proceedings Ser.: Vol. 93-17). 1120p. 1993. 66.00 (*1-56677-060-2*) Electrochem Soc.

Proceedings of the International Symposium on Electrochemical Processing of Tailored Materials, 2nd. Ed. by R. C. Alkire et al. LC 93-70057. (Proceedings Ser.: Vol. 93-12). 312p. 1993. 37.00 (*1-56677-027-0*) Electrochem Soc.

Proceedings of the International Symposium on Electrochemical Technology Applications in Electronics, 2nd. Ed. by L. T. Romankiw et al. LC 93-70065. (Proceedings Ser.: Vol. 93-20). 560p. 1993. 54.00 (*1-56677-062-9*) Electrochem Soc.

Proceedings of the International Symposium on Electrochemistry in Mineral & Metal Processing. International Symposium on Electrochemistry in Min. Ed. by P. E. Richardson et al. LC 84-81900. (Electrochemical Society Proceedings Ser.: No. 84-10). (Illus.). 685p. reprint ed. pap. 200.00 (*0-7837-4706-3*, 205248800002) Bks Demand.

Proceedings of the International Symposium on Fibre Reinforced Concrete: Madras, India, 16-19 December, 1987, 3 vols. 1500p. 1988. text 252.00 (*90-6191-796-4*, Pub. by A A Balkema) Ashgate Pub Co.

Proceedings of the International Symposium on Gold Metallurgy. G. W. McDonald & Canadian Mineral Processors Staff. Ed. by R. S. Salter et al. (Proceedings of Metallurgical Society of Canadian Institute of Mining & Metallurgy Ser.: Vol. 1). 408p. 1987. 127.25 (*0-08-035882-9*, Pergamon Pr) Elsevier.

Proceedings of the International Symposium on High Temperature Lamp Chemistry, 3rd. Ed. by J. M. Ranish & C. W. Struck. LC 93-72869. (Proceedings Ser.: Vol. 93-16). 280p. 1993. 37.00 (*1-56677-040-8*) Electrochem Soc.

Proceedings of the International Symposium on In-Beam Nuclear Spectroscopy, Debrecen, Hungary, May 14-18, 1984. Ed. by Dombradi & T. Fenyes. 820p. 1984. 520.00 (*0-569-08841-0*, Pub. by Collets) St Mut.

Proceedings of the International Symposium on InBeam Nuclear Spectroscopy, 2 vols., Set, Vols. 1 & 2. Z. S. Dombradi & T. Fenyes. 820p. (C). 1984. 195.00 (*963-05-3993-4*, Pub. by Akade Kiado) St Mut.

Proceedings of the International Symposium on Ionic & Mixed Conducting Ceramics, 2nd. Ed. by T. A. Ramanarayanan et al. LC 94-70844. (Proceedings Ser.: Vol. 94-12). 622p. 1994. 68.00 (*1-56677-044-0*) Electrochem Soc.

*__Proceedings of the International Symposium on Laboratory Automation & Robotics, 1997.__ (Illus.). 801p. 1998. pap. 75.00 (*0-931565-15-4*) Zymark Corp.

Proceedings of the International Symposium on Magnetic Materials, Processe & Devices, 3rd. Ed. by L. T. Romankiw & D. A. Herman, Jr. LC 93-72865. (Proceedings Ser.: Vol. 94-06). 312p. 1994. 48.00 (*1-56677-036-X*) Electrochem Soc.

Proceedings of the International Symposium on Management Strategies for Exploited Fish Populations: Lowell Wakefield Fisheries Symposium. Ed. by G. Kruse et al. (Report Ser.: No. AK-SG-93-01). (Illus.). 870p. (C). 1994. text 30.00 (*1-56612-021-7*) AK Sea Grant CP.

Proceedings of the International Symposium on Molten Salt Chemistry & Technology. Ed. by H. Kojima et al. LC 93-70058. (Proceedings Ser.: Vol. 93-9). 648p. 1993. 68.00 (*1-56677-028-9*) Electrochem Soc.

Proceedings of the International Symposium on Molten Salts, 9th. Ed. by C. L. Hussey et al. LC 94-70845. (Proceedings Ser.: Vol. 94-13). 860p. 1994. 92.00 (*1-56677-045-9*) Electrochem Soc.

Proceedings of the International Symposium on Multiparticle Dynamics, XXI: Wu-han, China, 23-27 September, 1991. Liu Lianshou. Ed. by Wu Yuanfang. LC 92-11996. 700p. 1992. text 137.00 (*981-02-0949-5*) World Scientific Pub.

Proceedings of the International Symposium on Natural Antioxidants: Molecular Mechanisms & Health Effects. Ed. by Lester Packer et al. LC 96-15468. (Illus.). xiii, 705 p. 1996. 150.00 (*0-935315-69-1*) Am Oil Chemists.

Proceedings of the International Symposium on North Pacific Flatfish: Lowell Wakefield Fisheries Symposium Series. (Alaska Sea Grant Report Ser.: Vol. 95-04). (Illus.). 664p. 1995. 25.00 (*1-56612-034-9*) AK Sea Grant CP.

Proceedings of the International Symposium on Pergolesi. Ed. by Francesco Degrada. (Pergolesi Studies: Vol. 2). (ENG & ITA.). 1989. pap. text 54.00 (*88-221-0443-9*) Pendragon NY.

Proceedings of the International Symposium on Plant Aging & Life Prediction of Corrodible Structures. Ed. by T. Shoji & T. Shibata. 1000p. 1997. pap. 130.00 (*1-57590-006-8*, 37401) NACE Intl.

Proceedings of the International Symposium on Plasma Processing, 10th. Ed. by G. S. Mathad et al. LC 94-70852. (Processing Ser.: Vol. 94-20). 620p. 1994. 64.00 (*1-56677-077-7*) Electrochem Soc.

Proceedings of the International Symposium on Plasma Processing, 9th. Ed. by G. S. Mathad & D. W. Hess. LC 92-82777. (Proceedings Ser.: Vol. 92-18). 670p. 1992. 60.00 (*1-56677-020-3*) Electrochem Soc.

Proceedings of the International Symposium on Process Physics & Modeling in Semiconductor Technology, 3rd. Ed. by G. R. Srinivasan et al. LC 93-70053. (Proceedings Ser.: Vol. 93-6). 628p. 1993. 60.00 (*1-56677-064-5*) Electrochem Soc.

Proceedings of the International Symposium on Quantum Confinement, 2nd: Physics & Applications. Ed. by M. Cahay et al. LC 94-70849. (Proceedings Ser.: Vol. 94-17). 427p. 1994. 78.00 (*1-56677-049-1*) Electrochem Soc.

Proceedings of the International Symposium on Reception Facilities for Noxious Liquid Substances. International Maritime Organization Staff. 1987. text 150.00 (*0-89771-971-9*, Pub. by Intl Maritime Org) St Mut.

Proceedings of the International Symposium on Redox Mechanisms & Interfacial Properties of Molecules of Biological Importance, 5th. Ed. by F. Shultz et al. LC 93-70076. (Proceedings Ser.: Vol. 93-11). 460p. 1993. 55.00 (*1-56677-029-7*) Electrochem Soc.

Proceedings of the International Symposium on Rheology & Soil Mechanics. International Symposium on Rheology & Soil Mechani. Ed. by P. M. Sirieys & J. Kravtchenko. (ENG & FRE., Illus.). 1966. 125.95 (*0-387-03652-0*) Spr-Verlag.

Proceedings of the International Symposium on Runaway Reactions & Pressure Relief Design. Ed. by AIChE Design Institute for Emergency Relief System et al. (DIERS Proceedings Ser.). 764p. 1995. 115.00 (*0-8169-0676-9*, P-78) Am Inst Chem Eng.

Proceedings of the International Symposium on Semiconductor Wafer Bonding, 2nd: Science, Technology, & Applications. Ed. by M. A. Schmidt et al. LC 93-70070. (Proceedings Ser.: Vol. 93-29). 484p. 1994. 56.00 (*1-56677-068-8*) Electrochem Soc.

Proceedings of the International Symposium on Silicon Materials Science & Technology, 7th. Ed. by H. R. Huff et al. LC 94-70842. (Proceedings Ser.: Vol. 94-10). 1296p. 1994. 95.00 (*1-56677-042-4*) Electrochem Soc.

Proceedings of the International Symposium on Solid Oxide Fuel Cells, 3rd. Ed. by H. Iwahara & S. C. Singhal. LC 93-70055. (Proceedings Ser.: Vol. 93-4). 980p. 1993. 84.00 (*1-56677-073-4*) Electrochem Soc.

Proceedings of the International Symposium on Stress Waves in Anelastic Solids, Providence, 1963. International Symposium on Stress Waves in Anelast. Ed. by H. Kolsky & W. Prager. (Illus.). 1964. 94.95 (*0-387-03221-5*) Spr-Verlag.

Proceedings of the International Symposium on Table Grape Production. Ed. by Joanne M. Rantz. LC 95-137769. (Illus.). (C). 1994. pap. text 40.00 (*0-9630711-1-4*) Am Soc Enology.

Proceedings of the International Symposium on the Trade of Bear Parts for Medicinal Use, University of Washington, Seattle, Washington, U. S. A., September 9-11, 1994. International Symposium on the Trade of Bear Parts. Ed. by Debra A. Rose & Andrea L. Gaski. LC 95-20608. (Illus.). 173p. 1995. pap. 53.70 (*0-608-04964-6*, 206554300004) Bks Demand.

Proceedings of the International Symposium on Trends in Continuum Physics, Trecop' 98, Pozna N, Poland, 17-20 August 1998. Bodgan Maruszewski. LC 98-53243. 350p. 1999. 98.00 (*981-02-3760-X*) World Scientific Pub.

Proceedings of the International Symposium on Ultra Large Scale Integration Science & Technology, 4th. Ed. by G. K. Celler et al. LC 93-70066. (Proceedings Ser.: Vol. 93-13). 320p. 1993. 42.00 (*1-56677-063-7*) Electrochem Soc.

Proceedings of the International Symposium on Water Resources in the Middle East Policy & Institutional Aspects, Held October 24-27, 1993 at the University of Illinois Urbana, IL. Ed. by Glenn E. Stout & Radwan A. Al-Weshah. 285p. 1993. 20.00 (*0-923227-06-7*) Intl Water Resc.

*__Proceedings of the International Topical Meeting on Probabilistic Safety Assessment: Washington, DC, August 22-25, 1999.__ 1999. 225.00 (*0-89448-640-3*, 700263) Am Nuclear Soc.

Proceedings of the International Workshop "Dubna Deuteron-91" Dubna 11-13 June, 1991. Intro. by B. Kuehn. 306p. 1992. pap. text 25.00 (*0-911767-57-6*) Hadronic Pr Inc.

Proceedings of the International Workshop on Advanced Topics in Multivariate Approximation. 420p. 1996. lib. bdg. 67.00 (*981-02-2852-X*) World Scientific Pub.

Proceedings of the International Workshop on Applications of Neural Networks to Telecommunications, Vol. 2. Ed. by Josh Alspector et al. (Neural Networks: The INNS Series of Texts, Monographs, & Proceedings). 320p. 1993. text 79.95 (*0-8058-1560-0*) L Erlbaum Assocs.

Proceedings of the International Workshop on Applications of Neural Networks to Telecommunications, Vol. 2. Ed. by Josh Alspector et al. 384p. 1995. text 79.95 (*0-8058-2084-1*) L Erlbaum Assocs.

P

An Asterisk (*) at the beginning of an entry indicates that the title is appearing for the first time.

Proceedings of the International Workshop on Applications of Neural Networks to Telecommunications 3. Ed. by Joshua Alspector et al. LC 97-13153. 296p. 1997. 79.95 (*0-8058-2900-8*) L Erlbaum Assocs.

Proceedings of the International Workshop on Lie Theory & Its Applications in Physics. LC 97-129938. 300p. 1996. lib. bdg. 47.00 (*981-02-2882-1*) World Scientific Pub.

Proceedings of the International Workshop on Memory Technology, Design & Testing. IEEE International Workshop on Memory Technology et al. LC 97-202128. ix, 103p. 1997. write for info. (*0-8186-8101-2*) IEEE Comp Soc.

Proceedings of the International Workshop on Photoionization 1992, Berlin, Germany, August 24-28, 1992. Ed. by Uwe Becker & Ulrich Heinzmann. LC 93-4230. (Studies of Vacuum Ultraviolet & X-Ray Processes: No. 1). 204p. 1993. 75.00 (*0-404-69951-0*) AMS Pr.

Proceedings of the IRRA Spring Meeting: 1996 Saint Louis. 570p. (C). 1996. pap. 5.00 (*0-913447-66-8*) Indus Relations Res.

Proceedings of the ISA Conference & Exhibit, Niagara Falls, New York, October 17-20, 1977, Pt. 1. Instrument Society of America Staff. LC 56-29277. (Advances in Instrumentation Ser.: Vol. 32). 287p. 1977. reprint ed. pap. 89.00 (*0-608-09981-3*, 205162800001) Bks Demand.

Proceedings of the ISA Conference & Exhibit, Niagara Falls, New York, October 17-20, 1977, Pt. 3. Instrument Society of America Staff. LC 56-29277. (Advances in Instrumentation Ser.: Vol. 32). 234p. 1977. reprint ed. pap. 72.60 (*0-608-09982-1*, 205162800003) Bks Demand.

Proceedings of the ISSAT 4th International Conference: Reliability & Quality in Design. Ed. by Hoang Pham & Ming-Wei Lu. 1998. pap. text 60.00 (*0-9639998-3-4*) ISSAT.

Proceedings of the ISSAT International Conference: Reliability & Quality in Design. Hoang Pham. 436p. (Orig.). (C). 1994. pap. text 60.00 (*0-9639998-0-X*) ISSAT.

Proceedings of the 1st European Conference on Cormac McCarthy. Ed. by David Holloway. 72p. 1999. ring bd. 10.00 (*0-9671049-0-4*) C McCarthy Socy.

Proceedings of the Italian National Program for Antarctica Research. Ed. by Juan Albaiges. 250p. 1994. pap. text 883.00 (*2-88449-008-6*) Gordon & Breach.

Proceedings of the IVth Indian Geological Congress Varanasi. Ed. by A. K. Bhattacharya et al. (Current Trends in Geology Ser.: Vols. 7-8). 900p. 1985. 95.00 (*1-55528-005-6*) Scholarly Pubns.

Proceedings of the IX UOEH International Symposium & the First Pan Pacific Cooperative Symposium: Industrialization & Emerging Environmental Health Issues: Risk Assessment & Risk Management. Ed. by Takesumi Yoshimura et al. (Toxicology & Industrial Health Ser.: Vol. 7, No. 5-6). (Illus.). 1991. pap. text 60.00 (*0-911131-25-6*) Specialist Journals.

Proceedings of the Joint Contractors Meeting, FE/EE Advanced Turbine System Conference & FE Fuel Cells & Coal-Fired Heat Engines Conference (Aug. 1993) Ed. by D. W. Geiling. (Fuel Cell Information Ser.: Vol. II). 505p. 1996. lib. bdg. 185.00 (*0-89934-302-3*, BT958) Bus Tech Bks.

Proceedings of the Joint U. S.-France Workshop on Recent Advances in Geomechanical, Geotechnical & Geo Environmental Engineering. F. Darve et al. (Illus.). 190p. (C). 1993. 175.00 (*2-7108-0644-4*, Pub. by Edits Technip) Enfield Pubs NH.

Proceedings of the J.R.R. Tolkien Centenary Conference, 1992: Proceedings of the Conference Held at Keble College, Oxford, England, 17th-24th August 1992 To Celebrate The Centenary Of The Birth Of Professor J.r.r. Tolkien, Incorporating The 23rd Mythopoeic Conference (mythcon Xxiii) & Oxonmoot 1992. J. R. R. Tolkien Centenary Conference Staff et al. LC 96-140796. (Mythlore Ser.). 458 p. 1995. write for info. (*1-887726-04-7*) Mythopoeic Press.

Proceedings of the L'Aquila Conference on Categorical Topology: (1994) Ed. by Eraldo Giuli. LC 96-13180. 280p. (C). 1996. text 144.00 (*0-7923-4049-3*) Kluwer Academic.

Proceedings of the Laser & the Electron Beam in Welding, Cutting & Surface Treatment - State of the Art, 1993. 1993. 70.00 (*0-939997-16-9*) Bakish Mat.

Proceedings of the Laser vs. the Electron Beam in Welding, Cutting & Surface Treatment: State of the Art, 1987. 334p. 1990. 70.00 (*0-939997-02-9*) Bakish Mat.

Proceedings of the Laser vs. the Electron Beam in Welding, Cutting & Surface Treatment: State of the Art, 1989. 344p. 1990. 70.00 (*0-939997-06-1*) Bakish Mat.

Proceedings of the Lunar & Planetary Science Conference, 10th, Houston, Texas, March 19-23, 1979, 3 vols. Lunar & Planetary Institute Staff. LC 79-22554. (Illus.). 3200p. 1980. 400.00 (*0-08-025128-5*, Pergamon Pr) Elsevier.

Proceedings of the Lunar & Planetary Science Conference, 12th, Houston, Texas, March 16-20, 1981. Lunar & Planetary Institute Staff. (Geochimica & Cosmochimica Acta Ser.: No. 16). (Illus.). 2000p. 1982. 235.00 (*0-08-028074-9*, Pergamon Pr) Elsevier.

Proceedings of the Lunar & Planetary Science Conference, 9th, Houston, Texas, 1978, 3 vols., Set. Lunar & Planetary Institute Staff. (Geochimica & Cosmochimica Acta Ser.: Suppl. 10). 1979. 450.00 (*0-08-022966-2*, Pergamon Pr) Elsevier.

Proceedings of the Massachusetts Historical Society, Index, Vols. 41-60. 1941. 50.00 (*0-934909-31-8*, Pub. by Mass Hist Soc) NE U Pr.

Proceedings of the Massachusetts Historical Society, 1791-1992, Index, Vols. 61-80. 1987. 75.00 (*0-934909-32-6*, Pub. by Mass Hist Soc) NE U Pr.

Proceedings of the Meeting of Experts on Forest Research, Rome, 1992. (ENG, FRE & SPA.). 262p. 1993. 21.00 (*92-5-003359-1*, F33591, Pub. by FAO) Bernan Associates.

Proceedings of the Meeting of the American Society for Stereotactic & Functional Neurosurgery, Pittsburgh, PA, June 1991, Pt. 1: Journal: Stereotactic & Functional Neurosurgery, Vol. 58, Nos. 1-4, 1992. Ed. by L. D. Lunsford et al. (Illus.). vi, 214p. 1992. pap. 188.00 (*3-8055-5684-5*) S Karger.

Proceedings of the Meeting of the American Society for Stereotactic & Functional Neurosurgery, Pittsburgh, PA, June 1991, Pt. 2: Journal: Stereotactic & Functional Neurosurgery, Vol. 59, Nos. 1-4, 1992. Ed. by L. D. Lunsford et al. (Illus.). vi, 210p. 1992. pap. 188.00 (*3-8055-5688-8*) S Karger.

Proceedings of the Meeting of the Leksell Gamma Knife Society, Buenos Aires, March 1992: Journal: Stereotactic & Functional Neurosurgery, Vol. 61, Suppl. 1, 1993. Ed. by J. C. Ganz et al. (Illus.). iv, 188p. 1993. pap. 59.25 (*3-8055-5945-3*) S Karger.

Proceedings of the Membrane Processes for Industry Symposium, May 19-20, 1986. Membrane Processes for Industry Symposium Staff. Ed. by Charles E. Feazel & Robert E. Lacey. LC 66-30620. (Illus.). 268p. 1966. pap. 5.00 (*0-940824-00-0*) S Res Inst.

Proceedings of the Meson-, Photo-, & Electroproduction at Low & Intermediate Energies Symposium, Bonn, 1970. Meson-, Photo-, & Electroproduction at Low & Inter. LC 25-9130. (Tracts in Modern Physics Ser.: Vol. 59). 1971. 71.95 (*0-387-05494-4*) Spr-Verlag.

Proceedings of the Michigan Morphometrics Workshop. Ed. by Fred L. Bookstein. (Special Publications: No. 2). viii, 380p. (C). 1990. pap. text 17.50 (*0-9628499-0-1*); pap. text 25.00 incl. disk (*0-685-38831-X*) U MI Mus Zool.

Proceedings of the Microscopy Society of America. (Illus.). 1993. 10.00 (*0-614-11175-7*) San Francisco Pr.

Proceedings of the Modeling of Casting, Welding, & Advanced Solidification Processes VIII: Eighth International Conference on Modeling of Casting & Welding Processes, Held in San Diego, California on June 7-12, 1998. International Conference on Modeling of Casting & Engineering Foundation (U.S.) Staff. Ed. by Brian G. Thomas & Christoph Beckermann. LC 98-66197. xxiii, 1267 p. 1998. write for info. (*0-87339-407-0*) Minerals Metals.

Proceedings of the MUMPS Users' Group Meeting. MUMPS Users' Group Staff. Ed. by Judith R. Faulkner. 1979. 20.00 (*0-918118-06-9*) M Technol.

Proceedings of the MUMPS Users' Group Meeting, 1974. MUMPS Users' Group Staff. Ed. by Joan Zimmerman. 1974. 20.00 (*0-918118-01-8*) M Technol.

Proceedings of the MUMPS Users' Group Meeting, 1978. MUMPS Users' Group Staff. Ed. by Pat Zimmerman. 1978. pap. 20.00 (*0-918118-05-0*) M Technol.

Proceedings of the Myopia International Conference, 3rd, Copenhagen, 1980. Myopia International Conference Staff. Ed. by H. C. Fledelius et al. (Documenta Ophthalmologica Proceedings Ser.: No. 28). 266p. 1981. text 191.50 (*90-6193-725-6*) Kluwer Academic.

Proceedings of the N. P. A. Resin & Blending Seminar. 115p. 1990. 40.00 (*0-935018-53-0*, 7365) Forest Prod.

Proceedings of the NAIC. Ed. by Karen Montalto. 1286p. (Orig.). (C). 1996. pap. 325.00 (*0-89382-423-2*, PRC-2C) Nat Assn Insurance.

Proceedings of the NAIC. rev. ed. Ed. by Karen Montalto. 980p. (Orig.). (C). 1997. 325.00 (*0-89382-439-9*, PRC-ZS) Nat Assn Insurance.

Proceedings of the NAIC: 1996 Third Quarter. Ed. by Karen Montalto. 858p. (C). 1997. 180.00 (*0-89382-490-9*, PRC-ZS) Nat Assn Insurance.

Proceedings of the NAIC: 1996 Third Quarter, Vol. II. Ed. by Karen Montalto. 586p. (C). 1997. 180.00 (*0-89382-491-7*, PRC-ZS) Nat Assn Insurance.

Proceedings of the NAIC: 1996 2nd Quarter. Ed. by Karen Montalto. 1152p. (C). 1997. 325.00 (*0-89382-467-4*, PRC-ZS) Nat Assn Insurance.

Proceedings of the NAIC, 1994, 4th Quarter. rev. ed. Ed. by Karen Montalto. 1350p. (C). 1996. 325.00 (*0-89382-378-3*, PRC-25) Nat Assn Insurance.

Proceedings of the NAIC, 1995, 2nd Quarter. annuals rev. ed. Ed. by Karen Montalto. 920p. (Orig.). (C). 1996. 325.00 (*0-89382-409-7*, PRC-ZS) Nat Assn Insurance.

Proceedings of the NAIC 1997 First Quarter. rev. ed. Ed. by Karen Montalto. 1164p. (C). 1999. 180.00i (*0-89382-578-6*, PRC-ZS97-1) Nat Assn Insurance.

Proceedings of the NASA-UCLA Workshop on Laser Propagation in Atmospheric Turbulence. Ed. by A. V. Balakrishnan & Russell Butts. (COMCON Conferences Proceedings Ser.). (Illus.). 200p. 1996. pap. text 68.00 (*0-911575-68-5*) Optimization Soft.

Proceedings of the Nassau Mossbauer Conference, 2nd. Clive Wynter & Esen E. Alp. LC 95-126361. 216p. (C). 1994. text. write for info. (*0-697-26825-X*, WCB McGr Hill) McGrw-H Hghr Educ.

Proceedings of the National Academy of the Avant Garde. National Academy of the Avant Garde Staff. Ed. by Henry J. Korn. 1975. pap. 5.00 (*0-915066-62-9*) Assembling Pr.

*__Proceedings of the National Association for Multicultural Education Seventh Annual Name Conference.__ Ed. by Carl A. Grant. 504p. 1999. pap. 74.95 (*0-8058-3420-6*) L Erlbaum Assocs.

Proceedings of the National Association of Insurance Commissioners. 1176p. 1995. 75.00 (*0-89382-357-0*) Nat Assn Insurance.

Proceedings of the National Association of Insurance Commissioners. rev. ed. Ed. by Karen Montalto. 950p. (Orig.). 1996. 325.00 (*0-89382-388-0*) Nat Assn Insurance.

Proceedings of the National Association of Insurance Commissioners: 1993 First Quarter, 4 vols., Set. 506p. 1994. 300.00 (*0-89382-253-1*) Nat Assn Insurance.

Proceedings of the National Association of Insurance Commissioners: 1995 3rd Quarter. Ed. by Karen Montalto. 1130p. (Orig.). (C). 1996. 325.00 (*0-89382-413-5*, PRC-ZS) Nat Assn Insurance.

Proceedings of the National Association of Insurance Commissioners Cumulative Index, 1980-1989. 362p. (C). 1991. 150.00 (*0-89382-169-1*) Nat Assn Insurance.

Proceedings of the National Association of Insurance Commissioners, 1986, Vol. I. 892p. (C). 1986. 125.00 (*0-89382-166-7*) Nat Assn Insurance.

Proceedings of the National Association of Insurance Commissioners, 1986, Vol. II. 901p. (C). 1986. 125.00 (*0-89382-167-5*) Nat Assn Insurance.

Proceedings of the National Association of Insurance Commissioners, 1988, Vol. II. 902p. (C). 1988. 125.00 (*0-89382-171-3*) Nat Assn Insurance.

Proceedings of the National Association of Insurance Commissioners, 1989, Vol. I. 1041p. (C). 1989. 125.00 (*0-89382-173-X*) Nat Assn Insurance.

Proceedings of the National Association of Insurance Commissioners, 1989, Vol. II. 941p. (C). 1990. 125.00 (*0-89382-172-1*) Nat Assn Insurance.

Proceedings of the National Association of Insurance Commissioners, 1990, Set, Vols. IA & B. 1269p. (C). 1990. 125.00 (*0-89382-174-8*) Nat Assn Insurance.

Proceedings of the National Association of Insurance Commissioners, 1991, Vol. II. Ed. by Karen Montalto. 1343p. (C). 1992. 125.00 (*0-89382-176-4*) Nat Assn Insurance.

Proceedings of the National Association of Insurance Commissioners, 1992, Vol. I. 1654p. (C). 1992. 125.00 (*0-89382-186-1*) Nat Assn Insurance.

Proceedings of the National Association of Insurance Commissioners, 1992, 2 vols., Vols. IIA-IIB. 1300p. (C). 1993. 125.00 (*0-89382-212-4*) Nat Assn Insurance.

Proceedings of the National Association of Insurance Commissioners 1993, 2 vols., Vols. IA & B. 1573p. 1993. 300.00 (*0-89382-226-4*) Nat Assn Insurance.

Proceedings of the National Association of Insurance Commissioners 1993 Fourth Quarter, 4 vols., Set. annuals 965p. (C). 1995. 75.00 (*0-89382-299-X*) Nat Assn Insurance.

Proceedings of the National Association of Insurance Commissioners 1993 Third Quarter, 4 vols., Set. annuals 816p. (C). 1994. 75.00 (*0-89382-296-5*) Nat Assn Insurance.

Proceedings of the National Association of Insurance Commissioners 1993 2nd Quarter. annuals 1152p. (C). 1994. 300.00 (*0-89382-266-3*) Nat Assn Insurance.

Proceedings of the National Association of Insurance Commissioners 1994: Second Quarter - 4 Volumes Annually. 1166p. (C). 1995. 75.00 (*0-89382-354-6*) Nat Assn Insurance.

Proceedings of the National Association of Insurance Commissioners 1994 First Quarter. 795p. (C). 1995. 75.00 (*0-89382-330-9*) Nat Assn Insurance.

Proceedings of the National Athletic Trainers' Association 48th Annual Meeting & Clinical Symposia. National Athletic Trainers' Association Staff. 276p. 1997. pap. 20.00 (*0-88011-826-1*) Human Kinetics.

Proceedings of the National Bioash Utilization Conference (1996) Ed. by Eric A. Vance. (Illus.). 161p. 1999. pap. text 35.00 (*0-7881-7625-0*) DIANE Pub.

Proceedings of the National Child Labor Committee, 1905, Vol. 1. National Child Labor Committee. Ed. by Robert H. Bremner. LC 74-1699. (Children & Youth Ser.). 1974. 36.95 (*0-405-05976-0*) Ayer.

Proceedings of the National Communications Forum, Vol. 44, 1990. fac. ed. National Communications Forum Staff. LC 86-642827. (Illus.). 1058p. 1990. reprint ed. pap. 200.00 (*0-7837-7723-X*, 202917300044) Bks Demand.

Proceedings of the National Communications Forum, Vol. 45, 1991. fac. ed. National Communications Forum Staff. LC 86-642827. (Illus.). 783p. 1991. reprint ed. pap. 200.00 (*0-7837-7724-8*, 202917300045) Bks Demand.

Proceedings of the National Communications Forum, 1984, Vol. 38. National Communications Forum Staff. LC 45-8478. 714p. reprint ed. pap. 200.00 (*0-608-15244-7*, 202917300038) Bks Demand.

Proceedings of the National Communications Forum, 1988, Vol. XXXXII. Intro. by Bernard F. Sergesketter. (Illus.). 1933p. 1988. 139.00 (*0-933217-04-8*) Prof Educ Intl.

Proceedings of the National Communications Forum, 1988, Vol. XXXXIII. Intro. by James A. Eibel. (Illus.). 1283p. 1989. 139.00 (*0-933217-05-6*) Prof Educ Intl.

Proceedings of the National Communications Forum, 1990, Vol. XXXXIV. Intro. by Samuel E. Leftwich. (Illus.). 1042p. 1990. 139.00 (*0-933217-06-4*) Prof Educ Intl.

Proceedings of the National Communications Forum, 1991, Vol. XXXXV. Intro. by Joseph S. Colson. (Illus.). 771p. 1991. 139.00 (*0-933217-07-2*) Prof Educ Intl.

Proceedings of the National Conference on Decennial Census Data for Transportation Planning. (Special Reports: No. 206). 180p. 1985. 20.00 (*0-309-03766-2*) Transport Res Bd.

Proceedings of the National Database & 4th Generation Language Symposium. Ed. by George Schussel. 500p. 1986. pap. text 250.00 (*0-318-21393-1*) Digit Consult MA.

Proceedings of the National Earthquake Prediction Evaluation Council (1991) V. A. Frizzell, Jr. 148p. (Orig.). (C). 1994. pap. text 60.00 (*0-7881-0436-5*) DIANE Pub.

Proceedings of the National Earthquake Prediction Evaluation Council (1992) V. A. Frizzell, Jr. (Illus.). 161p. (Orig.). (C). 1995. pap. text 40.00 (*0-7881-2546-X*) DIANE Pub.

Proceedings of the National Energy Modeling System Conference. (Illus.). 1027p. (Orig.). (C). 1994. pap. text 175.00 (*0-7881-0315-6*) DIANE Pub.

Proceedings of the National Heart, Lung & Blood Institute Symposium on Rapid Identification & Treatment of Acute Myocardial Infarction: Issues & Answers. Ed. by Judith H. LaRosa et al. (Illus.). 157p. (Orig.). 1996. pap. text 25.00 (*0-7881-2825-6*) DIANE Pub.

Proceedings of the National Integrated Pest Management Forum, June 17-19, 1992. Ed. by A. Ann Sorensen. (Illus.). 86p. (C). 1998. pap. text. write for info. (*0-7881-7515-7*) DIANE Pub.

Proceedings of the National Negro Conference, 1909. National Negro Conference Staff. LC 69-18544. (American Negro: His History & Literature. Series 2). 1968. reprint ed. 18.95 (*0-405-01890-8*) Ayer.

Proceedings of the National Passive Solar Conference, 3rd, San Jose, 1979. National Passive Solar Conference Staff. Ed. by Harry Miller et al. 1979. pap. text 80.00 (*0-89553-015-5*) Am Solar Energy.

Proceedings of the National Passive Solar Conference, 5th, Amherst, 1980, 2 vols., Set. National Passive Solar Conference Staff. Ed. by John Hayes & Rachel Snyder. (Illus.). 1980. pap. text 60.00 (*0-89553-025-2*) Am Solar Energy.

Proceedings of the National Quarantine & Sanitary Convention, 1st-4th: Original Anthology. National Quarantine & Sanitary Convention Staff. Ed. by Barbara G. Rosenkrantz. LC 76-40668. (Public Health in America Ser.). 1977. reprint ed. lib. bdg. 89.95 (*0-405-09877-4*) Ayer.

Proceedings of the National Symposium on Dairy Goat Production & Marketing. Ed. by Terry Gipson et al. 200p. (Orig.). (C). 1992. 25.00 (*1-880667-01-0*) Lang U Agri Res & Ext.

Proceedings of the National Symposium on the Future Availability of Ground Water Resources. National Symposium on the Future Availability of G. Ed. by Robert C. Borden & William L. Lyke. LC 92-70847. (AWRA Technical Publication: No. TPS-92-1). 485p. reprint ed. pap. 150.40 (*0-7837-6283-6*, 204599800010) Bks Demand.

Proceedings of the National Tax-Association Tax Institute of America Annual Conference, 88th, 1995. Ed. by Robert D. Ebel & Frederick D. Stocker. 280p. 1996. pap. 25.00 (*0-318-68997-9*) Natl Tax.

Proceedings of the National Workshop on Soil Fertility Management Action Plan for Ghana: Held at Cape Coast, Ghana, 2nd to 5th, July, 1996. F. Ofori et al. LC 98-28351. 15p. 1998. pap. write for info. (*0-88090-117-9*) Intl Fertilizer.

Proceedings of the Naval Court Martial in the Case of Alexander Slidell Mackenzie: A Facsimile Reproduction with an Introduction by Hugh Egan. LC 92-17893. 392p. 1992. 60.00 (*0-8201-1465-0*) Schol Facsimiles.

Proceedings of the Neo-Classicism Conferences, 1967-1968. Modern Language Association of America Staff. Ed. by Paul J. Korshin. (Studies in the Eighteenth Century: No. 1). reprint ed. 34.50 (*0-404-07949-0*) AMS Pr.

Proceedings of the Nevada Newspaper Conference. Intro. by Karen R. Gash & Helen M. Blue. 118p. 1990. lib. bdg. 32.50 (*1-56475-350-6*); fiche. write for info. (*1-56475-351-4*) U NV Oral Hist.

Proceedings of the New York State Historical Associaton Vol. 6: The Seventh Annual Meeting with the Constitution, By-Laws, & List of Members Including Indian Geographical Names by E. M. Ruttenber. New York State Historical Association Staff. (Illus.). 243p. 1995. reprint ed. pap. text 20.00 (*0-7884-0224-2*) Heritage Bk.

Proceedings of the New York University Conference on Practice & Procedure Under the Immigration & Nationality Act (McCarran-Walter Act) Held on June 13,1953: Proceedings. New York University, Division of General Education. Ed. by Henry Sellin. LC 54-7877. xii, 145p. reprint ed. lib. bdg. 22.50 (*0-8371-7684-0*, NYUP) Greenwood.

Proceedings of the 1988 IEEE International Conference on Systems, Man & Cybernetics, August 8-12, 1988, Beijing & Shenyang, China, 2. IEEE International Conference on Systems Staff & Xinsong Jiang. LC 89-3813. 1989. write for info. (*0-08-037528-6*, Pergamon Pr) Elsevier.

Proceedings of the Nineteen Eighty-Four Vancouver Conference on Algebraic Geometry. Carrell et al. LC 85-28720. (Proceedings, Canadian Mathematical Society Ser.: Vol. 6). 503p. 1986. reprint ed. pap. 72.00 (*0-8218-6010-0*, CMSAMS/6) Am Math.

Proceedings of the 1980 Hokan Languages Workshop, Held at University of California, Berkeley. Ed. by J. E. Redden. (Occasional Papers on Linguistics: No. 9). 135p. 1981. reprint ed. pap. text 15.00 (*1-55567-488-7*) Coyote Press.

Proceedings of the Nineteen Eighty-Nine International Conference on Parallel Processing, 3 vols., Set. Ed. by Peter M. Kogge. LC 79-640377. 1989. lib. bdg. 100.00 (*0-271-00675-7*) Pa St U Pr.

P

An Asterisk (*) at the beginning of an entry indicates that the title is appearing for the first time.

Proceedings of the 1981 Hokan Languages Workshop & Penutian Languages Conference. Ed. by J. E. Redden. (Occasional Papers on Linguistics: No. 10). 87p. 1982. reprint ed. pap. text 10.00 (*1-55567-487-9*) Coyote Press.

Proceedings of the Nineteen Eighty-Seven Conference of the American Academy of Advertising. Ed. by Florence Feasley. 1987. pap. 25.00 (*0-931030-10-2*) Am Acad Advert.

Proceedings of the Nineteen Eighty-Six Conference of the American Academy of Advertising. Ed. by Ernest F. Larkin. 1986. pap. 25.00 (*0-931030-09-9*) Am Acad Advert.

***Proceedings of the 1983-98 International Conference on Very Large Databases (VLDB)** 600p. 1998. pap. 40.00 (*1-55860-566-5*) Morgan Kaufmann.

Proceedings of the 1997 U. S. Workshop on the Physics & Chemistry of Li-Vi Materials. Paul M. Amirtharaj. LC 98-66949. ix, 819 p. 1998. write for info. (*0-87339-410-0*) Minerals Metals.

Proceedings of the 1998 International Computer Music Conference. (Illus.). 600p. 1998. pap. write for info. (*0-9667927-0-X*) Internatl Computer Music Assn.

Proceedings of the 1998 SAE Aerospace Manufacturing Technology Conference. 1998. pap. 85.00 (*0-7680-0230-3*, P-324) Soc Auto Engineers.

Proceedings of the 1998 SAE Aerospace Automated Fastening Conference. 200p. 1998. pap. 79.00 (*0-7680-0255-9*, P-326) Soc Auto Engineers.

Proceedings of the 1998 Airframe/Engine Maintenance & Repair Conference. LC 98-86383. 200p. 1998. pap. 60.00 (*0-7680-0284-2*, P-329) Soc Auto Engineers.

Proceedings of the 1998 International Body Engineering Conference & Exposition, 6 Volumes. 1998. pap. 425.00 (*0-7680-0292-3*, P-336) Soc Auto Engineers.

Proceedings of the 1998 SAE Southern Automotive Manufacturing Technology Conference. 200p. 1998. pap. 69.00 (*0-7680-0316-4*, P-337) Soc Auto Engineers.

Proceedings of the 1998 Total Life Cycle Conference. 600p. 1998. pap. 119.00 (*0-7680-0317-2*, P-339) Soc Auto Engineers.

Proceedings of the 1998 Brake Colloquim. 160p. 1998. pap. 49.00 (*0-7680-0276-1*, P-327) Soc Auto Engineers.

Proceedings of the 1998 ASSE Behavioral Safety Symposium. E. Scott Geller et al. 200p. 1998. pap. 28.95 (*1-885581-12-2*, 4366) ASSE.

Proceeding of the 1998 Sugar Processing Research Conference. Mary A. Godshall. (Illus.). 563p. (Orig.). 1998. pap. text 100.00 (*1-883326-07-9*) Sugar Process Res.

***Proceedings of the 1998 ARMA International Conference: Houston.** 472p. 1998. pap. 30.00 (*0-933887-82-5*) ARMA Intl.

Proceedings of the 1995 International Computer Music Conference. (Illus.). 605p. write for info. (*0-9667927-5-0*) Internatl Computer Music Assn.

Proceedings of the 1995 Industrial Power Conference, April 2-5, 1995, Orlando, Florida. Ed. by N. C. Francovigli & Bibb & Associates, Inc. LC 89-46157. (PWR Ser.: Vol. 27). 159p. 1995. 88.00 (*0-7918-1215-4*, 100378) ASME.

Proceedings of the 1995 DOE-NREL Hydrogen Program Review (April 18-21, 1995), Vols. A & B. Compiled by National Renewable Energy Laboratory Staff. (Hydrogen Fuel Information Ser.: Vol. II). (Illus.). 880p. 1996. lib. bdg. 385.00 (*0-89934-294-9*, BT954) Bus Tech Bks.

Proceedings of the 1995 International Symposium on Language Teaching & Testing: Beijing-Xi'An. Ed. by Fritz Konia et al. 349p. (C). 1997. lib. bdg. 25.00 (*0-9641511-5-4*) Assn Text Study.

Proceedings of the 1994 ASME IEEE Joint Railroad Conference. LC 89-46368. (Rail Transportation Division Ser.: Vol. 7). 157p. 1994. pap. 45.00 (*0-7918-1207-3*) ASME.

Proceedings of the 1994 International Computer Music Conference. (Illus.). 500p. write for info. (*0-9667927-6-9*) Internatl Computer Music Assn.

Proceedings of the Nineteen Ninety-Four Joint Symposium on Computer-Aided Control System Design. IEEE, Control Systems Society Staff. Ed. by IEEE, Institute of Electrical & Electronics Engine. LC 93-81032. 500p. 1994. pap. write for info. (*0-7803-1800-5*, 94TH0619-7); fiche. write for info. (*0-7803-1801-3*) Inst Electrical.

Proceedings of the Nineteen Ninety International Conference on Nuclear Waste: Management & Environmental Remediation, 3 vols. LC 87-45827. 1994. pap. 185.00 (*0-7918-0691-X*) ASME Pr.

Proceedings of the 1999 Noise & Vibration Conference. (Proceedings Ser.). 1750p. 1999. pap. 323.00 (*0-7680-0410-1*, P-342) Soc Auto Engineers.

Proceedings of the 1999 Advances in Aviation Safety Conference. (Proceedings Ser.). 250p. 1999. pap. 87.00 (*0-7680-0392-X*, P-343) Soc Auto Engineers.

Proceedings of the 1999 International Conference on Lightning & Statis Electricity (ICOLSE) (Proceedings Ser.). 850p. 1999. pap. 134.00 (*0-7680-0393-8*, P-344) Soc Auto Engineers.

***Proceedings of the 1999 ARMA International Conference.** 558p. 1999. pap. 60.00 (*0-933887-87-6*) ARMA Intl.

***Proceedings of the 1999 International Computer Music Conference.** (Illus.). 615p. 1999. write for info. (*0-9667927-1-8*) Internatl Computer Music Assn.

Proceedings of the 1999 Atmospheric Flight Mechanics Conference. 320.00 (*1-56347-300-3*) AIAA.

***Proceedings of the 1999 SAE Southern Automotive Manufacturing Conference & Exposition.** (Proceedings Ser.). 148p. 1999. 64.00 (*0-7680-0494-2*, P-351) Soc Auto Engineers.

***Proceedings of the 1999 Airframe/Engine Maintenance & Repair Conference.** (Proceedings Ser.). 42p. 1999. 23.00 (*0-7680-0501-9*, P-352) Soc Auto Engineers.

***Proceedings of the 1999 SAE Aerospace Automated Fastener Conference.** (Proceedings Ser.). 164p. 1999. 75.00 (*0-7680-0461-6*, P-347) Soc Auto Engineers.

***Proceedings of the 1999 SAE Small Engine Technology Conference.** (Proceedings Ser.). 776p. 1999. 162.00 (*0-7680-0462-4*, P-348) Soc Auto Engineers.

***Proceedings of the 1999 Brake Colloquium.** (Proceedings Ser.). 148p. 1999. 56.00 (*0-7680-0463-2*, P-349) Soc Auto Engineers.

Proceedings of the 1999 Georgia Water Resources Conference. Ed. by Kathryn J. Hatcher. (Illus.). 550p. 1999. pap. 25.00 (*0-935835-06-7*) Univ GA Eco.

***Proceedings of the 1998 National Conference on Environmental Remediation Science & Technology.** Ed. by G. A.. Uzochukwu & G. B. Reddy. LC 99-14312. 1999. 75.00 (*1-57477-069-1*) Battelle.

Proceedings of the 1991 International Computer Music Conference. (Illus.). 594p. write for info. (*0-9667927-9-3*) Internatl Computer Music Assn.

Proceedings of the 1997 National Conference on Object Oriented Technology (NCOOT '97), August 22-24, 1997. National Conference on Object Oriented Technology Staff et al. LC 97-914243. x, 125 p. 1997. write for info. (*81-7023-630-4*) Allied Pubs.

Proceedings of the 1997 Wireless Communications Conference, August 11-13, 1997, Regal Harvest House, Boulder, Colorado. Wireless Communication Conference & IEEE Microwave Theory & Techniques Society Staff. LC 97-80023. vii, 258 p. 1997. write for info. (*0-7803-4195-3*) Inst Electrical.

Proceedings of the 1997 2nd IEEE-CAS Region 8 Workshop on Analog & Mixed IC Design: Baveno, Italy, 12-13 September, 1997. IEEE-CAS Region 8 Workshop on Analog and Mixed IC Design et al. LC 97-80101. ix, 129p. 1997. write for info. (*0-7803-4241-0*) IEEE Standards.

Proceedings of the 1997 GASS Reliability Workshop: October 12, 1997, Anaheim, California. GAAS Reliability Workshop Staff et al. LC 98-193590. v, 116p. 1998. pap. write for info. (*0-7803-4313-1*) IEEE Standards.

Proceedings of the 1997 Brake Colloquim. 114p. 1997. pap. 45.00 (*0-7680-0101-3*) Soc Auto Engineers.

Proceedings of the 1997 International Computer Music Conference. (Illus.). 492p. write for info. (*0-9667927-3-4*) Internatl Computer Music Assn.

Proceedings of the 1997 Undergraduate Symposium on Research in Astronomy. Ed. by Thomas Balonek. (C). 1998. pap. text. write for info. (*1-882334-07-8*) Keck NE Astron.

Proceedings of the 1997 Rapid Excavation Tunneling Conference. Ed. by J. E. Carlson & T. H. Budd. LC 96-72547. (Illus.). 874p. 1997. 83.00 (*0-87335-148-7*, 148-7) SMM&E Inc.

***Proceedings of the 1997 International Conference on Simulation in Engineering Education (ICSEE '97) Held in Phoenix, Arizona - January, 1997.** Ed. by Darush Davani & Clark C. Guest. (Simulation Ser.: Vol. 29, No. 2). 232p. 1998. 100.00 (*1-56555-104-4*, SS-29-2) Soc Computer Sim.

Proceedings of the 1997 Summer Computer Simulation Conference Held in Arlington, Virginia July, 1997. Ed. by Mohammad S. Obaidat & John Illgen. 957p. 1998. 180.00 (*1-56555-123-0*, SCSC-97) Soc Computer Sim.

Proceedings of the 1997 International Conference on Intelligent Systems & Semiotics: A Learning Perspective, ISAS '97. Ed. by A. M. Meystel. 587p. 1997. pap. write for info. (*1-886843-02-3*, PB 98122880) Ntl Inst Stndrds.

Proceedings of the 1996 DOE-NREL 1996 DOE-NREL Hydrogen Program Review. Compiled by National Renewable Energy Laboratory Staff. (Hydrogen Fuel Information Ser.: No. III, Pts. A & B). (Illus.). 885p. 1997. lib. bdg. 405.00 (*0-89934-326-0*, BT968) Bus Tech Bks.

Proceedings of the 1996 European Joint Conference on Engineering Systems Design & Analysis, Montpellier, France, June 9-14, 1996, Vol. 1. (PD Ser.: Vol. 73). 260p. 1996. 130.00 (*0-7918-1496-3*, G00991) ASME Pr.

Proceedings of the 1996 European Joint Conference on Engineering Systems Design & Analysis, Montpellier, France, June 9-14, 1996, Vol. 2. (PD Ser.: Vol. 74). 284p. 1996. 130.00 (*0-7918-1497-1*, G00992) ASME Pr.

Proceedings of the 1996 European Joint Conference on Engineering Systems Design & Analysis, Montpellier, France, June 9-14, 1996, Vol. 3. (PD Ser.: Vol. 75). 312p. 1996. 130.00 (*0-7918-1498-X*, G00993) ASME Pr.

Proceedings of the 1996 European Joint Conference on Engineering Systems Design & Analysis, Montpellier, France, June 9-14, 1996, Vol. 5. (PD Ser.: Vol. 77). 252p. 1996. 130.00 (*0-7918-1500-5*, G00995) ASME Pr.

Proceedings of the 1996 European Joint Conference on Engineering Systems Design & Analysis, Montpellier, France, June 9-14, 1996, Vol. 6. (PD Ser.: Vol. 78). 224p. 1996. 130.00 (*0-7918-1501-3*, G00996) ASME Pr.

Proceedings of the 1996 European Joint Conference on Engineering Systems Design & Analysis, Montpellier, France, June 9-14, 1996, Vol. 7. (PD Ser.: Vol. 79). 232p. 1996. 130.00 (*0-7918-1502-1*, G00997) ASME Pr.

Proceedings of the 1996 European Joint Conference on Engineering Systems Design & Analysis, Montpellier, France, June 9-14, 1996, Vol. 8. (PD Ser.: Vol. 80). 264p. 1996. 130.00 (*0-7918-1503-X*, G00998) ASME Pr.

Proceedings of the 1996 European Joint Conference on Engineering Systems Design & Analysis, Montpellier, France, June 9-14, 1996, Vol. 9. (PD Ser.: Vol. 81). 308p. 1996. 130.00 (*0-7918-1504-8*, G00990) ASME Pr.

Proceedings of the 1996 International Computer Music Conference. (Illus.). 514p. write for info. (*0-9667927-4-2*) Internatl Computer Music Assn.

Proceedings of the 1996 International Joint Power Generation Conference - Environmental Control - Fuels & Combustion Technologies, Houston, Texas, October 31-17, 1996, Vol. 1. (EC Ser.: Vol. 3). 516p. 1996. 140.00 (*0-7918-1795-4*, H01076) ASME Pr.

Proceedings of the 1996 International Joint Power Generation Conference, Houston, Texas, October 13-17, 1996, Vol. 3. (NE Ser.: Vol. 20). 80p. 1996. 60.00 (*0-7918-1798-9*, H01079) ASME Pr.

Proceedings of the 1996 World Congress on Coastal & Marine . . . Experiences in Management & Development. Ed. by Marc L. Miller & Jan Auyong. LC 98-85252. (Illus.). 336p. 1998. pap. text 35.00 (*0-934539-17-0*, WSGWO98-02WASHU) Wash Sea Grant.

Proceedings of the 1993 Georgia Water Resources Conference. LC 92-76060. 1993. 20.00 (*0-935835-03-2*) Univ GA Eco.

Proceedings of the 1993 International Computer Music Conference. (Illus.). 486p. write for info. (*0-9667927-7-7*) Internatl Computer Music Assn.

Proceedings of the 1992 International Computer Music Conference. (Illus.). 497p. write for info. (*0-9667927-8-5*) Internatl Computer Music Assn.

Proceedings of the 1978 Hokan Languages Workshop. Ed. by J. E. Redden. (Occasional Papers on Linguistics: No. 5). 96p. 1979. reprint ed. pap. text 10.94 (*1-55567-490-9*) Coyote Press.

Proceedings of the 1979 Hokan Languages Workshop, Held at University of California, Los Angeles. Ed. by J. E. Redden. (Occasional Papers on Linguistics: No. 7). 83p. 1980. reprint ed. pap. text 9.38 (*1-55567-489-5*) Coyote Press.

Proceedings of the 1977 Hokan-Yuman Languages Workshop, Held at University of Utah, Salt Lake City. Ed. by J. E. Redden. (Occasional Papers on Linguistics: No. 2). 95p. 1978. reprint ed. pap. text 10.63 (*1-55567-492-5*) Coyote Press.

Proceedings of the 1976 Hokan-Yuman Languages Workshop Held at University of California. Ed. by J. E. Redden. (Occasional Papers on Linguistics: No. 11). 99p. 1977. reprint ed. pap. text 11.25 (*1-55567-494-1*) Coyote Press.

Proceedings of the 19th Annual Boston University Conference on Language Development, 2 vols. Ed. by Dawn MacLaughlin & Susan McEwen. (BUCLD Proceedings Ser.: Vol. 19). (Illus.). 688p. (C). 1995. pap. 42.00 (*1-57473-002-9*); lib. bdg. 92.00 (*1-57473-102-5*) Cascadilla Pr.

Proceedings of the Nineteenth Annual Conference of the Cognitive Science Society. Cognitive Science Society Staff. 1128p. 1997. pap. 150.00 (*0-8058-2941-5*) L Erlbaum Assocs.

Proceedings of the Nineteenth Annual SAS User's Group International Conference. 1728p. (C). 1994. pap. 12.50 (*1-55544-611-6*, BR55148) SAS Publ.

Proceedings of the 19th Annual Simulation Symposium. Ed. by Kimbler. 256p. 1986. pap. 48.00 (*0-8186-0715-7*, ANS19-1) Soc Computer Sim.

Proceedings of the 19th Colloquium on the Law of Outer Space, October 1-15, 1976, Anaheim, California. International Institute of Space Law of the International Astronautical Federation Staff. 419p. 1977. pap. 27.50 (*0-8377-0414-6*, Rothman) W S Hein.

Proceedings of the Nineteenth International Astronautical Congress, New York, 1968, 4 vols., Set. M. Lunc & P. Contensou. LC 58-23647. 1970. 909.00 (*0-08-006933-9*, Pub. by Pergamon Repr) Franklin.

Proceedings of the Nineteenth International Technical Conference on Coal Utilization & Fuel Systems (1994) 874p. 1995. 395.00 (*0-932066-19-4*) Coal Slurry Tech.

Proceedings of the Nineteenth Meeting of the French Colonial Historical Society, Providence, R. I., May, 1993. Ed. by James Pritchard.Tr. of Actes du Dix-Neuvieme Colloque de la Societe D'Histoire Coloniale Francaise, Providence, R. I., Mai 1993. (ENG & FRE., Illus.). v, 228p. (C). 1994. text 30.00 (*1-884679-01-3*) Fr Colonial Hist.

Proceedings of the 9th Biennial Conference. ICHCA Staff. (C). 1988. 50.00 (*0-7855-6158-7*, Pub. by ICHCA) St Mut.

Proceedings of the Ninth Annual ACM-SIAM Symposium on Discrete Algorithms. Ed. by Howard Karloff. (Proceedings in Applied Mathematics Ser.: Vol. 95). (Illus.). xii, 704p. 1998. pap. 79.00 (*0-89871-410-9*, PR95) Soc Indus-Appl Math.

Proceedings of the Ninth Annual Battery Conference on Applications & Advances, 1994. IEEE, Aerospace & Electronic Systems Society Staff. Ed. by IEEE, Institute of Electrical & Electronics Engine. LC 93-80939. 470p. 1994. pap. write for info. (*0-7803-1795-5*, 94TH0617-1); fiche. write for info. (*0-7803-1796-3*) Inst Electrical.

Proceedings of the 9th Annual Control Engineering Conference: Held as Part of the Control Engineering Conference & Exposition, O'Hare Exposition Center, Rosemont, Illinois, May 22-24, 1990. Ed. by Henry M. Morris. (Illus.). 500p. (Orig.). (C). 1990. pap. text 120.00 (*0-914331-59-0*, Control Engrng) Cahners Busn Des Plaines.

Proceedings of the Ninth Annual IEEE International ASIC Conference & Exhibit. IEEE (Rochester Section) Staff. Ed. by IEEE (Institute of Electrical & Electronics Engine. 500p. 1996. 128.00 (*0-7803-3303-9*, 96TH8186); pap. 128.00 (*0-7803-3302-0*, 96TH8186) Inst Electrical.

Proceedings of the Ninth Annual International Conference on Veterinary Acupuncture. Ed. by David H. Jaggar. 86p. (Orig.). 1983. pap. text 30.00 (*0-318-19687-5*) Intl Vet Acup.

Proceedings of the Ninth Annual Meeting of the Geoscience Information Society, November 18, 1974, Miami Beach, Florida, Vol. 5. Geoscience Information Society Staff. LC 73-16672. 99p. reprint ed. pap. 30.70 (*0-608-14456-8*, 202504800041) Bks Demand.

Proceedings of the 9th Annual UCLA Indo-European Conference Los Angeles, 1997. Ed. by Marlene Jones-Bley et al. LC 98-202087. (Journal of Indo-European Studies Monograph Ser.: Vol. 28). (Illus.). 1998. pap. text 46.00 (*0-941694-65-8*) Inst Study Man.

***Proceedings of the Ninth Biennial Southern Silvicultural Research Conference.** Ed. by Thomas A. Waldrop. (Illus.). 628p. (C). 2000. reprint ed. pap. text. write for info. (*0-7881-8579-9*) DIANE Pub.

Proceedings of the 9th Colloquium on the Law of Outer Space, October 14, 1966, Madrid Spain. International Institute of Space Law of the International Astronautical Federation Staff. 221p. 1967. pap. 27.50 (*0-8377-0403-0*, Rothman) W S Hein.

Proceedings of the Ninth Danube-European Conference on Soil Mechanics & Foundation Engineering: Budapest, Oct. 2-5, 1990. G. Petrasovits. (GER., Illus.). 555p. (C). 1990. 220.00 (*963-05-5898-X*, Pub. by Akade Kiado) St Mut.

Proceedings of the 9th Ethylene Producers' Conference. Ed. by John Burke & Ethylene Producers Staff. (Ethylene Producers Ser.). 850p. 1997. 170.00 (*0-8169-0743-9*, T-104) Am Inst Chem Eng.

Proceedings of the Ninth European Conference on Artificial Intelligence. Ed. by Luigia C. Aiello. 785p. 1998. pap. text 45.00 (*0-273-08822-X*) Morgan Kaufmann.

Proceedings of the 9th International Symposium on Continuum Models & Discrete Systems: 29 June-3 July 1998, Istanbul, Turkey. International Symposium on Continuum Models of Discrete Systems Staff. Ed. by Konstantine Z. Markov & Esin Inan. LC 98-42146. 1998. write for info. (*981-02-3669-7*) World Scientific Pub.

***Proceedings of the 9th International Colloquium on Differential Equations: Plovdiv, Bulgaria, 18-23 August 1998.** D. Bainov. 460p. 1999. 210.00 (*90-6764-296-7*, Pub. by VSP) Coronet Bks.

Proceedings of the Ninth International Conference on Composite Materials: ICCM-9, 6 vols., Set. International Conference on Composite Materials St. (Illus.). 1993. pap. 299.95 (*1-85573-140-1*) Technomic.

Proceedings of the Ninth International Conference on Composite Materials Vol. 1: ICCM-9: Metal Matrix Composites. International Conference on Composite Materials St. (Ninth International Conference on Composite Materials Ser.: Vol. 1). 928p. 1993. pap. 170.00 (*1-85573-134-7*, Pub. by Woodhead Pubng) Am Educ Systs.

Proceedings of the Ninth International Conference on Composite Materials Vol. 2: ICCM-9: Ceramic Matrix Composites & Other Systems. International Conference on Composite Materials St. Ed. by J. P. Singh. (Ninth International Conference on Composite Materials Ser.). 920p. 1993. pap. 170.00 (*1-85573-135-5*, Pub. by Woodhead Pubng) Am Educ Systs.

Proceedings of the Ninth International Conference on Composite Materials Vol. 3: ICCM-9: Composites: Modelling & Processing Science. International Conference on Composite Materials St. (Ninth International Conference on Composite Materials Ser.: Vol. 3). 832p. 1993. pap. 170.00 (*1-85573-136-3*, Pub. by Woodhead Pubng) Am Educ Systs.

Proceedings of the Ninth International Conference on Composite Materials Vol. 4: ICCM-9: Composites Design. International Conference on Composite Materials St. (Ninth International Conference on Composite Materials Ser.: Vol. 4). 864p. 1993. pap. 170.00 (*1-85573-137-1*, Pub. by Woodhead Pubng) Am Educ Systs.

Proceedings of the Ninth International Conference on Composite Materials Vol. 5: ICCM-9: Composites Behaviour. International Conference on Composite Materials St. (Ninth International Conference on Composite Materials Ser.: Vol. 5). 944p. 1993. pap. 170.00 (*1-85573-138-X*, Pub. by Woodhead Pubng) Am Educ Systs.

Proceedings of the Ninth International Conference on Composite Materials Vol. 6: ICCM-9: Composites Properties & Applications. International Conference on Composite Materials St. (Ninth International Conference on Composite Materials Ser.: Vol. 6). 944p. 1993. pap. 170.00 (*1-85573-139-8*, Pub. by Woodhead Pubng) Am Educ Systs.

Proceedings of the Ninth International Conference on the Study of Shamanism & Alternate Modes of Healing: Held at the St. Sabina Center, San Rafael, California, September 5-7, 1992. Ed. by Ruth-Inge Heinze. LC 92-47429. (Illus.). 340p. (C). 1993. pap. 21.75 (*0-945875-09-6*) Independent Scholars Asia Inc.

Proceedings of the Ninth International Conference on Vehicle Structural Mechanics & CAE. 410p. 1995. pap. 79.00 (*1-56091-657-5*, P290) Soc Auto Engineers.

***Proceedings of the Ninth International Congress on Hyperbaric Medicine.** Ed. by Ian P. Unsworth & Frederick S. Cramer. LC 93-70913. (Illus.). 228p. 1998. 38.00 (*0-941332-34-9*, B0485) Best Pub Co.

Proceedings of the Ninth International Symposium on Cyclodextrins, Santiago de Compostela, Spain, May 31-June 3, 1998. International Symposium on Cyclodextrins Staff. Ed. by J. J. Torres Labandeira & J. L. Vila-Jato. LC 99-24918. 707p. 1999. 297.00 (*0-7923-5721-3*) Kluwer Academic.

P

An Asterisk (*) at the beginning of an entry indicates that the title is appearing for the first time.

Proceedings of the Ninth International Symposium on Human Factors in Telecommunications, 1980, Redbank, N. J., U. S. A. 265p. 1980. 75.00 (*1-56851-091-8*, 125409) Info Gatekeepers.

Proceedings of the Ninth International Symposium Trace Elements in Man & Animals (Tema-9) Ed. by P. W. Fischer et al. 677p. 1997. 120.00 (*0-660-16404-3*, Pub. by NRC Res Pr) Accents Pubns.

Proceedings of the Ninth Midwest Artificial Intelligence & Cognitive Science Conference. Ed. by Martha W. Evens. (Technical Reports). (Illus.). 145p. 1998. pap. text 35.00 (*1-57735-045-6*, CF-98-01) AAAI Pr.

Proceedings of the 9th (1999) International Offshore & Polar Engineering Conference, 4 vols. Incl. Vol. I. Proceedings of the 9th (1999) International Offshore & Polar Engineering Conference., **4 vols.** (Illus.). 826p. 1999. pap. 130.00 (*1-880653-40-0*); Vol. II. Proceedings of the 9th (1999) International Offshore & Polar Engineering Conference., **4 vols.** (Illus.). 725p. 1999. pap. 130.00 (*1-880653-41-9*); Vol. III. Proceedings of the 9th (1999) International Offshore & Polar Engineering Conference., **4 vols.** (Illus.). 830p. 1999. pap. 130.00 (*1-880653-42-7*); Vol. IV. Proceedings of the 9th (1999) International Offshore & Polar Engineering Conference., **4 vols.** (Illus.). 680p. 1999. pap. 130.00 (*1-880653-43-5*); (Illus.). 3061p. 1999. Set pap. 380.00 (*1-880653-39-7*) ISOPE.

Proceedings of the 9th (1999) International Offshore & Polar Engineering Conference see Proceedings of the 9th (1999) International Offshore & Polar Engineering Conference

Proceedings of the 9th Quadrennial IAGOD Symposium Held in Beijing, China, August 12-18, 1994. Ed. by R. D. Hagni. xiv, 620p. 1994. 142.00 (*3-510-65180-4*, Pub. by E Schweizerbartsche) Balogh.

Proceedings of the 9th RID National Convention, 1985: Interpreting: The Art of Cross-Cultural Mediation. Ed. by Marina L. McIntire. 192p. (C). 1990. reprint ed. pap. 10.95 (*0-916883-05-1*) RID Pubns.

Proceedings of the Ninth Session of the Committee on Natural Resources. 387p. 35.00 (*92-1-119231-5*) UN.

Proceedings of the 9th Symposium on Space Nuclear Power Systems. Ed. by Mohamed S. El-Genk. (AIP Conference Proceedings Ser.: No. 246). 352p. 1992. 95.00 (*1-56396-007-9*) Am Inst Physics.

Proceedings of the 9th Symposium on Space Nuclear Power Systems. Ed. by Mohamed S. El-Genk & Mark D. Hoover. LC 91-58793. (AIP Conference Proceedings Ser.: No. 246). (Illus.). 1403p. 1992. pap. write for info. (*1-56396-026-5*); Set boxed set 195.00 (*1-56396-027-3*) Am Inst Physics.

Proceedings of the 9th Symposium on Space Nuclear Power Systems see Proceedings of the 9th Symposium on Space Nuclear Power Systems

Proceedings of the 9th Symposium on Space Nuclear Power Systems, Pt. 1. Ed. by Mohamed S. El-Genk & Mark D. Hoover. LC 91-58793. (AIP Conference Proceedings Ser.: No. 246). (Illus.). 1403p. 1992. pap. write for info. (*1-56396-020-6*) Am Inst Physics.

Proceedings of the 9th Symposium on Space Nuclear Power Systems, Pt. 2. Ed. by Mohamed S. El-Genk & Mark D. Hoover. LC 91-58793. (AIP Conference Proceedings Ser.: No. 246). (Illus.). 1403p. 1992. pap. write for info. (*1-56396-022-2*) Am Inst Physics.

Proceedings of the 9th Symposium on Space Nuclear Power Systems, Pt. 3. Ed. by Mohamed S. El-Genk & Mark D. Hoover. LC 91-58793. (AIP Conference Proceedings Ser.: No. 246). (Illus.). 1403p. 1992. pap. write for info. (*1-56396-024-9*) Am Inst Physics.

Proceedings of the Ninth West Coast Conference on Formal Linguistics. Ed. by Aaron L. Halpern. (Proceedings of the West Coast Conference on Formal Linguistics Ser.: Vol. 9). 603p. 1991. pap. 27.95 (*0-937073-64-4*, WCCFL 9) CSLI.

P

*__Proceedings of the Ninth World Congress on Pain.__ Ed. by Marshall Devor et al. (Progress in Pain Research & Management Ser.: No. 16). (Illus.). xxiv, 1154p. 2000. 80.00 (*0-931092-31-0*) Intl Assn Study Pain.

Proceedings of the Norbert Wiener Centenary Congress, 1994: Michigan State University, November 27-December 3, 1994. V. R. Mandrekar & Pesi R. Masani. LC 96-43346. (Proceedings of Symposia in Applied Mathematics Ser.: Vol. 52). 566p. 1996. text 99.00 (*0-8218-0452-9*, PSAPM/52) Am Math.

Proceedings of the North Pacific Symposium on Invertebrate Stock Assessment & Management. Ed. by G. S. Jamieson & A. Campbell. 462p. 1998. pap. 81.50 (*0-660-17221-6*) NRC Res Pr.

Proceedings of the Northwestern Homotopy Theory Conference. Ed. by Haynes R. Miller et al. LC 83-9941. (Contemporary Mathematics Ser.: Vol. 19). 454p. 1983. pap. 42.00 (*0-8218-5020-2*, CONM/19) Am Math.

Proceedings of the OECD/CSNI Workshop on Transient Thermal-Hydraulic & Neutronic Codes Requirements: Held in Annapolis, Maryland, United States of America, November 5-8, 1996. Government Printing Office Staff. 825p. 1997. per. 57.00 (*0-16-054684-2*) USGPO.

Proceedings of the Open Forum on Laboratory Accreditation. Ed. by Walter Leight & Lawrence Galowin. 175p. (Orig.). (C). 1997. pap. text 40.00 (*0-7881-3899-5*) DIANE Pub.

Proceedings of the Order-Disorder Transformations in Alloys International Symposium, Tubinger, Germany, September 1973. Order-Disorder Transformations in Alloys Internati. Ed. by H. Warlimont. (Reine Uno Angewandte Metallkunde in Einzel-Darstellungen Ser.: Vol. 24). (Illus.). viii, 556p. 1974. 94.95 (*0-387-06766-3*) Spr-Verlag.

Proceedings of the Ordinary Differential Equations Symposium, Minneapolis, May 1972. Ordinary Differential Equations Symposium Staff. Ed. by W. A. Harris, Jr. & Y. Sibuya. LC 72-97022. (Lecture Notes in Mathematics Ser.: Vol. 312). (Illus.). 204p. 1973. 37.95 (*0-387-06146-0*) Spr-Verlag.

Proceedings of the Pacific Rim/ASME International Intersociety Electronic & Photonic Packaging Conference, Kohala Coast, Hawaii, 1997: Advances in Electronic Packaging 1997, 2 vols. Pacific Rim/ASME Staff. Ed. by E. Suhir et al. LC 97-73292. 2223p. 1997. pap. 500.00 (*0-7918-1559-5*) ASME.

Proceedings of the PCTE '94 Conference. Ed. by Timothy Lindquist & Harry Koehnemann. (PCTE Technical Journal Ser.: No. 2). 1994. pap. 50.00 (*0-9644599-0-6*) Mark V Systs.

Proceedings of the Perma-Flow PerFCT Investigators Meeting. Ed. & Illus. by Silent Partners, Inc. Staff. 292p. (Orig.). 1997. pap. write for info. (*1-878353-41-1*) Silent Partners.

Proceedings of the Princeton Symposium on Mathematical Programming. Princeton Symposium on Mathematical Programming St. Ed. by Harold W. Kuhn. LC 75-140280. (Illus.). 626p. 1970. reprint ed. pap. 194.10 (*0-608-06611-7*, 206680800009) Bks Demand.

Proceedings of the Probabilistic Track of the 8th Annual SAE RMS Workshop (1996) 80p. 1996. 29.00 (*1-56091-720-2*, P-297) Soc Auto Engineers.

Proceedings of the Protein-Ligand Interactions Symposium, University of Konstanz, Germany, Sept. 1974. Protein-Ligand Interactions Symposium Staff. Ed. by Gideon Blauer & Horst Sund. (C). 1975. 188.50 (*3-11-004881-7*) De Gruyter.

Proceedings of the RadTech '96 International North America UV/EB Conference & Exhibition, Vol. 1. (Orig.). Date not set. pap. write for info. (*1-878664-14-X*) RadTech Intl North Amer.

Proceedings of the RadTech '96 International North America UV/EB Conference & Exhibition, Vol. 2. (Orig.). Date not set. pap. write for info. (*1-878664-15-8*) RadTech Intl North Amer.

Proceedings of the RadTech '96 International North America UV/EB Conference & Exhibition, 2 vols., Vols. I & II. (Orig.). pap. 125.00 (*1-878664-16-6*) RadTech Intl North Amer.

Proceedings of the Rand Project Air Force Workshop on Transatmospheric Vehicles. Daniel Gonzalez et al. LC 97-29214. (Illus.). 19p. 1997. pap. 13.00 (*0-8330-2547-3*, MR-890-AF) Rand Corp.

Proceedings of the Rapid Excavation & Tunneling Conference, 1993. Ed. by L. D. Bowerman & J. E. Monsees. LC 93-83948. (Illus.). 1308p. 1993. 82.00 (*0-87335-127-4*, 127-4) SMM&E Inc.

Proceedings of the Raymond L. Orbach Symposium on 35 Years of Condensed Matter & Related Physics. LC 97-109561. 300p. 1996. lib. bdg. 56.00 (*981-02-2822-8*) World Scientific Pub.

Proceedings of the Recent & Fossil Marine Diatoms Symposium, 1st, 1972. Reimer Simonsen. 1972. 250.00 (*3-7682-5439-9*) Lubrecht & Cramer.

Proceedings of the Recent & Fossil Marine Diatoms, 2nd, 1974. Reimer Simonsen. 1974. 150.00 (*3-7682-5445-3*) Lubrecht & Cramer.

Proceedings of the Recent & Fossil Marine Diatoms, 3rd Symposium, 1975. Reimer Simonsen. 1975. 150.00 (*3-7682-5453-4*) Lubrecht & Cramer.

Proceedings of the Regional Seminar on Satellite Communication Applications for Distance Education. 198p. 25.00 (*92-1-119872-0*) UN.

Proceedings of the Regional Seminar on Systems Analysis for Water Resources Development: ST-ESCAP-SER.F-61. (Water Resources Ser.: No. 61). 163p. 1986. pap. 19.50 (*92-1-119407-5*, E.86.II.F.13) UN.

Proceedings of the Regional Workshop on Environmental Health Management in Refugee Areas. (WHO/EMRO Technical Publication Ser.: No. 19). 1994. pap. text 18.00 (*92-9021-185-7*) World Health.

Proceedings of the Research Conference on Geriatric Blindness & Severe Visual Impairment, September, 7-8, 1967, Washington, D. C. Research Conference on Geriatric Blindness & Severe Visual Impairment Staff. Ed. by Leslie L. Clark. LC RE0091.R4. 91p. reprint ed. pap. 30.00 (*0-7837-0134-9*, 204042300016) Bks Demand.

Proceedings of the Retina Research Foundation Symosia Vol. 1: Cellular & Molecular Biology of the Retina. Ed. by Dominic M. Lam & Charles D. Gilbert. (Illus.). 200p. 1991. pap. text 45.00 (*0-262-62083-9*) MIT Pr.

Proceedings of the Royal Institution, Vol. 65. Ed. by Peter Day & Richard Catlow. (Illus.). 274p. 1994. text 59.00 (*0-19-855836-8*) OUP.

Proceedings of the Royal Institution of Great Britain, Vol. 66. Ed. by Peter Day & Richard Catlow. (Illus.). 302p. 1995. 80.00 (*0-19-855896-1*) OUP.

Proceedings of the Royal Institution of Great Britain, Vol. 67. Ed. by Peter Day. (Illus.). 344p. 1996. text 110.00 (*0-19-855938-0*) OUP.

Proceedings of the Royal Institution of Great Britain, Vol. 68. Ed. by Peter Day. (Illus.). 386p. 1997. text 125.00 (*0-19-850084-X*) OUP.

Proceedings of the Royal Institution of Great Britain, Vol. 69. Ed. by Peter Day. (Illus.). 348p. 1999. text 125.00 (*0-19-850366-0*) OUP.

*__Proceedings of the Royal Institution of Great Britain, Vol. 70.__ Ed. by P. Day. (Illus.). 360p. 1999. text 130.00 (*0-19-850539-6*) OUP.

Proceedings of the RPA, NIDDK Meeting 1994 Joint Annual Meeting in Conjunction with Renal Physicians, Association Annual Membership Meeting. Ed. by M. J. Scherbenske et al. (Journal: Blood Purification Ser.: Vol. 12 No. 1, 1994). (Illus.). 84p. 1994. pap. 47.00 (*3-8055-6029-X*) S Karger.

*__Proceedings of the St. Petersburg Mathematical Society, Vol. VI.__ Ed. by N. N. Uraltseva. (TRANS2 Ser.: Vol. 199). 238p. 2000. 99.00 (*0-8218-2112-1*) Am Math.

Proceedings of the Savard-Lee International Symposium on Bath Smelting, Montreal, Quebec, 1992. Savard-Lee International Symposium on Bath Smeltin. Ed. by J. K. Brimacombe. LC 92-61283. 682p. 1992. reprint ed. pap. 200.00 (*0-608-03828-8*, 206279000004) Bks Demand.

Proceedings of the Scandinavian Clinical Symposium on the CarboMedics Prosthetic Heart Valve. Ed. & Illus. by Silent Partners, Inc. Staff. 147p. (Orig.). 1991. pap. write for info. (*1-878353-20-9*) Silent Partners.

Proceedings of the Science & Technology Alliance Materials Conference '93. Ed. by J. Sankar. LC 94-61717. 420p. 1994. text 69.95 (*1-56676-232-4*) Technomic.

Proceedings of the Scientific Workshop on the Health Effects of Electric & Magnetic Fields on Workers. Ed. by Philip J. Bierbaum & John M. Peters. (Illus.). 229p. (Orig.). (C). 1994. pap. text 60.00 (*0-7881-0227-3*) DIANE Pub.

Proceedings of the SCOPE Workshop on Soil & Groundwater Pollution: Fundamentals, Risk Assessment & Legislation: Cesky Krumlov, Czech Rebublic, June 6 & 7, 1994. Ed. by Alexander J. Zehnder. LC 95-38221. (Soil & Environment Ser.: Vol. 4). 176p. (C). 1995. text 81.00 (*0-7923-3743-3*) Kluwer Academic.

Proceedings of the Second Annual ACM-SIAM Symposium on Discrete Algorithms. Ed. by Alok Aggarwal et al. (Proceedings in Applied Mathematics Ser.: No. 49). xiv, 482p. 1991. pap. 59.50 (*0-89871-271-8*) Soc Indus-Appl Math.

Proceedings of the Second Annual Battery Conference on Applications & Advances, January 14-16, 1986: California State University - Long Beach, Long Beach, California. Battery Conference on Applications & Advances Staf. Ed. by R. L. Das et al. LC 87-83054. (Electrochemical Society Proceedings Ser.: No. 87-16). (Illus.). 286p. reprint ed. pap. 88.70 (*0-7837-4422-6*, 205248200012) Bks Demand.

Proceedings of the Second Annual Conference on Genetic Programming. Ed. by John Koza. 200p. (C). 1997. pap. text 79.00 (*1-55860-483-9*) Morgan Kaufmann.

Proceedings of the Second ASME-JSME Joint Conference on Nuclear Engineering, 2 vols. Ed. by P. F. Peterson. 1993. 200.00 (*0-685-70661-3*, IX0343) ASME.

Proceedings of the Second ASME-JSME Joint Conference on Nuclear Engineering, Vol. 1. Ed. by P. F. Peterson. 772p. 1993. write for info. (*0-7918-0636-7*, I0343A) ASME.

Proceedings of the Second ASME-JSME Joint Conference on Nuclear Engineering, Vol. 2. Ed. by P. F. Peterson. 916p. 1993. write for info. (*0-7918-0637-5*, I0343B) ASME.

Proceedings of the Second Champlain Valley Symposium, 1982. Ed. by Dennis M. Lewis. 38p. 1982. pap. 5.00 (*1-890402-05-2*) Clinton Cnty Hist.

Proceedings of the 2nd Columbia River Basalt Symposium. Ed. by Ernest H. Gilmour & Dale Stradling. 333p. (Orig.). 1970. pap. 6.25 (*0-910055-03-3*) East Wash Univ.

Proceedings of the 2nd Conference on Acoustic Emission: Microseismic Activity in Geologic Structures & Materials. H. Reginald Hardy & Frederick W. Leighton. (Rock & Soil Mechanics Ser.). (Illus.). 500p. (C). 1980. 70.00 (*0-87849-032-9*, Pub. by Trans T Pub) Enfield Pubs NH.

Proceedings of the Second Conference on Artificial Intelligence Planning Systems. Ed. by Kristian J. Hammond. LC 94-219906. (Illus.). 360p. (Orig.). 1994. pap. text 45.00 (*0-929280-56-3*) AAAI Pr.

Proceedings of the Second Conference on Natural Gas Research & Technology Sponsored by American Gas Association & Institute of Gas Technology, Atlanta, Georgia, June 5-7, 1972. Conference on Natural Gas Research & Technology (2. Ed. by Jack W. White & Maryann Kragulski. LC TP0350.C65. 987p. reprint ed. pap. 200.00 (*0-608-12450-8*, 202423600036) Bks Demand.

Proceedings of the Second Conference on the Use of Computers in the Coal Industry, April 15-17, the University of Alabama, Tuscaloosa, Alabama. fac. ed. Conference on the Use of Computers in the Coal Ind. Ed. by Thomas Novak et al. LC 85-70438. (Illus.). 487p. 1985. reprint ed. pap. 151.00 (*0-7837-7840-6*, 204759900007) Bks Demand.

Proceedings of the Second Euromicro Conference on Software Maintenance & Reengineering, Florence, Italy, March 8-11, 1998. Euromicro Conference on Software Maintenance and Reengineering et al. LC 98-84087. xiv, 239 p. 1998. write for info. (*0-8186-8423-2*) IEEE Comp Soc.

*__Proceedings of the Second European Conference on Cognitive Modelling (ECCM-98)__ Tr. by Frank E. Ritter & Richard M. Young. 215p. 1999. pap. 90.00 (*1-897676-67-0*, Pub. by Nottingham Univ Pr) St Mut.

Proceedings of the Second European Conference on Computer-Supported Cooperative Work - ECSCW 1991. Liam Bannon. 364p. (C). 1991. pap. text 171.00 (*0-7923-1439-5*) Kluwer Academic.

Proceedings of the 2nd Glacier Bay Science Symposium. Ed. by A. M. Milner & James D. Wood, Jr. LC 90-5862. (Illus.). (Orig.). (C). 1990. pap. write for info. (*0-943475-03-1*) Natl Pk AK.

Proceedings of the Second Governors Meeting. 171p. 1994. write for info. (*92-806-3132-2*) U N I C E.

Proceedings, of the Second IEEE Workshop on Future Trends of Distributed Computing Systems, September 30-October 2, 1990, Cairo, Egypt. IEEE Workshop on Future Trends of Didtributed Computing Systems & IEEE Computer Society. LC 90-55484. xii, 542p. 1990. pap. write for info. (*0-8186-6088-0*) IEEE Comp Soc.

*__Proceedings of the 2nd International Conference on Information Fusion (FUSION99),__ Incl. . Proceedings of the 2nd International Conference on Information Fusion Vol. II. (Illus.). 626p. (C). 1999. pap. 100.00 (*0-9671429-2-X*); Vol. I. Proceedings of the 2nd International Conference on Information Fusion. (Illus.). 670p. (C). 1999. pap. 100.00 (*0-9671429-1-1*); (Illus.). 1296p. (C). 1999. Set pap. 200.00 (*0-9671429-3-8*) Intl Socy Info Fusn.

Proceedings of the 2nd International Symposium on Contamination Control (ICCCS) 75.00 (*0-685-63218-0*) IEST.

Proceedings of the 2nd International Symposium on Runaway Reactions, Pressure Relief Design & Effluent Handling. Design Institute for Emergency Releif Systems User. Ed. by G. A. Melhem & H. G. Fisher. (Illus.). 694p. 1998. 125.00 (*0-8169-0761-7*, P-90) Am Inst Chem Eng.

Proceedings of the 2nd International Conference on Visual Information Systems. Ed. by Knowledge Systems Institute Staff. (Illus.). 1997. pap. 65.00 (*0-9641699-8-3*) Knowldge Systs.

Proceedings of the 2nd International Lewis Carroll Conference. Ed. by Charles Lovett. LC 94-73512. (Illus.). 191p. 1994. 25.00 (*0-930326-10-5*) L Carroll Soc.

Proceedings of the 2nd International Conference on Shape Memory & Superelastic Technologies (SMST-97) Alan Pelton et al. 636p. (C). 1997. 100.00 (*0-9660508-1-9*) MIAS.

Proceedings of the 2nd International Congress of Dipterology. Ed. by L. Weismann et al. (Illus.). 367p. 1991. 97.00 (*90-5103-059-2*, Pub. by SPB Acad Pub) Balogh.

Proceedings of the 2nd International Conference on Information Fusion see Proceedings of the 2nd International Conference on Information Fusion (FUSION99)

Proceedings of the 2nd International Conference on Human-Computer Interaction, Honlulu, HI, USA, 10-13 August 1987, Vol. 5. 7th C.O.S.P.A.R International Space Science Symposium et al. Ed. by A. H. Brown & F. G. Favorite. (Advances in Human Factors/Ergonomics Ser.: Vol. 10). 1969. 19.75 (*0-7204-1364-8*) Elsevier.

Proceedings of the 2nd International Conference on Ground Water Ecology: Atlanta, GA, March 27-30, 1994. International Conference on Ground Water Ecology Staff. Ed. by Jack A. Stanford & H. Maurice Valett. LC 94-70722. (American Water Resources Association Technical Publication Ser.: Vol. 94-1). (Illus.). 400p. reprint ed. pap. 124.00 (*0-608-09838-8*, 207080800007) Bks Demand.

Proceedings of the Second International Clinical Symposium (CarboMedics) Ed. & Illus. by Silent Partners, Inc. Staff. 145p. (Orig.). 1990. pap. write for info. (*1-878353-12-8*) Silent Partners.

Proceedings of the Second International Colloquium on Numerical Analysis. Ed. by D. Bainov & V. Covachev. 204p. 1994. 115.00 (*90-6764-168-5*) Coronet Bks.

Proceedings of the Second International Conference on Adaptive Structures. Ed. by Yuji Matsuzaki & Ben K. Wada. LC 92-54123. 890p. 1992. text 39.95 (*0-87762-932-3*) Technomic.

Proceedings of the Second International Conference on Calorimetry in High Energy Physics: Capri, Italy, 14-18 October 1991. A. Ereditato. LC 92-10271. 400p. 1992. text 109.00 (*981-02-0916-9*) World Scientific Pub.

Proceedings of the Second International Conference on Civil & Structural Engineering Computing, Set. Civil Comp Editors. 1985. pap. 245.00 (*0-948749-00-8*, Pub. by Civil-Comp) St Mut.

Proceedings of the Second International Conference on Document Analysis & Recognition, October 20-22, 1993, Tsukuba Science City, Japan. International Association for Pattern Recognition Staff. LC 93-79398. xx, 963 p. 1993. pap. write for info. incl. 5.25 hd (*0-8186-4961-5*) IEEE Comp Soc.

Proceedings of the Second International Conference on Electronic Materials: Materials Research Society Conference Proceedings, Vol. ICEM-2. Ed. by R. P. H. Chang et al. 664p. 1991. text 17.50 (*1-55899-092-5*) Materials Res.

Proceedings of the Second International Conference on Intelligent Materials. Craig A. Rogers & Gordon G. Wallace. (Illus.). 1409p. 1994. 319.95 (*1-56676-171-9*) Technomic.

Proceedings of the Second International Conference on Intelligent Systems for Molecular Biology. Ed. by Russ Altman. (Illus.). 408p. (Orig.). 1995. pap. text 45.00 (*0-929280-68-7*) AAAI Pr.

Proceedings of the Second International Conference on Knowledge Discovery & Data Mining. Ed. by Evangelos Simoudis et al. (Illus.). 400p. (Orig.). 1996. pap. text 55.00 (*1-57735-004-9*) AAAI Pr.

Proceedings of the Second International Conference on Mathematical & Numerical Aspects of Wave Propagation. Ed. by Ralph E. Kleinman et al. LC 93-8109. (Proceedings in Applied Mathematics Ser.: No. 69). xi, 473p. 1993. pap. 86.50 (*0-89871-318-8*) Soc Indus-Appl Math.

Proceedings of the Second International Conference on Multiagent Systems. Ed. by Edmund Durfee & Mario Tokoro. (Illus.). 476p. (Orig.). 1996. pap. text 59.95 (*1-57735-013-8*) AAAI Pr.

An Asterisk (*) at the beginning of an entry indicates that the title is appearing for the first time.

*__Proceedings of the Second International Conference on Remediation of Chrlorinated & Recalcitrant Compounds, May 22-25, 2000, Monterey, California, 7 vols., Set.__ Ed. by Godage B. Wickramanayake & Arun R. Gavaskar. 2000. 399.50 (*1-57477-094-2*) Battelle.

Proceedings of the Second International Conference on Requirements Engineering: April 15-18, 1996, Colorado Springs, Colorado International Conference on Requirements Engineering Staff & IEEE Computer Society Staff. LC 96-76124. xvi, 257 p. 1996. write for info. (*0-8186-7254-4*) IEEE Comp Soc.

Proceedings of the Second International Conference on Reservoir Limnology & Water Quality. Ed. by Vera Straskrabova & J. F. Tailing. (Advances in Limnology Ser.: Vol. 40). (GER., Illus.). viii, 294p. 1994. pap., teacher ed. 105.00 (*3-510-47041-9*, Pub. by E Schweizerbartsche) Balogh.

Proceedings of the Second International Conference on Senior Tourism: Selected Materials, May 1997. 89p. 1997. 20.00 (*92-844-0213-1*, WTO2013, Pub. by Wrld Tourism Org) Bernan Associates.

Proceedings of the Second International Conference on Space Charge in Solid Dielectrics. IEEE (Dielectrics & Electrical Insulation Society). Ed. by IEEE (Institute of Electrical & Electronics Engine. 700p. 1995. pap. write for info. (*0-7803-2649-0*, 95TH8072); mic. film. write for info. (*0-7803-2650-4*, 95TM8072) Inst Electrical.

Proceedings of the Second International Conference on the Study of Shamanism, 1985, Santa Sabina Center, San Rafael, California, August 31-September 2, 1985. Ed. by Ruth-Inge Heinze. (Illus.). 253p. (C). 1985. pap. 21.75 (*0-945875-06-1*) Independent Scholars Asia Inc.

Proceedings of the Second International Congress on Cancer Pain, Rye, NY, 1988. International Congress on Cancer Pain Staff. Ed. by Kathleen M. Foley et al. LC 89-70121. (Advances in Pain Research & Therapy Ser.: Vol. 16). 559p. 1990. reprint ed. pap. 173.30 (*0-608-03408-8*, 206410500008) Bks Demand.

Proceedings of the Second International Forum on Applications of Neural Networks to Power Systems. IEEE, Neural Networks Council & Tokyo Section Staf. Ed. by Institute of Electrical & Electronics Engineers, I. LC 93-77241. 480p. 1993. pap. write for info. (*0-7803-1217-1*, 93TH0532-2); fiche. write for info. (*0-7803-1218-X*, 93TH0532-2) Inst Electrical.

Proceedings of the Second International Hindukush Cultural Conference. Ed. by Elena Bashir & Israr-Ud-Din. (Hindukush & Karakoram Studies: No. 1). (Illus.). 534p. 1997. text 65.00 (*0-19-577571-6*) OUP.

Proceedings of the Second International ISA Food Instrumentation Division Symposium, Montreal, 1972. Food & Beverage Instrumentation Symposium Staff. Ed. by David S. Harding. LC 72-90018. (Instrumentation in the Food & Beverage Industry Ser.: Vol. 2). (Illus.). 133p. reprint ed. pap. 41.30 (*0-608-15167-X*, 205216500046) Bks Demand.

Proceedings of the Second International Scientific Meeting Microwaves in Medicine 1993. IEEE, Italy Section Staff. Ed. by Institute of Electrical & Electronics Engineers, I. LC 93-61233. 320p. 1993. pap. write for info. (*0-7803-1468-9*, 93TH0591-8); fiche. write for info. (*0-7803-1469-7*) Inst Electrical.

*__Proceedings of the Second International Topical Meeting on Nuclear Applications of Accelerator Technology: Gatlinburg, Tennessee, September 20-23, 1998.__ 720p. 1998. pap. 90.00 (*0-89448-633-0*, 700253) Am Nuclear Soc.

Proceedings of the 2nd ISSAT International Conference: Reliability & Quality in Design. Ed. by Hoang Pham. (Orig.). (C). 1995. pap. text 60.00 (*0-9639998-1-8*) ISSAT.

Proceedings of the Second National Conference on Citizens with Mental Retardation & the Law. 52p. 1987. write for info. (*1-55672-050-5*) US HHS.

Proceedings of the 2nd (1997) Ocean Mining Symposium. Ed. by Jin S. Chung et al. LC 97-74490. (Illus.). 201p. 1997. pap. 100.00 (*1-880653-33-8*) ISOPE.

*__Proceedings of the 2nd (1999) ISOPE European Offshore Mechanics Symposium: Pipeline.__ Ed. by Jin S. Chung et al. (ENG & RUS., Illus.). 135p. 1999. pap. 50.00 (*1-880653-44-3*) ISOPE.

*__Proceedings of the Second Palestinian International Conference on Mathematics: Birzeit & An-Najah University, Nablus, Palestine, August 19-23, 1998.__ Ed. by Palestinian International Conference on Mathematics Staff & Saber N. Elaydi. LC 00-20881. 2000. write for info. (*981-02-4220-4*) World Scientific Pub.

Proceedings of the 2nd Scandinavian Symposium on Aspectology. Lars-Gunnar Larsson. (Studia Uralica et Altaica Upsaliensia: No. 19). 130p. (Orig.). 1989. pap. 37.50 (*91-554-2412-0*) Coronet Bks.

Proceedings of the Second Sudden Infant Death Syndrome International Conference. Ed. by National SIDS Council of Australia Staff et al. (Illus.). 1993. pap. 50.00 (*0-916859-52-5*) Perinatology.

Proceedings of the 2nd Symposium on the Botany of the Bahamas. Ed. by R. R. Smith. 65p. (Orig.). (C). 1987. pap. 12.00 (*0-935909-26-5*) Bahamian.

Proceedings of the Second Symposium of the International Working Group on Plant Viruses with Fungal Vectors. Ed. by Chuji Hiruki. (Illus.). 156p. (Orig.). 1993. pap. 10.00 (*0-9639572-0-1*) Am Soc Sugarbeet.

Proceedings of the 2nd Symposium on Southeastern Fox Squirrels. Ed. by Nancy D. Moncrief et al. 90p. 1993. pap. 15.00 (*0-9625801-6-3*) VA Mus Natl Hist.

Proceedings of the Second Symposium on Social Aspects & Recreation Research. Ed. by Deborah J. Chavez. (Illus.). 186p. (C). 1997. reprint ed. pap. text 40.00 (*0-7881-3768-9*) DIANE Pub.

Proceedings of the Second Symposium on the Geology of Rocky Mountain Coal, 1977. Ed. by Helen E. Hodgson. (Resource Ser.: No. 4). (Illus.). 219p. (Orig.). 1978. pap. 2.00 (*1-884216-26-9*) Colo Geol Survey.

Proceedings of the Second U. S. National Conference on Earthquake Engineering: Held at Stanford University, August 22-24, 1979. 1170p. 1979. 36.00 (*0-685-14405-4*) Earthquake Eng.

Proceedings of the Second Workshop on Environments & Tools for Parallel Scientific Computing. Ed. by Jack J. Dongarra & Bernard Tourancheau. LC 94-36849. (Proceedings in Applied Mathematics Ser.: Vol. 74). x, 292p. 1994. pap. 43.50 (*0-89871-343-9*) Soc Indus-Appl Math.

Proceedings of the 2nd Workshop on Folyl & Antifolyl Polyglumates. Ed. by I. David Goldman. LC 85-3531. 416p. 1985. 79.50 (*0-275-91314-7*, C1314, Praeger Pubs) Greenwood.

Proceedings of the Second Workshop on Hadronics Mechanics Held in Villa Olmo Centro a Volta Como, Italy Aug. 3-Aug. 6, 1984, 2 vols., Set. Ed. by J. Fronteau et al. 1984. pap. 140.00 (*0-911767-29-0*) Hadronic Pr Inc.

Proceedings of the Second Workshop on Hadronics Mechanics Held in Villa Olmo Centro a Volta Como, Italy Aug. 3-Aug. 6, 1984, 2 vols., Vol. 1. Ed. by J. Fronteau et al. 375p. 1984. pap. 70.00 (*0-317-14022-1*) Hadronic Pr Inc.

Proceedings of the Second Workshop on Hadronics Mechanics Held in Villa Olmo Centro a Volta Como, Italy Aug. 3-Aug. 6, 1984, 2 vols., Vol. 2. Ed. by J. Fronteau et al. 375p. 1984. pap. 70.00 (*0-317-14023-X*) Hadronic Pr Inc.

Proceedings of the Second Workshop on Measurement of Microbial Activity in the Carbon Cycle of Aquatic Ecosystems. Ed. by Juergen Overbeck et al. (Advances in Limnology Ser.: Vol. 19). (GER., Illus.). xii, 316p. 1984. pap. text 82.00 (*3-510-47017-6*, Pub. by E Schweizerbartsche) Balogh.

Proceedings of the 2nd Workshop on Neural Networks, 1991: Academic-Industrial-NASA-Defense. Ed. by Mary L. Padgett. 816p. 1991. pap. 100.00 (*0-911801-77-4*, WNN91-1) Soc Computer Sim.

Proceedings of the Second Workshop on Radon Monitoring in Radioprotection, Environmental, & or Earth Sciences: ICTP, Trieste, Italy, 25 November-6 December 1991. Ed. by G. Furlan & L. Tommasino. LC 92-36777. 588p. 1993. text 178.00 (*981-02-1226-7*) World Scientific Pub.

Proceedings of the Second Workshop on Road-Vehicle-Systems & Related Mathematics June 20-25, 1987, ISI Torino. Ed. by Helmut Neunzert. (C). 1989. text 171.00 (*0-7923-0243-5*) Kluwer Academic.

*__Proceedings of the Second World Conference on Structural Control.__ World Conference on Structural Control et al. Ed. by Yutaka Inoue et al. LC 98-48786. (Illus.). 2552p. 1999. write for info. (*0-471-98310-1*) Wiley.

Proceedings of the Second (1992) International Offshore & Polar Engineering Conference, 4 vols., Set. Ed. by Jin S. Chung et al. LC 91-78280. 2900p. (Orig.). 1992. pap. 340.00 (*1-880653-00-1*) ISOPE.

Proceedings of the Second (1992) International Offshore & Polar Engineering Conference, Vol. I. Ed. by Jin S. Chung et al. LC 91-78280. 729p. (Orig.). 1992. pap. 100.00 (*1-880653-01-X*) ISOPE.

Proceedings of the Second (1992) International Offshore & Polar Engineering Conference, Vol. II. Ed. by Michael S. Triantafyllou et al. LC 91-78280. 825p. (Orig.). 1992. pap. 100.00 (*1-880653-02-8*) ISOPE.

Proceedings of the Second (1992) International Offshore & Polar Engineering Conference, Vol. III. Ed. by Jin S. Chung et al. LC 91-78280. 724p. (Orig.). 1992. pap. 100.00 (*1-880653-03-6*) ISOPE.

Proceedings of the Second (1992) International Offshore & Polar Engineering Conference, Vol. IV. Ed. by Ram S. Puthli et al. LC 91-78280. 628p. (Orig.). 1992. pap. 100.00 (*1-880653-04-4*) ISOPE.

Proceedings of the Seminaire de Probabilities, 9th, Universite de Strasbourg. Seminaire Pierre Lelong Staff. Ed. by P. A. Meyer. (Lecture Notes in Mathematics Ser.: Vol. 465). 598p. 1975. 50.95 (*0-387-07178-4*) Spr-Verlag.

Proceedings of the Seminar: Conservation & Development of Tank Irrigation for Livelihood Promotion. C. R. Shanmugham et al. (Illus.). 101p. 1998. spiral bd. write for info. (*0-9662380-2-8*) Conserv & Devel.

Proceedings of the Seminar on Natural Family Planning & Family Life Education. Ed. by Ramon Ruiz. 320p. (C). 1990. pap. text 32.50 (*962-209-260-8*, Pub. by HK Univ Pr) Coronet Bks.

Proceedings of the Seminar on Regional Statistics Baden, 1996 Vol. 2: Specific Reports. Eurostat Staff. 375p. 1997. pap. 30.00 (*92-827-9236-6*, CA-77-96-002ENC, Pub. by Comm Europ Commun) Bernan Associates.

Proceedings of the Seminar on Reliability Growth, Management, Testing & Modeling. LC 62-38584. (Illus.). 1978. pap. text 50.00 (*0-915414-57-0*) IEST.

Proceedings of the Seminar on the Use of Administrative Sources for Statistical Luxembourg 15-16 January, 1997. LC 98-125011. (Statistical Document Ser.). 277p. 1997. 55.00 (*92-828-1151-4*, CA-05-97-123ENC, Pub. by Comm Europ Commun) Bernan Associates.

Proceedings of the Seminar on Water Quality Monitoring in the Asian & Pacific Region, State of the Art, Regional Overview & Country Reports. (Water Resources Ser.: No. 67). 345p. 1991. 37.00 (*0-685-41904-5*, 91.II.F.9) UN.

*__Proceedings of the Senate Task Force on Economic Sanctions.__ Ed. by Mitch McConnell & Joe Biden. (Illus.). 192p. 2000. reprint ed. pap. text 35.00 (*0-7881-8505-5*) DIANE Pub.

Proceedings of the Session on Tropical Forestry for People of the Pacific. Seventeenth Pacific Science Congress. Ed. by C. Eugene Conrad & Leonard A. Newell. (Illus.). 88p. (Orig.). (C). 1994. pap. text 35.00 (*0-7881-0364-4*) DIANE Pub.

Proceedings of the 17th Biennial Conference. ICHCA Staff. (C). 1988. 270.00 (*0-7855-6155-2*, Pub. by ICHCA) St Mut.

Proceedings of the 17th Annual Conference. APLIC International Staff. Ed. by Carann G. Turner. LC 76-643241. 121p. (Orig.). 1985. pap. 15.00 (*0-933438-10-9*) APLIC Intl.

Proceedings of the Seventeenth Annual Conference of the Cognitive Science Society. Cognitive Science Society Staff. 1995. cd-rom. write for info. (*1-56321-191-2*) L Erlbaum Assocs.

Proceedings of the Seventeenth Annual Conference of the Cognitive Science Society. Cognitive Science Society Staff. Ed. by Jill F. Lehman & Johanna D. Moore. 824p. 1995. pap. 150.00 (*0-8058-2159-7*) L Erlbaum Assocs.

Proceedings of the Seventeenth Annual SAS User's Group International Conference. 1632p. (C). 1992. pap. 12.50 (*1-55544-505-5*, BR56055) SAS Publ.

Proceedings of the 17th Colloquium on the Law of Outer Space, October 1-4, 1974, Amsterdam, The Netherlands. International Institute of Space Law of the International Astronautical Federation Staff. vi, 401p. 1975. pap. 27.50 (*0-8377-0412-X*, Rothman) W S Hein.

Proceedings of the Seventeenth International Conference on the Physics of Semiconductors. Ed. by J. D. Chadi & W. A. Harrison. (Illus.). 1600p. 1985. 219.00 (*0-387-96108-9*) Spr-Verlag.

Proceedings of the Seventeenth International Technical Conference on Coal Utilization & Slurry Technologies (1992) 910p. 1992. 325.00 (*0-932066-17-8*) Coal Slurry Tech.

Proceedings of the Seventeenth Meeting of the French Colonial Historical Society, Chicago, May 1991. Ed. by Patricia Galloway. 138p. (C). 1993. lib. bdg. 38.00 (*0-8191-8930-8*) U Pr of Amer.

Proceedings of the 17th National Online Meeting May, 1996. 412p. 1996. pap. 59.00 (*1-57387-026-9*) Info Today Inc.

Proceedings of the Seventeenth West Coast Conference on Formal Linguistics. Ed. by Kimary N. Shahin et al. 720p. (C). 1999. text 74.95 (*1-57586-185-2*) CSLI.

Proceedings of the Seventh Annual ACM-SIAM Symposium on Discrete Algorithms. Ed. by E. Tardos. (Proceedings in Applied Mathematics Ser.: No. 81). x, 586p. 1996. pap. 66.50 (*0-89871-366-8*) Soc Indus-Appl Math.

Proceedings of the 7th Annual Control Engineering Conference: Held as Part of the Control Engineering Conference & Exposition Center, Rosemont, IL June 7-9, 1988. Intro. by Byron K. Ledgerwood. (Illus.). (Orig.). (C). 1988. pap. 100.00 (*0-914331-57-4*, Control Engrng) Cahners Busn Des Plaines.

Proceedings of the Seventh Annual IEEE International Conference on Wafer Scale Integration, 1995. IEEE, Components, Packaging & Manufacturing Techno. Ed. by IEEE Staff. 400p. 1995. pap. write for info. (*0-7803-2466-8*, 95CH35742); lib. bdg. write for info. (*0-7803-2467-6*, 94CH35742); fiche. write for info. (*0-7803-2468-4*, 95CH35742) Inst Electrical.

Proceedings of the Seventh Annual Meeting of the Geoscience Information Society, November 13, 1972, Minneapolis, Minnesota. Geoscience Information Society Staff. LC QE0048.85.G4. (Geoscience Information Society Proceedings Ser.: Vol. 3). 68p. reprint ed. pap. 30.00 (*0-7837-5624-0*, 204553300005) Bks Demand.

Proceedings of the Seventh ASTM-Euratom Symposium on Reactor Dosimetry, Strasbourg, France, 27-31 August 1990. Ed. by G. Tsotridis et al. LC 92-15198. 976p. (C). 1992. text 468.50 (*0-7923-1792-0*) Kluwer Academic.

Proceedings of the 7th Conference on Fluid Machinery, Vol. 1. Ed. by L. Kisbocskoi & A. Szabo. 484p. 1983. 258.00 (*963-05-3462-2*, Pub. by Akade Kiado) St Mut.

Proceedings of the 7th Conference on Fluid Machinery, 2 vols., Vol. 2. Ed. by L. Kisbocskoi & A. Szabo. 485p. (C). 1983. 258.00 (*963-05-3464-9*, Pub. by Akade Kiado) St Mut.

*__Proceedings of the Seventh Conference on Subregional Economic Cooperation.__ Asian Development Bank Staff. 196p. 1999. pap. 35.00 (*971-561-154-0*, Pub. by Asian Devel Bank) Paul & Co Pubs.

Proceedings of the 7th International Conference on Creep & Fracture of Engineering Materials & Structures. Ed. by J. C. Earthman & F. A. Mohamed. LC 97-73307. (Illus.). 799p. 1997. 214.00 (*0-87339-379-1*, 3791) Minerals Metals.

Proceedings of the 7th International Symposium of Celtic Studies. Ed. by D. Ellis-Evans & J. G. Griffith. 324p. 1986. pap. 30.00 (*0-9511269-0-3*) David Brown.

Proceedings of the 7th International Snow Leopard Symposium. Ed. by Joseph L. Fox & Du Jizeng. (Illus.). 332p. 1994. pap. text 25.00 (*0-913934-22-4*) Intl Snow Leopard.

Proceedings of the 7th International Congress of Myriapodology. Ed. by Alessandro Minelli. LC 89-9901. xv, 480p. 1989. 201.00 (*90-04-08972-1*) Brill Academic Pubs.

Proceedings of the Seventh International Colloquium on Differential Equations: Plovdiv, Bulgaria, 18-23 August, 1996. Ed. by D. Bainov. (Illus.). 480p. 1997. 199.00 (*90-6764-233-9*, Pub. by VSP) Coronet Bks.

Proceedings of the Seventh International Conference of Racing Analysts & Veterinarians. Ed. by Thomas Tobin et al. 1990. 95.00 (*0-9626367-0-3*) Univ KY Vet Sci.

Proceedings of the Seventh International Conference on Composite Materials, 3 vols., Set. Ed. by Wu Yunshu et al. LC 89-15967. (International Academic Publishers Ser.). 2026p. 1990. 505.00 (*0-08-037537-5*, Pub. by IAP) Elsevier.

Proceedings of the Seventh International Conference on Genetic Algorithms: Michigan State University, East Lansing, MI, July 19-23, 1997. Ed. by Thomas Baeck. LC 97-25149. 800p. (C). 1997. pap. text 49.95 (*1-55860-487-1*) Morgan Kaufmann.

*__Proceedings of the Seventh International Conference on Intelligent Systems for Molecular Biology.__ Ed. by Thomas Lengauer et al. (Illus.). 324p. 1999. pap. text 45.00 (*1-57735-083-9*) AAAI Pr.

Proceedings of the Seventh International Conference on Jojoba & Its Uses. Ed. by A. R. Baldwin. 453p. 1989. 40.00 (*0-935315-22-5*) Am Oil Chemists.

Proceedings of the Seventh International Conference on Low Temperature Physics, University of Toronto, Canada, 29th August-3rd September, 1960. International Conference on Low Temperature Physic. Ed. by G. M. Graham & Hollis A. Hallett. LC QC0278.I5. 745p. reprint ed. pap. 200.00 (*0-608-13069-9*, 201422300095) Bks Demand.

Proceedings of the Seventh International Conference on Software Engineering & Knowledge Engineering. Ed. by Knowledge Systems Institute Staff. (Illus.). 502p. 1995. pap. 65.00 (*0-9641699-2-4*) Knowldge Systs.

Proceedings of the Seventh International Conference on the Study of Shamanism & Alternate Modes of Healing, 1990, Santa Sabina Center, San Rafael, California, September 1-3, 1990. Ed. by Ruth-Inge Heinze. LC 91-6513. (Illus.). 429p. (C). 1991. pap. 21.75 (*0-945875-07-X*) Independent Scholars Asia Inc.

Proceedings of the Seventh International Congress of Logic, Methodology & Philosophy of Science. Paul Weingartner et al. (Studies in Logic & the Foundations of Mathematics: Vol. 114). xiv,738p. 1986. 358.50 (*0-444-87656-1*) Elsevier.

Proceedings of the Seventh International Congress of the Phonetic Sciences, Montreal, 22-28 August 1971-Actes Du Septieme Congres International Des Sciences Phonetiques. Ed. by Andre Rigault & Rene Charbonneau. (Janua Linguarum, Series Major: No. 57). (Illus.). 1972. 346.15 (*90-279-2311-6*) Mouton.

Proceedings of the Seventh International Coral Reef Symposium, 2 vols. Ed. by Robert H. Richmond. Incl. Vol. 1. (Illus.). (C). 1994. (*1-881629-01-5*); Vol. 2. (Illus.). (C). 1994. (*1-886129-02-9*); 1993. 125.00 (*1-881629-03-1*) Univ Guam Pr.

Proceedings of the Seventh International Symposium on Human Factors in Telecommunications, 1974, Montreal, Canada. 750p. 1974. pap. 95.00 (*1-56851-093-4*, 125407) Info Gatekeepers.

Proceedings of the Seventh International Symposium on Inorganic Ring Systems, IRIS VII. Ed. by Tristan Chivers. 448p. 1995. pap. text 1095.00 (*2-88449-168-6*) Gordon & Breach.

Proceedings of the Seventh International Workshop on Inelastic Ion-Surface Collisions, Krakow, Poland, September 1988: A Special Issue of the Journal Radiation Effects & Defects in Solids. M. Szymonski & R. Pedrys. xii, 328p. 1989. pap. text 907.00 (*0-677-22300-5*) Gordon & Breach.

Proceedings of the Seventh North American Crane Workshop, Vol. 7. unabridged ed. Ed. by Richard P. Urbanek & Dale W. Stahlecker. LC 97-68410. (Illus.). 262p. (C). 1997. pap. 25.00 (*0-9659324-0-0*) North Crane.

Proceedings of the 7th Quadrennial Symposium, Lulea/Sweden, Aug. 18-22, 1986. Ed. by E. Zachrisson. (International Association on the Genesis of Ore Deposits (IAGOD) Symposia Ser.). (Illus.). x, 694p. 1988. lib. bdg. 140.00 (*3-510-65137-5*, Pub. by E Schweizerbartsche) Balogh.

Proceedings of the Seventh Scientific Meeting of the Inter-American Society. Ed. by Edgar Haber. LC 73-2001. (Hypertension Monographs: No. 4). 235p. 1988. 16.80 (*0-87493-653-5*) Am Heart.

Proceedings of the Seventh SIAM Conference on Parallel Processing for Scientific Computing. SIAM Conference on Parallel Processing for Scientific Computing Staff. Ed. by David H. Bailey. LC 95-1405. (SIAM Proceedings in Applied Mathematics Ser.: Vol. 75). (Illus.). xviii, 875p. 1995. pap. text 105.00 (*0-89871-344-7*, PR0075) Soc Indus-Appl Math.

*__Proceedings of the 7th Symposium on the Natural History of the Bahamas.__ Thomas K. Wilson. (Illus.). 136p. 1998. pap. text 25.00 (*0-935909-66-4*) Bahamian.

Proceedings of the Seventh Symposium on the Geology of the Bahamas. Ed. by Mark R. Boardman. (Illus.). 74p. (Orig.). (C). 1995. pap. text 16.00 (*0-935909-55-9*) Bahamian.

Proceedings of the 7th UCLA Indo-European Conference, Los Angeles, 1995. Henning Andersen et al. Ed. by Angela Della Volpe. LC 99-165919. (Journal of Indo-European Studies Monograph Ser.: No. 27). 248p. (C). 1998. pap. text 46.00 (*0-941694-64-X*) Inst Study Man.

Proceedings of the Seventy-Eighth Convention of the International Association of Fish & Wildlife Agencies, 1988. Ed. by Kenneth J. Sabol. 330p. 1991. lib. bdg. 20.00 (*0-932108-15-6*) IAFWA.

Proceedings of the Seventy-Fifth Convention: International Association of Fish & Wildlife Agencies, 1985. Ed. by Kenneth J. Sabol. 325p. 1989. lib. bdg. 20.00 (*0-932108-12-1*) IAFWA.

Proceedings of the Seventy-Fourth Convention: International Association of Fish & Wildlife Agencies 1984. Kenneth J. Sabol. 300p. 1986. lib. bdg. 20.00 (*0-932108-11-3*) IAFWA.

P

Proceedings of the Seventy-Seventh Convention, International Association of Fish & Wildlife Agencies, 1987. Kenneth J. Sabol. 325p. 1990. lib. bdg. 20.00 (*0-932108-14-8*) IAFWA.

Proceedings of the Seventy-Sixth Convention, International Association of Fish & Wildlife Agencies, 1986. Ed. by Kenneth J. Sabol. 325p. (Orig.). 1989. lib. bdg. 20.00 (*0-932108-13-X*) IAFWA.

Proceedings of the Short Parliament, 1640. E. S. Cope. (Camden Fourth Ser.: Vol. 19). 343p. 27.00 (*0-901050-37-7*) David Brown.

Proceedings of the 16th Biennial Conference. ICHCA Staff. (C). 1988. 210.00 (*0-7855-6156-0*, Pub. by ICHCA) St Mut.

Proceedings of the Sixteenth Annual Conference of the Cognitive Science Society: Atlanta, Georgia, 1994. Ed. by Ashwin Ram & Kurt Eiselt. 1016p. 1994. pap. 180.00 (*0-8058-1803-0*) L Erlbaum Assocs.

Proceedings of the Sixteenth Annual Users' Group International Conference. 1784p. (C). 1991. pap. 12.50 (*1-55544-438-5*, BR56053) SAS Publ.

Proceedings of the 16th Colloquium on the Law of Outer Space, October 7-13, 1973, Baku, U. S. S. R. International Institute of Space Law of the International Astronautical Federation Staff. vi, 408p. 1974. pap. 27.50 (*0-8377-0411-1*, Rothman) W S Hein.

Proceedings of the 16th International Conference on Offshore Mechanics & Arctic Engineering, Yokohama, Japan, April 13-17, 1997 Vol. I, Pts. A & B: Offshore Technology. Ed. by S. Chakrabarti et al. 684p. 1997. 230.00 (*0-7918-1799-7*, HX1080) ASME Pr.

Proceedings of the 16th International Conference on Offshore Mechanics & Arctic Engineering, Yokohama, Japan, April 13-17, 1997 Vol. II: Safety & Reliability. Ed. by C. Guedes-Soares et al. 362p. 1997. 170.00 (*0-7918-1800-4*, H01081) ASME Pr.

Proceedings of the 16th International Conference on Offshore Mechanics & Arctic Engineering, Yokohama, Japan, April 13-17, 1997 Vol. III: Materials Engineering. Ed. by M. M. Salama et al. 404p. 1997. 170.00 (*0-7918-1801-2*, H01082) ASME Pr.

Proceedings of the 16th International Conference on Offshore Mechanics & Arctic Engineering, Yokohama, Japan, April 13-17, 1997 Vol. IV: Arctic - Polar Technology. Ed. by H. Yamaguchi et al. 488p. 1997. 180.00 (*0-7918-1802-0*, H01083) ASME Pr.

Proceedings of the 16th International Conference on Offshore Mechanics & Arctic Engineering, Yokohama, Japan, April 13-17, 1997 Vol. V: Pipeline Technology. Ed. by R. Bruschi et al. 256p. 1997. 120.00 (*0-7918-1803-9*, H01084) ASME Pr.

Proceedings of the 16th International Conference on Offshore Mechanics & Arctic Engineering, Yokohama, Japan, April 13-17, 1997 Vol. VI: Ocean Space Utilization. 16th ed. Ed. by Y. Ohkawa et al. 304p. 1997. 120.00 (*0-7918-1804-7*, H01085) ASME Pr.

Proceedings of the Sixteenth International Technical Conference on Coal & Slurry Technologies (1991) 760p. 1991. 225.00 (*0-932066-16-X*) Coal Slurry Tech.

Proceedings of the Sixteenth Meeting of the French Colonial Historical Society: Mackinac Island, May 1990. Ed. by Patricia Galloway. 200p. (C). 1992. lib. bdg. 42.50 (*0-8191-8505-1*) U Pr of Amer.

***Proceedings of the 16th National Convention: Honoring Our Past, Creating Our Future Together.** (Illus.). 280p. 1999. pap. 24.95 (*0-916883-27-2*) RID Pubns.

Proceedings of the 16th National Online Meeting, 1995. 448p. 1995. pap. 55.00 (*1-57387-004-8*) Info Today Inc.

Proceedings of the Sixteenth West Coast Conference on Formal Linguistics. Ed. by Emily Curtis et al. (Proceedings of the West Coast Conference on Formal Linguistics Ser.). 624p. (C). 1998. text 75.00 (*1-57586-143-7*); pap. text 27.95 (*1-57586-142-9*) CSLI.

Proceedings of the 6th Bienniel Conference. ICHCA Staff. (C). 1988. 22.00 (*0-7855-6159-5*, Pub. by ICHCA) St Mut.

Proceedings of the 6th Annual ACM-SIAM Symposium on Discrete Algorithms (1995: San Francisco, California) (Proceedings in Applied Mathematics Ser.: No. 76). viii, 654p. 1995. pap. 68.50 (*0-89871-349-8*) Soc Indus-Appl Math.

Proceedings of the 6th Annual Control Engineering Conference, 1987. Ed. & Intro. by Byron K. Ledgerwood. (Control Engineering Conference Ser.). 703p. 1987. pap. 100.00 (*0-914331-56-6*, Control Engrng) Cahners Busn Des Plaines.

Proceedings of the Sixth Annual IEEE International ASIC Conference & Exhibit. IEEE Rochester Section Staff. Ed. by IEEE Staff. 600p. 1993. pap. write for info. (*0-7803-1375-5*, 93TH0570-2); fiche. write for info. (*0-7803-1376-3*, 93TH0570-2) Inst Electrical.

Proceedings of the 6th Asian Logic Conference Beijing, China, 20-24 May 1996. Ed. by C. T. Chong et al. 350p. 1998. 68.00 (*981-02-3432-5*) World Scientific Pub.

Proceedings of the Sixth Budapest Conference of Soil Mechanics & Foundation Engineering. G. Petrasovits. (ENG & GER.). 640p. (C). 1984. 175.00 (*963-05-3962-4*, Pub. by Akade Kiado) St Mut.

Proceedings of the Sixth Complement Genetics Workshop & Conference, Mainz, July 1989. Ed. by C. Rittner et al. (Illus.). vi, 142p. 1990. reprint ed. 113.25 (*3-8055-5342-0*) S Karger.

Proceedings of the Sixth Conference of the Comitbe Arctique International, 13-15 May 1985. Comite Arctique International Staff et al. LC 88-34085. vii, 637p. 1989. 243.00 (*90-04-08281-6*) Brill Academic Pubs.

Proceedings of the 6th Conference on Fluid Machinery, 2 vols., Set. Ed. by L. Kisbocskoi & A. Szabo. 1324p. (C). 1979. 345.00 (*963-05-2082-6*, Pub. by Akade Kiado) St Mut.

Proceedings of the 6th European Meeting on Ferroelectricity. Ed. by B. Hilczer. ccxii, 1380p. 1988. pap. text 2929.00 (*2-88124-301-0*) Gordon & Breach.

Proceedings of the Sixth IEEE Digital Signal Processing Workshop. IEEE, Signal Processing Society Staff. Ed. by IEEE, Institute of Electrical & Electronics Engine. LC 94-76188. 320p. 1994. pap. write for info. (*0-7803-1948-6*, 94TH0658-5); fiche. write for info. (*0-7803-1949-4*) Inst Electrical.

***Proceedings of the 6th International Conference on Processing & Fabrication of Advanced Materials (PFAM VI), Singapore, November 1997, 2 vols., Set.** Ed. by K. A. Khor et al. 2020p. 1999. 300.00 (*1-86125-039-8*, Pub. by Inst Materials) Ashgate Pub Co.

Proceedings of the 6th International Conference on Soil Mechanics & Foundation Engineering, 1965, Montreal, Vol. 1. International Conference on Soil Mechanics & Foundation Engineering Staff. 434p. reprint ed. pap. 134.60 (*0-608-09983-X*, 2026392) Bks Demand.

Proceedings of the 6th International Conference on Soil Mechanics & Foundation Engineering, 1965, Montreal, Vol. 2. International Conference on Soil Mechanics & Foundation Engineering Staff. 602p. reprint ed. pap. 186.70 (*0-608-09984-8*) Bks Demand.

Proceedings of the 6th International Conference on Soil Mechanics & Foundation Engineering, 1965, Montreal, Vol. 3. International Conference on Soil Mechanics & Foundation Engineering Staff. reprint ed. pap. 154.80 (*0-608-09985-6*) Bks Demand.

***Proceedings of the 6th International Conference on Distributed Multimedia Systems, DMS'99: Systems, DMS'99.** Ed. by Knowledge Systems Institute Staff. (Illus.). viii, 272p. 1999. pap. 65.00 (*1-891706-02-0*) Knowldge Systs.

Proceedings of the Sixth International Colloquium on Differential Equations. Ed. by D. Bainov. 424p. 1996. 187.50 (*90-6764-203-7*, Pub. by VSP) Coronet Bks.

Proceedings of the Sixth International Conference on Computer Communications & Networks, September 22-25, 1997, Las Vegas, Nevada. International Conference on Computer Communications and Networks et al. LC 97-218420. xviii, 551 p. 1997. write for info. (*0-8186-8188-8*) IEEE Comp Soc.

***Proceedings of the Sixth International Conference on Facility Operation - Safeguards Inter-care: Jackson Hole, Wyoming, September 20-24, 1999.** 1999. cd-rom 75.00 (*0-89448-642-X*, 700265) Am Nuclear Soc.

Proceedings of the Sixth International Conference on Intelligent Systems for Molecular Biology. Ed. by Janice Glasgow et al. (Illus.). 234p. 1998. pap. text 45.00 (*1-57735-053-7*) AAAI Pr.

Proceedings of the Sixth International Conference on Software Engineering & Knowledge Engineering. Ed. by Knowledge Systems Institute Staff. 534p. 1994. pap. 65.00 (*0-9641699-0-8*) Knowldge Systs.

Proceedings of the Sixth International Conference on Soil Mechanics & Foundation Engineering, 1965: Montreal, 3 vols., 1. International Conference on Soil Mechanics & Found. LC TA0710.A115. 434p. reprint ed. pap. 134.60 (*0-608-16719-3*, 202639200001) Bks Demand.

Proceedings of the Sixth International Conference on Soil Mechanics & Foundation Engineering, 1965: Montreal, 3 vols., 2. International Conference on Soil Mechanics & Found. LC TA0710.A115. 602p. reprint ed. pap. 186.70 (*0-608-16720-7*, 202639200002) Bks Demand.

Proceedings of the Sixth International Conference on Soil Mechanics & Foundation Engineering, 1965: Montreal, 3 vols., 3. International Conference on Soil Mechanics & Found. LC TA0710.A115. 619p. reprint ed. pap. 191.90 (*0-608-16721-5*, 202639200003) Bks Demand.

Proceedings of the Sixth International Conference on the Study of Shamanism & Alternate Modes of Healing, 1989, Santa Sabina Center, San Rafel, California, September 2-4, 1989. Ed. by Ruth-Inge Heinze. LC 90-4220. (Illus.). 402p. (C). 1990. pap. 21.75 (*0-945875-04-5*) Independent Scholars Asia Inc.

Proceedings of the 6th International Kant Congress, Vol. I. Ed. by Gerhard Funke & Thomas M. Seebohm. (Current Continental Research Ser.: No. 601). 354p. (C). 1991. lib. bdg. 71.00 (*0-8191-8153-6*) U Pr of Amer.

Proceedings of the Sixth International Kant Congress, Vol. II, Pt. 1: Group Sessions Sections A & B. Ed. by Gerhard Funke & Thomas M. Seebohm. LC 88-37036. (Current Continental Research Ser.: No. 602). 444p. (Orig.). (C). 1989. pap. text 46.00 (*0-8191-7446-7*); lib. bdg. 74.00 (*0-8191-7445-9*) U Pr of Amer.

Proceedings of the Sixth International Kant Congress, Vol. II, Pt. 2: Two Group Sessions Sections C Through J. Ed. by Gerhard Funke & Thomas M. Seebohm. LC 88-37036. (Current Continental Research Ser.: No. 603). 630p. (Orig.). (C). 1989. pap. text 53.00 (*0-8191-7402-5*); lib. bdg. 87.00 (*0-8191-7401-7*) U Pr of Amer.

Proceedings of the 6th International Symposium on Artificial Heart & Assist Devices, July 30-31, 1996 Tokyo, Japan No. 6. Contrib. by E. Asan. LC 97-41992. (Illus.). xx, 524p. 1998. 260.00 (*4-431-70209-1*) Spr-Verlag.

Proceedings of the Sixth International Symposium on Liquid Crystals & Ordered Fluids: A Special Issue of the Journal Molecular Crystals & Liquid Crystals. A. C. Griffin & R. S. Porter. x, 660p. 1988. pap. text 1082.00 (*2-88124-267-7*) Gordon & Breach.

Proceedings of the Sixth International Symposium on Magnetic Bearings. Ed. by Paul E. Allaire & David L. Trumper. LC 98-86736. 760p. 1998. 189.95 (*1-56676-710-5*) Technomic.

Proceedings of the Sixth International Workshop on Computer-aided Software Engineering, Case '93, Singapore, July 19-23 International Workshop on Computer-Aided Scheduling of Public Transport Staff et al. LC 93-217163. xix, 419 p. 1993. pap. write for info. incl. fiche (*0-8186-3482-0*) IEEE Comp Soc.

Proceedings of the Sixth Japan-U. S. Conference on Composite Materials. Ed. by K. L. Reifsnider & M. W. Hyer. LC 92-85213. 875p. 1993. text 219.95 (*1-56676-021-6*) Technomic.

Proceedings of the 6th Lunar Science Conference. R. B. Merrill. 1975. 1655.00 (*0-08-020566-6*, Pub. by Pergamon Repr) Franklin.

Proceedings of the 6th Plains Archeological Conference, 1948. Jesse D. Jennings. (Utah Anthropological Papers: No. 11). reprint ed. 32.00 (*0-404-60611-3*) AMS Pr.

Proceedings of the Sixth Plains Archeological Conference. fac. ed. Ed. by Jesse Jennings. (University of Utah, Department of Anthropology, Anthropological Papers: No. 11). (Illus.). 175p. (C). 1950. reprint ed. pap. text 18.75 (*1-55567-864-5*) Coyote Press.

Proceedings of the 6th Quadrennial Symposium Held in Tbilisi, U. S. S. R., September 6-12, 1982, Vol. I. Ed. by T. V. Janelidze & A. G. Tvalchrelidze. (International Association on the Genesis of Ore Deposits (IAGOD) Symposia Ser.). (Illus.). viii, 544p. 1984. text 73.00 (*3-510-65095-6*, Pub. by E Schweizerbartsche) Balogh.

Proceedings of the Sixth Southeastern Safety & Health Conference & Exhibition, 1992. Ed. by Leigh F. McElvaney. 227p. 1993. 40.00 (*0-9624647-7-5*) GA Tech Rsch Inst.

Proceedings of the 6th Symposium on the Geology of the Bahamas. Ed. by Brian White. 222p. (Orig.). (C). 1993. pap. text 20.00 (*0-935909-43-5*) Bahamian.

Proceedings of the Sixth Symposium on the Natural History of the Bahamas. Ed. by N. Elliott et al. (Illus.). 165p. (C). 1996. pap. text 12.00 (*0-935909-60-5*) Bahamian.

Proceedings of the 6th Tihany Symposium of Radiation Chemistry. Peter Hedvig. 890p. (C). 1987. 545.00 (*0-569-09066-0*, Pub. by Collets) St Mut.

Proceedings of the 6th Tihany Symposium on Radiation Chemistry: Balatonszeplak, Hungary, 21-26, Sept. 1986. Ed. by Peter Hedvig et al. 889p. (C). 1987. 234.00 (*963-05-4643-4*, Pub. by Akade Kiado) St Mut.

Proceedings of the Sixth Tihany Symposium on Radiation Chemistry, Held in Balatonszeplak, Hungary, 1986, 2 vols., Set. R. Schiller et al. 889p. 1987. 234.00 (*0-7855-2768-0*, Pub. by Akade Kiado) St Mut.

Proceedings of the Sixth Topical Meeting on Emergency Preparedness & Response: San Francisco, California, April 22-25, 1997. 764p. 1997. pap. 80.00 (*0-89448-623-3*, 700256) Am Nuclear Soc.

Proceedings of the Sixth (1996) International Offshore & Polar Engineering Conference, 4 vols. Ed. by Jin S. Chung. Incl. Vol. 1. LC 95-82077. (Illus.). 625p. 1996. pap. 110.00 (*1-880653-23-0*); Vol. 2. LC 95-82077. (Illus.). 625p. 1996. pap. 110.00 (*1-880653-24-9*); Vol. 3. LC 95-82077. (Illus.). 625p. 1996. pap. 110.00 (*1-880653-25-7*); Vol. 4. LC 95-82077. (Illus.). 625p. 1996. pap. 110.00 (*1-880653-26-5*); LC 95-82077. 2326p. 1996. Set pap. 360.00 (*1-880653-22-2*) ISOPE.

Proceedings of the 60th Annual Meeting of the American Society of Information Science (ASIS) November 1-6, 1997. Ed. by Candy Schwarte & Mark Rorvig. 426p. 1997. pap. 49.50 (*1-57387-048-X*) Info Today Inc.

***Proceedings of the 62nd Annual Meeting of the American Society for Information Science.** 750p. 1999. pap. 49.50 (*1-57387-091-9*) Info Today Inc.

***Proceedings of the Solar 99 Conference: Including Proceedings of ASES Annual Conference - Proceedings of the 24th National Passive Solar Conference.** Ed. by R. Campbell-Howe & B. Wilkins-Crowder. (Proceedings of the American Solar Energy Society Conference Ser.). (Illus.). 766p. 1999. pap. 150.00 (*0-89553-171-2*) Am Solar Energy.

Proceedings of the Southeastern Safety & Health Conference & Exhibition, 1993. Ed. by Leigh F. McElvaney. 318p. 1993. 40.00 (*0-9624647-8-3*) GA Tech Rsch Inst.

Proceedings of the Soviet-British Puppetry Conference: Glasgow, November 1989, Vol. 1, Part 1. Ed. by Malcolm Knight. (Contemporary Theatre Review Ser.). 96p. 1992. pap. text 15.00 (*3-7186-5269-2*, Harwood Acad Pubs) Gordon & Breach.

Proceedings of the Special Offshore Symposium China: SOSC 1994 (PACOMS '94) Ed. by Yu-cheng Li & Jin S. Chung. 797p. 1994. 100.00 (*1-880653-15-X*) ISOPE.

Proceedings of the Specialist Symposium on Fluid Dynamics, Fourth Meeting, Munich, September, 1977. European Geophysical Society Staff. Ed. by P. A. Davies & P. H. Roberts. 156p. 1978. pap. text 129.00 (*0-677-40115-9*) Gordon & Breach.

Proceedings of the Spring Meeting: April, 1997, New York City. 1997. write for info. (*0-913447-69-2*) Indus Relations Res.

Proceedings of the St. Petersburg Mathematical Society, Vol. I. Ed. by O. A. Ladyzhenskaya & A. M. Vershik. (Translations Ser.: Series 2, Vol. 155). 223p. 1993. text 99.00 (*0-8218-7505-1*, TRANS2/155C) Am Math.

Proceedings of the St. Petersburg Mathematical Society Volume IV, Vol. IV. O. A. Ladyzhenskaya. (American Mathematical Society Translations Ser. 2: Vol. 188). 250p. 1998. 115.00 (*0-8218-0613-0*) Am Math.

Proceedings of the State-of-the-Art Program on Compound Semiconductor & the Symposium on Materials & Processing Issues for Large Scale Integrated Electronic & Photonic Arrays, 16th. Ed. by D. N. Buckley et al. LC 92-61520. (Proceedings Ser.: Vol. 92-20). 312p. 1992. 40.00 (*1-56677-019-X*) Electrochem Soc.

Proceedings of the State-of-the-Art Program on Compound Semiconductors, 15th. Ed. by A. Katz et al. LC 92-73945. (Proceedings Ser.: Vol. 92-19). 212p. 1992. 38.00 (*1-56677-021-1*) Electrochem Soc.

Proceedings of the State-of-the-Art Program on Compound Semiconductors, 18th. Ed. by S. N. G. Chu et al. LC 93-70071. (Proceedings Ser.: Vol. 93-27). 452p. 1993. 41.00 (*1-56677-069-6*) Electrochem Soc.

Proceedings of the Steamship College: C. A. Stephens Sesquicentennial Lectures. Ed. by Larry S. Glatz. 88p. (Orig.). 1996. pap. 25.00 (*1-888853-01-8*, CAS-001) Frnds C A Stephens.

Proceedings of the Summer 1986 Intensive Workshop in Chinese & Russian. Ed. by Albert Leong. 1987. 15.00 (*0-87114-177-9*) U Oreg Russian Dept.

Proceedings of the Symposia on Chlor-Alkali & Chlorate Production & New Mathematical & Computational Methods in Electrochemical Engineering. Ed. by T. C. Jeffery et al. LC 93-70074. (Proceedings Ser.: Vol. 93-14). 448p. 1993. 40.00 (*1-56677-025-4*) Electrochem Soc.

Proceedings of the Symposia on Interconnects, Contact Metallization, & Multilevel Metallization & Reliability for Semiconductor Devices, Interconnects, & Thin Insulator Materials. Ed. by T. O. Herndon et al. LC 93-70069. (Proceedings Ser.: Vol. 93-25). 494p. 1993. 55.00 (*1-56677-067-X*) Electrochem Soc.

Proceedings of the Symposium of the International Society for Corneal Research. Ed. by J. Francois et al. (Documenta Ophthalmologica Proceedings Ser.: No. 20). 1979. text 141.50 (*90-6193-157-6*) Kluwer Academic.

Proceedings of the Symposium on Advanced Manufacturing, 1987. Symposium on Advanced Manufacturing Staff. Ed. by R. William De Vore & R. G. Edwards. (Illus.). 142p. (Orig.). 1987. pap. 10.00 (*0-89779-069-3*, UKY BU144) OES Pubns.

Proceedings of the Symposium on Atomic Collisions Held 1994, Oak Ridge, TN: A Symposium in Honor of Christopher Bottcher 1945-1993. Ed. by D. R. Schultz et al. LC 95-78689. (AIP Conference Proceedings Ser.: No. CP 347). (Illus.). 298p. 1995. 120.00 (*1-56396-322-1*) Am Inst Physics.

Proceedings of the Symposium on Batteries & Fuel Cells for Stationary & Electric Vehicle Applications. Ed. by A. R. Landgrebe & Z. R. Takehara. LC 93-70052. (Proceedings Ser.: Vol. 93-8). 342p. 1993. 43.00 (*1-56677-055-6*) Electrochem Soc.

Proceedings of the Symposium on Chemical Aspects of High-Tc Superconductors. D. Carlson. vii, 412p. 1990. text 1229.00 (*2-88124-450-5*) Gordon & Breach.

Proceedings of the Symposium on Chemical Sensors II. Ed. by M. Butler et al. LC 93-70059. (Proceedings Ser.: Vol. 93-7). 864p. 1993. 77.00 (*1-56677-030-0*) Electrochem Soc.

Proceedings of the Symposium on Compatability of Biomedical Implants. Ed. by P. K. Kovacs & N. S. Istephanous. LC 94-70847. (Proceedings Ser.: Vol. 94-15). 390p. 1994. 50.00 (*1-56677-047-5*) Electrochem Soc.

Proceedings of the Symposium on Contamination Control & Defect Reduction in Semiconductor Manufacturing I. Ed. by D. N. Schmidt. LC 92-73946. (Proceedings Ser.: Vol. 92-21). 512p. 1992. 55.00 (*1-56677-022-X*) Electrochem Soc.

Proceedings of the Symposium on Contamination Control & Defect Reduction in Semiconductor Manufacturing II. Ed. by R. Novak et al. LC 93-70066. (Proceedings Ser.: Vol. 94-03). 346p. 1994. 43.00 (*1-56677-065-3*) Electrochem Soc.

Proceedings of the Symposium on Contamination Control & Defect Reduction in Semiconductor Manufacturing III. Ed. by D. N. Schmidt. LC 94-70841. (Proceedings Ser.: Vol. 94-09). 440p. 1994. 56.00 (*1-56677-041-6*) Electrochem Soc.

Proceedings of the Symposium on Corrosion, Electrochemistry, & Catalysis of Metastable Metals & Intermetallics. Ed. by C. R. Clayton & K. Hashimoto. LC 93-70061. (Proceedings Ser.: Vol. 93-30). 420p. 1994. 43.00 (*1-56677-057-2*) Electrochem Soc.

Proceedings of the Symposium on Corrosion Protection by Coatings & Surface Modification. Ed. by M. W. Kendig et al. LC 93-70062. (Proceedings Ser.: Vol. 93-28). 252p. 1994. 36.00 (*1-56677-058-0*) Electrochem Soc.

Proceedings of the Symposium on Electrochemical Deposited Thin Films. Ed. by M. Paunovic et al. LC 93-70064. (Proceedings Ser.: Vol. 93-26). 426p. 1993. 60.00 (*1-56677-061-0*) Electrochem Soc.

Proceedings of the Symposium on Electrochromic Materials II. Ed. by K. C. Ho & D. A. MacArthur. LC 93-72868. (Proceedings Ser.: Vol. 94-02). 380p. 1994. 42.00 (*1-56677-039-4*) Electrochem Soc.

Proceedings of the Symposium on Electroresponsive Molecular & Polymeric Systems, Set, Pts. 1 & 2. T. A. Skotheim. 568p. 1990. pap. text 1696.00 (*2-88124-451-3*) Gordon & Breach.

Proceedings of the Symposium on Environmental Aspects of Electrochemistry & Photoelectrochemistry. Ed. by M. Tomkiewicz et al. LC 93-70072. (Proceedings Ser.: Vol. 93-18). 252p. 1993. 40.00 (*1-56677-070-X*) Electrochem Soc.

Proceedings of the Symposium on Giant Sequoias: Their Place in the Ecosystem & Society. Ed. by Philip S. Aune. (Illus.). 170p. (C). 1997. reprint ed. pap. text 40.00 (*0-7881-4165-1*) DIANE Pub.

Proceedings of the Symposium on High Strength Sheet Steels for the Automotive Industry: Held in Conjunction with the 36th Mechanical Working &

P

An Asterisk (*) at the beginning of an entry indicates that the title is appearing for the first time.

Steel Processing Conference, Baltimore, MD, October 16-19, 1994. Symposium on High Strength Sheet Steels for the Au. Ed. by R. Pradhan. LC 94-77829. 284p. 1994. reprint ed. pap. 88.10 (0-608-00482-0, 206130100007) Bks Demand.

Proceedings of the Symposium on Highly Selective Dry Etching & Damage Control. Ed. by G. S. Mathad & Yasuhiro Horiike. LC 93-70068. (Proceedings Ser.: Vol. 93-21). 440p. 1993. 60.00 (1-56677-066-1) Electrochem Soc.

Proceedings of the Symposium on International & Transboundary Water Resources Issues. Symposium on International & Transboundary Water R. Ed. by John E. FitzGibbon. LC 90-80550. (American Water Resources Association Technical Publication Ser.: No. TPS-90-1). (Illus.). 664p. reprint ed. pap. 200.00 (0-7837-1094-1, 204162600021) Bks Demand.

Proceedings of the Symposium on Liquid Crystals & Ordered Fluids: A Special Issue of the Journal Molecular Crystals & Liquid Crystals. Ed. by A. C. Griffin et al. 565p. 1984. 946.00 (0-685-47158-6) Gordon & Breach.

Proceedings of the Symposium on Lithium Batteries. Ed. by N. Doddapaneni & A. R. Landgrebe. LC 93-72862. (Proceedings Ser.: Vol. 94-04). 312p. 1994. 43.00 (1-56677-033-5) Electrochem Soc.

Proceedings of the Symposium on Lithium Batteries. Ed. by S. Surapudi & V. R. Koch. LC 93-84541. (Proceedings Ser.: Vol. 93-24). 160p. 1993. 42.00 (1-56677-050-5) Electrochem Soc.

Proceedings of the Symposium on Logic & Functional Devices for Photonics & the State-of-the-Art Program on Compound Semiconductors, 17th. Ed. by D. N. Buckley et al. LC 92-74537. (Proceedings Ser.: Vol. 93-10). 312p. 1993. 40.00 (1-56677-054-8) Electrochem Soc.

Proceedings of the Symposium on Low Temperature Electronics & High Temperature Superconductivity. Ed. by S. I. Raider et al. LC 93-70073. (Proceedings Ser.: Vol. 93-22). 600p. 1993. 58.00 (1-56677-071-8) Electrochem Soc.

Proceedings of the Symposium on Metal Deposition & Dissolution. Ed. by D. T. Chin et al. LC 92-74474. (Proceedings Ser.: Vol. 92-23). 342p. 1992. 43.00 (1-56677-024-6) Electrochem Soc.

Proceedings of the Symposium on Microscopic Models of Electrode-Electrolyte Interfaces. Ed. by J. W. Halley & L. Blum. LC 92-74539. (Proceedings Ser.: Vol. 93-5). 352p. 1993. 47.00 (1-56677-052-1) Electrochem Soc.

Proceedings of the Symposium on Microstructures & Microfabricated Systems. Ed. by P. J. Hesketh et al. LC 94-70846. (Proceedings Ser.: Vol. 94-14). 252p. 1994. 44.00 (1-56677-046-7) Electrochem Soc.

Proceedings of the Symposium on Mining, Hydrology, Sedimentology & Reclamation, 1987. Symposium on Mining, Hydrology, Sedimentology & Re. Ed. by R. William De Vore & Donald H. Graves. LC 83-60966. (Illus.). 438p. (Orig.). 1987. pap. 10.00 (0-89779-070-7, UKY BU145) OES Pubns.

Proceedings of the Symposium on "Molecules in Motion", University of Kentucky, Lexington, May 20-21, 1984: Transactions of the American Crystallographic Association, 1984, Vol. 20. Ed. by John J. Stezowski. (Transactions of the American Crystallographic Association Ser.: Vol. 20, 1984). 166p. 1985. pap. 25.00 (0-937140-28-7) Polycrystal Bk Serv.

Proceedings of the Symposium on "Neutron Diffraction," University of Texas, Austin, March 16, 1987. Ed. by Bryan M. Craven. (Transactions of the American Crystallographic Association Ser.: Vol. 23). 104p. 1988. pap. 25.00 (0-937140-31-7) Polycrystal Bk Serv.

Proceedings of the Symposium on New Developments in the Chemistry & Properties of Low-Dimensional & Conducting Solids: A Special Issue of the Journal Molecular Crystals & Liquid Crystals Incorporating Nonlinear Optics. Ed. by J. M. Williams & H. Kuroda. viii, 368p. 1990. pap. text 1137.00 (2-88124-432-7) Gordon & Breach.

Proceedings of the Symposium on New Sealed Rechargeable Batteries & Supercapacitors. Ed. by B. M. Barnett et al. LC 93-70060. (Proceedings Ser.: Vol. 93-23). 532p. 1993. 54.00 (1-56677-056-4) Electrochem Soc.

Proceedings of the Symposium on Nonpoint Pollution: Policy, Economy, Management, & Appropriate Technology, 1988. Symposium on Nonpoint Pollution: Policy, Economy,. Ed. by Vladimir Novotny. LC 88-72279. (American Water Resources Association Technical Publication Ser.: No. TPS-88-4). (Illus.). 336p. reprint ed. pap. 104.20 (0-7837-1093-3, 204162500021) Bks Demand.

Proceedings of the Symposium on Order in Polymeric Materials: A Special Issue of the Journal Molecular Crystals & Liquid Crystals, 2 vols., Set. D. Sandman & P. Cukor. xiv, 619p. 1984. 958.00 (0-685-47159-4) Gordon & Breach.

Proceedings of the Symposium on Oxide Films on Metals & Alloys. Ed. by B. R. MacDougall et al. LC 92-74173. (Proceedings Ser.: Vol. 92-22). 624p. 1992. 55.00 (1-56677-023-8) Electrochem Soc.

Proceedings of the Symposium on Partial Evaluation & Semantics-Based Program Manipulation, PEPM '91, Yale University, New Haven, Connecticut, U. S. A., June 17-19, 1991: A Symposium. Symposium on Partial Evaluation and Semantics-Based Program Manipulation Staff et al. LC 92-231893. v, 333p. 1991. write for info. (0-89791-433-3) Assn Compu Machinery.

Proceedings of the Symposium on Photoinduced Charge Transfer. E. Conwell. iv, 362p. 1991. pap. text 1300.00 (2-88124-483-1) Gordon & Breach.

Proceedings of the Symposium on Quality Management in Industrial Electrochemistry. Ed. by D. Hall et al. LC 93-70075. (Proceedings Ser.: Vol. 93-19). 252p. 1993. 36.00 (1-56677-026-2) Electrochem Soc.

Proceedings of the Symposium on Sandalwood in the Pacific. Ed. by Lawrence Hamilton & C. Eugene Conrad. (Illus.). 84p. (Orig.). (C). 1994. pap. text 35.00 (0-7881-1076-4) DIANE Pub.

Proceedings of the Symposium on "Structure Determination With Synchrotron Radiation" at Stanford University, Stanford, CA August 19-20, 1985. Ed. by Benno P. Schoenborn. (Transactions of the American Crystallographic Association Ser.: Vol. 21, 1985). v, 55p. (Orig.). 1986. pap. 25.00 (0-937140-29-5) Polycrystal Bk Serv.

Proceedings of the Symposium on Terrestrial & Aquatic Ecological Studies of the Northwest. Ed. by Rollins D. Andrews, III et al. 397p. (Orig.). 1977. pap. 10.00 (0-910055-04-1) East Wash Univ.

Proceedings of the Symposium on the Degradation of Electronic Devices Due to Device Operation As Well As Crystalline & Process-Induced Defects. Ed. by H. J. Queisser et al. LC 93-72866. (Proceedings Ser.: Vol. 94-01). 328p. 1994. 37.00 (1-56677-037-8) Electrochem Soc.

Proceedings of the Symposium on the Great Lakes: Living with North America's Inland Waters. fac. ed. Ed. by David H. Hickcox. LC 88-72278. (American Water Resource Association, Technical Publication Ser.: No. TPS-88-3). (Illus.). 310p. 1988. reprint ed. pap. 96.10 (0-608-00997-0, 206185500012) Bks Demand.

Proceedings of the Symposium on the Small-Angle Scattering: University of Missouri, Columbia, March, 1983. Ed. by Paul W. Schmidt. (Transactions of the American Crystallographic Association Ser.: Vol. 19). 92p. 1984. pap. 25.00 (0-937140-27-9) Polycrystal Bk Serv.

Proceedings of the Symposium on Thin Film Transistor Technologies, 1st. Ed. by Y. Kuo. LC 92-74538. (Proceedings Ser.: Vol. 92-24). 328p. 1993. 36.00 (1-56677-053-X) Electrochem Soc.

Proceedings of the Symposium on Water Purification by Photocatalytic, Photoelectrochemical, & Electrochemical Processes. Ed. by T. L. Rose et al. LC 94-70851. (Proceedings Ser.: Vol. 94-19). 384p. 1994. 48.00 (1-56677-076-9) Electrochem Soc.

Proceedings of the Symposium on Water-Use Data for Water Resources Management. Symposium on Water-Use Data for Water Resources Ma. Ed. by Marvin Waterstone & R. John Burt. LC 88-71321. (American Water Resources Association Technical Publication Ser.: No. TPS-88-2). 874p. reprint ed. pap. 200.00 (0-7837-6282-8, 204599700010) Bks Demand.

Proceedings of the Symposium the Oskar Klein Centenary. Ulf Lindstrom. 225p. 1995. text 58.00 (981-02-2332-3) World Scientific Pub.

Proceedings of the Tenth Annual ACM-SIAM Symposium on Discrete Algorithms. LC 93-46264. (Proceedings Ser.: Vol. 97). viii, 992p. 1999. pap. 93.00 (0-89871-434-6) Soc Indus-Appl Math.

Proceedings of the 10th Annual Congress on Veterinary Acupuncture. Ed. by David H. Jaggar. 213p. (Orig.). 1984. pap. text 35.00 (0-318-19690-5) Intl Vet Acup.

Proceedings of the 10th Annual Control Engineering Conference: Held As Part of the Control Engineering Conference & Exposition, O'Hare Exposition Center, Rosemont, IL May 21-23, 1991. Ed. by Henry Morris. (Illus.). 500p. (Orig.). (C). 1991. pap. write for info. (0-914331-60-4, Control Engrng) Cahners Busn Des Plaines.

Proceedings of the 10th Colloquium on the Law of Outer Space, September 24-29, 1967, Belgrade Yugoslavia. International Institute of Space Law of the International Astronautical Federation Staff. 279p. 1968. pap. 27.50 (0-8377-0405-7, Rothman) W S Hein.

Proceedings of the 10th Ethylene Producers Conference. (AIChE Technical Manual: Vol. 7). 1998. pap. 175.00 (0-8169-0777-3, T-107) Am Inst Chem Eng.

***Proceedings of the 10th European Symposium on the Reliability of Electron Devices, Failure Physics & Analysis (ESREF'99)** Ed. by N. Labat & A. Touboul. 450p. 1999. pap. 91.00 (0-08-043419-3); pap. text 152.00 (0-08-043421-5) Elsevier.

Proceedings of the 10th International Diatom Symposium, Joensuu, Finland, August 28-September 2, 1998. Ed. by Heikki Simola. (Illus.). v, 592p. 1991. 299.20 (3-87429-307-6, 041703, Pub. by Koeltz Sci Bks) Lubrecht & Cramer.

Proceedings of the 10th International Conference on Mechanics in Medicine & Biology, Honolulu, Hawaii, March 2-5, 1998. Ed. by J. A. Ashton-Miller. 1998. write for info. (0-9652469-5-7) Pac Ctr Thermal.

Proceedings of the 10th International Conference on Software Engineering & Knowledge Engineering, SEKE, '98. Ed. by Knowledge Systems Institute Staff. (Illus.). 464p. 1998. pap. 65.00 (0-9641699-9-1) Knowldge Systs.

Proceedings of the Tenth International Conference on Composite Materials: Proceedings of the Tenth International Conference on Composite Materials, Whistler, B.C., Canada, August 14-18, 1995, 6 vols. Ed. by Anoush Poursartip & Ken Street. 4906p. 1995. pap. 299.95 (1-85573-221-1, 732211) Technomic.

Proceedings of the Tenth International Conference on Composite Materials Vol. 1: Fatigue & Fracture. International Conference on Composite Materials St. (ICCM-10 Ser.). 800p. 1995. 170.00 (1-85573-222-X, Pub. by Woodhead Pubng) Am Educ Systs.

Proceedings of the Tenth International Conference on Composite Materials Vol. 2: Metal Matrix Composites. International Conference on Composite Materials St. (ICCM-10 Ser.). 816p. 1995. 170.00 (1-85573-223-8, Pub. by Woodhead Pubng) Am Educ Systs.

Proceedings of the Tenth International Conference on Composite Materials Vol. 3: Processing & Manufacturing. International Conference on Composite Materials St. (ICCM-10 Ser.). 768p. 1995. 170.00 (1-85573-224-6, Pub. by Woodhead Pubng) Am Educ Systs.

Proceedings of the Tenth International Conference on Composite Materials Vol. 4: Characterization & Ceramic Matrix Composites. International Conference on Composite Materials St. (ICCM-10 Ser.). 816p. 1995. 170.00 (1-85573-225-4, Pub. by Woodhead Pubng) Am Educ Systs.

Proceedings of the Tenth International Conference on Composite Materials Vol. 5: Structures. International Conference on Composite Materials St. (ICCM-10 Ser.). 768p. 1995. 170.00 (1-85573-226-2, Pub. by Woodhead Pubng) Am Educ Systs.

Proceedings of the Tenth International Conference on Composite Materials Vol. 6: Microstructures, Degradation & Design. International Conference on Composite Materials St. (ICCM-10 Ser.). 736p. 1995. 170.00 (1-85573-227-0, Pub. by Woodhead Pubng) Am Educ Systs.

Proceedings of the Tenth International Conference on the Study of Shamanism & Alternate Modes of Healing, 1993, Santa Sabina Center, San Rafael, California, September 4-6, 1998. Ed. by Ruth-Inge Heinze. LC 94-2722. (Illus.). 381p. (C). 1994. pap. 21.75 (0-945875-10-X) Independent Scholars Asia Inc.

Proceedings of the Tenth International Conference on Vehicle Structural Mechanics & CAE. LC 97-66289. 1997. pap. 80.00 (0-7680-0010-6, P-308) Soc Auto Engineers.

Proceedings of the Tenth International Congress on Hyperbaric Medicine. Ed. by D. J. Bakker. 201p. (C). 1992. 35.50 (0-941332-24-1, D450) Best Pub Co.

***Proceedings of the 10th International Symposium on Insect-Plant Relations.** Stephen J. Simpson et al. LC 99-27067. (Series Entomologica). 1999. write for info. (0-7923-5773-6) Kluwer Academic.

Proceedings of the Tenth International Symposium on Human Factors in Telecommunications, 1983, Helsinki, Finland. 270p. 1983. pap. text 75.00 (951-46-6741-7, 125410) Info Gatekeepers.

Proceedings of the Tenth Meeting of the French Colonial Historical Society, April 12-14, 1984. Ed. by Philip P. Boucher. LC 76-644752. (Illus.). 290p. (Orig.). 1986. pap. 59.00 (0-8191-4916-0); pap. text 27.00 (0-8191-4917-9) U Pr of Amer.

***Proceedings of the Tenth Midwest Artificail Intelligense & Cognitive Science Conference.** Uta Priss. (Technical Reports). (Illus.). 115p. 1999. pap. 35.00 (1-57735-082-0) AAAI Pr.

Proceedings of the Tenth MSIS National Users Group Conference - Issues in Patient Tracking. Ed. by Linda J. Kline & Carl Cappello. (Orig.). 1987. pap. 20.00 (0-936934-06-9) N S Kline Inst.

Proceedings of the 10th Oil Shale Symposium. Ed. by John Rubens & J. H. Gary. LC 75-17946. (Illus.). 256p. 1977. pap. 3.50 (0-918062-01-2) Colo Sch Mines.

***Proceedings of the Tenth (2000) International Offshore & Polar Engineering Conference, 4 vols., Set.** Ed. by Jin S. Chung et al. (Illus.). 2662p. 2000. pap. 420.00 incl. cd-rom (1-880653-46-X) ISOPE.

***Proceedings of the Tenth (2000) International Offshore & Polar Engineering Conference, Vol. I.** Ed. by Jin S. Chung et al. (Illus.). 775p. 2000. pap. 130.00 (1-880653-47-8) ISOPE.

***Proceedings of the Tenth (2000) International Offshore & Polar Engineering Conference, Vol. II.** Ed. by Jin S. Chung et al. (Illus.). 688p. 2000. pap. 130.00 (1-880653-48-6) ISOPE.

***Proceedings of the Tenth (2000) International Offshore & Polar Engineering Conference, Vol. III.** Ed. by Jin S. Chung et al. (Illus.). 704p. 2000. pap. 130.00 (1-880653-49-4) ISOPE.

***Proceedings of the Tenth (2000) International Offshore & Polar Engineering Conference, Vol. IV.** Ed. by Paul Grundy et al. (Illus.). 495p. 2000. pap. 130.00 (1-880653-50-8) ISOPE.

Proceedings of the 3rd & 4th International Symposium on Arctic & Alpine Mycology. Gary A. Laursen. Ed. by Orlando Petrini. (Bibliotheca Mycologica: Vol. 150). (GER., Illus.). xiv, 270p. 1993. 53.00 (3-443-59051-9, Pub. by Gebruder Borntraeger) Balogh.

Proceedings of the Third Annual ACM-SIAM Symposium on Discrete Mathematics. (Proceedings in Applied Mathematics Ser.: No. 60). xiv, 472p. 1992. pap. 65.50 (0-89871-293-9) Soc Indus-Appl Math.

***Proceedings of the 3rd Annual Symposium of the Institute of Islamic & Arabic Sciences in America, 14-15 Dhul-Qidah, 1415 A. H., April 15-16, 1995 C. E. Islamic Studies in American Universities.** Institute of Islamic & Arabic Sciences in America Staff. LC 99-34949. 1999. write for info. (1-56923-021-8) Inst Islamic.

Proceedings of the Third European Conference on Computer-Supported Cooperative Work - ECSCW '93. Ed. by Giorgio De Michelis. LC 93-26848. 380p. (C). 1993. lib. bdg. 166.50 (0-7923-2447-1) Kluwer Academic.

Proceedings of the Third European Conference on Mathematics in Industry. Ed. by J. Manley et al. (C). 1990. text 226.50 (0-7923-0807-7) Kluwer Academic.

Proceedings of the 3rd European Simulation Congress. Ed. by J. Stephenson et al. 846p. 1989. 90.00 (0-911801-60-X, EURO-89) Soc Computer Sim.

Proceedings of the Third Finnish-Soviet Conference on Probability Theory & Mathematical Statistics. Ed. by H. Niemi et al. (Frontiers in Pure & Applied Probability Ser.: Vol. 1). 306p. 1994. 175.00 (90-6764-156-1) Coronet Bks.

Proceedings of the Third Florida Artificial Intelligence Research Symposium. Ed. by Mark B. Fishman. 330p. (Orig.). (C). 1990. pap. 30.00 (0-9620173-2-9) FL AI Research.

Proceedings of the Third Forum on Research & Technology Advances in Digital Libraries, ADL '96, May 13-15 1996, Washington, D. C. Goddard Space Flight Center Staff. LC 96-76268. xi, 151 p. 1996. write for info. (0-8186-7404-0) IEEE Comp Soc.

Proceedings of the 3rd Glacier Bay Science Symposium, 1993. Ed. by Daniel R. Engstrom & Thetus H. Smith. LC 95-41705. (Illus.). 337p. (Orig.). 1995. pap. write for info. (0-941555-01-1) Natl Pk AK.

Proceedings of the Third IEEE International Symposium on Requirements Engineering, January 6-10, 1997, Annapolis, Maryland, U. S. A. IEEE Computer Society Staff et al. LC 98-191003. xv, 267p. 1997. pap. write for info. (0-8186-7742-2) IEEE Comp Soc.

Proceedings of the Third IEEE International Symposium on Spready Spectrum & Applications, 1994. IEEE, Communications Society Staff et al. LC 93-80347. 500p. 1994. pap. write for info. (0-7803-1750-5, 94TH0604-9); fiche. write for info. (0-7803-1751-3, 94TH0604-9) Inst Electrical.

Proceedings of the 3rd International Conference on Principles of Knowledge Representation & Reasoning. Ed. by Bernhard Nebel et al. LC 92-34433. (Representation & Reasoning Ser.). 615p. (C). 1992. pap. text 49.95 (1-55860-262-3) Morgan Kaufmann.

Proceedings of the Third International Clinical Symposium (CarboMedics) Ed. & Illus. by Silent Partners, Inc. Staff. 156p. (Orig.). 1992. pap. write for info. (1-878353-24-1) Silent Partners.

Proceedings of the Third International Colloquium on Differential Equations. Ed. by D. Bainov & V. Covachev. 236p. 1993. 125.00 (90-6764-153-7) Coronet Bks.

Proceedings of the Third International Colloquium on Numerical Analysis. Ed. by D. Bainov & V. Covachev. 236p. 1995. 135.00 (90-6764-193-6, Pub. by VSP) Coronet Bks.

Proceedings of the Third International Colloquium on Paratuberculosis. Rodrick J. Chiodini & J. Kreeger. (C). 1992. pap. text 145.00 (0-9633043-0-5) Intl Assn Paratuber.

Proceedings of the Third International Conference on Adaptive Structures. Ed. by M. Natori et al. LC 93-60100. 735p. 1993. text 79.95 (1-56676-028-3) Technomic.

Proceedings of the Third International Conference on Boiotian Antiquities. Ed. by John M. Fossey & Hubert Giroux. (McGill University Monographs in Classical Archaeology & History: No. 2). (Illus.). viii, 198p. (C). 1985. 60.00 (90-70265-66-4, Pub. by Gieben) J Benjamins Pubng Co.

Proceedings of the Third International Conference on Civil & Structural Engineering Computing, Set. Civil Comp Editors. 1987. pap. 245.00 (0-948749-03-2, Pub. by Civil-Comp) St Mut.

Proceedings of the Third International Conference on Intelligent Systems for Molecular Biology. Ed. by Christopher Rawlings et al. (Illus.). 512p. (Orig.). 1995. pap. text 50.00 (0-929280-83-0) AAAI Pr.

Proceedings of the Third International Conference on Knowledge Discovery & Data Mining. Ed. by Usama M. Fayyad & Ramasamy Uthurusamy. LC 95-222496. (Illus.). 348p. (Orig.). 1995. pap. text 50.00 (0-929280-82-2) AAAI Pr.

Proceedings of the Third International Conference on Knowledge Discovery & Data Mining. Ed. by David Heckerman et al. 325p. 1997. pap. text 60.00 (1-57735-027-8) AAAI Pr.

Proceedings of the Third International Conference on Pervaporation Processes in the Chemical Industry. 532p. 1990. 120.00 (0-939997-05-3) Bakish Mat.

Proceedings of the Third International Conference on the Study of Shamanism & Alternate Modes of Healing, 1986, Santa Sabina Center, San Rafael, California, August 31-September 1, 1986. Ed. by Ruth-Inge Heinze. (Illus.). 349p. (C). 1987. pap. 21.75 (0-945875-00-2) Independent Scholars Asia Inc.

Proceedings of the Third International Iron & Steel Congress, 16-20 April 1978, Chicago, Illinois - Sponsored by the American Society for Metals & the Iron & Steel Society of AIME. International Iron & Steel Congress, 3rd, 1978, Ch. LC 79-4097. 768p. reprint ed. pap. 200.00 (0-608-16558-1, 202704900053) Bks Demand.

Proceedings of the 3rd International Magnesium Conference. G. W. Lorimer. (Illus.). 760p. 1997. 200.00 (1-86125-013-4, Pub. by Inst Materials) Ashgate Pub Co.

Proceedings of the Third International Offshore & Polar Engineering Conference, 1993, 4 vols., 1. Ed. by Jin S. Chung et al. LC 92-76219. 709p. (Orig.). 1993. pap. 100.00 (1-880653-06-0) ISOPE.

Proceedings of the Third International Offshore & Polar Engineering Conference, 1993, 4 vols., 2. Ed. by Jin S. Chung et al. LC 92-76219. 784p. (Orig.). 1993. pap. 100.00 (1-880653-07-9) ISOPE.

Proceedings of the Third International Offshore & Polar Engineering Conference, 1993, 4 vols., 3. Ed. by Jin S. Chung et al. LC 92-76219. 740p. (Orig.). 1993. pap. 100.00 (1-880653-08-7) ISOPE.

Proceedings of the Third International Offshore & Polar Engineering Conference, 1993, 4 vols., 4. Ed. by Ram S. Puthli et al. LC 92-76219. 732p. (Orig.). 1993. pap. 100.00 (1-880653-09-5) ISOPE.

P

Proceedings of the Third International Offshore & Polar Engineering Conference, 1993, 4 vols., Set. Ed. by Jin S. Chung et al. LC 92-76219. 2965p. (Orig.). 1993. pap. 340.00 (*1-880653-05-2*) ISOPE.

Proceedings of the Third International Symposium on Acoustic Emission from Composite Materials (AECM-3) July 17-21, 1989, Paris, France: July 17-21, 1989, Paris, France. American Society for Nondestructive Testing (ASNT). (Illus.). 441p. (Orig.). (C). 1989. pap. 31.00 (*0-931403-88-X*, 770) Am Soc Nondestructive.

Proceedings of the Third International Symposium on Domain Decomposition Methods for Partial Differential Equations. Ed. by T. F. Chan et al. LC 90-34097. (Proceedings in Applied Mathematics Ser.: No. 43). xx, 491p. 1990. pap. 62.00 (*0-89871-253-X*) Soc Indus-Appl Math.

Proceedings of the Third International Symposium on Magnetic Bearings. Ed. by Paul E. Allaire. LC 92-64061. 620p. 1992. text 89.95 (*0-87762-976-5*) Technomic.

Proceedings of the Third International Symposium on the Chrysomelidae, Beijing, 1992. Ed. by D. G. Furth. (Illus.). 150p. 1994. 60.00 (*90-73348-32-3*, Pub. by Backhuys Pubs) Balogh.

Proceedings of the Third International Symposium on the Edwards Duromedics Bileaflet Valve. Ed. & Illus. by Silent Partners, Inc. Staff. 123p. (Orig.). 1987. pap. write for info. (*1-878353-05-5*) Silent Partners.

Proceedings of the Third International Symposium on the Use of Ozone in Aquatic Systems. 49.00 (*0-685-65155-X*) Pan Am Intl Ozone.

Proceedings of the Third International Symposium on the Use of Ozone in Aquatic Systems. 1992. 49.00 (*0-685-70331-2*) Pan Am Intl Ozone.

Proceedings of the Third International Workshop on Multistrategy Learning. Ed. by Ryszard S. Michalski & Janusz Wnek. 348p. 1996. pap. text 40.00 (*1-57735-010-3*) AAAI Pr.

Proceedings of the Third International Workshop on Phosphorus in Sediments. Ed. by P. C. Boers et al. LC 92-46549. (Developments in Hydrobiology Ser.: Vol. 84). 416p. (C). 1993. text 289.50 (*0-7923-2126-X*) Kluwer Academic.

Proceedings of the Third International Workshop on Transducers for Sonics & Ultrasonics. Ed. by Michele D. McCollum et al. LC 92-62615. 420p. 1992. text 119.95 (*0-87762-993-5*) Technomic.

Proceedings of the 3rd ISSAT International Conference: Reliability & Quality in Design. Ed. by Hoang Pham. (Orig.). (C). 1997. pap. text 60.00 (*0-9639998-2-6*) ISSAT.

***Proceedings of the 3rd (1999) ISOPE Ocean Mining Symposium.** Ed. by Jin S. Chung & Rahul Sharma. (Illus.). 288p. 1999. pap. 100.00 (*1-880653-45-1*) ISOPE.

Proceedings of the 3rd Pacific Islands Conference of Leaders: Regional Cooperation with Emphasis on Private Sector Development: April 9-11, 1990, Big Island of Hawaii, Hawaii. Ed. by Sitiveni Halapua & Barbara Naudain. LC 92-7872. 1992. write for info. (*0-86638-150-3*) EW Ctr HI.

Proceedings of the 3rd Round Table with European Ombudsmen (Florence, 1991) Council of Europe Staff. (Human Rights & Democracy Ser.). 1992. 18.00 (*92-871-2153-2*, Pub. by Council of Europe) Manhattan Pub Co.

Proceedings of the Third Symposium of Societas Celtologica Nordica, Nov. 1991. Ed. by Ailbhe O. Corrain & Jan E. Rekdal. LC 95-109124. (Studia Celtica Upsaliensia: No. 1). 149p. (Orig.). 1994. pap. 40.00 (*91-554-3325-1*) Coronet Bks.

Proceedings of the 3rd Symposium of the International Working Group. Ed. by J. L. Sherwood & C. M. Rush. 1996. write for info. (*0-926195-02-6*) TX AES.

Proceedings of the Third Symposium on Technical Diagnostics, Moscow, October 3-5, 1983. Ed. by Collet's Holdings, Ltd. Staff. 512p. 1984. pap. 410.00 (*0-7855-1184-9*) St Mut.

Proceedings of the 3rd Symposium on the Geology of the Bahamas. Ed. by H. Allen Curran. 250p. 1987. pap. text 18.00 (*0-935909-24-9*) Bahamian.

Proceedings of the 3rd Symposium on the Botany of the Bahamas. Ed. by Robert R. Smith. (Illus.). 83p. (Orig.). (C). 1990. pap. text 12.00 (*0-935909-36-2*) Bahamian.

***Proceedings of the third Topical Meeting on DOE Spent Nuclear Fuel & Fissile Materials Management: Charleston, South Carolina, September 8-11, 1998, 2.** 810p. 1998. pap. 125.00 incl. cd-rom (*0-89448-638-1*, 700261) Am Nuclear Soc.

Proceedings of the 3rd U. S.-Japan Workshop on Seismic Retrofit of Bridges. Shigeki Unjoh. (Illus.). 446p. (C). 1999. reprint ed. pap. text 50.00 (*0-7881-7874-1*) DIANE Pub.

Proceedings of the Third Workshop on Future Trends of Distributed Computing Systems, April 14-16, 1992, Taipei, Taiwan. IEEE Workshop on Future Trends of Didtributed Computing Systems & IEEE Computer Society. LC 91-78036. xiii, 426p. 1992. write for info. (*0-8186-2757-3*) IEEE Comp Soc.

Proceedings of the 3rd Workshop on Neural Networks. Ed. by Mary L. Padgett. 662p. 1993. pap. 90.00 (*1-56555-007-2*, WNN92-1) Soc Computer Sim.

Proceedings of the 3rd World Conference on Detergents: Global Perspectives. Ed. by Arno Cahn. LC 94-8065. (Illus.). vii, 279 p. 1994. lib. bdg. 120.00 (*0-935315-52-7*, PCWC93) Am Oil Chemists.

Proceedings of the Third World Congress on Pain, Edinburgh, Scotland, 1981. World Congress on Pain Staff. Ed. by John J. Bonica et al. LC 82-16673. (Advances in Pain Research & Therapy Ser.: Vol. 5). 990p. 1983. reprint ed. pap. 200.00 (*0-608-04686-8*, 206540700004) Bks Demand.

Proceedings of the Thirteenth & Fourteenth Meetings of the French Colonial Historical Society. Ed. by Philip P. Boucher. (Illus.). 248p. (C). 1990. lib. bdg. 49.00 (*0-8191-7637-0*) U Pr of Amer.

Proceedings of the 13th Annual Conference. APLIC International Staff. Ed. by Adele B. Burns. LC 76-643241. 157p. 1980. pap. 13.00 (*0-933438-05-2*) APLIC Intl.

Proceedings of the Thirteenth Annual Conference of the Cognitive Science Society. Ed. by Kristian J. Hammond & Dedre Gentner. 984p. 1991. pap. 125.00 (*0-8058-1138-9*) L Erlbaum Assocs.

Proceedings of the Thirteenth Annual International Conference on Soil Mechanics & Foundations Engineering, New Dehli, January 1994. Publications Committee XIII ICSMFE Ser. (Illus.). 3500p. (C). 1994. text 970.00 (*90-5410-370-1*, Pub. by A A Balkema) Ashgate Pub Co.

Proceedings of the 13th Colloquium on the Law of Outer Space, October 4-10, 1970, Constance, Germany. International Institute of Space Law of the International Astronautical Federation Staff. iii, 381p. 1971. pap. 27.50 (*0-8377-0408-1*, Rothman) W S Hein.

Proceedings of the 13th International Vacuum Web Coating Conference, Vol. 13. Ed. by Robert Bakish. (Illus.). 250p. 2000. pap. 80.00 (*0-939997-23-1*) Bakish Mat.

Proceedings of the 13th International Congress of Archives: Beijing 2-7 September, 1996. LC 98-182855. (Archivum Ser.: Vol. XLIII). 300p. 1997. write for info. (*3-598-21244-5*) K G Saur Verlag.

Proceedings of the Thirteenth International Conference of Offshore Mechanics & Arctic Engineering (OMAE 1994), Vol. 2: Safety & Reliability. LC 82-70515. (Offshore Mechanics & Arctic Engineering Ser.). 404p. 1994. pap. 55.00 (*0-7918-1265-0*, H00897) ASME Pr.

Proceedings of the Thirteenth International Conference on Coal & Slurry Technology. LC 86-6147. (Illus.). 797p. 1988. 175.00 (*0-932066-13-5*) Coal Slurry Tech.

Proceedings of the Thirteenth International Conference on Offshore Mechanics & Arctic Engineering (OMAE 1994), Vol. 1: Offshore Technology. LC 82-70515. (Offshore Mechanics & Arctic Engineering Ser.). 492p. 1994. pap. 75.00 (*0-7918-1264-2*) ASME Pr.

Proceedings of the Thirteenth International Conference on Offshore Mechanics & Arctic Engineering (OMAE 1994), Vol. 3: Materials Engineering. LC 82-70515. (Offshore Mechanics & Arctic Engineering Ser.). 440p. 1994. pap. 60.00 (*0-7918-1266-9*, H00898) ASME Pr.

Proceedings of the Thirteenth International Conference on Offshore Mechanics & Arctic Engineering (OMAE 1994), Vol. 4: Artice - Polar Technology. LC 82-70515. (Offshore Mechanics & Arctic Engineering Ser.). 136p. 1994. pap. 45.00 (*0-7918-1267-7*, H00899) ASME Pr.

Proceedings of the Thirteenth International Conference on Offshore Mechanics & Arctic Engineering (OMAE 1994), Vol. 5: Pipeline Technology. LC 82-70515. (Offshore Mechanics & Arctic Engineering Ser.). 376p. 1994. pap. 55.00 (*0-7918-1268-5*, H00900) ASME Pr.

Proceedings of the Thirteenth International Conference on Soil Mechanics & Foundation Engineering, New Dehli. (Illus.). 315p. 1996. 181.00 (*90-5410-376-0*, Pub. by A A Balkema) Ashgate Pub Co.

Proceedings of the 13th Oil Shale Symposium. Ed. by James H. Gary. LC 80-18711. (Oil Shale Ser.). (Illus.). 391p. (Orig.). 1980. pap. 12.00 (*0-918062-39-X*) Colo Sch Mines.

Proceedings of the Thirteenth West Coast Conference on Formal Linguistics Vol. 13 (WCCFL 13) Proceedings of the West Coast Conference on Formal Linguistics. Ed. by Raul Aranovich et al. 1995. pap. 26.95 (*1-881526-76-3*) CSLI.

Identification I see Hollander Interchange Manual: ID/Body

Proceedings of the 13th World Congress: Adaptive Control see IFAC '96: 13th World Congress Proceedings

Proceedings of the 13th World Congress: Aerospace, Transportation Systems see IFAC '96: 13th World Congress Proceedings

Proceedings of the 13th World Congress: Automotive, Marine, Autonomous Vehicles see IFAC '96: 13th World Congress Proceedings

Proceedings of the 13th World Congress: Chemical Process Control, Mineral, Mining, Metals see IFAC '96: 13th World Congress Proceedings

Proceedings of the 13th World Congress: Control Design I see IFAC '96: 13th World Congress Proceedings

Proceedings of the 13th World Congress: Control Design II, Optimization see IFAC '96: 13th World Congress Proceedings

Proceedings of the 13th World Congress: Education, Robust Control I see IFAC '96: 13th World Congress Proceedings

Proceedings of the 13th World Congress: Fault Detection, Pulp & Paper, Biotechnology see IFAC '96: 13th World Congress Proceedings

Proceedings of the 13th World Congress: Identification II, Discrete Event Systems see IFAC '96: 13th World Congress Proceedings

Proceedings of the 13th World Congress: Manufacturing, Social Effects, Bio-Production, Biomedical, Environment see IFAC '96: 13th World Congress Proceedings

Proceedings of the 13th World Congress: Nonlinear Systems I see IFAC '96: 13th World Congress Proceedings

Proceedings of the 13th World Congress: Nonlinearr Systems II see IFAC '96: 13th World Congress Proceedings

Proceedings of the 13th World Congress: Plenary Volume see IFAC '96: 13th World Congress Proceedings

Proceedings of the 13th World Congress: Power Plants & Systems, Computer Control see IFAC '96: 13th World Congress Proceedings

Proceedings of the 13th World Congress: Robotics, Components & Instruments see IFAC '96: 13th World Congress Proceedings

Proceedings of the 13th World Congress: Robust Control II, Stochatic Systems see IFAC '96: 13th World Congress Proceedings

Proceedings of the 13th World Congress: Systems Engineering & Management see IFAC '96: 13th World Congress Proceedings

Hollander Interchange Manual, No. 1, Identification see IFAC '96: 13th World Congress Proceedings

***Proceedings of the Thirtieth Child Language Research Forum.** Ed. by Eve V. Clark. LC 99-462363. 300p. (C). 2000. pap. 24.95 (*1-57586-242-5*, Pub. by CSLI); text 64.95 (*1-57586-241-7*, Pub. by CSLI) Cambridge U Pr.

Proceedings of the Thirty-Eighth Annual Technical Conference of the Society of Vacuum Coaters, 1995. 1995. pap. 110.00 (*1-878068-14-8*) Vacuum Coaters.

Proceedings of the 38th Colloquium on the Law of Outer Space Held October, 1995, Oslo, Norway. 408p. 1996. 84.95 (*1-56347-213-9*, P961(9991)) AIAA.

Proceedings of the Thirty-Ninth Annual Convention of the American Association of Equine Practitioners, Held in San Antonio, Texas, December 5-8, 1993. American Association of Equine Practitioners Staff. LC 79-2671. 310p. 1993. reprint ed. pap. 96.10 (*0-608-01730-2*, 206238700002) Bks Demand.

Proceedings of the Thirty-Second Annual Professional Development Conference. Intro. by Gary H. Barnett. (Illus.). 275p. (Orig.). 1993. pap. 12.95 (*0-939874-92-X*, 431093) ASSE.

Proceedings of the 32nd National Heat Transfer Conference, Baltimore, Maryland, August 8-12, 1997, Vol. 1. Ed. by K. Vafai & J. L. Chen. (HTD Ser.: Vol. 339). 252p. 1997. 100.00 (*0-7918-1806-3*, H01087) ASME Pr.

Proceedings of the 32nd National Heat Transfer Conference, Baltimore, Maryland, August 8-12, 1997, Vol. 2. Ed. by G. S. Dulikravich & K. A. Woodbury. (HTD Ser.: Vol. 340). 172p. 1997. 80.00 (*0-7918-1807-1*, H01088) ASME Pr.

Proceedings of the 32nd National Heat Transfer Conference, Baltimore, Maryland, August 8-12, 1997, Vol. 3. Ed. by L. A. Gritzo & J. P. Delplanque. (HTD Ser.: Vol. 341). 208p. 1997. 90.00 (*0-7918-1808-X*, H01089) ASME Pr.

Proceedings of the 32nd National Heat Transfer Conference, Baltimore, Maryland, August 8-12, 1997, Vol. 4. Ed. by S. G. Kandlikar & C. H. Amon. (HTD Ser.: Vol. 342). 204p. 1997. 90.00 (*0-7918-1809-8*, H01090) ASME Pr.

Proceedings of the 32nd National Heat Transfer Conference, Baltimore, Maryland, August 8-12, 1997, Vol. 5. Ed. by C. Amon et al. (HTD Ser.: Vol. 343). 148p. 1997. 70.00 (*0-7918-1810-1*, H01091) ASME Pr.

Proceedings of the 32nd National Heat Transfer Conference, Baltimore, Maryland, August 8-12, 1997, Vol. 6. Ed. by M. V. Bianchi et al. (HTD Ser.: Vol. 344). 148p. 1997. 70.00 (*0-7918-1811-X*, H01092) ASME Pr.

Proceedings of the 32nd National Heat Transfer Conference, Baltimore, Maryland, August 8-12, 1997, Vol. 7. Ed. by D. Kaminski et al. (HTD Ser.: Vol. 345). 104p. 1997. 60.00 (*0-7918-1812-8*, H01093) ASME Pr.

Proceedings of the 32nd National Heat Transfer Conference, Baltimore, Maryland, August 8-12, 1997, Vol. 9. Ed. by T. Bergman et al. (HTD Ser.: Vol. 347). 340p. 1997. 100.00 (*0-7918-1814-4*, H01095) ASME Pr.

Proceedings of the 32nd National Heat Transfer Conference, Baltimore, Maryland, August 8-12, 1997, Vol. 10. Ed. by R. Clarksean et al. (HTD Ser.: Vol. 348). 144p. 1997. 70.00 (*0-7918-1815-2*, H01096) ASME Pr.

Proceedings of the 32nd National Heat Transfer Conference, Baltimore, Maryland, August 8-12, 1997, Vol. 11. Ed. by K. Goodson et al. (HTD Ser.: Vol. 349). 212p. 1997. 90.00 (*0-7918-1816-0*, H01097) ASME Pr.

***Proceedings of the 37th annual Meeting, Easter Academy of Management: Profits & People.** Ed. by Jean Forray & Steven Meisel. 2000. Price not set. (*0-916958-20-5*) Eastrn Acad Mgmt.

Proceedings of the Thirty-Seventh Annual Technical Conference of the Society of Vacuum Coaters, 1994. (Orig.). (C). 1994. pap. 105.00 (*1-878068-13-X*) Vacuum Coaters.

Proceedings of the Thirty-Third IEEE Conference on Decision & Control. IEEE Control System Society Staff. Ed. by IEEE Staff. 4000p. 1994. pap. text. write for info. (*0-7803-1968-0*); lib. bdg. write for info. (*0-7803-1969-9*, 94CH3460-3); fiche. write for info. (*0-7803-1970-2*) Inst Electrical.

***Proceedings of the Topical Meeting on Risk-gases Performance Assessment & Decision Making: Richland, Washington, April 5-8, 1998.** 392p. 1998. pap. 55.00 (*0-89448-636-5*, 700258) Am Nuclear Soc.

***Proceedings of the topical Meeting on Safety of Operating Reactors: San Francisco, California, October 11-14, 1998.** 530p. 1998. pap. 90.00 (*0-89448-630-6*, 700250) Am Nuclear Soc.

Proceedings of the Tra Vinh (Vietnam) Aid Management & Coordination Seminar. Ed. by Michael Etherton. (Illus.). 54p. (C). 1998. pap. text 20.00 (*0-7881-7217-4*) DIANE Pub.

Proceedings of the Transgenic Animal Research Workshop. Ed. by Joan Hopper et al. (Studies in Technology & Social Change: No. 10). 167p. (Orig.). (C). 1989. pap. 15.00 (*0-945271-14-X*) ISU-CIKARD.

Proceedings of the Trees & Buildings Conference. R. Dan Neely & Gary Watson. 191p. (C). 1995. pap. text 45.00 (*1-881956-15-6*) Int Soc Arboricult.

Proceedings of the Trenton City Museum Symposia & Exhibition "When Trenton Baseball Roared Like Thunder" Ed. by Harvey R. Kornberg. LC 96-162583. (C). 1995. lib. bdg. write for info. (*0-9649452-0-7*) Trenton City Mus.

Proceedings of the Tulane Tidelands Institute Staff, 7. Tulane Tidelands Institute Staff. Ed. by R. Slovenko. 1963. 7.50 (*0-685-01112-7*) Claitors.

Proceedings of the Tulane Tidelands Institute Staff, Vols. 1-6. Tulane Tidelands Institute Staff. Ed. by R. Slovenko. 1963. 25.00 (*0-685-01111-9*) Claitors.

Proceedings of the Twelfth Annual Conference of the Cognitive Science Society. Cognitive Science Society Staff. 1112p. 1990. pap. 150.00 (*0-8058-0938-4*) L Erlbaum Assocs.

Proceedings of the Twelfth Biennial University Government Industry Microelectronics Symposium. IEEE, Electron Devices Society Staff. Ed. by Institute of Electrical & Electronics Engineers, I. 1997. pap. text. write for info. (*0-7803-3790-5*, 97CH36030); lib. bdg. write for info. (*0-7803-3791-3*, 97CB36030); fiche. write for info. (*0-7803-3792-1*, 97CH36030) Inst Electrical.

Proceedings of the 12th Colloquium on the Law of Outer Space, October 5-10, 1969, Mar Del Plata, Argentina. International Institute of Space Law of the International Astronautical Federation Staff. iii, 336p. 1970. pap. 27.50 (*0-8377-0407-3*, Rothman) W S Hein.

Proceedings of the 12th International Vacuum Web Coating Conference. Robert Bakish. (Illus.). 1999. pap. 70.00 (*0-939997-22-3*) Bakish Mat.

***Proceedings of the 12th International Conference on Software Engineering & Knowledge Engineering.** Ed. by Shi-Kuo Chang. (Illus.). 376p. 2000. pap. 65.00 (*1-891706-05-5*) Knowldge Systs.

Proceedings of the 12th International Congress on Hyperbaric Medicine. Ed. by G. Oriani & F. Wattel. LC 97-73095. (Illus.). 320p. 1998. 64.00 (*0-941332-63-2*, D938) Best Pub Co.

Proceedings of the XII International Congress on Mathematical Physics, Vol. 12. Ed. by David Dewitt et al. (Series in Mathematical Physics: Vol. 12). (Illus.). 411p. 1998. 42.00 (*1-57146-055-1*, 1CMP12) Intl Pr Boston.

Proceedings of the Twelfth International Conference on the Study of Shamanism & Alternate Modes of Healing 1995, Santa Sabina Center, San Rafael, California, September 2-4, 1990, Vol. XII. Ed. by Ruth-Inge Heinze. LC 95-50127. (Illus.). 327p. (C). 1995. pap. 21.75 (*0-945875-15-0*) Independent Scholars Asia Inc.

***Proceedings of the Twelfth International Florida Artificial Intelligence Research Society Conference.** Ed. by Amruth Kumar & Ingrid Russell. (Illus.). 560p. 1999. pap. text 50.00 (*1-57735-080-4*) AAAI Pr.

Proceedings of the Twelfth International Symposium on Earth Tides Held in Beijing, China on August 4-7, 1993. Ed. by H. T. Hsu. 586p. 1996. 52.00 (*7-03-004768-0*, Pub. by Sci Pr) Lubrecht & Cramer.

Proceedings of the Twelfth International Zeolite Conference, 4 vols. Ed. by M. M. Treacy et al. LC 98-46348. 3360p. 1999. 245.00 (*1-55899-463-7*) Materials Res.

Proceedings of the Twelfth National Convention of the Registry of Interpreters for the Deaf. Ed. by Jean Plant-Moeller. 224p. (Orig.). (C). 1992. pap. 3.50 (*0-916883-11-6*) RID Pubns.

Proceedings of the 12th Oil Shale Symposium. Ed. by J. H. Gary. 395p. 1979. 11.00 (*0-918062-08-X*) Colo Sch Mines.

***Proceedings of the 12th Toyota Conference: Challenge of Plant & Agricultural Sciences to the Crisis of Biosphere on the Earth in the 21st Century.** Toyota Conference Staff et al. LC 99-34880. (Environmental Intelligence Unit Ser.). 378p. 1999. 89.00 (*1-57059-616-6*) Landes Bioscience.

***Proceedings of the 12th Toyota Conference: Challenge of Plant & Agricultural Sciences to the Crisis of Biosphere on the Earth in the 21st Century.** Kazuo Watanabe & Atsushi Komamine. 378p. 2000. 99.00 (*1-58706-015-9*, Pub. by Eurekah) Landes Bioscience.

Proceedings of the Twelfth West Coast Conference on Formal Linguistics (WCCFL 12) Proceedings of the West Coast Conference on Formal Linguistics, Vol. 12. Ed. by Erin Duncan et al. 611p. 1995. pap. 24.95 (*1-881526-33-X*) CSLI.

Proceedings of the 12th FEBS Meeting, Dresden 1978, 6 vols., Set. Federation European Staff & S. Rapoport. 1979. 903.00 (*0-08-023165-9*, Pub. by Pergamon Repr) Franklin.

Proceedings of the 23rd Annual Boston University Conference on Language Development. Ed. by Annabel Greenhill et al. (BUCLD Proceedings Ser.: Vol. 23). (Illus.). 775p. (C). 1999. pap. 50.00 (*1-57473-042-8*); lib. bdg. 96.00 (*1-57473-142-4*) Cascadilla Pr.

Proceedings of the Twentieth Annual Conference of the Cognitive Science Society. Cognitive Science Society Staff. 1280p. 1998. pap. 180.00 (*0-8058-3231-9*) L Erlbaum Assocs.

Proceedings of the Twentieth Annual SAS Users Group International Conference. 1592p. (C). 1995. pap. 12.50 (*1-55544-211-0*, BR55326) SAS Publ.

P

An Asterisk (*) at the beginning of an entry indicates that the title is appearing for the first time.

Proceedings of the 20th Colloquium on the Law of Outer Space, September 25-October 1, 1977, Prague, Czechoslovakia. International Institute of Space Law of the International Astronautical Federation Staff. v, 524p. 1977. pap. 32.50 (*0-8377-0439-1*, Rothman) W S Hein.

Proceedings of the 20th Congress of the International Council of the Aeronautical Sciences held September, 1996, Sorrento, Italy, 2 vols. 2728p. 1996. pap. 220.00 (*1-56347-219-8*, 20-ICAS(9991)) AIAA.

Proceedings of the Twentieth International Congress of Papyrologists. Adam B. Jacobsen. (Illus.). 656p. 1994. 88.00 (*87-7289-264-1*, Pub. by Mus Tusculanum) Paul & Co Pubs.

Proceedings of the 20th Lunar & Planetary Science Conference. Ed. by Graham Ryder. LC 87-643480. (Illus.). 533p. 1990. 50.00 (*0-942862-04-X*) Lunar & Planet Inst.

Proceedings of the Twentieth Meeting of the French Colonial Historical Society, Cleveland, Ohio, May, 1994 Actes du Vingtieme Colloque de la Societe d'Histoire Coloniale Francaise. Cleveland, Ohio, Mai 1994. Ed. by A. J. Johnston. (ENG & FRE., Illus.). v, 147p. 1996. text 30.00 (*1-884679-02-1*) Fr Colonial Hist.

Proceedings of the Twentieth World Congress of Philosophy Vol. 1: Ethics, Vol. 1. Ed. by Klaus Brinkmann. 288p. (C). 1999. 45.00 (*1-889680-05-2*) Philos Document.

***Proceedings of the Twentieth World Congress of Philosophy Vol. II: Metaphysics.** Ed. by Tom Rockmore. LC 99-66878. 256p. (C). 1999. 45.00 (*1-889680-06-0*) Philos Document.

***Proceedings of the Twentieth World Congress of Philosophy Vol. III: Philosophy of Education.** Ed. by David Steiner. LC 99-66878. 210p. (C). 1999. 45.00 (*1-889680-07-9*) Philos Document.

***Proceedings of the Twentieth World Congress of Philosophy Vol. 4: Philosophies of Religion, Art & Creativity.** Ed. by Kevin Stoehr. 250p. (C). 1999. 45.00 (*1-889680-08-7*) Philos Document.

***Proceedings of the Twentieth World Congress of Philosophy Vol. V: Epistemology.** Ed. by Richard Cobb-Stevens. 250p. (C). 1999. 45.00 (*1-889680-09-5*) Philos Document.

***Proceedings of the Twentieth World Congress of Philosophy Vol. VI: Analytic Philosophy & Logic.** Ed. by Akihiro Kanamori. LC 99-66878. 250p. (C). 2000. 45.00 (*1-889680-10-9*) Philos Document.

***Proceedings of the Twentieth World Congress of Philosophy Vol. VII, Pt. I: Modern Philosophy: The Enlightenment & Its Critics.** Ed. by Mark Gedney. 250p. (C). 2000. 45.00 (*1-889680-11-7*) Philos Document.

***Proceedings of the Twentieth World Congress of Philosophy Vol. VIII, Pt. II: Contemporary Philosophy: The Enlightenment & Its Critics.** Ed. by Daniel Dahlstrom. LC 99-66878. 250p. (C). 2000. 45.00 (*1-889680-12-5*) Philos Document.

***Proceedings of the Twentieth World Congress of Philosophy Vol. IX: Philosophy of Mind & Philosophy of Psychology.** Ed. by Bernard Elevitch. 250p. (C). 2000. 45.00 (*1-889680-13-3*) Philos Document.

***Proceedings of the Twentieth World Congress of Philosophy Vol. X: Philosophy of Science.** Ed. by Tian Yu Cao. LC 99-66878. 250p. (C). 2000. 45.00 (*1-889680-14-1*) Philos Document.

***Proceedings of the Twentieth World Congress of Philosophy Vol. XI: Social & Political Philosophy.** Ed. by David Rasmussen. LC 99-66878. 250p. (C). 2000. 45.00 (*1-889680-15-X*) Philos Document.

***Proceedings of the Twentieth World Congress of Philosophy Vol. XII: Intercultural/Non-Western.** Ed. by David Eckel. 250p. (C). 2000. 45.00 (*1-889680-16-8*) Philos Document.

Proceedings of the 24th International Conference on Parallel Processing Vol. 1: Architecture. Ed. by Tse-yun Feng. 256p. 1995. per. 84.95 (*0-8493-2615-X*, 2615) CRC Pr.

Proceedings of the Twenty-Eighth Annual Child Language Research Forum. Ed. & Intro. by Eve V. Clark. 308p. (C). 1997. 69.95 (*1-57586-063-5*); pap. 24.95 (*1-57586-062-7*) CSLI.

Proceedings of the 25th Annual Simulation Symposium. Ed. by Abrams. 248p. 1988. pap. 48.00 (*0-8186-0845-5*, ANS21-1) Soc Computer Sim.

Proceedings of the Twenty-Fifth Annual Child Language Research Forum. Intro. by Eve V. Clark. 1993. 54.95 (*1-881526-32-1*); pap. 23.95 (*1-881526-31-3*) CSLI.

***Proceedings of the 25th Annual International Congress on Veterinary Acupuncture.** Gary Allen et al. (Illus.). 240p. 1999. spiral bd. 30.00 (*0-9616627-0-0*) Intl Vet Acup.

Proceedings of the 25th Annual Simulation Symposium. Ed. by Kubiak. 360p. 1992. 80.00 (*1-56555-011-0*, ANSS25-1) Soc Computer Sim.

***Proceedings of the Twenty-First Annual Conference of the Cognitive Science Society.** Ed. by Martin Hahn & Scott C. Stoness. 848p. 1999. pap. 150.00 (*0-8058-3581-4*) L Erlbaum Assocs.

Proceedings of the Twenty-First Annual SAS Users Group International Conference. 1716p. (C). 1996. pap. 12.50 (*1-55544-747-3*, BR55540) SAS Publ.

Proceedings of the 21st Colloquium on the Law of Outer Space, October 1-8, 1978, Dubrovnik, Yugoslavia. International Institute of Space Law of the International Astronautical Federation Staff. v, 291p. 1979. pap. 32.50 (*0-8377-0440-5*, Rothman) W S Hein.

Proceedings of the 21st Plenary Meeting of COSPAR, Innsbruck, Austria, May-June 1978. Ed. by Michael J. Rycroft. (Advances in Space Research Ser.: Vol. 19). 642p. 1979. 145.00 (*0-08-023417-8*, Pergamon Pr) Elsevier.

Proceedings of the Twenty-Fourth Annual Child Language Research Forum. Ed. by Eve V. Clark. LC 92-43908. ix, 288p. 1993. 49.95 (*1-881526-05-4*); pap. 19.95 (*1-881526-04-6*) CSLI.

***Proceedings of the Twenty-Fourth Annual SAS Users Group International Conference.** (C). 1999. pap. 50.00 (*1-58025-447-0*) SAS Publ.

Proceedings of the 24th International Technical Conference on Coal Utilization & Fuel Systems. (Illus.). 1100p. 1999. pap. 395.00 (*0-932066-23-2*) Coal Slurry Tech.

Proceedings of the 24th International Conference on Parallel Processing Vol. 2: Software. Ed. by Tse-yun Feng. 256p. 1995. per. 84.95 (*0-8493-2616-8*, 2616) CRC Pr.

Proceedings of the 24th International Conference on Parallel Processing Vol. 3: Algorithms & Applications. Ed. by Tse-yun Feng. 256p. 1995. per. 84.95 (*0-8493-2617-6*, 2617) CRC Pr.

Proceedings of the 24th International Conference on Parallel Processing Vol. 4: Workshop on Recent Advances in Parallel Processing. Ed. by Tse-yun Feng. 168p. 1995. per. 84.95 (*0-8493-2618-4*, 2618) CRC Pr.

Proceedings of the Twenty-Ninth Annual Child Language Research Forum. Ed. by Eve Clark. 310p. (C). 1998. 64.95 (*1-57586-119-4*); pap. 24.95 (*1-57586-118-6*) CSLI.

Proceedings of the 29th International Geological Congress Pt. C: Siliceous, Phosphatic & Glauconitic Sedmiments of the Tertiary & Mesozoic. Ed. by A. Iijima et al. 252p. 1994. 115.00 (*90-6764-175-8*, Pub. by VSP) Coronet Bks.

Proceedings of the 29th International Geological Congress Pt. D: Circum-Pacific Ophiolites. Ed. by A. Ishiwatari et al. 292p. 1994. 127.50 (*90-6764-176-6*, Pub. by VSP) Coronet Bks.

Proceedings of the 29th International Geological Congress Pt. A: Metamorphic Reactions; Sandstone Petrology; Evaporite & Desert Environment. Ed. by T. Nishiyama et al. (Illus.). 316p. 1994. 140.00 (*90-6764-173-1*, Pub. by VSP) Coronet Bks.

Proceedings of the 29th International Geological Congress Pt. B: Reconstruction of the Paleo-Asian Ocean; Quarternary Environmental Changes. Ed. by R. G. Coleman & E. H. Juvigne. 326p. 1994. 140.00 (*90-6764-174-X*, Pub. by VSP) Coronet Bks.

Proceedings of the 22nd Annual Boston University Conference on Language Development, 2 vols. Ed. by Annabel Greenhill et al. (BUCLD Proceedings Ser.: Vol. 22). (Illus.). 796p. 1998. pap. 50.00 (*1-57473-032-0*) Cascadilla Pr.

Proceedings of the 22nd Annual Boston University Conference on Language Development. Ed. by Annabel Greenhill et al. (BUCLD Proceedings Ser.: Vol. 22). (Illus.). 796p. (C). 1998. lib. bdg. 96.00 (*1-57473-132-7*) Cascadilla Pr.

Proceedings of the 22nd Annual Simulation Symposium. Ed. by Rutan. 194p. 1989. pap. 48.00 (*0-685-66803-7*, ANS22-1) Soc Computer Sim.

Proceedings of the 22nd Annual SAS Users Group International Conference. SAS Institute, Inc. Staff. 1648p. 1997. pap. 25.00 (*1-58025-448-9*, BR57304) SAS Publ.

Proceedings of the Twenty-Second Annual SAS User's Group International Conference. 1996. pap. 15.00 (*1-58025-180-3*, BR55620) SAS Publ.

Proceedings of the Twenty-Sixth Annual Child Language Research Forum. Ed. & Intro. by Eve V. Clark. 261p. 1995. pap. 22.95 (*1-881526-57-7*) CSLI.

Proceedings of the Twenty-Third Annual SAS(R) Users Group International Conference. 1664p. (C). 1998. pap. 12.50 (*1-58025-149-8*, BR56565) SAS Publ.

Proceedings of the 23rd Annual Users Group International Conference. SAS Institute, Inc. Staff. 1664p. (C). 1998. pap. 12.50 (*1-55544-961-1*, BR55782) SAS Publ.

***Proceedings of the 2000 Advances in Aviation Safety Conference.** (Proceedings Ser.). 300p. 2000. 98.00 (*0-7680-0607-4*, P-355) Soc Auto Engineers.

***Proceedings of the 2000 Automotive Dynamics & Stability Conference.** (Proceedings Ser.). 500p. 2000. 143.00 (*0-7680-0605-8*, P-354) Soc Auto Engineers.

***Proceedings of the 2000 International Computer Music Conference.** 2000. write for info. (*0-9667927-2-6*) Internatl Computer Music Assn.

***Proceedings of the 2000 Total Life Cycle Conference.** (Proceedings Ser.). 600p. 2000. 140.00 (*0-7680-0539-6*, P-353) Soc Auto Engineers.

Proceedings of the U. S. - Italy - Japan Workshop - Symposium on Structural Control & Intelligent Systems. Ed. by George W. Housner et al. LC 92-38057. 282p. 1992. 25.00 (*0-9628908-1-2*) USC Schl EDCE.

Proceedings of the U. S. Geological Survey Global Change Research Forum. Ed. by John A. Kelmelis & Mitchell Snow. (Illus.). 121p. (Orig.). (C). 1994. pap. text 35.00 (*0-7881-0299-0*) DIANE Pub.

Proceedings of the U. S. National Workshop on Structural Control Research. Ed. by Sami F. Masri. LC 91-2839. 300p. 1991. 25.00 (*0-9628908-0-4*) USC Schl EDCE.

Proceedings of the UBC International Conference on Phonological Acquisition. Ed. by Barbara Bernhardt et al. (Illus.). 292p. (C). 1996. pap. 25.00 (*1-57473-009-6*); lib. bdg. 54.00 (*1-57473-109-2*) Cascadilla Pr.

Proceedings of the United Nations Conference on Trade & Development, Seventh Session, (Geneva) Vol. I: Report & Annexes. 147p. 1987. 45.00 (*92-1-112240-6*, E.88.II.D.1) UN.

Proceedings of the United Nations Conference on Trade & Development, Seventh Session, 1987, Vol. II. 1988. 55.00 (*0-685-39207-4*, 88.II.D.2) UN.

Proceedings of the United States Nuclear Regulatory Commission: Twenty-Fourth Water Reactor Safety Information Meeting, Plenary Session, High Burnup Fuel, Containment & Structural Aging, Vol. 1. Susan Monteleone. 372p. 1997. per. 33.00 (*0-16-063014-2*) USGPO.

***Proceedings of the U.S.-Japan Earthquake Policy Symposium, 16-18 Sept., 1996.** (Illus.). 308p. 2000. reprint ed. pap. text 45.00 (*0-7881-8650-7*) DIANE Pub.

Proceedings of the U.S.-Mexico Conference on Women[0012]s Health: Health Without Boundaries/Salud Sin Fronteras (1995) 274p. pap. text 35.00 (*0-7881-8470-9*) DIANE Pub.

Proceedings of the USAID Latin America Caribbean Region Biosafety Workshop (1993) Karen Maredia & Bruce Bedford. (Illus.). 39p. (Orig.). (C). 1994. pap. text 25.00 (*0-7881-1504-9*) DIANE Pub.

Proceedings of the USENIX 1998 Annual Technical Conference. (Illus.). 282p. 1998. pap. 40.00 (*1-880446-94-4*) USENIX Assn.

Proceedings of the V. Wigner Symposium: Vienna, Austria 25-29 August, 1997. Ed. by Peter Kasperkovitz. 600p. 1998. 96.00 (*981-02-3464-3*) World Scientific Pub.

***Proceedings of the VI Congreso Latinoamericano De Botanica, Mar Del Plata, Argentina, 2-8 October 1994.** Congreso Latinoamericano de Botanica et al. LC 99-191737. (Illus.). 1998. write for info. (*0-915279-58-4*) Miss Botan.

Proceedings of the Virgin Islands' Seminar on Unification Theology. Ed. by Darrol M. Bryant. LC 80-52594. (Conference Ser.: No. 6). (Illus.). xv, 323p. (Orig.). 1980. pap. text 9.95 (*0-932894-06-2*) Unif Theol Seminary.

Proceedings of the Virginia Historical Society Annual Meeting, Dec. 21-22, 1891. Virginia Historical Society Annual Meeting Staff. Ed. by R. A. Brock. LC 73-592. (Virginia Historical Society. Collections First Ser.: No. 11). reprint ed. 27.50 (*0-404-57661-3*) AMS Pr.

Proceedings of the Virginia State Convention of 1861, 4 vols., Set. Ed. by George H. Reese. LC 65-7459. 1965. text 79.95 (*0-88490-057-6*) Library of VA.

Proceedings of the VIth World Congress Vol. 2: Water for World Development, Ottawa, Canada, 4 vols., Vols. 1-4. 2814p. 1988. 35.00 (*0-614-10759-8*) Intl Water Resc.

Proceedings of the West Coast Conference on Formal Linguistics, Vol. 6. Ed. by Megan Crowhurst. 347p. (Orig.). 1987. pap. 13.95 (*0-937073-31-8*) CSLI.

Proceedings of the Western Conference on Linguistics Vol. 2: WECOL '89. Ed. by Vida Samiian. (C). 1998. pap. 16.00 (*1-879890-00-3*) CSU Linguistics.

Proceedings of the Western Conference on Linguistics Vol. 3: WECOL '90. Ed. by Vida Samiian. (C). 1998. pap. 16.00 (*1-879890-01-1*) CSU Linguistics.

Proceedings of the Western Conference on Linguistics Vol. 4: WECOL '91. Ed. by Vida Samiian. (C). 1998. pap. 16.00 (*1-879890-03-8*) CSU Linguistics.

Proceedings of the Western Conference on Linguistics Vol. 5: WECOL '92. Ed. by Vida Samiian. (C). 1998. pap. 16.00 (*1-879890-04-6*) CSU Linguistics.

Proceedings of the Western Conference on Linguistics Vol. 6: WECOL '93. Ed. by Vida Samiian. (C). 1998. pap. 16.00 (*1-879890-05-4*) CSU Linguistics.

Proceedings of the Western Conference on Linguistics Vol. 7: WECOL '94. Ed. by Vida Samiian. (C). 1998. pap. 16.00 (*1-879890-06-2*) CSU Linguistics.

Proceedings of the Western Conference on Linguistics Vol. 8: WECOL '95. Ed. by Vida Samiian. (C). 1998. pap. 16.00 (*1-879890-07-0*) CSU Linguistics.

Proceedings of the Western Conference on Linguistics Vol. 9: WECOL '96. Ed. by Vida Samiian. (C). 1998. pap. 16.00 (*1-879890-08-9*) CSU Linguistics.

Proceedings of the Winter Simulation Conference, 1991. Nelson et al. 1262p. 1991. 150.00 (*0-685-66846-0*, WSC-91) Soc Computer Sim.

Proceedings of the Winter, 1990, International Joint Conference on Neural Networks, 2 Vols., Set. Ed. by Maureen Caudill. 1590p. (C). 1990. pap. text 220.00 (*0-8058-0754-3*) L Erlbaum Assocs.

Proceedings of the Workshop on Advances in Experimental Pharmacology of Hydergine Basel, December 1976. Workshop on Advances in Experimental Pharmacology. LC 71-114908. (Select Bibliographies Reprint Ser.). 1977. 31.95 (*0-8369-5313-4*) Ayer.

Proceedings of the Workshop on Direct Methanol-Air Fuel Cells. Ed. by A. R. Landgrebe et al. LC 92-81870. (Proceedings Ser.: Vol. 92-14). 224p. 1992. 46.00 (*1-56677-015-7*) Electrochem Soc.

Proceedings of the Workshop on Elderly, the Elderly Disabled & Technology (1994) Ed. by Jan Ekberg. (Illus.). 123p. (Orig.). (C). 1994. pap. text 40.00 (*0-7881-1607-X*) DIANE Pub.

Proceedings of the Workshop on Engineering Controls for Preventing Airborne Infections in Workers in Health Care & Related Facilities. 184p. pap. text 40.00 (*0-7881-3921-5*) DIANE Pub.

Proceedings of the Workshop on Gammasphere Physics. LC 97-102566. 300p. 1996. lib. bdg. 55.00 (*981-02-2797-3*) World Scientific Pub.

Proceedings of the Workshop on General Population Exposure to Gasoline: (Gasoline Assessment of Human Exposure) Ed. by Edo Pellizari. (Journal of Exposure Analysis & Environmental Epidemiology Ser.: Vol. 2, No. 1). (Illus.). 1992. pap. text 65.00 (*0-911131-28-0*) Specialist Journals.

Proceedings of the Workshop on High Integrity Software. Dolores R. Wallace et al. (Illus.). 80p. (Orig.). (C). 1994. pap. text 30.00 (*0-7881-0626-0*) DIANE Pub.

Proceedings of the Workshop on Measurement of Microbial Activities in the Carbon Cycle of Freshwaters. Ed. by Juergen Overbeck. (Advances in Limnology Ser.: Vol. 12). (GER., Illus.). vi, 170p. (Orig.). 1979. 38.00 (*3-510-47010-9*, Pub. by E Schweizerbartsche) Balogh.

Proceedings of the Workshop on Neutron Scattering Studies of Polymers: A Special Issue of the Journal Molecular Crystals & Liquid Crystals Incorporating Nonlinear Optics. D. K. Hyer & M. Aldissi. 165p. 1990. pap. text 568.00 (*2-88124-434-3*) Gordon & Breach.

Proceedings of the Workshop on Random Media & Composites. Ed. by Robert Kohn & Graeme Milton. LC 89-26092. (Proceedings in Applied Mathematics Ser.: No. 40). 214p. 1989. pap. 32.00 (*0-89871-246-7*) Soc Indus-Appl Math.

Proceedings of the Workshop on Research Methodologies & Applications for Pacific Island Agroforestry. Ed. by Bill Raynor & Roger R. Bay. (Illus.). 86p. (Orig.). (C). 1994. pap. text 25.00 (*0-7881-1073-X*) DIANE Pub.

Proceedings of the World Bank Annual Conference on Development Economics 1993. Ed. by Michael Bruno & Boris Pleskovic. 496p. 1994. pap. 22.00 (*0-8213-2558-2*, 12558) World Bank.

Proceedings of the World Conference on Biotechnology for the Fats & Oils Industry. Ed. by Thomas H. Applewhite. 364p. 1988. 40.00 (*0-935315-20-9*) Am Oil Chemists.

Proceedings of the World Conference on Earthquake Engineering, 10th: 19-24 July, 1922, Madrid, Spain, 11 vols., Set. (Illus.). 7500p. (C). 1992. text 1000.00 (*90-5410-060-5*, Pub. by A A Balkema) Ashgate Pub Co.

Proceedings of the World Conference on Lauric Oils: Sources, Processing & Applications. Ed. by Thomas H. Applewhite. (Illus.). 192p. 1994. lib. bdg. 135.00 (*0-935315-56-X*, PCWC94) Am Oil Chemists.

Proceedings of the World Conference on Oilseed Technology & Utilization. Ed. by Thomas H. Applewhite. LC 93-3191. (Illus.). 512p. 1993. lib. bdg. 130.00 (*0-935315-45-4*, PCWC92) Am Oil Chemists.

Proceedings of the World Conference on Palm & Coconut Oils for the 21st Century--Sources, Processing, Applications, & Competition. World Conference on Palm and Coconut Oils for the 21st Century: Sources Staff et al. LC 99-18140. 176p. 1999. write for info. (*0-935315-99-3*) Am Oil Chemists.

Proceedings of the World Congress on Expert Systems: Orlando, FL, December 16-19, 1991. World Congress on Expert Systems Staff. Ed. by Jay Liebowitz. LC 92-185988. 782p. 1991. reprint ed. pap. 200.00 (*0-608-04555-1*, 206529700001) Bks Demand.

Proceedings of the World Congress on Expert Systems Vol. 2: Orlando, FL, December 16-19, 1991. World Congress on Expert Systems Staff. Ed. by Jay Liebowitz. LC 92-185988. 731p. 1991. reprint ed. pap. 200.00 (*0-608-04556-X*, 206529700002) Bks Demand.

Proceedings of the World Congress on Expert Systems Vol. 3: Orlando, FL, December 16-19, 1991. World Congress on Expert Systems Staff. Ed. by Jay Liebowitz. LC 92-185988. 752p. 1991. reprint ed. pap. 200.00 (*0-608-04557-8*, 206529700003) Bks Demand.

Proceedings of the World Congress on Expert Systems Vol. 4: Orlando, FL, December 16-19, 1991. World Congress on Expert Systems Staff. Ed. by Jay Liebowitz. LC 92-185988. 860p. 1991. reprint ed. pap. 200.00 (*0-608-04558-6*, 206529700004) Bks Demand.

Proceedings of the World Congress on Vegetable Protein Utilization in Human Foods & Animal Feedstuffs. Ed. by Thomas H. Applewhite. 588p. 1989. 130.00 (*0-935315-25-X*) Am Oil Chemists.

Proceedings of the XIth Congress of the International Society of Biometeorology. Ed. by D. Driscoll et al. (Illus.). xvi, 407p. 1989. pap. 125.00 (*90-5103-036-3*, Pub. by SPB Acad Pub) Balogh.

Proceedings of the XIX International Mineral Processing Congress, 4 vols. Intro. by J. A. Herbst. Incl. Vol. 1. Comminution & Simulation Control. LC 95-70770. (Illus.). 306p. (Orig.). 1995. pap. 40.00 (*0-87335-139-8*); Vol. 2. Physical & Chemical Processing. LC 95-70770. (Illus.). 266p. (Orig.). 1995. pap. 40.00 (*0-87335-140-1*); Vol. 3. Flotation Operating Practices & Fundamentals. LC 95-70770. (Illus.). 312p. (Orig.). 1995. pap. 40.00 (*0-87335-141-X*); Vol. 4. Precious Metals Processing & Mineral Waste & the Environment. LC 95-70770. (Illus.). 190p. (Orig.). 1995. pap. 40.00 (*0-87335-142-8*); LC 95-70770. 1995. Set pap. 99.00 (*0-87335-134-7*) SMM&E Inc.

Proceedings of the XV Symposium Neuroradiologicum. M. Takahashi & Y. Korogi. 624p. 1995. suppl. ed. 302.00 (*3-540-58755-1*) Spr-Verlag.

Proceedings of the XVIth International Congress of Dermatology, May 23-28, 1982, Tokyo, Japan. International Congress of Dermatology Staff. Ed. by Atsushi Kukita & Makoto Seiji. LC 84-101911. 902p. 1983. reprint ed. pap. 200.00 (*0-608-01238-6*, 206192600001) Bks Demand.

Proceedings of the XXIX International Conference on High Energy Physics: Vancouver, Canada 23-29, 2 Vol. ALAN ASTBURY. 1600p. 1999. 148.00 (*981-02-3772-3*) World Scientific Pub.

Proceedings of the XXVII International Conference on High Energy Physics, 21-27 July 1994, Glasgow, Scotland, U. K., Vol. 2. Ed. by P. J. Bussey & I. G. Knowles. LC 95-6174. (Illus.). 1528p. 1995. 670.00 (*0-7503-0125-2*) IOP Pub.

Proceedings of the 1st Annual Symposium of the Institute of Islamic & Arabic Sciences in America, 2-3 Shaban, 1413 AH, 24025 January 1993 CE. Institute of Islamic & Arabic Sciences in America. LC 95-16190. (Symposia

P

An Asterisk (*) at the beginning of an entry indicates that the title is appearing for the first time.

& Seminars Ser.: No. 1). Orig. Title: Proceedings of the 1st Annual Symposium on Islamic & Arabic Studies in American Universities, 1993. (ARA & ENG.). 1995. pap. write for info. (*1-56923-017-X*) Inst Islamic.

Proceedings of the 1st Annual Symposium on Islamic & Arabic Studies in American Universities, 1993 see Proceedings of the 1st Annual Symposium of the Institute of Islamic & Arabic Sciences in America, 2-3 Shaban, 1413 AH, 24025 January 1993 CE

*__Proceedings of the 1st International Conference on Smarandache Type Notions in Number Theory.__ Ed. by C. Dumitrescu & V. Seleacu. LC 98-185610. (Smarandache Bks.). (ENG & FRE., Illus.). 250p. (C). 1998. pap. 39.95 incl. VHS (*1-879585-58-8*) Erhus Univ Pr.

Proceedings of the 1st International ISA Food Instrumentation Division Symposium, Montreal, 1972. Food & Beverage Instrumentation Symposium Staff. Ed. by E. Nobrega. LC 72-90018. (Instrumentation in the Food & Beverage Industry Ser.: Vol. 1). 94p. 1972. reprint ed. pap. 30.00 (*0-608-09980-5*, 205111900001) Bks Demand.

Proceedings of the 1st International Specalist Meeting on Amorphous Carbon. S. Silva. LC 98-214545. 1998. 58.00 (*981-02-3449-X*) World Scientific Pub.

Proceedings of the 1st Southeastern Pole Conference. 216p. 1994. 45.00 (*0-935018-68-9*, 7314) Forest Prod.

Proceedings of the 11th International Conference on Phosphorus Chemistry. A. Aaviksaar. xiv, 470p. 1990. text 2001.00 (*2-88124-438-6*) Gordon & Breach.

Proceedings of the 11th International Conference on Wear of Materials, 1997. Ed. by D. Rigney & R. G. Bayer. 740p. 1997. 281.00 (*0-08-042841-X*, Pergamon Pr) Elsevier.

Proceedings of the 11th Meeting of the World Society for Stereotactic & Functional Neurosurgery, Ixtapa, Mexico, October 1993, Pt. I. Ed. by Philip L. Gildenberg et al. (Journal Ser.: Vol. 62, No. 1-4, 1994). (Illus.). viii, 320p. 1995. pap. 201.75 (*3-8055-6159-8*) S Karger.

Proceedings of the 12th International Conference on Soil Mechanics & Foundation Engineering, Rio de Janeiro, 13-18 August 1989, 5 vols. Ed. by Publications Committee of the XII ICSMFE Staff. 2500p. (C). 1989. text 1288.00 (*90-6191-890-1*, Pub. by A A Balkema) Ashgate Pub Co.

Proceedings of the 13th International Diatom Symposium. D. Marino & M. Montresor. 566p. 1995. 165.00 (*0-948737-35-2*, Pub. by Biopress) Balogh.

Proceedings of the 13th RID National Convention, 1993: A Confluence of Diverse Relationships. 220p. 1993. pap. 16.95 (*0-916883-14-0*) RID Pubns.

Proceedings of the 14th Collegium Internationale Neuro-Psychopharmacologium Congress, Florence, Italy, 1984. Collegium Internationale Neuro-Psychopharmacologic. Ed. by Giorgio Racagni et al. LC RM0315.. (Clinical Neuropharmacology Ser.: Vol. 7, Supplement 1). 1008p. 1984. reprint ed. pap. 200.00 (*0-608-00439-1*, 206115400007) Bks Demand.

Proceedings of the 14th U. S. Army Symposium on Solid Mechanics: 16-18 October 1996, Myrtle Beach, South Carolina. Iyer & S. C. Chou. LC 97-25158. 1997. write for info. (*1-57477-038-1*) Battelle.

Proceedings of the 14th West Coast Conference on Formal Linguistics. Ed. by Jose Camacho et al. 600p. (C). 1996. pap. 28.95 (*1-57586-042-2*) CSLI.

Proceedings of the 15th International Conference on Physics Held in Collison, 1995. Ed. by M. Rozanska & K. Rybicki. LC 96-3255. 540p. 1996. write for info. (*981-02-2587-3*) World Scientific Pub.

Proceedings of the 15th Meeting of the French Colonial Historical Society: Martinique & Guadeloupe. Ed. by Patricia Galloway & Philip Boucher. 240p. (C). 1991. lib. bdg. 49.50 (*0-8191-8322-9*) U Pr of Amer.

Proceedings of the 17th Annual Fall Technical Conference of the ASME Internal Combustion Engine Division Vol. 25-1: New Technology & Design, 4 vols., Set. Ed. by J. A. Caton. LC 95-80398. 132p. 1995. pap. 76.00 (*0-7918-1485-8*, G0980A) ASME.

Proceedings of the 17th Annual Fall Technical Conference of the ASME Internal Combustion Engine Division Vol. 25-2: New Technology & Design. J. A. Caton. LC 95-80398. 156p. 1995. pap. 84.00 (*0-614-16881-3*, G0980B) ASME.

Proceedings of the 17th Annual Fall Technical Conference of the ASME Internal Combustion Engine Division Vol. 25-3: New Technology & Design. J. A. Caton. LC 95-80398. 132p. 1995. 76.00 (*0-614-16878-3*, G0980C) ASME.

Proceedings of the 17th Biennial Waste Processing Conference. 500p. 1996. 150.00 (*0-7918-1227-8*, I00390) ASME.

Proceedings of the 18th Annual International Conference of the IEEE Engineering in Medicine & Biology Society. IEEE, Engineering in Medicine & Biology Society St. Ed. by Institute of Electrical & Electronics Engineers, I. 2435p. 1997. pap. text. write for info. (*0-7803-3811-1*, 96CH36036); lib. bdg. write for info. (*0-7803-3812-X*, 96CH36036); fiche. write for info. (*0-7803-3813-8*, 96CH36036) Inst Electrical.

Proceedings of the 18th International Astronautical Congress Belgrade 1967, 4 vols., Set. M. Lunc & P. Contensou. (Interntional Astronautical Congress Ser.). 1968. reprint ed. 735.00 (*0-08-013012-7*, Pub. by Pergamon Repr) Franklin.

Proceedings of the 1975 Clay Conference. International Clay Conference Staff. Ed. by Sturges W. Bailey. LC 75-32132. (Illus.). 1976. 55.00 (*0-915834-02-2*) Applied Pub.

Proceedings of the 1980 National Literacy Forum. limited ed. Ed. by John R. Batten. 182p. 1980. pap. text 3.00 (*0-942717-13-9*) Intl Inst Rural.

Proceedings of the 1982 Conference on Far Western American Indian Languages, Held at University of California, Santa Cruz. Ed. by J. E. Redden. (Occasional Papers on Linguistics: No. 11). (Illus.). 61p. (C). 1983. reprint ed. pap. text 7.19 (*1-55567-486-0*) Coyote Press.

Proceedings of the 1984 Dusseldorf Conference on Piezo- & Pyroelectric PVDF Films. Ed. by R. Betz. iv, 84p. 1987. pap. text 201.00 (*2-88124-284-7*) Gordon & Breach.

Proceedings of the 1985 Conference of the American Academy of Advertising. Ed. by Nancy Stephens. 1985. pap. 25.00 (*0-931030-08-0*) Am Acad Advert.

Proceedings of the 1987 International Conference on Parallel Processing. Ed. by Sartaj Sahni. LC 87-43026. 943p. 1987. 85.00 (*0-271-00608-0*) Pa St U Pr.

Proceedings of the 1989 Conference of the American Academy of Advertising. Ed. by Kim B. Rotzoll. 1989. pap. 25.00 (*0-931030-12-9*) Am Acad Advert.

Proceedings of the 1989 Food Processing Waste Conference. Ed. by G. Edward Valentine & Charles C. Ross. (Illus.). 592p. (C). 1989. 60.00 (*0-685-29077-8*) GA Tech Rsch Inst.

Proceedings of the 1989 Georgia Water Resources Conference. Ed. by Kathryn J. Hatcher. LC 89-84386. (Illus.). 250p. (Orig.). (C). 1989. pap. text 20.00 (*0-935835-01-6*) Univ GA Eco.

Proceedings of the 1990 AMA Microcomputers in Marketing Education Conference: March 31-April 2, 1990, New Orleans, Louisiana. American Marketing Association Staff. Ed. by Barry Berman et al. LC 90-189871. (Illus.). 265p. 1990. reprint ed. pap. 82.20 (*0-608-04084-3*, 206481600011) Bks Demand.

Proceedings of the 1990 Undergraduate Symposium on Research in Astronomy. Ed. by Frederick R. Chromey. 74p. (C). 1991. pap. text. write for info. (*1-882334-00-0*) Keck NE Astron.

Proceedings of the 1991 Asheville Institute on General Education. Ed. by Merritt Moseley. 87p. (Orig.). 1992. pap. 15.00 (*0-911696-54-7*) Assn Am Coll.

Proceedings of the 1991 Georgia Water Resources Conference. Ed. by Kathryn J. Hatcher. LC 91-70247. 356p. (Orig.). (C). 1991. pap. text 20.00 (*0-935835-02-4*) Univ GA Eco.

Proceedings of the 1991 International Mozart Symposium. Ebisawa & Colyer. 1998. text 54.00 (*1-57647-005-9*) Pendragon NY.

Proceedings of the 1991 National Legal Conference on Immigration & Refugee Policy see In Defense of the Alien Series: Proceedings of the National Legal Conference on Immigration & Refugee Policy

Proceedings of the 1991 Undergraduate Symposium on Research in Astronomy. Ed. by Jay M. Pasachoff. 120p. (C). 1992. pap. text. write for info. (*1-882334-01-9*) Keck NE Astron.

Proceedings of the 1992 U. S. Workshop on the Physics & Chemistry of Mercury Cadmium Telluride & Other IR Materials: 13-15 October 1992, Danvers, Massachusetts. U. S. Workshop on the Physics & Chemistry of Mercu. Ed. by James R. Waterman & Ralph P. Ruth. LC 93-86220. 312p. 1993. reprint ed. pap. 96.80 (*0-608-00767-6*, 206156500010) Bks Demand.

Proceedings of the 1992 Undergraduate Symposium on Research in Astronomy. Ed. by Stephen Boughn. 120p. (C). 1993. pap. text. write for info. (*1-882334-02-7*) Keck NE Astron.

Proceedings of the 1993 Conference of the American Academy of Advertising. Ed. by Esther Thorson. 1993. pap. 25.00 (*0-931030-16-1*) Am Acad Advert.

Proceedings of the 1993 Connectionist Models Summer School. Ed. by David S. Touretzky et al. 424p. 1994. text 89.95 (*0-8058-1590-2*) L Erlbaum Assocs.

Proceedings of the 1993 Industrial Power Conference. Ed. by F. N. Coon. LC 89-46157. (PWR Ser.: Vol. 20). 120p. 1993. pap. 40.00 (*0-7918-0679-0*, I00342) ASME.

Proceedings of the 1993 International Forum on Dimensional Tolerancing & Metrology. Ed. by Vijay Srinivasan & Herbert B. Voelcker. 325p. 1994. pap. 60.00 (*0-7918-0697-9*) ASME.

Proceedings of the 1993 International Symposium on Language Teaching Methodology, Beijing - Hohhot. Ed. by Fritz Konig et al. LC 97-172452. 498p. (C). 1995. lib. bdg. 25.00 (*0-9641511-2-X*) Assn Text Study.

Proceedings of the 1993 NSF Design & Manufacturing Systems Conference: The University of North Carolina at Charlotte, Mechanical Engineering & Engineering Science Department, Precision Engineering Laboratory, Charlotte, North Carolina, January 6-8, 1993, Vol. I. NSF Design & Manufacturing Systems Conference Staf. LC 92-64413. (Illus.). 981p. 1993. reprint ed. pap. 200.00 (*0-7837-9728-1*, 206045900001) Bks Demand.

Proceedings of the 1993 NSF Design & Manufacturing Systems Conference: The University of North Carolina at Charlotte, Mechanical Engineering & Engineering Science Department, Precision Engineering Laboratory, Charlotte, North Carolina, January 6-8, 1993, Vol. II. NSF Design & Manufacturing Systems Conference Staf. LC 92-64413. (Illus.). 972p. 1993. reprint ed. pap. 200.00 (*0-7837-9729-X*, 206045900002) Bks Demand.

Proceedings of the 1993 Professional Case Conference. (Proceedings of the Professional Case Conference Ser.: No. 5). (Illus.). 336p. (Orig.). 1994. pap. 34.50 (*1-885029-00-4*) Intl Homeopathy.

Proceedings of the 1993 Undergraduate Symposium on Research in Astronomy. Ed. by Priscilla J. Benson. 118p. (C). 1994. pap. text. write for info. (*1-882334-03-5*) Keck NE Astron.

Proceedings of the 1994 Canadian Conference on Electrical & Computer Engineering. IEEE (Region 7) Staff. Ed. by IEEE (Institute of Electrical & Electronics Engine. 800p. 1994. pap. write for info. (*0-7803-2416-1*); fiche. write for info. (*0-7803-2417-X*, 94TH8023) Inst Electrical.

Proceedings of the 1994 Conference of the American Academy of Advertising. Ed. by Karen W. King. 1994. pap. text, per. 25.00 (*0-931030-17-X*) Am Acad Advert.

Proceedings of the 1994 DOE/NREL Hydrogen Program Review (April 18-21, 1994) Thomas Cawthon. Ed. by National Renewable Energy Laboratory Staff. (Hydrogen Fuel Information Ser.: Vol. I). (Illus.). 476p. 1996. lib. bdg. 195.00 (*0-89934-262-0*, BT938) Bus Tech Bks.

Proceedings of the 1994 First International Joint Conference of the North American Fuzzy Information Processing Society. IEEE, Neural Networks Council Staff. Ed. by IEEE Staff. LC 94-78757. 420p. 1994. pap. write for info. (*0-7803-2125-1*); fiche. write for info. (*0-7803-2126-X*, 94TH8006) Inst Electrical.

Proceedings of the 1994 Professional Case Conference. Ed. by Stephen King et al. (Proceedings of the Professional Case Conference Ser.: No. 6). (Illus.). 400p. (Orig.). 1995. 34.50 (*1-885029-01-2*) Intl Homeopathy.

Proceedings of the 1994 Undergraduate Symposium on Research in Astronomy. Ed. by John E. Gaustad. 115p. (Orig.). (C). 1995. pap. text. write for info. (*1-882334-04-3*) Keck NE Astron.

Proceedings of the 1994 World Congress on Adventure Travel & Ecotourism. World Congress on Adventure Travel & Eco-Tourism S. Ed. by Adventure Travel Society Staff. (Illus.). 270p. (Orig.). 1995. pap. 50.00 (*1-885789-03-3*) Advent Trvl Soc.

Proceedings of the 1995 Aerofast Conference. 1995. pap. 69.00 (*1-56091-696-6*, P-295) Soc Auto Engineers.

Proceedings of the 1995 ASME-IEEE Joint Railroad Conference. IEEE (Vehicular Technology Society) Staff. Ed. by IEEE Staff et al. LC 90-644036. (ASME RTD Ser.: Vol. 9). 168p. 1995. pap. 86.00 (*0-7803-2556-7*, 95CH35766) Inst Electrical.

Proceedings of the 1995 ASME-IEEE Joint Railroad Conference. IEEE (Vehicular Technology Society) Staff. Ed. by IEEE Staff. LC 90-644036. 168p. 1995. lib. bdg. write for info. (*0-7803-2557-5*, 95CH35766); mic. film. write for info. (*0-7803-2558-3*, 95CH35766) Inst Electrical.

Proceedings of the 1995 Georgia Water Resources Conference: April 11-12, 1995, Athens, Georgia. Ed. by Kathryn J. Hatcher. LC 95-68015. 1995. write for info. (*0-935835-04-0*) Univ GA Eco.

Proceedings of the 1995 Global Vehicle Development Conference. LC 95-71541. 1995. pap. 34.00 (*1-56091-740-7*, P-298) Soc Auto Engineers.

Proceedings of the 1995 IEEE International Frequency Control Symposium. IEEE, Ultrasonics, Ferroelectrics & Frequency Cont. LC 87-654207. 930p. 1995. pap. text 146.00 (*0-7803-2500-1*, 95CH35752); lib. bdg. 146.00 (*0-7803-2501-X*, 95CB35752); fiche 146.00 (*0-7803-2502-8*, 95CM35752) Inst Electrical.

Proceedings of the 1995 IEEE International Symposium on Intelligent Control. IEEE Staff. LC 90-655042. 654p. 1995. pap. text 126.00 (*0-7803-2722-5*, 95CH35815); lib. bdg. 126.00 (*0-7803-2723-3*, 95CB35815) Inst Electrical.

Proceedings of the 1995 IEEE/Nagoya University World Wisepersons Workshop. IEEE Staff. Ed. by Institutes of Electrical & Electronics Engineers,. 150p. 1995. pap. text 92.00 (*4-9900266-2-4*, 95TH8148) Inst Electrical.

Proceedings of the 1995 IEEE/Nagoya University World Wisepersons Workshop. IEEE Staff. Ed. by Institute of Electrical & Electronics Engineers, I. 150p. 1995. fiche 92.00 (*0-7803-3097-8*, 95TM8148) Inst Electrical.

Proceedings of the 1995 International Computers in Engineering Conference & 1995 ASME Database Symposium: September 17-20, 1995 Boston, Massachusetts. Ed. by Ahmed A. Busnaina & Ravi Rangan. LC 95-80498. 1264p. 1995. 380.00 (*0-7918-1701-6*, H009) ASME.

Proceedings of the 1995 International Joint Power Generation Conference Vol. 1: Minneapolis, Minnesota - October 8-12, 1995, EC-Vol. 3/FACT-Vol. 20. Ed. by Scott M. Smouse & William F. Frazier. LC 95-80547. (EC Ser.: Vol. 3). 524p. 1995. 160.00 (*0-7918-1486-6*, G00981) ASME.

Proceedings of the 1995 International Joint Power Generation Conference Vol. 2: October 8-12, 1995 Minneapolis, Minnesota, NE-Vol. 17. Ed. by R. T. Laudenat. LC 95-80547. (NE Ser.: Vol. 17). 144p. 1995. 70.00 (*0-7918-1487-4*, G00982) ASME.

Proceedings of the 1995 International Joint Power Generation Conference Vol. 3: October 8-12, 1995 Minneapolis, Minnesota, PWR-Vol. 28. Ed. by I. Fruchtman et al. LC 95-80547. (PWR Ser.: Vol. 28). 548p. 1995. 168.00 (*0-7918-1488-2*, G00983) ASME.

Proceedings of the 1995 International Joint Power Generation Conference Vol. 4: October 8-12, 1995 Minneapolis, Minnesota, PWR-Vol. 29. Ed. by D. A. Kennedy. LC 95-80547. (PWR Ser.: Vol. 29). 164p. 1995. 80.00 (*0-7918-1489-0*, G00984) ASME.

Proceedings of the 1995 International Symposium & Workshop on Systems Engineering of Computer Based Systems. IEEE (Computer Society) Staff. Ed. by IEEE Staff. LC 95-75167. 400p. 1995. pap. write for info. (*0-7803-2531-1*, 95TH8053); mic. film. write for info. (*0-7803-2532-X*, 95TM8053) Inst Electrical.

Proceedings of the 1995 National Heat Transfer Conference: August 6-9, 1995, Portland, Oregon, Vol. 1. Ed. by Y. Bayazitoglu et al. 96p. 1995. 72.00 (*0-7918-1714-8*, H00996) ASME.

Proceedings of the 1995 National Heat Transfer Conference: August 6-9, 1995, Portland, Oregon, Vol. 1. Ed. by W. J. Bryan & J. V. Beck. 196p. 1995. 100.00 (*0-7918-1711-3*, H00993) ASME.

Proceedings of the 1995 National Heat Transfer Conference: August 6-9, 1995, Portland, Oregon, Vol. 1. Ed. by F. B. Cheung et al. 128p. 1995. 76.00 (*0-7918-1715-6*, H00997) ASME.

Proceedings of the 1995 National Heat Transfer Conference: August 6-9, 1995, Portland, Oregon, Vol. 1. Ed. by Kem M. Obasih et al. 108p. 1995. 72.00 (*0-7918-1712-1*, H00994) ASME.

Proceedings of the 1995 National Heat Transfer Conference: August 6-9, 1995, Portland, Oregon, Vol. 1. Ed. by A. Ortega & S. P. Mulay. 164p. 1995. 88.00 (*0-7918-1702-4*, H00984) ASME.

Proceedings of the 1995 National Heat Transfer Conference: August 6-9, 1995, Portland, Oregon, Vol. 1. Ed. by V. Sernas et al. 192p. 1995. 100.00 (*0-7918-1713-X*, H00995) ASME.

Proceedings of the 1995 National Heat Transfer Conference: August 6-9, 1995, Portland, Oregon, Vol. 3. Ed. by S. S. Sadhal et al. 200p. 1995. 100.00 (*0-7918-1704-0*, H00986) ASME.

Proceedings of the 1995 National Heat Transfer Conference: August 6-9, 1995, Portland, Oregon, Vol. 4. Ed. by R. L. Mahajan. 264p. 1995. 112.00 (*0-7918-1705-9*, H00987) ASME.

Proceedings of the 1995 National Heat Transfer Conference: August 6-9, 1995, Portland, Oregon, Vol. 5. Ed. by S. Downing et al. 156p. 1995. 88.00 (*0-7918-1706-7*, H00988) ASME.

Proceedings of the 1995 National Heat Transfer Conference: August 6-9, 1995, Portland, Oregon, Vol. 6. Ed. by V. K. Dhir. 156p. 1995. 88.00 (*0-7918-1707-5*, H00989) ASME.

Proceedings of the 1995 National Heat Transfer Conference: August 6-9, 1995, Portland, Oregon, Vol. 7. M. L. Hunt. 108p. 1995. 72.00 (*0-7918-1708-3*, H00990) ASME.

Proceedings of the 1995 National Heat Transfer Conference: August 6-9, 1995, Portland, Oregon, Vol. 8. Ed. by I. S. Habib et al. 204p. 1995. 100.00 (*0-7918-1709-1*, H00991) ASME.

Proceedings of the 1995 National Heat Transfer Conference: August 6-9, 1995, Portland, Oregon, Vol. 9. Ed. by G. C. Vradis & K. A. Woodbury. 208p. 1995. 100.00 (*0-7918-1710-5*, H00992) ASME.

Proceedings of the 1995 National Heat Transfer Conference Vol. 2: August 6-9, 1995, Portland, Oregon, Vol. 2. Ed. by R. B. Peterson et al. 148p. 1995. 80.00 (*0-7918-1703-2*, H00985) ASME.

Proceedings of the 1995 Noise & Vibration Conference. 1234p. 1995. 149.00 (*1-56091-666-4*, P-291) Soc Auto Engineers.

Proceedings of the 1995 Particle Accelerator Conference. IEEE (Nuclear & Plasma Sciences Society) Staff. LC 88-647453. 3780p. 1995. pap. text 388.00 (*0-7803-2934-1*, 95CH35843); lib. bdg. 388.00 (*0-7803-2935-X*, 95CB35843); fiche 388.00 (*0-7803-2936-8*, 95CM35843) Inst Electrical.

Proceedings of the 1995 Professional Case Conference, No. 7. Ed. by Stephen King et al. (Illus.). 387p. (Orig.). 1996. pap. 34.50 (*1-885029-02-0*) Intl Homeopathy.

Proceedings of the 1995 Rapid Excavation Tunneling Conference. Ed. by G. Williamson & I. M. Gowring. LC 95-67821. (Illus.). 844p. 1995. text 83.00 (*0-87335-132-0*, 132-0) SMM&E Inc.

Proceedings of the 1995 SAE Alternative Fuels Conference. 386p. 1995. 85.00 (*1-56091-686-9*, P-294) Soc Auto Engineers.

Proceedings of the 1995 Small Engine Technology Conference. 498p. 1995. 99.00 (*1-56091-673-7*, P-292) Soc Auto Engineers.

Proceedings of the 1995 Undergraduate Symposium on Research in Astronomy. Ed. by Debra M. Elmegreen. 1995. pap. text. write for info. (*1-882334-05-1*) Keck NE Astron.

Proceedings of the 1995 World Congress on Neural Networks, 3 vols. Ed. by INNS Staff. (INNS Series of Texts, Monographs, & Proceedings). 1995. pap. 325.00 (*0-8058-2240-2*) L Erlbaum Assocs.

Proceedings of the 1995 21st Annual Northeast Bioengineering Conference. IEEE (Engineering in Medicine & Biology Society) S. Ed. by IEEE (Institute of Electrical & Electronics Engine. LC 88-646567. 150p. 1995. pap. text. write for info. (*0-7803-2692-X*, 95CH35807); lib. bdg. write for info. (*0-7803-2693-8*, 95CH35807); mic. film. write for info. (*0-7803-2694-6*, 95CH35807) Inst Electrical.

Proceedings of the 1996 Aerofast Conference. 1996. 69.00 (*1-56091-860-8*, P-302) Soc Auto Engineers.

Proceedings of the 1996 ASME/IEEE Joint Railroad Conference. IEEE (Vehicular Technology Society) Staff. Ed. by IEEE Staff. LC 90-644036. 260p. 1996. pap. text 108.00 (*0-7803-3351-9*, 96CH35947); lib. bdg. 108.00 (*0-7803-3352-7*, 96CB35947); fiche 108.00 (*0-7803-3353-5*, 96CM35947) Inst Electrical.

Proceedings of the 1996 Distributed Multimedia Systems Workshop. Ed. by Knowledge Systems Institute Staff. (Illus.). 300p. (Orig.). 1996. pap. 25.00 (*0-9641699-4-0*) Knowldge Systs.

Proceedings of the 1996 Dubai International Equine Symposium: The Equine Athlete: Tendon, Ligament & Soft Tissue Injuries. Ed. by Norman W. Rantanen & Michael L. Hanser. (Illus.). 448p. 1996. write for info. (*0-9656603-0-3*) M R Rantanen.

Proceedings of the 1996 IEEE International Frequency Control Symposium. IEEE Staff. 1000p. 1996. write for info. (*0-7803-3311-X*); pap. text. write for info. (*0-7803-3309-8*); lib. bdg. write for info. (*0-7803-3310-1*) Inst Electrical.

An Asterisk (*) at the beginning of an entry indicates that the title is appearing for the first time.

Proceedings of the 1996 IEEE International Symposium on Intelligent Control. IEEE (Control Systems Society) Staff. Ed. by IEEE Staff. 800p. 1996. pap. text 142.00 (0-7803-2978-3, 96CH35855); lib. bdg. 142.00 (0-7803-2979-1, 96CB35855); mic. film 142.00 (0-7803-2980-5, 96CM35855) Inst Electrical.

Proceedings of the 1996 IEEE National Radar Conference. IEEE (Aerospace & Electronic System Society) Staff. LC 88-652183. 500p. 1996. pap. text 118.00 (0-7803-3145-1, 96CH35891); lib. bdg. 118.00 (0-7803-3146-X, 96CB35891); fiche 118.00 (0-7803-3147-8, 96CM35891) Inst Electrical.

Proceedings of the 1996 International Conference on Outdoor Recreation & Education (ICORE) Back to the Basics. (Illus.). 250p. 1997. pap. 30.00 (1-891101-00-5) O R C A.

Proceedings of the 1996 IPC Conference & Exposition. 192p. 1996. 74.00 (1-56091-828-4, P-300) Soc Auto Engineers.

Proceedings of the 1996 National Sensor Conference, Delft, The Netherlands. Ed. by M. R. Wolffenbuttel. (Illus.). x, 245p. 1996. pap. 67.50 (90-407-1321-9, Pub. by Delft U Pr) Coronet Bks.

Proceedings of the 1996 Professional Case Conference. Ed. by Stephen King et al. 336p. (Orig.). 1997. pap. text 34.00 (1-885029-03-9) Intl Homeopathy.

Proceedings of the 1996 Sugar Processing Research Conference. Ed. by Margaret A. Clarke. (Illus.). 534p. (Orig.). 1996. pap. text 100.00 (1-883326-05-2) Sugar Process Res.

Proceedings of the 1996 Undergraduate Symposium on Research in Astronomy. Ed. by Priscilla J. Benson. (Orig.). (C). 1996. pap. text. write for info. (1-882334-06-X) Keck NE Astron.

Proceedings of the 1996 Workshop on Data Encoding for Page-Oriented Optical Memories. Ed. by Pericles A. Mitkas. (Illus.). (C). 1997. pap. text 40.00 (0-9624477-1-4) CSU Coll Eng.

Proceedings of the 1996 World Congress on Neural Networks. International Neural Network Society Staff. (INNS Series of Texts, Monographs, & Proceedings). 1424p. 1996. pap. 395.00 (0-8058-2608-4) L Erlbaum Assocs.

Proceedings of the 1997 Dubai International Equine Symposium: The Diagnosis & Treatment of Respiratory Disease. Ed. by Norman W. Rantanen & Michael L. Hanser. (Illus.). 460p. 1997. write for info. (0-9656603-1-1) M R Rantanen.

Proceedings of the 1997 Fuel Tank Flammability Conference. 1997. pap. 49.00 (0-7680-0111-0) Soc Auto Engineers.

Proceedings of the 1997 Georgia Water Resources Conference: March 20-22, 1997 Athens, Georgia. Ed. by Kathryn J. Hatcher. LC 97-71355. 1997. write for info. (0-935835-05-9) Univ GA Eco.

Proceedings of the 1997 International Topical Meeting on LWR Fuel Performance: Portland, Oregon, March 2-6, 1997. International Topical Meeting on LWR Fuel Performance et al. LC 97-216081. (Illus.). 1997. write for info. (0-89448-616-0) Am Nuclear Soc.

Proceedings of the 1997 Noise & Vibration Conference. 1997. 269.00 (0-7680-0012-2, P-309) Soc Auto Engineers.

Proceedings of the 1997 Professional Case Conference, Vol. IX. Ed. by Lucy Vaughter. (Illus.). 400p. (Orig.). 1998. pap. 34.50 (1-885029-04-7) Intl Homeopathy.

Proceedings of the 1997 SAE Aerospace Automated Fastening Conference. LC 97-217906. 1997. pap. 69.00 (0-7680-0100-5) Soc Auto Engineers.

Proceedings of the 1997 Sensors & Electron Devices Symposium. Ed. by Kelly McVey. (Illus.). 425p. (Orig.). 1997. pap. write for info. (0-9603590-8-7) ERI MI.

Proceedings of the 1997 Total Life Cycle Conference, 2 pts. Total Life Cycle Conference Staff. Incl. Procedings of the 1997 Total Life Cycle Conference Pt. I: Life Cycle Management & Assessment. LC 97-66290. 1997. 79.00 (0-7680-0017-3, P-310); Procedings of the 1997 Total Life Cycle Conference Pt. II: Design for the Environment, Recycling & Environmental Act. LC 97-66290. 1997. 79.00 (0-7680-0018-1, P-311); LC 97-66290. Set text 125.00 (0-7680-0019-X) Soc Auto Engineers.

Proceedings of the 1998 Advances in Aviation Safety Conference. LC 97-81109. 1998. pap. 129.00 (0-7680-0130-7) Soc Auto Engineers.

Proceedings of the 1998 Aerospace Power Systems Conference. 1998. pap. 85.00 (0-7680-0188-9) Soc Auto Engineers.

***Proceedings of the 1998 ANS Radiation Protectino & Shielding Division Topical Conference, Technologies for the New Century: Nashville, Tennessee, april 19-23, 1998, 2.** 1178p. 1998. pap. 125.00 (0-89448-637-3, 700259) Am Nuclear Soc.

Proceedings of the 1998 IAM Conference & Exposition. 1998. pap. 55.00 (0-7680-0195-1, P-323) Soc Auto Engineers.

Proceedings of the 1998 Icpp Workshops: Architectural & Os Support for Multimedia Applications : Flexible Communication Systems : Wireless Networks & Mobile Computing, Minneapolis, Minnesota, August 14, 1998. IEEE Computer Society Staff et al. LC 98-86578. vii, 155 p. 1998. write for info. (0-8186-8660-X) IEEE Comp Soc.

***Proceedings of the 1998 IEEE Hong Kong Electron Devices Meeting: 29 August, 1998, Hong Kong University of Science & Technology** IEEE Hong Kong Electron Devices Meeting Staff et al. LC 98-85263. vii, 164 p. 1998. pap. write for info. (0-7803-4933-4) Inst Electrical.

Proceedings of the 1998 Second IEEE International Caracas Conference on Devices, Circuits & Systems, Isla De Margarita, Venezuela, March 2-4, 1998. IEEE Electron Devices Society Staff & Universidad Simbon Bolbivar Staff. LC 97-81048. xix, 461 p. 1998. pap. write for info. (0-7803-4435-9) IEEE Standards.

Proceedings of the 2nd Annual Symposium on Operating Systems Design & Implementation (OSDI '96) Ed. by Karin Petersen & Willy Zwaenepoel. 300p. (Orig.). 1996. pap. 27.00 (1-880446-82-0) USENIX Assn.

Proceedings of the 2nd International Conference on Principles of Knowledge Representation & Reasoning. Ed. by James Allen et al. (Representation & Reasoning Ser.). 602p. (C). 1991. pap. text 44.95 (1-55860-165-1) Morgan Kaufmann.

***Proceedings of the 2nd Topical Meeting on Decontamination, Decommissioning & Reutilization of Commercial & Governemtn Facilites: Knoxville, Tennessee, September 12-16, 1999.** 1999. cd-rom 100.00 (0-89448-645-4, 700269) Am Nuclear Soc.

Proceedings of the 20th Annual Boston University Conference on Language Development. Ed. by Andy Stringfellow et al. (BUCLD Proceedings Ser.: Vol. 20). (Illus.). 872p. (C). 1996. pap. 50.00 (1-57473-012-6); lib. bdg. 96.00 (1-57473-112-2) Cascadilla Pr.

Proceedings of the 20th Century British Dielectrics Society Meeting on Ferroelectrics & Related Dielectric Phenomena in Ordered Material. D. K. Das Gupta & S. B. Lang. 260p. 1987. pap. text 533.00 (2-88124-276-6) Gordon & Breach.

Proceedings of the 20th International Conference on Parallel Processing 1991, Vol. I: Architecture, Set. Chuan-Lin Wu & Tse-Yun Feng. 760p. 1991. boxed set 79.95 (0-8493-0191-2) CRC Pr.

Proceedings of the 20th International Conference on Parallel Processing 1991, Vol. II: Software, Vol. 2. Herbert D. Schwetman & Tse-Yun Feng. 330p. 1991. boxed set 69.95 (0-8493-0192-0) CRC Pr.

Proceedings of the 20th International Conference on Parallel Processing 1991, Vol. III: Algorithms & Applications, Vol. 3. Tse-Yun Feng. Ed. by Kimming So. 336p. 1991. boxed set 69.95 (0-8493-0193-9) CRC Pr.

Proceedings of the 20th International Symposium on Shock Waves, 2 vols. 2000p. 1997. lib. bdg. write for info. (981-02-2957-7); lib. bdg. write for info. (981-02-2958-5) World Scientific Pub.

Proceedings of the 20th International Technical Conference on Coal Utilization & Fuel Systems. (Illus.). 780p. 1995. pap. text 395.00 (0-932066-20-8) Coal Slurry Tech.

Proceedings of the 21st Annual Boston University Conference on Language Development. Ed. by Elizabeth Hughes et al. (BUCLD Proceedings Ser.: Vol. 21). (Illus.). 739p. (C). 1997. pap. 50.00 (1-57473-022-3); lib. bdg. 96.00 (1-57473-122-X) Cascadilla Pr.

Proceedings of the 21st Century Chinese Astronomy Conference Dedicated to Professor C. C. Lin. Ed. by K. L. Chan & K. S. Cheng. 600p. 1997. text 86.00 (981-02-3226-8) World Scientific Pub.

Proceedings of the 21st European Conference on Optical Communication. IEEE (Lasers & Electro-Optics Society & Electron D. Ed. by IEEE (Institute of Electrical & Electronics Engine. 1150p. 1995. pap. write for info. (0-614-07779-6, 95TH8127) Inst Electrical.

Proceedings of the 21st International Technical Conference on Coal Utilization & Fuel Systems. 21st ed. Ed. by Barbara A. Sakkestad. (Illus.). 843p. 1996. pap. text 395.00 (0-932066-21-6) Coal Slurry Tech.

Proceedings of the 22nd European Conference on Optical Communication: ECOC 96. IEEE (Lasers & Electro-Optics Society) Staff. Ed. by IEEE (Institute of Electrical & Electronics Engine. 1100p. 1996. pap. write for info. (0-614-18164-X, 96TH8217); fiche. write for info. (0-7803-3603-8, 96TH8217) Inst Electrical.

Proceedings of the 22nd International Technical Conference on Coal Utilization & Fuel Systems. (Illus.). 966p. 1997. pap. text 395.00 (0-932066-22-4) Coal Slurry Tech.

Proceedings of the 23rd International Conference on Parallel Processing (ICPP) Vols. I-III, Set. Ed. by Tse-yun Feng. 1040p. 1994. 169.95 (0-8493-2496-3, 2496) CRC Pr.

Proceedings of the 24th International Conference on Parallel Processing, Set, Vols. 1-4. Ed. by Tse-yun Feng. 1995. write for info. (0-8493-2619-2, 2619) CRC Pr.

Proceedings of the 26th International Symposium on Application of Computers & Operations Research in the Mineral Industry. Ed. by R. V. Ramani. LC 96-69563. (Illus.). 548p. 1996. 95.00 (0-87335-137-1) SMM&E Inc.

Proceedings of the 27th Annual Child Language Research Forum. Eve Clark. 241p. 1996. 69.95 (1-57586-021-X); pap. 22.95 (1-57586-020-1) CSLI.

Proceedings of the 28th International Conference on High Energy Physics. 1600p. 1997. lib. bdg. 92.00 (981-02-2874-0) World Scientific Pub.

Proceedings of the 29th International Congress of the International Society for Applied Ethology. Ed. by S. M. Rutter et al. 250p. 1995. pap. 100.00 (0-900767-92-8, Pub. by Univs Fed Animal Welfare) St Mut.

Proceedings of the 3rd DARPA Message Understanding Evaluation & Conference. (C). 1998. pap. text 40.00 (1-55860-236-4) Morgan Kaufmann.

Proceedings of the 3rd International Conference on Rare Earth Development & Applications Held in Baotou, Inner Mongolia, China on August 21-25, 1995 by the Chinese Society of Rare Earths, Vols. 1 & 2. Ed. by Xu Guangxian et al. 1301p. 1996. 185.00 (7-5024-1748-6, Pub. by Sci Pr) Lubrecht & Cramer.

Proceedings of the 3rd International Congress on Neo-Adjuvant Chemotherapy. Ed. by P. Banzet et al. (Illus.). 477p. 1992. 174.00 (0-387-55039-9) Spr-Verlag.

Proceedings of the 3rd International Symposium on Coal Combustion Science & Technology. Ed. by Xuchang Xu & Lixing Zhou. 652p. 1996. 78.50 (7-03-004954-3, Pub. by Sci Pr) Lubrecht & Cramer.

Proceedings of the 3rd International Symposium on Reservoir Wettability & Its Effect on Oil Recovery. Norman R. Morrow. (Illus.). viii, 200p. 1996. 50.00 (0-941570-17-7) U of Wyoming.

Proceedings of the 30th Annual International Carnahan Conference on Security Technology. IEEE (Aerospace & Electronic Systems Society) Staf. Ed. by IEEE (Institute of Electrical & Electronics Engine. LC 79-644630. 250p. 1996. pap. text. write for info. (0-7803-3537-6, 96CH35975); lib. bdg. write for info. (0-7803-3538-4, 96CB35975); fiche. write for info. (0-7803-3539-2, 96CM35975) Inst Electrical.

Proceedings of the 30th International Geological Congress, 26 vols. Incl. Energy & Mineral Resources for the 21st Century: Vol.9: Geology of Mineral Deposits & Mineral Economics. Ed. by Pei Rongfu. LC 99-496385. (Illus.). 521p. 1998. 149.50 (90-6764-264-9, Pub. by VSP); Geology of Fossil Fuels Vol. 18, Pt. A: Oil & Gas. Ed. by Sun Zhaocai. LC 99-496383. (Illus.). 368p. 1997. 115.00 (90-6764-234-7, Pub. by VSP); Geology of Fossil Fuels Vol. 18, Pt. B: Coal. Ed. by Yang Qi. LC 99-496375. (Illus.). 166p. 1997. 82.50 (90-6764-238-X, Pub. by VSP); Geosciences & Human Survival Vols. 2 & 3: Environment, Natural Hazards & Global Change. Ed. by Zhang Zonghu. LC 99-496370. (Illus.). 380p. 1998. 115.00 (90-6764-260-6, Pub. by VSP); Structure of the Lithosphere & Deep Processes. Ed. by Hong Dawei. LC 99-496410. (Illus.). 176p. 1997. 82.50 (90-6764-261-4, Pub. by VSP); Vol. 1. Origin & History of the Earth. Ed. by Hongzhen Wang. LC 99-496380. (Illus.). 224p. 1997. 95.00 (90-6764-248-7, Pub. by VSP); Vol. 5. Contemporary Lithospheric Motion in Seismic Geology. Ed. by Ye Hong. LC 99-496372. (Illus.). 264p. 1997. 99.50 (90-6764-269-X, Pub. by VSP); Vol. 6. Global Tectonic Zones, Supercontinent Formation & Disposal. Ed. by Xiao Xuchang & Liu Hefu. LC 99-496376. (Illus.). 174p. 1997. 85.00 (90-6764-262-2, Pub. by VSP); Vol. 7. Orogenic Belts & Geological Mapping. Ed. by Hemin Koyi. LC 99-496374. (Illus.). 176p. 1997. 82.50 (90-6764-263-0, Pub. by VSP); Vol. 8. Basin Analysis & Global Sedimentary Geology. Ed. by Liu Baojun & Li Sitian. LC 99-496386. (Illus.). 374p. 1997. 115.00 (90-6764-244-4, Pub. by VSP); Vol. 10. New Technology for Geosciences. Ed. by Guo Huadong. LC 99-496392. (Illus.). 274p. 1997. 99.50 (90-6764-265-7, Pub. by VSP); Vol. 11. Stratigraphy. Ed. by Wang Naiwen & J. Remane. LC 99-496378. (Illus.). 246p. 1997. 95.00 (90-6764-274-6, Pub. by VSP); Vol. 12. Palaeontology & Historical Geology. Ed. by Jin Yu-Gan & D. Dineley. LC 99-496391. (Illus.). 198p. 1997. 92.50 (90-6764-257-6, Pub. by VSP); Vol. 13. Marine Geology & Palaeoceanography. Ed. by Wang Pingxian & W. A. Berggren. LC 99-496379. (Illus.). 148p. 1997. 72.50 (90-6764-242-8, Pub. by VSP); Vol. 14. Structural Geology & Geomechanics. Ed. by Zheng Yadong. LC 99-496364. (Illus.). 322p. 1997. 110.00 (90-6764-249-5, Pub. by VSP); Vol. 15. Igneous Tetrology. Ed. by Li Zhaonai. LC 99-496389. (Illus.). 220p. 1998. 92.50 (90-6764-246-0, Pub. by VSP); Vol. 16. Mineralogy. Ed. by Huang Yunhui & Cao Yawen. LC 99-496390. (Illus.). 308p. 1997. 105.00 (90-6764-266-5, Pub. by VSP); Vol. 17. Precambrian Geology & Metamorphic Petrology. Ed. by Qian Xianglin. LC 99-496382. (Illus.). 356p. 1998. 120.00 (90-6764-275-4, Pub. by VSP); Vol. 19. Geochemistry. Ed. by Xie Xuejing. LC 99-496377. (Illus.). 394p. 1997. 97.50 (90-6764-267-3, Pub. by VSP); Vol. 20. Geophysics. Ed. by Liu Guangding. LC 99-496387. (Illus.). 194p. 1997. 87.50 (90-6764-241-X, Pub. by VSP); Vol. 21. Quaternary Geology. Ed. by An Zhisheng & Zhou Weijian. LC 99-496397. (Illus.). 176p. 1997. 82.50 (90-6764-243-6, Pub. by VSP); Vol. 22. Hydrogeology. Ed. by Fei Jin & N. C. Krothe. LC 99-496395. (Illus.). 324p. 1997. 115.00 (90-6764-253-3, Pub. by VSP); Vol. 23. Engineering Geology. Ed. by Wang Sijing & P. Marinos. (Illus.). 544p. 1997. 152.00 (90-6764-240-1, Pub. by VSP); Vol. 24. Environmental Geology. Ed. by Yuan Daoxian. LC 99-496373. (Illus.). 304p. 1997. 99.50 (90-6764-239-8, Pub. by VSP); Vol. 25. Mathematical Geology & Geoinformatics. Ed. by Zhao Pengda. LC 99-496371. (Illus.). 170p. 1998. 79.50 (90-6764-268-1, Pub. by VSP); Vol. 26. Comparative Planetology, Geological Education & History of Geosciences. Ed. by Wang Hongzhen. LC 99-496381. 316p. 1997. 110.00 (90-6764-254-1, Pub. by VSP); 1895.00 (90-6764-276-2, Pub. by VSP) Coronet Bks.

Proceedings of the 30th Intersociety Energy Conversion Engineering Conference. IEEE (Electron Devices Society & Aerospace & Elect. Ed. by IEEE (Institute of Electrical & Electronics Engine. 2400p. 1995. lib. bdg. 350.00 (0-7803-2771-3, 95CB35829); mic. film 350.00 (0-7803-2772-1, 95CM35829) Inst Electrical.

Proceedings of the 30th Intersociety Energy Conversion Engineering Conference, 3 vols. IEEE (Electron Devices Society & Aerospace & Elect. Ed. by IEEE (Institute of Electrical & Electronics Engine et al. LC 94-25069. 1962p. 1995. pap. 350.00 (0-7918-1221-9, 95CH35829) Inst Electrical.

Proceedings of the 31st Meeting of the European High Pressure Research Group. Ed. by Brendan Austin. 368p. 1995. pap. text 653.00 (2-88449-024-8) Gordon & Breach.

Proceedings of the 32nd Annual Meeting of the Institute of Environmental Sciences: Environmental Technology-Coming of Age. 569p. 1986. 125.00 (0-915414-26-0) IEST.

Proceedings of the 33rd Annual Highway Geology Symposium: Engineering Geology & Environmental Constraints in Vail, Colorado, 1982. Ed. by Jeffrey L. Hynes. (Special Publications: No. 22). (Illus.). 286p. (Orig.). 1983. pap. 7.00 (1-884216-42-0) Colo Geol Survey.

***Proceedings of the 33rd Intersociety Energy Conversion Engineering Conference - IECEC '98: Colorado Springs, Colorado, August 2-8, 1998.** 1998. cd-rom 320.00 (0-89448-639-X, 700262) Am Nuclear Soc.

Proceedings of the 34th IEEE Conference on Decision & Control. IEEE (Control Systems Society) Staff. Ed. by IEEE (Institute of Electrical & Electronics Engine. LC 79-640961. 4712p. 1995. pap. text 426.00 (0-7803-2685-7, 95CH35803); lib. bdg. 426.00 (0-7803-2686-5, 95CB35803); fiche 426.00 (0-7803-2687-3, 95CM35803) Inst Electrical.

Proceedings of the 34th SICE Annual Conference. IEEE (Industrial Electronics Society, Tokyo Sectio. Ed. by IEEE (Institute of Electrical & Electronics Engine. 1995. fiche 114.00 (0-7803-2782-9, 95TM8107) Inst Electrical.

Proceedings of the 35th IEEE Conference on Decision & Control. IEEE (Control Systems Society) Staff. Ed. by IEEE (Institute of Electrical & Electronics Engine. LC 79-640961. 4000p. 1997. pap. text. write for info. (0-7803-3590-2, 96CH35989); lib. bdg. write for info. (0-7803-3591-0, 96CB35989); fiche. write for info. (0-7803-3592-9, 96CM35989) Inst Electrical.

Proceedings of the 36th Annual Conference of the American Translators Association (ATA) - 1995. Ed. by Peter W. Krawutschke. 508p. 1995. pap. 50.00 (1-57387-023-4) Info Today Inc.

Proceedings of the 38th Midwest Symposium on Circuits & Systems. IEEE (Circuits & Systems Society) Staff. Ed. by IEEE Staff. LC 79-645128. 1700p. 1996. pap. text 214.00 (0-7803-2972-4, 95CH35853); lib. bdg. 214.00 (0-7803-2973-2, 95CB35853); fiche 214.00 (0-7803-2974-0, 95CM35853) Inst Electrical.

Proceedings of the 39th Colloquium on the Law of Outer Space: Beijing, China. 381p. 1997. 94.95 (1-56347-251-1) AIAA.

Proceedings of the 39th Staff Car Crash Conference. 480p. 1995. pap. 89.00 (1-56091-741-5, P-299) Soc Auto Engineers.

Proceedings of the 4th Annual L5 Space Development Conference, Apr. 25-28, 1985, Washington, D.C. Ed. by Frank Hecker. (Science & Technology Ser.: Vol. 68). (Illus.). 268p. 1988. pap. 35.00 (0-87703-273-4, Am Astronaut Soc) Univelt Inc.

Proceedings of the 4th Experimental Chaos Conference: Boca Raton, Florida, USA, 6-8 August ,1997. M. Z. Ding. 1999. 86.00 (981-02-3743-X) World Scientific Pub.

Proceedings of the 4th International Congress of Acarology, Saalfelden, Austria. E. Piffl. (ENG, FRE & GER.). 752p. (C). 1979. 180.00 (963-05-1695-0, Pub. by Akade Kiado) St Mut.

Proceedings of the 4th Rio de Janeiro International Workshop on Relativistic Aspects of Nuclear Physics: August 28-30, 1995, Centro Brasileiro de Pesquisas Fisicas, Rio de Janeiro, Brasil. Takeshi Kodama. LC 96-21776. 540p. 1996. write for info. (981-02-2734-5) World Scientific Pub.

Proceedings of the 4th Workshop on Thermal Field Theories & Their Applications. Ed. by X. Y. Gui et al. LC 96-16480. 472p. 1996. write for info. (981-02-2649-7) World Scientific Pub.

Proceedings of the 41st Annual ISA Analysis Division Symposium Vol. 29: 1996: Presented at Sheraton Tara Hotel, Framingham, MA, April 21-24, 1996. ISA Analysis Division Symposium Staff. LC 63-25575. (Analysis Division Ser.: No. 29). (Illus.). 368p. 1996. reprint ed. pap. 114.10 (0-608-04251-X, 206500700012) Bks Demand.

Proceedings of the 42nd International Instrumentation Symposium: Presented at Catamaran Resort Hotel, San Diego, CA, May 5-9, 1996, Sponsored by Aerospace Industries Division & Test Measurement Division of the Instrument Society of America. International Instrumentation Symposium Staff. LC 63-25575. (Illus.). 652p. reprint ed. pap. 200.00 (0-608-20413-7, 207166600002) Bks Demand.

Proceedings of the 42nd International Instrumentation Symposium: Presented at Catamaran Resort Hotel, San Diego, California, May 5-9, 1996. International Instrumentation Symposium Staff. LC 63-25575. (Illus.). 652p. 1996. reprint ed. pap. 200.00 (0-608-04244-7, 206500000012) Bks Demand.

Proceedings of the 48th Industrial Waste Conference: Purdue University, May 1993. Ed. by Ronald F. Wukasch & Cynthia S. Dalton. 896p. 1993. lib. bdg. 129.00 (1-56670-063-9, L1063) Lewis Pubs.

Proceedings of the 5th Biennial Conference of the International Society for Scientometrics & Informetrics (ISSI) Ed. by Michael E. Koenig & Abraham Bookstein. 703p. 1995. pap. 79.00 (1-57387-010-2) Info Today Inc.

Proceedings of the 5th Ethylene Producers Conference. Ed. by Ethylene Producers' Committee of AIChE's Fuels & P. (Technical Manual - Ethylene Producers Ser.: Vol. 2). 584p. 1994. 50.00 (0-8169-0648-3, T-92) Am Inst Chem Eng.

Proceedings of the 5th International Conference on Molton Slags, Fluxes & Salts '97: June 5-8, 1997, Sydney, Australia. LC 96-78210. (Illus.). 894p. 1996. pap. 200.00 (0-608-05571-9, 206603100006) Bks Demand.

Proceedings of the 5th International Symposium on the Biology of the Zygaenidae (Insecta, Lepidoptera) Grietherbusch (Germany) 10-12 September 1993. Ed. by W. Gerald Tremewan et al. (Theses Zoologicae Ser.: Vol. 30). (Illus.). 289p. 1998. text 90.00 (3-87429-409-9, Pub. by Koeltz Sci Bks) Lubrecht & Cramer.

P

Proceedings of the 5th U. S. National Conference on Earthquake Engineering. (Illus.). 4000p. 1994. 200.00 (0-943198-46-1, NCP-5) Earthquake Eng.

Proceedings of the 5th Workshop on the Chemistry & Fate of Modern Pesticides. Ed. by Juan Albaiges. 342p. 1996. pap. text 60.00 (90-5699-074-8) Gordon & Breach.

Proceedings of the 50th Purdue Industrial Waste Conference. Ed. by Ronald F. Wukasch & Cynthia S. Dalton. (Purdue Industrial Waste Conference Ser.). 855p. (C). 1997. ring bd. 94.95 (1-57504-022-0) CRC Pr.

Proceedings of the 51st Purdue Industrial Waste Conference. Ed. by Ronald F. Wukasch & Cynthia S. Dalton. (Purdue Industrial Waste Conference Ser.). 850p. (C). 1997. ring bd. 94.95 (1-57504-052-2) CRC Pr.

Proceedings of the 58th Annual Meeting of the American Society for Information Science (ASIS) Ed. by Thomas E. Kinney. 258p. 1995. pap. 45.00 (1-57387-017-X) Info Today Inc.

Proceedings of the 6th Ethylene Producers Conference. Ed. by Ethylene Producers' Committee of AIChE's Fuels & P. (Technical Manual - Ethylene Producers Ser.: Vol. 3). 714p. 1994. 50.00 (0-8169-0662-9, T-95) Am Inst Chem Eng.

Proceedings of the 6th International Mine Ventilation Symposium. Ed. by Raja V. Ramani. LC 96-72548. (Illus.). 568p. 1997. text 95.00 (0-87335-146-0, 146-0) SMM&E Inc.

Proceedings of the 6th U. S. Mine Ventilation Symposium: June 21-23, 1993, Salt Lake City, Utah. fac. ed. Mine Ventilation Symposium Staff. LC 93-83949. (Illus.). 652p. 1993. reprint ed. pap. 200.00 (0-7837-7869-4, 204762600007) Bks Demand.

Proceedings of the 7th Biennial Conference on Computational Techniques & Applications: CTAC '95. 896p. 1996. lib. bdg. 106.00 (981-02-2820-1) World Scientific Pub.

Proceedings of the 7th Ethylene Producers Conference. Ed. by Ethylene Producers' Committee of AIChE's Fuels & P. (Technical Manual - Ethylene Producers Ser.: Vol. 4). 520p. 1995. 50.00 (0-8169-0686-6, T-98) Am Inst Chem Eng.

Proceedings of the 7th International Congress of Accountants, 1957. (Foundations of Accounting Ser.). 720p. 1988. reprint ed. text 20.00 (0-8240-6142-X) Garland.

Proceedings of the 7th International Symposium on Trichoptera, Ume, Sweden, 3-8 August 1992. Ed. by C. Otto. (Illus.). 312p. 1993. 105.00 (90-73348-27-7, Pub. by Backhuys Pubs) Balogh.

Proceedings of the 7th International Workshop on Multiparticle Production: Correlations & Fluctuations. 400p. 1997. lib. bdg. 64.00 (981-02-2887-2) World Scientific Pub.

Proceedings of the 7th U. S. Mine Ventilation Symposium. Ed. & Intro. by A. M. Wala. LC 95-67820. (Illus.). 524p. 1995. text 105.00 (0-87335-133-9, 133-9) SMM&E Inc.

Proceedings of the 7th U. S. Mine Ventilation Symposium Held in Lexington, Kentucky on June 5-7, 1995. Mine Ventilation Symposium Staff. Ed. by A. M. Wala. LC 95-67820. (Illus.). 524p. 1995. reprint ed. pap. 162.50 (0-608-01703-5, 206235800002) Bks Demand.

Proceedings of the 7th World Congress on Pain. Ed. by Gerald F. Gebhart et al. LC 94-12699. (Progress in Pain Research & Management Ser.: Vol. 2). (Illus.). 950p. 1994. 40.00 (0-931092-07-8, PPRM2) Intl Assn Study Pain.

*Proceedings of the 77th Annual Meeting Technical Program of the FSCT. Federation of Societies for Coatings Technology, D. (Illus.). 567p. 1999. pap. 109.00 (0-934010-45-5) Fed Soc Coat Tech.

Proceedings of the 78th Annual Meeting Technical Program of the FSCT. Date not set. pap. write for info. (0-934010-46-3) Fed Soc Coat Tech.

Proceedings of the 8th Ethylene Producers Conference, with Selected Papers from the 5th World Congress. Ed. by Ethylene Producers' Committee of AIChE's Fuels & P & C. R. Risinger. (Technical Manual - Ethylene Producers Ser.: Vol. 5). 644p. 1996. 50.00 (0-8169-0714-5, T-101) Am Inst Chem Eng.

Proceedings of the 8th GIFCO Conference, Cosmic Physics in the Year 2000: Scientific Perspectives & New Instrumentation: Como, 8-10 April 1997. Conferenza GIFCO Staff et al. LC 97-224591. (Conference Proceedings/Italian Physical Society Ser.). 326p. 1997. write for info. (88-7794-097-2) Compositori IT.

Proceedings of the 8th International Conference on Software Engineering & Knowledge Engineering. Ed. by Knowledge Systems Institute Staff. (Illus.). 612p. (Orig.). 1996. pap. 65.00 (0-9641699-3-2) Knowldge Systs.

Proceedings of the 8th International Symposium on the Trichoptera. Ed. by Ralph W. Holzenthal & Oliver S. Flint, Jr. LC 96-70955. (Illus.). 498p. 1997. boxed set 70.00 (0-86727-122-1) Ohio Bio Survey.

Proceedings of the 9th International Conference on Software Engineering & Knowledge Engineering, SEKE '97. Ed. by Knowledge Systems Institute Staff. (Illus.). 598p. 1997. pap. 65.00 (0-9641699-5-9) Knowldge Systs.

Proceedings of the 9th International Symposium on Insect-Plant Relationships. Erich Stadler et al. LC 96-22087. (Series Entomologica: Vol. 53). 336p. 1996. text 239.50 (0-7923-4127-9) Kluwer Academic.

Proceedings of the 9th International Symposium on Soil Biology & Conservation of the Biosphere: Held at the Sopron University of Forestry & Timber Industry, August 17-30, 1985. Ed. by J. Segi. 944p. (C). 1987. 275.00 (963-05-4759-7, Pub. by Akade Kiado) St Mut.

Proceedings of the '94 Annual Pittsburgh Employment Conference for Augmented Communicators Vol. 2. 150p. pap. 35.00 (0-9638380-1-6) SHOUT.

Proceedings of the '95 Annual Pittsburgh Employment Conference for Augmented Communications, Vol. 3. 150p. 1995. pap. write for info. (0-9638380-2-4) SHOUT.

Proceedings of Third China-Japan Seminar on Numerical Mathematics. Ed. by Zhongci Zhi & Masatake Mori. (Illus.). 313p. (C). 1998. text 80.00 (1-880132-30-3) Sci Pr NY.

Proceedings of Third International Conference on Vacuum Web Coating. 232p. 1989. 70.00 (0-939997-07-X) Bakish Mat.

*Proceedings of 29th International Symposium on Fault-Tolerant Computing Held in Madison, Wisconsin, 1999. 357p. 1999. pap. 135.00 (0-7695-0213-X) IEEE Comp Soc.

Proceedings of Unified International Technical Conference on Refractories: Fifth Biennial Worldwide Congress: Refractories, A Worldwide Technology. American Ceramic Society Staff. LC 97-31094. 1997. 245.00 (1-57498-048-3, G033) Am Ceramic.

Proceedings of Users 1 Conference on Building Energy Simulation: HVAC. Ed. by Kerckhoffs et al. (Illus.). 310p. 1988. pap. text 60.00 (0-911801-41-3, USER1-1) Soc Computer Sim.

Proceedings of Waste Stream Minimization & Utilization Innovative Concepts Vol. 1: An Experimental Technology Exchange: Industrial Solid Waste Processing & Municipal Waste Reduction-Recycling. (Illus.). 73p. (Orig.). (C). 1994. pap. text 40.00 (0-7881-1275-9) DIANE Pub.

Proceedings of Workshop on Advances in Control & Its Applications. Ed. by Hassan K. Khalil et al. (Lecture Notes in Control & Information Sciences: Vol. 208). 319p. 1995. pap. 64.95 (3-540-19993-4) Spr-Verlag.

Proceedings of XI European Congress of Perinatal Medicine. Ed. by E. V. Cosmi & G. C. Di Renzo. xvi, 874p. 1989. pap. text 249.00 (3-7186-4919-5) Gordon & Breach.

Proceedings of 3rd International Conference on Adhesive Joining & Coating Technology in Electronics Manufacturing 1998: Presented at Adhesives'98 Binghamton, New York, September 28-30, 1998. International Conference on Adhesive Joining and Coating Technology in Electronics Manufacturing Staff et al. LC 98-85262. xvi, 365p. 1998. pap. write for info. (0-7803-4935-0) IEEE Standards.

Proceedings on an International Symposium on Engineering Sciences & Mechanics, Dec. 29-31, Tainan, Taiwan. Ed. by Han-Min Hsia et al. LC 57-43769. (Advances in the Astronautical Sciences Ser.: Vol. 50). (Illus.). 1570p. 1983. 120.00 (0-87703-176-2, Am Astronaut Soc) Univelt Inc.

Proceedings on Banach Algebras & Several Complex Variables Conference. Ed. by F. Greenleaf & Denny Gulick. LC 84-18443. (Contemporary Mathematics Ser.: Vol. 32). 295p. 1985. pap. 40.00 (0-8218-5034-2, CONM/32) Am Math.

Proceedings on Conference on Simulators V. Clymer & Amico. (Simulation Ser.: Vol. 19, No. 4). 488p. 1988. 40.00 (0-911801-34-0, SS19-4) Soc Computer Sim.

Proceedings on Discrete Event Simulation & Operations Research (ESM 1987, Austria) 156p. 1987. 30.00 (0-911801-22-7, EMC87-1) Soc Computer Sim.

Proceedings on the International Conference on Number Theory, Moscow, 1971. Ed. by I. M. Vinogradov et al. LC 75-14189. (Proceedings of the Steklov Institute of Mathematics Ser.: Vol. 132). 298p. 1975. pap. 84.00 (0-8218-3032-5, STEKLO/132) Am Math.

Proceedings on the United Nations Conference on Trade & Development: 8th Session. 213p. 70.00 (92-1-113291-6) UN.

Proceedings on the United Nations Conference on Trade & Development: 9th Session. 70p. 20.00 (92-1-112408-5) UN.

Proceedings Principally in the County of Kent, in Connection with the Parliaments Called in 1640, & Especially with the Committee of Religion Appointed in That Year. Ed. by Lambert B. Larking. (Camden Society, London. Publications, First Ser.: No. 80a). reprint ed. 70.00 (0-404-50180-X) AMS Pr.

Proceedings, Qualitative Reasoning: The Tenth International Workshop, WS-96-01. Ed. by Yumi Iwasaki & Adam Farquhar. (Technical Reports). (Illus.). 174p. (Orig.). 1998. pap. text 30.00 (1-57735-001-4) AAAI Pr.

Proceedings, Santa Cruz Conference on Finite Groups, Vol. 37. Ed. by Bruce Cooperstein & Geoffrey Mason. LC 80-26879. (Proceedings of Symposia in Pure Mathematics Ser.). 634p. 1981. text 62.00 (0-8218-1440-0, PSPUM/37) Am Math.

Proceedings 2nd Annual Technology Advancement Contractor Review Meeting (Sept. 19-20, 1994) Compiled by South Coast Air Quality Management District Staff. (Electric Vehicle Information Ser.: Vol. 17). (Illus.). 404p. 1996. lib. bdg. 155.00 (0-89934-274-4, BT944) Bus Tech Bks.

Proceedings Second Annual Technology Advancement Contractor Review Meeting (Sept. 19-20, 1994) Compiled by South Coast Air Quality Management District Staff. (Electric Vehicle Information Ser.: Vol. 17). (Illus.). 404p. 1996. pap. 105.00 (0-89934-273-6, BT044) Bus Tech Bks.

Proceedings, Second International Enterprise Distributed Object Computing Workshop: 3-5 November 1998, la Jolla, California USA. International Enterprise Distributed Object Computing Staff & Object Management Group Staff. LC 98-88034. vii, 391 p. 1998. write for info. (0-7803-5159-2) Inst Electrical.

Proceedings, 2nd National Conference & Workshop on Tailoring Applications of the DOD: Streamlining Initiative in Acquisition Programs. 355p. 1985. 75.00 (0-915414-89-9) IEST.

Proceedings, 1770-1776, Vol. 1. 1986. 60.00 (0-87413-284-3) U Delaware Pr.

Proceedings Seventh Annual IEEE International ASIC Conference & Exhibit. IEEE, Rochester Section Staff. Ed. by IEEE Staff. 600p. 1994. pap. write for info. (0-7803-2020-4, 94TH0685-8); fiche. write for info. (0-7803-2021-2) Inst Electrical.

Proceedings, 7th European Simulation Symposium, ESS, '95. Ed. by Mario D. Chin et al. (Illus.). 806p. 1995. 180.00 (1-56555-083-8, ESS-95) Soc Computer Sim.

Proceedings Sixth International Congress of Pharmacology, Helsinki 1975, 6 vols., Set. J. Tuomisto & M. Paasonen. 1976. 780.00 (0-08-020458-9, Pub. by Pergamon Repr) Franklin.

Proceedings, Symposium on Surface Mining, Hydrology, Sedimentology, & Reclamation, 1982. Ed. by R. William DeVore & Donald H. Graves. LC 82-51182. (Illus.). 728p. (Orig.). 1982. pap. 10.00 (0-89779-054-5, UKY BU129) OES Pubns.

Proceedings Symposium on Value Distribution Theory in Several Complex Variables. Ed. by Wilhelm Stoll. (Mathematical Lectures: No. 12). (C). 1992. pap. text 17.50 (0-268-01512-0) U of Notre Dame Pr.

Proceedings Third Annual Technology Advancement Contractor Review Meeting (Sept. 26-27, 1995) Compiled by South Coast Air Quality Management District Staff. (Electric Vehicle Information Ser.: Vol. 20). (Illus.). 54p. 1996. pap. 75.00 (0-89934-279-5, BT047); lib. bdg. 115.00 (0-89934-280-9, BT947) Bus Tech Bks.

Proceedings 3rd Lunar Science Conference, Houston 1-72: Physical Properties, Vol. 3. Lunar & Planetary Institute Staff & D. Criswell. 1972. write for info. (0-318-69664-9, Pub. by Pergamon Repr) Franklin.

Proceedings, 24th Annual Simulation Symposium. Ed. by Alan Rutan. LC 71-149514. 338p. 1991. pap. 58.00 (0-8186-2169-9, ANSS-24) Soc Computer Sim.

Proceedings Twenty-Ninth Annual 1995 International Carnahan Conference on Security Technology. IEEE (Aerospace & Electronic Systems Society) Staf. Ed. by IEEE (Institute of Electrical & Electronics Engine. LC 79-644630. 280p. 1995. pap. text 116.00 (0-7803-2627-X, 95CH35788); lib. bdg. 116.00 (0-7803-2628-8, 95CB35788); fiche 116.00 (0-7803-2629-6, 95CM35788) Inst Electrical.

Proceedings, 27th Annual Simulation Symposium. Ed. by Patrick W. Dowd. LC 71-149514. 264p. 1994. pap. 90.00 (0-8186-5620-4, ANSS-27) Soc Computer Sim.

Proceedings, 26th Annual Simulation Symposium. Ed. by John A. Miller. LC 71-149514. 352p. 1993. pap. text 80.00 (0-8186-3620-3, ANSS-26) Soc Computer Sim.

Proceedings, 23rd Annual Simulation Symposium. Ed. by Ben Pinkowski. LC 71-149514. (Illus.). 167p. 1990. pap. text 48.00 (0-8186-2067-6, ANSS-23) Soc Computer Sim.

Proceedings Volume, Basin & Range Province Seismic-Hazards Summit. Ed. by Basin & Range Province Seismic-Hazards Summit Staff & Western States Seismic Policy Council Staff. LC 99-167786. (Miscellaneous Publication / Utah Geological Survey Ser.: 98-2). (Illus.). 204p. 1998. pap. 15.00 (1-55791-623-3) Utah Geological Survey.

Proceedings-Workshop on Needle Exchange & Bleach Distribution Programs. National Research Council, Panel on Needle Exchange & Institute of Medicine Staff. 320p. (Orig.). (C). 1994. pap. text 39.00 (0-309-05084-7) Natl Acad Pr.

Proceedings, World Zionist Organization. Jerusalem Ideological Conference Hebrew University. 1972. reprint ed. lib. bdg. 85.00 (0-8371-4120-6, WOZO, Greenwood Pr) Greenwood.

Proceedings, 1979 Symposium on Surface Mining Hydrology, Sedimentology, & Reclamation. Ed. by R. William De Vore & Stanley B. Carpenter. LC 79-91553. (Illus.). 353p. (Orig.). 1979. pap. 10.00 (0-89779-024-3, UKY BU119) OES Pubns.

Proceedings, 1980 Symposium on Surface Mining, Hydrology, Sedimentology, & Reclamation. Ed. by R. William De Vore & Donald H. Graves. LC 80-84399. (Illus.). 490p. 1980. 10.00 (0-89779-044-8, UKY BU123) OES Pubns.

Proceedings 1981 International Symposium on Urban Hydrology, Hydraulics & Sediment Control. Ed. by R. William De Vore & Don J. Wood. LC 81-82243. (Illus.). 473p. (Orig.). 1981. pap. 10.00 (0-89779-047-2, UKY BU125) OES Pubns.

Proceedings, 1981 Symposium on Surface Mining, Hydrology, Sedimentology & Reclamation. Ed. by R. William De Vore & Donald H. Graves. LC 81-84944. (Illus.). 558p. (Orig.). 1981. 10.00 (0-89779-050-2, UKY BU126) OES Pubns.

Proceedings, 1983 International Symposium on Urban Hydrology, Hydraulics & Sediment Control. Ed. by R. William De Vore. LC 83-60965. (Illus.). 531p. (Orig.). 1983. pap. 10.00 (0-89779-056-1, UKY BU 131) OES Pubns.

Proceedings, 1983 Symposium on Surface Mining, Hydrology, Sedimentology & Reclamation. Ed. by R. William De Vore & Donald H. Graves. LC 83-60966. (Illus.). 554p. (Orig.). 1983. pap. 10.00 (0-89779-058-8, UKY BU 133) OES Pubns.

Proceedings, 1984 Carnahan Conference on Security Technology. Ed. by R. William DeVore & J. S. Jackson. LC 82-64615. (Illus.). 218p. 1984. pap. 10.00 (0-89779-059-6, UKY BU134) OES Pubns.

Proceedings 1989 Congressional International Solar Energy Society, Kobe City, 4-8 September 1989: Proceedings of the 1989 Congress of the International Solar Energy Society, Kobe City, Japan, 4-8 September 1989, 3 vols., Set. Ed. by T. Horigome et al. LC 90-7152. (International Solar Energy Society Proceedings Ser.). (Illus.). 2426p. 1990. 1436.00 (0-08-037193-0, Pub. by Pergamon Repr) Franklin.

Proceedings 1996 IEEE International Conference on Robotics & Automation. IEEE Robotics & Automation Society Staff. Ed. by IEEE Staff. LC 90-640158. 4004p. 1996. pap. text 406.00 (0-7803-2988-0, 96CH35857); lib. bdg. 406.00 (0-7803-2989-9, 96CB35857); fiche 406.00 (0-7803-2990-2, 96CM35857) Inst Electrical.

Proceedings 21st Session, 1994 of the International Commission for Uniform Methods of Sugar Analysis. ICUMSA Staff. 1995. pap. 280.00 (0-905003-14-4, Pub. by ICUMSA) St Mut.

Proceedings, 23rd Euromicro Conference: New Frontiers of Information Technology : Short Contributions : Budapest, Hungary, September 1-4, 1997. Symposium on Microprocessing & Microprogramming et al. LC 97-81043. 1997. write for info. (0-8186-8131-4) IEEE Comp Soc.

Proceedings 9th International Conference on Vacuum Web Coating. (Illus.). 400p. 1996. write for info. (0-939997-19-3) Bakish Mat.

Proceedings/Memoria Conference on Books in Spanish for Young Readers, Fifth Annual. Claudia Quigg & Pedro G. Rodriguez. Ed. by Isabel Schon. (SPA.). 23p. (Orig.). (C). 1995. pap. 5.00 (0-9639354-4-5) Ctr Bks Spanish.

Proceedings/Memoria Conference on Books in Spanish for Young Readers, Fourth Annual. Jose E. Pacheco & David W. Foster. Ed. by Isabel Schon. 23p. (Orig.). (C). 1994. pap. 5.00 (0-9639354-3-7) Ctr Bks Spanish.

Proces. Franz Kafka. (FRE.). 384p. 1987. pap. 10.95 (0-7859-2540-6, 2070378403) Fr & Eur.

Proces de Rastatt (1946-1954) Le Jugement des Crimes de Guerre en Zone Francaise d'Occupation en Allemagne. Yveline Pendaries. (Contacts Ser.: Series II, Vol. 16). (FRE.). 396p. 1995. 55.95 (3-906754-18-9, Pub. by P Lang) P Lang Pubng.

Proces D'impiete Intentes Aux Philosophes a Athenes Au Vme & Au Ivme Siecles. Eudore Derenne. LC 75-13260. (History of Ideas in Ancient Greece Ser.). (FRE.). 1976. reprint ed. 19.95 (0-405-07302-X) Ayer.

Proces du Roman: Ecriture et Contrefacon Chez Charles Sorel. Martine Debaisieux. LC 89-84499. (Stanford French & Italian Studies: Vol. 63). (FRE.). 196p. 1989. pap. 56.50 (0-915838-78-8) Anma Libri.

Proces-Verbal. J. M. Le Clezio. (FRE.). 1973. pap. 11.95 (0-8288-3707-4) Fr & Eur.

Proces-Verbal. J. M. Le Clezio. (Folio Ser.: No. 353). (FRE.). pap. 9.95 (2-07-036353-8) Schoenhof.

Procesamiento Digital de Imagenes. R. C. Gonzalez. (SPA.). 800p. (C). 1996. pap. text 32.00 (0-201-62576-8) Addison-Wesley.

Procesion de los Ardientes. Pedro G. Valderrama. (SPA.). 127p. 1981. pap. 4.00 (84-85859-10-3, 2007) Ediciones Norte.

Proceso a Darwin. Phillip E. Johnson. (SPA.). 240p. 1995. pap. 8.99 (0-8254-1361-3, Edit Portavoz) Kregel.

Proceso Administrativo en la Iglesia (The Administrative Process in the Church) Ines J. Figueroa. (What You Need to Know about ... in 12 Lessons Ser.). (ENG & SPA.). 240p. 9.99 (0-89922-498-9) Caribe Betania.

Proceso Colonial en el Alto Orinoco-Rio Negro (Siglos XVI a XVIII) Mariano Useche. (SPA., Illus.). 208p. 1987. pap. 8.50 (1-877812-30-7, BR028) UPLAAP.

Proceso de Produccion de Espacios y Estructuras en Teotihuacan. Noel Morelos. 285p. 1993. pap. 21.00 (968-29-5105-4, IN033) UPLAAP.

Proceso del las Ideas Politicas en Cuba. Humberto Pinera et al. (SPA.). 132p. (Orig.). 1988. pap. 15.00 (0-89729-489-0, Pub. by Laurenty Pub Inc) Ediciones.

Proceso Democratico de Mexico. Jose F. Ruiz Massieu. (SPA.). pap. 8.99 (968-16-4424-7, Pub. by Fondo) Continental Bk.

Proceso Historico Prehispanico de San Agustin en el Valle de Laboyos (Pitalito-Huila) Hector Llanos. (SPA., Illus.). 122p. 1990. pap. 8.50 (1-877812-31-5, BR029) UPLAAP.

Process. Brion Gysin. LC 86-43064. 344p. 1987. 22.95 (0-87951-277-6, Pub. by Overlook Pr) Penguin Putnam.

Process. Brion Gysin. 344p. 1989. pap. 13.95 (0-87951-297-0, Pub. by Overlook Pr) Penguin Putnam.

Process: A Tomato Project. (Illus.). 160p. 1997. pap. 34.95 (3-927258-50-4) Gingko Press.

Process: Identify, Attract & Retain Customers. 1997. write for info. (0-614-25480-9, N281) Econ Intel.

Process: Roman. Franz Kafka. Ed. by Malcolm Pasley. (GER.). 304p. 1994. pap. 13.50 (3-596-12443-3, Pub. by Fischer Tasch) Intl Bk Import.

Process: 1,100 Days That Changed the Middle East. Uri Savir. (Illus.). 352p. 1999. pap. 15.00 (0-679-74561-0) Knopf.

Process Algebra. J. C. Baeten & W. P. Weijland. (Cambridge Tracts in Theoretical Computer Science Ser.: No. 17). (Illus.). 256p. (C). 1990. text 44.95 (0-521-40043-0) Cambridge U Pr.

Process Analysis & Optimization of Direct Horizontal-Flow Roughing Filtration. Tanveer Ahsan. (Illus.). 194p. (C). 1995. pap. text 52.00 (90-5410-635-2, Pub. by A A Balkema) Ashgate Pub Co.

Process Analysis Workbook for Government: How to Achieve More with Less. Gerard Bruno. LC 94-19797. 219p. 1995. pap. 35.00 (0-87389-259-3, H0814) ASQ Qual Pr.

Process Analytical Chemistry: Control, Optimization, Quality, Economy. K. H. Koch. (Illus.). 230p. 1999. 125.00 (3-540-65337-6) Spr-Verlag.

Process Analytical Instruments. Donald Gillum. (C). 1995. pap. text 25.07 (1-56870-138-1) RonJon Pub.

Process Analyzer Technology. Kenneth J. Clevett. LC 85-26302. 960p. 1986. 265.00 (0-471-88316-6) Wiley.

P

An Asterisk (*) at the beginning of an entry indicates that the title is appearing for the first time.

Process & Business Control Technologies for the Forest Products Industry. (Illus.). 130p. 1997. pap. 40.00 (*0-935018-58-1*, 7281) Forest Prod.

Process & Device Simulation for MOS-VLSI Circuits. Ed. by Paolo Antognetti. 1983. text 255.50 (*90-247-2824-X*) Kluwer Academic.

***Process & Equipment Control in Microelectronic Manufacturing.** Ed. by Kevin Yallup & Murali K. Narasimhan. (Europto Ser.: Vol. 3742). 214p. 1999. pap. text 62.00 (*0-8194-3222-9*) SPIE.

Process & Expression in Architectural Form. Gunnar Birkerts. LC 93-40030. (Bruce Alonzo Goff Series in Creative Architecture: Vol. 1). (Illus.). 192p. 1994. 39.95 (*0-8061-2642-6*); pap. 17.95 (*0-8061-2645-0*) U of Okla Pr.

Process & Form in Geomorphology. Ed. by D. R. Stoddart. LC 95-52607. (Illus.). 432p. (C). 1996. 140.00 (*0-415-10527-7*) Routledge.

Process & Fundamental Considerations of Selected Hydrometallurgical Systems. Ed. by Martin C. Kuhn. LC 79-57685. (Illus.). 400p. 1981. pap. 124.00 (*0-7837-7841-4*, 204760000007) Bks Demand.

Process & Metaphors in the Evolutionary Paradigm. Ed. by Mae-Wan Ho & Sidney Fox. LC 87-25445. 346p. 1988. 333.00 (*0-471-91801-6*, Wiley-Interscience) Wiley.

Process & Organization of Government Planning. John D. Millett. LC 76-38753. (FDR & the Era of the New Deal Ser.). 188p. 1972. reprint ed. lib. bdg. 29.50 (*0-306-70444-7*) Da Capo.

***Process & Organizational Redesign: Leading Change in Colleges & Universities.** Ed. by Barbara S. Butterfield et al. 132p. 1998. pap. 29.99 (*1-878240-68-4*) Coll & U Personnel.

Process & Pattern. Cobb. (C). 1985. mass mkt., teacher ed. 5.00 (*0-534-03706-2*) Heinle & Heinle.

Process & Pattern in Evolution. Charlotte J. Avers. (Illus.). 608p. (C). 1989. text 57.00 (*0-19-505275-7*) OUP.

Process & Politics in Library Research: A Model for Course Design. Deborah Fink. 211p. 1989. pap. text 8.00 (*0-8389-0519-6*) ALA.

Process & Portfolios in Writing Instruction. 2nd ed. Ed. by Kent Gill. (Classroom Practices in Teaching English Ser.: Vol. 26). 99p. 1993. pap. 11.95 (*0-8141-3724-5*) NCTE.

Process & Practice: A Guide for Developing Writers. 4th ed. Ed. by Philip Eggers. LC 97-14414. 370p. (C). 1997. pap. text 52.00 (*0-321-01215-1*) Addson-Wesley Educ.

Process & Practice in Family Therapy. 2nd ed. Gerald H. Zuk. 202p. (C). 1986. 32.95 (*0-89885-276-5*, Kluwer Acad Hman Sci) Kluwer Academic.

Process & Practice of Radio Programming. Joanna R. Lynch & Greg Gillispie. LC 98-4847. 336p. (C). 1998. pap. 39.00 (*0-7618-1045-5*) U Pr of Amer.

Process & Practice with Readings. Philip Eggers. LC 94-32172. 448p. (C). 1997. pap. 24.00 (*0-673-46810-0*) HarpC.

Process & Product Quality Conference, 1995: Airport Hilton, Montreal, Quebec, October 23-26. Technical Association of the Pulp & Paper Industry. LC 93-146404. (TAPPI Proceedings Ser.). 171p. reprint ed. pap. 53.10 (*0-608-09156-1*, 208251600002) Bks Demand.

Process & Product Quality Conference, 1992: Paper Valley Hotel, Appleton, WI, October 26-29. Technical Association of the Pulp & Paper Industry. LC TS1109.P76. (TAPPI Proceedings Ser.). 124p. reprint ed. pap. 38.50 (*0-7837-3971-0*, 204380000011) Bks Demand.

Process & Product Quality Conference, 1994: Hyatt Regency, Savannah, GA, October 17-20. Technical Association of the Pulp & Paper Industry. LC 93-146404. (TAPPI Proceedings Ser.). (Illus.). 162p. 1994. pap. 50.30 (*0-608-05382-1*, 208244200011) Bks Demand.

Process & Reality: An Essay in Cosmology. 2nd rev. ed. Alfred North Whitehead. 416p. 1979. pap. 16.95 (*0-02-934570-7*) Free Pr.

Process & Result in Language: A Study of Aspect in the English Verb. Yishai Tobin. LC 92-555. (Linguistics Library). 1993. write for info. (*0-582-06832-0*) Longman.

Process & Structure in Human Decision Making. Ed. by Henry Montgomery & Ola Svenson. LC 88-33788. 335p. 1989. reprint ed. pap. 103.90 (*0-608-04603-5*, 206537300003) Bks Demand.

***Process & Structure of Crime.** Ed. by Robert F. Meier et al. (Criminal Events & Crime Analysis Advances in Criminological Theory Ser.: Vol. 9). 317p. 2000. 44.95 (*0-7658-0004-7*) Transaction Pubs.

Process Approach for Teaching Skills. 2nd ed. Barbara F. Tea. 148p. (C). 1990. pap. 37.60 (*0-536-57828-1*) Pearson Custom.

Process Approach for Teaching Skills. 3rd ed. Avril Garscadden. 180p. (C). 1994. text 37.40 (*0-536-58654-3*) Pearson Custom.

Process Approach for Teaching Skills. 4th ed. Avril Garscadden. 194p. (C). 1995. text 45.00 (*0-536-59034-6*) Pearson Custom.

Process Approach to Public Speaking. David Burns & B. Bruce Wagener. 448p. (C). 1995. pap. text, per. 37.95 (*0-8403-9750-X*) Kendall-Hunt.

Process Approach to Public Speaking. David Burns & B. Bruce Wagener. 416p. (C). 1996. pap. text, per. 37.95 (*0-7872-3230-0*) Kendall-Hunt.

Process Architecture No. 115: Prague. Atsuko Tanaka. (Illus.). 155p. 1994. pap. 37.95 (*4-89331-155-7*, Pub. by Process Archit) Bks Nippan.

Process Architecture No. 120: EDAW: The Integrated World. Ed Miyakada. 1994. pap. 37.95 (*4-89331-120-4*, Pub. by Process Archit) Bks Nippan.

Process Architecture No. 133: Cityscape of Hong Kong. Naonori Matsuda. (Illus.). 144p. 1997. pap. 37.95 (*4-89331-133-6*, Pub. by Process Archit) Bks Nippan.

Process Architecture No. 134: Landscape of Balmori. Diana Balmori. (Illus.). 144p. 1997. pap. 37.95 (*4-89331-134-4*, Pub. by Process Archit) Bks Nippan.

Process Capability Indices in Theory & Practice. Ed. by Sam Kotz & Cyndi Lovelace. LC 98-232699. (An Arnold Publication). (Illus.). 320p. 1998. text 70.00 (*0-340-69177-8*, Pub. by E A) OUP.

Process Catholicism: An Exercise in Ecclesial Imagination. Robert L. Kinast. LC 98-54387. 144p. 1999. 45.00 (*0-7618-1339-X*); pap. 25.50 (*0-7618-1340-3*) U Pr of Amer.

Process-Centered Enterprise: The Power of Commitments. Gabriel A. Pall. LC 99-48848. 325p. 1999. boxed set 29.95 (*1-57444-239-2*) St Lucie Pr.

Process-Centered Health Care Organizations. Suzanne P. Smith & Dominick L. Flarey. LC 99-18270. 400p. 1999. 59.00 (*0-8342-1249-8*, 12498) Aspen Pub.

Process Centered Logical Analysis for Writers. William M. Specht, 3rd. 121p. 1995. pap. text 32.00 (*0-931889-09-X*) Epistemology Pubs.

Process-Centered Organizations. LC 97-47375. 1998. pap. 39.95 (*0-89806-181-4*, SHSCMP) Eng Mgmt Pr.

Process-Centered Requirements Engineering. Klaus Pohl. LC 96-3339. (Advanced Software Development Ser.). 342p. 1996. 84.95 (*0-86380-193-5*) Wiley.

Process-Centered School: Sustaining a Renaissance Community. Arthur L. Costa & Rosemarie M. Liebmann. (Illus.). 264p. 1997. 69.95 (*0-8039-6313-0*); pap. 32.95 (*0-8039-6314-9*) Corwin Pr.

Process-Centered Software Engineering Environments. Pankaj K. Garg & Mehdi Jazayeri. LC 95-7576. 424p. 1995. pap. 50.00 (*0-8186-7103-3*) IEEE Comp Soc.

Process Cheese. Vincent Zehren & D. D. Nusbaum. 364p. 1993. 58.00 (*0-9634946-0-0*) Cheese Reporter.

Process Chemistry. Multimedia Development Services Staff. (Plant Fundamentals Ser.: Vol. II, Module II). (Illus.). 80p. 1995. student ed. 30.00 (*1-57431-005-4*) Tech Trng Systs.

Process Chemistry, Vol. II, Module II. Multimedia Development Services Staff. (Plant Fundamentals Ser.). (Illus.). (Orig.). 1995. teacher ed. 49.95 (*1-57431-045-3*) Tech Trng Systs.

***Process Chemistry in the Pharmaceutical Industry** Kumar G. Gadamasetti. LC 99-26854. (Illus.). 504p. 1999. text 195.00 (*0-8247-1981-6*) Dekker.

Process Chemistryar Energy, Vol. 4. C. E. Stevenson et al. 1970. 115.00 (*0-08-013401-7*, Pergamon Pr) Elsevier.

Process Christology. David R. Griffin. LC 89-71369. 280p. (C). 1990. reprint ed. pap. text 25.00 (*0-8191-7686-9*) U Pr of Amer.

Process Chromatography: A Guide to Validation. Lars-Erik Nystrom & Gail K. Sofer. (Illus.). 800p. 1991. text 48.00 (*0-12-654267-8*) Acad Pr.

Process Chromatography: A Practical Guide. Ed. by Gail K. Sofer & Lars-Erik Nystom. 145p. 1989. text 62.00 (*0-12-654268-6*) Acad Pr.

***Process Color Manual: 24,000 CMYK Combinations for Design, Prepress, & Printing.** rev. expanded ed. Michael Rogondino & Pat Rogondino. (Illus.). 256p. 2000. spiral bd. 35.00 (*0-8118-2757-7*) Chronicle Bks.

Process Compressor Technology, Vol. 2. Ronald P. Lapina. LC 82-3124. 351p. 1983. reprint ed. pap. 108.90 (*0-608-01575-X*, 206199500002) Bks Demand.

***Process Consultation.** 446p. (C). 2000. 52.00 (*0-536-60747-8*) Pearson Custom.

Process Consultation: Its Role in Organization Development. Edgar H. Schein. LC 76-91149. (Organization Development Ser.). (Orig.). (C). 1969. pap. text 16.25 (*0-201-06733-1*) Addison-Wesley.

Process Consultation: It's Role in Organization Development, Vol. 1. 2nd ed. Edgar H. Schein. 204p. (C). 1988. pap. text 40.00 (*0-201-06736-6*) Addison-Wesley.

Process Consultation: Lessons for Managers & Consultants, Vol. II. Edgar H. Schein. LC 76-91149. (Organization Development Ser.). (Illus.). 208p. (C). 1987. pap. text 40.00 (*0-201-06744-7*) Addison-Wesley.

Process Consultation Vol. I: Its Role in Organization Development. 2nd ed. Edgar H. Schein. (Illus.). 192p. (C). 1988. pap. text. write for info. (*0-318-62689-6*) Addison-Wesley.

Process Consultation Revisited: Building the Helping Relationship, Vol. III. Edgar H. Schein. LC 98-24926. 204p. (C). 1998. pap. text 40.00 (*0-201-34596-X*, Prentice Hall) P-H.

Process Control. A. E. Marlin. 1995. text, wbk. ed. 35.00 (*0-07-040493-3*) McGraw.

Process Control. Multimedia Development Services Staff. (Plant Fundamentals Ser.: Vol. VIII, Module I). (Illus.). 1995. teacher ed. 49.95 (*1-57431-065-8*); student ed. 30.00 (*1-57431-025-9*) Tech Trng Systs.

Process Control: A Literature Review. Glen Havelock. (Pira Reviews of Pulp & Paper Technology Ser.). 87p. 1993. pap. 120.00 (*1-85802-029-8*, TS1120, Pub. by Pira Internatl) Bks Intl VA.

Process Control: A Primer for the Non-Specialist & Newcomer. 2nd rev. ed. George Pratt. LC 98-18882. (Illus.). 200p. 1998. pap. 35.00 (*1-55617-633-3*, RA633-3) ISA.

Process Control: Designing Processes & Control Systems for Dynamic Performance. E. Thomas Marlin. 1994. pap. text, teacher ed. write for info. (*0-07-040492-5*) McGraw.

Process Control: Designing Processes & Control Systems for Dynamic Performance. Thomas E. Marlin. LC 94-45967. (Chemical Engineering Ser.). 640p. (C). 1995. 93.75 (*0-07-040491-7*) McGraw.

***Process Control: Designing Processes & Control Systems for Dynamic Performance.** 2nd ed. Thomas E. Marlin. LC 99-26739. 1056p. 2000. 93.75 (*0-07-039362-1*) McGraw.

Process Control & Automation in Extractive Metallurgy: Proceedings of an International Symposium. fac. ed. Materials, Metals & Materials Society Staff. Ed. by E. H. Partelpoeg & D. C. Himmesoete. LC 88-63685. (Illus.). 233p. reprint ed. pap. 72.30 (*0-7837-6968-7*, 205252500003) Bks Demand.

Process Control & Identification. W. Fred Ramirez. (Illus.). 424p. 1993. text 73.00 (*0-12-577240-8*) Acad Pr.

Process Control & Management. P. L. Lee et al. LC 97-77204. 752p. 1997. write for info. (*0-7514-0457-8*) Kluwer Academic.

Process Control & Sensors for Manufacturing, Vol. 3399. Ed. by Richard H. Bossi & David M. Pepper. 258p. 1998. 69.00 (*0-8194-2848-5*) SPIE.

***Process Control & Sensors for Manufacturing II.** Ed. by David M. Pepper. 188p. 1999. pap. text 62.00 (*0-8194-3059-5*) SPIE.

Process Control Charting with Quattro Pro for Windows. Peter McReynolds. 250p. 1993. pap. 39.95 (*1-883327-41-5*) TitleWave Pr.

Process Control Conference, 1987: Proceedings of TAPPI, Opryland Hotel, Nashville, TN, March 22-25. Technical Association of the Pulp & Paper Industry. LC TS1109.. (Illus.). 167p. pap. 51.80 (*0-608-17488-2*, 202998400067) Bks Demand.

Process Control Conference, 1989: Peabody Hotel, Orlando, FL, Feb. 16-March 2. Technical Association of the Pulp & Paper Industry. LC TS1117.6.P73. (TAPPI Proceedings Ser.). (Illus.). 133p. reprint ed. pap. 41.30 (*0-8357-6340-4*, 203561200096) Bks Demand.

Process Control Conference, 1991 TAPPI - ISA PUPID: Walt Disney World Dolphin Hotel, Lake Buena Vista, FL, March 3-7. Technical Association of the Pulp & Paper Industry. LC TS1116.. (TAPPI Proceedings Ser.). 157p. pap. 48.70 (*0-7837-0257-4*, 204056600017) Bks Demand.

Process Control Conference, 1992: Atlanta, GA, March 3-5. Technical Association of the Pulp & Paper Industry. LC TS1117.6.P73. (TAPPI Notes Ser.). 102p. reprint ed. pap. 31.70 (*0-7837-2054-8*, 204232900004) Bks Demand.

Process Control, Diagnostics & Modeling in Semiconductor Manufacturing I. Ed. by M. Meyyappan et al. LC 97-211633. (Proceedings Ser.: Vol. 97-9). 348p. 1997. 75.00 (*1-56677-136-6*) Electrochem Soc.

Process Control, Diagnostics & Modeling in Semiconductor Manufacturing I. M. Meyyappan et al. LC 95-60437. (Proceedings Ser.: Vol. 95-2). 630p. 1995. pap. 62.00 (*1-56677-096-3*) Electrochem Soc.

Process Control Digest. 304p. 1993. pap. 70.00 (*1-881369-32-3*) Water Environ.

Process Control Engineering. V. Epple & M. Helm. Ed. by M. Polke. LC 94-30443. 475p. 1994. 230.00 (*3-527-28689-6*, Wiley-VCH) Wiley.

Process Control Engineering: A Textbook for Chemical, Mechanical & Electrical Engineers. Ming Rao & Haiming Qiu. 410p. 1993. text 81.00 (*2-88124-628-1*) Gordon & Breach.

Process Control Fundamentals, 3 vols. J. P. Jerald & D. W. Powers. (Illus.). (C). 1981. teacher ed. 595.00 (*0-87683-009-2*) GP Courseware.

Process Control Fundamentals, 3 vols., Set. J. P. Jerald & D. W. Powers. (Illus.). (C). 1981. 195.00 (*0-87683-005-X*) GP Courseware.

Process Control Fundamentals, 3 vols., Vol. 1. J. P. Jerald & D. W. Powers. (Illus.). 157p. (C). 1981. ring bd. 95.00 (*0-87683-006-8*) GP Courseware.

Process Control Fundamentals, 3 vols., Vol. 2. J. P. Jerald & D. W. Powers. (Illus.). 306p. (C). 1981. ring bd. 79.50 (*0-87683-007-6*) GP Courseware.

Process Control Fundamentals, 3 vols., Vol. 3. J. P. Jerald & D. W. Powers. (Illus.). 313p. (C). 1981. 79.50 (*0-87683-008-4*) GP Courseware.

Process Control Fundamentals for the Pulp & Paper Industry. Ed. by Nancy J. Sell. (Illus.). 612p. 1995. 115.00 (*0-89852-294-3*, 0101R249) TAPPI.

***Process Control Instrumentation in Australia: A Strategic Entry Report, 1996.** Compiled by Icon Group International Staff. (Illus.). 133p. 1999. ring bd. 1330.00 incl. audio compact disk (*0-7418-1357-2*) Icon Grp.

Process Control Instrumentation in Vietnam: A Strategic Entry Report, 1998. Compiled by Icon Group International Staff. (Country Industry Report). (Illus.). 156p. 1999. ring bd. 1560.00 incl. audio compact disk (*0-7418-0522-7*) Icon Grp.

***Process Control Instrumentation Technology.** 6th ed. Johnson. LC 99-24235. 678p. 1999. 105.00 (*0-13-938200-3*) P-H.

Process Control Markets Instrumentation. Market Intelligence Staff. Ed. by Milmoth Hammersley. 230p. 1992. pap. text 995.00 (*1-56753-910-6*) Frost & Sullivan.

***Process Control Modules: A Software Laboratory for Control Design.** Doyle. LC 99-56390. 174p. 1999. pap. text 49.00 (*0-13-021107-9*) P-H.

Process Control Source, 1994. Market Intelligence Staff. 250p. 1994. 545.00 (*0-7889-0041-2*) Frost & Sullivan.

Process Control, State-of-the-Art Printing Technology, Software Engineering & Management, Statistical Modeling & Reliability Techniques, Computers in Education see Computers in Engineering, 1982

Process Control Strategy & Profitability. Page S. Buckley. LC 92-4130. 107p. 1992. pap. 28.00 (*1-55617-371-7*, TP155) ISA.

Process Control Symposium, 1985: Notes of TAPPI. Technical Association of the Pulp & Paper Industry. LC TS1109.. 131p. reprint ed. pap. 40.70 (*0-608-12801-5*, 202528300043) Bks Demand.

Process Control Symposium, 1994: Fairmont Hotel, New Orleans, Louisiana, February 7-10. Technical Association of the Pulp & Paper Industry. LC TS0156.8.P76. (TAPPI Proceedings Ser.). 193p. 1994. reprint ed. pap. 59.90 (*0-608-05353-8*, 208240100004) Bks Demand.

Process Control Systems. 2nd ed. F. Jovic. 1991. 84.95 (*0-442-31457-4*) Chapman & Hall.

Process Control Systems: Application, Design & Tuning. 4th ed. F. Greg Shinskey. LC 95-47576. (Illus.). 439p. 1996. 79.00 (*0-07-057101-5*) McGraw.

Process Control Valves in Australia: A Strategic Entry Report, 1998. Compiled by Icon Group International Staff. (Country Industry Report). (Illus.). 136p. 1999. ring bd. 1360.00 incl. audio compact disk (*0-7418-0523-5*) Icon Grp.

Process Controls & Instrumentation in Germany: A Strategic Entry Report, 1998. Compiled by Icon Group International Staff. (Country Industry Report). (Illus.). 106p. 1999. ring bd. 1060.00 incl. audio compact disk (*0-7418-0283-X*) Icon Grp.

Process Controls in Sweden: A Strategic Entry Report, 1998. Compiled by Icon Group International Staff. (Country Industry Report). (Illus.). 94p. 1999. ring bd. 940.00 incl. audio compact disk (*0-7418-0524-3*) Icon Grp.

Process Cost Accounting Practice Case: PC Processors. Carter. 1998. pap. 30.95 (*0-87393-819-4*) Dame Pubns.

Process Data Presentation for Control Valves: ISA Standard RP75.21. ISA Staff. 1989. pap. 25.00 (*1-55617-206-0*, RP75.21) ISA.

Process Design Case Studies. Ron Scott & Norman Macleod. 118p. 1991. pap. 25.00 (*0-85295-276-7*, 9CH14, Pub. by IChemE) Gulf Pub.

Process Design for Reliable Operations. 2nd ed. Norman P. Lieberman. LC 88-1463. (Illus.). 263p. 1988. reprint ed. pap. 81.60 (*0-608-07949-9*, 206792200012) Bks Demand.

***Process Design in a Changing Environment: Identification of Quality Demands Governing the Design Process.** Paulien Herder. (Illus.). 222p. 1999. pap. 55.00 (*90-407-1818-0*, Pub. by Delft U Pr) Coronet Bks.

Process Design Principles. Seider. 840p. 1998. text 115.95 incl. cd-rom (*0-471-32416-7*) Wiley.

***Process Design Principles.** Seider. 1999. 1.95 (*0-471-33306-9*) Wiley.

Process Design Principles: Synthesis, Analysis, & Evaluation. Warren D. Seider et al. LC 98-18846. (Illus.). 824p. 1998. text 102.95 (*0-471-24312-4*) Wiley.

***Process Design Tools for the Environment.** Subhas K. Sikdar & Mahmoud M. El-Halwagi. LC 00-22007. 2000. write for info. (*1-56032-824-X*) Taylor & Francis.

Process Development: Fine Chemicals from Grams to Kilograms. Stan Lee & Graham Robinson. (Oxford Chemistry Primers Ser.: No. 30). (Illus.). 92p. (C). 1995. pap. text 12.95 (*0-19-855824-4*) OUP.

Process Development in Antibiotic Fermentations. C. T. Calam. (Cambridge Studies in Biotechnology: No. 4). (Illus.). 228p. 1987. text 69.95 (*0-521-30490-3*) Cambridge U Pr.

Process Diagnostics: Materials, Combustion, Fusion. Alan C. Eckbreth & G. Campbell. Ed. by A. K. Hays et al. (Symposium Proceedings Ser.: Vol. 117). 1988. text 17.50 (*0-931837-87-1*) Materials Res.

Process Discipline: How to Maximize Profitability & Quality Through Manufacturing Consistency. Norman M. Edelson & Carole L. Bennett. LC 98-22048. 1998. 34.95 (*0-527-76345-4*) Productivity Inc.

Process-Driven Business: Managerial Perspectives on Policy Management. William E. Eureka & Nancy E. Ryan. 138p. 1993. 19.50 (*0-941243-12-5*) ASI Pr.

Process Dynamics: Modeling, Analysis & Simulation. Wayne B. Bequette. LC 97-36052. 640p. (C). 1998. lab manual ed. 99.00 (*0-13-206889-3*) P-H.

Process Dynamics & Control: A Self-Instructional Problem Workbook. P. T. Vasudevan. (Illus.). 370p. (Orig.). (C). 1996. pap. text 60.00 (*1-882767-20-9*) ETS.

Process Dynamics Estimation & Control. A. Johnson. (IEE Control Engineering Ser.: No. 27). 188p. 1985. boxed set 82.00 (*0-86341-032-4*, CE027) INSPEC Inc.

Process Dynamics in Environmental Systems. Walter J. Weber, Jr. & Francis A. DiGiano. LC 94-49669. 943p. 1996. 87.95 (*0-471-01711-6*) Wiley.

Process Dynamics, Modeling, & Control. Babatunde A. Ogunnaike & W. Harmon Ray. (Topics in Chemical Engineering Ser.). (Illus.). 1296p. (C). 1994. text 92.00 (*0-19-509119-1*) OUP.

Process Edge: Creating Value Where It Counts. Peter G.W. Keen. LC 96-48382. 208p. 1997. 24.95 (*0-87584-588-6*) Harvard Busn.

Process Education: The New Direction for Elementary-Secondary Schools. Henry P. Cole. LC 79-178843. 288p. 1972. 37.95 (*0-87778-030-7*) Educ Tech Pubns.

Process Energy Conservation Manual. Fairmont Press Staff. 154p. 1984. text 37.00 (*0-915586-73-8*) Fairmont Pr.

Process Engineering Analysis in Semiconductor Device Fabrication. Stanley Middleman & Arthur K. Hochberg. (Illus.). 672p. (C). 1993. 98.75 (*0-07-041853-5*) McGraw.

Process Engineering & Design for Air Pollution Control. Jaime Benitez. LC 92-20982. (C). 1992. 63.00 (*0-13-723214-4*) Prntice Hall Bks.

P

Process Engineering Calculations: Material & Energy Balances. Mack Tyner. LC 60-7613. 414p. reprint ed. pap. 128.40 (*0-608-11286-0*, 201246000081) Bks Demand.

Process Engineering Control. Mack Tyner & Frank P. May. LC 67-21681. (Illus.). 478p. reprint ed. 148.20 (*0-8357-9962-X*, 201244100081) Bks Demand.

Process Engineering Data Book. Paul N. Cheremisinoff & Nicholas P. Cheremisinoff. LC 94-61845. (Process Engineering Handbook Ser.). 360p. 1995. pap. text 29.95 (*1-56676-224-3*) Technomic.

Process Engineering for Pollution Control & Waste Minimization. Ed. by Donald L. Wise & Debra J. Trantolo. (Environmental Science & Pollution Ser.: Vol. 7). (Illus.). 744p. 1994. text 235.00 (*0-8247-9161-4*) Dekker.

Process Engineering Handbook. Ed. by L. Butts. 168p. (Orig.). 1991. pap. 72.00 (*0-89852-421-0*, 0101R184) TAPPI.

Process Engineer's Absorption Pocket Handbook. Robert N. Maddox. LC 85-852. 96p. 1985. reprint ed. pap. 30.00 (*0-608-01336-6*, 206208000001) Bks Demand.

Process Engineer's Pocket Handbook, Vol. 1. Carl Branan. LC 76-1680. (Illus.). 144p. 1976. reprint ed. pap. 44.70 (*0-608-07937-5*, 206791000001) Bks Demand.

Process Engineer's Pocket Handbook, Vol. 3. Carl Branan. LC 76-1680. (Illus.). 176p. 1976. reprint ed. pap. 54.60 (*0-608-07562-0*, 206161700003) Bks Demand.

Process Engineer's Pocket Handbook Vol. 2: Process Systems Development. Carl Branan. LC 76-1680. 109p. 1983. reprint ed. pap. 33.80 (*0-608-00828-1*, 206161700002) Bks Demand.

Process, Enhanced & Multiphase Heat Transfer: A Festschrift for A. E. Bergles. Arthur E. Bergles et al. LC 96-36955. 1996. write for info. (*1-56700-079-7*) Begell Hse.

Process, Equipment & Materials Control in Integrated Circuit Manufacturing II, Vol. 2876. Ed. by Armando Iturralde & Te-Hua Lin. 266p. 1996. 66.00 (*0-8194-2274-6*) SPIE.

Process, Equipment & Materials Control in Integrated Circuit Manufacturing III, Vol. 3213. Ed. by Abe Ghanbari & Anthony J. Toprac. LC 98-122092. 280p. 1997. 69.00 (*0-8194-2645-8*) SPIE.

Process, Equipment & Materials Control in Integrated Circuit Manufacturing IV. Ed. by Anthony J. Toprac & Kim Dang. LC 98-233179. (Proceedings of SPIE Ser.: Vol. 3507). 330p. 1998. 89.00 (*0-8194-2966-X*) SPIE.

***Process, Equipment & Materials Control in Integrated Circuit Manufacturing V.** Ed. by Anthony J. Toprac & Kim Dang. 318p. 1999. pap. text 72.00 (*0-8194-3479-5*) SPIE.

Process Equipment Design: Vessel Design. Lloyd E. Brownell & Edwin H. Young. 420p. 1959. 235.00 (*0-471-11319-0*) Wiley.

Process Ethics: A Constructive System. Kenneth Cauthen. LC 84-16662. (Toronto Studies in Theology: Vol. 18). 365p. 1983. lib. bdg. 99.95 (*0-88946-764-1*) E Mellen.

Process Evaluation & Economic Analysis. Carl Branan & John Mills. LC 76-1680. (Process Engineer's Pocket Handbook Ser.: Vol. 3). 168p. (Orig.). 1984. pap. 15.00 (*0-87201-715-X*, 1715) Gulf Pub.

***Process Evaluation Handbook.** Donald J. Wheeler. 260p. 2000. text 35.00 (*0-945320-55-8*, SPC Pr) Stat Process Contrl.

Process Experience Language Classroom. Michael Legutke & Howard Thomas. (Applied Linguistics & Language Ser.). 332p. (C). 1995. pap. text 34.74 (*0-582-01654-1*) Longman.

Process Flow Scheduling. Steven F. Bolander & Sam G. Taylor. 1994. pap. 26.00 (*1-55822-109-3*) Am Prod & Inventory.

Process Fluid Mechanics. Morton M. Denn. 1979. text 67.60 (*0-13-723163-6*) P-H.

Process for Learning, Sharing & Selling. Frank M. Munson. (Illus.). iii, 55p. (Orig.). 1997. pap. 134.95 (*1-891156-01-2*) HSR Pub.

Process for Profit: The How to Approach of TQM. Erna Marquis & Karen Silva. 176p. (C). 1996. pap. text, spiral bd. 32.95 (*0-7872-1995-9*, 41199501) Kendall-Hunt.

Process for System Development: A Practical Guide to Requirements & Architecture Modeling. Derek J. Hatley et al. (Illus.). 528p. 2000. 59.95 (*0-932633-41-2*) Dorset Hse Pub Co.

Process, Form & Substance: A Rhetoric for Advanced Writers. 2nd ed. Richard M. Coe. LC 89-29676. 448p. (C). 1990. text 36.80 (*0-13-326604-4*) P-H.

Process Geomorphology. 3rd ed. Dale F. Ritter & R. Craig Kochel. 560p. (C). 1994. text. write for info. (*0-697-07632-6*, WCB McGr Hill) McGrw-H Hghr Educ.

Process Geomorphology. 3rd ed. Dale F. Ritter et al. LC 94-72474. 560p. (C). 1995. text. write for info. (*0-697-27127-7*, WCB McGr Hill) McGrw-H Hghr Educ.

Process Geomorphology. 4th ed. Ritter. 1999. text 58.50 (*0-697-34410-X*) McGraw.

Process Guide for School Improvement. Herbert J. Klausmeier. LC 85-20193. (Illus.). 258p. (Orig.). 1985. pap. text 25.00 (*0-8191-4942-X*) U Pr of Amer.

Process Heat Transfer. G. F. Hewitt. 1072p. (C). 1994. boxed set 110.95 (*0-8493-9918-1*) CRC Pr.

Process, Image & Meaning: A Realistic Model of the Meaning of Sentences & Narrative Texts. Wolfgang Wildgen. LC 94-31087. (Pragmatics & Beyond Ser.: No. 31). xii, 281p. 1994. lib. bdg. 67.00 (*1-55619-298-3*) J Benjamins Pubng Co.

Process Improvement: A Guide for Teams. Richard Beans et al. 225p. 1993. pap. 44.95 (*0-944533-06-X*) Coopers Total Qlty.

Process Improvement: A Handbook for Managers. Sarah Cook. 176p. 1996. 61.95 (*0-566-07633-0*, Pub. by Gower) Ashgate Pub Co.

Process Improvement: Enhancing Your Organization's Effectiveness. Eileen Flanagan & Jon Scott. Ed. by Chris Carrigan. LC 95-67042. (Fifty-Minute Ser.). (Illus.). 106p. (Orig.). 1995. pap. 10.95 (*1-56052-322-0*) Crisp Pubns.

Process Improvement: The Dsmc Approach (prima) Mary-jo Hall. 178p. 1995. per. 15.00 (*0-16-048298-4*) USGPO.

Process Improvement & Organizational Learning: The Role of Collaboration Technologies. Ned F. Kock. LC 98-51559. 198p. 1999. pap. 49.95 (*1-878289-58-6*) Idea Group Pub.

Process Improvement in Higher Education. Tromp et al. 110p. (C). 1997. per. 11.95 (*0-7872-3903-8*) Kendall-Hunt.

Process Improvement in the Electronics Industry. Yefim Fasser & Donald Brettner. LC 91-23312. (Series in Systems Engineering). 544p. 1992. 145.00 (*0-471-53638-5*) Wiley.

Process in Architecture: A Documentation in Six Examples. Lance Laver et al. LC 79-88539. (Illus.). 144p. (Orig.). 1979. pap. 4.00 (*0-938437-00-3*) MIT List Visual Arts.

Process in Cybernetics & Systems Research, Vol. 7. F. R. A. Pichler. 1981. 80.00 (*0-07-049847-4*) McGraw.

Process in Neurobiology, Vol. 21. Ed. by G. A. Kerkut & J. W. Phillis. (Illus.). 360p. 1985. 150.00 (*0-08-032321-9*, Pergamon Pr) Elsevier.

***Process in the Arts Therapies.** Ed. by Ann Cattanach. LC 98-45891. 224p. 1999. 69.95 (*1-85302-624-7*, Pub. by Jessica Kingsley) Taylor & Francis.

Process in the Arts Therapies. Ann Cattanach. LC 98-45891. 1999. pap. 26.95 (*1-85302-625-5*) Jessica Kingsley.

Process-Induced Chemical Changes in Food: Proceedings of Pacifichem 95 Held in Honolulu, Hawaii, December 18-22, 1995. Ed. by Fereidoon Shahidi et al. LC 98-15604. (Advances in Experimental Medicine & Biology Ser.: No. 434). (Illus.). 372p. 1998. 110.00 (*0-306-45824-1*, Kluwer Plenum) Kluwer Academic.

Process-Industrial Instruments & Controls Handbook. 4th ed. Douglas M. Considine. (Illus.). 1008p. 1991. 99.50 (*0-07-012445-0*, 6394U) McGraw.

Process Industries Corrosion: The Theory & Practice. Ed. by B. J. Moniz & Walter I. Pollock. LC 86-62318. (Illus.). 858p. 1986. 58.00 (*0-915567-46-6*) NACE Intl.

Process Industries (PID) (1995 ASME International Mechanical Engineering Congress & Exposition Ser.). 1995. 10.00 (*0-614-16714-0*, 95-WA/NCA-1) ASME.

Process Industry Economics. Brennan. 1998. 75.00 (*0-85295-391-7*, 53917) Gulf Pub.

Process Industry Reprints. Ed. by S. G. Taylor et al. LC 83-71088. 216p. 1984. pap. 10.00 (*0-935406-41-7*, 40641) Am Prod & Inventory.

Process Industry Specific Industry Software Requirements Guide. American Production & Inventory Control Society St. 64p. 1991. 15.00 (*1-55822-079-8*) Am Prod & Inventory.

Process Industry Symposium: Dynamic Performance Through Innovation. American Production & Inventory Control Society St. 122p. 1991. 25.00 (*1-55822-049-6*) Am Prod & Inventory.

Process Industry Symposium: Dynamic Performance Through Innovation. American Production & Inventory Control Society St. 115p. 1992. 25.00 (*1-55822-092-5*) Am Prod & Inventory.

Process Industry Symposium: Forum for Change. American Production & Inventory Control Society St. 88p. 1993. 25.00 (*1-55822-102-6*) Am Prod & Inventory.

Process Industry Symposium: Productivity Through Innovation. (Illus.). 180p. 1990. 25.00 (*1-55811-055-0*) Am Prod & Inventory.

Process Innovation. Davenport. 220p. 1992. pap. 29.95 (*0-07-103382-3*) McGraw.

Process Innovation: Reengineering Work Through Information Technology. Thomas H. Davenport. LC 92-21959. 337p. (C). 1993. 34.95 (*0-87584-366-2*) Harvard Busn.

Process Innovation & Automation in Small & Medium Sized Business. Ed. by E. Poutsma et al. 146p. (Orig.). 1987. pap. 33.50 (*90-6275-365-5*, Pub. by Delft U Pr) Coronet Bks.

Process Instrumentation & Control Fundamentals. R. J. Howarth & D. W. Powers, Jr. (Illus.). 380p. 1976. teacher ed. 395.00 (*0-87683-324-5*); ring bd. 95.00 (*0-87683-323-7*) GP Courseware.

Process Instrumentation Applications Manual. Bob Connell. LC 95-22624. 364p. 1995. 84.95 (*0-07-012353-5*) McGraw.

Process Instrumentation Manifolds: Their Selection & Use, a Handbook. enl. ed. John E. Hewson. LC 85-5177. (Illus.). 369p. reprint ed. pap. 114.40 (*0-7837-4522-2*, 205248700001) Bks Demand.

***Process Intensification for the Chemical Industry: Smaller, Cheaper & Safer.** Ed. by A. Green. (BHR Group Conference Ser.: No. 38). 233p. 1999. 266.00 (*1-86058-215-X*) Prof Eng Pubng.

Process Is the Punishment: Handling Cases in a Lower Criminal Court. Malcolm M. Feeley. LC 79-7349. (Illus.). 330p. 1979. 34.95 (*0-87154-253-6*) Russell Sage.

Process Is the Punishment: Handling Cases in a Lower Criminal Court. Malcolm M. Feeley. (Illus.). 1992. pap. 12.95 (*0-87154-255-2*) Russell Sage.

Process Kit, Getting a Job. 3rd ed. Robert H. Zedlitz. (CA - Career Development Ser.). 1992. pap. 11.95 (*0-538-61337-8*) S-W Pub.

Process Level Instrumentation & Control. Nicholas P. Cheremisinoff. LC 80-21922. (Engineering Measurements & Instrumentation Ser.: No. 2). 264p. reprint ed. pap. 81.90 (*0-7837-0920-X*, 204122500019) Bks Demand.

Process Management to Quality Improvement: The Way to Design, Document & Reengineer Business Systems. Gary Born. 304p. 1994. 95.00 (*0-471-94283-9*) Wiley.

Process Mapping: How to Reengineer Your Business Processes. Daniel V. Hunt. LC 95-25495. 288p. 1996. 39.95 (*0-471-13281-0*) Wiley.

Process Mastering: How to Establish & Document the Best Known Way to Do a Job. Ray W. Wilson & Paul Harsin. LC 97-47365. 168p. 1998. 24.00 (*0-527-76344-6*) Productivity Inc.

Process Math, Vol. II, Module I. Multimedia Development Services Staff. (Plant Fundamentals Ser.). (Illus.). 92p. (Orig.). 1995. student ed. 30.00 (*1-57431-004-6*) Tech Trng Systs.

Process Math Vol., Vol. II, Module I. Multimedia Development Services Staff. (Plant Fundamentals Ser.). (Illus.). (Orig.). 1995. teacher ed. 49.95 (*1-57431-044-5*) Tech Trng Systs.

Process Measurement & Control. American Chemical Society Staff. 280p. 1989. 455.00 incl. audio (*0-685-25943-9*, A8); student ed. 42.00 (*0-685-25944-7*) Am Chemical.

***Process Measurement & Control: Introduction to Sensors, Communication, Adjustment & Control.** Roy E. Fraser. LC 00-27088. 224p. 2000. 87.00 (*0-13-022211-9*) P-H.

Process Measurement Fundamentals, 3 vols. E. M. Eacho et al. (Illus.). 1981. teacher ed., ring bd. 595.00 (*0-87683-004-1*) GP Courseware.

Process Measurement Fundamentals, 3 vols., Set. E. M. Eacho et al. (Illus.). 1981. 195.00 (*0-87683-000-9*) GP Courseware.

Process Measurement Fundamentals, 3 vols., Vol. 1. E. M. Eacho et al. (Illus.). 177p. 1981. ring bd. 95.00 (*0-87683-001-7*) GP Courseware.

Process Measurement Fundamentals, 3 vols., Vol. 2. E. M. Eacho et al. (Illus.). 29p. 1981. ring bd. 79.50 (*0-87683-002-5*) GP Courseware.

Process Measurement Fundamentals, 3 vols., Vol. 3. E. M. Eacho et al. (Illus.). 175p. 1981. student ed., ring bd. 79.50 (*0-87683-003-3*) GP Courseware.

Process Metaphysics: An Introduction to Process Philosophy. Nicholas Rescher. LC 95-8784. (SUNY Series in Philosophy). 213p. (C). 1996. text 36.50 (*0-7914-2817-6*); pap. text 17.95 (*0-7914-2818-4*) State U NY Pr.

Process Mineralogy: Extractive Metallurgy, Mineral Exploration, Energy Resources: Proceedings of a Symposium Held at the 110th AIME Annual Meeting, Chicago, IL, February 22-26, 1981. Metallurgical Society of AIME Staff. Ed. by Donald M. Hausen & Won C. Park. LC 81-82942. (Conference Proceedings Ser.). 727p. reprint ed. pap. 200.00 (*0-8357-2516-2*, 205239600013) Bks Demand.

Process Mineralogy Vol. XI: Characterization of Metallurgical & Recyclable Products: Proceedings That Were Presented in Sessions Held at the Minerals, Metals, & Materials Society (TMS) Annual Meeting in New Orleans, LA, Feb. 24-28, 1991. Ed. by Donald M. Hausen et al. LC 91-51004. 241p. 1991. reprint ed. pap. 74.80 (*0-608-03821-0*, 206278300004) Bks Demand.

Process Mineralogy VIII: Applications of Mineralogy to Mineral Beneficiation Technology, Metallurgy, & Mineral Exploration & Evaluation, with Emphasis on Precious Metal Ores: Proceedings of a Symposium Presented in Six Sessions on Process Mineralogy Held During the Minerals, Metals & Materials Society Annual Meeting, Phoenix, Arizona, January 25-28, 1988. fac. ed. Minerals, Metals & Materials Society Staff. Ed. by Andreas H. Vassiliou & David J. Carson. LC 88-63682. (Illus.). 405p. 1988. pap. 125.60 (*0-7837-8607-7*, 205253800008) Bks Demand.

Process Mineralogy IX: Applications to Mineral Beneficiation, Metallurgy, Gold, Diamonds, Ceramics, Environment & Health. International Symposium on Applied Mineralogy (198. Ed. by William Petruk et al. LC 90-61328. 685p. 1990. reprint ed. pap. 200.00 (*0-608-00772-2*, 206157000010) Bks Demand.

Process Mineralogy VII: Applications to Mineral Beneficiation Technology & Mineral Exploration, with Special Emphasis on Disseminated Carbonaceous Gold Ores: Proceedings of a Symposium Presented in Seven Sessions on Process Mineralogy Held During the Metallurgical Society Annual Meeting, Denver, Colorado, February 23-27, 1987. fac. ed. Metallurgical Society of AIME Staff. Ed. by Andreas H. Vassiliou et al. LC 87-42880. 663p. 1987. reprint ed. pap. 200.00 (*0-7837-8302-7*, 204908800010) Bks Demand.

Process Mineralogy VI: Proceedings of a Symposium Presented in Six Sessions on Process Mineralogy Held During the Metallurgical Society Annual Meeting, New Orleans, Louisiana, March 2-6, 1986. fac. ed. Metallurgical Society of AIME Staff. Ed. by Richard D. Hagni. LC 86-23576. 647p. 1986. reprint ed. pap. 200.00 (*0-7837-8300-0*, 204908600010) Bks Demand.

Process Mineralogy XII: Applications to Environment, Precious Metal, Mineral Beneficiation, Pyrometallurgy, Coal & Refractories. Ed. by William Petruk & Albert R. Rule. LC 94-75561. (Illus.). 411p. 1994. 10.00 (*0-87339-273-6*, 2736) Minerals Metals.

Process Mineralogy II: Applications in Metallurgy, Ceramics, & Geology: Proceedings of a Symposium Held at the AIME Annual Meeting in Dallas, Texas, February 14-18, 1982. Metallurgical Society of AIME Staff. Ed. by Richard D. Hagni. LC 82-61494. 517p. reprint ed. pap. 160.30 (*0-8357-2517-0*, 205239700013) Bks Demand.

Process Mineralogy XIII - Proceedings: Process Mineralogy Symposia at the Annual Meetings of the Minerals, Metals & Materials Society (1995: Las Vegas, Nevada) Ed. by R. D. Hagni. LC 94-73625. (Illus.). 330p. 1995. 10.00 (*0-87339-248-5*, 2485) Minerals Metals.

Process Modeling - Fundamentals & Applications to Metals: Proceedings of American Society for Metals Process Modelling Sessions. American Society for Metals Staff. LC 80-12489. (Material-Metalworking Technology Ser.). 456p. reprint ed. 141.40 (*0-608-17141-7*, 202698500053) Bks Demand.

Process Modeling & Control in Chemical Engineering. Ed. by Kaddour Najim. (Chemical Industries Ser.: Vol. 38). (Illus.). 504p. 1989. text 210.00 (*0-8247-8204-6*) Dekker.

***Process Modeling & Control of Enhanced Coagulation.** S. J. Stanley. LC 99-53856. 2000. write for info. (*1-58321-050-4*) Am Water Wks Assn.

Process Modeling of Forest Growth Responses to Environmental Stress. William G. Warren. Ed. by Robert K. Dixon et al. LC 89-20657. 450p. 1990. text 54.95 (*0-88192-152-1*) Timber.

Process Modeling, Simulation & Control. 2nd ed. William L. Luyben. (Chemical Engineering Ser.). 725p. (C). 1989. 98.13 (*0-07-039159-9*) McGraw.

Process Modeling Tools: Proceedings of American Society for Metals Process Modeling Sessions Processes Congress 1980. Materials & Processes Congress. LC 81-52303. (Materials-Metalworking Technology Ser.). 224p. reprint ed. pap. 69.50 (*0-608-16435-6*, 202703500053) Bks Demand.

Process Modelling & Computer Aided Design in Chemical Engineering. Norman. 93.00 (*0-471-93870-X*); pap. 37.00 (*0-471-96761-0*) Wiley.

Process Modelling & Landform Evolution. Stefan Hergarten & Horst Neugebauer. LC 98-41660. (Lecture Notes in Earth Sciences). 1998. pap. 99.00 (*3-540-64932-8*) Spr-Verlag.

Process Modelling for Metal Forming & Thermomechanical Treatment. C. R. Boer et al. (Materials Research & Engineering Ser.). (Illus.). xv, 410p. 1986. 131.95 (*0-387-16401-4*) Spr-Verlag.

***Process Monitoring with Optical Fibers & Harsh Sensors, Vol. #353.** Ed. by Michael A. Marcus & Anbo Wang. 1999. 89.00 (*0-8194-2999-6*) SPIE.

Process of Absorption of New Immigrants in Israel. Samuel N. Eisenstadt. (Reprint Series in Social Sciences). (C). 1993. reprint ed. pap. text 5.00 (*0-8290-3501-X*, S-78) Irvington.

Process of Admission to Ordained Ministry Vol. 2: Reformed, Anglican, Lutheran, & Wesylan Rites. James F. Puglisi. Tr. by Mary M. Misrahi. (Reformed Anglican, Lutheran, & Wesleyan Rites Ser.). 252p. (Orig.). 1997. pap. text 39.95 (*0-8146-6129-7*, Pueblo Bks) Liturgical Pr.

Process of Admission to Ordained Ministry Vol. 3: A Comparative Study: The Contemporary Rites & General Conclusions. James F. Puglisi. 1999. pap. 39.95 (*0-8146-6130-0*, M Glazier) Liturgical Pr.

Process of Admission to Ordained Ministry, a Comparative Study Vol. 1: Epistemological Principles & Roman Catholic Rites. James F. Puglisi. Tr. by Michael S. Driscoll & Mary M. Misrahi. (Process of Admission to Ordained Ministry Ser.). 278p. (Orig.). 1996. pap. 39.95 (*0-8146-6128-9*, M Glazier) Liturgical Pr.

Process of Argument. Michael Boylan. 122p. (C). 1993. reprint ed. pap. text 18.50 (*0-8191-9065-9*) U Pr of Amer.

Process of Art: Studies In Nineteenth-Century Literature & Art Offered to Alan Raitt. Michael Freeman. (Illus.). 248p. 1999. text 72.00 (*0-19-815953-6*) OUP.

Process of Awakening: An Overview, Vol. 1. Diane K. Pike. LC 85-8083. (Illus.). 75p. (Orig.). 1985. pap. 9.95 (*0-916192-29-6*) L P Pubns.

Process of Becoming Multicultural. Terry Ford. Ed. by Joe Kincheloe & Shirley R. Steinberg. 200p. Date not set. pap. text 18.95 (*0-8153-2325-5*) Garland.

Process of Breastfeeding, Module 2. Rebecca F. Black et al. LC 97-25569. (Nursing Ser.). 264p. 1997. spiral bd. 39.95 (*0-7637-0195-5*) Jones & Bartlett.

Process of Business Planning: A Practical Hands-On Text. 3rd ed. Andrew J. Batchelor, Sr. & Andrew J. Batchelor, Jr. (Illus.). 261p. (C). 1997. pap. text 55.00 (*0-9623374-6-3*) Tangent Pub.

***Process of Business/Environmental Collaborations: Partnering for Sustainability.** Alissa J. Stern & Timothy Hicks. LC 99-59613. 224p. 2000. 67.50 (*1-56720-292-6*, Praeger Pubs) Greenwood.

Process of Change. Peggy Papp. LC 83-12814. (Guilford Family Therapy Ser.). 248p. 1983. lib. bdg. 39.95 (*0-89862-052-X*) Guilford Pubns.

Process of Change. Peggy Papp. LC 83-12814. 248p. 1994. pap. text 22.00 (*0-89862-501-7*) Guilford Pubns.

Process of Change in American Banking: Political Economy & the Public Purposes. Jeremy F. Taylor. LC 89-24328. 240p. 1990. 62.95 (*0-89930-504-0*, TPB/, Quorum Bks) Greenwood.

Process of Change in Early Modern Europe: Essays in Honor of Miriam Usher Chrisman. Ed. by Phillip N. Bebb & Sherrin D. Marshall. LC 88-19497. (Illus.). 250p. 1988. lib. bdg. 36.95 (*0-8214-0900-X*) Ohio U Pr.

***Process of Community Health Education & Promotion.** Eva Doyle & Susan Ward. LC 00-33244. 2000. write for info. (*0-7674-1561-2*) Mayfield Pub.

***Process of Competition.** Jackie Kraft. LC 00-20573. 208p. 2000. text 80.00 (*1-84064-212-2*) E Elgar.

An Asterisk (*) at the beginning of an entry indicates that the title is appearing for the first time.

Process of Composition. Joy M. Reid. (Illus.). 224p. (C). 1982. pap. text 11.95 (*0-13-723015-X*) P-H.

Process of Composition. 2nd ed. Joy M. Reid. (Illus.). 256p. (C). 1988. pap. text 33.27 (*0-13-723065-6*) P-H.

***Process of Composition.** 3rd ed. Joy M. Reid. LC 99-38017. 368p. 1999. pap. text 33.27 (*0-13-021317-9*) P-H.

***Process of Confession: Spokenword.** Gno. LC 98-94869. 106 p. 1999. write for info. (*0-7392-0061-5*) Morris Pubng.

Process of Counseling & Therapy. 3rd ed. Janet Moursund. LC 92-12024. 240p. (C). 1992. pap. 33.40 (*0-13-720657-7*) P-H.

Process of Democratization. Georg Lukacs. Tr. by Susanne Bernhardt & Norman Levine from GER. LC 90-47554. (SUNY Series in Contemporary Continental Philosophy). 189p. (C). 1991. pap. text 19.95 (*0-7914-0762-4*) State U NY Pr.

Process of Democratization: A Comparative Study of 147 States, 1980-88. Tatu Vanhanen. (Illus.). 250p. (C). 1990. text 65.00 (*0-8448-1640-X*); pap. text 55.00 (*0-8448-1641-8*) Taylor & Francis.

Process of Development of Societies. Kanjirathara C. Alexander. LC 94-4732. 1994. 32.00 (*0-8039-9171-1*) Sage.

Process of Discovery: A Writer's Workshop. R. J. Willey & Jennifer Berne. LC 96-23361. 288p. (C). 1996. pap. 22.81 (*0-07-070316-7*) McGraw.

Process of Divorce: Helping Couples Negotiate Settlements. Kenneth Kressel. LC 96-46468. 376p. 1997. pap. 40.00 (*0-7657-0049-2*) Aronson.

Process of Drama. John O'Toole. LC 92-7785. (Illus.). 272p. (C). 1992. pap. 25.99 (*0-415-08244-7*, A9664) Routledge.

Process of Economic Development. James M. Cypher & James L. Dietz. LC 96-38305. 576p. (C). 1997. 110.00 (*0-415-11027-0*); pap. 32.99 (*0-415-11028-9*) Routledge.

Process of Education. Jerome S. Bruner. LC 60-15235. 113p. 1976. pap. 12.95 (*0-674-71001-0*) HUP.

Process of Elimination. Carolyn Keene. (Nancy Drew & Hardy Boys Super Mystery Ser.: No. 36). (YA). (gr. 6 up). 1998. per. 3.99 (*0-671-00739-4*) PB.

Process of Elimination. Carolyn Keene. (Nancy Drew & Hardy Boys Super Mystery Ser.: No. 36). (YA). (gr. 6 up). 1998. 9.09 (*0-606-13651-7*, Pub. by Turtleback) Demco.

Process of Elimination: The Bathroom, the Kitchen, & the Aesthetics of Waste. Ellen Lupton & J. Abbott Miller. (Illus.). 80p. (Orig.). 1992. pap. 19.95 (*0-938437-42-9*) MIT List Visual Arts.

Process of Excelling: The Practical How-To Guide for Today's Leaders. 2nd ed. Roger E. Herman. LC 98-145636. (Illus.). 248p. 1997. 22.95 (*1-886939-22-5*); pap. 16.95 (*1-886939-04-7*, Pub. by OakHill Pr VA) ACCESS Pubs Network.

Process of Financial Liberalization in India. Kunal Sen & Rajendra R. Vaidya. LC 98-902986. (Illus.). 228p. 1998. text 22.95 (*0-19-564260-0*) OUP.

Process of Fine Grinding. B. Beke. 1981. text 99.50 (*90-247-2462-7*) Kluwer Academic.

Process of Forgiveness. William A. Meninger. 156p. 1997. pap. 12.95 (*0-8264-1008-1*) Continuum.

Process of Government: A Study of Social Pressures. rev. ed. Arthur F. Bentley. 520p. (C). 1994. pap. 24.95 (*1-56000-778-8*) Transaction Pubs.

Process of Government under Jefferson. Noble E. Cunningham. LC 77-85535. 371p. 1978. reprint ed. pap. 115.10 (*0-608-04569-1*, 206534100003) Bks Demand.

***Process of Group Psychotherapy: Systems for Analyzing Change.** Ed. by Araidne P. Beck & Carol M. Lewis. 494p. 2000. 49.95 (*1-55798-658-4*, 4318930) Am Psychol.

Process of Healing. Alice M. Givens. LC 90-61517. 1991. pap. 12.95 (*0-87212-241-7*) Libra.

Process of Historical Inquiry: Everyday Lives of Working Americans. Erik W. Austin et al. (Illus.). 248p. 1989. pap. text 21.00 (*0-231-06967-7*) Col U Pr.

Process of Human Development: A Holistic Life-Span Approach. 3rd ed. Clara S. Schuster & Shirley S. Ashburn. (Illus.). 992p. 1992. text 47.95 (*0-397-54881-8*) Lppncott W & W.

Process of Industrialization & Technological Alternatives. Ed. by Yoginder K. Alagh. (C). 1988. 34.00 (*81-7062-044-9*, Pub. by Lancer International) S Asia.

***Process of Industrialization & the Role of Labor Law in Asian Countries.** Ed. by Roger Blanpain et al. (Bulletin of Comparative Labour Relations Ser.: Vol. 34). 172p. 1999. pap. 60.00 (*90-411-1047-X*) Kluwer Law Intl.

Process of Innovation in Education. LC 72-12724. (Educational Technology Reviews Ser.: Vol. 2). 144p. 1973. pap. 29.95 (*0-87778-050-1*) Educ Tech Pubns.

Process of International Arbitration. Kenneth S. Carlston. LC 74-152591. 318p. 1972. reprint ed. lib. bdg. 65.00 (*0-8371-6024-3*, CAIA, Greenwood Pr) Greenwood.

Process of Investigation: Concepts & Strategies for the Security Professional. Charles A. Sennewald. 255p. 1991. 44.95 (*0-7506-9222-7*) Buttrwrth-Heinemann.

Process of Islamic Revolution. S. Abul Ala Maududi. 1990. pap. 3.00 (*1-56744-195-5*) Kazi Pubns.

Process of Language Understanding. Ed. by G. B. Flores d'Arcais & R. J. Jarvella. LC 82-23754. 356p. reprint ed. pap. 110.40 (*0-7837-0124-1*, 204040700016) Bks Demand.

Process of Legal Research. C. Peter Erlinder et al. 384p. (C). 1986. 17.95 (*0-316-50728-8*, Aspen Law & Bus) Aspen Pub.

Process of Legal Research. 4th ed. Ann L. Bateson. 1996. pap. text 34.95 (*0-7355-0633-7*) Panel Pubs.

Process of Legal Research. 4th ed. Christina L. Kunz et al. LC 96-75340. 533p. 1996. pap. 29.95 (*0-316-50732-6*) Aspen Pub.

Process of Legal Research: Successful Strategies, Vol. 1. 3rd ed. Christina L. Kunz. LC 92-71001. 1992. 27.95 (*0-316-50720-2*, Aspen Law & Bus) Aspen Pub.

***Process of Legal Research: With Teacher's Manual.** 5th ed. Christina L. Kunz et al. (Legal Research & Writing Text Ser.). 530p. 2000. pap., teacher ed. write for info. (*0-7355-1223-X*, 1223X) Panel Pubs.

Process of Management. T. S. McAlpine. 1973. pap. 26.95 (*0-8464-0765-5*) Beekman Pubs.

Process of Media Writing. Beverley J. Pitts. LC 96-22525. 325p. 1996. pap. text 48.00 (*0-205-15636-3*) Allyn.

Process of Media Writing. Beverley J. Pitts et al. (C). 1996. pap. text, teacher ed. write for info. (*0-205-26344-5*, T6344-0) Allyn.

Process of Moral Choice. Benito F. Reyes. (Ethics 101 Ser.). 142p. 1967. pap. 10.00 (*0-939375-28-1*) World Univ Amer.

Process of Neurologic Care in Medical Practice. Thomas H. Glick. LC 83-12899. (Illus.). 373p. 1984. 52.50 (*0-674-71080-0*) HUP.

Process of New Drug Discovery & Development. Charles G. Smith. 160p. 1992. boxed set 131.95 (*0-8493-4211-2*, RM301) CRC Pr.

Process of Paragraph Writing. 2nd ed. Joy M. Reid. 272p. (C). 1994. pap. text 33.27 (*0-13-101205-3*) P-H.

Process of Parenting. 5th rev. ed. Jane B. Brooks. LC 98-39378. (Illus.). 556p. 1999. pap. text 47.95 (*0-7674-0215-4*, 0215-4) Mayfield Pub.

Process of Parenting Instructor's Manual. 5th rev. ed. Jane B. Brooks. 147p. (C). 1999. pap. text, teacher ed. write for info. (*0-7674-1044-0*, 1044-0) Mayfield Pub.

Process of Political Domination in Ecuador. Agustin Cueva. Tr. by Danielle Salti. LC 79-809. 109p. 1981. 34.95 (*0-87855-338-X*) Transaction Pubs.

Process of Presentational Speaking. 2nd ed. William S. Howell & Ernest G. Bormann. 240p. (C). 1997. pap. text 50.00 (*0-06-042929-1*) Addson-Wesley Educ.

***Process of Professional Financial Planning.** Milton. 2001. pap. 30.00 (*0-324-02030-9*) Sth-Wstrn College.

***Process of Professional Financial Planning.** Milton. 2001. pap. 55.00 (*0-324-02029-5*) Thomson Learn.

Process of Program Evaluation. 672p. write for info. (*0-318-59908-2*, NIDSP) Am Soc Train & Devel.

Process of Psychotherapy: An Integration of Clinical Experiences & Empirical Research. John R. Thompson. 424p. (Orig.). 1987. pap. text 34.00 (*0-8191-6603-0*); lib. bdg. 58.50 (*0-8191-6602-2*) U Pr of Amer.

Process of Psychotherapy: Matter of Mind. Welch. LC 98-19881. (Counseling Ser.). 1998. pap. 46.95 (*0-534-34413-5*) Wadsworth Pub.

Process of Ratemaking, 2 vols. Leonard S. Goodman. LC 98-6253. 1600p. 1998. 299.00i (*0-910325-70-7*) Public Util.

Process of Reading: A Cognitive Analysis of Fluent Reading & Learning to Read. Don C. Mitchell. LC 81-21912. 258p. reprint ed. pap. 80.00 (*0-7837-0126-8*, 204040900016) Bks Demand.

Process of Recreation Programming Theory & Technique. 3rd ed. Patricia Farrell & Herberta M. Lundegren. LC 91-65114. 367p. 1991. text 28.95 (*0-910251-40-1*) Venture Pub PA.

Process of Regeneration: Change. Oletha M. Pinkston. LC 90-82451. 112p. (Orig.). 1991. pap. 9.95 (*0-9627055-0-0*) Pinkston.

Process of Religion: Essays in Honor of Dean Shailer Mathews. Ed. by Miles H. Krumbine. LC 71-38776. (Essay Index Reprint Ser.). 1977. reprint ed. 20.95 (*0-8369-2667-6*) Ayer.

Process of Rural Transformation: Eastern Europe, Latin America & Australia. Ed. by Ivan Volgyes et al. LC 79-10190. (Policy Studies). 1980. 100.00 (*0-08-023110-1*, Pergamon Pr) Elsevier.

Process of Science. Saunders. (C). 1998. pap. text, wbk. ed. write for info. (*0-03-021007-0*) Harcourt Coll Pubs.

Process of Science: Contemporary Philosophical Approaches to Understanding Scientific Practice. Ed. by Nancy J. Nersessian. (Science & Philosophy Ser.: No. 3). 234p. 1987. lib. bdg. 151.50 (*90-247-3425-8*, Pub. by M Nijhoff) Kluwer Academic.

Process of Science: Discovering Biology. Brace Jovanovich Harcourt. 1998. 37.00 (*0-03-021008-9*) Harcourt Coll Pubs.

Process of Sculpture. Anthony T. Padovano. (Illus.). 352p. 1986. pap. 17.95 (*0-306-80273-2*) Da Capo.

Process of Socio-Economic Development. K. N. Dubey. (C). 1992. text 22.00 (*81-7033-164-1*, Pub. by Rawat Pubns) S Asia.

Process of Speech: Puritan Religious Writing & Paradise Lost. Boyd M. Berry. LC 75-36933. 320p. reprint ed. pap. 99.20 (*0-608-14661-7*, 202583000046) Bks Demand.

Process of Spermatogenesis in Animals. Edward C. Roosen-Runge. LC 76-9169. (Developmental & Cell Biology Ser.: 5). 222p. reprint ed. pap. 63.30 (*0-608-16855-6*, 2027239) Bks Demand.

Process of Standardization & Certification in Mexico: A Strategic Entry Report, 1997. Compiled by Icon Group International Staff. (Illus.). 142p. 1999. ring bd. 1420.00 incl. audio compact disk (*0-7418-1027-1*) Icon Grp.

Process of Transnationalization & Transnational Mergers. (UNCTC Current Studies A: No. 8). 91p. 1989. 12.00 (*92-1-104310-7*, E.89.II.A.4) UN.

Process of Waking Up - A Psychotherapy of Awakening. Jerry Fankhauser. 170p. (Orig.). 1990. pap. 12.00 (*0-9617006-5-3*) J Fankhauser.

Process of War: Advancing the Scientific Study of War. Ed. by Stuart Bremer & Thomas Cusack. 255p. 1996. text 20.00 (*2-88449-176-7*); pap. text 12.00 (*2-88449-177-5*) Gordon & Breach.

Process of Writing. Roberta Allen & Marcia Mascolini. 144p. (C). 1996. pap. text 30.40 (*0-13-182114-8*) P-H.

***Process of Writing.** Mary Riordan-Kirlsson. (Illus.). 76p. 1999. pap., teacher ed. 9.95 (*1-57690-473-3*, TCM2473) Tchr Create Mat.

Process of Writing. A. D. Van Nostrand. (C). 1995. pap. text 26.36 (*0-395-72175-X*) HM.

Process of Writing: What Works for Teachers & Students. (GED Staff Development Videotape Ser.). 307.40 incl. VHS (*0-8092-4746-1*) NTC Contemp Pub Co.

Process Operator. Multimedia Development Services Staff. (Plant Fundamentals Ser.). (Illus.). (Orig.). 1995. student ed. 30.00 (*1-57431-001-1*) Tech Trng Systs.

Process Operator Vol., Vol. 1, Module 1. Multimedia Development Services Staff. (Plant Fundamentals Ser.). (Illus.). (Orig.). 1995. teacher ed. 49.95 (*1-57431-041-0*) Tech Trng Systs.

Process Optimization: With Applications in Metallurgy & Chemical Engineering. Willis H. Ray & Julian Szekely. LC 73-936. (Wiley-Interscience Publications). (Illus.). 382p. reprint ed. pap. 118.50 (*0-7837-3465-4*, 205779300008) Bks Demand.

Process-Oriented Group Therapy: For Men & Women Sexually Abused in Childhood. Carolyn Knight. LC 96-231197. 192p. (Orig.). 1996. pap. 26.95 (*1-55691-123-8*, 238) Learning Pubns.

Process-Oriented Instruction: Verbal & Pictorial Aid & Comprehension Strategies. Frank P. De Jong & Bernadette H. Van Hout-Wolters. LC 94-205367. 200p. 1994. pap. 32.50 (*90-5383-256-4*, Pub. by VU Univ Pr) Paul & Co Pubs.

Process Patterns: Building Large-Scale Systems Using Object Technology Series. Scott W. Ambler. LC 99-160053. (Managing Object Technology Ser.: No. 15). 300p. (C). 1998. 39.95 (*0-521-64568-9*) Cambridge U Pr.

***Process Philosophy: A Survey of Basic Issues.** Nicholas Rescher. 120p. 2000. 27.50 (*0-8229-4142-2*) U of Pittsburgh Pr.

Process Philosophy & Christian Thought. Delwin Brown et al. LC 74-127586. 1971. pap. 17.50 (*0-672-60799-9*, Bobbs) Macmillan.

Process Philosophy & Political Ideology: The Social & Political Thought of Alfred North Whitehead & Charles Hartshorne. Randall C. Morris. LC 89-49229. 289p. (C). 1991. pap. text 21.95 (*0-7914-0416-1*) State U NY Pr.

Process Physics. Multimedia Development Services Staff. (Plant Fundamentals Ser.). (Illus.). 64p. (Orig.). 1995. student ed. 30.00 (*1-57431-006-2*) Tech Trng Systs.

Process Physics Vol., Vol. II, Module III. Multimedia Development Services Staff. (Plant Fundamentals Ser.). (Illus.). (Orig.). 1995. teacher ed. 49.95 (*1-57431-046-1*) Tech Trng Systs.

Process Physics & Modeling in Semiconductor Devices: 4th International Symposium. Ed. by G. R. Srinivasan et al. LC 95-83752. (Proceedings Ser.: Vol. 96-4). (Illus.). 528p. 1996. 66.00 (*1-56677-154-4*) Electrochem Soc.

Process Physics & Modeling in Semiconductor Technology: Proceedings of the Second International Symposium, Montreal, Quebec, 1990. International Symposium on Process Physics & Model. Ed. by G. R. Srinivasan et al. LC 90-85817. (Electrochemical Society Proceedings Ser.: No. 91-4). 816p. 1991. reprint ed. pap. 200.00 (*0-608-00279-8*, 205254300008) Bks Demand.

***Process Physics & Modeling in Semiconductor Technology: 5th International Symposium.** International Symposium on Process Physics and Modeling in Semiconductor Technology et al. Ed. by C. S. Murthy et al. LC 99-62162. (Illus.). 230p. 1999. 54.00 (*1-56677-224-9*, PV 99-2) Electrochem Soc.

Process Pipe & Tube Welding: A Guide to Welding Process Options, Techniques, Equipment, NDT & Codes of Practice. Ed. by W. Lucas. (Illus.). 160p. 1991. 135.00 (*1-85573-012-X*, Pub. by Woodhead Pubng) Am Educ Systs.

***Process Pipe Drafting.** Terence M. Shumaker. LC 94-28111. (Illus.). 354p. 1999. text 34.64 (*1-56637-535-5*) Goodheart.

Process Planning Technology. Mark A. Curtis. LC 87-34605. 253p. 1988. text 27.95 (*0-471-83254-5*) P-H.

Process Plant & Equipment Cost Estimating. O. P. Kharbanda. 1979. 19.00 (*0-910460-68-X*) Craftsman.

Process Plant Commissioning: A User Guide. Ed. by David Horsley & John Parkinson. 109p. 1990. 35.00 (*0-85295-260-0*, 9CH35, Pub. by IChemE) Gulf Pub.

Process Plant Construction Equipment Standards, 1994: Sitework Piling Concrete, Vol. 1. 34th ed. Richardson Engineering Services, Inc. Staff. (Illus.). 950p. 1994. write for info. (*1-881386-14-7*) Richardson Eng.

Process Plant Construction Estimating Standards: 1994 - Masonry, Metals, Carpentry, Doors, Finishes, Windows, Specialties, Vol. 2. 34th ed. Richardson Engineering Services, Inc. Staff. (Illus.). 782p. 1994. write for info. (*1-881386-15-5*) Richardson Eng.

Process Plant Construction Estimating Standards, 1994, 4 vols., Set. 33rd ed. Richardson Engineering Services, Inc. Staff. (Illus.). 4048p. 1994. 457.00 (*1-881386-13-9*) Richardson Eng.

Process Plant Construction Estimating Standards, 1994: Mechanical & Electrical, Vol. 3. 34th ed. Richardson Engineering Services, Inc. Staff. (Illus.). 1026p. 1994. write for info. (*1-881386-16-3*) Richardson Eng.

Process Plant Construction Estimating Standards, 1994: Process Equipment, Vol. 4. 34th ed. Richardson Engineering Services, Inc. Staff. (Illus.). 1290p. 1994. write for info. (*1-881386-17-1*) Richardson Eng.

Process Plant Construction Estimating Standards, 1995. 1995. 457.00 (*1-881386-22-8*) Richardson Eng.

***Process Plant Control Room Resource Management Training.** (Illus.). 2000. reprint ed. spiral bd. 39.95 (*1-57431-169-7*) Tech Trng Systs.

Process Plant Designer's Pocket Handbook of Codes & Standards. C. R. Burklin. LC 79-17599. 184p. 1979. reprint ed. pap. 57.10 (*0-608-00832-X*, 206162200010) Bks Demand.

Process Plant Layout & Piping Design. Ed Bausbacher & Roger Hunt. LC 93-9725. (Illus.). 464p. (C). 1993. text 67.60 (*0-13-138629-8*) P-H.

Process Plant Machinery. Heinz P. Bloch. (Illus.). 493p. 1989. text 125.00 (*0-409-90087-7*) Buttrwrth-Heinemann.

Process Plant Machinery. 2nd ed. Heinz Bloch. LC 98-10447. 512p. 1998. 95.00 (*0-7506-7081-9*) Buttrwrth-Heinemann.

Process, Praxis, & Transcendence. James L. Marsh. LC 98-16746. (SUNY Series in the Philosophy of the Social Sciences). 384p. (C). 1999. text 73.50 (*0-7914-4073-7*); pap. text 24.95 (*0-7914-4074-5*) State U NY Pr.

***Process Pumps Selection: A Systems Approach.** 2nd ed. John Davidson & Otto Von Bertele. 202p. 2000. 112.00 (*1-86058-180-3*) Prof Eng Pubng.

Process, Purpose, Practice: A Basic Writer's Guide. Carole Moses. 411p. (C). 1991. teacher ed. 2.66 (*0-669-19819-6*); pap. text 36.76 (*0-669-19818-8*); teacher ed. 37.96 (*0-669-24709-X*) HM Trade Div.

Process, Quality & Information Control in the Worldwide Pulp & Paper Industry. Pulp & Paper Magazine Editors. (Illus.). 189p. 1996. pap. 59.00 (*0-87930-400-6*, 510) Miller Freeman.

Process Quality Control. 3rd ed. Ott et al. LC 00-37255. (Illus.). 500p. 2000. pap. 74.95 (*0-07-135010-1*) McGraw-Hill Prof.

Process Quality Management & Improvement Guidelines. 2nd rev. ed. Roger Ackerman et al. Ed. by Susan Annitto. (AT&T Quality Library). (Illus.). 102p. (Orig.). 1988. reprint ed. pap. 29.95 (*0-932764-32-0*, 500-049) AT&T Customer Info.

Process Quality Management & Improvement Guidelines. 2nd rev. ed. Roger Ackerman et al. Ed. by Susan Annitto. (AT&T Quality Library). (Illus.). 102p. (Orig.). 1988. pap. 24.95 (*0-614-07666-8*) AT&T Customer Info.

Process Qualtiy Control. 2nd ed. Schilling. 1997. 38.25 (*0-07-365509-0*) McGraw.

Process Reactor Design. Ning H. Chen. 512p. (C). 1983. teacher ed. write for info. (*0-318-57278-8*, H79049) P-H.

Process Reader. Bishop. 2000. text 26.00 (*0-07-237939-1*) McGraw.

Process Reading & Writing: A Literature-Based Approach. Ed. by Shelly B. Wepner et al. (Language & Literacy Ser.: No. 6). 296p. (C). 1991. text 47.00 (*0-8077-3118-8*); pap. text 19.95 (*0-8077-3117-X*) Tchrs Coll.

Process Redesign: The Implementation Guide for Managers. Irving J. Detoro & Arthur R. Tenner. (Engineering Process Improvement Ser.). 352p. (C). 1996. 42.00 (*0-201-63391-4*) Addison-Wesley.

Process Redesign & Management: Beyond Reengineering. Douglas C. Montgomery et al. LC 96-60496. (Illus.). x, 262p. 1996. write for info. (*0-9652178-0-9*) Windham Brannon.

Process Reengineering: The Key to Achieving Breakthrough Success. Lon Roberts. LC 93-45264. 195p. 1994. text 33.00 (*0-87389-274-7*, H0830) ASQ Qual Pr.

Process Reengineering in Action: A Practical Guide to Achieving Breakthrough Results. Richard Y. Chang. (Quality Improvement Ser.). (Illus.). 120p. 1995. pap. 14.95 (*0-7879-5096-3*) R Chang Assocs.

Process Reengineering, Organizational Change & Performance Improvement. Soumitra Dutta & J. F. Manzoni. LC 98-19210. (INSEAD Global Management Ser.). 1998. write for info. (*0-07-709436-0*) McGraw.

Process Reengineering Workbook: Practical Steps to Working Faster & Smarter Through Process Improvement. Jerry L. Harbour. LC 94-14109. (Illus.). 147p. 1994. pap. 22.50 (*0-527-76240-7*) Productivity Inc.

Process Risk Management Systems. W. F. Kenney. 373p. 1993. 120.00 (*0-471-18791-7*, Wiley-VCH) Wiley.

Process Risk Management Systems. William F. Kenney. LC 93-7879. 1993. 65.00 (*1-56081-045-9*, Wiley-VCH) Wiley.

Process Safety Analysis. Bob Skelton. 215p. 1997. 75.00 (*0-88415-666-4*, 5666) Gulf Pub.

Process Safety Management. Ian S. Sutton. 470p. 1997. pap. 55.00 (*1-57502-528-0*) Morris Pubng.

***Process Safety Management Overview.** (Illus.). 200p. 2000. reprint ed. spiral bd. 39.95 (*1-57431-187-5*, PSMO) Tech Trng Systs.

Process Safety Management Program. Mark M. Moran. (OSHA Written Compliance Programs Ser.: No. 22). (Illus.). 60p. 1992. ring bd. 169.00 (*1-890966-16-9*) Moran Assocs.

Process Safety Management Standard Inspection Manual. 2nd ed. Occupational Safety & Health Administration Staff. 120p. 1994. pap. text 69.00 (*0-86587-427-1*) Gov Insts.

Process Safety Pocket Guide, 10 copies. Donald Pierce. Ed. by Catherine Franklin et al. (Illus.). 84p. (Orig.). 1993. pap. text 41.80 (*0-931690-56-0*) Genium Pub.

Process Scale Liquid Chromatography. Ed. by G. Subramanian. LC 94-24799. 225p. 1995. 160.00 (*3-527-28672-1*, Wiley-VCH) Wiley.

Process Selection: From Design to Manufacture. K. G. Swift & J. D. Booker. 224p. 1997. pap. text 39.95 (*0-340-69249-9*, TJ230) Wiley.

Process Selection: From Design to Manufacture. Ken Swift & Julian Booker. LC 97-189228. 214p. 1997. pap. 64.95 (*0-470-23774-0*) Wiley.

Process Server. Jack Rudman. (Career Examination Ser.: C-620). 1994. pap. 23.95 (*0-8373-0620-5*) Nat Learn.

P

Process Server's Handbook & Legal Reference Directory: Technical & Legal Aspects of Successfully Serving Legal Papers. Jody Ball. 1997. spiral bd. 38.00 (*1-891247-01-8*) Thomas Investigative.

Process Serving for Pros. Nelson Tucker. 67p. (Orig.). (C). 1997. pap. 35.00 (*0-918487-95-1*) Thomas Investigative.

Process Simulation & Control in Iron & Steelmaking. Ed. by J. M. Uys & H. L. Bishop. LC 65-27847. (Metallurgical Society Conference Ser.: Vol. 32). 350p. reprint ed. pap. 108.50 (*0-608-11272-0*, 200152000079) Bks Demand.

Process Skills Development in Ambulatory Family Practice. CSOF (Grime) Staff. 246p. 1999. ring bd. 47.96 (*0-7872-5591-2*, 41559101) Kendall-Hunt.

Process Skipping: Mechanisms Which Lock in Addictive Patterns. Edwin M. McMahon & Peter A. Campbell. 32p. 1996. pap. text 3.00 (*1-55612-513-5*, LL1513) Sheed & Ward WI.

Process Studies in Hillslope Hydrology. Ed. by M. G. Anderson & T. P. Burt. LC 90-12111. 550p. 1990. 360.00 (*0-471-92714-7*) Wiley.

Process Synthesis & Design: A Self Instructional Problem Workbook. D. Kauffman. 264p. (C). 1992. pap. text 60.00 (*1-882767-08-X*) ETS.

Process Systems Analysis & Control. 2nd ed. Donald R. Coughanower. 640p. (C). 1991. 92.50 (*0-07-013212-7*) McGraw.

Process Technologies for Water Treatment. Ed. by S. Stucki. LC 88-21918. (Illus.). 262p. 1988. 79.50 (*0-306-43002-9*, Plenum Trade) Perseus Pubng.

Process Technology. Ed. by Elisabetta Di Notto & Alfonso Fuggetta. LC 97-39191. 140p. 1998. text 127.50 (*0-7923-8090-8*) Kluwer Academic.

Process Technology: A Compilation of Recent Engineering Conference Papers on Process Control & Simulation. Technical Association of the Pulp & Paper Industry. LC TS1117.6. 192p. reprint ed. pap. 59.60 (*0-608-13334-5*, 202556500044) Bks Demand.

Process Technology Conference: Eighth Proceedings, Dearborn Meeting, October 23-26, 1988, Vol. 8. Iron & Steel Society of AIME Staff. LC 82-197229. (Illus.). 103p. reprint ed. pap. 32.00 (*0-7837-6138-4*, 204569700008) Bks Demand.

Process Technology Conference: Fifth Proceedings, Detroit Meeting, April 15-17, 1985, Vol. 5. Iron & Steel Society of AIME Staff. LC 82-197229. (Illus.). 251p. reprint ed. pap. 77.90 (*0-7837-6136-8*, 204569500005) Bks Demand.

Process Technology Conference: Fourth Proceedings, Chicago Meeting, April 3-4, 1984, Vol. 4. Iron & Steel Society of AIME Staff. LC 82-197229. (Illus.). 201p. reprint ed. pap. 62.40 (*0-7837-6135-X*, 204569400004) Bks Demand.

Process Technology Conference: Proceedings, Chicago Meeting, Feburary 23-25, 1981 Sponsered by the Process Technology Division, Iron & Steel Society of AIME, Vol. 2. Iron & Steel Society of AIME Staff. LC TS0307.P67. 323p. reprint ed. pap. 100.20 (*0-608-14763-X*, 202418700035) Bks Demand.

Process Technology Conference: Proceedings, Washington, D. C. Meeting, March 25-26, 1980, Vol. 1. Iron & Steel Society of AIME Staff. LC 80-138368. 194p. reprint ed. pap. 60.20 (*0-608-14469-X*, 201923700001) Bks Demand.

Process Technology Conference: Sixth Proceedings, Washington Meeting, April 6-9, 1986. Iron & Steel Society of AIME Staff. LC 82-197229. (Illus.). 1225p. reprint ed. pap. 200.00 (*0-7837-6137-6*, 204569600006) Bks Demand.

Process Technology Conference: Third Proceedings, Pittsburgh Meeting, March 28-31, 1982, Vol. 3. Iron & Steel Society of AIME Staff. LC 82-197229. (Illus.). 305p. reprint ed. pap. 94.60 (*0-7837-6134-1*, 204569300003) Bks Demand.

Process Technology Conference: 12th Proceedings - Environmental Concerns in the Iron & Steel Industry. Iron & Steel Society of AIME Staff. LC 82-197229. (Illus.). 389p. reprint ed. pap. 120.60 (*0-608-09066-2*, 206970100012) Bks Demand.

Process Technology Conference - Effect of Residuals on Steel Products & Processing, Vol. 15. 244p. 1997. 90.00 (*1-886362-22-X*, P-PC98/083) Iron & Steel.

Process Technology Conference, 14th: Proceedings Ladle Processing: Metallurgy & Operations, Orlando Meeting, November 12-15, 1995. Iron & Steel Society of AIME Staff. LC 82-197229. (Illus.). 195p. reprint ed. pap. 60.50 (*0-608-08081-0*, 206904000003) Bks Demand.

Process Technology Conference, 9th, Proceedings, Detroit Meeting, March 25-28, 1990 Vol. 9: Use of Instrumentation to Optimize the Continuous Casting Process. AIME, Iron & Steel Society Staff. LC 82-197229. 203p. pap. 63.00 (*0-7837-2203-6*, 204254100004) Bks Demand.

Process Technology Conference, 10th Proceedings: Second International Symposium on Modeling in the Iron & Steel Industry, Toronto Meeting, April 5-18, 1992, Vol. 10. Iron & Steel Society of AIME Staff. LC 82-197229. (Illus.). 472p. 1992. reprint ed. pap. 146.40 (*0-608-05892-0*, 206622700010) Bks Demand.

Process Technology for Semiconductor Lasers: Crystal Growth & Microprocesses. Kenichi Iga & Susumu Kinoshita. LC 95-48999. (Springer Series in Materials Science: Vol. 30). (Illus.). 169p. 1996. 79.00 (*3-540-58972-4*) Spr-Verlag.

Process Technology Handbook. Charles E. Thomas. (Illus.). xi, 420p. 1997. pap. text 49.15 (*0-9665515-0-8*) Uhai Publ.

Process Technology Handbook Instructor's Guide. Charles E. Thomas. (Illus.). xi, 300p. 1997. ring bd. 36.45 (*0-9665515-1-6*) Uhai Publ.

Process Technology of Cement Manufacturing. VDZ Congress Staff. (ENG, FRE & GER.). 693p. 1987. 295.00 (*0-8288-0225-4*, M7678) Fr & Eur.

Process Theology: A Basic Introduction. C. Robert Mesle & John B. Cobb, Jr. LC 93-9204. 160p. (Orig.). 1993. pap. 12.99 (*0-8272-2945-3*) Chalice Pr.

Process Theology: An Introductory Exposition. John B. Cobb, Jr. & David R. Griffin. LC 76-10352. 192p. 1976. pap. 18.95 (*0-664-24743-1*) Westminster John Knox.

Process Theology & Secularization. Edwin C. Garvey. 21p. 1972. pap. 0.75 (*0-912414-14-6*) Lumen Christi.

Process Theology & the Christian Tradition. Illtyd Trethowan. LC 84-26240. (Studies in Historical Theology: Vol. 5). 124p. 1985. pap. 14.95 (*0-932506-44-5*) St Bedes Pubns.

Process Theory of Medicine: Problems in Contemporary Philosophy. Ed. by Marcus P. Ford. LC 87-7865. (Problems in Contemporary Philosophy Ser.: Vol. 5). 240p. 1987. lib. bdg. 89.95 (*0-88946-328-X*) E Mellen.

***Process Think: Wining Perspectives for Business Change in the Information Age.** Ed. by Varun Grover & William J. Kettinger. LC 99-44627. (Illus.). 416p. 2000. 149.95 (*1-878289-68-3*) Idea Group Pub.

Process to Product. Ioannides. 136p. (C). 1998. pap. text 10.45 (*0-536-01517-1*) Pearson Custom.

Process to Product 10. 152p. (C). 1999. pap. text 10.45 (*0-536-02407-3*) Pearson Custom.

Process Tomography: Principles, Techniques, & Applications. Ed. by R. A. Williams & M. S. Beck. LC 94-41070. (Illus.). 384p. 1995. text 125.00 (*0-7506-0744-0*) Buttrwrth-Heinemann.

Process Utility Systems: Introduction to Design, Operation, & Maintenance. Ed. by Jack Broughton. 282p. 1994. 55.00 (*0-85295-322-4*, 9CH89) Gulf Pub.

Process Validation for Business Success. Robert G. Launsby et al. 150p. 1995. pap. text 49.95 (*0-9636093-4-3*) Launsby Cnslting.

Process Writing Portfolio Program Teacher Handbook. Charles Skidmore. (Secondary Writing Ser.). (Illus.). 80p. 1993. pap. 22.47 (*0-201-62391-9*) Addison-Wesley.

Process Your Thoughts. Marianne Phinney. (College ESL Ser.). (J). 1994. pap. 23.95 (*0-8384-5289-2*) Heinle & Heinle.

***Processed Food in Brazil: A Strategic Entry Report, 1996.** Compiled by Icon Group International Staff. (Illus.). 171p. 1999. ring bd. 1710.00 incl. audio compact disk (*0-7418-1217-7*) Icon Grp.

Processed Food in Russia: A Strategic Entry Report, 1997. Compiled by Icon Group International Staff. (Illus.). 168p. 1999. ring bd. 1680.00 incl. audio compact disk (*0-7418-0839-0*) Icon Grp.

Processed Foods & the Consumer: Additives, Labeling, Standards, & Nutrition. Vernal S. Packard. LC 75-32670. 367p. reprint ed. pap. 113.80 (*0-7837-2930-8*, 205752400006) Bks Demand.

***Processed Foods in Pakistan: A Strategic Entry Report, 1999.** Compiled by Icon Group International. (Illus.). 193p. 1999. ring bd. 1930.00 incl. audio compact disk (*0-7418-1824-8*) Icon Grp.

Processed Foods Packaging. Ed. by Peter Allen. 200p. 1986. pap. 985.00 (*0-685-09455-3*) FIND-SVP.

Processed Foodstuffs, Vol. I-7. Conrad Caspari. (Single Market Review Ser.). 1998. 80.00 (*0-7494-2311-0*) Kogan Page Ltd.

Processed Fruits & Vegetables Market. M. Laverty. 800p. 1997. 1195.00 (*0-318-00496-8*) Busn Trend.

Processed Lives: Gender & Technology in Everyday Life. Ed. by Jennifer Terry & Melodie Calvert. LC 96-26628. (Illus.). 264p. (C). 1997. 75.00 (*0-415-14931-2*); pap. 22.99 (*0-415-14932-0*) Routledge.

***Processed Meats.** Albert M. Pearson. 464p. 1998. pap. 95.00 (*0-8342-1304-4*) Aspen Pub.

Processed Words. Louis M. Cole. 36p. 1998. pap. 7.95 (*0-9663293-5-X*) Main St Rag.

Processed Words. Tom Savage. (Morning Coffee Chapbook Ser.). (Illus.). 15p. (Orig.). 1990. pap. 20.00 (*0-918273-65-X*) Coffee Hse.

Processes & Environments of Glacial Margins. American Quaternary Association. 173p. 1986. 10.00 (*0-318-22004-0*) Am Quaternary Assn.

Processes & Lists see Technical Bulletins of Dianetics & Scientology

Processes & Materials of Manufacture. 4th ed. Roy A. Lindberg. (Illus.). 848p. (C). 1989. text 63.00 (*0-205-11817-8*, H18179) P-H.

Processes & Materials of Manufacture. 4th ed. Roy A. Lindberg. (Illus.). 848p. 1990. teacher ed. write for info. (*0-318-63888-6*, H18187); teacher ed. write for info. (*0-318-63887-8*, H18195) P-H.

Processes & Products of Collaborative Problem Solving Vol. 13, No. 4: Some Interdisciplinary Perspectives. Ed. by Celia Hoyles & Ellice A. Forman. 112p. 1995. pap. 17.50 (*0-8058-9936-7*) L Erlbaum Assocs.

Processes, Beliefs & Questions: Essays on Formal Semantics of Natural Language & Natural Language Processing. Ed. by Stanley Peters & Esa Saarinen. 252p. 1981. text 149.50 (*90-277-1314-6*, D Reidel) Kluwer Academic.

Processes Controlling the Composition of Clastic Sediments. Ed. by M. J. Johnsson & A. Basu. (Special Papers: No. 284). 1994. pap. 56.25 (*0-8137-2284-5*) Geol Soc.

Processes for Major Addition-Type Plastics & Their Monomers. 2nd ed. Lyle F. Albright. LC 80-12568. 304p. 1985. lib. bdg. 37.50 (*0-89874-074-6*) Krieger.

Processes in Continental Lithospheric Deformation. Ed. by Sydney P. Clark, Jr. et al. LC 87-37344. (Geological Society of America Ser.: Vol. 218). (Illus.). 220p. 1988. reprint ed. pap. 68.20 (*0-608-07744-5*, 206783200010) Bks Demand.

Processes in Cutaneous Epidermal Differentiation. Ed. by I. A. Bernstein. LC 87-10327. 400p. 1987. 105.00 (*0-275-92406-8*, C2406, Praeger Pubs) Greenwood.

Processes in Individual Differences. Colin Cooper & Ved P. Varma. LC 96-52970. (Illus.). 192p. (C). 1997. 75.00 (*0-415-14119-2*) Routledge.

Processes in Karst Systems Physics, Chemistry, & Geology. W. Dreybrodt. (Physical Environment Ser.: Vol. 4). (Illus.). 325p. 1988. 185.95 (*0-387-18839-8*) Spr-Verlag.

Processes in Non-Linear Media. 1993. write for info. (*0-8493-7723-4*) CRC Pr.

Processes in Photoreactive Polymers. V. V. Krongauz. LC 94-3136. 1994. 89.95 (*0-412-98401-6*) Chapman & Hall.

Processes in Photoreactive Polymers. Ed. by V. V. Krongauz & A. D. Trifunac. LC 94-3136. 1994. 89.95 (*0-442-03891-7*) Chapman & Hall.

Processes of Adult Education. Ed. by Coolie Verner & Thurman White. 57p. 1965. 3.50 (*0-88379-028-9*) A A A C E.

Processes of Cognitive Growth: Infancy. Jerome S. Bruner. LC 68-27831. (Heinz Werner Lectures: No. 3). 1968. 9.00 (*0-8271-6810-1*) Clark U Pr.

Processes of Constitutional Decision Making. 3rd ed. Paul Brest & Sanford Levinson. 1632p. 1992. 59.00 (*0-316-10787-5*, Aspen Law & Bus) Aspen Pub.

Processes of Constitutional Decision Making, 1986: Supplement. Paul Brest & Sanford Levinson. 250p. (C). 1986. pap. text 12.00 (*0-316-10789-1*, Aspen Law & Bus) Aspen Pub.

Processes of Constitutional Decisionmaking: Cases & Materials. 3rd ed. Paul Brest. 1632p. 1992. teacher ed. write for info. (*0-316-10850-2*, 08502) Aspen Law.

Processes of Constitutional Decisionmaking: Cases & Materials. 3rd ed. Paul Brest. 1632p. 1995. suppl. ed. 26.95 (*0-316-10625-9*, 06259) Aspen Law.

***Processes of Constitutional Decisionmaking: Cases & Materials.** 4th ed. Paul Brest. LC 99-87802. 2000. 64.00 (*0-7355-1250-7*) Panel Pubs.

Processes of Diesel Engine Combustion. (Special Publications). 210p. 1999. pap. 95.00 (*0-7680-0376-8*, SP-1444) Soc Auto Engineers.

Processes of Dispute Resolution: The Role of Lawyers. 2nd ed. John S. Murray et al. (University Casebook Ser.). 854p. 1996. text 42.95 (*1-56662-330-8*) Foundation Pr.

Processes of Fossilization. Ed. by Stephen K. Donovan. 256p. 1991. text 68.00 (*0-231-07674-6*) Col U Pr.

Processes of Literary Creation: Flaubert & Proust. Marion Schmid. (Legenda Ser.). 229p. (Orig.). 1998. pap. 49.50 (*1-900755-06-8*, Pub. by E H R C) David Brown.

***Processes of Manufacturing.** R. Thomas Wright. LC 86-29563. (Illus.). 464p. 1999. text 39.96 (*1-56637-533-9*) Goodheart.

Processes of Ongoing Human Evolution. Ed. by Gabriel W. Lasker. LC 60-12566. 113p. reprint ed. pap. 35.10 (*0-7837-3783-1*, 204360200010) Bks Demand.

Processes of Organic Evolution. 3rd ed. G. Ledyard Stebbins. (Illus.). 1977. pap. text 15.95 (*0-13-723452-X*) P-H.

Processes of Stratification in Science. Paul D. Allison. Ed. by Harriet Zuckerman & Robert K. Merton. LC 80-13567. (Dissertations on Sociology Ser.). 1980. lib. bdg. 25.95 (*0-405-12946-7*) Ayer.

Processes of the Cranial Midline: International Symposium Vienna, Austria, May 21-25, 1990. Ed. by Wolfgang T. Koos & B. Richling. (Acta Neurochirugica - Supplementum Ser.: Supplement 53). (Illus.). viii, 205p. 1991. 168.00 (*0-387-82309-3*) Spr-Verlag.

Processes of the World-System. Ed. by Terence K. Hopkins & Immanuel Wallerstein. LC 79-27385. (Political Economy of the World-System Annuals Ser.: No. 3). 320p. 1980. reprint ed. pap. 99.20 (*0-608-01459-1*, 205950300001) Bks Demand.

Processes of Tribal Unification & Integration: Case Study of the Bhils. S. L. Doshi. 1978. 11.00 (*0-8364-0291-X*) S Asia.

Processes of Urbanism: A Multidisciplinary Approach. Ed. by Joyce Aschenbrenner & Lloyd R. Collins. (World Anthropology Ser.). xiv, 424p. 1978. 58.50 (*90-279-7620-1*) Mouton.

Processes of Vegetation Change. Colin Burrows. 340p. 1990. pap. 49.95 (*0-04-580013-8*) Thomson Learn.

***Process/industrial Instruments & Controls Handbook, 5th Ed.** 5th ed. Gregory K. McMillan. LC 99-29591. 1999. 173.75 (*0-07-012582-1*) Datapro Res.

Processing & Applications of High Tc Superconductors: Proceedings of the Northeast Regional Meeting of the Metallurgical Society Held at Rutgers - the State University of New Jersey, May 9-11, 1988. Metallurgical Society of AIME Staff. Ed. by William E. Mayo. LC 88-62259. (Illus.). 269p. 1988. reprint ed. pap. 83.40 (*0-7837-9134-8*, 204993400004) Bks Demand.

Processing & Characterization of Materials Using Ion Beams, Vol. 128. Ed. by F. A. Smidt et al. (Materials Research Society Symposium Proceedings Ser.). 760p. 1989. text 17.50 (*1-55899-001-1*) Materials Res.

Processing & Design Issues in High Temperature Materials. Ed. by N. S. Stoloff & R. H. Jones. LC 96-80050. (Illus.). 450p. 1997. 105.00 (*0-87339-357-0*, 3570) Minerals Metals.

Processing & Fabrication of Advanced Materials, No. V. Ed. by T. S. Srivatsan & J. J. Moore. (Illus.). 703p. 1996. 334.00 (*0-87339-349-X*, 349X) Minerals Metals.

Processing & Fabrication of Advanced Materials: Proceedings of a Symposiumon Processing & Fabrication of Advanced Materials (7th: 1998: Rosemont, Illinois) T. S. Srivatsan et al. LC 98-67359. xiii, 523 p. 1998. 156.00 (*0-87339-415-1*) Minerals Metals.

Processing & Fabrication of Advanced Materials for High Temperature Applications: Proceedings of a Symposium Sponsored by the Structural Materials Division (SMD), Held at the TMS/ASM Fall Meeting in Cincinnati, OH, October 1991. Minerals, Metals & Materials Society Staff. Ed. by V. A. Ravi & T. S. Srivatsan. LC 92-60673. (Illus.). 390p. 1992. reprint ed. pap. 120.90 (*0-608-05696-0*, 206621100007) Bks Demand.

Processing & Fabrication of Advanced Materials IV. Ed. by T. S. Srivatsan & J. J. Moore. (Illus.). 926p. 1995. 20.00 (*0-87339-337-6*) Minerals Metals.

Processing & Handling of Powders & Dusts. Ed. by T. P. Battle & H. Henein. LC 96-79954. (Illus.). 296p. 1997. 64.00 (*0-87339-359-7*, 3597) Minerals Metals.

***Processing & Printing.** Julien Busselle. LC 99-40277. (B & W Photo-Lab Ser.). 128p. 2000. 29.95 (*1-883403-67-7*, Silver Pixel Pr) Saunders Photo.

***Processing & Printing Black & White for Effect.** Julien Busselle. 1999. pap. 29.95 (*2-88046-427-7*) Watsn-Guptill.

Processing & Properties for Powder Metallurgy Composites: Proceedings of a Symposium Sponsored by the P-M Committee of TMS-AIME Held at the Annual Meeting of the Metallurgical Society in Denver, Colorado, February 1987. Metallurgical Society of AIME Staff. Ed. by A. M. Ritter et al. LC 87-43115. 180p. reprint ed. pap. 55.80 (*0-7837-1439-4*, 205241300016) Bks Demand.

Processing & Properties of High TC Superconductors: Bulk Materials, Vol. 1. S. Jin. 492p. 1993. text 124.00 (*981-02-1165-1*) World Scientific Pub.

Processing & Properties of High TC Superconductors II: Thin Films & Applications. Sung-Ho Jin & D. K. Christen. 500p. 1997. text 162.00 (*981-02-1670-X*) World Scientific Pub.

Processing & Properties of Low Carbon Steel. Ed. by J. M. Gray. LC 73-172124. 425p. reprint ed. pap. 131.80 (*0-608-30958-3*, 201265300083) Bks Demand.

Processing & Properties of Nanocrystalline Materials. Ed. by Suryanarayana J. Singh & F. H. Froes. (Illus.). 494p. 1996. 20.00 (*0-87339-335-X*) Minerals Metals.

Processing & Property Enhancement Utilizing Modifiers & Additives in Polymers: First International Conference - Sponsored by Polymer Modifiers & Additives Division, the Marriot Hotel, Newark Airport, Newark, NJ, Nov. 6-7, 1985. Society of Plastics Engineers Staff. LC TP1142.P7. 226p. reprint ed. pap. 70.10 (*0-608-17118-2*, 202769500056) Bks Demand.

Processing & Synthesis of Hydrogeological Data. A. Gheorghe. (Abacus Bks.). 390p. 1978. text 179.00 (*0-85626-107-6*) Gordon & Breach.

Processing & Testing of Reaction Injection Molding Urethanes - STP 788. Ed. by Ashe, pseud & Dunleavy. 95p. 1982. pap. 13.95 (*0-8031-0779-X*, STP788) ASTM.

Processing & Use of Organic Sludge & Liquid Agricultural Wastes. P. L. L'Hermite. 1986. text 256.00 (*90-277-2338-9*) Kluwer Academic.

Processing & Use of Sewage Sludge. Ed. by P. L. L'Hermite & H. Ott. 600p. 1984. text 252.50 (*90-277-1727-3*) Kluwer Academic.

Processing & Utilization of Sorghum: Selected Bibliographical Reference (with Abstracts) from 1990 to 1996. D. Cox et al. 98p. 1997. pap. 75.00 (*0-85954-477-X*, Pub. by Nat Res Inst) St Mut.

Processing Auditory Messages Exactly & Totally. Jean G. DeGaetano. 60p. 1994. pap. text 22.00 (*1-886143-22-6*) Grt Ideas Tching.

Processing Data: The Survey Example. Linda B. Bourque & Virginia A. Clark. LC 92-9653. (Quantitative Applications in the Social Sciences Ser.: Vol. 85). 96p. (C). 1992. pap. text 10.95 (*0-8039-4741-0*) Sage.

Processing Declarative Knowledge: International Workshop PDK '91 Kaiserslautern, Germany, July 1-3, 1991 Proceedings. Ed. by H. Boley et al. (Lecture Notes in Artificial Intelligence Ser.: Vol. 567). xii, 427p. 1991. 58.95 (*0-387-55033-X*) Spr-Verlag.

Processing, Design & Performance of Composite Materials: 1994 International Mechanical Engineering Congress & Exposition, Chicago, Illinois - November 6-11, 1994. (MD Ser.: Vol. 52). 300p. 1994. 90.00 (*0-7918-1426-2*, G00921) ASME.

Processing Digital Images in GIS: A Tutorial Featuring ArcView & Arc-Info. David L. Verbyla & Kang-tsung Chang. LC 97-16685. 312p. (C). 1997. pap. 57.95 (*1-56690-135-9*) Thomson Learn.

***Processing East Asian Languages: A Special Issue of the Journal Language & Cognitive Processes.** Hsuan-Chih Chen Staff & Xiaolin Zhou. 288p. 1999. 54.95 (*0-86377-660-4*) Psychol Pr.

Processing, Fabrication & Application of Advanced Composites: Proceedings of ASM International's 1993 Conference. Ed. by Kamleshwar Upadhya. LC 93-73187. 400p. 1993. 104.00 (*0-87170-473-0*, 6326) ASM.

Processing, Fabrication & Application of Advanced Composites: Proceedings of the Conference on Processing Fabrication & Application of Advanced Composites, Held August 9-11, 1993, in Long Beach, CA. Ed. by Kamleshwar Upadhya. LC 93-73187. (Illus.). 229p. 1993. reprint ed. pap. 71.00 (*0-608-02618-2*, 206327600004) Bks Demand.

Processing, Fabrication, & Manufacturing of Composite Materials - 1992. Ed. by T. S. Srivatsan & E. J. Lavernia. (MD Ser.: Vol. 35). 272p. 1992. 62.50 (*0-7918-1089-5*, G00733) ASME.

Processing Foods: Quality Optimization & Process Assessment. Fernanda A. R. Oliveira & Jorge C. Oliveira. LC 98-46086. (Food Engineering & Manufacturing Ser.). 1999. 99.95 (*0-8493-7905-9*) CRC Pr.

An Asterisk (*) at the beginning of an entry indicates that the title is appearing for the first time.

Processing Fruits Vol. 1: Science & Technology: Biology, Principles & Applications. Ed. by Laszlo P. Somogyi et al. LC 95-62013. 518p. 1996. 179.95 (*1-56676-362-2*, 763622) Technomic.

Processing Fruits Vol. 2: Science & Technology: Major Processed Products. Ed. by Laszlo P. Somogyi et al. 520p. 1996. 179.95 (*1-56676-383-5*, 763835) Technomic.

***Processing Function Standard Operating Procedures.** Government Printing Office Staff. 739p. 1998. pap. text 60.00 (*0-16-049340-4*) USGPO.

Processing Government Loans. Mortgage Bankers Assn. of America Staff. 260p. (C). 1997. pap. 145.00 (*1-57599-015-6*) Mortgage Bankers.

Processing Images of Faces. Ed. by Vicki Bruce et al. (Tutorial Monographs in Cognitive Science: Vol. 2). 272p. (C). 1992. text 73.25 (*0-89391-684-6*) Ablx Pub.

Processing Images of Faces. Vicki Bruce & Mike Burton. Ed. by Nigel Shadbolt. (Tutorial Monographs in Cognitive Science: Vol. 2). 272p. (C). 1992. pap. 39.50 (*0-89391-771-0*) Ablx Pub.

Processing Interclausal Relationships in the Production & Comprehension of Text: Studies in the Production & Comprehension of Text. Ed. by Jean Costermans & Michael Fayol. 344p. 1996. 59.95 (*0-8058-1846-4*); pap. 29.95 (*0-8058-1847-2*) L Erlbaum Assocs.

Processing Medical Documents. 2nd ed. Robert P. Poland. LC 98-49590. 256p. 1998. 38.95 (*0-02-804745-1*) Glencoe.

Processing Medical Documents Using WordPerfect. Robert P. Poland. LC 94-12977. 1995. write for info. (*0-02-802536-9*) Glencoe.

Processing Metonymy & Metaphor. Dan Fass. LC 97-23756. (Series in Artificial Intelligence). (Illus.). 300p. 1997. text 78.50 (*1-56750-231-8*); pap. text 39.50 (*1-56750-232-6*) Ablx Pub.

Processing, Microstructure & Properties of HSLA Steels: Proceedings of International Symposium Held November 3-5, 1987 in Pittsburgh, Pennsylvania. Minerals, Metals & Materials Society Staff. Ed. by Anthony J. DeArdo, Jr. LC 88-62439. 523p. reprint ed. pap. 162.20 (*0-7837-1443-2*, 205241700016) Bks Demand.

Processing Mortgage-Backed Securities. Louis J. Karcher. 128p. (C). 1989. text 39.50 (*0-13-723685-9*) NY Inst Finance.

***Processing Near-Surface Seismic-Reflection Data: A Primer.** Gregory S. Baker. Ed. by Roger A. Young. (Course Notes Ser.: Vol. 11). (Illus.). 77p. 1999. 75.00 (*1-56080-090-9*) Soc Expl Geophys.

Processing of Complex Sounds by the Auditory System: Proceedings of a Royal Society Discussion Meeting Held on 4-5 December 1991. Ed. by R. P. Carlyon et al. LC 92-28567. (Illus.). 146p. (C). 1993. text 55.00 (*0-19-852272-X*, Clarendon Pr) OUP.

Processing of Composites. Raju S. Dave & Alfred C. Loos. LC 99-27337. (Progress in Polymer Processing Ser.). 1999. write for info. (*1-56990-226-7*) Hanser-Gardner.

Processing of Environmental Information in Vertebrates. Ed. by M. H. Stetson. (Illus.). 330p. 1987. 196.00 (*0-387-96558-0*) Spr-Verlag.

Processing of Information & Structure. Wendall R. Garner. LC 73-22174. 208p. (C). 1974. text 39.95 (*0-89859-119-8*) L Erlbaum Assocs.

Processing of Medical Information in Aging Patients: Cognitive & Human Factors Perspectives. Ed. by Denise C. Park et al. LC 98-30256. 344p. 1999. 69.95 (*0-8058-2889-3*) L Erlbaum Assocs.

Processing of Metal & Ceramic Powders: Proceedings of a Symposium, Sponsored by the Powder Metallurgical Society of AIME & Basic Science Division of the American Ceramic Society ...Louisville, KY, October 12-14, 1981. AIME, Metallurgical Society Staff. Ed. by Randall M. German & K. W. Lay. LC 82-61009. 345p. reprint ed. pap. 107.00 (*0-608-16944-7*, 205614700050) Bks Demand.

Processing of Metals & Advanced Materials: Modeling, Design & Properties. Ed. by B. Q. Li. LC 97-75877. (Illus.). 306p. 1998. 90.00 (*0-87339-395-3*, 3953) Minerals Metals.

Processing of Multidimensional Signals. Alexandre J. Smirnov. Ed. by A. Lacroix & A. N. Venetsanopoulos. LC 98-55109. (Digital Signal Processing Ser.). (Illus.). 276p. 1999. 89.95 (*3-540-65449-6*) Spr-Verlag.

***Processing of Reusable Surgical Textiles for Use in Health Care Facilities: ANSI/AAMI ST65:2000.** (Illus.). 2000. pap. 100.00 incl. cd-rom (*1-57020-128-5*) Assn Adv Med Instrn.

Processing of RNA. D. Apirion. LC 82-22834. 360p. 1983. 203.00 (*0-8493-6510-4*, CRC Reprint) Franklin.

Processing of Structural Metals by Rapid Solidification: Proceedings of a Seven Session Symposium on Enhanced Properties in Structural Metals Via Rapid Solidification. ASM International Staff. Ed. by F. H. Froes & S. J. Savage. LC 87-81828. (Conference Proceedings Ser.). (Illus.). 483p. 1987. reprint ed. pap. 149.80 (*0-608-02612-3*, 206327000004) Bks Demand.

Processing of Utilization of High-Sulfur Coals, Vol. 5. Ed. by B. K. Parekh & J. G. Groppo. (Coal Science & Technology Ser.: Vol. 21). 644p. 1993. 471.75 (*0-444-81476-0*) Elsevier.

Processing of Wide Bandgap Semiconductors S. J. Pearton. LC 99-27325. 1999. 145.00 (*0-8155-1439-5*) Noyes.

Processing Procedures for Canned Food Products see Complete Course in Canning & Related Processes

***Processing Program: Using Language Webs & Altered Auditory Input to Improve Comprehension, 2 vols.** Sandra McKinnis. LC 00-21012. 2000. pap. write for info. (*1-888222-47-6*) Thinking Pubns.

Processing, Properties & Applications of Cast Metal Matrix Composites. Ed. by P. K. Rohatgi & P. A. Khan. (Illus.). 200p. 1996. 68.00 (*0-87339-344-9*, 3449) Minerals Metals.

Processing Science of Advanced Ceramics Vol. 155: Materials Research Society Symposium Proceedings, Vol. 155. Ed. by I. Aksay et al. 387p. 1989. text 17.50 (*1-55899-028-3*) Materials Res.

Processing Structures for Perception & Action. Ed. by H. Marko et al. LC 87-34522. 279p. 1988. 145.00 (*3-527-27705-6*) Wiley.

Processing Technician. Jack Rudman. (Career Examination Ser.: C-3534). 1994. pap. 27.95 (*0-8373-3534-5*) Nat Learn.

Processing the Computer Conspiracy. Matt Tullos. LC 97-40331. (Summit High Ser.: Vol. 2). 144p. (Orig.). (J). (gr. 7-9). 1998. pap. 4.99 (*0-8054-0181-4*) Broadman.

Processing the Experience: Enhancing & Generalizing Learning. 2nd ed. John L. Luckner & Reldan S. Nadler. 464p. 1997. per. 36.95 (*0-7872-1000-5*, 41100001) Kendall-Hunt.

Processing the Facial Image: Proceedings of a Royal Society Discussion Meeting Held on 9-10 July 1991. Ed. by V. Bruce et al. (Illus.). 138p. 1992. text 85.00 (*0-19-852261-4*) OUP.

Processing the News: How People Tame the Information Tide. 2nd ed. Doris A. Graber. 314p. (C). 1994. reprint ed. pap. text 29.50 (*0-8191-9098-5*) U Pr of Amer.

Processing the Plan of God Through Prayer. Mark Brazee. 107p. 1998. pap. 7.00 (*0-934445-07-9*) Eternal Word.

Processing Unemployment Insurance Claims. Cornelia Spanier. (Orig.). 1986. pap. 39.95 (*0-938545-01-9*) Jennings & Keefe.

Processing Vegetables: Science & Technology. Ed. by D. S. Smith et al. LC 97-60163. 430p. 1997. text 104.95 (*1-56676-507-2*) Technomic.

Procession. Kahlil Gibran. 1972. pap. 4.95 (*0-8065-0274-6*, Citadel Pr) Carol Pub Group.

Procession des Pierres. Thierry Vila. (FRE.). 220p. 1989. pap. 39.95 (*0-7859-4463-X*, 2715807511) Fr & Eur.

Procession of Friends: Quakers in a America. Daisy Newman. LC 79-160875. 460p. (C). 1972. pap. 17.00 (*0-913408-59-X*) Friends United.

Procession of Holy Spirit: An Insight to the Triadic Relationship of the Divinity. Volodymyr Owcharuk. Ed. by Raphael Masterjohn & Nicholas C. Eliopoulos. 112p. 1999. pap. text 12.00 (*1-893760-01-4*) Eliopoulos.

Procession of Masks. Herbert S. Gorman. LC 77-99698. (Essay Index Reprint Ser.). 1977. 21.95 (*0-8369-1352-3*) Ayer.

Procession of Prayers: Meditations & Prayers from Around the World. John Carden. 320p. 1997. pap. 25.00 (*0-304-70139-4*) Continuum.

Procession of Prayers: Meditations & Prayers from Around the World. John Carden. LC 97-46455. 352p. 1998. pap. 16.95 (*0-8192-1752-2*) Morehouse Pub.

Procession of Saints. James Brodrick. LC 72-5436. (Biography Index Reprint Ser.). 1977. reprint ed. 22.95 (*0-8369-8134-0*) Ayer.

Processionals & Recessionals for Traditional Weddings: Guidebook & Cassette. David Perkoff et al. (Illus.). 20p. (Orig.). 1990. pap. 15.95 (*0-9631377-0-0*) Seven Veils Recs.

Processions of God: The Significance of Ceremony. J. E. Leonard. 60p. 1995. pap. 5.95 (*1-884454-03-8*) Laudemont Pr.

Processo de Cartas de Amores. Juan De Segura. Tr. by Edwin B. Place. LC 70-134270. (Northwestern Humanities Ser.: No. 23). 1970. reprint ed. 22.00 (*0-404-50723-9*) AMS Pr.

***Processor Architecture: From Dataflow to Superscalar & Beyond.** J. Silc et al. LC 99-15706. 410p. 1999. pap. 49.00 (*3-540-64798-8*) Spr-Verlag.

Processual & Postprocessual Archaeologies: Multiple Ways of Knowing the Past. Ed. by Robert W. Preucel. LC 90-84175. (Center for Archaeological Investigations Occasional Paper Ser.: No. 10). (Illus.). xii, 324p. (Orig.). 1991. pap. 25.00 (*0-88104-074-6*) Center Archaeol.

Processus Bernardi Delitiosi: The Trial of Father Bernard Delicieux, 3 September-8 December 1319. Alan Friedlander. LC 94-76685. (Transactions Ser.: Vol. 86, Pt. 1). 393p. (C). 1996. pap. 30.00 (*0-87169-861-7*, T861-fra) Am Philos.

Prochatechisis & Mystagogical Catechesis see Oglasytel' Nija i Tajnovodstennija Pouchenija

Prochatechisis & Mystagogical Catechesis of St. Cyril of Jerusalem see Oglasytel'nija I Tajnovodstvennija Pouchenija Svjatago Kirilma Jerusalimskago

Proche-Orient Eclate. Georges Corm. (FRE.). 559p. 1991. pap. 18.95 (*0-7859-1675-X*, 2070326144) Fr & Eur.

Proche-Orient Ottoman (1517-1918) et Postottoman (1918-1930) see Peuples et les Civilisations du Proche-Orient: Essai d'une Histoire Comparee, des Origines a nos Jours

ProCite in Libraries: Applications in Bibliographic Database Management. Ed. by Deb R. Biggs. 221p. 1995. 39.50 (*0-938734-90-3*) Info Today Inc.

Proclaim Good Tidings: Evangelism for the Faith Community. Vernard Eller. LC 86-20697. 59p. 1987. reprint ed. pap. 30.00 (*0-608-02158-X*, 206282700004) Bks Demand.

Proclaim His Marvelous Deeds: How to Give a Personal Testimony. Patti G. Mansfield. 93p. (Orig.). 1987. pap. 3.75 (*0-940535-06-8*, UP107) Franciscan U Pr.

Proclaim Jubilee! A Spirituality for the Twenty-First Century. Maria Harris. 144p. (Orig.). 1996. pap. 16.95 (*0-664-25661-9*) Westminster John Knox.

Proclaim My Word: Insights to Inspire Confidence in Members & Missionaries. S. Shane Littlefield. LC 95-61399. 140p. 1995. 9.95 (*0-9647847-1-8*) Timpanogos UT.

Proclaim Peace: Christian Pacifism from Unexpected Quarters. Theron F. Schlabach & Richard T. Hughes. LC 96-1006. 304p. 1997. text 34.95 (*0-252-02262-9*); pap. text 14.95 (*0-252-06588-3*) U of Ill Pr.

Proclaim Praise: Daily Prayer for Parish & Home. LC 93-29357. 128p. 1995. pap. 5.00 (*0-929650-94-8*, PRAYER) Liturgy Tr Pubns.

Proclaim Salvation: Preaching the Church Year. David Ewert. LC 92-72909. 160p. (Orig.). 1992. pap. 9.99 (*0-8361-3608-X*) Herald Pr.

Proclaim the Word: Pronunciation Guide for Catholic Lay Lectors. 79p. 1998. pap. 12.95 (*1-885057-13-X*) C E Hugenberger.

Proclaiming a Classic: The Canonization of Orlando Furioso. Daniel Javitch. 208p. 1991. text 39.50 (*0-691-06549-7*, Pub. by Princeton U Pr) Cal Prin Full Svc.

Proclaiming & Sustaining Excellence: Assessment As a Faculty Role. Karen M. Schilling & Karl L. Schilling. Ed. by Jonathan D. Fife. LC 98-85236. (ASHE-ERIC Higher Education Reports: Vol. 26). 100p. 1998. pap. 24.00 (*1-878380-83-4*, 26-3) GWU Grad Schl E&HD.

Proclaiming Bible Truth: Evangelistic Sermons. 388p. 1992. 19.95 (*1-882449-15-0*) Messenger Pub.

Proclaiming Bible Truth: Pastoral Sermons, Vol. 2. Elizabeth Williams. 381p. 1993. 19.95 (*1-882449-23-1*) Messenger Pub.

Proclaiming God's Love in Song. Eugene A. Walsh. (Illus.). 96p. (Orig.). 1994. pap. 4.95 (*0-915531-22-4*) OR Catholic.

Proclaiming God's Love in Word & Deed. Eugene A. Walsh. (Illus.). 96p. (Orig.). 1994. pap. text 4.95 (*0-915531-21-6*) OR Catholic.

Proclaiming God's Message: A Study in the Theology of Preaching. Domenico Grasso. LC 65-14739. (University of Notre Dame Liturgical Studies). 306p. 1968. reprint ed. pap. 94.90 (*0-608-00879-6*, 206167300010) Bks Demand.

Proclaiming God's Truth: 25 Years at Christian Light Publications, 1969-1994. John Coblentz et al. 1994. pap. 7.95 (*0-87813-558-8*) Christian Light.

Proclaiming God's Word Today: Preaching God's Word Today. Stanley S. Harakas. 1989. pap. 6.95 (*0-937032-69-7*) Light&Life Pub Co MN.

Proclaiming Harmony. Tr. by William O. Hennessey from CHI. LC 81-18143. (Michigan Monographs in Chinese Studies: No. 41). 180p. (Orig.). 1981. pap. text 15.00 (*0-89264-041-3*) Ctr Chinese Studies.

Proclaiming Shalom: Lectionary Introductions to Foster the Catholic & Jewish Relationship. Philip Cunningham. 152p. (Orig.). 1995. pap. text 16.95 (*0-8146-6142-4*, Pueblo Bks) Liturgical Pr.

Proclaiming the Good News: Evangelistic Expository Messages. Stephen F. Olford. (Stephen Olford Biblical Preaching Library). 128p. 1998. pap. 10.99 (*0-8010-9061-X*) Baker Bks.

Proclaiming the Gospel of Life. William N. Seifert et al. 128p. 1996. pap. 7.95 (*0-8198-5898-6*) Pauline Bks.

***Proclaiming the Messiah: The Life & Letters of Paul of Tarsus, Envoy the Nations.** Hugh Schonfield. 245p. 1999. pap. 18.95 (*1-871871-32-8*, Pub. by Open Gate Pr) Paul & Co Pubs.

Proclaiming the Pro-Life Message: Christian Leaders Address the Abortion Issue. Larry L. Lewis. 192p. 1997. pap. 10.95 (*0-929292-84-7*) Hannibal Bks.

Proclaiming the Resurrection: Papers from the Firt Oak Hill College Annual School of Theology. Ed. by Peter M. Head. xiv, 130p. 1998. reprint ed. pap. 20.00 (*0-85364-824-7*, Pub. by Paternoster Pub) OM Literature.

***Proclaiming the Scandal: Reflections on Post-Modern Ministry.** Jerome E. Bruce. 96p. 2000. pap. 12.00 (*1-56338-332-2*) TPI PA.

Proclaiming the Whole Counsel of God: Suggestions for Planning & Preparing Doctrinal Sermons. Jerry E. Oswalt. 66p. (Orig.). (C). 1993. pap. text 18.00 (*0-8191-9011-X*) U Pr of Amer.

Proclamadion for the Marchauntes Adventurers see Proclamations II

Proclamation. Gloria Taylor-Edwards. 240p. (Orig.). 1992. 20.00 (*1-56411-125-3*); pap. 10.95 (*1-56411-049-4*) Untd Bros & Sis.

Proclamation Agaynst Breaking Monumentes of Antiquitie see Proclamations II

Proclamation from Prophecy & Pattern: Lucan Old Testament Christology. Darrell L. Bock. (JSNT Supplement Ser.: No. 12). 413p. 1987. 85.00 (*1-85075-000-9*, Pub. by Sheffield Acad) CUP Services.

Proclamation of Baha'u'llah. Baha'u'llah. LC 72-237435. 127p. 1967. pap. 4.95 (*0-87743-065-9*, 103-013) Bahai.

Proclamation of Jesus. Bruce Chilton & Craig A. Evans. LC 97-38945. (Arbeiten zur Geschichte des Antiken Judentums und des Urchristentums Ser.: No. 39). xi, 572p. 1997. 193.00 (*90-04-10746-0*) Brill Academic Pubs.

***Proclamation of the Good News: A Study of Lk 24 in Tiv Context.** Terwase H. Akaabiam. LC 99-39759. (European University Studies: Series 23). XI, 184p. (C). 1999. pap. text 37.95 (*0-8204-4363-8*) P Lang Pubng.

Proclamation of the Gospel in a Pluralistic World: Essays on Christianity & Culture. George W. Forell. LC 73-79354. 144p. (Orig.). reprint ed. pap. 44.70 (*0-608-16843-2*, 202686500052) Bks Demand.

Proclamation Six Series A: Pentecost One. K. C. Hanson. 1995. pap. 5.00 (*0-8006-4212-0*) Augsburg Fortress.

Proclamation Six Series A: Pentecost Three. William Klassen. 1995. pap. 5.00 (*0-8006-4214-7*) Augsburg Fortress.

Proclamations, Broadsides, Ballads & Poems, 1357-1830: The Halliwell-Phillipps Collection in Cheetham's Library, Manchester. Ed. by Anne Snape. 28p. 1990. pap. 29.95 (*0-7201-2111-6*) Continuum.

Proclamations of the Soul. Rich Work. 400p. 1999. pap. 25.00 (*0-9648002-2-5*) Asini Publns.

Proclamations of the Tudor Kings. Rudolph W. Heinze. LC 75-22983. 329p. reprint ed. pap. 93.80 (*0-608-15258-7*, 2029220) Bks Demand.

Proclamations of the Tudor Queens. Frederic A. Youngs. LC 75-30442. 291p. reprint ed. pap. 83.00 (*0-608-15278-1*, 2029225) Bks Demand.

Proclamations II, 2 vols., Set. Incl. No. 243. King's Maiesties Declaration Concerning Lawfull Sports. 1971. reprint ed. (*90-221-0377-3*); No. 368. Proclamadion for the Marchauntes Adventurers. 1971. reprint ed. No. 369. By the Queene, Forbidding Unlicensed Plays. 1971. reprint ed. (*90-221-0369-2*); No. 370. Proclamation Agaynst Breaking Monumentes of Antiquitie. 1971. reprint ed. (*90-221-0370-6*); No. 371. By the Queene, Forbidding Export of Armour to Russia. 1971. reprint ed. (*90-221-0371-4*); No. 372. This Is the Ordinance for the Quenes Swannes. 1971. reprint ed. No. 373. By the Queene, Against Ill-Treatment of "Informers" 1971. reprint ed. (*90-221-0372-2*); No. 374. By the Queene, Against the Earl of Northumberland. 1971. reprint ed. (*90-221-0373-0*); No. 375. By the Queene, a Proclamation Concerning Hattes & Cappes. 1971. (*90-221-0374-9*); No. 376. By the Queene, for Discovering Authors of Libels. 1971. reprint ed. (*90-221-0375-7*); No. 377. By the Queene, for Sowing Lands with Flax. 1971. reprint ed. (*90-221-0376-5*); (Chronological Ser.: Nos. 243, 368-377). 1971. 21.00 (*90-221-0368-4*) Walter J Johnson.

Proclaming Bible Truth Vol. 3: Sermons for Hurting People. Joseph Clark. 1997. 19.95 (*1-882449-27-4*, 130124) Messenger Pub.

Procli Diadochi. Ed. by Manitius. (GER & GRE.). 1974. reprint ed. 53.50 (*3-519-01732-6*, T1732, Pub. by B G Teubner) U of Mich Pr.

Procli Diadochi. Ed. by Pasquali. (GER & GRE.). 1994. reprint ed. 35.00 (*3-8154-1731-7*, T1731, Pub. by B G Teubner) U of Mich Pr.

Proclus: Neoplatonic Philosophy & Science. Lucas Siorvanes. LC 96-22687. 364p. 1997. 37.50 (*0-300-06806-9*) Yale U Pr.

Proclus' Commentary on Plato's "Parmenides" Proclus. Tr. by Glenn R. Morrow & John M. Dillon. 664p. 1987. pap. text 39.50 (*0-691-02089-2*, Pub. by Princeton U Pr) Cal Prin Full Svc.

Proclus' Commentary on the Pythagorean Golden Verses. Ibn At-Tayyib. Ed. by Neil Linley. (Arethusa Monographs: No. 10). xi, 105p. 1984. pap. 10.00 (*0-930881-07-9*) Dept Classics.

Proclus' Commentary on the Timaeus of Plato, Vol. I. Tr. by Thomas Taylor. (Thomas Taylor Ser.: Vol. 15). 530p. 1998. 45.00 (*1-898910-14-6*, Pub. by Prometheus) Minerva CA.

Proclus' Commentary on the Timaeus of Plato, Vol. II. Tr. by Thomas Taylor. (Thomas Taylor Ser.: Vol. 16). 539p. 1998. 45.00 (*1-898910-15-4*, Pub. by Prometheus) Minerva CA.

Proclus' Elements of Theology. Tr. by Thomas Taylor. (Thomas Taylor Ser.: No. 1). 1994. 24.00 (*1-898910-00-6*, Pub. by Prometheus) Minerva CA.

***Proclus et la Theologie Platonicienne: Actes du Colloque International de Louvain (13-16 mai 1998) En L'honneur de H.D. Saffrey et L.G. Westerink.** Ed. by A. Ph. Segonds & C. M. Steel. (Ancient & Medieval Philosophy de Wulf-Mansion Centre Series: xxvi, 1). 741p. 2000. 99.50 (*90-5867-020-1*, Pub. by Leuven Univ) Coronet Bks.

Proclus the Neoplatonic Philosopher: Ten Doubts Concerning Providence & a Solution of Those Doubts & on the Substance of Evil. Thomas Taylor. 175p. 1992. reprint ed. pap. 13.95 (*1-56459-123-9*) Kessinger Pub.

Proclus the Neoplatonic Philosopher: Two Treatises. T. Taylor. 175p. 1980. pap. 15.00 (*0-89005-329-4*) Ares.

Proclus' Theology of Plato. Tr. by Thomas Taylor. (Thomas Taylor Ser.: Vol. 8). 1995. 50.00 (*1-898910-07-3*, Pub. by Prometheus) Minerva CA.

***Procol Harum: Beyond the Pale.** Claes Johansen. 2000. pap. 18.95 (*0-946719-28-4*) Interlink Pub.

Procomm Plus for Windows: The Visual Learning Guide. Grace J. Beatty. 1995. pap. 19.95 (*1-55958-740-7*) Prima Pub.

ProComm Plus 2 for Windows for Dummies. Wallace Wang. LC 94-79838. 384p. 1994. pap. 19.99 (*1-56884-219-8*) IDG Bks.

Procompsognatus: A Dinosaur from the Triassic Period see New Dinosaur Collection

Procopii Caesariensis Vol. IV: Indices. Ed. by Haury. (GRE.). 1964. reprint ed. 43.50 (*3-322-00245-4*, T1737, Pub. by B G Teubner) U of Mich Pr.

Procopius. Averil Cameron. 312p. (C). 1996. pap. 27.99 (*0-415-14294-6*) Routledge.

Procopius. J. A. Evans. LC 78-120500. (Twayne's World Authors Ser.). 162p. (C). 1972. lib. bdg. 20.95 (*0-8290-1748-8*) Irvington.

Procrastination: Don't Let It Ruin Your Life. Danton H. O'Day. (Illus.). 8p. (Orig.). 1996. pap. 2.50 (*1-884241-70-0*, SPS0022) Energeia Pub.

Procrastination: Using Psychological Type Concepts to Help Students. Judith A. Provost. 11p. 1988. 5.00 (*0-935652-14-0*) Ctr Applications Psych.

Procrastination: Why You Do It, What to Do about It. Jane B. Burka. 1990. pap. 12.00 (*0-201-55089-X*) Addison-Wesley.

Procrastination: Why You Do It, What to Do about It. Jane B. Burka. 1990. pap. 6.95 (*0-201-57037-8*) Addison-Wesley.

Procrastination: Why You Do It, What to Do about It. Jane B. Burka & Lenora Yuen. (Illus.). 256p. 1983. pap. 9.95 (*0-201-10191-2*) Addison-Wesley.

P

An Asterisk (*) at the beginning of an entry indicates that the title is appearing for the first time.

Procrastination & Blocking: A Novel, Practical Approach. Robert Boice. LC 96-20684. 240p. 1996. 57.95 (*0-275-95657-1*, Praeger Pubs) Greenwood.

Procrastination & Task Avoidance: Theory, Research, & Treatment. Joseph R. Ferrari et al. LC 94-48365. (Social-Clinical Psychology Ser.). (Illus.). 288p. (C). 1995. 47.50 (*0-306-44842-4*, Plenum Trade) Perseus Pubng.

Procrastinator's Guide to Success. Lynne Lively. LC 99-14473. 254p. 1999. pap. 12.95 (*0-07-038307-3*) McGraw.

***Procrastinator's Guide to Wills & Estates.** Eric Matlin. 2001. pap. 12.95 (*1-57071-617-X*) Sourcebks.

***Procrastinator's Handbook: Mastering the Art of Doing It Now.** Rita Emmett. 2000. 20.00 (*0-8027-1356-4*); pap. 12.00 (*0-8027-7598-5*) Walker & Co.

Procrastinator's Success Kit. Alyce P. Cornyn-Selby. 172p. 1987. pap. 12.95 (*0-941383-01-6*) Beynch Pr.

Procrastinator's Success Kit: How to Get What You Really Want from Yourself. rev. ed. Alyce P. Cornyn-Selby. LC 86-33444. (Illus.). 196p. 1987. reprint ed. pap. 12.95 (*0-941383-03-2*) Beynch Pr.

Procrastinator's Workshop: A Manual for Running Groups to Overcome Procrastination. Edward Zuckerman. (Clinician's Toolbox Ser.). 150p. (Orig.). (C). 1992. pap. text 75.00 (*0-9622281-1-7*) Three Wishes.

Procreation & Parenthood see Handbook of Sexology

Procreation or Pleasure? Sexual Attitudes in American History. Ed. by Thomas L. Altherr. LC 83-12. 180p. (C). 1983. pap. text 12.75 (*0-89874-609-4*) Krieger.

Procreative Man. William Marsiglio. LC 97-21089. 1998. text 55.00 (*0-8147-5578-X*); pap. text 19.00 (*0-8147-5579-8*) NYU Pr.

Procreative Pen: Sir Philip Sidney & the Circulation of Manuscripts, 1558-1640. H. R. Woudhuysen. LC 95-39313. (Illus.). 530p. (C). 1996. text 95.00 (*0-19-812966-1*, Clarendon Pr) OUP.

Procrustes. Bernard Evslin. (Monsters of Mythology Ser.). (Illus.). 104p. 1987. lib. bdg. 19.95 (*1-55546-239-1*) Chelsea Hse.

Procter R. Hug: Recollections of My Life in Education, in Politics, & in the Senate in Nevada. Intro. by Mary E. Glass. 336p. 1973. lib. bdg. 51.50 (*1-56475-129-5*); fiche. write for info. (*1-56475-130-9*) U NV Oral Hist.

Proctor & Gamble: The WetFeet.com Insider Guide. 5th ed. WetFeet.com Staff. (Insider Guides Ser.). 35p. 1999. spiral bd. 25.00 (*1-58207-050-4*) WetFeet.

Proctor & Gamble Company: A Report on the Company's Environmental Policies & Practices. (Illus.). 82p. (C). 1994. reprint ed. pap. text 40.00 (*0-7881-0929-4*, Coun on Econ) DIANE Pub.

Proctor & Hughes' Chemical Hazards of the Workplace. 4th ed. Gloria J. Hathaway et al. (Industrial Health & Safety Ser.). 720p. 1996. 130.00 (*0-471-28702-4*, VNR) Wiley.

Proctor's Accounts of Peter Lewis, 1564-5. Ed. by Raymond Gillespie. 128p. 1996. 39.50 (*1-85182-218-6*, Pub. by Four Cts Pr) Intl Spec Bk.

Procudural Skills for Internal Medicine, Individual Version. Robert S. Wigton & Thomas G. Tape. 148p. (C). 1997. write for info. (*0-8151-9410-2*) Mosby Inc.

Procuratori Di San Marco & the Ventian Credit Market: A Study of the Development of Credit & Banking in the Trecento. Reinhold C. Mueller. Ed. by Stuart Bruchey. LC 77-77181. (Dissertations in European Economic History Ser.). 1978. lib. bdg. 40.95 (*0-405-10794-3*) Ayer.

Procurement Agent. Jack Rudman. (Career Examination Ser.: C-621). 1994. pap. 23.95 (*0-8373-0621-3*) Nat Learn.

Procurement & Disbursement Manual for Projects with Community Participation. Gita Gopal. LC 95-46379. (Discussion Paper Ser.). 42p. 1995. pap. 22.00 (*0-8213-3492-1*, 13492) World Bank.

Procurement & Public Management: The Fear of Discretion & the Quality of Government Performance. Steven Kelman. 150p. (C). 1990. 29.75 (*0-8447-3712-7*, AEI Pr) Am Enterprise.

Procurement Clerk. Jack Rudman. (Career Examination Ser.: C-2623). 1994. pap. 23.95 (*0-8373-2623-0*) Nat Learn.

Procurement Coordinator. Jack Rudman. (Career Examination Ser.: C-2368). 1994. pap. 34.95 (*0-8373-2368-1*) Nat Learn.

Procurement Ethics Desktop Reference. 355p. 1991. ring bd. 156.00 (*1-56726-044-6*) Mgmt Concepts.

Procurement in the Process Industry. L. Lester & B. Benning. 258p. 1989. 400.00 (*0-7855-5755-5*, Pub. by Inst Pur & Supply) St Mut.

Procurement Law for Construction & Engineering Works & Services. R.W. Craig. LC 98-52407. 1999. write for info. (*0-632-04927-8*) Blackwell Sci.

Procurement Management. Didactic Systems Staff. (Simulation Game Ser.). 1975. pap. 26.25 (*0-89401-080-8*) Didactic Syst.

Procurement Marketing: A Strategic Concept. U. Koppelmann. LC 98-29120. xii, 183p. 1998. 69.95 (*3-540-64459-8*) Spr-Verlag.

Procurement of Commodities. (Dossier Type d'Appel d'Offres Ser.).Tr. of Procurement of Commodities: Fertilizers & Fertilizer Raw materials - Standard Bidding Documents. (FRE.). 59p. 1993. pap. 22.00 (*0-8213-2438-1*, 12438) World Bank.

Procurement of Commodities - Fertilizers & Fertilizer Raw Materials: Sample Bidding Documents. Compiled by World Bank Staff. 48p. 1988. pap. 22.00 (*0-8213-1002-X*, 11002) World Bank.

Procurement of Commodities: Fertilizers & Fertilizer Raw materials - Standard Bidding Documents see Procurement of Commodities

Procurement of Goods: Standard Bidding Documents. LC 95-147722. 88p. 1995. pap. 22.00 (*0-8213-3237-6*, 13237) World Bank.

Procurement of Goods: Standard Bidding Documents. (SPA.). 104p. 1995. pap. 22.00 (*0-8213-3486-7*, 13486) World Bank.

Procurement of Goods: Standard Bidding Documents. (FRE.). 96p. 1995. pap. 22.00 (*0-8213-3536-7*, 13536) World Bank.

Procurement of Pancreatic Islets, Vol. I. Ed. by Robert P. Lanza & William L. Chick. 130p. 1994. 94.00 (*1-57059-133-4*, LN9133) CRC Pr.

Procurement of Practices of the Mexican Affiliates of Selected United States Automobile Firms. Guillermo S. Edelberg. Ed. by Stuart Bruchey & Eleanor Bruchey. LC 76-5005. (American Business Abroad Ser.). (Illus.). 1976. reprint ed. lib. bdg. 23.95 (*0-405-09274-1*) Ayer.

Procurement of Services for the Non-Acoustic Anti-Submarine Warfare Program Through the Tennessee Valley Authority. (Illus.). 78p. (Orig.). (C). 1995. pap. text 20.00 (*0-7881-2540-0*) DIANE Pub.

Procurement of Works: Major Equipment & Industrial Installations: Standard Prequalification Documents. 61p. 1993. pap. 22.00 (*0-8213-2447-0*, 12447) World Bank.

Procurement of Works: Smaller Contracts. 108p. 1995. pap. 22.00 (*0-8213-3361-5*, 13361) World Bank.

Procurement of Works: Standard Bidding Documents. LC 99-203079. 240p. 1995. pap. 22.00 (*0-8213-3309-7*, 13309) World Bank.

Procurement Opportunities: A Small Business Guide to Procurement Reform. Jere W. Glover. 57p. 1996. pap. 4.50 (*0-16-048698-X*) USGPO.

Procurement, Preservation & Allocation of Vascularized Organs. Ed. by G. M. Collins et al. LC 96-38863. 384p. 1997. lib. bdg. 275.00 (*0-7923-4299-2*) Kluwer Academic.

Procurement Reengineering. Ben Laaper. LC 97-40468. (Orig.). 1998. pap. 14.95 (*0-945456-31-X*) PT Pubns.

Procurement Supervisor. Jack Rudman. (Career Examination Ser.: C-2711). 1994. pap. 29.95 (*0-8373-2711-3*) Nat Learn.

Procurement Systems: A Guide to Best Practice in Construction. Ed. by Steve Rowlinson & Peter McDermott. LC 98-49878. (Illus.). 264p. (C). (gr. 13). 1999. 100.00 (*0-419-24100-0*, D6635, E & FN Spon) Routledge.

Procurement Works: Civil Law. (FRE.). 192p. 1997. pap. 22.00 (*0-8213-3846-3*, 13846) World Bank.

Procuring Organs for Transplant: The Debate over Non-Heart-Beating Cadaver Protocols. Ed. by Stuart J. Youngner et al. 252p. 1995. text 55.00 (*0-8018-5100-9*); pap. text 24.95 (*0-8018-5101-7*) Johns Hopkins.

Prod. Oper. Manag. 8th ed. Chase. 1997. 89.06 (*0-07-561278-X*) McGraw.

Prod. Oper. Manag. 8th ed. Chase. 240p. 1998. pap. 30.00 (*0-07-292737-2*) McGraw.

Prod. Oper. Management. Schrage. 1997. teacher ed. write for info. (*0-02-407794-1*) P-H.

Prodcom List, 1998. European Communities Staff. (E. C. Comprehensive Standing Order English Editions Ser.: Vol. 81450000). 614p. 1997. pap. 110.00 (*92-828-1587-0*, CA-08-97-476ENC, Pub. by Comm Europ Commun) Bernan Associates.

***Prodcom List, 2000.** European Communities Staff. 614p. 2000. pap. 95.00 (*92-828-8196-2*, CA26-99-077-EN-C, Pub. by Comm Europ Commun) Bernan Associates.

Prodi-Gull. Ronald E. Griego Jr. (Illus.). 60p. (Orig.). (YA). 1994. pap. 5.95 (*1-886045-06-2*) Covenant Marriages.

Prodigal. Stephen Guschov. 1999. pap. 3.50 (*1-57514-335-6*, 1180) Encore Perform Pub.

Prodigal. rev. ed. Larry Barkdull & Marvin Payne. (Keepsake Bookcards Ser.). 16p. (Orig.). 1988. pap. 1.95 (*0-929985-04-4*) Jackman Pubng.

Prodigal Brothers. I. K. Hoh. (Evans Africa Plays Ser.). 29p. 1991. pap. write for info. (*0-237-49776-X*) EVNI UK.

***Prodigal Cat.** Janette Oke. (Oke Children's Classics Ser.). (Illus.). 160p. (Orig.). (J). (gr. 3 up). 1998. pap. 5.99 (*0-934998-19-1*) Bethany Hse.

***Prodigal Cat.** Janette Oke. (Janette Oke's Animal Friends Ser.). (Illus.). (J). 2000. pap. 5.99 (*0-7642-2406-9*) Bethany Hse.

Prodigal Children. Barbara Centilli. 104p. 1998. pap. 4.95 (*1-891903-11-X*) St Andrew Prodns.

Prodigal Church: How You Can Restore the Power & Intimacy Shared by Early Christians. Mike Dowgiewicz & Sue Dowgiewicz. (Illus.). 38p. 1997. pap. 3.00 (*1-890592-01-3*) Restrtion Minist.

Prodigal Daughter. Jeffrey Archer. 496p. 1993. mass mkt. 7.50 (*0-06-100714-5*, Harp PBks) HarpC.

Prodigal Daughter. Janet Dailey. (Superromance Ser.). 1979. per. 1.25 (*0-373-70775-4*, 1-70775-1) Harlequin Bks.

***Prodigal Daughter.** Ginna Gray. 384p. 2000. mass mkt. 5.99 (*1-55166-603-0*, 1-66603-1, Mira Bks) Harlequin Bks.

Prodigal Daughter: A Biography of Sherwood Bonner. Hubert H. McAlexander. LC 98-40283. (Illus.). 272p. 1999. reprint ed. pap. text 20.00 (*1-57233-049-X*, Pub. by U of Tenn Pr) U Ch Pr.

Prodigal Daughter: A Maundy Thursday Reconciliation Service. Maxine Dudley. 1992. pap. 3.75 (*1-55673-563-4*, 9310) CSS OH.

***Prodigal Daughters: Catholics Women Come Home to the Church.** Donna Steichen. 1999. pap. 14.95 (*0-89870-732-3*) Ignatius Pr.

***Prodigal Father: A True Story of Tragedy, Survival & Reconciliation in an American Family.** Jon Du Pre. LC 99-59123. (Illus.). 304p. 2000. pap. 13.95 (*1-56170-674-4*, 5010) Hay House.

Prodigal Father: Reuniting Fathers & Their Children. Mark A. Bryan. LC 98-13497. 278p. 1998. pap. 14.00 (*0-609-80203-8*, Three Riv Pr) Crown Pub Group.

Prodigal Genius. 1992. 12.00 (*0-685-52651-8*) Tesla Bk Co.

Prodigal Genius: The Life & Mind of Nikola Tesla. J. J. O'Neil. (Nikola Tesla Ser.). 1986. lib. bdg. 79.95 (*0-8490-3839-1*) Gordon Pr.

Prodigal Genius: The Life of Nikola Tesla. John J. O'Neill. 326p. reprint ed. 12.00 (*0-913022-40-3*) Angriff Pr.

Prodigal Genius: The Life of Nikola Tesla. unabridged ed. John J. O'Neill. 326p. 1978. reprint ed. 25.00 (*0-945001-22-3*) GSG & Assocs.

Prodigal Genius: The Life of Nikola Tesla. unabridged ed. John J. O'Neill. 326p. 1978. reprint ed. pap. 15.00 (*0-945001-21-5*) GSG & Assocs.

Prodigal Girl. Grace Livingston Hill. 24.95 (*0-89190-358-5*) Amereon Ltd.

Prodigal Girl. Grace Livingston Hill. (Grace Livingston Hill Ser.: Vol. 56). 1996. mass mkt. 5.99 (*0-8423-5039-X*) Tyndale Hse.

Prodigal Groom: The Wedding Night. Karen Leabo. (Desire Ser.). 1996. per. 3.50 (*0-373-76007-8*, 1-76007-3) Silhouette.

Prodigal Husband. Pamela Dalton. (Romance Ser.). 1993. per. 2.75 (*0-373-08957-0*, 5-08957-8) Silhouette.

Prodigal People: Coming Home to Right Relationships. Woodrow M. Kroll & Don Hawkins. 216p. 1995. pap. 11.99 (*0-8254-3050-X*) Kregel.

Prodigal Press: The Anti-Christian Bias of the American News Media. Marvin N. Olasky. LC 87-72951. (Turning Point Christian Worldview Ser.). 256p. 1988. pap. 14.99 (*0-89107-476-7*) Crossway Bks.

Prodigal Principle: The Essential Handbook for Managing & Professional Change. Martis Jones. LC 94-61929. (Illus.). 80p. (Orig.). 1995. pap. 14.95 (*0-9644607-1-8*) Worth Bk Pub.

Prodigal Psalms. Harald Wyndham. 160p. (Orig.). 1991. pap. 12.00 (*0-937179-07-8*) Blue Scarab.

***Prodigal Saint: John of Kronstadt & the Russian People** Nadieszda Kizenko. LC 99-28363. (Studies of the Harriman Institute). (Illus.). 384p. 2000. 23.00 (*0-271-01976-X*) Pa St U Pr.

Prodigal Soldiers: How the Generation of Officers Born of Vietnam Revolutionized the American Style of War. James Kitfield. LC 97-15273. 478p. 1997. reprint ed. pap. 23.95 (*1-57488-123-X*) Brasseys.

Prodigal Soldiers: How the Generation of Officers Born of Vietnam Revolutionized the American Style of War. 2nd rev. ed. Joseph M. Siegman. LC 97-19449. (Association of the U. S. Army Book Ser.). (Illus.). 246p. 1997. 29.95 (*1-57488-128-0*) Brasseys.

Prodigal Son see Stories Jesus Told

Prodigal Son. LC 96-133002. (Arch Bks.). (J). (gr. k-4). 1996. 1.99 (*0-570-07522-X*, 59-1495) Concordia.

Prodigal Son. Heather Amery. (Bible Tales Readers Ser.). (Illus.). 16p. 1999. pap. text 4.50 (*0-7460-2971-3*, Usborne) EDC.

Prodigal Son. Heather Amery. (Illus.). 16p. (J). (ps-3). 1999. 12.95 (*1-58086-176-8*) EDC.

Prodigal Son. Georges Chevrot. 56p. 1999. pap. 2.95 (*0-906138-48-5*) Scepter Pubs.

Prodigal Son. John Wheatcroft. 5.95 (*0-8453-6734-X*, Cornwall Bks) Assoc Univ Prs.

Prodigal Son. Tim Wood & Kath Mellentin. (Illus.). 12p. (J). (ps). 1998. 9.99 (*1-884628-50-8*, Flyng Frog) Allied Pub MD.

Prodigal Son. Andre Gide. 1992. reprint ed. lib. bdg. 18.95 (*0-89966-958-1*) Buccaneer Bks.

Prodigal Son: Dancing for Balanchine in a World of Pain & Magic. Edward Villella & Larry Kaplan. LC 97-45770. (Dance Ser.). (Illus.). 317p. 1998. pap. 17.95 (*0-8229-5666-7*) U of Pittsburgh Pr.

***Prodigal Son: Oh, Brother!** Mike Thaler & Dennis Adler. LC 99-31548. (Heaven & Mirth Ser.). 32p. 1999. 12.99 (*0-7814-3263-4*) Chariot Victor.

***Prodigal Son: Vasilii Shukshin in Soviet Russia Culture.** John Givens. (Studies in Russian Literature & Theory). (Illus.). 2000. write for info. (*0-8101-1770-3*) Northwestern U Pr.

Prodigal Son - Elder Brother: Interpretation & Alterity in Augustine, Petrarch, Kafka, Levinas. Jill Robbins. LC 90-19722. (Religion & Postmodernism Ser.). 190p. 1991. 29.95 (*0-226-72110-8*) U Ch Pr.

Prodigal Son Narratives, 1480-1980. Ellen D'Oench. LC 97-218076. 1995. pap. 5.00 (*0-89467-070-0*) Yale Art Gallery.

Prodigal Sons: A Study in Authorship & Authority. David Wyatt. LC 79-22930. 196p. reprint ed. pap. 60.80 (*0-8357-6630-6*, 203527600094) Bks Demand.

Prodigal Son's Journey. Concordia Publishing Staff. (Illus.). 10p. (J). (ps-k). 1998. bds. 3.99 (*0-570-05466-4*, 56-1965GJ) Concordia.

Prodigal Souls: A Novel. Harriet R. Ackert. LC 97-32023. 240p. 1998. pap. 14.95 (*1-56474-248-2*) Fithian Pr.

Prodigal Spy. Joseph Kanon. LC 98-35767. 416p. 1998. 25.00 (*0-7679-0142-8*) Broadway BDD.

Prodigal Spy. Joseph Kanon. 537p. 1999. mass mkt. 7.50 (*0-440-22534-5*) Dell.

Prodigal Spy. Joseph Kanon. LC 99-19336. 1999. write for info. (*1-56895-715-7*) Wheeler Pub.

***Prodigal Summer.** Barbara Kingsolver. 450p. 2000. 26.00 (*0-06-019965-2*) HarpC.

***Prodigal Summer.** large type ed. Barbara Kingsolver. Ed. by Gaudinier. 2000. write for info. (*0-06-019966-0*) HarpC.

Prodigal Years. Gary J. Grappo. (Illus.). 72p. 1993. mass mkt. 5.95 (*1-58193-018-6*) Brown Bag Prods.

***Prodigality, Liberality & Meanness: The Prodigal Son in Graeco-Roman Perspective.** David A. Holgate. (Journal for the Study of the New Testament, Supplement Ser.: No. 187). 299p. 1999. 82.00 (*1-84127-025-3*, Pub. by Sheffield Acad) CUP Services.

Prodigals: Two Short Plays. Don Evans. 1977. pap. 5.25 (*0-8222-0919-5*) Dramatists Play.

Prodigals & Those Who Love Them. Ruth Bell Grahm. LC 99-14366. 158p. (gr. 13). 1999. pap. 11.99 (*0-8010-5897-X*) Baker Bks.

Prodigals Do Come Home. 2nd rev. ed. Robert Steinkamp. 87p. 1993. reprint ed. pap. 5.95 (*1-886045-08-9*) Covenant Marriages.

Prodigious Birds: Moas & Moa-Hunting in New Zealand. Atholl Anderson. (Illus.). 256p. (C). 1990. text 95.00 (*0-521-35209-6*) Cambridge U Pr.

Prodigious Builders. Bernard Rudofsky. (Illus.). 383p. (C). 1977. text 59.50 (*0-8290-0986-8*) Irvington.

Prodigious Thrust. William Everson. LC 96-21543. 325p. (C). 1996. 27.50 (*1-57423-008-5*); pap. 15.00 (*1-57423-007-7*) Black Sparrow.

Prodigy. Jan Clark. 1997. mass mkt. 5.99 (*0-451-45615-7*, ROC) NAL.

Prodigy. Noel Hynd. LC 97-72053. 336p. 1998. 23.00 (*1-57566-240-X*, Knsington) Kensgtn Pub Corp.

Prodigy. Noel Hynd. 352p. 1999. mass mkt. 5.99 (*0-7860-0614-5*) Kensgtn Pub Corp.

***Prodigy.** Paul Lester. (Illustrated Story Ser.). (Illus.). 80p. 2000. pap. 9.95 (*0-600-59511-0*, Pub. by P HM) Trafalgar.

Prodigy: Adventures with the Voodoo Crew. Martin James. (Illus.). 181p. 1998. pap. 17.95 (*0-09-186088-1*) Ebury Pr.

Prodigy: An Illustrated Biography. Stuart Coles. (Illus.). 1998. pap. text 12.95 (*0-7119-6718-0*) Omnibus NY.

***Prodigy: Fat of the Land.** 1998. pap. 16.95 (*0-7935-9172-4*) H Leonard.

Prodigy: The Fat of the Land. Martin Roach. (Illus.). 128p. (C). 1997. pap. 24.95 (*1-897783-12-4*, MR 55645, Pub. by Indep Music Pr) Music Sales.

Prodigy: Wolfgang Amadeus Mozart (Musical) Mary H. Surface. 50p. (J). 1988. 6.00 (*0-87602-281-6*) Anchorage.

Prodigy for Dummies. Gus Venditto. 384p. 1995. pap. 19.99 (*1-56884-936-2*) IDG Bks.

Prodigy Quick Reference Guide. Amanda Heartland. Ed. by Kathy M. Berkemeyer. (DDC Quick Reference Guides Ser.). (Illus.). 140p. 1993. spiral bd. 12.00 (*1-56243-106-4*, P-18) DDC Pub.

Prodomus Flora Nepalensis. D. Don. 256p. (C). 1976. text 100.00 (*0-89771-597-7*, Pub. by Intl Bk Distr) St Mut.

Prodomus Florae Penninsulae Indian Orientalis. R. Wight. 480p. (C). 1976. text 350.00 (*0-89771-675-2*, Pub. by Intl Bk Distr) St Mut.

ProDOS Inside & Out. Dennis Doms & Tom Weishaar. (Illus.). 270p. 1986. 24.95 (*0-8306-0245-3*) McGraw-Hill Prof.

ProDOS Technical Reference Manual. write for info. (*0-318-59720-9*) Addison-Wesley.

PRODOS 8TECH REF MNL DSK. Apple Computer, Inc. Staff. 1985. 29.95 (*0-201-17757-9*) Addison-Wesley.

Prodromi, Theodori. 9th ed. Ed. by Marcovich. (GRE.). 1992. 92.50 (*3-8154-1703-1*, T1703, Pub. by B G Teubner) U of Mich Pr.

Prodromus der Algenflora von Boehmen. A. Hansgirg. LC 86-6303. (From: Archiv F. Naturw. Landesdurchf (Boehmens) Ser.). (GER.). 1979. reprint ed. lib. bdg. 120.00 (*3-7682-0922-9*) Lubrecht & Cramer.

Prodromus der Moosgesellschaften Zentraleuropas. Alex Von Huesbchmann. (Bryophytorum Bibliotheca Ser.: No. 32). (GER., Illus.). 414p. 1986. 96.00 (*3-443-62004-3*, Pub. by Gebruder Borntraeger) Balogh.

Prodromus Einer Flora Von Sudwestafrika. H. Merxmuller. (C). 1988. text 720.00 (*0-7855-3159-9*, Pub. by Scientific) St Mut.

Prodromus Flora Novae-Hollandiae et Insulae Van Dieman (Now Australia & Tasmania) R. Brown. 1960. reprint ed. 120.00 (*3-7682-0033-7*) Lubrecht & Cramer.

Prodromus Florae Hepaticarum Polynesiae. H. A. Miller & H. O. Whittier. (Bryophytorum Bibliotheca Ser.: Vol. 25). 422p. 1983. lib. bdg. 128.00 (*3-7682-1373-0*) Lubrecht & Cramer.

Prodromus Florae Hispanicae Seu Synopsis Methodica Omnium Plantarum in Hispania Sponte Nascentium Vel Frequentius Cultarum Quae Innotuerunt, 1861-1880, Vols. I-III. Mauritio Willkomm & Joanni Lange. (Botanical Bks.). (GER., Illus.). 2140p. 1972. reprint ed. 312.00 (*3-510-65030-1*, Pub. by E Schweizerbartsche) Balogh.

Prodromus Florae Muscorum Polynesiae with a Key to Genera. H. A. Miller et al. 1978. lib. bdg. 65.00 (*3-7682-1115-0*) Lubrecht & Cramer.

Prodromus Florae Nepalensis. Ed. by D. Don. 256p. 1976. reprint ed. 135.00 (*0-7855-5990-6*, Pub. by Intl Bk Distr) St Mut.

Prodromus Florae Peninsulae Balcanicae Vol. 1: Pteridophyta, Gymnospermae, Dicotyledoneae (Apetalae et Chiropetalae) August V. Hayek. (Feddes Repertorium Ser.: Vol. XXX, 1). (Illus.). 317p. 200.00 (*3-87429-086-7*, Pub. by Koeltz Sci Bks) Lubrecht & Cramer.

Prodromus Florae Peninsulae Indiae Orientalis, Vol. 1. Ed. by R. Wight. (C). 1988. text 60.00 (*0-7855-3144-0*, Pub. by Scientific) St Mut.

Prodromus Florae Penninsular. R. Wirght. 480p. (C). 1976. reprint ed. 250.00 (*0-7855-3092-4*, Pub. by Intl Bk Distr) St Mut.

Prodromus to Class Loculoascomycetes. Margaret E. Barr. (Illus.). 168p. 1987. spiral bd. 18.00 (*0-934454-51-5*) Lubrecht & Cramer.

Prodrugs: Topical & Ocular Drug Delivery. Ed. by Kenneth B. Sloan. (Drugs & the Pharmaceutical Sciences Ser.: Vol. 53). (Illus.). 336p. 1992. text 155.00 (*0-8247-8629-7*) Dekker.

An Asterisk (*) at the beginning of an entry indicates that the title is appearing for the first time.

Produce & Conserve, Share & Play Square: The Grocer & the Consumer on the Home Front Battlefield During World War II. Ed. by Barbara M. Ward. LC 93-4304. (Illus.). 240p. 1994. pap. 24.95 (0-87451-655-2) U Pr of New Eng.

Produce Facts: What Your Mother Maybe Didn't Tell You. Frank R. Comella. LC 95-92209. 207p. 1995. spiral bd. 12.95 (0-9646221-0-6) Comella Pr.

Produce Handling for Direct Marketing, Vol. 51. James A. Bartsch & Roger Kline. (Illus.). 26p. 1992. pap. text 7.00 (0-935817-31-X, NRAES-51) NRAES.

Produce Identification Guide. 27p. 1987. pap. 15.00 (0-317-01514-1) Produce Mktg Assn.

***Produce Manager.** Angela McHaney Brown. LC 99-51703. (Workers You Know Ser.). 32p. (J). 2000. lib. bdg. 22.83 (0-8172-5594-X) Raintree Steck-V.

Produce Marketing Association Membership Directory & Buyer's Guide. 405p. 1988. 45.00 (0-318-35250-8) Produce Mktg Assn.

Produced Water Vol. 1: Technological/Environmental Issues & Solutions. J. P. Ray & F. R. Engelhardt. (Environmental Science Research Ser.: Vol. 46). (Illus.). 632p. (C). 1993. 155.00 (0-306-44358-9, Plenum Trade) Perseus Pubng.

Produced Water 2: Environmental Issues & Mitigation Technologies. Ed. by Mark Reed & Stale Johnsen. (Environmental Science Research Ser.: Vol. 52). (Illus.). 549p. (C). 1996. 167.00 (0-306-45308-8, Plenum Trade) Perseus Pubng.

***Producer Compensation: A Profile of Pay & Performance.** 186p. 1999. pap. 39.50 (1-878204-61-0) APIS Inc.

Producer Cooperatives & Labor-Managed Systems, 2 vols., Set. Ed. by David L. Prychitko & Jaroslav Vanek. LC 95-42011. (International Library of Critical Writings in Economics: Vol. 62). 864p. 1996. 325.00 (1-85898-189-1) E Elgar.

***Producer Responsibility: Packaging Law.** David Brown. 224p. 2000. pap. write for info. (1-902558-12-X, Pub. by Palladian Law) Gaunt.

Producer's Broadway Journey. Stuart Ostrow. LC 97-46533. 232p. 1999. 19.95 (0-275-95866-3, Praeger Pubs) Greenwood.

***Producer's Business Handbook.** John J. Lee, Jr. LC 99-87181. 210p. 2000. pap. 39.95 (0-240-80396-5, Focal) Buttrwrth-Heinemann.

***Producer's Directory.** Hollywood Creative Directory Staff. 2000. pap. 59.95 (1-928936-04-0) Hollywood Creat Dir.

Producers' English: English-French Vocabulary of the Cinema & Audiovisual. Nicolas Robert. (ENG & FRE.). 292p. 1995. 95.00 (0-7859-9941-8) Fr & Eur.

***Producers 411 2000: Variety's Guide to Film & Television Executives & Producers.** 300p. 2000. pap. 49.00 (1-879930-18-8, Pub. by LA Four-Eleven) SCB Distributors.

Producer's Guide to Interactive Videodiscs. Martin Perlmutter. 160p. 1991. pap. text 56.95 (0-86729-173-7, Focal) Buttrwrth-Heinemann.

Producer's Master-Guide, 1983: The International Production Manual for Motion Picture, Television, Commercials, Cable & Videotape Industries in the United States & Canada. 3rd ed. Shmuel Bension. LC 83-641703. 624p. (Orig.). (C). 1982. pap. 58.00 (0-935744-02-9) Prod Mstrguide.

Producer's Masterguide, 1986: The International Production Manual for Motion Picture, Broadcast Television, Commercials, Cable & Videotape Industries in the United States, Canada, the United Kingdom, Ireland, The Caribbean Islands & Bermuda. 6th ed. Shmuel Bension. LC 83-641703. 600p. (Orig.). 1986. pap. 69.95 (0-935744-05-3) Prod Mstrguide.

Producer's Masterguide, 1987: The International Production Manual for Motion Picture, Broadcast Television, Commercials, Cable & Videotape Industries Throughout the United States, Canada, the United Kingdom, The Caribbean Islands & Bermuda, Ireland & New Zealand. 7th ed. Shmuel Bension. LC 83-641703. 600p. 1987. 79.95 (0-935744-06-1) Prod Mstrguide.

Producer's Masterguide, 1988: The International Production Manual for Motion Picture, Broadcast Television, Commercials, Cable & Videotape Industries Throughout the United States, Canada, the United Kingdom, the Caribbean Islands & Bermuda, Israel, Australia & New Zealand. 8th ed. Shmuel Bension. LC 83-641703. 500p. 1988. 79.95 (0-935744-07-X) Prod Mstrguide.

Producer's Masterguide, 1989: The International Production Manual for Motion Picture, Broadcast Television, Commercials, Cable & Videotape Industries Throughout the United States, Canada, the United Kingdom, the Caribbean Islands & Bermuda, Israel, Australia & New Zealand. 9th ed. Shmuel Bension. LC 83-641703. 500p. 1989. 89.95 (0-935744-08-8) Prod Mstrguide.

Producer's Masterguide, 1984: The International Production Manual for Motion Picture, Television, Commercials, Cable & Videotape Industries in the United States, Canada & the United Kingdom. 4th ed. Shmuel Bension. LC 83-641703. 770p. 1985. pap. 69.95 (0-935744-03-7) Prod Mstrguide.

Producer's Masterguide, 1985: The International Production Manual for Motion Picture, Television, Commercials, Cable & Videotape Industries in the United States, Canada & the United Kingdom. 5th ed. Shmuel Bension. LC 83-641703. 700p. (Orig.). 1985. pap. 69.95 (0-935744-04-5) Prod Mstrguide.

Producer's Masterguide, 1997/1998: The International Production Manual for Motion Picture, Broadcast-Television, Commercials, Cable, & Videotape Industries Throughout the U. S., Canada, the U. K., the Caribbean Islands, Mexico, Israel, Australia, & New Zealand, Europe, South America, & the Far East. Shmuel Bension. 500p. 1997. pap. 125.00 (0-935744-16-9) Prod Mstrguide.

Producer's Masterguide, 1996: The International Production Manual for Motion Picture, Broadcast-Television, Commercials, Cable, & Videotape Industries Throughout the U. S., Canada, the U. K., the Caribbean Islands, Mexico, Israel, Australia, & New Zealand, Europe, South America, & the Far East. 15th ed. Shmuel Bension. 500p. 1996. pap. 125.00 (0-935744-15-0) Prod Mstrguide.

Producer's Masterguide, 1995: The International Production Manual for Motion Picture, Broadcast Television, Commercials, Cable & Videotape Industries Throughout the U. S., Canada, U. K., Caribbean Islands, Bermuda, Israel, Australia, New Zealand, Austria, Norway, Philippines & Mexico. 14th ed. Shmuel Bension. 400p. 1995. pap. 120.00 (0-935744-13-4) Prod Mstrguide.

Producer's Masterguide, 1990: The International Production Manual for Motion Picture, Broadcast Television, Commercials, Cable & Videotape Industries Throughout the United States, Canada, the United Kingdom, the Caribbean Islands & Bermuda, Israel, Australia & New Zealand, Austria & Mexico. 10th ed. Shmuel Bension. LC 83-641703. 500p. 1990. 98.95 (0-935744-09-6) Prod Mstrguide.

Producer's Masterguide, 1991: The International Production Manual for Motion Picture, Broadcast Television, Commercials, Cable & Videotape Industries Throughout the United States, Canada, the United Kingdom, the Caribbean Islands & Bermuda, Israel, Australia & New Zealand, Austria & Mexico. 11th ed. Shmuel Bension. LC 83-641703. 500p. 1991. 98.95 (0-935744-10-X) Prod Mstrguide.

Producer's Masterguide, 1992: The International Production Manual for Motion Picture, Broadcast Television, Commercials, Cable & Videotape Industries Throughout the United States, Canada, the United Kingdom, the Caribbean Islands & Bermuda, Israel, Australia & New Zealand, Austria, Philippines & Mexico. 12th ed. Shmuel Bension. 400p. 1992. pap. 98.95 (0-935744-11-8) Prod Mstrguide.

Producer's Masterguide, 1993/94: The International Production Manual for Motion Picture, Broadcast Television, Commercials, Cable & Videotape Industries Throughout the United States, Canada, the United Kingdom, the Caribbean Islands, Israel, Europe, Australia, Austria, Japan, Philippines, & Mexico. 13th ed. Shmuel Bension. 400p. 1993. pap. 115.00 (0-935744-12-6) Prod Mstrguide.

Producer's Masterguide, 2000: The International Production Manual for Motion Picture, Broadcast-Television, Feature Films, Commercials, Cable, & Videotape Industries Throughout the U. S., Canada, the United Kingdom, the Caribbean Islands, Mexico, Israel, Australia, New Zealand, Europe, South America, the Far East & Africa. 18th ed. Shmuel Bension. LC 83-641703. 500p. 2000. pap. 125.00 (0-935744-17-7) Prod Mstrguide.

Producers, Proletarians, & Politicians: Workers & Party Politics in Evansville & New Albany, Indiana, 1850-87. Lawrence M. Lipin. LC 92-41298. 336p. 1993. text 42.50 (0-252-02019-7) U of Ill Pr.

Producers Versus Capitalists: Constitutional Conflict in Antebellum America. Tony A. Freyer. LC 93-34186. (Constitutionalism & Democracy Ser.). 288p. (C). 1994. text 37.50 (0-8139-1496-5) U Pr of Va.

Producibility-Machinability of Space-Age & Conventional Materials. Ed. by Raymond E. Howe. LC 68-56154. (American Society of Tool & Manufacturing Engineers Manufacturing Data Ser.). 372p. reprint ed. pap. 115.40 (0-608-11558-4, 201600200097) Bks Demand.

Producible Interpretation: Eight English Plays, 1675-1707. Ed. by Judith Milhous & Robert D. Hume. LC 84-5634. (Illus.). 352p. 1985. text 36.95 (0-8093-1167-4) S Ill U Pr.

Producing a First-Class Newsletter: A Guide to Planning, Writing, Editing, Designing, Photography, Production & Printing. Barbara Fanson. (Reference Ser.). 192p. 1994. pap. 14.95 (0-88908-296-0) Self-Counsel Pr.

Producing a National Curriculum: Plans & Paranoia. Colin Marsh. LC 95-106398. 160p. 1994. pap. 24.95 (1-86373-741-3, Pub. by Allen & Unwin Pty) Paul & Co Pubs.

Producing a Quality Family History. Patricia L. Hatcher. LC 96-8240. 286p. 1996. pap. 19.95 (0-916489-64-7) Ancestry.

Producing a Quality Plan: Pharmaceutical Automation: A Systems-Based Approach. Tony Simmons. (Illus.). Date not set. 49.50 (1-930114-21-4) Serentec Pr.

Producing a School Newsletter Parents Will Read! A Simple, Yet Complete Guide to Producing a School Newsletter for Today's Busy Families. Rhonda Jones. (Illus.). 160p. 1994. pap. 18.95 (0-9641008-3-5) Image Cntrl.

***Producing Affordable Housing: Partnerships for Profit.** National Association of Home Builders Staff. LC 99-42067. (Illus.). 1999. write for info. (0-86718-486-8) Home Builder.

***Producing Against Poverty: Female & Male & Micro-Etrepeneurs in Lima, Peru.** Annelou Ypeij. (Illus.). 216p. (C). 2000. pap. text 32.50 (90-5356-377-6, Pub. by Amsterdam U Pr) U of Mich Pr.

Producing American Races: Henry James, William Faulkner, Toni Morrison. Patricia McKee. LC 98-32346. (New Americanists Ser.). 1999. write for info. (0-8223-2329-X) Duke.

***Producing American Races: Henry James, William Faulkner, Toni Morrison.** Patricia McKee. LC 98-32346. (New Americanists Ser.). 1999. 17.95 (0-8223-2363-X) Duke.

Producing & Directing Drama for the Church. Robert M. Rucker. 208p. Date not set. pap. 19.99 (0-8341-9726-X) Nazarene.

Producing & Directing the Short Film & Video. Peter W. Rea & David K. Irving. (Illus.). 304p. 1995. pap. 39.95 (0-240-80188-1, Focal) Buttrwrth-Heinemann.

***Producing & Directing the Short Film & Video.** 2nd ed. Peter Rea & David K. Irving. (Illus.). 384p. 2000. pap. 39.95 (0-240-80394-9, Focal) Buttrwrth-Heinemann.

Producing & Marketing Prints. 2nd ed. Sue Viders. 96p. 1997. pap. 14.95 (0-942011-10-4) S Viders.

Producing & Reducing Disaffection. Ed. by Tony Booth & David Coulby. (Curricula All Ser.). 288p. 1987. 113.00 (0-335-15976-1); pap. 33.95 (0-335-15975-3) OpUniv Pr.

***Producing Animation.** Catherine Winder & Zahra Dowlatabadi. (Illus.). 288p. 2001. pap. 29.95 (0-240-80412-0, Focal) Buttrwrth-Heinemann.

Producing Beauty Pageants: A Director's Guide. Anna Stanley. 360p. 1989. pap. 24.95 (0-9621972-0-3) Box Ideas Pub.

Producing Business Documents: Integrated Projects & In-Basket Exercises, Practice set. James Labarre & William M. Mitchell. 1992. pap. text 20.95 (1-56118-361-X) Paradigm MN.

Producing Business Documents: Integrated Projects & In-Basket Exercises, Instructor's guide. James LaBarre et al. 1992. teacher ed. 9.95 (1-56118-362-8) Paradigm MN.

Producing Contracts for Market Testing IS-IT Services. 84p. 1994. pap. 30.00 (0-11-330646-6, HM06466, Pub. by Statnry Office) Bernan Associates.

Producing Corrugated Containers Profitably. Elliot S. Rohde. LC 94-7893. (Illus.). 256p. 1995. reprint ed. 81.00 (0-9616302-7-2) Jelmar Pub.

Producing Digital Video. Lou Wallace. 1997. 65.00 (1-56830-338-6) Brady Pub.

Producing Farm Crops. 4th ed. L. V. Boone et al. 392p. 1991. 44.95 (0-8134-2874-2); teacher ed. 9.95 (0-8134-2875-0) Interstate.

Producing, Financing & Distributing Film: A Comprehensive Legal & Business Guide. rev. ed. Paul A. Baumgarten et al. LC 91-43708. 240p. 1992. reprint ed. pap. 17.95 (0-87910-107-5) Limelight Edns.

***Producing for Hollywood: A Guide for the Independent Producer.** Paul Mason & Don Gold. 256p. 2000. pap. 19.95 (1-58115-065-2, Pub. by Allworth Pr) Watsn-Guptill.

***Producing for the Web.** Jason Whittaker. LC 00-23759. 2000. pap. write for info. (0-415-23114-0) Routledge.

Producing Fruit or Just Working! A Primary Study on the Fruit of the Spirit. Ralph W. Szasz. 100p. (Orig.). 1997. pap. 10.00 (1-57502-481-0, PO1438) Morris Pubng.

***Producing Great Sound for Digital Video.** Jay Rose. LC 99-43323. (Illus.). 349p. 1999. pap. 39.95 incl. cd-rom, audio compact disk (0-87930-597-5, Pub. by Miller Freeman) Publishers Group.

Producing Guanxi: Sentiment, Self, & Subculture in a North China Village. Andrew B. Kipnis. LC 96-36851. (Illus.). 264p. 1997. pap. text 16.95 (0-8223-1873-3); lib. bdg. 49.95 (0-8223-1883-0) Duke.

Producing Hegemony: The Politics of Mass Production & American Global Power. Mark Rupert. (Studies in International Relations: No. 38). (Illus.). 277p. (C). 1995. pap. text 19.95 (0-521-46650-4) Cambridge U Pr.

Producing High-Impact Learning Tools: A Practical Guide to Developing Effective Training Material. Pamela A. Wade. (High-Impact Training Ser.). (Illus.). 120p. 1995. pap. 14.95 (0-7879-5100-5) R Chang Assocs.

Producing Jazz: The Experience of an Independent Record Company. Herman Gray. LC 88-15925. 184p. (C). 1988. 19.95 (0-87722-574-5) Temple U Pr.

Producing Legality: Law & Socialism in Cuba. Marjorie S. Zati. LC 94-8847. (After the Law Ser.). 320p. (C). 1994. pap. 25.99 (0-415-90857-4) Routledge.

Producing Lower Income Housing: Local Initiatives. James Pickman et al. LC 86-26424. 389p. reprint ed. pap. 120.60 (0-7837-4608-3, 204432700002) Bks Demand.

Producing Macintosh(R) Graphics from SAS/GRAPH(R) Output. (Technical Report Ser.: No. P-186). 1988. pap. 3.00 (1-55544-317-6, BR5929) SAS Publ.

Producing Newsletters for New Literates Action-Learning Manual: A Guide for Literacy Practitioners. (Literacy Linkage Series Manuals). 19p. (Orig.). 1996. pap. 3.50 (0-932288-93-6) Ctr Intl Ed U of MA.

Producing Patient-Centered Health Care: Patient Perspectives about Health & Illness & the Physician/Patient Relationship. James Monroe Smith. LC 99-12474. 240p. 1999. 65.00 (0-86569-293-9, Auburn Hse) Greenwood.

Producing Pop: Culture & Conflict in the Popular Music Industry. Keith Negus. 192p. 1995. pap. text 16.95 (0-340-57512-3, B0097, Pub. by E A) OUP.

Producing Power: Ethnicity, Gender, & Class in a Caribbean Workplace. Kevin A. Yelvington. 320p. (Orig.). (C). 1995. pap. text 24.95 (1-56639-286-1) Temple U Pr.

Producing Power: Ethnicity, Gender, & Class in a Caribbean Workplace. Kevin A. Yelvington. 320p. (Orig.). (C). 1995. lib. bdg. 69.95 (1-56639-285-3) Temple U Pr.

Producing Precious Metals at Home: A. - Q.E.D. (Alchemy - Which Was to Be Proved) Joe E. Champion. Ed. by Roger C. Briggs. LC 94-70366. (Illus.). 410p. 1994. 69.95 (1-884928-32-3) Discov Pubng.

Producing Public Television, Producing Public Culture. Barry Dornfeld. LC 97-39819. 248p. 1998. text 55.00 (0-691-04468-6, Pub. by Princeton U Pr); pap. text 17.95 (0-691-04467-8, Pub. by Princeton U Pr) Cal Prin Full Svc.

Producing Quality Radiographs. Angeline Cullinan. (Illus.). 289p. 1987. text 41.50 (0-397-50778-X, Lippnctt) Lppncott W & W.

Producing Quality Radiographs. 2nd ed. Angeline Cullinan. 352p. 1993. text 51.00 (0-397-55031-6) Lppncott W & W.

Producing Quality Whitetails. 3rd rev. ed. Al Brothers & Murphy E. Ray, Jr. Ed. by Charly McTee. (Illus.). 1997. 29.95 (0-9661411-0-5); pap. 19.95 (0-9661411-1-3); lthr. 99.95 (0-9661411-2-1) Tex Wildlife.

***Producing Ridden Show Ponies.** (Allen Photographic Guides Ser.). (Illus.). 24p. 2000. pap. 10.95 (0-85131-664-6, Pub. by J A Allen) Trafalgar.

Producing Speech, Contemporary Issues: For Katherine Safford Harris. Ed. by Fredericka Bell-Berti & Lawrence J. Raphael. LC 95-12369. (Modern Acoustics & Signal Processing Ser.). 567p. (C). 1995. 69.95 (1-56396-286-1, AIP Pr) Spr-Verlag.

Producing Target Models at a Central Facility: Assessment Methodology. Myron Hura & Gary W. McLeod. LC 94-19225. 1994. pap. 7.50 (0-8330-1550-8, MR-425-AF) Rand Corp.

Producing the Musical: A Guide for School, College & Community Theatres. Haller Laughlin & Randy Wheeler. LC 83-22704. (Illus.). 151p. 1984. lib. bdg. 47.95 (0-313-24100-7, LPM/, Greenwood Pr) Greenwood.

Producing the Past: Aspects of Antiquarian Culture & Practice (1700-1850) Ed. by Martin Myrone & Lucy Peltz. LC 98-53016. (Illus.). 298p. 1999. text 86.95 (1-84014-275-8) Ashgate Pub Co.

***Producing the Promise.** Liberty Savard. LC 99-64055. (Keys of the Kingdom Trilogy Ser.). 212p. 1999. pap. 11.99 (0-88270-780-9, Logos NJ) Bridge-Logos.

Producing the Sacred: An Essay on Public Religion. Robert Wuthnow. LC 93-8934. (Public Expressions of Religion in America Ser.). 184p. 1994. text 24.95 (0-252-01920-2); pap. text 12.95 (0-252-06401-1) U of Ill Pr.

Producing the Small to Midsize Festival. International Festivals & Events Assoc. Staff. 70p. 1997. pap. 44.95 (1-891202-04-9) Intl Festivals.

Producing Theatre: A Comprehensive Legal & Business Guide. rev. ed. Donald C. Farber. LC 86-27312. 432p. 1997. reprint ed. pap. 25.00 (0-87910-103-2) Limelight Edns.

Producing TV Movies. Everett Chambers. (Illus.). 229p. (C). 1988. reprint ed. pap. 12.00 (0-9620587-0-X) ECP Inc.

Producing Vegetable Crops. 4th ed. John M. Swiader et al. (Illus.). 626p. (YA). (gr. 9-12). 1992. 53.25 (0-8134-2903-X) Interstate.

***Producing Vegetable Crops.** 5th ed. John M. Swiader & George W. Ware. (Illus.). 640p. 2001. 66.25 (0-8134-3203-0) Interstate.

Producing Videos: A Complete Guide. Martha Mollison. LC 97-186974. (Illus.). 528p. 1997. pap. 35.00 (0-642-24528-2, Pub. by Allen & Unwin Pty) Paul & Co Pubs.

Producing Women & Progress in Zimbabwe: Narratives of Identity & Work from the 1980s. Christine Sylvester. LC 99-28369. 296p. 2000. 65.00 (0-325-00070-0) Greenwood.

Producing Workers: The Politics of Gender, Class & Culture in the Calcutta Jute Mills. Leela Fernandes. LC 96-6524. (Critical Histories Ser.). 224p. 1997. text 42.50 (0-8122-3401-4); pap. text 22.50 (0-8122-1597-4) U of Pa Pr.

Producing Your Own Brochure - Catalog. Allan Smith. (Illus.). 72p. 1990. pap. 8.00 (0-931113-36-9) Success Publ.

Product. Daniel Davidson. 40p. 1991. 6.00 (0-938979-37-X) EG Bksellers.

Product & Process: An Index to the Way Things Work. Robert Finnegan. LC 88-6691. 254p. 1988. 26.50 (0-8108-2113-3) Scarecrow.

Product & Process Development in the Food Industry. Ed. by Mary D. Earle. xvi, 296p. 1985. text 141.00 (3-7186-0241-5) Gordon & Breach.

Product & Process Integration: Advanced Technology. LC 97-81301. 171p. 1998. 99.00 (0-7680-0157-9) Soc Auto Engineers.

Product & Process Modelling in the Building Industry: Proceedings of the First European Conference, Dresden, 5-7 October, 1994. Ed. by R. J. Scherer. (Illus.). 800p. Date not set. text 149.00 (90-5410-533-X, Pub. by A A Balkema) Ashgate Pub Co.

Product & Process Modelling in the Building Industry: Proceedings of the 1st European Conference, Dresden, 5-7 October 1994. Ed. by R. J. Scherer. 620p. 1995. 115.00 (90-5410-548-8, Pub. by A A Balkema) Ashgate Pub Co.

Product Assurance Principles: Integrating Design Assurance & Quality Assurance. E. R. Carubba & R. D. Gordon. 278p. 1988. 53.00 (0-07-010148-5) McGraw.

***Product Book.** Ed. by Catherine McDermott. (D & AD Mastercraft Ser.). (Illus.). 176p. 1999. 55.00 (2-88046-394-7, Rotovision) Watsn-Guptill.

***Product Costing: Concepts & Applications.** 3rd ed. Ralph S. Polimeni. (C). 1999. pap. 66.56 (0-07-239084-0) McGrw-H Hghr Educ.

P

Product Costing in Lean Manufacturing Operations Costing (Module) Ansari. 1999. pap. text 6.00 (*0-256-26715-4*, Irwn McGrw-H) McGrw-H Hghr Educ.

Product Costing Manual. 1981. 100.00 (*0-7855-1059-1*) St Mut.

***Product Costing Scenarios Made Easy.** SAP Labs, Inc. Staff. (R-Three Made Easy Guidebks.). (Illus.). 256p. 1999. pap. 30.00 (*1-893570-82-7*) SAP Labs.

Product-Country Images: Impact & Role in International Marketing. Ed. by Nicolas Papadopoulos & Louise A. Heslop. 477p. 1993. pap. 29.95 (*1-56024-237-X*) Haworth Pr.

Product-Country Images: Impact & Role in International Marketing. Nicolas Papadopoulos & Louise A. Heslop. LC 91-35947. (Illus.). 480p. 1993. lib. bdg. 79.95 (*1-56024-236-1*) Haworth Pr.

Product Data Exchange. Susan Bloor & Jon Owen. LC 94-42780. 320p. 1994. 49.95 (*1-85728-279-5*, Pub. by UCL Pr Ltd) Taylor & Francis.

Product Data Interfaces in CAD-CAM Applications. Ed. by Jose L. Encarnacao et al. (Symbolic Computation Ser.). (Illus.). 270p. 1986. 109.95 (*0-387-15118-4*) Spr-Verlag.

***Product Design.** Kevin Otto & Kristin Wood. 800p. 2000. 81.00 (*0-13-021271-7*, Prentice Hall) P-H.

Product Design: Fundamentals & Methods. N. F. Roozenburg & J. Eekels. 422p. 1995. pap. 85.00 (*0-471-95465-9*) Wiley.

Product Design & Development. Eppinger. 1994. teacher ed. 35.00 (*0-07-065812-9*) McGraw.

Product Design & Development. Karl T. Ulrich & Steven D. Eppinger. LC 94-20358. 1994. text 80.75 (*0-07-065811-0*) McGraw.

Product Design & Development. 2nd ed. Karl T. Ulrich. LC 99-27708. 384p. 1999. 74.06 (*0-07-229647-X*) McGraw.

Product Design & Manufacture. John R. Lindbeck & Robert M. Wygant. LC 94-20422. 352p. 1994. 96.00 (*0-13-034257-2*) P-H.

Product Design & Technological Innovation. Ed. by Robin Roy & David Wield. 320p. 1986. 79.95 (*0-335-15110-8*); pap. 34.95 (*0-335-15109-4*) OpUniv Pr.

Product Design & Testing of Polymeric Materials. Nicholas P. Cheremisinoff. (Illus.). 576p. 1990. text 199.00 (*0-8247-8261-5*) Dekker.

Product Design Engineering for Quality Improvement. Ed. by Roger N. Wright & Don A. Lucca. LC 83-60541. (Manufacturing Update Ser.). (Illus.). 272p. reprint ed. pap. 84.40 (*0-8357-6479-6*, 203585000097) Bks Demand.

Product Design 5, No. 5. Joe Dolce. LC 92-10433. 240p. 1992. 60.00 (*0-86636-185-5*) PBC Intl Inc.

***Product Design for Key Stage 3 Course Guide: Pupil's Book.** Andy Biggs et al. (Design & Make It Ser.). (Illus.). 144p. (YA). (gr. 6-9). 2000. pap. 22.50 (*0-7487-4429-0*, Pub. by S Thornes Pubs) Trans-Atl Phila.

***Product Design for Key Stage 3 Course Guide: Teacher Support Pack.** Andy Biggs et al. (Design & Make It Ser.). (Illus.). 223p. (YA). (gr. 6-9). 2000. pap. 99.50 (*0-7487-4430-4*, Pub. by S Thornes Pubs) Trans-Atl Phila.

***Product Design for Key Stage 3 Course Guide: Teacher Support Pack CD-Rom.** Andy Biggs et al. (Design & Make It Ser.). (Illus.). 144p. (YA). (gr. 6-9). 2000. audio compact disk 187.50 (*0-7487-5455-5*, Pub. by S Thornes Pubs) Trans-Atl Phila.

Product Design for Manufacture & Assembly. Geoffrey Boothroyd et al. LC 93-43398. (Illus.). 552p. 1994. text 165.00 (*0-8247-9176-2*) Dekker.

Product Design Management: An Annotated Bibliography. Timothy Warner & Patrick J. Noon. 220p. 1988. text 61.95 (*0-566-05466-3*, Pub. by Gower) Ashgate Pub Co.

***Product Design Methods & Practices.** Henry W. Stoll. LC 99-15459. (Illus.). 400p. 1999. text 99.75 (*0-8247-7565-1*) Dekker.

Product Design Review: A Method for Error-Free Product Development. Ed. by Edward C. Voigt. LC 96-3637. (ENG & JPN.). 274p. 1996. 65.00 (*1-56327-041-2*) Productivity Inc.

Product Design 6. Tucker Viemeister. 239p. 1994. 60.00 (*0-86636-280-0*) PBC Intl Inc.

Product Design with Plastics: A Practical Manual. Joseph B. Dym. LC 82-3091. (Illus.). 288p. (C). 1982. 32.95 (*0-8311-1141-0*) Indus Pr.

Product Development. Paisley College Staff. (Marketing For Manufacturing Managers Ser.). 1989. 105.00 (*0-08-037125-6*) Elsevier.

Product Development see Marketing for Manufacturing Managers

Product Development: Meeting the Challenge of the Design-Marketing Interface. Ed. by Margaret Bruce & Wim G. Biemans. LC 94-41380. 362p. 1995. 115.00 (*0-471-95353-9*) Wiley.

Product Development: Prospering in a Rapidly Changing World. Ed. by Thomas P. Hustad. 129p. (C). 1990. pap. 20.00 (*0-9622586-2-8*) Prod Dev Mgt Assn.

Product Development & Production Engineering in Manufacturing Industries. Ed. by Claude Foulard. 400p. 1990. 115.00 (*0-89116-799-4*) Hemisp Pub.

***Product Development & Production Networks: The Practice of Concurrent Engineering - Optimizing Time to Market - Technical & Social Requirements.** Ed. by U. Jurgens. LC 99-58790. 350p. 1999. 124.00 (*3-540-64172-6*) Spr-Verlag.

Product Development & Research Guidance Testing with Special Consumer Groups, Vol. 2. Ed. by L. S. Wu & Ayn D. Gelinas. (Special Technical Publication Ser.: No. STP 1155). (Illus.). 100p. 1992. text 32.00 (*0-8031-1479-6*, STP1155) ASTM.

Product Development & the Environment. Paul Burall. LC 95-40205. 232p. 1996. 69.95 (*0-566-07659-4*, Pub. by Gower) Ashgate Pub Co.

Product Development Challenge. Clark. 1995. 32.50 (*0-07-103619-9*) McGraw.

Product Development Challenge: Competing Through Speed, Quality, & Creativity. Kim B. Clark & Steven C. Wheelwright. LC 94-44895. (Harvard Business Review Book Ser.). 448p. 1995. 32.50 (*0-87584-609-2*) Harvard Busn.

Product Development for the Service Sector. Scott Edgett. 1999. write for info. (*0-201-36097-7*) Addison-Wesley.

Product Development for the Service Sector: Lessons from Market Leaders. Scott J. Edgett & Robert G. Cooper. 256p. 1999. 30.00 (*0-7382-0105-7*, Pub. by Perseus Pubng) HarpC.

Product Development Performance: Strategy, Organization, & Management in the World Auto Industry. Kim B. Clark & Takahiro Fujimoto. 409p. 1991. 35.00 (*0-87584-245-3*) Harvard Busn.

Product Development Planning for Healthcare Products Regulated by the FDA. Elaine Whitmore. LC 96-48101. 159p. 1997. 35.00 (*0-87389-416-2*, H0957) ASQ Qual Pr.

***Product Development Section Monograph.** (SOA Monographs: No. M-AS99-3). (Illus.). 1999. pap. text 20.00 (*0-938959-63-8*) Soc Actuaries.

Product Devlopment Performance. Clark. 350p. 1991. 39.95 (*0-07-103291-6*) McGraw.

***Product Engineering & Manufacturing.** Patrick F. Cunniff et al. LC 99-210799. (Illus.). 344p. 1998. pap. text 42.60 (*0-9655911-3-1*) College Hse.

Product Engineering Design Manual. Ed. by Douglas C. Greenwood. LC 80-23595. (Illus.). 342p. (C). 1982. reprint ed. text 34.50 (*0-89874-273-0*) Krieger.

Product Esthetics: An Interpretation for Designers. Zdzislaw M. Lewalski. (Illus.). 240p. (Orig.). 1988. pap. 17.95 (*0-944327-04-4*) Design & Dev Engineering Pr.

Product Evolution Mad World. Bach & Dolkas. 1997. text 29.95 (*0-07-002039-6*) McGraw.

Product Export Riches Opportunities. 220p. 1996. 35.00 (*0-317-55713-0*) B Klein Pubns.

***Product Focused Software Process Improvement: Second International Conference Profes 2000, Oulu, Finland, June 20-22, 2000 Proceedings.** International Conference Profes 2000 Staff et al. LC 00-44014. 2000. write for info. (*3-540-67688-0*) Spr-Verlag.

Product Formation in Cultures of Microbes & the Microbial Growth Process. Ed. by S. John Pirt. (C). 1994. 75.00 (*1-874685-15-0*, Pub. by Pirtferm Ltd) St Mut.

Product Formula for Surgery Obstructions. J. W. Morgan. LC 78-4581. (Memoirs Ser.: No. 14/201). 90p. 1978. pap. 19.00 (*0-8218-2201-2*, MEMO/14/201) Am Math.

Product Formulas, Nonlinear Semigroups, & Addition of Unbounded Operators. Paul R. Chernoff. LC 73-22235. (American Mathematical Society Ser.: No. 140). 128p. 1974. pap. 39.70 (*0-608-05170-5*, 205259100001) Bks Demand.

Product Formulas, Nonlinear Semigroups & Addition of Unbounded Operators. Paul R. Chernoff. LC 73-22235. (Memoirs Ser.: No. 1/140). 121p. 1974. pap. 18.00 (*0-8218-1840-6*, MEMO/1/140) Am Math.

***Product Graphs: Structure & Recognition.** Wilfried Imrich & Sandi Klavzar. LC 99-59409. 360p. 2000. 84.95 (*0-471-37039-8*) Wiley.

Product Improvement Through Environmental Science: Proceedings of the Annual Meeting of the Institute of Environmental Sciences, 8th, 1962. Annual Meeting of the Institute of Environmental S. LC 62-38584. (Illus.). 1962. pap. text 75.00 (*0-915414-02-3*) IEST.

Product Innovation: An Annotated Bibliography: Short Abstracts of Important Articles & a Section Listing Recent Books. Axel Johne & Damian Brown. 77p. (Orig.). 1989. pap. 20.00 (*0-9622586-1-X*) Prod Dev Mgt Assn.

Product Innovation & Directions of International Trade. Louis T. Wells, Jr. Ed. by Stuart Bruchey. LC 80-602. (Multinational Corporations Ser.). (Illus.). 1981. lib. bdg. 24.95 (*0-405-13392-8*) Ayer.

Product Innovation & Eco-Efficiency. Ed. by Judith E. Klostermann et al. LC 97-39896. 304p. 1998. text 151.00 (*0-7923-4761-7*) Kluwer Academic.

Product Innovation Strategy, Pure & Simple: How Winning Companies Outpace Their Competitors. Michel Robert. LC 95-11855. 174p. 1995. 24.95 (*0-07-053132-3*) McGraw.

Product Juggernauts. Deschamps. 1995. 29.95 (*0-07-103614-8*) McGraw.

Product Juggernauts: How Companies Mobilize to Generate a Stream of Market Winners. Jean-Philippe Deschamps & P. Ranganath Nayak. LC 94-39670. 480p. 1995. 29.95 (*0-87584-341-7*) Harvard Busn.

Product Labeling & Health Risks. Ed. by Louis A. Morris et al. LC 80-22728. (Banbury Report: Vol. 6). 344p. 1980. reprint ed. pap. 106.70 (*0-608-01801-5*, 206245400003) Bks Demand.

***Product Leadership: Creating & Launching Superior New Products.** Robert G. Cooper. 336p. 1999. pap. text 20.00 (*0-7382-0156-1*, Pub. by Perseus Pubng) HarpC.

Product Liability. John S. Allee. 550p. 1984. ring bd. 90.00 (*0-318-20280-8*, 00587) NY Law Pub.

Product Liability. Ellen E. Beerworth. 220p. 1989. pap. 48.00 (*1-86287-011-X*, Pub. by Federation Pr) Gaunt.

Product Liability. James Henderson. 1992. 54.00 (*0-316-35622-0*, Aspen Law & Bus) Aspen Pub.

Product Liability. J. G. Roche. (Illus.). xxviii, 200p. 1990. 70.95 (*0-387-51819-3*) Spr-Verlag.

Product Liability. Chris Wright. 220p. 1989. pap. 38.00 (*1-85431-036-4*, Pub. by Blackstone Pr) Gaunt.

Product Liability: Law & Insurance. Ed. by Mark Mildred & Evans B. Wade. ring bd. 185.00 (*1-85044-595-8*) LLP.

Product Liability: Prevention, Practice & Process in Europe & the United States. R. Hulsenbek & D. Campbell. 208p. 1989. pap. 63.00 (*90-6544-454-8*) Kluwer Law Intl.

Product Liability: The New Law under the Consumer Protection Act, 1987. Rodney Nelson-Jones & P. Stewart. 208p. (C). 1988. 90.00 (*1-85190-049-7*, Pub. by Fourmat Pub) St Mut.

Product Liability: The New Law under the Consumer Protection Act 1987. Rodney Nelson-Jones & Peter Stewart. 208p. 1987. 128.00 (*1-85190-034-9*, Pub. by Fourmat Pub) St Mut.

Product Liability - The New Pocket Liability Law in Germany: Tochtergesellschaften Deutscher Unternehmen in den U. S. A. 1994-95. Peter Bleutge. (ENG & GER.). 80p. 1993. 25.00 (*0-86640-049-4*) German Am Chamber.

Product Liability Actions by Foreign Plaintiffs in the United States. Warren Freedman. 312p. 1988. 95.00 (*90-6544-325-8*) Kluwer Law Intl.

Product Liability & Innovation: Managing Risk in an Uncertain Environment. National Academy of Engineering Staff. Ed. by Janet R. Hunziker & Trevor O. Jones. 216p. (C). 1994. text 37.95 (*0-309-05130-4*) Natl Acad Pr.

Product Liability & Safety. 3rd ed. David G. Owen & Mary J. Davis. (University Casebook Ser.). 204p. (C). 1997. pap. text, teacher ed. write for info. (*1-56662-580-7*) Foundation Pr.

Product Liability Case Digest. annuals Scott Baldwin et al. 400p. pap. 60.00 (*0-316-08015-2*, 80152) Aspen Law.

Product Liability Casebook. Ed. by J. S. Ashworth. (C). 1984. 365.00 (*0-7855-4058-X*, Pub. by Witherby & Co) St Mut.

Product Liability Desk Reference: A Fifty-State Compendium. annuals Ed. by Morton F. Daller. 496p. pap. 109.00 (*0-316-17241-3*, 72413) Aspen Law.

***Product Liability Desk Reference: 1999 Edition.** Morton F. Daller. 544p. 1999. pap. 122.00 (*0-7355-0508-X*) Panel Pubs.

***Product Liability for the Professional.** Hart & Kinzie. (C). 2001. pap. 39.75 (*0-7668-2035-1*) Thomson Learn.

Product Liability in Australia. S. W. Cavanaugh & C. S. Phegan. 1983. 82.00 (*0-409-49101-2*, AT, MICHIE) LEXIS Pub.

Product Liability in Europe. Association Europeene D'etudes Juridiques et Fisca. Ed. by Paul Strom. 160p. 1975. pap. 21.00 (*90-268-0815-1*) Kluwer Academic.

Product Liability in the Construction Industry. Norman Palmer & Ewan McKendrick. 326p. 1993. 100.00 (*1-85044-530-3*) LLP.

Product Liability in the United States: A Primer for Japanese Manufacturers & Their Employees. Perkins Coie Product Liability Practice Group Staf & Keith Gerrard. Ed. by Mark Lough. LC 91-60104. (Illus.). 96p. (C). 1991. pap. text 9.95 (*1-879650-01-0*) Perkins Coie.

Product Liability in the United States: A Primer for Korean Manufacturers & Their Employees. Keith Gerrard & Perkins Cole Liability Law Group Staff. Ed. by Anne Airy. (KOR., Illus.). 96p. 1995. pap. text 9.95 (*1-879650-04-5*) Perkins Coie.

Product Liability in the United States: A Primer for Manufacturers & Their Employees. Perkins Coie Product Liability Law Practice Group & Keith Gerrard. Ed. by Laurie Winfield. LC 91-60104. (Illus.). 96p. (C). 1991. pap. text 9.95 (*1-879650-00-2*) Perkins Coie.

Product Liability Law: A Guide for Managers. Michael H. Whincup. (C). 1985. 240.00 (*0-7855-4057-1*, Pub. by Witherby & Co) St Mut.

Product Liability Law in Illinois. Charles W. Chapman & Thomas E. Hoffman. 142p. 1994. text 75.00 (*0-910095-00-0*) Law Bulletin.

Product Liability Law in Texas. James B. Sales. LC 85-18150. xv, 700p. 1985. 39.50 (*0-913797-09-X*) Houston Law Review.

Product Liability of Manufacturers, 1989. 379p. 1989. 15.00 (*0-685-69478-X*) PLI.

***Product Liability Prevention: A Strategic Guide.** Randall L. Goodden. LC 00-25299. 2000. write for info. (*0-87389-482-0*) ASQ Qual Pr.

Product Liability Problems, 1996 Edition for Use with Products Liability & Safety, Cases & Materials. 3rd ed. David G. Owen et al. (University Casebook Ser.). 243p. 1996. pap. text. write for info. (*1-56662-426-6*) Foundation Pr.

Product Liability Reform: Hearing Before the Committee on the Judiciary, House of Representatives, 105th Congress, 1st Session, April 10, 1997. USGPO Staff. LC 97-194986. iii, 255p. 1997. pap. write for info. (*0-16-055306-7*) USGPO.

Product Liability Reform: Hearing Before the Committee on the Judiciary, U. S. House of Representatives. Ed. by Henry J. Hyde. (Illus.). 255p. (C). 1998. pap. text 40.00 (*0-7881-7248-4*) DIANE Pub.

***Product Liability Reform & Consumer Access to Life-Saving Products: Congressional Hearings.** Ed. by W. J. Tauzin. 160p. (C). 1999. reprint ed. pap. text 30.00 (*0-7881-8303-6*) DIANE Pub.

Product Liability Rules in OECD Countries. OECD Staff. LC 96-161803. 58p. (Orig.). 1995. pap. 18.00 (*92-64-14439-0*, Pub. by Org for Econ) OECD.

Product Liability Trial Practice (1992) 15p. 1992. pap. text 15.00 (*1-56986-004-1*) Federal Bar.

Product Liability Update, 1990. (Litigation & Administrative Practice Course Handbook, 1983-84 Ser.). 593p. 1990. 17.50 (*0-685-69479-8*) PLI.

Product Life-Cycle Assessment to Reduce Health Risks & Environmental Impacts. Gregory A. Keoleian et al. LC 94-3808. (Illus.). 295p. 1994. 109.00 (*0-8155-1354-2*) Noyes.

Product Life Cycles & Product Management. Sak Onkvisit & John J. Shaw. LC 88-26509. 172p. 1989. 55.00 (*0-89930-319-6*, OKV, Quorum Bks) Greenwood.

Product-Line Performance Evaluation Systems for Financial Depositories. Kenneth J. Thygerson. LC 96-32509. 168p. 1997. 59.95 (*1-56720-104-0*, Quorum Bks) Greenwood.

Product Management. Donald R. Lehman & Russell S. Winer. LC 93-10645. 464p. (C). 1993. text 68.95 (*0-256-11623-7*, Irwn McGrw-H) McGrw-H Hghr Educ.

Product Management. 2nd ed. Donald R. Lehmann. 512p. (C). 1996. text 68.95 (*0-256-21439-5*, Irwn McGrw-H) McGrw-H Hghr Educ.

Product Management: A Reader. Patrick M. Dunne & Susan Obenhouse. LC 80-22355. 182p. reprint ed. pap. 56.50 (*0-608-12626-8*, 202542700043) Bks Demand.

***Product Management: Sharpening the Competitive Edge.** John Legge. 2000. pap. 52.95 (*0-7329-5408-8*, Pub. by Macmill Educ) Paul & Co Pubs.

Product Management/Marketing. Michael Baker. LC 96-25428. 550p. (C). 1998. pap. 49.00 (*0-13-065368-3*) P-H.

Product Manager. Jehiel Zif & Aval Igal. 64p. (C). 1989. pap. text 12.75 (*0-13-724121-6*) P-H.

Product Manager's Handbook: The Complete Product Management Resource. Linda Gorchels. (Illus.). 288p. 1995. 37.95 (*0-8442-3669-1*, NTC Business Bks) NTC Contemp Pub Co.

***Product Manager's Handbook: The Complete Product Management Resource.** 2nd ed. Linda Gorchels. LC 99-57181. (Illus.). 320p. 2000. 39.95 (*0-658-00135-3*, 001353) NTC Contemp Pub Co.

***Product Marketing Handbook for Software.** 3rd ed. Merrill R. Chapman. Ed. by Gail Ostrow. (Illus.). 424p. 1999. pap. 59.95 (*0-9672008-0-6*) Aegis Resources.

Product, Music Gallery, Business Simulation. 9th ed. Caldwell. (GB - Basic Business Ser.). 1990. 20.95 (*0-538-60196-5*) S-W Pub.

Product of Love: From the Bottom Up. Denise Nickell. LC 96-61917. 176p. (Orig.). 1997. pap. 12.95 (*1-883893-94-1*) WinePress Pub.

Product of Two Normally Distributed Random Variables. William Q. Meeker, Jr. et al. LC 74-6283. (Selected Tables in Mathematical Statistics Ser.: No. 7). 256p. 1982. text 34.00 (*0-8218-1907-0*, TABLES 7) Am Math.

Product Offering: The Right Mix. R. Craig Palubiak. (Business Person's Handbook Ser.: Vol. 11). 20p. (Orig.). 1998. pap. 8.95 (*1-893308-10-3*) Optim Consult Grp.

Product Operations Management. 6th ed. Stevenson. 1998. text 67.00 (*0-256-24866-4*) McGrw-H Hghr Educ.

Product P. Don Debelak. LC 96-36095. (Entrepreneur Magazine Small Business Ser.). 384p. 1997. pap. 19.95 (*0-471-15750-3*) Wiley.

Product Placement Im Kinospielfilm. Florian Asche. (GER.). 156p. 1996. 35.95 (*3-631-30254-1*) P Lang Pubng.

Product Planning & Management: Designing & Delivering Value. William L. Moore & Edgar A. Pessemier. LC 92-13522. (Marketing Ser.). (C). 1993. text 66.25 (*0-07-043046-2*) McGraw.

***Product Planning Essentials.** Kenneth B. Kahn. LC 00-9514. 2000. pap. write for info. (*0-7619-1999-6*) Sage Pub.

Product Planning Practices in the Software Industry: Benchmarks & Best Practices. Joseph G. Kormos & Culpepper & Associates Staff. (Illus.). 420p. 1997. 795.00 (*1-58128-010-6*, WR) Culpepper.

Product Policy: Cases & Concepts. Richard N. Cardozo. LC 78-67939. 1979. text. write for info. (*0-201-00888-2*) Addison-Wesley.

Product Policy in Europe: New Environmental Perspectives. Frans Oosterhuis et al. LC 96-16837. (Environment & Policy Ser.). 320p. (C). 1996. text 166.00 (*0-7923-4078-7*, D Reidel) Kluwer Academic.

***Product Recall Planning Guide.** 2nd ed. American Society for Quality Staff. LC 99-17454. xvii, 84p. 1999. write for info. (*0-87389-457-X*) ASQ Qual Pr.

Product Release Engineering for Software Engineering. Michael Bays. LC 99-16017. 256p. (C). 1999. 48.00 (*0-13-636564-7*) P-H.

Product Reliability, Maintainability, & Supportability Handbook. Ed. by Michael G. Pecht. LC 95-5257. 448p. 1995. boxed set 104.95 (*0-8493-9457-0*, 9457) CRC Pr.

Product Risk Labeling: A Federal Responsibility. W. Kip Viscusi. LC 92-35079. (Studies in Regulation & Federalism). 50p. (Orig.). 1993. pap. 9.75 (*0-8447-3820-4*, AEI Pr) Am Enterprise.

Product Safety: Management Guidelines. National Safety Council Staff. LC 88-61858. (Illus.). 199p. (Orig.). 1989. reprint ed. pap. 61.70 (*0-608-01653-5*, 206230500002) Bks Demand.

Product Safety - Legislation, Regulation & Consumerism: Index of New Information with Authors, Subjects & References. Science & Life Consultants Association Staff. 150p. 1996. 47.50 (*0-7883-1264-2*); pap. 44.50 (*0-7883-1265-0*) ABBE Pubs Assn.

Product Safety & Surveillance: Index of New Information, Reference & Research Guidance with Post-Marketing Activity. Christian B. Kassover. 150p. 1997. 47.50 (*0-7883-1350-9*); pap. 44.50 (*0-7883-1351-7*) ABBE Pubs Assn.

Product Safety Evaluation. Ed. by Alan M. Goldberg. (Alternative Methods in Toxicology Ser.: Vol. 1). 376p. 1983. text 191.00 (*0-913113-00-X*) M Liebert.

An Asterisk (*) at the beginning of an entry indicates that the title is appearing for the first time.

Product Safety Evaluation Handbook. Gad. (Drug & Chemical Toxicology Ser.: Vol. 6). (Illus.). 664p. 1988. text 275.00 (*0-8247-7829-4*) Dekker.

Product Safety Evaluation Handbook. 2nd ed. Ed. by Gad. LC 99-30388. (Illus.). 712p. 1999. text 195.00 (*0-8247-1971-9*) Dekker.

Product Safety in America. Michael F. Colley & Roscoe Pound-American Trial Lawyers Assn. Staff. LC 85-60392. (Annual Chief Justice Earl Warren Conference on Advocacy in the U.S. Ser.). 127p. (Orig.). 1985. pap. 25.00 (*0-933067-00-3*) Roscoe Pound Inst.

Product Safety Management & Engineering. 2nd ed. Willie Hammer. (Illus.). 311p. (C). 1993. 84.95 (*0-939874-90-3*, 4342) ASSE.

Product Safety Management Guidelines. 2nd ed. National Safety Council Staff. LC 96-42201. 189p. 1996. 43.95 (*0-87912-193-9*, 17655-0000) Natl Safety Coun.

Product Side of Pollution Prevention: Evaluating the Potential for Safe Substitutes. Environmental Protection Agency Staff. 208p. 1995. pap. text 69.00 (*0-86587-479-5*) Gov Insts.

Product Standards for Internationally Integrated Goods Markets. Alan O. Sykes. (Integrating National Economies Ser.). 235p. (C). 1995. 34.95 (*0-8157-8296-9*); pap. 14.95 (*0-8157-8295-0*) Brookings.

***Product Strategy for High Technology Companies.** 2nd ed. Michael E. McGrath. (Illus.). 320p. 2000. 49.95 (*0-07-136246-0*) McGraw.

Product Strategy for High-Technology Companies: How to Achieve Growth, Competitive Advantage, & Increased Profits. Michael E. McGrath. LC 94-27340. 284p. 1994. text 42.50 (*0-7863-0146-5*, Irwn Prfssnl) McGraw-Hill Prof.

Product Support: Buy Words for the 80's. Associated Equipment Distributors Staff. 48p. 1985. reprint ed. 10.00 (*0-318-19179-2*) Assn Equip Distrs.

Product Tampering: A Worldwide Problem: A Crisis Communications Tool for Newsrooms & Corporations. Deborah Lowe et al. Ed. by Doug Ramsey & John Warner. (Illus.). 28p. 1993. pap. 7.95 (*0-910755-00-0*) Foun Am Comm.

Product Testing & Sensory Evaluation of Foods: Marketing & R&D Approaches. H. R. Moskowitz. 605p. 1983. 87.00 (*0-917678-16-8*) Food & Nut Pr.

Product Testing with Consumers for Research Guidance. Ed. by Louise S. Wu. LC 89-6901. (Special Technical Publication Ser.: No. STP 1035). (Illus.). 100p. 1989. pap. text 24.00 (*0-8031-1256-4*, STP1035) ASTM.

Product Variety Management: Research Advances. Teck-Hua Ho & Christopher S. Tang. LC 98-8736. (International Series in Operations Research & Management Science). 1998. 115.00 (*0-7923-8226-9*) Kluwer Academic.

Product Video Center Narrative: Keeping Financial Records. 7th ed. Harold Baron & Steinfeld. (BB - Record Keeping I Ser.: Vol. 1). 1991. 26.95 (*0-538-60479-4*) S-W Pub.

***Product Warnings, Defects & Hazards.** 2nd ed. James T. O'Reilly. LC 98-47268. 1999. ring bd. 164.00 (*0-7355-0299-4*) Aspen Law.

Product Warranties & Servicing: Responsive Business Approaches to Consumer Needs. 35p. 1993. pap. 3.50 (*0-16-040600-5*) USGPO.

Product Warranty Handbook. Ed. by Wallace R. Blischke & D. N. Murthy. (Illus.). 952p. 1995. text 225.00 (*0-8247-8955-5*) Dekker.

***Production.** Wu. 1998. pap. text 31.00 (*0-471-32418-3*) Wiley.

Production: How to Organize Your Production Office, Increase Efficiency & Make Informed Production Decision. Cook Communications Ministries International Staff. (Interlit Imprint Ser.: Unit 10). 40p. 1995. pap. text 6.00 (*1-884752-15-2*, 44099) Cook Min Intl.

Production: Planning, Control & Integration. Daniel Sipper & Robert Bulfin. LC 96-36137. (McGraw-Hill Series in Industrial Engineering & Management Science). 640p. (C). 1997. 90.00 (*0-07-057682-3*) McGraw.

Production - Operations Management. T. Hill. 384p. (C). 1983. 200.00 (*0-7855-5729-6*, Pub. by Inst Pur & Supply) St Mut.

Production - Operations Management. Jack Rudman. (ACT Proficiency Examination Program (PEP) Ser.: Vol. 24). 43.95 (*0-8373-5574-5*) Nat Learn.

Production - Operations Management. 4th ed. William J. Stevenson. LC 92-28905. 1992. teacher ed. write for info. (*0-256-11768-3*, Irwn McGrw-H) McGrw-H Hghr Educ.

Production Activity Control: A Practical Guide. Steven A. Melnyk & Phillip L. Carter. (APICS Series in Production Management). 200p. 1987. text 47.50 (*0-87094-970-5*, Irwn Prfssnl) McGraw-Hill Prof.

Production Activity Control Instructor Guide Kit. American Production & Inventory Control Society St. 1991. 600.00 (*1-55822-070-4*) Am Prod & Inventory.

Production Activity Control Reprints. rev. ed. Ed. by APICS Production Activity Control Committee of the. LC 88-82787. (Illus.). 169p. 1993. pap. 21.00 (*1-55822-039-9*) Am Prod & Inventory.

Production Activity Control Student Guide. American Production & Inventory Control Society St. 1991. 37.00 (*1-55822-071-2*) Am Prod & Inventory.

Production, Analysis & Upgrading of Oils from Biomass. American Chemical Society, Division of Fuel Chemis. LC TP0324.P7. (Preprints of Papers: Vol. 32, No. 2). (Illus.). 334p. reprint ed. pap. 103.60 (*0-608-18396-2*, 202998800067) Bks Demand.

Production & Consumption of Foodgrains in India. J. S. Sarma & V. P. Gandhi. 115p. 1990. 10.00 (*0-89629-084-0*) Intl Food Policy.

Production & Cost Functions: Specification, Measurement & Applications. Ed. by Erkin I. Bairam. LC 98-71456. 144p. 1998. text 55.95 (*1-84014-378-9*, Pub. by Ashgate Pub) Ashgate Pub Co.

Production & Cost Models of a Multi-Product Firm: A Mathematical Programming Approach. Niels Knudsen. (Odense Studies in History & Social Sciences: No. 13). 300p. (Orig.). 1973. pap. 30.00 (*87-7492-085-5*, Pub. by Odense Universitets Forlag) Coronet Bks.

Production & Decay of Light Mesons: Proceedings of the Workshop Organized by the Laboratoire National Satume. Ed. by F. Fleury. 256p. 1989. text 75.00 (*9971-5-0677-7*) World Scientific Pub.

***Production & Distribution of Assistive Devices for People with Disabilities, Vol. 5.** Economic & Social Commission for Asia & the Pacific Staff. 100p. 1998. pap. 50.00 (*92-1-119775-9*) UN.

Production & Distribution Theories. George J. Stigler. LC 93-36977. 400p. (C). 1993. pap. text 24.95 (*1-56000-710-9*) Transaction Pubs.

Production & Economic Dynamics. Ed. by Michael A. Landesmann & Robert Scazzieri. (Illus.). 373p. (C). 1996. text 69.95 (*0-521-46251-7*) Cambridge U Pr.

Production & Improvement of Crops for Dryland. Ed. by U. S. Gupta. 462p. 1995. text 88.00 (*1-886106-17-7*) Science Pubs.

Production & Industrial Systems: Proceedings of the 4th International Conference on Production Research, Tokyo, 1977. Ed. by R. Muramatsu & N. A. Dudley. 1340p. 1978. 187.00 (*0-85066-138-2*) Taylor & Francis.

Production & Inventory Control: Applications. George W. Plossl. LC 83-81732. (Illus.). 320p. 1983. 45.00 (*0-926219-04-9*) G P Ed Serv.

Production & Inventory Control: Principles & Techniques. 2nd ed. George W. Plossl & Oliver W. Wright. (Illus.). 448p. 1985. 96.00 (*0-13-725144-0*) P-H.

Production & Inventory Control Handbook. 3rd ed. James H. Greene. LC 96-39980. (Illus.). 1200p. 1997. 95.00 (*0-07-024428-6*) McGraw.

Production & Inventory Management. 2nd ed. Donald W. Fogarty et al. 752p. (C). 1990. mass mkt. 75.95 (*0-538-07461-2*, G46) S-W Pub.

Production & Inventory Management. 3rd ed. Blackstone. (GC - Principles of Management Ser.). (C). 2001. mass mkt. 42.00 (*0-538-83909-0*) S-W Pub.

Production & Inventory Management in the Computer Age. Oliver W. Wight. LC 83-21645. 284p. 1988. reprint ed. 40.00 (*0-939246-06-6*) Wiley.

Production & Inventory Management Manual. 2nd ed. Fogarty & Hoffmann. (SWC-Management Ser.). (C). 1991. teacher ed. 20.00 (*0-538-28473-0*) S-W Pub.

Production & Management of Therapeutic Power in Zionist Churches Within a Zulu City. J. P. Kiernan. LC 90-45943. (Studies in African Health & Medicine: Vol. 4). 300p. 1990. lib. bdg. 89.95 (*0-88946-283-6*) E Mellen.

Production & Marketing of Milkfish in Taiwan: An Economic Analysis. Chaur-Shyan Lee. (ICLARM Technical Reports: No. 6). (Illus.). 41p. (Orig.). 1983. pap. text 9.50 (*0-89955-390-7*, Pub. by ICLARM) Intl Spec Bk.

Production & Marketing of Off-Season Vegetables. D. V. Singh. 1990. 32.50 (*81-7099-197-8*, Pub. by Mittal Pubs Dist) S Asia.

Production & Marketing of Potato in India: A Caste Study of Uttar Pradesh. S. S. Sangwan. (C). 1991. 18.50 (*81-7099-243-5*, Pub. by Mittal Pubs Dist) S Asia.

***Production & Marketing of Pulses.** R. S. Tripathi. (Illus.). xxiii, 255p. 1998. 30.00 (*81-7099-704-6*, Pub. by Mittal Pubns) Nataraj Bks.

Production & Neutralization of Negative Ion & Beams. Ed. by James G. Alessi. LC 85-71695. (Conference Proceeding Ser.: No. 158). 784p. 1987. lib. bdg. 85.00 (*0-88318-358-7*) Am Inst Physics.

Production & Neutralization of Negative Ions & Beams. Ed. by Ady Herschcovitch. LC 90-53316. (AIP Conference Proceedings Ser.: No. 210). (Illus.). 840p. 1990. 99.00 (*0-88318-775-2*) Am Inst Physics.

Production & Neutralization of Negative Ions & Beams: International Symposium, Brookhaven, 1983. 3rd ed. Ed. by Krsto Prelec. LC 84-70379. (AIP Conference Proceedings Ser.: No. 111). 778p. 1984. lib. bdg. 53.75 (*0-88318-310-2*) Am Inst Physics.

Production & Neutralization of Negative Ions & Beams: Seventh International Symposium/Production & Application of Light Negative Ions: Sixth European Workshop: A Joint Meeting. Ed. by Krsto Prelec. (AIP Conference Proceedings Ser.: No. 380). (Illus.). 624p. 1996. 155.00 (*1-56396-565-8*, AIP Pr) Spr-Verlag.

Production & Neutralization of Negative Ions & Beams - Production & Application of Light Negative Ions: Eighth International Symposium - Seventh European Workshop A Joint Meeting. Ed. by Claude Jacquot. LC 98-72695. (Conference Proceedings Ser.: Vol. 439). (Illus.). 304p. 1998. 90.00 (*1-56396-737-5*) Spr-Verlag.

Production & Operation Management. 5th ed. Dilworth. 1993. student ed. 28.75 (*0-07-016992-6*) McGraw.

Production & Operations Management. 6th ed. Norman Gaither. (SWC-Business Statistics). 948p. (C). 1995. mass mkt. 55.75 (*0-534-51020-5*) Wadsworth Pub.

Production & Operations Analysis. Steven Nahmias. (C). 1992. 57.00 (*0-256-05550-5*, Irwn McGrw-H) McGrw-H Hghr Educ.

Production & Operations Analysis. 2nd ed. Steven Nahmias. LC 92-23790. 800p. (C). 1992. text 74.65 (*0-256-10664-9*, Irwn McGrw-H) McGrw-H Hghr Educ.

Production & Operations Analysis. 3rd ed. Steven Nahmias. LC 96-28689. 864p. (C). 1996. text 74.65 (*0-256-19508-0*, Irwn McGrw-H) McGrw-H Hghr Educ.

Production & Operations Management. Lee. LC 93-78633. (C). 1993. pap. text 77.56 (*0-395-56084-5*) HM.

Production & Operations Management. Lee. (C). 1993. pap. 9.96 (*0-395-69233-4*) HM.

Production & Operations Management. Lee. (C). 1994. pap. text, student ed. 20.76 (*0-395-56085-3*) HM.

Production & Operations Management. L. Lockyer et al. 576p. (C). 1988. 185.00 (*0-7855-5728-8*, Pub. by Inst Pur & Supply) St Mut.

Production & Operations Management. L. Lockyer et al. 576p. (C). 1989. 147.00 (*0-7855-4641-3*, Pub. by Inst Pur & Supply) St Mut.

Production & Operations Management. Morton. (GC - Principles of Management Ser.). 720p. (C). 1999. 83.95 (*0-87709-524-8*) Course Tech.

Production & Operations Management. Howard J. Weiss & Mark E. Gershon. 816p. 1989. boxed set 55.00 (*0-205-11724-4*, H17247) Allyn.

Production & Operations Management. Howard J. Weiss & Mark E. Gershon. 816p. 1989. teacher ed. write for info. (*0-318-63860-6*, H18211); student ed. 19.00 (*0-685-44210-1*, H18245); disk. write for info. (*0-685-22009-5*, H18237) P-H.

Production & Operations Management. 5th ed. James B. Dilworth. (C). 1992. text 70.00 (*0-07-016987-X*) McGraw.

Production & Operations Management. 5th ed. William J. Stevenson. 296p. (C). 1996. text, student ed. 26.25 (*0-256-20851-4*, Irwn McGrw-H) McGrw-H Hghr Educ.

Production & Operations Management. 5th ed. Ray Wild. 928p. 1998. pap. 49.95 incl. cd-rom (*0-304-70403-2*) Continuum.

Production & Operations Management. 6th ed. Norman Gaither. 948p. (C). 1993. text 57.75 (*0-685-71987-1*) Dryden Pr.

Production & Operations Management. 7th ed. Gaither. (Business Statistics Ser.). 1996. mass mkt., student ed. 19.50 (*0-534-51147-3*) Wadsworth Pub.

Production & Operations Management. 7th ed. Norman Gaither. (C). 1995. mass mkt. 67.75 (*0-534-51000-0*) PWS Pubs.

Production & Operations Management. 8th ed. Richard Chase & Nicholas Aquilano. LC 97-36919. 880p. (C). 1997. text 65.50 (*0-256-22556-7*, Irwn McGrw-H) McGrw-H Hghr Educ.

Production & Operations Management. 8th ed. Gaither. LC 98-23075. (SWC-Management Ser.). 1998. pap. 68.00 (*0-538-89108-4*) S-W Pub.

Production & Operations Management. 8th ed. Gaither. (SWC-Management Ser.). Date not set. student ed. 79.00 (*0-324-08704-7*) Sth-Wstn College.

Production & Operations Management: An Applied Modern Approach. Joseph S. Martinich. LC 96-28170. 944p. 1996. text 105.95 (*0-471-54632-1*) Wiley.

Production & Operation's Management Class Notes. 210p. (C). 1996. text 29.80 (*0-536-59403-1*) Pearson Custom.

Production & Operations Management: Manufacturing & Services. 5th ed. Lawrence P. Ettkin & James B. Dilworth. (C). 1993. pap., student ed. 27.50 (*0-07-016989-6*) McGraw.

Production & Operations Management: Manufacturing & Services. 8th ed. Richard B. Chase et al. LC 97-36919. 1997. write for info. (*0-256-26921-1*, Irwn Prfssnl) McGraw-Hill Prof.

Production & Operations Management: Manufacturing Services. 7th ed. Richard B. Chase & Nicholas J. Aquilano. LC 94-31409. 896p. (C). 1994. text 73.75 (*0-256-14023-5*, Irwn McGrw-H) McGrw-H Hghr Educ.

Production & Operations Management: Strategy & Tactics. 2nd ed. Jay Heizer & Barry Render. 850p. 1991. text 55.00 (*0-205-12717-7*, H27170) Allyn.

Production & Operations Management: Text & Cases. 5th ed. Ray Wild. LC 93-40674. (Illus.). 800p. 1995. pap. 55.00 (*0-304-33077-9*) Continuum.

Production & Operations Management: Total Quality & Responsiveness. Hamid Noori & Russell Radford. LC 94-33821. (C). 1994. pap. text, wbk. ed. 70.25 (*0-07-912037-7*) McGraw.

Production & Operations Management (Prosim W/350 Package) 7th ed. Richard B. Chase et al. (C). 1996. pap., text 85.75 incl. disk (*0-256-21563-4*, Irwn McGrw-H) McGrw-H Hghr Educ.

Production & Operations Management Study Guide. 7th ed. Richard B. Chase et al. 254p. (C). 1995. text, student ed. 30.00 (*0-256-18752-5*, Irwn McGrw-H) McGrw-H Hghr Educ.

***Production & Operations Management 2000-2001: Production & Operations Management 00/01.** P. K. Shukla. (Annual Editions Ser.). 240p. (C). 1999. pap. 16.56 (*0-07-233373-1*) McGrw-H Hghr Educ.

***Production & Packaging of Non-Carbonated Fruit Juices & Fruit Beverages.** 2nd ed. Philip R. Ashurst. 429p. 1998. 165.00 (*0-8342-1289-7*) Aspen Pub.

Production & Productivity in the Service Industries. Ed. by Victor R. Fuchs. (Studies in Income & Wealth: No. 34). 404p. 1969. 105.90 (*0-87014-489-8*) Natl Bur Econ Res.

Production & Properties of Knitted & Woven Fabrics. M. S. Burnip & J. H. Thomas. 139p. 1969. 90.00 (*0-7855-7214-7*) St Mut.

Production & Properties of Knitted Fabrics. J. D. Turner. 159p. 1971. 75.00 (*0-7855-7213-9*) St Mut.

Production & Properties of Non-Woven Fabrics. A. Newton & J. E. Ford. 93p. 1973. 70.00 (*0-7855-7215-5*) St Mut.

Production & Properties of Staple-Fibre Yarns Made by Recently Developed Techniques. L. Hunter. 168p. 1978. 95.00 (*0-7855-7151-5*) St Mut.

Production & Properties of Warp-Knitted Fabrics. N. Gottlieb. 100p. 1975. 90.00 (*0-7855-7216-3*) St Mut.

Production & Properties of Weft-Knitted Fabrics. J. A. Smirfitt. 113p. 1973. 85.00 (*0-7855-7217-1*) St Mut.

Production & Properties of Wool & Other Animal Fibres. M. L. Ryder. 63p. 1975. 85.00 (*0-7855-7218-X*) St Mut.

Production & Separation of U-233: Collected Papers. AEC Technical Information Center Staff. Ed. by Leonard I. Katzin. (National Nuclear Energy Ser.: Div. IV, Vol. 17b). 323p. 1952. pap. 44.50 (*0-87079-383-7*, TID-5223); fiche 9.00 (*0-87079-341-1*, TID-5223) DOE.

Production & Separation of U-233: Survey. AEC Technical Information Center Staff. Ed. by Leonard I. Katzin & Glenn Theodore Seaborg. (National Nuclear Energy Ser.: Div. IV, Vol. 17A). 236p. 1951. pap. 36.50 (*0-87079-384-5*, TID-5222); mic. film 9.00 (*0-87079-342-X*, TID-5222) DOE.

***Production & Testing of the Revised Vitamin- B6 Fine-Group & the Bugle-93 Broad-Group Neutron/Photon Cross-Section Libraries: Derived from End F/B-VI. 3 Nuclear Data.** J. E. White. 183p. 2000. per. 18.00 (*0-16-059224-0*) USGPO.

Production & Use of Carbon-Based Materials for Environmental Cleanup: Microscopic Studies of Coal & Carbon: The Chemistry of Carbon in Coal Fly Ash Formation, Control & Utilization; Modified Asphalts; General Papers; Preprints of Papers Presented at the 216th ACS National Meeting, August 22-27, 1998, Boston, MA. American Chemical Society, Division of Fuel Chemistry Staff. LC 71-17970. (American Chemical Society, Division of Fuel Chemistry, Preprints of Papers: Vol. 43, No. 4). 398p. 1998. reprint ed. pap. 123.40 (*0-608-10663-1*, 207126800009) Bks Demand.

Production & Use of Double Skinned Hardboard Panels for Furniture. 1974. 39.00 (*0-7855-1091-5*) St Mut.

Production & Use of Interferon for the Treatment & Prevention of Human Virus Infections. Ed. by Charity Waymouth. (In Vitro Monographs: No. 3). 74p. 1974. 15.00 (*0-317-36064-7*) Soc In Vitro Biol.

Production & Use of Microalgae. Ed. by W. E. Becker. (Ergebnisse der Limnologie Ser.: Heft 20). (GER., Illus.). vi, 198p. 1985. pap. 57.00 (*3-510-47018-4*, Pub. by E Schweizerbartsche) Balogh.

Production & Utilisation of Protein in Oilseed Crops. Ed. by E. S. Bunting. 390p. 1981. text 195.50 (*90-247-2532-1*) Kluwer Academic.

Production & Utilization of Polyaluminum Sulfate. (Illus.). 92p. 1994. pap. 52.00 (*0-89867-740-8*, 90586) Am Water Wks Assn.

Production & Utilization of Radiation Vaccines Against Helminthic Diseases. (Technical Reports: No. 30). (Illus.). 84p. 1964. pap. 16.00 (*92-0-115164-0*, IDC30, Pub. by IAEA) Bernan Associates.

Production Automation & Numerical Control. William C. Leone. LC 67-21679. (Illus.). 245p. reprint ed. pap. 76.00 (*0-608-11695-5*, 201241900081) Bks Demand.

Production Checklist for Builders & Superintendents. John J. Haasl & Peter Kuchinsky, II. LC 90-4909. 72p. 1990. pap. 30.00 (*0-86718-351-9*) Home Builder.

Production Checklist for Builders & Superintendents. 2nd rev. ed. John J. Haasl & Peter Kuchinsky, II. LC 96-48692. 108p. 1997. pap. 30.00 (*0-86718-425-6*) Home Builder.

Production Conditions in Indian Agriculture: A Study Based on Farm Management Surveys. Krishna Bharadwaj. LC 78-176251. (University of Cambridge, Dept of Applied Economics, Occasional Papers: 33). 138p. reprint ed. pap. 39.40 (*0-608-12291-2*, 2024413) Bks Demand.

Production, Consumption & Trade of Wood Products in India. A. S. Gularia. 1989. 165.00 (*0-7855-6546-9*, Pub. by Intl Bk Distr) St Mut.

Production Control: A Structural & Design Oriented Approach. J. W. Bertrand et al. (Manufacturing Research & Technology Ser.: No. 11). 622p. 1990. 177.25 (*0-444-88122-0*) Elsevier.

Production Control in Construction: Different Approaches to Control, Use of Information & Automated Data Processing. B. Melles. 334p. 1997. pap. 57.50 (*90-6275-937-8*, Pub. by Delft U Pr) Coronet Bks.

Production Control in the Process Industry: Proceedings of the IFAC Workshop, Osaka, 29-31 October 1989 & Kariya, Japan, 1-2 November 1989. E. Oshima & C. F. Van Rijn. (IFAC Workshop Ser.: No. 9008). 258p. 1991. 142.00 (*0-08-036929-4*, Pergamon Pr) Elsevier.

Production Costs Here & Abroad: A Comparative Study of the Experience of American Manufacturers. Theodore R. Gates & Fabian Linden. Ed. by Stuart Bruchey & Eleanor Bruchey. LC 76-5012. (American Business Abroad Ser.). (Illus.). 1976. 19.95 (*0-405-09280-6*) Ayer.

***Production Design & Art Direction.** Peter Ettedgui. (Screencraft Ser.). (Illus.). 208p. 2000. pap. 39.95 (*0-240-80400-7*, Focal) Buttrwrth-Heinemann.

Production Design in the Contemporary American Film: A Critical Study of 23 Movies & Their Designers. Beverly Heisner. LC 96-45719. (Illus.). 181p. 1997. lib. bdg. 31.50 (*0-7864-0267-9*) McFarland & Co.

***Production Diseases in Farm Animals.** T. Wensing. 390p. 1999. pap. 83.00 (*90-74134-60-2*) Wageningen Pers.

Production, Distribution, & Growth in Transitional Economies. M. Katherine Perkins. LC 87-29292. 172p. 1988. 57.95 (*0-275-92104-2*, C2104, Praeger Pubs) Greenwood.

Production, Distribution, & Readership of a Conservative Journal of the Early French Revolution: The Ami du Roy of the Abbe Royou. Harvey Chisick. LC 91-57945. (Memoirs Ser.: Vol. 198). 233p. (C). 1992. pap. 20.00 (*0-87169-198-1*, M198-CHH) Am Philos.

***Production du Corps.** M. Godelier & M. Panoff. (Ordres Sociaux Ser). (FRE.). 400p. 1998. pap. text 50.00 (*90-5709-002-3*, edit archives) Gordon & Breach.

Production Ecology of Wetlands: The IBP Synthesis. Ed. by D. F. Westlake et al. LC 98-15359. (Illus.). xix, 568 p. (C). 1999. 130.00 (*0-521-22822-0*) Cambridge U Pr.

P

Production Economics: Mathematical Development & Applications. John F. Yanagida & Chauncey T. Ching. (Illus.). 330p. 1984. 49.95 (*0-88738-016-6*) Transaction Pubs.

Production Economics: Theory with Applications. 2nd ed. John P. Doll & Frank Orazem. LC 92-18812. 480p. (C). 1992. reprint ed. lib. bdg. 56.50 (*0-89464-769-5*) Krieger.

Production Efficiency in Domesday England, 1086. John McDonald. LC 97-12877. (Explorations in Economic History Ser.). 256p. (C). 1998. 85.00 (*0-415-16187-8*) Routledge.

Production, Employment & Wages in the Coffee Processing Sector of Brazil. Intl Labour Office Staff & Gustavo Maia Gomes. LC 91-187629. viii, 26 p. 1989. write for info. (*92-2-107202-9*) Intl Labour Office.

Production Engineering. Benjamin W. Neibel & Maurice S. Gjesdahl. (Illus.). 148p. 1971. text 14.75 (*92-833-1003-9*, 310039); pap. text 11.00 (*92-833-1004-7*, 310047) Productivity Inc.

Production Engineering, Estimating & Costing. M. Adithan & B. S. Pabla. 216p. 1990. text 25.00 (*81-220-0143-2*, Pub. by Konark Pubs Pvt Ltd) Advent Bks Div.

Production Essentials. Adobe Systems Inc. Staff et al. (Orig.). 1994. pap. text 39.95 (*0-685-75281-X*, Adobe) Hayden.

Production Factors in Cost Accounting & Works Management. Alexander H. Church. LC 75-18461. (History of Accounting Ser.). (Illus.). 1979. reprint ed. 18.95 (*0-405-07545-6*) Ayer.

Production Flow Analysis for Planning Group Technology. John L. Burbidge. (Oxford Series on Advanced Manufacturing: No. 8). (Illus.). 304p. 1989. 69.95 (*0-19-859183-7*) OUP.

Production Flow Analysis for Planning Group Technology. John L. Burbidge. (Oxford Series on Advanced Manufacturing: No. 8). (Illus.). 188p. 1997. reprint ed. pap. text 44.95 (*0-19-856459-7*) OUP.

Production Fly Tying: A Collection of Ideas, Notions, Hints & Variations on the Techniques of Fly Tying. A. K. Best. LC 89-37103. (Illus.). 177p. 1989. pap. 29.95 (*0-87108-792-8*) Pruett.

Production for Graphic Designers. 2nd ed. Alan Pipes. LC 97-19717. (Illus.). 224p. 1998. 45.00 (*0-87951-815-4*, Pub. by Overlook Pr) Penguin Putnam.

Production for Graphic Designers. 2nd ed. Alan Pipes. 240p. (C). 1997. pap. text 53.33 (*0-13-642380-9*) P-H.

Production for the Graphic Designer. James Craig. (Illus.). 208p. 1990. 29.95 (*0-8230-4416-5*) Watsn-Guptill.

Production from Fractured Shales. Society of Petroleum Engineers Staff. LC 97-163284. (Reprint Ser.). 269 p. 1996. write for info. (*1-55563-071-5*) Soc Petrol Engineers.

Production Frontiers. Rolf Fare et al. LC 92-34098. (Illus.). 312p. (C). 1994. text 54.95 (*0-521-42033-4*) Cambridge U Pr.

Production Function, Demand Function & Location Theory of the Firm. Noboru Sakashita. (Discussion Papers: No. 15). 1967. pap. 7.50 (*1-55869-100-6*) Regional Sci Res Inst.

Production Gas Carburizing. G. Parrish & G. S. Harper. (Materials Engineering Practice Ser.). (Illus.). 250p. 1985. 142.00 (*0-08-027312-2*, Pub. by Pergamon Repr) Franklin.

Production in Format Radio Handbook. Michael C. Keith. 218p. (Orig.). 1984. pap. text 22.00 (*0-8191-3887-8*) U Pr of Amer.

***Production-Integrated Environmental Protection & Waste Management in the Chemical Industry.** Ed. by Claus Christ. 212p. 1999. 135.00 (*3-527-28854-6*) Wiley.

***Production Line: Reproduction & Growing Up.** Sarah Angliss. (Human Machine Ser.). (Illus.). 32p. (J). 1999. lib. bdg. 15.95 (*1-929298-20-X*, Pub. by Thameside Pr) Smart Apple.

Production Line to Frontline. O'Leary. 1998. 19.95 (*1-85532-703-1*, 847845Q, Pub. by Ospry) Stackpole.

Production Logging. (SPE Reprint Ser.). 376p. 1985. reprint ed. pap. 13.00 (*0-89520-328-6*, COMPLRPT019) Soc Petrol Engineers.

Production Makers Source, Vol. 1. Peter Glenn Staff. 1998. 44.95 (*0-87314-275-6*) Peter Glenn.

Production Management: Concepts & Analysis for Operation & Control. Irving Abramowitz. LC 66-16835. (Illus.). 372p. reprint ed. pap. 115.40 (*0-608-11523-1*, 201244000081) Bks Demand.

Production Management Control Forms. (Illus.). 52p. 1990. 35.95 (*0-318-14966-4*, NP202) NAPL.

Production Management for Film & Video. 2nd ed. Richard Gates. 192p. 1995. pap. 34.95 (*0-240-51415-7*, Focal) Buttrwrth-Heinemann.

***Production Management for Film & Video.** 3rd ed. Richard Gates. LC 99-462555. (Illus.). 167p. 1999. pap. 35.95 (*0-240-51553-6*, Focal) Buttrwrth-Heinemann.

Production Management for Small & Medium Scale Furniture Manufacturing Firms in Developing Countries. 121p. 1990. 20.00 (*92-1-106246-2*, 90.III.E.8) UN.

Production Management Methods: Proceedings of the IFIP WG5.7 Working Conference on Evaluation of Production Management Methods, Gramado, Brazil, 21-24 March 1994, B-19. Working Conference on Evaluation of Production Man. Ed. by Claudio Walter et al. LC 94-28392. (IFIP Transactions B: Applications in Technology Ser.). 382p. 1994. 139.50 (*0-444-81910-X*, North Holland) Elsevier.

Production Management Systems: An Integrated Perspective. 2nd ed. Browne et al. LC 95-26032. 425p. (C). 1996. 72.95 (*0-201-42297-2*) Addison-Wesley.

Production Mangement for Small & Medium-Scale Furniture Manufacturers: A Manual for Developing Countries. 119p. pap. 10.00 (*92-1-106258-6*) UN.

Production, Marketing & Consumpton of Alcoholic Beverages since the Late Middle Ages: Proceedings of the Tenth International Economic History Congress, Leuven, Belgium, August 1990. Ed. by E. Aerts et al. (Studies in Social & Economic History: No. 18). 148p. (Orig.). 1990. pap. 32.50 (*90-6186-390-2*, Pub. by Leuven Univ) Coronet Bks.

Production Methods & Workability of Concrete. Ed. by Bartos. LC 96-209718. (Illus.). 560p. (C). 1996. 150.00 (*0-419-22070-4*, E & FN Spon) Routledge.

Production Notebooks: Theatre in Process, Vol. 1. Ed. & Intro. by Mark Bly. LC 95-45987. (Illus.). 280p. (Orig.). 1995. pap. 16.95 (*1-55936-110-7*) Theatre Comm.

***Production Notebooks Vol. 2: Theatre in Process.** Mark Bly. Vol. 2. (Illus.). 268p. 2001. pap. 17.95 (*1-55936-189-1*) Theatre Comm.

***Production Occupations.** Government Printing Office Staff. 34p. 1998. pap. 3.25 (*0-16-049369-2*) USGPO.

Production of Amorphous Silicon Spectrally Selective Surfaces for Copper Based Solar Thermal Energy Convertors. 98p. 1983. write for info. (*0-318-60082-X*, 331A) Intl Copper.

Production of Aquatic Animals: Crustaceans, Molluscs, Amphibians & Reptiles. Ed. by C. E. Nash. (World Animal Science Ser.: Vol. C4). 244p. 1991. 203.25 (*0-444-88312-6*) Elsevier.

Production of Aquatic Animals: Fishes. Ed. by C. E. Nash & A. J. Novotny. (World Animal Science Ser.: Vol. C8). 422p. 1995. 259.25 (*0-444-81950-9*) Elsevier.

Production of Basic Diagnostic Laboratory Reagents. M. El-Nageh & C. Heuck. LC 96-168047. (WHO Regional Publications, Eastern Mediterranean Series: No. 11). 1995. pap. text 15.00 (*92-9021-189-X*) World Health.

Production of Black Cinema. Watkins. LC 97-43151. 316p. 1999. pap. text 17.00 (*0-226-87489-3*) U Ch Pr.

Production of Black Cinema. S. Craig Watkins. LC 97-43151. (Illus.). 352p. 1998. 30.00 (*0-226-87488-5*) U Ch Pr.

Production of Culture. Ed. by Richard A. Peterson. LC 76-41102. (Sage Contemporary Social Science Issues Ser.: No. 33). 144p. 1976. reprint ed. pap. 44.70 (*0-608-01460-5*, 205950400001) Bks Demand.

Production of Culture: Media & the Urban Arts, No. 1. Diana Crane. (Foundations of Popular Culture Ser.: Vol. 1). 220p. (C). 1992. text 42.00 (*0-8039-3693-1*) Sage.

Production of Culture, Cultures of Production. Ed. by Paul Du Gay. LC 97-65516. (Culture, Media & Identities Ser.). 368p. 1997. 75.00 (*0-7619-5435-X*); pap. 24.95 (*0-7619-5436-8*) Sage.

Production of Economic Fruits in South-East Asia. Othman Yaacob & Suranant Subhadrabandhu. (Illus.). 444p. 1995. pap. 65.00 (*967-65-3046-8*) OUP.

Production of English Renaissance Culture. Ed. by David L. Miller et al. (Illus.). 336p. 1994. text 42.50 (*0-8014-2961-7*); pap. text 16.95 (*0-8014-8201-1*) Cornell U Pr.

Production of Fine Wool in Northern China: Effect of Nutrition & Helminth Infections. N. Anderson et al. 80p. 1995. pap. 114.00 (*1-86320-143-2*, Pub. by ACIAR) St Mut.

Production of Florist Azaleas. Roy A. Larson. Ed. by Allan M. Armitage. LC 92-41795. (Growers Handbook Ser.: Vol. 6). (Illus.). 160p. 1993. pap. 17.95 (*0-88192-230-7*) Timber.

Production of Houses. Christopher Alexander & Howard Davis. LC 82-14097. (Center for Environmental Structure Ser.: Vol. 4). (Illus.). 383p. (C). 1985. 45.00 (*0-19-503223-3*) OUP.

Production of Human Capital: A Study of Minority Achievement. Donald R. Winkler. Ed. by Stuart Bruchey. LC 76-45125. (Nineteen Seventy-Seven Dissertations Ser.). (Illus.). 1977. lib. bdg. 34.95 (*0-405-09936-3*) Ayer.

Production of Industrial Materials in World Wars I & II. Geoffrey H. Moore. (Occasional Papers: No. 18). 84p. 1944. reprint ed. 21.90 (*0-87014-333-6*) Natl Bur Econ Res.

Production of Inequality: Gender & Exchange among Kewa. L. Josephides. 288p. (Orig.). 1985. 35.00 (*0-422-79720-0*, 9608, Pub. by Tavistock) Routldge.

Production of Iron, Steel & High Quality Product Mix: Latest Technological Innovations & Processes. Ed. by B. R. Nijhawan. LC 92-82923. (Conference Proceedings Ser.). (Illus.). 325p. 1992. reprint ed. pap. 100.80 (*0-608-02636-0*, 206329400004) Bks Demand.

Production of Isotopes: A Portion of the Proceedings of the All-Union Scientific & Technical Conference on Applications of Radioactive Isotopes. Consultants Bureau Staff. LC 59-14487. 139p. reprint ed. pap. 43.10 (*0-608-10233-4*, 202065500018) Bks Demand.

Production of Juvenile Atlantic Salmon, Salmo Salar, in Natural Waters. Ed. by R. J. Gibson & R. E. Cutting. 262p. 1993. 56.50 (*0-660-14954-0*) NRC Res Pr.

Production of Landscape Plants. rev. ed. Carl E. Whitcomb. (Illus.). 487p. 1989. 35.00 (*0-9613109-3-6*) Lacebark.

Production of Man-Made Fibres. A. J. Hughes et al. 177p. 1976. 70.00 (*0-7855-7219-8*) St Mut.

Production of Micro-Forms, Vol. 5, Part 1. Reginald Hawkins. Ed. & Pref. by Ralph Shaw. LC 75-17838. (State of the Library Art Ser.: Vol. 5, Pt . 1). 208p. 1975. reprint ed. lib. bdg. 59.50 (*0-8371-8235-2*, HAPM, Greenwood Pr) Greenwood.

Production of N-Mesons in Proton-Neutron Collisions. Stina Haggstrom. (Uppsala Dissertations from the Faculty of Science Ser.: Vol. 13). (Illus.). 128p. 1997. pap. 42.50 (*91-554-3955-1*, Pub. by Almqvist Wiksell) Coronet Bks.

Production of New Potato Varieties: Technological Advances. D. E. Richardson. Ed. by G. J. Jellis. 384p. 1987. text 90.00 (*0-521-32458-0*) Cambridge U Pr.

Production of Nucleotides & Nucleosides by Fermentation, Vol.1. Sadao Teshiba & Akira Furuya. (Japanese Technology Reviews Ser.). viii, 104p. 1989. text 96.00 (*2-88124-287-1*) Gordon & Breach.

Production of Pathogen Tested Sweet Potato. P. Beetham & A. Mason. 1992. pap. 69.00 (*1-86320-063-0*, Pub. by ACIAR) St Mut.

Production of Personal Life: Class, Gender & the Psychological in Hawthorne's Fiction. Joel Pfister. LC 91-16686. 288p. 1991. pap. 15.95 (*0-8047-1948-9*) Stanford U Pr.

Production of Pipeline Gas by Hydrogasification of Coal, 1954-1964. E. J. Pyrcioch et al. (Research Bulletin Ser.: No. 39). iv, 225p. 1972. pap. 50.00 (*1-58222-039-5*) Inst Gas Tech.

Production of Pipeline Gas by Hydrogasification of Oil Shale. E. B. Schultz et al. Ed. by W. G. Blair. (Research Bulletin Ser.: No. 36). iv, 109p. 1966. pap. 25.00 (*1-58222-040-9*) Inst Gas Tech.

Production of Pipeline Gas from Crude Oil Feedstocks. Institute of Gas Technology Staff. 63p. pap. 5.00 (*0-318-12686-9*, F40100) Am Gas Assn.

Production of Pot Roses. H. Brent Pemberton et al. LC 96-27599. (Growers Handbook Ser.). 130p. 1997. 17.95 (*0-88192-379-6*) Timber.

Production of Quality Woollen Yarn. Ed. by Wira Staff. 1984. 40.00 (*0-7855-1000-1*) St Mut.

Production of Radionuclides at Intermediate Energies, Subvol. D, Interactions of Protons with Nuclei see Crystal & Solid State Physics: Group III

Production of Radionuclides at Intermediate Energies, Subvol. E, Interaction of Pions & Antiprotons with Nuclei see Nuclear Particles & Physics: Group I

Production of Radionuclides at Intermediate Energies Vol. G: Interaction of a-Particles with Targets He to Rb. Ed. by H. Schopper & W. Martienssen. (Landolt-Bornstein - Numerical Data & Functional Relationships in Science & Technology Series, Group I: Vol. 13). vi, 407p. 1996. 1647.00 (*3-540-60324-7*) Spr-Verlag.

Production of Radionuclides at Intermediate Energies Vol. H: Interactions of a-Particles with Targets from Sr to Cf. Ed. by H. Schopper & W. Martienssen. (Landolt-Bornstein - Numerical Data & Functional Relationships in Science & Technology Series, Group I: Vol. 13). vii, 407p. 1996. 1647.00 (*3-540-61045-6*) Spr-Verlag.

Production of Reality: Essays & Readings on Social Interaction. 2nd ed. Jodi O'Brien & Peter Kollock. LC 96-15615. 608p. (C). 1996. pap. 37.95 (*0-7619-8500-X*) Pine Forge.

Production of Society: A Marxian Foundation for Social Theory. Michael E. Brown. 176p. (C). 1986. 58.00 (*0-8476-7472-X*) Rowman.

Production of Space. Henri Lefebvre. Tr. by Donald Nicholson-Smith. 500p. 1991. pap. text 31.95 (*0-631-18177-6*) Blackwell Pubs.

Production of Specific United States Gemstones. Gordon Austin. 45p. 1995. pap. 6.50 (*0-16-061630-1*) USGPO.

Production of Speech. Ed. by P. F. MacNeilage. (Illus.). 302p. 1983. 107.00 (*0-387-90735-1*) Spr-Verlag.

Production of Spoken Discourse: A Computational Model. Ed. by George Houghton. LC 96-38041. (Advances in Discourse Processes Ser.: Vol. 62). 1997. pap. 39.50 (*1-56750-151-6*); text 73.25 (*1-56750-150-8*) Ablx Pub.

Production of Sugarcane: Theory & Practice. Gururaj Hunsigi. LC 93-14008. (Advanced Series in Agricultural Sciences: 21). (Illus.). 254p. 1993. 186.95 (*0-387-56552-3*) Spr-Verlag.

Production of Synthetic-Polymer Fibres. E. M. Hicks, Jr. et al. 127p. 1971. 70.00 (*0-7855-7220-1*) St Mut.

Production of Textile Yarns by the False-Twist Technique. D. K. Wilson. 66p. 1978. 70.00 (*0-7855-7221-X*) St Mut.

Production of Textured Yarns by Methods Other That the False-Twist Technique. D. K. Wilson. 55p. 1977. 70.00 (*0-7855-7222-8*) St Mut.

Production of Woven Fabrics. D. C. Snowden. 94p. 1972. 110.00 (*0-7855-7224-4*) St Mut.

Production Operation Management. Mabert. 1997. write for info. (*0-02-373032-3*) P-H.

***Production Operation Management.** 9th ed. Chase. 2000. pap. text 23.50 (*0-07-239279-7*) McGraw.

Production Operation Management CTB IBM. Mabert. 1997. write for info. (*0-02-373035-8*) P-H.

Production Operation Management TB. Mabert. 1997. write for info. (*0-02-373034-X*) P-H.

Production Operations, 2 vols., Set. Thomas O. Allen & Alan P. Roberts. 720p. 1993. 120.00 (*0-930972-18-X*) Oil & Gas.

Production Operations, Vol. 1. 4th ed. Thomas O. Allen & Alan P. Roberts. 374p. 1993. 64.00 (*0-930972-19-8*) Oil & Gas.

Production Operations, Vol. 2. 4th ed. Thomas O. Allen & Alan P. Roberts. 346p. 1993. 64.00 (*0-930972-20-1*) Oil & Gas.

Production Operations Analysis. 4th ed. Nahmias. 2000. 70.74 (*0-07-231265-3*) McGraw.

Production-Operations Management. T. Hill. 384p. (C). 1989. 210.00 (*0-7855-4642-1*, Pub. by Inst Pur & Supply) St Mut.

Production-Operations Management. Jack Rudman. (ACT Proficiency Examination Program Ser.: PEP-24). 1994. pap. 23.95 (*0-8373-5524-9*, PEP-24) Nat Learn.

Production-Operations Management. 5th ed. William J. Stevenson. (Irwin Series in Production Operations Management). 896p. (C). 1995. text 73.75 (*0-256-13900-8*, Irwn McGrw-H) McGrw-H Hghr Educ.

Production Operations Management. 6th ed. William J. Stevenson. LC 98-24796. 1998. write for info. (*0-07-366112-0*) McGraw.

Production Operations Management: An Applied Analytical Approach & Wall Street Journal Interactive Guide. Martinich. 1008p. 1997. text 71.00 (*0-471-28215-4*) Wiley.

Production-Operations Management: From Inside Out. 5th ed. Roger W. Schmenner. 825p. (C). 1992. text 78.67 (*0-02-406871-3*, Macmillan Coll) P-H.

Production-Operations Management Curricula: Thoughts from Practitioners & Professors. Nancy M. Levenburg. (E & R Foundation Research Papers). 38p. (Orig.). 1996. pap. 25.00 (*1-55822-156-5*) Am Prod & Inventory.

Production Optimization Using Nodal Analysis. H. Dale Beggs. 411p. 1991. 64.00 (*0-930972-14-7*, P7479) Oil & Gas.

Production Order Specifications - EDI (PROSE) Ed. by Alan Kotok. 58p. 1992. 125.06 (*0-933505-26-4*) Graph Comm Assn.

***Production Places & Environment.** Ray Hudson. 432p. 1999. pap. 32.95 (*0-582-36940-1*) Longman.

Production Planning & Control. William Bolton. (Illus.). 192p. (Orig.). 1994. pap. 39.50 (*0-582-22820-4*, Pub. by Addison-Wesley) Trans-Atl Phila.

Production Planning & Control: An Introduction to Quantitative Methods. J. R. King. 1975. 182.00 (*0-08-017721-2*, Pub. by Pergamon Repr) Franklin.

Production Planning & Control Procedures for Cellular Manufacturing Systems Concepts & Practices. Urban Wemmerlov. 120p. 1988. 25.00 (*1-55822-004-6*) Am Prod & Inventory.

Production Planning & Controlling: A Problem-Based Approach. Gordon Minty. LC 97-39024. (Illus.). 370p. (YA). (gr. 9-12). 1999. pap. text 37.28 (*1-56637-449-9*) Goodheart.

Production Planning & Inventory Control. 2nd ed. Seetharama L. Narasimhan et al. LC 94-22418. 752p. (C). 1994. text 74.20 (*0-13-186214-6*) P-H.

Production Planning & Scheduling for Long Line Prestress Products. 64p. 1977. 18.00 (*0-318-16191-5*, JR184) P-PCI.

Production Planning & Scheduling in Flexible Assembly Systems. Tadeusz Sawik. LC 98-49870. 207p. 1999. 69.95 (*3-540-64998-0*) Spr-Verlag.

Production Planning in Automated Manufacturing. Yves Crama et al. LC 94-11600. (Lecture Notes in Economics & Mathematical Systems Ser.: Vol. 414). 1994. 49.95 (*0-387-58082-4*) Spr-Verlag.

Production Planning in Automated Manufacturing. 2nd ed. Yves Crama et al. LC 96-28430. 239p. 1996. 84.95 (*3-540-61359-5*) Spr-Verlag.

Producion, Pollution, Protection. Ed. by J. S. Weiner et al. (Wykeham Science Ser.: No. 19). 368p. 1972. pap. 18.00 (*0-85109-250-0*) Taylor & Francis.

Production, Pollution, Protection. W. B. Yapp & M. I. Smith. (Wykeham Science Ser.: No. 19). 196p. (C). 1972. 18.00 (*0-8448-1121-1*, Crane Russak) Taylor & Francis.

Production, Power, & World Order: Social Forces in the Making of History. Robert W. Cox. Ed. by John G. Ruggie. (Political Economy of International Change Ser.). 301p. 1989. pap. text 23.00 (*0-231-05809-8*) Col U Pr.

Production Problems in the Men's Clothing Manufacturing Industry. 16p. 1953. 10.00 (*0-318-19654-9*) Clothing Mfrs.

Production Process & Technical Change. Mario Morroni. (Illus.). 234p. (C). 1992. text 54.95 (*0-521-41001-0*) Cambridge U Pr.

Production Processes: The Productivity Handbook. 5th ed. Roger W. Bolz. LC 81-6494. 1089p. 1981. 60.00 (*0-8311-1088-0*) Indus Pr.

Production Register: The John Deere Model "G" Tractor. Ed. by Jack D. Cherry. 190p. (Orig.). 1997. pap. 16.95 (*1-887446-03-6*) Two-Cylinder.

Production, Release & Paracrine Action of Acetylcholine in the Anterior Pituitary of the Rat. P. Carmeliet. No. 10. 123p. (Orig.). 1989. pap. 32.50 (*90-6186-316-3*, Pub. by Leuven Univ) Coronet Bks.

Production Research. Kathy Chater. LC 97-151437. 160p. 1998. pap. 29.95 (*0-240-51466-1*, Focal) Buttrwrth-Heinemann.

Production Rig Equipment. (Well Servicing & Workover Ser.: Lesson 6). (Illus.). 39p. (Orig.). 1971. pap. text 12.00 (*0-88698-062-3*, 3.70610) PETEX.

Production Safety in Film & Video. Robin Small. LC 00-35461. (Illus.). 367p. 2000. pap. 37.95 (*0-240-51531-5*, Focal) Buttrwrth-Heinemann.

Production Sharing: A Conference with Peter Drucker. Ed. by Richard L. Bolin. LC 77-649702. 156p. (C). 1988. reprint ed. pap. text 40.00 (*0-945951-00-0*) Flagstaff Inst.

Production Sharing: Use of United States Components & Materials in Foreign Assembly Operations. 1996. lib. bdg. 255.99 (*0-8490-5959-3*) Gordon Pr.

Production, Stability & Dynamic Symmetry: The Selected Essays of Ryuzo Sato, vol. 2. 20th ed. Ryuzo Sato. LC 98-55934. (Economists of the Twentieth Century Ser.). 320p. 1999. 95.00 (*1-85898-969-8*) E Elgar.

Production Structure & International Trade. M. Tawada. (Lecture Notes in Economics & Mathematical Systems Ser.: Vol. 327). (Illus.). xiv, 206p. 1980. pap. 25.70 (*0-318-41904-1*) Spr-Verlag.

Production System: An Efficient Integration of Resources. Ed. by R. Hollier & J. M. Moore. 768p. 1977. 110.00 (*0-85066-103-X*) Taylor & Francis.

Production System Models of Learning & Development. Ed. by David Klahr et al. (Computational Models of Cognition & Perception Ser.). (Illus.). 478p. 1987. 60.00 (*0-262-11114-4*, Bradford Bks) MIT Pr.

An Asterisk (*) at the beginning of an entry indicates that the title is appearing for the first time.

Production System Version of the Hearsay-II Speech Understanding System. Donald L. McCracken. Ed. by Harold Stone. LC 81-7459. (Computer Science: Artificial Intelligence Ser.: No. 2). 151p. 1981. reprint ed. pap. 46.90 (*0-8357-1197-8*, 207004400063) Bks Demand.

Production Systems & Hierarchies of Centres. J. Gunnarsson. (Studies in Applied Regional Science). 1977. pap. text 72.50 (*90-207-0688-8*) Kluwer Academic.

Production Systems for Architects & Designers. Fred A. Stitt. (Illus.). 304p. 1994. text 79.95 (*0-442-00920-8*, VNR) Wiley.

Production Systems for Architects & Designers: A Handbook. Fred A. Stitt. 349p. 1993. 99.00 (*0-471-28452-1*, VNR) Wiley.

Production Systems Technology. Henry R. Harms & Dennis K. Kroon. (Illus.). (gr. 6-12). 1999. student ed., wbk. ed. 7.30 (*0-02-667593-5*) Glencoe.

Production Systems Technology. William Shakespeare & Henry R. Harms. Ed. by Stephen Ogrel. 1991. 40.50 (*0-02-667591-9*) Glencoe.

Production Systems Technology: Teacher's Annotated Edition. annot. ed. Henry R. Harms & Krooh. 1999. teacher ed. 45.05 (*0-02-667594-3*) Glencoe.

Production Technology. Stanley A. Komacek. (Tech & Industrial Education Ser.). 1992. 54.95 (*0-8273-4955-6*); text 36.95 (*0-8273-4837-1*) Delmar.

Production Technology Computerized Testmaker & Testbank for IBM & Compatible Computers. Stanley A. Komacek. 1992. 115.95 incl. disk (*0-8273-5379-0*) Delmar.

Production Technology of Vegetable Crops. K. G. Shanmugavelu. (C). 24.00 (*81-204-0414-9*, Pub. by Oxford IBH) S Asia.

Production Testing of a Chromium-Free Carburizing Grade Gear Steel. Dale H. Breen & T. Cameron. (Nineteen Eighty-Seven Fall Technical Meeting Ser.: Vol. 87FTM11). (Illus.). 12p. 1987. pap. text 30.00 (*1-55589-487-9*) AGMA.

Production Theory & Indivisible Commodities. Charles R. Frank. LC 68-29383. (Princeton Studies in Mathematical Economics: No. 3). (Illus.). 153p. reprint ed. pap. 47.50 (*0-7837-4328-9*, 204403200012) Bks Demand.

Production to near Net Shape: Source Book: A Collection of Outstanding Articles from the Technical Literature. American Society for Metals Staff. Ed. by C.J Van Tyne & B. Avitzur. LC 82-73611. (Illus.). 413p. reprint ed. pap. 128.10 (*0-608-18679-1*, 203307700083) Bks Demand.

Production to Order. N. P. Dellaert. (Lecture Notes in Economics & Mathematical Systems Ser.: Vol. 333). vii, 158p. 1989. 30.10 (*0-387-51309-4*) Spr-Verlag.

Production Trends in the United States since 1870. Arthur F. Burns. xxxii, 363p. 1964. reprint ed. 49.50 (*0-678-00024-7*) Kelley.

Production Trends in the United States since 1870. Arthur F. Burns. (General Ser.: No. 23). 396p. 1934. reprint ed. 103.00 (*0-87014-022-1*) Natl Bur Econ Res.

Production Typing Projects. D. Sue Rigby & Robert N. Hanson. 1980. text 10.12 (*0-07-052836-5*) McGraw.

Production Well Analysis: New Methods & a Computer Program in Well Hydraulics. Michael Kasenow. 350p. 1996. 85.00 (*0-918334-99-3*, PWELL) WRP.

Production Work Flow: Concepts & Techniques. Ed. by Prentice-Hall Staff. LC 99-33025. 479p. (C). 1999. pap. 61.00 (*0-13-021753-0*) P-H.

Production, Work, Territory. Allen J. Scott & Michael Storper. 352p. 1986. text 60.00 (*0-04-338126-X*); pap. text 21.95 (*0-04-338127-8*) Routledge.

***Production/Operations Management.** 6th ed. William Stevenson. 272p. (C). 1998. pap. 28.75 (*0-07-290664-2*) McGrw-H Hghr Educ.

***Production/Operations/Management.** 6th ed. William J. Stevenson. LC 98-24796. (Illus.). 1999. write for info. (*0-07-115856-1*, Irwn Prfssnl) McGraw-Hill Prof.

***Production/Operations/Management.** 6th ed. William J. Stevenson. LC 98-24796. (Illus.). 1999. write for info. (*0-07-366113-9*) McGrw-H Hghr Educ.

Productions & Operations Management. Carol Kanar. (C). 1993. pap., teacher ed. 7.96 (*0-395-69367-5*) HM.

Productions & Operations Management. Noori. 1995. text 75.25 (*0-07-912257-4*) McGraw.

Productions & Operations Management. 6th ed. Finch. (SWC-Business Statistics). 1994. pap., student ed. 15.50 (*0-534-51021-3*) Wadsworth Pub.

Productions & Operations Management: Total Quality & Responsiveness. Hamid Noori & Russell Radford. LC 94-33821. 1994. text 61.75 (*0-07-046923-7*) McGraw.

Productions of Time: Tradition History in the Old Testament Scholarship. Knud Jeppesen & Benedikt Otzen. (Almond Press Individual Titles Ser.). 169p. 1984. 52.50 (*0-907459-36-6*, Pub. by Sheffield Acad); pap. text 19.95 (*0-907459-37-4*, Pub. by Sheffield Acad) CUP Services.

Productions-Operations Management. 2nd ed. William J. Stevenson. (Irwin Series in Production Operations Management). 416p. (C). 1995. student ed., per. 35.50 (*0-256-20692-9*, Irwn McGrw-H) McGrw-H Hghr Educ.

Productions-Operations Management: University of South Florida. 3rd ed. William Stevenson. (C). 1991. text 19.50 (*0-256-10965-6*, Irwn McGrw-H) McGrw-H Hghr Educ.

Productive Agriculture & a Quality Environment. National Research Council Staff. LC S 0601.N28. 335p. reprint ed. pap. 103.90 (*0-608-13707-3*, 205529000013) Bks Demand.

Productive Bankers & Profitable Banks: The Grand Slam of Banking. Janet L. Myers. LC 91-61867. (Illus.). 176p. 1992. 49.95 (*1-880023-44-X*) Dearborn Busn Pr.

Productive Capacity of Locality As a Function of Soil & Climate with Particular Reference to Forest Land. M. S. Czarnowski. LC 64-16087. (Louisiana State University Studies, Biological Science Ser.: No. 5). 192p. reprint ed. pap. 59.60 (*0-608-14376-6*, 205187800013) Bks Demand.

Productive Christians in an Age of Guilt Manipulators: A Biblical Response to Ronald J. Sider. 3rd ed. David Chilton. LC 90-44055. 439p. 1990. reprint ed. 25.00 (*0-930464-38-9*); reprint ed. pap. 12.50 (*0-930464-04-4*) Inst Christian.

Productive Conflict Management: Perspectives for Organizations. Dean R. Tjosvold & David W. Johnson. 1989. write for info. (*0-939603-09-8*) Team Media.

***Productive Edge: A New Strategy for Economic Growth.** Richard K. Lester. 368p. 2000. pap. 16.95 (*0-393-32038-3*) Norton.

Productive Edge: How U. S. Industries Are Pointing the Way to a New Era of Economic Growth. Richard K. Lester. LC 97-35029. 350p. 1998. 29.95 (*0-393-04574-9*) Norton.

Productive Educational Change. Michael G. Fullan. (School Development & the Management of Change Ser.: No. 10). 224p. 1993. pap. 26.95 (*1-85000-826-4*, Falmer Pr) Taylor & Francis.

Productive Efficiency of Chinese Enterprises: An Empirical Study. Yanrui Wu. (Studies on the Chinese Economy). 220p. 1996. text 75.00 (*0-312-12832-0*) St Martin.

Productive Electrician. Michael Sammaritano. (Illus.). 200p. 1996. ring bd. 39.00 (*1-887720-23-5*) Contracting Pubns.

Productive Labour & Effective Demand, Including a Critique of Keynesian Economics. Sydney H. Coontz. LC 66-15567. (Illus.). ix, 174p. 1966. 35.00 (*0-678-06511-X*) Kelley.

Productive Living Series: Building a Meaningful Lifestyle. Walter Shepperd. LC 98-90379. 220p. 1999. pap. 30.00 (*0-9660256-1-X*) W Shepperd.

Productive Living Strategies for People with AIDS. Ed. by Jerry A. Johnson & Michael Pizzi. (Occupational Therapy in Health Care Ser.). 249p. 1991. 39.95 (*1-56024-024-5*) Haworth Pr.

Productive Living Strategies for People with AIDS. Ed. by Jerry A. Johnson & Michael Pizzi. (Occupational Therapy in Health Care Ser.). 249p. 1994. pap. text 19.95 (*0-918393-83-3*) Haworth Pr.

Productive Meetings: How to Structure & Conduct Committee or Group Meetings. 2nd rev. ed. Martin Management Books Staff. LC 97-74894. 90p. 1997. pap. 14.95 (*1-878500-08-2*) Martin Mgmt.

Productive Men & Reproductive Man: The Agrarian Household & the Emergence of Separate Spheres during the German Enlightenment. Marion W. Gray. LC 99-19028. (Illus.). 370p. 2000. 69.95 (*1-57181-171-0*) Berghahn Bks.

Productive Men & Reproductive Women: The Agrarian Household & the Emergence of Separate Spheres during the German Enlightenment. Marion W. Gray. LC 99-19028. (Illus.). 384p. 2000. pap. 24.00 (*1-57181-172-9*) Berghahn Bks.

Productive Objects: An Applied Software Project Management Framework. Robert J. Muller. LC 97-15396. 600p. 1997. pap. text 49.95 (*1-55860-437-5*) Morgan Kaufmann.

Productive Performance. Charles W. Lachenmeyer. (Analysis Ser.). 51p. (Orig.). 1980. pap. text 18.00 (*0-938526-01-4*) Inst Analysis.

Productive Performance Appraisals. Randi T. Sachs. LC 92-20830. 108p. 1992. pap. 10.95 (*0-8144-7796-8*) AMACOM.

Productive Personnel: California Employment, Training, & Management. Gregory J. Pozovich. 200p. 1994. pap. 14.95 (*0-9640592-0-7*) Pacific St Pubng.

Productive Roles in an Older Society. National Research Council Staff & Institute of Medicine Staff. (America's Aging Ser.). 168p. 1986. pap. text 19.95 (*0-309-03637-2*) Natl Acad Pr.

Productive Speech Communication for Business & the Professions. rev. ed. James N. Holm. (Illus.). 495p. (C). 1985. pap. text 27.95 (*0-89641-149-4*) American Pr.

Productive Supervisor: A Program of Practical Managerial Skills. Charles MacDonald & Richard Pierce. Incl. Career Counseling Skills. 1985. lab manual ed. 5.00 (*0-914234-36-6*); Career Counseling Skills. 1985. (*0-87425-006-4*); Coaching Skills. 1985. lab manual ed. 5.00 (*0-914234-34-X*); Coaching Skills. 1985. (*0-87425-004-8*); Controlling Skills. 1985. lab manual ed. 5.00 (*0-87425-001-3*); Delegating Skills. 1985. (*0-914234-93-5*); Delegating Skills. 1985. (*0-87425-013-7*); Feedback Skills. 1985. lab manual ed. 5.00 (*0-87425-003-X*); Group Communication Skills. 1985. (*0-914234-39-0*); Group Communication Skills. 1985. (*0-87425-009-9*); Managing by Standards Skills. 1985. (*0-914234-96-X*); Managing by Standards Skills. 1985. (*0-87425-016-1*); Motivative Skills. 1985. lab manual ed. 5.00 (*0-914234-37-4*); Motivative Skills. 1985. (*0-87425-007-2*); Performance Appraisal Skills. 1985. lab manual ed. 5.00 (*0-914234-35-8*); Performance Appraisal Skills. 1985. (*0-87425-005-6*); Person-to-Person Communication Skills. 1985. (*0-914234-38-2*); Person-to-Person Communication Skills. 1985. (*0-87425-008-0*); Planning Skills. 1985. lab manual ed. 5.00 (*0-914234-30-7*); Planning Skills. 1985. (*0-87425-000-5*); Priority Setting Skills. 1985. (*0-914234-92-7*); Priority Setting Skills. 1985. (*0-87425-012-9*); Problem-Solving Skills. 1985. lab manual ed. 5.00 (*0-914234-32-3*); Problem-Solving Skills. 1985. (*0-87425-002-1*); Public Relations Skills. 1985. (*0-914234-60-9*); Public Relations Skills. 1985. (*0-87425-011-0*); Self-Development Skills. 1985. (*0-914234-95-1*); Self-Development Skills. 1985. (*0-87425-015-3*); Time Management Skills. 1985. (*0-914234-94-3*); Time Management Skills. 1985. (*0-87425-014-5*); Written Communication Skills. 1985. (*0-87425-010-2*); 1985. write for info. (*0-318-59244-4*) HRD Press.

Productive Supervisor: A Program of Practical Managerial Skills. Charles Macdonald & Richard Pierce. 1985. pap. 85.00 (*0-685-73696-2*) HRD Press.

Productive Teaching in the Christian School. Carl D. Herbster. (Illus.). 91p. (Orig.). 1988. pap. 5.95 (*0-89084-463-1*, 042895) Bob Jones Univ.

Productive Tension of Hawthorne's Art. Claudia D. Johnson. LC 80-15634. 170p. 1981. pap. 52.70 (*0-7837-8386-8*, 205919600009) Bks Demand.

Productive Thinking. Annette Geistfeld & Joyce E. Juntune. 45p. (Orig.). 1983. pap. 5.00 (*0-912773-01-4*) One Hund Twenty Creat.

Productive Thinking. enl. ed. Max Wertheimer. LC 82-10913. (Phoenix Ser.). 318p. (C). 1996. pap. text 11.00 (*0-226-89376-6*) U Ch Pr.

Productive Thinking Activities. Faye Day & Annette Geistfeld. 56p. (Orig.). 1985. pap. 6.25 (*0-912773-11-1*) One Hund Twenty Creat.

Productive Use of Saline Land. Ed. by Neil Davidson & Richard P. Galloway. 124p. (Orig.). 1993. pap. 99.00 (*1-86320-078-9*) St Mut.

***Productive Water Points in Dryland Areas: Guidelines on Integrated Planning for Rural Water Supply.** Chris Lovell. 208p. 2000. pap. 22.00 (*1-85339-516-1*, Pub. by Intermed Tech) Stylus Pub VA.

Productive Workplaces: Organizing & Managing for Dignity, Meaning, & Community. Marvin R. Weisbord. LC 87-45425. (Management Ser.). 433p. 1991. reprint ed. pap. 30.00 (*1-55542-370-1*) Jossey-Bass.

Productivite Morphologique et Emprunt: Etude des Derives Deverbaux Savants en Francais Moderne. Wiecher Zwanenburg. Ed. by Jean C. Chevalier et al. (Lingvisticae Investigationes Supplementa Ser.: No. 10). (FRE.). x, 199p. 1983. 59.00 (*90-272-3120-6*) J Benjamins Pubng Co.

Productivity. Ed. by A. Dale Timpe. LC 88-21849. (Art & Science of Business Management Ser.: Vol. 7). 383p. 1989. reprint ed. pap. 118.80 (*0-608-02815-0*, 206388200007) Bks Demand.

Productivity. 2nd ed. (Open Learning Super Ser.). 1991. pap. text 26.00 (*0-08-041662-4*, Pergamon Pr) Elsevier.

Productivity: A Practical Program for Improving Efficiency. Clair F. Vough & Bernard Asbell. LC 79-12562. xii, 223p. 1986. reprint ed. 30.00 (*0-9616778-0-5*) Productivity Rsch.

Productivity: International Comparisons of Economic Growth, Vol. 2. Dale W. Jorgenson. LC 94-22733. Vol. 2. (Illus.). 442p. 1995. 55.00 (*0-262-10050-9*) MIT Pr.

Productivity: Postwar U. S. Economic Growth, 2 vols., Vol. 1. Dale W. Jorgenson. LC 94-22733. Vol. 1. 1995. 55.00 (*0-262-10049-5*) MIT Pr.

Productivity: Problems, Prospects, & Policies. Sar A. Levitan & Diane Werneke. LC 83-22184. (Policy Studies in Employment & Welfare: Vol. 40). 143p. 1984. reprint ed. pap. 44.40 (*0-608-03717-6*, 206454200009) Bks Demand.

Productivity: The Human Side: A Social Dynamics Approach. Robert R. Blake & Jane S. Mouton. LC 80-69695. 143p. reprint ed. pap. 44.40 (*0-608-30692-4*, 202261900028) Bks Demand.

Productivity: The Link to Social & Economic Progress. Ed. by Curtis Prendergast. LC 76-19833. (Swedish-American Exchange of Views Ser.). 55p. 1976. pap. text 3.50 (*0-89361-000-3*) Work in Amer.

Productivity: The New Economic Context. Kathleen Newland. LC 82-50699. (Worldwatch Papers). 1982. pap. 5.00 (*0-916468-48-8*) Worldwatch Inst.

Productivity - Improving Performance. Didactic Systems Staff. (Simulation Game Ser.). 1975. pap. 26.25 (*0-89401-081-6*) Didactic Syst.

Productivity Analysis: An Empirical Investigation. rev. ed. Doris Y. Wang. LC 95-47463. (Studies on Industrial Productivity). (Illus.). 152p. 1996. text 61.00 (*0-8153-2015-9*) Garland.

Productivity Analysis at the Organizational Level. Ed. by Nabil R. Adam & Ali Dogramaci. (Productivity Analysis Studies). 192p. 1981. lib. bdg. 71.50 (*0-89838-038-3*) Kluwer Academic.

Productivity & American Leadership: The Long View. Ed. by William J. Baumol et al. (Illus.). 408p. 1991. pap. text 21.50 (*0-262-52163-6*) MIT Pr.

Productivity & Creativity: Studies in General & Descriptive Linguistics in Honour of E. M. Uhlenbeck. Ed. by Mark Janse. (Trends in Linguistics Ser.). 268p. 1998. 168.00 (*3-11-016217-2*) De Gruyter.

Productivity & Economic Progress. Frederick C. Mills. (Occasional Papers: No. 38). 46p. 1952. reprint ed. 20.00 (*0-87014-353-0*) Natl Bur Econ Res.

Productivity & Employee Ownership: The Case of Sweden. Barbara W. Lee. (Studia Oeconomiae Upsaliensia: No. 16). 110p. (Orig.). 1989. pap. 36.00 (*91-554-2424-4*, Pub. by Umea U Bibl) Coronet Bks.

Productivity & Employment: Challenges of the 1990's. 1992. lib. bdg. 85.95 (*0-8490-5489-3*) Gordon Pr.

Productivity & Growth. Nicholas Oulton & Mary O'Mahony. (National Institute of Economic & Social Research Occasional Papers: No. 46). (Illus.). 333p. (C). 1994. text 64.95 (*0-521-45345-3*) Cambridge U Pr.

***Productivity & Growth in Chinese Agriculture.** K. P. Kalirajan. LC 98-44052. (Studies on the Chinese Economy). 1999. text 79.95 (*0-312-21935-0*) St Martin.

Productivity & Growth in Indian Manufacturing. Isher Judge Ahluwalia. (Illus.). 260p. 1992. 27.00 (*0-19-562763-6*) OUP.

Productivity & Higher Education: Improving the Effectiveness of Faculty, Facilities, & Financial Resources. Ed. by Joel W. Meyerson & Richard Anderson. LC 91-22290. 144p. 1991. 27.95 (*1-56079-090-3*) Petersons.

Productivity & Performance in the Paper Industry: Labour, Capital & Technology in Britain & America, 1860-1914. Gary B. Magee. LC 96-26082. (Cambridge Studies in Modern Economic History: No. 4). 309p. 1997. text 59.95 (*0-521-58197-4*) Cambridge U Pr.

Productivity & Prices: The Consequences of Industrial Concentration. Steven Lustgarten. LC 83-17133. (AEI Studies: No. 392). (Illus.). 62p. reprint ed. pap. 30.00 (*0-8357-4526-0*, 203739000008) Bks Demand.

Productivity & Public Policy. Ed. by Marc Holzer & Stuart S. Nagel. LC 84-4862. (Sage Yearbooks in Politics & Public Policy Ser.: No. 12). (Illus.). 296p. reprint ed. pap. 91.80 (*0-8357-4808-1*, 203774500009) Bks Demand.

Productivity & Quality Improvement. Johnson A. Edosomwan. 200p. 1989. 64.00 (*0-387-50452-4*) Spr-Verlag.

Productivity & Quality Management Frontiers IV, 2 vols., Set. Ed. by David J. Sumanth et al. 1993. 90.00 (*0-89806-125-3*, PQMF94) Eng Mgmt Pr.

Productivity & Quality Through People: Practices of Well-Managed Companies. Ed. by Y. Krishna Shetty & Vernon M. Buehler. LC 84-24930. (Illus.). 351p. 1985. 72.95 (*0-89930-115-0*, BPY/, Quorum Bks) Greenwood.

Productivity & Quality Through Science & Technology. Ed. by Y. Krishna Shetty & Vernon M. Buehler. LC 87-32595. 467p. 1988. 79.50 (*0-89930-344-7*, SYQ/, Quorum Bks) Greenwood.

Productivity & Sustainability of Southern Forest Ecosystems in a Changing Environment. Ed. by R. A. Mickler & S. Fox. LC 97-10648. (Ecological Studies: Vol. 128). (Illus.). 944p. 1998. 164.00 (*0-387-94851-1*) Spr-Verlag.

Productivity & Technical Change: With an Addendum by W. B. Reddaway. W. E. Salter. (Cambridge University, Department of Applied Economics, Paper in Industrial Relations & Labour Ser.: No. 6). 234p. reprint ed. pap. 66.70 (*0-608-12201-7*, 2024543) Bks Demand.

Productivity & Technological Progress in Japanese Agriculture. Keizo Tsuchiya. LC 77-356355. 285p. 1976. reprint ed. pap. 88.40 (*0-608-01563-6*, 206198000001) Bks Demand.

Productivity & Technology in the Metallurgical Industries: Proceedings of the International Symposium on Productivity & Technology in the Metallurgical Industries. International Symposium on Productivity & Technolo. Ed. by Michael Koch & John C. Taylor. LC 89-61032. (Illus.). 972p. reprint ed. pap. 200.00 (*0-7837-6757-9*, 205251700011) Bks Demand.

Productivity & the Business Cycle: Three Essays on U. S. & Polish Manufacturing. rev. ed. Domenico Marchetti, Jr. LC 96-39992. (Studies on Industrial Productivity). (Illus.). 94p. 1997. text 33.00 (*0-8153-2722-6*) Garland.

Productivity & the Economy. 1994. lib. bdg. 250.95 (*0-8490-5811-2*) Gordon Pr.

Productivity & the Economy: A Chartbook. (Illus.). 76p. (Orig.). (YA). (gr. 12 up). 1994. pap. text 30.00 (*0-7881-0793-3*) DIANE Pub.

Productivity & the Quality of Working Life. Steven Parnes. (Studies in Productivity: Highlights of the Literature Ser.: Vol. 2). 43p. 1978. pap. 55.00 (*0-89361-014-3*) Work in Amer.

Productivity & the Social System - The U. S. S. R. & the West. Abram Bergson. LC 77-15493. 288p. 1978. 37.95 (*0-674-71165-3*) HUP.

Productivity & the Technological Change in Electric Power Generating Plants. Paul H. Nowill. Ed. by Stuart Bruchey. LC 78-22703. (Energy in the American Economy Ser.). (Illus.). 1979. lib. bdg. 19.95 (*0-405-12005-2*) Ayer.

Productivity & U. S. Economic Growth. Dale W. Jorgenson et al. LC 87-12098. (Economic Studies: No. 159). (Illus.). 504p. 1988. 32.00 (*0-674-71175-0*) HUP.

Productivity & Value: The Political Economy of Measuring Progress. Folke Dovring. LC 87-2347. 201p. 1987. 57.95 (*0-275-92668-0*, C2668, Praeger Pubs) Greenwood.

P

Productivity at the Workstation: Wellness & Fitness at Your Desk. Robert R. Dvorak. Ed. by Michael G. Crisp. LC 89-82344. (Fifty-Minute Ser.). (Illus.). 100p. (Orig.). 1990. pap. 10.95 (*1-56052-041-8*) Crisp Pubns.

Productivity Benchmarks: Sheetfed Printers Production Characteristics. 129.00 (*0-614-25554-6*, 00BT44676) Print Indus Am.

Productivity Change, Public Goods & Transaction Costs: Essays at the Boundaries of Microeconomics. Yoram Barzel. (Economists of the Twentieth Century Ser.). 512p. 1995. 110.00 (*1-85898-076-3*) E Elgar.

Productivity Differences Within the Service Sector. Victor R. Fuchs & Jean A. Wilburn. (Occasional Papers: No. 102). 125p. 1967. reprint ed. 32.50 (*0-87014-443-X*) Natl Bur Econ Res.

Productivity Dilemma: Roadblock to Innovation in the Automobile Industry. William J. Abernathy. LC 78-1034. (Illus.). 279p. reprint ed. pap. 86.50 (*0-8357-6751-5*, 203540700095) Bks Demand.

Productivity, Education & Training: Facts & Policies in International Perspective. S. J. Prais. (National Institute of Economic & Social Research Occasional Papers). 154p. 1995. pap. text 18.95 (*0-521-55667-8*) Cambridge U Pr.

Productivity Effects of Cropland Erosion in the United States. Pierre R. Crosson & Anthony T. Stout. LC 83-19094. 103p. 1983. pap. 11.00 (*0-8018-3207-1*) Resources Future.

Productivity Engineering. Sumanth. 1999. 54.24 (*0-07-234792-9*) McGraw.

An Asterisk (*) at the beginning of an entry indicates that the title is appearing for the first time.

Productivity Growth & the Competitiveness of the American Economy. Ed. by Stanley W. Black. (C). 1989. lib. bdg. 80.00 (*0-7923-9001-6*) Kluwer Academic.

Productivity, Growth & U. S. Competitiveness. Ed. by William J. Baumol & Kenneth McLennan. (CED Supplementary Paper). 228p. 1985. lib. bdg. 19.95 (*0-87186-245-X*) Comm Econ Dev.

***Productivity Growth in Developing Countries: The Role of Efficiency.** Vaishali Mamgain. LC 99-44756. (Studies on Industrial Productivity). 1999. write for info. (*0-8153-3551-2*) Garland.

Productivity Growth in Japan & the United States. Ed. by Charles R. Hulten. (National Bureau of Economic Research Studies in Income & Wealth: Vol. 53). (Illus.). 456p. 1991. lib. bdg. 72.00 (*0-226-36059-8*) U Ch Pr.

Productivity Hoax! & Auto Workers' Real Needs! 1970. pap. 0.65 (*0-87898-056-3*) New Outlook.

Productivity Improvement in Construction. Clarkson H. Oglesby et al. 1988. pap. text, teacher ed. write for info. (*0-07-047803-1*) McGraw.

Productivity Improvement in IS. Ed. by Robert E. Umbaugh. 1993. pap. 49.95 (*0-685-69681-2*, HMIX) Warren Gorham & Lamont.

Productivity Improvement Management. Jacques Bialek. LC 87-6557. (Illus.). 339p. (Orig.). 1987. pap. 18.00 (*0-941883-01-9*, HD56.B49) CA Mgmt Pr.

Productivity Improvement Manual. Alan Lawlor. LC 85-12194. (Illus.). 306p. 1986. 59.95 (*0-89930-148-7*, LPY/, Quorum Bks) Greenwood.

Productivity Improvement Programs. (Personnel Policies Forum Surveys Ser.: No. 138). 36p. 1984. 30.00 (*0-87179-972-3*) BNA.

Productivity Improvement Through QC Circles in Service Industry. Surasak Nananukool et al. (Productivity Ser.: No. 21). (Illus.). 27p. 1987. pap. text 7.50 (*92-833-1711-4*, 317114) Productivity Inc.

Productivity Improvements Through TPM: The Philosophy & Application of Total Productive Maintenance. R. K. Davis. LC 94-31925. 160p. 1995. pap. text 45.00 (*0-13-133034-9*) P-H.

Productivity in Academia: Scientific Publishing at Norwegian Universities. Svein Kyvik. 256p. 1991. pap. 6.00 (*82-00-21410-9*) Scandnvan Univ Pr.

Productivity in Aquatic Ecosystem. Helms. 1997. 1.50 (*0-7167-9348-2*) W H Freeman.

Productivity in Foodservice. Lynne N. Robertson. LC 90-46631. (Illus.). 96p. 1991. reprint ed. pap. 30.00 (*0-608-07180-3*, 206740500009) Bks Demand.

Productivity in Japan. Ed. by Kageyu Noro. (Ergonomics Special Issue Ser.: Vol. 28, No. 6). 1985. pap. 23.00 (*0-85066-986-3*) Taylor & Francis.

Productivity in Marketing. Louis P. Bucklin. LC 78-24445. 130p. reprint ed. pap. 40.30 (*0-608-14408-8*, 202152100022) Bks Demand.

Productivity in Natural Resource Industries. Ed. by R. David Simpson. LC 99-21300. (Illus.). 220p. 1999. text 45.00 (*0-915707-99-3*) Resources Future.

Productivity in Organizations: New Perspectives from Industrial & Organizational Psychology. John P. Campbell et al. LC 88-42780. (Management Ser.). 477p. 1988. text 43.95 (*1-55542-100-8*) Jossey-Bass.

Productivity in Public & Non-Profit Organizations. Evan M. Berman. LC 97-33869. 1998. write for info. (*0-7619-1030-1*); pap. write for info. (*0-7619-1031-X*) Sage.

***Productivity in the Age of Competitiveness.** S. Balan. 1998. pap. 125.00 (*81-86982-78-7*, Pub. by Business Pubns) St Mut.

Productivity in the Blast-Furnace & Open-Hearth Segments of the Steel Industry, 1920-1946. William T. Hogan. LC 51-454. (Illus.). 168p. reprint ed. pap. 52.10 (*0-7837-5578-3*, 204536400005) Bks Demand.

***Productivity, Innovation & Economic Performance.** Ed. by Ray Barrell et al. LC 99-87220. (National Institute of Economic & Social Research Economic & Social Studies). (Illus.). 304p. 2000. text 74.95 (*0-521-78031-4*) Cambridge U Pr.

Productivity, Innovation, Management & Development: A Study in the Productivity Cultures of Nations & System Renewal. P. N. Rastogi. 273p. (C). 1988. text 28.00 (*0-8039-9563-6*) Sage.

Productivity Investment & Import Substitution in India Industries. N. C. Gupta. 176p. 1987. 48.00 (*81-7041-066-5*, Pub. by Scientific Pubs) St Mut.

Productivity Issues in Services at the Micro Level: A Special Issue of the Journal of Productivity Analysis. Ed. by Zvi Griliches & Jacques Mairesse. LC 93-20547. 236p. (C). 1993. lib. bdg. 194.50 (*0-7923-9335-X*) Kluwer Academic.

Productivity Management. Ed. by Vana Prewitt. (ACCRUE Ser.: Level II). 175p. 1991. ring bd. 63.00 (*1-879907-01-1*) Am Soc Hlth-Syst.

Productivity Management: A Practical Handbook. Joseph Prokopenko. xiv, 287p. (Orig.). 1992. pap. 36.00 (*92-2-105901-4*) Intl Labour Office.

Productivity Management for Nutrition Care. American Dietetic Association Staff. LC RA0975.5.D5. 61p. 1986. reprint ed. pap. 30.00 (*0-608-03562-9*, 205256000009) Bks Demand.

Productivity Management in Hospitality & Tourism. Ed. by Nick Johns. LC 95-22057. 224p. 1996. 100.00 (*0-304-33445-6*) Continuum.

Productivity Management in the Development of Computer Applications. John F. Keane. write for info. (*0-318-58197-3*) P-H.

Productivity Manual: Methods & Activities for Involving Employees in Productivity Improvement. 2nd ed. Elizabeth A. Smith. LC 95-17972. (Building Blocks of Human Potential Ser.). (Illus.). 220p. 1995. pap. 36.95 (*0-88415-652-4*, 5652) Gulf Pub.

P

Productivity Measurement: A Guide for Managers & Evaluators. Robert O. Brinkerhoff & Dennis E. Dressler. (Applied Social Research Methods Ser.: Vol. 19). (Illus.). 160p. (C). 1989. text 42.00 (*0-8039-3151-4*); pap. text 18.95 (*0-8039-3152-2*) Sage.

Productivity Measurement: An Evolving Art. Irving H. Siegel. (Studies in Productivity: Vol. 16). 34p. (Orig.). 1982. pap. 55.00 (*0-08-029497-9*) Work in Amer.

Productivity Measurement: An International Review of Concepts, Techniques, Programmes & Current Issues. Tony Hubert. Ed. by David Bailey. 284p. 1981. text 69.95 (*0-566-02230-3*, Pub. by Gower) Ashgate Pub Co.

Productivity Measurement & Improvement. 2nd ed. Lawrence S. Aft. 400p. (C). 1991. text 54.00 (*0-13-728759-3*) P-H.

Productivity Measurement & Improvement: Organizational Case Studies. Ed. by Robert D. Pritchard. LC 94-32932. 400p. 1995. 79.50 (*0-275-93907-3*) Greenwood.

Productivity Measurement & Management at the Company Level: The Japanese Experience. K. Kurosawa. (Advances in Industrial Engineering Ser.: Vol. 14). 582p. 1991. 214.25 (*0-444-87437-2*) Elsevier.

Productivity Measurement in Organizations Private Firms & Public Agencies. Irving H. Siegel. (Studies in Productivity: Highlights of the Literature Ser.: Vol. 43). 1985. 55.00 (*0-08-034312-0*) Work in Amer.

Productivity Measurement in Regulated Industries. Ed. by T. G. Cowing & R. E. Stevenson. LC 80-1685. (Economic Theory, Econometrics & Mathematical Economics Ser.). 1981. text 119.95 (*0-12-194080-2*) Acad Pr.

Productivity Measurement System for Administrators of Social Work Programs in Health Care. Shirley M. Keller et al. LC 92-48852. 72p. (Orig.). 1993. pap. text 37.50 (*0-87258-625-1*, 187151) Am Hospital.

Productivity Measures for Selected Industries & Government Services. (Illus.). 139p. (C). 1994. pap. text 40.00 (*0-7881-0583-3*) DIANE Pub.

Productivity Measures for Selected Industries & Government Services. 1992. lib. bdg. 79.95 (*0-8490-5536-9*) Gordon Pr.

Productivity Measures for Selected Industries & Government Services. 1997. lib. bdg. 251.95 (*0-8490-6102-4*) Gordon Pr.

Productivity Measures for Selected Industries & Government Services, July 1996. Government Printing Office Staff. 149p. 1996. pap. text 14.00 (*0-16-048744-7*) USGPO.

Productivity of America's Forests & Climate Change. Ed. by Linda A. Joyce. (Illus.). 70p. (Orig.). 1996. pap. text 20.00 (*0-7881-2764-0*) DIANE Pub.

Productivity of Biocenoses in Coastal Regions of Japan. Ed. by Kinji Hogetsu et al. LC 79-301742. (JIBP Synthesis Ser.: No. 14). 402p. 1977. reprint ed. pap. 124.70 (*0-608-01211-4*, 206190000001) Bks Demand.

Productivity of Cities. Sung Jong Kim. LC 97-70890. (Bruton Center for Development Studies Ser.). (Illus.). 144p. 1997. text 58.95 (*1-85972-542-2*, Pub. by Ashgate Pub) Ashgate Pub Co.

Productivity of Communities in Japanese Inland Waters. Ed. by Syuiti Mori & G. Yamamoto. LC 77-377170. (JIBP Synthesis Ser.: No. 10). 444p. 1975. reprint ed. pap. 137.70 (*0-608-01248-3*, 206193600001) Bks Demand.

Productivity of Health Care & Pharmaceuticals: An International Comparison. H. E. Frech & Richard D. Miller. LC 98-48714. xi, 97 p. 1999. pap. 14.95 (*0-8447-7124-4*, AEI Pr) Am Enterprise.

Productivity of Labor in Peace & War. Solomon Fabricant. (Occasional Papers: No. 7). 32p. 1943. reprint ed. 20.00 (*0-87014-322-0*) Natl Bur Econ Res.

Productivity of Labor in the Rubber Tire Manufacturing Industry. John D. Gaffey. LC 68-58577. (Columbia University. Studies in the Social Sciences: No. 472). reprint ed. 20.00 (*0-404-51472-3*) AMS Pr.

Productivity Plus. John G. Belcher, Jr. LC 87-9222. 240p. 1987. 26.95 (*0-87201-451-7*, 1451) Gulf Pub.

Productivity Policy: Key to the Nation's Economic Future. Committee for Economic Development. (CED Statement on National Policy Ser.). 108p. (Orig.). 1983. 10.50 (*0-87186-776-1*); pap. 8.50 (*0-87186-076-7*) Comm Econ Dev.

Productivity Power: Two Hundred Fifty Ideas for Being More Productive. Jim Temme. Ed. by Kelly Scanlon. (Self-Study Sourcebook Ser.). (Illus.). 186p. (Orig.). 1994. pap. 15.95 (*1-878542-31-1*, 13-0002) SkillPath Pubns.

Productivity Principle. David H. Barber. 140p. (Orig.). (C). 1986. pap. text, write for info. (*0-915667-08-8*) Spectra Pub Co.

Productivity Race: British Manufacturing in International Perspective, 1850-1990. S. N. Broadberry. LC 96-49929. (Illus.). 478p. (C). 1997. text 74.95 (*0-521-58440-X*) Cambridge U Pr.

Productivity Research in the Behavioral & Social Sciences. Ed. by Arthur P. Brief. LC 84-5877. 301p. 1984. 59.95 (*0-275-91132-2*, C1132, Praeger Pubs) Greenwood.

Productivity Sand Traps & Tar Pits: How to Detect & Avoid Them. Mike Walsh. LC 91-21441. (Illus.). 216p. (Orig.). 1991. pap. 27.95 (*0-932633-21-8*) Dorset Hse Pub Co.

Productivity, Societal Well-Being & Public Policy. Ed. by Rita M. Kelly. (Orig.). 1985. pap. 15.00 (*0-918592-74-7*) Pol Studies.

Productivity Software Guide. Edward G. Martin. LC 94-68687. 84p. (C). 1994. pap. text 14.50 (*0-03-015288-7*) Harcourt Coll Pubs.

Productivity Software Guide: Database Management with Paradox 5.0 for Windows. 95th ed. Edward G. Martin et al. 112p. (C). 1995. pap. text 9.75 (*0-03-011079-3*) Dryden Pr.

Productivity Statistics for Federal Government Functions: Fiscal Years, 1967-94. Arthur Young et al. (Illus.). 96p. (C). 1998. reprint ed. pap. text 25.00 (*0-7881-4566-5*) DIANE Pub.

Productivity Statistics for Federal Government Functions, Fiscal Years 1967-94. Government Printing Office Staff. 104p. 1996. pap. text 7.00 (*0-16-048582-7*) USGPO.

Productivity Through Consultancy in Small Industrial Enterprises. Ed. by Asian Productivity Organization Staff. (Illus.). 504p. 1974. pap. text 17.25 (*92-833-1026-8*, 310268) Productivity Inc.

Productivity Through People 1e. William B. Werther, Jr. et al. (SWC-Management). (Illus.). 550p. (C). 1986. pap. text 41.00 (*0-314-95573-9*) West Pub.

Productivity Through Work Innovation: Executive Summary. Work in America Institute, Inc. Staff. 48p. 1982. pap. 7.00 (*0-685-07115-4*, Pergamon Pr) Elsevier.

Productivity Through Work Innovations. 161p. 1982. 15.00 (*0-685-05560-4*, L120, Pergamon Pr) Elsevier.

Productivity Through Work Innovations: Complete Study. Jerome M. Rosow & Robert Zager. 161p. 1982. 18.25 (*0-08-029545-2*) Work in Amer.

Productivity Through Work Innovations: Executive Summary. Jerome M. Rosow & Robert Zager. 48p. 1982. pap. 7.75 (*0-08-029546-0*) Work in Amer.

Productivity Trends: Capital & Labor. John W. Kendrick. (Occasional Papers: No. 53). 28p. 1956. reprint ed. 20.00 (*0-87014-367-0*) Natl Bur Econ Res.

Productivity Trends in a Sectoral Macroeconomic Model: A Study of American Agriculture & Supporting Industries, 1919-1964. W. F. Gossling. (Illus.). xxii, 296p. 1972. lib. bdg. 175.00 (*0-678-08072-0*) Kelley.

Productivity Trends in the Goods & Service Sectors, 1929-61: A Preliminary Survey. Victor R. Fuchs. (Occasional Papers: No. 89). 60p. 1964. reprint ed. 20.00 (*0-87014-403-0*) Natl Bur Econ Res.

Productivity Trends in the United States. John W. Kendrick. LC 75-19715. (National Bureau of Economic Research Ser.). (Illus.). 1975. reprint ed. 53.95 (*0-405-07595-2*) Ayer.

Productivity Trends in the United States. John W. Kendrick & Maude R. Pech. (General Ser.: No. 71). 682p. 1961. reprint ed. 160.00 (*0-87014-070-1*) Natl Bur Econ Res.

Productivity vs. OSHA & EPA Regulations. Wayne B. Gray. Ed. by Richard Farmer. LC 85-28873. (Research for Business Decisions Ser.: No. 86). 131p. reprint ed. 40.70 (*0-8357-1721-6*, 207038100088) Bks Demand.

Product/Market Strategies of Small & Medium-Sized Enterprises. Ed. by Ingold Bamberger. 435p. 1994. 96.95 (*1-85628-963-X*, Pub. by Avebry) Ashgate Pub Co.

Productos de Mexico. Laura Conlon. (Al Sur de Nuestra Frontera Ser.).Tr. of Products of Mexico. 24p. (J). (gr. k-4). 1994. lib. bdg. 17.27 (*1-55916-074-8*) Rourke Bk Co.

***Products & Plans for Universal Homes: Over 1700 Products from Over 450 Manufacturers Plus 51 Plans for Universal Homes.** Home Planners Editors. 128p. 2000. pap. 15.95 (*1-881955-65-6*) Home Planners.

Products & Structure of Kilavea. J. B. Stone. (BMB Ser.). 1974. reprint ed. 25.00 (*0-527-02136-9*) Periodicals Srv.

Products Certified for Canada Directory, 1996, 2 vols. (C). 1996. pap. text 30.00 (*1-55989-968-9*) Underwrtrs Labs.

Products Certified for Canada Directory, 1996, 2 vols. 2nd ed. (C). 1996. pap. text 30.00 (*1-55989-969-7*) Underwrtrs Labs.

Products Certified for Canada Directory 1997, 2 vols. (C). 1996. pap. text 36.00 (*0-7629-0104-7*) Underwrtrs Labs.

Products Certified for Canada Directory, 1997, 2 vols. 2nd ed. (C). 1996. pap. text 30.00 (*0-7629-0111-X*) Underwrtrs Labs.

Products Comaparison Manual for Trademark Users: 1998 Cumulative Supplement. Francis M. Pinckney. LC 86-9732. 584p. 1998. pap., suppl. ed. 85.00 (*0-87179-501-9*, 9813-PR8) BNA Books.

Products Evaluated in Accordance with International, Regional & Foreign National Standards. (C). 1997. pap. text 8.00 (*0-7629-0109-8*) Underwrtrs Labs.

Products for World Markets. Design Council Staff. 60p. 1994. pap. 78.95 (*0-566-07624-1*) Ashgate Pub Co.

Products Liability. 35.00 (*0-317-29530-6*, #CO3182) Harcourt.

Products Liability. James L. Branton et al. (Trial Lawyer's Ser.: Vol. 9). 510p. 1992. ring bd. 135.00 (*1-878337-29-7*) Knowles Pub Inc.

Products Liability, 11 vols. Louis R. Frumer & Melvin I. Friedman. 1960. 2380.00 (*0-8205-1560-4*) Bender.

Products Liability. 2nd ed. David A. Fischer. Ed. by William C. Powers, Jr. 173p. 1994. pap. text, teacher ed. write for info. (*0-318-72895-8*) West Pub.

Products Liability. 2nd rev. ed. Steven Finz. LC 97-228835. (Smith's Review Ser.). 226p. (Orig.). 1996. pap. text 13.95 (*1-56542-165-5*) E Pub Corp.

Products Liability, 3 vols. 3rd ed. Ed. by Lexis Law Publishing Staff. 1998. lib. bdg. 240.00 (*0-327-00792-3*) LEXIS Pub.

Products Liability, Vol. 1. 3rd ed. Jerry J. Phillips & Robert E. Pryor. LC 98-88875. 550p. 1998. 240.00 (*0-327-00746-X*, 6081612) LEXIS Pub.

Products Liability: Adaptable to Courses Utilizing Owen, Montgomery & Keeton's Casebook on Products Liability & Safety. Casenotes Publishing Co., Inc. Staff. Ed. by Norman S. Goldenberg et al. (Legal Briefs Ser.). 1996. pap. write for info. (*0-87457-113-8*, 1431) Casenotes Pub.

Products Liability: Cases & Materials. 3rd ed. Harvey Sklaw. 322p. 1983. ring bd. 35.00 (*0-685-14665-0*) NJ Inst CLE.

Products Liability: Cases, Materials, Problems, 1994. Jerry J. Phillips. 1994. text 54.00 (*1-55834-136-6*) Bender.

Products Liability: Cases, Materials, Problems, 1998 Supplement. Frank J. Vandall et al. (Continuing Legal Education Ser.). 180p. 1998, pap. text. write for info. (*0-327-00289-1*, 1272210) LEXIS Pub.

Products Liability: Design & Manufacturing Defects. Lewis Bass. 587p. 1986. text 50.00 (*0-07-004036-2*) Shepards.

Products Liability: Prevention & Defense. Ed. by Benton. 1993. write for info. (*1-56257-341-1*, MICHIE) LEXIS Pub.

Products Liability: Problems & Process. James A. Henderson, Jr. & Aaron D. Twerski. 912p. 1987. 42.00 (*0-316-35612-3*, Aspen Law & Bus) Aspen Pub.

Products Liability: Problems & Process. 3rd ed. James A. Henderson & Aaron D. Twerski. LC 97-169579. 770p. 1997. teacher ed. write for info. (*1-56706-490-6*, 64906) Panel Pubs.

***Products Liability: Problems & Process.** 4th ed. James A. Henderson & Aaron D. Twerski. LC 00-20550. 2000. boxed set 64.00 (*0-7355-1316-3*) Panel Pubs.

Products Liability: Recreation & Sports Equipment. Jeffrey D. Wittenberg. 380p. 1985. ring bd. 90.00 (*0-318-20293-X*, 00591) NY Law Pub.

Products Liability: 1985 Pocket Part. Stuart M. Madden. 130p. 1985. pap. text. write for info. (*0-318-59390-4*) West Pub.

Products Liability & Safety, Cases & Materials. 2nd ed. W. Page Keeton et al. (University Casebook Ser.). 1050p. 1989. text 43.95 (*0-88277-648-7*) Foundation Pr.

Products Liability & Safety, Cases & Materials: Statutory Supplement. 3rd ed. David G. Owen et al. (University Casebook Ser.). 469p. 1996. pap. text. write for info. (*1-56662-419-3*) Foundation Pr.

Products Liability & Safety, Cases & Materials: Teacher's Manual. 2nd ed. W. Page Keeton et al. (University Casebook Ser.). 205p. 1990. pap. text, teacher ed. write for info. (*0-88277-808-0*) Foundation Pr.

Products Liability & Safety, Cases & Materials, Products Liability Problems 1996 Edition for Use in Conjunction With. 3rd ed. Montgomery Owen & Keeton Owen. Ed. by Paul A. LeBel. (University Casebook Ser.). 164p. Date not set. pap. text. write for info. (*1-56662-422-3*) Foundation Pr.

Products Liability & Safety, Cases & Materials, 1993: Case & Statutory Supplement To. 2nd ed. W. Page Keeton et al. (University Casebook Ser.). 535p. 1993. pap. text. write for info. (*1-56662-074-0*) Foundation Pr.

Products Liability & Safety, Cases & Materials, 1997 Case & Statutory Supplement To. David G. Owen & Mary J. Davis. (University Casebook Ser.). 589p. 1997. pap. text. write for info. (*1-56662-567-X*) Foundation Pr.

PRODUCTS LIABILITY & SAFETY 3E. 3rd ed. David G. Owen et al. LC 96-5863. (Paralegal). 1105p. (C). 1996. text 42.00 (*1-56662-341-3*) Foundation Pr.

Products Liability & the Economics of Pharmaceuticals & Medical Devices. Steven Garber. LC 93-6414. 1993. pap. 15.00 (*0-8330-1450-1*, R-4285-ICJ) Rand Corp.

Products Liability & the Food Consumer. Reed Dickerson. LC 77-139130. 339p. 1972. reprint ed. lib. bdg. 69.50 (*0-8371-5746-3*, DIPL, Greenwood Pr) Greenwood.

Products Liability & the Search for Justice. Marshall S. Shapo. LC 92-76164. 228p. 1993. 37.95 (*0-89089-536-8*) Carolina Acad Pr.

Products Liability & Toxic Tort Law in New Jersey: A Practitioner's Guide (1988) William A. Dreier et al. 639p. 1988. suppl. ed. 30.00 (*0-685-65976-3*) NJ Inst CLE.

Products Liability & Toxic Tort Law in New Jersey: A Practitioner's Guide (1988) 6th ed. William A. Dreier et al. 639p. 1988. ring bd., suppl. ed. 75.00 (*0-685-65975-5*) NJ Inst CLE.

Products Liability Anthology. Ed. & Comment by Anita Bernstein. LC 94-45933. 257p. 1995. pap. 29.95 (*0-87084-704-X*) Anderson Pub Co.

Products Liability Cases & Materials: 1997 Supplement. annuals 2nd ed. David A. Fischer & William C. Powers. 85p. 1997. pap. text, suppl. ed. write for info. (*0-314-22800-4*) West Pub.

Products Liability Citations. Shepard's Citations, Inc. Staff. 1983. 270.00 (*0-685-23134-8*) Shepards.

Products Liability Guide Reference: Law Citator. LC 94-72503. 1994. 135.00 (*0-614-07296-4*) West Group.

Products Liability in a Nutshell. 4th ed. Jerry J. Phillips. LC 93-1654. (NutShell Ser.). 322p. (C). 1993. pap. text 16.00 (*0-314-02252-X*) West Pub.

Products Liability in a Nutshell. 5th ed. Jerry J. Phillips. (Paralegal). 300p. 1998. pap. text 15.00 (*0-314-22585-4*) West Pub.

Products Liability in Florida. 3rd ed. Florida Bar Members. LC 95-60844. 200p. 1995. ring bd. 60.00 (*0-945979-74-6*, 260) FL Bar Legal Ed.

Products Liability Law: The 1984 National Conference. 381p. 1988. student ed. 95.00 (*1-55917-583-4*, 1019B) Natl Prac Inst.

Products Liability Law: The 1985 National Conference. 218p. 1988. student ed. 95.00 (*1-55917-586-9*, 5322B) Natl Prac Inst.

Products Liability Law: The 1986 National Conference. 198p. 1988. student ed. 95.00 (*1-55917-589-3*, 6321B) Natl Prac Inst.

Products Liability Law: The 1987 National Conference. 291p. 1988. 95.00 (*1-55917-592-3*, 7328B) Natl Prac Inst.

Products Liability Litigation, 4 vols. Susan E. Loggans et al. LC 88-19303. 1988. ring bd. 500.00 (*0-685-24501-2*) West Group.

An Asterisk (*) at the beginning of an entry indicates that the title is appearing for the first time.

Products Liability, 1998 Cumulative Supplement & 1998 Supplement, 2 vols., Set. 2nd ed. Jerry J. Phillips & Robert E. Pryor. 150p. 1998. pap., suppl. ed. write for info. (*0-327-00747-8*, 6082315) LEXIS Pub.

Products Liability, 1998 Cumulative Supplement, Vol. 2. 2nd ed. Jerry J. Phillips & Robert E. Pryor. 150p. 1998. pap., suppl. ed. write for info. (*0-327-00748-6*, 6082515) LEXIS Pub.

Products Liability, 1998 Supplement, Vol. 3. 2nd ed. Jerry J. Phillips & Robert E. Pryor. 150p. 1998. pap., suppl. ed. write for info. (*0-327-00749-4*, 6082615) LEXIS Pub.

Products Liability, 1996, Vol. 3. 2nd ed. Phillips & Pryor. 736p. 1997. text 80.00 (*1-55834-578-7*, 60818-11, MICHIE) LEXIS Pub.

Products Liability, 1993, 3 vols., Vol. 1. 2nd ed. Jerry J. Phillips et al. 519p. 1993. text 240.00 (*1-55834-109-9*, 60816-11, MICHIE) LEXIS Pub.

Products Liability Practice Guide, 5 vols. John Vargo. 1988. 820.00 (*0-8205-1547-7*) Bender.

Products Liability Problems 1995 Edition for Use in Conjunction with Products Liability & Safety, Cases & Materials. 2nd ed. Paul A. LeBel. 171p. 1995. pap. text 10.95 (*1-56662-260-3*) Foundation Pr.

Products Liability Resource Manual: An Attorney's Guide to Analyzing Issues, Developing Strategies, & Winning Cases. LC 93-70906. 344p. 1993. pap. 59.95 (*0-89707-875-6*, 515-0228, ABA Genl Prac) Amer Bar Assn.

Products Liability with 1991 Cumulative Supplement, 3 vols., Set. Robert E. Cartwright & Jerry J. Phillips. 1986. text 240.00 (*0-930273-41-9*, 60815-10, MICHIE) LEXIS Pub.

Products of Alska. Lynn M. Stone. LC 93-40429. (North to Alaska Discovery Library). 24p. (J). (gr. k-4). 1994. lib. bdg. 15.93 (*1-55916-027-6*) Rourke Bk Co.

Products of Automata. F. Gecseg. (EATCS Monographs on Theoretical Computer Science: Vol. 7). (Illus.). 180p. 1986. 49.95 (*0-387-13719-X*) Spr-Verlag.

Products of Conjugacy Classes in Groups. Ed. by Z. Arad & M. Herzog. (Lecture Notes in Mathematics Ser.: Vol. 1112). v, 244p. 1985. 37.95 (*0-387-13916-8*) Spr-Verlag.

Products of Groups. Bernhard Amberg et al. LC 92-19244. (Oxford Mathematical Monographs). 232p. 1993. text 85.00 (*0-19-853575-9*, Clarendon Pr) OUP.

Products of Mexico see Productos de Mexico

Products of Mexico. Laura Conlon. LC 94-15907. (South of the Border Discovry Library). 24p. (J). (gr. k-4). 1994. lib. bdg. 15.93 (*1-55916-053-5*) Rourke Bk Co.

***Products of Our Time.** David Redhead. LC 99-89524. (Illus.). 144p. 2000. pap. 38.00 (*3-7643-6234-0*, Pub. by Birkhauser) Princeton Arch.

Products of Random Matrices in Statistical Physics. Andrea Crisanti et al. LC 93-15234. (Solid-State Sciences Ser.: Vol. 104). 1993. 75.95 (*0-387-56575-2*) Spr-Verlag.

Products of Reflections in U(P,Q) D. Z. Djokovic & Jerry G. Malzan. LC 81-20544. (Memoirs Ser.: No. 37/259). 82p. 1982. pap. 16.00 (*0-8218-2259-4*, MEMO/37/259) Am Math.

Products of Sugarbeet & Sugarcane: Proceedings of Workshop on Products of Sugarbeet & Sugarcane, 1994. Ed. & Intro. by Margaret A. Clarke. (Workshop of Sugar Processing Research Institute (since 1984) Ser.). (Illus.). 307p. (Orig.). 1995. pap. text 100.00 (*1-883326-03-6*) Sugar Process Res.

Produits Tensoriels Topologiques et Espaces Nucleaires. Alexander Grothendieck. LC 52-42839. (Memoirs Ser.: No. 1/16). 336p. 1990. reprint ed. pap. 26.00 (*0-8218-1216-5*, MEMO/1/16) Am Math.

Produits TensorielsTopologiques et Espaces Nucleaires. Alexander Grothendieck. LC 52-42839. (American Mathematical Society Ser.: Vol. 16). (FRE.). 342p. reprint ed. pap. 106.10 (*0-608-10503-1*, 205278600009) Bks Demand.

Produktion und Logistik. 1995. 26.00 (*3-540-59194-X*) Spr-Verlag.

Produktivitatseffekte der Offentlichen Infrastruktur Vol. VIII: Mebkonzepte und Empirische Befunde fur Hamburg. Ulrich Hofmann. (Europaische Hochschulschriften: Reihe 5: Bd. 1945). (GER., Illus.). VIII, 135p. 1996. pap. 32.95 (*3-631-30397-1*) P Lang Pubng.

***Produktverantwortung und Ihre Durchsetzung: Eine Kartellrechtliche Beurteilung von Selbstverpflichtungen Im Umweltrecht Aus Deutscher und Europaischer Sicht Unter Besonderer Berucksichtigung der Altautoentsorgung.** Kerstin Andrea Muller. (Frankfurter Wirtschaftsrechtliche Studien. : Bd. 31). 324p. 1999. 52.95 (*3-631-35399-5*) P Lang Pubng.

Proective Clothing. Richard K. Miller et al. (Market Research Survey Ser.: No. 252). 50p. 1996. 200.00 (*1-55865-282-5*) Future Tech Surveys.

Proelivm Hastinge-Nse. M. C. Greenstock. (C). 1982. pap. text 60.00 (*0-900269-06-5*, Pub. by Old Vicarage) St Mut.

Proem see Art of Organ Building

Proems & Poems. Ruth Slonim. LC 91-42039. (Washington State University Press Art Ser.). 63p. 1992. 15.95 (*0-87422-084-X*); pap. 9.95 (*0-87422-077-7*) Wash St U Pr.

Pro/Engineer & Plastic Design. Norman Ladouceur & John McKeen. LC 98-54937. (Illus.). 400p. (C). 1999. pap. 68.95 (*1-56690-188-X*) Thomson Learn.

Pro/ENGINEER Release 20 Exercise Manual. Steven G. Smith. (Illus.). 120p. 1998. pap. 59.95 (*0-9669251-0-6*) CADquest.

Pro/Engineer Sheetmetal Design - Release 2.0. Steven G. Smith. (Illus.). 235p. 1999. pap. text 79.95 (*0-9669251-2-2*) CADquest.

Pro/Engineer Solutions Advanced Techniques & Workarounds. Robert Townsend & Gregory R. Schmidt. LC 98-55575. (Illus.). 448p. (C). 1999. pap. text 59.95 (*1-56690-163-4*) Thomson Learn.

***Pro/Engineer Tutorial & MultiMedia CD: A Click-by-Click Primer.** Roger Toogood & Jack Zecher. 244p. 2000. pap. 59.95 (*1-58503-022-8*, SDC Pubns) Schroff Dev Corp.

***Pro/Engineer Tutorial & Multimedia CD: Release 20/2001.** Roger Toogood. (Illus.). 255p. 1999. pap. 59.95 incl. cd-rom (*1-887503-93-5*) Schroff Dev Corp.

Pro/Engineer Tutorial Module for Engineering Design Communication. Herling. (C). 1999. pap. text. write for info. (*0-201-38039-0*) Addison-Wesley.

Prof. MicroMax Internet: CD Rom with activity book, IBM. MicroMax International A.S. Staff. 49.95 incl. cd-rom (*0-8219-1657-2*) EMC-Paradigm.

Prof. MicroMax Windows 95: CD Rom with teacher's guide, IBM. MicroMax International A.S. Staff. 49.95 incl. cd-rom (*0-8219-1660-2*) EMC-Paradigm.

Prof Prepress Printing & Publisher. Romano. LC 98-50144. 656p. 1999. 59.99 (*0-13-099744-7*) P-H.

Profane & Sacred Dances. Douglas Anderson. 71p. 1989. pap. 7.95 (*0-912549-16-5*) Bread & Butter.

Profane Art: Essays & Reviews. Joyce Carol Oates. 212p. 1985. reprint ed. pap. 9.95 (*0-89255-095-3*) Persea Bks.

Profane Friendship. Harold Brodkey. 1994. 23.00 (*0-374-23544-9*) FS&G.

Profane Illumination: Walter Benjamin & the Paris of Surreal Revolution. Margaret Cohen. LC 92-36861. (Weimar & Now Ser.: Vol. 5). 1993. 45.00 (*0-520-08023-8*, Pub. by U CA Pr) Cal Prin Full Svc.

Profane Illumination: Walter Benjamin & the Paris of Surrealist Revolution. Margaret Cohen. (Weimar & Now: German Cultural Criticism Ser.: Vol. 5). (Illus.). 271p. 1995. pap. 15.95 (*0-520-20150-7*, Pub. by U CA Pr) Cal Prin Full Svc.

Profane Justice: A Comprehensive Guide to Asserting Your Parental Rights. Suzanne Shell. LC 99-208745. 209p. 1997. pap. 17.00 (*0-9660254-0-7*) Sage Wis Pr.

Profane Mythology: The Savage Mind of the Cinema. Yvette Birbo. LC 81-48384. 158p. reprint ed. pap. 49.00 (*0-7837-6096-5*, 205914200008) Bks Demand.

Profane Passions: Politics & Culture in the Americas. Jean Franco et al. LC 98-20723. 1999. 69.95 (*0-8223-2231-5*); pap. 22.95 (*0-8223-2248-X*) Duke.

Profane Scriptures: Reflections on the Dialogue with the Bible in Modern Hebrew Poetry. Ruth Kartun-Blum. LC 99-10451. (Illus.). 108p. 1999. 21.95 (*0-87820-054-1*, Pub. by Hebrew Union Coll Pr) Wayne St U Pr.

***Profane Scriptures: Reflections on the Dialogue with the Bible in Modern Hebrew Poetry.** Ruth Kartun-Blum. (Illus.). 110p. 1999. 21.95 (*0-8143-2881-4*) Wayne St U Pr.

Profane, the Civil, & the Godly: The Reformation of Manners in Orthodox New England, 1679-1749. Richard P. Gildrie. LC 92-46614. 256p. (C). 1994. 45.00 (*0-271-01065-7*); pap. 18.95 (*0-271-01068-1*) Pa St U Pr.

Profaners. rev. ed. Lloyd E. Miller, Jr. 175p. (Orig.). 1995. pap. 4.95 (*0-9639322-1-7*) Literary Prods.

Profangeschichte in der Heilsgeschichte: Quellenuntersuchungen zu den Incidentien der, Christherre-Chronik. Monika Schwabbauer. (Vestigia Bibliae, Jahrbuch des Deutschen Bibel-Archivs Hamburg Ser.: Bd. 15 & 16, 1993-1994). (GER.). 414p. 1997. 85.95 (*3-906757-61-7*, Pub. by P Lang) P Lang Pubng.

Profanity in Relation to U. S. Federal & State Law & the Great Commission: 8 Principles of Tactical Warfare Needed to Eliminate Pornography from Your Community. Michael D. Juzwick. 1995. 3.50 (*1-887412-06-9*) Light Eternal Pubns.

Profecia. Aventura. 1996. mass mkt. 9.99 (*0-446-67300-5*, Pub. by Warner Bks) Little.

Profecia: Llave al Futuro. Duane S. Crowther. 1995. pap. 18.98 (*0-88290-532-5*) Horizon Utah.

Profecia Biblica en 12 Lecciones (Bible Prophecy in 12 Lessons) Max Anders. (What You Need to Know about ... in 12 Lessons Ser.). (ENG & SPA.). 192p. 8.99 (*0-89922-467-9*) Caribe Betania.

Profecia Celestina: Una Aventura. James Redfield. (SPA.). 320p. 1996. 16.95 (*0-446-52057-8*, Pub. by Warner Bks) Little.

Profecia de los Cuatro "Sietes" en la Biblia. Witness Lee.Tr. of Prophecy of the Four "Sevens" in the Bible, The. (SPA.). 97p. 1995. per. 5.50 (*0-87083-856-3*, 10-060-002) Living Stream Ministry.

Profecia y Luz en la Poesia de Maya Islas. Mireya Robles. Ed. by Juan Cardenas. (SPA.). 40p. (Orig.). 1987. pap. 6.00 (*0-913983-05-5*) M & A Edns.

Profecias de Nostradamus y San Malaquias. H. Forman. (SPA.). 1997. pap. text 4.98 (*968-15-0347-3*) Ed Mex.

***Profecias de Saint Germain Para el Nuevo Milenio.** Elizabeth Clare Prophet. (SPA.). 2000. pap. 12.95 (*968-19-0605-5*) Aguilar.

***Profecias del Milenio (The Millennium Book of Prophecies)** John Hogue. (SPA.). 480p. 1999. pap. 16.95 (*0-553-06106-2*, Pub. by Plaza) Random.

Profecias Mayas. A. Gilbert.Tr. of Mayan Prophecies. 1998. pap. text 17.95 (*970-05-0673-8*) Lectorum Pubns.

Profecias Para el Mundo Moderno. Dwight Pentecost.Tr. of Prophecy for Today. (SPA.). 1990. 4.99 (*0-945792-86-7*, 497703) Editorial Unilit.

Profecias para el Mundo Moderno. John D. Pentecost.Tr. of Prophecy for Today. (SPA.). 228p. 1989. pap. write for info. (*0-614-27118-5*) Editorial Unilit.

Profegiendo lo Nuestro: Pueblos Indigenas y Biodiversidad see Protecting What's Ours: Indigenous Peoples & Biodiversity

Profesor in Africa: Jurnal Eurocan. Florentin Smarandache. LC PC0840.29.M2. (RUM.). 52p. reprint ed. pap. 30.00 (*0-608-20526-5*, 207177800002) Bks Demand.

Profesor in Africa: Jurnal Marocan. Florentin Smarandache. Ed. by Xiquan Publishing House Staff. (RUM.). 100p. (Orig.). 1995. pap. 9.99 (*1-879585-24-3*) Erhus Univ Pr.

Profesor Ziper y La Fabulosa Guitarra Electrica. Juan Villoro. 1998. pap. text 9.95 (*968-29-4003-6*) Libros Fronteras.

Professeur Taranne & Pique-Nique en Campagne. Arthur Adamov & Arrabal Fernando. Ed. by Peter Norrish. 128p. (C). 1990. pap. 17.99 (*0-415-01713-0*) Routledge.

Professinal Business Communication. 2nd ed. 444p. (C). 1998. 30.75 (*0-536-01519-8*) Pearson Custom.

Professing Linguistic Historiography. E. F. K. Koerner. LC 95-43672. (Studies in the History of the Language Sciences: Vol. 79). viii, 274p. 1995. lib. bdg. 68.00 (*1-55619-615-6*) J Benjamins Pubng Co.

Professing Literature: An Institutional History. Gerald Graff. LC 86-16023. 324p. (C). 1989. pap. text 13.00 (*0-226-30604-6*) U Ch Pr.

Professing Literature: An Institutional History. Gerald Graff. LC 86-16023. 328p. (C). 1996. 29.95 (*0-226-30603-8*) U Ch Pr.

Professing the Faith: Christian Theology in a North American Context. Douglas J. Hall. LC 97-104873. 560p. 1996. pap. 28.00 (*0-8006-2548-X*, 1-2548, Fortress Pr) Augsburg Fortress.

Professing the New Rhetorics: A Sourcebook. Ed. by Theresa Enos & Stuart S. Brown. LC 93-20931. 490p. (C). 1993. pap. text 28.40 (*0-13-014317-0*) P-H.

Profession & Practice of Adult Education: An Introduction. Sharan B. Merriam & Ralph G. Brockett. LC 96-22517. (Higher & Adult Education Ser.). 334p. 1996. 32.95 (*0-7879-0290-X*) Jossey-Bass.

Profession & Practice of Educational Psychology: Future Directions. Ed. by Sheila Wolfendale et al. 208p. 1992. pap. text 31.95 (*0-304-32347-0*) Continuum.

Profession & Practice of Health Education. David A. Bedworth & Albert E. Bedworth. 496p. (Orig.). (C). 1991. text. write for info. (*0-697-12160-7*) Brown & Benchmark.

Profession & Practice of Program Evaluation. Scarvia B. Anderson & Samuel Ball. LC 78-1154. (Jossey-Bass Series in Social & Behavioral Science & in Higher Education). (Illus.). 272p. reprint ed. pap. 84.40 (*0-8357-4798-0*, 203773500009) Bks Demand.

Profession de Foi du Vicaire Savoyard. Jean-Jacques Rousseau. Ed. by Andre Robinet. (FRE.). 1978. pap. 24.95 (*0-685-73323-8*, 2711606678) Fr & Eur.

Profession '80: Selected Articles from the Bulletins of the Association of Departments of English & the Association of Foreign Languages. fac. ed. Modern Language Association of America Staff. LC LB2365.L4P7. (Illus.). 50p. 1980. reprint ed. pap. 30.00 (*0-7837-8023-0*, 204777900008) Bks Demand.

Profession '88. fac. ed. Modern Language Association of America Staff. Ed. by Carol Zuses & Phyllis FRanklin. LC LB2365.L4P7. 83p. 1988. reprint ed. pap. 30.00 (*0-7837-8029-X*, 204778500008) Bks Demand.

Profession '85. Richard I. Brod & Phyllis Franklin. 54p. (Orig.). 1985. pap. text 7.50 (*0-87352-320-2*) Modern Lang.

Profession '84. Ed. by Richard I. Brod & Phyllis Franklin. iv, 43p. (Orig.). 1984. pap. text 7.50 (*0-87352-319-9*) Modern Lang.

Profession '89. Ed. by Phyllis Franklin. 60p. (Orig.). 1989. pap. text 7.50 (*0-87352-324-5*, W3820) Modern Lang.

Profession '81: Selected Articles from the Bulletins of the Association of Departments of English & the Association of Departments of Foreign Languages. fac. ed. Modern Language Association of America Staff. LC LB2365.L4P7. (Illus.). 49p. 1981. reprint ed. pap. 30.00 (*0-7837-8024-9*, 204778000008) Bks Demand.

Profession '87. Ed. by Phyllis Franklin. 65p. (Orig.). 1987. pap. text 7.50 (*0-87352-322-9*, W380) Modern Lang.

Profession '83. Richard I. Brod & Phyllis Franklin. 52p. (Orig.). 1983. pap. text 7.50 (*0-87352-318-0*) Modern Lang.

Profession '82: Selected Articles from the Bulletins of the Association of Departments of English & the Association of Departments of Foreign Languages. fac. ed. Modern Language Association of America Staff. LC LB2365.L4P7. 56p. 1982. reprint ed. pap. 30.00 (*0-7837-8025-7*, 204778100008) Bks Demand.

Profession Journalist: A Study on the Working Conditions of Journalists. G. Bohere. Orig. Title: Fr.. ix, 177p. 1984. pap. 22.50 (*92-2-103531-X*) Intl Labour Office.

Profession '90. Ed. by Phyllis Franklin. 80p. (Orig.). 1990. pap. text 7.50 (*0-87352-624-4*, W3830) Modern Lang.

Profession '95. Ed. by Phyllis Franklin. 114p. (Orig.). 1995. pap. text 7.50 (*0-87352-670-8*) Modern Lang.

Profession '94. Ed. by Phyllis Franklin. 105p. (Orig.). 1994. pap. text 7.50 (*0-87352-669-4*) Modern Lang.

Profession '91. Ed. by Phyllis Franklin. 64p. (Orig.). 1991. pap. text 7.50 (*0-87352-633-3*, W3840) Modern Lang.

Profession '97. Ed. by Phyllis Franklin. 274p. (Orig.). 1997. pap. 7.50 (*0-87352-691-0*) Modern Lang.

Profession '96. Ed. by Phyllis Franklin. 219p. (Orig.). 1996. pap. 7.50 (*0-87352-683-X*) Modern Lang.

Profession '93. Ed. by Phyllis Franklin. 71p. (Orig.). 1993. pap. text 7.50 (*0-87352-660-0*) Modern Lang.

Profession '92. Ed. by Phyllis Franklin. 78p. (Orig.). 1992. pap. text 7.50 (*0-87352-652-X*) Modern Lang.

Profession of a Chartered Accountant & Other Lectures: Delivered to the Institute of Chartered Accountants in England & Wales. Francis W. Pixley. Ed. by Richard P. Brief. LC 77-87285. (Development of Contemporary Accounting Thought Ser.). 1978. reprint ed. lib. bdg. 26.95 (*0-405-10913-X*) Ayer.

Profession of Authorship in America, 1800-1870. William Charvat. 368p. 1992. text 57.50 (*0-231-07076-4*); pap. text 20.00 (*0-231-07077-2*) Col U Pr.

***Profession of City Planning: Changes, Images & Challenges, 1950-2000.** Ed. by Lloyd Rodwin & Bishwapriya Sanyal. 416p. 2000. text 49.95 (*0-88285-166-7*) Ctr Urban Pol Res.

Profession of City Planning: Changes, Images & Challenges, 1950-2000. Ed. by Lloyd Rodwin & Bishwapriya Sanyal. LC 99-33272. 416p. (C). 2000. pap. text 29.95 (*0-88285-165-9*) Ctr Urban Pol Res.

Profession of Conscience: The Making & Meaning of Life-Sciences Liberalism. Robert H. Sprinkle. LC 94-9662. 272p. 1994. text 32.50 (*0-691-03365-X*, Pub. by Princeton U Pr) Cal Prin Full Svc.

Profession of Counseling. 3rd ed. Frank A. Nugent. LC 99-32596. (Illus.). 506p. (C). 1999. 59.00 (*0-13-260944-4*, Macmillan Coll) P-H.

Profession of Dietetics. Ester A. Winterfeldt et al. LC 97-42006. 352p. 1998. 49.00 (*0-8342-0888-1*) Aspen Pub.

***Profession of Dietetics.** 2nd ed. Payne & Palaci. LC 99-32799. (Illus.). 192p. 1999. pap. text 32.00 (*0-13-646886-1*) P-H.

Profession of Faith. Lebert. 1995. pap. 4.95 (*0-8091-9443-0*) Paulist Pr.

Profession of Ignorance: With Constant Reference to Socrates. Martin McAvoy. LC 99-20590. 344p. 1999. 49.00 (*0-7618-1387-X*) U Pr of Amer.

Profession of Letters: A Study of the Relation of Author to Patron Publisher, & Public 1780-1832. A. S. Collins. LC 77-134832. 279p. 1973. reprint ed. lib. bdg. 39.50 (*0-678-00789-6*) Kelley.

Profession of Local Government Management: Management Expertise & the American Community. Roy E. Green. LC 89-3945. (Illus.). 268p. 1989. 65.00 (*0-275-93276-1*, C3276, Praeger Pubs) Greenwood.

Profession of Medicine: A Study of the Sociology of Applied Knowledge. Eliot Freidson. 440p. 1988. pap. text 16.95 (*0-226-26228-6*) U Ch Pr.

Profession of One's Own: Organized Medicine's Opposition to Chiropractic. Susan L. Smith-Cunnien. LC 97-38181. 224p. (C). 1997. 39.00 (*0-7618-0943-0*) U Pr of Amer.

Profession of Poetry, & Other Lectures. Heathcote W. Garrod. LC 67-302142. (Essay Index Reprint Ser.). 1977. 20.95 (*0-8369-0469-9*) Ayer.

Profession of Politics. Max Weber. Ed. & Tr. by Simona Draghici from GER. LC 89-22924.Tr. of Politik als Beruf. (Illus.). 98p. (Orig.). (C). 1989. pap. text 4.95 (*0-943045-04-5*) Plutarch Pr OR.

Profession of the Playwright: British Theatre, 1800-1900. John R. Stephens. 274p. (C). 1992. text 69.95 (*0-521-25913-4*) Cambridge U Pr.

Profession '79: Selected Articles from the Bulletins of the Association of Departments of English & the Association of Departments of Foreign Languages. fac. ed. Modern Language Association of America Staff. Ed. by Jasper P. Neel & Richard I. Brod. LC LB2365.L4P7. 65p. 1979. reprint ed. pap. 30.00 (*0-7837-8022-2*, 204777800008) Bks Demand.

Professional A. C. T. Acting, Communication, Technique. Mary Stark. (Illus.). 128p. (Orig.). 1993. pap. 12.95 (*1-55552-033-2*) Metamorphous Pr.

Professional Academic Writing in the Humanities & Social Sciences. Susan P. MacDonald. LC 93-11093. 256p. (C). 1994. 31.95 (*0-8093-1930-6*) S Ill U Pr.

***Professional Access 2000 Programming.** Felipe Martins et al. 800p. 2000. pap. 49.99 (*1-86100-408-7*) Wrox Pr Inc.

Professional Accident Investigation: Executive Investigator Training. Raymond L. Kuhlman. LC 78-56971. Date not set. ring bd. write for info. (*0-88061-014-X*) Intl Loss Cntrl.

Professional Accident Investigation: Investigator's Field Workbook. Raymond L. Kuhlman. LC 77-77275. Date not set. ring bd., wbk. ed. write for info. (*0-88061-013-1*) Intl Loss Cntrl.

Professional Accident Investigation: Methods & Techniques. Raymond L. Kuhlman. LC 77-77275. (Illus.). 262p. 1977. ring bd. 75.00 (*0-88061-012-3*) Intl Loss Cntrl.

Professional Accident Investigation: Supervisory Training. Raymond L. Kuhlman. LC 77-77275. Date not set. ring bd. write for info. (*0-88061-015-8*) Intl Loss Cntrl.

Professional Accountants: An Historical Sketch. Beresford Worthington. Ed. by Richard P. Brief. LC 77-87293. (Contemporary Accounting Thought Ser.). 1978. reprint ed. lib. bdg. 19.95 (*0-405-10920-2*) Ayer.

***Professional Accounting & Audit in Australia, 1880-1900.** Ed. by Garry D. Carnegie & Robert H. Parker. LC 99-33042. (New Works in Accounting History). 288p. 1999. reprint ed. 71.00 (*0-8153-3446-X*) Garland.

Professional Accounting Practice Management. Joseph T. Kastantin. LC 87-32261. 223p. 1988. 62.95 (*0-89930-290-4*, KPL/, Quorum Bks) Greenwood.

Professional Acting in Television Commercials: Techniques, Exercises, Copy & Storyboards. Pat Dougan. LC 94-33838. (Illus.). 214p. 1995. pap. 19.95 (*0-435-08659-6*, 08659) Heinemann.

***Professional Action: Teaching Student with Special Needs.** 1999. write for info. (*0-205-32011-2*) Allyn.

Professional Active Server Pages. Darren Gill et al. (Illus.). 500p. (Orig.). 1997. pap. 44.95 (*1-86100-072-3*) Wrox Pr Inc.

***Professional Active Server Pages 3.0.** Richard Anderson et al. 1200p. 1999. pap. 59.99 (*1-86100-261-0*) Wrox Pr Inc.

Professional Active Server Pages 2.0. 2nd ed. Brian Francis et al. LC 99-203426. (Professional Ser.). (Illus.). 1000p. 1998. pap. 59.95 (*1-86100-126-6*) Wrox Pr Inc.

Professional Activity Director: Be All You Want to Be. Marge Knoth. (Vital Handbook for Activity Directors Ser.). (Illus.). 164p. 1989. per. 16.99 (*0-927935-00-7*) Valley Pr IN.

Professional Activity Director: Be All You Want to Be. Marge Knoth. (Vital Handbook for Activity Directors Ser.). 164p. 1995. reprint ed. 16.99 (*0-927935-07-4*) Valley Pr IN.

Professional Activity Manager & Consultant. Ed. by Anne D'Antonio-Nocera et al. (Illus.). 452p. (Orig.). 1996. pap. 45.00 (*1-882883-24-1*, 297) Idyll Arbor.

Professional ADO & RDS Programming with ASP. Matt Brown et al. 585p. 1999. pap. 49.99 (*1-86100-164-9*, Pub. by Wrox Press) Wrox Pr Inc.

***Professional ADO 2.5 Programming.** David Sussman et al. (Professional Ser.). 800p. 1999. pap. 59.99 (*1-86100-275-0*) Wrox Pr Inc.

***Professional ADO 2.5 RDS Programming with ASP 3.0.** Charles Crawford Caison, Jr. et al. 700p. 1999. pap. 49.99 (*1-86100-324-2*) Wrox Pr Inc.

***Professional ADSI Programming.** Wrox Development Staff & Simon Robinson. 774p. 1999. pap. text 49.99 (*1-86100-226-2*) Wrox Pr Inc.

Professional Advertising Photography. Dave Saunders. (Illus.). 160p. 1990. 29.95 (*0-8442-3246-7*, NTC Business Bks) NTC Contemp Pub Co.

Professional Air Conditioning & Heating Labor Guide, 1989-91. Chilton Automotive Editorial Staff. 1920p. 1991. pap. 17.00 (*0-8019-8222-7*) Nichols Pub.

Professional Air Conditioning & Heating, 1989-91. 2112p. 1991. pap. 97.00 (*0-8019-8151-4*) Nichols Pub.

Professional Alcohol & Drug Counselor Supervisor's Handbook. 2nd ed. Lawrence Clayton & Randy Van Nostrand. Date not set. pap. 18.95 (*1-55691-159-9*) Learning Pubns.

Professional Altruist: The Emergence of Social Work As a Career, 1880-1930. Roy Lubove. LC 65-12786. (Publication of the Center for the Study of the History of Liberty in America, Harvard University Ser.). 299p. reprint ed. pap. 92.70 (*0-7837-4117-0*, 205794000011) Bks Demand.

Professional Amateur: A Handbook for the Variety Arts Performer. Toby Travis. 80p. 1996. pap. 15.00 (*1-57502-312-1*, P01060) Morris Pubng.

Professional Amateur: The Biography of Charles Franklin Kettering. Thomas A. Boyd. LC 72-5036. (Technology & Society Ser.). (Illus.). 242p. 1980. reprint ed. 20.95 (*0-405-04689-8*) Ayer.

Professional & Administrative Career Examination (PACE) Gary R. Gruber. (Exam Preparation Ser.). 300p. (C). 1976. pap. 6.95 (*0-685-04451-3*) S&S Trade.

Professional & Administrative Career Examination (PACE) Jack Rudman. (Admission Test Ser.). 43.95 (*0-8373-5126-X*) Nat Learn.

Professional & Administrative Career Examination (PACE) Jack Rudman. (General Aptitude & Abilities Ser.: No. CS-28). pap. 23.95 (*0-8373-6728-X*, CS-28) Nat Learn.

Professional & Administrative Career Examination (PACE) Jack Rudman. (Admission Test Ser.: Vol. ATS-26). 1994. pap. 23.95 (*0-8373-5026-3*) Nat Learn.

Professional & Business Guide to Creative Services '97. 1993. 170.00 (*0-9518494-0-9*, Pub. by Janvier Pubng Ltd) St Mut.

Professional & Business Guide to Design Services '97. Lanre. 1993. 250.00 (*0-9518494-1-7*, Pub. by Janvier Pubng Ltd) St Mut.

Professional & Continuing Education in Hong Kong: Issues & Perspectives. Lee Ngok & Agnes Lam. 184p. 1994. pap. 32.50 (*962-209-348-5*, Pub. by HK Univ Pr) Coronet Bks.

Professional & Ethical Issues in Psychology: Foundations of Practice. Walter B. Pryzwansky. LC 99-26042. 256p. 1999. 39.00 (*0-393-70285-5*) Norton.

Professional & Occupational Licensing Directory: A Descriptive Guide to State & Federal Licensing Registration, & Certification Requirements. 2nd ed. David J. Bianco. Ed. by Amanda Moran. 439p. 1995. 105.00 (*0-8103-9050-7*, 030306) Gale.

Professional & Occupational Licensure in the United States: An Annotated Bibliography & Professional Resource. Robert L. Hollings & Christal A. Pike-Nase. LC 97-39638. 176p. 1997. lib. bdg. 67.95 (*0-313-30440-8*, Greenwood Pr) Greenwood.

***Professional & Patient Responsibilities in Home Health Care Nursing.** Catherine Marrone. LC 99-31118. (Studies in Health & Human Services: Vol. 34). 196p. 1999. text 89.95 (*0-7734-7975-9*) E Mellen.

Professional & Personal Responsibilities of the Lawyer. John T. Noonan, Jr. & Richard W. Painter. (University Casebook Ser.). 171p. (C). 1997. pap. text. write for info. (*1-56662-577-7*) Foundation Pr.

Professional & Scholarly Publishing in the Digital Age. Professional/Scholarly Publishing Division, Electr. Ed. by Czeslaw J. Grycz. 144p. 1997. per. 25.00 (*0-933636-34-2*) AAP.

Professional & Student Portfolios for Physical Education. Vincent J. Melograno. LC 97-45626. (Illus.). 208p. 1998. pap. text 22.00 (*0-88011-809-1*, BMEL0809) Human Kinetics.

Professional & Technical Careers: A Guide from World Book. Ed. by World Book Staff. LC 97-20404. (Illus.). 496p. (YA). (gr. 7 up). 1998. write for info. (*0-7166-3311-6*) World Bk.

Professional & Technical Writing Strategies: Communicating in Technology & Science. 4th ed. Judith S. Vanalstyne. LC 98-13106. 673p. 1998. pap. text 61.00 (*0-13-954736-3*) P-H.

Professional & Vocational Regulations see Alaska Administrative Code--Register 150 Supplement (July 1999)

Professional & Vocational Regulations see Alaska Administrative Code 4/99 Supplement

Professional & White Collar Employment see History of Women in the United States: Topically Arranged Articles on the Evolution of Women's History in the United States

***Professional Apache.** Peter C. Wainwright. (Professional Ser.). 800p. 1999. pap. 49.99 (*1-86100-302-1*) Wrox Pr Inc.

Professional AppCenter Programming. Matt Odhner & Wrox Press Inc., Staff. 800p. Date not set. pap. 49.99 (*1-86100-447-8*) Wrox Pr Inc.

Professional Applicant Test Battery (CIA) (Career Examination Ser.: C-3587). pap. 29.95 (*0-8373-3587-6*) Nat Learn.

Professional Applied Ethics. Boylan. LC 99-46652. 210p. 1999. pap. text 23.80 (*0-13-674292-0*) P-H.

Professional Aquatic Management. 2nd ed. Robert D. Clayton & David G. Thomas. LC 88-8221. (Illus.). 208p. 1989. text 30.00 (*0-87322-217-2*, BCLA0217) Human Kinetics.

Professional Archery Technique. Kirk Ethridge. (Illus.). 128p. (Orig.). 1995. pap. 12.95 (*0-9646312-0-2*) Diff Dens Pubns.

Professional Architectural Photography. 2nd ed. Michael Harris. LC 98-8666. (Professional Photography Ser.). 192p. 2000. pap. text 32.95 (*0-240-51532-3*, Focal) Buttrwrth-Heinemann.

Professional Army Officer in a Changing Society. Sam C. Sarkesian. LC 74-10917. 264p. 1974. text 42.95 (*0-911012-62-1*) Burnham Inc.

Professional Arranger Composer, Bk. 1. Russ Garcia. 1954. 14.95 (*0-910468-05-2*) Criterion Mus.

Professional Arranger Composer, Bk. 2. Russ Garcia. LC 78-83425. 1978. 14.95 (*0-910468-06-0*) Criterion Mus.

Professional Articles for Elementary Counselors. Ed. by Priscilla A. Lorah. 1996. 126.55 (*1-55631-265-2*) Chron Guide.

Professional Artists' Resume, Biography, Cover Letter & Statement. Stanley Sporny & Laurel Williamson. Ed. by Mary Starnes & Drew Steis. (Art Calendar Guide Ser.). (Illus.). 98p. 1999. pap. 12.95 (*0-945388-14-4*) Art Calendar.

***Professional ASP Components.** Wrox Press Inc., Staff. 800p. 2000. pap. 49.99 (*1-86100-349-8*) Wrox Pr Inc.

***Professional ASP Data.** James De Carli et al. 500p. 2000. pap. 49.99 (*1-86100-392-7*) Wrox Pr Inc.

***Professional ASP E-Commerce Development with SiteServer.** Joe Stagner. 600p. 2000. pap. 49.99 (*1-86100-334-X*) Wrox Pr Inc.

Professional ASP MTS Web Security. Richard Harrison. 500p. 1998. 75.00 (*1-86100-182-7*, Pub. by Wrox Press) Wrox Pr Inc.

***Professional ASP N-Tier Applications.** 800p. 2000. pap. 49.99 (*1-86100-393-5*) Wrox Pr Inc.

***Professional ASP Site Indexing with Index Server 2.0.** Wrox Press Inc., Staff. 600p. 2000. pap. 49.99 (*1-86100-335-8*) Wrox Pr Inc.

Professional ASP Techniques for Webmasters. Alex Homer. LC 99-235659. 500p. 1998. pap. 49.99 (*1-86100-179-7*, Pub. by Wrox Press) Wrox Pr Inc.

***Professional ASP 3 Performance Tuning.** Juan T. Llibre. 600p. 2000. pap. 49.99 (*1-86100-309-9*) Wrox Pr Inc.

***Professional ASP UML.** Jake Sturm. 600p. 2000. pap. 49.99 (*1-86100-310-2*) Wrox Pr Inc.

***Professional ASP XML.** Bill Kropog et al. 750p. 2000. pap. 49.99 (*1-86100-402-8*) Wrox Pr Inc.

Professional Assistant: A Guide to Success for Real Estate Assistants. Monica Reynolds & Linda Rosen. LC 95-50124. 1996. pap. 34.95 (*0-7931-1774-7*, 1550-0101, Real Estate Ed) Dearborn.

Professional Associations & Municipal Innovation. Richard D. Bingham et al. LC 80-5119. 197p. 1981. reprint ed. pap. 61.10 (*0-608-01918-6*, 206257000003) Bks Demand.

Professional ATL COM Programming. Richard Grimes. LC 99-225818. 800p. 1998. pap. 59.99 (*1-86100-140-1*) Wrox Pr Inc.

Professional Audio Recording at Home. Jay Gluck. 100p. 1992. pap. text 9.95 (*1-882731-00-X*) Cactus Pub.

Professional Awareness in Software Engineering: Or Should a Software Engineer Wear a Suit? Ed. by Colin Myers. LC 94-45888. 1995. write for info. (*0-07-707837-3*) McGraw.

Professional Baking. Wayne Gisslen. 8p. 1996. pap. text 39.95 (*0-471-14541-6*) Wiley.

Professional Baking. 2nd ed. Wayne Gisslen. LC 84-26988. 400p. 1993. 54.95 (*0-471-59509-8*); pap., student ed. 25.00 (*0-471-30617-7*) Wiley.

Professional Baking. 2nd ed. Wayne Gisslen. LC 93-12377. (Illus.). 400p. 1993. 49.95 (*0-471-59508-X*) Wiley.

Professional Baking. 2nd ed. Wayne Gisslen. 160p. 1993. pap. text, teacher ed. write for info. (*0-471-30462-X*) Wiley.

***Professional Baking.** 3rd ed. Wayne Gisslen. LC 00-35180. 574p. 2000. write for info. (*0-471-34647-0*) Wiley.

Professional Baking: College Version. 3rd ed. Gisslen. 574p. (C). 2000. text 41.00 (*0-471-34646-2*) Wiley.

Professional Baking, College Version & Study Guide. 2nd ed. Walter Enders. 544p. 1993. student ed. 67.95 (*0-471-03999-3*) Wiley.

Professional Balance: The Careerstyle Approach to Balanced Achievement. Rick Griggs. Ed. by Elaine Fritz. 209p. 1989. 24.95 (*0-922530-00-9*) Tantalus Bks.

Professional Barber Styling State Board Exam Review. 1980. pap. 11.50 (*0-87350-502-6*) Milady Pub.

Professional Bartender's Educator. Jerry R. Elliott. (Illus.). 93p. (Orig.). 1982. pap. 5.95 (*0-317-00648-7*) J R Elliott.

Professional Bartending Basics see Mr. Austin's Commercial Bartending Basics

Professional Baseball in North Carolina: An Illustrated City-By-City History, 1901-1996. Chris Holaday. LC 98-17879. (Illus.). 259p. 1998. boxed set 35.00 (*0-7864-0532-5*) McFarland & Co.

Professional Baseball Rules Index. Jim Evans. 48p. 1991. pap. 9.95 (*0-9630626-1-1*) J Evans Acad.

Professional Baseball Trainers' Fitness Book. Major League Baseball Training Staff & Lee Lowenfish. (Orig.). 1988. mass mkt. 12.95 (*0-446-38751-7*, Pub. by Warner Bks) Little.

***Professional Behaviors in Athletic Training.** Susan Hannam. 160p. (C). 2000. pap. text 24.00 (*1-55642-409-4*) SLACK Inc.

Professional Beverage Management. Bob Lipinski & Kathie Lapinski. (Culinary Arts Ser.). 500p. 1996. text 46.95 (*0-442-02176-3*, VNR) Wiley.

Professional Beverage Management. Bob Lipinski & Kathie Lipinski. (Culinary Arts Ser.). 496p. 1996. 54.95 (*0-471-28737-7*, VNR) Wiley.

***Professional BizTalk.** Wrox Press Inc., Staff & Stephen F. Mohr. 800p. 2000. pap. 49.99 (*1-86100-329-3*) Wrox Pr Inc.

Professional Blackjack. Stanford Wong. 352p. 1994. pap. 19.95 (*0-935926-21-6*) Pi Yee Pr.

Professional Blues Guitar Transcriptions, No. 1. 19.95 (*1-56922-096-4*, 07-4058) Creat Cncpts.

Professional Blues Guitar Transcriptions, No. 2. 19.95 (*1-56922-099-9*, 07-4061) Creat Cncpts.

Professional Blues Guitar Transcriptions, No. 3. 19.95 (*1-56922-113-8*, 07-4067) Creat Cncpts.

Professional Bondsman: How to Start & Operate Your Own Bail Bond Agency. 2nd ed. Richard Wills. Ed. by Maureen Twyman. (Illus.). 114p. (Orig.). 1996. pap. 21.95 (*0-9622822-7-8*) Dragon Marina.

Professional Budo: Ethics, Chivalry & the Samurai Code for Lawyers, Doctors, Managers. George A. Katchmer, Jr. Ed. by Andrew D. Murray. LC 95-60694. 208p. (Orig.). (C). 1995. pap. 12.95 (*0-940871-31-9*, B023/319) YMAA Pubn.

Professional Burnout in Human Services Organizations. Cary Cherniss. LC 80-12136. 318p. 1980. 37.95 (*0-275-90462-8*, C0462, Praeger Pubs) Greenwood.

Professional Burnout in Medicine & the Helping Professions. T. Wessells, Jr. et al. LC 88-28409. (Loss, Grief & Care Ser.: Vol. 3, Nos. 1 & 2). (Illus.). 123p. 1989. text 39.95 (*0-86656-785-2*) Haworth Pr.

Professional Business Communication. 508p. (C). 1997. 40.00 (*0-536-00398-X*) Pearson Custom.

Professional by Choice: Milady's Career Development Guide. Harper & Victoria Harper. LC 93-32170. (SalonOvations Ser.). 143p. 1994. pap. 20.95 incl. audio (*1-56253-148-4*) Milady Pub.

Professional Visual C++ ISAPI Programming. Michael Tracy. LC 96-61409. 1996. pap. 39.95 (*1-874416-66-4*) Wrox Pr Inc.

Professional C++ Programmer. Marshall. (ITCP-UK Computer Science Ser.). 1997. pap. 42.99 (*1-85032-296-1*) ITCP.

Professional Cameraman's Handbook. 4th rev. ed. Sylvia E. Carlson & Verne Carlson. (Illus.). 578p. 1994. 52.95 (*0-240-80080-X*, Focal) Buttrwrth-Heinemann.

Professional Care for the Elderly Mentally Ill. Ed. by L. Matthew. 288p. 1995. pap. 44.75 (*1-56593-327-3*, 0657) Singular Publishing.

Professional Careers in Administrative & Technical Services. Jack Rudman. (Career Examination Ser.: C-2068). 1994. pap. 23.95 (*0-8373-2068-2*) Nat Learn.

Professional Careers in the Natural Sciences. Jack Rudman. (Career Examination Ser.: C-2386). 1994. pap. 23.95 (*0-8373-2386-X*) Nat Learn.

***Professional Careers Sourcebook.** 6th ed. 1000p. 1999. 105.00 (*0-7876-2646-5*) Gale.

Professional Careers Test (PCT) Jack Rudman. (Career Examination Ser.: C-622). 1994. pap. 23.95 (*0-8373-0622-1*) Nat Learn.

Professional Cemetery. Johnny Masiulewicz. LC 97-211041. 80p. 1997. pap. 10.00 (*0-9615879-4-6*) Puddinhead Pr.

Professional Certification & Registration for Water Resources & Related Disciplines. Ed. by A. Ivan Johnson. LC TD0357.P76. (AWRA Special Publication: Vol. 89-4). 64p. 1989. reprint ed. pap. 30.00 (*0-7837-9229-8*, 204998000004) Bks Demand.

Professional Certification Implications for Adult Education & HRD. Michael W. Galbraith & Jerry W. Gilley. (Eric Information Analysis Ser.). 38p. 1986. 6.00 (*0-318-22351-1*, IN 307) Ctr Educ Trng Employ.

***Professional Chaplaincy: What Is Happening to It During Health Care Reform?** Larry VandeCreek. 120p. (C). 2000. 49.95 (*0-7890-1172-7*); pap. text 22.95 (*0-7890-1173-5*, Haworth Pastrl) Haworth Pr.

Professional Charcuterie: Sausage Making, Curing, Terrines & Pates. John Kinsella & David T. Harvey. LC 95-43662. (Illus.). 304p. 1996. 49.95 (*0-471-12237-8*) Wiley.

Professional Charges for Building Surveying Services. Surveyors Publications Staff. (C). 1988. text 60.00 (*0-85406-402-8*, Pub. by Surveyors Pubns) St Mut.

Professional Chassis Electronic Service Manual European Cars, 89-91. 1344p. 1991. text 97.00 (*0-8019-8188-3*) Nichols Pub.

Professional Chef: Student Manual. Educational Foundation of the National Restaurant. 83p. (Orig.). 1992. pap., student ed. write for info. (*0-915452-91-X*) Educ Found.

Professional Chef No. 6: Exploring Wine Set. CIA Staff. 1997. 75.95 (*0-442-02303-0*, VNR) Wiley.

Professional Chef's Art of Garde Manger. 5th ed. John F. Nicolas. LC 92-23801. (Illus.). 286p. 1993. text 49.95 (*0-442-01153-9*, VNR) Wiley.

Professional Chef's Knife. Culinary Institute of America Staff. LC 77-26689. (Illus.). 64p. 1978. pap. 33.95 (*0-8436-2125-7*, VNR) Wiley.

Professional Chef's Knife. Culinary Institute of America Staff. (Professional Chef's Photo-Text Ser.). (Illus.). 64p. 1983. pap. 34.95 (*0-471-28986-8*, VNR) Wiley.

Professional Chef's Knife Kit. 2nd ed. CIA Staff. LC 99-24635. 160p. 1999. pap. 34.95 (*0-471-34997-6*) Wiley.

Professional Chef's Techniques of Healthy Cooking. Culinary Institute of America Staff & Mary D. Donovan. 640p. 1992. 49.95 (*0-471-28483-1*, VNR) Wiley.

Professional Chef's Techniques of Healthy Cooking. Culinary Institute of America Staff & Mary D. Donovan. LC 92-19495. (Illus.). 614p. 1992. 49.95 (*0-442-01126-1*, VNR); pap. 34.95 (*0-442-02555-6*, VNR) Wiley.

Professional Chef's Techniques of Healthy Cooking. Culinary Institute of America Staff & Mary D. Donovan. 640p. 1997. pap. 34.95 (*0-471-28836-5*, VNR) Wiley.

Professional Chef's Techniques of Healthy Cooking. 2nd ed. Culinary Institute of America Staff. LC 98-52145. 656p. 2000. 59.95 (*0-471-33269-0*) Wiley.

Professional Chiller System Monitoring. K. Calder. (C). 1994. pap. 60.00 (*0-86022-369-8*, Pub. by Build Servs Info Assn) St Mut.

Professional Choices: Values at Work. Ann A. Abbott. LC 87-34901. 163p. 1988. 18.95 (*0-87101-159-X*) Natl Assn Soc Wkrs.

Professional Cleaner's Personal Handbook. Don A. Aslett. Ed. by Carol Cartaino. (Illus.). 197p. (Orig.). 1994. pap. 10.00 (*0-937750-11-5*) Marsh Creek Pr.

Professional Cleaning & Building Maintenance: How to Organize a Money Saving Business or Department for Floor & Building Care. Bill Clarke. Ed. by William R. Griffin. 344p. 1965. reprint ed. pap. 25.00 (*0-944352-04-9*) Cleaning Cons.

Professional Codes: A Sociological Analysis to Determine Applications to the Educational Profession. Benson Y. Landis. LC 70-176974. (Columbia University. Teachers College. Contributions to Education Ser.: No. 267). reprint ed. 37.50 (*0-404-55267-6*) AMS Pr.

Professional Codes of Conduct in the United Kingdom: A Directory. Nigel G. Harris. 320p. 1989. text 130.00 (*0-7201-2017-9*) Continuum.

Professional Codes of Conduct in the United Kingdom: A Directory. 2nd rev. ed. Nigel G. Harris. 448p. 1996. 170.00 (*0-7201-2235-X*) Continuum.

Professional Collaboration: A Team Approach to Health Care. Carol M. Frattali. Ed. by Leah C. Lorendo. (Clinical Ser.: Vol. 11). 84p. (Orig.). Date not set. pap. text 9.00 (*0-910329-80-X*, 0111969) Am Speech Lang Hearing.

Professional Collection for Elementary Educators: A Selection Aid Focusing on Professional Material for Library Media Specialists & Elementary Teachers. Patricia P. Wilson. 295p. 1996. 38.00 (*0-8242-0874-9*) Wilson.

Professional COM Control Applications with ATL. Sing Li & Panos Economopolous. LC 99-494991. 500p. 1998. pap. 49.99 (*1-86100-170-3*) Wrox Pr Inc.

***Professional Com Patterns.** Keith Bottner. 400p. 1998. pap. 49.99 (*1-86100-137-1*) Wrox Press.

***Professional COM+ with VCC++** 500p. 2000. pap. 59.99 (*1-86100-320-X*) Wrox Pr Inc.

Professional Com Programming with IDL3 MIDL. Frank Bendroth. 500p. 1998. pap. 49.99 (*1-86100-225-4*) Wrox Press.

Professional Commitment: Issues & Ethics in Nursing. Carroll A. Quinn & Michael D. Smith. 208p. 1987. pap. text 32.00 (*0-7216-1098-6*, W B Saunders Co) Harcrt Hlth Sci Grp.

Professional Commodity Trader. Stanley Kroll. 181p. 1995. reprint ed. pap. 19.95 (*0-934380-26-0*, 72-S) Traders Pr.

Professional Communcation Workbook. 2nd ed. Sutton & Brown. 72p. (C). 1998. pap. text, wbk. ed. 12.70 (*0-536-01254-7*) Pearson Custom.

Professional Communication 70p. (C). 1996. text 17.20 (*0-536-59667-0*) Pearson Custom.

Professional Communication: The Social Perspective. Nancy Blyler & Charlotte Thralls. (Illus.). 320p. (C). 1992. 46.00 (*0-8039-3934-5*); pap. 19.95 (*0-8039-3935-3*) Sage.

Professional Communication Skills Pt. 1: Getting Your Ideas Across. rev. ed. James C. Campbell. (Skill Centered Leadership Ser.). 8p. 1997. pap., wbk. ed. 12.95 incl. audio (*1-891161-50-4*) ClamShell Pub.

Professional Communication Skills Pt. 2: Leading by Listening. rev. ed. James C. Campbell. (Skill Centered Leadership Ser.). 8p. 1997. pap., wbk. ed. 12.95 incl. audio (*1-891161-51-2*) ClamShell Pub.

Professional Communications in Eye Care. Ellen R. Ettinger. (Illus.). 272p. 1993. pap. text 49.50 (*0-7506-9306-1*) Buttrwrth-Heinemann.

Professional Competence & Higher Education: The ASSET Programme. Richard Winter & Maire Maisch. LC 96-11921. 224p. 1996. 79.95 (*0-7507-0556-6*, Falmer Pr); pap. 29.95 (*0-7507-0557-4*, Falmer Pr) Taylor & Francis.

Professional Competence & Quality Assurance in the Caring Professions. Ed. by Roger Ellis. 280p. 1988. lib. bdg. 55.00 (*0-7099-5313-5*, Pub. by C Helm) Routldge.

Professional Competence & Quality Assurance in the Caring Professions. Ed. by Roger Ellis. 256p. 1990. 29.95 (*0-412-34080-1*, A4447) Chapman & Hall.

Professional Competencies - Technology & the Librarian. Clinic on Library Applications of Data Processing. Ed. by Linda C. Smith. LC 84-6047. (Illus.). 144p. reprint ed. pap. 44.70 (*0-7837-1176-X*, 204170400022) Bks Demand.

Professional Competition & Professional Power. Ed. by Yves Dezalay & David Sugarman. LC 94-28910. 304p. (C). 1995. 85.00 (*0-415-09362-7*, C0444) Routledge.

***Professional ColdFusion 4.5.** Wrox Press Inc., Staff. 1000p. 2000. pap. 39.99 (*1-86100-454-0*) Wrox Pr Inc.

Professional Conduct: A Handbook for Chartered Surveyors. Ed. by Richard Chalkley. (C). 1991. 110.00 (*0-7855-6631-7*, Pub. by Surveyors Pubns) St Mut.

Professional Conduct & Discipline in Psychology. Larry J. Bass et al. LC 96-8182. 330p. 1996. pap. text 24.95 (*1-55798-372-0*) Am Psychol.

Professional Conduct & Practical Background. (Legal Skills for the 1990s Ser.). 1990. pap. 49.00 (*1-85431-101-8*, Pub. by Blackstone Pr) Gaunt.

Professional Conduct & Practical Background. Ed. by Blackstone Press Ltd. Staff. (C). 1991. text 65.00 (*1-85431-160-3*, Pub. by Blackstone Pr) Gaunt.

Professional Conduct Investigator. Jack Rudman. (Career Examination Ser.: C-2315). 1994. reprint ed. pap. 27.95 (*0-8373-2315-0*) Nat Learn.

Professional Conduct Manual. 2nd ed. National Association of School Psychologists. 1992. pap. text 12.00 (*0-932955-12-6*) Natl Assn Schl Psych.

Professional Conduct, 1998-99. 3rd ed. Debbie Abrahamson et al. LC 98-181977. (Inns of Court School of Law Ser.). 366p. 1998. pap. 42.00 (*1-85431-773-3*) Gaunt.

Professional Conduct, 1997-98. 2nd ed. Debbie Abrahamson et al. (Inns of Court School of Law Ser.). 362p. 1997. pap. 40.00 (*1-85431-680-X*, Pub. by Blackstone Pr) Gaunt.

Professional Conduct, 1996-97. 332p. 1996. pap. 38.00 (*1-85431-576-5*, Pub. by Blackstone Pr) Gaunt.

Professional Construction Management. 3rd ed. Donald S. Barrie & Boyd C. Paulson. 672p. (C). 1991. 79.38 (*0-07-003889-9*) McGraw.

Professional Contributions, No. 7. L. W. Leroy & Robert J. Weimer. 1984. pap. 2.00 (*0-685-09169-4*) Colo Sch Mines.

Professional Cooking. Wayne Gisslen. LC 82-2610. 179p. (C). 1983. pap. 16.00 (*0-471-89521-0*) Wiley.

Professional Cooking. 2nd ed. Wayne Gisslen. LC 88-818817. 187p. 1989. pap., teacher ed. 12.50 (*0-471-50091-7*) Wiley.

Professional Cooking. 3rd ed. Wayne Gisslen. 864p. (C). 1994. 60.00 (*0-471-59301-X*) Wiley.

Professional Cooking. 3rd ed. Wayne Gisslen. 1995. 39.95 (*0-471-14368-5*) Wiley.

Professional Cooking. 4th ed. Wayne Gisslen. LC 98-2773. 896p. 1998. 65.00 (*0-471-24563-1*); 60.00 (*0-471-23997-6*) Wiley.

Professional Cooking & Baking. Mary F. Ray & Beda Dondi. (Illus.). 450p. (C). 1981. teacher ed. 14.65 (*0-02-665440-7*); text 31.99 (*0-02-665430-X*); student ed. 7.77 (*0-02-665450-4*) Glencoe.

Professional Copy of Microeconomics. 6th ed. Robert Ekelund. (C). 2000. pap. text. write for info. (*0-201-63539-9*) Addison-Wesley.

Professional Copy of Economics. 6th ed. Robert Ekelund. (C). 2000. write for info. (*0-201-65755-4*) Addison-Wesley.

Professional Copy of Elementary Statistics. 3rd ed. Neil A. Weiss. (C). 1995. text. write for info. (*0-201-87765-1*) Addison-Wesley.

Professional Copy of Macroeconomics. 6th ed. Robert Ekelund. (C). 2000. pap. text. write for info. (*0-201-63540-2*) Addison-Wesley.

Professional Copy to Developmental Mathematics. 4th ed. Marvin L. Bittinger. (C). 1995. pap. text. write for info. (*0-201-88078-4*) Addison-Wesley.

Professional Copy to Elementary & Intermediate Algebra: Combined. Marvin L. Bittinger. (C). 1995. pap. text. write for info. (*0-201-88080-6*) Addison-Wesley.

Professional Copy to Prealgebra. 2nd ed. Marvin L. Bittinger. (C). 1996. pap. text. write for info. (*0-201-88079-2*) Addison-Wesley.

*__Professional CORBA.__ Wrox Press Inc., Staff. 1200p. 2000. pap. 59.99 (*1-86100-367-6*) Wrox Pr Inc.

Professional Core Cases for Teacher Decision Making. Gordon E. Greenwood & H. Thompson Fillmer. (C). 1996. pap. text 37.00 (*0-13-432840-X*, Merrill Pub Co) Macmillan.

Professional Corporate Guide: Organization, Administration, Termination, Employee Benefits, Forms & Laws. Prentice-Hall Staff. 1983. write for info. (*0-318-57211-7*) P-H.

Professional Corporations & Associations, 6 vols., Vols. 17, 17a, 17b, 17c, 17d & 17e. B. C. Eaton. 1970. 1140.00 (*0-8205-1563-9*) Bender.

Professional Correctness: Literary Studies & Political Change. Stanley Eugene Fish. 1999. pap. text 14.95 (*0-674-71220-X*) HUP.

Professional Correctness: Literary Studies & Political Change. Stanley Eugene Fish. (Clarendon Lectures in Economics). 160p. 1996. 25.00 (*0-19-812373-6*) OUP.

Professional Cosmetologist. John W. Dalton. (Illus.). 552p. (C). 1989. reprint ed. pap. text, teacher ed. 6.25 (*0-314-77883-7*); reprint ed. pap. text, teacher ed., student ed. 20.50 (*0-314-77879-9*) West Pub.

Professional Cosmetologist. 3rd ed. John W. Dalton. (Illus.). 552p. (C). 1989. reprint ed. text 35.50 (*0-314-77877-2*); reprint ed. pap. text 27.25 (*0-314-77878-0*) West Pub.

Professional Cosmetologist. 4th ed. John W. Dalton. 1992. text 42.50 (*0-314-73042-7*) West Pub.

Professional Cost Estimating. rev. ed. Walter W. Stoeppelwerth. 167p. 1990. pap. 37.50 (*1-882379-09-8*) HomeTech Info Systs.

*__Professional Counseling: Transitioning into the Next Millennium.__ Ed. by Charlotte G. Dixon & William G. Emener. LC 99-30363. (Illus.). 178p. 1999. 36.95 (*0-398-06985-9*); pap. 24.95 (*0-398-06986-7*) C C Thomas.

Professional Counseling Forms. 2nd rev. ed. Joseph R. Pfeiffer. 61p. 1996. 54.99 (*0-9655865-0-2*) Landscapes Pub.

Professional Counselor. 3rd ed. Garcia. 384p. 1995. pap. text, student ed. 26.00 (*0-205-19543-1*) P-H.

Professional Counselor: A Process Guide to Helping. Sherilyn N. Cormier & Harold L. Hackney. (Illus.). 352p. (C). 1987. text 27.95 (*0-13-725508-X*) P-H.

Professional Counselor: A Process Guide to Helping. 3rd ed. Harold L. Hackney & L. Sherilyn Cormier. LC 95-23597. 384p. 1995. 71.00 (*0-205-19192-4*) Allyn.

*__Professional Counselor: A Process Guide to Helping.__ 4th ed. Hackney & Cormier. 384p. 2000. 66.00 (*0-205-32934-9*) Allyn.

Professional Counselor: Competencies, Performance Guidelines & Assessment. 2nd ed. Dennis W. Engels & Joseph Dameron. 167p. 1990. pap. text 23.95 (*1-55620-075-7*, 72524) Am Coun Assn.

*__Professional Counselors in Private Practice.__ Richard Sinacola. 175p. 2000. pap. text 19.95 (*1-55691-174-2*) Learning Pubns.

Professional Crafter's Business Management & Marketing Guide. Barbara Brabec. (Illus.). 304p. 2000. pap. 16.95 (*0-87131-903-9*) M Evans.

*__Professional Crafter's Business Management & Marketing Guide.__ Barbara Brabec. LC 99-49966. (Illus.). 304p. 2000. 21.95 (*0-87131-902-0*) M Evans.

Professional Crime in India. P. K. Rao. 256p. 1983. text 27.50 (*0-685-14724-X*) Coronet Bks.

Professional Criminals. Ed. by Dick Hobbs. (International Library of Criminology, Criminal Justice & Penology). 424p. 1995. text 169.95 (*1-85521-414-8*, Pub. by Dartmth Pub) Ashgate Pub Co.

Professional Curiosity of a Martyr. J. Chester Johnson. 1988. pap. 5.95 (*0-914426-05-2*) Juliet Pr.

Professional Dance Musician & His Audience. Howard S. Becker. (Reprint Series in Sociology). (C). 1993. reprint ed. pap. text 5.00 (*0-8290-2620-7*, S-10) Irvington.

*__Professional Data Warehousing with SQL Server 7.0 & OLAP Services.__ Wrox Press Staff & Sakhr Youness. 600p. 2000. pap. 49.99 (*1-86100-281-5*) Wrox Pr Inc.

Professional Database Programming with Visual C++ 6.0. Wendy Sarrett. 400p. 1998. pap. text 49.99 (*1-86100-241-6*, Pub. by Wrox Press) Wrox Pr Inc.

Professional DCOM Programming. Richard Grimes. 1997. 49.95 (*1-86100-060-X*) Wrox Pr Inc.

Professional Degree Programs in the Visual & Performing Arts 1999. 5th ed. Peterson's Guides Staff. (Peterson's Guides). 591p. 1998. pap. text 26.95 (*0-7689-0112-X*) Petersons.

*__Professional Degree Programs in the Visual & Performing Arts 2001.__ 6th ed. Peterson's Guides Staff. 603p. 2000. pap. text 26.95 (*0-7689-0442-0*) Petersons.

Professional Dental Hygiene. Gurenlian. Date not set. text. write for info. (*0-7216-5005-8*) Harcourt.

Professional Developer's Guide to Visual C++ Que Development Staff. 1998. 49.99 (*0-7897-1457-4*) Que.

*__Professional Development.__ LC 99-170996. (S. Hrg. Ser.). iii, 39p. 1998. write for info. (*0-16-057634-2*) USGPO.

Professional Development. Ed. by Esther A. Meacham & Mabel M. Sarbaugh. 113p. (Orig.). (C). 1979. pap. text 9.00 (*0-89894-022-2*) Advocate Pub Group.

Professional Development. Ed. by Roberta Tovey. (Focus Ser.: No. 4). 36p. 1998. pap. 9.95 (*1-883433-05-3*) Harv Educ Letter.

Professional Development. 4th ed. Wilkes. (Freshman Orientation/College Success Ser.). Date not set. teacher ed. 2.25 (*0-534-51158-9*) Wadsworth Pub.

Professional Development. 4th ed. Wilkes. (Freshman Orientation Ser.). 1991. 38.25 (*0-534-51157-0*) Wadsworth Pub.

Professional Development: International & National Perspectives. Linda Darling-Hammond et al. 60p. 1995. pap. 12.00 (*1-56377-041-5*, SC9501) Am Assn Higher Ed.

*__Professional Development: Residencies, ASHP Midyear Clinical Meeting, & More.__ Katherine P. Smith & Sandra Baldinger. 70p. 1999. pap. text. write for info. (*1-58528-008-9*) Am Soc Hlth-Syst.

Professional Development: The Dynamics of Success. 5th ed. Mary Wilkes-Hull & C. Bruce Crosswait. 496p. (C). 1995. 68.95 (*0-534-51160-0*) Wadsworth Pub.

Professional Development & Educational Technology. LC 80-81616. 1980. 15.00 (*0-89240-036-6*) Assn Ed Comm Tech.

Professional Development As Transformative Learning: New Perspectives for Teachers of Adults. Patricia Cranton. LC 95-36272. (Higher & Adult Education Ser.). 226p. 1996. 34.95 (*0-7879-0197-0*) Jossey-Bass.

Professional Development Education. Kydd et al. LC 96-32326. (Leadership & Management in Education Ser.). 176p. 1996. 108.00 (*0-335-19812-0*); pap. 29.95 (*0-335-19811-2*) OpUniv Pr.

Professional Development for Cooperative Learning: Issues & Approaches. Ed. by Celeste M. Brody & Neil Davidson. LC 97-37732. (Illus.). 320p. (C). 1998. text 59.50 (*0-7914-3849-X*); pap. text 19.95 (*0-7914-3850-3*) State U NY Pr.

Professional Development for Educators of Adults: A Bibliography. Alexander N. Charters & Donald Holmwood. 1977. 8.00 (*0-87060-078-8*, CRE 3) Syracuse U Cont Ed.

Professional Development for Quality Care. Paul Shanahan. LC 96-21185. 1996. pap. text 50.00 (*0-443-05331-6*) Church.

Professional Development for Teachers: The Public's View. Steve Farkas & Will Friedman. 17p. (Orig.). 1995. pap. 7.50 (*1-889483-11-7*) Public Agenda.

Professional Development for Teachers of Mathematics: 1994 Yearbook. Ed. by Douglas B. Aichele. (Illus.). 248p. 1994. 22.95 (*0-87353-366-6*) NCTM.

Professional Development for Technicians. Johnson. (Heating, Ventilation & Air Conditioning Ser.). 1997. 110.00 (*0-8273-7349-X*); 15.95 (*0-8273-7350-3*); 12.00 (*0-8273-7351-1*) Delmar.

*__Professional Development Guide for Educators.__ Martha Green. LC 00-41887. (Multicultural Resource Ser.). 2000. write for info. (*0-8106-2012-X*) NEA.

Professional Development Guidelines for Registrars: A Self Audit. 192p. 1987. 15.00 (*0-614-23450-6*, 1241) Am Assn Coll Registrars.

Professional Development in Education: New Paradigms & Practices. Ed. by Thomas R. Guskey & Michael Huberman. 304p. (C). 1995. text 51.00 (*0-8077-3426-8*); pap. text 23.95 (*0-8077-3425-X*) Tchrs Coll.

Professional Development in General Practice. Ed. by David Pendleton & John Hasler. (Oxford General Practice Ser.: No. 37). (Illus.). 192p. 1996. pap. text 55.95 (*0-19-262532-2*) OUP.

*__Professional Development in Higher Education: New Dimensions & Directions.__ Gill Nicholls. 160p. 2000. pap. 29.95 (*0-7494-3207-1*, Pub. by Kogan Page Ltd) Stylus Pub VA.

Professional Development in Nursing: A Handbook for Practice. Ed. by Frank Quinn & John Humphreys. 1998. pap. 28.95 (*0-7487-3333-7*, Pub. by S Thornes Pubs) Trans-Atl Phila.

Professional Development in School. Joan Dean. (Developing Teachers & Teaching Ser.). 192p. 1991. pap. 35.95 (*0-335-09590-9*) OpUniv Pr.

Professional Development of Educators of Adults. Alexander N. Charters. (MS Ser.). (SPA.). 1977. 3.50 (*0-686-52209-5*, MSS 2) Syracuse U Cont Ed.

Professional Development of Graduate Teaching Assistants. Ed. by Michele Marincovich et al. 300p. 1998. 35.95 (*1-882982-24-X*) Anker Pub.

*__Professional Development Program: A Curriculum Guide for Teaching Career Enhancement Skills, Instructor's Guide.__ 1999. teacher ed. 24.95 (*0-933263-35-X*) Voc Indus Clubs.

*__Professional Development Program: A Curriculum Guide for Teaching Career Enhancement Skills, U. S. A. - VICA Instructor's Manual.__ 1999. teacher ed. write for info. (*0-933263-43-0*) Voc Indus Clubs.

*__Professional Development Program: Enhancing Your Career Skills, Special Projects Level.__ 1999. write for info. (*0-933263-41-4*) Voc Indus Clubs.

*__Professional Development Program: Enhancing Your Career Skills, Starter Kit.__ 1999. write for info. (*0-933263-42-2*) Voc Indus Clubs.

Professional Development Program: Enhancing Your Career Skills, U. S. A. - VICA Student Workbook. 1999. wbk. ed. write for info. (*0-933263-44-9*) Voc Indus Clubs.

*__Professional Development Program Level 1: Enhancing Your Career Skills, Student Workbook.__ 1999. wbk. ed. write for info. (*0-933263-36-8*) Voc Indus Clubs.

*__Professional Development Program Level 2: Enhancing Your Career Skills, Student Workbook.__ 1999. wbk. ed. write for info. (*0-933263-37-6*) Voc Indus Clubs.

*__Professional Development Program Level 3: Enhancing Your Career Skills, Student Workbook.__ 1999. wbk. ed. write for info. (*0-933263-38-4*) Voc Indus Clubs.

*__Professional Development Program Level 4: Enhancing Your Career Skills, Student Workbook.__ 1999. wbk. ed. write for info. (*0-933263-39-2*) Voc Indus Clubs.

*__Professional Development Program Level 5: Enhancing Your Career Skills, Student Workbook.__ 1999. wbk. ed. write for info. (*0-933263-40-6*) Voc Indus Clubs.

*__Professional Development School Partnership: Conflict & Collaboration.__ Renee W. Campoy. LC 99-89268. 160p. 2000. 62.50 (*0-89789-705-6*, Bergin & Garvey) Greenwood.

Professional Development Schools: A Directory of Projects in the United States. 2nd ed. Ismat Abdal-Haqq. 1995. 18.00 (*0-89333-130-9*) AACTE.

Professional Development Schools: Combining School Improvement & Teacher Preparation. Ed. by Lucinda Chance. LC 97-34895. (NEA School Restructuring Ser.). 1997. pap. write for info. (*0-8106-1869-9*, NEA Prof Lib) NEA.

Professional Development Schools: Schools for Developing a Professional. Ed. by Linda Darling-Hammond. LC 93-31823. (Series on School Reform). 240p. (C). 1994. text 45.00 (*0-8077-3320-2*); pap. text 19.95 (*0-8077-3319-9*) Tchrs Coll.

Professional Development Schools: Weighing the Evidence. Ismat Abdal-Haqq. LC 97-21137. (Critical Issues in Teacher Education Ser.). 96p. 1997. 39.95 (*0-8039-6349-1*); pap. 16.95 (*0-8039-6350-5*) Corwin Pr.

Professional Development Schools Policy & Financing: A Guide for Policymakers. Richard W. Clark. 1997. pap. 7.00 (*0-89333-152-X*) AACTE.

Professional Development Through Action Research in Educational Settings. Ed. by Christine O'Hanlon. LC 96-12656. 224p. 1996. 79.95 (*0-7507-0507-8*, Falmer Pr); pap. 29.95 (*0-7507-0508-6*, Falmer Pr) Taylor & Francis.

*__Professional Development with VISIO 2000.__ David Edson. (Illus.). 700p. 1999. pap. 49.99 (*0-672-31813-X*) Sams.

Professional Developments in Policy Studies, 297. Stuart S. Nagel. LC 91-38209. (Contributions in Political Science Ser.: No. 297). 288p. 1993. 69.50 (*0-313-28429-6*, NPV, Greenwood Pr) Greenwood.

Professional Development/Technology. Johnson. (Career Education Ser.). 1997. 28.95 (*0-8273-7347-3*) Delmar.

*__Professional DHTML.__ Wrox Press Staff. (Professional Ser.). 1200p. 2000. pap. 59.99 (*1-86100-284-X*) Wrox Pr Inc.

*__Professional DHTML Solutions.__ Wrox Press Inc., Staff. 800p. 2000. pap. 49.99 (*1-86100-292-0*) Wrox Pr Inc.

Professional Dictionary. Beverly L. Ritter. (Realtime Machine Shorthand Ser.). 279p. (Orig.). (C). 1992. pap. text 40.00 (*0-938643-12-6*) Stenotype Educ.

Professional Dictionary: Accounting/Tax/Banking/EPD. 4th ed. Arthur Anderson. 232p. 1996. 95.00 (*0-7859-9463-7*) Fr & Eur.

Professional Dietitian's Natural Fiber Diet. Margaret B. Salmon. LC 79-1262. 1981. pap. 4.95 (*0-725341-9*) Techkits.

Professional Digital Photography. Katrin Eismann & John McIntosh. 300p. 1997. 49.99 (*1-56830-374-2*) Hayden.

Professional Digital Photography. Frank J. Romano & Bill Erickson. LC 99-18428. (Illus.). 336p. 1999. 49.99 (*0-13-099745-5*) P-H.

Professional Dining Room Management. 2nd ed. Carol A. King. 224p. 1988. pap. 44.95 (*0-471-28934-5*, VNR) Wiley.

Professional Dining Room Management. 2nd ed. Carol A. King. (Illus.). 464p. 1988. text 36.95 (*0-442-24706-0*, VNR) Wiley.

Professional Directory, 1985. LC 72-623255. 220p. 25.00 (*0-685-43339-0*) Amer Inst Chem.

Professional Directory, 1988. 272p. 1987. 50.00 (*0-939293-02-1*) Amer Inst Chem.

Professional Directory, 1989. 250p. 1989. 50.00 (*0-939293-03-X*) Amer Inst Chem.

Professional Directory, 1987. rev. ed. Ed. by David A. Roethel. 225p. 1987. pap. 50.00 (*0-939293-01-3*) Amer Inst Chem.

Professional Discipline for Lawyers & Judges. 168p. 1979. pap. 19.95 (*0-685-07162-6*, 720-0014) Amer Bar Assn.

Professional Discipline in Nursing, Midwifery, & Health Visiting: Including a Treatise on Professional Regulation. 3rd ed. Reginald H. Pyne. LC 97-23059. 1997. pap. 34.95 (*0-632-04086-6*) Blackwell Sci.

Professional Dispensing for Opticianry. 2nd ed. Opticians Association of America Staff. 1996. text 80.00 (*0-7506-9889-6*) Buttrwrth-Heinemann.

Professional Diver's Log Book. Ed. by Best Publishing Co. Staff. 224p. (C). 1986. text 21.00 (*0-941332-01-2*, D019) Best Pub Co.

Professional Diver's Manual on Wet-Welding. David Keats. (Illus.). 80p. 1990. spiral bd. 59.95 (*1-85573-006-5*, Pub. by Woodhead Pubng) Am Educ Systs.

Professional Domesticity in the Victorian Novel: Women, Work & Home. Monica F. Cohen. LC 97-11305. (Studies in Nineteenth-Century Literature & Culture: No. 14). 230p. (C). 1998. text 54.95 (*0-521-59141-4*) Cambridge U Pr.

Professional Driver Workbook: Tractor Trailer Driver Training Workbook Based on the DOT Model Curriculum. Lewis J. Grill. (Illus.). 86p. (C). 1994. 13.25 (*1-881912-08-6*) Atlantic Pac Res.

*__Professional E-Commerce Site Security.__ Brian Matsik. 500p. 2000. pap. 59.99 (*1-86100-339-0*) Wrox Pr Inc.

Professional Edition JK Lasser Your Income Tax, 1995. Lasser Institute Staff. 1994. pap. 40.00 (*0-671-89880-9*) S&S Trade.

Professional Education. Peter Jarvis. 160p. 1983. pap. 16.95 (*0-7099-1456-3*, Pub. by C Helm) Routldge.

Professional Education for General Practice. Peter Havelock et al. (Oxford General Practice Ser.: No. 31). (Illus.). 200p. 1995. pap. text 49.95 (*0-19-262607-8*) OUP.

Professional Education for Social Work in Britain: An Historical Account. Marjorie J. Smith. 1965. 40.00 (*0-7855-2907-1*, Pub. by Natl Inst Soc Work) St Mut.

Professional Education in Public Works - Environmental Engineering & Administration. 71p. 1974. 5.00 (*0-917084-32-2*) Am Public Works.

Professional Education in the United States: Experiential Learning, Issues, & Prospects. Ed. by Solomon Hoberman & Sidney Mailick. LC 94-1148. 240p. 1994. 59.95 (*0-275-93386-5*, Praeger Pubs) Greenwood.

Professional Education of Elementary Teachers in the Field of Arithmetic. Arthur E. Robinson. LC 78-177196. (Columbia University. Teachers College. Contributions to Education Ser.: No. 672). reprint ed. 37.50 (*0-404-55672-8*) AMS Pr.

Professional Educator. Charles B. Myers. (Education Ser.). 1995. student ed. 17.50 (*0-534-20575-5*) Wadsworth Pub.

Professional Educator: A NEW Introduction to Teaching & Schools. rev. ed. Charles B. Myers & Lynn K. Myers. LC 94-23321. 634p. 1995. 88.95 (*0-534-20574-7*) Wadsworth Pub.

*__Professional Educators' Communications Guide: An Effective Tool for the Primary & Secondary Administrator, Teacher or Counselor.__ 2nd rev. ed. Joseph R. Sullivan & Fred Lealgren. Ed. by Jack Kennevan & Jeanne Kennevan. 109p. 1999. pap. 15.00 (*1-929112-05-X*) Personality Res.

*__Professional Effectiveness Through Supervision.__ P. Osborne & E. Van Ooijen. (Illus.). 320p. 2000. pap. write for info. (*0-443-05842-3*, W B Saunders Co) Harcrt Hlth Sci Grp.

Professional Engineer (PE) Jack Rudman. (Admission Test Ser.: Vol. 35). 89.95 (*0-8373-5135-9*) Nat Learn.

Professional Engineer (PE) Jack Rudman. (Admission Test Ser.: ATS-35). 1994. pap. 69.95 (*0-8373-5035-2*) Nat Learn.

Professional Engineers (Civil) License Reviewer (Solved Problems) Charles Li & Franquintin Talania. LC 89-81648. (Illus.). 300p. 1990. pap. 34.00 (*0-929176-07-3*) Burdick & Landreth Co.

Professional English Marketing. Maggie Jo St. John. 112p. 1993. pap. text 20.40 (*0-13-720046-3*) P-H.

Professional Enterprise Message Queing with C++ Srini Krishnamurthy. 500p. 1999. pap. 49.99 (*1-86100-187-8*, Pub. by Wrox Press) Wrox Pr Inc.

Professional Entry Test (PET) Jack Rudman. (Career Examination Ser.: C-3404). 1994. pap. 23.95 (*0-8373-3404-7*) Nat Learn.

P

Professional Environmental Auditors' Guidebook. Paul N. Cheremisinoff & Nicholas P. Cheremisinoff. LC 93-31337. (Illus.). 257p. 1993. 98.00 (*0-8155-1335-6*) Noyes.

Professional Environmental Management & Auditing. 238p. 1994. 39.95 (*0-934165-34-3*, 65349) Gulf Pub.

Professional Estheticians. 7th ed. Gerson. (SKIN). 1992. pap., wbk. ed. 22.50 (*1-56253-040-2*) Thomson Learn.

Professional Estheticians. 7th rev. ed. Joel Gerson. (Skin Ser.). 1992. pap. 43.25 (*1-56253-129-8*) Milady Pub.

Professional Estheticians: Answer Key. 7th ed. Gerson. (Cosmetology Ser.). 1992. wbk. ed. 30.00 (*1-56253-038-0*, VNR) Wiley.

Professional Ethics, Vol. 2.1. Ed. by Richard Franklin. (Studies in Christian Ethics). 134p. (Orig.). 1989. pap. 23.95 (*0-567-29169-3*, Pub. by T & T Clark) Bks Intl VA.

Professional Ethics: A Guide for Rehabilitation Professionals. Scott. (Illus.). 240p. (C). (gr. 13). 1998. pap. text 29.95 (*0-8151-2525-9*, 31051) Mosby Inc.

Professional Ethics & Civic Morals. Emile Durkheim. Tr. by Cornelia Brookfield. LC 83-12653. 228p. (C). 1983. reprint ed. lib. bdg. 75.00 (*0-313-24114-7*, DUPR, Greenwood Pr) Greenwood.

Professional Ethics & Civic Morals. 2nd ed. Emile Durkheim. (Illus.). 304p. (C). 1992. pap. 24.99 (*0-415-06225-X*) Routledge.

***Professional Ethics & Insignia.** 2nd ed. John Stierman et al. 766p. 2000. 125.00 (*0-8108-3620-3*) Scarecrow.

Professional Ethics & Organisational Change in Education & Health. Ed. by Christine Henry & Jane Pritchard. 143p. 1995. pap. 40.95 (*0-340-60142-6*, Pub. by E A) Routldge.

Professional Ethics & Organizational Change in Health Care & Educational Management. Ed. by Christine Henry. 160p. 1994. pap. text 40.99 (*1-56593-396-6*, 0818) Singular Publishing.

Professional Ethics & Practice in Organizational Development: A Systematic Analysis of Issues, Alternatives, & Approaches. Louis P. White & Kevin Wooten. LC 85-9523. 235p. 1985. 55.00 (*0-275-90007-X*, C0007, Praeger Pubs) Greenwood.

Professional Ethics & Primary Care Medicine: Beyond Dilemmas & Decorum. Harmon L. Smith & Larry R. Churchill. LC 85-16098. viii, 118p. (Orig.). 1986. text 39.95 (*0-8223-0521-6*); pap. text 16.95 (*0-8223-0540-2*) Duke.

Professional Ethics & Social Responsibility. Daniel E. Wueste. 240p. (Orig.). (C). 1994. pap. text 23.95 (*0-8476-7816-4*); lib. bdg. 62.50 (*0-8476-7815-6*) Rowman.

Professional Ethics & the Education Professoriate. Ed. by Ayers Bagley. (SPE Monographs). 1984. 10.00 (*0-933669-24-0*) Soc Profs Ed.

Professional Ethics for Accountants. 2nd ed. Brooks. LC 99-38151. (SWC-Accounting). 316p. 1999. pap. 40.95 (*0-324-01316-7*) Thomson Learn.

Professional Ethics for Audiologists & Speech-Language Pathologists. David M. Resnick. LC 92-34723. (Illus.). 196p. (Orig.). (C). 1993. pap. text 39.95 (*1-56593-087-8*, 0392) Thomson Learn.

Professional Ethics for Sport Managers. Earle F. Zeigler. (Monograph Series on Sport & Physical Education). 41p. (C). 1992. pap. text 4.80 (*0-87563-392-7*) Stipes.

Professional Ethics in Accounting. Leonard J. Brooks. LC 95-1648. 300p. (C). 1995. pap. 28.75 (*0-314-04603-8*) West Pub.

Professional Ethics in Health Care Services. Ed. by Eugene W. Kelly. LC 88-27691. (Illus.). 230p. (Orig.). (C). 1989. pap. text 22.00 (*0-8191-7211-1*); lib. bdg. 45.00 (*0-8191-7210-3*) U Pr of Amer.

Professional Ethics in Librarianship: A Real Life Casebook. Fay Zipkowitz. LC 96-11702. 173p. 1996. lib. bdg. 35.00 (*0-7864-0223-7*) McFarland & Co.

Professional Ethics in Nursing. Joyce E. Thompson. LC 89-2667. 232p. (Orig.). 1990. 23.50 (*0-89464-352-5*) Krieger.

Professional Ethics of Public Accounting. John L. Carey. Ed. by Richard P. Brief. LC 80-1476. (Dimensions of Accounting Theory & Practice Ser.). 1980. reprint ed. lib. bdg. 17.95 (*0-405-13506-8*) Ayer.

Professional Ethics of the Florida Bar. 2nd ed. Florida Bar Members. 1390p. 1996. ring bd. 50.00 (*0-910373-89-2*, 289) FL Bar Legal Ed.

Professional Evaluation: Social Impact & Political Consequences. Ernest R. House. LC 92-39718. (Illus.). 232p. (C). 1993. text 49.95 (*0-8039-4995-2*) Sage.

Professional Examination Study Guides Electives: International Purchasing. Institute of Purchasing & Supply Staff. (C). 1991. 250.00 (*0-7855-5700-8*, Pub. by Inst Pur & Supply) St Mut.

Professional Examination Study Guides Electives: Marketing. Institute of Purchasing & Supply Staff. (C). 1990. 250.00 (*0-7855-5704-0*, Pub. by Inst Pur & Supply) St Mut.

Professional Examination Study Guides Electives: Materials & Production Management. Institute of Purchasing & Supply Staff. (C). 1990. 250.00 (*0-7855-5705-9*, Pub. by Inst Pur & Supply) St Mut.

Professional Examination Study Guides Electives: Projects & Construction Management. Institute of Purchasing & Supply Staff. (C). 1990. 250.00 (*0-7855-5703-2*, Pub. by Inst Pur & Supply) St Mut.

Professional Examination Study Guides Electives: Public Services. Ed. by Institute of Purchasing & Supply Staff. (C). 1991. 250.00 (*0-7855-5702-4*, Pub. by Inst Pur & Supply) St Mut.

Professional Examination Study Guides Electives: Retail Merchandise Management. Institute of Purchasing & Supply Staff. (C). 1991. 250.00 (*0-7855-5701-6*, Pub. by Inst Pur & Supply) St Mut.

Professional Examination Study Guides Foundation Stage: Introduction to Purchasing & Supply Management. Institute of Purchasing & Supply Staff. (C). 1990. 250.00 (*0-7855-5710-5*, Pub. by Inst Pur & Supply) St Mut.

Professional Examination Study Guides Professional Stage: Purchasing & Supply Management I: Planning, Policy & Organisation. Institute of Purchasing & Supply Staff. (C). 1990. 250.00 (*0-7855-5709-1*, Pub. by Inst Pur & Supply) St Mut.

Professional Examination Study Guides Professional Stage: Purchasing & Supply Management II: Provisioning. Institute of Purchasing & Supply Staff. (C). 1990. 250.00 (*0-7855-5708-3*, Pub. by Inst Pur & Supply) St Mut.

Professional Examination Study Guides Professional Stage: Purchasing & Supply Management III: Logistics. Institute of Purchasing & Supply Staff. (C). 1990. 250.00 (*0-7855-5707-5*, Pub. by Inst Pur & Supply) St Mut.

Professional Examination Study Guides Professional Stage: Purchasing & Supply Management IV: Legal Applications. Institute of Purchasing & Supply Staff. (C). 1991. 250.00 (*0-7855-5706-7*, Pub. by Inst Pur & Supply) St Mut.

***Professional Excel 2000 Programming.** Stephen Bullen. 600p. 2000. pap. 49.99 (*1-86100-336-6*) Wrox Pr Inc.

Professional Excellence: System for Managing Professionals. Peter H. Burgher. LC 85-7296. 160p. 1986. 29.95 (*0-936033-00-2*) Agnes Press.

Professional Excellence for Secretaries: Practical Proven Techniques for Professional Development. Marilyn Manning & Carolyn Barnes. Ed. by Michael G. Crisp. LC 87-73561. (Fifty-Minute Ser.). (Illus.). 71p. 1988. pap. 10.95 (*0-931961-52-1*) Crisp Pubns.

***Professional Exchange 2000 Server Programming.** 600p. 2000. write for info. (*1-86100-400-1*) Wrox Pr Inc.

Professional F. E. Teacher: Staff Development & Training in the Corporate College. Ed. by Jocelyn Robson. 160p. 1996. 66.95 (*1-85972-113-3*, Pub. by Avebry) Ashgate Pub Co.

Professional Farm Manager. Robert C. Suter. LC 92-80663. (Illus.). 672p. 1992. 45.00 (*0-9632285-1-X*) RETUS.

Professional Feature Writing. Ed. by Bruce Garrison. (Communication Ser.). 416p. (C). 1989. text 79.95 (*0-8058-0483-8*) L Erlbaum Assocs.

Professional Feature Writing. 2nd ed. Bruce Garrison. (LEA's Communication Ser.). 528p. 1994. pap. 36.00 (*0-8058-1477-9*); text 89.95 (*0-8058-1476-0*) L Erlbaum Assocs.

Professional Feature Writing. 3rd ed. Bruce Garrison. LC 98-30121. (LEA's Communication Ser.). 480p. 1998. write for info. (*0-8058-3017-0*); pap. 45.00 (*0-8058-3018-9*) L Erlbaum Assocs.

Professional Financial Planner's Diary & Guide: 1998 Edition. Ed. by Jonathan D. Pond. Date not set. 40.95 (*1-57987-015-5*) Faulkner & Gray.

Professional Floral Design Manual. Ed. by Jim Morley. (Illus.). 72p. (C). 1989. text 24.95 (*0-944074-01-4*) AFS Education.

Professional Floristry Techniques. Malcolm Ashwell & Sally Pearson. (Illus.). 300p. text 49.95 (*0-85236-275-7*, Pub. by Farming Pr) Diamond Farm Bk.

Professional Football: The Official Pro Footbal of Fame Bibliography, 1. Myron J. Smith, Jr. LC 92-42677. (Bibliographies & Indexes on Sports History Ser.: No. 1). 432p. 1993. lib. bdg. 89.50 (*0-313-28928-X*, GR8928, Greenwood Pr) Greenwood.

Professional Forestry in the United States. Henry Clepper. LC 70-171107. 349p. reprint ed. pap. 108.20 (*0-7837-3139-6*, 201573700097) Bks Demand.

***Professional Foundations for Masterful Coaches: Expanding the Ordinary to Achieve the Extraordinary.** Lee Smith & Jeannine Sandstrom. (Illus.). 200p. 1999. pap. 35.00 (*0-9672175-0-4*) CoachWorks.

Professional Frenchman. Mac Wellman. (Blue Corner Drama Ser.). 70p. (Orig.). 1990. pap. 7.95 (*1-55713-115-5*) Sun & Moon CA.

***Professional Gambler's Handbook.** LC 00-41343. (Illus.). 2000. write for info. (*1-56980-166-5*) Barricade Bks.

Professional Gambler's Handbook: Beating the System by Hook & by Crook. Weasel Murphy. LC 97-136647. (Illus.). 208p. 1997. pap. 17.00 (*0-87364-915-X*) Paladin Pr.

Professional Garde Manger: A Guide to the Arts of the Buffett. David P. Larousse. LC 95-41073. (Illus.). 440p. 1996. 65.00 (*0-471-10603-8*) Wiley.

Professional Gentlemen: A Culture of Work & Its Reconstruction in Nineteenth-Century Ontario. R. D. Gidney & W. P. Millar. (Ontario Historical Studies). 508p. 1994. text 60.00 (*0-8020-0619-1*); pap. text 24.95 (*0-8020-7580-0*) U of Toronto Pr.

Professional Goldsmithing: A Contemporary Guide to Traditional Jewelry Techniques. Alan Revere. LC 90-35140. 1991. text 62.95 (*0-442-23898-3*) Chapman & Hall.

Professional Goldsmithing: A Contemporary Guide to Traditional Jewelry Techniques. 4th ed. Alan Revere. (Illus.). 240p. Date not set. reprint ed. 69.95 (*0-9651049-0-7*, Revere Acad) RAJA.

Professional Golf Shop. (Illus.). 106p. 1998. pap. 50.00 (*1-57701-166-X*, 99GCM03) Natl Golf.

Professional Grooming & Care of the Racehorse. T. A. Landers. Ed. & Illus. by Equine Research, Inc. Research Staff. 480p. (C). 1995. text 48.00 (*0-935842-10-1*) Equine Res.

***Professional GroupWise.** Bob Good et al. 750p. 2000. pap. 49.99 (*1-86100-395-1*) Wrox Pr Inc.

Professional Growth Activities for Teachers: Ready-to-Use Materials for Training. Michael Koehler. LC 99-19059. (C). 1999. pap. text 34.95 (*0-13-679812-8*, Macmillan Coll) P-H.

Professional Guide. Kathleen L. Pond. (Illus.). 250p. 1993. text 46.95 (*0-442-00148-7*, VNR) Wiley.

Professional Guide: Dynamics of Tour Guiding. Kathleen L. Pond. 288p. 1992. 59.95 (*0-471-28386-X*, VNR) Wiley.

Professional Guide for Young Engineers. William E. Eickenden. 52p. 1967. 2.00 (*0-318-12197-2*, EC43) Accred Bd Eng & Tech.

Professional Guide to Alcoholic Beverages. Kathleen A. Lipinski & Robert A. Lipinski. (Illus.). 548p. (C). 1989. text 55.95 (*0-442-25837-2*, VNR) Wiley.

Professional Guide to Bartending: An Encyclopedia of American Mixology. 2nd ed. Robert A. Plotkin. LC 91-60296. (Illus.). 183p. (C). 1991. pap. 29.95 (*0-945562-10-1*) PSD Pub.

Professional Guide to Diseases. 6th ed. Springhouse Publishing Company Staff. LC 97-42712. 1360p. 1998. 39.95 (*0-87434-926-5*) Springhouse Corp.

***Professional Guide to Management in the Public Sector.** Malcolm Prowle. LC 00-26417. 288p. 2000. 99.95 (*0-566-08216-0*, Pub. by Ashgate Pub) Ashgate Pub Co.

Professional Guide to Office 97. Gini Courter. 1997. pap. text 39.99 (*0-7821-2062-8*) Sybex.

Professional Guide to Signs & Symptoms. 2nd ed. Springhouse Publishing Company Staff. Ed. by Patricia Schull. LC 96-69114. (Illus.). 864p. 1996. 39.95 (*0-87434-856-0*) Springhouse Corp.

***Professional Guide to Signs & Symptoms.** 3rd ed. LC 00-30053. 2001. write for info. (*1-58255-074-3*) Springhouse Corp.

Professional Gun Dealing: Buying, Selling, & Trading Firearms for Fun & Profit. Ryan K. Kephart. (Illus.). 224p. 1993. pap. 20.00 (*0-87364-723-8*) Paladin Pr.

Professional Handbook of Diagnostic Tests. Matt Cahill. LC 94-39918. (Illus.). 704p. 1995. 32.95 (*0-87434-775-0*) Springhouse Corp.

Professional Headshots: How to Make Money Shooting Portfolios for Actors. John Hart. LC 94-15148. (Illus.). 144p. 1994. pap. 22.50 (*0-8174-5606-6*) Watsn-Guptill.

Professional Healthy Cooking. Sandy Kapoor. LC 94-37924. 341p. 1995. 54.95 (*0-471-53839-6*) Wiley.

***Professional Housekeeper.** 4th ed. Madelin Schneider et al. LC 98-16187. 320p. 1998. 59.95 (*0-471-29193-5*) Wiley.

***Professional Housekeeper Im.** Schneider. 1999. pap. text 0.01 (*0-471-35082-6*) Wiley.

Professional Hungarian Artists Outside Hungary. Leslie Konnyu. Ed. by E. Gy Kasas. LC 77-94982. (Illus.). 1978. pap. 10.50 (*0-911862-03-X*) Hungarian Rev.

Professional Hypnotism Manual. rev. ed. John G. Kappas. LC 78-107043. (Illus.). 276p. 1987. pap. 17.95 (*0-937671-53-3*) Panorama Van Nuys.

Professional Hypnotism Manual: Introducing Physical & Emotional Suggestibility & Sexuality. rev. ed. John G. Kappas. 1978. pap. 17.95 (*0-87505-250-9*) Panorama Van Nuys.

***Professional ICD-9-CM Code Bk,1999-2000, Vols.1-3.** St. Anthony's Publishing Staff. (Medical Assisting Ser). (C). 1999. pap. 56.00 (*1-56329-656-X*) Thomson Learn.

Professional Ideals of the Lawyer: A Study of Legal Ethics. Henry W. Jessup. xlii, 292p. 1986. reprint ed. 47.50 (*0-8377-2301-9*, Rothman) W S Hein.

Professional Illustration for Chemistry & Physics. 2nd ed. (C). 1983. write for info. (*0-8087-8430-7*) Pearson Custom.

Professional Imaginative Writing in England, 1670-1740: Hackney for Bread. Brean S. Hammond. 358p. 1997. text 85.00 (*0-19-811299-8*) OUP.

Professional Income of Engineers, 1998. Engineering Workforce Commission Staff. 175p. (Orig.). 1998. pap. 130.00 (*0-87615-204-3*) AAES.

Professional Instructor Exam Review. Howe St.John. (Career Development Ser.). 128p. 1995. 16.25 (*1-56253-315-0*) Thomson Learn.

Professional Instructor Workbook. Howe & Milady Publishing Company Staff. (Career Development Ser.). 1994. wbk. ed. 20.00 (*1-56253-232-4*) Thomson Learn.

Professional Instrument Flight Review Guide. Michael Dempsey. 112p. pap. write for info. (*1-57087-067-5*) Prof Pr NC.

Professional Integration: A Guide for Students from the Developing World. Mary A. Hood & Kevin Schieffer. LC 83-63519. 143p. (Orig.). 1983. pap. text 15.00 (*0-912207-02-7*) NAFSA Washington.

Professional Interactions: Oral Communication Skills of Science, Technology & Medicine. Matthews & Marino. 320p. 1990. pap. text 23.80 (*0-13-726084-9*) P-H.

Professional Interior Photography. 2nd ed. Michael G. Harris. LC 98-12353. 192p. 1998. pap. text 32.95 (*0-240-51475-0*, Focal) Buttrwrth-Heinemann.

Professional Interpersonal Skills for Nurses: A Practitioner's Handbook. C. Kagan & B. Kay. (Illus.). 288p. 1994. pap. text 39.95 (*1-56593-151-3*, 0463) Thomson Learn.

Professional Interviewing. Rob Millar et al. (International Series on Communication Skills). (Illus.). 224p. (C). 1991. pap. 27.99 (*0-415-04085-X*, A6297) Routledge.

Professional Issue Software Engineering. 2nd ed. Bott. 256p. 1995. pap. 29.95 (*1-85728-450-X*, Pub. by UCL Pr Ltd) Taylor & Francis.

Professional Issues for Translators & Interpreters. Ed. by Deanna L. Hammond. (ATA Scholarly Monographs Ser.: No. VII). viii, 216p. 1994. lib. bdg. 45.00 (*1-55619-626-1*) J Benjamins Pubng Co.

Professional Issues in Learning Disabilities: Practical Strategies & Relevant Research Findings. William Bender. 533p. 1998. text 43.00 (*0-89079-781-1*, 8554) PRO-ED.

***Professional Issues in Software Engineering.** 3rd ed. Frank Bott. LC 00-37780. 2000. pap. write for info. (*0-7484-0951-3*) Taylor & Francis.

Professional Issues in Speech & Language. Silverman. LC 98-29863. 210p. 1999. pap. text 33.00 (*0-205-27470-6*) Allyn.

Professional Issues in Speech-Language Pathology & Audiology. Carol Frattali. Ed. by Rosemary Lubinski. LC 93-44521. 396p. 1994. 55.00 (*1-56593-171-8*, 0480) Thomson Learn.

Professional Issues in Speech Language Pathology/ Audiology. 2nd ed. Lubinski. 2000. pap. 57.95 (*0-7693-0002-2*) Singular Publishing.

***Professional Java Corba.** 2000. write for info. (*1-86100-416-8*) Wrox Pr Inc.

***Professional Java Data.** 600p. 2000. write for info. (*1-86100-410-9*) S&S Trade.

Professional Java Fundamentals. Shy Cohen. LC 96-60892. 500p. 1996. pap. 35.00 (*1-86100-038-3*) Wrox Pr Inc.

***Professional Java MS Interoperability.** Naufal Khan et al. 900p. 2000. pap. 49.99 (*1-86100-289-0*) Wrox Pr Inc.

Professional Java Networking. Harish Rawat & Deepak Veliath. 1000p. Date not set. pap. 49.99 (*1-86100-460-5*) Wrox Pr Inc.

***Professional Java Programming.** (Illus.). 2000. pap. 49.99 (*1-86100-382-X*) Wrox Pr Inc.

Professional Java Programming Kit. Rizwan Virk. 2600p. 1996. pap. text 129.99 incl. audio compact disk (*1-57521-133-5*) Sams.

Professional JAVA Script Objects. Tom Myers. 450p. 1998. pap. text 49.99 (*1-86100-189-4*, Pub. by Wrox Press) Wrox Pr Inc.

***Professional Java Server Programming.** Danny Ayers et al. (Illus.). 1121p. 1999. pap. 59.99 (*1-86100-277-7*) Wrox Pr Inc.

***Professional Java Server Programming.** 2nd ed. Jason Diamond et al. 1200p. 2000. pap. 59.99 (*1-86100-465-6*) Wrox Pr Inc.

***Professional Java Swing Components.** Kenneth Krutsch. 600p. 2000. pap. 49.99 (*1-86100-364-1*) Wrox Pr Inc.

***Professional Java XML Programming with Servlets & JSP.** Tom Myers & Alexander Nakhimovsky. 400p. 1999. pap. 49.99 (*1-86100-285-8*) Wrox Pr Inc.

***Professional JavaScript.** Nigel McFarlane et al. (Professional Ser.). 1200p. 1999. pap. 49.99 (*1-86100-270-X*) Wrox Pr Inc.

***Professional JavaServer Pages.** Wrox Press Inc., Staff et al. 800p. 2000. pap. 49.99 (*1-86100-362-5*) Wrox Pr Inc.

***Professional Jini & JavaSpaces Programming.** Sing Li. 500p. 2000. pap. 49.99 (*1-86100-355-2*) Wrox Pr Inc.

Professional Job Changing System: An Easier Way to Find the Right Job. Bob Gerberg. LC 96-92340. (Illus.). 112p. 1996. 15.00 (*1-882885-08-2*); mass mkt. 4.95 (*1-882885-09-0*) Prince-Mstrs.

***Professional J2EE Programming with BEA Web Logic Server.** Francisco Gomez & Peter A. Zadrozny. 1000p. 2000. pap. 49.99 (*1-86100-299-8*) Wrox Pr Inc.

Professional Judgment: A Reader in Clinical Decision Making. Ed. by J. Dowie & Arthur S. Elstein. (Illus.). 584p. 1988. pap. text 38.95 (*0-521-34696-7*) Cambridge U Pr.

Professional Kitchen Design. Murray Shaw. (Illus.). 176p. (Orig.). 1996. pap. 24.50 (*1-57218-014-5*) Craftsman.

Professional Knowledge (Combined) Jack Rudman. (National Teacher Examination Ser.: NC-7). 1994. pap. 23.95 (*0-8373-8467-2*) Nat Learn.

Professional Knowledge Economy: The Management & Integration of Professional Services in Business Organizations. Pieter P. Tordoir. 1995. lib. bdg. 125.00 (*0-7923-3668-2*) Kluwer Academic.

Professional Landscape Management. David L. Hensley. (Illus.). 344p. (Orig.). (C). 1994. pap. text 26.80 (*0-87563-521-0*) Stipes.

Professional Law Enforcement Codes: A Documentary Collection. Compiled by John Kleining. LC 92-42673. 288p. 1993. lib. bdg. 75.00 (*0-313-28701-5*, GR8701, Greenwood Pr) Greenwood.

Professional Leadership: HSM 465. California College for Health Sciences Staff. 225p. (C). 1991. ring bd. write for info. (*0-933195-24-9*) CA College Health Sci.

Professional Learning Communities at Work: Best Practices for Enhancing Student Achievement. Richard Dufour & Robert Eaker. LC 98-160769. xx, 338p. 1998. pap. text 24.95 (*1-879639-60-2*) Natl Educ Serv.

***Professional Legal Ethics: Critical Interrogations.** Donald Nicolson & Julian S. Webb. LC 99-48741. 344p. 2000. text 85.00 (*0-19-876471-5*) OUP.

Professional Liability. James L. Branton & Jim D. Lovett. (Trial Lawyer's Ser.: Vol. 5). (Illus.). 349p. 1988. ring bd. 135.00 (*1-878337-13-0*) Knowles Pub Inc.

Professional Liability: An Economic Analysis. Roger Bowles & Philip Jones. (David Hume Papers: No. 11). 92p. 1989. pap. text 14.00 (*0-08-037962-1*, Pub. by Aberdeen U Pr) Macmillan.

Professional Liability: Guidelines in Obstetrics & Gynecology. Roberts. 1991. 275.00 (*0-8016-3357-5*) Mosby Inc.

Professional Liability: Insurance Text & Course Guide, 1997. Robert A. Bregman et al. (Registered Professional Liability Underwriter (RPLU) Ser.: Vol. II). 498p. 1997. ring bd. 115.00 (*1-886813-26-4*) Intl Risk Mgt.

Professional Liability: Law & Insurance. Ray W. Hodgin. LC 99-162114. (Lloyd's Commercial Law Library). lix, 703 p. 1996. write for info. (*1-85978-034-2*) LLP.

Professional Liability: Medical Text & Course Guide, 1997. Robert A. Bregman et al. (Registered Professional Liability Underwriter (RPLU) Ser.: Vol. IV). 374p. 1997. ring bd. 115.00 (*1-886813-28-0*) Intl Risk Mgt.

An Asterisk (*) at the beginning of an entry indicates that the title is appearing for the first time.

Professional Liability: Non-Medical Text & Course Guide, 1997. Robert A. Bregman et al. (Registered Professional Liability Underwriter (RPLU) Ser.: Vol. III). 540p. 1997. ring bd. 115.00 (1-886813-27-2) Intl Risk Mgt.

Professional Liability & Risk Management. Ed. by Bruce E. Bennett et al. LC 90-1199. 128p. (Orig.). 1990. pap. text 19.95 (1-55798-101-9) Am Psychol.

Professional Liability Insurance. 1990. 284.00 (1-886813-13-2) Intl Risk Mgt.

Professional Liability Insurance in Texas. Todd M. Baker. (Working Paper Ser.: No. 68). 27p. 1992. pap. 5.50 (0-89940-550-9) LBJ Sch Pub Aff.

Professional Liability of Architects. Pilling. 224p. 1998. pap. 59.50 (0-419-17900-3) Thomson Learn.

Professional Liability of Lawyers. Ed. by Dennis Campbell & Christian Campbell. 400p. 1995. 175.00 (1-85044-869-8) LLP.

Professional Liability of Lawyers in Florida. Florida Bar Members. LC 89-81848. 378p. 1993. ring bd. 30.00 (0-945979-05-3, 203) FL Bar Legal Ed.

Professional Liability-Risk Management: A Manual for Surgeons. Ed. by Paul F. Nora. 240p. 1991. pap. text. write for info. (0-9620370-8-7) Am Coll Surgeons.

Professional Liability-Risk Management: A Manual for Surgeons. 2nd ed. Paul F. Nora & American College of Surgeons Staff. LC 96-35880. 1997. pap. write for info. (1-880696-08-8) Am Coll Surgeons.

***Professional Liability to Third Parties.** Jay M. Feinman. LC 00-35536. 2000. write for info. (1-57073-781-9) Amer Bar Assn.

Professional Library Examination. Jack Rudman. (Career Examination Ser.: C-623). 1994. pap. 29.95 (0-8373-0623-X) Nat Learn.

Professional Life of Mr. Dibdin, Written by Himself, 4 vols. in 2. Charles Dibdin. LC 80-2272. reprint ed. 150.00 (0-404-18835-4) AMS Pr.

Professional Lifeguard Textbook. American Red Cross Staff. 96p. (C). (gr. 13). 1994. pap. text 10.00 (0-8016-7554-5) Mosby Inc.

Professional Lighting Handbook. 2nd ed. Verne Carlson & Sylvia E. Carlson. (Illus.). 256p. 1991. 52.95 (0-240-80020-6, Focal) Buttrwrth-Heinemann.

***Professional Linux Deployment.** Michael Boerner et al. (Professional Ser.). 1000p. 1999. pap. 49.99 (1-86100-287-4) Wrox Pr Inc.

***Professional Linux Programming.** Jens Axboe et al. 750p. 2000. pap. 49.99 (1-86100-301-3) Wrox Pr Inc.

Professional Lives in America: Structure & Aspiration, 1750-1850. Daniel H. Calhoun. LC 65-22042. (Center for the Study of the History of Liberty in America Ser.). (Illus.). 247p. reprint ed. 76.60 (0-8357-9174-2, 201774500007) Bks Demand.

Professional Locksmithing Techniques. Bill Phillips. (Illus.). 400p. 1991. pap. 25.95 (0-8306-3523-8) McGraw-Hill Prof.

Professional Locksmithing Techniques. 2nd ed. Bill Phillips. 426p. 1996. pap. 36.95 (0-07-049867-9) McGraw.

Professional Look at S & P Day Trading. Donald Trivette. (Illus.). 72p. 1998. pap. 29.00 (0-934380-49-X, 1394) Traders Pr.

***Professional Macromedia Generator Programming.** Branden Hall et al. 800p. 2000. pap. 49.99 (1-86100-455-9) Wrox Pr Inc.

Professional Magic for Amateurs. Walter B. Gibson. (Illus.). 223p. 1974. reprint ed. pap. 6.95 (0-486-23012-0) Dover.

Professional Management of Housekeeping Operations. 2nd ed. Robert J. Martin & Tom Jones. LC 91-34407. 480p. 1992. 59.95 (0-471-54779-4); pap., teacher ed. write for info. (0-471-55825-7) Wiley.

***Professional Management of Housekeeping Operations.** 3rd ed. Robert J. Martin. LC 97-29029. 528p. 1998. 59.95 (0-471-19862-5) Wiley.

Professional-Managerial Class: Contemporary British Management in the Pursuer Mode. Ed. by Ian Glover & Michael Hughes. 336p. (C). 1996. 77.95 (1-85972-027-7, Pub. by Avebry) Ashgate Pub Co.

Professional Manicure Bible. Betty Morgan. LC 85-63875. (Illus.). 300p. 1985. pap. text 45.00 (0-936789-01-8) Ramif HI.

Professional Manuscript Paper. (Twelve Stave Bks.). 1990. 3.95 (0-685-32062-6, G068) Hansen Ed Mus.

Professional Mediation of Civil Disputes. Robert Coulson. LC 84-72418. 62p. 1984. pap. 7.50 (0-943001-18-8) Am Arbitration.

Professional Medical Assistant: Clinical Practice. Bonnie J. Lindsey & Francis M. Rayburn. LC 92-18589. 316p. 1990. pap. 34.95 (0-8273-4150-4) Delmar.

Professional Medical Assistant: Clinical Practice CTB. Bonnie J. Lindsey. (Medical Assisting Ser.). 1993. 62.95 (0-8273-5901-2) Delmar.

Professional Medical Assistant Clinical Practice: Instructor's Resource Guide. Bonnie J. Lindsey & Francis M. Rayburn. 216p. 1990. pap., teacher ed. 18.00 (0-8273-4151-2) Delmar.

Professional Medical Assistant Clinical Practice: Workbook. Bonnie J. Lindsey & Francis M. Rayburn. 134p. 1991. pap., wbk. ed. 16.95 (0-8273-4155-5) Delmar.

Professional Medical Secretary. Aurandt. 1984. teacher ed. 30.95 (0-87350-336-8) Milady Pub.

Professional Medical Secretary. Aurandt. 1989. text 29.95 (0-87350-333-3) Milady Pub.

Professional Medical Secretary Student Transcripts. Aurandt. (General Business & Business Education Ser.). 1986. pap. 28.00 (0-87350-608-1, VNR) Wiley.

***Professional Medicolegal Death Investigator Series Training Module A: Interacting with Federal, State & Local Agencies.** Ed. by Steven C. Clark. 2000. wbk. ed. 5.50 (0-9651299-2-6) Occupat Res.

***Professional Medicolegal Death Investigator Series Training Module B: Communicating.** Ed. by Steven C. Clark. 2000. 9.50 (0-9651299-3-4) Occupat Res.

***Professional Medicolegal Death Investigator Series Training Module C: Interacting with Families.** Ed. by Steven C. Clark. 2000. 5.50 (0-9651299-4-2) Occupat Res.

***Professional Medicolegal Death Investigator Series Training Module D: Investigating Deaths.** Ed. by Steven C. Clark. 2000. 10.50 (0-9651299-5-0) Occupat Res.

***Professional Medicolegal Death Investigator Series Training Module E: Identifying & Preserving Evidence.** Ed. by Steven C. Clark. 2000. 3.50 (0-9651299-6-9) Occupat Res.

***Professional Medicolegal Death Investigator Series Training Module F: Maintaining Ethical & Legal Responsibilities.** Ed. by Steven C. Clark. 2000. 5.50 (0-9651299-7-7) Occupat Res.

***Professional Medicolegal Death Investigator Series Training Module G: Demonstrating Scientific Knowledge.** Ed. by Steven C. Clark. (Illus.). 2000. 7.50 (0-9651299-8-5) Occupat Res.

***Professional Medicolegal Death Investigator Series Training Module H: Coping with Job-Related Stress.** Ed. by Steven C. Clark. (Illus.). 2000. 1.50 (0-9651299-9-3) Occupat Res.

***Professional Medicolegal Death Investigator Series Training Modules.** Ed. by Steven C. Clark. (Illus.). 2000. 49.00 (0-9651299-1-8) Occupat Res.

Professional Meeting Planner's Start-Up Guide. International Society of Meeting Planners Staff. 72p. (Orig.). Date not set. pap. 65.00 (0-614-23688-6) Todd Pub.

***Professional Metadata: With DTDs, XML Schemas, Topic Maps, RDF, WebDav, XML Servers.** David Dobbs. 1000p. 2000. pap. 59.99 (1-86100-451-6) Wrox Pr Inc.

***Professional MFC with Visual C++ 6.0.** Mike Blaszczak. 1203p. 1999. 64.99 (1-86100-015-4) Wrox Pr Inc.

Professional Microphone Techniques. David Miles Huber. LC 98-67693. 1998. pap. 39.95 (0-87288-685-9) Intertec Pub.

Professional Military Education: An Asset for Peace & Progress. William J. Taylor, Jr. LC 97-164277. (CSIS Report Ser.). 1997. pap. text 21.95 (0-89206-297-5) CSIS.

Professional Military Education for Air Force Officers: Comments & Criticisms. Richard L. Davis & Frank P. Donnini. LC 91-15110. (Illus.). 136p. 1991. pap. 9.00 (1-58566-039-6) Air Univ.

***Professional Military Education in the United States: A Historical Dictionary.** William E. Simons. LC 99-43507. 408p. 2000. lib. bdg. 95.00 (0-313-29749-5) Greenwood.

***Professional Mobile Computing.** Ackerman. (Illus.). 2000. pap. 49.99 (1-86100-389-7) Wrox Pr Inc.

Professional Modelmaking: A Handbook of Techniques & Materials for Architects & Designers. Norman Trudeau. LC 94-42679. (Illus.). 176p. 1995. pap. 35.00 (0-8230-4098-4, Whitney Lib) Watsn-Guptill.

Professional Model's Handbook: A Comprehensive Guide to Modeling & Related Fields. Linda Balhorn. (Career Development Ser.). (Illus.). 512p. 1990. 34.50 (0-87350-376-7) Thomson Learn.

Professional MTS & MSMQ Programming with VB & ASP. Alex Homer & David Sussman. 512p. 1998. pap. 49.99 (1-86100-146-0) Wrox Pr Inc.

***Professional Musician's Internet Guide.** Ron Simpson. 2000. pap. 34.95 (0-87288-738-3) Intertec Pub.

Professional MySQL Programming. Wrox Press Inc., Staff. 1000p. Date not set. pap. 49.99 (1-86100-428-1) Wrox Pr Inc.

Professional Nanny. Bassett. (Early Childhood Education Ser.). 1997. teacher ed. 10.50 (0-8273-7385-6) Delmar.

Professional Nanny. Monica M. Bassett. LC 97-7422. (Early Childhood Education Ser.). 380p. (C). 1997. pap. 49.95 (0-8273-7384-8) Delmar.

Professional Natural History Photography. Nigel Hicks. LC 99-223817. (Illus.). 182p. 1999. pap. text 32.95 (0-240-51521-8, Focal) Buttrwrth-Heinemann.

***Professional NDS.** Wrox Press Inc., Staff. 800p. 2000. pap. 49.99 (1-86100-396-X) Wrox Pr Inc.

Professional Negligence. A. M. Dugdale & K. M. Stanton. (C). 1988. 500.00 (0-7855-4056-3, Pub. by Witherby & Co) St Mut.

Professional Negligence. Ashley Underwood & Stephen Holt. 1981. 85.00 (0-7855-7322-4, Pub. by Fourmat Pub) St Mut.

Professional Negligence. 2nd ed. A. M. Dugdale et al. 1989. 140.00 (0-406-17911-5, U.K., MICHIE) LEXIS Pub.

Professional Negligence: Malpractice Law in New Jersey. 3rd ed. Albert Cohn & Barry Knopf. 547p. 1991. 75.00 (0-685-65977-1) NJ Inst CLE.

Professional Negligence & Insurance Law. Jones, Neil F., & Co. Staff. Ed. by Jeffrey C. Brown. (Lloyd's List Practical Guide Ser.). 200p. 1994. 95.00 (1-85044-515-X) LLP.

Professional Negligence & Insurance Law: A Lloyd's of London Press Industry Report. Ed. by Jeffrey C. Brown. 96p. 1991. pap. 160.00 (1-85044-348-3) LLP.

Professional Negligence (Underwood & Holt's) 2nd ed. Hilton Harrop-Griffiths & J. Bennington. (C). 1985. 110.00 (0-7855-4055-5, Pub. by Witherby & Co) St Mut.

Professional Negotiations for Media-Library Professionals: District & School. Rolland G. Billings & Errol Goldman. LC 80-67724. 70p. 1980. pap. 8.50 (0-89240-037-4) Assn Ed Comm Tech.

Professional Netscape Visual Javascript. 1997. 39.99 (0-7897-1501-5) Que.

Professional Networker's Handbook. 560p. 1999. 35.00 (1-57870-186-4) Cisco Press.

Professional News Reporting. Bruce Garrison. (Communication Textbooks, Journalism Subseries). 352p. (C). 1992. pap. 39.95 (0-8058-1021-8); text 69.95 (0-8058-1020-X) L Erlbaum Assocs.

Professional News Writing. Bruce Garrison. (Communication Ser.). 312p. (C). 1990. student ed., wbk. ed. 17.50 (0-8058-0970-8); pap. 42.00 (0-8058-0827-2); text 99.95 (0-8058-0734-9) L Erlbaum Assocs.

Professional News Writing. Bruce Garrison. (Communication Ser.). (C). 1991. teacher ed. write for info. (0-8058-0971-6) L Erlbaum Assocs.

Professional NT Internet Information Server 2 Admin. Christian Gross & Sohail Gani. LC 96-60893. 550p. 1996. pap. 40.00 (1-86100-048-0) Wrox Pr Inc.

Professional NT Services. Kevin Miller. 450p. 1998. pap. 49.99 (1-86100-130-4, Pub. by Wrox Press) Wrox Pr Inc.

Professional Nurse. Jack Rudman. (Career Examination Ser.: C-624). 1994. pap. 29.95 (0-8373-0624-8) Nat Learn.

Professional Nurse: Coping with Change, Now & the Future. M. Bowman. (Illus.). 272p. 1994. pap. text 44.95 (1-56593-297-8, 0621) Singular Publishing.

Professional Nurse: Coping with Change, Now & the Future. Michael Bowman. LC 94-72657. 246p. 1995. pap. 41.50 (0-412-47100-0) Chapman & Hall.

Professional-Nurse Handbook. 3rd ed. Melodie Chenevert. (Illus.). 192p. (C). (gr. 13). 1996. pap. text 22.00 (0-8151-1215-7, 29588) Mosby Inc.

Professional Nursing: Concepts & Challenges. 2nd ed. Kay K. Chitty. Ed. by Maura Connor. (Illus.). 576p. 1996. pap. text 32.00 (0-7216-6882-8, W B Saunders Co) Harcrt Hlth Sci Grp.

Professional Nursing: Concepts & Challenges. 2nd ed. Kay K. Chitty. (Illus.). 575p. 1997. pap., teacher ed. write for info. (0-7216-6883-6, W B Saunders Co) Harcrt Hlth Sci Grp.

Professional Nursing Practice. Marilyn H. Oermann. (Orig.). (C). 1996. pap. text 32.95 (0-8385-8114-5, A8114-9) Appleton & Lange.

Professional Nursing Practice: A Conceptual Approach. Marilyn H. Oermann. LC 90-6351. (Illus.). 347p. 1991. reprint ed. pap. 107.60 (0-608-05811-4, 205977600007) Bks Demand.

Professional Nursing Practice: Concepts & Perspectives. 3rd ed. Barbara Kozier. LC 96-17922. 470p. (C). 1996. pap. text 51.00 (0-8053-3523-4) Addison-Wesley.

Professional Office Procedures. Jolene Scriven et al. 1992. teacher ed. 14.04 (0-02-650864-8) Glencoe.

Professional Office Procedures. 2nd ed. Cooperman. LC 98-30199. 270p. 1998. pap. text 48.00 (0-13-979576-6) P-H.

***Professional Oracle 8i Programming.** Wrox Press Inc., Staff. 750p. 2000. pap. 59.99 (1-86100-353-6) Wrox Pr Inc.

***Professional Oracle 8i XML.** Wrox Press Inc., Staff. 500p. 2000. pap. 49.99 (1-86100-399-4) Wrox Pr Inc.

***Professional Orientation to Counseling.** 3rd ed. Nicolas Vacc. 2000. 45.95 (1-56032-851-7) Taylor & Francis.

***Professional Outlook 2000 Programming.** Ken Slovak et al. 651p. 1999. pap. 49.99 (1-86100-331-5) Wrox Pr Inc.

Professional Painted Finishes: A Guide to the Art & Business of Decorative Painting. Ina B. Marx et al. (Illus.). 240p. 1991. 45.00 (0-8230-4418-1, Whitney Lib) Watsn-Guptill.

***Professional Palm Programming.** Wrox Press Inc., Staff. 1200p. 2000. pap. 49.99 (1-86100-450-8) Wrox Pr Inc.

Professional Paralegal Job Search: A Guide for Launching Your Legal Career. Christopher French. 224p. 1995. pap. text 24.95 (0-316-29436-5, Aspen Law & Bus) Aspen Pub.

Professional Paranoid: How to Fight Back If Stalked, Surveilled, Investigated or Targeted by Any Agency, Organization, or Individual. H. Michael Sweeney. (Illus.). 220p. 1998. pap. 12.95 (0-922915-54-7) Feral Hse.

Professional Partnerships: The Student Teaching Experience. 3rd ed. Billie Enz et al. 192p. (C). 1996. pap. text, per. 31.95 (0-7872-2672-6, 41267201) Kendall-Hunt.

Professional Pastry Chef. B. Friberg. (Illus.). 1154p. 1996. text 59.95 (0-442-01597-6, VNR) Wiley.

Professional Pastry Chef. 3rd ed. Bo Friberg. 1184p. 1995. 59.95 (0-471-28576-5, VNR) Wiley.

Professional Pattern Grading. Jack Handford. LC 79-91230. (Illus.). 1980. 25.95 (0-916434-34-6) Plycon Pr.

Professional Pattern Making for Designer's of Women's Wear & Men's Casual Wear. Jack Handford. LC 74-78635. (Illus.). 1984. spiral bd. 25.95 (0-916434-20-6) Plycon Pr.

***Professional Patterns for Tie-Backs.** Catherine Merrick. 1999. pap. 25.00 (0-9516841-3-2) Merk & Day.

Professional People Puppets. David Cole & Elaine Cole. (Illus.). 32p. (Orig.). 1994. pap. 12.95 (1-883426-08-1) Chldrns Outrch.

***Professional Perl Programming.** Simon Cozens et al. 1100p. 2000. pap. 59.99 (1-86100-449-4) Wrox Pr Inc.

***Professional Perspectives on Indexing.** Fabozzi. 1998. text 75.00 incl. audio (0-07-067687-9) McGraw-Hill Prof.

Professional Perspectives on Indexing. Ed. by Frank J. Fabozzi. (Illus.). 253p. 1997. 75.00 (1-883249-32-5) F J Fabozzi.

Professional Pet Sitter: Your Guide to Starting & Operating a Successful Service. Lori Mangold & Scott Mangold. 108p. 1994. pap. 29.95 (0-9635442-1-7) Paws-itive Pr.

Professional Philosophy. Thomas D. Perry. 256p. 1985. pap. text 61.50 (90-277-2072-X, D Reidel); lib. bdg. 107.50 (90-277-2071-1, D Reidel) Kluwer Academic.

Professional Photocopier Troubleshooting & Repair. Eric Kuaimoku. 1993. 29.95 (0-07-035889-3) McGraw.

Professional Photocopier Troubleshooting & Repair. Eric Kuaimoku. 1993. 29.95 (0-8306-4308-7) McGraw-Hill Prof.

Professional Photographer's Guide to Shooting & Selling Nature & Wildlife Photos. Jim Zuckerman. (Illus.). 134p. 1991. pap. 24.99 (0-89879-460-9, Wrtrs Digest Bks) F & W Pubns Inc.

Professional Photographers Management Handbook. Ann Monteith. LC 99-19351. (Illus.). 144p. 1999. pap. text. write for info. (0-9658571-3-1) Marathon NE.

Professional Photographic Illustration. 2nd ed. Eastman Kodak Company Staff. (Illus.). 160p. (Orig.). (C). 1998. pap. 24.95 (0-87985-756-0, O-16, Kodak) Saunders Photo.

***Professional Photoshop 5.0: The Classic Guide to Color Correction.** Dan Margulis. LC 98-39148. 336p. 1998. pap. 64.99 (0-471-32308-X) Wiley.

***Professional PHP Programming.** Jesus Castagnetto et al. (Professional Ser.). (Illus.). 850p. 1999. pap. 49.99 (1-86100-296-3) Wrox Pr Inc.

Professional Pianist's Christmas Fake Book. L. Evans. 208p. 1992. per. 22.95 (0-7935-1056-2, 00240040) H Leonard.

Professional Pianist's Fake Book. 264p. 1990. spiral bd. 24.95 (0-7935-0079-6, 00290084) H Leonard.

Professional Playscript Format Guidelines & Sample (Booklet) 1991. pap. 4.95 (0-937657-13-1) Feedbk Theabks & Prospero.

Professional Playwrights: Massinger, Ford, Shirley, & Brome. Ira Clark. LC 91-45853. 240p. 1992. 29.95 (0-8131-1787-9) U Pr of Ky.

Professional Plumbing Techniques--Illustrated & Simplified. Arthur J. Smith. (Illus.). 294p. 1993. pap. 14.95 (0-8306-1763-9, 1763) McGraw-Hill Prof.

Professional Poker Dealer's Handbook. Dan Paymar et al. Ed. by Paula Cizmar. LC 99-163450. (Illus.). 247p. 1998. pap. 19.95 (1-880685-18-3) Two Plus NV.

Professional Pool & Spa Technicians' Guide to pH, Alkalinity, Water Testing, & Water Balance. Robert W. Lowry & David Dickman. 64p. 1988. pap. 6.95 (0-685-29431-5) Serv Industry Pubns.

Professional Porfolios for School Administrators: Documenting Performance for Evaluation & Career Advancement. Sandra M. Evans. (Illus.). 150p. 1996. 32.95 (1-888793-03-1) Tchrs Little Secrets.

Professional Portfolio Models: Applications in Education. Maureen McLaughlin et al. 215p. (C). 1998. pap. text 29.95 (0-926842-74-9) CG Pubs Inc.

Professional Portfolios: A Collection of Articles. Ed. by Kay Burke. LC 96-77237. 192p. (Orig.). 1996. pap. 23.95 (1-57517-013-2, 1462) SkyLght.

Professional Portfolios: Documenting & Presenting Performance Excellence. Sandra M. Evans. (Illus.). 127p. 1995. 29.95 (1-888793-02-3) Tchrs Little Secrets.

Professional Portfolios for New & Aspiring Teachers. Sandra M. Evans. (Illus.). 130p. 1997. write for info. (1-888793-05-8) Tchrs Little Secrets.

***Professional Portfolios for Teachers: A Guide for Learners, Experts & Scholars.** Bonita L. Wilcox & Lawrence A. Tomei. LC 98-74794. 267p. 1999. pap. text, teacher ed. 36.95 (0-926842-92-7, 790) CG Pubs Inc.

***Professional Portfolios for the Development, Licensure & Employment of Teachers.** Sandra M. Evans et al. (Illus.). 164p. 1999. write for info. (1-888793-07-4) Tchrs Little Secrets.

Professional Potpourri: Seeds Are Sown. Margaret A. Golton. (Illus.). (Orig.). 1984. pap. 9.95 (0-685-08751-4) Frank Pubns.

Professional Power & the Need for Health Care. Ian Rees Jones. LC 99-72601. (Developments in Nursing & Health Care Ser.). 174p. 1999. text 56.95 (1-85972-626-7, Pub. by Ashgate Pub) Ashgate Pub Co.

Professional Power, Personal Excellence: 7 Integrated Steps to Accelerate Your Career! Gary K. Yamamoto. (Illus.). 1996. 24.95 (1-878182-14-5) Dynamic Pathways.

Professional Powerbuilder 4.O Programming. Paul Bukauskas. LC 96-35304. 512p. (C). 1997. pap. 39.95 (0-13-508145-9) P-H.

Professional Powers: A Study of the Institutionalization of Formal Knowledge. Eliot Freidson. xviii, 260p. 1988. pap. text 13.95 (0-226-26225-1) U Ch Pr.

Professional Practice: A Handbook for Interior Design. Ronald M. Veitch et al. (Illus.). 152p. (Orig.). (C). 1990. pap. 34.95 (0-920541-37-2) Peguis Pubs Ltd.

Professional Practice: A South African Nursing Perspective. Charlotte Searle. 346p. 1987. pap. text 45.00 (0-409-10906-1) Buttrwrth-Heinemann.

Professional Practice Builders Kit, 3 vols. 9th ed. Alan Weisman. 101p. 1998. pap. 100.00 (1-56150-246-4) Intl Wealth.

Professional Practice Builders Kit. 10th ed. Alan Weisman. 101p. 1999. pap. 100.00 (1-56150-297-9) Intl Wealth.

***Professional Practice Builders Kit.** 11th ed. Alan Weisman. 101p. 2000. pap. 100.00 (1-56150-357-6) Intl Wealth.

Professional Practice Builders Kit, 3 vols., Set. Alan Weisman. 101p. 1996. pap. 100.00 (1-56150-196-4) Intl Wealth.

Professional Practice Development: Meeting the Competitive Challenge. E. W. Brody. LC 88-28574. 273p. 1989. 69.50 (0-275-93102-1, C3102, Praeger Pubs) Greenwood.

Professional Practice for Interior Design. 2nd ed. Christine M. Piotrowski. (Illus.). 448p. 1994. text 52.95 (0-442-01684-0, VNR) Wiley.

Professional Practice for Interior Designers. 2nd ed. Christine M. Piotrowski. (Interior Design Ser.). 448p. 1994. 64.95 (0-471-28597-8, VNR) Wiley.

P

***Professional Practice for Landscape Architects.** Tennant et al. 224p. 2001. 32.95 (*0-7506-4818-X*, Architectural Pr) Buttrwrth-Heinemann.

Professional Practice Guide to Cost Engineering in Aerospace & Aviation. Ed. by Sarwan A. Samad. (Illus.). 250p. 1998. ring bd. 43.50 (*1-885517-12-2*) AACE Intl.

***Professional Practice Guide to Cost Engineering in the Utility Industries.** Ed. by David Hayes. (Illus.). 400p. 2000. cd-rom 53.50 (*1-885517-23-8*) AACE Intl.

Professional Practice Guide to Risk. Ed. by Michael Curan. (Illus.). 1100p. 1998. ring bd. 245.00 (*1-885517-10-6*) AACE Intl.

Professional Practice in Design Consultancy: A Design Business Association Guide. Ed. by Liz Lydiate. (Illus.). 208p. (C). 1992. pap. 46.95 (*0-85072-304-3*, Pub. by Design Council Bks) Ashgate Pub Co.

Professional Practice in Health Care Marketing. Ed. by William J. Winston. LC 85-22036. (Health Marketing Quarterly Ser.: Vol. 3, Nos. 2 & 3). 224p. 1986. 49.95 (*0-86656-549-3*) Haworth Pr.

Professional Practice of Architectural Detailing. 3rd ed. Osamu A. Wakita & Richard M. Linde. LC 98-25194. 512p. 1999. 69.95 (*0-471-18016-5*) Wiley.

Professional Practice of Architectural Working Drawings. 2nd ed. Osamu A. Wakita & Richard M. Linde. 672p. 1994. pap. 75.00 (*0-471-59663-9*) Wiley.

Professional Practice of Architectural Working Drawings. 2nd ed. Osamu A. Wakita & Richard M. Linde. 190p. 1994. pap., student ed. 30.50 (*0-471-04068-1*) Wiley.

Professional Practice of Architectural Working Drawings. 2nd ed. Osamu A. Wakita & Richard M. Linde. 672p. 1994. 85.00 (*0-471-04070-3*) Wiley.

Professional Practice of Environmental Management. R. S. Dorney. (Environmental Management Ser.). (Illus.). 220p. 1991. 96.95 (*0-387-96907-1*) Spr-Verlag.

Professional Practice of Landscape Architecture: A Complete Guide to Starting & Running Your Own Firm. Walter Rogers. 448p. 1996. 75.00 (*0-471-28680-X*, VNR) Wiley.

Professional Practice of Landscape Architecture: A Complete Guide to Starting & Running Your Own Firm. Walter Rogers. LC 96-24289. (Landscape Architecture Ser.). (Illus.). 422p. 1996. text 59.95 (*0-442-01964-5*, VNR) Wiley.

Professional Practice of Nursing Administration. Lillian M. Simms et al. LC 84-2209. 379p. 1989. text 36.95 (*0-8273-4364-7*) Delmar.

Professional Practice of Nursing Administration. 3rd ed. Lillian M. Simms et al. 685p. 61.95 (*0-7668-0790-8*, Pub. by Delmar) Thomson Learn.

Professional Practice of Psychology. Georgiana S. Tryon. Ed. by Glenn R. Caddy. LC 85-13433. (Developments in Clinical Psychology Ser.). 320p. 1986. text 73.25 (*0-89391-163-1*) Ablx Pub.

Professional Practice of Urban & Rural Planning in Canada. George Rich. LC 92-41583. 172p. 1993. pap. 59.95 (*0-7734-1942-X*) E Mellen.

Professional Practice 101: A Compendium of Business & Management Strategies in Architecture. Andy Pressman. LC 96-54601. 368p. 1997. pap. 49.95 (*0-471-13015-X*) Wiley.

Professional Practice Schools: Integrating School Reform & Teacher Education. Ed. by Marsha Levine. 192p. (C). 1992. text 38.00 (*0-8077-3176-5*); pap. text 17.95 (*0-8077-3175-7*) Tchrs Coll.

Professional Practices: Commitment & Capability in a Changing Environment. Tony Becher. 289p. 1999. 34.95 (*1-56000-414-2*) Transaction Pubs.

Professional Practices in Association Management. John B. Cox & American Society of Association Executives Staff. LC 98-106191. vi, 352 p. 1997. 49.95 (*0-88034-113-0*) Am Soc Assn Execs.

Professional Practicum Manual: Experiential Education in Recreation & Leisure Services: A Workbook for the Recreation & Leisure Studies Practicum. 2nd ed. David L. Jewell. LC 96-50487. 178p. 1996. spiral bd. 30.95 (*0-398-06755-4*) C C Thomas.

Professional Presence: The Total Program for Gaining That Extra Edge in Business by America's Top Corporate Image Consultant. 288p. text 23.00 (*0-7881-9125-X*) DIANE Pub.

Professional Presentations: How to Succeed in International Business. Tracy Henninger-Chiang & Judee Reel. (Illus.). 168p. (C). 1998. pap. text 18.95 (*0-472-08447-X*, 08447) U of Mich Pr.

Professional Presentations: Using Technology. Ed. by Pat R. Graves & Joyce Kupsh. LC 99-199894. (Illus.). 144p. (Orig.). 1999. pap. text 30.00 (*1-881530-12-4*) Delta Pi Epsilon.

Professional Press, Editorial & PR Photography. Jon Tarrant. LC 98-162047. (Professional Photography Ser.). (Illus.). 192p. 1998. pap. text 32.95 (*0-240-51520-X*, Focal) Buttrwrth-Heinemann.

Professional Prevention in Dentistry: Advances in Dentistry 1. Contrib. by International Health Care Foundation et al. LC 94-20962. 1945. write for info. (*0-683-00201-5*) Lppncott W & W.

Professional Print Buying. Phil Green. LC 96-72412. (Illus.). 192p. 1997. text 75.00 (*0-88362-197-5*, 1436) GATFPress.

Professional Print Buying. Pira Staff. 1998. 80.00 (*1-85802-137-5*, Pub. by Pira Pub) Bks Intl VA.

Professional Printing Estimating. Gerald A. Silver. LC 91-92964. (Illus.). 156p. (C). 1991. pap. 45.00 (*1-880472-04-X*) Edit Enter.

Professional Procurement Practices: A Guide for Dietary Managers. DMA Staff. 220p. 1997. per. 35.00 (*0-7872-3755-8*, 41375501) Kendall-Hunt.

Professional Professoriate: Unionization, Bureaucratization & the AAUP. Philo A. Hutcheson. LC 99-6509. (Issues in Higher Education Ser.). 288p. (C). 1999. pap. 23.95 (*0-8265-1348-4*) Vanderbilt U Pr.

***Professional Professoriate: Unionization, Bureaucratization & the AAUP.** Philo A. Hutcheson. LC 99-6509. (Issues in Higher Education Ser.). (C). 1999. 48.00 (*0-8265-1323-9*) Vanderbilt U Pr.

Professional Profile of Management Consultants: A Body of Expertise, Skills & Attributes. rev. ed. Association of Management Consulting Firms Staff. 40p. (C). 1992. 15.00 (*0-614-00301-6*) ACME.

Professional Program Proceedings: Electro 98, June 9-11, 1998, Bayside Exposition Center, Boston, Ma, Usa. Electro 98 et al. LC 98-85330. 273 p. 1998. pap. write for info. (*0-7803-4942-3*) IEEE Standards.

Professional Project Management. M. Dean Martin & John Adams. 154p. 1957. 28.00 (*0-317-54778-X*) Univ Tech.

Professional Proposal Writing. Jane Fraser. 262p. 1995. 74.95 (*0-566-07536-9*, Pub. by Gower) Ashgate Pub Co.

Professional Psychologist Today: New Developments in Law, Health Insurance, & Health Practice. Herbert Dorken et al. LC 75-24011. (Jossey-Bass Behavioral Science Ser.). 416p. reprint ed. pap. 129.00 (*0-608-15898-4*, 203081300070) Bks Demand.

Professional Psychologist's Handbook. Ed. by Bruce D. Sales. 780p. 1983. 110.00 (*0-306-40934-8*, Plenum Trade) Perseus Pubng.

Professional Psychology in Canada. Ed. by K. Dobson & D. Dobson. (Illus.). 480p. 1993. text 49.00 (*0-88937-043-5*) Hogrefe & Huber Pubs.

Professional Psychology in Transition: Meeting Today's Challenges. Herbert Dorken et al. LC 85-45900. (Jossey-Bass Social & Behavioral Science Ser.). 440p. reprint ed. pap. 136.40 (*0-7837-2512-4*, 204267100006) Bks Demand.

Professional Psychology of Long-Term Care. Ed. by Victor Molinari. LC 99-37326. (CE Book Ser.). 214p. 1999. pap. 39.95 (*1-57826-035-3*, Pub. by Hatherleigh) Norton.

Professional Public Executives. Chester A. Newland. LC 80-81209. (PAR Classics Ser.: No. 1). 222p. reprint ed. pap. 68.90 (*0-8357-4219-9*, 203700400003) Bks Demand.

Professional Public Relations & Political Power. Stanley Kelley. LC 56-8492. 263p. reprint ed. pap. 81.60 (*0-608-11880-X*, 202311100032) Bks Demand.

Professional Publishing with Ventura. Jonathan Press. (Orig.). 1989. 29.95 (*0-317-93951-3*); pap. 19.95 (*0-317-93952-1*) Jonathan Pr.

Professional Purchasing. Lars-Erik Gadde & Hakan Hakansson. LC 92-18933. (Bus Press-Previous Routledge). 208p. (C). (gr. 13). 1993. pap. 57.95 (*0-415-07933-0*, A9859) Thomson Learn.

Professional Purchasing. Lars-Erik Gadde & Hakan Hakansson. LC 93-49098. (Bus Press-Previous Routledge). 288p. (C). 1994. pap. 28.95 (*0-415-10397-5*, B4301) Thomson Learn.

***Professional Python.** Wrox Press Inc., Staff. 1000p. 2000. pap. 59.99 (*1-86100-427-3*) Wrox Pr Inc.

Professional Quest for Truth: A Social Theory of Science & Knowledge. Stephan Fuchs. LC 91-3095. (SUNY Series in Science, Technology, & Society). (Illus.). 254p. (C). 1992. text 21.50 (*0-7914-0923-6*); pap. text 21.95 (*0-7914-0924-4*) State U NY Pr.

Professional Raccoon Trapping. 3rd rev. ed. David A. Avant, III. LC 78-57404. (Illus.). 61p. pap. 4.95 (*0-317-03287-9*) LAvant Studios.

Professional Real Estate Development: The ULI Guide to the Business. Dean Schwanke & Richard B. Peiser. LC 92-4662. 414p. 1992. 59.95 (*0-7931-0392-4*, P37) Urban Land.

Professional Real Estate Investment Guidebook. J. T. Ferguson. 1982. 17.95 (*0-201-04074-3*) Addison-Wesley.

Professional Real Estate Problem Solving Using the HP 12C. 2nd rev. ed. John A. Tirone. 316p. 1996. spiral bd. 28.95 (*0-9624236-4-5*) J A Tirone.

Professional Real Estate Problem Solving Using the HP 17BII. John A. Tirone. 340p. 1994. spiral bd. 29.95 (*0-9624236-3-7*) J A Tirone.

Professional Records Management. Jeffrey R. Stewart. LC 93-45985. 1994. 33.95 (*0-02-801028-0*) Glencoe.

Professional Records Management. Jeffrey R. Stewart. 1995. teacher ed. 16.87 (*0-02-801030-2*) Glencoe.

Professional Records Management: Projects. Jeffrey R. Stewart. 1995. teacher ed. 6.50 (*0-02-801027-2*) Glencoe.

Professional Reference Collection ESL. 1990. 101.40 (*0-201-52807-X*) Addison-Wesley.

Professional Regulation in Marital & Family Therapy. Douglas K. Sturkie. (C). 2000. 36.67 (*0-205-27306-8*) Allyn.

Professional Regulations see Alaska Administrative Code--Register 151 Supplement (October 1999)

Professional Remodeler's Manual: Save Time, Avoid Mistakes, Increase Profits. R. Dodge Woodson. LC 95-9260. 1995. write for info. (*0-07-071974-8*) McGraw.

Professional Remodeler's Manual: Save Time, Avoid Mistakes, Increase Profits. R. Dodge Woodson. 400p. 1996. 50.00 (*0-07-071797-4*) McGraw.

Professional Remodeling Management. Walter W. Stoeppelwerth. 232p. 1990. pap. 37.50 (*1-882379-08-X*) HomeTech Info Systs.

Professional Report Writing. Simon Mort. 300p. 1992. 69.95 (*0-566-02712-7*, Pub. by Gower) Ashgate Pub Co.

Professional Report Writing. Simon Mort. 240p. 1995. pap. 33.95 (*0-566-07669-1*, Pub. by Gower) Ashgate Pub Co.

Professional Rescuer. 2nd ed. Amercian Red Cross Staff. (C). (gr. 13). 1997. write for info. (*0-8151-1253-X*) Mosby Inc.

Professional Rescuer. 2nd ed. American Red Cross Staff. (C). (gr. 13). 1997. teacher ed. write for info. (*0-8151-1254-8*) Mosby Inc.

Professional Rescuer: Instructor-Trainer Guide. 2nd ed. American Red Cross Staff. (C). (gr. 13). 1997. teacher ed. write for info. (*0-8151-1255-6*) Mosby Inc.

***Professional Rescuer CPR Instructor's Manual.** American Academy of Orthopaedic Surgeons Staff. (Illus.). 40p. (C). 1998. pap. text, teacher ed. 20.00 (*0-7637-0889-5*) JB Pubns.

Professional Responsibilities in Protecting Children: A Public Health Approach to Child Sexual Abuse, 9. Ed. by Ann Maney & Susan Wells. LC 87-32798. 237p. 1988. 55.00 (*0-275-92966-3*, C2966, Praeger Pubs) Greenwood.

Professional Responsibility. (Quick Study Law School Ser.). 4p. pap. 4.95 (*1-57222-290-5*) Barcharts.

Professional Responsibility. Theresa Gabaldon. (Professor Ser.). 251p. 1998. pap. text 17.95 (*1-56542-195-7*) E Pub Corp.

***Professional Responsibility.** James E. Moliterno. LC 99-39533. (Roadmap Ser.). 384p. 1999. pap. text 20.95 (*1-56706-536-8*) Panel Pubs.

***Professional Responsibility.** 2nd rev. ed. Lazar Emanuel et al. (Siegel's Ser.). 205p. (C). 2000. pap. text 15.95 (*1-56542-355-0*) E Pub Corp.

Professional Responsibility. 2nd rev. ed. Percy Luney. (Quick Review Ser.). 227p. (C). 1996. pap. text 18.95 (*1-57793-008-8*) Sum & Substance.

Professional Responsibility. 3rd ed. Kimm Walton. (Law in a Flash Ser.). 950p. 1997. 32.95 (*1-56542-570-7*) E Pub Corp.

***Professional Responsibility.** 6th ed. Buchanan. 526p. 1999. pap. text 44.00 (*0-536-02763-3*) Pearson Custom.

Professional Responsibility: A Problem Approach. 2nd ed. Norman Redlich. 288p. 1983. 23.00 (*0-316-73657-0*, Aspen Law & Bus) Aspen Pub.

Professional Responsibility: Anthology. Ed. by Thomas B. Metzloff. LC 94-15848. 267p. 1994. pap. 29.95 (*0-87084-573-X*) Anderson Pub Co.

Professional Responsibility: Cases & Materials. Maynard E. Pirsig & Kenneth F. Kirwin. LC 84-7566. 107p. 1986. pap. text, teacher ed. write for info. (*0-314-98583-2*) West Pub.

Professional Responsibility: Cases & Materials. 4th ed. Maynard E. Pirsig & Kenneth F. Kirwin. LC 84-7566. 603p. (C). 1984. reprint ed. 45.50 (*0-314-83001-4*) West Pub.

Professional Responsibility: Ethics by the Pervasive Method. Deborah Rhode. 1994. teacher ed. 40.00 (*0-316-66508-8*, 65088) Aspen Law.

Professional Responsibility: Ethics by the Pervasive Method. Deborah Rhode. LC 93-80778. 912p. 1994. pap. 35.00 (*0-316-74232-5*, 42325) Aspen Law.

Professional Responsibility: Ethics by the Pervasive Method. 2nd ed. Deborah L. Rhode. LC 97-51275. 1998. pap. text 40.00 (*1-56706-542-2*) Aspen Law.

Professional Responsibility: Problems of Practice & the Profession. Nathan Crystal. LC 95-80363. 736p. 1996. teacher ed. write for info. (*0-316-16379-1*, 63791) Aspen Law.

***Professional Responsibility: Problems of Practice & the Profession.** 2nd ed. Nathan M. Crystal. LC 00-20258. 2000. text 58.00 (*0-7355-1207-8*) Panel Pubs.

Professional Responsibility: Standards, Rules & Statutes (1995-1996 Ed) Ed. & Selected by John S. Dzienkowski. 996p. (C). pap. 19.00 (*0-314-06788-4*) West Pub.

Professional Responsibility: Standards, Rules & Statutes, 1998-1999. abr. ed. John S. Dzienkowski. (Miscellaneous Ser.). 650p. 1998. 16.00 (*0-314-23247-8*) West Pub.

Professional Responsibility for Government Attorneys: Who Is the Client & What Are Your Responsibilities to Your Client? 99p. 1995. 30.00 (*1-56986-258-3*, ETH-95-99) Federal Bar.

Professional Responsibility for Government Attorneys (1994) 40p. 1994. 15.00 (*1-56986-241-9*) Federal Bar.

Professional Responsibility for Lawyers: Cases & Materials. John F. Sutton, Jr. & John S. Dzienkowski. (American Casebook Ser.). 839p. (C). 1989. reprint ed. 57.50 (*0-314-54867-X*) West Pub.

Professional Responsibility in a Nutshell. 2nd ed. Robert H. Aronson & Donald T. Weckstein. (Nutshell Ser.). 514p. (C). 1991. reprint ed. pap. 23.50 (*0-314-83121-5*) West Pub.

Professional Responsibility in New Jersey (1992) David Dugan, III et al. 900p. ring bd. 85.00 (*0-685-65974-7*) NJ Inst CLE.

Professional Responsibility of Lawyers. 2nd ed. Sutton. (Casebook Ser.). Date not set. text. write for info. (*0-314-06597-0*) West Pub.

Professional Responsibility of Lawyers: Cases & Materials on, Teacher's Manual to Accompany. John F. Sutton, Jr. & John S. Dzienkowski. (American Casebook Ser.). 374p. 1990. pap. text. write for info. (*0-314-77058-5*) West Pub.

Professional Responsibility, Problems & Materials On. 5th ed. Thomas D. Morgan & Ronald D. Rotunda. 571p. 1990. text 34.50 (*0-88277-861-7*) Foundation Pr.

Professional Responsibility, Problems, Cases & Materials. Robert H. Aronson et al. LC 84-27029. (American Casebook Ser.). 745p. 1988. reprint ed. teacher ed., student ed. write for info. (*0-314-39543-1*); reprint ed. text 42.50 (*0-314-87537-9*) West Pub.

Professional Responsibility, Revised Teacher's Manual to Accompany. 5th ed. Thomas D. Morgan & Ronald D. Rotunda. (University Casebook Ser.). 363p. 1993. pap. text. write for info. (*1-56662-123-2*) Foundation Pr.

Professional Responsibility, Selected Standards on, 1997. Thomas D. Morgan & Ronald D. Rotunda. 639p. (C). 1996. pap. text. write for info. (*1-56662-501-7*) Foundation Pr.

Professional Responsibility Standards, Rules & Statutes. 11th abr. ed. John S. Dzienkowski. 500p. (C). 1997. pap. text, suppl. ed. write for info. (*0-314-21225-6*) West Pub.

Professional Responsibility Standards, Rules & Statutes, 1996-97. abr. ed. John Dzinkowski. 500p. 1996. pap. text. write for info. (*0-314-09975-1*) West Pub.

Professional Responsibility Standards, Rules & Statutes, 1996-97 Edition. Ed. by John S. Dzienkowski. 975p. 1996. pap. text. write for info. (*0-314-09976-X*) West Pub.

Professional Responsibility Standards, Rules & Statutes, 1997-1998 Edition. 10th ed. John S. Dyienkowski. 1031p. (C). 1997. pap. text. write for info. (*0-314-21220-5*) West Pub.

Professional Responsibility, Standards, Rules, & Statutes, 1998-1999 Edition. John S. Dzienkowski. (Pamphlet Ser.). 1000p. 1998. 21.00 (*0-314-23246-X*) West Pub.

Professional Responsibility the Criminal Lawyer. John W. Hall, Jr. LC 87-83036. 1987. 120.00 (*0-685-59847-0*) West Group.

Professional Responsibility to Courses Utilizing Morgan & Rotunda. Casenotes Publishing Co., Inc. Staff. Ed. by Norman S. Goldenberg et al. (Orig.). (C). 1995. pap. text. write for info. (*0-87457-169-3*, 1092) Casenotes Pub.

Professional Responsiblity: Standards, Rules & Statutes (1995-1996 Ab.Ed) abr. ed. Ed. & Selected by John S. Dzienkowski. 492p. (C). Date not set. pap. 14.00 (*0-314-06839-2*) West Pub.

Professional Restaurant Service. Ecole Technique Hoteliere Tsuji Staff. LC 90-24651. 188p. 1991. 59.95 (*0-471-53828-0*) Wiley.

Professional Resume Writing Techniques. James F. Baker. (Illus.). 105p. (C). 1984. 37.95 (*0-916780-26-0*) CES Assocs.

***Professional Resumes for Accounting, Tax, Finance & Law: A Special Gallery of Quality Resumes by Professional Resume Writers.** David F. Noble. Ed. by Virginia D. Noble. LC 99-43465. 416p. 1999. pap. 19.95 (*1-56370-605-9*, J6059) Park Ave.

Professional Resumes for Executives, Managers & Other Administrators: A New Gallery of Best Resumes by Professional Resume Writers. David F. Noble. LC 98-20676. 624p. 1998. pap. 19.95 (*1-56370-483-8*, J4838) JIST Works.

***Professional Resumes for Tax & Accounting Occupations.** David F. Noble. LC 99-40714. (Illus.). 2000. pap. write for info. (*1-56370-604-0*) JIST Works.

Professional Retouching with Photoshop. 280p. 1999. 39.99 (*1-56830-422-6*) Hayden.

Professional Review Action Group (PRAG) Model: A User's Guide. Peg M. Hess & Gail Folaron. 1993. pap. 5.50 (*0-87868-581-2*) Child Welfare.

Professional Review Guide for the CCS & CCS-P Examinations: 1998 Edition. 4th rev. ed. Patricia Schnering et al. 250p. (C). 1993. pap. text 39.95 (*0-9656386-3-4*) Prof Review Guides.

***Professional Review Guide for the CCS & CCS-P Examinations, 1999 Edition.** 2nd rev. ed. Patricia Schnering et al. 528p. (Orig.). 1999. pap. text 49.95 (*0-9656386-5-0*, PRG Pub) Prof Review Guides.

***Professional Review Guide for the RRA & ART Examinations: 1999 Edition.** 5th rev. ed. Patricia Schnering et al. 360p. 1999. pap. text 49.95 (*0-9656386-4-2*, PRG Pub) Prof Review Guides.

Professional Roof Cutter's Handbook. Marc B. Greene. (Illus.). 206p. 1988. 19.95 (*0-9619901-0-4*) M B Greene.

Professional Sales Management. Anderson et al. 1998. 69.95 (*0-87393-751-1*) Dame Pubns.

Professional Sales Management. 2nd ed. Anderson. 1992. teacher ed. 50.00 (*0-07-001688-7*) McGraw.

Professional Sales Management. 2nd ed. Rolph E. Anderson et al. 1992. pap. text. write for info. incl. disk (*0-07-836702-6*); boxed set, suppl. ed. write for info. (*0-07-001687-9*) McGraw.

Professional Sales Management. 2nd ed. Rolph E. Anderson et al. (C). 1992. text 66.25 (*0-07-001686-0*) McGraw.

Professional SAS Program Secrets. Rick Aster & Rhena Seidman. 1991. 24.95 (*0-8306-1600-4*) McGraw-Hill Prof.

Professional SAS Programmer's Pocket Reference. 2nd ed. Rick Aster. (Illus.). 192p. 1998. pap. 16.00 (*1-891957-02-3*, BR56646, Breakfast) Brkfst Commn Corp.

***Professional SAS Programmers Pocket Reference.** 2nd ed. Rick Aster. 192p. 1998. pap. 25.00 (*1-58025-148-X*, BR56602) SAS Publ.

***Professional SAS Programmer's Pocket Reference.** 3rd ed. Rick Aster. 239p. 2000. pap. 18.00 (*1-891957-07-4*, Breakfast) Brkfst Commn Corp.

Professional SAS Programming Secrets: Updated with New Features of Releases 6.08-6.10. 2nd ed. Rick Aster & Rhena Seidman. LC 96-17754. (Illus.). 592p. 1996. pap., pap. text 49.95 incl. cd-rom (*0-07-913095-X*, BR56279) McGraw.

Professional Seafood Demonstrator's Handbook. Northwest Seafood Consultant Staff. Ed. by Jay Lane. (How-To Ser.). (Illus.). 80p. 1988. pap. text 5.00 (*0-934363-06-4*) Lance Pubns.

Professional Seafood Demonstrator's Handbook. rev. ed. Northwest Seafood Consultant Staff et al. (Illus.). 48p. (Orig.). 1989. pap. text 5.95 (*0-934363-07-2*) Lance Pubns.

Professional Secrecy & the Journalist see International Press Institute Surveys

P

An Asterisk (*) at the beginning of an entry indicates that the title is appearing for the first time.

Professional Secretaries International Complete Office Handbook: The Definitive Reference for Today's Electronic Office. Susan Jaderstrom et al. (Illus.). 573p. 1998. reprint ed. pap. text 16.00 (*0-7881-5892-9*) DIANE Pub.

Professional Secretary, Vol. 1. John Spencer & Adrian Pruss. LC 94-43428. (Management Skills-ISM Ser.). (Illus.). 160p. 1995. pap. 17.95 (*0-304-33151-1*) Continuum.

Professional Secretary, Vol. 2. John Spencer & Adrian Pruss. (Illus.). 160p. 1995. pap. 26.95 (*0-304-33153-8*) Continuum.

Professional Secretary's Book of Lists & Tips. Mary A. De Vries. 448p. (C). 1994. text 29.95 (*0-13-149345-0*) P-H.

Professional Secretary's Encyclopedic Dictionary. 5th ed. Mary DeVries. LC 94-28490. 608p. 1994. text 29.95 (*0-13-030453-0*) P-H.

Professional Secretary's Handbook. 3rd ed. American Heritage Dictionary Editors. LC 95-12835. (Illus.). 592p. 1995. 18.95 (*0-395-69621-6*, AHD & Ref) HM.

Professional Secretary's Handbook: Communication Skills. John Spencer & Adrian Pruss. LC 96-41843. 224p. 1997. pap. 11.95 (*0-7641-0023-8*) Barron.

Professional Secretary's Handbook: Management Skills. John Spencer & Adrian Pruss. LC 96-42919. 208p. 1997. pap. 11.95 (*0-7641-0024-6*) Barron.

Professional Secretary's Survival Guide: Failsafe Tactics for the Corporate Jungle. Dartnell Editors. 159p. 1992. pap. 12.95 (*0-85013-206-1*) Dartnell Corp.

Professional Secrets: How to Do Extension Hair Braiding by Songa. Moremi Songa & Barbara Terry. Ed. by Rhonda Evans. LC 85-63072. (Illus.). 44p. (Orig.). 1986. pap. 15.00 (*0-936017-00-7*) Songa Pubns.

Professional Secrets for Photographing Children. Douglas A. Box. LC 98-72978. (Illus.). 128p. 1999. pap. 29.95 (*0-936262-76-1*) Amherst Media.

Professional Secrets of Advertising Photography. Paul Markow. (Illus.). 128p. 1999. pap. 29.95 (*0-936262-79-6*) Amherst Media.

***Professional Secrets of Natural Light Portrait Photography: Techniques & Images.** Douglas Allen Box. (Illus.). 128p. 2000. pap. 29.95 (*1-58428-045-X*, Pub. by Amherst Media) IPG Chicago.

***Professional Secrets of Nature Photography.** Judy Holmes. (Illus.). 128p. 2000. pap. 29.95 (*1-58428-021-2*) Amherst Media.

***Professional Secrets of Nude & Beauty Photography: Techniques & Images in Black & White.** Bill Lemon. (Illus.). 128p. 2000. pap. 29.95 (*1-58428-044-1*, Pub. by Amherst Media) IPG Chicago.

Professional Secrets of Performing Great Oral Sex on Men: Advanced Techniques for Liberated Lovers, Vol. 4. (Sex Masters Collection). (Illus.). 84p. (Orig.). 1997. pap. write for info. (*1-890677-03-5*) Delphi Pr.

Professional Secrets of Performing Great Oral Sex on Women: Advanced Techniques for Liberated Lovers, Vol. 5. (Sex Masters Collection). (Illus.). 78p. (Orig.). 1997. pap. write for info. (*1-890677-04-3*) Delphi Pr.

Professional Secrets of Wedding Photography. Douglas Allen Box. 128p. 1999. pap. text 29.95 (*0-936262-92-3*, Pub. by Amherst Media) IPG Chicago.

Professional Secrets to Nail Art: Expert Nail Art Techniques-What to Use & How to Use It! Antoinette Brennan. LC 93-74394. (Illus.). 190p. (Orig.). 1995. pap. 24.95 (*1-884609-19-8*) Alyssa Prince.

Professional Selling. 2nd ed. B. Robert Anderson. (Illus.). 400p. 1981. text 19.95 (*0-13-725960-3*) P-H.

Professional Selling. 2nd ed. Oberhau. LC 94-70733. (C). 1995. write for info. (*0-03-000639-2*) Harcourt Coll Pubs.

Professional Selling. 2nd ed. Oberhaus. (C). 1997. pap. text 63.50 (*0-15-504405-2*) Harcourt Coll Pubs.

Professional Selling: A Consultative Approach. Karl Gretz et al. LC 95-49443. 576p. (C). 1995. text 51.45 (*0-256-14384-6*, Irwn McGrw-H) McGrw-H Hghr Educ.

Professional Selling: A Relationship Management Process. John I. Coppett & William A. Staples. 512p. (C). 1990. text. write for info. (*0-538-80367-3*, SD60AA) S-W Pub.

Professional Selling: A Relationship Process. 2nd ed. Mary A. Oberhaus et al. LC 92-75903. 344p. (C). 1995. pap. text, teacher ed. 82.25 incl. trans. (*0-03-010221-9*) Dryden Pr.

Professional Selling: A Relationship Process, Test bank. 2nd ed. Mary A. Oberhaus et al. LC 92-75903. 272p. (C). 1995. pap. text, teacher ed. 40.00 (*0-03-010222-7*) Dryden Pr.

Professional Selling: Practical Secrets for Successful Sales. Rebecca Morgan. Ed. by Michael G. Crisp. LC 87-72479. (Fifty-Minute Ser.). (Illus.). 91p. (Orig.). 1988. pap. 10.95 (*0-931961-42-4*) Crisp Pubns.

Professional Selling in the 21st Century. Ed. by Cooper. (C). 1999. text. write for info. (*0-321-01410-3*) Addson-Wesley Educ.

***Professional Selling in the 21st Century.** 1999. write for info. (*0-673-98303-X*) Addison-Wesley.

Professional Selling Skills. Avila. (C). 1995. pap. text, wbk. ed. 37.00 (*0-03-016332-3*) Harcourt Coll Pubs.

Professional Selling Workbook. Avila. (C). 1995. pap. text, teacher ed. 28.00 (*0-03-017482-1*) Harcourt Coll Pubs.

Professional Service Corporations in Kentucky. Scott W. Dolson. x, 186p. 1993. pap. 41.00 (*1-58757-004-1*, BM015) Univ of KY.

Professional Service Firm50. Tom Peters. LC 99-33616. 1999. 15.95 (*0-375-40771-5*) Knopf.

Professional Services Marketing: Strategy & Tactics. F. G. Crane. LC 91-36043. 131p. 1993. pap. 14.95 (*1-56024-241-8*) Haworth Pr.

Professional Services Marketing: Strategy & Tactics. F. G. Crane. LC 91-36043. (Illus.). 142p. 1993. lib. bdg. 39.95 (*1-56024-240-X*) Haworth Pr.

Professional Sightsinging Technique Vol. I: An Intuitive & Structural Approach to Diatonic & Chromatic Sightsinging in Popular Music & Jazz, Intervals - Basic & Altered. Martin Grusin. LC 97-93846. (Illus.). xviii, 192p. 1998. 53.95 (*0-9659219-8-0*) Jubal Pr.

***Professional Singer's Christmas Fake Book.** 120p. 1998. per. 19.95 (*0-7935-6014-4*); per. 19.95 (*0-7935-6015-2*) H Leonard.

Professional Singer's Country Fake Book: High Voice. (Illus.). 224p. 1997. otabind 19.95 (*0-7935-5992-8*, HL00240093) H Leonard.

Professional Singer's Country Fake Book: Low Voice. (Illus.). 224p. 1997. otabind 19.95 (*0-7935-5991-X*, HL00240092) H Leonard.

Professional Singer's Fake Book - High Key. spiral bd. 22.95 (*0-7935-4692-3*, 00240057) H Leonard.

Professional Singer's Fake Book - Low Voice. spiral bd. 22.95 (*0-7935-4693-1*, 00240060) H Leonard.

Professional Singer's Handbook. Gloria Rusch. 216p. 1998. per. 19.95 (*0-7935-8851-0*) H Leonard.

Professional Singer's Pop/Rock Fake Book. Leonard, Hal, Corporation Staff. 168p. 1998. per. 19.95 (*0-7935-5989-8*); per. 19.95 (*0-7935-5990-1*) H Leonard.

***Professional Site Server 3.0 Personalization & Membership.** Nick Apostolopoulos et al. 1000p. 1999. pap. text 59.99 (*1-86100-269-6*) Wrox Pr Inc.

Professional Site Server 3.0 Personalization & Membership. Robert Howard. 500p. 1998. pap. 49.99 (*1-86100-194-0*) Wrox Pr Inc.

***Professional Site Server 3.0: Commerce Edition.** Marco Tabini. 750p. 1999. pap. text 49.99 (*1-86100-250-5*) Wrox Pr Inc.

Professional Skills. Charles Brady & Gillian Perry. 120p. 1992. pap. 26.50 (*1-85811-000-9*, Pub. by CLT Prof) Gaunt.

Professional Skills for Lawyers: A Student's Guide. 464p. 1994. pap. text 33.00 (*0-406-02128-7*, UK, MICHIE) LEXIS Pub.

Professional Skills of the Small Business Lawyer. Harry J. Haynsworth. LC 84-72250. 255p. 1984. 22.50 (*0-8318-0459-9*, B459) Am Law Inst.

Professional Skills, or How to Start & Run a Genealogy Business for Profit. Arlene H. Eakle. 110p. 1986. pap. 25.50 (*0-940764-33-4*) Genealog Inst.

Professional Smithing: Traditional Techniques for Decorative Ironwork, Whitesmithing, Hardware, Toolmaking, & Locksmithing. Donald Streeter. (Illus.). 144p. 1995. pap. 22.95 (*1-879335-66-2*) Astragal Pr.

Professional SMT Component & Land Pattern Book, 2 vols., Set, Vols. 1 & 2. James C. Blankenhorn. (C). 1992. text 299.95 (*1-882812-07-7*) SMT Plus.

Professional Social Work Education & Health Care: Challenges for the Future. Ed. by Mildred D. Mailick & Phyllis Caroff. LC 96-30654. (Social Work in Health Care Ser.: Vol. 24, Nos. 1/2). 158p. (C). 1996. 39.95 (*0-7890-0010-5*) Haworth Pr.

Professional Software: Programming Practice, Vol. 2. Henry F. Ledgard. (C). 1987. pap. text 18.36 (*0-201-12232-4*) Addison-Wesley.

Professional Software: Software Engineering Concepts, Vol. 1. Henry F. Ledgard. LC 87-1760. (C). 1987. pap. text 24.75 (*0-201-12231-6*) Addison-Wesley.

Professional Solidarity among the Teachers of England. Donna F. Thompson. LC 68-57584. (Columbia University. Studies in the Social Sciences: No. 228). reprint ed. 31.50 (*0-404-51288-7*) AMS Pr.

***Professional Sound Reinforcement Techniques.** Jim Yakabuski. 140p. 2000. pap. 24.95 (*0-87288-759-6*) Intertec Pub.

Professional Sports: The Challenges Facing the Future of the Industry: Hearing Before the Committee on the Judiciary U. S. Senate. Composed by Diane Publishing Staff. 154p. (C). 1998. pap. text 35.00 (*0-7881-4920-2*) DIANE Pub.

Professional Sports: The Community College Connection. Manque Winters. Ed. by Jessie Levine & Helen Curtis. (Illus.). 201p. (Orig.). 1984. 19.95 (*0-9613253-0-5*); pap. 13.95 (*0-9613253-1-3*) Winmar Pr.

Professional Sports & Antitrust. Warren Freedman. LC 87-2499. 153p. 1987. 65.00 (*0-89930-191-6*, FBS/, Quorum Bks) Greenwood.

Professional Sports & the Law. Lionel S. Sobel. 850p. (C). 1977. 55.00 (*0-317-67881-7*); text, student ed. 22.50 (*0-317-67882-5*) Law Arts.

Professional Sports & the Law. Lionel S. Sobel. LC 76-51948. 1981. suppl. ed. 75.00 (*0-88238-060-5*) Law Arts.

Professional Sports Statistics: A North American Team-by-Team, & Major Non-Team Events, Year-by-Year Reference, 1876 Through 1996. K. Michael Gaschnitz. LC 97-13593. 1352p. 1997. lib. bdg. 99.50 (*0-7864-0299-7*) McFarland & Co.

***Professional SQL Server 7 Performance Tuning.** Guy Van Den Berg. 600p. 2000. pap. 49.99 (*1-86100-326-9*) Wrox Pr Inc.

***Professional SQL Server 7 Programming.** Rob Vieira. 1000p. 1999. pap. 49.99 (*1-86100-231-9*) Wrox Pr Inc.

***Professional SQL Server 7 Stored Procedures.** Wrox Press Staff & Dejan Sunderic. 500p. 2000. pap. 49.99 (*1-86100-325-0*) Wrox Pr Inc.

Professional SQL Server 6.5 Admin. Sharon Dooley. LC 96-60557. 800p. 1996. pap. 44.95 (*1-874416-49-4*) Wrox Pr Inc.

***Professional SQL Server 2000 Programming.** Rob Vieira. 1200p. 2000. pap. 59.99 (*1-86100-448-6*) Wrox Pr Inc.

***Professional SQL Server 2000 XML.** Jonathan Langdale. 800p. 2000. pap. 49.99 (*1-86100-446-X*) Wrox Pr Inc.

Professional SQL Server 7.0. Frank Abendroth. 500p. 1998. pap. 49.99 (*1-86100-177-0*, Pub. by Wrox Press) Wrox Pr Inc.

Professional Stage Hypnotism. Ormond McGill. (Illus.). 203p. 1994. reprint ed. pap. 14.95 (*0-930298-03-9*) Westwood Pub Co.

Professional Standards for Teaching Mathematics. NCTM Commission on Teaching Standards for School M. LC 90-26154. (Illus.). 196p. 1991. pap. 29.50 (*0-87353-307-0*) NCTM.

Professional Standards for the Superintendency. John Hoyle. 16p. 1993. pap. 3.96 (*0-87652-202-9*, 21-00423) Am Assn Sch Admin.

Professional Standards Review Act: A Legislative History of Title Eleven of the Social Securities Amendments of 1972 Pub. Law No. 92-603, 2 vols., Set. Ed. by Bernard D. Reams, Jr. LC 89-84259. (Federal Health Law Ser.: Part 4). 1636p. 1990. lib. bdg. 150.00 (*0-89941-694-2*, 305950) W S Hein.

Professional Standards Training Manual. 60p. 3.50 (*0-318-15190-1*, 111-793) Natl Assoc Realtors.

Professional Stockmaking. D. Wesbrook. 1993. 54.00 (*1-879356-15-5*) Wolfe Pub Co.

Professional Storywriter's Handbook. Edwin A. Peeples. LC 60-6901. 1960. 8.50 (*0-9600080-0-4*) Peeples.

Professional Stranger: An Informal Introduction to Ethnography. 2nd ed. Michael Agar. (Illus.). 296p. 1996. pap. text 34.95 (*0-12-044470-4*) Acad Pr.

Professional Strategies, Nursing. Jack Rudman. (ACT Proficiency Examination Program (PEP) Ser.: Vol. 50). 43.95 (*0-8373-5925-2*) Nat Learn.

Professional Strategies, Nursing. Jack Rudman. (ACT Proficiency Examination Program Ser.: PEP-50). 1994. pap. 23.95 (*0-8373-5900-7*) Nat Learn.

Professional Strategies, Nursing. Jack Rudman. (Regents External Degree (REDP) Ser.: Vol. REDP-26). 1994. pap. 23.95 (*0-8373-5626-1*) Nat Learn.

Professional Strategies (Nursing) Jack Rudman. (Regents External Degree (REDP) Ser.: Vol. 26). 43.95 (*0-8373-5676-8*) Nat Learn.

Professional Style Sheets with HTML & XML. Frank Boumphrey. 500p. 1998. pap. 39.99 (*1-86100-165-7*, Pub. by Wrox Press) Wrox Pr Inc.

Professional Stylings for the Solo Pianist. Noreen Sauls. 1993. pap. 14.95 (*0-943748-59-3*) Ekay Music.

Professional Surveyor's Manual. Robert C. Vernon. LC 96-2758. (Illus.). 400p. 1997. 44.95 (*0-07-067419-1*) McGraw.

***Professional Symbian Programming.** Martin Tasker et al. 850p. 2000. pap. 49.99 (*1-86100-303-X*) Wrox Pr Inc.

Professional Table Service. Sylvia Meyer. (Illus.). 464p. 1991. text 52.95 (*0-442-23982-3*, VNR) Wiley.

Professional Table Service. Sylvia Meyer et al. Tr. by Heinz Holtmann. 464p. 1990. 64.95 (*0-471-28926-4*, VNR) Wiley.

Professional Tax Planning Using Multiplan. Mitchell H. Jacobs. write for info. (*0-318-58207-4*) P-H.

Professional Tax Planning Using 1-2-3. Mitchell H. Jacobs. write for info. (*0-318-58204-X*) P-H.

Professional Teacher: Preparation & Nurturance of the Reflective Practioner. Charles W. Case & Kay A. Norlander-Case. LC 99-6257. (Agenda for Education in a Democracy Ser.). 208p. 1999. pap. 39.95 (*0-7879-4560-9*) Jossey-Bass.

Professional Teaching Techniques: A Handbook for Teaching Adults Any Subject. rev. ed. Elizabeth Nelson. LC 98-91328. 106p. (Orig.). 1998. pap. 15.00 (*0-918328-21-7*) We Unlimited.

Professional Techniques for the Wedding Photographer. George Schaub. (Illus.). 144p. 1985. pap. 18.95 (*0-8174-5601-5*, Amphoto) Watsn-Guptill.

Professional Tennis Drills. United States Tennis Association Staff & Lewis Brewer. 192p. (J). (gr. 7 up). 1985. pap. 13.95 (*0-684-18298-X*) S&S Trade.

Professional Thief: Annotated & Interpreted by Edwin Hardin Sutherland. Edwin H. Sutherland. 270p. 1988. pap. text 16.95 (*0-226-78051-1*, Midway Reprint) U Ch Pr.

Professional Thieves & the Detective. Allan Pinkerton. LC 73-156031. reprint ed. 72.50 (*0-404-09133-4*) AMS Pr.

Professional Tiling. Edwin M. Field. 240p. 1993. pap. 25.00 (*0-02-537741-8*, Pub. by Macmillan) S&S Trade.

***Professional Touch: How to Think, Act, Write & Look Your Professional Best.** rev. ed. Eve Cappello. 108p. 2000. pap. text 10.95 (*0-9639037-2-1*, Dr Eve Pub) Eve Cappello.

Professional Trading System. R. C. Allen. (Illus.). 97p. 1983. pap. 45.00 (*0-930233-21-2*, Pub. by Windsor) Natl Bk Netwk.

Professional Trainee. Jack Rudman. (Career Examination Ser.: C-625). 1994. pap. 23.95 (*0-8373-0625-6*) Nat Learn.

Professional Trainer: A Human Resource Training & Development Guide. Robert H. Vaughn. (Illus.). 200p. 1999. pap. 28.00 (*1-893435-10-5*) Lakeshore Comm.

Professional Training for Feminist Therapists: Personal Memoirs. Esther D. Rothblum & Ellen Cole. LC 90-26555. (Women & Therapy Ser.). 129p. 1991. text 39.95 (*1-56024-123-3*) Haworth Pr.

Professional Treatment of the Subject Matter of Arithmetic for Teacher-Training Institutions. Elias A. Bond. LC 75-176576. (Columbia University. Teachers College. Contributions to Education Ser.: No. 525). reprint ed. 37.50 (*0-404-55525-X*) AMS Pr.

Professional Turnover: The Case of Nurses. James L. Price & Charles W. Mueller. (Health Systems Management Ser.). 218p. (C). 1980. 25.00 (*0-88331-184-4*) R B Luce.

Professional Updating of Personnel-Industrial Relations Training. Charles M. Rehmus. (Occasional Publications: No. 146). 11p. 1983. 1.00 (*0-318-04753-5*) U Hawaii.

Professional Values & Individual Autonomy: The United States Supreme Court & Lawyer Advertising. J. Gordon Hylton. LC 98-87269. 216p. 1998. pap. 25.00 (*0-89089-786-7*) Carolina Acad Pr.

Professional VB Distributed Systems. Robert Hambright & Michael Z. Brown. 400p. 1998. pap. 49.99 (*1-86100-224-6*, Pub. by Wrox Press) Wrox Pr Inc.

***Professional VB6 Com.** Thomas Lewis. 500p. 1999. pap. 39.99 (*1-86100-213-0*) Wrox Press.

***Professional Visual Basic 6 MTS Programming.** Thomas Robbins. 500p. 1998. pap. text 49.99 (*1-86100-244-0*) Wrox Pr Inc.

***Professional Vegetarian Cooking.** Ken Bergeron. LC 98-47051. 448p. 1999. 44.95 (*0-471-29235-4*) Wiley.

Professional Video & Audio Equipment, UL 1419. 2nd ed. (C). 1997. pap. text 135.00 (*0-7629-0162-4*) Underwrtrs Labs.

Professional Video Poker. 2nd ed. Stanford Wong. (Illus.). 159p. (Orig.). 1991. reprint ed. pap. 14.95 (*0-935926-15-1*) Pi Yee Pr.

Professional Video Production. 2nd ed. Ingrid Wiegand & Ben Bogossian. (Illus.). 215p. 1993. 37.95 (*0-86729-311-X*, Focal) Buttrwrth-Heinemann.

Professional Visual Basic for Windows CE Programming. Larry Roof. LC 99-494990. 450p. 1998. pap. 49.99 (*1-86100-162-2*) Wrox Pr Inc.

***Professional Visual Basic SAP R/3 Programming.** Oleg Ovanesyan. (Professional Ser.). 500p. 1999. pap. 59.99 (*1-86100-278-5*) Wrox Pr Inc.

Professional Visual Basic 6 Database. Charles Williams. 800p. 1999. pap. 49.99 (*1-86100-202-5*) Wrox Pr Inc.

***Professional Visual Basic 6.0 Business Objects.** Rockford Lhotka. 700p. 1998. pap. 59.99 (*1-86100-107-X*) Wrox Pr Inc.

***Professional Visual Basic 6 Project Management.** Jake Sturm. (Professional Ser.). 600p. 1999. pap. 49.99 (*1-86100-293-9*) Wrox Pr Inc.

Professional Visual Basic 6 Web Programming. Pierre Boutquin et al. 1081p. 1999. pap. text 49.99 (*1-86100-222-X*) Wrox Pr Inc.

Professional Visual C++ MTS Programming. Richard Grimes. (Professional Ser.). 500p. 1999. pap. 49.99 (*1-86100-239-4*) Wrox Pr Inc.

Professional Visual C++ 6 Windows Shell Programming. Dino Espisito. 450p. 1998. pap. 39.99 (*1-86100-184-3*, Pub. by Wrox Press) Wrox Pr Inc.

Professional Visual InterDev 7.0. Wrox Press Inc., Staff. 1000p. Date not set. pap. 59.99 (*1-86100-453-2*) Wrox Pr Inc.

***Professional Visual Interdev 6 Programming.** Ian Blackburn et al. (Professional Ser.). 700p. 1999. pap. 49.99 (*1-86100-264-5*) Wrox Pr Inc.

Professional Vocalist: A Handbook for Commercial Singers & Teachers. Rachel L. Lebon. LC 98-30718. 144p. 1999. text 39.50 (*0-8108-3565-7*) Scarecrow.

***Professional Vocalist: A Handbook for Commercial Singers & Teachers.** Rachel L. Lebon. LC 98-30718. 144p. 1999. pap. 29.50 (*0-8108-3566-5*) Scarecrow.

***Professional Voice: Science & Art of Clinic Care.** 3rd ed. Sataloff. 2002. pap. 316.75 (*0-7693-0166-5*, Pub. by Singular Publishing) Thomson Learn.

Professional Voice: The Science & Art of Clinical Care. Robert T. Sataloff. LC 90-9022. (Illus.). 560p. reprint ed. pap. 173.60 (*0-608-09716-0*, 206988200007) Bks Demand.

Professional Voice: The Science & Art of Clinical Care. 2nd ed. Ed. by Robert T. Sataloff. (Illus.). 585p. 1997. pap. 325.00 (*1-56593-728-7*, 1416) Singular Publishing.

***Professional WAP.** Wrox Press Inc., Staff. 1000p. 2000. pap. 49.99 (*1-86100-404-4*) Wrox Pr Inc.

Professional Way to Sell Automobiles. Brad Kerfoot. 117p. 1992. text 21.95 (*0-9636090-0-9*) B Kerfoot Prods.

Professional Web Design: Theory & Technique at the Cutting Edge. Molly Holzschlag. LC 96-69006. 384p. 1996. per. 40.00 (*0-7615-0759-0*) Prima Pub.

Professional Web Site Optimization. Scott Ware. 1997. pap. 40.00 (*1-86100-074-X*) Wrox Pr Inc.

***Professional WebObjects with Java.** Wrox Press Inc., Staff. 600p. 2000. pap. 49.99 (*1-86100-431-1*) Wrox Pr Inc.

Professional Window Washing. William Thomas. (Illus.). 88p. (C). 1993. lib. bdg. 35.00 (*0-614-10727-X*) Marsh-Wentworth.

***Professional Windows DNA 2000 Development.** Wrox Press Inc., Staff. 1000p. 2000. pap. 59.99 (*1-86100-445-1*) Wrox Pr Inc.

Professional Wine Reference. Frank E. Johnson. (Illus.). 354p. 1983. pap. 9.95 (*0-9602566-0-1*) Beverage Media.

Professional Wine Reference. deluxe ed. Frank E. Johnson. (Illus.). 354p. 1983. 35.00 (*0-9602566-1-X*) Beverage Media.

Professional Women at Work: Interactions, Tacit Understandings & the Non-Trivial Nature of Trivia in Bureaucratic Settings. Jerry Jacobs. LC 93-37848. 160p. 1994. 52.95 (*0-89789-380-8*, Bergin & Garvey) Greenwood.

***Professional Women Painters in Nineteenth-Century Scotland: Commitment, Friendship & Pleasure.** Janice Helland. LC 00-36347. 2000. write for info. (*0-7546-0068-8*) Ashgate Pub Co.

Professional Wordsworth: Law, Labor, & the Poet's Contract. Mark Schoenfield. LC 95-4679. 1996. 50.00 (*0-8203-1791-8*) U of Ga Pr.

Professional Workers As Learners: The Scope, Problem, & Accountability of Continuing Professional Education in the 1990s. 1996. lib. bdg. 250.99 (*0-8490-6904-1*) Gordon Pr.

Professional Workstation: Requirements & Marketing Opportunities in the Engineering Environment. Williamson & York, Inc. Staff. 250p. 1983. write for info. (*0-318-57948-0*) C I M Systems.

Professional Wrestling: Sport & Spectacle. Sharon Mazer. LC 97-42266. (Performance Studies Ser.). (Illus.). 192p. 1998. 45.00 (*1-57806-020-6*); pap. 18.00 (*1-57806-021-4*) U Pr of Miss.

P

Professional Wrestling As Ritual Drama in American Popular Culture. Michael R. Ball. LC 90-44431. (Studies in Sociology: Vol. 8). 200p. 1990. lib. bdg. 79.95 (*0-88946-112-0*) E Mellen.

*Professional Wrestling Collectibles.** Kristian Pope & Ray Whebbe, Jr. LC 99-68109. (Illus.). 160p. 2000. pap. 21.95 (*0-87341-878-6*, PWRES) Krause Pubns.

Professional Wrestling Trivia Book. 2nd ed. Robert Myers. Ed. by Adolph Caso. LC 99-12748. (Illus.). 140p. 1999. pap. 9.95 (*0-8283-2045-4*) Branden Bks.

Professional Writer: A Guide for Advanced Technical Writing. Gerald J. Alred et al. LC 90-71628. 426p. (Orig.). (C). 1991. pap. text 46.95 (*0-312-00248-3*) St Martin.

Professional Writer's Organization Kit. Diana Gregory. (Illus.). 192p. (Orig.). 1989. pap. 14.95 (*0-944494-07-2*) Lifeboat Bks.

Professional Writing: Processes, Strategies, & Tips for Publishing in Educational Journals. Roger Hiemstra & Ellen M. Brier. LC 93-7439. 152p. (Orig.). (C). 1993. 19.50 (*0-89464-660-5*) Krieger.

Professional Writing for Lawyers: Skills & Responsibilities. Margaret Z. Johns. LC 98-86436. 256p. 1998. pap. 15.00 (*0-89089-804-9*) Carolina Acad Pr.

Professional Writing for the Human Services. Ed. by Linda Beebe. LC 92-39534. 325p. (C). 1993. 31.95 (*0-87101-199-9*) Natl Assn Soc Wkrs.

Professional Writing in Context: Lessons from Teaching & Consulting in Worlds of Work. Ed. by Lynn V. Sadler et al. 192p. 1995. 45.00 (*0-8058-1726-3*); pap. 22.50 (*0-8058-1727-1*) L Erlbaum Assocs.

Professional Writing Online. Y. Porter. (C). 2000. 40.00 (*0-205-27918-X*, Macmillan Coll) P-H.

*Professional Writing Online: Website.** 2000. write for info. (*0-205-27919-8*) Allyn.

Professional Writing Skills: A Self-Paced Training Program. 2nd rev. ed. Diane Lutovich & Janis F. Chan. 217p. (Orig.). 1997. pap. 45.00 (*0-9637455-4-9*) Adv Comm Designs.

Professional Writing Tasks for Undergraduate Student in Teaching. 2nd ed. 356p. (C). 1997. text 28.50 (*0-536-00457-9*) Pearson Custom.

*Professional XML.** Mark Birbeck et al. 2000. pap. 49.99 (*1-86100-311-0*) Wrox Pr Inc.

Professional XML Applications. Trevor Jenkins. 400p. 1998. pap. 49.99 (*1-86100-152-5*) Wrox Pr Inc.

*Professional XML Databases.** Wrox Press Inc., Staff. 800p. 2000. pap. 49.99 (*1-86100-358-7*) Wrox Pr Inc.

Professional XML Design & Implementation. Paul Spencer. (Professional Ser.). (Illus.). 420p. 1999. pap. 39.99 (*1-86100-228-9*) Wrox Pr Inc.

*Professional XML Schema Design.** Stephen F. Mohr. 800p. 2000. pap. 49.99 (*1-86100-356-0*) Wrox Pr Inc.

*Professional XSL.** 800p. 2000. pap. 49.99 (*1-86100-357-9*) Wrox Pr Inc.

Professionalism. Driscoll. (PJE Ser.: Vol. 73, No. 1). 1998. pap. 20.00 (*0-8058-9837-9*) L Erlbaum Assocs.

Professionalism: How to Enhance & Enrich Your Profession. Elmer W. Mattson. LC 82-99894. (Illus.). (Orig.). 1982. pap. 4.95 (*0-9609084-0-4*) Motiv Unltd.

Professionalism & Community: Perspectives on Reforming Urban Schools. Karen S. Louis & Sharon D. Kruse. LC 94-46409. (Illus.). 272p. 1995. 65.95 (*0-8039-6252-5*); pap. 29.95 (*0-8039-6253-3*) Corwin Pr.

*Professionalism & Ethics in Teaching.** David Carr. LC 99-23908. 304p. (C). 1999. text. write for info. (*0-415-18459-2*) Routledge.

Professionalism & Ethics in Teaching. David Carr. LC 99-23908. (Professional Ethics Ser.). 304p. 2000. pap. 25.99 (*0-415-18460-6*) Routledge.

Professionalism & Law Enforcement Accreditation: The First Ten Years. John W. Bizzack. 1993. pap. 32.95 (*0-9630878-7-8*) Autumn Hse KY.

Professionalism & Originality. Frank H. Hayweare. LC 73-14156. (Perspectives in Social Inquiry Ser.). 278p. 1974. reprint ed. 19.95 (*0-405-05502-1*) Ayer.

Professionalism & Pastoral Care. Alastair V. Campbell. Ed. by Don S. Browning. LC 84-48710. (Theology & Pastoral Care Ser.). 119p. reprint ed. pap. 36.90 (*0-608-18363-6*, 203304700083) Bks Demand.

Professionalism & the Early Childhood Practitioner. Ed. by Donald L. Peters et al. (Early Childhood Education Ser.). 216p. (C). 1988. text 36.95 (*0-8077-2896-9*); pap. text 18.95 (*0-8077-2895-0*) Tchrs Coll.

*Professionalism Boundaries & the Workplace.** Ed. by Nigel Malin. LC 99-17035. 288p. (C). 2000. text. write for info. (*0-415-19262-5*) Routledge.

*Professionalism Boundaries & Workplace.** Nigel Malin. LC 99-17035. 2000. pap. write for info. (*0-415-19263-3*) Routledge.

Professionalism in Basic Nursing. Lois Harrion. (C). 1991. mass mkt. 24.50 (*0-8273-3680-2*) Delmar.

Professionalism in Pentecostal Education. Bernard Rossier. 96p. 1992. pap. 7.95 (*0-930401-50-6*) Artex Pub.

Professionalism in Practice. (Conference Proceedings Ser.). 128p. (Orig.). 1988. pap. 15.00 (*1-882147-08-1*) Am Art Therapy.

Professionalism in Public Administration. Ed. by S. P. Rao & V. M. Sinha. 1990. text 27.50 (*0-685-31755-2*, Pub. by Assoc Pub Hse) Advent Bks Div.

Professionalism in Teaching. Hurst & Reding. 75p. 1999. pap. text 8.00 (*0-13-022551-7*) P-H.

Professionalism, Patronage & Public Service in Victorian London: Metropolitan Board of Works Staff, 1856. Gloria C. Clifton. LC 92-10363. 192p. (C). 1992. text 80.00 (*0-485-11387-2*, Pub. by Athlone Pr) Humanities.

Professionalism Reborn: Theory, Prophecy & Policy. Eliot Freidson. LC 94-7503. 248p. 1994. pap. text 16.95 (*0-226-26221-9*); lib. bdg. 42.00 (*0-226-26220-0*) U Ch Pr.

Professionalization & Activism in Social Work. Linda C. Reeser & Irwin Epstein. 196p. 1990. text 44.00 (*0-231-06788-7*) Col U Pr.

Professionalization & Professionalism of Catholic Priests. Hernan Vera & George Ritzer. LC 82-6886. (University of Florida Social Sciences Monographs: No. 68). xii, 116p. 1982. pap. 16.95 (*0-8130-0713-5*) U Press Fla.

Professionalization & Professionalism of Catholic Priests. Hernan Vera. LC 82-6886. (University of Florida Monographs: Vol. 68). 128p. 1982. reprint ed. pap. 39.70 (*0-608-04476-8*, 206522100001) Bks Demand.

Professionalization of Dental Students. M. L. Helfrich & E. L. Quarantelli. 1974. pap. 16.95 (*0-8084-0382-6*) NCUP.

Professionalization of Economics: Alfred Marshall & the Dominance of Orthodoxy. John Maloney. 248p. (C). 1990. pap. 24.95 (*0-88738-345-9*) Transaction Pubs.

Professionalization of Nursing: Current Issues & Trends. 3rd ed. Patricia M. Schwirian. LC 97-45687. 352p. 1998. pap. text 27.95 (*0-7817-1045-6*) Lppncott W & W.

Professionalization of Peacekeeping. David Wurmser & Nancy Beargdyke. Ed. by Robert B. Oakley et al. 71p. (Orig.). (C). 1994. pap. text 30.00 (*0-7881-0813-1*) DIANE Pub.

Professionalization of Peacekeeping: A Study Group Report. 72p. 1993. pap. text 40.00 (*1-57979-248-0*) DIANE Pub.

*Professionalization of Poverty: Social Work & the Poor in the Twentieth Century.** Ed. by Gary R. Lowe & P. Nelson Reid. LC 99-45674. (Modern Applications of Social Work Ser.). 272p. 1999. pap. text 18.95 (*0-202-36112-8*); lib. bdg. 37.95 (*0-202-36111-X*) Aldine de Gruyter.

Professionalization of Psychology in Nazi Germany. Ulfried Geuter. Tr. by Richard Holmes. (Studies in the History of Psychology). (Illus.). 359p. (C). 1992. text 59.95 (*0-521-33297-4*) Cambridge U Pr.

Professionalization of Sociology: A Comparative Study, Germany - U. S. A. Bert Hardin. 196p. 1982. text 50.00 (*3-593-32206-4*) Irvington.

Professionalization of Soviet Society. Alexander Simirenko. Ed. by Cheryl A. Kern-Simirenko. LC 80-21210. 225p. 1982. 39.95 (*0-87855-419-X*) Transaction Pubs.

Professionalization of Teaching: Is It Truly Much Ado about Nothing? Robert Engvall. LC 96-3422. 176p. 1996. pap. text 28.00 (*0-7618-0494-3*) U Pr of Amer.

Professionalization of Teaching: Is It Truly Much Ado about Nothing? Robert Engvall. LC 96-3422. 176p. 1997. lib. bdg. 47.00 (*0-7618-0493-5*) U Pr of Amer.

Professionalization of the English Church from 1560 to 1700: Ambassadors for Chirst. Stewart Dippel. LC 99-23102. (Studies in Religion & Society: Vol. 44). 272p. 1999. text 89.95 (*0-7734-7982-1*) E Mellen.

Professionalization of the Senior Chinese Officer Corps: Trends & Implications. James C. Mulvenon. LC 97-31081. 109p. 1997. pap. 15.00 (*0-8330-2543-0*, MR-901-OSD) Rand Corp.

Professionalization of Young Hockey Players. Edmund W. Vaz. LC 81-12938. (Illus.). 224p. reprint ed. pap. 69.50 (*0-7837-6182-1*, 204590400009) Bks Demand.

Professionalization, Partnership, & Power: Building Professional Development Schools. Ed. by Hugh G. Petrie. LC 94-39617. (SUNY Series, Frontiers in Education). 310p. (C). 1995. text 59.50 (*0-7914-2605-X*); pap. text 19.95 (*0-7914-2606-8*) State U NY Pr.

*Professionalizing Elemenatary Science Instruction.** (C). 2001. pap. text 0.00 (*0-321-02324-2*) HEPC Inc.

Professionalizing Modern Medicine: Paris Surgeons & Medical Science & Institutions in the Eighteenth Century, 6. Toby Gelfand. LC 79-8955. (Contributions in Medical History Ser.: No. 6). (Illus.). 271p. 1980. 59.95 (*0-313-21488-3*, GPM/) Greenwood.

Professionalizing the Organization: Reducing Bureaucracy to Enhance Effectiveness. Guy Benveniste. LC 86-27567. (Jossey-Bass Management Ser.). 316p. reprint ed. pap. 98.00 (*0-7837-6532-0*, 204564400007) Bks Demand.

Professionally Speaking: A Marketing & Management Handbook for Dental & Medical Professionals. Neil H. Shulkin & Glenn H. Shulkin. (Illus.). 182p. (Orig.). 1994. pap. 79.95 (*0-9640863-0-1*) Dental Store.

Professionally Speaking: Public Speaking for Health Professionals. Arnold Melnick. LC 98-22026. (Illus.). 113p. 1998. 39.95 (*0-7890-0600-6*); pap. 19.95 (*0-7890-0601-4*) Haworth Pr.

Professionally Spoken. 2nd ed. Thomas & Blocher. 164p. (C). 1998. per. 34.95 (*0-7872-5140-2*) Kendall-Hunt.

Professionally Yours: A Book for the Amateur Producer. Pat Trevor. LC 93-48192. 1994. 15.00 (*0-88734-645-6*) Players Pr.

*Professionals: Magnates, Entrepreneurs & Career Women.** Jillian Hanson. LC 00-27198. (Remarkable Women Ser.). (Illus.). (J). 2000. 27.12 (*0-8172-5726-8*) Raintree Steck-V.

Professionals Against Populism: The Peres Government & Democracy. Michael Keren. LC 95-11831. (SUNY Series in Israeli Studies). 147p. (C). 1995. text 49.50 (*0-7914-2563-0*); pap. text 16.95 (*0-7914-2564-9*) State U NY Pr.

Professionals & Managers Public. M. Exworthy. LC 98-13170. 1998. pap. 29.95 (*0-335-19819-8*); pap. 95.00 (*0-335-19820-1*) OpUniv Pr.

Professionals & Paraprofessionals. Michael J. Austin. LC 77-26273. 295p. 1978. text 41.95 (*0-87705-305-7*, Kluwer Acad Hman Sci) Kluwer Academic.

Professionals & Their Addictions: Charter Peachford Hospital National Interdisciplinary Forum, 1989. Ed. by Thomas W. Hester. 176p. (Orig.). 1989. pap. text. write for info. (*0-318-66521-2*) Charter Med.

Professional's Book of Budgerigars. Maja Muller-Bierl. Tr. by T.F.H. Publications Staff from GER. (Illus.). 144p. 1991. lib. bdg. 11.95 (*0-86622-076-3*, TS-138) TFH Pubns.

Professional's Book of Conures. John Coborn. (Illus.). 144p. 1991. 17.95 (*0-86622-421-1*, TS-159) TFH Pubns.

Professional's Book of Gerbils. Bob Bernhard. (Illus.). 160p. 1993. 17.95 (*0-86622-669-9*, TS-120) TFH Pubns.

Professional's Book of Koi. Anmarie Barrie. (Illus.). 160p. 1998. text 17.95 (*0-86622-528-5*, TS-158) TFH Pubns.

Professional's Book of Lovebirds. John Coborn. (Illus.). 160p. 1991. text 17.95 (*0-86622-604-4*, TS155) TFH Pubns.

Professional's Book of Rottweilers. Anna K. Nicholas. (TS Ser.). (Illus.). 448p. 1991. lib. bdg. 89.95 (*0-86622-625-7*, TS-147) TFH Pubns.

Professional's Business Guide for Proprietor & Partnerships. rev. ed. Luanna C. Blagrove. LC 81-65223. (Illus.). 185p. (C). 1981. 29.95 (*0-9604466-5-6*) Blagrove Pubns.

Professional's Business Handbook: A Guide to Successful Planning. Edward Poll. Ed. & Des. by Harald Johnson. 74p. 1997. pap. 29.95 (*0-9654948-2-9*) E Poll & Assocs.

*Professional's Guide Block Scheduling.** Sara Davis Powell. (Illus.). 76p. 1999. pap., teacher ed. 9.95 (*1-57690-478-4*, TCM 2478) Tchr Create Mat.

*Professional's Guide Standards in the Classroom.** Sara Davis Powell. 776p. 1999. pap., teacher ed. 9.95 (*1-57690-482-2*, TCM 2482) Tchr Create Mat.

Professional's Guide to a Fresh Look at Writing: Professional's Guide. Donald Graves. 61p. 1994. pap. text 6.00 (*0-435-08833-5*, 08833) Heinemann.

Professionals Guide to Auto Repossession. Chris Cantrell. 1997. pap. 35.00 (*1-891247-03-4*) Thomas Investigative.

Professional's Guide to Background Investigations. Ralph D. Thomas. 1999. spiral bd. 35.00 (*1-891247-30-1*) Thomas Investigative.

*Professional's Guide to Doing Business on the Internet with CD-ROM.** Alan S. Gutterman et al. 500p. 2000. pap. 99.00 incl. cd-rom (*0-15-607215-7*) Harcourt Prof.

Professional's Guide to Effective Communication: How to Speak & Write Clearly. LC 89-61561. 1989. 27.50 (*1-887024-68-9*) Bisel Co.

Professional's Guide to Ending Violence Quickly: How Bouncers, Bodyguards, & Other Security Professionals Handle Ugly Situations. Marc A. MacYoung. LC 96-216344. (Illus.). 256p. 1996. pap. 21.00 (*0-87364-899-4*) Paladin Pr.

Professional's Guide to Finance & Insurance: A Career Success Plan for Building F&I Profits Through Custom... Gart Sutton. Ed. by Ronda Eckhardt. (Illus.). (Orig.). Date not set. pap. 50.00 (*0-9626008-2-2*) G Sutton & Assoc.

Professional's Guide to Finance & Insurance: A Career Success Plan for Building F&I Profits Through Custom... Gart Sutton. Ed. by Ronda Eckhardt. (Illus.). 150p. (Orig.). 1994. pap. text 50.00 (*0-9626008-0-6*) G Sutton & Assoc.

Professional's Guide to Fitness: Staying Fit While Staying on Track. Lawrence Schwartz. LC 99-36583. 1999. pap. 12.95 (*0-87833-161-1*) Taylor Pub.

Professional's Guide to Fund Raising, Corporate Giving, & Philanthropy: People Give to People. Lynda L. Adams-Chau. LC 87-32263. 192p. 1988. 52.95 (*0-89930-251-3*, ACP/, Quorum Bks) Greenwood.

Professional's Guide to Practicing Private Investigation: A Field Manual & Training Guide. Greg Hauser. 522p. 1997. pap. 45.00 (*0-918487-04-8*) Thomas Investigative.

Professional's Guide to Publicity. 3rd rev. ed. Richard Weiner. LC 78-52626. 176p. (C). 1982. 9.50 (*0-913046-07-8*) Public Relations.

Professional's Guide to QuarkXPress3 3.3 for the Macintosh: The Essential Sourcebook for Designers, Typographers, & Creative Directors. Kim Baker & Sunny Baker. LC 94-25276. 624p. 1995. pap. 39.95 incl. cd-rom (*0-471-11439-1*) Wiley.

Professional's Guide to Reflexology. Shelley Hess. Ed. by Annette D. Danaber. (Milady - Cosmetology). (Illus.). 174p. (C). 1996. pap. 26.95 (*1-56253-334-7*) Thomson Learn.

*Professional's Guide to Retirement Financial Management.** Gerald J. Robinson. (Illus.). 381p. 1999. pap. 139.00 incl. cd-rom (*0-15-606757-9*) Harcourt.

Professional's Guide to Robust Spreadsheets. Ronny Richardson & Manning Publications Staff. 400p. (C). 1996. pap. text 39.95 (*0-13-262320-X*) P-H.

Professional's Guide to Robust Spreadsheets: Using Examples in Lotus 1-2-3 & Microsoft Excel. Ronny Richardson. LC 96-15537. xxi, 281 p. 1996. write for info. (*1-884777-19-8*) Manning Pubns.

Professional's Guide to Sales Management: A Career Success Plan for Managing Retail Vehicle Salespeople. Gart Sutton. Ed. by Fernando Belair. (Illus.). Date not set. pap. 40.00 (*0-9626008-1-4*) G Sutton & Assoc.

Professional's Guide to Successful Management: The Eight Essentials for Running Your Firm, Practice or Partnership. Carol A. O'Connor. LC 94-27726. 1994. write for info. (*0-07-707999-X*) McGraw.

Professional's Guide to Systems Analysis. 2nd ed. Martin E. Modell. (Illus.). 458p. 1996. 55.00 (*0-07-042948-0*) McGraw.

*Professional's Guide to Understanding Gay & Lesbian Domestic Violence: Understanding Practice Interventions.** Joan C. McClennen & John Gunther. LC 99-45504. (Symposium Ser.: Vol. 56). 356p. 1999. text 99.95 (*0-7734-7892-2*) E Mellen.

*Professional's Guide to Value Pricing with CD-ROM.** Ronald J. Baker. 400p. 2000. pap. 99.00 incl. cd-rom (*0-15-607224-6*) Harcourt Prof.

Professional's Guide to Value Pricing 2000. Ronald J. Baker. 400p. 1999. pap. text 99.00 (*0-15-606993-8*) Harcourt.

*Professional's Guide to Value Pricing 2000.** Ronald J. Baker. 460p. 1999. pap. 99.00 (*0-15-606992-X*) Harcourt.

*Professional's Handbook of Financial Risk Management.** Ed. by Lev Borodovsky & Marc Lore. LC 99-88517. 832p. 2000. 299.00 (*0-7506-4111-8*) Buttrwrth-Heinemann.

Professionals in Distress: Issues, Syndromes, & Solutions in Psychology. Ed. by Richard R. Kilburg et al. LC 85-18487. 299p. 1986. 29.95 (*0-912704-43-8*) Am Psychol.

Professionals in Organizations: Debunking a Myth. Mary E. Guy. LC 85-509. 208p. 1985. 57.95 (*0-275-90111-4*, C0111, Praeger Pubs) Greenwood.

Professional's Job Finder. Daniel Lauber. LC 96-92660. (Illus.). 520p. (Orig.). 1997. 36.95 (*1-884587-07-0*); pap. 18.95 (*1-884587-04-6*) Planning Comns.

Professionals on the Front Line: Two Decades of the All-Volunteer Force. J. Eric Fredland. Ed. by Curtis L. Gilroy et al. (Association of the U. S. Army Book Ser.). 336p. 1996. 37.00 (*1-57488-003-9*) Brasseys.

Professionals on Workplace Stress: The Essential Facts. Alex Roney & Cary L. Cooper. LC 97-23239. (Essential Facts Ser.). 1997. pap. text 46.50 (*0-471-97651-2*) Wiley.

Professionals, Power & Solidarity in Poland: A Critical Sociology of Soviet-Type Society. Michael D. Kennedy. (Cambridge Russian, Soviet & Post-Soviet Studies: No. 79). (Illus.). 437p. (C). 1991. text 69.95 (*0-521-39083-4*) Cambridge U Pr.

Professional's Tax Desk Manual. Executive Reports Corporation Editorial Staff. 1971. 89.50 (*0-13-725432-6*) Exec Reports.

Professional's TV News Handbook. Charles Coates. (Illus.). 285p. 1994. 29.95 (*1-56625-006-4*) Bonus Books.

*Professional's TV News Handbook.** Charles Coates. 2000. pap. 29.95 (*1-56625-148-6*) Bonus Books.

*Professional/Trade Organization Laboratory Accreditation/Designation Programs.** Charles W. Hyer. 131p. 2000. pap. 12.00 (*0-16-059028-0*) USGPO.

Professionelles Programmieren mit Microsoft Basic PDS. Peter Monadjemi. (GER.). (C). 1991. text. write for info. (*0-201-55940-4*) Addison-Wesley.

Professions: Roles & Rules. Wilbert E. Moore. LC 78-104184. 316p. 1970. 39.95 (*0-87154-604-3*) Russell Sage.

Professions Accounting: A Business Simulation. 2nd ed. Swinney. (BA - Accounting - First Year Ser.). 1992. mass mkt. 17.95 (*0-538-61048-4*) S-W Pub.

Professions & Disciplines. Daniel W. Rossides. LC 97-12148. 352p. 1997. pap. text 38.60 (*0-13-619982-8*) P-H.

Professions & Occupations see Burns Indiana Statutes Annotated 1999 Cumulative Supplement Set: Pocket Part

Professions & Patriarchy. Anne Witz. (International Library of Sociology Ser.). 224p. (C). 1992. pap. 24.99 (*0-415-07044-9*); text 85.00 (*0-415-05008-1*) Routledge.

Professions & Professional Ideologies in America. Ed. by Gerald L. Geison. LC 83-5853. 157p. 1983. reprint ed. pap. 48.70 (*0-7837-9891-1*, 206061700006) Bks Demand.

Professions & Public Policy. Ed. by Philip Slayton & Michael J. Trebilcock. LC 79-302151. (Illus.). 356p. reprint ed. pap. 110.40 (*0-8357-8286-7*, 203399700088) Bks Demand.

Professions & Services in the European Economic Community. Dominik Lasok. LC 86-15274. 396p. 1986. 133.00 (*90-6544-253-7*) Kluwer Law Intl.

Professions & the French State, 1700-1900. Ed. by Gerald L. Geison. LC 83-14700. (Shelby Cullom Davis Center Ser.). 352p. 1984. 62.50 (*0-8122-7912-3*) U of Pa Pr.

Professions & the Public Interest: Medical Power, Altruism & Alternative Medicine. Mike Saks. LC 94-9582. 272p. (C). 1994. 90.00 (*0-415-01805-6*, B4657) Routledge.

Professions & the State: The Mexican Case. Peter S. Cleaves. LC 87-5911. (PROFMEX Ser.). 147p. 1987. 28.95 (*0-8165-1016-4*) U of Ariz Pr.

Professions & the State Expertise & Autonomy in the Soviet Union & Eastern Europe. Ed. by Anthony Jones. (Labor & Social Change Ser.). 256p. 1991. 49.95 (*0-87722-801-9*) Temple U Pr.

Professions at Bay. Ed. by Ian Glover & Michael Hughes. (Stirling School of Management Ser.). 356p. 1999. text 74.95 (*1-85972-030-7*, Pub. by Avebry) Ashgate Pub Co.

Professions, Businesses & Trades see Tennessee Code Annotated 1999 Supplement

Professions in the Nuclear Age. Sandra Sewell et al. 282p. (C). 1990. pap. 60.00 (*0-86439-077-7*, Pub. by Boolarong Pubns) St Mut.

Professions in Theory & History: Rethinking the Study of the Professions. Ed. by Michael Burrage & Rolf Torstendahl. (SCASSS Ser.). 248p. (C). 1990. text 45.00 (*0-8039-8252-6*) Sage.

Professions, Information Technology & Management in Hospitals. Mike Dent. LC 96-84597. xii, 212 p. 1996. pap. 63.95 (*1-85628-869-2*, Pub. by Avebry) Ashgate Pub Co.

Professions, Law & Social Change. Ed. by J. S. Gandhi. (C). 1994. 14.00 (*81-241-0232-5*, Pub. by Har-Anand Pubns) S Asia.

Professions of a Lucky Jew. Benno W. Varon. LC 91-55276. (Illus.). 456p. 1992. 24.50 (*0-8453-4837-X*, Cornwall Bks) Assoc Univ Prs.

Professions of Authorship: Essays in Honor of Matthew J. Bruccoli. Matthew J. Bruccoli. Ed. by Richard Layman & Joel Myerson. LC 96-10095. 258p. 1996. text 34.95 (*1-57003-144-4*) U of SC Pr.

P

An Asterisk (*) at the beginning of an entry indicates that the title is appearing for the first time.

Professions of Desire: Lesbian & Gay Studies in Literature. Ed. by George E. Haggerty & Bonnie Zimmerman. LC 94-28342. xii, 246p. (Orig.). 1995. pap. 19.75 (*0-87352-563-9*, T128P); lib. bdg. 37.50 (*0-87352-562-0*, T128C) Modern Lang.

Professions of Dramatist & Player in Shakespeare's Time, 1590-1642. Gerald E. Bentley. LC 83-43059. 658p. reprint ed. pap. 200.00 (*0-7837-4327-0*, 204403100012) Bks Demand.

Professions of Taste: Henry James, British Aesteticism, & Commodity Culture. Jonathan Freedman. 337p. (C). 1993. pap. 16.95 (*0-8047-2178-5*) Stanford U Pr.

Professions of Taste: Henry James, British Aestheticism, & Commodity Culture. Jonathan Freedman. LC 90-9773. (Illus.). 337p. 1990. 42.50 (*0-8047-1784-2*) Stanford U Pr.

Professions, Work & Careers. Anselm L. Strauss. 313p. 1975. 34.95 (*0-87855-128-X*) Transaction Pubs.

***Professor.** Charlotte Bronte. (Twelve-Point Ser.). 250p. 1999. lib. bdg. write for info. (*1-58287-095-0*) North Bks.

Professor. Charlotte Bronte. Ed. by Margaret Smith & Herbert Rosengarten. (Clarendon Edition of the Novels of the Brontes Ser.). (Illus.). 390p. 1987. 110.00 (*0-19-812694-8*) OUP.

Professor. Charlotte Bronte. Ed. by Margaret Smith & Herbert Rosengarten. (World's Classics Ser.). 336p. 1991. pap. 5.95 (*0-19-282741-3*) OUP.

Professor. Charlotte Bronte. Ed. by Margaret Smith & Herbert Rosengarten. (Oxford World's Classics Ser.). 330p. 1998. pap. 6.95 (*0-19-283511-4*) OUP.

Professor. Charlotte Bronte. Ed. & Intro. by Heather Glen. 320p. 1989. pap. 8.95 (*0-14-043311-2*, Penguin Classics) Viking Penguin.

Professor. Charlotte Bronte. (Classics Library). 215p. 1998. pap. 3.95 (*1-85326-208-0*, 2080WW, Pub. by Wrdsworth Edits) NTC Contemp Pub Co.

***Professor & The Madman.** unabridged ed. Simon Winchester. 1999. audio 29.95 (*0-694-52243-0*) HarperAudio.

Professor & the Madman: A Tale of Murder, Insanity & the Making of the Oxford English Dictionary. Simon Winchester. LC 98-10204. 256p. (YA). (gr. 8 up). 1998. 22.00 (*0-06-017596-6*) HarpC.

Professor & the Madman: A Tale of Murder, Insanity & the Making of the Oxford English Dictionary. Simon Winchester. (Illus.). 242p. (YA). 1999. pap. 13.00 (*0-06-099486-X*) HarpC.

Professor & the Madman: A Tale of Murder, Insanity & the Making of the Oxford English Dictionary. large type ed. Simon Winchester. LC 98-50794. (YA). 1999. 28.95 (*0-7838-8500-8*, G K Hall & Co) Mac Lib Ref.

***Professor & The Madman: Jones,&Simon.** abr. ed. Simon Winchester. 1998. audio 18.00 (*0-694-52066-7*) HarperAudio.

***Professor & the Madman, The - Intl edition.** abr. ed. Simon Winchester. 256p. 1999. mass mkt. 7.99 (*0-06-103022-8*) HarpC.

***Professor & the Nanny: An Older Man.** Phyllis Halldorson. (Romance Ser.: Bk. 1452). 2000. per. 3.50 (*0-373-19452-8*, 1-19452-1) Silhouette.

***Professor & the Profession.** Robert B. Heilman. LC 99-25129. 368p. 1999. 39.95 (*0-8262-1232-8*) U of Mo Pr.

Professor & the Prophets - Chinese Edition. Moody Institute of Science Staff. Tr. by CRM Staff. (CHI.). 15p. 1982. pap. 0.50 (*1-56582-064-9*) Christ Renew Min.

Professor & the Public: The Role of the Scholar in the Modern World. Goldwin A. Smith. LC 72-2088. (Franklin Memorial Lectures Ser.: Vol. 20). 124p. reprint ed. 38.50 (*0-608-17020-8*, 202760800055) Bks Demand.

Professor Anderson's Tax Guide, 1989: Step by Step Approach for Tax Return Preparation Forms 1040, 1040A & 1040EZ. Tracey A. Anderson. (Orig.). (C). 1989. pap. 8.00 (*0-685-29801-9*) Samco Educ Series.

Professor Anderson's Tax Guide, 1990: Step-By-Step Approach for Tax Return Preparation, 1989 Forms 1040, 1040A, & 1040EZ. Tracey A. Anderson. Ed. by Sue A. Anderson. 100p. (Orig.). 1990. pap. text 9.95 (*0-9624939-0-2*) Samco Educ Series.

Professor at Bay. Burges Johnson. LC 73-107718. (Essay Index Reprint Ser.). 1977. 20.95 (*0-8369-1520-8*) Ayer.

Professor at Large. Stephen P. Duggan. LC 72-4507. (Essay Index Reprint Ser.). 1977. reprint ed. 30.95 (*0-8369-2942-X*) Ayer.

Professor at Play: Essays. Robert Wexelblatt. LC 90-28863. 225p. (C). 1991. pap. 12.95 (*0-8135-1719-2*); text 40.00 (*0-8135-1718-4*) Rutgers U Pr.

Professor at the Breakfast Table: With the Story of the Iris. Oliver W. Holmes. x, 332p. 1968. reprint ed. 18.00 (*0-403-00068-8*) Scholarly.

Professor Bernhardi. Arthur Schnitzler. Tr. by Hetty Landstone. LC 77-175444. reprint ed. 37.50 (*0-404-05616-4*) AMS Pr.

Professor Bernhardi & Other Plays. Arthur Schnitzler. Tr. by G. J. Weinberger. LC 93-7274. (Studies in Austrian Literature, Culture, & Thought. Translation Ser.). 1993. pap. 28.50 (*0-929497-70-8*) Ariadne CA.

Professor Bubbles' Official Bubble Handbook. Richard Favery & John Javna. (Illus.). 96p. (Orig.). (J). 1988. pap. 5.95 (*0-913319-05-8*) Sunstone Pubns.

Professor Business: A Teaching Primer for Faculty. Barbara J. Flood & Joy K. Moll. 228p. 1990. 29.95 (*0-938734-45-8*); pap. 22.50 (*0-938734-41-5*) Info Today Inc.

Professor Challenger Adventures: The Lost World & the Poison Belt. Arthur Conan Doyle. LC 89-7204. 300p. (C). 1989. pap. 9.95 (*0-87701-620-8*) Chronicle Bks.

Professor Challenger in Secrets of the Dreamlands. Ralph E. Vaughan. (Orig.). 1997. pap. 9.95 (*0-936071-66-4*) Gryphon Pubns.

Professor David Zolotnitsky: A Festschrift. David Zolotnitsky. (Contemporary Theatre Review Ser.: Vol. 4, Pt. 1). 107p. 1995. pap. text 20.00 (*3-7186-5597-7*, ECU15, Harwood Acad Pubs) Gordon & Breach.

Professor Dirk Durrer: 35 Years of Cardiology in Amsterdam. Ed. by F. L. Meijler & H. B. Burchell. 648p. 1986. text 135.00 (*0-444-85656-0*); pap. text. write for info. (*0-444-85654-4*) Elsevier.

Professor, Dr. Jur. Max Sorensen: A Bibliography. Ellen M. Sorenson et al. 80p. (C). 1988. pap. 11.95 (*87-7288-194-1*, Pub. by Aarhus Univ Pr) David Brown.

Professor E. McSquared's Calculus Primer. enl. ed. 264p. (YA). (gr. 10 up). 1989. pap. 19.95 (*0-939765-12-8*, GK110) Janson Pubns.

***Professor Eli & the Bible Bunch.** rev. ed. Cornelius L. Barker & Claudette J. Searchwell. Orig. Title: Professor Wyser & the Applic Bunch. (Illus.). 38p. 2000. pap. 15.95 (*0-9678378-2-0*) Cordet Bks.

Professor Farlow's Guide to RVing. Bill Farlow. 176p. 1998. pap. 14.95 (*0-937877-26-3*) Cottage Pubns Inc.

Professor Filarsky's Miraculous Invention. Eric Vos. (J). 1980. 6.00 (*0-87602-182-8*) Anchorage.

Professor Fred & the Fid Fuddlephone. Donna L. Pape. LC 68-56825. (Sound Ser.). (Illus.). 48p. (J). (gr. 2-5). 1968. lib. bdg. 10.95 (*0-87783-032-0*) Oddo.

Professor Googol Flying Time Machine & Atomic Space Capsule Math Primer. Samuel W. Valenza. (gr. 7-12). 1974. 10.95 (*0-936918-00-4*) Intergalactic NJ.

Professor Gulu's Just Our Secret: A Childhood Sexual Abuse Story. Karl A. Floyd. (Illus.). 24p. 1995. pap. 12.95 (*0-8059-3787-0*) Dorrance.

***Professor Hein J.J. Wellens: 33 Years of Cardiology & Arrhythmology.** J. Smeets et al. 700p. 2000. 160.00 (*0-7923-6209-8*, Kluwer Plenum) Kluwer Academic.

Professor, How Could You! Anne Coulter Martens. 96p. 1939. pap. 5.25 (*0-87129-874-0*, P39) Dramatic Pub.

Professor How Could You! Harry Leon Wilson. (Collected Works of Harry Leon Wilson). 340p. 1999. reprint ed. lib. bdg. 98.00 (*1-58201-882-0*) Classic Bks.

Professor James Beart Simonds: A Great British Veterinarian Forgotten. Iain Pattison. 172p. 1990. 64.00 (*0-85131-491-0*, Pub. by J A Allen) St Mut.

Professor Kane's Contribution to Charmasastra Literature. Ed. by S. G. Moghe. xii, 380p. 1997. 35.00 (*81-246-0075-9*, Pub. by D K Printwrld) Nataraj Bks.

Professor Lasio's The Office Passalong: Round Tuits & Other Silliness. Lasio. Ed. by F. J. Sharp. LC 91-71394. (Illus.). 50p. 1991. 5.00 (*0-9629202-0-7*) Co Called W.

***Professor Longhair Collection.** 128p. 1999. otabind 19.95 (*0-7935-9334-4*) H Leonard.

Professor Lord Acton. Owen Chadwick. 56p. 1995. pap. 5.00 (*1-880595-04-4*) Acton Inst Stu Rel.

Professor Martens' Departure. Jaan Kross. 304p. 1995. pap. 13.95 (*1-56584-111-5*, Pub. by New Press NY) Norton.

Professor Martens' Departure. Joan Kross. Tr. by Anselm Holla. LC 93-83812. 304p. 1994. 25.00 (*1-56584-110-7*, Pub. by New Press NY) Norton.

Professor Mayo's College: A History of East Texas State University. Donald E. Reynolds. (Illus.). 212p. 1993. 24.95 (*0-9637092-0-8*) E TX Mayo Pr.

Professor McGee's Solution: And Other Light & Whimsical Verse. 2nd rev. ed. William J. Middleton. LC 98-96253. (Illus.). 56p. 1998. pap. 5.00 (*1-886467-35-8*) WJM Press.

***Professor Miyagawa's Diary: StarFestival CD-ROM.** (Illus.). 2000. pap. 35.00 (*1-929724-14-4*) StarFestival.

Professor Mmaa's Lecture. Stefan Themerson. LC 74-21585. 226p. 1976. 22.50 (*0-87951-029-3*, Pub. by Overlook Pr) Penguin Putnam.

Professor Mmaa's Lecture. Stefan Themerson. LC 74-21585. 226p. 1984. pap. 11.95 (*0-87951-966-5*, Pub. by Overlook Pr) Penguin Putnam.

Professor Noah Thingertoo & His Bible Fact Book: Old Testament. Christopher Gray. LC 97-104625. 32p. (J). 1996. 10.99 (*1-56476-554-7*, Victor Bks) Chariot Victor.

Professor Noah Thingertoo's & His Bible Fact Book: Old Testament. Christopher Gray. LC 97-104618. (J). 1996. 10.99 (*1-56476-555-5*, Victor Bks) Chariot Victor.

Professor Noah's Spaceship. Brian Wildsmith. (Illus.). 32p. (J). (ps-3). 1987. pap. 11.95 (*0-19-272149-6*) OUP.

Professor of Aesthetics. Christopher T. Leland. LC 93-38225. 160p. 1994. 18.95 (*0-944072-37-2*) Zoland Bks.

Professor of Desire. Philip Roth. 1994. pap. 12.00 (*0-679-74900-4*) Vin Bks.

Professor of Education: An Assessment of Conditions. Ed. by Ayers Bagley. (SPE Monographs). 125p. 1975. 10.00 (*0-933669-15-1*) Soc Profs Ed.

Professor of Light. Marina Budhos. LC 98-33904. 254p. 1999. 23.95 (*0-399-14473-0*, G P Putnam) Peng Put Young Read.

Professor on the Loose. Loren Reid. LC 92-96967. (Illus.). vi, 334p. (Orig.). 1992. pap. 13.95 (*0-9634518-0-4*) Longinus Pr.

Professor Patulli Sing-a-Long. abr. ed. Joe Loesch. Ed. by Cheryl J. Hutchinson. (Bible Stories for Kids Ser.). (Illus.). 16p. (J). (gr. 1-6). 1997. 7.95 incl. audio (*1-887729-16-X*) Toy Box Prods.

Professor Phonics Gives Sound Advice: An Intensive, Comprehensive Phonics Book & Reader. 13th ed. Monica Fohzer. (Illus.). 112p. (J). (gr. k-3). 1965. reprint ed. pap. text 15.00 (*0-9607918-0-9*, A 505419) Prof Phonics-EduCare.

Professor Phonics Gives Sound Advice: Manual of Instructions. 8th ed. Monica Foltzer. 32p. 1984. pap. text 7.00 (*0-9607918-1-7*, 653531) Susan M Greve.

Professor Phonics Gives Sound Advice: Student's Book. An Intesive Comprehensive Phonics Book & Reader. Monica Foltzer. (Professor Phonics System Ser.). (Illus.). 112p. (J). (gr. k-3). 1965. pap., student ed. 15.00 (*0-9665307-0-5*) Prof Phonics-EduCare.

Professor Phonics Gives Sound Advice: Teacher's Manual. Monica Foltzer. (Professor Phonics System Ser.). (Illus.). 1965. pap., teacher ed. 7.00 (*0-9665307-1-3*) Prof Phonics-EduCare.

Professor Pishposh & the Robots. Adelaide Altman. (Illus.). 48p. (J). (ps-2). 1988. 12.95 (*0-933905-05-X*); pap. 9.95 (*0-933905-16-5*) Claycomb Pr.

Professor Popkin's Prodigious Polish: A Tale of Coven Tree. Bill Brittain. LC 89-78221. (Illus.). 160p. (J). (gr. 3-7). 1991. 13.95 (*0-06-020726-4*) HarpC Child Bks.

Professor Protein's Book of F. H. H. A. R. T. Steve Parker. (Illus.). 48p. 1996. pap. 6.95 (*0-7613-0500-9*, Copper Beech Bks) Millbrook Pr.

Professor Protein's Fitness, Health, Hygiene & Relaxation Tonic. Steve Parker. (Illus.). 48p. (YA). (gr. 5 up). 1996. lib. bdg. 23.90 (*0-7613-0494-0*, Copper Beech Bks) Millbrook Pr.

Professor Puffendorf's Secret Potions. Robin Tzannes. (Illus.). 40p. (J). (ps-5). 1992. 16.95 (*1-56288-267-8*) Checkerboard.

Professor Puffendorf's Secret Potions. Robin Tzannes & Korky Paul. (Illus.). 40p. (J). 1998. pap. 9.95 (*0-19-521446-3*) OUP.

Professor Romeo. Anne Bernays. LC 96-29913. (Hardscrabble Bks.). 287p. 1997. reprint ed. pap. 14.95 (*0-87451-809-1*) U Pr of New Eng.

Professor Rubin. Jim O'Neal. 118p. (Orig.). 1993. pap. text 10.95 (*1-883457-00-9*) J ONeal Publng.

Professor Skinner, Alias Montagu Norman. J. Hargrave. 1974. 69.95 (*0-8490-0895-6*) Gordon Pr.

Professor Sniff & the Lost Spring Breezes. Alex Shearer. LC 97-36065. (Illus.). 102p. (J). (gr. 2-4). 1998. pap. 14.95 (*0-531-30079-X*) Orchard Bks Watts.

Professor Sniff & the Lost Spring Breezes. Alex Shearer. LC 97-36065. (Illus.). 102p. (J). (gr. 3-7). 1998. lib. bdg. 15.99 (*0-531-33079-6*) Orchard Bks Watts.

Professor Solomon Snickerdoodle Looks at Air. Peter Murray. LC 95-7608. (Umbrella Bks.). (Illus.). 32p. (J). (gr. 2-6). 1997. lib. bdg. 19.93 (*1-56766-082-7*) Childs World.

Professor Solomon Snickerdoodle Looks at Light. Peter Murray. LC 95-10203. (Umbrella Bks.). (Illus.). 32p. (J). (gr. 2-6). 1997. lib. bdg. 19.93 (*1-56766-148-3*) Childs World.

Professor Swami: Dream Interpretations Plus Mole Significance. Amading S. Abad. Ed. & Tr. by Angelie Bliss. LC 96-84086. (Illus.). 112p. (Orig.). 1996. pap. 12.95 (*0-9651438-4-8*, Forever Yng Club) Air & Water King.

Professor T. S. C. Lowe & His Mountain Railway. Maria S. Burden. 1993. pap. 5.50 (*0-87505-402-1*) Borden.

Professor, the Institute, & DNA. Rene Jules Dubos. LC 76-26812. (Illus.). 262p. 1976. 15.00 (*0-87470-022-1*) Rockefeller.

Professor Von Cluck. (J). pap. 8.00 (*0-614-18219-0*) Let Us Tch Kids.

Professor Weissman's Laugh with Math. rev. ed. Martin Weissman & Keith Monse. (Illus.). 94p. 1995. pap. 19.95 (*0-9632003-0-5*) Laugh & Lrn.

Professor Wellstone Goes to Washington: The Inside Story of a Grassroots U. S. Senate Campaign. Dennis J. McGrath & Dane Smith. LC 94-41361. (Illus.). 328p. 1995. 24.95 (*0-8166-2662-6*); pap. 17.95 (*0-8166-2663-4*) U of Minn Pr.

Professor Wormbog in Search for the Zipperump-a-Zoo. Mercer Mayer. (Illus.). 48p. (J). (ps up). 1992. pap. 5.95 (*1-879920-04-2*) Rain Bird Prods.

Professor Wyser & the Applic Bunch see Professor Eli & the Bible Bunch

Professor X. Peter Kalu. 288p. 1996. pap. 9.95 (*1-874509-17-4*) LPC InBook.

Professor Zuccini's Traveling Tales: Folk Tales in Commedie Style. Sylvia Ashby. 44p. (J). (gr. k up). 1983. pap. 4.00 (*0-88680-208-3*) I E Clark.

Professorenroman in America: A Study in Cultural Crosscurrents, Popular Acclaim, & Literary Survival. Edward J. Danis. 184p. (C). 1993. lib. bdg. 44.00 (*0-8191-9104-3*) U Pr of Amer.

Professorial Vitality: A Critical Issue in Higher Education. Dennis D. Gooler. LC 91-8871. 263p. (Orig.). 1991. lib. bdg. 16.95 (*1-879528-00-2*) Ed Studies Pr.

Professoriate: Challenges & Promises. Ed. by Paul V. Bredeson & Jay P. Scribner. LC 95-70738. (NCPEA Yearbook Ser.). 285p. 1998. 49.95 (*1-56676-353-3*) Scarecrow.

***Professors Are from Mars Students Are from Snickers.** Ronald A. Berk. 1998. pap. 19.95 (*0-912150-52-1*) Atwood Pub LLC.

Professors As Teachers. Kenneth E. Eble. LC 78-186579. (Jossey-Bass Series in Higher Education). 218p. reprint ed. pap. 67.60 (*0-8357-4940-1*, 203787000009) Bks Demand.

Professors As Writers: A Self-Help Guide to Productive Writing. Robert Boice. LC 89-63465. 180p. 1989. pap. 19.95 (*0-913507-13-X*) New Forums.

Professor's Attitude & Performance. Rafael Colon Cora. LC 78-12813. 161p. 1981. pap. 5.00 (*0-8477-2450-6*) U of PR Pr.

Professor's Book of First Names. Thomas V. Busse. LC 83-80773. (Illus.). 120p. (Orig.). 1984. pap. 5.95 (*0-9610950-1-6*) Green Ball Pr.

Professors Can Preach. Joe E. Trull. LC 88-81871. 140p. (Orig.). 1988. pap. 10.00 (*0-914520-26-1*) Insight Pr.

Professor's Duties: Ethical Issues in College Teaching. Peter J. Markie. (Issues in Academic Ethics Ser.). 224p. (C). 1994. pap. text 22.95 (*0-8476-7952-7*); lib. bdg. 58.50 (*0-8476-7951-9*) Rowman.

***Professor's House.** Willa Cather. Ed. by Frederick M. Link. (Willa Cather Scholarly Edition Ser.). (Illus.). 2001. text 75.00 (*0-8032-1428-6*) U of Nebr Pr.

Professor's House. Willa Cather. 1976. 23.95 (*0-8488-0456-2*) Amereon Ltd.

Professor's House. Willa Cather. LC 90-50269. (Vintage Classics Ser.). 283p. 1990. pap. 11.00 (*0-679-73180-6*) Vin Bks.

Professor's House. large type ed. Willa Cather. (All-Time Favorites Ser.). 299p. 1993. reprint ed. lib. bdg. 19.95 (*1-56054-484-8*) Thorndike Pr.

Professor's House. Willa Cather. (Collected Works of Willa Cather). 283p. 1998. reprint ed. lib. bdg. 88.00 (*1-58201-574-0*) Classic Bks.

Professor's Love-Story, Etc. see Works of J. M. Barrie: Peter Pan Edition

Professors of Education & Education Librarians. Ed. by Ayers Bagley. (SPE Monographs). 1985. 10.00 (*0-933669-34-8*) Soc Profs Ed.

Professors of Teaching: An Inquiry. Ed. by Richard Wisniewski & Edward R. Ducharme. LC 88-12655. (SUNY Series, Teacher Preparation & Development). 172p. (C). 1989. text 64.50 (*0-88706-901-0*); pap. text 21.95 (*0-88706-902-9*) State U NY Pr.

***Professors of the Law: Barristers & English Legal Culture in the Eighteenth Century.** David Lemmings. (Illus.). 408p. 2000. text 88.00 (*0-19-820721-2*) OUP.

Professors of War: The Naval War College & the Development of the Naval Profession. Ronald H. Spector. LC 77-7155. (Historical Monographs: No. 3). (Illus.). 187p. (C). 1977. reprint ed. pap. 8.00 (*0-9637973-2-8*) Naval War Coll.

Professors on Guard: The First AAUP Investigations. Ed. by Walter P. Metzger. LC 76-55213. (Academic Profession Ser.). 1977. lib. bdg. 29.95 (*0-405-10040-X*) Ayer.

Professors, Patronage & Politics: The Aberdeen Universities in the Eighteenth Century. Roger L. Emerson. (Quincentennial Studies in the History of the University of Aberdeen). (Illus.). 200p. 1992. pap. text 15.25 (*0-08-040916-4*, Pub. by Aberdeen U Pr) Macmillan.

Professors, Politics & Pop. Jon Wiener. 380p. (gr. 13). 1994. pap. 20.00 (*0-86091-672-3*, Pub. by Verso) Norton.

Professor's Stick Book & Toy. Richard Aspen. 16p. (J). (gr. 3 up). 1993. pap. text 19.95 (*1-883737-01-X*) Matey Pr.

Professors Who Believe: The Spiritual Journeys of Christian Faculty. Ed. by Paul M. Anderson. LC 98-27832. 252p. 1998. pap. 14.99 (*0-8308-1599-6*, 1599) InterVarsity.

Professor's Work. Matthew Melko. LC 98-29101. (Illus.). 268p. 1998. 54.00 (*0-7618-1216-4*); pap. 36.50 (*0-7618-1217-2*) U Pr of Amer.

Professorship in Educational Administration. Ed. by Donald J. Willower & Jack A. Culbertson. 105p. (C). 1964. text 5.00 (*1-55996-103-1*, W4) Univ Council Educ Admin.

Profeta. Kahlil Gibran. 1998. pap. text 60.00 (*0-679-78500-0*) Knopf.

Profeta. Kahlil Gibran. 1999. pap. 7.99 (*0-375-70162-1*) Vin Bks.

Profeta. Frank E. Peretti.Tr. of Prophet. (SPA.). 480p. 1993. pap. 14.99 (*0-8297-1840-0*) Vida Pubs.

Profeta Elias. Yiye Avila.Tr. of Prophet Elijah. (SPA.). 50p. 3.50 (*0-7899-0074-2*, 550042) Editorial Unilit.

Profetas de Israel. Leon J. Wood. (SPA.). 424p. 1995. pap. 12.99 (*0-8254-1901-8*, Edit Portavoz) Kregel.

Profetas de la Revolucion. Peter A. Gonzalez.Tr. of Prophets of the Revolution. (SPA.). 279p. 1989. pap. 1.99 (*0-945792-88-3*, 497705) Editorial Unilit.

Profetas Del Antiguo Testamento (Preaching from the Prophets) K. M. Yates. Tr. by Simon Corona from ENG.Tr. of Preaching from the Prophets. (SPA.). 336p. 1978. reprint ed. pap. 14.50 (*0-311-04026-8*) Casa Bautista.

Profetas Menores. Charles L. Feinberg.Tr. of Minor Prophets. (SPA.). 384p. 1989. pap. 13.99 (*0-8297-1088-4*) Vida Pubs.

Profetas y Reyes. Ellen G. White. (SPA.). 400p. Date not set. pap. 11.99 (*1-883012-85-6*) Remnant Pubns.

Profetizar En Las Reuniones De La Iglesia Para La Edificacion Organica De La Iglesia Como El Cuerpo De Cristo, El (Bosqu. Witness Lee.Tr. of PROPHESYING IN THE CHURCH MEETINGS FOR THE ORGANIC BUILDING UP OF THE CHURCH AS THE BODY OF CHRIST (OUTLINES). (SPA.). 71p. 1989. pap. 4.50 (*0-87083-487-8*, 12-017-002) Living Stream Ministry.

Proffered Crown: Saint-Simonianism & the Doctrine of Hope. Robert B. Carlisle. LC 87-45481. (Johns Hopkins University Studies in Historical & Political Science: Series 105, No. 3). 286p. 1987. reprint ed. pap. 88.70 (*0-608-06706-7*, 206690300009) Bks Demand.

Proffesional Travel Agency Management. Chuck Y. Gee & Dexter J. L. Choy. (C). 1989. text 57.00 (*0-13-725557-8*) P-H.

***Proffesional VB 6 XML.** Wrox Press Inc., Staff. 2000. pap. text 49.99 (*1-86100-332-3*) Wrox Pr Inc.

Proffessionally Speaking: Managing Your English in Bussiness. Lees, Smith, Osborne. 1995. disk 121.00 (*0-471-95410-1*) Wiley.

Proficiency, Curriculum, Articulation: The Ties That Bind. Ed. by Alice C. Omaggio. (Reports of the Northeast Conference on the Teaching of Foreign Languages). 220p. 1985. pap. 10.95 (*0-915432-85-4*) NE Conf Teach Foreign.

Proficiency in Counterpoint: A College Worktext. Paul Fontaine. LC 67-13407. (Illus.). (Orig.). 1967. pap. text 22.95 (*0-89197-360-5*) Irvington.

Proficiency in Oral English Communication: An Assessment of Accented Speech. 2nd ed. Lorna D. Sikorski. (Illus.). (YA). (gr. 7 up). 1997. pap. 79.95 (*1-883574-00-5*, 3601) LDS & Asocs.

Proficiency, Policy & Professionalism in Foreign Language Education. Ed. by Robert DiDonato. (Central States Ser.). pap. 14.21 (*0-8442-9319-9*, VF9319-9) NTC Contemp Pub Co.

Proficiency Testing in Analytical Chemistry. Ed. by R. E. Lawn et al. 122p. 1997. pap. 47.00 (*0-85404-432-9*) Am Chemical.

***Proficient Motorcycling for Men & Women: The Ultimate Guide to Riding Well.** David L. Hough. LC 00-8873. (Illus.). 264p. 2000. pap. 24.95 (*1-889540-53-6*) Bowtie Press.

Proficient Pilot. enl. rev. ed. Barry J. Schiff. (Illus.). 320p. 1985. 21.95 (*0-02-607150-9*) Macmillan.

Proficient Pilot, Vol. 1. Barry J. Schiff. LC 94-14249. 1994. 24.95 (*1-56566-075-7*) Thomasson-Grant.

Proficient Pilot, Vol. 2. rev. enl. ed. Barry J. Schiff. (Illus.). 302p. 1995. 24.95 (*1-56566-079-X*, ASA-HSCH-PP2, Pub. by Thomasson-Grant) ASA Inc.

Proficient Pilot: #ASA-PP-1, Vol. 1. rev. ed. Barry Schiff. LC 94-14249. (Illus.). 330p. 1998. pap. 19.95 (*1-56027-281-3*, ASA-PP-1) ASA Inc.

Proficient Reader, 2 vols. Epstein. (C). 1993. pap. 3.96 (*0-395-63178-5*) HM.

Proficient Reader, 2 vols. 2nd ed. Epstein. (C). 1992. pap. text 38.36 (*0-395-63177-7*) HM.

***Proficient Reader** 3rd ed. Ira D. Epstein & Ernest B. Nieratka. LC 98-72021. xxvi, 524p. 1999. write for info. (*0-395-87794-6*) HM.

Proficient Reading. Evelyn Hodge & Acquanet Bracy. 490p. (C). 1999. per. 41.95 (*0-7872-5477-0*, 41547701) Kendall-Hunt.

Profil du Succes: L'Ascension Sociale de Population d'Afrique, d'Asie et d'Amer. 68p. 1995. write for info. (*92-806-3168-3*) U N I C E.

Profil Perdu. Francoise Sagan. (FRE.). 224p. 1974. pap. 6.95 (*0-7859-1490-0*, 2277117021); pap. 3.95 (*0-686-55394-2*) Fr & Eur.

***Profile.** C. J. Koehler. 2000. per. 5.99 (*0-373-26345-7*) Harlequin Bks.

Profile: A Guide to Military Lifestyles. (Illus.). 59p. (Orig.). 1993. pap. text 20.00 (*0-7881-0148-X*) DIANE Pub.

***Profile: The Architects' Sourcebook.** 2300p. (C). 1999. 149.00 (*0-9651113-6-9*, 62139) Construct Mkt Data.

Profile: The Architects Sourcebook. rev. ed. Ed. by Dorothy A. DeGennaro. 2000p. 1997. pap. 149.00 (*0-9651113-3-4*) Construct Mkt Data.

Profile: The Architects Sourcebook. 12th rev. ed. Ed. by Dorothy A. DeGennaro. 2000p. 1997. 175.00 (*0-9651113-2-6*) Construct Mkt Data.

Profile: The Architects Sourcebook. 13th rev. ed. Ed. by Dorothy A. DeGennaro. (Illus.). 2000p. 1998. 175.00 (*0-9651113-5-0*); pap. 149.00 (*0-9651113-4-2*) Construct Mkt Data.

ProFile: The Sourcebook of U. S. Architectural Design Firms. 11th rev. ed. Ed. by Dorothy A. DeGennaro. 1800p. 1996. pap. 149.00 (*0-9651113-1-8*); boxed set 175.00 (*0-9651113-0-X*) Construct Mkt Data.

Profile & Longitudinal Corrections on Involute Gears. H. Sigg. (Technical Papers: Vol. P109.16). (Illus.). 8p. 1965. pap. text 30.00 (*1-55589-211-6*) AGMA.

***Profile f the Fossil Fuel Electric Power Generation Industry.** Government Printing Office Staff. 162p. 1998. per. 14.00 (*0-16-049399-4*) USGPO.

Profile for Profitability: Using Cost Control & Profitability Analysis. Thomas S. Dudick. LC 72-4353. (Wiley Systems & Controls for Financial Management Ser.). 271p. reprint ed. 84.10 (*0-8357-9963-8*, 201561900095) Bks Demand.

Profile in Alternative Medicine: The Eclectic Medical College of Cincinnati, 1835-1942. John S. Haller. LC 98-43302. (Illus.). 224p. 1999. text 35.00 (*0-87338-610-8*) Kent St U Pr.

Profile in Photography. Brooks Institute Staff. Ed. by Tony Corbell. (Illus.). 224p. 1991. boxed set 50.00 (*0-9628858-0-0*) Serbin Commns.

Profile Makers. Linda Bierds. 1997. 25.00 (*0-614-29408-8*); 23.00 (*0-8050-5535-5*); pap. 12.00 (*0-614-29409-6*); pap. 12.95 (*0-8050-5536-3*) H Holt & Co.

Profile of a Collector: The Collection of Muriel Bultman Francis. Edward P. Caraco. LC 85-43432. (Illus.). 132p. 1985. pap. 18.95 (*0-89494-024-4*) New Orleans Mus Art.

Profile of a Computer Hacker. Nicolas Chantler. Ed. by Winn Schwartau. (Illus.). 400p. (Orig.). 1997. pap. 24.95 (*0-9628700-2-1*) Inter Pact Pr.

Profile of a Leader: A Facilitator's Resource Kit. Samuel E. Dotson & James A. Griffin. (Illus.). 176p. 1996. ring bd. 195.00 (*0-9662588-1-9*) DaySpring Lrdrship.

Profile of a Manic Depressive. Isabel Bingham. 1997. pap. write for info. (*1-57553-637-4*) Watermrk Pr.

Profile of a Metropolis: A Case Book. Robert J. Mowitz & Deil S. Wright. LC 62-14069. (Illus.). 691p. reprint ed. pap. 200.00 (*0-7837-3604-5*, 204346900009) Bks Demand.

Profile of Abuse: Breaking the Cycle Of... Dee Frances. 179p. Date not set. pap. 20.00 (*1-885519-08-7*, Pub. by DDDD Pubns) Baker & Taylor.

Profile of an Opportunity: The Risks & Rewards of Investing in China. Ed. & Arranged by Dennis Bloodworth. LC 95-948213. 296p. 1995. pap. 22.50 (*981-210-076-8*, Pub. by Times Academic) Intl Spec Bk.

Profile of Brigadier General Alfred N. A. Duffie. Thomas S. Reed. 53p. 1982. pap. text 23.00 (*0-89126-109-5*) MA-AH Pub.

***Profile of California Computer & Internet Users.** Rosa Maria Moller. 21p. 2000. pap. write for info. (*1-58703-123-X*, CRB-00-002) CA St Libry.

Profile of Children in United States School Districts. Government Printing Office Staff. 152p. 1996. pap. 12.00 (*0-16-048782-X*) USGPO.

Profile of Correctional Effectiveness & New Directions for Research. Ted Palmer. LC 93-24925. (New Directions in Crime & Justice Studies). 339p. (C). 1994. pap. text 21.95 (*0-7914-1910-X*) State U NY Pr.

Profile of Correctional Effectiveness & New Directions for Research. Ted Palmer. LC 93-24925. (SUNY Series in New Directions in Crime & Justice Studies). 339p. (C). 1994. text 64.50 (*0-7914-1909-6*) State U NY Pr.

Profile of Courts in Canada 1995. Canadian Centre for Justice Statistics. LC 96-151252. v, 227p. 1996. write for info. (*0-660-15593-1*) Can7 Govern Pub.

Profile of Courts in Canada, 1987-1988. Canadian Centre for Justice Statistics. LC 90-110409. 161 p. 1989. write for info. (*0-660-12543-9*) Can7 Govern Pub.

Profile of Current Developments in Atomic Spectroscopy: Dedicated to Kurt Laqua on the Occasion of His 65th Birthday. Ed. by P. W. Boumans et al. 400p. 1985. pap. 91.00 (*0-08-031447-3*, Pergamon Pr) Elsevier.

Profile of Economic Plants. Ed. by John C. Roecklein & PingSun Leung. 608p. 1987. 89.95 (*0-88738-167-7*) Transaction Pubs.

Profile of Eighth Graders in Catholic Schools. Penny A. Sebring & Eric M. Camburn. (Illus.). 55p. (Orig.). 1992. pap. 4.80 (*1-55833-116-6*) Natl Cath Educ.

Profile of European Packaging Machinery Manufacturers. 541p. 1996. spiral bd. 1950.00 (*0-7889-0572-4*, 3003-21) Frost & Sullivan.

Profile of Horace. D. R. Shackleton Bailey. 152p. 1982. 32.50 (*0-674-71325-7*) HUP.

Profile of Indian Culture. Krishana Chaitanya. 1975. 15.95 (*0-318-36956-7*) Asia Bk Corp.

Profile of Jawaharlal Nehru. K. T. Char. 1965. 49.50 (*0-614-01827-7*) Elliots Bks.

Profile of Jonathan Miller. Ed. by Michael Romain. (Illus.). 251p. (C). 1991. pap. 22.95 (*0-521-40953-5*); text 69.95 (*0-521-40137-2*) Cambridge U Pr.

Profile of Lake St. Clair. Thomas A. Edsall & John E. Gannon. (Great Lakes Profile Ser.). (Illus.). 15p. (Orig.). 1991. pap. 1.00 (*1-885756-01-1*, MICHU-SG91-701) MI Sea Grant.

Profile of Legal Malpractice: A Statistical Study of Determinative Characteristics of Claims Asserted Against Attorneys. LC 86-210693. 81p. 1979. pap. 40.00 (*0-89707-254-5*, 414-0003) Amer Bar Assn.

Profile of Love. Ferdinand Campbell. LC 78-62758. 96p. reprint ed. 10.95 (*0-912444-16-9*) DARE Bks.

Profile of 1994-95 State Assessment Systems & Reported Results National Education Goals Panel. Ed. by Leslie Lawrence. (Illus.). 140p. (C). 1999. reprint ed. pap. text 30.00 (*0-7881-7695-1*) DIANE Pub.

Profile of North Carolina's African American & Native American Populations. Nicole Curbeam et al. (Illus.). 74p. 1994. write for info. (*0-9633115-2-2*) NC Inst Min Econ Devel.

Profile of Policies & Practices for Limited English Proficient Students: Screening Methods, Program Support & Teacher Training (SASS 1993- 94) Mei Han. 65p. 1997. pap. 4.75 (*0-16-048976-8*) USGPO.

Profile of Runaway Slaves in Virginia & South Carolina from 1730 Through 1787. rev. ed. Lathan A. Windley. LC 95-32389. (Studies in African American History & Culture). (Illus.). 224p. 1995. text 15.00 (*0-8153-1018-8*) Garland.

Profile of Rural Older Americans. 1995. pap. 8.00 (*0-910883-81-5*, 4193) Natl Coun Aging.

***Profile of San Bernardino County, CalWORKs Caseload.** James N. Dertouzos & Patricia A. Ebener. ix, 47p. 2000. pap. 12.00 (*0-8330-2864-2*, DB-304) Rand Corp.

Profile of Some Indian Tribes: An Anthropo-Nutritional Micro Study. Tilak Bagchi. LC 94-902403. (C). 1995. 44.00 (*81-85094-73-X*, Pub. by Punthi Pus) S Asia.

Profile of St. Mary's River. Thomas A. Edsall & John E. Gannon. (Great Lakes Profile Ser.). (Illus.). 20p. (Orig.). 1993. pap. 1.00 (*1-885756-03-8*, MICHU-SG93-700) MI Sea Grant.

Profile of State Chartered Banking. Ellen C. Lamb. 300p. 1996. spiral bd. 60.00 (*0-614-13712-8*) Conf St Bank.

Profile of State-Chartered Banking. 11th rev. ed. Conference of State Bank Supervisors. 1995. ring bd. 60.00 (*0-916361-01-2*) Conf St Bank.

Profile of Teachers in the U.S., 1996. 3rd rev. ed. C. Emily Feistritzer. Ed. by David T. Chester. (Illus.). 80p. (Orig.). 1996. pap. 35.00 (*1-928665-01-2*) Natl Ctr Ed Info.

***Profile of the Aerospace Industry: EPA Office of Compliance Sector Notebook Project.** Ed. by Carol M. Browner. (Illus.). 122p. (C). 2000. reprint ed. pap. text 30.00 (*0-7567-0068-X*) Branden Bks.

***Profile of the Air Transportation Industry.** Government Printing Office Staff. 100p. 1998. per. 7.50 (*0-16-042735-5*) USGPO.

***Profile of the City Council, 1996.** Evelina R. Moulder & International City/County Management Association Staff. LC 98-217153. (Special Data Issue Ser.). 85p. 1998. write for info. (*0-87326-811-3*) Intl City-Cnty Mgt.

Profile of the Dry Cleaning Industry. 1997. lib. bdg. 250.75 (*0-8490-7620-X*) Gordon Pr.

Profile of the Dry Cleaning Industry. Government Printing Office Staff. 91p. 1995. per. 7.00 (*0-16-048268-2*) USGPO.

Profile of the Electronics & Computer Industry. 1997. lib. bdg. 260.95 (*0-8490-7740-0*); lib. bdg. 250.99 (*0-8490-7619-6*) Gordon Pr.

Profile of the Electronics & Computer Industry. Government Printing Office Staff. 154p. 1995. per. 12.00 (*0-16-048269-0*) USGPO.

Profile of the European Connector Industry: Market Prospects to 1999. 6th ed. Compiled by Andrew Fletcher. 200p. 1995. pap. 710.50 (*1-85617-254-6*, Pergamon Pr) Elsevier.

Profile of the European Mobile Communications Industry: Market Prospects to 2000. 3rd ed. Ed. by Andrew Fletcher. LC 96-117453. 307p. 1995. pap. 1176.00 (*1-85617-262-7*) Elsevier.

Profile of the European Motors & Drives Industry. G. Weaver. LC 95-135055. 1994. 1011.75 (*1-85617-220-1*) Elsevier.

Profile of the Fabricated Metal Products Industry. 1997. lib. bdg. 250.99 (*0-8490-7609-9*) Gordon Pr.

Profile of the Fabricated Metal Products Industry. Government Printing Office Staff. 156p. 1995. per. 12.00 (*0-16-048274-7*) USGPO.

***Profile of the Ground Transportation Industry: Trucking, Railroad & Pipeline.** Government Printing Office Staff. 133p. 1998. per. 10.00 (*0-16-049394-3*) USGPO.

Profile of the Inorganic Chemical Industry. 1997. lib. bdg. 250.95 (*0-8490-7615-3*) Gordon Pr.

Profile of the Inorganic Chemical Industry. Government Printing Office Staff. 126p. 1995. per. 9.50 (*0-16-048271-2*) USGPO.

Profile of the International Filtration & Separation Industry. LC 96-116405. 482p. 1995. pap. text 680.00 (*1-85617-264-3*) Elsevier.

Profile of the International Fluid Sealing Industry: Market Prospects to 1999. Ed. by Roisin Reidy. LC 95-215107. 204p. 1995. spiral bd. 855.00 (*1-85617-227-9*) Elsevier.

Profile of the International Membranes Industry. LC 97-127986. Date not set. text 835.00 (*1-85617-317-8*, Pergamon Pr) Elsevier.

Profile of the International Pump Industry: Market Prospects to 1988. 2nd ed. Compiled by Roisin Reidy. LC 95-117280. 280p. 1994. pap. 855.00 (*1-85617-225-2*, Pergamon Pr) Elsevier.

Profile of the International Pump Industry: Prospects to 2000. 3rd ed. LC 97-190457. 1997. 1000.00 (*1-85617-330-5*, R100, Pub. by Elsvr Adv Tech) Elsevier.

Profile of the International Technical Textiles Industry. Profile Staff. 1996. 630.00 (*1-85617-194-9*, Pergamon Pr) Elsevier.

Profile of the International Valve Industry. Profile Staff. LC 96-115956. 1995. 776.75 (*1-85617-265-1*, Pub. by Elsvr Adv Tech) Elsevier.

Profile of the Iron & Steel Industry. 1997. lib. bdg. 250.95 (*0-8490-7613-7*) Gordon Pr.

Profile of the Iron & Steel Industry. Government Printing Office Staff. 120p. 1995. per. 8.50 (*0-16-048272-0*) USGPO.

Profile of the Last Puritan: Jonathon Edwards, Self-Love, & the Dawn of the Beatific. David Brand. 165p. 1991. 24.95 (*1-55540-582-7*, 01 01 73); pap. 14.95 (*1-55540-583-5*, 01 01 73) OUP.

Profile of the Lumber & Wood Products Industry. 1997. lib. bdg. 250.95 (*0-8490-7607-2*) Gordon Pr.

Profile of the Lumber & Wood Products Industry. Government Printing Office Staff. 130p. 1995. per. 9.50 (*0-16-048273-9*) USGPO.

***Profile of the Metal Casting Industry.** Government Printing Office Staff. 159p. 1998. per. 13.00 (*0-16-049396-X*) USGPO.

Profile of the Metal Mining Industry. 1997. lib. bdg. 250.99 (*0-8490-7621-8*) Gordon Pr.

Profile of the Metal Mining Industry. Government Printing Office Staff. 140p. 1995. per. 11.00 (*0-16-048275-5*) USGPO.

Profile of the Motor Vehicle Assembly Industry. 1997. lib. bdg. 251.99 (*0-8490-7618-8*) Gordon Pr.

Profile of the Motor Vehicle Assembly Industry. Government Printing Office Staff. 150p. 1995. per. 12.00 (*0-16-048276-3*) USGPO.

Profile of the Nation: An American Portrait. 10th rev. ed. Ed. by Nancy R. Jacobs et al. (Information Plus Reference Ser.). (Illus.). 176p. 1998. pap. text 26.95 (*1-57302-066-4*) Info Plus TX.

Profile of the Negro in American Dentistry. Foster Kidd. LC 79-16159. (Illus.). 224p. 1979. 16.95 (*0-88258-034-5*) Howard U Pr.

Profile of the New Home Buyer, 1991: Based on 1990 Home Buyers. National Association of Home Builders Staff. 150p. 1991. pap. 65.00 (*0-86718-467-1*) Home Builder.

Profile of the Non-Fuel, Non-Metal Mining Industry. 1997. lib. bdg. 250.95 (*0-8490-7614-5*) Gordon Pr.

Profile of the Non-fuel, Non-Metal Mining Industry. Government Printing Office Staff. 102p. 1995. per. 7.00 (*0-16-048278-X*) USGPO.

Profile of the Nonferrous Metals Industry. 1997. lib. bdg. 250.95 (*0-8490-7606-4*) Gordon Pr.

Profile of the Nonferrous Metals Industry. Government Printing Office Staff. 140p. 1995. per. 9.50 (*0-16-048277-1*) USGPO.

Profile of the Northeast Ohio Cultural Community. William H. Keller et al. LC 97-77009. (Illus.). 97p. 1998. pap. 14.95 (*0-9630961-2-5*) CL Cultural.

Profile of the Organic Chemical Industry. 1997. lib. bdg. 250.99 (*0-8490-7617-X*) Gordon Pr.

Profile of the Organic Chemicals Industry. Government Printing Office Staff. 140p. 1995. per. 12.00 (*0-16-048279-8*) USGPO.

Profile of the Petroleum Refining Industry. 1997. lib. bdg. 250.95 (*0-8490-7616-1*) Gordon Pr.

Profile of the Petroleum Refining Industry. Government Printing Office Staff. 152p. 1995. per. 12.00 (*0-16-048280-1*) USGPO.

***Profile of the Pharmaceutical Manufacturing Industry.** Government Printing Office Staff. 157p. 1998. per. 13.00 (*0-16-049397-8*) USGPO.

***Profile of the Plastic Resin & Man-Made Fiber Industry.** Government Printing Office Staff. 189p. 1998. per. 15.00 (*0-16-049398-6*) USGPO.

Profile of the Printing Industry. 1997. lib. bdg. 250.95 (*0-8490-7608-0*) Gordon Pr.

Profile of the Printing Industry. Government Printing Office Staff. 116p. 1995. per. 8.00 (*0-16-048281-X*) USGPO.

***Profile of the Public Service of Singapore No. 8 in the Series: Current Good Practices & New Development in Public Service Management.** 116p. 2000. pap. 16.95 (*0-85092-574-6*, Pub. by Comm Sec) Stylus Pub VA.

Profile of the Pulp & Paper Industry. 1997. lib. bdg. 250.99 (*0-8490-7629-3*) Gordon Pr.

Profile of the Pulp & Paper Industry. Government Printing Office Staff. 140p. 1995. per. 12.00 (*0-16-048282-8*) USGPO.

Profile of the Rubber & Plastics Industry. 1997. lib. bdg. 251.99 (*0-8490-6244-6*); lib. bdg. 250.95 (*0-8490-7611-0*) Gordon Pr.

Profile of the Rubber & Plastics Industry. Government Printing Office Staff. 146p. 1995. per. 12.00 (*0-16-048283-6*) USGPO.

***Profile of the Shipbuilding & Repair Industry.** Government Printing Office Staff. 137p. 1998. per. 9.50 (*0-16-049400-1*) USGPO.

Profile of the Stone, Clay, Glass & Concrete Products Industry. Government Printing Office Staff. 118p. 1995. pap. 8.00 (*0-16-048284-4*) USGPO.

Profile of the Stone, Clay, Glass, & Concrete Products Industry. 1997. lib. bdg. 250.95 (*0-8490-7612-9*) Gordon Pr.

***Profile of the Textile Industry.** Government Printing Office Staff. 147p. 1998. per. 10.00 (*0-16-049401-X*) USGPO.

Profile of the Transportation Cleaning Industry. 1997. lib. bdg. 250.95 (*0-8490-7610-2*) Gordon Pr.

Profile of the Transportation Equipment Cleaning Industry. Government Printing Office Staff. 70p. 1995. pap. 6.00 (*0-16-048285-2*) USGPO.

***Profile of the Water Transportation Industry.** Government Printing Office Staff. 95p. 1998. per. 7.50 (*0-16-049395-1*) USGPO.

Profile of the Wood Furniture & Fixtures Industry. 1997. lib. bdg. 250.95 (*0-8490-7628-5*) Gordon Pr.

Profile of the Wood Furniture & Fixtures Industry. Government Printing Office Staff. 126p. 1995. per. 8.50 (*0-16-048270-4*) USGPO.

Profile of the Working Poor. 1994. lib. bdg. 250.00 (*0-8490-5691-8*) Gordon Pr.

Profile of the Worldwide Capacitor Industry: Market Prospects to 1998. 4th ed. Compiled by Andrew Fletcher. 240p. 1995. pap. 793.50 (*1-85617-253-8*, Pergamon Pr) Elsevier.

Profile of the Worldwide Resistor Industry to 1997. A. J. Fletcher. 220p. 1993. 776.75 (*1-85617-176-0*, Pergamon Pr) Elsevier.

Profile of the Worldwide Semiconductor: Market Prospects to 1999. 7th ed. Ed. by Andrew Fletcher. 500p. 1995. pap. 933.50 (*1-85617-263-5*) Elsevier.

Profile of the Worldwide Telecommunications Industry. Date not set. pap. text 950.00 (*1-85617-299-6*) Elsevier.

Profile of Three Theories: Erikson, Maslow, Piaget. Carol Tribe. 120p. (C). 1995. pap. text, per. 19.95 (*0-8403-2800-1*) Kendall-Hunt.

Profile of Twentieth-Century American Poetry. Ed. by Jack Myers & David Wojahn. LC 90-37757. 336p. (C). 1991. text 18.95 (*0-8093-1349-9*) S Ill U Pr.

Profile of Undergraduates in United States Postsecondary Education Institutions: 1992-93, with an Essay on Undergraduates at Risk. Laura J. Horn. 177p. 1995. per. 13.00 (*0-16-048410-3*) USGPO.

***Profile of Undergraduates in United States Postsecondary Education Institutions: 1995-96, with an Essay on.** Laura J. Horn. 184p. 1998. pap. 15.00 (*0-16-049577-6*) USGPO.

Profile of Western North America: Indicators of an Emerging Economic Region. Philip M. Burgess & Michael Kelly. LC 94-31787. (Economic Regions: Statistical Handbook Ser.). 1994. 39.95 (*1-55591-907-3*) Fulcrum Pub.

Profile of Work Motivation Attitudes of Apparel Workers. Emma W. Bragg. LC 79-17776. 1979. 18.00 (*0-8357-0460-2*) E W Bragg.

Profile of Young Australians: Facts, Figures & Issues. Ed. by Peter Boss et al. LC 94-49559. 1995. text 55.00 (*0-443-05257-3*) Church.

Profile Your Lifestyle: Questions to Ask Yourself Before Building, Buying or Remodeling a Home. June Curran. LC 78-72187. (C). 1979. pap. 7.95 (*0-932370-00-4*) Brooks Pub Co.

***Profiled Sheet Roofing & Cladding: A Guide to Good Practice.** 3rd ed. N.W. Spons. LC 98-45204. 1999. pap. 47.00 (*0-419-23940-5*) Routledge.

Profiles. Isabella Alden. (Grace Livingston Hill Ser.: Vol. 16). 1997. pap. 5.99 (*0-8423-3192-1*) Tyndale Hse.

Profiles. Glyn Jones & John Rowlands. 330p. (C). 1982. text 55.00 (*0-85088-713-5*, Pub. by Gomer Pr) St Mut.

Profiles. Kenneth Tynan. 1998. pap. 20.00 (*0-679-75639-6*) Random.

Profiles. deluxe limited ed. Baron Wolman. LC 74-81290. (Illus.). 1974. 35.00 (*0-916290-02-6*) Squarebooks.

Profiles, No. 2. 2nd ed. California Design Publications Staff. (Illus.). 288p. 1989. pap. 14.95 (*0-929374-00-2*) CA Design Pubns.

Profiles: A Language Skill Kit. Workman. (EC - HS Communication/English Ser.). 1995. 85.95. (*0-538-62784-0*) S-W Pub.

Profiles: Architecture Landscape Architecture Interior Design. (Illus.). 208p. (Orig.). 1986. pap. 14.95 (*0-317-89908-2*) CA Design Pubns.

Profiles: Architecture, 1990. 2nd ed. Ed. by California Design Publications Staff. (Illus.). 136p. 1989. pap. 24.95 (*0-929374-04-5*) CA Design Pubns.

Profiles: Giants in Medicine. Frederick Eberson. LC 80-53139. (Illus.). 116p. (Orig.). 1980. pap. 10.00 (*0-934616-11-6*) Valkyrie Pub Hse.

Profiles & Letters K. Natwar-Singh. LC 97-913667. xii, 244p. 1998. write for info. (*81-207-2066-0*) Sterling Pub.

P

An Asterisk (*) at the beginning of an entry indicates that the title is appearing for the first time.

Profiles & Profiling. Hitchcock. Date not set. pap. text. write for info. (*0-582-05214-9*, Pub. by Addison-Wesley) Longman.

Profiles & Training for Senior Officials of Local & Regional Authorities (Barcelona, 1990) Council of Europe Staff. (Congress of Local & Regional Authorities of Europe Ser.: No. 20). 1991. 15.00 (*92-871-1983-X*, Pub. by Council of Europe) Manhattan Pub Co.

Profiles & Trends: Hospital Inpatient & Ambulatory Care in Southern New York, Vol. II. Compiled by Division of Research, Analysis, & Planning Staff. 43p. 1985. 15.00 (*0-934459-07-X*) United Hosp Fund.

Profiles Cut from the Wave: CSS Sixth Collection of Poetry. Rebecca S. Bell & C. Sherman Severin. (Collection of National Poetry Ser.). (Illus.). 200p. 1984. pap. 9.95 (*0-942170-06-7*) CSS Pubns.

Profiles for Success. Richard F. Edlich. (Illus.). 176p. 1998. pap. 16.95 (*0-918339-49-9*) Vandamere.

Profiles for Success: Lessons in Teaching, Healing Caring & Living. Richard F. Edlich. 16.95 (*0-918339-53-7*) Vandamere.

Profiles in African Heritage. Edward L. Jones. 1972. pap. 18.00 (*0-9602458-0-4*) Ed-Lynne Jones.

Profiles in American History, 8 vols. Incl. Civil Rights Movement to the Present: Significant Events & the People Who Shaped Them. Joyce Moss & George Wilson. 200p. (J). 1994. text 39.00 (*0-8103-9215-1*, UXL); Great Depression to the Cuban Missile Crisis: Significant Events & the People Who Shaped Them. Joyce Moss & George Wilson. 200p. 1994. text 39.00 (*0-8103-9214-3*, UXL); Profiles in American History Vol. 1: Exploration to Revolution. Ed. by Joyce Moss & George Wilson. (Illus.). 280p. 1993. text 39.00 (*0-8103-9208-9*, M89334-101917, UXL); Profiles in American History Vol. 2: Constitutional Convention to the Louisiana Purchase. Ed. by Joyce Moss & George Wilson. (Illus.). 280p. 1994. text 39.00 (*0-8103-9209-7*, M89334-101918, UXL); Profiles in American History Vol. 3: Indian Removal to the Abolition Movement. Ed. by Joyce Moss & George Wilson. (Illus.). 280p. 1994. text 39.00 (*0-8103-9210-0*, M89334-101919); Profiles in American History Vol. 4: Westward Expansion to the Civil War. Joyce Moss & George Wilson. LC 94-6677. 280p. 1994. text 39.00 (*0-8103-9211-9*, UXL); Profiles in American History Vol. 5: Reconstruction to the Spanish American War. Joyce Moss & George Wilson. 280p. (J). 1994. text 39.00 (*0-8103-9212-7*, UXL); Profiles in American History Vol. 6: Chinese Exclusion to the Women's Rights Movement. Joyce Moss & George Wilson. 280p. 1994. text 39.00 (*0-8103-9213-5*, UXL); LC 94-6677. 2240p. 1993. Set text 270.00 (*0-8103-9207-0*, UXL) Gale.

Profiles in American History, Vol. 1, Exploration to Revolution see Profiles in American History

Profiles in American History, Vol. 2, Constitutional Convention to the Louisiana Purchase see Profiles in American History

Profiles in American History, Vol. 3, Indian Removal to the Abolition Movement see Profiles in American History

Profiles in American History, Vol. 4, Westward Expansion to the Civil War see Profiles in American History

Profiles in American History, Vol. 5, Reconstruction to the Spanish American War see Profiles in American History

Profiles in American History, Vol. 6, Chinese Exclusion to the Women's Rights Movement see Profiles in American History

Profiles in Belief: The Religious Bodies of the United States & Canada, Vols. 3 & 4. Arthur C. Piepkorn. Incl. Vol. 3. Holiness & Pentecostal Bodies. 1990. Vol. 4. Evangelical, Fundamental, & Other Christian Bodies. 1990. LC 89-45748. 1990. 24.95 (*0-06-066581-5*) Harper SF.

Profiles in Business & Management: An International Directory of Scholars & Their Research Version 2.0, 2 vols., Set. Ed. by Claudia Bruce. 2720p. 1996. 495.00 (*0-87584-517-7*) Harvard Busn.

Profiles in Caregiving: The Unexpected Career. Leonard I. Pearlin et al. LC 95-3498. (Illus.). 408p. 1995. pap. text 42.00 (*0-12-059540-0*) Acad Pr.

Profiles in Caring: Advocates for the Elderly. Val J. Halamandaris. (Illus.). 409p. 1990. 25.00 (*0-9628363-0-3*) Caring Pub.

Profiles in Caring: The Most Caring People in America. W. Halamandaris. (Illus.). 175p. 1991. 25.00 (*0-9628363-1-1*) Caring Pub.

Profiles in Character. Jeb Bush & Brian Yablonski. LC 95-83319. 288p. (Orig.). 1996. pap. 15.00 (*0-9650912-0-1*) J M Inst.

Profiles in Character. Members of the U.S. Congress. 288p. 1996. 19.99 (*0-7852-7356-5*) Nelson.

Profiles in Character: Hubris & Heroism in the U. S. Senate, 1789-1990. Joseph M. Hernon. LC 96-8940. 262p. (C). (gr. 13). 1996. 38.95 (*1-56324-937-5*) M E Sharpe.

Profiles In Character: Hubris & Heroism In the U.S. Senate, 1789-1990. Joseph Martin Hernon. LC 96-8940. (Illus.). 262p. 2000. pap. 19.95 (*1-56324-938-3*) M E Sharpe.

Profiles in Childhood Education, 1931-1960: Project of ACEI Later Leaders Committee. LC 92-30308. 1992. 14.00 (*0-87173-127-4*) ACEI.

Profiles in Cognitive Aging. Douglas H. Powell & Dean K. Whitla. LC 94-18126. (Illus.). 256p. 1994. text 46.95 (*0-674-71331-1*, POWPRO) HUP.

Profiles in Connecting Learning & Work: State Initiatives. 220p. 1996. pap. 30.00 (*0-614-30586-1*, LW-96-2) Ed Comm States.

Profiles in Courage. John F. Kennedy. 272p. 1998. 17.98 (*1-57912-014-8*) Blck Dog & Leventhal.

Profiles in Courage. John F. Kennedy. 1983. 12.10 (*0-606-03338-6*, Pub. by Turtleback) Demco.

Profiles in Courage. John F. Kennedy. LC 83-48678. 304p. 1988. reprint ed. mass mkt. 7.00 (*0-06-080698-2*, P 698, Perennial) HarperTrade.

***Profiles in Courage: Commemorative Edition.** John F. Kennedy. LC 99-57061. (Perennial Classics Ser.). 272p. 2000. pap. 12.00 (*0-06-095544-9*, Perennial) HarperTrade.

Profiles in Courage: Commemorative Edition. large type ed. John F. Kennedy. LC 93-36524. 1993. lib. bdg. 22.95 (*0-8161-5886-X*, G K Hall Lrg Type) Mac Lib Ref.

Profiles in Courage: Commemorative Edition. large type ed. John F. Kennedy. LC 93-36524. 1994. pap. 14.95 (*0-8161-5887-8*, G K Hall Lrg Type) Mac Lib Ref.

Profiles in Courage: Curriculum Unit. Center for Learning Network Staff & John F. Kennedy. (Novel Ser.). 104p. (YA). (gr. 9-12). 1990. spiral bd. 18.95 (*1-56077-127-5*) Ctr Learning.

***Profiles in Courage: Kennedy,&John F.Jr., Set.** abr. ed. John F. Kennedy. 2000. audio 18.00 (*0-89845-793-9*, CPN 2110) HarperAudio.

***Profiles in Courage of Ghetto Mothers: The Unique Task Facing Ghetto Moms Raising Kids.** Ricardo Scott. (Ras Cardo Exclusing Reggae Archives Speaks Ser.). (Illus.). 85p. 2000. pap. 30.00 (*1-58470-041-6*, CARDO9949, RAS Cardo Prodn) Crnerstone GA.

Profiles in Courageous Manhood. Edwin Louis Cole. 224p. 1998. pap. 11.99 (*1-57778-087-6*, Pub. by Albury Pub) Appalach Bk Dist.

Profiles in Cultural Evolution: Papers from a Conference in Honor of Elman R. Service. Ed. by A. Terry Rambo & Kathleen Gillogly. LC 90-25676. (Anthropological Papers Ser.: No. 85). xviii, 450p. (Orig.). 1991. pap. 20.00 (*0-915703-23-8*) U Mich Mus Anthro.

Profiles in Democracy: A New Generation of Latin American Leaders. Gil Dorland & Clara Ospina. 182p. 1995. 20.00 (*0-9646531-0-9*) New Continents.

Profiles in Democracy: New Generation of Latin-American Leaders. Gil Dorland & Clara Ospina. Tr. by Luis Zalamea from ENG. 182p. 1995. pap. 12.00 (*0-9646531-1-7*) New Continents.

Profiles in Diversity: Jews in a Changing Europe, 1750-1870. Frances Malino & David J. Sorkin. LC 97-37514. 352p. 1997. pap. 18.95 (*0-8143-2715-X*) Wayne St U Pr.

Profiles in Diversity: Women in the New South Africa. Patricia Romero. LC 98-20674. 235p. 1994. pap. 24.95 (*0-87013-447-7*) Mich St U Pr.

Profiles in Ethnology. 3rd ed. Elman R. Service. (Illus.). 495p. (C). 1997. pap. text 62.00 (*0-06-045912-3*) Addson-Wesley Educ.

Profiles in Excellence. Ed. by Jill Muehrcke. (Leadership Ser.). 147p. 1993. spiral bd. 35.00 (*0-614-07102-X*) Soc Nonprofit Org.

Profiles in Female Poverty. Leela Gulati. 179p. 1981. 19.95 (*0-318-37068-9*) Asia Bk Corp.

Profiles in Female Poverty. Leela Gulati. 1986. 17.00 (*0-8364-1777-1*, Pub. by Usha) S Asia.

Profiles in Flowers: The Story of San Diego County Floriculture. Robert Melvin. Ed. by Paul Ecke, Jr. 168p. 1989. write for info. (*0-9623551-0-0*) P Ecke Ranch Pr.

Profiles in Gerontology: A Biographical Dictionary. W. Andrew Achenbaum & Daniel M. Albert. LC 95-8002. 416p. 1995. lib. bdg. 95.00 (*0-313-29274-4*, Greenwood Pr) Greenwood.

Profiles in Greatness. Swami Sastrananda. 153p. (Orig.). 1988. pap. 3.95 (*0-87481-582-7*, Pub. by Ramakrishna Math) Vedanta Pr.

Profiles in Growth Management. Douglas R. Porter et al. LC 96-61397. 230p. 1996. pap. text 49.95 (*0-87420-795-9*, P02) Urban Land.

Profiles in International Social Work. Ed. by M. C. Hokenstad et al. LC 92-11051. 207p. 1992. 24.95 (*0-87101-215-4*) Natl Assn Soc Wkrs.

Profiles in Jazz: From Sidney Bechet to John Cultrane. Raymond Horricks. 256p. (C). 1991. 34.95 (*0-88738-432-3*) Transaction Pubs.

Profiles in Leadership: A History of the Spence School. Mary D. Edmondson. LC 91-14757. 160p. 1991. 25.00 (*0-914659-52-9*) Phoenix Pub.

Profiles in Management. Ed. by Deanna La Valle. Date not set. text 695.00 incl. cd-rom (*0-07-912243-4*) McGraw.

Profiles in Management. Ed. by Deanna La Valle. 1994. text 595.00 incl. cd-rom (*0-07-103610-5*); text 495.00 (*0-07-103609-1*) McGraw.

Profiles in Management. 2nd ed. Ed. by Deanna La Valle. 1995. 595.00 incl. cd-rom (*0-07-103639-3*) McGraw.

Profiles in Management: Roles of the Value-Adding Manager. Nils L. Dailey. Ed. by Deborah Cannarella. (Illus.). 100p. (Orig.). 1987. pap. text 14.95 (*0-941837-00-9*) N L Dailey Assocs.

Profiles in Medical History, Vol. I. Glenn M. Bruss. (Illus.). 120p. 1997. pap. 12.00 (*0-8059-4215-7*) Dorrance.

Profiles in Murder: An FBI Legend Dissects Killers & Their Crimes. Told to Russell Vorpagel & Joseph Harrington. LC 98-28440. (Illus.). 294p. (C). 1998. 26.95 (*0-306-45980-9*, Plenum Trade) Perseus Pubng.

Profiles in Music, 6 bks., Reading Level 6. Nancy Loewen. (Illus.). 602p. (J). (gr. 5 up). 1989. 83.70 (*0-685-58764-9*) Rourke Corp.

Profiles in Music, 4 bks., Set, Reading Level 6. Nancy Loewen. (Illus.). 602p. (YA). (gr. 5 up). 1989. lib. bdg. 101.07 (*0-86592-604-2*) Rourke Enter.

Profiles in Oriental Diagnosis: What Dietetics, Face Reading, Nine Star Ki, & the I Ching Reveal about Art, Creativity, & Genius. Alex Jack. (Illus.). 144p. (Orig.). 1996. pap. 10.95 (*1-882984-16-1*) One Peaceful World.

Profiles in Personality: Personality Enlightenment Which Provokes the Mind & Feelings. Jacob Bell. 40p. (Orig.). 1988. pap. 9.95 (*0-9621090-0-2*) Bell Pub MA.

Profiles in Populism. W. A. Carto. 1982. 12.95 (*0-8159-6518-4*); pap. 7.95 (*0-8159-6519-2*) Devin.

Profiles in Poverty. Judith L. Birch. Ed. by Jack Goodman. LC 90-24740. (Orig.). 1992. pap. 13.95 (*0-87949-308-9*) Ashley Bks.

Profiles in Power: The Antinuclear Movement & the Dawn of the Solar Age. Jerry B. Brown. LC 97-26458. 1997. 33.00 (*0-8057-3879-7*) Macmillan.

Profiles in Quality: Learning from the Masters. Louis E. Schultz. LC 94-32836. 268p. 1994. text 33.95 (*0-527-76238-5*, 762385) Productivity Inc.

***Profiles in Saltwater Angling: A History of the Sport - Its People & Places, Tackle & Techniques.** 2nd rev. ed. George Reiger. LC 99-35356. 470p. 1999. 24.95 (*0-89272-449-8*) Down East.

Profiles in Stress. James H. Humphrey. LC 86-48066. (Stress in Modern Society Ser.: No. 2). 1986. 32.50 (*0-404-63252-1*) AMS Pr.

Profiles in Success. Ed. by Robert E. Bahruth & Phillip N. Venditti. LC 90-84156. (Illus.). 320p. reprint ed. pap. 99.20 (*0-608-20517-6*, 207176900002) Bks Demand.

Profiles in Success: People's Progress in Africa, Asia & Latin America. 68p. 1995. write for info. (*92-806-3167-5*) U N I C E.

Profiles in Success: Reflections on the Community College Experience. Ed. by Robert E. Bahruth & Phillip Venditti. 1990. pap. 10.00 (*0-87117-220-8*, 1313) Comm Coll Pr Am Assn Comm Coll.

Profiles in Terrorism: Twenty Years of Anti-Abortion Violence. Frederick Clarkson. 2000. 20.00 (*1-56751-165-1*); pap. 10.00 (*1-56751-164-3*) Common Courage.

Profiles in Terrorism in the Twentieth Century. Arthur E. Gerringer. LC 98-93293. 466p. 1998. ring bd. 69.00 (*0-9665628-0-1*) Inst Strategic Studs.

Profiles in the American Dream. Timothy P. Cahill. LC 94-71215. (Illus.). 1994. 16.95 (*0-8158-0501-2*) Chris Mass.

Profiles in Wesleyan Theology, 3 vols., Set. Leslie D. Wilcox. 74.99 (*0-88019-191-0*) Schmul Pub Co.

Profiles in World History: British World Influence to Seeking Alternatives to Capitalism (1750-1900), 8 vols. Joyce Moss & George Wilson. (Profiles in World History Ser.: Vol. 5). 246p. (J). 1995. text 39.00 (*0-7876-0469-0*, 5 of 8, UXL) Gale.

Profiles in World History: Significant Events & the People Who Shaped Them, 8 vols. Joyce Moss & George Wilson. (Profiles in World History Ser.). 1968p. (J). 1995. text 270.00 (*0-7876-0464-X*, UXL) Gale.

Profiles in World History Vol. 1: Beginnings of Civilization to Expansion of World Powers (3100-200 B.C.), 8 vols. Joyce Moss & George Wilson. (Profiles in World History Ser.: Vol. 1). 246p. (J). 1995. text 39.00 (*0-7876-0465-8*, 1 of 8, UXL) Gale.

Profiles in World History Vol. 2: Experimenting with Governments to Viking Invasion of England (200 B. C. - A. D. 1066), 8 vols. Joyce Moss & George Wilson. (Profiles in World History Ser.: Vol. 2). 246p. (J). 1995. text 39.00 (*0-7876-0466-6*, 2 of 8, UXL) Gale.

Profiles in World History Vol. 3: The Crusades to Building Empires in the Americas, 8 vols. Joyce Moss & George Wilson. (Profiles in World History Ser.: Vol. 3). 246p. (J). 1995. text 39.00 (*0-7876-0467-4*, 3 of 8, UXL) Gale.

Profiles in World History Vol. 4: The Age of Discovery to Industrial Revolution (1400-1830) Joyce Moss & George Wilson. (Profiles in American History Ser.: Vol. 4). 246p. (J). 1995. text 39.00 (*0-7876-0468-2*, UXL) Gale.

Profiles in World History Vol. 6: Social Reform to World Wars (1880-1945), 8 vols. Joyce Moss & George Wilson. (Profiles in World History Ser.: Vol. 6). 246p. (J). 1995. text 39.00 (*0-7876-0470-4*, 6 of 8, UXL) Gale.

Profiles in World History Vol. 7: Reshaping Europe to Cold War (1945-1970), 8 vols. Joyce Moss & George Wilson. (Profiles in World History Ser.: Vol. 7). 246p. (J). 1995. text 39.00 (*0-7876-0471-2*, 7 of 8, UXL) Gale.

Profiles in World History Vol. 8: Middle East Crisis to Innovations in Technology (1960-1995), 8 vols. Joyce Moss & George Wilson. (Profiles in World History Ser.: Vol. 8). 246p. (J). 1995. text 39.00 (*0-7876-0472-0*, 8 of 8, UXL) Gale.

Profiles 1998. Terri McGrath. (Illus.). 700p. 1998. reprint ed. ring bd. 1245.00 (*1-877750-68-9*) Integrated Circuit.

***Profiles '98: Salary Report; Research Report #19.** Ed. by International Facility Management Association Staf. 68p. 1998. pap. 100.00 (*1-883176-25-5*, 146016) Intl Facility Mgmt Assn.

Profiles of a Leader: The Characteristics of Spiritual Leadership. Judson Cornwall. LC 80-85161. 227p. (Orig.). 1980. pap. 8.99 (*0-88270-503-2*) Bridge-Logos.

Profiles of a Lost World: Memoirs of East European. Hirsz Abramowicz. LC 98-27168. (Raphael Patai Series of Jewish Folklore & Anthropology). 1999. text 39.95 (*0-8143-2784-2*) Wayne St U Pr.

Profiles of Activities to Reduce Perinatal Transmission of HIV: Assessing the Response. Michelle Renaud & Elizabeth Kresse. (Illus.). 115p. (C). 1998. pap. text 25.00 (*0-7881-7379-0*) DIANE Pub.

***Profiles of African American Stage Performers & Theatre People, 1816-1960.** Bernard L. Peterson, Jr. LC 99-88456. 400p. 2000. lib. bdg. 95.00 (*0-313-29534-4*, GR9534, Greenwood Pr) Greenwood.

Profiles of America: An Informational, Statistical, & Relocation Encyclopedia of All U. S. Cities, Towns, & Counties, 16 vols., Set. (Illus.). 9474p. (Orig.). 1995. pap. text 1312.00 (*1-884925-03-0*) Toucan Valley.

Profiles of America: Midwest Region, Vol. 1. (Illus.). 576p. (Orig.). 1995. pap. text 82.00 (*1-884925-21-9*) Toucan Valley.

Profiles of America: Midwest Region, Vol. 2. (Illus.). 546p. (Orig.). 1995. pap. text 82.00 (*1-884925-22-7*) Toucan Valley.

Profiles of America: Midwest Region, Vol. 3. (Illus.). 634p. (Orig.). 1995. pap. text 82.00 (*1-884925-23-5*) Toucan Valley.

Profiles of America: Midwest Region, Vol. 4. (Illus.). 646p. (Orig.). 1995. pap. text 82.00 (*1-884925-24-3*) Toucan Valley.

Profiles of America: Midwest Region, Vol. 5. (Illus.). 409p. (Orig.). 1995. pap. text 82.00 (*1-884925-25-1*) Toucan Valley.

Profiles of America: Midwest Region, Vol. 6. (Illus.). 510p. (Orig.). 1995. pap. text 82.00 (*1-884925-26-X*) Toucan Valley.

Profiles of America: Northeast Region, Vol. 1. (Illus.). 534p. (Orig.). 1995. pap. text 82.00 (*1-884925-41-3*) Toucan Valley.

Profiles of America: Northeast Region, Vol. 2. (Illus.). 576p. (Orig.). 1995. pap. text 82.00 (*1-884925-42-1*) Toucan Valley.

Profiles of America: Northeast Region, Vol. 3. (Illus.). 458p. (Orig.). 1995. pap. text 82.00 (*1-884925-43-X*) Toucan Valley.

Profiles of America: South Region, Vol. 1. (Illus.). 724p. (Orig.). 1995. pap. text 82.00 (*1-884925-31-6*) Toucan Valley.

Profiles of America: South Region, Vol. 2. (Illus.). 654p. (Orig.). 1995. pap. text 82.00 (*1-884925-32-4*) Toucan Valley.

Profiles of America: South Region, Vol. 3. (Illus.). 586p. (Orig.). 1995. pap. text 82.00 (*1-884925-33-2*) Toucan Valley.

Profiles of America: South Region, Vol. 4. (Illus.). 664p. (Orig.). 1995. pap. text 82.00 (*1-884925-34-0*) Toucan Valley.

Profiles of America: South Region, Vol. 5. (Illus.). 526p. (Orig.). 1995. pap. text 82.00 (*1-884925-35-9*) Toucan Valley.

Profiles of America: West Region, Vol. 1. (Illus.). 697p. (Orig.). 1995. pap. text 82.00 (*1-884925-11-1*) Toucan Valley.

Profiles of America: West Region, Vol. 2. (Illus.). 707p. (Orig.). 1995. pap. text 82.00 (*1-884925-12-X*) Toucan Valley.

Profiles of American Artists. rev. ed. Lynn Bettman. 1984. pap. 25.00 (*0-317-26926-7*) Kennedy Gall.

***Profiles of American Colleges.** 24th abr. ed. Barron's Educational Staff. (Profiles of American Colleges Ser.). 2000. pap. 24.95 (*0-7641-7294-8*) Barron.

***Profiles of American Colleges, Northeast.** 14th ed. Barron's Educational Editors. (Profiles of American Colleges Ser.). 2000. pap. text 14.95 (*0-7641-1319-4*) Barron.

Profiles of American Culture. 206p. (C). 1996. text 30.60 (*0-536-58932-1*) Pearson Custom.

Profiles of American Labor Unions. 2nd ed. 1998. 285.00 (*0-8103-9059-0*) Gale.

Profiles of Anabaptist Women: Sixteenth-Century Reforming Pioneers. Ed. by C. Arnold Snyder & Linda A. Hecht. LC 96-932001. (Illus.). 448p. 1990. pap. 29.95 (*0-88920-277-X*) W Laurier U Pr.

Profiles of Black Mayors in America. Joint Center for Political Studies Staff. 245p. 1976. pap. 10.00 (*0-87485-074-6*) Johnson Chicago.

Profiles of Black Success: Thirteen Creative Geniuses Who Changed the World. Gene N. Landrum. LC 96-39376. (Illus.). 402p. 1997. 25.95 (*1-57392-119-X*) Prometheus Bks.

Profiles of Canada. Kenneth G. Pryke. (C). 1992. pap. text 33.95 (*0-7730-5188-0*) Addison-Wesley.

Profiles of College & University Distance Learning Programs. Primary Research Group Staff. 100p. Date not set. 80.00 (*1-57440-009-6*) Primary Research.

Profiles of Companies in the World Drug Delivery System Markets. Frost & Sullivan Staff. LC 98-168764. 581p. 1996. spiral bd. 1995.00 (*0-7889-0445-0*, 3263-54) Frost & Sullivan.

***Profiles of Criminal Justice Systems in Europe & North America, 1990-1994.** Ed. by Kristiina Kangaspunta. (Illus.). 493p. 1999. pap. text 30.00 (*951-53-1919-6*, Pub. by Willow Tree NY) Lib Res.

Profiles of Deception. Reed Irvine & Cliff Kincaid. 256p. 1989. write for info. (*0-318-66581-6*) Bk Distributors.

Profiles of Eleven. Melech Epstein. 386p. (C). 1987. reprint ed. pap. text 32.50 (*0-8191-5493-8*) U Pr of Amer.

Profiles of Eleven: Profiles of Eleven Men Who Guided the Destiny of An Immigrant Society & Stimulated Social Consciousness among the American People. Melech Epstein. LC 65-20760. 380p. reprint ed. pap. 108.30 (*0-7837-3648-7*, 2043519) Bks Demand.

Profiles of Eminent American Chemists. Raymond B. Seymour & Charles H. Fisher. LC 86-82985. (Discovering the Discoverers Ser.: Vol. I). 600p. 1988. text 29.95 (*0-937557-05-6*) Litarvan Lit.

Profiles of Eminent Goans, Past & Present. J. Clement Vaz. LC 97-905326. 347 p. 1997. write for info. (*81-7022-619-8*) Concept.

Profiles of Erudite Jewish Physicians & Scholars: Biographical Essays. Ed. by Harry A. Savite. LC 72-96332. 84p. (C). 1973. 7.95 (*0-935982-04-3*, AS-01) Spertus Coll.

Profiles of European Adhesive, Sealant & Related Product Manufacturers. Frost & Sullivan Staff. 624p. 1995. spiral bd. 1950.00 (*0-7889-0308-X*, 3186-39) Frost & Sullivan.

P

An Asterisk (*) at the beginning of an entry indicates that the title is appearing for the first time.

Profiles of European Analytical Instrument Manufacturers: Area of Company Focus: Recession, Competition & Changing Technology. Frost & Sullivan Staff. 689p. 1995. spiral bd. 1195.00 (*0-7889-0310-1*, 3211-30) Frost & Sullivan.

Profiles of European Automotive Component Suppliers. Frost & Sullivan Staff. 537p. 1996. spiral bd. 1995.00 (*0-7889-0468-X*, 3248-18) Frost & Sullivan.

Profiles of European Clinical Diagnostic Industry. Market Intelligence Staff. 313p. 1993. 1500.00 (*0-685-71265-6*) Frost & Sullivan.

Profiles of European Computer Equipment & Service Suppliers. Market Intelligence Staff. 253p. 1994. 975.00 (*0-7889-0007-2*) Frost & Sullivan.

Profiles of European Datacommunications Equipment & Service Suppliers. Market Intelligence Staff. 364p. 1994. 950.00 (*1-56753-995-5*) Frost & Sullivan.

Profiles of European Diagnostic Imaging Equipment & Contrast Media Companies. Frost & Sullivan Staff. 400p. 1995. spiral bd. 1995.00 (*0-7889-0314-4*, 31744-50) Frost & Sullivan.

Profiles of European Electro-Mechanical Component Suppliers. Market Intelligence Staff. 350p. 1994. 895.00 (*0-685-71483-7*) Frost & Sullivan.

Profiles of European Electronic Chemical Companies. Market Intelligence Staff. 305p. 1995. spiral bd. 1500.00 (*0-7889-0246-6*, 3089-39) Frost & Sullivan.

Profiles of European Electronic Test & Measurement Suppliers. Market Intelligence Staff. 366p. 1994. 950.00 (*1-56753-984-X*) Frost & Sullivan.

Profiles of European Environmental Monitoring Instrument Suppliers. Frost & Sullivan Staff. 548p. 1996. spiral bd. 1950.00 (*0-7889-0492-2*, 3237-15) Frost & Sullivan.

Profiles of European Food Manufacturers: Processed Foods Offer Greatest Convenience, Variety. Frost & Sullivan. 653p. 1996. 1950.00 (*0-7889-0518-X*, 3012-88) Frost & Sullivan.

Profiles of European Industrial Food Processing Equipment Markets. Frost & Sullivan. 588p. 1996. spiral bd. 1995.00 (*0-7889-0604-6*, 3383-21) Frost & Sullivan.

Profiles of European Information Technology (IT) Companies: Product Innovation & Pricing Major Competitive Factors. Frost & Sullivan Staff. 629p. 1996. spiral bd. 1995.00 (*0-7889-0516-3*, 3197-78) Frost & Sullivan.

Profiles of European Office Equipment Manufacturers. Frost & Sullivan Staff. 607p. 1996. spiral bd. 1995.00 (*0-7889-0491-4*, 3223-73) Frost & Sullivan.

Profiles of European OTC Pharmaceutical Manufacturers & Suppliers: Continued Growth in a 45 Billion Dollar Industry. Market Intelligence Staff. 300p. 1993. 1495.00 (*1-56753-557-7*) Frost & Sullivan.

Profiles of European Patient Monitoring Equipment Manufacturers. Ed. by Frost & Sullivan Staff. 542p. 1996. spiral bd. 1995.00 (*0-7889-0409-4*, 3206-56) Frost & Sullivan.

Profiles of European Patient Monitoring Equipment Manufacturers: Detailed Profiles of 50 Pan-European Players. Frost & Sullivan Staff. 542p. Date not set. write for info. (*0-614-97068-7*, 3206-56) Frost & Sullivan.

Profiles of European Petrochemical Producers. Frost & Sullivan Staff. 367p. 1995. spiral bd. 1995.00 (*0-7889-0302-0*, 3030-39) Frost & Sullivan.

Profiles of European Pharmaceutical Wholesalers & Distributors. Frost & Sullivan. 430p. 1996. spiral bd. 1995.00 (*0-7889-0615-1*, 3336-49) Frost & Sullivan.

Profiles of European Pipe & Fitting Manufacturers: Plastics Develop Niches As Metals Consolidate. 615p. 1996. spiral bd. 1950.00 (*0-7889-0560-0*, 3125-21) Frost & Sullivan.

Profiles of European Pneumatic & Hydraulic Equipment Suppliers. Market Intelligence Staff. (Orig.). 1994. 950.00 (*0-7889-0116-8*) Frost & Sullivan.

Profiles of European Power Transmission Industry Manufacturers. Frost & Sullivan Staff. 443p. 1995. spiral bd. 1995.00 (*0-7889-0315-2*, 3182-17) Frost & Sullivan.

P

Profiles of European Printed Circuit Board Manufacturers: A Market Assessment. Market Intelligence Staff. 225p. 1993. 695.00 (*1-56753-564-X*) Frost & Sullivan.

Profiles of European Sensor Suppliers. Frost & Sullivan Staff. 502p. 1996. spiral bd. 1995.00 (*0-7889-0479-5*, 3181-32) Frost & Sullivan.

Profiles of European Suppliers of Process Control Instrumentation. Market Intelligence Staff. 364p. 1994. 995.00 (*1-56753-955-6*) Frost & Sullivan.

Profiles of EuropeanHospital Disposable Suppliers. Ed. by Frost & Sullivan Staff. 594p. 1997. spiral bd. 1995.00 (*0-7889-0688-7*, 3333-51) Frost & Sullivan.

Profiles of Excellence: Achieving Success in the Nonprofit Sector. E. B. Knauft et al. LC 90-23637. (Nonprofit Sector-Public Administration Ser.). 197p. 1991. text 28.95 (*1-55542-337-X*) Jossey-Bass.

Profiles of Faith. Charles E. Bradshaw. 1984. 9.95 (*0-911866-01-9*) LifeSprings Res.

***Profiles of Faith: Histories of Religious Communities of Howard County.** (Illus.). 428p. 1999. pap. 10.00 (*0-9658386-2-5*) Simple Gifts.

Profiles of Faith: The Religious Beliefs of Eminent Americans. C. Bernard Ruffin. LC 97-15972. 416p. (Orig.). 1997. pap. 18.00 (*0-7648-0106-6*, Liguori Triumph) Liguori Pubns.

Profiles of Female Genius: Thirteen Creative Women Who Changed the World. Gene N. Landrum. LC 94-7579. (Illus.). 437p. (C). 1994. 25.95 (*0-87975-892-9*) Prometheus Bks.

Profiles of Foreign Direct Investment in U. S. Energy. 1996. lib. bdg. 250.95 (*0-8490-6007-9*) Gordon Pr.

Profiles of Foreign Direct Investment in United States Energy, 1993. 45p. 1995. pap. 3.75 (*0-16-063467-9*) USGPO.

Profiles of Genius: Thirteen Creative Men Who Changed the World. Gene N. Landrum. LC 93-18637. 263p. (C). 1993. 25.95 (*0-87975-832-5*) Prometheus Bks.

Profiles of Great African-Americans. Consumer Guide Editors. 1998. mass mkt. 6.99 (*0-451-19275-3*, Sig) NAL.

Profiles of Great Black Americans, 10 vols., Set. Ed. by Richard S. Rennert. (Illus.). (J). (gr. 3 up). 1993. lib. bdg. 149.50 (*0-7910-2050-9*) Chelsea Hse.

Profiles of Indian Prime Minister: Nehru to Narasimha Rao. Shashi Ahluwalea. (C). 1991. 34.00 (*81-7099-326-1*, Pub. by Mittal Pubs Dist) S Asia.

Profiles of Leading Biotechnology Companies. 665p. 1996. spiral bd. 1995.00 (*0-7889-0562-7*, 3332-43) Frost & Sullivan.

Profiles of Learning. Geofferey Masters. (C). 1990. pap. 55.00 (*0-86431-067-6*, Pub. by Aust Council Educ Res) St Mut.

Profiles of National Standards-Related Activities. Robert B. Toth. 192p. 1997. per. 17.00 (*0-16-054646-X*) USGPO.

Profiles of North American Automotive Hard Parts Manufacturers: Expanded Strategic Analysis of 50 Suppliers. Frost & Sullivan Staff. 1996. spiral bd. 995.00 (*0-7889-0531-7*, 5510-18) Frost & Sullivan.

Profiles of Nurse Healers. Lynn Keegan & Barbara Dossey. LC 97-7960. (Professional Reference - Nursing Ser.). 256p. (C). 1997. mass mkt. 21.95 (*0-8273-7958-7*) Delmar.

Profiles of Orogenic Belts. Ed. by N. Rast & F. M. Delaney. (Geodynamics Ser.: Vol. 10). 310p. 1983. 36.00 (*0-87590-510-2*) Am Geophysical.

***Profiles of Partnership: 50 Years of Nepal-India Co-Operation.** H. B. Jha. 1998. pap. 34.00 (*0-7855-7625-8*) St Mut.

Profiles of PCB Manufacturers. Market Intelligence Staff. 298p. 1994. 995.00 (*0-7889-0140-0*) Frost & Sullivan.

Profiles of Pentecostal Missionaries. Mary H. Wallace. LC 86-15919. (Illus.). 250p. 2000. reprint ed. pap. 6.95 (*0-932581-00-5*) Word Aflame.

***Profiles of Play the Process.** Chazan. 2000. 40.00 (*0-465-09540-2*, Pub. by Basic) HarpC.

Profiles of Power: How the Governors Run Our 50 States. Allen H. Neuharth et al. (Illus.). 1988. 9.95 (*0-944347-14-2*) USA Today Bks.

Profiles of Power & Success: Fourteen Geniuses Who Broke the Rules. Gene N. Landrum. LC 95-54002. (Illus.). 412p. 1996. 25.95 (*1-57392-052-5*) Prometheus Bks.

Profiles of Power Electronics. Jai P. Agrawal. (C). 2000. 68.00 (*0-13-442864-1*, Macmillan Coll) P-H.

Profiles of Preservice Teacher Education: Inquiry into the Nature of Programs. Ed. by Kenneth R. Howey & Nancy L. Zimpher. LC 88-19995. (SUNY Series, Teacher Preparation & Development). 273p. (C). 1989. pap. text 24.95 (*0-88706-974-6*) State U NY Pr.

Profiles of Preservice Teacher Education: Inquiry into the Nature of Programs. Ed. by Kenneth R. Howey & Nancy L. Zimpher. LC 88-19995. (SUNY Series, Teacher Preparation & Development). 273p. (C). 1989. text 74.50 (*0-88706-973-8*) State U NY Pr.

Profiles of Progress: A Photographic Journal of Ketchikan-Saxman- Matlakatla Southeast Alaska. David R. Dillman. 240p. (C). 1989. 65.00 (*0-945848-02-1*); pap. 25.00 (*0-945848-01-3*) Prince Wales Pub.

Profiles of Progress: A Photographic Journal of Prince of Wales Island Southeast Alaska. David R. Dillman. LC 88-60289. 144p. (C). 1988. pap. 15.00 (*0-945848-00-5*) Prince Wales Pub.

Profiles of Regulatory Agencies in the U. S. & Canada, Yearbook 1994-1995. 537p. 1995. 50.00 (*0-317-05195-4*) NARUC.

Profiles of Rural Poverty. Intro. by Antoinette Beguin. (Illus.). v, 50p. (Orig.). 1979. pap. 6.75 (*92-2-102142-4*) Intl Labour Office.

Profiles of Satellite Earth Station & Component Manufacturers. Frost & Sullivan Staff. 659p. 1996. spiral bd. 995.00 (*0-7889-0490-6*, 2876-60) Frost & Sullivan.

Profiles of Students With Disabilities As Identified In Nels: 88. Robert Rossi. LC 97-223433. 141p. 1997. pap. 14.00 (*0-16-049099-5*) USGPO.

Profiles of Success: The Best of Christian Businessmen's Magazine, Vol. 1. Ed. by Ronnie Belanger & Brian Mast. LC 99-64057. (Illus.). 170p. 1999. pap. 15.99 (*0-88270-775-2*, Pub. by Bridge-Logos) Spring Arbor Dist.

Profiles of Success in the Human Resource Management Profession. Gloria W. White. 98p. 1991. 15.00 (*1-878240-03-X*) Coll & U Personnel.

***Profiles of the California Governors.** Bennett Jacobstein. (California Government Ser.). (Illus.). 48p. (J). (gr. 4-10). 1999. pap. text 14.95 (*1-884925-98-7*) Toucan Valley.

Profiles of the Joseph Medworth & Mary Pratt Family: Descendants in United States, 1840-1984. Ilyff Schalliol & Frances Edwards. (Illus.). 278p. (Orig.). 1985. pap. 10.00 (*0-9605732-2-4*) Belle Pubns.

Profiles of the Newly Licensed Nurse. Delroy Louden et al. 120p. 1997. 29.95 (*0-88737-756-4*, 19-7564, NLN Pr) Natl League Nurse.

Profiles of the Systems Professional. (Bookshelf Ser.). 1984. 6.00 (*0-934356-15-7*); 15.00 (*0-686-00304-7*) Assn Syst Mgmt.

Profiles of U. N. Organizations Working in Population. Cynthia P. Green. Ed. by Shanti R. Conly. 60p. 1996. 8.00 (*1-889735-01-9*) Population Action.

Profiles of U. S. Adhesive & Sealant Manufacturers. 363p. 1995. spiral bd. 695.00 (*0-7889-0371-3*, 2779-39) Frost & Sullivan.

Profiles of U. S. Call Center Hardware & Software Manufacturers. Frost & Sullivan Staff. 751p. 1996. spiral bd. 995.00 (*0-7889-0593-7*, 2444-62) Frost & Sullivan.

Profiles of U. S. Chemical Distributors. Ed. by Susan Rich. LC 81-83812. 265p. 1981. pap. 277.00 (*0-917148-77-0*) Kline.

Profiles of U. S. Hospitals. 1995. write for info. (*1-880678-66-7*) HCIA.

Profiles of U. S. Hospitals. 1996. write for info. (*1-57372-031-3*) HCIA.

Profiles of U. S. Hospitals, 1997. 1997. pap. 299.00 (*1-57372-063-1*) HCIA.

Profiles of U. S. Industrial Chemical & Gas Sensor Manufacturers. 289p. 1995. spiral bd. 995.00 (*0-7889-0324-1*, 2778-32) Frost & Sullivan.

Profiles of U. S. Polymer & Fine Chemical Manufacturers. Market Intellience Staff. 372p. 1995. spiral bd. 995.00 (*0-7889-0242-3*, 2803-39) Frost & Sullivan.

Profiles of U. S. Test & Measurement Equipment Manufacturers. Market Intelligence Staff. 308p. 1994. 995.00 (*1-56753-969-6*) Frost & Sullivan.

Profiles of Western Greek Mouldings. L. T. Shoe. 191p. 1952. 20.00 (*0-271-00460-6*); 20.00 (*0-271-00461-4*) Am Acad Rome.

Profiles of Wind, Temperature, & Humidity over the Arabian Sea. Franklin I. Badgley et al. LC 70-129539. (International Indian Ocean Expedition. Meteorological Monographs: No. 6). 68p. reprint ed. pap. 30.00 (*0-7837-3987-7*, 204381700011) Bks Demand.

Profiles of Women: Astro-Data. 5th enl. rev. ed. Lois M. Rodden. (Astro-Data Ser.: Vol. 1). 416p. 1996. pap. 46.00 (*0-9633716-3-0*) Data News Pr.

Profiles of Women Past & Present: Women's History Monologues for Group Presentations, Vol. 1. rev. ed. AAUW, Thousand Oaks, CA Branch Members. LC 96-86656. (Illus.). 96p. (Orig.). 1996. pap. 14.95 (*0-9637756-2-6*) AAUW.

Profiles of Women Past & Present: Women's History Monologues for Group Presentations, Vol. 2. AAUW, Thousand Oaks, CA Branch Members. LC 93-72554. (Illus.). 96p. (Orig.). 1996. pap. 14.95 (*0-9637756-1-8*) AAUW.

Profiles of World Telecom & Datacom Test Equipment Manufacturers. Frost & Sullivan Staff. 466p. 1996. spiral bd. 995.00 (*0-614-15985-7*, 5370-30) Frost & Sullivan.

***Profiles of Worldwide Government Leaders.** 5th ed. 825p. 1999. 306.00 (*1-886994-24-2*) Wrldwide Govt.

***Profiles of Worldwide Government Leaders.** 6th ed. Gale Group. 850p. 2000. 312.00 (*1-886994-31-5*, Pub. by Wrldwide Govt) Gale.

Profiles of Worldwide Government Leaders, 1998. 4th ed. Ed. by Ken Gause. 850p. 1998. 297.00 (*1-886994-12-9*, 111526) Wrldwide Govt.

Profiles on Women Artists. Alexander Russo. LC 84-27015. 258p. 1985. lib. bdg. 59.95 (*0-313-27049-X*, U7049, Greenwood Pr) Greenwood.

Profiles U. S. A. American Immigrants in Canada: An Analysis of Selected Demographic & Socio-Economic Characteristics. Statistics Canada Staff. LC 98-225873. (Immigration Research Ser.). 11p. 1996. write for info. (*0-662-62489-0*, Pub. by Can7 Govern Pub) Intl Spec Bk.

Profiles of U. S. Hospitals, 1998. 1997. pap. 299.00 (*1-57372-101-8*) HCIA.

Profiling & Utilizing Learning Style. James W. Keefe et al. 52p. (Orig.). 1988. 8.00 (*0-88210-207-9*) Natl Assn Principals.

Profiling Fabrics: Properties, Performance & Construction Techniques. Debbie A. Gioello. LC 80-68747. (Language of Fashion Ser.). (Illus.). 319p. reprint ed. pap. 98.90 (*0-608-08787-4*, 206942600004) Bks Demand.

Profiling in Policy & Practice. Ed. by David Canter & Laurence J. Alison. LC 98-74579. (Offender Profiling Ser.). 280p. 1999. 30.95 (*1-84014-782-2*); text 74.95 (*1-84014-779-2*) Ashgate Pub Co.

Profiling in Primary Schools: A Handbook for Teachers. Ed. by Ron Ritchie. 176p. 1992. spiral bd. 50.00 (*0-304-32450-7*) Continuum.

Profiling Property Crimes. Laurence J. Alison & D. V. Canter. 70.95 (*1-84014-785-7*); 30.95 (*1-84014-787-3*) Ashgate Pub Co.

Profiling Rape & Murder. Laurence J. Alison & D. V. Canter. 30.95 (*1-84014-495-5*); 70.95 (*1-85521-388-5*) Ashgate Pub Co.

Profiling the Lethal Employee: Case Studies of Violence in the Workplace. Michael D. Kelleher. LC 96-26280. 176p. 1997. 55.00 (*0-275-95756-X*, Praeger Pubs) Greenwood.

Profiling Violent Crimes: An Investigative Tool. 2nd ed. Ronald M. Holmes & Stephen T. Holmes. 224p. 1995. 33.00 (*0-8039-7238-5*); pap. 14.99 (*0-8039-7239-3*) Sage.

Profiling Violent Crimes: An Investigative Tools. Ronald M. Holmes. 136p. (C). 1989. text 42.00 (*0-8039-3681-8*); pap. text 19.95 (*0-8039-3682-6*) Sage.

Profilo Ideologico del Novecento see Ideological Profile of Twentieth-Century Italy

Profils des Francais: Intermediate. (FRE.). (C). pap., teacher ed. 35.95 (*0-8442-1474-4*, VF1474-4) NTC Contemp Pub Co.

***Profinite Groups.** L. Ribes & P. Zalesskii. (Ergebnisse der Mathematik und Ihrer Grenzgebiete Ser.: Vol. 40). 450p. 2000. 109.00 (*3-540-66986-8*) Spr-Verlag.

Profinite Groups. John S. Wilson. LC 99-196877. (London Mathematical Society Monographs: No. 19). (Illus.). 296p. 1999. text 115.00 (*0-19-850082-3*) OUP.

Profit & Loss of Dying. Clyde Irion. 1969. pap. 12.95 (*0-87516-030-1*) DeVorss.

***Profit & Pleasure: Sexual Identities in Late Capitalism.** Rosemary Hennessy. LC 99-86840. 2000. 85.00 (*0-415-92425-1*); pap. 22.99 (*0-415-92426-X*) Routledge.

Profit & Responsibility: Issues in Business & Professional Ethics. Ed. by Patricia Werhane & Kendall D'Andrade. LC 84-27279. (Studies in Religion & Society: Vol. 12). 295p. 1985. lib. bdg. 89.95 (*0-88946-862-1*) E Mellen.

Profit & the Practice of Law: What's Happened to the Legal Profession. Michael H. Trotter. LC 96-16168. 256p. 1997. 29.95 (*0-8203-1875-2*) U of Ga Pr.

***Profit Building: Cutting Costs Without Cutting People.** Perry J. Ludy. 200p. 2000. 27.95 (*1-57675-108-2*, Pub. by Berrett-Koehler) Publishers Group.

Profit by Design. Design Council Staff. (C). 1989. pap. text 60.00 (*0-85072-261-6*) St Mut.

Profit by Electional Astrology. Doris C. Doane. 1990. pap. 28.95 (*0-86690-340-2*, 3034-014) Am Fed Astrologers.

Profit by Quality. Peter W. Moir. (Industry & Applied Technology Ser.). 108p. 1988. text 36.95 (*0-470-21143-1*) P-H.

Profit Centers in Industrial Ecology: The Business Executive's Approach to the Environment. Ronald S. Smith. LC 98-6016. 288p. 1998. 65.00 (*1-56720-209-8*, Quorum Bks) Greenwood.

Profit Cycles, Oligopoly & Regional Development. Ann R. Markusen. 336p. 1985. 44.00 (*0-262-13201-X*) MIT Pr.

Profit-Driven Project Management. Richard E. Westney & N. Lavinga. (Total Cost Management Ser.). Date not set. write for info. (*0-8247-9929-1*) Dekker.

Profit Fever: The Drive to Corporatize Health Care & How to Stop It. Charles Andrews. 150p. 1995. text 29.95 (*1-56751-057-4*) Common Courage.

Profit Fever: The Drive to Corporatize Health Care & How to Stop It. Charles Andrews. 150p. 1995. pap. text 11.95 (*1-56751-056-6*) Common Courage.

Profit for the Poor: Cases in Micro-finance. Malcolm Harper. LC 98-901706. viii, 188p. 1998. write for info. (*81-204-1229-X*) Oxford & IBH Pubng.

Profit Forecasts: How They Are Made, Reviewed & Used. Ed. by C. A. Westwick. 264p. 1983. text 64.95 (*0-566-02207-9*) Ashgate Pub Co.

Profit from Experience. Michael J. O'Brien & Larry Shook. 192p. 1998. pap. 10.00 (*0-425-16219-2*) Berkley Pub.

Profit from Experience: The National Semiconductor Story of Transformation Management. Gil F. Amelio & William Simon. LC 97-25041. 352p. 1997. per. 14.00 (*0-684-83702-1*, Touchstone) S&S Trade Pap.

Profit from Experience: The National Semiconductor Story of Transformation Management. Gil F. Amelio & William L. Simon. (Industrial Engineering Ser.). 312p. 1995. 26.95 (*0-471-28704-0*, VNR) Wiley.

Profit from Experience: The National Semiconductor Story of Transformation Management. Gil F. Amelio et al. LC 95-35688. (Industrial Engineering Ser.). 312p. 1995. 26.95 (*0-442-02055-4*, VNR) Wiley.

***Profit from Home Using a Computer: How to Turn Your Computer into a Cash Machine.** Bill Mauger. 63p. 1999. pap. 109.00 (*0-9686587-0-9*) IV-DS.

Profit from Legal Insider Trading: Invest Today on Tomorrow's News. Jonathan Moreland. 224p. 2000. pap. 18.95 (*0-7931-2723-8*) Dearborn.

Profit from Property You Can't Sell. Harvey Sherman & Patricia J. Sherman. 1976. 7.95 (*0-686-19133-1*) Sherman.

Profit from Real Estate. Betty L. Randolph. Ed. by Success Education Institute International Staff. (Specialized Sales Ser.). 1989. 14.98 incl. audio (*1-55909-214-9*, 80PM) Randolph Tapes.

Profit from the IBM PC: A Non-Technical Guide to Selling User Services. Dan W. Post. LC 83-82632. (Illus.). 192p. 1984. 14.95 (*0-911160-89-2*) Post Group.

Profit from Your Money-Making Ideas: How to Build a New Business or Expand an Existing One. Herman R. Holtz. LC 80-65880. 380p. reprint ed. pap. 117.80 (*0-608-12966-6*, 202392100034) Bks Demand.

Profit from Your PC: How to Use a Personal Computer to Buy & Sell Shares. David Linton. 1998. pap. text 19.95 (*0-7134-8397-0*, Pub. by B T B) Branford.

Profit Game: How to Play - How to Win. Barry R. Schimel & Gary R. Kravitz. LC 98-29091. (Illus.). 176p. 1998. 24.95 (*1-892123-01-0*) Capital VA.

Profit in Our Own Country. J. Lawrence. 139p. 1994. pap. 30.00 (*1-86320-119-X*, Pub. by ACIAR) St Mut.

Profit in Power Washing: How to Start & Run a Pressure Washing Service - A Business Start-Up Manual. 2nd ed. Jon E. Herman. vii, 168p. 1998. pap. 22.95 (*0-9666114-1-1*) Carved Stone.

Profit in Power Washing: How to Start & Run Your Own Pressure Washing Service - A Business Start-Up Manual. Jon E. Herman. 164p. 1997. pap. 16.95 (*0-9666114-0-3*) Carved Stone.

Profit Is Not a Four-Letter Word: The Real Truth about What Is Is, Where It Comes from, How It Improves the Quality of Life for Everyone. John A. Steiber. LC 97-32858. (Illus.). 88p. 1998. pap. 10.95 (*0-8144-7983-9*) AMCOM.

***Profit Magic of Stock Transaction Timing.** J. M. Hurst. (Illus.). 223p. 2000. reprint ed. pap. text 25.00 (*0-934380-62-7*, 77) Traders Pr.

Profit Maximization: The Ethical Mandate of Business. Patrick Primeaux & John A. Stieber. (Illus.). 118p. 1995. 44.95 (*1-57292-025-4*); pap. 24.95 (*1-57292-024-6*) Austin & Winfield.

Profit Measurement & Price Changes. Kenneth Lacey. LC 82-48370. (Accountancy in Transition Ser.). 148p. 1982. text 10.00 (*0-8240-5323-0*) Garland.

An Asterisk (*) at the beginning of an entry indicates that the title is appearing for the first time.

Profit Minded Florist: A Financial Manual for Retail Florists. Floral Finance, Inc. (Illus.). 192p. 1987. pap. 69.95 (*0-317-61828-8*) Source Okla.

Profit Motive & Patient Care: The Changing Accountability of Doctors & Hospitals. Bradford H. Gray. LC 90-5119. (Twentieth Century Fund Study). (Illus.). 448p. 1991. 51.95 (*0-674-71337-0*, GRAPRM) HUP.

Profit Motive & Patient Care: The Changing Accountability of Doctors & Hospitals. Bradford H. Gray. 456p. 1991. pap. 23.95 (*0-674-71338-9*) HUP.

Profit on the Dotted Line: Coupons & Rebates. LC 84-71637. (Illus.). 200p. 1984. 24.95 (*0-913247-00-6*) CCH INC.

Profit on the Farm: A Marketing Guide to Help the Farmer Sell Better. Sherry Lorton & Don White. 132p. (Orig.). (C). 1994. pap. text 14.95 (*0-87563-501-6*) Stipes.

Profit on the Farm II: The One Habit of Top-Third Sellers. Sherry Lorton & Don White. 138p. (Orig.). (C). 1994. pap. text 14.95 (*0-87563-625-X*) Stipes.

Profit over People: Neoliberalism & Global Order. Noam Chomsky. LC 98-35985. 288p. 1998. pap. 15.95 (*1-888363-82-7*) Seven Stories.

Profit over People: Neoliberalism & Global Order. Noam Chomsky. LC 98-35985. 288p. 1998. 32.00 (*1-888363-89-4*) Seven Stories.

Profit Patterns: A Field Guide. Adrian J. Slywotsky. Date not set. pap. 20.00 (*0-8129-3377-X*, Times Bks) Crown Pub Group.

***Profit Patterns: 30 Ways to Anticipate & Profit from Strategic Changes Reshaping Your Business.** Adrian J. Slywotzky et al. LC 98-31337. (Illus.). 432p. 1999. 27.50 (*0-8129-3118-1*, Times Business) Random.

***Profit Planning.** 2nd ed. Peter Harris. (Professional Hospitality Guides). 195p. 1999. 29.95 (*0-7506-4528-8*) Buttrwrth-Heinemann.

Profit Planning & Control. T. S. McAlpine. (Illus.). 164p. 1969. pap. 24.95 (*0-8464-1122-9*) Beekman Pubs.

Profit Planning & Decision Making in the Hospitality Industry. Charles Ilvento. 264p. (C). 1996. text 57.95 (*0-7872-1794-8*, 41179401) Kendall-Hunt.

Profit, Plots & Lynching: The Creation of Nevada Territory. C. W. Bayer. LC 95-67579. 200p. 1995. pap. 30.00 (*0-9628890-3-2*) Purple Mntn.

Profit Potential: Taking High Performance to the Bottom Line. Carol J. McNair. (Illus.). 224p. (C). 1994. 75.00 (*0-939246-66-X*) Wiley.

Profit Potential: Taking High Performance to the Bottom Line. Carol J. McNair. 272p. 1995. 29.95 (*0-471-13178-4*) Wiley.

Profit, Principle & Apartheid, 1948-1994: The Conflict of Economic & Moral Issues in United States-South African Relations. Benjamin Kline. LC 97-12603. (Studies in African Economic & Social Development: No. 10). 232p. 1997. text 89.95 (*0-7734-8606-2*) E Mellen.

Profit Project Summary Reports. Reservoir Characterization near Well Flow. Norwegian Petroleum Directorate Staff. 355p. 1995. pap. 250.00 (*82-7257-443-8*, Pub. by Oljedirektoratet) St Mut.

***Profit RX.** John S. Haskell. 313p. 2000. 19.95 (*1-890009-70-9*) Exec Excell.

Profit Sharing & Gain Sharing. Ed. by Myron J. Roomkin. LC 90-8777. (Institute of Management & Labor Relations Ser.: No. 2). (Illus.). 190p. 1990. 35.00 (*0-8108-2335-7*) Scarecrow.

Profit-Sharing & Industrial Co-Partnership in British Industry, 1880-1920: Class Conflict or Class Collaboration. Jihang Park. (Modern European History Ser.). 512p. 1987. text 15.00 (*0-8240-7827-6*) Garland.

Profit Sharing & Profitability: How Profit Sharing Promotes Business Success. D. Wallace Bell & Charles G. Hanson. 128p. (C). 1987. 108.00 (*1-85091-303-X*) St Mut.

Profit Sharing Between Employer & Employee: A Study in the Evolution of the Wages System. Nicholas P. Gilman. LC 78-165635. (Select Bibliographies Reprint Ser.). 1977. reprint ed. 29.95 (*0-8369-5944-2*) Ayer.

Profit Sharing: Does It Make a Difference? The Productivity & Stability Effects of Employee Profit-Sharing Plans. Douglas L. Kruse. LC 93-23240. 240p. 1993. text 37.00 (*0-88099-138-0*); pap. text 19.00 (*0-88099-137-2*) W E Upjohn.

Profit Sharing in Canada: The Complete Guide to Designing & Implementing Plans That Really Work. David E. Tyson. 256p. 1996. pap. 75.00 (*0-471-64146-4*) Wiley.

Profit Strategies: Unlocking Trading Performance with Money Management. David Stendahl. 82p. 1999. pap. 19.95 (*1-883272-30-0*) Traders Lib.

Profit Strategies for Business. Robert Rachlin. LC 79-88674. 127p. 1980. 14.95 (*0-938712-01-2*) Marr Pubns.

Profit Theory & Capitalism. Mark Obrinsky. LC 82-40482. (Illus.). 176p. 1983. pap. text 20.95 (*0-8122-1147-2*) U of Pa Pr.

Profit Through Association Marketing. Gary C. Teagno. LC 93-14387. 288p. 1993. text 37.50 (*1-55623-836-3*, Irwn Prfssnl) McGraw-Hill Prof.

Profit Without Honor. Stephen M. Rosoff & Henry N. Pontell. LC 97-12923. 448p. (C). 1997. pap. text 19.95 (*0-13-669664-3*) P-H.

Profit Without Honor: White Collar Crime & the Looting of America. Stephen M. Rosoff & Henry N. Pontell. LC 97-12923. 436p. 1997. 28.60 (*0-13-103722-6*) P-H.

Profit Zone: How Strategic Business Design Will Lead You to Tomorrow's Profits. Adrian J. Slywotzky & David J. Morrison. 1998. text 32.00 (*0-471-98391-8*) Wiley.

Profit Zone: How Strategic Business Design Will Lead You to Tomorrow's Profits. Adrian J. Slywotzky et al. LC 97-27496. 320p. 1997. 25.00 (*0-8129-2900-4*, Times Bks) Crown Pub Group.

PROFITAB: Farm Record System. 144p. 1983. pap. 29.95 (*0-932250-20-3*) Red Wing Busn.

Profitability & Economic Choice. Paul H. Jaynes. LC 67-28033. (Illus.). 632p. reprint ed. pap. 196.00 (*0-8357-0412-2*, 202982300065) Bks Demand.

Profitability & Economic Choice. Paul H. Jeynes. LC 67-28033. (Illus.). 632p. reprint ed. pap. 180.00 (*0-608-17354-1*, 2029823) Bks Demand.

Profitability by Line by State. 270p. 1996. pap. 150.00 (*0-89382-434-8*, PBL-PB) Nat Assn Insurance.

Profitability by Line by State in 1997. rev. ed. Ed. by Jim Bugenhagen. 376p. 1998. ring bd. 150.00i (*0-89382-593-X*, PBL-PB) Nat Assn Insurance.

Profitability by Line by State, 1991. 270p. (C). 1992. spiral bd. 100.00 (*0-89382-217-5*) Nat Assn Insurance.

Profitability by Line by State Report for 1996. rev. ed. Ed. by Jim Bugenhagen. 375p. (C). 1997. ring bd. 150.00i (*0-89382-505-0*, PBL-PB97) Nat Assn Insurance.

***Profitability, Financing & Growth of the Firm: Goals, Relationships & Measurement Methods.** Sven-Erik Johansson. 166p. 1998. 25.00 (*87-16-13443-5*, Pub. by Copenhagen Busn Schl) Bks Intl VA.

Profitability in Swedish Manufacturing: Trends & Explanations. Lennart Erixon. (Swedish Institute for Social Research Ser.: No. 4). 267p. (Orig.). 1987. pap. text 53.00 (*91-7604-027-5*) Coronet Bks.

Profitability, Mechanization & Economies of Scale. Dudley Jackson. LC 97-77386. (Illus.). 332p. 1998. text 76.95 (*1-84014-302-9*, Pub. by Ashgate Pub) Ashgate Pub Co.

Profitability of Major Oil Companies: Normal Returns or Windfall Profits? Gerald D. Keim et al. 16p. 1980. 1.00 (*0-86599-003-4*) PERC.

Profitable Acquistions: Guidelines for Buying & Selling Companies for Businessmen & Financiers. deluxe ed. Thomas H. Hopkins. LC 83-61892. (Illus.). 138p. 1984. reprint ed. 92.50 (*0-9611864-1-0*) McTaggart.

Profitable Acquistions: Guidelines for Buying & Selling Companies for Businessmen & Financiers. Thomas H. Hopkins. LC 83-61892. (Illus.). 138p. 1984. reprint ed. 24.95 (*0-9611864-0-2*) McTaggart.

Profitable & Necessarie Booke of Observations. William Clowes. LC 73-171740. (English Experience Ser.: No. 366). 1971. reprint ed. 33.50 (*90-221-0366-8*) Walter J Johnson.

Profitable Asset-Based Lending. Clyde Draughon, Jr. & Richard G. Kemmer. 352p. 1990. per. 55.00 (*1-55520-077-X*, Irwn Prfssnl) McGraw-Hill Prof.

Profitable Calendar Photography. 1988. 4.95 (*0-89816-113-4*) Embee Pr.

Profitable Catering. Bruce H. Axler. 1974. pap. 3.95 (*0-672-96118-0*, Bobbs) Macmillan.

Profitable Child Care: How to Start & Run a Successful Business. Nan L. Howkins & Heidi K. Rosenholtz. 288p. 1993. 33.95 (*0-8160-2236-4*) Facts on File.

Profitable Coexistence: A New Strategy in Foreign Affairs. James D. Blum. LC 97-69937. 58p. 1998. 12.95 (*1-887750-74-6*) Rutledge Bks.

Profitable Color Postcard Photography. 1989. 4.95 (*0-89816-049-9*) Embee Pr.

Profitable Color Poster Photography. 1988. 4.95 (*0-89816-100-2*) Embee Pr.

Profitable Company: Milestones & Monuments of the Signers of the Declaration of Independence. Archibald Laird. LC 84-71719. 1987. 19.50 (*0-8158-0425-3*) Chris Mass.

Profitable Computer Aided Engineering. N. W. Sandland. 304p. 1992. 95.00 (*1-85573-082-0*, Pub. by Woodhead Pubng) Am Educ Systs.

Profitable Condition Monitoring. Ed. by B. K. Rao. 330p. 1992. text 279.50 (*0-7923-2098-0*) Kluwer Academic.

Profitable Construction Photography. 1988. 4.95 (*0-89816-120-7*) Embee Pr.

Profitable Consulting: Helping American Managers Face the Future. Robert O. Metzger. 144p. 1988. 17.26 (*0-201-09539-4*) Addison-Wesley.

Profitable Consumer Lending. Sarah E. Hutchinson & Stacey Sawyer. 1991. text 30.00 (*0-07-413136-2*, Irwn McGrw-H) McGrw-H Hghr Educ.

Profitable Consumer Lending: A Guide to Lending, Collection & Compliance. Robert D. Hall, Jr. & F. Blake Cloonen. LC 84-319. (Bankers Lending Ser.). 192p. 1991. text 30.00 (*0-87267-047-3*, Irwn Prfssnl) McGraw-Hill Prof.

Profitable Corporate Report Photography. 1988. 4.95 (*0-89816-103-7*) Embee Pr.

Profitable Customers: How to Identify, Develop & Retain Them. Charles Wilson. (Marketing & Sales Ser.). 1999. pap. 24.95 (*0-7494-1930-X*) Kogan Page Ltd.

Profitable Customers: Making Sense of Emu & What It Means For You. Charles Wilson. 1999. pap. 24.95 (*0-7494-2825-2*) Kogan Page Ltd.

Profitable Dance Studio Photography. 1990. 4.95 (*0-89816-033-2*) Embee Pr.

Profitable Direct Mail for Travel Agencies. 2nd ed. Douglas Thompson. 150p. 1992. ring bd. 29.95 (*0-936831-06-5*) Dendrobium Bks.

***Profitable Direct Marketing.** Iain Maitland. LC 98-149379. (Bus Press-New). 256p. 1998. pap. 24.95 (*1-86152-145-6*) Thomson Learn.

Profitable Direct Marketing. 2nd ed. Jim Kobs. (Illus.). 288p. 1994. 49.95 (*0-8442-3029-4*, NTC Business Bks) NTC Contemp Pub Co.

Profitable Distribution of Low-Cost CAD-CAE Hardware, Software & Systems: Vendor Strategies, Third-Party Channels, Retail Outlets. Summit Strategies Staff. (Illus.). 199p. 1986. 1231.00 (*0-914849-06-9*) TBC Inc.

Profitable Earthworm Farming: Complete Manual of Worm Production, Storage, Selling & Shipping. Charlie Morgan. 1975. pap. 8.00 (*0-914116-06-1*) Shields.

Profitable Estimating for Constructions Firms: A Guide for Contractors, Subcontractors, Builders, & Developers. Carleton Coulter, III. (Illus.). 120p. (C). 1986. 37.50 (*1-55538-012-3*) Pract Mgmt Assocs.

Profitable Export Marketing: A Strategy for U. S. Business. Marta Ortiz-Buonafina. LC 92-15752. 1992. pap. 29.50 (*0-8191-8733-X*) U Pr of Amer.

Profitable Food Plan & Operation Set. Greene. (Hospitality, Travel & Tourism Ser.). 1991. write for info. (*0-442-00710-8*, VNR) Wiley.

Profitable Footwear Retailing. William Rossi. 322p. 1988. 43.00 (*0-87005-630-1*) Fairchild.

Profitable Free Range Egg Production. Mick Dennett. (Illus.). 128p. 1995. 22.95 (*1-85223-835-6*, Pub. by Cro1wood) Trafalgar.

Profitable Grain Trading. Ralph M. Ainsworth. LC 80-53316. (Illus.). 256p. 1980. reprint ed. text 25.00 (*0-934380-04-X*, 32) Traders Pr.

Profitable Herb Growing at Home. Betty E. Jacobs. 1976. pap. 5.95 (*0-88266-087-X*) Storey Bks.

Profitable Home Ownership: Building Wealth Through Home Ownership. Eric Richardson. Ed. & Illus. by Margaret Coleman. (Decisions/Decisions Ser.: No. 3). 256p. (Orig.). 1997. pap. 12.95 (*0-9659992-0-3*) Getting Ahead.

Profitable Investing: Fundamentals of the Science of Investing. John Moody. LC 75-2651. (Wall Street & the Security Market Ser.). 1975. reprint ed. 28.95 (*0-405-06976-6*) Ayer.

Profitable Law Office Handbook: Attorney's Guide to Successful Business Planning. Illus. by Harald Johnson. 74p. (Orig.). 1996. pap. 29.95 (*0-9654948-1-0*) E Poll & Assocs.

Profitable Legal Aid. John Clegg & Stephen Dawson. 283p. 1991. 110.00 (*1-85190-124-8*, Pub. by Tolley Pubng) St Mut.

Profitable Legal Aid. Ed. by John Clegg & Stephen Dawson. 335p. 1994. 175.00 (*0-85459-950-9*, Pub. by Tolley Pubng) St Mut.

***Profitable Mail Order Made E-Z.** Made E-Z Staff. 316p. 2000. pap. 17.95 (*1-56382-442-6*) E-Z Legal.

Profitable Marching Band Photography. 1991. 4.95 (*0-89816-048-0*) Embee Pr.

Profitable Menu Planning. 2nd ed. John A. Drysdale. LC 97-26733. 378p. (C). 1997. pap. text 82.00 (*0-13-646944-2*) P-H.

Profitable Model Photography. Art Ketchum. 128p. 1992. pap. 18.95 (*0-929667-12-3*, 10300) Images NY.

***Profitable Negotiation.** Gavin Kennedy. 192p. 1999. pap. 13.95 (*0-7528-1357-9*, Pub. by Orion Pubng Grp) Trafalgar.

Profitable No-Load Mutual Fund Trading Techniques: For the Individual Investor. Norman Mallory. (Illus.). 153p. 1988. pap. 37.95 (*0-930233-11-5*, Pub. by Windsor) Natl Bk Netwk.

Profitable Organic Farming. Jon Newton. LC 95-24181. 1995. pap. 38.95 (*0-632-03929-9*) Blackwell Sci.

***Profitable Partnering in Construction Procurement: CIB W 92 (Procurement Systems) CIB TG 23 (Culture in Construction) Joint Symposium.** Stephen O. Ogunlana et al. LC 98-53113. (CIB Proceedings Ser.). xii, 735 p. 1999. text. write for info. (*0-419-24760-2*, E & FN Spon) Routledge.

Profitable Patterns for Stock Trading. Larry Pesavento. (Illus.). 224p. 1999. 49.00 (*0-934380-47-3*) Traders Pr.

Profitable Penalties: How to Cut Both Crime Rates & Costs. Daniel Glaser. LC 97-4599. 240p. (Orig.). (C). 1997. pap. text 21.95 (*0-7619-8534-4*) Pine Forge.

Profitable Personnel Services: Start & Run a Money-Making Business. Kristi L. Mishel & John J. Thomas. 1995. pap. text 18.95 (*0-07-042369-5*) McGraw-Hill Prof.

Profitable Pet Photography. 1988. 4.95 (*0-89816-110-X*) Embee Pr.

Profitable Photo Insurance Business. 1988. 4.95 (*0-89816-118-5*) Embee Pr.

Profitable Photographic Ventures. unabridged ed. Mark Baczynsky. (Illus.). 44p. 1990. spiral bd. 24.95 (*0-89816-006-5*) Embee Pr.

Profitable Photography: Start & Run a Money-Making Business. Geza Szurovy. 1995. pap. text 19.95 (*0-07-063022-4*) McGraw.

Profitable Portrait Photography. Roger Berg. LC 97-75208. (Illus.). 128p. 1998. pap. 29.95 (*0-936262-65-6*) Amherst Media.

Profitable Practice Management. Peter Barrett. LC 92-38837. 1993. mass mkt. 49.95 (*0-419-15590-2*, E & FN Spon) Routledge.

Profitable Printing Management. (Illus.). 240p. 1996. text 31.95 (*0-9618281-1-0*) Practical Print Mgmt.

Profitable Product Management: Powerful Techniques for Improving Products & Performance for Maximizing Profits. Richard A. Collier. (Marketing Ser.). (Illus.). 304p. 1995. pap. text 39.95 (*0-7506-1888-4*) Buttrwrth-Heinemann.

Profitable Promises: Essays on Women, Science & Health. Ruth Hubbard. LC 94-37839. 150p. (Orig.). 1994. pap. 11.95 (*1-56751-040-X*); lib. bdg. 29.95 (*1-56751-041-8*) Common Courage.

Profitable Purchasing Management: A Guide for Small Business Owners-Managers. William A. Messner. LC 81-69367. 317p. reprint ed. pap. 98.30 (*0-608-12967-4*, 202392200034) Bks Demand.

Profitable Purchasing Strategies: Breakthrough Purchasing. Paul T. Steele & Brian Court. LC 95-38512. 228p. 1996. 34.95 (*0-07-709214-7*) McGraw.

Profitable Restaurant Management. 2nd ed. Kenneth L. Solomon & Norman Katz. LC 80-25007. 298p. 1981. 60.00 (*0-13-728816-6*, Busn) P-H.

Profitable Risk Control: The Winning Edge. William W. Allison. 197p. 1986. 14.95 (*0-939874-71-7*) ASSE.

Profitable Roadside Retailing: Making It Happen. Gerald Lewis & Bill Simmons. 131p. 10.00 (*0-685-65572-5*) Mkters Assn of Am.

Profitable Sales Management & Marketing for Growing Businesses. Robert J. Calvin. 326p. (C). reprint ed. pap. 15.00 (*0-685-29363-7*) Mgmt Dimensions.

Profitable School Port: Photography. 1990. 4.95 (*0-89816-138-X*) Embee Pr.

Profitable Self-Publishing: The Entrepreneur's Guide to Gathering & Selling How-to Information. Jerry Buchanan. 93p. 1993. lib. bdg. 14.95 (*0-930668-08-1*) Towers Club.

Profitable Selling. John Lidstone. 240p. 1986. pap. text 22.95 (*0-7045-0524-X*, Pub. by Gower) Ashgate Pub Co.

Profitable Sheep Farming. 5th ed. M. McG. Cooper & R. J. Thomas. (Illus.). 192p. 1982. 32.95 (*0-85236-117-3*, Pub. by Farming Pr) Diamond Farm Bk.

Profitable Small Product Photography. 1988. 4.95 (*0-89816-105-3*) Embee Pr.

Profitable Solutions for Quality Drying of Softwoods & Hardwoods. 150p. 1994. 45.00 (*0-935018-70-0*, 7311) Forest Prod.

Profitable Speculations: Essays on Current Philosophical Themes. Nicholas Rescher. LC 97-17812. 300p. 1997. 71.50 (*0-8476-8677-9*); pap. 26.95 (*0-8476-8678-7*) Rowman.

Profitable Time Management. rev. ed. James C. Campbell. (Skill Centered Leadership Ser.). 5p. 1997. pap., wbk. ed. 12.95 incl. audio (*1-891161-71-7*) ClamShell Pub.

Profitable Trucking. American Trucking Association, National Freight Cl. 161p. 1994. pap. text 12.95 (*0-88711-267-6*) Am Trucking Assns.

Profitable Woodworking - Turning Your Hobby into a Profession. Martin Edic. LC 96-21057. (Illus.). 160p. 1996. pap. 19.95 (*1-56158-122-4*, 070253) Taunton.

Profitable Worke to This Whole Kingdome Concerning the Mending of All Highways, As Also for Waters & Iron Workes. Thomas Procter. LC 77-7425. (English Experience Ser.: No. 885). 1977. reprint ed. lib. bdg. 15.00 (*90-221-0885-6*) Walter J Johnson.

Profitably Managing Your Rental Properties. R. Dodge Woodson. LC 92-6198. 240p. 1992. pap. 19.95 (*0-471-57565-8*) Wiley.

Profiteer. S. Andrew Swann. 352p. (Orig.). 1995. pap., mass mkt. 4.99 (*0-88677-647-3*, Pub. by DAW Bks) Penguin Putnam.

Profiting by Phone: No Nonsense Skills & Techniques for Selling & Getting Leads by Telephone. Jim Domanski. 248p. 1997. pap. 29.00 (*1-881081-08-7*, PBP) Busn By Phone.

Profiting for People, by People: The New Management Paragon for the 21st Century. Anthony J. Garbowski. (Illus.). (Orig.). 1995. pap. text 25.00 (*1-888223-00-6*) Sigler Print.

Profiting from a Geographic Information System. Ed. by Gilbert H. Castle, III. (Illus.). 414p. 1993. pap. 37.95 (*0-9625063-7-0*) GIS World Bks.

***Profiting from a Geographic Information System.** Ed. by Gilbert H. Castle, III. 415p. 1998. pap. 90.00 (*0-471-32984-3*) Wiley.

Profiting from a Parade of Homes: A Guide for Builders & Sponsoring Associations. Judith S. Kincaid & Peggy L. Golden. LC 90-49689. (Illus.). 110p. (Orig.). 1990. pap. 7.50 (*0-86718-354-3*) Home Builder.

Profiting from Diversity. Trevor J. Bentley & Susan Clayton. LC 97-42339. 192p. 1998. 69.95 (*0-566-07931-3*, Pub. by Gower) Ashgate Pub Co.

Profiting from Emerging Market Stocks. Mitchell Posner. 352p. 1998. text 30.00 (*0-7352-0023-8*) PH Pr.

Profiting from Financial Statements: A Business Analysis System. Robert J. Brinson. (Orig.). 1992. pap. text 25.00 (*1-878870-04-1*) Halcyon Grp SC.

Profiting from Financial Statements: Fiscal Key Disk & Manual. Robert J. Brinson. (C). 1995. pap. text 25.00 incl. disk (*1-878870-03-3*) Halcyon Grp SC.

Profiting from Financial Statements: Fiscal Key Disk & Manual, 3.5 Inch Disk. Robert J. Brinson. (C). 1990. pap. text 15.00 (*1-878870-02-5*) Halcyon Grp SC.

Profiting from Financial Statements: Fiscal Key Disk & Manual, 5.25 Inch Disk. Robert J. Brinson. (C). 1990. pap. text 15.00 (*1-878870-00-9*) Halcyon Grp SC.

Profiting from Gene-Based Diagnostics. Ed. by CTB Diagnostic Intelligence Group Staff. 82p. 1996. spiral bd. 637.00 (*1-887566-04-X*, RPG-01) CTB Intl.

***Profiting from Human Genome Stocks: Bigger Than the Internet.** Paul Ruggieri. 145p. 2000. pap. 39.95 (*1-893756-07-6*) M Gordon Pubng.

Profiting from Industry Analysis. Wanetick. (C). 1997. 25.00 (*0-13-246349-0*, Macmillan Coll) P-H.

Profiting from Innovation: The Report of the Three-Year Study from the National Academy of Engineering. Ed. by William G. Howard, Jr. & Bruce R. Guile. 150p. 1991. 29.95 (*0-02-922385-7*) Free Pr.

***Profiting from Intellectual Capital: Extracting Value from Innovation.** Ed. by Patrick H. Sullivan. LC 97-34975. (Intellectual Property Ser.). 384p. 1998. 65.00 (*0-471-19302-X*) Wiley.

Profiting from IPOs & Small Cap Stocks. Brown. (C). 1998. 24.95 (*0-13-679804-7*, Macmillan Coll) P-H.

Profiting from IPOs & Small Cap Stocks. Norman H. Brown. LC 98-17862. 256p. 1998. text 26.00 (*0-7352-0029-7*) PH Pr.

Profiting from Low-Grade Heat: Thermodynamic Cycles for Low-Temperature Heat Sources, Watt Committee on Energy Report. Ed. by A. W. Crook. (Energy Ser.: No. 7). 200p. 1993. boxed set 77.00 (*0-85296-835-3*, EN007) INSPEC Inc.

P

An Asterisk (*) at the beginning of an entry indicates that the title is appearing for the first time.

***Profiting from Multiple Intelligence in the Workplace.** Joyce Martin. LC 00-39393. 232p. 2000. 84.95 (*0-566-08312-4*, Pub. by Ashgate Pub) Ashgate Pub Co.

Profiting from Quality: Outcomes Strategies for Medical Practice. Steven F. Isenberg & Richard E. Gliklich. LC 99-12557. 256p. 1999. 49.95 (*0-7879-4624-9*) Jossey-Bass.

Profiting from Radio Ratings: A Manual for Radio Managers, Sales Managers, & Programmers. James E. Fletcher & Mark E. Dorminy. 275p. 1989. pap. 49.95 (*0-8058-1047-1*) L Erlbaum Assocs.

Profiting from Real Estate Rehab. Sandra M. Brassfield. LC 91-15775. 256p. 1992. pap. 39.95 (*0-471-54858-8*) Wiley.

Profiting from Technical Analysis. (C). 1999. 39.95 (*0-13-956673-2*, Macmillan Coll) P-H.

***Profiting from Teleservices: An Operational Guide to Call Center Technologies.** Charles E. Day. (Illus.). 528p. 2000. pap. 65.00 (*0-07-016430-4*) McGraw.

Profiting from the Bank & S&L Crisis: How Anyone Can Find Bargains at America's Greatest Garage Sale. Stephen Pizzo & Paul Muolo. LC 92-53369. 256p. 1993. 23.00 (*0-88730-596-2*, HarpBusn) HarpInfo.

Profiting from the Word. Arthur W. Pink. 1977. pap. 5.99 (*0-85151-032-9*) Banner of Truth.

Profiting from Tomorrow's Customers. Prod. by Editorial Board Staff. (Publishing in the 21st Century Research Ser.). 76p. 1997. pap. 149.00 (*0-9525566-3-4*, Pub. by Vista Comp Serv) Vista Comp Serv.

Profiting with Futures Options. David L. Caplan. 48p. (Orig.). 1994. pap. 7.95 (*0-915513-56-0*) Ctr Futures Ed.

Profits & Morality. Ed. by Robin Cowan & Mario J. Rizzo. (Illus.). 192p. 1995. 27.50 (*0-226-11632-8*) U Ch Pr.

Profits & Politics: Beaverbrook & the Gilded Age of Canadian Finance. Gregory P. Marchildon. (Illus.). 352p. 1996. text 39.00 (*0-8020-0740-6*) U of Toronto Pr.

Profits & Politics in Paradise: The Development of Hilton Head Island. Michael N. Danielson. LC 95-4364. 323p. 1995. pap. 19.95 (*1-57003-039-1*) U of SC Pr.

***Profits & Principles: Global Capitalism & Human Rights in China.** Michael Santoro. LC 99-85912. (Illus.). 320p. 2000. 26.00 (*0-8014-3501-3*) Cornell U Pr.

Profits & Professions: Essays in Business & Professional Ethics. Ed. by Wade L. Robison et al. LC 82-23399. (Contemporary Issues in Biomedicine, Ethics, & Society Ser.). 343p. 1983. 49.50 (*0-89603-039-3*) Humana.

Profits & the Cost of Capital to the U. S. Trunk Airline Industry under CAB Regulation. B. Starr McMullen. LC 92-38639. (Government & the Economy Ser.). 128p. 1993. text 10.00 (*0-8153-1230-X*) Garland.

Profits Are in Order. Frank E. Bird, Jr. 90p. 1992. pap. text 35.00 (*0-88061-128-6*) Intl Loss Cntrl.

Profits, Dividends & the Law: Profits Available for Dividends from Standpoint of Law & Best Accounting Practice. Prosper Reiter, Jr. LC 75-18481. (History of Accounting Ser.). (Illus.). 1979. reprint ed. 23.95 (*0-405-07563-4*) Ayer.

***Profits from Natural Resources: How to Make Big Money Investing in Metals, Food, & Energy.** Roland A. Jansen. LC 98-16188. (Trading Advantage Ser.). 296p. 1998. 59.95 (*0-471-29523-X*) Wiley.

Profits from Power: Readings in Protection Rent & Violence-Controlling Enterprises. Frederick C. Lane. LC 79-13860. 128p. (C). 1979. pap. text 19.95 (*0-87395-420-3*) State U NY Pr.

Profits from Preempts. C. C. Wei & Ron Andersen. 162p. 1977. pap. 8.95 (*0-87643-035-3*) Barclay Bridge.

Profits from Preempts, No. 3. (Bidding Precisely Ser.). 162p. (Orig.). 1977. pap. 8.95 (*0-686-36625-5*) M Lisa Precision.

Profits from Successful Management or Working for Profits. Warren F. Purdy. Ed. by Penny T. Purdy. (Illus.). 353p. Date not set. 99.50 (*0-9661965-0-3*) W F Purdy.

Profits from Your Backyard Herb Garden. Lee Sturdivant. (Bootstrap Guide Ser.). (Illus.). 120p. 1995. pap. 10.95 (*0-9621635-3-8*) San Juan Naturals.

Profits Hidden, Profits Found: 12 Steps to Making a Big Fortune in Any Business. Pete Lisoskie. (Orig.). 1995. pap. 14.95 (*1-879141-13-2*) Busn Toolbox.

Profits in Building Spec Homes. William Maddox. (Illus.). 232p. (Orig.). 1994. pap. 27.25 (*0-934041-93-8*) Craftsman.

Profits in Buying & Renovating Homes. Lawrence Dworin. 304p. (Orig.). 1990. pap. 19.75 (*0-934041-57-1*) Craftsman.

Profits in the British Economy, 1909-1938. George D. Worswick & D. G. Tipping. LC 67-5122. 155p. 1967. 35.00 (*0-678-06264-1*) Kelley.

Profits in the Long Run. Dennis C. Mueller. (Illus.). 400p. 1986. text 85.00 (*0-521-30693-0*) Cambridge U Pr.

Profits in the Modern Economy: Selected Papers. Conference on Understanding Profits (1964: Macales. Ed. by Harold W. Stevenson & J. Russell Nelson. LC 67-13120. 214p. reprint ed. pap. 66.40 (*0-608-15957-3*, 203323800084) Bks Demand.

Profits in the Stock Market. H. M. Gartley. 446p. 1935. 120.00 (*0-939093-07-3*) Lambert Gann Pub.

Profits in the Wilderness: Entrepreneurship & the Founding of New England Towns in the Seventeenth Century. John F. Martin. LC 91-2945. xvi, 363p. (C). 1991. 45.00 (*0-8078-2001-6*); pap. 18.95 (*0-8078-4346-6*) U of NC Pr.

Profits in Volume: Equivolume Charting. Richard Arms, Jr. (Illus.). 158p. 1999. 39.95 (*1-883272-25-4*) Traders Lib.

Profits of Death: An Insider Exposes the Death Care Industries; Learn How to Cut Funeral Costs in Half. Darryl J. Roberts. Ed. by Paul M. Howey. LC 96-53657. 224p. 1997. pap. 12.95 (*1-877749-21-4*) Five Star AZ.

Profits of Peace: The Political Economy of Anglo-German Appeasement. Scott Newton. LC 95-30149. (Illus.). 226p. (C). 1996. text 60.00 (*0-19-820212-1*, Clarendon Pr) OUP.

Profits of Persuasion: Speaking Effectively for Your Company. Leonard H. Roller. (Illus.). 224p. 1988. 18.95 (*0-914598-24-4*) Intl Resources.

***Profits of Religion.** Upton Sinclair. (Great Minds Ser.). 315p. 2000. pap. 12.95 (*1-57392-844-5*) Prometheus Bks.

Profits of Religion. Upton Sinclair. LC 73-120566. 1970. reprint ed. 37.50 (*0-404-06093-5*) AMS Pr.

***Profits of Religion.** Upton Sinclair. (Collected Works of Upton Sinclair). 315p. 1999. reprint ed. lib. bdg. 98.00 (*1-58201-831-6*) Classic Bks.

Profits of the National Banks. Keith Powlison. Ed. by Stuart Bruchey. LC 80-1166. (Rise of Commercial Banking Ser.). (Illus.). 1981. reprint ed. lib. bdg. 15.95 (*0-405-13676-5*) Ayer.

Profits of War: Inside the Secret U.S. Israeli Arms Network. Ari Ben-Menashe. (Illus.). 410p. 1992. 24.95 (*1-879823-01-2*) Sheridan Sq Pr.

Profits, Politics & Drugs. Duncan W. Reekie & Michael H. Weber. LC 78-24496. 185p. 1979. 49.50 (*0-8419-0461-8*) Holmes & Meier.

Profits, Power, & Prohibition: American Alcohol Reform & the Industrializing of America, 1800-1930. John J. Rumbarger. LC 88-1884. (SUNY Series in New Social Studies on Alcohol & Drugs). 272p. 1989. text 24.50 (*0-88706-782-4*) State U NY Pr.

Profits, Priests, & Princes: Adam Smith's Emancipation of Economics from Politics & Religion. Peter Minowitz. LC 93-18798. 364p. (C). 1993. 47.50 (*0-8047-2166-1*) Stanford U Pr.

Profits, Profitability, & the Oil Industry. Edward R. Lehman. Ed. by Stuart Bruchey. LC 78-22694. (Energy in the American Economy Ser.). (Illus.). 1979. lib. bdg. 25.95 (*0-405-11997-6*) Ayer.

Profit's Prophet: Garet Garrett, 1878-1954. Carl Ryant. LC 88-43110. (Illus.). 128p. 1989. 28.50 (*0-945636-04-0*) Susquehanna U Pr.

Profits, Taxes & the State. Richard Jankowski. LC 97-34755. 208p. 1998. 59.95 (*0-275-96081-1*, Praeger Pubs) Greenwood.

Profits Through Association. Gary C. Teagno. 50p. (Orig.). 1991. pap. text 39.00 (*0-9630461-0-1*) Profits.

Profits, Wages & Productivity in the Business Cycle: A Kaldorian Analysis. Mitsuhiko Iyoda. LC 96-40418. 160p. 1997. lib. bdg. 99.00 (*0-7923-9868-8*) Kluwer Academic.

Profits Without Panic: Investment Psychology for Personal Wealth. Jonathan Myers. LC 99-11373. (Illus.). 312p. 1999. 25.00 (*1-85788-217-2*) Nicholas Brealey.

Profits Without Products: How to Transform Your Product Business into a Service. Mack Hanan. LC 92-27376. 160p. 1992. 24.95 (*0-8144-5132-2*) AMACOM.

ProForms NYSBA Electronic Legal Forms. New York State Bar Association Staff. 55p. 1994. pap. text 140.00 (*0-942954-71-8*) NYS Bar.

Profound & the Profane: An Inquiry into Spiritual Awakening. Christopher Titmuss. 95p. 1995. pap. 14.95 (*0-946672-27-X*, Pub. by Buddhist Pub) Assoc Pubs Grp.

Profound Buddhism: From Hinayana to Vajrayana. Kalu Rinpoche. Tr. by Christiane Buchet from FRE. LC 95-78919. (Illus.). 200p. 1995. pap. text 15.95 (*0-9630371-5-3*) ClearPoint.

Profound Deafness & Speech Communication. Karl-Grik Spens. Ed. by Geoff Plant. 600p. (Orig.). (C). 1995. 75.00 (*1-56593-492-X*, 0715) Singular Publishing.

Profound Honesty: Get it All/Outcompete God & Government. 620p. 1996. pap. 69.95 (*0-911752-78-1*) Neo-Tech Pub.

Profound Mystery: The Use of the Old Testament in Ephesians. Thorsten Moritz. (Novum Testamentum, Supplements Ser.: No. 85). xiv, 252p. 1996. 101.50 (*90-04-10556-5*) Brill Academic Pubs.

Profound Retardation & Multiple Impairment Vol. 3: Medical & Physical Care & Management. Ed. by James C. Hogg et al. 250p. 1990. pap. 36.95 (*0-412-34630-3*, A4456) Chapman & Hall.

Profound Though Special Erudition: Justin Winsor as Historian of Discovery. William A. Koelsch. 39p. 1983. reprint ed. pap. 5.50 (*0-912296-62-3*) Am Antiquarian.

Profound Thoughts from the World's Deepest Thinkers. Fred Maes. (Illus.). (Orig.). 1997. pap. write for info. (*1-890462-03-9*) J Francisco.

Profound Wisdom of the Heart Sutra: And Other Teachings. Bokar Rinpoche. Tr. by Christiane Buchet from FRE. LC 94-68742. (Illus.). 96p. (Orig.). 1994. pap. text 10.95 (*0-9630371-3-7*) ClearPoint.

Profound Writings, East & West. Illus. by Cecy Rose. 242p. 1988. 14.00 (*1-878683-05-5*) TAT Found.

ProfScam. Charles J. Sykes. 304p. 1989. pap. 10.95 (*0-312-03916-6*) St Martin.

ProfScam: Professors & the Demise of Higher Education. Charles J. Sykes. LC 88-21942. 250p. 1988. 18.95 (*0-89526-559-1*) Regnery Pub.

Profugo de la Sal. Luis Mario. LC 78-56759. 1978. pap. 5.00 (*0-89729-206-5*) Ediciones.

Profumi Mignon see Perfume Bottles: Profumi Mignon

Profunctional Stage of First Language Acquisition: A Crosslinguist Study. Ianthi-Maria Tsimpli. Ed. by Laurence Horn. LC 96-32080. (Linguistics Ser.). 250p. 1996. text 65.00 (*0-8153-2561-4*) Garland.

Profundas Verdades de la Biblia. Kay H. De Friederichsen. Orig. Title: God's Word Made Plain. (SPA.). 256p. 1958. mass mkt. 5.99 (*0-8254-1248-X*, Edit Portavoz) Kregel.

Profundity: A Universal Value. Jean G. Harrell. 192p. 1992. 35.00 (*0-271-00849-0*) Pa St U Pr.

Profusion: Whatever One May Think of It: Analysis & Commentary on the Economic, Social & Literary Impact of the Blackman's Guide to Understanding the Blackwoman on the National African Community. H. Khalif Khalifah. 75p. (Orig.). 1990. pap. 5.95 (*1-56411-000-1*) Untd Bros & Sis.

Profusion of Spires: Religion in Nineteenth-Century Ontario. John W. Grant. (Illus.). 319p. 1988. text 30.00 (*0-8020-5798-5*) U of Toronto Pr.

Prog Frince: A Mixed-Up Tale. C. Drew Lamm. LC 98-12379. (Illus.). 32p. (J). (ps-2). 1999. 16.95 (*0-531-30135-4*); lib. bdg. 17.99 (*0-531-33135-0*) Orchard Bks Watts.

Prog GD Sound & CD Win/Mac. Tim Kientzle. LC 97-29920. 464p. (C). 1997. pap. text 39.95 (*0-201-41972-6*) Addison-Wesley.

Prog Ibm Persn Comp:ibm C Lang. Duffy. (C). 1987. pap. text 25.00 (*0-03-071481-8*) Harcourt Coll Pubs.

Progam Guide to Calculus with Analytic Geometry. 4th ed. Swokowski. (Mathematics Ser.). 1988. 18.50 (*0-87150-149-X*) PWS Pubs.

Proganasauria, Bolosauria, Placedontia, Aeraeoscelidia, Trilophosauria, Weigeltisauria, Millerosauria, Rhincocephalia, Protorosauria. O. Kuhn. (Encyclopedia of Paleoherpetology Ser.: Pt. 9). (Illus.). 74p. 1969. text 50.70 (*3-437-30027-X*) Lubrecht & Cramer.

***Progay/antigay: The Rhetorical War Over Sexuality.** Ralph R. Smith & Russel R. Windes. LC 99-50766. (Rhetoric & Society Ser.: Vol. 4). 240p. 2000. 59.95 (*0-7619-1646-6*) Sage.

Progeny. Martha D. Ogburn. LC 98-40784. 288p. 1999. pap. 10.99 (*0-8054-1889-X*) Broadman.

***Progeny BC 2000 AD: Nothing New under the Sun.** Helen Gordon. 277p. 2000. 18.00 (*1-930520-01-8*) H Gordon.

***Progeny of Ghosts.** D. Manicom. LC 98-199377. 252p. 1998. text 34.95 (*0-88982-170-4*, Pub. by Oolichan Bks); pap. text 19.95 (*0-88982-168-2*, Pub. by Oolichan Bks) Genl Dist Srvs.

Progeny 2.0. 5th rev. ed. CCH Inc. Staff. 1992. 4.49 (*0-943293-01-4*) ViewPlan.

Progesterone Receptors in Normal & Neoplastic Tissues. fac. ed. Ed. by William L. McGuire et al. LC 77-72065. (Progress in Cancer Research & Therapy Ser.: No. 4). (Illus.). 357p. pap. 110.70 (*0-7837-7353-6*, 204716200005) Bks Demand.

***Progestins & Antiprogestins in Clinical Practice.** Ed. by Regine Sitruk-Ware & Daniel R. Mishell. 410p. 2000. 165.00 (*0-8247-8291-7*) Dekker.

Progetto Universale: A Proposal Towards Love, Peace, & Freedom in the Universe! 4th ed. Michael Jerome Pardo et al. 320p. 1998. reprint ed. 35.00 (*0-9666633-0-6*, 9603001) Universal Way.

Progmg Discret Sim. Pollatschek. 1995. pap. text 40.00 (*0-13-234584-6*) P-H.

Progne y Filomena de Francisco de Rojas Zorrilla: Edicion, Introduccion y Notas de Dr. Alfred Rodriguez y Saul Roll-Velez. Francisco D. Rojas Zorrilla. Ed. by Alfred Rodriguez & Saul Roll-Velez. LC 93-2531. (Iberica Ser.: No. 8). 147p. (C). 1994. text 38.95 (*0-8204-2080-8*) P Lang Pubng.

Progno 1.0: Prognostic Models in Fertility Practice. M. A. Wiegerinck. 1996. 150.00 incl. disk (*1-85070-794-4*) Prthnon Pub.

Prognose und Verlauf Ersthospitalisierter Schizophrener: Unter Mitarbeit von Wolfgang Brauer, Dagmar Laubenstein, Michael Handel & Martin Volz. Eibe-Rudolf Rey & Josef Bailer. (Illus.). 199p. 1997. 38.95 (*3-631-30074-3*) P Lang Pubng.

Prognoserechung. 5th ed. 1995. 91.00 (*0-387-00758-X*) Spr-Verlag.

Prognosis: Fair. John M. Dorn. 1993. pap. 14.95 (*1-56883-004-1*) Colonial Pr AL.

***Prognosis & Outcome Expectancy of Surgical Diseases.** Daniel P. McKellar et al. LC 99-27978. 465p. 1999. 85.00 (*1-57626-101-8*) Quality Med Pub.

Prognosis & Risk Assessment in Cardiovascular Disease. Ed. by Amar S. Kapoor & Bramah N. Singh. (Illus.). 578p. 1992. text 110.00 (*0-443-08768-7*) Church.

Prognosis & Treatment of Cardiomyopathies & Myocarditis: Cardiomyopathy Update 5. Ed. by Morie Sekiguchi & Peter J. Richardson. 412p. 1995. 250.00 (*0-86008-511-2*, Pub. by U of Tokyo) Col U Pr.

Prognosis in Neurology. James M. Gilchrist. LC 97-52638. 496p. 1998. text 87.50 (*0-7506-9888-8*) Buttrwrth-Heinemann.

Prognosis in the Rheumatic Diseases. Ed. by Nicholas Bellamy. 528p. 1991. text 279.50 (*0-7923-8958-1*) Kluwer Academic.

Prognosis of Coronary Heart Disease-Progression of Coronary Arteriosclerosis. Ed. by H. Roskamm. (Illus.). 248p. 1983. 48.95 (*0-387-12367-9*) Spr-Verlag.

Prognosis of Diabetes in Children. Ed. by Z. Laron. (Pediatric & Adolescent Endocrinology Ser.: Vol. 18). xiv, 304p. 1989. 216.75 (*3-8055-4702-1*) S Karger.

***Prognosis of Neurological Disorders.** 2nd ed. Ed. by Randolph W. Evans et al. LC 99-19078. (Illus.). 776p. 2000. text 99.50 (*0-19-511936-3*) OUP.

***Prognosis 2000: Evaluation of Current Trends.** Lawrance George Lux. LC 99-91198. 1999. 25.00 (*0-7388-0660-9*); pap. 18.00 (*0-7388-0661-7*) Xlibris Corp.

Prognostic & Predictive Value of p53: European School of Oncology Scientific Updates, Vol. 1. Ed. by J. G. Klijn. LC 97-29349. 174p. 1997. 95.00 (*0-444-82832-X*) Elsevier.

Prognostic Astronomy: The Scientific Basis of Astrology. Sepharial. 77p. 1996. pap. 7.00 (*0-89540-302-1*, SB-302) Sun Pub.

Prognostic Factors in Cancer. International Union Against Cancer Staff & M. K. Gospodarowicz. Ed. by D. E. Henson et al. LC 95-19216. (Illus.). 250p. 1997. 64.95 (*3-540-58688-1*) Spr-Verlag.

Prognostic Value of a Primary Group Test: A Study of Intelligence & Relative Achievement in the First Grade. Bess V. Cunningham. LC 70-176683. (Columbia University. Teachers College. Contributions to Education Ser.: No. 139). reprint ed. 37.50 (*0-404-55139-4*) AMS Pr.

***Prognostic Variables in Node-Negative & Node-Positive Breast Cancer.** Ed. by Giampietro Gasparini. 428p. 1998. 290.00 (*0-7923-8447-4*) Kluwer Academic.

Prognostication Euerlasting of Ryght Goode Effecte: Lately Corrected & Augmented by Thomas Digges, His Sonne. Leonard Digges. LC 74-28846. (English Experience Ser.: No. 727). 1975. reprint ed. 15.00 (*90-221-0727-2*) Walter J Johnson.

***Program.** Stephen Walsh White. LC 00-24029. 2001. 24.95 (*0-385-49903-5*) Doubleday.

Program Administration, Vol. 1. Larry Cooper & Yvonne Harrison. (Restorative Nursing for Long Term Care Ser.). 544p. 1994. ring bd. 60.00 (*1-885506-02-3*) Cooper & Harrison.

Program Administrator. Jack Rudman. (Career Examination Ser.: C-2868). 1994. pap. 34.95 (*0-8373-2868-3*) Nat Learn.

Program Advocacy: Power, Publicity, & the Teacher-Librarian. Ken Haycock. xii, 105p. 1990. lib. bdg. 20.00 (*0-87287-781-7*) Libs Unl.

Program Analysis for State & Local Governments. 2nd ed. Harry P. Hatry et al. LC 87-27372. (Illus.). 184p. 1988. pap. text 18.50 (*0-87766-409-9*) Urban Inst.

Program & Abstract Book. Paul A. Anderson et al. 180p. (C). 1990. pap. 22.00 (*0-9627560-0-8*) U of MD Physical Therapy.

Program & Problem Solving C++ Test Item File. Nell Dale et al. (Computer Science Ser.). 1996. pap., teacher ed. 10.00 (*0-669-29775-5*) Jones & Bartlett.

Program Applicants As a Comparison Group in Evaluating Training Programs. Stephen H. Bell et al. LC 95-37399. 184p. (C). 1995. pap. text 15.00 (*0-88099-157-7*) W E Upjohn.

Program Architecture for Improved Maintainability in Software Engineering. John Einbu. (Information Technology Ser.). 1989. text 39.95 (*0-470-21538-0*) P-H.

Program Assessment. Timothy R. Cline. LC 98-21988. (AWL Series on Managing Human Resources). 320p. (C). 1998. pap. 47.00 (*0-201-32259-5*, Prentice Hall) P-H.

Program Assessment in Speech Communication. Ed. by Ellen A. Hay. 46p. (Orig.). (C). 1992. pap. text 10.00 (*0-944811-11-6*) Natl Comm Assn.

Program Bank, 12 vols., Set. 85.00 (*0-686-96119-6*) USCJE.

Program Bits 'n Pieces. Helen Eikamp. 42p. 1985. pap. 2.50 (*0-614-24789-6*) Tesseract SD.

Program Budgeting: Program Analysis & the Federal Budget. 2nd ed. Ed. by David Novick. LC 68-1604. (Rand Corporation Research Studies). (Illus.). 406p. 1967. 38.50 (*0-674-71350-8*) HUP.

Program Budgeting for Primary & Secondary Public Education: Current Status & Prospects in Los Angeles. Werner Z. Hirsch et al. LC 72-83569. (Special Studies in U. S. Economic, Social & Political Issues). 1972. 42.50 (*0-89197-907-7*) Irvington.

Program Budgeting for School District Planning. Sue A. Haggart et al. LC 76-170027. 320p. 1972. 37.95 (*0-87778-026-9*) Educ Tech Pubns.

Program Budgeting for Urban Police Services: With Special Reference to Los Angeles. Donald C. Shoup & Stephen L. Mehay. LC 72-83009. (Special Studies in U. S. Economic, Social & Political Issues). 1972. 42.50 (*0-275-28676-2*) Irvington.

Program CC: Introductory Version. Peter M. Thompson & Bahram Shahian. (Illus.). 160p. (C). 1993. pap. text 23.95 (*0-03-097347-3*) OUP.

***Program Comprehension: Proceedings: International Workshop on Program Comprehension (7th: 1999: Pittsburgh, Pennsylvania)** 227p. 1999. 110.00 (*0-7695-0179-6*) IEEE Comp Soc.

Program Comprehension, 5th International Workshop: Proceedings of the 5th International Workshop on Program Comprehension, Dearborn, Michigan, 1997. LC 10-928138. 264p. 1997. 115.00 (*0-8186-7993-X*) IEEE Comp Soc.

Program Comprehension, 4th Workshop on (WPC '96) LC 95-81853. 264p. 1996. 50.00 (*0-8186-7283-8*, PRO7283) IEEE Comp Soc.

Program Construction. R. G. Stone & D. J. Cooke. (Cambridge Computer Science Texts Ser.: No. 22). (Illus.). 382p. 1987. pap. text 38.95 (*0-521-31883-1*) Cambridge U Pr.

Program Construction: International Summer School. Ed. by F. L. Bauer & Manfred Broy. (Lecture Notes in Computer Science Ser.: Vol. 69). 1982. 47.00 (*0-387-09251-X*) Spr-Verlag.

Program Consultation with Human Service Programs: A Clinical Perspective. Barbara L. Blackwell & Lillian K. Cartwright. LC 88-50021. 238p. 1988. pap. 15.95 (*0-89914-026-2*) Third Party Pub.

Program Controllers. 4th ed. Richard Cox. (Electrical Trades Ser). (C). 2000. pap. 43.50 (*0-7668-1427-0*) Thomson Learn.

Program Correctness over Abstract Data Types, with Error State Semantics. J. V. Tucker & J. I. Zucker. (CWI Monographs: Vol. 6). 212p. 1988. 97.75 (*0-444-70340-3*, North Holland) Elsevier.

Program Derivation: The Development of Programs from Specifications. R. Geoff Dromey. 432p. (C). 1989. pap. text 29.95 (*0-201-41624-7*) Addison-Wesley.

P

An Asterisk (*) at the beginning of an entry indicates that the title is appearing for the first time.

Program Design & Construction. David A. Higgins. LC 78-31097. (Personal Computing Ser.). (Illus.). 1979. pap. text 28.95 (*0-13-729525-1*) P-H.

Program Design & Data Structures with C++ Kenneth A. Lambert & Thomas L. Naps. LC 95-45571. 550p. (C). 1996. mass mkt. 67.95 (*0-314-07340-X*) West Pub.

Program Design & Development Using C++ Gary J. Bronson. LC 96-47078. (Illus.). 991p. 1997. pap. 69.95 (*0-314-20338-9*) West Pub.

Program Design Calculi. Ed. by Manfred Broy. LC 93-34001. (NATO ASI Series F: Computer & Systems Sciences, Special Programme AET: Vol. 118). viii, 409p. 1993. 107.95 (*0-387-56943-X*) Spr-Verlag.

Program Design for Personal Trainers: Bridging Theory into Application. Douglas Brooks. LC 98-25930. (Illus.). 328p. 1998. 30.00 (*0-7360-0079-8*, BBRO0079) Human Kinetics.

Program Design with Modula-2. Susan Eisenbach & Chris Sadler. (Illus.). 250p. (C). 1989. pap. text 32.25 (*0-201-17567-3*) Addison-Wesley.

Program Design with Pseudocode. 2nd ed. T. E. Bailey & Kris Lundgaard. LC 85-15170. 200p. (C). 1985. mass mkt. 14.50 (*0-534-05574-5*) Brooks-Cole.

Program Development. Terry R. Bacon. (Illus.). 114p. 1994. write for info. (*1-57740-004-6*, ILW004) Intl LrningWrk.

Program Development by Refinement: Case Studies Using the B Method. Emil Sekerinski & Kaisa Sere. LC 98-25801. (Formal Approaches to Computing & Information Technology Ser.). 1998. write for info. (*1-85233-053-8*) Spr-Verlag.

Program Development by Specification & Transformation: A Methodology Language Family System. Ed. by Berthold Hoffmann & Bernd Krieg-Bruckner. LC 93-29020. (Lecture Notes in Computer Science Ser.: Vol. 680). xv, 623p. 1993. 87.95 (*0-387-56733-X*) Spr-Verlag.

Program Development for Community AIDS Outreach. Ed. by Rebecca S. Ashery. 70p. (Orig.). (C). 1994. pap. text 20.00 (*0-7881-1488-3*) DIANE Pub.

Program Development Handbook for the Holistic Assessment of Writing. Norbert Elliot & Maximino Plata. Ed. by Paul Zelhart. 154p. (Orig.). (C). 1990. pap. text 19.00 (*0-8191-7705-9*); lib. bdg. 38.00 (*0-8191-7704-0*) U Pr of Amer.

Program Development in Continuing Education. Allen E. Goody & Charles E. Kozoll. LC 94-47469. (Professional Practices Ser.). (Illus.). 160p. (C). 1995. 19.50 (*0-89464-852-7*) Krieger.

Program Development in Java. Robert Ekelund. LC 00-36277. 464p. (C). 2000. 49.95 (*0-201-65768-6*) Addison-Wesley.

Program Development Manual. 1985. 4.00 (*0-686-31455-7*) Parents Anon.

Program Development Process Pt. I: The Individual Programmer. Joel D. Aron. (IBM Systems Programming Ser.). (Illus.). 280p. 1974. text. write for info. (*0-201-14451-4*) Addison-Wesley.

Program Development Process Pt. II: The Programming Team. Joel D. Aron. LC 74-2847. (Illus.). 704p. 1983. text. write for info. (*0-201-14463-8*) Addison-Wesley.

Program Director's Handbook. Bob Paiva. (Illus.). 168p. (Orig.). 1983. pap. 16.95 (*0-8306-1363-3*, 1363) McGraw-Hill Prof.

Program Efficiencies at the U.s. Department of Transportation: Hearing Before the Committee on Commerce, Science, & Transportation, United States Senate, One Hundred Fifth Congress, First Session, May 21, 1997. United States. LC 98-160349. iii, 69 p. 1998. write for info. (*0-16-056349-6*) USGPO.

Program Evaluation. M. E. Gredler. LC 95-7420. 374p. 1995. 76.00 (*0-02-346246-9*, Macmillan Coll) P-H.

Program Evaluation. 2nd ed. John M. Owen & Patricia Rogers. 272p. 1998. pap. 35.00 (*1-86448-784-4*, Pub. by Allen & Unwin Pty) Paul & Co Pubs.

Program Evaluation. 2nd ed. Blaine Worthen. (C). 1997. pap. text, teacher ed. write for info. (*0-8013-2004-6*) Addison-Wesley.

Program Evaluation: A Compilation of Articles from the Journal of Health Education. Des. by Randall R. Cottrell et al. (Illus.). 124p. 1997. pap. 15.95 (*0-88314-607-X*) AAHPERD.

Program Evaluation: A Field Guide for Administrators. Robert L. Schalock & Craig V. D. Thornton. (Illus.). 286p. (C). 1988. 49.50 (*0-306-42840-7*, Plenum Trade) Perseus Pubng.

Program Evaluation: A Self-Study Manual. Christopher Smith. 216p. (Orig.). 1987. pap. text. write for info. (*0-916671-70-4*) TRR.

Program Evaluation: Alternative Approaches & Practical Guidelines. 2nd ed. Blaine Worthen. LC 96-28952. (C). 1997. pap. text 57.19 (*0-8013-0774-0*) Longman.

Program Evaluation: An Introduction. 2nd ed. David Royse & Bruce A. Thyer. 230p. 1996. pap. text 49.95 (*0-8304-1415-0*) Thomson Learn.

*__Program Evaluation: An Introduction.__ 3rd ed. David D. Royse. LC 00-33740. 2000. write for info. (*0-8304-1536-X*) Burnham Inc.

Program Evaluation: Forms & Approaches. John M. Owen. 176p. 1994. pap. 22.95 (*1-86373-462-7*, Pub. by Allen & Unwin Pty) Paul & Co Pubs.

Program Evaluation: Improving the Flow of Information to the Congress. (Illus.). 84p. (Orig.). (C). 1995. pap. text 30.00 (*0-7881-1671-1*) DIANE Pub.

Program Evaluation: Methods & Case Studies. 5th ed. Emil Posavac & Raymond G. Carey. LC 96-3291. 305p. (C). 1996. 56.00 (*0-13-255332-5*) P-H.

Program Evaluation: Patterns & Directions. Intro. by Eleanor Chelimsky. (Illus.). 316p. 1985. pap. text 14.95 (*0-936678-08-9*) Am Soc Pub Admin.

Program Evaluation & Review Technique: Applications in Education. Desmond L. Cook. LC 78-57981. 1978. pap. text 16.00 (*0-8191-0657-7*) U Pr of Amer.

Program Evaluation & the Management of Government. Ed. by Ray C. Rist. 378p. 1989. 39.95 (*0-88738-297-5*) Transaction Pubs.

*__Program Evaluation & the Management of Government.__ Ed. by Ray C. Rist. 193p. 1999. pap. 24.95 (*0-7658-0600-2*) Transaction Pubs.

Program Evaluation at HEW: Research Versus Reality, 3 pts., Pt. 1. Ed. by James G. Abert. LC 79-17495. (Public Administration & Public Policy Ser.: No. 8). (Illus.). 423p. reprint ed. pap. 131.20 (*0-8357-3507-9*, 203451500001) Bks Demand.

Program Evaluation at HEW: Research Versus Reality, 3 pts., Pt. 2. Ed. by James G. Abert. LC 79-17495. (Public Administration & Public Policy Ser.: No. 8). (Illus.). 407p. reprint ed. pap. 126.20 (*0-8357-3508-7*, 203451500002) Bks Demand.

Program Evaluation at HEW: Research Versus Reality, 3 pts., Pt. 3. Ed. by James G. Abert. LC 79-17495. (Public Administration & Public Policy Ser.: No. 8). (Illus.). 328p. reprint ed. pap. 101.70 (*0-8357-3509-5*, 203451500003) Bks Demand.

*__Program Evaluation for Exercise Leaders.__ Anita M. Myers. LC 99-33757. (Illus.). 168p. 1999. pap. 28.00 (*0-88011-709-5*) Human Kinetics.

Program Evaluation for SportDirectors. James L. Kestner. LC 95-24267. (Illus.). 128p. (Orig.). 1995. pap. text 22.00 (*0-88011-505-X*, PKES0505) Human Kinetics.

Program Evaluation Grants. Foundation Center Staff. 70p. 1998. 75.00 (*0-87954-810-X*, PEG) Foundation Ctr.

Program Evaluation Guide. 21p. 1996. per. 12.00 (*0-16-048508-8*) USGPO.

Program Evaluation Handbook. Robert C. Serow. LC 98-202434. 80p. (C). 1998. pap. text 14.95 (*0-536-01053-6*) Pearson Custom.

Program Evaluation in Moral Education. Hugh F. Cline & Robert A. Feldmesser. 1988. 10.00 (*0-317-67889-2*) Educ Testing Serv.

Program Evaluation in the Health Fields, Vol. II. Ed. by Herbert C. Schulberg et al. LC 78-102679. 467p. 1979. 54.95 (*0-87705-339-1*, Kluwer Acad Hman Sci) Kluwer Academic.

Program Evaluation in the Human Services. Michael Smith. LC 89-26318. (Social Work Ser.: Vol. 16). 168p. 1990. 28.95 (*0-8261-6590-7*) Springer Pub.

Program Evaluation in the Public Sector. Ed. by Albert C. Hyde et al. LC 78-19742. (Praeger Special Studies). 380p. 1979. 69.50 (*0-275-90368-0*, C0368, Praeger Pubs) Greenwood.

Program Evaluation Specialist. Jack Rudman. (Career Examination Ser.: C-2699). 1994. pap. 34.95 (*0-8373-2699-0*) Nat Learn.

Program Evaluation Standards: How to Assess Evaluations of Educational Programs. 2nd ed. Joint Committee on Standards for Educational Progr & James R. Sanders. LC 94-1178. 272p. (C). 1994. text 46.00 (*0-8039-5731-9*); pap. text 21.00 (*0-8039-5732-7*) Sage.

Program Evaluation Study Guide. 2nd ed. Blaine Worthen. (C). 1997. pap. text, teacher ed. 19.69 (*0-8013-1985-4*) Addison-Wesley.

Program Evolution: Processes of Software Change. M. M. Lehman & L. A. Belady. (APIC Studies in Data Processing). 1985. pap. text 62.00 (*0-12-442441-4*) Acad Pr.

Program Examiner. Jack Rudman. (Career Examination Ser.: C-2655). 1994. pap. 34.95 (*0-8373-2655-9*) Nat Learn.

Program FARSEP: A Program for Determination of the Far Postbuckling Section of the Secondary Equilibrium Path of Marine Risers. Theodore Kokkinis & Michael M. Bernitsas. LC VM0605.. (University of Michigan, Dept. of Naval Architecture & Marine Engineering, Report Ser.: No. 278). 46p. reprint ed. pap. 30.00 (*0-608-12941-0*, 202468300038) Bks Demand.

Program Flow Analysis: Theory & Application. Steven S. Muchnick & Neil D. Jones. (Software Ser.). (Illus.). 448p. (C). 1981. 50.00 (*0-13-729681-9*) P-H.

Program for Athletic Coaches' Education Instructor's Guide, No. 1. Ed. by Vern Seefeldt. 1991. VHS 110.00 (*1-884125-42-5*) Cooper Pubng.

Program for Athletic Coaches' Education Instructor's Guide, No. 2. Ed. by Vern Seefeldt. 1991. VHS 110.00 (*1-884125-43-3*) Cooper Pubng.

Program for Athletic Coaches' Education Reference Manual & Study Guide. Ed. by Vern Seefeldt & Eugene Brown. LC 89-45908. (Illus.). 400p. 1996. reprint ed. pap. text 30.00 (*1-884125-52-2*) Cooper Pubng.

Program for Better Vision: How to See Better in Minutes a Day. Martin Sussman. LC 97-38016. (Illus.). 202p. 1998. pap. 19.95 (*1-55643-257-7*) North Atlantic.

Program for Destruction. Franklin W. Dixon. Ed. by Ann Greenberg. (Hardy Boys Mystery Stories Ser.: No. 87). (J). (gr. 3-6). 1987. pap. 3.99 (*0-671-64895-0*, Minstrel Bks) PB.

Program for Higher Education in the Church of the Brethren. John S. Noffsinger. LC 78-177711. (Columbia University. Teachers College. Contributions to Education Ser.: No. 172). (C). reprint ed. 37.50 (*0-404-55172-6*) AMS Pr.

Program for Living Longer. Carlton Fredericks. 1983. 9.95 (*0-686-44866-9*, Fireside) S&S Trade Pap.

Program for Monetary Stability. Milton Friedman. LC 60-9782. xv, 110p. 1983. pap. 15.00 (*0-8232-0371-9*) Fordham.

Program for Mother's Day & Other Poems see Programas del Dia de la Madre y Poesias

Program for Personal & Cultural Change: Modules on Smoking, Nutrition, Weight Control, Physical Fitness, & Stress, 5 vols. Robert F. Allen. (Illus.). 60p. (C). 1981. reprint ed. pap. 8.95 (*0-941703-03-7*) Healthyculture.

Program for Personal & Cultural Change on Nutrition. Robert F. Allen. LC 81-17569. (Illus.). 40p. (C). 1990. reprint ed. pap., student ed. 8.95 (*0-941703-07-X*) Healthyculture.

Program for Personal & Cultural Change on Physical Fitness. Robert F. Allen. LC 81-15029. (C). 1990. reprint ed. pap., student ed. 8.95 (*0-941703-08-8*) Healthyculture.

Program for Personal Change on Smoking. Robert F. Allen. LC 81-15025. (Illus.). 40p. (C). 1990. reprint ed. pap., student ed. 8.95 (*0-941703-04-5*) Healthyculture.

Program for Personal Change on Stress Resolution. Robert F. Allen. LC 81-15041. (Illus.). 40p. (C). 1990. reprint ed. pap., student ed. 8.95 (*0-941703-05-3*) Healthyculture.

Program for Personal Change on Weight Control. Robert F. Allen. LC 81-15026. 40p. 1990. reprint ed. pap., student ed. 8.95 (*0-941703-06-1*) Healthyculture.

Program for Progress: Proceedings & Communications of Regional Meetings of the Sister-Formation Conferences, 1965. Sister Formation Conferences Staff. Ed. by Mary H. Valentine. LC 58-10465. (Sister Formation Ser.). 299p. reprint ed. pap. 92.70 (*0-7837-0477-1*, 204080000018) Bks Demand.

Program for Research in Military Nursing: Progress & Future Direction. Contrib. by Institute of Medicine Staff. 128p. (Orig.). (C). 1996. pap. text 19.00 (*0-309-05490-7*) Natl Acad Pr.

Program for Self Psychoanalysis, Vols. 3-12. Arnold Goldberg. 1994. pap. 250.00 (*0-88163-210-4*) Analytic Pr.

Program for Special Days see Programas para Dias Especiales

Program for Staying Fit after Chelation. Arline Brecher. Ed. by Harold Brecher. 80p. (Orig.). 1989. pap. 29.95 (*0-927839-13-X*) HlthSavers Pr.

Program for Strengthening Security & Reducing the Risk of War in the Asian-Pacific Region. International Strategic Institute at Stanford Staf & Institute of Far Eastern Studies of Soviet Academy. (Special Report of the Center for International Security & Arms Control, Stanford University Ser.). 20p. (Orig.). 1988. pap. 5.00 (*0-935371-17-6*) CFISAC.

Program for the Assessment & Instruction of Swallowing (PAIS) Virginia A. Mulpeter & Judith F. Rosenfield. 24p. (Orig.). (C). 1993. teacher ed. 55.00 (*0-937857-39-4*, 1529) Speech Bin.

Program for Writing Winning Business Plans. Richard H. Buskirk et al. 88p. 1991. pap. 9.95 (*0-944303-04-8*) Entre Ed Fndtn.

Program for You: A Guide to the Big Book's Design for Living. Carolyn Barnes. 183p. (Orig.). pap. 10.00 (*0-89486-741-5*, 5122A) Hazelden.

Program Generators With Java & XML. (C). 2000. pap. 49.99 (*0-13-025878-4*) P-H.

Program Guide for CIM Implementation: A Project of the CASA - SME Technical Council. Ed. by Charles M. Savage. LC 85-72355. (Illus.). 168p. reprint ed. pap. 52.10 (*0-8357-6497-4*, 203586800097) Bks Demand.

Program Guide for CIM Implementation: A Project of the CASA - SME Technical Council. 2nd ed. Ed. by Leonard Bertain & Lee Hales. LC 87-62381. (Illus.). 216p. reprint ed. pap. 67.00 (*0-7837-6280-1*, 204599500010) Bks Demand.

Program Guide for Infants & Toddlers with Neuromotor & Other Developmental Disabilities. Frances P. Connor et al. LC 77-28188. 408p. 1978. pap. 21.95 (*0-8077-2546-3*) Tchrs Coll.

Program Guide to Calculus. 2nd ed. Campbell. (Mathematics Ser.). 1979. 6.75 (*0-87150-271-2*) PWS Pubs.

Program Guide to Federally Funded Environment & Natural Resources R & D. 3rd ed. Ed. by John H. Gibbons. (Illus.). 87p. (C). 1998. pap. text 25.00 (*0-7881-7432-0*) DIANE Pub.

Program Guide to Fundamentals of College Algebra. 4th ed. Swokowski. (Mathematics Ser.). 1978. 6.75 (*0-87150-270-4*) PWS Pubs.

Program Guide to Fundamentals of Trigonometry. 4th ed. Swokowski. (Mathematics Ser.). 1979. 6.75 (*0-87150-273-9*) PWS Pubs.

Program Guidelines for Hearing Impaired Individuals. California Department of Education Staff. 64p. 1986. pap. 10.00 (*0-8011-0309-6*) Calif Education.

Program Guidelines for Individuals Who Are Deaf-Blind. California Department of Education Staff. 94p. 1990. pap. 10.00 (*0-8011-0886-1*) Calif Education.

Program Guidelines for Individuals Who Are Severely Orthopedically Impaired. California Department of Education Staff. 112p. 1992. pap. 10.00 (*0-8011-1032-7*) Calif Education.

Program Guidelines for Visually Impaired Individuals. California Department of Education Staff. 88p. 1997. pap. 10.00 (*0-8011-1289-3*) Calif Education.

Program Handbook for Women's Ministries. Compiled by Berniece Garsee. 88p. 1984. pap. 14.99 (*0-8341-0924-7*) Beacon Hill.

Program HYDCYL: A Database for Calculation of Hydrodynamic Loading of Circular Cylinders. Michael M. Bernitsas & S. Guha-Thakurta. LC VM0605.. (University of Michigan, Dept. of Naval Architecture & Marine Engineering, Report Ser.: No. 267). 41p. reprint ed. pap. 30.00 (*0-608-12942-9*, 202468200038) Bks Demand.

Program Implementation in Preventive Trials. Joseph A. Durlak. Ed. by Joseph R. Ferrari. LC 98-3323. 94p. 1998. 29.95 (*0-7890-0523-9*) Haworth Pr.

Program Information Package for Technology Reinvestment Project FY95 Competition: Technology Reinvestment Project. 79p. pap. text 30.00 (*0-7881-4315-8*) DIANE Pub.

Program Isapi with Visual Basic 5. Wayne Freeze. LC 97-66158. 504p. 1997. pap., per. 40.00 incl. cd-rom (*0-7615-0914-3*) Prima Pub.

Program Logic Controll Act Manual. 1989. 27.27 (*0-07-049688-9*) McGraw.

Program Logic for Business. 3rd ed. Saret. 1992. teacher ed. 79.06 (*0-07-054909-5*) McGraw.

Program Manager. Jack Rudman. (Career Examination Ser.: C-985). 1994. pap. 34.95 (*0-8373-0985-9*) Nat Learn.

Program Manager: The Bull Leading the Charge. Richard Hardy. 147p. 1998. pap. 12.95 (*0-9656945-3-4*) LHA Bks.

Program Manager, the Journal of the Defense Systems Management College. Government Printing Office Staff. 1983. pap. 19.00 (*0-16-010264-2*) USGPO.

Program Manager's Notebook, August 1995. 538p. 1995. ring bd. 40.00 (*0-16-061180-6*) USGPO.

Program Materials for Family Law for the General Practitioner: August 22, 1986, Savannah, Georgia-August 29, 1986, Atlanta, Georgia. Institute of Continuing Legal Education in Georgia. LC 86-623177. 1986. 9.00 (*0-685-18649-0*) ICLE Georgia.

Program Materials for Real Property Law Institute: May 8-10, 1986, St. Simons, May 22-23, 1986, Atlanta. Real Property Law Institute & Institute of Continuing Legal Education, Georgia S. LC 86-623182. 1986. 23.00 (*0-685-18536-2*) ICLE Georgia.

Program Materials for Seminar on Employee Benefit Plans, April 11, 1986, Atlanta Georgia. LC 86-621897. 1986. 16.00 (*0-685-17604-5*) ICLE Georgia.

Program Materials for Seminar on Ethics & Malpractice, December 19, 1985, Atlanta, Georgia. LC 86-621678. 1985. 6.50 (*0-685-17605-3*) ICLE Georgia.

Program Materials for Seminar on Georgia Law School: March 21, 1986, Atlanta, Georgia. Georgia Council of School Board Attorneys & Georgia Institute of Continuing Legal Education St. LC 86-194719. 1986. 9.00 (*0-685-17618-5*) ICLE Georgia.

Program Materials for Seminar on Real Property Law: April 21, 22,23, 1983, St. Simons Island, Georgia. Ed. by Institute of Continuing Legal Education, Georgia S. LC 83-623096. (Illus.). 16.00 (*0-685-08689-5*) ICLE Georgia.

Program Materials for Seminar on Special Real Estate Issues: Multi-Owners Development, February 21, 1986, Atlanta, Georgia. Institute of Continuing Legal Education Staff. LC 86-621680. 1986. 13.00 (*0-685-18556-7*) ICLE Georgia.

Program Modification. Jean-Dominique Warnier. 152p. 1978. pap. text 72.50 (*90-207-0777-9*) Kluwer Academic.

Program Monitoring & Visualization: An Exploratory Approach. Clinton L. Jeffery. LC 98-31161. (Illus.). 209p. 1999. 59.95 incl. cd-rom (*0-387-98644-8*) Spr-Verlag.

Program Notes for the Singer's Repertoire. Berton Coffin & Werner Singer. LC 60-7265. 230p. 1962. 32.00 (*0-8108-0169-8*) Scarecrow.

Program Notes for the Solo Tuba. Compiled by Gary Bird. LC 93-34073. (Illus.). 160p. (C). 1994. 19.95 (*0-253-31189-6*) Ind U Pr.

Program of Financial Research. (NBER Bulletin Ser.: No. 64). 22p. 1937. reprint ed. 20.00 (*0-685-61182-5*) Natl Bur Econ Res.

Program of Financial Research Vol. 1: Report of the Exploratory Committee on Financial Research. Exploratory Committee on Financial Research. (Financial Research Program Ser.: No. 1). 95p. 1937. reprint ed. 24.70 (*0-87014-458-8*) Natl Bur Econ Res.

Program of Financial Research Vol. 2: Inventory of Current Research on Financial Problems. Exploratory Committee on Financial Research. (Financial Research Program Ser.: No. 1). 264p. 1937. reprint ed. 68.70 (*0-87014-459-6*) Natl Bur Econ Res.

Program of the Communist Party of the Soviet Union. Kommunisticheskaia Partiia Staff & Sovetskogo Soiuza Staff. LC 74-10423. 143p. 1974, reprint ed. lib. bdg. 55.00 (*0-8371-7685-9*, KHCP, Greenwood Pr) Greenwood.

Program Officer (Aging Services) (Career Examination Ser.: C-3644). pap. 29.95 (*0-8373-3644-9*) Nat Learn.

*__Program Operations Series, 9 vols.__ Incl. Creating Housing for People with Special Needs: A Complete Overview of the Skills & Rules Needed for Developing & Managing Supportive Housing. Wendy Shaia. 44p. 1999. pap. (*0-942901-48-7*, Pub. by Enterprise Fnd); Creating Multifamily Rental Housing Through Renovation: A Complete Overview of the Skills & Finances Needed to Run a Successful Program. Bob Santucci. 1999. pap. (*0-942901-44-4*, Pub. by Enterprise Fnd); Developing & Managing Scattered-Site Rental Housing: A Complete Overview of the Skills & Finances Needed to Run a Successful Program. Matt Perrenod. 20p. 1999. pap. (*0-942901-46-0*, Pub. by Enterprise Fnd); Developing Multifamily Housing with New Construction: A Complete Overview of the Skills & Finances Needed to Buy a Successful Program. Matt Perrenod. 40p. 1999. pap. (*0-942901-45-2*, Pub. by Enterprise Fnd); Developing Single-Family Subdivisions: A Complete Overview of the Skills & Finances Needed to Run a Successful Program. Armand Magnelli & Deborah Webster. 1999. pap. (*0-942901-41-X*, Pub. by Enterprise Fnd); New Construction of Single-Family Housing for Infill: A Complete Overview of the Skills & Finance Needed to Run a Successful Program. Bob Santucci. 16p. 1999. pap. (*0-942901-43-6*, Pub. by Enterprise Fnd); Operating a Home Improvement Program: A Complete Overview of the Skills & Finances Need to Run a Successful Program. Bob Santucci. 16p. 1999.

P

pap. (*0-942901-47-9*, Pub. by Enterprise Fnd); Successful Single-Family Acquisition & Rehabilitation: A Complete Overview of the Skills & Finances Needed for Running a Successful Program. Bill Batko. 20p. 1999. pap. (*0-942901-16-9*, Pub. by Enterprise Fnd); Understanding the Home Investment Partnership Program: A Guide for Nonprofit Housing Developers. Bill Batko. 16p. 1999. pap. (*0-942901-49-5*, Pub. by Enterprise Fnd); 1999. pap. write for info. (*0-942901-40-1*, Pub. by Enterprise Fnd) BookMasters.

Program Operations Specialist. (Career Examination Ser.: C-3584). pap. 34.95 (*0-8373-3584-1*) Nat Learn.

Program Opportunities for Academically Talented Students. rev. ed. Ed. by JHU Center for Talented Youth Staff. 111p. 1996. pap. text 12.00 (*1-881622-06-1*) JHU IAAY.

Program Outcome Evaluation: A Step-by-Step Handbook. Kristine L. Mika. LC 96-44909. 106p. 1996. pap. 16.95 (*0-87304-286-7*) Manticore Pubs.

Program Outreach Specialist. Jack Rudman. (Career Examination Ser.: C-3405). 1994. pap. 29.95 (*0-8373-3405-5*) Nat Learn.

Program Planning: A Real Life Quantitative Approach. Mitchell L. Springer. LC 97-45961. 1998. 45.95 (*1-55753-129-3*, Ichor Busn Bks) Purdue U Pr.

Program Planning about World Affairs. Carole E. Baumann. 70p. 1991. pap. 10.00 (*0-944675-47-6*) Amer Forum.

Program Planning & Evaluation for Blind & Visually Impaired Students: National Guidelines for Educational Excellence. Ed. by Jack Hazekamp & Kathleen M. Huebner. LC 89-6970. 128p. 1989. pap. 24.95 (*0-89128-155-X*) Am Foun Blind.

Program Planning & Evaluation for the Public Manager. 2nd rev. ed. Ronald D. Sylvia et al. LC 97-205450. (Illus.). 208p. (C). 1996. pap. text 20.95 (*0-88133-920-2*) Waveland Pr.

Program Planning for Health Education & Promotion. 2nd ed. Mark Dignan & Patricia A. Carr. (Illus.). 176p. 1993. pap. 27.95 (*0-8121-1554-6*) Lppncott W & W.

Program Planning for the Training & Continuing Education of Adults: North American Perspectives. Ed. by Peter S. Cookson. LC 97-35031. (Illus.). 528p. (C). 1998. 63.50 (*0-89464-767-9*) Krieger.

Program Planning Guide for AgriScience & Technology Education. 2nd rev. ed. Jasper S. Lee. LC 99-175508. 106p. 1998. pap. 29.95 (*0-8134-2999-4*, 2999) Interstate.

Program Power I: How It Was, What Happened, What It's Like Now. T. Allen. 104p. 1994. pap. 6.00 (*0-317-05543-7*, 93-90586) Tenavision.

Program-Related Investments: A Guide to Funders & Trends. Loren Renz & Cynthia W. Massarsky. 189p. 1995. 45.00 (*0-87954-558-5*, PRI) Foundation Ctr.

Program-Related Investments: A Technical Manual for Foundations. Christie I. Baxter. LC 96-46710. (Nonprofit Law, Finance, & Management Ser.). (Illus.). 475p. 1997. 140.00 (*0-471-17833-0*) Wiley.

Program Research Analyst. Jack Rudman. (Career Examination Ser.: C-1704). 1994. pap. 34.95 (*0-8373-1704-5*) Nat Learn.

Program Research Specialist. Jack Rudman. (Career Examination Ser.: C-3200). 1994. pap. 34.95 (*0-8373-3200-1*) Nat Learn.

Program Review & Educational Quality in the Major. (Liberal Learning & the Arts & Sciences Major Ser.: Vol. 3). viii, 32p. 1992. pap. 10.00 (*0-911696-53-9*) Assn Am Coll.

Program Solos Lul. 3. 48p. (YA). 1985. pap. 6.50 (*0-7692-1451-7*, FPL00770) Wrner Bros.

Program Specialist. Jack Rudman. (Career Examination Ser.: C-2861). 1994. pap. 34.95 (*0-8373-2861-6*) Nat Learn.

Program Specialist (Aging Services) Jack Rudman. (Career Examination Ser.: C-2820). 1994. pap. 29.95 (*0-8373-2820-9*) Nat Learn.

Program Specialist (Correction) Jack Rudman. (Career Examination Ser.: C-1997). 1994. pap. 34.95 (*0-8373-1997-8*) Nat Learn.

Program Specification, Aarhus, Denmark, 1981: Proceedings. Ed. by J. Staunstrup. (Lecture Notes in Computer Science Ser.: Vol. 134). 426p. 1982. 36.00 (*0-387-11490-4*) Spr-Verlag.

Program STARI-3D: A Program for Static Risers, 3-Dimensional Analysis. A. Imron & Michael M. Bernitsas. LC VM0605., (University of Michigan, Dept. of Naval Architecture & Marine Engineering, Report Ser.: No. 280). 46p. reprint ed. pap. 30.00 (*0-608-12939-9*, 202468400038) Bks Demand.

Program Trading & Systematic Risk. A. J. Sanchack, Jr. & John D. Martin. (Orig.). 1990. pap. text 20.00 (*0-943205-09-3*) RFICFA.

Program Transformation & Programming Environments. Ed. by P. Pepper. (NATO ASI Series F: Computer & Systems Sciences, Special Programme AET: No. 8). 400p. 1984. 82.95 (*0-387-12932-4*) Spr-Verlag.

Program Translation Fundamentals: Methods & Issues. Peter Calingaert. (C). 1988. text 37.60 (*0-7167-8146-8*, Computer Sci Pr) W H Freeman.

Program Verification: Fundamental Issues in Computer Science. Ed. by Timothy R. Colburn et al. LC 92-26748. (Studies in Cognitive Systems: Vol. 14). 471p. (C). 1993. lib. bdg. 289.50 (*0-7923-1965-6*, Pub. by Kluwer Academic) Kluwer Academic.

Program Verifier. James C. King. LC 76-127837. 262p. 1969. 19.00 (*0-403-04510-X*) Scholarly.

***Program with MS Visl Basic 7.0: Object-Oriented Approach.** Ekedahl. (Programming Language Ser.). (C). 2000. text 37.25 (*0-619-01658-2*) Course Tech.

Program with UNIX System Calls. UNIX System Laboratories Staff. 608p. 1993. pap. text 32,00 (*0-13-177239-2*, Pub. by P-H) S&S Trade.

Program Your IBM PC to Program Itself. David D. Busch. 1991. 24.95 (*0-8306-6630-3*) McGraw-Hill Prof.

Program Yourself for Success. Herschel L. Scott, Jr. 12p. 1982. pap. 3.50 (*0-88083-007-7*) Poverty Hill Pr.

Programa De Accion Para Enfrentar la Crisis Economica Que Se Avecina. 2nd ed. Ed. by Doug Jenness. (SPA., Illus.). 42p. 1989. reprint ed. pap. 3.50 (*0-87348-534-3*) Pathfinder NY.

Programa de Capacitacion para el Desarrollo de Ministerios Hispanos: Modulo I. Saul Trinidad. (ENG & SPA.). 148p. 1996. pap. 12.95 (*0-88177-163-5*, DR163) Discipleship Res.

Programa de Desarrollo del TPM. Seiichi Nakajima. (SPA., Illus.). 428p. (Orig.). 1991. pap. 65.00 (*84-87022-82-0*) Productivity Inc.

Programa de Infraestructura para America Latina y el Caribe. (SPA.). 76p. 1995. pap. 22.00 (*0-8213-3029-2*, 13029) World Bank.

Programa del Salud para los Grados Escolares Medios: Recursos para Maestros, 15 bks., Set. ETR Staff. (SPA.). 1996. 39.00 (*1-56071-500-6*, H640) ETR Assocs.

Programa para el Mejoramiento del Aprovechamiento del Estudiante: Guia - Guidebook. National School Services Staff. (SPA.). (C). 1994. student ed. 25.00 (*0-932957-67-6*) Natl School.

Programa para el Mejoramiento del Aprovechamiento del Estudiante - Training Manual. National School Services Staff. (SPA.). (C). 1993. teacher ed. 125.00 (*0-932957-74-9*) Natl School.

Programa para Ti: Una Guia Disenada del Libro Grande. Tr. of Guide to the Big Book's Design for Living. (SPA.). 190p. pap. 10.00 (*0-89486-874-8*) Hazelden.

Programa para Todo el Pueblo. Felix Ojeda. (SPA.). 1966. pap. 0.25 (*0-87898-013-X*) New Outlook.

Programacion Basica con Foxpro 2.5. Ramon M. Chorda. (SPA.). (C). 1993. pap. text 32.00 (*0-201-64192-5*) Addison-Wesley.

Programacion de las Tarjetas Graficas. 1993. write for info. (*0-201-62503-2*) Addison-Wesley.

Programacion de Riego - Irrigation Scheduling: Un Manual Bilingue - A Bilingual Manual. rev. ed. George Hargreaves & Zohrab Samani. 86p. 1992. reprint ed. spiral bd. 22.50 (*1-884512-23-2*) Two Eagles.

Programacion en Pascal Computer Graphing Lab Manual. 2nd ed. (SPA.). 400p. (C). 1995. 21.33 (*0-201-65372-9*) P-H Intl.

Programacion Estructurada, 4 Vol. Set, Vol. 1. Nilda R. Rivera. (SPA., Illus.). 133p. (C). 1994. pap. text. write for info. (*1-879185-02-4*) CompuConsultants.

Programacion Estructurada y Cobol, 4 vol. set. rev. ed. Nilda R. Rivera. (Programacion Estructurada Ser.). (SPA., Illus.). 133p. 1994. pap. text 19.95 (*1-879185-01-6*) CompuConsultants.

Programacion Financiera Aplicada: El Caso de Colombia. Instituto del FMI Staff. xvii, 311p. 1984. 20.00 (*0-939934-35-3*); pap. 12.50 (*0-939934-39-6*) Intl Monetary.

Programacion Grafica con Turbo C++ Ben Ezzell. (SPA.). 608p. (C). 1993. pap. text 31.00 (*0-201-60114-1*) Addison-Wesley.

Programacion Orientada a Objectos. Brad J. Cox. (SPA.). 384p. (C). 1993. pap. text 17.00 (*0-201-60112-5*) Addison-Wesley.

Programas del Dia de la Madre y Poesias. Tr. of Program for Mother's Day & Other Poems. (SPA.). 62p. 1961. reprint ed. pap. 4.99 (*0-311-07303-4*) Casa Bautista.

Programas para Dias Especiales, Vol. I. A. Lopez Munoz.Tr. of Program for Special Days. (SPA.). 107p. 1986. reprint ed. pap. 5.50 (*0-311-07005-1*) Casa Bautista.

Programas para Dias Especiales, Vol. II. A. Lopez Munoz.Tr. of Program for Special Days. (SPA.). 64p. 1969. reprint ed. pap. 4.99 (*0-311-07006-X*) Casa Bautista.

Programing Excellence: Self Power Balance: The Revolution of Psychology, Bk. 4. Rose A. Parvin. LC 95-35695. 288p. 1995. write for info. (*1-885917-03-1*) Univrsl Pubng.

***Programing with Visual Basic 6.0 Comprehension: An Object Oriented Approach.** Ekedahl & Newman. (Programming Ser.). (C). 1999. pap. 49.95 (*0-7600-1076-5*) Course Tech.

Programmable Assembly. Ed. by W. B. Heginbotham. (International Trends in Manufacturing Technology Ser.). (Illus.). 349p. 1984. 100.95 (*0-387-13479-4*) Spr-Verlag.

Programmable Controller Circuits. Roger M. Bertrand. LC 95-17503. 240p. (C). 1995. mass mkt. 39.95 (*0-8273-7066-0*) Delmar.

Programmable Controller Circuits. Roger M. Bertrand. (Electrical Trades Ser.). 104p. 1995. teacher ed. 18.00 (*0-8273-7067-9*) Delmar.

Programmable Controllers. Denis Collins & Eamonn Lane. LC 95-9892. 1995. write for info. (*0-07-709017-9*) McGraw.

Programmable Controllers. Geller. LC 99-49447. 336p. 1999. 82.00 (*0-13-096208-2*) P-H.

Programmable Controllers. Richard K. Miller & Terri C. Walker. LC 88-81656. (Survey on Technology & Markets Ser.: No. 65). 50p. 1989. pap. text 200.00 (*1-55865-064-4*) Future Tech Surveys.

Programmable Controllers. Tel-A-Train, Inc. Staff. 1984. student ed. 28.50 (*1-56355-100-4*) Tel-A-Train.

Programmable Controllers. Thomas A. Hughes. LC 89-39267. (Resources for Measurement & Control Ser.). (Illus.). 268p. reprint ed. pap. 83.10 (*0-608-08599-5*, 206912200003) Bks Demand.

Programmable Controllers. 2nd ed. Thomas A. Hughes. LC 97-2872. (Resources for Measurement & Control Ser.). 1997. 76.00 (*1-55617-610-4*) ISA.

Programmable Controllers: An Engineer's Guide. Andrew Parr. LC 92-30189. (Illus.). 256p. 1993. text 69.95 (*0-7506-0498-0*) Buttrwrth-Heinemann.

Programmable Controllers: Hardware, Software & Applications. 2nd ed. George J. Batten. LC 93-48744. (Illus.). 281p. 1994. 39.00 (*0-07-004214-4*) McGraw.

Programmable Controllers: Hardware, Software & Applications. 2nd ed. George L. Batten. 1994. 39.00 (*0-07-442144-1*) McGraw.

Programmable Controllers: Theory & Implementation. 2nd ed. L. A. Bryan & E. A. Bryan. Ed. by Stephanie Phillipo. LC 96-49350. (Illus.). 1050p. 1997. pap. 88.00 incl. VHS (*0-944107-32-X*, 206) Indust Text.

Programmable Controllers & Designing Sequential Logic. Robert F. Filer & George Leinonen. 410p. (C). 1992. text 68.50 (*0-03-032322-3*, Pub. by SCP) Harcourt.

Programmable Controllers for Factory Automation. Johnson. (Manufacturing Engineering & Materials Processing Ser.: No. 20). (Illus.). 280p. 1987. text 135.00 (*0-8247-7674-7*) Dekker.

Programmable Controlles & Industrial Automation. Liam Henry. (C). 1999. pap. text. write for info. (*0-201-34295-2*) Addison-Wesley.

Programmable Hearing Aids: The Art & Science. H. Gustav Mueller & Dennis Hampton. 1997. 38.00 incl. audio (*1-58041-009-X*, 0112074) Am Speech Lang Hearing.

Programmable Logic Controllers. Constanzo. (Food Science & Technology Ser.). 1997. pap. text 23.95 (*0-340-69258-8*, VNR) Wiley.

***Programmable Logic Controllers.** S. Brian Morriss. LC 99-12358. (Illus.). 735p. 1999. 98.00 (*0-13-095565-5*, Prentice Hall) P-H.

Programmable Logic Controllers. Frank D. Petruzella. 216p. 1989. text 67.12 (*0-07-049687-0*) McGraw.

Programmable Logic Controllers. Ed. by Prentice-Hall Staff. (Advanced Electronical Topics Ser.). (C). 1998. pap. text 20.00 (*0-13-909961-1*) P-H.

Programmable Logic Controllers. Ed. by Prentice-Hall Staff. 104p. (C). 1999. text, teacher ed. write for info. (*0-13-022119-8*) P-H.

Programmable Logic Controllers. Colin Simpson. 350p. (C). 1993. text 61.60 (*0-13-735861-X*) P-H.

Programmable Logic Controllers. 2nd ed. Frank Petruzella. 1996. 53.50 (*0-02-802661-6*) Glencoe.

Programmable Logic Controllers. 2nd ed. Frank D. Petruzella. 1997. teacher ed. 15.00 (*0-02-802663-2*) Glencoe.

***Programmable Logic Controllers.** 3rd ed. Bill Bolton. 192p. 2000. pap. 32.95 (*0-7506-4746-9*, Newnes) Buttrwrth-Heinemann.

Programmable Logic Controllers: Activities Manual. 2nd ed. Petruzella. (Illus.). (gr. 6-12). 1999. student ed. 25.00 (*0-02-802662-4*) Glencoe.

Programmable Logic Controllers: Principles & Applications. 4th ed. John W. Webb & Ronald A. Reis. LC 98-13424. 443p. (C). 1998. 100.00 (*0-13-679408-4*) P-H.

Programmable Logic Controllers: Video Guide & Workbook. unabridged ed. L. A. Bryan & E. A. Bryan. Ed. by L. B. Thompson. (Illus.). 417p. 1992. pap. text 57.00 incl. VHS (*0-944107-02-8*, 561) Indust Text.

Programmable Logic Controllers & Robotics. Mike R. Khier. (C). 2001. 69.00 (*0-13-230509-7*, Macmillan Coll) P-H.

Programmable Logic Controllers & Their Engineering Applications. 2nd ed. Alan J. Crispin. LC 96-27718. 1996. pap. write for info. (*0-07-709317-8*) McGraw.

***Programmable Logic Controllers 20505.** NCCER Staff. 1998. pap. text 20.00 (*0-13-909979-4*, Prentice Hall) P-H.

Programmable Logic Data Book. Texas Instruments Engineering Staff. 714p. 1992. 20.00 (*0-685-62497-8*, SRPD001A) Tex Instr Inc.

Programmable Logic Handbook. Ashok K. Sharma. LC 98-10726. (Illus.). 500p. 1998. 69.50 (*0-07-057852-4*) McGraw.

Programmable Logic Handbook. 2nd ed. Geoff Bostock. LC 92-27737. (EDN Ser.). (Illus.). 256p. 1993. pap. text 66.95 (*0-7506-0808-0*) Buttrwrth-Heinemann.

Programmable Logic PLDs & FPGAs. R. C. Seals & G. F. Whapshott. LC 97-166764. (Illus.). 300p. 1997. 55.00 (*0-07-057260-7*) McGraw.

Programmatic Elements in the Works of Schoenberg. Walter B. Bailey. LC 83-18310. (Studies in Musicology: No. 74). (Illus.). 200p. reprint ed. pap. 62.00 (*0-8357-1480-2*, 207033600085) Bks Demand.

Programme. 1980. 23.50 (*0-8176-0604-1*) Birkhauser.

Programme: Lowell Musicale & Musical Portrait of the Spindle City. Susanne M. Robertson. (Illus.). 131p. (Orig.). 1986. pap. 8.95 (*0-9616315-0-3*) Euterpe Pr.

Programme d'Action Pour Faire Face a la Crise Economique Qui Vient. Ed. by Doug Jenness. (FRE.). 57p. 1996. pap. 5.50 (*0-87348-832-6*) Pathfinder NY.

Programme de Sante Hippocrate: Ou Comment Vivre Sainement avec l'Alimentation Vivante. Brian R. Clement. 114p. 1990. 9.95 (*2-920083-48-1*) Edns Roseau.

Programme Design. Thomas L. Naps. Date not set. pap. text, teacher ed., lab manual ed. write for info. (*0-314-01818-2*) West Pub.

Programme Evaluation in ELT. Cyril Weir & Jon Roberts. (Applied Language Studies). (Illus.). 304p. 1994. 61.95 (*0-631-16571-1*); pap. 26.95 (*0-631-16572-X*) Blackwell Pubs.

Programme for the 1990 World Census of Agriculture. 55p. 1991. 9.00 (*92-5-103062-6*, F0626, Pub. by FAO) Bernan Associates.

Programme for the 1990 World Census of Agriculture: Supplement for Asia & the Pacific. 58p. 1990. 9.00 (*92-5-102911-3*, F9113, Pub. by FAO) Bernan Associates.

Programme for the Third World War. C. H. Douglas. 1972. 59.95 (*0-8490-0896-4*) Gordon Pr.

Programme Management Case Studies. 138p. 1995. pap. 75.00 (*0-11-330666-0*, HM06660, Pub. by Statnry Office) Bernan Associates.

Programme Management Demystified: Managing Multiple Projects Successfully. Geoff Reiss. LC 95-72359. (Illus.). 272p. (Orig.). 1996. pap. 34.99 (*0-419-21350-3*, E & FN Spon) Routledge.

Programme Music in the Last Four Centuries. Frederick Niecks. LC 68-25299. (Studies in Music: No. 42). 1969. reprint ed. lib. bdg. 75.00 (*0-8383-0311-0*) M S G Haskell Hse.

Programme Music in the Last Four Centuries: A Contribution to the History of Musical Expression. Frederick Niecks. 548p. 1990. reprint ed. lib. bdg. 99.00 (*0-7812-9122-4*) Rprt Serv.

Programme of Action Against Corruption. 1997. 18.00 (*92-871-3208-9*, Pub. by Council of Europe) Manhattan Pub Co.

Programme of Training on Conflict Resolution, Crisis Prevention & Management & Confidence-Building among African States: Workshop for Senior African Military & Civilian Officials. 222p. (Orig.). (C). 1994. pap. text 50.00 (*0-7881-1072-1*) DIANE Pub.

Programme Qualite' Totale d'AT&T. 2nd rev. ed. Randall R. Willie et al. (AT&T Quality Library). (Illus.). 20p. (Orig.). 1992. pap. 7.50 (*0-932764-39-8*) AT&T Customer Info.

Programme Sponsorship & New Forms of Commercial Promotion on Television. Council of Europe Staff. (Mass Media Files Ser.: No. 9). 1991. 18.00 (*92-871-1879-5*, Pub. by Council of Europe) Manhattan Pub Co.

Programmed Alternative Reading of the Genetic Code. Philip Farabaugh. LC 96-29924. (Molecular Biology Intelligence Unit Ser.). 257p. 1997. 99.00 (*1-57059-430-9*) Landes Bioscience.

Programmed Approach to Human Genetics. Allen Vegotsky & Cynthia A. White. LC 73-22395. 166p. (C). reprint ed. 51.50 (*0-8357-9964-6*, 201187800079) Bks Demand.

Programmed Approach to the Circulatory System. George I. Sackheim. (Illus.). 1960. pap. 10.80 (*0-87563-014-6*) Stipes.

Programmed Arabic-Islamic Reader, Bk. I. Raji M. Rammuny. 1991. audio 65.00 (*0-86685-545-9*) Intl Bk Ctr.

Programmed Arabic-Islamic Reader II. Raji M. Rammuny. 320p. 1994. pap., teacher ed. 5.95 (*0-86685-747-8*) Intl Bk Ctr.

Programmed Arabic-Islamic Reader II, Bk. 2. Raji M. Rammuny. (ARA & ENG.). 1988. teacher ed. 5.95 (*0-86685-635-8*); pap. 24.95 (*0-86685-431-2*); audio 99.95 (*0-86685-546-7*) Intl Bk Ctr.

Programmed Arabic-Islamic Reader I. Raji M. Rammuny. (Illus.). 206p. 1987. pap., teacher ed. 5.95 (*0-86685-746-X*) Intl Bk Ctr.

Programmed Arabic-Islamic Reader I. Raji M. Rammuny. 1991. pap. 19.95 (*0-86685-412-6*) Intl Bk Ctr.

Programmed Blueprint Reading. 3rd ed. Shriver L. Coover. 1975. text 22.92 (*0-07-013063-9*) McGraw.

Programmed Business Mathematics, Bk. 1. 4th ed. Harry Huffman. 1980. text 20.30 (*0-07-030901-9*) McGraw.

Programmed Business Mathematics, Bk. 1. 5th ed. Harry Huffman. 200p. 1986. text 28.92 (*0-07-030917-5*) McGraw.

Programmed Business Mathematics, Bk. 2. 4th ed. Harry Huffman. (Illus.). 256p. 1980. text 17.46 (*0-07-030902-7*) McGraw.

Programmed Business Mathematics, Bk. 2. 5th ed. Harry Huffman. 244p. 1986. text 30.48 (*0-07-030918-3*) McGraw.

Programmed Business Mathematics, Bk. 3. 4th rev. ed. Harry Huffman. (Illus.). 192p. 1980. text 17.46 (*0-07-030903-5*) McGraw.

Programmed Business Mathematics, Bk. 3. 5th ed. Harry Huffman. 200p. 1986. text 30.48 (*0-07-030919-1*) McGraw.

Programmed Capitalism: A Computer-Mediated Global Society. Maurice F. Estabrooks. LC 88-4476. 224p. (C). (gr. 13). 1988. text 72.95 (*0-87332-480-3*) M E Sharpe.

Programmed Cell Death: Proceedings of an International Symposium Held in Shanghai, China, September 8-12, 1996. Ed. by Yun Bo Shi et al. LC 97-22246. 180p. 1997. 79.50 (*0-306-45680-X*, Kluwer Plenum) Kluwer Academic.

Programmed Cell Death: The Cellular & Molecular Biology of Apoptosis. Ed. by Martin Lavin & Dianne Watters. LC 93-27865. xviii, 331p. 1993. text 129.00 (*3-7186-5461-X*) Gordon & Breach.

Programmed College Algebra. Robert D. Hackworth & Joseph W. Howland. (Programmed Algebra Ser.). (Illus.). 535p. 1991. pap. text 51.95 (*0-943202-11-6*) H & H Pub.

Programmed College Vocabulary. 5th ed. George W. Feinstein. LC 97-6329. 346p. (C). 1997. pap. text 38.80 (*0-13-255613-8*) P-H.

Programmed College Vocabulary 3600. 3rd ed. George W. Feinstein. 336p. (C). 1986. pap. text 14.95 (*0-13-729427-1*) P-H.

Programmed Course in Modern Literary Arabic Phonology & Script. Raji M. Rammuny & Ernest N. McCarus. 1995. 14.95 (*0-86685-384-7*, UM02X) Intl Bk Ctr.

Programmed Dynamic Analysis Structures. Bhatt. (Civil Engineering Ser.). 1999. pap. 55.00 (*0-419-15610-0*) Thomson Learn.

Programmed Ear Training: Intervals; Melody & Rhythm. 2nd ed. Leo Horacek & Gerald Lefkoff. 479p. (C). 1989. pap. text 5.00 (*0-15-572028-7*); audio. write for info. (*0-318-64535-1*) Harcourt Coll Pubs.

An Asterisk (*) at the beginning of an entry indicates that the title is appearing for the first time.

Programmed Ear Training: Intervals; Melody & Rhythm, Vol. I. 2nd ed. Leo Horacek & Gerald Lefkoff. 479p. (C). 1989. pap. text 43.00 (*0-15-572026-0*, Pub. by Harcourt Coll Pubs) Harcourt.

Programmed for Peril. C. K. Cambray. 336p. (Orig.). 1993. mass mkt. 4.99 (*0-671-73540-3*) PB.

Programmed French Readers, 4 bks. Hugh D. Campbell & Camille Bauer. Incl. Bk. 1. Contes pour Debutants., **001** (C). 1972. pap. 25.56 (*0-395-04258-5*); (C). pap. write for info. (*0-318-53416-9*) HM.

Programmed Guide T-A 6FAT. 6th ed. Dobyns. (C). 1986. mass mkt. 14.75 (*0-87150-984-9*, 33L2985) PWS Pubs.

Programmed Guide T-A 6FCA. 6th ed. Dobyns. (C). 1986. mass mkt. 13.50 (*0-87150-920-2*, 33L3015) PWS Pubs.

Programmed Guide to Accompany Fundamentals of Algebra & Trigonometry. 4th ed. Roy A. Dobyns. 1978. pap. text 6.75 (*0-87150-258-5*, PWS 2075) PWS Pubs.

Programmed Guide to Tax Research. 4th ed. Marshall & Misiwicz. (SWC-Taxation). (C). 1992. pap. 43.25 (*0-538-82383-6*) Thomson Learn.

Programmed Hebrew Series, 2 vols. Ed. by David Bridger. Incl. Vol. 1. 1971. pap. text 3.50 (*0-87441-079-7*); 62p. pap. write for info. (*0-318-51048-0*) Behrman.

Programmed Instruction. Donald H. Bullock. Ed. by Danny G. Langdon. LC 77-25108. (Instructional Design Library). (Illus.). 112p. 1978. 27.95 (*0-87778-118-4*) Educ Tech Pubns.

Programmed Instruction: Bold New Venture. Ed. by Allen D. Calvin. LC 69-15993. 260p. reprint ed. pap. 80.60 (*0-608-30289-9*, 205012100059) Bks Demand.

Programmed Instruction: Radiation Therapy. Pilapil & Studva. (gr. 13). 1980. 11.00 (*0-89352-099-3*) Mosby Inc.

Programmed Instruction in West Africa & the Arab States: A Report on Two Training Workshops (UNESCO) P. Kenneth Komoski & Edward J. Green. (Education Studies & Documents: No. 52). 1974. reprint ed. pap. 25.00 (*0-8115-1376-9*) Periodicals Srv.

Programmed Introduction to Dynamics, 2 vols. 2nd ed. Clyde E. Work. LC 75-37492. (Illus.). 1976. 26.50 (*0-916572-00-5*) Aylsworth.

Programmed Introduction to Gas-Liquid Chromatography. 2nd ed. James B. Pattison. LC QD0271.P33. (Illus.). 320p. reprint ed. pap. 99.20 (*0-608-17586-2*, 203042700069) Bks Demand.

Programmed Introduction to General & Physical Chemistry. Derrick E. Hoare. LC 67-27670. (Illus.). 149p. (C). reprint ed. 46.20 (*0-8357-9965-4*, 201398200088) Bks Demand.

Programmed Introduction to Infrared Spectroscopy. B. W. Cook & K. Jones. LC 72-189960. (Illus.). 216p. reprint ed. pap. 67.00 (*0-8357-3052-2*, 203930800012) Bks Demand.

Programmed Introduction to Medical Terminology. Marie L. Kotter. 48p. (C). 1995. 10.23 (*0-7872-1698-4*) Kendall-Hunt.

Programmed Introduction to Statics, 2 vols. 3rd ed. Clyde E. Work. LC 75-37493. (Illus.). (C). 1978. pap. text 25.50 (*0-916572-01-3*) Aylsworth.

Programmed Introduction to Upper Gastrointestinal Radiology. Stephen L. Gammill. 1977. pap. text 22.00 (*0-316-30294-5*, Little Brwn Med Div) Lppncott W & W.

Programmed Journalism Editing. James P. Alexander. LC PN4785.A43. 183p. 1979. reprint ed. pap. 56.80 (*0-608-00302-6*, 206084800008) Bks Demand.

Programmed Learning Guide to Finance. Marianne Hite. LC 95-31234. 320p. (C). 1995. text 46.75 (*0-256-17908-5*, Irwn Prfssnl) McGraw-Hill Prof.

Programmed Manual for Nursing Home Administrator Examinees. 11th ed. Edmond Boudreaux. 172p. (Orig.). (C). 1991. pap. text 35.00 (*1-878199-02-1*) Pro Exam Review.

Programmed Manual for Nursing Home Administrator Examinees. 12th ed. Edmond Boudreaux. 160p. (Orig.). (C). 1995. pap. text 35.00 (*1-878199-07-2*) Pro Exam Review.

Programmed Mathematics for Nurses. 8th ed. George I. Sackheim & Lewis Robins. (Illus.). 320p. 1995. pap. text 24.95 (*0-07-105398-0*) McGraw-Hill HPD.

***Programmed Mathematics of Drugs & Solutions.** 6th ed. Virginia Poole Arcangelo. 224p. 1999. pap. text 19.95 Lppncott W & W.

Programmed Mathematics Series, Bks. 9-15. 2nd ed. Sullivan Associates Staff. 1975. 6.64 (*0-685-73381-5*) McGraw.

Programmed Medical Language. Myrna LaFleur Brooks & Danielle LaFleur. (Illus.). 352p. (C). (gr. 13). 1995. spiral bd. 27.00 (*0-8016-7835-8*, 07835) Mosby Inc.

***Programmed Medical Language.** Myrna LaFleur Brooks & Danielle LaFleur. 1998. write for info. (*0-8151-5417-8*); teacher ed. write for info. (*0-8151-7852-2*); text. write for info. (*0-323-00112-2*); text. write for info. incl. audio (*0-323-00113-0*) Mosby Inc.

Programmed Medical Language Packaged with Accompanying Audiotape. Myrna LaFleur-Brooks & Danielle LaFleur. 1996. pap. text 31.00 incl. audio (*0-8151-1278-5*) Mosby Inc.

Programmed Proofreading. 2nd ed. Thadys J. Dewar & H. Frances Daniels. 208p. (C). 1987. mass mkt. 22.95 (*0-538-23020-7*, WO2) S-W Pub.

Programmed Proofreading. 3rd ed. Daniels & Dewar. (PS - Communication/English Ser.). (C). 1991. mass mkt. 19.00 (*0-538-70392-X*) S-W Pub.

Programmed Review for Electrical Engineering: For the Professional Engineer's Exam. 3rd ed. James H. Bentley. (Illus.). 238p. 1999. pap. 44.50 (*1-57645-034-1*, 341) Engineering.

Programmed Rudiments of Music. 2nd ed. Robert W. Ottman & Frank D. Mainous. LC 92-46702. 352p. (C). 1993. pap. text 65.00 (*0-13-138042-7*) P-H.

Programmed Spelling Demons. 4th ed. George W. Feinstein. LC 97-7663. 218p. 1997. pap. text 38.80 (*0-13-255621-9*) P-H.

Programmed Study Guide for Introduction to Probability & Statistics. 4th ed. Robert J. Beaver & William Mendenhall. 1975. pap. 6.75 (*0-87872-095-2*) PWS Pubs.

Programmed Text to Learn Gujarati. 2nd rev. ed. Bharat S. Shah. (Setubandh Language Ser.: Vol. 1). 300p. (Orig.). (J). (gr. 6 up). 1999. pap. text 15.00 (*0-9623674-2-7*) Setubandh Pubns.

Programmed Text to Learn Gujarati, Set. Bharat S. Shah. (Language Ser.). 300p. (Orig.). (J). (gr. 6 up). 1990. pap. text 18.00 (*0-9623674-0-0*) Setubandh Pubns.

Programmed to Learn: An Essay on the Evolution of Culture. H. Ronald Pulliam & Christopher Dunford. LC 79-17941. (Illus.). 1980. text 41.00 (*0-231-04838-6*) Col U Pr.

Programmed Word Attack for Teachers. 6th ed. Robert Wilson & Maryanne Hall. LC 96-19716. 95p. (C). 1996. pap. text 20.00 (*0-13-249146-X*) P-H.

Programmed Writing: A Self-Administered Approach for Intervention with Individuals, Couples & Families. Luciano L'Abate & Janet Cox. LC 90-27793. 300p. (C). 1992. text 80.95 (*0-534-14484-5*) Brooks-Cole.

Programmed Writing Skills. George W. Feinstein. 1976. teacher ed. 1.95 (*0-13-730515-X*) P-H.

Programmer. Jack Rudman. (Career Examination Ser.: C-1430). 1994. pap. 27.95 (*0-8373-1430-5*) Nat Learn.

Programmer Aptitude Test (PAT) Jack Rudman. (Career Examination Ser.: C-643). 1994. pap. 23.95 (*0-8373-0643-4*) Nat Learn.

Programmer Trainee. Jack Rudman. (Career Examination Ser.: C-1431). 1994. pap. 23.95 (*0-8373-1431-3*) Nat Learn.

Programmer/Programmer Analyst. Jack Rudman. (Career Examination Ser.: C-1439). 1994. pap. 27.95 (*0-8373-1439-9*) Nat Learn.

Programmers & Managers: The Routinization of Computer Programming in the United States. Philip Kraft. LC 77-1667. (Illus.). 1984. 43.95 (*0-387-90248-1*) Spr-Verlag.

Programmer's Assistants: A User's Guide. Ronald Kashden. (Illus.). 150p. 1990. 99.95 (*1-878777-01-7*) Aladdin Systs.

Programmer's COBOL: A Complete Reference. Marjorie Berk. LC 70-20656. xxviii, 320 p. 1970. write for info. (*0-07-004895-9*) McGraw.

Programmer's Desk Reference for Your Commodore 64. Mona Reinhardt. write for info. (*0-318-58214-7*) P-H.

Programmer's Guide. Common Desktop Environment Documentation Group Sta. LC 95-11123. (Common Desktop Environment 1.0 Ser.). 208p. (C). 1995. pap. 29.95 (*0-201-48954-6*) Addison-Wesley.

Programmer's Guide: Ansi C & Programming Support Tools. UNIX Staff. 800p. 1992. pap. 47.20 (*0-13-020629-6*) P-H.

***Programmer's Guide for Internet Streaming SIMD Extensions.** Shreekant S. Thakkar. 2000. pap. text 49.99 (*0-471-37524-1*) Wiley.

Programmer's Guide to C. John Lees & Stephanie Rosenhaum. write for info. (*0-318-58252-X*) P-H.

Programmer's Guide to C++ Adrian P. Robson. LC 96-36943. 296p. 1997. pap. 34.50 (*0-8058-2681-5*) L Erlbaum Assocs.

Programmer's Guide to F. Walter S. Brainerd et al. LC 96-60076. 388p. (Orig.). (C). 1996. pap. 30.00 (*0-9640135-1-7*) Unicomp.

Programmer's Guide to Fortran 90. 3rd ed. W. S. Brainerd. 445p. 1995. 39.95 (*0-387-94570-9*) Spr-Verlag.

Programmer's Guide to Internet Mail: SMTP, POP, IMAP & LDAP. John Rhoton. LC 99-36739. 291p. 1999. pap. 39.95 (*1-55558-212-5*, Digital DEC) Buttrwrth-Heinemann.

***Programmers Guide to Java Certification: A COmprehensive Primer.** Muchal. LC 99-40779. 800p. (C). 1999. pap. text 44.95 (*0-201-59614-8*) Addison-Wesley.

***Programmer's Guide to Java Smart Cards.** Zhiqun Chen. 352p. 2000. pap. 39.95 (*0-201-70329-7*) Addison-Wesley.

Programmer's Guide to Object-Oriented Programming in Common LISP. Sonya E. Keene. (Illus.). 288p. (C). 1989. pap. text 37.95 (*0-201-17589-4*) Addison-Wesley.

Programmer's Guide to Online Resources. Bob Kochem. LC 95-38014. 354p. 1995. pap. 24.95 (*0-471-12852-X*) Wiley.

Programmer's Guide to Pen Services for Microsoft Windows 95. Microsoft Corporation Staff. LC 95-1474. (Professional Editions Ser.). 544p. 1995. 27.95 (*1-55615-835-1*) Microsoft.

Programmer's Guide to Reserved Microsoft Windows API Functions. Andrew Schulman & David Maxey. 736p. 1992. pap. 44.95 (*0-201-60834-0*) Pearson Custom.

***Programmer's Guide to Scsi.** (C). 1998. write for info. (*0-201-37933-3*) Addison-Wesley.

Programmer's Guide to SCSI. Brian Sawert. LC 97-44773. 320p. (C). 1998. pap. 42.95 (*0-201-18538-5*) Addison-Wesley.

Programmer's Guide to Segment Geometry. Skip Kittredge. (Illus.). 181p. (Orig.). 1991. pap. text 9.95 (*0-9622531-0-3*) American Segment.

Programmer's Guide to the EGA & VGA Cards. Richard F. Ferraro. 1988. pap. text 26.95 (*0-201-12692-3*) Addison-Wesley.

Programmer's Guide to the EGA, VGA & Super VGA Cards: Includes Graphics Accelerators! 3rd ed. Richard F. Ferraro. 1632p. (C). 1994. pap. text 44.95 (*0-201-62490-7*) Addison-Wesley.

Programmer's Guide to the Hercules Graphics Cards. David B. Doty. 1988. pap. 24.95 (*0-201-11885-8*) Addison-Wesley.

Programmer's Guide to the NCP (Netware Core Protocol) Steve Conner & Diane Conner. 650p. 1996. mass mkt. 49.95 (*0-929392-31-0*) Annabooks.

Programmer's Guide to ZPL. Lawrence Snyder. LC 98-34702. (Scientific & Engineering Computation Ser.). (Illus.). 200p. 1999. pap. text 30.00 (*0-262-69217-1*) MIT Pr.

PROGRAMMERS GUIDE 3D GRA. Richard F. Ferraro. (C). 1996. pap. text 49.95 (*0-201-48324-6*) Addison-Wesley.

Programmers' Handbook of Computer Printer Commands: For Printer Models Through 1984. Ed. by Mary Lou East & Fred B. East. 1985. pap. 37.95 (*0-932065-00-7*) Cardinal Pt.

Programmers' Handbook of Computer Printer Commands-11: For Printer Models As New As 1985, Vol. 2. Ed. by Mary Lou East & Fred B. East. 196p. (Orig.). (C). 1986. pap. 26.95 (*0-932065-25-2*) Cardinal Pt.

Programmer's Introduction to SNOBOL. Ward D. Maurer. LC 75-26837. (Programming Languages Series Elsevier Computer Science Library). 151p. reprint ed. pap. 46.90 (*0-608-16357-0*, 202627000049) Bks Demand.

Programmer's Introduction to the MacIntosh Family. (C). 1990. pap. text. write for info. (*0-201-41715-4*) Addison-Wesley.

***Programmer's Introduction to Windows DNA.** Christian Gross. LC 00-25266. 700p. 2000. pap. 59.95 incl. cd-rom (*1-893115-17-8*, Pub. by APress L P) Spr-Verlag.

Programmer's Job Handbook: The Skills You Need to Stay Ahead in the 90s. Eugene Wang. 304p. 1995. pap. text 24.95 (*0-07-882137-1*) McGraw.

Programmer's Online Companion Inside Macintosh. Steve Capps. LC 70-991. 1970. 2995.00 (*0-201-12214-6*) Addison-Wesley.

Programmer's Overview. Common Desktop Environment Documentation Group Sta. LC 95-11124. (Common Desktop Environment 1.0 Ser.). 112p. (C). 1995. pap. 27.95 (*0-201-48953-8*) Addison-Wesley.

Programmer's Problem Solver for the IBM PC, XT & AT. Robert L. Jourdain. (Illus.). 320p. 1986. pap. 22.95 (*0-89303-787-7*) Brady Pub.

Programmer's Supplement for Release 6 of the Window System. Ed. by Adrian Nye. (Illus.). 452p. 1995. pap. 29.95 (*1-56592-089-9*) Thomson Learn.

Programmer's Technical Reference: Data & FAX Communications. Robert L. Hummel. (Technical Reference...Ser.). 912p. 1993. pap. 39.95 (*1-56276-077-7*, Ziff-Davis Pr) Que.

Programmer's View of Computer Architecture: With Assembly Language Examples from the Mips Risc Architecture. James Goodman & Karen Miller. (Illus.). 416p. (C). 1993. text 72.95 (*0-19-513109-6*) OUP.

Programmer's View of Computer Architecture: With Assembly Language Examples from the MIPS RISC Architecture. Karen Miller. (Illus.). 132p. (C). 1993. pap. write for info. (*0-03-006314-0*) OUP.

Programmer's Workbench Buch Zu Microsoft Basic Pds. Peter Monadjemi. (GER.). (C). 1991. text. write for info. (*0-201-55939-0*) Addison-Wesley.

***Programmes & Services of Training & Promotion Centres for Adolescents.** R. G. Ros. (SPA.). 86p. 1999. write for info. (*92-806-3516-6*) U N I C E.

Programmes of Analysis of Mortality Trends & Levels: Proceedings of the U. N.-WHO Meeting, Geneva, 1968. U. N. Staff & World Health Organization Staff. (Technical Reports: No. 440). 1970. pap. text 5.00 (*92-4-120440-0*, 1100440) World Health.

Programmes to Promote Breastfeeding. Ed. by Derrick B. Jelliffe & Patrice E. Jelliffe. (Illus.). 514p. 1988. pap. 60.00 (*0-19-261457-6*) OUP.

Programmieren in C++ 1995. 26.00 (*3-540-59037-4*) Spr-Verlag.

Programmieren in C. Kruger. (GER.). (C). 1992. text. write for info. (*0-201-55991-9*) Addison-Wesley.

Programmierung Neuronaler Netze. Mechler. (GER.). (C). 1991. text. write for info. (*0-201-55942-0*) Addison-Wesley.

Programming: An Introduction to Computer Techniques. 2nd rev. ed. Ward D. Maurer. LC 70-188126. (Illus.). (C). 1972. text 32.95 (*0-8162-5453-2*) Holden-Day.

Programming--fortran. D. J. Malcolme-Lawes. LC 78-109582. v, 122p. 1970. write for info. (*0-08-015508-1*, Pergamon Pr) Elsevier.

Programming Abstractions. Eric S. Roberts. LC 97-15248. 819p. (C). 1997. pap. text 73.00 (*0-201-54541-1*) Addison-Wesley.

***Programming Active Directory Services.** Charles J. Oppermann. 400p. 2000. 49.99 (*0-7356-1037-1*) Microsoft.

Programming Ada. 3rd ed. John G. Barnes. (Illus.). (C). 1989. pap. text 39.75 (*0-201-17566-5*) Addison-Wesley.

***Programming & Customizing the AVR Microcontroller.** Dhananjay V. Gadre. 2000. pap. 39.95 (*0-07-134666-X*) McGraw.

Programming & Customizing the BASIC Stamp Computer. Scott Edwards. LC 98-17952. 350p. 1998. 44.95 incl. cd-rom (*0-07-913683-4*); pap. 34.95 incl. cd-rom (*0-07-913684-2*) McGraw.

Programming & Customizing the 8051 Microcontroller. Myke Predko. LC 98-48076. 1999. 49.95 (*0-07-134195-1*) Osborne-McGraw.

***Programming & Customizing the 8051 Microcontroller.** Myke Predko. LC 98-48076. (Tab Electronics Technician Library Ser.). (Illus.). 541p. 1999. pap. 34.95 incl. cd-rom (*0-07-134192-7*) Osborne-McGraw.

***Programming & Customizing the HC11 Microcontroller.** Thomas Fox. LC 99-53271. 1999. 125.00 incl. audio compact disk (*0-07-134405-5*) McGraw.

Programming & Customizing the PIC-Microcontroller. Michael Predko. LC 97-21762. (Illus.). 352p. 1997. pap. 39.95 (*0-07-913646-X*) McGraw.

***Programming & Customizing the Picmicro.** 2nd ed. Myke Predko. (TAB Electronics Technician Library). (Illus.). 600p. 2000. pap. text 44.95 (*0-07-136172-3*) McGraw.

***Programming & Customizing the 68HCHC11 Microcontroller.** Tom Fox. LC 99-53271. (Illus.). 268p. 1999. pap. 39.95 (*0-07-134406-3*) McGraw.

Programming & Deploying Mobile Agents with Java Aglets. Danny Lange. LC 98-20525. 256p. (C). 1998. pap. text 37.95 (*0-201-32582-9*) Addison-Wesley.

Programming & Design for Dementia: Development of a 50 Person Residential Environment. Gerald D. Weisman et al. (Publications in Architecture & Urban Planning: No. R90-3). (Illus.). 107p. (C). 1992. reprint ed. per. 12.00 (*0-938744-72-0*) U of Wis Ctr Arch-Urban.

Programming & Design Handbook-80386. Penn Brumm & Don Brumm. (Illus.). 448p. 1987. pap. 19.95 (*0-8306-2937-8*) McGraw-Hill Prof.

Programming & Interregional Input-Output Analysis: An Application to the Problem of Industrial Location in India. A. Ghosh. LC 72-76092. (University of Cambridge, Dept. of Applied Economics, Occasional Papers: 22). 112p. reprint ed. pap. 32.00 (*0-608-12511-3*, 2024461) Bks Demand.

Programming & Mathematical Method. Manfred Broy. LC 92-26379. (NATO ASI Series F: Computer & Systems Sciences, Special Programme AET: Vol. 88). viii, 428p. 1992. 124.00 (*0-387-55558-7*) Spr-Verlag.

Programming & Mathematical Techniques in Physics. Y. Yu Lobanov & E. P. Zhidkov. 324p. 1994. text 109.00 (*981-02-1706-4*) World Scientific Pub.

Programming & Meta-Programming in Scheme. J. Pearce. Ed. by D. Gries & F. B. Schneider. LC 97-28476. (Undergraduate Texts in Computer Science Ser.). 340p. 1997. 39.95 (*0-387-98320-1*) Spr-Verlag.

***Programming & Operating CNC Routers.** Mike Lynch. (Illus.). 224p. 1999. pap. text. write for info. (*1-930861-12-5*) C N C Con.

Programming & Problem Solving: A Second Course with Pascal. Lawrence H. Miller. 624p. (C). 1986. teacher ed. write for info. (*0-201-05579-1*); text 39.75 (*0-201-05531-7*) Addison-Wesley.

Programming & Problem-Solving in ALGOL 68. Andrew J. Colin. LC 78-306642. (Computer Science Ser.). 251p. 1977. write for info. (*0-333-21716-0*) Macmillan.

Programming & Problem Solving in C++ 2nd ed. Nell B. Dale et al. LC 99-25436. 1999. write for info. (*0-7637-1063-6*) Jones & Bartlett.

Programming & Problem Solving Test Item File. Nell Dale et al. (Computer Science Ser.). 1994. pap. 10.00 (*0-669-29362-8*) Jones & Bartlett.

Programming & Problem Solving with ADA. Nell B. Dale et al. (Computer Science Ser.). 887p. (C). 1994. pap., teacher ed. 10.00 (*0-669-29361-X*) Jones & Bartlett.

Programming & Problem Solving with ADA. Nell Dale et al. LC 93-78374. 887p. 1996. pap. 56.25 (*0-7637-0293-5*) Jones & Bartlett.

***Programming & Problem Solving with ADA.** 2nd ed. Nell Dale et al. LC 99-49488. (Illus.). 896p. (C). 2000. pap. text 60.00 (*0-7637-0792-9*) Jones & Bartlett.

***Programming & Problem Solving with C++** Nell Dale et al. (Illus.). 1312p. (C). 1998. text 63.75 (*0-7637-0812-7*) JB Pubns.

Programming & Problem Solving with C++ Nell Dale et al. LC 96-223831. 1155p. 1996. pap. 58.75 (*0-7637-0292-7*) Jones & Bartlett.

***Programming & Problem Solving with Java.** Nell Dale et al. (Illus.). 1184p. (C). 2000. pap. text 63.75 (*0-7637-1064-4*) Jones & Bartlett.

Programming & Promotion see Radio Book

Programming & Proof System ATES: Advanced Techniques Integration into Efficient Scientific Software. Ed. by A. Puccetti. (Research Reports ESPRIT, Project 1158: Vol. 1). viii, 341p. 1991. 39.00 (*0-387-54188-8*) Spr-Verlag.

Programming & Q Basic. Susan K. Baumann. Date not set. pap. text, teacher ed. 16.95 (*0-314-02538-3*) West Pub.

***Programming Applications for Microsoft Windows.** Jeffrey M. Richter. LC 99-40456. 1999. pap. 59.99 (*1-57231-996-8*) Microsoft Pr.

Programming Applications for Netscape Servers. Kaveh Bassiri. LC 98-23135. 1008p. (C). 1998. pap. text 49.95 (*0-201-41970-X*) Addison-Wesley.

Programming Applications with the Wireless Application Protocol: The Complete Developer's Guide. Steve Mann. LC 99-42181. 256p. 1999. 49.99 incl. cd-rom (*0-471-32754-9*) Wiley.

Programming Approach to Formal Methods. Chris Casey. LC 94-20022. (International Series in Software Engineering). 1994. 16.95 (*0-07-707968-X*) McGraw.

Programming As If People Mattered: Friendly Programs, Software Engineering, & Other Noble. Nathaniel S. Borenstein. 200p. 1992. pap. text 16.95 (*0-691-03763-9*, Pub. by Princeton U Pr) Cal Prin Full Svc.

Programming Assembler Language: IBM 370 Architecture & Assembly Language. 3rd ed. Peter Abel. 528p. (C). 1989. text 44.20 (*0-13-728924-3*) P-H.

Programming Assembly Language. Driver. Date not set. pap. text, teacher ed. write for info. (*0-314-01316-4*) West Pub.

P

An Asterisk (*) at the beginning of an entry indicates that the title is appearing for the first time.

Programming Author Visits. Jan Watkins. LC 95-53270. (ALSC Program Support Publications). 16p. 1996. pap. 8.00 (*0-8389-5766-8*) ALA.

***Programming AutoCAD Using Object ARX.** Charles McAuley. LC 99-48556. (Illus.). 678p. 2000. pap. 44.95 (*0-7668-0643-X*, AutoDesk Pr) Delmar.

Programming BASIC. 2nd ed. Stewart M. Venit. Date not set. pap. text, teacher ed. write for info. (*0-314-70532-5*) West Pub.

Programming Basic Apple. Susan K. Baumann. Date not set. pap. text, teacher ed. 21.95 (*0-314-72072-3*) West Pub.

Programming Basics. 2nd ed. Stewart M. Venit. Date not set. pap. text, teacher ed. write for info. (*0-314-08395-2*) West Pub.

Programming Bots, Spiders & Intelligent Agents in Microsoft Visual C++ David Pallman. LC 99-10774. 500p. 1999. pap. 49.99 (*0-7356-0565-3*) Microsoft.

***Programming Business Applications with Microsoft Visual Basic: Version 6.0.** 3rd ed. William E. Burrows & Joseph D. Langford. LC 99-89329. 2000. write for info. (*0-07-238408-5*) McGraw.

Programming Business Applications with Visual Basic. Joseph D. Langford & William E. Burrows. (Illus.). 512p. (C). 1996. pap. text 50.00 (*0-07-036435-4*) McGraw.

Programming Business Applications with Visual Basic. 2nd ed. William E. Burrows & Joseph D. Langford. LC 97-50038. 688p. 1998. pap. 56.88 (*0-07-012143-5*) McGraw.

Programming by Case Studies: An Algol Primer. Olaf B. Chedzoy & Sandra E. Ford. LC 76-490790. (Introductory Monographs in Mathematics). vi, 90 p. 1969. write for info. (*0-333-10146-4*) Macmillan.

Programming Byte by Byte: Structured FORTRAN. 3rd rev. ed. Bijan Mashaw. 550p. (C). 1992. pap. text 37.45 (*0-934433-08-9*) Am Comp Pr.

Programming Byte by Byte: Structured FORTRAN 77. 2nd rev. ed. Bijan Mashaw. 540p. (Orig.). (C). 1987. reprint ed. pap. 32.20 (*0-934433-02-X*) Am Comp Pr.

Programming Classics PHA: Implementing the World's Best Algorithms. Ian Oliver. LC 93-32080. 500p. 1994. text 60.00 (*0-13-100413-1*) Prntice Hall Bks.

Programming Components with Microsoft Visual Basic 6.0. Guy Eddon & Henry Eddon. LC 98-30228. 416p. 1998. 44.99 incl. cd-rom (*1-57231-966-6*) Microsoft.

Programming Concepts & Methods: Procomet 98. Chapman & Hall Staff. text 239.00 (*0-412-83760-9*) Chapman & Hall.

Programming Concepts, Methods & Calculi: Proceedings of the IFIP TC2/WG2.1/WG2.2/WG2.3 Working Conference on Programming Concepts, Methods, & Calculi (PROCOMET '94), San Miniato, Italy, 6-10 June 1994. Ed. by Ernst R. Olderog. LC 94-36660. (IFIP Transactions & Computer Science & Technology Ser.). 602p. 1994. 178.50 (*0-444-82020-5*) Elsevier.

Programming Concepts with the ADA Reference Manual. Roy S. Freedman. (Illus.). 128p. 1982. pap. text 12.95 (*0-89433-190-6*) Petrocelli.

Programming Discrete Solutions. Moshe A. Pollatschek. 350p. 1996. 39.95 incl. disk (*0-87930-449-9*) C M P Books.

***Programming Distributed Applications with COM+ & Microsoft Visual Basic.** 2nd ed. Ted Pattisön. LC 00-20234. (DV-MPS Programming Ser.). (Illus.). 2000. pap. text 49.99 (*0-7356-1010-X*) Microsoft.

Programming Distributed Applications with COM & Microsoft Visual Basic 6.0. Ted Pattison. LC 98-39267. 500p. 1998. 44.99 incl. cd-rom (*1-57231-961-5*) Microsoft.

Programming Distributed Systems. H. E. Bal. 290p. (Orig.). 1990. pap. 29.95 (*0-929306-05-8*) Silicon Pr.

***Programming Domino 4.6 Java: Groupware for the Internet.** Bob Balaban. LC 98-10610. 480p. 1998. 49.99 (*1-55851-583-6*, MIS Pr) IDG Bks.

Programming Effective Human Services: Strategies for Institutional Change & Client Transition. Ed. by Walter P. Christian et al. 538p. 1984. 75.00 (*0-306-41526-7*, Plenum Trade) Perseus Pubng.

***Programming Embedded System in C & C++** Michael Barr et al. Ed. by Andy Oram. (Illus.). 174p. (Orig.). 1999. pap. 29.95 (*1-56592-354-5*) OReilly & Assocs.

Programming Embedded Systems for Microsoft Windows CE. Kathy H. DeGraaf. 1999. pap. text 49.99 (*0-7356-0548-3*) Microsoft.

Programming Environments for High-Level Scientific Problem Solving. P. W. Gaffney & Elias N. Houstis. (IFIP Transactions A: Vol. 2). xiv, 406p. 1992. pap. 145.00 (*0-444-89176-5*, North Holland) Elsevier.

Programming Environments for Massively Parallel Distributed Systems: Working Conference of the IFIP WG10.3, April 25-29, 1994. Ed. by K. M. Decker & R. M. Rehmann. LC 94-30359. (Monte Verita Ser.). 400p. 1994. 89.50 (*0-8176-5090-3*) Birkhauser.

Programming Expert Systems in OPS5: An Introduction to Rule-Based Programming. Lee Browston et al. (Artificial Intellegence Ser.). (C). 1985. text 49.50 (*0-201-10647-7*) Addison-Wesley.

Programming Expert Systems in Turbo Prolog. Daniel H. Marcellus. (Illus.). 256p. (C). 1989. text 34.00 (*0-13-295841-4*) P-H.

Programming for Aggressive & Violent Students. Richard L. Simpson et al. (Exceptional Children at Risk Ser.). 42p. 1991. pap. text 9.00 (*0-86586-207-9*, P350) Coun Exc Child.

Programming for Architecture. R. Hershberger. 1987. pap. write for info. (*0-442-23701-4*, VNR) Wiley.

Programming for Artificial Intelligence. Wolfgang Kreutzer. Ed. by Bruce McKenzie. 600p. (C). 1990. text 36.33 (*0-201-41621-2*) Addison-Wesley.

Programming for Computer Science. C. M. Dawe. 1994. pap. 35.00 (*3-540-19811-3*) Spr-Verlag.

Programming for Design: From Theory to Practice. Edith Cherry. LC 98-15978. 352p. 1998. 54.95 (*0-471-19645-2*) Wiley.

Programming for Everyone in Java. Per Brinch Hansen. LC 98-51800. (Illus.). 238p. 1999. pap. 29.95 (*0-387-98683-9*) Spr-Verlag.

Programming for Graphics Files: In C & C Plus Plus. John R. Levine. 512p. 1994. pap. 49.95 incl. disk (*0-471-59856-9*); disk 20.00 (*0-471-59857-7*) Wiley.

Programming for Graphics Files: In C & C Plus Plus. John R. Levine. 512p. 1994. pap. 29.95 (*0-471-59854-2*) Wiley.

Programming for Introducing Adults to Children's Literature. Carole D. Fiore. LC 93-33364. (ALSC Program Support Publications). 16p. (Orig.). 1993. pap. text 8.00 (*0-8389-5762-5*) ALA.

Programming for Librarians: A How-to-Do-It Manual. Barbara J. Brown. (How-to-Do-It Ser.). 130p. 1992. 45.00 (*1-55570-112-4*) Neal-Schuman.

***Programming for Mathematicians.** R. Seroul. LC 99-57204. (Universitext Ser.). viii, 395p. 2000. pap. 42.00 (*3-540-66422-X*) Spr-Verlag.

Programming for Memory Efficiency. David Loshin. LC 97-12176. 304p. (C). 1997. pap. text. write for info. (*0-201-44212-4*) Addison-Wesley.

Programming for Parks, Recreation, & Leisure Services: A Servant Leadership Approach. Donald G. DeGraaf et al. LC 98-88780. 340p. 1999. 37.95 (*0-910251-99-1*, No. DEG104) Venture Pub PA.

Programming for Serving Children with Special Needs. Cynthia K. Richey. LC 93-33365. (ALSC Program Support Publications). 19p. (Orig.). 1993. pap. text 8.00 (*0-8389-5763-3*) ALA.

Programming for Software Sharing. D. T. Muxworthy. 1983. pap. text 70.50 (*90-277-1547-5*) Kluwer Academic.

Programming for Staff Development: Fanning the Flame. Ed. by Peter Burke et al. 224p. 1990. pap. 34.95 (*1-85000-752-7*, Falmer Pr) Taylor & Francis.

Programming for Students with Special Needs. Eric Alberta. LC 96-206208. 1995. write for info. (*0-7732-1834-3*) APAB.

Programming for Technology Students Using Visual Basic. Peter Spasov. LC 98-2693. 702p. (C). 1998. pap. text 90.00 (*0-13-622044-4*) P-H.

Programming for the Java Virtual Machine. Joshua Engel. LC 99-22853. 512p. 1999. pap. text 39.95 (*0-201-30972-6*) Addison-Wesley.

Programming for the Liberal Arts: An Introduction to PL-C. Cynthia Spencer. LC 85-11775. 120p. pap. 19.00 (*0-8226-0391-8*) Littlefield.

***Programming for the Masses.** 250p. (C). 2000. 27.00 (*0-536-60313-8*) Pearson Custom.

Programming for the Social Sciences: Algorithms & FORTRAN 77 Coding. Ed. by Richard S. Lehman. 592p. (C). 1986. text 99.95 (*0-89859-588-6*) L Erlbaum Assocs.

Programming for the Whole World: A Guide to Internationalization. Sandra Martin. 320p. (C). 1994. pap. text 33.00 (*0-13-722190-8*) P-H.

Programming for the Year 2000. Conor Sexton. LC 99-203981. 167p. 1998. pap. text 49.95 (*0-7506-3919-9*, Digital DEC) Buttrwrth-Heinemann.

Programming for TV, Radio & Cable. Edwin T. Vane & Lynne S. Gross. LC 93-21554. (Illus.). 400p. 1994. pap. 44.95 (*0-240-80128-8*, Focal) Buttrwrth-Heinemann.

Programming for Very Young Children. Carole D. Fiore. LC 95-50875. (ALSC Program Support Publications). 1996. pap. 8.00 (*0-8389-5757-9*) ALA.

***Programming for Web Authors.** NWECT Staff. (C). 1999. pap. text 81.00 (*0-03-029284-0*, Pub. by Harcourt Coll Pubs) Harcourt.

Programming Visual FoxPro 3.O. Whil Hentzen. 912p. 1995. pap. text 39.95 (*1-56276-325-3*, Ziff-Davis Pr) Que.

Programming Games in C. Robert Marmelstein. LC 94-22465. 89p. 1994. pap. 34.95 incl. disk (*1-55851-380-9*, M&T Bks) IDG Bks.

Programming Guide for Emotional Disturbance. Lynn Boreson. 168p. (C). 1994. pap. text 27.00 (*1-57337-018-5*) WI Dept Pub Instruct.

Programming Halo Graphics in C. Robert J. Traister, Sr. (Illus.). 128p. (C). 1986. 21.95 (*0-13-729310-0*) P-H.

Programming IBM Assembly Language. Paul Massie. (Illus.). 500p. 1985. pap. text. write for info. (*0-8087-6405-5*) Macmillan.

Programming in Ada. Jean-Paul Tremblay & John DeDourek. 489p. (C). 1989. pap. 54.69 (*0-07-065180-9*) McGraw.

Programming in Ada. 2nd ed. John G. Barnes. 300p. (Orig.). 1983. pap. 25.95 (*0-201-13799-2*) Addison-Wesley.

Programming in Ada 95. John G. Barnes. LC 95-38017. (International Computer Science Ser.). 702p. (C). 1996. pap. text 44.95 (*0-201-87700-7*, QA76.73) Addison-Wesley.

Programming in Adapted Physical Education. Elisabeth Evans. (C). 1993. student ed. 28.98 (*1-56870-092-X*) RonJon Pub.

Programming in Advanced Revelation Training Manual. Revelation Technologies Staff. 150p. 1990. 50.00 (*0-923387-22-6*) Revelation Sftware.

Programming in Advanced Revelation Training Manual (Instructor Manual) Revelation Technologies Staff. 75p. 1990. 100.00 (*0-923387-23-4*) Revelation Sftware.

Programming in Algol. J. S. Rohl. LC 79-555612. 112 p. 1970. write for info. (*0-7190-0443-8*) Manchester Univ Pr.

Programming in ANSI C. deluxe rev. ed. Stephen G. Kochan. LC 93-83485. 534p. 1994. 29.95 (*0-672-30339-6*) Sams.

Programming in Assembly Language. Heath Company Staff. (Illus.). 1979. 49.95 (*0-87119-085-0*, EC-1108) Heathkit-Zenith Ed.

Programming in Assembly Language: Macro-11. Edward F. Sowell. LC 83-3774. (Computer Science Ser.). (Illus.). 512p. 1984. text 31.16 (*0-201-07788-4*) Addison-Wesley.

Programming in Assembly Language: VAX 11. Edward F. Sowell. LC 86-26577. (C). 1987. text 43.25 (*0-201-10886-0*) Addison-Wesley.

Programming in Assembly Language on the IBM PC. Richard Tropper. Ed. by Robert J. Gordon. 648p. (C). 1992. text 63.00 (*0-314-93382-4*) West Pub.

Programming in Basic. N. L. Sarda. 298p. 1992. 65.00 (*81-209-0648-9*, Pub. by Pitambar Pub) St Mut.

Programming in Basic. N. L. Sarda. 256p. 1996. pap. 50.00 (*81-209-0013-8*, Pub. by Pitambar Pub) St Mut.

Programming in BASIC. John Cookson & Iain Richmond. LC 85-621. 128p. reprint ed. pap. 39.70 (*0-8357-2770-X*, 203989500014) Bks Demand.

Programming in BASIC: Problem Solving with Structure & Style. 2nd ed. Stewart M. Venit. Ed. by Mixter. 433p. (Orig.). (C). 1990. pap. text 50.75 (*0-314-66435-1*) West Pub.

Programming in BASIC for Microcomputers. Bruce Bosworth & Harry L. Nagel. 1992. teacher ed. write for info. (*0-02-800294-6*) Glencoe.

Programming in C++ Nell Dale et al. (Illus.). 320p. (C). 1996. pap. text 10.00 (*0-7637-0711-2*) Jones & Bartlett.

Programming in C++ Nell Dale et al. LC 98-3359. (Computer Science Ser.). 645p. 1998. pap. 50.00 (*0-7637-0537-3*) Jones & Bartlett.

Programming in C. J. Gray. (C). 1994. text 35.95 (*1-85032-257-0*) ITCP.

Programming in C++ Habib Kashani. LC 97-17979. 348p. 1997. pap. text 87.00 (*0-13-228818-4*) P-H.

Programming in C. Todd Knowlton. (J). 1996. mass mkt. 43.95 (*0-538-64886-4*) S-W Pub.

Programming in C. Michael F. Marek. (Introduction to Computing Ser.). 1988. pap. 29.95 (*0-8273-2950-4*) Delmar.

Programming in C. Edward Yourdon. (C). 2001. 32.00 (*0-13-725664-7*, Macmillan Coll) P-H.

Programming in C. rev. ed. Stephen G. Kochan. (UNIX Library). (Illus.). 476p. 1988. 29.95 (*0-672-48420-X*) Sams.

Programming in C++ 2nd ed. Stephen C. Dewhurst & Kathy T. Stark. LC 95-2776. 320p. (C). 1995. pap. 42.00 (*0-13-182718-9*) P-H.

Programming in C for Engineers. Kamal B. Rojiani. 500p. (C). 1995. text 74.00 (*0-13-726498-4*) P-H.

Programming in C for UNIX. C. Schirmer. (Computers & Their Applications Ser.). 250p. 1987. text 33.95 (*0-470-20768-X*) P-H.

Programming in C++ rev. ed. Knowlton. LC 96-37463. (Computer Programming Ser.). 1998. pap. 49.95 (*0-538-67600-0*) S-W Pub.

***Programming in C++** 2nd ed. Nell B. Dale et al. LC 00-44385. 2000. write for info. (*0-7637-1424-0*) Jones & Bartlett.

Programming in Clipper: The Definitive Guide to the Clipper dBASE Compiler. Stephen J. Straley. (Apple Technical Library). 1988. pap. 29.95 (*0-201-11993-5*) Addison-Wesley.

Programming in Clipper 5.O. Mike Schinkel. 976p. (C). 1991. pap. text 32.95 (*0-201-57018-1*) Addison-Wesley.

Programming in COBOL/400. Nancy B. Stern et al. LC 96-45970. 800p. 1997. pap. 73.95 (*0-471-12722-1*) Wiley.

Programming in dBase 5.O DOS. James Pratt. (Computer Applications Ser.). 1996. pap. 40.95 (*0-7895-0075-2*) Course Tech.

Programming in Dylan, Vol. XI. I. D. Craig. LC 96-36945. (Illus.). 254p. 1996. pap. 34.95 (*3-540-76053-9*) Spr-Verlag.

***Programming in Emacs Lisp: An Introduction, Edition 1.05.** Robert J. Chassell. 273p. 1999. per. 20.00 (*1-882114-42-6*) Free Software.

***Programming in F.** Miles Ellis. LC 98-3580. 640p. (C). 1998. pap. text 52.50 (*0-201-17991-1*) Addison-Wesley.

Programming in FORTRAN. Heath Company Staff. (Illus.). 616p. 1981. 99.95 incl. audio (*0-87119-084-2*, EC-1101) Heathkit-Zenith Ed.

***Programming in Fortran for Engineers & Scientists.** 640p. 1999. teacher ed. write for info. (*0-02-422740-4*, Macmillan Coll) P-H.

Programming in FORTRAN IV. William F. Schallert & Carol R. Clark. LC 78-74039. 1979. pap. text. write for info. (*0-201-06716-1*) Addison-Wesley.

Programming in FORTRAN 90: A First Course for Engineers & Scientists. I. M. Smith. 220p. 1995. pap. 64.99 (*0-471-94185-9*) Wiley.

Programming in FORTRAN 77. Jean-Paul Tremblay. 448p. 1988. pap. text 19.95 (*0-07-065179-5*) McGraw.

Programming in FORTRAN 77. 3rd ed. V. J. Calderbank. 1989. 55.00 (*0-412-30500-3*, A3298) Chapman & Hall.

Programming in HyperCard. Susan K. Baumann & Steven L. Mandell. LC 93-25651. 1994. mass mkt. 34.25 (*0-314-02735-1*) West Pub.

Programming in IBM PC DOS Pascal. David M. Chess. (Illus.). 240p. 1986. 27.95 (*0-13-730292-4*) P-H.

Programming in Martin-Lof's Type Theory: An Introduction. Bengt Nordstrom et al. (International Series of Monographs on Computer Science: No. 7). 232p. 1990. 55.00 (*0-19-853814-6*) OUP.

Programming in Mathematica. Roman E. Maeder. 1989. 35.50 (*0-685-31411-1*) Addison-Wesley.

Programming in Mathematica. 2nd ed. Roman E. Maeder. (Advanced Book Program Ser.). (Illus.). 304p. (C). 1991. 46.95 (*0-201-54877-1*) Addison-Wesley.

Programming in Mathematica. 2nd ed. Roman E. Maeder. 1995. 31.25 (*0-201-54578-0*) Addison-Wesley.

Programming in Mathematica. 3rd ed. Roman E. Maeder. LC 96-5714. 384p. (C). 1996. pap. text 34.95 (*0-201-85449-X*) Addison-Wesley.

Programming in Mathematics. Roman E. Maeder. 1989. text 35.50 (*0-201-51002-2*) Addison-Wesley.

Programming in Mathematics. 2nd ed. Roman E. Maeder. 304p. (C). 1991. pap. text 36.95 (*0-201-54878-X*) Addison-Wesley.

Programming in Matlab. 464p. pap. 60.95 (*0-534-36880-8*, Pub. by Brooks-Cole) Thomson Learn.

Programming in Microsoft BASIC. Heath Company Staff. (Illus.). 920p. 1981. 99.95 incl. audio (*0-87119-086-9*, EC-1110) Heathkit-Zenith Ed.

***Programming in Microsoft Visual Basic 6.0.** (C). 1999. pap. text 0.00 (*0-201-61190-2*) HEPC Inc.

Programming in Modula-3: An Introduction in Programming with Style. Laszlo Boszormenyi & Carsten Weich. LC 96-38492. 1996. 39.00 (*3-540-57912-5*) Spr-Verlag.

Programming in Modula 2. 1986. teacher ed. write for info. (*0-02-378294-3*, Macmillan Coll) P-H.

Programming in Modula-2. 3rd ed. Niklaus Wirth. (Texts & Monographs in Computer Science). iv, 192p. 1985. 29.95 (*0-387-15078-1*) Spr-Verlag.

Programming in Modula-2. 3rd ed. Niklaus Wirth. 1989. 45.95 (*0-387-50150-9*) Spr-Verlag.

Programming in Occam, No. 2. 2nd ed. Geraint Jones & M. Goldsmith. 336p. (C). 1989. pap. text 47.00 (*0-13-730334-3*) P-H.

Programming in Parlog. Tom Conlon. (Illus.). (C). 1989. text 33.50 (*0-201-17450-2*) Addison-Wesley.

Programming in Pascal. Nell Dale. (Computer Science Ser.). 624p. 1997. pap. 51.25 (*0-7637-0484-9*) Jones & Bartlett.

Programming in Pascal. Nell B. Dale. 515p. (C). 1990. teacher ed. write for info. (*0-318-70087-5*) HM Trade Div.

Programming in Pascal. Nell B. Dale. (Computer Science Ser.). 515p. (C). 1990. pap. 51.25 (*0-669-20042-5*) Jones & Bartlett.

Programming in Pascal. Heath Company Staff. (Illus.). 513p. 1981. 99.95 (*0-87119-093-1*, EC-1111) Heathkit-Zenith Ed.

Programming in Pascal. N. L. Sarda. 336p. 1996. pap. 75.00 (*81-209-0014-6*, Pub. by Pitambar Pub) St Mut.

Programming in Pascal. rev. ed. Peter Grogono. LC 79-24640. (Illus.). 384p. 1980. pap. text. write for info. (*0-201-02775-5*) Addison-Wesley.

Programming in Pascal: Computer Science. 2nd ed. Peter Grogono. (Illus.). 512p. 1984. pap. text 34.50 (*0-201-12070-4*) Addison-Wesley.

***Programming in Pascal for Engineers & Scientists.** 640p. 1999. write for info. (*0-02-422750-1*, Macmillan Coll) P-H.

Programming in Pascal with an Early Introduction to Procedures. Nell B. Dale. (Computer Science Ser.). 523p. (C). 1990. pap. 50.00 (*0-669-20249-5*); pap. 10.00 (*0-669-20246-0*); pap., teacher ed. 10.00 (*0-669-20244-4*) Jones & Bartlett.

Programming in Pascal with Pascal 1000. Peter Grogono. (C). 1980. pap. text. write for info. (*0-201-02889-1*) Addison-Wesley.

Programming in POP-2. Rod M. Burstall et al. LC 71-850175. viii, 290 p. 1971. write for info. (*0-85224-197-6*) Edinburgh U Pr.

Programming in Prolog. W. F. Clocksin & C. S. Mellish. 300p. 1993. pap. 29.00 (*0-387-17539-3*) Spr-Verlag.

Programming in Prolog. 4th ed. W. F. Clocksin & C. S. Mellish. LC 94-31331. 1994. 34.00 (*0-387-58350-5*) Spr-Verlag.

Programming in Prology. 4th ed. W. F. Clocksin & C. S. Mellish. 281p. 1994. text 34.95 (*3-540-58350-5*) Spr-Verlag.

Programming in Q-Basic for Engineering Technology. Kenneth A. Craven. LC 98-9672. 451p. (C). 1998. pap. text 86.00 (*0-13-622748-1*) P-H.

Programming in QuickBASIC. James Quasney. (Shelly Cashman Ser.). (C). 1991. pap., teacher ed. 18.50 (*0-87835-798-X*) Course Tech.

Programming in QuickBASIC. James S. Quasney. (Shelly Cashman Ser.). 128p. (C). 1991. pap., teacher ed. 10.50 (*0-87835-777-7*) Course Tech.

Programming in QuickBASIC with Structure & Style. Stewart M. Venit. Ed. by Mixter. 418p. (C). 1991. pap. text 54.25 (*0-314-78410-1*) West Pub.

Programming in REXX. Charles Daney. 299p. 1990. 49.00 (*0-07-015305-1*) McGraw.

Programming in RPG IV. rev. ed. Judy Yaeger. LC 97-4868. 435p. 1997. pap. text 65.00 (*1-882419-79-0*) News Four-Hund.

***Programming in RPG IV.** 2nd ed. Bryan Meyers & Judy Yaeger. (Illus.). 450p. 2000. pap. text 65.00 (*1-58304-074-9*) News Four-Hund.

Programming in RPG/400. 2nd ed. Judy Yaeger. LC 95-11169. 481p. (C). 1995. pap. text 65.00 (*1-882419-23-5*) News Four-Hund.

Programming in Scheme: Learn Scheme Through Artificial Intelligence. Mark Watson. LC 96-10599. (Illus.). 238p. 1996. pap. text, student ed. 39.95 (*0-387-94681-0*) Spr-Verlag.

Programming in Standard. Unix System Laboratories Staff. 816p. 1993. pap. text 33.00 (*0-13-177247-3*, Pub. by P-H) S&S Trade.

Programming in Style: An Introduction to Programming with Modula-3. L. Boszormenyi. (Illus.). 592p. 1996. 39.00 (*0-387-57912-5*) Spr-Verlag.

Programming in Sybase Open Server. David Van Couvering. (C). 1997. text. write for info. (*0-201-82078-1*) Addison-Wesley.

P

An Asterisk (*) at the beginning of an entry indicates that the title is appearing for the first time.

Programming in the 1990s: An Introduction to the Calculation of Programs. E. Cohen. Ed. by David Gries. (Texts & Monographs in Computer Science). 288p. 1990. 48.95 (*0-387-97382-6*) Spr-Verlag.

Programming in True Basic. 2nd ed. Venit. LC 98-34943. (West Computer Science Ser.). (C). 1998. mass mkt. 59.95 (*0-534-95351-4*) Wadsworth Pub.

Programming in True BASIC: Problem Solving with Structure & Style, Macintosh Version. Stewart M. Venit & Sandra M. Schleiffers. Ed. by Mixter. 536p. (C). 1991. mass mkt. 40.00 (*0-314-93446-4*) West Pub.

Programming in Turbo & Apple Pascal. Michel Boillot & Mickey G. Settle. LC 86-19098. (Illus.). 571p. (Orig.). (C). 1987. text 50.75 (*0-314-28510-5*); pap. text 49.75 (*0-314-34801-8*); pap. text, student ed. 26.00 (*0-314-34839-5*) West Pub.

Programming in VAX-BASIC. Bryant College Staff & E. Joseph Guay. LC 84-14602. 288p. (C). 1986. write for info. (*0-201-11568-9*) Addison-Wesley.

Programming in Visual BASIC. P. K. MacBridge. 208p. 1994. pap. 59.95 (*1-85805-092-8*, Pub. by DP Publns) St Mut.

Programming in Visual Basic TB. Bradley. 1995. 11.25 (*0-697-20275-5*, WCB McGr Hill) McGrw-H Hghr Educ.

Programming in Visual BASIC Version 5.0. Julia C. Bradley & A. C. Millspaugh. LC 97-21935. 1997. 45.75 (*0-256-25941-0*, Irwn Prfssnl) McGraw-Hill Prof.

Programming in Visual BASIC, Version 4.0 & Microsoft Visual BASIC 4.0. Julia C. Bradley & Anita Millspaugh. (C). 1996. text, pap. text 53.65 incl. cd-rom (*0-256-24731-5*, Irwn McGrw-H) McGrw-H Hghr Educ.

Programming in Your Words: With Any Database Program, Expert or Novice, Custom-Make Your Programs, Linguistic Technique, Filing & Accounting System. Raymond C. Rothman. LC 87-81413. 254p. (Orig.). (C). 1989. pap. text 9.95 (*0-9618666-2-4*) DUIMINT.

Programming Industrial Control Systems Using IEC 1131-3. R. W. B. Lewis. (IEE Control Engineering Ser.: No. 50). xiv, 281p. 1995. boxed set 77.00 (*0-85296-827-2*) INSPEC Inc.

***Programming Industrial Strength Windows.** Petter Hesselberg. 528p. 2000. pap. 44.95 incl. cd-rom (*0-87930-605-X*, Pub. by C M P Books) Publishers Group.

Programming Informix SQL-4GL: A Step-by-Step Approach. 2nd ed. Cathy Kipp. LC 97-34776. 512p. (C). 1997. pap. text 49.95 (*0-13-675919-X*) P-H.

Programming Intelligent Agent for the Internet. Mark Watson. (Illus.). 52p. 1996. pap., pap. text 39.95 incl. disk (*0-07-912206-X*) McGraw.

Programming Intelligent Agents for Distributed Systems. Michael Knapik. LC 97-24364. 389p. 1997. pap. 39.95 (*0-07-035011-6*) McGraw.

Programming Internet Controls. Markus W. Pope. LC 96-70103. 480p. 1996. per. 45.00 (*0-7615-0773-6*) Prima Pub.

Programming Internet E-Mail. Dave Wood. Ed. by Mark Stone. (Illus.). 400p. 1999. pap. 34.95 (*1-56592-479-7*) OReilly & Assocs.

***Programming Interviews Exposed: Secrets to Landing Your Next Job.** John Mongan & Noah Suojanen. LC 00-28304. 272p. 2000. pap. 24.99 (*0-471-38356-2*) Wiley.

Programming-Java: Beta Edition. Rick Decker. LC 97-29138. (Miscellaneous/Catalogs Ser.). (C). 1997. mass mkt. 36.95 (*0-534-95588-6*) Wadsworth Pub.

Programming Java Beans 1.1. Reaz Hoque. LC 98-17833. (Hands-On Web Development Ser.). 524p. 1998. pap. text 49.95 incl. cd-rom (*0-07-913704-0*) McGraw.

***Programming KDE 2.0: Creating Linux Desktop Applicatons.** Lotsi Boloni & Tom Genereaux. 432p. 2000. pap. 49.95 incl. cd-rom (*1-929629-13-3*, Pub. by C M P Books) Publishers Group.

Programming Language. Kenneth E. Iverson. LC 62-15180. 286p. reprint ed. pap. 88.70 (*0-608-17770-9*, 205655200072) Bks Demand.

Programming Language ADA: A Reference Manual, Proposed Standard. (Lecture Notes in Computer Science Ser.: Vol. 106). 243p. 1983. 27.00 (*0-387-10693-6*) Spr-Verlag.

Programming Language ADA: Reference Manual. (Lecture Notes in Computer Science Ser.: Vol. 155). 331p. 1990. 43.95 (*0-387-12328-8*) Spr-Verlag.

Programming Language Concepts. 3rd ed. Carlo Ghezzi & Mehdi Jazayeri. LC 97-1905. 448p. 1997. text 74.95 (*0-471-10426-4*) Wiley.

Programming Language Concepts & Paradigms. Watt. (C). 1993. pap. text 39.95 (*0-13-728866-2*) P-H.

Programming Language Concepts & Paradigms. David A. Watt. 320p. 1990. boxed set 37.00 (*0-13-728874-3*) P-H.

Programming Language for Industrial Robots. rev. ed. C. Blume & W. Jakob. (Symbolic Compilation - Artificial Intelligence Ser.). 330p. 1986. 91.00 (*0-387-16319-0*) Spr-Verlag.

Programming Language for Today, Compiler: RPG. Doris B. Cable & Trident Software Staff. 544p. (C). 1992. lib. bdg., ring bd. 81.75 incl. disk (*0-697-20998-9*, Irwn McGrw-H) McGrw-H Hghr Educ.

Programming Language Implementation. Patrick D. Terry. 416p. (C). 1986. pap. text. write for info. (*0-318-61720-X*) Addison-Wesley.

Programming Language Implementation & Logic Programming: Fifth International Symposium, PLILP '93, Tallinn, Estonia, August 1993, Proceedings. Ed. by Maurice Bruynooghe & Jaan Penjam. LC 93-11822. (Lecture Notes in Computer Science Ser.: Vol. 714). 1993. 60.00 (*0-387-57186-8*) Spr-Verlag.

Programming Language Implementation & Logic Programming: International Workshop PLILP '90 Linkoping, Sweden, August 20-22, 1990 Proceedings. Ed. by P. Deransart et al. (Lecture Notes in Computer Science Ser.: Vol. 456). viii, 401p. 1990. 43.00 (*0-387-53010-X*) Spr-Verlag.

Programming Language Implementation & Logic Programming: Proceedings of the Sixth International Symposium, PHLILP '94, Madrid, Spain, September 14-16, 1994. Ed. by Jean Penjam & M. Hermenegildo. (Lecture Notes in Computer Science Ser.: Vol. 844). 469p. 1994. 65.95 (*3-540-58402-1*) Spr-Verlag.

Programming Language Implementation & Logic Programming: 3rd International Symposium, PLILP '91, Passau, Germany, August 26-28, 1991 Proceedings. Ed. by Jan Maluszynski et al. (Lecture Notes in Computer Science Ser.: Vol. 528). xi, 433p. 1991. 44.95 (*0-387-54444-5*) Spr-Verlag.

Programming Language Implementation & Logic Programming: 4th International Symposium, PLILP '92, Leuven, Belgium, August 26-28, 1-92: Proceedings. Ed. by Maurice Bruynooghe & M. Wirsing. LC 92-26380. (Lecture Notes in Computer Science Ser.: Vol. 631). xi, 492p. 1992. 76.95 (*0-387-55844-6*) Spr-Verlag.

Programming Language Pragmatics. Michael L. Scott. LC 99-47125. 700p. 1999. text 69.95 (*1-55860-442-1*, Pub. by Morgan Kaufmann) Harcourt.

***Programming Language Processors in Java: Compilers & Interpreters.** David A. Watt & Deryck F. Brown. LC 99-50395. 436p. 2000. pap. 52.00 (*0-13-025786-9*) P-H.

Programming Language Translation: A Practical Approach. Patrick D. Terry. 416p. (C). 1986. pap. text. write for info. (*0-318-61555-X*) Addison-Wesley.

Programming Languages. Appleby. 1991. teacher ed. 27.50 (*0-07-002574-6*) McGraw.

Programming Languages. Ravi Sethi. (C). 1989. text. write for info. (*0-201-50372-7*) Addison-Wesley.

***Programming Languages.** Tucker. 2001. 57.00 (*0-07-238111-6*) McGraw.

Programming Languages. M. Woodman. (Illus.). 400p. 1995. mass mkt. 43.00 (*0-412-58930-3*) Chapman & Hall.

Programming Languages. Ed. by Mark Woodman. 1996. mass mkt. 48.95 (*1-85032-186-8*) ITCP.

Programming Languages: Abstraction, Representation & Implementation. Daniel P. Friedman. 448p. (C). 1992. 82.81 (*0-07-022443-9*) McGraw.

Programming Languages: Concepts & Constructs. 2nd ed. Ravi Sethi. Ed. by Tom Stone. LC 95-40528. 624p. (C). 1995. 82.00 (*0-201-59065-4*) Addison-Wesley.

Programming Languages: Design & Implementation. 3rd ed. Terrence W. Pratt & Marvin V. Zelkowitz. 654p. 1995. 74.00 (*0-13-678012-1*) P-H.

***Programming Languages: Design & Implementation.** 4th ed. Terry Pratt & Marvin V. Zelkowitz. 660p. 2000. 74.00 (*0-13-027678-2*, Prentice Hall) P-H.

Programming Languages: Implementations, Logics, & Programs - 8th International Symposium, PLILP '96, Aachen, Germany, September 24-27, 1996 - Proceedings, Vol. 114. S. D. Swierstra. LC 96-36464. (Lecture Notes in Computer Science Ser.). xi, 479p. 1996. 75.00 (*3-540-61756-6*) Spr-Verlag.

Programming Languages: Implementations, Logics & Programs: 7th International Symposium, PLILP '95, Utrecht, The Netherlands, September 20-22, 1995 - Proceedings. Ed. by M. Hermenegildo et al. LC 95-232662. (Lecture Notes in Computer Science Ser.: Vol. 982). xi, 467p. 1995. pap. 75.00 (*3-540-60359-X*) Spr-Verlag.

Programming Languages: Paradigm & Practice. Doris Appleby. (C). 1991. text 48.50 (*0-07-557904-9*) McGraw.

Programming Languages: Paradigm & Practice. 2nd ed. Doris Appleby & Julius Vandekopple. LC 96-36525. (Illus.). 444p. (C). 1996. pap. 64.06 (*0-07-005315-4*) McGraw.

Programming Languages: Paradigm & Practice. 2nd ed. Richard Hull. (C). 1996. pap. text 17.00 (*0-07-005317-0*) McGraw.

Programming Languages: Paradigm & Practice - Ada Mini-Manual. Doris Appleby. (C). 1991. pap. text 20.00 (*0-07-002578-9*) McGraw.

Programming Languages: Paradigm & Practice - C Mini-Manual with C Plus Plus Supplement. Maryam Hastings. (C). 1991. pap. text 15.00 (*0-07-002576-2*) McGraw.

Programming Languages: Paradigm & Practice - PC Scheme Mini-Manual. Hull. (C). 1991. pap. text 16.00 (*0-07-002577-0*) McGraw.

Programming Languages: Paradigm & Practice - PROLOG Mini-Manual. Tom Hawkins & Thom Luce. (C). 1991. pap. text. write for info. (*0-07-002579-7*) McGraw.

Programming Languages: Paradigm & Practice - Turbo Pascal Mini-Manual. Doris Appleby. (C). 1991. mass mkt. 17.74 (*0-07-002575-4*) McGraw.

Programming Languages: Pascal, Modula, Chill, & Ada. C. H. Smedema et al. 160p. 1983. 16.95 (*0-685-08596-1*) P-H.

Programming Languages: Principles & Practice. Kenneth C. Louden. 641p. 1993. mass mkt. 69.95 (*0-534-93277-0*) PWS Pubs.

Programming Languages: Principles & Practice. 2nd ed. Kenneth C. Louden. (Computer Science Ser.). (C). 2000. 55.75 (*0-534-95341-7*) PWS Pubs.

Programming Languages: Structures & Models. Herbert L. Dershem & Michael J. Jipping. 413p. (C). 1990. text 55.95 (*0-534-12900-5*) PWS Pubs.

Programming Languages: The Computer Professional's Quick Reference. Marius S. Vassiliou. 1993. 30.00 (*0-07-067218-0*); pap. 19.95 (*0-07-067219-9*) McGraw.

Programming Languages Minimanual: Paradigm & Practice C++ 2nd ed. William Hastings. (C). 1996. pap., teacher ed. 23.44 (*0-07-005321-9*) McGraw.

Programming Languages Prolog Minimanual: Paradigm & Practice. 2nd ed. Tom Hankins. (C). 1996. pap. text 17.00 (*0-07-005319-7*) McGraw.

Programming Languages - Implementations, Logics, & Programs: Proceedings, 9th International Symposium, PLILP '97, Including a Special Track on Declarative Programming Languages in Education, Southampton, U. K., September 3-5, 1997. Pieter H. Hartel et al. Ed. by Henning Grann & Herbert Kuchen. LC 97-13426. (Lecture Notes in Computer Science Ser.: Vol. 1292). xi, 425p. pap. 67.00 (*3-540-63398-7*) Spr-Verlag.

Programming Languages & Data Structures (BASIC, Cobol, Pascal, FORTRAN, ADA, Lisp) Ed. by Pradip Bose. (C). 1989. 100.00 (*0-89771-388-5*, Pub. by Current Dist) St Mut.

Programming Languages & System Architectures: Proceedings of the International Conference, Zurich, Switzerland, March 2-4, 1994. Ed. by Jurg Gutknecht. LC 94-4694. (Lecture Notes in Computer Science Ser.: Vol. 782). x, 344p. 1994. 55.95 (*0-387-57840-4*) Spr-Verlag.

***Programming Languages & Systems: Proceedings of the Ninth European Symposium on Programming, ESOP 2000.** Ed. by G. Smolka. (Lecture Notes in Computer Science Ser.: Vol. 1782). xiii, 429p. 2000. pap. 69.00 (*3-540-67262-1*) Spr-Verlag.

Programming Languages & Systems: 7th European Symposium on Programming, ESOP'98, Held As Part of the Joint European Conferences on Theory & Practice of Software, ETAPS'98, Lisbon, Portugal, March 28-April 4, 1998, Proceedings. Ed. by Chris Hankin et al. LC 98-14853. (Lecture Notes in Computer Science: Vol. 1381). x, 283p. 1998. pap. 49.00 (*3-540-64302-8*) Spr-Verlag.

Programming Languages & Systems: 8th European Symposium on Programming, ESOP'99 Held as Part of the Joint European Conferences on Theory & Practice of Software, ETAPS'99 Asterdam, the Netherlands, March 22-28, 1999 Proceedings. Ed. by S. D. Swierstra et al. LC 99-24736. (Lecture Notes in Computer Science Ser.: Vol. 1576). x, 307p. 1999. pap. 56.00 (*3-540-65699-5*) Spr-Verlag.

Programming Languages & Systems, ESOP '94: Fifth European Symposium on Programming, Edinburgh, U.K., April 1994. Ed. by Donald Sanella. LC 94-8472. (Lecture Notes in Computer Science Ser.: Vol. 788). 1994. 73.95 (*0-387-57880-3*) Spr-Verlag.

Programming Languages & Systems, ESOP '96: Proceedings of the 6th European Symposium on Programming, Link Oping, Sweden, April 22-24, 1996. Ed. by Hanne R. Nielson. (Lecture Notes in Computer Science Ser.: Vol. 1058). 405p. 1996. pap. 68.00 (*3-540-61055-3*) Spr-Verlag.

Programming Languages & Their Definition: H. Bekic (1936-1982) Ed. by C. B. Jones. (Lecture Notes in Computer Science Ser.: Vol. 177). xxxii, 254p. 1985. 33.00 (*0-387-13378-X*) Spr-Verlag.

Programming Languages Implementation & Logic Programming. Ed. by P. Deransart et al. (Lecture Notes in Computer Science Ser.: Vol. 348). 299p. 1989. 44.95 (*0-387-50820-1*) Spr-Verlag.

Programming Languages Pragmatics. Michael Scott. 1997. 49.95 (*0-387-94897-X*) Spr-Verlag.

Programming Linguistics. David Gelernter & Suresh J. Jag. 434p. 1990. 49.50 (*0-262-07127-4*) MIT Pr.

Programming Logic Marjorie Leeson. LC 82-16790. x, 358p. 1983. write for info. (*0-574-21420-8*) SRA.

Programming Logic for Business. 3rd ed. Laura Saret. 450p. (C). 1992. pap. 55.31 (*0-07-054908-7*) McGraw.

Programming Logowriter & Teacher Professional Development. Peter Evans. (ECRG Papers: No. 16). 166p. 1995. pap. 28.00 (*0-949823-55-4*, Pub. by Deakin Univ) St Mut.

Programming Manual: C Mini-Manual. 2nd ed. Appleby. 1996. 18.25 (*0-07-005320-0*) McGraw.

***Programming Mapobjects with Visual Basic.** Scott Hofmann. 350p. 1999. pap. 49.95 (*1-879102-54-4*) ESR Inst.

***Programming Mental Ray.** Ed. by T. Driemeyer & R. Herken. (Mental Ray Handbks.: Vol. 2). (Illus.). 480p. 2000. 99.00 (*3-211-83404-4*) Spr-Verlag.

Programming Methodology: A Collection of Articles by Members of IFIP WG 2.3. Ed. by David Gries. LC 78-16539. (Texts & Monographs in Computer Science). (Illus.). 1978. 65.00 (*0-387-90329-1*) Spr-Verlag.

Programming Microcontrollers in C. Ted Van Sickle. LC 94-75549. (Illus.). 416p. 1994. pap. 39.95 (*1-878707-14-0*) LLH Tech Pub.

***Programming Microcontrollers in C.** 2nd ed. Ted Van Sickle. (Illus.). 336p. 2000. pap. 49.95 incl. cd-rom (*1-878707-57-4*, Pub. by LLH Tech Pub) IPG Chicago.

Programming Microsoft Access 2000. Rick Dobson. LC 99-13032. (Illus.). 550p. 1999. pap. 49.99 incl. cd-rom (*0-7356-0500-9*) Microsoft.

***Programming Microsoft Internet Explorer 5.** Scott Roberts. LC 99-27216. 1999. pap. text 49.99 (*0-7356-0781-8*) Microsoft.

Programming Microsoft Office 2000 Web Components. Dave Stearns. LC 99-36327. 1999. pap. 49.99 (*0-7356-0794-X*) Microsoft.

Programming Microsoft Outlook & Microsoft Exchange, 1. Thomas Rizzo. LC 99-13555. (Illus.). 684p. 1999. pap. 49.99 (*0-7356-0509-2*) Microsoft.

***Programming Microsoft Outlook & Microsoft Exchange.** 2nd ed. Microsoft Press Staff. LC 00-28169. (DV-MPS Programming Ser.). (Illus.). 2000. pap. text 49.99 (*0-7356-1019-3*) Microsoft.

Programming Microsoft Visual Basic 6.0. Francesco Balena. LC 99-20381. (Programming Ser.). (Illus.). 1276p. 1999. pap. 59.99 (*0-7356-0558-0*) Microsoft.

Programming Microsoft Windows 2000 Unleashed. Mickey Williams. LC 98-87346. (Sams Unleashed Series). (Illus.). 1040p. 1999. pap. 49.99 incl. cd-rom (*0-672-31486-X*) Sams.

Programming Mobile Objects with Java. Jeff Nelson. LC 98-50956. 601p. 1999. pap. 49.99 incl. cd-rom (*0-471-25406-1*) Wiley.

Programming Models for Massively Parallel Computers 1997. LC 98-84701. 1998. pap. text 60.00 (*0-8186-8427-5*) Inst Electrical.

Programming Models for Parallel Systems. Shirley A. Williams. LC 89-70543. (Parallel Computing Ser.). 182p. 1990. text 110.00 (*0-471-92304-4*) Wiley.

Programming MS Exchange Server. Nik Okuntseff. (Illus.). 318p. 1999. pap. 39.95 incl. cd-rom (*0-87930-567-3*, Pub. by C M P Books) Publishers Group.

PROGRAMMING M68000. 2nd ed. Tim King & Brian Knight. 288p. 1987. pap. text 32.25 (*0-8053-5550-2*) Benjamin-Cummings.

Programming Netscape Plug-Ins. Zan Oliphant. LC 96-67543. 448p. 1996. 39.99 (*1-57521-098-3*) Sams.

Programming of Computer Numerical Controlled Machines. John Polywka & Stanley Gabrel. (Illus.). 288p. 1992. 36.95 (*0-8311-3035-0*) Indus Pr.

Programming on Purpose: Essays on Programming Design. P. J. Plauger. LC 92-45905. (Illus.). 256p. (C). 1993. pap. text 24.80 (*0-13-721374-3*) P-H.

***Programming 101: A Basic Introduction to Computer Programming.** James E. Potter. 140p. (C). 1999. spiral bd. 26.95 (*1-885587-66-X*) Bridge Lrn Systs.

Programming Opportunities for Students Gifted & Talented in the Visual Arts. Gilbert A. Clark & Enid Zimmerman. 51p. 1998. reprint ed. pap. text 20.00 (*0-7881-7210-7*) DIANE Pub.

Programming Outlook 2000. Bob Lavinger. 1999. 29.99 (*0-672-31549-1*) Sams.

Programming Outreach for Children. (ALSC Program Support Publications). 16p. (Orig.). 1994. pap. text 8.00 (*0-8389-5764-1*) ALA.

Programming Paradigms in Graphics '95. Ed. by Remco C. Veltkamp & E. H. Blake. (Eurographics Ser.). (Illus.). 184p. 1996. pap. 59.00 (*3-211-82788-9*) Spr-Verlag.

***Programming Pearls.** 2nd ed. Patrick Chan. LC 99-46520. 256p. (C). 1999. pap. text 24.95 (*0-201-65788-0*) Addison-Wesley.

Programming Perl. 2nd rev. ed. Tom Christiansen et al. (Illus.). 670p. 1996. pap. 39.95 (*1-56592-149-6*) Thomson Learn.

***Programming Perl.** 3rd ed. Larry Wall. 2000. pap. 44.95 (*0-596-00027-8*) OReilly & Assocs.

***Programming Perl/TK.** Andrew L. Johnson & Randy Kobes. (Illus.). 400p. 2000. pap. 39.95 (*1-884777-93-7*, Pub. by Manning Pubns) IPG Chicago.

Programming, Pitfalls & Puppy-Dog Tales. Gyeorgos C. Hatonn. 234p. 1993. pap. 7.95 (*1-56935-001-9*) Phoenix Source.

Programming Plug in Applications. Ziff Davis Development Group Staff. 1996. pap. text 49.99 incl. cd-rom (*1-56276-459-4*, Ziff-Davis Pr) Que.

Programming Post Occupancy Evaluation & the Financial Success of the Architect. Edward T. White. (Illus.). 24p. 1988. pap. 6.00 (*1-928643-16-7*) Archit Media.

Programming Primer a Guide to Programming Fundamentals. John Ribar. 1994. pap. text 16.95 (*0-07-881999-7*) McGraw.

Programming Proverbs Henry F. Ledgard. LC 74-22058. (Hayden Computer Programming Ser.). 134p. 1975. write for info. (*0-8104-5522-6*) Sams.

Programming Proverbs for FORTRAN Programmers Henry F. Ledgard. LC 74-22074. (Hayden Computer Programming Ser.). 130p. 1975. write for info. (*0-8104-5820-9*) Sams.

Programming Push Technologies Unleashed. 1997. 49.99 (*1-57521-357-5*) Sams.

Programming Python: Object-Oriented Scripting. Mark Lutz. LC 97-102075. (Illus.). 904p. (Orig.). 1996. pap. 44.95 (*1-56592-197-6*) Thomson Learn.

Programming Real Time Games on the TRS-80. P. Pellier. Tr. by Laurent Martres from FRE. 112p. write for info. (*0-318-57946-4*) Blue Cat.

***Programming Services for Microsoft Windows.** Jason Clark & Jeffrey M. Richter. 2000. pap. 49.99 (*0-7356-0753-2*) Microsoft.

***Programming SQL Server 2000 with XML.** Krishna Sankar. 400p. 2000. pap. 49.99 (*0-7356-1175-0*) Microsoft.

Programming Starter Kit for Macintosh. Jim Trudeau. (Illus.). 600p. 1995. 45.00 (*1-56830-174-X*, Alpha Ref) Macmillan Gen Ref.

Programming Subfiles in COBOL/400. Jerry Goldson. 204p. 1992. pap. 79.00 (*1-882419-42-1*) News Four-Hund.

Programming Techniques. Blaise W. Liffick. LC 78-8649. 1978. write for info. (*0-931718-12-0*) Byte Pubns Inc.

Programming Techniques for Object-Based Statistical Analysis with SAS Software. Tanya Kolosova & Samuel Berestizhevsky. 148p. 1998. pap. 25.95 (*1-58025-198-6*, P55869) SAS Publ.

***Programming Techniques in EMACS.** Prima Publishing Staff. 400p. 2000. pap. 39.99 (*0-7615-2446-0*) Prima Pub.

Programming the Apple II in BASIC. Paul Tebbe. LC 83-10895. (Illus.). 176p. 1983. pap. 26.95 (*0-13-729749-1*) P-H.

Programming the BE Operating System. Dan P. Sydow. Ed. by Andy Oram. (Illus.). 400p. 1999. pap. 34.95 (*1-56592-467-3*) OReilly & Assocs.

P

Programming the Boundary Elements. Beer. 1969. text. write for info. (*0-471-85722-X*) Wiley.

Programming the Display PostScript System with X. Adobe Systems Inc. Staff. LC 93-7455. 624p. (C). 1993. pap. text 29.95 (*0-201-62203-3*) Addison-Wesley.

Programming the 80286, 80386, 80486, & Pentium-Based Personal Computer. Barry B. Brey. LC 95-32795. 786p. 1995. 115.00 (*0-02-314263-4*, Macmillan Coll) P-H.

Programming the Finite Element Method. I. M. Smith & D. V. Griffiths. LC 96-54905. 546p. 1997. pap. 64.95 (*0-471-96543-X*) Wiley.

Programming the Futaba Super 7 for Aircraft & Sailplanes. unabridged ed. Don Edberg. (Illus.). vi, 90p. 1995. pap. 15.00 (*1-892556-02-2*, DM109C) Dynamic Model.

Programming the IBM Personal Computer: Fundamentals of BASIC. Neill Graham. (Illus.). 304p. 1995. pap. text 33.95 (*0-03-059561-4*) OUP.

Programming, the Impossible Challenge. B. Walraet. 464p. 1988. 133.25 (*0-444-87128-4*, North Holland) Elsevier.

***Programming the Internet with Java.** 2nd rev. ed. Freeman & Ince. LC 98-231995. 400p. (C). 1998. pap. text 51.00 (*0-201-39844-3*) Addison-Wesley.

Programming the I386-I486. Automata Publishing Staff. 1994. text. write for info. (*0-442-01427-9*, VNR) Wiley.

Programming the Lotus Notes API. Carolyn Kraut & Mitch Allen. LC 94-44830. 528p. 1995. pap. text 44.95 incl. disk (*0-471-11776-5*) Wiley.

Programming the Matrix Analysis of Skeletal Structures. Bhatt. (Civil & Mechanical Engineering Ser.). 1986. text 59.95 (*0-470-20310-2*) P-H.

***Programming the Microsoft Windows Driver Model.** Walter Oney. LC 99-33878. (C). (gr. 8). 1999. pap. 49.99 (*0-7356-0588-2*) Microsoft.

Programming the Microsoft WIN32 Driver Model. Brian Catlin. 1998. pap. 44.99 (*1-57231-850-3*) Microsoft.

***Programming the Motorola M68HC12 Family.** Gordon Doughman. (Illus.). 576p. 2000. pap. 39.95 (*0-929392-67-1*, Pub. by Annabooks) Coriolis Grp.

Programming the OS-2 Kernel. T. Godfrey. 1990. pap. 40.00 (*0-13-723776-6*) P-H.

Programming the OS/23 WARP Version 3 GPI. Stephen A. Knight & Jeffrey M. Ryan. 406p. 1995. pap. 39.95 incl. disk (*0-471-10718-2*) Wiley.

Programming the Parallel Port: Interfacing the PC for Data Acquisition & Process Control. Dhananjay Gadre. 312p. (Orig.). 1997. pap. 44.95 incl. disk (*0-87930-513-4*) C M P Books.

Programming the Perl DBI: Database Programming for Perl & CGI. Alligator Descartes & Tim Bunce. Ed. by Linda Mui. (Illus.). 356p. 1999. pap. 34.95 (*1-56592-699-4*) OReilly & Assocs.

Programming the PowerPC. Don Sydow. LC 94-37488. 400p. 1994. pap. 39.95 incl. disk (*1-55851-400-7*, M&T Bks) IDG Bks.

Programming the 65816 Microprocessor: Including 6502 & 65C02. David Eyes & Ron Lichty. 512p. 1985. pap. 22.95 (*0-317-37797-3*) S&S Trade.

Programming the Windows 95 User Interface: A Practical Insider's Guide to Coding the New UI Features. Nancy W. Cluts. (Programming Ser.). 408p. 1995. pap. 34.95 incl. cd-rom (*1-55615-884-X*) Microsoft.

***Programming the World Wide Web.** 2000. write for info. (*0-201-70484-6*) Addison-Wesley.

Programming the X Image Extension. James B. Fahy. 1996. pap. write for info. (*0-201-63376-0*) Addison-Wesley.

Programming the 8086 & 8088. Michael Thorne. (C). 1986. pap. text. write for info. (*0-201-14525-1*) Addison-Wesley.

Programming under Mach. Joseph Boykin et al. (Illus.). 480p. (C). 1993. pap. 58.95 (*0-201-52739-1*) Addison-Wesley.

***Programming Using the Tuxedo System.** Edward Felt. (C). 2000. text. write for info. (*0-201-30999-8*) Addison-Wesley.

Programming Using VAX Basic. Wayne Muller. 320p. 1985. pap. text 18.95 (*0-317-38895-9*) P-H.

Programming Visual Basic 6.0. Bradley. LC 98-43108. 704p. 1998. pap. 54.38 (*0-07-231190-8*) McGraw.

Programming Visual C++ 5th ed. David J. Kruglinski et al. LC 98-27329. 1153p. 1998. 49.99 incl. cd-rom (*1-57231-857-0*) Microsoft.

Programming Visual InterDev 6.0. 2nd ed. Nicholas D. Evans et al. LC 98-31911. 600p. 1999. 49.99 incl. cd-rom (*1-57231-814-7*) Microsoft.

Programming VisualAge for Java Version 2. Luc Chamberland. 1998. pap. text 49.99 (*0-471-31730-6*) Wiley.

Programming Web Advertising. Becker. (C). 1998. text. write for info. (*1-55860-522-3*) Morgan Kaufmann.

Programming Web Components. Hoque. 810p. 1998. 64.95 (*0-07-913776-8*) McGraw.

***Programming Web Graphics with Perl & GNU Software.** Shawn P. Wallace. Ed. by Richard Koman. (Illus.). 470p. 1999. pap. 32.95 (*1-56592-478-9*) OReilly & Assocs.

Programming Web Server Applications. Eric Richardson. LC 96-70101. 480p. 1996. per. 40.00 (*0-7615-0780-9*) Prima Pub.

***Programming Web Store Applications with Microsoft Exchange Server 2000.** Mindy Martin. 2000. pap. 49.99 (*0-7356-0772-9*) Microsoft.

Programming Windows. 5th ed. Charles Petzold. LC 98-42529. 1100p. 1998. 59.99 incl. cd-rom (*1-57231-995-X*) Microsoft.

Programming Windows CE. Douglas Boling. LC 98-39279. 650p. 49.99 incl. cd-rom (*1-57231-856-2*) Microsoft.

Programming Windows in Japanese. Franklin B. Murch. (JPN.). (C). 2001. pap. text 34.00 (*0-13-447723-5*) P-H.

Programming Windows 95: The Definitive Developer's Guide to the Windows 95 API. 4th ed. Charles Petzold. 1120p. 1996. pap. 67.95 incl. cd-rom (*1-55615-676-6*) Microsoft.

Programming Windows 95 Unleashed. (Illus.). 1120p. 1995. 49.99 (*0-672-30602-6*) Sams.

Programming Windows 95 with MFC: Create Object-Oriented Programs Quickly with the Microsoft Foundation Class Library. Jeff Prosise. 1024p. 1996. pap. 49.95 incl. cd-rom (*1-55615-902-1*) Microsoft.

***Programming Windows Services: Implementing Application Servers.** Randy Charles Morin. 432p. 2000. pap. 49.99 incl. audio compact disk (*0-471-38576-X*) Wiley.

Programming Windows with Borland C++ 4.0. William Roetzheim. LC 95-125997. (Programming Ser.). (Illus.). 496p. (Orig.). 1995. pap. 39.95 incl. disk (*1-56276-269-9*, Ziff-Davis Pr) Que.

***Programming Windows with JAVA & WFC With CDROM.** Bruce Krell. LC 99-26381. (Illus.). 720p. 1999. pap. 49.99 (*0-7645-3272-3*) IDG Bks.

Programming Windows with MFC. 2nd ed. Jeff Prosise. LC 99-13028. 1200p. 1998. 49.99 incl. cd-rom (*1-57231-695-0*) Microsoft.

***Programming Windows 2000: A Practical Guide for the C/c++ Programmer.** Robert J. Oberg. 600p. 2000. pap. 49.99 (*0-13-027953-6*, Prentice Hall) P-H.

***Programming Windows 32 Api & Unix System Services.** (C). 2001. 49.99 (*0-13-025969-1*) S&S Trade.

Programming with ANSI C. B. J. Holmes. 512p. 1995. pap. 59.95 (*1-85805-117-7*, Pub. by DP Publns) St Mut.

***Programming With C++** John Hubbard. 1999. pap. text 8.95 (*0-07-052713-X*) McGraw-Hill Pubng.

Programming with C. Siday. (De-Computer Science Ser.). (C). 1995. pap. 27.50 (*0-340-60035-7*) Routledge.

***Programming with C++** 2nd ed. John Hubbard. LC 00-38016. (Schaum's Outlines Ser.). (Illus.). 448p. 2000. pap. 16.95 (*0-07-135346-1*) McGraw.

Programming with C++ 10th ed. 480p. (C). 1998. pap. 45.95 (*0-7600-5044-9*) Course Tech.

Programming with C++ Course Technology. 608p. (C). 1998. teacher ed. 49.95 (*0-7600-5069-4*) Course Tech.

Programming with C++ Using, Modifying & Implementing Object Classes. Rick Mercer. LC 99-27204. 1998. pap. 49.95 (*1-887902-39-2*) Franklin Beedle.

Programming with Class: A Practical Introduction to Object-Oriented Programming with C++ Rudolf Kruse et al.Tr. of Fuzzy Systeme. 638p. 1994. pap. text 80.00 (*0-471-94350-9*) Wiley.

Programming with Comal 1: Lab Pack 1. James MacDonald et al. Ed. by Bonnie Schroeder. (Illus.). teacher ed. 19.95 (*1-56177-131-7*, TE403-1); student ed. 9.95 (*1-56177-125-2*, 403-1); teacher ed., student ed. 159.95 incl. disk (*1-56177-129-5*, L403-1); disk 6.95 (*0-685-45809-1*, D403-1) CES Compu-Tech.

Programming with Comal 1: Lab Pack 2. James MacDonald et al. Ed. by Bonnie Schroeder. (Illus.). teacher ed. 19.95 (*0-685-45810-5*, T403-2); student ed. 9.95 (*1-56177-126-0*, 403-2); teacher ed., student ed. 159.95 incl. disk (*1-56177-130-9*, L403-2); disk 6.95 (*1-56177-128-7*, D403-2) CES Compu-Tech.

Programming with Constraints: An Introduction. Kim Marriott & Peter J. Stuckey. LC 97-40549. (Illus.). 476p. 1998. 49.50 (*0-262-13341-5*) MIT Pr.

Programming with Curses. John Strang. (Computer Science). 76p. 1986. pap. 12.95 (*0-937175-02-1*) Thomson Learn.

Programming with Data. J. M. Chambers. LC 98-13049. (Illus.). 480p. 1998. pap. 44.95 (*0-387-98503-4*) Spr-Verlag.

Programming with Data Structures Modula-2 Version. Robert L. Kruse. 1988. 32.00 (*0-13-729188-4*) P-H.

Programming with dBASE II. Cary N. Prague & James E. Hammitt. (Illus.). 288p. (Orig.). 1984. 26.95 (*0-8306-0776-5*, 1776); pap. 16.60 (*0-8306-1776-0*, 1776P) McGraw-Hill Prof.

Programming with dBASE III Plus. Cary N. Prague & James E. Hammitt. (Illus.). 384p. 1986. pap. 19.95 (*0-8306-2726-X*) McGraw-Hill Prof.

Programming with dBASE III Plus. Cary N. Prague & James E. Hammitt. 1991. 24.95 (*0-8306-6632-X*) McGraw-Hill Prof.

Programming with dBASE III (IBM PC) James E. Hammitt & Cary N. Prague. 1991. 24.95 (*0-8306-6626-5*) McGraw-Hill Prof.

Programming with Enterprise JavaBeans, Jts, & OTS: Building Distributed Transactions with Java & C++ Andreas Vogel & Madhavan Rangarao. LC 99-26921. (Illus.). 368p. 1999. pap. 39.99 (*0-471-31972-4*) Wiley.

Programming with GNU Software: Tools from Cygnus Support. Mike Loukides & Andy Oram. LC 97-115579. 260p. 1996. pap. 39.95 (*1-56592-112-7*) Thomson Learn.

Programming with IBM PC BASIC. David Clark. 1991. 24.95 (*0-8306-6732-6*) McGraw-Hill Prof.

Programming with Java. 608p. (C). 1997. pap. 34.25 (*0-7600-5043-0*) Course Tech.

Programming with Java: Course Technology. 608p. (C). 1998. teacher ed. 49.95 (*0-7600-5067-8*) Course Tech.

Programming with JFC. Scott Weiner & Stephen Asbury. LC 98-14347. 576p. 1998. pap. 49.99 incl. cd-rom (*0-471-24731-6*) Wiley.

Programming with Latino Children's Materials: A How-to-Do-It Manual. Tim Wadham. LC 98-52056. (How-to-Do-It Manuals for Librarians Ser.: Vol. 89). 225p. 1999. pap. 39.95 (*1-55570-352-6*) Neal-Schuman.

Programming with Logo: Lab Pack. Yvonne Mullen & Susan Weinman. Ed. by Bonnie Schroeder. (Illus.). 97p. 1990. teacher ed. 19.95 (*1-56177-100-7*, TE394-6); teacher ed., student ed. 149.95 incl. disk (*1-56177-099-X*, L394-6); disk 15.95 (*1-56177-098-1*, D394-6) CES Compu-Tech.

Programming with Microsoft BASIC. 2nd ed. Wayne M. Zage. (C). 1990. text 15.25 (*0-07-072879-8*) McGraw.

Programming with Microsoft RPC. John Shirley. 1995. pap. 24.95 (*1-56592-070-8*) Thomson Learn.

Programming with Microsoft Visual Basic 5.0 for Windows. Diane Zak. 800p. (C). 1997. pap. 36.50 (*0-7600-5016-3*) Course Tech.

Programming with Microsoft Visual Basic 5.0 for Windows. Diane Zak. 800p. (C). 1997. pap., teacher ed. 49.95 (*0-7600-5017-1*) Course Tech.

***Programming with Microsoft Visual Basic 7.0.** Zak. (C). 2000. text 37.25 (*0-619-01662-0*) Course Tech.

Programming with Motif. Keith D. Gregory. LC 92-17576. (Illus.). 672p. 1993. 58.95 (*0-387-97877-1*) Spr-Verlag.

Programming with MS DOS & PC DOS Interrupts in Assembly Language. Thomas Hogan & Roger Chapman. 1986. pap. 23.95 (*0-89303-788-5*) P-H.

Programming with MS DOS & PC DOS Interrupts in Assembly Language. Thomas Hogan & Roger Chapman. write for info. (*0-318-59642-3*) S&S Trade.

***Programming with Oracle SQL.** Rajshekhar Sunderraman. LC 98-28914. 336p. (C). 1998. pap. 32.46 (*0-201-35753-4*) Addison-Wesley.

Programming with OSF-MOTIF. Kee Hinckley & Brian R. Holt. (Illus.). 512p. (C). 1999. pap. text. write for info. (*0-201-50959-8*) Addison-Wesley.

Programming with Posix Threads. David Butenhof. LC 97-6635. 400p. (C). 1997. pap. text 39.95 (*0-201-63392-2*) Addison-Wesley.

Programming with Purpose: Developing a Process for Programming. Kim Anderson & Troy Murphy. LC 97-34170. (Student Impact Ser.). (Illus.). 176p. (Orig.). 1997. pap. 14.99 (*0-310-20129-2*) Zondervan.

***Programming with Python.** Tim Altom. 1999. pap. 34.99 (*0-7615-2334-0*) Prima Pub.

Programming with QBasic. (Prisma Be an Expert! Ser.). (Illus.). 192p. (Orig.). (J). 1995. pap. 12.95 (*1-85365-346-2*, Pub. by Spectrum) Seven Hills Bk.

Programming with Qt: Write Portable GUI Applications on UNIX & WIN32. Matthias K. Dalheimer. (Illus.). 361p. 1999. pap. 32.95 (*1-56592-588-2*) OReilly & Assocs.

Programming with R: BASE for DOS. Cary N. Prague et al. (Orig.). 1991. 24.95 (*0-8306-6676-1*); 24.95 (*0-8306-9575-3*) McGraw-Hill Prof.

Programming with R: Base 5000. James E. Hammitt & Cary N. Prague. 1991. 24.95 (*0-8306-6628-1*) McGraw-Hill Prof.

Programming with R: Base 5000. Cary N. Prague & James E. Hammitt. (Illus.). 304p. 1986. 28.95 (*0-8306-0366-2*, 2666) McGraw-Hill Prof.

Programming with SeeLogo: Lab Pack. Dan Novak & Paula Weinberger. Ed. by Catherine Doheny & Bonnie Schroeder. (Illus.). teacher ed., student ed. 149.95 incl. disk (*1-56177-051-5*, L194-6) CES Compu-Tech.

Programming with Sets: An Introduction to SETL. Ed. by Jacob T. Schwartz et al. (Texts & Monographs in Computer Science). (Illus.). 465p. 1986. 98.95 (*0-387-96399-5*) Spr-Verlag.

Programming with Specifications: An Introduction to ANNA: A Language for Specifying Ada Programs. David C. Luckham. (Texts & Monographs in Computer Science). (Illus.). 440p. 1990. text 55.00 (*0-387-97254-4*) Spr-Verlag.

Programming with Structured Flowcharts. Krishna K. Agarwal. 142p. 1984. pap. text 13.50 (*0-89433-226-0*) Petrocelli.

Programming with the Java Media Framework. Sean Sullivan et al. Tr. by Deanna Brown. LC 97-52389. 384p. 1998. pap., pap. text 39.99 incl. cd-rom (*0-471-25169-0*) Wiley.

Programming with Turbo C. S. Scott Zimmerman & Beverly B. Zimmerman. (C). 1989. pap. 27.66 (*0-673-38092-0*, Scott Frsmn) Addison-Wesley Educ.

Programming with Turbo Vision. Blake Watson. LC 94-12690. 600p. 1994. pap. 39.95 incl. disk (*1-55851-399-X*, M&T Bks) IDG Bks.

Programming with Turing: With Object Oriented Turing for Windows. Peter Grogono. LC 95-10802. (Illus.). 390p. 1995. 44.95 (*0-387-94517-2*) Spr-Verlag.

Programming with UNIX Threads. Charles J. Northrup. LC 95-35799. 416p. 1996. pap. 44.99 (*0-471-13751-0*) Wiley.

***Programming with VisiBroken.** Erik Bleifield et al. LC 97-37943. 464p. 1998. pap. 49.99 incl. cd-rom, audio compact disk (*0-471-23901-1*) Wiley.

***Programming with VisiBroker.** 2nd ed. Hoffmann. 560p. 2000. pap. text 49.99 (*0-471-37682-5*) Wiley.

Programming with Visual C++ Richard Leinecker. 448p. (C). 1999. mass mkt., teacher ed. 49.95 (*0-7600-5019-8*) Course Tech.

Programming with Visual C++ 10th ed. Richard Leinecker. 656p. (C). 1998. pap. 51.95 (*0-7600-5018-X*) Course Tech.

Programming with VisualAge for Java Version 2, 2nd Edtion. 2nd ed. John Akerley. 500p. 1999. pap. text 49.99 (*0-13-021298-9*) P-H.

***Programming W/MS Vb 6.0.** Zak. (Programming Ser.). (C). 1998. pap. 49.95 (*0-7600-1071-4*) Course Tech.

***Programming Workflow Applications with Domino.** Daniel Giblin & Richard Lam. (Illus.). 384p. 2000. pap. 44.95 incl. cd-rom (*1-929629-06-0*) C M P Books.

***Programming wth Microsoft Visual C++ 7.0.** Gosselin. (Programming Language Ser.). (C). 2000. text 37.25 (*0-619-01657-4*) Course Tech.

***Programming wth Perl on Windows.** Harry S. Singh & Edward Syrett. 650p. 2000. pap. 49.99 (*0-13-022000-0*) P-H.

Programming Your Adam Computer with Ready-to-Run Programs. Susan E. Sutphin. 176p. 1985. pap. 21.95 (*0-13-729377-1*) P-H.

Programming Your Texas Instruments Computer in TI BASIC. F. D'Ignazio. 256p. 1984. pap. 9.95 (*0-07-016897-0*, BYTE Bks) McGraw.

Programming 80486. Penn Brumm et al. 1991. 29.95 incl. disk (*0-8306-3543-2*) McGraw-Hill Prof.

PROGRAMMING 8086/8088. Michael Thorne. 1987. pap. text 25.95 (*0-8053-5004-7*) Benjamin-Cummings.

Programowanie Maszyn CNC: Tokarki, Frezarici Pionowe, Frezarki Moryzontalne. unabridged ed. Ed. by Zbigniew Kruczalak. (POL., Illus.). 200p. 1997. pap. text 9.95 (*0-9659518-0-4*) D&Z Hse Bks.

Programs & Celebrations. Judy G. Smith. 124p. (Orig.). 1995. pap. 10.95 (*1-877871-83-4*, 5196) Ed Ministries.

Programs & Centers in Comparative & International Education: An International Inventory. Compiled by Philip G. Altbach & Eng Thye Jason Tan. LC 94-13234. (Special Studies in Comparative Education: No. 34). 1994. 15.00 (*0-937033-57-X*) Grad Schl of Educ.

Programs & Data Structures in C: Based on ANSI C & C Plus Plus. 2nd ed. Leendert Ammeraal. 284p. 1992. pap. 64.00 (*0-471-93123-3*) Wiley.

Programs & Machines: An Introduction to the Theory of Computation. Richard Bird. LC 75-38893. (Wiley Series in Computing). 224p. reprint ed. pap. 69.50 (*0-7837-3213-9*, 204323100007) Bks Demand.

Programs & Manifestos on 20th-Century Architecture. Ed. by Ulrich Conrads. 1975. pap. text 14.50 (*0-262-53030-9*) MIT Pr.

Programs & Practices: Writing Across the Secondary School Curriculum. Ed. by Pamela B. Farrell-Childers et al. LC 93-5996. 280p. (J). 1994. pap. text 25.00 (*0-86709-334-X*, 0334, Pub. by Boynton Cook Pubs) Heinemann.

Programs & Subroutines for the IBM. John C. Craig & Jeff Bretz. 1991. 19.95 (*0-8306-6619-2*) McGraw-Hill Prof.

Programs at Higher Education Institutions for Disadvantaged Precollege Students. Bradford Chaney et al. (Illus.). 97p. (C). 1998. reprint ed. pap. text 20.00 (*0-7881-3929-0*) DIANE Pub.

Programs at Higher Education Institutions for Disadvantaged Students. 1996. lib. bdg. 250.75 (*0-8490-6056-7*) Gordon Pr.

Programs for Advent & Christmas, Vol. 3. Ed. by Elizabeth W. Gale. 64p. (Orig.). 1989. pap. 11.00 (*0-8170-1149-8*) Judson.

Programs for At-Risk Students: A Guide to Evaluation. Rita G. O'Sullivan & Cheryl V. Tennant. (Essential Tools for Educators Ser.). 96p. 1993. pap. 24.95 (*0-8039-6043-3*) Corwin Pr.

Programs for At-Risk Youth: A Review of the American, Canadian & British Literature since 1984. Ed. by Margaret Batten & Jean Russell. 1995. pap. 75.00 (*0-86431-179-6*, Pub. by Aust Council Educ Res) St Mut.

Programs for Digital Signal Processing. Ed. by Digital Signal Processing Committee. LC 79-89028. 592p. 1979. audio 85.00 (*0-686-96748-8*) Inst Electrical.

Programs for Ladies Vol. 2: Themes, Dramas, Games, Puzzles, Activities for Ladies' Meetings, Large or Small Banquets, Retreats, Conventions, Showers, Special Services. Barbara Westberg. LC 89-49113. (Illus.). 208p. (Orig.). 1993. pap. 9.99 (*1-56722-010-X*) Word Aflame.

Programs for Lent & Easter, Vol. 3. Ed. by Elizabeth G. Wright. 64p. 1990. pap. 11.00 (*0-8170-1164-1*) Judson.

Programs for Older Americans: Evaluations by Academic Gerontologists. Ed. by Gordon F. Streib. LC 81-11645. (Center for Gerontological Studies & Programs Ser.: Vol. 1). (Illus.). xi, 268p. (Orig.). 1981. pap. 19.95 (*0-8130-0705-4*) U Press Fla.

Programs for People in Crisis: A Guide for Educators, Administrators, & Clinical Trainers. Lee A. Hoff. LC 87-12317. 213p. (C). 1987. text 18.45 (*0-89801-012-8*) NE Univ Pub.

Programs for Productivity & Quality of Work Life. Richard A. Guzzo. (Studies in Productivity: No. 32). 38p. 1984. pap. 55.00 (*0-08-030964-X*) Work in Amer.

Programs for Special Days. Ed. & Compiled by Pat Fittro. 64p. 1999. 5.99 (*0-7847-0914-9*, 08702) Standard Pub.

Programs for Spouses of Foreign Students. Rosalie Berg et al. 25p. 1986. 12.00 (*0-912207-28-0*) NAFSA Washington.

Programs for the TI-81 & TI-82 Calculators. Stuart W. Ball. (Illus.). 1995. pap. text 14.95 (*0-914534-12-2*) Stokes.

Programs in Aid of the Poor. rev. ed. Sar A. Levitan. LC 84-28890. 176p. 1990. pap. text 12.95 (*0-8018-4040-6*) Johns Hopkins.

Programs in Aid of the Poor. 5th ed. Sar A. Levitan. LC 84-28890. 165p. reprint ed. pap. 51.20 (*0-8357-6904-6*, 203796200009) Bks Demand.

Programs in Aid of the Poor. 6th rev. ed. Sar A. Levitan. LC 84-28890. 176p. 1990. text 29.50 (*0-8018-4039-2*) Johns Hopkins.

Programs in Aid of the Poor. 7th ed. Sar A. Levitan. Ed. by Garth L. Mangum & Stephen L. Mangum. LC 97-15768. 264p. 1998. pap. text 13.95 (*0-8018-5713-9*) Johns Hopkins.

Programs in Aid of the Poor. 7th ed. Sar A. Levitan. Ed. by Garth L. Mangum & Stephen L. Mangum. LC 97-15768. 264p. 1999. text 35.00 (*0-8018-5688-4*) Johns Hopkins.

P

An Asterisk (*) at the beginning of an entry indicates that the title is appearing for the first time.

Programs in Aid of the Poor for the 1980's. 4th ed. Sar A. Levitan. LC 80-8093. (Policy Studies in Employment & Welfare: No. 1). 169p. reprint ed. pap. 52.40 (*0-608-15001-0*, 202588500046) Bks Demand.

Programs of Medieval Illumination. Robert G. Calkins. LC 84-51249. (Franklin D. Murphy Lectures: No. 5). (Illus.). 158p. 1984. 12.00 (*0-913689-12-2*) Spencer Muse Art.

Programs That Work. Ed. by Linda Shirato. (Library Orientation Ser.: No. 28). 1997. pap. 40.00 (*0-87650-348-2*) Pierian.

Programs That Work: Models & Methods for Writing Across the Curriculum. Ed. by Toby Fulwiler & Art Young. LC 89-15430. 327p. (Orig.). (C). (gr. 13). 1989. pap. text 29.50 (*0-86709-248-3*, 0248, Pub. by Boynton Cook Pubs) Heinemann.

Programs to Examine Phonetic & Phonologic Evaluation Records, 1990. Lawrence D. Shriberg. 1990. ring bd. 495.00 incl. disk (*1-56321-047-9*) LEA S&AM.

Programs to Strengthen Families: A Resource Guide. Ed. by Kathryn Goetz. 200p. 1992. pap. 30.00 (*1-885429-04-5*) Family Resource.

Progres des Nations. 1995. 6.95 (*92-806-3172-1*) U N I C E.

Progres des Nations 94. (FRE.). 1994. 6.95 (*92-806-3104-7*) U N I C E.

Progres du Traitement des Images (Progress in Picture Processing) Ed. by H. Maitre & J. Zinn-Justin. LC 96-17001. 376p. 1996. 207.00 (*0-444-82407-3*) Elsevier.

Progres et Pauvrete-Progress & Poverty. (FRE.). 1991. pap. 3.00 (*0-911312-03-X*) Schalkenbach.

Progres, Pauvrete et Exclusion: Histoire Economique de l'Amerique Latine au 20e Siecle. Rosemary Thorp. (SPA.). 400p. 1998. pap. text 24.95 (*1-886938-49-0*) IADB.

Progresa Con las Matematicas. N. Alvarado & Cicely Banks. (SPA., Illus.). 448p. (J). (gr. 8-9). 1994. text, student ed. 48.00 (*0-9624192-0-6*) N Bacchus.

Progresa con las Matematicas. Cicely Banks & Noemi Alvarado. 80p. 1999. pap. text, teacher ed. 12.00 (*0-9624192-4-9*) N Bacchus.

Progresa con las Matematicas. Arthur Gordon et al. (SPA.). 80p. (J). (gr. 7-8). 1999. pap., wbk. ed. 12.00 (*0-9624192-2-2*) N Bacchus.

Progresion de Aquitania. Robert Ludlum. 1998. pap. 9.95 (*84-08-00023-3*) Planeta.

***Progresiones de Acordes.** Orig. Title: Chord Progressions. (SPA.). 48p. 1998. pap. 5.95 (*0-7935-9013-2*) H Leonard.

Progreso de las Naciones. 1995. 6.95 (*92-806-3171-3*) U N I C E.

Progreso Del Peregrino: Pilgrims Progress. John Bunyan & L. P. Leavell. Tr. by Hiram F. Duffer, Jr. from ENG. (SPA.). 1968. reprint ed. pap. 7.50 (*0-311-37006-3*) Casa Bautista.

Progreso Del Peregrino Ilustrado. John Bunyan. Orig. Title: Pilgrim's Progress Illustrated. (SPA., Illus.). 256p. 1981. mass mkt. 5.99 (*0-8254-1096-7*, Edit Portavoz) Kregel.

Progreso Economico y Social en America Latina: Informe, 1994. Inter-American Development Bank Staff. (SPA.). 290p. 1994. pap. text 24.95 (*0-940602-89-X*) IADB.

Progreso Economico y Social en America Latina: Informe, 1995. Inter-American Development Bank Staff. LC 74-648164. 328p. (C). 1995. pap. text 24.95 (*1-886938-00-8*) IADB.

Progreso Economico y Social en America Latina: Informe, 1996. Inter-American Development Bank Staff. (SPA.). 430p. 1996. pap. text 24.95 (*1-886938-11-3*) IADB.

Progreso Economico y Social en America Latina, Informe, 1997: America Latina Tras una Decada de Reformas. Inter-American Development Bank Staff. (SPA.). 317p. 1997. pap. text 24.95 (*1-886938-26-1*) IADB.

Progreso, Pobreza y Exclusion: Una Historia Economica de America Latina en el Siglo XX. Rosemary Thorp. (SPA.). 404p. 1998. pap. text 24.95 (*1-886938-39-3*) IADB.

Progreso y Miseria-Progress & Poverty. (SPA.). 1996. pap. 14.00 (*0-911312-07-2*) Schalkenbach.

Progress. Doug Lucie. 1985. pap. 5.25 (*0-8222-0920-9*) Dramatists Play.

Progress. Barrett Watten. LC 85-61016. (Roof Bks.). 120p. (Orig.). 1985. pap. text 7.50 (*0-937804-16-9*) Segue NYC.

Progress: Critical Thinking about Historical Change. Raymond D. Gastil. LC 92-35340. 224p. 1993. 52.95 (*0-275-94283-X*, C4283, Praeger Pubs) Greenwood.

Progress: Fact or Illusion? Ed. by Leo Marx & Bruce Mazlish. LC 95-50970. 248p. (C). 1996. text 47.50 (*0-472-10676-7*, 10676) U of Mich Pr.

Progress: Fact or Illusion? Ed. by Leo Marx & Bruce Mazlish. 248p. (C). 1998. pap. text 24.95 (*0-472-08509-3*, 08509) U of Mich Pr.

Progress - Hepatic Encephalopath & Metabolic Nitrogen, 7th International. Bengt Jeppsson & Bengts. 1991. 89.95 (*0-685-48460-2*, 180, CRC Reprint) Franklin.

Progress Achieved in the Development of Informatics Capabilities in Arab Countries. 100p. 1990. 20.00 (*92-1-128121-0*, 90.II.L.11) UN.

Progress after Referendum. Ken Kalonde. LC 97-950425. (Poetry Ser.). 90p. 1996. write for info. (*99908-42-00-0*) Sunrise Prods.

Progress after Statehood: A Book of Readings. Ed. by Pamela J. Bennett. 570p. 1974. 9.95 (*1-885323-26-3*); pap. 4.95 (*1-885323-27-1*) IN Hist Bureau.

Progress Against the Tide. E. Dorian Gadsden. 1989. 16.95 (*0-533-08385-0*) Vantage.

Progress along the Way: Life, Service & Realization. Hua-Ching Ni. (Self Development Ser.). (Orig.). 1994. pap. 4.00 (*0-937064-79-3*) SevenStar Comm.

Progress Analytical. Borchard. 1996. 73.00 (*3-7985-0910-7*) Spr-Verlag.

***Progress & a Mexican American Community's Struggle for Existence: Phoenix's Gold Gate Barrio, Ser. 21.** Pete R. Dimas. LC 97-48961. (American University Studies XXI: Vol. 10). XVIII, 175p. (C). 1999. pap. text 30.00 (*0-8204-2353-X*) P Lang Pubng.

Progress & Hard Feelings. Doug Lucie. 86p. (Orig.). (C). 1988. pap. 8.95 (*0-413-57760-0*, A0229) Heinemann.

Progress & History: Essays. Ed. by Francis S. Marvin. LC 78-84326. (Essay Index Reprint Ser.). 1977. 20.95 (*0-8369-1096-6*) Ayer.

Progress & Human Value. Ed. by Peter M. Schuller. (Orig.). 1979. 15.65 (*0-89894-007-9*) Advocate Pub Group.

Progress & Intelligence of Americans: Collateral Proof of Slavery, from the First to the Eleventh Chapter of Genesis, As Founded on Organic Law. M. T. Wheat. LC 77-83882. (Black Heritage Library Collection). 1977. 30.95 (*0-8369-8684-9*) Ayer.

Progress & Its Problems: Towards a Theory of Scientific Growth. Larry Laudan. LC 76-24586. 1977. pap. 17.95 (*0-520-03721-9*, Pub. by U CA Pr) Cal Prin Full Svc.

Progress & Opportunities in Southern Hemisphere Optical Astronomy: CTIO Twenty-Fifth Anniversary Symposium. Ed. by Victor M. Blanco & Mark M. Phillips. (Astronomical Society of the Pacific Conference Ser.: Vol. 1). (Illus.). 438p. 1988. 34.00 (*0-937707-18-X*) Astron Soc Pacific.

Progress & Performance. Edwin T. Cornelius, Jr. (New Technology English Ser.: Vol. 3). (Illus.). 125p. 1984. text 8.95 (*0-89209-164-9*); pap. text 6.25 (*0-89209-402-8*); audio 17.00 (*0-89209-165-7*) Pace Grp Intl.

Progress & Peril: Black Children in America. Black Community Crusade for Children Staff. 156p. (Orig.). 1993. pap. 6.00 (*0-938008-99-4*) Childrens Defense.

Progress & Perspectives in the Treatment of Lung Cancer. Ed. by P. Van Houtte & P. Rocmans. LC 98-35108. (Illus.). 200p. 1999. 199.00 (*3-540-62548-8*) Spr-Verlag.

Progress & Pessimism: Religion, Politics & History in Late Nineteenth Century Britain. Jeffrey P. Von Arx. (Historical Studies: No. 104). 256p. 1985. 25.00 (*0-674-71375-3*) HUP.

Progress & Poetry of the Movies: A Second Book of Film Criticism, No. 2. Vachel Lindsay. Ed. & Comment by Myron Lounsbury. LC 94-16749. 490p. 1995. 92.00 (*0-8108-2917-7*) Scarecrow.

Progress & Poverty. (HEB.). 1991. 4.00 (*0-911312-05-6*); pap. 3.00 (*0-911312-57-9*) Schalkenbach.

Progress & Poverty. abr. ed. Henry George. LC 85-43339. 274p. 1998. pap. 10.00 (*0-911312-10-2*) Schalkenbach.

Progress & Poverty. Henry George. (Notable American Authors Ser.). 1992. reprint ed. lib. bdg. 75.00 (*0-7812-2914-6*) Rprt Serv.

Progress & Poverty. unabridged ed. Henry George. LC 79-12191. 599p. 1996. pap. 15.00 (*0-911312-58-7*) Schalkenbach.

Progress & Poverty: An Economic & Social History of Britain 1700-1850. Martin Daunton. (Illus.). 636p. 1995. text 85.00 (*0-19-822282-3*); pap. text 24.00 (*0-19-822281-5*) OUP.

Progress & Poverty: An Inquiry into the Cause of Industrial Depressions & of Increase of Want with Increase of Wealth ... the Remedy. Henry George. LC 79-12191. 1979. 10.00 (*0-914016-60-1*) Phoenix Pub.

Progress & Poverty: Centenary Edition. Henry George. 599p. 1992. 25.00 (*0-911312-79-X*) Schalkenbach.

Progress & Power. Carl L. Becker. LC 83-45701. reprint ed. 32.50 (*0-404-20023-0*) AMS Pr.

Progress & Pragmatism: James, Dewey, Beard & the American Idea of Progress, 9. David W. Marcell. LC 72-818. (Contributions in American Studies: No. 9). 402p. 1974. 79.50 (*0-8371-6387-0*, MPR/, Greenwood Pr) Greenwood.

Progress & Problems in Atmospheric Chemistry. Ed. by J. R. Barker. (Advanced Series in Physical Chemistry: Vol. 3). 1000p. 1995. pap. 95.00 (*981-02-2113-4*) World Scientific Pub.

Progress & Problems in Information Retrieval. David Ellis. 220p. 1997. 80.00 (*1-85604-123-9*, Pub. by Library Association) Bernan Associates.

Progress & Problems in Lichenology in the Eighties: Proceedings of an International Symposium Held at the University of Munster, 16-21.3.1986. Ed. by Elisabeth Peveling et al. (Bibliotheca Lichenologica: Vol. 25). (GER., Illus.). xv, 497p. 1987. pap. 89.00 (*3-443-58004-1*, Pub. by Gebruder Borntraeger) Balogh.

Progress & Problems in Lichenology in the Nineties: Proceedings of the Third Symposium of the International Association for Lichenology (IAL3) Held at the University of Salzburg, Salzburg, Austria on 1-7, September 1996. Roman Tuerk & Roberto Zorer. (Bibliotheca Lichenologica Ser.: Vol. 68). (GER., Illus.). 252p. 1997. pap. 98.00 (*3-443-58047-5*, Pub. by Gebruder Borntraeger) Balogh.

Progress & Problems in Medical & Dental Education: Federal Support Versus Federal Control. Carnegie Council on Policy Studies in Higher Educa. LC 76-11964. (Carnegie Council Ser.). 192p. reprint ed. pap. 59.60 (*0-608-12272-6*, 202378000034) Bks Demand.

Progress & Problems in Medieval England: Essays in Honour of Edward Miller. Ed. by Richard Britnell & John Hatcher. (Illus.). 344p. (C). 1996. text 64.95 (*0-521-55036-X*) Cambridge U Pr.

Progress & Problems of Genetic Improvement of Tropical Forest Trees, 2 Vols. D. G. Nikles et al. 1978. 165.00 (*0-85074-020-7*) St Mut.

Progress & Prospects in Evolutionary Biology: The Drosophila Model. Jeffrey R. Powell. LC 96-12478. (Illus.). 576p. 1997. text 45.00 (*0-19-507691-5*) OUP.

Progress & Prospects of Pottery Industry in India: A Case Study of U. P. K. C. Gupta. 250p. (C). 1988. 35.00 (*81-7099-051-3*, Pub. by Mittal Pubs Dist) S Asia.

Progress & Prosperity. Earl Beach. LC 99-10. 202p. 1999. 13.00 (*1-55212-242-5*) Trafford Pub.

Progress & Prosperity. Richard M. Wagner & Roy J. Wright. (Cincinnati Streetcars Ser.: No. 7). 100p. 1976. pap. 13.95 (*0-914196-27-8*) JAS Pubng.

Progress & Rationality in Science. Ed. by Robert S. Cohen et al. (Boston Studies in the Philosophy of Science: No. 58). 426p. 1978. lib. bdg. 117.50 (*90-277-0921-1*) Kluwer Academic.

Progress & Religion. Christopher Dawson. 287p. 1991. pap. 12.95 (*0-89385-038-1*) Sugden.

Progress & Religion, an Historical Enquiry. Christopher H. Dawson. LC 79-104266. 254p. 1970. reprint ed. lib. bdg. 38.50 (*0-8371-3917-1*, DAPR, Greenwood Pr) Greenwood.

Progress & Survival: An Essay on the Future of Mankind. Emile Benoit. Ed. by Jack B. Gohn. LC 80-14423. 130p. 1980. 47.95 (*0-275-90452-0*, C0452, Praeger Pubs) Greenwood.

Progress & the Quest for Meaning: A Philosophical & Historical Inquiry. John A. Bernstein. LC 92-52717. 224p. 1993. 36.50 (*0-8386-3503-2*) Fairleigh Dickinson.

Progress & Tradition. Anscar J. Chupungco. (Worship Ser.). 312p. 1995. pap. text 14.95 (*1-56929-051-2*, Pastoral Press) OR Catholic.

Progress & Trends in Rheology, Vol. II. Ed. by H. Giesekus & M. F. Hibberd. (Rheologica Acta Ser.: Vol. 27). 456p. 1988. 217.00 (*0-387-91329-7*) Spr-Verlag.

Progress & Trends in Rheology V No. V: Proceedings of the Fifth European Rheology Conference. Ed. by I. Emri & R. Cvelbar. 620p. 1998. 112.00 (*3-7985-1128-4*) Spr-Verlag.

Progress & Welfare in Southeast Asia: A Comparison of Colonial Policy & Practice. John S. Furnivall. LC 75-30055. (Institute of Pacific Relations Ser.). reprint ed. 32.50 (*0-404-59525-1*) AMS Pr.

Progress Chemistry. Laszlo Zechmeister. 1988. 219.95 (*0-387-82074-4*) Spr-Verlag.

Progress Developer's Guide. 1995. 49.99 incl. disk (*0-672-30749-9*) Macmillan USA.

Progress for Food or Food for Progress? The Political Economy of Agricultural Growth & Development. Folke Dovring. 330p. 1988. 65.00 (*0-275-92904-3*, C2904, Praeger Pubs) Greenwood.

Progress, Hunger & Envy: Commercial Agriculture, Marketing & Social Transformation in the Venezuelan Andes. Monica L. De Montoya. (Stockholm Studies in Social Anthropology: No. 36). (Illus.). 270p. (Orig.). 1996. pap. 67.50 (*91-7153-522-5*) Coronet Bks.

Progress in Acarology Vols. I & II: Proceedings of the International Congress on Acarology, Bongalore, 1986, 2 vols., Set. I.C.A. Staff. (C). 1988. 84.00 (*81-204-0348-7*, Pub. by Oxford IBH) S Asia.

Progress in Adjusting Differences of Amount of Educational Opportunity Offered Under the County Unit Systems of Maryland & Utah. Leonard J. Nuttall. LC 72-177122. (Columbia University. Teachers College. Contributions to Education Ser.: No. 43). reprint ed. 37.50 (*0-404-55431-8*) AMS Pr.

Progress in Aerospace Science, 16 vols., Vol. 4. Kucheman. 1976. pap. 29.00 (*0-08-019609-8*, Pergamon Pr) Elsevier.

Progress in Aerospace Science, Vol. 10. D. Kuchemann. 1970. 165.00 (*0-08-013117-4*, Pergamon Pr) Elsevier.

Progress in Aerospace Science, Vol. 12. D. Kuchemann. 1972. 165.00 (*0-08-016656-3*, Pergamon Pr) Elsevier.

Progress in Aerospace Science, Vol. 13. D. Kuchemann. 1972. 165.00 (*0-08-017012-9*, Pergamon Pr) Elsevier.

Progress in Aerospace Science, Vol. 14. D. Kuchemann. 1973. 165.00 (*0-08-017138-9*, Pergamon Pr) Elsevier.

Progress in Aerospace Science, Vol. 15. D. Kuchemann. 1974. 165.00 (*0-08-017838-3*) Elsevier.

Progress in Aerospace Sciences, Vol. 18, No. 1. Ed. by J. A. Bagley & P. J. Finley. LC 74-618347. 1977. pap. 35.00 (*0-08-022133-5*, Pergamon Pr) Elsevier.

Progress in Aerospace Sciences, Vol. 19. Ed. by P. J. Finley. (Illus.). 320p. 1982. 145.00 (*0-08-029097-3*, A140, A999, Pergamon Pr) Elsevier.

Progress in Aerospace Sciences, Vol. 20. Ed. by A. D. Young. (Illus.). 332p. 1985. 145.00 (*0-08-032756-7*, Pub. by PPL) Elsevier.

Progress in Aerospace Sciences, Vol. 21. Ed. by A. D. Young. (Illus.). 350p. 1986. 132.00 (*0-08-033202-1*, Pub. by PPL) Elsevier.

Progress in Aerospace Sciences (Incorporating Progress in Astronautical Sciences), Vols. 7-8, 10-16. Incl. Vol. 8. LC 74-618347. pap. LC 74-618347. pap. write for info. (*0-318-55189-6*, Pub. by Pergamon Repr) Franklin.

Progress in Agricultural Geography. Ed. by Michael Pacione. (Progress in Geography Ser.). 288p. 1986. 55.00 (*0-7099-2095-4*, Pub. by C Helm) Routldge.

Progress in Agricultural Physics & Engineering. Ed. by John Matthews. (Illus.). 352p. 1991. text 130.00 (*0-85198-705-2*) OUP.

Progress in AIDS Pathology. Heidrum Rotterdam. 1989. 75.00 (*0-938607-21-9*) Field & Wood Inc Medical.

Progress in AIDS Pathology, Vol. 2. Heidrum Rotterdam. 1990. 109.00 (*0-938607-35-9*) Field & Wood Inc Medical.

Progress in Alcohol Research Vol. 1: Alcohol Nutrition & the Nervous System. Ed. by S. H. Parvez et al. 340p. 1985. lib. bdg. 135.00 (*90-6764-050-6*, Pub. by VSP) Coronet Bks.

Progress in Alcohol Research Vol. 2: Alcohol & Behaviour: Basic & Clinical Aspects. Ed. by H. Parvez et al. 285p. 1990. 160.00 (*90-6764-124-3*, Pub. by VSP) Coronet Bks.

Progress in Algebraic Combinatorics. Ed. by E. Bannai & A. Munemasa. LC 96-178157. (Advanced Studies in Pure Mathematics: No. 24). 453p. 1996. 88.00 (*4-314-10119-9*, Pub. by Kinokuniya) Am Math.

Progress in Allergy see Idiotypes in Biology & Medicine

Progress in Allergy, 26. Ed. by P. Kallos et al. (Illus.). 1979. 86.25 (*3-8055-2934-1*) S Karger.

Progress in Allergy, 27. Ed. by P. Kallos et al. (Illus.). 1979. 100.00 (*3-8055-3053-6*) S Karger.

Progress in Allergy, Vol. 13. Ed. by P. Kallos et al. (Illus.). 300p. 1969. 94.00 (*3-8055-0378-4*) S Karger.

Progress in Allergy, Vol. 14. Ed. by P. Kallos & B. H. Waksman. 1970. 74.00 (*3-8055-0379-2*) S Karger.

Progress in Allergy, Vol. 15. Ed. by P. Kallos & B. H. Waksman. 1971. 95.75 (*3-8055-1238-4*) S Karger.

Progress in Allergy, Vol. 16. Ed. by P. Kallos et al. (Illus.). 1972. 111.50 (*3-8055-1335-6*) S Karger.

Progress in Allergy, Vol. 17. Ed. by P. Kallos et al. (Illus.). 300p. 1973. 84.50 (*3-8055-1539-1*) S Karger.

Progress in Allergy, Vol. 18. Ed. by P. Kallos et al. 300p. 1974. 162.75 (*3-8055-1660-6*) S Karger.

Progress in Allergy, Vol. 19. Ed. by P. Kallos. (Illus.). 300p. 1975. 111.50 (*3-8055-2033-6*) S Karger.

Progress in Allergy, Vol. 20. Ed. by P. Kallos & B. H. Waksman. (Illus.). 1975. 111.50 (*3-8055-2189-8*) S Karger.

Progress in Allergy, Vol. 21. Ed. by P. Kallos et al. (Illus.). 1976. 133.25 (*3-8055-2342-4*) S Karger.

Progress in Allergy, Vol. 22. Ed. by P. Kallos et al. 1977. 82.75 (*3-8055-2419-6*) S Karger.

Progress in Allergy, Vol. 23. Ed. by P. Kallos et al. (Illus.). 1977. 128.75 (*3-8055-2665-2*) S Karger.

Progress in Allergy, Vol. 24. Ed. by P. Kallos et al. (Illus.). 1977. 129.75 (*3-8055-2781-0*) S Karger.

Progress in Allergy, Vol. 25. Ed. by P. Kallos et al. (Illus.). 1978. 86.25 (*3-8055-2849-3*) S Karger.

Progress in Allergy & Clinical Immunology: Kyoto, Vol. 2. Minoru Okuda. Ed. by Terumasa Miyamoto. LC 92-53196. (Illus.). 747p. 1992. text 50.00 (*0-88937-087-7*) Hogrefe & Huber Pubs.

***Progress in Allergy & Clinical Immunology: Volume S. Sydney.** Ed. by C. Katelaris. 2000. 58.00 (*0-88937-230-6*) Hogrefe & Huber Pubs.

Progress in Allergy & Clinical Immunology Vol. 1: Montreux. Ed. by W. J. Pichler et al. LC 89-1678. 580p. 1989. 48.00 (*0-920887-45-7*) Hogrefe & Huber Pubs.

Progress in Allergy & Clinical Immunology Vol. 3: Stockholm Proceedings of the 15th International Congress of Allergology & Clinical Immunology, & the 1994 Annual Meeting of the European Academy of Allergology & Clinical Immunology Stockholm, June 7-July 1, 1994. Ed. by S. G. Johansson. LC 94-74177. 352p. 1995. text 56.00 (*0-88937-122-9*) Hogrefe & Huber Pubs.

Progress in Allergy & Clinical Immunology Vol. 4: Cancun. A. Oehling. LC 97-73937. 436p. 1997. 58.00 (*0-88937-179-2*) Hogrefe & Huber Pubs.

Progress in Alzheimer's & Parkinson's Diseases: Proceedings of the 4th International Conference Held in Eilat, Israel, May 18-23, 1997. Ed. by Abraham Fisher et al. LC 98-26174. (Advances in Behavioral Biology Ser.: Vol. 49). (Illus.). 912p. 1998. 175.00 (*0-306-45903-5*, Kluwer Plenum) Kluwer Academic.

Progress in Alzheimer's Disease & Similar Conditions. Ed. by Leonard L. Heston. LC 96-26156. (American Psychopathological Association Ser.). (Illus.). 326p. 1997. text 49.50 (*0-88048-760-7*, 8760) Am Psychiatric.

***Progress in Ambulatory Assessment.** Ed. by Jochen Fahrenberg. 2001. 49.50 (*0-88937-225-X*) Hogrefe & Huber Pubs.

Progress in Analytical Atomic Spectroscopy, 2 vols., Set. C. L. Chakrabarti. (Illus.). 282p. 1981. 100.00 (*0-08-027126-X*, Pergamon Pr) Elsevier.

Progress in Analytical Atomic Spectroscopy, Vol. 1, Pt. 1. Ed. by C. L. Chakrabarti. 1978. 44.00 (*0-08-022924-7*, Pergamon Pr) Elsevier.

Progress in Analytical Atomic Spectroscopy, Vol. 3. Ed. by C. L. Chakrabarti. 368p. 1981. 92.00 (*0-08-029081-7*, E130, Pergamon Pr) Elsevier.

Progress in Analytical Atomic Spectroscopy, Vol. 4. Ed. by C. L. Chakrabarti. 440p. 1982. 125.00 (*0-08-029659-9*, Pergamon Pr) Elsevier.

Progress in Analytical Atomic Spectroscopy Vol. 5. Ed. by C. L. Chakrabarti. (Illus.). 470p. 1983. 125.00 (*0-08-030418-4*, Pergamon Pr) Elsevier.

Progress in Analytical Atomic Spectroscopy, Vol. 6. Ed. by C. L. Chakrabarti & R. E. Sturgeon. (Illus.). 444p. 1985. 145.00 (*0-08-032307-3*, Pergamon Pr) Elsevier.

Progress in Analytical Atomic Spectroscopy, Vol. 7. Ed. by C. L. Chakrabarti & R. E. Sturgeon. (Illus.). 426p. 1986. 132.00 (*0-08-034141-1*, Pub. by PPL) Elsevier.

Progress in Analytical Luminescence, STP 1009. Ed. by DeLyle Eastwood & L. J. Cline Love. LC 88-17615. (Special Technical Publication (STP) Ser.). (Illus.). 120p. 1988. pap. text 32.00 (*0-8031-1178-9*, STP1009) ASTM.

Progress in Analytical Ultracentrifugation. Ed. by W. Borchard et al. (Progress in Colloid & Polymer Science Ser.: Vol. 86). 200p. 1992. 69.95 (*0-387-91407-2*) Spr-Verlag.

Progress in Anatomy, Vol. 2. Ed. by Richard J. Harrison et al. 228p. reprint ed. pap. 70.70 (*0-608-09986-4*, 2031668) Bks Demand.

Progress in Anatomy, Vol. 3. Ed. by Richard J. Harrison et al. 273p. reprint ed. pap. 84.70 (*0-608-09987-2*) Bks Demand.

Progress in Animal Biometeorology, Vol 1, Pt. 1. Ed. by H. D. Johnson. 624p. 1976. 140.00 (*0-685-26764-4*) Taylor & Francis.

Progress in Animal Biometeorology, Vol 1, Pt. 2. Ed. by H. D. Johnson. 322p. 1976. 70.00 (*0-685-44681-6*) Taylor & Francis.

Progress in Animal Biometeorology: The Effects of Weather & Climate on Animals; Vol 1 Period 1963-1973, 2 pts. H. D. Johnson. Incl. Effect of Light, High Actitude, Noise, Electric, Magnetic & Electro-Magnetic Fields, Ionization, Gravity & Air

P

Pollutions on Animals. 322p. 1976. text 116.00 (*90-265-0235-4*); Pt. 1. Effects of Temperature on Animals: Including Effects of Humidity, Radiation & Wind. 624p. 1976. text 233.00 (*90-265-0196-X*); (Progress in Biometeorology Ser.). 1976. write for info. (*0-318-55899-8*) Swets.

Progress in Animal Hygiene. F. Kovacs & P. Rafai. 502p. (C). 1975. 75.00 (*963-05-0942-3*, Pub. by Akade Kiado) St Mut.

Progress in Animal Retroviruses. Ed. by D. Gaudry & W. Hennessen. (Developments in Biological Standardization Ser.: Vol. 72). (Illus.). x, 394p. 1990. pap. 61.00 (*3-8055-5271-8*) S Karger.

Progress in Anterior Eye Segment: Research & Practice. Ed. by Otto Hockwin & W. B. Rathbun. (Documenta Ophthalmologica Proceedings Ser.: No. 18). (Illus.). 1979. pap. text 239.50 (*90-6193-158-4*) Kluwer Academic.

Progress in Anti-Cancer Chemotherapy. Ed. by Gabriel N. Hortobagyi & David Khayat. LC 97-15125. 1997. 75.00 (*0-86542-564-7*) Blackwell Sci.

Progress in Anti-Cancer Chemotherapy, Vol. 2. Ed. by Gabriel N. Hortobagyi & David Khayat. (Illus.). 322p. 1998. 99.95 (*0-632-04408-X*) Blackwell Sci.

***Progress in Anti-Cancer Chemotherapy, Vol. 3.** Ed. by Gabriel N. Hortobagyi & David Khayat. 200p. 1999. 124.00 (*2-287-59666-6*, Pub. by Sp1 France Editions) Spr-Verlag.

***Progress in Anti-Cancer Chemotherapy, Vol. 4.** Ed. by Gabriel N. Hortobagyi & David Khayat. x, 269p. 2000. pap. 89.00 (*2-287-59692-5*, Pub. by Sp1 France Editions) Spr-Verlag.

Progress in Aphasiology. fac. ed. Ed. by F. Clifford Rose. LC 84-15979. (Advances in Neurology Ser.: No. 42). (Illus.). 382p. pap. 118.50 (*0-7837-7269-6*, 204703600005) Bks Demand.

Progress in Applied Mechanics: The Chien Wei-Zang Anniversary Volume. Ed. by Yeh Kai-Yuan. 1987. text 326.50 (*90-247-3249-2*) Kluwer Academic.

Progress in Applied Social Psychology, Vol. 1, 1981. Ed. by G. M. Stephenson & J. H. Davis. LC 83-641069. (Wiley Series on Progress in Applied Social Psychology). 402p. reprint ed. pap. 124.70 (*0-7837-3220-1*, 204323800001) Bks Demand.

Progress in Applied Social Psychology, Vol. 2, 1984. Ed. by G. M. Stephenson & J. H. Davis. LC 83-641069. (Wiley Series in Progress in Applied Social Psychology). 337p. reprint ed. pap. 104.50 (*0-7837-3221-X*, 204323800002) Bks Demand.

Progress in Approximation Theory: An International Perspective. Ed. by A. A. Gonchar et al. LC 92-24316. (Computational Mathematics Ser.: No. 19). 480p. 1992. 99.95 (*0-387-97901-8*) Spr-Verlag.

Progress in Artificial Intelligence: Iberamia 98 : Proceedings of the 6th Ibero-American Conference on AI, Lisbon, Portugal, October 5-9, 1998. Ibero-American Conference on Artificial Intelligence Staff & Helder Coelho. LC 98-41924. (Lecture Notes in Computer Science Ser.). xiii, 420p. 1998. pap. write for info. (*3-540-64992-1*) Spr-Verlag.

Progress in Artificial Intelligence: 6th Portuguese Conference, EPIA '93, Porto, Portugal, October 1993 Proceedings. Ed. by Miguel Filgueiras & Luis Damas. LC 93-34003. (Lecture Notes in Computer Science, Lecture Notes in Artificial Intelligence Ser.: Vol. 727). 1993. 54.00 (*0-387-57287-2*) Spr-Verlag.

Progress in Artificial Intelligence: 7th Portuguese Conference on Artificial Intelligence, EPIA '95, Funchal, Madeira Island, Portugal, October 3-6, 1995 - Proceedings. Nuno J. Mamede et al. (Lecture Notes in Computer Science Subseries: Lecture Notes in Artificial Intelligence: Vol. 990). xiv, 487p. 1995. pap. 81.00 (*3-540-60428-6*) Spr-Verlag.

Progress in Artificial Intelligence: 8th Portuguese Conference on Artificial Intelligence, EPIA '97, Coimbra, Portugal, October 6-9, 1997 : Proceedings. Ed. by Ernesto Costa et al. LC 97-40472. (Lecture Notes in Computer Science Ser.: Vol. 1323). xiv, 388p. 1997. pap. 67.00 (*3-540-63586-6*) Spr-Verlag.

***Progress in Artificial Intelligence: 9th Portuguese Conference on Artificial Intelligence, EPIA '99, Evora, Portugal, September 22-24, 1999, Proceedings.** Ed. by P. Barahona & J. J. Alferes. LC 99-49082. (Lecture Notes in Artificial Intelligence Ser.: Vol. 1695). xi, 385p. 1999. pap. 62.00 (*3-540-66548-X*) Spr-Verlag.

***Progress in Asian Social Psychology, Vol. 1.** Kwok Leung et al. Tr. by Yoshihisa Kashima. 1998. 55.00 (*0-471-24865-7*) Wiley.

Progress in Assessment of Morbidity Due to Schistosomiasis: Reviews of Recent Literature. K. Mott & M. Chen. (Document Published by WHO Parasitic Diseases Programme Ser.). 56p. 1989. pap. text 20.00 (*0-9510869-4-4*) World Health.

Progress in Atmospheric Physics. Ed. by R. G. Rodrigo et al. (C). 1988. text 162.50 (*90-277-2753-8*) Kluwer Academic.

Progress in Atomic Spectroscopy, 4 vols., Pt. C. Ed. by W. Hanle & Hans Kleinpoppen. LC 78-18230. (Physics of Atoms & Molecules Ser.). 626p. 1984. 140.00 (*0-306-41300-0*, Plenum Trade) Perseus Pubng.

Progress in Atomic Spectroscopy, 4 vols., Pt. D. Ed. by W. Hanle & Hans Kleinpoppen. LC 78-18230. (Physics of Atoms & Molecules Ser.). (Illus.). 538p. (C). 1987. text 179.00 (*0-306-42528-9*, Kluwer Plenum) Kluwer Academic.

Progress in Atomic Spectroscopy, 4 vols., Pt. A. Ed. by W. Hanle & Hans Kleinpoppen. LC 78-18230. (Physics of Atoms & Molecules Ser.). 756p. 1978. 135.00 (*0-306-31115-1*, Plenum Trade) Perseus Pubng.

Progress in Atomic Spectroscopy, 4 vols., Pt. B. Ed. by W. Hanle & Hans Kleinpoppen. LC 78-18230. (Physics of Atoms & Molecules Ser.). 820p. 1978. 125.00 (*0-306-31116-X*, Plenum Trade) Perseus Pubng.

Progress in Atrial Peptide Research. Ed. by Barry M. Brenner & John H. Laragh. LC 89-10468. (American Society of Hypertension Symposium Ser.: No. 3). (Illus.). 715p. 1989. reprint ed. pap. 200.00 (*0-608-00600-9*, 206118700007) Bks Demand.

Progress in Automatic Signature Verification. Plamondon. 180p. 1994. text 74.00 (*981-02-1852-4*) World Scientific Pub.

Progress in Behavior Modification, Vol. 3. Michel Hersen & Richard M. Eisler. 300p. 1995. pap. 66.95 (*0-534-26304-6*) Brooks-Cole.

Progress in Behavior Modification, Vol. 21. Ed. by Michel Hersen et al. LC 75-646720. 262p. reprint ed. pap. 81.30 (*0-7837-6596-7*, 204616100021) Bks Demand.

Progress in Behavior Modification, Vol. 22. Progress in Behavior Modification Staff. Ed. by Michel Hersen et al. LC 75-646720. (Illus.). 286p. reprint ed. pap. 88.70 (*0-608-09793-4*, 206996700022) Bks Demand.

Progress in Behavior Modification, Vol. 23. Ed. by Michel Hersen et al. 320p. (C). 1988. text 65.00 (*0-8039-3315-0*) Sage.

Progress in Behavior Modification, Vol. 23, 1988. Progress in Behavior Modification Staff. Ed. by Michel Hersen et al. LC 75-646720. (Illus.). 230p. reprint ed. pap. 71.30 (*0-608-09794-2*, 206996700023) Bks Demand.

Progress in Behavior Modification, Vol. 24. Ed. by Michael Hersen et al. 320p. (C). 1989. text 65.00 (*0-8039-3212-X*) Sage.

Progress in Behavior Modification, Vol. 24, 1989. Progress in Behavior Modification Staff. Ed. by Michel Hersen et al. LC 75-646720. (Illus.). 260p. reprint ed. pap. 80.60 (*0-608-09795-0*, 206996700024) Bks Demand.

Progress in Behavior Modification, Vol. 25. Ed. by Michel Hersen et al. (Illus.). 224p. (C). 1990. text 65.00 (*0-8039-3701-6*) Sage.

Progress in Behavior Modification, Vol. 25, 1990. Progress in Behavior Modification Staff. Ed. by Michel Hersen et al. LC 75-646720. (Illus.). 224p. reprint ed. pap. 69.50 (*0-608-09796-9*, 206996700025) Bks Demand.

Progress in Behavior Modification, Vol. 26. Ed. by Michael Hersen. 230p. (C). 1990. text 65.00 (*0-8039-3942-6*) Sage.

Progress in Behavior Modification, Vol. 26. Ed. by Michel Hersen et al. (Illus.). 320p. (C). 1990. 65.00 (*0-8039-3927-2*) Sage.

Progress in Behavior Modification, Vol. 26, 1990. Progress in Behavior Modification Staff. Ed. by Michel Hersen et al. LC 75-646720. (Illus.). 230p. reprint ed. pap. 71.30 (*0-608-09797-7*, 206996700026) Bks Demand.

Progress in Behavior Modification, Vol. 27. Michel Hersen et al. (Illus.). 248p. 1991. 65.00 (*0-8039-4196-X*) Sage.

Progress in Behavior Modification, Vol. 27, 1991. Progress in Behavior Modification Staff. Ed. by Michel Hersen et al. LC 75-646720. (Illus.). 168p. reprint ed. pap. 52.10 (*0-608-09798-5*, 206996700027) Bks Demand.

Progress in Behavior Modification, Vol. 28. Ed. by Michel Hersen et al. 250p. (C). 1991. text 34.95 (*0-9625233-5-6*) Sycamore Pub.

Progress in Behavior Modification, Vol. 29. Ed. by Michel Hersen et al. 250p. (C). 1993. text 34.95 (*0-9625233-6-4*) Sycamore Pub.

Progress in Behavior Modification, Vol. 29. Ed. by Michel Hersen et al. 155p. (C). 1994. 41.00 (*0-534-23838-6*) Thomson Learn.

Progress in Behavioral Social Work. Ed. by Bruce A. Thyer & Walter W. Hudson. LC 87-19819. (Journal of Social Service Research: Vol. 10, Nos. 2-4). 194p. 1988. text 39.95 (*0-86656-656-2*) Haworth Pr.

Progress in Behavioral Studies, Vol. I. Ed. by Aaron J. Brownstein et al. 144p. 1989. 29.95 (*0-89859-511-8*) L Erlbaum Assocs.

Progress in Biomedical Polymers. Ed. by Charles G. Gebelein & R. L. Dunn. LC 90-7298. (Illus.). 420p. 1990. 115.00 (*0-306-43523-3*, Plenum Trade) Perseus Pubng.

Progress in Biometeorology Vol. 12: Phenology in Seasonal Climates. Ed. by H. Lieth & M. D. Schwartz. LC 97-218588. (Illus.). 143p. (C). 1997. pap. 43.00 (*90-73348-79-X*, Pub. by Backhuys Pubs) Balogh.

Progress in Biophysics, Vol 19 1/2. Butler. (Progress in Biophysics & Molecular Biology Ser.). 1969. 98.00 (*0-08-006523-6*) Elsevier.

Progress in Biophysics & Molecular Biology. Butler. (Progress in Biophysics & Molecular Biology Ser.: 30). 1975. pap. 24.00 (*0-08-019972-0*, Pergamon Pr) Elsevier.

Progress in Biophysics & Molecular Biology, Vol. 1. Butler. 1950. 125.00 (*0-08-009001-X*, Pergamon Pr) Elsevier.

Progress in Biophysics & Molecular Biology, 29 vols., Vol. 1. Butler. 1975. pap. 24.00 (*0-08-019719-1*, Pergamon Pr) Elsevier.

Progress in Biophysics & Molecular Biology, Vol. 5. Butler. 1955. 185.00 (*0-08-009026-5*, Pergamon Pr) Elsevier.

Progress in Biophysics & Molecular Biology, Vol. 6. Butler. 1956. 175.00 (*0-08-009034-6*, Pergamon Pr) Elsevier.

Progress in Biophysics & Molecular Biology, Vol. 7. Butler. 1957. 175.00 (*0-08-009065-6*, Pergamon Pr) Elsevier.

Progress in Biophysics & Molecular Biology, Vol. 8. Butler. 1958. 175.00 (*0-08-009096-6*, Pergamon Pr) Elsevier.

Progress in Biophysics & Molecular Biology, Vol. 9. Butler. 1959. 165.00 (*0-08-009176-8*, Pergamon Pr) Elsevier.

Progress in Biophysics & Molecular Biology, Vol. 10. Butler. 1960. 105.00 (*0-08-009293-4*, Pergamon Pr) Elsevier.

Progress in Biophysics & Molecular Biology, Vol. 15. Butler. 1965. 76.00 (*0-08-011041-X*, Pergamon Pr) Elsevier.

Progress in Biophysics & Molecular Biology, Vol. 17. Butler. 1967. 100.00 (*0-08-012046-6*, Pergamon Pr) Elsevier.

Progress in Biophysics & Molecular Biology, Vol. 19. Butler. 1969. 48.00 (*0-08-006522-8*, Pergamon Pr) Elsevier.

Progress in Biophysics & Molecular Biology, Vol. 20. Butler. 1970. 94.50 (*0-08-006627-5*, Pergamon Pr) Elsevier.

Progress in Biophysics & Molecular Biology, Vol. 21. Butler. 1970. 100.00 (*0-08-015696-7*, Pergamon Pr) Elsevier.

Progress in Biophysics & Molecular Biology, Vol. 22. Butler. 1971. 100.00 (*0-08-016348-3*, Pergamon Pr) Elsevier.

Progress in Biophysics & Molecular Biology, Vol. 24. Butler. 1972. 76.00 (*0-08-016868-X*, Pergamon Pr) Elsevier.

Progress in Biophysics & Molecular Biology, Vol. 25. Butler. 1972. 100.00 (*0-08-016935-X*, Pergamon Pr) Elsevier.

Progress in Biophysics & Molecular Biology, Vol. 26. Butler. 1973. 100.00 (*0-08-017048-X*, Pergamon Pr) Elsevier.

Progress in Biophysics & Molecular Biology, Vol. 27. Butler. 1973. 100.00 (*0-08-017142-7*, Pergamon Pr) Elsevier.

Progress in Biophysics & Molecular Biology, Vol. 28. Butler. 1974. 100.00 (*0-08-018005-1*, Pergamon Pr) Elsevier.

Progress in Biophysics & Molecular Biology, Vol. 29. Butler. 1976. 100.00 (*0-08-020201-2*, Pergamon Pr) Elsevier.

Progress in Biophysics & Molecular Biology, Vol. 30. Butler. 1976. 100.00 (*0-08-020207-1*, Pergamon Pr) Elsevier.

Progress in Biophysics & Molecular Biology, Vol. 34. D. Noble. 1979. 76.00 (*0-08-024858-6*, Pergamon Pr) Elsevier.

Progress in Biophysics & Molecular Biology, Vol. 35. Ed. by D. Noble & T. L. Blundell. (Illus.). 206p. 1981. 76.00 (*0-08-027122-7*, Pergamon Pr) Elsevier.

Progress in Biophysics & Molecular Biology, Vol. 36, Nos. 1-3 Complete. D. Noble & T. L. Blundell. (Illus.). 130p. 1981. 83.00 (*0-08-028394-2*, Pergamon Pr) Elsevier.

Progress in Biophysics & Molecular Biology, Vol. 37. Ed. by D. Noble & T. L. Blundell. (Illus.). 229p. 1982. 95.00 (*0-08-029120-1*, Pergamon Pr) Elsevier.

Progress in Biophysics & Molecular Biology, Vol. 38. Ed. by D. Noble & T. L. Blundell. (Illus.). 210p. 1982. 94.00 (*0-08-029683-1*, Pergamon Pr) Elsevier.

Progress in Biophysics & Molecular Biology, Vol. 39. Ed. by D. Noble & T. L. Blundell. (Illus.). 230p. 1983. 86.00 (*0-08-030015-4*, Pergamon Pr) Elsevier.

Progress in Biophysics & Molecular Biology, Vol. 41. Ed. by D. Noble & T. L. Blundell. (Illus.). 260p. 1983. 99.00 (*0-08-031020-6*, Pergamon Pr) Elsevier.

Progress in Biophysics & Molecular Biology, Vol. 42. Ed. by D. Noble & T. L. Blundell. LC 50-11295. (Illus.). 202p. 1984. 99.00 (*0-08-031691-3*, Pergamon Pr) Elsevier.

Progress in Biophysics & Molecular Biology, Vol. 43. Ed. by D. Noble & T. L. Blundell. (Illus.). 268p. 1985. 110.00 (*0-08-032324-3*, Pergamon Pr) Elsevier.

Progress in Biophysics & Molecular Biology, Vol. 44. D. Noble & T. L. Blundell. (Illus.). 288p. 1985. 110.00 (*0-08-033210-2*, Pub. by PPL) Elsevier.

Progress in Biophysics & Molecular Biology, Vol. 45. D. Noble. LC 50-11295. (Illus.). 256p. 1986. 102.00 (*0-08-033225-0*, Pub. by PPL) Elsevier.

Progress in Biophysics & Molecular Biology, Vols. 5-11, & 13-30. Incl. Vol. 6. Ed. by J. A. Butler & D. Noble. 1956. Vol. 7. Ed. by J. A. Butler & D. Noble. 1957. Vol. 8. Ed. by J. A. Butler & D. Noble. 1958. Vol. 9. Ed. by J. A. Butler & D. Noble. 1959. Vol. 10. Ed. by J. A. Butler & D. Noble. 1960. Vol. 11. Ed. by J. A. Butler & D. Noble. 1961. Vol. 13. Ed. by J. A. Butler & D. Noble. 1964. 140.00 (*0-08-010028-7*); Vol. 14. Ed. by J. A. Butler & D. Noble. 1964. 155.00 (*0-08-010612-9*); Vol. 15. Ed. by J. A. Butler & D. Noble. 1965. Vol. 31, Pt. 2. 1976. pap. 23.00 (*0-08-021415-0*); Vol. 31, Pt. 3. 1977. pap. 23.00 (*0-08-021522-X*); Vol. 32. 1978. 76.00 (*0-08-020295-0*); Vol. 32, Pt. 1. 1977. pap. 25.00 (*0-08-021547-5*); Pt. 2. 1977. pap. 25.00 (*0-08-021554-8*); Pt. 3. 1978. pap. 25.00 (*0-08-022656-6*); Pt. 1. 1978. pap. 25.00 (*0-08-022675-2*); Pt. 2. 1978. pap. 25.00 (*0-08-023166-7*); Pt. 3. 1978. pap. 25.00 (*0-08-023184-5*); write for info. (*0-318-55191-8*) Elsevier.

Progress in Botanical Research: Proceedings of the 1st Balkan Botanical Congress: Proceedings of the 1st Balkan Botanical Congress. Ioannes Tsekos. LC 98-42546. 1998. 280.00 (*0-7923-5305-6*) Kluwer Academic.

Progress in Botany, Vol. 51. Ed. by H. D. Bebnek et al. (Illus.). 455p. 1990. 257.95 (*0-387-51785-5*) Spr-Verlag.

***Progress in Botany, Vol. 61.** Ed. by K. Esser et al. (Illus.). 330p. 1999. 176.00 (*3-540-64991-3*) Spr-Verlag.

Progress in Botany: Genetics - Cell Biology & Physiology - Systematics & Comparative Morphology - Ecology & Vegetation Science, Vol. 60. Ed. by K. Esser et al. (Illus.). xii, 544p. 1998. 249.00 (*3-540-64689-2*) Spr-Verlag.

Progress in Botany: Structural Botany, Physiology, Genetics, Taxonomy, Geobotany, 57, Vol. 57. Ed. by H. Behnke et al. 424p. 1996. 230.00 (*3-540-59460-4*) Spr-Verlag.

Progress in Botany: Structural Botany, Physiology, Genetics, Taxonomy, Geobotany Fortschritte der Botanik, Vol. 52. Ed. by H. D. Behnke et al. (Illus.). xv, 420p. 1991. 238.95 (*0-387-53471-7*) Spr-Verlag.

Progress in Botany: Structural Botany, Physiology, Genetics, Taxonomy, Geobotany Fortschritte der Botanik, Vol. 53. Ed. by H. D. Behnke et al. (Illus.). 450p. 1992. 272.95 (*0-387-54734-7*) Spr-Verlag.

Progress in Botany: Structural Botany, Physiology, Genetics, Taxonomy, Geobotany Fortschritte der Botanik, Vol. 55. Ed. by H. D. Behnke et al. (Illus.). 470p. 1994. 238.95 (*0-387-57321-6*) Spr-Verlag.

Progress in Caries Prevention: European Organization for Caries Research (ORCA) - 25th Anniversary. Ed. by Y. Ericsson. (Caries Research Ser.: Vol. 12, Suppl. 1). (Illus.). 1978. pap. 27.00 (*3-8055-2920-1*) S Karger.

Progress in Case-Based Reasoning: First United Kingdom Workshop, Salford, UK, January 1995, Proceedings. Ed. by Ian D. Watson. LC 95-47438. (Lecture Notes in Artificial Intelligence: No. 1202). 209p. 1995. 43.00 (*3-540-60654-8*) Spr-Verlag.

Progress in Catalysis: Proceedings of the 12th Canadian Symposium on Catalysis, Banff, Alberta, Canada, May 25-28, 1992. Ed. by K. J. Smith & E. C. Sanford. LC 92-5598. (Studies in Surface Science & Catalysis: Vol. 73). 406p. 1992. 239.50 (*0-444-89556-6*) Elsevier.

Progress in Catalyst Deactivation. J. L. Figueiredo. 1982. text 171.00 (*90-247-2690-5*) Kluwer Academic.

***Progress in Cell Cycle Research.** Laurent Meijer et al. 256p. 2000. 120.00 (*0-306-46305-9*, Kluwer Plenum) Kluwer Academic.

Progress in Cell Cycle Research, Vol. 1. Ed. by Laurent Meijer & Silvana Guidet. (Illus.). 384p. 1996. 95.00 (*0-306-45280-4*, Kluwer Plenum) Kluwer Academic.

Progress in Cell Cycle Research, Vol. 2. Ed. by Laurent Meijer et al. 292p. (C). 1997. text 95.00 (*0-306-45507-2*, Kluwer Plenum) Kluwer Academic.

Progress in Cell Cycle Research, Vol. 3. L. Meijer et al. 326p. 1998. 95.00 (*0-306-45810-1*, Kluwer Plenum) Kluwer Academic.

Progress in Ceramic Science, Vol. 4. J. E. Burke. 1966. 133.00 (*0-08-011842-9*, Pub. by Pergamon Repr) Franklin.

Progress in Cerebrovascular Disease: Papers Presented at the XIVth World Congress of Neurology, New Delhi, 22-27 Oct., 1989. Ed. by H. Lechner et al. 142p. 1990. 108.75 (*0-444-81421-3*) Elsevier.

Progress in Chemical Fibrinolysis & Thrombolysis, Vol. 3. Ed. by John F. Davidson et al. LC 78-643573. (Illus.). 631p. reprint ed. pap. 195.70 (*0-7837-7144-4*, 204715000003) Bks Demand.

Progress in Chemistry of Fats & Other Lipids, Vol. 7. R. J. Holman. LC 52-13359. 1964. 140.00 (*0-08-011236-6*, Pub. by Pergamon Repr) Franklin.

Progress in Clinical Biochemistry. 1989. 94.95 (*0-387-51097-4*) Spr-Verlag.

Progress in Clinical Biochemistry & Medicine Vol. 11: Immobilized Enzymes in Medicine. V. P. Torchilin. Ed. by International Board of Experts Staff & John A. Kellen. (Illus.). viii, 206p. 1991. 158.95 (*0-387-52778-8*) Spr-Verlag.

Progress in Clinical Immunology. Ed. by Gianni Marone & M. Ricci. (Monographs in Allergy: Vol. 18). (Illus.). x, 314p. 1983. 142.75 (*3-8055-3697-6*) S Karger.

Progress in Clinical Pacing 1990: Proceedings of the International Symposium on Progress in Clinical Pacing, Rome, Italy, 5-8 December, 1990. Ed. by M. Santini et al. (Current Clinical Practice Ser.: No. 55). 516p. 1990. text 255.00 (*90-219-9885-8*, Excerpta Medica) Elsevier.

Progress in Clinical Parasitology, Vol. 2. Tsieh Sun. 1990. 110.00 (*0-938607-36-7*) Field & Wood Inc Medical.

Progress in Clinical Parasitology, Vol. 3. Ed. by T. Sun. (Illus.). 216p. 1992. 140.00 (*0-387-97860-7*) Spr-Verlag.

Progress in Clinical Parasitology, Vol. 4. Ed. by Tsieh Sun. 192p. 1994. lib. bdg. 149.00 (*0-8493-7647-5*, 7647) CRC Pr.

Progress in Clinical Pathology, Vol. 6. Ed. by Mario Stefanini. LC 66-11412. (Illus.). 352p. 1975. 99.50 (*0-8089-0894-4*, 794316, Grune & Strat) Harcrt Hlth Sci Grp.

Progress in Clinical Pathology, Vol. 7. Ed. by Mario Stefanini. (Progress in Clinical Pathology Ser.). 1978. 99.50 (*0-8089-1037-X*, 794317, Grune & Strat) Harcrt Hlth Sci Grp.

Progress in Clinical Pathology, Vol. 8. Ed. by Mario Stefanini & Ellis S. Benson. (Illus.). 352p. 1981. text 78.00 (*0-8089-1310-7*, 794318, Grune & Strat) Harcrt Hlth Sci Grp.

Progress in Clinical Pathology, Vol. 9. Ed. by Mario Stefanini et al. 288p. 1983. text 83.00 (*0-8089-1614-9*, 794319, Grune & Strat) Harcrt Hlth Sci Grp.

Progress in Clinical Psychiatry. Ed. by Malcolm P. Weller & Daniel P. Van Kammen. (Illus.). 361p. 1997. pap. 63.00 (*0-7020-2270-5*, Pub. by W B Saunders) Saunders.

Progress in Communication Sciences, Vol. 1. Ed. by Brenda Dervin. (Communication & Information Science Ser.). 208p. 1979. text 78.50 (*0-89391-010-4*) Ablx Pub.

Progress in Communication Sciences, Vol. 2. Ed. by Melvin J. Voigt & Brenda Dervin. (Communication & Information Science Ser.). 368p. 1980. text 78.50 (*0-89391-060-0*) Ablx Pub.

Progress in Communication Sciences, Vol. 3. Ed. by Brenda Dervin. (Communication & Information Science Ser.). 368p. (C). 1982. text 78.50 (*0-89391-081-3*) Ablx Pub.

Progress in Communication Sciences, Vol. 4. Ed. by Brenda Dervin. (Communication & Information Science Ser.). 288p. 1984. text 78.50 (*0-89391-102-X*) Ablx Pub.

P

An Asterisk (*) at the beginning of an entry indicates that the title is appearing for the first time.

Progress in Communication Sciences, Vol. 5. Ed. by Brenda Dervin. (Communication & Information Science Ser.). 336p. 1984. text 78.50 (*0-89391-141-0*) Ablx Pub.

Progress in Communication Sciences, Vol. 6. Ed. by Brenda Dervin. (Progress in Communication Science Ser.). 336p. 1985. text, teacher ed. 78.50 (*0-89391-306-5*) Ablx Pub.

Progress in Communication Sciences, Vol. 7. Ed. by Brenda Dervin. (Communication & Information Science Ser.). 288p. 1986. text 78.50 (*0-89391-325-1*) Ablx Pub.

Progress in Communication Sciences, Vol. 8. Ed. by Brenda Dervin. (Communication & Information Science Ser.). 320p. 1986. text 78.50 (*0-89391-392-8*) Ablx Pub.

Progress in Communication Sciences, Vol. 9. Ed. by Brenda Dervin. (Communication & Information Science Ser.). 320p. (C). 1989. text 78.50 (*0-89391-474-6*) Ablx Pub.

Progress in Communication Sciences, Vol. 10. Ed. by Brenda Dervin. 336p. 1991. text 78.50 (*0-89391-645-5*) Ablx Pub.

Progress in Communication Sciences, Vol. 11. Ed. by Brenda Dervin. 348p. (C). 1993. text 78.50 (*0-89391-723-0*) Ablx Pub.

Progress in Communication Sciences, Vol. 12. Ed. by George Barnett & William D. Richards. 304p. 1993. 78.50 (*1-56750-067-6*); pap. 39.50 (*1-56750-068-4*) Ablx Pub.

Progress in Communication Sciences, Vol. 14. George Barnett. Ed. by Mark T. Palmer. 300p. 1998. 78.50 (*1-56750-347-0*); pap. 39.50 (*1-56750-365-9*) Ablx Pub.

Progress in Communication Sciences Vol. 13: Advances in Persuasion. Ed. by George Barnett & Franklin J. Boster. (Illus.). 300p. 1997. text 78.50 (*1-56750-277-6*) Ablx Pub.

Progress in Communication Sciences Vol. 13: Advances in Persuasion. Ed. by Frank Boster. 262p. 1997. pap. 39.50 (*1-56750-360-8*) Ablx Pub.

Progress in Communications: Advances in Telecommunications, Vol. 15. Harmeet Sawhney & George A. Barnett. 300p. 1999. 78.50 (*1-56750-399-3*); pap. 39.50 (*1-56750-400-0*) Ablx Pub.

Progress in Community Child Health Care. 2nd ed. Spencer. (C). 1997. pap. text 42.95 (*0-443-05584-X*) Church.

Progress in Community Child Health Care, Vol. 1. Spencer. (C). 1995. pap. text 46.00 (*0-443-05197-6*, W B Saunders Co) Harcrt Hlth Sci Grp.

Progress in Community Mental Health, Vol. 1. Ed. by Leopold Bellak & Harvey H. Barten. LC 69-15739. 280p. 1969. text 63.00 (*0-8089-0047-1*, 790501, Grune & Strat) Harcrt Hlth Sci Grp.

Progress in Comparative Placentology. Ed. by K. S. Ludwig & H. Hartels. (Illus.). 1973. 35.00 (*3-8055-1365-8*) S Karger.

Progress in Computational Analysis of Inelastic Structures. Ed. by E. Stein. (CISM International Centre for Mechanical Sciences Ser.: Vol. 321). (Illus.). vi, 287p. 1993. 86.95 (*0-387-82429-4*) Spr-Verlag.

Progress in Computational Physics of Matter: Methods, Software & Applications. L. Reatto & F. Manghi. LC 96-146973. 300p. 1995. text 76.00 (*981-02-2404-4*) World Scientific Pub.

Progress in Computer-Assisted Function Analysis. J. L. Willems et al. 442p. 1988. 152.00 (*0-444-70384-5*, North Holland) Elsevier.

Progress in Connectionist-Based Information Systems: Proceedings of the 1997 International Conference on Neural Information Processing & Intelligent Information Systems. Ed. by N. Kasabov et al. 1400p. 1998. pap. 110.00 (*981-3083-64-6*) Spr-Verlag.

Progress in Construction Science & Technology, Vol. 1. Ed. by Roger A. Burgess. LC TA0145.P76. 330p. reprint ed. pap. 102.30 (*0-608-09988-0*, 201550200001) Bks Demand.

Progress in Construction Science & Technology, Vol. 2. Ed. by Roger A. Burgess. LC TA0145.P7. 251p. reprint ed. pap. 77.90 (*0-608-09989-9*, 201550200002) Bks Demand.

Progress in Cosmology. Ed. by Arnold W. Wolfendale. 1982. text 176.50 (*90-277-1441-X*) Kluwer Academic.

Progress in Crop Physiology. Ed. by U. S. Gupta. (C). 1988. 26.50 (*81-204-0281-2*, Pub. by Oxford IBH) S Asia.

Progress in Crystal Growth, Vol. 2, Complete. Ed. by Brian R. Pamplin. (Illus.). 404p. 1981. 140.00 (*0-08-026040-3*, Pergamon Pr) Elsevier.

Progress in Crystal Growth & Characterization, Pt. 2. Ed. by Brian R. Pamplin. 1978. pap. 28.00 (*0-08-023050-4*, Pub. by Pergamon Repr) Franklin.

Progress in Crystal Growth & Characterization, Pt. 3. Ed. by Brian R. Pamplin. 1978. pap. 28.00 (*0-08-023051-2*, Pub. by Pergamon Repr) Franklin.

Progress in Crystal Growth & Characterization, Pt. 4. Ed. by Brian R. Pamplin. 1979. pap. 21.00 (*0-08-023083-0*, Pub. by Pergamon Repr) Franklin.

Progress in Crystal Growth & Characterization, Vol. 1. Ed. by Brian R. Pamplin. (Illus.). 248p. 1980. 140.00 (*0-08-026013-6*, Pergamon Pr) Elsevier.

Progress in Crystal Growth & Characterization, Vol. 3, No. 2-3. Ed. by Brian R. Pamplin. (Illus.). 166p. 1981. pap. 72.00 (*0-08-027149-9*, Pergamon Pr) Elsevier.

Progress in Crystal Growth & Characterization, Vol. 4. Ed. by Brian R. Pamplin. (Illus.). 345p. 1982. 160.00 (*0-08-029681-5*, Pergamon Pr) Elsevier.

Progress in Crystal Growth & Characterization, Vol. 5. Ed. by Brian R. Pamplin. (Illus.). 425p. 1983. 155.00 (*0-08-031011-7*, Pergamon Pr) Elsevier.

Progress in Crystal Growth & Characterization, Vol. 6. Ed. by Brian R. Pamplin. (Illus.). 424p. 1984. 155.00 (*0-08-030997-6*, Pergamon Pr) Elsevier.

Progress in Crystal Growth & Characterization, Vol. 8. Ed. by Brian R. Pamplin. (Illus.). 475p. 1985. 180.00 (*0-08-032736-2*, Pub. by PPL) Elsevier.

Progress in Crystal Growth & Characterization, Vol. 9. Ed. by Brian R. Pamplin. (Illus.). 385p. 1985. 180.00 (*0-08-032737-0*, Pub. by PPL) Elsevier.

Progress in Crystal Growth & Characterization Vol. 10: Proceedings of the 6th International Conference on Ternary & Multinary Compounds, Car acas, Venezuela, 15-17 August 1984. Ed. by Brian R. Pamplin et al. (Illus.). 430p. 1985. 180.00 (*0-08-032344-8*, Pergamon Pr) Elsevier.

Progress in Crystal Growth & Characterization, Vol. 23 see Role of Crystal Growth for Device Development

Progress in Cybernetics & Systems Research, Vol. 8. Ed. by Robert Trappl. 1982. text 110.00 (*0-07-065068-3*) McGraw.

Progress in Dairy Science. Ed. by C. J. Phillips. (A CAB International Publication). (Illus.). 416p. 1996. text 110.00 (*0-85198-974-8*) OUP.

Progress in Decision, Utility & Risk Theory. Ed. by Atilla Chikan. (C). 1991. lib. bdg. 194.00 (*0-7923-1211-2*) Kluwer Academic.

Progress in Development Administration: Selected Papers from "Public Administration & Development", 1981-1991. Ed. by Brian Smith. LC 91-84949. 249p. 1992. reprint ed. pap. 77.20 (*0-608-02604-2*, 206326200004) Bks Demand.

Progress in Diagnostics & Therapy of Prostatic Cancer. Ed. by W. B. Peeling et al. (Illus.). 80p. 1996. pap. 49.00 (*3-540-60195-3*) Spr-Verlag.

Progress in Diatom Studies: Contributions to Taxonomy, Ecology & Nomenclature. Ed. by Patricia A. Sims et al. (Nova Hedwigia Beihefte Ser.: Vol. 106). (Illus.). xiv, 377p. 1993. pap. 112.00 (*3-443-51028-0*, Pub. by Gebruder Borntraeger) Balogh.

Progress in Diet & Nutrition. Ed. by C. Horwitz & P. Rozen. (Frontiers of Gastrointestinal Research Ser.: Vol. 14). (Illus.). x, 226p. 1988. 168.75 (*3-8055-4608-4*) S Karger.

Progress in Digital Angiocardiography. Ed. by Paul H. Heintzen & J. H. Bursch. (Developments in Cardiovascular Medicine Ser.). (C). 1988. text 282.00 (*0-89838-965-8*) Kluwer Academic.

Progress in Distributed Operating Systems & Distributed Systems Management: European Workshop, Berlin, FRG, April 18-19, 1989 Proceedings. Ed. by W. Schroder-Preikschat et al. (Lecture Notes in Computer Science Ser.: Vol. 433). vi, 206p. 1990. 30.00 (*0-387-52609-9*) Spr-Verlag.

Progress in Drug Metabolism, 1. Ed. by James W. Bridges & L. F. Chasseaud. LC 75-19446. (Illus.). 300p. reprint ed. pap. 85.50 (*0-608-18830-1*, 2030485) Bks Demand.

Progress in Drug Metabolism, 2. Ed. by James W. Bridges & L. F. Chasseaud. LC 75-19446. (Illus.). 360p. reprint ed. pap. 102.60 (*0-608-18831-X*, 2030485) Bks Demand.

Progress in Drug Metabolism, 3. Ed. by James W. Bridges & L. F. Chasseaud. LC 75-19446. (Illus.). 385p. reprint ed. pap. 109.80 (*0-608-18832-8*, 2030485) Bks Demand.

Progress in Drug Metabolism, 4. Ed. by James W. Bridges & L. F. Chasseaud. LC 75-19446. (Illus.). 347p. reprint ed. pap. 98.90 (*0-608-18833-6*, 2030485) Bks Demand.

Progress in Drug Metabolism, 5. Ed. by James W. Bridges & L. F. Chasseaud. LC 75-19446. (Illus.). 372p. reprint ed. pap. 106.10 (*0-608-18834-4*, 2030485) Bks Demand.

Progress in Drug Metabolism, 6. Ed. by James W. Bridges & L. F. Chasseaud. LC 75-19446. (Illus.). 331p. reprint ed. pap. 94.40 (*0-608-18835-2*, 2030485) Bks Demand.

Progress in Drug Metabolism, Vol. 13. Ed. by G. Gordon Gibson. 360p. 1992. 145.00 (*0-7484-0012-5*, Pub. by Tay Francis Ltd) Taylor & Francis.

Progress in Drug Research. Ed. by Ernst Jucker. (Progress in Drug Research Ser.: Vol. 27). 400p. (C). 1983. text 164.95 (*3-7643-1365-X*) Birkhauser.

Progress in Drug Research, Vol. 4. Ed. by Ernst Jucker. vii, 322p. 1994. 276.50 (*0-8176-5042-3*) Birkhauser.

Progress in Drug Research, Vol. 14. Ed. by Ernst Jucker. 408p. 1993. 324.50 (*0-8176-2925-4*) Birkhauser.

Progress in Drug Research, Vol. 23. Ernst Jucker. 320p. 1980. 195.00 (*0-8176-1070-7*) Birkhauser.

Progress in Drug Research, Vol. 24. Ed. by Ernst Jucker. 300p. 1980. 241.00 (*0-8176-1148-7*) Birkhauser.

Progress in Drug Research, Vol. 26. Ed. by Ernst Jucker. 412p. 1982. 269.50 (*0-8176-1261-0*) Birkhauser.

Progress in Drug Research, Vol. 28. Ernst Jucker. 1984. 232.00 (*0-8176-1556-3*) Birkhauser.

Progress in Drug Research, Vol. 29. Ed. by Ernst Jucker. 503p. 1986. 299.00 (*0-8176-1672-1*) Birkhauser.

Progress in Drug Research, Vol. 30. Ed. by Ernst Jucker. 580p. 1986. 446.50 (*0-8176-1752-3*) Birkhauser.

Progress in Drug Research, Vol. 31. Ed. by Ernst Jucker. 480p. 1988. 492.50 (*0-8176-1837-6*) Birkhauser.

Progress in Drug Research, Vol. 32. Ernst Jucker & Urs A. Meyer. 500p. 1988. 399.00 (*0-8176-1943-7*) Birkhauser.

Progress in Drug Research, Vol. 33. Ernst Jucker & Urs A. Meyer. 550p. 1989. 399.00 (*0-8176-2306-X*) Birkhauser.

Progress in Drug Research, Vol. 34. Ernst Jucker. 544p. 1990. 399.00 (*0-8176-2351-5*) Birkhauser.

Progress in Drug Research, Vol. 35. Ed. by Ernst Jucker. 600p. 1990. 419.00 (*0-8176-2499-6*) Birkhauser.

Progress in Drug Research, Vol. 36. Ed. by Ernst Jucker. vii, 475p. 1991. 343.50 (*0-8176-2582-8*) Birkhauser.

Progress in Drug Research, Vol. 37. Ed. by Ernst Jucker. ix, 410p. 1991. 324.50 (*0-8176-2626-3*) Birkhauser.

Progress in Drug Research, Vol. 38. Ed. by Ernst Jucker. 380p. 1992. 296.50 (*0-8176-2705-7*) Birkhauser.

Progress in Drug Research, Vol. 39. Ed. by Ernst Jucker. ix, 398p. 1992. 324.50 (*0-8176-2717-0*) Birkhauser.

Progress in Drug Research, Vol. 40. Ed. by Ernst Jucker. vii, 204p. 1993. 258.00 (*0-8176-2850-9*) Birkhauser.

Progress in Drug Research, Vol. 42. Ernst Jucker. 464p. 1994. 349.00 (*0-8176-2995-5*) Birkhauser.

Progress in Drug Research, Vol. 44. Ed. by Ernst Jucker. (Illus.). 352p. 1995. 269.00 (*0-8176-5149-7*) Birkhauser.

Progress in Drug Research, Vol. 45. Ed. by Ernst Jucker. (Illus.). vii, 374p. 1996. 290.00 (*3-7643-5212-4*) Birkhauser.

Progress in Drug Research, Vol. 48. Ed. by E. Jucker. (Illus.). 288p. 1997. 249.00 (*3-7643-5671-5*) Spr-Verlag.

Progress in Drug Research, Vol. 49. Ed. by E. Jucker. 373p. 1997. text 250.00 (*3-7643-5672-3*) Birkhauser.

Progress in Drug Research, Vol. 50. Ed. by E. Jucker. 300p. 1998. student ed. 250.00 (*3-7643-5821-1*) Birkhauser.

Progress in Drug Research, Vol. 52. Ed. by Ernst Jucker. 300p. 1999. 265.00 (*3-7643-5979-X*) Birkhauser.

***Progress in Drug Research, Vol. 53.** Ed. by E. Jucker. (Illus.). 250p. 1999. 265.00 (*3-7643-6028-3*, Pub. by Birkhauser) Spr-Verlag.

***Progress in Drug Research, Vol. 54.** Ed. by E. Jucker. (Illus.). 250p. 2000. 249.00 (*3-7643-6113-1*, Pub. by Birkhauser) Spr-Verlag.

Progress in Drug Research Vol. 51. Ed. by E. Jucker. 400p. 1998. 250.00 (*3-7643-5822-X*) Birkhauser.

Progress in Durability Analysis of Composite Systems: Proceedings of the International Conference on the Subject, DURACOSYS 95, Brussels, 16-21 July 1995. Ed. by A. H. Cardon et al. (Illus.). 336p. (C). 1996. text 136.00 (*90-5410-809-6*, Pub. by A A Balkema) Ashgate Pub Co.

Progress in Durability Analysis of Composite Systems: Proceedings of the 2nd International Conference, Blacksburg, Virginia, 14-17 September 1997. Ed. by K. L. Reifsnider. 500p. 1998. 101.00 (*90-5410-960-2*, Pub. by A A Balkema) Ashgate Pub Co.

Progress in Ecology Vol. I: Progress of Plant Ecology in India. Ed. by R. Mishra et al. (Illus.). 162p. 1973. 20.00 (*0-88065-160-1*) Scholarly Pubns.

Progress in Ecology Vol. VIII: Ecological & Anatomical Marvels of the Himalayan Orchids. Purushotam Kaushik. 124p. 1983. 65.00 (*1-55528-028-5*, Pub. by Today Tomorrow) Scholarly Pubns.

Progress in Electrochemistry. Ed. by D. A. Rand et al. (Studies in Physical & Theoretical Chemistry). 470p. 1981. reprint ed. 141.00 (*0-444-41955-1*) Elsevier.

Progress in Electrodermal Research. J. C. Roy et al. LC 93-11397. (NATO ASI Ser.: Vol. 249). (Illus.). 360p. (C). 1993. text 110.00 (*0-306-44536-0*, Kluwer Plenum) Kluwer Academic.

***Progress in Electromagnetics Research Symposium, 2000: Proceedings.** (Illus.). viii, 1178p. 2000. write for info. (*0-9679674-0-6*) Electromagnetics.

Progress in Electron Properties of Solids: Festschrift in the Honour of Franco Bassani. Ed. by R. Girlanda et al. (C). 1989. lib. bdg. 251.50 (*0-7923-0337-7*) Kluwer Academic.

Progress in Electrorheology: Science & Technology of Electrorheological Materials. K. O. Havelka & F. E. Filisko. (Illus.). 382p. (C). 1995. text 125.00 (*0-306-45074-7*, Kluwer Plenum) Kluwer Academic.

Progress in Elliptic & Parabolic Partial Differential Equations. A. Alvino. (Pitman Research Notes in Mathematics Ser.). 1995. lib. bdg. 55.95 (*0-582-25970-3*) Longman.

Progress in Emission Control Technologies. LC 94-67932. 264p. 1994. pap. 74.00 (*1-56091-565-X*, SP1053) Soc Auto Engineers.

Progress in Energy & Combustion Science, 3 vols., Vol. 3. Chigier. 1978. pap. 22.00 (*0-08-022706-6*, Pergamon Pr) Elsevier.

Progress in Energy & Combustion Science, Vol. 4. Norman A. Chigier. 224p. 1980. 140.00 (*0-08-024257-X*, Pergamon Pr) Elsevier.

Progress in Energy & Combustion Science, Vol. 6. Ed. by Norman A. Chigier. (Illus.). 388p. 1981. 145.00 (*0-08-027153-7*, Pergamon Pr) Elsevier.

Progress in Energy & Combustion Science, Vol. 6, Pt. 2. Ed. by Norman A. Chigier. 102p. 1980. pap. 30.00 (*0-08-026059-4*, Pergamon Pr) Elsevier.

Progress in Energy & Combustion Science, Vol. 7. Ed. by Norman A. Chigier. (Illus.). 316p. 1982. 160.00 (*0-08-029124-4*, Pergamon Pr) Elsevier.

Progress in Energy & Combustion Science, Vol. 8. Ed. by Norman A. Chigier. 354p. 1983. 160.00 (*0-08-031041-9*, Pergamon Pr) Elsevier.

Progress in Energy & Combustion Science, Vol. 9. Ed. by Norman A. Chigier. (Illus.). 378p. 1984. 160.00 (*0-08-031727-8*, Pergamon Pr) Elsevier.

Progress in Energy & Combustion Science, Vol. 10. Ed. by Norman A. Chigier. (Illus.). 478p. 1986. 162.00 (*0-08-033677-9*, B110, Pub. by PPL) Elsevier.

Progress in Energy & Combustion Science, Vols. 1-2. Incl. Vol. 1, Complete. Pollution Formation & Destruction in Flames. LC 75-24822. 1976. 140.00 (*0-08-020307-8*); Vol. 1, Pt. 1. LC 75-24822. 1976. pap. 24.00 (*0-08-019931-3*); Vol. 1, Pts. 2-3. LC 75-24822. 1976. pap. 39.00 (*0-08-021023-6*); Vol. 1, Pt. 4. LC 75-24822. 1976. pap. 35.00 (*0-08-021041-4*); Vol. 2, Pt. 1. LC 75-24822. 1976. pap. 22.00 (*0-08-021211-5*); Vol. 2, Pt. 2. LC 75-24822. 1976. pap. 22.00 (*0-08-021213-1*); Vol. 2, Pt. 3. LC 75-24822. 1977. pap. 19.75 (*0-08-021215-8*); Vol. 2. LC 75-24822. 1978. 140.00 (*0-08-021219-0*); Vol. 2, Pt. 4. LC 75-24822. 1977. pap. 19.75 (*0-08-021217-4*); LC 75-24822. 1978. pap. write for info. (*0-318-55200-0*, Pergamon Pr) Elsevier.

Progress in Engineering Optimization, 1981: Presented at the ASME Design Engineering Technical Conferences, Hartford, Connecticut, September 20-23, 1981. American Society of Mechanical Engineers Staff. Ed. by R. W. Mayne & K. M. Ragsdell. LC 81-68332. (Illus.). 157p. reprint ed. pap. 48.70 (*0-8357-2837-4*, 203907300010) Bks Demand.

Progress in Environmental Remote Sensing Research & Application: Proceedings of the 15th EARSEL Symposium Basel, 1995. Ed. by E. Parlow. (Illus.). 670p. (C). 1996. text 155.00 (*90-5410-598-4*, Pub. by A A Balkema) Ashgate Pub Co.

Progress in Ergometry: Quality Control & Test Criteria, Fifth International Seminar on Ergometry. Ed. by H. Loellgen & H. Mellerowicz. (Illus.). 260p. 1984. 54.95 (*0-387-13570-7*) Spr-Verlag.

Progress in Essential Oil Research: Proceedings of the International Symposium on Essential Oils, Holzminden-Neuhaus, Federal Republic of Germany, September 18-21, 1985. Ed. by Ernst-Joachim Brunke. (Illus.). xvi, 668p. 1986. 211.55 (*3-11-010614-0*) De Gruyter.

Progress in Evolutionary Computation: AI '93 & AI '94 Workshop on Evolutionary Computation, Melbourne, Victoria, Australia, November 16, 1993, Armidale, NSW, Australia, November 21-22, 1994, Selected Papers, Vol. VIII. Ed. by Joerg H. Siekmann et al. LC 95-34610. (Lecture Notes in Artificial Intelligence: Vol. 956). 314p. 1995. 56.00 (*3-540-60154-6*) Spr-Verlag.

***Progress in Experimental & Theoretical Studies of Clusters.** Tamotsu Kondow. (Advanced Series in Physical Chemistry). 1999. 103.00 (*981-02-3893-2*) World Scientific Pub.

Progress in Experimental Personality & Psychopathology Research, Vol. 15. Ed. by Elaine F. Walker et al. 336p. 1992. 49.95 (*0-8261-6090-5*) Springer Pub.

Progress in Experimental Personality & Psychopathology Research, Vol. 16. Ed. by Loren J. Chapman et al. 304p. 1992. 49.95 (*0-8261-6091-3*) Springer Pub.

Progress in Experimental Personality & Psychopathology Research, Vol. 17. Ed. by Don C. Fowles et al. (Special Focus on Antisocial Personality Ser.). 344p. 1994. 49.95 (*0-8261-6092-1*) Springer Pub.

Progress in Experimental Tumor Research, Vols. 27-28. (Illus.). xxxii, 500p. 1984. 204.50 (*3-8055-3857-X*) S Karger.

Progress in Extractive Metallurgy Series, Vol. 1. Fathi Habashi. 248p. 1973. 82.00 (*0-677-12220-9*) Gordon & Breach.

Progress in Family Law. John S. Bradway. Ed. by Richard D. Lambert. LC 71-81088. (Annals Ser.: No. 383). 1969. 28.00 (*0-87761-116-5*); pap. 18.00 (*0-87761-115-7*) Am Acad Pol Soc Sci.

Progress in Fast Neutron Physics: Proceedings of the International Conference, Houston, TX, 1963. International Conference on Fast Neutron Physics S. Ed. by G. C. Phillips & Jerry B. Marion. LC 63-18849. (Rice University Semicentennial Publications). 411p. reprint ed. pap. 127.50 (*0-608-10000-5*, 20202040016) Bks Demand.

Progress in Fatigue & Fracture, Vol. 8 No. 1. Ed. by H. Liebowitz. 1976. pap. 73.00 (*0-08-020866-5*, Pergamon Pr) Elsevier.

Progress in Fibrin Sealing. Ed. by H. W. Waclawiczek. (Illus.). 168p. 1989. 103.00 (*0-387-50797-3*) Spr-Verlag.

Progress in Fibromyalgia & Myofascial Pain. Henning Vaery & Harold Merskey. LC 93-7696. (Pain Research & Clinical Management Ser.: Vol. 6). 476p. 1993. 299.50 (*0-444-89536-1*) Elsevier.

Progress in Flaw Growth & Fracture Toughness Testing: Proceedings of the 1972 National Symposium on Fracture Mechanics, Philadelphia, PA, 28-30, 1972. American Society for Testing & Materials Staff. LC 73-76198. (American Society for Testing & Materials Special Technical Publication Ser.: No. 536). 501p. reprint ed. pap. 155.40 (*0-608-11427-8*, 202254600028) Bks Demand.

Progress in Fluid Flow Research: Turbulence & Applied MHD. Herman Branover & Yeshajahu Unger. (Progress in Astronautics & Aeronautics Ser.: Vol. 182). 942p. 1998. 109.95 (*1-56347-284-8*) AIAA.

Progress in Fluidization & Fluid Particle Systems. Desmond King et al. LC 96-35283. (AICHE Symposium Ser.). 130p. 1996. 35.00 (*0-8169-0718-8*) Am Inst Chem Eng.

Progress in Flying Machines. unabridged ed. Octave Chanute. LC 97-38658. (Illus.). 320p. 1998. reprint ed. pap. 10.95 (*0-486-29981-3*) Dover.

Progress in Food & Nutrition Science. Ed. by R. K. Chandra. (Illus.). 198p. 1984. pap. 92.00 (*0-08-030928-3*, Pergamon Pr) Elsevier.

Progress in Food & Nutrition Science, Vol. 1, Pts. 1-10 & Vol. 2, Pts. 1-9. Incl. Vol. 1, Pt. 1. LC 75-7734. 1975. pap. 15.75 (*0-08-019697-7*); Vol. 1, Pt. 2. LC 75-7734. 1975. pap. 19.75 (*0-08-019782-5*); Vol. 1, Pt. 3. LC 75-7734. 1975. pap. 19.75 (*0-08-019786-8*); Vol. 1, Pt. 4. LC 75-7734. 1975. pap. 15.75 (*0-08-019789-2*); Vol. 1, Pt. 5. LC 75-7734. 1975. pap. 19.75 (*0-08-019876-7*); Vol. 1, Pt. 6. LC 75-7734. 1975. pap. 15.75 (*0-08-019878-3*); Vol. 1, Pts. 7-8. LC 75-7734. 1975. pap. 35.00 (*0-08-019880-5*); Vol. 1, Pt. 9. LC 75-7734. 1975. pap. 20.00 (*0-08-019942-9*); Vol. 1, Pt. 10. LC 75-7734. 1975. pap. 17.25 (*0-08-019944-5*); Vol. 2, Pt. 1. LC 75-7734. 1976. pap. 15.75 (*0-08-021025-2*); Vol. 2, Pts. 2-3. LC 75-7734. 1976. pap. 29.00 (*0-08-021287-5*); Vol. 2, Pt. 4. LC 75-7734. 1977. pap. 13.25 (*0-08-021764-8*); Vol. 2, Pt. 5. LC 75-7734. 1977. pap. 15.50 (*0-08-021777-X*); Vol. 2, Pt. 6. LC 75-7734. 1977. pap. 15.75 (*0-08-021921-7*); Vol. 2, Pt. 7. LC 75-7734. 1977. pap. 13.25 (*0-08-021519-X*); Vol. 2, Pt. 8. LC 75-7734. 1977. pap. 13.25 (*0-08-021532-7*); Vol. 2, Pt. 9. LC 75-7734. 1977. pap. 13.25 (*0-08-021537-8*); LC 75-7734. 1977. pap. write for info. (*0-318-55201-9*) Elsevier.

Progress in Food & Nutrition Science, Vol. 2, No. 11-12. H. M. Sinclair. LC 75-7734. (Illus.). 70p. 1979. pap. 28.00 (*0-08-023758-4*, Pergamon Pr) Elsevier.

Progress in Forensic Genetics 7. Ed. by Bjonar Olaisen et al. 580p. 1998. 244.00 (*0-444-82965-2*, Excerpta Medica) Elsevier.

Progress in Fourier Transform Spectroscopy: 10th International Conference, August 27-September 1, 1995, Budapest. Ed. by J. Mink et al. (Mikrochimica Acta Ser.: Suppl. 14). (Illus.). 800p. 1997. pap., suppl. ed. 213.00 (*3-211-82931-8*) Spr-Verlag.

P

An Asterisk (*) at the beginning of an entry indicates that the title is appearing for the first time.

Progress in Fuel Systems to Meet New Fuel Economy & Emissions Standards: 1995 International Congress & Exposition Meeting. 156p. 1995. pap. 36.00 (*1-56091-634-6*, SP1084) Soc Auto Engineers.

Progress in Functional Psychoses. Ed. by Robert Cancro et al. LC 78-31828. (Illus.). 250p. 1979. 44.95 (*0-88331-185-2*) R B Luce.

Progress in Fuzzy Sets & Systems. Ed. by Wolfgang H. Janko. (C). 1990. text 155.00 (*0-7923-0730-5*) Kluwer Academic.

Progress in Gastroenterology, Vol. 4. Ed. by George B. Glass & Paul Sherlock. 624p. 1983. text 190.00 (*0-8089-1555-X*, 791564, Grune & Strat) Harcrt Hlth Sci Grp.

Progress in Gestural Interaction Vol. VI: Proceedings of Gesture Workshop '96. Ed. by Philip A. Harling & Alistair D. Edwards. LC 96-36953. (Illus.). 251p. 1997. pap. 59.95 (*3-540-76094-6*) Spr-Verlag.

Progress in Gynecology & Endocrinology. Ed. by Andrea R. Genazzani et al. 944p. (C). 1990. 125.00 (*1-85070-299-3*) Prthnon Pub.

Progress in Haematology No. 2. Ed. by C. Pallister & C. Dunn. (Illus.). 208p. 1999. pap. text 45.00 (*1-900151-79-0*) OUP.

Progress in Handwriting Recognition. S. Impedovo. 650p. 1997. text 76.00 (*981-02-3084-2*) World Scientific Pub.

Progress in Heat & Mass Transfer, Vol. 2. Irvine. 1969. 130.00 (*0-08-006514-7*, Pergamon Pr) Elsevier.

Progress in Heat & Mass Transfer, Vol. 3. Eckert. 1971. 130.00 (*0-08-006852-9*, Pergamon Pr) Elsevier.

Progress in Heat & Mass Transfer Vol. 19, No. 10: Alan Ede Memorial Issue: Developments in Heat & Mass Transfer. Ed. by D. Brian Spalding. 1977. pap. 39.00 (*0-08-021285-9*, Pergamon Pr) Elsevier.

Progress in Heat Transfer Pt. I: Laminar Boundary Layer Flow in Transparent - And Gray Media, Pt. II: Equipment for the Preparation of Seminconductor Materials. Ed. by P. K. Konakov. Tr. by James S. Wood from RUS. LC 65-26629. 167p. reprint ed. pap. 51.80 (*0-608-30581-2*, 202067200018) Bks Demand.

Progress in Hemostasis & Thrombosis, Vol. 10. Barry S. Coller. (Illus.). 368p. 1990. text 180.00 (*0-7216-3445-1*, W B Saunders Co) Harcrt Hlth Sci Grp.

Progress in Hepatic Encephalopathy & Metabolic Nitrogen Exchange Proceedings: Seventh International Symposium on Ammonia. Finn Bengtsson et al. (Illus.). 576p. 1991. 324.00 (*0-8493-0180-7*, 180FV, CRC Reprint) Franklin.

***Progress in Hepatocellular Carcinoma Treatment.** Ed. by K. Okita. LC 99-48955. xii, 112p. 2000. 79.00 (*4-431-70257-1*) Spr-Verlag.

Progress in Hepatology Vol. 4: Liver Cirrhosis Update; Proceedings. Takahashi Memorial Forum on Progress in Hepatology, Liver Cirrhosis Update (1997: Tokyo, Japan) (International Congress Ser.: Vol. 1163). 146p. 1998. 132.00 (*0-444-82940-7*) Elsevier.

***Progress in Hepatology 5 - Liver & Immunology.** Ed. by M. Yamanaka et al. (International Congress Ser.). 144p. 1999. 114.00 (*0-444-50344-7*, Excerpta Medica) Elsevier.

Progress in Heterocyclic Chemistry. rev. ed. Hans Suschitzky & E. F. Scriven. LC 89-8531. (Progress in Heterocyclic Chemistry Ser.: Vol. 1). 320p. 1989. 157.00 (*0-08-037044-6*, Pub. by Pergamon Repr) Franklin.

Progress in Heterocyclic Chemistry, Vol. 6. E. Suschitzky. 352p. 1994. text 173.00 (*0-08-042086-9*, Pergamon Pr) Elsevier.

Progress in Heterocyclic Chemistry, Vol. 9. G. W. Gribble & T. L. Gilchrist. 376p. 1997. pap. 21.50 (*0-08-042802-9*, Pergamon Pr) Elsevier.

Progress in Heterocyclic Chemistry, Vol. 9. Gribble & Gilchrist. 366p. 1997. 168.50 (*0-08-042801-0*, Pergamon Pr) Elsevier.

Progress in Heterocyclic Chemistry: A Critical Review of the 1992 Literature Preceded by Two Chapters on Current Heterocyclic Topics. Ed. by Hans Suschitzky & E. F. Scriven. (Progress in Heterocyclic Chemistry Ser.: Vol. 5). 350p. 1993. 165.00 (*0-08-042074-5*, Pergamon Pr) Elsevier.

Progress in Heterocyclic Chemistry: A Critical Review of the 1996 Literature. Hans Suschitzky & G. Gribble. (Progress in Heterocyclic Chemistry Ser.: Vol. 8). 366p. 1996. 149.50 (*0-08-042795-2*, Pergamon Pr) Elsevier.

Progress in Heterocyclic Chemistry Vol. 2: Crit. Revised 1989 Lit. Preceded by 1 Chapter on Curriculum Heteroc. Topic. Hans Suschitzky & E. F. Scriven. LC 89-8531. 1990. 140.00 (*0-08-037069-1*, Pub. by Pergamon Repr) Franklin.

Progress in Heterocyclic Chemistry Vol. 4: Critical Review 1991 Lit. Preceded by 2 Chapters on Curriculum Heterocyclic Topic. Hans Suschitzky & E. F. Scriven. LC 89-8531. 1992. 141.00 (*0-08-040612-2*, Pub. by Pergamon Repr) Franklin.

Progress in Heterocyclic Chemistry Vol. 10: A Critical Review of the 1997 Literature Preceded by Two Chapters on Current Heterocyclic Topics. Ed. by G. W. Gribble & T. L. Gilchrist. 370p. 1998. 163.00 (*0-08-043402-9*, Pergamon Pr) Elsevier.

***Progress in Heterocyclic Chemistry II, Vol. 11.** Gribble & Gilchrist. 372p. 1999. 150.00 (*0-08-043407-X*, Pergamon Pr) Elsevier.

Progress in Heterocyclic Chemistry, Vol. 3: A Critical Review of the 1990 Literature Preceded by Two Chapters on Current Heterocyclic Topics, Vol. 3. Hans Suschitky & E. F. Scriven. LC 89-8531. 324p. 1991. 158.00 (*0-08-040589-4*, Pub. by Pergamon Repr) Franklin.

Progress in High Energy Physics: Proceedings of the Spring School & International Conference on Medium & High Energy Nuclear Physics, 2nd, Held in Taiwan, Republic of China, May 8-18, 1990. Ed. by P. W. Hwang et al. 400p. 1991. 145.00 (*0-444-01588-4*) P-H.

Progress in High Energy Physics & Progress in Nuclear Physics, Set, Pts. A & B. W. Y. Hwang et al. 1991. 264.00 (*0-444-01589-2*) P-H.

Progress in Holomorphic Dynamics. Ed. by Hartje Kriete. (Pitman Research Notes in Mathematics Ser.: No. 387). 200p. 1998. pap. 42.00 (*0-582-32388-6*, LM2388, Chap & Hall CRC) Addison-Wesley.

Progress in HPLC Vol. 1: Gel Permeation & Ion-Exchange Chromatography of Proteins & Peptides. Ed. by Y. Kato et al. 231p. 1985. lib. bdg. 117.50 (*90-6764-048-4*, Pub. by VSP) Coronet Bks.

Progress in HPLC Vol. 2: Electromechanical Detection in Medicine & Chemistry. Ed. by S. H. Parvez et al. 480p. 1987. lib. bdg. 190.00 (*90-6764-062-X*, Pub. by VSP) Coronet Bks.

Progress in HPLC Vol. 3: Flow Through Radioactivity Detection in HPLC. Ed. by A. R. Reich et al. 214p. 1988. 115.00 (*90-6764-114-6*, Pub. by VSP) Coronet Bks.

Progress in HPLC Vol. 4: Supercritical Fluid Chromatography & Microbore-HPLC. Ed. by M. Yoshioka et al. 300p. 1988. 120.00 (*90-6764-113-8*, Pub. by VSP) Coronet Bks.

***Progress in Human African Trypanosomiasis, Sleeping Sickness.** Michael Dumas. LC 98-31567. 1998. 159.00 (*2-287-59655-0*) Spr-Verlag.

Progress in Human Auditory & Vestibular Histopathology. Salvatore Iurato & Jan E. Veldman. LC 96-38655. 1997. 115.00 (*90-6299-151-3*) Kugler Pubns.

Progress in Hydrogen Energy. Ed. by R. P. Dahiya. 1987. text 169.00 (*90-277-2440-7*) Kluwer Academic.

Progress in Hydrogeochemistry: Organics - Carbonate Systems - Silicate Systems - Microbiology - Models. Ed. by P. Hirsch et al. (Illus.). xxix, 544p. 1992. 163.95 (*0-387-54034-2*) Spr-Verlag.

Progress in Hypertension: Antihypertensive Drugs Today, Vol. 2. Ed. by H. Saito et al. 383p. 1992. 127.50 (*90-6764-140-5*) Coronet Bks.

Progress in Hypertension Vol. 1: Neurotransmitters As Modulators of Blood Pressure. Ed. by H. Saito et al. 380p. 1987. lib. bdg. 150.00 (*90-6764-100-6*, Pub. by VSP) Coronet Bks.

Progress in Hypertension Vol. 3: New Advances in SHR Research. Pathophysiology & Pharmacology. Ed. by H. Saito et al. 240p. 1995. 125.00 (*90-6764-198-7*, Pub. by VSP) Coronet Bks.

Progress in Image Analysis & Processing: Proceedings of the 5th International Conference. Virginio Cantoni et al. 804p. 1990. text 147.00 (*981-02-0061-7*) World Scientific Pub.

Progress in Image Analysis & Processing II: Proceedings of the 6th International Conference. Ed. by Virginio Cantoni et al. 600p. (C). 1992. text 143.00 (*981-02-0800-6*) World Scientific Pub.

Progress in Image Analysis & Processing III: Proceedings of the 7th International Conference on Image Analysis & Processing. S. Impedovo. 760p. 1994. text 189.00 (*981-02-1552-5*) World Scientific Pub.

Progress in Immunodeficiency: Proceedings of the 7th Meeting of the European Society of Immunodeficiencies, June 6-9, 1996, Goteborg, Sweden, Vol. 1. European Society of Immunodeficiencies Staff et al. LC 96-49576. (Advances in the Biosciences Ser.). 140p. 1996. 129.50 (*0-444-82462-6*) Elsevier.

Progress in Immunology, Vol. VII. Ed. by F. Melchers et al. (Illus.). 1408p. 1989. 207.00 (*0-387-51053-2*) Spr-Verlag.

Progress in Immunology 8: Proceedings of the 8th International Congress of Immunology, Budapest 1992. Ed. by J. Gergely. (Illus.). 987p. 1993. 181.00 (*0-387-56401-2*) Spr-Verlag.

Progress in In Vitro Toxicology, Vol. 6. (Alternative Methods in Toxicology Ser.). 350p. 1988. 191.00 (*0-913113-16-6*) M Liebert.

Progress in Industrial Gas Chromatography: Proceedings of the Gas Chromatography Institute, 3rd Annual, Buffalo, N. Y., April 4-6, 1961, Vol. 1. Gas Chromatography Institute Staff. LC 61-15520. 239p. reprint ed. pap. 74.10 (*0-608-11382-4*, 202070000001) Bks Demand.

Progress in Industrial Mathematics at ECMI '94. Ed. by Morten Brons et al. LC 98-139547. 449 p. 1997. write for info. (*3-519-02607-4*) B G Teubner.

Progress in Infancy Research. Ed. by Carolyn Rovee-Collier et al. 264p. 2000. write for info. (*0-8058-3493-1*) L Erlbaum Assocs.

Progress in Inflammation Research & Therapy. Ed. by N. R. Ackerman et al. (Agents & Actions Supplements Ser.: Vol. 35). (Illus.). 208p. 1991. 128.50 (*0-8176-2529-1*) Birkhauser.

Progress in Infrared Spectroscopy Vol. 2: Based on Lectures from the Sixth & Seventh Infrared Spectroscopy Institutes Held at Canisius College, Buffalo, New York, 1962 & 1963. Ed. by Herman A. Syzmanski. LC 62-13472. (Illus.). 304p. reprint ed. pap. 94.30 (*0-608-10885-5*, 201940500002) Bks Demand.

Progress in Inorganic Chemistry, Vol. 1. LC 59-13035. 576p. reprint ed. pap. 178.60 (*0-608-10888-X*, 200712100061) Bks Demand.

Progress in Inorganic Chemistry, 8 vols., Vol. 35. Stephen J. Lippard. (Progress in Inorganic Chemistry Ser.). 660p. 1987. 275.00 (*0-471-84291-5*, Wiley-Interscience) Wiley.

Progress in Inorganic Chemistry, 8 vols., Vol. 37. Stephen J. Lippard. (Progress in Inorganic Chemistry Ser.). 613p. 1989. 275.00 (*0-471-62297-4*) Wiley.

Progress in Inorganic Chemistry, 8 vols., Vol. 38. Stephen J. Lippard. (Progress in Inorganic Chemistry Ser.). 535p. 1991. pap. 98.95 (*0-471-52945-1*) Wiley.

Progress in Inorganic Chemistry, Vol. 40. Ed. by Stephen J. Lippard. LC 59-13035. 608p. 1992. 275.00 (*0-471-57191-1*) Wiley.

Progress in Inorganic Chemistry, Vol. 41. Ed. by Kenneth D. Karlin. 848p. 1993. 175.00 (*0-471-59699-X*) Wiley.

Progress in Inorganic Chemistry, Vol. 42. Kenneth D. Karlin. (Progress in Inorganic Chemistry Ser.: Vol. 42). 606p. 1994. 170.00 (*0-471-04693-0*) Wiley.

Progress in Inorganic Chemistry, Vol. 43. Ed. by Kenneth D. Karlin. LC 59-13035. 592p. 1995. 165.00 (*0-471-12336-6*) Wiley.

Progress in Inorganic Chemistry, Vol. 45. Ed. by Kenneth D. Karlin. LC 59-13035. (Progress in Inorganic Chemistry Ser.). 510p. 1996. 159.00 (*0-471-16357-0*, Wiley-Interscience) Wiley.

Progress in Inorganic Chemistry, Vol. 46. Ed. by Kenneth D. Karlin. LC 59-13035. (Progress in Inorganic Chemistry Ser.). 488p. 1997. 159.00 (*0-471-17992-2*) Wiley.

Progress in Inorganic Chemistry, Vol. 47. Ed. by Kenneth D. Karlin. 992p. 1997. 175.00 (*0-471-24039-7*) Wiley.

Progress in Inorganic Chemistry, Vol. 48. Ed. by Kenneth D. Karlin. 616p. 1999. 145.00 (*0-471-32623-2*) Wiley.

Progress in Inorganic Chemistry: Molecular Level Artificial Photosynthetic Materials, Vol. 44. Gerald Meyer. LC 59-13035. (Progress in Inorganic Chemistry Ser.). 421p. 1996. 175.00 (*0-471-12535-0*) Wiley.

Progress in Inorganic Chemistry, Vol. 33, 8 vols., Vol. 33. Stephen J. Lippard. (Progress in Inorganic Chemistry Ser.). 533p. 1985. 275.00 (*0-471-80334-0*, Wiley-Interscience) Wiley.

Progress in Inorganic Chemistry, Vol. 34, 8 vols., Vol. 34. Stephen J. Lippard. (Progress in Inorganic Chemistry Ser.). 701p. 1986. 275.00 (*0-471-81948-4*, Wiley-Interscience) Wiley.

Progress in Inorganic Chemistry, Vol. 39, 8 vols., Vol. 39. Stephen J. Lippard. (Progress in Inorganic Chemistry Ser.). 544p. 1991. 275.00 (*0-471-54489-2*) Wiley.

Progress in Intercalation Research. Ed. by W. Muller-Warmuth & R. Schollhorn. LC 93-4586. (Physics & Chemistry of Materials with Low-Dimensional Structures Ser.: Vol. 17). 544p. 1993. text 336.00 (*0-7923-2357-2*) Kluwer Academic.

Progress in International Organization. Manley O. Hudson. ix, 162p. 1981. reprint ed. 35.00 (*0-8377-0637-8*, Rothman) W S Hein.

Progress in International Research on Thermodynamic & Transport Properties: Papers Presented at Second Symposium on Thermophysical Properties, Princeton, NJ, 1962. Thermophysical Properties Symposium Staff. Ed. by Joseph F. Masi & Donald H. Tsai. LC 62-11754. 772p. reprint ed. pap. 200.00 (*0-608-14758-3*, 202111500020) Bks Demand.

Progress in Inventory Research: A Selection of Papers Presented at the Fourth International Syumposium on Inventories, Budapest, August 25-19, 1986. Attila Chikan. 446p. (C). 1989. 125.00 (*963-05-4900-X*, Pub. by Akade Kiado) St Mut.

Progress in Inverse Spectral Geometry. S. I. Andersson & Michel L. Lapidus. LC 97-35734. (Trends in Mathematics Ser.). (ENG & FRE.). 1997. write for info. (*3-7643-5755-X*) Birkhauser.

Progress in Ion Exchange: Advances & Applications, Proceedings. Conference on Progress in Ion Exchange (1995: Wrex. Ed. by A. Dyer et al. 498p. 1997. text 174.00 (*0-85404-791-3*, QD562) Am Chemical.

Progress in Iron Research. C. Hershko et al. (Advances in Experimental Medicine & Biology Ser.: Vol. 356). (Illus.). 412p. (C). 1994. text 125.00 (*0-306-44729-0*, Kluwer Plenum) Kluwer Academic.

Progress in Laboratory Diagnosis. 1997. text 19.00 (*3-540-99546-3*) Spr-Verlag.

Progress in Land Evaluation. Ed. by J. C. Haans et al. (Illus.). 320p. (C). 1984. text 123.00 (*90-6191-545-7*, Pub. by A A Balkema) Ashgate Pub Co.

Progress in Language Planning: International Perspectives, No. xi. Ed. by Juan Cobarrubias & Joshua A. Fishman. LC 82-22310. (Contributions to the Sociology of Language Ser.: No. 31). 383p. 1983. 93.85 (*90-279-3358-8*); pap. 41.95 (*90-279-3388-X*) Mouton.

Progress in Language, with Special Reference to English. Otto Jespersen. LC 93-36955. (Amsterdam Classics in Linguistics Ser.: No. 17). xviii, 186p. 1993. 59.00 (*1-55619-314-9*) J Benjamins Pubng Co.

Progress in Laser Therapy: Selected Papers from the October 1990 ILTA Congress. Ed. by Toshio Ohshiro & R. G. Calderhead. LC 91-24452. (Illus.). 246p. 1991. reprint ed. pap. 76.30 (*0-608-01640-3*, 206222500002) Bks Demand.

Progress in Leaf Protein Research. (Current Trends in Life Sciences Ser.: Vol. 11). (Illus.). 525p. 1984. 79.00 (*1-55528-046-3*, Pub. by Today Tomorrow) Scholarly Pubns.

Progress in Linguistic Historiography: Papers from the International Conference on the History of the Language Sciences, Ottawa, 28-31 August 1978. Ed. by E. Konrad Koerner. (Studies in History of the Language Sciences: 20). xiv, 421p. 1980. 78.00 (*90-272-4501-0*) J Benjamins Pubng Co.

Progress in Linguistics: A Collection of Papers. Ed. by Manfred Bierwisch & Karl E. Heidolph. LC 78-123127. (Janua Linguarum, Ser.: No. 43). 1970. text 63.10 (*90-279-0723-4*) Mouton.

Progress in Lipid Research, Vol. 17. Ed. by Ralph T. Holman. 396p. 1980. 84.00 (*0-08-023797-5*, Pergamon Pr) Elsevier.

Progress in Lipid Research, Vol. 18. Ed. by Ralph T. Holman. (Illus.). 180p. 1981. 91.00 (*0-08-027129-4*, Pergamon Pr) Elsevier.

Progress in Lipid Research, Vol. 22. Ed. by Ralph T. Holman. (Illus.). 306p. 1984. 150.00 (*0-08-031507-0*, Pergamon Pr) Elsevier.

Progress in Lipid Research: Golden Jubilee International Conference, Minnesota, May 4-7, 1980, Vol. 20. Ed. by R. J. Holman. (Illus.). 968p. 1982. 415.00 (*0-08-028011-0*, H115, H125, Pub. by Pergamon Repr) Franklin.

Progress in Liquid Physics. Ed. by Clive A. Croxton. LC 76-40166. 602p. 1978. reprint ed. pap. 186.70 (*0-608-08311-9*, 203054100069) Bks Demand.

Progress in Littorinid & Muricid Biology. Ed. by K. Johannesson et al. (C). 1990. text 273.00 (*0-7923-0695-3*) Kluwer Academic.

Progress in Liver Diseases, Vol. 9. Fenton Schaffner & Arthur N. Popper. (Illus.). 736p. 1990. text 235.00 (*0-7216-2940-7*, W B Saunders Co) Harcrt Hlth Sci Grp.

Progress in Liver Transplantation. Ed. by Chris H. Gips. (Developments in Gastroenterology Ser.). 1985. text 215.00 (*0-89838-726-4*) Kluwer Academic.

Progress in Love on the Slow Side. Jean Paulhan. Tr. by Christine M. Laennec & Michael Syrotinski. LC 94-1316. (French Modernist Library). xxii, 146p. 1994. text 35.00 (*0-8032-3705-7*) U of Nebr Pr.

Progress in Low Temperature Physics, Vol. XIV. Ed. by W. P. Halperin. 482p. 1995. 244.00 (*0-444-82233-X*, North Holland) Elsevier.

Progress in Machine Translation. Ed. by S. Nirenburg. LC 92-3503. 334p. 1992. 70.00 (*90-5199-074-X*, Pub. by IOS Pr) IOS Press.

Progress in Managing Medicine. Sanderson. (C). 1998. pap. text. write for info. (*0-443-05655-2*) Church.

Progress in Marketing. Ed. by J. A. Dawson et al. 224p. 1989. 39.00 (*0-86187-961-9*) St Martin.

Progress in Material Handling & Logistics Vol. 2: Material Handling '90. Ed. by J. A. White, Jr. & I. W. Pence. x, 580p. 1991. 141.95 (*0-387-53442-3*) Spr-Verlag.

Progress in Material Science, Vol. 24. Ed. by J. W. Christian et al. (Illus.). 346p. 1980. 115.00 (*0-08-027107-3*, Pergamon Pr) Elsevier.

Progress in Materials Handling & Logistics. Ed. by J. A. White & I. W. Pence, Jr. (Illus.). x, 345p. 1989. 128.95 (*0-387-51836-3*) Spr-Verlag.

Progress in Materials Science, Vol. 14. B. Chalmers. 1969. pap. 45.00 (*0-08-006404-3*, Pergamon Pr) Elsevier.

Progress in Materials Science, Vol. 14. B. Chalmers. 1971. 115.00 (*0-08-016136-7*, Pergamon Pr) Elsevier.

Progress in Materials Science, Vol. 23. Ed. by B. Chalmers. 280p. 1980. 115.00 (*0-08-024846-2*, Pergamon Pr) Elsevier.

Progress in Materials Science, Vol. 25. J. W. Christian et al. 1982. 120.00 (*0-08-029096-5*, Pergamon Pr) Elsevier.

Progress in Materials Science, Vol. 26. Ed. by J. W. Christian et al. (Illus.). 420p. 1982. 145.00 (*0-08-029122-8*, Pergamon Pr) Elsevier.

Progress in Materials Science, Vol. 27. Ed. by J. W. Christian et al. (Illus.). 460p. 1983. 145.00 (*0-08-030029-4*, Pergamon Pr) Elsevier.

Progress in Materials Science, Vol. 28. Ed. by J. W. Christan et al. (Illus.). 450p. 1985. 170.00 (*0-08-032741-9*, Pub. by PPL) Elsevier.

Progress in Materials Science, Vol. 29. Ed. by J. W. Christian et al. (Illus.). 394p. 1986. 156.00 (*0-08-034154-3*, Pub. by PPL) Elsevier.

Progress in Materials Science, Vols. 6-10, 12-13. Incl. Vol. 9, Pt. 3. Effects of Environment on Mechanical Properties of Metals. 1961. pap. 22.00 (*0-08-009471-6*); Vol. 10, Pt. 1. Alloy Phases of the Noble Metals. 1962. pap. 20.00 (*0-08-009618-2*); Vol. 15, Pt. 1. 1970. pap. 24.00 (*0-08-015869-2*); Vol. 15, Pt. 2. 1972. pap. 24.00 (*0-08-016824-8*); Vol. 15, Pt. 3. 1972. pap. 24.00 (*0-08-016877-9*); Vol. 16. 1972. (*0-08-016866-3*); Vol. 18. 1974. 115.00 (*0-08-017155-9*); Vol. 19. 1974. 115.00 (*0-08-017964-9*); Vol. 20. 1977. 485.00 (*0-08-021143-7*); Vol. 21, Pt. 1. 1975. pap. 18.75 (*0-08-018172-4*); Vol. 21, Pt. 2. 1976. pap. 24.00 (*0-08-019831-7*); Vol. 21, Pts. 3 & 4. 1976. pap. 52.00 (*0-08-019987-9*); Vol. 21, Complete. 1977. 115.00 (*0-08-018171-6*); Vol. 9, Pt. 1. 1961. pap. Vol. 9, Pt. 2. 1962. pap. Vol. 9, Pt. 4. 1962. pap. Vol. 9, Pt. 5. 1962. pap. Vol. 12, Pt. 1. 1963. pap. Vol. 13, Pt. 1. pap. pap. write for info. (*0-318-55203-5*, Pub. by Pergamon Repr) Franklin.

Progress in Materials Science, Vols. 15-21. Incl. Vol. 9, Pt. 3. Effects of Environment on Mechanical Properties of Metals. 1961. pap. 22.00 (*0-08-009471-6*); Vol. 10, Pt. 1. Alloy Phases of the Noble Metals. 1962. pap. 20.00 (*0-08-009618-2*); Vol. 15, Pt. 1. 1970. pap. 24.00 (*0-08-015869-2*); Vol. 15, Pt. 2. 1972. pap. 24.00 (*0-08-016824-8*); Vol. 15, Pt. 3. 1972. pap. 24.00 (*0-08-016877-9*); Vol. 16. 1972. (*0-08-016866-3*); Vol. 18. 1974. 115.00 (*0-08-017155-9*); Vol. 19. 1974. 115.00 (*0-08-017964-9*); Vol. 20. 1977. 485.00 (*0-08-021143-7*); Vol. 21, Pt. 1. 1975. pap. 18.75 (*0-08-018172-4*); Vol. 21, Pt. 2. 1976. pap. 24.00 (*0-08-019831-7*); Vol. 21, Pts. 3 & 4. 1976. pap. 52.00 (*0-08-019987-9*); Vol. 21, Complete. 1977. 115.00 (*0-08-018171-6*); Vol. 9, Pt. 1. 1961. pap. Vol. 9, Pt. 2. 1962. pap. Vol. 9, Pt. 4. 1962. pap. Vol. 9, Pt. 5. 1962. pap. Vol. 12, Pt. 1. 1963. pap. Vol. 13, Pt. 1. pap. pap. write for info. (*0-318-55202-7*, Pub. by Pergamon Repr) Franklin.

Progress in Mathematical Programming. Ed. by Nimrod Megiddo. (Illus.). x, 158p. 1988. 79.95 (*0-387-96847-4*) Spr-Verlag.

Progress in Mathematics, 4 vols. Incl. Vol. 10. Mathematical Analysis. Tr. by J. S. Wood. LC 67-27902. 117p. pap. 36.30 (*0-608-08313-5*, 202472100010); Vol. 11. Probability Theory, Mathematical Statistics, & Theoretical Cybernetics. Tr. by J. S. Wood. LC

P

An Asterisk (*) at the beginning of an entry indicates that the title is appearing for the first time.

67-27902. 132p. pap. 41.00 (*0-608-08314-3*, 202472100011); Vol. 12. Algebra & Geometry. Tr. by Nasli H. Choksy. LC 67-27902. 264p. pap. 81.90 (*0-608-08315-1*, 202472100012); Vol. 13. Probability Theory, Mathematical Statistics & Theoretical Cybernetics. Tr. by J. S. Wood. LC 67-27902. 118p. pap. 36.60 (*0-608-16086-5*, 202472100013); LC 67-27902. reprint ed. write for info. (*0-608-18690-2*, 2024721) Bks Demand.

Progress in Mathematics, Vol. 2. Progress in Mathematics Staff. Ed. by R. V. Gamkrelidze. LC 67-27902. (RUS.). 169p. 1968. reprint ed. pap. 52.40 (*0-608-08312-7*, 202630500002) Bks Demand.

***Progress in Mathematics, Grade 5, Skills Update Practice Book.** Rose Anita McDonnell et al. (Progress in Mathematics Ser.: Vol. 7). (Illus.). 32p. (J). (gr. 5-6). 2000. pap. 1.95 (*0-8215-2645-6*) Sadlier.

***Progress in Mathematics, Grade 5, Skills Update Practice Book, Teacher's Edition.** Rose Anita McDonnell et al. (Progress in Mathematics Ser.: Vol. 7). (Illus.). 32p. 2000. pap., teacher ed. 3.00 (*0-8215-2655-3*) Sadlier.

***Progress in Mathematics, Grade 5, Student Text.** Rose Anita McDonnell et al. (Progress in Mathematics Ser.: Vol. 7). (Illus.). 516p. (J). (gr. 5-6). 2000. text 39.12 (*0-8215-2605-7*) Sadlier.

***Progress in Mathematics, Grade 5, Student Test Booklet.** Rose Anita McDonnell et al. (Progress in Mathematics Ser.: Vol. 7). (Illus.). 32p. (J). (gr. 5-6). 2000. pap. write for info. (*0-8215-2665-0*) Sadlier.

***Progress in Mathematics, Grade 5, Teacher's Edition.** Rose Anita McDonnell et al. (Progress in Mathematics Ser.: Vol. 7). (Illus.). 646p. 2000. teacher ed., spiral bd. 67.50 (*0-8215-2615-4*) Sadlier.

***Progress in Mathematics, Grade 5, Workbook.** Rose Anita McDonnell et al. (Progress in Mathematics Ser.: Vol. 7). (Illus.). 160p. (J). (gr. 5-6). 2000. pap., wbk. ed. 9.60 (*0-8215-2625-1*) Sadlier.

***Progress in Mathematics, Grade 5, Workbook, Teacher's Edition.** Rose Anita McDonnell et al. (Progress in Mathematics Ser.: Vol. 7). (Illus.). 160p. 2000. pap., teacher ed., wbk. ed. 10.59 (*0-8215-2635-9*) Sadlier.

***Progress in Mathematics, Grade 4, Skills Update Practice Book.** Rose Anita McDonnell et al. (Progress in Mathematics Ser.: Vol. 7). (Illus.). 32p. (J). (gr. 4-5). 2000. pap. 1.95 (*0-8215-2644-8*) Sadlier.

***Progress in Mathematics, Grade 4, Skills Update Practice Book, Teacher's Edition.** Rose Anita McDonnell et al. (Progress in Mathematics Ser.: Vol. 7). (Illus.). 32p. 2000. pap., teacher ed. 3.00 (*0-8215-2654-5*) Sadlier.

***Progress in Mathematics, Grade 4, Student Text.** Rose Anita McDonnell et al. (Progress in Mathematics Ser.: Vol. 7). (Illus.). 520p. (J). (gr. 4-5). 2000. text 38.40 (*0-8215-2604-9*) Sadlier.

***Progress in Mathematics, Grade 4, Student Test Booklet.** Rose Anita McDonnell et al. (Progress in Mathematics Ser.: Vol. 7). (Illus.). 32p. (J). (gr. 4-5). 2000. pap. write for info. (*0-8215-2664-2*) Sadlier.

***Progress in Mathematics, Grade 4, Teacher's Edition.** Rose Anita McDonnell et al. (Progress in Mathematics Ser.: Vol. 7). (Illus.). 640p. 2000. teacher ed., spiral bd. 67.50 (*0-8215-2614-6*) Sadlier.

***Progress in Mathematics, Grade 4, Workbook.** Rose Anita McDonnell et al. (Progress in Mathematics Ser.: Vol. 7). (Illus.). 160p. (J). (gr. 4-5). 2000. pap., wbk. ed. 9.60 (*0-8215-2624-3*) Sadlier.

***Progress in Mathematics, Grade 4, Workbook, Teacher's Edition.** Rose Anita McDonnell et al. (Progress in Mathematics Ser.: Vol. 7). (Illus.). 160p. 2000. pap., teacher ed., wbk. ed. 10.59 (*0-8215-2634-0*) Sadlier.

***Progress in Mathematics, Grade K, Student Text.** Rose Anita McDonnell et al. (Progress in Mathematics Ser.: Vol. 7). (Illus.). 320p. (J). (gr. k-1). 2000. pap. text 16.35 (*0-8215-2600-6*) Sadlier.

***Progress in Mathematics, Grade K, Teacher's Edition.** Rose Anita McDonnell et al. (Progress in Mathematics Ser.: Vol. 7). (Illus.). 464p. 2000. teacher ed., spiral bd. 61.50 (*0-8215-2610-3*) Sadlier.

***Progress in Mathematics, Grade K, Workbook.** Rose Anita McDonnell et al. (Progress in Mathematics Ser.: Vol. 7). (Illus.). 128p. (J). (gr. k). 2000. pap. text, wbk. ed. 7.50 (*0-8215-2620-0*) Sadlier.

***Progress in Mathematics, Grade K, Workbook, Teacher's Edition.** Rose Anita McDonnell et al. (Progress in Mathematics Ser.: Vol. 7). (Illus.). 128p. 2000. pap., teacher ed., wbk. ed. 8.49 (*0-8215-2630-8*) Sadlier.

***Progress in Mathematics, Grade 1, Skills Update Practice Book.** Rose Anita McDonnell et al. (Progress in Mathematics Ser.: Vol. 7). (Illus.). 32p. (J). 2000. pap. 1.95 (*0-8215-2641-3*) Sadlier.

***Progress in Mathematics, Grade 1, Skills Update Practice Book, Teacher's Edition.** Rose Anita McDonnell et al. (Progress in Mathematics Ser.: Vol. 7). (Illus.). 32p. 2000. pap., teacher ed. 3.00 (*0-8215-2651-0*) Sadlier.

***Progress in Mathematics, Grade 1, Student Text.** Rose Anita McDonnell et al. (Progress in Mathematics Ser.: Vol. 7). (Illus.). 506p. (J). (gr. 1-2). 2000. pap. text 21.12 (*0-8215-2601-4*) Sadlier.

***Progress in Mathematics, Grade 1, Student Test Booklet with Answer Booklet.** Rose Anita McDonnell et al. (Progress in Mathematics Ser.: Vol. 7). (Illus.). 32p. (J). (gr. 1-2). 2000. pap. write for info. (*0-8215-2661-8*) Sadlier.

***Progress in Mathematics, Grade 1, Teacher's Edition.** Rose Anita McDonnell et al. (Progress in Mathematics Ser.: Vol. 7). (Illus.). 496p. 2000. teacher ed., spiral bd. 61.50 (*0-8215-2611-1*) Sadlier.

***Progress in Mathematics, Grade 1, Workbook.** Rose Anita McDonnell et al. (Progress in Mathematics Ser.: Vol. 7). (Illus.). 160p. (J). 2000. pap., wbk. ed. 7.50 (*0-8215-2621-9*) Sadlier.

***Progress in Mathematics, Grade 1, Workbook, Teacher's Edition.** Rose Anita McDonnell et al. (Progress in Mathematics Ser.: Vol. 7). (Illus.). 160p. 2000. pap., teacher ed., wbk. ed. 8.49 (*0-8215-2631-6*) Sadlier.

***Progress in Mathematics, Grade 6, Skills Update Practice Book.** Rose Anita McDonnell et al. (Progress in Mathematics Ser.: Vol. 7). (Illus.). 32p. (YA). (gr. 6-7). 2000. pap. 1.95 (*0-8215-2646-4*) Sadlier.

***Progress in Mathematics, Grade 6, Skills Update Practice Booklet, Teacher's Edition.** Rose Anita McDonnell et al. (Progress in Mathematics Ser.: Vol. 7). (Illus.). 32p. 2000. pap., teacher ed. 3.00 (*0-8215-2656-1*) Sadlier.

***Progress in Mathematics, Grade 6, Student Text.** Rose Anita McDonnell et al. (Progress in Mathematics Ser.: Vol. 7). (Illus.). 546p. (YA). (gr. 6-7). 2000. text 39.96 (*0-8215-2606-5*) Sadlier.

***Progress in Mathematics, Grade 6, Student Test Book.** Rose Anita McDonnell et al. (Progress in Mathematics Ser.: Vol. 7). (Illus.). 32p. (YA). (gr. 6-7). 2000. pap. write for info. (*0-8215-2666-9*) Sadlier.

***Progress in Mathematics, Grade 6, Teacher's Edition.** Rose Anita McDonnell et al. (Progress in Mathematics Ser.: Vol. 7). (Illus.). 672p. 2000. teacher ed., spiral bd. 69.00 (*0-8215-2616-2*) Sadlier.

***Progress in Mathematics, Grade 6, Workbook.** Rose Anita McDonnell et al. (Progress in Mathematics Ser.: Vol. 7). (Illus.). 176p. (YA). (gr. 6-7). 2000. pap., wbk. ed. 9.60 (*0-8215-2626-X*) Sadlier.

***Progress in Mathematics, Grade 6, Workbook, Teacher's Edition.** Rose Anita McDonnell et al. (Progress in Mathematics Ser.: Vol. 7). (Illus.). 176p. 2000. pap., teacher ed., wbk. ed. 10.59 (*0-8215-2636-7*) Sadlier.

***Progress in Mathematics, Grade 3, Skills Update Practice Book.** Rose Anita McDonnell et al. (Progress in Mathematics Ser.: Vol. 7). (Illus.). 32p. (J). (gr. 3-4). 2000. pap. 1.95 (*0-8215-2643-X*) Sadlier.

***Progress in Mathematics, Grade 3, Skills Update Practice Book, Teacher's Edition.** Rose Anita McDonnell et al. (Progress in Mathematics Ser.: Vol. 7). (Illus.). 32p. 2000. pap., teacher ed. 3.00 (*0-8215-2653-7*) Sadlier.

***Progress in Mathematics, Grade 3, Student Text.** Rose Anita McDonnell et al. (Progress in Mathematics Ser.: Vol. 7). (Illus.). 500p. (J). (gr. 3-4). 2000. text 38.40 (*0-8215-2603-0*) Sadlier.

***Progress in Mathematics, Grade 3, Student Test Booklet.** Rose Anita McDonnell et al. (Progress in Mathematics Ser.: Vol. 7). (Illus.). 32p. (J). (gr. 3-4). 2000. pap. write for info. (*0-8215-2663-4*) Sadlier.

***Progress in Mathematics, Grade 3, Teacher's Edition.** Rose Anita McDonnell et al. (Progress in Mathematics Ser.: Vol. 7). (Illus.). 640p. 2000. teacher ed., spiral bd. 67.50 (*0-8215-2613-8*) Sadlier.

***Progress in Mathematics, Grade 3, Workbook.** Rose Anita McDonnell et al. (Progress in Mathematics Ser.: Vol. 7). (Illus.). 160p. (J). (gr. 3-4). 2000. pap., wbk. ed. 9.60 (*0-8215-2623-5*) Sadlier.

***Progress in Mathematics, Grade 3, Workbook, Teacher's Edition.** Rose Anita McDonnell et al. (Progress in Mathematics Ser.: Vol. 7). (Illus.). 160p. 2000. pap., teacher ed., wbk. ed. 10.59 (*0-8215-2633-2*) Sadlier.

***Progress in Mathematics, Grade 2, Skills Update Practice Book.** Rose Anita McDonnell et al. (Progress in Mathematics Ser.: Vol. 7). (Illus.). 32p. (J). (gr. 2-3). 2000. pap. 1.95 (*0-8215-2642-1*) Sadlier.

***Progress in Mathematics, Grade 2, Skills Update Practice Book, Teacher's Edition.** Rose Anita McDonnell et al. (Progress in Mathematics Ser.: Vol. 7). (Illus.). 32p. 2000. pap., teacher ed. 3.00 (*0-8215-2652-9*) Sadlier.

***Progress in Mathematics, Grade 2, Student Text.** Rose Anita McDonnell et al. (Progress in Mathematics Ser.: Vol. 7). (Illus.). 496p. (J). (gr. 2-3). 2000. pap. text 21.12 (*0-8215-2602-2*) Sadlier.

***Progress in Mathematics, Grade 2, Student Test Booklet.** Rose Anita McDonnell et al. (Progress in Mathematics Ser.: Vol. 7). (Illus.). 32p. (J). (gr. 2-3). 2000. pap. 29.47 (*0-8215-2662-6*) Sadlier.

***Progress in Mathematics, Grade 2, Teacher's Manual.** Rose Anita McDonnell et al. (Progress in Mathematics Ser.: Vol. 7). (Illus.). 640p. 2000. teacher ed., spiral bd. 61.50 (*0-8215-2612-X*) Sadlier.

***Progress in Mathematics, Grade 2, Workbook.** Rose Anita McDonnell et al. (Progress in Mathematics Ser.: Vol. 7). (Illus.). 160p. (J). (gr. 2-3). 2000. pap., wbk. ed. 7.50 (*0-8215-2622-7*) Sadlier.

***Progress in Mathematics, Grade 2, Workbook, Teacher's Edition.** Rose Anita McDonnell et al. (Progress in Mathematics Ser.: Vol. 7). (Illus.). 160p. 2000. pap., teacher ed., wbk. ed. 8.49 (*0-8215-2632-4*) Sadlier.

Progress in Medical Genetics, Vol. 1. Arthur G. Steinberg et al. LC 75-21151. (Illus.). 300p. 1976. text. write for info. (*0-7216-8586-2*) W B Saunders.

Progress in Medical Genetics, Vol. III. Arthur G. Steinberg et al. LC 60-53514. (Illus.). 1979. text. write for info. (*0-7216-8599-4*) W B Saunders.

Progress in Medical Genetics, Vols. II-III & VI-X. Ed. by Arthur G. Steinberg & Alexander G. Bearn. Incl. Vol. II. LC 60-53514. (Illus.). 384p. 1962. 54.50 (*0-8089-0479-5*, W B Saunders Co); Vol. III. LC 60-53514. (Illus.). 272p. 1963. 80.00 (*0-8089-0480-9*, W B Saunders Co); LC 60-53514. write for info. (*0-318-52861-4*, Grune & Strat) Harcrt Hlth Sci Grp.

Progress in Medical Radiation Physics, Vol. 1. Ed. by Colin G. Orton. 402p. 1982. 95.00 (*0-306-40713-2*, Plenum Trade) Perseus Pubng.

Progress in Medical Radiation Physics, Vol. 2. Ed. by Colin G. Orton. 248p. 1985. 95.00 (*0-306-41789-8*, Plenum Trade) Perseus Pubng.

Progress in Medical Radioisotope Scanning: Proceedings. Ed. by Ralph M. Kniseley & Gould A. Andrews. (AEC Symposium Ser.). 539p. 1963. pap. 6.25 (*0-685-01483-5*); fiche 9.00 (*0-87079-314-4*, TID-7673) DOE.

Progress in Medical Terminology. Ed. by Alexandre Manuila. (Illus.). xii, 116p. 1981. pap. 68.75 (*3-8055-2112-X*) S Karger.

Progress in Medical Virology, Vol. 12. Ed. by Joseph L. Melnick. 1970. 75.00 (*3-8055-0409-8*) S Karger.

Progress in Medical Virology, Vol. 13. Ed. by Joseph L. Melnick. 1971. 95.75 (*3-8055-1181-7*) S Karger.

Progress in Medical Virology, Vol. 14. Ed. by Joseph L. Melnick. 1972. 82.75 (*3-8055-1291-0*) S Karger.

Progress in Medical Virology, Vol. 16. Ed. by Joseph L. Melnick. (Illus.). 1973. 85.25 (*3-8055-1601-0*) S Karger.

Progress in Medical Virology, Vol. 17. Ed. by Joseph L. Melnick. 400p. 1974. 85.25 (*3-8055-1642-8*) S Karger.

Progress in Medical Virology, Vol. 20. Ed. by Joseph L. Melnick. (Illus.). 400p. 1975. 86.25 (*3-8055-2161-8*) S Karger.

Progress in Medical Virology, Vol. 22. Ed. by Joseph L. Melnick. 250p. 1976. 103.50 (*3-8055-2315-7*) S Karger.

Progress in Medical Virology, Vol. 23. Ed. by Joseph L. Melnick. (Illus.). 1977. 95.75 (*3-8055-2423-4*) S Karger.

Progress in Medical Virology, Vol. 24. Ed. by Joseph L. Melnick. (Illus.). 1978. 94.00 (*3-8055-2810-8*) S Karger.

Progress in Medical Virology, Vol. 25. Ed. by Joseph L. Melnick. (Illus.). 1979. 77.50 (*3-8055-2978-3*) S Karger.

Progress in Medical Virology, Vol. 26. Ed. by Joseph L. Melnick. (Illus.). viii, 240p. 1980. 129.75 (*3-8055-0702-X*) S Karger.

Progress in Medical Virology, Vol. 28. Ed. by Joseph L. Melnick. (Illus.). x, 234p. 1982. 128.75 (*3-8055-2983-X*) S Karger.

Progress in Medical Virology, Vol. 29. Ed. by Joseph L. Melnick. (Illus.). x, 246p. 1984. 128.75 (*3-8055-3618-6*) S Karger.

Progress in Medical Virology, Vol. 30. Ed. by Joseph L. Melnick & K. Hummeler. (Illus.). viii, 212p. 1984. 135.00 (*3-8055-3851-0*) S Karger.

Progress in Medical Virology, Vol. 31. Ed. by Joseph L. Melnick. (Illus.). x, 234p. 1984. 142.75 (*3-8055-3909-6*) S Karger.

Progress in Medical Virology, Vol. 33. Ed. by Joseph L. Melnick. (Illus.). viii, 182p. 1986. 129.75 (*3-8055-4155-4*) S Karger.

Progress in Medical Virology, Vol. 34. Ed. by Joseph L. Melnick. (Illus.). x, 206p. 1987. 150.50 (*3-8055-4468-5*) S Karger.

Progress in Medical Virology, Vol. 35. Ed. by Joseph L. Melnick. (Illus.). viii, 220p. 1988. 173.25 (*3-8055-4711-0*) S Karger.

Progress in Medical Virology, Vol. 36. Ed. by Joseph L. Melnick. (Illus.). viii, 210p. 1989. 164.50 (*3-8055-4834-6*) S Karger.

Progress in Medical Virology, Vol. 37. Ed. by Joseph L. Melnick. (Illus.). x, 250p. 1990. 197.50 (*3-8055-5077-4*) S Karger.

Progress in Medical Virology, Vol. 39. Ed. by Joseph L. Melnick. (Illus.). x, 270p. 1992. 231.50 (*3-8055-5428-1*) S Karger.

Progress in Medical Virology, Vol. 40. Ed. by Joseph L. Melnick. (Illus.). viii, 224p. 1993. 230.50 (*3-8055-5600-4*) S Karger.

***Progress in Medicinal Chemistry.** Ed. by F. D. King & A. W. Oxford. 310p. 1999. 177.50 (*0-444-50090-1*) Elsevier.

Progress in Medicinal Chemistry, 6 vols., 1. Ed. by G. P. Ellis & G. B. West. LC 62-2712. 272p. reprint ed. pap. 84.40 (*0-608-08317-8*, 202576400001) Bks Demand.

Progress in Medicinal Chemistry, 6 vols., 2. Ed. by G. P. Ellis & G. B. West. LC 62-2712. 211p. reprint ed. pap. 65.50 (*0-608-08318-6*, 202576400002) Bks Demand.

Progress in Medicinal Chemistry, 6 vols., 3. Ed. by G. P. Ellis & G. B. West. LC 62-2712. 417p. reprint ed. pap. 129.30 (*0-608-08319-4*, 202576400003) Bks Demand.

Progress in Medicinal Chemistry, 6 vols., 4. Ed. by G. P. Ellis & G. B. West. LC 62-2712. 231p. reprint ed. pap. 71.70 (*0-608-08320-8*, 202576400004) Bks Demand.

Progress in Medicinal Chemistry, 6 vols., 5. Ed. by G. P. Ellis & G. B. West. LC 62-2712. 401p. reprint ed. pap. 124.40 (*0-608-08321-6*, 202576400005) Bks Demand.

Progress in Medicinal Chemistry, 6 vols., 6. Ed. by G. P. Ellis & G. B. West. LC 62-2712. 384p. reprint ed. pap. 119.10 (*0-608-08322-4*, 202576400006) Bks Demand.

Progress in Medicinal Chemistry, 33. Ed. by G. P. Ellis & D. K. Luscombe. 406p. 1996. 205.50 (*0-444-82057-4*) Elsevier.

Progress in Medicinal Chemistry, Vol. 29. G. P. Ellis & D. K. Luscombe. viii,350p. 1992. 206.50 (*0-444-89472-1*) Elsevier.

Progress in Medicinal Chemistry, Vol. 31. Ed. by M. Iqbal Choudhary. (Studies in Medicinal Chemistry). 400p. 1996. text 90.00 (*3-7186-5795-3*, Harwood Acad Pubs) Gordon & Breach.

Progress in Medicinal Chemistry, Vol. 31. Ed. by G. P. Ellis et al. 362p. 1994. text 238.00 (*0-444-81807-3*) Elsevier.

Progress in Medicinal Chemistry, Vol. 34. Ed. by G. P. Ellis et al. 406p. 1996. 187.00 (*0-444-82310-7*) Elsevier.

Progress in Medicinal Chemistry, Vol. 34. Ed. by D. K. Luscombe et al. 270p. 1998. 198.50 (*0-444-82632-7*) Elsevier.

Progress in Medicinal Chemistry, Vol. 35. Ed. by G. P. Ellis et al. 270p. 1998. 198.50 (*0-444-82909-1*) Elsevier.

Progress in Medicinal Chemistry 30, 31. Ed. by G. P. Ellis & D. K. Luscombe. 474p. 1993. 216.00 (*0-444-89989-8*) Elsevier.

Progress in Medicine. Iago Galdston. LC 76-39166. (Essay Index Reprint Ser.). 1977. 23.95 (*0-8369-2689-7*) Ayer.

Progress in Medium Energy Physics: Chinese-German Symposium. W. Y. Hwang & J. Speth. 308p. (C). 1989. text 130.00 (*9971-5-0914-8*) World Scientific Pub.

Progress in Membrane Biotechnology. Ed. by David J. Chapman et al. (Advances in Life Sciences Ser.). 352p. 1991. 110.00 (*0-8176-2666-2*) Birkhauser.

Progress in Metal Physics. B. Chalmers & R. King. (Progress in Materials Science Ser.: Vol. 5). 1954. 156.00 (*0-08-009012-5*, Pub. by Pergamon Repr) Franklin.

Progress in Metamorphic & Magmatic Petrology: A Memorial Volume in Honour of D. S. Korzhinskiy. Ed. by L. L. Perchuk. (Illus.). 519p. (C). 1991. text 140.00 (*0-521-39077-X*) Cambridge U Pr.

Progress in Metaphysics see Fortschritte der Metaphysik

Progress in Microcirculation Research. Niimi. LC 94-26568. 540p. 1994. 173.00 (*0-08-042503-8*, Pergamon Pr) Elsevier.

Progress in Microemulsions. Ed. by S. Martellucci & Arthur N. Chester. (Ettore Majorana International Science Series, Life Sciences: Vol. 41). (Illus.). 302p. 1989. 95.00 (*0-306-43212-9*, Plenum Trade) Perseus Pubng.

Progress in Micropaleontology: Papers in Honor of Professor Kiyoshi Asano. Ed. by T. Takayanagi & T. Saito. (Micropaleontology Special Publications). 422p. 1976. 35.00 (*0-686-84247-2*) Am Mus Natl Hist.

Progress in Mineral Processing Technology: Proceedings of the 5th International Mineral Processing Symposium, Cappadocia, Turkey, 6-8 September 1994. Ed. by Halim Demirel & Salih Ersayin. (Illus.). 596p. (C). 1994. text 142.00 (*90-5410-513-5*, Pub. by A A Balkema) Ashgate Pub Co.

Progress in Modern Cholinergic Biology: Model Cholinergic Synapses. Ed. by Israel Hanin & Alan M. Goldberg. LC 80-5249. (Illus.). 381p. 1982. reprint ed. pap. 118.20 (*0-608-00373-5*, 206108600007) Bks Demand.

Progress in Modern Psychology: The Legacy of American Functionalism. Ed. by D. Alfred Owens & Mark Wagner. LC 92-15990. 352p. 1992. 69.50 (*0-275-93055-6*, C3055, Praeger Pubs) Greenwood.

Progress in Molecular & Subcellular Biology, Vol. II. Ed. by W. E. Muller. (Illus.). 215p. 1990. 99.00 (*0-387-51832-0*) Spr-Verlag.

Progress in Molecular & Subcellular Biology, Vol. 4. (Illus.). 300p. 1976. 60.95 (*0-387-07487-2*) Spr-Verlag.

Progress in Molecular & Subcellular Biology, Vol. 8. Ed. by F. E. Hahn. (Illus.). 160p. 1983. 71.95 (*0-387-12590-6*) Spr-Verlag.

Progress in Molecular & Subcellular Biology, Vol. 9. (Illus.). 180p. 1985. 103.95 (*0-387-15071-4*) Spr-Verlag.

Progress in Molecular & Subcellular Biology, Vol. 12. Ed. by P. Jeanteur et al. (Illus.). ix, 137p. 1991. 103.95 (*0-387-53900-X*) Spr-Verlag.

Progress in Molecular & Subcellular Biology, Vol. 17. Ed. by W. E. Muller et al. LC 96-3924. (Progress in Molecular & Subcellular Biology Ser.: No. 17). (Illus.). 224p. 1996. 149.50 (*3-540-60796-X*) Spr-Verlag.

Progress in Molecular & Subcellular Biology: Biological Response Modifiers Interferone, Double-Stranded RNA & 2-5 Adenylate, Vol. 14. Ed. by W. E. G. Muller et al. (Illus.). 1994. 136.00 (*0-387-57285-6*) Spr-Verlag.

Progress in Molecular & Subcellular Biology: Molecular & Cellular Enzymology, Vol. 13. Ed. by Y. Kuchino et al. (Illus.). 1994. 136.00 (*0-387-57337-2*) Spr-Verlag.

Progress in Molecular Spectroscopy. Ed. by R. Salzer et al. (Teubner Physics Texts Ser.: Vol. 20). 271p. 1989. pap. 45.00 (*3-322-00702-2*, Wiley-VCH) Wiley.

Progress in Motor Control: Bernstein's Traditions in Movement Studies, Vol. 1. Ed. by Mark L. Latash. LC 97-44950. (Illus.). 408p. 1998. text 49.00 (*0-88011-674-9*, BLAT0674) Human Kinetics.

Progress in Multiple Sclerosis Research. Ed. by H. J. Bauer. (Illus.). 630p. 1980. 68.95 (*0-387-09867-4*) Spr-Verlag.

Progress in Neural Information Processing: ICONIP'96: Proceedings of the International Conference on Neural Information Processing, Hong Kong, 24-27 September 1996. Shunichi Amari & Asian Pacific Neural Network Assembly Staff. LC 96-27442. 1997. 59.95 (*981-3083-04-2*); pap. 59.95 (*981-3083-03-4*) Spr-Verlag.

Progress in Neural Information Processing Set: Proceedings of the International Conference on Neural Information Processing (ICONIP '96), Hong Kong, 2 vols. Ed. by S. I. Amari et al. (Illus.). 700p. 1997. pap. 102.00 (*981-3083-05-0*) Spr-Verlag.

Progress in Neurobiology, Vol. 1. G. A. Kerkut. 1973. 125.00 (*0-08-017711-5*, Pergamon Pr) Elsevier.

Progress in Neurobiology, Vol. 2. G. A. Kerkut. 1975. 125.00 (*0-08-017882-0*, Pergamon Pr) Elsevier.

Progress in Neurobiology, Vol. 3. G. A. Kerkut. 1975. 125.00 (*0-08-017963-0*, Pergamon Pr) Elsevier.

Progress in Neurobiology, Vol. 11. Ed. by G. A. Kerkut & J. W. Phillis. 1979. 125.00 (*0-08-024857-8*, Pergamon Pr) Elsevier.

Progress in Neurobiology, Vol. 12. G. A. Kerkut. (Illus.). 312p. 1980. 125.00 (*0-08-024888-8*, Pergamon Pr) Elsevier.

Progress in Neurobiology, Vol. 13, Complete. Ed. by G. A. Kerkut. (Illus.). 440p. 1980. 125.00 (*0-08-026039-X*, Pergamon Pr) Elsevier.

Progress in Neurobiology, Vol. 14 Complete. Ed. by G. A. Kerkut & J. W. Phillis. 344p. 1980. 125.00 (*0-08-027114-6*, Pergamon Pr) Elsevier.

Progress in Neurobiology, Vol. 15. Ed. by G. A. Kerkut & J. W. Phillis. (Illus.). 344p. 1981. 130.00 (*0-08-029084-1*, H999, Pergamon Pr) Elsevier.

Progress in Neurobiology, Vol. 15, No.4. 1981. pap. 32.00 (*0-08-027148-0*, Pergamon Pr) Elsevier.

P

An Asterisk (*) at the beginning of an entry indicates that the title is appearing for the first time.

Progress in Neurobiology, Vol. 16. Ed. by G. A. Kerkut & J. W. Phillis. (Illus.). 320p. 1982. 125.00 (*0-08-029105-8*) Elsevier.

Progress in Neurobiology, Vol. 17. Ed. by G. A. Kerkut & J. W. Phillus. 289p. 1983. 125.00 (*0-08-029697-1*, Pergamon Pr) Elsevier.

Progress in Neurobiology, Vol. 18. Ed. by G. A. Kerkut & J. W. Phillis. (Illus.). 338p. 1983. 130.00 (*0-08-031046-X*, Pergamon Pr) Elsevier.

Progress in Neurobiology, Vol. 19. Ed. by G. A. Kerkut & J. W. Phillis. (Illus.). 370p. 1984. 130.00 (*0-08-031508-9*, Pergamon Pr) Elsevier.

Progress in Neurobiology, Vol. 20. Ed. by G. A. Kerkut & J. W. Phillis. LC 72-12616. (Illus.). 348p. 1984. 130.00 (*0-08-031706-5*, Pergamon Pr) Elsevier.

Progress in Neurobiology, Vol. 22. Ed. by G. A. Kerkut & J. W. Phillis. LC 72-12616. (Illus.). 374p. 1985. 150.00 (*0-08-032757-5*, Pub. by PPL) Elsevier.

Progress in Neurobiology, Vol. 23. Ed. by G. A. Kerkut & J. W. Phillis. LC 72-12616. (Illus.). 358p. 1985. 150.00 (*0-08-033211-0*, Pub. by PPL) Elsevier.

Progress in Neurobiology, Vol. 24. Ed. by G. A. Kerkut & J. W. Phillis. (Illus.). 350p. 138.00 (*0-08-033679-5*, H140, H110, Pub. by PPL) Elsevier.

Progress in Neurobiology, Vols. 1-7. Incl. Vol. 2. LC 72-12616. 1973. pap. 24.00 (*0-08-017688-7*); Vol. 2, Pt. 1. LC 72-12616. 1973. pap. 24.00 (*0-08-017752-2*); Pt. 2. LC 72-12616. 1974. pap. 24.00 (*0-08-017812-X*); Pt. 3. LC 72-12616. 1974. pap. 24.00 (*0-08-017929-0*); Vol. 3, Pt. 1. LC 72-12616. 1974. pap. 24.00 (*0-08-017956-8*); Pt. 2. LC 72-12616. 1974. pap. 24.00 (*0-08-018009-4*); Pt. 3. LC 72-12616. 1974. pap. 24.00 (*0-08-018023-X*); Pt. 4. LC 72-12616. 1974. pap. 24.00 (*0-08-018092-2*); Pt. 1. LC 72-12616. 1975. pap. 19.75 (*0-08-018093-0*); Pt. 2. LC 72-12616. 1974. pap. 29.00 (*0-08-018127-9*); Pt. 3. LC 72-12616. 1975. pap. 24.00 (*0-08-018157-0*); Pt. 4. LC 72-12616. 1975. pap. 24.00 (*0-08-018208-9*); Vol. 5. LC 72-12616. 1976. 125.00 (*0-08-018973-3*); Pt. 1. LC 72-12616. 1975. pap. 22.00 (*0-08-018969-5*); Pt. 2. LC 72-12616. 1975. pap. 17.25 (*0-08-018970-9*); Pt. 3. LC 72-12616. 1975. pap. 22.00 (*0-08-018971-7*); Pt. 4. LC 72-12616. 1975. pap. 29.00 (*0-08-018972-5*); Vol. 6. LC 72-12616. 1976. 125.00 (*0-08-020319-1*); Pt. 1. LC 72-12616. 1976. pap. 24.00 (*0-08-020615-8*); Pt. 2. LC 72-12616. 1976. pap. 24.00 (*0-08-020966-1*); Pts. 3-4. LC 72-12616. 1976. pap. 44.00 (*0-08-020976-9*); LC 72-12616. pap. write for info. (*0-318-55210-8*) Elsevier.

Progress in Neuroendocrinology Vol. 1: Neuroendricrinology of Hormone-Transmitter Interactions. Ed. by H. Parvez et al. 315p. 1985. lib. bdg. 127.50 (*90-6764-049-2*, Pub. by VSP) Coronet Bks.

Progress in Neurological Surgery, Vol. 5. H. Krayenbuehl et al. (Illus.). 500p. 1973. 149.75 (*3-8055-1499-9*) S Karger.

Progress in Neuropathology, 1983, Vol. 5. Ed. by Harry M. Zimmerman. LC 80-640739. 355p. 1983. reprint ed. pap. 110.10 (*0-608-00343-3*, 206106000005) Bks Demand.

Progress in Neuropathology, 1986, Vol. 6. Ed. by Harry M. Zimmerman. LC 80-640739. 296p. 1986. reprint ed. pap. 91.80 (*0-608-00344-1*, 206106000006) Bks Demand.

Progress in Neuropeptide Research. K. D. Dohler & M. Pawlikowski. (Congress Reports: No. 3). 185p. 1989. 52.00 (*0-8176-2268-3*) Birkhauser.

***Progress in Neuropharmacology & Neurotoxicology of Pesticides & Drugs.** Ed. by D. Beadle. 217p. 1999. 160.00 (*0-85404-729-8*, Pub. by Royal Soc Chem) Spr-Verlag.

Progress in Neuropsychopharmacology, Vol. 4, No. 6. Ed. by C. Radouco-Thomas & F. Garcin. (Illus.). 110p. 1981. pap. 31.00 (*0-08-027157-X*, Pergamon Pr) Elsevier.

Progress in Neuroscience. Ed. by Richard F. Thompson. LC 85-16120. (Scientific American Reader Ser.). (Illus.). 151p. (C). 1985. pap. text 16.95 (*0-7167-1727-1*) W H Freeman.

Progress in Neuroscience. Ed. by Richard F. Thompson. LC 85-16120. (Scientific American Reader Ser.). (Illus.). 151p. (C). 1985. text 17.60 (*0-7167-1726-3*) W H Freeman.

Progress in Neutron Capture Therapy for Cancer. Ed. by B. J. Allen et al. (Illus.). 702p. (C). 1992. text 186.00 (*0-306-44104-7*, Kluwer Plenum) Kluwer Academic.

Progress in New Cosmologies: Beyond the Big Bang. H. C. Arp et al. (Illus.). 376p. (C). 1994. text 110.00 (*0-306-44635-9*, Kluwer Plenum) Kluwer Academic.

Progress in New Crops. Ed. by Jules Janick. (New Crops Ser.). (Illus.). 660p. 1996. lib. bdg. 139.95 (*0-9615027-3-8*) Am Soc Horticult.

Progress in Nickel Toxicology. Brown & F. William Sunderman. 1991. 55.00 (*0-632-01355-9*) CRC Pr.

Progress in Nitrogen Cycling: Proceedings of the 8th Nitrogen Fixation Workshop, University of Ghent, Belgium, 5-8 September 1994. A. Vermoesen & G. Hofman. Ed. by O. Van Cleemput. LC 96-52087. (Development in Plant & Soil Sciences Ser.). 728p. (C). 1997. text 478.50 (*0-7923-3962-2*) Kluwer Academic.

Progress in NMR Spectroscopy, Vol. 11. Ed. by James W. Emsley & L. H. Sutcliffe. LC 66-17931. 282p. 1978. 105.00 (*0-08-020325-6*, Pergamon Pr) Elsevier.

Progress in Non-Histone Protein Research, Vol. I. Ed. by Isaac Bekhor. 224p. 1985. 130.00 (*0-8493-5528-1*, QP552, CRC Reprint) Franklin.

Progress in Non-Histone Protein Research, Vol. II. Ed. by Isaac Bekhor. 240p. 1985. 137.00 (*0-8493-5529-X*, CRC Reprint) Franklin.

Progress in Non-Histone Protein Research, Vol. III. Ed. by Isaac Bekhor. 224p. 1989. 121.00 (*0-8493-5530-3*, QP552, CRC Reprint) Franklin.

Progress in Nonlinear Optics. Jerome D. Swalen. 213p. 1994. pap. text 193.00 (*2-88124-952-3*) Gordon & Breach.

Progress in Nonmammalian Brain Research, 3 Vols., III. Ed. by Giuseppe Nistico & Liana Bolis. 1983. 146.00 (*0-8493-6352-7*, CRC Reprint) Franklin.

Progress in Nonmammalian Brain Research, 3 Vols., Vol. I. Ed. by Giuseppe Nistico & Liana Bolis. 208p. 1983. 114.00 (*0-8493-6350-0*, QP376, CRC Reprint) Franklin.

Progress in Nonmammalian Brain Research, 3 Vols., Vol. II. Ed. by Giuseppe Nistico & Liana Bolis. 240p. 1983. 135.00 (*0-8493-6351-9*, CRC Reprint) Franklin.

Progress in Nuclear Energy, Series 9. Ed. by H. A. Elion & D. C. Stewart. Incl. Vol. 9. LC 59-8283. 1969. 86.00 (*0-08-012716-9*); Vol. 11. LC 59-8283. 1972. 86.00 (*0-08-016920-1*); Vol. 12, Pt. 1. LC 59-8283. 1975. 10.25 (*0-08-018967-9*); LC 59-8283. write for info. (*0-318-55211-6*, Pub. by Pergamon Repr) Franklin.

Progress in Nuclear Energy, Vol. 3. Ed. by M. M. Williams. (Illus.). 252p. 1979. 115.00 (*0-08-024875-6*, Pergamon Pr) Elsevier.

Progress in Nuclear Energy, Vol. 3, No. 2. Ed. by M. M. Williams. (Illus.). 92p. 1979. pap. 47.00 (*0-08-024253-7*, Pergamon Pr) Elsevier.

Progress in Nuclear Energy, Vol. 3, No. 3. Ed. by M. M. Williams. 96p. 1979. pap. 47.00 (*0-08-024844-6*, Pergamon Pr) Elsevier.

Progress in Nuclear Energy, Vol. 5 Complete. Ed. by M. M. Williams. (Illus.). 292p. 1980. 115.00 (*0-08-027115-4*, Pergamon Pr) Elsevier.

Progress in Nuclear Energy, Vol. 7. Ed. by M. M. Williams & Norman J. McCormick. (Illus.). 228p. 1981. 125.00 (*0-08-029090-6*, A999, B120, Pergamon Pr) Elsevier.

Progress in Nuclear Energy, Vol. 7, No. 1. Ed. by M. M. Williams & Norman J. McCormick. (Illus.). 71p. 1981. pap. 36.00 (*0-08-027146-4*, Pergamon Pr) Elsevier.

Progress in Nuclear Energy, Vol. 8. Ed. by M. R. Williams & Norman J. McCormick. 318p. 1982. 145.00 (*0-08-029684-X*, Pergamon Pr) Elsevier.

Progress in Nuclear Energy, Vol. 10. Ed. by M. M. Williams & Norman J. McCormick. (Illus.). 408p. 1983. 130.00 (*0-08-030420-6*, Pergamon Pr) Elsevier.

Progress in Nuclear Energy, Vol. 11. Ed. by M. M. Williams & Norman J. McCormick. (Illus.). 310p. 1984. 130.00 (*0-08-031029-X*, Pergamon Pr) Elsevier.

Progress in Nuclear Energy, Vol. 12. Ed. by M. M. Williams & Norman J. McCormick. (Illus.). 300p. 1985. 130.00 (*0-08-031695-6*, Pergamon Pr) Elsevier.

Progress in Nuclear Energy, Vol. 13. Ed. by M. M. Williams & Norman J. McCormick. (Illus.). 300p. 1985. 150.00 (*0-08-032322-7*, Pergamon Pr) Elsevier.

Progress in Nuclear Energy, Vol. 14. Ed. by M. M. Williams & Norman J. McCormick. (Illus.). 260p. 1985. 150.00 (*0-08-032323-5*, Pub. by PPL) Elsevier.

Progress in Nuclear Energy, Vol. 16. Ed. by M. M. Williams & Norman J. McCormick. (Illus.). 322p. 138.00 (*0-08-034139-X*, Pub. by PPL) Elsevier.

Progress in Nuclear Energy: New Series, Vol. 1, No. 1. Ed. by M. M. Williams & R. Sher. (Illus.). 1977. pap. 33.00 (*0-08-022118-1*, Pergamon Pr) Elsevier.

Progress in Nuclear Energy: New Series, Vol. 2, No. 1. Ed. by M. M. Williams & R. Sher. (Illus.). 1978. pap. 32.00 (*0-08-022710-4*, Pergamon Pr) Elsevier.

Progress in Nuclear Energy: New Series, Vol. 2, No. 4. Ed. by M. M. Williams & R. Sher. (Illus.). 1978. pap. 23.00 (*0-08-023260-4*, Pergamon Pr) Elsevier.

Progress in Nuclear Energy: Selected Staff Reports to the President's Commission on the Accident at Three Mile Island, Vol. 6. Ed. by M. M. Williams & Norman J. McCormick. (Illus.). 436p. 1981. 115.00 (*0-08-027124-3*, Pergamon Pr) Elsevier.

Progress in Nuclear Energy: The Role of the Boltzmann Transport Equation in Radiation Damage Calculations, Vol. 3, No. 1. M. M. Williams. LC 77-25743. (Progress in Nuclear Energy Ser.). (Illus.). 66p. 1979. pap. 47.00 (*0-08-024243-X*, Pergamon Pr) Elsevier.

Progress in Nuclear Magnetic Reasonance Spectroscopy, Vol. 16. Ed. by James W. Emsley et al. 382p. 1985. 150.00 (*0-08-033238-2*, Pub. by PPL) Elsevier.

Progress in Nuclear Magnetic Resonance Spectroscopy, Vol. 13. 1980. 105.00 (*0-08-026027-6*, Pergamon Pr) Elsevier.

Progress in Nuclear Magnetic Resonance Spectroscopy, Vol. 14. Ed. by James W. Emsley et al. 370p. 1982. 140.00 (*0-08-029698-X*, Pergamon Pr) Elsevier.

Progress in Nuclear Magnetic Resonance Spectroscopy, Vol. 15. Ed. by James W. Emsley et al. (Illus.). 430p. 1984. 130.00 (*0-08-031510-0*, Pergamon Pr) Elsevier.

Progress in Nuclear Magnetic Resonance Spectroscopy, Vols. 1-10. Ed. by James W. Emsley & L. H. Sutcliffe. Incl. Vol. 2. 1967. 76.00 (*0-08-012208-6*); Vol. 4. 1969. pap. 213.00 (*0-08-012717-7*); Vol. 5. 1970. pap. 105.00 (*0-08-012834-3*); Vol. 6. 1971. pap. Vol. 7. 1971. pap. 234.00 (*0-08-016267-3*); Vol. 8., **3 pts.** 1972. 105.00 (*0-08-017018-8*); Pt. 1., **3 pts.** 1972. pap. 24.00 (*0-08-016662-8*); Pt. 2., **3 pts.** 1972. pap. 24.00 (*0-08-016757-8*); Pt. 3., **3 pts.** 1972. pap. 24.00 (*0-08-016857-4*); Vol. 9., **3 pts.** 1975. 130.00 (*0-08-017704-2*); Pt. 1. 1975. pap. 12.75 (*0-08-017703-4*); Pt. 2. 1976. pap. 22.00 (*0-08-019463-X*); pap. write for info. (*0-318-55212-4*, Pub. by Pergamon Repr) Franklin.

Progress in Nuclear Physics. Ed. by D. M. Brink & J. Mulvey. Incl. Vol. 10. 1969. 98.00 (*0-08-012682-0*); Vol. 11. 1970. 98.00 (*0-08-006360-8*); Vol. 12, Pt. 1. 1970. pap. 24.00 (*0-08-015766-1*); Vol. 12, Pt. 2. 1970. pap. 24.00 (*0-08-016394-7*); write for info. (*0-318-55214-0*) Elsevier.

Progress in Nuclear Physics, Vol. 2. Ed. by O. R. Frisch. 1952. 98.00 (*0-08-013329-0*, Pub. by Pergamon Repr) Franklin.

Progress in Nuclear Physics, Vol. 3. O. R. Frisch. 1953. 125.00 (*0-08-009004-4*, Pub. by Pergamon Repr) Franklin.

Progress in Nuclear Physics, Vol. 5. Ed. by O. R. Frisch. 1956. 98.00 (*0-08-009043-5*, Pub. by Pergamon Repr) Franklin.

Progress in Nuclear Physics, Vol. 7. Ed. by O. R. Frisch. 1959. 98.00 (*0-08-009186-5*, Pub. by Pergamon Repr) Franklin.

Progress in Nuclear Physics, Vol. 8. Ed. by O. R. Frisch. 1963. 89.00 (*0-685-04013-5*, Pub. by Pergamon Repr) Franklin.

Progress in Nuclear Physics, Vol. 9. Ed. by O. R. Frisch. 1963. 98.00 (*0-08-010063-5*, Pub. by Pergamon Repr) Franklin.

Progress in Nuclear Physics: Proceedings of the Spring School & International Conference on Medium & High Energy Nuclear Physics, 2nd, Held in Taiwan, Republic of China, May 8-18, 1990. Ed. by P. W. Hwang et al. 624p. 1991. 185.00 (*0-444-01603-1*) P-H.

Progress in Nuclear Physics, Vol. 13: Rudolf Peierls & Theoretical Physics - Proceedings of the Peierls Symposium. Ed. by Ian J. Aitchison & J. E. Paton. 1977. 89.00 (*0-08-020606-9*, Pergamon Pr); pap. 18.25 (*0-08-021621-8*, Pergamon Pr) Elsevier.

***Progress in Nucleic Acid Research & Molecular Biology.** Kivie Moldave. (Progress in Nucleic Acid Research & Molecular Biology Ser.: Vol. 65). 375p. 2000. 99.95 (*0-12-540065-9*) Acad Pr.

Progress in Nucleic Acid Research & Molecular Biology, Vol. 5. Ed. by Waldo E. Cohn & Kivie Moldave. (Illus.). 345p. (C). 1995. text 90.00 (*0-12-540050-0*) Acad Pr.

Progress in Nucleic Acid Research & Molecular Biology, Vol. 5. Ed. by Kivie Moldave. (Illus.). 404p. (C). 1997. text 89.95 (*0-12-540058-6*) Morgan Kaufmann.

Progress in Nucleic Acid Research & Molecular Biology, Vol. 27. Ed. by Waldo E. Cohn & Kivie Moldave. (Illus.). 408p. (C). 1994. text 104.00 (*0-12-540047-0*) Acad Pr.

Progress in Nucleic Acid Research & Molecular Biology, Vol. 33. Ed. by Waldo E. Cohn & Kivie Moldave. (Illus.). 401p. (C). 1996. text 85.00 (*0-12-540053-5*) Acad Pr.

Progress in Nucleic Acid Research & Molecular Biology, Vol. 48. Ed. by Waldo E. Cohn & Kivie Moldave. (Illus.). 379p. (C). 1994. text. write for info. (*0-12-540048-9*) Acad Pr.

Progress in Nucleic Acid Research & Molecular Biology, Vol. 51. Ed. by Waldo E. Cohn & Kivie Moldave. (Illus.). 369p. (C). 1995. text 90.00 (*0-12-540051-9*) Acad Pr.

Progress in Nucleic Acid Research & Molecular Biology, Vol. 52. Ed. by Waldo E. Cohn & Kivie Moldave. (Illus.). 370p. (C). 1996. text 85.00 (*0-12-540052-7*) Acad Pr.

Progress in Nucleic Acid Research & Molecular Biology, Vol. 54. Ed. by Waldo E. Cohn & Kivie Moldave. (Illus.). 387p. (C). 1996. text 85.00 (*0-12-540054-3*) Acad Pr.

Progress in Nucleic Acid Research & Molecular Biology, Vol. 55. Ed. by Waldo E. Cohn & Kivie Moldave. (Illus.). 291p. (C). 1996. text 85.00 (*0-12-540055-1*) Acad Pr.

Progress in Nucleic Acid Research & Molecular Biology, Vol. 57. Ed. by Kivie Moldave. (Illus.). 348p. (C). 1997. text 89.00 (*0-12-540057-8*) Morgan Kaufmann.

Progress in Nucleic Acid Research & Molecular Biology, Vol. 59. Ed. by Kivie Moldave. (Illus.). 373p. (C). 1997. text 89.95 (*0-12-540059-4*) Morgan Kaufmann.

Progress in Nucleic Acid Research & Molecular Biology, Vol. 60. Ed. by Kivi Moldave. (Illus.). 353p. (C). 1998. text 89.95 (*0-12-540060-8*) Acad Pr.

Progress in Nucleic Acid Research & Molecular Biology, Vol. 61. Ed. by Kivie Moldave. (Illus.). 431p. (C). 1998. text 89.95 (*0-12-540061-6*) Acad Pr.

Progress in Nucleic Acid Research & Molecular Biology, Vol. 62. Ed. by Kivie Moldave. (Illus.). 407p. 1998. text 89.95 (*0-12-540062-4*) Acad Pr.

***Progress in Nucleic Acid Research & Molecular Biology, Vol. 64.** Kivie Moldave. Vol. 64. 392p. 2000. 99.95 (*0-12-540064-0*) Acad Pr.

***Progress in Nucleic Acid Research & Molecular Biology Vol. 63.** Ed. by Kivie Moldave. 350p. 1999. 99.95 (*0-12-540063-2*) Acad Pr.

Progress in Obesity Research, No. 7. Angel. 784p. 122.00 (*0-86196-532-9*, Pub. by J Libbey Med) Bks Intl VA.

Progress in Obesity Research, No. 8. B. Guy-Grand. 880p. 149.00 (*0-86196-581-7*, Pub. by J Libbey Med) Bks Intl VA.

Progress in OB/GYN. 12th ed. Studd. 1996. pap. text 60.00 (*0-443-05307-3*, W B Saunders Co) Harcrt Hlth Sci Grp.

Progress in Obstetrics & Gynaecology, No. 7. Ed. by John W. Studd. (Illus.). 412p. 1989. pap. text 40.00 (*0-443-03885-6*) Church.

Progress in Obstetrics & Gynaecology, Vol. 6. Ed. by John W. Studd. LC 81-21699. (Illus.). 456p. 1987. pap. text 54.00 (*0-443-03572-5*) Church.

Progress in Obstetrics & Gynaecology, Vol. 8. Ed. by John W. Studd. (Illus.). 416p. 1990. pap. text 40.00 (*0-443-04170-9*) Church.

Progress in Obstetrics & Gynaecology, Vol. 9. Ed. by John W. Studd. (Illus.). 412p. 1991. pap. text 54.00 (*0-443-04412-0*) Church.

***Progress in Obstetrics/Gynecology.** 13th ed. Studd. (C). 1999. text 60.00 (*0-443-05868-7*, W B Saunders Co) Harcrt Hlth Sci Grp.

Progress in Oceanography, Vol. 4. Ed. by M. Sears & Bruce A. Warren. LC 63-15353. 1967. 98.00 (*0-08-012124-1*, Pub. by Pergamon Repr) Franklin.

Progress in Oceanography, Vol. 5. Ed. by M. Sears & Bruce A. Warren. LC 63-15353. 1969. 98.00 (*0-08-012631-6*, Pub. by Pergamon Repr) Franklin.

Progress in Oceanography, Vol. 6. Ed. by M. Sears & Bruce A. Warren. LC 63-15353. 1974. 98.00 (*0-08-017707-7*, Pub. by Pergamon Repr) Franklin.

Progress in Oceanography, Vol. 7. Ed. by Mary Swallow. Incl. Pt. 1. Midwater Fishes in the Eastern North Atlantic. LC 63-15353. 1976. pap. 13.25 (*0-08-020877-0*); Pt. 2. Mixing & Spreading of Medoc. LC 63-15353. 1976. pap. 11.75 (*0-08-020888-6*); Pt. 4. Observations of Rossby Waves Near Site D. LC 63-15353. 1977. pap. 10.75 (*0-08-020892-4*); Pt. 3. LC 63-15353. 1977. pap. 11.50 (*0-08-020890-8*); Pts. 5 & 6. LC 63-15353. 1979. pap. 25.00 (*0-08-022069-X*); Vol. 7 Complete. LC 63-15353. 1980. 98.00 (*0-08-020329-9*); LC 63-15353. pap. write for info. (*0-318-55216-7*) Elsevier.

Progress in Oceanography, Vol. 8. M. V. Angel. (Illus.). 296p. 1980. 125.00 (*0-08-022963-8*, Pergamon Pr) Elsevier.

Progress in Oceanography, Vol. 9, Nos. 1-4. M. V. Angel & J. J. O'Brien. (Illus.). 246p. 1982. 125.00 (*0-08-027116-2*, Pergamon Pr) Elsevier.

Progress in Oceanography, Vol. 10. Ed. by M. V. Angel & J. J. O'Brien. (Illus.). 226p. 1982. 115.00 (*0-08-029121-X*, Pergamon Pr) Elsevier.

Progress in Oceanography, Vol. 12. Ed. by M. V. Angel & J. J. O'Brien. (Illus.). 470p. 1984. 165.00 (*0-08-031504-6*, Pergamon Pr) Elsevier.

Progress in Oceanography, Vol. 13. Ed. by M. V. Angel & J. J. O'Brien. (Illus.). 520p. 1985. 175.00 (*0-08-032724-9*, Pergamon Pr) Elsevier.

Progress in Oceanography, Vol. 13, Nos. 3-4. H. S. Roe. (Illus.). 276p. 1984. pap. 83.00 (*0-08-031735-9*, Pergamon Pr) Elsevier.

Progress in Oceanography, Vols. 1 & 4-6. Ed. by M. Sears & Bruce A. Warren. 1974. text. write for info. (*0-318-55215-9*, Pub. by Pergamon Repr) Franklin.

Progress in Old World Palaeoethnobotany: A Retrospective View on the Occasion of 20 Years of the International Work Group for Palaeoethnobotany. Ed. by W. Van Zeist et al. (Illus.). 352p. (C). 1990. text 123.00 (*90-6191-881-2*, Pub. by A A Balkema) Ashgate Pub Co.

Progress in Oncology. David Khayat & Gabriel N. Hortobagyi. LC 99-19801. (Progress in Anti-cancer Chemotherapy Ser.). 1999. write for info. (*3-540-59666-6*) Spr-Verlag.

Progress in Operations Research, Vol. 1. Russell L. Ackoff. LC 61-10415. (Operations Research Ser.: No. 5). 517p. reprint ed. 160.30 (*0-8357-9966-2*, 205157500089) Bks Demand.

Progress in Opioid Research. J. Cros et al. (Advances in the Biosciences Ser.: 75). (Illus.). 812p. 1989. 141.00 (*0-08-037362-3*, Pergamon Pr) Elsevier.

Progress in Optics. Ed. by E. Wolf. (Applied Optics Ser.: Vol. XXXII). 404p. 1993. 157.00 (*0-444-81592-9*, North Holland) Elsevier.

Progress in Optics. Ed. by E. Wolf. 570p. 1998. 181.00 (*0-444-82907-5*, North Holland) Elsevier.

***Progress in Optics.** Ed. by E. Wolf. (Progress in Optics Ser.). 522p. 1999. 147.00 (*0-444-50104-5*, North Holland) Elsevier.

Progress in Optics, Vol. X. Ed. by E. Wolf. 506p. 1994. 188.50 (*0-444-81839-1*, North Holland) Elsevier.

Progress in Optics, Vol. XX. Ed. by E. Wolf. xviii, 400p. 1983. 148.25 (*0-444-86736-8*) Elsevier.

Progress in Optics, Vol. XXVII. Ed. by E. Wolf. xx, 438p. 1990. 185.25 (*0-444-88439-4*, PIO 28) Elsevier.

Progress in Optics, Vol. XXVIII. Ed. by E. Wolf. xx, 420p. 1989. 194.50 (*0-444-87425-9*) Elsevier.

Progress in Optics, Vol. XXIX. Ed. by E. Wolf. xx, 438p. 1991. 188.50 (*0-444-88951-5*, North Holland) Elsevier.

Progress in Optics, Vol. XXX. Ed. by E. Wolf. xx, 376p. 1992. 179.25 (*0-444-89544-2*, North Holland) Elsevier.

Progress in Optics, Vol. XXXI. Ed. by E. Wolf. 454p. 1993. 170.50 (*0-444-89836-0*, North Holland) Elsevier.

Progress in Optics, Vol. XXXIV. Ed. by E. Wolf. 442p. 1995. 163.75 (*0-444-82140-6*) Elsevier.

Progress in Optics, Vol. XXXV. Ed. by E. Wolf. 494p. Date not set. 176.00 (*0-444-82309-3*, North Holland) Elsevier.

Progress in Optics, Vol. XXXVI. E. Wolf. 338p. 1996. 140.75 (*0-444-82530-4*, North Holland) Elsevier.

Progress in Optics, Vol. XXXVII. Ed. by E. Wolf. 454p. 1997. 155.00 (*0-444-82796-X*, North Holland) Elsevier.

***Progress in Optics, Vol. 40.** Ed. by E. Wolf. 496p. 2000. 144.00 (*0-444-50305-6*, North Holland) Elsevier.

Progress in Optimization: Contributions from Australasia Andrew Eberhard. LC 99-22863. (Applied Optimization Ser.). 1999. write for info. (*0-7923-5733-7*) Kluwer Academic.

***Progress in Optimization: Contributions from Australasia.** Alistair I. Mees et al. 354p. 2000. 149.00 (*0-7923-6286-1*) Kluwer Academic.

Progress in Organosilicon Chemistry. Ed. by Bogdan Marciniec. 560p. 1995. text 121.00 (*2-88449-122-8*) Gordon & Breach.

Progress in Pacific Polymer Science: Proceedings of the First Pacific Polymer Conference Maui, Hawaii, U. S. A., 12-15 December 1989. Ed. by B. C. Anderson & Y. Imanishi. xi, 431p. 1991. 122.95 (*0-387-52222-0*) Spr-Verlag.

Progress in Pacific Polymer Science 3. K. P. Ghiggino. (Progress in Pacific Polymer Science 3 Ser.). 448p. 1994. 157.95 (*0-387-57621-5*) Spr-Verlag.

Progress in Pacific Polymer Science 2: Proceedings of the Second Pacific Polymer Conference, Otsu, Japan, November 26-29, 1991. Ed. by Y. Imanishi. LC 92-24756. viii, 359p. 1992. 98.00 (*3-540-55659-1*); 111.95 (*0-387-55659-1*) Spr-Verlag.

Progress in Palynology: Cumulation of Journal of Palynology, 2 vols. in 4 pts., Vols. 1-20. P. K. Nair. 3500p. 1986. 300.00 (*1-55528-077-3*, Pub. by Today Tomorrow) Scholarly Pubns.

An Asterisk (*) at the beginning of an entry indicates that the title is appearing for the first time.

Progress in Parkinson Research. Ed. by F. Hefti & William J. Weiner. (Illus.). 238p. 1989. 69.50 (*0-306-43096-7*, Plenum Trade) Perseus Pubng.

Progress in Partial Differential Equations: Pont-A-Mousson 1997. Ed. by H. Amann et al. 208p. 1998. ring bd. 55.95 (*0-582-31708-8*, LM1708, Chap & Hall CRC) CRC Pr.

Progress in Partial Differential Equations: The Metz Surveys. Ed. by Michel Chipot & J. Saint-Jean Paulin. LC 90-28942. (Pitman Research Notes in Mathematics Ser.: Vol. 249). 212p. 1991. reprint ed. pap. 65.80 (*0-608-03603-X*, 206442600009) Bks Demand.

Progress in Partial Differential Equations: The Metz Surveys 2. M Chipot. LC 92-205887. 1993. lib. bdg. 59.95 (*0-582-22769-0*, Pub. by Addison-Wesley) Longman.

Progress in Partial Differential Equations: The Metz Surveys 3. M. Chipot. LC 92-205887. 1994. lib. bdg. 69.95 (*0-582-25380-2*, Pub. by Addison-Wesley) Longman.

Progress in Partial Differential Equations: The Metz Surveys 4. Michel Chipot. (Pitman Research Notes in Mathematics Ser.). 1996. lib. bdg. 58.95 (*0-582-27730-2*) Longman.

Progress in Partial Differential Equations Vol. 2: Pont-A-Mousson. Ed. by H. Amann et al. 224p. 1998. ring bd. 55.95 (*0-582-31709-6*, LM1709, Chap & Hall CRC) CRC Pr.

*__Progress in Particle & Nuclear Physics.__ Ed. by A. Faessler. (Progress in Particle & Nuclear Physics Ser.: Vol. 42). 372p. 1999. 251.50 (*0-444-50246-7*, Pergamon Pr) Elsevier.

Progress in Particle & Nuclear Physics, Vol. 3. Ed. by Denys Wilkinson. 1980. 98.00 (*0-08-025020-3*, Pergamon Pr) Elsevier.

Progress in Particle & Nuclear Physics, Vol. 4. Ed. by Denys Wilkinson. (Illus.). 600p. 1980. 98.00 (*0-08-025039-4*, Pergamon Pr) Elsevier.

Progress in Particle & Nuclear Physics, Vol. 5. Ed. by Denys Wilkinson. (Illus.). 280p. 1981. 98.00 (*0-08-027109-X*, Pergamon Pr) Elsevier.

Progress in Particle & Nuclear Physics, Vol. 6. Ed. by Denys Wilkinson. 350p. 1981. 98.00 (*0-08-027117-0*, Pergamon Pr) Elsevier.

Progress in Particle & Nuclear Physics, Vol. 7. Ed. by Denys Wilkinson. (Illus.). 270p. 1981. 100.00 (*0-08-027152-9*, Pergamon Pr) Elsevier.

Progress in Particle & Nuclear Physics, Vol. 12. Ed. by Denys Wilkinson. (Illus.). 470p. 1984. 110.00 (*0-08-031500-3*, Pergamon Pr) Elsevier.

Progress in Particle & Nuclear Physics, Vol. 14. Ed. by Armand Faessler. (Illus.). 300p. 1985. 110.00 (*0-08-032300-6*, Pub. by PPL) Elsevier.

Progress in Particle & Nuclear Physics, Vol. 16. Ed. by Armand Faessler. 268p. 1985. 140.00 (*0-08-033667-1*, Pub. by PPL) Elsevier.

Progress in Particle & Nuclear Physics, Vol. 21. Ed. by Armand Faessler. (Illus.). 472p. 1988. 203.00 (*0-08-036881-6*, Pergamon Pr) Elsevier.

Progress in Particle & Nuclear Physics, Vol. 23. Ed. by Armand Faessler. (Illus.). 472p. 1989. 190.25 (*0-08-040148-1*, Pub. by PPL) Elsevier.

Progress in Particle & Nuclear Physics, Vol. 24. Ed. by Armand Faessler. 390p. 1990. 272.50 (*0-08-040761-7*, Pergamon Pr) Elsevier.

Progress in Particle & Nuclear Physics, Vol. 25. Ed. by Armand Faessler. (Illus.). 360p. 1990. 272.50 (*0-08-040773-0*, Pergamon Pr) Elsevier.

Progress in Particle & Nuclear Physics, Vol. 26. Ed. by Armand Faessler. 322p. 1991. 297.00 (*0-08-041140-1*, Pergamon Pr) Elsevier.

Progress in Particle & Nuclear Physics, Vol. 27. Ed. by Armand Faessler. 336p. 1991. 297.00 (*0-08-041163-0*, Pergamon Pr) Elsevier.

Progress in Particle & Nuclear Physics, Vol. 28. Armand Faessler. 542p. 1992. 3.00 (*0-08-041860-0*, Pergamon Pr) Elsevier.

Progress in Particle & Nuclear Physics, Vol. 29. Ed. by Armand Faessler. 536p. 1992. 350.50 (*0-08-042040-0*, Pergamon Pr) Elsevier.

Progress in Particle & Nuclear Physics, Vol. 30. Ed. by Armand Faessler. 1993. 386.00 (*0-08-042194-6*, Pergamon Pr) Elsevier.

Progress in Particle & Nuclear Physics, Vol. 31. Ed. by Armand Faessler. 1993. 386.00 (*0-08-042328-0*, Pergamon Pr) Elsevier.

Progress in Particle & Nuclear Physics, Vol. 33. Ed. by Armand Faessler. 870p. 1994. 482.50 (*0-08-042499-6*, Pergamon Pr) Elsevier.

Progress in Particle & Nuclear Physics, Vol. 34. A. Faessler. 1995. write for info. (*0-08-042628-X*) Elsevier.

Progress in Particle & Nuclear Physics, Vol. 41. Ed. by A. Faessler. 382p. 1998. 373.50 (*0-444-50018-9*, Pergamon Pr) Elsevier.

*__Progress in Particle & Nuclear Physics, Vol. 43.__ Ed. by A. Faessler. 848p. 1999. 251.50 (*0-444-50306-4*) Elsevier.

Progress in Particle & Nuclear Physics: Mesons, Isobars, Quarks & Nuclear Excitations, Vol. 11. Ed. by Denys Wilkinson. (Illus.). 630p. 1984. 110.00 (*0-08-031489-9*, Pergamon Pr) Elsevier.

Progress in Particle & Nuclear Physics: Neutrinos in Cosmology, Astro, Particle & Nuclear Physics: Proceedings of the International School of Nuclear Physics, Erice, 8-17 September, 1993. Ed. by Armand Faessler. (Progress in Particle & Nuclear Physics Ser.: Vol. 32). 438p. 1994. 482.50 (*0-08-042490-2*) Elsevier.

Progress in Particle & Nuclear Physics: Nuclear & Subnuclear Degrees of Freedom & Lepton Nucleus Scattering, Vol. 13. Ed. by Armand Faessler. (Illus.). 540p. 1985. 110.00 (*0-08-031743-X*, Pergamon Pr) Elsevier.

Progress in Particle & Nuclear Physics: Nucleus-Nucleus Collisions from the Coulomb Barrier to the Quark-Gluon Plasma, Vol 15. Ed. by Armand Faessler. 1985. 140.00 (*0-08-034005-9*, Pub. by PPL) Elsevier.

Progress in Passive Solar Energy Systems Vol. 7: The World Turns to Solar. Ed. by John Hayes. 1985. pap. text 50.00 (*0-89553-035-X*) Am Solar Energy.

Progress in Pathology, Vol. 1. Kirkham. 1995. pap. text 58.00 (*0-443-05013-9*, W B Saunders Co) Harcrt Hlth Sci Grp.

Progress in Pathology, Vol. 3. 3rd ed. Nigel Kirkham. 1997. pap. text 63.00 (*0-443-05583-1*) Church.

Progress in Pediatric Neurology I. J. Gordon Millichap. LC 91-90076. 598p. 1991. text 57.95 (*0-9629115-0-X*) PNB Pub.

Progress in Pediatric Neurology III. J. Gordon Millichap. LC 94-1233. 611p. (C). 1997. 64.95 (*0-9629115-6-9*) PNB Pub.

Progress in Pediatric Neurology II. J. Gordon Millichap. LC 94-66683. (Illus.). 550p. 1994. 64.95 (*0-9629115-8-5*) PNB Pub.

Progress in Penal Reform. Ed. by Louis Blom-Cooper. 1975. 59.00 (*0-19-825325-7*) OUP.

Progress in Peptic Ulcer. T. Javor & Gy Mozsik. 774p. (C). 1976. 150.00 (*963-05-1210-6*, Pub. by Akade Kiado) St Mut.

Progress in Peptide Research, Vol. 2. Ed. by Saul Lande. LC 76-153298. x, 394p. 1972. text 510.00 (*0-677-13610-2*) Gordon & Breach.

Progress in Perinatal Medicine, Vol. 9. D. F. Hawkins. (Ettore Majorana International Life Science Ser.). 350p. 1990. text 160.00 (*3-7186-5054-1*, Harwood Acad Pubs) Gordon & Breach.

Progress in Pesticide Biochemistry, Vol. 1. Ed. by D. H. Hutson & T. R. Roberts. LC 80-41419. 358p. pap. 111.00 (*0-7837-0194-2*, 204049000001) Bks Demand.

Progress in Pesticide Biochemistry & Toxicology, Vol. 2. fac. ed. Progress in Pesticide Biochemistry & Toxicology St. LC 80-41419. (Wiley-Interscience Publications). (Illus.). 238p. pap. 73.80 (*0-7837-7379-X*, 204329500002) Bks Demand.

Progress in Pesticide Biochemistry & Toxicology, Vol. 3. fac. ed. Ed. by D. H. Hutson & T. R. Roberts. LC 83-647760. (Wiley-Interscience Publications). 463p. 1983. pap. 143.60 (*0-7837-8642-5*, 204329500003) Bks Demand.

Progress in Pesticide Biochemistry & Toxicology, Vol. 4, 1985. Ed. by D. H. Hutson & T. R. Roberts. LC 83-647760. (Wiley-Interscience Publications). 382p. reprint ed. pap. 118.50 (*0-7837-3275-9*, 204329500004) Bks Demand.

Progress in Pesticide Biochemistry & Toxicology: Environmental Behaviour of Agrochemicals, Vol. 9, Environmental Behaviour of Agrochemicals. Ed. by T. R. Roberts & Philip C. Kearney. LC 83-647760. (Progress in Pesticide Biochemistry & Toxicology Ser.: Vol. 9). 418p. 1995. 305.00 (*0-471-95301-6*) Wiley.

Progress in Pesticide Biochemistry & Toxicology: The Mammalian Metabolism of Agrochemicals, Vol. 8, The Mammalian Metabolism of Agrochemicals. Ed. by Gaylord D. Paulson & D. H. Hutson. LC 83-647760. (Progress in Pesticide Biochemistry & Toxicology Ser.: Vol. 8). 384p. 1995. 275.00 (*0-471-95155-2*) Wiley.

Progress in Petroleum Technology: A Collection of the Papers of the Symposium, New York, 1951. Twenty-Five Years of Progress in Petroleum Technol. LC 51-6844. (Advances in Chemistry Ser.: No. 5). (Illus.). 392p. reprint ed. pap. 121.60 (*0-608-08323-2*, 205018200080) Bks Demand.

Progress in Photochemistry & Photophysics, Vol. V. Jan F. Rabek. 208p. 1992. lib. bdg. 169.00 (*0-8493-4045-4*, QD714) CRC Pr.

Progress in Photochemistry & Photophysics, Vol. VI. Jan F. Rabek. 256p. 1992. lib. bdg. 199.00 (*0-8493-4046-2*) CRC Pr.

Progress in Photosynthesis Research, 4 vols., Set. Ed. by J. Biggins. 1986. text 1668.50 (*90-247-3449-5*) Kluwer Academic.

Progress in Phycological Research. Ed. by F. E. Round & D. J. Chapman. (Progress in Phycological Research Ser.: Vol. 8). (Illus.). 278p. 1992. lib. bdg. 90.00 (*0-948737-17-4*, Pub. by Biopress) Balogh.

Progress in Phycological Research, Vol. 4. Ed. by F. E. Round & D. J. Chapman. (Illus.). 481p. 1986. lib. bdg. 90.00 (*0-948737-00-X*, Pub. by Biopress) Balogh.

Progress in Phycological Research, Vol. 5. F. E. Round & D. J. Chapman. (Illus.). 299p. 1987. lib. bdg. 90.00 (*0-948737-03-4*, Pub. by Biopress) Balogh.

Progress in Phycological Research, Vol. 6. F. E. Round & D. J. Chapman. (Illus.). 286p. 1988. lib. bdg. 90.00 (*0-948737-07-7*, Pub. by Biopress) Balogh.

Progress in Phycological Research, Vol. 7. Ed. by F. E. Round & D. J. Chaoman. (Illus.). 330p. 1990. lib. bdg. 90.00 (*0-948737-13-1*, Pub. by Biopress) Balogh.

Progress in Phycological Research, Vol. 9. Ed. by F. E. Round & D. J. Chapman. (Illus.). 376p. 1993. lib. bdg. 120.00 (*0-948737-19-0*, Pub. by Biopress) Balogh.

Progress in Phycological Research, Vol. 10. Ed. by F. E. Round & D. J. Chapman. (Illus.). 209p. 1994. lib. bdg. 128.00 (*0-948737-20-4*, Pub. by Biopress) Balogh.

Progress in Phycological Research, Vol. 11. Ed. by F. E. Round & D. J. Chapman. 1995. 120.00 (*0-948737-40-9*, Pub. by Biopress) Balogh.

Progress in Phycological Research, Vol. 12. Ed. by F. E. Round & D. J. Chapman. 324p. 1997. 120.00 (*0-948737-50-6*, Pub. by Biopress) Balogh.

*__Progress in Phycological Research, Vol. 13.__ Ed. by F. E. Round & D. J. Chapman. (Illus.). 201p. 1999. 99.00 (*0-948737-55-7*, Pub. by Biopress) Balogh.

Progress in Physical Organic Chemistry, Vol. 17. Ed. by Robert W. Taft. 336p. 1990. 220.00 (*0-471-50912-4*) Wiley.

Progress in Physical Organic Chemistry, Vol. 19. Ed. by Robert W. Taft. LC 63-19364. 349p. 1993. 220.00 (*0-471-52442-5*) Wiley.

Progress in Phytochemistry, 1. Ed. by L. Reinhold & Y. Liwschitz. LC 68-24347. 731p. 1968. reprint ed. pap. 200.00 (*0-608-08324-0*, 201617700001) Bks Demand.

Progress in Phytochemistry, 2. Ed. by L. Reinhold & Y. Liwschitz. LC 68-24347. 523p. 1970. reprint ed. pap. 162.20 (*0-608-08325-9*, 201617700002) Bks Demand.

Progress in Phytochemistry, 2 vols., 5. Ed. by L. Reinhold et al. LC 68-24347. 1978. 105.00 (*0-08-022645-0*, Pub. by Pergamon Repr) Franklin.

Progress in Pig Science. Ed. by J. Wiseman et al. 617p. 1999. 240.00 (*1-897676-26-3*, Pub. by Nottingham Univ Pr) St Mut.

Progress in Planetary Exploration. Ed. by R. W. Shorthill. (Advances in Space Research Ser.: Vol. 1, No. 8). (Illus.). 224p. 1981. pap. 35.00 (*0-08-028384-5*, Pergamon Pr) Elsevier.

Progress in Planning, Vol. 9. Ed. by Donald R. Diamond & J. B. McLoughlin. 300p. 1979. 61.00 (*0-08-025221-4*, Pergamon Pr) Elsevier.

Progress in Planning, Vol. 10. Ed. by Donald R. Diamond & J. B. McLoughlin. (Illus.). 247p. 1980. 61.00 (*0-08-025788-7*, Pergamon Pr) Elsevier.

Progress in Planning, Vol. 11. Ed. by Donald R. Diamond & J. B. McLoughlin. (Illus.). 280p. 1980. 61.00 (*0-08-025802-6*, Pergamon Pr) Elsevier.

Progress in Planning, Vol. 12. Ed. by Donald R. Diamond & J. B. McLoughlin. 224p. 1980. 61.00 (*0-08-026100-0*, Pergamon Pr) Elsevier.

Progress in Planning, Vol. 13, (complete) Donald R. Diamond & J. B. McLoughlin. (Illus.). 174p. 1981. 68.00 (*0-08-028398-5*, Pergamon Pr) Elsevier.

Progress in Planning, Vol. 17. Ed. by Donald R. Diamond & J. B. McLoughlin. 268p. 1982. 68.00 (*0-08-029701-3*, Pergamon Pr) Elsevier.

Progress in Planning, Vol. 18. Ed. by Donald R. Diamond & J. B. McLoughlin. (Illus.). 384p. 1983. 66.00 (*0-08-030415-X*, Pergamon Pr) Elsevier.

Progress in Planning, Vol. 19. Ed. by Donald R. Diamond & J. B. McLoughlin. (Illus.). 280p. 1983. 66.00 (*0-08-031035-4*, Pergamon Pr) Elsevier.

Progress in Planning, Vol. 20. Ed. by Donald R. Diamond. (Illus.). 260p. 1984. 66.00 (*0-08-031490-2*, Pergamon Pr) Elsevier.

Progress in Planning, Vol. 21. Ed. by Donald R. Diamond & J. B. McLoughlin. (Illus.). 230p. 1985. 66.00 (*0-08-032325-1*, Pergamon Pr) Elsevier.

Progress in Planning, Vol. 22. Ed. by Donald R. Diamond & J. B. McLoughlin. LC 73-66. (Illus.). 266p. 1985. 66.00 (*0-08-033206-4*, Pub. by PPL) Elsevier.

Progress in Planning, Vol. 23. Ed. by Donald R. Diamond. (Illus.). 260p. 1985. 66.00 (*0-08-033213-7*, Pub. by PPL) Elsevier.

Progress in Planning, Vol. 24. Ed. by Donald R. Diamond & J. B. McLoughlin. (Illus.). 250p. 1986. 60.00 (*0-08-034144-6*, Pub. by PPL) Elsevier.

Progress in Planning, Vols. 1-8. Incl. Vol. 1, Pt. 1. Education for Planning: The Development of Knowledge & Capability for Urban Governance. C. C. Cockburn. 1973. pap. 16.75 (*0-08-017179-6*); Vol. 1, Pt. 2. Office Linkages & Location. John B. Goddard. 1973. pap. 16.75 (*0-08-017180-X*); Vol. 1, Pt. 3. Planning & the Innovative Process. R. Jefferson. 1973. pap. 16.75 (*0-08-017181-8*); Vol. 1, Pt. 4. Transportation Planning & Public Policy. D. Starkie. 1973. pap. 16.75 (*0-08-017698-4*); Vol. 2, Pt. 1. Urban Planning Law in East Africa. G. W. Kanyeihamba. 1973. pap. 16.75 (*0-08-017754-9*); Vol. 2, Pt. 2. Towards Measures of Spatial Opportunity. Michael Breheny. 1974. pap. 16.75 (*0-08-017933-9*); Vol. 2, Pt. 3. Planning & Change. P. Healey. 1974. pap. 16.75 (*0-08-017944-4*); Vol. 2, Pt. 4. Labor Market Areas. M. W. Smart. 1974. pap. 16.75 (*0-08-018019-1*); Vol. 3. Journey to Work. P. H. O'Farrell. 1979. 61.00 (*0-08-018059-0*); Vol. 3, Pt. 1. City Centre Redevelopment. Ian C. Alexander. 1974. pap. 16.75 (*0-08-018058-2*); Vol. 3, Pt. 2. Local Authorities & the Attraction of Industry. M. M. Camina. 1974. pap. 16.75 (*0-08-018082-5*); Vol. 3, Pt. 3. Journey to Work. P. H. O'Farrell. 1975. pap. 16.75 (*0-08-018083-3*); Vol. 4. Impact of Regional Policy: A Case Study of Manufactturing Employment in the Northern Region. M. E. Frost. 1979. 61.00 (*0-08-018770-6*); Vol. 4, Pt. 1. Urban Networks: The Structure of Activity Patterns. I. Cullen & V. Godson. 1975. pap. 16.75 (*0-08-018768-4*); Vol. 4, Pt. 2. Underdevelopment & Spatial Inequality: Approaches to the Problems of Regional Planning in the Third World. D. Slater. 1975. pap. 12.75 (*0-08-018769-2*); Vol. 4, Pt. 3. Impact of Regional Policy: A Case Study of Manufactturing Employment in the Northern Region. M. E. Frost. 1975. pap. 12.75 (*0-08-019924-0*); Vol. 5, Road Traffic Noise. 1979. 61.00 (*0-08-019928-3*); Vol. 5, Pt. 1. Exploratory Study in Strategic Monitoring. F. Wedgwood-Oppenheim. 1976. pap. 12.75 (*0-08-019925-9*); Vol. 5, Pt. 2. Participation & the Community. A. R. Long. 1976. pap. 18.75 (*0-08-019926-7*); Vol. 5 Pt. 3. Road Traffic Noise. 1976. pap. 15.25 (*0-08-019927-5*); Vol. 6. Critique of Urban Modelling. 1979. 61.00 (*0-08-020331-0*); Vol. 6, Pt. 1. Communications Factor in Office Decentralization. 1976. pap. 15.25 (*0-08-021349-9*); Vol. 6, Pt. 2. New Building & Housing Need. 1977. pap. 12.00 (*0-08-021483-5*); Vol. 6, Pt. 3. Critique of Urban Modelling. 1977. pap. 13.25 (*0-08-021485-1*); Vol. 7. Transport Modelling: Sensitivity Analysis & Policy Testing. 1979. 61.00 (*0-08-020333-7*); Vol. 7, Pt. 1. Theoretical Perspectives on Planning Participation. 1977. pap. 13.25 (*0-08-021355-3*); Vol. 7, Pt. 2. Input-Output Methods in Urban & Regional Planning: A Practical Guide. 1977. pap. 13.25 (*0-08-021858-X*); Vol. 7, Pt. 3. Transport Modelling: Sensitivity Analysis & Policy Testing. 1977. pap. 13.25 (*0-08-022233-1*); Vol. 8, Pt. 1. Migration Dynamics & Labour Market Turnover. 1977. pap. 13.25 (*0-08-022256-0*); Vol. 1 (complete). 1973. 61.00 (*0-08-017805-7*); Vol. 2 (complete). 1974. 61.00 (*0-08-017941-X*); pap. write for info. (*0-318-55217-5*) Elsevier.

Progress in Planning: Recent Research in Urban & Regional Planning, 3 pts., Vol. 10. Incl. Pt. 1. Internal Migration & the Australian Urban System. J. McKay & J. S. Whitelaw. 1979. pap. 15.75 (*0-08-023704-5*); Pt. 2. Employment Decentralisation: Policy Instruments for Large Cities in Less Developed Countries. P. M. Townroe. 1979. pap. 15.75 (*0-08-023705-3*); Pt. 3. Geography of Industrial Reorganisation. Doreen Massey & Richard A. Meegan. 1979. pap. 17.25 (*0-08-023706-1*); (Illus.). 1979. write for info. (*0-318-55218-3*) Elsevier.

Progress in Plant Cellular & Molecular Biology. Ed. by H.J. Nijkamp et al. (Current Plant Science & Biotechnology in Agriculture Ser.). (C). 1990. lib. bdg. 257.00 (*0-7923-0873-5*) Kluwer Academic.

Progress in Plant Growth Regulation: Proceedings of the 14th International Conference on Plant Growth Substances 21-26 July 1991, Amsterdam, the Netherlands. Ed. by C. M. Karssen. (Current Plant Science & Biotechnology in Agriculture Ser.). 984p. (C). 1992. text 567.00 (*0-7923-1617-7*) Kluwer Academic.

Progress in Plant Research: Cumulation of New Botanist, Vol. 3, Pt. I. Ed. by T. N. Khoshoo & P. K. Nair. (Illus.). 1800p. 1986. 120.00 (*1-55528-078-1*) Scholarly Pubns.

Progress in Plant Research: Silver Jubilee Publication of NBRI, 2 vols., Set. Ed. by T. N. Khoshoo & P. K. Nair. 1979. 90.00 (*0-88065-144-X*) Scholarly Pubns.

Progress in Plant Research Vol. 1: Applied Morphology & Allied Subjects, Vol. 1. Ed. by T. N. Khoshoo & P. K. Nair. 320p. 1979. 50.00 (*0-88065-145-8*) Scholarly Pubns.

Progress in Plant Research Vol. 2: Plant Improvement & Horticulture, Vol. 2. Ed. by T. N. Khoshoo & P. K. Nair. 248p. 1979. 50.00 (*0-88065-146-6*) Scholarly Pubns.

Progress in Plasma Processing of Materials, 1997: Proceedings of the Fourth International Thermal Plasma Processes Conference, Athens, Greece, July 15-18, 1996. Pierre Fauchais. LC 97-42148. 1997. write for info. (*1-56700-093-2*) Begell Hse.

Progress in Plasma Processing of Materials 1999: Proceedings of the Fourth International Thermal Plasma Processes Conference, St. Petersburg, Russia, July 13-16, 1998. Jacques Amouroux & Pierre Fauchais. LC 98-55121. 1999. write for info. (*1-56700-126-2*) Begell Hse.

Progress in Polyamine Research: Novel Biochemical, Pharmacological, & Clinical Aspects. Ed. by V. Zappia & Anthony E. Pegg. (Illus.). 796p. 1988. 135.00 (*0-306-43144-0*, Plenum Trade) Perseus Pubng.

*__Progress in Polyimide Chemistry I.__ Ed. by H. R. Kricheldorf. (Advances in Polymer Science Ser.: Vol. 140). (Illus.). 190p. 1999. 139.00 (*3-540-64962-X*) Spr-Verlag.

*__Progress in Polyimide Chemistry II.__ Ed. by H. R. Kricheldorf. (Advances in Polymer Science Ser.: Vol. 141). 240p. 1999. 169.00 (*3-540-64963-8*) Spr-Verlag.

Progress in Polymer Science, 5 vols., Vol. 2. Jenkins. 1977. pap. 13.25 (*0-08-019475-3*, Pergamon Pr) Elsevier.

Progress in Polymer Science, Vol. 8. Ed. by A. D. Jenkins & V. T. Stannett. (Illus.). 490p. 1983. 125.00 (*0-08-031007-9*, Pergamon Pr) Elsevier.

Progress in Polymer Science, Vol. 9. Ed. by A. D. Jenkins. (Illus.). 380p. 1984. 145.00 (*0-08-031734-0*, Pergamon Pr) Elsevier.

Progress in Polymer Science, Vol. 10. Ed. by A. D. Jenkins & V. T. Stannett. (Illus.). 364p. 1985. 145.00 (*0-08-032721-4*, Pergamon Pr) Elsevier.

Progress in Population Genetics & Human Evolution. Ed. by Peter J. Donnelly & E. Simon Tavare. LC 96-49167. (IMA Volumes in Mathematics & Its Applications Ser.: Vol. 87). (Illus.). 336p. 1997. 59.95 (*0-387-94944-5*) Spr-Verlag.

Progress in Post-War International Relations. Emanuel Adler & Beverly Crawford. 1991. text 61.50 (*0-231-07278-3*) Col U Pr.

Progress in Post War International Relations. Emanuel Adler & Beverly Crawford. 497p. 1995. pap. 22.00 (*0-231-07279-1*) Col U Pr.

Progress in Powder Metallurgy, Vol. 17. (Illus.). 195p. 1961. 5.00 (*0-918404-03-7*) Metal Powder.

Progress in Powder Metallurgy, Vol. 23. (Illus.). 62p. 1967. pap. 5.00 (*0-918404-08-8*) Metal Powder.

Progress in Powder Metallurgy, Vol. 25. (Illus.). 143p. 1969. pap. 5.00 (*0-918404-11-8*) Metal Powder.

Progress in Powder Metallurgy see Progress in Powder Metallurgy, 1977: Proceedings

Progress in Powder Metallurgy, Vol. 38. Ed. by James G. Bewley & S. W. McGee. (Illus.). 634p. 1982. pap. 20.00 (*0-918404-58-4*) Metal Powder.

Progress in Powder Metallurgy, Vol. 39. Ed. by H. S. Nayer et al. (Illus.). 696p. 1983. pap. 20.00 (*0-918404-61-4*) Metal Powder.

Progress in Powder Metallurgy, Vol. 41. Ed. by Howard I. Sanderow et al. 870p. 1985. pap. 40.00 (*0-918404-69-X*) Metal Powder.

Progress in Powder Metallurgy, Vol. 42. Ed. by G. Gaines. (Illus.). 808p. 1986. pap. 40.00 (*0-918404-71-1*) Metal Powder.

Progress in Powder Metallurgy, Vol. 43. Ed. by H. Hjort. (Illus.). 944p. 1987. pap. 40.00 (*0-918404-73-8*) Metal Powder.

P

An Asterisk (*) at the beginning of an entry indicates that the title is appearing for the first time.

Progress in Powder Metallurgy: Proceedings, National Powder Metallurgy Conference, Los Angeles & Cincinatti, 1978 & 1979 see Progress in Powder Metallurgy, 1977: Proceedings

Progress in Powder Metallurgy: Proceedings of the Twenty-Fourth Annual Powder Metallurgy Conference, Chicago, IL, April 22-25, 1968, Vol. 24. Progress in Powder Metallurgy Staff. LC 79-18458. (Illus.). 96p. reprint ed. pap. 30.00 (*0-7837-1559-5*, 204185100024) Bks Demand.

Progress in Powder Metallurgy, 1960: Proceedings of the 16th Annual Meeting of the Metal Powder Industries Federation. Progress in Powder Metallurgy Staff. LC 79-18458. (Progress in Powder Metallurgy Ser.: Vol. 16). (Illus.). 215p. reprint ed. pap. 66.70 (*0-7837-1552-8*, 204184500016) Bks Demand.

Progress in Powder Metallurgy, 1962: Proceedings of the Eighteenth Annual Powder Metallurgy Technical Conference & Magnetic Inductance Core Conference Held at the Hotel Sheraton, Philadelphia, PA, April 23-25, 1962. Powder Metallurgy Technical Conference Staff. LC TN0695.P68. (Progress in Powder Metallurgy Ser.: Vol. 18). (Illus.). 243p. reprint ed. pap. 75.40 (*0-7837-1553-6*, 204184600018) Bks Demand.

Progress in Powder Metallurgy, 1963: Proceedings of the Nineteenth Annual Powder Metallurgy Technical Conference Held at the Hotel Sheraton-Cadillac, Detroit, MI, April 29-May 1, 1963. Powder Metallurgy Technical Conference Staff. LC TN0695.P68. (Progress in Powder Metallurgy Ser.: Vol. 19). (Illus.). 204p. reprint ed. pap. 63.30 (*0-7837-1554-4*, 204184700019) Bks Demand.

Progress in Powder Metallurgy, 1964: Proceedings of the Twentieth Annual Powder Metallurgy Technical Conference Magnetic Inductance Core Conference Held at the Drake Hotel, Chicago, IL, April 27-29, 1964. Powder Metallurgy Technical Conference Staff. LC TN0695.P68. (Progress in Powder Metallurgy Ser.: Vol. 20). (Illus.). 333p. reprint ed. pap. 103.30 (*0-7837-1555-2*, 204184800020) Bks Demand.

Progress in Powder Metallurgy, 1969: Proceedings of the Twenty-Fifth Annual Powder Metallurgy Conference Sponsored by the Metal Powder Industries Federation & Presented at the New York Park Sheraton Hotel, May 5-7, 1969, New York, NY. Powder Metallurgy Technical Conference Staff. (Progress in Powder Metallurgy Ser.: No. 25). 147p. reprint ed. pap. 41.90 (*0-7837-3166-3*, 2042812) Bks Demand.

Progress in Powder Metallurgy, 1977: Proceedings, Vol. 33. Incl. Vol. 37. Progress in Powder Metallurgy. Ed. by Joseph Capus & Donald L. Dyke. (Illus.). 418p. (Orig.). 1981. pap. 22.00 (*0-918404-56-8*); Vols. 34-35. Progress in Powder Metallurgy: Proceedings, National Powder Metallurgy Conference, Los Angeles & Cincinatti, 1978 & 1979. Ed. by W. Cebulak. (Illus.). 439p. (Orig.). 1979. pap. 20.00 (*0-918404-49-5*); 283p. 1977. Set pap. text 15.00 (*0-918404-43-6*) Metal Powder.

Progress in Precision Engineering: Proceedings of the International Precision Engineering Seminar, 6th, IPES6 - International Conference on Ultraprecision in Manufacturing Engineering, 2nd, UME2, May 1991, Braunschweig, FRG. Ed. by P. Seyfried et al. (Illus.). xii, 417p. 1991. 118.95 (*0-387-53986-7*) Spr-Verlag.

Progress in Preventing AIDS? Dogma, Dissent & Innovation - Global Perspectives. Ed. by David Buchanan & George Cernada. LC 97-1804. (Health Services Ser.). 360p. 1998. pap. text 46.95 (*0-89503-176-0*) Baywood Pub.

Progress in Protistology. Ed. by David J. Patterson & John O. Corliss. (Illus.). 299p. 1989. 70.00 (*0-948737-08-5*, Pub. by Biopress) Balogh.

Progress in Protistology, Vol. 1. J. O. Corliss & D. J. Patterson. (Illus.). 419p. 1986. lib. bdg. 70.00 (*0-948737-01-8*, Pub. by Biopress) Balogh.

Progress in Protistology, Vol. 2. J. O. Corliss & D. J. Patterson. (Illus.). 390p. 1987. lib. bdg. 70.00 (*0-948737-04-2*, Pub. by Biopress) Balogh.

Progress in Protozoology: Proceedings of the IX International Congress of Protozoology, Berlin, 1993. Klaus Hausmann. Ed. by Nobert Hulsmann. (Illus.). x, 136p. 1994. 78.00 (*3-437-30762-2*) Balogh.

Progress in Psychobiology & Physiological Psychology, Vol. 15. Ed. by Alan N. Epstein & Adrian R. Morrison. (Illus.). 309p. (C). 1992. text 115.00 (*0-12-542115-X*) Acad Pr.

Progress in Psychobiology & Physiological Psychology, Vol. 16. Ed. by Steven J. Fluharty et al. (Illus.). 231p. (C). 1995. text 99.95 (*0-12-542116-8*) Acad Pr.

Progress in Public Health. Scally. 1998. pap. text. write for info. (*0-443-05938-1*) Church.

Progress in Quantitative Coronary Arteriography. Ed. by Johan H. Reiber & Patrick W. Serruys. LC 94-13374. (Developments in Cardiovascular Medicine Ser.: Vol. 155). 432p. (C). 1994. text 251.00 (*0-7923-2814-0*) Kluwer Academic.

Progress in Quantum Electronics, Vol. 6, Complete. T. S. Moss & Stig Stenholm. (Illus.). 292p. 1981. 88.00 (*0-08-028387-X*, Pergamon Pr) Elsevier.

Progress in Quantum Electronics, Vol. 8. Ed. by T. S. Moss et al. (Illus.). 278p. 1985. 140.00 (*0-08-031718-9*, Pub. by PPL) Elsevier.

Progress in Quantum Electronics, Vol. 9. Ed. by T. S. Moss et al. (Illus.). 346p. 126.00 (*0-08-034010-5*, Pub. by PPL) Elsevier.

Progress in Quantum Electronics, Vols. 1-4. Incl. Vol. 1, Pt. 1. Parametric Processes. J. H. Sanders & Stig Stenholm. 1969. pap. 24.00 (*0-08-006632-1*); Vol. 1, Pt. 2. Light Propagation & Light Shifts in Optical Pumping Experiments. Ed. by J. H. Sanders & Stig Stenholm. 1970. pap. 24.00 (*0-08-006795-6*); Vol. 1, Pt. 3. Non-Resonant Feedback in Lasers. Ed. by J. H. Sanders & Stig Stenholm. 1970. pap. 24.00 (*0-08-015645-2*); Vol. 1, Pt. 4. Semiclassical Theory of the Gas Laser. Ed. by J. H. Sanders & Stig Stenholm. 1971. pap. 24.00 (*0-08-016409-9*); Vol. 1, Pt. 5. Laser Lines in Atomic Species. Ed. by J. H. Sanders & Stig Stenholm. 1971. pap. 24.00 (*0-08-016652-0*); Vol. 2, Pt. 1. Photon Counting & Photon Statistics. Ed. by J. H. Sanders & Stig Stenholm. 1972. pap. 24.00 (*0-08-016865-5*); Vol. 2, Pt. 2. Nonlinear Spectroscopy of Molecules. Ed. by J. H. Sanders & Stig Stenholm. 1972. pap. 24.00 (*0-08-016880-9*); Vol. 2, Pt. 3. Collision Broadening of Spectral Lines by Neutral Atoms. Ed. by J. H. Sanders & Stig Stenholm. 1972. pap. 24.00 (*0-08-016881-7*); Vol. 2, Pt. 4. Quantum Theory of Josephson Radiation. Ed. by J. H. Sanders & Stig Stenholm. 1973. pap. 24.00 (*0-08-017743-3*); Vol. 3, Pt. 1. Three-Level Gas System & Their Interaction with Radiation. Ed. by J. H. Sanders & Stig Stenholm. 1975. 92.00 (*0-08-017765-4*); Vol. 3, Pt. 2. Mode-Locking of Lasers. Ed. by J. H. Sanders & Stig Stenholm. 1974. pap. 24.00 (*0-08-017852-9*); Vol. 3, Pt. 3. Quantum Theory of the Laser. Ed. by J. H. Sanders & Stig Stenholm. 1974. pap. 24.00 (*0-08-017923-1*); Vol. 4, Pt. 1. Self-Focusing: Experimental & Theory. Ed. by J. H. Sanders & Stig Stenholm. 1975. pap. 24.00 (*0-08-018946-6*); Vol. 4, Pt. 2. Nonlinear Narrow Optical Resonance by Laser Radiation. Ed. by J. H. Sanders & Stig Stenholm. 1975. pap. 24.00 (*0-08-018947-4*); Vol. 4, Pt. 3. Far Infrared Generation by Optical Mixing. Ed. by J. H. Sanders & Stig Stenholm. 1976. pap. 24.00 (*0-08-019461-3*); Vol. 1 (complete). Ed. by J. H. Sanders & Stig Stenholm. 1971. 92.00 (*0-08-016776-4*); Vol. 2 (complete). Ed. by J. H. Sanders & Stig Stenholm. 1974. 92.00 (*0-08-017818-9*); Vol. 3 (complete). Ed. by J. H. Sanders & Stig Stenholm. 1975. text 76.00 Vol. 4 (complete). Ed. by J. H. Sanders & Stig Stenholm. 1977. pap. 19.75 (*0-08-019462-1*); pap. write for info. (*0-318-55219-1*) Elsevier.

Progress in Radiation Processing: Proceedings of the International Meeting, 5th, San Diego, California, October 24-26, 1984. S. Nablo. 916p. 1985. pap. 205.00 (*0-08-032620-X*, Pub. by PPL) Elsevier.

Progress in Radio-Oncology II. Ed. by Karl-Heinz Karcher et al. LC 81-40545. 509p. 1982. reprint ed. pap. 157.80 (*0-608-00377-8*, 206109100007) Bks Demand.

Progress in Radiopharmacology, 1985. Ed. by Peter H. Cox et al. LC 85-13774. (Developments in Nuclear Medicine Ser.). 1985. text 191.00 (*0-89838-745-0*) Kluwer Academic.

Progress in Radiopharmacology 3. Peter H. Cox. 1982. text 141.50 (*90-247-2768-5*) Kluwer Academic.

Progress in Radiopharmacy. Ed. by Peter H. Cox et al. (Developments in Nuclear Medicine Ser.). 1986. lib. bdg. 314.00 (*0-89838-823-6*) Kluwer Academic.

Progress in Radiopharmacy. Ed. by P. August Schubiger & Gerrit Westera. (Developments in Nuclear Medicine Ser.). 256p. (C). 1992. text 137.50 (*0-7923-1525-1*) Kluwer Academic.

Progress in Rational Emotive Behavior Therapy. Windy Dryden. 150p. 1994. pap. 39.50 (*1-56593-369-9*, 0725) Singular Publishing.

Progress in Reaction Kinetics, Vol. 5. Porter. 1970. 140.00 (*0-08-013035-6*, Pergamon Pr) Elsevier.

Progress in Reaction Kinetics, Vol. 6-7. Incl. Vol. 6, Pt. 2. Chemi-Ionization Reactions in the Gas Phase. LC 61-1784. 1971. pap. 24.00 (*0-08-016658-X*); Vol. 6, Pt. 3. Salt & Medium Effects on Reaction Rates in Concentrated Solutions of Acids & Bases. LC 61-1784. 1971. pap. 24.00 (*0-08-016721-7*); Vol. 6, Pt. 4. Chemical Applications of Metasable Rare Gas Atoms. LC 61-1784. 1971. pap. 24.00 (*0-08-016722-5*); Vol. 6, Pt. 5. Primary Salt-Effect in Aqueous Solutions. LC 61-1784. 1971. pap. 24.00 (*0-08-016759-4*); Vol. 6, Pt. 1. LC 61-1784. 1971. pap. 24.00 (*0-08-016657-1*); Vol. 6. LC 61-1784. 1972. 84.00 (*0-08-016873-6*); Vol. 7, Pts. 1 & 2. LC 61-1784. 1973. pap. 24.00 (*0-08-017037-4*); Vol. 7. LC 61-1784. 1973. pap. 24.00 (*0-08-017151-6*); LC 61-1784. pap. write for info. (*0-318-55220-5*) Elsevier.

Progress in Reaction Kinetics, Vol. 7. K. R. Jennings & R. Cundall. LC 61-1784. 1975. 94.00 (*0-08-017807-3*, Pub. by Pergamon Repr) Franklin.

Progress in Reaction Kinetics, Vol. 9. Ed. by K. R. Jennings & R. B. Cundall. 368p. 1980. 92.00 (*0-08-020343-4*, Pergamon Pr) Elsevier.

Progress in Reaction Kinetics, Vol. 10 Complete. Ed. by K. R. Jennings & R. B. Cundall. 402p. 1981. 100.00 (*0-08-027155-3*, Pergamon Pr) Elsevier.

Progress in Reaction Kinetics, Vol. 12. Ed. by K. R. Jennings et al. (Illus.). 268p. 1985. 130.00 (*0-08-032326-X*, Pergamon Pr) Elsevier.

Progress in Reaction Kinetics, Vol. 13. Ed. by K. R. Jennings et al. (Illus.). 314p. 120.00 (*0-08-033228-5*, E120, E115, E12, Pub. by PPL) Elsevier.

Progress in Refrigeration Science & Technology, Munich Conference, 3 vols., Set. International Institute of Refrigeration. 1965. 802.00 (*0-08-011439-3*, Pub. by Pergamon Repr) Franklin.

Progress in Regional Cancer Therapy. Ed. by R. Jakesz & H. Rainer. (Illus.). 360p. 1990. 118.00 (*0-387-51259-4*) Spr-Verlag.

Progress in Relaxin Research: Proceedings of the 2nd International Congress on the Hormone Relaxin. Ed. by Alastair H. MacLennan et al. LC 94-31284. 696p. 1995. text 106.00 (*981-3049-02-2*) World Scientific Pub.

Progress in Reproductive & Urinary Tract Pathology. Ivan Damjanov. 1989. 70.00 (*0-938607-13-8*) Field & Wood Inc Medical.

Progress in Reproductive & Urinary Tract Pathology, Vol. 2. Ivan Damjanov. 1990. 89.00 (*0-938607-29-4*) Field & Wood Inc Medical.

Progress in Reproductive Medicine, Vol. 2. Ed. by Richard H. Asch & John W. Studd. (Illus.). 304p. 1995. 65.00 (*1-85070-574-7*) Prthnon Pub.

Progress in Resource Management & Environmental Planning, 4 vols., Vol. 1. Ed. by Timothy O'Riordan. LC 80-646092. 335p. reprint ed. pap. 103.90 (*0-8357-4623-2*, 203755500001) Bks Demand.

Progress in Resource Management & Environmental Planning, 4 vols., Vol. 2. Ed. by Timothy O'Riordan. LC 80-646092. 256p. reprint ed. pap. 79.40 (*0-8357-4624-0*, 203755500002) Bks Demand.

Progress in Resource Management & Environmental Planning, 4 vols., Vol. 3. Ed. by Timothy O'Riordan. LC 80-646092. 340p. reprint ed. pap. 105.40 (*0-8357-4625-9*, 203755500003) Bks Demand.

Progress in Resource Management & Environmental Planning, 4 vols., Vol. 4. Ed. by Timothy O'Riordan. LC 80-646092. 322p. reprint ed. pap. 99.90 (*0-8357-4626-7*, 203755500004) Bks Demand.

Progress in Retinal Research, Vol. 1. Ed. by Neville N. Osborne & Gerald J. Chader. (Illus.). 245p. 1982. 95.75 (*0-08-028901-0*, Pergamon Pr) Elsevier.

Progress in Retinal Research, Vol. 2. Ed. by Neville N. Osborne. (Illus.). 337p. 1983. 84.75 (*0-08-030773-6*, 07, Pergamon Pr) Elsevier.

Progress in Retinal Research, Vol. 3. Ed. by Neville N. Osborne & G. J. Chader. (Illus.). 358p. 1984. 81.00 (*0-08-031701-4*, Pergamon Pr) Elsevier.

Progress in Retinal Research, Vol. 4. Ed. by Neville N. Osborne & Gerald J. Chader. (Illus.). 330p. 1985. 120.00 (*0-08-031738-3*, Pergamon Pr) Elsevier.

Progress in Retinopathy of Prematurity. Ed. by A. Reibaldi et al. (Illus.). xii, 234p. (Orig.). 1997. pap. 71.50 (*90-6299-146-7*) Kugler Pubns.

Progress in Rural Geography. Ed. by Michael Pacione. LC 82-22756. (Illus.). 268p. (C). 1983. text 41.50 (*0-389-20358-0*, N7218) B&N Imports.

Progress in Self Psychology, Vol. 1. Goldberg. 1995. 45.00 (*0-88163-214-7*) L Erlbaum Assocs.

Progress in Self Psychology, Vol. 2. Goldberg. 1995. 45.00 (*0-88163-215-5*) L Erlbaum Assocs.

Progress in Sensory Physiology, Vol. 5. (Illus.). 175p. 1985. 79.95 (*0-387-15339-X*) Spr-Verlag.

Progress in Sensory Physiology, Vol. 9. Ed. by W. D. Willis, Jr. et al. (Illus.). 225p. 1989. 107.00 (*0-387-50282-3*) Spr-Verlag.

Progress in Sensory Physiology, Vol. 12. Ed. by H. Autrum et al. (Illus.). 260p. 1991. 136.00 (*0-387-52985-3*) Spr-Verlag.

Progress in Sensory Physiology: Ionic & Volume Changes in the Microenvironment of Nerve & Receptor Cells, Vol. 13. Ed. by H. Autrum et al. (Illus.). 176p. 1992. 123.00 (*0-387-54553-0*) Spr-Verlag.

Progress in Sexual Biology & Strategy Studies, Vol. 9A, Progress in Male Gamete Ultrastructure an. Adiyodi. 286p. 1999. 225.00 (*0-471-97163-4*) Wiley.

Progress in Shape Memory Alloys. Ed. by Stephan Eucken. (Illus.). 316p. 1992. 102.00 (*3-88355-178-3*, Pub. by DGM Metallurgy Info) IR Pubns.

Progress in Social Psychology, Vol. 1. M. Fishbein. LC 79-67453. (Illus.). 240p. 1980. text 49.95 (*0-89859-005-1*) L Erlbaum Assocs.

Progress in Solar Energy: Proceedings of the American Section of the International Solar Energy Society, Vol. 6. Ed. by G. E. Franta. 1500p. 1984. reprint ed. pap. 60.00 (*0-89553-126-7*) Am Solar Energy.

Progress in Solar Energy Vol. 5: The Renewable Challenge. Ed. by Gregory E. Franta & Keith W. Haggard. 1985. pap. text 60.00 (*0-89553-034-1*) Am Solar Energy.

Progress in Solar Energy Technologies. Ed. by H. Hubbard. 64p. 1994. pap. 20.00 (*0-89553-300-6*) Am Solar Energy.

Progress in Solar Engineering. Yogi Goswami. 378p. 1986. 125.00 (*0-89116-560-6*) Hemisp Pub.

Progress in Solar Physics. Ed. by C. De Jager & Z. Svestka. 1986. text 273.50 (*90-277-2180-7*) Kluwer Academic.

Progress in Solar-Terrestrial Physics. J. G. Roederer. 1983. text 296.00 (*90-277-1559-9*) Kluwer Academic.

Progress in Solid State Chemistry, Vol. 5. Ed. by H. Reiss et al. 1971. 98.00 (*0-08-015846-3*, Pub. by Pergamon Repr) Franklin.

Progress in Solid State Chemistry, Vol. 6. Ed. by H. Reiss et al. 1971. 98.00 (*0-08-016723-3*, Pub. by Pergamon Repr) Franklin.

Progress in Solid State Chemistry, Vol. 7. Ed. by H. Reiss et al. 1972. 98.00 (*0-08-016916-3*, Pub. by Pergamon Repr) Franklin.

Progress in Solid State Chemistry, Vol. 13. Ed. by G. M. Rosenblatt & W. L. Worrell. (Illus.). 376p. 1982. 140.00 (*0-08-029712-9*, Pergamon Pr) Elsevier.

Progress in Solid State Chemistry, Vol. 14. Ed. by G. M. Rosenblatt & W. L. Worrell. (Illus.). 302p. 1983. 130.00 (*0-08-030998-4*, Pergamon Pr) Elsevier.

Progress in Solid State Chemistry, Vol. 15. Ed. by G. M. Rosenblatt & W. L. Worrell. (Illus.). 374p. 1985. 145.00 (*0-08-033664-7*, E115, E125, C140, Pub. by PPL) Elsevier.

Progress in Solid State Chemistry, Vols. 8-10. Incl. Vol. 10, Pt. 2. Heterogeneous Catalysis by Metals. John H. Sinfelt. LC 63-11362. 1975. pap. 12.75 (*0-08-019480-X*); Vol. 8. Ed. by J. O. McCaldin & Gabor A. Sommorjai. LC 63-11362. 1973. 98.00 (*0-08-017147-8*); Vol. 9. Ed. by J. O. McCaldin & Gabor A. Sommorjai. LC 63-11362. 1975. 98.00 (*0-08-018067-1*); Vol. 10, Pt. 1. Ed. by J. O. McCaldin & Gabor A. Sommorjai. LC 63-11362. 1975. pap. 12.75 (*0-08-019479-6*); Vol. 10, Pt. 3. Ed. by J. O. McCaldin & Gabor A. Sommorjai. LC 63-11362. 1975. pap. 19.75 (*0-08-019481-8*); Vol. 10, Pt. 4. Ed. by J. O. McCaldin & Gabor A. Sommorjai. LC 63-11362. 1976. pap. 24.00 (*0-08-019482-6*); LC 63-11362. pap. text. write for info. (*0-318-55221-3*, Pub. by Pergamon Repr) Franklin.

Progress in Standardization in Health Care Informatics. Ed. by G. De Moor et al. (Studies in Health Technology & Informatics: Vol. 6). 225p. (YA). (gr. 12). 1993. 98.00 (*90-5199-114-2*, Pub. by IOS Pr) IOS Press.

Progress in Standardization of Aquatic Toxicity Tests. Amadeu M. V. M. Soares. 224p. 1993. lib. bdg. 95.00 (*0-87371-845-3*, L845) Lewis Pubs.

Progress in Statistical Mechanics. Ed. by C. K. Hu. 416p. (C). 1988. pap. 52.00 (*9971-5-0737-4*); text 125.00 (*9971-5-0714-5*) World Scientific Pub.

Progress in Statistical Physics: Proceedings of the International Conference on Statistical Physics in Memory of Professor Soon-Tahk Choh Seoul, Korea. Ed. by Wokyung Sung et al. (Illus.). 400p. 1998. 78.00 (*981-02-3525-9*) World Scientific Pub.

Progress in Stellar Spectral Line Formation Theory. Ed. by John E. Beckman & Lucio Crivellari. 1985. text 203.00 (*90-277-2007-X*) Kluwer Academic.

Progress in Structural Engineering. Ed. by Donald E. Grierson et al. 648p. (C). 1991. text 253.00 (*0-7923-1396-8*) Kluwer Academic.

Progress in Surface Science, 8 vols., Vol. 1. Davison. 1977. pap. 15.25 (*0-08-021765-6*, Pergamon Pr) Elsevier.

Progress in Surface Science, Vol. 10, No. 1. Ed. by S. G. Davison. (Illus.). 164p. 1981. pap. 31.00 (*0-08-027154-5*, Pergamon Pr) Elsevier.

Progress in Surface Science, Vol. 11. Ed. by S. G. Davison. LC 77-141188. 378p. 1983. 115.00 (*0-08-030875-9*, 17, Pergamon Pr) Elsevier.

Progress in Surface Science, Vol. 12. Ed. by S. G. Davison. 436p. 1984. 120.00 (*0-08-030876-7*, Pergamon Pr) Elsevier.

Progress in Surface Science, Vol. 13. Ed. by S. G. Davison. LC 77-141188. 355p. 1985. 120.00 (*0-08-030886-4*, Pergamon Pr) Elsevier.

Progress in Surface Science, Vol. 14. Ed. by S. G. Davison. LC 77-141188. 423p. 1985. 120.00 (*0-08-030887-2*, Pergamon Pr) Elsevier.

Progress in Surface Science, Vol. 15. Ed. by S. G. Davison. 494p. 1985. 120.00 (*0-08-030894-5*, Pub. by PPL) Elsevier.

Progress in Surface Science, Vol. 16. Ed. by S. G. Davison. 1985. 120.00 (*0-08-030904-6*, Pub. by PPL) Elsevier.

Progress in Surface Science, Vol. 17. Ed. by S. G. Davison. LC 77-141188. 328p. 1986. 126.00 (*0-08-030905-4*, Pub. by PPL) Elsevier.

Progress in Surface Science, Vol. 18. Ed. by S. G. Davison. LC 77-141188. 541p. 1986. 126.00 (*0-08-030906-2*, Pub. by PPL) Elsevier.

Progress in Surface Science, Vols. 1-7 & 9. Incl. Vol. 1., **4 pts.** 1972. 110.00 (*0-08-016878-7*); Pt. 1., **4 pts.** 1971. pap. 24.00 (*0-08-016549-4*); Pt. 2., **4 pts.** 1971. pap. 24.00 (*0-08-016629-6*); Pt. 3., **4 pts.** 1971. pap. 24.00 (*0-08-016815-9*); Pt. 4., **4 pts.** 1971. pap. 24.00 (*0-08-016792-6*); Vol. 2., **4 pts.** 1972. 110.00 (*0-08-017135-4*); Pt. 1., **4 pts.** 1972. pap. 24.00 (*0-08-016934-1*); Pt. 2., **4 pts.** 1972. pap. 24.00 (*0-08-016879-5*); Pt. 3., **4 pts.** 1972. pap. 24.00 (*0-08-016944-9*); Pt. 4., **4 pts.** 1972. pap. 24.00 (*0-08-016952-X*); Vol. 3., **4 pts.** 1973. 110.00 (*0-08-017150-8*); Pt. 1., **4 pts.** 1972. pap. 24.00 (*0-08-016981-3*); Pt. 2., **4 pts.** 1972. pap. 24.00 (*0-08-017045-5*); Pt. 3., **4 pts.** 1972. pap. 24.00 (*0-08-017046-3*); Pt. 4., **4 pts.** 1973. pap. 24.00 (*0-08-017127-3*); Vol. 4., **3 pts.** 1974. 110.00 (*0-08-017778-6*); Pt. 1., **3 pts.** 1973. pap. 24.00 (*0-08-017790-5*); Pt. 2., **3 pts.** 1974. pap. 24.00 Pt. 3., **3 pts.** 1974. pap. 24.00 (*0-08-017798-0*); Vol. 5., **4 pts.** 1975. 110.00 (*0-08-017791-3*); Pt. 1., **4 pts.** 1974. pap. 24.00 (*0-08-017904-5*); Pt. 2., **4 pts.** 1974. pap. 24.00 (*0-08-017792-1*); Pt. 3., **4 pts.** 1974. pap. 24.00 (*0-08-018051-5*); Pt. 4., **4 pts.** 1975. pap. 24.00 (*0-08-018150-3*); Vol. 6-7., **3 pts.** 1978. 220.00 (*0-08-019460-5*); Pt. 1., **3 pts.** 1975. pap. 12.75 (*0-08-018223-2*); Pt. 2., **3 pts.** 1975. pap. 35.00 (*0-08-018974-1*); Pt. 3., **3 pts.** 1975. pap. 19.75 (*0-08-018975-X*); Pt. 1., **3 pts.** 1976. pap. 15.75 (*0-08-018977-6*); Pt. 2., **3 pts.** 1976. pap. 18.75 (*0-08-018978-4*); Pt. 3., **3 pts.** 1976. pap. 17.25 (*0-08-018979-2*); Vol. 9 Complete. 273p. 1981. 110.00 (*0-08-026052-7*); pap. write for info. (*0-318-55222-1*) Elsevier.

Progress in Surgery, 2 vols., 11. Ed. by M. Allgoewer et al. (Illus.). 1972. 57.50 (*3-8055-1379-8*) S Karger.

Progress in Surgery, 2 vols., 12. Ed. by M. Allgoewer et al. (Illus.). 1973. 85.25 (*3-8055-1617-7*) S Karger.

Progress in Surgery, Vol. 10. Ed. by M. Allgoewer et al. (Illus.). x, 132p. 1971. 48.00 (*3-8055-1285-6*) S Karger.

Progress in Surgery, Vol. 13. Ed. by M. Allgoewer et al. 300p. 1974. 121.00 (*3-8055-1741-6*) S Karger.

Progress in Surgery, Vol. 14. Ed. by M. Allgoewer et al. x, 192p. 1975. 80.00 (*3-8055-2181-2*) S Karger.

Progress in Surgery, Vol. 15. Ed. by U. F. Gruber et al. 1977. 60.00 (*3-8055-2365-3*) S Karger.

Progress in Surgery of the Liver, Pancreas & Biliary System. Ed. by Stig Bengmark. (Developments in Surgery Ser.). (C). 1988. text 271.50 (*0-89838-956-9*) Kluwer Academic.

Progress in Surgical Pathology. 1992. 149.00 (*0-387-54130-6*) Spr-Verlag.

Progress in Surgical Pathology, Vol. 6. Cecilia M. Fenoglio-Preiser et al. 400p. (C). 1988. text. write for info. (*0-938607-00-6*) Macmillan.

Progress in Surgical Pathology, Vol. 9. Cecilia M. Fenoglio-Preiser. 1989. 75.00 (*0-938607-11-1*) Field & Wood Inc Medical.

Progress in Surgical Pathology, Vol. 10. Cecilia M. Fenoglio-Preiser. 1989. 75.00 (*0-938607-14-6*) Field & Wood Inc Medical.

An Asterisk (*) at the beginning of an entry indicates that the title is appearing for the first time.

Progress in Surgical Pathology, Vol. 11. Cecilia M. Fenoglio-Preiser. 1990. 85.00 (*0-938607-31-6*) Field & Wood Inc Medical.

Progress in Synthetic Fuels. G. Imarisio & J. M. Bemtgen. (C). 1989. text 178.50 (*1-85333-161-9*) Kluwer Academic.

***Progress in System & Robot Analysis & Control Design.** S. G. Tzafestas & G. Schmidt. LC 98-46939. (Lecture Notes in Control & Information Sciences Ser.: Vol. 243). (Illus.). 596p. 1999. pap. 125.00 (*1-85233-123-2*, Pub. by Spr-Verlag) Spr-Verlag.

Progress in Temperate Fruit Breeding. Ed. by Hanna Schmidt. LC 94-21241. (Developments in Plant Breeding Ser.: Vol. 1). 472p. (C). 1994. text 281.00 (*0-7923-2947-3*) Kluwer Academic.

Progress in the Characterization of Venoms & Standardization of Antivenoms. WHO Staff. (WHO Offset Publications: No. 58). 44p. 1981. 6.00 (*92-4-170058-0*) World Health.

Progress in the Chemistry of Aza-Analogs of SO-2, Vol. 2. R. Bussas et al. 162p. 1983. pap. text 277.00 (*3-7186-0153-2*) Gordon & Breach.

Progress in the Chemistry of Fats & Other Lipids, Vol. 7. R. J. Holman. 1964. pap. 45.00 (*0-08-010088-0*, Pergamon Pr) Elsevier.

Progress in the Chemistry of Fats & Other Lipids, Vol. 8. R. J. Holman. 1965. pap. 45.00 (*0-08-011150-5*, Pergamon Pr) Elsevier.

Progress in the Chemistry of Fats & Other Lipids, Vol. 8. R. J. Holman. 1965. pap. 24.00 (*0-08-011359-1*, Pergamon Pr) Elsevier.

Progress in the Chemistry of Fats & Other Lipids, Vol. 8. R. J. Holman. LC 53-22998. 1966. 188.00 (*0-08-011920-4*, Pub. by Pergamon Repr) Franklin.

Progress in the Chemistry of Fats & Other Lipids, Vols. 5-14. Incl. Vol. 9, Pt. 1. Polyunsaturated Acids. Ed. by Ralph T. Holman. LC 53-22998. 1966. pap. 24.00 (*0-08-011797-X*); Vol. 14, Pt. 2. Lipids of Fungi. Ed. by Ralph T. Holman. LC 53-22998. 1974. pap. 24.00 (*0-08-017880-4*); Vol. 14, Pt. 3. Infrared Absorption Spectroscopy of Normal & Substituted Long-Chain Fatty Acids & Esters in Solid State. H. Fischmeister. LC 53-22998. 1975. pap. 23.00 (*0-08-018073-6*); Vol. 14, Pt. 4. Lipid Metabolism Membrane Functions of the Mammary Gland. S. Patton & R. G. Jensen. LC 53-22998. 1975. pap. 24.00 (*0-08-018222-4*); Pt. 1. Ralph T. Holman. LC 53-22998. 1964. pap. 24.00 (*0-08-010087-2*); Vol. 9. Ralph T. Holman. LC 53-22998. 1971. 84.00 (*0-08-016041-7*); Pt. 2. Ralph T. Holman. LC 53-22998. 1968. pap. 24.00 (*0-08-012632-4*); Pt. 3. Ralph T. Holman. LC 53-22998. 1967. pap. 24.00 (*0-08-013239-1*); Pt. 4. Ralph T. Holman. LC 53-22998. 1968. pap. 24.00 (*0-08-015971-0*); Pt. 5. Ralph T. Holman. LC 53-22998. 1970. pap. 24.00 (*0-08-016111-1*); Vol. 10, Pts. 1-4. Ralph T. Holman. LC 53-22998. 1970. 84.00 (*0-08-016040-9*); Pt. 1. Ralph T. Holman. LC 53-22998. 1967. pap. 24.00 (*0-08-012292-2*); Pt. 2. Ralph T. Holman. LC 53-22998. 1969. pap. 24.00 (*0-08-012996-X*); Pt. 3. Ralph T. Holman. LC 53-22998. 1969. pap. 24.00 (*0-08-012997-8*); Pt. 4. Ralph T. Holman. LC 53-22998. 1969. pap. 24.00 (*0-08-013990-6*); Vol. 11, Pts. 1-3. Ralph T. Holman. LC 53-22998. 1972. 84.00 (*0-08-016795-0*); Pt. 1. Ralph T. Holman. LC 53-22998. 1970. pap. 24.00 (*0-08-015847-1*); Pt. 2. Ralph T. Holman. LC 53-22998. 1970. pap. 24.00 (*0-08-016150-2*); Pt. 3. Ralph T. Holman. LC 53-22998. 1971. pap. 24.00 (*0-08-016571-0*); Vol. 12. Ralph T. Holman. LC 53-22998. 1972. 84.00 (*0-08-016758-6*); Vol. 13, Pts. 1-4. Ralph T. Holman. LC 53-22998. 1973. 84.00 (*0-08-017146-X*); Pt. 1. Ralph T. Holman. LC 53-22998. 1973. pap. 24.00 (*0-08-016942-2*); Pt. 2. Ralph T. Holman. LC 53-22998. 1973. pap. 24.00 (*0-08-017043-9*); Pt. 3. Ralph T. Holman. LC 53-22998. 1973. pap. 24.00 (*0-08-017176-1*); Pt. 4. Ralph T. Holman. LC 53-22998. 1973. pap. 24.00 (*0-08-017129-X*); Vol. 14, Pt. 1. Ralph T. Holman. LC 53-22998. 1973. pap. 24.00 (*0-08-017130-3*); LC 53-22998. pap. write for info. (*0-318-55223-X*, Pub. by Pergamon Repr) Franklin.

Progress in the Chemistry of Organic Natural Products. (Fortschritte der Chemie Organischer Naturstoffe Ser.: Vol. 72). (Illus.). 330p. 1997. 219.00 (*3-211-82879-6*) Spr-Verlag.

Progress in the Chemistry of Organic Natural Products. Ed. by W. Herz et al. (The Zechmeister Ser.: Vol. 67). 200p. 1996. 174.00 (*3-211-82695-5*) Spr-Verlag.

Progress in the Chemistry of Organic Natural Products. Ed. by W. Herz et al. (Illus.). 350p. 1996. 230.00 (*3-211-82597-5*) Spr-Verlag.

Progress in the Chemistry of Organic Natural Products. L. Wechmeister. Ed. by W. Heerz. 250p. 1996. 198.00 (*3-211-82824-9*) Spr-Verlag.

Progress in the Chemistry of Organic Natural Products. Ed. by L. Zechmeister et al. Vol. 76. (Illus.). 220p. 1998. 169.00 (*3-211-83165-7*) Spr-Verlag.

Progress in the Chemistry of Organic Natural Products, Vol. 35. Ed. by W. Herz et al. LC 39-1015. 1978. 206.95 (*0-387-81460-4*) Spr-Verlag.

Progress in the Chemistry of Organic Natural Products, Vol. 36. Ed. by W. Herz et al. (Illus.). 1979. 157.95 (*0-387-81472-8*) Spr-Verlag.

Progress in the Chemistry of Organic Natural Products, Vol. 37. Ed. by W. Herz et al. LC 39-1015. (Illus.). 1979. 142.95 (*0-387-81528-7*) Spr-Verlag.

Progress in the Chemistry of Organic Natural Products, Vol. 38. Ed. by W. Herz et al. (Illus.). 450p. 1980. 156.95 (*0-387-81529-5*) Spr-Verlag.

Progress in the Chemistry of Organic Natural Products, Vol. 39. Ed. by W. Herz et al. (Illus.). 330p. 1980. 126.95 (*0-387-81530-9*) Spr-Verlag.

Progress in the Chemistry of Organic Natural Products, Vol. 40. Ed. by W. Herz et al. (Illus.). 300p. 1981. 126.95 (*0-387-81624-0*) Spr-Verlag.

Progress in the Chemistry of Organic Natural Products, Vol. 41. Ed. by W. Herz et al. (Illus.). 373p. 1982. 157.95 (*0-387-81690-9*) Spr-Verlag.

Progress in the Chemistry of Organic Natural Products, Vol. 42. Ed. by W. Herz et al. 330p. 1983. 131.95 (*0-387-81706-9*) Spr-Verlag.

Progress in the Chemistry of Organic Natural Products, Vol. 43. Ed. by W. Herz et al. (Illus.). 383p. 1983. 167.95 (*0-387-81741-7*) Spr-Verlag.

Progress in the Chemistry of Organic Natural Products, Vol. 46. (Illus.). 280p. 1985. 151.95 (*0-387-81804-9*) Spr-Verlag.

Progress in the Chemistry of Organic Natural Products, Vol. 54. Ed. by W. Herz et al. (Illus.). 350p. 1988. 256.95 (*0-387-82086-8*) Spr-Verlag.

Progress in the Chemistry of Organic Natural Products, Vol. 59. Ed. by W. Herz et al. (Illus.). 200p. 1992. 168.95 (*0-387-82278-X*) Spr-Verlag.

Progress in the Chemistry of Organic Natural Products, Vol. 61. Ed. by W. Herz et al. (Illus.). 200p. 1993. 175.95 (*0-387-82388-3*) Spr-Verlag.

Progress in the Chemistry of Organic Natural Products, Vol. 62. Laszlo Zechmeister. Ed. by W. Herz et al. (Illus.). 320p. 1993. 224.95 (*0-387-82402-2*) Spr-Verlag.

Progress in the Chemistry of Organic Natural Products, Vol. 63. Ed. by W. Herz et al. 250p. 1995. 143.00 (*0-387-82443-X*) Spr-Verlag.

Progress in the Chemistry of Organic Natural Products, Vol. 65. Ed. by W. Herz et al. (Zechmeister Ser.). (Illus.). 600p. 1995. write for info. (*0-387-82576-2*) Spr-Verlag.

Progress in the Chemistry of Organic Natural Products, Vol. 74. Ed. by W. Herz et al. (Illus.). 320p. 1998. 199.00 (*3-211-83033-2*) Spr-Verlag.

***Progress in the Chemistry of Organic Natural Products, Vol. 77.** Ed. by W. Herz et al. 250p. 1999. 156.00 (*3-211-83264-5*) Spr-Verlag.

***Progress in the Chemistry of Organic Natural Products, Vol. 78.** Ed. by W. Herz et al. (Illus.). 180p. 1999. 149.00 (*3-211-83311-0*) Spr-Verlag.

***Progress in the chemistry of Organic Natural Products, Vol. 79.** Ed. by W. Herz et al. 250p. 2000. (*3-211-83361-7*) Spr-Verlag.

***Progress in the Chemistry of Organic Natural Products, Vol. 80.** Ed. by W. Herz et al. (Illus.). 250p. 2000. 159.00 (*3-211-83428-1*) Spr-Verlag.

Progress in the Chemistry of Organic Natural Products, Vols. 21-31. Incl. Vols. 1-20. Cumulative Index. 1964. 86.95 (*0-387-80677-6*); Vol. 21. 1963. 87.95 (*0-387-80638-5*); Vol. 22. 1964. 105.95 (*0-387-80678-4*); Vol. 23. 1965. 111.95 (*0-387-80716-0*); Vol. 24. 1966. 129.95 (*0-387-80757-8*); Vol. 25. 1967. 91.95 (*0-387-80811-6*); Vol. 26. 1968. 146.95 (*0-387-80864-7*); Vol. 27. 1970. 129.95 (*0-387-80909-0*); Vol. 28. 1971. 142.95 (*0-387-80975-9*); Vol. 29. 1972. 167.95 (*0-387-81024-2*); Vol. 31. 1974. 203.95 (*0-387-81172-9*); Vol. 5. 1948. 97.95 (*0-387-80047-6*); Vol. 6. 1950. 91.95 (*0-387-80140-5*); Vol. 7. 1950. 79.95 (*0-387-80141-3*); Vol. 8. 1951. 91.95 (*0-387-80204-5*); Vol. 9. 1952. 124.95 (*0-387-80253-3*); Vol. 10. 1953. 124.95 (*0-387-80300-9*); Vol. 11. 1954. 107.95 (*0-387-80336-X*); Vol. 12. 1955. 128.95 (*0-387-80371-8*); Vol. 16. 1958. 55.95 (*0-387-80475-7*); Vol. 17. 1959. 118.95 (*0-387-80510-9*); Vol. 18. 1960. 140.95 (*0-387-80540-0*); Vol. 19. 1961. 100.95 (*0-387-80577-X*); Vol. 20. 1962. 118.95 (*0-387-80605-9*); write for info. (*0-318-55815-7*) Spr-Verlag.

Progress in the Chemistry of Organic Natural Products: Fortschritte der Chemie Organischer Naturstoffe, Vol. 68. Ed. by W. Herz et al. (Zechmeister Ser.). 490p. 1996. 226.00 (*3-211-82702-1*) Spr-Verlag.

Progress in the Chemistry of Organic Natural Products Vol. 70: Fortschritte der Chemie Organischer Naturstoffe. Ed. by W. Herz et al. 250p. 1997. 229.00 (*3-211-82825-7*) Spr-Verlag.

Progress in the Chemistry of Organic Natural Products (Fortschritte der Chemie Organischer Naturstoffe), Vol. 73. W. Herz et al. 250p. 1998. 150.00 (*3-211-83019-7*) Spr-Verlag.

Progress in the Chemistry of Organic Natural Products (Fortschritte der Chemie Organischer Naturstoffe), Vol. 75. Ed. by W. Herz et al. (Illus.). 250p. 1998. 159.00 (*3-211-83053-7*) Spr-Verlag.

Progress in the Development & Use of Antiviral Drugs & Interferon. (Technical Reports: No. 754). 25p. 1987. pap. 5.00 (*92-4-120754-X*, 1100754) World Health.

Progress in the Development of Cost-Effective Treatment for Drug Abusers. 1986. lib. bdg. 175.00 (*0-8490-3517-1*) Gordon Pr.

Progress in the Greece of Thucydides. W. Den Boer. (Mededelingen der Koninklijke Nederlandse Akademie van Wetenschappen, Afd. Letterkunde Ser.: No. 40(2)). 82p. 1977. pap. text 22.00 (*0-7204-8455-3*) Elsevier.

Progress in the Management of the Menopause: Proceedings of the 8th International Congress, Sydney, Australia, 3-7 November, 1996. Ed. by Barry G. Wren. LC 97-34442. (Illus.). 508p. 1997. 90.00 (*1-85070-799-5*) Prthnon Pub.

Progress in the Physics of Clusters. G. N. Chuev et al. 500p. 1998. 88.00 (*981-02-3660-3*) World Scientific Pub.

***Progress in the Reduction, Refinement & Replacement of Animal Experimentation.** Michael Balls et al. LC 00-42978. (Developments in Animal & Veterinary Science Ser.). (Illus.). 2000. write for info. (*0-444-50529-6*) Elsevier.

Progress in the Science & Technology of the Rare Earths. Leroy Eyring. write for info. (*0-318-57473-X*, Pergamon Pr) Elsevier.

Progress in the Study of Point Defects. Ed. by Masao Doyama & Sho Yoshida. LC 78-303785. (Illus.). 448p. 1977. reprint ed. pap. 138.90 (*0-608-01196-7*, 206188500001) Bks Demand.

Progress in the Treatment of Fluency Disorders. Ed. by Lena Rustin et al. 330p. 1987. 62.25 (*1-56593-545-4*, 0066) Singular Publishing.

Progress in the Treatment of Parkinsonism. fac. ed. Ed. by Donald B. Calne. LC 73-180269. (Advances in Neurology Ser.: No. 3). (Illus.). 342p. pap. 106.10 (*0-7837-7356-0*, 204716500005) Bks Demand.

Progress in the Understanding & Prevention of Corrosion: 10th European Corrosion Congress. A. D. Mercer. Ed. by J. M. Costa. 960p. 1993. 160.00 (*0-901716-36-7*, Pub. by Inst Materials) Ashgate Pub Co.

Progress in Theoretical & Computational Fluid Mechanics. G. P. Galdi. 1994. lib. bdg. 54.95 (*0-582-24466-8*, Pub. by Addison-Wesley) Longman.

Progress in Theoretical Physics: Tenth Annual Montreal-Rochester-Syracuse-Toronto Meeting on HEP. T. Barnes et al. 240p. 1988. text 77.00 (*9971-5-0775-7*) World Scientific Pub.

Progress in Thyroid Research: Proceedings of the 10th International Thyroid Conference, the Hague, 4-8 February 1991. Ed. by A. Gordon et al. 930p. 1991. 175.00 (*90-5410-028-1*, Pub. by A A Balkema) Ashgate Pub Co.

Progress in Tourism, Recreation & Hospitality Management, Vol. 1. Ed. by C. P. Cooper. (Progress in Tourism, Recreation & Management Ser.: Vol. 1). 224p. 1993. 185.00 (*0-471-94509-9*) Wiley.

Progress in Tourism, Recreation & Hospitality Management, Vol. 4. C. P. Cooper. Ed. by A. Lockwood. (Progress in Tourism, Recreation & Management Ser.: Vol. 4). 224p. 1993. 195.00 (*0-471-94512-9*) Wiley.

Progress in Tourism, Recreation & Hospitality Management, Vol. 5. Ed. by C. P. Cooper & A Lockwood. (Progress in Tourism, Recreation & Management Ser.: Vol. 5). 327p. 1994. 185.00 (*0-471-94433-5*) Wiley.

Progress in Tourism, Recreation & Hospitality Management, Vol. 6. Ed. by C. P. Cooper & A. Lockwood. (Progress in Tourism, Recreation & Management Ser.: Vol. 6). 314p. 1995. 185.00 (*0-471-94859-4*) Wiley.

Progress in Transfusion Medicine, No. 3. Ed. by John D. Cash. (Illus.). 232p. 1988. text 144.00 (*0-443-03721-3*) Church.

Progress in Transputer & Occam Research. R. E. Miles & A. Chalmers. LC 94-75912. 229p. (gr. 12). 1994. pap. 70.00 (*90-5199-163-0*) IOS Press.

Progress in Tryptophan & Serotonin Research: Proceedings - Fifth Meeting of the International Study Group for Tryptophan Research (ISTRY) Ed. by Walter Kochen et al. 430p. (C). 1987. text 215.40 (*3-11-011164-0*) De Gruyter.

Progress in Tryptophan & Serotonin Research: Proceedings - Fourth Meeting of the International Study Group for Tryptophan Research (ISTRY) Ed. by H. G. Schlossberger et al. LC 84-1719. xix, 889p. 1984. 219.25 (*3-11-009760-5*) De Gruyter.

Progress in Two-Stroke Engines & Emissions Control: 1996 International Congress & Exposition. LC 96-207939. (Special Publications). 164p. 1996. pap. 55.00 (*1-56091-761-X*, SP-1131) Soc Auto Engineers.

***Progress in Understanding Reading: Scientific Foundations & New Frontiers.** Keith E. Stanovich. 524p. 2000. 54.95 (*1-57230-564-9*, C0564); pap. 34.95 (*1-57230-565-7*, C0565) Guilford Pubns.

Progress in Underwater Acoustics. Ed. by Harold Merklinger. 816p. 1987. 145.00 (*0-306-42552-1*, Plenum Trade) Perseus Pubng.

Progress In Unity Vol. 18: Fifty Years of Theology within the World Council of Churches, 1945-1995. Martien E. Brinkman. (Louvain Theological & Pastoral Monographs). 188p. 1995. pap. 25.00 (*0-8028-0557-4*) Eerdmans.

Progress in Urban Economics: The Work of the Committee on Urban Economics, 1959-1968, & the Development of the Field. Irving Hoch. LC 74-88793. 152p. reprint ed. pap. 47.20 (*0-7837-3126-4*, 204286100006) Bks Demand.

Progress in Urban Geography. Ed. by Michael Pacione. LC 82-22757. (Illus.). 296p. (C). 1983. text 46.00 (*0-389-20357-2*, N7217) B&N Imports.

Progress in Utility & Risk Theory. Ole Hagen & Fred Wenstop. (Theory & Decision Library). 288p. 1984. lib. bdg. 147.50 (*90-277-1731-1*) Kluwer Academic.

Progress in Vaccinology, Vol. 2. Ed. by Gursaran P. Talwar. (Illus.). 495p. 1989. 265.00 (*0-387-96734-6*) Spr-Verlag.

Progress in Vacuum Microbalance Techniques: Proceedings of the Ninth Conference on Vacuum Microbalance Techniques, Technical University, Berlin, Germany, June, 1970, Vol. 1. Conference on Vacuum Microbalance Techniques (9th:. Ed. by Erich Robens & T. Gast. LC 72-82129. 419p. reprint ed. pap. 129.90 (*0-608-18636-8*, 202402200001) Bks Demand.

Progress in Vacuum Microbalance Techniques: Proceedings of the 10th Conference on Vacuum Microbalance Techniques, Brunal University, Uxbridge, England, June 1972, Vol. 2. Conference on Vacuum Microbalance Techniques (9th:. Ed. by Stanley C. Bevan & S. J. Gregg. LC 72-82129. 266p. reprint ed. pap. 82.50 (*0-608-14057-0*, 202402300002) Bks Demand.

Progress in Vacuum Microbalance Techniques: Proceedings of the 12th Conference on Vacuum Microbalance Techniques, Lyon University, Lyon, France, September 1974, Vol. 3. Conference on Vacuum Microbalance Techniques (9th:. Ed. by C. Eyraud & M. Escoubes. LC 72-82129. 461p. reprint ed. pap. 143.00 (*0-608-14058-9*, 202402400003) Bks Demand.

Progress in Variational Methods in Hamiltonian Systems & Elliptic Equations. Ed. by M. Girardi et al. LC 91-28967. (Pitman Research Notes in Mathematics Ser.: No. 243). 195p. 1991. pap. 60.50 (*0-608-05231-0*, 206576800001) Bks Demand.

Progress in Very High Pressure Research: Proceedings of an International Conference. Conference on Very High Pressure. Ed. by F. P. Bundy et al. LC 61-13156. 333p. reprint ed. pap. 103.30 (*0-608-16820-3*, 205617800054) Bks Demand.

***Progress in Water Quality: The Impact of the 1972 Clean Water Act.** Stoddard. 400p. 2000. 80.00 (*0-471-24360-4*) Wiley.

Progress in Water Technology, Vols. 1-7. Ed. by S. H. Jenkins. Incl. Pts. 2-6. Atlanta Conference Proceedings., **2 vols.** LC 73-1162. 1976. 537.00 (*0-08-020225-X*); Vol. 3. Water Quality: Management & Pollution Control Problems. LC 73-1162. 1973. pap. Vol. 4. Marine, Municipal & Industrial Waste Water Disposal: Proceedings, Sorrento, Italy. LC 73-1162. 1979. pap. (*0-08-018070-1*); Vol. 6. Instrumentation, Control & Automation for Waste Water Treatment Systems. LC 73-1162. 1974. pap. 258.00 (*0-08-017976-2*); LC 73-1162. pap. write for info. (*0-318-55224-8*, Pub. by Pergamon Repr) Franklin.

Progress in Water Technology: Journal International Association on Water Pollution Research. S. H. Jenkins. (Progress in Water Technology Ser.: Vol. 7, Nos. 3 & 4). 1975. 198.00 (*0-08-019840-6*, Pub. by Pergamon Repr) Franklin.

Progress in Zeolite & Microporous Materials: Proceedings of the 11th International Zeolite Conference, Seoul, Korea, August 12-17, 1996, Vol. 105. Zeolite Conference Staff et al. LC 96-48237. (Studies in Surface Science & Catalysis: 105). 2502p. 1996. 546.00 (*0-444-82344-1*) Elsevier.

Progress in Zeolites Science: A China Perspective. R. R. Xu et al. 195p. 1995. text 59.00 (*981-02-2130-4*) World Scientific Pub.

Progress into the Past: The Rediscovery of Mycenaean Civilization. 2nd ed. William A. McDonald & Carol G. Thomas. LC 89-45196. (Illus.). 558p. Date not set. reprint ed. pap. 173.00 (*0-608-20562-1*, 205447600002) Bks Demand.

Progress Notes. Laskin. 1994. text 65.00 (*0-7216-5964-0*, W B Saunders Co) Harcrt Hlth Sci Grp.

Progress Notes on a State of Mind. Patricia Fillingham. 55p. 1980. pap. 2.00 (*0-942292-07-3*) Warthog Pr.

Progress of a Race. J. L. Nichols & William H. Crogman. LC 69-18552. (American Negro: His History & Literature. Series 2). 1969, reprint ed. 21.95 (*0-405-01883-5*) Ayer.

Progress of a Race: Or, Remarkable Advancement of the American Negro. J. W. Gibson & William H. Crogman. LC 79-81118. (Black Heritage Library Collection). 1977. 34.95 (*0-8369-8578-8*) Ayer.

Progress of Afro-American Women: A Selected Bibliography & Resource Guide. Compiled by Janet L. Sims. LC 79-8948. 378p. 1980. lib. bdg. 49.95 (*0-313-22083-2*, SAF/, Greenwood Pr) Greenwood.

Progress of an Image: The East in English Literature, Vol. 181. Naji B. Oueijan. (American University Studies: Ser. IV). 152p. (C). 1996. 39.95 (*0-8204-2712-8*) P Lang Pubng.

Progress of an Object in Motion Pictures. Curtis Gillespie. LC 98-134015. 1997. pap. text 12.95 (*1-55050-119-4*, Pub. by Coteau) Genl Dist Srvs.

Progress of Animal Magnetism. Charles Poyen. (Hypnosis & Altered States of Consciousness Ser.). 1982. reprint ed. lib. bdg. 25.00 (*0-306-76163-7*) Da Capo.

Progress of Another Pilgrim. Frances J. Roberts. 1970. 11.99 (*0-932814-10-7*); pap. 8.50 (*0-932814-11-5*) Kings Farspan.

Progress of Continental Law in the 19th Century. A. Alvarez et al. Tr. by L. B. Register. (Continental Legal History Ser.: Vol. 11). (Illus.). xlix, 558p. 1969. reprint ed. 85.00 (*0-8377-1900-3*, Rothman) W S Hein.

Progress of Cybernetics, Vol. 2. J. Rose. xvi, 438p. 1970. 314.00 (*0-685-47155-1*) Gordon & Breach.

Progress of Dulness Pt. 1: The Rare Adventures of Tom Brainless. John Trumbull. (Notable American Authors). 1999. reprint ed. lib. bdg. 125.00 (*0-7812-9822-9*) Rprt Serv.

Progress of Dulness Pt. 2: The Life & Character of Dick Hairbrain. John Trumbull. (Notable American Authors Ser.). 1999. reprint ed. lib. bdg. 125.00 (*0-7812-9823-7*) Rprt Serv.

Progress of Dulness Pt. 3: The Adventures of Miss Harriet Simper. John Trumbull. (Notable American Authors). 1999. reprint ed. lib. bdg. 125.00 (*0-7812-9824-5*) Rprt Serv.

Progress of Economics: A History of Economic Thought. Warren B. Catlin. LC 61-15681. 788p. 1962. text 67.50 (*0-8290-0200-6*) Irvington.

Progress of Experiment: Science & Therapeutic Reform in the United States, 1900-1990. Harry M. Marks. LC 96-38997. (Cambridge History of Medicine Ser.). 271p. (C). 1997. text 59.95 (*0-521-58142-7*) Cambridge U Pr.

***Progress of Experiment: Science & Therapeutic Reform in the United States, 1900-1990.** Harry M. Marks. (Cambridge Studies in the History of Medicine). 271p. 2000. text. write for info. (*0-521-78561-8*) Cambridge U Pr.

P

Progress of Greek Epigraphy, 1937-1953. Marcus N. Tod. 1979. 35.00 (*0-89005-292-1*) Ares.

Progress of India, Japan & China in the 19th Century. Richard Temple. (C). 1990. reprint ed. text 17.50 (*81-85418-84-5*, Pub. by BR Pub) S Asia.

Progress of Insight: A Treatise on Satipatthana Meditation. Mahasi Sayadaw. 64p. 1994. 3.60 (*955-24-0090-2*, Pub. by Buddhist Pub Soc) Vipassana Res Pubns.

Progress of Japan, 1853-1871. John H. Gubbins. LC 79-137237. reprint ed. 49.50 (*0-404-02939-6*) AMS Pr.

***Progress of Love.** Alice Munro. 2000. pap. 13.00 (*0-375-72470-2*) Knopf.

Progress of Love. Alice Munro. 320p. 1987. pap. 6.95 (*0-14-009879-8*, Penguin Bks) Viking Penguin.

Progress of Management: Process & Behavior in a Changing Environment. 3rd ed. Jerome E. Schnee et al. (Illus.). 1977. pap. text 22.75 (*0-13-730622-9*) P-H.

Progress of Medicine. O. V. Jones. 317p. (C). 1984. pap. 20.00 (*0-86383-131-1*, Pub. by Gomer Pr) St Mut.

Progress of Miracles. Lynne H. DeCourcy. Ed. by Kathleen Iddings. LC 92-61244. 90p. (Orig.). 1993. per. 10.00 (*0-931289-11-4*) San Diego Poet Pr.

Progress of Music. George Dyson. LC 79-93334. (Essay Index Reprint Ser.). 1977. 20.95 (*0-8369-1287-X*) Ayer.

Progress of Nations. 54p. 1994. write for info. (*92-806-3128-4*) U N I C E.

Progress of Nations. 1995. 6.95 (*92-806-3170-5*) U N I C E.

Progress of Nations: The Nations of the World Ranked According to Their Achievements in Child Health, Nutrition, Education, Family Planning, & Progress for Women. 56p. pap. 6.95 (*92-806-3224-8*) UN.

***Progress of Nations, 1999.** UNICEF Switzerland Staff. (RUS.). 48p. 1999. write for info. (*92-806-3496-8*) U N I C E.

Progress of Nations 94. 1994. 6.95 (*92-806-3110-1*); 6.95 (*92-806-3107-1*) U N I C E.

***Progress of Nations '99.** EPS, HQ, UNICEF Staff. 48p. 1999. write for info. (*92-806-3472-0*) U N I C E.

Progress of Nucleic Acid Research & Molecular Biology, Vol. 56. Ed. by Waldo E. Cohn & Divie Moldave. (Illus.). 391p. (C). 1997. text 89.00 (*0-12-540056-X*) Morgan Kaufmann.

Progress of Passion. Alison Kelly. (Presents Ser.: Bk. 108). 1999. mass mkt. 3.75 (*0-373-18708-4*, 1-18708-7) Harlequin Bks.

Progress of Physics During 33 Years, 1875-1908. Arthur Schuster. LC 74-26289. (History, Philosophy & Sociology of Science Ser.). 1975. reprint ed. 17.95 (*0-405-06615-5*) Ayer.

Progress of Redemption: From Creation to the New Jerusalem. William A. Van Gemeren. (Biblical & Theological Classics Library: Vol. 8). 544p. 1995. reprint ed. pap. 9.99 (*0-85364-710-0*, Pub. by Paternoster Pub) OM Literature.

Progress of Redemption: The Story of Salvation from Creation to the New Jerusalem. William A. Van Gemeren. 432p. 1988. 24.99 (*0-310-23130-2*, 10868) Zondervan.

Progress of Redemption: The Story of Salvation from Creation to the New Jerusalem. Willem VanGemeren. 544p. 1996. reprint ed. pap. 19.99 (*0-8010-2081-6*) Baker Bks.

Progress of Romance: The Politics of Popular Fiction. Ed. by Jean Radford. 224p. 1987. 32.50 (*0-7102-0717-4*, 07174, Routledge Thoemms); pap. 12.95 (*0-7102-0963-0*, 09630, Routledge Thoemms) Routledge.

Progress of Seismology of the Sun & Stars: Proceedings of the Oji International Seminar Held at Hakone, Japan, December 11-14, 1989. Ed. by Yuji Osaki et al. (Lecture Notes in Physics Ser.: Vol. 367). xiii, 467p. 1990. 59.00 (*0-387-53091-6*) Spr-Verlag.

Progress of Sentiments: Reflections on Hume's Treatise. Annette C. Baier. LC 90-5124. (Illus.). 352p. 1991. 53.50 (*0-674-71385-0*, BAIPRO) HUP.

Progress of Sentiments: Reflections on Hume's Treatise. Annette C. Baier. 352p. 1994. pap. 22.95 (*0-674-71386-9*) HUP.

Progress of Slavery in the United States. George M. Weston. LC 73-83952. (Black Heritage Library Collection). 1977. 18.95 (*0-8369-8683-0*) Ayer.

Progress of Slavery in the United States. George M. Weston. LC 78-92448. 1857. 11.00 (*0-403-00175-7*) Scholarly.

Progress of Society. Robert Hamilton. LC 68-55729. (Reprints of Economic Classics Ser.). xix, 411p. 1969. reprint ed. 49.50 (*0-678-00451-X*) Kelley.

Progress of Society in Europe: A Historical Outline from the Subversion of the Roman Empire to the Beginning of the 16th Century. William Robertson. Ed. by Felix Gilbert & Leonard Krieger. LC 75-190283. (Classic European Historians Ser.). 224p. 1994. lib. bdg. 14.00 (*0-226-72133-7*) U Ch Pr.

Progress of Stories. Laura R. Jackson. LC 70-167469. (Short Story Index Reprint Ser.). 1980. reprint ed. 23.95 (*0-8369-3995-6*) Ayer.

Progress of Stories: A New, Enlarged Edition with Commentary by Laura (Riding) Jackson. Laura Riding. 414p. 1994. reprint ed. pap. 15.00 (*0-89255-203-4*) Persea Bks.

Progress of Superpave (Superior Performing Asphalt Pavement) Evaluation & Implementation, Vol. 132. Ed. by Robert N. Jester. LC 97-29520. (STP 1322 Ser.). (Illus.). 225p. 1997. text 49.00 (*0-8031-2418-X*, STP1322) ASTM.

Progress of the African Race since Emancipation & Prospects for the Future. Tony Martin. x, 28p. 1998. pap. text 5.00 (*0-912469-35-8*) Majority Pr.

Progress of the Breed: A History of U. S. Holsteins. Richard H. Mansfield. Ed. by Robert H. Hastings. LC 85-60730. 350p. 1985. 34.95 (*0-9614711-0-7*) Holstein-Friesian.

Progress of the Jesuits (1556-79) James Brodrick. LC 86-2864. 357p. (C). 1986. reprint ed. 12.95 (*0-8294-0523-2*, Jesuit Way) Loyola Pr.

Progress of the Marbling Art. Josef Halfer. (Illus.). 256p. 1989. reprint ed. 95.00 (*0-9623586-0-6*) Fresh Ink Pr.

Progress of the Nation: In Its Various Social & Economic Relations from the Beginning of the 19th Century. George R. Porter. LC 77-85189. (Reprints of Economic Classics Ser.). xvi, 735p. 1970. reprint ed. 65.00 (*0-678-00538-9*) Kelley.

***Progress of the Pilgrim Mouse: An Adaption of the Pilgrim's Progress.** Alan Parry. (J). 2000. pap. 9.99 (*0-8024-2930-0*) Moody.

Progress of the Seasons: Forty Years of Baseball in Our Town. George V. Higgins. (Spectator Ser.). 1990. pap. 9.95 (*0-685-46178-5*) P-H.

Progress of the United States in Population & Wealth: As Exhibited by the Decennial Census. George Tucker. LC 63-23040. (Reprints of Economic Classics Ser.). 278p. 1964. reprint ed. 49.50 (*0-678-00033-6*) Kelley.

Progress of the United States in Population & Wealth in Fifty Years. George Tucker. (Notable American Authors). 1999. reprint ed. lib. bdg. 125.00 (*0-7812-9836-9*) Rprt Serv.

Progress of Underdeveloped Areas. Ed. by Bert F. Hoselitz. LC 52-14480. 1993. lib. bdg. 20.00 (*0-226-35406-7*) U Ch Pr.

Progress on Biomechanics. Nuri Akkas. (NATO Advanced Study Institutes Ser.). 395p. 1979. text 122.00 (*90-286-0479-0*) Kluwer Academic.

Progress on Family Problems: A Nationwide Study of Clients' & Counselors' Views on Family Agency Services. Dorothy F. Beck & Mary A. Jones. LC 73-81256. 205p. reprint ed. pap. 63.60 (*0-8357-2760-2*, 203988400014) Bks Demand.

Progress on Pest Management in Field Vegetables: Proceedings of the CEC-IOBC Experts' Group Meeting, Rennes, November 20-22, 1985. Ed. by R. Cavalloro & C. Pelerents. (Illus.). 312p. 1988. lib. bdg. 97.00 (*90-6191-759-X*, Pub. by A A Balkema) Ashgate Pub Co.

Progress or Catastrophe: The Nature of Biological Science & Its Impact on Human Society. Bentley Glass. 286p. 1985. 65.00 (*0-275-90107-6*, C0107, Praeger Pubs) Greenwood.

Progress Payments: A Probus Guide to Subcontract Project Management & Control. Quentin W. Fleming. 250p. 1992. 47.50 (*1-55738-283-2*, Irwn Prfssnl) McGraw-Hill Prof.

Progress Plant Protoplasm. K. J. Puite. 1988. lib. bdg. 185.00 (*90-247-3688-9*, Pub. by M Nijhoff) Kluwer Academic.

Progress, Poverty & Exclusion: An Economic History of Latin America in the 20th Century. Rosemary Thorp. LC 98-73731. 370p. 1998. pap. text 24.95 (*1-886938-35-0*) IADB.

Progress, Poverty & Population: Re-Reading Condorcet, Godwin & Malthus. John Avery. 168p. (C). 1997. pap. text 19.50 (*0-7146-4404-8*, Pub. by F Cass Pubs) Intl Spec Bk.

Progress, Poverty & Population: Re-Reading Condorcet, Godwin & Malthus. John Avery et al. LC 97-30117. 168p. (C). 1997. text 47.50 (*0-7146-4750-0*, Pub. by F Cass Pubs) Intl Spec Bk.

Progress Problems in Atmospheric Chemistry. John R. Barker. (Advanced Series in Physical Chemistry). 1000p. 1995. text 177.00 (*981-02-1868-0*) World Scientific Pub.

Progress Psychbiology & Physiological Psychology, Vol. 17. Adrian R. Morrison. Ed. by Steven J. Fluharty. (Illus.). 208p. (C). 1998. boxed set 99.95 (*0-12-542117-6*) Acad Pr.

Progress Report: An Investigation to Determine Whether the Built Environment Affects Patient's Medical Outcomes. Haya R. Rubin & Amanda J. Owens. 48p. (C). 1996. pap. text 19.00 (*0-9638938-3-1*) Ctr for Hlth.

Progress Report of Gear Rating Coordinating Committee. AGMA Technical Committee. (Technical Papers: Vol. P101.04). (Illus.). 28p. 1952. pap. text 30.00 (*1-55589-131-4*) AGMA.

Progress Report of Gear Rating Coordinating Committee Pt. I: Proposed Practice for Beam Strength of Spur Gears. R. P. Van Zandt. (Technical Papers: Vol. P229.01). (Illus.). 56p. 1951. pap. text 30.00 (*1-55589-139-X*) AGMA.

Progress Report of Gear Rating Coordinating Committee Pt. II: Propsed Practice for Beam Strength of Bevel Gears. W. Coleman. (Technical Papers: Vol. 229.01A). (Illus.). 49p. 1951. pap. text 30.00 (*1-55589-140-3*) AGMA.

Progress Report on Civilization: Burk Uzzle. Brooks Johnson. LC 92-90322. (Illus.). 36p. 1992. pap. 12.00 (*0-940744-65-1*) Chrysler Museum.

Progress Report on the Reforms in D. C. Public Schools: Hearing Before the Subcommittee on Oversight of Government Management, Restructuring & the District of Columbia of the Committee on Governmental Affairs, United States Senate, One Hundred Fifth Congress, First Session, September 8, 1997. LC 98-161320. (S. Hrg. Ser.). iii, 101p. 1998. write for info. (*0-16-056230-9*) USGPO.

Progress Report, Section 1, Bending Stress of Spur & Helical Gears. AGMA Technical Committee. (AGMA Technical Papers: Vol. 101.02). (Illus.). 18p. 1951. pap. text 30.00 (*1-55589-129-2*) AGMA.

Progress Report, Section 2, Scoring Factor (PVT) Values of Gear Teeth. AGMA Technical Committee. (Technical Papers: Vol. P101.02A). (Illus.). 24p. 1951. pap. text 30.00 (*1-55589-130-6*) AGMA.

Progress Through High School. John Ainley & Michael Sheret. (C). 1992. pap. 65.00 (*0-86431-138-9*, Pub. by Aust Council Educ Res) St Mut.

Progress Through Pioneer Evangelism. Dan Beller. pap. 2.00 (*0-911866-80-9*) LifeSprings Res.

***Progress Through the Teacher Pipeline: 1992- 93 College Graduates & Elementary & Secondary School Teaching as of 1997.** Robin R. Henke. 198p. 2000. per. 18.00 (*0-16-050259-4*) USGPO.

Progress to Proficiency. 1993. teacher ed. 16.95 (*0-521-42574-3*) Cambridge U Pr.

Progress to Proficiency. 314p. 1993. pap. text 17.95 (*0-521-42575-1*) Cambridge U Pr.

Progress Towards a Male Contraceptive. Ed. by S. L. Jeffcoate & M. Sandler. LC 82-2789. (Current Topics in Reproductive Endocrinology Ser.: No. 2). (Illus.). 266p. reprint ed. pap. 82.50 (*0-8357-8640-4*, 203506400092) Bks Demand.

Progress Towards Health for All: Statistics of Member States, 1994. 191p. 1994. pap. text 15.30 (*0-614-08052-5*, 1930051) World Health.

Progress, War & Reaction, 1900-1933. Ed. by David R. Ross et al. LC 78-101951. (Structure of American History Ser.: Vol. 5). (C). 1970. pap. text 6.95 (*0-88295-759-7*) Harlan Davidson.

Progress Western Style. Robert Whitelaw. pap. 1.49 (*0-87377-112-5*) GAM Pubns.

Progress with Human Factors in Automotive Design: Seating Comfort, Visibility, & Safety. 1997. 86.00 (*1-56091-954-X*, SP-1242) Soc Auto Engineers.

Progress with Nucleic Acid Research & Molecular Biology, Vol. 49. Ed. by Waldo E. Cohn & Kivie Moldave. (Illus.). 394p. (C). 1994. text 100.00 (*0-12-540049-7*) Acad Pr.

Progress with Profits: The Development of Rural Banking in Indonesia. Richard H. Patten & Jay K. Rosengard. 114p. 1991. pap. 14.95 (*1-55815-140-0*) ICS Pr.

Progress with Puppets: Speech & Language Activities & a Guide for Using Puppets. unabridged ed. Joanne C. Hanson. (Illus.). 57p. 1998. pap. 15.95 (*0-9667099-0-X*) Bldg Blocks Ther.

Progress Without Loss of Soul: A Wholistic Approach to Modernization Planning. Theodor Abt. Tr. by Boris L. Matthews from GER. LC 89-890. (Illus.). 428p. 1989. 9.95 (*0-933029-36-5*); pap. 3.95 (*0-933029-19-5*) Chiron Pubns.

Progress Without People - In Defense of Luddism. David F. Noble. 156p. (C). 1993. pap. 15.00 (*0-88286-218-9*) C H Kerr.

Progress Without Planning: The Economic History of Ontario from Confederation to the Second World War. Ian M. Drummond. (Ontario Historical Studies). 525p. 1987. pap. 19.95 (*0-8020-6661-5*); text 45.00 (*0-8020-2614-1*) U of Toronto Pr.

Progress Without Punishment: Effective Approaches for Learners with Behavior Problems. Anne M. Donnellan et al. (Special Education Ser.). 192p. (C). 1988. pap. text 17.95 (*0-8077-2911-6*) Tchrs Coll.

Progressed Horoscope (1923) Alan Leo. 378p. 1998. reprint ed. pap. 15.95 (*0-7661-0552-0*) Kessinger Pub.

Progressed Horoscope Simplified. Leigh H. Milburn. 180p. 1936. 17.00 (*0-86690-131-0*, M1339-014) Am Fed Astrologers.

Progresses & Public Processions of Queen Elizabeth, 3 vols. John Nichols. LC 03-17051. reprint ed. 435.00 (*0-404-04770-X*) AMS Pr.

Progresses of Aging: Social & Psychological Perspectives, 2 vols. Ed. by Richard H. Williams et al. LC 79-8692. (Growing Old Ser.). 1980. reprint ed. lib. bdg. 113.95 (*0-405-12811-8*) Ayer.

Progresses, Processions & Magnificent Festivities of King James First, His Royal Consort, Family & Court, 4 vols., Set. John Nichols. LC 03-29463. reprint ed. 310.00 (*0-404-04780-7*) AMS Pr.

Progressi Nella Ricerca e Nella Terapia Con Nitrati - Advances in Nitrate Research & Therapy Pt. 1. Ed. by J. S. Alpert et al. (Journal: Cardiology: Vol. 84, Suppl. 1, 1994). (Illus.). iv, 72p. 1994. pap. 23.50 (*3-8055-5893-7*) S Karger.

Progressing Cavity Pumps. Henri Cholet. LC 98-132907. 128p. 1997. pap. 160.00 (*2-7108-0724-6*, Pub. by Edits Technip) Enfield Pubs NH.

Progressing Public-Private Sector Partnerships in International Agricultural Research & Development. Clive James. (ISAAA Briefs Ser.: Vol. 4). (Illus.). vii, 32p. 1997. pap. 10.00 (*1-892456-05-2*) Agri-Biotech.

***Progressing to Distributed Multi-Processing.** Harinder S. Singh. 350p. (C). 1998. 58.00 (*0-13-095683-X*, Macmillan Coll) P-H.

Progressing with AutoCAD. Bob McFarlane. 186p. 1997. pap. 49.95 (*0-470-24436-4*) Wiley.

Progression: The Afterlife. D. Jeff Burton. 80p. 1992. pap. 8.95 (*0-9623160-5-9*) IVE Inc.

Progression & Regression in Language: Sociocultural, Neuropsychological, & Linguistic Perspectives. Ed. by Kenneth Hyltenstam & Ake Viberg. LC 92-46241. 501p. (C). 1994. pap. text 30.95 (*0-521-43874-8*) Cambridge U Pr.

Progression Blackjack: Exposing the Cardcounting Myth. Donald Dahl. LC 92-38085. 1993. pap. 11.95 (*0-8065-1396-9*) Carol Pub Group.

Progression in Learning. Ed. by Martin Hughes. LC 95-23851. (BERA Dialogues Ser.: No. 11). 139p. 1995. 69.00 (*1-85359-310-9*, Pub. by Multilingual Matters); pap. 24.95 (*1-85359-309-5*, Pub. by Multilingual Matters) Taylor & Francis.

***Progression in Primary Design & Technology.** Christine Bold. 1999. pap. text 27.95 (*1-85346-605-0*) David Fulton.

Progression in Primary Science: A Guide to the Nature & Practice of Science. Martin Hollins. LC 98-179048. 170p. 1998. pap. 27.95 (*1-85346-498-8*, Pub. by David Fulton) Taylor & Francis.

Progression of Chronic Renal Diseases. Ed. by H. Koide. (Contributions to Nephrology Ser.: Vol. 118). (Illus.). x, 270p. 1996. 198.25 (*3-8055-6243-8*) S Karger.

***Progressions.** Dina Daniel. 300p. 2001. pap. 13.95 (*1-57532-275-7*, Pub. by Press-Tige Pub) Barnes & Noble Inc.

Progressions. Mark Dunster. 38p. (Orig.). (YA). (gr. 9-12). 1996. pap. 5.00 (*0-89642-323-9*) Linden Pubs.

Progressions. Nordquist. pap. text. write for info. (*0-312-08415-3*) St Martin.

Progressions. 4th ed. Barbara F. Clouse. LC 98-4574. 528p. (C). 1998. pap. text 42.00 (*0-205-28157-5*) Allyn.

Progressions & Other Poems. Albert S. Cook. LC 63-11976. 128p. reprint ed. pap. 39.70 (*0-608-13693-X*, 205534800017) Bks Demand.

***Progressive.** Jerry Lucky. (20th Century Rock & Roll Ser.). 2000. pap. 13.95 (*1-896522-20-3*) CN06.

Progressive Answer to the Fiscal Deficit. Arne Anderson. 38p. 1989. 10.00 (*0-944826-09-1*) Economic Policy Inst.

Progressive Approach to Coordinated Independence Jazz Drummer Technique. R. Spagnardi. 128p. 1997. spiral bd. 12.95 (*0-7935-7992-9*) H Leonard.

Progressive Architecture of Frederick G. Scheibler, Jr. Martin Aurand. LC 93-40788. (Illus.). 184p. 1994. text 37.50 (*0-8229-3781-6*) U of Pittsburgh Pr.

Progressive Assault on Laissez Faire: Robert Hale & the First Law & Economics Movement. Barbara Fried. LC 97-39972. 448p. 1999. 55.00 (*0-674-77527-9*) HUP.

Progressive Bengali English Dictionary. Progressive Staff. 1992. reprint ed. 29.95 (*0-8288-8474-9*) Fr & Eur.

Progressive Business Man or How the Right Mental Attitude & Reciprocity Are Revolutionizing Business. Orison S. Marden. 166p. 1997. pap. 15.00 (*0-89540-390-0*) Sun Pub.

Progressive Careers. Rosemary Wallner. (Women Today Ser.). (J). 1991. 17.27 (*0-685-59205-7*); lib. bdg. 17.95 (*0-86593-123-2*) Rourke Corp.

Progressive Casting & Splinting. Cusick. 1998. 58.00 (*0-12-784576-3*) Acad Pr.

Progressive Casting & Splinting: For Lower Extremity Deformities in Children with Neuromotor Dysfunction. Beverly D. Cusick. (Illus.). 410p. (C). 1990. pap. text 59.00 (*0-7616-4182-3*) Commun Skill.

Progressive Cavity Pump Handbook. James M. Revard. LC 95-10764. 1995. 79.95 (*0-87814-445-5*) PennWell Bks.

Progressive Celestial Navigation. Hewitt Schlereth. 400p. 1994. 30.00 (*0-393-03645-6*) Norton.

Progressive Censoring: Theory, Methods & Applications. R. Aggarwala & N. Balakrishnan. (Statistics for Industry & Technology Ser.). 256p. 2000. 69.95 (*0-8176-4001-0*) Birkhauser.

Progressive Cities: The Commission Government Movement in America, 1901-1920. Bradley R. Rice. LC 77-8458. 180p. reprint ed. pap. 55.80 (*0-7837-1013-5*, 204132400020) Bks Demand.

Progressive City: Planning & Participation, 1969-1984. Pierre Clavel. 300p. (C). 1986. pap. text 17.00 (*0-8135-1120-8*) Rutgers U Pr.

Progressive Class Piano. 2nd ed. Elmer Heerema. 352p. 1984. pap. 28.50 (*0-88284-297-8*, 1599) Alfred Pub.

Progressive Classical Guitar Method. Jason Waldron. 1997. pap. 16.95 (*0-947183-12-4*) Koala Pubns.

Progressive Cleric. Gregory J. Reed. 170p. 1992. text 35.00 (*1-882806-09-3*); pap. text 35.00 (*1-882806-10-7*) New Natl Pub.

Progressive Constitutionalism: Reconstructing the Fourteenth Amendment. Robin West. LC 94-17146. (Constitutional Conflicts Ser.). 368p. 1994. text 42.95 (*0-8223-1525-4*) Duke.

Progressive Democracy. Herbert Croly & Sidney A. Pearson. LC 97-24833. 460p. 1997. pap. text 29.95 (*1-56000-963-2*) Transaction Pubs.

Progressive Development for Marginal Fields. W. G. Edward. 1989. 125.00 (*90-6314-572-1*, Pub. by Lorne & MacLean Marine) St Mut.

Progressive Development for Marginal Fields. Ed. by W. G. Edwards. (C). 1989. 120.00 (*0-89771-741-4*, Pub. by Lorne & MacLean Marine) St Mut.

***Progressive Development of Practical Skills in Chemistry: A Guide to Early-Undergraduate Experimental Work.** Ed. by S. W. Bennett & K. O'Neale. 186p. 1999. pap. 29.95 (*0-85404-950-9*, Pub. by Royal Soc Chem) Spr-Verlag.

Progressive Dies: Principles & Practices of Design & Construction. Ed. by Donald A. Peterson. LC 94-65575. (Illus.). 464p. 1994. 88.00 (*0-87263-448-5*) SME.

***Progressive Dispensationalism.** Craig Biaising. 2000. pap. 19.99 (*0-8010-2243-6*) Baker Bks.

Progressive Dispensationalism. Craig A. Blaising & Darrell L. Bock. LC 93-23467. 336p. (gr. 12). 1993. 20.99 (*0-8010-2117-0*, Bridgept Bks) Baker Bks.

Progressive Double Bass Drumming, Vol. 1. B. Burgett. 88p. 1994. otabind 10.95 (*0-7935-3155-1*, 06621767) H Leonard.

Progressive Dressage. Andre Jousseaume. 152p. 1990. pap. 30.00 (*0-85131-231-4*, Pub. by J A Allen) St Mut.

Progressive Drum Method. Craig Laurisen. (Progressive Ser.). 1997. pap. 14.95 (*1-875726-18-7*) Koala Pubns.

Progressive Education: A Marxist Interpretation. Gilbert G. Gonzalez. LC 81-5787. (Studies in Marxism: Vol. 8). 199p. 1982. 19.95 (*0-930656-15-6*); pap. 9.95 (*0-930656-16-4*) MEP Pubns.

P

An Asterisk (*) at the beginning of an entry indicates that the title is appearing for the first time.

Progressive Education Across the Continents: A Handbook. Herman R. O'hrs & Volker Lenhart. LC 95-23815. (Heidelberger Studien zur Erziehungswissenschaft Ser.: Bd. 44). 446p. 1995. 69.95 (*0-8204-2914-7*, 68705) P Lang Pubng.

Progressive Education Across the Continents: A Handbook. Ed. by Hermann Rohrs & Volker Lenhart. 446p. 1995. 69.95 (*3-631-48917-X*) P Lang Pubng.

Progressive Education at the Crossroads. Boyd H. Bode. LC 71-165707. (American Education Ser., No. 2). 1972. reprint ed. 17.95 (*0-405-03696-5*) Ayer.

Progressive Education in the 1990's: Transforming Practice. Ed. by Kathe Jervis & Carol Montag. 224p. (C). 1991. text 39.00 (*0-8077-3133-1*); pap. text 19.95 (*0-8077-3132-3*) Tchrs Coll.

Progressive English-Bengali Dictionary. Progressive Staff. 1992. reprint ed. 29.95 (*0-8288-8475-7*) Fr & Eur.

Progressive Environmentalism: Principles for Regulatory Reform. Kent Jeffreys. 45p. 1995. pap. 10.00 (*1-56808-059-X*, 194) Natl Ctr Pol.

Progressive Environmentalism: Task Force Report. 1991. pap. 10.00 (*0-943802-65-2*, 162) Natl Ctr Pol.

Progressive Environmentalism: What We've Learned about Progress for Individuals, Government, Business & Society. Lynn Scarlett. 41p. 1995. pap. 10.00 (*1-56808-067-0*, 201) Natl Ctr Pol.

Progressive Era. Ed. by Lewis L. Gould. LC 73-20783. (Illus.). 270p. (C). 1974. pap. text 17.95 (*0-8156-2164-7*) Syracuse U Pr.

Progressive Era: The Limits of Reform. 2nd ed. James R. Giese. (Public Issues Ser.). (Illus.). 68p. 1989. teacher ed. 2.00 (*0-89994-351-9*); pap. 3.50 (*0-89994-350-0*) Soc Sci Ed.

Progressive Era & the Great War, 1896-1920. 2nd ed. William M. Leary, Jr. LC 78-70030. (Goldentree Bibliographies Series in American History). (C). 1978. text 24.95 (*0-88295-574-8*); pap. text 14.95 (*0-88295-575-6*) Harlan Davidson.

Progressive Era in Minnesota, 1899-1918. Carl H. Chrislock. LC 79-178677. (Public Affairs Center Publications). (Illus.). xiii, 242p. 1971. 8.95 (*0-87351-067-4*) Minn Hist.

Progressive Filing. 9th ed. Jeffrey R. Stewart, Jr. et al. Ed. by Ella Pezzuti. LC 79-26178. (Illus.). 160p. (gr. 9-12). 1980. text 18.56 (*0-07-061445-8*) McGraw.

Progressive Fly Fishing for Salmon. Alexander Keachie. (Illus.). 208p. 1997. 45.00 (*1-86126-048-2*, Pub. by Cro1wood) Trafalgar.

Progressive Grammar of the English Tongue. William Swinton. LC 91-21192. 240p. 1991. 50.00 (*0-8201-1457-X*) Schol Facsimiles.

Progressive Grammar of the Malayam Language. L. J. Frohnmeyer. (ENG & MAL.). 322p. 1989. 39.95 (*0-8288-8438-2*, M10933) Fr & Eur.

Progressive Guide to Alternative Media & Activism. Project Censored Staff. LC 98-30137. (Open Media Pamphlet Ser.: No. 8). 128p. 1999. pap. 10.00 (*1-888363-84-3*) Seven Stories.

Progressive Historians: Turner, Beard, Parrington. Richard Hofstadter. LC 79-12591. 1992. pap. text 14.95 (*0-226-34818-0*, P841) U Ch Pr.

Progressive in Particle & Nuclear Physics: Collective Bands in Nuclei, Vol. 9. Ed. by Denys Wilkinson. (Illus.). 563p. 1983. 110.00 (*0-08-030036-7*, Pergamon Pr) Elsevier.

Progressive Intellectuals & the Dilemmas of Democratic Commitment. Leon Fink. LC 97-25506. (Illus.). 384p. 1998. 39.95 (*0-674-66160-5*) HUP.

Progressive Intellectuals & the Dilemmas of Democratic Commitment. Leon Fink. 384p. 1999. pap. 19.95 (*0-674-71390-7*) HUP.

Progressive Masks: Letters of Oliver Wendell Holmes, Jr., & Franklin Ford. Ed. by David H. Burton. LC 80-54787. 144p. 1982. 27.50 (*0-87413-188-X*) U Delaware Pr.

Progressive Mind. (C). 1981. write for info. (*0-8087-5978-7*) Pearson Custom.

Progressive Movement. 1999. per. write for info. (*0-8057-3858-4*, Twyne) Mac Lib Ref.

Progressive Movement. Stromquist. 1996. 26.95 (*0-8057-3857-6*, Twyne) Mac Lib Ref.

Progressive Movement, Its Principles & Its Programme. S. J. Duncan-Clark. LC 72-164808. reprint ed. 36.50 (*0-404-02217-0*) AMS Pr.

Progressive Movement, 1900-1917 see Perspectives on History Series

Progressive Movement of Nineteen Twenty-Four & the Development of Interest Group Liberalism. rev. ed. David L. Waterhouse. LC 91-10859. (Modern American History Ser.). 192p. 1991. text 15.00 (*0-8240-1892-3*) Garland.

Progressive Nature of Epileptogenesis. U. Heinemann. LC 96-41409. (Epilepsy Research Ser.). 408p. 1996. 284.50 (*0-444-82270-4*) Elsevier.

Progressive Nature of Renal Disease. 2nd ed. William E. Mitch. (Contemporary Issues in Nephrology Ser.: Vol. 26). 288p. 1992. text 89.00 (*0-443-08819-5*) Church.

Progressive Nature of Renal Diseases: Myths & Facts. Ed. by L. Oldrizzi. (Contributions to Nephrology Ser.: Vol. 75). (Illus.). viii, 218p. 1989. 29.75 (*3-8055-5021-9*) S Karger.

Progressive Neuromuscular Diseases. Ed. by M. R. Dimitrijevic et al. (Limited Volume Series 1-4: Recent Achievements in Restorative Neurology: Vol. 2). (Illus.). xii, 360p. 1986. 242.75 (*3-8055-4222-4*) S Karger.

Progressive Neutralism: A Philosophical Aspect of American Education. R. M. Barral. Ed. by Sebastian A. Matczak. LC 72-80678. (Philosophical Questions Ser.: No. 6). 1970. 35.00 (*0-912116-03-X*) Learned Pubns.

Progressive Organ Solos, Bk. 2. Albert De Vito. 1964. pap. 7.95 (*0-934286-39-6*) Kenyon.

Progressive Organ Solos, Bk. 4. Albert De Vito. 1965. pap. 7.95 (*0-934286-41-8*) Kenyon.

Progressive Organ Solos I. Albert De Vito. 1964. pap. 7.95 (*0-934286-38-8*) Kenyon.

Progressive Periodicals Directory. 2nd ed. Craig T. Canan. Orig. Title: U.S. Progressive Periodicals Directory. 52p. 1989. 16.00 (*0-935396-03-9*) Prog Educ.

Progressive Phonics, Level 1. Ernest H. Christman. LC 90-71304. (Illus.). 84p. (J). 1990. per. 15.95 (*0-912329-06-8*) Tutorial Press.

Progressive Phonics, Level 2. Ernest H. Christman. LC 90-71304. (Illus.). 48p. (J). 1990. per. 12.95 (*0-912329-03-3*) Tutorial Press.

Progressive Phonics, Level 3. Ernest H. Christman. LC 90-71304. (Illus.). 44p. (J). 1990. per. 10.95 (*0-912329-09-2*) Tutorial Press.

Progressive Phonics, Level 4. Ernest H. Christman. LC 90-71304. (Illus.). 48p. (J). 1990. per. 10.95 (*0-912329-12-2*) Tutorial Press.

Progressive Phonics, Level 5. Ernest H. Christman. LC 90-71304. (Illus.). 40p. (J). 1990. per. 10.95 (*0-912329-15-7*) Tutorial Press.

Progressive Politics & the Training of America's Persuaders. Katherine Adams. LC 98-41195. 184p. 1999. 39.95 (*0-8058-3236-X*); pap. 19.95 (*0-8058-3237-8*) L Erlbaum Assocs.

Progressive Presidents: Theodore Roosevelt, Woodrow Wilson, Franklin D. Roosevelt, Lyndon B. Johnson. John M. Blum. 224p. (C). 1982. pap. 14.00 (*0-393-00063-X*) Norton.

Progressive Printmakers: Wisconsin Artists & the Print Renaissance. Warrington Colescott & Arthur Hove. LC 98-51818. 1999. 39.95 (*0-299-16110-2*) U of Wis Pr.

Progressive Relaxation: A Physiological & Clinical Investigation of Muscular States & Their Significance in Psychology & Medical Practice. 3rd rev. ed. Edmund Jacobson. LC 38-13310. (Midway Reprint Ser.). xvii, 494p. 1993. reprint ed. pap. text 22.00 (*0-226-39059-4*) U Ch Pr.

Progressive Renaissance: America & the Reconstruction of Italian Education, 1943-1962. Steven F. White. LC 91-31238. (Modern European History II Ser.). 232p. 1991. text 15.00 (*0-8153-0672-5*) Garland.

Progressive Resistance: Building Muscular Strength & Endurance. Judson Biasiotto & Wilbur Campbell. Ed. by Uef Kirchdorfer. (Illus.). 124p. (Orig.). (C). 1996. pap. 19.95 (*0-9648775-1-1*) Solaris GA.

Progressive Revelation of Jesus As Savior, Lord & King. Austin Ridenour. LC 98-92241. 390p. 1998. pap. 14.95 (*0-7392-0027-5*, PO2787) Morris Pubng.

Progressive Rock Drumming & Soloing Methods. Rob Leytham. 36p. 1997. pap. 9.95 incl. audio compact disk (*0-7866-2854-5*, 96670BCD) Mel Bay.

***Progressive Rock Files.** 4th ed. Jerry Lucky. 1998. pap. 26.95 (*1-896522-10-6*) CN06.

***Progressive Scale Studies for Cello: Intermediate Level.** John Bauer. 100p. 1998. spiral bd. 14.95 (*0-7866-2969-X*, 96746) Mel Bay.

***Progressive Scale Studies for Viola: Intermediate Level.** John Bauer. 104p. 1998. spiral bd. 14.95 (*0-7866-2970-3*, 96745) Mel Bay.

***Progressive Scale Studies for Violin: Intermediate Level.** John Bauer. 104p. 1998. spiral bd. 14.95 (*0-7866-2971-1*, 96744) Mel Bay.

Progressive Shorthand Passages, Bk. 1. Marie Quint. LC 80-42139. (Longman Secretarial Studies). 30p. 1981. reprint ed. pap. 30.00 (*0-608-09990-2*, 202522600043) Bks Demand.

Progressive Shorthand Passages, Bk. 2. Marie Quint. LC 80-42139. (Longman Secretarial Studies). 32p. 1981. reprint ed. pap. 30.00 (*0-608-09991-0*, 202522600002) Bks Demand.

Progressive Shorthand Passages, Bk. 3. Marie Quint. LC 80-42139. (Longman Secretarial Studies). 35p. 1982. reprint ed. pap. 30.00 (*0-608-09992-9*, 202522600003) Bks Demand.

Progressive Shorthand Passages, Bk. 4. Marie Quint. LC 80-42139. (Longman Secretarial Studies). 30p. 1982. reprint ed. pap. 30.00 (*0-608-09993-7*, 202522600004) Bks Demand.

Progressive Sight Reading: Exercises for Piano. H. Smith. 96p. 1986. pap. 8.95 (*0-7935-5262-1*) H Leonard.

Progressive Soccer. M. Smith & Marion L. Johnson. (Illus.). 196p. (Orig.). (C). 1991. pap. text 17.95 (*0-89641-211-3*) American Pr.

Progressive Socialism. Gary Coyle. 56p. (Orig.). (C). 1984. pap. 2.50 (*0-9591792-1-6*) Proutist Universal.

Progressive Sound Game. Genevieve Arnold. 1973. text 3.00 (*0-686-09405-0*) Expression.

Progressive Steps to a New Voice. Helen Emerson & Barbara Witteman. LC 95-61111. 61p. 1996. spiral bd. 25.00 (*0-9631439-4-8*) Vanderbilt Wilkerson.

Progressive Supranuclear Palsy: Clinical & Research Approaches. Ed. by Irene Litvan & Yves Agid. (Illus.). 304p. 1992. text 67.50 (*0-19-507229-4*) OUP.

Progressive Techniques for Tuba. D. Knaub. 128p. 1985. per. 14.95 (*0-7935-1780-X*, 00123244) H Leonard.

Progressive Typewriting Speed Practice. 4th ed. Beatrice E. Hansen & Lorrine B. Skaff. 1976. text 14.24 (*0-07-026061-3*) McGraw.

Progressive Typewriting Speed Practice. 5th ed. Lorrine B. Skaff & Beatrice E. Hansen. 96p. 1988. pap. text 13.56 (*0-07-057775-7*) McGraw.

Progressive Vision: The Planning of Downtown Cleveland 1903-1930. Holly M. Rarick. LC 86-12950. 96p. 1986. pap. 16.95 (*0-910386-86-2*) Cleveland Mus Art.

Progressive Women in Conservative Times: Racial Justice, Peace, & Feminism, 1945-1960s. Susan Lynn. LC 92-7978. 220p. (C). 1993. text 40.00 (*0-8135-1867-9*); pap. text 17.00 (*0-8135-1868-7*) Rutgers U Pr.

Progressive Yankees: Republican Reformers in New Hampshire, 1906-1916. James E. Wright. LC 86-40553. 287p. 1987. reprint ed. pap. 89.00 (*0-608-02298-5*, 206293900004) Bks Demand.

Progressive Years, 1901 to 1933. Rose Blue & Corinne J. Naden. LC 97-14710. (Who's That in the White House? Ser.). 96p. (J). (gr. 7-8). 1998. lib. bdg. 28.55 (*0-8172-4303-8*) Raintree Steck-V.

Progressives. Ed. by Carl Resek. (Orig.). (C). 1967. pap. write for info. (*0-672-60084-6*, AHSJ4, Bobbs) Macmillan.

Progressives & Prohibitionists: Texas Democrats in the Wilson Era. Lewis L. Gould. LC 92-22783. (Fred H. & Ella Mae Moore Texas History Reprint Ser.). 364p. 1992. pap. 19.95 (*0-87611-121-5*) Tex St Hist Assn.

Progressives & the Slums. Roy Lubove. LC 74-4843. (Illus.). 284p. 1974. reprint ed. lib. bdg. 59.75 (*0-8371-7487-2*, LUPS, Greenwood Pr) Greenwood.

Progressivism. Arthur S. Link & Richard L. McCormick. Ed. by A. S. Eisenstadt & John H. Franklin. LC 82-15857. (American History Ser.). 164p. (C). 1983. pap. text 11.95 (*0-88295-814-3*) Harlan Davidson.

Progressivism & the New Democracy. Ed. by Sidney M. Milkis & James J. Mileur. LC 99-19459. (Political Development of the American Nation Ser.). 312p. 1999. 50.00 (*1-55849-192-9*); pap. 16.95 (*1-55849-193-7*) U of Mass Pr.

Progressivism & the World of Reform: New Zealand & the Origins of the American Welfare State. Peter J. Coleman. LC 87-6187. xiv, 248p. 1987. 29.95 (*0-7006-0321-2*) U Pr of KS.

Progressivism at Risk: Electing a President in 1912, 134. Francis L. Broderick. LC 88-38547. (Contributions in American History Ser.: No. 134). 244p. 1989. 59.95 (*0-313-26400-7*, BPX, Greenwood Pr) Greenwood.

***Progressivism, the Great Depression & the New Deal 1901-1941.** Christopher Collier. (Drama of American History Ser.). (Illus.). (J). 2000. 29.93 (*0-7614-1054-6*, Benchmark NY) Marshall Cavendish.

Progresso e Poverta (Progress & Poverty) (ITA.). 1991. pap. 3.00 (*0-911312-06-4*) Schalkenbach.

Progresso, Pobreza e Exclusao: Una Historia Eonomica Da America Latina No Seculo XX. Rosemary Thorp. (SPA.). 387p. 1998. pap. text 24.95 (*1-886938-50-4*) IADB.

Progrowth Politics: Change & Governance in Houston. Robert D. Thomas & Richard W. Murray. LC 91-11571. 430p. (Orig.). (C). 1991. pap. 16.95 (*0-87772-327-3*) UCB IGS.

Progulka V Durnoe Obshcestvo. Igor Dolinjak. Ed. by Gina Levin. LC 90-61124.Tr. of A Walk into Bad Company. (RUS.). 66p. 1992. pap. text 14.98 (*0-914265-14-8*) New Eng Pub MA.

Progulki Vokrug Baraka. Igor Guberman. LC 88-24422. (Russian Ser.). 189p. (Orig.). 1988. pap. 10.00 (*0-938920-95-2*) Hermitage Pubs.

Prohias Spy. Antonio Prohias. 1999. mass mkt. 2.95 (*0-446-34565-2*, Pub. by Warner Bks) Little.

***Prohibited.** Luis Royo. 1999. 12.95 (*1-882931-51-3*) Heavy Metal Magazine.

***Prohibition.** Renee C. Rebman. LC 98-34225. (World History Ser.). (J). (gr. 4-12). 1998. lib. bdg. 23.70 (*1-56006-444-7*) Lucent Bks.

Prohibition: America Makes Alcohol Illegal. Daniel Cohen. LC 94-37756. (Spotlight on American History Ser.). (Illus.). 64p. (J). (gr. 4-6). 1995. lib. bdg. 21.90 (*1-56294-529-7*) Millbrook Pr.

Prohibition: The Lie of the Land. Dennis Cashman. 1981. 17.95 (*0-317-30516-6*) Free Pr.

Prohibition: Thirteen Years That Changed America. Edward Behr. LC 96-24063. 256p. 1996. 24.45 (*1-55970-356-3*, Pub. by Arcade Pub Inc) Time Warner.

Prohibition: Thirteen Years That Changed America. Edward Behr. LC 96-24063. (Illus.). 272p. 1997. pap. 13.45 (*1-55970-394-6*, Pub. by Arcade Pub Inc) Time Warner.

Prohibition - The Eighteenth Amendment, the Volstead Act, the Twenty-First Amendment. LC 86-16306. (Milestone Documents in the National Archives Ser.). (Illus.). 20p. (Orig.). 1986. pap. text 1.00 (*0-911333-48-7*, 200107) National Archives & Recs.

Prohibition & Politics: The Life of Bishop James Cannon, Jr. Robert A. Hohner. (Illus.). 384p. 1999. 45.00 (*1-57003-281-5*) U of SC Pr.

Prohibition & Politics: Turbulent Decades in Tennessee. Paul E. Isaac. LC 65-17347. 314p. reprint ed. pap. 97.40 (*0-608-18674-0*, 202317000032) Bks Demand.

***Prohibition Enforcement: Charting a New Mission.** Martin Alan Greenberg. LC 99-35710. (Illus.). 310p. 1999. 53.95 (*0-398-06997-2*); pap. 39.95 (*0-398-06998-0*) C C Thomas.

Prohibition in Kansas: A History. Robert S. Bader. LC 86-231. (Illus.). xiv, 322p. 1986. 15.95 (*0-7006-0298-4*) U Pr of KS.

Prohibition Legal & Illegal. Howard L. McBain. LC 72-67. (Select Bibliographies Reprint Ser.). 1977. reprint ed. 15.95 (*0-8369-9963-0*) Ayer.

Prohibition of Benami Transaction. A. N. Saha. (C). 1989. 45.00 (*0-7855-4743-6*) St Mut.

Prohibition of Federal Government Funding of Human Cloning Research: Hearing Before the Committee on Science, Subcommittee on Technology, U.S. House of Representatives, One Hundred Fifth Congress, First Session, July 22, 1997. United States Government. LC 98-142482. iii, 156 p. 1997. write for info. (*0-16-056112-4*) USGPO.

Prohibition of Nuclear Weapons: The Relevance of International Law. Elliott L. Meyrowitz. 350p. 1990. 75.00 (*0-941320-53-7*) Transnatl Pubs.

Prohibition on Financial Transactions with Countries Supporting Terrorism Act of 1997: Hearing Before the Subcommittee on Crime of the Committee on the Judiciary, House of Representatives, one Hundred Fifth Congress, First Session, on H.r. 748 ... June 10, 1997. United States. LC 98-194355. iii, 64 p. 1997. write for info. (*0-16-057001-8*) USGPO.

Prohibition's Second Failure: The Quest for a Rational & Humane Drug Policy. Theodore R. Vallance. LC 92-35957. 192p. 1993. 52.95 (*0-275-94482-4*, C4482, Praeger Pubs) Greenwood.

Prohibitive Policy: Implementing the Federal Endangered Species Act. Steven L. Yaffee. LC 82-43. (Studies in American Politics & Public Policy: Vol. 9). 240p. 1982. 30.00 (*0-262-24024-6*) MIT Pr.

Prohrama Zajriat u Svitlychkac Dlia Ditej see Lessons for Nurseries for English-Speaking Children

Proie. Naomi Horton. (Amours d'Aujourd'Hui Ser.). 1999. mass mkt. 4.99 (*0-373-38331-2*, 1-38331-4) Harlequin Bks.

***Proinflammatory & Antiinflammatory Peptides.** Sami Said & Federation of American Societies for Experimental. LC 97-47124. (Lung Biology in Health & Disease Ser.). (Illus.). 760p. 1998. text 195.00 (*0-8247-0120-8*) Dekker.

PROJ ANAL CASEBK & 3.5DISK-SYS. David Harris. 252p. (C). 1994. pap. text 25.00 (*0-03-011618-X*) Harcourt Coll Pubs.

Projecoes da Consciencia: Diario de Experiencias Fora do Corpo Fisico see Projections of the Consciousness: A Diary of Out-of-Body Experiences

Project. Zev Chafets. 272p. 1998. mass mkt. 6.50 (*0-446-60542-5*, Pub. by Warner Bks) Little.

Project. large type ed. Zev Chafets. LC 97-12439. (Core Ser.). 286p. 1997. lib. bdg. 25.95 (*0-7838-8207-6*, G K Hall Lrg Type) Mac Lib Ref.

Project. Michael Brodsky. (Illus.). 224p. 1991. reprint ed. pap. 10.95 (*0-941062-51-1*) Begos & Rosenberg.

Project: A Perfect. Gary Paulsen. (J). 1996. pap. 4.99 (*0-440-91113-3*) BDD Bks Young Read.

Project: A Perfect World. Gary Paulsen. (World of Adventure Ser.). 1996. 9.09 (*0-606-08851-2*, Pub. by Turtleback) Demco.

***Project: Daddy: Baby Boom.** Patricia Knoll. (Romance Ser.: Bk. 3610). 2000. per. 3.50 (*0-373-03610-8*, 1-03610-2) Harlequin Bks.

Project: Earth. Roy B. Bliven. Ed. by Bookcrafters Staff. (Illus.). 128p. 1998. pap. 13.00 (*0-9663387-0-7*) I Am NY.

***Project Vol. 456: Daddy.** large type ed. Patricia Knoll. Vol. 456. 2000. mass mkt. 3.50 (*0-373-15856-4*) Harlequin Bks.

Project A-Ko, Vol. 1. Tim Eldred. (Illus.). 112p. 1995. pap. 12.95 (*1-56219-900-5*, CMX 0234) Central Pk Media.

Project A-Ko, Vol. 2. Tim Eldred. (Illus.). 104p. 1995. pap. 12.95 (*1-56219-902-1*, CMX 8234) Central Pk Media.

Project Air Force Analysis of the Air War in the Gulf: An Assessment of Strategic Airlift Operational Efficiency. John Lund et al. LC 93-3532. 1993. pap. 10.00 (*0-8330-1351-3*, R-4269/4-AF) Rand Corp.

Project Air Force Assessment of Operation Desert Shield: The Buildup of Combat Power. Project Air Force Desert Shield Assessment Team St. LC 94-7952. 1994. pap. text 13.00 (*0-8330-1521-4*, MR-356-AF) Rand Corp.

Project Alberta: The Preparation of Atomic Bombs for Use in World War II. Harlow W. Russ. (Illus.). 200p. (Orig.). 1990. pap. 34.95 (*0-944482-01-5*) Except Bks NM.

Project Alpha, Vol. 1. Sedgwick Tourison. 1997. mass mkt. 6.99 (*0-312-96262-2*) St Martin.

***Project Analysis & Financing.** Gerald Pollio. 1999. 70.00 (*0-7506-4383-8*) Buttrwrth-Heinemann.

Project & Cost Engineers' Handbook. 3rd enl. rev. ed. Ed. by Kenneth K. Humphreys & Lloyd M. English. LC 92-29095. (Cost Engineering Ser.: Vol. 19). (Illus.). 312p. 1992. text 69.75 (*0-8247-8746-3*) Dekker.

Project & Infrastructure Finance in Asia. 2nd ed. Asia Law & Practice Staff. 303p. 1996. 240.00 (*962-7708-80-1*) Am Educ Systs.

P

Project & Production Scheduling. Quentin W. Fleming et al. 325p. 1986. text 47.50 (*0-917253-63-9*, Irwn Prfssnl) McGraw-Hill Prof.

***Project & Program Management: Managing Complex Projects.** 7th ed. Richard Billows. (Illus.). 322p. 2000. pap. 65.00 (*0-9642865-9-9*) Hampton Grp.

Project & Program Management: Managing Complex Projects with PC Software. Richard A. Billows. LC 94-96302. (Illus.). 178p. (Orig.). 1994. pap. text 30.00 (*0-9642865-0-5*) Hampton Grp.

Project & Program Management: People, Budgets & Software. Dick Billows. (Illus.). 250p. (Orig.). 1996. pap. text 49.95 (*0-9642865-2-1*) Hampton Grp.

***Project & Program Management: People, Budgets & Software.** Richard Billows. (Illus.). 153p. 1999. pap. 39.95 incl. cd-rom (*0-9642865-8-0*) Hampton Grp.

Project & Program Risk Management: A Guide to Managing Project Risks & Opportunities. Ed. by R. Max Wideman. LC 92-3336. 120p. 1992. pap. 32.95 (*1-880410-06-0*) Proj Mgmt Inst.

Project Apollo. Diane M. Sipiera. (True Bks.). (J). 1998. pap. text 6.95 (*0-516-26273-4*) Childrens.

Project Apollo. Diane M. Sipiera & Paul P. Sipiera. LC 96-38141. (True Bk.). (J). 1997. 21.00 (*0-516-20435-1*) Childrens.

***Project Apollo.** Ray Spangenburg & Diane Moser. LC 00-27089. (Out of This World Ser.). (Illus.). 2001. write for info. (*0-531-11761-8*) Watts.

Project Appraisal & Macroeconomic Policy. Tajalle Van der Burg. LC 95-40137. 264p. (C). 1997. lib. bdg. 140.50 (*0-7923-3800-6*) Kluwer Academic.

Project Appraisal & Policy Review. Ed. by Timothy O'Riordan & W. R. Sewell. LC 80-40847. (Wiley Series on Studies in Environmental Management & Resource Development). (Illus.). 316p. reprint ed. pap. 98.00 (*0-8357-4622-4*, 203755400008) Bks Demand.

Project Appraisal for Development Administration. Philip C. Packard. LC 74-75576. (Publications of the Institute of Social Studies: No. 12). 158p. 1974. pap. text 24.65 (*90-279-3452-5*) Mouton.

Project Aries: Astronomy I see Aries Exploring the Earth in Motion: Daylight, Sun, & Shadow Patterns: Science Journal

Project Aries: Astronomy I see Aries Exploring the Earth in Motion: Daylight, Sun, & Shadow Patterns: Teacher Manual

Project Aries: Light & Color see Aries Exploring Light & Color: Filters, Lenses, & Cameras: Science Journal

Project Aries: Light & Color see Aries Exploring Light & Color: Filters, Lenses, & Cameras: Teacher Manual

Project Aries: Time see Aries Exploring Time: Sundials, Water Clocks, & Pendulums: Science Journal

Project Aries: Time see Aries Exploring Time: Sundials, Water Clocks, & Pendulums: Teacher Manual

Project ASTRO How-To Manual for Teachers & Astronomers. Jessica Richter & Andrew Fraknoi. (Illus.). 42p. 1996. pap. 5.00 (*1-886733-99-6*) Astron Soc Pacific.

Project Avalon. B. Alexander Howerton. LC 98-60540. 217p. 1998. pap. 12.95 (*0-9663729-0-5*) Space Avail.

Project B. U. G. S. Gary A. Dunn. (Illus.). 128p. 1994. pap. 9.95 (*1-884256-13-9*) Yng Entomol.

Project Based Group Work Facilitator's Manual: Participation in Practice. Andy Gibson. 200p. 1994. pap. 27.00 (*1-85302-169-5*) Taylor & Francis.

***Project-Based Learning Using Information Technology.** David G. Moursund. LC 99-236301. (Illus.). 160p. 1998. spiral bd. 24.95 (*1-56484-145-6*) Intl Society Tech Educ.

***Project-Based Multimedia Instruction.** John D. Foshay. (Fastback Ser.: No. 445). 56p. 1999. pap. 3.00 (*0-87367-645-9*, FB# 445) Phi Delta Kappa.

Project Black Bear. Lissa H. Johnson. (China Tate Ser.: No. 3). (J). (gr. 6-11). 1994. pap. 5.99 (*1-56179-283-7*) Focus Family.

Project Blue Book Exposed. Kevin Randle. 288p. 1998. pap. 14.95 (*1-56924-691-2*) Marlowe & Co.

Project BREED (Breed Rescue Efforts & Education) Directory - Green Book Edition: A Nationwide Source Book for Rescue & Adoption of All Breeds of Dogs & Other Species. Shirley Weber & Lori Levin. (Orig.). 1998. pap. write for info. (*0-938073-04-4*) Network Anti-Males & Females.

Project BREED (Breed Rescue Efforts & Education) Directory, Red Book Edition: A Nationwide Source Book for Rescue of All Breeds of Dogs & Other Species. Shirley Weber. 168p. (Orig.). 1993. per. 25.00 (*0-938073-03-6*) Network Anti-Males & Females.

Project BREED (Breed Rescue Efforts & Education) Directory, Vol. I, No. 1: Project BREED Directory: A Nationwide Source Book for Rescue & Adoption of All Breeds of Dogs. Shirley Weber. 291p. (Orig.). 1989. per. 15.95 (*0-938073-02-8*) Network Anti-Males & Females.

Project Brochure Fall Meeting 1981 Philadelphia, Pennsylvania. Incl. Project Brochure Fall Meeting 1982 Denver, Colorado. 1982. pap. 13.25 Project Brochure Fall Meeting 1983 Miami Beach, Florida. 1983. pap. 13.25 1981. Set pap. 15.00 (*0-317-06719-2*, P-34) Urban Land.

Project Brochure Fall Meeting 1982 Denver, Colorado see Project Brochure Fall Meeting 1981 Philadelphia, Pennsylvania

Project Brochure Fall Meeting 1983 Miami Beach, Florida see Project Brochure Fall Meeting 1981 Philadelphia, Pennsylvania

Project Brochure Spring Meeting 1981 Portland, Oregon. Incl. Project Brochure Spring Meeting 1982 Houston, Texas. 1982. pap. 13.25 Project Brochure Spring Meeting 1983 Seattle, Washington. 1983. pap. 15.00 Project Brochure Spring Meeting 1984 San Antonio, Texas. 1984. pap. 15.00 1981. Set pap. 15.00 (*0-317-06714-1*, P-30) Urban Land.

Project Brochure Spring Meeting 1982 Houston, Texas see Project Brochure Spring Meeting 1981 Portland, Oregon

Project Brochure Spring Meeting 1983 Seattle, Washington see Project Brochure Spring Meeting 1981 Portland, Oregon

Project Brochure Spring Meeting 1984 San Antonio, Texas see Project Brochure Spring Meeting 1981 Portland, Oregon

***Project BTB.** E. G. Ross. 2000. pap. 19.95 (*1-891519-24-7*) Premiere Edits.

Project Budgeting for Buildings. Donald E. Parker & Alphonse Dell'Isola. (Illus.). 256p. (gr. 13). 1991. text 57.95 (*0-442-00483-4*) Chapman & Hall.

Project-by-Project Approach to Quality: A Practical Handbook for Individuals, Teams, & Organizations. Richard Capper. LC 97-20129. 277p. 1998. 96.95 (*0-566-07925-9*, Pub. by Gower) Ashgate Pub Co.

Project Change Management: Applying Change Management to Improvement Projects. H. James Harrington & Darryl R. Conner. LC 99-45942. (H. James Harrington Performance Improvement Ser.). (Illus.). 200p. 1998. 71.95 incl. cd-rom (*0-07-027104-6*) McGraw-Hill Prof.

Project Checklist. J. Hardy LeGwin. 10p. 1991. pap. 15.00 (*1-55701-308-X*) BNI Pubns.

Project Clear: Social Research & the Desegregation of the United States Army. Ed. by Leo Bogart. 396p. (C). 1991. 44.95 (*0-88738-424-2*) Transaction Pubs.

Project Cockroach. 96p. (J). 1991. write for info. (*1-55513-357-6*, Chariot Bks) Chariot Victor.

Project Coldfeet: Secret Mission to a Soviet Ice Station. William M. Leary & Leonard A. LeSchack. LC 96-38262. (Special Warfare Ser.). (Illus.). 240p. 1996. 28.95 (*1-55750-514-4*) Naval Inst Pr.

Project Controls: Needs & Solutions. Ed. by C. W. Ibbs & David B. Ashley. 120p. 1987. 5.00 (*0-87262-601-6*) Am Soc Civil Eng.

Project Cool Guide to Enhancing Your Web Site. Teresa A. Martin & Glenn Davis. LC 97-31836. 416p. 1998. pap. 29.99 (*0-471-19457-3*) Wiley.

Project Cool Guide to HTML. Teresa A. Martin & Glenn Davis. LC 96-35308. 272p. 1996. pap. 19.95 (*0-471-17371-1*) Wiley.

Project Cool Guide to XML for Web Designers. Teresa A. Martin. LC 99-18992. (Illus.). 298p. 1999. pap. 34.99 (*0-471-34401-X*) Wiley.

Project Coordinator. Jack Rudman. (Career Examination Ser.: C-2589). 1994. pap. 29.95 (*0-8373-2589-7*) Nat Learn.

***Project COPE.** Boy Scouts of America Staff. (Illus.). 152p. 1999. pap. 25.95 (*0-8395-4371-9*) BSA.

Project Cost Control for Managers. Bill G. Tompkins. LC 84-22443. (Illus.). 175p. 1985. reprint ed. pap. 54.30 (*0-608-07291-5*, 206751900009) Bks Demand.

Project Cost Control in Action. 2nd ed. E. A. Stallworthy et al. 320p. 1987. text 78.95 (*0-291-39742-5*, Pub. by Gower) Ashgate Pub Co.

Project Cost Estimating. Ed. by Nigel J. Smith. LC 95-202426. 108p. 1995. 5.00 (*0-7277-2032-5*) Am Soc Civil Eng.

Project Cost Estimating: Principles & Practice. Jack Sweeting. 180p. 1997. 40.00 (*0-85295-380-1*, 53801) IChemE.

Project Cycle. rev. ed. Warren C. Baum. 16p. 1978. pap. write for info. (*0-8213-0022-9*, 10022) World Bank.

Project Cycle. rev. ed. Warren C. Baum. (FRE.). 25p. 1982. pap. write for info. (*0-8213-0134-9*, 10134); pap. write for info. (*0-8213-0135-7*, 10135) World Bank.

Project Cycle Paper. Ed. by Mohamed T. El-Ashry. (C). 1996. pap. text 6.95 (*1-884122-16-7*) Global Environ.

Project Cyclops: A Design Study of a System for Detecting Extraterrestrial Intelligence. 2nd ed. Cyclops Design Team Staff. Ed. by Bernard M. Oliver & John Billingham. (Illus.). 256p. 1996. pap. 20.00 (*0-9650707-0-0*) SETI League.

Project Delivery Systems. David Royall. 224p. 15.00 (*0-614-05190-8*, PEC09931.5M) ASFE.

***Project Delta: After Action Reports Det B-52 (1964-1970)** Stephen Sherman. (Illus.). 1500p. 1999. 59.99 incl. audio compact disk (*1-929932-01-4*) Radix Pr.

Project Delta: Special Forces Vietnam Recon Manual. (Illus.). 40p. 1990. pap. 8.00 (*0-87364-554-5*) Paladin Pr.

Project Delta - A Study of Multiple UFO. Richard F. Haines. (Illus.). 175p. (Orig.). 1994. pap. 9.95 (*0-9618082-4-1*) LDA Pr CA.

Project Design & Recommendations for Watershed Reforestation & Fuelwood Development in Sri Lanka. William H. Bollinger et al. (Illus.). 122p. 1979. pap. 15.00 (*0-936130-03-2*) Intl Sci Tech.

Project Design for Agricultural Development. Nicholas Maddock & Frank Wilson. 236p. 1994. 72.95 (*1-85628-413-1*, Pub. by Avebry) Ashgate Pub Co.

Project Development Coordinator. Jack Rudman. (Career Examination Ser.: C-1432). 1994. pap. 29.95 (*0-8373-1432-1*) Nat Learn.

Project Development for Gas Processing Plants & Facilities. Richard W. Donnelly. Ed. by Karen I. Stelzner. (Illus.). 347p. 1982. ring bd. 45.00 (*0-88698-047-X*, 3.80020) PETEX.

***Project Documentation: Debt Finance.** George K. Miller. 120p. 2000. pap. text 350.00 (*1-85564-789-3*, Pub. by Euromoney) Am Educ Systs.

Project Earth Science: Astronomy. P. Sean Smith. (Illus.). 160p. 1992. pap. text 21.95 (*0-87355-108-7*) Natl Sci Tchrs.

Project Earth Science: Meteorology. P. Jean Smith & Brent A. Ford. 240p. 1994. pap. 21.95 (*0-87355-123-0*) Natl Sci Tchrs.

Project Earth Science: Physical Oceanography. P. Sean Smith & Brent A. Ford. LC 95-67461. (Illus.). 224p. 1995. pap. text 21.95 (*0-87355-130-3*, PB114X) Natl Sci Tchrs.

Project Earth Science Geology. Brent Ford. (Project Earth Science Ser.). (Illus.). 224p. (YA). (gr. 5-10). 1996. pap. 21.95 (*0-87355-131-1*) Natl Sci Tchrs.

Project Earth Science Series, 4 vols., Vols. 1-4. (J). (gr. 6-10). 1996. pap. text 69.00 (*0-614-25417-5*) Natl Sci Tchrs.

Project EASE. Karl Pillemer et al. 36p. 1993. 18.00 (*1-57753-104-3*, 321 EASE) Corn Coop Ext.

Project Elvyn: An Experiment in Electronic Journal Delivery. Jack Meadows. LC 94-185519. (British Library Research). 200p. 1995. 60.00 (*1-85739-161-6*) Bowker-Saur.

Project Energy, '93: Conference Proceedings. Ed. by Roger E. Billings. LC 93-61304. (Illus.). 528p. 1993. 40.00 (*0-9631634-4-2*) Intl Acad Science.

Project Engineering: Computer-Oriented Planning & Operational Decision Making. A. Pagnoni. 256p. 1990. 42.95 (*0-387-52475-4*) Spr-Verlag.

Project Engineering of Process Plants. Howard F. Rase & M. H. Barrow. LC 57-5929. 708p. reprint ed. pap. 200.00 (*0-608-13184-9*, 205594700040) Bks Demand.

Project Epiphany. Richard Boylan. 296p. (Orig.). 1996. pap. 12.95 (*1-885395-21-3*) Book Tree.

Project Evaluation: An Integrated Financial & Economic Analysis. Axel Sell. 300p. 1991. text 85.95 (*1-85628-228-7*, Pub. by Avebry) Ashgate Pub Co.

Project Evaluation: Collected Papers. Arnold C. Harberger. (Midway Reprint Ser.). 342p. 1976. pap. text 31.00 (*0-226-31593-2*) U Ch Pr.

Project Evaluation: Techniques & Practices for Developing Countries. Heng-Kang Sang. 261p. 1995. 82.95 (*1-85972-105-2*, Pub. by Avebry) Ashgate Pub Co.

Project Evaluation: Techniques & Practices for Developing Countries. Heng-Kang Sang. 350p. (C). 1988. 32.50 (*0-9617304-0-4*) H K Sang.

Project Evaluation in Building Economics. Marshall & Flanagan. (Foundations of Building Economics Ser.). (Illus.). 256p. 1999. pap. 65.00 (*0-419-19240-9*) Thomson Learn.

Project Factorisations in Partial Evaluation. John Launchbury. (Distinguished Dissertations in Computer Science Ser.: No. 1). 175p. (C). 1991. text 52.95 (*0-521-41497-0*) Cambridge U Pr.

Project Factors & Influences Integral to the Development of Fire Protection Solutions. John W. McCormick. 1984. 4.35 (*0-318-03821-8*, TR84-4) Society Fire Protect.

Project Farcry. Pauline Ashwell. 1996. mass mkt. 5.99 (*0-8125-3446-8*) Tor Bks.

Project File: (A Short Course on Project Work for Students & Their Teachers) Domino Books Ltd Staff. (C). 1987. 150.00 (*0-7855-2247-6*, Pub. by Domino Bks Ltd); pap. 100.00 (*0-7855-2248-4*, Pub. by Domino Bks Ltd) St Mut.

Project Finance. Clifford Chance. 117p. 1995. reprint ed. pap. 138.00 (*1-873446-45-4*, Pub. by IFR Pub) Am Educ Systs.

Project Finance: A Legal Guide. 2nd ed. Graham D. Vinter. LC 98-218513. xxxii, 306 p. 1998. write for info. (*0-421-57530-1*) Sweet & Maxwell.

Project Finance: Ifc's Lessons of Experience International Finance Corporation Staff. LC 99-21713. (Lessons of Experience Ser.). 112p. 1999. pap. 22.00 (*0-8213-4434-X*) World Bank.

Project Finance: Practical Case Studies. Henry A. Davis. 1996. pap. 215.00 (*1-85564-460-6*, Pub. by Euromoney) Am Educ Systs.

Project Finance: Selected Issues in Choice of Law. Skadden et al. (Project Finance Strategic Reports). 1996. pap. 225.00 (*1-85564-524-6*, Pub. by Euromoney) Am Educ Systs.

Project Finance at the World Bank: An Overview of Policies & Instruments. Philippe Benoit. LC 95-48254. (Technical Papers: No. 312). 124p. 1996. pap. 22.00 (*0-8213-3521-9*, 13521) World Bank.

Project Finance in Europe. Ed. by Haydn Shaughnessy. LC 94-35583. (Business Boundaries Ser.). 192p. 1995. pap. 496.95 (*0-471-94381-9*) Wiley.

Project Finance in Latin America. Euromoney Books Staff. 215p. 2000. pap. 225.00 (*1-85564-628-5*, Pub. by Euromoney) Am Educ Systs.

Project Finance Training Manual. Thomas H. Pyle. 1995. 295.00 (*1-85564-355-3*, Pub. by Euromoney) Am Educ Systs.

Project Finance Yearbook, 1991-92. (C). 1990. 400.00 (*1-85564-064-3*) St Mut.

***Project Finance Yearbook 1999/2000.** Euromoney Books Staff. 1999. pap. 195.00 (*1-85564-719-2*, Pub. by Euromoney) Am Educ Systs.

Project Financing. 6th ed. Frank J. Fabozzi & Peter Nevitt. 412p. 1995. pap. 170.00 (*1-85564-299-9*, Pub. by Euromoney) Am Educ Systs.

***Project Financing.** 7th ed. Frank J. Fabozzi & Peter Nevitt. 2000. pap. 195.00 (*1-85564-791-5*, Pub. by Euromoney) Am Educ Systs.

Project Financing: Asset Based Financial Engineering. John D. Finnerty. LC 96-26913. 400p. 1996. 79.95 (*0-471-14631-5*) Wiley.

***Project Financing & the International Financial Markets** Esteban C. Buljevich & Yoon S. Park. LC 99-31824. 1999. write for info. (*0-7923-8524-1*) Kluwer Academic.

Project Financing from Domestic to International: Building Infrastructure Projects in Developing Markets. (Commercial Law & Practice Course Handbook Ser.). 304p. 1994. pap. 99.00 (*0-614-17142-3*, A4-4460) PLI.

Project Financing in Asia. Larry H. Lang. LC 98-13337. (Advances in Finance, Investment, & Banking Ser.). 1998. write for info. (*0-444-82804-4*) Elsevier.

Project Financing, 1996: Building Infrastructure Projects in Developing Markets. (Commercial Law & Practice Course Handbook Ser.). Date not set. pap. 99.00 (*0-614-17161-X*, A4-4494) PLI.

Project Financing, 1992: Power Generation, Waste Recovery & Other Industrial Facilities. (Commercial Law & Practice Ser.). 818p. 1992. pap. text 70.00 (*0-685-56868-7*, A4-4368) PLI.

Project Financing, 1991: Power Generation, Waste Recovery & Other Industrial Facilities. Robert T. Smith. (Commercial Law & Practice Ser.). 981p. 1991. pap. text 17.50 (*0-685-49875-1*, A4-4328) PLI.

Project Flexability, Agency & Competition: New Developments in the Theory & Application of Real Options. Ed. by Michael J. Brennan & Lenos Trigeorgis. LC 98-40655. (Illus.). 368p. (C). 1999. text 49.95 (*0-19-511269-5*) OUP.

Project Focus, '93: Conference on Work-Related Injury. 77p. (Orig.). 1994. pap. 25.00 (*0-912452-96-X*, P-107) Am Phys Therapy Assn.

Project Follow Through: A Case Study of Contingencies Influencing Instructional Practices of the Educational Establishment. Cathy L. Watkins. LC 97-78162. (Behavior Monographs). 103p. 1997. pap. 16.95 (*1-881317-04-8*) Cambdge Ctr Behav.

Project for Orthodox Renewal: Key Issues Facing Orthodox Christians in the U. S. A. S. Sfekas & G. Matsoukas. 1993. pap. 12.95 (*0-937032-95-6*) Light&Life Pub Co MN.

***Project For Precalculus.** Andersen. (C). 1999. pap. text, teacher ed. 33.50 (*0-03-028261-6*, Pub. by Harcourt Coll Pubs) Harcourt.

Project for Precalculus, Instructor. Hungerf. 1997. pap. text, teacher ed. 22.50 (*0-03-024966-X*) Harcourt.

Project for the Theatre. Ingmar Bergman. Ed. by Frederick J. Marker & Lise-Lone Marker. 192p. 1987. pap. text 11.95 (*0-8044-6040-X*) F Ungar Bks.

Project Focus, '96: The Conference on Sports Related Injury. Ed. by Holtzman, Robert, & Assoc, Inc. Staff. (Illus.). 84p. 1997. pap. 17.95 (*0-9628807-1-X*) FPT VA.

Project 4 - Badge of Honor: Pepon Osorio. Joseph Jacobs et al. Tr. by Felix Cortes. (Illus.). 20p. (Orig.). 1996. pap. 10.00 (*0-932828-33-7*) Newark Mus.

Project Funny Bone: A Curriculum on Humor. Tami L. Fern. (Illus.). 30p. 1990. pap. 9.95 (*0-936386-56-8*) Creative Learning.

Project Gemini. Diane M. Sipiera. (True Bks.). (J). 1998. pap. text 6.95 (*0-516-26274-2*) Childrens.

Project Gemini. Diane M. Sipiera & Paul P. Sipiera. LC 96-50002. (True Bk.). 47p. (J). (gr. 2-4). 1997. 21.00 (*0-516-20441-6*) Childrens.

***Project Gemini.** Ray Spangenburg & Diane Moser. LC 00-27007. (Out of This World Ser.). 2001. pap. write for info. (*0-531-11762-6*) Watts.

Project Girl. Janet McDonald. LC 98-23281. 256p. 1999. 23.00 (*0-374-23757-3*) FS&G.

***Project Girl.** Janet McDonald. LC 99-86211. 231p. 2000. pap. 15.95 (*0-520-22345-4*, Pub. by U CA Pr) Cal Prin Full Svc.

Project Haystack: The Search for Life in the Galaxy. SETI Institute Staff. (Life in the Universe Ser.). 264p. 1997. pap. text 55.50 incl. vdisk (*1-56308-328-0*, B280) Teacher Ideas Pr.

Project Head Start: Models, Strategies & Issues for the Twenty-First Century. Valora Washington & Ura J. Bailey. LC 94-36041. (Source Books on Education: Vol. 38). (Illus.). 216p. 1994. pap. text 24.95 (*0-8153-1207-5*) Garland.

Project Head Start: Models, Strategies & Issues for the Twenty-First Century. Valora Washington & Ura J. Bailey. LC 94-36041. (Source Books on Education: Vol. 38). (Illus.). 216p. 1995. text 40.00 (*0-8153-0800-0*, SS827) Garland.

Project Heritage, Wood County, Ohio: Index of the Federal Manuscript Census, 1860. James Q. Graham et al. 441p. 1978. write for info. incl. mic. film (*0-932690-00-9*) Ctr for Arch Collects.

Project Hula: Secret Soviet-American Cooperation in the War Against Japan. Richard A. Russell. 50p. 1998. pap. 5.50 (*0-16-049376-5*) USGPO.

Project Hula: Secret Soviet-American Naval Cooperation in the War Against Japan. Richard A. Russell. LC 97-7022. (U. S. Navy in the Modern World Ser.). 1997. write for info. (*0-945274-35-1*) Naval Hist Ctr.

Project Hydrogen, '91: Technical Proceedings. Ed. by T. Nejat Veziroglu & R. E. Billings. 394p. 1992. 25.00 (*0-9631634-1-8*) Intl Acad Science.

Project ILPs: Individualized Learning Plans for Life-Based Projects. Philip G. Kapfer & Miriam B. Kapfer. Ed. by Danny G. Langdon. LC 77-25409. (Instructional Design Library). (Illus.). 96p. 1978. 27.95 (*0-87778-119-2*) Educ Tech Pubns.

Project Impact: Disseminating Innovation in Undergraduate Education Conference Proceedings. Ed. by Ann McNeal. (Illus.). 116p. (C). 1996. reprint ed. pap. text 35.00 (*0-7881-3124-9*) DIANE Pub.

Project Impact - Disseminating Innovation in Undergraduate Education: Abstracts of Projects: Things That Work. Ed. by Ann McNeal. 303p. 1998. reprint ed. pap. text 40.00 (*0-7881-4241-0*) DIANE Pub.

Project Infrastructure Development Handbook. Donna Hanousk et al. LC 89-51453. 178p. (Orig.). 1989. text 56.95 (*0-87420-692-8*, P43) Urban Land.

***Project Insider.** Thomas LaMarre. LC 00-190792. 311p. 2000. 25.00 (*0-7388-1862-3*); pap. 18.00 (*0-7388-1863-1*) Xlibris Corp.

Project Journal. Paulette Morrissey. (Fast, Fun & Easy Ser.: Bk. 6). (Illus.). 28p. 1996. spiral bd. 8.95 (*1-893502-05-8*) Morrissey Co.

Project Korea: The British Soldier in Korea 1950-53. David Smurthwaite & Linda Washington. 1997. pap. 23.00 (*1-873376-88-X*, Pub. by Spellmnt Pubs) St Mut.

Project Kuzbas: American Workers in Siberia, 1921-1926. J. P. Morray. LC 83-12607. (Illus.). 204p. 1983. pap. 4.75 (*0-7178-0606-5*) Intl Pubs Co.

Project L. U. C. I. D. The Beast 666 Universal Human Control System. Texe Marrs. (Illus.). 224p. (Orig.). 1996. pap. 12.95 (*1-884302-02-5*) Living Truth Pubs.

Project Lambda. Paul O. Welles. Ed. by Billie Young. LC 78-11353. 1979. 22.95 (*0-87949-146-9*) Ashley Bks.

Project Leadership. 2nd ed. Wendy Briner et al. 176p. 1996. 59.95 (*0-566-07714-0*, Pub. by Gower) Ashgate Pub Co.

Project Leadership: From Theory to Practice. Jeffrey K. Pinto et al. 300p. 1998. pap. 39.95 (*1-880410-10-9*) Proj Mgmt Inst.

Project Leadership 2nd Edition. Briner. 176p. 1996. pap. 29.95 (*0-566-07785-X*) Ashgate Pub Co.

Project LEAP, Grade 1. Ruth Yarrow. (Learning about Ecology, Animals & Plants Ser.). (Illus.). 124p. (J). (gr. 1). 1995. teacher ed., ring bd. 50.00 (*1-57753-178-7*, 137LEAP1) Corn Coop Ext.

Project LEAP, Grade 2, 6 vols. Ruth Yarrow. (Learning about Ecology, Animals, & Plants Ser.). (Illus.). 126p. 1995. teacher ed., ring bd. 50.00 (*1-57753-179-5*, 137LEAP2) Corn Coop Ext.

Project LEAP, Grade 3. Ruth Yarrow. (Learning about Ecology, Animals & Plants Ser.). (Illus.). 96p. (J). (gr. 3). 1996. teacher ed., ring bd. 50.00 (*1-57753-180-9*, 137LEAP3) Corn Coop Ext.

Project LEAP, Kindergarten. Ruth Yarrow. (Learning about Ecology, Animals & Plants Ser.). (Illus.). 125p. 1995. teacher ed., ring bd. 50.00 (*1-57753-177-9*, 137LEAP) Corn Coop Ext.

P

An Asterisk (*) at the beginning of an entry indicates that the title is appearing for the first time.

Project Learning for the Multiple Intelligences Classroom. Sally Berman. LC 97-77116. 159p. 1997. pap. 32.95 (*1-57517-077-9*) SkyLght.

Project Lessons in Orchestration. Arthur E. Heacox. LC 74-28557. reprint ed. 35.00 (*0-404-13381-9*) AMS Pr.

***Project Looking Forward: Sketching the Future of Copyright in a Networked World, Final Report.** I. Trotter Hardy. 304p. 1998. per. 23.00 (*0-16-061821-5*, Library of Cong) USGPO.

Project Maldon. Chris Atack. 384p. 1997. per. 5.99 (*0-671-87786-0*) Baen Bks.

***Project Management.** (Ten Minute Guides Ser.). 192p. 2000. pap. 10.95 (*0-02-863966-9*) Macmillan Gen Ref.

Project Management. Robert Ambrieno. (Illus.). 300p. 1997. lib. bdg. 295.00 (*1-890299-06-5*) Gov Technology.

***Project Management.** Andy Bruce. (Illus.). 72p. 2000. pap. 6.95 (*0-7894-5971-X*) DK Pub Inc.

Project Management. Erich Draeger. 400p. (C). 2000. 49.95 (*0-201-39835-4*) Addison-Wesley.

Project Management. Mike Field & Laurie Keller. LC 98-123443. 480p. 1998. pap. 26.99 (*1-86152-274-6*) Thomson Learn.

Project Management. Gray. LC 99-27905. 1999. pap. text 63.25 (*0-07-365812-X*) McGraw.

Project Management. Harvard Business School Press Staff. 100p. 1991. pap. 1995.00 (*0-07-103324-6*) McGraw.

Project Management. Patrick Healey. LC 98-145753. 300p. 1998. pap. text 41.95 (*0-7506-8943-9*) Buttrwrth-Heinemann.

Project Management. Hebert. (Business Statistics Ser.). 2000. pap. 49.25 (*0-534-52965-8*) PWS Pubs.

***Project Management.** Peter Hobbs. (Self-Development for Success Ser.: Vol. 14). 96p. 2000. pap. 12.95 (*0-8144-7067-X*) AMACOM.

Project Management. Kerzner. 1999. text, student ed. 83.95 (*0-471-34428-1*) Wiley.

Project Management. D. Lock. 300p. (C). 1989. 115.00 (*0-7855-6110-2*, Pub. by Inst Pur & Supply) St Mut.

Project Management. D. Roman. 240p. 1985. 42.25 (*0-444-00966-3*) P-H.

Project Management. Manuel P. Spinner. 308p. (C). 1996. 73.00 (*0-13-436437-6*) P-H.

***Project Management.** 2nd ed. Harvey Maylor. (Illus.). 302p. 1999. pap. 57.50 (*0-273-63829-7*, Pub. by F T P-H) Trans-Atl Phila.

Project Management. 3rd ed. Burke. LC 99-13356. 2000. pap. text 42.00 (*0-471-98762-X*) Wiley.

Project Management. 3rd ed. Rory Burke. pap. text, teacher ed. write for info. (*0-471-72036-4*) Wiley.

Project Management. 6th ed. Kerznerh. (Business Technology Ser.). (C). 1997. pap., wbk. ed. 22.95 (*0-442-02607-2*, VNR) Wiley.

Project Management. 6th ed. Dennis Lock. LC 96-29673. 522p. 1996. pap. 69.95 (*0-470-23723-6*) Wiley.

***Project Management.** 7th ed. Dennis Lock. LC 99-57302. 592p. 2000. 87.95 (*0-566-08223-3*, Pub. by Gower); pap. 43.95 (*0-566-08225-X*, Pub. by Gower) Ashgate Pub Co.

Project Management: A Managerial Approach. 3rd ed. Jack R. Meredith & Samuel J. Mantel. (Series in Production-Operations Management). 784p. 1995. text 95.95 (*0-471-01626-8*) Wiley.

***Project Management: A Managerial Approach.** 4th ed. Meredith. 640p. 1999. text 98.95 (*0-471-29829-8*) Wiley.

Project Management: A Reference for Professionals. Robert L. Kimmons & James H. Loweree. (Illus.). 1136p. 1989. text 110.00 (*0-8247-7676-3*) Dekker.

Project Management: A Strategic Approach. Larry L. Richman. (Illus.). 152p. 1996. ring bd. 39.95 (*0-941846-04-0*) Centry Pub.

Project Management: A Systems Approach to Planning, Scheduling, & Controlling. 5th ed. Harold Kerzner. (Industrial Engineering Ser.). 1152p. 1995. text 60.95 (*0-442-01907-6*, VNR) Wiley.

Project Management: A Systems Approach to Planning, Scheduling & Controlling. 6th ed. Harold Kerzner. 1200p. 1997. 65.00 (*0-471-28835-7*, VNR); text 59.95 (*0-442-02551-3*, VNR) Wiley.

Project Management: A Systems Approach to Planning, Scheduling & Controlling. 6th ed. Harold Kerzner. 384p. 1997. pap., wbk. ed. 27.95 (*0-471-29271-0*, VNR) Wiley.

***Project Management: A Systems Approach to Planning, Scheduling & Controlling.** 7th ed. Harold Kerzner. LC 00-36802. 2000. write for info. (*0-471-39342-8*) Wiley.

***Project Management: An International Focus.** Ralph F. Keeling. LC 99-88129. 2000. text 65.00 (*0-312-23291-8*) St Martin.

Project Management: As If People Mattered. rev. ed. Robert J. Graham. LC 89-24230. (Illus.). 234p. 1989. pap. text 19.95 (*0-926282-00-X*) Primavera Syst.

Project Management: Construction Monitoring. Surveyors Publications Staff. (C). 1988. text 80.00 (*0-85406-408-7*, Pub. by Surveyors Pubns) St Mut.

Project Management: Engineering, Technology, & Implementation. Avraham Shtub et al. LC 93-32078. 656p. (C). 1994. 95.00 (*0-13-556458-1*) P-H.

Project Management: From Idea to Implementation. 2nd rev. ed. Marion E. Haynes. Ed. by Elaine Fritz. LC 96-86236. 120p. 1997. pap. 10.95 (*1-56052-418-9*) Crisp Pubns.

Project Management: Getting It Right. A. Reid & Tripatra Engineers Staff. 200p. 1999. boxed set 63.00 (*1-85573-420-6*) Am Educ Systs.

***Project Management: Getting It Right.** Arnold P. Reid. LC 99-38743. 1999. write for info. (*0-8493-0645-0*) CRC Pr.

Project Management: How to Plan & Manage Successful Projects. Joan Knutson et al. 250p. 1991. 55.00 (*0-8144-5043-1*) AMACOM.

Project Management: Orientation for Decision Makers. J. Dingle. LC 97-204382. 288p. 1997. pap. text 34.95 (*0-340-67770-8*, T56) Wiley.

Project Management: Orientation for Decision Makers. John Dingle. 279p. 1997. pap. 54.95 (*0-470-23759-7*) Wiley.

***Project Management: Planning & Control Techniques.** 3rd ed. Rory Burke. 346p. 2000. pap. 29.95 (*0-620-23414-8*) Red Roof Design.

Project Management: Strategic Design & Implementation. 2nd ed. David I. Cleland. 1994. 49.00 (*0-07-011351-3*) McGraw.

Project Management: Strategic Design & Implementation. 3rd ed. David I. Cleland. LC 98-25720. (Illus.). 575p. 1998. 64.95 (*0-07-012020-X*) McGraw.

Project Management: Techniques in Planning & Controlling Construction Projects. 2nd ed. Hira N. Ahuja et al. 520p. 1994. 99.00 (*0-471-59168-8*) Wiley.

***Project Management: The CommonSense Approach: Using Earned Value to Balance the Triple Constraint.** Lee R. Lambert & Erin Lambert. 2000. pap. 24.99 (*0-9626397-8-8*) L R Lambert & Assocs.

***Project Management: The Managerial Process.** Clifford F. Gray. 1999. 81.88 (*0-07-237786-4*) McGraw.

Project Management: The Next Century: Proceedings of the 28th Annual Project Management Institute Seminars & Symposium, Chicago, IL, September 26-October 2, 1997. Project Management Institute Staff. LC 97-33556. 1997. pap. 169.95 (*1-880410-33-8*) Proj Mgmt Inst.

***Project Management: The People Challenge.** Bee & Bee. 168p. 2000. pap. 56.95 (*0-8464-5135-2*) Beekman Pubs.

Project Management-Advanced Techniques Handbook. rev. ed. Ed. by Thomas C. Charland. (Illus.). 403p. (C). 1999. spiral bd. 59.95 (*0-9610754-3-0*) Manage Co In.

Project Management & Project Network Techniques. 6th ed. Keith Lockyer & James Gordon. 288p. (Orig.). 1995. pap. 57.50 (*0-273-61454-1*, Pub. by Pitman Pub) Trans-Atl Phila.

Project Management & Teamwork. Karl Smith. LC 99-59497. (Business Communication Ser.). 128p. 2000. pap. text 19.38 (*0-07-012296-2*) McGrw-H Hghr Educ.

Project Management Basics. R. Pat Webb. 256p. 1991. 29.95 (*0-8306-2502-X*) McGraw-Hill Prof.

Project Management Basics: A Step by Step Approach. Robert L. Kimmons. (Illus.). 352p. 1990. text 79.75 (*0-8247-8391-3*) Dekker.

Project Management Casebook. Ed. by David I. Cleland et al. LC 97-3116. (Illus.). 626p. (Orig.). 1998. pap. 69.95 (*1-880410-45-1*) Proj Mgmt Inst.

Project Management Casebook Instructor's Manual. David I. Cleland & A. Yaroslav Vlasak. Ed. by Karen M. Busic & Richard J. Puerzer. LC 97-10752. 196p. 1998. pap., teacher ed. 29.95 (*1-880410-18-4*) Proj Mgmt Inst.

Project Management Competence: Building Key Skills for Individuals, Teams, & Organizations. Davidson & J. Davidson Frame. LC 99-31823. 256p. 1999. text 34.95 (*0-7879-4662-1*) Jossey-Bass.

Project Management Demystified. Geoff Reiss. 1992. pap. text 30.95 (*0-419-16920-2*, E & FN Spon) Routledge.

Project Management Demystified: Today's Tools & Techniques. 2nd ed. Geoff Reiss. (Illus.). 240p. 1995. pap. 29.99 (*0-419-20750-3*, E & FN Spon) Routledge.

***Project Management Experience & Knowledge Self-Assessment Manual.** Project Management Institute Staff. LC 00-27972. 2000. write for info. (*1-880410-24-9*) Proj Mgmt Inst.

Project Management for Building Designers & Owners. 2nd ed. Howard G. Birnberg. LC 98-17157. 256p. 1998. boxed set 54.95 (*0-8493-1265-5*) CRC Pr.

***Project Management for Business Professionals: A Comprehensive Guide.** Joan Knutson. 464p. 2001. 65.00 (*0-471-38033-4*) Wiley.

Project Management for Clinical Trials. Nancy J. Stark. (Safety, Efficacy & Performance of Medical Devices Ser.). 300p. 1999. ring bd. 200.00 (*1-889160-05-9*) Clinical Design.

Project Management for Developing Countries: International Seminar. Ed. by K. R. Saxena. (C). 1991. 48.50 (*81-204-0647-8*, Pub. by Oxford IBH) S Asia.

***Project Management for Dummies.** Stanley Portny. 384p. 2000. pap. 19.99 (*0-7645-5283-X*) IDG Bks.

Project Management for Engineering & Construction. 2nd ed. James A. Bent & Albert Thumann. LC 93-29879. 1993. write for info. (*0-88173-182-X*) Fairmont Pr.

Project Management for Engineering Construction. 2nd ed. Oberlander. LC 99-53231. 384p. 2000. 76.56 (*0-07-039360-5*) McGraw.

Project Management for Engineers. Garold Oberlender. 448p. (C). 1993. 76.56 (*0-07-048150-4*) McGraw.

Project Management for Environmental, Health & Safety Professionals: 18 Steps to Success. F. David Pierce. LC 97-37709. (Illus.). 264p. 1998. text 69.00 (*0-86587-598-7*, 598) Gov Insts.

Project Management for Health Care Professionals. Kathleen Roberts & Carol Ludvigsen. LC 98-213326. (Illus.). 224p. 1998. pap. text 35.00 (*0-7506-3405-7*) Buttrwrth-Heinemann.

Project Management for Its Professionals. Ed. by Prentice-Hall Staff. 280p. (C). 2000. 39.99 (*0-13-021914-2*) P-H.

***Project Management for Managers.** Mihaly Gorog & Nigel J. Smith. LC 98-40818. 175p. (Orig.). 1998. pap. 32.95 (*1-880410-54-0*) Proj Mgmt Inst.

Project Management for Product Development. G. Brickell. Date not set. write for info. (*0-8247-9931-3*) Dekker.

***Project Management for Product Innovation.** 2nd ed. Alan Webb. LC 00-20999. 424p. 2000. 129.95 (*0-566-08262-4*, Pub. by Ashgate Pub) Ashgate Pub Co.

Project Management for the General Manager. Training Management Corp. Staff & Harry M. Stuart. Ed. by Jane A. Silverman. LC 97-5425. (Illus.). 150p. (Orig.). Date not set. pap. text. write for info. (*1-882390-08-3*) Princeton Trng.

Project Management for the 21st Century. 2nd ed. Ed. by Bennet P. Lientz & Kathryn Rea. (Illus.). 339p. 1998. pap. text 44.95 (*0-12-449966-X*) Acad Pr.

Project Management Handbook. Ed. by D. Lock. 625p. (C). 1987. 475.00 (*0-7855-5711-3*, Pub. by Inst Pur & Supply) St Mut.

Project Management Handbook. 2nd ed. Ed. by David Cleland & William R. King. 1008p. 1988. 110.00 (*0-471-29384-9*, VNR) Wiley.

Project Management Handbook: Proceedings of the Third International Symposium. 22nd ed. David I. Cleland. LC 87-23151. 1988. text 88.95 (*0-442-22114-2*, VNR) Wiley.

***Project Management Handbook for Building Services.** Ed. by C. J. Parsloe & L. J. Wild. 220p. 1998. pap. 120.00 (*0-86022-502-X*, Pub. by Build Servs Info Assn) St Mut.

Project Management Handbook for Object-Oriented Software Development. Edward V. Berard. (C). 2001. 36.75 (*0-13-138611-5*, Macmillan Coll) P-H.

Project Management Handbook 1999 Paul C. Tinnirello. LC 99-24921. 512p. 1999. boxed set 79.95 (*0-8493-9998-X*) CRC Pr.

Project Management in Construction. 2nd ed. Sidney M. Levy. LC 93-21585. 310p. 1992. 59.95 (*0-07-037590-9*) McGraw.

Project Management in Construction. 3rd ed. Levy. LC 99-36049. 352p. 1999. 64.95 (*0-07-134230-3*) McGraw.

Project Management in Construction. 3rd ed. Anthony Walker. LC 96-33862. 304p. 1996. pap. text 44.95 (*0-632-04071-8*) Blackwell Sci.

Project Management in Manufacturing & High Technology Operations. 2nd ed. Adedeji B. Badiru. LC 95-46164. (Wiley Series in Engineering & Technology). 600p. 1996. 110.00 (*0-471-12721-3*) Wiley.

Project Management in Russia: Basic Notions, History, Achievements, Perspectives. Vladimir Voropajev. LC 97-9206. (Illus.). 240p. (Orig.). 1997. pap. 44.95 (*1-880410-02-8*) Proj Mgmt Inst.

Project Management in the Fast Lane: Applying the Theory of Constraints Management. Robert C. Newbold. LC 97-48806. (APICS Series on Constraints Management). 320p. 1998. boxed set 44.95 (*1-57444-195-7*) St Lucie Pr.

Project Management in the Process Industries. Roy Whittaker. 384p. 1996. 109.95 (*0-471-96040-3*) Wiley.

Project Management Institute Project Management Handbook. Ed. by Jeffrey K. Pinto. LC 98-12381. (Business & Management Ser.). 544p. 1998. 74.95 (*0-7879-4013-5*) Jossey-Bass.

Project Management Made Simple: A Guide to Successful Management of Computer Systems Projects. Yourdon Press Staff & David King. 128p. 1991. pap. 48.00 (*0-13-717729-1*, 270801) P-H.

Project Management Memory Jogger: A Pocket Guide for Project Teams. Paula Martin & Karen Tate. Ed. by Francine Oddo. (Illus.). 164p. 1997. spiral bd. 7.95 (*1-57681-001-1*, 103SE) GOAL-QPC.

Project Management Methodology: A Practical Guide for the Next Millennium. Ralph L. Kliem et al. LC 97-4019. (Illus.). 288p. 1997. text 110.00 (*0-8247-0088-0*) Dekker.

Project Management Module+Software - Parsifal Workbench. Morton. (GC - Principles of Management Ser.). (C). 1998. pap. 29.95 (*0-87709-531-0*) S-W Pub.

Project Management Office: Gaining the Competitive Edge. Melvin Deguzman. (Project Management Nuts & Bolts Ser.: Vol. 2). 1999. pap. 32.00 (*1-890367-13-3*) ESI Int.

Project Management Paradigm. Ken Burnett. LC 98-2641. (Practitioner Ser.). xiv, 266p. 1998. pap. 79.95 (*3-540-76238-8*) Spr-Verlag.

***Project Management Pocketbook.** Keith Posner & Mike Applegarth. 112p. 2000. pap. 8.95 (*1-57922-004-5*) Stylus Pub VA.

Project Management Practitioner's Handbook. Ralph L. Kleim. LC 98-22616. 360p. 1998. 78.95 (*0-8144-0396-4*) AMACOM.

Project Management Software & Systems. P. Rohrer. 1989. text. write for info. (*0-442-27707-5*, VNR) Wiley.

Project Management Software Survey, 1998. Project Management Institute Staff. LC 99-230980. 100p. 1998. pap. 249.95 (*1-880410-52-4*) Proj Mgmt Inst.

***Project Management Success Stories: Lessons of Project Leaders.** Alexander Laufer & Edward J. Hoffman. 240p. 2000. text 44.95 (*0-471-36007-4*) Wiley.

Project Management Techniques. Alfred O. Awani. (Illus.). 192p. 1983. text 24.95 (*0-89433-197-3*) Petrocelli.

Project Management Terms: A Working Glossary. Ed. by J. Leroy Ward. 182p. 1997. pap. 29.95 (*1-890367-04-4*) ESI Int.

Project Management Tools. Eugene G. Spiegle & John T. Wilhelm. 90p. 1994. ring bd. 39.95 (*1-885318-00-6*) Cambridge Grp.

Project Management Using the SAS System, Version 6. 180p. (C). 1993. pap. 39.95 (*1-55544-557-8*, BR56575) SAS Publ.

Project Management with CPM, Pert & Precedence Diagramming. 3rd ed. Joseph J. Moder et al. (Illus.). 389p. (C). 1995. pap. text 40.00 (*0-9606344-8-7*) Blitz Pub Co.

Project Management Workbook. Harold Kerzner. (Industrial Engineering Ser.). 1996. pap., wbk. ed. 24.95 (*0-442-02229-8*, VNR) Wiley.

***Project Management Workshop.** James Taylor. (Trainer's Workshop Ser.: Vol. 4). 300p. 2000. pap. 39.95 (*0-8144-7044-0*) AMACOM.

Project Manager. Jack Rudman. (Career Examination Ser.: C-1433). 1994. pap. 29.95 (*0-8373-1433-X*) Nat Learn.

Project Manager As Change Agent: Leadership, Influence & Negotiation. Ed. by J. Rodney Turner et al. LC 96-562. 1996. write for info. (*0-614-97200-0*) McGraw.

Project Manager's CADD Survival Guide. Stephen M. Benz & American Society Of Civil Engineers Staff. LC 97-16679. 184p. 1997. 22.00 (*0-7844-0247-7*) Am Soc Civil Eng.

Project Manager's Desk Reference: A Comprehensive Guide to Project Planning, Evaluation & Control. James P. Lewis. 525p. 1995. 29.95 (*1-55738-896-2*, Irwn Prfssnl) McGraw-Hill Prof.

Project Manager's Desk Reference: A Comprehensive Guide to Project Planning, Evaluation & Control. 2nd ed. Lewis. LC 99-32834. 546p. 1999. 70.00 (*0-07-134750-X*) McGraw.

Project Manager's Desk Reference: A Comprehensive Guide to Project Planning, Scheduling, Evaluation, Control & Systems. James P. Lewis. 475p. 1993. text 60.00 (*1-55738-461-4*, Irwn Prfssnl) McGraw-Hill Prof.

Project Manager's Desk Reference: Guide to the Project Management Body of Knowledge. 8th ed. A. J. Thomas. (Project & Program Management Ser.). 335p. 1999. pap. 75.00 (*0-9642865-4-8*) Hampton Grp.

***Project Manager's MBA: How to Translate Project Decisions Into Business Success.** Dennis J. Cohen. 2000. 34.95 (*0-7879-5256-7*) Jossey-Bass.

Project Manager's Partner: A Step-by-Step Guide to Project Management. Michael Greer. 1996. 39.95 (*0-87425-397-7*) HRD Press.

***Project Manager's Portable Handbook.** David I. Cleland. 464p. 1999. pap. 54.95 (*0-07-135263-5*) McGraw.

***Project Manager's Portable Handbook.** David I. Cleland & Lewis R. Ireland. LC 99-54562. 1999. write for info. (*0-07-135233-3*) McGraw-Hill Sch.

Project Manager's Survival Guide: The Handbook for Real-World Project Management. Donald Penner. LC 93-4016. 100p. 1994. pap. text 14.95 (*0-935470-72-7*) Battelle.

Project Managinot: Guideplans for Music Education Lesson Plans & Learning Activities for Nursery-Grade 6. 1992. pap., teacher ed. 20.00 (*0-8074-0489-6*, 241150) UAHC.

Project Materials Management Handbook. Ed. by Bureau of Engineering Research The University of T. 372p. 1989. text 75.00 (*0-685-31295-X*, CPMMH) Am Soc Civil Eng.

Project Megalon. Richard Hodes. 250p. (Orig.). 1999. pap. 12.95 (*1-881542-36-X*) Book World Inc.

Project Mercury. Diane M. Sipiera. (True Bks.). (J). 1998. pap. text 6.95 (*0-516-26275-0*) Childrens.

Project Mercury. Diane M. Sipiera & Paul P. Sipiera. LC 96-37919. (True Bk.). 47p. (J). (gr. 2-4). 1997. 21.00 (*0-516-20443-2*) Childrens.

***Project Mercury.** Ray Spangenburg & Diane Moser. LC 00-27010. (Out of This World Ser.). 2001. write for info. (*0-531-11763-4*) Watts.

Project Mind: The Conscious Conquest of Man & Matter Through Accelerated Thought. T. Kun. LC 92-41961. 1993. 14.95 (*1-880646-02-1*) Unimedia.

Project Mindshift: The Re-Education of the American Public Concerning Extraterrestrial Life 1947-1997. Michael Mannion. LC 98-6510. 256p. 1998. 19.95 (*0-87131-856-3*) M Evans.

***Project Mindshift: The Re-Education of the American Public Concerning Extraterrestrial Life 1947-1997.** Michael Mannion. (Illus.). 304p. 2000. pap. 14.95 (*0-87131-907-1*) M Evans.

Project Modelling in Construction: Seeing Is Believing. Norman Fisher et al. LC 97-182856. 88p. 1997. 92.00 (*0-7277-2581-5*) Am Soc Civil Eng.

Project Monitoring & Evaluation in Agriculture. Dennis J. Casley & Krishna Kumar. LC 87-22632. 174p. 1987. reprint ed. pap. 54.00 (*0-608-03653-6*, 206447900009) Bks Demand.

***Project Monitoring Plan: Results Framework, Results Indicators, Worksheets, Coastal Resources Management Project II.** Alan Desbonnet & Lynne Z. Hale. (Coastal Management Report Ser.: Vol. 2209). (Illus.). 1998. pap. write for info. (*1-885454-09-0*) Coastal Res.

Project Moon Dust: Beyond Roswell--Exposing the Government's Continuing Covert UFO Investigation. Kevin D. Randle. 328p. 1999. mass mkt. 6.99 (*0-380-80603-7*, Avon Bks) Morrow Avon.

Project 19: A Mission Most Secret. John W. Swancara. (Aviation History Ser.). (Illus.). 304p. (Orig.). 1997. 29.95 (*1-885354-07-X*); pap. 19.95 (*1-885354-04-5*) Honoribus Pr.

***Project 98.** ENI Publishing Ltd. Staff. (Pasaporte Ser.). 2000. pap. text 15.95 (*2-84072-900-8*); pap. text 7.95 (*2-84072-924-5*) ENI Publng.

***Project 98 - Intermediate.** Ed. by Ron Pronk. (Illus.). 220p. 1998. pap. 20.00i (*1-58264-091-2*) ActiveEd.

Project 98 - Introduction. Ed. by Ron Pronk. (Illus.). 200p. 1998. pap. 20.00 (*1-58264-042-4*, 163) ActiveEd.

Project Nirvana. Keith Bush. Date not set. 12.95 (*1-881542-62-9*) Book World Inc.

Project Notebook: Basic Edition. J. Hardy LeGwin. 1990. ring bd. 29.95 (*1-55701-310-1*) BNI Pubns.

Project Notebook: Professional Edition. J. Hardy LeGwin. Ed. by Susan J. Bicknell. 1991. ring bd. 59.95 (*1-55701-307-1*) BNI Pubns.

***Project of a Permanent Court of International Justice & Resolutions of the Advisory Committee of Jurists: Report & Commentary.** James Brown Scott. LC 99-48872. 2000. write for info. (*1-57588-610-3*) W S Hein.

P

Project of Prose in Early Modern Europe & the New World. Ed. by Elizabeth Fowler & Roland Greene. LC 96-51159. (Cambridge Studies in Renaissance Literature & Culture: No. 16). (Illus.). 219p. (C). 1997. text 59.95 (0-521-44112-9) Cambridge U Pr.

Project Office: A Key to Managing Projects Effectively. Thomas A. Block & J. Davidson Frame. Ed. by Bill Christopher. LC 97-68245. (Management Library: No. 12). 88p. 1997. pap. text 12.95 (1-56052-443-X) Crisp Pubns.

Project Omega: Eye of the Beast. James E Acre. LC 99-31093. 216p. 1999. pap. text 13.95 (1-55571-511-7, Hellgate Pr) PSI Resch.

Project Opportunity Pt. A: Curriculum for Training Providers - Mentors & Field Placement Providers - Supervisors. Phylis Benner & Sandra Gellert. 52p. 1998. ring bd. 150.00 (1-884093-08-6) Chldrns Fnd.

Project Opportunity Pt. B: Parent-Education Enhanced Basic Family Child Care Provider Training Course. Phylis Benner et al. 276p. 1998. ring bd. 500.00 (1-884093-09-4) Chldrns Fnd.

Project Organizer. (Believer's Life System Women's Edition Ser.). 1998. ring bd. 3.50 (0-8024-6976-0) Moody.

Project Overview: The Subject of Thinking. Sydney Tyler-Parker. 74p. (Orig.). (gr. k-6). 1982. pap. text 10.00 (0-912781-09-2) Thomas Geale.

Project Pain, Project Gain, Vol. I. Deborah Isom. 67p. pap. text. write for info. (0-9640273-0-5) ISOM Pubns.

Project Partnering for the Design & Construction Industry: In the Planning, Design, & Construction Business. Ralph J. Stephenson. LC 95-39866. 441p. 1995. 90.00 (0-471-10716-6) Wiley.

Project Partnering Manual for Design & Construction. William C. Ronco. LC 95-46348. (Construction Engineering Ser.). 312p. 1995. 59.95 (0-07-053669-4) McGraw.

Project Performance of IRD Programs in Sierra Leone & Malawi. Michael Johnny et al. 182p. 1986. pap. text 19.95 (3-87895-297-X) Transaction Pubs.

Project Phsyics. Rutherford. 1981. text 67.00 (0-03-055141-2) Holt R&W.

Project Planner. Dennis Lock. (Illus.). 168p. 1990. text 189.95 (0-566-02845-X, Pub. by Gower) Ashgate Pub Co.

***Project Planning.** 416p. (C). 1999. 55.00 (0-536-60389-8) Pearson Custom.

Project Planning & Computer Models. Raz. 1995. pap. 32.95 (0-442-01843-6, VNR) Wiley.

Project Planning & Control see Project Scheduling Management Construction

***Project Planning & Control.** 3rd ed. Albert Lester. 448p. 2000. 66.95 (0-7506-4261-0) Buttrwrth-Heinemann.

Project Planning & Control. 3rd ed. Albert Lester. (Illus.). 256p. 2000. 91.95 (0-7506-1100-6) Buttrwrth-Heinemann.

***Project Planning & Implementation.** (C). 1999. write for info. (0-536-60379-0); 56.00 (0-536-60242-5) Pearson Custom.

Project Planning & Income Distribution. F. Leslie & C. H. Helmers. (Studies in Development & Planning: Vol. 9). 1979. lib. bdg. 71.50 (0-89838-010-3) Kluwer Academic.

Project Planning & Management: An Integrated System for Improving Productivity. Louis J. Goodman. (Illus.). 320p. (gr. 13). 1987. text 71.95 (0-442-22762-0) Chapman & Hall.

Project Planning & Management in the People's Republic of China: Sharing of Development Experience. Asian Development Bank Staff. 98p. 1998. pap. 15.00 (971-561-135-4, Pub. by Asian Devel Bank) Paul & Co Pubs.

Project Planning for Developing Economies. W. W. Shaner. LC 79-13225. (Praeger Special Studies). 235p. 1979. 55.00 (0-275-90422-9, C0422, Praeger Pubs) Greenwood.

Project Planning for I. R. D. P. P. N. Sharma. 341p. (C). 1989. 250.00 (81-85009-34-1, Pub. by Print Hse) St Mut.

***Project Planning, Scheduling & Control.** 3rd ed. James P. Lewis. 350p. 2000. 50.00 (0-07-136050-6, Schaums Outlne) McGraw-Hill Prof.

Project Planning, Scheduling & Control: A Hands-on Guide to Bringing Projects in on Time & on Budget. 2nd rev. ed. James P. Lewis. 300p. 1995. 45.00 (1-55738-869-5, Irwn Prfssnl) McGraw-Hill Prof.

Project Planning, Scheduling & Control in Construction: An Encyclopedia of Terms & Applications. Calin M. Popescu & Chotchai Charoenngam. LC 94-35464. 573p. 1995. 110.00 (0-471-02858-4) Wiley.

***Project Planning Toolkit.** Prosci Research Staff. (Illus.). 1999. 189.00 (1-930885-00-8, RTA 1) Prosci Rsrch.

Project Plans. rev. ed. Ed. by Michael Kirchwehm. (Illus.). 84p. 1998. reprint ed. pap. 3.99 (0-934039-45-3) Hme Dsgn Altntves.

Project Preparation. (Open Learning for Supervisory Management Ser.). 1987. pap. text 19.50 (0-08-034977-3, Pergamon Pr) Elsevier.

Project Preparation. 2nd ed. (Open Learning Super Ser.). 1991. pap. text 26.00 (0-08-041610-1, Pergamon Pr) Elsevier.

Project Preparation & Appraisal Material & Techniques for Co-Operative Management Training. 130p. 1990. 31.50 (92-2-102446-6) Intl Labour Office.

Project Programming: A Growing Architectural Service. Edward T. White. (Illus.). 26p. 1991. pap. 6.00 (1-928643-13-2) Archit Media.

Project Puffin: How We Brought Puffins Back to Egg Rock. Stephen W. Kress. LC 95-47805. (National Audubon Society Book). (Illus.). 40p. (J). (gr. 3-6). 1997. 16.95 (0-88448-170-0) Tilbury Hse.

Project Puffin: How We Brought Puffins Back to Egg Rock. Stephen W. Kress. (National Audubon Society Bks.). (Illus.). 40p. (J). (gr. 3-6). 1999. pap. 7.95 (0-88448-171-9) Tilbury Hse.

Project-Readiness: A Guide to Family Emergency Preparedness. rev. ed. Louise E. Nelson. 272p. 1999. pap. 18.95 (0-88290-657-7) Horizon Utah.

Project Rehabilitation in Adverse Environments. Michael Yaffey & Michael A. Tribe. 170p. 1992. 82.95 (1-85628-341-0, Pub. by Avebry) Ashgate Pub Co.

***Project Relative to a Court of Arbitral Justice: Draft Convention & Report Adopted by the 2nd Hague Peace Conference of 1907.** International Peace Conference Staff. LC 99-48871. 1999. write for info. (1-57588-609-X) W S Hein.

Project Remember: A National Index of Grave Sites of Notable Americans. Arthur S. Koykka. Ed. by Keith Irvine. LC 83-42530. 598p. 1986. 64.00 (0-917256-22-0) Ref Pubns.

Project Renewal in Israel: Urban Revitalization Through Partnership. Paul King et al. 194p. (Orig.). 1987. pap. text 24.00 (0-8191-5347-8) U Pr of Amer.

Project RIDE Program Manual: Early Childhood Version. 2nd ed. Great Falls Public Schools Staff. (Project RIDE Ser.). 112p. 1997. pap. text. write for info. (1-57035-135-X) Sopris.

Project RIDE Program Manual: Elementary/Middle School Version. Great Falls Public Schools Staff. (Project RIDE Ser.). 120p. 1997. pap. text. write for info. (1-57035-139-2) Sopris.

Project RIDE Program Manual: Secondary Version. 3rd ed. Ray Beck. (Project RIDE Ser.). (Illus.). 128p. 1996. pap. text. write for info. (1-57035-110-4) Sopris.

Project Risk Management: Processes, Techniques & Insights. Chris B. Chapman. LC 96-30345. 344p. 1996. 79.95 (0-471-95804-2) Wiley.

Project Rooms: Mischa Kuball. Mischa Kuball & Gerard A. Goodrow. LC 98-199690. 147p. 1998. write for info. (3-88375-305-X) Walther Konig.

Project SAEFP Workbook. 2nd ed. Society of Teachers of Family Medicine Staff. (Illus.). 489p. 1991. 75.00 (0-942295-24-2, 80) Soc Tchrs Fam Med.

Project Scheduling: Recent Models, Algorithms, & Applications. Jan Weglarz. LC 98-30712. (International Series in Operations Research & Management Science). 1998. 179.95 (0-7923-8268-4) Kluwer Academic.

Project Scheduling for Construction Contracting see Advantage Contractor TM Business Success Series

Project Scheduling Management Construction. 3rd rev. ed. David R. Pierce, Jr. LC 99-162329. Orig. Title: Project Planning & Control. 250p. 1998. 64.95 (0-87629-533-2, 67247A) R S Means.

***Project Scheduling under Limited Resources: Models, Methods & Applications.** Shonke Hartmann. LC 99-41942. (Lecture Notes in Economics & Mathematical Systems Ser.: Vol. 478). (Illus.). xii, 221p. 2000. pap. 61.00 (3-540-66392-4) Spr-Verlag.

Project SEARCH: The Struggle for Control of Criminal Information in America, 23. Gordon K. Zenk. LC 78-67654. (Contributions in Political Science Ser.: No. 23). (Illus.). 176p. 1979. 52.95 (0-313-20639-2, ZEP/, Greenwood Pr) Greenwood.

Project Seasons: Hands-On Activities for Discovering the Wonders of the World. 2nd ed. Deborah Parrella. (Illus.). 336p. 1999. pap. 24.95 (0-9642163-0-2, Pub. by Shelburne Farms) Chelsea Green Pub.

Project Seek: Onassis, Kennedy & the Gemstone Thesis. Gerald A. Carroll. LC 94-2937. (Illus.). 310p. (Orig.). (C). 1994. pap. 16.95 (0-9640104-0-2) Bridger Hse.

Project Self Discovery: Artistic Alternatives for High Risk Youth. Harvey Milkman et al. 200p. 1996. pap. 49.95 (0-471-16241-8) Wiley.

Project Self-Esteem: A Parent-Involvement Program for Children Grades K-6. rev. ed. Sandy McDaniel & Peggy Bielen. Ed. by Janet Lovelady. LC 89-84056. (Creative Teaching & Parenting Ser.). (Illus.). 408p. (J). (gr. k-6). 1990. reprint ed. pap. 39.95 (0-915190-59-1, JP9059-1) Jalmar Pr.

Project Services Specialist. Jack Rudman. (Career Examination Ser.: C-1660). 1994. pap. 29.95 (0-8373-1660-X) Nat Learn.

Project Set Strategies. Frans G. Derkinderen & Roy L. Crum. (Nijenrode Studies in Business: Vol. 4). 1979. lib. bdg. 73.50 (0-89838-014-6) Kluwer Academic.

Project Site Safety & Security for Construction Contracting see Advantage Contractor TM Business Success Series

Project Skills. Sam Elbeik. 192p. 2000. pap. text 19.95 (0-7506-3978-4) Buttrwrth-Heinemann.

Project Skyline: Modern - Moderne Modernistic Miami Beach Hotel Architecture. Jewel Stern. 1982. pap. 20.00 (0-905836-33-2, Pub. by Museum Modern Art) St Mut.

Project Smart: Local Manufacturing Industry Skill Standards April 1996. Joyce M. Smith & Joseph Ippolito. Ed. by Jennifer Roscoe et al. 146p. 1996. pap. text. write for info. (0-89292-283-4) Educ Dev Ctr.

Project Smart: Work-Based Learning in the Manufacturing Firm. Joyce Malyn-Smith et al. 125p. 1997. pap. 19.95 (0-89292-285-0) Educ Dev Ctr.

Project SOAR: Stress on Analytical Reasoning. J. W. Carmichael et al. 186p. (C). 1989. pap. text 11.80 (0-87563-354-4) Stipes.

Project SPICA: A Teacher Resource to Enhance Astronomy Education. Harvard College Staff. 288p. (C). 1994. spiral bd. 25.95 (0-8403-9366-0, 40936601) Kendall-Hunt.

***Project Sponsor Guide.** Neil A. Love & Joan Brant-Love. LC 00-23371. 2000. write for info. (1-880410-15-X) Proj Mgmt Inst.

Project STAR: The Universe in Your Hands. 7th ed. Harvard Observatory Staff. 400p. 1995. 34.90 (0-8403-7715-0) Kendall-Hunt.

***Project Studies: A Late Modern University Reform?** Ed. by Henning Salling Olesen & Jens Hojgaard Jensen. 305p. 1999. 34.00 (87-16-13482-6, Pub. by Copenhagen Busn Schl) Bks Intl VA.

***Project Studios.** Philip Newell. LC 99-43615. 224p. 1999. pap. 47.95 (0-240-51573-0, Focal) Buttrwrth-Heinemann.

Project Sunlight. June Strong. LC 80-13011. 1980. pap. 1.99 (0-8127-0289-1) Review & Herald.

Project Surveying: General Adjustment & Optimization Techniques with Applications to Engineering Surveying. Peter Richardus. 640p. (C). 1984. text 194.00 (90-6191-519-8, Pub. by A A Balkema); pap. text 110.00 (90-6191-526-0, Pub. by A A Balkema) Ashgate Pub Co.

Project TALENT Data Bank Handbook. rev. ed. Lauress L. Wise et al. 1979. pap. 14.50 (0-89785-606-6) Am Inst Res.

Project Techniques for Product & Service Improvement. Andrew Greasley. LC 97-24160. 176p. 1997. pap. text 39.95 (0-7506-3769-2) Buttrwrth-Heinemann.

Project the Right Image: A Practical Handbook for Christian Bookstall Organisers. Eric A. Thom. (C). 1989. 26.00 (0-9510086-2-5, Pub. by Jay Bks) St Mut.

Project 3.O for Windows. 1993. 49.95 (1-56877-063-4); teacher ed. 49.95 (1-56877-064-2) Catapult WA.

Project to Develop a Model Anti-Stalking Code for States. (Illus.). 117p. (Orig.). (C). 1994. pap. text 35.00 (0-7881-0689-9) DIANE Pub.

Project Turn-Around. Larry Dixon. LC 84-61674. 61p. 1985. ring bd. 49.95 (0-914607-20-0) Master Tchr.

Project Twilight. Wolf White Wolf Publishing Staff & Christopher Howard. (Werewolf Ser.). 96p. 1995. pap. 12.00 (1-56504-310-3, 3064) White Wolf.

Project 2015: Power & Progress. Ed. by Patrick M. Cronin. (Illus.). 157p. (C). 1997. pap. text 30.00 (0-7881-4646-7) DIANE Pub.

Project 2061: Education for a Changing Future. Jana J. Zinser. (State Legislative Reports: Vol. 17, No. 17). 6p. 1992. pap. text 15.00 (1-55516-289-4, 7302-1717) Natl Conf State Legis.

Project UFO. Raymond A. Montgomery. (Choose Your Own Adventure Ser.: No. 143). (J). (gr. 4-8). 1994. 9.09 (0-606-05981-4, Pub. by Turtleback) Demco.

***Project Utopia.** Carl Bowen et al. (Aberrant Ser.). (Illus.). 144p. 1999. pap. 19.95 (1-56504-631-5, 8504) White Wolf.

Project VIP (Violence Is Preventable), Level 1. Doug Stevens & Amy Keller. 24p. (Orig.). (J). 1995. wbk. ed. 69.95 (1-56688-264-8) Bur For At-Risk.

Project VIP (Violence Is Preventable), Level 2. Doug Stevens & Amy Keller. 24p. (Orig.). (YA). 1995. wbk. ed. 69.95 (1-56688-265-6) Bur For At-Risk.

Project VIP (Violence Is Preventable), Level 3. Doug Stevens & Amy Keller. 24p. (Orig.). (YA). 1995. wbk. ed. 69.95 (1-56688-266-4) Bur For At-Risk.

Project W. I. Z. E. (Wildlife Inquiry Through Zoo Education) Environmental Education Department. 1993. reprint ed. teacher ed. write for info. (0-9635151-1-X); reprint ed. teacher ed. write for info. (0-9635151-0-1); reprint ed. student ed. write for info. (0-9635151-2-8) NY Zoological.

Project Water Science: General Science Secondary Level. Judy Wheatley. Ed. by Rita S. Sudman. (Illus.). 37p. (YA). (gr. 7-12). 1996. pap. text 20.00 (1-893246-76-0) Water Educ.

Project Work. Diana L. Fried-Booth. (Illus.). 96p. 1986. pap. text 13.95 (0-19-437092-5) OUP.

Project Workbench Whiz's Sourcebook: Everything You Always Wanted to Know about 3.0, but Couldn't Find in the User Manuals. William S. Ruggles & Mukunda S. Murthy. (Illus.). 200p. (Orig.). 1989. spiral bd. 24.95 (0-685-30021-8) W S Ruggles & Assocs.

***Project Workout: A Toolkit for Reaping the Rewards of All You.** 2nd ed. Robert Buttrick. 450p. 2000. pap. text 34.00 (0-273-64436-X) F T P H.

Project Workout: A Toolkit to Drive Change & Improve the Health of Your Business. Robert Buttrick. (Illus.). 250p. (Orig.). 1997. pap. text 25.00 (0-273-62680-9) F T P-H.

Project World Evacuation: UFOs to Assist in the "Great Exodus" of Human Souls off This Planet. Tuella. 160p. 1993. 14.00 (0-938294-37-7) Inner Light.

Project X: The Search for the Secrets of Immortality. Gene Savoy. LC 76-44670. (Illus.). 279p. 1977. text 35.00 (0-672-52181-4) Intl Comm Christ.

Project Zero Framework Vol. I: Building on Children's Strengths - The Experience of Project Spectrum. Ed. by Mara Krechevsky et al. LC 98-30414. 192p. 1998. pap. text 17.95 (0-8077-3766-6) Tchrs Coll.

Project Zero Framework Vol. II: Project Spectrum - Learning Activities Guide. Ed. by Jie-Qi Chen. LC 98-30414. 264p. 1998. pap. text 18.95 (0-8077-3767-4) Tchrs Coll.

Project Zero Framework Vol. III: Project Spectrum - Preschool Assessment Handbook. Ed. by Mara Krechevsky. LC 98-30414. 256p. 1998. pap. text 18.95 (0-8077-3768-2) Tchrs Coll.

Project Zero Frameworks for Early Childhood Education. Howard Gardner et al. LC 98-30414. 192p. 1998. text 36.00 (0-8077-3817-4) Tchrs Coll.

Project 3.0 Advanced. Computer Confidence Staff. (Illus.). 150p. 1993. spiral bd. 29.95 incl. disk (1-57533-057-1) Comput Confidence.

Project 3.0 Windows Introduction. Computer Confidence Staff. (Illus.). 150p. 1993. spiral bd. 29.95 incl. disk (1-57533-056-3) Comput Confidence.

Project 4.0 Advanced. Computer Confidence Staff. (Illus.). 160p. 1994. spiral bd. 29.95 incl. disk (1-57533-055-5) Comput Confidence.

Project 4.0 Introduction. Computer Confidence Staff. (Illus.). 160p. 1994. spiral bd. 29.95 incl. disk (1-57533-054-7) Comput Confidence.

Project/Contract Management Techniques Handbook. rev. ed. Ed. by Thomas C. Charland. (Illus.). 221p. (C). 2000. spiral bd. 29.95 (0-9610754-2-2) Manage Co In.

Projected Chemical Weapons Convention: A Guide to the Negotiations in the Conference on Disarmament. 330p. 1990. 50.00 (92-9045-041-X, GV.90.0.3) UN.

Projected Costs of Generating Electricity: Update 1998. NEA Staff. LC 98-222889. 244p. 1998. pap. 66.00 (92-64-16162-7, 6698161P) OECD.

Projected Dynamical Systems & Variational Inequalities with Applications. Anna Nagurney & Ding Zhang. (International Series in Operations Research & Management Science: Vol. 2). 320p. (C). 1995. lib. bdg. 121.00 (0-7923-9637-5) Kluwer Academic.

Projected Pulp & Paper Mills in the World, 1989-1999. 148p. 1990. 17.00 (92-5-102957-1, F9571, Pub. by FAO) Bernan Associates.

Projected Pulp & Paper Mills in the World, 1990-2000. 158p. 1991. 20.00 (92-5-103058-8, F0588, Pub. by FAO) Bernan Associates.

Projected Pulp & Paper Mills in the World, 1995-2000. (Illus.). 150p. 1996. pap. 14.00 (92-5-103867-8, F38678, Pub. by FAO) Bernan Associates.

***Project50.** Tom Peters. LC 99-33615. 208p. 1999. 15.95 (0-375-40773-1) Knopf.

Projectile Point Typology for Pennsylvania & the Northeast. Gary L. Fogelman. (Illus.). 221p. (Orig.). 1988. pap. 11.00 (0-941777-77-4) Fogelman Pub.

***Projectile Points of the Midwest: A Field Guide.** Noel D. Justice & Suzanne Kudlaty. (Illus.). 60p. 1999. pap. 12.00 (0-9678154-0-1) Timelines Arch Res.

Projectile Technology. H. Knecht. LC 97-34477. (Interdisciplinary Contributions to Archaeology Ser.). (Illus.). 428p. (C). 1997. 71.00 (0-306-45716-4, Plenum Trade) Perseus Pubng.

Projecting a Positive Image. Marilyn Pincus. (Barron's Business Success Ser.). 112p. 1993. pap. 4.95 (0-8120-1455-3) Barron.

Projecting a Positive Image Through Public Relations: Including a Communication Audit for School Media Centers. Cosette N. Kies. LC 78-21250. (School Media Centers: Focus on Trends & Issues Ser.: No. 2). 84p. reprint ed. pap. 30.00 (0-7837-5959-2, 204575900007) Bks Demand.

Projecting Beirut: Episodes in the Construction & Reconstruction of a Modern City. Ed. by Peter C. Rowe & Hashim Sarkis. LC 98-11909. (Illus.). 300p. 1998. pap. 35.00 (3-7913-1938-8) te Neues.

Projecting California's Fiscal Future. Stephen Carroll et al. 111p. (Orig.). 1996. pap. text 13.00 (0-8330-2364-0, MR-570-LE) Rand Corp.

Projecting Capitalism: A History of the Internationalization of the Construction Industry, 158. Marc Linder. LC 93-50546. (Contributions in Economics & Economic History Ser.). 288p. 1994. 65.00 (0-313-29293-0, Greenwood Pr) Greenwood.

Projecting Environmental Trends. Meyer Lyons. 59.95 (1-84014-194-8) Ashgate Pub Co.

Projecting Illusion: Film Spectatorship & the Impression of Realliity. Richard Allen. (Cambridge Studies in Film). (Illus.). 188p. 1997. pap. text 17.95 (0-521-58715-8) Cambridge U Pr.

***Projecting Post-Fordism: Capital, Class & Technology in Contemporary American Culture.** Nick Heffernan. LC 00-9740. 2001. write for info. (0-7453-1104-0) Pluto GBR.

Projecting the Adjective: The Syntax & Semantics of Gradability & Comparison. Christopher Kennedy. LC 98-49253. (Outstanding Disc Linguistics Ser.). 262p. 1999. 61.00 (0-8153-3349-8) Garland.

Projecting the Past: Ancient Rome, Cinema & History. Maria Wyke. LC 96-35995. (Illus.). 224p. (C). 1997. 75.00 (0-415-90613-X); pap. 19.99 (0-415-90614-8) Routledge.

Projecting the Shadow: The Cyborg Hero in American Film. Janice H. Rushing & Thomas S. Frentz. LC 95-30431. 274p. 1995. lib. bdg. 45.00 (0-226-73166-9) U Ch Pr.

Projecting the Shadow: The Cyborg Hero in American Film. Janice H. Rushing & Thomas S. Frentz. LC 95-30431. (Illus.). 224p. 1995. pap. 14.95 (0-226-73167-7) U Ch Pr.

Projection: A Novel. Keith Russell Ablow. LC 99-21637. 320p. 1999. 24.00 (0-679-44212-X) Pantheon.

***Projection: A Novel.** Keith Russell Ablow. 2000. mass mkt. 6.99 (0-312-97574-0) St Martin.

Projection & Religion: An Anthropological & Psychological Study of the Phenomena of Projection in the Various Religions. Fokke Sierksma. Tr. by Jacob Faber from DUT. LC BV4637.S52. 182p. reprint ed. pap. 56.50 (0-8357-4712-3, AU0040800009) Bks Demand.

***Projection Displays.** Edward H. Stupp & Matthew S. Brennesholtz. LC 98-22038. (SID Series in Display Technology). 438p. 1998. 135.00 (0-471-98253-9) Wiley.

Projection Displays III, Vol. 3013. Ed. by Ming H. Wu. LC 97-209076. 248p. 1997. 59.00 (0-8194-2424-2) SPIE.

Projection Displays IV, Vol. 3296. Ed. by Ming H. Wu. 274p. 1998. 69.00 (0-8194-2736-5) SPIE.

Projection for the Performing Arts. Graham Walne. LC 94-24063. (Illus.). 192p. 1995. pap. text 52.95 (0-240-51390-8, Focal) Buttrwrth-Heinemann.

Projection, Identification, Projective Identification. Ed. by Joseph Sandler. 1987. 35.00 (0-8236-4370-0) Intl Univs Pr.

P

Projection-Iterative Methods for Solution of Operator Equations. Ed. by N. S. Kurpel. LC 76-17114. (Translations of Mathematical Monographs: No. 46). 196p. 1976. text 60.00 (0-8218-1596-2, MMONO/46) Am Math.

Projection Methods for Systems of Equations. Claude Brezinski. LC 97-43588. (Studies in Computational Mathematics). 408p. 1997. 143.50 (0-444-82777-3) Elsevier.

Projection of Arguments: Lexical & Compositional Factors. Ed. by Miriam Butt & Wilhem Geuder. LC 97-45090. (Lecture Notes Ser.: Vol. 83). 360p. (C). 1998. text 64.95 (1-57586-111-9); pap. text 24.95 (1-57586-110-0) CSLI.

Projection of Britain: British Overseas Publicity & Propaganda, 1919-1939. Philip M. Taylor. LC 80-42274. 379p. reprint ed. pap. 108.10 (0-608-15613-2, 2031733) Bks Demand.

Projection of the Astral Body. Sylvan Muldoon & Hereward Carrington. (Illus.). 336p. 1973. reprint ed. pap. 12.95 (0-87728-069-X) Weiser.

Projection of the Astral Body. Sylvan J. Muldoon & Hereward Carrington. (Collector's Library of the Unknown). 242p. 1990. reprint ed. write for info. (0-8094-8062-X); reprint ed. lib. bdg. write for info. (0-8094-8063-8) Time-Life.

Projection Operator Techniques in Nonequilibrium Statistical Mechanics. H. Grabert. (Tracts in Modern Physics Ser.: Vol. 95). (Illus.). 220p. 1982. 66.95 (0-387-11635-4) Spr-Verlag.

Projection Stenciling. Linda Buckingham & Leslie Bird. LC 99-43780. (Illus.). 224p. 1999. pap. 24.95 (0-88179-180-6, Pub. by Hartley & Marks) Andrews & McMeel.

Projection Transformation Method for Nearly Singular Surface Boundary Element Integrals. 2nd ed. K. Hayami. Ed. by Carlos A. Brebbia & S. A. Orszag. (Lecture Notes in Engineering Ser.: Vol. 73). (Illus.). viii, 456p. 1992. 120.95 (0-387-55000-3) Spr-Verlag.

Projection TV Troubleshooting & Repair. Joseph Desposito. (Illus.). 336p. 1998. pap. 34.95 (0-7906-1134-1) Prompt Publns.

Projectionists' Programmed Primer. (Illus.). 1982. 6.25 (0-9601006-0-1) G T Yeamans.

Projections. Eckhard Gerdes. 52p. (Orig.). 1986. pap. 16.95 (1-884097-00-6) Depth Charge.

***Projections, Vol. 11.** Tod Lippy. Vol. 11. (Illus.). 304p. 2000. pap. 20.00 (0-571-20591-7) Faber & Faber.

***Projections: Brief Reading on America Culture.** Warner. (C). 1999. pap. text 40.50 (0-15-505373-6) Harcourt.

Projections: Film-Makers on Film-Making, No. 6. Ed. by John Boorman & Walter Donohue. (Illus.). 304p. (Orig.). 1996. pap. 16.95 (0-571-17853-7) Faber & Faber.

***Projections: Poems from Hollywood.** Mark Dunster. 11p. 1999. pap. 5.00 (0-89642-710-2) Linden Pubs.

Projections: The Photomontages of Romare Bearden. LC 96-46959. (Illus.). 1997. pap. write for info. (0-87427-104-5) Whitney Mus.

Projections & Interface Conditions: Essays on Modularity. Ed. by Anna-Maria Di Sciullo. (Illus.). 272p. 1997. text 65.00 (0-19-510414-5) OUP.

Projections 8: Film-Makers on Film-Making. John Boorman. 1998. pap. 19.95 (0-571-19355-2) Faber & Faber.

Projections 5: Film-Makers on Film-Making. John Boorman. Ed. by Walter Donohue. LC 96-210403. 304p. 1996. pap. 18.95 (0-571-17811-1) Faber & Faber.

Projections 4: Film-Makers on Film-Making. Ed. by John Boorman et al. (Projections Ser.: Vol. 4). (Illus.). 288p. (Orig.). 1995. pap. 18.95 (0-571-17363-2) Faber & Faber.

Projections 4 & 1/2: Film-Makers on Film-Making. Ed. by John Boorman & Walter Donohue. (Projections Ser.). 288p. 1995. pap. 16.95 (0-571-17609-7) Faber & Faber.

Projections 9: Film-Makers on Film-Making. Ed. by John Boorman & Walter Donohue. (Illus.). 384p. 1999. pap. 21.95 (0-571-19356-0) Faber & Faber.

Projections 92 by County. 1992. 25.00 (0-317-05659-X, P92011PRO) Assn Bay Area.

Projections of Consciousness: A Diary of Out-of-Body Experiences. 2nd ed. Waldo Vieira. Tr. by Kevin De La Tour et al. (Illus.). 226p. 1997. reprint ed. pap. 11.95 (85-86019-25-9) Intl Inst Proj.

***Projections of Education Statistics to 2009.** (Illus.). 198p. (C). 2000. pap. text 35.00 (0-7881-8720-1) DIANE Pub.

***Projections of Education Statistics to 2008.** Debra E. Gerald. 214p. 1998. per. 25.00 (0-16-049597-0) USGPO.

***Projections of Education Statistics to 2009.** Debra E. Gerald et al. (Illus.). 220p. 1999. per. 21.00 (0-16-050145-8, Pub. by USGPO) Bernan Associates.

Projections of Education Statistics to 2007. 26th ed. Debra E. Gerald & William J. Hussar. (Illus.). 192p. (C). 1997. pap. text 35.00 (0-7881-4278-X) DIANE Pub.

***Projections of Education Statistics to 2008.** 27th ed. Debra E. Gerald & William J. Hussar. (Illus.). 192p. (C). 1999. reprint ed. pap. text 40.00 (0-7881-8364-8) DIANE Pub.

Projections of Education Statistics to the Year 2000. 1990. lib. bdg. 75.00 (0-8490-4033-7) Gordon Pr.

Projections of Education Statistics to 2005 (1995) Debra E. Gerald & William J. Hussar. (Illus.). 200p. (Orig.). (C). 1995. pap. text 40.00 (0-7881-2039-5) DIANE Pub.

Projections of Education Statistics to 2006. 25th ed. William J. Hussar & Debra E. Gerald. (Illus.). 202p. (C). 1997. pap. text 40.00 (0-7881-4012-4) DIANE Pub.

***Projections of Femininity in the Fiction of Mexican Writer Rosario Castellanos.** Nuala Finnegan. LC 00-21119. (Hispanic Literature Ser.: Vol. 54). 196p. 2000. text 79.95 (0-7734-7732-2) E Mellen.

Projections of National Health Expenditures. (Illus.). 57p. (Orig.). (C). 1993. pap. text 20.00 (1-56806-367-9) DIANE Pub.

***Projections of Psychic Reality: A Centennial of Film & Psychoanalysis.** Ed. by Diana Diamond & Harriet K. Wrye. (Psychoanalytic Inquiry Ser.: Vol. 18, No. 2). 1998. pap. 20.00 (0-88163-931-1) Analytic Pr.

Projections of the Consciousness: A Diary of Out-of-Body Experiences. Waldo Vieira. Tr. by Alvarado Salgado et al from POR. Orig. Title: Projecoes da Consciencia: Diario de Experiencias Fora do Corpo Fisico. (Illus.). 240p. (Orig.). 1995. pap. 11.95 (85-86019-01-1, Pub. by Inst Intl Projeciologia) Intl Inst Proj.

Projections of United States Agricultural Production & Demand: An Original Anthology. LC 75-29757. (World Food Supply Ser.). (Illus.). 1976. 36.95 (0-405-07782-3) Ayer.

Projections of War: Hollywood, American Culture, & World War II. Thomas Doherty. 1994. pap. 19.00 (0-231-08245-2) Col U Pr.

Projections of War: Hollywood & American Culture. Thomas Doherty. LC 99-461853. 1999. pap. 17.00 (0-231-11635-7) Col U Pr.

Projections onto Translation-Invariant Subspaces of Lp(G) H. P. Rosenthal. LC 52-42839. (Memoirs Ser.: No. 1/63). 84p. 1966. pap. 16.00 (0-8218-1263-7, MEMO/1/63) Am Math.

Projections 7: Film-Makers on Film-Making. Ed. by John Boorman & Walter Donohue. (Illus.). 304p. (Orig.). 1997. pap. 16.95 (0-571-19033-2) Faber & Faber.

***Projections 10: Hollywood Film-makers on Film-making.** Ed. by Mike Figgis. (Illus.). 304p. 2000. pap. 20.00 (0-571-19357-9) Faber & Faber.

Projections 3: A Year in Film. Ed. by John Boorman & Walter Donohue. (Illus.). 288p. 1994. pap. 19.95 (0-571-17047-1) Faber & Faber.

Projections to the Spinal Cord of the Rat During Development: A Time-Table of Descent. E. A. Lakke. LC 96-39080. (Advances in Anatomy, Embryology & Cell Biology Ser.). 1997. pap. write for info. (3-540-61878-3) Spr-Verlag.

Projections 92. 307p. 1992. 75.00 (0-317-05658-1, P92005PRO); 20.00 (0-317-05660-3, P92008PRO) Assn Bay Area.

Projective & Euclidean Geometry. 2nd ed. W. T. Fishback. LC 76-81329. 312p. (C). reprint ed. 96.80 (0-8357-9967-0, 205160200097) Bks Demand.

Projective & Introjective Identification & the Use of the Therapist's Self. Jill S. Scharff. LC 91-26070. 344p. 1992. 50.00 (0-87668-530-0) Aronson.

Projective Assessment of Aging Method, Set. Bernard Starr et al. LC 79-13358. (Adulthood & Aging Ser.: Vol. 4). 1979. student ed. 44.95 (0-8261-2440-2) Springer Pub.

Projective Cast: Architecture & Its Three Geometries. Robin Evans. (Illus.). 451p. 1995. 65.00 (0-262-05049-8) MIT Pr.

***Projective Cast: Architecture & Its Three Geometries.** Robin Evans. (Illus.). 456p. (C). 2000. reprint ed. pap. 39.95 (0-262-55038-5) MIT Pr.

***Projective Chronometry.** Sung Ho Kim & Tina Yuan. Ed. by Christopher Genter & Adam Dum. LC 99-97232. (Illus.). 98p. 1999. pap. text 2.50 (0-9676300-0-2) Sungho.

Projective Differential Geometry of Submanifolds. M. A. Akivis & V. V. Goldberg. LC 93-10725. (North-Holland Mathematical Library: No. 49). (Illus.). 374p. 1993. 149.50 (0-444-89771-2, North Holland) Elsevier.

Projective Genogramming. Florence W. Kaslow. LC 95-18287. (Practitioner's Resource Ser.). 45p. (Orig.). 1995. pap. 14.45 (1-56887-013-2, Prof Resc Pr) Pro Resource.

Projective Geometries over Finite Fields. 2nd ed. James Hirschfeld. (Oxford Mathematical Monographs). (Illus.). 570p. 1998. text 125.00 (0-19-850295-8) OUP.

Projective Geometry. P. Samuel. (Undergraduate Texts in Mathematics Ser.). (Illus.). 160p. 1988. 49.95 (0-387-96752-4) Spr-Verlag.

Projective Geometry. Olive Whicher. 292p. 1986. pap. 31.95 (0-85440-245-4, Pub. by R Steiner Pr) Anthroposophic.

Projective Geometry. 2nd ed. H. S. Coxeter. (Illus.). xii, 162p. 1994. reprint ed. 52.95 (0-387-96532-7) Spr-Verlag.

Projective Geometry: From Foundations to Applications. Albrecht Beutelspacher & Ute Rosenbaum. LC 97-18012. (Illus.). 268p. (C). 1998. text 64.95 (0-521-48277-1); pap. text 24.95 (0-521-48364-6) Cambridge U Pr.

Projective Geometry & Modern Algebra. Lars Kadison & Matthias T. Kromann. LC 95-47840. 1995. write for info. (3-7643-3900-4) Birkhauser.

Projective Geometry & Modern Algebra. Lars Kadison & Matthias T. Kromann. LC 95-47840. 208p. 1996. 44.50 (0-8176-3900-4) Birkhauser.

Projective Geometry with Applications. Edoardo Ballico. LC 94-27247. (Lecture Notes in Pure & Applied Mathematics Ser.: Vol. 166). (Illus.). 256p. 1994. pap. text 125.00 (0-8247-9278-5) Dekker.

Projective Identification & Psychotherapeutic Technique. Thomas H. Ogden. LC 81-67124. 256p. 1982. 45.00 (0-87668-446-0) Aronson.

Projective Modules & Complete Intersections, Vol. 167. Satya Mandal. Ed. by A. Dold & F. Takens. LC 97-37176. (Lecture Notes in Mathematics Ser.: Vol. 1672). viii, 114p. 1997. pap. text 27.00 (3-540-63564-5) Spr-Verlag.

Projective Modules over Lie Algebras of Cartan Type. Daniel Ken Nakano. LC 92-12518. (Memoirs Ser.: No. 470). 84p. 1992. pap. 24.00 (0-8218-2530-5, MEMO/98/470) Am Math.

Projective Ornament. Claude Bragdon. (Illus.). 96p. 1992. reprint ed. pap. 3.95 (0-486-27117-X) Dover.

Projective Ornament (1915) Claude Bragdon. 80p. 1998. reprint ed. pap. 14.95 (0-7661-0177-0) Kessinger Pub.

Projective Planes. Frederick W. Stevenson. LC 92-7736. (Illus.). 415p. (C). 1992. reprint ed. 32.00 (0-936428-13-9) Polygonal Pub.

Projective Planes: Proceedings of the International Conference Held at Washington State University, April 25-28, 1973. International Conference on Projective Planes Staf. Ed. by M. J. Kallaher & T. G. Ostrom. LC 74-162885. 297p. reprint ed. pap. 92.10 (0-8357-8287-5, 203410300088) Bks Demand.

Projective Probability. James Logue. (Oxford Philosophical Monographs). (Illus.). 184p. 1995. text 45.00 (0-19-823959-9) OUP.

Projective Psychodiagnostic Assessment. H. Stephen Caldwell & Stacey L. Dixon. 185p. (Orig.). 1992. pap. text 12.95 (0-929240-49-9) EMIS.

Projective Relativity Cosmology & Gravitation. Giuseppe Arcidiacono. 295p. 1986. pap. text 60.00 (0-911767-39-8) Hadronic Pr Inc.

Projective Representations of the Symmetric Groups: Q-Functions & Shifted Tableaux. P. N. Hoffman & J. F. Humphreys. (Mathematical Monographs). (Illus.). 318p. 1992. text 74.00 (0-19-853556-2) OUP.

Projective Techniques. Boris Semeonoff. LC 75-37872. (Illus.). 346p. reprint ed. pap. 107.30 (0-608-17692-3, 203041200069) Bks Demand.

Projective Techniques & Cross-Cultural Research. Gardner Lindzey. LC 61-15951. (Century Psychology Ser.). 1976. reprint ed. 32.75 (0-89197-361-3); reprint ed. pap. text 12.95 (0-89197-908-5) Irvington.

Projective Techniques for Adolescents & Children. Albert I. Rabin. (Illus.). 384p. 1986. 44.95 (0-8261-4920-0) Springer Pub.

Projective Testing & Psychoanalysis. Roy Schafer. LC 67-15418. 229p. 1967. 34.50 (0-8236-4380-8) Intl Univs Pr.

Projective Use of Mother-&-Child Drawings: A Manual for Clinicians. Jacquelyn Gillespie. LC 94-11439. (Illus.). 168p. 1994. text 32.95 (0-87630-736-5) Brunner-Mazel.

Projectizing the Governance Approach to Civil Service Reform: An Environmental Assessment for Preparing a Sectoral Adjustment Loan in the Gambia. Rogerio F. Pinto. LC 94-28328. (World Discussion Papers Africa Technical Department: 252). 120p. 1994. pap. 22.00 (0-8213-2966-9) World Bank.

Projects. Brian Clarke. 1999. 49.95 (1-891475-13-4) T Shafrazi.

Projects: A Guide to Their Use & Design. Ernest J. Ingram. 180p. (Orig.). (C). 1989. pap. text 17.95 (0-920490-88-3) Temeron Bks.

Projects: Calculus: The Language of Change. 2nd ed. K. D. Stroyan. LC 98-19464. (C). 1998. pap. text 34.95 (0-12-673031-8) Acad Pr.

***Projects: Cv/Visual Arts Research - Works in Catalogue.** deluxe ed. Illus. by Philip James. (Visual Arts Research Ser.: Vol. 6). 80p. (C). 1999. pap. 24.00 (1-901161-77-3) Cv Pubns.

Projects: For the EFL Classroom. Simon Haines. 1992. pap. text. write for info. (0-17-555736-5) Addison-Wesley.

Projects & Investigations for Advanced Physics: Teacher's Guide. Jim Breithaupt. 1998. pap. 49.50 (0-7487-2954-2) St Mut.

Projects & Layouts. Libby Nelson. (J). (gr. 4-7). pap. 5.95 (0-8225-9831-0) Lerner Pub.

Projects & Layouts. Libby Nelson & Kari A. Cornell. LC 97-8482. (California Missions Ser.). (J). 1997. lib. bdg. 23.93 (0-8225-1931-3) Lerner Pub.

Projects & Monuments in the Period of the Roman Baroque. Ed. by Susan S. Munshower. LC 83-43269. (Papers in Art History: Vol. I). (Illus.). 168p. (Orig.). 1984. pap. 20.00 (0-915773-00-7) Penn St Univ Dept Art Hist.

Projects & Procedures for Serials Administration. Ed. by Diane Stine. LC 85-60593. (Current Issues in Serials Management Ser.: No. 5). 334p. 1985. 45.00 (0-87650-190-0) Pierian.

***Projects As Arenas for Renewal & Learning Processes.** Rolf A. Lundin & Christopher Midler. LC 98-26076. 29p. 1998. write for info. (0-7923-8124-6) Kluwer Academic.

***Projects as Business Constituents & Guiding Motives.** Rolf A. Lundin & Francis T. Hartman. 280p. 2000. 120.00 (0-7923-7834-2) Kluwer Academic.

Projects Assisting Older Workers in European Countries: A Review of the Findings of Eurowork Age. European Commission. LC 98-222849. (Employment & Social Affairs Ser.). 328p. 1998. write for info. (92-827-9481-4) Comm Europ Commun.

Projects at Warp Speed with QRPD: The Definitive Guidebook to Quality Rapid Product Development. 8th unabridged ed. Orion Kopelman & Cinda Voegtli. LC 99-191938. (Illus.). 480p. 1998. text 69.95 (1-885261-16-0) Global Brain.

Projects 5: Frank Majore: Dreamsville. Ileen Sheppard. Ed. by Kathleen G. Chilson. LC 90-64088. 32p. (Orig.). 1990. pap. 10.00 (0-916758-32-X) Ringling Mus Art.

Projects for a Healthy Planet: Simple Environmental Experiments for Kids. Shar Levine & Allison Grafton. LC 91-42406. (Illus.). 96p. (J). 1992. pap. 10.95 (0-471-55484-7) Wiley.

Projects for Accounting Systems. 3rd ed. Robert Harper. 114p. (C). 1998. spiral bd. 35.95 (0-7872-5419-3, 41541901) Kendall-Hunt.

Projects for Creative Woodcarving. Ian Norbury. LC 94-32689. (Illus.). 187p. 1994. reprint ed. pap. 19.95 (0-941936-30-9) Linden Pub Fresno.

Projects for Microsoft Office 2000: Professional Brief Edition. Tim Duffy. (Duffy Lab Series). 542p. (C). 1999. spiral bd. 49.00 (0-201-61202-X) Addison-Wesley.

Projects for New Technologies in Education. Norma Heller. xiv, 154p. (J). (gr. 6-9). 1994. pap. text 23.50 (1-56308-083-4) Teacher Ideas Pr.

***Projects for Office 2000 Ms Certified Edition.** (C). 2000. write for info. (0-201-69966-4) Addison-Wesley.

Projects for Office 2000, Brief Edition: Projects for Office 2000, Microsoft Certified Edition , Brief Edition. Johnson Toliver. (Select Lab Series). 572p. (C). 1999. spiral bd. 47.67 (0-201-61201-1) Addison-Wesley.

***Projects for Office 2000, Brief Edition: Projects for Office 2000, Microsoft Certified Edition , Brief Edition.** Pamela R. Toliver & Yvonne Johnson. 943p. 1999. spiral bd. 61.33 (0-201-61187-2) Addison-Wesley.

Projects for Piano Pedagogy, Vol. 1. R. Fred Kern & Marguerite Miller. 80p. 1989. pap. text 8.95 (0-8497-9340-8, WP170) Kjos.

Projects for Piano Pedagogy, Vol. 2. R. Fred Kern & Marguerite Miller. 80p. 1989. pap. text 8.95 (0-8497-9374-2, WP171) Kjos.

***Projects For Precalculus.** Andersen. (C). 1999. pap. text, student ed. 17.00 (0-03-027061-8) Harcourt Coll Pubs.

Projects for Precalculus. Hungerford. (C). 1996. pap. text 16.00 (0-03-020444-5) Harcourt.

Projects for Preschoolers: A Super Fun Collection of Games, Crafts & Guided Activities for Young Children. Suzan W. Allen & Karen H. Talbot. 72p. (Orig.). 1981. pap. 19.98 (0-88290-161-3, 2048) Horizon Utah.

Projects for Preschoolers Arts & Crafts. Judy Nayer. (Projects for Preschoolers Ser.). 48p. (J). (ps-1). 1999. mass mkt. 4.99 (0-7681-0080-1, McClanahan Book) Learn Horizon.

Projects for Preschoolers Make-Believe. Judy Nayer. (Projects for Preschoolers Ser.). 48p. (J). (ps-1). 1999. mass mkt. 4.99 (0-7681-0081-X, McClanahan Book) Learn Horizon.

Projects for Preschoolers-Nature. Judy Nayer. (Projects for Preschoolers Ser.). 48p. (J). (ps-1). 1999. mass mkt. 4.99 (0-7681-0079-8, McClanahan Book) Learn Horizon.

Projects for Preschoolers-Science. Judy Nayer. (Projects for Preschoolers Ser.). 48p. 1999. mass mkt. 4.99 (0-7681-0078-X, McClanahan Book) Learn Horizon.

Projects for the Home Craftsman. Reader's Digest Editors. (Woodworking Ser.). 264p. 1999. pap. 14.95 (0-7621-0196-2, Pub. by RD Assn) Penguin Putnam.

Projects for the Netscape Communicator 4.0: Select Lab Series Plus. Gillian Hall. LC 98-176629. 352p. (C). 1997. pap. text 39.00 (0-201-31566-1, Prentice Hall) P-H.

Projects for Windows for Beginners. Philippa Wingate. (Computer Guides Ser.). (Illus.). 48p. (YA). (gr. 5 up). 1996. lib. bdg. 17.95 (0-88110-853-7, Usborne) EDC.

Projects for Windows for Beginners. Philippa Wingate. (Computer Guides Ser.). (Illus.). 48p. (YA). (gr. 5 up). 1996. pap. 9.95 (0-7460-2337-5, Usborne) EDC.

Projects for Woodworkers. John Birchard. Ed. by Robert J. Beckstrom. LC 94-69603. (Illus.). 96p. (Orig.). 1995. pap. 9.95 (0-87921-258-6, 05994, Ortho Bks) Meredith Bks.

Projects for Woodworkers. Ortho Books Staff. (Illus.). 96p. 1995. pap. 9.95 (0-89721-258-4) Meredith Bks.

Projects in Biofeedback. George D. Fuller. (Orig.). 1980. pap. 16.95 (0-686-27974-3) Biofeed Pr.

Projects in Business Record Keeping. 6th ed. Swinney. (BA - Accounting - First Year Ser.). 1992. mass mkt. 24.95 (0-538-61239-8) S-W Pub.

Projects in Business Record Keeping No. 1: Shopping Made Easy. 6th ed. Swinney. (BA - Accounting - First Year Ser.). 1992. mass mkt. 8.95 (0-538-62376-4) S-W Pub.

Projects in Business Record Keeping No. 1: Wagon Wheel Apartments. 6th ed. Swinney. (BA - Accounting - First Year Ser.). 1992. mass mkt. 8.95 (0-538-62377-2) S-W Pub.

Projects in Business Record Keeping No. 3: The Pizza Stop. 6th ed. Swinney. (BA - Accounting - First Year Ser.). 1992. mass mkt. 8.95 (0-538-62378-0) S-W Pub.

Projects in Business Record Keeping No. 4: The Trading Post. 6th ed. Swinney. (BA - Accounting - First Year Ser.). 1992. mass mkt. 8.95 (0-538-62379-9) S-W Pub.

Projects in Business Record Keeping No. 5: Sound Sensational. 6th ed. Swinney. (BA - Accounting - First Year Ser.). 1992. mass mkt. 8.95 (0-538-62380-2) S-W Pub.

Projects in Business Record Keeping No. 6: Max's Market. 6th ed. Swinney. (BA - Accounting - First Year Ser.). 1992. mass mkt. 6.75 (0-538-62381-0) S-W Pub.

Projects in Linguistics: A Practical Guide to Researching Language. Alison Wray et al. LC 98-14557. (An Arnold Publication). (Illus.). 320p. 1998. text 65.00 (0-340-70002-5); pap. text 19.95 (0-340-65210-1) OUP.

Projects in Scientific Computation. R. Crandall. 470p. 1996. 54.95 incl. disk (3-540-97808-9) Spr-Verlag.

***Projects in Scientific Computation.** Richard Crandall. (Illus.). 496p. 2000. pap. 39.95 incl. disk (0-387-95009-5, Telos) Spr-Verlag.

Projects in Space Science. Robert Gardner. (Robert Gardner's Science Activity Bks.). (Illus.). 136p. (J). (gr. 4-8). 1988. pap. 5.95 (0-671-65993-6, Julian Messner) Silver Burdett Pr.

Projects 1: Doug & Mike Starn, The Christ Series. Joseph Jacobs. 16p. 1987. pap. 4.95 (0-916758-24-9) Ringling Mus Art.

Projects Patterns & Poems for Early Education. Marion C. Ruppert. LC 87-31202. (Illus.). 175p. (Orig.). 1989. lib. bdg. 29.95 (0-89334-226-2, 2262030) Humanics Ltd.

Projects pour un Stade Olympique Bagdad & Other Buildings & Projects 1953. Ed. by Allen H. Brooks. (Le Corbusier Archive Ser.). 1984. text 95.00 (0-8240-5076-2) Garland.

P

Projects Procured by Privately Financed Concession Contracts, Vol. 1. Asia Law & Practice Staff. 320p. 1996. pap. 225.00 (*962-7708-73-9*) Am Educ Systs.
Projects Procured by Privately Financed Concession Contracts, Vol. 2. Asia Law & Practice Staff. 280p. 1996. pap. 225.00 (*962-7708-74-7*) Am Educ Systs.
Projects Science. Vaughn-Steck Staff. (Illus.). 96p. (gr. 7-13). 1997. pap. text 9.95 (*0-8172-6345-4*) Raintree Steck-V.
Projects 6. Ed. & Intro. by Joe Rice. LC 95-74799. (Illus.). 250p. 1995. 35.00 (*0-941653-19-6*) Village Pr Pubns.
Projects That Explore Energy. Martin J. Gutnik & Natalie Browne-Gutnik. LC 93-7787. (Investigate! Ser.). (Illus.). 72p. (J). (gr. 5-8). 1994. lib. bdg. 21.40 (*1-56294-334-0*) Millbrook Pr.
Projects 2. Ed. by Joe D. Rice. 200p. 1988. 24.95 (*0-941653-03-X*) Village Pr Pubns.
Projects 2: Allan McCollum, Perfect Vehicles 1988. Joseph Jacobs. 16p. 1988. pap. 4.95 (*0-916758-25-7*) Ringling Mus Art.
Projects with People: The Practice of Participation in Rural Development. Peter Oakley et al. xv, 284p. 1991. pap. 29.25 (*92-2-107282-7*) Intl Labour Office.
Projektionen des Geschichtlichen: Ernst Jungers Arbeit an den Fassungen von in Stahlgewittern. Wojciech Kunicki. (GER.). XI, 372p. 1993. 54.80 (*3-631-45929-7*) P Lang Pubng.
Projektive Ebenen. 2nd ed. G. Pickert. LC 75-9953. (Grundlehren der Mathematischen Wissenschaften Ser.: Vol. 80). (Illus.). 371p. 1975. 108.95 (*0-387-07280-2*) Spr-Verlag.
Projektive Geometrie. 3rd ed. W. Blaschke. (Mathematische Reihe Ser.: No. 17). (Illus.). 197p. 1980. 39.00 (*0-8176-0032-9*) Birkhauser.
***Projet ACE: Des Ressources Electroniques du Projet ACE.** Ed. by Lisa Handley et al. (FRE., Illus.). 96p. 1999. pap. text. write for info. (*1-879720-38-8*) Intl Fndt Elect.
Projet de Lexique Minier Russe-Francais. Ed. by N. N. Ersov & A. N. Komarov. (FRE & RUS.). 183p. 1972. pap. 39.95 (*0-8288-6418-7*, M-6468) Fr & Eur.
Projet pour une Revolution a New York. Alain Robbe-Grillet. (FRE.). 20.50 (*0-685-37077-1*) Fr & Eur.
Prokaryotes. Evert. 1998. 1.50 (*0-7167-9358-X*) W H Freeman.
Prokaryotes. A Handbook on Habitats. Isolation, & Identification of Bacteria., 2 pts., Set. Ed. by M. P. Starr et al. (Illus.). 2624p. 1989. 550.00 (*0-387-08871-7*) Spr-Verlag.
Prokaryotes: A Handbook on the Biology of Bacteria: Ecophysiology, Isolation, Identification, Applications, 4 vols., Set. Ed. by A. Balows et al. (Illus.). clxxii, 4770p. 1991. 2635.95 (*0-387-97258-7*) Spr-Verlag.
Prokaryotes: An Evolving Electronic Resource for the Microbiological Community. 3rd ed. Ed. by M. Dworkin. 1999. 295.00 (*0-387-14254-1*) Spr-Verlag.
Prokaryotic Cells. Helms. 1997. 1.50 (*0-7167-9309-1*) W H Freeman.
***Prokaryotic Development.** Ed. by Yves V. Brun & Lawrence J. Skimkets. LC 99-44864. (Illus.). 475p. 2000. 89.95 (*1-55581-158-2*) ASM Pr.
Prokaryotic Gene Expression. Ed. by Simon Baumberg. LC 98-52907. (Frontiers in Molecular Biology Ser.). (Illus.). 346p. 1999. text 125.00 (*0-19-963604-4*) OUP.
Prokaryotic Gene Expression. Ed. by Simon Baumberg. LC 98-52907. (Frontiers in Molecular Biology Ser.: No. 21). (Illus.). 346p. 1999. pap. text 55.00 (*0-19-963603-6*) OUP.
Prokaryotic Genetics: Gene Transfer in Prokaryotes. F. Joset & J. Guespin. (Illus.). 416p. 1993. pap. 54.95 (*0-632-02728-2*) Blackwell Sci.
***Prokaryotic Nitrogen Fixation: A Model System for the Analysis of a Biological Process.** Ed. by Eric W. Triplett. 850p. 2000. 199.99 (*1-898486-19-0*, Pub. by Horizon Sci) Intl Spec Bk.
Prokaryotic Structure & Function: A New Perspective. Ed. by J. A. Cole et al. (Society for General Microbiology Symposium Ser.: No. 47). (Illus.). 452p. (C). 1992. text 125.00 (*0-521-41570-5*) Cambridge U Pr.
***Prokofiev.** Wendy Lynch. LC 99-37331. (Lives & Times Ser.). 2000. lib. bdg. write for info. (*1-57572-220-8*) Heinemann Lib.
Prokofiev. Israel V. Nestyev. Tr. by Florence Jonas from RUS. LC 60-11631. 556p. 1960. reprint ed. pap. 30.00 (*0-7837-1224-3*, 204175500023) Bks Demand.
Prokofiev: The Illustrated Lives of the Great Composers. David Gutman. (Illustrated Lives of the Great Composers Ser.). (Illus.). 144p. 1996. 17.95 (*0-7119-2083-4*, OP 45681) Omnibus NY.
Prokofiev Cinderella Suite see Classical Connections: Complete Program
Prokop Divorce Adjustment Inventory: Divorce Test for Children. M. S. Prokop. 1986. audio 10.40 (*0-933879-30-X*) Alegra Hse Pubs.
Prokoviev. Claude Samuel. Tr. by Miriam John from FRE. LC 97-47310. (Illus.). 192p. 1998. reprint ed. pap. 15.00 (*0-7145-0490-4*) M Boyars Pubs.
Prolactin & Prolactinomas. Ed. by George Tolis et al. LC 83-8657. (Illus.). 504p. 1983. reprint ed. pap. 156.30 (*0-7837-9537-8*, 206028600005) Bks Demand.
Prolactin Lesions in Breasts, Uterus, Prostate. Ed. by Hiroshi Nagasawa. 272p. 1988. 138.00 (*0-8493-6836-7*, RC280, CRC Reprint) Franklin.
Prolactinomas. Ed. by Jerrold M. Olefsky & Richard J. Robbins. (Contemporary Issues in Endocrinology & Metabolism Ser.: Vol. 2). (Illus.). 230p. 1985. text 42.00 (*0-443-08406-8*) Church.
Prolactinomas: An Interdiciplinary Approach. Ed. by L. M. Auer et al. (Illus.). x, 439p. 1985. 134.65 (*3-11-010153-X*) De Gruyter.
Prolego-mena to In Memoriam. Thomas Davidson. (Notable American Authors Ser.). 1992. reprint ed. lib. bdg. 75.00 (*0-7812-2619-8*) Rprt Serv.
Prolegomena. Ed. by Joachim Latacz. (GRE.). 100p. 1998. pap. 19.95 (*3-519-04300-9*, T4300, Pub. by B G Teubner) U of Mich Pr.
Prolegomena: Questions to Be Settled before the Study of an Author or a Text. Jaap Mansfeld. LC 94-16216. (Philosophia Antiqua Ser.: Vol. 61). vii, 246p. 1994. 75.00 (*90-04-10084-9*) Brill Academic Pubs.
Prolegomena: The Relation of Theology to Modern Thought-Forms. Helmut Thielicke. (Evangelical Faith Ser.: Vol. 1). 420p. 1997. pap. text 30.00 (*1-57312-161-4*) Smyth & Helwys.
Prolegomena Vol. I(A), Fascicle 1: Text with Critical Apparatus & Translation. Tr. by Joachim Latacz. (GRE.). 70p. 1998. pap. 15.95 (*3-519-04301-7*, T4301, Pub. by B G Teubner) U of Mich Pr.
Prolegomena Ad Homerum. Friedrich A. Wolf. viii, 307p. 1963. reprint ed. write for info. (*0-318-71063-3*) G Olms Pubs.
Prolegomena & Prehistory. (Cambridge Ancient History Ser.: Vol. 1, Pt. 1). 780p. 1971. text 135.00 (*0-521-07051-1*) Cambridge U Pr.
Prolegomena Critica. Virgil. (GER.). xxxiii, 467p. write for info. (*0-318-70513-3*) G Olms Pubs.
Prolegomena Critica. Virgil. Ed. by Otto Ribbeck. xxxiii, 467p. write for info. (*0-318-71242-3*) G Olms Pubs.
Prolegomena Mathematica: From Apollonius of Perga to Late Neoplatonism: With an Appendix on Pappus & the History of Platonism. Jaap Mansfeld. LC 98-38382. (Philosphia Antiqua). viii, 182p. 1998. 68.00 (*90-04-11267-7*) Brill Academic Pubs.
***Prolegomena to a Christian Theology of Religions.** Heung-Gyu Kim. 224p. 2000. 42.50 (*0-7618-1702-6*) U Pr of Amer.
Prolegomena to a Critical Grammar. Jacquelyn Schachter. Tr. & Frwd. by Paul Foulkes. LC 72-77879. (Vienna Circle Collection: Vol. 2). Orig. Title: Prolegomena Zu Einer Kritischen Grammatik. 186p. 1973. pap. text 59.00 (*90-277-0301-9*, D Reidel); lib. bdg. 80.00 (*90-277-0296-9*, D Reidel) Kluwer Academic.
Prolegomena to a Middlebrow Arithmetic of Curves of Genus 2. J. W. Cassels & V. Flynn. (London Mathematical Society Lecture Note Ser.: No. 230). (Illus.). 232p. (C). 1996. pap. text 42.95 (*0-521-48370-0*) Cambridge U Pr.
Prolegomena to a New Text of Lucian's Vitarum Auctio & Piscator. Joel B. Itzkowitz. (Spudasmata Ser.: Vol. XXXVIII). (GER.). xi, 465p. 1986. 57.20 (*3-487-07785-X*) G Olms Pubs.
Prolegomena to a Nineteen Eighty-Five Philosophiae Naturalis Principia Mathematica. F. S. Northrop. LC 84-27350. xvi, 73p. 1986. 30.00 (*0-918024-35-8*) Ox Bow.
Prolegomena to a Theory of Language. rev. ed. Louis Hjelmslev. Tr. by Francis J. Whitfield. LC 62-7095. 152p. reprint ed. pap. 47.20 (*0-8357-4749-2*, 203767100009) Bks Demand.
Prolegomena to a Theory of Practical Reasoning. Robert J. Richman. 208p. 1983. text 121.50 (*90-277-1548-3*, D Reidel) Kluwer Academic.
Prolegomena to All Future Metaeconomics: Formation & Deformation of Economic Thought. Paul K. Crosser. LC 72-13845. (Illus.). 240p. 1974. 10.00 (*0-87527-099-9*) Green.
Prolegomena to Any Future: A Liberal Arts Novel. Mark A. Fenton. 147p. (Orig.). 1986. pap. 5.00 (*0-9616217-0-2*) M A Fenton.
Prolegomena to Any Future Historiography of Cultures & Civilizations: Historiography of Cultures & Civilizations. Daya Krishna. (C). 1997. 26.50 (*81-215-0764-2*, Pub. by M Manoharial) Coronet Bks.
Prolegomena to Any Future Metaphysics: Kant. Carcus Mahaffy & Lewis W. Beck. (C). 1950. pap. text 8.60 (*0-02-319330-1*, Pub. by P-H) S&S Trade.
Prolegomena to Any Future Metaphysics That Will Be Able to Come Forward As Science. Immanuel Kant. Ed. by James W. Ellington. Tr. by Paul Carus from GER. LC 76-51051. (HPC Classics Ser.). 154p. (C). 1977. 24.95 (*0-915144-33-6*); pap. 6.95 (*0-915144-25-5*) Hackett Pub.
Prolegomena to Ethics. Thomas Hill Green. 1986. reprint ed. pap. 31.95 (*0-935005-58-7*); reprint ed. lib. bdg. 47.95 (*0-935005-57-9*) Lincoln-Rembrandt.
Prolegomena to Formal Logic. B. H. Slater. (Avebury Series in Philosophy). 300p. 1988. text 82.95 (*0-566-05693-3*, Pub. by Avebry) Ashgate Pub Co.
Prolegomena to History: The Relation of History to Literature, Philosophy, & Science, Vol. 4. Frederick J. Teggart. LC 73-14184. (Perspectives in Social Inquiry Ser.). 142p. 1974. reprint ed. 11.95 (*0-405-05528-5*) Ayer.
Prolegomena to Homer, 1795. Friedrich A. Wolf. Tr. by Anthony Grafton et al. LC 84-42907. 280p. 1985. reprint ed. pap. 86.80 (*0-608-02739-1*, 206340400004) Bks Demand.
Prolegomena to Inferential Discourse Processing. Roger G. Van de Velde. LC 84-24476. (Pragmatics & Beyond Ser.: Vol. 5:2). vii, 100p. 1985. pap. 35.00 (*0-915027-40-2*) J Benjamins Pubng Co.
Prolegomena to Library Classification, Vol. I. S. R. Ranganathan. 640p. 1990. reprint ed. pap. 30.00 (*81-85273-16-2*, Pub. by Sarada Ranganathan Endowment for Library Science) Advent Bks Div.
Prolegomena to Relativity Economics. Ralph W. Souter. LC 68-58623. (Columbia University. Studies in the Social Sciences: No. 391). reprint ed. 29.50 (*0-404-51391-3*) AMS Pr.
Prolegomena to Religious Pluralism: Reference & Realism. Peter Byrne. LC 95-10839. 265p. 1995. text 69.95 (*0-312-12843-6*) St Martin.
Prolegomena to the History of Israel. Julius Wellhausen. LC 93-40279. (Reprints & Translations Ser.). 567p. 1994. reprint ed. pap. 44.95 (*1-55540-938-5*, 000717) Duke.
Prolegomena to the Law of War & Peace. Hugo Grotius. Tr. by Francis W. Kelsey. 1957. pap. 2.80 (*0-672-60240-7*, LLA65, Bobbs) Macmillan.
Prolegomena to the Metaphysics of Islam. Syed Muhammad Naquib al-Attas. 358p. (C). 1997. text 42.00 (*0-934905-86-X*, Library of Islam) Kazi Pubns.
Prolegomena to the Psychological Study of Religion. Benjamin Beit-Hallahmi. LC 88-48020. 128p. 1989. 28.50 (*0-8387-5159-8*) Bucknell U Pr.
Prolegomena to the Qur'an. Tr. by Abdulaziz Sachedina. LC 97-7034. 288p. 1998. text 65.00 (*0-19-511675-5*) OUP.
Prolegomena to the Sources on the History of Pre-Islamic... J. Harmatta. 1979. pap. 148.00 (*963-05-1651-9*, Pub. by Akade Kiado) St Mut.
Prolegomena to the Study of Greek Religion. Jane E. Harrison. (Mythos: The Princeton - Bollingen Series in World Mythology). (Illus.). 704p. 1991. pap. text 22.95 (*0-691-01514-7*, Pub. by Princeton U Pr) Cal Prin Full Svc.
Prolegomena to the Study of Greek Religion. Jane E. Harrison. LC 75-10639. (Ancient Religion & Mythology Ser.). (Illus.). 1979. reprint ed. 49.95 (*0-405-07018-7*) Ayer.
Prolegomena to the Study of the Later Irish Bards, 1200-1500. E. C. Quiggin. (Studies in Irish Literature). 1970. reprint ed. pap. 19.95 (*0-8383-0064-2*) M S G Haskell Hse.
Prolegomena Zu Einer Kritischen Grammatik see Prolegomena to a Critical Grammar
Prolegomena zur Altesten Geschichte des Islam: Verschiedenes (Unveraenderter Photomechanischer Nachdruck der 1. Auflage 1899) Julius Wellhausen. (Skizzen und Vorarbeiten Ser.: 6 Heft). (GER.). viii, 260p. 1985. 93.85 (*3-11-002215-X*) De Gruyter.
Prolegomena Zur Bestimmung des Gottesbegriffes Bei Kant. Kumetaro Sasao. (Abhandlungen Zur Philosophie und Ihrer Geschichte Ser.: Bd. 13). (GER.). 71p. 1980. reprint ed. write for info. (*3-487-06775-7*) G Olms Pubs.
Prolegomenes D'ebn-Khaldoun, 3 vols., Set. M. Quatremere. (ARA.). 105.00 (*0-86685-165-8*) Intl Bk Ctr.
Proleptic Priests: Priesthood in the Epistle to the Hebrews. John M. Scholer. (JSNT Supplement Ser.: Vol. 49). 243p. 1991. 70.00 (*1-85075-266-4*, Pub. by Sheffield Acad) CUP Services.
Proletarian Journey: New England, Gastonia, Moscow. Fred E. Beal. LC 73-179505. (Select Bibliographies Reprint Ser.). 1977. reprint ed. 26.95 (*0-8369-6634-1*) Ayer.
Proletarian Moment: The Controversy over Leftism in Literature. James F. Murphy. 240p. 1991. text 27.50 (*0-252-01788-9*) U of Ill Pr.
Proletarian Performance in Weimar Berlin: Agitprop, Chorus, & Brecht. Richard Bodek. LC 97-15691. (GERM Ser.). 210p. 1998. 55.00 (*1-57113-126-4*) Camden Hse.
Proletarian Philosophers: Problems in Socialist Culture in Britain, 1900-1940. Jonathan Ree. (Illus.). 182p. (C). 1984. text 39.95 (*0-19-827261-8*) OUP.
Proletarian Power: Shanghai in the Cultural Revolution. Elizabeth Perry & Xun Li. LC 96-42940. (Transitions: Asia & Asian America Ser.). (C). 1996. pap. 25.00 (*0-8133-2165-4*, Pub. by Westview) HarpC.
Proletarian Science: Marxism in Britain, 1917-1933. Stuart MacIntyre. (C). 1986. pap. 22.50 (*0-85315-667-0*, Pub. by Lawrence & Wishart) NYU Pr.
Proletarian Tales. Wayne Pounds. (Illus.). 59p. (Orig.). 1987. 10.95 (*0-941720-50-0*); pap. 4.95 (*0-941720-51-9*) Slough Pr TX.
Proletarians & African Capitalism: The Kenyan Case, 1960-1972. Richard Sandbrook. LC 73-91818. (Perspectives on Development Ser.: Vol. 4). 232p. reprint ed. pap. 66.20 (*0-608-12202-5*, 2024545) Bks Demand.
Proletarians & Politics: Socialism, Protest, & the Working Class in Germany Before the First World War. Richard J. Evans. LC 90-46985. 208p. 1991. text 55.00 (*0-312-05652-4*) St Martin.
Proletarians & Protest: The Roots of Class Formation in an Industrializing World, 17. Ed. by Michael Hanagan & Charles Stephenson. LC 85-5596. (Contributions in Labor Studies: No. 17). (Illus.). 263p. 1986. 65.00 (*0-313-23217-2*, STI/) Greenwood.
Proletarians of the North: Mexican Industrial Workers in Detroit in the Midwest, 1917-1933. Zaragosa Vargas. LC 92-9122. (Latinos in American Society & Culture Ser.). 299p. 1993. 45.00 (*0-520-07156-5*, Pub. by U CA Pr) Cal Prin Full Svc.
***Proletarians of the North: Mexican Industrial Workers in Detroit in the Midwest, 1917-1933.** Zaragosa Vargas. 299p. 1999. pap. 18.95 (*0-520-21962-7*, Pub. by U CA Pr) Cal Prin Full Svc.
Proletariat: A Challange to Western Civilization. Goetz A. Briefs. LC 74-25742. (European Sociology Ser.). 320p. 1975. reprint ed. 26.95 (*0-405-06498-5*) Ayer.
Proletariat of the World Unite! . . . So We United! 1989, a Year to Remember. Nikolai Cvetkov. (Illus.). 38p. (Orig.). 1990. pap. 12.95 (*0-945490-01-1*) Carolina Pacific.
Proletariato e la Borghesia Nel Movimento Socialista Italiano: Saggio Di Scienza Sociografico-Politica: Proletariat & Bourgeoisie Within the Socialist Movement: a Sociographic Political Essay. Robert Michels. LC 74-25769. (European Sociology Ser.). 404p. 1975. reprint ed. 33.95 (*0-405-06523-X*) Ayer.
Proleterianizing of the Fonctionnaires: Civil Service Workers & the Labor Movement under the Third Republic. Judith Wishnia. LC 90-6064. 408p. reprint ed. pap. 126.50 (*0-608-09816-7*, 206998400007) Bks Demand.
***Prolife Answers to Pro-Choice Arguments.** Randy Alcorn. 2000. pap. 10.99 (*1-57673-751-9*) Multnomah Pubs.
Prolife Answers to Prochoice Arguments. Randy Alcorn. Ed. by Rod Morris. LC 92-15392. 294p. 1992. pap. 10.99 (*0-88070-472-1*, Multnomah Bks) Multnomah Pubs.
Prolife Feminism: Yesterday & Today. Rachel MacNair et al. 380p. (Orig.). 1995. pap. 14.99 (*0-945819-62-5*) Sulzburger & Graham Pub.
Proliferated Autonomous Weapons: An Example of Cooperative Behavior. David Frelinger et al. LC 98-215967. (Illus.). 92p. 1998. pap. text 6.00 (*0-8330-2625-9*, DB-239-AF) Rand Corp.
Proliferating Talent: Essays on Politics, Thought, & Education in the Meiji Era. Yukihiko Motoyama. Ed. by J. S. Elisonas & Richard Rubinger. LC 97-779. 440p. 1997. text 48.00 (*0-8248-1846-6*) UH Pr.
Proliferation: Threat & Response. 88p. 1997. pap. 10.00 (*0-16-042727-4*) USGPO.
Proliferation: Threat & Response. William J. Perry. (Illus.). 63p. 1997. pap. text 25.00 (*0-7881-4219-4*) DIANE Pub.
Proliferation: Threat & Response. United States. LC 96-146464. vi, 63p. 1996. write for info. (*0-16-048591-6*) USGPO.
Proliferation & Export Controls. Ed. by Kathleen Bailey & Robert Rudney. LC 92-23886. 138p. (Orig.). (C). 1992. pap. text 18.50 (*0-8191-8720-8*); lib. bdg. 44.00 (*0-8191-8719-4*) U Pr of Amer.
Proliferation & U.S. Export Controls: Hearing Before the Subcommittee on International Security, Proliferation & Federal Services of the Committee on Governmental Affairs, United States Senate, One Hundred Fifth Congress, First Session, June 11, 1997. United States Government. LC 98-139342. (S. Hrg. Ser.). iii, 53 p. 1997. write for info. (*0-16-055864-6*) USGPO.
Proliferation Concerns: Assessing U.S. Efforts to Help Contain Nuclear & Other Dangerous Materials & Technologies in the Former Soviet Union. National Research Council Staff. 160p. (Orig.). 1997. pap. 36.00 (*0-309-05741-8*, Joseph Henry Pr) Natl Acad Pr.
Proliferation of Land-Based Technologies: Implications for Local Military Balances. Steven J. Rosen. (CISA Working Papers: No. 12). 35p. (Orig.). 1978. pap. 15.00 (*0-86682-011-6*) Ctr Intl Relations.
Proliferation of Rights: Moral Progress or Empty Rhetoric? Carl Wellman. LC 98-28117. 200p. 1998. pap. text 24.00 (*0-8133-2821-7*, Pub. by Westview) HarpC.
***Proliferation of Rights: Moral Progress or Empty Rhetoric?** Carl Wellman. LC 98-28117. 200p. 1998. text 65.00 (*0-8133-2820-9*, Pub. by Westview) HarpC.
Proliferation of Weapons for Mass Destruction & Cooperation on Defence System. K. Goebel. (Science & Culture Ser.). 316p. 1993. text 109.00 (*981-02-1493-6*) World Scientific Pub.
Proliferation of Weapons of Mass Destruction: Assessing the Risks. 1994. lib. bdg. 250.00 (*0-8490-8557-8*) Gordon Pr.
Proliferation, Politics, & the IAEA: The Issue of Nuclear Safeguards. Ed. by Aspen Institute Staff. 42p. (Orig.). 1985. pap. text 10.50 (*0-8191-5849-6*) U Pr of Amer.
Proliferation Puzzle: Why Nuclear Weapons Spread & What Results. Ed. by Zachary S. Davis & Benjamin Frankel. LC 93-28873. (Illus.). 357p. (C). 1994. pap. text 32.50 (*0-7146-4108-1*, Pub. by F Cass Pubs) Intl Spec Bk.
Proliferation Russian Case Studies: Hearing Before the Subcommittee on International Security, Proliferation & Federal Services of the Committee on Governmental Affairs, United States Senate, One Hundred Fifth Congress, First Session, June 5, 1997. United States Government. LC 98-139070. (S. Hrg. Ser.). iii, 47 p. 1997. write for info. (*0-16-055868-9*) USGPO.
Proliferation, Theater Missile Defense, & U. S. Security. LC 93-49046. 1994. 8.95 (*0-89549-103-6*) Inst Foreign Policy Anal.
Proliferative Vitreoretinopathy - Epidemiology of Glaucoma. Ed. by W. Straub. (Developments in Ophthalmology Ser.: Vol. 16). (Illus.). viii, 118p. 1989. 99.25 (*3-8055-4853-2*) S Karger.
Proliferative Vitreoretinopathy (PVR) Ed. by H. M. Freeman & F. I. Tolentio. (Illus.). 225p. 1988. 140.00 (*0-387-96806-7*) Spr-Verlag.
Prolific & the Devourer. W. H. Auden. LC 93-2409. 1993. 18.00 (*0-88001-345-1*) HarpC.
Prolific And The Devourer. W. H. Auden. (Illus.). 101p. 1996. reprint ed. pap. 11.00 (*0-88001-465-2*) HarpC.
Prolific Knitting Machine. Catherine Cartwright-Jones. LC 90-4592. (Illus.). 208p. (Orig.). 1990. pap. 17.95 (*0-934026-58-0*) Interweave.
Prolific Pencil. Percy F. Rex. Ed. by Fredrika A. Burrows & Stephen W. Sullwold. LC 80-51482. (Illus.). 312p. 1980. 15.00 (*0-88492-037-2*) W S Sullwold.
***Prolific Poisoner: An Heimdal Nacht Mystery.** Gary J. Gunning. LC 99-91199. 1999. 25.00 (*0-7388-0662-5*); pap. 18.00 (*0-7388-0663-3*) Xlibris Corp.
Prolific Sheep. Ed. by M. H. Fahmy. (A CAB International Publication). (Illus.). 560p. 1996. text 130.00 (*0-85198-983-7*) OUP.
Prolific Survivors: Population Change in Cambodia, 1975-1993. Jacqueline Desbarats. LC 98-127600. (Illus.). 250p. (Orig.). 1995. pap. text 19.95 (*1-881044-13-0*) ASU Prog SE Asian.

An Asterisk (*) at the beginning of an entry indicates that the title is appearing for the first time.

Prolo Your Arthritis Pain Away! Curing Disabling & Disfiguring Arthritis Pain with Prolotherapy. Ross A. Hauser & Marion A. Hauser. (Illus.). 200p. 2000. pap. 19.95 (*0-9661010-5-7*, Pub. by Mann Daniel) BookWorld.

Prolo Your Back Pain Away! Curing Chronic Lower Back Pain with Prolo Therapy. Ross A. Hauser & Marion A. Hauser. (Illus.). 200p. 2000. pap. 19.95 (*0-9661010-2-2*, Pub. by Mann Daniel) BookWorld.

Prolo Your Fibromyalgia Pain Away! Curing the Disabling Pain of Fibromyalgia with Prolotherapy. Ross A. Hauser & Marion A. Hauser. (Illus.). 128p. 2000. pap. 19.95 (*0-9661010-4-9*, Pub. by Mann Daniel) BookWorld.

Prolo Your Headaches & Neck Pain Away! Curing Migraines & Chronic Neck Pain with Prolotherapy. Ross A. Hauser & Marion A. Hauser. (Illus.). 128p. 2000. pap. 19.95 (*0-9661010-3-0*, Pub. by Mann Daniel) BookWorld.

Prolo Your Pain Away: Curing Chronic Pain with Prolotherapy. Ross A. Hauser et al. LC 99-166478. (Illus.). 252p. (Orig.). 1997. pap. 24.95 (*0-9661010-0-6*) Mann Daniel.

Prolo Your Sports Injuries Away! Curing Sports Injuries & Enhancing Athletic Performance with Prolotherapy. Ross A. Hauser & Marion A. Hauser. (Illus.). 800p. 2001. 99.00 (*0-9661010-1-4*, Pub. by Mann Daniel) BookWorld.

Prolog. Francis Giannesini. (ICSS Ser.). 320p. (C). 1986. text 27.95 (*0-201-12911-6*) Addison-Wesley.

PROLOG: A Logical Approach. Anthony Dodd. (Illus.). 568p. 1990. pap. 39.95 (*0-19-853821-9*) OUP.

Prolog: Sophisticated Applications in Artificial Intelligence. Ramachandran Bharath. (Illus.). 220p. 1989. pap. 17.95 (*0-8306-9392-0*, 3092) McGraw-Hill Prof.

Prolog: The Standard: Reference Manual. Pierre Deransart et al. LC 96-15173. 300p. 1996. pap. text 44.95 (*3-540-59304-7*) Spr-Verlag.

PROLOG & Databases: Implementation & New Directions. Peter Gray et al. 312p. 1988. text 52.95 (*0-470-21221-7*) P-H.

Prolog & Expert Systems. Kenneth Bowen. 448p. (C). 1991. pap. 54.69 (*0-07-006731-7*) McGraw.

Prolog & Its Applications. Fumio Mizoguchi. (C). 1990. mass mkt. 67.50 (*0-412-37770-5*) Chapman & Hall.

Prolog & Natural Language Analysis. Fernando C. Pereira & Stuart M. Shieber. LC 87-70774. (Center for the Study of Language & Information-Lecture Notes Ser.: No. 10). 268p. (Orig.). 1987. 39.95 (*0-937073-17-2*); pap. 18.95 (*0-937073-18-0*) CSLI.

Prolog for Computer Science. C. M. Dawe. 189p. 1994. 29.00 (*0-387-19811-3*) Spr-Verlag.

Prolog for Natural Language Processing. Patrick Saint-Dizier et al. 320p. 1991. pap. 125.00 (*0-471-93012-1*) Wiley.

Prolog Multiprocessors. Michael Wise. (Illus.). 160p. 1987. text 34.00 (*0-13-730755-1*) P-H.

Prolog Primer. Jean B. Rogers. LC 85-22846. 214p. (C). 1986. pap. text 23.75 (*0-201-06467-7*) Addison-Wesley.

PROLOG Programming for Artificial Intelligence. Ivan Bratko. 272p. (C). 1986. pap. text 29.25 (*0-201-14224-4*) Addison-Wesley.

Prolog Programming for Artificial Intelligence. 2nd ed. Ivan Bratko. 597p. (C). 1990. pap. text 42.19 (*0-201-41606-9*) Addison-Wesley.

Prolog Programming for Students. D. H. Callear. 256p. 1994. pap. 59.95 (*1-85805-093-6*, Pub. by DP Publns) St Mut.

Prolog Programming in Depth. Michael A. Covington & Donald Nute. LC 96-1642. 516p. (C). 1996. pap. 36.80 (*0-13-138645-X*) P-H.

Prolog Programming in Depth. Michael A. Covington et al. LC 96-1642. 1997. write for info. (*0-614-12747-5*) P-H.

Prolog Spanish. (SPA.). (C). 1989. text 15.33 (*0-201-64409-6*) Addison-Wesley.

PROLOG User's Handbook: A Library of Utility Programs. Filipi & Bogdan. 1988. text 41.95 (*0-470-21297-7*) P-H.

Prolog vs. You. A. L. Johansson et al. (Illus.). x, 297p. 1989. 42.95 (*0-387-17577-6*) Spr-Verlag.

Prologos. unabridged ed. Jonathan Bayliss. LC 98-74560. (Gloucesterman Ser.). 1091p. 1999. pap. 24.95 (*0-9667807-0-1*) Basilicum Pr.

Prologue see Filipinos Fight for Freedom

Prologue: A Drama of John Hus. Bob Jones, Jr. (Illus.). 85p. 1968. pap. 5.95 (*0-89084-195-0*, 020701) Bob Jones Univ.

Prologue: A Novel for the 1860s. Nikolai G. Chernyshevsky. Tr. & Intro. by Michael R. Katz. LC 95-18082. (Studies in Russian Literature & Theory). (RUS.). 416p. 1995. text 59.95 (*0-8101-1180-2*); pap. text 19.95 (*0-8101-1165-9*) Northwestern U Pr.

Prologue: The Novels of Black American Women, 1891-1965, 79. Carole M. Watson. LC 84-21265. (Contributions in American Studies: No. 79). (Illus.). 168p. 1985. 45.00 (*0-313-23630-5*, WPG/, Greenwood Pr) Greenwood.

Prologue & Epilogues of William Caxton. William Caxton. Ed. by W. J. Crotch. (EETS, OS Ser.: No. 176). 1974. reprint ed. 45.00 (*0-527-00173-2*) Periodicals Srv.

Prologue & Gospel: The Theology of the Fourth Evangelist. Elizabeth Harris. LC 95-109958. (JSNT Supplement Ser.: No. 107). 224p. 1994. 65.00 (*1-85075-504-3*, Pub. by Sheffield Acad) CUP Services.

Prologue & Performances. Morris Morrison. 32p. 1972. write for info. (*0-318-64130-5*) Poets Pr.

Prologue in the Old French & Provencal Mystery. David H. Carnahan. LC 68-55160. (Studies in French Literature: No. 45). 1969. reprint ed. lib. bdg. 75.00 (*0-8383-0519-9*) M S G Haskell Hse.

Prologue of the Gospel of St. John: Esoteric Studies. E. C. Marion-Wild. Tr. by Helga Roboz & Steven Roboz from GER. 19p. 1984. pap. 3.75 (*0-919924-22-0*) Anthroposophic.

Prologue to "Ask the Dust" limited ed. John Fante. (Illus.). 36p. 1990. 1500.00 (*0-942067-02-9*) Okeanos Pr.

Prologue to Manifest Destiny: Anglo-American Relations in the 1840s. Ed. by Howard Jones & Donald A. Rakestraw. LC 96-42450. (Illus.). 358p. 1997. pap. 18.95 (*0-8420-2498-0*, SR Bks); text 50.00 (*0-8420-2488-3*, SR Bks) Scholarly Res Inc.

Prologue to National Development Planning, 70. Jamshid Gharajedaghi. LC 86-9921. (Contributions in Economics & Economic History Ser.: No. 70). 223p. 1986. 55.00 (*0-313-25285-8*, GPG/, Greenwood Pr) Greenwood.

Prologue to Performance: Spanish Classical Theater Today. Ed. by Louise Fothergill-Payne & Peter Fothergill-Payne. LC 90-55886. 168p. 1992. 32.50 (*0-8387-5206-3*) Bucknell U Pr.

Prologue to Revolution: Cuba, 1898-1958. Jorge Ibarra. LC 97-49324. (Studies in Cuban History). 235p. 1998. pap. 18.95 (*1-55587-792-3*); lib. bdg. 48.00 (*1-55587-791-5*) L Rienner.

Prologue to Revolution: The Political Career of George Grenville, 1712-1770. Allen S. Johnson. LC 96-44589. 366p. 1997. 49.50 (*0-7618-0600-8*) U Pr of Amer.

Prologue to the Canterbury Tales of Chaucer. E. F. Willoughby. 1972. 59.95 (*0-8490-0898-0*) Gordon Pr.

Prologue to the Chinese Revolution: The Transformation of Ideas & Institutions in Hunan Province, 1891-1907. Charlton M. Lewis. (East Asian Monographs: No. 70). 216p. 1976. 21.00 (*0-674-71441-5*) HUP.

Prologues & Epilogues of John Dryden. William B. Gardner & John Dryden. 381p. reprint ed. 15.00 (*0-911858-14-8*) Appel.

Prolongation of Life: Optimistic Studies. Elie Metchnikoff. Ed. by Robert J. Kastenbaum. Tr. by P. Chalmers Mitchell. LC 76-19583. (Death & Dying Ser.). (Illus.). 1977. reprint ed. lib. bdg. 34.95 (*0-405-09579-1*) Ayer.

Prolonged Connections: The Rise of the Extended Family in Nineteenth-Century England & America. Steven Ruggles. LC 87-6079. (Social Demography Ser.). 303p. reprint ed. pap. 94.00 (*0-608-20473-0*, 207172500002) Bks Demand.

Prolonged Echoes Vol. 1: Old Norse Myths in Medieval Northern Society: The Myths. Margaret C. Ross. 325p. 1994. 37.00 (*87-7838-008-1*, Pub. by Odense Univ) Intl Spec Bk.

***Prolonged Echoes Vol. 2: Old Norse Myths in Medieval Northern Society: The Reception of Norse Myths in Medieval Island.** Margaret C. Ross. 222p. 1998. 32.00 (*87-7838-332-3*, Pub. by Odense Univ) Intl Spec Bk.

Prolonged Wars: A Post-Nuclear Challenge. Karl P. Magyar. Ed. by Constantine P. Danopo. LC 94-32131. 475p. pap. 27.00 (*1-58566-056-6*) Air Univ.

Prolucid Dreaming. Akhter Ahsen. 312p. (C). 1992. pap. text 25.00 (*0-913412-43-0*) Brandon Hse.

Prolyl Hydroxylase, Protein Disulfide Isomerase, & Other Structurally Related Proteins. Norberto A. Guzman. LC 97-24479. (Illus.). 544p. 1997. text 185.00 (*0-8247-9831-7*) Dekker.

Prom. Nicholas Pine. (Terror Academy Ser.: No. 9). 192p. (Orig.). (YA). 1994. mass mkt. 3.99 (*0-425-14153-5*) Berkley Pub.

Prom: Short Vowel II Sequence. Ellis Richardson & Barbara DiBenedetto. (Read Aloud Ser.: Bk. 11). 32p. (Orig.). 1991. pap. text 4.00 (*1-56775-028-1*, SVIIS11-6) ISM Teach Systs.

Prom Date. Diane Hoh. 274p. (J). (gr. 6-10). 1996. pap. text 3.99 (*0-590-54429-2*) Scholastic Inc.

Prom Date. R. L. Stine, pseud. (Fear Street Seniors Ser.: No. 11). 176p. (YA). (gr. 8-12). 1999. pap. 3.99 (*0-307-24715-5*) Gldn Bks Pub Co.

Prom Dress. Lael J. Littke. 176p. (YA). (gr. 7-9). 1989. pap. 3.50 (*0-590-44237-6*) Scholastic Inc.

Prom Night. Jesse Osburn. 160p. (Orig.). 1995. mass mkt. 3.99 (*0-380-77318-X*, Avon Bks) Morrow Avon.

Prom Night. Fred Saberhagen et al. Ed. by Nancy Springer. 320p. 1999. mass mkt. 6.99 (*0-88677-840-9*, Pub. by DAW Bks) Penguin Putnam.

***Prom Night: Youth & Popular Culture.** Amy Best. 2000. pap. 19.99 (*0-415-92428-6*) Routledge.

***Prom Night: Youth Schools & Popular Culture.** Amy Best. 224p. 2000. text 75.00 (*0-415-92427-8*) Routledge.

Prom Nite: How the Local Photographer Can Compete. Michael R. Santomenna. (Illus.). 30p. 1996. 15.95 (*0-9643407-1-2*, 11560) WindSpirit.

Prom Queen. R. L. Stine, pseud. (Fear Street Ser.: No. 11). 176p. (YA). (gr. 7 up). 1992. mass mkt. 3.99 (*0-671-72485-1*, Archway) PB.

Prom Queen. R. L. Stine, pseud. (Fear Street Ser.: No. 11). (YA). (gr. 7 up). 1992. 9.09 (*0-606-02008-X*, Pub. by Turtleback) Demco.

Prom Time. Bobbi J. G. Weiss & David Cody Weiss. (Sabrina, the Teenage Witch Ser.: No. 21). 176p. (YA). (gr. 7-12). 1999. mass mkt. 4.50 (*0-671-02816-2*, Archway) PB.

***Pro/Manufacturing Tutor (Release 2000i)** 3rd ed. Paul E. Funk & Loren Begley, Jr. (Illus.). 98p. 1999. pap. 39.95 (*1-58503-014-7*, SDC Pubns) Schroff Dev Corp.

***Pro/Mechanica Tutorial Structure (Release 2000i) A Click-by-Click Primer.** 3rd ed. Roger Toogood. (Illus.). 283p. (C). 1999. pap. 49.95 (*1-58503-015-5*, SDC Pubns) Schroff Dev Corp.

Promenade: A Voyeur's Guide to America. Art Hazelwood. LC 94-149615. (Illus.). 30p. 1994. pap. 12.95 (*0-9640208-2-3*) Epigone Pr.

Promenade & Other Plays. Maria I. Fornes. 1987. pap. 13.95 (*1-55554-014-7*) PAJ Pubns.

Promenade Home: Macrobiotics & Women's Health. Gale Jack & Alex Jack. LC 87-82910. (Illus.). 240p. 1988. 18.95 (*0-87040-697-3*) Japan Pubns USA.

Promenades a Cambridge. Frank A. Reeve. (Cambridge Town, Gown & County Ser.: Vol. 26). (FRE., Illus.). 1978. pap. 4.95 (*0-900891-43-2*) Oleander Pr.

Promenades dans Rome, 3 vols. Stendhal, pseud. 150.00 (*0-686-55078-1*) Fr & Eur.

Promenades dans Rome, 3 vols. Stendhal, pseud. Ed. by Ernest Abravanel & Victor Del Litto. (Illus.). 9.95 (*0-685-73324-6*) Fr & Eur.

Promenades dans Rome, 3 tomes, Set. Stendhal, pseud. 47.90 (*0-685-35015-0*) Fr & Eur.

Promenades et Souvenirs see Oeuvres

Promenades et Souvenirs. Gerard Enerval. Ed. by Lemaitre. (Class. Garnier Ser.). pap. write for info. Schoenhof.

Promenades of an Impressionist. James G. Huneker. LC 73-134097. (Essay Index Reprint Ser.). 1977. 26.95 (*0-8369-1959-9*) Ayer.

Promenades 1. G. McConnell. 1981. text 22.20 (*0-201-18671-3*); pap. text 12.16 (*0-201-18672-1*) Addison-Wesley.

Promenades 2. G. McConnell. 1982. pap. text 22.20 (*0-201-18681-0*); pap. text 12.16 (*0-201-18682-9*) Addison-Wesley.

Promeneuse au Jasmin. Roland Morisseau. (Collection Voix: No. 7). (FRE.). 70p. 1988. pap. write for info. (*2-89135-021-9*) Guernica Editions.

Promesa. Steel Publishing Company Staff. pap. 6.95 (*950-04-0064-2*) Emece.

Promesa Cumplidas: Lucy & the Loner. Elizabeth Bevarly. (Deseo Ser.: Vol. 122).Tr. of Fulfilled Promises. 1998. per. 3.50 (*0-373-35252-2*, 1-35252-5) Harlequin Bks.

Promesa de Dios a Abraham. Tr. of God's Promise to Abraham. (SPA.). 30p. (J). 1994. pap. write for info. (*0-614-27119-3*) Editorial Unilit.

Promesa de Dios a Abraham (God's Promise to Abraham) (SPA.). 30p. (J). 1994. write for info. (*0-614-24399-8*) Editorial Unilit.

Promesa de Sanidad. Richard L. Mayhue. (SPA.). 256p. 1995. pap. 8.99 (*0-8254-1472-5*, Edit Portavoz) Kregel.

Promesa Rota. Kate William. Tr. by Maruja Del Pozo. (Sweet Valley High Ser.: No. 12).Tr. of When Love Dies. (YA). (gr. 7 up). 1993. 13.05 (*0-606-10463-1*, Pub. by Turtleback) Demco.

Promesa se Pasion (Promise of Passion) Natalie Fox. (Bianca Ser.). (SPA.). 1997. per. 3.50 (*0-373-33393-5*, 1-33393-9) Harlequin Bks.

Promesas: Geography of the Impossible. Gloria Vando. LC 92-28053. 96p. (Orig.). 1993. pap. 8.00 (*1-55885-059-7*); text 16.95 (*1-55885-061-9*) Arte Publico.

Promesas de Aliento. Harold Shaw. (Serie Guia de Bolsillo - Pocket Guides Ser.).Tr. of Promise of Encouragement. (SPA.). 88p. 1991. pap. 2.79 (*1-56063-639-4*, 498393) Editorial Unilit.

Promesas de Dios para Cada una de Sus Necesidades. Tr. of God's Promises for Your Every Need. (SPA.). 1996. 14.99 (*0-89922-574-8*) Caribe Betania.

Promesas de Dios para Cada una de Sus Necesidades. Tr. of God's Promises for Your Every Need. (SPA.). 1996. pap. 3.99 (*0-8499-5175-5*) Word Pub.

***Promesas de Dios para el Hombre (Bible Promises for Men)** (SPA.). 1999. pap. 3.99 (*0-8297-1976-8*) Vida Pub.

Promesas de Dios Para La Mujer. Vida Pubs Staff. (Bible Promises Ser.). 1999. pap. text 3.99 (*0-8297-1975-X*) Vida Pubs.

***Promesas de Dios Para Ninos.** Ed. by Vida Publishers Staff. (Bible Promises Ser.). (SPA.). 2000. pap. 3.99 (*0-8297-2370-6*) Vida Pubs.

***Promesas de Dios Para Ti de la NVI.** Ed. by Vida Publishers Staff. (Bible Promises Ser.). (SPA.). 160p. 2000. pap. 3.99 (*0-8297-2753-1*) Vida Pubs.

Promesas de Jesus. David Wilkerson.Tr. of Jesus' Person Promise Book. (SPA.). 96p. 1989. pap. 3.99 (*0-945792-36-0*, 490207) Editorial Unilit.

Promesas del Pasado. Vanessa Grant. Orig. Title: Yesterday's Vows. (SPA.). 1996. per. 3.50 (*0-373-33353-6*) Harlequin Bks.

***Promesas Dignas de Cumplirse: Spanish Journal.** Tr. by Elvira Ramirez. (Nineteen Ninety-Nine 50-Day Spiritual Adventure Ser.). 64p. 1998. 7.00 (*1-57849-106-1*) Mainstay Church.

Promesas Florales (Flower Promises) Scandinavia Staff. (SPA.). 4.50 (*0-685-74975-4*, 491399) Editorial Unilit.

Promesas para Cada Dia. (Serie Libro Nueva Vida - New Life Bks.).Tr. of Promises for Every Day. (SPA.). 12p. 1986. pap. 1.00 (*0-8423-6463-3*, 490269) Editorial Unilit.

***Promesas Para Corazoncitos.** Elena Kucharik. (SPA.). (J). (gr. 4-7). 1999. per. 6.99 (*0-7899-0664-3*) Spanish Hse Distributors.

Promesas para Estudiantes. Harold Shaw. (Serie Guia de Bolsillo - Pocket Guides Ser.).Tr. of Student Promise Pocketbook. (SPA.). 1991. 2.79 (*1-56063-641-6*, 498390); pap. write for info. (*0-614-27121-5*) Editorial Unilit.

Promesas para los Abuelos. Harold Shaw. (Serie Guia de Bolsillo - Pocket Guides Ser.).Tr. of Promise for Grandparents. (SPA.). 60p. 1991. pap. 2.79 (*1-56063-642-4*, 498394) Editorial Unilit.

Promesas para los Padres. Harold Shaw. (Serie Guia de Bolsillo - Pocket Guides Ser.).Tr. of Parent's Promise Pocketbook. (SPA.). 1991. 2.79 (*1-56063-640-8*, 498391); pap. write for info. (*0-614-27123-1*) Editorial Unilit.

Promesas para Personas Activas. Harold Shaw. (Serie Guia de Bolsillo - Pocket Guides Ser.).Tr. of Promises for People on the Go. (SPA.). 1991. 2.79 (*1-56063-638-6*, 498392); pap. write for info. (*0-614-27120-7*) Editorial Unilit.

Promesas Personales de la Biblia. Tr. of Personal Promise Pocketbook. (SPA.). 128p. 1988. pap. write for info. (*0-614-27122-3*) Editorial Unilit.

Promesas Personales de la Biblia. Luis Palau. (Serie Guia de Bolsillo - Pocket Guides Ser.).Tr. of Personal Promises of the Bible. (SPA.). 2.79 (*0-945792-29-8*, 490208) Editorial Unilit.

Promesse de l'Aube. Romain Gary. (FRE.). 370p. 1976. pap. 11.95 (*0-7859-2309-8*, 2070363732) Fr & Eur.

Promesse de l'Aube. Romain Gary. (Folio Ser.: No. 373). (FRE.). 1966. pap. 9.95 (*2-07-036373-2*) Schoenhof.

***Promesse pour l'An 2000.** Ellen James. (FRE.). 2000. mass mkt. 5.50 (*0-373-38350-9*) Harlequin Bks.

Promesse Rompue. Susanne McCarthy. (Azur Ser.: No. 783). (FRE.). 1999. mass mkt. 3.99 (*0-373-34783-9*, 1-34783-0) Harlequin Bks.

Promesse Trahie. Morgan Hayes. (Amours d'Aujourd'Hui Ser.: No. 319). (FRE.). 1999. mass mkt. 4.99 (*0-373-38319-3*, 1-38319-9) Harlequin Bks.

Prometeos Modernos. Julio M. Benito. (Ciencia para Todos Ser.). (SPA.). pap. 6.99 (*968-16-4212-0*, Pub. by Fondo) Continental Bk.

***Promethea.** Alan Moore. (Illus.). 160p. (J). 2000. 24.95 (*1-56389-655-9*, Pub. by DC Comics) Time Warner.

Promethean & Epimethean Continuum of Art. 2nd ed. Shlomo G. Shoham. LC 98-17970. 40p. 1998. pap. text 2.00 (*0-943123-34-8*) Arjuna Lib Pr.

Promethean Fire: Reflections on the Origin of Mind. Charles J. Lumsden & Edward O. Wilson. (Illus.). 224p. 1983. 30.00 (*0-674-71445-8*) HUP.

Promethean Fire: Reflections on the Origin of Mind. Charles J. Lumsden & Edward O. Wilson. (Illus.). 224p. 1983. pap. text 11.50 (*0-674-71446-6*) HUP.

Promethean Politics of Milton, Blake, & Shelley. Linda M. Lewis. (Illus.). 240p. (C). 1992. text 34.95 (*0-8262-0805-3*) U of Mo Pr.

Prometheans. Ben Bova. (Illus.). 288p. (Orig.). 1986. pap. 2.95 (*0-8125-3219-8*, Pub. by Tor Bks) St Martin.

Prometheans: Ancient & Moderns. Burton Rascoe. LC 70-156707. (Essay Index Reprint Ser.). 1977. reprint ed. 20.95 (*0-8369-2855-5*) Ayer.

Promethee Mal Enchaine: Nouvelles. Andre Gide. pap. 8.95 (*0-685-34154-2*) Fr & Eur.

Promethee: ou La Vie de Balzac. Andre Maurois. 27.50 (*0-685-36955-2*) Fr & Eur.

Promethee: ou La Vie de Balzac; Olympio: ou La View de Victor Hugo. Andre Maurois. (FRE.). 1993. pap. 60.00 (*0-7859-3406-5*) Fr & Eur.

Prometheus. (GRE.). 1992. pap. 13.95 (*3-519-01018-6*, T1018, Pub. by B G Teubner) U of Mich Pr.

***Prometheus.** William R. Forstchen. 1999. mass mkt. 6.99 (*0-671-57795-6*) S&S Trade.

Prometheus. Marcello Maia. LC 96-44344. (Illus.). 96p. 1997. 13.00 (*0-312-15166-7*, Stonewall Inn) St Martin.

Prometheus. James H. Sutton. LC 94-43771. 88p. 1995. pap. 19.95 (*0-7734-2750-3*, Mellen Poetry Pr) E Mellen.

Prometheus see Greek Mythology

Prometheus: A Play. Mark Dunster. 10p. (Orig.). (J). 1995. pap. 5.00 (*0-89642-284-4*) Linden Pubs.

Prometheus: The Life of Balzac. Andre Maurois. 573p. 1983. pap. 11.95 (*0-88184-023-8*) Carroll & Graf.

Prometheus Pt. 1: Archetypal Image of Human Existence, Vol. 65. Carl Kerenyi. Tr. by R. Manheim from GER. LC 99-218299. (Mythos Ser.). 178p. 1997. pap. text 14.95 (*0-691-01907-X*, Pub. by Princeton U Pr) Cal Prin Full Svc.

Prometheus & Adam: Enduring Symbols of the Human Situation. Larry Kreitzer. 224p. (C). 1992. lib. bdg. 45.00 (*0-8191-8497-7*) U Pr of Amer.

Prometheus & Agamemnon of Aeschylus: Translated into English Verse. Henry W. Herbert. (Notable American Authors Ser.). 1992. reprint ed. lib. bdg. 75.00 (*0-7812-3096-9*) Rprt Serv.

Prometheus & Faust: The Promethean Rebellion in Drama from Classical Antiquity to Goethe, 62. Timothy R. Wutrich. LC 94-46944. (Contributions to the Study of World Literature Ser.: No. 62). 192p. 1995. 55.00 (*0-313-29244-2*, Greenwood Pr) Greenwood.

Prometheus & the Story of Fire. I. M. Richardson. LC 82-15979. (Illus.). 32p. (J). (gr. 4-8). 1983. lib. bdg. 18.60 (*0-89375-859-0*) Troll Communs.

Prometheus Bedeviled: Science & the Contradictions of Contemporary Culture. Norman Levitt. LC 98-37628. 420p. (C). 1999. 32.00 (*0-8135-2652-3*) Rutgers U Pr.

Prometheus Bound see Seven Famous Greek Plays

Prometheus Bound see Ten Greek Plays in Contemporary Translations

Prometheus Bound. Aeschylus. Tr. by Elizabeth Barrett Browning from GRE. LC 92-53873. 70p. 1992. pap. 7.00 (*0-88734-252-3*) Players Pr.

Prometheus Bound. Photos by Mark Griffith. LC 82-1301. (Cambridge Greek & Latin Classics Ser.). (Illus.). 328p. 1983. pap. text 24.95 (*0-521-27011-1*) Cambridge U Pr.

Prometheus Bound. Aeschylus. Ed. by W. R. Connor. LC 78-18612. (Greek Texts & Commentaries Ser.). (Illus.). 1979. reprint ed. lib. bdg. 20.95 (*0-405-11451-6*) Ayer.

Prometheus Bound. unabridged ed. Aeschylus. (Thrift Editions Ser.). 64p. 1996. reprint ed. pap. text 1.00 (*0-486-28762-9*) Dover.

Prometheus Bound: Science in a Dynamic Steady State. John M. Ziman. LC 93-5922. 299p. (C). 1994. 26.95 (*0-521-43430-0*) Cambridge U Pr.

Prometheus Bound: The Changing Relationship Between Government & Higher Education in Western Europe. Frans van Vught. Ed. by Guy Neave. (Comparative & International Education Ser.). (Illus.). 284p. 1991. text 84.75 (*0-08-037246-5*, Pergamon Pr) Elsevier.

Prometheus Bound: The Mythic Structure of Karl Marx's Scientific Thinking. fac. ed. Leonard P. Wessell. LC 84-5740. (Illus.). 326p. 1984. reprint ed. pap. 101.10 (*0-7837-7754-X*, 204751000007) Bks Demand.

P

Prometheus Bound & Other Plays. Aeschylus. Tr. by Philip Vellacott. Incl. Persians. (Orig.). 1961. pap. Seven Against Thebes. 1961. pap. Suppliants. 1961. pap. (Classics Ser.). 160p. (Orig.). 1961. Set pap. 8.95 (*0-14-044112-3*, Penguin Classics) Viking Penguin.

Prometheus Bound & the Fragments of Prometheus Loosed. Aeschylus. Ed. by N. Wecklein. (College Classical Ser.). (GRE.). iv, 178p. (Orig.). (C). 1981. reprint ed. pap. text 16.00 (*0-89241-126-0*); reprint ed. lib. bdg. 32.50 (*0-89241-358-1*) Caratzas.

Prometheus Bound of Aischylos: A New Presentation. James M. Pryse. 207p. 1996. reprint ed. spiral bd. 18.00 (*0-7873-0681-9*) Hlth Research.

***Prometheus Deception.** Robert Ludlum. 384p. 2000. 27.95 (*0-312-25346-X*) St Martin.

Prometheus Design, No. 5. Sondra Marshak. 1990. pap. 5.50 (*0-671-72366-9*) S&S Trade.

***Prometheus in Bondage: or All the Girls I Should Have Kissed.** Kent D. Boklan. 2000. pap. 14.95 (*1-929613-21-0*) Avid MI.

Prometheus on Fifth Avenue. Brett Rutherford. 62p. 1987. 6.00 (*0-318-64165-8*) Poets Pr.

Prometheus Reborn. Michael J. Johnson. LC 76-52144. 1977. 15.00 (*0-87212-073-2*) Libra.

Prometheus Revisited. William H. Sheldon. 225p. 1974. 24.95 (*0-87073-808-9*) Schenkman Bks Inc.

Prometheus Rising. 2nd ed. Robert A. Wilson. LC 83-81665. (Illus.). 288p. 1993. pap. 14.95 (*1-56184-056-4*) New Falcon Pubns.

Prometheus Syndrome. Bettina L. Knapp. LC 78-69803. x, 286p. 1979. 35.00 (*0-87875-147-5*) Whitston Pub.

Prometheus the Awakener: An Essay on the Archetypal Meaning of the Planet Uranus. Richard Tarnas. LC 94-29645. (Dunquin Ser.: Vol. 21). 160p. (Orig.). 1994. pap. 14.50 (*0-88214-221-6*) Spring Pubns.

Prometheus the Firebringer (1985) (Poetry Ser.). 85.00 (*0-9604252-2-5*) Parpaglion.

Prometheus Trilogy. Ruth F. Birnbaum & Harold F. Birnbaum. 1978. 10.00 (*0-87291-125-X*) Coronado Pr.

Prometheus 2000 - Truth - Vision - Power Creativity, Innovation, Entrepreneurship: Derivation of Success & Power & the Use & Abuse of Libidinal Energy. Gene N. Landrum. 421p. 1997. pap. 14.95 (*0-9659355-0-7*) Genie-Vision.

Prometheus Unbound: An Interpretation. Carl H. Grabo. LC 68-19149. 214p. 1968. reprint ed. 50.00 (*0-87752-045-3*) Gordian.

***Prometheus Wired.** Darin Barney. 2000. 29.00 (*0-226-03745-2*) U Ch Pr.

***Prometheus Wired: The Hope for Democracy in the Age of Network Technology.** Darin Barney. LC 00-23239. 2000. write for info. (*0-226-03746-0*) U Ch Pr.

Promethium Technology. James Wheelwright. (ANS Monographs). 416p. 1973. 30.00 (*0-89448-002-2*, 300006) Am Nuclear Soc.

***Prominence of Tense, Aspect & Mood.** D. N. S. Bhat. LC 99-11172. (Studies in Language Companion Ser.: Vol. 49). xii, 198p. 1999. 65.00 (*1-55619-935-X*) J Benjamins Pubng Co.

***Prominent Families of the United States of America.** Arthur M. Burke. 510p. 1999. pap. 37.50 (*0-8063-1308-0*) Clearfield Co.

Prominent Indians of Victorian Age: A Biographical Dictionary. T. Lethbride. 600p. 1986. 120.00 (*0-7855-1827-4*, Pub. by Archives Pubs) St Mut.

Prominent Scientists: An Index to Collective Biographies. 3rd ed. Paul A. Pelletier. 390p. 1994. 65.00 (*1-55570-114-0*) Neal-Schuman.

Prominent Sisters: Mary Lamb, Dorothy Wordsworth & Sarah Disraeli. Michael Polowetzky. LC 96-21316. 176p. 1996. 55.00 (*0-275-95716-0*, Praeger Pubs) Greenwood.

Prominent Visitors to the California Missions, 1986-1842. Ed. by J. Weber. 220p. 1991. 30.00 (*0-87461-933-5*) Dawsons.

Prominent Women of the 20th Century, 4 vols., Set. Ed. by Peggy Saari. (Illus.). 1034p. (J). (gr. 5-10). 1995. text 120.00 (*0-7876-0646-4*, UXL) Gale.

Prominent Women of the 20th Century, Vol. 1. Peggy Saari. (J). (gr. 5-10). 1995. write for info. (*0-7876-0647-2*, UXL) Gale.

Prominent Women of the 20th Century, Vol. 2. Peggy Saari. (J). (gr. 5-10). 1995. write for info. (*0-7876-0648-0*) Gale.

Prominent Women of the 20th Century, Vol. 3. Peggy Saari. (J). (gr. 5-10). 1995. write for info. (*0-7876-0649-9*) Gale.

Prominent Women of the 20th Century, Vol. 4. Peggy Saari. (J). (gr. 5-10). 1995. write for info. (*0-7876-0650-2*) Gale.

***Prominenzbasierte Methode Zur Prosodieanalyse und Synthese.** Barbara Heuft. (Sprache, Sprechen und Computer Ser.). 164p. 1999. 31.95 (*3-631-34083-4*) P Lang Pubng.

Prominica. Ahmad Nawaz. LC 98-70828. (BEN.). xiv, 79p. 1998. pap. 10.00 (*1-58225-146-0*) Ananta Prakashani.

Promiscuities. Naomi Wolf. 320p. 1999. pap. 13.95 (*0-449-90764-3*) Fawcett.

***Promiscuities.** Naomi Wolf. 1999. pap. 13.95 (*0-449-45915-2*) Fawcett.

***Promiscuity: An Evolutionary History of Sperm Competition & Sexual Conflict.** Tim R. Birkhead. (Illus.). 280p. 2000. 24.95 (*0-674-00445-0*) HUP.

Promiscuous Plasmids of Gram Negative Bacteria. Ed. by C. M. Thomas. 320p. 1989. text 94.00 (*0-12-688480-3*) Acad Pr.

Promiscuous Winds. Noelle Vial. (Irish Literature Ser.). 108p. (Orig.). 1995. pap. 10.95 (*1-885266-13-8*) Story Line.

Promise. 1996. pap. 6.99 (*1-85078-206-7*, Pub. by Sheffield Acad) CUP Services.

Promise. Aleksei Arbuzov. Tr. by Ariadne Nicolaeff. 1998. pap. 5.25 (*0-8222-0921-7*) Dramatists Play.

Promise. Fred Bell. 1992. 15.00 (*0-938294-07-5*) Inner Light.

***Promise.** Donna Boyd. 2000. mass mkt. 6.99 (*0-380-79096-3*) Morrow Avon.

Promise. Pearl Synderstricker Buck. LC 97-6889. 248p. (Orig.). 1997. pap. 9.95 (*1-55921-209-8*) Moyer Bell.

***Promise.** Friedrich Durrenmatt. 2000. pap. 10.00 (*0-226-17440-9*) U Ch Pr.

Promise. T. Evans. (SPA.). 1997. pap. 14.99 (*0-8297-0471-X*) Vida Pubs.

Promise. Steven Farley. (Young Black Stallion Ser.: No. 1). (J). (gr. 4-6). 1998. pap. 3.99 (*0-679-89141-2*) Random.

Promise. Steven Farley. (Young Black Stallion Ser.: No. 1). (J). (gr. 4-6). 1998. lib. bdg. 11.99 (*0-679-99141-7*, Pub. by Random Bks Yng Read) Random.

Promise. Andrew R. Gault. 144p. mass mkt. 4.99 (*1-55197-007-4*) Picasso Publ.

Promise. Maria Hodges. LC 98-55227. (Illus.). 128p. 1999. 14.95 (*1-58182-017-8*) Cumberland Hse.

Promise. Mike Kalibabky. (Illus.). 49p. (Orig.). (J). (gr. 3). 1993. pap. text 10.00 (*0-9640212-0-X*) Moonlight MN.

Promise. Mandalyn Kaye. 448p. 1995. mass mkt. 4.99 (*0-8217-0087-1*, Zebra Kensgtn) Kensgtn Pub Corp.

Promise. Pamela Keavney. LC 89-26896. (Charlotte Zolotow Bk.). (Illus.). 32p. (J). (ps-3). 1992. lib. bdg. 14.89 (*0-06-023020-7*) HarpC Child Bks.

Promise. Jackie French Koller. LC 98-39420. 1999. lib. bdg. 17.99 (*0-679-99484-X*) Knopf.

Promise. Jackie French Koller. LC 98-39420. (J). 1999. 15.95 (*0-679-89484-5*, Pub. by Knopf Bks Yng Read) Random.

Promise. Kasey Michaels. 1997. per. 5.99 (*0-671-50114-3*, Pocket Books) PB.

Promise. Chaim Potok. 384p. 1985. mass mkt. 6.99 (*0-449-20910-5*, Crest) Fawcett.

Promise. Chaim Potok. 1997. pap. 12.00 (*0-449-00116-4*) Fawcett.

Promise. J. R. Rodriguez. 192p. 1999. pap. 12.95 (*1-56279-118-4*) Mercury Hse Inc.

Promise. Mary Ryan. LC 99-24818. 1999. text 22.95 (*0-312-20571-6*) St Martin.

Promise. Danielle Steel. 288p. (YA). (gr. 7 up). 1989. mass mkt. 6.99 (*0-440-17079-6*) Dell.

Promise. Danielle Steel. 1978. 11.09 (*0-606-00555-2*, Pub. by Turtleback) Demco.

Promise. Robert Westall. (Illus.). 176p. (J). (gr. 7-9). 1991. 13.95 (*0-590-43760-7*, Scholastic Hardcover) Scholastic Inc.

Promise. large type ed. Jane Peart. LC 98-53621. 1999. 23.95 (*0-7862-1804-5*) Thorndike Pr.

Promise. large type ed. Chaim Potok. LC 98-23278. 515p. 1998. 25.95 (*0-7838-0256-0*, G K Hall & Co) Mac Lib Ref.

***Promise, Vol. 1.** Donna Boyd. LC 99-20949. 352p. 1999. 23.00 (*0-380-97450-9*, Avon Bks) Morrow Avon.

Promise, Vol. 10. Virginia Jacober. LC 93-74546. (Jaffray Collection of Missionary Portraits). 211p. 1994. pap. 9.99 (*0-87509-547-X*) Chr Pubns.

Promise: Experiencing God's Greatest Gift: the Holy Spirit. Tony Evans. 1999. 18.99 (*0-8024-3921-7*, 258) Moody.

Promise: Junior Jaffray Edition. Hope Marston. (Junior Jaffray Collection: Vol. 10). 30p. (J). (ps-2). 1994. pap. 3.99 (*0-87509-548-8*) Chr Pubns.

Promise: The Celebration of the Birth of Christ. Michael Card. Ed. by David Hazard. (Illus.). 48p. 1991. 10.95 (*0-917143-07-8*) Sparrow TN.

Promise: The Sequel to the Proud Tree. Luane Roche. LC 96-82112. (Illus.). 64p. (J). (gr. 3-5). 1996. pap. 3.95 (*0-89243-877-0*) Liguori Pubns.

***Promise: The Story of Noah's Ark.** Kelly S. Heaps & Susan Dunn. LC 99-43478. (Holy Bear's Travel Ser.). (Illus.). 32p. (J). (gr. k-5). 1999. pap. 7.95 (*1-885628-30-7*) Buckaroo Bks.

Promise Ahead: A Vision of Hope & Action for Humanity's Future. Duane Elgin. LC 99-87191. (Illus.). 256p. 2000. 23.00 (*0-688-17191-5*, Wm Morrow) Morrow Avon.

***Promise & Dilemma: Perspectives on Racial Diversity & Higher Education.** Eugene Y. Lowe. LC 98-45778. 1999. 29.95 (*0-691-00489-7*, Pub. by Princeton U Pr) Cal Prin Full Svc.

Promise & Paradox of Civil Service Reform. Ed. by Patricia W. Ingraham & David H. Rosenbloom. LC 92-5668. (Policy & Institutional Studies). 384p. (C). 1992. text 49.95 (*0-8229-3716-6*) U of Pittsburgh Pr.

***Promise & Paradox of Freedom.** A. Field & McAllister. 2002. pap. 30.00 (*0-534-53560-7*) Thomson Learn.

Promise & Performance: A Study of Student Progress at University Level (Australia) Fred J. Schonell et al. 1962. 79.50 (*0-317-27537-2*) Elliots Bks.

Promise & Performance: Choosing & Implementing an Environmental Policy, 39. Alfred A. Marcus. LC 79-8290. (Contributions in Political Science Ser.: No. 39). 204p. 1980. 57.95 (*0-313-20707-0*, MPT/, Greenwood Pr) Greenwood.

Promise & Performance in Managed Care: The Prepaid Group Practice Model. Donald K. Freeborn & Clyde R. Pope. LC 94-6176. 1994. text 42.50 (*0-8018-4819-9*) Johns Hopkins.

Promise & Performance of American Democracy: Brief. 5th ed. Richard A. Watson. LC 84-25691. 632p. (C). 1985. pap. 48.00 (*0-02-424640-9*, Macmillan Coll) P-H.

Promise & Peril of Environmental Justice. Christopher H. Foreman, Jr. LC 98-25431. 160p. 1998. 22.95 (*0-8157-2878-6*) Brookings.

***Promise & Peril of Environmental Justice.** Christopher H. Foreman. 192p. 2000. pap. 16.95 (*0-8157-2877-8*) Brookings.

Promise & Peril of Genetic Screening. National Conference of Catholic Bishops. (Science & the Catholic Church Ser.). 6p. (Orig.). (C). 1997. pap. 1.00 (*1-57455-076-4*) US Catholic.

Promise & Peril of Human Purpose: The New Relevance of Purpose & Existence. William Horosz. LC 71-93793. 350p. 1970. 12.75 (*0-87527-018-2*) Green.

Promise & Perils of Biotechnology: Genetic Testing. Contrib. by Valli T. McDougle. 1996. pap., teacher ed. 70.00 (*0-87969-494-7*) Cold Spring Harbor.

Promise & Power: The Life & Times of Robert McNamara. Deborah Shapley. (Illus.). 734p. 1998. reprint ed. 30.00 (*0-7881-5181-9*) DIANE Pub.

Promise & Pragmatism of Adult Education. T. White. (Tolley Medal Ser.: No. 7). 1979. 2.50 (*0-686-63884-0*) Syracuse U Cont Ed.

Promise & Reality of European Security Cooperation: States, Interests & Institutions. Ed. by Mary M. McKenzie & Peter H. Loedel. LC 97-33705. 216p. 1998. 59.95 (*0-275-95949-X*, Praeger Pubs) Greenwood.

Promise & the Paradox of Civil Service Reform. Ed. by Patricia W. Ingraham & David Rosenbloom. LC 92-5668. (Policy & Institutional Studies). 384p. (C). 1992. pap. 19.95 (*0-8229-5496-6*) U of Pittsburgh Pr.

Promise & the Price: Essays on Women & Organisations. Clare Burton. 208p. 1991. pap. text 18.95 (*0-04-442286-5*, Pub. by Allen & Unwin Pty) Paul & Co Pubs.

Promise at Dawn. Romain Gary. Tr. by John M. Beach from FRE. LC 86-23737. (New Directions Classics Ser.).Tr. of La/Promesse de L'Aube. 352p. 1987. reprint ed. pap. 10.95 (*0-8112-1016-2*, NDP635, Pub. by New Directions) Norton.

Promise at the Alamo. Dorothy Hoobler & Thomas Hoobler. (Her Story Ser.). (Illus.). 64p. (J). (gr. 4-6). 1992. lib. bdg. 9.95 (*0-382-24147-9*) Silver Burdett Pr.

Promise at the Alamo: The Story of a Texas Girl. Dorothy Hoobler & Thomas Hoobler. (Her Story Ser.). (Illus.). 64p. (J). (gr. 4-6). 1992. pap. 3.95 (*0-382-24352-8*) Silver Burdett Pr.

Promise Bible see Biblia de Promesas

Promise Box. large type ed. Louise James. 1990. 27.99 (*0-7089-2234-1*) Ulverscroft.

***Promise Breaker.** Robert Elmer. LC 99-51014. (Promise of Zion Ser.: Vol. 1). 144p. (J). (gr. 4-7). 2000. pap. 5.99 (*0-7642-2296-1*) Bethany Hse.

Promise Builders: Study Series see Aplicando las Siete Promesas

Promise Clinic. Robert Saxton et al. 806p. 1995. pap. 13.95 (*1-870612-39-6*, Pub. by Enitha Pr) Dufour.

Promise Continues: Empire State College - the First Twenty-Five Years. Richard F. Bonnabeau. LC 96-4381. 1996. write for info. (*0-89865-966-3*) Donning Co.

Promise for Breanna. Al Lacy. (Angel of Mercy Ser.: Vol. 1). 321p. 1985. pap. 10.99 (*0-88070-797-6*, Multnomah Bks) Multnomah Pubs.

Promise for Grandparents see Promesas para los Abuelos

Promise for Tomorrow. Judith Pella & Tracie Peterson. LC 97-45442. (Ribbons of Steel Ser.). 368p. 1998. pap. 10.99 (*1-55661-864-6*) Bethany Hse.

Promise for Tomorrow. large type ed. Sheila Lewis. (Linford Romance Library). 304p. 1997. pap. 16.99 (*0-7089-5178-3*) Ulverscroft.

Promise Fulfilled. Carlo-Maria Martini. 176p. 1996. pap. 39.95 (*0-85439-481-8*, Pub. by St Paul Pubns) St Mut.

Promise Fulfilled: A Portrait of Norwegian Americans Today. Odd Sverre Lovoll & Norwegian-American Historical Association. LC 98-4000. 352p. 1998. 29.95 (*0-8166-2832-7*); pap. write for info. (*0-8166-2833-5*) U of Minn Pr.

Promise Given. Samantha James. LC 97-93789. 384p. 1998. mass mkt. 5.99 (*0-380-78608-7*, Avon Bks) Morrow Avon.

***Promise Given.** Lois Richer. (Castles of the Heart Ser.). 2000. pap. 12.99 (*0-8054-2182-3*) Broadman.

***Promise Given.** Anita Wall. (Zebra Splendor Historical Romances Ser.). 2000. mass mkt. 4.99 (*0-8217-6599-X*, Zebra Kensgtn) Kensgtn Pub Corp.

Promise-Giving & Treaty-Making: Homer & the Near East. Peter Karavites. (Mnemosyne Ser.: Supplement 119). xii, 224p. 1991. 89.50 (*90-04-09567-5*) Brill Academic Pubs.

Promise in the Storm: Grieving & Dying with Hope. Nancy Marrocco. 312p. 1996. teacher ed., spiral bd. 24.95 (*0-88489-367-7*, 1226) St Marys.

Promise in the Storm: Grieving & Dying with Hope. Nancy Marrocco. LC 97-169638. 208p. 1997. pap. 15.20 (*0-88489-366-9*) St Marys.

Promise Is. Kip Zegers. LC 84-14. (Vox Humana Ser.). 96p. 1985. 14.95 (*0-89603-081-4*); pap. 11.95 (*0-89603-087-3*) Humana.

Promise Is a Promise. Ellsworth. 1997. pap. 11.99 (*0-85234-387-6*, Pub. by Evangelical Pr) P & R Pubng.

Promise Is a Promise. Robert Munsch. (J). 1988. 11.15 (*0-606-04380-2*, Pub. by Turtleback) Demco.

Promise Is a Promise. Robert Munsch & Michael A. Kusugak. (Illus.). 32p. (J). (gr. k-3). 1988. pap. 5.95 (*1-55037-008-1*, Pub. by Annick); lib. bdg. 15.95 (*1-55037-009-X*, Pub. by Annick) Firefly Bks Ltd.

Promise Is a Promise. Robert Munsch & Michael A. Kusugak. 1995. 3.95 (*0-87129-493-1*, P72) Dramatic Pub.

Promise Is a Promise: An Almost Unbelievable Story of a Mother's Unconditional Love & What It Can Teach Us. Wayne W. Dyer & Marcelene Dyer. LC 96-9125. 112p. 1996. 14.00 (*1-56170-348-6*, 831) Hay House.

Promise Is a Promise: Inuktitut Editon. 1988. pap. 4.95 (*1-55037-031-6*, Pub. by Annick) Firefly Bks Ltd.

***Promise Is Forever, 12.** Robin Jones Gunn. (Christy Miller Ser.: Vol. 12). 160p. (J). (gr. 7-13). 1999. pap. text 5.99 (*1-56179-733-2*) Focus Family.

Promise Is to Keep. Nan H. Agle. 160p. 1985. pap. 7.95 (*0-310-41591-8*, 9290P) Zondervan.

***Promise Is to Keep.** Mary Teegardin. 264p. 2000. pap. 10.99 (*0-87508-490-7*, 490) Chr Lit.

***Promise Is to Keep.** Mary Teegardin. 264p. 1999. pap. 10.99 (*1-929122-03-9*) OMF Bks.

Promise Keeper at Work. Bob Horner. LC 98-55368. (Orig.). 1998. pap. 6.99 (*0-8499-3731-0*) Word Pub.

Promise Keepers: Another Trojan Horse: They Really Are Breaking down the Walls. Phil Arms. LC 96-71761. 416p. 1997. 25.95 (*1-890058-00-9*); pap. 15.95 (*1-890058-01-7*) P Arms Minist.

Promise Keepers: Essays on Masculinity & Christianity. Ed. by Dane S. Claussen. LC 99-38799. 352p. 1999. lib. bdg. 46.50 (*0-7864-0700-X*) McFarland & Co.

Promise Keepers: Playing God. Nancy Novosad. (Illus.). 250p. 1999. 24.95 (*1-57392-700-7*) Prometheus Bks.

Promise Keepers: Politics & Promises. Bryan W. Brickner. LC 99-10349. 160p. 1999. 59.00 (*0-7391-0008-4*); pap. 22.95 (*0-7391-0059-9*) Lxngtn Bks.

Promise Keepers Beware!, Vol. I. David W. Cloud. 44p. 1995. pap. 2.50 (*1-58318-045-1*, WOL481B) Way of Life.

Promise Keepers Beware!, Vol. II. David W. Cloud. (Illus.). 53p. Date not set. pap. 4.00 (*1-58318-046-X*, WOL490B) Way of Life.

***Promise Kept.** LC 96-69803. iv, 284p. 2000. 22.95 (*0-9654922-0-6*) Salt Islnd Publns.

Promise Kept. J. Robertson McQuilkin. LC 98-16753. 1998. 14.99 (*0-8423-5099-3*) Tyndale Hse.

***Promise Kept.** large type ed. Annabel Murray. 320p. 2000. pap. 20.99 (*1-85389-946-1*, Dales) Ulverscroft.

Promise Kids on the Promise Path: Children's Journal. Linda Washington. (Nineteen Ninety Nine Fifty-Day Spiritual Adventure Ser.). (Illus.). 64p. (J). 1998. 7.00 (*1-57849-108-8*) Mainstay Church.

Promise Land. Frederick K. Price. 27p. (Orig.). 1993. pap. 1.99 (*1-883798-03-5*) Faith One.

Promise Land Cinema. Kristin Thompson. pap. 0.00 (*0-691-00860-4*) Princeton U Pr.

Promise Made. Catherine Lanigan. 496p. (Orig.). 1990. mass mkt. 4.95 (*0-380-75694-3*, Avon Bks) Morrow Avon.

Promise Makers. 115p. (Orig.). 1998. pap. 10.00 (*0-9665811-1-3*) Prosperity & You.

Promise Me. Margaret Allison. 1997. per. 5.99 (*0-671-56327-0*) PB.

Promise Me. Robyn Amos. 256p. 1997. mass mkt. 4.99 (*0-7860-0444-4*, Pinncle Kensgtn) Kensgtn Pub Corp.

Promise Me. Kathleen Harrington. 416p. (Orig.). 1995. mass mkt. 5.50 (*0-380-77833-5*, Avon Bks) Morrow Avon.

***Promise Me.** large type ed. Angela Noel. 320p. 1999. pap. 20.99 (*1-85389-925-9*, Dales) Ulverscroft.

***Promise Me a Rainbow.** Cheryl Reavis. 1999. 25.95 (*0-7862-2200-X*) Five Star.

Promise Me Anything. Meryl Sawyer. 464p. 1996. reprint ed. 24.00 (*0-7278-4865-8*) Severn Hse.

Promise Me Forever. Debbie Macomber. 256p. 1999. mass mkt. write for info. (*1-55166-052-0*, 0-66052-2, Mira Bks) Harlequin Bks.

Promise Me Forever. Cara Miles. 1992. mass mkt. 4.50 (*0-380-76451-2*, Avon Bks) Morrow Avon.

Promise Me Forever. Janelle Taylor. 1992. mass mkt. 5.99 (*0-8217-3764-3*, Zebra Kensgtn) Kensgtn Pub Corp.

Promise Me Forever. large type ed. Janelle Taylor. LC 96-42515. (Star-Romance Ser.). 554p. 1997. 23.95 (*0-7862-0905-4*) Five Star.

Promise Me Forever. Connie Mason. 384p. 1998. reprint ed. mass mkt. 5.50 (*0-505-52246-2*, Love Spell) Dorchester Pub Co.

Promise Me Heaven. Connie Brockway. 384p. (Orig.). 1994. mass mkt. 4.50 (*0-380-77550-6*, Avon Bks) Morrow Avon.

Promise Me Law: A Preview of a Brighter Tomorrow. Anna Van Gogh. LC 88-33667. 800p. 1986. pap. 14.95 (*0-913829-02-1*); text 29.95 (*0-685-09109-0*) Lucy Mary Bks.

Promise Me Life: A Preview of a Brighter Tomorrow. Anna Van Gogh. (Illus.). 424p. (Orig.). (C). 1996. pap. 19.95 (*0-913829-35-8*); boxed set 29.95 (*0-913829-34-X*) Lucy Mary Bks.

Promise Me Light: A Preview of a Brighter Tomorrow. Anna Van Gogh. 1991. pap. 19.95 (*0-913829-18-8*); lib. bdg. 29.95 (*0-913829-17-X*) Lucy Mary Bks.

***Promise Me Love.** Elizabeth Graham. (Zebra Splendor Historical Romances Ser.). 2000. mass mkt. 4.99 (*0-8217-6600-7*, Zebra Kensgtn) Kensgtn Pub Corp.

Promise Me Love: A Preview of a Brighter Tomorrow. Anna Van Gogh. LC 93-19936. (Illus.). 608p. 1993. pap. 19.95 (*0-913829-19-6*); boxed set 29.95 (*0-913829-20-X*) Lucy Mary Bks.

Promise Me Moonlight. Carol Finch, pseud. 448p. 1993. mass mkt. 5.99 (*0-8217-4057-1*, Zebra Kensgtn) Kensgtn Pub Corp.

Promise Me Paradise. Ellen T. Marsh. 400p. 1998. mass mkt. 5.99 (*0-8439-4426-9*, Leisure Bks) Dorchester Pub Co.

Promise Me Series: A Preview of a Brighter Tomorrow. Anna Van Gogh. (Promise Me War; -Law; -Love; -Life; -Light Ser.). 1991. pap. 60.00 (*0-913829-06-4*); lib. bdg. 75.00 (*0-913829-05-6*) Lucy Mary Bks.

***Promise Me Spring.** Robin L. Hatcher. 448p. 1999. reprint ed. mass mkt. 5.99 (*0-8439-4662-8*, Pub. by Dorchester Pub Co) CMG.

Promise Me the Moon. Joyce A. Barnes. LC 95-53085. 176p. (YA). 1997. 14.99 (*0-8037-1798-9*, Dial Yng Read) Peng Put Young Read.

Promise Me the Moon. Joyce A. Barnes. LC 95-53085. (YA). 1999. pap. 14.89 (*0-8037-1799-7*, Dial Yng Read) Peng Put Young Read.

Promise Me the Moon. Joyce A. Barnes. 144p. (gr. 3-7). 1999. pap. 4.99 (*0-14-038040-X*) Viking Penguin.

P

Promise Me Today. large type ed. Lori Copeland. LC 93-17004. 401p. 1993. lib. bdg. 17.95 (*1-56054-735-9*) Thorndike Pr.

*__Promise Me Tomorrow.__ Candace Camp. 408p. 2000. mass mkt. 6.50 (*1-55166-607-3*, 1-66607-2, Mira Bks) Harlequin Bks.

Promise Me Tomorrow. Leigh Michaels. (Romance Ser.: No. 141). 1991. per. 2.75 (*0-373-03141-6*) Harlequin Bks.

Promise Me Tomorrow. Lori Wick. LC 97-9439. (Rocky Mountain Memories Ser.). 400p. 1997. pap. 10.99 (*1-56507-695-8*) Harvest Hse.

Promise Me Tomorrow. large type ed. Lori Copeland. LC 94-599. (Orig.). 1994. pap. text 22.95 (*1-56895-064-0*) Wheeler Pub.

Promise Me Tomorrow. large type ed. Lori Wick. LC 98-10561. 1998. 23.95 (*0-7862-1404-X*) Thorndike Pr.

Promise Me War: A Preview of a Brighter Tomorrow. Anna Van Gogh. LC 84-3876. 424p. 1984. 29.95 (*0-913829-03-X*, UA23); pap. 14.95 (*0-913829-00-5*, V26) Lucy Mary Bks.

Promise Me You'll Sing Mud. Ian Wallace. (Orig.). pap. 11.95 (*0-7145-3594-X*) Riverrun NY.

Promise Me You'll Stop Me: Distress Call 911. 7th ed. Diane L. Carey. (Distress Call 911 Ser.: No. 7). (YA). 1997. per. 3.99 (*0-671-00097-7*) PB.

Promise Not to Tell. Jane Futcher. 192p. (Orig.). (J). (gr. 4-5). 1991. pap. 2.95 (*0-380-76037-1*, Avon Bks) Morrow Avon.

Promise Not to Tell. Beverly Hastings. 256p. (Orig.). (YA). 1995. mass mkt. 4.50 (*0-425-14945-5*) Berkley Pub.

Promise Not to Tell. Carolyn Polese. LC 84-19767. (Illus.). 66p. (J). (gr. 3 up). 1985. 16.95 (*0-89885-239-0*, Kluwer Acad Hman Sci) Kluwer Academic.

Promise of a New Day. Karen Casey & Martha Vanceburg. (Illus.). 400p. (Orig.). pap. 10.00 (*0-89486-203-0*) Hazelden.

Promise of a New Day: A Book of Daily Meditations. Karen Casey & Martha Vanceburg. LC 96-188316. 416p. (Orig.). 1996. pap. 5.99 (*0-06-255268-6*, Pub. by Harper SF) HarpC.

Promise of a New Day/Night Light. Karen Casey et al. LC 97-75630. 784p. 1998. reprint ed. 8.98 (*1-56731-261-6*, MJF Bks) Fine Comms.

Promise of Alliance: NATO & the Political Imagination. Ian Q. Thomas. LC 97-14246. 320p. 1997. 71.00 (*0-8476-8580-2*); pap. 26.95 (*0-8476-8581-0*) Rowman.

Promise of America. (Little Remembrance Gift Editions Ser.). (J). (gr. 5-11). 6.95 (*0-87741-008-9*) Makepeace Colony.

Promise of America: A History of the Norwegian-American People. Odd Sverre Lovoll. LC 83-27350. (Illus.). 248p. 1984. pap. 17.95 (*0-8166-1334-6*) U of Minn Pr.

*__Promise of America: A History of the Norwegian-American People.__ Odd Sverre Lovoll. LC 99-10492. 1999. pap. write for info. (*0-8166-3350-9*) U of Minn Pr.

Promise of American Industry: An Alternative Assessment of Problems & Prospects. Donald L. Losman & Shu-Jan Liang. LC 89-24329. 296p. 1990. 59.95 (*0-89930-508-3*, LAB/, Quorum Bks) Greenwood.

Promise of American Life. Herbert Croly. LC 92-9926. 502p. (C). 1992. pap. 29.95 (*1-56000-628-5*) Transaction Pubs.

Promise of American Life. Herbert Croly. 468p. 1989. reprint ed. pap. text 18.95 (*1-55553-062-1*) NE U Pr.

Promise of American Politics: Principles & Practice after Two Hundred Years. Ed. by Robert L. Utley, Jr. LC 88-20892. 318p. (Orig.). (C). 1989. pap. text 26.50 (*0-8191-7191-3*); lib. bdg. 41.00 (*0-8191-7190-5*) U Pr of Amer.

Promise of Another Tomorrow. Cheryl L. Ellis. 88p. 1973. write for info. (*0-318-64131-3*) Poets Pr.

*__Promise of Bible Prophecy.__ Hal Lindsey. 192p. 1999. pap. 9.99 (*0-7369-0310-0*) Harvest Hse.

Promise of Cognitive Psychology. Richard E. Mayer. (Illus.). 136p. (C). 1990. reprint ed. pap. text 17.50 (*0-8191-7653-2*) U Pr of Amer.

Promise of Critical Theology: Essays in Honour of Charles Davis. Ed. by Marc P. Lalonde. LC 96-110739. xii, 146p. (C). 1995. pap. 21.95 (*0-88920-254-0*) W Laurier U Pr.

Promise of Dawn: The Eschatology of Lewis Sperry Chafer. Jeffrey J. Richards. 280p. (C). 1991. pap. 28.00 (*0-8191-8197-8*); lib. bdg. 52.00 (*0-8191-8196-X*) U Pr of Amer.

Promise of Deliverance. Dan Wilson. (C). 1983. pap. 4.00 (*0-87574-060-X*) Pendle Hill.

Promise of Deliverance in Time of Trouble. E. Willis. 1978. 2.00 (*0-89858-023-4*) Fill the Gap.

Promise of Destiny: Children & Women in the Stories of Louisa May Alcott, 2. Joy A. Marsella. LC 82-15573. (Contributions to the Study of Childhood & Youth Ser.: No. 2). 166p. 1983. 47.95 (*0-313-23603-8*, MLO/, Greenwood Pr) Greenwood.

Promise of Eden: A Novel. Eric Durchholtz. 208p. 1999. pap. 14.95 (*0-9670297-0-8*, 10018) Concrete Bks.

Promise of Eden: The Canadian Expansionist Movement & the Idea of the West, 1856-1900. Doug Owram. LC 80-491231. 276p. reprint ed. pap. 85.60 (*0-608-12873-2*, 202365800033) Bks Demand.

Promise of Eden: The Canadian Expansionist Movement & the Idea of the West, 1856-1900. Doug Owram. (Reprints in Canadian History Ser.). 288p. 1992. reprint ed. pap. text 22.95 (*0-8020-7390-5*) U of Toronto Pr.

Promise of Educational Psychology: Learning in the Content Areas. Richard E. Mayer. LC 98-9789. 280p. (C). 1998. pap. text 32.00 (*0-13-913013-6*, Merrill Coll) P-H.

Promise of Encouragement see Promesas de Aliento

Promise of Eternity: A Look Through the Door of Time. Karel Untermeyer. LC 98-86933. 128p. 1998. 18.95 (*0-9664348-0-3*) Ocean Pr Fla.

*__Promise of Flowers.__ Delia Parr. 272p. 2000. mass mkt. 5.99 (*0-312-97505-8*) St Martin.

Promise of Forever. Judith Gale. 112p. 1997. pap. 10.00 (*0-8059-4085-5*) Dorrance.

Promise of Forever: A Novel. Anita Stansfield. LC 96-49276. 1997. pap. 11.95 (*1-57734-060-4*, 01112716) Covenant Comms.

Promise of Friendship: A Collection of Memories Shared among Family & Friends. Roxie Kelley. 1999. 14.95 (*0-8362-7852-6*) Andrews & McMeel.

*__Promise of Glory.__ C. X. Moreau. 304p. 2000. text 24.95 (*0-312-87272-0*) Forge NYC.

Promise of Glory. Catherine Nerney. 1985. pap. 1.25 (*0-8091-9334-5*) Paulist Pr.

*__Promise of God: A Novel.__ David Shapiro. LC 99-56095. 335p. 2000. pap. 12.95 (*1-55874-744-3*, Simcha Press) Health Comm.

*__Promise of God's Name.__ A. L. Gill & Joyce Gill. (Illus.). 251p. 2000. pap. 9.99 (*0-88368-625-2*) Whitaker Hse.

Promise of God's Presence. Chris Bigaham. 1999. pap. text 9.99 (*0-8474-1713-1*) Back to Bible.

Promise of Good Things - The Apostolic Fathers. Ed. by Oliver Davies. (Spirituality of the Fathers Ser.). 120p. (Orig.). 1993. pap. 7.95 (*1-56548-019-8*) New City.

Promise of Greatness. Sar A. Levitan & Robert Taggart. 325p. 1977. pap. 17.00 (*0-674-71456-3*) HUP.

Promise of Green Politics: Environmentalism & the Public Sphere. Douglas Torgerson. LC 98-56543. 240p. 1999. pap. 17.95 (*0-8223-2370-2*) Duke.

*__Promise of Green Politics: Environmentalism & the Public Sphere.__ Douglas Torgerson. LC 98-56543. 240p. 1999. 49.95 (*0-8223-2337-0*) Duke.

Promise of Group Therapy: How to Build a Vigorous Training & Organizational Base for Group Therapy in Managed Behavioral Healthcare. Bill Roller. LC 96-48494. 252p. 1997. 34.95 (*0-7879-0842-8*) Jossey-Bass.

Promise of Happiness. large type ed. Paula Lindsay. 288p. 1988. 27.99 (*0-7089-1868-9*) Ulverscroft.

Promise of Healing. Geoffrey F. Spencer. LC 93-316. 150p. (Orig.). 1993. pap. text 4.00 (*0-8309-0634-7*) Herald Pub Hse.

*__Promise of Heaven.__ Ed. by Good News Publishers Staff. 2000. pap. 8.50 (*5-550-02701-1*) Nairi.

*__Promise of Heaven: Discovering Our Eternal Home.__ Douglas Connelly. 128p. 2000. 11.99 (*0-8308-2231-3*) InterVarsity.

*__Promise of Hermeneutics.__ Roger Lundin et al. LC 99-12924. 272p. 1999. pap. 20.00 (*0-8028-4635-1*) Eerdmans.

Promise of His Coming: Interpreting New Testament Statements Concerning the Time of Christ's Appearance. R. C. Leonard & J. E. Leonard. 223 p. (Orig.). 1996. pap. 12.95 (*1-884454-05-4*) Laudemont Pr.

Promise of His Glory. Marvene Brooks. LC 98-90369. 1998. 13.95 (*0-533-12769-6*) Vantage.

Promise of History: Essays in Political Philosophy. Ed. by Athanasios Moulakis. (European University Institute, Series C (Political & Social Science): No. 2). vi, 206p. 1985. 69.25 (*3-11-010043-6*) De Gruyter.

Promise of Jenny Jones. Maggie Osborne. 384p. 1997. reprint ed. mass mkt. 6.50 (*0-446-60441-0*, Pub. by Warner Bks) Little.

Promise of Joy. Winston Press Editorial Staff. (Joy Ser.). 1991. reprint ed. teacher ed. 29.95 (*1-55944-021-X*, 2533651) Franciscan Comns.

Promise of Justice: The Eighteen Year Fight to Save Four Innocent Men. David Protess & Robert Warden. LC 97-36431. 288p. (J). 1998. 23.95 (*0-7868-6294-7*, Pub. by Hyperion) Time Warner.

Promise of Liberalism: A Comparative Analysis of Consensus Politics. Ed. by Mike Mills & Fraser King. LC 95-16699. 256p. 1995. 77.95 (*1-85521-481-4*, Pub. by Dartmth Pub) Ashgate Pub Co.

*__Promise of Light.__ Paul Watkins. 2000. pap. 13.00 (*0-312-26766-5*, Picador USA) St Martin.

Promise of Love. Alice B. Bradshaw. 208p. 1996. pap. 20.00 (*1-55630-884-1*) Brentwood Comm.

Promise of Love. Karen Ranney. 384p. 1997. mass mkt. 4.99 (*0-8217-5750-4*, Zebra Kensgtn) Kensgtn Pub Corp.

Promise of Love. large type ed. Sarah Westbury. (Linford Romance Library). 1991. pap. 16.99 (*0-7089-7102-4*) Ulverscroft.

Promise of Love. Mary Renault. 382p. reprint ed. lib. bdg. 26.95 (*0-89244-079-1*) Amereon Ltd.

Promise of Lutheran Ethics. Ed. by Karen L. Bloomquist & John R. Stumme. LC 98-34165. 256p. 1998. pap. 18.00 (*0-8006-3132-3*, 1-3132) Augsburg Fortress.

Promise of Mediation: Responding to Conflict Through Empowerment & Recognition. Robert A. Bush et al. LC 94-27217. (Management Ser.). 336p. 1994. text 34.95 (*0-7879-0027-3*) Jossey-Bass.

Promise of Modern Life: An Interrelational View. Dilman W. Gotshalk. LC 58-8735. 128p. reprint ed. pap. 39.70 (*0-608-10015-3*, 201459700096) Bks Demand.

Promise of Morning: Writings from Arizona Prisons. Ed. by Williams Aberg. 1982. pap. 4.95 (*0-933188-21-8*) Blue Moon Pr.

Promise of Multiculturalism: Education & Autonomy in the 21st Century: A New Political Science Reader. George N. Katsiaficas & Teodros Kiros. LC 98-7406. (Illus.). 256p. (C). 1998. pap. 21.99 (*0-415-92126-0*) Routledge.

Promise of Murder. Mignon G. Eberhart. 21.95 (*0-89190-538-3*) Amereon Ltd.

Promise of Narrative Theology: Recovering the Gospel in the Church. George W. Stroup. 288p. 1997. pap. 25.00 (*1-57910-053-8*) Wipf & Stock.

Promise of Nature: Ecology & Cosmic Purpose. John F. Haught. LC 92-41353. 160p. 1993. pap. 9.95 (*0-8091-3396-2*) Paulist Pr.

Promise of Neural Networks. J. G. Taylor. (Perspectives in Neural Computing Ser.). (Illus.). 170p. 1993. pap. write for info. (*3-540-19773-7*) Spr-Verlag.

Promise of Neural Networks. J. G. Taylor. LC 93-25443. (Perspectives in Neural Computing Ser.). 1993. 69.00 (*0-387-19773-7*) Spr-Verlag.

Promise of Oregon. Benjamin C. Dodson. 118p. (Orig.). (YA). (gr. 7-12). 1989. pap. 6.75 (*0-9620550-3-4*) Dodson Assocs.

Promise of Paradise. large type ed. Karen Lawton Barrett. (Black Satin Romance Ser.). 255p. 1997. 27.99 (*1-86110-035-3*) Ulverscroft.

Promise of Paradise: A Woman's Intimate Life with "Bhagwan" Osho Rajneesh. Satya B. Franklin. 400p. 1992. 24.95 (*0-88268-139-7*) Station Hill Pr.

Promise of Paradise: Recreational & Retirement Communities in the United States since 1950. Hubert B. Stroud. LC 94-13228. (Creating the North American Landscape Ser.). (Illus.). 220p. 1995. text 35.00 (*0-8018-4926-8*) Johns Hopkins.

Promise of Paradise: Utopian Communities in British Columbia. Andrew Scott. (Illus.). 224p. 1997. pap. 14.95 (*1-55110-622-1*) Whitecap Bks.

Promise of Peace: Economic Cooperation Between Egypt & Israel. Henry J. Bruton. 1981. pap. 6.95 (*0-8157-1125-5*) Brookings.

Promise of Perfection. Andrew Cohen. 1998. pap. 6.00 (*1-883929-21-0*) Moksha Pr.

Promise of Photography: The DG Bank Art Collection. Ed. by Luminita Sabau. (Illus.). 390p. 1998. 75.00 (*3-7913-1995-7*) te Neues.

Promise of Power: Reflections in the Toltec Warrior's Dialogue from the Collected Works of Carlos Castaneda. Tomas. 762p. 1995. pap. 18.95 (*1-57174-024-4*) Hampton Roads Pub Co.

Promise of Power: The Emergence of the Legal Profession in Massachusetts, 1760-1840, 6. Gerald W. Gawalt. LC 78-57764. (Contributions in Legal Studies: No. 6). 254p. 1979. 59.95 (*0-313-20612-0*, GPP/, Greenwood Pr) Greenwood.

Promise of Power to Serve. E. Willis. 1978. 2.00 (*0-89858-024-2*) Fill the Gap.

Promise of Pragmatism: Modernism & the Crisis of Knowledge & Authority. John P. Diggins. LC 93-11686. 530p. 1994. 29.95 (*0-226-14878-5*) U Ch Pr.

Promise of Pragmatism: Modernism & the Crisis of Knowledge & Authority. John P. Diggins. 528p. 1995. pap. 22.00 (*0-226-14879-3*) U Ch Pr.

Promise of Prayer. Guideposts Staff. 192p. 1995. 7.99 (*0-517-10323-0*) Random.

Promise of Presence: Studies in Honor of David N. Power, OMI. Ed. by Michael Downey & Richard Fragomeni. 283p. (Orig.). 1992. pap. 24.95 (*0-912405-92-9*, Pastoral Press) OR Catholic.

Promise of Presence: Weekly Reflections & Daily Prayer Activities. Bridget M. Meehan & Regina M. Oliver. LC 99-62047. 232p. 1999. pap. 9.95 (*0-87946-200-0*, 283) ACTA Pubns.

*__Promise of Prevention: Leading Crime Prevention Programs.__ P. Grabosky & M. James. LC 96-207962. 47p. 1999. pap. 75.00 (*0-642-22768-3*, Pub. by Aust Inst Criminology) Advent Bks Div.

Promise of Private Pensions: The First Hundred Years. Steven A. Sass. LC 96-37847. (Illus.). 384p. 1996. 41.50 (*0-674-94520-4*) HUP.

Promise of Productive Aging. Butler & Oberlink. 176p. 1990. 38.95 (*0-8261-6270-3*) Springer Pub.

Promise of Rain. Shana Abe. 384p. 1998. mass mkt. 5.99 (*0-553-57788-3*) Bantam.

Promise of Rain: Bilingual Collection of Selected Hebrew Poems with English Translations. Moshe D. Shafrir-Stillman. LC 95-2584.Tr. of Ha-Havtahah le-Geshem. (ENG & HEB.). 72p. 1996. pap. 14.95 (*0-7734-2719-8*, Mellen Poetry Pr) E Mellen.

Promise of Reinhold Niebuhr. rev. ed. Gabriel Fackre. 89p. (C). 1994. reprint ed. pap. text 18.50 (*0-8191-9535-9*) U Pr of Amer.

Promise of Representative Bureaucracy: Diversity & Responsiveness in a Government Agency. Sally Coleman-Selden. LC 97-12695. (Bureaucracies, Public Administration, & Public Policy Ser.). 172p. (C). (gr. 13). 1998. pap. text 29.95 (*0-7656-0056-0*) M E Sharpe.

Promise of Representative Bureaucracy: Diversity & Responsiveness in a Government Agency. Sally C. Selden. LC 97-12695. (Bureaucracies, Public Administration, & Public Policy Ser.). 172p. (C). (gr. 13). 1997. text 60.95 (*0-7656-0055-2*) M E Sharpe.

Promise of Rest. Reynolds Price. 368p. 1996. per. 13.00 (*0-684-82510-4*) S&S Trade.

*__Promise of Roses.__ Heidi Betts. 320p. 2000. pap. 4.99 (*0-8439-4738-1*, Leisure Bks) Dorchester Pub Co.

Promise of Schooling: Education in Canada, 1800-1914. Paul Axelrod. LC 97-159155. (Themes in Canadian Social History Ser.). 155p. 1997. text 45.00 (*0-8020-0825-9*, LA411) U of Toronto Pr.

Promise of Shelter. Robyn Sarah. LC 98-138090. 128p. 1997. pap. write for info. (*0-88984-192-6*) Porcup Quill.

Promise of Sleep: A Pioneer in Sleep Medicine Explores the Vital Connection Between Health, Happiness, & a Good Nights Sleep. William C. Dement & Christopher Vaughan. LC 98-23527. 540p. 1999. 24.95 (*0-385-32008-6*) Delacorte.

*__Promise of Sleep: A Pioneer in Sleep Medicine Explores the Vital Connection Between Health, Happiness & a Good Nights Sleep.__ William C. Dement & Christopher Vaughan. 560p. 2000. pap. 14.95 (*0-440-50901-7*, Dell Trade Pbks) Dell.

Promise of Summer. large type ed. Lynn Bulock. 154p. 1993. reprint ed. pap. 13.95 (*1-56054-677-8*) Thorndike Pr.

Promise of Tax Reform. Ed. by Joseph A. Pechman. LC 85-1236. 1985. 15.95 (*0-13-731092-7*) Am Assembly.

*__Promise of the City: Space, Identity & Politics in Contemporary Social Thought.__ Kian Tajbakhsh. LC 99-56668. 250p. 2000. pap. 17.95 (*0-520-22278-4*, Pub. by U CA Pr) Cal Prin Full Svc.

*__Promise of the City: Space, Identity, & Politics in Contemporary Social Thought.__ Kian Tajbakhsh. LC 99-56668. 250p. 2000. 45.00 (*0-520-22277-6*, Pub. by U CA Pr) Cal Prin Full Svc.

Promise of the Father. Frank Bailey. 76p. 1998. pap. 6.00 (*1-879451-05-0*) Carpenters Pub.

Promise of the Father. Phoebe Palmer. pap. 19.99 (*0-88019-099-X*) Schmul Pub Co.

*__Promise of the Father: God, Jesus & the New Community.__ Marianne Meye Thompson. 200p. 2000. pap. 16.95 (*0-664-22197-1*, Pub. by Westminster John Knox) Presbyterian Pub.

Promise of the Fountain: Health Secrets for Life, Longevity & Freedom from Fear of Disease. Michael Capria. (Illus.). 264p. (Orig.). 1993. pap. text 15.95 (*0-9638492-0-4*) Plumosa Pr.

*__Promise of the Gun.__ Sam Gort. 256p. 1999. 18.99 (*1-85389-948-8*) Ulverscroft.

Promise of the Harvest: A Novel, No. 4. Jean Grant. LC 95-34692. (Salinas Valley Saga Ser.: Bk. 4). 228p. 1996. pap. 10.99 (*0-7852-8105-3*) Nelson.

Promise of the Land: The Inheritance of the Land of Canaan by the Israelites. Moshe Weinfeld. (Taubman Lectures in Jewish Studies: No. 3). 384p. (C). 1992. 45.00 (*0-520-07510-2*, Pub. by U CA Pr) Cal Prin Full Svc.

Promise of the Land As Oath: A Key to the Formation of the Pentateuch. Suzanne Boorer. (Beiheft zur Zeitschrift fuer die Alttestamentliche Wissenschaft Ser.: No. 205). xvi, 470p. (C). 1992. lib. bdg. 141.55 (*3-11-013505-1*) De Gruyter.

Promise of the New South: Life after Reconstruction. Edward L. Ayers. (Illus.). 592p. (C). 1993. reprint ed. pap. text 18.95 (*0-19-508548-5*) OUP.

Promise of the Rose. Brenda Joyce. LC 93-90339. 448p. (Orig.). 1993. mass mkt. 6.99 (*0-380-77140-3*, Avon Bks) Morrow Avon.

Promise of the Rose Stone. Claudia McKay. LC 86-62343. 238p. 1986. pap. 7.95 (*0-934678-09-X*) New Victoria Pubs.

Promise of the Spirit. Andrew Murray. 1990. pap. 4.99 (*0-7208-0748-4*) Zondervan.

Promise of the West: The Greek World, Rome & Judaism. Alan E. Samuel. 500p. 1988. lib. bdg. 95.00 (*0-415-00274-5*) Routledge.

Promise of Theory: Education & the Politics of Cultural Change. C. A. Bowers. LC 86-23056. (John Dewey Lecture Ser.: No. 19). 128p. 1987. reprint ed. pap. 39.70 (*0-608-04167-X*, 206490100011) Bks Demand.

Promise of Theory: Education & the Politics of Cultural Change. C. A. Bowers. 128p. (C). 1986. reprint ed. text 21.00 (*0-8077-2840-3*) Tchrs Coll.

Promise of Thunder. Connie Mason. 448p. (Orig.). 1996. mass mkt. 5.99 (*0-8439-4194-4*) Dorchester Pub Co.

Promise of Tomorrow. Ed. by Rick Schaub. LC 98-146508. 1998. 69.95 (*1-57553-610-2*) Watermrk Pr.

Promise of Tomorrow. large type ed. Honor Vincent. (Linford Romance Library). 1990. pap. 16.99 (*0-7089-6831-7*, Linford) Ulverscroft.

Promise of Total Protection. E. Willis. 1978. 2.00 (*0-89858-022-6*) Fill the Gap.

Promise of Trinitarian Theology. Colin E. Gunton. 202p. 1993. pap. text 25.95 (*0-567-29224-X*, Pub. by T & T Clark) Bks Intl VA.

Promise of Trinitarian Theology. 2nd expanded rev. ed. Colin E. Gunton. 224p. pap. 25.95 (*0-567-08574-0*, Pub. by T & T Clark) Bks Intl VA.

Promise of Virtue. Eugene F. Hemrick. LC 98-40704. 160p. 1999. pap. 12.95 (*0-87793-671-4*) Ave Maria.

Promise of Winter: Quickening the Spirit on Ordinary Days & in Fallow Seasons. Martin Marty & Micah Marty. (Illus.). 111p. (Orig.). 1997. pap. 16.00 (*0-8028-4436-7*) Eerdmans.

Promise of Youth: Follow-up Studies of a Thousand Gifted Children. Barbara S. Burks et al. (Genetic Studies of Genius: Vol. III). xiv, 508p. 1930. 65.00 (*0-8047-0011-7*) Stanford U Pr.

Promise or Pretence? A Christian's Guide to Sexual Morals. A. E. Harvey. 1994. pap. 13.00 (*0-334-01283-X*) TPI PA.

Promise Pending. Gail MacMillan. LC 98-96066. 192p. 1998. 18.95 (*0-8034-9292-8*) Bouregy.

*__Promise Prevails.__ David G. Keane. 140p. 1999. pap. 9.95 (*0-9669771-0-6*) Royal Pubg.

Promise Quilt. Candice F. Ransom. LC 99-13053. (Illus.). 32p. (J). (gr. 2-4). 1999. 15.95 (*0-8027-8694-4*); lib. bdg. 16.85 (*0-8027-8695-2*) Walker & Co.

*__Promise Remains: A Love Story.__ Travis Thrasher. 2000. 12.99 (*0-8423-3621-4*) Tyndale Hse.

Promise Renewed: Jesuit Higher Education for a New Millennium. Ed. by Martin R. Tripole. LC 98-36980. 500p. 1999. pap. 19.95 (*0-8294-1292-1*) Loyola Pr.

Promise Song. Linda Holeman. LC 96-61149. 264p. (J). (gr. 6-9). 1997. pap. 6.95 (*0-88776-387-1*) Tundra Bks.

*__Promise Switchback.__ Jo Bannister. 1999. 25.00 (*0-7278-5489-5*, Pub. by Severn Hse) Chivers N Amer.

Promise That Was America. Edwin C. Anderson. LC 97-32193. 1998. write for info. (*0-9660522-2-6*) Jerns Mont Pr.

Promise to Akiko: A Mother's Notes. Tsunekio Kunou. 160p. 1998. 23.50 (*0-88739-180-X*) Creat Arts Bk.

P

An Asterisk (*) at the beginning of an entry indicates that the title is appearing for the first time.

Promise to Aleiko: A Mother's Notes. Tsuneko Kunou. LC 97-66000. 160p. 1998. reprint ed. pap. 13.50 (*0-88739-153-2*) Creat Arts Bk.

Promise to Catie. Judd Holt. LC 92-9905. 242p. 1992. 14.95 (*0-929398-41-6*) UNTX Pr.

Promise to Deliver. Rhonda Kanan & Philip Golabuk. Date not set. pap. 21.95 (*1-893064-50-6*, WOW Women Ink) Creative Consort Inc.

Promise to Keep. large type ed. Marlene E. McFadden. LC 97-94871. (Nightingale Ser.). 143p. 1998. pap. 18.95 (*0-7838-8411-7*, G K Hall & Co) Mac Lib Ref.

Promise to Pay. R. McNair Wilson. 1972. 250.00 (*0-8490-0899-9*) Gordon Pr.

Promise to Protect. large type ed. Abigail Gordon. 288p. 1996. 23.99 (*0-263-14618-9*, Pub. by Mills & Boon) Ulverscroft.

Promise to Repay. Amanda Browning. (Presents Ser.: No. 432). 1992. pap. 2.79 (*0-373-11432-X*, 1-11432-1) Harlequin Bks.

Promise to Wake Me. Evelene Steele. LC 95-78576. 151p. pap. 8.95 (*0-9646592-5-5*) Kiamichi.

Promise Unbroken: A Battle of Destiny. Al Lacy. (Battles of Destiny Ser.: Vol. 1). 320p. 1993. pap. 9.99 (*0-88070-581-7*, Multnomah Bks) Multnomah Pubs.

Promise Unfilled: Consumer Protection. 50p. 1970. 8.00 (*0-943136-16-4*) Ctr Analysis Public Issues.

***Promise You Won't Get Mad: And Other Read-Aloud Plays for Young Adults.** Amy Rider. 80p. (YA). (gr. 7-10). 2000. pap. 15.95 (*1-877673-39-0*) Cottonwood Pr.

Promise You Won't Tell Nobody. 2nd rev. ed. Kimberly T. Matthews. 130p. 1998. pap. 11.00 (*0-9667609-0-5*) Kissed Pubns.

Promise You'll Stop Me. D.L. Carey. (Distress Call 911 Ser.). (J). 1997. 9.09 (*0-606-11263-4*, Pub. by Turtleback) Demco.

Promised Brides. Mary Jo Putney et al. 1994. per. 4.99 (*0-373-83296-6*, 1-83296-3) Harlequin Bks.

Promised Child. Jane Taylor. 1997. pap. text 2.99 (*1-85792-297-2*, Pub. by Christian Focus) Spring Arbor Dist.

Promised Child. Avner Gold. Ed. by Y. Y. Reinman. LC 85-72493. (Ruach Ami Ser.: No.1). (Illus.). 128p. (J). (gr. 7-11). 1985. reprint ed. 12.95 (*0-935063-10-2*); reprint ed. pap. 7.95 (*0-935063-00-5*) CIS Comm.

Promised City: New York's Jews, 1870-1914. Moses Rischin. (Illus.). 342p. 1972. pap. 17.00 (*0-674-71501-2*) HUP.

Promised Day Is Come. Shoghi Effendi. 219p. 1994. pap. 3.95 (*0-87743-244-9*) Bahai.

Promised End: Essays & Reviews, 1942-1962. Stanley E. Hyman. 380p. 1977. 22.95 (*0-8369-2597-1*) Ayer.

Promised God-Man Is Here: The Extraordinary Life-Story, the Crazy Teaching Work & the Divinely Emerging World-Blessing Work of the Divine World-Teacher of the Late-Time, Ruchira Avatar Adi Da Samraj. Carolyn Lee. LC 98-89626. (Illus.). 856p. 1998. pap. 9.95 (*1-57097-059-9*) Dawn Horse Pr.

Promised Land. Mary Antin & Werner Sollors. LC 96-26048. 196p. 1997. pap. 10.95 (*0-14-018985-8*) Viking Penguin.

Promised Land. Pat Cadigan. (Lost in Space (Digest) Ser.). 208p. 1999. mass mkt. 5.99 (*0-06-105909-9*) HarpC.

Promised Land. Howard Convers. LC 96-225333. (Illus.). 185p. (Orig.). 1996. pap., per. 23.95 (*0-9653430-0-6*) H Convers.

Promised Land. John Culea. LC 98-17112. 350p. 1998. 11.99 (*1-56476-722-1*) SP Pubns.

Promised Land. Abba Eban. LC 97-73069. 168p. 1997. 49.99 (*1-57866-007-6*) Galahad Bks.

Promised Land. Cynthia Felice & Connie Willis. LC 96-31436. 240p. 1997. 21.95 (*0-441-00405-9*) Ace Bks.

Promised Land. Isabelle Holland. LC 94-42284. 176p. (J). (gr. 3-7). 1996. 15.95 (*0-590-47176-7*) Scholastic Inc.

Promised Land. Nicholas Lemann. 320p. 1992. pap. 16.00 (*0-679-73347-7*) McKay.

***Promised Land.** New Leaf Press Staff. (Awsome Adventure Bible Stories Ser.). (Illus.). (J). 2000. pap. 5.99 (*0-89051-327-9*) Master Bks.

Promised Land. Robert B. Parker. 224p. 1983. mass mkt. 6.99 (*0-440-17197-0*) Dell.

***Promised Land.** Ray L. Vander. 1999. pap., teacher ed. 27.99 (*0-310-67856-0*) Zondervan.

Promised Land. Ruhama Veltfort. LC 98-21805. 300p. 1998. 23.95 (*1-57131-022-3*) Milkweed Ed.

Promised Land. Connie Willis & Cynthia Felice. 1998. mass mkt. 5.99 (*0-441-00543-8*) Ace Bks.

***Promised Land.** large type ed. Caroline Gray. 408p. 1999. 31.99 (*0-7089-4158-3*) Ulverscroft.

Promised Land. large type ed. Michele Guinness. 1989. 27.99 (*0-7089-2104-3*) Ulverscroft.

Promised Land. Mary Antin. Ed. by Annette K. Baxter. LC 79-8768. (Signal Lives Ser.). 1980. reprint ed. lib. bdg. 48.49 (*0-405-12818-5*) Ayer.

Promised Land. Mary Antin. (History - United States Ser.). 373p. 1993. reprint ed. lib. bdg. 89.00 (*0-7812-4849-3*) Rprt Serv.

Promised Land. 2nd ed. Mary Antin. LC 84-42936. 397p. 1985. reprint ed. pap. 123.10 (*0-7837-8159-8*, 204786400008) Bks Demand.

Promised Land: Adventures & Encounters in Wild America. rev. ed. Michael Frome. LC 94-4691. (Illus.). 360p. 1994. pap. 19.95 (*0-87049-851-7*) U of Tenn Pr.

Promised Land: And Other Courthouse Adventures. American Bar Association, Litigation Staff. LC 87-70688. 176p. 1987. pap. 14.50 (*0-89707-300-2*, 531-0054) Amer Bar Assn.

Promised Land: Base Christian Communities & the Struggle for the Amazon. Madeleine C. Adriance. LC 94-42607. (SUNY Series in Religion, Culture, & Society). 202p. (C). 1995. text 59.50 (*0-7914-2649-1*); pap. text 19.95 (*0-7914-2650-5*) State U NY Pr.

***Promised Land: Feminist Writing in the German Democratic Republic.** Lorna Martens. (C). 2001. pap. text 19.95 (*0-7914-4860-6*) State U NY Pr.

***Promised Land: Feminist Writing in the German Democratic Republic.** Lorna Martens. (C). 2001. text 59.50 (*0-7914-4859-2*) State U NY Pr.

Promised Land: Homestead Memories. O. Ray Dodson. 191p. (Orig.). 1989. pap. 10.95 (*0-9620550-4-2*) Dodson Assocs.

Promised Land: Italian Poetry after 1975, Vol. 156. Ed. by Luigi Ballerini et al. (Sun & Moon Classics Ser.). 1999. pap. text 25.95 (*1-55713-316-6*, Pub. by Sun & Moon CA) Consort Bk Sales.

Promised Land: Poems from the Journey. Katriel. 51p. 1998. pap. 10.00 (*0-9665863-0-1*) One Night Pub.

Promised Land: The Church. G. J. Zondervan. 1999. student ed. 6.99 (*0-310-67896-X*) Zondervan.

Promised Land: The Great Black Migration & How It Changed America. Nicholas Lemann. 1992. pap. 13.00 (*0-685-57357-5*) Vin Bks.

Promised Land: The South since 1945. David R. Goldfield. Ed. by A. S. Eisenstadt & John H. Franklin. LC 86-16243. (American History Ser.). 280p. (C). 1987. pap. 21.95 (*0-88295-850-X*); pap. text 13.95 (*0-88295-843-7*) Harlan Davidson.

Promised Land, Crusader State. Walter A. McDougall. 288p. 1998. pap. 14.00 (*0-395-90132-4*) HM.

Promised Land, Crusader State: The American Encounter with the World since 1776. Walter A. McDougall. LC 96-35467. 286p. 1997. 26.00 (*0-395-83085-0*) HM.

Promised Land, El Salvador. Beth Cagan & Steve Cagan. (Illus.). 220p. (C). 1991. 24.95 (*0-8135-1679-X*) Rutgers U Pr.

Promised Land Instructions. Robert D. Shackelford. 224p. (Orig.). 1987. pap. 7.95 (*0-9618308-1-6*) R Shackelford.

Promised Land, the Life & Times of Henry Dodge, First Territorial Governor of Wisconsin: A Historical Drama. Edna Meudt. Ed. by John E. Westburg. LC 80-54737. 56p. 1980. pap. 8.00 (*0-87423-026-8*) Westburg.

Promised Lands. Jane Rogers. LC 96-29265. 388p. 1997. 24.95 (*0-87951-753-0*, Pub. by Overlook Pr) Penguin Putnam.

Promised Lands. Jane Rogers. 376p. 1998. pap. 14.95 (*0-87951-866-9*, Pub. by Overlook Pr) Penguin Putnam.

Promised Lands: A Novel of the Texas Rebellion. Elizabeth Crook. LC 94-45348. (Southwest Life & Letters Ser.). 528p. 1995. pap. 12.95 (*0-87074-385-6*) SMU Press.

Promised Lands: The Low Countries under Burgundian Rule, 1369-1530. Willem P. Blockmans & Walter Prevenier. LC 98-48565. 1999. 19.95 (*0-8122-1382-3*) U of Pa Pr.

Promised Lands The Low Countries Under Burgundian Rule, 1369-1530. Wim Blockmans. LC 98-48565. 1999. 42.50 (*0-8122-3130-9*) U of Pa Pr.

Promised Lands Vol. 3: Subdivisions & the Law. Patricia A. Simko et al. Ed. by Jean M. Halloran. LC 77-90919. 548p. reprint ed. pap. 169.90 (*0-7837-0333-3*, 204065200003) Bks Demand.

Promised Land/Tierra De Promisio'n: Hispanic Literature, No.45. Jose Eustasio Rivera. Tr. by Carl W. Cobb from SPA. LC 98-31827. 128p. 1999. 59.95 (*0-7734-8277-6*) E Mellen.

Promised Messiah. Philip Ledger. 96p. 1998. pap. 8.00 (*0-89328-144-1*, 65/1867R) Lorenz Corp.

Promised Messiah: The First Coming of Christ. Bruce R. McConkie. LC 78-3478. (Messiah Ser.). 636p. 1990. reprint ed. pap. 11.95 (*0-87579-402-5*) Deseret Bk.

Promised Ones Are Alive & Well on Planet Earth. 1986. write for info. (*0-318-60643-7*) Port Love Intl.

Promised Paradise: Angha Jan - Sufism's Secret Divulged. Avideh Shashaani. LC 93-28463. 115p. (Orig.). (C). 1993. 41.00 (*0-8191-9254-6*) U Pr of Amer.

Promised Paradise: Angha Jan - Sufism's Secret Divulged. 2nd ed. Avideh Shashaani. LC 93-28463. 115p. (Orig.). 1997. reprint ed. pap. 12.50 (*0-8191-9255-4*) U Pr of Amer.

Promised Pony. Kathleen Kieffer. (Illus.). 32p. (J). (gr. 4-6). 2000. pap. 14.95 (*1-57532-270-6*) Press-Tige Pub.

***Promised Savior: A Jesse Tree Christmas Devotional.** 2nd rev. ed. Marilyn Kok & Denise Gaskins. Orig. Title: The Jesse Tree: A Christmas Devotional. (Illus.). 100p. 2000. pap. 10.95 (*1-892083-15-9*) Tabletop Acad.

***Promised Splendor.** Connie Mason. 448p. (Orig.). 1999. pap. 5.99 (*0-8439-4608-3*, Leisure Bks) Dorchester Pub Co.

Promised to a Stranger. Linda O'Brien. 384p. 1998. mass mkt. 5.99 (*0-380-80206-6*, Avon Bks) Morrow Avon.

Promised Verse: Poets in the Society of Augustan Rome. Peter White. LC 93-9190. 348p. 1993. 55.50 (*0-674-71525-X*) HUP.

Promiseland: A Century of Life in a Negro Community. Elizabeth R. Bethel. LC 97-27292. 346p. 1997. reprint ed. pap. 16.95 (*1-57003-229-7*) U of SC Pr.

Promises. Peggy Darty. LC 97-26591. 280p. (Orig.). 1997. pap. 9.99 (*1-57673-149-9*, Palisades OR) Multnomah Pubs.

Promises. Roger Elwood. 1997. per. 4.50 (*0-373-87008-6*, 1-87008-8) Harlequin Bks.

***Promises.** Illus. by Betsy Lewin. LC 99-27186. 32p. (J). (gr. k-3). 2000. 16.00 (*0-395-82272-6*, Clarion Bks) HM.

Promises. Kimberly C. Lyons. 203p. 1998. pap. 10.00 (*0-9666027-0-6*) Lyons Den MI.

Promises. Created by Francine Pascal. (Sweet Valley High Ser.: No. 15). 160p. (YA). (gr. 7 up). 1984. mass mkt. 3.99 (*0-553-27940-8*) Bantam.

Promises. Belva Plain. 464p. 1997. mass mkt. 7.50 (*0-440-21687-7*) Dell.

Promises. Belva Plain. 1996. pap. 6.99 (*0-440-29544-0*) Doubleday.

Promises. Nancy A. Richardson. (Star Wars: No. 3). (Orig.). (J). (gr. 4-7). 1999. mass mkt. 4.50 (*0-425-16955-3*) Berkley Pub.

Promises. Nancy A. Richardson. (Star Wars: No. 3). 128p. (Orig.). (J). (gr. 3-5). 1996. mass mkt. 4.50 (*1-57297-097-9*) Blvd Books.

Promises. Katherine Stone. 512p. 1996. mass mkt. 6.99 (*0-8217-5248-0*, Zebra Kensgtn) Kensgtn Pub Corp.

Promises. Kate William. (Sweet Valley High Ser.: No. 15). (YA). (gr. 7 up). 1985. 8.35 (*0-606-01263-X*, Pub. by Turtleback) Demco.

Promises. large type ed. Belva Plain. LC 96-20236. 1996. lib. bdg. 27.95 (*0-7838-1842-4*, G K Hall Lrg Type) Mac Lib Ref.

Promises. large type ed. Belva Plain. LC 96-20236. 1997. pap. 25.95 (*0-7838-1841-6*, G K Hall Lrg Type) Mac Lib Ref.

Promises. Charlotte Vale Allen. 369p. 1980. reprint ed. pap. 20.00 (*1-892738-26-0*) Isld Nation.

Promises: A Daily Guide to Supernatural Living. Bill Bright. 384p. 1998. reprint ed. 14.99 (*1-56399-043-1*) NewLife Pubns.

***Promises: A Gallery of Biblical Portraits, Vol. 4.** Steve Stephens. (Story Teller Ser.). (Illus.). 2000. pap. text 9.99 (*1-57748-851-2*) Barbour Pub.

Promises: A Teen's Guide to Pregnancy. Ginny Brinkley & Sherry Sampson. (Illus.). 48p. (YA). (gr. 7-12). 1993. pap. text. write for info. (*0-9622585-4-7*) Pink Inc.

Promises & Beginnings. Jack W. Hayford. LC 94-166329. (Spirit-Filled Life Study Guide Ser.). 1994. pap. 6.99 (*0-8407-8515-1*) Nelson.

Promises & Performance: Presidential Campaigns As Policy Predictors. Michael G. Krukones. LC 84-13208. 158p. (Orig.). 1984. pap. text 20.50 (*0-8191-4214-X*); lib. bdg. 43.75 (*0-8191-4213-1*) U Pr of Amer.

Promises & Pitfalls: A Briefing Paper on Internet Publishing. Ed. by Czeslaw J. Grycz. 76p. 1994. pap. 40.00 (*0-933636-28-8*) AAP.

Promises Broken: Courtship, Class, & Gender in Victorian England. Ginger S. Frost. LC 95-7637. (Victorian Literature & Culture Ser.). 304p. (C). 1995. text 35.00 (*0-8139-1610-0*) U Pr of Va.

Promises Broken, Promises Kept. Janet Q. Bedley. LC 91-6306. 224p. (J). 1991. pap. 6.99 (*1-55513-609-5*, 36095, LifeJourney) Chariot Victor.

Promises Broken, Promises Kept: Continued Writings to God's Glory. Grace O. Weindorf. Ed. by Laura Reynolds. 58p. 1998. 8.95 (*0-9661661-2-4*) Write Designs.

Promises by the Dozen. Tom Carter. LC 87-71393. 160p. (Orig.). 1988. pap. 7.99 (*0-88270-635-7*) Bridge-Logos.

Promises Daily Devotions for Successful Living. Bill Bright. 400p. 1996. pap. 14.99 (*1-56399-054-7*) NewLife Pubns.

Promises de Dios. M. Countryman. (SPA.). 320p. 1987. pap. 3.95 (*0-937347-12-4*) C & D Intl.

Promises for Dads: Encouragement for Standing Strong. Gene Eble & John Waldrop. LC 96-6994. (Pocketpac Bks.). 80p. 1996. pap. 2.99 (*0-87788-633-4*, H Shaw Pubs) Waterbrook Pr.

Promises for Every Day see **Promesas para Cada Dia**

Promises for Little Hearts. James C. Galvin & Tyndale House Publishers Staff. LC 96-46020. (Illus.). (J). 1997. 9.99 (*0-8423-4992-8*) Tyndale Hse.

Promises for People on the Go see **Promesas para Personas Activas**

***Promises for Spirit-Led Living.** Smith Wigglesworth. LC 99-12794. 1999. pap. 6.97 (*1-56955-114-6*) Servant.

Promises for Spiritual Battle: Encouragement in Daily Warfare. Compiled by Anna Trimiew. (Pocketpac Bks.). 96p. 1996. pap. 2.99 (*0-87788-749-7*, H Shaw Pubs) Waterbrook Pr.

Promises from God's Word. LC 96-60098. 256p. 1996. 14.99 (*0-529-10627-2*, GW20) World Publng.

Promises from Proverbs. David Carder. 1984. pap. 11.70 (*0-310-36782-4*, 12732P) Zondervan.

Promises in a New Life: Available to All Who Walk a Twelve Step Path. Linda Macuga. 346p. 1998. pap. 12.95 (*1-891929-03-8*) Four Seasons.

Promises in Poetry, Vol. 1. abr. ed. Nancy Marthaler. (Illus.). 100p. (C). 1989. reprint ed. pap. 8.50 (*0-9624310-9-5*) Words From the Heart Pub.

Promises in the Attic. Elisabeth H. Friedmood. LC 60-12790. 240p. (YA). (gr. 6-9). 1996. reprint ed. pap. 6.95 (*0-913428-14-0*) Landfall Pr.

Promises in the Dust. Bill Bauer. LC 94-43704. 64p. (Orig.). 1995. pap. 10.00 (*1-886157-01-4*) BkMk.

Promises in the Promised Land: Mobility & Inequality in Israel, 89. Vered Kraus & Robert W. Hodge. LC 89-23264. (Contributions in Sociology Ser.: No. 89). 216p. 1990. 57.95 (*0-313-26784-7*, KPF/, Greenwood Pr) Greenwood.

Promises Kept. Martha Culton. (Illus.). 264p. 1995. text 18.99 (*0-9645306-0-0*) United Gospel.

Promises Kept: Memoirs of a Missionary Priest. Fred Julien & Richard Pezdirtz. LC 96-91861. ix, 311p. 1996. 20.00 (*0-9654494-0-8*, 1000) Pez-Tex.

Promises Kept: The Life of an Issei Man. Akemi Kikumura. LC 91-22060. xii, 132p. 1991. 17.95 (*0-88316-563-5*); pap. text 9.95 (*0-88316-562-7*) Chandler & Sharp.

Promises Lost. Audrey Howard. 476p. 1996. 27.00 (*0-340-60951-6*, Pub. by Hodder & Stought Ltd) Trafalgar.

Promises Lost. Audrey Howard. 512p. 1997. mass mkt. 10.95 (*0-340-66601-3*, Pub. by Hodder & Stought Ltd) Trafalgar.

***Promises Made Clear: A Modern Day Catechism Companion.** H. Burnell Baldwin. 44p. 1999. pap. 6.00 (*0-7880-1525-7*) CSS OH.

Promises Made, Promises Kept: The Source of Staying Power in Marriage. E. Scott Mabry. 208p. (Orig.). 1996. pap. 12.95 (*1-883893-50-X*) WinePress Pub.

Promises, Morals, & Law. Patrick S. Atiyah. 214p. 1983. pap. text 24.95 (*0-19-825479-2*) OUP.

Promises Not Kept: The Betrayal of Social Change in the Third World. 4th ed. John Isbister. LC 97-53264. (Illus.). xii, 288p. (C). 1998. pap. 21.95 (*1-56549-078-9*) Kumarian Pr.

Promises of Encouragement. Ed. by Carol Plueddemann. (Pocketpac Bks.). 96p. 1991. pap. text 2.99 (*0-87788-650-4*, H Shaw Pubs) Waterbrook Pr.

***Promises of Glass.** Michael Palmer. LC 99-88019. 128p. 2000. 21.95 (*0-8112-1443-5*, Pub. by New Directions) SPD-Small Pr Dist.

Promises of God. (Walk with Jesus Ser.). 245p. 1990. pap. 30.00 (*1-57277-431-2*) Script Rsch.

Promises of God. Ed. by Thomas A. Jones. 136p. 1998. pap. 7.99 (*1-57782-055-X*) Discipleshp.

Promises of God. Lester Sumrall. 88p. (C). 1987. pap. text 10.00 (*0-937580-73-2*) Sumrall Pubng.

Promises of God: A Promise a Day Keeps the Devil Away. Lester Sumrall. 129p. (Orig.). 1988. pap. text 3.95 (*0-937580-15-5*) Sumrall Pubng.

Promises of God Daybrightners: Catholic Edition. Date not set. 7.95 (*0-88271-576-3*, 10320) Regina Pr.

Promises of God's Abundance for a More Meaningful Life. Kathy Collard Miller. LC 98-86023. (God's Abundance Ser.). 208p. 1998. pap. 9.95 (*0-914984-09-8*, Pub. by Starburst) Natl Bk Netwk.

Promises of Heaven. Lil Copan. (Pocket Pac Ser.). 1997. pap. text 2.99 (*0-87788-618-0*, H Shaw Pubs) Waterbrook Pr.

Promises of Hope. B. Honour. Date not set. pap. 4.99 (*0-906731-72-0*, Pub. by Christian Focus) Spring Arbor Dist.

Promises of Infinity. rev. ed. James I. Mystery. LC 97-94735. (Illus.). 454p. (YA). (gr. 8 up). Date not set. 24.95 (*0-9661550-0-9*, Tomorrow) INEDIN.

Promises of Joy for a Woman of Faith, NIV. gif. ed. LC 97-221572. (Women of Faith Ser.). 128p. 1997. 7.99 (*0-310-97389-9*, Zondervan Gifts) Zondervan.

Promises of Love. Sylvie F. Sommerfield. 1994. pap. 5.99 (*0-7860-0062-7*) Kensgtn Pub Corp.

***Promises of the Heart.** JoAnn Jolley. LC 00-43057. 2000. write for info. (*1-57734-716-1*) Covenant Comms.

Promises of the Past: A History of Indian Education in the United States. David H. DeJong. LC 93-10469. 304p. 1993. 24.95 (*1-55591-905-7*) Fulcrum Pub.

Promises of the Proverbs. Compiled by Michael Beck. 256p. 1998. lthr. 4.97 (*1-57748-202-6*) Barbour Pub.

Promises of the Psalms. Ed. by Ellen Caughey. LC 98-119958. 192p. 1997. lthr. 4.97 (*1-57748-077-5*) Barbour Pub.

Promises of the Sacred Heart. Lawrence G. Lovasik. (Saint Joseph Picture Bks.). (Illus.). 1976. pap. 1.25 (*0-89942-303-5*, 303-00) Catholic Bk Pub.

Promises on Prior Obligations at Common Law, 85. Kevin M. Teeven. LC 97-53289. (Contributions in Legal Studies: Vol. 85). 240p. 1998. 65.00 (*0-313-30652-4*, Greenwood Pr) Greenwood.

Promises, Promises. Laura Peyton Roberts. (Clearwater Crossing Ser.). 224p. (YA). (gr. 7 up). 1998. mass mkt. 3.99 (*0-553-57127-3*) BDD Bks Young Read.

***Promises, Promises.** Laura Peyton Roberts. (Clearwater Crossing Ser.). (YA). (gr. 5-8). 1998. 9.09 (*0-606-13281-3*, Pub. by Turtleback) Demco.

***Promises Promises.** Scanlan. 2000. pap. 8.95 (*0-553-81288-2*, Pub. by Transworld Publishers Ltd) Trafalgar.

Promises, Promises! A Review: 6-7 Economic Summit Declarations on Environment & Development. James N. Barnes. (Illus.). 110p. (Orig.). 1994. pap. 10.00 (*0-913890-40-5*) Friends of Earth.

Promises! Promises! Adventures of Sargento Tico, Cataluna to California, 1766-1802. Betty L. Britton. LC 96-95504. (ENG & SPA., Illus.). 302p. 1997. lib. bdg. 28.50 (*0-9655914-0-9*) Juanez Bks.

***Promises, Promises: Contracts in Russia & Other Post-Communist Economies.** Paul H. Rubin. LC 97-38256. (Shaftesbury Papers: Vol. 11). 96p. (C). 1998. pap. 15.00 (*1-85898-558-7*) E Elgar.

Promises, Promises: Vocal Selections. Ed. by Carol Cuellar. 52p. (Orig.). (C). 1989. pap. text 9.95 (*0-7692-0915-7*, VF1536) Wrner Bros.

***Promises, Promises: Writing On Psychoanalysis And Literature.** Adam Phillips. 280p. 2000. 26.00 (*0-465-05677-6*, Pub. by Basic) HarpC.

Promises, Pumpkins & Prince Charming: Do You Take This Stranger? Karen R. Smith. 1998. per. 3.50 (*0-373-19332-7*, 1-19332-5) Silhouette.

***Promises to Keep.** 140p. (J). (gr. 5-8). 1999. pap. 5.99 (*0-9673794-1-5*) Small Miracles.

Promises to Keep. George Bernau. 1989. mass mkt. 5.95 (*0-446-35605-0*, Pub. by Warner Bks) Little.

Promises to Keep. T. Davis Bunn. 4p. (Orig.). 1991. pap. 10.99 (*1-55661-213-3*) Bethany Hse.

Promises to Keep. Marjorie Eatock. 512p. 1994. mass mkt. 4.99 (*0-8217-4527-1*, Zebra Kensgtn) Kensgtn Pub Corp.

Promises to Keep. Millie H. Griswold. 24p. 1985. student ed. 1.95 (*1-881909-13-1*) Advent Christ Gen Conf.

Promises to Keep. Kathleen Iddings. 68p. (Orig.). 1997. pap. write for info. (*0-942424-12-3*) W Anglia Pubns.

Promises to Keep. Josie Metcalfe. (Romance Ser.: Vol. 429). 1999. mass mkt. 3.50 (*0-373-17429-2*, 1-17429-1, Harlequin) Harlequin Bks.

Promises to Keep. Ernest Michel. LC 93-13550. (Illus.). 320p. 1993. 22.00 (*0-9623032-4-0*) Barricade Bks.

Promises to Keep. Jane Peart. 1998. per. 4.50 (*0-373-87043-4*, 1-87043-5) Harlequin Bks.

P

An Asterisk (*) at the beginning of an entry indicates that the title is appearing for the first time.

Promoting the National Spatial Data Infrastructure Through Partnerships. National Research Council, Mapping Science Committ. LC 94-66772. 113p. (Orig.). (C). 1995. pap. text 24.00 (*0-309-05141-X*) Natl Acad Pr.

Promoting the Profession: A Resource Guide for Marketing & Publicizing Occupational Therapy. Ed. by Suzanne Carlton & Crystal W. Brockington. 129p. (Orig.). 1993. pap. text 16.00 (*1-56900-002-6*) Am Occup Therapy.

Promoting the Professions: Which Way Do We Go? Neville Eldridge & Peter Carvell. 151p. (C). 1986. text 85.00 (*0-85406-304-8*, Pub. by Surveyors Pubns) St Mut.

Promoting the Well-Being of the Elderly: A Community Diagnosis. Thomas T. Wan et al. LC 82-9209. 227p. (C). 1982. text 49.95 (*0-917724-38-0*); pap. text 4.95 (*0-917724-39-9*) Haworth Pr.

Promoting Third-World Development & Food Security. Ed. by Luther G. Tweeten & Donald McClelland. LC 96-47613. 280p. 1997. 59.95 (*0-275-95815-9*, Praeger Pubs) Greenwood.

Promoting Tissue Regeneration Potency & Mechanism of Natural Products: Muscle Regeneration. Xuhui Wang & Sophie Chen. (CHI., Illus.). (Orig.). 1993. pap. 65.00 (*0-9636432-0-7*) Int Med Res.

Promoting Tourism in Rural America: A Bibliography. Ed. by Dorothy A. Heise. 74p. (Orig.). (C). 1995. pap. text 20.00 (*0-7881-2178-2*) DIANE Pub.

Promoting U. S. Economic Relations with Africa: Report of an Independent Task Force. Contrib. by Peggy Dulany et al. 1998. pap. 5.00 (*0-87609-215-6*) Coun Foreign.

Promoting Women. HMSO Staff. 50p. 1992. pap. 13.00 (*0-11-321537-1*, HM15371, Pub. by Statnry Office) Bernan Associates.

***Promoting Work Opportunities for Older Americans.** Committee for Economic Development. LC 99-45902. 1999. write for info. (*0-87186-135-6*) Comm Econ Dev.

Promoting World Recovery: A Statement on Global Economic Strategy. Institute for International Economics Staff. LC 82-84529. 48p. reprint ed. pap. 30.00 (*0-608-12182-7*, 202479200038) Bks Demand.

Promoting Your Acting Career. Glenn Alterman. LC 98-70412. 224p. 1998. pap. 18.95 (*1-880559-97-8*) Allworth Pr.

Promoting Your Business with Free Publicity. Donna G. Albrecht. 1996. pap. text 16.95 (*0-89384-305-9*) P-H.

Promoting Your Professional Practice. Jack Gottschalk. 356p. 1992. pap. 24.95 (*0-929543-14-9*) Round Lake Pub.

Promoting Your Professional Services. Jack Gottschalk. 300p. 1991. write for info. (*0-318-68316-4*, Irwn Prfssnl) McGraw-Hill Prof.

Promoting Your School: A Public Relations Handbook. Irene Lober. LC 92-62396. 325p. 1997. text 39.95 (*0-87762-687-1*) Scarecrow.

Promoting Your School: Going Beyond PR. Carolyn Warner. 200p. 1994. pap., student ed. 32.95 (*0-8039-6120-0*) Corwin Pr.

Promoting Your Web Site. DDC Publishing Staff. 1999. pap. text 18.00 (*1-56243-833-6*) DDC Pub.

Promoting Yourself: 50 Ways to Increase Your Prestige, Power, & Paycheck. Marlene Caroselli. Ed. by Kelly Scanlon. LC 95-68998. (Illus.). 139p. (Orig.). 1995. 15.95 (*1-878542-89-3*) SkillPath Pubns.

Promotion. Gerald J. Boudreau. LC 97-90905. 245p. 1998. pap. 12.95 (*0-533-12508-1*) Vantage.

ProMotion: How Today's Creators Broke into Comics & Their Advice to You! Brian Saner-Lamken. (Illus.). 180p. (Orig.). 1995. pap. 14.95 (*0-9649237-0-X*) Harbor Pr PA.

Promotion: Analysis,strategy ,creativity. William P. Dommermuth. LC 84-970. (SWC-Marketing). 745p. (C). 1984. mass mkt. 45.00 (*0-534-03106-4*) PWS Pubs.

Promotion & Control of Industry in Postwar France. John Sheahan. LC 63-7592. 314p. 1963. 37.95 (*0-674-71550-0*) HUP.

Promotion & Development of Traditional Medicine: Report of a WHO Meeting, 1978. (Technical Report Ser.: No. 622). 40p. 1978. pap. text 5.00 (*92-4-120622-5*, 1100622) World Health.

***Promotion & Integrated Marketing Communication.** Semenik et al. (Swc-Marketing Ser.). (C). 2001. text 62.50 (*0-324-06253-2*) Sth-Wstrn College.

Promotion & Marketing for Broadcasting & Cable. 3rd ed. Susan T. Eastman et al. LC 98-56532. (Illus.). 248p. 1999. pap. 29.95 (*0-240-80342-6*, Focal) Buttrwrth-Heinemann.

Promotion & Tenure: Community & Socialization in Academe. William G. Tierney & Estela M. Bensimon. LC 96-10349. (SUNY Series, Frontiers in Education). 161p. (C). 1996. pap. text 16.95 (*0-7914-2978-4*) State U NY Pr.

Promotion Day Program Builder. 32p. 1961. 4.99 (*0-8341-9727-8*, MP-501) Lillenas.

Promotion Design, Vol. 1. Ed. by B. Martin Pedersen. (Illus.). 256p. 1999. text 70.00 (*1-888001-61-5*, Pub. by Graphis US) Watsn-Guptill.

Promotion for Sport Directors. John R. Johnson. LC 95-34843. (Illus.). 152p. 1995. pap. text 22.00 (*0-87322-722-0*, PJOH0722) Human Kinetics.

Promotion Management. Burnett. (C). 1992. pap., teacher ed. 4.76 (*0-395-56554-5*) HM.

Promotion Management. John J. Burnett. (C). 1992. text 75.96 (*0-395-56553-7*) HM.

***Promotion of Architecture Some Lessons from France.** Sebastian Loew. LC 99-236613. 40p. (Orig.). 1998. pap. text 12.00 (*1-901092-02-X*) Andreas Papadakis.

Promotion of Continence in Adult Nursing. D. Colborn. 192p. 1994. 32.99 (*1-56593-192-0*, 0507) Singular Publishing.

Promotion of Education & Awareness in the Area of Copyright & Neighbouring Rights Concerning Creativity (Recommendation & Explanatory Memorandum), No. R(94)3. 1995. 12.00 (*92-871-2732-8*, Pub. by Council of Europe) Manhattan Pub Co.

Promotion of Exports from Texas. Sidney Weintraub. (Policy Research Project Report Ser.: No. 46). 195p. 1981. pap. 5.95 (*0-89940-648-3*) LBJ Sch Pub Aff.

Promotion of Investment in Countries in the Early Stages of Tourism Development: Mongolia, Myanmar, Nepal & Viet Nam. (Studies in Trade & Investment: No. 14). 140p. 22.00 (*92-1-119720-1*) UN.

Promotion of Medical Practitioners' Interest in Preventive Medicine. (Technical Report Ser.: No. 269). 22p. 1964. pap. text 3.00 (*92-4-120269-6*) World Health.

Promotion of Mental Health, 1995. Ed. by Colin Reed & Dennis R. Trent. (Mental Health Promotion Unit Ser.: No. 5). 429p. 1996. pap. 87.95 (*1-85972-284-9*, Pub. by Avebry) Ashgate Pub Co.

Promotion of Mental Health, 1996. Ed. by Denis R. Trent & Colin A. Reed. 368p. 1997. text 83.95 (*1-85972-652-6*, Pub. by Avebry) Ashgate Pub Co.

Promotion of Mental Health, 1991, Vol. 1. Dennis R. Trent. (Mental Health Promotion Unit Ser.). 356p. 1992. 75.95 (*1-85628-307-0*, Pub. by Avebry) Ashgate Pub Co.

Promotion of Mental Health, 1992, Vol. 2. Dennis R. Trent & Colin Reed. 662p. 1993. 85.95 (*1-85628-430-1*, Pub. by Avebry) Ashgate Pub Co.

Promotion of Mental Health, 1994, Vol. 4. Ed. by Colin Reed & Dennis R. Trent. (Mental Health Promotion Unit Ser.). 560p. 1995. 101.95 (*1-85972-065-X*, Pub. by Avebry) Ashgate Pub Co.

Promotion of Mental Health 1993, Vol. 3. Trent & Reed. 432p. 1994. 82.95 (*1-85628-619-3*) Ashgate Pub Co.

Promotion of Pharmaceuticals: Issues, Trends, Options. Ed. by Dev S. Pathak et al. LC 92-49617. (Journal of Pharmaceutical Marketing & Management: Vol. 7, No. 1). (Illus.). 203p. 1993. pap. text 19.95 (*1-56024-384-8*); lib. bdg. 49.95 (*1-56024-383-X*) Haworth Pr.

Promotion of Physical Activity in the Community: A Manual for Community Health Professionals. 2nd ed. Health Promotion Resource Center Staff. Ed. by Abby C. King et al. 86p. 1991. reprint ed. pap. 19.50 (*1-879552-19-1*) SCRDP.

Promotion of Public Library Use: An Experiment in Promotion & National Survey of Activities. Roger G. Woodhouse & J. Neill. LC 81-188099. (Occasional Papers/Department of Librarianship, Newcastle upon Tyne Polytechnic). 62p. 1978. write for info. (*0-905984-35-8*) Brit Lib R & D.

Promotion of Small- & Medium-Sized Enterprises in Europe. 1994. 12.00 (*92-871-2549-X*, Pub. by Council of Europe) Manhattan Pub Co.

Promotion of the Rights of Patients in Europe: Proceedings of a WHO Consultation. Ed. by World Health Organization Staff. LC 95-31704. 164p. (C). 1995. lib. bdg. 57.50 (*90-411-0100-4*) Kluwer Academic.

***Promotion of Wellness in Children & Adolescents.** Dante Cicchetti. LC 00-30364. 2000. write for info. (*0-87868-791-2*, CWLA Pr) Child Welfare.

Promotion of Women's Participation in Water Resources Development. (Natural Resources/Water Ser.: No. 25). 63p. pap. 12.00 (*92-1-104354-9*, 90.II.A.24) UN.

Promotion Outreach Efforts for Census 2000: Hearing Before the Subcommittee on National Security, International Affairs & Criminal Justice of the Committee on Government Reform & Oversight, House of Representatives, 105th Congress, First Session, April 29, 1997. LC 98-160466. iii, 75p. 1998. write for info. (*0-16-056311-9*) USGPO.

Promotion Planning All Year 'Round. 2nd ed. Claudia Hannaford & Ruth S. Smith. LC 75-6857. (Guide Ser.: No. 2). (Illus.). 68p. 1996. pap. 11.00 (*0-915324-09-1*) CSLA.

Promotion Planning Process: Sales Promotion vs. Advertising. Roger A. Strang. LC 80-18848. 127p. 1980. 55.00 (*0-275-90558-6*, C0558, Praeger Pubs) Greenwood.

Promotion Point Accelerator: The Consolidated Army Correspondence Course Program. 2nd rev. ed. Richard Morales. Ed. by Janine H. Hornung. LC 97-141123. (Fast Mover Ser.: Vol. 97-1). Orig. Title: The Promotion Point Accelerator: TRADOC Correspondence Courses & Subcourses. (Illus.). 92p. 1997. pap. 19.95 (*0-9654788-0-7*) Non Com Pub.

Promotion Point Accelerator: TRADOC Correspondence Courses & Subcourses see Promotion Point Accelerator: The Consolidated Army Correspondence Course Program

Promotion Strategies. Vilma Barr. (Architecture Ser.). 182p. 1995. 39.95 (*0-471-28559-5*, VNR) Wiley.

Promotion Strategies for Design & Construction. V. Barr. 1995. pap. 39.95 (*0-442-01439-2*, VNR) Wiley.

Promotion Test Battery. Jack Rudman. (Career Examination Ser.: Vol. C-3815). 1997. pap. 29.95 (*0-8373-3815-8*) Nat Learn.

Promotional Copy. Robin Kahn. 1994. pap. 20.00 (*1-881616-16-9*) Dist Art Pubs.

Promotional Culture: Advertising & Symbolic Expression in Late Capitalism. Andrew Wernick. (Theory, Culture & Society Ser.). (Illus.). 256p. 1992. 59.95 (*0-8039-8390-5*); pap. 22.95 (*0-8039-8391-3*) Sage.

Promotional Edge: The Complete Guide to the Successful Oral Interview. 3rd rev. ed. Ronald S. Bateman & Harry C. Mounts, Jr. LC 98-91379. ii, 167p. 1998. pap. text 12.95 (*0-9663652-0-8*) Promot Edge Pub.

Promotional Feats: The Role of Planned Events in the Marketing Communications Mix. Eric J. Soares. LC 91-7809. 240p. 1991. 57.95 (*0-89930-515-6*, SJF/, Quorum Bks) Greenwood.

Promotional Marketing. 2nd ed. William Robinson & Christine Hauri. Ed. by Anne Knudsen. (Illus.). 192p. (Orig.). 1995. pap. 23.95 (*0-8442-3151-7*, NTC Business Bks) NTC Contemp Pub Co.

Promotional Marketing: Ideas & Techniques for Success in Sales Promotion. William A. Robinson & Christine Hauri. Orig. Title: Strategic Sales Promotion. (Illus.). 192p. 1992. 39.95 (*0-8442-3150-9*, NTC Business Bks) NTC Contemp Pub Co.

Promotional Material: Birthday Postcard. (Church Music for Children Ser.). (Illus.). (J). 3.00 (*0-687-00293-1*) Abingdon.

Promotional Material: "Miss You" Postcard. (Church Music for Children Ser.). (J). 3.00 (*0-687-00324-5*) Abingdon.

Promotional Material: Promotion Certificate. (Church Music for Children Ser.). (J). 3.25 (*0-687-00182-X*) Abingdon.

Promotional Material: Recognition Certificate. (Church Music for Children Ser.). (J). 3.25 (*0-687-00183-8*) Abingdon.

Promotional Plans in the High School. Will French. LC 72-176787. (Columbia University. Teachers College. Contributions to Education Ser.: No. 587). reprint ed. 37.50 (*0-404-55587-X*) AMS Pr.

***Promotional Practice 1998-99.** Ace. 208p. 2000. pap. text 34.95 (*0-7506-4031-6*) Buttrwrth-Heinemann.

Promotional Practices & Policies. Paul M. Connolly. (Studies in Productivity: Highlights of the Literature Ser.: Vol. 41). 1985. 55.00 (*0-08-029515-0*) Work in Amer.

Promotional Publishing: Turn Wary Prospects into Trusting Clients by Packaging Your Knowledge, Experience & Expertise. Keith F. Luscher. LC 94-78028. 40p. (Orig.). 1994. pap. 4.75 (*0-9625977-0-8*) K & L Pubns.

Promotional Strategy: Managing the Marketing Communications Process. 8th ed. James F. Engel et al. LC 93-48793. (Marketing Ser.). 640p. (C). 1994. text 69.30 (*0-256-12240-7*, Irwn McGrw-H) McGrw-H Hghr Educ.

Promotional Strategy: Marketing Communications in Practice. L. Koekemoer et al. 464p. 1999. pap. 32.50 (*0-7021-4370-7*, Pub. by Juta & Co) Intl Spec Bk.

Promotional Strategy, International: Managing the Marketing Communications Process. 7th ed. James Engel et al. (C). 1991. text, student ed. 32.50 (*0-256-11408-0*, Irwn McGrw-H) McGrw-H Hghr Educ.

Promotional Test Questions. Daniel M. Del Bagno & R. Spina. 420p. 1991. 25.95 (*0-87526-381-X*) Gould.

Promotionals, 1934-1983: Dealership Vehicles in Miniature. Steve Butler. LC 97-185823. (Illus.). 1997. write for info. (*0-89538-090-0*) L-W Inc.

Promoviendo un Futuro Saludable: Manual de Entrenamiento para Jovenes Promotores de Salud. Carmen Duran & Paloma Cuchi.Tr. of Promoting a Healty Future. (SPA., Illus.). 200p. 1997. pap. text. write for info. (*0-9658448-1-1*) LatAm Youth.

Promoviendo un Futuro Saludable: Manual de Entrenamiento para Jovenes Promotores de Salud. unabridged ed. Carmen Duran & Paloma Cuchi.Tr. of Promoting a Healty Future. (SPA., Illus.). 200p. 1997. text. write for info. (*0-9658448-0-3*) LatAm Youth.

Prompt a Day! 360 Thought-Provoking Writing Prompts Keyed to Every Day of the School Year. Jacqueline Sweeney. 1998. pap. text 14.95 (*0-590-18738-4*) Scholastic Inc.

Prompt & Utter Destruction: Truman & the Use of Atomic Bombs Against Japan. J. Samuel Walker. LC 96-52038. (Illus.). 160p. (gr. 13). 1997. pap. 15.95 (*0-8078-4662-7*) U of NC Pr.

Prompter. Aaron Hill & William Popple. Ed. by William W. Appleton & Kalman A. Burnim. LC 65-16247. (Illus.). 1972. 23.95 (*0-405-08615-6*) Ayer.

Prompter Is a Royal Publisher. Myungkark Park. 100p. 1996. pap. write for info. (*1-877974-28-5*) Prompter Pubns.

Prompting the Age: Poems Early & Late. A. L. Rowse. (C). 1989. text 60.00 (*1-85022-056-5*, Pub. by Dyllansow Truran) St Mut.

***Promptings from Paradise.** J. Philip Newell. LC 99-88940. 80p. 2000. pap. 7.95 (*0-8091-3935-9*) Paulist Pr.

Promptings of Desire: Creativity & the Religious Impulse in the Works of D. H. Lawrence, 49. Paul Poplawski. LC 92-42429. (Contributions to the Study of World Literature Ser.: No. 49). 224p. 1993. 52.95 (*0-313-28789-9*, GM8789, Greenwood Pr) Greenwood.

Promptorium Parvulorum: The First English-Latin Dictionary. Ed. by A. L. Mayhew. (EETS. ES Ser.: No. 102). 1974. reprint ed. 75.00 (*0-527-00306-9*) Periodicals Srv.

Promptorium Parvulorum Sive Clericorum, Lexicon Anglo-Latinum Princeps, 3 vols. Anglicus Galfridus. LC 70-168091. (Camden Society, London. Publications, First Ser.: Nos. 25, 54, 89). (LAT.). reprint ed. 145.00 (*0-404-50209-1*) AMS Pr.

Prompts: Readings for ESL Composition. Bruce Leeds. (Illus.). 78p. (Orig.). (C). 1990. pap. text 9.95 (*0-916177-68-8*) Am Eng Pubns.

Promulgation of Universal Peace: Talks Delivered by Abdu'l-Baha During His Visit to the United States & Canada in 1912. 2nd ed. Abdu'l-Baha. LC 81-21689. 513p. 1982. 16.95 (*0-87743-172-8*, 103-039) Bahai.

Promus & Cassandra, Pts. 1 & 2. George Whetstone. (Tudor Facsimile Texts. Old English Plays Ser.: No. 52). reprint ed. 49.50 (*0-404-53352-3*) AMS Pr.

Promus of Formularies & Elegancies Illustrated & Elucidated by Passages from Shakespeare. Henry Pott. 648p. 1997. reprint ed. pap. 45.00 (*0-7661-0084-7*) Kessinger Pub.

Prone Body Under. Rick London. 1982. pap. 3.00 (*0-917588-05-3*) Trike.

Prone to Violence Erin Pizzey & Jeff Shapiro. LC 98-168194. 252p. 1982. write for info. (*0-600-20551-7*) P HM.

Pronghorn Home Ranges, Movements, & Habitat Selection in Central Arizona: Arizona Game & Fish Department Technical Report, No. 13. A. Alexander et al. (Illus.). 80p. (Orig.). 1994. pap. 5.00 (*0-917563-18-2*) AZ Game & Fish.

***Pronghorns.** Aaron Frisch. LC 99-36195. (Kings of the Mountain Ser.). 2001. lib. bdg. write for info. (*1-58340-054-0*) Smart Apple.

PRonline: Acceso Remoto a Leyes, Legislaciun, Reglamentos y Decisiones. write for info. (*0-614-05951-8*, MICHIE) LEXIS Pub.

Pronomical Reference. Lawrence Solan. 1983. text 160.50 (*90-277-1495-9*) Kluwer Academic.

Pronoms et Visages: Lecture de'Emmanuel Levinas. Michel Dupuis. (Phaenomenologica Ser.: No. 134). 240p. (C). 1996. lib. bdg. 118.00 (*0-7923-3655-0*, Pub. by Kluwer Academic) Kluwer Academic.

Prononciation du Francais Standard. Monique Leon. (Coll. Linguistique Appliquee). 16.50 (*0-685-36699-5*); 39.95 (*0-8288-7873-0*, F139430); audio 59.95 (*0-685-36700-2*) Fr & Eur.

***Pronoun Envy: Literary Uses of Linguistic Gender.** Anna Livia. (Studies in Language & Gender). 272p. 2000. pap. 29.95 (*0-19-513853-8*); text 55.00 (*0-19-513852-X*) OUP.

***Pronoun Music.** Richard Cohen. 260p. 2000. pap. write for info. (*1-929355-03-3*) Pleasure Boat.

Pronounce It Perfectly in English. Jean Yates. LC 95-12841. (Barron's Educational Ser.). 160p. 1995. pap. 24.95 incl. audio (*0-8120-8244-3*) Barron.

Pronounce It Perfectly in French. Christopher Kendris. LC 93-44387. (Pronounce It Perfectly Ser.). (FRE & ENG.). 140p. 1994. pap. 19.95 incl. audio (*0-8120-8038-6*) Barron.

Pronounce It Perfectly in German, 2 cassettes. Annegret Decker. LC 93-49850. (Pronounce It Perfectly Ser.). (ENG & GER.). 140p. 1994. pap. 39.95 incl. audio (*0-8120-8034-3*) Barron.

Pronounce It Perfectly in Italian! Marcel Danesi. (Pronounce It Perfectly Ser.). (ITA & ENG.). 140p. 1994. pap. 16.95 incl. audio (*0-8120-8015-7*) Barron.

Pronounce It Perfectly in Japanese. Charles Inouye & Charles S. Inouye. LC 94-23498. (JPN & ENG.). 250p. 1994. pap. 16.95 incl. audio (*0-8120-8035-1*) Barron.

Pronounce It Perfectly in Russian, 2 cass., Set. Thomas R. Beyer, Jr. LC 93-49857. (Pronounce It Perfectly Ser.). (RUS & ENG.). 140p. 1994. pap. 16.95 incl. audio (*0-8120-8016-5*) Barron.

Pronounce It Perfectly in Spanish. Jean Yates. LC 93-45376. (ENG.). 1994. write for info. (*0-8120-1658-0*) Barron.

Pronounciation Dictionary see Dictionnaire de la Prononciation

Pronounciation of Contrast English. Nilson. 112p. 1987. pap. text 19.93 (*0-13-730938-4*) P-H.

Pronouncing American English. 2nd ed. Orion. (College ESL Ser.). (J). 1998. mass mkt., suppl. ed. 6.00 (*0-8384-6334-7*) Heinle & Heinle.

Pronouncing American English. 2nd ed. Getrude F. Orion. LC 96-51549. (College ESL Ser.). (J). 1997. pap. 32.95 (*0-8384-6332-0*) Heinle & Heinle.

Pronouncing American English: Sounds, Stress, & Intonation. Gertrude Orion. 321p. (J). 1987. pap., teacher ed. 11.95 (*0-8384-2696-4*, Newbury) Heinle & Heinle.

Pronouncing & Defining Dictionary of Music. William S. Mathews & Emil Liebling. LC 78-173059. reprint ed. 42.00 (*0-404-07210-0*) AMS Pr.

Pronouncing & Persevering. Susan F. Hirsch. LC 97-45178. 376p. 1998. pap. text 19.00 (*0-226-34464-9*) U Ch Pr.

***Pronouncing & Persevering.** Susan F. Hirsch. LC 97-45178. 376p. 1998. lib. bdg. 48.00 (*0-226-34463-0*) U Ch Pr.

Pronouncing Arabic 1. T. F. Mitchell. (Illus.). 180p. 1990. text 55.00 (*0-19-815151-9*) OUP.

Pronouncing Arabic 2. T. F. Mitchell. (Illus.). 322p. 1993. text 70.00 (*0-19-823989-0*) OUP.

Pronouncing Dictionary of American English. John S. Kenyon & Thomas A. Knott. LC 53-1416. 544p. 1995. reprint ed. 15.95 (*0-87779-047-7*) Merriam-Webster Inc.

Pronouncing Dictionary of California Names in English & Spanish. Martha L. Marshall. (Shorey Historical Ser.). 41p. 1925. reprint ed. pap. 10.00 (*0-8466-0155-9*, S-155) Shoreys Bkstore.

Pronouncing Dictionary of Musical Terms, Giving the Meaning, Derivation & Pronunciation. A. Mason Clarke. 121p. 2000. reprint ed. lib. bdg. 69.00 (*0-7812-0750-9*) Rprt Serv.

Pronouncing Dictionary of Musical Terms, Giving the Meaning Derivation & Pronunciation of Italian, German, French & Other Words. Hugh A. Clarke. 1977. reprint ed. 39.00 (*0-403-07492-4*) Scholarly.

Pronouncing Dictionary of Proper Names: Pronunciations of the Names of Notable People, Places & Things. 2nd ed. John Bollard. LC 97-23664. 1997. lib. bdg. 110.00 (*0-7808-0098-2*) Omnigraphics Inc.

Pronouncing Dictionary of Scottish Gaelic. Compiled by Henry C. Dieckhoff. (C). 1989. 75.00 (*1-871901-18-9*, Pub. by Gairm Pubns) St Mut.

Pronouncing Musical Dictionary. Dudley Buck. 1988. reprint ed. lib. bdg. 49.00 (*0-7812-0257-4*) Rprt Serv.

***Pronouncing Shakespeare's Words: A Guide from A to Zounds.** Ed. by Dale F. Coye. 744p. 1998. pap. text 100.00 (*1-57958-081-5*) Fitzroy Dearborn.

Pronouncing Shakespeare's Words: A Guide from A to Zounds. Dale F. Coye. LC 97-44868. 744p. 1998. lib. bdg. 99.50 (*0-313-30655-9*, Greenwood Pr) Greenwood.

Pronouns. 1981. 3.00 (*0-939418-41-X*) Ferguson-Florissant.

P

Pronouns: A Collection of Forty Dances for the Dancers-February 3rd to March 22nd 1964. Jackson MacLow. LC 79-64919. 88p. 1979. pap. 15.00 (*0-930794-06-0*) Station Hill Pr.

Pronouns: A Collection of Forty Dances for the Dancers-February 3rd to March 22nd 1964. deluxe limited ed. Jackson MacLow. LC 79-64919. 88p. 1979. boxed set 50.00 (*0-930794-74-5*) Station Hill Pr.

Pronouns of Address in Modern Standard French. Catherine A. Maley. LC 74-17218. (Romance Monographs: No. 10). 1974. 22.00 (*84-399-2792-4*) Romance.

Pronouns Through Pictures. Harris Winitz. (Language Through Pictures Ser.). (Illus.). 40p. (YA). (gr. 2-12). 1982. pap. 5.00 (*0-939990-31-8*) Intl Linguistics.

Pronto. Elmore Leonard. 272p. 1998. pap. 9.95 (*0-385-33290-4*) Doubleday.

Prontuario Historico de Puerto Rico. Tomas Blanco. LC 80-67412. (Obras Completas de Tomas Blanco Ser.). 166p. 1981. pap. 7.25 (*0-940238-34-9*) Ediciones Huracan.

Pronunciacion Simplificada del Ingles Con un Resumen de la Gramatica Inglesa. Serafin Aleman. LC 94-71460. (Coleccion Textos). 176p. 1994. pap. 19.00 (*0-89729-734-2*) Ediciones.

Pronunciation. 282p. 1990. text 35.95 (*0-19-437086-0*) OUP.

Pronunciation. Christiane Dalton & Barbara Seidhofer. Ed. by H. G. Widdowson & C. N. Candlin. 206p. 1995. pap. text 14.95 (*0-19-437197-2*) OUP.

Pronunciation. Clement Laroy. 160p. 1995. pap. text 13.95 (*0-19-437087-9*) OUP.

Pronunciation & Reading of Ancient Greek: A Practical Guide. 2nd rev. ed. Stephen G. Daitz. LC 85-740005. (Living Voice of Greek & Latin Ser.). 20p. 1985. pap. 34.95 incl. audio (*0-88432-138-X*, S23660) Audio-Forum.

Pronunciation & Reading of Classical Latin: A Practical Guide. Stephen G. Daitz. LC 85-740004. (Living Voice of Classical Latin Ser.). 1984. pap. 34.95 incl. audio (*0-88432-125-8*, S23675) Audio-Forum.

Pronunciation Book: Student Centered Activities for Pronunciation Work. T. Bowen & J. Marles. (Pilgrims Longman Resource Bks.). 85p. 1995. pap. text 22.39 (*0-582-06491-0*, 79849) Addison-Wesley.

Pronunciation Dictionary for Radio & Television Workers. 5th ed. F. L. Ageenko. (RUS.). 810p. 1984. 49.95 (*0-8288-1317-5*, M15226) Fr & Eur.

Pronunciation Dictionary of Artists' Names: The Art Institute of Chicago. 3rd rev. ed. Ed. by Debra Edelstein. LC 93-6130. 112p. (Orig.). 1993. pap. 11.95 (*0-8212-2025-X*, Pub. by Bulfinch Pr) Little.

Pronunciation Exercises for Advanced Learners of English As a Second Language. rev. ed. Gary Esarey. LC 95-61937. 144p. 1996. pap. text 16.95 (*0-472-08376-7*, 08376) U of Mich Pr.

Pronunciation Exercises for Beginning Chinese. James Liang. 1978. 1.75 (*0-88710-059-7*) Yale Far Eastern Pubns.

Pronunciation Exercises for Beginning Chinese. James Liang. 1978. 8.95 incl. audio (*0-88710-060-0*) Yale Far Eastern Pubns.

Pronunciation Exercises for English As a Second Language. 2nd ed. Gary Esarey. LC 95-61937. (Pitt Series in English As a Second Language). (Illus.). 144p. (C). 1997. audio 60.00 (*0-472-00250-3*, 00250) U of Mich Pr.

Pronunciation Exercises for English as a Second Language. 2nd ed. Gary Esarey. (Illus.). 144p. (C). 1997. pap. text 70.00 (*0-472-08382-1*, 08382) U of Mich Pr.

Pronunciation Exercises in English. Lolita Dixson & Elizabeth Woods. (C). 1987. 53.00 (*0-13-730870-1*, Macmillan Coll) P-H.

Pronunciation Exercises in English. rev. ed. M. Elizabeth Clarey & Robert J. Dixson. 144p. 1987. pap. text 18.07 (*0-13-730854-X*) P-H.

Pronunciation Games. Mark Hancock. LC 97-108039. (Illus.). 112p. (C). 1996. pap. text 32.95 (*0-521-46735-7*) Cambridge U Pr.

Pronunciation Guide for Astrology. T. Patrick Davis. 16p. 1973. 4.50 (*0-86690-180-9*, D1055-014) Am Fed Astrologers.

Pronunciation Guide for Choral Literature: French, German, Hebrew, Italian, Latin, Spanish. William V. May & Craig Tolin. 100p. (Orig.). 1987. pap. 20.00 (*0-940796-47-3*, 1040) MENC.

Pronunciation in Action. Linda L. Taylor. LC 93-14344. 1993. pap. 12.25 (*0-13-017864-0*) P-H.

*Pronunciation in American English: Workbook & Audio Cassettes.** Kathy L. Hans. (Illus.). 136p. 2000. pap., wbk. ed. 50.00 incl. audio (*0-9678379-1-X*) AmEnglish.

Pronunciation Manual. 1993. text. write for info. (*0-8013-0575-6*) Addison-Wesley.

Pronunciation Matters: Communicative, Story-Based Activities for Mastering North American English. Lynn E. Henrichsen et al. LC 99-188768. (Illus.). 408p. (C). 1998. pap. text 18.95 (*0-472-08491-7*, 08491) U of Mich Pr.

Pronunciation Models. Adam Brown. 135p. 1991. pap. 28.50 (*9971-69-157-4*, Pub. by Sngapore Univ Pr) Coronet Bks.

Pronunciation of English. Charles W. Kreidler. (Illus.). 400p. 1989. pap. text 28.95 (*0-631-16219-4*) Blackwell Pubs.

Pronunciation of English. 4th ed. Daniel Jones. 256p. (C). 1956. pap. text 27.95 (*0-521-09369-4*) Cambridge U Pr.

*Pronunciation of English: A Workbook.** Joanne Kenworthy. (An Arnold Publication). 192p. 2000. pap. 29.95 (*0-340-73123-0*, Pub. by E A) OUP.

Pronunciation of English in Metropolitan Chicago. Lee A. Pederson. (Publications of the American Dialect Society: No. 44). 87p. 1967. pap. text 8.70 (*0-8173-0644-7*) U of Ala Pr.

Pronunciation of English in the Atlantic States: Based Upon the Collections of the Linguistic Atlas of the Eastern U. S. Hans Kurath & Raven I. McDavid. LC 60-5671. 192p. 1982. pap. 59.60 (*0-7837-8390-6*, 205920100009) Bks Demand.

Pronunciation of English Vowels, 1400-1700. R. E. Zachrisson. LC 71-158215. reprint ed. 39.50 (*0-404-07074-4*) AMS Pr.

Pronunciation of English Words see Preliminary Announcement

Pronunciation of Greek & Latin. Edgar H. Sturtevant. 192p. 1975. pap. 15.00 (*0-89005-087-2*) Ares.

Pronunciation of Standard American English. James G. Luter. 131p. (Orig.). (C). 1988. pap. text 10.50 (*0-939085-00-3*) Garrett.

Pronunciation of Standard American English. James G. Luter, Jr. Ed. by Kathleen B. Beaufait. pap. text 14.50 (*0-939085-01-1*, GPC-002) Garrett Pub Co.

Pronunciation of Standard English in America. George P. Krapp. LC 76-97891. reprint ed. 30.00 (*0-404-03780-1*) AMS Pr.

Pronunciation of Ten Thousand Proper Names: Giving Geographical & Biographical Names, Names of Books, Works of Art, Characters in Fiction, Foreign Titles, Etc. Mary S. Mackey & Maryette G. Mackey. LC 89-71138. xiii, 329p. 1993. reprint ed. lib. bdg. 48.00 (*1-55888-918-3*) Omnigraphics Inc.

Pronunciation of the French Spoken at Brunswick, Maine. W. N. Locke. (Publications of the American Dialect Society: No. 12). 201p. 1949. pap. text 8.25 (*0-8173-0612-9*) U of Ala Pr.

Pronunciation Pairs: An Introductory Course for Students of English. Ann Baker & Sharon Goldstein. (Illus.). 158p. (C). 1990. pap. text, student ed. 16.95 (*0-521-34972-9*) Cambridge U Pr.

Pronunciation Pairs: An Introductory Course for Students of English. Ann Baker & Sharon Goldstein. (Illus.). 137p. (C). 1990. pap. text, teacher ed. 17.95 (*0-521-34973-7*) Cambridge U Pr.

Pronunciation Pedagogy & Theory: New Views, New Directions. Ed. by Joan Morley. 115p. 1994. pap. 15.95 (*0-939791-55-2*) Tchrs Eng Spkrs.

Pronunciation Plus: Practice Through Interaction. Martin Hewings & Sharon Goldstein. 144p. 45.95 incl. audio (*0-521-57795-0*) Cambridge U Pr.

Pronunciation Plus: Practice Through Interaction - In North American English. Martin Hewings & Sharon Goldstein. (Illus.). 160p. (C). 1998. teacher ed. 17.95 (*0-521-57796-9*) Cambridge U Pr.

Pronunciation Plus: Practice Through Interaction - In North American English. Martin Hewings & Sharon Goldstein. LC 98-3653. (Illus.). 152p. (C). 1998. pap. text, student ed. 16.95 (*0-521-57797-7*) Cambridge U Pr.

Proof. Mamie Dundas. 40p. 1986. 40.00 (*0-7223-1993-2*, Pub. by A H S Ltd) St Mut.

Proof. Dick Francis. 368p. 1997. mass mkt. 6.99 (*0-515-12120-7*, Jove) Berkley Pub.

*Proof.** Dick Francis. 1999. 34.95 (*0-7540-7529-X*) Chivers N Amer.

Proof. large type ed. Dick Francis. 1993. 39.95 (*0-7066-1001-6*, Pub. by Remploy Pr) St Mut.

Proof: God Exists! Ronald Roth. (Illus.). iv, 36p. 1998. pap. text 5.95 (*0-9663810-0-9*) Ark of Prose Bks.

Proof: Los Angeles Art & the Photograph, 1960-1980. Ed. & Contrib. by Charles Desmarais. LC 92-72754. (Illus.). 144p. 1992. pap. 45.00 (*0-911291-20-2*, Pub. by Fellows Cont Art) RAM Publications.

Proof: Photographs by Jean-Philipe Reverdot. Photos by Jean-Philipe Reverdot. (Illus.). 60p. 1998. 45.00 (*1-899235-50-7*, 811032, Pub. by Dewi Lewis) Dist Art Pubs.

*Proof: There Is a God!** Steve Martin. (Illus.). vi, 136p. 2000. pap. 9.95 (*0-9678383-0-4*) J Trombly.

*Proof Vol. 1: The Magazine of Virtuous Reality.** Neil Martinson et al. (Illus.). 68p. 1999. pap. 5.95 (*0-9673621-0-5*) Proof Press.

Proof & Computation. H. Schwichtenberg. (NATO ASI F Computer & Systems Sciences Ser.: Vol. 139). 464p. 1995. 112.00 (*3-540-58581-8*) Spr-Verlag.

Proof & Explanation: The Virginia Lectures by John Wisdom. Ed. by Stephen F. Barker. 242p. (Orig.). (C). 1991. pap. text 26.50 (*0-8191-8042-4*); lib. bdg. 49.00 (*0-8191-8041-6*) U Pr of Amer.

Proof Before You Publish: 21 Checklists for Proofreading Genealogy Publications. Corinne P. Earnest. LC 98-115878. 40p. (Orig.). 1997. pap. 12.80 (*1-879311-10-0*) R D Earnest.

Proof Coins Struck at the U. S. Mints: Updated. W. Breen. 1983. reprint ed. pap. 10.00 (*0-915262-94-0*) S J Durst.

Proof Complexity & Feasible Arithmetics: Dimacs Workshop, April 21-24, 1996. Ed. by Paul W. Beame & Samuel R. Buss. LC 97-29122. (DIMACS: Series in Discrete Mathematics & Theoretical Computer Science: Vol. 39). 320p. 1997. text 59.00 (*0-8218-0577-0*) Am Math.

Proof Corrections: Z39.22-1989. rev. ed. National Information Standards Organization Staff. (National Information Standards Ser.). 38p. 1991. pap. 45.00 (*0-88738-949-X*) Transaction Pubs.

Proof from Prophecy: A Study in Justin Martyr's Proof-Text Tradition: Text-Type, Provenance, Theological Profile. Oskar Skarsaune. (Novum Testamentum, Supplements Ser.: Supplement 56). xiv, 508p. 1987. 145.00 (*90-04-07468-6*) Brill Academic Pubs.

Proof, Herbs Against Cancer. Cynthia J. Sommers. LC 93-85420. (Illus.). 140p. (Orig.). 1993. pap. 13.95 (*0-9640193-0-2*) Red Wing Pubng.

Proof in Competitive Business Litigation. Ed. by William C. Steffin et al. LC 92-76049. 790p. 1993. ring bd. 167.00 (*0-88124-590-9*, CP-31930) Cont Ed Bar-CA.

Proof in the VDM: A Practitioner's Guide. Juan C. Bicarregui. LC 93-23655. (Formal Approaches to Computing & Information Technology Ser.). 1993. 50.95 (*0-387-19813-X*) Spr-Verlag.

Proof in VDM: Case Studies. Ed. by J. C. Bicarregui. LC 97-29213. (Formal Approaches to Computing & Information Technology Ser.). (Illus.). xvi, 228p. 1998. pap. 69.95 (*3-540-76186-1*) Spr-Verlag.

Proof It! A Competency-Based Approach to Proofreading & Editing Skills. George S. Amsbury. LC 93-18927. (C). 1994. mass mkt. 15.00 (*0-538-70944-8*) S-W Pub.

*Proof, Language & Interaction: Essays in Honour of Robin Milner.** Robin Milner. Ed. by George Plotkin et al. LC 99-27800. (Foundations of Computing Ser.). (Illus.). 700p. 2000. 60.00 (*0-262-16188-5*) MIT Pr.

Proof, Logic & Formalization. Michael Detlefsen. LC 91-17469. 272p. (C). 1992. 85.00 (*0-415-02335-1*, A6498) Routledge.

Proof Methods for Modal & Intuitionistic Logic. Melvin Fitting. 561p. 1983. text 247.50 (*90-277-1573-4*, D Reidel) Kluwer Academic.

Proof of Cases in Massachusetts, 2 vols. 2nd ed. Gabriel V. Mottla. LC 66-24570. 1780p. 1993. suppl. ed. 60.00 (*0-317-03185-6*) West Group.

Proof of Cases in Massachusetts, 2 vols. 3rd ed. Gabriel V. Mottla. LC 66-24570. 1780p. 220.00 (*0-317-00489-1*) West Group.

Proof of Eminence: The Life of Sir John Hawkins. Bertam H. Davis. LC 72-75389. 466p. reprint ed. pap. 144.50 (*0-608-30311-9*, 201581400097) Bks Demand.

Proof of God. Ian McCrimmon. (C). 1992. text 19.00 (*0-9514698-5-1*, Pub. by Cosmatom) St Mut.

*Proof of Immortality: A Rational Basis for Spirituality.** Geoffrey Hamilton. LC 99-97642. 120p. 2000. pap. 14.95 (*0-9654915-1-X*, High Ground) Northwoods Cnslting.

Proof of Our Reincarnation: Now You Can Live Forever. Arthur Trice. 300p. (Orig.). 1991. pap. 13.50 (*1-886217-00-9*) W O A Pubng.

Proof of Our Reincarnation: Now You Can Live Forever. 2nd ed. Arthur Trice. 250p. (Orig.). 1992. pap. 13.50 (*1-886217-01-7*) W O A Pubng.

Proof of Our Reincarnation: Now You Can Live Forever. 4th ed. Arthur Trice. 300p. (Orig.). 1994. pap. 13.50 (*1-886217-03-3*) W O A Pubng.

Proof of Our Reincarnation: Now You Can Live Forever. 5th ed. Arthur Trice. 300p. (Orig.). 1995. pap. 13.50 (*1-886217-04-1*) W O A Pubng.

Proof of Our Reincarnation: Now You Can Live Forever. 6th ed. Arthur Trice. 300p. (Orig.). 1995. pap. 13.50 (*1-886217-05-X*) W O A Pubng.

Proof of Our Reincarnation: Now You Can Live Forever, 6 vols., Set. Arthur Trice. (Orig.). 1995. pap. write for info. (*1-886217-07-6*) W O A Pubng.

*Proof of Performance: How to Build a Career Portfolio to Land a Great New Job.** Rick Nelles. 2000. pap. 17.95 (*1-57023-148-6*) Impact VA.

Proof of Proofs, They Live. Brown Landone. 149p. 1996. reprint ed. spiral bd. 14.00 (*0-7873-0526-X*) Hlth Research.

Proof of the Pudding. Phoebe Atwood Taylor. 192p. 1991. pap. 6.00 (*0-88150-193-X*, Foul Play) Norton.

*Proof of the Pudding: What Has Worked for Us: A Three-Way Approach to Successful Long-Term Investing.** Herbert Hart. LC 99-88815. 2000. pap. write for info. (*0-87034-136-7*) Fraser Pub Co.

Proof of the Q-Macdonald-Morris Conjecture for BCn. Kevin W. Kadell. LC 93-48293. (Memoirs of the American Mathematical Society Ser.: Vol. 516). 80p. 1994. pap. 31.00 (*0-8218-2552-6*, MEMO/108/516) Am Math.

Proof of the Truth: The Spiritual Journey of Dr. Grace Lightfoot Faus. Dorothy Elder. LC 94-94329. 96p. 1994. pap. 8.95 (*0-9631673-1-6*) Doriel Pub.

Proof of the Truth of Past Life Therapy. Ruth E. Norman. 212p. 1988. 11.00 (*0-935097-13-9*) Unarius Acad Sci.

Proof of Things Invisible. G. L. Sundance. Ed. by Gloria D. Ladd & James E. Gilliland. 64p. 1997. 12.95 (*1-890668-04-4*) Electronic Books.

*Proof of Vedic Culture's Global Existence.** Stephen Knapp. LC 98-61106. 350p. 2000. pap. 14.95 (*0-9617410-6-6*, Pub. by World Relief) New Leaf Dist.

Proof Positive. Werner G. Marx. 1992. pap. 8.95 (*1-55673-462-X*, 7915) CSS OH.

*Proof Positive.** Philip Singerman. 2001. text. write for info. (*0-312-87686-6*) St Martin.

Proof Positive: Developing Significant Volunteer Recordkeeping Systems. rev. ed. Susan J. Ellis & Katherine H. Noyes. LC 90-82887. (Volunteer Energy Ser.: No. 1). (Illus.). 60p. 1990. pap. 12.95 (*0-940576-10-4*) Energize.

Proof Positive: Forty Years of Contemporary American Printmaking at Ulae, 1957-1997. Intro. by Jack Cowart. (Illus.). 272p. 1998. pap. 60.00 (*0-8109-6351-5*, Pub. by Abrams) Time Warner.

Proof Positive: Forty Years of Contemporary American Printmaking at ULAE, 1957-1997. Jack Cowart et al. LC 98-155075. (Illus.). 1997. write for info. (*0-88675-049-0*) Corcoran.

Proof Positive: How to Find Errors Before They Embarrass You. Karen Anderson. Ed. by Kelly Scanlon. LC 96-67393. (Self-Study Sourcebook Ser.). (Illus.). 193p. 1996. pap. 15.95 (*1-57294-043-3*, 13-0016) SkillPath Pubns.

Proof Positive: How to Reliably Combat Diseases & Achieve Optimal Health. Neil Nedley. Ed. by David De Rose. (Illus.). 560p. 1998. text 49.00 (*0-9661979-3-3*) Nedley Publishing.

Proof That God Exists: Sixties Biographies. 2nd ed. Alan K. Gorg. Ed. by Gwyn Yates. LC 95-81498. (Illus.). 145p. (Orig.). 1996. pap. 12.95 (*0-9642754-0-6*) Media Associates.

Proof Theory. Ed. by Peter Aczel et al. (Illus.). 316p. (C). 1993. text 59.95 (*0-521-41413-X*) Cambridge U Pr.

Proof Theory. W. Pohlers. (Lecture Notes in Mathematics Ser.: Vol. 1407). vi, 213p. 1996. pap. 39.95 (*0-387-51842-8*) Spr-Verlag.

Proof Theory. K. Schuette. Tr. by J. N. Crossley from GER. LC 76-45768. (Grundlehren der Mathematischen Wissenschaften Ser.: Vol. 225). 1977. 59.00 (*3-540-07911-4*) Spr-Verlag.

Proof Theory & Automated Deduction. LC 97-18876. 1997. text 174.00 (*0-7923-4593-2*) Kluwer Academic.

Proof Theory & Logical Complexity. J. Y. Girard. (Studies in Proof Theory: Vol. 1). 504p. 1990. 136.00 (*0-444-98715-0*) Elsevier.

Proof Theory for General Unification. W. Snyder. (Progress in Computer Science & Applied Logic Ser.: Vol. 11). vi, 175p. 1991. 54.50 (*0-8176-3593-9*) Birkhauser.

Proof Theory of Modal Logic. Heinrich Wansing. LC 96-9019. (Applied Logic Ser.: Vol. 2). 317p. 1996. text 130.50 (*0-7923-4120-1*) Kluwer Academic.

Proof Theory Symposium Keil 1974: Proceedings. Proof Theory Symposium Staff. Ed. by G. H. Muller & J. Diller. (Lecture Notes in Mathematics Ser.: Vol. 500). 1976. 28.95 (*0-387-07533-X*) Spr-Verlag.

Proofreading. Souder. (C). 1995. pap. 18.36 (*0-395-73720-6*); pap. text 21.56 (*0-395-66038-6*) HM.

Proofreading & Editing Business Documents. 2nd ed. Patricia E. Seraydarian. 208p. 1993. teacher ed. 9.95 (*1-56118-582-5*); pap. text 16.95 (*1-56118-581-7*) Paradigm MN.

Proofreading & Editing Precision. 3rd ed. Ellis Jones & David Kane. (EC - HS Communication/English Ser.). 1995. mass mkt. 17.95 (*0-538-62840-5*) S-W Pub.

*Proofreading & Editing Precision.** 4th ed. Ellis Jones & David Kane. 2000. pap. 21.95 (*0-538-69250-2*) Thomson Learn.

*Proofreading at the Computer.** Barbara Norstrom & Mary V. Cole. 80p. 1999. pap. 19.95 (*0-538-68925-0*) Sth-Wstrn College.

Proofreading At The Computer:10 Hour Series. Alison D. Norstrom. LC 99-14154. 76p. 1999. 16.95 (*0-538-68924-2*) Thomson Learn.

Proofreading for Word Processing. 2nd ed. Jo A. Lee. LC 93-43962. 248p. (C). 1994. pap. text 31.00 (*0-03-098011-9*) Dryden Pr.

Proofreading for Word Processing. 2nd ed. Jo A. Lee. LC 93-43962. 68p. (C). 1994. pap. text, teacher ed. 34.00 (*0-03-098012-7*) Dryden Pr.

Proofreading for Wordprocessing. Jo A. Lee. 184p. (C). 1988. pap. text 29.50 (*0-15-572260-3*); pap. text, teacher ed. 3.00 (*0-15-572261-1*) Dryden Pr.

Proofreading Plain & Simple. Debra H. May. LC 97-8273. (In Plain English Ser.). 192p. (Orig.). 1997. pap. 11.99 (*1-56414-291-4*) Career Pr Inc.

Proofreading Precision. Jones Staff. (EC - HS Communication/English Ser.). 1982. mass mkt. 18.95 (*0-538-11200-X*) S-W Pub.

Proofreading the Histories. Nora Mitchell. 72p. (Orig.). 1996. pap. 9.95 (*1-882295-10-2*) Alice James Bks.

Proofreading Written Work. Larry Mikulecky. 1990. mass mkt. 9.00 (*0-13-852260-X*) P-H.

Proofreading/Editing Precision. 2nd ed. Kane Jones. (C). 1989. text 66.25 (*0-538-11212-3*) Sth-Wstrn College.

Proofreading/Editing Precision. 2nd ed. Jones Staff. (EC - HS Communication/English Ser.). 1989. mass mkt. 18.95 (*0-538-11211-5*) S-W Pub.

Proofs & Confirmations: The Story of the Alternating Sign Matrix Conjecture. David M. Bressoud. LC 99-20232. (Spectrum Ser.). (Illus.). 256p. (C). 1999. 74.95 (*0-521-66170-6*) Cambridge U Pr.

*Proofs & Confirmations: The Story of the Alternating Sign Matrix Conjecture.** David M. Bressoud. (Spectrum Ser.). (Illus.). 256p. (C). 1999. pap. 29.95 (*0-521-66646-5*) Cambridge U Pr.

Proofs & Fundamentals: A First Course in Abstract Mathematics. Ethan D. Bloch. 432p. 1999. 49.50 (*0-8176-4111-4*) Birkhauser.

*Proofs & Fundamentals: A First Course in Abstract Mathematics.** Ethan D. Bloch. LC 00-23309. 2000. write for info. (*3-7643-4111-4*) Birkhauser.

Proofs & Refutations. E. Lakatos. Ed. by J. Worrall. LC 75-32478. 174p. 1976. pap. text 23.95 (*0-521-29038-4*) Cambridge U Pr.

Proofs & Theories Essays. Louise Gluck. 1994. 22.00 (*0-88001-369-9*) HarpC.

Proofs & Theories Essays. Louise Gluck. 152p. 1995. pap. 12.00 (*0-88001-442-3*) HarpC.

Proofs for Eternity, Creation & the Existence of God. Herbert A. Davidson. 430p. 1996. 49.95 (*0-614-21187-5*, 989) Kazi Pubns.

Proofs from "The Book" Martin Aigner & G. M. Ziegler. LC 98-34262. (Illus.). 210p. 1998. 29.00 (*3-540-63698-6*) Spr-Verlag.

Proofs of a Conspiracy. John Robison. 1979. lib. bdg. 59.95 (*0-8490-2987-2*) Gordon Pr.

Proofs of a Conspiracy. unabridged ed. John Robison. 304p. reprint ed. pap. 12.00 (*0-945001-32-0*) GSG & Assocs.

Proofs of Affection. large type ed. Rosemary Friedman. 1990. 27.99 (*0-7089-2152-3*) Ulverscroft.

Proofs of the Corruption of Gen. James Wilkinson & of His Connexion with Aaron Burr, with a Full Refutation of His Slanderous Allegations in Relation to the Character of the Principal Witness Against Him. Daniel Clark. LC 70-146383. (First American Frontier Ser.). 1971. reprint ed. 34.95 (*0-405-02834-2*) Ayer.

P

An Asterisk (*) at the beginning of an entry indicates that the title is appearing for the first time.

Proofs of the Corruption of General James Wilkinson, & of His Connexion with Aaron Burr. Daniel Clark. LC 70-117868. (Select Bibliographies Reprint Ser.). 1977. 34.95 (*0-8369-5321-5*) Ayer.

Proofs of the Spirit World (1920) L. Chevreuil. 300p. 1998. reprint ed. pap. 24.95 (*0-7661-0510-5*) Kessinger Pub.

Proofs Without Words: Exercises in Visual Thinking. Roger B. Nelsen. LC 93-86338. (Classroom Resource Materials Ser.). 160p. (Orig.). 1993. pap. text 34.95 (*0-88385-700-6*, PWW) Math Assn.

ProofWriter, Bk. 1. Michelle Waters & Marybeth A. Mehlmann. Ed. by Joan Ostacher. (Illus.). 120p. (Orig.). 1987. 17.95 (*0-913935-40-9*) ERA-CCR.

ProofWriter, Bk. 2. Michelle Waters & Marybeth A. Mehlmann. Ed. by Joan Ostacher. (Illus.). 120p. (Orig.). 1990. 17.95 (*0-913935-41-7*) ERA-CCR.

Prop Builder's Mask Making Handbook. 1996. lib. bdg. 255.75 (*0-8490-8300-1*) Gordon Pr.

Prop Builder's Mask-Making Handbook. Thurston James. (Illus.). 204p. 1990. pap. 19.99 (*1-55870-166-4*, Betrwy Bks) F & W Pubns Inc.

Prop Builder's Molding & Casting Handbook. 1996. lib. bdg. 265.75 (*0-8490-8308-7*) Gordon Pr.

Prop Builder's Molding & Casting Handbook. Thurston James. 238p. 1989. pap. 19.99 (*1-55870-128-1*, Betrwy Bks) F & W Pubns Inc.

Prop Perfection: Restored Propliners & Warbirds. Graham Robson. LC 97-52134. (Illus.). 112p. 1997. pap. 24.95 (*0-7603-0511-0*) MBI Pubg.

***Prop Shop Crafts Leader Manual: Grades 1-6.** (Holyword Studios VBS Ser.). 2000. pap., teacher ed. 9.99 (*0-7644-2175-1*) Group Pub.

Prop Talk: Understanding & Optimizing Propeller Performance for Model Electric Aircraft. unabridged ed. Donald W. Brooks. (Illus.). v, 98p. (Orig.). 1997. pap., spiral bd. 17.95 (*0-9657014-0-9*, ARPI-0100) ARPI Bks.

***Prop Us Up: On Every Leaning Side, a Collection of Poetry.** L. G. Thomas. (Illus.). 88p. (Orig.). 1999. pap. 10.00 (*1-890676-36-5*, Pub. by Beavers Pond) Bookman Bks.

Propa Propaganda. Benjamin Zephaniah. LC 97-155221. 80p. 1997. pap. 15.95 (*1-85224-372-4*, Pub. by Bloodaxe Bks) Dufour.

Propachlor. (Environmental Health Criteria Ser.: No. 147). (ENG, FRE & SPA.). 110p. 1993. pap. text 26.00 (*92-4-157147-0*, 1160147) World Health.

Propachlor Health & Safety Guide. (Health & Safety Guides Ser.: No. 77). 26p. 1992. pap. text 5.00 (*92-4-151077-3*, 1860077) World Health.

Propaedeutics to Comparative Neurology see Central Nervous System of Vertebrates: A General Survey of Its Comparative Anatomy with an Introduction to Pertinent Fundamental Biologic & Logical Concepts

Propaganda. David Huberman. 36p. 1991. pap., per. 3.00 (*1-886206-04-X*) Venom Pr.

Propaganda. Ed. by Robert Jackall. LC 94-7500. (Main Trends of the Modern World Ser.). 320p. (C). 1994. text 50.00 (*0-8147-4196-7*); pap. text 18.50 (*0-8147-4197-5*) NYU Pr.

Propaganda. Bertrand Taithe. Ed. by Tim Thornton. (Orig.). 2000. pap. text 27.95 (*0-7509-2029-7*) Sutton Pub Ltd.

Propaganda: A Pluralistic Perspective. Ed. by Ted J. Smith, III. LC 89-33975. (Media & Society Ser.). 198p. 1989. 49.95 (*0-275-92743-1*, C2743, Praeger Pubs) Greenwood.

Propaganda: Political Rhetoric & Identity, 1300-2000. Bertrand Taithe. 1999. 92.00 (*0-7509-2028-9*) A Sutton.

Propaganda: The Formation of Men's Attitudes. Jacques Ellul. 352p. 1973. pap. 11.00 (*0-394-71874-7*) Vin Bks.

Propaganda Analysis. Alexander L. George. (WV Encore Edition Ser.). (C). 1996. pap. text 23.50 (*0-8133-0142-4*) Westview.

Propaganda Analysis, 5 vols., Set. Institute for Propaganda Analysis Staff. 1977. lib. bdg. 1500.00 (*0-8490-2486-2*) Gordon Pr.

Propaganda & Aesthetics: The Literary Politics of African-American Magazines in the Twentieth Century. Abby A. Johnson & Ronald M. Johnson. LC 90-19935. 272p. (Orig.). (C). 1994. pap. 17.95 (*0-87023-402-1*) U of Mass Pr.

Propaganda & Culture in Mao's China: Deng Tuo & the Intelligentsia. Timothy Cheek. LC 97-7811. (Studies on Conemporary China). (Illus.). 406p. 1998. text 85.00 (*0-19-829066-7*) OUP.

Propaganda & Democracy: The American Experience of Media & Mass Persuasion. J. Michael Sproule. (Studies in the History of Mass Communciations). (Illus.). 344p. 1996. text 64.95 (*0-521-47022-6*) Cambridge U Pr.

Propaganda & Dictatorship: A Collection of Papers. Ed. by Harwood L. Childs. LC 72-4659. (International Propaganda & Communications Ser.). 153p. 1972. reprint ed. 13.95 (*0-405-04742-8*) Ayer.

Propaganda & Dreams: Photographing the 1930s in the U. S. S. R. & U. S. A. Ed. by Leah Bendavid-Val. (Illus.). 1999. 55.00 (*3-908161-80-0*) Abbeville Pr.

Propaganda & Empire: The Manipulation of British Public Opinion, 1880-1960. John M. MacKenzie. LC 83-25325. (Illus.). 320p. (C). 1988. text 32.00 (*0-7190-1869-2*, Pub. by Manchester Univ Pr) St Martin.

Propaganda & Myth in Time of War. Charles H. Hamlin. LC 77-147725. (Library of War & Peace; the Character & Causes of War). 1977. lib. bdg. 46.00 (*0-8240-0261-X*) Garland.

Propaganda & National Power: The Organization of Public Opinion for National Politics. Eugen Hadamovsky. Tr. by Alice Mavrogordato & Ilse De Witt from GER. LC 72-4667. (International Propaganda & Communications Ser.). 204p. 1976. reprint ed. 16.95 (*0-405-04748-7*) Ayer.

Propaganda & Nationalism in Wartime Russia: The Jewish Anti-Fascist Committee in the U. S. S. R., 1941-1948. Shimon Redlich. (East European Monographs: No. 108). 236p. 1982. text 55.50 (*0-88033-001-5*, Pub. by East Eur Monographs) Col U Pr.

Propaganda & Persuasion. 2nd ed. Garth S. Jowett. 296p. (C). 1992. text 54.00 (*0-8039-4677-5*); pap. text 24.50 (*0-8039-4678-3*) Sage.

***Propaganda & Persuasion.** 3rd ed. Garth Jowett & Victoria O'Donnell. LC 99-6010. 430p. 1999. 59.95 (*0-7619-1146-4*) Sage.

Propaganda & Persuasion. 3rd ed. Garth Jowett & Victoria O'Donnell. LC 99-6010. 1999. write for info. (*0-7619-1147-2*) Sage.

Propaganda & Promotional Activities: An Annotated Bibliography. Ed. by Harold D. Lasswell et al. LC 75-77979. 474p. reprint ed. pap. 147.00 (*0-608-11161-9*, 202010000016) Bks Demand.

***Propaganda & the Cold War.** 2000. write for info. (*0-582-31294-9*) Pearson Educ.

Propaganda & the Cold War: A Princeton University Symposium. Ed. by John B. Whitton. LC 83-22551. 119p. 1984. reprint ed. lib. bdg. 55.00 (*0-313-24304-2*, WHPR, Greenwood Pr) Greenwood.

Propaganda & the News: Or, What Makes You Think So. William H. Irwin. LC 70-98841. 325p. 1970. reprint ed. lib. bdg. 65.00 (*0-8371-2818-8*, IRPN, Greenwood Pr) Greenwood.

Propaganda & the Role of the State in Inter-War Britain. Mariel Grant. (Oxford Historical Monographs). (Illus.). 296p. 1995. text 65.00 (*0-19-820444-2*) OUP.

Propaganda by Short Wave. Ed. by Harwood L. Childs & John B. Whitton. LC 72-4660. (International Propaganda & Communications Ser.). (Illus.). 365p. 1972. reprint ed. 26.95 (*0-405-04743-6*) Ayer.

Propaganda, Cultural Imperialism & Population Control: Ideological Communications in the Southern Hemisphere. Information Project for Africa, Inc. Staff. (I. P. F. A. Foreign Policy Ser.). 152p. 1993. pap. text 26.00 (*1-886719-03-9*) Info Proj for Afr.

Propaganda for War: How the United States Was Conditioned to Fight the Great War of 1914-1918. Stewart H. Ross. LC 95-25927. (Illus.). 351p. 1996. lib. bdg. 46.50 (*0-7864-0111-7*) McFarland & Co.

Propaganda from China & Japan: A Case Study in Propaganda Analysis. Bruno Lasker & Agnes Roman. LC 75-30126. (Institute of Pacific Relations Ser.). reprint ed. 39.50 (*0-404-59537-5*) AMS Pr.

Propaganda Gap. Walter Joyce. LC 74-20076. 144p. 1975. reprint ed. lib. bdg. 55.00 (*0-8371-7843-6*, JOPG, Greenwood Pr) Greenwood.

Propaganda in an Open Society: The Roosevelt Administration & the Media, 1933-1941, 111. Richard W. Steele. LC 84-27931. (Contributions in American History Ser.: No. 111). 231p. 1985. 59.95 (*0-313-24830-3*, SNS/, Greenwood Pr) Greenwood.

Propaganda in the English Reformation: Heroic & Villainous Images of King John. Carole Levin. LC 87-31949. (Studies in British History: Vol. 11). 306p. 1988. lib. bdg. 99.95 (*0-88946-463-4*) E Mellen.

Propaganda in the Next War. Sidney Rogerson. LC 72-4678. (International Propaganda & Communications Ser.). 188p. 1972. reprint ed. 17.95 (*0-405-04762-2*) Ayer.

Propaganda in the 20th Century: Contributions to Its History. Ed. by Jurgen Wilke. LC 98-12289. (IAMCR Bks.). (Illus.). 172p. (C). 1998. text 45.00 (*1-57273-120-6*); pap. text 19.95 (*1-57273-121-4*) Hampton Pr NJ.

Propaganda in Twentieth Century War & Politics: An Annotated Bibliography. Robert Cole. LC 96-27825. (Magill Bibliographies Ser.). 416p. 1996. 48.50 (*0-8108-3196-1*) Scarecrow.

Propaganda in War & Crisis. Ed. by Daniel Lerner. LC 72-4669. (International Propaganda & Communications Ser.). 516p. 1978. reprint ed. 30.95 (*0-405-04754-1*) Ayer.

Propaganda, Inc. Selling America's Culture to the World. Nancy Snow. LC 97-52614. (The Open Media Pamphlet Ser.: Vol. 6). (Illus.). 64p. 1998. pap. 5.95 (*1-888363-74-6*) Seven Stories.

Propaganda Novel. M. Waldman. 1972. 75.00 (*0-8490-0900-6*) Gordon Pr.

Propaganda of a Seed. Christopher Butters. 72p. 1990. pap., per. 6.00 (*0-943594-10-3*) Cardinal Pr.

Propaganda of Power: The Role of Panegyric Late Antiquity. Mary Whitby. LC 98-16226. (Mnemosyne, Bibliotheca Classica Batava Ser.). 1998. 111.00 (*90-04-10571-9*) Brill Academic Pubs.

Propaganda, Politics, & Violence in Cambodia: Democratic Transition Under United Nations Peace-Keeping. Ed. by Steve Heder & Judy Ledgerwood. LC 95-31350. (Illus.). 298p. (C). (gr. 13). 1995. text 79.95 (*1-56324-664-3*, East Gate Bk); pap. text 32.95 (*1-56324-665-1*, East Gate Bk) M E Sharpe.

***Propaganda Postcards of World War II.** Ron Menchene. (Illus.). 160p. 2000. pap. 21.95 (*1-58221-024-1*, Antique Trader) Krause Pubns.

Propaganda Warriors: America's Crusade Against Nazi Germany. Clayton D. Laurie. LC 95-26321. (Modern War Studies). (Illus.). 321p. (C). 1996. 35.00 (*0-7006-0765-X*) U Pr of KS.

Propagate Your Own Plants, Vol. 1. Wilma R. James. LC 78-18248. (Illus.). 149p. 1978. pap. 10.95 (*0-87961-072-7*) Naturegraph.

Propagating. (Taylor's Weekend Gardening Guide Ser.). 1997. pap. 12.95 (*0-614-27241-6*) HM.

Propagating Australian Plants. Alec M. Blombery & Betty Maloney. (Illus.). 120p. (Orig.). 1995. pap. 14.95 (*0-86417-613-9*) Seven Hills Bk.

Propagating the Word of Irish Dissent, 1650-1800. Ed. by Kevin Herlihy. LC 99-176190. 144p. 1998. pap. 20.00 (*1-85182-412-X*, Pub. by Four Cts Pr); boxed set 39.50 (*1-85182-411-1*, Pub. by Four Cts Pr) Intl Spec Bk.

Propagation & Imaging Through the Atmosphere. Ed. by Luc R. Bissonnette & Christopher Dainty. x, 458 p. 1997. pap. 99.00 (*0-8194-2547-8*) SPIE.

Propagation & Imaging Through the Atmosphere II, Vol. 3433. Ed. by Luc R. Bissonnette. LC 99-200354. 1998. 99.00 (*0-8194-2888-4*) SPIE.

***Propagation & Imaging Through the Atmosphere III.** Ed. by Michael C. Roggemann & Luc R. Bissonnette. 1999. pap. text 72.00 (*0-8194-3249-0*) SPIE.

Propagation & Instabilities in Plasmas: Proceedings of the Lockheed Symposium on Magnetohydrodynamics, Palo Alto, Calif, 1962. 7th ed. Lockheed Symposium on Magnetohydrodynamics Staff. LC 63-19236. 155p. reprint ed. pap. 48.10 (*0-608-11828-1*, 200031800025) Bks Demand.

Propagation & Interaction of Singularities in Nonlinear Hyperbolic Problems. Michael Beals. (Progress in Nonlinear Differential Equations & Their Applications Ser.: No. 3). 150p. 1989. 42.50 (*0-8176-3449-5*) Birkhauser.

Propagation & Polarization of Radiation in Cosmic Media. A. Z. Dolginov et al. 400p. 1995. text 154.00 (*2-88124-987-6*) Gordon & Breach.

Propagation & Practice of Important Indian Trees. Ram Parkash. 460p. (C). 1991. pap. 250.00 (*81-7089-112-4*, Pub. by Intl Bk Distr) St Mut.

Propagation & Reflection of Shock Waves. LC 97-3964. 300p. 1997. 45.00 (*981-02-3010-9*) World Scientific Pub.

Propagation du Francais en France Jusqu'a la Fin de l'Ancien Regime see Histoire de la Langue Francaise des Origines a nos Jours

Propagation Handbook: Basic Techniques for Gardeners. Geoff Bryant. LC 94-37457. 1995. 12.95 (*0-8117-3065-4*) Stackpole.

Propagation in Systems Far from Equilibrium. Ed. by J. E. Wesfreid et al. (Synergetics Ser.: Vol. 41). (Illus.). 430p. 1988. 78.95 (*0-387-19473-8*) Spr-Verlag.

Propagation of a Curved Shock & Nonlinear Ray Theory. P. Prasad. 1993. lib. bdg. 54.95 (*0-582-07253-0*) Longman.

Propagation of Alpine Plants & Dwarf Bulbs. Brian Halliwell. (Illus.). 208p. 1992. 24.95 (*0-88192-254-4*) Timber.

Propagation of Alpines. Lawrence D. Hills. (Illus.). 1976. reprint ed. write for info. (*0-913728-11-X*) Theophrastus.

Propagation of Electromagnetic Signals. F. Harmuth Henning & G. M. Hussain. 350p. 1994. text 81.00 (*981-02-1689-0*) World Scientific Pub.

Propagation of Electromagnetic Waves in Multiconductor Tras. P. Kuznetsov & Rouslan L. Stratonovich. LC 61-11528. 1964. 91.00 (*0-08-013559-5*, Pub. by Pergamon Repr) Franklin.

Propagation of Electromagnetic Waves in Plasmas. 2nd rev. ed. Vitaly L. Ginzburg. 1964. 278.00 (*0-08-015569-3*, Pub. by Pergamon Repr) Franklin.

Propagation of Horticultural Plants. 2nd ed. Guy W. Adriance & Fred R. Brison. LC 79-9753. 308p. 1979. reprint ed. lib. bdg. 37.00 (*0-88275-965-5*) Krieger.

Propagation of Intensive Laser Radiation in Clouds. O. A. Volkovitsky et al. (PAAS Ser.: Vol. 138). 339p. 1992. 92.95 (*1-56347-020-9*, V-138) AIAA.

Propagation of Light. Leszek Balczewski. LC 97-90062. 42p. 1998. pap. 10.95 (*0-533-12698-3*) Vantage.

Propagation of Mammalian Cells in Culture, Vol. I. J. D. Roth et al. 1976. text 39.50 (*0-8422-7290-9*) Irvington.

Propagation of Pacific Northwest Native Plants. Robin Rose et al. LC 97-41008. (Illus.). 256p. 1998. pap. 21.95 (*0-87071-428-7*) Oreg St U Pr.

Propagation of Power in the Medieval West: Selected Proceedings of the International Conference, Groningen, 20-23 November 1996. Ed. by Martin Gosman et al. (Mediaevalia Groningana Ser.: Vol. XXIII). xii, 438p. 1997. pap. 82.00 (*90-6980-107-8*, Pub. by Egbert Forsten) Hod1der & Stoughton.

Propagation of Radiowaves. Ed. by M. P. Hall et al. 450p. 1996. boxed set 95.00 (*0-85296-819-1*, EW501) INSPEC Inc.

Propagation of Shock Waves in Solids: Presented at the Applied Mechanics Conference, Salt Lake City, Utah, June 14-17, 1976. Applied Mechanics Conference Staff. LC 76-12662. (American Society of Mechanical Engineers, Applied Mechanics Division Ser.: Vol. 17). 122p. reprint ed. pap. 37.90 (*0-608-12667-5*, 202418500035) Bks Demand.

Propagation of Short Radio Waves. Ed. by D. E. Kerr. (Electromagnetic Waves Ser.: No. 24). 738p. 1987. 115.00 (*0-86341-099-5*, EW024) INSPEC Inc.

Propagation of Short Radio Waves. Donald E. Kerr. LC 87-63304. 756p. 1989. reprint ed. 53.95 (*0-932146-20-1*) Peninsula CA.

Propagation of Sound in Porous Media: Modelling Sound Absorbing Materials. J. F. Allard. (Illus.). 300p. (C). (gr. 13). 1994. text 94.95 (*0-412-53470-3*, Chap & Hall NY) Chapman & Hall.

Propagation of the Houbara Bustard. Ed. by M. Saint Jalme & Y. Von Heezik. LC 95-14864. 1995. 76.50 (*0-7103-0518-4*) Routledge.

Propagation of Tropical & Subtropical Horticultural Crops. T. K. Bose & S. K. Mitra. 580p. (C). 1986. 82.50 (*81-85109-40-0*, Pub. by Naya Prokash) S Asia.

Propagation of Waves in Hydrodynamic Flows. Y. A. Stepanyants & A. L. Fabrikant. LC 98-29453. (Series on Nonlinear Science). 287p. 1997. text 61.00 (*981-02-2052-9*) World Scientific Pub.

Propagation Programs: A Review of Current Forecasting Software. Jacques D'Avignon. Ed. by Bob Grove. (Illus.). 48p. (Orig.). 1992. 9.95 (*0-944543-06-5*) Grove Enterp.

Propagation, Scattering & Dissipation of Electromagnetic Waves. A. S. Ilyinski et al. (Electromagnetic Waves Ser.: No. 36). x, 276p. 1993. boxed set 99.00 (*0-86341-283-1*, EW036) INSPEC Inc.

Propagations: Thirty Years of Influence from the Mental Research Institute. Ed. by Wendel A. Ray & John H. Weakland. LC 94-32743. 310p. (C). 1995. lib. bdg. 49.95 (*1-56024-936-6*) Haworth Pr.

Propagators for Many-Particle Systems. R. L. Mills. xiii, 128p. 1969. text 220.00 (*0-677-02040-6*) Gordon & Breach.

Propagator's Handbook: Fifty Foolproof Recipes - 100s of Plants for Your Garden. Peter Thompson. (Illus.). 144p. 1993. 27.50 (*0-943955-69-6*, Trafalgar Sq Pub) Trafalgar.

Propagator's Handbook: Fifty Foolproof Recipes--Hundreds of Plants for Your Garden. Peter Thompson. (Illus.). 144p. 1996. reprint ed. pap. 16.95 (*1-57076-040-3*, Trafalgar Sq Pub) Trafalgar.

***Propagator's Handbook: Fifty Foolproof Recipes, Hundreds of Plants for Your Garden.** Peter Thompson. (Illus.). 144p. 1999. 17.95 (*0-7153-0426-7*, Pub. by D & C Pub) Sterling.

Propane, Butane & 2-Methylpropane see Solubility Data Series

Propashchaia Dusha (Lost Soul) Stikhotvoreniia i Poemy, 1987-1996 (Poems, 1987-1996) David Shrayer-Petrov. (RUS., Illus.). 1997. pap. 7.95 (*1-888244-00-3*) APKA Pubs.

Propecia: The Hair Restoration Breakthrough. Othneil J. Seiden. LC 98-12168. 256p. 1998. per. 14.00 (*0-7615-1536-4*) Prima Pub.

Propedeutics of Children's Diseases. V. Molchanov et al. Tr. by Mir Publishers Staff from RUS. (Illus.). 392p. (C). 1975. 29.00 (*0-8464-0768-X*) Beekman Pubs.

Propellant Profiles. 3rd ed. Ed. by Dave Wolfe. (Illus.). 158p. 1991. 16.95 (*1-879356-01-5*) Wolfe Pub Co.

Propellants Manufacture, Hazards, & Testing: A Symposium. Carl Boyars. LC 75-87208. (Advances in Chemistry Ser.: No. 88). 405p. reprint ed. pap. 125.60 (*0-608-17750-4*, 205225100074) Bks Demand.

Propeller Handbook. Dave Gerr. 128p. 1989. 32.95 (*0-07-157323-2*) McGraw.

Propeller Handbook: The Boatowner's Reference for Choosing, Installing, & Understanding Propellers. Dave Gerr. 128p. 1989. text 32.95 (*0-87742-988-X*) Intl Marine.

Propeller Island. Jules Verne. lib. bdg. 22.95 (*0-8488-2049-5*) Amereon Ltd.

Propeller Log: #ASA-SP-L. rev. ed. ASA Staff. (Logbook Ser.). (Illus.). 20p. 1998. pap. 4.95 (*1-56027-202-3*, ASA-SP-L) ASA Inc.

Propeller Making for the Amateur. (Illus.). 7.00 (*0-614-13165-0*, 21-37713) EAA Aviation.

Propensity of Things: Toward a History of Efficacy in China. Francois Jullien. Tr. by Janet Lloyd. LC 94-30660. (Illus.). 320p. (C). 1995. 24.95 (*0-942299-94-9*) Zone Bks.

***Propensity of Things: Towards a History of Efficacy in China.** Francois Jullien. 1999. pap. 18.00 (*0-942299-95-7*) Zone Bks.

Propensity to Protect: Butter, Margarine & the Rise of Urban Culture in Canada. W. H. Heick. 288p. (C). 1991. text 39.95 (*0-88920-994-4*) W Laurier U Pr.

Propensity to Self-Subversion. Albert O. Hirschman. LC 94-46737. (Illus.). 264p. (C). 1995. 41.50 (*0-674-71557-8*); pap. 19.50 (*0-674-71558-6*) HUP.

Proper Acadian. Mary A. Downie & George Rawlyk. 64p. (J). 1980. pap. 4.96 (*0-919964-29-X*) Kids Can Pr.

***Proper Ambition of Science.** M. W. Stone & Jonathan Wolff. LC 99-39024. (London Studies in the History of Philosophy). 200p. 2000. 75.00 (*0-415-18617-X*) Routledge.

Proper & Improper Forcing. 2nd ed. Saharon Shelah. LC 97-46606. (Perspectives in Mathematical Logic Ser.). 1050p. (C). 1998. 189.00 (*3-540-51700-6*) Spr-Verlag.

Proper Attitudes Toward Leadership. Robyn Gool. 144p. 1987. pap. 6.99 (*0-88144-073-6*) Christian Pub.

Proper BASIC. Brian C. Walsh. LC 82-17447. 411p. reprint ed. pap. 127.50 (*0-608-18451-9*, 203266700080) Bks Demand.

Proper Bostonian: or Sex & Birth Control. Horatio R. Storer. Incl. Is It I? A Book for Every Man, Boston, 1867. LC 73-20653. 1974. Why Not? A Book for Every Woman, Boston, 1868. LC 73-20653. 1974. LC 73-20653. (Sex, Marriage & Society Ser.). 258p. 1974. reprint ed. 26.95 (*0-405-05813-6*) Ayer.

Proper Bostonians. Cleveland Amory. 384p. 1984. reprint ed. pap. 9.95 (*0-940160-25-0*) Parnassus Imprints.

Proper Burial. Pat Welch. (Helen Black Mystery Ser.). 176p. 1993. pap. 9.95 (*1-56280-033-7*) Naiad Pr.

Proper Care & Feeding of Church Volunteers. Gary Petri. LC 97-148992. 72p. 1996. pap. 8.95 (*1-55612-916-5*) Sheed & Ward WI.

Proper Care of Amphibians. John Coborn. (TW Ser.). (Illus.). 256p. 1993. text 16.95 (*0-86622-346-0*, TW116) TFH Pubns.

Proper Care of Aquarium Plants. Mary E. Sweeney. 256p. 16.95 (*0-86622-792-X*, TW-134) TFH Pubns.

Proper Care of Bichon Frise. Ann Hearn. 256p. 1995. 16.95 (*0-7938-1965-2*, TW136) TFH Pubns.

***Proper Care of Bichon Frises.** Ann Hearn. 256p. 2000. pap. 12.95 (*0-7938-3161-X*, Pub. by TFH Pubns) K K & B.

Proper Care of Budgies. Dennis Kelsey-Wood. (Illus.). 256p. 1992. text 16.95 (*0-86622-192-1*, TW104) TFH Pubns.

P

Proper Care of Canaries. John Coborn. (Illus.). 256p. 1994. 16.95 (*0-86622-447-5*, TW114) TFH Pubns.

Proper Care of Cats. Christopher Burris. (TW Ser.). (Illus.). 256p. 1991. text 16.95 (*0-86622-403-3*, TW-103) TFH Pubns.

Proper Care of Chow Chows, AKC Rank No. 17. Bob Banghart & Love Banghart. (Illus.). 256p. 1996. 16.95 (*0-7938-1967-9*, TW138) TFH Pubns.

Proper Care of Cockatiels. Karl-Herbert Delpy. (Illus.). 256p. 1992. text 16.95 (*0-86622-189-1*, TW105) TFH Pubns.

Proper Care of Cockatoos. Helmut Pinter. (TW Ser.). (Illus.). 256p. 1993. text 16.95 (*0-86622-387-8*, TW-126) TFH Pubns.

Proper Care of Cocker Spaniels, AKC Rank No. 6. Frank DeVito & Joseph Serrano. (Illus.). 256p. (J). (gr. 5). 1996. 16.95 (*0-7938-1970-9*, TW141) TFH Pubns.

Proper Care of Dalmatians. Sylvian Howason. (Illus.). 256p. 1995. text 16.95 (*0-7938-1966-0*, TW137) TFH Pubns.

Proper Care of Discus. Bernd Degen. (Illus.). 256p. 1995. 16.95 (*0-86622-548-X*, TW130) TFH Pubns.

Proper Care of Dogs. Christopher Burris. (TW Ser.). (Illus.). 256p. 1991. text 16.95 (*0-86622-402-5*, TW-102) TFH Pubns.

***Proper Care of Dogs.** Christopher Burris. (Illus.). 2000. 12.95 (*0-7938-3155-5*) TFH Pubns.

Proper Care of Dwarf Rabbits. Michael Mettler. (Illus.). 256p. 1992. text 16.95 (*0-86622-443-2*, TW-121) TFH Pubns.

Proper Care of Fancy Rats. Nick Mays. (Illus.). 256p. 1993. 16.95 (*0-86622-340-1*, TW122) TFH Pubns.

Proper Care of Finches. Phillip St. Blazey. (TW Ser.). (Illus.). 256p. 1991. text 16.95 (*0-86622-400-9*, TW-100) TFH Pubns.

***Proper Care of Finches.** Phillip St. Blazey. (Proper Care Of... Ser.). (Illus.). 1999. pap. 12.95 (*0-7938-3153-9*) TFH Pubns.

Proper Care of German Shepherds. Carmelo L. Battaglia. 256p. 1998. 16.95 (*0-7938-0495-7*, TW144) TFH Pubns.

Proper Care of Golden Retrievers, AKC Rank No. 4. Nona K. Bauer. (Illus.). 256p. 1996. 16.95 (*0-7938-2082-0*, TW143) TFH Pubns.

Proper Care of Goldfish. James Geran. (Illus.). 256p. 1992. text 16.95 (*0-86622-186-7*, TW107) TFH Pubns.

***Proper Care of Goldfish.** James Geran. 256p. 2000. pap. 12.95 (*0-7938-3158-X*, Pub. by TFH Pubns) K K & B.

Proper Care of Guinea Pigs. Peter Gurney. (Illus.). 256p. 1992. text 16.95 (*0-86622-195-6*, TW108) TFH Pubns.

***Proper Care of Guinea Pigs.** Peter Gurney. (Proper Care Of... Ser.). (Illus.). 1999. pap. 12.95 (*0-7938-3151-2*) TFH Pubns.

Proper Care of Guppies. S. Shubel. (Illus.). 256p. 1995. 16.95 (*0-86622-615-X*, TW133) TFH Pubns.

Proper Care of Koi. Dennis K. Wood. (Illus.). 256p. 16.95 (*0-7938-1964-4*, TW-135) TFH Pubns.

Proper Care of Labrador Retrievers. Dennis Livesay. (Illus.). 256p. (J). (gr. 5). 1995. 16.95 (*0-7938-1969-5*, TW140) TFH Pubns.

Proper Care of Lovebirds. Murray Greenleaf. (Illus.). 256p. 1993. 16.95 (*0-86622-190-5*, TW109) TFH Pubns.

Proper Care of Malawi Cichlids. Mary E. Sweeney. (TW Ser.). (Illus.). 256p. 1993. text 16.95 (*0-86622-367-3*, TW124) TFH Pubns.

Proper Care of Marine Aquaria. Scott B. Meyer. (TW Ser.). (Illus.). 256p. 1992. 16.95 (*0-86622-347-9*, TW117) TFH Pubns.

***Proper Care of Marine Aquarium.** Scott B. Meyer. (Illus.). 2000. 12.95 (*0-7938-3156-3*) TFH Pubns.

Proper Care of Parrots. Martin Skinner. (TW Ser.). (Illus.). 256p. 1992. 16.95 (*0-86622-401-7*, TW101) TFH Pubns.

Proper Care of Rabbits. Darlene Campbell. 256p. 1992. 16.95 (*0-86622-196-4*, TW110) TFH Pubns.

Proper Care of Reptiles. John Coborn. (TW Ser.). (Illus.). 256p. 1993. text 16.95 (*0-86622-345-2*, TW115) TFH Pubns.

Proper Care of Rottweilers. Joan R. Klem. (Illus.). 256p. 1995. 16.95 (*0-7938-1971-7*, TW142) TFH Pubns.

Proper Care of Shetland Sheepdogs, AKC Rank No. 13. Sandy Ganz & Rick Thompson. (Illus.). 256p. 1996. 16.95 (*0-7938-1968-7*, TW139) TFH Pubns.

Proper Care of Snakes. Armin Geus. (Illus.). 256p. 1992. text 16.95 (*0-86622-185-9*, TW111) TFH Pubns.

Proper Care of Tarantulas. Ann Webb. (TW Ser.). (Illus.). 256p. 1992. text 16.95 (*0-86622-446-7*, TW-123) TFH Pubns.

Proper Care of Turtles. John Coborn. (Illus.). 256p. 1993. 16.95 (*0-86622-534-X*, TW132) TFH Pubns.

Proper Companion. Candice Hern. 208p. (Orig.). 1995. pap. text 4.50 (*0-515-11526-6*, Jove) Berkley Pub.

Proper Conduct of Marriage in Islam (Adab An-Nikah) Book 12 of Ihya Ulumud-Din, Vol. 1. Imam Al-Ghazali. Tr. by Muhtar Holland from ARA. LC 98-84302. 120p. 1998. pap. 16.00 (*1-882216-14-8*) Al-Baz Pub.

Proper Confidence: Faith, Doubt, & Certainty in Christian Discipleship. Lesslie Newbigin. 110p. (Orig.). 1995. pap. 10.00 (*0-8028-0856-5*) Eerdmans.

Proper Deafinitions: Collected Theorograms. Betsy Warland. 144p. 1990. pap. 11.95 (*0-88974-021-6*, Pub. by Press Gang Pubs) LPC InBook.

Proper Distinction Between Law & Gospel. Carl F. Walther. Tr. by W. H. Dau. 448p. 1969. 22.00 (*0-570-03248-2*, 15-1601) Concordia.

Proper Distribution of Expense Burden. Alexander H. Church, Jr. Ed. by Alfred D. Chandler. LC 79-7538. (History of Management Thought & Practice Ser.). 1980. reprint ed. lib. bdg. 15.95 (*0-405-12323-X*) Ayer.

Proper English: Myths & Misunderstandings about Language. Ronald Wardhaugh. LC 98-24577. (Language Library). 208p. 1999. 49.95 (*0-631-21268-X*); pap. 19.95 (*0-631-21269-8*) Blackwell Pubs.

Proper Food Combining Cookbook. rev. ed. Lee DuBelle. 200p. 1987. pap. 20.00 (*0-9618703-0-3*) L DuBelle.

Proper Food Combining Works - Living Testimony. rev. ed. Lee Dubelle. 115p. 1987. pap. 12.00 (*0-9618703-1-1*) L DuBelle.

Proper Forcing. 1997. 189.00 (*0-387-51700-6*) Spr-Verlag.

Proper Fuss. Brian Louis Pearce. 105p. pap. write for info. (*3-7052-0785-7*, Pub. by Poetry Salzburg) Intl Spec Bk.

Proper Garden: On Perennials in the Border. Elisabeth Sheldon. LC 88-38732. (Illus.). 224p. 1989. 19.95 (*0-8117-0711-3*) Stackpole.

Proper Gentleman. Vernon Scannell. LC 78-312973. 160p. 1977. write for info. (*0-903895-86-2*) Robson Bks.

Proper Institution: Guaranteeing Televised Presidential Debates - A Twentieth Century Fund Paper. John B. Anderson. 61p. 1988. 18.95 (*0-87078-253-3*); pap. 8.95 (*0-87078-252-5*) Century Foundation.

Proper Lady & the Woman Writer: Ideology As Style in the Writings of Mary Wollstonecraft, Mary Shelley, & Jane Austen. Mary Poovey. LC 83-3664. 287p. (C). 1985. pap. text 10.95 (*0-226-67528-9*) U Ch Pr.

Proper Lady & the Woman Writer: Ideology As Style in the Writings of Mary Wollstonecraft, Mary Shelley, & Jane Austen. Mary Poovey. LC 83-3664. 287p. (C). 1992. lib. bdg. 20.00 (*0-226-67527-0*) U Ch Pr.

Proper Mark Twain. Leland Krauth. LC 98-51168. 304p. 1999. 29.95 (*0-8203-2106-0*) U of Ga Pr.

Proper Marriage. Lessing. 1969. pap. text 3.95 (*0-586-02116-7*) HarpC.

Proper Marriage: A Novel. Doris Lessing. LC 95-33114. (Children of Violence Ser.). 448p. 1995. pap. 15.00 (*0-06-097663-2*, Perennial) HarperTrade.

Proper Match. Dorothea Donley. 224p. 1998. mass mkt. 4.99 (*0-8217-5827-6*, Zebra Kensgtn) Kensgtn Pub Corp.

***Proper Match.** Sherry-Anne Jacobs. 256p. 2000. mass mkt. 5.99 (*1-929613-50-4*, Echoes MI) Avid MI.

Proper Me! The Way to Be. Florette Morgan. 70p. 1997. pap. 15.00 (*0-9653163-8-6*) Character Dev.

Proper Motions & Galactic Astronomy: Proceedings of a Workshop Held at the University of Minnesota, Minneapolis, December 12-13, 1996. Ed. by Roberta M. Humphreys. (ASP Conference Series Proceedings: Vol. 127). 197p. 1997. 34.00 (*1-886733-47-3*) Astron Soc Pacific.

Proper Myth. William F. Van Wert. LC 97-25369. 64p. (J). 1998. pap. 12.95 (*0-914061-67-4*) Orchises Pr.

Proper Name & Other Stories. Bernadette Mayer. 144p. (Orig.). 1996. pap. 13.95 (*0-8112-1325-0*, NDP824, Pub. by New Directions) Norton.

Proper Name Speller. Jean Emerich. Ed. by Diana Gregory. 240p. (Orig.). 1990. pap. 11.95 (*0-944494-11-0*) Lifeboat Bks.

Proper Names. Emmanuel Levinas. Tr. by Michael B. Smith. (Meridian: Crossing Aesthetics Ser.). 208p. 1997. 35.00 (*0-8047-2351-6*); pap. 15.95 (*0-8047-2352-4*) Stanford U Pr.

Proper Names Master Index: A Comprehensive Index of More Than 200,000 Proper Names That Appear As Entries in Standard Reference Works, 2 vols., Set. Ed. by Frank R. Abate. LC 94-22479. 1600p. 1994. lib. bdg. 125.00 (*1-55888-837-3*) Omnigraphics Inc.

Proper Noun Speller. Jean Emerich. Ed. by Diana Gregory. 320p. 1988. 16.95 (*0-944494-10-2*) Lifeboat Bks.

Proper Noun Speller: A Word Book of Names. 2nd ed. Ed. by Jean Emerich & Diana Gregory. 288p. 1992. pap. write for info. (*0-944494-16-1*) Lifeboat Bks.

Proper Pattern for Pentecostal Postsecondary Education. Bernard Rossier. 96p. 1992. pap. text 7.95 (*0-930401-53-0*) Artex Pub.

Proper Pig's Guide to Mealtime Manners. Sally S. Stamp & L. A. Kowal. Ed. by Paul M. Howey. (Illus.). 56p. 1996. pap. 15.95 (*1-877749-20-6*) Five Star AZ.

***Proper Polly's Perfect Pet.** Jane West. (J). 2001. write for info. (*0-9701025-3-4*) Haylett Pubng.

***Proper Polly's Playroom.** Jane West. (Illus.). (J). 2001. write for info. (*0-9701025-2-6*) Haylett Pubng.

Proper Puppy Guides: Six Handbooks for Raising a Proper Puppy, 6 booklets, Set. September B. Morn. (Illus.). 96p. (Orig.). 1996. pap. 18.00 (*0-9633884-8-7*) Pawprince Pr.

Proper Reply to a Late Scurrilous Libel Intitled Sedition & Defamation Display'd (1731) No. 2: British Ideas & Issues, 1660-1820. William P. Bath et al. LC 97-42766. 1998. 24.50 (*0-404-59652-5*) AMS Pr.

Proper Role of Government. Ezra Taft Benson. 32p. 1975. reprint ed. pap. 2.50 (*0-89036-122-3*) Liahona Pub Trust.

Proper Roller Techniques. Kip Productions, Inc. Staff. (Cosmetology Ser.). 1980. 44.95 (*0-87350-455-0*) Milady Pub.

Proper Schooling: And Other Poems. Aonghas MacNeacail. 88p. 1996. pap. 13.95 (*0-7486-6218-9*, Pub. by Polygon) Subterranean Co.

Proper Sphere: Woman's Place in Canadian Society. Ed. by G. Ramsay Cook & Wendy Mitchinson. 1976. pap. 8.95 (*0-19-540272-3*) OUP.

Proper Standard. large type ed. Brenda H. English. 1989. 27.99 (*0-7089-2053-5*) Ulverscroft.

Proper Stitch: A Guide for Counted Thread. Needle's Prayse Staff & Darlene O'Steen. Ed. by Barbara Cockerham. (Illus.). 144p. 1994. 39.95 (*0-932437-03-6*) Symbol Exc Pubs.

Proper Study of Mankind. rev. ed. Stuart Chase & Edmund de S. Brunner. LC 78-87. 327p. 1978. reprint ed. lib. bdg. 35.00 (*0-313-20261-3*, CHPS, Greenwood Pr) Greenwood.

Proper Study of Mankind: An Annotated Bibliography of Manuscript Sources on Anthropology & Archeology in the Library of the American Philosophical Society. David K. Van Keuren. LC 86-71011. (American Philosophical Society Library Publication Ser.: No. 10). 89p. reprint ed. pap. 30.00 (*0-8357-3411-0*, 203966800013) Bks Demand.

Proper Study of Mankind: An Anthology of Essays. Isaiah Berlin. Ed. by Henry Hardy & Roger Hausheer. LC 97-43470. 672p. 1998. 35.00 (*0-374-23750-6*) FS&G.

***Proper Study of Mankind: An Anthology of Essays.** Isaiah Berlin. Ed. by Henry Hardy & Roger Hausheer. 672p. 2000. pap. 16.00 (*0-374-52717-2*) FS&G.

Proper-T-Care: How to Win at Real Estate! K. K. McNulty, Sr. (One of the Answers Ser.). (Illus.). 320p. 1989. 19.95 (*0-935025-02-2*) Data & Res Tech.

Proper Taming. Joan E. Overfield. 224p. (Orig.). 1994. mass mkt. 3.99 (*0-380-77401-1*, Avon Bks) Morrow Avon.

Proper Use of Standardized Tests. James W. Deuink. (Illus.). 64p. (Orig.). 1986. pap. 4.95 (*0-89084-355-4*, 030858) Bob Jones Univ.

Proper Use of the Watchmaker's Graver. Homer A. Barkus. (Illus.). 1992. pap. 5.00 (*0-930163-29-X*) Arlington Bk.

Proper Way to Breed Tropical Fish. TFH Pubns. Staff. (Illus.). 256p. 16.95 (*0-86622-775-X*, TW-128) TFH Pubns.

Proper Wife. Sandra Marton. 1997. per. 3.50 (*0-373-11860-0*, 1-11860-3) Silhouette.

Proper Wife. large type ed. Sandra Marton. (Harlequin Romance Ser.). 283p. 1997. 20.95 (*0-263-14910-2*) Mac Lib Ref.

Properjohn. large type ed. Terence Kelly. (General Fiction Ser.). 256p. 1993. 27.99 (*0-7089-2958-3*) Ulverscroft.

Properti. 4th rev. ed. Ed. by Fedeli. (LAT.). 1994. 43.50 (*3-519-01740-7*, T1740, Pub. by B G Teubner) U of Mich Pr.

Properti: Poemata. Ed. by Westerink. (GRE.). 1992. 125.00 (*3-8154-1662-0*, T1662, Pub. by B G Teubner) U of Mich Pr.

Propertiana. D. R. Shackleton-Bailey. 339p. 1956. reprint ed. lib. bdg. 47.50 (*0-685-13670-1*, Pub. by AM Hakkert) Coronet Bks.

Properties. Ed. by D. H. Mellor & Alex Oliver. LC 97-164761. (Oxford Readings in Philosophy). 288p. 1997. text 60.00 (*0-19-875177-X*); pap. text 19.95 (*0-19-875176-1*) OUP.

Properties: A Play for Voices. E. G. Burrows. (QRL Poetry Bks.: Vol. XX). 1978. 20.00 (*0-614-06366-3*) Quarterly Rev.

Properties & Applications of Diamonds. John Wilks & Eileen Wilks. 525p. 1994. pap. 85.00 (*0-7506-1915-5*) Buttrwrth-Heinemann.

Properties & Applications of Perovskite-Type Oxides. L. G. Tejuca & J. L. G. Fierro. (Chemical Industries Ser.: Vol. 50). (Illus.). 408p. 1992. text 199.00 (*0-8247-8786-2*) Dekker.

Properties & Applications of Zeolites, No. 33. Royal Society of Chemistry Staff. 1988. 44.00 (*0-85186-670-0*) CRC Pr.

Properties & Characterization of Amorphous Carbon Films. Ed. by J. J. Pouch & S. A. Alterovitz. 714p. (C). 1990. text 213.00 (*0-87849-604-1*, Pub. by Trans T Pub) Enfield Pubs NH.

Properties & Evaluation of Carpenter Pyrowear Alloy 53 for Extended Gear Life. W. E. Burd. (1984 Fall Technical Meeting Ser.: Vol. 84FTM10). 9p. 1984. pap. text 30.00 (*1-55589-092-X*) AGMA.

Properties & Growth of Diamond. Ed. by G. Davies. (EMIS Datareviews Ser.: No. 9). xx, 435p. 1994. boxed set 245.00 (*0-85296-875-2*, EM009) INSPEC Inc.

Properties & Interactions of Hyperons: Proceedings of the U. S.-Japan Seminar. Ed. by P. D. Barnes & B. F. Gibson. 328p. 1994. text 99.00 (*981-02-1764-1*) World Scientific Pub.

Properties & Interactions of Interplanetary Dust. Ed. by R. H. Giese & P. Lamy. 1985. text 220.00 (*90-277-2115-7*) Kluwer Academic.

Properties & Management of Forest Soils. 2nd ed. William L. Pritchett & Richard F. Fisher. LC 86-22421. 512p. 1987. text 109.95 (*0-471-89572-5*) Wiley.

Properties & Management of Vertisols. M. E. Probart et al. 36p. (Orig.). 1987. pap. text 45.00 (*0-85198-601-3*) OUP.

Properties & Performance of Materials in the Coal Gasification Environment: Proceedings of a Conference Held 8-10 September 1980, Pittsburgh, PA - Sponsored by the Gas Research Institute... et al. American Society for Metals Staff. Ed. by V. L. Hill & Herbert L. Black. LC 81-67327. (Materials-Metalworking Technology Ser.). 831p. reprint ed. pap. 200.00 (*0-608-16500-X*, 202704100053) Bks Demand.

Properties & Processing of Vapor-Deposited Coatings, Vol. 555. Ed. by Roger N. Johnson et al. LC 99-14571. (Materials Research Society Symposium Proceedings Ser.). 427p. 1999. 80.00 (*1-55899-461-0*) Materials Res.

Properties & Production Spectra of Elementary Particles see Nuclear Particles & Physics: Group I

Properties & Reactions of Bonds in Organic Molecules. K. F. Reid. LC 79-365421. 570p. reprint ed. pap. 176.70 (*0-608-10832-4*, 200455100043) Bks Demand.

Properties & Selection: Irons & Steels. American Society for Metals Staff. LC 78-14934. (Metals Handbook Ser.: No. 1). 818p. reprint ed. pap. 200.00 (*0-7837-2771-2*, 204316200006) Bks Demand.

Properties & Selection: Nonferrous Alloys & Pure Metals. American Society for Metals Staff. LC 79-21644. (Metals Handbook Ser.: Vol. 2). 871p. reprint ed. pap. 200.00 (*0-7837-2773-9*, 204316400006) Bks Demand.

Properties & Selection: Nonferrous Alloys & Special-Purpose Materials. 10th ed. (Metals Handbook Ser.: Vol. 2). 1300p. 1990. 118.00 (*0-8169-0536-3*, X-119) Am Inst Chem Eng.

Properties & Selection: Stainless Steels, Tool Materials & Special-Purpose Metals. American Society for Metals Staff. LC 80-26336. (Metals Handbook Ser.: Vol. 3). 900p. reprint ed. pap. 200.00 (*0-7837-2774-7*, 204316500006) Bks Demand.

Properties & Selection of Tool Materials. American Society for Metals Staff & Victor A. Kortesoja. LC 75-26829. 320p. reprint ed. pap. 99.20 (*0-608-13111-3*, 201948300013) Bks Demand.

Properties & Uses of Ferrous & Nonferrous Metals. rev. ed. Hercules C. Kazanas. LC 78-70035. (Illus.). (C). 1979. pap. 9.95 (*0-911168-39-7*); pap., teacher ed. 3.50 (*0-911168-40-0*) Prakken.

Properties As Processes: A Synoptic Study of Wilfrid Sellars' Nominalism. Johanna Seibt. xiv, 338p. (Orig.). 1990. pap. text 20.00 (*0-917930-59-2*); lib. bdg. 38.00 (*0-917930-99-1*) Ridgeview.

Properties Concrete w/3.5 disk. Sandor Popovics. LC 97-31766. 535p. 1998. 120.00 incl. disk (*0-471-14903-9*) Wiley.

Properties, Evaluation & Control of Engineering Materials. William A. Cordon. 550p. (C). 1979. 108.44 (*0-07-013123-6*) McGraw.

Properties, Evaluation & Testing of P-M Materials - Preprint of a Seminar Held at the 1988 International Powder Metallurgy Conference, Orlando, FL, June 8, 1988. Metal Powder Industries Federation Staff. LC TN0695.P651. (Illus.). 128p. reprint ed. pap. 39.70 (*0-7837-1564-1*, 204185600024) Bks Demand.

***Properties of Advanced Semiconductor Materials: G An, Aln, Inn, Bn, Sic, Sige.** Mikhail Levinshtein. 165p. 2001. 74.95 (*0-471-35827-4*) Wiley.

Properties of Aluminium Gallium Arsenide. Ed. by S. Adachi. (EMIS Datareviews Ser.: No. 7). 340p. 1993. boxed set 195.00 (*0-85296-558-3*, EM007) INSPEC Inc.

***Properties of Aluminum Alloys: Tensile, Creep & Fatigue Data at High & Low Temperatures.** J. G. Kaufman. LC 99-41789. 305p. 1999. write for info. (*0-87170-632-6*) ASM.

Properties of Amorphous Silicon & Its Alloys. Ed. by T.M. Searle. (EMIS Datareviews Ser.: No. 19). 440p. 1998. 245.00 (*0-85296-922-8*, EM019) INSPEC Inc.

Properties of Aqueous Solutions of Electrolytes. Ed. by Ivan D. Zaytsev & Georgiy G. Aseyev. 1729p. 1992. lib. bdg. 459.00 (*0-8493-9314-0*, QD565) CRC Pr.

Properties of Asphalt Cements. V. P. Puzinauskas. 72p. 1980. 15.00 (*0-318-13396-2*, RR-80-2) Asphalt Inst.

Properties of Austenitic Stainless Steels & Their Weld Metals: Influence of Slight Chemistry Variations - STP 679. Ed. by C. R. Brinkman & H. W. Garvin. 153p. 1979. pap. 13.50 (*0-8031-0537-1*, STP679) ASTM.

Properties of Biomaterials in the Physiological Environment. Stephen D. Bruck. 160p. 1980. 110.00 (*0-8493-5685-7*, R857, CRC Reprint) Franklin.

Properties of Breath. Jean H. Korelitz. 1989. pap. 12.95 (*1-85224-069-5*, Pub. by Bloodaxe Bks) Dufour.

Properties of Building Materials. H. J. Eldridge. LC TA0403.6.P76. (Illus.). 121p. reprint ed. pap. 37.60 (*0-608-30722-X*, 201962700013) Bks Demand.

Properties of Ceramic Raw Materials. 2nd ed. W. Ryan. (Illus.). 120p. (C). 1992. reprint ed. 55.00 (*1-878907-29-8*) TechBooks.

Properties of Chemically Interesting Potential Energy Surfaces. Deitmar Heidrich et al. (Lecture Notes in Chemistry Ser.: Vol. 56). viii, 182p. 1991. 35.95 (*0-387-54286-8*) Spr-Verlag.

Properties of Chlorine in SI Units. Chlorine Institute Staff. LC 81-67483. (Illus.). 87p. 1986. pap. text 27.00 (*0-940230-02-X*) Chlorine Inst.

Properties of Complex Inorganic Solids: Proceedings of the First International Alloy Conference Held in Athens, Greece, June 16-21, 1996. A. Gonis et al. LC 97-15429. (Illus.). 524p. (C). 1997. text 162.00 (*0-306-45606-0*, Kluwer Plenum) Kluwer Academic.

Properties of Concrete. 4th ed. Neville. LC 95-31843. 1995. pap. text. write for info. (*0-582-23070-5*, Pub. by Addison-Wesley) Longman.

Properties of Concrete: The Final Edition. 4th ed. Adam M. Neville. LC 97-148152. 844p. 1996. pap. 99.00 (*0-470-23527-6*) Wiley.

Properties of Copper. Ed. by Helmut Sigel & Astrid Sigel. LC 81-12587. (Metal Ions in Biological Systems Ser.: Vol. 12). (Illus.). 377p. reprint ed. pap. 116.90 (*0-608-08587-1*, 206911000012) Bks Demand.

Properties of Diamond. Ed. by J. E. Field. 1979. text 275.00 (*0-12-255350-0*) Acad Pr.

Properties of Doped Semiconducting Materials. Ed. by V. S. Zemskov. 277p. 1992. text 165.00 (*1-56072-064-6*) Nova Sci Pubs.

Properties of Double Stars: A Survey of Parallaxes & Orbits. Leendert Binnendijk. LC 58-8011. 357p. reprint ed. pap. 110.70 (*0-608-30344-5*, 205527900012) Bks Demand.

Properties of Earth & Planetary Materials at High Pressure & Temperature. Ed. by M. H. Manghnani & Takehiko Yagi. LC 97-46529. (Geophysical Monograph Ser.: Vol. 101). 1997. pap. 90.00 (*0-87590-084-4*) Am Geophysical.

Properties of Earth & Planetary Materials at High Pressure & Temperature, Vol. 101. Ed. by M. H. Manghnani & Takehiko Yagi. LC 97-46529. (Geophysical Monograph Ser.). 1997. 90.00 (*0-87590-083-6*) Am Geophysical.

Properties of Electrodeposited Metals & Alloys. 550p. 1986. 82.00 (*0-936569-00-X*) Am Electro Surface.

An Asterisk (*) at the beginning of an entry indicates that the title is appearing for the first time.

Properties of Electrodeposits, Their Measurement & Significance. Ed. by Richard Sard et al. LC 74-84702. (Illus.). 436p. reprint ed. pap. 135.20 (*0-608-11676-9*, 205124300092) Bks Demand.

Properties of Elemental & Compound Semiconductors: Proceedings. Ed. by Harry C. Gatos. LC 60-10585. (Metallurgical Society Conference Ser.: Vol. 5). 353p. reprint ed. pap. 109.50 (*0-608-30577-4*, 200066800038) Bks Demand.

Properties of Emerging P-M Materials, Vol. 8. 400p. 1992. 100.00 (*1-878954-27-X*) Metal Powder.

Properties of Engineering Materials. Raymond A. Higgins. (Illus.). 559p. 1990. pap. text 14.95 (*0-340-17909-0*, A3147, Pub. by E A) Routldge.

Properties of Engineering Materials. rev. ed. Raymond A. Higgins. LC 77-22284. 448p. 1980. reprint ed. pap. 23.00 (*0-89874-250-1*) Krieger.

Properties of Engineering Materials. 2nd ed. write for info. (*0-340-60033-0*, Pub. by E A) Routldge.

Properties of Engineering Materials. 2nd ed. Raymond A. Higgins. LC 93-47970. 480p. 1994. 36.95 (*0-8311-3055-5*) Indus Pr.

Properties of Estimators for the Gamma Distribution. K. O. Bowman & L. R. Shenton. (Statistics: Textbooks & Monographs: Vol. 89). (Illus.). 288p. 1987. text 127.50 (*0-8247-7556-2*) Dekker.

Properties of Fibrous Raw Materials & Their Preparation for Pulping. 3rd ed. Ed. by C. F. Stevens & Michael J. Kocurek. LC 90-70774. (Pulp & Paper Manufacture Ser.: Vol. 1). 1983. pap. 35.00 (*0-919893-07-4*, 0202MS01) TAPPI.

Properties of Flexible Pavement Materials - STP 807. Ed. by John J. Emery. LC 82-83521. 178p. 1983. text 25.00 (*0-8031-0257-7*, STP807) ASTM.

Properties of Galactic Carbon Stars. Zenta Alksne et al. Tr. by Christine A. Gallant from RUS. (Orbit Ser.). (Illus.). 172p. (C). 1991. 48.50 (*0-89464-034-8*) Krieger.

Properties of Gallium Arsenide. Ed. by M.R. Brozel & G. E. Stillman. (EMIS Datareviews Ser.: No. 16). 1000p. 1996. 395.00 (*0-85296-885-X*, EM016) INSPEC Inc.

Properties of Gallium Arsenide. 2nd rev. ed. 1990. 295.00 (*0-85296-485-4*, EM002) INSPEC Inc.

Properties of Gases & Liquids. 4th ed. Robert C. Reid et al. (Illus.). 741p. 1987. 110.00 (*0-07-051799-1*) McGraw.

***Properties of Gases & Liquids.** 5th ed. Bruce E. Poling. (Illus.). 2000. 115.00 (*0-07-011682-2*) McGraw.

Properties of Global Attractors of Partial Differential Equations. Ed. by A. V. Babin & M. I. Vishik. LC 91-640741. (Advances in Soviet Mathematics Ser.: Vol. 10). 172p. 1992. text 106.00 (*0-8218-4109-2*, ADVSOV/10C) Am Math.

Properties of Group III Nitrides. Ed. by James H. Edgar. (EMIS Datareviews Ser.: No. 11). 280p. 1994. boxed set 165.00 (*0-85296-818-3*) INSPEC Inc.

Properties of Hazardous Industrial Materials. Andre R. Cooper, Sr. 1998. 250.00 (*1-56670-236-4*, L1236) CRC Pr.

Properties of High Temperature Alloys, with Emphasis on Environmental Effects: Proceedings of the Symposium. Symposium on Properties of High Temperature Alloys. Ed. by Z. A. Foroulis. LC 76-29569. (Electrochemical Society Proceedings Ser.: No. 77-1). (Illus.). 863p. reprint ed. pap. 200.00 (*0-8357-8289-1*, 205229300087) Bks Demand.

Properties of Hot, Luminous Stars: Boulder-Munich II. Ed. by Ian D. Howarth. (ASP Conference Series Proceedings: Vol. 131). 456p. 1998. 34.00 (*1-886733-51-1*) Astron Soc Pacific.

Properties of Hot Luminous Stars: Boulder-Munich Workshop. Ed. by C. D. Germany. (ASP Conference Series Proceedings: Vol. 7). 362p. 1990. 34.00 (*0-937707-24-4*) Astron Soc Pacific.

Properties of II-VI Semiconductors - Bulk Crystals, Epitaxial Films, Quantum Well Structures, & Dilute Magnetic Systems Vol. 161: Materials Research Symposium Proceedings. Ed. by J. F. Schetzina et al. 516p. 1990. text 17.50 (*1-55899-049-6*) Materials Res.

Properties of Impurity States in Superlattice Semiconductors. Ed. by C. Y. Fong et al. LC 88-25348. (NATO ASI Series B, Physics: Vol. 183). (Illus.). 366p. 1988. 105.00 (*0-306-43009-6*, Plenum Trade) Perseus Pubng.

Properties of Incramute I Castings. Ampco Metal Division Staff. 85p. 1974. 12.75 (*0-317-34541-9*, 209) Intl Copper.

Properties of Indium Phosphide. (EMIS Datareviews Ser.: No. 6). 495p. 1991. 285.00 (*0-85296-491-9*, EM006) INSPEC Inc.

Properties of Inorganic & Organic Fluids. Peter E. Liley et al. (CINDAS Data Series on Material Properties: Vol. V[00ad]1). 309p. 1988. 165.00 (*0-89116-802-8*) Hemisp Pub.

Properties of Inorganic Compounds, Version 2.0. 56p. 1997. cd-rom 142.00 (*0-8493-0407-5*) CRC Pr.

Properties of Intermetallic Alloys Vol. 1: Aluminides. James E. Payne & Pramod D. Desai. LC 94-39757. 1994. 400.00 (*0-931682-48-7*) Purdue U Pubns.

Properties of Intermetallic Alloys Vol. 2: Silicides. Brian F. Gilp & Pramod D. Desai. LC 94-39757. 1994. 150.00 (*0-931682-49-5*) Purdue U Pubns.

Properties of Intermetallic Alloys Vol. III: Beryllides & Miscellaneous Intermetallis Alloys. (MIAC Databook Ser.: Vol. 3). 150.00 (*0-931682-50-9*, 2509) Purdue U Pubns.

Properties of Lattice-Matched & Strained Indium Gallium Arsenide. Ed. by P. Bhattacharya. (EMIS Datareviews Ser.: No. 8). 360p. 1993. boxed set 225.00 (*0-85296-865-5*) INSPEC Inc.

***Properties of Light: A Novel of Love, Betrayal & Quantum Physics.** Rebecca Goldstein. LC 99-49994. 224p. 2000. 23.00 (*0-395-98659-1*) HM.

Properties of Liquid see Advanced Treatise on Physical Chemistry

Properties of Liquids & Solutions. John N. Murrell & E. A. Boucher. LC 81-21921. 298p. reprint ed. pap. 92.40 (*0-8357-6983-6*, 205236000009) Bks Demand.

Properties of Liquids & Solutions. 2nd ed. J. N. Murrell & A. D. Jenkins. 316p. 1994. pap. 69.95 (*0-471-94419-X*) Wiley.

Properties of Liquids & Solutions. 2nd ed. John N. Murrell & A. D. Jenkins. LC 93-46721. (Illus.). 315p. 1994. reprint ed. pap. 97.70 (*0-608-05294-9*, 206583200001) Bks Demand.

Properties of Love. Felicity Brett. (Rainbow Romances Ser.: No. 906). 160p. 1994. 14.95 (*0-7090-4989-7*) Parkwest Pubns.

Properties of Materials. Mary Anne White. LC 98-38204. (Illus.). 352p. (C). 1999. pap. text 45.00 (*0-19-511331-4*) OUP.

Properties of Materials for Electrical Engineers. K. J. Pascoe. LC 72-8612. (Illus.). 336p. reprint ed. pap. 104.20 (*0-7837-1877-2*, 204207800001) Bks Demand.

Properties of Materials for Liquified Natural Gas Tankage - STP 579. 424p. 1975. 39.75 (*0-8031-0538-X*, STP579) ASTM.

Properties of Matter. C. Suits & H. Way. LC 60-7068. (Collected Works of Irving Langmuir: Vol. 8). 1961. 125.00 (*0-08-009360-4*, Pub. by Pergamon Repr) Franklin.

Properties of Matter, Custom Pub. 5th ed. Thomas C. Pollock. (Texas A&M Core Engineering Ser.). 472p. (C). 1995. pap. 41.56 (*0-07-050439-3*) McGraw.

Properties of Metal Silicides. Ed. by Karen Maex & Marc Van Rossum. (EMIS Datareviews Ser.: No. 14). 380p. 1995. boxed set 195.00 (*0-85296-859-0*) INSPEC Inc.

Properties of Narrow-Gap Cadmium-Based Compounds. Ed. by Peter Capper. (EMIS Datareviews Ser.: No. 10). 650p. 1994. boxed set 295.00 (*0-85296-880-9*) INSPEC Inc.

Properties of Natural & Synthetic Diamond. Ed. by J. E. Field. (Illus.). 728p. 1992. text 227.00 (*0-12-255352-7*) Acad Pr.

Properties of Nonmetallic Fluid Elements. Ed. by Y. S. Touloukian & C. Y. Ho. (CINDAS Data Series on Material Properties: Vol. III[00ad]2). 208p. 1989. 165.00 (*0-89116-871-0*) Hemisp Pub.

Properties of Nuclei. 2nd ed. Geraint A. Jones. (Oxford Physics Ser.). (Illus.). 204p. 1987. pap. text 21.00 (*0-19-851869-2*) OUP.

Properties of Optical Glass. 1995. 169.95 (*3-540-58357-2*) Spr-Verlag.

Properties of Optical Glass. Ed. by H. Bach et al. 330p. 1995. 168.00 (*0-387-58357-2*) Spr-Verlag.

Properties of Ordinary Water-Substances in All Its Phases: Water-Vapor, Water, & All the Ices. rev. ed. Noah E. Dorsey. LC 68-19563. (American Chemical Society Symposium Ser.: No. 81). 687p. reprint ed. pap. 200.00 (*0-608-10137-0*, 201523700094) Bks Demand.

Properties of Organic Compounds. Lide. 1995. cd-rom 179.00 (*0-8493-0449-0*); cd-rom 550.00 (*0-8493-0450-4*); cd-rom 2900.00 (*0-8493-0451-2*); cd-rom 3800.00 (*0-8493-0452-0*) CRC Pr.

Properties of Organic Compounds: Pers Edition. Lide. 48p. 1996. 139.95 incl. cd-rom (*0-8493-0408-3*) CRC Pr.

Properties of Organic Compounds 5.0. Ed. by David R. Lide, Jr. & G. W. Milne. 50p. 1995. 1049.95 incl. cd-rom (*0-8493-0447-4*, 447) CRC Pr.

Properties of Organic Solvents. 48p. 1996. lib. bdg. 139.00 (*0-8493-0406-7*) CRC Pr.

Properties of "Othello" James L. Calderwood. LC 88-27767. 176p. 1989. 25.00 (*0-87023-666-0*) U of Mass Pr.

Properties of Paper: An Introduction. 2nd ed. William E. Scott et al. LC 95-4070. 192p. 1989. student ed. 68.00 (*0-89852-062-2*, 0102B052) TAPPI.

Properties of Pesticides: User's Guide. G. W. Milne. 48p. 1995. 264.95 (*0-8493-2448-3*, 2448) CRC Pr.

Properties of Petroleum Fluids. 2nd ed. William D. McCain, Jr. 596p. 1990. 99.95 (*0-87814-335-1*) PennWell Bks.

Properties of Planar Graphs with Uniform Vertex & Face Structure. Joseph Malkevitch. LC 52-42839. (Memoirs Ser.: No. 1/99). 116p. 1970. pap. 16.00 (*0-8218-1299-8*, MEMO/1/99) Am Math.

Properties of Planar Graphs with Uniform Vertex & Face Structure. Joseph Malkevitch. LC 52-42839. (American Mathematical Society Ser.: Vol. 99). (Illus.). 120p. reprint ed. pap. 37.20 (*0-608-09607-5*, 205276500007) Bks Demand.

Properties of Polymers: Their Correlation with Chemical Structure; Their Numerical Estimation & Prediction from Additive Group Contributions. 3rd rev. ed. D. W. Van Krevelen. 898p. pap. 123.50 (*0-444-82877-X*, North Holland) Elsevier.

Properties of Polymers: Their Correlation with Chemical Structure; Their Numerical Estimation & Prediction from Additive Group Contributions. 3rd rev. ed. D. W. Van Krevelen. 898p. 1990. 475.75 (*0-444-88160-3*) Elsevier.

Properties of Porous Silicon. Ed. by L. Canham. (EMIS Datareviews Ser.: No. 18). 424p. 1997. 245.00 (*0-85296-932-5*, EM018) INSPEC Inc.

Properties of Reactor Structural Alloys after Neutron or Particle Irradiation - STP 570. 631p. 1976. 59.50 (*0-8031-0539-8*, STP570) ASTM.

Properties of Reservoir Rocks: Core Analysis. Robert P. Monicard. (Illus.). 184p. 1980. 330.00 (*2-7108-0387-9*, Pub. by Edits Technip) Enfield Pubs NH.

Properties of Roofing Asphalts. 102p. 1982. 15.00 (*0-318-17745-5*, RR-82-1) Asphalt Inst.

Properties of Selected Ferrous Alloying Elements. Ed. by Y. S. Touloukian & C. Y. Ho. (CINDAS Data Series on Material Properties: Vol. III[00ad]1). 269p. 1989. 165.00 (*0-89116-872-9*) Hemisp Pub.

Properties of Silicon Carbide. Ed. by Gary L. Harris. (EMIS Datareviews Ser.: No. 13). 304p. 1995. 195.00 (*0-85296-870-1*, EM013) INSPEC Inc.

***Properties of Silicon Germanium & SiGe: Carbide.** Ed. by Erich Kasper & Klara Lyutovich. 372p. 2000. 195.00 (*0-85296-783-7*, Pub. by IEE) SPIE.

Properties of Solids see Advanced Treatise on Physical Chemistry

Properties of Solvents. Y. Marcus. LC 98-18212. (Series in Solution Chemistry). 254p. 1998. 170.00 (*0-471-98369-1*) Wiley.

Properties of Steam. Ed. by V. V. Sytchev & A. A. Aleksandrov. 872p. 1987. 155.00 (*0-306-42159-3*, Plenum Trade) Perseus Pubng.

Properties of Steel Weldments for Elevated Temperature Pressure Containment Applications: Presented at the Winter Annual Meeting of the American Society of Mechanical Engineers, San Francisco, California, December 10-15, 1978. American Society of Mechanical Engineers Staff. Ed. by George V. Smith. LC 78-60045. (MPC Ser.: No. 9). (Illus.). 211p. reprint ed. pap. 65.50 (*0-8357-2899-4*, 203913500011) Bks Demand.

Properties of Strained & Relaxed Silicon Germanium. Ed. by Erich Kasper. (EMIS Datareviews Ser.: No. 12). 248p. 1995. boxed set 165.00 (*0-85296-826-4*, EM012) INSPEC Inc.

Properties of Susy Particles. L. Cifarelli & V. A. Khoze. 500p. 1994. text 121.00 (*981-02-1424-3*) World Scientific Pub.

Properties of the Poet. Paul Kavanagh. 143p. (C). 1990. 30.00 (*0-7259-0586-7*, Pub. by Pascoe Pub) St Mut.

Properties of III-V Quantum Wells & Superlattices. Ed. by P. K. Bhattacharya. (EMIS Datareviews Ser.: No. 15). 420p. 1996. 195.00 (*0-85296-881-7*, EM015) INSPEC Inc.

Properties of Water & Steam. 1976. 16.95 (*0-387-04675-5*) Spr-Verlag.

Properties of Water & Steam. 1996. text 99.50 (*3-540-09601-9*) Spr-Verlag.

Properties of Water & Steam: Proceedings of the 11th International Conference. Ed. by M. Pichal & O. Sifner. 704p. 1990. 220.00 (*1-56032-042-7*) Hemisp Pub.

Properties of Water & Steam: The Industrial Standard IAPWS-IF97 for the Thermodynamic Properties & Supplementary Equations for Other Properties: Tables Based on These Equations. W. Wagner. LC 98-20104. (Illus.). 350p. 1998. 120.00 (*3-540-64339-7*) Spr-Verlag.

Properties of Water & Steam IAPWS-IF97. H. J. Kretzschmar. 1998. 10.00 (*3-540-64375-3*) Spr-Verlag.

Properties of Water & Steam in SI-Units. 3rd rev. ed. Ed. by H. Grigull. (Illus.). 194p. 1996. 99.50 (*0-387-09601-9*) Spr-Verlag.

Properties of Water in Foods in Relation to Quality & Stability. Ed. by D. Simatos & J. L. Multon. 1985. text 344.50 (*90-247-3153-4*) Kluwer Academic.

Properties of Wide Bandgap II-VI Semiconductors. Ed. by R. Bhargava. (EMIS Datareviews Ser.: No. 17). 320p. 1996. 195.00 (*0-85296-882-5*, EM017) INSPEC Inc.

Properties of Writing: Ideological Discourse in Modern Italian Fiction. Robert S. Dombroski. LC 94-16037. 208p. 1995. text 35.00 (*0-8018-4919-5*) Johns Hopkins.

***Properties, Processing, & Applications of Glass & Rare Earth-Doped Glasses for Optical Fibres, Vol. PM82.** Ed. by D. W. Hewak. 400p. 1998. 195.00 (*0-85296-952-X*, Pub. by IEE) SPIE.

***Properties, Processing & Applications of Indium Phosphide.** Ed. by George T. P. Pearsall. (EMIS Datareviews Ser.: No. 21). 325p. 1999. boxed set 175.00 (*0-85296-949-X*) INSPEC Inc.

Properties Related to Fracture Toughness - STP 605. Ed. by W. R. Warke et al. 150p. 1976. pap. 15.00 (*0-8031-0540-1*, STP605) ASTM.

Properties, Types & Meaning: Foundational Issues. Ed. by Gennaro Chierchia et al. 264p. (C). 1988. lib. bdg. 122.00 (*1-55608-067-0*, Pub. by Kluwer Academic) Kluwer Academic.

Properties, Types & Meaning: Foundational Issues. Gennaro Chierchia et al. 578p. (C). 1988. lib. bdg. 129.00 (*1-55608-088-3*, Pub. by Kluwer Academic) Kluwer Academic.

Properties, Types & Meaning: Foundational Issues, Vol. I. Gennaro Chierchia et al. 578p. (C). 1988. pap. text 47.50 (*1-55608-089-1*, Pub. by Kluwer Academic) Kluwer Academic.

Properties, Types & Meaning, Vol. II: Semantic Issues. Gennaro Chierchia et al. 314p. (C). 1988. lib. bdg. 130.00 (*1-55608-069-7*, Pub. by Kluwer Academic) Kluwer Academic.

Propertional Representation: The Case for a Better Election System. Douglas J. Amy. LC 97-68972. (Illus.). 50p. (Orig.). 1997. pap. 2.95 (*0-9659456-3-4*) Crescent St Pr.

Propertius. Ed. by E. H. Warmington. (Loeb Classical Library: No. 18). (ENG & LAT.). 528p. 1991. 18.95 (*0-674-99021-8*) HUP.

Propertius: Elegies. Ed. by G. P. Goold. (Loeb Classical Library). 528p. 1990. text 15.50 (*0-674-99020-X*) HUP.

Propertius: Elegies, Bk. IV. Propertius. Ed. by W. R. Connor & W. A. Camps. LC 78-67126. (Latin Texts & Commentaries Ser.). (ENG & LAT.). 1979. reprint ed. lib. bdg. 20.95 (*0-405-11597-0*) Ayer.

Propertius: Elegies II, Bk. II. Ed. by W. A. Camps. (Bristol Latin Texts Ser.). (LAT.). 255p. 1985. reprint ed. 25.95 (*0-86292-148-1*, Pub. by Brist Class Pr) Focus Pub-R Pullins.

Propertius: Elegies III, Bk. III. Ed. by W. A. Camps. (Bristol Latin Texts Ser.). (LAT.). 188p. 1986. reprint ed. 25.95 (*0-86292-116-3*, Pub. by Brist Class Pr) Focus Pub-R Pullins.

Propertius: Modernist Poet of Antiquity. D. Thomas Benediktson. LC 88-10115. 176p. (C). 1989. text 26.95 (*0-8093-1453-3*) S Ill U Pr.

Property. Jesse Dukeminier & James E. Krier. 1344p. 1993. teacher ed. write for info. (*0-316-19524-3*, 95243) Aspen Law.

Property. Steven L. Emanuel. 465p. 1993. pap. text 17.95 (*1-56542-091-8*) E Pub Corp.

Property. Calvin Massey. (Professor Ser.). 410p. 1998. pap. text 17.95 (*1-56542-130-2*) E Pub Corp.

Property. Allan Ryan. LC 87-25538. (Concepts in Social Thought Ser.). 143p. (Orig.). 1988. pap. 13.95 (*0-8166-1670-1*) U of Minn Pr.

Property see Burns Indiana Statutes Annotated 1999 Cumulative Supplement Set: Pocket Part

Property. 2nd ed. Roger H. Bernhardt. 388p. (C). 1991. pap., text, pap. text 24.50 (*0-314-86227-7*) West Pub.

Property. 2nd rev. ed. Julian C. Juergensmeyer. (Quick Review Ser.). 258p. (C). 1996. pap. text 18.95 (*1-57793-009-6*) Sum & Substance.

Property. 3rd ed. Roger H. Bernhardt & Ann M. Burkhart. LC 97-35462. (Black Letter Ser.). 403p. (C). 1997. pap., suppl. ed. 24.50 incl. disk (*0-314-22795-4*) West Pub.

Property. 3rd ed. Jesse Dukeminier. 1344p. 1993. 56.00 (*0-316-19523-5*, Aspen Law & Bus) Aspen Pub.

Property. 4th ed. Jesse Dukeminier & James E. Krier. LC 97-33583. 1998. boxed set 64.00 (*1-56706-648-8*) Aspen Law.

Property: A Study in Social Psychology. Ernest Beaglehole. LC 73-14147. (Perspectives in Social Inquiry Ser.). 332p. 1974. reprint ed. 20.95 (*0-405-05493-9*) Ayer.

Property: Adaptable to Courses Utilizing Casner & Leach's Casebook on Property. Casenotes Publishing Co., Inc. Staff. Ed. by Norman S. Goldenberg & Peter Tenen. (Legal Briefs Ser.). 1985. pap. write for info. (*0-87457-115-4*, 1030) Casenotes Pub.

Property: Adaptable to Courses Utilizing Cribbet, Johnson, Findley & Smith's Casebook on Property. Casenotes Publishing Co., Inc. Staff. Ed. by Norman S. Goldenberg et al. (Legal Briefs Ser.). 1996. pap. write for info. (*0-87457-116-2*, 1031) Casenotes Pub.

Property: Adaptable to Courses Utilizing Donohue, Kauper, & Martin's Casebook on Property. Casenotes Publishing Co., Inc. Staff et al. (Legal Briefs Ser.). (Orig.). 1993. pap. text. write for info. (*0-87457-208-8*, 1037) Casenotes Pub.

Property: Adaptable to Courses Utilizing Dukeminier & Krier's Casebook on Property. Casenotes Publishing Co., Inc. Staff. Ed. by Norman S. Goldenberg et al. (Legal Briefs Ser.). 1998. pap. write for info. (*0-87457-117-0*, 1035) Casenotes Pub.

Property: Adaptable to Courses Utilizing Haar & Liebman's Casebook on Property & Law. Casenotes Publishing Co., Inc. Staff. Ed. by Norman S. Goldenberg & Peter Tenen. (Legal Briefs Ser.). 1985. pap. write for info. (*0-87457-118-9*, 1034) Casenotes Pub.

Property: Adaptable to Courses Utilizing Materials by Browder. 2nd ed. Olin L. Browder. LC 87-130233. (Legalines Ser.). 355p. 13.50 (*0-685-19023-4*) Harcourt.

Property: Adaptable to Courses Utilizing Nelson, Stoebuck & Whitman's Casebook on Basic Property Law. Casenotes Publishing Co., Inc. Staff. Ed. by Norman S. Goldenberg et al. (Legal Briefs Ser.). 1996. pap. write for info. (*0-87457-114-6*, 1033) Casenotes Pub.

Property: Adaptable to Courses Utilizing Rabin & Kwall's Casebook on Real Property Law. Casenotes Publishing Co., Inc. Staff. Ed. by Norman S. Goldenberg & Peter Tenen. (Legal Briefs Ser.). 1992. pap. write for info. (*0-87457-119-7*, 1032) Casenotes Pub.

Property: Cases & Statutes. Roger Bernhardt. LC 99-202244. (American Casebook Ser). 969p. 1999. 44.25 (*0-314-23232-X*) West Pub.

Property: Land Ownership & Use. 4th ed. Curtis J. Berger & Joan Williams. 1300p. 1997. teacher ed., boxed set 60.00 (*1-56706-509-0*, 65090) Panel Pubs.

Property: Mainstream & Critical Positions. Ed. by C. B. Macpherson. LC 78-2311. (Controversy Ser.). 216p. 1978. pap. text 15.95 (*0-8020-6336-5*) U of Toronto Pr.

Property: Manual to Accompany Cases & Materials. 6th ed. John E. Cribbet et al. 268p. 1990. pap. text, teacher ed. write for info. (*0-88277-849-8*) Foundation Pr.

Property: Teacher's Manual to Accompany Cases & Materials on. 7th ed. John E. Cribbet et al. (University Casebook Ser.). 252p. (C). 1996. pap. text, student ed. write for info. (*1-56662-352-9*) Foundation Pr.

Property - Casualty Risk-Based Capital Report Including Overview & Instructions for Companies. annuals 104p. (C). 1994. pap. write for info. (*0-89382-303-1*) Nat Assn Insurance.

Property, a Constitutional Right. T. D. Mudliar. (C). 1988. 150.00 (*0-7855-4744-4*) St Mut.

Property Adaptable to Courses Utilizing Kurtz & Hovenkamps Casebook on American Property Law. Casenotes Publishing Co., Inc. Staff et al. Ed. by Norman S. Goldenberg et al. (Legal Briefs Ser.). 1993. pap. write for info. (*0-87457-159-6*, 1036) Casenotes Pub.

Property, an Introduction to the Concept & the Institution, Teacher's Manual to Accompany Cases & Materials On. 3rd ed. Charles Donahue, Jr. et al. (American Casebook Ser.). 332p. 1993. pap. text, teacher ed. write for info. (*0-314-02806-4*) West Pub.

Property Analyzer: A Program for the HP 17BII & HP 19BII Financial Calculators. Ed. by Edric Cane. 54p. (Orig.). 1991. pap. text 14.95 incl. disk (*0-916785-08-4*) E Cane Sem.

P

Property & Casualty General Insurance Primer. rev. ed. Ed. by Craig A. Carter. LC 95-61702. 240p. 1999. pap. text 24.95 (*1-884803-05-9*) Werbel Pub.

Property & Casualty Insurance. 34th rev. ed. Philip Gordis. Ed. by Diana Kowatch & Bruce Hicks. 608p. 1998. text 59.95 (*1-56461-254-6*, 26520) Rough Notes.

Property & Casualty Insurance: Core Book. Franklin Moore & Bradley S. Moore. 600p. (Orig.). 1996. pap. 50.00 (*1-56461-155-8*) Rough Notes.

***Property & Casualty Insurance: State Legislation.** Robert E. Mackin. 220p. 1999. pap. 75.00 (*0-8080-0323-2*) CCH INC.

Property & Casualty Insurance: Study Guide. Franklin L. Moore. 1991. student ed. 50.00 (*0-942326-25-3*, 26629) Rough Notes.

Property & Casualty Insurance Principles & Practices. 5th ed. Dearborn Financial Institute Staff. 359p. 1999. pap. 26.00 (*0-7931-2752-1*) Dearborn.

Property & Casualty State Law Study Guide: Pennsylvania. Ed. by Franklin L. Moore & Bradley S. Moore. 50p. 1996. student ed. write for info. (*1-56461-172-8*) Rough Notes.

***Property & Construction Accounting.** Eccles & Sayce. 1999. pap. write for info. (*0-415-12507-3*) Thomson Learn.

Property & Construction Economics. Eccles & Sayce. LC 99-182005. (ITBP Textbooks Ser.). 1998. text 18.99 (*1-86152-158-8*) Thomson Learn.

Property & Construction in Asia Pacific, Hong Kong - Japan - Singapore. A. Walker & Roger Flanagan. (Illus.). 244p. 1991. 99.95 (*0-632-02715-0*) Blackwell Sci.

Property & Freedom. Richard Pipes. LC 98-41728. 384p. 1999. 30.00 (*0-375-40498-8*) Knopf.

***Property & Freedom.** Richard Pipes. 352p. 2000. pap. 15.00 (*0-375-70447-7*) Vin Bks.

Property & Freedom: The Constitution, the Courts & Land-Use Regulation. Bernard H. Siegan. LC 97-19241. (Studies in Social Philosophy & Policy). 275p. 1997. text 34.95 (*1-56000-323-5*); pap. text 21.95 (*1-56000-974-8*) Transaction Pubs.

Property & Inequality in Victorian Ontario: Structural Patterns & Cultural Communities in the 1871 Census. Gordon Darroch & Lee Soltow. (Social History of Canada Ser.). (Illus.). 256p. (C). 1994. text 45.00 (*0-8020-0516-0*); pap. text 19.95 (*0-8020-6952-5*) U of Toronto Pr.

Property & Justice. Jim Harris. 414p. (C). 1996. text 90.00 (*0-19-825957-3*) OUP.

Property & Kinship: Inheritance in Early Connecticut, 1750-1820. Toby L. Ditz. LC 86-5051. 230p. 1986. reprint ed. pap. 71.30 (*0-608-03297-2*, 206381500007) Bks Demand.

Property & Land Reform: Consitutional & Jurisprudential Perspectives. S. B. Gutto. LC 95-229851. 104p. Date not set. pap. write for info. (*0-409-02946-7*, MICHIE) LEXIS Pub.

Property & Law. 2nd ed. Charles M. Haar & Lance M. Liebman. LC 84-81025. 1534p. (C). 1985. 60.00 (*0-316-33682-3*, Aspen Law & Bus) Aspen Pub.

Property & Liability Insurance. 4th ed. Solomon S. Heubner & Kenneth Black. 690p. 1995. 96.00 (*0-13-191586-X*) P-H.

***Property & Liability Insurance Principles.** 3rd ed. Constance M. Luthardt et al. LC 99-73210. (Illus.). 312p. (C). 1999. pap. text 31.00 (*0-89462-132-7*) IIA.

Property & Liability Reinsurance Management: A Recognized Text on P. & L. Reinsurance. Robert C. Reinarz. LC 68-59174. (C). 1969. 15.95 (*0-916910-01-6*) Mission Pub.

Property & Participation: Employee Ownership & Workplace Democracy in Three New England Firms. David Toscano. Ed. by George P. Garrett. 202p. 1983. text 29.00 (*0-8290-0553-6*) Irvington.

Property & Pecuniary Insurance. Mark S. Dacey. 115p. (C). 1987. pap. 60.00 (*0-948691-70-0*, Pub. by Witherby & Co) St Mut.

Property & Pecuniary Insurance. Mark S. Dacey. 115p. (C). 1989. pap. 75.00 (*0-948691-85-9*, Pub. by Witherby & Co) St Mut.

Property & Politics, 1870-1914: Ideology & Urban Development in England. Avner Offer. (Modern Revivals in History Ser.). 445p. 1992. 72.95 (*0-7512-0066-2*, Pub. by Gregg Revivals) Ashgate Pub Co.

Property & Politics "No Problem" A Smart Shopper's Guide to Buying or Developing Real Estate. L. L. Thompson. LC 96-93045. (Illus.). vi, 94p. (Orig.). 1997. pap. 16.95 (*0-9656497-0-9*) Pen & Ink Pub.

Property & Power. Leszek Nowak. 1983. pap. text 79.50 (*90-277-1595-5*); lib. bdg. 152.00 (*90-277-1351-0*) Kluwer Academic.

Property & Power in Social Theory: A Study in Intellectual Rivalry. Dick Pels. LC 98-23828. (Studies in Social & Political Thought : No. 14). (Illus.). 336p. (C). (gr. 13). 1998. 100.00 (*0-415-18780-X*, D6275) Routledge.

Property & Power in the Early Middle Ages. Ed. by Wendy Davies & Paul Fouracre. 336p. (C). 1995. text 59.95 (*0-521-43419-X*) Cambridge U Pr.

Property & Prices: Towards a Unified Theory of Value. Andre Burgstaller. (Illus.). 254p. (C). 1995. text 59.95 (*0-521-41903-4*) Cambridge U Pr.

Property & Prophets: The Evolution of Economic Institutions & Ideologies. 5th ed. E. K. Hunt. 256p. (C). 1985. pap. 19.66 (*0-06-043037-0*) Addson-Wesley Educ.

***Property & Prophets: The Evolution of Economic Institutions & Ideologies.** 8th ed. E. K. Hunt. (Illus.). 328p. 2000. 68.95 (*0-7656-0608-9*) M E Sharpe.

Property & Riches in the Early Church. Martin Hengel. Tr. by John Bowden. viii, 96p. Date not set. pap. text 12.00 (*1-888961-03-1*, 1031) Sigler Pr.

Property & Riches in the Early Church: Aspects of a Social History of Early Christianity. Martin Hengel. Tr. by John Bowden from GER. LC 75-305658. 104p. reprint ed. pap. 32.30 (*0-608-16837-8*, 202685600052) Bks Demand.

***Property & the Constitution.** Ed. by Janet McLean. 304p. 1999. 45.00 (*1-84113-055-9*, Pub. by Hart Pub) Intl Spec Bk.

Property & the Family in Biblical Law. Raymond Westbrook. (Journal for the Study of the Old Testament Supplement Ser.: No. 113). 177p. (C). 1991. 52.50 (*1-85075-271-0*, Pub. by Sheffield Acad) CUP Services.

"Property" & the Making of the International System. Kurt Burch. LC 97-21297. (Critical Perspectives Ser.). 195p. 1998. 49.95 (*1-55587-622-6*) L Rienner.

Property & Value. Hugh Hood. (New Age Ser.). 249p. 1990. pap. 24.95 (*0-88784-160-0*, Pub. by Hse of Anansi Pr) Genl Dist Srvs.

***Property & Values: Alternatives to Public & Private Ownership.** Ed. by Charles C. Geisler & Gail Daneker. 336p. 2000. pap. 35.00 (*1-55963-766-8*) Island Pr.

Property Anthology. 2nd ed. Ed. by Richard H. Chused. 625p. (C). 1997. pap. 29.95 (*0-87084-735-X*) Anderson Pub Co.

Property Appraisal & Assessment Administration. Ed. by Joseph K. Eckert et al. (Illus.). 716p. (C). 1991. text 100.00 (*0-88329-080-4*); pap. text 75.00 (*0-88329-081-2*) IAAO.

Property Appraisal Deskbook: A Working Guide. T. Herbert Stevenson. 1991. text 125.00 (*1-55738-304-9*, Irwn Prfssnl) McGraw-Hill Prof.

Property As a Guarantor of Liberty. James M. Buchanan. (Shaftesbury Papers: Vol. 1). 72p. 1993. pap. 13.00 (*1-85278-733-3*) E Elgar.

Property Assessment Valuation. 478p. 1996. 55.00 (*0-88329-156-8*); pap. 40.00 (*0-88329-157-6*) IAAO.

Property Asset Management. 2nd ed. Douglas Scarrett. (Illus.). 288p. (C). 1995. pap. 29.99 (*0-419-19310-3*, E & FN Spon) Routledge.

Property, Bureaucracy & Culture. Mike Savage et al. 288p. (C). 1995. pap. 27.99 (*0-415-13009-3*) Routledge.

Property, Cases & Materials On. 6th ed. John E. Cribbet et al. 1441p. 1991. reprint ed. text 46.95 (*0-88277-782-3*) Foundation Pr.

Property, Cases On. 5th ed. John E. Cribbet & Corwin W. Johnson. (University Casebook Ser.). 32.00 (*0-685-08785-9*) Foundation Pr.

Property Casualty Insurance Investment Management Handbook. (C). 1991. 115.00 (*0-13-724204-2*, Macmillan Coll) P-H.

Property Claims. 2nd ed. Barry Zalma. 1998. pap. 195.00 (*1-884770-19-3*) ClaimSchool.

Property Claims - Investigation. Barry Zalma. 171p. 1997. per. 38.95 (*1-884770-17-7*) ClaimSchool.

Property Claims - Weapons to Fight Fraud. Barry Zalma. 200p. 1998. pap. 38.95 (*1-884770-18-5*) ClaimSchool.

Property Clerk. Jack Rudman. (Career Examination Ser.: C-3465). 1994. pap. 23.95 (*0-8373-3465-9*) Nat Learn.

Property Concepts of the Navaho Indians. Berard Haile. LC 76-43726. reprint ed. 29.50 (*0-404-15566-9*) AMS Pr.

Property Conservation Workbook. 169p. 30.00 (*0-318-14059-4*, P7917) Factory Mutual.

Property Control & Social Strategies: Settlers on a Middle Eastern Plain. Barbara C. Aswad. (Anthropological Papers Ser.: No. 44). 1971. pap. 2.00 (*0-932206-42-5*) U Mich Mus Anthro.

Property Control Coordinator. (Career Examination Ser.: C-3645). pap. 29.95 (*0-8373-3645-7*) Nat Learn.

Property Crime Victims: An Analysis of Needs & Services in Texas. Laura Lein & Robert C. Rickards. (Special Project Reports). 55p. 1992. pap. 9.50 (*0-89940-872-9*) LBJ Sch Pub Aff.

Property Damage Accident: The Neglected Part of Safety. Frank E. Bird, Jr. & George L. Germain. (Illus.). 325p. 1997. 70.00 (*0-9656516-3-0*) FEBCO.

Property Development. Cadman. 1997. 39.95 (*0-419-14850-7*, E & FN Spon) Routledge.

Property Disposition: Information on HUD's Acquisition & Disposition of Single-Family Properties. (Illus.). 46p. (Orig.). (C). 1996. pap. text 20.00 (*0-7881-2941-4*) DIANE Pub.

Property Disputes in Practice. Susan Blake et al. 151p. 1998. pap. 48.00 (*1-85431-719-9*, Pub. by Blackstone Pr) Gaunt.

Property Disputes in Practice. 2nd ed. Susan Blake et al. 151p. 1999. pap. 50.00 (*1-85431-903-5*, Pub. by Blackstone Pr) Gaunt.

***Property Disputes in Practice.** 3rd ed. Susan Blake et al. 149p. 2000. pap. 46.00 (*1-84174-006-3*, Pub. by Blackstone Pr) Gaunt.

Property Disrepair & Dilapidations: A Guide to the Law. Rosy Thornton. 225p. (C). 1992. 150.00 (*1-85190-182-5*, Pub. by Tolley Pubng) St Mut.

Property Division at Marriage Dissolution Cases. Joan M. Krauskopf. LC 83-23464. (American Casebook Ser.). 250p. (C). 1983. reprint ed. pap. 18.50 (*0-314-80327-0*) West Pub.

Property Enhancement with Modifiers & Additives: Technical Papers; Regional Technical Conference, October 18-19, 1994, Hyatt Regency Hotel, New Brunswick, NJ. Society of Plastics Engineers Staff. LC TP1140,. (Illus.). 211p. reprint ed. pap. 65.50 (*0-7837-9707-9*, 206043800005) Bks Demand.

Property Futures & Securitisation: The Way Ahead. Julian Roche. 208p. 1995. 155.00 (*1-85573-180-0*, Pub. by Woodhead Pubng) Am Educ Systs.

Property in Cyprus. large type ed. Robert MacLeod. 1978. 27.99 (*0-7089-0092-5*) Ulverscroft.

Property in Economic Context No. 14: Monographs in Economic Anthropology. Ed. by Robert C. Hunt & Antonio Gilman. LC 98-10501. (Society for Economic Anthropology Ser.: Vol. 52). 392p. 1998. 69.00 (*0-7618-1063-3*) U Pr of Amer.

Property in Economic Context No. 14: Monographs in Economic Anthropology, No. 14. Ed. by Robert C. Hunt & Antonio Gilman. LC 98-10501. (Society for Economic Anthropology Ser.: Vol. 52). 392p. 1998. pap. 44.50 (*0-7618-1064-1*) U Pr of Amer.

Property in Girl Scouting. Girl Scouts of the U. S. A. Staff. 62p. 1987. pap. 9.50 (*0-88441-456-6*, 26-186) Girl Scouts USA.

Property in, Taxes on, Agricultural Land. Gene Wunderlich. (LTC Papers: No. 153). 29p. 1995. 4.00 (*0-934519-71-4*) U of Wis Land.

Property Inspection. John A. Simpson. LC 97-3831. 1997. 27.50 (*0-922154-36-8*) Appraisal Inst.

Property Insurance: Some Points to Consider. 3rd ed. R. Sinclair Taylor. (C). 1985. 60.00 (*0-7855-4054-7*, Pub. by Witherby & Co) St Mut.

Property Insurance: Some Points to Consider in Relation to the Proper Cover of Risks. RICS Staff. (C). 1985. text 39.00 (*0-85406-288-2*, Pub. by Surveyors Pubns) St Mut.

Property Insurance: Some Points to Consider in Relation to the Property Cover of Risks. RICS Staff. 1995. pap. 40.00 (*0-85406-703-5*, Pub. by R-I-C-S Bks) St Mut.

Property Insurance Annotations: Fire & Extended Coverages. LC 94-71351. 344p. 1994. ring bd. 99.95 (*0-89707-998-1*, 5190238) Amer Bar Assn.

Property Insurance Annotations: Fire & Extended Coverages. 3rd ed. Stephen E. Goldman. LC 98-29641. vii, 530p. 1998. 109.95 (*1-57073-596-4*) Amer Bar Assn.

Property Insurance Coverage Disputes: Issues & Techniques for Managing First-Party Claims. LC 92-74871. 262p. 1993. pap. 54.95 (*0-89707-837-3*, 519-0217, ABA Tort) Amer Bar Assn.

Property Insurance Risk Assessment & Control. James Sanderson. 120p. (C). 1992. 69.00 (*1-85609-030-2*, Pub. by Witherby & Co) St Mut.

Property Interests in North Carolina City Streets. David M. Lawrence. LC 86-621832. 59p. (C). 1985. 7.00 (*1-56011-131-3*) Institute Government.

Property Investment. 2nd ed. Squire L. Speedy. 177p. 1990. pap. 59.00 (*0-409-60081-4*, NZ, MICHIE) LEXIS Pub.

Property Investment & the Capital Markets. G. R. Brown. (Illus.). 350p. 1991. pap. 52.00 (*0-419-15530-9*) Thomson Learn.

Property Investment Appraisal. 2nd ed. Baum. (ITBP Textbooks Ser.). 1998. pap. 19.99 (*1-86152-396-3*) Thomson Learn.

Property Investment Appraisal. 2nd ed. Andrew Baum & Neil Crosby. 304p. (C). 1995. pap. 31.95 (*0-415-09328-7*, C0136) Thomson Learn.

Property Investment Decisions. Hargitay. (Illus.). 336p. (C). 1993. pap. 45.00 (*0-419-16780-3*, E & FN Spon) Routledge.

Property Investments & Their Financing. Patrick Rowland. 288p. 1993. pap. 55.00 (*0-455-21167-1*, Pub. by LawBk Co) Gaunt.

Property Law. Phillip H. Kenny. (Student Statutes Ser.). 304p. 1994. pap. text 20.00 (*0-406-03145-2*, UK, MICHIE) LEXIS Pub.

Property Law. Roger Smith. LC 96-454. (Longman Law Ser.). 1996. write for info. (*0-582-09011-3*, Pub. by Addison-Wesley); pap. write for info. (*0-582-09140-3*, Pub. by Addison-Wesley) Longman.

Property Law. 2nd ed. Roger Smith. LC 97-44085. (Law Ser.). 1998. pap. write for info. (*0-582-32746-6*) Longman.

Property Law. 5th ed. Olin L. Browder et al. (American Casebook Ser.). 1386p. (C). 1989. reprint ed. text 55.00 (*0-314-54012-1*) West Pub.

Property Law, 2 vols., 1. Ed. by Elizabeth Mensch & Alan Freeman. LC 92-33815. (International Library of Essays in Law & Legal Theory: Vol. 14). (C). 1993. lib. bdg. 125.00 (*0-8147-5488-0*) NYU Pr.

Property Law, 2 vols., 2. Ed. by Elizabeth Mensch & Alan Freeman. LC 92-33815. (International Library of Essays in Law & Legal Theory: Vol. 14). (C). 1993. lib. bdg. 125.00 (*0-8147-5489-9*) NYU Pr.

Property Law, 2 vols., Set. Ed. by Elizabeth Mensch & Alan Freeman. LC 92-33815. (International Library of Essays in Law & Legal Theory: Vol. 14). (C). 1993. lib. bdg. 250.00 (*0-8147-5475-9*) NYU Pr.

Property Law: Cases & Materials. 4th ed. C. Rossiter et al. 1988. 109.00 (*0-409-49287-6*, AT, MICHIE); pap. 94.00 (*0-409-49288-4*, AT, MICHIE) LEXIS Pub.

Property Law: Cases, Materials & Problems 2E" 2nd ed. Sandra H. Johnson et al. LC 98-11098. (Paralegal). 1200p. 1998. lib. bdg. 42.75 (*0-314-22762-8*) West Pub.

***Property Law: Current Issues & Debates.** Ed. by Paul Jackson & David C. Wilde. LC 99-49169. 344p. 2000. 105.95 (*0-7546-2040-9*, Pub. by Ashgate Pub) Ashgate Pub Co.

Property Law: Rules, Policies, & Practices. 2nd ed. Joseph W. Singer. 1580p. 1997. teacher ed., boxed set 60.00 (*1-56706-521-X*, 6521X) Panel Pubs.

Property Law: Texts & Materials. Allison Clark & Paul Kohler. 480p. 1996. pap. text 52.95 (*0-406-05191-7*, MICHIE) LEXIS Pub.

Property Law Act Victoria. Stanley Robinson. 616p. 1992. 157.50 (*0-455-21050-0*, Pub. by LawBk Co) Gaunt.

Property Law & Policy: A Comparative Institutional Perspective. John P. Dwyer & Peter S. Menell. LC 97-30646. (University Casebook Ser.). 1060p. 1998. text 41.25 (*1-56662-533-5*) Foundation Pr.

Property Law & the Public Interest. Gordon Hylton et al. LC 98-85099. 1998. 55.00 (*0-327-00111-9*, 12218-10) LEXIS Pub.

Property Law, Cases, Materials & Problems. Sandra H. Johnson, Jr. et al. (American Casebook Ser.). 237p. 1992. pap. text. write for info. (*0-314-00968-X*) West Pub.

Property Law, Cases, Materials & Problems. Thomas L. Shaffer et al. (American Casebook Ser.). 908p. (C). 1992. text 47.00 (*0-314-00340-1*) West Pub.

Property Law in Contemporary Russia. Viktor P. Mozolin. 174p. 1993. 40.00 (*0-935328-75-0*) Intl Law Inst.

Property Law in Contemporary Russia. Viktor P. Mozolin. 174p. 1993. ring bd. 75.00 (*90-411-0994-3*) Kluwer Law Intl.

Property Law in the Arab World. Farhat J. Ziadeh. 112p. 1979. lib. bdg. 87.50 (*0-86010-112-6*) G & T Inc.

Property Law Innovation in Latin America, with Recommendations. Steven E. Hendrix. (LTC Paper Ser.: Vol. 149). viii, 65p. (C). 1993. pap. 7.00 (*0-934519-67-6*, LTC149) U of Wis Land.

Property Law on the Threshold of the 21st Century. Ed. by G. E. Van Maanen & A. J. Van der Walt. 687p. 1997. 158.00 (*90-6215-541-3*, Pub. by Maklu Uitgev) Gaunt.

Property Loss Adjusting, 2 vols. 2nd ed. Robert G. Anderson et al. Ed. by James J. Markham. LC 95-77155. (C). 1995. pap. 41.00 (*0-89462-091-6*, 3502/3503) IIA.

Property, Mainstream & Critical Positions. Ed. by Crawford B. Macpherson. LC 78-2311. 217p. reprint ed. pap. 67.30 (*0-8357-8290-5*, 203406200088) Bks Demand.

Property Management. Joseph W. DeCarlo. LC 96-41969. 368p. (C). 1996. pap. text 39.80 (*0-13-257262-1*) P-H.

Property Management. Dwight E. Norris. (Illus.). 512p. (C). 1998. pap. text 39.95 (*0-934772-09-6*) Ashley Crown Systems Inc.

Property Management. 5th ed. Robert C. Kyle & Floyd M. Baird. LC 94-37589. 458p. 1995. pap. 37.95 (*0-7931-1067-X*, 1551-1005, Real Estate Ed) Dearborn.

***Property Management.** 6th ed. Robert C. Kyle. LC 99-28188. 472p. 1999. pap. 40.95 (*0-7931-3117-0*) Dearborn.

Property Management & Managing Risk Robert C. Kyle & Floyd M. Baird. LC 98-209526. 72p. 1998. write for info. (*0-7931-2951-6*, Real Estate Ed) Dearborn.

Property Management in California. 2nd ed. Joseph W. DeCarlo. (Illus.). (Orig.). 1987. pap. 24.95 (*0-317-61553-X*) JD Pub & Seminars.

Property Management in California. 6th ed. Joseph W. DeCarlo. (Illus.). (Orig.). (C). 1996. pap. 24.95 (*0-937841-01-3*) JD Pub & Seminars.

Property Management in Girl Scouting. LC 99-176950. 120 p. 1998. write for info. (*0-88441-493-0*) Girl Scouts USA.

Property Management in Mexico see Administracion de Inmuebles

Property Management Manual for Massachusetts Rental Owners: The Hap Manual. 3rd ed. H. John Fisher et al. (Illus.). 250p. 1998. reprint ed. pap. 25.00 (*1-884540-41-4*) Haleys.

***Property Manager Companion: An Insiders Guide on "How to Manage Residential Rental Property"** Steven T. Vivaldi. Ed. by Peter Andrew. (Illus.). 160p. 1998. ring bd. 125.00 St Mut.

Property Matters. James V. DeLong. LC 96-48280. 352p. 1997. 27.00 (*0-684-87437-7*) S & S Enterprises.

Property Of. Alice Hoffman. 304p. 1993. mass mkt. 7.50 (*0-425-13903-4*) Berkley Pub.

***Property Of.** Alice Hoffman. 288p. 2000. reprint ed. pap. 12.95 (*0-425-17435-2*) Berkley Pub.

Property of a Gentleman: The Formation, Organisation & Dispersal of the Private Library, 1620-1920. M. Harris. LC 96-43049. 1996. 35.00 (*1-884718-29-9*) Oak Knoll.

Property of a Lady. Elizabeth A. Adler. 576p. 1991. mass mkt. 6.50 (*0-440-21014-3*) Dell.

Property of the Folsom Wolf. Don Lasseter. 512p. 1995. mass mkt. 4.99 (*0-7860-0090-2*, Pinnacle Kensgtn); mass mkt. 4.99 (*0-8217-0090-1*, Zebra Kensgtn) Kensgtn Pub Corp.

***Property Offences.** 3rd ed. D. R. Williams. 393p. 1999. pap. write for info. (*0-455-21681-9*, Pub. by LBC Info Servs) Gaunt.

Property Ownership, 1995. Robert G. Natelson. 1995. suppl. ed. 80.00 (*0-316-59932-8*, Aspen Law & Bus) Aspen Pub.

Property Ownership Set. Robert G. Natelson. 779p. 1990. 125.00 (*0-316-59871-2*) Little.

Property, Paternalism, & Power: Class & Control in Rural England. Howard Newby et al. LC 78-20301. 432p. reprint ed. pap. 134.00 (*0-8357-6797-3*, 203547300095) Bks Demand.

Property, Planning & Compensation Reports, 1950-1993, 72 vols., Set. 1949. 8640.00 (*0-8377-9131-6*, Rothman) W S Hein.

Property, Politics & Urban Planning: A History of Australian City Planning. Leonie Sandercock. 292p. (C). 1990. 39.95 (*0-88738-335-1*) Transaction Pubs.

Property Portfolio Management: An Introduction. Nigel Dubben & Sarah Sayce. 336p. (C). (gr. 13). 1991. pap. 75.95 (*0-415-05123-1*, A5779); pap. 27.95 (*0-415-05124-X*, A5783) Thomson Learn.

Property, Power & American Democracy. David Schultz. 376p. (C). 1992. 44.95 (*1-56000-038-4*) Transaction Pubs.

Property, Principles of the Law Of. 3rd ed. John E. Cribbet & Corwin W. Johnson. (University Textbook Ser.). 481p. 1991. reprint ed. text 27.50 (*0-88277-718-1*) Foundation Pr.

Property Problems: From Genes to Pension Funds. J. W. Harris. LC 98-183460. 322p. 1998. lib. bdg. 100.00 (*90-411-9643-9*) Kluwer Law Intl.

P

An Asterisk (*) at the beginning of an entry indicates that the title is appearing for the first time.

Property, Production & Family in Neckarhausen, 1700-1870. David W. Sabean. (Cambridge Studies in Social & Cultural Anthropology: No. 73). (Illus.). 537p. (C). 1991. text 95.00 (*0-521-38538-5*); pap. text 25.95 (*0-521-38692-6*) Cambridge U Pr.

Property Qualifications of Members of Parliament. Helen E. Witmer. LC 68-58644. (Columbia University. Studies in Social Sciences: No. 498). reprint ed. 29.50 (*0-404-51498-7*) AMS Pr.

Property Relations: Renewing the Anthropological Tradition. C. M. Hann. LC 97-35811. 288p. (C). 1998. text 59.95 (*0-521-59389-1*) Cambridge U Pr.

Property Relations: Renewing the Anthropological Tradition. Ed. by C. M. Hann. 287p. (C). 1998. pap. text 21.95 (*0-521-59636-X*) Cambridge U Pr.

Property Relations, Incentives, & Welfare: Proceedings of a Conference Held in Barcelona, Spain. Ed. by John E. Roemer. LC 96-7681. (IEA Conference Ser.: No. 115). 384p. 1997. text 79.95 (*0-312-15926-9*) St Martin.

Property Rights: Philosophic Foundations. Lawrence C. Becker. 148p. 1980. pap. 14.95 (*0-7100-0606-3*, Routledge Thoemms) Routledge.

Property Rights: Understanding Government Takings & Environmental Regulation. Nancie G. Marzulla & Roger J. Marzulla. LC 96-47384. 325p. 1997. text 79.00 (*0-86587-554-5*) Gov Insts.

***Property Rights & Economic Development in Southeast Asia & Oceania.** Ed. by Toon Von Meijl & Franz Von Benda-Beckmann. 300p. 1999. 110.00 (*0-7103-0641-5*, Pub. by Kegan Paul Intl) Col U Pr.

Property Rights & Economic Reform in China Jean C. Oi & Andrew G. Walder. LC 99-11806. 1999. 22.95 (*0-8047-3788-6*) Stanford U Pr.

***Property Rights & Economic Reform in China.** Ed. by Jean C. Oi & Andrew G. Walder. LC 99-11806. 354p. 1999. 60.00 (*0-8047-3456-9*) Stanford U Pr.

Property Rights & Eminent Domain. Ellen F. Paul. 276p. 1987. 39.95 (*0-88738-094-8*) Transaction Pubs.

Property Rights & Indian Economies. Ed. by Terry L. Anderson. 320p. (C). 1992. text 48.50 (*0-8476-7708-7*) Rowman.

***Property Rights & Political Development in Ethiopia & Eritrea.** Sandra F. Joireman. (Eastern African Studies). 192p. (C). 2000. text 44.95 (*0-8214-1363-5*); pap. text 21.95 (*0-8214-1364-3*) Ohio U Pr.

Property Rights & Poverty: Political Argument in Britain, 1605-1834. Thomas A. Horne. LC 89-77791. x, 296p. (C). 1990. 49.95 (*0-8078-1912-3*) U of NC Pr.

Property Rights & Regulatory Systems in Fisheries. David Symes. LC 97-17308. 1997. 99.95 (*0-85238-249-9*) Blackwell Sci.

Property Rights & the Constitution: Shaping Society Through Land Use Regulation. Dennis J. Coyle. LC 92-16680. (SUNY Series in the Constitution & Economic Rights). 382p. (C). 1993. text 64.50 (*0-7914-1443-4*); pap. text 21.95 (*0-7914-1444-2*) State U NY Pr.

***Property Rights & the Environment.** Giuliano d'Auria et al. (IEA Studies on the Environment: No. 13). 55p. 1999. pap. 15.95 (*0-255-36471-7*, Pub. by Inst Economic Affairs) Coronet Bks.

Property Rights & the Environment: Social & Ecological Issues. Ed. by Susan Hanna & Mohan Munasinghe. LC 95-35031. 172p. 1995. pap. 22.00 (*0-8213-3415-8*, 13415) World Bank.

Property Rights & the Limits of Democracy. Ed. by Charles K. Rowley. (Shaftesbury Papers). 404p. 1993. 100.00 (*1-85278-529-2*) E Elgar.

***Property Rights, Economics & the Environment.** Michael D. Kaplowitz. LC 00-22076. (Economics of Legal Relationship Ser.). 2000. write for info. (*0-7623-0646-7*) Jai Pr.

Property Rights in a Social & Ecological Context: Case Studies & Design Applications. Ed. by Susan Hanna & Mohan Munasinghe. LC 95-35029. 216p. 1995. pap., wbk. ed. 22.00 (*0-8213-3416-6*, 13416) World Bank.

Property Rights in American History: From the Colonial Era to the Present, 6 vols. Incl. Vol. 1. Property Rights in the Colonial Era & Early Republic. Ed. by James W. Ely, Jr. LC 97-18634. 432p. 1997. reprint ed. text 83.00 (*0-8153-2683-1*); Vol. 2. Property Rights in the Age of Enterprise. Ed. by James W. Ely, Jr. LC 97-14432. (Illus.). 440p. 1997. reprint ed. text 83.00 (*0-8153-2684-X*); Vol. 3. Reform & Regulation of Property Rights. Ed. by James W. Ely, Jr. LC 97-14492. (Illus.). 416p. 1997. reprint ed. text 95.00 (*0-8153-2685-8*); Vol. 4. Contract Clause in American History. Ed. by James W. Ely, Jr. LC 97-14491. 440p. 1997. reprint ed. text 83.00 (*0-8153-2686-6*); Vol. 5. Contemporary Property Rights Issues. James W. Ely, Jr. LC 97-16139. 432p. 1997. reprint ed. text 83.00 (*0-8153-2687-4*); Vol. 6. Main Themes in the Debate over Property Rights. Ed. by James W. Ely, Jr. LC 97-16118. 425p. 1997. reprint ed. text 83.00 (*0-8153-2688-2*); LC 97-18634. 1997. 690.00 (*0-8153-2682-3*) Garland.

Property Rights in the Age of Enterprise see Property Rights in American History: From the Colonial Era to the Present

Property Rights in the Colonial Era & Early Republic see Property Rights in American History: From the Colonial Era to the Present

Property Rights in Transition. Ed. by Don A. Derr & Leslie Small. 243p. (C). 1977. text 32.50 (*0-8422-5252-5*); pap. text 11.95 (*0-8422-0554-3*) Irvington.

Property Rights of Unmarried Cohabitees. John Mee. 388p. 1999. 54.00 (*1-901362-76-0*, Pub. by Hart Pub) Northwestern U Pr.

Property Rules: Political Economy in Chicago, 1833-1872. Robin L. Einhorn. LC 91-7781. (Illus.). 314p. 1991. 39.95 (*0-226-19484-1*) U Ch Pr.

Property, Substance & Effect: Anthropological Essays on Persons & Things. Marilyn Strathern. LC 99-14804. 1999. write for info. (*0-485-12149-2*, Pub. by Athlone Pr) Humanities.

Property System Approach to the Electromagnetic Spectrum: A Legal-Economic-Engineering Study. Arthur S. De Vany et al. (Cato Papers: No. 10). 87p. 1980. pap. 1.00 (*0-932790-11-9*) Cato Inst.

Property Tax: An International Comparative Review. 2nd ed. Ed. by William McCluskey. LC HJ4113.P758 1999. 482p. 1999. text 86.95 (*1-85972-517-1*) Ashgate Pub Co.

Property Tax & Its Administration. Ed. by Arthur D. Lynn, Jr. LC 69-16110. 260p. 1969. reprint ed. pap. 80.60 (*0-608-01925-9*, 206258000003) Bks Demand.

***Property Tax California Style.** LC 98-96213. (Illus.). 427p. 2000. pap. 79.95 (*0-9663310-7-9*) Santiago Press.

Property Tax Collection in North Carolina. 4th ed. William A. Campbell. LC 98-132171. 286p. 1998. pap. text 34.00 (*1-56011-302-2*, 97.04) Institute Government.

***Property Tax Collection in North Carolina: 2000 Supplement.** William A. Campbell. (C). 2000. pap. write for info. (*1-56011-375-8*) Institute Government.

Property Tax Consultant's Guide. Lynn Tylczak & Christopher R. Malburg. LC 92-20840. 1992. write for info. (*0-13-720202-4*) Prntice Hall Bks.

Property Tax Consultant's Guide. Lynn Tylczak & Christopher R. Malburg. LC 92-20840. (C). 1992. ring bd. 129.00 (*0-13-013541-0*) Prntice Hall Bks.

Property Tax in Anglophone Africa: A Practical Manual. Simon H. Keith. LC 93-34790. (Technical Paper, Africa Technical Department Ser.: No. 209). 136p. 1993. pap. 22.00 (*0-8213-2486-1*, 12486) World Bank.

Property Tax in Singapore. Leung Y. Kwong. 256p. 1985. pap. 55.00 (*0-409-99510-X*, MICHIE) LEXIS Pub.

Property Tax in Singapore & Malaysia 2nd ed. Leung Y. Kwong & Mani Usilappan. LC 98-474084. xxviii, 322p. 1997. write for info. (*0-409-99867-2*) Buttrwrth-Heinemann.

Property Tax Lien Foreclosure: Forms & Procedures. 5th ed. William A. Campbell. (C). 1999. pap. text 19.00 (*1-56011-323-5*) Institute Government.

Property Tax Planning. 3rd ed. Philip Spencer. 1994. pap. write for info. (*0-406-03286-6*, MICHIE) LEXIS Pub.

Property Tax Planning Manual. 2nd ed. Philip Spencer. 1989. pap. 60.00 (*0-406-51080-6*, UK, MICHIE) LEXIS Pub.

Property Tax Reform in Developing Countries. Jay K. Rosengard. LC 97-38894. 232p. 1998. lib. bdg. 104.50 (*0-7923-8095-9*) Kluwer Academic.

Property Tax Relief. Steven D. Gold. LC 79-1723. 349p. reprint ed. pap. 108.20 (*0-7837-5758-1*, 204542000006) Bks Demand.

Property Tax Slashing Guide. George Thompson. (Orig.). pap. 19.95 (*1-884350-51-8*) Alpha Pubng.

Property Taxation & the Finance of Education. Ed. by Richard W. Lindholm. LC 73-2046. (Publications of the Committee on Taxation, Resources & Economic Development: Vol. 7). 345p. 1974. reprint ed. pap. 107.00 (*0-608-01896-1*, 206254800003) Bks Demand.

Property Taxation, Land Use & Public Policy: Proceedings of a Symposium Sponsored by the Committee on Taxation, Resources & Economic Development (TRED) at the University of Wisconsin-Madison, 1973. Ed. by Arthur D. Lynn, Jr. LC 75-12210. (Publications of the Committee on Taxation, Resources & Economic Development: Vol. 8). 267p. 1976. reprint ed. pap. 82.80 (*0-608-01960-7*, 206261500003) Bks Demand.

Property Taxation, U. S. A. Proceedings of a Symposium Sponsored by the Committee on Taxation, Resources & Economic Development (TRED) at the University of Wisconsin, Milwaukee, 1965. Ed. by Richard W. Lindholm. LC 67-20762. 327p. 1969. reprint ed. pap. 101.40 (*0-608-01929-1*, 206258400003) Bks Demand.

Property Taxes, 11 vols. (Information Services Ser.). 1987. 948.00 (*0-685-07434-X*); write for info. (*0-318-57358-X*); ring bd. 1062.00 (*0-685-07433-1*) P-H.

Property Taxes & Homeowner Associations: Property Taxes & Homeowner Associations. rev. ed. George R. Grasser. (GAP Reports: Vol. 6). 1995. pap. 17.50 (*0-944715-28-1*) CAI.

Property Taxes & Homeowner Associations No. 6: GAP Reports. 3rd ed. George R. Grasser. 16p. 1995. pap. 17.50 (*0-944715-38-9*) CAI.

Property Taxes & Local Economic Development: Pennsylvania, 1976-1980. rev. ed. Donna M. Kish-Goodling. LC 95-38867. (Studies in Entrepreneurship Ser.). (Illus.). 138p. 1995. text 15.00 (*0-8153-2173-2*) Garland.

Property Taxes & Tax Revolts: The Legacy of Proposition 13. Arthur O'Sullivan et al. (Illus.). 171p. (C). 1995. text 47.95 (*0-521-46159-6*) Cambridge U Pr.

Property to the People: The Struggle for Radical Economic Reform in Russia. Lynn D. Nelson & Irina Y. Kuzes. LC 93-5692. 280p. (C). (gr. 13). 1994. text 85.95 (*1-56324-273-7*) M E Sharpe.

Property to the People: The Struggle for Radical Economic Reform in Russia. Lynn D. Nelson et al. LC 93-5692. 280p. (gr. 13). 1994. pap. text 36.95 (*1-56324-274-5*) M E Sharpe.

Property Valuation: The Five Methods. Douglas Scarrett. (Illus.). 232p. (C). 1991. pap. 35.00 (*0-419-13780-7*, E & FN Spon) Routledge.

Property Valuation & Investment Analysis: A Cash Flow Approach. Jon Robinson. vii, 161p. 1989. pap. 36.50 (*0-455-20830-1*, Pub. by LawBk Co) Gaunt.

Property Values & Open Space in Northwest Philadelphia: An Empirical Analysis. Robert E. Coughlin & Tatsuhiko Kawashima. (Discussion Papers: No. 64). 1973. pap. 10.00 (*1-55869-101-4*) Regional Sci Res Inst.

Property Values & Race: Studies in Seven Cities. Luigi Laurenti. LC 76-5437. (Illus.). 256p. 1976. reprint ed. lib. bdg. 69.50 (*0-8371-8795-8*, LAPV, Greenwood Pr) Greenwood.

Property, Women & Politics: Subjects or Objects? Donna Dickenson. LC 97-21504. 210p. 1997. 48.00 (*0-8135-2457-1*); pap. 18.00 (*0-8135-2458-X*) Rutgers U Pr.

PROPERTY 7E. 7th ed. John E. Cribbet et al. LC 96-3610. (Paralegal). 1345p. (C). 1996. text 45.00 (*1-56662-334-0*) Foundation Pr.

Prophecies. Alfons Paquet. Tr. & Intro. by H. M. Waidson. LC 82-84465. (GERM Ser.: Vol. 10). (Illus.). xxii, 130p. 1983. 35.00 (*0-938100-08-4*) Camden Hse.

Prophecies. Lawrence Tyler. 107p. 1990. pap. 10.00 (*0-9615879-1-1*) Puddinhead Pr.

Prophecies. 2nd ed. Wladyslaw Biernacki. Tr. by Nellie Dzierzynski & Henryk Szewczyk from POL. (Illus.). 84p. 1992. pap. text 8.50 (*0-933731-07-8*) Children of Mary.

Prophecies: Can You See into the Future? Gerald Bailey. 96p. (J). (gr. 4 up). 1998. pap. 5.95 (*1-901881-40-7*, Pub. by Element MA) Penguin Putnam.

Prophecies - 2000: Predictions, Revelations, & Visions for the New Millennium. Matthew Bunson. LC 98-51027. 160p. 1999. per. 12.00 (*0-671-01917-1*, WSP) PB.

Prophecies & Transformations. Kosrof Chantikian. LC 75-35012. 88p. (Orig.). 1978. pap. 12.95 (*0-916426-01-7*) KOSMOS.

Prophecies for the End of This Age. B. L. Cochrell et al. LC 98-92940. 425p. 1998. pap. write for info. (*1-57502-807-7*, PO2225) Morris Pubng.

Prophecies for the New Millennium: Psychics, Seers, & Oracles Tell You What to Expect from the Next 1000 Years. James Manning. LC 97-10762. 128p. 1997. 15.00 (*0-06-270211-4*) HarpC.

Prophecies in Parables As Recorded in the Gospels of Matthew, Mark, Luke & John. (Walk with Jesus Ser.). 133p. 1989. pap. 20.00 (*1-57277-327-8*) Script Rsch.

Prophecies of Daniel see Daniel

Prophecies of Daniel. Gordon Lindsay. 1969. per. 4.95 (*0-89985-052-9*) Christ for the Nations.

Prophecies of Great World Changes. George B. Brownell. 53p. 1989. pap. 4.00 (*0-89540-176-2*, SB-176) Sun Pub.

Prophecies of His Devine Grace Daniel Clay. Daniel Clay. LC 85-876299. 305p. 1998. pap. 16.95 (*0-9667877-0-6*, 84743) Haas Pubns.

Prophecies of Jesus. Michael Sours. (Illus.). 224p. (Orig.). 1994. pap. 18.95 (*1-85168-025-X*, Pub. by Onewrld Pubns) Penguin Putnam.

Prophecies of Joseph Smith: Over Four Hundred Prophecies by & about Joseph Smith, & Their Fulfillment. Duane S. Crowther. LC 83-80664. 413p. 1873. 19.98 (*0-88290-221-0*) Horizon Utah.

Prophecies of Melchi-Zedek in the Great Pyramid & the Seven Temples. Brown Landone. 179p. 1996. reprint ed. pap. 14.50 (*0-7873-0523-5*) Hlth Research.

Prophecies of Mother Shipton. 1983. reprint ed. pap. 4.95 (*0-916411-22-2*, Sure Fire) Holmes Pub.

Prophecies of Nostradamus. Nostradamus & Erika Cheetham. LC 74-155828. 426p. 1973. write for info. (*0-85435-152-3*) C W Daniel.

***Prophecies of Nostradamus: And the World's Greatest Seers & Mystics.** Francis King & Stephen Skinner. 304p. 2000. pap. 15.95 (*1-85868-454-4*, Pub. by Carlton Bks Ltd) Natl Bk Netwk.

Prophecies of Nostradamus & a Scientific Approach to Scripture see Science & Religion Series

Prophecies of Nostradamus in Historical Order. H. G. Erickstad. 236p. 27.95 (*1-85756-247-X*, Pub. by Janus Pubng) Paul & Co Pubs.

Prophecies of Paracelsus. Philippus Aureolus Paracelsus. Tr. by J. Kohn from GER. 1992. reprint ed. pap. 8.95 (*1-55818-188-1*) Holmes Pub.

Prophecies of St. Malachy. Peter Bander. LC 74-125419. (Illus.). 1993. reprint ed. pap. 7.00 (*0-89555-038-5*) TAN Bks Pubs.

Prophecies of St. Malachy & St. Columbkille. 5th ed. Peter Bander et al. 142p. 1995. pap. 9.95 (*0-86140-386-X*, Pub. by Smyth) Dufour.

***Prophecies of the Bible.** Daymond R. Duck. Ed. by Larry Richards. (God's Word for the Biblically-Inept Ser.: No. 8). 352p. 2000. pap. 16.95 (*1-892016-22-2*, Pub. by Starburst) Natl Bk Netwk.

Prophecies of the Brahan Seer. rev. ed. Elizabeth Sutherland. (Illus.). 156p. 1998. pap. 15.95 (*0-09-478460-4*, Pub. by Constable & Co) Trafalgar.

Prophecies of the End-Times: God's Call to Prayer, Repentance, & Revival. exp. ed. Intro. by R. C. Schaffter. 200p. 1992. pap. 9.99 (*0-9633026-0-4*) Clar Call WI.

Prophecies of the Holy Quran. Hingora. 1989. pap. 9.50 (*1-56744-196-3*) Kazi Pubns.

Prophecies of the Presidents: The Spiritual Destiny of America Revealed! Timothy G. Beckley & Arthur Crockett. 1992. 15.00 (*0-938294-39-3*) Inner Light.

Prophecies on World Events by Nostradamus. 4th ed. Tr. by Stewart Rodd. (Illus.). (Orig.). 1991. pap. 8.95 (*0-87140-220-3*, Pub. by Liveright) Norton.

Prophecies to America. Warren A. Reed. 24p. 1996. pap. 7.00 (*0-8059-4000-6*) Dorrance.

***Prophecy.** K. A. Applegate. (Animorphs Ser.: No. 34). 141p. (J). (gr. 4-7). 1999. pap. 4.99 (*0-439-07034-1*, Pub. by Scholastic Inc) Penguin Putnam.

***Prophecy.** Elizabeth Haydon. LC 00-26836. 448p. 2000. 27.95 (*0-312-86751-4*, Pub. by Tor Bks) St Martin.

Prophecy. W. Edmund Hood. (Illus.). 342p. (Orig.). (YA). (gr. 7 up). 1995. pap. 12.50 (*0-9647539-0-1*) QDP Pubng.

Prophecy. J. C. Ryle. Date not set. 8.99 (*1-871676-64-9*, Pub. by Christian Focus) Spring Arbor Dist.

Prophecy. Bertrand O. Taithe & Tim Thornton. LC 97-156907. 224p. 1997. pap. 22.95 (*0-7509-1332-0*, Pub. by Sutton Pub Ltd) Intl Pubs Mktg.

Prophecy see Animorphs

Prophecy: A Novel of Sai Baba. 280p. 1994. 15.95 (*0-929839-02-1*) Wisdom Works Pr.

Prophecy: Book Five of the Blending. Sharon Green. LC 98-94801. (Blending Ser.: Bk. 5). 416p. 1999. mass mkt. 6.50 (*0-380-78811-X*, Eos) Morrow Avon.

Prophecy: Essays Presented to Georg Fohrer on His Sixty-Fifth Birthday. Ed. by J. A. Emerton. (Beiheft zur Zeitschrift fuer die Alttestamentliche Wissenschaft Ser.: No. 155). 240p. (C). 1980. text 83.10 (*3-11-007761-2*) De Gruyter.

Prophecy: From Beginning to Finality. viii, 313p. 1994. per. 14.95 (*0-9656530-0-5*) W Oxner.

Prophecy: Key to the Future. rev. ed. Duane S. Crowther. 368p. 1996. 19.98 (*0-88290-583-X*) Horizon Utah.

Prophecy: Reflections on Life & Love from a Black Perspective. Jamarhl Carlton Crawford. v, 127p. 1997. pap. 10.00 (*0-9678559-0-X*) Prophecy Comns.

Prophecy: The Year 2000 & Beyond. Gene Fadeley. 96p. 1998. pap. 7.00 (*0-9646041-2-4*) Anchor Pubng.

***Prophecy Bk. III: Masquerade Cycle.** Vance Moore. (Magic Ser.: Vol. 3). 320p. 2000. pap. 6.99 (*0-7869-1570-6*) TSR Inc.

Prophecy & Apocalypticism: The Postexilic Social Setting. Stephen L. Cook. LC 95-23148. 240p. 1995. pap. 23.00 (*0-8006-2839-X*, 1-2839) Augsburg Fortress.

Prophecy & Canon: A Contribution to the Study of Jewish Origins. Joseph Blenkinsopp. LC 76-22411. 206p. 1986. pap. 13.00 (*0-268-01559-7*) U of Notre Dame Pr.

Prophecy & Diplomacy: The Moral Doctrine of John Paul II - A Jesuit Symposium. Ed. by John J. Conley & Joseph W. Koterski. LC 99-41405. 306p. 1999. 35.00 (*0-8232-1975-5*, Pub. by Fordham) BookMasters.

***Prophecy & Diplomacy: The Moral Doctrine of John Paul II - A Jesuit Symposium.** Ed. by John J. Conley & Joseph W. Koterski. LC 99-41405. 306p. 1999. pap. 17.50 (*0-8232-1976-3*, Pub. by Fordham) BookMasters.

Prophecy & Ethics: Isaiah & the Ethical Traditions of Israel. Eryl W. Davies. (JSOT Supplement Ser.: No. 16). 185p. 1981. 57.50 (*0-905774-26-4*, Pub. by Sheffield Acad) CUP Services.

Prophecy & Hermeneutics in Early Christianity: New Testament Essays. E. Earle Ellis. 306p. 1978. lib. bdg. 62.50 (*3-16-138742-2*) Coronet Bks.

Prophecy & History in Luke-Acts. David L. Tiede. LC 79-8897. 176p. reprint ed. pap. 54.60 (*0-608-15330-3*, 202961600061) Bks Demand.

Prophecy & Inspired Speech in Early Christianity & It's Hellenistic Environment. Christopher Forbes. 378p. 1997. pap. 19.95 (*1-56563-269-9*) Hendrickson MA.

Prophecy & Millenarianism: Essays in Honour of Marjorie Reeves. Ed. by Ann Williams. LC 81-109635. (Illus.). 367p. reprint ed. pap. 113.80 (*0-7837-1598-6*, 204189000024) Bks Demand.

Prophecy & Modern Times. W. Cleon Skousen. 170p. (C). 1980. pap. 6.95 (*0-910558-47-7*) Ensign Pub.

Prophecy & Mysticism: The Heart of the Postmodern Church. Mary C. Grey. (Scottish Journal of Theology Current Issues in Theology Ser.). 76p. 1997. pap. 19.95 (*0-567-08587-2*, Pub. by T & T Clark) Bks Intl VA.

Prophecy & People in Renaissance Italy. Ottavia Niccoli. Tr. by Lydia G. Cochrane from ITA. (Illus.). 214p. (C). 1990. pap. text 16.95 (*0-691-00835-3*, Pub. by Princeton U Pr) Cal Prin Full Svc.

Prophecy & Power among the Dogrib Indians. June Helm. LC 94-11841. (Studies in the Anthropology of North American Indians). (Illus.). xiv, 173p. 1994. text 45.00 (*0-8032-2373-0*) U of Nebr Pr.

Prophecy & Prediction. Dewey M. Beegle. 274p. 1978. write for info. (*0-933462-00-X*); pap. text 8.95 (*0-933462-01-8*) Pryor Pettengill.

Prophecy & Prediction in the 20th Century. Charles Gattey. 1988. pap. 12.95 (*0-85030-830-5*, Pub. by Aqrn Pr) Harper SF.

Prophecy & Providence. Meir S. Sokolovsky. 1991. 17.95 (*0-87306-578-6*) Feldheim.

***Prophecy & Religion: Studies in the Life of Jeremiah.** John Skinner. 368p. 1999. pap. 30.00 (*1-57910-309-X*) Wipf & Stock.

Prophecy & Revolution. Nathaniel Ndiokwere. 350p. 1996. pap. 32.50 (*0-7618-0602-4*) U Pr of Amer.

Prophecy & Society in Ancient Israel. Robert R. Wilson. LC 78-14677. 336p. 1980. pap. 24.00 (*0-8006-1814-9*, 1-1814, Fortress Pr) Augsburg Fortress.

***Prophecy & Teaching: Prophetic Authority, Form Problems & the Use of Traditions in the Book of Malachi.** Karl William Weyde. LC 00-24026. (Beihefte Zur Zeitschrift Fur die Alttestamentliche Wissenschaft Ser.). 2000. write for info. (*3-11-016692-5*) De Gruyter.

Prophecy & the Biblical Prophets. rev. ed. John F. Sawyer. LC 92-44095. (Oxford Bible Ser.). 192p. 1993. 47.00 (*0-19-826210-8*) OUP.

Prophecy & the Biblical Prophets. 2nd rev. ed. John F. Sawyer. LC 92-44095. (Oxford Bible Ser.). 192p. 1993. pap. text 19.95 (*0-19-826209-4*) OUP.

Prophecy & the Comet: Biblical Impact of Shoemaker-Levy 9. Daniel R. Walsh. LC 96-85222. (Illus.). 96p. (Orig.). 1996. pap. 8.95 (*0-9652590-0-5*) Celtica.

Prophecy & the Philosophy of Mind: Traditions of Blake & Shelley. Terence A. Hoagwood. LC 83-6896. (Illus.). 264p. 1985. pap. 81.90 (*0-7837-8381-7*, 205919100009) Bks Demand.

Prophecy & the Quest for the Holy Grail: Critiquing Knowledge in the Vulgate Cycle. Katheryn Karczewska. LC 97-20816. (Studies in the Humanities: Vol. 37). XVI, 279p. (C). 1998. text 51.95 (*0-8204-3852-9*) P Lang Pubng.

P

An Asterisk (*) at the beginning of an entry indicates that the title is appearing for the first time.

Prophecy & the World. George D. Ding. LC 88-90464. (Illus.). 258p. (Orig.). 1988. pap. 8.95 (*0-9621732-0-7*); lib. bdg. 14.95 (*0-9621732-1-5*) G D D Ding.

Prophecy & War in Ancient Israel: Studies in the Oracles Against the Nations. Duane L. Christensen. LC 88-71437. (BIBAL Monographs: No. 3). Orig. Title: Transformations of the War Oracle in Old Testament Prophecy. 310p. 1989. reprint ed. pap. 14.95 (*0-941037-06-1*, BIBAL Press) D & F Scott.

Prophecy As Literature: A Text-Linguistic & Rhetorical Approach to Isaiah 2-4. Bertil Wiklander. (Coniectanea Biblica. Old Testament Ser.: No. 22). (Orig.). 1984. pap. 49.00 (*0-317-65786-0*) Coronet Bks.

Prophecy Blessings. George O. McCalep, Jr. 140p. 1997. mass mkt. write for info. (*0-9652262-6-3*) Orman Pr.

Prophecy for a Queen. large type ed. Dilys A. Gater. 1995. 27.99 (*0-7089-3294-0*) Ulverscroft.

Prophecy for Today see Profecias para el Mundo Moderno

Prophecy for Today see Profecias Para el Mundo Moderno

Prophecy for Today. Edward Connor. LC 83-70408. 135p. 1984. reprint ed. pap. 5.50 (*0-89555-212-4*) TAN Bks Pubs.

Prophecy for Today: God's Purpose & Plan for Our Future. J. Dwight Pentecost. 224p. 1989. pap. 10.99 (*0-929239-11-3*) Discovery Hse Pubs.

Prophecy Guide. 102p. (Orig.). 1996. pap. 10.00 (*0-9652845-0-6*) Thirteen Enter.

Prophecy Handbook. William E. Biederwolf. 728p. 1991. pap. 14.99 (*0-529-06991-1*, PHB) World Publng.

Prophecy Handbook: A Theologian Looks at Millennial Myths & Scriptural Truths. George Monta. LC 99-218659. 181p. 1998. pap. 14.95 (*1-883179-10-6*) Weston Bible.

Prophecy in Ancient Israel. Johannes Lindblom. LC 63-907. 480p. reprint ed. pap. 148.80 (*0-608-15450-4*, 202929800060) Bks Demand.

Prophecy in Early Christianity. David E. Aune. 522p. 1991. pap. 25.00 (*0-8028-0635-X*) Eerdmans.

Prophecy in Islam: Philosophy & Orthodoxy. Fazlur Rahman. LC 78-66082. (Midway Reprint Ser.). 1992. pap. text 9.00 (*0-226-70282-0*) U Ch Pr.

Prophecy in Islam: Philosophy & Orthodoxy. Fazlur Rahman. LC 78-66082. (Midway Reprint Ser.). 118p. reprint ed. pap. 36.60 (*0-608-09506-0*, 205430700005) Bks Demand.

Prophecy in Our Time. Martin Ebon. 1971. pap. 2.50 (*0-87980-125-5*) Wilshire.

Prophecy in the Christian Era: A Study of Bob Dylan's Work from 1961 to 1967 Emphasizing His Use of Enigma to Teach Ethics & Comparing Him to Dante Alighieri & Other Poets. Jenny Ledeen. LC 95-92819. (Illus.). 250p. (Orig.). (C). 1996. pap. text 18.00 (*0-9650542-0-9*) Peaceberry Pr.

***Prophecy in the Hebrew Bible: Selected Studies from Vetus Testamentum.** David E. Orton. LC 99-51406. (Brill's Readers in Biblical Studies). 1999. write for info. (*90-04-11160-3*) Brill Academic Pubs.

Prophecy Knowledge Handbook. John Walvoord. 800p. 1990. text 31.99 (*0-89693-509-4*, 6-1509, Victor Bks) Chariot Victor.

Prophecy Marked Reference Study Bible. Ed. by Grant R. Jeffrey. LC 98-61553. 2000. 34.99 (*0-310-90862-0*) Zondervan.

Prophecy of Amos & Hosea. Christina Bucher. LC 97-19277. (Covenant Bible Studies). (Orig.). 1997. pap. 5.95 (*0-87178-008-9*) Brethren.

Prophecy of Berchan: Irish & Scottish High-Kings of the Early Middle Ages, 54. Benjamin T. Hudson. LC 95-34159. (Contributions to the Study of World History Ser.). 288p. 1996. 65.00 (*0-313-29567-0*, Greenwood Pr) Greenwood.

Prophecy of Daniel: A Brief Look at How an Ancient Prophecys Fulfillment Is Still Awaited Today. Thomas W. Petrisko. 54p. 1997. pap. 4.95 (*1-891903-03-9*) St Andrew Prodns.

***Prophecy of Daniel: A Commentary.** Edward J. Young. 330p. 1998. pap. 35.00 (*1-57910-179-8*) Wipf & Stock.

Prophecy of Darkness. Stella Howard. (Xena: Warrior Princess Ser.). 224p. 1997. mass mkt. 5.99 (*1-57297-249-1*) Blvd Books.

***Prophecy of Isaiah: An Introduction & Commentary.** J. Alec Motyer. LC 93-17815. 544p. 1999. pap. 19.99 (*0-8308-1593-7*, 1593) InterVarsity.

Prophecy of the Four "Sevens" in the Bible. Witness Lee. 96p. 1990. per. 5.50 (*0-87083-548-3*, 10-060-001) Living Stream Ministry.

Prophecy of the Four "Sevens" in the Bible, The see Profecia de los Cuatro "Sietes" en la Biblia

Prophecy of the Russian Epic: How the Holy Mountains Released the Mighty Russian Heroes from Their Rocky Caves. Sergei O. Prokofieff. Tr. by Simon B. De Lange from RUS. 64p. 1993. pap. 10.95 (*0-904693-49-X*, Pub. by Temple Lodge) Anthroposophic.

Prophecy of the Seventy Weeks of the Book of Daniel: A Critical Review of the Prophecy as Viewed by Three Major Theological Interpretations & the Impact of the Book of Daniel on Christology. Michael Kalafian. 276p. (C). 1991. lib. bdg. 47.00 (*0-8191-8299-0*) U Pr of Amer.

***Prophecy of the Soul Sorcerer, Bk. 1.** Eric Dean Seaton. (Illus.). 120p. 2000. pap. 10.95 (*1-930315-00-7*) Arcane.

***Prophecy of the Soul Sorcerer, 4 bks., Set.** Eric Dean Seaton. 128p. 2000. pap. 10.95 (*1-930315-99-6*) Arcane.

***Prophecy of the Soul Sorcerer, 4 bks., Set.** Ed. by Eric Dean Seaton. (Illus.). 128p. (YA). 2000. pap. 10.95 (*1-930315-98-8*) Arcane.

Prophecy of the Swan: The Upper Peace River Fur Trade of 1794-1823. David V. Burley et al. 1996. pap. 25.95 (*0-7748-0545-5*) U of Wash Pr.

Prophecy on the Mount: Mark 13 & the Gathering of the New Community. Keith D. Dyer. (International Theological Studies: Vol. 2). 338p. (C). 1998. pap. text 50.95 (*3-906759-71-7*) P Lang Pubng.

Prophecy, Poetry & Hosea. Gerald Morris. (JSOT Supplement Ser.: No. 219). 167p. 1996. 52.50 (*1-85075-599-X*, Pub. by Sheffield Acad) CUP Services.

Prophecy Rock. Rob MacGregor. LC 94-33163. 208p. (YA). (gr. 7 up). 1995. mass mkt. 16.00 (*0-689-80056-8*) S&S Bks Yung.

Prophecy Rock. Rob MacGregor. (J). 1998. 9.60 (*0-606-13725-4*, Pub. by Turtleback) Demco.

Prophecy Rock. Rob MacGregor. 208p. (YA). (gr. 7 up). 1998. reprint ed. mass mkt. 4.50 (*0-440-22738-0*, LLL BDD) BDD Bks Young Read.

***Prophecy Study Bible.** 2000. 39.99 (*0-89957-924-8*); 47.99 (*0-89957-925-6*); 64.99 (*0-89957-926-4*); 72.99 (*0-89957-927-2*); 64.99 (*0-89957-928-0*); 72.99 (*0-89957-929-9*); 74.99 (*0-89957-932-9*); 82.99 (*0-89957-933-7*); 74.99 (*0-89957-934-5*); 82.99 (*0-89957-935-3*) AMG Pubs.

Prophecy Study Bible, Supersaver ed. Prophecy Study Staff. 1999. 19.97 (*0-7852-0736-8*) Nelson.

Prophecy Study Bible, Supersaver ed. Prophecy Study Staff. 1999. 29.97 (*0-7852-0107-6*) Nelson.

Prophecy Study Marked Reference. Prophecy Study Staff. 1999. 69.99 (*0-310-92066-3*); 79.99 (*0-310-92070-1*) Zondervan.

Prophecy, Things to Come. James L. Boyer. pap. 7.99 (*0-88469-006-7*) BMH Bks.

***Prophecy to Presidency. Ralph DePucchio. v, 46p. 2000. per. 7.99 (*0-9676558-0-3*) Deeds of Christ.**
God spake & I believe. I have created & have acted on what I believe God has called me to to. That is to give a declaration to a nation that has totally red lined the mandates that God has given to His creation. The book includes warnings to four specific groups, the church being one of them. Do not be deceived, God is not mocked. The sin that has become prevalent throughout this nation has reached its point of judgment. That is to say predominant, widely existing, generally practiced & accepted. Before this devasting judgment, enlighten your heart & come to know that God is God of order. That life is a gift. A precious gift that is given to us by God.
Publisher Paid Annotation.

Prophecy, 2000. David A. Lewis. LC 90-60310. (Illus.). 432p. 1990. pap. 11.95 (*0-89221-179-2*) New Leaf.

Prophesied Band: The Saga of the Prodigal Band Continues. Deborah Lagarde. (Prodigal Band Trilogy Ser.: Vol. 2). 112p. (Orig.). 1998. pap. 13.95 (*0-9649566-1-6*) OmegaBooks.

Prophesy. 5.95 (*0-913343-65-X*) Inst Psych Inc.

Prophesy. Tony Higton. 1998. pap. text 9.95 (*0-281-05106-2*) Intl Pubs Mktg.

Prophesy & Dissent, 1914-16. Ed. by Richard A. Rempel et al. (The Collected Papers of Bertrand Russell: Vol. 13). 774p. 1988. 140.00 (*0-415-10463-7*, A9421) Routledge.

Prophesy Deliverance! An Afro-American Revolutionary Christianity. Cornel West. LC 82-13483. 186p. 1982. pap. 19.95 (*0-664-24447-5*) Westminster John Knox.

Prophesy to the Land. Les Lawrence. LC 96-101189. 238p. (Orig.). 1994. pap. 10.99 (*1-56043-802-9*, Treasure Hse) Destiny Image.

***Prophesy to These Bones: These Bones Can Live!** Leon Carter Price. 144p. 1999. pap. 7.95 (*1-58169-038-X*, Gazelle Pr) Genesis Comm Inc.

PROPHESYING IN THE CHURCH MEETINGS FOR THE ORGANIC BUILDING UP OF THE CHURCH AS THE BODY OF CHRIST (OUTLINES) see Profetizar En Las Reuniones De La Iglesia Para La Edificacion Organica De La Iglesia Como El Cuerpo De Cristo, El (Bosqu

Prophesying the Past: The Use of Israel's History in the Book of Hosea. Else Kragelund Holt. (JSOT Supplement Ser.: No. 194). 160p. 1995. 52.50 (*1-85075-540-X*, Pub. by Sheffield Acad) CUP Services.

Prophesying Tragedy: Sign & Voice in Sophocles' Theban Plays. Rebecca W. Bushnell. LC 87-47857. 155p. reprint ed. pap. 48.10 (*0-608-20879-5*, 207197800003) Bks Demand.

Prophesying upon the Bones: J. Reuben Clark & the Foreign Debt Crisis, 1933-39. Gene A. Sessions. 168p. (C). 1992. text 24.95 (*0-252-01927-X*) U of Ill Pr.

Prophet see Profeta

***Prophet.** (French Audiobooks Ser.).Tr. of The Prophet. 2000. 14.95 incl. audio (*2-89517-050-9*, Pub. by Coffragants) Penton Overseas.

Prophet. Kahlil Gibran. 1999. 16.95 (*0-627-02372-X*, Pub. by J L Van Schaik) BHB Intl.

Prophet. Kahlil Gibran. (Illus.). 1923. 15.00 (*0-394-40428-9*) Knopf.

Prophet. Kahlil Gibran. (Illus.). 1966. 15.00 (*0-394-40427-0*) Knopf.

Prophet. Kahlil Gibran. (Kahlil Gibran Pocket Library). 1995. 14.00 (*0-679-44067-4*) Knopf.

Prophet. Kahlil Gibran. 1998. pap. 2.95 (*0-375-70411-6*) Knopf.

Prophet. Kahlil Gibran. 1999. pap. 6.95 (*0-375-70140-0*) Knopf.

Prophet. Kahlil Gibran. (Classics of World Literature Ser.). 80p. 1997. pap. 5.95 (*1-85326-485-7*, 4587WW, Pub. by Wrdsworth Edits) NTC Contemp Pub Co.

Prophet. Kahlil Gibran. 1999. write for info. (*0-316-30847-1*) Little.

Prophet. Kahlil Gibran. 128p. 1999. pap. 10.95 (*0-14-019586-6*) Viking Penguin.

Prophet. Gibran Kahlil. 1999. write for info. (*0-316-30899-4*) Little.

Prophet. Frank E. Peretti. LC 92-4850. 416p. 1992. pap. 12.99 (*0-89107-618-2*) Crossway Bks.

Prophet. deluxe ed. Kahlil Gibran. (Illus.). 1952. 35.00 (*0-394-40426-2*) Knopf.

Prophet. deluxe ed. Kahlil Gibran. LC 97-50638. 112p. 1999. 4.99 (*0-517-20275-1*) Random Hse Value.

Prophet. large type ed. Kahlil Gibran. 1986. pap. 9.95 (*0-8027-2532-5*) Walker & Co.

Prophet: A Tragedy. Bayard Taylor. (Notable American Authors). 1999. reprint ed. lib. bdg. 125.00 (*0-7812-8992-0*) Rprt Serv.

Prophet: Francis of Assisi: Early Documents, Vol. 3. Ed. by Regis J. Armstrong et al. Tr. by Wayne J. Hellmann et al from ITA. 638p. 1999. 49.00 (*1-56548-115-1*) New City.

Prophet: Francis of Assisi: Early Documents, Vol. 3. Ed. by Regis J. Armstrong et al. Tr. by Wayne J. Hellmann et al from ITA. (Francis of Assisi: Early Documents Ser.). (Illus.). 638p. 2001. pap. 29.95 (*1-56548-114-3*) New City.

Prophet: Friend of God. rev. ed. Ed Dufresne. 86p. 1993. pap. 6.00 (*0-940763-05-2*) E Dufresne Minist.

Prophet: The Inner Meaning of Prayer see Torkington Trilogy on Prayer

***Prophet: The Life & Times of Kahil Gibran.** Robin Waterfield. (Illus.). 288p. 2000. pap. 14.95 (*0-312-25409-1*) St Martin.

Prophet: The Life & Times of Kahlil Gibran. Robin Waterfield. LC 98-30880. 384p. 1998. 25.95 (*0-312-19319-X*, Thomas Dunne) St Martin.

Prophet & a Pilgrim. Herbert W. Schneider & George Lawton. LC 78-134433. (Illus.). reprint ed. 36.50 (*0-404-05610-5*) AMS Pr.

Prophet & His Work: Essays from General Authorities on Joseph Smith & the Restoration. LC 96-22251. x, 158p. 1996. 14.95 (*1-57345-193-2*) Deseret Bk.

***Prophet & Other Stories.** Yi Chong-jun. Tr. by Julie Pickering from KOR. LC 99-232443. (Illus.). 208p. (C). 1998. 18.70 (*1-885445-61-X*); pap. 11.90 (*1-885445-01-6*) Cornell East Asia Pgm.

Prophet & Other Stories. Samuel Rawet. Tr. by Nelson Vieira. LC 98-23096. (Jewish Latin American Ser.). 86p. 1998. 29.95 (*0-8263-1837-1*); pap. 12.95 (*0-8263-1952-1*) U of NM Pr.

Prophet & Peacemaker: The Life of Adolphe Monod. James L. Osen. (Illus.). 420p. 1984. pap. text 31.00 (*0-8191-3826-6*); lib. bdg. 60.50 (*0-8191-3825-8*) U Pr of Amer.

Prophet & the Age of the Caliphates: The Islamic Near East from the Sixth to the Eleventh Century. Intro. by Hugh Kennedy. (History of the Near East Ser.). 440p. (C). 1989. pap. 48.00 (*0-582-49313-7*, 73573) Longman.

Prophet & Witness of Charity, (Tommaso Maria Fusco) Ed. by Margherita Marchione. LC 74-127109. 170p. 1973. write for info. (*0-614-10144-1*) Am Inst Ital Stud.

Prophet Annie. Ellen Recknor. LC 98-54331. 336p. 1999. pap. 12.00 (*0-380-79513-2*, Avon Bks) Morrow Avon.

***Prophet Annie.** Ellen Recknor. 352p. 2000. mass mkt. 6.99 (*0-380-81122-7*, Avon Bks) Morrow Avon.

Prophet Annie, Vol. 1. Ellen Recknor. LC 99-14979. 1999. 26.95 (*0-7862-1992-0*) Thorndike Pr.

Prophet Armed: Trotsky: 1879-1921. 254p. 1997. reprint ed. lib. bdg. 39.95 (*0-7351-0014-4*) Replica Bks.

Prophet Crying in the Wilderness. Bonnie L. Wright et al. Ed. by John Donohue et al. 164p. 1986. pap. 6.98 (*0-9616309-0-6*) Mountain Pubs.

Prophet Dance of the Northwest & Its Derivatives: The Source of the Ghost Dance. Leslie Spier. LC 76-43853. reprint ed. 37.50 (*0-404-15708-4*) AMS Pr.

Prophet Elijah see Profeta Elias

Prophet for Our Times: The Life & Teachings of Peter Deunov. Ed. by David Lorimer. 208p. 1993. pap. 14.95 (*1-85230-211-9*, Pub. by Element MA) Penguin Putnam.

Prophet for the Archangels. Ann R. Colton & Jonathan Murro. LC 64-6257. (Illus.). 257p. 1964. pap. 9.95 (*0-917187-06-7*) A R Colton Fnd.

***Prophet for the Priesthood.** John A. Hardon. 174p. 1998. pap. 8.95 (*0-9672989-3-8*) Eternal Life Inc.

Prophet from Harlem Speaks: Sermons & Essays. Wyatt Tee Walker. LC 97-72368. 1997. write for info. (*0-937644-30-7*) M L King Pr.

Prophet Harris, the "Black Elijah" of West Africa. abr. ed. David A. Shank. Ed. by Jocelyn Murray. LC 94-26022. (Studies of Religion in Africa: 10). 1994. 148.00 (*90-04-09980-8*) Brill Academic Pubs.

Prophet in Exile: Joseph Mazzini in England, 1837-1868. William Roberts. (Studies in Modern European History). IX, 153p. (C). 1989. text 37.50 (*0-8204-1051-9*) P Lang Pubng.

Prophet in the House. J. Ronald Miller. LC 93-73155. 171p. (Orig.). 1993. pap. 10.00 (*0-9638451-0-1*) Commun Church.

Prophet in the Marketplace: Thoreau's Development as a Professional Writer. Steven Fink. LC 99-24878. 1999. pap. text 18.95 (*0-8142-5040-8*) Ohio St U Pr.

Prophet Jeremia. Paul Volz. (Kommentar Zum Alten Testament Ser.: No. 10). (GER.). iii, 450p. 1983. write for info. (*3-487-07189-4*) G Olms Pubs.

Prophet Joseph: Essays on the Life & Mission of Joseph Smith. Ed. by Larry C. Porter & Susan E. Black. LC 88-22638. viii, 359p. 1988. 17.95 (*0-87579-177-8*) Deseret Bk.

Prophet King. Ray L. Vander. Date not set. pap., teacher ed. 17.99 (*0-310-67857-9*) Zondervan.

Prophet King: A New Look at the Historical Jesus. Richard Lamb. 195p. (Orig.). 1997. pap. 13.95 (*0-9657750-0-3*) Earth Heart Pr.

Prophet Motive: Examining the Reliability of the Biblical Prophets. Kenny Barfield. 340p. 1995. pap. 12.99 (*0-89225-458-0*, G54580) Gospel Advocate.

Prophet Muhammad: History & Character of His Life. Faizul R. Khan. LC 96-47531. 146p. 1998. pap. 10.00 (*0-9627854-9-0*) Writers Inc.

Prophet Muhammad: The Infinite Light, Vol. 1. M. Fethullah Gulen. 278p. 8.95 (*975-7388-47-5*) Fountain Pub.

Prophet Muhammad: The Infinite Light, Vol. 2. M. Fethullah Gulen. 282p. 1996. pap. 8.95 (*975-7388-45-9*) Fountain Pub.

***Prophet Muhammad As Commander.** M. Fethullah Gulen. 126p. 1998. pap. 5.95 (*975-7388-46-7*) Fountain Pub.

Prophet Next Door. Odimumba Kwamdela, pseud. LC 81-83794. 57p. 1981. pap. 5.00 (*0-941266-01-X*) Kibo Bks.

Prophet Next Door. 2nd ed. Odimumba Kwamdela, pseud & J. Ashton Brathwaite. LC 92-72601. 61p. 1992. pap. text 5.00 (*0-941266-10-9*) Kibo Bks.

Prophet of Akhran. Margaret Weis & Tracy Hickman. 1989. pap. 4.50 (*0-318-42578-5*, Spectra) Bantam.

Prophet of Community: The Romantic Socialism of Gustav Landauer. Eugene Lunn. 434p. 1973. 35.00 (*0-88286-136-0*) C H Kerr.

Prophet of Compostela: A Novel Apprenticeship & Initiation. Henri Vincenot. LC 95-41044. (Illus.). 248p. 1996. pap. 19.95 (*0-89281-524-8*) Inner Tradit.

Prophet of Death. Pete Earley. (Illus.). 450p. 1998. reprint ed. 32.95 (*0-7351-0045-4*) Replica Bks.

Prophet of Death: The Mormon Blood-Atonement Killings. Pete Earley. (Illus.). 448p. 1993. mass mkt. 4.99 (*0-380-71502-3*, Avon Bks) Morrow Avon.

Prophet of Doom. Warren Murphy. (Destroyer Ser.: Vol. 111). 1998. per. 5.99 (*0-373-63226-6*, 1-63226-4, Wrldwide Lib) Harlequin Bks.

Prophet of Hope see O Profeta da Esperanca

Prophet of Hope. F. B. Meyer. 1997. pap. 8.99 (*1-898787-28-X*) Emerald House Group Inc.

Prophet of Islam in Old French: "The Romance of Muhammad" (1258) & "The Book of Muhammad's Ladder" (1264) Tr. by Reginald Hyatte. LC 96-39811. (Studies in Intellectual History: No. 75). (Illus.). viii, 208p. 1997. 76.00 (*90-04-10702-9*, NLG 115) Brill Academic Pubs.

Prophet of Islam, the Ideal Husband. Syed Abu Zafar Zain. 1983. pap. 3.95 (*0-935782-14-1*) Kazi Pubns.

Prophet of Islam, the Ideal Husband. Syed A. Zain. 64p. 1996. pap. 3.95 (*0-614-21094-1*, 992) Kazi Pubns.

Prophet of Islam, the Ideal Husband. Syed A. Zain. 64p. (J). (gr. 7-8). 1996. pap. 3.95 (*0-614-21039-9*, 992) Kazi Pubns.

Prophet of Joy. Gamaliel Bradford. LC 77-179506. (Select Bibliographies Reprint Ser.). 1977. reprint ed. 19.95 (*0-8369-6635-X*) Ayer.

Prophet of Justice: Understanding the Book of Amos. William J. Doorly. 1989. pap. 5.95 (*0-8091-3089-0*) Paulist Pr.

Prophet of Justice, Prophet of Life: Essays on William Stringfellow. Ed. by Robert B. Slocum. LC 97-34272. 175p. 1997. 22.95 (*0-89869-269-5*) Church Pub Inc.

Prophet of Light. Ahmad Nawaz. LC 98-70773. xiv, 44p. 1998. pap. 10.00 (*1-58225-029-4*) Ananta Prakashani.

***Prophet of Light.** Ahmad Nawaz. LC 00-131826. 50p. 2000. pap. 10.00 (*1-58225-228-9*) Ananta Prakashani.

Prophet of Love: Understanding the Book of Hosea. William J. Doorley. 1991. pap. 8.95 (*0-8091-3241-9*) Paulist Pr.

Prophet of Orthodoxy: The Wisdom of G. K. Chesterton. Russell Sparkes. 370p. 1997. pap. 14.95 (*0-00-628037-4*) HarpC.

Prophet of Prohibition: Neal Dow & His Crusade. F. L. Byrne. 1990. 16.50 (*0-8446-0533-6*) Peter Smith.

Prophet of Rage: A Life of Louis Farrakhan & His Nation. Arthur J. Magida. 1997. pap. 13.00 (*0-465-06437-X*, Pub. by Basic) HarpC.

Prophet of the Coming Day. O. Robertson. 1995. pap. 8.99 (*0-85234-335-3*, Pub. by Evangelical Pr) P & R Pubng.

Prophet of the Dead Sea Scrolls: The Essenes & the Early Christians - One & the Same People, Their Seven Devout Practices. 3rd rev. ed. Upton C. Ewing. LC 94-15771. (Illus.). 175p. 1994. pap. 11.95 (*0-930852-26-5*) Tree Life Pubns.

Prophet of the Great Smoky Mountains. Mary N. Murfree. LC 76-110350. reprint ed. 34.50 (*0-404-04542-1*) AMS Pr.

Prophet of the Great Smoky Mountains. Mary N. Murfree. (BCL1-PS American Literature Ser.). 308p. 1992. reprint ed. lib. bdg. 89.00 (*0-7812-6804-4*) Rprt Serv.

Prophet of the Great Smoky Mountains. Mary N. Murfree. (Notable American Authors Ser.). 1999. reprint ed. lib. bdg. 125.00 (*0-7812-4594-X*) Rprt Serv.

Prophet of the Jubilee, Vol. 10. Ed. & Tr. by Ronald Dennis. LC 96-71245. 1997. 28.95 (*1-57008-296-0*) Bookcraft Inc.

Prophet of the New Drama: William Archer & the Ibsen Campaign, 20. Thomas Postlewait. LC 85-9878. (Contributions in Drama & Theatre Studies: No. 20). (Illus.). 210p. 1986. 55.00 (*0-313-24540-1*, POW/, Greenwood Pr) Greenwood.

Prophet of the People: A Biography of Padre Pio. 12th ed. Dorothy M. Gaudiose. LC 74-7123. (Illus.). 237p. reprint ed. pap. 14.95 (*0-8189-0351-1*) Alba.

***Prophet of the Plains.** Robert H. Tessier. 78p. 1999. pap. 11.95 (*1-896754-09-0*) Sh1oreline.

Prophet on the Payroll: When Pulpit & Pew Clash. John R. Bodo. LC 98-46475. 188p. 1999. pap. 19.95 (*1-57249-156-6*, Burd St Pr) White Mane Pub.

Prophet on the Screen: Computerized Description & Literary Interpretation of Ishinic Texts. Eep Talstra & A. L. Van Wieringen. 152p. 1993. pap. text 34.50 (*90-5383-120-7*, Pub. by VU Univ Pr) Paul & Co Pubs.

Prophet Outcast: Trotsky, 1929-1940. Isaac Deutscher. 559p. 1997. reprint ed. lib. bdg. 39.95 (*0-7351-0016-0*) Replica Bks.

Prophet Pasqual. Robert Wintner. LC 98-34204. 240p. 1999. 24.00 (*1-57962-050-7*) Permanent Pr.

Prophet, Pastor, Protestant: The Work of Huldrych Zwingli after Five Hundred Years. Ed. by E. J. Furchs & H. Wayne Pipkin. LC 84-14723. (Pittsburgh Theological Monographs, New Ser.: No. 11). (Orig.). 1984. pap. 10.00 (*0-915138-64-6*) Pickwick.

Prophet Puzzle: Interpretive Essays on Joseph Smith. Ed. & Intro. by Bryan Waterman. LC 98-47222. (Essays on Mormonism Ser.: No. 9). 365p. (Orig.). 1999. pap. 18.95 (*1-56085-121-X*) Signature Bks.

Prophet Reads Scripture: Allusion in Isaiah 40-66. Benjamin D. Sommer. LC 98-20169. (Contraversions Ser.). xiii, 355p. 1998. 49.50 (*0-8047-3216-7*) Stanford U Pr.

Prophet, Son, Messiah: Narrative Form & Function in Mark 14-16. Edwin K. Broadhead. LC 94-212245. (JSNTS Ser.: Vol. 97). 336p. 1994. 85.00 (*1-85075-476-4*, Pub. by Sheffield Acad) CUP Services.

Prophet Stathopulos: Right Living. Max. 50p. 1997. pap. 40.00 (*0-9720707-41-5*) M Tecton Pub.

Prophet Unarmed: Trotsky: 1921-1929. Isaac Deutscher. 504p. 1997. lib. bdg. 39.95 (*0-7351-0015-2*) Replica Bks.

Prophet und Prophetenbuch: Festschrift fur Otto Kaiser Zum 65, Geburtstag: Beiheft zur Zeitschrift fur die Alttestamentliche Wissenschaft, Vol. 185. Ed. by Volkmar Fritz et al. vii, 284p. (C). 1989. lib. bdg. 115.40 (*3-11-011339-2*) De Gruyter.

Prophet with Honor: The Billy Graham Story. William Martin. (Illus.). 760p. 1992. pap. 15.00 (*0-688-11906-9*, Quil) HarperTrade.

Prophet with Honor: The Career of Andrew Jackson Downing, 1815-1852. Ed. by George B. Tatum & Elisabeth B. MacDougall. LC 88-13943. (Dumbarton Oaks Colloquium on the History of Landscape Architecture Ser.: No. 11). (Illus.). 332p. 1990. 35.00 (*0-88402-178-5*, TAPR, Dumbarton Rsch Lib) Dumbarton Oaks.

Prophet with Honor: The Career of Andrew Jackson Downing, 1815-1852. Ed. by George B. Tatum & Elizabeth B. MacDugall. 1989. 35.00 (*0-685-45280-8*) Athenaeum Phila.

Prophetae Maiores: In Dialecto Linguae Aegyptiacae Memphitica Seu Coptica. Ed. by Henricus Tattam. (GER.). x, 978p. 1989. reprint ed. 298.00 (*3-487-09186-0*) G Olms Pubs.

Prophete: Le Jardin du Prophete. Kahlil Gibran. (FRE.). 1992. pap. 16.95 (*0-7859-2730-1*) Fr & Eur.

Prophetess. Barbara Wood. 1997. mass mkt. 188.73 (*0-446-16418-6*) Warner Bks.

Prophetess. Barbara Wood. 496p. 1997. reprint ed. mass mkt. 6.99 (*0-446-60380-5*, Pub. by Warner Bks) Little.

Prophetess: Conversations with Rana. Thea Alexander. 48p. (Orig.). 1972. pap. 10.00 (*0-913080-08-X*) Macro Bks.

Prophetess of Health see Prophetess of Health: Ellen G. White & the Origins of Seventh-Day Adventist Health Reform

Prophetess of Health: Ellen G. White & the Origins of Seventh-Day Adventist Health Reform. Ronald L. Numbers. LC 91-22807. Orig. Title: Prophetess of Health. (Illus.). 408p. (C). 1992. reprint ed. pap. text 19.95 (*0-87049-713-8*); reprint ed. lib. bdg. 49.95 (*0-87049-712-X*) U of Tenn Pr.

Prophetess of the Earth & the Apocalypso: Drahcira's Last Dance. Richard E. Kuykendall. LC 92-3182. 128p. (Orig.). 1992. pap. 12.95 (*0-932727-54-9*, N Paradigm Bks); lib. bdg. 19.95 (*0-932727-55-7*, N Paradigm Bks) Hope Pub Hse.

Prophethood in Islam. Abdul H. Siddiqui. 1992. pap. 5.00 (*1-56744-197-1*) Kazi Pubns.

***Prophethood of All Believers: A Study in Luke's Charismatic Theology.** Roger Stronstad. (Journal of Pentecostal Theology Supplement Ser.: No. 16). 136p. 1999. pap. 13.95 (*1-84127-005-9*, Pub. by Sheffield Acad) CUP Services.

Prophethood of Black Believers: An African-American Political Theology for Ministry. J. Deotis Roberts. LC 93-32901. 192p. (Orig.). 1994. pap. 19.95 (*0-664-25488-8*) Westminster John Knox.

Prophetia Merlini of Geoffrey of Monmouth: A Fifteenth Century English Commentary. Ed. by Caroline D. Eckhardt. 1982. pap. 12.00 (*0-910956-74-X*) Medieval Acad.

Prophetic. Barbara Hines. 144p. 1997. pap. 8.95 (*0-9660600-0-8*) Peculiar Treas.

Prophetic Analyst: Erich Fromm's Contributions to Psychoanalysis. Ed. by Maruicio Cortina & Michael Maccoby. 480p. 1996. 50.00 (*1-56821-621-1*) Aronson.

Prophetic & the Preacher see Sentido Profetico del Predicador

Prophetic Bible Time Intervals. Kathryn Gever. 1997. pap. write for info. (*1-57074-374-6*) Greyden Pr.

Prophetic Book of Mormon. Hugh Nibley. LC 88-30986. (Collected Works of Hugh Nibley: Vol. 8). xi, 595p. 1989. 26.95 (*0-87579-179-4*) Deseret Bk.

***Prophetic Books & Their Theological Witness.** Odil Hannes Steck. Tr. by James D. Nogalski. 280p. 2000. pap. 29.99 (*0-8272-2957-7*) Chalice Pr.

Prophetic Charisma: The Psychology of Revolutionary Religious Personalities. Len Oakes. LC 97-20929. xiii, 246p. 1997. pap. 19.95 (*0-8156-0398-3*) Syracuse U Pr.

Prophetic Charisma: The Psychology of Revolutionary Religious Personalities. Len Oakes. 192p. 1997. 39.95 (*0-8156-2700-9*) Syracuse U Pr.

Prophetic Christianity & the Liberation Movement in South Africa. Peter Walshe. LC 95-50810. 180p. (C). 1998. pap. text 14.00 (*0-9583807-9-1*) U of Notre Dame Pr.

Prophetic Church. Terry M. Crist, Jr. Ed. by Phyllis Mackall. (Illus.). (Orig.). (C). 1989. pap. 5.95 (*0-9623768-0-9*) SpiritBuilder.

***Prophetic Church Seminar.** Frank Damazio. 2000. pap. text 13.00 (*1-886849-52-8*) City Bible Pub.

Prophetic Commands. Bill Panko & Margaret Panko. 150p. (Orig.). Date not set. pap. 14.95 (*1-885342-25-X*) Creative Ways.

Prophetic Community. Earl Paulk. 140p. (Orig.). 1995. pap. 9.99 (*1-56043-841-X*, Treasure Hse) Destiny Image.

Prophetic Conflict: Its Effect upon Israelite Religion. James L. Crenshaw. (Beiheft zur Zeitschrift fuer die Alttestamentliche Wissenschaft Ser.: No. 124). 134p. (C). 1971. 66.15 (*3-11-003363-1*) De Gruyter.

***Prophetic Cry of Wisdom.** Dilley Nadesan. 1999. pap. write for info. (*0-7392-0481-5*, PO3820) Morris Pubng.

***Prophetic Deliverence.** Timothy C. Mather. 128p. 2000. pap. 7.99 (*1-930027-01-X*) Insight Intl.

Prophetic Destinies: Who Is Israel? Who Is the Church? (ENG & IND.). 1993. pap. write for info. (*0-934920-53-2*, B-39IN) Derek Prince.

Prophetic Destiny: The Saints in the Rocky Mountains. Paul Thomas Smith. 96p. 1996. 2.97 (*1-55503-918-9*, 01112171) Covenant Comms.

Prophetic Development: Insights to Maturing in the Prophetic Anointing & It's How. John Tetsola. (Prophetic Ser.: Vol. 2). (Illus.). 189p. (Orig.). 1999. pap. 11.99 (*1-889389-21-8*, Pub. by End-Time Wave) Spring Arbor Dist.

Prophetic Drama in the Old Testament. David Stacey. 1991. pap. 24.00 (*0-7162-0470-3*) Epworth Pr.

Prophetic Element in Modern Art. Dorothea Blom. LC 66-28100. (C). 1966. pap. 4.00 (*0-87574-148-7*) Pendle Hill.

Prophetic Element in the Church: As Conceived in the Theology of Karl Rahner. David Lowry. 258p. (C). 1990. lib. bdg. 50.50 (*0-8191-7857-8*) U Pr of Amer.

***Prophetic End Time Temple.** large type ed. Carol Crook. (Illus.). 78p. (C). 1999. ring bd. 22.95 (*0-939399-30-X*) Bks of Truth.

***Prophetic Etiquette: Helpful Guidelines for Giving & Receiving Prophecy.** Michael Sullivant. 2000. pap. 12.99 (*0-88419-675-5*) Creation House.

Prophetic Events. E. C. Hadley. 74p. pap. 4.95 (*0-88172-146-8*) Believers Bkshelf.

Prophetic Faith in Isaiah. Sheldon H. Blank. LC 57-9887. (Wayne Bks.: No. WB24). 253p. reprint ed. pap. 78.50 (*0-7837-3646-0*, 204351500009) Bks Demand.

Prophetic Families: or The Negro: His Origin, Destiny & Status. J. Troup Taylor. LC 70-89442. (Black Heritage Library Collection). 1977. 14.95 (*0-8369-8664-4*) Ayer.

Prophetic Figures in Late Second Temple Jewish Palestine: The Evidence from Josephus. Rebecca Gray. LC 92-22896. 256p. 1993. text 65.00 (*0-19-507615-X*) OUP.

Prophetic Flow. John J. Eckhardt & Tanya C. Stokes. 57p. (Orig.). 1991. pap. write for info. (*0-9627849-9-0*) Temperance Pub Hse.

Prophetic Flow. John J. Eckhardt. 57p. (Orig.). reprint ed. 5.00 (*0-9630567-5-1*) Crusaders Minist.

Prophetic Fragments. Cornel West. 315p. (C). 1988. 17.95 (*0-86543-085-3*); pap. write for info. (*0-86543-086-1*) Africa World.

Prophetic Genesis, Vol. 1. 2nd ed. E. Bernard Jordan. Ed. by Deborah Jones. (Illus.). 100p. (Orig.). 1992. reprint ed. pap. 10.00 (*0-939241-08-0*) Faith Print.

Prophetic Gospel: A Study of John & the Old Testament. Anthony T. Hanson. 400p. 55.95 (*0-567-09583-5*, Pub. by T & T Clark) Bks Intl VA.

Prophetic History of Christendom. R. K. Campbell. 7.95 (*0-88172-012-7*) Believers Bkshelf.

Prophetic Imagination. Walter Brueggemann. LC 78-54546. 128p. 1978. pap. 14.00 (*0-8006-1337-6*, 1-1337, Fortress Pr) Augsburg Fortress.

Prophetic Insight: The Higher Education & Pedagogy of African Americans. Ernest N. Bracey. LC 99-22439. 160p. 1999. pap. 26.50 (*0-7618-1384-5*) U Pr of Amer.

***Prophetic Insight: The Higher Education & Pedagogy of African Americans.** Ernest N. Bracey. LC 99-22439. 160p. 1999. 45.00 (*0-7618-1383-7*) U Pr of Amer.

Prophetic Inspiration after the Prophets: Maimonides & Other Medieval Authorities. Abraham Joshua Heschel. Ed. by Morris Faierstein. LC 94-13623. 1995. 24.95 (*0-88125-346-4*) Ktav.

***Prophetic Intercession: Letting God Lead Your Prayers.** Barbara Wentroble. LC 99-37027. 181p. 1999. pap. 9.99 (*0-8307-2376-5*, Regal Bks) Gospel Lght.

***Prophetic Invocations: Adhkar al-Sabah W'l-Masa'** Imam Abdallah Ibn Alawi. Tr. by Mostafa Al-Badawi. 80p. 2000. pap. 10.99 (*1-929694-10-5*) Starlatch Pr.

Prophetic Life: Powerful Truths for Powerful Leadership. Michael Lattiboudeaire. LC 96-72018. 400p. 1998. 19.95 (*1-889448-08-7*); pap. 14.95 (*1-889448-05-2*); pap. 6.99 (*1-889448-04-4*); pap. 6.99 (*1-889448-09-5*); pap., wbk. ed. 15.95 (*1-889448-06-0*); lib. bdg. 19.95 (*1-889448-07-9*); lib. bdg. 19.95 (*1-889448-11-7*); mass mkt. 14.95 (*1-889448-10-9*) NBN Publishers Group.

Prophetic Life: Powerful Truths for Powerful Leadership, 14 vols., No. 1. Michael Lattiboudeaire. LC 96-72018. 400p. 1998. 19.95 (*1-889448-03-6*) NBN Publishers Group.

Prophetic Medical Sciences. Sehban Ul-Hind. Tr. by Badr Azimabadi. 350p. 1989. 29.00 (*1-56744-360-5*) Kazi Pubns.

Prophetic Memory in Wordsworth's "Ecclesiastical Sonnets" Anne L. Rylestone. LC 89-26352. 160p. (C). 1991. 21.95 (*0-8093-1643-9*) S Ill U Pr.

Prophetic Milton. William Kerrigan. LC 74-6118. 297p. reprint ed. pap. 92.10 (*0-8357-9813-5*, 201696400004) Bks Demand.

Prophetic Ministry. Howard H. Brinton. (C). 1950. pap. 4.00 (*0-87574-054-5*) Pendle Hill.

Prophetic Ministry. Rick Joyner. 222p. 1997. 15.00 (*1-878327-62-3*, RJ1-021) Morning NC.

***Prophetic Ministry.** Rick Joyner. 200p. 1999. pap. 10.99 (*1-878327-90-9*) Morning NC.

***Prophetic Ministry.** T. A. Sparks. 144p. 2000. pap. 11.99 (*0-7684-4000-9*) McFarland & Co.

Prophetic Ministry & the Voices of the Prophets. T. A. Sparks. 280p. 1994. pap. text 11.20 (*1-883137-14-4*) Christ Stewards.

Prophetic Moment: An Essay on Spenser. Angus Fletcher. LC 73-130587. 1994. lib. bdg. 20.00 (*0-226-25332-5*) U Ch Pr.

Prophetic Mysteries Revealed: The Prophetic Significance of the Parables of Matthew 13 & the Letters of Revelation 2-3. Lehman Strauss. LC 80-17540. 256p. 1980. 14.99 (*0-87213-832-1*) Loizeaux.

Prophetic Novel. Molly A. Daniels. LC 91-17983. (American University Studies: English Language & Literature: Ser. IV, Vol. 166). XI, 158p. (C). 1991. text 34.95 (*0-8204-1266-X*) P Lang Pubng.

Prophetic Operations: Walking Through Prophetic Ministry. 2nd ed. Jonas Clark. (Illus.). 124p. (Orig.). 1996. reprint ed. pap. 8.00 (*1-886885-02-8*) Spirit Life.

Prophetic Oracles of Salvation in the Old Testament. Claus Westermann. Tr. by K. R. Crim. 252p. 1998. pap. 24.95 (*0-567-29197-9*, Pub. by T & T Clark) Bks Intl VA.

Prophetic Pastoral Practice. Charles V. Gerkin. LC 90-21916. 1991. pap. 7.50 (*0-687-34373-9*) Abingdon.

Prophetic Pentecostalism in Chile: A Case Study on Religion & Development Policy. Frans H. Kamsteeg. LC 97-43226. (Studies in Evangelicalism: No. 15). 240p. 1998. 59.50 (*0-8108-3440-5*) Scarecrow.

Prophetic Persona: Jeremiah & the Language of the Self. Timothy Polk. (JSOT Supplement Ser.: No. 32). 1984. 70.00 (*0-905774-70-1*, Pub. by Sheffield Acad); pap. 23.75 (*0-905774-71-X*, Pub. by Sheffield Acad) CUP Services.

Prophetic Picture Language: A Study in Parabolic Expressions. Marilyn J. Wright. (Illus.). 70p. (C). 1994. pap. 12.50 (*0-9632748-4-8*) Majesty Pubns.

Prophetic Pictures: Nathaniel Hawthorne's Knowledge & Uses of the Visual Arts, 99. Rita K. Gollin et al. LC 91-9554. (Contributions in American Studies: No. 99). 240p. 1991. 59.95 (*0-313-27573-4*, IPR/, Greenwood Pr) Greenwood.

Prophetic Power. Lam Kam Chuen. 1996. pap. 7.99 (*1-56229-471-7*) Pneuma Life Pub.

Prophetic Revelations of Paul Solomon: Earthward Toward a Heavenly Light. W. Alexander Wheeler. LC 94-31408. 320p. (Orig.). 1994. pap. 12.95 (*0-87728-831-3*) Weiser.

Prophetic Romance. Fuchsia Pickett. 154p. (Orig.). 1996. pap. 10.99 (*0-88419-423-X*) Creation House.

Prophetic Secrets & the New World Order. David A. Miller. LC 97-60986. 192p. 1997. per. 7.95 (*1-57258-089-5*) Teach Servs.

***Prophetic Sense of History in Medieval & Renaissance Europe: From Jerusalem to Cyprus.** Marjorie Reeves. LC 99-31184. (Variorum Collected Studies). 1999. 97.95 (*0-86078-805-9*) Ashgate Pub Co.

Prophetic Significance of the Different Church Doctrines: The Prophecies of Jesus, Peter & Paul. Wayne Brown. LC 97-40894. 203p. 2000. pap. 27.00 (*1-56072-480-3*, Nova Troitsa Bks) Nova Sci Pubs.

Prophetic Song. LaMar Boschman. 115p. 1999. write for info. (*1-883092-01-9*) L Boschman Minist.

Prophetic Song: The Psalms As Moral Discourse in Late Medieval England. Michael P. Kuczynski. LC 94-44651. (Middle Ages Ser.). (Illus.). 336p. 1995. text 37.50 (*0-8122-3271-2*) U of Pa Pr.

Prophetic Song of Songs. 3rd ed. Marian G. Berry. (Illus.). 283p. 1992. pap. 15.00 (*0-945383-43-6*) Teach Servs.

Prophetic Sons & Daughters: Female Preaching & Popular Religion in Industrial England. Deborah M. Valenze. LC 85-42755. 329p. 1985. reprint ed. pap. 102.00 (*0-608-03308-1*, 206402000008) Bks Demand.

***Prophetic Spirit of Catechesis: How We Share the Fire in Our Hearts.** Anne Marie Mongoven. LC 99-49017. 320p. 2000. pap. 22.95 (*0-8091-3922-7*) Paulist Pr.

***Prophetic Statements on Food Storage for Latter-Day Saints.** Neil H. Leash. 192p. 1999. pap. 13.98 (*0-88290-665-8*, 1255) Horizon Utah.

Prophetic Strain: The Greater Lyric in the Eighteenth Century. Anne Williams. LC 83-24103. (Orig.). 1995. lib. bdg. 26.50 (*0-226-89916-0*) U Ch Pr.

Prophetic Strain: The Greater Lyric in the Eighteenth Century. Anne Williams. LC 83-24103. 200p. (Orig.). 1996. pap. text 12.95 (*0-226-89917-9*) U Ch Pr.

Prophetic Stream. William Taber. LC 84-61291. (Orig.). 1984. pap. 1.00 (*0-87574-256-4*) Pendle Hill.

Prophetic Strength: Understanding the Prophetic Anointing As a Battle Axe for War. John Tetsola. (Prophetic Ser.: Vol. 4). (Illus.). 87p. (Orig.). 1999. pap. 8.99 (*1-889389-23-4*, Pub. by End-Time Wave) Spring Arbor Dist.

Prophetic Thought: Essays & Addresses. Sheldon H. Blank. LC 77-5898. (Jewish Perspectives Ser.: No. 2). 179p. reprint ed. pap. 55.50 (*0-7837-1398-3*, 204157900021) Bks Demand.

***Prophetic Tradition & Radical Rhetoric in America.** James Darsey. 1999. pap. text 19.00 (*0-8147-1924-4*) NYU Pr.

Prophetic Tradition & Radical Rhetoric in America. James F. Darsey. LC 97-4772. 1997. text 45.00 (*0-8147-1876-0*) NYU Pr.

Prophetic Tradition in American Poetry, 1835-1900. Aaron Kramer. 416p. 1975. 45.00 (*0-8386-6774-0*) Fairleigh Dickinson.

Prophetic Training Manual: A Comprehensive Guide & Training Manual for the Development of the Prophetic Anointing, the Training of Strong Prophetic Teams & the Establishment of Prophetic Ministry. John Tetsola. (Illus.). 394p. 1999. pap. 25.99 (*1-889389-18-8*, Pub. by End-Time Wave) Spring Arbor Dist.

Prophetic Vision for the 21st Century. Rick Joyner. LC 99-36562. 247p. 1999. pap. 14.99 (*0-7852-6936-3*, RJ1-029) Nelson.

Prophetic Visions & Economic Realities: Protestants, Jews, & Catholics Confront the Bishops' Letter on the Economy. Ed. by Charles R. Strain. LC 88-25842. 271p. reprint ed. pap. 84.10 (*0-7837-5562-7*, 204533700005) Bks Demand.

Prophetic Visions of the Future. Diane Stein. LC 99-33917. Orig. Title: Dreaming the Past, Dreaming the Future. 240p. 1999. pap. 16.95 (*1-58091-046-7*) Crossing Pr.

Prophetic Voice. Brian E. Fidler. (YA). (gr. 9-12). 1991. teacher ed. 25.00 (*1-881678-13-X*) CSEE.

Prophetic Voice for the Kingdom. Gregory L. Jackson. Ed. by Ross E. Paulson. LC 86-71907. (Augustana Historical Society Publications: No. 35). 239p. 1986. text 19.95 (*0-910184-35-6*) Augustana.

Prophetic Voice in the City: Meditations on the Prophet Jeremiah. Carlo M. Martini. Tr. by Vera Castelli Theisen from ITA. LC 97-14655. 160p. 1997. pap. 11.95 (*0-8146-2412-X*) Liturgical Pr.

Prophetic Voices. Ed. by Ruth W. Schuler et al. (Illus.). 288p. (Orig.). 1991. pap. 12.00 (*0-910083-20-7*) Heritage Trails.

Prophetic Voices: Black Preachers Speak on Behalf of Children. Black Community Crusade for Children Staff. 76p. (Orig.). 1993. pap. 10.95 (*1-881985-00-8*) Childrens Defense.

Prophetic Words of Hosea: A Morphological Study. Martin J. Buss. (Beiheft zur Zeitschrift fuer die Alttestamentliche Wissenschaft Ser.: No. 111). (C). 1969. 66.15 (*3-11-002579-5*) De Gruyter.

Prophetic Worlds: Indians & Whites on the Columbia Plateau. Christopher L. Miller. 180p. (C). 1985. text 35.00 (*0-8135-1084-8*) Rutgers U Pr.

***Prophetic Worship.** R. Loren Sandford. Ed. by Bill Miller. 132p. 1999. pap. 10.95 (*0-7392-0213-8*, PO3236) Morris Pubng.

Prophetic Worship. Marilyn J. Wright. (Illus.). 76p. (C). 1993. pap. 12.00 (*1-886232-20-2*) Majesty Pubns.

Prophetic Worship: Releasing the Presence of God. Vivien Hibbert. Date not set. pap. 15.95 (*1-892976-03-X*) Cuington Pr.

Prophetic Writings of Lady Eleanor Davies. Eleanor Davies. Ed. by Esther S. Cope. (Women Writers in English 1350-1850 Ser.). (Illus.). 400p. (C). 1995. text 65.00 (*0-19-507875-6*, 4537) OUP.

Prophetic Writings of Lady Eleanor Davies. Eleanor Davies. Ed. by Esther S. Cope. (Women Writers in English 1350-1850 Ser.). (Illus.). 400p. (C). 1995. pap. 26.00 (*0-19-508717-8*, 74) OUP.

Prophetic Writings of William Blake, 2 vols., Set. William Blake. (BCL1-PR English Literature Ser.). 1992. reprint ed. lib. bdg. 150.00 (*0-7812-7442-7*) Rprt Serv.

Prophetie des Andes. Tr. of Celestine Prophecy. (FRE.). pap., boxed set 16.95 incl. audio (*2-921997-17-7*, Pub. by Coffragants) Penton Overseas.

Prophetie et Royaute au Retour de l'Exil: Les Origines Litteraires de la Forme Massoretique du Livre de Jeremie. Yohanan Goldman. (Orbis Biblicus et Orientalis Ser.: Vol. 118). (FRE.). 259p. 1992. text 52.50 (*3-7278-0814-4*, Pub. by Presses Univ Fribourg) Eisenbrauns.

Prophetie im Streit vor dem Untergang Judas: Erzahlkommunikative Studien zur Entstehungssituation der Jesaja-und Jeremiaerzahlungen in II Reg 18-20 und Jer 37-40. Christof Hardmeier. (Beiheft zur Zeitschrift fuer die Alttestamentliche Wissenschaft Ser.: Band 187). xvii, 506p. 1990. lib. bdg. 136.95 (*3-11-011735-5*) De Gruyter.

Prophetie und Deuteronomium: Die Rezeption Prophetischer Theologie Durch das Deuteronomium. Konstantin Zobel. (Beiheft zur Zeitschrift fuer die Alttestamentliche Wissenschaft Ser.: Vol. 199). (GER.). vii, 267p. (C). 1992. lib. bdg. 83.10 (*3-11-012838-1*, 258-91) De Gruyter.

Prophets. (Bible People Ser.). 80p. 1996. pap. text 4.95 (*0-687-05528-8*) Abingdon.

Prophets. (Interpreting Biblical Texts Ser.). 2001. 18.95 (*0-687-00844-1*) Abingdon.

Prophets. Timothy Bryan. (Bible People Ser.). 1996. pap. 5.95 (*0-687-07415-0*) Abingdon.

Prophets, 3. (Following God Ser.). 1999. pap. 16.99 (*0-89957-302-9*) AMG Pubs.

Prophets, 2 vols., Vol. 1. Abraham Joshua Heschel. 256p. 1969. pap. 15.00 (*0-06-131421-8*, TB1421, Torch) HarpC.

Prophets, 2 vols., Vol. 2. Abraham Joshua Heschel. 320p. 1971. pap. 15.00 (*0-06-131557-5*, TB1557, Torch) HarpC.

Prophets see Oxford Illustrated Old Testament: With Drawings by Contemporary Artists

***Prophets: A Liberation-Critical Reading.** Carol J. Dempsey. LC 99-58914. 2000. pap. text 20.00 (*0-8006-3116-1*) Augsburg Fortress.

Prophets: A Sheffield Reader. Philip R. Davies. (Biblical Seminar Ser.: No. 42). 388p. 1996. pap. 19.95 (*1-85075-788-7*, Pub. by Sheffield Acad) CUP Services.

An Asterisk (*) at the beginning of an entry indicates that the title is appearing for the first time.

Prophets: God's Truth Tellers. Vinita H. Wright. (Fisherman Bible Studyguide Ser.). 80p. 1994. pap. text 4.99 (*0-87788-665-2*, H Shaw Pubs) Waterbrook Pr.

Prophets: Hearing the Word of the Lord. Clarence Vos. LC 93-23850. (Revelation Ser.). 1993. pap., student ed. 4.95 (*1-56212-040-9*) CRC Pubns.

Prophets: Hearing the Word of the Lord. Sierd Woudstra. (Revelation Ser.). 1995. pap., teacher ed. 6.75 (*1-56212-083-2*) CRC Pubns.

Prophets: Models for Humanity. Alia N. Athar. 240p. (YA). 1993. pap. 14.50 (*1-56744-425-3*) Kazi Pubns.

Prophets: The Assyrian Age, Vol. 1. Klaus Koch. Tr. by Margaret Kohl from GER. LC 79-8894. 192p. (C). 1982. pap. 20.00 (*0-8006-1648-0*, 1-1648, Fortress Pr) Augsburg Fortress.

Prophets: The Babylonian & Persian Period, Vol. 2. Klaus Koch. LC 79-8894. Vol. 2. 228p. 1984. pap. 20.00 (*0-8006-1756-8*, 1-1756, Fortress Pr) Augsburg Fortress.

Prophets & Conspirators in Prerevolutionary Russia. Adam B. Ulam. LC 98-5462. 418p. 1998. pap. text 29.95 (*0-7658-0443-3*) Transaction Pubs.

Prophets & Emperors: Human & Divine Authority from Augustus to Theodosius. David Potter. LC 94-25982. (Revealing Antiquity Ser.: 7). (Illus.). 344p. 1994. text 50.95 (*0-674-71565-9*, POTPRO) HUP.

Prophets & Kings. Ellen Gould Harmon White. 752p. 1917. 14.99 (*0-8163-0040-2*, 16642-1) Pacific Pr Pub Assn.

Prophets & Kings: The Rise & Fall of a Nation. Ellen Gould Harmon White. (Bible Study Companion Set Ser.: Vol. 2). 448p. (C). 1997. pap. 11.99 (*1-883012-51-1*) Remnant Pubns.

***Prophets & Kings of Israel, 2 vols.** Zondervan Publishing Staff. 1999. pap., student ed. 6.99 (*0-310-67897-8*) Zondervan.

Prophets & Markets. Morris Silver. 1982. lib. bdg. 85.50 (*0-89838-112-6*) Kluwer Academic.

Prophets & Our Times. R. Gerald Culleton. 1994. reprint ed. pap. 13.50 (*0-89555-050-4*) TAN Bks Pubs.

Prophets & Paradigms: Essays in Honor of Gene M. Tucker. Ed. by Stephen B. Reid. (JSOTS Ser.: No. 229). 248p. 1996. 70.00 (*1-85075-630-9*, Pub. by Sheffield Acad) CUP Services.

Prophets & Patrons: The French University & the Emergence of the Social Sciences. Terry N. Clark. LC 72-93947. (Illus.). 320p. 1973. 37.95 (*0-674-71580-2*) HUP.

Prophets & Paupers: Religion in the California Gold Rush, 1848-1869. Harland Hogue. 1996. 69.95 (*1-57309-083-2*) Intl Scholars.

Prophets & Paupers: Religion in the California Gold Rush, 1848-1869. Harland Hogue & Ray L. Welles. 182p. 1996. pap. 49.95 (*1-57309-082-4*) Intl Scholars.

Prophets & Personal Prophecy. Bill Hamon. 240p. (Orig.). 1987. pap. 13.99 (*0-939868-03-2*) Destiny Image.

Prophets & Pioneers. Beth Lefgren & Jennifer Jackson. 1996. pap. 8.95 (*1-57008-280-4*) Bookcraft Inc.

Prophets & Politics: A Handbook on the Washington Offices of the U. S. Churches. Roy Beck. (Illus.). 193p. (Orig.). 1994. pap. 8.95 (*1-881780-08-2*) Social Contract.

Prophets & Professors: Essays on the Lives & Works of Modern Poets. Bruce Bawer. 352p. 1995. 26.95 (*1-885266-05-7*); pap. 15.95 (*1-885266-04-9*) Story Line.

Prophets & Profits: What's to Be Learned from Daddy Grace. Paul E. Hunter. (Illus.). 89p. (Orig.). 1995. reprint ed. pap. 5.00 (*0-9642820-3-8*) Revelation NY.

Prophets & Prophecies of the Old Testament. 2nd ed. Duane S. Crowther. LC 66-25508. (Illus.). 656p. 1993. reprint ed. 25.98 (*0-88290-022-6*) Horizon Utah.

Prophets & Prophecy: Seven Key Messengers. Frank H. Seilhamer. LC 76-62603. 95p. (Orig.). reprint ed. pap. 30.00 (*0-608-17172-7*, 202787800056) Bks Demand.

Prophets & Prophecy in Today's Church. James O. Murphy & Carolyn S. Murphy. 281p. 1994. reprint ed. pap. 10.95 (*1-893921-01-8*) Hundred Fold.

Prophets & Prophethood. Muhammad A. Sabuni. LC 98-28000. 1998. write for info. (*1-881963-66-7*) Al-Saadawi Pubns.

Prophets & Prophetic Leaders: Understanding the Heart, the Character & Characteristics of Prophetic Leadership. John Tetsola. (Prophetic Ser.: Vol. 1). 107p. (Orig.). 1999. pap. 9.99 (*1-889389-20-X*, Pub. by End-Time Wave) Spring Arbor Dist.

Prophets & the Prophetic Movement, Vol. 2. Bill Hamon. 252p. (Orig.). 1990. pap. 13.99 (*0-939868-04-0*) Destiny Image.

Prophets & the Rise of Judaism. Adolphe Lods. Tr. by Samuel H. Hooke. LC 77-109772. (Illus.). 378p. (C). 1971. reprint ed. lib. bdg. 69.50 (*0-8371-4262-8*, LOPR, Greenwood Pr) Greenwood.

Prophets & Their Times. rev. ed. John M. Smith. Ed. by William A. Irwin. LC 25-6864. 1941. lib. bdg. 20.00 (*0-226-76356-0*) U Ch Pr.

Prophet's Army: Trotskyists in America, 1928-1941, 56. Constance A. Myers. LC 76-15330. (Contributions in American History Ser.: No. 56). 281p. 1977. 59.95 (*0-8371-9030-4*, MPA/, Greenwood Pr) Greenwood.

Prophets As Preachers: An Introduction to the Hebrew Prophets. Gary V. Smith. 1998. pap. text 29.99 (*0-8054-1860-1*) Broadman.

Prophet's Biography Series for Children, Nos. 1-10. Abdulhamid Jodah Al Sahhar. Ed. by Mary Shahnaz & Hamid Quinlan. Tr. by Outaiba Elhuwaib from ARA. LC 82-70350. Orig. Title: Kasas Alsyrah. (Illus.). 16p. 1982. pap. 2.00 (*0-89259-025-4*) Am Trust Pubns.

Prophets' Bread. John G. Lynch. 1989. pap. 7.25 (*1-55673-131-0*, 9856) CSS OH.

Prophet's Children: Travels on the American Left. Tim Wohlforth. LC 93-26388. (Historical Memories Ser.). (Illus.). 360p. (C). 1994. pap. 18.50 (*0-391-03802-8*); text 49.95 (*0-391-03819-2*) Humanities.

Prophet's Daughters. Geraldine Brooks. 1992. write for info. (*0-679-41245-X*) McKay.

Prophets for a Day of Judgment. Albert E. Baker. LC 72-90605. (Essay Index Reprint Ser.). 1977. 19.95 (*0-8369-1390-6*) Ayer.

Prophets for a New Day. Margaret Walker. LC 78-130304. 32p. (YA). (gr. 12). 1970. pap. 7.00 (*0-910296-21-9*) Broadside Pr.

Prophets for the End of Time. Marcos Donnelly. 1998. mass mkt. 5.99 (*0-671-57775-1*) S&S Trade.

Prophets for Young People. Esta Cassway. LC 94-2498. 376p. (J). 1994. 50.00 (*1-56821-148-1*) Aronson.

Prophet's Friend. Clarin D. Ashby. 436p. pap. 14.95 (*1-55517-210-5*) CFI Dist.

***Prophets Have Spoken** Eric Bateman. LC 99-23282. 1999. write for info. (*1-57345-503-2*) Deseret Bk.

Prophets in Babylon: Five California Novelists in the 1930s. Margaret C. Jones. LC 91-32462. (American University Studies: American Literature: Ser. XXIV, Vol. 28). 156p. (C). 1992. text 33.95 (*0-8204-1750-5*) P Lang Pubng.

Prophets in Their Own Country: Living Saints & the Making of Sainthood in the Later Middle Age. Aviad M. Kleinberg. 1997. pap. text 12.95 (*0-226-43972-0*) U Ch Pr.

Prophets in Their Own Country: Living Saints & the Making of Sainthood in the Later Middle Ages. Aviad M. Kleinberg. LC 91-38561. 200p. 1992. 30.50 (*0-226-43971-2*) U Ch Pr.

Prophets of a New Age: The Politics of Hope in 1800, 1900, & 2000. Martin Green. (Illus.). 288p. 1992. text 25.00 (*0-684-19316-7*) S&S Trade.

Prophets of Agroforestry: Guarani Communities & Commercial Gathering. Richard K. Reed. LC 94-10634. (Illus.). 264p. (C). 1995. text 37.50 (*0-292-77067-7*) U of Tex Pr.

Prophets of Allah, Vol. I. Suhaib H. Ghazi. Ed. by Abidullah Ghazi & Tasneema Ghazi. LC 95-76089. (Illus.). 67p. (J). (gr. 2 up). 1992. pap. text 7.00 (*1-56316-350-0*) Iqra Intl Ed Fdtn.

Prophets of Allah, Vol. 2. Mildred El-Amin. Ed. by Suhaib H. Ghazi & Huda Quraishi. (Prophets of Allah Ser.). (Illus.). 67p. (J). (gr. 2 up). 1993. text 7.00 (*1-56316-357-8*) Iqra Intl Ed Fdtn.

Prophets of Allah, Vol. III. unabridged ed. Suhaib Ghazi & Mildred El-Amin. Ed. by Huda Quraishi. LC 95-82409. (Illus.). 174p. (J). (gr. 3-5). 1997. 7.00 (*1-56316-378-0*) Iqra Intl Ed Fdtn.

Prophets of Allah V. unabridged ed. Suhaib Ghazi. Ed. by Mahlaqa Patel & Carolyn Baugh. LC 95-80224. (Illus.). 132p. (J). (gr. 1-5). 1996. 7.00 (*1-56316-356-X*) Iqra Intl Ed Fdtn.

Prophets of Allah IV. Suhaib H. Ghazi. Ed. by Mahlaqa Patel. LC 95-76089. (Illus.). 80p. (J). (gr. 1-5). 1995. text 7.00 (*1-56316-371-3*) Iqra Intl Ed Fdtn.

Prophets of Deceit. J. L. Davidson. 1960. 5.25 (*0-88027-016-0*) Firm Foun Pub.

Prophets of Deceit: A Study of the Techniques of the American Agitator. 2nd ed. Leo Lowenthal & Norbert Guterman. LC 68-31291. (Paperbounds Ser.: No. PB-8). (Illus.). xx, 164p. 1970. pap. 1.95 (*0-87015-182-7*) Pacific Bks.

Prophets of Decline. 1996. 25.00 (*0-02-914581-3*) Free Pr.

Prophets of Doom: Literature As a Socio-Political Phenomenon in Modern Iran. Mohammad R. Ghanoonparvar. LC 84-17304. 242p. 1985. pap. text 22.50 (*0-8191-4293-X*); lib. bdg. 52.00 (*0-8191-4292-1*) U Pr of Amer.

Prophets of Doom: Millennium Edition. Daniel Cohen. LC 98-38462. 144p. (YA). (gr. 7 up). 1999. 20.90 (*0-7613-1317-6*, Copper Beech Bks) Millbrook Pr.

Prophets of Doom in an Age of Optimism. V. Kerry Inman. (Orig.). 1981. pap. 4.95 (*0-934688-02-8*) Great Comm Pubns.

Prophets of Extremity: Nietzsche, Heidegger, Foucault, Derrida. Allan Megill. 1985. pap. 17.95 (*0-520-06028-8*, Pub. by U CA Pr) Cal Prin Full Svc.

Prophets of Fire: The Elijah Message for the End Time. Brian Jones. LC 98-31887. 1999. 11.99 (*0-8163-1704-6*) Pacific Pr Pub Assn.

Prophets of Heaven & Hell. Charles R. Buxton. LC 78-100796. 1970. reprint ed. pap. 75.00 (*0-8383-0086-3*) M S G Haskell Hse.

Prophets of Hope Model: A Weekend Workshop. Carmen Cervantes et al. LC 96-71261. (Prophets of Hope Ser.: Vol. 3).Tr. of Modelo Profetas de Esperanza. (Illus.). 72p. (Orig.). 1997. pap. 4.95 (*0-88489-451-7*) St Marys.

Prophets of Israel. Leon J. Wood. 416p. (C). 1998. pap. 19.99 (*0-8010-2198-7*) Baker Bks.

Prophets of Israel: And Their Place in History to the Close of the Eighth Century, B.C. William Robertson Smith. LC 77-87666. 504p. reprint ed. 61.50 (*0-404-16403-X*) AMS Pr.

Prophets of Joy. Steven C. Warner. pap. write for info. (*1-58459-051-3*, 7215) Wrld Lib Pubns.

Prophets of Joy: A Spirituality for the Baptized. Jean Miller. 1990. pap. 9.95 (*0-87193-268-7*) Dimension Bks.

Prophets of Modern Indian Nationalism: Raja Rammohun Roy, Swami Dayananda Saraswati, Ishwar Chandra Vidyasagar, Bankim Chandra Chatterji, Swami Vivekananda, Dababhai Naoroji, Mahadev Govind-Ranade & Pherozeshah Mehta. Arun Bhattacharjee. viii, 213p. 1993. 25.00 (*81-7024-535-4*, Pub. by Ashish Pub Hse) Nataraj Bks.

Prophets of Old & the Day of the End: Zechariah, the Book of Watchers, & Apocalyptic. Eibert J. Tigchelaar. 1995. 99.50 (*90-04-10356-2*) Brill Academic Pubs.

Prophets of Order: The Rise of the New Class, Technocracy & Socialism in America. Donald Stabile. LC 84-50939. 296p. 1984. 35.00 (*0-89608-230-X*); pap. 10.50 (*0-89608-229-6*) South End Pr.

Prophets of Past Time: Seven British Autobiographers, 1880-1914. Carl Dawson. LC 87-30025. 280p. 1988. reprint ed. pap. 86.80 (*0-608-03725-7*, 206455000009) Bks Demand.

***Prophets of Peace: Pacifism & Cultural Identity in Japan's New Religions.** Robert Kisala. LC 99-35260. (Illus.). 254p. 1999. text 49.00 (*0-8248-2228-5*); pap. text 24.95 (*0-8248-2267-6*) UH Pr.

Prophets of Prosperity: America's First Political Economists. Paul K. Conkin. LC 79-3251. 347p. reprint ed. pap. 107.60 (*0-608-18249-4*, 205669700081) Bks Demand.

***Prophets of Rage: The Black Freedom Struggle in San Francisco, 1945-1969.** Daniel E. Crowe. LC 00-22424. (Studies in African American History & Culture). 2000. write for info. (*0-8153-3766-3*) Garland.

Prophets of Rebellion: Millenarian Protest Movements Against the European Colonial Order. Michael Adas. LC 78-26775. 271p. reprint ed. pap. 84.10 (*0-7837-2453-5*, 204260600005) Bks Demand.

Prophets of Recognition: Ideology & the Individual in Novels by Ralph Ellison, Toni Morrison, Saul Bellow & Eudora Welty. Julia Eichelberger. LC 99-20908. (Southern Literary Studies). 248p. 1999. text 49.95 (*0-8071-2358-7*); pap. text 24.95 (*0-8071-2528-8*) La State U Pr.

Prophets of Regulation. Thomas K. McCraw. (Illus.). 416p. 1986. pap. text 16.50 (*0-674-71608-6*) Belknap Pr.

Prophets of Regulation: Charles Francis Adams, Louis D. Brandeis, James M. Landis, Alfred E. Kahn. Thomas K. McCraw. LC 84-296. 416p. 1984. 32.00 (*0-674-71607-8*) Belknap Pr.

Prophets of the Bible. Lester Sumrall. 86p. (C). 1988. pap. text 10.00 (*0-937580-14-7*) Sumrall Pubng.

Prophets of the Dark Side. Paul Davids. LC 94-137284. (Star Wars: No. 6). 128p. (YA). (gr. 4-7). 1993. pap. 4.50 (*0-553-15892-9*) Bantam.

Prophets of the Dark Side. Paul Davids. (Star Wars: No. 6). (YA). 1993. 9.09 (*0-606-05557-6*, Pub. by Turtleback) Demco.

Prophets of the Dark Side see **Star Wars**

Prophets of the Jews. Norman Bull. (Bible Story & Its Background Ser.: Vol. 3). 204p. (J). (gr. 2-7). 1984. pap. 12.95 (*0-7175-0979-6*) Dufour.

Prophets of the Left: American Socialist Thought in the Twentieth Century, 109. Robert Hyfler. LC 83-18327. (Contributions in Political Science Ser.: No. 109). 187p. 1984. 52.95 (*0-313-23390-X*, HYP/, Greenwood Pr) Greenwood.

Prophets of the Lord. Mary Evans. 267p. (Orig.). 1992. reprint ed. pap. 17.95 (*0-85364-483-7*, Pub. by Paternoster Pub) OM Literature.

***Prophets of the Obvious: Under Your Nose, in Your Face Life Tactics.** Lisa Bell & Beverly Lerner. (Illus.). 2000. 19.95 (*1-893569-09-8*) Accolade Pub Co.

Prophets of the Restoration: Portraits of Latter-Day Saint Presidents in Counted Cross Stitch. Jean D. Crowther. 24p. (Orig.). 1988. pap. 8.98 (*0-88290-321-7*) Horizon Utah.

Prophets of the Revolution see **Profetas de la Revolucion**

Prophets of the Soul. Joseph M. Gray. LC 71-156655. (Essay Index Reprint Ser.). 1977. reprint ed. 20.95 (*0-8369-2277-8*) Ayer.

Prophets of Yesterday & Their Message for Today. John Kelman. LC 74-152181. (Essay Index Reprint Ser.). 1977. 19.95 (*0-8369-2193-3*) Ayer.

Prophets or Profits? Elizabeth Baron. Ed. by Sandra Frazier-Delsignore. 187p. (Orig.). 1993. pap. 12.95 (*1-884039-01-4*) Mystic-Art Media.

Prophets, Pitfalls & Principles: God's Prophetic People Today. Bill Hamon. 238p. (Orig.). 1991. pap. 13.99 (*0-939868-05-9*) Destiny Image.

Prophets, Poets, Priests, & Kings. F. Washington Jarvis. (YA). (gr. 8-12). 1989. reprint ed. pap. text 16.00 (*1-877653-05-5*) Wayside Pub.

Prophets, Poets, Priests, & Kings: The Old Testament Story. F. Washington Jarvis. 288p. 1984. 8.95 (*0-8164-2089-0*) Harper SF.

Prophet's Power. Sean Wesley Smith. (Unreal Ser.: No. 2). 1998. per. 5.99 (*0-671-01882-5*) PB.

Prophets, Priesthood Keys, & Succession. Hoyt W. Brewster, Jr. LC 91-32110. 154p. 1991. 10.95 (*0-87579-560-9*) Deseret Bk.

Prophet's Pulpit. Patrick D. Gaffney. 408p. 1996. pap. 20.00 (*0-614-21474-2*, 993) Kazi Pubns.

Prophet's Pulpit: Islamic Preaching in Contemporary Egypt. Patrick D. Gaffney. LC 93-34827. (Comparative Studies on Muslim Societies: No. 20). 1994. 58.00 (*0-520-08471-3*, Pub. by U CA Pr); pap. 24.95 (*0-520-08472-1*, Pub. by U CA Pr) Cal Prin Full Svc.

Prophet's Return: God's Missions & the Manners of Men. Dennis A. Doeing. LC 96-94680. iv, 666p. (Orig.). 1997. pap. 26.00 (*0-9654224-1-0*) Ionisus Pr.

Prophet's Return from Exile. Ruth W. Schuler. (Illus.). 84p. (Orig.). (C). 1984. pap. 4.00 (*0-910083-17-7*) Heritage Trails.

Prophets Speak to Our Time. George Drew. 62p. (Orig.). 1981. pap. 7.95 (*0-940754-09-6*) Ed Ministries.

Prophet's Speech at Tabuk. abr. ed. Abdullah. 16p. (Orig.). 1984. pap. 1.00 (*0-916157-02-4*) African Islam Miss Pubns.

Prophets Still Speak: Messiah in Both Testaments. Fred J. Meldau. 1988. 8.95 (*0-915540-42-8*) Frnds Israel.

Prophet's Story: Buy Those Who Knew Him. Sophia Johanson. 160p. (Orig.). 1995. pap. text 12.50 (*1-885186-00-2*) Amber Pr OK.

Prophets True & False. Oswald G. Villard. LC 75-93384. (Essay Index Reprint Ser.). 1977. 30.95 (*0-8369-1386-8*) Ayer.

***Prophet's Way: Touching the Power of Life.** Thom Hartmann. 2000. 24.00 (*0-609-60549-6*) Harmony Bks.

Prophet's Way: Touching the Power of Life. Thom Hartmann. 333p. 1997. pap. 12.95 (*0-9655728-0-3*) Mythical Bks.

Prophets Without Honour: Freud, Kafka, Einstein, & Their World. Frederic V. Grunfeld. Ed. by Joshua Sitzer & Philip Turner. (Kodansha Globe Ser.). (Illus.). 368p. 1996. pap. 15.00 (*1-56836-107-6*, Kodansha Globe) Kodansha.

***Prophets Without Vision: Subjectivity & the Sacred in Contemporary American Writing.** Hedda Ben-Bassat. LC 99-54765. 216p. 2000. 38.50 (*0-8387-5433-3*) Bucknell U Pr.

Prophets' Words & Actions. Henry R. Rust. 1990. pap. 5.95 (*0-940754-89-4*, 3553) Ed Ministries.

Prophezei: Humanismus und Reformation in Zurich Ausgewahlte Aufsatze und Vortrage Zu Seinem 70. Geburtstag Am 12. Februar 1993. Fritz Busser. Ed. by Alfred Schindler. (Zurcher Beitrage Zur Reformationsgeschichte Ser.: Bd. 17). (GER.). 241p. 1994. 48.95 (*3-906752-60-7*, Pub. by P Lang) P Lang Pubng.

Prophylaxis of Infectious & Other Diseases by Means of Vaccination & the Use of Immunoglobulins. Ed. by T. M. Inderbitzin. (Monographs in Allergy: Vol. 9). (Illus.). 300p. 1975. 66.25 (*3-8055-1779-3*) S Karger.

Propiedad, Tenencia y Redistribucion de Tierras en la Legislacion de America Central y Mexico. (SPA.). 166p. 1986. 20.00 (*92-5-302472-0*, Pub. by FAO) Bernan Associates.

Propliners: A Half Century of the Worlds Great Propeller-Driven Airliners. Clinton H. Groves. (Enthusiast Color Ser.). (Illus.). 96p. 1994. pap. 13.95 (*0-87938-866-8*) MBI Pubg.

Propogation of Electromagnetic Waves in Plasmas. Vitaly L. Ginzburg & V. A. Fock. LC 63-10136. (International Series of Monographs on Electronics & Instrumentation: Vol. 7). 1964. 248.00 (*0-08-010073-2*, Pub. by Pergamon Repr) Franklin.

Propolis: Nature's Energizer. Carlson Wade. (Good Health Guide Ser.). 32p. (Orig.). 1987. pap. 2.95 (*0-87983-329-7*, Keats Publng) NTC Contemp Pub Co.

Propolis Power-Plus. Joan A. Friedrich & Carlson Wade. Ed. by Don R. Bensen. (Good Health Guides Ser.). 48p. 1996. pap. 3.95 (*0-87983-698-9*, 36989K, Keats Publng) NTC Contemp Pub Co.

Proponents of Limited Monarchy in Sixteenth Century France. Beatrice Reynolds. LC 68-58616. (Columbia University. Studies in the Social Sciences: No. 334). reprint ed. 22.50 (*0-404-51334-4*) AMS Pr.

Proportion: Philosophy, Science & Architecture. Richard Padovan. LC 98-49274. 1999. pap. 39.99 (*0-419-22780-6*, E & FN Spon) Routledge.

Proportion & Style in Ancient Egyptian Art. Gay Robins. LC 93-65. (Illus.). 296p. (Orig.). 1994. pap. 19.95 (*0-292-77064-2*); text 40.00 (*0-292-77060-X*) U of Tex Pr.

Proportion of Industrial Gears. G. E. Katzenmeyer. (Technical Papers: Vol. P81). (Illus.). 14p. 1922. pap. text 30.00 (*1-55589-178-0*) AGMA.

Proportional Form in the Sonnets of the Sidney Circle: Loving in Truth. Tom W. Parker. (Oxford English Monographs). (Illus.). 268p. 1998. text 75.00 (*0-19-818443-3*) OUP.

***Proportional Reasoning.** Sheldon Erickson. Ed. by Betty Cordel. (Illus.). ix, 212p. (YA). (gr. 6-9). 1999. teacher ed. 16.95 (*1-881431-78-9*, 1317) AIMS Educ Fnd.

Proportional Representation: Critics of the British Electoral System 1820-1945. Jenifer Hart. 320p. 1992. text 69.00 (*0-19-820136-2*) OUP.

Proportional Representation: With Chapters on the Initiative, the Referendum & Primary Elections. 2nd ed. John R. Commons. LC 66-21662. xi, 369p. 1967. reprint ed. 45.00 (*0-678-00222-3*) Kelley.

Proportional Representation in Presidential Nominating Politics. Paul T. David & James W. Ceaser. LC 79-4387. 314p. reprint ed. pap. 97.40 (*0-8357-2708-4*, 203982100013) Bks Demand.

Proportioning Concrete Mixes. American Concrete Institute Staff. LC 74-18167. (ACI Publication: No. SP-46). (Illus.). 519p. reprint ed. pap. 160.90 (*0-7837-5217-2*, 204494800005) Bks Demand.

Proportionsproblem in der Architekturanschauung: Frankreich, 18. Horst Mellenthin. (Studien Zur Kunstgeschichte Ser.: Vol. 90). (GER.). 347p. 1995. write for info. (*3-487-09958-6*) G Olms Pubs.

Propos. deluxe ed. Alain. (Pleiade Ser.: Vol. 2). (FRE.). 1408p. 1973. 95.00 (*0-7859-4642-X*, F33650) Fr & Eur.

Propos, Vol. 1. deluxe ed. Alain. (Pleiade Ser.). (FRE.). 1424p. 1956. 95.00 (*0-7859-4636-5*, F21170) Fr & Eur.

Propos de Paris. Henri Cartier-Bresson. (Illus.). 168p. 1998. pap. 35.00 (*0-8212-2496-4*, Pub. by Bulfinch Pr) Little.

Propos Spectacle: Etudes de Pragmatique Theatrale. Sanda Golopentia. (Studies in the Humanities: Vol. 20). (FRE.). VIII, 255p. (C). 1996. text 57.95 (*0-8204-2855-8*) P Lang Pubng.

Propos sur la Litterature Outaouaise & Franco-Ontarienne. Rene Dionne. LC 79-361598. (Documents de Travail due Centre de Recherche en Civilisation Canadienne-Francaise Ser.: Vol. 11). (FRE.). 211p. 1978. reprint ed. pap. 65.50 (*0-608-02181-4*, 206285000004) Bks Demand.

***Proposal.** K. A. Applegate. (Animorphs Ser.: No. 35). (J). (gr. 3-7). 1999. mass mkt. 4.99 (*0-439-07035-X*, Pub. by Scholastic Inc) Penguin Putnam.

Proposal. Adapted by C. Archer. LC 95-53078. (Christy Fiction Ser.: Vol. 5). 128p. (J). (gr. 5-9). 1995. mass mkt. 4.99 (*0-8499-3918-6*) Tommy Nelson.

Proposal. John Maloney. LC 98-54307. 112p. 1999. pap. 13.00 (*1-58195-004-7*, Pub. by Zoland Bks) Consort Bk Sales.

Proposal. Margaret E. Porter. 384p. 1998. mass mkt. 5.99 (*0-380-79557-4*, Avon Bks) Morrow Avon.

P

An Asterisk (*) at the beginning of an entry indicates that the title is appearing for the first time.

Proposal. Linda Turner. Vol. 847. 1998. per. 4.25 (*0-373-07847-1*, 1-07847-6) Silhouette.

Proposal: Key to an Effective Foreign Policy. Max F. Millikan & Walt W. Rostow. LC 76-39842. 170p. 1977. reprint ed. lib. bdg. 49.75 (*0-8371-9346-X*, MIAPR, Greenwood Pr) Greenwood.

Proposal Development: How to Respond & Win the Bid. 3rd rev. ed. Bud Porter-Roth. LC 98-21244. (Illus.). 264p. 1998. pap. 21.95 (*1-55571-431-5*, PROPP) PSI Resch.

Proposal for a Charter to Build a Railroad from Lake Michigan to the Pacific Ocean. Hartwell Carver. 50p. 1987. pap. 6.95 (*0-87770-410-4*) Ye Galleon.

Proposal for Gearing Velocity Standard. R. L. Benford. (Technical Papers: Vol. P109.17). (Illus.). 16p. 1966. pap. text 30.00 (*1-55589-181-0*) AGMA.

Proposal for Putting Reform to the Vote Throughout the Kingdom. Percy Bysshe Shelley. LC 74-30280. (Shelley Society, Extra Ser.: No. 5). reprint ed. 29.50 (*0-404-11523-3*) AMS Pr.

Proposal for the Load/Capacity Calculation Formulae of Bevel Gears. L. Gui-Ming. (1984 Fall Technical Meeting Ser.: Vol. 84FTM11). 5p. 1984. pap. text 30.00 (*1-55589-093-8*) AGMA.

Proposal Planning & Writing. 2nd ed. Lynn E. Miner et al. LC 98-16683. 184p. 1998. pap. 34.50 (*1-57356-141-X*) Oryx Pr.

Proposal Preparation. 2nd ed. Rodney D. Stewart & Ann L. Stewart. LC 91-41581. 384p. 1992. 125.00 (*0-471-55269-0*) Wiley.

Proposal Preparation for Technical Staff Contributors. Dave Adamy. 110p. 1990. pap. 19.95 (*1-885897-01-4*) Lynx Pubng.

Proposal Savvy: A Guide for Journalists, Public Relations, & Advertising Writers. Elise K. Parsigian. LC 95-41789. 240p. 1996. 45.00 (*0-7619-0026-8*); pap. 21.95 (*0-7619-0027-6*) Sage.

Proposal to Require Traffic Alert & Collision Avoidance Systems on Cargo Aircraft. LC 98-107828. v, 237 p. 1997. write for info. (*0-16-055393-8*) USGPO.

Proposal Writer's Swipe File. Ed. by Susan Ezell-Kalish et al. LC 81-50258. 162p. 1993. pap. 21.95 (*0-914756-45-1*, 600025) Taft Group.

Proposal Writers Workshop. V. C. League. Ed. by Odessa Bethea. LC 98-93880. 350p. 1998. pap. 24.95 (*0-9636195-5-1*) Curry-Co Pubns.

Proposal Writing. Soraya M. Coley. (Human Services Guides Ser.: Vol. 63). 160p. (C). 1990. pap. text 18.95 (*0-8039-3232-4*) Sage.

Proposal Writing. Pfeiffer. LC 99-33817. (Illus.). 335p. 1999. pap. text 34.80 (*0-13-658213-3*) P-H.

Proposal Writing & Costing Techniques Handbook. rev. ed. Ed. by Thomas C. Charland. (Illus.). 118p. (C). 1998. spiral bd. 29.95 (*0-9610754-1-4*) Manage Co In.

Proposals for Carrying on Certain Public Works in the City of Edinburgh. Gilbert Elliot. LC 78-72778. (Scottish Enlightenment Ser.). reprint ed. 37.50 (*0-404-17629-1*) AMS Pr.

Proposals That Win Federal Contracts: How to Plan, Price, Write & Negotiate to Get Your Fair Share of Government Business. Barry L. McVay. LC 88-62678. (Federal Contracting Ser.). 334p. (Orig.). 1989. pap. 24.95 (*0-912481-08-0*) Panoptic Ent.

Proposals That Work: A Guide for Planning Dissertations & Grant Proposals. 3rd ed. Lawrence F. Locke et al. (Illus.). 320p. (C). 1993. text 52.00 (*0-8039-5066-7*); pap. text 22.95 (*0-8039-5067-5*) Sage.

***Proposals That Work: A Guide for Planning Dissertations & Grant Proposals.** 4th ed. Lawrence F. Locke. LC 99-6594. 350p. 2000. 59.95 (*0-7619-1706-3*) Sage.

***Proposals to Provide Rights to Victims of Crime: Congressional Hearings.** Ed. by Henry J. Hyde. 125p. (C). 1999. reprint ed. pap. text 25.00 (*0-7881-8289-7*) DIANE Pub.

Proposed Absorbtion of Mexico in 1847-48. Edward G. Bourne. (Works of Edward Gaylord Bourne). 1989. reprint ed. lib. bdg. 79.00 (*0-7812-2009-2*) Rprt Serv.

Proposed Acceptance Process for Commercial Off-the-Shelf Software in Reactor Applications. 1997. lib. bdg. 250.95 (*0-8490-7737-0*) Gordon Pr.

Proposed Amendments. U. S. Library of Congress, Legislative Reference S. Ed. by Charles C. Tansill. LC 75-35363. (U. S. Government Documents Program Ser.). 148p. 1976. reprint ed. lib. bdg. 65.00 (*0-8371-8606-4*, USPA, Greenwood Pr) Greenwood.

Proposed Amendments to the Constitution: A Monograph on the Resolutions Introduced in Congress Proposing Amendments to the Constitution of the United States of America, 2nd sess. House. Doc. 551--551. Michael A. Musmanno. LC 75-35374. (U. S. Government Documents Program Ser.). 253p. 1976. reprint ed. lib. bdg. 65.00 (*0-8371-8610-2*, MUPAC) Greenwood.

Proposed Amendments to the Federal Rules of Evidence. Litigation Section Staff. 155p. 1985. 25.00 (*0-685-14430-5*, 531-0047) Amer Bar Assn.

Proposed Application Factors for Industrial & High Speed Gearing. Darle W. Dudley. (Technical Papers: Vol. P159.02). (Illus.). 16p. 1969. pap. text 30.00 (*1-55589-204-3*) AGMA.

Proposed Audit & Accounting Guide Audits of Employee Benefit Plans. 3rd rev. ed. American Institute of Certified Public Accountants. LC HD7105.4.A9. (Exposure Draft Ser.). 227p. pap. 70.40 (*0-7837-0072-5*, 204032100016) Bks Demand.

Proposed Audit & Accounting Guide for Consideration of the Internal Control Structure in a Financial Statement Audit: August 21, 1989. American Institute of Certified Public Accountants. LC HF5667.. (Exposure Draft Ser.). 229p. reprint ed. pap. 71.00 (*0-8357-4259-8*, 203705100007) Bks Demand.

Proposed Constitutional Amendments & Referred Laws, 1968. Ronald Schmidt. 1968. 1.00 (*1-55614-097-5*) U of SD Gov Res Bur.

Proposed Constitutional Amendments to Balance the Federal Budget. United States Government Printing Office Staff. LC 95-144466. (S. Prt. Ser.). xiii, 2383 p. 1994. write for info. (*0-16-046743-8*); write for info. (*0-16-046436-6*); write for info. (*0-16-046371-8*); write for info. (*0-16-046370-X*) USGPO.

Proposed Durability & Strength Rating Practices for Enclosed Drive Spiral Bevel Gears. E. J. Wellauer & Donald L. Borden. (Technical Papers: Vol. P229.09). (Illus.). 13p. 1965. pap. text 30.00 (*1-55589-276-0*) AGMA.

Proposed Dynamic Balancing Tolerances for High Speed Gear Couplings. L. Filepp. (Technical Papers: Vol. P519.01). (Illus.). 10p. 1967. pap. text 30.00 (*1-55589-436-4*) AGMA.

Proposed Estate Plan for Mr. & Mrs. Richard Harry Black III. rev. ed. A. James Casner. (C). 1983. ring bd. 26.00 (*0-316-13162-8*, Aspen Law & Bus) Aspen Pub.

***Proposed Fiscal Year 1999 Budget Request for the Department of the Interior: Hearing Before the Committee on Energy & Natural Resources, United States Senate, One Hundred Fifth Congress, Second Session, on the Proposed Fiscal Year 1999 Budget Request for the Department of the Interior, March 5, 1998.** USGPO Staff. LC 98-212945. (S. Hrg. Ser.). iii, 105 p. 1998. write for info. (*0-16-057218-5*) USGPO.

***Proposed Fiscal Year 1999 Budget Request for the Forest Service: Hearing Before the Committee on Energy & Natural Resources, United States Senate, One Hundred Fifth Congress, Second Session, on the Forest Service Fiscal Year 1999 Budget, March 3, 1998.** USGPO Staff. LC 98-207500. (S. Hrg. Ser.). iii, 149 p. 1998. write for info. (*0-16-057146-4*) USGPO.

Proposed Fissile-Material Production Cutoff: Next Steps. Brian G. Chow et al. LC 95-12856. 60p. 1996. pap. text 15.00 (*0-8330-2359-4*, MR-586-1-OSD) Rand Corp.

Proposed Guidelines for Collecting & Interpreting Technological Innovation Data: The Oslo Manual. OECD Staff. LC 97-180546. (Measurement of Scientific & Technological Activities Ser.). 124p. (Orig.). 1997. pap. 23.00 (*92-64-15464-7*, 92-97-03-1, Pub. by Org for Econ) OECD.

Proposed Idea Regulations: Joint Hearing Before the Committee on Labor & Human Resources, United States Senate & the Committee on Education & the Workforce, House of Representatives, 105th Congress, Second Session ... April 22, 1998. LC 98-213852. (S. Hrg. Ser.). iv, 90 p. 1998. write for info. (*0-16-057301-7*) USGPO.

Proposed Income Tax Benefits for Charitable Gifts of Social Security & Pension Payments. Ken Ransford. (Issue Paper #3-97 Ser.). 19p. 1997. pap. text 8.00 (*1-57655-155-5*) Independ Inst.

Proposed Model for Visual Information Processing in the Human Brain. Matthew Kabrisky. LC 66-10343. 114p. reprint ed. pap. 35.40 (*0-608-16247-7*, 201493700094) Bks Demand.

Proposed Modifications to the Harmonized Tariff Schedule of the U. S. 116p. (Orig.). (C). 1995. pap. text 30.00 (*0-7881-2581-8*) DIANE Pub.

Proposed National Strategies for the Prevention of Leading Work-Related Diseases & Injuries: 1988 Edition. 196p. (C). 1994. reprint ed. pap. text 50.00 (*0-7881-0452-7*) DIANE Pub.

Proposed 1985 Farm Bill Changes: Taking the Bias Out of Farm Policy: Symposium Proceedings. Ed. by William Lockeretz. 54p. 1985. pap. 6.00 (*1-893182-12-6*) H A Wallace Inst.

Proposed Reorganization of U. S. International Trade Relief Laws. (Illus.). 398p. (C). 1996. reprint ed. pap. text 65.00 (*0-7881-3424-8*) DIANE Pub.

Proposed Revision on Tooth Proportions for Enlarged Pinions. G. L. Breur. (Technical Papers: Vol. P209.10). (Illus.). 17p. 1971. pap. text 30.00 (*1-55589-233-7*) AGMA.

Proposed Standard for Acoustic Emission Examinations During Application of Pressure. 1975. pap. text 2.50 (*0-685-62574-5*, E00096) ASME.

Proposed Standard International Acupuncture Nomenclature: Report of a WHO Scientific Group. WHO Staff. 30p. 1991. 9.00 (*92-4-154417-1*) World Health.

Proposed Stock Transfer Rules under Sections 367(a) & 367(b), 1991. 70p. 1991. pap. text 17.00 (*1-56986-181-1*) Federal Bar.

Proposed Uniform Accountancy Act, December 2, 1990. American Institute of Certified Public Accountants. LC KF1357.. 72p. reprint ed. pap. 30.00 (*0-7837-1051-8*, 204152800021) Bks Demand.

Proposed Yosemite National Park: Treasures & Features. John Muir. Ed. by William R. Jones. (Illus.). 64p. 1976. reprint ed. pap. text 2.00 (*0-89646-003-7*) Vistabooks.

Proposicion Inocente. Elizabeth Bevarly. (Deseo Ser.). 1996. per. 3.50 (*0-373-35145-3*, 1-35145-1) Harlequin Bks.

Proposing a Balanced Budget Amendment to the Constitution of the U. S. Hearing Before the Committee on the Judiciary, U. S. House of Representatives. Ed. by Henry J. Hyde. 141p. (C). 1998. pap. text 30.00 (*0-7881-7296-4*) DIANE Pub.

Proposing a New Scientific Method & Biosocial Theory to Explain Western Society. Ed. by F. Mervin Baker. LC 98-8629. 176p. 1998. text 79.95 (*0-7734-8310-1*) E Mellen.

***Proposing Empirical Research: A Guide to the Fundamentals.** Mildred L. Patten. 138p. 1999. pap. text 23.95 (*1-884585-25-6*) Pyrczak Pub.

Proposing Men: Dialectics of Gender & Class in the Eighteenth-Century English Periodical. Shawn L. Maurer. LC 98-16809. 320p. 1998. 49.50 (*0-8047-3353-8*); pap. write for info. (*0-8047-3357-0*) Stanford U Pr.

Proposing to Win. David G. Pugh et al. (Illus.). 240p. 1994. write for info. (*1-57740-006-2*, ILW005) Intl LrningWrk.

Proposing to Win - Workbook. Terry R. Bacon et al. (Illus.). 180p. 1994. wbk. ed. write for info. (*1-57740-023-2*, ILW057) Intl LrningWrk.

***Proposition.** Judith Ivory. LC 99-94816. 384p. 1999. mass mkt. 6.50 (*0-380-80260-0*, Avon Bks) Morrow Avon.

***Proposition.** large type ed. Judith Ivory. LC 00-36981. 473p. 2000. pap. 29.95 (*0-7838-9057-5*, G K Hall & Co) Mac Lib Ref.

Proposition Marriage. Eileen Wilks. (Desire Ser.: No. 1239). 1999. per. 3.75 (*0-373-76239-9*, 1-76239-2) Silhouette.

Proposition Thirteen: A Ten-Year Retrospective. Ed. by Frederick D. Stocker. 201p. (Orig.). 1991. pap. text 17.50 (*1-55844-108-5*) Lincoln Inst Land.

Proposition 13 in Recession & Recovery. Steven M. Sheffrin & Terri A. Sexton. LC 98-40449. (Illus.). xx, 90p. 1998. 10.00 (*1-58213-003-5*) Pub Policy Inst.

Proposition 13 in the 1978 California Primary: A Post-Election Bibliography. Ronald J. Heckart & Terry J. Dean. LC 80-27111. (Occasional Bibliographies Ser.: No. 2). 176p. reprint ed. pap. 54.60 (*0-608-20117-0*, 207138900011) Bks Demand.

***Proposition 218 after Two Years.** Dean J. Misczynski. 16p. 1998. pap. write for info. (*1-58703-095-0*, CRB-98-016) CA St Libry.

Propositional Attitudes: An Essay on Thoughts & How We Ascribe Them. Mark Richard. (Studies in Philosophy). (Illus.). 285p. (C). 1990. pap. text 26.95 (*0-521-38819-8*) Cambridge U Pr.

Propositional Attitudes: The Role of Content in Logic, Language, & Mind. C. Anthony Anderson & Joseph Owens. LC 90-34223. (CSLI Lecture Notes Ser.: No. 20). 342p. (C). 1990. 49.95 (*0-937073-51-2*); pap. 17.95 (*0-937073-50-4*) CSLI.

Propositional Logic: Deduction & Algorithms. Hans K. Buning & T. Letterman. LC 98-38806. (Cambridge Tracts in Theoretical Computer Science Ser.: No. 48). (Illus.). 420p. (C). 1998. 74.95 (*0-521-63017-7*) Cambridge U Pr.

Propositional Logic of Avicenne. Avicenna. LC 73-75642. (Synthese Historical Library: No. 7). 309p. 1973. text 191.50 (*90-277-0360-4*, D Reidel) Kluwer Academic.

Propositional Logical Thinking & Comprehension of Language Connectives: A Developmental Analysis. Scott G. Paris. LC 74-75824. (Janua Linguarum, Series Minor: No. 216). (Illus.). 101p. 1975. pap. text 23.10 (*90-279-3197-6*) Mouton.

***Propositional Logics.** Epstein. 2000. pap. 26.00 (*0-534-55847-X*) Wadsworth Pub.

Propositional Logics: Propositional Logics. 2nd ed. Richard L. Epstein. (The Semantic Foundations of Logic Ser.). 512p. (C). 1995. text 80.00 (*0-19-508761-5*) OUP.

Propositional Structure & Illocutionary Force: A Study of the Contribution of Sentence Meaning to Speech Acts. Ed. by Katz. (C). 1930. pap. text. write for info. (*0-690-00883-X*) Addison-Wesley.

Propositional Structure & Illocutionary Force: A Study of the Contribution of Sentence Meaning to Speech Acts. Jerrold J. Katz. (Language & Thought Ser.). (Illus.). 264p. 1980. pap. 18.00 (*0-674-71615-9*) HUP.

Propositionale Wahreitsbegriff im 14. Jahrundert. Dominik Perler. (Quellen und Studien zur Philosophie: Bd. 33). (GER.). x, 387p. (C). 1992. lib. bdg. 144.65 (*3-11-013415-2*) De Gruyter.

Propositions & Attitudes. Ed. by Nathan Salmon & Scott Soames. (Oxford Readings in Philosophy Ser.). 296p. (C). 1989. 55.00 (*0-19-875092-7*) OUP.

Propositions Concerning Protection & Free Trade. Willard Phillips. LC 67-29515. (Reprints of Economic Classics Ser.). xv, 233p. 1968. reprint ed. 39.50 (*0-678-00369-6*) Kelley.

Proposito! Frank Medley. 1992. mass mkt. 15.95 (*0-8384-2399-X*) Heinle & Heinle.

Proposito! Anne Nerenz & Ariew. 1992. mass mkt. 16.95 (*0-8384-2369-8*) Heinle & Heinle.

Proposito del Formativo. Ed. by M. Teresa Castillo. 136p. 1993. pap. 6.00 (*968-29-5114-3*, IN060) UPLAAP.

Proposito en la Vida: Hacer la Voluntad de Dios. D. S. Prince.Tr. of Objective for Living: To Do God's Will. (SPA.). 28p. 1996. 3.50 (*0-7899-0208-7*, 550088) Editorial Unilit.

Propped & Cantilevered Rigid Walls. 104p. 1986. 40.00 (*0-7277-0271-8*, Pub. by T Telford) RCH.

Proprietary Burglar Alarm Units & Systems, UL 1076. 5th ed. (C). 1995. pap. text 95.00 (*1-55989-878-X*) Underwrtrs Labs.

Proprietary Claims & Remedies. Malcolm Cope. 218p. 1997. 64.00 (*1-86287-253-8*, Pub. by Federation Pr) Gaunt.

Proprietary Schools: Programs, Policies, & Prospects. John B. Lee & Jamie P. Merisotis. Ed. by Jonathan D. Fife. LC 91-60263. (ASHE-ERIC Higher Education Reports: No. 90-5). 90p. 1990. pap. 24.00 (*1-878380-02-8*) GWU Grad Schl E&HD.

Propriete Fonciere en Grece Jusqua a Conquete Romaine. Paul Guiraud. Ed. by Gregory Vlastos. LC 78-19357. (Morals & Law in Ancient Greece Ser.). 1979. reprint ed. lib. bdg. 50.95 (*0-405-11549-0*) Ayer.

Propriete Privee. Paule Constant. (FRE.). 248p. 1989. pap. 11.95 (*0-7859-2130-3*, 2070382036) Fr & Eur.

Proprieties & Vagaries: A Philosophical Thesis from Science, Horse Racing, Sexual Customs, Religion, & Politics. Albert L. Hammod. LC 61-13245. 282p. pap. 87.50 (*0-608-10087-0*, 200386700037) Bks Demand.

Proprietor: The Screenplay & Story Behind the Film. Ismail Merchant. LC 96-31367. (Illus.). 224p. 1996. 24.95 (*1-55704-306-X*, Pub. by Newmarket) Norton.

Proprietor, Proprietary. abr. ed. Intro. by Luanna C. Blagrove. (Illus.). 250p. 1988. 24.95 (*0-939776-19-7*) Blagrove Pubns.

Proprietors. Jeffrey Archer. 1995. 25.00 (*0-614-96259-5*) HarpC.

Proprietor's Daughter. Lewis Orde. 1988. 18.95 (*0-316-67340-4*) Little.

Proprietors of Carolina. William S. Powell. (Illus.). vi, 70p. 1968. reprint ed. pap. 4.00 (*0-86526-101-6*) NC Archives.

Proprietors, Patronage, & Paper Money: Legislative Politics in New Jersey, 1703-1776. Thomas L. Purvis. LC 85-27895. 360p. 1986. lib. bdg. 45.00 (*0-8135-1161-5*) Rutgers U Pr.

Proprietors Records, Newbury, Massachusetts, 1720-1768. Stephen P. Hale. 101p. (Orig.). 1995. pap. 15.00 (*1-878545-01-9*) ACETO Bookmen.

***Proprietor's Records of the Town of Lunenburg, Massachusetts: Including Fitchburg & a Portion of Ashby 1729-1833.** Walter C. Davis. 392p. 2000. reprint ed. pap. 30.00 (*0-7884-1456-9*, 1456) Heritage Bk.

Proprietorship of Maryland: A Documented Account. Vera F. Rollo. LC 87-43200. 550p. 1988. 49.75 (*0-917882-26-1*) MD Hist Pr.

***Propriety & Permissiveness in Bourbon Mexico.** Juan Pedro Viqueira Albban. Tr. by Sonya Lipsett-Riviera from SPA. LC 99-19888. 280p. 1999. 55.00 (*0-8420-2466-2*) Scholarly Res Inc.

Propriety & Permissiveness in Bourbon Mexico. Juan Pedro Viqueira Albban et al. LC 99-19888. (Latin American Silhouettes Ser.). 280p. 1999. pap. 19.95 (*0-8420-2467-0*) Scholarly Res Inc.

Propriety Interests in Commercial Transactions. Sarah Worthington. LC 96-31402. 318p. 1997. text 95.00 (*0-19-826275-2*) OUP.

***Proprioception & Neuromuscular Control in Joint Stability.** Ed. by Scott M. Lephart & Freddie H. Fu. (Illus.). 464p. 1999. 59.00 (*0-88011-864-4*) Human Kinetics.

Proprioceptive Neuromuscular Facilitation. 3rd ed. Dorothy E. Voss & Marjorie K. Ionta. LC 84-25958. (Illus.). 370p. 1985. text 42.00 (*0-06-142595-8*, Lippnctt) Lppncott W & W.

Propriums. Mark Dunster. 30p. (Orig.). (YA). (gr. 9-12). 1995. pap. 5.00 (*0-89642-293-3*) Linden Pubs.

***Propuestas Escenicas de Fin de Siglo: Fit 1998.** Ed. by Juan Villegas. LC 99-73730. (Coleccion Historia del Teatro: No. 3). (SPA.). 1999. write for info. (*0-9656914-3-8*) Gestos-Actas.

Propulsion. Edward Stever. 50p. 1992. pap. 8.00 (*0-925062-07-3*) Writers Ink Pr.

Propulsion Combustion: Fuels to Emissions. G. D. Roy. LC 97-24299. (Combustion Ser.). 376p. 1997. 95.00 (*1-56032-431-7*) Taylor & Francis.

Propulsion Techniques: Action & Reaction. Peter J. Turchi. LC 97-43740. 1998. write for info. (*1-56347-115-9*) AIAA.

Propylaia of the Akropolis in Athens: The Project of Mnesikles. Jos De Waele. (Publications of the Netherlands Institute at Athens: Vol. 1). 106p. 1991. 94.00 (*90-5063-059-6*, Pub. by Gieben) J Benjamins Pubng Co.

Propylaia to the Athenian Akropolis: The Predecessors, Vol. 1. William B. Dinsmoor, Jr. LC 79-9232. (Illus.). xviii, 69p. 1980. 25.00 (*0-87661-940-5*) Am Sch Athens.

Propylene Oxide. (Environmental Health Criteria Ser.: No. 56). 53p. 1986. pap. text 11.70 (*92-4-154196-2*, 1160056) World Health.

Propylene Oxide Health & Safety Guide. WHO Staff. (Health & Safety Guides: No. 15). 32p. 1988. 5.00 (*92-4-154338-8*) World Health.

Prorsvs Taliter. Louis Kelly. (C). 1982. pap. text 60.00 (*0-900269-27-8*, Pub. by Old Vicarage) St Mut.

Pros & Cons. Bethany Campbell. 1994. per. 3.59 (*0-373-45171-7*) Harlequin Bks.

Pros & Cons: A Debater's Handbook. 18th ed. Trevor Sather. 192p. 1999. 60.00 (*0-415-19547-0*); pap. 18.99 (*0-415-19548-9*) Routledge.

***Pros & Cons: Social Policy Debates of Our Times.** S. C. Kim. LC 99-87087. 304p. 2000. pap. 22.00 (*0-205-29840-0*) Allyn.

Pros & Cons: The Criminals Who Play in the NFL. Jeff Benedict & Don Yaeger. 432p. 1999. mass mkt. 7.99 (*0-446-60747-9*, Pub. by Warner Bks) Little.

Pros & Cons: The Criminals Who Play in the NFL. Jeff Benedict & Don Yaeger. LC 98-28090. 317p. 1998. 24.00 (*0-446-52403-4*, Pub. by Warner Bks) Little.

Pros & Cons in Financial Management for Professionals. Victor I. Eber. LC 71-166924. (Illus.). 1971. 12.95 (*0-912458-00-3*) Finan Pr FL.

Pros & Cons of EMU. 1997. 295.00 (*0-614-25484-1*, P519) Econ Intel.

Pros & Cons of EMU. (Research Reports: No. P519). 1997. 295.00 (*0-85058-922-3*, P519) Economist Intell.

Pros & Cons of International Weapons Procurement Collaboration. Mark Lorell & Julie Lowell. LC 95-16550. 54p. 1995. pap. text 7.50 (*0-8330-1655-5*, MR-565-OSD) Rand Corp.

Pros & Cons of Third World Multinationals: A Case Study of India. Jamuna P. Agarwal. 115p. 1985. lib. bdg. 42.50 (*3-16-344994-8*, Pub. by JCB Mohr) Coronet Bks.

Pro's Edge: Vision Training for Golf. Lawrence D. Lampert. Ed. by Erica Orloff. (Illus.). 176p. 1998. pap. 14.95 (*1-885843-06-2*) Saturn Press.

***Pro's Poetry.** Estella Provencher. 1999. pap. write for info. (*1-58235-197-X*) Watermrk Pr.

P

Prosa de Luis Lloren Torres: Estudio y Antologia. Daisy Caraballo. LC 83-27416. xiv, 286p. 1986. pap. 10.50 (*0-8477-3802-7*) U of PR Pr.

Prosa de Luis Rafael Sanchez: Texto y Contexto. Alvin J. Figueroa. (University of Texas Studies in Contemporary Spanish-American Fiction: Vol. 2). (SPA.). XXIV, 220p. (C). 1989. text 38.00 (*0-8204-0723-2*) P Lang Pubng.

Prosa der Gegenwart. Gudrum Isaak & Susan Ray. 96p. 1985. pap. 17.50 (*3-468-49789-X*) Langenscheidt.

Prosa Hispanoamericana: Evolucion y Antologia. Ed. by Jose Promis & Jorge Roman-Lagunas. LC 88-18742. 502p. (Orig.). (C). 1988. lib. bdg. 64.00 (*0-8191-7098-4*) U Pr of Amer.

Prosareden des Jeremiabuches. Helga Weippert. LC 72-76045. (Beiheft zur Zeitschrift fuer die Alttestamentliche Wissenschaft Ser.: No. 132). (GER.). (C). 1973. 113.85 (*3-11-003867-6*) De Gruyter.

Prosas Para Sonreir, Pensar y Refrescar. Calva Morales. (SPA.). 1997. pap. text 7.50 (*968-409-763-8*) Edamex.

Prose. Paul Claudel. Ed. by Petit & Charles Galperine. (Bibliotheque de la Pleiade Ser.). 1965. 80.95 (*0-685-11455-4*) Fr & Eur.

Prose. Edward R. Sill. LC 70-117844. (Essay Index Reprint Ser.). 1977. 23.95 (*0-8369-1683-2*) Ayer.

Prose. Yang Jiang. (CHI.). pap. 12.95 (*7-5339-0761-2*, Pub. by China Intl Bk) Distribks Inc.

Prose. unabridged ed. Aleksandr Pushkin. (World Classic Literature Ser.). (RUS.). pap. 8.95 (*2-87714-270-1*, Pub. by Bookking Intl) Distribks Inc.

Prose see Oeuvres Completes

Prose: Essays & Personal Letters. C. Liegh McInnis. 153p. 1999. per. 15.00 (*0-9655775-5-4*) Psychedelic Lit.

Prose & Cons. Richard Mendes. 128p. 1993. pap. 8.95 (*1-880365-41-3*) Prof Pr NC.

Prose & Cons: The Do's & Don'ts of Technical & Business Writing. Carol M. Barnum. 156p. 1986. pap. text 9.95 (*0-935920-29-3*, Ntl Pubs Blck) P-H.

Prose & Poetry. Stephen Crane. Ed. by J. C. Levenson. LC 83-19908. 1379p. 1984. 35.00 (*0-940450-17-8*, Pub. by Library of America) Penguin Putnam.

Prose & Poetry. Alice C. Meynell. LC 76-117824. (Essay Index Reprint Ser.). 1977. 20.95 (*0-8369-1983-1*) Ayer.

Prose & Poetry, 100 Vols. Rainer Maria Rilke. Ed. by Egon Schwarz. LC 77-6951. (The German Library). 264p. 1984. 39.50 (*0-8264-0286-0*) Continuum.

Prose & Poetry, Vol. 4, No. 1. Ed. by Ann L. Dunnington. 1978. pap. 2.50 (*0-916912-33-7*) Hellcoal Pr.

Prose & Poetry, 100 Vols., Vol. 7. Rainer Maria Rilke. LC 80-7563. (German Library). 264p. 1984. pap. 19.95 (*0-8264-0287-9*) Continuum.

Prose & Poetry: Maggie: A Girl of the Streets; The Red Badge of Courage; George's Mother; The Third Violet; Journalism, Poetry, Tales, & Sketches. Stephen Crane. Ed. by J. C. Levenson. (Library of America College Editions). 1379p. (C). 1996. pap. text 15.95 (*1-883011-39-6*, Pub. by Library of America) Penguin Putnam.

Prose & Poetry by Sonia Savage. Norton Savage. (Illus.). 64p. 1999. 13.95 (*1-58244-025-5*) Rutledge Bks.

Prose & Poetry of Andree Chedid: Selected Poems, Short Stories, & Essays. Andree Chedid. Ed. & Tr. by Renee Linkhorn from FRE. LC 90-70298. (Illus.). 214p. 1990. lib. bdg. 24.95 (*0-917786-78-5*) Summa Pubns.

Prose & Poetry of Modern Sweden: An Intermediate Swedish Reader. Gosta Franzen. LC 70-78815. (SWE.). 165p. 1969. reprint ed. pap. 51.20 (*0-608-01854-6*, 206250400003) Bks Demand.

Prose & Poetry of the American West. James C. Work. LC 90-32944. xv, 733p. 1991. pap. text 29.95 (*0-8032-9718-1*, Bison Books) U of Nebr Pr.

Prose & Poetry of the Millennium. Julie Y. Luna. 1998. pap. 18.00 (*1-57553-934-9*) Watermrk Pr.

Prose & the Passion: Children & Their Reading. Ed. by Morag Styles et al. LC 95-197197. (Education Ser.). (Illus.). 256p. 1994. pap. 35.00 (*0-304-32771-9*) Continuum.

Prose & Travel Books in Prose & Verse. W. H. Auden. Ed. by Edward Mendelson. LC 95-38162. (Complete Works of W. H. Auden: Vol. 1). (Illus.). 952p. 1997. text 59.50 (*0-691-06803-8*, Pub. by Princeton U Pr) Cal Prin Full Svc.

P

Prose Brut: The Development of a Middle English Chronicle. Lister M. Matheson. LC 98-11574. (Medieval & Renaissance Texts & Studies: Vol. 180). 424p. 1998. 30.00 (*0-86698-222-1*, MR180) MRTS.

Prose by Victorian Women: An Anthology. Ed. by Andrea Broomfield & Sally Mitchell. LC 95-24400. 752p. 1995. pap. text 32.95 (*0-8153-1967-3*, H1893) Garland.

Prose by Victorian Women: An Anthology. Andrea Broomfield & Sally Mitchell. LC 95-24400. (Garland Reference Library of the Humanities: Vol. 1893). 752p. 1995. reprint ed. text 95.00 (*0-8153-1970-3*, H1893) Garland.

Prose Comprehension Beyond the Word. Arthur C. Graesser. (Illus.). 310p. 1981. 88.95 (*0-387-90544-8*) Spr-Verlag.

Prose-Conversations on Some of the Old Poets. James Russell Lowell. (Notable American Authors Ser.). 1999. reprint ed. lib. bdg. 125.00 (*0-7812-3892-7*) Rprt Serv.

Prose Edda of Snorri Sturluson: Tales from Norse Mythology. Snorri Sturluson. Tr. by Jean I. Young from ICE. 1964. pap. 13.95 (*0-520-01232-1*, Pub. by U CA Pr) Cal Prin Full Svc.

Prose, Essays, Poems. Gottfried Benn. Ed. by Richard Becker & Volkmar Sander. LC 80-7563. (German Library: Vol. 73). 320p. (C). 1987. 39.50 (*0-8264-0310-7*); pap. 19.95 (*0-8264-0311-5*) Continuum.

Prose Fiction of Shakespeare's Time. Ed. by Mary E. Morrison. (Shakespeariana Ser.). xiii, 35p. (Orig.). 1989. 15.00 (*0-8357-0888-8*) Univ Microfilms.

Prose Fiction of the Cuban Revolution. Seymour Menton. LC 75-5993. (Latin American Monographs: No. 37). 364p. reprint ed. pap. 112.90 (*0-8357-7713-8*, 203607000002) Bks Demand.

Prose Fiction of Veniamin A. Kaverin. Hongor Oulanoff. v, 203p. 1976. pap. 19.95 (*0-89357-032-X*) Slavica.

Prose Fiction of W. B. Yeats: The Search for 'Those Simple Forms' Richard J. Finneran. LC 92-150112. 42 p. 1973. write for info. (*0-85105-217-7*) Smyth.

Prose from the Book That Was Not Published in 1968. Lev Navrozov. 112p. (Orig.). 1984. pap. 14.00 (*0-914265-00-8*) New Eng Pub MA.

Prose-Legends of New England in Prose & Verse. John Greenleaf Whittier. (Notable American Authors Ser.). 1999. reprint ed. lib. bdg. 125.00 (*0-7812-9968-3*) Rprt Serv.

Prose Life of Alexander from the Thorton Ms. (EETS, OS Ser.: No. 143). 1974. reprint ed. 45.00 (*0-527-00139-2*) Periodicals Srv.

Prose Literature of the Gaelic Revival, 1881-1921: Ideology & Innovation. Philip O'Leary. LC 92-47013. 544p. (C). 1994. 80.00 (*0-271-01063-0*); pap. 25.00 (*0-271-01064-9*) Pa St U Pr.

Prose Lives of Women Saints of Our Contrie of England. Ed. by C. Horstmann. (EETS, OS Ser.: No.86). 1974. reprint ed. 45.00 (*0-685-02860-7*) Periodicals Srv.

Prose Masterpieces from Modern Essayists, 3 Vols. LC 79-121500. (Essay Index Reprint Ser.). 1977. 60.95 (*0-8369-1773-1*) Ayer.

***Prose Merlin.** Ed. by John Conlee. (Teams Middle English Text Ser.). 1998. pap. text 20.00 (*1-58044-015-0*) Medieval Inst.

Prose Models. 9th ed. Gerald Levin. 576p. (C). 1992. pap. text, teacher ed. 5.00 (*0-15-500297-X*) Harcourt Coll Pubs.

Prose Models. 10th ed. Levin. (C). 1995. pap. text 35.50 (*0-15-502167-2*, Pub. by Harcourt Coll Pubs); pap. text, teacher ed. 30.00 (*0-15-502168-0*) Harcourt Coll Pubs.

Prose Observations. Samuel Butler. Ed. by Hugh De Quehen. (Oxford English Texts Ser.). (Illus.). 470p. 1980. text 110.00 (*0-19-812728-6*) OUP.

Prose of Alexander of Robert Thornton: The Middle English Text with a Modern English Translation. Tr. by Julie Chappel from ENM. LC 90-24425. (American University Studies: English Language & Literature: Ser. IV, Vol. 131). 291p. (C). 1992. text 49.95 (*0-8204-1508-1*) P Lang Pubng.

Prose of Jorge Luis Borges: Existentialism & the Dynamics of Surprise. Ion T. Agheana. LC 84-47694. (American University Studies: Romance Languages & Literature: Ser. II, Vol. 13). XIII, 320p. (Orig.). (C). 1984. pap. text 31.85 (*0-8204-0130-7*) P Lang Pubng.

Prose of Life: Sketches from Victorian Canada. Ed. by Carole Gerson & Kathy Mezel. 261p. (C). 1981. pap. text 5.00 (*0-920802-27-3*, Pub. by ECW) Genl Dist Srvs.

Prose of the English Renaissance. Ed. by J. William Hebel et al. 1952. 59.00 (*0-89197-362-1*) Irvington.

Prose of the Minor Connecticut Wits, 3 vols., Set. Ed. by Benjamin Franklin. LC 74-11124. 1500p. 1974. reprint ed. 200.00 (*0-8201-1132-5*) Schol Facsimiles.

Prose of the Victorian Period, 001. Ed. by William E. Buckler. (YA). (gr. 9 up). 1958. pap. 13.96 (*0-395-05128-2*, RivEd) HM.

Prose of the World. Maurice Merleau-Ponty. Ed. by Claude Lefort. Tr. by John O'Neill from FRE. LC 72-96699. (Studies in Phenomenology & Existential Philosophy). 154p. (C). 1973. pap. 15.95 (*0-8101-0615-9*); text 26.95 (*0-8101-0412-1*) Northwestern U Pr.

Prose of Vachel Lindsay, Vol. 1. Vachel Lindsay. Ed. by Dennis Camp. 340p. 1989. 24.95 (*0-944024-08-4*) Spoon Riv Poetry.

Prose Papers. John Drinkwater. 259p. 1969. 20.95 (*0-8369-1205-5*) Bks for Libraries.

Prose Poem in France: Theory & Practice. Ed. by Mary A. Caws & Hermine Riffaterre. LC 82-20691. 256p. 1983. text 69.00 (*0-231-05434-3*); pap. text 23.00 (*0-231-05435-1*) Col U Pr.

Prose Poems & Selections. Robert G. Ingersoll. (Notable American Authors Ser.). 1992. reprint ed. lib. bdg. 75.00 (*0-7812-3333-X*) Rprt Serv.

Prose Poems from Les Illuminations of Arthur Rimbaud. Jean N. Rimbaud. Tr. by Helen Rootham. LC 77-11478. reprint ed. 29.50 (*0-404-16339-4*) AMS Pr.

Prose, Poetry & Drama for Oral Interpretation, First Ser. Ed. by William J. Farma. LC 73-139759. (Granger Index Reprint Ser.). 1977. 29.95 (*0-8369-6213-3*) Ayer.

Prose, Poetry & Drama for Oral Interpretation, Second Ser. Ed. by William J. Farma. LC 73-139759. (Granger Index Reprint Ser.). 1977. 29.95 (*0-8369-6223-0*) Ayer.

Prose, Poetry, & Dramatic Interpretation. Betty Whitlock & Kathy Owens. iv, 91p. (Orig.). (YA). (gr. 7-12). 1995. pap. text 24.00 (*1-889510-18-1*) Chmpionship Debate.

Prose, Poetry & Dreams. Willard A. Faust. (Illus.). 186p. (Orig.). 1990. pap. 13.95 (*0-9625027-0-7*) W A Faust.

Prose Quotations from Socrates to Macaulay. Samuel A. Allibone. 1972. 59.95 (*0-8490-0902-2*) Gordon Pr.

Prose Quotations from Socrates to Macaulay. Samuel A. Allibone. (Principle Works of Samuel Austin Allibone). 1989. reprint ed. lib. bdg. 79.00 (*0-7812-1788-1*) Rprt Serv.

Prose Reader: Essays for College Writers. Kim Flachmann & Michael Flachmann. LC 86-25424. (Illus.). 576p. (C). 1987. pap. text 19.33 (*0-13-731209-1*) P-H.

Prose Reader: Essays for Thinking, Reading & Writing. 5th ed. Kim Flachmann. LC 98-24266. 688p. 1998. pap. text 35.40 (*0-13-095406-3*) P-H.

Prose-Rhythm of Demosthenes. rev. ed. Donald F. McCabe. Ed. by W. R. Connor. LC 80-2658. (Monographs in Classical Studies). 203p. 1981. lib. bdg. 35.95 (*0-405-14044-4*) Ayer.

Prose Romances of Edgar Allan Poe. Edgar Allan Poe. (Notable American Authors Ser.). 1999. reprint ed. lib. bdg. 125.00 (*0-7812-8755-3*) Rprt Serv.

Prose Sketches & Poems: Written in the Western Country. Albert Pike. Ed. by David J. Weber. LC 86-29994. (Southwest Landmark Ser.: No. 6). (Illus.). 336p. 1987. reprint ed. 27.50 (*0-89096-305-3*) Tex A&M Univ Pr.

Prose Sketches & Poems: Written in the Western Country. Albert Pike. Ed. by David J. Weber. LC 86-29994. (Southwest Landmark Ser.: No. 6). (Illus.). 336p. 1987. reprint ed. pap. 15.95 (*0-89096-323-1*) Tex A&M Univ Pr.

Prose Sketches & Poems Written in the Western Country. Albert Pike. (Notable American Authors Ser.). 1999. reprint ed. lib. bdg. 125.00 (*0-7812-8748-0*) Rprt Serv.

Prose Solomon & Saturn: Adrian & Ritheus. James E. Cross & Thomas D. Hill. Ed. by British Library Manuscripts Staff. LC 82-217040. (McMaster Old English Studies & Texts: No. 1). 200p. reprint ed. pap. 62.00 (*0-7837-2047-5*, 204232200004) Bks Demand.

***Prose-Specimen Days & Collect.** Walt Whitman. (Notable American Authors Ser.). 1999. reprint ed. lib. bdg. 125.00 (*0-7812-9953-5*) Rprt Serv.

Prose Style: A Contemporary Guide. 2nd ed. Robert Miles et al. 224p. (C). 1990. pap. text 31.60 (*0-13-713181-X*) P-H.

Prose Style of Emerson. Andre Celieres. 1972. 59.95 (*0-8490-0903-0*) Gordon Pr.

Prose Style of Emerson. Andre Celieres. (BCL1-PS American Literature Ser.). 87p. 1993. reprint ed. lib. bdg. 59.00 (*0-7812-6962-8*) Rprt Serv.

Prose Tales of Alexander Pushkin. Aleksandr Pushkin. Tr. by T. Keane from RUS. LC 78-150484. (Short Story Index Reprint Ser.). 1977. reprint ed. 24.95 (*0-8369-3825-9*) Ayer.

***Prose, Verse & Truth-Telling in the Thirteenth Century: An Essay on Form & Function in Selected Texts, Accompanied by an Edition of the Prose Thebes as Found in the Histoire Ancienne Jusqu'a Cesar.** Molly Lynde-Recchia. LC 99-75745. (Edward C. Armstrong Monographs on Medieval Literature: Vol. 10). 206p. 2000. pap. 34.50 (*0-917058-92-5*) French Forum.

Prose Volgari Inedite e Poesi Latine e Greche Edite e Inedite. Angelo Poliziano. (Illus.). xxxv, 568p. 1976. reprint ed. write for info. (*3-487-06101-5*) G Olms Pubs.

Prose Works. Henry Wadsworth Longfellow. (Notable American Authors Ser.). 1999. reprint ed. lib. bdg. 125.00 (*0-7812-3835-8*) Rprt Serv.

Prose Works, 8 vols. Richard Wagner. Ed. by William A. Ellis. Incl. In Paris & Dresden. 1966. reprint ed. lib. bdg. 42.50 (*0-8450-2107-9*); Posthumous. (Illus.). 1967. reprint ed. lib. bdg. 42.50 (*0-8450-2108-7*); (GER.). 1966. reprint ed. Set lib. bdg. 250.00 (*0-8450-2100-1*) Broude.

Prose Works see Complete Works of Algernon Charles Swinburne

Prose Works, 1892, 2 vols. Ed. by Walt Whitman & Floyd Stovall. Incl. Vol. 2. Collect & Other Prose. LC 60-15980. 445p. (C). 1984. text 130.00 (*0-8147-0443-3*); LC 60-15980. (Illus.). 75.00 (*0-685-03618-9*) NYU Pr.

Prose Works of Alexander Pope Vol. II: The Major Works, 1725-1744. Ed. by Rosemary Cowler. LC 86-3625. xv, 529p. (C). 1986. lib. bdg. 57.50 (*0-208-02059-4*, Archon Bks) Shoe String.

Prose Works of Fulke Greville, Lord Brooke. Fulke Greville. Ed. by John Gouws. 346p. 1986. text 79.00 (*0-19-812746-4*) OUP.

Prose Works of Jonathan Swift, 12 vols., Set. Jonathan Swift. Ed. by Temple Scott. LC 79-179300. 495.00 (*0-404-10050-3*) AMS Pr.

Prose Works of Percy Bysshe Shelley, Vol. I. Percy Bysshe Shelley. Ed. by E. B. Murray. (Illus.). 644p. 1993. text 98.00 (*0-19-812748-0*) OUP.

Prose Works of Robert Burns. Robert Burns. LC 79-144501. reprint ed. 51.00 (*0-404-08509-1*) AMS Pr.

Prose Works of Saint-John Perse: Towards an Understanding of His Poetry. Richard L. Sterling. LC 92-31123. (Currents in Romance Languages & Literature Ser.: Vol. 8). XIII, 160p. (C). 1994. text 42.95 (*0-8204-1917-6*) P Lang Pubng.

Prose Works of William Byrd of Westover: Narratives of a Colonial Virginian. William Byrd. Ed. by Louis B. Wright. LC 66-11359. (Illus.). 450p. reprint ed. pap. 139.50 (*0-7837-4456-0*, 205798600012) Bks Demand.

Prose Works of William Wordsworth, 3 vols. William Wordsworth. Ed. by Alexander B. Grosart. LC 29-24298. reprint ed. 215.00 (*0-404-07050-7*) AMS Pr.

Prose Works, Other Than Science & Health with Key to the Scriptures. Mary Baker Eddy. reprint ed. 55.00 (*0-87952-074-4*) Writings of Mary Baker.

Prose Writers of America. Ed. by Rufus W. Griswold. (C). 1972. reprint ed. lib. bdg. 25.00 (*0-8422-8064-2*) Irvington.

Prose Writers of America. Rufus W. Griswold. (C). 1986. reprint ed. pap. text 10.95 (*0-8290-1870-0*) Irvington.

***Prose Writing, 1940-1990.** Ed. by Sacvan Bercovitch. (Cambridge History of American Literature Ser.). 800p. (C). 1999. 85.00 (*0-521-49732-9*) Cambridge U Pr.

Prose Writings. Thomas O. Davis. 1977. text 18.95 (*0-8369-8153-7*, 8293) Ayer.

Prose Writings. Nathaniel P. Willis. Ed. by Henry A. Beers. LC 70-128984. reprint ed. 34.00 (*0-404-06990-8*) AMS Pr.

Prose Writings. Nathaniel P. Willis. (BCL1-PS American Literature Ser.). 365p. 1992. reprint ed. lib. bdg. 89.00 (*0-7812-6905-9*) Rprt Serv.

Prose Writings of Heinrich Heine. Heinrich Heine. Ed. by Havelock Ellis. LC 73-2205. (Jewish People; History, Religion, Literature Ser.: His History & Literature, Ser. No. 2). 1973. reprint ed. 29.95 (*0-405-05270-7*) Ayer.

Prose Writings of James Clarence Mangan. James C. Mangan. Ed. by David J. O'Donoghue. LC 75-28826. reprint ed. 49.50 (*0-404-13818-7*) AMS Pr.

Prosea, Vol. II. PUDOC Staff. Ed. by E. Westphal & P. C. Jansen. 324p. (C). 1991. text 650.00 (*0-89771-634-5*, Pub. by Intl Bk Distr) St Mut.

PROSEA Vol. I: (Pulses) PUDOC Staff. Ed. by L. J. Van Maesen. 108p. (C). 1991. text 250.00 (*0-89771-632-9*, Pub. by Intl Bk Distr) St Mut.

PROSEA Vol. III: (Plant Resources of South-East Asia) PUDOC Staff. Ed. by J. S. Siemonsma & N. Wolijarni-SoetJipto. 337p. (C). 1991. text 695.00 (*0-89771-635-3*, Pub. by Intl Bk Distr) St Mut.

PROSEA Vol. IV: (Forages) L. T. Mannetje & R. M. Jones. Ed. by PUDOC Staff. 250p. (C). 1991. text 500.00 (*0-89771-636-1*, Pub. by Intl Bk Distr) St Mut.

Prosea Plant Resources of South-East Asia: Essential-Oil Plants. Ed. by L. P. Oyen & Nguyen Xuan Dung. (Illus.). 277p. 1999. 95.00 (*90-5782-010-2*, Pub. by Backhuys Pubs) Balogh.

***PROSEA (Plant Resources of South-East Asia 12 (1) Medicinal & Poisonous Plants (1)** L. S. Padua et al. (Illus.). 711p. 1999. 185.00 (*90-5782-042-0*, Pub. by Backhuys Pubs) Balogh.

Prosecuting a Civil RICO Case. 70p. 1992. 15.00 (*0-317-05914-9*, PB15) Natl Attys General.

Prosecuting Child Abuse: An Evaluation of the Government's Speedy Progress Policy. Joyce Plotnikoff & Richard Woolfson. LC 96-189240. 109p. 1995. pap. 33.00 (*1-85431-404-1*, Pub. by Blackstone Pr) Gaunt.

Prosecuting Crime in the Renaissance: England, Germany, France. John H. Langbein. LC 73-81670. (Studies in Legal History). (Illus.). 330p. reprint ed. pap. 102.30 (*0-7837-4165-0*, 205901300012) Bks Demand.

***Prosecuting Nazi War Criminals.** Alan S. Rosenbaum. 144p. 1999. reprint ed. pap. text 17.00 (*0-7881-6753-7*) DIANE Pub.

Prosecuting War Crimes & Genocide: The Twentieth-Century Experience. Howard Ball. LC 99-22186. (Illus.). 304p. 1999. 35.00 (*0-7006-0977-6*) U Pr of KS.

***Prosecution.** 2nd ed. Weinreb. (C). 1998. pap. 21.00 (*1-56662-710-9*) Foundation Pr.

Prosecution: A Legal Thriller. Dudley W. Buffa. LC 99-13417. 256p. 1999. 25.00 (*0-8050-6107-X*, J Macrae Bks) H Holt & Co.

Prosecution & Adjudication. 4th ed. Frank W. Miller et al. 1260p. 1991. pap. text 23.25 (*0-88277-882-X*) Foundation Pr.

Prosecution & Defense of Criminal Conspiracy Cases, 2 vols. Paul Marcus. 1978. ring bd. 175.00 (*0-8205-1365-2*) Bender.

Prosecution & Defense of Forfeiture Cases, 2 vols. David B. Smith. 1985. 355.00 (*0-8205-1099-8*) Bender.

Prosecution & Defense of Sex Crimes. Anthony B. Morosco. 1976. 250.00 (*0-8205-1562-0*) Bender.

Prosecution & Defense of the Sexual Abuse Case. 271p. 1995. 30.00 (*0-614-26677-7*, 1061) NYS Bar.

Prosecution & the Public Interest. T. Hetherington. 192p. 1989. 49.95 (*0-08-033110-6*) Macmillan.

Prosecution in Common Law Jurisdictions. Ed. by Andrew Sanders. (International Library of Criminology, Criminal Justice & Penology). (Illus.). 416p. 1996. 139.95 (*1-85521-460-1*, Pub. by Dartmth Pub) Ashgate Pub Co.

Prosecution of Economic Crimes in the U. S. S. R., 1954-1984. Fridrikh Neznansky. Ed. by Andrew A. Michta. (Orig.). 1985. pap. text 75.00 (*1-55831-031-2*) Delphic Associates.

Prosecution of False Memory. Makram K. Girgis. 2000. pap. write for info. (*0-87527-528-1*) Green.

Prosecution of International Crimes: A Critical Study of the International Tribunal for the Former Yugoslavia. Ed. by Roger Clark & Madeleine Sann. 491p. 1996. text 49.95 (*1-56000-269-7*) Transaction Pubs.

Prosecution of the Mentally Disturbed: Dilemmas of Identification & Discretion. D. Chiswick et al. 192p. 1984. text 35.90 (*0-08-028481-7*, Pergamon Pr) Elsevier.

Prosecution Responds: An O. J. Simpson Trial Prosecutor Reveals What Really Happened. Hank Goldberg. (Illus.). 288p. 1996. 21.95 (*1-55972-361-0*, Birch Ln Pr) Carol Pub Group.

Prosecution Without Trial. J. B. Bishop. 1989. 59.00 (*0-409-49478-X*, AT, MICHIE) LEXIS Pub.

Prosecutor. large type ed. Thomas Chastain. LC 92-44635. (General Ser.). 293p. 1993. reprint ed. lib. bdg. 17.95 (*1-56054-656-5*) Thorndike Pr.

Prosecutor. Ed. by William F. McDonald. LC 79-14388. (Sage Criminal Justice System Annuals Ser.: No. 11). 279p. 1979. reprint ed. pap. 86.50 (*0-608-01504-0*, 205954800001) Bks Demand.

Prosecutor: An Inquiry into the Exercise of Discretion. Brian A. Grosman. LC 78-322270. (Canadian University Paperbooks Ser.). 135p. reprint ed. pap. 41.90 (*0-8357-3639-3*, 203636800003) Bks Demand.

Prosecutor As Problem Solver. Ronald Goldstock. Ed. by Graham Hughes. (Occasional Papers: No. X). (Orig.). 1991. pap. 5.00 (*1-878429-59-0*) NYU Ctr for Rsch in Crime Justice.

Prosecutor Disclosure & Judicial Reform: The Omnibus Hearing in Two Courts. Raymond T. Nimmer. LC 75-13605. vii, 117p. 1986. 25.00 (*0-910058-72-5*, 305010); pap. 20.00 (*0-910058-71-7*, 305010) W S Hein.

Prosecutorial Misconduct. Bennett L. Gershman. LC 84-12399. (Civil Rights Ser.). 1984. ring bd. 135.00 (*0-87632-443-X*) West Group.

***Prosecutorial Misconduct.** 2nd ed. Bennett L. Gershman. LC 99-46527. 1999. write for info. (*0-8366-1386-4*) West Group.

An Asterisk (*) at the beginning of an entry indicates that the title is appearing for the first time.

***Prosecutorial Misconduct.** 2nd ed. Joseph F. Lawless, Jr. 1219p. 1999. 120.00 (*0-327-04963-4*, 6424111) LEXIS Pub.

Prosecutorial Misconduct: Law, Procedure, Forms. Joseph F. Lawless, Jr. 812p. 1985. 120.00 (*0-930273-06-0*, 64241-10, MICHIE) LEXIS Pub.

Prosecutorial Relationships in Criminal Justice see Roles & Functions of the Prosecutor

Prosecutorial Response to Heavy Drug Caseloads: Comprehensive Problem-Reduction Strategies. Kerry M. Healey & Barbara Boland. (Illus.). 106p. (Orig.). (C). 1994. pap. text 35.00 (*0-7881-1304-6*) DIANE Pub.

Prosecutors & Computers: Automating Major Operations - What a Prosecutor Needs to Know. Barbara Boland. (Illus.). 79p. (Orig.). (C). 1994. pap. text 25.00 (*0-7881-1486-7*) DIANE Pub.

Prosecutor's Manual for Arrest, Search & Seizure. James A. Adams & Daniel D. Blinka. LC 98-85666. xvi, 648 p. 1998. 105.00 (*0-327-00210-7*, 60074-10) LEXIS Pub.

Prosecutor's Manual for Arrest, Search & Seizure, 1999 Supplement. James A. Adams & Daniel D. Blinka. 70p. 1999. write for info. (*0-327-01499-7*, 6007310) LEXIS Pub.

***Prosecutors Will be Violated: No Matter What Crime You Committed, It's Not Your Fault.** Archibald Spencer. LC 98-96908. 235p. 1999. 23.00 (*0-9666271-6-4*) Trigance Press.

Proselytism & Orthodoxy in Russia. Ed. by John Witte, Jr. LC 99-21682. (Religion & Human Rights Ser.). 400p. 1999. pap. 25.00 (*1-57075-262-1*) Orbis Bks.

Proselytization & Communal Self-Determination in Africa. rev. ed. Ed. by Abdullahi A. An-Na'Im. LC 99-37929. (Religion & Human Rights Ser.). 400p. 1999. pap. 25.00 (*1-57075-261-3*) Orbis Bks.

***Proselytizer: The Diaries of Panos T. Zachariou.** Philemon Zachariou. 280p. 1999. pap. 15.00 (*1-892525-05-4*) ACW Press.

Prosentential Theory of Truth. Dorothy Grover. 264p. 1992. text 49.50 (*0-691-07399-6*, Pub. by Princeton U Pr) Cal Prin Full Svc.

Proserpina, the Duck That Came to School. Constantine Georgiou. (J). (gr. 3-6). 1992. pap. write for info. (*0-9637111-0-5*) C Georgiou.

Proserpine see Chefs-d'Oeuvre Classiques de l'Opera Francais

Proses: On Poems & Poets. Carolyn Kizer. LC 93-31586. 208p. (Orig.). 1994. pap. 12.00 (*1-55659-045-8*) Copper Canyon.

Proses Texte et Musique, Precedees d'une Etude see Melanges de Musicologie Critique

PROSIM see PROSIM 3 for Windows: A Production Management Simulation

PROSIM 3 for Windows: A Production Management Simulation. 3rd rev. ed. Chao-Hsien Chu et al. LC 96-14308. Orig. Title: PROSIM. 224p. (C). 1996. text 25.60 (*0-256-21435-2*, Irwn McGrw-H) McGrw-H Hghr Educ.

PROSIM 3 for Windows: A Production Management Simulation. 5th rev. ed. Chao-Hsien Chu et al. LC 96-9318. Orig. Title: PROSIM. 1996. teacher ed. write for info. (*0-256-21436-0*, Irwn McGrw-H) McGrw-H Hghr Educ.

Prosimetrum: Crosscultural Perspectives on Narrative in Prose & Verse. Ed. by Joseph Harris & Karl Reichl. 448p. 1997. 75.00 (*0-85991-475-5*, DS Brewer) Boydell & Brewer.

Proslavery: A History of the Defense of Slavery in America, 1701-1840. Larry E. Tise. LC 86-14671. (Illus.). 528p. 1990. pap. 25.00 (*0-8203-1228-2*) U of Ga Pr.

ProSlavery Thought, Ideology, & Politics. Ed. by Paul Finkelman. (Articles on American Slavery Ser.). 536p. 1990. reprint ed. text 20.00 (*0-8240-6792-4*) Garland.

Proslogion A Third Interpretation of Anselm's Argument, Vols. II & III. Richard R. La Croix. LC 73-157410. xii, 137 p. 1972. write for info. (*90-04-03436-6*) Brill Academic Pubs.

Prosocial Behavior. Ed. by Margaret S. Clark. (Review of Personality & Social Psychology Ser.: Vol. 12). (Illus.). 320p. (C). 1990. text 58.00 (*0-8039-4071-8*); pap. text 26.00 (*0-8039-4072-6*) Sage.

Prosocial Behavior. Ed. by Margaret S. Clark. LC 80-649712. (Review of Personality & Social Psychology Ser.: No. 12). (Illus.). 327p. 1991. reprint ed. pap. 101.40 (*0-608-04305-2*, 206508400012) Bks Demand.

Prosocial Development in Children Caring, Helping & Cooperating: A Bibliographic Resource Guide. Alice S. Honig & Donna S. Wittmer. LC 91-36676. (Reference Books on Family Issues: Vol. 19). 384p. 1992. text 59.00 (*0-8240-7846-2*, SS538) Garland.

Prosocial Gang: Implementing Aggression Replacement Therapy. Arthur Goldstein et al. LC 94-8569. 120p. 1994. 38.00 (*0-8039-5770-X*); pap. 16.50 (*0-8039-5771-8*) Sage.

Prosocial Guidance for the Preschool Child. Janice J. Beaty. LC 98-6519. (C). 1998. pap. text 32.00 (*0-13-633512-8*, Scribners Ref) Mac Lib Ref.

Prosodia Rationalis: or An Essay Towards Establishing the Melody & Measure of Speech, to Be Expressed & Perpetuated by Peculiar Symbols. 2nd enl. ed. Joshua Steele. (Anglistica & Americana Ser.: No. 125). xvii, 243p. 1971. reprint ed. 76.70 (*3-487-04156-1*) G Olms Pubs.

Prosodic Cues for Segments. Ed. by K. J. Kohler. (Journal: Phonetica: Vol. 43, No. 1-3). (Illus.). 154p. 1986. pap. 106.25 (*3-8055-4474-X*) S Karger.

Prosodic Features & Prosodic Structure: The Phonology of Suprasegmentals. Anthony Fox. (Illus.). 416p. 2000. text 90.00 (*0-19-823785-5*) OUP.

Prosodic Model of Sign Language Phonology. Diane Brentari. LC 97-50053. (Language, Speech & Communication Ser.). (Illus.). 384p. 1999. 45.00 (*0-262-02445-4*, Bradford Bks) MIT Pr.

Prosodic Phonology. Marina Nespor & G. Vogel. (Studies in Generative Grammar). xiv, 328p. 1986. pap. 80.80 (*90-6765-242-3*) Mouton.

Prosodic Phonomorphology Issues at the Interface. Anjanee Sethi. LC 97-901382. xii, 245p. 1997. write for info. (*81-85163-72-3*) Kalinga.

Prosodic Structure of Lithuanian. Steven R. Young. 110p. (Orig.). (C). 1991. pap. text 19.00 (*0-8191-8144-7*); lib. bdg. 38.00 (*0-8191-8143-9*) U Pr of Amer.

Prosodies along the Way. Oscar Washington. LC 89-90679. 124p. 1989. pap. text 6.95 (*1-883069-00-9*) NESB Pubs.

***Prosody & Focus in European Portuguese.** Sonia Frota. LC 00-27739. (Outstanding Dissertations in Linguistics Ser.). 2000. write for info. (*0-8153-3776-0*) Garland.

Prosody & Information Structure. Ed. by W. J. Barry et al. (Journal: Phonetica: Vol. 50, No. 3, 1993). (Illus.). 72p. 1993. pap. 21.75 (*3-8055-5878-3*) S Karger.

Prosody & Parsing. Warren. 1996. 79.95 (*0-86377-942-5*) L Erlbaum Assocs.

Prosody & Poetics in the Early Middle Ages: Essays in Honour of C. B. Hieatt. Ed. by M. J. Toswell. 222p. 1995. text 65.00 (*0-8020-0653-1*) U of Toronto Pr.

Prosody & Purpose in the English Renaissance. O. B. Hardison. LC 88-22598. 360p. 1989. reprint ed. pap. 111.60 (*0-608-06727-X*, 206692400009) Bks Demand.

Prosody & Speech Recognition. Alex Waibel. (Research Notes in Artificial Intelligence Ser.). 212p. 1988. pap. text 34.95 (*0-934613-70-2*) Morgan Kaufmann.

Prosody at the Cafe du Coin. Jeff Bien. 112p. 1996. 14.95 (*1-55082-173-3*, Pub. by Quarry Pr) LPC InBook.

Prosody, Focus, & Word Order. Maria L. Zubizarreta. LC 98-15459. (Linguistic Inquiry Monograph 33 Ser.). (Illus.). 232p. 1998. pap. text 20.00 (*0-262-74021-4*) MIT Pr.

Prosody, Focus, & Word Order. Maria L. Zubizarreta. LC 98-15459. (Linguistic Inquiry Monograph 33 Ser.). (Illus.). 232p. 1998. 40.00 (*0-262-24041-6*) MIT Pr.

Prosody in Conversation: Interactional Studies. Ed. by Elizabeth Couper-Kuhlen & Margret Selting. (Studies in International Sociolinguistics: No. 12). 480p. (C). 1996. text 74.95 (*0-521-46075-1*) Cambridge U Pr.

Prosody in Speech Understanding Systems. Ralf Kompe. Ed. by J. G. Carbonell & J. Siekmann. LC 97-39890. (Lecture Notes in Computer Science Ser.: Vol. 1307). xix, 357p. 1997. pap. 59.00 (*3-540-63580-7*) Spr-Verlag.

Prosody Management of Communicative Disorders. Patricia M. Hargrove & Nancy S. McGarr. (Illus.). 332p. (Orig.). (C). 1993. pap. text 49.95 (*1-879105-88-8*, 0351) Thomson Learn.

Prosody-Morphology Interface. 2nd ed. Ed. by Rene Kager et al. LC 98-35819. (Studies in Natural Language Processing). (Illus.). 420p. (C). 1999. text 69.95 (*0-521-62108-9*) Cambridge U Pr.

Prosody of Chaucer & His Followers: Supplementary Chapters to "Verses of Cadence" James G. Southworth. LC 77-16835. 96p. 1978. reprint ed. lib. bdg. 49.50 (*0-313-20008-4*, SOPC, Greenwood Pr) Greenwood.

Prosody of Greek Speech. A. M. Devine & Laurence D. Stephens. (Illus.). 584p. 1994. text 60.00 (*0-19-508546-9*) OUP.

Prosody of Mandarin Chinese. Susan Xiao-nan Shen. 1990. pap. 20.00 (*0-520-09750-5*, Pub. by U CA Pr) Cal Prin Full Svc.

Prosody of the Persians, According to Saifi, Jami & Other Writers. Henry F. Blochmann. 1976. lib. bdg. 59.95 (*0-8490-2487-0*) Gordon Pr.

***ProsoftTraining.com Technology Terms A4.** ProsoftTraining.com Staff. 2000. pap. write for info. (*1-58143-104-X*) Prosoft I-net.

***ProsoftTraining.com Technology Terms.** ProsoftTraining.com Staff. 2000. pap. write for info. (*1-58143-103-1*) Prosoft I-net.

Prosopografia Isiaca, 2 vols., Set. Fabio Mora. (Etudes Preliminaires aux Religions Orientales dans l'Empire Romain Ser.: Vol. 113). (ITA., Illus.). 1990. 245.50 (*90-04-09232-3*) Brill Academic Pubs.

Prosopografia Isiaca, 2 vols., Vol. I. Fabio Mora. (Etudes Preliminaires aux Religions Orientales dans l'Empire Romain Ser.: Vol. 113). (ITA., Illus.). xxii, 526p. 1990. 178.50 (*90-04-09233-1*) Brill Academic Pubs.

Prosopografia Isiaca, 2 vols., Vol. II. Fabio Mora. (Etudes Preliminaires aux Religions Orientales dans l'Empire Romain Ser.: Vol. 113). (ITA., Illus.). 1990. 67.00 (*90-04-09235-8*) Brill Academic Pubs.

Prosopographia Attica. J. Sundwall. 177p. 1981. suppl. ed. 25.00 (*0-89005-383-9*) Ares.

Prosopographia Attica, 2 vols., Set. Ed. by J. Kirchner. 1340p. 1981. reprint ed. 140.00 (*0-89005-387-1*) Ares.

Prosopographia Imperii Romani, Pt. 5, Fascicle 2. (LAT.). 121p. 1983. 103.10 (*3-11-008902-5*) De Gruyter.

***Prosopographia Imperii Romani Saec. I. II. III. Editio altera, Pars VII. Fasciculus 1.** Leiva Petersen et al. 144p. 2000. 61.00 (*3-11-016743-3*) De Gruyter.

Prosopographia Lacaedaemoniorum. P. Poralla. 1985. reprint ed. pap. 15.00 (*0-89005-521-1*) Ares.

Prosopographia Macedonica. D. Kanatzoulis. 183p. 1979. 30.00 (*0-89005-316-2*) Ares.

Prosopographiae Graecae Minores: A Prosopographical "Corpus" of the Minor Greek States. Ed. by John M. Fossey. Date not set. write for info. (*0-89005-564-5*) Ares.

Prosopographical Study of the Ancient Persians Royal & Noble, 550-450 B.C. Jack M. Balcer. LC 93-27367. 380p. 1993. write for info. (*0-7734-9372-7*) E Mellen.

***Prosopographie der mittelbyzantinischen Zeit.** Herausgegeben von der Berlin & Brandenburgischen Akademie der Wissenschaften. 2000. 161.00 (*3-11-016672-0*) De Gruyter.

Prosopography of Ptolemaic Cyprus. Nicolaou I. Michalidou. (Studies in Mediterranean Archaeology: Vol. XLIV). 165p. (Orig.). 1976. pap. 29.50 (*91-85058-70-X*) P Astroms.

Prosopography of the Later Roman Empire, Vol. 2, A.D. 395-527. Ed. by J. R. Martindale. LC 77-118859. (Illus.). 1355p. 1980. text 285.00 (*0-521-20159-4*) Cambridge U Pr.

Prosopography of the Later Roman Empire, A.D. 527-641, Vol. 3. Ed. by J. R. Martindale. 1626p. (C). 1992. text 375.00 (*0-521-20160-8*) Cambridge U Pr.

***Prosopography of the Neo-Assyrian Empire: B-G, Vol. 1, Pt. 2.** Ed. by Karen Radner. 241p. 1999. pap. text 50.00 (*951-45-8645-X*, Pub. by Neo-Assyrian Text) Eisenbrauns.

Prospect: Photography in Contemporary Art. Peter Weiermair. LC 97-115551. 1996. 55.00 (*3-908162-19-X*, Pub. by Edit Stemmle) Dist Art Pubs.

Prospect: The Journey of an Artist. Anne Truitt. LC 95-26194. 221p. 1997. pap. 12.95 (*0-14-026768-9*) Viking Penguin.

Prospect & Perspective: Recent Art from Chile. Justo P. Mellado. Ed. & Intro. by Beverly Adams. (Illus.). 48p. 1997. pap. write for info. (*1-883502-09-8*) San Ant Mus Art.

Prospect & Retrospect: Selected Essays of James Britton. James N. Britton. Ed. by Gordon M. Pradl. LC 82-14608. 218p. (C). 1982. pap. text 21.50 (*0-86709-043-X*, 0043, Pub. by Boynton Cook Pubs) Heinemann.

Prospect Before Her. Olwen Hufton. LC 96-39158. 1998. pap. 18.00 (*0-679-76818-1*) Random.

Prospect Before Her, Vol. 2. Olwen Hufton. 1998. pap. write for info. (*0-679-76819-X*) Knopf.

Prospect Before Her Vol. 1: A History of Women in Western Europe, 1500-1800. Olwen Hufton. LC 96-39158. 638p. 1996. 40.00 (*0-679-45030-0*) Random.

Prospect Births, Marriages & Deaths, 1753 to 1871 (Marriages 1816-1832 Not Included) Compiled by E. H. Sweetser. (Illus.). 179p. 1997. reprint ed. pap. 23.00 (*0-8328-5900-1*) Higginson Bk Co.

Prospect for Metaphysics: Essays of Metaphysical Exploration. Ed. by Ian T. Ramsey. LC 72-97318. 240p. 1970. reprint ed. lib. bdg. 59.50 (*0-8371-2557-X*, RAME, Greenwood Pr) Greenwood.

Prospect of Detachment. Lindsley Cameron. 1991. pap. 8.95 (*0-312-05496-3*) St Martin.

***Prospect of Immortality.** Kelly R. Nicholson. 400p. 1999. pap. 34.95 (*0-9668911-1-2*, Pub. by Homeward Bnd) ACCESS Pubs Network.

Prospect of Liberal Democracy. Ed. by William S. Livingston. LC 79-63171. 239p. reprint ed. pap. 74.10 (*0-7837-1015-1*, 204132600020) Bks Demand.

Prospect of Release. Tom Mandel. 64p. (Orig.). 1996. pap. 11.00 (*0-925904-16-3*) Chax Pr.

Prospect of Release. Tom Mandel. LC 96-13879. (Orig.). 1996. write for info. (*0-925904-11-2*) Chax Pr.

Prospect of Southwell: An Architectural History of the Church & Domestic Buildings of the Collegiate Foundation. Norman Summers. LC 75-329229. 152 p. 1974. write for info. (*0-85033-181-1*) Phillimore & Co.

Prospect of Sutherland: The Building of a Castle & the Making of a Duchess. Gilbert T. Bell. LC 96-143384. (Illus.). 234p. pap. 17.95 (*1-874744-25-4*, Pub. by Birlinn Ltd) Dufour.

Prospect of War: Studies in British Defence Policy, 1847-1942. John Gooch. 174p. 1981. 32.50 (*0-7146-3128-0*, Pub. by F Cass Pubs) Intl Spec Bk.

Prospect Research: A How-To-Guide. Ed. by Bobbie J. Strand & Susan Hunt. (Illus.). 150p. (Orig.). 1986. pap. 17.00 (*0-89964-244-6*, 26701) Coun Adv & Supp Ed.

Prospect Researcher's Guide to Biographical Research Collections: A Detailed Look at Special Libraries Serving the Fund Raising Professionals. Ed. by Jane Kokernak. 339p. 1991. 85.00 (*0-930807-26-X*, 600312) Fund Raising.

Prospect Spirit of Creative Poetry. Walter Moore. 72p. 1999. pap. 8.00 (*0-8059-4444-3*) Dorrance.

Prospecting: From Reader Response to Literary Anthropology. Wolfgang Iser. LC 88-46065. 304p. 1989. text 45.00 (*0-8018-3792-8*) Johns Hopkins.

Prospecting: From Reader Response to Literary Anthropology. Wolfgang Iser. 328p. 1993. reprint ed. pap. text 15.95 (*0-8018-4593-9*) Johns Hopkins.

Prospecting: Prospects: How to Find 'Em, Sign 'Em & What To Do with 'Em in Multilevel. Venus C. Andrecht. Ed. by Summer Andrecht. 120p. (Orig.). 1995. pap. 12.95 (*0-941903-13-3*) Ransom Hill.

Prospecting: The Key to Sales Success. Virden Thornton. Ed. by Robert Racine. LC 93-73211. (Fifty-Minute Ser.). (Illus.). 90p. (Orig.). 1994. pap. 10.95 (*1-56052-271-2*) Crisp Pubns.

Prospecting & Exploration of Mineral Deposits. 2nd rev. ed. M. Kuzvart & M. Bohmer. 508p. 1986. 264.25 (*0-444-99515-3*) Elsevier.

Prospecting for Drugs in Ancient & Medieval European Texts: A Scientific Approach. Ed. by Bart K. Holland. 182p. 1996. text 39.00 (*3-7186-5928-X*, Harwood Acad Pubs) Gordon & Breach.

Prospecting for Gold: From Dogtown to Virginia City, 1852-1864. Granville Stuart. (American Biography Ser.). 272p. 1991. reprint ed. lib. bdg. 69.00 (*0-7812-8372-8*) Rprt Serv.

Prospecting for Gold: 101 Ways to Market Yourself & Strike Gold in Sales. Thomas O. Metcalf. (Illus.). 163p. 1999. pap. 14.95 (*1-55571-483-8*, Oasis Pr) PSI Resch.

Prospecting for Lode Gold. 2nd ed. Gregory V. Stone. (Illus.). 56p. 1994. pap. 10.95 (*0-8059-3537-1*) Dorrance.

Prospecting for Successful Selling. abr. ed. Mark Victor Hansen. (Self-Help Ser.). 9.95 incl. audio (*0-07-026054-0*, TDM 1111, Caedmon) McGraw.

Prospecting in Alaska. R. Steinart. (Shorey Prospecting Ser.). 28p. reprint ed. pap. 10.00 (*0-8466-0038-2*, S38) Shoreys Bkstore.

***Prospecting International Relations: Conjectures at the Millennium International Studies Review Millennium Special Issue.** Ed. by Davis B. Bobrow. 172p. 1999. pap. text 32.95 (*0-631-21829-7*) Blackwell Pubs.

Prospecting of Deepwater Leads in the Portuguese Basin. Rui Vieira. 1989. 130.00 (*90-6314-582-9*, Pub. by Lorne & MacLean Marine) St Mut.

Prospecting of Deepwater Leads in the Portuguese Basin. Ed. by Rui Vieira. (C). 1989. 110.00 (*0-89771-733-3*, Pub. by Lorne & MacLean Marine) St Mut.

Prospecting Our Past: Gold, Silver & Tungsten Mills of Boulder County. 2nd rev. ed. Harrison S. Cobb. Ed. by Silvia Pettem. LC 99-233864. (Illus.). 160p. 1998. pap. 19.95 (*1-891274-02-3*) Book Lode.

Prospecting the Client: How to Target & Find the New Financial Services Customer. Laurie Brannen. 200p. 1991. text 24.95 (*1-55738-188-7*, Irwn Prfssnl) McGraw-Hill Prof.

Prospecting Your Way to Sales Success: How to Find New Business by Phone. Bill Good. 224p. 1986. 21.95 (*0-684-18620-9*) S&S Trade.

Prospecting Your Way to Sales Success: How to Find New Business by Phone, Fax & Internet. Bill Good. LC 97-18085. 1997. 27.00 (*0-684-84203-3*) S&S Trade.

Prospective Changes in Payment Systems: Implications for Credit Unions. David A. Humphrey. 61p. 1997. pap. 100.00 (*1-880572-29-X*, 1752-33) Filene Res.

Prospective City: Economic, Population, Energy, & Environmental Developments. Ed. by Arthur P. Solomon. (MIT-Harvard Joint Center for Urban Studies). 511p. 1981. pap. text 16.95 (*0-262-69071-3*) MIT Pr.

Prospective Community Studies in Developing Countries. Ed. by Monica Das Gupta et al. (International Studies in Demography). (Illus.). 358p. 1998. text 85.00 (*0-19-829209-0*) OUP.

Prospective Development of the Northern Seaboard. European Communities Staff. LC 96-122433. 220p. 1995. pap. 35.00 (*92-826-8828-3*, CX-85-94-535ENC, Pub. by Comm Europ Commun) Bernan Associates.

Prospective Financial Statements Documentation Manual. Larry L. Perry. 432p. 1988. ring bd. 69.95 (*0-13-731373-X*, Busn) P-H.

Prospective Issues in Infancy Research. Ed. by Kathleen Bloom. LC 80-17479. 208p. 1981. text 39.95 (*0-89859-059-0*) L Erlbaum Assocs.

Prospective Memory: Theory & Applications. Ed. by Maria Brandimonte et al. 432p. 1996. text 79.95 (*0-8058-1536-8*) L Erlbaum Assocs.

Prospective Payment for Ambulatory Services. Norbert Goldfield & William P. Kelly. LC 99-26845. 1999. write for info. (*0-8342-1640-X*) Aspen Pub.

Prospective Payment for Home Health Agencies. Judith J. Baker. 522p. Date not set. ring bd. 159.00 (*0-8342-1313-3*, 13133) Aspen Pub.

Prospective Payment for Home Health Agencies. Judith J. Baker. LC 98-38051. 300p. 1998. 69.00 (*0-8342-1111-4*, 11114) Aspen Pub.

***Prospective Payment for Long Term Care: An Annual Guide, 2000 Edition.** Baker. 2000. write for info. (*0-8342-1799-6*) Aspen Pub.

Prospective Payment for Long Term Care: An Annuel Guide. Judith J. Baker. 300p. 1998. 69.00 (*0-8342-1142-4*, 11424) Aspen Pub.

Prospective Payment Reimbursement: The Costs to Nursing. Ed. by Marian M. Pettengill & Lu Ann Young. 150p. (Orig.). 1988. pap. 12.50 (*0-942146-16-6*) Midwest Alliance Nursing.

Prospective Payment Systems for Inpatient Hospital Services Fiscal Year 1998 Regulations & Rates: Final Rule with Provider Reimbursement Provisions from the Balanced Budget Act of 1997. Ed. by CCH Editorial Staff. LC 98-170465. 256p. 1997. pap. 18.00 (*0-8080-0158-2*) CCH INC.

Prospective Payments & Hospital Discharge Planning with Older Adults. rev. ed. Cynthia Stuen. LC 91-30937. (Studies on the Elderly in America). 208p. 1991. text 30.00 (*0-8153-0516-8*) Garland.

Prospective Purchaser Agreements: Reducing the Liability Risks of Contaminated Property Elizabeth G. Geltman. LC 97-73770. xiii, 424 p. 1997. write for info. (*1-57073-502-6*) ABA Prof Educ Pubns.

Prospective Studies of Crime & Deliquency. Katherine Teilmann Van Dusen & Sarnoff A. Mednick. LC 83-178. (Longitudinal Research in the Behavioral, Social, & Medical Sciences Ser.). 1983. lib. bdg. 139.50 (*0-89838-131-2*) Kluwer Academic.

Prospectives: Celebrating 40 Years of AD Nursing Education. Ed. by Jean A. Simmons. 1993. 9.95 (*0-88737-576-6*, 23-2517) Natl League Nurse.

Prospector. J. M. G. Le Clezio. Tr. by Carol Marks from FRE. (Verba Mundi Ser.). 352p. 1993. 22.95 (*0-87923-976-X*) Godine.

Prospector: North of Sixty. Ted Nagle & Jordan Zinovich. 1989. pap. 14.95 (*0-919433-67-7*) Lone Pine.

Prospector's Field Book & Guide. 1996. lib. bdg. 360.95 (*0-8490-8329-X*) Gordon Pr.

Prospector's Gold & Canyon Walls. Zane Grey. (Illus.). 196p. 1990. pap. 3.50 (*0-8125-0536-0*, Pub. by Tor Bks) St Martin.

Prospects... Study of American Literature. Ed. by Richard Kopley. LC 97-15555. 1997. text 55.00 (*0-8147-4666-7*) NYU Pr.

Prospects & Challenges for the Caribbean. Steven B. Webb. LC HC11.W377 1977. (World Bank Latin America & Caribbean Studies). 40p. 1997. pap. 22.00 (*0-8213-3946-X*, 13946) World Bank.

Prospects & Policy for Europe-Wide Specialized Satellite Services. (Illus.). 25p. (Orig.). (C). 1993. pap. text 30.00 (*0-7881-0160-9*) DIANE Pub.

Prospects & Strategies for Nuclear Power: Global Boon or Dangerous Diversion? Peter Beck. 144p. (C). 1994. pap. 19.95 (*1-85383-217-0*) Brookings.

Prospects for a Common Morality. Ed. by Gene Outka & John P. Reeder, Jr. LC 92-5681. 296p. 1992. text 65.00 (*0-691-07418-6*, Pub. by Princeton U Pr); pap. text 18.95 (*0-691-02093-0*, Pub. by Princeton U Pr) Cal Prin Full Svc.

Prospects for a Natural Theology. Ed. by Eugene T. Long. LC 91-41756. (Studies in Philosophy & the History of Philosophy: Vol. 25). 242p. 1992. text 51.95 (*0-8132-0755-X*) Cath U Pr.

Prospects for a New Structuralism. Ed. by Hans-Heinrich Lieb. LC 92-33520. (Current Issues in Linguistic Theory Ser.: No. 96). vii, 275p. 1992. 59.00 (*1-55619-158-8*) J Benjamins Pubng Co.

Prospects for Adjustment in Argentina, Brazil, & Mexico: Responding to the Debt Crisis. Ed. by John Williamson. LC 83-81496. 71p. reprint ed. pap. 30.00 (*0-608-12179-7*, 202479100038) Bks Demand.

Prospects for Antisense Nucleic Acid Therapy of Cancer & AIDS. Eric Wickstrom. LC 91-22880. 284p. 1991. 175.00 (*0-471-56880-5*, Wiley-Liss) Wiley.

Prospects for Artificial Intelligence: Proceedings of AISB '93, 29 March-2 April 1993, Birmingham, U. K. Ed. by A. Sloman et al. LC 93-77459. 300p. (gr. 12). 1993. pap. 98.00 (*90-5199-126-6*, Pub. by IOS Pr) IOS Press.

Prospects for Change in Bibliographic Control: Proceedings of the 38th Annual Conference of the Graduate Library School, November 8-9, 1976. Ed. by Abraham Bookstein et al. LC 77-23767. (University of Chicago Studies in Library Science). 138p. Date not set. reprint ed. pap. 42.80 (*0-608-20593-1*, 205455800003) Bks Demand.

Prospects for Change in Socialist Systems: Challenges & Responses. Ed. by Charles J. Bukowski & Mark A. Cichock. LC 86-30614. 157p. 1987. 49.95 (*0-275-92434-3*, C2434, Praeger Pubs) Greenwood.

Prospects for Conservatives. rev. ed. Russell Kirk. LC 88-31812. 289p. 1989. pap. 11.95 (*0-89526-761-6*) Regnery Pub.

Prospects for Constitutional Democracy: Essays in Honor of R. Taylor Cole. Ed. by John H. Hallowell. LC 76-4220. 222p. reprint ed. pap. 68.90 (*0-608-12737-X*, 202339500033) Bks Demand.

Prospects for Container Shipping & Port Development: ASEAN Subregion. 50p. 20.00 (*92-1-119266-8*) UN.

Prospects for Container Shipping & Port Development: East Asia Subregion. 73p. 20.00 (*92-1-119267-6*) UN.

Prospects for Container Shipping & Port Development: South Asia Subregion. 60p. 20.00 (*92-1-119734-1*) UN.

Prospects for Democracy: North, South, East, West. David Held. LC 92-62583. 424p. (C). 1993. 52.50 (*0-8047-2192-0*); pap. 17.95 (*0-8047-2193-9*) Stanford U Pr.

***Prospects for Democracy in China.** Weller. LC 99-21971. 192p. 1999. 60.00 (*0-8133-3685-6*, Pub. by Westview) HarpC.

Prospects for Democracy in Mexico. enl. ed. Ed. by George W. Grayson. 338p. 1990. 39.95 (*0-88738-809-4*) Transaction Pubs.

Prospects for Democratic Development in Africa. Larry Diamond. LC 96-6718. (Essays in Public Policy Ser.: No. 74). 1996. pap. 5.00 (*0-8179-5792-8*) Hoover Inst Pr.

Prospects for East-West Relations. William G. Hyland et al. (Triangle Papers: No. 31). 1986. pap. 6.00 (*0-930503-00-7*) Trilateral Comm.

Prospects for Europe's Automotive Components Market. LC 96-232925. (Research Reports: No. R337). 1996. 875.00 (*0-85058-883-9*) Economist Intell.

Prospects for Europe's Automotive Components Market No. R317: An Assessment of Original Equipment & Aftermarket Demand by Product to 1997. 1994. 770.00 (*0-85058-731-X*) Economist Intell.

Prospects for Functional Programming in Software Engineering. J. P. Banatre et al. Ed. by Commission of the European Community Staff. (Research Reports ESPRIT, Project 302: Vol. 1). ix, 210p. 1991. 34.95 (*0-387-53852-6*) Spr-Verlag.

Prospects for Growth: Changing Expectations for the Future. Ed. by Kenneth D. Wilson. LC 77-14567. (Praeger Special Studies). 349p. 1977. 59.95 (*0-275-90278-1*, C0278, Praeger Pubs); pap. 19.95 (*0-03-041441-5*, Praeger Pubs) Greenwood.

Prospects for Hard Coal in Europe. Mike Parker. 75p. (C). pap. 14.95 (*0-905031-79-2*) Brookings.

Prospects for Hardware Foundations: ESPRIT Working Group 8533: NADA - New Hardware Design Methods, Survey Chapters. Ed. by Bernhard Moller & J. V. Tucker. LC 98-52459. x, 468p. 1998. pap. 69.00 (*3-540-65461-5*) Spr-Verlag.

Prospects for Implementation of Dayton Agreements & the New Nato Mission in Bosnia: Hearing Before the Committee on International Relations, House of Representatives, 105th Congress, Second Session, March 12, 1998. LC 98-207002. iii, 59 p. 1998. write for info. (*0-16-057188-X*) USGPO.

Prospects for International Engineering Practice: Proceedings of a Session Held in Conjunction with Structures, 1990. Ed. by Richard N. Wright. LC 90-34272. 65p. 1990. pap. text 5.00 (*0-87262-753-5*) Am Soc Civil Eng.

Prospects for Interstellar Travel. John H. Mauldin. LC 57-43769. (Science & Technology Ser.: Vol. 80). (Illus.). 390p. 1992. 50.00 (*0-87703-344-7*, Am Astronaut Soc) Univelt Inc.

Prospects for Korean Reunification. Ed. by Jay Speakman & Chae-Jin Lee. LC 93-15179. (Keck Center for International & Strategic Studies: No. 4). viii, 136p. 1993. pap. 10.95 (*0-930607-15-5*) Keck Ctr.

Prospects for Metropolitan Water Management. M. B. McPherson. 240p. 1970. pap. 3.00 (*0-87262-026-3*) Am Soc Civil Eng.

Prospects for Middle Eastern & North African Countries. Nemat Shafik. LC 97-13672. 240p. 1998. text 68.00 (*0-312-17633-3*) St Martin.

Prospects for Mining to the Year 2000. 256p. 95.00 (*92-1-100371-7*) UN.

Prospects for North Korea's Survival, Vol. 323. David Reese. LC 99-200844. (International Institute for Strategic Studies: 323). 96p. 1999. pap. text 26.95 (*0-19-922379-3*) OUP.

Prospects for Partnership: Industrialization & Trade Policies in the 1970's. Ed. by Helen Hughes. LC 72-12369. 310p. reprint ed. pap. 96.10 (*0-7837-4234-7*, 204392300012) Bks Demand.

Prospects for Peace & Development in Southern Africa in the 1990s: Canadian & Comparative Perspectives. Ed. by Larry A. Swatuk & Timothy M. Shaw. 321p. (C). 1991. pap. text 28.00 (*0-8191-8156-0*); lib. bdg. 49.00 (*0-8191-8155-2*) U Pr of Amer.

Prospects for Peace in the Middle East: An Israeli-Palestinian Dialogue (Helsinki Encounter) 142p. pap. 17.50 (*92-1-100493-4*, E.92.I.25) UN.

Prospects for Peace with Justice in Bosnia: Hearing Before the Committee on International Relations, House of Representatives, 104th Congress, 2nd Session, February 1, 1996. USGPO Staff. LC 96-152237. iii, 60 p. 1996. pap. write for info. (*0-16-052545-4*) USGPO.

Prospects for Peacemaking: A Citizen's Guide to Safer Nuclear Strategy. Ed. by Harlan Cleveland & Lincoln P. Bloomfield. LC 87-2622. 176p. 1987. 20.00 (*0-262-03131-0*) MIT Pr.

Prospects for People with Learning Disabilities. Ed. by Stanley S. Segal & Ved P. Varma. 224p. 1991. 90.00 (*1-85346-155-5*, Pub. by David Fulton) Taylor & Francis.

Prospects for Photovoltaic Power Supplies in Building. D. P. Gregory. (C). 1987. 105.00 (*0-86022-154-7*, Pub. by Build Servs Info Assn) St Mut.

Prospects for Photovoltaics: Commercialization, Mass Production & Application for Development. (ATAS Bulletin Ser.: No. 8). 304p. 25.00 (*92-1-104391-3*) UN.

Prospects for Post-Holocaust Theology: Israel in the Theologies of Karl Barth, Jurgen Moltmann & Paul VanBuren. Stephen Haynes. (American Academy of Religion Academy Ser.). 318p. (C). 1991. 29.95 (*1-55540-651-3*, 010177); pap. 19.95 (*1-55540-652-1*, 010177) OUP.

Prospects for Privatization. (Proceedings of the Academy of Political Science Ser.: Vol. 36, No. 3). 1987. pap. 12.95 (*0-614-04169-4*) Acad Poli Sci.

Prospects for Recovery & Sustainable Development in Africa, 169. Aguibou Y. Yansane. LC 93-49712. (Contributions in Afro-American & African Studies: No. 169). 384p. 1996. 65.00 (*0-313-28995-6*, Greenwood Pr) Greenwood.

Prospects for Russian Military R&D. Sharon Leiter. 95p. 1996. pap. text 15.00 (*0-8330-2362-4*, MR-709-A) Rand Corp.

Prospects for Sexing Mammalian Sperm. Ed. by Rupert P. Amann & George E. Siedel, Jr. LC 82-70138. (Illus.). 306p. reprint ed. pap. 94.90 (*0-7837-0549-2*, 204088300019) Bks Demand.

Prospects for Social Security Reform. Olivia S. Mitchell. LC 98-41908. 1999. 49.95 (*0-8122-3479-0*) U of Pa Pr.

***Prospects for Sustainable Development in the Chinese Countryside: The Political Economy of Chinese Ecological Agriculture.** Richard Sanders. 240p. 1999. text 69.95 (*1-84014-924-8*, Pub. by Ashgate Pub) Ashgate Pub Co.

Prospects for Sustainable Energy: A Critical Assessment. Edward S. Cassedy. LC 99-11969. (Illus.). 345p. (C). 2000. 69.95 (*0-521-63120-3*) Cambridge U Pr.

Prospects for the British Economy. Cockerell Brown. 59.95 (*1-85628-844-7*) Ashgate Pub Co.

***Prospects for the Development of a Peripheral Electricity Market in the Balkan.** 209p. 1999. 50.00 (*92-828-2620-1*, CS-11-97-455-EN-C, Pub. by Comm Europ Commun) Bernan Associates.

Prospects for the Development of the Central & Capital Cities & Regions. 266p. 1996. pap. 40.00 (*92-826-8808-9*, CX85-94-567-ENC, Pub. by Comm Europ Commun) Bernan Associates.

Prospects for the Nation: Recent Essays in British Landscape, 1750-1880, Vol. 4. Michael Rosenthal. LC 97-60730. (Studies in British Art: Vol. 4). 335p. 1997. 50.00 (*0-300-06383-0*) Yale U Pr.

Prospects for the Study of American Literature: A Guide for Scholars & Students. Richard Kopley. LC 97-15555. 1997. pap. text 19.50 (*0-8147-4698-5*) NYU Pr.

Prospects for the Textile & Clothing Sector of the ESCAP Region in the Post-Uruguay Round Context. (Studies in Trade & Investment: No. 17). 52p. pap. 15.00 (*92-1-119808-9*) UN.

Prospects for the World Cocoa Market until the Year 2005. 297p. 1991. 45.00 (*92-1-112295-3*) UN.

***Prospects for the World Economy.** Richard N. Cooper. (New Ser.: Vol. 26). 26p. 2000. pap. 15.00 (*0-86682-112-0*) Ctr Intl Relations.

Prospects for Tourism Is Chhekampar. Bishnu Bhandari. 1998. pap. 27.00 (*0-7855-7481-6*, Pub. by Ratna Pustak Bhandar) St Mut.

Prospects for Western Hemisphere Free Trade. Jeffrey J. Schott. 80p. 2000. pap. 15.95 (*0-88132-275-X*) Inst Intl Eco.

Negotiations on a Free Trade Area of the Americas (FTAA) were officially launched at the Santiago Summit in April 1998. This study examines the prospects for the FTAA in light of the new challenges to trade negotiations posed by the global financial crisis. It first focuses on the policy reforms instituted throughout Latin America since the Miami Summit & then assesses the "readiness" of countries to participate in a broad hemisphere-wide free trade zone. It includes updated "readiness indicators" originally developed by Hufbauer & Schott in their 1194 study, Western Hemisphere Economic Integration. *Publisher Paid Annotation.*

Prospects in Aging. Ed. by J. C. Dall et al. (Sandoz Lectures in Gerontology). (Illus.). 314p. 1993. text 101.00 (*0-12-200745-X*) Acad Pr.

Prospects in Complex Geometry: Proceedings of the 25th Taniguchi International Symposium Held in Katata, & the Conference held in Kyoto, July 31-August 9, 1989. Ed. by J. Noguchi & T. Ohsawa. (Lecture Notes in Mathematics Ser.: Vol. 1468). vii, 421p. 1991. 62.95 (*0-387-54053-9*) Spr-Verlag.

Prospects in Complex Geometry: Proceedings of the 25th Taniguchi International Symposium Held in Katata & the Conference Held in Kyoto, July 31-August 9, 1989. Junjireo Noguchi et al. LC 91-202464. 421p. 1991. write for info. (*3-540-54053-9*) Spr-Verlag.

Prospects in Diagnosis & Treatment of Breast Cancer. Ed. by Manfred Schmitt et al. LC 94-13767. (International Congress Ser.: No. 1050). 252p. 1994. 178.50 (*0-444-81707-7*, Excerpta Medica) Elsevier.

Prospects in Mathematics: Invited Talks on the Occasion of the 250th Anniversary of Princeton University. Ed. by Hugo Rossi. LC 98-36451. 154p. 1998. 29.00 (*0-8218-0975-X*) Am Math.

Prospects in Modern Acoustics: Education & Development. Ed. by G. Budzynski & A. S. Sliwinski. 472p. (C). 1987. text 144.00 (*9971-5-0379-4*) World Scientific Pub.

Prospects in Nanotechnology: Toward Molecular Manufacturing. Ed. by Markus Krummenacker & James Lewis. LC 94-5710. 297p. 1995. 59.99 (*0-471-30914-1*) Wiley.

Prospects in Topology: Proceedings of a Conference in Honor of William Browder. Ed. by Frank Quinn. LC 95-25751. (Annals of Mathematics Studies: No. 138). 340p. 1996. pap. text 29.95 (*0-691-02728-5*, Pub. by Princeton U Pr) Cal Prin Full Svc.

Prospects In Trade Investing & Business. Van Hoa. LC 99-37581. 1999. text 69.95 (*0-312-22656-X*) St Martin.

***Prospects, Independent Power Production in Brazil: A Strategic Entry Report, 1996.** Compiled by Icon Group International Staff. (Illus.). 162p. 1999. ring bd. 1620.00 incl. audio compact disk (*0-7418-1204-5*) Icon Grp.

Prospects of a U. S.-Chile Free Trade Agreement. Dean C. Alexander. (Nijhoff Law Specials Ser.). 164p. (C). 1994. pap. text 60.00 (*0-7923-2885-X*, Pub. by M Nijhoff) Kluwer Academic.

Prospects of American Industrial Recovery. John E. Ullmann. LC 84-15923. (Illus.). 244p. 1985. 65.00 (*0-89930-063-4*, UED/, Quorum Bks) Greenwood.

Prospects of Democracy: A Study of 172 Countries. Tatu Vanhanen. LC 96-26285. 392p. (C). 1997. 90.00 (*0-415-14405-1*); pap. 29.99 (*0-415-14406-X*) Routledge.

Prospects of Democracy & Other Essays. Alfred E. Zimmern. LC 68-8506. (Essay Index Reprint Ser.). 1977. 21.95 (*0-8369-1017-6*) Ayer.

Prospects of Economic Development Through Co-Operation in North-East Asia. (Studies in Trade & Investment: No. 7). 143p. 30.00 (*92-1-119647-7*, E.94.II.F.15) UN.

Prospects of Eternity. Russell. 188p. 1982. 10.95 (*0-85435-394-1*, Pub. by C W Daniel) Natl Bk Netwk.

Prospects of Eternity: Debunking Death. Edward W. Russell. 164p. (Orig.). pap. 16.95 (*0-8464-4274-4*) Beekman Pubs.

Prospects of Heart Surgery. Alan Radley. (Contributions to Psychology & Medicine Ser.). (Illus.). 250p. 1988. 105.95 (*0-387-96721-4*) Spr-Verlag.

Prospects of Humanism. Lawrence Hyde. LC 77-94273. (Select Bibliographies Reprint Ser.). 1977. 24.95 (*0-8369-5047-X*) Ayer.

Prospects of Industrial Civilization. Russell. LC 96-222613. 264p. (C). 1996. 60.00 (*0-415-13602-4*) Routledge.

Prospects of Industrial Civilization. Bertrand Russell. 1996. lib. bdg. 251.75 (*0-8490-5942-9*) Gordon Pr.

Prospects of Industrial Civilization. Bertrand Russell & Dora Russell. LC 96-222613. 264p. (C). 1996. pap. 18.99 (*0-415-13133-2*) Routledge.

Prospects of Mathematical Science. Ed. by Kenji Nagasaka et al. 284p. (C). 1988. pap. 40.00 (*9971-5-0465-0*); text 98.00 (*9971-5-0454-5*) World Scientific Pub.

Prospects of Part-time Work: Preparing to Evaluate the Back to Work Bonus : A Study Carried Out On Behalf of the Department of Social Security Alison Smith. LC 99-170067. (In-House Report Ser.). 1998. write for info. (*1-85197-862-3*) Dept of Social Security.

Prospects of Power: Tragedy, Satire, the Essay, & the Theory of Genre. John Snyder. LC 90-38952. 248p. 1991. text 32.00 (*0-8131-1724-0*) U Pr of Ky.

Prospects of the Heart. large type ed. Rosemary Gill. (Linford Romance Library). 1989. pap. 16.99 (*0-7089-6780-9*, Linford) Ulverscroft.

Prospects of World Urbanization, 1988. (Population Studies: No. 112). 204p. 23.00 (*92-1-151182-8*, E.89.XIII.8) UN.

Prospects of World Urbanization, 1984-85: Revised. rev. ed. (Population Studies: No. 101). 269p. 1987. pap. 34.00 (*92-1-151163-1*, E.87.XIII.3) UN.

Prospects, Thresholds, Interiors: Watercolours from the National Collection at The Victoria & Albert Museum. Lewis Johnson. LC 93-3423. (Illus.). 270p. (C). 1994. pap. text 31.95 (*0-521-44927-8*) Cambridge U Pr.

Prospects, Thresholds, Interiors: Watercolours from the National Collection at The Victoria & Albert Museum. Lewis Johnson. LC 93-3423. (Illus.). 270p. (C). 1994. text 80.00 (*0-521-44488-8*) Cambridge U Pr.

Prospectus. Bruce Braunstein. 1986. 89.95 incl. audio (*0-317-52217-5*) Tetragrammaton.

Prospectus d'un Nouveau Dictionnaire de Commerce. Andre Morellet. (Economistes Francais du XVIIIe Siecle Ser.). 1990. reprint ed. pap. 44.00 (*0-8115-3802-8*) Periodicals Srv.

Prospectus for the Triumph of Realism. Thomas A. Russman. LC 86-28646. 208p. (C). 1987. 24.95 (*0-86554-232-5*, MUP-H205) Mercer Univ Pr.

Prospectus of a System of General Geography. Charles Brockden Brown. (Works of Charles Brockden Brown). 1989. reprint ed. lib. bdg. 79.00 (*0-685-44731-6*) Rprt Serv.

ProSpeech: American Diction for Men & Women in Business, How to Speak for Success. Geoffrey G. Forward. (Illus.). 325p. (Orig.). 1995. pap. 39.95 (*0-944200-04-4*) Forward CA.

Prosper. Mark Dunster. 24p. (Orig.). 1995. pap. 5.00 (*0-89642-266-6*) Linden Pubs.

Prosper Lucas's "On the Heredity of Mental Illness" (1850) Prosper Lucas. Ed. by Charles D. Mellon. Tr. by Linda F. Mellon from FRE. LC 96-94516. (Illus.). 83p. 1996. 29.50 (*0-9653362-1-2*) Genetics Heritage.

Prosper Merimee. Maxwell A. Smith. LC 72-1485. (Twayne's World Authors Ser.). 200p. (C). 1972. lib. bdg. 20.95 (*0-8290-1747-X*) Irvington.

Prosper Merimee: A Concise Study of Carmen & His Other Novels, with a Short Biography. George H. Yu. Tr. by Sun L. Yu from FRE. LC 91-72150. (Illus.). 240p. 1997. 21.95 (*1-878756-90-7*); pap. 14.95 (*1-878756-91-5*) YCP Pubns.

Prosper of Aquitaine - De Providentia Dei: Text, Translation & Commentary. Miroslav Marcovich. LC 89-36313. (Supplements to Vigiliae Christianae Ser.: No. X). xii, 137p. 1989. text 54.00 (*90-04-09090-8*) Brill Academic Pubs.

Prosper Through Environmental Leadership: Succeeding in Tough Times. Joseph R. Jablonski. LC 93-94312. 192p. 1994. 19.95 (*1-878821-08-3*) Tech Man Consortium.

Prosperidad. Charles Fillmore. LC 97-45117.Tr. of Prosperity. (SPA.). 234p. 1998. 12.95 (*0-87159-215-0*) Unity Bks.

Prosperidad: Es Posible - Sociedad en Crisis?Tr. of Prosperity: Possible/Society in Crisis?. (SPA.). 1990. 3.99 (*1-56063-063-9*, 498025); pap. write for info. (*0-614-27124-X*) Editorial Unilit.

Prospering in Private Practice: A Handbook for Speech-Language Pathology & Audiology. Katharine G. Butler. LC 86-10828. 320p. (C). 1986. 75.00 (*0-87189-368-1*) Aspen Pub.

Prospering Parachurch: Enlarging the Boundaries of God's Work. Wesley K. Willmer et al. LC 98-25331. (Religion in Practice Ser.). 256p. 1998. 21.95 (*0-7879-4198-0*) Jossey-Bass.

Prospering Power of Love. rev. ed. Catherine Ponder. LC 66-25849. 126p. 1984. reprint ed. pap. 6.95 (*0-87516-525-7*) DeVorss.

Prospering Power of Prayer. Catherine Ponder. 80p. 1983. pap. 6.95 (*0-87516-516-8*) DeVorss.

Prosperites du Vice. Marquis De Sade, pseud. (FRE.). 320p. 1969. pap. 16.95 (*0-7859-5569-0*, 2264008393) Fr & Eur.

Prosperity see Prosperidad

Prosperity. Charles Fillmore. Ed. by Michael Maday. LC 98-33938. 217p. 2000. 12.95 (*0-87159-107-3*) Unity Bks.

***Prosperity: A Woman's Guide to Achieving Spiritual, Financial & Emotional Strength.** Ross. 208p. 2000. 7.98 (*1-56731-389-2*, MJF Bks) Fine Comms.

Prosperity: Coming Twenty-Year Boom & What it Means. Bob Davis. LC 97-44858. 1998. 27.50 (*0-8129-2819-9*, Times Bks) Crown Pub Group.

Prosperity; The Choice Is Yours. Kenneth Copeland. 35p. 1985. pap. 3.95 (*0-88114-728-1*) K Copeland Pubns.

Prosperity: The Coming Twenty Year Boom & What It Means to You. Bob Davis. 324p. 1999. pap. 14.00 (*0-8129-3200-5*, Times Bks) Crown Pub Group.

Prosperity Aerobics. Cary Bayer. 80p. 7.95 (*0-9644224-0-9*, Pub. by Bayer Commun) New Leaf Dist.

***Prosperity & Danger: Das Gesellschaftsbild Amerikanischer Intellektueller in Den 1950 Jahren.** Arndt Schnoring. (Europaische Hochschulschriften Geschichte und Ihre Hilfswissenschaften Ser.). 262p. 1999. 42.95 (*3-631-35610-2*) P Lang Pubng.

Prosperity & Depression: A Theoretical Analysis of Cyclical Movements. 4th ed. Gottfried Haberler. LC 59-6133. (Economic Studies: No. 105). (Illus.). 535p. 1964. 35.00 (*0-674-71750-3*) HUP.

Prosperity & Parenthood. Banks. 248p. 1993. 56.95 (*0-7512-0267-3*) Ashgate Pub Co.

An Asterisk (*) at the beginning of an entry indicates that the title is appearing for the first time.

Prosperity & Public Spending: Transformation Growth & the Role of Government. Edward J. Nell. (Studies in International Political Economy). 224p. 1988. text 37.95 (*0-04-339044-7*); pap. text 17.95 (*0-04-339045-5*) Routledge.

Prosperity & Sustainable Development for Canada: Advice to the Prime Minister of Canada. Ronald L. Doering & David Runnalls. 37p. (Orig.). 1996. pap. text 20.00 (*0-7881-2801-9*) DIANE Pub.

Prosperity & the Christian-Owned Business. Os Hillman. 1996. 4.95 (*1-888582-03-0*) Aslan Pubng.

Prosperity & the Coming Apocalypse. Jim Bakker. LC 98-39749. 256p. 1998. 19.99 (*0-7852-7458-8*) Nelson.

Prosperity & Violence. Robert Bates. 22.95 (*0-393-05038-6*) Norton.

Prosperity Cards. Deborah Thornton. 52p. 1994. 15.99 (*0-9636638-2-8*) Inspirat Prayer.

Prosperity Consciousness. 2nd rev. ed. Martha B. Beveridge. Ed. by Terrisa Bruce-Phipps. 28p. 1994. pap. 3.50 (*1-889237-04-3*) Options Now.

Prosperity Consciousness: How to Tap Your Unlimited Wealth. Fredric Lehrman. 1995. 16.00 incl. audio (*0-671-52975-7*) S&S Trade.

Prosperity Consciousness Consultation. Leonard D. Orr. 1990. 20.00 (*0-945793-10-3*) Inspir Univ.

Prosperity Decade: From War to Depression 1917-1929. George Soule. LC 89-10694. (The Economic History of the United States Ser.). 380p. (gr. 13). 1977. pap. text 34.95 (*0-87332-098-0*) M E Sharpe.

Prosperity, Depression, & War, 1920-1945. 2nd expanded rev. ed. Alan Brinkley. (New American History Ser.). 26p. (C). 1997. reprint ed. pap. 5.00 (*0-87229-090-5*) Am Hist Assn.

Prosperity for Beginners. Yvon Morris. 51p. 1996. pap. 9.98 (*1-888139-02-1*) Y Morris Carib.

Prosperity Forever: The New World Order. J. Ray Estefania. (Victory Ser.: No. 3). 1993. 19.95 (*0-945542-01-1*) Park & Park Pub.

***Prosperity from Technology: A New Approach to Industrial Production, Money & the Environment.** David Rudd. LC 99-201234. x, 409 p. 1999. write for info. (*1-85776-362-9*, Pub. by Book Guild Ltd) Gannon.

***Prosperity Gap: Why Americans Are Falling Behind: A Posterbook.** Barry Bluestone et al. (Illus.). 64p. 1999. pap. 16.95 (*1-56584-479-3*, Pub. by New Press NY) Norton.

Prosperity God's Way! Keith E. Johnson, Jr. (Illus.). 63p. 1997. pap. 5.00 (*0-9662283-7-5*) Life-N-Faith.

Prosperity God's Way. Lester Sumrall. 50p. (C). 1985. pap. text 6.00 (*0-937580-66-X*) Sumrall Pubng.

Prosperity Gospel see IVP Booklets

***Prosperity Gospel, 5 vols.** Charles E. Hummel. 32p. (Orig.). 1999. pap. 4.95 (*0-8308-6586-1*) InterVarsity.

Prosperity Handbook: A Guide to Personal & Financial Success. Michael Fries & C. Holland Taylor. Ed. by Diane Frank. LC 83-72180. (Illus.). 512p. 1984. 16.95 (*0-9611910-0-7*); pap. 9.95 (*0-9611910-4-X*) Comm Res.

Prosperity Handbook: Winning the Money Game. Paul De Haas & Surya Lovejoy. 150p. 1994. 34.95 (*0-566-07447-8*, Pub. by Gower) Ashgate Pub Co.

Prosperity, How to Attract It. Orison S. Marden. 325p. 1998. pap. 28.00 (*0-89540-392-7*, SB-392) Sun Pub.

Prosperity in the Information Age: Creating Value with Technology - from Mailrooms to Boardrooms. James K. Ho. 308p. 1995. pap. 25.00 (*1-885058-08-X*) Infotomics.

Prosperity Instructors' Course Guide. Charles Fillmore. 1998. ring bd. 17.95 (*0-87159-985-6*, 2114, Unity Schl Relgs Studies) Unity Bks.

***Prosperity is More than an Attitude A Practical Use of the Law.** Alyce B. Soden. 1998. pap. text 9.95 (*1-57087-397-6*) Prof Pr NC.

Prosperity Learners' Workbook. Charles Fillmore. (Orig.). 1998. pap. text 14.95 (*0-87159-984-8*, 2115, Unity Schl Relgs Studies) Unity Bks.

Prosperity Lovers Guide: "Or Better" Holly Hogue & Rick Hogue. 64p. 1994. pap. text. write for info. (*1-881571-05-X*) Letters Etcetera.

Prosperity Magick: How-to Transform Your World into a Luxuriantly Abundant Environment of Your Own. Zuriel. (Illus.). 60p. (C). 1991. pap. 9.95 (*1-57555-004-0*, Monster Bks) Cedar Bay Pr.

Prosperity on God's Terms. Frederick K. Price. 112p. (Orig.). 1990. pap. 5.99 (*0-89274-670-X*, HH670) Harrison Hse.

Prosperity 101: The Key to Your Future. Jane Vincent. LC 96-65956. 1997. mass mkt., per. 12.95 (*1-889131-08-3*) CasAnanda.

Prosperity Plan. Albert A. Van Petten. LC 89-51500. 216p. (Orig.). 1990. 14.95 (*1-878357-16-6*) Van Petten Co.

Prosperity Plan: Starter Kit: A Metaphysical Catalyst to Health, Wealth & Happiness. 2nd rev. ed. C. A. Lofton. (Illus.). 84p. 1997. 25.95 (*0-9659321-2-5*); pap. 14.00 (*0-9659321-0-9*); lib. bdg. 16.00 (*0-9659321-1-7*) Lofton Publ.

Prosperity: Possible/Society in Crisis? see Prosperidad: Es Posible - Sociedad en Crisis?

Prosperity, Poverty, & Pollution: The Emergence of Global Economic Responsibility. Nurnberger. LC 98-32145. 480p. 1999. pap. 27.50 (*1-85649-731-3*) St Martin.

Prosperity Power Tools. Richard Ervasti & Mary Ervasti. 168p. 1997. reprint ed. pap. 14.95 (*0-9658081-0-6*) Ervasti & Co.

Prosperity Promises. Kenneth Copeland. 48p. 1985. pap. 2.50 (*0-88114-731-1*) K Copeland Pubns.

Prosperity Promises. expanded ed. Kenneth Copeland & Gloria Copeland. 288p. 1997. pap. 6.95 (*1-57562-036-7*) K Copeland Pubns.

***Prosperity, Region & Institutions in Maritime China: The South Fukien Pattern, 946-1368.** Billy K. L. So. 2000. 49.50 (*0-674-00371-3*) HUP.

Prosperity Restored by the State Rate Tax Plan. Edward A. Ellison. LC 85-10104. write for info. (*0-934005-00-1*) Free State Constitution.

Prosperity Secrets of the Ages. rev. ed. Catherine Ponder. LC 64-16436. 344p. 1986. reprint ed. pap. 14.95 (*0-87516-567-2*) DeVorss.

Prosperity Through Thought Force. Bruce MacLelland. 158p. 1997. pap. 12.00 (*0-89540-276-9*, SB-276) Sun Pub.

Prosperity Versus Planning: How Government Stifles Economic Growth. David Osterfeld. (Illus.). 288p. (C). 1992. pap. text 26.95 (*0-19-507614-1*) OUP.

Prosperity with Purpose. Marc Carr. Ed. by Florence K. Biros. (Mini Teaching Ser.). 96p. (Orig.). 1987. pap. 3.95 (*0-936369-13-2*) Son-Rise Pubns.

Prosperity Without Inflation. Arthur F. Burns. LC 58-7634. (Millar Lectures). 102p. reprint ed. pap. 31.70 (*0-7837-5570-8*, 204534800005) Bks Demand.

Prosperity Without Pollution: The Prevention Strategy for Industry & Consumers. Joel S. Hirschhorn & Kirsten U. Oldenburg. 400p. 1990. pap. 49.95 (*0-471-28395-9*, VNR) Wiley.

Prosperity Without Pollution: The Prevention Strategy for Industry & Consumers. Joel S. Hirschhorn & Kirsten U. Oldenburg. 1991. pap. 38.95 (*0-442-00225-4*, VNR) Wiley.

Prosperity's Promise: The Amazon Rubber Boom & Distorted Economic Development. Bradford L. Barham & Oliver T. Coomes. LC 96-8820. (Dellplain Latin American Studies). (C). 1996. pap. 75.00 (*0-8133-8996-8*, Pub. by Westview) HarpC.

Prosperity's Ten Commandments. Georgiana T. West. Ed. by Michael Maday. 170p. 2000. reprint ed. 12.95 (*0-87159-125-1*, 16) Unity Bks.

Prospero & Caliban: The Psychology of Colonization. Octave Mannoni. 224p. 1990. text 49.50 (*0-472-09430-0*, 09430); pap. text 18.95 (*0-472-06430-4*, 06430) U of Mich Pr.

Prospero Drill. Carl A. Posey. 288p. 1988. per. 3.95 (*0-373-97052-8*) Harlequin Bks.

***Prospero in Therapy.** Dancing Bear Staff. 40p. 1999. pap. 5.00 (*0-9659307-1-8*) Dream Horse Pr.

Prospero's Almanac, 1997 Vol. 1: The Theatre Lover's Guide to the World at Large. Prospero Press Staff. (Illus.). 96p. (Orig.). 1996. mass mkt. 7.95 (*0-937657-21-2*) Feedbk Theabks & Prospero.

Prospero's Cell: A Guide to the Landscape & Manners of the Island of Corfu. Lawrence Durrell. LC 96-24352. 150p. 1996. pap. 10.95 (*1-56924-766-8*) Marlowe & Co.

***Prospero's Children.** Jan Siegel. 368p. 2000. 24.00 (*0-345-43901-5*, Del Rey) Ballantine Pub Grp.

Prospero's Daughter: The Prose of Rosario Castellanos. Joanna O'Connell. LC 95-3795. (Texas Pan American Ser.). 288p. (Orig.). 1995. 35.00 (*0-292-76041-8*); pap. 17.95 (*0-292-76042-6*) U of Tex Pr.

Prospero's Kitchen: Mediterranean Cooking of the Ionian Islands from Corfu to Kythera. Diana F. Louis & June Marinos. LC 94-49418. (Illus.). 256p. 1995. 21.95 (*0-87131-782-6*) M Evans.

***Prospero's Magic: Active Learning Strategies for the Teaching of Literature.** rev. ed. Ed. by Michael Degen. 120p. 2000. pap. 17.95 (*0-9665125-4-5*) Telemachos Pub.

Prospero's Mirror: A Translator's Portfolio of Latin American Short Fiction. Ed. by Ilan Stavans. LC 97-16443. 327p. (Orig.). 1997. pap. 17.95 (*1-880684-49-7*) Curbstone.

Prospero's Palace. Christopher Manson. Date not set. pap. write for info. (*0-8050-4865-0*) H Holt & Co.

Prospero's Staff: Acting & Directing in the Contemporary Theatre. Charles Marowitz. LC 85-45887. (Indiana Studies in Theatre & Drama). 213p. 1986. pap. 66.10 (*0-608-05032-6*, 205969300004) Bks Demand.

Prosperous Ending. Bint Al-Huda. Tr. by Fatemeh Talebian. 156p. (J). 1997. pap. 12.95 (*1-871031-72-9*) Kazi Pubns.

Prosperous Few & the Restless Many. Noam Chomsky. LC 93-35814. (Real Story Ser.). 95p. (Orig.). 1994. pap. 7.00 (*1-878825-03-8*) Odonian Pr.

Prosperous Paupers & Other Population Problems. Nicholas Eberstadt. 256p. 1999. 34.95 (*1-56000-423-1*) Transaction Pubs.

Prosperous Retirement: Guide to the New Reality. Michael K. Stein. LC 98-92621. (Illus.). 320p. 1998. pap. 19.95 (*0-9663381-0-3*, E98101, EMSTCO Pr) EMSTCO.

Prosperous Soul. Miriam Hellman. 109p. 1991. pap. 10.00 (*1-891309-01-3*) Prophetic DC.

Prosperous Years: The Economic History of Ontario, 1939-1975. Kenneth J. Rea. (Ontario Historical Studies). 304p. 1985. pap. 14.95 (*0-8020-6592-9*) U of Toronto Pr.

Prosperous Years: The Economic History of Ontario, 1939-1975. Kenneth J. Rea. LC 86-182022. (Ontario Historical Studies). 301p. reprint ed. pap. 93.40 (*0-8357-3771-3*, 203650000003) Bks Demand.

Prosser & Keeton on Torts: Lawyers Edition. 5th ed. William L. Prosser & Page Keeton. LC 83-19714. (Hornbook Ser.). 1456p. 1985. reprint ed. text. write for info. (*0-314-74442-8*) West Pub.

Prosser, 1910-1920: Going Back. Paul Fridlund. 172p. 1985. 19.95 (*0-87770-367-1*) Ye Galleon.

Prost! The Story of German Beer. Horst D. Dornbusch. LC 97-18237. (Illus.). 160p. 1998. pap. 14.95 (*0-937381-55-1*, Siris Bks) Brewers Pubns.

Prostacyclin & Hypertension. Gerd Bonner & K. H. Rahn. (Illus.). xii, 90p. 1990. 17.95 (*0-387-52140-2*) Spr-Verlag.

***Prostacyclin & Its Receptors.** Helen D. Wise & Robert L. Jones. LC 99-52122. 1999. write for info. (*0-306-46308-3*, Kluwer Plenum) Kluwer Academic.

Prostacyclin in Pregnancy. Ed. by Peter J. Lewis et al. LC 83-42597. (Illus.). 246p. 1983. reprint ed. pap. 76.30 (*0-7837-9559-9*, 206030800005) Bks Demand.

Prostaglandin. 1988. 69.95 (*0-387-50098-7*) Spr-Verlag.

Prostaglandin & Fertility Regulation. Ed. by M. Toppozada et al. (Advances in Reproductive Health Care Ser.). 1984. text 225.00 (*0-85200-804-X*) Kluwer Academic.

Prostaglandin & Lipid Metabolism in Radiation Injury. Ed. by T. L. Walden, Jr. & H. N. Hughes. LC 87-32663. (Illus.). 434p. 1988. 110.00 (*0-306-42793-1*, Plenum Trade) Perseus Pubng.

Prostaglandin Inhibitors in Tumor Immunology & Immunotherapy. Jules E. Harris. 256p. 1994. lib. bdg. 249.00 (*0-8493-6903-7*, QR188) CRC Pr.

Prostaglandins: Biology & Chemistry of Prostaglandins & Related Eicosanoids. Ed. by P. B. Curtis-Prior. (Illus.). 720p. 1988. text 250.00 (*0-443-02519-3*) Church.

Prostaglandins & Arachidonate Metabolites. Ed. by Sidney P. Colowick & William E. Lands. LC 82-6791. (Methods in Enzymology Ser.: Vol. 86). 1982. text 188.00 (*0-12-181986-8*) Acad Pr.

Prostaglandins & Cardiovascular Disease. Ed. by Ruth J. Hegyeli. LC 80-5411. (Atherosclerosis Reviews Ser.: No. 8). (Illus.). 217p. 1981. reprint ed. pap. 67.30 (*0-7837-7098-7*, 204692700004) Bks Demand.

Prostaglandins & Control of Vascular Smooth Muscle Cell Proliferation. Ed. by K. Schror et al. (Agents & Actions Supplements Ser.: Vol. 48). 129p. 1997. 56.50 (*3-7643-5689-8*) Birkhauser.

Prostaglandins & Eicosanoids. Curtis. text. write for info. (*0-471-48984-0*) Wiley.

Prostaglandins & Immunity. Ed. by James S. Goodwin. LC 85-4989. (Prostaglandins, Leukotrienes, & Cancer Ser.: No. 4). 1985. text 113.50 (*0-89838-723-X*) Kluwer Academic.

Prostaglandins & Inflammation. Ed. by Kim D. Rainsford & A. Ford-Hutchinson. (Agents & Actions Supplements Ser.: No. 6). (Illus.). 242p. 1980. 63.00 (*0-8176-1132-0*) Birkhauser.

Prostaglandins & Membrane Ion Transport. Ed. by Pierre Braquet et al. LC 84-24949. (Advances in Ion Transport Regulation Ser.: No. 1). (Illus.). 430p. 1985. reprint ed. pap. 133.30 (*0-608-00658-0*, 206124600007) Bks Demand.

Prostaglandins & Other Eicosanoids in the Cardiovascular System. Ed. by K. Schroer. (Illus.). xiv, 570p. 1985. pap. 143.50 (*3-8055-4007-8*) S Karger.

Prostaglandins & Perinatal Medicine. fac. ed. Ed. by Flavio Coceani & Peter M. Olley. LC 77-17758. (Advances in Prostaglandin, Thromboxane Research Ser.: No. 4). 428p. pap. 132.70 (*0-7837-7538-5*, 204696600005) Bks Demand.

Prostaglandins & Related Compounds: Seventh International Conference, Florence, Italy. Ed. by Bengt Samuelsson et al. LC 83-645438. (Advances in Prostaglandin, Thromboxane, & Leukotriene Research Ser.: Vol. 21A). 528p. 1991. reprint ed. pap. 163.70 (*0-608-03445-2*, 206414600008) Bks Demand.

Prostaglandins & Related Compounds: Sixth International Conference, Florence, Italy, Vol. 17A. fac. ed. Ed. by Bengt Samuelsson et al. LC 87-4286. (Advances in Prostaglandin, Thromboxane, & Leukotriene Research Ser.: No. 17A-B). 624p. pap. 177.90 (*0-7837-7436-2*, 2047231) Bks Demand.

Prostaglandins & Related Compounds: Sixth International Conference, Florence, Italy, Vol. 17B. fac. ed. Ed. by Bengt Samuelsson et al. LC 87-4286. (Advances in Prostaglandin, Thromboxane, & Leukotriene Research Ser.: No. 17A-B). 620p. pap. 192.20 (*0-7837-7437-0*, 204723100002) Bks Demand.

Prostaglandins & Related Compounds: 9th International Conference, Florence, Italy. Ed. by Bengt Samuelsson et al. LC 83-645438. (Advances in Prostaglandin, Thromboxane, & Leukotriene Research Ser.: Vol. 23). 603p. 1995. reprint ed. pap. 187.00 (*0-608-07270-2*, 206749800009) Bks Demand.

Prostaglandins & the Cardiovascular System. Ed. by John A. Oates. LC 82-15035. (Advances in Prostaglandin, Thromboxane, & Leukotriene Research Ser.: No. 10). (Illus.). 400p. 1982. reprint ed. pap. 124.00 (*0-7837-9638-2*, 206039100005) Bks Demand.

Prostaglandins & the Kidney. Ed. by R. Horton & M. J. Dunn. (Journal: Mineral & Electrolyte Metabolism Ser.: Vol. 6, No. 1-2). (Illus.). 104p. 1981. pap. 61.00 (*3-8055-3406-X*) S Karger.

Prostaglandins & the Kidney: Biochemistry, Physiology, Pharmacology & Clinical Applications. Ed. by Michael J. Dunn et al. LC 82-18117. 438p. 1982. 95.00 (*0-306-41054-0*, Kluwer Plenum) Kluwer Academic.

Prostaglandins & the Uterus. Ed. by J. O. Drife & A. A. Calder. (Illus.). xiii, 301p. 1992. 159.00 (*0-387-19719-2*) Spr-Verlag.

Prostaglandins in Bone Resorption. Ed. by Wilson Harvey. 144p. 1987. 87.00 (*0-8493-5591-5*, QP88, CRC Reprint) Franklin.

Prostaglandins in Cancer Research: Proceedings. Ed. by E. Garaci et al. (Life Sciences Ser.). (Illus.). 300p. 1987. 107.95 (*0-387-17548-2*) Spr-Verlag.

Prostaglandins in Cardiovascular & Renal Function. Ed. by Alexander Scriabine et al. (Monographs of the Physiology. Soc. of Phila.: Vol. 6). (Illus.). 481p. 1980. text 75.00 (*0-88331-186-0*) R B Luce.

Prostaglandins in Clinical Medicine: Cardiovascular & Thrombotic Disorders: Proceedings of an International Symposium, "Prostaglandins in Cardiovascular & Thrombotic Disorders", Chicago, IL, May 7-9, 1981. Ed. by Kenneth K. Wu & Ennio C. Rossi. LC 81-23995. (Illus.). 427p. reprint ed. pap. 132.40 (*0-8357-7636-0*, 205695900096) Bks Demand.

Prostaglandins in Clinical Practice. Ed. by W. David Watkins et al. LC 83-42852. 278p. 1989. reprint ed. pap. 86.20 (*0-608-04742-2*, 206546300004) Bks Demand.

Prostaglandins in Reproduction. Norman L. Poyser. LC 81-181787. (Prostaglandins Research Studies Ser.: No. 2). (Illus.). 272p. reprint ed. pap. 84.40 (*0-8357-8996-9*, 203334800085) Bks Demand.

Prostaglandins in the Cardiovascular System. Ed. by K. Schror & Helmet F. Sinzinger. (Agents & Actions Supplements Ser.: Vol. 37). 390p. 1992. 109.50 (*0-8176-2701-4*) Birkhauser.

Prostaglandins, Leukotrienes, & Lipoxins. Ed. by J. Martyn Bailey. LC 85-16941. (GWUMC Department of Biochemistry Annual Spring Symposia Ser.). 722p. 1985. 150.00 (*0-306-41980-7*, Plenum Trade) Perseus Pubng.

***Prostaglandins, Leukotrienes & Other Eicosanoids: From Biogenesis to Clinical Application.** G. Furstenberger. Ed. by F. Marks. 408p. 1999. 154.95 (*3-527-29360-4*) Wiley.

Prostaglandins, Leukotrienes, Lipoxins & PAF: Mechanisms of Action, Molecular Biology & Clinical Applications. J. M. Bailey. (GWUMC Department of Biochemistry Annual Spring Symposium Ser.). (Illus.). 448p. (C). 1992. text 123.00 (*0-306-44055-5*, Kluwer Plenum) Kluwer Academic.

Prostaglandins, Organ & Tissue-Specific Actions. Ed. by Stan Greenberg et al. LC 82-5165. (Modern Pharmacology-Toxicology Ser.: No. 21). 476p. 1982. reprint ed. pap. 147.60 (*0-608-01289-0*, 206203500001) Bks Demand.

Prostaglandins, Prostacyclin, Thromboxanes Measurement. Ed. by J. M. Boeynaems & A. G. Herman. (Developments in Pharmacology Ser.: No. 1.). (Illus.). 209p. 1980. text 101.50 (*90-247-2417-1*) Kluwer Academic.

Prostanoids & Drugs. Ed. by Bengt Samuelsson et al. LC 89-22775. (NATO ASI Series A, Life Sciences: Vol. 177). (Illus.). 270p. 1990. 89.50 (*0-306-43330-3*, Plenum Trade) Perseus Pubng.

Prostatakarzinom: Spektrum der Kurativen Therapie. Ed. by H. Sommerkamp & J. E. Altwein. (Illus.). xiv, 334p. 1989. 105.25 (*3-8055-5099-5*) S Karger.

Prostate. Ed. by John M. Fitzpatrick & Robert J. Kane. (Illus.). 464p. 1989. text 95.00 (*0-443-03558-X*) Church.

Prostate: A Guide for Men & the Women Who Love Them. Patrick C. Walsh & Janet F. Worthington. LC 94-33397. (Health Bks.). (Illus.). 320p. 1995. text 39.95 (*0-8018-4988-8*) Johns Hopkins.

Prostate: A Guide for Men & the Women Who Love Them. Patrick C. Walsh & Janet F. Worthington. (Illus.). 464p. 1997. mass mkt. 6.99 (*0-446-60432-1*, Pub. by Warner Bks) Little.

Prostate: A Guide for Men & the Women Who Love Them. Janet F. Worthington & Patrick C. Walsh. LC 94-33397. (Health Bks.). (Illus.). 320p. 1995. pap. 15.95 (*0-8018-4989-6*) Johns Hopkins.

Prostate: Basic & Clinical Aspects. Rajesh K. Naz. LC 96-49184. 400p. 1997. boxed set 104.95 (*0-8493-3159-5*) CRC Pr.

Prostate: Facts & Misconceptions. Hernando Salcedo. (Illus.). 160p. 1993. 16.95 (*1-55972-189-8*, Birch Ln Pr) Carol Pub Group.

Prostate: Facts & Misconceptions. Hernando Salcedo. (Illus.). 136p. 1996. pap. 12.95 (*0-8065-1764-6*, Citadel Pr) Carol Pub Group.

Prostate: Guides to Clinical Aspiration Biopsy. Tilde S. Kline. LC 84-12957. (Illus.). 200p. 1985. 72.50 (*0-89640-106-5*) Igaku-Shoin.

Prostate: Questions You Have, Answers You Need. 2nd rev. ed. Sandra Salmans. (Illus.). 192p. 1996. pap. 12.95 (*1-882606-63-9*) Peoples Med Soc.

Prostate Accessory Male Sex Gland. S. Battaglia. (Journal: Applied Pathology: Vol. 3, No. 4). (Illus.). iv, 72p. 1986. pap. 52.25 (*3-8055-4464-2*) S Karger.

Prostate & Cancer: A Family Guide to Diagnosis, Treatment & Survival. Sheldon Marks. LC 95-17803. (Illus.). 352p. 1995. pap. 14.95 (*1-55561-078-1*) Fisher Bks.

Prostate & Cancer: A Family Guide to Diagnosis, Treatment & Survival. rev. ed. Sheldon Marks. LC 99-37432. (Illus.). 360p. 1999. pap. 14.95 (*1-55561-206-7*) Fisher Bks.

***Prostate & Cancer: A Family Guide to Diagnosis, Treatment & Survival.** rev. ed. Sheldon Marks. (Illus.). 352p. 2000. pap. 17.95 (*1-55561-262-8*) Fisher Bks.

***Prostate & Finasteride: Index of New Information with Authors, Subjects & References.** rev. ed. Patrick J. Mullin. LC 96-12486. 141p. 1999. 47.50 (*0-7883-2128-5*); pap. 44.50 (*0-7883-2129-3*) ABBE Pubs Assn.

Prostate & Male Health: Index of New Information with Authors & Subjects. Virginia L. Jensen. 180p. 1992. 47.50 (*1-55914-702-4*); pap. 44.50 (*1-55914-703-2*) ABBE Pubs Assn.

Prostate Answer Book. Roberta Altman. 176p. (Orig.). 1993. mass mkt. 5.50 (*0-446-36408-8*, Pub. by Warner Bks) Little.

Prostate Answer Book: Remedies & Cures for Every Man & What Your Doctor Never Tells You about Surgery. FC&A Staff. (Illus.). 384p. 2000. 27.96 (*1-890957-02-X*) FC&A Pub.

Prostate As an Endocrine Gland. Ed. by Richard J. Ablin. 232p. 1989. lib. bdg. 129.00 (*0-8493-5364-5*, QP257) CRC Pr.

Prostate Biopsy Interpretation. 2nd ed. Jonathan I. Epstein. LC 95-7308. (Biopsy Interpretation Ser.). (Illus.). 288p. 1995. text 104.00 (*0-7817-0325-5*) Lppncott W & W.

Prostate Book. rev. ed. Stephen N. Rous. 288p. 1995. pap. 13.00 (*0-393-30864-2*) Norton.

Prostate Book: Sound Advice on Symptoms & Treatment. Stephen N. Rous. (Illus.). 256p. 1992. 22.95 (*0-393-03387-2*) Norton.

P

An Asterisk (*) at the beginning of an entry indicates that the title is appearing for the first time.

Prostate Brachtherapy Made Complicated. large type ed. Kent Wallner et al. (Illus.). 325p. 1997. text 155.00 (*0-9648991-1-6*) SmartMedicine.

***Prostate Cancer.** Peter R. Carroll. (ACS Atlas of Clinical Oncology Ser.). 400p. 2000. boxed set 89.95 incl. cd-rom (*1-55009-130-1*) DEKR.

***Prostate Cancer.** Ed. by Leland W. K. Chung et al. (Contemporary Cancer Research Ser.). 550p. 2000. 145.00 (*0-89603-868-8*) Humana.

Prostate Cancer. Ed. by Nancy A. Dawson & Nicholas J. Vogelzang. 300p. 1994. 129.95 (*0-471-58834-2*, Wiley-Liss) Wiley.

Prostate Cancer. Richard E. Peschel. Ed. by Marc S. Ernstoff & John A. Heaney. 240p. 1998. 75.00 (*0-632-04317-2*) Blackwell Sci.

Prostate Cancer: A Doctor's Personal Triumph. Saralee Fine & Robert Fine. LC 99-22948. 256p. 1999. 24.95 (*0-8397-6808-7*, Pub. by Eriksson) IPG Chicago.

Prostate Cancer: A Guide for Men. Cary N. Robertson. Ed. by G. D. Webster. (Urology Ser.). (Illus.). 24p. (Orig.). 1996. pap. 2.95 (*1-885274-27-0*) Health InfoNet Inc.

Prostate Cancer: A Multidisciplinary Guide. Philip W. Kantoff et al. LC 96-39071. (Illus.). 281p. (Orig.). 1996. text 44.95 (*0-86542-456-X*) Blackwell Sci.

Prostate Cancer: A Non-Surgical Perspective. large type ed. Kent Wallner. LC 95-90687. (Illus.). 172p. (Orig.). 1996. pap. 15.95 (*0-9648991-0-8*) SmartMedicine.

***Prostate Cancer: A Non-Surgical Perspective.** 2nd rev. large type ed. Kent Wallner. LC 95-90687. (Illus.). 230p. (Orig.). 2000. pap. 18.95 (*0-9648991-3-2*, Pub. by SmartMedicine) Pathway Bk Serv.

Prostate Cancer: A Survivor's Guide. 3rd rev. ed. Donald F. Kaltenbach & Tim Richards. (Illus.). 296p. 1996. pap. 16.95 (*0-9640008-2-3*) Seneca Hse.

Prostate Cancer: All You Need to Know to Take an Active Part in Your Treatment. 2nd rev. ed. S. Larry Goldenberg. (Illus.). 197p. 1997. pap. text 24.95 (*0-9696125-3-2*) ITPG.

Prostate Cancer: Cell & Molecular Mechanisms in Diagnosis & Treatment. Ed. by J. T. Isaacs. (Cancer Surveys Ser.: Vol. 11). (Illus.). 287p. (C). 1991. text 60.00 (*0-87969-368-1*) Cold Spring Harbor.

Prostate Cancer: Current Issues, New Approaches. Ed. by R. S. Kirby. (Journal Ser.: Vol. 29, No. 2, 1996). (Illus.). iv, 136p. 1996. pap., suppl. ed. 50.50 (*3-8055-6314-0*) S Karger.

Prostate Cancer: Hormonal Treatment & Treatment of Advanced Disease. Ed. by Donald W. Newling. (Journal: European Urology: Vol. 26, Suppl. 1, 1994). (Illus.). iv, 34p. 1994. pap. 21.75 (*3-8055-6111-3*) S Karger.

Prostate Cancer: Making Survival Decisions. Sylvan Meyer & Seymour C. Nash. 284p. 1994. 19.95 (*0-226-56857-1*) U Ch Pr.

Prostate Cancer: New Approaches to Endocrine Therapy. Ed. by P. H. Smith. (Journal: European Urology: Vol. 18, Supplement 3, 1990). (Illus.). iv, 68p. 1990. pap. 21.75 (*3-8055-5336-6*) S Karger.

Prostate Cancer: Overcoming Denial with Action: A Guide to Screening, Treatment & Healing. Allen E. Salowe. 224p. 1998. pap. 14.95 (*0-312-18159-0*, St Martin Griffin) St Martin.

Prostate Cancer: Overcoming Denial with Action: A Guide to Screening, Treatment & Healing. Allen E. Salowe & Leon M. Lessinge. LC 96-50460. 205p. 1997. 15.00 (*1-57626-023-2*) Quality Med Pub.

Prostate Cancer: Potraits of Empowerment. Ed. by Nadine Jelsing. LC 98-45154. 256p. 1999. pap. 14.00 (*0-8133-6657-7*, Pub. by Westview) HarpC.

Prostate Cancer: Principles & Practice. Philip Kantoff et al. 800p. text 110.00 (*0-7817-2006-0*) Lppncott W & W.

Prostate Cancer: Questions & Answers. Colin Buck. (Illus.). 120p. 1995. pap. 10.95 (*1-873413-85-8*) Merit Pub Intl.

Prostate Cancer: Treatment & Recovery. Richard Y. Handy. LC 96-18737. 251p. 1996. pap. text 17.95 (*1-57392-074-6*) Prometheus Bks.

Prostate Cancer: What I Found Out & What You Should Know. Robert L. Maddox. LC 97-20186. 160p. 1997. pap. text 11.99 (*0-87788-566-4*, H Shaw Pubs) Waterbrook Pr.

Prostate Cancer & Bone Metastasis. J. P. Karr & H. Yamanaka. (Advances in Experimental Medicine & Biology Ser.: Vol. 324). (Illus.). 334p. (C). 1992. text 95.00 (*0-306-44314-7*, Kluwer Plenum) Kluwer Academic.

Prostate Cancer Answ. Bk. Marion Morra & Eve Potts. LC 96-5684. 93p. 1996. pap. 12.50 (*0-380-78564-1*, Avon Bks) Morrow Avon.

Prostate Cancer Detection & Cure. A. M. Durrani. Ed. by Pete Billac. LC 97-66581. (Illus.). 120p. (Orig.). 1997. pap. 9.95 (*0-943629-30-6*) Swan Pub.

Prostate Cancer. Kirby. 1996. text 110.00 (*0-7234-2050-5*) Wolfe Pubng AZ.

***Prostate Cancer Patient Outcomes & Choice of Providers: Development of an Infrastructure for Quality Assessment.** Mark Litwin et al. 205p. (C). 2000. pap. 25.00 (*0-8330-2873-1*) Rand Corp.

***Prostate Cancer Protection Plan: The Foods, Supplements, & Drugs That Could Save Your Life.** Bob Arnot. 352p. 2000. 24.95 (*0-316-05153-5*) Little.

Prostate Cancer Sourcebook: How to Make Informed Treatment Choices. Marcus H. Loo & Marian Betancourt. LC 97-33001. 256p. 1998. pap. 14.95 (*0-471-15927-1*) Wiley.

***Prostate Cancer Treatment Options: A Guide to the Basics.** Will Connell. LC 99-95100. (Illus.). xiv, 220p. 2000. pap. 19.95 (*0-9673892-1-6*) Edconco Pr.

Prostate Cancer 2000. Ed. by L. Denis. LC 94-30517. (Monographs European School of Oncology). 1994. write for info. (*3-540-58296-7*) Spr-Verlag.

Prostate Cancer 2000. Ed. by L. Denis. LC 94-30517. (Monographs of the European School of Oncology). 1994. 86.95 (*0-387-58296-7*) Spr-Verlag.

Prostate Cancers - Prevention & Control: Index of New Information for Medicine, Science & Research with New Update of Progress. rev. ed. Patrick J. Mullins. 151p. 1997. 47.50 (*0-7883-1616-8*); pap. 44.50 (*0-7883-1617-6*) ABBE Pubs Assn.

Prostate Cure: The Revolutionary natural Approach to Treating Enlarged Prostates. Harry G. Preuss & Brenda D. Adderly. LC 98-29437. 288p. 1998. 23.00 (*0-609-60323-X*) Crown Pub Group.

Prostate Disease: A Massachusetts General Hospital Book. W. Scott McDougal & Pat Skerrett. LC 95-15175. (Illus.). 368p. 1996. pap. 14.00 (*0-8129-2319-7*, Times Bks) Crown Pub Group.

Prostate Diseases. Ed. by Herbert Lepor & Russell K. Lawson. LC 92-49620. (Illus.). 512p. 1993. text 115.00 (*0-7216-4545-3*, W B Saunders Co) Harcrt Hlth Sci Grp.

Prostate Disorders. Tony Smith. (ACP Home Medical Guides). 96p. 2000. pap. 6.95 (*0-7894-4168-3*, D K Ink) DK Pub Inc.

Prostate Enlargement: Symptoms, Causes, Treatment & Recovery. 1991. lib. bdg. 79.00 (*0-8490-5155-X*) Gordon Pr.

Prostate Gland & Seminal Vesicle. G. Aumueller. (Handbuch der Mikroskopischen Anatomie Des Menschen Ser.: Vol. 7, Pt. 6). (Illus.). 1979. 191.00 (*0-387-09191-2*) Spr-Verlag.

Prostate Gland Troubles. Ed. by Health Research Staff. 24p. 1994. reprint ed. spiral bd. 10.00 (*0-7873-1261-4*) Hlth Research.

Prostate Guidebook. Date not set. pap. write for info. (*1-884350-65-8*) Alpha Pubng.

Prostate Health in 90 Days: Without Drugs Or Surgery. Larry Clapp. (Illus.). 323p. 1997. pap. 14.95 (*1-56170-460-1*) Hay House.

***Prostate Miracle.** Jesse A. Stoff. 2000. pap. text. write for info. (*1-57566-544-1*, Knsington) Kensgtn Pub Corp.

Prostate Problem. Chet Cunningham. 1995. pap. 8.95 (*0-8217-4892-0*) NAL.

Prostate Problems: Every Man's Fear: What Everyone Should Know About the Prostate. Martin K. Gelbard & William Bentley. LC 94-26400. (Illus.). 272p. 1995. per. 12.00 (*0-671-88465-4*, Fireside) S&S Trade Pap.

Prostate Problems & Elective Surgery. 1994. lib. bdg. 250.95 (*0-8490-5665-9*) Gordon Pr.

Prostate Problems & Their Treatment: Information & Advice for Sufferers. Jeremy Hamand. 1991. pap. 13.00 (*0-7225-2252-5*) Thorsons PA.

Prostate Research: Index of New Information with Authors & Subjects. rev. ed. Virginia L. Jensen. LC 94-33829. 163p. 1994. 47.50 (*0-7883-0248-5*); pap. text 44.50 (*0-7883-0249-3*) ABBE Pubs Assn.

Prostate Sourcebook. 3rd ed. Steven Morganstern & Allen Abrahams. LC 99-188320. 272p. 1998. pap. 16.00 (*1-56565-871-X*, 0871XW, Pub. by Lowell Hse) NTC Contemp Pub Co.

Prostate Sourcebook: Everything You Need to Know. Steven Morganstern. 252p. 1994. reprint ed. pap. 12.95 (*1-56565-117-0*) Lowell Hse.

Prostatic Cancer. Ed. by Richard J. Ablin. LC 81-12500. (Science & Practice of Surgery Ser.: No. 2). (Illus.). 341p. reprint ed. pap. 105.80 (*0-7837-0909-9*, 204121400019) Bks Demand.

Prostatic Carcinoma: Biology & Diagnosis. Ed. by E. S. Hafez & E. Spring-Mills. (Clinics in Andrology Ser.: No. 6). (Illus.). 200p. 1980. text 211.50 (*90-247-2379-5*) Kluwer Academic.

Prostatic Disease. Herbert Lepor. LC 99-48130. 1999. text. write for info. (*0-7216-7416-X*, W B Saunders Co) Harcrt Hlth Sci Grp.

Prostatic Diseases. 3rd ed. George S. White. 127p. 1996. reprint ed. spiral bd. 12.00 (*0-7873-0962-1*) Hlth Research.

Prostatic Disorders. Ed. by David F. Paulson. LC 88-9388. 397p. reprint ed. pap. 123.10 (*0-7837-2737-2*, 204311700006) Bks Demand.

Prostatic Hyperplasia: Etiology, Surgical & Conservative Management. Ed. by R. Ackermann & F. H. Schroder. (New Developments in Biosciences Ser.: No. 5). x, 154p. (C). 1989. pap. text 41.45 (*0-89925-528-0*) De Gruyter.

Prostatitis: Etiopathology, Diagnosis & Therapy. Ed. by Wolfgang Weidner et al. LC 93-29539. 1994. 149.00 (*0-387-56624-4*) Spr-Verlag.

Prostheses & Abdominal Wall Hernias. Ed. by Robert Bendavid. 500p. 1994. 205.00 (*1-879702-70-3*, R) CRC Pr.

Prosthesis. David Wills. LC 94-42467. (Meridian: Crossing Aesthetics Ser.). xiv, 350p. 1995. 49.50 (*0-8047-2459-8*); pap. 18.95 (*0-8047-2460-1*) Stanford U Pr.

Prosthesis: Caesarea. limited ed. Susan Gevirtz. 59p. (Orig.). 1994. 18.00 (*0-937013-51-X*) Potes Poets.

Prosthesis: Poems. Edison Dupree. LC 94-24525. 1994. 18.00 (*1-878325-10-8*); pap. 9.95 (*1-878325-11-6*) Bluestem Press.

Prosthetic Culture. Cecilia Lury. LC 98-120999. (International Library of Sociology Ser.). 256p. (C). 1998. 80.00 (*0-415-10293-6*); pap. 24.99 (*0-415-10294-4*) Routledge.

Prosthetic Dentistry: Principles & Treatment Strategies. Bengt Owall et al. (Illus.). 256p. 1995. text 96.95 (*0-7234-2046-7*, Pub. by Martin Dunitz) Mosby Inc.

Prosthetic Gait Training Program for Lower Extremity Amputees. Robert S. Gailey & Ann M. Gailey. (Rehabilitation Series for Lower Extremity Amputees: Vol. 1). (Illus.). 36p. (C). 1989. pap. text 7.00 (*1-888131-00-4*) Adv Rehab Therapy.

Prosthetic Knee Ligament Reconstruction. Marc J. Friedman & Richard D. Ferkel. 1988. text 115.00 (*0-7216-2559-2*, Grune & Strat) Harcrt Hlth Sci Grp.

Prosthetic Rehabilitation. Keith F. Thomas. (Illus.). 280p. 1994. text 130.00 (*1-85097-032-7*, B8810) Quint Pub Co.

Prosthetics: Methods of Producing Facial & Body Restorations. Carl D. Clarke. (Illus.). 336p. 1965. 40.00 (*0-911426-07-8*) Standard Arts.

***Prosthetics - Amputations - Orthotics - Orthopedics & Spinal Cord Injury & Other Neurological Disorders.** Ed. by Mindy L. Aisen. (Illus.). 59p. (C). 2000. pap. text 20.00 (*0-7881-8674-4*) DIANE Pub.

Prosthetics & Orthotics. Donald G. Shurr. (Illus.). 225p. (C). 1990. pap. text 45.00 (*0-8385-7977-9*, A7977-0) Appleton & Lange.

Prosthetics & Orthotics. 2nd ed. Shurr. (C). 1999. 45.00 (*0-8385-8133-1*) Appleton & Lange.

Prostho Plus. Piers Anthony. 224p. 1986. reprint ed. pap. 2.95 (*0-8125-3116-7*, Pub. by Tor Bks) St Martin.

Prosthodontic Treatment for Edentulous Patients. 11th ed. Boucher & George A. Zarb. LC 96-51006. (Illus.). 576p. (C). (gr. 13). 1997. text 76.00 (*0-8151-9899-X*, 24125) Mosby Inc.

***Prosthodontics for the Elderly: Diagnosis & Treatment.** Ejvind Budtz-Jorgensen. LC 99-38079. 266p. 1999. 89.00 (*0-86715-368-7*) Quint Pub Co.

***Prosthondontics for the Elderly: Diagnosis & Treatment.** Ejvind Budtz-Jergensen. (Illus.). 255p. 2000. 120.00 (*4-87417-607-0*, Pub. by QPC) Quint Pub Co.

Prostitucion Infantil. A. Martin. (Serie Actualidades - Actualities Ser.).Tr. of Child Prostitution. (SPA.). 40p. 1995. 2.29 (*1-56063-732-3*, 496254) Editorial Unilit.

Prostitute & Other Stories. J. P. Das. LC 95-905271. (C). 1995. 14.00 (*81-241-0262-7*, Pub. by Har-Anand Pubns) S Asia.

Prostitute & the Prophet: Hosea's Marriage in Literary-Theoretical Perspective. Yvonne M. Sherwood. LC 96-123995. (JSOT Supplement Ser.: No. 212, No. 2). 357p. 1996. 85.00 (*1-85075-581-7*, Pub. by Sheffield Acad); pap. 29.95 (*1-85075-777-1*, Pub. by Sheffield Acad) CUP Services.

Prostitute & the Social Reformer: Commercial Vice in the Progressive Era. LC 73-20647. (Sex, Marriage & Society Ser.). 394p. 1979. reprint ed. 36.95 (*0-405-05814-4*) Ayer.

Prostitute in the Family Tree: Discovering Humor & Irony in the Bible. Douglas Adams. LC 97-16943. 136p. 1997. pap. 12.00 (*0-664-25693-7*) Westminster John Knox.

Prostitutes & Prostitution in India. Deepa Das. (C). 1993. 30.00 (*0-7069-5957-4*, Pub. by Vikas) S Asia.

Prostitutes in Medical Literature: An Annotated Bibliography, 6. Compiled by Sachi S. Kantha. LC 91-3211. (Bibliographies & Indexes in Medical Studies: No. 6). 256p. 1991. lib. bdg. 65.00 (*0-313-27491-6*, KPQ, Greenwood Pr) Greenwood.

Prostitutes, Margarine & Handguns. Albert D. McCallum. viii, 216p. (Orig.). 1996. pap. 9.00 (*0-9651659-0-6*) Pragmatic Publns.

Prostitutes' Well-Being & Risk. W. M. Vanwesenbeeck. LC 94-241920. 224p. 1994. pap. 24.00 (*90-5383-301-3*, Pub. by VU Univ Pr) Paul & Co Pubs.

Prostitution. Pierre Guyotat & Maya Khosla. Tr. by Bruce Benderson from FRE. (French Ser.). 32p. 1995. pap. 4.00 (*0-87376-081-6*) Red Dust.

Prostitution see History of Women in the United States: Topically Arranged Articles on the Evolution of Women's History in the United States

Prostitution: An International Handbook on Trends, Problems, & Policies. Ed. by Nanette J. Davis. LC 92-27880. 424p. 1993. lib. bdg. 89.50 (*0-313-25754-X*, DIR/, Greenwood Pr) Greenwood.

Prostitution: On Whores, Hustlers, & Johns. Ed. by James E. Elias et al. LC 98-33520. (Illus.). 450p. 1998. 29.95 (*1-57392-229-3*) Prometheus Bks.

***Prostitution: Prevention & Reform in England, 1860-1914.** Paula Bartley. (Illus.). 224p. 2000. pap. 25.99 (*0-415-21457-2*) Routledge.

Prostitution: Regulation & Control. John F. Decker. (N. Y. U. Criminal Law Education & Research Center Publications: Vol. 13). xxvi, 572p. 1979. reprint ed. 65.00 (*0-8377-0507-X*, Rothman) W S Hein.

Prostitution - A Bibliographical Synthesis. B. Joardar. 131p. 1984. 14.95 (*0-318-37061-1*) Asia Bk Corp.

***Prostitution & Feminism.** Maggie O'Neill. 2001. 59.95 (*0-7456-1204-0*, Pub. by Polity Pr); pap. 24.95 (*0-7456-1921-5*, Pub. by Polity Pr) Blackwell Pubs.

Prostitution & Its Repression in New York City, 1900-1931. Willoughby C. Waterman. LC 68-54305. (Columbia University. Studies in the Social Sciences: No. 352). reprint ed. 22.50 (*0-404-51352-2*) AMS Pr.

***Prostitution & Sexuality in Shanghai: A Social History (1849-1949)** Christian Henriot. Tr. by Noel Castelino. LC 00-20001. (Illus.). 464p. 2000. text. write for info. (*0-521-57165-0*) Cambridge U Pr.

***Prostitution & the State in Italy, 1860-1915.** 2nd ed. Mary Gibson. LC 99-45873. (History of Crime & Criminal Justice Ser.). (Illus.). 277p. (C). 2000. pap. text 27.95 (*0-8142-5048-3*) Ohio St U Pr.

Prostitution & the Victorians. Trevor Fisher. LC 97-12257. 170p. 1997. text 35.00 (*0-312-17583-3*) St Martin.

Prostitution & Victorian Society: Women, Class & the State. Judith R. Walkowitz. LC 79-21050. 368p. 1982. pap. text 19.95 (*0-521-27064-2*) Cambridge U Pr.

Prostitution, Considered in Its Moral, Social & Sanitary Aspects in London & Other Large Cities & Garrison Towns. William Acton. 302p. 1972. reprint ed. 27.50 (*0-7146-2414-4*, BHA-02414, Pub. by F Cass Pubs) Intl Spec Bk.

Prostitution, Drugs, Gambling & Organized Crime see Crime & Justice in American History

Prostitution in America: Three Investigations, 1975. New York Committee of Fifteen et al. Ed. by Syracuse Moral Survey Committee. Tr. by Massachusetts Commission for Investigation of Whit. (Social Problems & Social Policy Ser.). 1976. 41.95 (*0-405-07511-1*) Ayer.

Prostitution in Elizabethan & Jacobean Comedy. Anne M. Haselkorn. LC 82-50415. viii, 158p. 1983. 39.00 (*0-87875-247-1*) Whitston Pub.

Prostitution in Europe. Abraham Flexner. LC 69-14924. (Criminology, Law Enforcement, & Social Problems Ser.: No. 30). 1969. reprint ed. 25.00 (*0-87585-030-8*) Patterson Smith.

Prostitution in Great Britain, 1485-1901: An Annotated Bibliography. Stanley D. Nash. LC 94-331. 267p. 1994. 34.50 (*0-8108-2734-4*) Scarecrow.

Prostitution in Hollywood Films: Plots, Critiques, Casts & Credits for 389 Theatrical & Made-for-Television Releases. James R. Parish. LC 91-51213. (Illus.). 616p. 1992. lib. bdg. 65.00 (*0-89950-677-1*) McFarland & Co.

Prostitution in Medieval Society: The History of an Urban Institution in Languedoc. Leah L. Otis. LC 84-16184. (Women in Culture & Society Ser.). (Illus.). 240p. 1987. pap. text 11.95 (*0-226-64033-7*) U Ch Pr.

Prostitution in Medieval Society: The History of an Urban Institution in Languedoc. Leah L. Otis. LC 84-16184. (Women in Culture & Society Ser.). (Illus.). 240p. 1993. lib. bdg. 22.50 (*0-226-64032-9*) U Ch Pr.

Prostitution in Paris, Considered Morally, Politically, & Medically: Prepared for Philanthropists & Legislators from Statistical Documents. Alexandre J. Parent-Duchatelet. LC 72-9671. reprint ed. 37.50 (*0-404-57488-2*) AMS Pr.

Prostitution of Our Constitution. (Illus.). xii, 340p. 1998. pap. write for info. (*0-9664618-0-0*, 01) Knimi Inc.

Prostitution of Sexuality. Kathleen Barry. (C). 1996. pap. text 19.00 (*0-8147-1277-0*) NYU Pr.

Prostitution of Sexuality. Kathleen L. Barry. 381p. (C). 1994. text 45.00 (*0-8147-1217-7*) NYU Pr.

Prostitution of Women & Girls. R. Barri Flowers. LC 98-12338. 263p. 1998. lib. bdg. 38.50 (*0-7864-0490-6*) McFarland & Co.

Prostitution, Power & Freedom. Julia O. Davidson. LC 98-43995. 240p. 1998. text 49.50 (*0-472-09695-8*, 09695) U of Mich Pr.

***Prostitution, Power & Freedom.** Julia O. Davidson. LC 98-43995. 240p. 1998. pap. text 19.95 (*0-472-06695-1*, 06695) U of Mich Pr.

Prostitution Prism. Gail Pheterson. (C). 1995. text 49.50 (*90-5356-185-4*, Pub. by Amsterdam U Pr) U of Mich Pr.

Prostitution Prism. Gail Pheterson. (C). 1996. pap. 29.95 (*90-5356-176-5*, Pub. by Amsterdam U Pr) U of Mich Pr.

Prostitution, Sexuality, & the Law in Ancient Rome. Thomas A. McGinn. 432p. 1998. text 55.00 (*0-19-508785-2*) OUP.

Prostranstuo I Uremja V Micromire see Space & Time in the Microworld

***Prostrate Humor: A Thinking (And Laughing) Man's Views on Prostate Surgery.** (Illus.). 20p. 2000. pap. 3.00 (*0-9653403-1-7*) R Olson.

Protactinium. 1969. 140.00 (*0-387-93172-4*) Spr-Verlag.

Protagonist Powers & the Third World. Wayne Wilcox. Ed. by Richard D. Lambert. LC 76-102760. (Annals of the American Academy of Political & Social Science Ser.: Vol. 386). 1969. 28.00 (*0-87761-122-X*); pap. 18.00 (*0-87761-121-1*) Am Acad Pol Soc Sci.

Protagoras. Plato. Tr. by C. C. Taylor. (The World's Classics Ser.). 122p. 1996. pap. 8.95 (*0-19-282330-2*) OUP.

Protagoras. Plato. Tr. by Stanley Lombardo & Karen Bell from GRE. LC 91-28322. (HPC Classics Ser.). 112p. (C). 1992. pap. text 6.95 (*0-87220-094-9*); lib. bdg. 27.95 (*0-87220-095-7*) Hackett Pub.

Protagoras. Plato. (College Classical Ser.). ix, 232p. (C). 1984. reprint ed. pap. text 17.50 (*0-89241-387-5*) Caratzas.

Protagoras. 2nd rev. ed. Plato. Tr. & Notes by C. C. Taylor. (Clarendon Plato Ser.). 266p. 1992. pap. text 35.00 (*0-19-823934-3*) OUP.

Protagoras & Meno. Plato. Tr. & Intro. by W. K. Guthrie. (Classics Ser.). 160p. 1957. pap. 9.95 (*0-14-044068-2*, Penguin Classics) Viking Penguin.

Protagoras, Philebus, & Gorgias. Plato. Tr. by Benjamin Jowett. (Great Books in Philosophy). 213p. 1996. pap. 7.95 (*1-57392-062-2*) Prometheus Bks.

Protagoras (Plato) Benjamin E. Jowett & Martin Oswald. 128p. (C). 1956. pap. text 5.60 (*0-02-361090-5*, Macmillan Coll) P-H.

***Proteaccae of New South Wales.** Ed. by Gwen Harden et al. (Illus.). 204p. 1999. pap. 35.00 (*0-86840-302-4*, Pub. by New South Wales Univ Pr) Intl Spec Bk.

Proteaceae of the Sydney Region. Alec M. Blombery & Betty Maloney. (Illus.). 216p. 1993. 37.50 (*0-86417-433-0*, Pub. by Kangaroo Pr) Seven Hills Bk.

***Proteaceae 2.** (Flora of Australia Ser.: Vol. 17B). (Illus.). 434p. 1999. 89.95 (*0-643-06454-0*, Pub. by CSIRO); pap. 69.95 (*0-643-06455-9*, Pub. by CSIRO) Accents Pubns.

Protean Behaviour: The Biology of Anarchization. P. M. Driver & D. A. Humphries. (Illus.). 360p. 1988. 69.00 (*0-19-857170-4*) OUP.

Protean Gate Structure & Plasticity of the Primary Nociceptive Analyzer: Structure & Plasticity of the Primary Nociceptive Analyzer. B. Csillik & E. Csillik-Knyihar. 294p. (C). 1986. 120.00 (*963-05-3928-4*, Pub. by Akade Kiado) St Mut.

Protean Scot: Multiple Voices in Eighteenth-Century Scottish Literature. Kenneth Simpson. 300p. 1989. text 34.00 (*0-08-036401-2*, Pub. by Aberdeen U Pr) Macmillan.

P

An Asterisk (*) at the beginning of an entry indicates that the title is appearing for the first time.

Protean Self: Human Resilience in an Age of Fragmentation. Robert Jay Lifton. LC 99-35389. 262p. 1999. pap. 15.00 (*0-226-48098-4*) U Ch Pr.

Protean Text: A Study of the Versions of the Medieval French Legend of "Doon & Olive" Kimberlee A. Campbell. LC 88-25078. (Garland Monographs in Medieval Literature: Vol. 1). 881028p. 1988. text 12.00 (*0-8240-4786-9*, 865) Garland.

Proteas in Hawaii. Kay Kepler & Jacob Mau. (Illus.). 80p. 1988. pap. 9.95 (*0-935180-66-4*) Mutual Pub HI.

Proteas of the World. Lewis Matthews. (Illus.). 256p. 1993. 45.00 (*0-88192-235-8*) Timber.

Proteas of Tropical Africa. John S. Beard. (Illus.). 112p. 1993. 65.00 (*0-86417-449-7*, Pub. by Kangaroo Pr) Seven Hills Bk.

Protease Inhibitors: Therapeutic Application & Development. Ed. by Norra Macready. (Biomedical Library). 1997. pap. 795.00 (*1-57936-022-X*) IBC USA.

Protease Inhibitors As Cancer Chemopreventive Agents. W. Troll & A. R. Kennedy. LC 93-24959. (Illus.). 334p. (C). 1993. text 95.00 (*0-306-44390-2*, Kluwer Plenum) Kluwer Academic.

Protease Inhibitors of Human Plasma-Biochemistry & Pathophysiology. Genesio Murano. (Reviews of Hematology: Vol. II). 1985. 69.95 (*0-915340-14-3*) PJD Pubns.

***Proteases: New Perspectives.** Ed. by V. Turk. LC 99-40887. (Molecular & Cell Biology Updates Ser.). (Illus.). 350p. 1999. 155.00 (*3-7643-5789-4*, Pub. by Birkhauser) Spr-Verlag.

***Proteases: New Perspectives.** Vito Turk. LC 99-40887. (Molecular & Cell Biology Updates Ser.). 1999. write for info. (*0-8176-5789-4*) Birkhauser.

Proteases: Potential Role in Health & Disease, Vol. 2. Ed. by Walter H. Horl & August Heidland. (Advances in Experimental Medicine & Biology Ser.: Vol. 240). (Illus.). 572p. 1988. 135.00 (*0-306-43018-5*, Plenum Trade) Perseus Pubng.

***Proteases as Targets for Therapy.** Ed. by M. Adel-Meguid et al. LC 99-45434. (Handbook of Experimental Pharmacology Ser.: Vol. 140). (Illus.). 500p. 1999. 325.00 (*3-540-66118-2*) Spr-Verlag.

Proteases of Infectious Agents. Ben Dunn. LC 98-89642. 282p. 1999. 69.95 (*0-12-420510-0*) Acad Pr.

Proteases of Retroviruses: Proceedings of The Colloqium C52, 14th International Congress of Biochemistry Prague, Czechoslovakia, July 10-15, 1988. Ed. by Vladimir Kostka. xii, 206p. (C). 1989. lib. bdg. 161.55 (*3-11-011820-3*) De Gruyter.

Proteases, Protease Inhibitors & Protease-Derived Peptides: Importance in Human Pathophysiology & Therapeutics. Ed. by J. C. Cheronis & J. E. Repine. LC 93-15611. (Agents & Actions Supplements Ser.: Vol. 42). viii, 248p. 1993. 84.50 (*0-8176-2868-1*) Birkhauser.

Proteasomes: Multicatalytic Proteinase Complexes. Ed. by S. Wilk. (Journal: Enzyme & Protein Ser.: Vol. 47, No. 4-6, 1993). (Illus.). 192p. 1994. pap. 59.25 (*3-8055-6081-8*) S Karger.

***Proteasomes: The World of Regulatory Proteolysis.** Wolfgang Hilt & Dieter H. Wolf. (Molecular Biology Intelligence Unit Ser.). 367p. 2000. 99.00 (*1-58706-011-6*, Pub. by Eurekah) Landes Bioscience.

***Proteasomes: The World of Regulatory Proteolysis.** Ed. by Wolfgang Hilt & Dieter H. Wolf. LC 99-57145. (Molecular Biology Intelligence Unit Ser.). 2000. write for info. (*1-57059-621-2*) Landes Bioscience.

Proteccion Espiritual. L. Lambert.Tr. of Spiritual Protection. (SPA.). 93p. 1995. 3.50 (*1-56063-432-4*, 550016) Editorial Unilit.

Proteccion Espiritual para Sus Hijos. N. Anderson.Tr. of Spiritual Protection for Your Children. (SPA.). 8.99 (*0-7899-0288-5*, 497513) Editorial Unilit.

Proteccion o Librecambio. rev. ed. Henry George. Tr. by Baldomero Argente del Castillo.Tr. of Protection or Free Trade. (SPA.). 384p. 1995. pap. 8.00 (*0-911312-16-1*) Schalkenbach.

***Proteccion Social Para la Equidad y el Crecimiento.** IADB Staff. (SPA.). 263p. 2000. 22.50 (*1-886938-77-6*) IADB.

Protect & Avenge: The 49th Fighter Group in World War II. S. W. Ferguson & William K. Pascalis. LC 94-68964. (Illus.). 320p. 1995. 49.95 (*0-88740-750-1*) Schiffer.

***Protect & Defend.** Eric L. Harry. 649p. 1999. mass mkt. 7.50 (*0-425-16814-X*) Berkley Pub.

***Protect & Defend.** Richard North Patterson. 2001. 26.95 (*0-679-45044-0*) Knopf.

Protect & Serve. Geoff Pass & Mike LaBossiere. (Cyberpunk Ser.). (Illus.). 96p. (Orig.). 1992. pap. 10.00 (*0-937279-25-0*, CP3171) Talsorian.

Protect It Now. Anthony J. Battaglia, Jr. 16p. 1992. pap., student ed. 15.00 incl. audio (*1-880254-04-2*) Vista.

Protect Me, Love. Alice H. Orr. 1996. per. 3.75 (*0-373-22398-6*, 1-22398-1) Harlequin Bks.

Protect Pro for Networks - Software, Workbook, & Guide: The Complete Network Protection Planning Kit for Computer Security, Disaster Recovery. Wayne D. Storkman. 1998. pap., wbk. ed. 475.00 incl. disk (*0-9653146-7-7*) Protectware.

Protect Pro Network Protection Guide: 80 Powerfuls Ways to Protect Computers & Data. Wayne D. Storkman. (Illus.). 1998. pap. 55.00 (*0-9653146-9-3*) Protectware.

Protect Pro Network Protection Plan & Tools Workbook: Computer Network Security & Disaster Recovery Planning. Wayne D. Storkman. 1998. pap., wbk. ed. 125.00 (*0-9653146-5-0*) Protectware.

Protect Shareholder Value: A Guide to Managing Financial Market Risk. Abraham M. George. 448p. 1995. 65.00 (*0-7863-0439-1*, Irwn Prfssnl) McGraw-Hill Prof.

Protect the Future of Your School District Client. NSBA Council of School Attorneys Members. 800p. 1995. pap. 200.00 (*0-88364-191-7*, 06-149) Natl Sch Boards.

Protect the Panda. Ladybird Staff. (J). 1999. pap. 4.99 (*0-7214-5722-3*, Ladybrd) Penguin Putnam.

Protect the President: Outrageous Editorials from the Ultra-Right Newspaper Publisher William Loeb. Ed. by Andrew Mayer et al. LC 79-87929. (Illus.). 1979. pap. 9.95 (*0-932400-01-9*) Intervale Pub Co.

Protect the Tiger. Ladybird Staff. (J). 1999. pap. 4.99 (*0-7214-5723-1*) Penguin Putnam.

Protect This Girl: Words of Inspiration from Girl to Girl. Zoe Stern. 32p. (YA). (gr. 7 up). 1999. pap. 9.95 (*1-883672-81-3*) Tricycle Pr.

***Protect This Girl's Journal.** Zoe Stern. (Illus.). 96p. (YA). (gr. 4). 2000. 12.95 (*1-58246-015-9*) Tricycle Pr.

Protect Us from All Anxiety: Meditations for the Depressed. William Burke. (Illus.). 274p. 1998. pap. 9.95 (*0-87946-184-5*, 274) ACTA Pubns.

Protect Your Assets: How to Avoid Falling Victim to the Government's Forfeiture Laws. Adam Starchild. 120p. 1996. pap. 15.00 (*0-87364-906-0*) Paladin Pr.

Protect Your Assets! Smart Strategies for Estate Planning & Asset Protection. Joe Scalone. 220p. 1992. 19.95 (*1-56681-111-2*) Am Strategies.

Protect Your Assets: The Nurses Self Defense Guide. Audrey Stephan. Ed. by Diane Dettmore. LC 93-60935. 104p. (C). 1993. pap. 12.95 (*1-880254-09-3*) Vista.

Protect Your Child from Sexual Abuse: A Parent's Guide. Janie Hart-Rossi. LC 84-60586. 64p. 1984. pap. 7.95 (*0-943990-06-8*); lib. bdg. 17.95 (*0-943990-07-6*) Parenting Pr.

Protect Your Child from Sexual Abuse Perpetrators. Dorothy M. Neddermeyer. 55p. 1995. pap. text 8.95 (*0-9647757-0-0*) Genesis Consult.

Protect Your Children from the Pain of Divorce: How to Avoid the Legal & Emotional Pitfalls. unabridged ed. Barbara M. Massa. 213p. 1998. pap. 14.95 (*0-9669228-0-8*) Check Pr.

Protect Your Dreams, Your Dollars & Your Sanity: or How to Deal with Contractors. Feurmin Industries Staff. (Illus.). 51p. 1985. 8.95 (*0-910531-08-0*) Wolcotts.

Protect Your Estate: A Personal Guide to Intelligent Estate Planning. Robert A. Esperti & Renno L. Peterson. LC 92-23828. 295p. 1993. pap. 14.95 (*0-07-019685-0*) McGraw.

Protect Your Estate: The Definitive Strategies for Estate & Wealth Planning from America's Leading. 2nd ed. Robert A. Esperti. 320p. 1999. pap. text 16.95 (*0-07-135198-1*) McGraw.

Protect Your Family Against AIDS. Jeffrey Wehr & Marlene Wehr. LC 94-78147. 160p. 1994. per. 7.95 (*1-57258-004-6*) Teach Servs.

Protect Your Family from Lead in Your Home. 14p. 1995. pap. 30.00 (*0-16-063318-4*) USGPO.

Protect Your Groundwater: Educating for Action. League of Women Voters Education Fund Staff. 64p. 1994. 6.95 (*0-89959-384-4*, 980) LWVUS.

Protect Your Home: A Common-Sense Guide to Home Security. Richard H. Geiger. LC 87-45010. (Illus.). 160p. (Orig.). 1987. pap. 8.95 (*0-88266-501-4*, Garden Way Pub) Storey Bks.

Protect Your Idea-Invention for under Thirty Dollars! Terry Cupples. LC 90-92959. 204p. 1990. write for info. (*0-9625726-0-8*) Why Didnt I.

Protect Your Life: A Health Handbook for Law Enforcement Professionals. Davidson C. Umeh. LC 99-15918. (Illus.). 250p. (C). 1999. pap. text, wbk. ed. 34.95 (*1-889031-23-2*) Looseleaf Law.

Protect Your Life in the Sun: How to Minimize Your Exposure to Ultraviolet Sunlight & Prevent Skin Cancer & Eye Disorders. Paul L. Gourley & Gail M. Gourley. LC 93-77915. (Illus.). 104p. (Orig.). 1993. pap. 9.95 (*0-9636297-1-9*) High Light Pub.

Protect Your Macintosh. Bruce Schneier. (Illus.). 350p. (C). 1995. pap. text 23.95 (*1-56609-101-2*) Peachpit Pr.

Protect Your Money: Strategies for a Worry Free Retirement. Lyle Allen. 192p. 2000. pap. 17.95 (*1-58501-000-6*) CeShore Pubg.

Protect Your Parents & Their Financial Health... Talk with Them Before It's Too Late. Susan C. Richards. LC 98-36975. 248p. 1999. pap. 19.95 (*0-7931-2762-9*, 56806701) Dearborn.

Protect Your Privacy on the Internet. Bryan Pfaffenberger. LC 96-30073. 336p. 1997. pap. 29.99 incl. cd-rom (*0-471-18143-9*) Wiley.

***Protect Your Prostate: The World-Renowned Colgan Institute Reveals Its Program for a Healthy Prostate.** Michael Colgan. 2000. pap. 12.95 (*1-896817-17-3*) ApPubng.

Protect Yourself Against Tuberculosis: A Respiratory Protection Guide for Health Care Workers. 1997. lib. bdg. 251.95 (*0-8490-8147-5*) Gordon Pr.

Protect Yourself Against Tuberculosis: Respiratory Protection for Health Care Workers. 31p. 1996. pap. 2.00 (*0-16-061557-7*) USGPO.

Protect Yourself & Your Family from Crime & Violence. Foundation for Crime & Prevention Education Staff. 267p. 1998. 24.95 (*0-9648903-1-3*) Safety Press.

Protect Yourself from Business Lawsuits: And Lawyers Like Me. Thomas A. Schweich. LC 98-6158. 224p. 1998. 24.00 (*0-684-85267-5*) Scribner.

***Protect Yourself from Business Lawsuits & Lawyers Like Me.** Thomas A. Schweich. LC 98-6158. (Illus.). 224p. 2000. per. 13.00 (*0-684-85655-7*) S&S Trade.

Protect Yourself from Contaminated Food. Carol Turkington. 1999. mass mkt. 5.99 (*0-345-42898-6*) Ballantine Pub Grp.

Protect Yourself from Pesticides: A Guide for Pesticide Handlers. (Illus.). 101p. (Orig.). (C). 1995. pap. text 30.00 (*0-7881-2388-2*) DIANE Pub.

Protect Yourself from Pesticides: A Guide for Pesticide Handlers. (Orig.). 1996. lib. bdg. 251.95 (*0-8490-6352-3*) Gordon Pr.

Protect Yourself from Pesticides - Protejase de los Pesticidas: Guide for Agricultural Workers - Guia Para los Trabajadores Agricolas. (SPA., Illus.). 43p. (C). 1995. pap. text 20.00 (*0-7881-2374-2*) DIANE Pub.

Protect Yourself from Pesticides - Protejase de los Pesticidas: Guide for Agricultural Workers - Guia Para los Trabajadores Agricolas. 1994. lib. bdg. 250.00 (*0-8490-5754-X*) Gordon Pr.

Protect Yourself, Your Family, Your Home: Checklists Against Crime. James B. Motley. 192p. 1994. pap. 9.95 (*0-02-881074-0*) Brasseys.

Protected Area Economics & Policy: Linking Conservation & Sustainable Development. Mohan Munasinghe & Jeffrey A. McNeely. LC 94-45272. 372p. 1995. pap. 22.00 (*0-8213-3132-9*, 13132) World Bank.

Protected Areas of the World Vol. 2: Palaearctic: A Review of National Systems. Ed. by IUCN Staff. 584p. 1991. 40.00 (*2-8317-0091-4*, Pub. by IUCN) Island Pr.

Protected Areas of the World Vol. 3: Afrotropical: A Review of National Systems. Ed. by IUCN Staff. 384p. 1991. 40.00 (*2-8317-0092-2*, Pub. by IUCN) Island Pr.

***Protected by the Enemy.** Annelore Maack. LC 00-102828. 2000. 19.95 (*1-880710-51-X*) Monterey Pacific.

***Protected by the Enemy.** Annelore Maack. 225p. 2000. 19.95 (*1-885003-51-X*, Pub. by R D Reed Pubs) Midpt Trade.

Protected by the Light: The Complete Book of Psychic Self-Defense. Bruce Goldberg. LC 98-11112. (Illus.). 264p. 1999. pap. 12.95 (*1-56718-316-6*) Llewellyn Pubns.

***Protected by the Light: The Complete Book of Psychic Self-Defense.** 2nd ed. Bruce Goldberg. 250p. 2000. pap. 13.95 (*1-58736-004-7*) Hats Off Bks.

Protected Mode Software Architecture. Tom Shanley. 336p. (C). 1996. pap. text 32.95 (*0-201-55447-X*) Addison-Wesley.

Protected Mode Software Architecture. Tom Shanley & Mindshare Inc. Staff. 1996. 29.95 (*0-614-14428-0*) Addison-Wesley.

Protected Persons & Their Property in New South Wales. B. E. Porter & M. B. Robinson. xvi, 176p. 1987. pap. 41.50 (*0-455-20719-4*, Pub. by LawBk Co) Gaunt.

***Protected Souls: A Former FBI Agent's Odyssey into the Realm of Protection, Intuition, Good & Evil.** LC 99-91363. 192p. 1999. pap. 14.95 (*0-9675784-0-X*) M Miles.

Protected Wildlife Species of Nepal: An Introductory Handbook. Nabina Shrestha. 1997. pap. 22.00 (*0-7855-7478-6*, Pub. by Ratna Pustak Bhandar) St Mut.

Protecting a Will. Shane Newton. 154p. 1994. 49.00 (*1-86287-142-6*, Pub. by Federation Pr) Gaunt.

Protecting Abused & Neglected Children. Michael S. Wald et al. LC 87-10208. 275p. 1988. 39.50 (*0-8047-1420-7*) Stanford U Pr.

Protecting Abused Children: Protective Services & Proceedings, Foster Care, Termination of Parental Rights. Ed. by Byrgen P. Finkelman. LC 95-753. (Child Abuse: a Multidisciplinary Survey Ser.: Vol. 7). 528p. 1995. text 88.00 (*0-8153-1819-7*) Garland.

***Protecting Against the Expropriation Risk in Investing Abroad.** Richard C. Allison & Jack J. Coe, Jr. 520p. 1999. ring bd. 245.00 (*1-57823-001-2*) Juris Pubng.

Protecting American Workers: An Assessment of Government Programs. Sar A. Levitan et al. LC 86-13681. 294p. 1986. reprint ed. pap. 91.20 (*0-608-00703-X*, 206147500009) Bks Demand.

***Protecting America's Fisheries.** 17p. 1999. pap. 8.00 (*0-16-049918-6*) USGPO.

Protecting & Exploiting New Technology & Designs. Keith Hodkinson. 400p. 1987. pap. 100.50 (*0-419-13810-2*) Thomson Learn.

Protecting & Exploring Biotechnological Inventions. Ed. by Rosa Greaves. 296p. 1991. text 131.00 (*2-88316-008-2*) Gordon & Breach.

Protecting Assets with Estate Planning. 9.95 (*0-9630356-5-7*) Makai.

***Protecting Biodiversity: Legal Mechanisms Concerning Access to & Compensation for the Use of Genetic Resources in the United States of America.** LC 99-202796. (Research Report Ser.). 82p. 1998. write for info. (*0-911937-77-3*) Environ Law Inst.

***Protecting Biodiversity: National Laws Regulating Access to Genetic Resources in the Americas.** Ed. by Susan Perkoff Bass & Manuel Ruiz Muller. 100p. 2000. pap. 17.95 (*0-88936-900-3*, Pub. by IDRC Bks) Stylus Pub VA.

Protecting Biological Diversity in the National Parks: Workshop Recommendations. Ed. by F. Dominic Dottavio et al. LC 90-6008. (NPS Transactions & Proceedings Ser.: No. 9). (Illus.). (Orig.). (C). 1990. pap. write for info. (*0-943475-04-X*) Natl Park GA.

Protecting Business Information: A Manager's Guide. James A. Schweitzer. LC 95-9549. 199p. 1995. text 44.95 (*0-7506-9658-3*) Buttrwrth-Heinemann.

***Protecting Business Information (1996) A Manager's Guide.** James A. Schweitzer. 199p. 2000. reprint ed. text 25.00 (*0-7881-9194-2*) DIANE Pub.

Protecting Children: A Practical Guide. Ed. by Janet Kay & Linda James. LC 64-15297. 192p. 1999. pap. 21.50 (*0-304-33415-4*) Continuum.

Protecting Children: Challenges & Change. Ed. by John Bates et al. LC 96-80033. 288p. 1997. text 64.95 (*1-85742-323-2*, Pub. by Arena) Ashgate Pub Co.

***Protecting Children: Challenges & Change.** Ed. by John Bates et al. 263p. 1999. pap. 34.95 (*0-7546-1129-9*) Ashgate Pub Co.

Protecting Children & Supporting Families: Promising Programs & Organizational Realities. Gary Cameron & Jim R. Vanderwoerd. LC 96-33570. (Modern Applications of Social Work Ser.). 301p. 1997. pap. text 22.95 (*0-202-36106-3*); lib. bdg. 45.95 (*0-202-36105-5*) Aldine de Gruyter.

Protecting Children & Young People. Colin Findlay & Anne P. Salter. LC 92-49353. (Skills for Caring Ser.). (Illus.). 48p. 1992. pap. text 9.95 (*0-443-04618-2*) Church.

Protecting Children from Abuse & Neglect: Developing & Maintaining Effective Support Systems for Families. James Garbarino et al. LC 79-24239. (Jossey-Bass Social & Behavioral Science Ser.). 242p. reprint ed. pap. 75.10 (*0-7837-2541-8*, 204270000006) Bks Demand.

Protecting Children from Abuse & Neglect: Foundations for a New National Strategy. Ed. by Gary B. Melton & Frank D. Barry. LC 94-18298. 451p. 1994. lib. bdg. 50.00 (*0-89862-265-4*, 2265) Guilford Pubns.

Protecting Children from Danger: Learning Self-Reliance & Emergency Skills. Bob Bishop & Matt Thomas. LC 93-5977. (Illus.). 192p. (Orig.). 1993. pap. 12.95 (*1-55643-159-7*) North Atlantic.

Protecting Children from Sexual Abuse. Marjorie S. Fink. (Family Forum Library). 16p. 1992. 1.95 (*1-56688-012-2*) Bur For At-Risk.

***Protecting Children from the Impacts of Substance Abuse on Families Receiving Welfare: Congressional Hearing.** Ed. by E. Clay Shaw, Jr. (Illus.). 99p. (C). 1999. reprint ed. pap. text 25.00 (*0-7881-8447-4*) DIANE Pub.

Protecting Children in Cyberspace. Stephen J. Kavanagh. Ed. by Tom Kavanagh & Andrew Kavanagh. (Illus.). 102p. 1997. pap. 11.95 (*0-9659132-0-1*) Behav Psychoth.

Protecting Children in Military Families: A Cooperative Response. Ralph Blanchard. 141p. (Orig.). (C). 1995. pap. text 35.00 (*0-7881-1827-7*) DIANE Pub.

Protecting Children in School: A Handbook for Developing Child Protection Training. Jane Wonnacott. 50p. 1996. pap. 22.50 (*1-874579-38-5*, Pub. by Natl Childrens Bur) Paul & Co Pubs.

Protecting Children in Substance-Abusing Families. Vickie Kropenske & Judy Howard. (Illus.). 128p. (Orig.). (C). 1995. pap. text 30.00 (*0-7881-1826-9*) DIANE Pub.

***Protecting Children, Strenghtening Families & Creating Caring Communities in Israel.** Family Resource Coalition Staff & International Initiative Staff. (Illus.). 2000. pap. write for info. (*1-885429-24-X*) Family Resource.

Protecting Civil Rights Should be an Urgent Conservative Issue. Clint Bolick. (Issue Paper #5-88 Ser.). 3p. 1988. pap. text 8.00 (*1-57655-025-7*) Independ Inst.

***Protecting Company Assets: Preventing Loss.** Joyce McDowell. Ed. by Debbie Woodbury. LC 99-80075. (Retailing Smarts Ser.: Vol. 9). (Illus.). 80p. 2000. pap., wbk. ed. 7.95 (*1-56052-574-6*) Crisp Pubns.

***Protecting Company Assets: Promoting Safety.** Joyce McDowell. Ed. by Debbie Woodbury. LC 99-80076. (Retailing Smarts Ser.: Vol. 10). (Illus.). 80p. 2000. pap., wbk. ed. 7.95 (*1-56052-575-4*) Crisp Pubns.

Protecting Competition from the Postal Monopoly. J. Gregory Sidak & Daniel F. Spulber. 208p. 1996. 39.95 (*0-8447-3950-2*, AEI Pr) Am Enterprise.

Protecting Computer Systems & Software. Ed. by Frank L. Huband & R. Duane Shelton. 1985. 50.00 (*0-317-29415-6*, #H43937) Harcourt.

Protecting Constitutional Freedoms: A Role for Federal Courts, 56. Daan Braveman. LC 89-7531. (Contributions in Legal Studies: No. 56). 217p. 1989. 55.00 (*0-313-26833-9*, BVF, Greenwood Pr) Greenwood.

Protecting Consumer Rights. 1987. text 95.00 (*0-07-034852-9*) Shepards.

***Protecting Consumers Against Slamming: Hearing Before the Subcommittee on Telecommunications, Trade & Consumer Protection of the Committee on Commerce, House Of Representatives, 105th Congress, 2nd Session, on H. R. 3050 & H. R. 3888, June 23, 1998.** USGPO Staff. LC 98-215882. iii, 129 p. 1998. write for info. (*0-16-057444-7*) USGPO.

Protecting Corporate America's Secrets in the Global Economy. 225p. 1992. 250.00 (*0-9633534-0-3*) Am Inst Busn Res.

Protecting Corporate Trade Secrets. J. Steele, Jr. Vol. IP1. text 82.00 (*0-8205-2416-6*) Bender.

Protecting Counter & Interviewing Staff from Client Aggression. B. Swanton & D. Webber. 64p. 1990. pap. 15.00 (*0-642-14974-7*, Pub. by Aust Inst Criminology) Advent Bks Div.

Protecting Critical Information & Technology: Fourth National Operations Security Conference Proceedings. (Illus.). 667p. (C). 1997. reprint ed. pap. text 50.00 (*0-7881-4506-1*) DIANE Pub.

Protecting Cultural Landscapes: Planning, Treatment & Management of Historic Landscapes. Charles A. Birnbaum. 20p. 1994. pap. 1.75 (*0-16-061666-2*) USGPO.

Protecting Danube River Basin Resources - Ensuring Access to Water Quality Data & Information: Proceedings of the NATO Advanced Research Workshop on an International Data-Sharing Programme for the Effective Management of Danube River Basin Resources, Budapest, Hungary, 27-30 May 1996. Ed. by Irene L. Murphy. LC 96-52350. (NATO Advanced Science Institutes Series: C). 236p. (C). 1997. text 144.00 (*0-7923-4382-4*) Kluwer Academic.

Protecting Designs - Law & Litigation. John Phillips. 425p. 1994. 110.00 (*0-455-21275-9*, Pub. by LawBk Co) Gaunt.

Protecting Endangered Species. F. Brooks. (Conservation Guides Ser.). (Illus.). 24p. (J). (gr. 2-5). 1991. lib. bdg. 12.95 (*0-88110-500-7*, Usborne) EDC.

Protecting Endangered Species: U. S. Trade Policy & the Cases of China & Taiwan. Robert Letovsky & Brian Dwyer. (Pew Case Studies in International Affairs). 50p. (C). 1997. pap. text 3.50 (*1-56927-218-2*) Geo U Inst Dplmcy.

Protecting Endangered Species at the San Diego Zoo. Georgeanne Irvine. (Zoo World Ser.). (Illus.). 48p. (J). (gr. 3-7). 1990. pap. 14.95 (*0-671-68776-X*) S&S Bks Yung.

Protecting Engineering Ideas & Inventions. 3rd ed. LC 88-64137. 373p. 1989. 56.00 (*0-944606-05-9*); pap. 46.00 (*0-944606-04-0*) Penn Inst.

Protecting Estuaries: The Mix of Land & Sea. Cheryl C. Runyon & Larry Morandi. 30p. 1993. 10.00 (*1-55516-376-9*, 4338) Natl Conf State Legis.

Protecting Floodplan Resources: A Guidebook for Communities. 2nd ed. Richard C. Smardon. (Illus.). 41p. 1996. pap. text 20.00 (*0-7881-3689-5*) DIANE Pub.

Protecting Foreign Investment under International Law: Legal Aspects of Political Risk. Paul E. Comeaux & N. Stephan Kinsella. LC 96-41023. 448p. 1997. text 105.00 (*0-379-21371-0*) Oceana.

Protecting Groups. P. J. Kocienski. LC 94-17462. (Foundations of Organic Chemistry Ser.). (Illus.). 256p. 1994. 85.00 (*0-86577-558-3*); pap. 45.00 (*0-86577-557-5*) Thieme Med Pubs.

Protecting Health Care Workers from HIV Infection. (State Legislative Reports: Vol. 15, No. 11). 9p. 1990. 15.00 (*1-55516-267-3*, 7302-1511) Natl Conf State Legis.

***Protecting His Own.** Molly Rice. 2000. per. 4.25 (*0-373-22562-8*) Harlequin Bks.

Protecting Historic Properties: A Guide to Research & Preservation. Martha Wolf et al. LC 84-72856. (Illus.). 150p. 1984. pap. 15.00 (*0-940540-03-7*) Brandywine Conserv.

Protecting Human Rights. Ed. by Frick W. Curry. (WVSS in Public Policy & Public Systems Ser.). (C). 1996. pap. text 18.50 (*0-8133-7156-2*) Westview.

Protecting Human Rights in Africa: Roles & Strategies of Non-Governmental Organizations. Claude E. Welch. (Pennsylvania Studies in Human Rights). (Illus.). 360p. 1995. text 39.95 (*0-8122-3330-1*) U of Pa Pr.

Protecting Human Subjects: Departmental Subject Pools & Institutional Review Boards. Ed. by Garvin Chastain & R. Eric Landrum. LC 99-22348. 228p. 1999. pap. 29.95 (*1-55798-575-8*, 431-617A) Am Psychol.

Protecting Individual Rights: The Role of State Constitutionalism: Report of the 1992 Forum for State Court Judges. Roscoe Pound Foundation Staff. Ed. by Barbara Wolfson. 82p. 1993. pap. 35.00 (*0-933067-14-3*) Roscoe Pound Inst.

Protecting Intellectual Property in Latin America. Ed. by Scott Studebaker. 1998. pap. 235.00 (*1-893323-15-3*) WorldTrade Exec.

Protecting Investors: A Half Century of Investment Company Regulation. Government Printing Office Staff. 563p. 1992. per. 40.00 (*0-16-037900-8*) USGPO.

Protecting Investors: A Half Century of Investment Company Regulation, 2 vols., Set. 1996. lib. bdg. 608.95 (*0-8490-6039-7*) Gordon Pr.

***Protecting Jennie.** Ann Collins. (Historical Ser.). 2000. mass mkt. 4.99 (*0-373-29142-6*, 1291426) Harlequin Bks.

Protecting Judgment-Impaired Adults: Issues, Interventions & Policies. Ed. by Edmund F. Dejowski. LC 90-45236. (Journal of Elder Abuse & Neglect). 178p. 1990. text 39.95 (*1-56024-054-7*) Haworth Pr.

***Protecting Kids Online: What Industry & Nonprofit Organizations Are Doing.** Ed. by Richard T. Kaplar. LC 99-75978. 161p. 1999. ring bd. 10.95 (*0-937790-62-1*) Media Institute.

Protecting LAN Resources: A Comprehensive Guide to Securing, Protecting & Rebuilding a Network. Gilbert Held. 214p. 1995. pap. 110.00 (*0-471-95407-1*) Wiley.

***Protecting Library Staff, Users, Collections, & Facilities: A How-to-Do-It Manual for Librarians.** (How-to-Do-It Manuals for Librarians Ser.). 200p. 2000. pap. 55.00 (*1-55570-392-5*) Neal-Schuman.

P

Protecting Life on Earth: Steps to Save the Ozone Layer. Cynthia P. Shea. 60p. (Orig.). (C). 1988. pap. 5.00 (*0-916468-88-7*) Worldwatch Inst.

Protecting Marie. (Assessment Packs Ser.). 15p. 1998. pap. text 15.95 (*1-58303-058-1*) Pthways Pubng.

Protecting Marie. Kevin Henkes. LC 94-16387. (Illus.). 208p. (YA). (gr. 7 up). 1995. 15.00 (*0-688-13958-2*, Grenwillow Bks) HarpC Child Bks.

Protecting Marie. Kevin Henkes. LC 96-23208. 1996. 9.09 (*0-606-10289-2*, Pub. by Turtleback) Demco.

Protecting Marie. Kevin Henkes. (Illus.). 208p. (J). (gr. 5-9). 1996. pap. 4.99 (*0-14-038320-4*) Viking Penguin.

Protecting Markets: U. S. Policy & the World Grain Trade. Ronald T. Libby. LC 91-55536. (Illus.). 176p. 1992. text 32.50 (*0-8014-2617-0*) Cornell U Pr.

Protecting Minnesota's Children: Public Issues. League of Women Voters of Minnesota Education Fund. (Illus.). 29p. 1986. pap. 2.50 (*0-9613566-2-6*) League Wmn Voters MN.

Protecting Molly McCulloch: Loving Dangerously. Dee Holmes. 1997. per. 3.99 (*0-373-70732-0*, 1-70732-2) Harlequin Bks.

Protecting Money. Patricia Armentrout. LC 96-3457. (Money Ser.). (Illus.). (J). 1996. lib. bdg. 14.60 (*1-57103-120-0*) Rourke Pr.

Protecting Motherhood: Women & the Family in the Politics of Postwar West Germany. Robert G. Moeller. (C). 1992. 50.00 (*0-520-07903-5*, Pub. by U CA Pr) Cal Prin Full Svc.

Protecting Motherhood: Women & the Family in the Politics of Postwar West Germany. Robert G. Moeller. LC 92-6622. 346p. (C). 1996. pap. 15.95 (*0-520-20516-2*, Pub. by U CA Pr) Cal Prin Full Svc.

Protecting Natural Resources with Remote Sensing. 504p. 1990. 8.00 (*0-944426-35-2*) ASP & RS.

Protecting Nature: Regional Reviews of Protected Areas. Ed. by Jeffrey A. McNeely. LC 95-194741. 376p. (C). 1994. pap. text 50.00 (*2-8317-0119-8*, Pub. by IUCN) Island Pr.

Protecting Networks with Satan. Martin Freiss. (Illus.). 128p. 1998. pap. 19.95 (*1-56592-425-8*) OReilly & Assocs.

Protecting Niagara: A History of the Niagara County Sheriff's Office. Christopher J. Carlin. Ed. by Paul G. Colangelo. (Illus.). 242p. (Orig.). 1995. 17.00 (*0-9645195-1-8*); pap. 10.00 (*0-9645195-4-2*); lib. bdg. 17.00 (*0-9645195-2-6*) AEGIS Pr.

***Protecting Nuclear Weapons Material in Russia.** National Research Council Staff. 64p. 1999. pap. 18.00 (*0-309-06547-X*) Natl Acad Pr.

Protecting Oil & Gas Lien & Security Interests: Use of Memorandum of Operating Agreement & Financing Statement. LC 87-81830. 128p. 1987. pap. 29.95 (*0-89707-315-0*, 535-0014-01) Amer Bar Assn.

Protecting One's Turf: Social Strategies for Maintaining Urban Neighborhoods. Judith N. DeSena. 168p. (C). 1990. lib. bdg. 38.00 (*0-8191-7716-4*) U Pr of Amer.

Protecting Ontario's Wilderness: A History of Changing Ideas & Preservation Politics, 1927-1973. George Warecki. LC 93-17232. (American University Studies: Regional Studies: Ser. XXI, Vol. 8). 344p. (C). 2000. 55.95 (*0-8204-2215-0*) P Lang Pubng.

***Protecting Our Children on the Internet: Towards a New Culture of Responsibility.** Jens Waltermann. 2000. 44.95 (*3-89204-474-0*) Bertelsmann Stiftung.

Protecting Our Children's Innocence: How to Help Children Guard Against Pornography. (Illus.). 100p. 1996. student ed., wbk. ed. 35.00 incl. audio (*0-9647169-1-7*) Yawna Pubns.

Protecting Our Feathered Friends. Dean T. Spaulding. LC 96-25117. (Birder's Bookshelf Ser.). (J). 1997. lib. bdg. 19.93 (*0-8225-3178-X*) Lerner Pub.

Protecting Our Forests. Rosa Costa-Pace. (Junior Library of Ecology). (Illus.). 32p. (J). (gr. 4 up). 1994. lib. bdg. 15.95 (*0-7910-2104-1*) Chelsea Hse.

***Protecting Our Kids from Disasters: Nonstructural Mitigation for Child Care Centers.** Institute for Business & Home Safety Staff. (Illus.). 60p. 1999. write for info. (*1-885312-20-2*) Inst for Busn.

***Protecting Our Personal Health Information: Privacy in the Electronic Age Congressional Hearings.** Ed. by Bill First. (Illus.). 198p. (C). 1999. reprint ed. pap. text 30.00 (*0-7881-8412-1*) DIANE Pub.

Protecting Our Planet - Primary Grades. Ava D. Drutman. 144p. (J). (gr. 1-3). 1991. 10.99 (*0-86653-619-1*, GA1338) Good Apple.

Protecting Our Planet (Early Childhood Version) Ave D. Drutman & Evelyn Deutsch. (Illus.). 128p. (J). (ps-1). 1992. 9.99 (*0-86653-665-5*, GA1400) Good Apple.

Protecting Our Planet (Intermediate) Ava Drutman & Susan Zuckerman. 144p. (J). (gr. 4-8). 1991. 10.99 (*0-86653-589-6*, GA1302) Good Apple.

Protecting Our Rights: What Goes on the Internet? NIF Staff. LC 99-210839. 28p. 1998. 6.00 (*0-7872-4880-0*); pap. 6.00 (*0-7872-5352-9*) Kendall-Hunt.

Protecting Our Rivers & Lakes. Rosa Costa-Pace. (Junior Library of Ecology). (Illus.). 32p. (J). (gr. 4 up). 1994. lib. bdg. 15.95 (*0-7910-2105-X*) Chelsea Hse.

Protecting Our World. F. Brooks. (Conservation Guides Ser.). (Illus.). 72p. (J). (gr. 2-5). 1992. pap. 10.95 (*0-7460-1082-6*, Usborne) EDC.

Protecting Paradise: Three Hundred Ways to Protect Florida's Environment. Peggy Cavanaugh & Margaret Spontak. 160p. 1992. pap. 11.95 (*0-9632566-5-3*) Phoenix Fla.

Protecting Paradise: Yosemite Rangers, 1898-1960. Shirley Sargent. LC 98-66429. (Illus.). 160p. 1998. pap. text 18.95 (*0-9642244-1-0*) Ponderosa CA.

Protecting Perishable Foods During Transport by Truck. 1991. lib. bdg. 75.00 (*0-8490-4387-5*) Gordon Pr.

Protecting Personnel at Hazardous Waste Sites. 2nd ed. Ed. by William F. Martin & Steven P. Levine. LC 93-28510. 592p. 1993. 79.95 (*0-7506-9457-2*) Buttrwrth-Heinemann.

***Protecting Personnel at Hazardous Waste Sites.** 3rd ed. Michael Gochfeld. LC 99-31223. 640p. 1999. 75.00 (*0-7506-7049-5*) Buttrwrth-Heinemann.

***Protecting Prisoners: The Standards of the European Committee for the Prevention of Torture in Context.** Rod Morgan & Malcolm E. Evans. LC 99-16151. 320p. 1999. text 90.00 (*0-19-829821-8*) OUP.

***Protecting Privacy.** Ed. by Basil Markesinis. (Clifford Chance Lecture Ser.). 260p. 1999. text 80.00 (*0-19-826885-8*) OUP.

Protecting Privacy in Computerized Medical Information. (Illus.). 168p. (Orig.). (C). 1994. pap. text 40.00 (*0-7881-0446-2*) DIANE Pub.

Protecting Privacy in Computerized Medical Information. (Orig.). 1994. lib. bdg. 250.00 (*0-8490-5769-8*) Gordon Pr.

Protecting Privacy in Surveillance Societies: The Federal Republic of Germany, Sweden, France, Canada, & the United States. David H. Flaherty. LC 89-4762. xxiv, 483p. 1992. pap. 24.95 (*0-8078-4352-0*) U of NC Pr.

Protecting Privacy in Two-Way Electronic Services. David H. Flaherty. LC 84-15492. (Professional Librarian Ser.). 173p. 1985. 40.00 (*0-86729-107-9*, Hall Reference) Macmillan.

Protecting, Promoting, & Supporting Breast-Feeding: The Special Role of Maternity Services, a Joint WHO-UNICEF Statement. (ARA, ENG, FRE & SPA.). iv, 32p. 1989. pap. text 6.00 (*92-4-156130-0*) World Health.

Protecting Public Health. United States Government Printing Office Staff. LC 97-216852. (S. Hrg. Ser.). iii, 47 p. 1997. write for info. (*0-16-055311-3*) USGPO.

Protecting Public Health & the Environment: Implementing the Precautionary Principle. Ed. by Carolyn Raffensperger & Joel Tickner. LC 99-19514. (Illus.). 350p. (C). 1999. pap. 30.00 (*1-55963-688-2*) Island Pr.

***Protecting Reliance: The Emergent Doctrine of Equitable Estoppel.** Michael Spence. 188p. 1999. 40.00 (*1-901362-62-0*) Hart Pub.

Protecting Religious Freedom after Boerne V. Flores: Hearing Before the Subcommittee on the Constitution of the Committee on the Judiciary, House of Representatives, One Hundred Fifth Congress, First Session, July 14, 1997. USGPO Staff. LC 98-211336. iii, 89 p. 1997. write for info. (*0-16-057402-1*) USGPO.

Protecting Residences from Wildfires: A Guide for Homeowners, Lawmakers, & Planners. Howard E. Moore. 44p. (Orig.). (C). 1993. pap. text 20.00 (*1-56806-971-5*) DIANE Pub.

Protecting Restaurant Profits. Stephen Miller. 1988. pap. 36.95 (*0-86730-252-6*) Lebhar Friedman.

Protecting Rivers & Seas. F. Brooks. (Conservation Guides Ser.). (Illus.). 24p. (J). (gr. 2-5). 1992. pap. 4.50 (*0-7460-0687-X*, Usborne); lib. bdg. 12.95 (*0-88110-529-5*, Usborne) EDC.

Protecting Scientific Ideas & Inventions. Ramon D. Foltz & Thomas A. Penn. 233p. 1988. 55.00 (*0-944606-03-2*, KF6032, CRC Reprint) Franklin.

Protecting Scientific Ideas & Inventions. 2nd ed. Ramon D. Foltz & Thomas A. Penn. 233p. 1990. 77.00 (*0-944606-06-7*, KF6032) CRC Pr.

Protecting Social Security Number Privacy: How States Can Protect Their Residents from Idenity theft. Robert E. Smith. (Issue Paper #5-97). 13p. 1997. pap. text 8.00 (*1-57655-157-1*) Independ Inst.

Protecting Soldiers & Mothers: The Political Origins of Social Policy in the United States. Theda Skocpol. 714p. 1995. pap. text 18.95 (*0-674-71766-X*, SKOPRX) Belknap Pr.

Protecting Soldiers & Mothers: The Political Origins of Social Policy in the United States. Theda Skocpol. (Illus.). 714p. 1992. text 46.95 (*0-674-71765-1*) HUP.

***Protecting Stream & River Corridors: Creating Effective Local Riparian Buffer.** Seth J. Wenger & Laurie Fowler. (Public Policy Research Ser.). 68p. 2000. pap. 13.75 (*0-89854-198-0*) U of GA Inst Govt.

Protecting Stream Corridors. Lee Nellis. 27p. 1993. pap. 10.00 (*0-86602-301-1*, Sage Prdcls Pr) Sage.

***Protecting Study Volunteers in Clinical Research.** Cynthia Dunn & Gary Chadwick. Ed. by Whitney Allen. 200p. 1999. pap. 59.00 (*0-9673029-1-9*) CenterWatch.

Protecting Superannuation Against Criminal Exploitation. Ed. by Adam Graycar. LC 98-118618. 70p. 1999. pap. 20.00 (*0-642-24023-X*, Pub. by Aust Inst Criminology) Advent Bks Div.

Protecting the Arctic: Indigenous Peoples & Cultural Survival. Mark Nuttall. (Studies in Environmental Anthropology: Vol. 3). 204p. 1998. text 42.00 (*90-5702-354-7*, Harwood Acad Pubs); pap. text 22.00 (*90-5702-355-5*, Harwood Acad Pubs) Gordon & Breach.

Protecting the Best Men: An Interpretive History of the Law of Libel. Norman L. Rosenberg. LC 85-1174. (Studies in Legal History). xi, 369p. (C). 1990. reprint ed. pap. text 22.50 (*0-8078-4290-7*) U of NC Pr.

Protecting the Built Environment: Cleaning for Health. Michael A. Berry. Ed. by Judith P. Stanton & Mary F. Ashley. (Illus.). 304p. 1994. pap. 50.00 (*0-9635715-0-8*) Tricomm TwntyFrst.

Protecting the Business Module, PACE Level 1: A Program for Acquiring Competence in Entrepreneurship, 3 levels. rev. ed. National Center for Research in Vocational Educati. 1983. 2.50 (*0-317-06082-1*, RD240CB18) Ctr Educ Trng Employ.

Protecting the Business Module, PACE Level 2: A Program for Acquiring Competence in Entrepreneurship, 3 levels. rev. ed. National Center for Research in Vocational Educati. 1983. 2.50 (*0-317-06083-X*, RD240BB18) Ctr Educ Trng Employ.

Protecting the Business Module, PACE Level 3: A Program for Acquiring Competence in Entrepreneurship, 3 levels. rev. ed. National Center for Research in Vocational Educati. 1983. 2.50 (*0-317-06084-8*, RD240CB18) Ctr Educ Trng Employ.

Protecting the Children: Strategies for Optimizing Emotional & Behavioral Development. Ed. by Raymond P. Lorion. LC 89-28933. (Prevention in Human Services Ser.: Vol. 7, No. 1). (Illus.). 275p. 1990. text 49.95 (*0-86656-970-7*) Haworth Pr.

***Protecting the Commons: A Framework for Resource Management in the Americas.** Ed. by Joanna Burger et al. (Illus.). 328p. 2000. 60.00 (*1-55963-737-4*, Shearwater Bks); pap. 30.00 (*1-55963-738-2*, Shearwater Bks) Island Pr.

Protecting the Confidentiality of Business Information Submitted to the Federal Government. Kevin McCarthy. Vol. G6. text 82.00 (*0-8205-2388-7*) Bender.

Protecting the Corporate Parent: Avoiding Liability for Acts of the Subsidiary. (Corporate Law & Practice Ser.). 241p. 1991. pap. text 17.50 (*0-685-56878-4*, B4-6980) PLI.

Protecting the Corporate Parent, 1992: Avoiding Liability for Acts of the Subsidiary. (Corporate Law & Practice Course Handbook, 1985-86 Ser.: Vol. 785). 235p. 1992. 70.00 (*0-685-65488-5*, B4-7010) PLI.

***Protecting the Cultural Heritage: National Legislations & International Conventions** S. S. Biswas. LC 99-931901. 263p. 1999. write for info. (*81-7305-150-X*, Pub. by Aryan Bks Intl) S Asia.

Protecting the Dispossessed: A Challenge for the International Community. Francis M. Deng. 175p. (C). 1993. 34.95 (*0-8157-1826-8*); pap. 14.95 (*0-8157-1825-X*) Brookings.

Protecting the Emotional Development of the Ill Child: The Essence of the Child Life Profession. Ed. by Jerome Oremland. LC 99-17720. 275p. 1999. 45.00 (*1-887841-20-2*, 64385, Psychosocial) Intl Univs Pr.

Protecting the Environment: Opportunities to Volunteer see Community Service for Teens

Protecting the European Environment: Enforcing EC Environmental Law. Ed. by Han Somsen. 313p. 1996. pap. 44.00 (*1-85431-604-4*, Pub. by Blackstone Pr) Gaunt.

Protecting the Family Jewels: How to Inventory Your Home Without Losing Your Mind. Kathleen Gura. 120p. 1987. pap. 12.95 (*0-939355-00-0*) Enterpress.

Protecting the Family Jewels: How to Inventory Your Home Without Losing Your Mind. 2nd ed. Kathleen Gura. 116p. 1987. pap. 12.95 (*0-939355-11-6*) Enterpress.

***Protecting the Future of Social Security: Congressional Hearing.** Ed. by John R. Kasich. 55p. (C). 1999. reprint ed. pap. text. write for info. (*0-7881-8444-X*) DIANE Pub.

***Protecting the Gift: Keeping Children & Teenagers Safe (And Parents Sane)** Gavin De Becker. 368p. 2000. pap. 11.95 (*0-440-50900-9*, Dell Trade Pbks) Dell.

Protecting the Gift: Keeping Children & Teenagers Safe (and Parents Sane) Gavin De Becker. LC 99-22006. 336p. 1999. 22.95 (*0-385-33309-9*) Doubleday.

Protecting the Growing Number of Older Workers: The Age Discrimination in Employment Act. Daniel P. O'Meara. LC 88-80365. (Labor Relations & Public Policy Ser.: No. 33). 384p. 1989. pap. 30.00 (*0-89546-069-6*) U PA Ctr Hum Res.

Protecting the Growing Numbers of Older Workers: The Age Discrimination in Employment Act, 1989-97, Supplement. rev. ed. Kristofer K. Strasser. (Labor Relations & Public Policy Ser.: Vol. 33). 91p. 1998. pap. 25.00 (*1-891496-08-5*) J M Olin.

Protecting the Gulf of Aqaba: A Regional Environmental Challenge. Ed. by Deborah Sandler et al. LC 93-495. 1993. 50.00 (*0-911937-46-3*) Environ Law Inst.

Protecting the Health of the Elderly: A Review of WHO Activities. M. Skeet. (Public Health in Europe Ser.: No. 18). 125p. 1983. pap. text 11.00 (*92-890-1154-8*) World Health.

Protecting the Human Environment. (United Nations Peaceful Settlement Ser.). 8.00 (*92-1-157002-6*, E.77.XV.PS/9) UN.

Protecting the Innocent: Enhancing the Humanitarian Role of the United Nations in Natural Disasters & Other Disaster Situations. Thomas E. Boudreau. 1983. pap. write for info. (*0-87641-310-6*) Carnegie Ethics & Intl Affairs.

Protecting the Nation's Ground Water from Contamination. OTA Staff. (C). 1987. text 125.00 (*81-85046-52-2*, Pub. by Scientific Pubs) St Mut.

Protecting the Nation's Groundwater from Contamination. Congress of the United States Office of Technology. 1986. 90.00 (*81-85046-53-0*, Pub. by Scientific) St Mut.

Protecting the Nation's Groundwater from Contamination, Vols. 1 & 2. Ed. by Congress of the United States Office of Technology. (C). 1986. text 300.00 (*0-685-74016-1*) Scientific.

Protecting the New Jersey Pinelands: A New Direction in Land-Use Management. Ed. by Beryl R. Collins & Emily W. Russell. (Illus.). 234p. 1988. pap. 18.95 (*0-8135-1275-1*); text 45.00 (*0-8135-1267-0*) Rutgers U Pr.

Protecting the Ozone Layer: Lessons, Models, & Prospects. Philippe G. Le Prestre et al. LC 98-30071. 1998. 99.95 (*0-7923-8245-5*) Kluwer Academic.

Protecting the Ozone Layer Vol. 1: Refrigerants, Vol. 1. 40p. pap. 15.00 (*92-807-1333-7*) UN.

Protecting the Ozone Layer Vol. 2: Solvents, Coatings & Adhesives, Vol. 2. 40p. pap. 15.00 (*92-807-1334-5*) UN.

Protecting the Ozone Layer Vol. 3: Fire Extinguishing Substances, Vol. 3. 32p. pap. 15.00 (*92-807-1335-3*) UN.

Protecting the Ozone Layer Vol. 4: Foams, Vol. 4. 40p. pap. 15.00 (*92-807-1337-X*) UN.

Protecting the Ozone Layer Vol. 5: Aerosols, Sterilants, Carbon Tetrachloride & Miscellaneous Uses, Vol. 5. 40p. pap. 15.00 (*92-807-1336-1*) UN.

Protecting the Ozone Layer Through Trade Measures: Reconciling the Trade Provisions of the Montreal Protocol & the Rules of the GATT. (Environment & Trade Ser.: No. 6). 120p. pap. 10.00 (*92-1-127010-3*) UN.

Protecting the Past. George S. Smith & John E. Ehrenhard. 420p. 1991. lib. bdg. 59.95 (*0-8493-8877-5*, E159) CRC Pr.

Protecting the Past from Natural Disasters. Carl L. Nelson et al. (Illus.). 192p. (Orig.). 1995. pap. 14.95 (*0-471-14416-9*) Wiley.

Protecting the Periphery. Steven Yearly. Ed. by Susan Baker & Kay Milton. 173p. (C). 1994. 45.00 (*0-7146-4584-2*, Pub. by F Cass Pubs); pap. 22.50 (*0-7146-4114-6*, Pub. by F Cass Pubs) Intl Spec Bk.

An Asterisk (*) at the beginning of an entry indicates that the title is appearing for the first time.

*Protecting the Polar Marine Environment: Law & Policy for Pollution Prevention.** Ed. by Davor Vidas. (Illus.). 288p. 2001. text. write for info. (*0-521-66311-3*) Cambridge U Pr.

Protecting the Privacy of Student Records: Guidelines for Education Agencies. Oona Cheung. 151p. 1997. pap. 14.00 (*0-16-049118-5*) USGPO.

***Protecting the Privacy of Student Records: Guidelines for Education Agencies.** Dona Cheung et al. 143p. (C). 1999. reprint ed. pap. text 25.00 (*0-7881-8129-7*) DIANE Pub.

***Protecting the Prostate: Relieving Symptoms Through the Integration of Diet & Lifestyle.** Jean-Yves Dionne & Karolyn A. Gazella. 32p. 2000. pap. 3.95 (*1-890694-30-4*) IMPAKT Communs.

Protecting the Pub: Brewers & Publicans Against Temperance. David W. Gutzke. (Royal Historical Society: Studies in History: No. 58). (Illus.). 234p. (C). 1989. 75.00 (*0-86193-215-3*) Boydell & Brewer.

Protecting the Public: Legal Issues in Injury Prevention. Tom Christoffel & Stephen P. Teret. LC 92-36159. (Illus.). 248p. 1993. text 45.00 (*0-19-507368-1*) OUP.

Protecting the Rain Forest. Mae Woods. LC 98-13432. (Rain Forest Ser.). (Illus.). 24p. (J). (gr. 2-4). 1999. lib. bdg. 18.60 (*1-57765-022-0*, Checkerboard Library) ABDO Pub Co.

Protecting the Right to Read: A How-to-Do-It Manual for School & Public Librarians. Ann K. Symons & Charles Harmon. (How-to-Do-It Manuals Ser.: Vol. 60). 215p. (Orig.). 1995. pap. 45.00 (*1-55570-216-3*) Neal-Schuman.

Protecting the Seeds. Terri Miskell. (Illus.). 40p. 1997. pap. 8.00 (*0-8059-3965-2*) Dorrance.

Protecting the Source. Steven E. Browne. 242p. 1996. pap. 14.95 (*0-914499-03-3*) Wilton Place.

Protecting the Space Shuttle from Meteoroids & Orbital Debris. National Research Council Staff. 70p. (C). Date not set. pap. text 15.00 (*0-309-05988-7*) Natl Acad Pr.

Protecting the Vulnerable: A Re-Analysis of Our Social Responsibilities. Robert E. Goodin. LC 85-1127. 248p. 1986. pap. 11.95 (*0-226-30299-7*) U Ch Pr.

Protecting the Vulnerable: A Re-Analysis of Our Social Responsibilities. Robert E. Goodin. LC 85-1127. xii, 236p. 1995. lib. bdg. 30.00 (*0-226-30298-9*) U Ch Pr.

***Protecting Trade Secrets.** Laurence H. Reece, III. LC 97-76383. 138p. 1998. write for info. (*1-57589-080-1*) Mass CLE.

Protecting Trade Secrets: Safeguard Your Business's Confidential Information. Nishan Swais. 208p. (Orig.). 1996. pap. 10.95 (*1-55180-053-5*) Self-Counsel Pr.

***Protecting Trade Secrets, Patents, Copyrights & Trademarks.** 3rd ed. Robert C. Dorr & Christopher H. Munch. LC 99-51534. 1999. ring bd. 165.00 (*0-7355-1155-1*) Panel Pubs.

Protecting Trade Secrets under the Uniform Trade Secrets Act: Practical Advice for Executives. Michael C. Budden. LC 96-3622. 192p. 1996. 57.95 (*1-56720-016-8*, Quorum Bks) Greenwood.

Protecting Trade Secrets, 1989. (Patents, Copyrights, Trademarks, & Literary Property Ser.). 783p. 1989. 17.50 (*0-685-69480-1*) PLI.

***Protecting Us from Ourselves.** Robert D. Grimes. 64p. 1999. pap. 8.00 (*0-8059-4567-9*) Dorrance.

Protecting Visibility in National Parks & Wilderness Areas. National Research Council, Committee on Haze in Na. 316p. (Orig.). (C). 1993. pap. text 38.00 (*0-309-04844-3*) Natl Acad Pr.

Protecting Water Quality. Ed. by Gary E. McCuen. (Ideas in Conflict Ser.). 180p. (YA). (gr. 7-12). 1986. lib. bdg. 15.95 (*0-86596-056-9*) G E M.

***Protecting Watershed Areas: Case of the Panama Canal.** Ed. by Mark S. Ashton et al. LC QH77.P357P76 1999. (Journal of Sustainable Forestry Ser.: Vol. 8, Nos. 3/4). 214p. (C). 1999. 49.95 (*1-56022-064-3*, Food Products); pap. 29.95 (*1-56022-066-X*, Food Products) Haworth Pr.

Protecting What's Ours: Indigenous Peoples & Biodiversity. Ed. & Compiled by David Rothschild. LC 96-71965.Tr. of Profégiendo lo Nuestro: Pueblos Indigenas y Biodiversidad. 1997. 10.83 (*0-9635396-0-4*) S & Meso-Am Ind.

Protecting What's Yours: How to Safeguard Your Assets & Maintain Your Personal Wealth. Andrew D. Westhem & Donald J. Korn. LC 94-16683. 256p. 1994. 18.95 (*1-55972-258-4*) Carol Pub Group.

Protecting Women: Labor Legislation in Europe, the United States, & Australia, 1880-1920. Ed. by Ulla Wikander et al. LC 94-44875. 392p. 1995. text 49.95 (*0-252-02175-4*) U of Ill Pr.

Protecting Women: Labor Legislation in Europe, the United States, & Australia, 1880-1920. Ed. by Ulla Wikander et al. 344p. (C). 1995. pap. text 19.95 (*0-252-06464-X*) U of Ill Pr.

Protecting Workers' Health in the Third World: National & International Strategies. Ed. by Michael R. Reich & Toshiteru Okubo. LC 92-6991. 328p. 1992. 59.95 (*0-86569-026-X*, T026, Auburn Hse) Greenwood.

Protecting Working Children. Ed. by William E. Myers. LC 91-13767. 192p. (C). 1991. text 62.50 (*1-85649-006-8*, Pub. by Zed Books); text 22.50 (*1-85649-007-6*, Pub. by Zed Books) St Martin.

Protecting Your Assets. Ed. by Richard L. Strohm. LC 96-48968. (Layman's Law Guides Ser.). 128p. 1999. 16.95 (*0-7910-4441-6*) Chelsea Hse.

Protecting Your Assets: How to Safeguard & Maintain Your Personal Wealth. Andrew D. Westhem & Donald J. Korn. 288p. 1996. pap. 14.95 (*0-8065-1760-3*, Citadel Pr) Carol Pub Group.

Protecting Your Assets: Strategies for a Successful Business Operation in a Litigious Society. Wayne S. Hyatt. 1997. pap. 44.95 (*0-87420-797-5*, P 11) Urban Land.

Protecting Your Baby to Be. Margie Profet. LC 97-7307. 1997. pap. 10.00 (*0-201-15492-7*) Addison-Wesley.

Protecting Your Baby-to-Be: Preventing Birth Defects in the First Trimester. Margie Profet. LC 95-4873. (Illus.). 168p. 1995. 20.00 (*0-201-40768-X*) Addison-Wesley.

Protecting Your Collection: A Handbook, Survey, & Guide for the Security of Rare Books, Manuscripts, Archives & Works of Art. Slade R. Gandert. LC 81-7004. (Library & Archival Security: Vol. 4, Nos. 1-2). 144p. 1982. text 39.95 (*0-917724-78-X*) Haworth Pr.

Protecting Your Collections: A Manual of Archival Security. Gregor Trinkaus-Randall. LC 95-16185. 84p. 1995. pap. 30.00 (*0-931828-83-X*) Soc Am Archivists.

Protecting Your Company Against Competitive Intelligence. John J. McGonagle & Carolyn M. Vella. LC 97-13402. 176p. 1998. 55.00 (*1-56720-117-2*, Quorum Bks) Greenwood.

***Protecting Your Company in the Information Age.** Ira Winkler. 2000. 29.00 (*0-7615-2836-9*) Prima Pub.

Protecting Your Family: Develop the Spiritual Strength Necessary to Withstand Today's Challenges. Charles Stanley. LC 99-173163. (In Touch Study Ser.). 120p. 1998. pap. 7.99 (*0-7852-7282-8*) Nelson.

Protecting Your Financial Future: The Inside Story on Wills, Living Trusts, Probate, Estate Taxes, & Asset Protection. 3rd rev. ed. Lee R. Phillips & Kristy S. Phillips. LC 98-67786. 364p. 1999. 24.95 (*0-9648965-2-4*) LegaLees.

***Protecting Your Health & the Environment Through Innovative Approaches to Compliance: Highlights from the Past 5 Years.** Government Printing Office Staff. 31p. 1999. pap. 2.75 (*0-16-049898-8*) USGPO.

Protecting Your Home from Radon: A Step-by-Step Manual for Radon Reduction. Ed. by D. L. Kladder et al. (Illus.). 163p. (Orig.). 1993. pap. text 45.00 (*0-9639434-0-5*) Colo Vintage.

Protecting Your Ideas: The Inventor's Guide to Patents. Joy L. Bryant. LC 98-86601. (Illus.). 222p. (C). 1998. pap. 25.00 (*0-12-138410-1*) Acad Pr.

Protecting Your Intellectual Property: How to Value, Maximize & Enhance Your Assets. Stacy A. Snowman. LC 97-144385. 472 p. 1997. 129.00 (*0-87224-309-5*) PLI.

Protecting Your Intellectual Property Assets. David H. Bernstein & Practising Law Institute Staff. LC 98-182398. (Patents, Copyrights, Trademarks, & Literary Property Course Handbook Ser.). 560 p. 1998. 129.00 (*0-87224-477-6*) PLI.

Protecting Your Legal Rights. Timothy Scott. (Illus.). 100p. (C). 1992. pap. text 15.00 (*1-877784-10-9*) T Scott Pub.

***Protecting Your Money: The Essential Guide to Personal Finance & Estate Planning for Gay & Lesbian Couples & Individuals.** Theodore E. Hughes & David Klein. LC 99-15318. xvii, 228p. 1999. pap. 14.95 (*1-55583-498-1*, Pub. by Alyson Pubns) Consort Bk Sales.

Protecting Your Organization's Tax-Exempt Status: A Guide for Nonprofit Managers. Mark Bookman. LC 91-36572. (Nonprofit Sector-Public Administration Ser.). 295p. 1992. text 51.95 (*1-55542-432-5*) Jossey-Bass.

Protecting Your Practice. Katherine Vessenes. LC 97-25544. (Professional Library). (Illus.). 512p. 1997. 50.00 (*1-57660-053-X*, Pub. by Bloomberg NJ) Norton.

Protecting Your Quilts: A Guide for Quilt Owners. rev. ed. American Quilter's Society Appraisal Certification. LC 96-214672. 32p. 1998. 6.95 (*0-89145-965-0*, No. 4779) Collector Bks.

Protecting Your Retirement Money: How to Avoid Swindles. Paul Koenigsmark. 144p. 1996. pap. text 14.95 (*0-9651603-0-0*) Covington Bks.

Protecting Your Savings & Investments in the Clinton Years. 1993. lib. bdg. 263.75 (*0-8490-8927-1*) Gordon Pr.

Protecting Your Web Sites with Firewalls. Marcus Gon Calves. LC 96-29766. 320p. (C). 1997. pap. 62.00 (*0-13-628207-5*) P-H.

***Protecting Yourself: HIV & AIDS in Health Care.** Charles A. Illian. (Illus.). 90p. 1999. pap. 29.95 (*1-888343-29-X*) Hartman Pub.

Protecting Yourself from Crime: What to Do If Attacked! B. A. Pogreba. (Illus.). 16p. (Orig.). 1997. pap. 3.95 (*1-891065-01-7*) Pogreba Pub.

Protecting Yourself Online: The Definitive Resource on Safety, Freedom & Privacy in Cyberspace. Bob Gelman et al. LC 97-32422. 224p. 1998. pap. 15.00 (*0-06-251512-8*) HarpC.

Protecting Youth at Work: Health, Safety, & Development of Working Children & Adolescents in the United States. Institute of Medicine Staff & National Research Council Staff. 200p. (C). 1998. text 34.95 (*0-309-06413-9*) Natl Acad Pr.

Protection. Chris Chandler & Phil Rockstroh. (Illus.). 96p. 1997. pap. 10.00 (*0-916620-30-1*) Portals Pr.

Protection: "The Sealed Book" 10th annot. ed. Joseph Meyer. Ed. & Illus. by Daniel R. Mead. LC 94-74310. 192p. 1999. pap. 12.95 (*0-934422-08-7*, BKS-100587) Mead Pub Corp.

Protection Against Anti-Union Discrimination. Bartolomei De la Cruz. vii, 123p. 1976. 18.00 (*92-2-101348-0*) Intl Labour Office.

Protection Against Atmospheric Corrosion: Theories & Methods. Karel Barton. Tr. by John R. Duncan. LC 75-26570. 204p. reprint ed. pap. 63.30 (*0-608-18827-1*, 203048200069) Bks Demand.

Protection Against Bombs & Incendiaries: For Business, Industrial & Educational Institutions. Earl A. Pike. (Illus.). 92p. 1973. 20.95 (*0-398-02517-7*) C C Thomas.

***Protection Against Genocide: Mission Impossible?** Neal Riemer. LC 99-46405. 208p. 2000. write for info. (*0-275-96515-5*, Praeger Pubs); pap. write for info. (*0-275-96516-3*, Praeger Pubs) Greenwood.

Protection Against Ionizing Radiation in the Teaching of Science. International Commission on Radiological Protectio. Ed. by F. D. Sowby. (International Commission of Radiological Protection Ser.: No. 36). 14p. 1983. pap. 11.75 (*0-08-029818-4*, Pergamon Pr) Elsevier.

Protection Against Ionizing Radiations: A Survey of Current World Legislation. (International Digest of Health Legislation Ser: Vol. 22, No. 4). 328p. 1972. pap. text 28.00 (*92-4-169224-3*, 1957201) World Health.

Protection Against Ischemia Reperfusion Damage of the Heart. Yasushi Abiko & M. Karmazyn. LC 98-6390. 1998. write for info. (*4-431-70226-1*) Spr-Verlag.

Protection Against Neutron Radiation. LC 73-138550. (Report Ser.: No. 38). 161p. 1971. pap. text 25.00 (*0-913392-20-0*) NCRP Pubns.

Protection Against Noise. Deepak Prasher. LC 99-169847. (Advances in Noise Research Ser.). 1998. 65.00 (*1-86156-076-1*) Whurr Pub.

Protection Against Radon-222 at Home & at Work. ICRP Staff. (International Commission on Radiological Protection Ser.: Vol. 65). 48p. 1994. pap. 54.50 (*0-08-042475-9*, Pergamon Pr) Elsevier.

Protection Against Trichothecene Mycotoxins. National Research Council (U. S.), Committee on Bi. LC 83-62917. (Illus.). 239p. reprint ed. pap. 74.10 (*0-8357-6813-9*, 203549600095) Bks Demand.

Protection & Conservation of Water Resources: A U. K. Perspective. Hadrian Cook. LC 97-41191. 354p. 1998. 165.00 (*0-471-97681-4*) Wiley.

Protection & Liberalization: A Review of Analytical Issues. W. Max Corden. (Occasional Papers: No. 54). 28p. 1987. pap. 7.50 (*0-939934-94-9*) Intl Monetary.

Protection & Management of Our Natural Resources, Wildlife & Habitat. 2nd ed. W. Jack Grosse. LC 96-44467. 416p. 1997. text 75.00 (*0-379-21380-X*) Oceana.

Protection & Politics: Conservative Economic Discourse, 1815-1852. Anna Gambles. LC 99-37129. (Studies in History). 288p. 1999. 75.00 (*0-86193-244-7*) Boydell & Brewer.

Protection & Politics in Bahrain, 1869-1915. Talal T. Farah. (Illus.). 256p. 1986. text 25.00 (*0-8156-6074-X*, Pub. by Am U Beirut) Syracuse U Pr.

Protection & Preservation of the Marine Environment: Protection & Preservation of the Marine Environment, Vol.3. (The Law of the Sea Ser.). 95p. pap. 12.00 (*92-1-133328-8*, E.90.V.3) UN.

***Protection & Security on the Information Highway.** Frederick B. Cohen. 301p. 1999. reprint ed. pap. text 20.00 (*0-7881-6550-X*) DIANE Pub.

Protection & Security on the Information Superhighway. Fredrick B. Cohen. LC 94-40488. 320p. 1995. pap. 24.95 (*0-471-11389-1*) Wiley.

Protection & Sustainable Use of Waters: Recommendations to ECE Governments. (ECE Water Ser.: No. 2). 48p. 24.00 (*92-1-116627-6*) UN.

***Protection As Prevention: Contraception for Sexually Active Teens.** Claire Brindis et al. 35p. 2000. pap. 5.00 (*1-58671-028-1*) Natl Cpgn Teen Preg.

Protection by Angels. E. Willis. 1982. 5.00 (*0-89858-041-2*) Fill the Gap.

***Protection Equipment & Counter Measure Devices: Congressional Hearing.** Ed. by Duncan Hunter. 211p. 2000. reprint ed. pap. text 35.00 (*0-7567-0114-7*) DIANE Pub.

Protection Financial International. White. LC 98-179594. 1998. pap. text 68.00 (*90-411-9647-1*) Kluwer Law Intl.

***Protection for Heart, Mind & Soul: Taking the Steps to Take Care of Yourself, Vol. 1.** Laura A. Hess. (Illus.). ii, 80p. 2000. pap. 24.95 (*1-930905-01-7*, 0001010) SPARCK.

Protection for Semiconductor Chip Masks in the United States: Analysis of the Semiconductor Chip Protection Art of 1984. Ed. by D. Ladd et al. (IIC Studies Ser.: Vol. 8). 99p. 1986. pap. 69.50 (*3-527-26003-X*, Wiley-VCH) Wiley.

Protection for the Machine Tool Industry: Domestic & International Negotiations for Voluntary Restraint Agreements. Richard Hooley. (Pew Case Studies in International Affairs). 50p. (C). 1992. pap. text 3.50 (*1-56927-120-8*) Geo U Inst Dplmcy.

Protection Formula: Thinking Like a Cop. Lyle Arnold. Ed. by Paul Lippman. LC 95-72860. (Illus.). 166p. (Orig.). 1996. pap. 12.95 (*0-9650241-7-2*) Philippi Pubng.

Protection from Deception. 1996. pap. 3.95 (*0-934920-68-0*, B-84); pap. write for info. (*0-934920-75-3*, B-84GE) Derek Prince.

Protection from Deception. (BUL & ENG.). 1997. pap. write for info. (*0-934920-91-5*, B-84BU) Derek Prince.

Protection from Potential Exposure: A Conceptual Framework. ICRP Staff. (International Commission on Radiological Protection Ser.: Vol. 64). 24p. 1993. 66.25 (*0-08-042205-5*, Pergamon Pr) Elsevier.

Protection from Power under English Law. Lord MacDermott. (Legal Reprint Ser.). viii, 196p. 1986. reprint ed. 35.00 (*0-421-37590-6*) W S Hein.

Protection from Power under English Law. Lord MacDermott. (Legal Reprint Ser.). viii, 196p. 1986. reprint ed. 25.00 (*0-8377-2430-9*, Rothman) W S Hein.

Protection in Nuclear Medicine & Ultrasound Diagnostic Procedures in Children. Intro. by Warren K. Sinclair. LC 83-61834. (Report Ser.: No. 73). 81p. 1983. pap. text 30.00 (*0-913392-63-4*) NCRP Pubns.

Protection Mutual Insurance Company: The First Hundred Years. Carole Presser. LC 87-61723. (Illus.). 72p. (Orig.). 1987. pap. write for info. (*0-916371-07-7*) Mobium Pr.

Protection of Aquatic Diversity Theme 3: Proceedings of the World Fisheries Congress, Athens, Greece. Ed. by David P. Philipp et al. 292p. 1996. text 79.00 (*1-886106-11-8*) Science Pubs.

Protection of Assets Manual. T. J. Walsh & Richard J. Healy. 1995. ring bd. 397.00 (*0-930868-04-8*) Silver Lake.

Protection of Biotechnological Matter: European & German Law. G. Bezold. LC 97-213163. 468p. 1997. pap. 125.00 (*3-527-28781-7*, Wiley-VCH) Wiley.

Protection of Brain from Ischemia, Vol. 3. Philip R. Weinstein & Alan I. Faden. 307p. 1990. 87.00 (*0-683-08908-0*) Lppncott W & W.

Protection of Chemical Inventions. Fritjoff Hirsch & Bernd Hansen. 530p. 1998. 150.00 (*3-527-28808-2*, Wiley-VCH) Wiley.

Protection of Children: State Intervention & Family Life. Robert Dingwall et al. 320p. 1995. 72.95 (*1-85628-586-3*, Pub. by Avebry) Ashgate Pub Co.

Protection of Coastal Areas of the Adriatic Sea: (Proceedings, Tirana, Albania, 27-29 October, 1994) (Environmental Encounters Ser.: No. 23). 1995. 12.00 (*92-871-2851-0*, Pub. by Council of Europe) Manhattan Pub Co.

***Protection of Coastal Fisheries under International Law.** Stefan A. Riesenfeld & Carnegie Endowment for International Peace Staff. LC 99-48873. (Carnegie Endowment for International Peace Monograph Ser.: No. 5). 308p. 2000. reprint ed. 47.50 (*1-57588-562-X*, 323940) W S Hein.

Protection of Computer Systems & Software. Frank L. Huband et al. LC 86-10271. 1986. 55.00 (*0-15-004393-7*) Harcourt.

Protection of Concrete: Proceedings of the International Conference, University of Dundee, September 1990. Ed. by R. Dhir & J. Green. (Illus.). 1136p. (C). 1990. 250.00 (*0-419-15490-6*, E & FN Spon) Routledge.

Protection of Confidential Information in Tax Matters. (Cahiers de Droit Fiscal International Ser.: Vol. LXXVIb). 1991. pap. 106.00 (*90-6544-558-7*) Kluwer Law Intl.

Protection of Corporate Names: A Country by Country Survey. annuals United States Trademark Association Staff. LC 82-4235. 1996. ring bd. 145.00 (*0-87632-404-9*) Intl Trademark.

Protection of Cultural Property in the Event of Armed Conflict: Commentary on the Convention for the Protection of Cultural Property in the Event of Armed Conflict & Its Protocol, Signed on 14 May, 1954 in the Hague, & on Other Instruments of International Law Concerning Such Protection. Jiri Toman. LC 95-46953. (UNESCO Ser.). (Illus.). 542p. 1996. pap. 54.95 (*1-85521-800-3*, Pub. by Dartmth Pub); text 82.95 (*1-85521-793-7*, Pub. by Dartmth Pub) Ashgate Pub Co.

Protection of Earth Slopes of Hydraulic Structures. V. S. Shaitan et al. (Geotechnika Ser.: Vol. 15). (Illus.). 500p. (C). 1997. text 123.00 (*90-5410-176-8*, Pub. by A A Balkema) Ashgate Pub Co.

Protection of Electricity Distribution Networks. J. Gers & E. J. Holmes. (Power Ser.: No. 28). 356p. 1998. 90.00 (*0-85296-923-6*, PO028) INSPEC Inc.

Protection of Electronic Circuits from over Voltages. Ronald B. Standler. LC 88-25879. 464p. 1989. 145.00 (*0-471-61121-2*) Wiley.

Protection of Ethnic Minorities: Comparative Perspectives. Ed. by Robert G. Wirsing. LC 80-25618. (Policy Studies on International Politics). 350p. 1981. 96.00 (*0-08-025556-6*, Pergamon Pr) Elsevier.

Protection of Foreign Interests, a Study in Diplomatic & Consular Practice. William M. Franklin. LC 69-13898. 328p. 1970. reprint ed. lib. bdg. 75.00 (*0-8371-0426-2*, FRFI, Greenwood Pr) Greenwood.

Protection of Foreign Investment: Six Procedural Studies. Richard B. Lillich. LC 65-15855. x, 222p. 1990. reprint ed. 42.00 (*0-89941-742-6*, 306600) W S Hein.

Protection of Foreign Investment, Property & Nationalisation in India. Hans Raj. (C). 1989. 250.00 (*0-7855-3709-0*) St Mut.

Protection of Foreign Investments: A Private Law Study of Safeguarding Devices in International Crisis Situations. Walter J. Kolvenbach. 462p. 1989. 110.00 (*90-6544-382-7*) Kluwer Law Intl.

Protection of Fundamental Rights by the Constitutional Court: Proceedings (Brioni, Croatia, 23-25 September, 1995) (Science & Technique of Democracy Ser.: No. 15). 1995. 25.00 (*92-871-2960-6*, Pub. by Council of Europe) Manhattan Pub Co.

Protection of Fundamental Social Rights in the European Union. LC 96-50081. 1996. lib. bdg. 86.00 (*90-411-0313-9*) Kluwer Academic.

Protection of Geographic Denominations of Goods & Services. Ed. by H. Cohen Jehoram. (Monographs in Industrial Property & Copyright Law: Vol. III). 216p. 1980. lib. bdg. 83.50 (*90-286-0090-6*) Kluwer Academic.

Protection of Global Biodiversity: Converging Strategies. Lakshman D. Guruswamy & Jeffrey A. McNeely. LC 97-46953. 1998. write for info. (*0-8223-2150-5*); pap. write for info. (*0-8223-2188-2*) Duke.

Protection of Historic Buildings & Their Artistic Contents Against Crime & Wilful Damage: Proceedings (Antwerp, Belgium, 3-6 November, 1992) (Cultural Heritage Ser.: No. 33). 1995. 18.00 (*92-871-2801-4*, Pub. by Council of Europe) Manhattan Pub Co.

Protection of Human Research Subjects: A Practical Guide to Federal Laws & Regulations. Dennis M. Maloney. LC 84-4873. (Illus.). 442p. 1984. 107.00 (*0-306-41522-4*, Kluwer Plenum) Kluwer Academic.

P

An Asterisk (*) at the beginning of an entry indicates that the title is appearing for the first time.

Protection of Human Rights in African Criminal Proceedings. Ed. by M. Cherif Bassiouni & Motala Ziyad. LC 94-16406. 1995. lib. bdg. 151.00 (*0-7923-2888-4*) Kluwer Academic.

Protection of Human Rights in Criminal Justice Administration: A Study of the Rights of Accused. Manjula Batra. (C). 1989. 250.00 (*0-7855-4774-6*) St Mut.

Protection of Human Rights in Criminal Justice Administration: A Study of the Rights of the Accused - Indian & Soviet Legal Systems. Manjula Batra. (C). 1990. 110.00 (*0-89771-186-6*) St Mut.

Protection of Human Rights in the Administration of Criminal Justice: A Compendium of United Nations Norms & Standards. M. Cherif Bassiouni. 529p. (C). 1994. lib. bdg. 105.00 (*0-941320-87-1*) Transnatl Pubs.

Protection of Human Rights in the Light of Scientific & Technological Progress in Biology & Medicine: 8th CIOMS Round Table Conference. 1974. pap. text 27.90 (*92-4-056007-6*, 0830008) World Health.

Protection of Industrial Power Systems. 2nd ed. T. Davies. LC 96-2720. (Illus.). 272p. 1998. pap. text 49.95 (*0-7506-2662-3*) Buttrwrth-Heinemann.

Protection of Know-How in Thirteen Countries: Reports to the VIIIth International Congress of Comparative Law, Pescara, 1970. Ed. by Carl Jehoram. 174p. 1972. 26.00 (*90-268-0586-1*) Kluwer Academic.

Protection of Laboratory Workers from Infectious Disease Transmitted by Blood, Body Fluids, & Tissue: Tentative Guideline (1991) 3rd ed. Contrib. by Stanley Bauer. 1991. 95.00 (*0-614-20212-4*, M29-T2) NCCLS.

Protection of Laboratory Workers from Instrument Biohazards. (Proposed Guideline Ser.). 1991. 75.00 (*1-56238-122-9*, I17-P) NCCLS.

Protection of Laboratory Workers from Instrument Biohazards & Infectious Disease Transmitted by Blood, Body Fluids, & Tissue: Approved Guideline (1997) 1997. 120.00 (*1-56238-339-6*, M29-A) NCCLS.

Protection of Love. Barbara Cartland. (Camfield Ser.: No. 142). 176p. 1995. pap. text 3.99 (*0-515-11640-8*, Jove) Berkley Pub.

Protection of Materials & Structures from the Low Earth Orbit Space Environment. Joseph I. Kleiman & Roderick C. Tennyson. LC 98-32286. 20p. 1999. write for info. (*0-7923-5540-7*) Kluwer Academic.

Protection of Medical Data: Recommendation No. R (97) 5 Council of Europe Staff & Project Group on Data Protection Staff. LC 98-136807. (Legal Issues Ser.). 65p. 1997. write for info. (*92-871-3334-4*) Council of Europe.

Protection of Metals from Corrosion in Storage & Transit. Donovan. 1986. text 71.95 (*0-470-20332-3*) P-H.

Protection of Minorities. (Science & Technique of Democracy Ser.: No. 9). 1994. 25.00 (*92-871-2647-X*, Pub. by Council of Europe) Manhattan Pub Co.

Protection of Minorities & Human Rights. Ed. by Yoram Dinstein. 544p. (C). 1992. lib. bdg. 185.50 (*0-7923-1437-9*) Kluwer Academic.

***Protection of Minority Rights Through Bilateral Treaties: The Case of Central & Eastern Europe.** A. Bloed. LC 99-40298. 1999. 130.00 (*90-411-1270-7*) Kluwer Law Intl.

Protection of Minority Shareholders. I. J. Dawson & I. S. Stephenson. 150p. 1993. 120.00 (*0-85459-816-2*, Pub. by Tolley Pubng) St Mut.

Protection of Minority Shareholders, Vol. AIJA. Ed. by Matthias W. Stecher. LC 97-14984. 1997. 215.00 (*90-411-0661-8*) Kluwer Law Intl.

Protection of Officials of Foreign States According to International Law. Franciszek Przetacznik. 1983. lib. bdg. 160.50 (*90-247-2721-9*) Kluwer Academic.

Protection of Participants in Sensitive Social Research: A Special Issue of Ethics & Behavior. Ed. by Gerald P. Koocher. 64p. pap. 20.00 (*0-8058-9819-0*) L Erlbaum Assocs.

Protection of Personal & Commercial Reputation: Study of the Law in Western Europe & the United States. Kunstadt. (IIC Studies Ser.). 98p. 1980. pap. 71.95 (*3-527-25697-0*) Wiley.

P

Protection of Personal Data in the Area of Telecommunication Services, with Particular Reference to Telephone Services (Recommendation & Explanatory Memorandum), No. R(95)4. LC 96-194056. 1996. 12.00 (*92-871-2895-2*, Pub. by Council of Europe) Manhattan Pub Co.

Protection of Personal Data Used for Employment Purposes (Recommendation), No. R(89)2. Council of Europe Staff. 1990. 18.00 (*92-871-1714-4*, Pub. by Council of Europe) Manhattan Pub Co.

Protection of Personal Data Used for Payment & Other Related Operations (Recommendation), No. R(90)19. Council of Europe Staff. 1993. 12.00 (*92-871-1922-8*, Pub. by Council of Europe) Manhattan Pub Co.

Protection of Persons Working at Home. Council of Europe Staff. 1989. 21.00 (*92-871-1718-7*, Pub. by Council of Europe) Manhattan Pub Co.

Protection of Public Health. 1993. 12.00 (*92-871-2216-4*, Pub. by Council of Europe) Manhattan Pub Co.

Protection of Public Water Supplies from Ground-Water Contamination. Ed. by Wayne A. Pettyjohn. LC 86-31173. (Pollution Technology Review Ser.: No. 141). (Illus.). 177p. 1987. 36.00 (*0-8155-1119-1*) Noyes.

Protection of Rights of Persons in the Church: Revised Report of the Canon Law Society of America on the Subject of Due Process. CLSA Committee on Procedures Staff. 55p. 1991. pap. 6.50 (*0-943616-56-5*) Canon Law Soc.

Protection of Technical Innovations & Design in Germany: Obtainment, Exploitation, Enforcement. Wilfried Stockmair. LC 94-196512. 297p. 1994. pap. 135.00 (*3-527-28656-X*, Wiley-VCH) Wiley.

Protection of the Architectural Heritage Against Earthquakes. Ed. by V. Petrini & M. Save. (CISM International Center for Mechanical Sciences Ser.: Vol. 359). (Illus.). ix, 325p. 1996. pap. 87.00 (*3-211-82805-2*) Spr-Verlag.

Protection of the Architectural Heritage Against Natural Disasters. Council of Europe Staff. (Cultural Heritage Ser.: No. 21). 1992. 12.00 (*92-871-2005-6*, Pub. by Council of Europe) Manhattan Pub Co.

Protection of the Heritage of Indigenous People Erica-Irene A. Daes & United Nations High Commissioner for Human Rights Staff. LC 98-160628. (Human Rights Study Ser.). vi, 30p. 1997. pap. write for info. (*92-1-154126-3*) UN.

Protection of the Insured. Ray W. Hodgin. 198p. 1989. 80.00 (*1-85044-205-3*) LLP.

Protection of the Library & Archive: An International Bibliography. Ed. by Martin H. Sable. LC 83-17169. (Library & Archival Security: Vol. 5, Nos 2-3). 183p. 1983. text 39.95 (*0-86656-246-X*) Haworth Pr.

Protection of the Patient in Diagnostic Radiology. International Commission on Radiological Protectio. Ed. by International Commission on Radiology Protection et al. (International Commission of Radiological Protection Ser.: No. 34). 88p. 1983. pap. 28.50 (*0-08-029797-8*, Pergamon Pr) Elsevier.

Protection of the Patient in Nuclear Medicine. International Commission on Radiological Protectio. (International Commission on Radiological Protection Ser.: No. 52). (Illus.). 46p. 1988. pap. 32.75 (*0-08-033188-2*, Pergamon Pr) Elsevier.

Protection of the Patient in Radiation Therapy. Ed. by F. D. Sowby. (International Commission of Radiological Protection Ser.: No. 44). (Illus.). 58p. pap. 32.75 (*0-08-032336-7*, Pergamon Pr) Elsevier.

Protection of the Patient in Radionuclide Investigations. International Commission on Radiological Protectio. (International Commission of Radiological Protection Ser.: No. 17). 1971. pap. 11.00 (*0-08-016773-X*, Pergamon Pr) Elsevier.

Protection of the Public in the Event of Radiation Accidents: Proceedings. United Nations Food & Agriculture Organization Staff et al. (ENG, FRE & RUS., Illus.). 370p. 1965. pap. text 34.00 (*92-4-156025-8*, 1150128) World Health.

Protection of the Thyroid Gland in the Event of Releases of Radioiodine. LC 77-82607. (Report Ser.: No. 55). 66p. 1977. pap. text 20.00 (*0-913392-37-5*) NCRP Pubns.

Protection of the Underwater Cultural Heritage: An Emerging Objective of the Contemporary Law of the Sea. Anastasia Strati. LC 94-22723. (Publications on Ocean Development: Vol. 23). 1995. lib. bdg. 184.50 (*0-7923-3052-8*) Kluwer Academic.

Protection of the Weak in the Talmud. Mordecai Katz. LC 26-5707. (Columbia University. Oriental Studies: No. 24). reprint ed. 27.50 (*0-404-50514-7*) AMS Pr.

Protection of Transboundary Waters: Guidance for Policy & Decision-Making. United Nations. Economic Commission for Europe. LC 97-168288. (ECE Water Ser.: No. 3). 44p. pap. 18.00 (*92-1-116658-6*) UN.

Protection of U. S. Forces Deployed Abroad: The Khobar Towers Terrorist Attack Report: Report to the President & Congress. (Illus.). 137p. (Orig.). (C). 1997. pap. text 40.00 (*0-7881-3910-X*) DIANE Pub.

Protection of Water Resources & Aquatic Ecosystems. (ECE Water Ser.: No. 1). 50p. 1993. 12.00 (*92-1-116571-7*) UN.

***Protection of Well-known Marks in Asia.** Christopher Heath. LC 99-87112. 256p. 2000. 95.00 (*90-411-9705-2*) Kluwer Law Intl.

Protection of Women under the Law. Anwarul Yaqin & B. Anwar. 200p. 1982. 18.95 (*0-318-37069-7*) Asia Bk Corp.

Protection of Workers Against Radio-Frequency & Microwave Radiation: A Technical Review. (Occupational Safety & Health Ser.: No. 57). ix, 72p. (Orig.). 1986. pap. 15.75 (*92-2-105604-X*) Intl Labour Office.

Protection of Workers' Claims in the Event of the Insolvency of Their Employers. Ed. by Edward Yemin & A. Bronstein. (Labour-Management Relations Ser.: No. 76). v, 149p. (Orig.). 1991. pap. 18.00 (*92-2-106477-8*) Intl Labour Office.

Protection of Workers' Personal Data: An ILO Code of Practice. International Labour Office Staff. LC 98-122238. 47p. (Orig.). 1999. pap. 20.00 (*92-2-110329-3*, Pub. by Statnry Office) Balogh.

Protection of Youth Against Physical & Moral Danger. Council of Europe Staff. 1990. 21.00 (*92-871-1835-3*, Pub. by Council of Europe) Manhattan Pub Co.

Protection Officer Guidebook. Christopher A. Hertig. 57p. 1992. spiral bd. 15.00 (*1-928987-55-9*) Intl Fdtn Protect.

***Protection Officer Survival.** 2nd ed. Christopher A. Hertig et al. 63p. 1999. spiral bd. 21.00 (*1-928987-52-4*) Intl Fdtn Protect.

Protection Officer's Training Manual. 6th ed. International Foundation for Protection Officers S. LC 97-18306. 288p. 1997. pap. 39.95 (*0-7506-9934-5*) Buttrwrth-Heinemann.

Protection Officer's Training Manual. 6th ed. International Foundation for Protection Officers S. LC 97-18306. 104p. 1998. pap., teacher ed. 18.95 (*0-7506-7015-0*, HV8291) Buttrwrth-Heinemann.

Protection or Free Trade see Proteccion o Librecambio

Protection or Free Trade. Henry George. LC 80-14436. 335p. 1992. 18.00 (*0-911312-83-8*); pap. 12.00 (*0-911312-84-6*) Schalkenbach.

Protection or Free Trade. Henry George. (Notable American Authors Ser.). 1992. reprint ed. lib. bdg. 75.00 (*0-7812-2917-0*) Rprt Serv.

Protection or Free Trade: An Examination of the Tariff Question with Especial Regard to the Interest's of Labor. Henry George. LC 80-14436. 352p. 1980. 10.00 (*0-914016-70-9*) Phoenix Pub.

Protection or Liberalization? A Policy Analysis of the Korean Beef Sector. Elke M. Forster. LC 96-2632. (Development Economics & Policy Ser.: Bd. 5). (Illus.). 209p. 1996. pap. 44.95 (*0-8204-2956-2*, HD9433) P Lang Pubng.

Protection or Punishment: The Detention of Asylum Seekers in Australia. Ed. by Mary Crock. 200p. 1993. pap. 24.00 (*1-86287-125-6*, Pub. by Federation Pr) Gaunt.

Protection ou Libre-Echange. (FRE.). 1991. 3.00 (*0-911312-14-5*) Schalkenbach.

Protection, Power & Display: Shields of Island Southeast Asia & Melanesia. Boston College Museum of Art Staff. Ed. & Intro. by Andrew Tavarelli. LC 95-79803. (Illus.). 108p. (Orig.). (C). 1995. pap. text 12.95 (*0-9640153-3-1*) McMullen Mus Art.

Protection Privee. Naomi Horton. (Rouge Passion Ser.: Bk. 490). 1999. mass mkt. 3.50 (*0-373-37490-9*, 1-37490-9) Harlequin Bks.

***Protection Promises.** Kenneth Copeland. 2000. pap. 9.99 (*1-57794-201-9*) Harrison Hse.

Protection Racket State: Elite Politics, Military Extortion, & Civil War in El Salvador. William Stanley. LC 95-20998. 384p. 1996. 69.95 (*1-56639-391-4*); pap. 24.95 (*1-56639-392-2*) Temple U Pr.

***Protection, Security & Safeguards: Practical Approaches & Perspectives.** Dale L. June. LC 00-39743. 2000. pap. write for info. (*0-8493-0093-2*) Auerbach.

Protection Spells & Charms. Jade. 43p. 1996. pap. 5.95 (*0-942272-48-X*) Original Pubns.

Protection Techniques in Electrical Energy Systems. Helmut Ungrad et al. Tr. by Peter G. Harrison. LC 95-32278. (Illus.). 399p. 1995. text 160.00 (*0-8247-9660-8*) Dekker.

Protection to Women in Matrimonial Home. Vijay Sharma. LC 94-900649. (C). 1994. 34.00 (*81-7100-589-6*, Pub. by Deep & Deep Pubns) S Asia.

Protectionism. Jagdish N. Bhagwati. (Illus.). 168p. 1988. 30.00 (*0-262-02282-6*) MIT Pr.

Protectionism. Jagdish N. Bhagwati. (Ohlin Lectures). 168p. 1989. reprint ed. pap. text 15.00 (*0-262-52150-4*) MIT Pr.

Protectionism: An Annotated Bibliography with Analytical Introductions. James M. Lutz. LC 88-15273. (Resources on Contemporary Issues Ser.: No. 2). 215p. 1988. pap. 40.00 (*0-87650-249-4*) Pierian.

Protectionism: Can American Business Overcome It? Ed. by Douglas Lamont. (ITT Key Issues Lecture). 127p. (Orig.). (C). 1986. pap. write for info. (*0-937137-01-4*) Bookscraft.

Protectionism: Regional Negotiation & Defence Strategies, No. 59. 261p. 1989. pap. 6.00 (*92-1-121142-5*, E.88.II.G.9) UN.

Protectionism & Economic Revival: The British Inter-War Economy. Michael Kitson & Solomos Solomou. (Illus.). 135p. (C). 1990. text 49.95 (*0-521-38267-X*) Cambridge U Pr.

Protectionism & Efficiency in Manufacturing: A Case Study of Pakistan. Syed Nawab Haider Naqvi & A. R. Kemal. 131p. 1991. pap. 19.95 (*1-55815-139-7*) ICS Pr.

Protectionism & the European Community. 2nd rev. ed. Ed. by Edmond L. Volker. 252p. 1988. pap. 67.00 (*90-6544-313-4*) Kluwer Law Intl.

Protectionism & the European Community, 1983. Ed. by Edmond L. Volker. 170p. 1983. pap. 28.00 (*90-6544-127-1*) Kluwer Academic.

Protectionism & the Future of International Shipping: The Nature, Development & Role of Flag Discriminations & Preferences, Cargo Reservations & Sabotage Restrictions, State Intervention & Maritime Subsidies. Ademuni-Odeke. LC 83-25055. 1984. lib. bdg. 215.50 (*90-247-2918-1*) Kluwer Academic.

Protectionism & World Welfare. Ed. by Dominick Salvatore. LC 92-34450. (Illus.). 461p. (C). 1993. text 64.95 (*0-521-41455-5*); pap. text 23.95 (*0-521-42489-5*) Cambridge U Pr.

Protectionism, Exchange Rates & the Macroeconomy. S. Sen. (Modern Revivals in Economics Ser.). 239p. 1992. 61.95 (*0-7512-0098-0*, Pub. by Gregg Pub) Ashgate Pub Co.

Protectionism in the World Economy. Ed. by Forrest H. Capie. (International Library of Macroeconomic & Financial History: Vol. 7). 584p. 1992. 240.00 (*1-85278-549-7*) E Elgar.

Protectionist Case in the 1840's. Derek Walker-Smith. LC 72-111294. (Reprints of Economic Classics Ser.). viii, 91p. 1970. reprint ed. 25.00 (*0-678-00614-8*) Kelley.

Protectionist Threat to Corporate America: The U. S. Trade Deficit & Management Responses. Louis E. Nevaer & Steven A. Deck. LC 88-39910. 239p. 1989. 62.95 (*0-89930-363-3*, NEW, Quorum Bks) Greenwood.

Protective & Decorative Coatings for Metals. H. Silman et al. 620p. 1991. 250.00 (*0-904477-03-7*) St Mut.

Protective & Preferential Import Duties: London School of Economics. A. C. Pigou. (LSE Scarce Tracts in Economics Ser.). 132p. (C). 1997. 60.00 (*0-415-14391-8*) Routledge.

Protective Clothing. Richard K. Miller & Marcia E. Rupnow. LC 90-83903. (Survey on Technology & Markets Ser.: No. 199). 50p. 1991. pap. text 200.00 (*1-55865-223-X*) Future Tech Surveys.

Protective Clothing. Shirley Inst. Staff. (C). 1983. 125.00 (*0-7855-4573-5*, Pub. by British Textile Tech) St Mut.

Protective Clothing & Equipment. 1995. lib. bdg. 255.75 (*0-8490-6641-7*) Gordon Pr.

Protective Clothing Systems & Materials. Ed. by Mastura Raheel. (Occupational Safety & Health Ser.: Vol. 25). (Illus.). 272p. 1994. text 155.00 (*0-8247-9118-5*) Dekker.

Protective Coatings: Processing & Characterization: Proceedings of 1989 TMS Northeast Regional Meeting Sponsored by the Minerals, Metals & Materials Society, 5th, Held in Hoboken, NJ, May 3-5, 1989. TMS Northeast Regional Meeting, Staff. Ed. by R. M. Yazici. LC 90-61857. (Illus.). 221p. 1990. reprint ed. pap. 68.60 (*0-608-00876-1*, 206167000010) Bks Demand.

Protective Coatings & Thin Films: Synthesis, Characterization & Applications. Ed. by Yves Pauleau. LC 96-52351. (NATO Advanced Science Institutes: Partnership Sub-Series: 3 High Technology). 680p. (C). 1997. text 364.50 (*0-7923-4380-8*) Kluwer Academic.

Protective Coatings for Bridge Steel. (National Cooperative Highway Research Program Report Ser.: No. 136). 107p. 1987. 11.00 (*0-309-04421-9*) Transport Res Bd.

Protective Coatings for Industrial Structures: Proceedings of the 1989 SSPC National Conference Seminars. Ed. by Janet Rex & Bernard R. Appleman. (Illus.). 140p. 1989. pap. text 45.00 (*0-938477-44-7*, SSPC 89-14) SSPC.

Protective Coatings for Metals. 3rd ed. Robert M. Burns & William W. Bradley. LC 67-20826. (ACS Monograph: No. 163). 1975. 59.95 (*0-8412-0285-0*); fiche. write for info. (*0-318-50482-0*) Am Chemical.

Protective Coatings for Pulp & Paper Mills. Ed. by Janet Rex & Bernard R. Appleman. 83p. 1988. pap. text 30.00 (*0-938477-37-4*) SSPC.

Protective Coatings for Pulp & Paper Mills: Proceedings of the Second Annual SSPC Pulp & Paper Industry Seminar (1989) Ed. by Janet Rex & Bernard R. Appleman. 69p. 1990. pap. text 30.00 (*0-938477-49-8*, SSPC 89-15) SSPC.

Protective Coatings for Weathering Steel Tower Joints. Bernard R. Appleman et al. (Illus.). 61p. 1987. pap. text 40.00 (*0-938477-32-3*, 87-03) SSPC.

Protective Coatings on Metals, Vol. 2. Grigorii V. Samonov. LC 69-12517. 220p. reprint ed. pap. 68.20 (*0-608-16669-3*, 205611300050) Bks Demand.

Protective Coatings on Metals, Vol. 10. Ed. by G. V. Samsonov. Tr. by A. Patani from RUS. (Illus.). 212p. (C). 1987. 42.50 (*81-7087-010-0*, Pub. by Oxford IBH) S Asia.

Protective Coatings on Metals, Vol. 11. Ed. by G. V. Samsonov. Tr. by K. M. Pai from RUS. (Illus.). 172p. (C). 1987. 28.00 (*81-7087-015-1*, Pub. by Oxford IBH) S Asia.

Protective Coatings on Metals, Vol. 12. V. I. Arakhov. 1986. 42.50 (*0-8364-2275-9*, Pub. by Oxford IBH) S Asia.

Protective Effect of BCG in Experimental Tuberculosis. Donald W. Smith. (Advances in Tuberculosis Research Ser.: Vol. 22). (Illus.). viii, 100p. 1985. 77.50 (*3-8055-4089-2*) S Karger.

Protective Gloves for Occupational Use. Mellstrom. 336p. 1994. boxed set 141.95 (*0-8493-7359-X*, RL244) CRC Pr.

Protective Groups in Organic Synthesis. 3rd ed. Ed. by Theodora Greene & Peter G. Wuts. LC 98-38182. 816p. 1999. 89.95 (*0-471-16019-9*) Wiley.

Protective Immediacy. Rod Smith. 93p. 1999. pap. 9.95 (*0-937804-78-9*, Pub. by Segue NYC) SPD-Small Pr Dist.

Protective Immediacy. limited ed. Rod Smith. 56p. (C). 1997. 26.00 (*0-937013-74-9*) Potes Poets.

Protective Interlocks. (Principles of Steam Generation Ser.: Module 17). (Illus.). 60p. 1982. spiral bd. 20.00 (*0-87683-267-2*) GP Courseware.

Protective Ixide Scales. Michael Schutze. Tr. by R. B. Waterhouse. LC 96-31942. 184p. 1997. 175.00 (*0-471-95904-9*) Wiley.

Protective Labor Legislation. Elizabeth Baker. 467p. 1993. reprint ed. lib. bdg. 99.00 (*0-7812-5243-1*) Rprt Serv.

Protective Labor Legislation, with Special Reference to Women in the State of New York. Elizabeth Baker. LC 76-82239. (Columbia University. Studies in the Social Sciences: No. 259). reprint ed. 22.50 (*0-404-51259-3*) AMS Pr.

Protective Medical Apparel & Accessories Markets. (Market Reports: No. 416). (Illus.). 163p. 1995. wbk. ed. 795.00 (*0-614-09920-X*) Theta Corp.

Protective Principle of International Criminal Jurisdiction. Iain Cameron. 412p. 1993. 87.95 (*1-85521-366-4*, Pub. by Dartmth Pub) Ashgate Pub Co.

Protective Relaying: Principles & Applications. 2nd ed. J. Lewis Blackburn. LC 97-33110. (Power Engineering Ser.: Vol. 2). (Illus.). 560p. 1997. text 99.75 (*0-8247-9918-6*) Dekker.

Protective Relaying for Power Systems, Vol. I. Ed. by S. H. Horowitz. LC 80-21776. 592p. 1981. pap. 79.95 (*0-87942-140-1*, PP01370) Inst Electrical.

Protective Relaying for Power Systems, 1981 & 1992, Vols. I & II. Ed. by Stanley H. Horowitz. (Illus.). 1184p. 1993. pap. 149.95 (*0-7803-0426-8*, PP4267) Inst Electrical.

Protective Relaying Systems, 1995. 128p. 220.00 (*1-55937-508-6*, SH94276) IEEE Standards.

Protective Relaying Theory & Applications. Ed. by Walter Elmore. LC 93-50097. (Illus.). 384p. 1994. text 99.75 (*0-8247-9152-5*) Dekker.

Protective Relays: Their Theory & Practice, 2 vols. Incl. Vol. 1, 2nd ed. A. R. Warrington. 484p. 1968. text 44.95 (*0-412-09060-0*, NO. 6310); Vol. 2, 3rd ed. by A. R. Warrington. 434p. 1978. 44.95 (*0-412-15380-7*, NO. 6311); write for info. (*0-318-54321-4*) Routledge.

Protective Relays: Their Theory & Practice, Vol. 1. 2nd ed. A. R. Warrington. LC 70-385616. 32.50 (*0-471-92118-1*) Halsted Pr.

An Asterisk (*) at the beginning of an entry indicates that the title is appearing for the first time.

Protective Relays: Their Theory & Practice, Vol. 2. 3rd ed. A. R. Warrington. 1978. 35.00 (0-470-26343-1) Halsted Pr.
Protective-Safety Clothing Materials-Markets, No. GB-142. Business Communications Co., Inc. Staff. 149p. 1991. 2250.00 (0-89336-812-1) BCC.
Protective Security Law. 2nd ed. Fred E. Inbau et al. LC 95-30395. 330p. 1995. 44.95 (0-7506-9279-0) Buttrwrth-Heinemann.
Protective Service Occupations & Compliance Inspectors. 19p. 1996. pap. 1.50 (0-16-048478-2) USGPO.
***Protective Service Occupations & Compliance Inspectors.** Government Printing Office Staff. 19p. 1998. pap. 2.00 (0-16-049364-1) USGPO.
Protective Services: A Manual for Police Escorts. 1991. lib. bdg. 77.96 (0-8490-4762-5) Gordon Pr.
Protective Shell in Children & Adults. Frances Tustin. 256p. 1990. pap. text 32.00 (0-946439-81-8, Pub. by H Karnac Bks Ltd) Other Pr LLC.
Protector. Larry Niven. 224p. (Orig.). 1987. mass mkt. 5.99 (0-345-35312-9, Del Rey) Ballantine Pub Grp.
Protector of the Faith: Cardinal Johannes de Turrecremata & the Defense of the Institutional Church. Thomas M. Izbicki. LC 81-1400. 220p. reprint ed. pap. 68.20 (0-608-18725-9, 202950400061) Bks Demand.
Protector of the Small, Vol. 1. Tamora Pierce. LC 98-30903. (J). 1999. lib. bdg. 17.99 (0-679-98914-5) Random.
Protector of the Small, Vol. 3. Tamora Pierce. (J). 2001. lib. bdg. 17.99 (0-679-98916-1) Random.
Protectorate & the Northumberland Conspiracy: Political Intrigue in the Reign of Edward VI. Daniel P. Brown. LC 80-65156. (European History Ser.: No. I-1001). (Illus.). 74p. (Orig.). 1982. reprint ed. pap. 4.15 (0-930860-02-0) Golden West Hist.
Protectors. David E. Brown. LC 98-93975. (Legend of the Golden Feather Ser.: Vol. 2). 270p. 1998. pap. 14.95 (1-878406-20-5) Parker Dstb.
Protectors. William Haggard. 20.95 (0-88411-666-2) Amereon Ltd.
Protectors: Harry J. Anslinger & the Federal Bureau of Narcotics, 1930-1962. John C. McWilliams. LC 88-40328. 256p. 1990. 40.00 (0-87413-352-1) U Delaware Pr.
Protectors & Praetorians? The Last Mamluk Sultans & Egypt's Waning as a Great Power. Carl F. Petry. LC 94-2925. (SUNY Series in Medieval Middle East History). 280p. (C). 1994. text 59.50 (0-7914-2139-2); pap. text 19.95 (0-7914-2140-6) State U NY Pr.
Protectors for Coaxial Communications Circuits: UL 497-C. 1998. write for info. (0-7629-0262-0, UL 497C) Underwrtrs Labs.
Protectors for Data Communication & Fire Alarm Circuits, UL 497B. 3rd ed. (C). 1999. pap. text 95.00 (1-55989-512-8) Underwrtrs Labs.
Protectors for Paired Conductor Communications Circuits, UL 497. 6th ed. (C). 1995. pap. text 95.00 (1-55989-825-9) Underwrtrs Labs.
Protector's Handbook: Reducing the Risk of Child Sexual Abuse & Helping Children Recover. Gerrilyn Smith. 190p. 1997. pap. 13.95 (0-7043-4417-3, Pub. by Womens Press) Trafalgar.
Protectors of Privilege: Red Squads & Police Repression in Urban America. Frank Donner. LC 89-20290. 496p. 1990. 45.00 (0-520-05951-4, Pub. by U CA Pr) Cal Prin Full Svc.
Protectors of Privilege: Red Squads & Police Repression in Urban America. Frank Donner. 1992. pap. 17.95 (0-520-08035-1, Pub. by U CA Pr) Cal Prin Full Svc.
Protectors of the Land: An Environmental Journey to Understanding the Conservation Ethic. Richard L. Burrill. Ed. by Regina Macias. (Illus.). 354p. (J). (gr. 3-12). 1994. pap. text 22.95 (1-878464-02-7) Anthro Co.
Protectors of the Land & Water: Environmentalism in Wisconsin, 1961-1968. Thomas R. Huffman. LC 93-32479. (Illus.). xii, 252p. (C). 1994. text 45.00 (0-8078-2138-1); pap. text 18.95 (0-8078-4445-4) U of NC Pr.
Protectors or Perpetrators? The Institutional Crisis of the Salvadoran Police. William Stanley. Ed. by George Vickers & Jack Spence. Tr. by Juan L. Guiller from SPA. 40p. pap. 4.50 (0-929513-33-9) WOLA.
Protee. Paul Claudel. (FRE.). 1972. 8.95 (0-8288-9113-3, F94450) Fr & Eur.
***Protege.** George Clidienst. LC 99-90156. 310p. 1999. 24.00 (0-9670459-0-8) Odin Pr AZ.
Protege. Robert Harbinson. 207p. 1988. pap. 9.95 (0-85640-413-6, Pub. by Blackstaff Pr) Dufour.
Protegee. C. C. Avram. LC 93-83905. 1993. 22.00 (1-883545-00-5) Shields Pub.
***Protegee of Jack Hamlin's.** Bret Harte. (Works of Bret Harte: Vol. 120). 438p. 1999. reprint ed. lib. bdg. 90.00 (0-7812-7852-X) Rprt Serv.
Protein - DNA Interactions. Ed. by John N. Abelson et al. (Methods in Enzymology Ser.: Vol. 208). (Illus.). 700p. 1991. text 125.00 (0-12-182109-9) Acad Pr.
Protein Analysis see Laboratory Manual of Analytical Methods of Protein Chemistry (Including Polypeptides)
Protein Analysis & Purification. I. Rosenberg. 560p. 1996. 120.00 (0-8176-3717-6) Birkhauser.
Protein Analysis & Purification: Benchtop Techniques. I. Rosenberg. 434p. 1996. pap. 59.95 (0-8176-3665-X) Birkhauser.
Protein & Amino Acid Metabolism in Cancer Cachexia. Murray F. Brennan & Peter W. Pisters. LC 95-24641. (Medical Intelligence Unit Ser.). 213p. 1995. 99.00 (1-57059-291-8) Landes Bioscience.
Protein & Energy: A Study of Changing Ideas in Nutrition. Kenneth J. Carpenter. LC 93-32130. (Illus.). 296p. (C). 1994. text 42.95 (0-521-45209-0) Cambridge U Pr.
Protein & Peptide Analysis by Mass Spectrometry. Ed. by John R. Chapman. (Methods in Molecular Biology Ser.: Vol. 61). 360p. 1996. 79.50 (0-89603-345-7) Humana.
***Protein Architecture.** Yurij Lvov & H. Mhohwald. LC 99-38871. 394p. 1999. 175.00 (0-8247-8236-4) Dekker.
Protein Architecture: A Practical Approach. Ed. by Arthur M. Lesk. (Practical Approach Ser.). (Illus.). 312p. 1991. pap. 45.00 (0-19-963055-0) OUP.
Protein Based Materials. David Kaplan & Kevin Mcgrath. LC 96-28021. 1996. write for info. (3-7643-3848-2) Birkhauser.
Protein-Based Materials. Ed. by Kevin P. McGrath & David Kaplan. LC 96-28021. (Bioengineering of Materials Ser.). 330p. 1997. 79.95 (0-8176-3848-2) Birkhauser.
Protein Binders in Paper & Paperboard Coating: A Project of the Coating Committee. Technical Association of the Pulp & Paper Industry. Ed. by R. Strauss. LC 75-929. (TAPPI Monographs: No. 36). 148p. reprint ed. pap. 45.90 (0-608-13838-X, 202030400016) Bks Demand.
Protein Biosynthesis: In Focus. H. R. Arnstein & R. H. Cox. (In Focus Ser.). (Illus.). 128p. (C). 1992. pap. text 19.95 (0-19-963040-2) OUP.
Protein Biosynthesis & Problems of Heredity Development & Aging. Zhores A. Medvedev. LC 67-71423. 606p. reprint ed. pap. 187.90 (0-608-13803-7, 202070200018) Bks Demand.
Protein Biosynthesis in Bacterial Systems. Ed. by Jerold A. Last & Allen I. Laskin. LC 78-160517. (Methods in Molecular Biology Ser.: No. 1). 349p. reprint ed. pap. 108.20 (0-7837-0745-2, 204106500019) Bks Demand.
Protein Biosynthesis in Nonbacterial Systems. Ed. by Jerold A. Last & Allen I. Laskin. LC 78-189798. (Methods in Molecular Biology Ser.: No. 2). (Illus.). 352p. reprint ed. pap. 109.20 (0-7837-0740-1, 204106200019) Bks Demand.
Protein Biotechnology. Gary Walsh & Dennis Headon. LC 93-50775. 382p. 1994. pap. 70.00 (0-471-94393-2) Wiley.
Protein Biotechnology: Isolation, Characterization & Stabilization. Ed. by Felix Franks. LC 93-3448. (Biological Methods Ser.). (Illus.). 608p. 1993. 125.00 (0-89603-230-2) Humana.
Protein Biotechnology & Biochemistry. Walsh. 1969. text. write for info. (0-471-89906-2); pap. text. write for info. (0-471-89907-0) Wiley.
Protein Blood Group Antigens of the Human Red Cell: Structure, Function, & Clinical Significance. Ed. by Peter C. Agre & Jean-Pierre Cartron. LC 92-49755. (Johns Hopkins Series in Hematology/Oncology). (Illus.). 281p. 1992. reprint ed. pap. 87.20 (0-608-05919-6, 206625500008) Bks Demand.
Protein Blotting: A Practical Approach. Ed. by Bonnie S. Dunbar. LC 93-42043. (Practical Approach Ser.: No. 140). (Illus.). 266p. 1994. pap. text 55.00 (0-19-963437-8) OUP.
Protein Blotting: Methodology, Research & Diagnostic Application. Ed. by B. A. Baldo & E. R. Tovey. (Illus.). viii, 168p. 1989. 97.50 (3-8055-4881-8) S Karger.
Protein C-Biochemical & Medical Aspects: Proceedings of the International Workshop, Titisee-Freiburg, Federal Republic of Germany, July 9-11, 1984. Ed. by Irene Witt. (Illus.). xiii, 191p. 1985. 123.10 (3-11-010222-6) De Gruyter.
Protein-Carbohydrate Interactions. Ed. by H. M. Einspahr. (Transactions of the American Crystallographic Association Ser.: Vol. 25). 1989. pap. 25.00 (0-685-51617-2) Polycrystal Bk Serv.
Protein Compartmentalization. Ed. by A. W. Strauss et al. (Molecular Biology Ser.). (Illus.). 170p. 1986. 68.00 (0-387-96292-1) Spr-Verlag.
Protein Conformation - Symposium No. 161. CIBA Foundation Staff. LC 91-22448. (CIBA Foundation Symposium Ser.: No. 161). 282p. 1991. 128.00 (0-471-92969-7, Wiley-Interscience) Wiley.
Protein Controlled Diet. Clara L. Gerwick. 40p. (Orig.). 1989. pap. text 7.25 (0-915187-05-1) Nutrition Ed.
Protein Counter. Annette B. Natow & Jo-Ann Helsin. 576p. 1997. per. 6.99 (0-671-00381-X, Pocket Books) PB.
Protein Crystallization: Techniques, Strategies & Tips. Ed. by Terese M. Bergfors. LC 98-75232. (Illus.). 250p. (C). 1999. lab manual ed. 69.95 (0-9636817-5-3) Intl Univ Line.
Protein Crystallography. T. L. Blundell & Louise Johnson. (Molecular Biology Ser.). 1976. text 264.00 (0-12-108350-0) Acad Pr.
Protein Data Bank CD-ROM. Ed. by Brookhaven National Laboratory Staff. 1992. 798.95 (0-387-14101-4); 325.00 (0-387-14102-2) Spr-Verlag.
Protein Degradation in Health & Disease. CIBA Foundation Staff. LC 80-15308. (CIBA Foundation Symposium: New Ser.: No. 75). 428p. reprint ed. pap. 132.70 (0-608-14283-2, 202219400024) Bks Demand.
Protein Delivery: Physical Systems. Ed. by Lynda M. Sanders & R. Wayne Hendron. LC 97-176. (Pharmaceutical Biotechnology Ser.: No. 10). (Illus.). 455p. (C). 1997. text 114.00 (0-306-45359-2, Kluwer Plenum) Kluwer Academic.
Protein Design & the Development of New Therapeutics & Vaccines. J. B. Hook & G. Poste. (Illus.). 512p. (C). 1990. text 120.00 (0-306-43463-6, Kluwer Plenum) Kluwer Academic.
Protein Drugs: Manufacturing Technologies. Philip Rotheim. LC 98-120872. (Report Ser.: No. B-114). 274p. 1997. 3450.00 (1-56965-384-4) BCC.
Protein Dynamics, Function & Design. Oleg Jardetzky et al. LC 98-41432. (NATO ASI Ser.). (Illus.). 230p. (C). 1998. text 125.00 (0-306-45939-6) Plenum.
Protein Dynamics Using NMR Relaxation. Kevin H. Mayo & Vladimir A. Daragan. 300p. 1998. 48.00 (1-86094-076-5, Pub. by Imperial College) World Scientific Pub.
***Protein Dysfunction in Human Genetic Disease.** D. Swallow. (Human Molecular Genetics Ser.). 258p. 1999. 105.00 (0-12-220444-1) Acad Pr.
Protein Electron Transfer. D. S. Bendall. (Illus.). 304p. (C). 1996. text, teacher ed., student ed. 130.00 (1-85996-040-5, Pub. by Bios Sci) Bks Intl VA.
Protein Engineering. Ed. by Dale L. Oxender & C. Fred Fox. LC 86-27741. 392p. 1987. 149.95 (0-471-63066-7) Wiley.
Protein Engineering: A Practical Approach. Ed. by Anthony R. Rees et al. LC 92-49381. (Practical Approach Ser.). (Illus.). 424p. (C). 1993. 95.00 (0-19-963139-5); pap. 55.00 (0-19-963138-7) OUP.
Protein Engineering: In Focus. A. J. Wilkinson & P. C. Moody. (In Focus Ser.). (Illus.). 96p. (C). 1991. pap. text 16.95 (0-19-963194-8) OUP.
Protein Engineering: Principles & Practice. Ed. by Jeffery Lynn Cleland & Charles S. Claik. LC 95-18093. 544p. 1996. 98.50 (0-471-10354-3) Wiley.
Protein Engineering: Protein Design in Basic Research, Medicine, & Industry: Proceedings of the Second International Conference on Protein Engineering, August 20-25, Kobe, Japan, 1989. Ed. by M. Ikehara. (Illus.). 368p. 1990. 79.95 (0-387-52887-3) Spr-Verlag.
Protein Engineering & Design. Ed. by Paul Carey. LC 96-2000. (Illus.). 361p. 1996. text 79.95 (0-12-159640-0) Acad Pr.
***Protein Engineering by Semisynthesis.** Wallace. LC 99-16241. 296p. 1999. boxed set 129.00 (0-8493-4727-0) CRC Pr.
***Protein Engineering for Industrial Biotechnology.** Ed. by Lilia Alberghina. 388p. 2000. text 110.00 (90-5702-412-8, Harwood Acad Pubs) Gordon & Breach.
Protein Engineering Methods & Protocols. Peter W. Goodenough. (Methods in Molecular Biology Ser.). 1999. 79.50 (0-89603-567-0) Humana.
Protein Evolution. Laszio Patthy. LC 98-46905. (Illus.). 228p. 1999. pap. 49.95 (0-632-04774-7) Blackwell Sci.
Protein Expression. Ed. by B. D. Hames & S. Higgins. LC 98-47316. (The Practical Approach Ser.: No. 202). (Illus.). 304p. 1999. text 120.00 (0-19-963624-9) OUP.
Protein Expression. Ed. by B. D. Hames & S. J. Higgins. LC 98-47316. (The Practical Approach Ser.: 202). (Illus.). 304p. 1999. pap. text 60.00 (0-19-963623-0) OUP.
Protein Expression in Animal Cells. Michael G. Roth. 1994. 53.00 (0-12-598560-6) Acad Pr.
Protein Folding. Ed. by Thomas E. Creighton. LC 92-10475. 547p. (C). 1992. pap. text 73.95 (0-7167-7027-X) W H Freeman.
Protein Folding. Ed. by C. M. Dobson & A. R. Fersht. LC 96-15183. (Illus.). 119p. (C). 1996. pap. text 29.95 (0-521-57636-9) Cambridge U Pr.
Protein Folding: Deciphering the Second Half of the Genetic Code. Ed. by Lila M. Gierasch & Jonathan King. LC 89-29567. (AAAS Miscellaneous Publications: No. 89-18S). (Illus.). 350p. reprint ed. pap. 108.50 (0-7837-6734-X, 204636200011) Bks Demand.
Protein Folding: In Vivo & in Vitro. Ed. by Jeffrey L. Cleland. LC 93-9740. (ACS Symposium Ser.: No. 526). (Illus.). 258p. 1993. text 59.00 (0-8412-2640-7, Pub. by Am Chemical) OUP.
Protein Folding Problem & Tertiary Structure Prediction. Ed. by Kenneth M. Merz, Jr. & Scott M. Le Grand. LC 93-41522. x, 581p. 1994. 87.50 (0-8176-3693-5) Birkhauser.
Protein Folds: A Distance Based Approach. Ed. by Henrik Bohr & Soren Brunak. 336p. 1995. boxed set 179.95 (0-8493-4009-8, 4009) CRC Pr.
***Protein Formulation & Delivery.** Eugene J. McNally. LC 99-40675. (Drugs & the Pharmaceutical Sciences Ser.). (Illus.). 278p. 1999. text 150.00 (0-8247-7883-9) Dekker.
Protein Function: A Practical Approach. 2nd ed. Ed. by T. E. Creighton. LC 97-6741. (The Practical Approach Ser.: No. 175). (Illus.). 360p. 1997. text 105.00 (0-19-963616-8); pap. text 55.00 (0-19-963615-X) OUP.
Protein Functionality in Food Systems. Ed. by Navam Hettiarachchy & Gregory Ziegler. LC 93-4799. (IFT Basic Symposium Ser.: Vol. 9). (Illus.). 536p. 1994. text 165.00 (0-8247-9197-5) Dekker.
Protein Functionality in Foods. Ed. by John P. Cherry. LC 81-97. (ACS Symposium Ser.: No. 147). 1981. 49.95 (0-8412-0605-8) Am Chemical.
Protein Functionality in Foods: Based on a Symposium. Ed. by John P. Cherry. LC 81-97. (ACS Symposium Ser.: Vol. 147). 343p. 1981. reprint ed. pap. 106.40 (0-608-03033-3, 206348600007) Bks Demand.
Protein Glycosylation. Kluwer Academic Publishing Staff. LC 98-42070. 1998. text 175.00 (0-7923-8337-0) Kluwer Academic.
***Protein Identification & Sequencing Using Tandem Mass Spectrometry.** Kinter. 400p. 2000. write for info. (0-471-32249-0) Wiley.
Protein Immobilization: Fundamentals & Applications. Ed. by Richard F. Taylor. (Bioprocess Technology Ser.: Vol. 14). (Illus.). 392p. 1991. text 175.00 (0-8247-8271-2) Dekker.
Protein Ingredients in Foods: A Western European Perspective. (Report Ser.: No. GA-094). 149p. 1996. 3000.00 (1-56965-113-2) BCC.
Protein Kinase C. Ed. by J. F. Kuo. LC 93-24246. (Illus.). 336p. (C). 1994. text 95.00 (0-19-508101-3) OUP.
Protein Kinase C. Peter J. Parker & Dekker. LC 96-50979. (Molecular Biology Intelligence Unit Ser.). 219p. 1997. 99.00 (1-57059-424-4) Landes Bioscience.
Protein Kinase C & Its Brain Substrates. W. H. Gispen & A. Routtenberg. (Progress in Brain Research Ser.: Vol. 89). xiv, 292p. 1991. 217.50 (0-444-81436-1) Elsevier.
Protein Kinase Factsbook. Hardie. 1995. pap. text 32.00 (0-12-324720-9); pap. text 32.00 (0-12-324721-7) Acad Pr.
Protein Kinase Factsbook, 2 vols., Set. Ed. by Grahame Hardie & Stephen Hanks. (Illus.). 663p. 1995. pap. 74.00 (0-12-324719-5) Acad Pr.
***Protein Kinase Functions.** Ed. by James Woodgett. (Frontiers in Molecular Biology Ser.: 29). (Illus.). 272p. 2000. pap. text 55.00 (0-19-963770-9) OUP.
***Protein Kinase Functions.** Ed. by James Woodgett. (Frontiers in Molecular Biology Ser.: No. 29). (Illus.). 272p. 2000. text 110.00 (0-19-963771-7) OUP.
Protein Kinase Protocols. Alastair D. Reith. (Methods in Molecular Biology Ser.: Vol. 124). (Illus.). 400p. 2000. 89.50 (0-89603-700-2) Humana.
Protein Kinases. Ed. by Hsien-Jien Kung. (Journal of Biomedical Science Ser.: Vol. 5, No. 2). (Illus.). 86p. 1998. pap. 21.00 (3-8055-6704-9) S Karger.
Protein Kinases: Frontiers in Molecular Biology 5. Ed. by James Robert Woodgett. (Frontiers in Molecular Biology Ser.). (Illus.). 292p. 1995. pap. text 49.95 (0-19-963408-4) OUP.
Protein Kinases in Blood Cell Function. Chi-Kuang Huang. 320p. 1993. lib. bdg. 199.00 (0-8493-6353-5, QP606) CRC Pr.
Protein Kinesis: Protein Trafficking & Stability. (Cold Spring Harbor Symposia on Quantitative Biology Ser.: Vol. LX). (Illus.). 843p. (C). 1996. text 115.00 (0-87969-069-0); pap. text 50.00 (0-87969-070-4) Cold Spring Harbor.
Protein-Ligand Interactions: Precise Molecular Dimensions & Thermal Motion. (American Crystallographic Association Program & Abstracts Ser. 2: Vol. 10, 2). 1982. pap. 10.00 (0-317-02525-2) Polycrystal Bk Serv.
Protein-Lipid Association in Wheat. Ferenc Bekes & Finlay MacRitchie. 1991. 129.95 (0-8493-5179-0, CRC Reprint) Franklin.
Protein-Lipid Interactions. Ed. by A. Watts. LC 93-1825. (New Comprehensive Biochemistry Ser.). 398p. 1993. 194.00 (0-444-81575-9) Elsevier.
Protein Lipidation Protocols. Michael H. Gelb. LC 98-50534. (Methods in Molecular Biology Ser.: Vol. 116). (Illus.). 256p. 1999. 89.50 (0-89603-534-4) Humana.
***Protein Liquid Chromatography.** Ed. by M. Kastner. (Journal of Chromatography Library). 974p. 1999. 380.50 (0-444-50210-6) Elsevier.
***Protein Liquid Chromatography.** Michael E. Kastner. LC 99-52197. (Journal of Chromatography Library). 974p. 1999. 165.00 (0-444-50211-4) Elsevier.
***Protein Localization by Fluorescence Microscopy: A Practical Approach.** Ed. by Victoria J. Allan. LC 99-37444. (The Practical Approach Ser.: No. 218). (Illus.). 256p. 2000. text 120.00 (0-19-963741-5); pap. text 55.00 (0-19-963740-7) OUP.
***Protein Metabolism & Nutrition.** G. E. Lobley. (Illus.). 284p. 1999. 85.00 (90-74134-69-6) Wageningen Pers.
Protein Metabolism & Nutrition: Proceedings of the International Symposium, 1st, Nottingham, England, 1974. International Symposium on Protein Metabolism & Nu. Ed. by D. J. Cole & K. N. Boorman. LC 77-357118. (European Association for Animal Production Publication Ser.: No. 16). 525p. reprint ed. pap. 162.80 (0-608-14854-7, 202574500046) Bks Demand.
Protein Metabolism During Infancy. Ed. by Niels C. Raiha. LC 94-1490. (Nestle Nutrition Workshop Ser.: Vol. 33). 272p. 1994. text 65.00 (0-7817-0215-1) Lppncott W & W.
Protein Metabolism in Farm Animals: Evaluation, Digestion, Absorption, & Metabolism. Ed. by H. D. Bock et al. (Illus.). 464p. 1990. 115.00 (0-19-854251-8) OUP.
Protein Metabolism in Renal Diseases. Ed. by Bradley J. Maroni. (Mineral & Electrolyte Metabolism Ser.: Vol. 24, No. 1, 1998). (Illus.). 102p. 1997. pap. 52.25 (3-8055-6573-9) S Karger.
Protein Metabolism in the Plant. Albert C. Chibnall. 1939. pap. 39.50 (0-685-69796-7) Elliots Bks.
Protein Metabolism of the Brain. Aleksandr V. Palladin et al. Tr. by Basill Haigh from RUS. LC 77-2307. (Studies in Soviet Science). (Illus.). 347p. 1977. reprint ed. pap. 107.60 (0-608-05495-X, 206596400006) Bks Demand.
Protein Metabolism of the Nervous System. Ed. by Abel Lajtha. LC 74-85373. 754p. reprint ed. pap. 200.00 (0-608-14551-3, 202471800038) Bks Demand.
Protein Methods. 2nd ed. Daniel M. Bollag et al. LC 96-14083. 432p. 1996. pap. 59.99 (0-471-11837-0, Wiley-Liss) Wiley.
Protein Methylation. Ed. by Woon K. Paik & Sangduk Kim. 432p. 1989. lib. bdg. 254.00 (0-8493-6818-9, QP551) CRC Pr.
Protein Modules in Signal Transduction. Ed. by A. J. Pawson et al. (Current Topics in Microbiology & Immunology Ser.: Vol. 228). (Illus.). 396p. 1997. text 179.00 (3-540-63396-0) Spr-Verlag.
Protein Molecule: Conformation, Stability & Folding. K. Hamaguchi. 270p. 1992. 82.95 (0-387-55915-9) Spr-Verlag.
Protein Motions. S. Subbiah. LC 96-5705. (Molecular Biology Intelligence Unit Ser.). 218p. 1996. 99.00 (1-57059-344-2) Landes Bioscience.
Protein NMR Spectroscopy: Principles & Practice. John Cavanaugh et al. LC 95-12822. (Illus.). 587p. 1995. text 70.00 (0-12-164490-1) Acad Pr.
Protein NMR Techniques. Ed. by David G. Reid. LC 97-17906. (Methods in Molecular Biology Ser.: Vol. 60). (Illus.). 429p. 1997. 79.50 (0-89603-309-0) Humana.
Protein-Nucleic Acid Interaction. Udo Heinema & W. Saenger. 1989. 88.00 (0-8493-7113-9, QH) CRC Pr.

Protein Nutrition & Mineral Absorption. Raul A. Wapnir. (Illus.). 352p. 1990. lib. bdg. 239.00 (*0-8493-5227-4*, QP533) CRC Pr.

Protein Nutrition in Ruminants. 2nd ed. E. R. Orskov. (Illus.). 175p. 1992. text 62.00 (*0-12-528481-0*) Acad Pr.

Protein Nutritional Quality of Foods & Feeds: Proceedings, 2 pts., Pt. 1. American Chemical Society Symposium on Chemical &. Ed. by Mendel Friedman. LC 74-335459. (Nutrition & Clinical Nutrition Ser.: No. 1). (Illus.). 648p. reprint ed. pap. 200.00 (*0-7837-0637-5*, 204098100001) Bks Demand.

Protein Nutritional Quality of Foods & Feeds: Proceedings, 2 pts., Pt. 2. American Chemical Society Symposium on Chemical &. Ed. by Mendel Friedman. LC 74-33549. (Nutrition & Clinical Nutrition Ser.: No. 1). (Illus.). 696p. reprint ed. pap. 200.00 (*0-7837-0638-3*, 204098100002) Bks Demand.

Protein Peptide Sequence Analysis Current Methodologies: Current Methodologies. Ed. by Ajit S. Bhown. LC 87-718. (Biochemists Ser.). 256p. 1988. 144.00 (*0-8493-6583-X*, QP551, CRC Reprint) Franklin.

Protein Pharmacokinetics & Metabolism. B. L. Ferraiolo et al. (Pharmaceutical Biotechnology Ser.: Vol. 1). (Illus.). 292p. (C). 1992. text 75.00 (*0-306-44151-9*, Kluwer Plenum) Kluwer Academic.

Protein Phosphatase Factsbook. Nick Tonks. 1997. pap. text 42.00 (*0-12-694955-7*) Acad Pr.

Protein Phosphatase Protocols. Ed. by John W. Ludlow. LC 98-15957. (Methods in Molecular Biology Ser.: Vol. 93). (Illus.). 336p. 1998. 79.50 (*0-89603-468-2*) Humana.

Protein Phosphatase Type-2A in Xenopus Laevis. M. Bosch. No. 90. 164p. (Orig.). 1994. pap. 47.50 (*90-6186-630-8*, Pub. by Leuven Univ) Coronet Bks.

Protein Phosphatase 2A Structure & ReEgulation. P. Hendrix. No. 57. 145p. (Orig.). 1992. pap. 42.50 (*90-6186-522-0*, Pub. by Leuven Univ) Coronet Bks.

Protein Phosphatases: Substrate Specificity & Enzyme Regulation by Second-Site Phosphorylation. P. Agostinis. No. 1. 92p. (Orig.). 1988. pap. 22.00 (*90-6186-260-4*, Pub. by Leuven Univ) Coronet Bks.

Protein Phosphatases of Xenopus Oocytes: Phosphotyrosyl Phosphatase Activation of the PCS Phosphatases. X. Cayla. No. 19. 133p. (Orig.). 1990. pap. 32.50 (*90-6186-355-4*, Pub. by Leuven Univ) Coronet Bks.

Protein Phosphorylation. Ed. by Friedrich Marks. (Illus.). 381p. 1996. 145.00 (*3-527-29241-1*, Wiley-VCH) Wiley.

Protein Phosphorylation, 2 bks. Ed. by Ora M. Rosen & Edwin G. Krebs. LC 81-10184. (Cold Spring Harbor Conferences on Cell Proliferation Ser.: Vol. 8). 1421p. (C). 1981. 177.00 (*0-87969-140-9*) Cold Spring Harbor.

Protein Phosphorylation. Ed. by Bartholomew M. Sefton & Tony Hunter. LC 98-149611. (Selected Methods in Enzymology Ser.). (Illus.). 675p. (C). 1998. boxed set 69.95 (*0-12-634490-6*) Acad Pr.

***Protein Phosphorylation: A Practical Approach.** 2nd ed. Ed. by Grahame Hardie. LC 99-32319. (The Practical Approach Ser.: No. 211). (Illus.). 448p. 2000. text 120.00 (*0-19-963729-6*); pap. text 55.00 (*0-19-963728-8*) OUP.

Protein Phosphorylation Pt. A: Protein Kinases, Assays, Purification, Antibodies, Functional Analysis, Cloning, & Expression. Ed. by Tony Hunter et al. (Methods in Enzymology Ser.: Vol. 200). (Illus.). 763p. 1991. text 125.00 (*0-12-182101-3*) Acad Pr.

Protein Phosphorylation Pt. B: Analysis of Protein Phosphorylation, Protein Kinase Inhibitors, & Protein Phosphatases. Ed. by John N. Abelson et al. (Methods in Enzymology Ser.: Vol. 201). (Illus.). 547p. (C). 1991. text 104.00 (*0-12-182102-1*) Acad Pr.

Protein Phosphorylation & Bio-Regulation. Ed. by J. Gordon et al. (Illus.). x, 234p. 1980. 71.50 (*3-8055-1168-X*) S Karger.

Protein Phosphorylation in Cell Regulation. Ed. by Michael Clemens. 368p. 1997. text 72.00 (*90-5702-030-0*, Harwood Acad Pubs); pap. text 22.00 (*90-5702-031-9*, Harwood Acad Pubs) Gordon & Breach.

Protein Phosphorylation in Heart Muscle. R. John Solaro. 192p. 1986. 102.00 (*0-8493-5133-2*, QP113, CRC Reprint) Franklin.

Protein Phosphorylation in Plants. Ed. by Peter R. Shewry et al. (Proceedings of the Phytochemical Society of Europe Ser.: Vol. 39). (Illus.). 338p. (C). 1996. text 135.00 (*0-19-857777-X*) OUP.

Protein Power: The Metabolic Breakthrough. Michael R. Eades & Mary D. Eades. LC 95-32738. (Illus.). 298p. 1996. 23.95 (*0-553-10183-8*) Bantam.

Protein Power: The Metabolic Breakthrough. Michael R. Eades & Mary D. Eades. 448p. 1997. mass mkt. 7.50 (*0-553-57475-2*) Bantam.

Protein Power: The Metabolic Breakthrough, 1. Michael R. Eades & Mary D. Eades. 448p. 1999. pap. 14.00 (*0-553-38078-8*) Broadway BDD.

Protein Power Lifeplan. Michael R. Eades & Mary D. Eades. LC 99-43052. 320p. 2000. 23.95 (*0-446-52576-6*, Pub. by Warner Bks) Little.

***Protein Power Lifeplan Gram Counter.** Michael R. Eades & Mary Dan Eades. 208p. 2000. mass mkt. 4.99 (*0-446-60824-6*, Pub. by Warner Bks) Little.

***Protein-Protein Recognition.** Ed. by Colin Kleanthous. (Frontiers in Molecular Biology Ser.: 31). (Illus.). 320p. 2000. text 115.00 (*0-19-963761-X*); pap. text 60.00 (*0-19-963760-1*) OUP.

Protein Protocols Handbook. Ed. by John M. Walker. (Illus.). 832p. 1996. 124.50 (*0-89603-338-4*) Humana.

Protein Purification: Design & Scale Up of Downstream Processing. Scott M. Wheelwright. 244p. 1993. 89.95 (*0-471-03723-0*) Wiley.

Protein Purification: From Molecular Mechanisms to Large-Scale Processes. Ed. by Michael R. Ladisch et al. LC 90-35551. (ACS Symposium Ser.: No. 427). (Illus.). 302p. 1990. text 75.00 (*0-8412-1790-4*, Pub. by Am Chemical) OUP.

Protein Purification: Principles & Practice. R. K. Scopes. (Advanced Texts in Chemistry Ser.). (Illus.). 345p. 1989. 49.00 (*0-387-96555-6*) Spr-Verlag.

Protein Purification: Principles & Practice. 3rd ed. R. K. Scopes. Ed. by Charles R. Cantor. (Advanced Texts in Chemistry Ser.). (Illus.). 380p. 1993. 54.95 (*0-387-94072-3*) Spr-Verlag.

Protein Purification: Principles, High Resolution Methods, & Application. 2nd ed. Jan-Christer Janson & Lars Ryden. LC 97-13875. 720p. 1998. 84.95 (*0-471-18626-0*) Wiley.

Protein Purification: Principles, High Resolution Methods, & Applications. Ed. by Jan-Christen Janson & Lars G. Ryden. LC 89-9134. 502p. 1989. 65.00 (*0-89573-122-3*, Wiley-VCH) Wiley.

Protein Purification: Principles, High Resolution Methods, & Applications. 2nd ed. Ed. by Jan-Christen Janson & Lars G. Ryden. 600p. 1997. write for info. (*1-56081-912-X*, Wiley-VCH) Wiley.

Protein Purification Applications: A Practical Approach. Ed. by E. L. Harris & S. Angal. (Practical Approach Ser.). (Illus.). 192p. 1990. pap. text 50.00 (*0-19-963023-2*) OUP.

Protein Purification Process Engineering. Ed. by Roger G. Harrison. (Bioprocess Technology Ser.: Vol. 18). (Illus.). 392p. 1993. text 185.00 (*0-8247-9009-X*) Dekker.

Protein Purification Protocols, Vol. 59. Ed. by Shawn Doonan. LC 96-3250. (Methods in Molecular Biology Ser.). (Illus.). 416p. 1996. 74.50 (*0-89603-336-8*) Humana.

Protein Quality & the Effects of Processing. R. Dixon Phillips & Finley. (Food Science & Technology Ser.: Vol. 29). (Illus.). 416p. 1988. text 145.00 (*0-8247-7984-3*) Dekker.

Protein Quality Evaluation: Report of the Joint FAO/WHO Expert Consultation, Bethesda, U. S. A., 1989. 70p. 1991. 12.00 (*92-5-103097-9*, F3979, Pub. by FAO) Bernan Associates.

Protein Refolding. Ed. by George Georgiou & Eliana De Bernardez-Clark. LC 91-22163. (ACS Symposium Ser.: No. 470). (Illus.). 216p. 1991. text 55.00 (*0-8412-2107-3*, Pub. by Am Chemical) OUP.

Protein Science. Wiley, John & Sons, Inc., Editorial Board Staff et al. LC 95-1030. 1995. 495.00 (*0-471-11184-8*) Wiley.

Protein Sequence Determination: Methods & Techniques. Stanley Blackburn. LC 77-130746. 301p. reprint ed. pap. 93.40 (*0-608-30332-1*, 205541000021) Bks Demand.

Protein Sequencing: A Practical Approach. J. B. Findlay & Michael J. Geisow. (Practical Approach Ser.). 212p. 1989. 75.00 (*0-19-963012-7*); pap. 45.00 (*0-19-963013-5*) OUP.

***Protein Skimming & Activated Carbon Secrets: Dialogue on Protein Skimming & Activated Carbon.** Bob Goemans. (Illus.). 1999. pap. 8.99 (*0-9664549-1-X*) M Weiss Cos.

Protein-Solvent Interactions. Ed. by Roger B. Gregory. (Illus.). 584p. 1995. text 195.00 (*0-8247-9239-4*) Dekker.

Protein-Sparing Diets: A Special Issue of Journal of Obesity & Weight Regulation. Ed. by Robert S. Sherwin & Jonathan K. Wise. 80p. 1984. pap. 14.95 (*0-89885-220-X*, Kluwer Acad Hman Sci) Kluwer Academic.

Protein Stability & Folding: A Collection of Thermodynamic Data. W. Pfeil. LC 98-13138. (Illus.). 500p. 1998. 250.00 (*3-540-63717-6*) Spr-Verlag.

Protein Stability & Folding: Theory & Practice. Ed. by Bret A. Shirley. LC 94-39996. (Methods in Molecular Biology Ser.: Vol. 40). (Illus.). 387p. 1995. pap. 74.50 (*0-89603-301-5*) Humana.

Protein Stability & Stabilization of Protein Function. Ciaran O. Fagain. LC 97-17143. (Biotechnology Intelligence Unit Ser.). 172p. 1997. text. write for info. (*1-57059-461-9*) Landes Bioscience.

Protein Stability & Stabilization of Protein Function. Ciaran O. Fagain. LC 97-17143. (Biotechnology Intelligence Unit Ser.). (Illus.). 172p. 1997. 99.95 (*3-540-63189-5*) Spr-Verlag.

Protein Staining & Identification Techniques. Robert Allen. Ed. by Bruce Budowle. LC 99-39668. (Molecular Laboratory Methods Ser.). (Illus.). 120p. 1999. 44.95 (*1-881299-08-2*) Eaton Pub Co.

Protein Structural Biology in Biomedical Research, 2 pts., Set. Ed. by E. Edward Bittar. (Advances in Molecular & Cell Biology Ser.: Vol. 22). 627p. 1997. 257.00 (*0-7623-0283-6*) Jai Pr.

Protein Structure. Ed. by R. Austin, Jr. et al. (Illus.). 1987. 124.00 (*0-387-96567-X*) Spr-Verlag.

Protein Structure. N. J. Darby & T. E. Creighton. LC 92-27978. (In Focus Ser.). (Illus.). 112p. 1994. pap. text 19.95 (*0-19-963310-X*) OUP.

Protein Structure. Max F. Perutz. LC 92-928. (C). 1992. text 36.80 (*0-7167-7021-0*) W H Freeman.

Protein Structure: A Practical Approach. 2nd ed. Ed. by T. E. Creighton. LC 97-162964. (The Practical Approach Ser.: No. 174). (Illus.). 408p. 1997. text 105.00 (*0-19-963619-2*); pap. text 55.00 (*0-19-963618-4*) OUP.

Protein Structure Analysis: Preparation & Characterization. Roza M. Kamp et al. LC 96-35790. (Springer Lab Manuals Ser.). (Illus.). 280p. 1997. lab manual ed. 69.95 (*3-540-61500-8*) Spr-Verlag.

Protein Structure & Engineering. Ed. by O. Jardetsky. LC 89-49339. (NATO ASI Series A, Life Sciences: Vol. 183). (Illus.). 396p. 1989. 115.00 (*0-306-43484-9*, Plenum Trade) Perseus Pubng.

Protein Structure & Evolution: Papers & Discussions. IUB Symposium on Protein Structure & Evolution Sta. Ed. by J. Lawrence Fox et al. LC 76-23583. (Illus.). 575p. reprint ed. pap. 178.30 (*0-7837-0898-X*, 204120300019) Bks Demand.

Protein Structure & Protein Engineering, 39: Colloquium der Gesellschaft Fur Biologische Chemie, 14-16 April, 1988 in Mosbach-Baden. Ed. by E. L. Winnacker & Reiner K. Huber. (Illus.). 150p. 1989. 56.95 (*0-387-50394-3*) Spr-Verlag.

Protein Structure & Protein Function: A Practical Approach, Two. 2nd ed. Ed. by T. E. Creighton. LC 97-6741. (Practical Approach Ser.: No. 174, 175). 1997. text 190.00 (*0-19-963617-6*); pap. text 95.00 (*0-19-963620-6*) OUP.

Protein Structure by Distance Analysis. H. Bohr & Soren Brunak. LC 94-75946. (YA). (gr. 12). 1994. 82.00 (*90-5199-161-4*) IOS Press.

Protein Structure-Function Relationship: Proceedings of the Fourth International Symposium Held in Karachi, Pakistan, January 20-25, 1995. Ed. by Zafar H. Zaidi & David L. Smith. LC 96-12998. 309p. (C). 1996. text 95.00 (*0-306-45285-5*, Kluwer Plenum) Kluwer Academic.

Protein Structure Prediction: A Practical Approach. Ed. by M. Sternberg. (The Practical Approach Ser.: No. 170). (Illus.). 318p. 1997. text 105.00 (*0-19-963497-1*); pap. text 49.95 (*0-19-963496-3*) OUP.

Protein Structure Prediction: Methods & Protocols. Ed. by David Webster. (Methods in Molecular Biology Ser.). 1999. 69.50 (*0-89603-711-8*) Humana.

Protein Structure Prediction: Methods & Protocols. David Webster. (Methods in Molecular Biology Ser.: Vol. 143). 430p. 2000. 79.50 (*0-89603-637-5*) Humana.

Protein Structure, Prediction & Design. Ed. by J. Kay et al. (Biochemical Society Symposium Ser.: Vol. 57). 158p. (C). 1991. text 110.50 (*1-85578-002-X*, Pub. by Portland Pr Ltd) Ashgate Pub Co.

Protein Structures. C. Suits & H. Way. LC 60-7068. (Collected Works of Irving Langmuir: Vol. 7). 1961. 121.00 (*0-08-009359-0*, Pub. by Pergamon Repr) Franklin.

Protein Synthesis. Ed. by Edwin H. McConkey. LC 75-155743. 400p. reprint ed. pap. 124.00 (*0-608-09995-3*, 202711200002) Bks Demand.

Protein Synthesis, Vol. 1. Ed. by Edwin H. McConkey. LC 74-155743. 314p. 1971. reprint ed. pap. 97.40 (*0-7837-0017-2*, 202711200001) Bks Demand.

Protein Synthesis: Methods & Protocols. Robin Martin. LC 98-27411. (Methods in Molecular Biology Ser.: Vol. 77). (Illus.). 456p. 1998. 79.50 (*0-89603-397-X*) Humana.

Protein Synthesis: Translational & Post-Translational Events. Ed. by Abraham K. Abraham et al. LC 83-26463. (Experimental Biology & Medicine Ser.). 477p. 1984. 125.00 (*0-89603-060-1*) Humana.

Protein Synthesis & Targeting in Yeast. Ed. by Alister J. Brown et al. LC 93-903. (NATO ASI Series H: Cell Biology: Vol. 71). 1993. 255.95 (*0-387-56521-3*) Spr-Verlag.

Protein Tailoring & Reagents for Food & Medical Uses. R. E. Feeney & J. R. Whitaker. 408p. 1986. 165.00 (*0-8247-7616-X*) Dekker.

Protein Targeting. Ed. by Stella M. Hurtley. (Frontiers in Molecular Biology Ser.: No. 16). (Illus.). 234p. 1996. text 110.00 (*0-19-963562-5*); pap. text 55.00 (*0-19-963561-7*) OUP.

Protein Targeting: A Practical Approach. Ed. by Anthony I. Magee. (Practical Approach Ser.). (Illus.). 288p. 1992. pap. text 49.95 (*0-19-963210-3*) OUP.

Protein Targeting & Secretion. Brian M. Austen & Olwyn M. Westwood. (Illus.). 96p. (C). 1991. pap. text 18.95 (*0-19-963217-0*, 126) OUP.

Protein Targeting & Translocation. Ed. by David Phoenix. (Portland Press Research Monograph Ser.: No. 12). (Illus.). 304p. 1998. text 127.50 (*1-85578-121-2*, Pub. by Portland Pr Ltd) Ashgate Pub Co.

***Protein Targeting & Translocation** David A. Phoenix. LC 99-189360. (Portland Press Research Monographs). xii, 292p. 1998. 85.00 (*0-691-00901-5*, Pub. by Princeton U Pr) Cal Prin Full Svc.

Protein Targeting Protocols. Ed. by Roger A. Clegg. (Methods in Molecular Biology Ser.: Vol. 88). (Illus.). 336p. 1998. 79.50 (*0-89603-450-X*); 99.50 (*0-89603-487-9*) Humana.

Protein Toxin Structure. Michael W. Parker. LC 96-21770. (Molecular Biology Intelligence Unit Ser.). 200p. 1996. 99.00 (*1-57059-368-X*) Landes Bioscience.

Protein Trafficking in Plant Cells. J. Soll. LC 98-34663. 1998. 175.00 (*0-7923-5237-8*) Kluwer Academic.

Protein Transport & Secretion. Ed. by Mary-Jane Gething. LC 85-167861. (Current Communications in Molecular Biology Ser.). 225p. (Orig.). reprint ed. pap. 69.80 (*0-7837-2082-3*, 204235600004) Bks Demand.

Protein Turnover. CIBA Foundation Staff. LC 72-96519. (CIBA Foundation Symposium: New Ser.: No. 9). 327p. reprint ed. pap. 101.40 (*0-608-13507-0*, 202214100024) Bks Demand.

Proteinases & Tumor Invasion. Ed. by Peter Strauli et al. LC 80-17634. (Monograph Series of the European Organization for Research on Treatment of Cancer: No. 6). (Illus.). 227p. 1980. reprint ed. pap. 70.40 (*0-7837-9522-X*, 206027100005) Bks Demand.

Proteinases in Inflammation & Tumor Invasion: Review Articles, Including Those from an International Conference, Bielefeld, Federal Republic of Germany, March 14-16, 1985. Ed. by Harald Tschesche. (Illus.). ix, 419p. 1986. lib. bdg. 196.15 (*3-11-010530-6*) De Gruyter.

Proteins. Jane Inglis. LC 92-26759. (J). (gr. 2-5). 1993. lib. bdg. 14.95 (*0-87614-780-5*, Carolrhoda) Lerner Pub.

Proteins. Renugopalakrishnan. 423p. 1991. text 245.00 (*90-72199-09-X*) Kluwer Academic.

Proteins. Alvin Silverstein et al. LC 91-41230. (Food Power Ser.). (Illus.). 48p. (J). (gr. 3-6). 1992. lib. bdg. 20.90 (*1-56294-209-3*) Millbrook Pr.

Proteins. Ed. by John M. Walker. LC 84-15696. (Methods in Molecular Biology Ser.: Vol. 1). 365p. 1984. 79.50 (*0-89603-062-8*); pap. 39.50 (*0-89603-106-3*) Humana.

Proteins: A Guide to Study by Physical & Chemical Methods. Rudy H. Haschemeyer & Audrey E. Haschemeyer. LC 72-13134. (Illus.). 457p. reprint ed. pap. 141.70 (*0-608-17415-7*, 205644900067) Bks Demand.

Proteins: A Theoretical Perspective of Dynamics, Structure & Thermodynamics. Charles L. Brooks et al. LC 87-15993. (Advances in Chemical Physics Ser.). 259p. 1988. 169.00 (*0-471-62801-8*) Wiley.

Proteins: A Theoretical Perspective of Dynamics, Structure & Thermodynamics. Charles L. Brooks et al. (Advances in Chemical Physics Ser.). 259p. 1990. pap. 79.95 (*0-471-52977-X*) Wiley.

Proteins: Analysis & Design. Ed. by Ruth H. Angeletti. LC 98-4746. (Illus.). 362p. 1998. boxed set 99.95 (*0-12-058785-8*) Acad Pr.

Proteins: Applications of Proteins, Vol. 15. Ed. by Geoffrey Allen. Date not set. 128.50 (*1-55938-685-1*) Jai Pr.

Proteins: Cell Surface Proteins, Vol. 11. Ed. by Geoffrey Allen. Date not set. 128.50 (*1-55938-681-9*) Jai Pr.

Proteins: Composition, Structure & Function, 5 vols. 2nd ed. Incl. Vol. 5. Metalloproteins. Ed. by Hans Neurath. 1970. 41.50 (*0-12-516265-0*); Vol. 4. Hans Neurath. 1966. 71.50 (*0-12-516264-2*); Vol. 3. Ed. by Hans Neurath. 1965. 48.50 (*0-12-516263-4*); write for info. (*0-318-50349-2*) Acad Pr.

Proteins: Major Non-Immune System Proteins of Blood Plasma, Vol. 5. Ed. by Geoffrey Allen. Date not set. 128.50 (*1-55938-675-4*) Jai Pr.

Proteins: Major Structural Proteins, Vol. 7. Ed. by Geoffrey Allen. Date not set. 128.50 (*1-55938-677-0*) Jai Pr.

Proteins: Nucleic Acid Binding Proteins, Vol. 13. Ed. by Geoffrey Allen. Date not set. 128.50 (*1-55938-683-5*) Jai Pr.

Proteins: Physical & Chemical Properties of, Vol. 2. Ed. by Geoffrey Allen. 1999. 128.50 (*1-55938-672-X*) Jai Pr.

Proteins: Plasma Membrane Transport Proteins, Vol. 10. Ed. by Geoffrey Allen. Date not set. 128.50 (*1-55938-680-0*) Jai Pr.

Proteins: Protein & the Immune System, Vol. 4. Ed. by Geoffrey Allen. Date not set. 128.50 (*1-55938-674-6*) Jai Pr.

Proteins: Protein Growth Factors & Cytokines, Vol. 6. Ed. by Geoffrey Allen. Date not set. 128.50 (*1-55938-676-2*) Jai Pr.

Proteins: Protein Synthesis & Degradation, Vol. 3. Ed. by Geoffrey Allen. Date not set. 128.50 (*1-55938-673-8*) Jai Pr.

Proteins: Protein Toxins & Defense Proteins, Vol. 14. Ed. by Geoffrey Allen. Date not set. 128.50 (*1-55938-684-3*) Jai Pr.

Proteins: Proteins in Oxidative Metabolism, Vol. 12. Ed. by Geoffrey Allen. Date not set. 128.50 (*1-55938-682-7*) Jai Pr.

Proteins: Proteins of the Cytoskeleton & Cell Motility, Vol. 9. Ed. by Geoffrey Allen. Date not set. 128.50 (*1-55938-679-7*) Jai Pr.

Proteins: Soluble Proteins of the Cytoplasm, Vol. 8. Ed. by Geoffrey Allen. Date not set. 128.50 (*1-55938-678-9*) Jai Pr.

Proteins: Structure & Function. J. J. L'Italien. 810p. 1987. 135.00 (*0-306-42299-9*, Plenum Trade) Perseus Pubng.

Proteins: Structures & Molecular Properties. 2nd ed. Thomas E. Creighton. LC 92-6664. 512p. (C). 1992. pap. text 80.95 (*0-7167-7030-X*) W H Freeman.

Proteins Vol. 1: Principles of Protein Structure. Geoffrey Allen. 360p. 1997. 128.50 (*1-55938-671-1*) Jai Pr.

Proteins, Ancient Greeks & T'ang Poetry. Richard Burton. 1994. pap. 18.95 (*0-7486-6173-5*, Pub. by Edinburgh U Pr) Col U Pr.

Proteins & Non-Protein Nitrogen in Human Milk. Ed. by Stephanie A. Atkinson. 256p. 1989. lib. bdg. 210.00 (*0-8493-6795-6*, QP246) CRC Pr.

Proteins & Peptides Hormones, Vol. 9, Proteins and Peptides. 3rd ed. Hans U. Bergmeyer. 572p. 1985. 320.00 (*3-527-26049-8*, Wiley-VCH) Wiley.

Proteins & Steroids in Early Pregnancy. Ed. by H. M. Beier & P. Karlson. (Illus.). 346p. 1982. 65.95 (*0-387-10457-7*) Spr-Verlag.

Proteins As Human Food: Proceedings. Easter School in Agricultural Science (14th 1967,. Ed. by R. A. Lawrie. LC 72-874133. 547p. reprint ed. pap. 169.60 (*0-608-14849-0*, 202574300046) Bks Demand.

Proteins at Interfaces: Fundaments & Applications. Ed. by Thomas A. Horbett & John L. Brash. LC 95-36863. (ACS Symposium Ser.: No. 602). (Illus.). 548p. 1995. text 140.00 (*0-8412-3304-7*, Pub. by Am Chemical) OUP.

Proteins at Interfaces: Physicochemical & Biochemical Studies. Ed. by John L. Brash & Thomas A. Horbett. LC 87-14394. (Symposium Ser.: No. 343). x, 715p. 1987. 99.95 (*0-8412-1403-4*) Am Chemical.

Proteins at Interfaces: Physicochemical & Biochemical Studies. Ed. by John L. Brash & Thomas A. Horbett. LC 87-14394. (ACS Symposium Ser.: Vol. 343). 716p. 1987. reprint ed. pap. 200.00 (*0-608-03536-X*, 206425500008) Bks Demand.

Proteins at Liquid Interfaces. D. Mobius & Reinhard Miller. LC 98-3512. (Studies in Interface Science). 1998. 258.50 (*0-444-82944-X*) Elsevier.

Proteins at Low Temperatures. Ed. by Owen R. Fennema. LC 79-16561. (Advances in Chemistry Ser.: No. 180). 1979. 43.95 (*0-8412-0484-5*) Am Chemical.

An Asterisk (*) at the beginning of an entry indicates that the title is appearing for the first time.

Proteins at Low Temperatures. Ed. by Owen R. Fennema. LC 79-16561. (Advances in Chemistry Ser.: Vol. 180). 240p. 1979. reprint ed. pap. 74.40 (*0-608-03853-9*, 206430000008) Bks Demand.

Proteins, Enzymes & Genes. Joseph S. Fruton. LC 98-38892. (Illus.). 752p. 1999. 45.00 (*0-300-07608-8*) Yale U Pr.

Proteins Labfax. Ed. by N. C. Price. (Labfax Ser.). (Illus.). 318p. 1996. text 70.00 (*0-12-564710-7*) Acad Pr.

Proteins of the Nervous System. 2nd fac. ed. Ed. by Ralph A. Bradshaw & Diana M. Schneider. LC 80-21584. (Illus.). 407p. pap. 126.20 (*0-7837-7165-7*, 204713200005) Bks Demand.

Proteins of the Placenta. Ed. by P. Bischof & A. Klopper. (Illus.). viii, 208p. 1985. 155.75 (*3-8055-4034-5*) S Karger.

***Proteins, Peptides & Amino Acids in Enternal Nutrition.** P. Furst & V. Young. (Nestle Nutrition Workshop Series : Clinical & Performance Programme: 3). (Illus.). 274p. 2000. 174.00 (*3-8055-7108-9*) S Karger.

Proteins, Transmitters & Synapses. D. Nicholls. (Illus.). 288p. 1994. pap. 49.95 (*0-632-03661-3*, Pub. by Blckwll Scitfc UK) Blackwell Sci.

Proteinuria. Ed. by M. M. Avram. LC 85-9305. (Illus.). 248p. 1985. 90.00 (*0-306-41956-4*, Kluwer Plenum) Kluwer Academic.

Proteinuria. Ed. by J. Brod et al. (Contributions to Nephrology Ser.: Vol. 1). (Illus.). 250p. 1975. 29.75 (*3-8055-2183-9*) S Karger.

Proteinuria: American Journal of Nephrology, Vol. 10, Suppl. 1. Ed. by Shaul G. Massry et al. (Illus.). iv, 166p. 1990. pap. 35.00 (*3-8055-5245-9*) S Karger.

Proteinuria: An Integrated Review. Amadeo J. Pesce & Martin R. First. LC 79-20352. (Kidney Disease Ser.: No. 1). (Illus.). 310p. reprint ed. pap. 96.10 (*0-7837-0633-2*, 204097700019) Bks Demand.

Proteja a Su Familia Del Plomo en Su Casa. Government Printing Office Staff. 14p. 1995. pap. 27.00 (*0-16-048319-0*) USGPO.

Protektor. Charles Platt. 1996. mass mkt. 5.99 (*0-380-78431-9*, Avon Bks) Morrow Avon.

Protelinase Action: Proceedings of the International Workshop, August 29-31, Debrecen, Hungary. P. Elodi. (Symposia Biologica Hungarica Ser.: No. 25). 474p. (C). 1984. 141.00 (*963-05-3887-3*, Pub. by Akade Kiado) St Mut.

Proteoglycans. Ed. by Pierre Jolles. LC 93-34616. (Experientia Supplementa Ser.: Vol. 70). 288p. 1993. 146.50 (*0-8176-2957-2*) Birkhauser.

***Proteoglycans: Structure, Biology & Molecular Interactions.** Renato V. Iozzo. LC 00-28153. (Illus.). 2000. write for info. (*0-8247-0334-0*) Dekker.

Proteolysis & Protein Turnover. LC 97-70209. (Biomedical & Health Research Ser.: No. 13). 250p. (gr. 12). 1997. 76.00 (*90-5199-322-6*) IOS Press.

Proteolysis & Protein Turnover. Ed. by J. S. Bond & A. J. Barrett. (Portland Press Proceedings Ser.: Vol. 6). (Illus.). 290p. (C). 1994. text 110.50 (*1-85578-039-9*, Pub. by Portland Pr Ltd) Ashgate Pub Co.

Proteolytic & Cellular Mechanisms in Prohormone Processing. Vivian Y. Hook. LC 98-28730. (Molecular Biology Intelligence Unit Ser.). 215p. 1998. 99.00 (*1-57059-553-4*) Landes Bioscience.

Proteolytic Enzymes see Methods in Enzymology

Proteolytic Enzymes, Pt. C. Ed. by Sidney P. Colowick & Laszlo Lorand. (Methods in Enzymology Ser.: Vol. 80). 1982. text 188.00 (*0-12-181980-9*) Acad Pr.

Proteolytic Enzymes, Pt. B. Colowick. (Methods in Enzymology Ser.: Vol. 45). 1976. text 199.00 (*0-12-181945-0*) Acad Pr.

Proteolytic Enzymes: A Practical Approach. R. J. Beynon & Judith S. Bond. (Practical Approach Ser.). (Illus.). 278p. 1989. pap. text 50.00 (*0-19-963059-3*) OUP.

Proteolytic Enzymes: Aspartic & Metallo Peptidases. Ed. by John N. Abelson et al. (Methods in Enzymology Ser.: Vol. 248). (Illus.). 873p. 1995. text 121.00 (*0-12-182149-8*) Acad Pr.

Proteolytic Enzymes: Serine & Cysteine Peptidases. Ed. by Alan J. Barrett et al. (Methods in Enzymology Ser.: Vol. 244). (Illus.). 765p. 1994. text 125.00 (*0-12-182145-5*) Acad Pr.

Proteolytic Enzymes: Tools & Targets. E. E. Sterchi & W. Stocker. LC 99-20523. 300p. 1997. pap. text 82.00 (*3-540-61233-5*) Spr-Verlag.

Proteolytic Enzymes in Cancer Invasion. Ed. by Liliana Ossowski & R. M. Lopez. (Journal Ser.: Vol. 49, No. 1-3, 1996). (Illus.). 182p. 1996. pap. 62.75 (*3-8055-6318-3*) S Karger.

Proteolytic Enzymes in Coagulation, Fibrinolysis, & Complement Activation Pt. A: Mammalian Blood Coagulation Factors & Inhibitors. Ed. by Laszlo Lorand et al. (Methods in Enzymology Ser.: Vol. 222). (Illus.). 613p. 1993. text 104.00 (*0-12-182123-4*) Acad Pr.

Proteolytic Enzymes in Coagulation, Fibrinolysis, & Complement Activation Pt. B: Complement Activation, Fibrinolysis, & Nonmammalian Blood Coagulation Factors & Inhibitors. Ed. by Laszlo Lorand et al. (Methods in Enzymology Ser.: Vol. 223). (Illus.). 433p. 1993. text 94.00 (*0-12-182124-2*) Acad Pr.

***Proteome & Protein Analysis.** Ed. by R. M. Kamp et al. LC 99-15549. (Illus.). 300p. 1999. 125.00 (*3-540-65891-2*) Spr-Verlag.

***Proteome Research: Mass Spectrometry.** P. James. LC 00-32205. (Principles & Practice Ser.). 2000. write for info. (*3-540-67256-7*) Spr-Verlag.

Proteome Research: New Frontiers in Functional Genomics. M. R. Wilkins. LC 97-30956. (Principles & Practice Ser.). 300p. 1997. write for info. (*3-540-62775-8*); pap. write for info. (*3-540-62753-7*) Spr-Verlag.

***Proteome Research: Two-Dimensional Gel Electrophoresis & Detection Methods.** Ed. by T. H. Rabilloud. LC 99-15544. (Principles & Practice Ser.). (Illus.). 250p. 1999. 109.00 (*3-540-65689-8*); pap. 62.00 (*3-540-65792-4*) Spr-Verlag.

***Proteomics: From Protein Sequence to Function.** S. Pennington & M. J. Dunn. (Illus.). 304p. 2000. pap. 45.00 (*0-387-91589-3*) Spr-Verlag.

***Proteomics in functional Genomics: Protein Structure Analysis.** Ed. by P. Jolles & H. Jornvall. (Experientia Supplementum Ser.: 88). 350p. 2000. (*3-7643-5885-8*) Birkhauser.

Proterozoic Biosphere: A Multidisciplinary Study. Ed. by J. William Schopf & Cornelius Klein. (Illus.). 1374p. (C). 1992. text 210.00 (*0-521-36615-1*) Cambridge U Pr.

Proterozoic Crustal Evolution. Ed. by K. C. Condie. LC 92-34776. (Developments in Precambrian Geology Ser.: No. 10). 538p. 1993. 192.50 (*0-444-88782-2*) Elsevier.

Proterozoic Geology: Selected Papers from an International Proterozoic Symposium, University of Wisconsin, Madison, 1981. International Proterozoic Symposium Staff. LC 83-16587. (Geological Society of America Ser.: Vol. 161). (Illus.). 323p. 1983. reprint ed. pap. 100.20 (*0-608-07712-7*, 206780000010) Bks Demand.

Proterozoic Geology of the Southern Rock Mountains. Ed. by Jeffrey A. Grambling & Barbara J. Tewksbury. LC 89-1092. (Geological Society of America Ser.: Vol. 235). (Illus.). 183p. 1989. reprint ed. pap. 56.80 (*0-608-07759-3*, 206784700010) Bks Demand.

Proterozoic Glaucophane-Schist Belt & Some Eclogites of North Yangtze Craton, Central China. Ed. by Dong Shenbao et al. 162p. 1996. 95.00 (*90-6764-221-5*, Pub. by VSP) Coronet Bks.

Proterozoic Kimberley Reef Placer in the Evander Goldfield, Witwatersrand, South Africa. Wolfgang Hirdes & Rudolf Saager. (Monograph Series on Mineral Deposits: No. 20). (Illus.). v, 100p. 1983. 46.00 (*3-443-12020-2*, Pub. by Gebruder Borntraeger) Balogh.

Proterozoic Lithospheric Evolution. A. Kroner. (Geodynamics Ser.: Vol. 17). 288p. 1987. 35.00 (*0-87590-517-X*) Am Geophysical.

Protest! see Single Titles Series

Protest! Kronwetter. 1996. write for info. (*0-8050-5278-X*) H Holt & Co.

Protest: Photographs, 1963-1993. Benedict J. Fernandez. (Illus.). 136p. 1996. 45.00 (*3-908162-35-1*, Pub. by Edit Stemmle) Dist Art Pubs.

Protest: Studies of Collective Behavior & Social Movements. John Lofland. 361p. 1991. 39.95 (*0-88738-031-X*); pap. 24.95 (*0-88738-876-0*) Transaction Pubs.

Protest & Change: Studies in Social Movements. T. K. Oommen. 304p. (C). 1990. text 32.50 (*0-8039-9652-7*) Sage.

Protest & Conflict in African Literature. Ed. by Cosmo Pieterse & Donald Munro. LC 77-80856. 127p. 1970. pap. 15.00 (*0-8419-0005-1*, Africana) Holmes & Meier.

Protest & Politics: Christianity & Contemporary Affairs. Ed. by Robert G. Clouse et al. 277p. 1968. 5.95 (*0-87921-000-1*) Attic Pr.

***Protest & Popular Culture.** Mary E. Triece. 325p. 2000. 69.00 (*0-8133-6819-7*, Pub. by Westview) HarpC.

Protest & Possibility in the Writing of Tillie Olsen. Mara Faulkner. LC 92-29062. 178p. 1993. text 35.00 (*0-8139-1417-5*) U Pr of Va.

Protest & Praise: Sacred Music of Black Religion. Jon M. Spencer. LC 89-23573. 276p. (Orig.). 1990. pap. 20.00 (*0-8006-2404-1*, 1-2404) Augsburg Fortress.

Protest & Prejudice: A Study of Belief in the Black Community. Gary T. Marx. LC 78-23898. 256p. 1979. reprint ed. lib. bdg. 65.00 (*0-313-20827-1*, MAPT, Greenwood Pr) Greenwood.

Protest & Reform: The British Social Narrative by Women, 1827-1867. Joseph A. Kestner. LC 84-40498. 252p. 1985. reprint ed. pap. 78.20 (*0-608-07010-6*, 206721700009) Bks Demand.

Protest & Survival: Essays in E. P. Thompson. Ed. by John Rule & Robert Malcolmson. LC 93-15823. 432p. 1993. 30.00 (*1-56584-114-X*, Pub. by New Press NY) Norton.

Protest Business: Mobilizing Campaign Groups. Grant Jordan & William A. Maloney. LC 96-38817. 213p. 1997. pap. 27.95 (*0-7190-4371-9*) St Martin.

Protest Businesses. Jordan. LC 96-38817. 1997. text 69.95 (*0-7190-4370-0*) St Martin.

Protest Experience under the Competition in Contracting Act. 115p. 1989. pap. 22.50 (*0-89707-504-8*, 539-0088) Amer Bar Assn.

Protest in Belgrade: Winter of Discontent. Ed. by Mladen Lazic. LC 99-35900. (Illus.). 200p. 1999. pap. 22.95 (*963-9116-45-9*) Ctrl Europ Univ.

***Protest in Belgrade: Winter of Discontent.** Ed. by Mladen Lazic. LC 99-35900. (Illus.). 200p. (C). 1999. 49.95 (*963-9116-72-6*) Ctrl Europ Univ.

Protest Is Not Enough: The Struggle of Blacks & Hispanics for Equality in Urban Politics. Rufus P. Browning et al. LC 83-15552. (Illus.). 311p. 1984. pap. 16.95 (*0-520-05730-9*, Pub. by U CA Pr) Cal Prin Full Svc.

Protest Makers: The British Nuclear Disarmament Movement 1958-1965, Twenty Years on. Richard Taylor & Colin Pritchard. (Illus.). 180p. 1982. text 95.00 (*0-08-025211-7*, Pub. by Pergamon Repr) Franklin.

Protest Movements in Colonial East Africa-Aspects of Early African Response to European Rule. Robert Strayer et al. LC 73-85549. (Foreign & Comparative Studies Program, Eastern Africa Ser.: No.12). 96p. 1973. pap. 3.00 (*0-915984-09-1*) Syracuse U Foreign Comp.

Protest Movements in Lagos, 1908-1930. Rina Okonkwo. LC 94-33462. (African Studies: Vol. 37). 134p. 1995. text 69.95 (*0-7734-9049-3*) E Mellen.

Protest Politics: Cause Groups & Campaigns, Vol. 7. Ed. by F. F. Ridley & Grant Jordan. LC 99-185239. (Hansard Society Series in Government & Politics: 7). 188p. 1998. pap. text 26.00 (*0-19-922374-2*) OUP.

Protest, Power, & Change: An Encyclopedia of Nonviolent Action from ACT-UP to Women's Suffrage. Roger S. Powers et al. LC 96-26869. (Illus.). 640p. 1997. text 95.00 (*0-8153-0913-9*, H1625) Garland.

Protest, Revolt, & Revolution: New Developments in Conflict Research. Ekkart Zimmermann. 250p. 1999. pap. 49.50 (*0-8133-0650-7*) Westview.

Protest und Propaganda: Demonstrationen in Berlin zur Zeit der Weimarer Republik. Marie-Luise Ehls. (Veroeffentlichungen der Historischen Kommission Zu Berlin Ser.). (GER.). 580p. (C). 1997. lib. bdg. 168.00 (*3-11-015618-0*) De Gruyter.

Protest, Violence & Social Change. J. Hanley et al. 1972. pap. 4.65 (*0-13-731406-X*) P-H.

Protestant & Catholic. Kenneth W. Underwood. LC 72-9051. (Illus.). 484p. 1972. reprint ed. lib. bdg. 75.00 (*0-8371-6567-9*, UNPC, Greenwood Pr) Greenwood.

Protestant & Catholic Women in Nazi Germany. J. Michael Phayer. LC 89-16574. (Illus.). 288p. (C). 1990. text 39.95 (*0-8143-2211-5*) Wayne St U Pr.

Protestant & Roman Catholic Ethics: Prospects for Rapprochement. James M. Gustafson. LC 77-21421. 204p. 1980. pap. text 19.50 (*0-226-31108-2*, P868) U Ch Pr.

Protestant & Roman Catholic Ethics: Prospects for Rapprochement. James M. Gustafson. LC 77-21421. 1992. 15.00 (*0-226-31107-4*) U Ch Pr.

Protestant Baroque Poet: Pierre Poupo. Ralph M. Hester. (Studies in French Literature: No. 10). 1970. 44.65 (*90-279-0537-1*) Mouton.

Protestant Biblical Interpretation. Bernard L. Ramm. Tr. by Silas Chan from ENG. (CHI.). (C). 1984. pap. write for info. (*0-941598-10-1*) Living Spring Pubns.

Protestant Biblical Interpretation: A Textbook of Hermeneutics. 3rd ed. Bernard Ramm. 328p. 1999. pap. 14.99 (*0-8010-2083-2*) Baker Bks.

Protestant, Catholic, Jew: An Essay in American Religious Sociology. Will Herberg. LC 83-9120. xvi, 328p. (C). 1983. reprint ed. pap. text 12.95 (*0-226-32734-5*) U Ch Pr.

Protestant Challenge to Corporate America: Issues of Social Responsibility. Roy W. Morano. LC 84-8514. (Research for Business Decisions Ser.: No. 69). 256p. reprint ed. pap. 79.40 (*0-8357-1592-2*, 207040800088) Bks Demand.

Protestant Christianity: Interpreted Through Its Development. 2nd ed. John Dillenberger & Claude Welch. 537p. (C). 1988. pap. text 32.20 (*0-02-329601-1*, Macmillan Coll) P-H.

Protestant Christianity College. Dillinbe. 1985. pap. 12.95 (*0-684-14719-X*) S&S Trade.

Protestant Church Music in America. Archibald Davison. 1972. 59.95 (*0-8490-0905-7*) Gordon Pr.

Protestant Clergy & Public Issues, Eighteen Twelve to Eighteen Forty-Eight. John R. Bodo. LC 79-12849. (Perspectives in American History Ser.: No. 52). xiv, 291p. 1980. reprint ed. lib. bdg. 45.00 (*0-87991-854-3*) Porcupine Pr.

Protestant Community on Modern Taiwan: Mission, Seminary, & Church. Ed. by Murray A. Rubinstein. LC 90-31312. (Taiwan in the Modern World). 214p. (C). (gr. 13). 1991. text 79.95 (*0-87332-658-X*, East Gate Bk) M E Sharpe.

Protestant Concepts of Church & State. Thomas G. Sanders. 1990. 20.00 (*0-8446-6185-6*) Peter Smith.

Protestant Crusade in Great Britain, 1829-1860. John Wolffe. (Oxford Historical Monographs). 384p. 1991. 98.00 (*0-19-820199-0*) OUP.

Protestant Crusade in Ireland, 1800-70: A Study of Protestant-Catholic Relations Between the Act of Union & Disestablishment. Desmond Bowen. 1978. 39.95 (*0-7735-0295-5*, Pub. by McG-Queens Univ Pr) CUP Services.

Protestant Denominations, Yesterday & Today. David W. Cloud. (Illus.). 45p. 1995. pap. 2.50 (*1-58318-023-0*, WOL471B) Way of Life.

Protestant Diplomacy & the Near East: Missionary Influence on American Policy, 1810-1927. Joseph L. Grabill. LC 70-153504. (Illus.). 417p. reprint ed. pap. 129.30 (*0-8357-8997-7*, 203322500085) Bks Demand.

Protestant Dissent & Controversy in Ireland: 1660-1714. Phil Kilroy. LC 94-177440. 1994. 43.95 (*1-85918-003-5*, Pub. by Cork Univ) Intl Spec Bk.

Protestant Era. abr. ed. Paul Johannes Tillich. Tr. by James L. Adams. 1957. pap. text 7.00 (*0-226-80342-2*, P19) U Ch Pr.

Protestant Establishment. E. Digby Baltzell. LC 86-24678. 429p. 1987. pap. 20.00 (*0-300-03818-6*) Yale U Pr.

Protestant Establishment Revisited. E. Digby Baltzell. Ed. by Howard G. Schneiderman. 336p. (C). 1991. 44.95 (*0-88738-419-6*) Transaction Pubs.

Protestant Establishment Revisited. E. Digby Baltzell. Ed. by Howard G. Schneiderman. 265p. 1999. pap. 24.95 (*0-7658-0664-9*) Transaction Pubs.

Protestant Ethic & the Spirit of Capitalism. Max Weber. 292p. 1997. pap. 12.95 (*0-89526-417-X*) Regnery Pub.

Protestant Ethic & the Spirit of Capitalism. Max M. Weber. 292p. (C). 1977. pap. text 50.00 (*0-02-424860-6*, Macmillan Coll) P-H.

Protestant Ethic & the Spirit of Capitalism. Max M. Weber. Tr. by Talcott Parsons. (Counterpoint Ser.). 292p. (C). pap. 14.95 (*0-04-331101-6*) Routledge.

Protestant Ethic & the Spirit of Capitalism. Max M. Weber. 310p. (C). (gr. 13). 1987. pap. 16.99 (*0-415-08434-2*, Pub. by Tavistock) Routldge.

Protestant Ethic & the Spirit of Capitalism. rev. ed. Max M. Weber. 1985. reprint ed. pap. 16.50 (*0-684-16489-2*) S&S Trade.

***Protestant Ethic & the Spirit of Capitalism.** 3rd ed. Max Weber. Tr. by Talcott Parsons from GER. 292p. 2000. pap. text 22.95 (*1-891487-43-4*) Roxbury Pub Co.

Protestant Ethic & the Spirit of Capitalism: Second Roxbury Edition. 2nd rev. ed. Max Weber. Tr. by Talcott Parsons. LC 97-34399. (Illus.). 300p. (C). 1998. pap. text 22.95 (*0-935732-90-X*) Roxbury Pub Co.

Protestant Evangelical Awakening. W. Reginald Ward. (Illus.). 388p. (C). 1992. text 69.95 (*0-521-41491-1*) Cambridge U Pr.

Protestant Evangelical Literary Culture & Contemporary Society, 51. Jan Blodgett. LC 96-53517. (Contributions to the Study of Religion Ser.: No. 51). 192p. 1997. 59.95 (*0-313-30395-9*, GM0395, Greenwood Pr) Greenwood.

Protestant Evangelism among Italians in America. Ed. by Francesco Cordasco. LC 74-17943. (Italian American Experience Ser.). (Illus.). 276p. 1975. reprint ed. 23.95 (*0-405-06414-4*) Ayer.

Protestant Experience in Gary, Indiana, 1906-1975: At Home in the City. James W. Lewis. LC 91-24752. (Illus.). 304p. (C). 1992. text 41.00 (*0-87049-737-5*) U of Tenn Pr.

Protestant Face of Anglicanism. Paul F. Zahl. 1997. pap. text 11.00 (*0-8028-4597-5*) Eerdmans.

Protestant Faith. George W. Forell. LC 74-26341. 336p. 1975. pap. 20.00 (*0-8006-1095-4*, 1-1095, Fortress Pr) Augsburg Fortress.

Protestant Family Bible. 1992. 85.00 (*0-911156-51-8*) Bern Porter.

Protestant Future. R. Kernohan. Date not set. 16.99 (*1-871676-67-3*, Pub. by Christian Focus); pap. text 10.99 (*1-871676-76-2*, Pub. by Christian Focus) Spring Arbor Dist.

Protestant History & Identity in Sixteenth-Century Europe, 2 vols., Set. Ed. by Bruce Gordon. (St. Andrews Studies in Reformation History). 400p. 1996. 135.95 (*1-85928-175-3*, Pub. by Scolar Pr) Ashgate Pub Co.

Protestant History & Identity in Sixteenth-Century Europe Vol. 1: The Medieval Inheritance. Ed. by Bruce Gordon. (St. Andrews Studies in Reformation History). 1996. 78.95 (*1-85928-294-6*, Pub. by Scolar Pr) Ashgate Pub Co.

Protestant History & Identity in Sixteenth-Century Europe Vol. 2: The Later Reformation. Ed. by Bruce Gordon. (St. Andrews Studies in Reformation History). 200p. 1996. 78.95 (*1-85928-295-4*, Pub. by Scolar Pr) Ashgate Pub Co.

Protestant Hour Classics: The Twelve Most Requested Sermons. John Claypool et al. LC 92-12752. 112p. (Orig.). 1992. pap. 2.69 (*0-687-34377-1*) Abingdon.

***Protestant Identities: Religion, Society & Self-Fashioning in Post-Reformation England** Muriel C. McClendon et al. LC 99-37228. 2000. 55.00 (*0-8047-3611-1*) Stanford U Pr.

Protestant Leadership Education Schools. Floy S. Hyde. LC 70-176892. (Columbia University. Teachers College. Contributions to Education Ser.: No. 965). reprint ed. 37.50 (*0-404-55965-4*) AMS Pr.

Protestant Legacy: Attitudes to Illness & Death among Older Aberdonians. Rory Williams. (Illus.). 384p. 1990. text 85.00 (*0-19-827736-9*) OUP.

Protestant Mind of the English Reformation, 1570-1640. Charles George & Katherine George. LC 61-7399. 464p. reprint ed. pap. 143.90 (*0-608-30477-8*, 200098600053) Bks Demand.

Protestant Mission Education in Zambia, 1880-1954. John P. Ragsdale. LC 85-40505. 192p. 1987. 36.50 (*0-941664-09-0*) Susquehanna U Pr.

Protestant Missionaries in the Philippines, 1898-1916: An Inquiry into the American Colonial Mentality. Kenton J. Clymer. LC 85-1278. (Illus.). 284p. 1986. text 29.95 (*0-252-01210-0*) U of Ill Pr.

***Protestant Non-Conformity & Roman Catholicism.** David Shorney. (Readers' Guides Ser.: No. 13). (Illus.). 126p. 1999. pap. 15.95 (*1-873162-27-8*, Pub. by PRO Pubns) Midpt Trade.

***Protestant Origins in India: Tamil Evangelical Christians, 1706-1835.** D. Dennis Hudson. 2000. 45.00 (*0-8028-3891-X*) Eerdmans.

***Protestant Origins in India: Tamil Evangelical Christians, 1706-1835.** D. Dennis Hudson. (Studies in the History of Christian Missions). 320p. 2000. 45.00 (*0-8028-4721-8*) Eerdmans.

Protestant Parish Minister: A Behavioral Science Interpretation. Samuel Blizzard. LC 85-50402. (Monographs: No. 5). 1985. pap. 8.00 (*0-932566-04-9*) Soc Sci Stud Rel.

Protestant Pastor Looks at Mary. Charles Dickson. LC 96-68286. 112p. 1996. pap. 7.95 (*0-87973-727-1*, 721) Our Sunday Visitor.

***Protestant Pentecostalism in Latin America: A Study in the Dynamics of Change.** Karl-Wilhelm Westmeier. LC 99-32705. 168p. 1999. 31.50 (*0-8386-3834-1*) Fairleigh Dickinson.

Protestant Pluralism & the New York Experience: A Study of Eighteenth-Century Religious Diversity. Richard W. Pointer. LC 87-45371. (Illus.). 224p. 1988. 11.95 (*0-253-34643-6*) Ind U Pr.

Protestant Poetics & the Seventeenth-Century Religious Lyric. Barbara K. Lewalski. LC 78-70305. (Illus.). 563p. reprint ed. pap. 174.60 (*0-8357-4284-9*, 203708300007) Bks Demand.

Protestant Politics: Jacob Sturm (1489-1553) & the German Reformation. Thomas A. Brady, Jr. LC 93-3015. (Studies in Central European Histories). 536p. (C). 1995. text 75.00 (*0-391-03823-0*) Humanities.

P

Protestant Presence in Twentieth-Century America: Religion & Political Culture. Phillip E. Hammond. LC 91-31731. (SUNY Series in Religion, Culture, & Society). 199p. (C). 1992. pap. text 21.95 (*0-7914-1122-2*) State U NY Pr.

Protestant Reformati. Ed. by Hans J. Hillerbrand. (Documentary History of Western Civilization Ser.). 320p. 1968. pap. 15.00 (*0-06-131342-4*, TB 1342, Torch) HarpC.

Protestant Reformation. Ed. by Hans J. Hillerbrand. (Orig.). 1992. 30.00 (*0-8446-6626-2*) Peter Smith.

Protestant Reformation 3rd rev. ed. 190p. (C). 1990. pap. 35.20 (*0-536-57840-0*) Pearson Custom.

Protestant Reformation in Europe. (Seminar Studies in History). 128p. (C). 1995. pap. 15.93 (*0-582-07020-1*) Longman.

Protestant Reformation in Ireland, 1590-1641. Alan Ford. LC 97-101114. 256p. 1997. pap. text 25.00 (*1-85182-282-8*, Pub. by Four Cts Pr); boxed set 65.00 (*1-85182-314-X*, Pub. by Four Cts Pr) Intl Spec Bk.

Protestant Reformation in Sixteenth-Century Italy. Salvatore Caponetto. Tr. by John Tedeschi & Anne C. Tedeschi from ITA. LC 98-3776. (Sixteenth Century Essays & Studies: No. 43). Orig. Title: La Riforma Protestante Nell'Italia del Cinquecento. (Illus.): 416p. 1999. 45.00 (*0-943549-67-1*) Truman St Univ.

Protestant Reformers in Elizabethan England. C. M. Dent. (Oxford Theological Monographs). 272p. (C). 1983. text 49.95 (*0-19-826723-1*) OUP.

Protestant Romance: Patterns of Reality in the Prose of Sir Giovanni Francesco Biondi. William M. Jones. 131p. 1980. 15.00 (*0-87291-138-1*) Coronado Pr.

***Protestant Scholasticism: Essays in Reassessment.** Ed. by Carl R. Trueman & R. S. Clarke. xx, 344p. 1999. pap. text 35.00 (*0-85364-853-0*, Pub. by Paternoster Pub) Eisenbrauns.

Protestant Search for Political Realism, 1919-1941. 2nd ed. Donald B. Meyer. LC 88-17509. 519p. reprint ed. pap. 160.90 (*0-608-09091-3*, 206972500005) Bks Demand.

Protestant Sensibility in the American Novel: An Annotated Bibliography. Leo F. O'Connor. LC 91-38034. 224p. 1991. text 10.00 (*0-8240-4605-6*, H1082) Garland.

***Protestant Spiritual Exercises: Theology, History & Practice.** Joseph D. Driskill. LC 99-12527. 152p. 1999. pap. 12.95 (*0-8192-1759-X*) Morehouse Pub.

Protestant Spiritual Traditions. Ed. by Frank C. Senn. 288p. (Orig.). 1986. pap. 9.95 (*0-8091-2761-X*) Paulist Pr.

Protestant Temperament: Patterns of Child-Rearing, Religious Experience, & the Self in Early America. Philip Greven. xiv, 446p. 1988. pap. text 15.95 (*0-226-30830-8*) U Ch Pr.

Protestant Theological Education in America: A Bibliography. Heather F. Day. LC 85-18300. (American Theological Library Association Monograph: No. 15). 523p. 1985. 45.00 (*0-8108-1842-6*) Scarecrow.

Protestant Thought. Karl Barth. LC 73-142606. (Essay Index Reprint Ser.). 1977. 32.95 (*0-8369-2102-X*) Ayer.

Protestant Thought & Natural Science. John Dillenberger. LC 88-23214. (C). 1988. pap. text 16.50 (*0-268-01575-9*) U of Notre Dame Pr.

Protestant Thought & Natural Science: A Historical Interpretation. John Dillenberger. LC 77-7200. 310p. 1977. reprint ed. lib. bdg. 35.00 (*0-8371-9670-1*, DIPT, Greenwood Pr) Greenwood.

Protestant Thought in the Nineteenth Century, Vol. 1. Claude Welch. LC 72-75211. 335p. (C). 1988. reprint ed. pap. 20.00 (*0-300-04200-0*) Yale U Pr.

Protestant Thought in the Nineteenth Century, Vol. 2. Claude Welch. LC 72-75211. 315p. (C). 1988. reprint ed. pap. 20.00 (*0-300-04201-9*) Yale U Pr.

Protestant Thought in the Nineteenth Century, 1870-1914 Vol. 2. Claude Welch. LC 72-75211. 328p. (C). 1985. 47.00 (*0-300-03369-9*) Yale U Pr.

Protestant Thought in the Twentieth Century: Whence & Whither? Ed. by Arnold S. Nash. LC 78-5860. 296p. 1978. reprint ed. lib. bdg. 65.00 (*0-313-20484-5*, NAPT, Greenwood Pr) Greenwood.

Protestant Throught in the Nineteenth Century, 1799-1870, Vol. 1. Claude Welch. LC 72-75211. 336p. reprint ed. 104.20 (*0-8357-9459-8*, 201320000086) Bks Demand.

Protestant vs. Catholic in Mid-Victorian England: Mr. Newdegate & the Nuns. Walter L. Arnstein. LC 81-11451. 288p. 1982. text 28.00 (*0-8262-0354-X*) U of Mo Pr.

Protestant Wedding Sourcebook: A Complete Guide for Developing Your Own Service. Sidney F. Batts. LC 92-19807. 192p. (Orig.). 1993. pap. 25.00 (*0-664-25303-2*) Westminster John Knox.

Protestant Work Ethic: The Psychology of Work-Related Beliefs & Behaviours. Adrian Furnham. LC 89-33213. 321p. reprint ed. pap. 99.60 (*0-608-20343-2*, 207159600002) Bks Demand.

Protestant Work Ethics: A Study of Work Ethical Theories in Contemporary Protestant Theology. Carl-Henric Grenholm. (Uppsala Studies in Social Ethics: No. 15). 349p. (Orig.). 1993. pap. 58.50 (*91-554-3041-4*) Coronet Bks.

Protestant Worship: Traditions in Transition. James F. White. 288p. (Orig.). 1989. pap. 28.95 (*0-664-25037-8*) Westminster John Knox.

Protestant Worship Music: Its History & Practice. Charles L. Etherington. LC 77-15990. (Illus.). 278p. 1978. reprint ed. lib. bdg. 65.00 (*0-313-20024-6*, ETPW, Greenwood Pr) Greenwood.

Protestantes/Protestants: Hispanic Christianity Within Mainline Traditions. David Maldonado, Jr. LC 98-31142. 400p. 1999. pap. 24.95 (*0-687-05509-1*) Abingdon.

***Protestantische Theologie und moderne Welt: Studien zur Geschichte der liberalen Theologie nach 1918.** Matthias Wolfes. 1999. 186.00 (*3-11-016639-9*) De Gruyter.

Protestantism. Ed. by William K. Anderson. LC 69-18918. (Essay Index Reprint Ser.). 1977. 20.95 (*0-8369-1018-4*) Ayer.

Protestantism & Jungian Psychology. Ed. by J. Marvin Spiegelman. LC 94-68555. (Religion & Psychology Ser.). 192p. (Orig.). 1994. pap. 12.95 (*1-56184-120-X*) New Falcon Pubns.

Protestantism & Latinos in the United States: An Original Anthology. Ed. by Carlos E. Cortes. LC 79-6266. (Hispanics in the United States Ser.). (Illus.). 1981. lib. bdg. 56.95 (*0-405-13173-9*) Ayer.

Protestantism & National Identity: Britain & Ireland, c. 1650-c. 1850. Ed. by Tony Claydon & Ian McBride. LC 99-211225. (Illus.). 330p. (C). 1999. text 64.95 (*0-521-62077-5*) Cambridge U Pr.

Protestantism & Patriotism: Ideologies & the Making of English Foreign Policy, 1650-1668. Steven C. Pincus. (Cambridge Studies in Early Modern British History). 518p. (C). 1996. text 74.95 (*0-521-43487-4*) Cambridge U Pr.

Protestantism & Politics in Eastern Europe & Russia: The Communist & Post-Communist Eras. Ed. by Sabrina P. Ramet. LC 92-9418. (Christianity under Stress Ser.: Vol. 3). 408p. 1993. text 46.95 (*0-8223-1241-7*) Duke.

Protestantism & Poor Relief in the "Genova of the North" Social Welfare Reform, in Early Modern Emden. Timothy G. Fehler. LC 98-52490. (St. Andrews Studies in Reformation History). (Illus.). 320p. 1999. text 86.95 (*1-85928-378-0*) Ashgate Pub Co.

***Protestantism & Progress: A Historical Study of the Relation of Protestantism to the Modern World.** Ernst Troeltsch & W. Montgomery. 220p. 1999. pap. 18.00 (*1-57910-226-3*) Wipf & Stock.

Protestantism & Regionalism see Modern American Protestantism & Its World

Protestantism & Repression: A Brazilian Case Study. Rubem A. Alves. Ed. by Jamie Wright. Tr. by John Drury. LC 82-3594.Tr. of Protestantismo e repressao. 255p. (Orig.). reprint ed. pap. 79.10 (*0-8357-8539-4*, 203484300091) Bks Demand.

Protestantism & Revolution in Cuba. Marcos A. Ramos. 168p. (C). 1989. pap. text 16.95 (*0-614-11068-8*) Transaction Pubs.

Protestantism & Social Christianity see Modern American Protestantism & Its World

Protestantism & the American University: An Intellectual Biography of William Warren Sweet. James L. Ash, Jr. LC 82-10629. (Illus.). 180p. 1982. 15.95 (*0-87074-183-7*) SMU Press.

Protestantism & the National Church in 16th Century England. Peter Lake & Maria Dowling. 224p. 1987. lib. bdg. 55.00 (*0-7099-1681-7*, Pub. by C Helm) Routldge.

Protestantism & the New South: North Carolina Baptists & Methodists in Political Crisis, 1894-1903. Frederick A. Bode. LC 75-1289. 184p. reprint ed. pap. 57.10 (*0-8357-2705-X*, 203981800013) Bks Demand.

Protestantism, Capitalism & Nature in America. Mark Stoll. LC 96-253251. 272p. 1997. 50.00 (*0-8263-1780-4*); pap. 24.95 (*0-8263-1781-2*) U of NM Pr.

Protestantism in Central America. Wilton M. Nelson. LC 84-13727. 96p. reprint ed. pap. 30.00 (*0-608-17708-3*, 203006900067) Bks Demand.

Protestantism in Guatemala: Living in the New Jerusalem. Virginia Garrard-Burnett. LC 97-49864. (Illus.). 280p. 1998. 30.00 (*0-292-72816-6*); pap. 14.95 (*0-292-72817-4*) U of Tex Pr.

Protestantism in Latin America see Protestantismo en America Latina

Protestantism in the Sangre de Cristos, 1850-1920. Randi J. Walker. LC 91-18285. (Illus.). 173p. 1991. reprint ed. pap. 53.70 (*0-608-07863-8*, 205404600011) Bks Demand.

Protestantismo e repressao see Protestantism & Repression: A Brazilian Case Study

Protestantismo en America Latina. Pablo Deiros.Tr. of Protestantism in Latin America. (SPA.). 1997. 8.99 (*0-89922-295-1*, C085-2951) Caribe Betania.

Protestantismus in Zentralamerika: Christliches Zeugnis Im Spannungsfeld von U. S.-Amerikanischem Fundamentalismus, Unterdruckung und Wiederbelebung "Indianischer" Kultur. Heinrich Schafer. (Studien zur Interkulturellen Geschichte des Christentums, 0170-9240, Studies in the Intercultural History of Christianity: Bd. 84). (GER., Illus.). 350p. 1992. 63.80 (*3-631-44655-1*) P Lang Pubng.

Protestants Against Poverty: Boston's Charities, 1870-1900, 9. Nathan I. Huggins. LC 70-105980. (Contributions in American History Ser.: No. 9). 225p. 1970. 55.00 (*0-8371-3307-6*, HUP/, Greenwood Pr) Greenwood.

Protestants & Catholics: Do They Now Agree? John Ankerberg & John Weldon. 1995. pap. 9.99 (*1-56507-314-2*) Harvest Hse.

Protestants & Pictures: Religion, Visual Culture & the Age of American Mass Production. David Morgan. LC 98-45312. (Illus.). 432p. 1999. 35.00 (*0-19-513029-4*) OUP.

Protestants & the Formation of Modern Korean Nationalism, 1885-1920: A Study of the Contributions of Horace G. Underwood & Sun Chu Kil. In Soo Kim. LC 94-10909. (Asian Thought & Culture Ser.: Vol. 16). VIII, 215p. (C). 1996. text 45.95 (*0-8204-2570-2*) P Lang Pubng.

Protestants & the Mexican Revolution: Missionaries, Ministers & Social Change. Deborah Baldwin. 216p. 1990. text 26.95 (*0-252-01659-9*) U of Ill Pr.

Protestants First: Orangeism in Nineteenth-Century Scotland. Elaine MacFarland. (Illus.). 224p. 1991. 55.00 (*0-7486-0202-X*, Pub. by Edinburgh U Pr) Col U Pr.

Protestants First: Orangeism in 19th Century Scotland. Elaine W. McFarland. (Illus.). 224p. 1992. pap. 28.00 (*0-7486-0216-X*, Pub. by Edinburgh U Pr) Col U Pr.

Protestants in a Catholic State: Ireland's Privileged Minority. Kurt Bowen. 240p. 1983. 55.00 (*0-7735-0412-5*, Pub. by McG-Queens Univ Pr) CUP Services.

***Protestants in America.** Mark Noll. (Religion in American Life Ser.). (Illus.). 144p. (YA). 2000. text 22.00 (*0-19-511034-X*) OUP.

Protestants in an Age of Science: The Baconian Ideal & Antebellum American Religious Thought. Theodore D. Bozeman. LC 76-25962. 259p. reprint ed. pap. 80.30 (*0-7837-0297-3*, 204061800018) Bks Demand.

Protestants in Russia. J. A. Hebly. Tr. by John Pott. LC 76-149. 192p. reprint ed. pap. 59.60 (*0-608-30408-5*, 201274100083) Bks Demand.

Protestants in the Ukrainian Lands of the Polish-Lithuanian Commonwealth. George H. Williams. 84p. 1994. write for info. (*0-940465-05-1*) Ukrainian Studies Fund.

Protestants Plea for a Socinian: Justifying His Doctrine from Being Opposite to Scripture or Church-Authority; & Him from Being Guilty of Heresie, or Schism, in Five Conferences. Abraham Woodhead. LC 92-25425. (Augustan Reprints Ser.: No. 243). 1987. reprint ed. 14.50 (*0-404-70243-0*, BT1480) AMS Pr.

Protestants Theologie. F. William Paterson. LC 77-362661. (English Recusant Literature, 1558-1640 Ser.). 309p. 1976. write for info. (*0-85967-330-8*) Scolar Pr.

Protestation of the Generall Assemblie Made in the High Kirk, & at the Mercate Crosse of Glasgow. LC 79-26239. (English Experience Ser.: No. 343). 1971. reprint ed. 7.00 (*90-221-0343-9*) Walter J Johnson.

Protestation Returns, 1641-1642 & Other Contemporary. J. S. W. Gibson & Alan Dell. 83p. 1995. pap. 10.00 (*0-8063-1564-4*) Genealog Pub.

Protesters on Trial: Criminal Justice in the Southern Civil Rights & Vietnam Antiwar Movements. Steven E. Barkan. (Crime, Law & Deviance Ser.). 190p. (C). 1985. text 35.00 (*0-8135-1108-9*) Rutgers U Pr.

Protestors for Paradise: The Story of Christian Reformers from the Thirteenth to the Twenty-First Century. Frances Gumley & Brian Redhead. (Illus.). 176p. 1994. 27.95 (*0-563-36478-5*, BBC-Parkwest) Parkwest Pubns.

***Protests & Appeals: A Competitor's Guide.** Willis. (Illus.). 95p. 2000. pap. 16.95 (*1-898660-17-4*, Pub. by Fernhurst Bks) Motorbooks Intl.

Protests & Visions: Peace Politics in 20th Century Britain. James Hinton. 1989. pap. 11.95 (*0-09-173005-8*, Pub. by Hutchnson) Trafalgar.

Proteus. Robert Adams. (C). Date not set. pap. write for info. (*0-393-09974-1*, Norton Paperbks) Norton.

Proteus. large type ed. Morris West. 510p. 1981. 27.99 (*0-7089-0642-7*) Ulverscroft.

Proteus Combined. Charles Sheffield. 496p. 1994. reprint ed. per. 5.99 (*0-671-87603-1*) Baen Bks.

Proteus Echo. Mather Byles. LC 86-31375. 224p. 1987. 50.00 (*0-8201-1420-0*) Schol Facsimiles.

Proteus in the Underworld. Charles Sheffield. 320p. 1995. mass mkt. 5.99 (*0-671-87659-7*) Baen Bks.

Proteus Operation. James Patrick Hogan. 480p. 1996. mass mkt. 5.99 (*0-671-87757-7*) Baen Bks.

Prothesis & Ekphora in Greek Geometric Art, Text & Figures, 2 vols. Gudrun Ahlberg. (Studies in Mediterranean Archaeology: Vol. XXXII). (Illus.). 385p. 1971. pap. 85.00 (*91-85058-50-5*, Pub. by P Astroms) Coronet Bks.

Prothesis und Ihre Bildausstattung in Byzanz Unter Besonderer Berucksichtigung der Denkmaler Griechenlands. Michael Altripp. Ed. by Peter Schreiner. (Studien und Texte Zur Byzantinistik Ser.: Vol. 4). (Illus.). XII, 334p. 1998. pap. 67.95 (*3-631-32382-4*) P Lang Pubng.

Prothrombin & Other Vitamin K Proteins, Vol. I. Ed. by Walter H. Seegers & Daniel A. Walz. LC 85-7869. 208p. 1986. 104.00 (*0-8493-6308-X*, QP93, CRC Reprint) Franklin.

Prothrombin & Other Vitamin K Proteins, Vol. II. Ed. by Daniel A. Walz & Walter H. Seegers. 192p. 1986. 94.00 (*0-8493-6309-8*, QP93) CRC Pr.

Prothrombin & Related Coagulation Factors. H. Coenraad Hemker. 1975. text 141.50 (*90-6021-236-3*) Kluwer Academic.

Protista I: Slime Molds,Eugleno. Evert. 1998. 1.50 (*0-7167-9360-1*) W H Freeman.

Protista II: Heterekonts & Gree. Evert. 1998. pap. 1.50 (*0-7167-9361-X*) W H Freeman.

Protistan Cell Surface. Ed. by R. Wetherbee et al. LC 94-33622. 1994. write for info. (*0-387-82621-1*) Spr-Verlag.

Protistan Cell Surface. Ed. by R. Wetherbee et al. LC 94-33622. 1995. 251.95 (*3-211-82621-1*) Spr-Verlag.

Proto-Dimensions, Vol. 1. Lester Smith. (Dark Conspiracy Ser.). 104p. (Orig.). (YA). 1992. pap. 12.00 (*1-55878-114-5*) Game Designers.

Proto-Draft Modules. Southwestern Staff. (Drafting Ser.). 1983. teacher ed. 21.44 (*0-538-33361-8*) S-W Pub.

Proto-Elamite Settlement at TUV. Ilene M. Nicholas. Ed. by William M. Sumner. (University Museum Monographs: Malayn Excavation Reports: No. 69, Report #1). (Illus.). xx, 164p. 1990. text 55.00 (*0-934718-86-5*) U Museum Pubns.

Proto-Finno-Ugric Antecedents of the Hungarian Phonetic Stock. Gyorgy Lako. LC 67-66163. (Uralic & Altaic Ser.: Vol. 80). 1966. reprint ed. spiral bd. write for info. (*0-87750-030-4*) Curzon Pr Ltd.

Proto-Gbaya. E. Peters. 1998. 51.00 (*90-6831-743-1*, Pub. by Peeters Pub) Bks Intl VA.

Proto-Historic India. K. P. Nautiyal. (C). 1989. 76.00 (*0-8364-2481-6*, Pub. by Agam) S Asia.

Proto-Historic Pottery of Indus Valley Civilisation: Study of Painted Motifs. Sudha Satyawadi. (C). 1994. 110.00 (*81-246-0030-9*, Pub. by DK Pubs Ind) S Asia.

Proto-Indo-European: The Archaeology of a Linguistic Problem: Papers in Honor of Marija Gimbutas. Ed. by Susan S. Skomal & Edgar C. Polome. 400p. 1994. pap. 52.00 (*0-941694-29-1*) Inst Study Man.

Proto-Indo-European Syntax: The Order of Meaningful Elements. Paul Friedrich. (Journal of Indo-European Studies: No. 1). 78p. (C). 1996. reprint ed. pap. 18.00 (*0-941694-25-9*) Inst Study Man.

Proto-Indo-European Trees: The Arboreal System of a Prehistoric People. Paul Friedrich. LC 70-104332. (C). 1994. lib. bdg. 16.00 (*0-226-26480-7*) U Ch Pr.

Proto-Industrialisation in Scandinavia: Craft Skills in the Industrial Revolution. Naths Isacson & lars Magnusson. LC 86-32062. 151p. 1987. 19.50 (*0-85496-514-9*) Berg Pubs.

Proto-Lima: A Middle Period Culture of Peru. Appendix: Cloths. Alfred L. Kroeber. LC 55-14208. (Chicago Natural History Museum Anthropology Ser.: Vol. 44, No. 1). (Illus.). 159p. 1954. reprint ed. pap. 49.30 (*0-608-02717-0*, 206338200004) Bks Demand.

Proto Lolo-Burmese. Robbins Burling. LC 66-64406. (General Publications: Vol. 43). (Orig.). 1967. pap. text 16.00 (*0-87750-131-9*) Res Inst Inner Asian Studies.

Proto-Oncogenes in Cell Development - Symposium No. 150. CIBA Foundation Staff. LC 90-11986. (CIBA Foundation Symposium Ser.: No. 150). 306p. 1990. 128.00 (*0-471-92686-8*) Wiley.

Proto Otomanguean Kinship. William R. Merrifield. LC 80-50558. (International Museum of Cultures Publications: No. 11). 400p. (Orig.). 1981. pap. 12.50 (*0-88312-161-1*) S I L Intl.

Proto-Romance & Sicilian. Michael L. Mazzola. 142p. 1976. pap. 21.00 (*90-316-0088-1*, Pub. by B R Gruner) Humanities.

Proto-Romance Morphology Vol. III: Comparative Romance Grammar. Robert A. Hall, Jr. (Current Issues in Linguistic Theory Ser.: No 30). xii, 304p. 1984. 65.00 (*90-272-3522-8*) J Benjamins Pubng Co.

Proto-Sinaitic Inscriptions & Their Decipherment. William F. Albright. LC 73-248003. (Harvard Theological Studies: No. 22). 50p. reprint ed. pap. 30.00 (*0-608-18593-0*, 201750500007) Bks Demand.

Proto-Slavic & Old Bulgarian Sound Changes. Boryana Velcheva. Tr. by Ernest A. Scatton from BUL. (Illus.). 187p. 1988. pap. 22.95 (*0-89357-189-X*) Slavica.

Proto-Takanan Phonology. Victor Girard. LC 76-631856. (U. C. Publ. in Linguistics Ser.: Vol. 70). 219p. reprint ed. 67.90 (*0-8357-9638-8*, 201509700092) Bks Demand.

Proto Thinker. Barker. 1997. 3.5 hd 11.00 (*0-534-53487-2*) Brooks-Cole.

Proto Witotoan. Richard P. Aschmann. LC 93-60089. (Publications in Linguistics Ser.: Vol. 114). viii, 168p. 1993. pap. 17.00 (*0-88312-189-1*) S I L Intl.

Protobiology: Physical Basis of Biology. Koichiro Matsuno. 272p. 1989. 136.00 (*0-8493-6403-5*, QH505, CRC Reprint) Franklin.

Protoceratops. Janet Riehecky. (Dinosaurs Bks.). (Illus.). 32p. (J). (gr. k-4). 1990. lib. bdg. 21.36 (*0-89565-634-5*) Childs World.

Protoceratops. Janet Riehecky. (Libros Sobre Dinosaurios! Ser.). (SPA., Illus.). 32p. (J). (gr. k-4). 1994. lib. bdg. 21.36 (*1-56766-144-0*) Childs World.

Protoceratops: A Dinosaur from the Cretaceous Period see New Dinosaur Collection

Protochlorophyllide Reduction & Greening. Ed. by C. Sironval & M. Brouers. (Advances in Agricultural Biotechnology Ser.). 1984. text 185.50 (*90-247-2954-8*) Kluwer Academic.

***Protocol.** April Christofferson. LC 99-33234. 304p. 1999. 23.95 (*0-312-86638-0*, Pub. by Forge NYC) St Martin.

***Protocol.** April Christofferson. 384p. 2000. mass mkt. 6.99 (*0-8125-6188-0*) Tor Bks.

***Protocol.** Steven Ford. 2000. mass mkt. 6.99 (*0-425-17402-6*) Berkley Pub.

Protocol: The Complete Handbook of Diplomatic Official & Social Usage. rev. ed. Maryjane McCaffree & Pauline B. Innis. LC 85-71131. (Illus.). 414p. 1998. reprint ed. pap. text 20.00 (*0-941402-04-5*) Devon Pub.

***Protocol Additional to the Geneva Conventions of 12 August 1949, & Relating to the Protection of Victims of International Armed Conflicts (Protocol I) Geneva, 8 June 1977.** (Treaty Series (Great Britain): Vol. 29, 1999). 76p. 1999. pap. 25.00 (*0-10-143382-4*, HM33824, Pub. by Statnry Office) Balogh.

Protocol Adjusting: The Agreement on the European Economic Area. 50p. 1994. pap. 8.00 (*92-824-1100-1*, RX-80-93-606ENC, Pub. by Comm Europ Commun) Bernan Associates.

Protocol Advantage. Jonathan R. Moller. LC 93-93668. (Illus.). 408p. (Orig.). 1993. pap. 110.00 (*1-884045-00-6*) Protocol Res.

Protocol Advantage: A Comprehensive Guide to Modern Protocol, Etiquette & Dignitary Management Techniques. rev. ed. Jonathan R. Moller. (Illus.). 400p. 1997. 60.00 (*1-884045-02-2*) Protocol Res.

Protocol Amending the European Social Charter & Explanatory Report. (Conventions & Agreements Ser.: No. 142). (ENG & FRE.). 1996. 12.00 (*92-871-2985-1*, Pub. by Council of Europe) Manhattan Pub Co.

Protocol Amending the European Social Charter (Turin, 1991) Council of Europe Staff. (Conventions & Agreements Ser.: No. 142). (ENG & FRE.). 1991. 12.00 (*92-871-2014-5*, Pub. by Council of Europe) Manhattan Pub Co.

An Asterisk (*) at the beginning of an entry indicates that the title is appearing for the first time.

Protocol Analysis: Verbal Reports As Data. rev. ed. K. Anders Ericsson & Herbert A. Simon. LC 92-33817. (Illus.). 420p. 1993. 45.00 (*0-262-05047-1*); pap. text 27.50 (*0-262-55023-7*) MIT Pr.

Protocol & Etiquette of Golf: The Golfer's Guide to Proper Behavior on the Golf Course. Bill Bailey. (Illus.). 112p. (Orig.). 1993. pap. 9.95 (*1-55958-358-4*) Prima Pub.

Protocol & Guidelines for Monotoring & Evaluation Procedures. Ed. by E. Leparsky & F. E. Nussel. xiii, 60p. 1987. pap. 32.70 (*0-387-18458-9*) Spr-Verlag.

Protocol & Procedures for Quality Assurance of Linear Accelerators. Chris Constantinou. (Illus.). (Orig.). (C). 1993. pap. write for info. (*0-9638266-0-3*); text. write for info. (*0-9638266-1-1*) CNC Med Physics.

Protocol Conformance Testing Using Unique Input/Output Sequences. LC 97-36332. 400p. 1997. lib. bdg. 42.00 (*981-02-2832-5*) World Scientific Pub.

Protocol Design for Local & Metropolitan Area Networks. Pawel Gburzynski. LC 95-11160. 730p. 1995. 52.60 (*0-13-554270-7*) P-H.

Protocol for a Kidnapping. Ross Thomas. 224p. 1993. mass mkt. 4.99 (*0-446-40176-5*, Pub. by Warner Bks) Little.

***Protocol for Clinical Reference Dosimetry of High-Energy Photon & Electron Beams No. 67: Report of the AAPM Radiation Therapy Committee TG No. 51.** Peter R. Almond et al. 22p. 2000. pap. text. write for info. (*1-888340-25-8*) AAPM.

Protocol for Improving Sheltered Instruction. Jana Echevarria & MaryEllen Vogt. LC 99-48623. 212p. (C). 1999. pap. text 27.00 (*0-205-29017-5*, Longwood Div) Allyn.

Protocol for Murder. Paul Nathan. LC 93-27529. 176p. 1994. 22.00 (*1-877946-46-X*); pap. 16.00 (*1-877946-64-8*) Permanent Pr.

Protocol for Phallometric Assessment: A Clinician's Guide. Deloris T. Roys & Pat Roys. Ed. by Euan Bear. 78p. (Orig.). 1999. pap., student ed. 10.00 (*1-884444-11-3*) Safer Soc.

Protocol for Profit: A Manager's Guide to Competing Worldwide, Vol. 1. Nelson. LC 98-218553. 256p. 1998. pap. 20.00 (*1-86152-314-9*) Thomson Learn.

Protocol for the International Collaborative Exercises within the International Quality Assurance Programme. 36p. 7.50 (*92-1-148110-4*) UN.

***Protocol for Touch.** Constance Merritt. Ed. by Scott Cairns. LC 99-54652. (Vassar Miller Prize in Poetry Ser.: Vol. 7). 86p. 1999. pap. 12.95 (*1-57441-083-0*, Pub. by UNTX Pr) Tex A&M Univ Pr.

***Protocol in Srimad Bhagawat.** Devi D. Aggarwal. LC 99-931371. 298p. 1999. write for info. (*81-7479-022-5*) S Asia.

***Protocol Management in Computer Networking.** Philippe Byrnes. LC 99-52313. (Telecommunications Library). 464p. 2000. 89.00 (*1-58053-069-9*) Artech Hse.

Protocol of Amendment to the European Convention for the Protection of Animals Kept for Farming Purposes (Strasbourg, 1992) Council of Europe Staff. (Conventions & Agreements Ser.: No. 145). (ENG & FRE.). 1992. 12.00 (*92-871-2062-5*, Pub. by Council of Europe) Manhattan Pub Co.

Protocol of Amendment to the Interamerican Treaty of Reciprocal Assistance (Rio Treaty) (Treaty Ser.: No. 46). (ENG, FRE, POR & SPA.). 14p. 1975. pap. text 1.00 (*0-8270-0540-7*) OAS.

Protocol of Neferyt, The Prophecy of Neferti. Hans Goedicke. LC 76-47371. (Johns Hopkins Near Eastern Studies). 214p. reprint ed. pap. 66.40 (*0-8357-6611-X*, 203525600094) Bks Demand.

Protocol of 1988 Relating to Solas, 1974. International Maritime Organization Staff. 1989. text 110.00 (*0-89771-857-7*, Pub. by Intl Maritime Org) St Mut.

Protocol of Nineteen Eighty-Eight Relating to the International Convention on Load Lines, 1966. International Maritime Organization Staff. 1989. text 80.00 (*0-89771-978-6*, Pub. by Intl Maritime Org) St Mut.

Protocol of the Gods: A Study of the Kasuga Cult in Japanese History. Allan G. Grapard. LC 92-16300. 1992. 55.00 (*0-520-07097-6*, Pub. by U CA Pr) Cal Prin Full Svc.

Protocol Packages. Sivasailam Thiagarajan. Ed. by Danny G. Langdon. LC 79-23503. (Instructional Design Library). 128p. 1980. 27.95 (*0-87778-151-6*) Educ Tech Pubns.

Protocol Specification & Testing. K. Tarnay. (Illus.). 392p. (C). 1991. 110.00 (*0-306-43574-8*, Plenum Trade) Perseus Pubng.

Protocol Specification & Testing Technical Sciences, Advances in Electronics 5. Katie Tarnay. 390p. 1991. 430.00 (*963-05-5861-0*, Pub. by Akade Kiado) St Mut.

Protocol Techniques in Cardiology. Simpson. (Illus.). 200p. 1998. pap. text. write for info. (*0-7020-1902-X*, W B Saunders Co) Harcrt Hlth Sci Grp.

Protocol to the Convention for the Protection of Human Rights & Fundamental Freedoms Restructuring the Control Machinery Established Thereby (Strasbourg, 1994), No. 11. (Conventions & Agreements Ser.: No. 155). (ENG & FRE.). 1994. 12.00 (*92-871-2513-9*, Pub. by Council of Europe) Manhattan Pub Co.

Protocol to the Convention for the Protection of Human Rights & Fundamental Freedoms (Strasbourg, 1992), No. 10. Council of Europe Staff. (Conventions & Agreements Ser.: No. 146). (ENG & FRE.). 1992. 12.00 (*92-871-2093-5*, Pub. by Council of Europe) Manhattan Pub Co.

Protocol to the Convention on Duties & Rights of States in the Event of Civil Strife. (Treaty Ser.: No. 7). (ENG, FRE, POR & SPA.). 1959. pap. 1.00 (*0-8270-0300-5*) OAS.

Protocol to the Convention on the Elaboration of a European Pharmacopoeia. Council of Europe Staff. (Conventions & Agreements Ser.: No. 134). (ENG & FRE.). 1989. 12.00 (*92-871-1781-0*, Pub. by Council of Europe) Manhattan Pub Co.

Protocol to the European Convention for the Prevention of Torture & Inhuman or Degrading Treatment or Punishment (Strasbourg, 1993), No. 1. (Conventions & Agreements Ser.: No. 151). (ENG & FRE.). 1993. 12.00 (*92-871-2454-X*, Pub. by Council of Europe) Manhattan Pub Co.

Protocol to the European Convention for the Prevention of Torture & Inhuman or Degrading Treatment or Punishment (Strasbourg, 1993), No. 2. (Conventions & Agreements Ser.: No. 152). (ENG & FRE.). 1993. 12.00 (*92-871-2455-8*, Pub. by Council of Europe) Manhattan Pub Co.

Protocol to the European Convention on Social Security. (Conventions & Agreements Ser.: No. 154). (ENG & FRE.). 1994. 12.00 (*92-871-2512-0*, Pub. by Council of Europe) Manhattan Pub Co.

Protocol to the European Convention on the Equivalence of Diplomas Leading to Admission to Universities. Council of Europe Staff. (Conventions & Agreements Ser.: No. 49). (ENG & FRE.). 1981. 12.00 (*92-871-0098-5*, Pub. by Council of Europe) Manhattan Pub Co.

Protocole Compassionnel. Herve Guibert. (Folio Ser.: No. 2481). (FRE.). 226p. 1991. pap. 29.95 (*2-07-038731-3*) Schoenhof.

***Protocols Acute Care Nurse Practice.** Barkley. 2001. pap. text. write for info. (*0-7216-8536-6*, W B Saunders Co) Harcrt Hlth Sci Grp.

Protocols by Invariants. A. Schoone. (International Series on Parallel Computation: No. 6). 200p. (C). 1996. text 49.95 (*0-521-44175-7*) Cambridge U Pr.

Protocols for Adapting Activities to the Changing Needs of People with Dementia. Ruth M. Griffin. 58p. (C). 1996. pap. text 11.00 (*0-935273-09-3*) Chess Pub.

Protocols for an All Taxa Biodiversity Inventory of Fungi in a Costa Rican Conservation Area: Report of the Fungus Twig Workshop 9-19 June 1995. Ed. by Amy Y. Rossman et al. LC 97-44635. (Illus.). xviii, 195p. (Orig.). (C). 1998. 35.00 (*1-887905-05-7*) Pkway Pubs.

Protocols for Application Communication. Keith Bearpark. LC 94-21734. 1994. write for info. (*0-07-709074-8*) McGraw.

Protocols for Evaluating Dehydrated Mueller-Hinton Agar: Approved Standard (1996) 1996. 75.00 (*1-56238-307-8*, M6-A) NCCLS.

Protocols for Evaluating Dehydrated Mueller-Hinton Agar: Tentative Standard, 1993. Contrib. by George L. Evans. 1993. 75.00 (*1-56238-215-2*, M6-T) NCCLS.

Protocols for Gene Analysis. Ed. by Adrian J. Harwood. LC 94-2365. (Methods in Molecular Biology Ser.: Vol. 31). (Illus.). 432p. 1994. pap., student ed. 69.50 (*0-89603-258-2*) Humana.

Protocols for Gene Trans in Ne. Ed. by P. R. Lowenstein & Lynn W. Enquist. LC 95-45487. 446p. 1996. pap. 229.95 (*0-471-95766-6*) Wiley.

Protocols for Gynecologic & Obstetric Health Care. Barger et al. 1987. pap. text 43.00 (*0-8089-1897-4*, Grune & Strat) Harcrt Hlth Sci Grp.

Protocols for Health Care Executive Behavior: A Factor for Success. Carson F. Dye. LC 93-14057. 231p. 1993. text 42.00 (*1-56793-000-X*, 0934) Health Admin Pr.

Protocols for High-Risk Pregnancies. 3rd ed. John T. Queenan et al. (Protocols in Obstetrics & Gynecology Ser.). 512p. 1995. pap. 49.95 (*0-86542-444-6*) Blackwell Sci.

***Protocols for Infectious Diseases in Obstetrics & Gynecology.** 2nd ed. Philip B. Mead et al. LC 99-30332. (Protocols in Obstetrics & Gynecology Ser.). (Illus.). 605p. 1999. pap. 49.95 (*0-632-04324-5*) Blackwell Sci.

Protocols for Neural Cell Culture. Ed. by Sergey Fedoroff & Arleen Richardson. LC 92-1532. (Illus.). 192p. 1992. 59.50 (*0-89603-228-0*) Humana.

Protocols for Neural Cell Culture. 2nd ed. Ed. by Sergey Fedoroff & Arleen Richardson. LC 96-41243. (Illus.). 280p. 1996. spiral bd. 69.50 (*0-89603-454-2*) Humana.

Protocols for Nucleic Acid Analysis by Nonradioactive Probes. Intro. by Peter G. Issac. LC 93-29390. (Methods in Molecular Biology Ser.: Vol. 28). (Illus.). 280p. 1993. pap. 64.50 (*0-89603-254-X*) Humana.

***Protocols for Nurse Practitioners in Gynecologic Settings.** 7th ed. Joellen Hawkins et al. (Illus.). 456p. (C). 1999. 45.00 (*0-913292-51-6*) Tiresias Pr.

Protocols for Office Gynecologic Surgery. Ed. by Philip D. Darney et al. (Protocols in Obstetrics & Gynecology Ser.). 400p. 1996. pap. 49.95 (*0-86542-374-1*) Blackwell Sci.

Protocols for Oligonucleotide Conjugates: Synthesis & Analytical Techniques. Ed. by Sudhir Agrawal. LC 93-23127. (Methods in Molecular Biology Ser.: Vol. 26). (Illus.). 390p. 1993. student ed., spiral bd. 99.50 (*0-89603-252-3*) Humana.

Protocols for Oligonucleotides & Analogs: Synthesis & Properties. Ed. by Sudhir Agrawal. LC 93-7121. (Methods in Molecular Biology Ser.: Vol. 20). 516p. 1993. 119.50 (*0-89603-281-7*); pap. 99.50 (*0-89603-247-7*) Humana.

Protocols for Recreation Therapy Programs. Alberta Hospital Edmonton, Recreation Therapy Staf. Ed. by Jill Kelland. LC 95-60642. 132p. (C). 1995. pap. 24.95 (*0-910251-73-8*, PRT79) Venture Pub PA.

Protocols for Secure Electronic Commerce. Ahmed Sehrouchni & Mostafa H. Sherif. (Advanced & Emerging Communications Technologies Ser.). 496p. 2000. boxed set 69.95 (*0-8493-9597-6*) CRC Pr.

Protocols for the Sex Abuse Evaluation. Richard A. Gardner. LC 94-39476. 431p. 1995. pap. text 40.00 (*0-933812-38-8*) Creative Therapeutics.

Protocols in Human Molecular Genetics. Ed. by Christopher G. Mathew. LC 91-25466. (Methods in Molecular Biology Ser.: Vol. 9). (Illus.). 472p. 1991. 89.50 (*0-89603-205-1*) Humana.

Protocols in Molecular Neurobiology, No. 13. Ed. by Alan Longstaff & Patricia Revest. LC 92-30701. (Methods in Molecular Biology Ser.: Vol. 13). (Illus.). 394p. 1992. spiral bd. 89.50 (*0-89603-199-3*) Humana.

Protocols in Molecular Parasitology. Ed. by John E. Hyde. LC 93-8540. (Methods in Molecular Biology Ser.: Vol. 21). (Illus.). 480p. 1993. 89.50 (*0-89603-239-6*) Humana.

Protocols in Neonatal Nursing: Physiological Perspective. 2nd ed. Carole A. Kenner. Ed. by Maura Connor. LC 97-48248. (Illus.). 704p. (C). 1998. pap. text 35.00 (*0-7216-6117-3*, W B Saunders Co) Harcrt Hlth Sci Grp.

Protocols in Primary Care Geriatrics. J. P. Sloan. (Illus.). 216p. 1993. 39.95 (*0-387-97395-8*) Spr-Verlag.

Protocols in Primary Care Geriatrics. 2nd ed. J. P. Sloan. 208p. 1996. pap. 36.00 (*0-387-94690-X*) Spr-Verlag.

Protocols of Reading. Robert Scholes. LC 89-5588. 192p. (C). 1989. 32.50 (*0-300-04513-1*) Yale U Pr.

Protocols of Reading. Robert Scholes. (Illus.). 192p. (C). 1991. reprint ed. pap. 14.00 (*0-300-05062-3*) Yale U Pr.

Protocols of the Learned Elders of Zion. Victor E. Marsden. pap. 7.95 (*0-685-17507-3*, Noontide Pr) Legion Survival.

Protocols of the Learned Elders of Zion. Tr. by Victor E. Marsden. 72p. 1996. pap. 4.00 (*0-944379-42-7*) CPA Bk Pub.

***Protocols of the Learned Elders of Zion.** Tr. by Victor E. Marsden. 299p. 1999. pap. 7.00 (*0-944379-41-9*) CPA Bk Pub.

Protocols of Zion. unabridged ed. Tr. by Nilus & Victor E. Marsden. 299p. 1934. reprint ed. pap. 12.00 (*0-945001-59-2*) GSG & Assocs.

Protoctist Glossary. Lynn Margulis et al. 1995. cd-rom 79.00 (*3-540-14199-5*) Spr-Verlag.

Protoctist Glossary. Lynn Margulis et al. 1995. 79.00 (*3-540-14510-9*) Spr-Verlag.

Protoctista Glossary. Lynn Margulis. 288p. (Orig.). (C). 1993. 53.75 (*0-86720-081-2*) Jones & Bartlett.

Protodynastic Egypt. Barbara Adams & Krzysztof Cialowicz. (Egyptology Ser.: No. 25). (Illus.). 64p. 1997. pap. 10.50 (*0-7478-0357-9*, Pub. by Shire Pubns) Parkwest Pubns.

Protogeometric Style: The First Greek Style. Robert L. Murray. (Studies in Mediterranean Archaeology: No. 2). (Illus.). 40p. 1975. pap. 14.95 (*91-85058-65-3*) P Astroms.

Protohistoric Period in the Mid-South, 1500-1700: Proceedings of the 1983 Mid-South Archaeological Conference. Ed. by David H. Dye & Ronald C. Brister. LC 86-620009. (Archaeological Report Ser.: No. 18). (Illus.). xiv, 102p. 1986. pap. text 5.00 (*0-938896-49-0*) Mississippi Archives.

Protohistoric Settlement on the Cittadella. Robert Leighton. (Morgantina Studies: No. 4). (Illus.). 265p. 1993. text 89.50 (*0-691-04015-X*, Pub. by Princeton U Pr) Cal Prin Full Svc.

Protohistoric Yamato: Archaeology of the First Japanese State. Gina L. Barnes. (Anthropological Papers Ser.: No. 78, Vol. 17). (Illus.). xx, 473p. (Orig.). (C). 1988. pap. text 19.95 (*0-915703-11-4*) U Mich Mus Anthro.

***Protokolliteratur in der DDR: Der Dokumentierte Alltag.** Reinhard Andress. (DDR-Studien/East German Studies: No. 14). (GER.). 232p. 2000. text 50.95 (*0-8204-4492-8*) P Lang Pubng.

Protomycetaceae of Switzerland: Life History & Biology. Gunther Von Buren. (C). 1987. 23.50 (*81-7087-007-0*, Pub. by Oxford IBH) S Asia.

Proton & Carbon NMR Spectra of Polymers. Pham. 1991. 330.00 (*0-8493-7728-5*, QC463) CRC Pr.

Proton-Antiproton Collider Physics. L. Diella & Guido Altarelli. (Advanced Series in Directions in High Energy Physics: Vol. 4). 416p. (C). 1989. text 99.00 (*9971-5-0562-2*); pap. text 52.00 (*9971-5-0563-0*) World Scientific Pub.

Proton-Antiproton Collider Physics: Madison, Wisconsin, 1982. American Institute of Physics. Ed. by V. Barger et al. LC 82-72141. (AIP Conference Proceedings Ser.: No. 85). 676p. 1982. lib. bdg. 42.00 (*0-88318-184-3*) Am Inst Physics.

Proton-Antiproton Collider Physics: Proceedings of the Sixth International Conference, Aachen, Germany, June 30-July 4, 1986. Ed. by K. Eggert et al. 872p. 1987. text 162.00 (*9971-5-0256-9*) World Scientific Pub.

Proton-Antiproton Collider Physics: Proceedings of the 7th Tropical Workshop. Ed. by Rajendran Raja & John Yoh. 912p. (C). 1989. text 138.00 (*9971-5-0754-4*) World Scientific Pub.

Proton-Antiproton Collider Physics: Proceedings of the 8th Tropical Workshop. Ed. by A. Scribano & G. Belletini. 700p. (C). 1990. text 173.00 (*981-02-0134-6*) World Scientific Pub.

Proton-Antiproton Collider Physics, 1985: Proceedings of the 5th Topical Workshop on Proton-Antiproton Collider Physics, Saint-Vincent Aosta Valley, 25 Feb.-March, 1985. Ed. by M. Greco. 700p. 1985. 125.00 (*9971-978-45-8*) World Scientific Pub.

Proton Conducting Membrane Fuel Cells. Ed. by A. R. Landgrebe et al. LC 95-61596. (Proceedings Ser.: Vol. 95-23). (Illus.). 318p. 1995. 61.00 (*1-56677-118-8*) Electrochem Soc.

***Proton Conducting Membrane Fuel Cells II.** International Symposium on Proton Conducting Membrane Fuel Cells et al. Ed. by Shimshon Gottesfeld & Thomas Francis Fuller. LC 99-201830. (Illus.). 506p. 1999. 87.00 (*1-56677-221-4*, PV 98-27) Electrochem Soc.

Proton Conductors: Solids, Membranes & Gels; Materials & Devices. Ed. by Philippe Colomban. (Chemistry of Solid State Materials Ser.: No. 3). (Illus.). 613p. (C). 1992. text 140.00 (*0-521-38317-X*) Cambridge U Pr.

***Proton Emitting Nuclei: PROCON '99 - First International Symposium.** Ed. by Jon C. Batchelder. LC 00-102142. (AIP Conference Proceedings Ser.: Vol. 518). (Illus.). xv, 351p. 2000. 110.00 (*1-56396-937-8*, Pub. by Am Inst Physics) Spr-Verlag.

Proton Microprobe: Applications in the Biomedical Field. Ed. by Ronald D. Vis. 208p. 1985. 121.00 (*0-8493-5718-7*, QH324, CRC Reprint) Franklin.

Proton Passage Across Cell Membranes. CIBA Foundation Staff. LC 88-25026. (CIBA Foundation Symposium Ser.: No. 139). 278p. 1988. 128.00 (*0-471-91903-9*) Wiley.

***Proton Pump Inhibitors.** Lars Olbe. LC 98-49154. (Milestones in Drug Therapy Ser.). 1999. write for info. (*0-8176-5897-1*) Birkhauser.

Proton Pump Inhibitors: Milestones in Drug Therapy. Ed. by L. Olbe. 250p. 1999. 138.00 (*3-7643-5897-1*) Birkhauser.

***Proton Therapy & Radiosurgery.** Hans Breuer & B. J. Smit. LC 99-35197. (Illus.). 305p. 1999. 146.00 (*3-540-64100-9*) Spr-Verlag.

Proton Transfer in Hydrogen-Bonded Systems. T. Bountis. (NATO ASI Ser.: Vol. 291). (Illus.). 379p. (C). 1992. text 120.00 (*0-306-44216-7*, Kluwer Plenum) Kluwer Academic.

Proton Transfer of Related Reactions see Comprehensive Chemical Kinetics

Protons & Muons in Materials Science. Ed. by E. A. Davis & S. F. Cox. 500p. 1996. 126.00 (*0-7484-0478-3*) Taylor & Francis.

Protooncogenes & Growth Factors in Steroid Hormone-Induced Growth & Differentiation. Ed. by Sohaib A. Khan & George M. Stancel. 288p. 1993. lib. bdg. 110.00 (*0-8493-8672-1*, SF105) CRC Pr.

Protophysics of Time: Constructive Foundation & history of Time Measurement. Peter Janich. Tr. by Robert Brown. (Boston Studies in the Philosophy of Science: No. 30). 264p. 1985. text 167.00 (*90-277-0724-3*) Kluwer Academic.

Protophysik: Entwurf einer Philosophie des Schopferischen. 1. Teil: Spezielle Relativitatstheorie. S. Muller-Markus. 438p. 1971. text 211.50 (*90-247-5106-3*) Kluwer Academic.

Protoplasts, 1983. 1984. 83.00 (*0-8176-1514-8*) Birkhauser.

Protoplasts Poster Proceedings 1983. Ed. by M. J. Norry et al. (Experientia Supplementa Ser.: Vol. 45). 388p. (C). 1983. pap. text 93.95 (*3-7643-1513-X*) Birkhauser.

Protoplasts Poster Proceedings 1983, Vol. 46. Ed. by M. J. Norry et al. (Experientia Supplementa Ser.: Vol. 45). 388p. (C). 1983. 70.95 (*3-7643-1514-8*) Birkhauser.

***Protostars & Planets IV.** Vincent Mannings. LC 99-50922. (Space Science Ser.). (Illus.). 1700p. 2000. 95.00 (*0-8165-2059-3*) U of Ariz Pr.

Prototractatus. Ludwig Josef Johann Wittgenstein. 264p. (C). 1997. 165.00 (*0-415-13667-9*) Routledge.

Prototype Action-Oriented School Health Curriculum for Primary Schools: National Guidelines. 1990. text, teacher ed. 43.20 (*92-9021-014-1*) World Health.

Prototype & Dream Cars. Dewar McLintock. (World of Wheels Ser.). (Illus.). (YA). (gr. 6 up). 19.95 (*0-614-21973-6*) Random.

***Prototype-Based Object-Oriented Programming: Concepts, Languages & Applications.** J. Noble et al. LC 98-50712. 324p. 1999. pap. 59.95 (*981-4021-25-3*) Spr-Verlag.

Prototype Church. Ruth S. Fajfr. pap. 2.49 (*1-56632-029-1*) Revival Lit.

Prototype of Hamlet & Other Shakespearian Problems. W. Preston Johnston. LC 71-170819. reprint ed. 31.50 (*0-404-03595-7*) AMS Pr.

Prototypes of Peacemaking: The First Forty Years of the U. N. Mary Allsebrook. 1987. 45.00 (*0-912289-72-4*) St James Pr.

Prototyping: An Approach to Evolutionary System Development. R. Budde et al. (Illus.). xi, 205p. 1992. 58.95 (*0-387-54352-X*) Spr-Verlag.

Prototyping a Microcomputer-Based Online Library Catalog. Susan S. Lazinger & Peretz Shoval. (Occasional Papers: No. 177). 1987. pap. 2.50 (*0-317-59035-9*) U of Ill Grad Sch.

Prototyping & Software Development. Malcolm Harrison. 1998. 49.95 (*0-387-98432-1*) Spr-Verlag.

Prototyping with Objects. Phillipe Krief & John Plaice. 250p. 1996. pap. 57.00 (*0-13-014713-3*) P-H.

Protozoa. 2nd ed. Theodore L. Jahn et al. (Pictured Key Nature Ser.). 304p. (C). 1978. text. write for info. (*0-697-04759-8*, WCB McGr Hill) McGrw-H Hghr Educ.

Protozoa: Ciliophora. B. L. Bhatia. (Fauna of British India Ser.). (Illus.). xxii, 522p. 1979. reprint ed. 30.00 (*0-88065-058-3*) Scholarly Pubns.

Protozoa: Sporozoa. B. L. Bhatia. (Fauna of British India Ser.). (Illus.). xx, 508p. 1979. reprint ed. 30.00 (*0-88065-103-2*) Scholarly Pubns.

Protozoa & Their Role in Marine Processes. Ed. by P. C. Reid et al. (NATO ASI Series G: Ecological Sciences: Vol. 25). x, 506p. 1991. 272.95 (*0-387-18565-8*) Spr-Verlag.

Protozoal Diseases: A Comprehensive Guide. Herbert M. Gilles. LC 98-55680. 740p. 2000. 195.00 (*0-340-74090-6*, Pub. by E A) OUP.

Protozoan Nucleus: Morphology & Evolution. I. B. Raikov. Tr. by Nicholas Bobrov & M. Verkhovsteva. (Cell Biology Monographs: Vol. 9). (Illus.). 450p. 1982. 216.95 (*0-387-81678-X*) Spr-Verlag.

Protozoan Parasites & Water, No. 168. Ed. by W. B. Betts et al. 260p. 1995. 99.95 (*0-85404-755-7*) CRC Pr.

P

An Asterisk (*) at the beginning of an entry indicates that the title is appearing for the first time.

Protozoan Parasites of Fishes. Iva Dykova & Jiri Lom. (Developments in Aquaculture & Fisheries Science Ser.: Vol. 26). 316p. 1992. 207.50 (*0-444-89434-9*) Elsevier.

Protozoan Parasites of Fishes. Jiri Lom & Iva Dykova. LC 92-15825. (Developments in Aquaculture & Fisheries Science Ser.: No. 24). 1992. 190.75 (*0-04-448943-9*) Elsevier.

Protozoan Phylum Apicomplexa, 2 vols., Vol. I. Ed. by Norman D. Levine. 240p. 1988. 124.00 (*0-8493-4653-3*, SF780, CRC Reprint) Franklin.

Protozoan Phylum Apicomplexa, 2 vols., Vol. II. Ed. by Norman D. Levine. 176p. 1988. 98.00 (*0-8493-4654-1*, CRC Reprint) Franklin.

Protozoology. K. Hausmann et al. LC 95-643. (Wehner Zoologie Ser.). (Illus.). 344p. 1995. text 59.00 (*0-86577-571-0*) Thieme Med Pubs.

Protozoology, 2 vols. 5th ed. Richard R. Kudo. (Illus.). 1188p. 1977. 171.95 (*0-398-01058-7*) C C Thomas.

Protractive Verse. Martin J. Rosenblum. 1976. pap. 0.50 (*0-89018-001-6*) Cats Pajamas.

Protreptici Quae Supersunt. Claudius Galenus. Ed. by Georg Kaibel. ix, 62p. 1963. write for info. (*3-296-12720-8*) G Olms Pubs.

Protura (Insecta) see Fauna of New Zealand Series

Protyping-Oriented Software Development: Concepts & Tools. Gustav Pomberger & W. Bischofberger. Ed. by David Gries. LC 92-18009. (Texts & Monographs in Computer Science). (Illus.). xi, 215p. 1992. 61.95 (*0-387-55448-3*) Spr-Verlag.

Proud. Fred Penner. (Illus.). 32p. (J). (ps-1). 1997. 10.95 (*1-56352-441-4*) Longstreet.

Proud Alliance. large type ed. Marion Carr. (Magna Large Print Ser.). 408p. 1996. 27.99 (*0-7505-0966-X*, Pub. by Mgna Lrg Print) Ulverscroft.

Proud American. Joe Foss & Donna W. Foss. (Illus.). 464p. 1993. reprint ed. mass mkt. 5.99 (*0-671-75746-6*, Pocket Star Bks) PB.

Proud & Ashamed. Laura Chester. 1977. 5.00 (*0-87922-128-3*) Christophers Bks.

Proud & the Free. Howard Fast. pap. write for info. (*0-318-57893-X*) HM.

Proud & the Free. large type ed. Janet Dailey. LC 94-42585. 647 p. 1995. 26.95 (*1-56895-167-1*) Wheeler Pub.

Proud Bastards. rev. ed. E. Michael Helms. LC 96-94726. vi, 226p. 1990. pap. 14.95 (*0-9653966-4-9*) Karmichael Pr.

Proud Beggars. Albert Cossery. Tr. by Thomas Cushing from FRE. LC 81-1095. 200p. (Orig.). 1981. 14.00 (*0-87685-451-X*); pap. 10.00 (*0-87685-450-1*) Black Sparrow.

Proud Beggars, signed ed. deluxe ed. Albert Cossery. Tr. by Thomas Cushing from FRE. LC 81-1095. 200p. (Orig.). 1981. 20.00 (*0-87685-452-8*) Black Sparrow.

Proud Child, Safer Child: A Handbook for Parents & Carers of Disabled Children. Merry Cross. 208p. 1999. pap. 15.95 (*0-7043-4561-7*, Pub. by Womens Press) Trafalgar.

Proud Citadel. large type ed. Theresa Charles. 336p. 1987. 27.99 (*0-7089-1697-X*) Ulverscroft.

Proud Citadel. large type ed. Stella Kent. (Linford Romance Library). 240p. 1993. pap. 16.99 (*0-7089-7408-2*, Linford) Ulverscroft.

Proud Decades: America in War & Peace, 1941-1960. John P. Diggins. (Illus.). (Orig.). (C). 1989. pap. 17.95 (*0-393-95656-3*) Norton.

Proud Donkey of Schaerbeek: Ade Bethune, Catholic Worker Artist. Judith Stoughton. LC 88-63680. (Illus.). 168p. 1988. 19.95 (*0-87839-051-0*) North Star.

Proud Frogs. Mirra Ginsburg. 1999. pap. write for info. (*0-14-050845-7*) NAL.

Proud Frogs. Mirra Ginsburg. 2000. write for info. (*0-670-82177-2*) Viking Penguin.

Proud Gun. Gordon D. Shirreffs. 128p. 1989. pap. 2.95 (*0-380-70641-5*, Avon Bks) Morrow Avon.

***Proud Heart, Fair Lady.** large type ed. Elayn Duffy. 352p. 1999. 31.99 (*0-7089-4087-0*) Ulverscroft.

Proud Hearts. Marylyle Rogers. Ed. by Carolyn Tolley. 352p. (Orig.). 1990. mass mkt. 5.50 (*0-671-70235-1*) PB.

Proud Helios, No. 9. Melissa Scott. Ed. by John Ordover. (Star Trek: Deep Space Nine Ser.). 288p. (Orig.). 1995. mass mkt. 5.50 (*0-671-88390-9*) PB.

Proud Heritage. Linda Bantel et al. Ed. by Terry A. Neff & Michael Sanden. (Two Centuries of American Art Ser.). (Illus.). 1987. write for info. (*0-932171-01-X*) Terra Found Arts.

Proud Heritage: An Illustrated History of Lake County, the Lower Flathead, Mission, & Jocko Valleys. Paul Fugleberg. LC 97-30603. (Illus.). 1997. write for info. (*1-57864-013-X*) Donning Co.

***Proud Heritage of AGCO Tractors.** Norm Swinford. (Illus.). 288p. 1999. text 39.95 (*1-892769-08-5*, H0499) Am Soc Ag Eng.

Proud Highway: Saga of a Desperate Southern Gentleman, 1955-1967. Hunter S. Thompson. Ed. by Douglas Brinkley. (Fear & Loathing Letters Ser.: Vol. 1). 720p. 1998. pap. 19.95 (*0-345-37796-6*) Ballantine Pub Grp.

Proud Highway: Saga of a Desperate Southern Gentleman, 1955-1967. Hunter S. Thompson. Ed. by Douglas Brinkley. (Fear & Loathing Letters Ser.: Vol. 1). 651p. 1997. pap. 29.95 (*0-375-75020-7*) Random.

Proud Highway: Saga of a Desperate Southern Gentleman, 1955-1967. Hunter S. Thompson. Ed. by Douglas Brinkley. LC 96-49846. (Fear & Loathing Letters Ser.: Vol. 1). 1997. 23.00 (*0-679-45285-0*) Villard Books.

Proud History: Durham, North Carolina, the Story of George Watts School Betsy Holloway. LC 98-66444. xvi, 121 p. 1998. write for info. (*0-9616500-2-8*) Persimmon Pr.

Proud Italians: Our Great Civilizers. Carl A. Pescosolido & Pamela Gleason. LC 90-64028. (Illus.). 200p. 1991. 19.95 (*0-9628757-0-8*) Latium Pub.

Proud Italians: Our Great Civilizers. 2nd ed. Carl A. Pescosolido & Pamela Gleason. (Illus.). 210p. 1995. pap. 11.95 (*0-9628757-1-6*) Latium Pub.

***Proud Jewels: A Book of Poetry.** 2000. pap. 9.95 (*0-9679923-0-3*) Sincere Prod.

Proud Journey. Wayne D. Overholser. 176p. 1989. pap. 2.75 (*0-380-70678-4*, Avon Bks) Morrow Avon.

Proud Knight Fair. Naomi Lewis. 1999. pap. 4.99 (*0-14-034038-6*) Viking Penguin.

***Proud Legions.** John Antal. (Illus.). 389p. 2000. mass mkt. 6.99 (*0-515-12784-1*, Jove) Berkley Pub.

Proud Legions. John Antal. LC 98-45437. (Illus.). 368p. 1999. 24.95 (*0-89141-667-6*, Pub. by Presidio Pr) Natl Bk Netwk.

Proud Leyte. D. L. Ferguson. (Orig.). 1997. pap. 6.95 (*0-9641760-1-7*) A B F Prods.

Proud Little Ant. Wayne Walker. (Illus.). (J). (gr. 1-6). 1999. write for info. (*0-944576-19-2*) Rocky River Pubs.

Proud Man. Katharine Burdekin. LC 93-22845. 360p. 1993. 35.00 (*1-55861-070-7*); pap. 14.95 (*1-55861-067-7*) Feminist Pr.

***Proud Mary.** Iris Gower. (J). 2000. pap. 8.95 (*0-552-12637-3*, Pub. by Transworld Publishers Ltd) Trafalgar.

Proud Mexicans. Robert Decker & Esther T. Marquez. (Illus.). 250p. (gr. 7-12). 1976. pap. 5.95 (*0-88345-254-5*, 18450) Prentice ESL.

Proud of Our Feelings. Lindsay Leghorn. LC 95-1039. (Illus.). 32p. (J). (ps-3). 1995. 11.95 (*0-945354-68-1*) Am Psychol.

Proud Ones. large type ed. Verne Athanas. 316p. 1975. 27.99 (*0-85456-340-7*) Ulverscroft.

Proud Ones: Poems by Koryne Ortega. Koryne Ortega. (Illus.). 46p. (Orig.). 1988. pap. 5.00 (*0-943557-00-3*) Esoterica Pr.

Proud Outcasts: The Gypsies of Spain. Merrill F. McLane. LC 86-70790. (Illus.). 192p. (Orig.). 1987. pap. 45.00 (*0-938813-03-X*) Carderock Pr.

Proud Paladin. Iris Morley. LC 70-144164. (Short Story Index Reprint Ser.). 1977. reprint ed. 20.95 (*0-8369-3779-1*) Ayer.

Proud, Peculiar New Orleans: The Inside Story. Gaspar J. Stall. 1984. 13.95 (*0-87511-679-5*) Claitors.

***Proud Pennsylvania Coloring Book.** Carole Marsh. (Pennsylvania Experience! Ser.). (Illus.). (J). (gr. k-5). 2000. pap. 3.95 (*0-7933-9591-7*) Gallopade Intl.

Proud People - A Proud Heritage: A History of Clarion County's Knox Township Area, Lucinda, Snydersburg, Huefner, & St. Joseph Parish. Margaret O. Wolbert et al. (Illus.). 272p. 1988. 30.00 (*0-9620183-0-9*) Hist Comm St Joseph.

Proud Prayer. R. Woodman. (Look 'N See Ser.). (J). 1995. 0.99 (*1-85792-173-9*, Pub. by Christian Focus) Spring Arbor Dist.

***Proud Quail of the San Joaquin.** Stephen Bly. LC 99-49704. (Old California Ser.: Vol. 3). 240p. 2000. pap. 10.99 (*1-58134-152-0*) Crossway Bks.

Proud Rooster & Little Hen. Carl Sommer. LC 99-35280. (Another Sommer-Time Story Ser.). (Illus.). 48p. (J). (ps-4). 1999. 9.95 (*1-57537-010-7*) Advance Pub.

Proud Rooster & Little Hen. Carl Sommer. (Another Sommer-Time Story Ser.). (Illus.). 48p. (J). (ps-4). 2000. lib. bdg. 14.95 (*1-57537-060-3*) Advance Pub.

Proud Servant: The Memoirs of a Career Ambassador. Ellis Briggs. LC 97-36506. (Illus.). 464p. 1998. 45.00 (*0-87338-588-8*) Kent St U Pr.

Proud Shoes: The Story of an American Family. Pauli Murray. LC 99-14164. 304p. 1999. pap. 16.00 (*0-8070-7209-5*) Beacon Pr.

Proud Sisters: The Wisdom & Wit of African-American Women. Ed. by Diane J. Johnson. (Gift Editions Ser.). (Illus.). 64p. 1995. 7.99 (*0-88088-472-X*) Peter Pauper.

Proud Spirit. limited ed. Rosemary Altea. 288p. 1997. 75.00 (*0-688-15510-3*, Wm Morrow) Morrow Avon.

Proud Spirit: Lessons, Insights & Healing from "The Voice of the Spirit World" Rosemary Altea. LC 96-40333. 288p. 1997. 19.95 (*0-688-14998-7*, Wm Morrow) Morrow Avon.

Proud Spirit: Lessons, Insights & Healing From 'the Voice Of The Spirit World' Rosemary Altea. LC 96-40333. 288p. 1998. pap. 10.00 (*0-688-16067-0*, Wm Morrow) Morrow Avon.

Proud Surgeon. large type ed. Lynne Collins. (Linford Romance Library). 224p. 1997. pap. 16.99 (*0-7089-5034-5*) Ulverscroft.

Proud Taste for Scarlet & Miniver. E. L. Konigsburg. LC 73-76320. (Illus.). 208p. (J). (gr. 5-9). 1973. 17.00 (*0-689-30111-1*) Atheneum Yung Read.

Proud Taste for Scarlet & Miniver. E. L. Konigsburg. 208p. (J). (gr. 5-8). 1985. pap. 4.99 (*0-440-47201-6*, YB BDD) BDD Bks Young Read.

Proud Taste for Scarlet & Miniver. E. L. Konigsburg. (J). 1973. 9.60 (*0-606-00556-0*, Pub. by Turtleback) Demco.

Proud That I'm Still Me. Kathlyn Messina & Vinny Dacquino. (Illus.). 21p. (Orig.). (J). 1992. pap. 3.95 (*0-910569-03-7*); teacher ed. 5.00 (*0-910569-06-1*) Hampton Court Pub.

Proud Threads: Twenty Years after Beating J. P. Stevens, What Have Textile Workers Won? Ed. by Eric R. Bates. (Southern Exposure Ser.). (Illus.). 64p. (Orig.). (C). 1994. pap. 5.00 (*0-943810-59-0*) Inst Southern Studies.

Proud to Be a Card-Carrying, Flag-Waving Patriotic American Liberal. Jean Hay. Ed. by David Bright. LC 96-94746. (Illus.). 208p. (Orig.). 1996. pap. 14.95 (*0-9657759-0-9*) Jean Hay.

Proud to Be a Poopini. Dave Sindrey. (Illus.). 32p. 1996. pap. text 7.95 (*0-929141-38-5*) Napoleon Publ.

Proud to Be Good! Kids of Character. Sherrie B. Keshner & Jennifer Richards. (Illus.). 39p. (J). (gr. k-5). 1995. spiral bd. 19.95 (*1-888562-00-5*, 95-1K) Proud to be Good.

Proud to Be Good! Color-Me Activity Book: Character-Building. Sherrie B. Keshner & Jennifer Richards. Ed. by Stephen G. Keshner. (Illus.). 44p. (Orig.). (J). (ps-3). 1996. pap., student ed. 5.00 (*1-888562-02-1*, PTBG021, Prd to be Good) Proud to be Good.

Proud to Be Good! Music Cassette & Color-Me Activity Book. Sherrie B. Keshner & Jennifer Richards. Ed. by Stephen G. Keshner. (Illus.). 44p. (Orig.). (J). (ps-3). 1996. pap. 12.00 incl. audio (*1-888562-03-X*, Prd to be Good) Proud to be Good.

Proud to Be Me, Peewee Platypus. Lisa Anderson. (Illus.). 40p. (Orig.). (J). (ps-4). 1990. pap. 12.95 (*0-9628323-0-8*) Ridge Enter.

Proud to Be Polite. Ann C. Humphries. 27p. (YA). (gr. 7-9). 1995. teacher ed. 99.95 incl. VHS (*0-9644556-6-8*) ETICON.

Proud to Be Polite, Vol. II. Ann C. Humphries. 52p. 1996. teacher ed. 19.95 (*0-9644556-7-6*) ETICON.

Proud to Be Polite: Activity Book. Ann C. Humphries. (Illus.). 67p. (J). (gr. k-3). 1995. wbk. ed. 19.95 (*0-9644556-3-3*) ETICON.

Proud to Be Polite: Activity Book, Vol. I. Ann C. Humphries. (Illus.). 68p. (J). (gr. 4-6). 1996. wbk. ed. 19.95 (*0-9644556-8-4*) ETICON.

Proud to Serve: The Saga of Wolfgang O'Neill. R. N. Price. Ed. by Lynne E. Lewis. LC 94-792250. 418p. (Orig.). 1996. pap. 12.95 (*1-885487-08-8*) Brownell & Carroll.

Proud Tower: A Portrait of the World Before the War, 1890-1914. Barbara W. Tuchman. LC 96-96511. (Illus.). 544p. 1996. pap. 14.00 (*0-345-40501-3*) Ballantine Pub Grp.

Proud Tradition, a Bright Future: A Sesquicentennial History of St. Johnsbury Academy. Richard Beck. LC 92-62022. (Illus.). 320p. 1992. 7.00 (*0-9634640-0-0*) St Johns Acad.

Proud Traditions & Future Challenges: Celebrates 150 Years. Ed. by David Ward. LC 99-19362. x, 224 p. 1999. pap. 9.95 (*0-9658834-2-6*, U Pubns) U Wis-Madison.

Proud Tree. Luane Roche. LC 98-38862. (Illus.). 48p. (J). 1999. pap. 11.95 (*0-7648-0377-8*) Liguori Pubns.

Proud Tree. rev. ed. Luane Roche. LC 94-73019. (Illus.). 64p. 1995. pap. 3.95 (*0-89243-769-3*) Liguori Pubns.

Proud Words on a Dusty Shelf. David G. Bick. 107p. (Orig.). 1990. pap. text 7.95 (*0-9625775-0-2*) Modern Printing.

Proudest Day: India's Long Road to Independence. Anthony Read & David Fisher. LC 98-10707. (Illus.). 566p. 1998. 35.00 (*0-393-04594-3*) Norton.

Proudest Day: India's Long Road to Independence. Anthony Read & David Fisher. (Illus.). 608p. 1999. pap. 17.50 (*0-393-31898-2*) Norton.

Proudflesh. Deborah Robertson. 1997. pap. 16.95 (*1-86368-205-8*, Pub. by Fremantle Arts) Intl Spec Bk.

Proudhon & His Age. John Ehrenberg. LC 95-19461. 216p. (C). 1996. text 45.00 (*0-391-03891-5*) Humanities.

Proudhon & His Bank of the People. Charles A. Dana. 1974. 59.95 (*0-8490-0906-5*) Gordon Pr.

Proudhon & His Bank of the People. Intro. by Paul Avrich. (Young America Ser.: No. 1). 80p. reprint ed. pap. 7.00 (*0-88286-066-6*) C H Kerr.

Proudhon & His Bank of the People: How to Solve the Current U. S. Financial Mess. C. A. Dana. 1992. lib. bdg. 75.00 (*0-8490-5457-5*) Gordon Pr.

Proudhon Marx Picasso. Raphael. (C). 1979. pap. 18.50 (*0-85315-549-6*, Pub. by Lawrence & Wishart) NYU Pr.

Proudhon's Solution of the Social Problem. P. J. Proudhon. Ed. by Henry E. Cohen. (Men & Movements in the History & Philosophy of Anarchism Ser.). 1980. lib. bdg. 250.00 (*0-87700-044-1*) Revisionist Pr.

Proudly Red & Black: Stories of Native & African Americans. William L. Katz & Paula A. Franklin. LC 92-36119. (Illus.). 96p. (J). (gr. 3-7). 1993. 15.00 (*0-689-31801-4*) Atheneum Yung Read.

Proudly Red & Black: Tales of Native & African Americans. William L. Katz & Paula A. Franklin. LC 92-36119. (YA). 1993. 13.95 (*0-684-31801-6*) Atheneum Yung Read.

Proudly We Serve: A Guide for Waiters & Waitresses. Gary J. Caulfield. (Illus.). 48p. (Orig.). 1987. pap. 3.95 (*0-912661-11-9*) Woodsong Graph.

Proudly We Served: The Men of the U.S.S. Mason. Mary Pat Kelly. 1999. pap. 15.95 (*1-55750-466-0*) Naval Inst Pr.

Proumenoir de Monsieur de Montaigne. Marie L. Gournay. LC 85-19662. 188p. 1985. reprint ed. 50.00 (*0-8201-1408-1*) Schol Facsimiles.

***Proust.** Brassai Brassai. 1998. 25.00 (*0-226-07144-8*) U Ch Pr.

Proust. Ghislain De Diesbach. 1997. write for info. (*0-679-42070-3*) Pantheon.

Proust. (Yale French Studies: No. 3). 1974. reprint ed. pap. 25.00 (*0-527-01736-1*) Periodicals Srv.

Proust: A Biography. Ronald Hayman. (Illus.). 588p. 1992. pap. 15.95 (*0-88184-818-2*) Carroll & Graf.

***Proust: A l'Ombre Des Jeunes Filles en Fleurs.** Ed. by Leighton Hodson. 96p. 1999. pap. 35.00 (*0-85261-444-6*, Pub. by U of Glasgow) St Mut.

Proust: Philosophy of the Novel. Vincent Descombes. Tr. by Catherine C. Macksey from FRE. 336p. (C). 1992. 42.50 (*0-8047-2000-2*) Stanford U Pr.

Proust: Portrait of a Genius. Andre Maurois. (Illus.). 336p. 1984. pap. 10.95 (*0-88184-104-8*) Carroll & Graf.

Proust: Questions D'Identite. Julia Kristeva. (Legenda Special Lecture Ser.). 37p. (Orig.). 1998. pap. 17.00 (*1-900755-08-4*, Pub. by E H R C) David Brown.

Proust: Speculative Scripture: The Reader of His Own Self. Peter S. Rogers. Ed. by Marshall C. Olds. (STCL Monographs: No. 2). 200p. (Orig.). 1992. pap. 4.40 (*0-9624892-1-2*) Studies Twentieth.

Proust: Swann's Way. Sheila Stern. (Landmarks of World Literature Ser.). (Illus.). 148p. (C). 1989. pap. text 11.95 (*0-521-31544-1*) Cambridge U Pr.

Proust: The Creative Silence. Angelo Caranfa. LC 88-43408. (Illus.). 208p. 1990. 36.50 (*0-8387-5165-2*) Bucknell U Pr.

***Proust among the Stars.** Malcolm Bowie. LC 98-8064. 348p. 1999. 28.50 (*0-231-11490-7*) Col U Pr.

***Proust among the Stars.** Malcolm Bowie. 352p. 2000. pap. text 16.95 (*0-231-11491-5*) Col U Pr.

***Proust & Signs.** Gilles Deleuze. LC 99-50616. (Theory Out of Bounds Ser.). 2000. write for info. (*0-8166-3258-8*) U of Minn Pr.

Proust & the Sense of Time. Julia Kristeva. Tr. & Intro. by Stephen Bann. LC 93-19359. 1993. 20.50 (*0-231-08478-1*) Col U Pr.

Proust & the Victorians: The Lamp of Memory. Robert G. Fraser. LC 93-26913. 1994. text 55.00 (*0-312-10364-6*) St Martin.

Proust & Venice: "Swann's Way" Peter Collier. (Landmarks of World Literature Ser.). (Illus.). 196p. (C). 1989. text 59.95 (*0-521-36206-7*) Cambridge U Pr.

Proust As Musician. Jean-Jacques Nattiez. Tr. by Derrick Puffett. 136p. (C). 1989. text 49.95 (*0-521-36349-7*) Cambridge U Pr.

Proust Between Two Centuries. Antoine Compagnon. Tr. by Richard E. Goodkin from FRE. 320p. 1992. text 44.00 (*0-231-07264-3*) Col U Pr.

Proust, Cole Porter, Michelangelo, Marc Almond & Me: Writings by Gay Men on Their Lives & Lifestyles. National Lesbian & Gay Survey Staff. LC 92-37658. 224p. (C). 1993. pap. 24.99 (*0-415-08914-X*, A9971) Routledge.

***Proust Screenplay: A la Recherche du Temps Perdu.** Harold Pinter et al. 192p. 1999. pap. 14.00 (*0-8021-3646-X*, Grove) Grove-Atltic.

Proust, the Body & Literary Form. Michael R. Finn. LC 98-35829. (Studies in French: No. 59). 224p. (C). 1999. text 59.95 (*0-521-64189-6*) Cambridge U Pr.

Proustian Fabric: Associations of Memory. Christie McDonald. LC 90-21940. xiv, 247p. 1991. text 45.00 (*0-8032-3150-4*) U of Nebr Pr.

Proustian Love: In Search of a Theory on the Nature of Love. I. A. Van Krotgen. 232p. 1992. 52.00 (*90-265-1237-6*) Swets.

Proustian Optics of Clothes: Mirrors, Masks, Mores. Diana Festa-McCormick. (Stanford French & Italian Studies: Vol. 29). 224p. 1984. pap. 56.50 (*0-915838-08-7*) Anma Libri.

***Proustian Passions: The Uses of Self-Justification for a La Recherche Du Temps Perdu.** Ingrid Wassenaar. 288p. 2000. text 60.00 (*0-19-816004-6*) OUP.

Proustian Quest. William C. Carter. (Illus.). 400p. (C). 1992. text 50.00 (*0-8147-1470-6*) NYU Pr.

Proustian Quest. William C. Carter. (C). 1994. pap. text 19.50 (*0-8147-1502-8*) NYU Pr.

Proustian Space. Georges Poulet. Tr. by Elliott Coleman. LC 76-47390. 120p. reprint ed. pap. 37.20 (*0-608-14759-1*, 202586400046) Bks Demand.

Proustk. Patrick Stubbins. LC 98-89871. 365p. 1999. 25.00 (*0-7388-0299-9*); pap. 15.00 (*0-7388-0300-6*) Xlibris Corp.

Prousts "A la Recherche du Temps Perdu" und die Form der Autobiographie: Zum Verhaltnis und Pragmatischer Erzahltexte. Ursula Link-Heer. (Beihefte zu Poetica Ser.: Vol. 18). (GER.). 348p. 1988. 56.00 (*90-6032-214-2*, Pub. by B R Gruner) Humanities.

***Proust's Gods: Christian & Mythological Figures of Speech in the Works of Marcel Proust.** Margaret Topping. (Oxford Modern Languages & Literature Monographs). 224p. 2000. text 60.00 (*0-19-816008-9*) OUP.

Proust's Lesbianism. Elisabeth Ladenson. LC 98-38248. 1999. 32.50 (*0-8014-3595-1*) Cornell U Pr.

Proust's Self-Reader: The Pursuit of Literature As Privileged Communication. Phillip Bailey. LC 97-67749. (Marcel Proust Ser.: Vol. 7). 182p. 1997. lib. bdg. 38.95 (*1-883479-15-0*) Summa Pubns.

***Proust's Way: A Field Guide to 'In Search of Lost Time'** Roger Shattuck. LC 99-58472. 288p. 2000. 26.95 (*0-393-04914-0*) Norton.

Prout: An Economic Solution to Poverty in the Third World. Ravi Batra. (Illus.). 220p. (Orig.). (C). 1989. pap. 9.95 (*0-88476-075-8*) Ananda Marga.

Prout & the End of Capitalism & Communism. M. B. Lokesh. 126p. (Orig.). (C). 1990. pap. 6.95 (*0-685-35763-5*) Proutist Universal.

Prout in a Nutshell, Pt. 1. Prabhat Rainjan Sarkar. Tr. by Acarya Vijayananda Avadhuta & Jayanta Kumar from BEN. 62p. (Orig.). (C). 1987. pap. 3.95 (*0-88476-050-2*) Ananda Marga.

Prout in a Nutshell, Pt. 2. Prabhat Rainjan Sarkar. Tr. by Acarya Vijayananda Avadhuta & Jayanta Kumar from BEN. 68p. (Orig.). (C). 1987. pap. text 3.95 (*0-88476-051-0*) Ananda Marga.

Prout in a Nutshell, Pt. 3. Prabhat Rainjan Sarkar. Tr. by Acarya Vijayananda Avadhuta & Jayanta Kumar from BEN. 64p. (Orig.). (C). 1987. pap. text 3.95 (*0-88476-052-9*) Ananda Marga.

Prout in a Nutshell, Pt. 4. 3rd ed. Prabhat Rainjan Sarkar. Tr. by Acarya Vijayananda Avadhuta & Jayanta Kumar from BEN. 53p. (Orig.). (C). 1987. pap. text 3.95 (*0-88476-053-7*) Ananda Marga.

Prout in a Nutshell, Pt. 5. Prabhat Rainjan Sarkar. Tr. by Acarya Vijayananda Avadhuta & Jayanta Kumar from BEN. 89p. (Orig.). (C). 1987. pap. 3.95 (*0-88476-054-5*) Ananda Marga.

An Asterisk (*) at the beginning of an entry indicates that the title is appearing for the first time.

Prout in a Nutshell, Pt. 6. Prabhat Rainjan Sarkar. Tr. by Acarya Vijayananda Avadhuta & Jayanta Kumar from BEN. 62p. (Orig.). (C). 1987. pap. 3.95 (*0-88476-055-3*) Ananda Marga.

Prout in a Nutshell, Pt. 7. Prabhat Rainjan Sarkar. Tr. by Acarya Vijayananda Avadhuta & Jayanta Kumar from BEN. 67p. (Orig.). (C). 1987. pap. 3.95 (*0-88476-056-1*) Ananda Marga.

Prout in a Nutshell, Pt. 8. Prabhat Rainjan Sarkar. Tr. by Acarya Vijayananda Avadhuta & Jayanta Kumar from BEN. 67p. (Orig.). (C). 1987. pap. 3.95 (*0-88476-057-X*) Ananda Marga.

Prout in a Nutshell, Pt. 9. Prabhat Rainjan Sarkar. Tr. by Acarya Vijayananda Avadhuta & Jayanta Kumar from BEN. 69p. (Orig.). (C). 1987. pap. 3.95 (*0-88476-058-8*) Ananda Marga.

Prout in a Nutshell, Pt. 10. Prabhat Rainjan Sarkar. Tr. by Acarya Vijayananda Avadhuta & Jayanta Kumar from BEN. 82p. (Orig.). (C). 1987. pap. 3.95 (*0-88476-059-6*) Ananda Marga.

Prout in a Nutshell, Pt. 11. Prabhat Rainjan Sarkar. Tr. by Acarya Vijayananda Avadhuta & Jayanta Kumar from BEN. 62p. (Orig.). (C). 1987. pap. 3.95 (*0-88476-060-X*) Ananda Marga.

Prout in a Nutshell, Pt. 12. Prabhat Rainjan Sarkar. Tr. by Acarya Vijayananda Avadhuta & Jayanta Kumar from BEN. 60p. (Orig.). (C). 1987. pap. 3.95 (*0-88476-061-8*) Ananda Marga.

Prout in a Nutshell, Pt. 13. Prabhat Rainjan Sarkar. Tr. by Acarya Vijayananda Avadhuta & Jayanta Kumar from BEN. 64p. (Orig.). (C). 1988. pap. 3.95 (*0-88476-062-6*) Ananda Marga.

Prout in a Nutshell, Pt. 14. Prabhat Rainjan Sarkar. Tr. by Acarya Vijayananda Avadhuta & Jayanta Kumar from BEN. 60p. (Orig.). (C). 1988. pap. 3.95 (*0-88476-063-4*) Ananda Marga.

Prout in a Nutshell, Pt. 15. Prabhat Rainjan Sarkar. Tr. by Acarya Vijayananda Avadhuta & Jayanta Kumar from BEN. 64p. (Orig.). (C). 1988. pap. 3.95 (*0-88476-064-2*) Ananda Marga.

Prouve. Jan Van Geest. 1994. pap. 19.99 (*3-8228-9751-5*) Taschen Amer.

Provability & Truth. Torkel Franzen. (Stockholm Studies in Philosophy: No. 9). 81p. (Orig.). 1987. pap. 35.00 (*91-22-01158-7*) Coronet Bks.

Provability, Complexity, Grammars. Lev D. Beklemishev et al. LC 99-20177. (Translations Ser.). 12p. 1999. write for info. (*0-8218-1078-2*) Am Math.

Provably Correct Systems: Modelling of Communication Languages & Design of Optimized Compilers. Jifeng He. LC 94-21071. (International Series in Software Engineering). 1994. write for info. (*0-07-709052-7*) McGraw.

Provacateur. Joel Lipman. (Bloody Twin Press Ser.). (Illus.). 24p. (Orig.). 1988. pap. 25.00 (*1-886350-33-7*) Bloody Twin Pr.

Prove All Things. Betty Miller. (Overcoming Life Ser.). 44p. 1994. pap. 5.00 (*1-57149-000-0*) Christ Unltd.

Prove All Things Workbook. Betty Miller. (Overcoming Life Ser.). 1995. pap. 10.00 (*1-57149-001-9*) Christ Unltd.

Prove Before Laying: Figuring the Word. Johanna Drucker. (Illus.). 30p. 1997. 300.00 (*1-887123-24-5*, Druckwerk) Granary Bks.

Prove It with Figures: Empirical Methods in Law & Litigation. Hans Zeisel & D. H. Kaye. LC 97-9827. 400p. 1997. 64.95 (*0-387-94892-9*) Spr-Verlag.

Prove the Nameless: An Owen Keane Mystery. Terence Faherty. (WWL Mystery Ser.). 1998. per. 4.99 (*0-373-26269-8*, 1-26269-0, Wrldwide Lib) Harlequin Bks.

Prove the Nameless: An Owen Keane Mystery. Terence Faherty. LC 96-24523. 304p. 1996. text 22.95 (*0-312-14706-6*) St Martin.

***Proven Cruise Routes of Alaska's Inside Passage: Seattle to Ketchikan.** Don Douglass & Kevin Monahan. (Illus.). 2000. 39.95 (*0-938665-49-9*) Fine Edge Prods.

Proven Garden Tips from Fine Gardening. Fine Gardening Magazine Editors. (Illus.). 128p. 1996. pap. 8.95 (*1-56158-157-7*, 070296) Taunton.

Proven Health Tips Encyclopedia. Michael Allen. 433p. (Orig.). 1997. pap. 18.95 (*0-9638596-6-8*) Amer Pubng.

Proven Herbal Blends. rev. ed. Daniel B. Mowrey. 1990. pap. 6.95 (*0-87983-524-9*, 35249K, Keats Publng) NTC Contemp Pub Co.

Proven Management Models. Sue Harding & Trevor Long. LC 96-8726. (Illus.). 250p. 1997. text 61.95 (*0-566-07674-8*, Pub. by Gower) Ashgate Pub Co.

Proven Performances: Recipes from Thoroughbred Racing Leaders. Ed. by Bobbee Ferrer. LC 85-51914. (Illus.). 248p. 1985. 13.50 (*0-9615869-0-7*) Proven Perf.

Proven Practice, Set, Vols. 1 & 2. 1993. 75.00 (*0-614-05011-1*, PSET) Capitol Publns.

Proven Practice, Vol. 1. 1994. 46.00 (*0-937925-86-1*, PRPR) Capitol Publns.

Proven Practice, Vol. 2. 1994. 48.00 (*1-56925-005-7*, PP2) Capitol Publns.

Proven Profits from Pollution Prevention: Case Studies in Resource Conservation & Waste Reduction. Donald Huisingh et al. LC 85-82638. 316p. 1986. pap. 25.00 (*0-917582-47-0*) Inst Local Self Re.

Proven Profits from Pollution Prevention: Case Studies in Resource Conservation & Waste Reduction, Vol. II. Larry Martin. Ed. by Diana White. LC 85-82638. 130p. 1989. pap. text 20.00 (*0-917582-40-3*) Inst Local Self Re.

Proven Promotions for Kitchen & Bathroom Businesses. Jim Krengel & Lori J. Krengel. (Illus.). 135p. (Orig.). 1997. pap. text 50.00 (*1-887127-05-4*, 5303) Natl Kit Bath.

Proven Proposal Strategies to Win More Business. Herman Holtz. LC 97-48649. 256p. 1998. 29.95 (*1-57410-088-2*) Dearborn.

Proven Radio Copy, 3 vols. Radio Ink Staff Writers. 651p. (Orig.). 1997. pap. text 197.00 (*1-886745-10-2*) Streamlne Pr.

Proven Radio Copy, Vol. 1. Radio Ink Staff Writers. 235p. (Orig.). 1997. pap. text 77.00 (*1-886745-07-2*) Streamlne Pr.

Proven Radio Copy: Automotive, Professional Services, Vol. 3. Radio Ink Staff Writers. 224p. (Orig.). 1997. pap. text 77.00 (*1-886745-09-9*) Streamlne Pr.

Proven Radio Copy: Entertainment, Food, Restaurants, Vol. 2. Radio Ink Staff Writers. 192p. (Orig.). 1997. pap. text 77.00 (*1-886745-08-0*) Streamlne Pr.

***Proven Resumes: Strategies That Increase Your Salary & Change Your Life!** Regina Pontow. LC 99-30493. 320p. 1999. 19.95 (*1-58008-080-4*) Ten Speed Pr.

Proven Resumes & Confidence Builders. Regina Pontow. LC 93-74727. (Orig.). 1994. pap. 19.95 (*1-884668-00-3*) Abrams & Smith.

Proven Resumes & Confidence Builders: A Complete Job Search Program. Regina Pontow. LC 96-168729. 300p. 1994. pap. 19.95 (*1-884668-05-4*) Abrams & Smith.

Proven Secrets to a Successful Marriage. LaSalle R. Vaughn & Portia B. Vaughn. 107p. 1997. pap. 10.00 (*1-886065-49-7*) N Life Christian.

Proven Strategies for Improving Learning & Achievement. Duane Brown. 307p. 1999. pap. text 26.95 (*1-56109-086-7*, EC 237) CAPS Inc.

Proven Successful Brochures & Methods for Direct Marketing. Research & Education Association Staff. 208p. Date not set. pap. text 29.95 (*0-87891-979-1*) Res & Educ.

Proven Whitetail Tactics. Greg Miller. LC 97-73037. (Illus.). 224p. 1997. pap. 19.95 (*0-87341-509-4*, AWII02) Krause Pubns.

Provenance. large type ed. Frank McDonald. 656p. 1983. 11.50 (*0-7089-8158-5*, Charnwood) Ulverscroft.

Provenance Evidence. 24p. 1988. pap. 10.50 (*0-8389-7239-X*) Assn Coll & Res Libs.

Provenance of Arenites. Ed. by G. G Zuffa. 1985. text 272.50 (*90-277-1944-6*) Kluwer Academic.

Provenance of Deuteronomy 32. Paul Sanders. LC 96-20377. (Oudtestamentische Studien). 1996. 174.50 (*90-04-10648-0*) Brill Academic Pubs.

Provenance Research in Book History. deluxe rev. ed. David Pearson. 352p. (C). 1998. reprint ed. 49.95 (*1-884718-79-5*, 53851RB) Oak Knoll.

Provenance Research in Book History. David Pearson. 352p. (C). 1998. reprint ed. pap. 29.95 (*1-884718-80-9*, 53852RB) Oak Knoll.

Provenance Research in Book History: A Handbook. David Pearson. (The British Library Studies in the History of the Book). (Illus.). 400p. 1994. 100.00 (*0-7123-0318-9*, Pub. by B23tish Library) U of Toronto Pr.

Provenance Research in Book History: A Handbook. David Pearson. (British Library Studies in the History of the Book). (Illus.). 336p. 1994. 90.00 (*0-7123-0344-8*) U of Toronto Pr.

Provencal & Eng. see Golden Chord

Provencal-Francais. 5th ed. E. Levy. 387p. 1973. pap. 70.00 (*3-533-01393-6*) IBD Ltd.

Provencal-French Dictionary with French-Provencal Vocabulary. fac. ed. J. T. Avril. (FRE & PRO.). 656p. 1990. pap. 95.00 (*0-7859-5214-4*, M14179) Fr & Eur.

Provencal-French, French-Provencal Dictionary: Lou Pichot Tresor: Dictionnaire Provencal-Francais et Francais-Provencal. Xavier D. Fourvieres. (FRE & PRO.). 1984. 39.95 (*0-8288-1720-0*, M4609) Fr & Eur.

Provencal Interiors: French Country Style in America. Betty L. Phillips. LC 98-17493. (Illus.). 150p. 1998. 39.95 (*0-87905-848-X*) Gibbs Smith Pub.

***Provencal Light: Traditional Recipes from Provence for Today's Healthy Lifestyles.** Martha Rose Shulman. LC 99-39649. 496p. 2000. pap. 16.00 (*0-688-17465-5*, Wm Morrow) Morrow Avon.

Provencal Literature & Language: Including the Local History of Southern France. Daniel C. Haskell. reprint ed. 45.00 (*0-404-08349-8*) AMS Pr.

Provencal Regionalism. Alphonse V. Roche. LC 74-128942. (Northwestern University. Humanities Ser.: No. 30). reprint ed. 37.50 (*0-404-50730-1*) AMS Pr.

Provencal Summer. large type ed. Suzanne Ebel. 277p. 1980. 27.99 (*0-7089-0497-1*) Ulverscroft.

Provencal Table. Jane Newdick & Maxine Clark. (Illus.). 108p. 1998. 24.95 (*0-09-182003-0*, Pub. by Ebury Pr) Trafalgar.

Provence. (Panorama Bks.). (FRE., Illus.). 3.95 (*0-685-11516-X*) Fr & Eur.

Provence. (Blue Guide Ser.). Date not set. pap. write for info. (*0-393-30972-X*, Norton Paperbks) Norton.

Provence. Lawrence Durrell. 192p. 1994. pap. 11.45 (*1-55970-247-8*, Pub. by Arcade Pub Inc) Time Warner.

Provence. Marie-Ange Guillaume. LC 93-9885. (Illus.). 180p. 1993. 45.00 (*1-55859-557-0*) Abbeville Pr.

***Provence.** Marie-Ange Guillaume. (Illus.). 288p. 2000. pap. write for info. (*0-7892-0487-8*) Abbeville Pr.

***Provence.** Richard Harteis. 300p. 2000. pap. 16.00 (*1-58776-030-4*) Vivisphere.

Provence. Insight Guides Staff. (Insight Guides). 1998. pap. text 7.95 (*0-88729-558-4*) Langenscheidt.

Provence. Knopf Guides Staff. LC 94-8366. (Knopf Guides Ser.). (Illus.). 400p. 1995. pap. 25.00 (*0-679-75066-5*) Knopf.

Provence. Illus. by Margaret Loxton. LC 93-5084. (Robert Stewart Bk.). 64p. 1993. 14.00 (*0-684-19664-6*) S&S Trade.

Provence. rev. ed. Compiled by Nelles Verlag. (Nelles Verlag Ser.). (Illus.). 256p. 1993. pap. 14.95 (*3-88618-388-2*, Pub. by Nelles Verlag) Seven Hills Bk.

***Provence.** 2nd ed. Dana Facaros. (City Guides Ser.). 2000. pap. text 19.95 (*1-86011-975-1*) Cadgn Bks.

Provence. 2nd ed. Ford Madox Ford. (Travel Ser.). 1992. pap. 12.95 (*0-88001-316-8*) HarpC.

Provence. 2nd ed. Insight Guides Staff. (Insight Guides). 1998. pap. text 12.95 (*0-88729-928-8*) Langenscheidt.

Provence. 3rd ed. Insight Guides Staff. (Insight Guides). 1998. pap. text 22.95 (*0-88729-744-7*) Langenscheidt.

Provence: A Book of Travel. 3rd ed. Ford Madox Ford. 1995. pap. 13.00 (*0-88001-413-X*) HarpC.

Provence: A Country Almanac. Louisa Jones. LC 92-40024. (Illus.). 176p. 1993. 24.95 (*1-55670-278-7*) Stewart Tabori & Chang.

***Provence: A Country Almanac.** Louisa Jones. LC 98-39754. (Illus.). 176p. 1999. text 24.95 (*1-55670-862-9*) Stewart Tabori & Chang.

Provence: The Art of Living. Sam Walden. (Illus.). 208p. 1996. 50.00 (*1-55670-449-6*) Stewart Tabori & Chang.

Provence: The Beautiful Cookbook. Photos by Peter Johnson & Michael Freeman. LC 93-55. (Illus.). 256p. 1993. 50.00 (*0-00-255154-3*) Collins SF.

***Provence: The Collected Traveler: An Inspired Anthology & Travel Resource.** Barry Kerper. 2001. pap. 14.00 (*0-609-80678-5*, Three Riv Pr) Crown Pub Group.

Provence: Walks, Motor Tours, Gazetteer, Where to Stay, Where to Eat, What to See, Plus Large-Scale IGN Maps. Institute Geographic Nationale Staff. (IGN Touring & Leisure Guides to France Ser.). (Illus.). 144p. (Orig.). 1991. pap. 19.95 (*1-85365-252-0*, Pub. by McCarta) Seven Hills Bk.

Provence - Cote D'Azur. 2nd rev. ed. Nelles Verlag Staff. (Nelles Guides Ser.). (Illus.). 256p. 1999. pap. 15.95 (*3-88618-034-4*) Hunter NJ.

Provence & Cote D'Azur. Paul Stirton. (Illus.). 256p. 1999. pap. 20.95 (*0-393-31931-8*) Norton.

Provence & Cote d'Azur. 2nd ed. Hans J. Mettler et al. (Travel Guides Ser.). (Illus.). 368p. 1998. pap. 21.95 (*2-89464-112-5*) Ulysses Travel.

***Provence & Cote D'Azur.** 3rd ed. Hans Jorg Mettler. (Travel Guide Ser.). (Illus.). 2001. pap. 21.95 (*2-89464-327-6*) Ulysses Travel.

Provence & Pound. Peter Makin. LC 77-76186. 442p. reprint ed. pap. 137.10 (*0-7837-4694-6*, 204444100003) Bks Demand.

Provence & The Cote D'Azur. Deni Bown. LC 94-44323. (Eyewitness Travel Guides Ser.). (Illus.). 264p. 1995. pap. 22.95 (*1-56458-860-2*) DK Pub Inc.

Provence & the Cote D'Azur. Roger MacDonald. 1995. pap. 16.95 (*0-8442-9938-3*, Passprt Bks) NTC Contemp Pub Co.

Provence & the Cote D'Azur. Roger Macdonald. (Regional Guides of France Ser.). (Illus.). 192p. 1994. pap. 16.95 (*0-8442-9087-4*, 90874, Passprt Bks) NTC Contemp Pub Co.

Provence & the Cote d'Azur. NTC Publishing Group Staff. (Passport Essential Guide Ser.). (Illus.). 128p. 1998. pap. 8.95 (*0-8442-0113-8*, 01138, Passprt Bks) NTC Contemp Pub Co.

Provence & the Cote D'Azur. Passport Books Editors. (Illus.). 120p. 1994. pap. 17.95 (*0-8442-9968-5*, Passprt Bks) NTC Contemp Pub Co.

Provence & the Cote D'Azur. 4th ed. Kate Ballie. 576p. 1999. pap. 17.95 (*1-85828-420-1*, Pub. by Rough Guides) Penguin Putnam.

***Provence-Art: Architecture & Landscape.** Contrib. by Koenemann Inc. Staff. (Illus.). 416p. 2000. 39.95 (*3-8290-2714-1*) Konemann.

Provence Gastronomique. Erica Brown. (Illus.). 160p. 1996. 29.95 (*0-7892-0038-4*) Abbeville Pr.

Provence Green Guide. Michelin Staff. (FRE.). 1996. pap. 19.95 (*0-7859-9168-9*) Fr & Eur.

Provence Green Guide: France (Regional Guides) 3rd ed. Ed. by Michelin Staff. 1996. per. 20.00 (*2-06-137503-0*, 1375) Michelin.

Provence Interiors. Lisa Lovatt-Smith. (Jumbo Ser.). (Illus.). 1996. 39.99 (*3-8228-8176-7*) Taschen Amer.

Provence Interiors. Taschen Staff. (SPA.). (J). Date not set. 39.99 (*3-8228-8062-0*, Pub. by Benedikt Taschen) Bks Nippan.

Provence on a Budget. Ed. by D. Delaforce. (C). 1989. text 29.95 (*0-948032-88-X*, Pub. by Rosters Ltd) St Mut.

Provence Pocket Guide. rev. ed. Text by Paul Murphy. LC 99-226248. (Illus.). 144p. 1999. 8.95 (*2-8315-7152-9*) Berlitz.

***Provence Welcomes You.** JEAN-MAX TIXIER. 1999. pap. text 35.00 (*2-911988-18-3*) BHB Intl.

Provence/Cote d'Azur Map. 1988. 8.95 (*2-06-700245-7*, 245) Michelin.

Provencial State: Politics in Canada's Provinces & Territories. Keith Brownsey. (C). 1992. pap. text 33.95 (*0-7730-5192-9*) Addison-Wesley.

Provenzalische Chrestomathie, Mit Abriss der Formenlehre & Glossar. 6th ed. Carl L. Appel. LC 71-38488. reprint ed. 27.50 (*0-404-08345-5*) AMS Pr.

Provenzalische Lautlehre: Mit Einer Karte. Carl L. Appel. LC 80-2165. (Provenzalische Chrestomathie Ser.). reprint ed. 37.50 (*0-404-19027-8*) AMS Pr.

***Proverb Iconography: An International Bibliography.** Wolfgang Mieder & Janet Sobieski. LC 98-52124. (Illus.). xix, 225p. (C). 1999. text 49.95 (*0-8204-4198-8*) P Lang Pubng.

Proverb in Mind: The Cognitive Science of Proverbial Wit & Wisdom. Richard P. Honeck. LC 97-1891. 150p. 1997. 65.00 (*0-8058-0231-2*) L Erlbaum Assocs.

Proverb Literature. W. Bonser & T. A. Stephens. 1972. 59.95 (*0-8490-0908-1*) Gordon Pr.

Proverb Literature: A Bibliography of Works Relating to Proverbs. Thomas A. Stephens. Ed. by Wilfred Bonser. (Folk-Lore Society, London Monographs: Vol. 89). 1974. reprint ed. pap. 55.00 (*0-8115-0535-9*) Periodicals Srv.

Proverb Lore. F. E. Hulme. 1972. 59.95 (*0-8490-0909-X*) Gordon Pr.

Proverb Stories. Louisa May Alcott. (Works of Louisa May Alcott). 1989. reprint ed. lib. bdg. 79.00 (*0-7812-1639-7*) Rprt Serv.

Proverb Wit & Widom. Louis A. Bergman. 560p. 1997. pap. 16.95 (*0-399-52273-5*, Perigee Bks) Berkley Pub.

Proverbes Bibliques et Proverbes Kongo: Etude Comparative de Proverbia 25-29 et de Quelques Proverbes Kongo. Philippe D. Nzambi. (Religionswissenschaft Ser.: Bd. 5). (FRE.). 767p. 1992. 107.80 (*3-631-44827-9*) P Lang Pubng.

***Proverbial Abraham Lincoln: An Index to Proverbs in the Works of Abraham Lincoln.** Wolfgang Mieder. LC 99-52371. 224p. 2000. text 49.95 (*0-8204-4955-5*) P Lang Pubng.

Proverbial Bernard Shaw: An Index to the Proverbs in the Works of George Bernard Shaw, 41. Ed. by George B. Bryan & Wolfgang Mieder. LC 93-41215. (Bibliographies & Indexes in World Literature Ser.: No. 41). 304p. 1994. lib. bdg. 75.00 (*0-313-29218-3*, Greenwood Pr) Greenwood.

Proverbial Bestiary. Warren Chappell et al. (Illus.). 64p. 1983. 10.95 (*0-931474-12-4*) Kennebec River.

Proverbial Bolt Blue. Jessica Freeman. 64p. 1995. pap. 7.00 (*1-886353-02-6*) B Downs Bks.

Proverbial Charles Dickens: An Index to Proverbs in the Works of Charles Dickens. Ed. by Wolfgang Mieder & George B. Bryan. LC 97-13446. (Dickens' Universe Ser.: Vol. 4). 319p. (C). 1997. text 39.95 (*0-8204-3837-5*) P Lang Pubng.

Proverbial Comparisons & Related Expressions in Spanish: Recorded in Los Angeles, California. Shirley Arora. LC 75-46053. (University of California Publications, Folklore Studies: No. 29). 530p. reprint ed. pap. 164.30 (*0-608-13908-4*, 202120800021) Bks Demand.

Proverbial Eugene O'Neill: An Index to Proverbs in the Works of Eugene Gladstone O'Neill, 21. Compiled by George B. Bryan & Wolfgang Mieder. LC 95-36073. (Bibliographies & Indexes in American Literature Ser.: No. 21). 376p. 1995. lib. bdg. 79.50 (*0-313-29794-0*, Greenwood Pr) Greenwood.

Proverbial Harry S. Truman: An Index to Proverbs in the Works of Harry S. Truman. Ed. by Wolfgang Mieder & George Bryan. LC 96-49836. XI, 247p. (C). 1997. text 39.95 (*0-8204-3748-4*) P Lang Pubng.

Proverbial Leroy. Jim Duriga. (Illus.). (Orig.). 1996. pap. text 4.95 (*1-889991-00-7*) Seneca-Secor.

Proverbial Winston S. Churchill: An Index to Proverbs in the Works of Sir Winston Churchill, 38. Ed. by Wolfgang Mieder & George B. Bryan. LC 95-2464. (Bibliographies & Indexes in World History Ser.: Vol. 38). 448p. 1995. lib. bdg. 85.00 (*0-313-29433-X*, Greenwood Pr) Greenwood.

***Proverbial Wisdom & Common Sense: A Messianic Jewish Approach to Today's Issues from the Proverbs.** Derek Leman. LC 99-32303. 248p. 1999. pap. 12.99 (*1-880226-78-2*, Pub. by M J Pubs) Spring Arbor Dist.

Proverbial Wisdom from Guyana. Victorine Solomon. 56p. 1997. pap. 8.00 (*0-8059-4150-9*) Dorrance.

***Proverbial Woman.** Robin Chaddock. LC 00-100228. 128p. 2000. pap. 10.95 (*1-57921-267-0*) WinePress Pub.

Proverbio al Giorno - A Proverb a Day. Caterina Cicogna. (Italian Linguistics & Language Pedagogy Ser.). (Illus.). 160p. (C). 1992. pap. text, teacher ed. 19.95 (*0-8020-7379-4*); pap. text, student ed. 19.95 (*0-8020-7678-5*) U of Toronto Pr.

Proverbios (Comentario Biblico Portavoz) Irving L. Jensen. Orig. Title: Proverbs (Everyman's Bible Commentary). (SPA.). 128p. 1995. pap. 6.99 (*0-8254-1356-7*, Edit Portavoz) Kregel.

Proverbios Morales of Santob de Carrion. Ed. by T. Anthony Perry. (Spanish Ser.: No. 21). (SPA.). xiii, 233p. 1986. 17.00 (*0-942260-63-5*) Hispanic Seminary.

Proverbios y Cantares. Ed. by Daniel Carro et al. (Comentario Biblico Mundo Hispano Ser.).Tr. of Proverbs & Chants. (SPA.). 374p. (Orig.). 1995. pap. 8.99 (*0-311-03109-9*, Edit Mundo) Casa Bautista.

Proverbios y la Mujer Moderna. Gloria Ricardo. (Estudio Biblico Para Mujeres Ser.). 76p. 1992. pap. 4.00 (*1-885630-26-3*) HLM Producciones.

Proverbs. (LifeChange Ser.). 156p. 1990. pap. 7.00 (*0-89109-348-6*) NavPress.

Proverbs. (Life Application Bible Study Guide Ser.). 128p. 1990. pap. 5.99 (*0-8423-2737-1*) Tyndale Hse.

Proverbs. K. T. Aitken. 1993. pap. 22.00 (*0-7152-0533-1*, Pub. by St Andrew) St Mut.

Proverbs. Charles Bridges. (Geneva Commentaries Ser.). 1979. 29.99 (*0-85151-088-4*) Banner of Truth.

Proverbs. Copelan. 1997. 14.99 (*0-89274-951-2*) Harrison Hse.

Proverbs. Roland C. Ehlke. (People's Bible Commentary Ser.). 336p. 1993. pap. 11.99 (*0-570-04617-3*, 12-8017) Concordia.

Proverbs. Roland C. Ehlke. LC 92-63030. (People's Bible Ser.). 322p. 1993. pap. 12.99 (*0-8100-0468-2*, 15N0497) Northwest Pub.

Proverbs. Roland C. Ehlke. LC 92-63030. (People's Bible Ser.). 40p. 1994. student ed. 4.00 (*0-8100-0518-2*, 22N0854) Northwest Pub.

Proverbs. Duane A. Garrett. LC 98-27116. (Shepherd's Notes Ser.). 1998. 5.95 (*0-8054-9016-7*) Broadman.

Proverbs. David A. Hubbard. (Communicator's Commentary Ser.: Vol. 15A). 496p. 1989. 22.99 (*0-8499-0421-8*) Word Pub.

Proverbs. David A. Hubbard. (Mastering the Old & New Testament Ser.: Vol. 15A). 1993. pap. 14.99 (*0-8499-3554-7*) Word Pub.

Proverbs. Donna Huisjen. LC 98-61557. (My Tall Bks.). (J). 2000. 6.99 (*0-310-91862-6*) Zondervan.

P

An Asterisk (*) at the beginning of an entry indicates that the title is appearing for the first time.

Proverbs. H. A. Ironside. LC 95-22994. (Ironside Commentaries Ser.). 281p. 1996. pap. 9.99 (*0-87213-404-0*) Loizeaux.

Proverbs. Derek Kidner. LC 75-23850. (Tyndale Old Testament Commentary Ser.). 192p. 1969. pap. 12.99 (*0-87784-266-3*, 266) InterVarsity.

Proverbs. Woodrow Kroll. 1999. pap. text 7.99 (*0-8474-1332-2*) Back to Bible.

Proverbs. James D. Martin. (Old Testament Guides Ser.: No. 16). 104p. 1995. pap. 12.50 (*1-85075-752-6*, Pub. by Sheffield Acad) CUP Services.

***Proverbs.** Thomas P. McCreesh. (Berit Olam (The Everlasting Covenant) Ser.). 2000. 0.00 (*0-8146-5071-6*) Liturgical Pr.

Proverbs. J. Vernon McGee. (Thru the Bible Commentary Ser.: Vol. 20). 1997. pap. 6.97 (*0-7852-0475-X*) Nelson.

Proverbs. Roland E. Murphy. (Biblical Commentary Ser.: Vol. 22). 450p. 1998. 29.99 (*0-8499-0221-5*) Word Pub.

Proverbs. Norman Whybray. (New Century Bible Ser.). 446p. 1994. pap. 24.95 (*0-551-02831-9*, Pub. by Sheffield Acad) CUP Services.

Proverbs. rev. ed. A. Cohen. 217p. 1985. 16.95 (*0-900689-33-1*) Soncino Pr.

***Proverbs: A Bible Commentary in the Wesleyan Tradition.** Stephen J. Lennox. LC 99-174410. 326 p. 1998. write for info. (*0-89827-197-5*) Wesleyan Pub Hse.

Proverbs: A Commentary. Richard J. Clifford. LC 98-50850. (Old Testament Library). 296p. 1999. 38.00 (*0-664-22131-9*) Westminster John Knox.

Proverbs: A Comparative Book of English, French, German, Italian, Spanish, & Russian Proverbs with a Latin Appendix. Ed. by J. Gluski. 486p. 1989. pap. 70.00 (*0-444-87350-3*) Elsevier.

Proverbs: Classic Library Edition. Marilyn Hickey. 1996. 24.95 (*1-56441-035-8*) M Hickey Min.

Proverbs: Critical Exegetical Commentary. Crawford H. Toy. Ed. by Samuel R. Driver et al. (International Critical Commentary Ser.). 592p. 1899. 39.95 (*0-567-05013-0*, Pub. by T & T Clark) Bks Intl VA.

***Proverbs: Everyday Wisdom for Everyone.** Eric Lane. 2000. pap. 14.99 (*1-85792-451-7*) Christian Focus.

***Proverbs: God's Abundance for Living.** Ed. by Kathy C. Miller. 240p. 2000. 19.95 (*1-892016-31-1*) Starburst.

Proverbs: God's Gift of Wisdom. (God's Word for Today Ser.). 1995. 5.50 (*0-570-09545-X*, 20-2653) Concordia.

Proverbs: God's Guide for Life's Choices. Woodrow M. Kroll. LC 96-146364. 222p. 1996. pap. text 9.99 (*0-8474-1467-1*) Back to Bible.

***Proverbs: Interpretation.** Leo G. Perdue. 2000. write for info. (*0-8042-3116-8*) Westminster John Knox.

Proverbs: Japanese-English Dictionary. Hokojiro Jona. (ENG & JPN.). 360p. 1997. boxed set 47.95 (*4-590-00955-2*, Pub. by Hokuseido Pr) Book East.

Proverbs: Learning to Live Wisely. William Mouser. (LifeGuide Bible Studies). 95p. (Orig.). 1990. pap., wbk. ed. 4.99 (*0-8308-1026-9*, 1026) InterVarsity.

Proverbs: Principles of Wisdom. Bob Yandian. (Illus.). 178p. 1997. pap. 7.99 (*1-880089-01-7*) Albury Pub.

Proverbs: Seventy-Five Proverbs from the Living Bible. Ed. by Timothy R. Botts. LC 94-12127. (Illus.). 160p. 1994. 16.99 (*0-8423-5034-9*) Tyndale Hse.

Proverbs: Study Guide. (Discover Life Ser.). 16p. pap., student ed. 3.25 (*1-56212-146-4*) CRC Pubns.

Proverbs: Wisdom for All Ages. Thomas L. Seals. 1981. 7.75 (*0-89137-529-5*) Quality Pubns.

Proverbs: Wisdom for Everyday Life. Walter C. Kaiser, Jr. (Great Books of the Bible). 64p. 1995. pap. 5.99 (*0-310-49861-9*) Zondervan.

Proverbs: Wisdom of the Wise & Foolish. David W. Cloud. Date not set. pap. 19.95 (*1-58318-007-9*, WOL Proverbs) Way of Life.

Proverbs: Wisdom That Works. Vinita H. Wright. (Fisherman Bible Studyguide Ser.). 80p. 1994. pap. 4.99 (*0-87788-668-7*, H Shaw Pubs) Waterbrook Pr.

Proverbs: 31 Days to a Lifetime of Wisdom. (Little Library Ser.). 48p. 1995. pap. text 0.99 (*1-55748-649-2*) Barbour Pub.

Proverbs - Ecclesiastes - Song of Solomon. (Complete Biblical Library: Vol. 11). 360p. 1998. 49.95 (*1-884642-35-7*) World Library.

Proverbs - Song of Solomon see Old Testament Commentaries

Proverbs - Song of Solomon see Layman's Bible Commentary

Proverbs & Be-Act-itudes. Plastow. 1995. pap. 24.95 (*1-57320-040-9*) PraiseGathering.

Proverbs & Chants see Proverbios y Cantares

Proverbs & Ecclesiastes, Vol. 18. Ed. by R. B. Scott. LC 65-13988. (Anchor Bible Ser.: No. 18). 312p. 1965. 32.50 (*0-385-02177-1*, Anchor NY) Doubleday.

Proverbs & How to Collect Them. Margaret M. Bryant. (Publications of the American Dialect Society: No. 4). 25p. 1945. pap. 2.50 (*0-8173-0604-8*) U of Ala Pr.

Proverbs & Parables: God's Wisdom for Living. LC 98-66069. 131 p. 1998. write for info. (*0-9665118-0-8*) New Creation Pub.

Proverbs & Parables: God's Wisdom for Living. Dee Brestin. (Fisherman Bible Studyguide Ser.). 75p. 1975. pap. 4.99 (*0-87788-694-6*, H Shaw Pubs) Waterbrook Pr.

Proverbs & People: A Midrash on the Hebrew Alphabet. Illus. by Stavroulakis & Gordon M. Freeman. 12.00 (*0-943376-19-X*) Magnes Mus.

Proverbs & Proverbial Expressions in the German Works of Martin Luther. James C. Cornette, Jr. Ed. by Wolfgang Mieder & Dorothee Racette. LC 97-184041. (Sprichworterforschung Ser.: Bd. 19). 236p. (C). 1997. 44.95 (*3-906757-48-X*, Pub. by P Lang) P Lang Pubng.

Proverbs & Sayings of the Oromo People of Ethiopia & Kenya with English Translations. George Cotter. LC 92-4367. (African Studies: Vol. 25). (Illus.). 612p. 1992. lib. bdg. 129.95 (*0-7734-9695-5*) E Mellen.

Proverbs East & West: An Anthology of Chinese, Korean & Japanese Sayings with Western Equivalents. Illus. by Lee Hyunjoo. 281p. 1998. 27.95 (*0-930878-09-4*) Hollym Intl.

***Proverbs, Ecclesiastes & the Song of Songs.** Ellen F. Davis. (Westminster Bible Companion Ser.). 272p. 2000. pap. 21.95 (*0-664-25522-1*, Pub. by Westminster John Knox) Presbyterian Pub.

Proverbs, Ecclesiastes, Song of Songs. Duane A. Garrett. LC 93-10279. (New American Commentary Ser.: Vol. 14). 1993. 27.99 (*0-8054-0114-8*, 4201-14) Broadman.

Proverbs, Ecclesiastes, Song of Songs & Nibcot 12. Roland Murphy & Elizabeth Huwiler. LC 98-54757. (New International Biblical Commentary Ser.). 325p. 1999. pap. 11.95 (*1-56563-221-4*) Hendrickson MA.

Proverbs (Everyman's Bible Commentary) see Proverbios (Comentario Biblico Portavoz)

***Proverbs Family Nights Tool Chest.** Jim Weidmann. (Heritage Builders Ser.). 128p. 2000. pap. 13.99 (*0-7814-3361-4*) Chariot Victor.

Proverbs for Children. Gwen G. Germain. 32p. (J). 1995. 12.00 (*1-887978-00-3*); text 21.00 (*1-887978-01-1*) Clockwise.

Proverbs for Children. Kathy White. Ed. by Betty B. Haynes. (Illus.). 64p. (J). (ps-3). 1985. pap. 6.95 (*0-9616130-0-9*) Naftaolh Pubns.

Proverbs for Graduates. Brent D. Earles. 160p. (YA). (gr. 9). 1984. 9.99 (*0-8010-3415-9*) Baker Bks.

Proverbs for Parenting: A Topical Guide for Child Raising from the Book of Proverbs King James Version. 2nd ed. Barbara Decker. LC 87-50633. 320p. 1989. 15.95 (*0-9618608-3-9*) Lynns Bookshelf.

Proverbs for Parenting: A Topical Guide for Child Raising from the Book of Proverbs New International Version. Barbara Decker. LC 87-50633. 336p. 1991. 15.95 (*0-9618608-5-5*) Lynns Bookshelf.

Proverbs for Promise Keeping. Bob Beasley & Gene Getz. (Illus.). 192p. 1996. pap. 12.99 (*1-885358-21-0*, DB46401) Rainbow CA.

Proverbs for the Initiated. Kenn Mitchell. iv, 76p. 1999. pap. 11.00 (*1-891812-06-8*) Cedar Hill Pubns.

Proverbs for the Young . . . And the Not So Young. David R. Burgest. (Illus.). 75p. (Orig.). (YA). (gr. 7-12). 1989. pap. write for info. (*0-318-65788-0*) Self-Taught Pubs.

Proverbs for Today. David Hocking. Ed. by M. B. Steele. 256p. (Orig.). 1991. pap. 9.95 (*0-939497-24-7*) Promise Pub.

***Proverbs for Today: 2001 Original Sayings.** Raymond Brunk. 256p. 2000. 4.97 (*1-57748-798-2*) Barbour Pub.

Proverbs from Around the World. Compiled by Norma Gleason. 160p. 1992. pap. 8.95 (*0-8065-1310-1*, Citadel Pr) Carol Pub Group.

Proverbs from Around the World, Vol. II. Kathy Davis. (Great Quotations Ser.). (Illus.). 64p. 1992. 9.95 (*1-56245-053-0*) Great Quotations.

Proverbs from North: Words of Wisdom-Vikings. Compiled by Joanne Asala. 63p. 1994. pap. 10.95 (*1-57216-022-5*) Penfield.

Proverbs from the Armenian. Tr. by P. M. Manuelian from ARM. LC 80-13387. (Illus.). 150p. 1980. 8.95 (*0-933706-20-0*) Ararat Pr.

Proverbs in African Orature: The Aniocha-Igbo Experience. Ambrose A. Monye. LC 95-51095. 224p. (C). 1996. lib. bdg. 44.00 (*0-7618-0244-4*) U Pr of Amer.

Proverbs in Medieval Occitan Literature. Wendy Pfeffer. LC 96-15389. 200p. 1997. 49.95 (*0-8130-1480-8*) U Press Fla.

Proverbs in World Literature: A Bibliography. Ed. by Wolfgang Mieder & George B. Bryan. XIV, 305p. (C). 1997. text 42.95 (*0-8204-3499-X*) P Lang Pubng.

***Proverbs-Malachi.** 1999. 28.99 (*0-521-51301-4*) Cambridge U Pr.

Proverbs of Africa: Human Nature in the Nigerian Oral Tradition. Ed. by Ryszard Pachocinski. 424p. 1996. 29.95 (*1-885118-01-5*); pap. 19.95 (*1-885118-02-3*) Prof World Peace.

Proverbs of Alfred. Helen P. South. LC 71-133287. (English Literature Ser.: No. 33). 1970. reprint ed. lib. bdg. 75.00 (*0-8383-1186-5*) M S G Haskell Hse.

Proverbs of Ancient Sumer: The World's Earliest Proverb Collections, 2 vols., Set. Bendt Alster. LC 97-37014. 970p. 1996. 90.00 (*1-883053-20-X*) CDL Pr.

Proverbs of Jesus: Issues of History & Rhetoric. Alan P. Winton. (JSNT Supplement Ser.: No. 35). 236p. 1990. 70.00 (*1-85075-219-2*, Pub. by Sheffield Acad) CUP Services.

Proverbs of Scotland. Alexander Hislop. 1972. 59.95 (*0-8490-0910-3*) Gordon Pr.

***Proverbs of Success: The Heart & Soul of Highly Effective People.** John Grogan. 96p. 2000. pap. 5.95 (*1-58169-045-2*, Evergrn Pr AL) Genesis Comm Inc.

Proverbs of the Meadow & the Mountain. Thomas A. Clark. Ed. by Laurie Clark. (Illus.). 62p. 1986. pap. 10.00 (*0-87924-059-8*) Membrane Pr.

Proverbs of the Pennsylvania Germans. Edwin M. Fogel. LC 95-200080. 231p. 1995. 55.95 (*3-906753-80-8*) P Lang Pubng.

Proverbs of the Russian People, 2 vols. V. Dal'. (RUS.). 1984. 49.95 (*0-8288-2287-5*, M15187) Fr & Eur.

Proverbs 1-9. Michael V. Fox. LC 99-30321. (Anchor Bible Ser.: Vol. 1). (Illus.). 720p. 2000. 42.50 (*0-385-26437-2*) Doubleday.

Proverbs or Adages. Desiderius Erasmus. Tr. by Richard Taverner & DeWitt T. Starnes. LC 55-11634. 160p. 1977. reprint ed. 50.00 (*0-8201-1232-1*) Schol Facsimiles.

Proverbs Prayers: Praying the Wisdom of Proverbs into Your Life-Every Day. John Mason. LC 99-73387. 144p. 1999. 12.99 (*1-890900-11-7*) Insight Intl.

Proverbs, Proverbial Expressions & Popular Rhymes of Scotland. Andrew Cheviot. 1972. 59.95 (*0-8490-0911-1*) Gordon Pr.

Proverbs, Sentences & Proverbial Phrases from English Writings Before 1500. Bartlett J. Whiting & Helen W. Whiting. LC 67-22874. 784p. 1968. 65.00 (*0-674-71950-6*) Belknap Pr.

Proverbs, Songs, Epic Narratives, Folktales of East Asia: Selected Texts, Parallel Analysis & Comparative Approach. Ping-Chiu Yen. LC 97-9252. 306p. 1997. 46.50 (*0-7618-0750-0*) U Pr of Amer.

Proverbs, Textuality, & Nativism in African Literature. Adeleke Adeeko. LC 97-40247. 176p. 1998. 49.95 (*0-8130-1562-6*) U Press Fla.

Proverbs Thirty-One Lady & Other Impossible Dreams. Marsha Drake. LC 84-6453. 192p. (Orig.). 1984. pap. 8.99 (*0-87123-595-1*) Bethany Hse.

Proverbs 31 Woman. E. R. Reid. 112p. 1993. pap. 8.99 (*1-56043-612-3*, Treasure Hse) Destiny Image.

***Proverbs to Grow By: A Bible Verse for Every Day, to Help Me Live a Better Way.** Nelson Word Publishing Staff. (Jesus in My Pocket Ser.). (Illus.). 64p. (J). (ps-3). 2000. pap. 2.99 (*0-7852-0025-8*) W1CL.

Proverbs to Live By: Wisdom from Ages Past. Jerome A. Meneely. 128p. 1998. pap. 6.98 (*0-88290-639-9*, 1094) Horizon Utah.

Proverbs Twisted with Wit & Humor for Laughs or Tumor. Vito C. Vanderbilt. LC 88-47610. 150p. 1990. 34.95 (*1-55914-144-1*); pap. 29.95 (*1-55914-145-X*) ABBE Pubs Assn.

ProversityTM: Getting Past Face Value & Finding the Soul of People--A Manager's Journey. Lawrence O. Graham. LC 97-152796. 196p. 1997. 19.95 (*0-471-17818-7*) Wiley.

Provide Audio & Visual Aids. (EUITS Ser.: No. C-2). 77p. 1991. spiral bd. 69.50 (*0-87683-506-X*) GP Courseware.

Provide Career Guidance to Girls & Women Module, Competency-Based Career Guidance (CBCG) - Category C: Implementing. National Center for Research in Vocational Educati. 1985. 7.95 (*0-317-03910-5*, CG100C13) Ctr Educ Trng Employ.

Provide for Employability Skill Development Module, Competency-Based Career Guidance (CBCG) - Category C: Implementing. National Center for Research in Vocational Educati. 1985. 7.95 (*0-317-03911-3*, CG100C08) Ctr Educ Trng Employ.

Provide for the Basic Skills Module, Competency-Based Career Guidance (CBCG) - Category C: Implementing. National Center for Research in Vocational Educati. 1985. 7.95 (*0-317-03909-1*, CG100C09) Ctr Educ Trng Employ.

Providence. Anita Brookner. 1994. pap. 12.00 (*0-679-73814-2*) Knopf.

Providence. John Calvin. 27p. pap. 2.99 (*0-9652883-1-5*) Audubon Pr.

Providence. Will D. Campbell. LC 91-77196. 336p. 1992. 19.95 (*1-56352-024-9*) Longstreet.

***Providence.** Reginald Garrigou-Lagrange. Tr. by Dom Bede Rose from FRE. LC 98-61399. Orig. Title: La Providence et la Confiance en Dieu. 389p. 1999. pap. 15.00 (*0-89555-633-2*, 1573) TAN Bks Pubs.

Providence. Miranda Jarrett. (Historical Ser.). 1993. per. 3.99 (*0-373-28801-8*, 1-28801-8) Harlequin Bks.

Providence see Summa Contra Gentiles

Providence: A Rhode Island Mosaic. Doug White et al. LC 96-19358. (Urban Tapestry Ser.). (Illus.). 224p. 1996. 39.50 (*1-881096-30-0*) Towery Pub.

Providence: Poems. deluxe ed. Stephen Wallin. (Burning Deck Poetry Chapbooks Ser.). 20p. 1981. pap. 15.00 (*0-930900-86-3*) Burning Deck.

Providence: The Story of a Fifty-Year Vision Quest. Daniel Quinn. 192p. (Orig.). 1996. pap. 13.95 (*0-553-37549-0*) Bantam.

Providence, a Citywide Survey of Historic Resources. W. McKenzie Woodward et al. (Statewide Historical Preservation Reports: No. P-P-7). (Illus.). 288p. (Orig.). 1986. pap. 14.95 (*0-685-17309-7*) RI Hist Preserv.

Providence & Liberty, Vol. I. Frederic Bastiat. Ed. & Tr. by Raoul Audouin. 91p. (C). 1991. pap. text 6.00 (*1-880595-00-1*) Acton Inst Stu Rel.

Providence & Love: Studies in Wordsworth, Channing, Myers, George Eliot & Ruskin. John Beer. LC 98-29841. (Illus.). 356p. 1999. text 80.00 (*0-19-818436-0*) OUP.

***Providence & Prayer: How Does God Work in the World?** Terrance L. Tiessen. LC 00-26316. 2000. pap. write for info. (*0-8308-1578-3*) InterVarsity.

Providence & the Problem of Evil. Richard Swinburne. 278p. 1998. text 65.00 (*0-19-823799-5*); pap. text 19.95 (*0-19-823798-7*) OUP.

Providence & the Raj: Imperial Mission & Missionary Imperialism. Gerald Studdert-Kennedy. LC 98-20644. 273p. 1998. 44.95 (*0-7619-9277-4*) Sage.

Providence as "Idee-Maitresse" in the Works of Bossuet. Georgiana Terstegge. LC 73-128931. (Catholic University of America Studies in Romance Languages & Literatures: No. 43). 257p. 1970. reprint ed. 37.50 (*0-404-50334-9*) AMS Pr.

Providence Births, 1871 to 1880, Inclusive Vol. IX: Alphabetical Index of the Births, Marriages & Deaths. Charles V. Chapin. 545p. 1995. reprint ed. lib. bdg. 57.00 (*0-8328-4722-4*) Higginson Bk Co.

Providence College - Then & Now. Photos by Brian Smith. (First Edition Ser.). (Illus.). 112p. 1992. 39.95 (*0-916509-89-3*) Harmony Hse Pub.

Providence Deaths from 1851-1870, Inclusive Vol. III: Alphabetical Index of the Births, Marriages & Deaths Recorded in Providence. Edwin M. Snow. (Illus.). 627p. 1996. lib. bdg. 65.00 (*0-8328-5118-3*) Higginson Bk Co.

***Providence Entertainment, 2000.** (Illus.). 678p. 1999. pap. 25.00 (*1-880248-61-1*, 00R1) Enter Pubns.

Providence File. Amanda K. Williams. 250p. (Orig.). 1991. pap. 8.95 (*0-941483-92-4*) Naiad Pr.

Providence in Colonial Times. Gertrude S. Kimball. LC 76-87452. (American Scene Ser.). (Illus.). 391p. 1972. reprint ed. lib. bdg. 65.00 (*0-306-71524-4*) Da Capo.

Providence in Colonial Times. Gertrude S. Kimball. (Illus.). 392p. 1992. reprint ed. lib. bdg. 45.00 (*0-8328-2261-2*) Higginson Bk Co.

Providence in Early Modern England. Alexandra Walsham. LC 99-17608. (Illus.). 408p. 1999. text 85.00 (*0-19-820655-0*) OUP.

***Providence Indexes to Early Town Records, from 4th & 5th Reports of the Record Commissioners, 2 vols.** 383p. 1999. reprint ed. pap. 37.50 (*0-8328-9896-1*) Higginson Bk Co.

Providence Island, 1630-1641: The Other Puritan Colony. Karen O. Kupperman. LC 92-35759. (Illus.). 409p. (C). 1993. text 74.95 (*0-521-35205-3*) Cambridge U Pr.

Providence Island, 1630-1641: The Other Puritan Colony. Karen O. Kupperman. (Illus.). 409p. (C). 1995. pap. text 20.95 (*0-521-55835-2*) Cambridge U Pr.

Providence of God see Contours of Christian Theology Series

Providence of God in History. Edward Panosian et al. 48p. 1996. pap. 3.25 (*0-89084-865-3*, 093286) Bob Jones Univ.

Providence of Jurisprudence Determined, 1832. John Austin. LC 99-33457. 2000. reprint ed. 75.00 (*1-58477-023-6*) Lawbk Exchange.

Providence of Wit: Aspects of Form in Augustan Literature & the Arts. Martin C. Battestin. x, 331p. (C). 1974. pap. text 16.50 (*0-8139-1235-0*) U Pr of Va.

(Providence) Owners & Occupants of the Lots, Houses & Shops in the Town of Providence in 1798: With Maps of Providence, 1650-1765-1770. Henry R. Chace. (Illus.). 66p. 1997. reprint ed. pap. 12.00 (*0-8328-6485-4*) Higginson Bk Co.

Providence 1649: The History & Archaeology of Anne Arundel County, Maryland. Al Luckenbach. LC 99-489351. (Studies in Local History). 1995. pap. 10.00 (*0-942370-41-4*) MD St Archives.

Providence Smiled: My Deaf Brother's Story. LC 97-93898. (Illus.). 360p. 1997. pap. 19.95 (*0-9659083-0-5*) JCM Pub.

***Providence Tales & the Birth of American Literature.** James D. Hartman. LC 98-36542. 216p. 1999. 38.50 (*0-8018-6027-X*) Johns Hopkins.

Provident Sea. D. H. Cushing. (Illus.). 336p. 1988. text 85.00 (*0-521-25727-1*) Cambridge U Pr.

Providential Accidents: An Autobiography. Geza Vermes. 288p. 1998. pap. 24.95 (*0-8476-9340-6*) Rowman.

Providential Aesthetic in Victorian Fiction. Thomas Vargish. LC 84-29098. 264p. reprint ed. pap. 81.90 (*0-7837-4351-3*, 204406100012) Bks Demand.

Providential Anti-Semitism: Nationalism & Polity in Nineteenth-Century Romania. William O. Oldson. LC 90-56109. (Memoirs Ser.: Vol. 193). (Illus.). 177p. (Orig.). (C). 1991. pap. 20.00 (*0-87169-193-0*, M193-OLW) Am Philos.

Providential Deliverance. W. A. Spicer. LC 96-60017. 128p. 1996. reprint ed. per. 7.95 (*1-57258-102-6*) Teach Servs.

Providential Order of the World. Alexander B. Bruce. LC 77-27225. (Gifford Lectures: 1897). 1978. reprint ed. 47.50 (*0-404-60455-2*) AMS Pr.

Provider. David Shobin. 320p. mass mkt. 6.99 (*0-312-97185-0*) St Martin.

Provider Report Cards: A Guide for Promoting Health Care Quality to the Public. Patrice L. Spath. LC 99-20309. xix, 154 p. 1999. pap. 32.00 (*1-55648-250-7*) AHPI.

Provider Sponsored Organizations: Emerging Opportunities for Growth. Fine & Colleen E. Dowd. LC 98-28499. 190p. 1998. 79.00 (*0-8342-1177-7*, 11777) Aspen Pub.

Providing a Foundation for Teaching Mathematics in the Middle Grades. Ed. by Judith T. Sowder & Bonnie P. Schappelle. LC 94-23451. (SUNY Series, Reform in Mathematics Education). 336p. (C). 1995. pap. text 19.95 (*0-7914-2534-7*) State U NY Pr.

Providing a Secure Environment for Learning. Antoine Bousquet. 84p. 1998. pap. 19.00 (*92-64-05756-0*, 95 98 01 3 P, Pub. by Org for Econ) OECD.

Providing Access for Large Trucks. (Special Reports: No. 223). 316p. 1989. 25.00 (*0-309-04751-X*) Transport Res Bd.

Providing Alternatives to Mortgage Disclosure: A Report to Congress. Charles A. Capone, Jr. et al. (Illus.). 176p. (Orig.). (C). 1996. pap. text 35.00 (*0-7881-2822-1*) DIANE Pub.

Providing & Receiving Consultation in Long-Term Care. Marylou Hughes. 1998. 29.50 (*0-929442-31-8*, 2137PP) Prof Prnting & Pub.

Providing Benchmarking Services for Internal Auditing Clients. Mark L. Frigo & Institute of Internal Auditors. Research Foundation. Ed. by Lee A. Campbell. LC 97-170363. 91p. 1997. pap. 65.00 (*0-89413-376-4*) Inst Inter Aud.

Providing Community-Based Services to the Rural Elderly. Ed. by John A. Krout. (Focus Editions Ser.: Vol. 165). (Illus.). 388p. (C). 1993. text 59.95 (*0-8039-4695-3*); pap. text 26.00 (*0-8039-4696-1*) Sage.

An Asterisk (*) at the beginning of an entry indicates that the title is appearing for the first time.

Providing Comprehensive Sexual Health Care in Spinal Cord Injury Rehabilitation: Continuing Education & Training for Health Care Professionals. Mitchell S. Tepper. 143p. 1997. ring bd. 95.00 (*0-9659185-0-5*) Sexual Hlth.

Providing Constructive Feedback. Jane Westberg & Hilliard Jason. 72p. (Orig.). (C). 1991. pap. text 15.00 (*0-938540-19-X*) CIS.

***Providing Continuity of Care: Death, Dying & Grief.** Sharon Edwards. (Illus.). 74p. 2000. pap. 29.95 (*1-888343-30-3*) Hartman Pub.

Providing Employment Support for People with Long-Term Mental Illness: Choices, Resources, & Practical Strategies. Laurie H. Ford. 352p. 1995. pap. 30.95 (*1-55766-190-1*) P H Brookes.

Providing Enterprise Development & Financial Services to Women: A Decade of Bank Experience in Asia. Lynn Bennett & Mike Goldberg. LC 93-21457. (Asia Technical Department Ser.: Vol. 236). 70p. 1993. pap. 22.00 (*0-8213-2682-1*, 12682) World Bank.

Providing Executive Protection (P. E. P.) Ed. by Richard W. Kobetz. LC 90-85357. (Illus.). 264p. 1991. 29.00 (*0-9628411-0-2*) Exec Protect Inst.

Providing Executive Protection (P. E. P.), Vol. II. Ed. by Richard W. Kobetz. LC 94-61208. (Illus.). 306p. 1994. 29.00 (*0-9628411-1-0*) Exec Protect Inst.

Providing Food Security for All. (IFAD Studies in Rural Poverty: No. 1). 269p. 1991. 22.00 (*92-1-190001-8*, 91.II.A.14) UN.

Providing Food Security for All. Mohivddin Alamgir & Poonam Arora. (Studies in Rural Poverty: An International Fund for Agricultural Development Ser.). 304p. (C). 1991. text 50.00 (*0-8147-0603-7*) NYU Pr.

Providing for Individual Differences in Student Learning: A Mastery Learning Approach. Jackson F. Lee, Jr. & K. Wayne Pruitt. (Illus.). 130p. 1984. pap. 20.95 (*0-398-06225-0*) C C Thomas.

Providing for Individual Differences in Student Learning: A Mastery Learning Approach. Jackson F. Lee, Jr. & K. Wayne Pruitt. (Illus.). 130p. (C). 1984. 33.95 (*0-398-05028-7*) C C Thomas.

Providing for the Preschool Child with Problems. rev. ed. 1986. 6.00 (*0-939418-29-0*) Ferguson-Florissant.

Providing Foreign Products to the Federal Government. 3rd rev. ed. Barry L. McVay. (Panoptic Federal Contracting Ser.). 35p. 1998. pap. 29.95 (*0-912481-14-5*) Panoptic Ent.

Providing Health Care: The Economics of Alternative Systems of Finance & Delivery. Ed. by Alistair McGuire et al. (Illus.). 312p. 1991. 75.00 (*0-19-828322-9*) OUP.

Providing Health Care Benefits in Retirement. Ed. by Judith F. Mazo et al. LC 94-13655. (Pensions Research Council Publications). 280p. (C). 1994. text 42.50 (*0-8122-3270-4*) U of Pa Pr.

Providing Home Care: A Textbook for Home Care Aides. William Leahy. Ed. by Jetta Fuzy & Julie Grafe. (Illus.). 368p. (C). 1998. pap. text 34.95 (*1-888343-22-2*, TEXT22-2) Hartman Pub.

Providing Hospital Services: The Changing Financial Environment. Gerard F. Anderson. LC 89-1855. (Johns Hopkins Studies in Health Care Finance & Administration: No. 2). (Illus.). 246p. 1989. reprint ed. pap. 76.30 (*0-608-05922-6*, 206625800008) Bks Demand.

Providing Learning Assistance in the Home, 4 modules, Module 3. Sharon K. Johnson & Clarence D. Johnson. (FAST (Families & Schools Together) Ser.). (Illus.). 42p. 1994. pap. write for info. (*1-57035-022-1*, 56MOD) Sopris.

Providing Library Services to Children & Young People: A Practical Handbook. Catherine Blanshard. 192p. 1997. pap. 80.00 (*1-85604-226-X*, LAP226X, Pub. by Library Association) Bernan Associates.

Providing Litigation Services. (MAS Technical Consulting Practice Aid Ser.). 1993. 16.50 (*0-685-18172-3*) Am Inst CPA.

Providing National Statistics on Health & Social Welfare Programs in an Era of Change: Summary of a Workshop. National Research Council Staff. Ed. by Constance F. Citro et al. LC 98-207848. 72p. 1998. pap. text 15.00 (*0-309-06040-0*) Natl Acad Pr.

Providing Palliative Care Services: Towards an Evidence Base. Nick Bosanquet & Chris Salisbury. LC 98-40982. 286p. 1999. pap. text 49.95 (*0-19-262991-3*) OUP.

Providing Personalized Customer Service. Robert Taggart. Ed. by Debbie Woodbury. LC 98-74370. (Retailing Smarts Ser.). (Illus.). 120p. 1998. pap. 19.95 (*1-56052-518-5*) Crisp Pubns.

Providing Programs for the Gifted/Talented Students see Reaching for the Stars Series: A Minicourse for Education of Gifted Students

Providing Quality Food & Beverage Services. unabridged ed. (NGF Info Pacs Ser.). (Illus.). 175p. (Orig.). 1998. pap. 45.00 (*1-57701-000-0*, 99LB007) Natl Golf.

Providing Recognition: A Handbook of Ideas. Recognition Systems Staff. 1974. ring bd. 24.90 (*0-89401-103-0*) Didactic Syst.

Providing Reference Service in Church & Synagogue Libraries. Jennifer Pritchett. LC 87-15776. (Guide Ser.: No. 15). 60p. 1987. pap. 9.75 (*0-915324-26-1*) CSLA.

Providing Reference Services for Archives & Manuscripts. Mary J. Pugh. (Archival Fundamentals Ser.). 124p. 1992. pap. 27.00 (*0-931828-82-1*) Soc Am Archivists.

***Providing Residential Services for Children & Young People: A Multidisciplinary Perspective.** Catherine Street. 258p. 1999. text 69.95 (*0-7546-1120-5*, Pub. by Inst Materials) Ashgate Pub Co.

Providing Safe Drinking Water in Small Systems: Technology, Operations & Economics. International Symposium on Safe Drinking Water in Small Systems Technology Operations Staff et al. LC 99-11450. 650p. 1999. 79.95 (*1-56670-393-X*) Lewis Pubs.

Providing Safe Health Care. National Education Association Staff. 1996. pap. 13.75 (*0-8106-1876-1*) NEA.

***Providing Security Services & Consulting.** Jody Ball & Anne Parker. 1999. spiral bd. 24.95 (*1-891247-32-8*) Thomas Investigative.

Providing Services for People with Vision Loss: A Multidisciplinary Perspective. Ed. by Susan L. Greenblatt. 1989. pap. 19.95 (*0-929718-02-X*) Resc Rehab.

Providing Supportive Services to the Frail Elderly in Federally Assisted Housing. Raymond J. Struyk et al. LC 89-5796. (Urban Institute Report: No. 89-2). (Illus.). 256p. 1989. pap. text 20.00 (*0-87766-462-5*) Urban Inst.

Providing the Home Court Advantage in the Classroom. Thomas J. Brown. LC 98-92866. 64p. 1998. 6.50 (*1-891404-01-6*, BA009); pap. 8.50 (*1-891404-03-2*, BH009) Brown & Assocs.

Providing 360-Degree Feedback: An Approach to Enhancing Individual & Organizational Performance. Mark R. Edwards & Ann J. Ewen. (Building Blocks Ser.: Vol. 31). (Illus.). 28p. (Orig.). 1996. pap. 24.95 (*1-57963-032-4*, A0231) Am Compensation.

Providing Useful Information for Deans & Department Chairs. Ed. by Mary K. Kinnick. LC 85-645339. (New Directions for Institutional Research Ser.: No. IR 84). 110p. (Orig.). 1994. pap. 22.00 (*0-7879-9989-X*) Jossey-Bass.

Province & Function of Law: Law As Logic, Justice & Social Control. A Study in Jurisprudence. 2nd ed. Julius Stone. LC 46-21845. lxi, 918p. 1973. reprint ed. lib. bdg. 55.00 (*0-930342-75-5*, 301560) W S Hein.

Province de Quebec. Andre Beaulieu & William F. Morley. LC 72-151555. (Canadian Local Histories to 1950: A Bibliography Ser.: No. 2). 436p. reprint ed. pap. 135.20 (*0-8357-8199-2*, 203400500088) Bks Demand.

Province in Rebellion: A Documentary History of the Founding of the Commonwealth of Massachusetts, 1774-1775. Ed. by L. Kinvin Wroth et al. (Harvard Audio Visual Materials Ser.). 343p. 1975. pap. 100.00 (*0-674-71955-7*) HUP.

Province of Administrative Law. Ed. by Michael Taggart. LC 98-130363. 424p. 1997. 90.00 (*1-901362-01-9*, Pub. by Hart Pub); pap. 40.00 (*1-901362-02-7*, Pub. by Hart Pub) Northwestern U Pr.

Province of Fire. Geraldine Connolly. LC 98-88641. xi, 82 p. 1998. write for info. (*0-916078-46-9*) Iris Pr.

Province of Jurisprudence - Determined & the Uses of the Study of Jurisprudence. John Austin. LC 98-30371. 432p. (C). 1998. reprint ed. pap. 16.95 (*0-87220-432-4*); reprint ed. lib. bdg. 37.95 (*0-87220-433-2*) Hackett Pub.

Province of Jurisprudence Determined. John Austin. LC 96-6122. (Classical Jurisprudence Ser.). (Illus.). 280p. 1996. text 68.95 (*1-85521-649-3*, Pub. by Dartmth Pub) Ashgate Pub Co.

***Province of Jurisprudence Determined.** John Austin. 410p. 2000. pap. 14.95 (*1-57392-845-3*) Prometheus Bks.

Province of New Jersey, 1664-1738. Edwin P. Tanner. LC 08-33297. (Columbia University. Studies in the Social Sciences: No. 80). reprint ed. 57.50 (*0-404-51080-9*) AMS Pr.

Province of Piety: Moral History in Hawthorne's Early Tales. Michael J. Colacurcio. LC 94-42365. 680p. 1995. pap. text 21.95 (*0-8223-1572-6*) Duke.

Province of Piety: Moral History in Hawthorne's Early Tales. Michael J. Colacurcio. LC 83-26586. 680p. 1984. 45.00 (*0-674-71957-3*) HUP.

Province of Quebec & the Early American Revolution: A Study in English-American Colonial History. Victor Coffin. 566p. 1995. reprint ed. pap. text 21.00 (*0-7884-0154-8*) Heritage Bk.

Province of Reason. Sam B. Warner, Jr. 320p. 1984. 32.00 (*0-674-71956-5*) Belknap Pr.

Province of Reason. Sam B. Warner, Jr. LC 84-7653. (Illus.). 320p. 1988. pap. text 12.50 (*0-674-71958-1*) Belknap Pr.

Province sous l'Ancien Regime, 2 vols., Vols. 1 - 2. Albert A. Babeau. LC 77-161720. 87.50 (*0-404-07506-1*) AMS Pr.

Provinces. Richard Grossinger. 1975. 5.00 (*0-913028-31-2*) North Atlantic.

Provinces. Czeslaw Milosz. Tr. by Robert Hass. 1991. 19.95 (*0-88001-317-6*) HarpC.

Provinces. Czeslaw Milosz. Tr. by Robert Hass. LC 92-44647. 1993. pap. 9.95 (*0-88001-321-4*) HarpC.

Provinces: Canadian Provincial Politics. Chris Dunn. 400p. 1996. pap. 27.95 (*1-55111-090-3*) Broadview Pr.

***Provinces & Cities of China.** Lynn M. Stone. LC 00-39006. 2000. write for info. (*1-55916-320-8*) Rourke Bk Co.

Provinces & Provincial Capitals of the World. 2nd ed. Compiled by Morris Fisher. LC 83-22125. 258p. 1985. 26.50 (*0-8108-1758-6*) Scarecrow.

Provinces of Early Mexico: Variants of Spanish American Regional Evolution. Ed. by James Lockhart & Ida Altman. LC 76-620055. (UCLA Latin American Studies: Vol. 36). (Illus.). 291p. 1984. pap. 17.95 (*0-87903-110-7*) UCLA Lat Am Ctr.

***Provinces of Night.** William Gay. LC 00-24214. 336p. 2000. 23.95 (*0-385-49927-2*) Doubleday.

Provinces of the Roman Empire: The European Provinces. Theodor Mommsen. Ed. by T. Robert Broughton. LC 68-16707. (Classic European Historians Ser.). (Illus.). 1968. pap. text 4.50 (*0-226-53395-6*, P305) U Ch Pr.

Provincetown, Vol. I. John Hardy Wright. (Images of America Ser.). 1997. pap. 16.99 (*0-7524-0484-9*) Arcadia Publng.

Provincetown, Vol. II. John Hardy Wright. LC 98-85879. (Images of America Ser.). (Illus.). 128p. 1998. pap. 16.99 (*0-7524-1218-3*) Arcadia Publng.

Provincetown! Questions You Don't Dare Ask (& Answers) Noel W. Beyle. (No. 18). (Illus.). 48p. (Orig.). 1983. pap. 0.95 (*0-912609-02-8*) First Encounter.

Provincetown & Other Poems. Leo Connellan. 77p. 1995. pap. 11.00 (*1-880684-29-2*) Curbstone.

Provincetown Art Association & Museum Collection. Tony Vevers et al. LC 98-67293. (Illus.). 160p. 1998. pap. 30.00 (*0-9666360-0-7*) Provincetown Arts.

Provincetown Arts: 1988 Annual. Ed. by Christopher Busa & Raymond S. Elman. (Robert Motherwell Cover Ser.). (Illus.). 184p. (Orig.). 1988. pap. 4.00 (*0-944854-00-1*) Provincetown Arts.

Provincetown Arts: 1990 Annual. Ed. by Christopher Busa. (Joel Meyerowitz Cover Ser.). (Illus.). 184p. (Orig.). 1990. pap. 5.00 (*0-944854-02-8*) Provincetown Arts.

Provincetown Arts: 1991 Annual. Ed. by Christopher Busa. (Long Point Artists Cover Ser.: Vol. 7). (Illus.). 184p. (Orig.). 1991. pap. 6.50 (*0-944854-03-6*) Provincetown Arts.

Provincetown Arts: 1992 Annual. Ed. by Christopher Busa. (Stanley Kunitz Cover Subject Ser.: Vol. 8). (Illus.). 184p. (Orig.). 1992. pap. 6.50 (*0-944854-04-4*) Provincetown Arts.

Provincetown Arts: 1993 Annual. Ed. by Christopher Busa. (Fine Arts Work Center in Provincetown Cover Subject Ser.: Vol. 9). (Illus.). 184p. (Orig.). 1993. pap. 6.50 (*0-944854-10-9*) Provincetown Arts.

Provincetown Arts: 1994 Annual. Ed. by Christopher Busa. (Illus.). 164p. (Orig.). 1994. pap. 6.50 (*0-944854-13-3*) Provincetown Arts.

Provincetown Arts: 1995 Annual. Ed. by Christopher Busa. (Mary Oliver Cover Subject Ser.). (Illus.). 164p. 1995. pap. 6.50 (*0-944854-21-4*) Provincetown Arts.

Provincetown Arts Annual: 1989 Annual. Ed. by Christopher Busa & Raymond S. Elman. (Annie Dillard Cover Ser.). (Illus.). 184p. (Orig.). 1990. pap. 5.00 (*0-944854-01-X*) Provincetown Arts.

Provincetown Arts, 1997 Annual. Ed. by Christopher Busa. (John Waters Cover Subject Ser.: Vol. 13). (Illus.). 164p. 1997. pap. 6.50 (*0-944854-32-X*) Provincetown Arts.

Provincetown Arts, 1996 Annual. Ed. by Christopher Busa. (Karen Finley Cover Ser.: Vol. 12). (Illus.). 164p. 1996. pap. 6.50 (*0-944854-30-3*) Provincetown Arts.

Provincetown Discovered. Edmund V. Gillon. LC 85-52374. (Illus.). 127p. 1986. pap. 12.95 (*0-88740-061-2*) Schiffer.

***Provincetown Dogs.** Susan Baker. LC 99-44080. (Illus.). 40p. 2000. pap. 12.95 (*1-58465-037-0*) U Pr of New Eng.

Provincetown Massachusetts Cemetery Inscriptions. Lurana H. Cook et al. 255p. (Orig.). 1980. pap. 20.00 (*0-917890-18-3*) Heritage Bk.

Provincetown: or Odds & Ends from the Tip End. Herman A. Jennings. (Illus.). 212p. 1993. reprint ed. lib. bdg. 27.50 (*0-8328-3178-6*) Higginson Bk Co.

Provincetown Plays, Second Series. LC 76-40392. (One-Act Plays in Reprint Ser.). 1976. reprint ed. 20.00 (*0-8486-2007-0*) Roth Pub Inc.

Provincetown Review, 2 vols., Nos. 1-7. reprint ed. 87.50 (*0-404-19544-X*) AMS Pr.

Provincetown Seafood Cookbook. Howard Mitcham. 288p. 1986. reprint ed. pap. 12.50 (*0-940160-33-1*) Parnassus Imprints.

Provincetown Summer. 4th ed. Lindsay Welsh. 1997. reprint ed. mass mkt. 6.50 (*1-56333-508-5*, Rosebud) Masquerade.

Provincetown Tales. Caleb Knight. 168p. 1998. pap. 10.00 (*0-9665917-0-4*, 987-1) Nocturnis Prodns.

Provincia Arabia, 3 vols., Vol. I. Rudolf E. Brunnow & Alfred V. Domaszewski. (Illus.). 532p. reprint ed. write for info. (*0-318-71491-4*) G Olms Pubs.

Provincial: Calvin Coolidge & His World, 1885-1895. Hendrik Booraem. LC 94-20106. 1995. 39.50 (*0-8387-5264-0*) Bucknell U Pr.

Provincial Administration of Siam, 1892-1915. Tej Bunnag. (East Asian Historical Monographs). 1978. 29.95 (*0-19-580343-4*) OUP.

Provincial America, 1690-1740. Evarts B. Greene. (BCL1 - U. S. History Ser.). 356p. 1991. reprint ed. lib. bdg. 89.00 (*0-7812-6097-3*) Rprt Serv.

Provincial America, 1690-1740, 6. Evarts B. Greene. LC 79-25852. (Field Museum of Natural History: Vol. 6). (Illus.). 356p. 1980. reprint ed. lib. bdg. 35.00 (*0-313-22242-8*, GRPR, Greenwood Pr) Greenwood.

Provincial American & Other Papers. Meredith Nicholson. LC 79-152205. (Essay Index Reprint Ser.). 1977. 20.95 (*0-8369-2211-5*) Ayer.

Provincial & Local Taxation in Canada. Solomon Vineberg. LC 70-76698. (Columbia University. Studies in the Social Sciences: No. 128). reprint ed. 29.50 (*0-404-51128-7*) AMS Pr.

***Provincial & National Park Campgrounds in British Columbia: A Complete Guide.** 2nd ed. Jayne Seagrave. (Illus.). 224p. 1998. pap. 16.95 (*1-895811-53-8*) Heritage Hse.

Provincial & State Papers, 18 vols., Set. New Hampshire State Legislature Staff. Ed. by Nathaniel Bouton & I. W. Hammond. LC 70-173073. reprint ed. 1690.00 (*0-404-07450-2*) AMS Pr.

Provincial & Territorial Legislatures in Canada. Ed. by Gary Levy & Graham White. 369p. 1989. pap. 18.95 (*0-8020-6734-4*) U of Toronto Pr.

Provincial Anecdotes. Aleksandr Vampilov. (Russian Theatre Archive Ser.). 56p. 1996. pap. text 4.00 (*3-7186-5838-0*, ECU5, Harwood Acad Pubs) Gordon & Breach.

Provincial at Rome: And Rome & the Balkans 80 B. C.-A. D. 14. Ronald Syme. Ed. by Anthony Birley. 256p. 1999. 69.95 (*0-85989-632-3*) Univ Exeter Pr.

Provincial Committees of Safety of the American Revolution. Agnes Hunt. LC 68-24986. (American History & Americana Ser.: No. 47). 1969. reprint ed. lib. bdg. 75.00 (*0-8383-0207-6*) M S G Haskell Hse.

Provincial Committees of Safety of the American Revolution. Agnes Hunt. (BCL1 - U. S. History Ser.). 180p. 1991. reprint ed. lib. bdg. 69.00 (*0-7812-6113-9*) Rprt Serv.

Provincial Councillors of Pennsylvania Who Held Office Before 1773-1776: And Those Earlier Councillors Who Were Some Time Chief Magistrates of the Province & Their Descendants. Charles P. Keith. LC 96-79573. 628p. 1997. reprint ed. 31.95 (*0-8063-1529-6*) Genealog Pub.

Provincial Deputation in Mexico: Harbinger of Provincial Autonomy, Independence, & Federalism. Nettie L. Benson. LC 91-43937. (Institute of Latin American Studies Special Publication). (Illus.). 239p. 1992. text 35.00 (*0-292-76531-2*) U of Tex Pr.

Provincial Elite in Early Modern Tuscany: Family & Power in the Creation of the State. Giovanna Benadusi. LC 95-44489. (Studies in Historical & Political Science, 112th Series (1994): Series 114, No. 3). 264p. (C). 1996. text 49.95 (*0-8018-5248-X*) Johns Hopkins.

Provincial Families of the Renaissance: Private & Public Life in the Veneto. James S. Grubb. LC 95-53072. 352p. 1996. text 45.00 (*0-8018-5321-4*) Johns Hopkins.

Provincial Inca: Archaeological & Ethnohistorical Assessment of the Impact of the Inca State. Ed. by Michael A. Malpass. LC 93-30296. (Illus.). 290p. 1993. pap. text 25.95 (*0-87745-426-4*) U of Iowa Pr.

Provincial Justice: Profiles in Upper Canadian Legal History from the D. C. B. Ed. by Robert Fraser. (Publications of the Osgoode Society). 512p. 1992. text 65.00 (*0-8020-2896-9*); pap. text 35.00 (*0-8020-7404-9*) U of Toronto Pr.

***Provincial Lady in America.** E. M. Delafield. (Illus.). 245p. 2000. reprint ed. pap. 16.95 (*0-89733-110-9*) Academy Chi Pubs.

Provincial Lady in London. E. M. Delafield. (Provincial Lady Ser.). (Illus.). 302p. 1999. pap. 15.00 (*0-89733-085-4*) Academy Chi Pubs.

Provincial Lady in Russia: I Visit the Soviets. E. M. Delafield. (Illus.). 344p. 1998. reprint ed. pap. 15.00 (*0-89733-156-7*) Academy Chi Pubs.

Provincial Lady in Wartime. E. M. Delafield. LC 86-22140. (Illus.). 349p. 1986. pap. 8.95 (*0-89733-210-5*) Academy Chi Pubs.

Provincial Leadership in China: The Cultural Revolution & Its Aftermath. Frederick C. Teiwes. (Cornell East Asia Ser.: No. 4). 169p. 1974. pap. 8.50 (*0-939657-04-X*) Cornell East Asia Pgm.

Provincial Leaderships in Syria, Fifteen Seventy-Five to Sixteen Fifty. Abdul-Rahim Abu-Husayn. 230p. 1985. text 29.95 (*0-8156-6072-3*, Pub. by Am U Beirut) Syracuse U Pr.

Provincial Letters. Blaise Pascal. 210p. 1997. pap. 18.00 (*1-57910-096-1*) Wipf & Stock.

Provincial Lives: Middle-Class Experience in the Antebellum Middle West. Timothy R. Mahoney. LC 98-35800. (Publications of the German Historical Institute, Washington, D. C.). (Illus.). 384p. (C). 1999. text 54.95 (*0-521-64092-X*) Cambridge U Pr.

Provincial Magistrates & Revolutionary Politics in France, 1789-1795. Philip Dawson. LC 74-182816. (Historical Monographs: No. 66). (Illus.). 436p. 1972. 30.00 (*0-674-71960-3*) HUP.

Provincial Mid-Decade Goals Completion of Work Plans. 464p. 1994. write for info. (*92-806-3133-0*) U N I C E.

Provincial Names & Folk Lore of British Birds. Charles Swainson. (English Dialect Society Publications: No. 47). 1974. reprint ed. pap. 30.00 (*0-8115-0471-9*) Periodicals Srv.

Provincial Party Financing in Quebec. Harold M. Angell. LC 95-39227. 124p. 1995. lib. bdg. 29.00 (*0-7618-0156-1*) U Pr of Amer.

Provincial Passages: Culture, Space, & the Origins of Chinese Communism. Wen-hsin Yeh. LC 95-38179. (Illus.). 410p. (C). 1996. 55.00 (*0-520-20068-3*, Pub. by U CA Pr) Cal Prin Full Svc.

Provincial Politics & the Pakistan Movement: The Growth of the Muslim League in North West & North East India, 1937-47. Ian Talbot. (Illus.). 174p. 1989. text 21.00 (*0-19-577387-X*) OUP.

Provincial Public Finance in Ontario: An Empirical Analysis of the Last Twenty-Five Years. David K. Foot. LC 78-303949. (Ontario Economic Council Research Studies: No. 12). 225p. reprint ed. pap. 69.80 (*0-8357-4024-2*, 203671600005) Bks Demand.

Provincial Society, 1690-1763. James T. Adams. (History - United States Ser.). 374p. 1991. reprint ed. lib. bdg. 99.00 (*0-7812-6093-0*) Rprt Serv.

Provincial Stock Exchanges. W. A. Thomas. (Illus.). 360p. 1973. 37.50 (*0-7146-2981-2*, Pub. by F Cass Pubs) Intl Spec Bk.

Provincial Strategies of Economic Reform in Post-Mao China: Leadership, Politics & Implementation. Ed. by Peter T. Cheung et al. LC 97-32756. (Studies on Contemporary China). 472p. (C). (gr. 13). 1998. pap. text 38.95 (*0-7656-0147-8*, East Gate Bk) M E Sharpe.

Provincial Strategies of Economic Reform in Post-Mao China: Leadership, Politics & Implementation. Ed. by Peter T. Y. Cheung et al. LC 97-32756. (Studies on Contemporary China). 472p. (C). (gr. 13). 1998. text 76.95 (*0-7656-0146-X*, East Gate Bk) M E Sharpe.

An Asterisk (*) at the beginning of an entry indicates that the title is appearing for the first time.

Provincial Tax Reforms: Options & Opportunities. Ed. by David Conklin & France St-Hilaire. 192p. 1990. pap. text 23.95 (*0-88645-111-6*, Pub. by Inst Res Pub) Ashgate Pub Co.

Provincial Token Coinage of the 18th Century. R. Dalton & S. H. Hamer. (Illus.). 1990. write for info. (*0-9627694-0-1*) Davissons Ltd.

Provincial Towns of Georgian England: A Study of the Building Process, 1740-1820. Christopher W. Chalklin. LC 74-82919. (Studies in Urban History: No. 3). 405p. reprint ed. pap. 125.60 (*0-7837-1037-2*, 204134800020) Bks Demand.

Provincial Types in American Fiction. Horace S. Fiske. (BCL1-PS American Literature Ser.). 264p. 1992. reprint ed. lib. bdg. 79.00 (*0-7812-6615-7*) Rprt Serv.

Provinciales. Jean Giraudoux. 9.95 (*0-686-54010-7*); 12.95 (*0-685-23908-X*); pap. 3.95 (*0-686-54011-5*) Fr & Eur.

Provinciales. Blaise Pascal. (FRE.). 1966. 10.95 (*0-8288-9947-9*, F40580) Fr & Eur.

Provincialisms of East Norfolk see English Dialect Society Publications, No. 1: Glossaries I-VII

Provincialisms of East Yorkshire see English Dialect Society Publications, No. 1: Glossaries I-VII

Provincialisms of the Midland Counties see English Dialect Society Publications, No. 1: Glossaries I-VII

Provincialisms of the Vale of Gloucester see English Dialect Society Publications, No. 1: Glossaries I-VII

Provincialisms of West Devonshire see English Dialect Society Publications, No. 1: Glossaries I-VII

***Provincializing Europe: Postcolonial Thought & Historical Difference.** Dipesh Chakrabarty. LC 99-87722. (Studies in Culture - Power - History). (Illus.). 336p. 2000. pap. 16.95 (*0-691-04909-2*, Pub. by Princeton U Pr) Cal Prin Full Svc.

***Provincializing Europe: Postcolonial Thought & Historical Difference.** Dipesh Chakrabarty. LC 99-87722. (Reprints of Economics Classics Ser.). (Illus.). 336p. 2000. 55.00 (*0-691-04908-4*) Princeton U Pr.

Provincials: A Personal History of Jews in the South. Eli N. Evans. LC 97-20931. 1997. per. 16.00 (*0-684-83412-X*) S&S Trade.

Proving. Thomas Szollosi. 224p. 1989. pap. 3.95 (*0-380-70788-8*, Avon Bks) Morrow Avon.

Proving & Defending Against Damages in Personal Injury Litigation 1993. (Litigation & Administrative Practice Course Handbook, 1983-84 Ser.: Vol. 465). 291p. 1993. 70.00 (*0-685-69739-8*, H4-5169) PLI.

Proving & Pricing Construction Claims, 1. 2nd ed. Robert F. Cushman. LC 96-585. 624p. 1997. boxed set 150.00 (*0-471-11424-3*) Wiley.

Proving Antitrust Damages: Legal & Economic Issues. LC 95-80580. 264p. 1996. pap. 65.00 (*1-57073-236-1*, 503-0277, ABA Antitrust) Amer Bar Assn.

***Proving Doctrine: The Uses of Scripture in Modern Theology.** David H. Kelsey. LC 99-21488. 240p. 1999. pap. 17.00 (*1-56338-283-0*) TPI PA.

Proving God: Triumphant Living Through Tithing. 2nd ed. Al Taylor. 144p. 1996. pap. 8.99 (*0-87148-975-9*) Pathway Pr.

Proving Ground. Gerald. 1997. pap. text 9.95 (*1-888103-10-8*) Trophy Pubng.

Proving Manhood: Reflections on Men & Sexism. Timothy Beneke. 183p. 1997. pap. text 17.95 (*0-520-21266-5*, Pub. by U CA Pr) Cal Prin Full Svc.

Proving Manhood: Reflections on Men & Sexism. Timothy Beneke. LC 97-1210. 183p. 1997. 48.00 (*0-520-20961-3*, Pub. by U CA Pr) Cal Prin Full Svc.

Proving Medical Diagnosis & Prognosis, 14 vols. Marshall Houts & Leonard Marmor. 1970. ring bd. 1560.00 (*0-8205-1564-7*) Bender.

Proving Operating Systems Correct. Richard A. Karp. LC 82-13378. (Computer Science: Systems Programming Ser.: No. 16). 171p. reprint ed. pap. 53.10 (*0-8357-1365-2*, 207039700088) Bks Demand.

Proving Punitive Damages: The Complete Handbook. Tom Riley. LC 81-2062. 347p. 1981. 37.50 (*0-13-731778-6*, Busn) P-H.

Proving Trail. Louis L'Amour. 224p. 1985. mass mkt. 4.50 (*0-553-25304-2*) Bantam.

Proving Your Arbitration Case. Boaz Siegel. LC 61-3879. (Illus.). 50p. reprint ed. pap. 30.00 (*0-608-15596-9*, 202966900062) Bks Demand.

Proving You're Qualified: Strategies for Competent People Without College Degrees. Charles D. Hayes. LC 94-96544. 176p. 1995. pap., per. 16.95 (*0-9621979-1-2*) Autodidactic Pr.

Provinzialwoerter: Deutsche Idiotismensammlungen des 18. Jahrhunderts. Ed. by Walter Haas. (Historische Wortforschung Ser.: Vol. 3). (GER.). lxvii, 945p. 1994. lib. bdg. 276.95 (*3-11-010852-6*) De Gruyter.

Provisao de Deus para a Cura see God's Provision for Healing

Provision & Maintenance of Public Personnel. J. Cheminais et al. LC 99-215250. 192p. 1998. pap. 39.95 (*0-7021-4380-4*) Intl Spec Bk.

Provision & Practice of Sacred Music at Cambridge Colleges & Selected Cathedrals, c. 1547-c. 1646: A Comparative Study of the Archival Evidence. Ian Payne. LC 92-43443. (Outstanding Dissertations in Music from British Universities Ser.). (Illus.). 480p. 1993. text 50.00 (*0-8153-0952-X*) Garland.

Provision for Children with Special Educational Needs in the Asia Region. James Lynch. LC 94-34138. (Technical Papers: No. 261). 116p. 1995. pap. 22.00 (*0-8213-3036-5*, 13036) World Bank.

Provision of Health Care Services to the Undocumented Population in Bexar County, Texas. Melissa Chabran et al. (Working Paper Ser.: No. 75). 54p. (C). 1994. pap. 5.50 (*0-89940-570-3*) LBJ Sch Pub Aff.

Provision of Mental Health Services in Britain: The Way Ahead. Ed. by Greg Wilkinson & Hugh Freeman. LC RA0790.7. (Gaskell Psychiatry Ser.). 209p. pap. 64.80 (*0-8357-7776-6*, 203613600002) Bks Demand.

Provision of Primary Experience: Winnicottian Work with Children & Adolescents. Barbara Dockar-Drysdale. LC 91-4536. 232p. 1991. 45.00 (*0-87668-525-4*) Aronson.

Provision of Spectacles at Low Cost. WHO Staff. 30p. 1987. 8.00 (*92-4-156108-4*) World Health.

Provisional Austrian Regime in Lombardy - Venetia, 1814-1815. Reuben J. Rath. LC 69-18808. 426p. reprint ed. pap. 132.10 (*0-8357-7756-1*, 203611400002) Bks Demand.

Provisional Central Product Classification. 304p. 35.00 (*92-1-161329-9*, 91.XVII.7) UN.

Provisional Checklist of Neotropical Rubiaceae. L. Andersson. (Scripta Botanica Belgica Ser.: Vol. 1). 199p. 1992. 64.00 (*90-72619-06-4*, Pub. by Natl Botanic Grdn Belgium) Balogh.

***Provisional City: Los Angeles Stories of Architecture & Urbanism.** Dana Cuff. (Illus.). 400p. 2000. 40.00 (*0-262-03276-7*) MIT Pr.

Provisional Constitution & Ordinances for the People of the United States. John Brown. 32p. 1969. 15.00 (*0-87730-001-1*) M & S Pr.

Provisional Court Protection in Administrative Matters (Recommendation & Explanatory Memorandum), No. R(89)8. Council of Europe Staff. 1990. 12.00 (*92-871-1807-8*, Pub. by Council of Europe) Manhattan Pub Co.

Provisional Guidelines on Statistics of International Tourism. pap. 5.00 (*0-685-12668-4*, E.78.XVII.6) UN.

Provisional Irish Republicans: An Oral & Interpretive History, 309. Robert W. White. LC 92-25806. (Contributions in Political Science Ser.: No. 309). 224p. 1993. 62.95 (*0-313-28564-0*, WGD, Greenwood Pr) Greenwood.

Provisional Maps: Critical Essays on David Malouf. Ed. by Amanda Nettlebeck. LC 94-213430. pap. 18.00 (*0-86422-300-5*, Pub. by Univ of West Aust Pr) Intl Spec Bk.

Provisional Patents: The Laymans Guide to Invention Security & Product Surety. Russell J. Rhea. (Illus.). 150p. (Orig.). 1996. pap. 29.95 (*0-9654309-0-1*) Surety Pr.

***Provisional Postage Stamps of Ukraine 1992-1995.** 2nd ed. Hryhoriy Lobko. Tr. by Andrew O. Martyniuk from UKR. LC 00-131213. (Illus.). 272p. 2000. pap. 30.00 (*1-889581-13-5*) Ukrnian Phltlc.

Provisional Regulations Relating to Littering & Pollution Caused by Petroleum Activities on the Norwegian Continental Shelf. Norwegian Petroleum Directorate Staff. 1998. pap. 75.00 (*82-7257-037-8*, Pub. by Oljedirektoratet) St Mut.

Provisional Remedies in International Commercial Arbitration: A Practitioner Handbook. Ed. by Axel Boesch. LC 94-27891. 830p. (C). 1994. lib. bdg. 290.80 (*3-11-012377-0*) De Gruyter.

Provisional Rules of Procedure of the Security Council: December, 1982. (Rules of Procedure Ser.). 14p. pap. 5.00 (*92-1-100087-4*, E.83.I.4) UN.

Provisional Sentence on Bills of Exchange, Cheques & Promissory Notes. F. R. Malan. 269p. 1986. pap. 92.00 (*0-409-04086-X*, SA, MICHIE) LEXIS Pub.

Provisioning (How-To for Pleasure Boaters) Patricia Miller. 2000. 12.95 (*0-9638470-2-3*) Pt Loma Pubng.

Provisioning Paris: Merchants & Millers in the Grain & Flour Trade During the Eighteenth Century. Steven L. Kaplan. LC 84-7004. (Illus.). 592p. 1984. text 62.50 (*0-8014-1600-0*) Cornell U Pr.

Provisions. Monifa Atungaye. LC 88-83009. 60p. (YA). (gr. 9-12). 1989. pap. 5.00 (*0-916418-68-5*) Lotus.

Provisions: A Reader from Nineteenth-Century American Women. Ed. by Judith Fetterley. LC 84-42840. 480p. 1985. 35.00 (*0-253-17040-0*); pap. 15.95 (*0-253-20349-X*, MB-349) Ind U Pr.

Provisions: One Hundred & Nine Great Places to Shop for Food in the Capital District. Peter Zaas et al. 144p. (Orig.). 1987. pap. 4.50 (*0-9605460-6-5*) Wash Park.

Provisions Concerning the Reporting of Incidents Involving Harmful Substances under Marpol 72-78. International Maritime Organization Staff. 1990. text 50.00 (*0-89771-951-4*, Pub. by Intl Maritime Org) St Mut.

Provisions for General Theory Courses in the Professional Education of Teachers. Obed J. Williamson. LC 78-177634. (Columbia University. Teachers College. Contributions to Education Ser.: No. 684). reprint ed. 37.50 (*0-404-55684-1*) AMS Pr.

Provisions of State Codes of Professional Responsibility Governing Lawyer Advertising & Solicitation. American Bar Association, Commission on Election L. 417p. 1990. pap. 75.00 (*0-89707-595-1*, 406-0011) Amer Bar Assn.

Provisions of the Internal Revenue Code & Treasury Regulations Pertaining to the Federal Taxation of Gifts, Trusts & Estates: 1983 Edition. Douglas A. Kahn & Lawrence W. Waggoner. (C). 1983. 18.00 (*0-316-48209-9*, Aspen Law & Bus) Aspen Pub.

Provisions of the 1996 Farm Bill. (Illus.). 21p. (Orig.). (C). 1997. pap. text 20.00 (*0-7881-3704-2*) DIANE Pub.

Provisions Relating to Digital Transmission of Geological & Reservoir Technical Data in Connection with the Final Report. Norwegian Petroleum Directorate Staff. 72p. 1998. pap. 100.00 (*82-7257-476-4*, Pub. by Oljedirektoratet) St Mut.

Provo Experiment in Delinquency Rehabilitation. LaMar T. Empey & Jerome Rabow. (Reprint Series in Social Sciences). (C). 1993. reprint ed. pap. text 5.00 (*0-8290-3739-X*, S-385) Irvington.

Provo International Conference on the Dead Sea Scrolls: Technological Innovations, New Texts, & Reformulated Issues. Donald Parry & Eugene C. Ulrich. LC 98-44346. (Studies on the Texts of the Desert of Judah). 1998. 184.00 (*90-04-11155-7*) Brill Academic Pubs.

Provo, Pioneer Mormon City. Writers Program, Utah Staff. LC 73-3654. (American Guide Ser.). 1942. reprint ed. 11.50 (*0-404-57954-X*) AMS Pr.

***Provocables! Dramatic Readings for Faith & Life.** Jerry Robbins. LC 99-55436. 2000. pap. 17.50 (*0-7880-1591-5*) CSS OH.

Provocateur, 6 Vols. Alluvial Staff. 1996. pap. text 125.00 (*0-9652009-6-5*) Alluvial Ent.

***Provocateur: Images of Women & Minorities in Advertising.** Anthony J. Cortese. LC 99-14501. 192p. 1999. 65.00 (*0-8476-9174-8*) Rowman.

Provocateur: Images of Women & Minorities in Advertising. Anthony J. Cortese. LC 99-14501. (Postmodern Social Futures Ser.). (Illus.). 192p. 1999. pap. 24.95 (*0-8476-9175-6*) Rowman.

Provocateurs Against the People. Art Shields. 32p. 1972. pap. 0.50 (*0-87898-079-2*) New Outlook.

Provocation & Responsibility. Jeremy Horder. LC 92-8424. (Oxford Monographs on Criminal Law & Justice). 224p. 1992. text 55.00 (*0-19-825696-5*, Clarendon Pr) OUP.

Provocation Testing in Clinical Practice. Ed. by Sheldon L. Spector. (Clinical Allergy & Immunology Ser.: Vol. 5). (Illus.). 816p. 1994. text 225.00 (*0-8247-9249-1*) Dekker.

Provocations. Ray DiPalma. LC 95-134043. 1995. pap. 11.00 (*0-937013-55-2*) Potes Poets.

Provocations: Spiritual Writings of Kierkegaard. Soren Kierkegaard. Ed. by Charles E. Moore. LC 99-28648. 160p. 2000. pap. 14.00 (*0-87486-981-1*, Pub. by Plough) Spring Arbor Dist.

Provocative Challenge Procedures: Bronchial Oral Nasal & Exercise. Sheldon L. Spector. LC 82-22655. 224p. 1983. 129.00 (*0-8493-6325-X*, CRC Reprint) Franklin.

Provocative Challenge Procedures Vol. 2: Bronchial Oral Nasal & Exercise. Sheldon L. Spector. LC 82-22655. 208p. 1983. 118.00 (*0-8493-6326-8*, CRC Reprint) Franklin.

Provocative Facts for West Coast Interpreters. Ed. by Phyllis Ford. 194p. 1983. 10.00 (*0-943272-05-X*) Inst Recreation Res.

Provocative Pens: Four Cleveland Cartoonists, 1900-1975. Rotraud Sackerlotzky & Carolyn S. Jirousek. LC 92-71847. (Illus.). 56p. (Orig.). 1992. pap. 5.00 (*0-9639562-1-3*) Clevelnd Art.

Provocative Shots. Alex Larg. (Pro-Lighting Ser.). 160p. 1999. pap. 35.00 (*2-88046-467-6*) Watsn-Guptill.

Provocative Therapy. Frank Farrelly & Jeff Brandsma. LC 74-78101. 1974. reprint ed. 19.95 (*0-916990-03-6*) META Pubns.

Provocative Thoughts & Pleasures in Poetry. Regina Conrath et al. (Illus.). 193p. 1992. per. 15.00 (*0-614-24755-1*) Tesseract SD.

Provokation Zum Leben: Gott Im Theologischen Werk Helmut Gollwitzers Mit Einem Geleitwort von H. Gollwitzer. Rolf Stieber-Westermann. (Europaische Hochschulschriften Ser.: Reihe 23, Bd. 473). (GER.). XI, 437p. 1993. 46.80 (*3-631-45653-0*) P Lang Pubng.

Provoke God with Your Giving. T. D. Jakes. (Orig.). 1997. pap. 9.90 (*1-890521-04-3*) Jakes Ent.

Provoked Husband. John Vanbrugh & Colley Cibber. Ed. by Peter Dixon. LC 79-128911. (Regents Restoration Drama Ser.). 194p. 1973. reprint ed. pap. 60.20 (*0-608-02044-3*, 206269700003) Bks Demand.

Provoked in Venice. Mark Rudman. LC 98-47527. (Wesleyan Poetry Ser.). 212p. 1999. pap. 14.95 (*0-8195-6354-4*, Wesleyan Univ Pr); text 30.00 (*0-8195-6353-6*, Wesleyan Univ Pr) U Pr of New Eng.

Provoked to Jealousy: The Origin & Purpose of the Jealousy Motif in Romans 9-11. Richard H. Bell. LC 94-212044. (Wissenschaftliche Untersuchungen Zum Neuen Testament Ser.: No. 2, Pt. 63). 493p. (Orig.). 1994. pap. 88.50 (*3-16-146091-X*, Pub. by JCB Mohr) Coronet Bks.

Provoked Wife. James Smith. (New Mermaid Ser.). (C). 1994. reprint ed. pap. text. write for info. (*0-393-90067-3*, Norton Paperbks) Norton.

Provoked Wife. John Vanbrugh. Ed. by Curt A. Zimansky. LC 69-12337. (Regents Restoration Drama Ser.). 167p. 1969. reprint ed. pap. 51.80 (*0-608-02668-9*, 206332100004) Bks Demand.

Provoker. Earl Paulk. Ed. by Tricia Weeks. 400p. (Orig.). 1986. pap. 9.95 (*0-917595-09-2*) Kingdom Pubs.

Provoking Agents: Theorizing Gender & Agency. Ed. by Judith K. Gardiner. LC 94-18086. 352p. 1995. text 44.95 (*0-252-02132-0*); pap. text 18.95 (*0-252-06418-6*) U of Ill Pr.

Provoking Feminisms. Carol Allen. 264p. 1999. pap. 20.00 (*0-226-01439-8*); lib. bdg. 39.00 (*0-226-01437-1*) U Ch Pr.

PROWAY-LAN Industrial Data Highway: ANSI-ISA Standard S72.01. 181p. 1986. pap. text 80.00 (*0-87664-896-0*, I896-0) ISA.

***Prowler.** Marion Campbell. 1999. 17.95 (*1-86368-251-1*, Pub. by Fremantle Arts) Intl Spec Bk.

Prowlpuss. Gina Wilson. LC 94-1598. (Illus.). (J). (ps up). 1995. 16.99 (*1-56402-483-0*) Candlewick Pr.

Prowlpuss. Gina Wilson. LC 94-1598. (Illus.). 32p. (J). (ps-3). 1997. reprint ed. pap. 5.99 (*0-7636-0287-6*) Candlewick Pr.

Prowrestling Stars Boxed Set. Chelsea House Publishing Staff. 1999. 287.20 (*0-7910-5440-3*) Chelsea Hse.

Proxies. Laura J. Mixon. LC 98-19417. 416p. 1998. 24.95 (*0-312-85467-6*, Pub. by Tor Bks) St Martin.

***Proxies.** Laura M. Mixon. 480p. 1999. mass mkt. 6.99 (*0-8125-2387-3*, Pub. by Tor Bks) St Martin.

***Proximate Causes.** Lyndsay Smith. 300p. 1999. pap. 17.95 (*1-55017-214-X*) Harbour Pub Co.

Proximity & Preference: Problems in the Multidimensional Analysis of Large Data Sets. Ed. by Reginald G. Golledge & John N. Rayner. LC 81-14634. 351p. 1982. reprint ed. pap. 108.90 (*0-7837-2955-3*, 205749900006) Bks Demand.

Proximity, Levinas, Blanchot, Bataille & Communication. Joseph Libertson. (Phaenomenologica Ser.: No. 87). 361p. 1982. lib. bdg. 171.00 (*90-247-2506-2*, Pub. by M Nijhoff) Kluwer Academic.

Proximity (Stolen Arrows) Charles Borkhuis. 1994. pap. 9.95 (*0-9623806-3-6*) SINK Pr.

Proximity to Death. William S. McFeely. LC 99-31293. 224p. 1999. text 23.95 (*0-393-04819-5*) Norton.

***Proximity to Death.** William McFeeley. 208p. 2000. reprint ed. pap. 13.95 (*0-393-32104-5*) Norton.

***Proximo Mover de Dios.** Luis A. Capdevila. 44p. 1999. mass mkt. write for info. (*0-7392-0218-9*, PO3245) Morris Pubng.

Proximo Paso. Jack T. Chick. (SPA., Illus.). 64p. 1983. pap. 3.50 (*0-937958-15-8*) Chick Pubns.

Proximo Paso. Barbara Mujica. (C). 1996. text 55.00 (*0-03-013388-2*) Harcourt Coll Pubs.

Proximos Pasos para Nuevos Creyentes. Kenneth N. Taylor.Tr. of Next Steps for New Christians. (SPA.). 188p. 1991. pap. 3.99 (*1-56063-144-9*, 498466) Editorial Unilit.

Proxy Contests & Corporate Control: Conducting the Proxy Campaign. Constance E. Bagley & David J. Berger. (Corporate Practice Ser.: No. 70). (Illus.). 1997. ring bd. 95.00 (*1-55871-351-4*) BNA.

Proxy Contests & Corporate Control: Strategic Considerations. Constance E. Bagley & David J. Berger. (Corporate Practice Ser.: No. 69). (Illus.). 1997. ring bd. 95.00 (*1-55871-349-2*) BNA.

Proxy Means Tests for Targeting Social Programs: Simulations & Speculation. Margaret E. Grosh & Judy L. Baker. (LSMS Working Papers: No. 118). 64p. 1995. pap. 22.00 (*0-8213-3313-5*, 13313) World Bank.

Proxy Regulation - with September Supplement. Michael D. Waters. 640p. 1992. 105.00 (*0-685-69481-X*) PLI.

Proxy Server Cram. Tittle. (Networking Ser.). (C). 1998. pap. text 15.60 (*0-619-00001-5*) Course Tech.

MCSE Test Success: Proxy Server 2. David Schaer. LC 98-86634. (MCSE Test Success Ser.). 1998. pap. 24.99 (*0-7821-2335-X*) Sybex.

Proxy Server 2 on Site: Street Knowledge for Technology in the Corporate Enterprise. Kevin Schuler. LC 98-13406. 600p. 1998. pap. text 39.99 (*1-57610-259-9*) Coriolis Grp.

Proxy Statements: Fifth Annual Institute. 35.00 (*0-317-29520-9*, #CO2283) Harcourt.

Proxy Statements: Strategy & Forms, 12 vols. Howard E. Deutch. 15,000p. 1985. ring bd. 975.00 (*0-917244-02-8*) Jefren Pub.

Proyeccion Astral: Experiences Fuera del Cuerpo Fisico. 2nd ed. Denning & Phillips. (SPA., Illus.). 260p. 1999. mass mkt. 8.95 (*1-56718-202-X*) Llewellyn Pubns.

Proyecciones de la Conciencia: Diario de Experiencias Fuera del Cuerpo Fisico. Waldo Vieira. Tr. by Luis I. Lopez & Oscar B. Traba from POR. (SPA., Illus.). 235p. 1995. pap. 11.95 (*85-86019-02-X*) Intl Inst Proj.

Proyecto Arqueologico Cancuen: Primera Temporada - 1999. Arthur A. Demarest et al. (Informe Preliminar Ser.: No. 1). (SPA., Illus.). 250p. 1999. spiral bd. 25.00 (*1-892940-07-8*) Vanderbilt Institute.

Proyecto Arqueologico Cancuen: Segunda Temporada - 2000. Arthur A. Demarest et al. (Informe Preliminar Ser.: No. 2). (SPA., Illus.). 450p. 2000. spiral bd. 35.00 (*1-892940-08-6*) Vanderbilt Institute.

Proyecto Arqueologico Punta de Chimino, 1996-97. Arthur A. Demarest et al. (Informe Preliminar Ser.). (SPA., Illus.). 210p. 1997. spiral bd. 20.00 (*1-892940-06-X*) Vanderbilt Institute.

Proyecto Arqueologico Regional Petexbatun: Cuarta Temporada - 1992. Arthur A. Demarest et al. (Informe Preliminar Ser.: No. 4). (SPA., Illus.). 393p. 1992. spiral bd. 30.00 (*1-892940-03-5*) Vanderbilt Institute.

Proyecto Arqueologico Regional Petexbatun: Primera Temporada - 1989. Arthur A. Demarest & Stephen D. Houston. (Informe Preliminar Ser.: No. 1). (Illus.). 248p. 1989. spiral bd. 20.00 (*1-892940-00-0*) Vanderbilt Institute.

Proyecto Arqueologico Regional Petexbatun: Quinta Temporada - 1993. Juan A. Valdes et al. (Informe Preliminar Ser.: No. 5). (SPA., Illus.). 200p. 1993. spiral bd. 20.00 (*1-892940-04-3*) Vanderbilt Institute.

Proyecto Arqueologico Regional Petexbatun: Segunda Temporada - 1990. Arthur A. Demarest & Stephen D. Houston. (Informe Preliminar Ser.: No. 2). (Illus.). 643p. 1990. spiral bd. 50.00 (*1-892940-01-9*) Vanderbilt Institute.

Proyecto Arqueologico Regional Petexbatun: Sexta Temporada - 1994. Arthur A. Demarest et al. (Informe Preliminar Ser.: No. 6). (SPA.). 766p. 1995. spiral bd. 45.00 (*1-892940-05-1*) Vanderbilt Institute.

Proyecto Arqueologico Regional Petexbatun: Tercera Temporada - 1991. Arthur A. Demarest et al. (Informe Preliminar Ser.: No. 3). (Illus.). 952p. 1991. spiral bd. 70.00 (*1-892940-02-7*) Vanderbilt Institute.

Proyecto Coatlan, Area Tonatico-Pilcaya. Raul M. Arana. 243p. 1990. pap. 14.00 (*968-6068-72-4*, IN029) UPLAAP.

Proyecto, Estatutos y Demas Documentos Relacionados al Establecimiento de la Real Academia de Pintura, Escultura y Arquitectura Denominada de San Carlos de Nueva Espana (1781-1802) LC 96-27990. (Coleccion Documenta Novae Hispaniae: Vol. B-7). (SPA.). 144p. 1984. 37.40 (*0-88653-007-5*) S Rolston-Bain.

P

An Asterisk (*) at the beginning of an entry indicates that the title is appearing for the first time.

Proyecto Futuro: Science & Mathematics Activities in English & Spanish. Ed. by Marsha L. Matyas & Estrella Triana. (Illus.). 450p. 1992. pap. write for info. (0-87168-507-8, 92-38B) AAAS.

*Proyectos con Macros en Excel en Espanol: Aprendiendo con Ejemplos Practicos. Claudio Sanchez. (PC Users Express Ser.). (SPA., Illus.). 239p. 1999. pap. 13.90 (987-97441-3-6, Pub. by MP Ediciones) Am Wholesale.

Proza: Kriticheskaia Proza Kn.1, Vol. 10. Mikhail A. Kuzmin. Ed. by George Cheron. (Modern Russian Literature & Culture Ser.: Vol. 38). (RUS., Illus.). 298p. 1998. pap. 30.00 (1-57201-041-X) Berkeley Slavic.

Proza Vol. 1: Pervaia Kniga Rasskazov. Mikhail A. Kuzmin. Ed. by Vladimir Markov. (Modern Russian Literature & Culture, Studies & Texts: Vol. 14). (RUS.). 329p. (Orig.). 1984. pap. 16.00 (0-933884-41-9) Berkeley Slavic.

Proza Vol. 2: Vtoraia Kniga Rasskazov. Mikhail A. Kuzmin. Ed. by Vladimir Markov. (Modern Russian Literature & Culture, Studies & Texts: Vol. 15). (RUS.). 391p. (Orig.). 1984. pap. 16.00 (0-933884-42-7) Berkeley Slavic.

Proza Vol. 3: Tret'ia Kniga Rasskazov. Mikhail A. Kuzmin. Ed. by Vladimir Markov. (Modern Russian Literature & Culture, Studies & Texts: Vol. 16). (RUS.). 437p. (Orig.). 1984. pap. 16.00 (0-933884-43-5) Berkeley Slavic.

Proza Vol. 4: Pokoinitsa v Dome, Zelenyi Solovei. Mikhail A. Kuzmin. Ed. by Vladimir Markov. (Modern Russian Literature & Culture, Studies & Texts: Vol. 17). (RUS.). 370p. (Orig.). 1985. pap. 16.00 (0-933884-44-3) Berkeley Slavic.

Proza Vol. 6: Tikhii Strazh; Babushkina Shkatulka. Mikhail A. Kuzmin. Ed. by Vladimir Markov. (Modern Russian Literature & Culture, Studies & Texts: Vol. 19). (RUS.). 374p. (Orig.). 1986. pap. 16.00 (0-933884-46-X) Berkeley Slavic.

Proza Vol. 7: Antrakt v Ovrage. Devstvennyi Viktor. Mikhail A. Kuzmin. Ed. by Vladimir Markov. (Modern Russian Literature & Culture, Studies & Texts: Vol. 20). (RUS.). 380p. 1987. pap. 16.00 (0-933884-47-8) Berkeley Slavic.

Proza Vol. 8: Nesobrannaia Proza. Mikhail A. Kuzmin. Ed. by Vladimir Markov. (Modern Russian Literature & Culture, Studies & Texts: Vol. 21). (RUS.). 392p. (Orig.). 1990. pap. 18.00 (0-933884-48-6) Berkeley Slavic.

Proza Vol. 9: Nesobrannaia Proza. Mikhail A. Kuzmin. Ed. by Vladimir Markov. (Modern Russian Literature & Culture, Studies & Texts: Vol. 22). (RUS.). 400p. (Orig.). 1990. pap. 18.00 (0-933884-49-4) Berkeley Slavic.

*Proza Vol. 11: Kriticheskaia Proza Kn.2. Mikhail Kuzmin. Ed. by George Cheron & Aleksandr Timofeev. (Modern Russian Literature & Culture: Vol. 39). (RUS., Illus.). 424p. 2000. pap. 40.00 (1-57201-042-8) Berkeley Slavic.

Proza Pushkina see Pushkin's Prose

Proza Rosyjska Epoki Obswiecenia: Nowe Odkrycia I Interpretacje : Tezy Referatbow Miqedzynarodowej Konferencji Naukowej, !bodbz, 19-21 Pabzdziernika, 1995 R. / Eliza Malek & Uniwersytet Lodzki, Zaklad Literatury Rosyjskiej. LC 96-216194. 50 p. 1995. write for info. (83-7016-871-X) Lodzki Univ Pr.

Proza, Vol. 5: Plavaiushchie-puteshestvuiushchie; Voennye Rasskazy. Mikhail A. Kuzmin. Ed. by Vladimir Markov. (Modern Russian Literature & Culture, Studies & Texts: Vol. 18). (RUS.). 381p. (Orig.). 1985. pap. 16.00 (0-933884-45-1) Berkeley Slavic.

Prozac: Panacea or Pandora?: "The Rest of the Story" on the New Class of SSRI Antidepressants (Prozac, Zoloft, Paxil, Lovan, Luvox, & More) Ann B. Tracy. (Illus.). 424p. 1994. pap. 15.95 (0-916095-59-2) Pubs Pr UT.

Prozac: Pros & Cons. rev. ed. Jim Parker. 1998. pap. 0.50 (0-89230-245-3) Do It Now.

Prozac: Questions & Answers. Ronald R. Fieve. 1994. mass mkt. 5.99 (0-380-77718-5, Avon Bks) Morrow Avon.

Prozac: The Controversial Cure. Helen C. Packard. LC 97-44529. (Drug Abuse Prevention Library). (Illus.), 64p. (YA). (gr. 7-9). 1998. lib. bdg. 17.95 (0-8239-2551-X) Rosen Group.

Prozac Alternative: Natural Relief from Depression with St. John's Wort, Kava, & Other Alternative Therapies. Ran Knishinsky. LC 98-25770. 176p. 1998. pap. 12.95 (0-89281-791-7, Heal Arts VT) Inner Tradit.

Prozac & Other Antidepressants. Steven L. Jaffe. LC 99-13185. (Illus.). 80p. (J). (gr. 4-8). 1999. lib. bdg. 19.95 (0-7910-5204-4) Chelsea Hse.

Prozac & Other Psychiatric Drugs: Everything You Need to Know. Lewis A. Opler & Carol Bialkowski. LC 96-222142. 1996. per. 6.99 (0-671-51070-3) PB.

*Prozac & the New Antidepressants: What You Need to Know about Prozac, Zoloft, Paxil, Luvox, Wellburtin, Effexor, Serzone, Selexa, St. John's Wart & Others. William S. Appleton. LC 99-44963. (Illus.). 2000. pap. 13.95 (0-452-28164-4, Plume) Dutton Plume.

*Prozac Backlash: Overcoming the Dangers of Prozac, Zoloft, Paxil & Other Antidepressants with Safe & Effective Alternatives. Joseph Glenmullen. LC 99-59911. 384p. 2000. 25.00 (0-684-86001-5) S&S Trade.

*Prozac Diary. Lauren Slater. 224p. 1999. pap. 11.95 (0-14-026394-2) Viking Penguin.

Prozac (Fluoxetine) - Side Effects & Harmful Reactions: New Information with Authors & Subjects. rev. ed. American Health Research Institute Staff. 1994. 47.50 (0-7883-0172-1); pap. 44.50 (0-7883-0173-X) ABBE Pubs Assn.

Prozac-Free: Homeopathic Medicine for Depression, Anxiety & Other Mental & Emotional Problems. Joseph Kandel et al. LC 98-47630. 304p. 1999. per. 17.00 (0-7615-1478-3) Prima Pub.

*Prozac Highway. Persimmon Blackbridge. 373p. 2000. pap. 14.95 (0-7145-3059-X) M Boyars Pubs.

Prozac Highway: A Novel. Persimmon Blackbridge. LC PR9199.3.B466P7 1997. 256p. 1997. pap. 14.95 (0-88974-078-X, Pub. by Press Gang Pubs) LPC InBook.

Prozac Nation: Young & Depressed in America. Elizabeth Wurtzel. LC 95-3984. 384p. 1995. pap. 12.95 (1-57322-512-6, Riverhd Trade) Berkley Pub.

*Prozac Nation: Young & Depressed in America. Elizabeth Wurtzel. 334p. 1999. 29.95 (0-7351-0137-X) Replica Bks.

Prozac Poetry: Prozac Poet. Pamela Holcombe et al. Ed. by Vickie Gordon. (Illus.). 57p. (Orig.). 1998. pap. 6.95 (1-891601-02-4, 724) Ladies Caliber.

Proze der Organisation. Peter Pelzer. 194p. 1995. text 81.00 (3-7186-5773-2, Harwood Acad Pubs); pap. text 40.00 (3-7186-5703-1, Harwood Acad Pubs) Gordon & Breach.

Prozeb, Kafka: Critical Monographs in English. William J. Dodd. 62p. 1993. pap. 32.00 (0-85261-323-7, Pub. by Univ of Glasgow) St Mut.

Prozeorientierte Mediendidaktik Im Fremdsprachenunterricht. Wilfried Gienow & Karlheinz Hellwig. (GER., Illus.). 188p. 1993. 33.95 (3-631-45773-1) P Lang Pubng.

Prozess Jesu Geht Weiter see Trial of Jesus Continues

PRPA: A Protein Controlling the Dual Specificy of Protein Phosphatase 2A. C. Van Hoof. No. 87. 140p. (Orig.). 1994. pap. 42.50 (90-6186-625-1, Pub. by Leuven Univ) Coronet Bks.

PRR: Hudson to Horseshoe. William D. Volkmer. (Illus.). 128p. 1994. 49.95 (1-878887-33-5) Morning NJ.

PRR Color Guide to Freight & Passenger Equipment. David R. Sweetland & Robert J. Yanosey. LC 91-62000. (Illus.). 128p. 1992. 45.00 (1-878887-07-6) Morning NJ.

PRR Color Guide to Freight & Passenger Equipment, Vol. 2. Ian S. Fischer. (Illus.). 128p. 1996. 49.95 (1-878887-55-6) Morning NJ.

*PRS Guitar Book: A Complete History of Paul Reed Smith Guitars. limited ed. Dave Burrluck. (Illus.). 126p. 1999. boxed set 75.00 (0-87930-593-2) Miller Freeman.

PRS 95: Parallel Rendering Symposium. 116p. 1996. pap. text 49.00 (0-89791-777-4, 428957) Assn Compu Machinery.

Prst, Ktery Se Nikdy Nedotkne see Fingers Pointing Somewhere Else

Prudden: Rev. Peter Prudden & His Descendants in America, 2 vols. Horton R. Prudden. 1351p. 1996. reprint ed. pap. 155.00 (0-8328-5613-4); reprint ed. lib. bdg. 175.00 (0-8328-5612-6) Higginson Bk Co.

*Prudence. Lucia Raatma. LC 99-48334. (Character Education Ser.). 24p. (J). (ps-3). 2000. lib. bdg. 15.93 (0-7368-0510-9, Bridgestone Bks) Capstone Pr.

Prudence. Don L. Taylor. (Illus.). 318p. 1993. 19.00 (0-9639286-2-7) Prairieville Pr.

Prudence & the Millers. Mildred A. Martin. (Miller Family Ser.). 190p. (J). (gr. 3-8). 1993. 9.50 (0-9627643-9-6) Green Psturs Pr.

Prudence & the Millers. 2nd rev. ed. Mildred A. Martin. (Miller Family Ser.). (Illus.). 192p. (J). (gr. 3-8). 1996. pap. 6.00 (1-884377-03-3) Green Psturs Pr.

*Prudence & Your Health: Workbook for Prudence & the Millers. Mildred Martin. Ed. by Don L. Martin. (Miller Family Ser.). (Illus.). 84p. (J). (gr. 3-6). 2000. pap., wbk. ed. 4.00 (1-884377-07-6) Green Psturs Pr.

Prudence Crandall: Woman of Courage. Elizabeth Yates. LC 93-74857. (Illus.). 256p. (J). (gr. 4 up). 1996. 16.95 (1-56397-391-X) Boyds Mills Pr.

Prudence in Victory: The Dynamics of Post-War Settlements. Nissan Oren. 16p. (Orig.). 1977. pap. text 11.00 (0-8191-5830-5) U Pr of Amer.

Prudence Palfrey. Thomas Bailey Aldrich. (Works of Thomas Bailey Aldrich). 1989. reprint ed. lib. bdg. 79.00 (0-7812-1672-9) Rprt Serv.

Prudence Valiant: Aviatrix Extraordinaire. Chris Majka & Sheilagh Hunt. (Illus.). 124p. (J). 1991. bds. 16.95 (0-88780-083-1, Pub. by Formac Publ Co) Formac Dist Ltd.

Prudence Valiant: Aviatrix Extraordinaire. Chris Majka & Sheilagh Hunt. (Illus.). 124p. (J). 1991. mass mkt. 6.95 (0-88780-082-3, Pub. by Formac Publ Co) Formac Dist Ltd.

*Prudence's Baby-sitter Book. Alona Frankel. LC 99-69086. (Joshua & Prudence Bks.). 48p. (J). (ps-k). 2000. 6.95 (0-694-01384-6, HarpFestival) HarpC Child Bks.

Prudence's Book of Food. Alona Frankel. LC 99-63973. (Joshua & Prudence Books Ser.). (Illus.). 48p. (J). (ps-k). 2000. 6.95 (0-694-01383-8, HarpFestival) HarpC Child Bks.

Prudence's Get Well Book. Blacklist Frankel & Alona Frankel. LC 99-69951. (Illus.). 48p. (J). (ps-k). 2000. 6.95 (0-694-01378-1, HarpFestival) HarpC Child Bks.

Prudence's Goodnight Book. Blacklist Frankel & Alona Frankel. LC 99-63975. (Joshua & Prudence Books Ser.). (Illus.). 48p. (J). (ps-k). 2000. 6.95 (0-694-01377-3, HarpFestival) HarpC Child Bks.

*Prudence's Moon & Stars. Alona Frankel. LC 99-69087. (J). 2001. 6.95 (0-694-01385-4, HarpFestival) HarpC Child Bks.

*Prudent Day Trader: Balancing Risk & Reward for Long-Term Success. James H. Lee. 2000. 34.95 (0-7615-2019-8) Prima Pub.

Prudent Heart. Timothy Steele. 39p. (Orig.). 1983. 25.00 (0-936576-08-1) Symposium Pr.

Prudent Investor: The Definitive Guide to Professional Investment Management. James P. Owen. 1990. text 32.50 (1-55738-106-2, Irwn Prfssnl) McGraw-Hill Prof.

Prudent Investor: The Definitive Guide to Professional Investment Management. James P. Owen. 200p. 1993. reprint ed. per. 21.95 (1-55738-490-8, Irwn Prfssnl) McGraw-Hill Prof.

Prudent Investor's Guide to Beating the Market. Carl Reinhardt et al. 1996. text 22.35 (0-7863-1160-6, Irwn Prfssnl) McGraw-Hill Prof.

Prudent Investor's Guide to Beating the Market. Reinhardt Werba Bowen Advisory Services Staff. 192p. 1996. pap. 30.00 (0-7863-0365-4, Irwn Prfssnl) McGraw-Hill Prof.

Prudent Investor's Guide to Beating the Market. 2nd ed. John J. Bowen. LC 98-6270. (Illus.). 200p. 1998. 24.95 (0-07-052760-1) McGraw.

*Prudent Investor's Guide to Hedge Funds: Profiting from Uncertainty & Volatility. James Owen. 288p. 2000. 49.95 (0-471-32336-5) Wiley.

Prudent Management of Modern U. S. Banks: Redefining Responsibility. Jeremy F. Taylor. LC 93-42759. 256p. 1994. 65.00 (0-89930-852-X, Quorum Bks) Greenwood.

*Prudent Match. Laura Matthews. (Regency Romance Ser.). 2000. mass mkt. 4.99 (0-451-20070-5, Sig) NAL.

Prudent Peace: Law As Foreign Policy. John A. Perkins. LC 81-1200. (C). 1993. 28.00 (0-226-65873-2) U Ch Pr.

Prudent Practice: A Guide for Managing Malpractice Risk. Mary K. Houston-Vega et al. LC 96-37035. (Illus.). 332p. (C). 1996. pap. text 42.95 (0-87101-267-7, 2677) Natl Assn Soc Wkrs.

Prudent Practices in the Laboratory: Handling & Disposal of Chemicals. National Research Council Staff. 448p. (C). 1995. text 69.95 (0-309-05229-7) Natl Acad Pr.

Prudent Revolutionaries: Portraits of British Feminists Between the Wars. Brian Harrison. (Illus.). 384p. 1987. 75.00 (0-19-820119-2) OUP.

Prudent Speculator: Al Frank on Investing. Al Frank. 327p. 1989. text 30.00 (1-55623-191-1, Irwn Prfssnl) McGraw-Hill Prof.

Prudential Regulation of Banks. Mathias Dewatripont & Jean Tirole. LC 94-30751. Vol. 1. (Illus.). 276p. 1994. 35.50 (0-262-04146-4) MIT Pr.

Prudential Regulation of Banks & Securities Firms: European & International Aspects. Ed. by Guido Ferrarini. LC 95-26615. 320p. 1996. 102.00 (90-411-0882-3) Kluwer Law Intl.

Prudentiall Ballance of Religion Richard Smith. LC 76-358539. (English Recusant Literature, 1558-1640 Ser.). 598p. 1975. write for info. (0-85967-269-7) Scolar Pr.

Prudentius on the Martyrs. Anne-Marie Palmer. (Oxford Classical Monographs). 336p. 1989. text 69.00 (0-19-814721-X) OUP.

Prudentius Psychomachia. Rosemary Burton. (Bryn Mawr Latin Commentaries Ser.). 106p. (Orig.). (C). 1989. pap. 7.00 (0-929524-61-6) Bryn Mawr Commentaries.

*Prudhoe Bay, Discovery to Recovery! Gene P. Rutledge. LC 98-60598. 1998. write for info. (0-932571-03-4) Wolfe Business Services.

Prudhoe Bay Governor: Alaska's Keith Miller. Keith H. Miller. LC 97-60349. (Illus.). 296p. 1997. 24.95 (1-878100-99-8) Todd Commns.

Prudhomme-Pure Magic. Paul Prud'Homme. LC 94-46213. (Illus.). 206p. 1995. 12.95 (0-688-14202-8, Wm Morrow) Morrow Avon.

Prudhomme's-Fork in T Ro. Paul Prud'Homme. LC 93-25836. 281p. 1993. 23.00 (0-688-12165-9, Wm Morrow) Morrow Avon.

Prud'Hon. Sylvain Laveissiere & Metropolitan Museum of Art (New York, N. Y.) Staff. LC 97-44759. (Illus.). 344p. 1998. 75.00 (0-8109-6520-8, Pub. by Abrams) Time Warner.

Prudy's Portraits of Santa. Prudy Vannier. (Illus.). (Orig.). 1994. pap. 10.95 (0-9641933-0-2) Prudys Studio.

Prudy's Spindle People. Prudy Vannien. (Illus.). 40p. (Orig.). 1994. pap. text 10.95 (0-9641933-1-0) Prudys Studio.

Prue & I. Harriot Curtis. (Works of Harriot Curtis). 1990. reprint ed. lib. bdg. 79.00 (0-7812-2465-9) Rprt Serv.

Prueba de Amor (Test of Love) Amanda Browning. (SPA.). 1997. per. 3.50 (0-373-33418-4, 1-33418-4) Harlequin Bks.

Prueba de Fuerza. Kate William. (Sweet Valley High Ser.: No. 4).Tr. of Power Play. (YA). (gr. 7 up). 1992. 13.05 (0-606-10466-6, Pub. by Turtleback) Demco.

*Pruefung der Vernuenftigen Gedancken des Herrn Hoff-Rath Wolffes von Gott, der Welt und der Seele des Menschen. M. Daniel Straehler. (Wolff, Christian, Gesammelte Werke Ser.: Vol. 53). (GER.). 352p. 1999. reprint ed. 150.00 (3-487-10803-8, Pub. by G Olms Verlag) Lubrecht & Cramer.

Prufen, Testen, Bewerten Im Modernen Fremdsprachenunterricht. Monica Gardenghi & Mary O'Connell. (Bayreuther Beitrage Zur Glottodidaktik Ser.: No. 6). (Illus.). 183p. 1997. 38.95 (3-631-31514-7) P Lang Pubng.

Prufer Domains: Recent Advances. Marco Fontana et al. LC 96-31586. (Pure & Applied Mathematics Ser.: Vol. 203). (Illus.). 344p. 1996. text 150.00 (0-8247-9816-3) Dekker.

Prufung der Kantischen Religionsphilosophie in Hinsicht auf die ihr Beygelegte Aehnlichkeit mit dem Reinen Mystizism. Reinhold B. Jachmann. (Europaea Memoria Ser.: Reihe II, Bd. 1). (GER.). 190p. 1999. reprint ed. 60.00 (3-487-10813-5, Pub. by G Olms Verlag) Lubrecht & Cramer.

Prufung der Untersuchungen Uber die Urbewohner Hispaniens Vermittelst der Baskischen Sprache. Wilhelm von Humboldt. viii, 192p. reprint ed. write for info. (0-318-71636-4) G Olms Pubs.

*Prulie. 2000. write for info. (0-9634890-8-9) B Lampen Knit.

Prune Book: The Forty-Five Toughest Financial Management Jobs in Washington. John H. Trattner. LC 92-30021. 288p. 1992. 34.95 (0-8191-8813-1) Madison Bks UPA.

Prune Book No. 2: The Sixty Toughest Science & Technology Jobs in Washington. John H. Trattner. 560p. 1992. 37.50 (0-8191-8419-5) Madison Bks UPA.

Prune Book No. 3: Forty-Five Financial Management Jobs in Washington. John H. Trattner. 1993. 34.95 (1-56833-002-2) Madison Bks UPA.

Pruner's Handbook: Practical Pruning Advice for Healthy. John Malins. (Illus.). 192p. 1996. pap. 19.95 (0-7153-0399-6, Pub. by D & C Pub) Sterling.

Prunes & Prism: With Other Odds & Ends. Charles H. Grandgent. LC 70-128251. (Essay Index Reprint Ser.). 1977. reprint ed. 19.95 (0-8369-2227-1) Ayer.

Pruning. (Taylor's Weekend Gardening Guide Ser.). 1997. pap. 12.95 (0-614-27236-X) HM.

Pruning. Kris Medic. LC 94-26692. (Rodale's Successful Organic Gardening Ser.). (Illus.). 1995. pap. 14.95 (0-87596-662-4) Rodale Pr Inc.

Pruning. David Squire. (Illus.). 112p. 1995. write for info. (1-57215-025-4) World Pubns.

Pruning. Sunset Books Staff. LC 97-80060. (Illus.). 128p. 1998. pap. text 12.95 (0-376-03606-0) Sunset Books.

Pruning: A Practical Guide. Peter McHoy. (Illus.). 240p. 1993. 35.00 (1-55859-634-8) Abbeville Pr.

Pruning: An Illustrated Guide to Pruning Ornamental Trees & Shrubs. 3rd rev. ed. Donald A. Rakow & Richard Weir, 3rd. (Information Bulletin Ser.). (Illus.). 28p. (Orig.). 1996. pap. 5.25 (1-57753-013-6, 1411B23) Corn Coop Ext.

Pruning: The Complete Guide to Perfect Pruning. Peter McHoy. (Illus.). 96p. 1997. pap. 12.95 (1-85967-463-1, Lorenz Bks) Anness Pub.

Pruning & Training Christopher Brickell. LC 98-32292. (Eyewitness Garden Handbks.). 160p. 1999. 18.95 (0-7894-4148-9) DK Pub Inc.

Pruning & Training Fruit Trees. Warren Somerville. LC 97-206442. 144p. 1997. pap. 36.95 (0-7506-8931-5) Buttrwrth-Heinemann.

Pruning Book. Lee Reich. LC 96-34301. (Illus.). 244p. 1997. 27.95 (1-56158-160-7, 070297) Taunton.

Pruning Book. Lee Reich. (Illus.). 244p. 1999. pap. 19.95 (1-56158-316-2, 070440) Taunton.

Pruning Handbook. Steve Bradley. (Illus.). 160p. 1997. pap. 24.95 (1-85223-981-6, Pub. by Crolwood) Trafalgar.

Pruning Made Easy. Lewis Hill. LC 97-32223. (Gardening Skills Illustrated Ser.). (Illus.). 1997. 28.95 (1-58017-007-2, Storey Pub); pap. text 19.95 (1-58017-006-4, Storey Pub) Storey Bks.

Pruning Made Easy. M. Lombardi & C. Serra Zanetti. LC 98-121205. (Illus.). 160p. 1998. pap. 14.95 (0-7063-7680-3, Pub. by WrLock) Sterling.

Pruning Made Simple. (Step-by-Step Visual Guide Ser.). 1997. pap. 6.95 (1-880281-14-7) NK Lawn & Garden.

Pruning of Trees, Shrubs & Conifers. George E. Brown et al. LC 94-46985. (Illus.). 374p. 1995. 29.95 (0-88192-319-2) Timber.

Pruning Shade Trees & Practicing Tree Surgery. (Shorey Lost Arts Ser.). 52p. reprint ed. pap. 10.00 (0-8466-6041-5, U41) Shoreys Bkstore.

Pruning Simplified. Lewis Hill. LC 85-45605. (Illus.). 208p. 1986. reprint ed. pap. 16.95 (0-88266-417-4) Storey Bks.

Pruning Techniques. Ed. by Alan D. Cook. (Plants & Gardens Ser.). (Illus.). 1994. per. 7.95 (0-945352-61-1) Bklyn Botanic.

Pruning the Bodhi Tree: The Storm over Critical Buddhism. Ed. by Jamie Hubbard & Paul L. Swanson. LC 97-5220. (Nanzan Library of Asian Religion & Culture). 1997. text 45.00 (0-8248-1908-X); pap. text 22.95 (0-8248-1949-7) UH Pr.

Pruning the Genealogical Tree: Procreation & Lineage in Literature, Law & Religion. Gian Balsamo. LC 99-13997. 320p. 1999. 46.50 (0-8387-5409-0) Bucknell U Pr.

Pruning Trees, Shrubs & Vine. S. Smith. 1983. pap. 2.95 (0-88266-229-5, Storey Pub) Storey Bks.

Pruning Word: The Parables of Flannery O'Connor. John R. May. LC 75-19878. 204p. reprint ed. pap. 63.30 (0-608-14225-5, 202207500024) Bks Demand.

Prunings-Accruings. deluxe limited ed. Richard Kostelanetz. 24p. 1978. pap. 35.00 (0-932360-22-X) Archae Edns.

*Prurient Interests: Gender, Democracy & Obscenity in New York City, 1909-1945. Andrea L. Friedman. LC 99-89010. (Trade Union Industrial Studies). 2000. 40.00 (0-231-11066-9); pap. text 17.50 (0-231-11067-7) Col U Pr.

Pruritis in Clinical Medicine: Pathology & Treatment. Stefano Gatti & Ferdinando Serri. 112p. 1990. text 45.00 (0-07-038776-1) McGraw-Hill HPD.

Prusia. (Arte & Arquitectura Ser.). (Illus.). 500p. 2000. 39.95 (3-8290-3282-X, 540543) Konemann.

Prussia. Giles MacDonogh. Date not set. pap. 12.99 (0-7493-2435-X) Heinemann.

*Prussia. Gert Streidt. 1999. 39.95 (3-8290-2590-4) Konemann.

Prussian-American Relations, Seventeen Seventy-Five to Eighteen Seventy-One. Henry M. Adams. LC 79-25884. 135p. 1980. reprint ed. lib. bdg. 49.50 (0-313-22270-3, ADPA, Greenwood Pr) Greenwood.

Prussian & Saxon Casualties of the Franco-Prussian War (1870-1871) Maralyn A. Wellauer. 31p. 1987. pap. 8.00 (0-932019-08-0) Roots Intl.

Prussian Army During the Napoleonic Wars Vol. 1: Infantry. George F. Nafziger. 122p. 1996. pap. 19.95 (1-58545-015-4) Nafziger Collection.

P

Prussian Army During the Napoleonic Wars Vol. 2: Guard & Landwehr. George F. Nafziger. (Illus.). 69p. 1996. pap. 19.95 (*1-58545-016-2*) Nafziger Collection.

Prussian Army During the Napoleonic Wars Vol. 3: Cavalry & Artillery. George F. Nafziger. 107p. 1996. pap. 19.95 (*1-58545-017-0*) Nafziger Collection.

Prussian Army, 1640-1871. Jonathan R. White. LC 95-39549. 378p. (C). 1996. pap. text 38.50 (*0-7618-0206-1*); lib. bdg. 64.50 (*0-7618-0205-3*) U Pr of Amer.

Prussian Cavalry of the Napoleonic Wars. Peter Hofschroer. (Men-at-Arms Ser.: No. 162). (Illus.). 48p. pap. 12.95 (*0-85045-575-8*, 9094, Pub. by Ospry) Stackpole.

Prussian Cavalry of the Napoleonic Wars, 1807-15, Vol. 2. Peter Hofschroer. (Men-at-Arms Ser.: No. 172). (Illus.). 48p. pap. 11.95 (*0-85045-683-5*, 9104, Pub. by Osprey) Stackpole.

Prussian Girls. P. N. Dedeaux. 223p. 1989. reprint ed. mass mkt. 4.95 (*0-929654-15-3*, 44) Blue Moon Bks.

Prussian Light Infantry, 1792-1815. Peter Hofschroer. (Men-at-Arms Ser.: No. 149). (Illus.). 48p. pap. 11.95 (*0-85045-540-5*, 9081, Pub. by Osprey) Stackpole.

Prussian Line Infantry, 1792-1815. Peter Hofschroer. (Men-at-Arms Ser.: No. 152). (Illus.). 48p. pap. 11.95 (*0-85045-543-X*, 9084, Pub. by Osprey) Stackpole.

Prussian Military Reforms, 1786-1813. William O. Shanahan. LC 73-182584. (Columbia University. Studies in the Social Sciences: No. 520). reprint ed. 39.50 (*0-404-51520-7*) AMS Pr.

Prussian Officer. D. H. Lawrence. (Penguin Twentieth-Century Classics). 1995. 17.30 (*0-606-12491-8*) Turtleback.

Prussian Officer & Other Stories. D. H. Lawrence. Ed. by Antony Atkins. (World's Classics Ser.). 308p. 1995. pap. 8.95 (*0-19-283181-X*) OUP.

Prussian Officer & Other Stories. D. H. Lawrence. Ed. by John Worthen. LC 95-220738. (Twentieth-Century Classics Ser.). 304p. 1995. pap. 12.95 (*0-14-018780-4*, Penguin Classics) Viking Penguin.

Prussian Officer & Other Stories. D. H. Lawrence. (Oxford World Classics Ser.). 2000. pap. text 8.95 (*0-19-283474-6*) OUP.

Prussian Officer & Other Stories. D. H. Lawrence. LC 72-160939. (Short Story Index Reprint Ser.). 1977. reprint ed. 23.95 (*0-8369-3918-2*) Ayer.

Prussian Poland in the German Empire, 1871-1900. Richard Blanke. (East European Monographs: No. 86). 268p. 1981. text 52.50 (*0-914710-80-X*, Pub. by East Eur Monographs) Col U Pr.

Prussian Reserve Foreign & Militia Troops, 1806-15. Peter Hofschroer. (Men-at-Arms Ser.: No. 192). (Illus.). 48p. 1987. pap. 11.95 (*0-85045-799-8*, 9125, Pub. by Osprey) Stackpole.

Prussian Schoolteachers: Profession & Office, 1763-1848. Anthony J. LaVopa. LC 79-24873. 230p. reprint ed. pap. 71.30 (*0-7837-0312-0*, 204063400018) Bks Demand.

Prussian Spirit: A Survey of German Literature & Politics, 1914-1940. S. D. Stirk. 1972. 59.95 (*0-8490-0912-X*) Gordon Pr.

Prussian Tradition, 1740-1890 see Sword & the Scepter: The Problem of Militarism in Germany

Prussian Welfare State Before 1740. Reinhold August Dorwart. LC 77-134954. (Illus.). 342p. 1971. 37.00 (*0-674-71975-1*) HUP.

***Prussian Welfare State Before 1740.** Reinhold August Dorwart. 344p. 1999. 28.95 (*0-7351-0177-9*) Replica Bks.

***Prutkys Travels to Ethiopia & Other Countries.** Nicholas Arrowsmith-Brown. 1998. 52.95 (*0-904180-30-1*) Ashgate Pub Co.

Prvy Znamy Bol Pribina. Zrubec. (SLO.). 176p. 1996. write for info. (*80-08-02185-3*, Pub. by Slov Pegagog Naklad) IBD Ltd.

Prydain Companion: A Reference Guide to Lloyd Alexander's Prydain Chronicles. Michael O. Tunnell. LC 88-7705. 274p. 1989. lib. bdg. 55.00 (*0-313-26585-2*, TPY, Greenwood Pr) Greenwood.

P

Prygoski's Quick Review Constitutional Law. 4th ed. Publishing West Staff. (Sum & Substance Quick Review Ser.). 1998. pap. 18.95 (*1-57793-051-7*) West Pub.

Prying Game: The Sex, Sleaze, & Scandals of Fleet Street & the Media Mafia. Christopher Browne. (Illus.). 160p. 1996. 25.95 (*0-86051-927-9*, Robson-Parkwest) Parkwest Pubns.

Prying Open the Door: Foreign Workers in Japan. Takashi Oka. LC 94-20944. (Contemporary Issue Papers: Vol. 2). 83p. (C). 1994. pap. 8.95 (*0-87003-053-1*) Carnegie Endow.

***Prymer: The Prayer Book of the Medieval Era Adapted for Contemporary Use.** Tr. by Robert Webber. 192p. 2000. pap. 14.95 (*1-55725-256-4*, 930-057) Paraclete MA.

Pryor Convictions: And Other Life Sentences. Richard Pryor & Todd Gold. (Illus.). 288p. 1997. pap. 12.00 (*0-375-70048-X*) Pantheon.

Pryor Convictions: 31 Insights into ABM. Tom Pryor. (Illus.). 52p. 1998. pap. 9.95 (*1-886933-05-7*) ICMS TX.

Pryor Rendering. Gary Reed. 1996. write for info. (*0-614-09427-5*, Dutt) Dutton Plume.

Przepowiednie Nostradamasa. Dagmara Choznacka. Ed. by Polish Book Fair, Inc. Staff. (Illus.). 144p. 1995. pap. 8.00 (*1-885889-62-3*) Home Tutor.

Przerwany Bieg. Stanislawa Pijanowska. (POL.). 1000p. (Orig.). 1988. pap. 18.95 (*0-930401-16-6*) Artex Pub.

Przewalski's Horse see Learning about Horses Series

Przewalski's Horse. Charlotte Wilcox. (Learning about Horses Ser.). (Illus.). (J). 1997. 19.00 (*0-516-20519-6*) Childrens.

Przewalski's Horse: The History & Biology of an Endangered Species. Ed. by Lee Boyd & Katherine A. Houpt. LC 93-2363. (SUNY Series in Endangered Species). (Illus.). 313p. (C). 1994. pap. text 21.95 (*0-7914-1890-1*) State U NY Pr.

Przewalski's Horse: The History & Biology of an Endangered Species. Ed. by Lee Boyd & Katherine A. Houpt. LC 93-2363. (SUNY Series in Endangered Species). (Illus.). 313p. (C). 1994. text 64.50 (*0-7914-1889-8*) State U NY Pr.

Przyczynek do Biografii see Still Alive: An Autobiographical Essay

PS: A Building By Eric Owen Moss. James Steele. 1998. 39.95 (*1-875498-79-6*) Images Aust AT.

PS: The Preventive Maintenance Monthly. Government Printing Office Staff. pap. 23.00 (*0-16-010270-7*) USGPO.

PS. - Herodian, de Figuris Ueberlieferungsgeschichte und Kritische Ausgabe; Der Attikistes des Moiris Quellenkritische Untersuchung und Edition, 2 vols. Ed. by Kerstin Hajdu & Dirk Hansen. (Sammlung Griechischer Und Lateinischer Grammatiker Ser.: Vols. 8 & 9). (GER.). 320p. 1997. lib. bdg. 200.00 (*3-11-014836-6*) De Gruyter.

P/S A-INTRO COLL ACCT: 1-14 2E, Chapters 1-14. 2nd ed. Bischoff. (C). 1992. pap. text, student ed. 20.50 (*0-15-541701-0*) Harcourt Coll Pubs.

Ps-algol Implementations. Cockshott. 1990. pap. text 36.00 (*0-13-741190-1*, Prentice Hall) P-H.

PS DW EX F7 CB. Toolkit Staff. 1995. pap. text 66.66 (*0-8053-6190-1*) Addison-Wesley.

PS God Loves You Too! Connie Witter. (PS God Loves You! Ser.). 160p. 1998. pap. 6.99 (*1-56292-452-4*) Honor Bks OK.

***P.S. I've Taken a Lover.** Patricia Lucas White. 2000. mass mkt. 7.99 (*1-57343-004-8*) LionHearted.

PSA: How a Simple Blood Test Can Save Your Life. Don Kaltenbach. 32p. 1998. pap. 5.00 (*0-9651827-5-4*) Proste Cancer.

PSA, 1986, Vol. 2. Ed. by Arthur Fine & Peter K. Machamer. LC 72-624169. 383p. 1988. 13.50 (*0-917586-25-5*) Philos Sci Assn.

PSA, 1990, Vol. 2. Ed. by Arthur Fine et al. 595p. 1991. 25.00 (*0-917586-31-X*) Philos Sci Assn.

PSA, 1976, Vol. 1. Ed. by F. Suppe & P. D. Asquith. LC 72-624169. 312p. 1976. 8.50 (*0-917586-02-6*) Philos Sci Assn.

PSA 'Ninety-Three: International Meeting on Proballistic Safety Assessment, Clearwater, FL, January 26-29, 1993, Set. 1476p. 1994. 165.00 (*0-89448-180-0*, 700190) Am Nuclear Soc.

PSA 1974: Proceedings of the Philosophy of Science Association, Biennial Meeting, 1974. Philosophy of Science Association Staff. Ed. by Alex C. Michalos & R. S. Cohen. (Synthese Library: No. 91). 747p. 1976. pap. text 148.50 (*90-277-0648-4*, D Reidel); lib. bdg. 187.00 (*90-277-0647-6*, D Reidel) Kluwer Academic.

PSA 1978, 2 vols., Vol. I. Ed. by Peter D. Asquith & Ian Hacking. LC 72-624169. 314p. 1978. pap. 6.00 (*0-917586-05-0*) Philos Sci Assn.

PSA 1978, 2 vols., Vol. II. Ed. by Peter D. Asquith & Ian Hacking. LC 72-624169. 478p. 1978. 22.50 (*0-917586-10-7*) Philos Sci Assn.

PSA 1980, 2 Vols., Vol. II. Ed. by Peter D. Asquith & Ronald Giere. 678p. 1981. 23.75 (*0-917586-16-6*) Philos Sci Assn.

PSA 1982, 2 Vols., I. Ed. by Peter D. Asquith & Thomas Nickles. 414p. 1982. 21.00 (*0-917586-18-2*) Philos Sci Assn.

PSA 1982, 2 Vols., Vol. II. Ed. by Peter D. Asquith & Thomas Nickles. 730p. 1983. 25.00 (*0-917586-19-0*) Philos Sci Assn.

PSA, 1984, Vol. 1. Ed. by Peter D. Asquith & Philip Kitcher. 223p. 1984. 15.50 (*0-917586-21-2*) Philos Sci Assn.

PSA, 1984, Vol. 2. Ed. by Peter D. Asquith & Philip Kitcher. 903p. 1985. 30.00 (*0-917586-24-7*) Philos Sci Assn.

PSA 1986, Vol. 1. Ed. by Arthur Fine & Peter K. Machamer. 521p. 1986. 20.00 (*0-917586-23-9*) Philos Sci Assn.

PSA, 1988, 2 vols., Vol. 1. Ed. by Arthur Fine & Jarrett Leplin. 344p. 1988. 16.00 (*0-917586-27-1*) Philos Sci Assn.

PSA, 1988, 2 vols., Vol. 2. Ed. by Arthur Fine & Jarrett Leplin. 517p. 1989. 21.50 (*0-917586-28-X*) Philos Sci Assn.

PSA 1990, Vol. 1. Ed. by Arthur Fine et al. 599p. 1990. 22.00 (*0-917586-30-1*) Philos Sci Assn.

PSA, 1992, Vol. 1. Ed. by David M. Hull et al. 582p. 1992. 22.00 (*0-917586-33-6*) Philos Sci Assn.

PSA, 1992, Vol. 2. Ed. by David M. Hull et al. 514p. 1994. 20.00 (*0-917586-34-4*) Philos Sci Assn.

PSA, 1994, Vol. 1. Ed. by David M. Hull et al. 554p. 1994. 22.00 (*0-917586-36-0*) Philos Sci Assn.

PSA, 1994, Vol. 2. Ed. by David M. Hull et al. 479p. 1995. 20.00 (*0-917586-37-9*) Philos Sci Assn.

Psalm & Homage to Winngenstein. Robert Lax. Tr. by Alfred Kuoni from GER. 91p. (Orig.). 1991. pap. text 15.00 (*3-85842-193-6*) Franciscan Inst.

Psalm & Story. James W. Watts. (JSOTS Ser.: Vol. 139). 244p. 1992. 70.00 (*1-85075-343-1*, Pub. by Sheffield Acad) CUP Services.

Psalm at Journey's End. Eric F. Hansen. Tr. by Joana Tate. LC 97-15049. 1997. pap. 13.00 (*0-15-600527-1*, Harvest Bks) Harcourt.

Psalm at Journey's End. Erik F. Hansen. Tr. by Joan Tate. LC 96-33811. 388p. 1996. 24.00 (*0-374-23868-5*) FS&G.

Psalm 8. deluxe limited ed. Illus. by Joyce Alexander. 1991. pap. 15.00 (*0-937686-18-2*) Turtles Quill.

Psalm 8 & Its Christological Re-Interpretations in the New Testament Context Vol. 577: An Inter-Contextual Study in Biblical Hermeneutics. Wenceslaus M. Urassa. LC 98-33928. (European University Studies: No. 23). (Illus.). 281p. 1998. pap. text 48.95 (*0-8204-3202-4*) P Lang Pubng.

Psalm for a Winter Twilight. Beatrice La Force. LC 97-221482. 91p. 1997. pap. 9.99 (*0-88092-320-2*, 3202) Royal Fireworks.

Psalm for Falconer, Vol. 1. Ian Morson. Date not set. write for info. (*0-312-96534-6*) Tor Bks.

Psalm in My Heart: Daily Devotionals from the Book of Psalms. deluxe ed. Leroy Brownlow. (Devotions for Today Ser.). 365p. 1989. 14.99 (*0-915720-32-9*) Brownlow Pub Co.

Psalm in Your Heart. George O. Wood. LC 97-71906. 304p. 1997. pap. 12.99 (*0-88243-685-6*, 02-0685) Gospel Pub.

***Psalm in Your Heart, Vol. 2.** George O. Wood. 304p. 1999. pap. 12.99 (*0-88243-785-2*, 02-0785) Gospel Pub.

Psalm Journal, Bk. II. Joan D. Chittister. 112p. (Orig.). 1988. pap. 6.95 (*0-934134-45-6*) Sheed & Ward WI.

Psalm Killer. Chris Petit. 1998. mass mkt. 6.99 (*0-345-42090-X*) Ballantine Pub Grp.

Psalm Killer. Chris Petit. 1998. mass mkt. 6.99 (*0-449-00289-6*, GM) Fawcett.

Psalm Killer. Chris Petit. LC 96-39157. 1997. 5.99 (*0-679-45126-9*) Knopf.

Psalm 91: An Illustrated Bible Chapter for Young Children. Ed. by David Meyer & Alice Meyer. LC 90-71556. (Illus.). 48p. (Orig.). (J). (ps-4). 1991. pap. 12.95 incl. audio (*1-879099-04-7*) Thy Word.

Psalm of Life. Patsy Hallman. LC 98-28264. (Illus.). vii, 166 p. 1998. 16.95 (*1-57168-270-8*, Eakin Pr) Sunbelt Media.

Psalm of Saiva. T. Isaac Tamby. 506p. 1986. reprint ed. 30.00 (*0-8364-1682-1*, Pub. by Abhinav) S Asia.

Psalm of the Gods. Molana Shah Maghsoud Sadegh Angha. LC 97-68912. 1997. write for info. (*0-910735-78-6*) MTO Printing & Pubn Ctr.

Psalm 1 Coloring Book. Illus. by Arlene L. Martin. 28p. (J). (ps-2). 1989. pap. 1.55 (*0-7399-0171-0*, 2929) Rod & Staff.

Psalm 1 Coloring Book. Illus. by Arlene L. Martin. (SPA.). 28p. (J). 1996. pap. 1.40 (*0-7399-0172-9*, 2929.1) Rod & Staff.

***Psalm 151: Humalong with the Spiritually Challenged.** Tom Hewitt. 125p. 1998. pap. text 9.99 (*1-900507-70-6*, Pub. by Solway) Eisenbrauns.

Psalm 148, Etc. Joyce Alexander & Dorsey Alexander. (Illus.). 1998. write for info. (*0-614-30683-3*) Turtles Quill.

Psalm 119: The Exaltation of Torah. David N. Freedman. LC 99-46630. (Biblical & Judaic Studies : Vol. 6). 140p. 1999. text 19.50 (*1-57506-038-8*) Eisenbrauns.

Psalm 119. Charles Bridges. 1977. 24.99 (*0-85151-176-7*) Banner of Truth.

Psalm 119, 3 vols. Thomas Manton. 580p. 1990. 79.99 (*0-85151-576-2*) Banner of Truth.

Psalm 119: A Journey into the Heart of God. Jeff Adams. 444p. 1993. 19.95 (*0-9643021-2-8*) Reality Living.

Psalm 119: Matrix, Form, & Setting. William M. Soll. LC 90-27610. 1989. 9.00 (*0-915170-22-1*, CMQMS22) Catholic Bibl Assn.

Psalm 104. deluxe limited ed. Illus. by Joyce Alexander. 32p. 1978. pap. 15.00 (*0-937686-27-1*) Turtles Quill.

Psalm 139: An Illustrated Bible Chapter for Young Children. Ed. by David Meyer & Alice Meyer. LC 91-90825. (Illus.). 48p. (Orig.). (J). (ps-4). 1991. pap. 12.95 incl. audio (*1-879099-03-9*) Thy Word.

Psalm-Poem & Psalter-Glosses: The Latin & Old English Psalter-Text Background to "Kentish Psalm 50" Sarah L. Keefer. LC 91-17449. (American University Studies: Theology & Religion: Ser. VII, Vol. 95). 177p. 1992. 36.95 (*0-8204-1479-4*) P Lang Pubng.

Psalm Prayers. David Haas. LC 94-232368. 96p. 1994. pap. 5.95 (*0-86716-233-3*) St Anthony Mess Pr.

Psalm-Prayers for Every Mood. Kevin Lyon. 176p. (Orig.). 1996. pap. 10.95 (*1-85607-164-2*, Pub. by Columba Press) Whitecap Bks.

Psalm Prayers for Morning & Evening. Intro. by Brian Magee. 65p. (Orig.). 1991. pap. 5.95 (*1-85390-121-0*, Pub. by Veritas Pubns) St Mut.

Psalm Refrains: Reproducible Calligraphic Expressions of Sunday Responsorials. Charles Lehman. LC 97-132308. (Illus.). 128p. (Orig.). 1996. pap. 19.95 (*1-55612-855-X*, LL1855) Sheed & Ward WI.

Psalm Services for Group Prayer. William Cleary. LC 92-81718. 96p. (Orig.). 1993. pap. 12.95 (*0-89622-526-7*) Twenty-Third.

Psalm Singer's Amusement. William Billings. LC 73-5100. (Earlier American Music Ser.: No. 20). 104p. 1974. reprint ed. lib. bdg. 25.00 (*0-306-70587-7*) Da Capo.

Psalm Songs Psalm Songs. David Ogden. 1998. pap. 23.95 (*0-225-66853-X*) Continuum.

Psalm-Structures: A Study of Psalms with Refrains. Paul R. Raabe. (JSOT Supplement Ser.: No. 104). 219p. 1990. 60.00 (*1-85075-262-1*, Pub. by Sheffield Acad) CUP Services.

Psalm to Remember. (Americana Bks.). (Illus.). 1980. 3.00 (*0-911410-49-X*) Applied Arts.

Psalm 23. Illus. by Tim Ladwig. LC 97-14082. 40p. (J). 1997. 16.00 (*0-8028-5160-6*, Eerdmans Bks); pap. 8.00 (*0-8028-5163-0*, Eerdmans Bks) Eerdmans.

Psalm 23: A Prescription to Relieve Stress. Clifford G. Hamil. 192p. 1998. pap. 10.95 (*1-57502-997-9*, PO2720) Morris Pubng.

Psalm Twenty-Three: An Anthology. Ed. by K. H. Strange & R. G. Sandbach. 144p. (C). 1989. 59.00 (*0-7855-6811-5*, Pub. by St Andrew); pap. 35.00 (*0-7855-6812-3*, Pub. by St Andrew) St Mut.

Psalm Twenty-Three: An Anthology. K. H. Strange & R. G. Sandbach. 144p. (C). 1988. text 45.00 (*0-7152-0624-9*); pap. text 25.00 (*0-7152-0623-0*) St Mut.

Psalm 23: An Illustrated Bible Chapter for Young Children. Ed. by David Meyer & Alice Meyer. (Illus.). 32p. (J). (ps-4). 1990. pap. 12.95 incl. audio (*1-879099-00-4*) Thy Word.

Psalm 23: Exploring the Parallels Between Sheep & Mankind. Beverly Hale-Watson. Ed. by Kimberly K. Tweed. (Illus.). 36p. (Orig.). 1995. pap. 5.75 (*0-9623647-5-4*) B H Watson.

Psalm 23: The Song of a Passionate Heart. David Roper. LC 94-9196. 168p. 1996. 12.99 (*1-57293-012-8*) Discovery Hse Pubs.

Psalm 118 see Psalm 118

Psalm 118. Theophan the Recluse.Tr. of Psalm 118. 496p. reprint ed. 22.00 (*0-317-28925-X*); reprint ed. pap. 17.00 (*0-317-28926-8*) Holy Trinity.

Psalm 119 see Salmo 119: Una Odisea Corazon de Dios

Psalm 23. David Roper. 168p. 1996. pap. 5.99 (*0-929239-86-5*, Pub. by Discovery Hse Pubs) Barbour Pub.

Psalmbook of the White Butterfly. Jay B. Fowler, Jr. LC 85-2887. 64p. (Orig.). 1985. pap. 5.00 (*0-914061-03-8*) Orchises Pr.

Psalmen. Georg Fohrer. (Studienbuch Ser.). (GER.). ix, 256p. 1993. pap. 44.65 (*3-11-013927-8*) De Gruyter.

Psalmen: Stilistische Verfahren und Aufbau mit besonderer Beruecksichtigung von Ps. 1-41. N. H. Ridderbos. Tr. by Karl E. Mittring from DUT. (Beiheft zur Zeitschrift fuer die Alttestamentliche Wissenschaft Ser.: No. 117). 305p. (C). 1972. 110.00 (*3-11-001834-9*) De Gruyter.

Psalmen in Einstimmigen Vokalen Uberlieferungen: Eine Vergleichende Untersuchung Judischer und Christlicher Traditionen, 2 vols. Regina Randhofer. (Europaische Hochschulschriften Ser.: Reihe 36, Bd. 131). (GER., Illus.). XII, 286p. 1995. 68.95 (*3-631-48037-7*) P Lang Pubng.

Psalmenkommentare aus der Katenenueberlieferung, Vol. 1. Ekkehard Muehlenberg. LC 73-91808. (Patristische Texte und Studien: Band 15). (GER.). (C). 1974. 157.70 (*3-11-004182-0*) De Gruyter.

Psalmenkommentare aus der Katenenueberlieferung, Vol. 2. Ekkehard Muehlenberg. (Patristische Texte und Studien: Vol. 16). (C). 1977. 157.70 (*3-11-005717-4*) De Gruyter.

Psalmenkommentare aus der Katenenueberlieferung: Untersuchungen zu den Psalmenkatenen, Vol. 3. Ekkehard Muehlenberg. (Patristische Texte und Studien: No. 19). (C). 1978. 108.50 (*3-11-006959-8*) De Gruyter.

Psalmist: Imagery & Style Collection. Patricia Williams. Ed. by Dewilda M. Williams. 124p. 1996. pap. 10.95 (*1-886493-09-X*) NBC Study Pub.

Psalmnary: Gradual Psalms for Cantor & Congregation. James E. Barrett. 196p. 1982. ring bd. 26.00 (*0-942466-04-7*); ring bd. 23.00 (*0-942466-03-9*) Hymnary Pr.

Psalms see Salmos I

Psalms. 181p. 1994. pap. 6.00 (*0-910424-29-2*) Concordant.

***Psalms.** 1999. pap. text 3.00 (*5-550-00793-2*); pap. text 3.00 (*5-550-00792-4*) Nairi.

Psalms. (Complete Biblical Library: Vol. 10). 733p. 1997. 49.95 (*1-884642-34-9*) World Library.

Psalms. Anthony L. Ash. LC 79-67300. 1984. 17.95 (*0-915547-42-2*) Abilene Christ U.

Psalms. Ronald Barany. LC 97-91812. x, 286p. 1997. 23.00 (*0-9657767-0-0*) Psilam Pub.

Psalms Bruce Boadt. 1999. text. write for info. (*0-312-22517-2*) St Martin.

***Psalms.** Bono. LC 99-482758. (Books of the Bible). 144p. 1999. pap. 2.95 (*0-8021-3675-3*, Pub. by Grove-Atltic) Publishers Group.

Psalms. Timothy R. Botts. 1998. pap. 9.99 (*0-8423-8817-6*) Tyndale Hse.

Psalms. John D. Bowman. (Covenant Bible Studies). 48p. (Orig.). 1989. pap. 4.95 (*0-87178-723-7*, 8237) Brethren.

***Psalms.** Dee Brestin. (Woman's Journey Through... Ser.). 2000. pap. 6.99 (*1-56476-767-1*) Chariot Victor.

Psalms. Craig Broyles. LC 99-40849. (New International Biblical Commentary Ser.: Vol. 11). 560p. 1999. pap. 11.95 (*1-56563-220-6*) Hendrickson MA.

Psalms. Concordia Publishing Staff. (God's Word for Today Ser.). 1994. pap. 5.50 (*0-570-09476-3*, 20-2641) Concordia.

Psalms. Jerome F. D. Creach. LC 98-48124. (Interpretation Bible Studies). 112p. 1998. pap. 7.95 (*0-664-50021-8*) Geneva Press.

Psalms. Mahmoud Darwish. Tr. by Ben Bennani. 70p. 1994. 15.00 (*0-89410-761-5*, Three Contnts); pap. 8.95 (*0-89410-762-3*, Three Contnts) L Rienner.

Psalms. J. Day. (Old Testament Guides Ser.: No. 15). 159p. 1990. pap. 12.50 (*1-85075-703-8*, Pub. by Sheffield Acad) CUP Services.

Psalms. Allan Harman. 1999. 29.99 (*1-85792-168-2*) Christian Focus.

Psalms. Donna Huisjen. LC 98-61558. (My Tall Bks.). (J). 2000. 6.99 (*0-310-91861-8*) Zondervan.

***Psalms.** David King. 2001. pap. 9.95 (*0-375-70552-X*, Pub. by Knopf) Random House.

***Psalms.** James Limburg. (Bible Companion Ser.). 448p. 2000. pap. 29.95 (*0-664-25557-4*) Westminster John Knox.

Psalms. Lawrence G. Lovasik. (Saint Joseph Picture Bks.). (Illus.). 1987. pap. 1.25 (*0-89942-398-1*, 398-00) Catholic Bk Pub.

Psalms. James L. Mays. LC 93-32887. (Interpretation, A Bible Commentary for Teaching & Preaching Ser.). 432p. 1994. 31.00 (*0-8042-3115-X*) Westminster John Knox.

***Psalms.** Frederick B. Meyer. (Classics Ser.). (Illus.). 190p. 1999. pap. 9.99 (*1-84030-056-6*) Emerald House Group Inc.

Psalms. Patrick Miller. (Interpreting Biblical Texts Ser.). 2001. 18.95 (*0-687-00845-X*) Abingdon.

An Asterisk (*) at the beginning of an entry indicates that the title is appearing for the first time.

Psalms. Kathleen Norris. LC 97-19048. 432p. 1997. pap. 12.95 (*1-57322-647-5*, Riverhd Trade) Berkley Pub.

Psalms. W. S. Plumer. (Geneva Commentaries Ser.). 1978. 59.99 (*0-85151-209-7*) Banner of Truth.

Psalms. Tr. by Joseph Rhymer. 448p. 1996. pap. 39.95 (*0-85439-474-5*, Pub. by St Paul Pubns) St Mut.

***Psalms.** Konrad Schaefer. (Berit Olam (The Everlasting Covenant) Ser.). 2000. 0.00 (*0-8146-5061-9*) Liturgical Pr.

Psalms. Charles H. Spurgeon. (Spurgeon Collection: Vol. 6). 231p. 1998. pap. 9.99 (*1-889893-16-1*) Emerald House Group Inc.

Psalms. Carroll Stuhlmueller. (Read & Pray Ser.). 1979. pap. 1.00 (*0-8199-0631-X*, Frncscn Herld) Franciscan Pr.

Psalms. David Dickson. (Geneva Commentaries Ser.). 1064p. 1985. reprint ed. 35.99 (*0-85151-481-2*) Banner of Truth.

Psalms. rev. ed. Irving L. Jensen. (Bible Self-Study Guides Ser.). 140p. (Orig.). 1968. pap. 7.99 (*0-8024-4463-6*, 433) Moody.

Psalms, Bk. 1, Chapters 1-50. Brian J. Bailey. Ed. by Paul G. Caram. 256p. (Orig.). (C). 1998. pap. text. write for info. (*0-9643924-3-7*) Zion Christian.

Psalms, Pt. I. J. Vernon McGee. (Thru the Bible Commentary Ser.: Vol. 17). 1997. pap. 6.97 (*0-7852-0444-X*) Nelson.

Psalms, Pt. II. J. Vernon McGee. (Thru the Bible Commentary Ser.: Vol. 18). 1997. pap. 6.97 (*0-7852-0458-X*) Nelson.

Psalms, Pt. III. J. Vernon McGee. (Thru the Bible Commentary Ser.: Vol. 19). 1997. pap. 6.97 (*0-7852-0461-X*) Nelson.

Psalms see Daily Study Bible for the Old Testament

Psalms, Vol. 1. John F. Brug. LC 88-62293. (People's Bible Ser.). 292p. 1988. pap. 11.99 (*0-8100-0299-X*, 15N0457) Northwest Pub.

Psalms, Vol. 1. John F. Brug. (The People's Bible Ser.). 64p. 1989. pap. text, student ed. 5.00 (*0-938272-61-6*, 22-2204) WELS Board.

Psalms, Vol. 1. G. A. Knight. 352p. 1993. pap. 22.00 (*0-7152-0520-X*, Pub. by St Andrew) St Mut.

Psalms, Vol. 1. S. Edward Tesh & Walter D. Zorn. LC 99-23687. (NIV Commentary Ser.). 500p. 1999. 26.99 (*0-89900-887-9*) College Pr Pub.

Psalms, Vol. I. abr. ed. Charles H. Spurgeon. LC 93-25952. (Classic Commentaries Ser.: Vol. 1). 384p. (C). 1993. pap. 17.99 (*0-89107-739-1*) Crossway Bks.

Psalms, Vol. 1, Pts. 1-72. John F. Brug. LC 88-62293. (People's Bible Ser.). 56p. 1989. student ed. 5.00 (*0-938272-62-4*, 22-2203) Northwest Pub.

Psalms, Vol. 2. Robert L. Alden. (Everyman's Bible Commentary Ser.). 1975. pap. 9.99 (*0-8024-2019-2*) Moody.

Psalms, Vol. 2. John F. Brug. LC 88-62293. (People's Bible Ser.). 285p. 1989. pap. 11.99 (*0-8100-0309-0*, 15N0468) Northwest Pub.

Psalms, Vol. II. Charles H. Spurgeon. LC 93-25952. (Classic Commentaries Ser.: Vol. 2). 384p. (C). 1993. pap. 17.99 (*0-89107-740-5*) Crossway Bks.

Psalms see Numerical Bible

Psalms, Vol. 13. L. Russ Bush. (The New American Commentary Ser.). 2000. 29.99 (*0-8054-0113-X*) Broadman.

***Psalms: A Bible Commentary in the Wesleyan Tradition.** Stephen J. Lennox. 1999. 24.95 (*0-89827-204-1*) Wesleyan Pub Hse.

Psalms: A Commentary. Artur Weiser. LC 62-16760. (Old Testament Library). 842p. 1962. 37.00 (*0-664-20418-X*) Westminster John Knox.

Psalms: A Devotional Commentary. Herbert Lockyer, Sr. LC 92-15243. 800p. 1993. pap. 27.99 (*0-8254-3137-9*) Kregel.

Psalms: A Guide to Prayer & Praise. Ronald Klug. (Fisherman Bible Studyguide Ser.). 80p. 1979. pap. 4.99 (*0-87788-699-7*, H Shaw Pubs) Waterbrook Pr.

Psalms: A Guide to Victorious Holy Living. Carl E. Foster. Ed. by Linda L. Foster. LC 87-51577. 275p. 1988. student ed. 15.00 (*0-9619962-1-8*) Victorious Holy Living.

***Psalms: A Journal: Spiritual Formation Through Personal Encounters with.** Kenneth Boa. LC 00-30517. 2001. write for info. (*1-57683-251-1*) NavPress.

Psalms: A Singing Version. Joseph Gelineau. 256p. 1968. pap. 14.95 (*0-8091-1669-3*) Paulist Pr.

***Psalms: A Thousand Years.** Laud O. Vaught. 2000. pap. 12.99 (*0-87148-944-9*) Pathway Pr.

Psalms: A Translation from the Hebrew. LC 96-40428. 1997. pap. write for info. (*0-8189-0795-9*) Alba.

***Psalms: An Artist's Impression.** Annie Kaai & Eugene H. Peterson. (Illus.). 56p. 1999. text 19.99 (*0-9535757-0-5*, Pub. by Piquant UK) OM Literature.

***Psalms: An Artist's Impression.** Eugene H. Peterson. (Illus.). 55p. 2000. 19.99 (*0-8308-2289-5*) InterVarsity.

Psalms: An Expositional Commentary, 3. James Montgomery Boice. 1998. 79.95 (*0-8010-1174-4*) Baker Bks.

Psalms: An Expositional Commentary (Psalms 42-106), 2. James M. Boice. LC 93-36246. 544p. 1996. 29.99 (*0-8010-1118-3*) Baker Bks.

***Psalms: An Invitation to Pray.** Kevin Perrotta. (Catholic Perspectives Six Weeks with the Bible). 83p. 2000. pap. 6.95 (*0-8294-1434-7*) Loyola Pr.

Psalms: Ancient Poetry of the Spirit. Ed. by Lawrence Boadt & F. F. Bruce. LC 99-28743. 192p. 1999. pap. 12.95 (*0-312-22109-6*, St Martins Paperbacks) St Martin.

Psalms: Chronologically Treated with a New Translation. rev. ed. Moses Buttenwieser. (Library of Biblical Studies). 1969. 79.50 (*0-87068-044-7*) Ktav.

Psalms: Critical & Exegetical Commentary, Vol. 1. Charles Briggs & Emile G. Briggs. Ed. by Samuel R. Driver et al. (International Critical Commentary Ser.). 532p. 1993. 39.95 (*0-567-05011-4*, Pub. by T & T Clark) Bks Intl VA.

Psalms: Critical & Exegetical Commentary, Vol. 2. Charles Briggs & Emile G. Briggs. Ed. by Samuel R. Driver et al. (International Critical Commentary Ser.). 580p. 1999. 39.95 (*0-567-05012-2*, Pub. by T & T Clark) Bks Intl VA.

Psalms: Daily Study of God's Word. Barbara Hilton. Ed. by Darlene Teague. (Bible Study Ser.). 96p. 1997. pap. text 4.95 (*0-89827-180-0*) Wesleyan Pub Hse.

Psalms: Deepening Your Relationship with God. Bill Hybels. (Small Group Ser.). 96p. (Orig.). 1997. pap. 5.99 (*0-310-21318-5*) Zondervan.

***Psalms: God's Abundance for Living.** Kathy Miller. 240p. 2000. 19.95 (*1-892016-30-3*) Starburst.

Psalms: Gratitude. St. Pauls Staff. 1992. pap. 24.95 (*0-7855-2654-4*, Pub. by St Paul Pubns) St Mut.

Psalms: Hebrew Text & Commentary with English Translation, Vol. 1 (Chaps. 1-41) Tr. by A. J. Rosenberg from HEB. LC 59-10454.Tr. of Sefer Tehillim. 352p. 1990. 20.95 (*0-910818-84-3*) Judaica Pr.

Psalms: Hebrew Text & Commentary with English Translation, Vol. 2 (Chaps. 42-89) Tr. by A. J. Rosenberg from HEB.Tr. of Sefer Tehillim. 432p. 1990. 20.95 (*0-910818-85-1*) Judaica Pr.

Psalms: Hebrew Text & Commentary with English Translation, Vol. 3 (Chaps. 90-150) Tr. by A. J. Rosenberg from HEB. LC 59-10454. (Books of the Prophets & Holy Writings).Tr. of Sefer Tehillim. 432p. 1990. 20.95 (*0-910818-86-X*) Judaica Pr.

Psalms: Hebrew Text, English Translation & Commentary Digest. rev. ed. A. Cohen. 495p. 1992. 14.95 (*1-871055-65-2*) Soncino Pr.

Psalms: Joy. St. Pauls Staff. 1992. pap. 24.95 (*0-7855-2653-6*, Pub. by St Paul Pubns) St Mut.

Psalms: Meditations for Every Day of the Year. Joan D. Chittister. LC 96-13864. 144p. (Orig.). 1996. pap. text 14.95 (*0-8245-1581-1*) Crossroad NY.

Psalms: Mercy. St. Pauls Staff. 1992. pap. 24.95 (*0-7855-2652-8*, Pub. by St Paul Pubns) St Mut.

Psalms: New American Bible 1991 Annotated Edition. annot. ed. 262p. (Orig.). 1992. pap. 9.95 (*0-8146-2156-2*, M Glazier) Liturgical Pr.

Psalms: New International Version, Vol. 1. 194p. write for info. (*0-614-00640-6*, 5290) LBW.

Psalms: New International Version, Vol. 2. 198p. write for info. (*0-614-00641-4*, 5295) LBW.

Psalms: Poems. April Bernard. 72p. 1995. pap. 9.00 (*0-393-31304-2*) Norton.

Psalms: Poems from Hollywood. Mark Dunster. 11p. 1999. pap. 5.00 (*0-89642-771-4*) Linden Pubs.

Psalms: Prayers of the Heart. Eugene H. Peterson. (LifeGuide Bible Studies). 64p. (Orig.). 1987. pap., wbk. ed. 4.99 (*0-8308-1034-X*, 1034) InterVarsity.

***Psalms: Prayers of the Heart.** 2nd ed. Eugene H. Peterson. (LifeGuide Bible Studies). 64p. (Orig.). 2000. pap. 4.99 (*0-8308-3034-0*) InterVarsity.

Psalms: Reading & Studying the Book of Praises. William H. Bellinger, Jr. LC 90-40913. 166p. 1990. pap. 9.95 (*0-943575-35-4*) Hendrickson MA.

***Psalms: Remembering Zion.** Alastair G. Hunter. LC 98-54242. (Old Testament Readings Ser.). 1999. pap. write for info. (*0-415-12770-X*); text. write for info. (*0-415-12769-6*) Routledge.

Psalms: Songs for the Way Home. Paul Glynn. 194p. (Orig.). 1997. pap. 9.95 (*0-85574-366-2*, Pub. by E J Dwyer) Morehouse Pub.

Psalms: Songs of Discipleship. Robert L. Alden. (Everyman's Bible Commentary Ser.: Vol. 3). 1975. pap. 9.99 (*0-8024-2020-6*) Moody.

Psalms: Songs of Tragedy, Hope, & Justice. J. David Pleins. LC 93-17541. (Bible & Liberation Ser.). 160p. (Orig.). 1993. pap. 15.00 (*0-88344-928-5*) Orbis Bks.

Psalms: Speaking Honestly with God (Leader Guide) Harvey Smit. 64p. 1998. pap. text, teacher ed. 6.75 (*1-56212-334-3*, 1312-8840) CRC Pubns.

Psalms: Speaking Honestly with God (Study) 2nd ed. Dale Cooper. LC 97-45091. (Revelation Series for Adults). 64p. 1998. pap. text, student ed. 4.95 (*1-56212-333-5*, 1312-8800) CRC Pubns.

Psalms: The Prayer Book of the Bible. 2nd ed. Dietrich Bonhoeffer. Tr. by James H. Burtness from GER. LC 73-101111.Tr. of Das/Gebetbuch der Bibel. 88p. 1970. pap. 6.99 (*0-8066-1439-0*, 10-5321, Augsburg) Augsburg Fortress.

Psalms: Translation & Commentary by Rabbi Samson Raphael Hirsch. Tr. by Gertrude Hirschler from GER. (Compact Ser.). 1978. 27.95 (*0-87306-135-7*) Feldheim.

Psalms: With Introduction to Cultic Poetry, Prt. I. Ed. by Erhard S. Gerstenberger. (Forms of the Old Testament Literature Ser.: Vol. XIV). 224p. (Orig.). 1988. pap. 20.00 (*0-8028-0255-9*) Eerdmans.

Psalms Bk. 2: Chapters 51-100. Brian J. Bailey. Ed. by Brian D. Alarid. 278p. pap. 12.00 (*1-890381-01-2*) Zion Christ.

Psalms Vol. 1: An Expositional Commentary (Psalms 1-41), 1. James M. Boice. LC 93-36246. 394p. 1994. 29.99 (*0-8010-1077-2*) Baker Bks.

Psalms Vol. II: My Long Journey Home. Philip Johnson. 51p. 1998. pap. 12.50 (*0-9668204-9-5*) Truth Publ.

Psalms Vol. 3: An Expositional Commentary Psalms 107-150, 3. James M. Boice. 480p. 1998. 29.99 (*0-8010-1164-7*) Baker Bks.

***Psalms - Chinese Edition: A Guide to Prayer & Praise.** Ron King. 101p. 1999. pap. 6.50 (*1-56582-132-7*) Christ Renew Min.

Psalms & Canticles. John T. Ferrier. 96p. 1935. text 9.00 (*0-900235-49-7*) Order Of The Cross.

***Psalms & Compassions: A Jesuit's Journey Through Cancer.** Timothy Brown. Ed. by Susan Hodges. LC 00-103822. 2000. pap. write for info. (*0-9668716-4-2*) Resonant Pubg.

Psalms & Hymns for Public Worship. William Allen. (Works of William Allen). 1989. reprint ed. lib. bdg. 79.00 (*0-7812-1770-9*) Rprt Serv.

Psalms & Hymns of Isaac Watts. Isaac Watts. LC 97-222707. 600p. 1997. reprint ed. 35.00 (*1-57358-069-4*) Soli Deo Gloria.

Psalms & Prayers for Congregational Participation: Series C (Common Consensus Lectionary) B. David Hostetter. (Common Consensus Lectionary Ser.: Series C). 1985. 8.25 (*0-89536-770-X*, 5865) CSS OH.

***Psalms & Proverbs.** 1998. text 14.99 incl. audio (*0-8423-5170-1*) Tyndale Hse.

Psalms & Proverbs. Alice J. Davidson. (Alice in Bibleland Storybooks). (Illus.). 32p. (J). (gr. 3 up). 1984. 5.95 (*0-8378-5069-X*) Gibson.

Psalms & Proverbs: Blueprints for 28 Messages Built upon God's Word. Sam E. Stone. (Sermon Starters Ser.). 64p. 1999. pap. 5.99 (*0-7847-0932-7*, 23010) Standard Pub.

***Psalms & Proverbs: For a Woman of Faith.** gif. ed. Zondervan Publishing Staff. (Women of Faith Ser.). 2000. 7.99 (*0-310-98092-5*) Zondervan.

Psalms & Proverbs: Perspective & Wisdom for Today. rev. ed. Marilyn Kunz & Catherine Schell. 112p. 1993. pap. 5.99 (*1-880266-05-9*) Neighborhood Bible.

Psalms & Proverbs on the Playing Field. Patsy Neal. LC 99-71677. (Illus.). 127p. (Orig.). 1999. pap. 9.95 (*0-9657561-7-3*, Pub. by Reflection TX) Spring Arbor Dist.

***Psalms & Readings for Every Season.** James Kraus. (Prayer Bks.). 1999. pap. 14.95 (*1-886510-33-4*) Treehaus Bks.

Psalms & the Life of Faith. Walter Brueggemann. Ed. by Patrick D. Miller. LC 95-21448. 240p. 1995. pap. 20.00 (*0-8006-2733-4*, Fortress Pr) Augsburg Fortress.

Psalms & the Transformation of Stress. Dennis Sylva. (Louvain Theological & Pastoral Monographs). 1995. pap. text 25.00 (*0-8028-0574-4*) Eerdmans.

Psalms & Their Readers: Interpretive Strategies for Psalm 18. Donald K. Berry. (JSOT Supplement Ser.: No. 153). 160p. 1993. 52.50 (*1-85075-399-7*, Pub. by Sheffield Acad) CUP Services.

Psalms Anew: In Inclusive Language. Nancy Schreck & Maureen Leach. LC 87-107847. 200p. 1986. spiral bd. 8.95 (*0-88489-174-7*) St Marys.

Psalms Are Yours. Roland E. Murphy. LC 93-15639. 160p. 1993. pap. 10.95 (*0-8091-3411-X*) Paulist Pr.

Psalms Beyond, 2000. Mark Link. (Illus.). 200p. (Orig.). 1996. pap. 12.95 (*0-88347-360-7*, 7360) Res Christian Liv.

Psalms Commentary of Gilbert of Poitiers: From Lectio Divina to the Lecture Room. Theresa Gross-Diaz. (Brill's Studies in Intellectual History: No. 68). 250p. 1995. 84.00 (*90-04-10211-6*) Brill Academic Pubs.

***Psalms 51-100.** Broadman & Holman Staff. LC 99-11544. (Shepherd's Notes Ser.). 100p. 1999. pap. 5.95 (*0-8054-9340-9*) Broadman.

Psalms 51-100. Marvin Tate. (Biblical Commentary Ser.: Vol. 20). 1991. 29.99 (*0-8499-0219-3*) Word Pub.

Psalms 56-85 see Tehillim: Psalms

Psalms for a Child's Heart. Sheryl Crawford. (Illus.). 64p. (J). (ps-2). 1997. 11.99 (*0-7814-3004-6*, Chariot Bks) Chariot Victor.

Psalms for a Child's Heart. Sheryl Ann Crawford. LC 97-7407. 64p. (J). (ps-2). 1997. write for info. (*0-7814-0022-8*, Chariot Bks) Chariot Victor.

Psalms for a Pilgrim People. Jim Cotter. LC 98-42301. 336p. 1998. pap. 17.95 (*0-8192-1778-6*) Morehouse Pub.

Psalms for a Woman's Life 7 Studies to Better Understand Our God, Ourselves & Our World. Jill Briscoe. 1999. pap. text 6.99 (*1-56476-774-4*) SP Pubns.

Psalms for All Seasons. John Craghan. 192p. (Orig.). 1993. pap. 6.95 (*0-8146-2205-4*) Liturgical Pr.

Psalms for Contemplation. rev. ed. Carlos G. Valles. LC 90-28647. 296p. 1991. reprint ed. pap. 12.95 (*0-8294-0709-X*) Loyola Pr.

Psalms for Feasts & Seasons: Revised & Augmented Full Music Edition. Composed by Christopher Willeock. 88p. 1998. reprint ed. pap. 15.95 (*1-57992-013-6*) OR Catholic.

Psalms for Feasts & Seasons Vol. 2: Reformed, Anglican, Lutheran, & Wesleyan Rites. Christopher Willcock. 88p. 1991. spiral bd. 29.95 (*0-8146-2055-8*) Liturgical Pr.

Psalms for Praise & Worship: A Complete Liturgical Psalter. S.T. Kimbough et al. Ed. by Carlton R. Young. 256p. (Orig.). 1992. pap. 15.95 (*0-687-09326-0*) Abingdon.

Psalms for Praying: An Invitation to Wholeness. Nan C. Merrill. LC 66-21737. 312p. 1997. pap. 16.95 (*0-8264-1045-6*) Continuum.

***Psalms for Praying: An Invitation to Wholeness.** Nan C. Merrill. 320p. 2000. 22.95 (*0-8264-1286-6*) Continuum.

Psalms for Teens. Eldon Weishei. 128p. (Orig.). (YA). 1993. pap. 6.99 (*0-570-04599-1*, 12-3185) Concordia.

Psalms for Teens, Bk. II. Eldon Weisheit. 128p. (YA). 1994. pap. 6.99 (*0-570-04687-4*, 12-3246) Concordia.

***Psalms for the Church Year, Vol. 9.** David Haas. 1999. 15.95 (*5-550-70806-X*); 12.50 (*5-550-71696-8*); pap. 10.95 (*5-550-70819-1*); pap. 11.50 (*5-550-71695-X*) Nairi.

Psalms for the Journey. Christopher Willcock. 65p. (Orig.). 1991. pap. text 24.95 (*0-8146-2053-1*) Liturgical Pr.

Psalms for the Journey: The Lord's Song in Ordinary Time. Larry R. Kalajainen. 128p. 1996. pap. 10.00 (*0-8358-0780-0*, UR780) Upper Room Bks.

***Psalms for the Millennium & Wee Words of Wisdom: A Collection of Psalms Paraphrased & Rhymed for New Century Living.** Roberta Brewer. LC 00-90012. 96p. 2000. pap. 12.95 (*1-58597-019-0*) Leathers Pub.

Psalms for the Single Mom. Lisa Hussey. LC 98-48289. 1999. pap. 9.99 (*1-56476-741-8*, Victor Bks) Chariot Victor.

***Psalms for the Soul: Psalms for the Heart.** Lula Varist. 70p. 1999. pap. 10.00 (*0-7392-0448-3*, P03741) Morris Pubng.

Psalms for the Tsar: A Minute Book of a Psalms-Society in the Russian Army, 1864-1867. Michael Stanislawski. LC 88-20611. (Illus.). 64p. 1988. 22.95 (*0-9620856-0-X*) Yeshiva U Lib.

Psalms for Times of Trouble. John Carmody. LC 94-60847. 176p. (Orig.). 1995. pap. 9.95 (*0-89622-614-X*) Twenty-Third.

***Psalms for Women.** Honor Books Publishing Staff. (Psalms Ser.). 128p. 2000. 15.99 (*1-56292-835-X*) Honor Bks OK.

Psalms for Worship Today. Dwight W. Vogel. LC 74-13761. 176 p. 1974. write for info. (*0-570-03239-3*) Concordia.

Psalms for Zero Gravity: Prayers for Life's Emigrants. Edward Hays. LC 98-39693. 264p. 1998. pap. 14.95 (*0-939516-42-X*) Forest Peace.

***Psalms from My Soul.** Mimi Crawford. LC 99-66345. 58p. 1999. pap. 7.99 (*1-891774-11-5*) Path Pubng.

Psalms from the Suburbs. Ed. by Brynmill Press Ltd. Staff. (C). 1989. 40.00 (*0-907839-27-4*, Pub. by Brynmill Pr Ltd) St Mut.

Psalms, Hymns & Spiritual Songs. 63p. 1998. pap. 4.00 (*0-9654955-3-1*) Founders Pr.

Psalms in Congregational Celebration. O. Palmer Robertson. 1995. pap. 14.99 (*0-85234-338-8*, Pub. by Evangelical Pr) P & R Pubng.

Psalms in Haiku. Richard Gwyn. LC 97-50453. (Illus.). 240p. 1998. pap. 14.00 (*1-56975-096-3*) Ulysses Pr.

Psalms in Inclusive Language. Joseph J. Arackel. 216p. (Orig.). 1993. pap. 12.95 (*0-8146-2024-8*) Liturgical Pr.

Psalms in Israel's Worship. Sigmund Mowinckel. (Biblical Seminar Ser.: No. 14). 335p. (C). 1992. 42.50 (*1-85075-333-4*, Pub. by Sheffield Acad) CUP Services.

Psalms in Scots. (Illus.). 1987. reprint ed. 7.45 (*0-317-59593-8*, Pub. by Aberdeen U Pr) Macmillan.

Psalms in Scots: Reprint of the Psalms - Frae Hebrew intil Scotis. P. Hately Waddell. (Illus.). 128p. 1987. reprint ed. pap. text 9.95 (*0-08-035075-5*, Pub. by Aberdeen U Pr) Macmillan.

Psalms in Song for the White Cavalry. 3rd ed. Frank M. Wakeman. (Illus.). 128p. 1979. 5.00 (*0-910840-19-9*) Kingdom.

***Psalms in the Early Irish Church.** Martin McNamara. (Journal for the Study of the Old Testament Supplement Ser.: No. 165). 500p. 2000. 85.00 (*1-85075-925-1*, Pub. by Sheffield Acad) CUP Services.

Psalms in the Life of God's People. Dermot Cox. (C). 1988. 60.00 (*0-85439-237-8*, Pub. by St Paul Pubns) St Mut.

Psalms in the Time of Trouble. Willie Mewborn. 110p. Date not set. pap. write for info. (*1-930070-37-3*) Words of Faith.

Psalms in Worship. Paul Miller & Jeff Wyatt. LC 98-155786. 1995. pap. 9.99 (*0-8341-9432-5*, MP-754) Nazarene.

Psalms Journal. Jim Newton. 65p. (Orig.). 1997. pap. 10.95 (*1-888555-09-2*) MGR Pr.

Psalms Now. Leslie F. Brandt. LC 96-14857. 224p. 1996. 12.99 (*0-570-04257-7*) Concordia.

Psalms of a Laywoman. 2nd gif. ed. Edwina Gateley. LC 98-37741. (Illus.). 142p. (Orig.). 1998. reprint ed. pap. 9.95 (*1-58051-052-3*) Sheed & Ward WI.

Psalms of a Sailor Jew: A Cycle of 18 Sea Poems. Ben Wilensky. LC 94-30511. 1995. pap. 12.95 (*0-7734-0005-2*) E Mellen.

Psalms of Asaph & the Pentateuch: Studies in the Psalter, III. Michael D. Goulder. (JSOTS Ser.: No. 233). 378p. 1997. 85.00 (*1-85075-639-2*, Pub. by Sheffield Acad) CUP Services.

Psalms of Children: Their Songs & Laments: Understanding & Healing the Scars on the Souls of Children. Ursula M. Anderson. LC 97-219682. (Illus.). v, 231p. (YA). 1997. 25.00 (*0-9655435-1-X*); pap. 15.95 (*0-9655435-0-1*) She-Bear Pubs.

Psalms of Friendship. St. Paul Publication Staff. 60p. (C). 1996. pap. 39.95 (*0-85439-359-5*, Pub. by St Paul Pubns) St Mut.

Psalms of Gods: Avaz-e-Khodayan. Moulana S. Maghsoud. Tr. by Nahid Angha from PER. (Illus.). 32p. (Orig.). 1991. pap. 8.00 (*0-918437-09-1*) Intl Sufism.

Psalms of Gratitude. St. Pauls Publication Staff. 60p. 1996. pap. 39.95 (*1-875570-18-7*, Pub. by St Paul Pubns) St Mut.

Psalms of Herod. Esther Friesner. (Illus.). 478p. (Orig.). 1995. pap. 5.99 (*1-56504-916-0*, 12025, Borealis) White Wolf.

Psalms of Joy. St. Pauls Publication Staff. 60p. 1996. pap. 39.95 (*1-875570-15-2*, Pub. by St Paul Pubns) St Mut.

Psalms of Joy & Faith. Kyle M. Yates. Orig. Title: Preaching from the Psalms. 216p. 1984. reprint ed. pap. 9.95 (*0-913029-03-3*) Stevens Bk Pr.

Psalms of Lament. Ann Weems. 128p. 1995. 16.95 (*0-664-22074-6*) Westminster John Knox.

***Psalms of Lament.** large type ed. Ann Weems. LC 98-44981. 128p. 1999. pap. 14.00 (*0-664-25831-X*) Westminster John Knox.

Psalms of Lamentation & the Enigma of Suffering. R. Kelvin Moore. LC 95-46887. (Biblical Press Ser.: Vol. 50). 144p. 1996. text 69.95 (*0-7734-2416-4*, Mellen Biblical Pr) E Mellen.

Psalms of Mercy. St. Pauls Publication Staff. 60p. 1996. pap. 39.95 (*1-875570-17-9*, Pub. by St Paul Pubns) St Mut.

Psalms of My Life. Joseph Bayly. LC 59-93301. 128p. 1992. pap. 6.99 (*0-7814-0933-0*, LifeJourney) Chariot Victor.

P

***Psalms of My Life.** Joseph Bayly. LC 99-41106. 80p. 2000. 12.99 (*1-56476-785-X*) SP Pubns.

Psalms of Peace. St. Paul Publication Staff. 60p. 1996. pap. 39.95 (*1-875570-16-0*, Pub. by St Paul Pubns) St Mut.

Psalms of Promise: Celebrating the Majesty & Faithfulness of God. 2nd ed. E. Calvin Beisner. 304p. 1994. reprint ed. pap. 9.99 (*0-87552-107-X*) P & R Pubng.

Psalms of Redemption. Kiarri T-H. Cheatwood. LC 82-83855. 50p. 1983. per. 5.00 (*0-916418-41-3*) Lotus.

Psalms of Reflection: A Selection of Psalm Verses for Those Who Mourn. Elmwood Publishing Company Staff. 1979. pap. 1.25 (*0-931396-00-X*) Elmwood Pub Co.

Psalms of Suffering. St. Pauls Publication Staff. 60p. (C). 1996. pap. 39.95 (*0-85439-360-9*, Pub. by St Paul Pubns) St Mut.

Psalms of Tenderness. St. Paul Publication Staff. 60p. (C). 1996. pap. 39.95 (*0-85439-361-7*, Pub. by St Paul Pubns) St Mut.

Psalms of the Early Buddhists. Tr. by C. A. Davids from PLI. (C). 1937. 73.50 (*0-86013-076-2*, Pub. by Pali Text) Elsevier.

Psalms of the Early Buddhists, 2 vols., Set. Carolina A. Davids. LC 78-72413. reprint ed. 67.50 (*0-404-17590-2*) AMS Pr.

Psalms of the Orthodox Liturgy: According to the Greek & Slav Usages. Michael Farrow. 200p. 1997. pap. 19.95 (*1-879038-93-5*) Oakwood Pubns.

Psalms of the Rabbi Physician. Eric R. Braverman. (Illus.). 112p. (Orig.). 1986. pap. 9.95 (*1-55630-003-4*) Brentwood Comm.

***Psalms of the Return (Book V, Psalms 107-150) Studies in the Psalter, IV.** Michael D. Goulder. LC 98-156811. (JSOT Supplement Ser.: No. 258). 352p. 1998. 85.00 (*1-85075-866-2*, Pub. by Sheffield Acad) CUP Services.

Psalms of the Sons of Korah. Michael D. Goulder. (JSOTS Ser.: Vol. 20). 302p. 1983. 85.00 (*0-905774-40-X*, Pub. by Sheffield Acad); pap. 24.50 (*0-905774-41-8*, Pub. by Sheffield Acad) CUP Services.

Psalms of the Still Country. Edward J. Ingebretsen. 1982. pap. 7.95 (*0-89390-036-2*) Resource Pubns.

Psalms of the Way & the Kingdom: A Conference with the Commentators. J. H. Eaton. LC 95-228765. (Journal for the Study of the Old Testament Supplement Ser.: Vol. 199). 120p. 1995. 46.50 (*1-85075-552-3*, Pub. by Sheffield Acad) CUP Services.

Psalms of Trust. St. Pauls Publication Staff. 60p. (C). 1996. pap. 39.95 (*0-85439-362-5*, Pub. by St Paul Pubns) St Mut.

Psalms 1. John F. Brug. (People's Bible Commentary Ser.). 292p. (Orig.). 1992. pap. 10.99 (*0-570-04584-3*, 12-8002) Concordia.

Psalms 1-72. Derek Kidner. LC 75-23852. (Tyndale Old Testament Commentary Ser.). 257p. 1973. pap. 12.99 (*0-87784-264-7*, 264) InterVarsity.

Psalms 101-150. Leslie C. Allen. (Biblical Commentary Ser.: Vol. 21). 1983. 29.99 (*0-8499-0220-7*) Word Pub.

***Psalms 101-150.** Dana Gould. LC 99-11545. (Shepherd's Notes Ser.). 100p. 1999. pap. 5.95 (*0-8054-9341-7*) Broadman.

Psalms 1 (1-72) (New Century Bible Ser.). 527p. 1972. pap. 28.50 (*0-551-00846-6*, Pub. by Sheffield Acad) CUP Services.

Psalms I, 1-50. Ed. by Mitchell Dahood. (Anchor Bible Ser.: Vol. 16). 384p. 1966. 29.00 (*0-385-02765-6*, Anchor NY) Doubleday.

Psalms 1-50. Peter C. Craigie. (Biblical Commentary Ser.: Vol. 19). 1983. 29.99 (*0-8499-0218-5*) Word Pub.

***Psalms 1-50.** Dana Gould. LC 98-48095. 1999. pap. text 5.95 (*0-8054-9339-5*) Broadman.

Psalms 1-59. Hans-Joachim Kraus. LC 87-19552. (Continental Commentary Ser.). 560p. 1987. 50.00 (*0-8006-9503-8*, 1-9503, Fortress Pr) Augsburg Fortress.

Psalms 1-72. Richard J. Clifford. (Collegeville Bible Commentary - Old Testament Ser.). 80p. 1986. pap. 4.95 (*0-8146-1479-5*) Liturgical Pr.

Psalms 1-72. Donald M. Williams. (Communicator's Commentary Ser.: Vol. 13). 493p. 1986. 24.99 (*0-8499-0419-6*) Word Pub.

Psalms 1-72. Donald M. Williams. (Mastering the Old & New Testament Ser.: Vol. 13). 1993. pap. 14.99 (*0-8499-3552-0*) Word Pub.

Psalms 1-30 see Tehillim: Psalms

Psalms, Prayers of Many Moods: Spiritual Enrichment through the Psalms. Ronald Quillo. LC 98-47843. 176p. 1999. pap. 19.95 (*0-8091-3843-3*) Paulist Pr.

Psalms Scroll of Qumran Cave XI, Vol. IV. Ed. by J. A. Sanders. (Discoveries in the Judaean Desert Ser.: No. IV). (Illus.). 132p. 1997. text 75.00 (*0-19-826313-9*) OUP.

Psalms 73-150. Derek Kidner. LC 75-7247. (Tyndale Old Testament Commentary Ser.). 234p. 1975. 19.99 (*0-87784-959-5*, 959) InterVarsity.

Psalms 73-150. Derek Kidner. LC 75-7247. (Tyndale Old Testament Commentary Ser.). 234p. 1975. pap. 12.99 (*0-87784-265-5*, 265) InterVarsity.

Psalms 73-150. Richard J. Clifford. (Collegeville Bible Commentary - Old Testament Ser.). 88p. 1986. pap. 4.95 (*0-8146-1480-9*) Liturgical Pr.

Psalms 73-150. Donald M. Williams. (Communicator's Commentary Ser.: Vol. 14). 543p. 1989. 25.99 (*0-8499-0420-X*) Word Pub.

Psalms 73-150. Donald W. Williams. (Mastering the Old & New Testament Ser.: Vol. 14). 1993. pap. 14.99 (*0-8499-3553-9*) Word Pub.

Psalms 60-150: A Continental Commentary. Kraus Hans-Joachim. Tr. by Hilton C. Oswald. LC 89-370. 596p. (C). 1989. 51.00 (*0-8006-9504-6*, 1-9504, Fortress Pr) Augsburg Fortress.

Psalms Speak. George T. Peck. 32p. (Orig.). 1991. pap. 4.00 (*0-87574-298-X*) Pendle Hill.

Psalms That Sing. T. Franklin Miller. (Eagle Bible Ser.). 1989. pap. 0.99 (*0-87162-553-9*, D9155) Warner Pr.

Psalms 31-55 see Tehillim: Psalms

Psalms III, 101-150. Ed. by Mitchell Dahood. LC 66-11766. (Anchor Bible Ser.: Vol. 17A). 544p. 1970. 35.00 (*0-385-00607-1*, Anchor NY) Doubleday.

Psalms Through Three Thousand Years: Prayerbook of a Cloud of Witnesses. William L. Holladay. 408p. 1996. pap. 29.00 (*0-8006-3014-9*, 1-3014, Fortress Pr) Augsburg Fortress.

***Psalms to Live & Love By: Daily Encouragement as Close as Your Heart, New King James Version, 1.** Nelson Word Publishing Staff. (Jesus in My Pocket Ser.). (Illus.). 64p. 2000. pap. 2.99 (*0-7852-0019-3*) W1CL.

Psalms to Sing. Ed. by Clarence R. Johnson. 290p. (Orig.). 1995. pap. 10.95 (*0-9645270-0-6*) Exhorter Pubns.

Psalms Translated & Explained see Commentary on Psalms

Psalms Translated from the Greek Septuagint. Leonidas C. Contos. Tr. by Jose M. De Vinck from GRE. LC 93-72528. 202p. 1993. 18.75 (*0-911726-60-8*, SPS) Alleluia Pr.

Psalms 23. rev. ed. James Wallace. 126p. 1990. pap. 4.95 (*0-934942-78-1*, 7072) White Wing Pub.

Psalms 2. John F. Brug. (People's Bible Commentary Ser.). 285p. (Orig.). 1992. pap. 10.99 (*0-570-04590-8*, 12-8008) Concordia.

Psalms II: Heart Cries to God. Juanita Ryan. (LifeGuide Bible Studies Ser.). (Orig.). 1995. pap., wbk. ed. 4.99 (*0-8308-1038-2*, 1038) InterVarsity.

Psalms II, 51-100. Ed. by Mitchell Dahood. LC 66-11766. (Anchor Bible Ser.: Vol. 17). 432p. 1968. 35.00 (*0-385-03759-7*, Anchor NY) Doubleday.

Psalms, 2000. Mark Link. 246p. 1996. pap. 8.95 (*0-7829-0633-8*) Res Christian Liv.

Psalms Were Made for Lent: Six Sermons & Worship Services. Robert G. McCreight. LC 95-39883. 66p. (Orig.). 1996. pap. 7.95 (*0-7880-0565-0*) CSS OH.

Psalms with Their Spoils. Jon Silkin. (Orig.). 1980. pap. 9.95 (*0-7100-0497-4*, Routledge Thoemms) Routledge.

Psalmthing for Everyone. Don Scheuerlein. 24p. (Orig.). 1991. pap., teacher ed. 7.50 (*0-8100-0362-7*, 22N0810); pap., student ed. 22.00 (*0-8100-0361-9*, 22N0809) Northwest Pub.

Psalter. Holy Transfiguration Monastery Staff. 300p. 1997. 22.00 (*0-943405-00-9*) Holy Trnsfgn.

Psalter: A Book of Hours. 100p. 1994. pap. 14.95 (*1-883938-10-4*) Dry Bones Pr.

Psalter: A Collection of Responsorial Psalms for Use at Mass. Ed. by Jeanette S. Dandurand. 1990. ring bd. 28.95 (*0-915866-16-1*) Am Cath Pr.

Psalter: A Faithful & Inclusive Rendering from the Hebrew into Contemporary English Poetry, Intended Primarily for Communal Song & Recitation. International Commission on English in the Liturgy. LC 93-29361. (Illus.). 336p. 1995. 25.00 (*0-929650-77-8*, C/150P); pap. 16.00 (*0-929650-88-3*, P/150P) Liturgy Tr Pubns.

Psalter: Psalms & Canticles for Singing. Westminster Press Staff. 1993. pap. 31.95 (*0-664-25445-4*) Westminster John Knox.

Psalter: 150 Psalms & 9 Canticles. Tr. by Monks of New Skete. 286p. 1984. 39.50 (*0-9607924-5-7*) Monks of New Skete.

Psalter & Hours of Yolande of Soissons. Karen Gould. LC 78-55888. 1978. 20.00 (*0-910956-78-2*, SAM4); pap. 12.00 (*0-910956-64-2*) Medieval Acad.

Psalter for the Christian People: An Inclusive Language Revision of the Psalter of the Book of Common Prayer 1979. Gail Ramshaw & Gordon W. Lathrop. 208p. (Orig.). 1993. pap. text 14.95 (*0-8146-6134-3*, Pueblo Bks) Liturgical Pr.

Psalter Hymnal: Worship Edition. 1120p. 1988. 15.95 (*0-930265-35-1*) CRC Pubns.

Psalter Hymnal: 1988 Edition. 880p. 1988. 12.95 (*0-930265-53-X*) CRC Pubns.

Psalter Hymnal: 1988 Edition. large type ed. 880p. 1989. pap. text 39.95 (*1-56212-017-4*) CRC Pubns.

Psalter Hymnal Handbook. Emily R. Brink & Bertus F. Polman. LC 97-39977. 1998. 59.95 (*1-56212-269-X*) CRC Pubns.

Psalter Hymnal Worship. 1100p. 1987. pap. 43.95 (*0-930265-84-X*) CRC Pubns.

Psalter of John. John M. Etheridge. LC 96-61003. 124p. 1996. pap. 12.95 (*0-87243-225-4*) Templegate.

***Psalter of Robert de Lisle.** Lucy F. Sandler. (Illus.). 144p. 1999. pap. text 35.00 (*1-872501-32-X*, Pub. by Harvey Miller) Gordon & Breach.

Psammic Algae from Praia Azul Brazil. Marines Garcia-Baptista. (Bibliotheca Phycologica Ser.: Vol. 94). (Illus.). vi, 167p. 1993. 65.00 (*3-443-60021-2*, Pub. by Gebruder Borntraeger) Balogh.

PSAT - Preliminary Scholastic Aptitude Test. Robert Bell. (Illus.). 750p. 1998. pap. text 15.95 (*0-87891-936-8*) Res & Educ.

PSAT/NMSQT Flash. Peterson's Guides Staff. LC 98-5109. 250p. 1998. pap. text 8.95 (*1-56079-989-7*) Petersons.

***PSAT/NMSQT Flash 2001.** 2nd ed. Shirley Tarbell & Cathy Fillmore Hoyt. 250p. 2000. pap. 9.95 (*0-7689-0512-5*) Petersons.

Psaumes: Traductions, 1918-1959. Jean Cocteau et al. (FRE., Illus.). 200p. 1988. 39.95 (*0-7859-4718-3*) Fr & Eur.

Psaumes Mesures a l'Antique de J. A. de Baif see Florilege du Concert Vocal de la Renaissance

***Pschology & Hamel: International Comtemporary Generator Psychology & Pschology.** 5th ed. Wade. (C). 1998. 73.00 (*0-201-53311-1*) Peachpit Pr.

Pschyrembel Klinisches Worterbuch. 1748p. 1997. text 44.00 (*3-11-014824-2*); pap. text 33.00 (*3-11-015676-8*) De Gruyter.

Pschyrembel Klinisches Worterbuch: Mit Klinischen Syndromen und Nomina Anatomica, 256, Neu Bearbeitete Auflage. xxi, 1876p. (C). 1989. lib. bdg. 52.35 (*3-11-010881-X*) De Gruyter.

Psciologia Escolar. Huguette Caglar. (Breviarios Ser.). (SPA.). pap. 6.99 (*968-16-4076-4*, Pub. by Fondo) Continental Bk.

Psychologies of 1930. Ed. by Carl Murchison. LC 73-2980. (Classics in Psychology Ser.). 1976. reprint ed. 34.95 (*0-405-05152-2*) Ayer.

PSE, 2. 4th ed. Raymond A. Serway. 1996. pap. 36.50 (*0-03-020044-X*) Harcourt Coll Pubs.

PSE, 3. 4th ed. Serway. 1996. pap. 34.00 (*0-03-020047-4*) Harcourt Coll Pubs.

PSE, 4. 4th ed. Raymond A. Serway. 1996. pap. 28.50 (*0-03-020048-2*) Harcourt Coll Pubs.

Pseaumes en Vers Mezurez, Deuxieme Fascicule see Maitres Musiciens de la Renaissance Francaise

Pseaumes en Vers Mezurez, Premier Fascicule see Maitres Musiciens de la Renaissance Francaise

Pseaumes en Vers Vezurez, Troisieme Fascicule see Maitres Musiciens de la Renaissance Francaise

Pseira I: The Minoan Buildings on the West Side of Area A. Ed. by Philip P. Betancourt & Costis Davaras. LC 95-25712. (University Museum Monographs: Vol. 90). (Illus.). 200p. 1995. 40.00 (*0-924171-40-5*) U Museum Pubns.

Pseira II: Building AC (the "Shrine") & Other Buildings in Area A. Philip P. Betancourt et al. LC 96-25365. (Illus.). xvi, 151p. 1997. 60.00 (*0-924171-44-8*) U Museum Pubns.

Pselaphidae of Oceania, with Special Reference to the Fiji Islands. O. Park. (BMB Ser.). 1974. reprint ed. pap. 25.00 (*0-527-02315-9*) Periodicals Srv.

Pselli, Michaelis: Orationes Forenses et Acta. Ed. by Littlewood. (GRE.). 1994. 75.00 (*3-8154-1667-1*, T1667, Pub. by B G Teubner) U of Mich Pr.

Pselli, Michaelis: Orationes Hagiographicae. Ed. by Fisher. (GRE.). 1994. 89.50 (*3-8154-1665-5*, T1665, Pub. by B G Teubner) U of Mich Pr.

Pselli, Michaelis: Orationes Panegyricae. Ed. by Dennis. (GRE.). 1994. 75.00 (*3-8154-1666-3*, T1666, Pub. by B G Teubner) U of Mich Pr.

Pselli, Michaelis: Oratoria Minora. Ed. by Littlewood. (GRE.). 1985. 75.00 (*3-322-00183-0*, T1660, Pub. by B G Teubner) U of Mich Pr.

Pselli, Michaelis Vol. I: Philosophica Minora. Ed. by Duffy. (GRE.). 1992. 95.00 (*3-8154-1955-7*, T1955, Pub. by B G Teubner) U of Mich Pr.

Pselli, Michaelis Vol. I: Theologica. Ed. by Gautier. (GRE.). 1989. 115.00 (*3-322-00456-2*, T1663, Pub. by B G Teubner) U of Mich Pr.

Pselli, Michaelis Vol. II: Philosophica Minora. Ed. by O'Meara. (GRE.). 1989. 75.00 (*3-322-00462-7*, T1661, Pub. by B G Teubner) U of Mich Pr.

Pseudacronis, Vol. II. Ed. by Keller. (LAT.). 1967. reprint ed. 49.50 (*3-519-01742-3*, T1742, Pub. by B G Teubner) U of Mich Pr.

Pseudepigrapha & Early Biblical Interpretation. Ed. by James H. Charlesworth & Craig A. Evans. (Journal for the Study of the Pseudepigrapha Supplement Ser.: No. 14). 319p. 1993. 60.00 (*1-85075-443-8*, Pub. by Sheffield Acad) CUP Services.

Pseudepigraphic Perspectives: The Apogrypha & Pseudepigrapha in Light of the Dead Sea Scrolls: Proceedings of the International Symposium of the Orion Center for the Study of the Dead Sea Scrolls & Associated Literature, 12-14 January, 1997. Orion Center for the Study of the Dead Sea Scrolls et al. LC 98-34509. (Studies on the Texts of the Desert of Judah). 1998. 94.50 (*90-04-11164-6*) Brill Academic Pubs.

***Pseudepigraphical Images in Early Art, Vol. 6.** Massimo Bernabo. (Dead Sea Scrolls & Christian Origins Library). (Illus.). 1999. pap. text. write for info. (*0-941037-85-1*) D & F Scott.

Pseudepigraphy & Ethical Arguments in the Pastoral Epistles. Lewis R. Donelson. 260p. 1986. lib. bdg. 82.50 (*3-16-145009-4*, Pub. by JCB Mohr) Coronet Bks.

Pseudo & Quasi-Random Point Sets, Vol. 138. Ed. by P. Hellekalek et al. LC 98-30563. (Lecture Notes in Statistics Ser.). 300p. 1998. pap. 39.95 (*0-387-98554-9*) Spr-Verlag.

Pseudo-Archytas ueber die Kategorien: Texte zur griechischen Aristoteles-Exegese. Thomas Slezak. (Peripatoi Ser.: Bd. 4). 184p. (C). 1972. 93.85 (*3-11-003676-2*) De Gruyter.

Pseudo-Athanasius, Contra Arianos Vol. IV: Eine Schrift Gegen Asterius von Kappadokien, Eusebius von Casarea, Markell von Ankyra & Photin von Sirmium. Markus Vinzent. (Vigiliae Christianae, Supplements Ser.: Vol. 36). (GER.). 480p. 1996. text 159.00 (*90-04-10686-3*, NLG250) Brill Academic Pubs.

Pseudo-Autobiography in the Fourteenth Century: Juan Ruiz, Guillaume de Machaut, Jean Froissart, & Geoffrey Chaucer. Laurence De Looze. LC 96-45075. 232p. 1997. 49.95 (*0-8130-1507-3*) U Press Fla.

Pseudo-Basilius: Adversus Eunomium IV-V: Einleitung, Ubersetzung und Kommentar. Franz X. Risch. LC 91-37162. (Supplements to Vigiliae Christianae Ser.: Vol. 16). 234p. 1992. 74.50 (*90-04-09558-6*) Brill Academic Pubs.

Pseudo-Boolean Methods for Bivalent Programming: Proceedings of the European Meeting, Warsaw, 1966. Institute of Management Sciences Staff & Econometric Institute Staff. Ed. by P. L. Ivanescu & S. Rudeanu. (Lecture Notes in Mathematics Ser.: Vol. 23). 1966. 32.95 (*0-387-03606-7*) Spr-Verlag.

Pseudo-Boolean Programming & Applications. Colloquium on Mathematics & Cybernetics in the Eco. Ed. by P. L. Ivanescu. (Lecture Notes in Mathematics Ser.: Vol. 9). 1965. 32.95 (*0-387-03352-1*) Spr-Verlag.

Pseudo Cool. Joseph E. Green. 192p. 1994. mass mkt. 4.95 (*0-87067-694-6*, BH694-6) Holloway.

Pseudo-Differential Boundary Value Problems, Conical Singularities, & Asymptotics. B. W. Schulze. LC 94-225763. (Mathematical Topics Ser.). 581p. 1994. 157.50 (*3-05-501597-5*) Wiley.

Pseudo-Differential Calculus & Mathematical Physics: Advances in Partial Differential Equations. Ed. by M. Demuth & E. Schrohe. LC 94-28611. (Mathematical Topics Ser.). 392p. 1994. 102.90 (*3-05-501625-4*) Wiley.

Pseudo-Differential Operators. Ed. by H. O. Cordes et al. (Lecture Notes in Mathematics Ser.: Vol. 1256). x, 479p. 1987. 62.95 (*0-387-17856-2*) Spr-Verlag.

Pseudo-Differential Operators. Hitoshi Kumano-Go. Tr. by Remi Vaillancourt & Michihiro Nagase from JPN. 560p. (C). 1982. 85.00 (*0-262-11080-6*) MIT Pr.

Pseudo-Differential Operators & Markov Processes. N. Jacob. 209p. 1996. pap. 120.75 (*3-05-501731-5*) Wiley.

Pseudo-Differential Operators, Singularities, Applications. Yuri V. Egorov & Bert-Wolfgang Schulze. LC 97-4312. (Operator Theory, Advances & Applications Ser.). 1997. pap. write for info. (*0-8176-5484-4*) Birkhauser.

Pseudo-Differential Operators, Singularities, Applications. Yuri V. Egorov & Bert-Wolfgang Schulze. LC 97-4312. (Operator Theory, Advances, & Applications Ser.). 1997. 139.50 (*3-7643-5484-4*) Birkhauser.

Pseudo-Dionysius: A Commentary on the Texts & an Introduction to Their Influence. Paul Rorem. LC 92-15353. 288p. (C). 1993. text 65.00 (*0-19-507664-8*) OUP.

Pseudo Dionysius: The Complete Works. Ed. by Colm Luibheid. (Classics of Western Spirituality Ser.: Vol. 54). 336p. 1987. pap. 22.95 (*0-8091-2838-1*) Paulist Pr.

Pseudo-Dionysius Aeropagite: The Divine Names & Mystical Theology. Tr. by John D. Jones. LC 80-82362. (Medieval Philosophical Texts in Translation Ser.: No. 21). 320p. 1980. pap. 25.00 (*0-87462-221-2*) Marquette.

Pseudo-Dionysius & the Metaphysics of Aquinas. Fran O'Rourke. LC 92-13959. (Studien und Texte zur Geistesgeschichte des Mittelalters Ser.: Vol. 32). xvi, 300p. 1992. 104.50 (*90-04-09466-0*) Brill Academic Pubs.

Pseudo-Dionysius of Tel-Mahre Pt. 3: Chronicle. Tr. by Witold Witakowski. 192p. (Orig.). 1996. pap. text 17.95 (*0-85323-760-3*) U of Pa Pr.

Pseudo Discipleship. Verwer. 91p. 1991. 2.25 (*0-9630908-0-1*) O M Lit.

Pseudo-Epiphanius Testimony Book. Ed. by Robert V. Hotchkiss. LC 74-15203. (Texts & Translations Ser.: No. 4). 90p. reprint ed. pap. 30.00 (*0-7837-5461-2*, 204522600005) Bks Demand.

Pseudo Ezekiel: Critical Studies. rev. ed. Charles C. Torrey & Shalom Spiegel. (Library of Biblical Studies). 1970. 25.00 (*0-87068-116-8*) Ktav.

Pseudo-Ezekiel & the Original Prophecy. Charles C. Torrey. LC 78-63562. (Yale Oriental Series: Researches: No. 18). reprint ed. 29.50 (*0-404-60288-6*) AMS Pr.

Pseudo-Gregorian Dialogues, Set, Vols. 1 & 2. F. Clark. (Studies in the History of Christian Thought: No. 37-38). 1987. 205.50 (*90-04-07773-1*) Brill Academic Pubs.

Pseudo-Hecateus "On the Jews" Legitimizing the Jewish Diaspora. Bezalel Bar-Kochva. LC 95-20939. (Hellenistic Culture & Society Ser.: Vol. XXI). (Illus.). 287p. (C). 1997. 60.00 (*0-520-20059-4*, Pub. by U CA Pr) Cal Prin Full Svc.

Pseudo-Iustinus: Cohortatio ad Graecos - De Monarchia - Oratio ad Graecos. Ed. by Miroslav Marcovich. (Patristische Texte Und Studien: Vol. 32). x, 161p. (C). 1990. lib. bdg. 90.80 (*3-11-012135-2*) De Gruyter.

Pseudo-Lukrezisches im Lukrez: Die Unechten Verse in Lukrezens "De Rerum Natura" Marcus Deufert. (Untersuchungen zur Antiken Literatur und Geschichte Ser.: Vol. 48). (GER.). ix, 343p. (C). 1996. lib. bdg. 161.50 (*3-11-015046-8*) De Gruyter.

Pseudo-Macarius: The Fifty Spiritual Homilies & the Great Letter. Tr. & Intro. by George A. Maloney. LC 92-4736. (Classics of Western Spirituality Ser.). 320p. 1992. 24.95 (*0-8091-0455-5*); pap. 17.95 (*0-8091-3312-1*) Paulist Pr.

Pseudo-Martyr. John Donne. 528p. 1993. 70.00 (*0-7735-0994-1*, Pub. by McG-Queens Univ Pr) CUP Services.

Pseudo-Martyr. John Donne. LC 74-16215. 450p. 1974. 75.00 (*0-8201-1140-6*) Schol Facsimiles.

Pseudo Maximum Likelihood Methode Und Generalised Estimating Equations Zur Analyse Korrelierter Daten. Andreas R. Ziegler. (Illus.). 117p. 1999. 26.95 (*3-631-34240-3*) P Lang Pubng.

Pseudo-Melesko: A Ukrainian Apocryphal Parliamentary Speech of 1615-1618. Bohdan A. Struminsky. (Ukrainian Research Institute Sources & Documents Ser.). 174p. 1984. 7.50 (*0-674-71980-8*, STRPSE) HUP.

Pseudo-Melesko: A Ukrainian Apocryphal Parliamentary Speech of 1615-1618. Bohdan A. Struminsky. LC 84-80992. (Harvard Ukrainian Research Institute Monograph). 175p. 1984. pap. text 14.00 (*0-916458-11-3*) Harvard Ukrainian.

Pseudo-Ovidian Ad Liviam de Morte Drusi: A Critical Text. Ed. by Henk Schoonhoven. xiv, 244p. 1992. 55.00 (*90-6980-050-0*, Pub. by Egbert Forsten) Hod1der & Stoughton.

Pseudo-Philo: Rewriting the Bible. Frederick J. Murphy. LC 92-44041. 336p. 1993. text 65.00 (*0-19-507622-2*) OUP.

Pseudo-Riemannian Symmetric Spaces. Michel Cahen & Monique Parker. LC 79-27541. (Memoirs Ser.: No. 24/229). 108p. 1992. pap. 17.00 (*0-8218-2229-2*, MEMO/24/229) Am Math.

An Asterisk (*) at the beginning of an entry indicates that the title is appearing for the first time.

Pseudo-Riemannian Symmetric Spaces. Michel Cahen. LC 79-27541. (American Mathematical Society Ser.: No. 229). 117p. reprint ed. pap. 36.30 (*0-608-20156-1*, 205280100011) Bks Demand.

Pseudo-Science & Society in Nineteenth Century America. Ed. by Arthur Wrobel. LC 87-12464. (Illus.). 256p. 1987. text 29.95 (*0-8131-1632-5*) U Pr of Ky.

Pseudo-Shakespearian Plays, 5 vols. in 1. Ed. by Karl Warnke & Ludwig Proescholdt. LC 74-148325. reprint ed. 57.50 (*0-404-06845-6*) AMS Pr.

Pseudo-Turpin. Ed. by Hamilton M. Smyser. (Mediaeval Academy of America Publications: Publ., Vol. 30). 1974. reprint ed. 30.00 (*0-527-01698-5*) Periodicals Srv.

***Pseudo-Zeno: The Anonymous Philosophical Treatise.** M. E. Stone et al. Tr. by J. Mansfield. 272p. 1999. 88.50 (*90-04-11524-2*) Brill Academic Pubs.

Pseudocapitalism & the Overpoliticized State: Reconciling Politics & Anthropology in Zaire. S. N. Sangmpam. (Making of Modern Africa Ser.). 272p. 1994. 82.95 (*1-85628-660-6*, Pub. by Avebry) Ashgate Pub Co.

Pseudocarcinoma of the Skin. Boris A. Berenbein. Tr. by V. E. Tatarchenko from RUS. LC 84-24988. (Illus.). 277p. 1985. reprint ed. pap. 85.90 (*0-608-05419-4*, 206588800006) Bks Demand.

Pseudococcidae (Insecta: Hemiptera) see Fauna of New Zealand Series

Pseudodifferential Analysis of Symmetric Cones. Andre Unterberger & Harald Upmeier. 224p. 1995. boxed set 89.95 (*0-8493-7873-7*, 7873) CRC Pr.

Pseudodifferential Operators. Michael E. Taylor. LC 80-8580. (Mathematical Ser.: No. 34). 468p. 1981. text 85.00 (*0-691-08282-0*, Pub. by Princeton U Pr) Cal Prin Full Svc.

Pseudodifferential Operators & Applications. Ed. by Francois Treves. LC 85-1419. (Proceedings of Symposia in Pure Mathematics Ser.: Vol. 43). 301p. 1985. text 60.00 (*0-8218-1469-9*, PSPUM/43) Am Math.

Pseudodifferential Operators & Nonlinear PDEs. M. E. Taylor. (Progress in Mathematics Ser.: Vol. 100). x, 203p. 1993. 52.00 (*0-8176-3595-5*) Birkhauser.

Pseudodifferential Operators & Spectral Theory. M. A. Shubin. (Soviet Mathematics Ser.). 305p. 1987. 165.00 (*0-387-13621-5*) Spr-Verlag.

Pseudoepileptic Seizures. Ed. by Lennart Gram et al. 192p. 1993. 65.00 (*1-871816-18-1*, Pub. by Wrightson Biomed) Taylor & Francis.

Pseudofunctors on Modules with Zero Dimensional Support. I-Chiau Huang. LC 94-43208. (Memoirs Ser.: Vol. 548). 53p. 1995. pap. 29.00 (*0-8218-2608-5*, MEMO/114/548) Am Math.

***PseudoGAP in High Temperature Superconductors.** Anant Narlikar. LC 99-22946. (Studies of High Temperature Superconductors: Vol. 27). 286p. 1999. lib. bdg. 89.00 (*1-56072-684-9*) Nova Sci Pubs.

Pseudolus see Pot of Gold & Other Plays

Pseudomonas. Ed. by T. C. Montie. (Biotechnology Handbooks Ser.: Vol. 10). (Illus.). 352p. (C). 1998. text 110.00 (*0-306-45849-7*, Kluwer Plenum) Kluwer Academic.

Pseudomonas Aeruginosa. Ed. by D. P. Speert & R. E. Hancock. (Antibiotics & Chemotherapy Ser.: Vol. 36). (Illus.). viii, 176p. 1985. 128.75 (*3-8055-3966-5*) S Karger.

Pseudomonas Aeruginosa: Ecological Aspects & Patient Colonization. fac. ed. Ed. by Viola M. Young. LC 76-56919. 155p. pap. 48.10 (*0-7837-7188-6*, 204711100005) Bks Demand.

Pseudomonas Aeruginosa - Infections & Treatment, No. 12. Ed. by Aldona L. Baltch & Raymond P. Smith. (Infectious Disease & Therapy Ser.: Vol. 12). (ITA., Illus.). 640p. 1994. text 215.00 (*0-8247-9210-6*) Dekker.

Pseudomonas Aeruginosa As an Opportunistic Pathogen. M. Campa et al. (Infectious Agents & Pathogenesis Ser.). (Illus.). 440p. (C). 1993. text 110.00 (*0-306-44265-5*, Kluwer Plenum) Kluwer Academic.

Pseudomonas Aeruginosa in Human Diseases. Ed. by J. Y. Homma et al. (Antibiotics & Chemotherapy Ser.: Vol. 44). (Illus.). x, 250p. 1991. 189.75 (*3-8055-5385-4*) S Karger.

Pseudomonas Aeruginosa Infection, 1988. Ed. by N. Hoiby et al. (Antibiotics & Chemotherapy Ser.: Vol. 42). (Illus.). 308p. 1989. 208.75 (*3-8055-5002-2*) S Karger.

Pseudomonas Aeruginosa the Opportunist: Pathogenesis & Disease. Ed. by Robert B. Fick, Jr. 272p. 1992. lib. bdg. 184.00 (*0-8493-4811-0*, QR201) CRC Pr.

Pseudomonas Infection & Alginates: Biochemistry, Genetics & Pathology. Ed. by Peter Gacesa & Nicholas Russell. 208p. 1990. 99.95 (*0-412-35840-9*, A4384) Chapman & Hall.

Pseudomonas Syringae Pathovars & Related Pathogens. Klaus-Peter Rudolph. LC 97-19457. (Developments in Plant Pathology Ser.: Vol. 9). 663p. 1997. text 327.50 (*0-7923-4601-7*) Kluwer Academic.

Pseudomorphic HEMT Technology & Applications. Ed. by R. Lee Ross et al. LC 95-48179. (NATO ASI Series E: Vol. 309). 350p. 1996. text 195.00 (*0-7923-3915-0*) Kluwer Academic.

Pseudonymous. (Illus.). 36p. (Orig.). (YA). (gr. 11 up). 1993. pap. 6.80 (*0-9642212-0-9*) Meroen Pr.

Pseudonyms & Nicknames Dictionary, 2 vols., Set. 3rd ed. Ed. by Jennifer Mossman. 2207p. 1986. 239.00 (*0-8103-0541-0*) Gale.

Pseudonyms of Authors. John E. Haynes. 1992. reprint ed. 38.00 (*1-55888-214-6*) Omnigraphics Inc.

***Pseudoperiodic Topology.** Ed. by Vladimir I. Arnold et al. LC 91-640741. (TRANS2 Ser.: Vol. 197). 179p. 2000. 85.00 (*0-8218-2094-X*) Am Math.

Pseudoscience & Mental Ability: The Origins & Fallacies of the IQ Controversy. Jeffrey Blum. LC 77-81371. 240p. 1979. pap. 10.00 (*0-85345-496-5*, Pub. by Monthly Rev) NYU Pr.

Pseudoscience & the Paranormal: A Critical Examination of the Evidence. Terence Hines. LC 87-43318. 384p. (Orig.). 1988. pap. 23.95 (*0-87975-419-2*) Prometheus Bks.

Pseudoscience in Biological Psychiatry: Blaming the Body. Ross Conlin & Pam Alvin. (Series in General & Clinical Psychology). 304p. 1994. 85.00 (*0-471-00776-5*) Wiley.

PSE,4E (VOL.5-MODERN PHYSICS), Vol. 5. 4th ed. Serway. (C). 1996. pap. text 33.50 (*0-03-020049-0*) Harcourt Coll Pubs.

PSI & Altered States of Consciousness: Proceedings of the International Conference on Hypnosis, Drugs, Dreams & Psi, France, June 9-12, 1967. International Conference on Hypnosis, Drugs, Dream. Ed. by Roberto Cavanna & Montague Ullman. LC 68-8909. 1968. 16.00 (*0-912328-11-8*) Parapsych Foun.

PSI & Clinical Practice: Proceedings, International Conference, London, England, Oct. 28-29, 1989. Ed. by Lisette Coly & Joanne D. McMahon. LC 93-85463. 1993. 20.00 (*0-912328-44-4*) Parapsych Foun.

PSI & States of Awareness. Proceedings of the International Conference, Paris, France, Aug. 24-26, 1977. International Conference, Paris Staff. Ed. by Betty Shapin & Lisette Coly. LC 78-50167. 1978. 17.00 (*0-912328-30-4*) Parapsych Foun.

PSI & the Mind: An Information Processing Approach. H. J. Irwin. LC 79-20587. 181p. 1979. 21.00 (*0-8108-1258-4*) Scarecrow.

PSI Delegation. Allan Conan. 298p. 1989. 15.95 (*0-922811-04-0*) Mid-List.

PSI Factors in Creativity: Proceedings of an International Conference, France, June 16-18, 1969. Ed. by Allan Angoff & Betty Shapin. LC 71-140141. 1970. 16.00 (*0-912328-18-5*) Parapsych Foun.

PSI Favorable States of Consciousness: Proceedings of an International Conference on Methodology in Psi Research, France, Sept. 2-6, 1968. Ed. by Roberto Cavanna. LC 75-97821. 1970. 16.00 (*0-912328-17-7*) Parapsych Foun.

PSI Magick Course. Charles Cosimano. Ed. by Thorguard Templar. 240p. 1993. 120.00 (*1-883147-94-8*) Intern Guild ASRS.

PSI Magick Course, 8 lessons, Set. Charles Cosimano. Ed. by Thorguard Templar. 240p. 1993. 120.00 (*1-883147-93-X*) Intern Guild ASRS.

***Psi-Man: Mind-Force Warrior.** Peter David. Vol. 1. (Illus.). 208p. 2000. mass mkt. 5.99 (*0-441-00705-8*) Ace Bks.

***Psi-Man No. 2: Deathscape.** Peter David. (PSI-Man Ser.: No. 2). 192p. 2000. mass mkt. 5.99 (*0-441-00710-4*) Ace Bks.

***Psi-Man No. 3: Main Street D. O. A.** Peter David. Vol. 3. 192p. 2000. mass mkt. 5.99 (*0-441-00717-1*) ACE.

***Psi-Man No. 4: The Chaos Kid.** Peter David. (PSI-Man Ser.: Vol. 4). 192p. 2000. mass mkt. 5.99 (*0-441-00745-7*) Ace Bks.

***Psi-Man No. 5: Stalker.** Peter David. (PSI-Man Ser.: Vol. 5). 192p. 2000. mass mkt. 5.99 (*0-441-00758-9*) Ace Bks.

***Psi-Man No. 6: Haven,** Peter David. (PSI-Man Ser.: Vol. 6). (Illus.). 192p. 2000. mass mkt. 5.99 (*0-441-00764-3*) Ace Bks.

Psi Model Curriculum for Office Careers. Psi. (Office Procedures Ser.). Date not set. 11.50 (*0-538-63279-8*) S-W Pub.

PSI Real Estate Sales Exam. Learning Express Staff. LC 98-37856. 256p. 1998. pap. 29.95 (*1-57685-151-6*) LrningExprss.

PSI Research Methodology: A Re-Examination: Proceedings, International Conference, Chapel Hill, N. C., Oct. 29-30, 1988. Ed. by Lisette Coly & Joanne D. McMahon. LC 93-85453. 1993. 20.00 (*0-912328-43-6*) Parapsych Foun.

PSI Student Study Guide to Calculus. 3rd ed. Murray H. Protter & Charles B. Morrey, Jr. LC 76-12800. (Mathematics Ser.). (C). 1977. student ed. 8.75 (*0-201-06036-1*) Addison-Wesley.

Psibot. James Eden. 245p. 1996. pap. 12.99 (*0-9654412-0-2*) Lester & Co Pub.

Psicoanalisis. C. Thompson. (Breviarios Ser.). (SPA.). pap. 8.99 (*968-16-0298-6*, Pub. by Fondo) Continental Bk.

Psicoanalisis y Existencialismo. Viktor E. Frankl. (Breviarios Ser.). (SPA.). pap. 9.99 (*968-16-0072-X*, Pub. by Fondo) Continental Bk.

Psicologia Cristiana en "Un Curso de Milagros" Kenneth Wapnick. LC 93-40954. (SPA.). 127p. 1994. pap. 5.00 (*0-933291-17-5*) Foun Miracles.

Psicologia de la Comunicacion. Ana M. O'Neill. (SPA.). 541p. 1987. reprint ed. 11.75 (*0-8477-2907-9*) U of PR Pr.

Psicologia de la Felicidad. Clyde M. Narramore.Tr. of This Way to Happiness. (SPA.). 92p. 1989. pap. write for info. (*0-614-27125-8*) Editorial Unilit.

Psicologia de la Felicidad. Clyde M. Narramore.Tr. of This Way to Happiness. (SPA.). 1990. 3.99 (*0-945792-82-4*, 497702) Editorial Unilit.

Psicologia de la Sensatez. Carlos Varona. (SPA.). 80p. (C). 1994. pap. 5.00 (*1-56328-063-9*) Edit Plaza Mayor.

Psicologia de la Vejez. Efrain Sanchez Hidalgo & Lydia De Sanchez Hidalgo. 211p. (C). 1980. pap. 8.25 (*0-8477-2905-2*) U of PR Pr.

Psicologia del Matrimonio. Cecil G. Osborne.Tr. of Art of Understanding Your Mate. (SPA.). 292p. 1989. pap. 4.99 (*0-945792-83-2*, 497704) Editorial Unilit.

Psicologia en Broma y en Serio. Carlos Varona. (SPA.). 112p. 1994. pap. 5.00 (*1-56328-062-0*) Edit Plaza Mayor.

Psicologia en Prevencion de Accidentes. 72p. 7.50 (*0-318-18012-X*) Inter-Am Safety.

Psicologia Latinoamericana. Carolina De la Torre. (SPA.). 160p. 1995. pap. write for info. (*0-929441-75-3*) Pubns Puertorriquenas.

***Psicologia Medica.** 2nd rev. ed. Roman de la Fuente. 547p. 1999. 14.99 (*968-16-3934-0*) Fondo CA.

***Psicologia Pastoral Para Toda la Familia.** Jorge A. Leon. 1998. pap. text 9.99 (*0-89922-426-1*) Caribe Betania.

Psicologia y Consejo Pastoral: Perspectives Hispanas. Ed. by Daniel S. Schipani & Pablo A. Jime'nez. (SPA.). 200p. 1997. pap. 14.95 (*0-9657839-0-1*) AETH Bks.

Psicologia 89. (SPA.). (C). 1997. pap. text 57.33 (*0-673-19327-6*) Addison-Wesley.

***Psicologo En Casa.** Bernabe Tierno. 1999. pap. 19.95 (*84-7880-965-1*) Planeta.

Psiconavegacion: Tecnicas Para Viajar Ma's All a Del Tiempo. John Perkins.Tr. of Psychonavigation. (SPA.). 136p. 1995. pap. 10.95 (*0-89281-461-6*) Inner Tradit.

Psilocybin: De-Mystifying "Magic Mushrooms" rev. ed. Rosemary Waltz. 1999. pap. 0.50 (*0-89230-209-7*) Do It Now.

Psilocybin: Magic Mushroom Grower's Guide. 2nd ed. O. T. Oss & O. N. Oeric. (Illus.). 81p. 1986. reprint ed. pap. 16.95 (*0-932551-06-8*) Quick Am Pub.

Psilocybin Mushrooms of the World: An Identification Guide. Paul Stamets. LC 96-15717. (Illus.). 245p. 1996. pap. 24.95 (*0-89815-839-7*) Ten Speed Pr.

Psilocybin Production. 2nd ed. Adam Gottlieb. (Illus.). 96p. (Orig.). 1998. pap. 9.95 (*0-914171-93-3*) Ronin Pub.

***PSI/NET.** Billy Dee Williams. 2000. mass mkt. 6.99 (*0-8125-7092-8*) Forge NYC.

PSI/Net. Billy Dee Williams & Rob MacGregor. LC 99-24477. 256p. 1999. 22.95 (*0-312-86766-2*, Pub. by Tor Bks) St Martin.

Psion. Joan D. Vinge. 288p. 1996. mass mkt. 5.99 (*0-446-60354-6*, Pub. by Warner Bks) Little.

Psionic Combat. Charles Cosimano. Ed. by Thorguard Templar. (Illus.). 112p. 1993. 65.00 (*1-883147-59-X*); 65.00 (*1-883147-60-3*) Intern Guild ASRS.

Psionic Gadget Book. Charles Cosimano. Ed. by Thorguard Templar. (Illus.). 110p. (Orig.). 1993. spiral bd. 29.95 (*1-883147-61-1*); spiral bd. 29.95 (*1-883147-62-X*) Intern Guild ASRS.

Psionic Path: Psychotronic Path. Charles Cosimano. (Illus.). 115p. 1997. 35.00 (*1-57179-058-6*) Intern Guild ASRS.

Psionics. Mayfair Games Staff. 1991. 12.00 (*0-923763-31-7*) Mayfair Games.

Psiquis la Hoz. St John Troya. 115p. (Orig.). 1986. pap. 7.95 (*0-89729-384-3*) Ediciones.

Psittacine Aviculture: Perspectives, Techniques & Research. Kevin J. Clubb et al. 200p. (C). 1992. write for info. (*0-9631424-0-2*) Avicult Breed Res.

Psittacosaurus. Frances Swann. (Dinosaur Library). (Illus.). 24p. (J). (gr. 3 up). 1989. 10.95 (*0-685-58285-X*) Rourke Corp.

Psittacosaurus (Cretaceous Period) see New Dinosaur Collection

Psittaculture. Tony Silva. (Illus.). 1991. 39.95 (*1-56465-177-0*, 16117) Tetra Pr.

Pskov Oblast: Economy, Industry, Government, Business. 2nd rev. ed. Russian Information & Business Center, Inc. Staff. (Russian Regional Business Directories Ser.). (Illus.). 200p. 1997. pap. 99.00 (*1-57751-408-4*) Intl Business Pubns.

***Pskov Oblast Regional Investment & Business Guide.** Global Investment & Business Center, Inc. Staff. (Russian Regional Investment & Business Guides Ser.: Vol. 61). (Illus.). 350p. 1999. pap. 99.00 (*0-7397-0859-7*) Intl Business Pubns.

***Pskov Oblast Regional Investment & Business Guide.** Contrib. by Global Investment & Business Center, Inc. Staff. (Russian Regional Investment & Business Guides Ser.: Vol. 60). (Illus.). 350p. 2000. pap. 99.95 (*0-7397-3009-6*) Intl Business Pubns.

Psm Alg W/trig For College Students. 2nd ed. Kaufmann. (Math). 1989. 14.00 (*0-534-91605-8*) Brooks-Cole.

Psm Algebra For College Students. 3rd ed. Kaufmann. (Math). 1989. student ed. 14.00 (*0-534-91614-7*) Brooks-Cole.

Psm College Algebra With Applications. 2nd ed. Hall. (Math). 1989. student ed. 17.50 (*0-534-91591-4*) Brooks-Cole.

Psm Elem Algebra For College Students. 3rd ed. Kaufmann. (Math). 1989. student ed. 14.00 (*0-534-91632-5*) Brooks-Cole.

Psm Intermediate Alg F/college Stdts. 3rd ed. Kaufmann. (Math). 1989. 14.00 (*0-534-91623-6*) Brooks-Cole.

Psm-precalculus. 2nd ed. Kaufmann. (Math). 1991. mass mkt., student ed. 17.50 (*0-534-92475-1*) PWS Pubs.

***PSM-RMP Auditing Handbook: A Checklist Approach.** David M. Einolf & Luverna Menghini. 337p. 1999. pap. text 79.00 (*0-86587-686-X*, 686) Gov Insts.

Psmith: Journalist. P. G. Wodehouse. 20.95 (*0-8488-0331-0*) Amereon Ltd.

Psmith in the City. P. G. Wodehouse. 160p. 1994. pap. 8.95 (*0-14-003207-X*, Penguin Bks) Viking Penguin.

Psmith in the City. P. G. Wodehouse. 402p. 1981. reprint ed. lib. bdg. 14.95 (*0-89968-222-7*, Lghtyr Pr) Buccaneer Bks.

Psmith, Journalist. P. G. Wodehouse. 187p. 1981. pap. 8.95 (*0-14-003214-2*, Penguin Bks) Viking Penguin.

Psmith, Journalist. P. G. Wodehouse. 1994. reprint ed. lib. bdg. 32.95 (*1-56849-363-0*) Buccaneer Bks.

PSOAS Book. 2nd enl. rev. ed. Liz Koch. LC 97-71684. (Illus.). 85p. 1997. reprint ed. pap. 22.95 (*0-9657944-0-7*) Guinea Pig.

Psocoptera of the Hawaiian Islands Pt. IV: The Endemic Genus Palistreptus (Elipsocidae): Systematics, Distribution & Evolution. Ian W. Thornton. (Bishop Museum Bulletin in Entomology Ser.: Vol. 4). (Illus.). 57p. (C). 1990. pap. 15.00 (*0-930897-48-X*) Bishop Mus.

Psocoptera of the Oriental Region - A Review. Tim R. New. (Oriental Insects Monographs: No. 6). 1977. pap. 30.00 (*1-877711-16-0*) Assoc Pubs FL.

Psocoptera, Phthiraptera, Thysanoptera. Laurence A. Mound et al. (Zoological Catalogue of Australia Ser.: Vol. 26). 417p. 1996. 79.95 (*0-643-05703-X*, Pub. by CSIRO) Accents Pubns.

Psoraisis & Eczema Solution: New Hope for Physical & Emotional Relief. Michael F. Holick et al. (Illus.). 200p. 1999. 21.95 (*1-890819-06-9*) TransMedia FL.

Psoralen DNA Photobiology, Vol. I. Ed. by Francis P. Gasparro. 160p. 1988. 88.00 (*0-8493-4379-8*, QP801, CRC Reprint) Franklin.

Psoralen DNA Photobiology, Vol. 2. Ed. by Francis P. Gasparro. LC 86-4216. 176p. 1988. 101.00 (*0-8493-4380-1*, QP801, CRC Reprint) Franklin.

Psoriasis. Charles Camisa. LC 93-11762. (Illus.). 368p. 1993. 99.95 (*0-86542-247-8*) Blackwell Sci.

Psoriasis. 3rd ed. Henry H. Roenigk & Howard I. Maibach. LC 98-16975. (Basic & Clinical Dermatology Ser.). (Illus.). 908p. 1998. text 225.00 (*0-8247-0108-9*) Dekker.

***Psoriasis: A Patient's Guide.** Nicholas Lowe. 91p. 1999. 14.95 (*1-85317-599-4*, Pub. by Martin Dunitz) Blackwell Sci.

***Psoriasis Cure: A Drug-Free Guide to Stopping & Reversing the Symptoms of Psoriasis.** Lisa LeVan. LC 99-28980. 154p. 1999. pap. 13.95 (*0-89529-917-8*, Avery) Penguin Putnam.

Psoriasis Handbook: A Self-Help Guide. Muriel K. MacFarlane. LC 95-61640. (Illus.). 224p. (Orig.). 1995. pap. 12.95 (*1-887053-01-8*) United Res CA.

Psoriatic Arthritis. Ed. by Lynn H. Gerber. 224p. 1985. text 72.00 (*0-8089-1709-9*, 791544, Grune & Strat) Harcrt Hlth Sci Grp.

PSpice. Susan Reidel. (C). 1996. pap. text. write for info. (*0-201-51055-3*) Addison-Wesley.

PSpice & Circuit Analysis. 3rd ed. John Keown. LC 97-6639. (Merrill's International Series in Engineering Technology). 615p. 1997. pap. text 50.00 (*0-13-235458-6*) P-H.

Pspice Manual for Electric Circuits Fundamentals. James S. Kang. (Illus.). 280p. (C). 1995. pap. text, lab manual ed. 20.95 (*0-03-003534-1*) OUP.

PSpice Student Version Disk: MacIntosh Compatible. Paul W. Tuinenga. 1989. 10.67 (*0-685-26607-9*) P-H.

PSpice Text-Manual: An Introduction. James J. Tart. (Engineering Technology Ser.). (Illus.). 91p. (Orig.). (C). 1993. pap. text. write for info. (*0-9635788-0-4*) Comp Prog Teach.

PSpice Text-Manual: An Introduction. 2nd ed. James J. Tart. (Engineering Technology Ser.). (Illus.). 252p. (Orig.). 1993. pap. text. write for info. (*0-9635788-1-2*) Comp Prog Teach.

PSSC Physics. 7th ed. Uri Haber-Schaim et al. 640p. 1991. 49.90 (*0-8403-6025-8*) Kendall-Hunt.

PSSC Physics: Test Item Bank. 7th ed. Uri Haber-Schaim et al. 160p. 1991. 44.90 (*0-8403-6391-5*) Kendall-Hunt.

PSSC Physics Laboratory Guide. 7th ed. Uri Haber-Schaim et al. 160p. 1991. pap. text, per. 13.90 (*0-8403-6026-6*) Kendall-Hunt.

PSSC Report. 1976. 30.00 (*0-7855-0565-2*, Pub. by Natl Inst Soc Work) St Mut.

PSSC, the Case History of an Advisory Non-Governmental Organisation, 1973-1980. Ed. by National Institute for Social Work Staff. 1981. 15.00 (*0-7855-0994-1*) St Mut.

Pssm - Applied Finite Math 4e. 4th ed. Soo T. Tan. (Math). 1994. mass mkt., student ed. 15.25 (*0-534-93514-1*) PWS Pubs.

Pssm - Elem & Int Alg-combined. Kaufmann. (Math). 1993. mass mkt., student ed. 19.50 (*0-534-93369-6*) PWS Pubs.

***Psssst It's Me The Bogeyman UK Edition.** (gr. k-3). 1999. per. 16.00 (*0-689-82742-3*) S&S Childrens.

Psst! It's Me The Bogeyman. Barbara Park. LC 97-10123. (Illus.). 40p. (J). (ps-4). 1998. 16.00 (*0-689-81667-7*) Atheneum Yung Read.

PS3569.L3. David R. Slavitt. LC 98-20570. 96p. 1998. pap. 12.95 (*0-8071-2301-3*); text 19.95 (*0-8071-2300-5*) La State U Pr.

Psybermagick: Advanced Ideas in Chaos Magick. 2nd ed. Peter J. Carroll. LC 96-68644. 128p. 1996. pap. 12.95 (*1-56184-092-0*) New Falcon Pubns.

Psyc & Life. 14th ed. Gerrig Zimbardo. 1997. pap. 78.00 (*0-673-98156-8*) Addison-Wesley.

Psyc Resrch Methd Stats. Ed. by Andrew M. Colman. LC 95-18117. (Essential Psychology Ser.). 123p. (C). 1995. pap. text 14.06 (*0-582-27801-5*, Pub. by Addison-Wesley) Longman.

Psycards Deck. Created by Maggie Kneen. 1997. boxed set 14.00 (*0-88079-401-1*) US Games Syst.

Psych Online '97. Patricia M. Wallace. 160p. (C). 1996. text 11.69 (*0-697-35168-8*) Brown & Benchmark.

Psychology Online '97: Abnormal, Clinical & Counseling Edition. annuals Patricia M. Wallace. 80p. (C). 1996. text 8.99 (*0-697-37543-9*) Brown & Benchmark.

Psychology Online, 97: Social & Applied Psychology Edition. Patricia M. Wallace. 50p. (C). 1996. text 8.99 (*0-697-37485-8*) Brown & Benchmark.

***Psych Symptoms & Their Treatment in Alzheimers Disease: Pocketbook Edition.** Devanand. 2000. 14.95 (*1-85317-918-3*, Pub. by Martin Dunitz) Blackwell Sci.

Psych Tech Notes. Eugene Galanter. Ed. by John Van Laer. (Illus.). 210p. (Orig.). (C). 1988. pap. 11.95 (*0-937431-02-8*) Adams Bannister Cox.

Psych Tech Notes, Version 2.1. 2nd rev. ed. Eugene Galanter & Alicia Walton. LC 94-22644. (Illus.). 249p. (C). 1994. pap. text 19.95 (*0-937431-05-2*) Adams Bannister Cox.

Psych Yourself to Better Tennis. Luszki. 1978. pap. 2.00 (*0-87980-246-4*) Wilshire.

***Psych Zone.** 1999. text. write for info. (*0-321-04986-1*) P-H.

Psychamok. Brian Lumley. 512p. (Orig.). 1993. mass mkt. 5.99 (*0-8125-2032-7*, Pub. by Tor Bks) St Martin.

P

Psychanalyse du Feu. Gaston Bachelard. (FRE.). 1985. pap. 12.95 (*0-7859-2799-9*) Fr & Eur.

Psychanalyse du Feu. Gaston Bachelard. (Folio Essais Ser.: No. 25). (FRE.). 184p. 1985. pap. 9.95 (*2-07-032325-0*) Schoenhof.

Psyche. Louis Couperus. Tr. by A. Teixeira de Mattos & John Gray from DUT. 150p. 1999. pap. 12.95 (*1-885586-10-8*, Pub. by Turtle Point Pr) Dist Art Pubs.

Psyche. Lindy Hough. 124p. (Orig.). 1974. pap. 3.00 (*0-913028-24-X*) North Atlantic.

Psyche see Chefs-d'Oeuvre Classiques de l'Opera Francais

Psyche: Invention of the Other. Jacques Derrida. 1993. pap. text 25.95 (*0-226-14310-4*); lib. bdg. 95.95 (*0-226-14309-0*) U Ch Pr.

Psyche: The Cult of Souls & Belief in Immortality Among the Greeks. Erwin Rohde. LC 75-37911. (Select Bibliographies Reprint Ser.). 1980. reprint ed. 57.95 (*0-8369-6749-6*) Ayer.

Psyche & Cerebrum, 1972. John N. Findlay. LC 72-76593. (Aquinas Lectures). 52p. 1972. 15.00 (*0-87462-137-2*) Marquette.

Psyche & Death. 2nd ed. Edgar Herzog. 224p. 2000. pap. 19.50 (*0-88214-515-0*, Pub. by Spring Pubns) Continuum.

Psyche & Eros: Mind & Gender in the Life Course. Gisela Labouvie-Vief. LC 93-21292. 345p. (C). 1994. text 59.95 (*0-521-43340-1*); pap. text 19.95 (*0-521-46824-8*) Cambridge U Pr.

Psyche & Family: Jungian Applications to Family Therapy. Ed. by Laura S. Dodson & Terrill L. Gibson. LC 96-25236. 164p. 1997. pap. 17.95 (*1-888602-02-3*, 023) Chiron Pubns.

***Psyche & Helix: Psychological Aspects of Genetic Counseling.** Seymour Kessler. 320p. 2000. 74.95 (*0-471-35055-9*) Wiley.

Psyche & Matter. Marie-Louise Von Franz. LC 91-53229. (C. G. Jung Foundation Bks.). 352p. (Orig.). 1992. pap. 18.00 (*0-87773-902-1*, Pub. by Shambhala Pubns) Random.

Psyche & Psychism, 2 vols., Set. 2nd ed. Torkom Saraydarian. LC 80-67684. 1982. 60.00 (*0-911794-06-9*) Saraydarian Inst.

Psyche & Schizophrenia: The Bond Between Affect & Logic. Luc Ciompi. Tr. by Deborah L. Schneider. LC 88-6768. (Illus.). 320p. 1988. 52.95 (*0-674-71990-5*) HUP.

Psyche & Society: Explorations in Psychoanalytic Sociology. Robert Endleman. LC 81-1646. 448p. 1981. text 69.50 (*0-231-04992-7*) Col U Pr.

***Psyche & Soma: Physicians & Metaphysicians on the Mind-body Problem from Antiquity to Enlightenment.** Ed. by John P. Wright & Paul Potter. LC 99-57195. 320p. 2000. write for info. (*0-19-823840-1*) OUP.

Psyche & Sports: Baseball, Hockey, Martial Arts, Running, Swimming, Tennis & Others. Ed. by Murray Stein & John Hollwitz. LC 94-28089. (Illus.). 248p. (Orig.). 1994. pap. 16.95 (*0-933029-79-9*) Chiron Pubns.

Psyche & Substance: Essays on Homeopathy in the Light of Jungian Psychology. 3rd rev. ed. Edward C. Whitmont. LC 82-22322. 300p. 1991. pap. 16.95 (*1-55643-106-6*) North Atlantic.

Psyche & Symbol. J. Campbell. pap. 15.00 (*0-06-092478-0*) HarpC.

Psyche & Symbol: A Selection from the Writings from C. G. Jung. C. G. Jung. Tr. by R. F. C. Hull from GER. LC 90-36021. (Bollingen Ser.). (Illus.). 384p. (C). 1990. pap. 16.95 (*0-691-01903-7*, Pub. by Princeton U Pr) Cal Prin Full Svc.

Psyche & Symbol in the Theater of Federico Garcia Lorca: Perlimplin, Verma, Blood Wedding. Rupert C. Allen. LC 74-4285. 234p. reprint ed. pap. 72.60 (*0-8357-7721-9*, 203607800002) Bks Demand.

Psyche & Text: The Sublime & the Grandiose in Literature, Psychopathology, & Culture. Henry Sussman. LC 92-30927. (SUNY Series in Psychoanalysis & Culture). 233p. (C). 1993. text 59.50 (*0-7914-1569-4*); pap. text 19.95 (*0-7914-1570-8*) State U NY Pr.

P

Psyche & the Social World: Developments in Group-Analytic Theory. Ed. by Dennis G. Brown & Louis Zinkin. LC 93-3918. (International Library of Group Psychotherapy & Group Process Ser.). 272p. (C). 1993. text 79.95 (*0-415-08708-2*, B0877) Routledge.

Psyche & the Social World: Developments in Group-Analytic Theory. Ed. by Dennis G. Brown & Louis Zinkin. LC 93-3918. (International Library of Group Psychotherapy & Group Process Ser.). 288p. (C). 1994. pap. 27.99 (*0-415-08709-0*, B0881) Routledge.

Psyche & the Split-Brain. Jenny L. Yates. (Illus.). 106p. (Orig.). (C). pap. text 19.50 (*0-8191-9447-6*); lib. bdg. 42.50 (*0-8191-9446-8*) U Pr of Amer.

Psyche As Hero: Female Heroism & Fictional Form. Lee R. Edwards. LC 83-21841. 319p. 1984. reprint ed. pap. 98.90 (*0-608-02316-7*, 206295700004) Bks Demand.

Psyche As Sacrament. John P. Dourley. 128p. 1995. pap. 16.00 (*0-919123-06-6*, Pub. by Inner City Bks) BookWorld.

Psyche at Work: Workplace Applications of Jungian Analytical Psychology. Ed. by Murray Stein & John Hollwitz. LC 92-12176. 248p. (Orig.). 1992. pap. 16.95 (*0-933029-61-6*) Chiron Pubns.

Psyche in Antiquity, Book 2: Gnosticism & Early Christian. Edward F. Edinger. 1999. pap. text 16.00 (*0-919123-87-2*) Inner City Bks.

Psyche in Medicine. Arthur Guirdham. 80p. (Orig.). pap. 12.95 (*0-8464-4275-2*) Beekman Pubs.

Psyche in Medicine. Arthur Guirdham. 109p. (Orig.). 1978. 8.25 (*0-85978-031-7*, Pub. by C W Daniel) Natl Bk Netwk.

Psyche in Scripture: The Idea of the Chosen People & Other Essays. Rivka Kluger. 128p. 1995. pap. 16.00 (*0-919123-71-6*, Pub. by Inner City Bks) BookWorld.

Psyche Reality: The Pleasurable Road to Your Own Reality. Volmar A. Franz. (Illus.). 150p. (Orig.). 1996. pap. 12.95 (*0-9655830-0-7*) Psyche Reality.

Psyche Reborn: The Emergence of H. D. Susan S. Friedman. LC 80-8378. (Illus.). 352p. (C). 1981. 31.50 (*0-253-37826-5*) Ind U Pr.

Psyche Reborn: The Emergence of H. D. Susan S. Friedman. LC 80-8378. (Illus.). 352p. (C). 1987. pap. 11.95 (*0-253-20449-6*, MB-449) Ind U Pr.

Psyche, Soul, & Spirit: A Search for the Meaning of Dreams & Visions. Dennis G. Twiggs. 94p. 1998. pap. 12.95 (*0-9662914-0-9*) Daystar Pr & Dist.

Psyche Speaks: A Jungian Approach to Self & World. Russell A. Lockhart. LC 87-18260. 130p. 1987. 29.95 (*0-933029-28-4*) Chiron Pubns.

Psyche Speaks: A Jungian Approach to Self & World. Russell A. Lockhart. LC 87-18260. 130p. 1987. pap. 15.95 (*0-933029-22-5*) Chiron Pubns.

Psyche Subversion. 128p. 1992. pap. 8.00 (*1-887151-01-X*) Andromeda CA.

Psyche, the Cult of Souls & Belief in Immortality among Ancient Greeks. Erwin Rohde. xvi, 626p. 1987. reprint ed. pap. 35.00 (*0-89005-477-0*) Ares.

Psyche-Therapy: How to Master Your Mind(s) & Emotions. I. Lovejoy. 250p. (Orig.). 1991. pap. 19.95 (*0-9601978-7-7*) Health Res Las Vegas.

Psyche Unbound. Heather Buck. LC 95-189497. 64p. 1995. pap. 14.95 (*0-85646-260-8*, Pub. by Anvil Press) Dufour.

Psyche, with Other Poems, 1811. Mary Tighe. LC 92-23244. (Revolution & Romanticism Ser.). 344p. 1992. reprint ed. 65.00 (*1-85477-110-8*) Continuum.

Psyched for Science, 6 vols. Incl. Energy & Motion. Allan B. Cobb. (Illus.). 48p. (YA). (gr. 5-8). 2000. lib. bdg. 17.95 (*0-8239-3116-1*, Rosen Central); Light & Optics. Allan B. Cobb. LC 99-51305. (Illus.). 48p. (YA). 1999. lib. bdg. 17.95 (*0-8239-3177-3*, Rosen Central); Oceans. Allan B. Cobb. LC 99-44867. (Illus.). 48p. (J). 1999. lib. bdg. 17.95 (*0-8239-3174-9*, Rosen Central); Super Science Projects About Animals in Their Habitats. Allan B. Cobb. LC 99-42687. (Illus.). 48p. (YA). 1999. lib. bdg. 17.95 (*0-8239-3175-7*, Rosen Central); Super Science Projects About Sound. Allan B. Cobb. LC 99-43237. (Illus.). 48p. (YA). 1999. lib. bdg. 17.95 (*0-8239-3176-5*, Rosen Central); Weather & Natural Forces. Lorraine Jones. LC 99-43742. (Illus.). 48p. (J). 2000. lib. bdg. 17.95 (*0-8239-3105-6*, Rosen Central); (Illus.). (YA). (gr. 5-8). Set lib. bdg. 107.70 (*0-8239-9087-7*, Rosen Central) Rosen Group.

Psyched on Bikes: The Bicycle Owner's Handbook. B. Andrew Renton. 184p. 1992. pap. 14.95 (*0-8306-1987-9*, 3668) McGraw-Hill Prof.

Psyched to Win. Robert M. Nideffer. LC 91-38529. 152p. 1992. pap. 14.95 (*0-88011-463-0*, PNID0463) Human Kinetics.

Psyched. 1.2 World Psy. Allyn. 1996. text 24.95 (*0-205-26173-6*) Allyn.

***Psychedelia.** Belmo. (20th Century Rock & Roll Ser.). 1999. pap. text 13.95 (*1-896522-40-8*) CN06.

Psychedelia: The Long Strange Trip. Martin Huxley. (CD Ser.). 1995. pap. 16.98 incl. audio (*1-56799-228-5*, Friedman-Fairfax) M Friedman Pub Grp Inc.

Psychedelic Chemistry. Michael V. Smith. (Illus.). x, 194 p. (Orig.). 1981. pap. text 19.95 (*0-915179-10-5*) Loompanics.

Psychedelic Chic: Artistic Fashions of the Late 1960s & Early 1970s. Roseann Ettinger. LC 99-14562. (Illus.). 176p. 1999. 39.95 (*0-7643-0811-4*) Schiffer.

***Psychedelic Daisy.** Andrews & McMeel Staff. 1999. 8.95 (*0-8362-8274-4*) Andrews & McMeel.

Psychedelic Drugs Reconsidered. 3rd ed. Lester Grinspoon & James B. Bakalar. (Drug Policy Classics Reprints Ser.: No. 1). 385p. 1997. reprint ed. pap. 12.95 (*0-9641568-5-7*) Open Soc Inst.

Psychedelic Experience: A Manual Based on the Tibetan Book of the Dead. Timothy Leary et al. 160p. 1995. pap. 10.95 (*0-8065-1652-6*, Citadel Pr) Carol Pub Group.

***Psychedelic Memoirs.** Steve Miller. Ed. by Jo Ann Yarak. (Illus.). 57p. 1998. pap. 9.95 (*1-893963-01-2*) YarakWorks Pub.

Psychedelic Prayers: And Other Meditations. 2nd ed. Timothy Leary. (Illus.). 128p. 1997. 20.00 (*0-914171-96-8*); pap. 12.95 (*0-914171-84-4*) Ronin Pub.

Psychedelic Reader. Ed. by Gunther M. Weil et al. 1971. reprint ed. pap. 3.95 (*0-8065-0255-X*, Citadel Pr) Carol Pub Group.

Psychedelic Reader: Classic Selections from the Psychedelic Review, the Revolutionary 1960s Forum of Psychopharmacological Substances. Ed. by Timothy Leary et al. (Illus.). 272p. 1993. pap. 12.95 (*0-8065-1451-5*, Citadel Pr) Carol Pub Group.

Psychedelic Reflections. Ed. by Lester Grinspoon & James B. Bakalar. 265p. 1983. 36.95 (*0-89885-129-7*, Kluwer Acad Hman Sci) Kluwer Academic.

Psychedelic Resource List. Jon Hanna. (Illus.). 120p. 1996. pap. 19.95 (*0-9654383-0-9*) Soma Graphics.

Psychedelic Resource List. 2nd rev. ed. Jon Hanna. (Illus.). 150p. 1998. pap. 19.95 (*0-9654383-1-7*) Soma Graphics.

Psychedelic Shamanism: The Cultivation, Preparation & Shamanic Use of Psychotropic Plants. Jim Dekorne. 1998. pap. text 19.95 (*0-9666932-5-6*) Breakout Prods Inc.

Psychedelic Source Book. Will Beifuss. (Illus.). 72p. (Orig.). 1996. pap., per. 12.95 (*0-9647946-2-4*) Flowers Pubng.

Psychedelics. Compiled by Thomas Lyttle. LC 93-19655. 272p. 1993. pap. 14.95 (*0-9623032-2-4*) Barricade Bks.

Psychedelics Encyclopedia. 3rd rev. ed. Peter Stafford. Ed. by Sigrid Radulovic & Sebastian J. Orfali. (Illus.). 420p. 1992. reprint ed. pap. 34.95 (*0-914171-51-8*) Ronin Pub.

Psychedelics Reimagined. Ed. by Thomas Little. 256p. 1999. pap. 14.00 (*1-57027-065-1*) Autonomedia.

Psycheresponse. Michael J. Asken. (C). 1992. pap. 21.00 (*0-89303-839-3*) P-H.

Psyche's Stories: Modern Jungian Interpretations of Fairy Tales, Vol. 1. Ed. by Murray Stein & Lionel Corbett. LC 90-26108. (Illus.). 184p. (Orig.). 1991. pap. 17.95 (*0-933029-39-X*) Chiron Pubns.

Psyche's Stories: Modern Jungian Interpretations of Fairy Tales, Vol. 2. Ed. by Murray Stein & Lionel Corbett. LC 90-26108. 192p. (Orig.). 1992. pap. 17.95 (*0-933029-56-X*) Chiron Pubns.

Psyche's Stories: Modern Jungian Interpretations of Fairy Tales, Vol. 3. Ed. by Murray Stein & Lionel Corbett. LC 90-26108. (Illus.). 136p. (Orig.). 1995. pap. 17.95 (*0-933029-90-X*) Chiron Pubns.

Psyche's Task: A Discourse Concerning the Influence of Superstition on the Growth of Institution. J. G. Frazer. 94p. 1997. reprint ed. 14.95 (*0-7661-0059-6*) Kessinger Pub.

Psycheye. Akhter Ahsen. 288p. 1977. 30.00 (*0-913412-47-3*) Brandon Hse.

Psychiatric - Mental Health Nursing. Jack Rudman. (Regents College Proficiency Examination Ser.: Vol. 34). 43.95 (*0-8373-5484-6*) Nat Learn.

Psychiatric - Mental Health Nursing. Jack Rudman. (ACT Proficiency Examination Program (PEP) Ser.: Vol. 40). 43.95 (*0-8373-5590-7*) Nat Learn.

Psychiatric & Behavioural Disorders in Developmental Disabilities & Mental Retardation. Ed. by Nick Bouras. LC 98-38465. (Illus.). 480p. (C). 1999. pap. text 59.95 (*0-521-64395-3*) Cambridge U Pr.

Psychiatric & Mental Health Nurse. Jack Rudman. (Certified Nurse Examination Ser.: CN-12). 1994. pap. 23.95 (*0-8373-6112-5*) Nat Learn.

Psychiatric & Mental Health Nursing CTB. Frisch. (Nursing Education Ser.). 1998. 47.95 (*0-8273-7235-3*) Delmar.

Psychiatric & Mental Health Nursing with Children & Adolescents. Ed. by Patricia West & Christina L. Evans. LC 91-26125. 446p. 1992. 64.00 (*0-8342-0240-9*) Aspen Pub.

Psychiatric & Paranormal Aspects of Ufology. Berthold E. Schwarz. (Illus.). 76p. 1999. pap. 7.95 (*0-940829-25-8*) Eagle Wing Bks.

Psychiatric Aspects of Abortion. Ed. by Nada L. Stotland. LC 90-14489. (Issues in Psychiatry Ser.). 210p. 1991. text 14.95 (*0-88048-451-9*, 8451) Am Psychiatric.

Psychiatric Aspects of AIDS & HIV Infection. Ed. by Stephen M. Goldfinger. LC 87-646993. (New Directions for Mental Health Services Ser.: No. MHS 48). 1990. pap. 25.00 (*1-55542-812-6*) Jossey-Bass.

Psychiatric Aspects of Cancer. Ed. by R. J. Goldberg. (Advances in Psychosomatic Medicine Ser.: Vol. 18). (Illus.). viii, 160p. 1988. 60.00 (*3-8055-4745-5*) S Karger.

Psychiatric Aspects of Chronic Pulmonary Disease. Ed. by Wendy L. Thompson & T. L. Thompson. (Advances in Psychosomatic Medicine Ser.: Vol. 14). (Illus.). x, 174p. 1985. 95.75 (*3-8055-4088-4*) S Karger.

Psychiatric Aspects of Epilepsy. Dietrich Blumer. LC 84-6236. (Illus.). 357p. 1984. reprint ed. pap. 110.70 (*0-608-06666-4*, 206686300009) Bks Demand.

Psychiatric Aspects of General Patient Care. 3rd rev. ed. Bonnie Fossett. Ed. by Barbara Halliburton. 186p. (C). 1996. pap. text 49.95 (*1-878025-92-9*) Western Schls.

Psychiatric Aspects of Juvenile Delinquency. L. Bovet. (WHO Monograph Ser.: No. 1). 90p. 1951. 5.00 (*92-4-140001-3*) World Health.

Psychiatric Aspects of Juvenile Delinquency. Lucien Bovet. LC 74-98747. 90p. 1970. reprint ed. lib. bdg. 55.00 (*0-8371-3019-0*, BOPA, Greenwood Pr) Greenwood.

Psychiatric Aspects of Opiate Dependence. A. Kurland. LC 77-18030. 272p. 1978. 161.00 (*0-8493-5056-5*, CRC Reprint) Franklin.

Psychiatric Aspects of Organ Transplantation. John Craven. Ed. by Gary M. Rodin. (Illus.). 256p. 1992. text 55.00 (*0-19-262073-8*) OUP.

Psychiatric Aspects of Personal Injury Claims. George Mendelson. (Illus.). 296p. 1988. pap. 40.95 (*0-398-06286-2*) C C Thomas.

Psychiatric Aspects of Personal Injury Claims. George Mendelson. (Illus.). 296p. (C). 1988. text 58.95 (*0-398-05411-8*) C C Thomas.

Psychiatric Aspects of Reproductive Technology. Ed. by Nada L. Stotland. LC 90-266. (Issues in Psychiatry Ser.). 168p. 1990. text 9.95 (*0-88048-316-4*, 8316) Am Psychiatric.

Psychiatric Aspects of Symptom Management in Cancer Patients. Ed. by William Breitbart & Jimmie C. Holland. LC 92-6969. (Clinical Practice Ser.: No. 25). 278p. 1993. text 14.95 (*0-88048-193-5*, 8193) Am Psychiatric.

Psychiatric Aspects of Terminal Illness. Ed. by Samuel C. Klagsbrun et al. LC 87-72173. 216p. 1988. pap. text 21.95 (*0-914783-23-8*) Charles.

Psychiatric Aspects of the Prevention of Nuclear War. Group for the Advancement of Psychiatry Staff. LC 64-7800. (Group for the Advancement of Psychiatry, Symposium Ser.: No. 57). 103p. reprint ed. pap. 32.00 (*0-7837-2121-8*, 204240300004) Bks Demand.

Psychiatric Aspects of Trauma. Ed. by Linda G. Peterson & G. J. O'Shanick. (Advances in Psychosomatic Medicine Ser.: Vol. 16). (Illus.). x, 238p. 1986. 66.75 (*3-8055-4219-4*) S Karger.

Psychiatric Assessment: Pre & Post Admission. Valerie A. Brown. LC 97-222449. (Forensic Focus Ser.: Vol. 8). 48p. 1997. pap. 36.95 (*1-85302-575-5*, Pub. by Jessica Kingsley) Taylor & Francis.

Psychiatric Attendant. Jack Rudman. (Career Examination Ser.: C-1434). 1994. pap. 23.95 (*0-8373-1434-8*) Nat Learn.

Psychiatric Care: Medical Malpractice, 1. Joseph T. Smith. (Medico-Legal Library Ser.). 664p. 1995. pap. 145.00 (*0-471-12892-9*) Wiley.

Psychiatric Care in the Nursing Home. Ed. by William E. Reichman & Paul R. Katz. (Illus.). 328p. 1996. text 49.95 (*0-19-508515-9*) OUP.

Psychiatric Care of the Medical Patient. 2nd ed. Ed. by Alan Stoudemire et al. LC 99-19105. (Illus.). 1240p. 2000. text 165.00 (*0-19-512452-9*) OUP.

Psychiatric Care Planning. Susan L. Krupnick & Andrew J. Wade. LC 92-2365. 320p. 1992. pap. 32.95 (*0-87434-399-2*) Springhouse Corp.

Psychiatric Care Planning. 2nd rev. ed. Susan Krupnick & Andrew J. Wade. LC 98-38122. 368p. 1998. 34.95 (*0-87434-953-2*) Springhouse Corp.

Psychiatric Care Plans: Guidelines for Planning & Documenting Client Care. 3rd ed. Marilynn E. Doenges et al. LC 97-24117. (Illus.). 532p. (C). 1997. pap. text 36.95 (*0-8036-0322-3*) Davis Co.

Psychiatric Claims in Workers' Compensation & Civil Actions, 2, Vol. 2. Herbert Lasky. (Personal Injury Library). 592p. 1993. boxed set 255.00 (*0-471-58490-8*) Wiley.

Psychiatric Clinical Pathways: An Interdisciplinary Approach. Patricia C. Dykes. LC 98-5909. 400p. 1998. 60.00 (*0-8342-1156-4*, 11564) Aspen Pub.

Psychiatric Comorbidity in Epilepsy: Basic Mechanisms, Diagnosis, & Treatment. Ed. by Harry W. McConnell & Peter J. Snyder. 416p. 1998. text 56.00 (*0-88048-853-0*, 8853) Am Psychiatric.

Psychiatric Consequences of Brain Disease in the Elderly: A Focus on Management. Ed. by D. K. Conn et al. (Illus.). 224p. 1989. 65.00 (*0-306-43216-1*, Plenum Trade) Perseus Pubng.

Psychiatric Consultation in Childbirth Settings: Parent- & Child-Oriented Approaches. R. L. Cohen. LC 88-6005. (Illus.). 298p. (C). 1988. text 57.50 (*0-306-42758-3*, Kluwer Plenum) Kluwer Academic.

Psychiatric Consultation in Mental Retardation. Group for the Advancement of Psychiatry Staff. LC 79-6358. (Group for the Advancement of Psychiatry, Symposium Ser.: Vol. 10, No. 104). 105p. reprint ed. pap. 32.60 (*0-7837-2104-8*, 204238100004) Bks Demand.

Psychiatric Consultation in Schools: A Report of the American Psychiatric Association. APA Committee on Psychiatry & Mental Health in Sch. LC 93-6913. 96p. 1993. text 9.95 (*0-89042-243-5*, 2243) Am Psychiatric.

Psychiatric Crisis Response Systems: A Descriptive Study. Beth A. Stroul. 106p. (C). 1999. reprint ed. pap. text 20.00 (*0-7881-7573-4*) DIANE Pub.

Psychiatric Diagnosis. 5th ed. Donald W. Goodwin & Samuel B. Guze. 384p. (C). 1996. text 39.95 (*0-19-510421-8*); pap. text 29.50 (*0-19-510422-6*) OUP.

Psychiatric Diagnosis: A Biopsychosocial Approach Using DSM-III-R. Jess Amchin. LC 90-874. (Illus.). 218p. 1991. reprint ed. pap. 67.60 (*0-608-06652-4*, 206684900009) Bks Demand.

Psychiatric Diagnosis: A World Perspective. Ed. by Juan E. Mezzich et al. LC 93-46006. 1994. 125.00 (*0-387-94221-1*) Spr-Verlag.

Psychiatric Dictionary. 7th ed. Robert J. Campbell. 840p. (C). 1996. text 67.50 (*0-19-510259-2*) OUP.

Psychiatric Differential Diagnosis. Jeremy M. Pfeffer & Gillian Waldron. LC 86-26356. (Illus.). 192p. (Orig.). (C). 1987. text 40.00 (*0-443-03703-5*) Church.

Psychiatric Dilemma of Adolescence. 2nd ed. James F. Masterson. LC 83-24039. 232p. 1986. reprint ed. text 38.95 (*0-87630-356-4*) Brunner-Mazel.

Psychiatric Dimensions of Medical Practice: What Primary-Care Physicians Should Know about Delirium, Demoralization, Suicidal Thinking, & Competence to Refuse Medical Advice. Phillip R. Slavney. LC 97-52406. 129p. 1998. 33.00 (*0-8018-5905-0*); pap. 15.95 (*0-8018-5906-9*) Johns Hopkins.

Psychiatric Disabilities, Employment, & the Americans with Disabilities Act. 1997. lib. bdg. 251.95 (*0-8490-8213-7*) Gordon Pr.

Psychiatric Disabilities, Employment & the Americans with Disabilities Act (ADA) (Illus.). 136p. (Orig.). (YA). (gr. 12 up). 1994. pap. text 20.00 (*0-7881-0860-3*) DIANE Pub.

Psychiatric Disorders. LC 94-33379. (Professional Care Guides Ser.). 224p. 1995. 24.95 (*0-87434-781-5*) Springhouse Corp.

Psychiatric Disorders in America. Ed. by Lee N. Robins & Darrel A. Regier. 400p. 1990. 60.00 (*0-02-926571-1*) Free Pr.

Psychiatric Disorders in Children: A Study of Individuals Known to have Attended both Child & Adult Psychiatric Departments of the Same Hospital. H. Zeitlin. (Maudsley Monographs: No. 29). (Illus.). 176p. 1986. 45.00 (*0-19-712153-5*) OUP.

Psychiatric Disorders with a Biochemical Basis: Including Pharmacology, Toxicology & Nutritional Aspects. David Donaldson. LC 97-7656. (Illus.). 252p. 1998. 45.00 (*1-85070-789-8*) Prthnon Pub.

Psychiatric Drugs. Jeffrey Leiberman & Allan Tasman. LC 99-44546. (Illus.). 255p. 2000. pap. text. write for info. (*0-7216-5884-9*, W B Saunders Co) Harcrt Hlth Sci Grp.

Psychiatric Emergencies. Ed. by William R. Dubin et al. (Clinics in Emergency Medicine Ser.: Vol. 4). (Illus.). 268p. 1984. text 42.00 (*0-443-08288-X*) Church.

Psychiatric Emergencies. Ed. by J. D. Pollitt. (C). 1987. text 82.00 (*0-85200-676-4*) Kluwer Academic.

Psychiatric Emergencies, No. 11. Stephen Merson & David Baldwin. (Oxford Handbooks in Emergency Medicine Ser.: Vol. 11). 134p. 1995. text 69.50 (*0-19-262478-4*); pap. text 35.00 (*0-19-262477-6*) OUP.

An Asterisk (*) at the beginning of an entry indicates that the title is appearing for the first time.

Psychiatry, 1982: The American Psychiatric Association Annual Review Psychiatry Update, Vol. 1. Ed. by Lester Grinspoon. Incl. Vol. 2. Psychiatry Update: The American Psychiatric Association Annual Review. (Illus.). 604p. 1983. text 15.00 (*0-88048-007-6*, 8007); Vol. 3. Psychiatry Update: The American Psychiatric Association Annual Review. (Illus.). 648p. 1984. text 15.00 (*0-88048-015-7*, 8015); 552p. 1982. 15.00 (*0-88048-000-9*, 8000) Am Psychiatric.

Psychiatry, 1995: Digging up the Bones, Vol. 6. Medical Review Staff. (Medical Review Ser.). (Illus.). 108p. 1997. pap. 18.95 (*0-07-038219-0*) McGraw-Hill HPD.

Psychiatry, 1999-2000 Edition: Current Clinical Strategies. rev. ed. Ed. by Rhoda K. Hahn et al. (Current Clinical Strategies Ser.). 129p. 1998. pap. 12.95 (*1-881528-65-0*) Current Clin Strat.

Psychiatry of Stroke. Ed. by D. Peter Birkett. LC 95-17692. 416p. 1996. 56.00 (*0-88048-540-X*, 8540) Am Psychiatric.

Psychiatry Pearls of Wisdom. Schmidt. (Pearls of Wisdom Ser.). 1999. pap. 88.00 (*1-890369-13-6*) Boston Medical.

Psychiatry, Psychoimmunology & Viruses. Ed. by A. Carlsson et al. (Key Topics in Brain Research Ser.). 180p. 1999. pap. 84.00 (*3-211-83249-1*) Spr-Verlag.

Psychiatry, Psychology, & Homosexuality. Ellen Herman. Ed. by Martin Duberman. LC 94-44952. (Issues in Gay & Lesbian Life Ser.). (Illus.). 154p. (YA). (gr. 9 up). 1995. 24.95 (*0-7910-2628-0*); pap. 12.95 (*0-7910-2977-8*) Chelsea Hse.

Psychiatry, Psychopharmacology, & Alternative Therapies: Trends for the 80s. Ed. by John J. Schwab. LC 81-15253. (Experimental & Clinical Psychiatry Ser.: No. 6). 243p. reprint ed. pap. 75.40 (*0-7837-0776-2*, 204109000019) Bks Demand.

Psychiatry Recall. Barbara Fadem & Steven S. Simring. LC 96-41667. 250p. 1997. write for info. (*0-683-18004-5*) Lppncott W & W.

Psychiatry Review. Cutler. 1999. pap. text. write for info. (*0-7216-6053-3*, W B Saunders Co) Harcrt Hlth Sci Grp.

Psychiatry Specialty Board Review for the DSM-IV. John C. Duffy & J. Bryce McLaulin. (Continuing Education in Psychiatry & Psychology Ser.: No. 5). 128p. 1996. pap. 22.95 (*0-87630-788-8*) Brunner-Mazel.

Psychiatry Takes to the Streets: Outreach & Crisis Intervention for the Mentally Ill. Ed. by Neal L. Cohen. LC 89-23741. 306p. 1990. lib. bdg. 42.00 (*0-89862-426-6*) Guilford Pubns.

Psychiatry Update: American Psychiatric Association Annual Review, Vol. 4. Ed. by Robert E. Hales & Allen J. Frances. 671p. 1985. text 15.00 (*0-88048-239-7*, 8239); pap. text 10.00 (*0-88048-039-4*, 8039) Am Psychiatric.

Psychiatry Update: American Psychiatric Association Annual Review, Vol. 6. Ed. by Robert E. Hales & Allen J. Frances. (Illus.). 852p. 1987. text 15.00 (*0-88048-243-5*, 8243); pap. text 10.00 (*0-88048-242-7*, 8242) Am Psychiatric.

Psychiatry Update: The American Psychiatric Association Annual Review see Psychiatry, 1982: The American Psychiatric Association Annual Review Psychiatry Update

Psychiatry Vade-Mecum. Basant Puri & Heather McKee. (An Arnold Publication). (Illus.). 288p. 1998. pap. text 24.95 (*0-340-69171-9*, Pub. by E A) OUP.

Psychiatry/Neurology: PreTest Self-Assessment & Review. 3rd rev. ed. Ed. by Joseph Friedman & James Duffy. LC 97-72. (Pretest Specialty Level Ser.). (Illus.). 348p. 1997. pap. text 45.00 (*0-07-052535-8*) McGraw-Hill HPD.

Psychic. 3rd rev. ed. Vern Overlee. Orig. Title: Let the Dead Speak of Their Lives. (Illus.). 204p. 1983. 11.95 (*0-9645230-1-9*) Mora Pr.

***Psychic: True Paranormal Experiences.** Hans Holzer. LC 99-19444. (Illus.). 560p. 1999. 24.98 (*0-7651-0953-0*) Smithmark.

Psychic Abilities: How to Train & Use Them. Marcia Pickands. LC 99-22982. 45p. 1999. pap. 9.95 (*1-57863-111-4*) Weiser.

Psychic Almanac, 1991 A. D. Gary Langford & Lauren Langford. 224p. (Orig.). pap. text 6.95 (*0-9627408-0-2*) Forest Light Pr.

Psychic & Paranormal Phenomena in the Bible: The True Story. (Orig.). 1998. 27.95 (*0-9654413-0-X*) psychicspacecom.

Psychic & Paranormal Phenomena in the Bible: The True Story. Ted Martin. LC 96-95063. 304p. (Orig.). 1998. pap. 22.95 (*0-9654413-1-8*) psychicspacecom.

Psychic & Religious Phenomena Limited: A Bibliographical Index. Compiled by Clyde S. King. LC 78-13535. 245p. 1978. lib. bdg. 99.50 (*0-313-20616-3*, KPR/, Greenwood Pr) Greenwood.

Psychic & Spirit Phenomena: Believers & Skeptics. John Burgess. 94p. (YA). (gr. 7-12). 1991. pap. 6.95 (*1-57515-008-5*) PPI Pubng.

Psychic & the Detective. Ann Druffel & Armand Marcotte. 176p. (Orig.). 1995. pap. 10.95 (*1-57174-029-5*) Hampton Roads Pub Co.

Psychic & the Spiritual: What's the Difference?, Set. Ed. by Frank C. Tribbe. (Spiritual Frontiers Fellowship Thirtieth Anniversary Booklet Ser.: Vol. I, No. 1). 1986. boxed set 12.00 (*0-317-68853-7*) Spirit Front Fellow.

Psychic & UFO Revelations in Last Days. 2nd ed. Timothy G. Beckley. (Illus.). 189p. 1989. pap. 15.00 (*0-938294-01-6*) Inner Light.

Psychic Animals: A Fascinating Investigation of Paranormal Behaviour. Dennis Bardens. (Illus.). 203p. (Orig.). 1995. pap. 21.95 (*1-898307-39-3*) Holmes Pub.

Psychic Autobiography. Amanda T. Jones. Ed. by Annette K. Baxter. LC 79-8798. (Signal Lives Ser.). (Illus.). 1980. reprint ed. lib. bdg. 53.95 (*0-405-12845-2*) Ayer.

Psychic Awareness. Compiled by Associations for Research & Enlightenment, Reading. (Library: Vol. 9). 400p. 1979. lib. bdg. 22.95 (*0-87604-109-8*, 1109) ARE Pr.

***Psychic Awareness.** Cassandra Eason. (Guides Ser.). 144p. 2000. pap. 6.95 (*0-7499-1932-9*, Pub. by Piatkus Bks) London Brdge.

***Psychic Battlefield: A History of the Military-Occult Complex.** Adam Mandelbaum. LC 99-55025. 336p. 2000. text 26.95 (*0-312-20955-X*) St Martin.

Psychic Beam to Beyond. Jane Boulton & Peter Boulton. LC 82-74522. 144p. 1983. pap. 6.95 (*0-87516-514-1*) DeVorss.

Psychic Being: Soul: Its Nature, Mission & Evolution. Sri Aurobindo & Mother. Ed. by A. S. Dalal. 223p. 1997. pap. 8.95 (*81-7058-138-9*, Pub. by SAA) E-W Cultural Ctr.

Psychic Being: The Soul in Evolution. Sri Aurobindo & The Mother. LC 89-85198. 223p. (Orig.). 1990. pap. 8.95 (*0-941524-56-6*) Lotus Pr.

Psychic Bible: The Apocryphal Scriptures of Genesis Porridge & Psychic TV. Ed. by J. A. Rapoza. LC 94-219874. 192p. 1994. pap. 14.99 (*0-9641136-0-0*) Mythword.

Psychic Book by Mae: Universal Understanding, Vol. 1. rev. ed. M. A. Eckels. (Revelation Ser.). 100p. 1998. pap. 9.95 (*0-9647790-7-2*) Exerbian Pr.

Psychic Breakthroughs Today. D. Scott Rogo. (Illus.). 240p. (Orig.). 1988. pap. 12.95 (*0-85030-570-5*, Pub. by Aqrn Pr) HarpC.

Psychic Case Book. Craig Hamilton-Parker. 1999. pap. 14.95 (*0-7137-2755-1*) Blandford Pr.

Psychic Certainties. H. F. Prevost Battersby. 230p. 1998. reprint ed. pap. 18.95 (*0-7661-0301-3*) Kessinger Pub.

Psychic Circle. Monte Farber & Amy Zerner. LC 92-41574. 32p. 1993. per. 25.00 (*0-671-86645-1*, Fireside) S&S Trade Pap.

***Psychic Close Encounters.** Albert Budden. (UFO Files Ser.). 2000. pap. 9.95 (*0-7137-2799-3*) Blandford Pr.

Psychic Connections: A Journey into the Mysterious World of Psychic. Lois Duncan. 272p. (YA). 1995. pap. 12.95 (*0-385-32072-8*) Delacorte.

***Psychic Counselor's Handbook: Ethics, Tools & Techniques.** (Illus.). 160p. 1999. pap. 14.95 (*0-9667683-0-2*) Inner Perceptions.

Psychic Deadness. Michael Eigen. LC 95-24825. 1996. 50.00 (*1-56821-735-8*) Aronson.

Psychic Detective. Nancy O. Weber & Iris Nevins. (Illus.). 179p. (Orig.). Date not set. pap. 12.50 (*0-9646118-0-5*) Unltd Mind.

Psychic Detective: Read-Along. Khoury. (Illus.). 32p. (J). (gr. 4-8). 1982. pap. 9.95 (*0-87386-306-2*) Jan Prods.

Psychic Detectives: The Story of Psychometry & Paranormal Crime Detection. Colin Wilson. LC 85-61405. 264p. (Orig.). 1989. reprint ed. pap. 10.95 (*0-916515-06-0*) Mercury Hse Inc.

Psychic Development. Compiled by Associations for Research & Enlightenment, Reading. (Library: Vol. 8). 327p. 1978. lib. bdg. 22.95 (*0-87604-108-X*, 1108) ARE Pr.

Psychic Development for Beginners: An Easy Guide to Releasing & Developing Your Psychic Abilities. William W. Hewitt. LC 95-49697. (Illus.). 216p. (Orig.). 1996. pap. 9.95 (*1-56718-360-3*) Llewellyn Pubns.

Psychic Development Workbook. Bruce Goldberg. (Illus.). 115p. 1996. 30.00 (*1-885577-93-1*) B Goldberg.

Psychic Development Workbook: How to Awaken & Use Your ESP. Rodney Davies. LC 97-201762. (Illus.). 128p. 1997. reprint ed. pap. 14.95 (*0-8069-9765-6*) Sterling.

Psychic Dictatorship in the U. S. A. Alex Constantine. 221p. 1995. pap. 12.95 (*0-922915-28-8*) Feral Hse.

Psychic Discoveries: The Iron Curtain Lifted. 2nd ed. Sheila Ostrander. 384p. 1997. pap. text 14.95 (*1-56924-750-1*) Marlowe & Co.

Psychic Empowerment: A Seven-Day Plan for Self-Development. Joe H. Slate. LC 95-1543. (Strategies for Success Ser.). (Illus.). 240p. 1999. pap. 12.95 (*1-56718-635-1*) Llewellyn Pubns.

Psychic Empowerment for Health & Fitness. Joe H. Slate. LC 96-12237. 256p. 1999. pap. 12.95 (*1-56718-634-3*) Llewellyn Pubns.

Psychic Energy: How to Change Your Desires into Realities. Joseph J. Weed. Orig. Title: Psychic Energy: Your Key to Transmute Desires into Realities. 1986. 10.95 (*0-13-732214-3*, Reward) P-H.

Psychic Energy: How to Change Your Desires into Realities. Joseph J. Weed. Orig. Title: Psychic Energy: Your Key to Transmute Desires into Realities. 1989. 6.95 (*0-13-732843-5*) P-H.

Psychic Energy: Its Source & Its Transformation. 2nd ed. M. Esther Harding. (Bollingen Ser.: Vol. 10). (Illus.). 520p. 1963. pap. 19.95 (*0-691-01790-5*, Pub. by Princeton U Pr) Cal Prin Full Svc.

Psychic Energy: The Magic Power of the Mind. Lloyd K. Ulery. LC 77-91279. 150p. 1978. 9.45 (*0-930984-02-1*) Psychic Bks.

Psychic Energy & Aggression. David M. Moriarity. 188p. (C). 1991. pap. 32.50 (*0-87527-486-2*) Green.

Psychic Energy Workbook: An Illustrated Course in Practical Psychic Skills. R. Michael Miller & Josephine M. Harper. (Workbook Ser.). (Illus.). 112p. 1987. pap. 14.95 (*0-85030-529-2*) Sterling.

Psychic Energy: Your Key to Transmute Desires into Realities see Psychic Energy: How to Change Your Desires into Realities

Psychic Envelopes. Ed. by Didier Anzieu. 280p. 1990. pap. text 29.00 (*0-946439-60-5*, Pub. by H Karnac Bks Ltd) Other Pr LLC.

Psychic Equilibrium & Psychic Change: Selected Papers of Betty Joseph. Ed. by Michael Feldman & Elizabeth B. Spillius. 240p. (C). 1989. pap. 29.99 (*0-415-04117-1*, A3644) Routledge.

Psychic Exhaustion & the Growth Process: An Appendix to Homosexuality: The Psychology of the Creative Process. Paul Rosenfels. LC 86-142957. (Ninth Street Center Monographs). (Orig.). 1976. pap. 3.95 (*0-932961-02-9*) Ninth St Ctr.

Psychic Experiences: A Bibliography. Rhea A. White & Rodger I. Anderson. (Bibliographies Ser.). 147p. (Orig.). 1990. pap. 20.00 (*0-944446-11-6*) EHE Network.

Psychic Factors of Civilization. Lester F. Ward. (Notable American Authors Ser.). 1999. reprint ed. lib. bdg. 125.00 (*0-7812-9876-8*) Rprt Serv.

Psychic for Life: How to Become Your Own Psychic Consultant. James R. Weiss. Ed. by Andrew De Simone. (Illus.). 180p. (Orig.). 1994. pap. text 19.95 (*0-9636041-4-7*) C B R Pubns.

Psychic Function of Religion in Mental Illness & Health. Group for the Advancement of Psychiatry Staff. LC 62-2872. (Group for the Advancement of Psychiatry, Symposium Ser.: Vol. 6, No. 67). 91p. reprint ed. pap. 30.00 (*0-7837-2118-8*, 204239800004) Bks Demand.

Psychic Growth: Dangers & Ecstasies. Kenneth J. Naysmith. 168p. 1977. pap. write for info. (*0-89540-037-5*, SB-037) Sun Pub.

***Psychic Handbook.** Betty F. Balcombe. 192p. 2000. pap. 12.95 (*1-57863-213-7*) Weiser.

Psychic Healing. Yogi Ramacharaka. reprint ed. 15.00 (*0-911662-07-3*) Yoga.

Psychic Healing Book. Amy Wallace & Bill Henkin. LC 77-16019. 224p. 1982. reprint ed. pap. 14.95 (*0-914728-34-2*) Wingbow Pr.

Psychic Healing with Spirit Guides & Angels. Diane Stein. LC 95-53703. (Illus.). 256p. (Orig.). 1996. pap. 18.95 (*0-89594-807-9*) Crossing Pr.

***Psychic History of the Cliff Dwellers, Their Origin & Destruction.** Emma F. Bullene. (LC History-America-E). 256p. 1999. reprint ed. lib. bdg. 89.00 (*0-7812-4314-9*) Rprt Serv.

Psychic Horoscopes: The Birth Charts & Biographies of Famous Psychics & Sensitives. Thomas Csere. LC 85-80043. (Illus.). 456p. (Orig.). 1986. 29.95 (*0-935283-01-3*); pap. 19.95 (*0-935283-00-5*) Empyreal Press.

Psychic Injuries, 3 vols., Vols. 12, 12a & 12b. Marvin E. Lewis & Robert L. Sadoff. (Courtroom Medicine Ser.). 1975. 580.00 (*0-8205-1256-7*) Bender.

Psychic Interaction. Fran De Aquino. 1994. 18.50 (*0-533-11114-5*) Vantage.

Psychic Investor. Marcus Goodwin. LC 99-27508. 256p. 1999. pap. 12.95 (*1-58062-197-X*) Adams Media.

Psychic Kitty. Cathy East Dubowski. (Sabrina, the Teenage Witch Ser.: No. 6). 96p. (J). (gr. 2-4). 1999. pap. 3.99 (*0-671-02382-9*) PB.

Psychic Life of Jesus. Maurice Elliott. 1972. 69.95 (*0-87968-185-3*) Gordon Pr.

Psychic Life of Power: Theories in Subjection. Judith Butler. LC 96-40851. 1997. pap. write for info. (*0-8047-2812-7*) Stanford U Pr.

Psychic Life of Power: Theories in Subjection. Judith P. Butler. LC 96-40851. 1997. write for info. (*0-8047-2811-9*) Stanford U Pr.

***Psychic Living: Tap Into Your Psychic Potential, 1.** Andrei Ridgeway. 192p. 1999. pap. 12.00 (*1-57566-415-1*) Kensgtn Pub Corp.

Psychic Magic. Raymond Ouellette. LC 74-78491. (Illus.). 343p. 1974. 12.95 (*0-936450-00-2*) Aero Pr.

Psychic Misfortune. rev. ed. Orig. Title: Nostradamus' Lost Predictions. 69p. 1997. write for info. (*0-9645601-3-5*) Scorpio Pub MA.

Psychic Murder Hunters: Real-Life Stories of Paranormal Detection. Andrew Boot. (Illus.). 384p. 1995. mass mkt. 11.95 (*0-7472-4302-6*, Pub. by Headline Bk Pub) Trafalgar.

Psychic or Charlatan? How to Interpret a Psychic Reading. Bruce Way. LC 97-38929. 1997. pap. 9.95 (*0-89087-846-3*) Celestial Arts.

Psychic Paradigm. Beverly Jaegers. LC 98-222969. 1998. mass mkt. 6.99 (*0-425-16509-4*) Berkley Pub.

Psychic Paradoxes. John Booth. LC 84-60005. (Illus.). 258p. (C). 1986. pap. 22.95 (*0-87975-358-7*) Prometheus Bks.

Psychic Pathway: A Guidebook to Developing Your Intuition & Spiritual Power. Sonia Choquette. LC 94-40628. 1995. pap. 18.00 (*0-517-88407-0*) Crown Pub Group.

Psychic Perception. Joseph Murphy. LC 94-70459. 241p. 1996. reprint ed. pap. 12.50 (*0-87516-670-9*) DeVorss.

Psychic Perspective. Robert R. Leichtman. (From Heaven to Earth Ser.). 1991. pap. 11.95 (*0-89804-081-7*) Ariel GA.

Psychic Pets: Supernatural True Stories of Paranormal Animals. rev. ed. John Sutton. LC 97-77586. (Illus.). 128p. (J). (gr. 5-7). 1998. pap. 7.95 (*1-885223-79-X*) Beyond Words Pub.

Psychic Pets & Spirit Animals: True Stories from the Files of FATE Magazine. Ed. by FATE Magazine Editorial Staff. LC 95-47294. 272p. 1999. mass mkt. 4.99 (*1-56718-299-2*) Llewellyn Pubns.

***Psychic Phenomena.** Rhiannon Lassiter. (Unexplained Ser.). 32p. (YA). (gr. 5 up). 1999. pap. 5.95 (*0-7641-1063-2*) Barron.

Psychic Phenomena of Jamaica. Joseph J. Williams. LC 78-32183. 309p. 1979. reprint ed. lib. bdg. 52.50 (*0-8371-5669-6*, WPP&, Greenwood Pr) Greenwood.

Psychic Philosophy As the Foundation of a Religion of Natural Law, 1921. Stanley De Breath. 880p. 1998. reprint ed. pap. 27.50 (*0-7661-0491-5*) Kessinger Pub.

***Psychic Pokemon: Abra, Kadabra, Alakazam.** Ed. by Readers Digest Children Staff. (Pokemon Elvolvers Bks.). (Illus.). (J). (gr. 4-7). 2000. pap. 3.99 (*1-57584-437-0*, RDYF) Rdrs Digest.

***Psychic Politics: An Aspect Psychology Book.** Jane Roberts. LC 99-48400. (Classics in Consciousness Ser.). 336p. 1999. pap. 15.95 (*0-9661327-4-2*, Pub. by Moment Pt Pr) ACCESS Pubs Network.

***Psychic Power.** Ted Andrews. Ed. by Pagyn Alexander-Harding & Diane Haugen. LC 00-100045. (Young Person's School of Magic & Mystery Ser.: Vol. 3). (Illus.). 220p. 2000. 17.95 (*1-888767-40-5*, Pub. by Dragonhawk Pubg) Partners Pubs Grp.

Psychic Power of Children. Cassandra Eason. (Illus.). 236p. 1992. pap. 13.95 (*0-7126-3619-6*, Pub. by Rider) Trafalgar.

Psychic Power of Children. 2nd ed. Cassandra Eason. 160p. 1994. pap. 14.95 (*0-572-02030-9*, Pub. by W Foulsham) Trans-Atl Phila.

Psychic Powers. (Mysteries of the Unknown Ser.). (Illus.). 144p. 1987. 14.95 (*0-8094-6308-3*); lib. bdg. 23.27 (*0-8094-6309-1*) Time-Life.

Psychic Powers. Helen Todd. (Theosophical Manual Ser.: No. 11). 1975. pap. 6.00 (*0-913004-38-3*) Point Loma Pub.

Psychic Protection. Ted Andrews. Ed. by Pagan Alexander-Harding & Diane Haugen. LC 98-84419. (Beginnings Ser.). (Illus.). 368p. 1998. pap. 12.95 (*1-888767-30-8*) Dragonhawk Pubg.

Psychic Protection. John Roger. LC 99-167071. 1998. mass mkt. 6.95 (*0-914829-69-6*) Mandeville LA.

Psychic Protection: Creating Positive Energies for People & Places. William Bloom. LC 97-18271. 1997. pap. text. write for info. (*0-7499-1603-6*) S&S Trade.

Psychic Protection: Creating Positive Energies for People & Places. William Bloom. LC 97-18271. 176p. 1997. per. 10.00 (*0-684-83519-3*) S&S Trade Pap.

Psychic Protection from Negativity. Bruce Goldberg. 1993. 12.00 incl. audio (*1-885577-29-X*) B Goldberg.

Psychic Reality: Developing Your Natural Abilities. Robert Cracknell. LC 99-71618. 200p. 1999. pap. 12.95 (*1-57174-132-1*) Hampton Roads Pub Co.

Psychic Reality & Psychoanalytic Knowing. Barnaby B. Barratt. LC 84-6353. (Advances in Psychoanalysis: Theory, Research, & Practice Ser.: No. 3). 316p. reprint ed. pap. 98.00 (*0-7837-4501-X*, 204427800001) Bks Demand.

Psychic Retreats: Pathological Organisations in Psychotic, Neurotic, & Borderline Patients. John Steiner. LC 92-48548. (New Library of Psychoanalysis Ser.: No. 19). 176p. (C). 1993. pap. 25.99 (*0-415-09924-2*, B0889) Routledge.

Psychic Roots: Serendipity & Intuition in Genealogy. Henry Z. Jones, Jr. LC 93-78363. (Illus.). 236p. 1996. pap. 14.95 (*0-8063-1388-9*, 3090) Genealog Pub.

Psychic Sasquatch: And Their UFO Connection. Jack Lapseritis. 300p. 1999. pap. 18.95 (*1-893183-14-9*, Pub. by Granite Pub) ACCESS Pubs Network.

Psychic Sasquatch: The UFO Connection. Jack Lapseritis. LC 98-13417. xxii, 225p. 1998. pap. 18.95 (*0-926524-17-8*) Granite WI.

Psychic Science & Survival. Hereward Carrington. 90p. 1993. reprint ed. spiral bd. 10.50 (*0-7873-0152-3*) Hlth Research.

Psychic Science & Survival: An Essay in Psychical Research. Hereward Carrington. 90p. 1996. reprint ed. pap. 8.95 (*1-56459-702-4*) Kessinger Pub.

***Psychic Secrets: Your Guide to Dreams, Hunches & Spirit Contact.** Joseph B. Mullen. LC 00-190723. 164p. 2000. 25.00 (*0-7388-1963-8*); pap. 18.00 (*0-7388-1964-6*) Xlibris Corp.

Psychic Self-Defense. Dion Fortune. LC 92-5952. 218p. 1992. reprint ed. pap. 9.95 (*0-87728-381-8*) Weiser.

Psychic Self Defense: Real Solutions. Jan Brodie. (Illus.). (Orig.). 1995. pap. 19.95 (*1-898307-36-9*, Pub. by Capall Bann Pubng) Holmes Pub.

Psychic Self Defense Manual, 2 vols. Darryl Williams. (Illus.). ii, 81p. 1998. pap. 16.95 (*0-9664945-0-4*) Mabon Tech.

Psychic Self-Defense Personal Training Manual. Marcia L. Pickands. LC 96-40272. (Illus.). 128p. (Orig.). 1997. pap. 9.95 (*1-57863-004-5*) Weiser.

Psychic Self-Reproach. Manly P. Hall. pap. 4.95 (*0-89314-344-8*) Philos Res.

***Psychic Senses: How to Develop Your Innate Powers.** Gloria Chadwick. LC 00-90910. 110p. 2000. pap. 11.95 (*1-883717-30-2*) Myst Mndscapes.

Psychic Sexual Command. Mark DeSade. Ed. by James Templar. LC 93-79465. 120p. (Orig.). 1993. pap. 25.00 (*1-883147-05-0*); pap. 25.00 (*1-883147-06-9*) Intern Guild ASRS.

Psychic Side of Dreams. Hans Holzer. LC 91-24523. (Fate Presents Ser.). 288p. 1999. reprint ed. mass mkt. 4.95 (*0-87542-369-8*) Llewellyn Pubns.

Psychic Side of Sports. Michael Murphy & Rhea White. (Illus.). 1978. 10.95 (*0-201-04728-4*) Addison-Wesley.

Psychic Sisters. Created by Francine Pascal. (Sweet Valley Twins Ser.: No. 70). 144p. (J). (gr. 3-7). 1993. pap. 3.50 (*0-553-48057-X*) Bantam.

Psychic Sisters. Jamie Suzanne. (Sweet Valley Twins Ser.: No. 70). (J). (gr. 3-7). 1993. 8.60 (*0-606-05650-5*, Pub. by Turtleback) Demco.

Psychic Skills: Lessons in Clairvoyance, Personal Magnetism, Auto-Suggestion, Concentration, & Mind Reading (1901) Psychic Research Co. Staff. 105p. 1996. reprint ed. pap. 14.95 (*1-56459-650-8*) Kessinger Pub.

Psychic Sleuths: ESP & Sensational Cases. Ed. by Joe Nickell. LC 93-43069. (Illus.). 251p. (C). 1994. 26.95 (*0-87975-880-5*) Prometheus Bks.

Psychic Sleuths: How Psychic Information Is Used to Solve Crimes. Jan Burgess. LC 93-40593. (J). 1994. pap. 5.95 (*0-382-24741-8*, New Dscvry Bks) Silver Burdett Pr.

Psychic Sleuths: How Psychic Information Is Used to Solve Crimes. Anita Larsen. LC 93-40593. (J). 1994. lib. bdg. 14.95 (*0-02-751645-8*, New Dscvry Bks) Silver Burdett Pr.

Psychic Songster (1907) G. Tabor Thompson. 65p. 1998. reprint ed. pap. 7.95 (*0-7661-0620-9*) Kessinger Pub.

P

Psychic Sourcebook: How to Choose & Use a Psychic. Frederick G. Levine. 368p. (Orig.). 1988. mass mkt. 9.95 (*0-446-38729-0*, Pub. by Warner Bks) Little.

Psychic Structure & Psychic Change: Essays in Honor of Robert S. Wallerstein, M.D. Ed. by Mardi J. Horowitz et al. LC 93-16491. 384p. 1993. 55.00 (*0-8236-5253-X*) Intl Univs Pr.

Psychic Surgeon. Solomon. 1998. pap. 13.00 (*0-7225-3461-2*) Thorsons PA.

Psychic Symbolism of Headaches, Insomnia & Upset Stomach. Manly P. Hall. pap. 4.95 (*0-89314-345-6*) Philos Res.

Psychic Tarot Book. Craig Junjulas. (Illus.). 128p. 1985. pap. 9.95 (*0-88079-300-7*, BK68) US Games Syst.

Psychic Tendencies of Today (1918) Alfred W. Martin. 172p. 1998. reprint ed. pap. 17.95 (*0-7661-0558-X*) Kessinger Pub.

***Psychic II.** (Pokemon Evolvers Ser.). (Illus.). 4p. (J). 2001. 3.99 (*1-57584-736-1*, Pub. by Rdrs Digest) S&S Trade.

***Psychic Unrest.** Lillian Allen. 112p. 2000. pap. 9.99 (*1-895837-55-3*) Insomniac.

Psychic Voyages. (Mysteries of the Unknown Ser.). (Illus.). 144p. 1988. 14.95 (*0-8094-6316-4*); lib. bdg. 23.27 (*0-8094-6317-2*) Time-Life.

***Psychic War: Parapsychology In Espionage & Beyond.** Elmar R. Gruber. LC 99-495094. 288p. 1999. pap. text 17.95 (*0-7137-2762-4*) Strlng Pub CA.

Psychic Warfare. Mark DeSade. Ed. by Thorguard Templar. 87p. (Orig.). 1993. 65.00 (*1-883147-91-3*); 65.00 (*1-883147-92-1*) Intern Guild ASRS.

Psychic Warfare: Fact or Fiction? John White. (Illus.). 224p. (Orig.). 1988. pap. 9.95 (*0-85030-644-2*, Pub. by Aqrn Pr) HarpC.

***Psychic Warrior.** Robert Doherty. 352p. 2000. mass mkt. 5.99 (*0-440-23625-8*) Dell.

Psychic Warrior, Vol. 1. David Morehouse. 1998. mass mkt. 6.99 (*0-312-96413-7*) St Martin.

Psychic Warrior: Inside the CIA's Stargate Program: The True Story of a Soldier's Espionage & Awakening. David Morehouse. (Illus.). 258p. 1999. reprint ed. text 24.00 (*0-7881-6203-9*) DIANE Pub.

Psychic Wholeness & Healing: Using All the Powers of the Human Psyche. Conrad W. Baars & Anna A. Terruwe. LC 81-4964. 278p. (Orig.). 1981. pap. 12.95 (*0-8189-0410-0*) Alba.

Psychic Within: True Psychic Stories. Dayle Schear. LC 94-3987. 270p. 1994. pap. 14.95 (*0-931892-90-2*) B Dolphin Pub.

Psychic Women. Antionette May. 1984. pap. 6.95 (*0-915689-03-0*) Hickman Systems.

***Psychic World of Derek Acorah.** Derek Acorah. 224p. 2000. pap. 14.95 (*0-7499-2024-6*, Pub. by Piatkus Bks) London Brdge.

Psychic Yellow Pages: The Very Best Psychics, Cardreaders, Mediums, Astrologers & Numerologists. Hans Holzer. LC 99-23682. (Illus.). 176p. 1999. pap. 12.00 (*0-8065-2095-7*, Citadel Pr) Carol Pub Group.

Psychical Research. W. F. Barrett. 255p. 1996. reprint ed. spiral bd. 20.00 (*0-7873-0073-X*) Hlth Research.

Psychical Research. W. F. Barrett. 255p. 1996. reprint ed. pap. 17.95 (*1-56459-658-3*) Kessinger Pub.

Psychical Research: The Science of the Super-Normal. Hans Driesch. Tr. by Theodore Besterman. LC 75-7376. (Perspectives in Psychical Research Ser.). 1975. reprint ed. 23.95 (*0-405-07026-8*) Ayer.

Psychical Research for the Plain Man. S. M. Kingsford. 269p. 1996. reprint ed. spiral bd. 16.50 (*0-7873-0496-4*) Hlth Research.

Psychical Research for the Plain Man (1920) S. M. Kingsford. 275p. 1996. reprint ed. pap. 14.95 (*1-56459-774-1*) Kessinger Pub.

Psychics. Ed. by Jim Hicks. (Mysteries of the Unknown Ser.). (Illus.). 144p. 1992. lib. bdg. 17.45 (*0-8094-6542-6*) Time-Life.

***Psychics: The Paranormal Investigators' Files.** Sarah Moran. 1999. 14.99 (*1-84100-295-X*) Quadrillion Pub.

Psychic's Casebook. large type ed. Dilys Gater. LC 97-28640. 1997. 20.95 (*0-7862-1227-6*) Thorndike Pr.

Psychicsphere: The Structure of Chaos. Michael Heidecke. (Illus.). 40p. 1999. pap. 8.00 (*0-8059-4592-X*) Dorrance.

Psychiczne Zrodla Komunizmu. rev. ed. Marian Wasilewski. Ed. & Illus. by Malgorzata Barton. (POL.). 80p. 1983. pap. 4.50 (*0-9612122-0-9*) Polish Am Ethnic.

Psyching. Judd Biasiotto. 80p. (Orig.). 1988. pap. 6.00 (*0-933079-08-7*) World Class Enterprises.

Psyching for Slalom: An Illustrated Guide to the Mind & Muscle of the Complete Skier. David Benzel. Ed. by Jo Robertson. (Illus.). 127p. (Orig.). (YA). 1989. pap. 15.95 (*0-944406-05-X*) World Pub FL.

Psyching Out Diabetes. 2nd rev. ed. Richard Rubin et al. 312p. 1997. pap. 16.00 (*1-56565-808-6*, Anodyne) Lowell Hse.

Psyching Out Diabetes: A Positive Approach to Your Negative Emotions. Richard Rubin et al. 288p. 1992. 22.95 (*0-929923-97-9*) Lowell Hse.

Psyching Out Diabetes: A Positive Approach to Your Negative Emotions. Richard Rubin et al. 312p. 1993. pap. 16.00 (*1-56565-088-3*, Anodyne) Lowell Hse.

Psyching out Diabetes: A Positive Approach to Your Negative Emotions. 3rd ed. Richard R. Rubin. 384p. 1999. pap. 16.95 (*0-7373-0258-5*, 02585W) NTC Contemp Pub Co.

Psyching Out Vegas. Marvin Karlins. (Illus.). 280p. 1983. 15.00 (*0-914314-03-3*) Gambling Times.

Psyching the Ads: The Case Book of Advertising; the Methods & Results of 180 Advertisements. Carroll Rheinstrom. LC 75-39271. (Getting & Spending:The Consumer's Dilemma Ser.). (Illus.). 1976. reprint ed. 31.95 (*0-405-08043-3*) Ayer.

Psychischen Storungen des Kindesalters. Hermann Emminghaus. LC 75-16701. (Classics in Psychiatry Ser.). (GER., Illus.). 1976. reprint ed. 25.95 (*0-405-07428-X*) Ayer.

Psycho. Robert Bloch. 224p. 1991. mass mkt. 5.99 (*0-8125-1932-9*, Pub. by Tor Bks) St Martin.

Psycho. Robert Bloch. reprint ed. lib. bdg. 21.95 (*0-88411-077-X*) Amereon Ltd.

Psycho. Robert Bloch. 1993. reprint ed. lib. bdg. 18.95 (*0-89968-420-3*, Lghtyr Pr) Buccaneer Bks.

Psycho: Behind the Scenes of the Classic Thriller. Janet Leigh & C. Nickens. 224p. 1995. 22.00 (*0-517-70112-X*) Harmony Bks.

Psycho-Analysis As History: Negation & Freedom in Freud. Michael S. Roth. LC 86-29192. 208p. 1987. 35.00 (*0-8014-1957-3*) Cornell U Pr.

Psycho-Analysis As History: Negation & Freedom in Freud. Michael S. Roth. 208p. 1995. pap. text 13.95 (*0-8014-8303-4*) Cornell U Pr.

Psycho-Analytic Explorations. Donald Woods Winnicott. Ed. by Clare Winnicott et al. (Illus.). 624p. 1992. pap. 24.50 (*0-674-72091-1*) HUP.

Psycho-Analytic Explorations. Donald Woods Winnicott et al. Ed. by Clare Winnicott et al. LC 88-21465. (Illus.). 616p. 1989. 50.00 (*0-674-72090-3*) HUP.

Psycho-Cosmic Symbolism of the Buddhist Stupa. Lama A. Govinda. LC 76-797. (Illus.). 120p. 1976. pap. 12.95 (*0-913546-36-4*) Dharma Pub.

Psycho-Cybernetics. Maxwell Maltz. 1973. pap. 10.00 (*0-87980-127-1*) Wilshire.

Psycho Cybernetics. Maxwell Maltz. 1989. per. 6.99 (*0-671-70075-8*) PB.

***Psycho-Cybernetics.** rev. ed. Maxwell Maltz Foundation Staff et al. 384p. 1999. 7.98 (*1-56731-306-X*, MJF Bks) Fine Comms.

Psycho-Cybernetics 2000. Maxwell Maltz Foundation Staff & Bobbe Sommer. 352p. 1993. 29.95 (*0-13-735903-9*) P-H.

Psycho Cybernetics, 2000. Bobbe Sommer. 352p. 1996. pap. text 12.95 (*0-13-263849-5*) P-H.

Psycho-Dictionary. F. H. Holl. (ENG & GER.). 255p. 1986. 95.00 (*0-8288-7812-9*) Fr & Eur.

***Psycho-Economics: Managed Care in Mental Health in the New Millennium.** Ed. by Robert D. Weitz. LC 99-47992. (Critical Strategies Ser.: Vol. 1, No. 1). 165p. (C). 1999. 39.95 (*0-7890-0780-0*); pap. text 19.95 (*0-7890-0815-7*) Haworth Pr.

Psycho Environmental Forces in Substance Abuse Prevention. L. B. Szalay et al. LC 99-17262. (A Volume in Cognition & Language). (Illus.). 364p. (C). 1999. 65.00 (*0-306-45963-9*) Kluwer Academic.

Psycho-Ethical Aspects of Abhidhamma. Rina Sircar. LC 98-32321. 182p. 1999. 48.00 (*0-7618-1322-5*); pap. 28.50 (*0-7618-1323-3*) U Pr of Amer.

Psycho-Harmonial Philosophy: Music, Mathematics & Geometry. P. Pearson. 1991. lib. bdg. 79.95 (*0-8490-5012-X*) Gordon Pr.

Psycho House. Robert Bloch. 1991. mass mkt. 4.95 (*0-8125-0919-6*, Pub. by Tor Bks) St Martin.

Psycho II. Robert Bloch. 1989. pap. 3.95 (*0-8125-0033-4*) Tor Bks.

Psycho II. Robert Bloch. 320p. 1982. mass mkt. 3.50 (*0-446-90804-5*, Pub. by Warner Bks) Little.

Psycho II. Robert Bloch. 224p. 1982. 16.00 (*0-918372-09-7*) Whispers.

Psycho II. limited ed. Robert Bloch. 224p. 1982. boxed set 36.00 (*0-918372-08-9*) Whispers.

Psycho-Immune-Neuroendocrine Integrative Mechanisms. Ed. by D. P. Cardinali & F. Fraschini. (Biological Signals & Receptors Ser.: Vol. 7, No. 1, 1998). (Illus.). 74p. 1998. pap. 33.25 (*3-8055-6685-9*) S Karger.

Psycho Kitty? Understanding Your Cat's "Crazy" Behavior. Pam Johnson-Bennett. LC 98-26916. 144p. 1998. pap. 12.95 (*0-89594-909-1*) Crossing Pr.

Psycho-Linguistics: THe Language of the Mind. Patrick K. Porter. Ed. by Jerry De Shazo. 240p. (Orig.). (C). 1993. pap. 19.98 (*0-963761-7-X*) Positive Chngs Hypnosis.

Psycho-Linguistics: The Language of the Mind. Patrick K. Porter. Ed. by Paul K. Massengill. LC 93-86045. 240p. (C). reprint ed. pap. 19.98 (*1-887630-02-3*) Renaissnce Pub.

Psycho-Logic. J. Smedslund. 130p. 1988. 44.00 (*0-387-18518-6*) Spr-Verlag.

Psycho-Marxism: Marxism & Psychoanalysis Late in the 20th Century. Robert Miklitsch. 1998. pap. 12.00 (*0-8223-6460-3*) Duke.

Psycho-Mathematics: The Key to the Universe, Set. William B. Conner. Incl. Vol. 1-Creativity through Calculator Harmonic Braiding. 140p. 1983. (*0-9603536-5-8*); Vol. 2-Creativity through Keyboard Harmonic Braiding. Orig. Title: Math's & Music's Metasonics. 213p. 1983. reprint ed. pap. 36.50 (*0-9603536-6-6*); Orig. Title: Math's & Music's Metasonics. (Orig.). 1983. Set pap. text 36.50 (*0-9603536-7-4*) Tesla Bk Co.

Psycho-Motor Breathscapes. unabridged ed. John Noto. 74p. (Orig.). 1996. pap. 7.95 (*0-9654877-0-9*) Vatic Hum Pr.

Psycho-Oncology. Ed. by Jimmie C. Holland. (Illus.). 1216p. 1998. text 139.50 (*0-19-510614-8*) OUP.

Psycho-Paths. Ed. by Robert Bloch. 320p. 1993. mass mkt. 4.99 (*0-8125-0340-6*) Tor Bks.

***Psycho Paths: Tracking the Serial Killer Through Contemporary American Film & Fiction.** Philip L. Simpson. LC 99-56666. (Illus.). 2000. 18.95 (*0-8093-2329-X*) S Ill U Pr.

Psycho-Physical Nature of Reality. J. H. Greidanus. (Verhandelingen der Koninklijke Nederlandse Akademie van Wetenschappen, Afd. Natuurkunde Ser.: No. 26(4)). 56p. 1972. pap. text 12.50 (*0-7204-8245-3*) Elsevier.

Psycho-Physiological Disorders: General & Medical Research Subject Directory with Bibliography. American Health Research Institute Staff. Ed. by John C. Bartone. LC 82-72012. 236p. 1982. 47.50 (*0-941864-40-5*); pap. 44.50 (*0-941864-41-3*) ABBE Pubs Assn.

Psycho-Physiological Disorders II: Medical Subject Analysis & Research Index with Bibliography. Ellen E. Sandison. LC 84-45993. 150p. 1985. 47.50 (*0-88164-308-4*); pap. 44.50 (*0-88164-309-2*) ABBE Pubs Assn.

Psycho-Physiology & Biofeedback: Index of New Information with Authors & Subjects. rev. ed. Tony A. Pellicano. LC 94-31239. 237p. 1994. write for info. (*0-7883-0258-2*); pap. write for info. (*0-7883-0259-0*) ABBE Pubs Assn.

Psycho-Physiology of Fatigue: Subject Analysis & Reference Guidebook with Bibliography. Martha G. Gorman. LC 84-45990. 150p. 1987. 47.50 (*0-88164-302-5*); pap. 44.50 (*0-88164-303-3*) ABBE Pubs Assn.

Psycho Pictography. Vernon Howard. 240p. (C). 1996. pap. text 9.95 (*0-13-231283-2*) P-H.

Psycho-Pictography. Vernon Howard. 1965. pap. 8.95 (*0-911203-29-X*) New Life.

Psycho-Political Muse: American Poetry since the Fifties. Paul Breslin. LC 87-10863. 280p. 1998. 33.00 (*0-226-07410-2*) U Ch Pr.

Psycho-Political Muse: American Poetry since the Fifties. Paul Breslin. LC 87-10863. 278p. reprint ed. pap. 86.20 (*0-608-09439-0*, 205423900005) Bks Demand.

Psycho-Politics & Cultural Desires. Jan Campbell. 1998. pap. text 24.95 (*1-85728-807-6*) Taylor & Francis.

***Psycho-Politics & Cultural Desires.** Jan Campbell. 240p. 1998. 75.00 (*1-85728-806-8*) Taylor & Francis.

Psycho-Politics in Government Vol. 1: A Dramatic Dialogue. Leon T. Newton. LC 93-85663. 52p. (Orig.). 1993. pap. 9.95 (*0-915885-02-6*) Playwright MI.

Psycho-Politics in Government Vol. 2: Theatre Version. rev. ed. Leon T. Newton. 52p. 1993. pap. 15.95 (*0-915885-03-4*) Playwright MI.

Psycho-Sales Analysis: The New Art of Self-Taught Sales Success. Jack Huttig. (Quality Paperback Ser.: No. 263). 232p. 1978. reprint ed. pap. 9.95 (*0-8226-0263-6*) Littlefield.

Psycho Shop. Alfred Bester & Roger Zelazny. LC 98-6111. 256p. 1998. pap. 12.00 (*0-679-76782-7*) Random.

Psycho-Social Aspects of Aging in India. Paramjeet K. Dhillon. (C). 1992. text 36.00 (*81-7022-426-8*, Pub. by Concept) S Asia.

Psycho-Social Dynamics of Leading & Following. Peter Gronn. 145p. (C). 1986. 48.00 (*0-7300-0411-2*, Pub. by Deakin Univ) St Mut.

Psycho-Spiritual Healing after Abortion. Douglas R. Crawford & Michael T. Mannion. LC 88-63847. 104p. (Orig.). 1989. pap. 6.95 (*1-55612-246-2*) Sheed & Ward WI.

Psycho Surgery. Mark A. J. O'Callaghan. 1983. lib. bdg. 124.00 (*0-942068-06-8*) Kluwer Academic.

Psycho-Therapeutics. Charles Lloyd Tuckey. 96p. 55.00 (*1-85506-678-5*) Thoemmes Pr.

Psycho-Yoga: The Practice of Mind Control. B. Edwin. 1969. reprint ed. pap. 2.95 (*0-8065-0071-9*, Citadel Pr) Carol Pub Group.

Psychoacoustics. J. Donald Harris. LC 74-10512. (Studies in Communicative Disorders). (C). 1974. pap. text. write for info. (*0-672-61332-8*, Bobbs) Macmillan.

Psychoacoustics. J. Donald Harris. reprint ed. pap. text 5.95 (*0-8290-0327-4*) Irvington.

Psychoacoustics: Facts & Models. H. Fastl & Eberhard Zwicker. LC 98-46050. (Illus.). 380p. 1999. pap. 64.95 (*3-540-65063-6*) Spr-Verlag.

Psychoacoustics: Facts & Models. E. Zwicker & H. Fastl. Ed. by T. S. Huang et al. (Information Sciences Ser.: Vol. 22). (Illus.). 352p. 1990. text 59.50 (*0-387-52600-5*) Spr-Verlag.

Psychoacoustics, Speech, & Hearing Aids: Proceedings of the Summer School & International Symposium, Bad Zwischenahn, 31 Aug-5 Sep 95. Ed. by B. Kollmeier. LC 96-6736. 372p. 1996. write for info. (*981-02-2561-X*) World Scientific Pub.

Psychoactive Drugs: Improving Prescribing Practices. H. Ghodse & I. Khan. 108p. 1988. 18.00 (*92-4-156112-2*) World Health.

Psychoactive Drugs: Including Combinations. Ed. by F. Wider. (Data Processing in Medicine Ser.: Vol. 3). 260p. 1974. 104.50 (*3-8055-1740-8*) S Karger.

***Psychoactive Drugs: The Street Pharmacopoeia.** Alasdair J. M. Forsyth. 192p. 2000. pap. 40.00 (*0-11-702475-9*, Pub. by Statnry Office) Balogh.

Psychoactive Drugs: Tolerance & Sensitization. Ed. by A. J. Goudie & M. W. Emmett-Oglesby. LC 89-11094. (Contemporary Neuroscience Ser.). 608p. 1989. 125.00 (*0-89603-148-9*) Humana.

Psychoactive Drugs & Harm Reduction: From Faith to Science. Heather. 366p. 1993. pap. 34.95 (*1-56593-246-3*, 0520) Singular Publishing.

Psychoactive Drugs & Sex. Ernest L. Abel. (Illus.). 242p. (C). 1985. 65.00 (*0-306-41869-X*, Plenum Trade) Perseus Pubng.

Psychoactive Medications in the Treatment of Adults & Adolescents. Frederick M. Jacobsen & Robert Golden. 400p. 1996. 45.00 (*0-471-55074-4*) Wiley.

Psychoalchemy. Oscar Ichazo. (Illus.). 54p. 1978. pap. 20.00 (*0-916554-08-2*) Arica Inst Pr.

Psychoanal Approaches to Myth. Daniel Merkur. Ed. by Robert A. Segal. (Theorists of Myth Ser.). 200p. Date not set. text 29.00 (*0-8240-5936-0*) Garland.

Psychoanalyse und Nationalsozialismus: Beitraege zur Bearbeitung eines unbewaeltigten Traaumas. Ed. by Hans-Martin Lohmann. (GER.). 288p. 1994. pap. 18.00 (*3-596-12231-7*, Pub. by Fischer Tasch) Intl Bk Import.

***Psychoanalyses & Feminisms.** Ed. by Peter L. Rudnytsky & Andrew M. Gordon. LC 99-45447. (C). 1999. pap. text 17.95 (*0-7914-4378-7*) State U NY Pr.

***Psychoanalyses/Feminisms.** Peter L. Rudnytsky & Andrew Gordon. LC 99-45447. 237p. (C). 1999. text 54.50 (*0-7914-4377-9*) State U NY Pr.

Psychoanalysis. Toews. 1997. 26.95 (*0-8057-8642-2*, Twyne); pap. 14.95 (*0-8057-8643-0*, Twyne) Mac Lib Ref.

Psychoanalysis. Eli Zaretsky. 1999. write for info. (*0-679-44654-0*) Knopf.

Psychoanalysis: A Contemporary Introduction. Robert M. Galatzer-Levy. 212p. 1998. pap. write for info. (*0-465-06492-2*) Basic.

Psychoanalysis: Clinical & Theoretical. Robert S. Wallerstein. LC 98-31872. 446p. 1999. 70.00 (*0-8236-5219-X*, 05219) Intl Univs Pr.

Psychoanalysis: Clinical Theory & Practice. Jacob A. Arlow. LC 91-20811. 450p. (C). 1991. 65.00 (*0-8236-5202-5*) Intl Univs Pr.

Psychoanalysis: Observation, Theory, Application: Selected Papers of Robert Waelder. Ed. by Samuel A. Guttman. LC 75-6432. 709p. 1976. 85.00 (*0-8236-5250-5*) Intl Univs Pr.

Psychoanalysis: Science & Profession. Maxwell Gitelson. LC 72-8789. xiv, 439p. 1973. 65.00 (*0-8236-5255-6*) Intl Univs Pr.

Psychoanalysis: The Impossible Profession. Janet Malcolm. LC 94-72518. 184p. 1994. 30.00 (*1-56821-342-5*) Aronson.

Psychoanalysis: The Impossible Profession. Janet Malcolm. LC 82-40036. 192p. 1982. pap. 13.00 (*0-394-71034-7*) Vin Bks.

***Psychoanalysis: The Major Concepts.** Burness E. Moore. (Illus.). 608p. 1999. 27.50 (*0-300-08078-6*) Yale U Pr.

Psychoanalysis: The Major Concepts. Ed. by Burness E. Moore & Bernard D. Fine. LC 95-173. 562p. 1995. 60.00 (*0-300-06329-6*) Yale U Pr.

Psychoanalysis: The Possible Profession. Ed. by Herbert S. Strean. LC 85-24757. (Current Issues in Psychoanalytic Practice Ser.: Vol. 2, No. 2). 102p. 1986. text 39.95 (*0-86656-509-4*) Haworth Pr.

Psychoanalysis: The Science of Mental Conflict - Essays in Honor of Charles Brenner. Ed. by Arnold D. Richards & Martin S. Willick. (Essays in Honor of Chas Brenner Ser.). 439p. 1986. text 55.00 (*0-88163-054-3*) Analytic Pr.

Psychoanalysis: The Vital Issues, 2 vols., Vol. 1. Ed. by John E. Gedo & George H. Pollock. LC 83-26429. (Emotions & Behavior Monographs: Nos. 2 & 3). 448p. 1983. 65.00 (*0-8236-5385-4*) Intl Univs Pr.

Psychoanalysis: The Vital Issues, 2 vols., Vol. 2. Ed. by John E. Gedo & George H. Pollock. LC 83-26429. (Emotions & Behavior Monographs: Nos. 2 & 3). 498p. 1985. 75.00 (*0-8236-5386-2*) Intl Univs Pr.

Psychoanalysis: Toward the Second Century. Arnold Cooper. 248p. (C). 1990. 40.00 (*0-300-04558-1*) Yale U Pr.

Psychoanalysis - A Theory in Crisis. Marshall Edelson. LC 88-1142. xxxvi, 428p. 1990. pap. text 22.00 (*0-226-18429-3*) U Ch Pr.

Psychoanalysis - A Theory in Crisis. Marshall Edelson. (Illus.). 416p. 1998. 39.95 (*0-226-18437-4*) U Ch Pr.

Psychoanalysis & ... Ed. by Richard Feldstein & Henry Sussman. 256p. 1989. 45.00 (*0-415-90152-9*, A3423) Routledge.

Psychoanalysis & American Literary Criticism. Louis Fraiberg. LC 59-11980. 275p. reprint ed. pap. 85.30 (*0-7837-3632-0*, 204349800009) Bks Demand.

Psychoanalysis & American Medicine, 1894-1918: Medicine, Science, & Culture. John C. Burnham. LC 67-31293. (Psychological Issues Monographs: No. 20, Vol. 5, No. 4). 249p. (Orig.). 1967. 37.50 (*0-8236-5100-2*) Intl Univs Pr.

Psychoanalysis & Anthropology. Geza Roheim. 496p. 1968. reprint ed. pap. 24.95 (*0-8236-8234-X*, 25120) Intl Univs Pr.

Psychoanalysis & Beyond. Charles Rycroft. 316p. (C). 1995. pap. text 15.00 (*0-226-73289-4*) U Ch Pr.

Psychoanalysis & Catholicism. Benjamin B. Wolman. LC 95-32605. (Master Works). 1995. 40.00 (*1-56821-715-3*) Aronson.

Psychoanalysis & Cinema: AFI Film Readers. Ed. by E. Ann Kaplan. 256p. 1989. 39.50 (*0-415-90028-X*) Routledge.

Psychoanalysis & Cinema: AFI Film Readers. Ed. by E. Ann Kaplan. 256p. (C). 1989. pap. 20.99 (*0-415-90029-8*) Routledge.

Psychoanalysis & Civilization. Paul Rosenfels. LC 62-18668. 1963. 10.95 (*0-87212-016-3*) Libra.

Psychoanalysis & Cognitive Science: A Multiple Code Theory. Wilma Bucci. LC 96-52825. (Illus.). 362p. 1997. lib. bdg. 44.00 (*1-57230-213-5*, 0213) Guilford Pubns.

Psychoanalysis & Contemporary Thought. Ed. by John D. Sutherland. LC 75-134139. (Essay Index Reprint Ser.). 1977. reprint ed. 18.95 (*0-8369-2373-1*) Ayer.

Psychoanalysis & Culture. Ed. by Lesley Caldwell. (New Formations Twenty-Six Ser.). 192p. (C). 1997. pap. 19.50 (*0-85315-813-4*, Pub. by Lawrence & Wishart) NYU Pr.

Psychoanalysis & Culture: Contemporary States of Mind. Rosalind Minsky. LC 98-23538. (C). 1998. text 50.00 (*0-8135-2585-3*); pap. text 20.00 (*0-8135-2586-1*) Rutgers U Pr.

Psychoanalysis & Culture at the Millennium. Nancy Ginsburg. LC 98-37423. (Illus.). 384p. 1999. 40.00 (*0-300-07190-6*) Yale U Pr.

P

Psychoanalysis & Development: Representations & Narratives. Ed. by Massimo Ammaniti & Daniel N. Stern. LC 94-14618. (Psychoanalytic Crosscurrents Ser.). 208p. (C). 1994. text 55.00 (*0-8147-0616-9*) NYU Pr.

***Psychoanalysis & Developmental Therapy.** Anne Hurry. 256p. 1998. pap. 31.00 (*1-85575-213-1*, Pub. by H Karnac Bks Ltd) Other Pr LLC.

Psychoanalysis & Developmental Therapy. Ed. by Anne Hurry. LC 99-25799. (Monograph Series of the Psychoanalysis Unit of University College London & the Anna Freud Centre : No. 3). 237p. 1999. 38.50 (*0-8236-5150-9*) Intl Univs Pr.

Psychoanalysis & Discourse. Patrick Mahony. Ed. by David Tuckett. (New Library of Psychoanalysis). 250p. (C). 1987. pap. 12.95 (*0-422-61720-2*, Pub. by Tavistock); lib. bdg. 42.50 (*0-422-61030-5*, Pub. by Tavistock) Routldge.

Psychoanalysis & Eating Disorders. Ed. by Jules R. Bemporad & David B. Herzog. 174p. 1989. lib. bdg. 30.00 (*0-89862-388-X*) Guilford Pubns.

Psychoanalysis & Ethics. Ernest Wallwork. LC 91-15276. 392p. 1991. 45.00 (*0-300-04878-5*) Yale U Pr.

Psychoanalysis & Ethics. Ernest Wallwork. 360p. 1994. pap. 20.00 (*0-300-06167-6*) Yale U Pr.

Psychoanalysis & Ethics. Lewis S. Feuer. LC 73-1433. 134p. 1973. reprint ed. lib. bdg. 59.75 (*0-8371-6795-7*, FEPE, Greenwood Pr) Greenwood.

Psychoanalysis & Family Therapy. Helm Stierlin. LC 77-2275. 355p. 1987. reprint ed. 50.00 (*0-87668-257-3*) Aronson.

***Psychoanalysis & Feminism.** Juliet Mitchell. 512p. 2000. pap. 18.00 (*0-465-04608-8*, Pub. by Basic) HarpC.

Psychoanalysis & Gender: An Introductory Reader. Rosalind Minsky. LC 95-16457. (Critical Readers in Theory & Practice Ser.). 336p. (C). 1996. 90.00 (*0-415-09220-5*); pap. 25.99 (*0-415-09221-3*) Routledge.

Psychoanalysis & Group Behavior: A Study of Freudian Group Psychology. Saul Scheidlinger. LC 77-141267. 245p. 1971. reprint ed. lib. bdg. 95.00 (*0-8371-5838-9*, SCPS, Greenwood Pr) Greenwood.

Psychoanalysis & Groups: History & Dialectics. David Rosenfeld. 212p. 1989. reprint ed. pap. text 15.00 (*0-946439-48-6*, Pub. by H Karnac Bks Ltd) Other Pr LLC.

Psychoanalysis & Human Values see Science & Psychoanalysis

Psychoanalysis & Hypnosis. Erika Fromm & Michael Nash. LC 96-43561. (Mental Health Library: Monograph 5). 318p. 1997. 50.00 (*0-8236-5181-9*, BN 05181) Intl Univs Pr.

Psychoanalysis & Infant Research. Joseph Lichtenberg. (Psychoanalytic Inquiry Bk.: Vol. 2). 280p. (C). 1991. pap. 24.95 (*0-88163-002-0*) Analytic Pr.

Psychoanalysis & Infant Research. Joseph Lichtenberg. (Psychoanalytic Inquiry Bk.: Vol. 2). 280p. (C). 1991. reprint ed. pap. 29.95 (*0-88163-145-0*) Analytic Pr.

Psychoanalysis & Its Discontents. John E. Gedo. LC 84-4615. 209p. 1984. lib. bdg. 31.50 (*0-89862-639-0*) Guilford Pubns.

Psychoanalysis & Language. Joseph H. Smith. LC 78-9156. (Psychiatry & the Humanities Ser.: No. 3). 432p. reprint ed. pap. 134.00 (*0-7837-2796-8*, 204318900006) Bks Demand.

Psychoanalysis & Male Homosexuality. Kenneth Lewes. LC 94-49189. 328p. 1995. pap. 50.00 (*1-56821-484-7*) Aronson.

Psychoanalysis & Male Sexuality. Ed. by Hendrik M. Ruitenbeek. 1966. pap. 15.95 (*0-8084-0256-0*) NCUP.

Psychoanalysis & Management. M. Hofmann & M. List. 392p. 1994. 95.95 (*3-7908-0795-8*) Spr-Verlag.

***Psychoanalysis & Mental Handicap.** Johan D. Groef & Evelyn Heinemann. 200p. 1999. 55.00 (*1-85343-432-9*, Pub. by Free Assoc Bks); pap. 25.00 (*1-85343-431-0*, Pub. by Free Assoc Bks) Intl Spec Bk.

Psychoanalysis & Moral Values. Heinz Hartmann. LC 58-9230. (New York Psychoanalytic Institute Freud Anniversary Lecture Ser.). 121p. 1960. 27.50 (*0-8236-5240-8*) Intl Univs Pr.

Psychoanalysis & Motivation. Joseph D. Lichtenberg. (Psychoanalytic Inquiry Bk.: Vol. 10). 440p. 1989. text 49.95 (*0-88163-084-5*) Analytic Pr.

Psychoanalysis & Pedagogy. Ed. by Stephen Appel. LC 98-38307. (Critical Studies in Education & Culture). 208p. 1999. 55.00 (*0-89789-502-9*, Bergin & Garvey) Greenwood.

Psychoanalysis & Philosophy. Ed. by Charles Hanly & Morris Lazerowitz. LC 73-138247. 362p. 1971. 55.00 (*0-8236-5185-1*) Intl Univs Pr.

Psychoanalysis & Politics: A Contribution to the Psychology of Politics & Morals. R. E. Money-Kyrle. LC 72-12143. 182p. 1973. reprint ed. lib. bdg. 75.00 (*0-8371-6714-0*, MOPS, Greenwood Pr) Greenwood.

Psychoanalysis & Psychology: Minding the Gap. Stephen Frosh. 304p. (C). 1989. text 18.00 (*0-8147-2595-3*) NYU Pr.

Psychoanalysis & Psychopathology. Philip S. Holzman. LC 95-15115. 224p. 1995. pap. 45.00 (*1-56821-588-6*) Aronson.

Psychoanalysis & Psychosis. Ed. by Ann-Louise S. Silver. (Illus.). 600p. 1989. 87.50 (*0-8236-5183-5*) Intl Univs Pr.

Psychoanalysis & Psychotherapy: Selected Papers. Frieda Fromm-Reichmann. Ed. by Dexter M. Bullard. LC 59-10746. 368p. 1997. reprint ed. pap. 15.95 (*0-226-26597-8*, P580) U Ch Pr.

Psychoanalysis & Psychotherapy, Selected Papers. Frieda Fromm-Reichmann. Ed. by Dexter M. Bullard. LC 59-10746. 368p. reprint ed. pap. 114.10 (*0-608-09304-1*, 205417800004) Bks Demand.

Psychoanalysis & Religion. Erich Fromm. (Terry Lectures Ser.). 1959. pap. 11.00 (*0-300-00089-8*, Y12) Yale U Pr.

Psychoanalysis & Religion. Ed. by Joseph H. Smith & Susan A. Handelman. LC 89-45492. (Psychiatry & the Humanities Ser.: Vol. 11). 276p. 1990. reprint ed. pap. 85.60 (*0-608-07321-0*, 206754900009) Bks Demand.

Psychoanalysis & Religious Experience. William W. Meissner. LC 83-51296. 254p. 1986. pap. 18.00 (*0-300-03751-1*, Y-599) Yale U Pr.

Psychoanalysis & Religious Mysticism. David C. McMlelland. (C). 1959. pap. 4.00 (*0-87574-104-5*) Pendle Hill.

Psychoanalysis & Severe Emotional Illness Vol. 18, No. 1: Journal of the American Academy of Psychoanalysis. Ed. by Ann-Louise S. Silver & Morton B. Cantor. 208p. 1990. lib. bdg. 30.00 (*0-89862-435-5*) Guilford Pubns.

Psychoanalysis & Social Theory: The Limits of Sociology. Ian Craib. LC 89-20163. 224p. (C). 1989. pap. 15.95 (*0-87023-702-0*); lib. bdg. 35.00 (*0-87023-701-2*) U of Mass Pr.

Psychoanalysis & Society: An Introduction. Scott Mann. 290p. 1994. pap. 27.95 (*0-614-13110-3*, Pub. by New South Wales Univ Pr) Intl Spec Bk.

Psychoanalysis & Spiritual Psychology. Rudolf Steiner. Tr. by May Laird-Brown from GER. 128p. 1990. 24.95 (*0-88010-351-5*) Anthroposophic.

Psychoanalysis & Spiritual Psychology. Rudolf Steiner & Robert J. Sardello. Tr. by May Laird-Brown from GER. 128p. 1990. pap. 12.95 (*0-88010-290-X*) Anthroposophic.

Psychoanalysis & Storytelling. Peter Brooks. (Bucknell Lectures in Literary Theory). 176p. 1994. pap. 19.95 (*0-631-19008-2*) Blackwell Pubs.

***Psychoanalysis & Synchronized Swimming & Other Writings on Art.** Jeanne Randolph. (Illus.). 184p. 1999. reprint ed. pap. 15.00 (*0-7881-6365-5*) DIANE Pub.

Psychoanalysis & the Bible: A Study in Depth of Seven Leaders. Dorothy F. Zeligs. 372p. 1988. 45.95 (*0-89885-389-3*, Kluwer Acad Hman Sci) Kluwer Academic.

Psychoanalysis & the Concept of a Rule: An Essay in the Philosophy of Psychoanalysis. A. Mooij. Tr. by S. Firth & J. H. Scheffer from DUT. 100p. 1991. 31.95 (*0-387-53573-X*) Spr-Verlag.

Psychoanalysis & the Future of Theory. Malcolm Bowie. (Bucknell Lectures in Literary Theory). (Illus.). 192p. 1993. pap. text 18.95 (*0-631-18926-2*) Blackwell Pubs.

Psychoanalysis & the Humanities. Ed. by Laurie Adams & Jacques Szaluta. (Psychoanalytic Practice Monographs: No. 6). (Illus.). 176p. 1996. text 26.95 (*0-87630-743-8*) Brunner-Mazel.

Psychoanalysis & the Nuclear Threat: Clinical & Theoretical Studies. Ed. by Howard B. Levine et al. 304p. 1988. text 34.50 (*0-88163-062-4*) Analytic Pr.

Psychoanalysis & the Occult. Ed. by George Devereux. 432p. 1970. pap. 24.95 (*0-8236-8240-4*, 25180) Intl Univs Pr.

Psychoanalysis & the Philosophy of Science: Collected Papers of Benjamin B. Rubinstein, M. D., Vol. 1. Ed. by Robert R. Holt. LC 96-42969. (Psychological Issues Monographs: Nos. 62 & 63). 1997. 95.00 (*0-8236-5245-9*) Intl Univs Pr.

Psychoanalysis & the Postmodern Impulse: Knowing & Being since Freud's Psychology. Barnaby B. Barratt. LC 92-36941. 272p. (C). 1993. text 47.00 (*0-8018-4547-5*) Johns Hopkins.

Psychoanalysis & the Scene of Reading. Mary Jacobus. (Illus.). 258p. 1999. 39.95 (*0-19-818434-4*) OUP.

Psychoanalysis & the Sciences. Andre Haynal. Tr. by Elizabeth Holder from FRE. LC 92-48742. (C). 1993. 35.00 (*0-520-08299-0*, Pub. by U CA Pr) Cal Prin Full Svc.

Psychoanalysis & the Social Sciences, Vol. 4. Ed. by Werner L. Muensterberger & S. Axelrad. LC 47-12480. 295p. 1955. reprint ed. pap. 91.50 (*0-608-09996-1*, 201045200070) Bks Demand.

Psychoanalysis & the Social Sciences, Vol. 5. Ed. by Werner L. Muensterberger & S. Axelrad. LC 47-12480. 307p. 1955. reprint ed. pap. 95.20 (*0-608-09997-X*, 201045200071) Bks Demand.

Psychoanalysis & the Zest for Living: Reflections & Psychoanalytic Writings in Memory of W. C. M. Scott. C. E. Benierakis et al. Ed. by Michel Grignon. (Illus.). 282p. 1998. pap. text 35.95 (*1-883881-27-7*, 27-7) S Freud RT&PF.

***Psychoanalysis & Woman: A Reader.** Shelley Saguaro. LC 99-56793. 2000. pap. text 22.50 (*0-8147-9771-7*) NYU Pr.

Psychoanalysis & Women: Contemporary Reappraisals. Ed. by Judith L. Alpert. 360p. 1994. reprint ed. pap. 29.95 (*0-88163-191-4*) Analytic Pr.

Psychoanalysis Around the World. Ed. by Reuben Fine. 174p. 1987. 5.95 (*0-86656-507-8*) Haworth Pr.

Psychoanalysis As a Human Science: Beyond Foundationalism. Bhargavi V. Davar & Parameshwar R. Bhat. LC 94-39606. 212p. 1995. text 22.50 (*0-8039-9196-7*) Sage.

Psychoanalysis As a Science. Leopold Bellack. 208p. (C). 1992. 67.00 (*0-205-13904-3*, Longwood Div) Allyn.

Psychoanalysis As Science: The Hixon Lectures on the Scientific Status of Psychoanalysis. Ed. by Eugene Pumpian-Mindlin. LC 70-106692. 174p. 1970. reprint ed. lib. bdg. 59.50 (*0-8371-3365-3*, PUMP, Greenwood Pr) Greenwood.

***Psychoanalysis at Its Limits: Navigating the Postmodern Turn.** Ed. by Anthony Elliott & Charles Spezzano. 320p. 1999. 55.00 (*1-85343-464-7*, Pub. by Free Assoc Bks); pap. 25.00 (*1-85343-465-5*, Pub. by Free Assoc Bks) Intl Spec Bk.

Psychoanalysis at One Hundred: An Issues in Ego Psychology Book. Ed. by Gerd H. Fenchel. (Commemorating the Thirtieth Anniversary of Washington Square Institute for Psychotherapy & Mental Health Ser.). 288p. (Orig.). (C). 1993. pap. text 36.00 (*0-8191-9243-0*); lib. bdg. 59.50 (*0-8191-9242-2*) U Pr of Amer.

Psychoanalysis at the Political Border: Essays in Honor of Rafael Moses. Ed. by Leo Rangell & Rena Moses-Hrushovski. 336p. 1996. 50.00 (*0-8236-5110-X*, BN 05110) Intl Univs Pr.

Psychoanalysis, Behavior Therapy, & the Relational World. Paul L. Wachtel. LC 96-53417. (APA Psychotherapy Integration Book Ser.: Vol. 1). 485p. 1997. 39.95 (*1-55798-409-3*, 4317850) Am Psychol.

Psychoanalysis, Feminism & the Future of Gender. Ed. by Joseph H. Smith & Afaf M. Mahfouz. LC 93-26632. (Psychiatry & the Humanities Ser.: Vol. 14). (C). 1994. text 40.00 (*0-8018-4711-7*) Johns Hopkins.

Psychoanalysis for Our Time: Exploring the Blindness of the Seeing I. Jeffrey B. Rubin. LC 98-58002. 230p. 1998. text 35.00 (*0-8147-7491-1*) NYU Pr.

Psychoanalysis for Teachers & Parents. Anna Freud. Tr. by Barbara Low from GER. 1979. reprint ed. pap. 7.95 (*0-393-00918-1*) Norton.

Psychoanalysis, Historiography, & Feminist Theory: The Search for Critical Method. Katherine Kearns. LC 96-47372. (Literature, Culture, Theory Ser.: Vol. 25). 183p. (C). 1997. text 59.95 (*0-521-58298-9*); pap. text 18.95 (*0-521-58754-9*) Cambridge U Pr.

Psychoanalysis in a New Context. Arnold H. Modell. LC 84-12965. xii, 294p. 1985. 45.00 (*0-8236-5212-2*, 05212) Intl Univs Pr.

***Psychoanalysis in Childhood & Adolescence.** Ed. by K. Von Klitzing et al. (Illus.). viii, 156p. 2000. 51.25 (*3-8055-6993-9*) S Karger.

Psychoanalysis in China: Literary Transformations, 1919-1949. Jingyuan Zhang. (Cornell East Asia Ser.: No. 55). 210p. (Orig.). (C). 1992. pap. 11.90 (*0-939657-55-4*) Cornell East Asia Pgm.

***Psychoanalysis in Colonial India.** Christine Hartnack. 242p. 2001. text 19.95 (*0-19-564542-1*) OUP.

Psychoanalysis in Contexts: Paths Between Theory & Modern Culture. Ed. by Anthony Elliott & Stephen Frosh. LC 94-14823. 288p. (Orig.). (C). 1994. 70.00 (*0-415-09703-7*, B7002) Routledge.

Psychoanalysis in Contexts: Paths Between Theory & Modern Culture. Ed. by Anthony Elliott & Stephen Frosh. LC 94-14823. 288p. (Orig.). (C). 1995. pap. 24.99 (*0-415-09704-5*, B7006) Routledge.

Psychoanalysis in France. Ed. by Serge Lebovici & K. Widlocher. Tr. by J. Diamanti from FRE. LC 79-2483. 620p. 1980. 70.00 (*0-8236-5210-6*) Intl Univs Pr.

Psychoanalysis in Our Time. Stefi Pedersen. LC 70-173220. 1973. 5.95 (*0-672-51411-7*, Bobbs) Macmillan.

Psychoanalysis in the Americas. Ed. by Robert E. Litman. LC 66-24394. 328p. 1966. 50.00 (*0-8236-5200-9*) Intl Univs Pr.

Psychoanalysis in Transition: A Personal View. Merton M. Gill. LC 94-17701. 200p. 1994. 29.95 (*0-88163-112-4*) Analytic Pr.

Psychoanalysis International: A Guide to Psychoanalysis Throughout the World, Vol. 1. Ed. by Peter Kutter. 344p. 1994. text 49.95 (*0-88163-119-1*) Analytic Pr.

Psychoanalysis International: A Guide to Psychoanalysis Throughout the World, Vol. 2. Ed. by Peter Kutter. 390p. 1995. text 49.95 (*0-88163-123-X*) Analytic Pr.

Psychoanalysis International Vols. 1 & 2: A Guide to Psychoanalysis Throughout the World, 2 vols., Set. Ed. by Peter Kutter. 764p. 1995. 75.00 (*0-88163-201-5*) Analytic Pr.

Psychoanalysis, Its Theories & Practical Application. A. A. Brill. LC 78-180559. (Medicine & Society in America Ser.). 346p. 1972. reprint ed. 23.95 (*0-405-03939-5*) Ayer.

Psychoanalysis, Language, & the Body of the Text. Martin J. Gliserman. LC 95-11053. 224p. (C). 1996. 39.95 (*0-8130-1416-6*) U Press Fla.

Psychoanalysis, Literature & War: Papers 1972-1995. Hanna Segal. Ed. & Intro. by John Steiner. LC 96-7559. (New Library of Psychoanalysis Ser.: Vol. 27). 192p. (C). 1997. 75.00 (*0-415-15328-X*); pap. 24.99 (*0-415-15329-8*) Routledge.

Psychoanalysis Never Lets Go. Francois Roustang. Tr. by Ned Lukacher from FRE. LC 82-10042. 176p. (C). 1982. text 30.00 (*0-8018-2674-8*) Johns Hopkins.

Psychoanalysis of a New Freeway. Jorn K. Bramann. LC 91-62671. (Illus.). 110p. (Orig.). 1992. pap. 7.00 (*0-945073-14-3*) Nightsun MD.

Psychoanalysis of Children. Melanie Klein. (Writings of Melanie Klein Ser.: Vol. 2). 352p. (C). 1984. 45.00 (*0-02-918430-4*) Free Pr.

Psychoanalysis of Culture & History. David Spisak. (Illus.). 368p. 1999. pap. 10.00 (*0-9670413-0-9*) D Spisak.

Psychoanalysis of Developmental Arrests: Theory & Treatment. Robert D. Stolorow & Frank M. Lachman. LC 79-53593. 211p. 1980. 32.50 (*0-8236-5146-0*) Intl Univs Pr.

Psychoanalysis of Fire. Gaston Bachelard. Tr. by A. C. Ross. 1964. pap. 15.50 (*0-8070-6461-0*) Beacon Pr.

Psychoanalysis of Organizations: A Psychoanalytic Approach to Behaviour in Groups & Organizations. Robert De Board. 158p. 1978. pap. 14.95 (*0-422-76530-9*, NO. 2731, Pub. by Tavistock) Routldge.

Psychoanalysis of Race. Christopher Lane. LC 97-38840. (Illus.). 1p. 1998. 52.00 (*0-231-10946-6*); pap. 19.50 (*0-231-10947-4*) Col U Pr.

Psychoanalysis of Racism, Revolution & Nationalism. Richard A. Koenigsberg. LC 76-16304. (Monograph). 58p. 1986. 25.00 (*0-915042-02-9*) Lib Soc Sci.

Psychoanalysis of the Sexual Functions of Women. Helene Deutsch. Ed. by P. Roazen. 149p. 1991. pap. text 25.00 (*0-946439-95-8*, Pub. by H Karnac Bks Ltd) Other Pr LLC.

Psychoanalysis of Young Adults. Ed. by Escoll. (Psychoanalytic Inquiry Ser.: Vol. 7, No. 1). 1995. 20.00 (*0-88163-967-2*) Analytic Pr.

Psychoanalysis on the Move: The Work of Joseph Sandler. Peter Fonagy. LC 98-47364. (New Library of Psychoanalysis Ser.). 1999. pap. 29.99 (*0-415-20549-2*) Routledge.

***Psychoanalysis on the Move: The Work of Joseph Sandler.** Peter Fonagy. LC 98-47364. (New Library of Psychoanalysis Ser.). 1999. 90.00 (*0-415-20548-4*) Routledge.

Psychoanalysis, Psychology & Literature: A Bibliography, 2 vols. 2nd ed. Ed. by Norman Kiell. LC 81-2475. 1296p. 1982. 89.50 (*0-8108-1421-8*) Scarecrow.

Psychoanalysis, Psychology & Literature: A Bibliography - Supplement to the Second Edition. Ed. by Norman Kiell. LC 89-70083. 599p. 1990. 71.00 (*0-8108-2178-8*) Scarecrow.

Psychoanalysis, Psychotherapy, & the New England Medical Scene, 1894-1944. Ed. by George E. Gifford. 1978. 40.00 (*0-88202-169-9*) Watson Pub Intl.

Psychoanalysis, Scientific Method & Philosophy. Ed. by Sidney Hook. 370p. 1990. pap. 24.95 (*0-88738-834-5*) Transaction Pubs.

Psychoanalysis Today. Ed. by Sandor Lorand. LC BF0175.L6. (Medical War Bks.). 420p. 1944. reprint ed. pap. 130.20 (*0-608-09998-8*, 201068800070) Bks Demand.

***Psychoanalysis with Children: History, Theory & Practice.** Leonardo S Rodriguez. 280p. 1999. 55.00 (*1-85343-439-6*, Pub. by Free Assoc Bks); pap. 25.00 (*1-85343-440-X*, Pub. by Free Assoc Bks) Intl Spec Bk.

Psychoanalyst & the Artist. Daniel E. Schneider. LC 50-7246. 332p. reprint ed. pap. 94.70 (*0-608-30634-7*, 2010689) Bks Demand.

Psychoanalyst & the Artist. Daniel E. Schneider. LC 50-7246. 332p. 1950. reprint ed. pap. 103.00 (*0-608-09999-6*, 201068900070) Bks Demand.

Psychoanalyst Explores the Alternate Therapies: Out in Inner Space. Stephen A. Appelbaum. LC 93-73987. 552p. 1994. pap. 50.00 (*1-56821-168-6*) Aronson.

Psychoanalyst in Psychiatry. Thomas Freeman. LC 87-10684. 208p. (C). 1988. 40.00 (*0-300-04071-7*) Yale U Pr.

Psychoanalysts Talk. Virginia Hunter. LC 93-40502. 456p. 1994. lib. bdg. 55.00 (*0-89862-373-1*) Guilford Pubns.

Psychoanalytic Anthropology after Freud: Essays on the 50th Anniversary of Freud's Death. Ed. by David H. Spain. 340p. (C). 1992. text 40.00 (*0-9622885-4-3*) Psyche Pr NY.

Psychoanalytic Approaches to Addiction. Ed. by Angelo Smaldino. LC 91-357. (Current Issues in Psychoanalytic Practice Ser.: No. 3). 128p. 1991. text 31.95 (*0-87630-644-X*) Brunner-Mazel.

Psychoanalytic Approaches to Literature & Film. Ed. by Maurice Charney & Joseph Reppen. LC 85-45931. 312p. 1987. 45.00 (*0-8386-3276-9*) Fairleigh Dickinson.

Psychoanalytic Approaches to Supervision. Ed. by Robert C. Lane. LC 90-1971. (Current Issues in Psychoanalytic Practice Ser.: No. 2). 224p. 1990. text 35.95 (*0-87630-603-2*) Brunner-Mazel.

Psychoanalytic Approaches to the Resistant & Difficult Patient. Ed. by Herbert S. Strean. LC 84-25210. (Current Issues in Psychoanalytic Practice Ser.: Vol. 1, No. 4). 140p. 1985. text 4.95 (*0-86656-340-7*) Haworth Pr.

Psychoanalytic Approaches to the Very Troubled Child: Therapeutic Practice Innovations in Residential & Educational Settings. Ed. by Barry L. Childress. LC 89-11010. (Residential Treatment for Children & Youth Ser.: Vol. 6, No. 4). 88p. 1989. text 39.95 (*0-86656-928-6*) Haworth Pr.

Psychoanalytic Approaches with the Hostile & Violent Patient. Ed. by Herbert S. Strean. LC 84-3784. (Current Issues in Psychoanalytic Practice Ser.: Vol. 1, No. 2). 83p. 1984. text 29.95 (*0-86656-319-9*) Haworth Pr.

Psychoanalytic Aspects of Fieldwork. Jennifer C. Hunt. (Qualitative Research Methods Ser.: Vol. 18). 96p. (C). 1989. pap. text 10.50 (*0-8039-3473-4*) Sage.

***Psychoanalytic Case Formulation.** Nancy McWilliams. LC 98-56044. 240p. 1999. 36.00 (*1-57230-462-6*) Guilford Pubns.

Psychoanalytic Case Studies. Ed. by G. Pirooz Sholevar & Jules Glenn. LC 90-36401. xiv, 286p. 1991. 42.50 (*0-8236-4405-7*, BN 04405) Intl Univs Pr.

***Psychoanalytic Century: Freud's Legacy for the Future.** David E. Scharff. LC 00-55076. 2000. write for info. (*1-892746-54-9*) Other Pr LLC.

***Psychoanalytic Clinical Practice.** Richard Chessick. 300p. 2000. 30.00 (*1-85343-479-5*, Pub. by Free Assoc Bks) Intl Spec Bk.

Psychoanalytic Concepts & the Structural Theory. Jacob A. Arlow & Charles Brenner. LC 64-16190. (Journal of the American Psychoanalytic Association Monograph Ser.: No. 3). 216p. (Orig.). 1964. 32.50 (*0-8236-5060-X*) Intl Univs Pr.

Psychoanalytic Core: Essays in Honor of Leo Rangell, M. D. Ed. by Harold P. Blum et al. LC 89-36104. 550p. 1989. 70.00 (*0-8236-4409-X*) Intl Univs Pr.

Psychoanalytic Criticism: A Reader. Ed. by Sue Vice. LC 95-37327. 320p. (C). 1996. text 64.95 (*0-7456-1049-8*, Pub. by Polity Pr); pap. text 24.95 (*0-7456-1050-1*, Pub. by Polity Pr) Blackwell Pubs.

Psychoanalytic Criticism: A Reappraisal. 2nd ed. Elizabeth Wright. LC 98-37098. 240p. (C). 1998. pap. 18.99 (*0-415-92145-7*) Routledge.

P

Psychoanalytic Criticism: A Reappraisal. 2nd rev. ed. Elizabeth Wright. LC 98-37098. 240p. (C). (gr. 13). 1998. 70.00 (*0-415-92144-9*, D5984) Routledge.

Psychoanalytic Criticism: Theory to Practice. Elizabeth Wright. (New Accents Ser.). 224p. (C). 1985. pap. 13.95 (*0-416-32660-9*, NO. 9253) Routledge.

Psychoanalytic Culture: Psychoanalytic Discourse in Western Society. Ian Parker. 304p. 1997. 45.00 (*0-7619-5642-5*); pap. 14.99 (*0-7619-5643-3*) Sage.

Psychoanalytic Diagnosis: Understanding Personality Structure in the Clinical Process. Nancy McWilliams. LC 94-8549. 398p. 1994. lib. bdg. 44.00 (*0-89862-199-2*) Guilford Pubns.

Psychoanalytic Dialogue. Stanley A. Leavy. LC 79-21796. 141p. 1987. pap. 15.00 (*0-300-04037-7*, Y-683) Yale U Pr.

Psychoanalytic Education & Research: The Current Situation & Future Possibilities. Stanley Goodman. LC 76-44638. 424p. 1977. 62.50 (*0-8236-4410-3*) Intl Univs Pr.

Psychoanalytic Explorations in Art. Ernst Kris. (Illus.). 377p. Date not set. 55.00 (*0-8236-4440-5*, 04440) Intl Univs Pr.

Psychoanalytic Explorations in Art. Ernst Kris. 2000. pap. text 29.95 (*0-8236-8220-X*) Intl Univs Pr.

Psychoanalytic Explorations in Music. Ed. by Stuart Feder et al. (Applied Psychoanalysis Monographs: No. 1). 540p. 1990. 77.50 (*0-8236-4407-3*) Intl Univs Pr.

Psychoanalytic Explorations in Music, Second Series. Ed. by Stuart Feder et al. LC 93-575. 324p. 1993. 47.50 (*0-8236-4408-1*) Intl Univs Pr.

Psychoanalytic Explorations of Technique: Discourse on the Theory of Therapy. Ed. by Harold P. Blum. LC 79-22349. 468p. 1980. 70.00 (*0-8236-5053-7*) Intl Univs Pr.

Psychoanalytic Group Dynamics: Basic Reading. Ed. by Saul Scheidlinger. LC 79-20604. 315p. 1980. 47.50 (*0-8236-4445-6*, 04445) Intl Univs Pr.

Psychoanalytic Group Theory & Therapy: Essays in Honor of Saul Scheidlinger, Ph.D. Ed. by Saul Tuttman. LC 90-5324. (American Group Psychotherapy Association Monographs: No. 7). 500p. 1991. 65.00 (*0-8236-4433-2*) Intl Univs Pr.

Psychoanalytic Group Therapy. Karl Konig & Wolf-Volker Lindnerer. LC 93-32905. 216p. 1994. 40.00 (*1-56821-119-8*) Aronson.

Psychoanalytic History of the Jews. Avner Falk. LC 95-2895. 856p. 1996. 95.00 (*0-8386-3660-8*) Fairleigh Dickinson.

Psychoanalytic Knowledge. Eugene B. Brody. 250p. 1990. 35.00 (*0-8236-4447-2*) Intl Univs Pr.

Psychoanalytic Literary Criticism. Maud Ellmann. LC 94-1983. (Critical Readers Ser.). 288p. (C). 1994. text 59.50 (*0-582-08348-6*, 76867, Pub. by Addison-Wesley) Longman.

Psychoanalytic Literary Criticism. Maud Ellmann. LC 94-1983. (Critical Readers Ser.). 288p. (C). 1995. pap. text 28.50 (*0-582-08347-8*, 76866) Longman.

Psychoanalytic Marxism: Groundwork. Eugene V. Wolfenstein. 468p. 1993. pap. 19.95 (*0-89862-590-4*) Guilford Pubns.

Psychoanalytic Mind. Marcia Cavell. 288p. 1996. pap. text 17.00 (*0-674-72096-2*) HUP.

Psychoanalytic Mind: From Freud to Philosophy. Marcia Cavell. LC 93-7325. 288p. 1993. 37.95 (*0-674-72095-4*) HUP.

Psychoanalytic Model of Attention & Learning. Fred Schwartz & Peter H. Schiller. LC 79-105070. (Psychological Issues Monographs: No. 23, Vol. 6, No. 3). 134p. (Orig.). 1970. 27.50 (*0-8236-4450-2*) Intl Univs Pr.

Psychoanalytic Movement: The Cunning of Unreason. Ernest Gellner. LC 96-17329. (Rethinking Theory Ser.). 241p. 1996. pap. 15.95 (*0-8101-1370-8*); text 39.95 (*0-8101-1369-4*) Northwestern U Pr.

***Psychoanalytic Mystic.** Michael Eigen. 220p. 1998. 25.00 (*1-85343-398-5*, Pub. by Free Assoc Bks) Intl Spec Bk.

Psychoanalytic Mystic. Michael Eigen. 220p. 1998. pap. text 29.95 (*1-883881-31-5*, 31-5) S Freud RT&PF.

Psychoanalytic Object Relations Theory & the Study of Religion: On Faith & the Imaging of God. John McDargh. 296p. (C). 1983. pap. text 25.00 (*0-8191-3511-9*); lib. bdg. 53.00 (*0-8191-3510-0*) U Pr of Amer.

Psychoanalytic Object Relations Therapy. Althea J. Horner. LC 91-3132. 304p. 1992. 50.00 (*0-87668-534-3*) Aronson.

Psychoanalytic Object Relations Therapy. Althea J. Horner. 304p. 1995. pap. text 40.00 (*1-56821-637-8*) Aronson.

Psychoanalytic Participation: Action, Interaction & Integration. Kenneth A. Frank. LC 99-24906. (Relational Perspectives Book Ser.: Vol. 16). 312p. 1999. 47.50 (*0-88163-273-2*) Analytic Pr.

Psychoanalytic Perspectives of Movement: An Original Anthology. Ed. by Martha Davis. LC 74-9161. (Body Movement Perspectives in Research Ser.). 164p. 1975. reprint ed. 33.95 (*0-405-06199-4*) Ayer.

Psychoanalytic Perspectives on Art, Vol. 2. Ed. by Mary M. Gedo. 360p. 1987. text 49.95 (*0-88163-058-6*) Analytic Pr.

Psychoanalytic Perspectives on Art, Vol. 3. Ed. by Mary M. Gedo. 331p. 1988. text 49.95 (*0-88163-078-0*) Analytic Pr.

Psychoanalytic Perspectives on Developmental Psychology. Ed. by Joseph M. Masling & Robert F. Bornstein. LC 96-30399. (Empirical Studies of Psychoanalytic Theories: Vol. 6). 351p. 1996. 49.95 (*1-55798-385-2*, 431-6810) Am Psychol.

Psychoanalytic Perspectives on Psychopathology. Ed. by Joseph M. Masling & Robert F. Bornstein. LC 93-26281. (Empirical Studies of Psychoanalytic Theories: Vol. 4). 309p. 1993. text 34.95 (*1-55798-211-2*) Am Psychol.

Psychoanalytic Perspectives on the Rorschach. Paul M. Lerner. LC 97-51640. 512p. 1998. 59.95 (*0-88163-234-1*) Analytic Pr.

Psychoanalytic Perspectives on Women. Ed. by Elaine V. Siegel. LC 91-43418. (Current Issues in Psychoanalytic Practice Ser.: No. 4). 160p. 1992. text 29.95 (*0-87630-655-5*) Brunner-Mazel.

Psychoanalytic Pioneers. Ed. by Franz Alexander et al. LC 94-41115. 1995. pap. 29.95 (*1-56000-815-6*) Transaction Pubs.

Psychoanalytic Politics: Jacques Lacan & Freud's French Revolution. 2nd ed. Sherry Turkle. LC 91-27658. (Critical Perspectives Ser.). 344p. 1992. reprint ed. pap. 18.95 (*0-89862-474-6*) Guilford Pubns.

Psychoanalytic Practice, 2 vols., Set. Helmut Thoma & Horst Kachele. LC 94-72375. 1116p. 1994. pap. text 140.00 (*1-56821-344-1*) Aronson.

Psychoanalytic Practice: Principles, Vol. 1. H. Kachele & Helmut Thoma. 440p. 1987. 87.95 (*0-387-16876-1*) Spr-Verlag.

Psychoanalytic Practice Vol. 1: Principles. Helmut Thoma & Horst Kachele. LC 94-72375. 448p. 1994. pap. 47.50 (*1-56821-346-8*) Aronson.

Psychoanalytic Practice Vol. 2: Clinical Studies. Helmut Thoma & H. Kachele. Tr. by M. Wilson from GER. xxii, 540p. 1991. 93.95 (*0-387-17515-6*) Spr-Verlag.

Psychoanalytic Practice Vol. 2: Clinical Studies. Helmut Thoma & Horst Kachele. LC 94-72375. 568p. 1994. pap. 47.50 (*1-56821-347-6*) Aronson.

Psychoanalytic Process: A Case Illustration. Paul A. Dewald. LC 93-74370. 682p. 1994. pap. 50.00 (*1-56821-194-5*) Aronson.

Psychoanalytic Process: Theory, Clinical Observation & Empirical Research. Joseph Weiss et al. LC 85-30548. 423p. 1986. lib. bdg. 58.00 (*0-89862-670-6*) Guilford Pubns.

Psychoanalytic Psychology: The Development of Freud's Thought. Raymond E. Fancher. LC 73-1273. (Illus.). (C). 1973. pap. text 15.50 (*0-393-09356-5*) Norton.

Psychoanalytic Psychology of Normal Development (1970-1980) Anna Freud. LC 81-11809. (Writings of Anna Freud: Vol. 8). 389p. 1981. 57.50 (*0-8236-6877-0*) Intl Univs Pr.

Psychoanalytic Psychotherapy in a College Context. Ed. by Robert May. LC 87-2836. 214p. 1988. 55.00 (*0-275-92733-4*, C2733, Praeger Pubs) Greenwood.

***Psychoanalytic Psychotherapy in Institutional Settings.** Julia Pestalozzi et al. 256p. 1998. pap. 32.00 (*1-85575-198-4*, Pub. by H Karnac Bks Ltd) Other Pr LLC.

***Psychoanalytic Psychotherapy in the Independent Tradition.** Sue Johnson & Stanley Ruszczynski. 204p. 1999. pap. 30.00 (*1-85575-176-3*, Pub. by H Karnac Bks Ltd) Other Pr LLC.

***Psychoanalytic Psychotherapy in the Kleinian Tradition.** S. Ruszczynsk & Johnson Ruszczynsk. 216p. 1999. pap. 30.00 (*1-85575-175-5*, Pub. by H Karnac Bks Ltd) Other Pr LLC.

***Psychoanalytic Psychotherapy of the Severely Disturbed Adolescent.** Dimitris Anastopoulos. 216p. 1999. pap. 31.50 (*1-85575-214-X*, Pub. by H Karnac Bks Ltd) Other Pr LLC.

Psychoanalytic Quarterly Cumulative Index, 1967-1976, Vols. XXXVI-XLV. LC 36-12164. 1977. 60.00 (*0-911194-03-7*) Psych Qtly.

Psychoanalytic Quarterly Cumulative Index, 1977-1986, Vols. LV-LXIV. LC 36-12164. 1990. 60.00 (*0-911194-04-5*) Psych Qtly.

Psychoanalytic Reader: An Anthology of Essential Papers with Critical Introductions. Ed. by Robert Fliess. 358p. (Orig.). 1969. reprint ed. 52.50 (*0-8236-4480-4*) Intl Univs Pr.

Psychoanalytic Reflections. Laurie W. Raymond & Susan Rosbrow-Reich. 40.00 (*0-87668-513-0*) Aronson.

Psychoanalytic Reflections on Current Issues. Ed. by Judith Lasky et al. 228p. (C). 1991. text 45.00 (*0-8147-7909-3*) NYU Pr.

Psychoanalytic Research: Three Approaches to the Experimental Study of Subliminal Processes. Ed. by Martin Mayman & Herbert J. Schlesinger. LC 73-2848. (Psychological Issues Monographs: 30, Vol. 8, No. 2). 116p. (C). 1975. 27.50 (*0-8236-4490-1*) Intl Univs Pr.

***Psychoanalytic Responses to Children's Literature.** Lucy Rollin & Mark I. West. LC 98-54256. 190p. 1999. lib. bdg. 34.50 (*0-7864-0674-7*) McFarland & Co.

Psychoanalytic Situation. Leo Stone. LC 61-18794. (New York Psychoanalytic Institute Freud Anniversary Lecture Ser.). 160p. 1961. 30.00 (*0-8236-4500-2*) Intl Univs Pr.

Psychoanalytic Sociology, 2 vols., set. Ed. by Jeffrey Prager & Michael Rustin. (Schools of Thought in Sociology Ser.: Vol. 10). (Illus.). 800p. 1993. 310.00 (*1-85278-336-2*) E Elgar.

Psychoanalytic Studies of Biography. Ed. by George Moraitis & George H. Pollock. LC 86-27750. (Emotions & Behavior Monographs: No. 4). 1987. 85.00 (*0-8236-4515-0*, BN#04515) Intl Univs Pr.

Psychoanalytic Studies of Religion: A Critical Assessment & Annotated Bibliography, 39. LC 96-18524. (Bibliographies & Indexes in Religious Studies: Vol. 39). 208p. 1996. lib. bdg. 69.50 (*0-313-27362-6*, Greenwood Pr) Greenwood.

Psychoanalytic Studies of the Personality. W. Ronald Fairbairn. LC 94-8493. 336p. (C). 1994. pap. 25.99 (*0-415-10737-7*, B4304) Routledge.

Psychoanalytic Studies of the Personality. W. Ronald Fairbairn. 1974. reprint ed. 37.50 (*0-7100-1361-2*, Routledge Thoemms) Routledge.

Psychoanalytic Studies on Goethe. Ed. by Silver. (Psychoanalytic Inquiry Ser.: Vol. 4, No. 4). 1995. 20.00 (*0-88163-976-1*) Analytic Pr.

Psychoanalytic Study of Literature. Ed. by Joseph Reppen & Maurice Charney. LC 84-16791. 296p. reprint ed. pap. 91.80 (*0-8357-2737-8*, 203984600013) Bks Demand.

Psychoanalytic Study of Society, 6 Vols., 1. Ed. by Werner L. Muensterberger et al. LC BF0175.P75. 384p. 1960. reprint ed. pap. 119.10 (*0-608-08326-7*, 201045100070) Bks Demand.

Psychoanalytic Study of Society, 6 Vols., 2. Ed. by Werner L. Muensterberger et al. LC BF0175.P75. 317p. 1960. reprint ed. pap. 98.30 (*0-608-08327-5*, 201045100071) Bks Demand.

Psychoanalytic Study of Society, 6 Vols., 3. Ed. by Werner L. Muensterberger et al. LC BF0175.P75. 408p. reprint ed. pap. 126.50 (*0-608-08328-3*, 201045100072) Bks Demand.

Psychoanalytic Study of Society, 6 Vols., 5. Ed. by Werner L. Muensterberger et al. LC BF0175.P75. 258p. 1960. reprint ed. pap. 80.00 (*0-608-08330-5*, 201045100074) Bks Demand.

Psychoanalytic Study of Society, 6 Vols., 6. Ed. by Werner L. Muensterberger et al. LC BF0175.P75. 320p. reprint ed. pap. 99.20 (*0-608-08331-3*, 201045100075) Bks Demand.

Psychoanalytic Study of Society, Vol. 4. Ed. by Werner L. Muensterberger et al. LC BF0175.P75. 350p. reprint ed. pap. 108.50 (*0-608-08329-1*, 201045100073) Bks Demand.

Psychoanalytic Study of Society, Vol. 8. Ed. by Werner L. Muensterberger et al. LC 61-486. (Illus.). 1979. 50.00 (*0-300-02257-3*) Yale U Pr.

Psychoanalytic Study of Society, Vol. 10. Ed. by Werner L. Muensterberger et al. (Muensterberger Ser.). 400p. 1983. text 39.95 (*0-88163-004-7*) Analytic Pr.

Psychoanalytic Study of Society: Essays in Honor of A. Irving Hallowell, Vol. 16. Ed. by L. Bryce Boyer & Ruth M. Boyer. 344p. 1991. 36.00 (*0-88163-140-X*) Analytic Pr.

Psychoanalytic Study of Society: Essays in Honor of George A. De Vos, Vol. 19. Ed. by L. Bryce Boyer et al. 392p. 1994. text 45.00 (*0-88163-183-3*) Analytic Pr.

Psychoanalytic Study of Society: Essays in Honor of George Devereux, Vol. 12. Ed. by L. Bryce Boyer & Simon A. Grolnick. (Muensterberger Ser.). 248p. (C). 1987. text 29.95 (*0-88163-069-1*) Analytic Pr.

Psychoanalytic Study of Society: Essays in Honor of Melford E. Spiro, Vol. 15. Ed. by L. Bryce Boyer & Simon A. Grolnick. (Muensterberger Ser.). 416p. 1990. text 39.95 (*0-88163-115-9*) Analytic Pr.

Psychoanalytic Study of Society: Essays in Honor of Paul Parin, Vol. 14. Ed. by L. Bryce Boyer & Simon A. Grolnick. (Muensterberger Ser.). 344p. 1989. 36.00 (*0-88163-085-3*) Analytic Pr.

Psychoanalytic Study of Society: Essays in Honor of Werner Muensterberger, Vol. 11. Ed. by L. Bryce Boyer & Simon A. Grolnick. (Muensterberger Ser.). 264p. (C). 1985. text 29.95 (*0-88163-032-2*) Analytic Pr.

Psychoanalytic Study of Society: Essays in Honor of Westo LaBarre, Vol. 13. Ed. by L. Bryce Boyer & Simon A. Grolnick. (Muensterberger Ser.). 200p. 1988. text 29.95 (*0-88163-079-9*) Analytic Pr.

Psychoanalytic Study of Society Vol. 17: Essays in Honor of George D. & Louise A. Spindler. Ed. by L. Bryce Boyer & Ruth Boyer. 384p. 1992. text 36.00 (*0-88163-151-5*) Analytic Pr.

Psychoanalytic Study of Society Vol. 18: Essays in Honor of Alan Dundes. L. Bryce Boyer et al. 522p. 1993. 45.00 (*0-88163-161-2*) Analytic Pr.

Psychoanalytic Study of the Child. Albert J. Solnit. 1995. 60.00 (*0-300-06471-3*) Yale U Pr.

***Psychoanalytic Study of the Child.** Albert J. Solnit. 392p. 1999. 60.00 (*0-300-08004-2*) Yale U Pr.

***Psychoanalytic Study of the Child, No. 55.** Ed. by Albert J. Solnit et al. 400p. 2000. 60.00 (*0-300-08371-8*) Yale U Pr.

Psychoanalytic Study of the Child, Vol. 1. Ed. by Ruth S. Eissler et al. LC 45-11304. 1945. text 65.00 (*0-8236-4520-7*) Intl Univs Pr.

Psychoanalytic Study of the Child, Vol. 2. Ed. by Ruth S. Eissler et al. LC 45-11304. 1946. text 65.00 (*0-8236-4540-1*) Intl Univs Pr.

Psychoanalytic Study of the Child, Vol. 5. Ed. by Ruth S. Eissler et al. LC 45-11304. 1949. text 65.00 (*0-8236-4580-0*) Intl Univs Pr.

Psychoanalytic Study of the Child, Vol. 6. Ed. by Ruth S. Eissler et al. LC 45-11304. 1950. text 65.00 (*0-8236-4600-9*) Intl Univs Pr.

Psychoanalytic Study of the Child, Vol. 7. Ed. by Ruth S. Eissler et al. LC 45-11304. 1951. text 65.00 (*0-8236-4620-3*) Intl Univs Pr.

Psychoanalytic Study of the Child, Vol. 8. Ed. by Ruth S. Eissler et al. LC 45-11304. 1952. text 65.00 (*0-8236-4640-8*) Intl Univs Pr.

Psychoanalytic Study of the Child, Vol. 10. Ed. by Ruth S. Eissler et al. LC 45-11304. 1954. text 65.00 (*0-8236-4700-5*) Intl Univs Pr.

Psychoanalytic Study of the Child, Vol. 11. Ed. by Ruth S. Eissler et al. LC 45-11304. 1995. text 65.00 (*0-8236-4720-X*) Intl Univs Pr.

Psychoanalytic Study of the Child, Vol. 12. Ed. by Ruth S. Eissler et al. LC 45-11304. 1956. text 65.00 (*0-8236-4740-4*) Intl Univs Pr.

Psychoanalytic Study of the Child, Vol. 13. Ed. by Ruth S. Eissler et al. LC 45-11304. 1957. text 65.00 (*0-8236-4760-9*) Intl Univs Pr.

Psychoanalytic Study of the Child, Vol. 14. Ed. by Ruth S. Eissler et al. LC 45-11304. 1958. text 65.00 (*0-8236-4780-3*) Intl Univs Pr.

Psychoanalytic Study of the Child, Vol. 15. Ed. by Ruth S. Eissler et al. LC 45-11304. 1959. text 65.00 (*0-8236-4800-1*) Intl Univs Pr.

Psychoanalytic Study of the Child, Vol. 16. Ed. by Ruth S. Eissler et al. LC 45-11304. 1960. text 65.00 (*0-8236-4820-6*) Intl Univs Pr.

Psychoanalytic Study of the Child, Vol. 17. Ed. by Ruth S. Eissler et al. LC 45-11304. 1961. text 65.00 (*0-8236-4840-0*) Intl Univs Pr.

Psychoanalytic Study of the Child, Vol. 18. Ed. by Ruth S. Eissler et al. LC 45-11304. 1962. text 65.00 (*0-8236-4860-5*) Intl Univs Pr.

Psychoanalytic Study of the Child, Vol. 19. Ed. by Ruth S. Eissler et al. LC 45-11304. 1963. text 65.00 (*0-8236-4880-X*) Intl Univs Pr.

Psychoanalytic Study of the Child, Vol. 21. Ed. by Ruth S. Eissler et al. LC 45-11304. 1965. text 65.00 (*0-8236-4920-2*) Intl Univs Pr.

Psychoanalytic Study of the Child, Vol. 22. Ed. by Ruth S. Eissler et al. LC 45-11304. 1967. text 65.00 (*0-8236-4940-7*) Intl Univs Pr.

Psychoanalytic Study of the Child, Vol. 23. Ed. by Ruth S. Eissler et al. LC 45-11304. 1968. text 65.00 (*0-8236-4960-1*) Intl Univs Pr.

Psychoanalytic Study of the Child, Vol. 24. Ed. by Ruth S. Eissler et al. LC 45-11304. 1969. text 65.00 (*0-8236-4961-X*) Intl Univs Pr.

Psychoanalytic Study of the Child, Vol. 25. Ed. by Ruth S. Eissler et al. LC 45-11304. 1970. text 65.00 (*0-8236-4962-8*) Intl Univs Pr.

Psychoanalytic Study of the Child, Vol. 27. Ed. by Ruth S. Eissler. 1974. 55.00 (*0-300-01780-4*) Yale U Pr.

Psychoanalytic Study of the Child, Vol. 28. Ed. by Ruth S. Eissler et al. Vol. 28. 1973. 60.00 (*0-300-01703-0*) Yale U Pr.

Psychoanalytic Study of the Child, Vol. 29. Ed. by Ruth S. Eissler et al. LC 45-11304. Vol. 29. 500p. 1974. 60.00 (*0-300-01796-0*) Yale U Pr.

Psychoanalytic Study of the Child, Vol. 30. Ed. by Ruth S. Eissler et al. LC 75-1934. Vol. 30. 800p. 1975. 60.00 (*0-300-01916-5*) Yale U Pr.

Psychoanalytic Study of the Child, Vol. 31. Ed. by Anna Freud et al. LC 45-11304. Vol. 31. 1976. 60.00 (*0-300-02025-2*) Yale U Pr.

Psychoanalytic Study of the Child, Vol. 32. Ed. by Ruth S. Eissler et al. LC 45-11304. Vol. 32. 1977. 60.00 (*0-300-02159-3*) Yale U Pr.

Psychoanalytic Study of the Child, Vol. 33. Ed. by Albert J. Solnit et al. LC 45-11304. 1978. 60.00 (*0-300-02297-2*) Yale U Pr.

Psychoanalytic Study of the Child, Vol. 34. Albert J. Solnit. Vol. 34. 1979. 60.00 (*0-300-02419-3*) Yale U Pr.

Psychoanalytic Study of the Child, Vol. 35. Ed. by Albert J. Solnit et al. LC 45-11304. Vol. 35. 600p. 1980. 60.00 (*0-300-02607-2*) Yale U Pr.

Psychoanalytic Study of the Child, Vol. 36. Ed. by Albert J. Solnit et al. LC 45-11304. Vol. 36. 468p. 1981. 60.00 (*0-300-02762-1*) Yale U Pr.

Psychoanalytic Study of the Child, Vol. 37. Albert J. Solnit et al. LC 45-11304. Vol. 37. 562p. 1982. 60.00 (*0-300-02909-8*) Yale U Pr.

Psychoanalytic Study of the Child, Vol. 38. Ed. by Albert J. Solnit et al. LC 45-11304. Vol. 38. 800p. 1983. 60.00 (*0-300-03127-0*) Yale U Pr.

Psychoanalytic Study of the Child, Vol. 39. Ruth S. Eissler & Peter B. Neubauer. Ed. by Albert J. Solnit et al. LC 45-11304. (Psychoanalytic Study of the Child Ser.: Vol. 39). 1984. 60.00 (*0-300-03260-9*) Yale U Pr.

Psychoanalytic Study of the Child, Vol. 40. Ed. by Albert J. Solnit et al. LC 45-11304. Vol. 40. 608p. 1986. 60.00 (*0-300-03503-9*) Yale U Pr.

Psychoanalytic Study of the Child, Vol. 41. Albert J. Solnit. LC 45-11304. Vol. 41. 667p. 1986. 60.00 (*0-300-03767-8*) Yale U Pr.

Psychoanalytic Study of the Child, Vol. 42. Ed. by Peter B. Neubauer & Albert J. Solnit. LC 45-11304. Vol. 42. 609p. 1987. 60.00 (*0-300-04057-1*) Yale U Pr.

Psychoanalytic Study of the Child, Vol. 43. Albert J. Solnit. Vol. 43. (C). 1988. 60.00 (*0-300-04341-4*) Yale U Pr.

Psychoanalytic Study of the Child, Vol. 44. Albert J. Solnit. LC 45-11304. Vol. 44. (C). 1989. 60.00 (*0-300-04594-8*) Yale U Pr.

Psychoanalytic Study of the Child, Vol. 45. Albert J. Solnit et al. Vol. 45. 544p. (C). 1990. 60.00 (*0-300-04908-0*) Yale U Pr.

Psychoanalytic Study of the Child, Vol. 47. Ed. by Albert J. Solnit et al. LC 45-11304. Vol. 47. 432p. (C). 1992. 60.00 (*0-300-05249-9*) Yale U Pr.

Psychoanalytic Study of the Child, Vol. 48. Ed. by Albert J. Solnit et al. Vol. 48. 416p. 1993. 60.00 (*0-300-05780-6*) Yale U Pr.

Psychoanalytic Study of the Child, Vols. 3-4. Ed. by Ruth S. Eissler et al. LC 45-11304. 1947. text 65.00 (*0-8236-4560-6*) Intl Univs Pr.

Psychoanalytic Study of the Child: Abstracts & Index, Vols. 1-25. Ed. by Ruth S. Eissler. LC 74-79973. 280p. 1975. 60.00 (*0-300-01778-2*) Yale U Pr.

Psychoanalytic Study of the Child Vol. 51: Anna Freud Anniversary Issue. Ed. by Albert J. Solnit et al. 464p. 1996. 60.00 (*0-300-06579-5*) Yale U Pr.

Psychoanalytic Study of the Child, 53. Ed. by Albert J. Solnit et al. 464p. 1998. 60.00 (*0-300-07556-1*) Yale U Pr.

Psychoanalytic Study of the Child, 52, Vol. 52. Ed. by Albert J. Solnit et al. (Illus.). 464p. 1997. 60.00 (*0-300-07136-1*) Yale U Pr.

Psychoanalytic Study of the Child, 49. Ed. by Albert J. Solnit et al. 544p. 1994. 60.00 (*0-300-06131-5*) Yale U Pr.

P

Psychoanalytic Study of the Myth of Dionysus & Apollo: Two Variants of the Son-Mother Relationship. Helene Deutsch. LC 70-85198. (New York Psychoanalytic Institute Freud Anniversary Lecture Ser.). 101p. 1969. 27.50 (*0-8236-4975-X*) Intl Univs Pr.

Psychoanalytic Supervision. Ed. by Levy & Kindler. (Psychoanalytic Inquiry Ser.: Vol. 15, No. 2). 1995. 20.00 (*0-88163-995-8*) Analytic Pr.

Psychoanalytic Supervision. Joan Fleming & Therese Benedek. Ed. by Chicago Institute for Psychanalysis Staff. LC 83-22763. (Classics in Psychoanalysis Monographs: No. 1). xii, 252p. (C). 1983. reprint ed. 37.50 (*0-8236-5041-3*) Intl Univs Pr.

Psychoanalytic Technique. Ed. by Herbert S. Strean. LC 87-30436. (Current Issues in Psychoanalytic Practice Ser.: Vol. 4, Nos. 3-4). (Illus.). 139p. 1988. text 39.95 (*0-86656-689-9*) Haworth Pr.

Psychoanalytic Technique & Psychic Conflict. Charles Brenner. LC 76-15047. 126p. (Orig.). 1976. 32.50 (*0-8236-5054-5*) Intl Univs Pr.

***Psychoanalytic Technique & the Creation of Analytic Patients.** A. Rothstein. 184p. 1998. pap. 25.50 (*1-85575-205-0*, Pub. by H Karnac Bks Ltd) Other Pr LLC.

Psychoanalytic Technique & the Creation of Analytic Patients. Arnold Rothstein. LC 95-46202. 137p. 1995. 27.50 (*0-8236-5057-X*, RC506) Intl Univs Pr.

Psychoanalytic Technique & the Creation of Analytic Patients. 2nd ed. Arnold Rothstein. LC 97-42836. 1997. 29.95 (*0-8236-5058-8*) Intl Univs Pr.

Psychoanalytic Terms & Concepts. Ed. by Burness E. Moore & Bernard D. Fine. LC 89-36223. 225p. (C). 1990. pap. 18.00 (*0-300-04701-0*) Yale U Pr.

Psychoanalytic Theories of Affect. Ruth Stein. LC 91-2762. 240p. 1991. 67.95 (*0-275-93984-7*, C3984, Praeger Pubs) Greenwood.

***Psychoanalytic Theories of Affect.** Ruth Stein. 240p. 1999. pap. 32.00 (*1-85575-231-X*, Pub. by H Karnac Bks Ltd) Other Pr LLC.

Psychoanalytic Theories of Development: An Integration. Phyllis Tyson & Robert L. Tyson. 414p. (C). 1993. reprint ed. pap. 20.00 (*0-300-05510-2*) Yale U Pr.

Psychoanalytic Theory: An Introduction. Anthony Elliott. 240p. 1994. pap. 27.95 (*0-631-18847-9*) Blackwell Pubs.

Psychoanalytic Theory & Clinical Relevance: What Makes a Theory Consequential for Practice? Louis S. Berger. 213p. 1985. 29.95 (*0-88163-042-X*) Analytic Pr.

Psychoanalytic Theory & the Rorschach. Paul M. Lerner. 1996. pap. 29.95 (*0-88163-255-4*) Analytic Pr.

Psychoanalytic Theory & the Rorschach. 2nd ed. Paul M. Lerner. 312p. 1990. text 39.95 (*0-88163-122-1*) Analytic Pr.

Psychoanalytic Theory of Art: A Philosophy of Art on Developmental Principles. Richard Kuhns. LC 82-23499. 192p. 1983. pap. text 20.50 (*0-231-05621-4*) Col U Pr.

Psychoanalytic Theory of Greek Tragedy. C. Fred Alford. LC 92-13469. 240p. (C). 1992. 37.50 (*0-300-05708-3*) Yale U Pr.

Psychoanalytic Theory of Neurosis. Otto Fenichel. 1945. 39.95 (*0-393-01019-8*) Norton.

Psychoanalytic Theory of Neurosis. 50th annot. ed. Otto Fenichel. 730p. 1995. 42.50 (*0-393-03890-4*) Norton.

Psychoanalytic Theory, Therapy & the Self. Harry Guntrip. LC 79-135563. 224p. 1973. pap. 18.50 (*0-465-09511-9*, Pub. by Basic) HarpC.

Psychoanalytic Therapy & Behavior Therapy: Is Integration Possible? Ed. by Hal Arkowitz & Stanley Messer. 370p. 1984. 62.50 (*0-306-41578-X*, Plenum Trade) Perseus Pubng.

Psychoanalytic Therapy & the Gay Man. Jack Drescher. LC 98-36101. 384p. 1998. 55.00 (*0-88163-208-2*) Analytic Pr.

Psychoanalytic Therapy as Health Care: Effectiveness & Economics in the 21st Century. Ed. by Harriette Kaley et al. LC 98-47699. 312p. 1999. 49.95 (*0-88163-202-3*) Analytic Pr.

Psychoanalytic Therapy in the Hospital Setting. Paul Janssen. Tr. by Dinah Cannell. LC 93-20497. (ENG & GER.). 224p. (C). 1994. text 74.95 (*0-415-07295-6*) Routledge.

***Psychoanalytic Treatment.** Robert Stolorow. 2000. 29.95 (*0-88163-330-5*) Analytic Pr.

Psychoanalytic Treatment: An Intersubjective Approach. Robert Stolorow et al. (Psychoanalytic Inquiry Book Ser.: Vol. 8). 200p. (C). 1987. text 29.95 (*0-88163-061-6*) Analytic Pr.

Psychoanalytic Understanding of the Dream. Paul Sloane. LC 79-50290. 288p. 1990. reprint ed. 40.00 (*0-87668-362-6*) Aronson.

Psychoanalytic Understanding of Violence & Suicide. Ed. by Rosine J. Perelberg. LC 98-25639. (New Library of Psychoanalysis Ser.). 200p. (C). (gr. 13). 1999. 95.00 (*0-415-19931-X*, D6659); pap. 29.99 (*0-415-19932-8*, D6663) Routledge.

Psychoanalytic Versions of the Human Condition: Philosophies of Life & Their Impact on Practice. Ed. by Paul Marcus & Alan Rosenberg. LC 98-6852. 424p. 1998. text 65.00 (*0-8147-5501-1*); pap. text 25.00 (*0-8147-5608-5*) NYU Pr.

Psychoanalytic Vocation: Rank, Winnicott, & the Legacy of Freud. Peter L. Rudnytsky. 224p. (C). 1991. 40.00 (*0-300-05067-4*) Yale U Pr.

Psychoanalytic Years. C. G. Jung. Tr. by R. F. C. Hull & Leopold Stein. LC 73-18935. (Princeton/Bollingen Paperbacks Ser.: No. 314). 185p. reprint ed. pap. 57.40 (*0-8357-4285-7*, 203708400007) Bks Demand.

Psychoanalytical Approaches to Sexual Problems. Ed. by Herbert S. Strean. LC 84-12961. (Current Issues in Psychoanalytic Practice Ser.: Vol. 1, No. 3). 100p. 1984. text 29.95 (*0-86656-341-5*) Haworth Pr.

Psychoanalytical Interpretations of All Aspects of Love in Persian Literature. Djavad Zamanzadeh. LC 94-75837. (PER.). 670p. 1994. 35.00 (*0-936347-52-X*) IBEX.

Psychoanalytical Method & the Doctrine of Freud, 2 Vols. Roland Dalbiez. Tr. by T. F. Lindsay from FRE. (Select Bibliographies Reprint Ser.). 1977. reprint ed. 52.95 (*0-8369-6715-1*) Ayer.

***Psychoanalytical Study of Lives over Time: Clinical & Research Perspectives on Children Who Return to Treatment in Adulthood.** Ed. by Jonathan Cohen. 320p. (C). 1999. pap. text 49.95 (*0-12-178410-X*) Acad Pr.

Psychoanalyzing: On the Order of the Unconscious & the Practice of the Letter. Serge Leclaire. Tr. by Peggy Kamauf from ENG. LC 97-21856. (Meridian, Crossing Aesthetics Ser.). 125p. 1998. 32.50 (*0-8047-2910-7*) Stanford U Pr.

Psychoanalyzing: On the Order of the Unconscious & the Practice of the Letter. Serge Leclaire. Tr. by Peggy Kamuf from ENG. LC 97-21856. (Meridian, Crossing Aesthetics Ser.). 125p. 1998. pap. 12.95 (*0-8047-2911-5*) Stanford U Pr.

Psychoanalyzing Psychoanalysis: Freud & the Hidden Fault of the Father. Marie Balmary. LC 81-18568. 208p. reprint ed. pap. 64.50 (*0-7837-2194-3*, 204253200004) Bks Demand.

Psychoanalyzing the Twelve Zodiacal Types. Manly P. Hall. pap. 4.95 (*0-89314-813-X*) Philos Res.

Psychobabbl Biobank. 4th ed. Wade. (C). 1997. 13.00 (*0-673-97467-7*) Addison-Wesley.

Psychobabble: The Failure of Modern Psychology - & the Biblical Alternative. Richard Ganz. LC 93-15883. 144p. 1993. pap. 12.99 (*0-89107-734-0*) Crossway Bks.

Psychobiographic Approach to Psychotherapy: A Study of the Power Structure of Psychotherapy. Herzel Yerushalmi. LC 97-21398. 1998. 45.00 (*1-887841-12-1*, Psychosocial) Intl Univs Pr.

Psychobiography & Life Narratives. Richard L. Ochberg. Ed. by Dan P. McAdams. LC 88-21922. 325p. 1988. pap. text 27.95 (*0-8223-0892-4*) Duke.

Psychobiological Approaches to Social Behavior. Ed. by P. Herbert Leiderman & David Shapiro. xv, 203p. 1964. 27.50 (*0-8047-0202-0*) Stanford U Pr.

Psychobiological Approaches to Social Behavior. fac. ed. Ed. by P. Herbert Leiderman & David Shapiro. LC 64-170178. (Illus.). 221p. 1964. pap. 30.00 (*0-7837-7913-5*, 204766900008) Bks Demand.

Psychobiological Aspects of Allergic Disorders. Ed. by Stuart H. Young et al. LC 85-19390. 399p. 1985. 75.00 (*0-275-91301-5*, C1301, Praeger Pubs) Greenwood.

Psychobiological Foundations of Psychiatric Care. Norman L. Keltner et al. LC 97-262. (Illus.). 368p. (C). (gr. 13). 1997. pap. text 36.95 (*0-8151-5658-8*, 28786) Mosby Inc.

Psychobiology. Sdorow. 1999. 17.50 (*0-697-10912-7*) McGraw.

Psychobiology: Psychophysiological & Psychohumoral Processes Combined. Ed. by P. Netter. (Journal: Neuropsychobiology: Vol. 28, No. 1-2, 1993). (Illus.). 112p. 1993. pap. 117.50 (*3-8055-5853-8*) S Karger.

Psychobiology: The Neuron & Behavior. Katherine B. Hoyenga & Kermit T. Hoyenga. LC 86-26837. 513p. (C). 1988. text 83.95 (*0-534-06978-9*) Brooks-Cole.

Psychobiology & Treatment of Anorexia Nervosa & Bulimia Nervosa. Ed. by Katherine A. Halmi. LC 92-17984. (American Psychopathological Association Ser.). 356p. 1992. text 49.50 (*0-88048-506-X*, 8506) Am Psychiatric.

Psychobiology of Affective Development. Ed. by Nathan A. Fox & Richard J. Davidson. 424p. (C). 1984. text 99.95 (*0-89859-269-0*) L Erlbaum Assocs.

Psychobiology of Affective Disorders. Ed. by J. Mendels. (Illus.). viii, 220p. 1981. pap. 34.00 (*3-8055-1400-X*) S Karger.

Psychobiology of Aggression: Engines, Measurement, Control. Ed. by Marc Hillbrand & Nathaniel J. Pallone. LC 94-45057. (Journal of Offender Rehabilitation: Vol. 21, No. 3-4). (Illus.). 260p. 1994. lib. bdg. 49.95 (*1-56024-715-0*) Haworth Pr.

Psychobiology of Aggression & Violence. fac. ed. Luigi Valzelli. LC 78-55807. (Illus.). 262p. pap. 81.30 (*0-7837-7246-7*, 204705900005) Bks Demand.

Psychobiology of Alcohol. Blum. (Substance & Alcohol Actions & Misuse). 1983. pap. 46.00 (*0-08-030949-6*, Pergamon Pr) Elsevier.

Psychobiology of Behavioral Development. Ronald Gandelman. (Illus.). 352p. (C). 1992. text 54.95 (*0-19-503941-6*) OUP.

Psychobiology of Bulimia. Ed. by James I. Hudson & Harrison G. Pope, Jr. LC 87-14431. (Progress in Psychiatry Ser.). (Illus.). 267p. 1987. reprint ed. pap. 82.80 (*0-608-06656-7*, 206685300009) Bks Demand.

Psychobiology of Bulimia Nervosa. Ed. by K. M. Pirke et al. (Illus.). 120p. 1988. pap. 53.00 (*0-387-18670-0*) Spr-Verlag.

Psychobiology of Cancer: Automatization & Boredom in Health & Disease. Augustin De la Pena. 240p. 1983. 49.95 (*0-275-90968-9*, C0968, Praeger Pubs) Greenwood.

Psychobiology of Consciousness. Ed. by Richard J. Davidson & Julian M. Davidson. LC 79-316. 508p. 1980. 80.00 (*0-306-40138-X*, Plenum Trade) Perseus Pubng.

Psychobiology of Down Syndrome. Ed. by Lynn Nadel. (Issues in the Biology of Language & Cognition Ser.). 496p. 1988. 44.00 (*0-262-14043-8*, Bradford Bks) MIT Pr.

Psychobiology of Emotions. J. G. Thompson. LC 88-5937. (Emotions, Personality, & Psychotherapy Ser.). (Illus.). 418p. (C). 1988. 59.50 (*0-306-42843-1*, Plenum Trade) Perseus Pubng.

Psychobiology of Human Motivation. Hugh Wagner. LC 98-41034. (Psychology Focus Ser.). 1999. write for info. (*0-415-19274-9*); pap. write for info. (*0-415-19275-7*) Routledge.

Psychobiology of Language. Ed. by Michael Studdert-Kennedy & David N. Caplan. (Series in Neurophyschology & Neurolinguistics). (Illus.). 272p. 1983. 30.50 (*0-262-19217-9*) MIT Pr.

Psychobiology of Parkinson's Disease. Keith F. Tipton. 1993. 64.95 (*3-211-82483-9*) Spr-Verlag.

Psychobiology of Parkinson's Disease. Keith F. Tipton & M. B. Youndim. LC 93-44011. (Journal of Neural Transmission: Suppl. 40). 130p. 1993. 64.95 (*0-387-82483-9*) Spr-Verlag.

Psychobiology of Post-Traumatic Stress Disorder. LC 97-21354. (Annual Academy of Sciences Ser.: Vol. 821). 1997. pap. 110.00 (*1-57331-079-4*) NY Acad Sci.

Psychobiology of Post-Traumatic Stress Disorder, Vol. 821. Ed. by Rachel Yehuda & Alexander C. McFarlane. LC 97-21354. 550p. 1997. 110.00 (*1-57331-078-6*) NY Acad Sci.

Psychobiology of Stress: Proceedings of the NATO Advanced Research Workshop Held in Sorrento, Italy, August 28 - September 2, 1988. Ed. by Stefan Puglisi-Allegra. (C). 1990. text 195.50 (*0-7923-0682-1*) Kluwer Academic.

Psychobiology of the Hand. Ed. by Kevin Connolly. (Clinics in Developmental Medicine Ser.: No. 147). (Illus.). 250p. (C). 1999. text 69.95 (*1-898683-14-X*, Pub. by Mc Keith Pr) Cambridge U Pr.

Psychobiology of the Human Newborn. Ed. by Peter Stratton. LC 81-14756. (Wiley Series in Developmental Psychology & Its Applications). (Illus.). 470p. reprint ed. pap. 145.70 (*0-8357-4324-1*, 203712300007) Bks Demand.

Psychobiology Prin. Ap. Sdorow. 1999. 48.74 (*0-697-10904-6*) McGraw.

Psychocriticism: An Annotated Bibliography, 1. Compiled by Joseph P. Natoli & Frederik L. Rusch. LC 84-4689. (Bibliographies & Indexes in World Literature Ser.: No. 1). 267p. 1984. lib. bdg. 59.95 (*0-313-23641-0*, NPL/, Greenwood Pr) Greenwood.

Psychocutaneous Diseases. Ed. by Caroline Koblenzer. 1987. text 82.00 (*0-8089-1865-6*, 792329, Grune & Strat) Harcrt Hlth Sci Grp.

Psychocybernetic Model of Art Therapy. Aina O. Nucho. (Illus.). 248p. 1987. 51.95 (*0-398-05339-1*); pap. 35.95 (*0-398-06646-9*) C C Thomas.

Psychodiagnosis: Selected Papers. Paul E. Meehl. LC 72-95440. (Illus.). 383p. 1973. reprint ed. pap. 118.80 (*0-608-00838-9*, 206162900010) Bks Demand.

Psychodiagnosis in Schizophrenia. Irving B. Weiner. 616p. 1996. 49.95 (*0-8058-2578-9*) L Erlbaum Assocs.

Psychodiagnostic Evaluation of Children: A Casebook Approach. Barbara R. Slater & John M. Thomas. LC 82-19146. (Illus.). 422p. 1983. pap. 130.90 (*0-608-05099-7*, 206565500005) Bks Demand.

Psychodiagnostic Evaluation of Children: A Casebook Approach. Barbara R. Slater & John M. Thomas. 402p. (C). 1983. pap. text 30.95 (*0-8077-2734-2*) Tchrs Coll.

Psychodiagnostics: A Diagnostic Test Based on Perception. 10th ed. Hermann Rorschach. 228p. 1998. pap. text 54.00 (*3-456-83024-6*) Hogrefe & Huber Pubs.

Psychodiagnostics & Personality Assessment: A Handbook. 2nd ed. Donald P. Ogdon. LC 66-29866. (Professional Handbook Ser.). 144p. (C). 1975. pap. 39.50 (*0-87424-095-6*, W-95) Western Psych.

Psychodick. unabridged ed. F. C. Wunderlich & Annie Laurie McEwen. Ed. by Paul S. Ewen. (Illus.). (Orig.). 1999. pap. 15.00 (*0-9649293-2-5*) Belle Terre.

Psychodietetics: Food As the Key to Emotional Health. Emanuel Cheraskin et al. LC 86-43196. 228p. 1987. pap. 7.95 (*0-8128-6266-X*, Scrbrough Hse) Madison Bks UPA.

Psychodrama, 3 vols. J. L. Moreno. Incl. Vol. 1. Collected Papers. pap. 20.00 Vol. 2. Foundations of Psychotherapy. 20.00 Vol. 3. Action-Therapy & Principles of Practice. 20.00 Vol. 3. Action-Therapy & Principles of Practice. pap. 19.00 write for info. (*0-318-51037-5*) Beacon Hse.

Psychodrama: Group Psychotherapy As Experimental Theater. Eva Roine. LC 98-137745. 224p. 1997. pap. 28.95 (*1-85302-494-5*, Pub. by Jessica Kingsley) Taylor & Francis.

Psychodrama: Resolving Emotional Problems Through Role-Playing. Lewis Yablonsky. LC 75-36385. 293p. 1992. text 45.95 (*0-87630-698-9*) Brunner-Mazel.

Psychodrama & Audience Attitude Change. Ira A. Greenberg. LC 68-54532. 1968. 10.00 (*0-911958-00-2*); pap. 5.95 (*0-685-06839-0*) Behavioral Studies.

Psychodrama & Sociodrama in American Education. J. L. Moreno. 14.00 (*0-685-22536-4*) Beacon Hse.

Psychodrama & Systemic Therapy. Chris Farmer. 136p. 1995. pap. 22.00 (*1-85575-089-9*, Pub. by H Karnac Bks Ltd) Other Pr LLC.

Psychodrama for the Timid Clinician see Clinician's Guide to Psychodrama

Psychodrama Since Moreno: Innovations in Theory & Practice. Ed. by Paul Holmes et al. LC 93-44657. (Lifeskills Library). (Illus.). 272p. (C). 1994. pap. 27.99 (*0-415-09351-1*, B4312) Routledge.

Psychodrama Since Moreno: Innovations in Theory & Practice. Ed. by William Dean Howells et al. LC 93-44657. (Lifeskills Library). (Illus.). 324p. (C). 1994. 80.00 (*0-415-09350-3*, B4308) Routledge.

***Psychodrama, Surplus Reality & the Art of Healing.** Zerka T. Moreno et al. LC 99-45591. 2000. write for info. (*0-415-22320-2*) Routledge.

Psychodynamic Approach to Adolescent Psychiatry: The Mount Sinai Experience. Ed. by Don R. Heacock. LC 80-27. (Experimental & Clinical Psychiatry Ser.: No. 2). 382p. reprint ed. 118.50 (*0-7837-0797-5*, 204111100019) Bks Demand.

***Psychodynamic Approaches to Sexual Problems.** Brian Daines & Angelina Perrett. LC 99-39401. 2000. pap. 25.95 (*0-335-20159-8*) OpUniv Pr.

Psychodynamic Concepts in General Psychiatry. Ed. by Harvey J. Schwartz et al. 544p. 1995. text 69.50 (*0-88048-536-1*, 8536) Am Psychiatric.

Psychodynamic Counselling in Action. Jacobs. 136p. 1988. pap. 21.50 (*0-8039-8046-9*) Sage.

Psychodynamic Group Psychotherapy. 2nd ed. J. Scott Rutan & Walter N. Stone. LC 93-15055. 274p. 1993. lib. bdg. 35.00 (*0-89862-096-1*) Guilford Pubns.

***Psychodynamic Group Psychotherapy.** 3rd ed. J. Scott Rutan & Walter N. Stone. 388p. 2000. lib. bdg. 45.00 (*1-57230-518-5*, C0518) Guilford Pubns.

***Psychodynamic Perspectives on Sickness & Health.** Paul Raphael Duberstein & Joseph M. Masling. LC 99-58549. 408p. 2000. 49.95 (*1-55798-668-1*) Am Psychol.

Psychodynamic Practice in a Managed Care Environment: A Strategic Guide for Clinicians. Michael B. Sperling et al. LC 99-48197. 160p. 1999. lib. bdg. 30.00 (*1-57230-133-3*, 0133) Guilford Pubns.

Psychodynamic Psychiatry in Clinical Practice. Glen O. Gabbard. LC 89-18405. 521p. 1990. reprint ed. pap. 161.60 (*0-608-02014-1*, 206267000003) Bks Demand.

***Psychodynamic Psychiatry in Clinical Practice.** 3rd ed. Glen O. Gabbard. LC 99-54484. 616p. 2000. 79.95 (*1-58562-002-5*) Am Psychiatric.

Psychodynamic Psychiatry in Clinical Practice: The DSM-IV Edition. 2nd ed. Glen O. Gabbard. LC 93-27939. 656p. 1994. text 75.00 (*0-88048-658-9*, 8658) Am Psychiatric.

***Psychodynamic Psychiatry in Clinical Practice, DSM-IV ed.** Glen O. Gabbard. 2000. pap. text 50.00 (*0-7657-0278-9*) Aronson.

Psychodynamic Psychiatry, Theory & Practice, 2 Vols., 1. John Frosch. 1990. 55.00 (*0-8236-5645-4*, BN 05645) Intl Univs Pr.

Psychodynamic Psychiatry, Theory & Practice, 2 Vols., 2. John Frosch. 1990. 75.00 (*0-8236-5646-2*, BN 05646) Intl Univs Pr.

***Psychodynamic Psychotherapy: Learning to Listen from Multiple Perspectives.** Jon Frederickson. LC 98-47697. 1998. pap. text 29.95 (*0-87630-962-7*) Brunner-Mazel.

Psychodynamic Psychotherapy: Listening from Multiple Perspectives. Jon Frederickson. LC 98-47697. 225p. 1998. 59.95 (*0-87630-961-9*) Brunner-Mazel.

Psychodynamic Psychotherapy of Borderline Patients. Otto F. Kernberg et al. LC 16-8. 224p. 1989. pap. 42.00 (*0-465-06643-7*, Pub. by Basic) HarpC.

Psychodynamic Psychotherapy of Children. Henry P. Coppolillo. 1987. 60.00 (*0-8236-4455-3*, BN#04455) Intl Univs Pr.

Psychodynamic Studies on Aging: Creativity, Reminiscing & Dying. Ed. by Sidney Levin & Ralph J. Kahana. LC 67-27427. 345p. 1967. 50.00 (*0-8236-5640-3*) Intl Univs Pr.

Psychodynamic Technique in the Treatment of the Eating Disorders. Ed. by C. Philip Wilson et al. LC 91-17197. 440p. 1992. 60.00 (*0-87668-622-6*) Aronson.

Psychodynamic Treatment of Anorexia Nervosa & Bulimia. Ed. by Craig L. Johnson. LC 90-13867. 404p. 1990. lib. bdg. 47.00 (*0-89862-550-5*) Guilford Pubns.

Psychodynamics & Cognition. Mardi J. Horowitz. (Illus.). xii, 402p. 1988. 33.00 (*0-226-35368-0*) U Ch Pr.

Psychodynamics of Culture: Abram Kardiner & Neo-Freudian Anthropology, 3. William C. Manson. LC 88-17778. (Contributions to the Study of Anthropology Ser.: No. 3). 162p. 1988. 55.00 (*0-313-26267-5*, MDY/, Greenwood Pr) Greenwood.

Psychodynamics of Drug Dependence. Ed. by Jack D. Blaine & Demetrios A. Julius. LC 93-35969. 196p. 1994. pap. 40.00 (*1-56821-157-0*) Aronson.

Psychodynamics of Family Life: Diagnosis & Treatment of Family Relationships. Nathan W. Ackerman. LC 94-72519. 396p. 1995. pap. text 50.00 (*1-56821-341-7*) Aronson.

Psychodynamics of Leadership. Edward B. Klein et al. LC 97-17770. 1998. 55.00 (*1-887841-13-X*, Psychosocial) Intl Univs Pr.

Psychodynamics of Organizations. Ed. by Larry Hirschhorn & Carole K. Barnett. LC 92-21061. 288p. 1993. 59.95 (*1-56639-020-6*); pap. 24.95 (*1-56639-021-4*) Temple U Pr.

Psychodynamics of the Black Experience. Quentin B. Huff. LC 95-83464. 172p. 1995. pap. 12.50 (*0-9649992-0-X*) Baraka Pubng.

Psychodynamics of the Emotionally Uncomfortable. David W. Shave. LC 79-50191. 489p. 1980. 27.75 (*0-87527-233-9*) Green.

Psychodynamics of Work & Organizations: Theory & Application. William M. Czander. LC 93-13405. 408p. 1993. lib. bdg. 48.00 (*0-89862-284-0*) Guilford Pubns.

Psychodynamics of Yoga. H. L. Sharma. 160p. 1981. 12.95 (*0-317-12326-2*) Asia Bk Corp.

***Psychoeducatioanl Assessment.** 3rd ed. Bracken. LC 99-23802. 488p. 1999. 78.00 (*0-205-29021-3*) Allyn.

***Psychoeducation: An Idea Whose Time Has Come.** Mary M. Wood et al. (What Works for Children & Youth with Emotional/Behavior Disorders Ser.). 46p. 1999. pap. 11.40 (*0-86586-349-0*) Coun Exc Child.

Psychoeducational Approach for Ending Wife/Partner Abuse: A Program Manual for Treating Individuals & Couples. R. Gettner & C. Mantooth. 1996. 29.95 (*1-882948-09-2*) Family Violence.

Psychoeducational Assessment of Hearing-Impaired Students: Infancy Through High School. Sharon Bradley-Johnson & Larry D. Evans. LC 90-27491. 251p. 1991. pap. text 29.00 (*0-89079-455-3*, 1949) PRO-ED.

P

Psychoeducational Assessment of Minority Group Children: A Casebook. Ed. by Reginald L. Jones. LC 87-20861. 429p. (Orig.). 1988. pap. text 24.95 (0-943539-00-5) Cobb & Henry Pubs.

Psychoeducational Assessment of Students Who Are Visually Impaired or Blind: Infancy Through High School. 2nd rev. ed. Sharon Bradley-Johnson. LC 93-23211. (Illus.). 253p. (C). 1994. pap. 29.00 (0-89079-599-1, 6693) PRO-ED.

Psychoeducational Groups. Nina W. Brown. LC 97-43840. 264p. 1998. pap. 24.95 (1-56032-676-X) Hemisp Pub.

Psychoeducational Groups for Patients with Schizophrenia: A Guide for Practitioners. Haya Ascher-Svanum & Audrey A. Krause. LC 90-14474. 308p. 1991. 93.00 (0-8342-0197-6) Aspen Pub.

Psychoeducational Practices see Perceptual & Learning Disabilities in Children

Psychoeducational Profile-Revised (PEP-R) Manual, Vol. I. Eric Schopler et al. LC 88-15316. (Illus.). 256p. 1979. 62.00 (0-89079-238-0, 1492) PRO-ED.

Psychoeducational Use & Interpretation of the Wechsler Adult Intelligence Scale. 2nd rev. ed. Hazel Z. Sprandel. LC 95-6679. 238p. (C). 1995. text 56.95 (0-398-06519-5); pap. text 38.95 (0-398-06520-9) C C Thomas.

Psychoendocrine Aspects of Epilepsy. Harold E. Simmons. 1974. pap. 5.00 (0-87312-004-3) Psychogenic Disease.

Psychoendocrinology of Human Sexual Behavior, 6. Harold Persky. LC 87-6976. (Sexual Medicine Ser.: Vol. 6). 280p. 1987. 95.00 (0-275-92526-9, C2526, Praeger Pubs) Greenwood.

Psychoenergetics: A Method of Self-Discovery & Healing. 2nd rev. ed. Jordan P. Weiss. (Illus.). 224p. 1995. pap. 15.95 (0-9638640-2-5) Oceanview Pub.

Psychofraud & Ethical Therapy. John D. Garcia. LC 73-92028. 200p. 1974. 6.95 (0-87426-032-9) Whitmore.

Psychogalvanic Reactions of Exceptional & Normal School Children. Robin D. Collmann. LC 79-176664. (Columbia University. Teachers College. Contributions to Education Ser.: No. 469). reprint ed. 37.50 (0-404-55469-5) AMS Pr.

Psychogenesis: Everything Begins in Mind. Jack E. Addington. LC 79-145391. 212p. 1994. reprint ed. pap. 12.95 (0-87516-672-5) DeVorss.

Psychogenesis: The Early Development of Gender Identity. Elizabeth R. Moberly. 120p. 1983. 29.95 (0-7100-9271-7, Routledge Thoemms) Routledge.

Psychogenesis & the History of Science. Jean Piaget & Rolando V. Garcia. Tr. by Helga Feider from FRE. (Illus.). 336p. 1989. text 64.50 (0-231-05992-2) Col U Pr.

***Psychogenetics: The Force of Heredity.** Chris Griscom. (Illus.). 2000. pap. 18.00 (0-9623696-7-5) Light Inst Fndtn.

Psychogenic Biochemical Aspects of Cancer. Harold E. Simmons. 1979. pap. 15.00 (0-87312-010-8) Psychogenic Disease.

Psychogenic Learning Disabilities: Psychodynamics & Psychotherapy. Richard A. Gardner. LC 94-12574. 675p. 1994. 40.00 (0-933812-34-5) Creative Therapeutics.

Psychogenic Theory of Disease: A New Approach to Cancer Research. Harold E. Simmons. 1966. pap. 15.00 (0-87312-000-0) Gen Welfare Pubns.

Psychogenic Voice Disorders. Butcher. 186p. 1993. pap. 47.50 (1-56593-238-2, 0557) Singular Publishing.

Psychogeriatric Care in the Community. (Public Health in Europe Ser.: No. 10). 119p. 1979. 11.00 (92-9020-129-0, 1320010) World Health.

Psychogeriatrics. K. Hasegawa & A. Homma. (Current Clinical Practice Ser.: Vol. 59). 1991. 148.75 (0-685-48202-2) Elsevier.

Psychogeriatrics: An Introduction to the Psychiatry of Old Age. 2nd ed. Brice Pitt. (Illus.). 224p. 1982. pap. text 24.00 (0-443-01598-8) Church.

Psychographics in Personal Growth. George Burtt. LC 72-95846. 1972. pap. 3.50 (0-913596-00-0) Vector Counsel.

Psychography: A Method of Self-Discovery. Church of Religious Research, Inc. Staff. Ed. by Helen Roberts & Isabel H. Pinkston. LC 90-60693. (Illus.). 232p. (Orig.). 1990. pap. 9.95 (0-915151-00-6) Religious Res Pr.

Psychography of the Child: Development of the Psychographic Capacity from Drawing to Writing, & the Means for its Improvement. Jonathan Shatil. (Illus.). 292p. (Orig.). (C). 1995. pap. text 32.50 (0-7618-0001-8); lib. bdg. 54.00 (0-7618-0000-X) U Pr of Amer.

PsychoHeresy: The Psychological Seduction of Christianity. Martin M. Bobgan & Deidre N. Bobgan. LC 87-80001. 272p. (Orig.). 1987. pap. 15.00 (0-941717-00-3) EastGate Pubs.

Psychohistory & Religion: The Case of Young Man Luther. Roger A. Johnson et al. LC 76-7870. 206p. reprint ed. pap. 63.90 (0-608-16386-4, 202689500053) Bks Demand.

***Psychohistry: Theory & Practice.** Jacques Szaluta. (American University Studies XIX). 296p. 1999. pap. text 32.95 (0-8204-4967-9) P Lang Pubng.

Psychoimmunology: CNS-Immune Interactions. Alan J. Husband. 192p. 1993. lib. bdg. 139.00 (0-8493-4879-X, QP356) CRC Pr.

Psychoimmunology of Human Cancer: Mind & Body in the Fight for Survival? Ed. by Jennifer Barraclough et al. LC 94-8027. (Illus.). 452p. 1995. text 89.50 (0-19-262365-6) OUP.

***Psychokinesiology: Doorway to the Subconscious.** Alexander S. Holub & Evelyn B. Michaels. LC 99-38726. 288p. 1999. pap. 16.95 (1-893157-06-7) Bridger Hse.

Psycholgy. Seamon & Kenrick. (C). 1996. student ed. 30.00 (0-13-711657-8) P-H.

Psycholinguistic Aspects of Foreign Accents (PAFAS) A Complete Personalized Program for Achieving Clear, Pleasant-Sounding Speech. Daniel P. Dato. 312p. 1988. pap. text, student ed. 39.95 (1-881336-04-2) Bilingual CI.

Psycholinguistic Aspects of Foreign Accents (PAFAT) A Complete Approach to Effective Accent Reduction. Daniel P. Dato. 318p. 1987. pap. text, teacher ed. 59.95 (1-881336-03-4) Bilingual CI.

Psycholinguistic Assessment of Children with Speech & Literacy Difficulties. Joy Stackhouse & Bill Wells. (Illus.). 200p. (Orig.). 1997. pap. 42.95 (1-56593-795-3, 1552) Singular Publishing.

Psycholinguistic Implications for Linguistic Relativity: A Case Study of Chinese. Ed. by R. Hoosain. 216p. (C). 1991. text 49.95 (0-8058-0898-1) L Erlbaum Assocs.

Psycholinguistic Learning Disabilities: Diagnosis & Remediation. Samuel A. Kirk & Winifred D. Kirk. LC 70-139805. 208p. 1971. pap. 12.50 (0-252-00142-7) U of Ill Pr.

Psycholinguistic Matrices Investigation into Osgood & Morris. Richard League. (Approaches to Semiotics Ser.: Vol. 47). (Illus.). 1977. 51.55 (90-279-3116-X) Mouton.

Psycholinguistic Models of Production. Ed. by Hans Dechert & Manfred Raupach. LC 87-17575. 320p. 1987. text 73.25 (0-89391-211-5) Ablx Pub.

Psycholinguistic Nature of the Reading Process: With a New Foreword. Ed. by Kenneth S. Goodman. LC 67-26383. (Illus.). 349p. reprint ed. pap. 108.20 (0-7837-3627-4, 204349300009) Bks Demand.

Psycholinguistic Studies in Language Processing. Ed. by Gert Rickheit & Michael Bock. (Research in Text Theory Ser.: Vol. 7). viii, 305p. 1983. 112.35 (3-11-008994-7) De Gruyter.

Psycholinguistic Study of Phonological Interference. Eugene J. Briere. LC 68-13339. (Janua Linguarum, Ser. Minor: No. 66). 1968. pap. text 42.35 (90-279-0594-0) Mouton.

Psycholinguistics. Joseph A. DeVito. LC 73-183112. (Studies in Communicative Disorders). 36p. (C). 1971. pap. write for info. (0-672-61277-1, Bobbs) Macmillan.

Psycholinguistics. Michael Garman. (Cambridge Textbooks in Linguistics Ser.). (Illus.). 532p. (C). 1990. pap. text 32.95 (0-521-27641-1) Cambridge U Pr.

Psycholinguistics. Insup Taylor. 436p. (C). 1990. text 53.20 (0-13-733817-1) P-H.

Psycholinguistics. Ed. by H. G. Widdowson. 148p. 1998. pap. text 11.25 (0-19-437213-8) OUP.

Psycholinguistics. Ed. by Charles E. Osgood & Thomas A. Sebeok. LC 76-2579. (Indiana Univ. Studies in the History & Theory of Linguistics). (Illus.). 307p. 1976. reprint ed. lib. bdg. 55.00 (0-8371-8730-3, OSPS, Greenwood Pr) Greenwood.

Psycholinguistics. 2nd ed. Glea Berko. (C). 1997. pap. text, teacher ed. 28.00 (0-15-504107-X) Harcourt.

Psycholinguistics. 2nd ed. Glea Berko. (C). 1997. text 71.00 (0-15-504106-1) Harcourt.

Psycholinguistics: An Introduction. 1979. 95.95 (0-387-90417-4) Spr-Verlag.

***Psycholinguistics: An Introduction.** Helen S. Cairns. LC 98-45758. 1999. pap. write for info. (0-89079-807-9) PRO-ED.

Psycholinguistics: An Introduction to Research & Theory. rev. ed. H. Hoermann. Tr. by Hans H. Stern & P. Leppmann. LC 79-18600. (Illus.). 342p. 1979. 42.90 (3-540-90417-4) Spr-Verlag.

Psycholinguistics: Psychology, Linguistics & the Study of Natural Language. Joseph F. Kess. LC 91-37929. (Current Issues in Linguistic Theory Ser.: No. 86). xiv, 360p. 1992. 59.00 (1-55619-141-3); pap. 24.95 (1-55619-142-1) J Benjamins Pubng Co.

Psycholinguistics & Aphasia. Harold Goodglass & Sheila Blumstein. LC 73-8667. 352p. reprint ed. pap. 109.20 (0-608-18672-4, 202310000032) Bks Demand.

Psycholinguistics in Clinical Practice. Ed. by Michael A. Simpson. LC 79-11813. 450p. 1980. text 42.50 (0-8290-0091-7) Irvington.

Psycholinguistics of Readable Writing: A Multidisciplinary Exploration. Alice S. Horning. LC 92-33489. (Communication & Information Science Ser.). 232p. 1993. pap. 39.50 (0-89391-997-7); text 73.25 (0-89391-896-2) Ablx Pub.

Psycholog An Introduction. 7th ed. Lahey. 1999. 42.00 (0-07-235829-7) McGraw.

Psychologia Osobnosti (Psychology of Personality) C. S. Hall & G. Lindzey. (SLO., Illus.). 512p. 1997. write for info. (80-08-00994-2, Pub. by Slov Pegagog Naklad) IBD Ltd.

Psychologic Foundations of Education: An Attempt to Show the Genesis of the Higher Education of the Mind. William T. Harris. LC 73-89187. (American Education: Its Men, Institutions, & Ideas. Series 1). 1977. reprint ed. 30.95 (0-405-01425-2) Ayer.

***Psychological Abuse in Domestically Violent Relations.** K. Daniel O'Leary & Roland D. Maiuro. LC 99-59298. 2000. write for info. (0-8261-1321-4) Springer Pub.

Psychological Abuse of Children in Health Care: The Issues. 2nd rev. ed. Ed. by Pat Azarnoff & Patricia Lindquist. (Issues in Pediatric Mental Health Ser.: No. 2). 130p. (C). 1997. spiral bd. 28.00 (0-912599-06-5) Pediatric Projects.

Psychological Activity in Homer: A Study of Phren. Shirley D. Sullivan. 303p. pap. 19.95 (0-88629-077-5, Pub. by McG-Queens Univ Pr) CUP Services.

Psychological Activity in Homer: A Study of Phren. Shirley Darcus Sullivan. 303p. 29.95 (0-88629-079-1, Pub. by McG-Queens Univ Pr) CUP Services.

Psychological Adaptations in Life & Work: Subject Analysis Index with Reference Bibliography. Denise J. Randall. LC 85-47866. 150p. 1987. 47.50 (0-88164-406-4); pap. 44.50 (0-88164-407-2) ABBE Pubs Assn.

Psychological Adjustment & Well-Being. Stanley L. Brodsky. (C). 1988. pap. text, teacher ed. 42.00 (0-03-013369-6) Harcourt Coll Pubs.

Psychological Adjustments: Human Relationships. 3rd ed. Calhoun. 1990. 14.06 (0-07-009769-0) McGraw.

Psychological Analysis & the Philosophy of John Stuart Mill. Fred Wilson. 336p. 1990. text 60.00 (0-8020-2714-8) U of Toronto Pr.

***Psychological & Behavioral Aspects of Diving.** Baruch Nevo & Stephen Breitstein. LC 98-89160. (Illus.). 192p. 1999. 19.95 (0-941332-73-X, B0993) Best Pub Co.

Psychological & Behavioral Aspects of Physical Disability: A Manual for Health Practitioners. James E. Lindemann et al. LC 81-17885. 452p. (C). 1981. 59.50 (0-306-40776-0, Plenum Trade) Perseus Pubng.

Psychological & Behavioral Assessment: Impact on Pediatric Care. Ed. by Phyllis R. Magrab. 384p. 1984. 70.00 (0-306-41697-2, Plenum Trade) Perseus Pubng.

Psychological & Biological Approaches to Emotion. Ed. by N. L. Stein et al. 456p. (C). 1990. pap. 55.00 (0-8058-0150-2); text 115.00 (0-8058-0149-9) L Erlbaum Assocs.

Psychological & Biological Assessment at the Turn of the Century. Ed. by John F. Clarkin & John P. Docherty. (Review of Psychiatry Ser.: Vol. 16, Sect. V). 144p. (Orig.). 1997. pap. text 25.00 (0-88048-449-7, 8449) Am Psychiatric.

Psychological & Demographic Factors Affecting Relationships with Financial Institutions. Lawrence Lepisto. 47p. 1994. pap. 100.00 (1-880572-12-5) Filene Res.

Psychological & Educational Testing: The User Friendly Text Book. Lynn McCutcheon. 144p. 1998. pap. text 24.95 (1-56226-389-7) CAT Pub.

Psychological & Ethical Aspects of Mormon Group Life. Ephraim E. Ericksen. LC 75-310523. (Bonneville Books Reprint Edition Ser.). 123p. reprint ed. pap. 38.20 (0-608-14815-6, 202590000047) Bks Demand.

Psychological & Ethical Ideas: What Early Greeks Say. Shirley D. Sullivan. LC 94-36311. (Mnemosyne, Bibliotheca Classica Batava, Supplementum, 0169-8958 Ser.: Vol. 144). xiii, 262p. 1995. 87.00 (90-04-10185-3) Brill Academic Pubs.

Psychological & Human Reproduction. James W. Selby et al. LC 80-1641. 1980. 24.95 (0-02-928690-5) Free Pr.

Psychological & Medical Aspects of Induced Abortion: A Selective, Annotated Bibliography, 1970-1986, 7. annot. ed. Compiled by Eugenia B. Winter. LC 88-194. (Bibliographies & Indexes in Women's Studies: No. 7). 177p. 1988. lib. bdg. 62.95 (0-313-26100-8, WPY/) Greenwood.

Psychological & Medical Well-Being & Their Relation in Adults with Insulin-Dependent Diabetes Mellitus. Bjorn Karlson. (Studia Psychologica et Pedagogica Ser.: Altera CXXVII). 106p. (Orig.). 1997. pap. 49.50 (91-22-01746-1, Pub. by Almqvist Wiksell) Coronet Bks.

Psychological & Neuropsychological Testing Terms: A Glossary in Nontechnical Language Version 1.0. Paul R. Lees-Haley. 1998. 19.95 (0-9668410-0-X) Lees-Haley Psych.

Psychological & Psychiatric Problems in Men. Joan Gomez. LC 93-7214. 1993. pap. write for info. (0-415-09713-4) Routledge.

***Psychological & Psychosocial Consequences of Combat & Deployment with Special Emphasis on the Gulf War.** David H. Marlowe. 2000. pap. 15.00 (0-8330-2685-2) Rand Corp.

Psychological & Scientific Evidence in Criminal Trials, 2 vols. Jane C. Moriarty. LC 95-52656. 1996. ring bd. write for info. (0-8366-1005-9) West Group.

Psychological & Social Aspects of Psychiatric Disability. Ed. by LeRoy Spaniol et al. LC 96-85675. 592p. 1997. pap. 44.95 (1-878512-06-4) Boston Univ Ctr Psy Rehab.

Psychological & Social Impact of Disability. 3rd ed. Ed. by Robert P. Marinelli & Arthur E. Dell Orto. LC 91-4809. 384p. (C). 1991. 39.95 (0-8261-2212-4) Springer Pub.

***Psychological & Social Impact of Disability.** 4th ed. Ed. by Robert P. Marinelli & Arthur E. Dell Orto. 384p. 1999. 49.95 (0-8261-2213-2) Springer Pub.

Psychological & Transcendental Phenomenology & the Confrontation with Heidegger (1927-1931) The Encyclopaedia Britannica Article, the Amsterdam Lectures "Phenomenology & Anthropology," & Husserl's Marginal Notes in Being, Time, Kant & the Problem of Metaphysics. Edmund Husserl et al. Ed. & Tr. by Thomas Sheehan & Richard E. Palmer from GER. LC 97-7798. (Husserliana Collected Works). 528p. 1997. text 240.50 (0-7923-4481-2) Kluwer Academic.

Psychological Androgny. Ellen P. Cook. (C). 1985. 25.95 (0-205-14432-2, Macmillan Coll) P-H.

Psychological Androgyny. Ellen Piel Cook. (General Psychology Ser.: No. 133). 256p. 1985. pap. text 25.00 (0-08-031612-3, Pergamon Pr) Elsevier.

Psychological Anthropology. Ed. by Philip K. Bock et al. LC 93-43434. 432p. 1994. pap. 32.50 (0-275-94956-7) Greenwood.

Psychological Anthropology. Erika Bourgui. (C). 1979. write for info. (0-03-034921-4) Harcourt Coll Pubs.

Psychological Anthropology. Ed. by Thomas R. Williams. (World Anthropology Ser.). (Illus.). xii, 656p. 1975. 58.50 (90-279-7729-1) Mouton.

Psychological Anthropology & Education: A Delineation of a Field of Inquiry. Charles Harrington. LC 78-18943. (Studies in Education: No. 5). 1979. 32.50 (0-404-16012-3) AMS Pr.

Psychological Anthropology Reconsidered. John M. Ingham. (Publications of the Society for Psychological Anthropology: No. 8). 320p. (C). 1996. text 59.95 (0-521-55107-2); pap. text 20.95 (0-521-55918-9) Cambridge U Pr.

Psychological Applications in Psychiatry. Ed. by Brendan P. Bradley & Chris Thompson. LC 85-9383. 259p. reprint ed. pap. 80.30 (0-7837-4411-0, 204415400012) Bks Demand.

Psychological Approach to Hospital-Acquired Infections. C. A. Bartzokas et al. LC 94-27126. 164p. 1995. text 79.95 (0-7734-9030-2) E Mellen.

Psychological Approaches in Psychiatric Nursing. Breda Kingston. 150p. 1987. pap. 24.50 (0-7099-1521-7, Pub. by C Helm) Routldge.

Psychological Approaches to Pain Management: A Practitioner's Handbook. Ed. by Robert J. Gatchel & Dennis C. Turk. LC 95-26230. (Illus.). 519p. 1996. lib. bdg. 62.00 (0-89862-292-1, 2292) Guilford Pubns.

Psychological Approaches to Sports Injury Rehabilitation. Jim Taylor & Shel Taylor. LC 97-20420. 302p. 1997. 52.00 (0-8342-0973-X) Aspen Pub.

Psychological Approaches to the Care of the Elderly. John Hodge. Ed. by Ian Hanley. 250p. 1984. 35.00 (0-416-00941-7, NO. 5077) Routledge.

Psychological Aspects of Abortion. Ed. by David Mall & Walter F. Watts. LC 79-88679. 156p. 1979. pap. 19.95 (0-313-27053-8, P7053, Greenwood Pr) Greenwood.

Psychological Aspects of Balance of Diabetes in Juvenile: Proceedings of the 3rd Beilinson Symposium, Pt. 2, Herzlyg, 1875. International Beilinson Symposium Staff. Ed. by Zvi Laron. (Pediatric & Adolescent Endocrinology Ser.: Vol. 3). (Illus.). 1977. 42.75 (3-8055-2631-8) S Karger.

Psychological Aspects of Cancer. Ed. by M. Watson & T. Morris. (Advances in the Biosciences Ser.: No. 49). (Illus.). 112p. 1985. pap. 28.50 (0-08-030791-4, Pergamon Pr) Elsevier.

Psychological Aspects of Cancer Care. Lawrence Goldie. 160p. 1996. pap. text 26.95 (1-85302-358-2, Pub. by Jessica Kingsley) Taylor & Francis.

Psychological Aspects of Caring in a Mixed Economy. Open Learning Foundation Staff. 130p. 1996. pap. write for info. (0-443-05733-8) Church.

Psychological Aspects of Critical Care Nursing. Barbara J. Riegel & Donna Ehrenreich. 352p. 1989. 62.00 (0-87189-799-7, 89799) Aspen Pub.

Psychological Aspects of Depression: Toward a Cognitive-Interpersonal Integration. Gotlib. 342p. 1995. pap. text 51.95 (0-471-96131-0) Wiley.

Psychological Aspects of Developmental & Physical Disabilities: A Case Book. Ed. by Michel Hersen & Vincent B. Van Hasselt. (Illus.). 280p. (C). 1990. text 45.00 (0-8039-3191-3); pap. text 22.95 (0-8039-3702-4) Sage.

Psychological Aspects of Developmental & Physical Disabilities: A Case Book. Ed. by Michel Hersen & Vincent B. Van Hasselt. LC 89-10763. (Illus.). 280p. 1990. reprint ed. pap. 86.80 (0-608-04314-1, 206509300012) Bks Demand.

Psychological Aspects of Diabetes in Children & Adolescents. Ed. by Z. Laron & A. Galatzer. (Pediatric & Adolescent Endocrinology Ser.: Vol. 10). xvi, 248p. 1983. 160.00 (3-8055-3575-9) S Karger.

Psychological Aspects of Early Breast Cancer. C. Ray & M Baum. (Contributions to Psychology & Medicine Ser.). (Illus.). 160p. 1985. 75.95 (0-387-96122-4) Spr-Verlag.

Psychological Aspects of Facial Form: Proceedings of a Sponsored Symposium Honoring Professor Robert E. Moyers, Held February 29 & March 1, 1980, in Ann Arbor, MI. Ed. by G. William Lucker et al. LC 83-132873. (Craniofacial Growth Monographs: No. 11). (Illus.). 233p. reprint ed. pap. 72.30 (0-8357-7560-7, 205232400097) Bks Demand.

Psychological Aspects of Genetic Counselling. Ed. by Alan E. Emery & Ian Pullen. 1984. text 104.00 (0-12-238220-X) Acad Pr.

Psychological Aspects of Health & Illness: A Life-Span Perspective. Ed. by Thomas L. Whitman et al. LC 98-21788. 300p. 1998. write for info. (0-8058-2771-4); pap. write for info. (0-8058-2772-2) L Erlbaum Assocs.

Psychological Aspects of Illness & Disease. California College for Health Sciences Staff. 166p. (C). 1992. spiral bd. 155.00 (0-933195-16-8) CA College Health Sci.

Psychological Aspects of Modernity. Ed. by Jerome Braun. LC 93-20297. 288p. 1993. 69.50 (0-275-94262-7, C4262, Praeger Pubs) Greenwood.

Psychological Aspects of Pauline Theology. Gerd Theissen. 448p. 1994. 59.95 (0-567-09479-0) Bks Intl VA.

Psychological Aspects of Pregnancy, Birthing, & Bonding. Barbara L. Blum. LC 80-14227. (New Directions in Psychotherapy Ser.: Vol. IV). 380p. 1980. 49.00 (0-87705-210-7, Kluwer Acad Hman Sci) Kluwer Academic.

Psychological Aspects of Radiation Therapy: The Patient, the Family & the Staff. Patricia Tretter & Lillian G. Kutscher. 1981. 21.95 (0-405-13096-1) Ayer.

Psychological Aspects of Rheumatoid Arthritis. M. L. Pritchard. (Recent Research in Psychology Ser.). (Illus.). xv, 208p. 1989. 59.95 (0-387-97116-5) Spr-Verlag.

Psychological Aspects of Serious Illness: Chronic Conditions, Fatal Diseases, & Clinical Care. Ed. by Paul T. Costa, Jr. & Gary R. VandenBos. 172p. 1990. pap. text 19.95 (1-55798-105-1) Am Psychol.

Psychological Aspects of Surgery. Ed. by Frederick G. Guggenheim. (Advances in Psychosomatic Medicine Ser.: Vol. 15). (Illus.). viii, 232p. 1986. 121.00 (3-8055-4090-6) S Karger.

Psychological Aspects of Terminal Care. Owens. pap. 30.00 (0-471-96621-5) Wiley.

Psychological Aspects of Terminal Care. Glynn R. Ownes. (Clinical Psychology Ser.). 300p. 1998. 65.00 (0-471-95291-5) Wiley.

An Asterisk (*) at the beginning of an entry indicates that the title is appearing for the first time.

Psychological Aspects of Women's Health Care: The Interface Between Psychiatry & Obstetrics & Gynecology. Ed. by Donna E. Stewart & Nada L. Stotland. LC 92-48771. 572p. 1993. text 74.50 (*0-88048-421-7*, 8421) Am Psychiatric.

*__Psychological Aspects of Women's Health Care: The Interface Between Psychiatry & Obstetrics & Gynecology.__ 2nd ed. Nada Logan Stotland & Donna E. Stewart. LC 00-33141. 2000. write for info. (*0-88048-831-X*) Am Psychiatric.

Psychological Aspects of Women's Reproductive Health. Ed. by Michael O'Hara et al. LC 94-36163. 368p. 1995. 43.95 (*0-8261-8660-2*) Springer Pub.

Psychological Assessment: A Conceptual Approach. Michael P. Maloney & Michael P. Ward. (Illus.). 422p. 1976. text 41.95 (*0-19-502027-8*) OUP.

Psychological Assessment: A Theory Systems Approach. James R. Barclay. LC 89-37230. 458p. (C). 1991. lib. bdg. 47.00 (*0-89464-405-X*) Krieger.

Psychological Assessment Children: Best Practices for School & Clinical Settings. 2nd ed. H. Booney Vance. LC 97-11277. 528p. 1997. 67.50 (*0-471-19301-1*) Wiley.

Psychological Assessment in Managed Care. Chris E. Stout. LC 96-45264. 276p. 1997. 75.00 (*0-471-17033-X*) Wiley.

Psychological Assessment in Medical Rehabilitation. Ed. by Laura A. Cushman & Marcia J. Scherer. LC 95-11109. (Measurement & Instrumentation in Psychology Ser.). 471p. 1995. text 29.95 (*1-55798-299-6*) Am Psychol.

Psychological Assessment in Medical Settings. Ronald H. Rozensky et al. LC 97-24814. (Applied Clinical Psychology Ser.). (Illus.). 340p. (C). 1997. 49.50 (*0-306-45551-X*, Plenum Trade) Perseus Pubng.

Psychological Assessment in Medicine. Ed. by Samuel E. Krug. LC 77-71889. 1977. 15.00 (*0-918296-07-2*) Inst Personality & Ability.

Psychological Assessment in the Schools. Ed. by James C. Impara & Linda L. Murphy. xv, 454p. (C). 1994. pap. 39.95 (*0-910674-37-X*) Buros Inst Mental.

Psychological Assessment of Abused & Traumatized Children. Francis D. Kelly. LC 98-31089. (Personality & Clinical Psychology Ser.). 272p. 1999. 29.95 (*0-8058-2973-3*) L Erlbaum Assocs.

Psychological Assessment of Adult Posttraumatic States. John Briere. LC 96-52132. (Psychotherapy Practitioner Resource Ser.). 251p. 1997. pap. text 24.95 (*1-55798-403-4*, 431-7840) Am Psychol.

Psychological Assessment of Dyslexia. Martin Turner. (Education). (Illus.). 374p. (Orig.). 1997. pap. 55.00 (*1-56593-782-1*, 1526) Thomson Learn.

Psychological Assessment of Mental & Physical Handicaps. Ed. by Peter Mittler. 886p. 1974. pap. 33.00 (*0-422-75600-8*, NO. 2819, Pub. by Tavistock) Routldge.

Psychological Assessment of Presidential Candidates. Stanley A. Renshon. 496p. (C). 1996. text 45.00 (*0-8147-7469-5*) NYU Pr.

Psychological Assessment of Presidential Candidates. Stanley A. Renshon. LC 98-11839. 528p. (C). 1998. reprint ed. pap. 24.99 (*0-415-92146-5*) Routledge.

Psychological Assessment of Reading. John R. Beech & Chris Singleton. LC 97-3684. (Routledge Assessment Library). (Illus.). 368p. (C). 1997. 85.00 (*0-415-12858-7*); pap. 29.99 (*0-415-12859-5*) Routledge.

Psychological Assessment, Psychiatric Diagnosis, & Treatment Planning. Stephen Hurt et al. LC 90-15146. 512p. 1991. text 61.95 (*0-87630-607-5*) Brunner-Mazel.

Psychological Assessment with the Millon Clinical Multiaxial Inventory (II) No. II: An Interpretive Guide. Robert J. Craig. LC 93-11583. 120p. 1993. pap. 26.00 (*0-911907-10-6*) Psych Assess.

Psychological Assessment with the MMPI. Alan Friedman et al. 424p. (C). 1989. text 55.00 (*0-8058-0310-6*); text, student ed. 65.00 (*0-8058-1066-8*) L Erlbaum Assocs.

*__Psychological Assessment with the MMPI-2.__ Alan F. Friedman. LC 99-87193. 2000. write for info. (*0-8058-1444-2*) L Erlbaum Assocs.

Psychological Astrology. G. Goodman & Grant Staff. 68p. 1974. 11.00 (*0-86690-107-8*, G1148-014) Am Fed Astrologers.

Psychological Astrology: A Synthesis of Jungian Psychology & Astrology. rev. ed. Karen Hamaker-Zondag. LC 90-77639. (Illus.). 224p. 1990. pap. 14.95 (*0-87728-718-X*) Weiser.

Psychological Atlas. David Katz. Tr. by Frank Gaynor. LC 68-28587. 142p. 1968. reprint ed. lib. bdg. 69.50 (*0-8371-0123-9*, KAPA, Greenwood Pr) Greenwood.

Psychological Attitude of Early Buddhist Philosophy. Lama A. Govinda. (C). 1991. reprint ed. 15.00 (*81-208-0952-1*, Pub. by Motilal Bnarsidass) S Asia.

Psychological Autopsy in the Courtroom. James Selkin. LC 87-90140. 112p. 1987. 19.95 (*0-318-23210-3*) J Selkin.

Psychological Autopsy in the Courtroom: Contributions of the Social Sciences to Resolving Issues Surrounding Equivocal Deaths. James Selkin. LC 87-90140. 112p. 1987. 19.95 (*0-8377-1150-9*, Rothman) W S Hein.

Psychological Backgrounds of Adult Education. Ed. by Raymond G. Kuhlen. (Notes & Essays Ser.: No. 40). 1970. pap. text 2.50 (*0-685-76691-8*, NES 40) Syracuse U Cont Ed.

Psychological Bases for Early Education. fac. ed. Anthony D. Pellegrini. LC 87-18995. (Wiley Series in Developmental Psychology & Its Applications). 296p. 1988. reprint ed. pap. 91.80 (*0-7837-8275-6*, 204905500009) Bks Demand.

Psychological Bases of Sport Injuries. Ed. by David Pargman. LC 92-73668. 315p. (C). 1993. 38.00 (*0-9627926-3-2*) Fit Info Tech.

*__Psychological Bases of Sport Injuries.__ 2nd rev. ed. Ed. by David Pargman. 376p. (C). 1999. text 39.00 (*1-885693-18-4*) Fit Info Tech.

Psychological Basis of Perfumery: Translation of the Expanded Fourth German Edition. 4th ed. Ed. by J. Stephan Jellinek. LC 96-85871. 288p. 1997. write for info. (*0-7514-0368-7*) Kluwer Academic.

Psychological Basis Underlying Common Stock Movements. Loren V. Corotto. LC 87-51166. 1987. pap. 14.95 (*0-941099-00-8*); lib. bdg. 17.95 (*0-941099-01-6*) Tourmaline Pub.

*__Psychological Biblical Criticism: Guides to Biblical Scholarship - Old Testament.__ D. Andrew Kille. 2000. pap. 21.00 (*0-8006-3246-X*, Fortress Pr) Augsburg Fortress.

Psychological Birth of the Human Infant. Margaret S. Mahler et al. LC 74-77255. 320p. 1975. pap. 37.50 (*0-465-06659-3*, Pub. by Basic) HarpC.

*__Psychological Birth of the Human Infant: Symbiosis & Individuation.__ Margaret S. Mahler. (Illus.). 2000. pap. 27.50 (*0-465-09554-2*, Pub. by Basic) HarpC.

Psychological Care During Pregnancy & the Postpartum Period. fac. ed. Walter A. Brown. LC 78-64644. 171p. pap. 53.10 (*0-7837-7505-9*, 204700100005) Bks Demand.

Psychological Care in Old Age. Nicholas R. Leng. 140p. 1990. 59.95 (*1-56032-049-4*) Taylor & Francis.

Psychological Care in Physical Illness. Keith A. Nichols. LC 84-71617. 204p. 1984. pap. text 21.95 (*0-914783-06-8*) Charles.

Psychological Care in Physical Illness. 2nd ed. Nichols. 248p. 1993. pap. 41.50 (*1-56593-134-3*, 0446) Singular Publishing.

Psychological Care in Physical Illness. 2nd ed. Keith A. Nichols. LC 92-49595. 1993. 34.95 (*0-412-43560-8*) Chapman & Hall.

Psychological Care of Infant & Child. John B. Watson. LC 75-169399. (Family in America Ser.). 206p. 1976. reprint ed. 13.95 (*0-405-03876-3*) Ayer.

Psychological Case Formulation in Clinical Practice. Glenn Waller & Liz Offen. 250p. 2000. 49.95 (*0-471-97568-0*); pap. 49.95 (*0-471-95726-7*) Wiley.

Psychological Chart. Paramhansa Yogananda. 44p. 1993. pap. 7.95 (*0-937134-06-6*) Amrita Found.

Psychological Cinemas: A Poetical Autobiography. Anthony Neal. 1998. pap. 15.95 (*1-890301-06-X*) M Bey.

Psychological Classification of the Adult Male Prison Inmate. Patricia Van Voorhis. LC 93-13292. (SUNY Series in New Directions in Crime & Justice Studies). 364p. 1994. text 64.50 (*0-7914-1793-X*); pap. text 21.95 (*0-7914-1794-8*) State U NY Pr.

Psychological Commentaries on the Teaching of Gurdjieff & Ouspensky, 6 vols. Maurice Nicoll & Gurdjieff Society of Washington D.C. Staff. LC 96-16548. 2030p. 1996. 150.00 (*0-87728-910-7*) Weiser.

Psychological Commentaries on the Teaching of Gurdjieff & Ouspensky, No. 1. Maurice Nicoll. LC 96-16548. 384p. 1996. reprint ed. 30.00 (*0-87728-899-2*) Weiser.

Psychological Commentaries on the Teaching of Gurdjieff & Ouspensky, Vol. 2. Maurice Nicoll. 416p. 1996. reprint ed. 25.00 (*0-87728-900-X*) Weiser.

Psychological Commentaries on the Teaching of Gurdjieff & Ouspensky, Vol. 3. Maurice Nicoll. 454p. 1996. reprint ed. 25.00 (*0-87728-901-8*) Weiser.

Psychological Commentaries on the Teaching of Gurdjieff & Ouspensky, Vol. 4. Maurice Nicoll. 280p. 1996. reprint ed. 25.00 (*0-87728-902-6*) Weiser.

Psychological Commentaries on the Teaching of Gurdjieff & Ouspensky, Vol. 5. Maurice Nicoll. 264p. 1996. reprint ed. 25.00 (*0-87728-903-4*) Weiser.

Psychological Commentaries on the Teaching of Gurdjieff & Ouspensky, Vol. 6. Maurice Nicoll. 216p. 1996. reprint ed. 25.00 (*0-87728-904-2*) Weiser.

Psychological Commentaries on the Teachings of Gurdjieff & Ouspensky, Vol. 3. Maurice Nicoll. LC 83-25194. 447p. (Orig.). 1984. pap. 24.95 (*0-394-72396-1*, Pub. by Shambhala Pubns) Random.

Psychological Comments & Queries. J. R. Kantor. 1984. 20.00 (*0-317-15914-3*) Principia Pr.

Psychological Concepts & Dissociative Disorders. Ed. by Raymond Klein & Benjamin Doane. 384p. 1994. text 89.95 (*0-8058-0516-8*) L Erlbaum Assocs.

Psychological Concomitants of Illness see Physican & the Mental Health of the Child

Psychological Consequences of Being a Black American: A Source Book of Research by Black Psychologists. Ed. by Roger N. Wilcox. LC 74-142720. 506p. (C). reprint ed. 156.90 (*0-8357-9968-9*, 205162200099) Bks Demand.

Psychological Consequences of Crowding. Uday Jain. 160p. (C). 1988. text 17.95 (*0-8039-9546-6*) Sage.

Psychological Consequences of Disasters: Prevention & Management. 24p. (Orig.). (C). 1993. pap. text 20.00 (*1-56806-774-7*) DIANE Pub.

Psychological Consultation: Introduction to Theiry & Practice. 4th ed. Brown & Pryzwansky. LC 97-39540. 448p. 1997. 62.00 (*0-205-26830-7*) P-H.

*__Psychological Consultation: Introduction to Theory & Practice.__ 5th ed. Duane Brown & Walter B. Pryzwansky. 384p. 2000. 60.00 (*0-205-32210-7*) Allyn.

Psychological Consultation: Perspectives & Applications. William A. Wallace & Donald L. Hall. (Counseling Ser.). 480p. 1995. 79.95 (*0-534-23094-6*) Brooks-Cole.

Psychological Consultation in Educational Settings. Judith L. Alpert et al. LC 82-8995. (Jossey-Bass Social & Behavioral Science Ser.). 359p. reprint ed. pap. 111.30 (*0-8357-4796-4*, 203773300009) Bks Demand.

Psychological Consultation in Educational Settings: Casebook for Working with Administrators, Teachers, Students. Judith L. Alpert et al. LC 94-45754. 362p. 1995. pap. 40.00 (*1-56821-485-5*) Aronson.

*__Psychological Consultation in Parental Rights Cases.__ Frank J. Dyer. LC 99-29101. 300p. 1999. lib. bdg. 35.00 (*1-57230-474-X*) Guilford Pubns.

Psychological Consultation to Business. Robert G. Rose. LC 94-8302. 195p. 1994. pap. 25.00 (*0-911907-15-7*) Psych Assess.

Psychological Consulting to Management: A Clinician's Perspective. Lester R. Tobias. LC 89-22098. 208p. 1990. text 29.95 (*0-87630-564-8*) Brunner-Mazel.

Psychological Contracts in Organizations: Understanding Written & Unwritten Agreements. Denise M. Rousseau. LC 95-11730. (Illus.). 242p. 1995. 48.00 (*0-8039-7104-4*); pap. 21.95 (*0-8039-7105-2*) Sage.

*__Psychological Coping Skills, Psychology & You.__ 3rd ed. Romano McMahon. 1999. pap. 12.00 (*0-538-42906-2*) S-W Pub.

Psychological Correlates of Entrepreneurship: What Makes a Winner. Wayne H. Stewart, Jr. LC 96-42263. (Studies in Entrepreneurship). 130p. 1996. text 51.00 (*0-8153-2648-3*) Garland.

Psychological Correlates of Infant Cognition: A Special Issue of "Developmental Neuropsychology" Ed. by Heikki Lyytinen. 1997. pap. 100.00 (*0-8058-9871-9*) L Erlbaum Assocs.

Psychological Counseling in a Small College. Eugenia Hanfmann et al. 144p. 1963. 18.95 (*0-87073-460-1*) Schenkman Bks Inc.

Psychological Counseling of Adolescents: The Proceedings. Catholic University of America Staff. Ed. by Raymond J. Steimel. LC 62-6111. 176p. reprint ed. pap. 54.60 (*0-608-11308-5*, 200521200051) Bks Demand.

Psychological Crime Thriller. Jerry Nachman. (*0-679-41275-1*) Random.

*__Psychological Debriefing: Theory, Practice & Evidence.__ Ed. by Beverley Raphael & John P. Wilson. LC 99-52565. (Illus.). 366p. 2000. text. write for info. (*0-521-64700-2*) Cambridge U Pr.

Psychological Decision Theory. Jozef Kozielecki. 1982. lib. bdg. 176.50 (*90-277-1051-1*) Kluwer Academic.

Psychological Defenses in Everyday Life. Robert W. Firestone & Joyce Catlett. (Insight Bk.). 256p. 1989. pap. 22.95 (*0-89885-454-7*, Kluwer Acad Hman Sci) Kluwer Academic.

Psychological Defenses in Everyday Life. rev. ed. Robert W. Firestone & Joyce Catlett. 264p. 1989. pap. 12.95 (*0-9676684-1-7*) Glendon Assn.

Psychological Deprivation: Index of New Information, with Authors, Subjects & Bibliography. Susanna L. Warren. LC 95-14594. 1995. write for info. (*0-7883-0700-2*); pap. write for info. (*0-7883-0707-X*) ABBE Pubs Assn.

Psychological Development. Speer. (C). 1996. pap. text, student ed. 17.75 (*0-15-500925-7*) Harcourt Coll Pubs.

Psychological Development. Kathleen M. Speer. (C). 1998. pap. text, teacher ed. 28.00 (*0-15-500924-9*); pap. text, teacher ed., suppl. ed. 28.00 (*0-15-500926-5*) Harcourt Coll Pubs.

Psychological Development: A Life-Span Approach. Paul H. Mussen et al. LC 78-11977. (C). 1979. text 30.33 (*0-06-044692-7*) Addson-Wesley Educ.

Psychological Development of Children. Faye B. Steuer. 1994. mass mkt., teacher ed. write for info. (*0-534-14769-0*) Brooks-Cole.

Psychological Development of Deaf Children. Marc Marschark. (Illus.). 288p. 1997. reprint ed. pap. text 24.95 (*0-19-511575-9*) OUP.

Psychological Development of High Risk Multiple Birth Children. V. Krall. xi, 148p. 1991. text 83.00 (*3-7186-0516-3*, Harwood Acad Pubs) Gordon & Breach.

Psychological Development of Low-Birthweight Children. Ed. by National Institutes of Child Health & Human Development Staff et al. (Advances in Applied Developmental Psychology Ser.: Vol. 6). 505p. (C). 1992. text 83.50 (*0-89391-855-5*) Ablx Pub.

Psychological Development of the Child. 3rd ed. Paul H. Mussen. (Foundations of Modern Psychology Ser.). (Illus.). 1979. text 17.95 (*0-13-732420-0*) P-H.

Psychological Differences: Causes, Consequences & Uses in Education & Guidance. James A. Wakefield & Nancy A. Goad. LC 82-71256. 1982. pap. 14.50 (*0-912736-27-5*) EDITS Pubs.

Psychological Dimensions of Near Eastern Studies. Ed. by L. Carl Brown & Norman Itzkowitz. LC 75-43499. 382p. 1977. 9.95 (*0-87850-028-6*) Darwin Pr.

Psychological Dimensions of Organizational Behavior. 2nd ed. Ed. by Barry M. Staw. LC 94-19440. 528p. 1994. 62.00 (*0-02-416153-5*, Macmillan Coll) P-H.

Psychological Dimensions of War. Ed. by Betty Glad. (Violence, Cooperation, & Peace Ser.). 384p. (C). 1990. text 55.00 (*0-8039-3940-X*); pap. text 24.95 (*0-8039-3941-8*) Sage.

Psychological Dimensions of War. Ed. by Betty Glad. LC 90-8755. (Violence, Cooperation, Peace Ser.). 384p. 1990. reprint ed. pap. 119.10 (*0-608-02772-3*, 206383800007) Bks Demand.

Psychological Disorders in General Medical Settings. Ed. by Norman Sartorius et al. LC 89-24611. 220p. (C). 1990. text 39.00 (*0-920887-59-7*) Hogrefe & Huber Pubs.

Psychological Disorders of Young Children. S. Dutta Ray. 259p. 1980. 19.95 (*0-318-36940-0*) Asia Bk Corp.

Psychological Disorders Related to Designer Drugs. Ed. by Carol C. Nadelson & Claire E. Reinburg. LC 99-13437. (Encyclopedia of Psychological Disorders Ser.). (Illus.). 144p. (YA). (gr. 7 up). 1999. lib. bdg. 24.95 (*0-7910-4957-4*) Chelsea Hse.

Psychological Disturbance in Adolescence. 2nd ed. Irving B. Weiner. LC 91-18344. (Series on Personality Processes: No. 1341). 496p. 1992. 95.00 (*0-471-82596-4*) Wiley.

Psychological Disturbances in Epilepsy. Ed. by J. Chris Sackellares & Stanley Berent. 272p. 1995. text 82.00 (*0-7506-9605-2*) Buttrwrth-Heinemann.

Psychological Disturbances in Y. Ed. by Micheal Rutter. 425p. 1997. pap. text 24.95 (*0-521-59873-7*) Cambridge U Pr.

Psychological Dog Training: Behavior Conditioning with Respect & Trust. C. W. Meisterfeld. (Illus.). 232p. (Orig.). (YA). (gr. 6 up). 1991. pap. 18.00 (*0-9601292-6-X*) M R K.

Psychological Dynamics of Religious Experience. Andre Godin. Tr. by Mary Turton from FRE. LC 85-2354. Orig. Title: Psychologie des Experiences Religieuses. 279p. 1985. pap. 18.95 (*0-89135-039-X*) Religious Educ.

*__Psychological Dynamics of Sport & Exercise.__ 2nd rev. ed. Diane L. Gill. LC 99-57712. (Illus.). 368p. 2000. 45.00 (*0-87322-956-8*) Human Kinetics.

Psychological Economics. Reth & Peter E. Earl. 1987. lib. bdg. 110.50 (*0-89838-234-3*) Kluwer Academic.

Psychological Economics. George Katona. LC 75-8272. 448p. reprint ed. pap. 138.90 (*0-608-16388-0*, 202627600049) Bks Demand.

Psychological Effects of Aerobic Fitness Training: Research & Theory. D. G. McDonald & J. A. Hodgdon. xi, 224p. 1991. 58.95 (*0-387-97603-5*) Spr-Verlag.

Psychological Effects of Cocaine & Crack Addiction. Ann Holmes & Claire E. Reinburg. Ed. by Carol C. Nadelson. LC 98-30975. (Encyclopedia of Psychological Disorders Ser.). 1998. 22.95 (*0-7910-4898-5*) Chelsea Hse.

Psychological Effects of Motherhood: A Study of First Pregnancy. Myra Leifer. LC 79-26179. 304p. 1980. 14.95 (*0-275-91691-X*, C1691, Praeger Pubs) Greenwood.

Psychological Effects of Police Work: A Psychodynamic Approach. P. Bonifacio. (Criminal Justice & Public Safety Ser.). (Illus.). 220p. (C). 1991. 42.50 (*0-306-43955-7*, Plenum Trade) Perseus Pubng.

Psychological Effects of U. S. Air Operations in Four Wars, 1941-1991: Lessons for U. S. Commanders. Stephen T. Hosmer. LC 95-46900. 225p. (Orig.). 1996. pap. text 15.00 (*0-8330-2336-5*, MR-576-AF) Rand Corp.

Psychological Effects of War & Violence on Children. Ed. by Lewis A. Leavitt & Nathan A. Fox. 392p. 1993. pap. 36.00 (*0-8058-1172-9*); text 89.95 (*0-8058-1171-0*) L Erlbaum Assocs.

Psychological Element in the English Sociological Novel of the 19th Century. Sijna De Vooys. LC 68-2022. (Studies in Fiction: No. 34). 1969. reprint ed. lib. bdg. 75.00 (*0-8383-0539-3*) M S G Haskell Hse.

Psychological Emergencies & Crisis. Brent Q. Hafen. 432p. 1995. pap. text 27.20 (*0-13-736406-7*) P-H.

Psychological Evaluation of Exceptional Children. Harold D. Love. (Illus.). 132p. 1985. 31.95 (*0-398-05045-7*); pap. 20.95 (*0-398-06247-1*) C C Thomas.

Psychological Evaluation of the Developmentally & Physically Handicapped. V. B. Van Hasselt & M. Hersen. LC 87-15275. (Illus.). 348p. (C). 1987. 80.00 (*0-306-42514-9*, Plenum Trade) Perseus Pubng.

Psychological Evaluations for the Courts: A Handbook for Mental Health Professionals & Lawyers. 2nd ed. Gary B. Melton et al. LC 97-10163. (Law & Behavior Ser.). 794p. 1997. lib. bdg. 75.00 (*1-57230-236-4*, 0236) Guilford Pubns.

Psychological Examination: A Guide for Clinicians. Paul W. Pruyser. LC 78-70234. 311p. 1979. 47.50 (*0-8236-5605-5*) Intl Univs Pr.

Psychological Examination of the Child. Theodore H. Blau. LC 90-39091. (Series on Personality Processes). 279p. 1991. 99.95 (*0-471-63559-6*) Wiley.

Psychological Experiences Connected with Different Parts of Speech. Ed. by Eleanor H. Rowland. (Psychology Monographs General & Applied: Vol. 8). 1974. reprint ed. pap. 55.00 (*0-8115-1407-2*) Periodicals Srv.

*__Psychological Experiments on the Internet.__ Michael H. Birnbaum. LC 99-68195. (Illus.). 352p. 1999. 59.95 (*0-12-099980-3*) Acad Pr.

*__Psychological Experts in Divorce Actions.__ 3rd ed. Marc J. Ackerman & Andrew W. Kane. LC 98-194251. xxxiii, 1190 p. 1998. boxed set 148.00 (*1-56706-922-3*) Aspen Law.

Psychological Experts in Personal Injury Actions, 1. 3rd ed. Marc J. Ackerman. LC 98-193425. 1156p. 1998. boxed set. write for info. (*1-56706-921-5*) Panel Pubs.

Psychological Explanations of Crime. Ed. by David P. Farrington. (International Library of Criminology & Criminal Justice). 484p. 1994. 194.95 (*1-85521-447-4*, Pub. by Dartmth Pub) Ashgate Pub Co.

Psychological Factors Affecting Medical Conditions. Alan Stoudemire. LC 94-27559. 240p. 1995. text 32.00 (*0-88048-708-9*, 8708) Am Psychiatric.

Psychological Factors in Competitive Sport. Don Davies & Malcom Armstrong. 180p. 1989. pap. 34.95 (*1-85000-607-5*, Falmer Pr) Taylor & Francis.

*__Psychological Factors in Emergency Medical Services for Children: Abstracts of the Psychological, Behavioral & Medical Literature, 1991-1998.__ Ed. by Lisa M. Horowitz et al. LC 99-39564. (Bibliographies in Psychology Ser.). 1999. pap. 19.95 (*1-55798-630-4*, 431-9220) Am Psychol.

P

An Asterisk (*) at the beginning of an entry indicates that the title is appearing for the first time.

Psychological Factors of Peace & War. Tom H. Pear. 262p. 1977. 18.95 (0-8369-2290-5) Ayer.

***Psychological First Aid Kit.** Darrell Franken. 318p. 1999. pap. 59.95 (0-934957-17-7) Wellness Pubns.

***Psychological First Aid Kit - Christian Teacher's Manual.** Darrell Franken. (Illus.). 90p. 1999. pap., teacher ed. 17.95 (0-934957-18-5) Wellness Pubns.

Psychological Foundations of Criminal Justice: Contemporary Perpectives on Forensic Psychiartry & Psychology, Vol. 2. Ed. by Harold J. Vetter & Robert W. Rieber. LC 78-18781. (Illus.). 416p. (C). 1980. 20.00 (0-89444-025-X) John Jay Pr.

Psychological Foundations of Criminal Justice: Historical Perspectives on Forensic Psychology, Vol. 1. Ed. by Robert W. Rieber & Harold J. Vetter. LC 78-18781. (Illus.). (C). 1978. 20.00 (0-89444-009-8); pap. 20.00 (0-89444-012-8) John Jay Pr.

Psychological Foundations of Economic Behavior. Ed. by Paul J. Albanese. LC 87-38476. 190p. 1988. 57.95 (0-275-92742-3, C2742, Praeger Pubs) Greenwood.

Psychological Foundations of Education. (National Teacher Examination Ser.: NC-1). pap. 23.95 (0-8373-8401-X) Nat Learn.

Psychological Foundations of Education: Readings. Ed. by Miriam Goldbert & Martha Werle. 350p. 1974. text 34.50 (0-8422-5187-1) Irvington.

Psychological Foundations of Moral Education & Character Development: An Integrated Theory of Moral Development. rev. ed. Ed. by Richard T. Knowles & George F. McLean. LC 92-56119. (Cultural Heritage & Contemporary Change Series VI: Foundations of Moral Education,: Vol. 2). 310p. (Orig.). 1992. pap. 17.50 (1-56518-002-X) Coun Res Values.

Psychological Foundations of Moral Education & Character Development: An Integrated Theory of Moral Development. 2nd rev. ed. Ed. by Richard T. Knowles & George F. McLean. LC 92-56119. (Cultural Heritage & Contemporary Change Series VI: Foundations of Moral Education,: Vol. 2). 310p. (Orig.). 1992. 45.00 (1-56518-003-8) Coun Res Values.

Psychological Foundations of Musical Behavior. 3rd ed. Rudolf E. Radocy & J. David Boyle. LC 96-31867. (Illus.). 408p. 1997. text 61.95 (0-398-06720-1); pap. text 44.95 (0-398-06721-X) C C Thomas.

Psychological Foundations of Sport. Ed. by John M. Silva & Robert S. Weinberg. LC 83-83239. (Illus.). 552p. 1984. reprint ed. pap. 171.20 (0-608-04283-8, 206506200012) Bks Demand.

Psychological Foundations of the Curriculum (UNESCO) (Education Studies & Documents: No. 26). 1974. reprint ed. pap. 25.00 (0-8115-1350-5) Periodicals Srv.

Psychological Healing: A Historical & Clinical Study, 2 vols., Set. Pierre M. Janet. LC 75-16710. (Classics in Psychiatry Ser.). 1976. reprint ed. 101.95 (0-405-07437-9) Ayer.

Psychological Healing: A Historical & Clinical Study, 2 vols., Vol. 1. Pierre M. Janet. LC 75-16710. (Classics in Psychiatry Ser.). 1977. reprint ed. 51.95 (0-405-07438-7) Ayer.

Psychological Healing: A Historical & Clinical Study, 2 vols., Vol. 2. Pierre M. Janet. LC 75-16710. (Classics in Psychiatry Ser.). 1977. reprint ed. 51.95 (0-405-07439-5) Ayer.

Psychological Immunity: Parent's First Line of Defense. K. L. Reddy. LC 95-69778. 218p. (Orig.). (C). 1995. pap. 16.95 (1-882792-11-4) Proctor Pubns.

Psychological Impact of Unemployment. N. T. Feather. (Illus.). xi, 285p. 1989. 96.95 (0-387-97027-4) Spr-Verlag.

***Psychological Interpretation of Ruth/Standing in the Sandals of Naomi: In the Light of Mythology, Legend & Kabbalah.** Yehezkel Kluger & Nomi Kluger-Nash. 1999. pap. 17.95 (3-85630-587-4, Pub. by Daimon Pubs) Cassell & Continuum.

***Psychological Intervention & Cultural Diversity.** 2nd ed. Ed. by Joseph F. Aponte & Julian Wohl. LC 99-37811. 320p. 1999. 66.67 (0-205-29474-X) Allyn.

Psychological Interventions: A Guide to Strategies. Ed. by Mary Ballou. LC 95-6939. 232p. 1995. 59.95 (0-275-94851-X, Praeger Pubs) Greenwood.

Psychological Interventions & Research with Latino Populations. Ed. by Jorge G. Garcia & Maria C. Zea. LC 96-19256. 284p. (C). 1996. 64.00 (0-205-16095-6) Allyn.

Psychological Issues in Biblical Lore: Explorations in the Old Testament. Albert I. Rabin. LC 98-17874. (Series on Social Work). 1998. 34.95 (0-8261-1212-9) Springer Pub.

Psychological Issues in Eyewitness Identification. Ed. by Siegfried L. Sporer et al. 328p. 1995. 69.95 (0-8058-1198-2); pap. 36.00 (0-8058-1865-0) L Erlbaum Assocs.

Psychological Issues Related to Child Maltreatment Vol. 24: Working Group Report by the Coordinating Committee on Child Abuse & Neglect, American Psychological Association. Ed. by Diane J. Willis. 101p. 1996. pap., suppl. ed. 20.00 (0-8058-9924-3) L Erlbaum Assocs.

Psychological Kinesiology: Changing the Body's Beliefs. rev. ed. William F. Whisenant. (Illus.). 400p. (Orig.). 1994. pap. 49.95 (1-880790-55-6) Monarch Butterfly.

Psychological Knowledge: A Social History & Philosophy. Martin Kusch. LC 98-35091. (Philosophical Issues in Science Ser.). (Illus.). 360p. (C). (gr. 13). 1999. 99.99 (0-415-19253-6, D6276) Routledge.

Psychological Learning for Instruction. 2nd ed. Driscoll. LC 99-35051. 448p. 1999. 52.00 (0-205-26321-6) Allyn.

Psychological Linguistics. J. R. Kantor. 1977. 15.00 (0-911188-53-3) Principia Pr.

Psychological Management of Chronic Headaches. Paul R. Martin. LC 92-48225. (Treatment Manuals for Practitioners Ser.). 266p. 1993. lib. bdg. 42.00 (0-89862-211-5) Guilford Pubns.

Psychological Management of Chronic Headaches. Paul R. Martin. LC 92-48225. (Treatment Manuals for Practitioners Ser.). 266p. 1996. pap. text 23.00 (1-57230-122-8, 0122) Guilford Pubns.

Psychological Management of Chronic Pain, 2 vols. 2nd ed. H. Clare Philips & Stanley J. Rachman. Incl. Psychological Management of Chronic Pain: A Treatment Manual. 2nd ed. (Illus.). 304p. 1996. 42.95 (0-8261-6111-1); Psychological Management of Chronic Pain: Patient Manual. 2nd ed. (Illus.). 80p. 1996. teacher ed. 14.95 (0-8261-6112-X); (Behavior Therapy & Behavioral Medicine Ser.). 1996. 52.00 (0-8261-6113-8, P4821) Springer Pub.

Psychological Management of Chronic Pain: A Treatment Manual see Psychological Management of Chronic Pain

Psychological Management of Chronic Pain: Patient Manual see Psychological Management of Chronic Pain

Psychological Management of Schizophrenia. Ed. by Max J. Birchwood & Nicholas Tarrier. LC 94-6698. 176p. 1994. pap. 65.95 (0-471-95056-4) Wiley.

Psychological Managements for Psychosomatic Disorders. J. W. Paulley & H. E. Pelser. (Illus.). 370p. 1989. 86.95 (0-387-19298-0) Spr-Verlag.

Psychological Managemnt of Chronic Tinnitus. 272p. (C). 2001. 50.00 (0-205-31365-5) Allyn.

Psychological Meaning of Chaos: Translating Theory into Practice. Ed. by Frank Masterpasqua & Phyllis A. Perna. LC 97-12954. 323p. 1997. text 39.95 (1-55798-429-8, 431-7910) Am Psychol.

Psychological Measurements in Psychopharmacology. Ed. by P. Pichot & R. Olivier-Martin. (Modern Problems of Pharmacopsychiatry Ser.: Vol. 7). (Illus.). 1974. 85.25 (3-8055-1630-4) S Karger.

***Psychological Mechanisms of Pain & Pain Modulation.** Donald D. Price. LC 99-39682. (Progress in Pain Research & Management Ser.). 248p. 1999. 69.00 (0-931092-29-9) Intl Assn Study Pain.

Psychological Medicine Insights: Treating Patients' Medical Psychological Problems. Harry Ireton. LC 85-73695. 80p. (Orig.). 1985. pap. text 15.00 (0-936787-00-7) Behavior Sci Systs.

Psychological Medicine of HIV Infection. Ed. by J. Catalan et al. (Illus.). 316p. 1996. text 85.00 (0-19-262202-1) OUP.

Psychological Methods in Criminal Investigation & Evidence. Ed. by David Raskin. 416p. 1989. 46.95 (0-8261-6450-1) Springer Pub.

Psychological Methods of Child Assessment. Jacquelin Goldman et al. LC 83-20889. 416p. 1984. text 47.95 (0-87630-348-3) Brunner-Mazel.

Psychological Methods of Testing Intelligence, 4. William L. Stern. Tr. by G. M. Whipple from GER. LC 77-72191. (Contributions to the History of Psychology Ser.). 494p. 1977. reprint ed. lib. bdg. 85.00 (0-313-26939-4, U6939, Greenwood Pr) Greenwood.

Psychological Milieu of Lytton Strachey. Martin Kallich. 1961. pap. 7.95 (0-8084-0408-3) NCUP.

Psychological Mindedness: A Contemporary Understanding. Ed. by Mary McCallum & William E. Piper. LC 97-2440. (Personality & Clinical Psychology Ser.). (Illus.). 375p. 1997. text. write for info. (0-8058-1722-0) L Erlbaum Assocs.

Psychological Models & Neural Mechanisms: An Examination of Reductionism in Psychology. Austen Clark. (CLLP Ser.). (Illus.). 216p. (C). 1980. text 70.00 (0-19-824422-3) OUP.

***Psychological Models of Communication in Collaborative Systems: Papers from the 1999 AAAI Symposium.** Ed. by Susan E. Brennan. 145p. 1999. pap. 25.00 (1-57735-105-3) AAAI Pr.

Psychological Mystique. Stewart Justman. LC 98-29522. (Rethinking Theory Ser.). 180p. 1998. 29.95 (0-8101-1601-4) Northwestern U Pr.

Psychological Needs of Adults: A Symposium. Gardner Murphy & Raymond G. Kuhlen. LC BF0727.A4M8. (Notes & Essays on Education for Adults Ser.: Vol. 12). 27p. reprint ed. pap. 30.00 (0-608-30830-7, 200041000025) Bks Demand.

Psychological, Neuropsychiatric, & Substance Abuse Aspects of AIDS. 1990. lib. bdg. 79.95 (0-87700-892-2) Revisionist Pr.

Psychological, Neuropsychiatric, & Substance Abuse Aspects of AIDS. fac. ed. Ed. by T. Peter Bridge et al. LC 87-42723. (Advances in Biochemical Psychopharmacology Ser.: No. 44). (Illus.). 281p. 1988. pap. 87.20 (0-7837-7271-8, 204703400005) Bks Demand.

Psychological Novel, 1900-1950. Leon Edel. 147p. (C). 1966. lib. bdg. 75.00 (0-8383-0657-8) M S G Haskell Hse.

Psychological Operations: Principles & Case Studies. Frank L. Goldstein. 376p. 1996. per. 21.00 (0-16-061365-5) USGPO.

Psychological Operations: Principles & Case Studies. Ed. by Frank L. Goldstein & Benjamin F. Findley. (Illus.). 376p. 1996. pap. 21.00 (1-58566-016-7) Air Univ.

Psychological Operations: Principles & Case Studies. Frank L. Goldstein & Benjamin F. Findley, Jr. (Illus.). 364p. 1997. pap. text 45.00 (0-7881-4667-X) DIANE Pub.

Psychological Operations & Political Warfare in Long-Term Strategic Planning. Janos Radvanyi. LC 90-31183. 168p. 1990. 47.95 (0-275-93623-6, C3623, Praeger Pubs) Greenwood.

Psychological Operations in Warfare. 1991. lib. bdg. 76.00 (0-8490-4117-1) Gordon Pr.

Psychological Organizations in Community & Culture. Coon. Date not set. pap. text. write for info. (0-314-81022-6) West Pub.

Psychological Patterns of Jesus Christ. Frank Jakubowsky. 342p. (Orig.). 1982. pap. 14.95 (0-932588-02-6) Jesus Bks.

Psychological Perspectives & the Religious Quest: Essays in Honor of Orlo Strunk, Jr. Ed. by Lallene J. Rector & Weaver Santaniello. LC 98-31582. 208p. 1998. 49.00 (0-7618-1292-X); pap. 26.50 (0-7618-1293-8) U Pr of Amer.

Psychological Perspectives in Education. Mark Fox. Ed. by Jonathan Solity. (Introduction to Education Ser.). (Illus.). 160p. 1993. 75.00 (0-304-32467-1); pap. 35.00 (0-304-32470-1) Weidner & Sons.

Psychological Perspectives of Essential Hypertension. W. Linden. (Biobehavioral Medicine Ser.: Vol. 3). (Illus.). x, 130p. 1984. pap. 60.00 (3-8055-3662-3) S Karger.

Psychological Perspectives of the Holocaust & of Its Aftermath. Ed. by Randolph L. Braham. (Holocaust Studies Series Social Science Monographs). 225p. 1988. text 69.50 (0-88033-960-8, Pub. by East Eur Monographs) Col U Pr.

Psychological Perspectives on Christian Ministry. Ed. by Leslie J. Francis & Susan H. Jones. 424p. 1997. pap. 29.95 (0-85244-332-3, 957, Pub. by Gra1cewing) Morehouse Pub.

Psychological Perspectives on Deafness. Ed. by Marc Marschark & M. Diane Clark. 400p. 1993. text 79.95 (0-8058-1054-4) L Erlbaum Assocs.

Psychological Perspectives on Deafness, Vol. II. Ed. by Marc Marschark & M. Diane Clark. 300p. 1998. write for info. (0-8058-2709-9); pap. write for info. (0-8058-2710-2) L Erlbaum Assocs.

Psychological Perspectives on Human Diversity in America. Ed. by Jacqueline D. Goodchilds. 192p. 1991. pap. text 14.95 (1-55798-122-1) Am Psychol.

Psychological Perspectives on Human Sexuality. Ed. by Lenore Szuchman & Frank Muscarella. LC 99-30531. 682p. 1999. 59.95 (0-471-24405-8) Wiley.

Psychological Perspectives on Intervention: A Case Study Approach to Prescriptions for Change. Rik C. D'Amato & Barbara A. Rothlisberg. (Illus.). 211p. (C). 1997. reprint ed. pap. text 15.95 (0-88133-974-1) Waveland Pr.

Psychological Perspectives on Justice: Theory & Applications. Ed. by Barbara A. Mellers & Jonathan Baron. LC 92-27263. (Series on Judgment & Decision Making). (Illus.). 360p. (C). 1993. text 59.95 (0-521-43199-9) Cambridge U Pr.

Psychological Perspectives on Lesbian & Gay Male Experiences. Ed. by Linda D. Garnets & Douglas C. Kimmel. 512p. 1993. pap. 31.50 (0-231-07885-4) Col U Pr.

Psychological Perspectives on Politics. Carol Barner-Barry & Robert Rosenwein. (Illus.). 342p. (C). 1991. reprint ed. pap. text 22.95 (0-88133-619-X) Waveland Pr.

Psychological Perspectives on Pregnancy & Childbirth. Sarah Clement. LC 97-36826. 1998. pap. text 29.50 (0-443-05760-5) Church.

***Psychological Perspectives on Self & Identity.** Ed. by Abraham Tesser et al. LC 00-21139. 272p. 2000. text 39.95 (1-55798-678-9, 431-8940) Am Psychol.

Psychological Perspectives on Sexual Problems: New Directions in Theory & Practice. Ed. by Jane M. Ussher & Christine D. Baker. LC 92-13346. (Illus.). 256p. (C). 1993. 85.00 (0-415-05508-3, A7777); pap. 27.99 (0-415-05509-1, A7781) Routledge.

***Psychological Perspectives on Stress & Health.** Ed. by Misra. 1999. 32.00 (81-7022-785-2, Pub. by Concept) S Asia.

Psychological Perspectives on the Life of Paul: An Application of the Methodology of Gerd Theissen. Terrence Callan. LC 90-33278. (Studies in the Bible & Early Christianity: Vol. 22). 172p. 1990. lib. bdg. 79.95 (0-88946-622-X) E Mellen.

Psychological Perspectives on the Self. Ed. by Jerry Suls. 248p. 1993. 59.95 (0-8058-1181-8) L Erlbaum Assocs.

Psychological Perspectives on the Self, Vol. 1. Ed. by Jerry Suls. LC 81-15108. 283p. reprint ed. pap. 87.80 (0-7837-0160-8, 204045700001) Bks Demand.

Psychological Perspectives on the Self, Vol. 2. Ed. by Jerry Suls & Anthony G. Greenwald. 408p. 1983. text 79.95 (0-89859-276-3) L Erlbaum Assocs.

Psychological Perspectives on the Self, Vol. 2, 1983. Ed. by Jerry M. Suls & Anthony G. Greenwald. LC 81-15108. (Illus.). 299p. reprint ed. pap. 92.70 (0-608-10412-4, 204045700002) Bks Demand.

Psychological Perspectives on the Self, Vol. 3. Ed. by Jerry Suls & G. Greenwald. 232p. (C). 1986. text 49.95 (0-89859-703-X) L Erlbaum Assocs.

Psychological Perspectives on the Self, Vol. 3, 1986. Ed. by Jerry M. Suls & Anthony G. Greenwald. LC 81-15108. (Illus.). 224p. reprint ed. pap. 69.50 (0-608-10413-2, 204045700003) Bks Demand.

Psychological Perspectives on Women's Health. Vincent J. Adesso. 360p. 1994. 27.95 (1-56032-335-3) Hemisp Pub.

Psychological Practice in a Changing Health Care System: Issues & New Directions. Ed. by Robert L. Glueckauf et al. LC 96-26099. (Illus.). 224p. 1996. 43.95 (0-8261-9280-7) Springer Pub.

Psychological Practice in Small Towns & Rural Areas. Intro. by Robert D. Weitz. LC 91-35398. (Psychotherapy in Private Practice Ser.: Vol. 10, No. 3, 1992). 137p. 1992. 39.95 (1-56024-280-9) Haworth Pr.

Psychological Principles & the Black Experience. Lawrence N. Houston. 194p. (Orig.). (C). 1990. pap. text 21.50 (0-8191-7957-4); lib. bdg. 40.50 (0-8191-7956-6) U Pr of Amer.

Psychological Problems Before & after Myocardial Infarction. Ed. by H. Denolin. (Advances in Cardiology Ser.: Vol. 29). viii, 156p. 1982. 85.25 (3-8055-3424-8) S Karger.

Psychological Problems in General Practice. A. F. Markus et al. (Oxford General Practice Ser.: No. 15). (Illus.). 424p. 1989. pap. 37.50 (0-19-261529-7) OUP.

Psychological Problems in the Father-Son Relationship. Harold A. Abramson. LC 71-81849. 1969. 7.50 (0-8079-0154-7) October.

Psychological Problems of Aging Assessment Treatment Care. Woods. LC 98-46227. (Wiley Series in Clinical Psychology). 368p. 1999. pap. 43.95 (0-471-97434-X) Wiley.

Psychological Process of Adjusting to Natural Disasters. Lewis Aptekar. 45p. (Orig.). (C). 1993. pap. text 25.00 (1-56806-972-3) DIANE Pub.

Psychological Processes & Advertising Effects: Theory, Research, & Applications. Ed. by Linda F. Alwitt & Andrew A. Mitchell. 320p. 1991. pap. 34.00 (0-89859-515-0) L Erlbaum Assocs.

Psychological Profiles of Conjoined Twins: Heredity, Environment, & Identity. J. David Smith. LC 88-1592. 171p. 1988. 57.95 (0-275-92965-5, C2965, Praeger Pubs) Greenwood.

Psychological Qualitative Research from a Phenomenological Perspective. Gunnar Karlsson. 147p. (Orig.). 1993. pap. 56.50 (91-22-01549-3) Coronet Bks.

Psychological Reflections: A New Anthology of His Writings, 1905-1961. C. G. Jung. Ed. by Jolande Jacobi & R. F. C. Hull. LC 88-177442. (Bollingen Ser.: Vol. 31). 332p. 1970. pap. 16.95 (0-691-01786-7, Pub. by Princeton U Pr) Cal Prin Full Svc.

Psychological Reflections: Students Seeing Themselves in Young Adult Literature. Sharon Stringer. LC 97-3489. (Young Adult Literature Ser.). 98p. (Orig.). 1997. pap. text 19.00 (0-86709-415-X, 0415, Pub. by Boynton Cook Pubs) Heinemann.

Psychological Reflections on Cinematic Terror: Jungian Archetypes in Horror Films. James F. Iaccino. LC 93-30997. 232p. 1994. 59.95 (0-275-94491-3, Praeger Pubs) Greenwood.

Psychological Report Writing. 4th ed. Norman Tallent. 336p. (C). 1992. text 48.00 (0-13-720319-5) P-H.

Psychological Reports: A Guide to Report Writing in Professional Psychology. 2nd rev. ed. Raymond L. Ownby. LC 91-70437. (Illus.). 198p. (C). 1991. pap. text 21.95 (0-88422-019-2) Clinical Psych.

Psychological Reports: A Guide to Report Writing in Professional Psychology. 3rd ed. Raymond L. Ownby. LC 96-20539. 209p. 1997. pap. 39.95 (0-471-16887-4) Wiley.

Psychological Research. Douglas Mook. (C). text. write for info. (0-393-97620-3) Norton.

Psychological Research: Innovative Methods & Strategies. John Haworth. (Illus.). 304p. (C). 1995. pap. 25.99 (0-415-11790-9) Routledge.

Psychological Research: Innovative Methods & Strategies. Ed. by John Haworth. (Illus.). 304p. (C). 1995. 80.00 (0-415-11789-5) Routledge.

Psychological Research: Methods for Discovery & Validation. Arlene C. Vadum & Neil O. Rankin. LC 97-29579. 432p. 1997. 48.13 (0-07-066787-X) McGraw.

Psychological Research with Human Subjects. Concettina N. M. Pagano. (C). lab manual ed. 20.00 (0-9678220-0-9) Luce Tech.

Psychological Responses to Social Change: Human Development in Changing Environments. Ed. by Peter Noack et al. (Prevention & Intervention in Childhood & Adolescence Ser.: No. 18). 264p. (C). 1994. lib. bdg. 64.95 (3-11-014343-7) De Gruyter.

Psychological Risks of Coronary Bypass Surgery. June B. Pimm & Joseph R. Feist. 226p. 1984. 59.50 (0-306-41586-0, Plenum Trade) Perseus Pubng.

Psychological Roots of Communism. Marian Wasilewski. Ed. by Malgorzata Barton. Tr. by Alexandra Chciuk-Celt from POL. 56p. (Orig.). 1987. pap. 7.50 (0-9612122-1-7) Polish Am Ethnic.

***Psychological Science.** Bolden, Jr. 304p. 1999. pap. text 21.00 (0-536-02814-1) Pearson Custom.

Psychological Science & Experiments for High School. Weaver & Johnson. 1997. pap. text 14.95 (0-697-35562-4) McGraw.

Psychological Science, the Study of Human Behavior. 4th ed. Wrightsman. (Psychology Ser.). 1975. pap. 14.75 (0-8185-0139-1) Brooks-Cole.

Psychological Scientific Study of Man. Sanford. (Psychology Ser.). 1970. student ed. 5.25 (0-534-02123-9) Brooks-Cole.

Psychological Sense of Community: Prospects for a Community Psychology. Seymour B. Sarason. LC 73-20962. (Jossey-Bass Behavioral Science Ser.). 304p. reprint ed. pap. 94.30 (0-7837-0187-X, 204048300017) Bks Demand.

Psychological Sense of Community: Prospects for a Community Psychology. rev. ed. Seymour B. Sarason. 290p. 1988. pap. text 19.95 (0-914797-47-6) Brookline Bks.

Psychological Services for Law Enforcement. 543p. (Orig.). (C). 1993. pap. text 50.00 (1-56806-876-X) DIANE Pub.

Psychological Services for Law Enforcement. Theodore H. Blau. 464p. 1994. 125.00 (0-471-55950-4) Wiley.

Psychological, Social, & Educational Dimensions of Deafness. Schirmer. (C). 2000. 40.53 (0-205-17513-9, Macmillan Coll) P-H.

***Psychological Statistics Using Spss for Windows.** Robert C. Gardner. 320p. 2000. pap. 40.00 (0-13-028324-X) P-H.

Psychological Storms. rev. ed. Thomas Parham. (Illus.). 91p. 1993. pap. 6.95 (0-913543-34-9) African Am Imag.

P

An Asterisk (*) at the beginning of an entry indicates that the title is appearing for the first time.

Psychological Strategy for Alternative Human Development: India's Performance since Independence. Prayag Mehta. LC 98-7051. 256p. 1998. 35.00 (0-7619-9257-X) Sage.

Psychological Stress in the Workplace. Terry A. Beehr. LC 94-9357. (Illus.). 288p. (C). (gr. 13). 1995. 75.00 (0-415-09426-7, A8201) Routledge.

Psychological Studies. 2nd ed. Theodor Lipps. LC 73-2972. (Classics in Psychology Ser.). 1974. reprint ed. 23.95 (0-405-05145-X) Ayer.

Psychological Studies see For the Teaching of Mathematics

Psychological Studies on Religious Man. T. Kallstad. 252p. 1978. pap. text 33.00 (91-554-0801-X) Coronet Bks.

Psychological Study of Delinquent & Non-Delinquent Negro Boys. Robert P. Daniel. LC 75-176718. (Columbia University. Teachers College. Contributions to Education Ser.: No. 546). reprint ed. 37.50 (0-404-55546-2) AMS Pr.

Psychological Study of Immigrant Children at Ellis Island. Bertha M. Boody. LC 79-129391. (American Immigration Collection. Series 2). 1970. reprint ed. 16.95 (0-405-00546-6) Ayer.

Psychological Study of Religion: Its Origin, Function, & Future. James H. Leuba. LC 75-98628. reprint ed. 49.50 (0-404-03969-3) AMS Pr.

Psychological Study of Tolstoy's Anna Karenina. Anthony Piraino. LC 93-29917. 172p. 1993. pap. 24.95 (0-7734-1943-8) E Mellen.

Psychological Symptoms. Frank J. Bruno. LC 92-28510. 288p. 1994. pap. 24.95 (0-471-01610-1) Wiley.

*****Psychological Technique of Martin Luther Thomas' Radio Addresses.** Theodor W. Adorno. LC 00-24888. 2000. pap. write for info. (0-8047-4003-8) Stanford U Pr.

Psychological Territories. Andrea F. Litkei. 176p. 1992. 14.95 (1-880165-00-7) Hanlit Pubns.

Psychological Testing. Lisa Friedenberg. 525p. 1995. 93.00 (0-205-14214-1) Allyn.

Psychological Testing. John R. Graham & Roy S. Lilly. (Illus.). 480p. (C). 1984. text 47.20 (0-13-732652-1) P-H.

Psychological Testing. K. Howard & J. Springall. 1996. pap. 129.00 (1-85953-076-1, Pub. by Tech Comm) St Mut.

Psychological Testing. Karen Howard & Joan Springall. (Financial Times Management Briefings Ser.). 1997. pap. 94.50 (0-273-63192-6, Pub. by F T P-H) Trans-Atl Phila.

Psychological Testing. Kaplan. (Psychology). 1982. teacher ed. write for info. (0-534-02118-2) Wadsworth Pub.

Psychological Testing. 2nd ed. Kaplan & Saccuzzo. (Psychology Ser.). 1989. student ed. 15.75 (0-534-09517-8) Brooks-Cole.

Psychological Testing. 3rd ed. Robert Kaplan & Dennis P. Saccuzzo. (Psychology Ser.). 1993. pap., wbk. ed. 22.95 (0-534-16233-9) Brooks-Cole.

Psychological Testing. 3rd ed. Robert Kaplan & Dennis P. Saccuzzo. 680p. (C). 1993. text 50.50 (0-534-16230-4) Brooks-Cole.

*****Psychological Testing.** 5th ed. Kaplan & Saccuzzo. 2000. pap. 22.25 (0-534-50412-4) Wadsworth Pub.

Psychological Testing. 7th ed. Anastasi. (C). 1997. pap. text, student ed. 26.20 (0-13-257321-0) P-H.

Psychological Testing. 7th ed. Anne Anastasi. LC 96-41155. 721p. (C). 1996. 89.00 (0-02-303085-2, Macmillan Coll) P-H.

*****Psychological Testing: A Manager's Guide.** Dulewicz Toplis & Fletcher. 240p. 2000. pap. 47.95 (0-8464-5136-0) Beekman Pubs.

Psychological Testing: A Manager's Guide. John Toplis et al. 144p. (C). 1991. 75.00 (0-85292-471-2, Pub. by IPM Hse) St Mut.

Psychological Testing: A Manager's Guide. 3rd ed. John Toplis et al. LC 98-178370. 240p. 1997. pap. 64.00 (0-85292-694-4, Pub. by IPM Hse) St Mut.

Psychological Testing: A Practical Guide to Aptitude & Other Tests. John Toplis et al. 112p. (C). 1987. 55.00 (0-85292-362-7, Pub. by IPM Hse) St Mut.

Psychological Testing: An Inside View. Ed. by Moshe Zeidner & Robert Most. LC 91-30493. 496p. 1992. pap. 32.95 (0-89106-051-0, 7399, Davies-Black Pub) Consulting Psychol.

Psychological Testing: An Introduction. George Domino. LC 99-19524. 657p. (C). 1999. 88.00 (0-13-020143-X) P-H.

Psychological Testing: Design, Analysis, & Use, with Test Bank. Lisa Friedenberg. (C). 1995. teacher ed. write for info. (0-205-16858-2, H6858-8) Allyn.

*****Psychological Testing: History Principals & Applications.** 3rd ed. 1999. teacher ed. write for info. (0-205-31487-2) Allyn.

Psychological Testing: History, Principles, & Applications. Robert J. Gregory. 768p. (C). 1992. text 32.95 (0-205-13264-2) Allyn.

*****Psychological Testing: History, Principles, & Applications.** 3rd ed. Robert J. Gregory. LC 99-25926. 697p. 1999. 83.00 (0-205-30479-6) Allyn.

Psychological Testing: Principles & Applications. 4th ed. Kevin R. Murphy & Charles O. Davidshofer. LC 97-9966. 602p. 1997. 77.00 (0-13-263815-0) P-H.

Psychological Testing: Principles, Applications, & Issues. Robert M. Kaplan & Dennis P. Saccuzzo. LC 81-38461. (Psychology Ser.). 1150p. (C). 1982. mass mkt. 34.00 (0-8185-0494-3) Brooks-Cole.

Psychological Testing: Principles, Applications, & Issues. 2nd ed. Robert M. Kaplan & Dennis P. Saccuzzo. LC 88-18755. 618p. (C). 1988. mass mkt. 52.25 (0-534-09516-X) Brooks-Cole.

Psychological Testing: Principles, Applications, & Issues. 4th ed. Robert M. Kaplan & Dennis P. Saccuzzo. LC 96-16325. (Psychology Ser.). 736p. (C). 1996. mass mkt. 95.95 (0-534-26364-X) Brooks-Cole.

Psychological Testing: Principles, Applications, & Issues, Test Items. 4th ed. Robert M. Kaplan & Dennis P. Saccuzzo. 1996. mass mkt. write for info. (0-534-34376-7) Brooks-Cole.

Psychological Testing: Student Workbook. 4th ed. Robert M. Kaplan & Dennis P. Saccuzzo. (C). 1996. mass mkt., wbk. ed. 20.00 (0-534-34375-9) Brooks-Cole.

Psychological Testing: Theory & Applications. Louis H. Janda. LC 97-33720. 455p. (C). 1997. 83.00 (0-205-19434-6) Allyn.

Psychological Testing & Assessment. 10th ed. Lewis R. Aiken. LC 99-13723. 501p. (C). 1999. 89.00 (0-205-29567-3) Allyn.

Psychological Testing & Assessment: An Introduction to Tests & Measurement. 4th ed. Ronald J. Cohen et al. LC 98-20417. xxvii, 769p. 1998. text 71.95 (0-7674-0509-9, 0509-9) Mayfield Pub.

*****Psychological Testing & What Those Tests Mean: Am I Okay?** Dwayne E. Pickels. LC 99-30473. (Encyclopedia of Psychological Disorders Ser.). (Illus.). 144p. 1999. 24.95 (0-7910-5319-9) Chelsea Hse.

Psychological Testing in American Society, 1890-1930. Michael M. Sokal. 220p. (Orig.). 1990. pap. text 16.00 (0-8135-1573-4) Rutgers U Pr.

Psychological Testing in Cultural Contexts. Theodora M. Abel. 1973. pap. 15.95 (0-8084-0364-8) NCUP.

Psychological Testing of American Minorities: Issues & Consequences. 2nd ed. Ronald J. Samuda. LC 97-33902. (Multicultural Aspects of Counseling Ser.). 1998. 52.00 (0-7619-1214-2); pap. 24.95 (0-7619-1215-0) Sage.

Psychological Testing of Children from Early Childhood through Adolescence: A Psychodynamic Approach. Miriam G. Siegel. 530p. 1987. 77.50 (0-8236-5615-2) Intl Univs Pr.

*****Psychological Testing of Hispanics.** Kurt F. Geisinger. 301p. 1998. pap. 19.95 (1-55798-538-3) Am Psychol.

Psychological Testing, Theory, & Applications: Instructor's Manual with Test Bank, with Test Bank. Louis Janda. 128p. (C). 1997. text, teacher ed. write for info. (0-205-28142-7, T8142-6) Allyn.

Psychological Tests & Testing: Index of New Information with Authors, Subjects & Bibliography. rev. ed. Rosalie F. Zoltano. LC 94-34893. 179p. 1994. 47.50 (0-7883-0252-3); pap. 44.50 (0-7883-0253-1) ABBE Pubs Assn.

Psychological Theories from a Structuralist Point of View. Ed. by H. Westmeyer. (Recent Research in Psychology Ser.). (Illus.). xiii, 213p. 1989. 56.95 (0-387-51904-1) Spr-Verlag.

*****Psychological Theories of Drinking & Alcoholism.** 2nd ed. Ed. by Kenneth E. Leonard & Howard T. Blane. LC 99-29558. (Substance Abuse Ser.). 467p. 1999. lib. bdg. 49.00 (1-57230-410-3) Guilford Pubns.

Psychological Theories of Human Learning. 2nd ed. Guy R. Lefrancois. LC 81-15511. (Psychology Ser.). 348p. (C). 1982. boxed set 39.95 (0-8185-0501-X) Brooks-Cole.

Psychological Theories of Learning. 3rd rev. ed. Guy R. Lefrancois. LC 94-30411. (Illus.). 380p. 1994. pap. 54.75 (0-534-23202-7) Brooks-Cole.

Psychological Theories of Learning & Teaching: An Analysis of the Use of the Psychology. David C. Payne. Ed. by Don Y. Lee. LC 87-82508. 270p. (C). 1988. 43.50 (0-939758-18-0) Eastern Pr.

Psychological Theories of Motivation. Arkes. (Psychology Ser.). 1977. mass mkt. 19.50 (0-8185-0216-9) Brooks-Cole.

Psychological Theories on Human Learning. Lefrancois. (Psychology Ser.). 1971. mass mkt. 18.50 (0-8185-0014-X) Brooks-Cole.

Psychological Theory of Bipolarity & Reflexivity. Vladimir A. Lefebvre. LC 92-21158. 120p. 1992. text 59.95 (0-7734-9226-7) E Mellen.

Psychological Theory of Work Adjustment: An Individual Differences Model & Its Applications. Rene V. Dawis & Lloyd H. Lofquist. LC 83-23381. (Illus.). 256p. reprint ed. pap. 79.40 (0-8357-7665-4, 205699300097) Bks Demand.

Psychological Time & Mental Illness. Matthew Edlund. LC 85-20577. 137p. 1987. text 29.95 (0-89876-122-0) Gardner Pr.

Psychological Tools: A Sociocultural Approach to Education. Alex Kozulin. LC 98-23168. (Illus.). 192p. 1998. 35.00 (0-674-72141-1) HUP.

Psychological Transactions & Other Posthumous Tracts, 1734-1744. 2nd ed. Emanuel Swedenborg. Ed. & Pref. by Alfred Acton. 282p. 1984. reprint ed. 14.95 (0-915221-62-4) Swedenborg Sci Assn.

Psychological Trauma. Bessel A. Van der Kolk. LC 86-14149. 237p. 1986. text 34.00 (0-88048-233-8, 8233) Am Psychiatric.

Psychological Trauma. Ed. by Rachel Yehuda. LC 98-10614. (Review of Psychiatry Ser.). 206p. 1998. pap. text 29.00 (0-88048-837-9, 8837) Am Psychiatric.

Psychological Trauma & the Adult Survivor: Theory, Therapy, & Transformation. I. Lisa McCann & Laurie A. Pearlman. LC 90-2336. (Psychosocial Stress Ser.: No. 21). 320p. 1990. text 43.95 (0-87630-594-X) Brunner-Mazel.

Psychological Treatment of Depression: A Guide to the Theory & Practice of Cognitive Behaviour Therapy. 2nd ed. J. Mark Williams. LC 92-49555. 1993. pap. write for info. (0-415-06744-8) Routledge.

Psychological Treatment of Depression: A Guide to Theory & Practice of Cognitive Behavior. 2nd ed. J. Mark & G. Williams. LC 94-44552. 312p. (C). 1995. pap. 24.99 (0-415-12874-9, A7433) Routledge.

Psychological Treatment of Mental Illness. Ed. by R. J. Daly & E. A. Sand. (Illus.). 170p. 1987. 79.95 (0-387-17596-2) Spr-Verlag.

Psychological Treatment of Older Adults: An Introductory Text. Ed. by Michel Hersen & Vincent B. Van Hasselt. LC 96-25547. (Adult Development & Aging Ser.). (Illus.). 333p. (C). 1996. 47.00 (0-306-45234-0, Kluwer Plenum) Kluwer Academic.

Psychological Treatment of Panic. David H. Barlow & Jerome A. Cerny. LC 87-19682. (Treatment Manuals for Practitioners Ser.). 227p. 1988. pap. text 22.00 (0-89862-507-6) Guilford Pubns.

Psychological Type: An Introduction. Alan W. Brownsword. 46p. (Orig.). (C). 1988. pap. text 8.00 (0-944393-01-2) Baytree Pubn.

Psychological Type in Action. Ed. by Patricia Cranton. (Illus.). 200p. 1998. pap. 19.95 (0-9661480-1-0) Psychol Type Pr.

Psychological Type in Schools: Applications for Educators. Sondra VanSant & Diane Payne. 1996. 135.00 (0-935652-28-0) Ctr Applications Psych.

Psychological Types. Joseph B. Wheelwright. 1973. pap. 3.00 (0-317-13548-1) C G Jung Frisco.

Psychological Types & the Seven Rays, Vol. 1. Kurt B. Abraham. LC 82-81863. 163p. (Orig.). 1983. pap. 15.00 (0-9609002-0-9) Lampus Pr.

Psychological Typology of Successful Entrepreneurs. John B. Miner. LC 97-8854. 304p. 1997. 69.50 (1-56720-115-6, Quorum Bks) Greenwood.

Psychological View of the Legal System. Linda A. Foley. 400p. (C). 1992. text. write for info. (0-697-12982-9) Brown & Benchmark.

Psychological Vision & Social Criticism in the Novels of Thomas Hardy. Lennart A. Bjork. 178p. (Orig.). 1987. pap. 40.00 (91-22-00868-3) Coronet Bks.

Psychological Vulnerability to Chronic Pain. Ed. by Roy C. Grzesiak & Donald Ciccone. LC 94-6565. 248p. 1994. 38.95 (0-8261-8070-1) Springer Pub.

Psychological Warfare. Paul M. Linebarger. LC 72-4671. (International Propaganda & Communications Ser.). (Illus.). 318p. 1977. reprint ed. 27.95 (0-405-04755-X) Ayer.

Psychological Warfare & Propaganda: Irgun Documentation. Ed. by Eli Tavin & Yonah Alexander. LC 81-52469. 265p. (C). 1982. pap. 17.95 (0-8420-2189-2); lib. bdg. 45.00 (0-8420-2188-4) Scholarly Res Inc.

Psychological Warfare Casebook. Johns Hopkins University Operations Research Offic & William E. Daughtery. 1979. 69.95 (0-405-10597-5) Ayer.

Psychological Warfare Casebook. William E. Daugherty. LC 58-2297. 904p. reprint ed. pap. 200.00 (0-608-30769-6, 200384800037) Bks Demand.

Psychological Well-Being of Nonhuman Primates. National Research Council Staff. LC 98-40103. 130p. (Orig.). (C). 1998. 35.00 (0-309-05233-5) Natl Acad Pr.

Psychological Work & Human Performance. 2nd ed. Robert D. Smithers. 640p. (C). 1997. 90.00 (0-06-501235-6) Addson-Wesley Educ.

Psychological Work & Human Performance: Case Book. 2nd ed. Robert D. Smithers. (C). 1997. pap., student ed. 24.00 (0-06-502060-X) Addson-Wesley Educ.

Psychological World of Natsume Soseki. Takeo Doi. Tr. & Intro. by William J. Tyler. (East Asian Monographs: No. 68). 250p. 1976. text 20.00 (0-674-72116-0) HUP.

Psychological Writings & Letters. Sigmund Freud. Ed. by Sander L. Gilman. (German Library). 324p. (C). 1995. 39.50 (0-8264-0722-6) Continuum.

Psychological Zodiac: The Roots of Self & Society. Angela Arnold. 384p. 1995. pap. 22.50 (0-9525539-3-7, Pub. by Waterweaver Pr) Trans-Atl Phila.

Psychologically Speaking: A Self-Assessment. Donovan Poulenez & Peter C. Rosato. 227p. 1996. pap. text 28.00 (0-205-16364-5, H6364-7) Allyn.

Psychologiche Perspektiven des Bluthochdrucks. W. Linden. (Illus.). vii, 132p. 1983. 58.50 (3-8055-3642-9) S Karger.

Psychologie. Jean Piaget. (FRE.). 1987. lib. bdg. 165.00 (0-7859-3854-0) Fr & Eur.

Psychologie. 2nd ed. Atkinson. (C). 1991. pap. write for info. (0-03-998273-4) Harcourt Coll Pubs.

Psychologie aus dem Begriff. Hermann Druee. (C). 1976. 150.00 (3-11-004603-2) De Gruyter.

Psychologie der Umweltpolitik: Transdisziplinare Erklarungen der Schwierigkeiten Beim Umweltschutz. Reinhard Steurer. (Illus.). 254p. 1998. pap. 45.95 (3-631-33054-5) P Lang Pubng.

Psychologie des Experiences Religieuses see Psychological Dynamics of Religious Experience

Psychologie des Pferdes und der Dressur. Stefan Von Maday. (Documenta Hippologica Ser.). (Illus.). 349p. 1997. reprint ed. 40.00 (3-487-08239-X) G Olms Pubs.

Psychologie des Sectes (Psychology of Sects) Scipio Sighele. Tr. by Louis Brandin from FRE. LC 74-25785. (European Sociology Ser.). 246p. 1975. reprint ed. 21.95 (0-405-06538-8) Ayer.

Psychologie et Pedagogie. Jean Piaget. (FRE.). 1988. pap. 12.95 (0-7859-2814-6) Fr & Eur.

Psychologie Genetique et Didactique des Sciences. 2nd ed. Ed. by Andre Giordan et al. (Exploration Ser.). (FRE., Illus.). 322p. 1997. 31.95 (3-906759-34-2, Pub. by P Lang) P Lang Pubng.

Psychologie-Lexikon. Uwe Tewes. (GER.). 428p. 1992. 75.00 (0-7859-8399-6, 3486209477) Fr & Eur.

Psychologie Ou Traite sur l'Ame, Contenant les Conoissances, Que nous en Donne l'Experience. Arranged by M. Wolff. (Materialien und Dokumente Ser.: Bd. 46). (GER.). xii, 340p. 1998. reprint ed. write for info. (3-487-10629-9) G Olms Pubs.

Psychologie Sociale. Cvetkov. (C). 1991. pap. write for info. (0-03-998283-1) Harcourt Coll Pubs.

Psychologie Sociale: Une Discipline en Mouvement. Denise Jodelet. (Textes de Sciences Sociales Ser.: No. 3). 1970. pap. 30.00 (90-279-6309-6) Mouton.

Psychologie Sociale et Experimentation. Gerard Lemaine & Jean-Marie Lemaine. (Textes de Sciences Sociales Ser.: No. 2). 1969. pap. 26.95 (90-279-6308-8) Mouton.

Psychologie Sociale Theorique et Experimentale. Claude Faucheux. (Recueil de Textes Choisis & Presentes Textes de Sciences Sociales Ser.: No. 8). 1971. pap. 26.95 (90-279-6920-5) Mouton.

Psychologie und Massenkommunikation, Planung, Durchfuhrung und Analyse Offentlicher Beeinflussung. Hans-Joachim Hoffmann. (Lehrbuch der Allgemeinen Geographie Ser. Vol. 12). (C). 1976. pap. 35.40 (3-11-006621-1) De Gruyter.

Psychologische Psychotherapie nach einem Schleudertrauma-Theorie & Praxis: Eine Falldarstellung zum Besseren Verstandnis des Therapeutischen Geschehens nach Milder Traumatischer Hirnschadigung. Annelis Wuthrich. (Europaische Hochschulschriften Ser.: Reihe 6, Bd. 624). 179p. 1999. 30.95 (3-906761-78-9, Pub. by P Lang) P Lang Pubng.

Psychologisches Woerterbuch. 9th ed. Friedrich Dorsch. (GER.). 784p. 1976. 95.00 (0-8288-5752-0, M7595) Fr & Eur.

Psychologisches Woerterbuch. 11th ed. Dorsch. (GER.). 921p. 1992. 135.00 (0-7859-7546-2, 3456816146) Fr & Eur.

Psychologism: A Case Study in the Sociology of Philosophical Knowledge. Martin Kusch. LC 94-43123. (Philosophical Issues in Science Ser.). 304p. (C). 1995. pap. 27.99 (0-415-12555-3, C0436) Routledge.

Psychologism: A Case Study in the Sociology of Philosophical Knowledge. Martin Kusch. LC 94-43123. (Philosophical Issues in Science Ser.). 304p. (C). (gr. 13). 1995. 85.00 (0-415-12554-5, B4886) Routledge.

Psychologism & Psychoaesthetics: A Historical & Critical View of Their Relations. John Fizer. (Linguistic & Literary Studies in Eastern Europe: Vol. 6). xvi, 278p. 1981. 65.00 (90-272-1506-5) J Benjamins Pubng Co.

*****Psychologist.** Darrell Franken. 435p. 1999. pap. 19.95 (0-934957-75-4) Wellness Pubns.

Psychologist. Jack Rudman. (Career Examination Ser.: C-627). 1994. pap. 34.95 (0-8373-0627-2) Nat Learn.

Psychologist & the Foreign Language Teacher. Wilga M. Rivers. LC 64-15809. 1993. reprint ed. pap. text 4.95 (0-226-72094-2, P741) U Ch Pr.

*****Psychologist as Detective: An Introduction to Conducting Research in Psychology.** 2nd ed. Randolph A. Smith & Stephen F. Davis. 518p. 2000. 68.00 (0-13-021982-7, Prentice Hall) P-H.

Psychologist As Expert Witness. 2nd ed. Theodore H. Blau. LC 98-2523. 596p. 1998. 95.00 (0-471-17870-5) Wiley.

Psychologist at Work. Mary R. Harrower. LC 71-102243. (Select Bibliographies Reprint Ser.). 1977. 26.95 (0-8369-5128-X) Ayer.

Psychologist in the Schools. Susan W. Gray. LC 63-13760. 1963. 24.95 (0-03-012220-1) Irvington.

Psychologist of Sorts: The Autobiography & Publications of the Inventor of the Porteus Maze Tests. Stanley D. Porteus. LC 68-31287. (Illus.). x, 325p. 1969. 27.95 (0-87015-174-6) Pacific Bks.

Psychologist Trainee. Jack Rudman. (Career Examination Ser.: C-2621). 1994. pap. 29.95 (0-8373-2621-4) Nat Learn.

Psychologists: Personal & Theoretical Pathways. Richard Coan. LC 79-13711. 224p. (C). 1979. text 22.50 (0-8290-0858-6) Irvington.

Psychologists As Detectives. Randolph A. Smith & Stephen F. Davis. 486p. (C). 1996. 73.00 (0-02-412581-4, Macmillan Coll) P-H.

*****Psychologist's Book of Personality Tests: 24 Revealing Tests to Identify & Overcome Your Personal...** Louis Janda. 224p. 2000. pap. 12.95 (0-471-37102-5) Wiley.

Psychologist's Book of Self-Tests: 25 Love, Sex, Intelligence, Career & Personality Tests Developed by Professionals to Reveal the Real You. Louis Janda. LC 95-49269. 240p. (Orig.). 1996. pap. 10.95 (0-399-52211-5, Perigee Bks) Berkley Pub.

Psychologists Caught: A Psycho-Logic of Psychology. Lewis W. Brandt. 248p. 1982. pap. 15.95 (0-8020-6508-2) U of Toronto Pr.

Psychologist's Companion: A Guide to Scientific Writing for Students & Researchers. 3rd ed. Robert J. Sternberg. 234p. (C). 1993. text 54.95 (0-521-45123-X); pap. text 16.95 (0-521-45756-4) Cambridge U Pr.

Psychologists' Desk Reference. Gerald P. Koocher et al. LC 98-5781. (Illus.). 648p. 1998. text 65.00 (0-19-511186-9) OUP.

Psychologist's Guide to an Academic Career. Harriet L. Rheingold. LC 94-532. 203p. 1994. pap. text 19.95 (1-55798-227-9) Am Psychol.

Psychologist's Guide to Licensure in the United States. Joseph J. Gillen. 90p. 1996. wbk. ed. 19.95 (0-9652543-0-5) Two Willow Pr.

Psychologist's Imagination & the Fantastic World of Imagery: A Handbook of Psycho-Imagination Therapy. Joseph E. Shorr. LC 98-23084. 240p. 1998. pap. 22.50 (1-56474-285-7) Fithian Pr.

Psychologists in Word & Image. Nicholas Wade. LC 94-31482. (Illus.). 260p. 1995. 45.00 (0-262-23180-8, Bradford Bks); pap. text 22.50 (0-262-73112-6, Bradford Bks) MIT Pr.

Psychologists on the March: Science, Practice, & Professional Identity in America, 1929-1969. James H. Capshew. LC 97-47526. (Studies in the History of Psychology). 304p. (C). 1998. 59.95 (0-521-56267-8); pap. 19.95 (0-521-56585-5) Cambridge U Pr.

*****Psychologist's Proactive Guide to Managed Mental Health Care.** Ed. by Alan J. Kent & Michel Hersen. LC 99-16478. 215p. 2000. write for info. (0-8058-2910-5) L Erlbaum Assocs.

P

An Asterisk (*) at the beginning of an entry indicates that the title is appearing for the first time.

***Psychologist's Proactve Guide to Managed Mental Health Care.** Ed. by Alan J. Kent & Michel Hensen. LC 99-16478. 171p. 2000. 19.95 (0-8058-3488-5) L Erlbaum Assocs.

Psychologist's Psychotropic Desk Reference. Louis A. Pagliaro. LC 98-26775. 1998. 59.95 (0-87630-964-3) Brunner-Mazel.

Psychologists Teach Critical Thinking Vol. 22, No. 1, 1995: A Special Issue of "Teaching of Psychology" Ed. by Diane F. Halpern & Susan G. Nummedal. 96p. 1995. pap. 20.00 (0-8058-9949-9) L Erlbaum Assocs.

Psychologist's Test File: An Illustrated Handbook of Sample Test Items. Patricia W. Clemens. 112p. 1983. 14.00 (0-87879-355-0) Acad Therapy.

Psychologist's Ventures in Faith: How God Guided & Preserved His Unworthy Servant, Psychologist Ray. From Nazi & Communist Europe to Ex-Christian America. Ratibor-Ray M Jurjevich. 250p. (Orig.). 1987. 18.95 (0-930711-05-X); pap. 11.95 (0-930711-04-1) Ichthys Bks.

Psychologizing of Modernity: Art - Architecture - History. Mark Jarzombek. LC 97-31087. (Illus.). 384p. (C). 1998. 60.00 (0-521-58238-5) Cambridge U Pr.

Psychologizing of the Faith. Bob Hoekstra. Ed. by Chuck Smith. (Calvary Basics Ser.). 74p. 1995. pap. 3.50 (0-936728-56-6) Word for Today.

Psychologue et L'Entreprise. Claude Levy-Leboyer. LC HF5548.8.P76. (Collection De Psychologie Appliquee). (FRE.). 175p. reprint ed. pap. 54.30 (0-7837-6951-2, 204678000003) Bks Demand.

Psychology. (C). 1997. 26.00 (0-06-501869-9); 26.00 (0-06-501868-0) Addson-Wesley Educ.

***Psychology.** 496p. 2000. teacher ed. write for info. (0-205-31816-9) Allyn.

Psychology. (Quick Study Academic Ser.). 4p. pap. 2.95 (1-57222-037-6) Barcharts.

Psychology. (Advanced Placement (AP) Test Ser.). 1997. pap. 23.95 (0-8373-6219-9, AP-19) Nat Learn.

***Psychology.** (C). 1999. 79.00 (0-13-030247-3) P-H.

***Psychology.** (C). 1999. 79.00 (0-13-030243-0); 79.00 (0-13-030246-5) P-H.

***Psychology.** (C). 2000. 29.00 (0-536-60901-2) Pearson Custom.

***Psychology.** 734p. (C). 1999. pap. text 30.00 (0-536-02307-7) S&S Trade.

Psychology. write for info. (0-8357-0657-5); write for info. (0-8357-0656-7); write for info. (0-8357-0655-9) Univ Microfilms.

Psychology. 1973. write for info. (0-8357-0098-4); write for info. (0-8357-0097-6) Univ Microfilms.

Psychology. 320p. 1995. pap. 27.95 (0-471-10778-6) Wiley.

Psychology. Don Baucum. LC 95-43647. (Barron's EZ-101 Study Keys Ser.). 1996. pap. 6.95 (0-8120-9580-4) Barron.

***Psychology.** Don Baucum. LC 98-54394. (Barron's College Review Ser.). 400p. 1999. pap. 14.95 (0-7641-0674-0) Barron.

Psychology, 4 vols. Douglas A. Bernstein. (C). Date not set. write for info. (0-395-78965-6) HM.

Psychology, 3 vols. Douglas A. Bernstein. (C). 1993. pap., teacher ed., suppl. ed. 6.76 (0-395-69047-1) HM.

Psychology, 3 vols. Douglas A. Bernstein. (C). 1993. pap., teacher ed. 6.76 (0-395-69046-3) HM.

Psychology. Douglas A. Bernstein et al. 784p. (C). 1987. write for info. (0-318-61892-3) HM.

Psychology, 4 bks. Lynne A. Bond et al. Ed. by Arthur W. Biddle. LC 86-82608. (Writer's Guide Ser.). 222p. (C). 2000. pap. text 24.36 (0-669-12004-9) HM Trade Div.

Psychology. Edmund Coleman. 272p. (C). 1994. pap. text, spiral bd., wbk. ed. 19.95 (0-8403-9565-5) Kendall-Hunt.

Psychology. Coon. Date not set. pap. text. write for info. (0-314-77166-2) West Pub.

Psychology. Stephen F. Davis & Joseph J. Palladino. (Illus.). 700p. (C). 1994. text 47.00 (0-02-327851-X, Macmillan Coll) P-H.

Psychology. T. M. Englehart & Louis Snellgrove. 1989. text 65.00 (0-15-374800-1) Harcourt.

Psychology. Ed. by Stephen Everson. (Companions to Ancient Thought Ser.: No. 2). 277p. (C). 1991. text 65.00 (0-521-35338-6); pap. text 22.95 (0-521-35861-2) Cambridge U Pr.

Psychology. Galliano. 416p. 1994. pap. text, student ed. 25.00 (0-02-340341-1, Macmillan Coll) P-H.

Psychology. Goldstein. 1994. teacher ed. write for info. (0-534-13610-9) Wadsworth Pub.

Psychology. Goldstein. 1994. write for info. (0-534-13612-5) Wadsworth Pub.

Psychology. Peter Gray. Ed. by Phyllis Fisher. (Illus.). 681p. (C). 1991. text 58.95 (0-87901-480-6) Worth.

Psychology. Peter Gray. Ed. by Phyllis Fisher. (Illus.). 287p. (C). 1991. student ed. 13.95 (0-87901-481-4) Worth.

Psychology. Don H. Hockenbury & Sandra E. Hockenbury. LC 96-60601. 768p. 1996. text 50.80 (1-57259-140-4); pap. text, student ed. 12.80 (1-57259-151-X) Worth.

Psychology. Saul M. Kassin. (C). Date not set. pap., student ed. 20.36 (0-395-72053-2) HM.

Psychology. Saul M. Kassin. LC 94-76518. (C). 1994. text 65.96 (0-395-52681-7) HM.

Psychology. Saul M. Kassin. (C). 1994. pap., teacher ed., suppl. ed. 11.96 (0-395-72055-9) HM.

Psychology. Saul M. Kassin. (C). 1995. pap., teacher ed. 11.96 (0-395-72054-0) HM.

Psychology. Kelley. 2000. pap. text 11.97 (0-395-97204-3) HM.

Psychology. Laird. (C). 1992. pap. 59.56 (0-395-63342-7) HM.

Psychology. Donald A. Laird. (C). 1991. pap. text, student ed. 21.16 (0-395-59231-3) HM.

Psychology. Donald A. Laird. (C). 1992. pap. text, teacher ed., suppl. ed. 5.96 (0-395-59233-X) HM.

Psychology. James D. Laird & Nicholas S. Thompson. (C). 1991. text 65.96 (0-395-47090-0) HM.

Psychology. James D. Laird & Nicholas S. Thompson. 561p. (C). 1992. text, teacher ed. 3.96 (0-395-59232-1) HM.

***Psychology.** Lester A. Lefton & Michael C. Boyes. 1999. pap., student ed. 26.60 (0-205-30740-X) P-H.

Psychology. Mcgee. Date not set. pap. text, teacher ed. write for info. (0-314-79143-4); pap. text, student ed. 17.75 (0-314-79144-2) West Pub.

Psychology. David G. Myers. 693p. 1986. text 34.95 (0-87901-311-7) Worth.

Psychology. Olf. 1994. pap. text 34.00 (0-443-05274-3, W B Saunders Co) Harcrt Hlth Sci Grp.

***Psychology.** Rathus. (C). 1999. pap. text 15.00 (0-15-507460-1) Harcourt Coll Pubs.

Psychology. Rubin. (C). Date not set. pap. 59.16 (0-395-65554-4) HM.

Psychology. Rubin. (C). 1992. pap. text 59.16 (0-395-65553-6); pap. text, student ed. 17.96 (0-395-60552-0) HM.

Psychology. Rubin. (C). 1993. pap., teacher ed., suppl. ed. 3.96 (0-395-60553-9) HM.

Psychology. Rubin. (C). 1993. pap. 3.16 (0-395-60551-2) HM.

Psychology. Z. Rubin. (C). 1992. text 65.96 (0-395-60550-4) HM.

Psychology. Jack Rudman. (Graduate Record Examination (GRE) Ser.: Vol. 17). 43.95 (0-8373-5267-3) Nat Learn.

Psychology. Jack Rudman. (Undergraduate Program Field Tests (UPFT) Ser.: Vol. 21). 43.95 (0-8373-6071-4) Nat Learn.

Psychology. Jack Rudman. (Graduate Record Examination Ser.: GRE-17). 1994. pap. 23.95 (0-8373-5217-7) Nat Learn.

Psychology. Jack Rudman. (National Teacher Examination (NTE) Ser.: Vol. NT-42). 1994. pap. 23.95 (0-8373-8452-4) Nat Learn.

Psychology. Jack Rudman. (Undergraduate Program Field Tests (UPFT) Ser.: Vol. UPFT-21). 1994. pap. 23.95 (0-8373-6021-8) Nat Learn.

Psychology. Samuels. 1996. text. write for info. (0-205-26744-0) Allyn.

Psychology. Santrock. 1998. teacher ed. 14.25 (0-07-230597-5) McGraw.

Psychology. Schultz & Hailstorks. 1995. pap. text, student ed. 27.00 (0-205-17418-3) Allyn.

Psychology. Simons. Date not set. pap. text, teacher ed. write for info. (0-314-35408-5); pap. text, student ed. 20.00 (0-314-35409-3) West Pub.

Psychology. Smith. 288p. 1997. pap., student ed. 21.88 (0-07-289144-0) McGraw.

Psychology. Smith. Date not set. pap. text, teacher ed. write for info. (0-314-02076-4) West Pub.

Psychology. Ronald Smith. 2001. student ed. 17.00 (0-07-232398-1) McGraw.

Psychology. Smith & Philip G. Zimbardo. 1994. pap., teacher ed. 11.00 (0-06-502354-4) Addson-Wesley Educ.

Psychology. Ed. by Uba. LC 97-32361. 700p. (C). 1998. 77.00 (0-321-01212-7, Prentice Hall) P-H.

Psychology. David Watson. 880p. (C). 1996. pap. text, per. 73.95 (0-7872-2091-4) Kendall-Hunt.

Psychology. David L. Watson. LC 91-33966. 500p. (C). 1992. pap., student ed. 18.95 (0-534-13009-7) Brooks-Cole.

Psychology. enl. rev. ed. Abraham P. Sperling. Ed. by Kenneth Martin. LC 93-44147. 300p. reprint ed. pap. 93.00 (0-608-07417-9, 206764400009) Bks Demand.

Psychology. Aristotle. LC 75-13253. (History of Ideas in Ancient Greece Ser.). (ENG & GRE.). 1976. reprint ed. 30.95 (0-405-07290-2) Ayer.

Psychology. David Hothersall. LC 83-63551. 686p. reprint ed. pap. 200.00 (0-7837-3008-X, 204293200006) Bks Demand.

Psychology. 2nd ed. (C). 1997. text 71.00 (0-321-80151-2) Addison-Wesley.

Psychology. 2nd ed. (C). 1997. text 72.67 (0-321-03237-3) Addison-Wesley.

***Psychology.** 2nd ed. (C). 1998. 84.33 (0-201-39361-1) Addison-Wesley.

***Psychology.** 2nd ed. (C). 1998. text 73.00 (0-201-39413-8) Addison-Wesley.

***Psychology.** 2nd ed. (C). 1998. 79.33 (0-201-39416-2); 60.66 (0-201-53317-0) Addison-Wesley.

***Psychology.** 2nd ed. 1998. write for info. (0-13-886185-4) P-H.

Psychology. 2nd ed. 150p. (C). 1999. pap. 16.80 (0-13-025675-7) P-H.

***Psychology.** 2nd ed. (C). 2000. write for info. (0-8087-1494-5) Pearson Custom.

Psychology. 2nd ed. Henry Gleitman. (C). Date not set. pap., teacher ed. write for info. (0-393-95534-6) Norton.

Psychology. 2nd ed. Peter Gray. 684p. 1993. text 53.40 (0-87901-464-4) Worth.

Psychology. 2nd ed. Hockenbury. LC 99-15582. 1999. pap. text 64.95 (1-57259-423-3) W H Freeman.

***Psychology.** 2nd ed. Hockenbury. 1999. pap. text, student ed. 19.95 (1-57259-825-5) Worth.

***Psychology.** 2nd ed. Hockenbury. 2001. pap. text, student ed. write for info. (1-57259-938-3) Worth.

Psychology. 2nd ed. Kassin. 1998. pap. text, student ed. 20.00 (0-13-884388-0) P-H.

Psychology. 2nd ed. Saul Kassin. LC 97-23212. 723p. (C). 1997. 81.00 (0-13-863887-X) P-H.

Psychology. 2nd ed. K. Martin. (Illus.). 256p. 1997. pap. text 19.95 (0-7506-3472-3) Buttrwrth-Heinemann.

Psychology. 2nd ed. Matlin. (C). 1994. pap. text, teacher ed. 35.00 incl. VHS (0-15-502107-9) Harcourt Coll Pubs.

Psychology. 2nd ed. Margaret W. Matlin. (C). 1994. pap. text, student ed. 25.00 (0-15-502108-7) Harcourt Coll Pubs.

Psychology. 2nd ed. David G. Myers. xxvi, 623p. (C). 1988. text 57.95 (0-87901-400-8) Worth.

Psychology. 2nd ed. Chris Peterson. LC 96-24666. 779p. (C). 1997. 84.00 (0-673-52414-0) Addison-Wesley.

Psychology. 2nd ed. Lester M. Sdorow. 864p. (C). 1993. disk. write for info. (0-318-69649-5) Brown & Benchmark.

Psychology. 2nd ed. Walker. 858p. 1996. write for info. (0-471-33514-2) Wiley.

Psychology. 2nd ed. Wayne Weiten. (Psychology Ser.). 1993. pap. 47.50 (0-534-19977-1) Brooks-Cole.

***Psychology.** 3rd ed. 480p. (C). 2000. text. write for info. (0-321-06052-0) Addson-Wesley Educ.

***Psychology.** 3rd ed. 400p. 2000. teacher ed. write for info. (0-205-30746-9) Allyn.

Psychology. 3rd ed. (C). 2000. text. write for info. (0-13-025953-5) P-H.

***Psychology.** 3rd ed. Robert Baron & Bruce Earhard. 398p. 2000. pap. 26.60 (0-205-30745-0) P-H.

Psychology. 3rd ed. Ludy T. Benjamin, Jr. et al. 880p. (C). 1993. text 52.00 (0-02-308290-9, Macmillan Coll) P-H.

Psychology, 3 vols. 3rd ed. Douglas A. Bernstein. LC 93-78678. (C). 1993. text 65.96 (0-395-64955-2) HM.

Psychology, 3 vols. 3rd ed. Douglas A. Bernstein. (C). 1993. pap. text, student ed. 20.36 (0-395-67540-5) HM.

Psychology. 3rd ed. Robert C. Carson. 688p. (C). 1999. pap. text. write for info. (0-321-03433-3) Addson-Wesley Educ.

***Psychology.** 3rd ed. Stephen F. Davis. LC 99-21562. 807p. 1999. 56.00 (0-13-932583-2) P-H.

Psychology. 3rd ed. Peter Gray. LC 98-85012. (Illus.). (C). 1998. text 51.00 (1-57259-414-4) Worth.

Psychology. 3rd ed. Peter Gray. (Illus.). (C). 1998. pap. text, student ed. 14.00 (1-57259-701-1) Worth.

***Psychology.** 3rd ed. Peter Gray. 1999. 70.95 (1-57259-943-X) Worth.

***Psychology.** 3rd ed. Kassin. 2001. pap. 21.33 (0-13-026946-8) P-H.

***Psychology.** 3rd ed. Saul Kassin. 832p. 2000. 77.33 (0-13-026926-3) P-H.

Psychology. 3rd ed. Gardner Lindzey et al. (C). 1988. text 55.95 (0-87901-361-3) Worth.

Psychology. 3rd ed. Gardner Lindzey et al. (C). 1988. pap., student ed. 12.95 (0-87901-354-0) Worth.

Psychology. 3rd ed. Matlin. (C). 1998. pap. text, teacher ed. 26.75 (0-15-508401-1) Harcourt Coll Pubs.

Psychology. 3rd ed. Margaret W. Matlin. LC 98-71493. (C). 1998. text 77.50 (0-15-505495-3, Pub. by Harcourt Coll Pubs) Harcourt.

Psychology. 3rd ed. McDermott. 316p. (C). 1998. pap. text 27.75 (0-536-01547-3) Pearson Custom.

Psychology. 3rd ed. David G. Myers. 636p. 1991. text 57.95 (0-87901-506-3) Worth.

Psychology. 3rd ed. David G. Myers. 636p. 1991. pap. text, student ed. 13.95 (0-87901-507-1) Worth.

Psychology. 3rd ed. Sdorow. 1995. pap. 30.62 (0-697-15064-X) McGraw.

Psychology. 3rd ed. Lester M. Sdorow. 792p. (C). 1994. text. write for info. (0-697-15062-3) Brown & Benchmark.

Psychology. 3rd ed. Lester M. Sdorow. (C). 1995. text, student ed. 15.62 (0-697-26756-3); text, student ed. 15.62 (0-697-26758-X) Brown & Benchmark.

Psychology. 3rd ed. Carole Wade & Carol Tavris. (C). 1997. pap., student ed. 29.00 (0-06-500519-8) Addson-Wesley Educ.

Psychology. 3rd ed. Carole Wade & Carol Tavris. LC 92-17531. (C). 1997. pap. 78.00 (0-06-500217-2) Addson-Wesley Educ.

Psychology. 3rd ed. Wayne Weiten & Wasden. (Psychology Ser.). 1994. mass mkt., student ed. 18.75 (0-534-24668-0) Brooks-Cole.

Psychology. 3rd ed. WGBH Educational Foundation Staff. (C). 1994. pap. text, student ed. 29.00 (0-15-502092-7, Pub. by Harcourt Coll Pubs) Harcourt.

***Psychology.** 3rd ed. Philip G. Zimbardo. 672p. (C). 1999. 52.67 (0-321-03432-5) Addson-Wesley.

Psychology. 4th ed. (C). 1997. pap. text 0.00 (0-673-99896-7) Addison-Wesley.

Psychology. 4th ed. (C). 1997. text 119.00 (0-673-97064-7, GoodYrBooks) Addson-Wesley Educ.

Psychology. 4th ed. (C). 1997. text 22.00 (0-673-97066-3) S&S Trade.

Psychology. 4th ed. (C). 1997. text 11.00 (0-673-97062-0) S&S Trade.

Psychology. 4th ed. Baron & Kalsher. LC 97-214036. 776p. 1997. 80.00 (0-205-26569-3) P-H.

Psychology. 4th ed. Baron & Kalsher. 1997. pap. text, student ed. 19.00 (0-205-27290-8) P-H.

Psychology. 4th ed. Bentley. 320p. (C). 1992. pap. text, student ed., wbk. ed. 18.80 (0-13-735176-3) P-H.

Psychology, 4 vols. 4th ed. Douglas A. Bernstein et al. LC 96-76573. 627p. (C). 1996. text 68.36 (0-395-77071-8) HM.

Psychology, 4 vols. 4th ed. Douglas A. Bernstein et al. (C). 1996. text, teacher ed. 11.96 (0-395-77985-5) HM.

Psychology. 4th ed. Henry Gleitman. (C). Date not set. text 50.00 incl. 5.25 hd (0-393-96690-9); text 52.00 incl. mac hd (0-393-96778-6); pap. write for info. (0-393-96950-9); pap. write for info. (0-393-96951-7); pap. write for info. (0-393-96952-5); pap. write for info. (0-393-96953-3) Norton.

Psychology. 4th ed. Spencer A. Rathus. 768p. (C). 1990. text 74.00 (0-03-034597-9, Pub. by Harcourt Coll Pubs) Harcourt.

Psychology. 4th ed. Roediger. 1991. mass mkt., student ed. 19.75 (0-314-94270-X) Wadsworth Pub.

Psychology. 4th ed. Henry L. Roediger. Date not set. pap. text, teacher ed. write for info. (0-314-09383-4) West Pub.

Psychology. 4th ed. Henry L. Roediger. 1996. mass mkt., student ed. 15.75 (0-314-08964-0) West Pub.

Psychology. 4th ed. Henry L. Roediger, III et al. LC 95-43775. 750p. (C). 1997. pap. 83.95 (0-314-06160-6) Thomson Learn.

Psychology. 4th ed. Sdorow. 1997. 48.74 (0-07-027347-2) McGraw.

Psychology. 4th ed. Sdorow. 400p. 1997. pap., student ed. 17.50 (0-697-25289-2) McGraw.

***Psychology.** 4th ed. Lester Sdorow. LC 97-70799. (Illus.). 1998. write for info. (0-07-115549-X, Irwn Prfssnl) McGraw-Hill Prof.

Psychology. 4th ed. Lester M. Sdorow. LC 97-70799. 768p. (C). 1997. per. write for info. (0-697-25285-X, WCB McGr Hill) McGrw-H Hghr Educ.

Psychology. 4th ed. Wortman. 1991. text 21.56 (0-07-071927-6) McGraw.

Psychology. 4th ed. Camille B. Wortman & Elizabeth F. Loftus. (C). 1991. pap. text, student ed. 20.00 (0-07-071922-5) McGraw.

Psychology. 4th ed. Camille B. Wortman & Elizabeth F. Loftus. (C). 1992. text 57.74 (0-07-071918-7) McGraw.

Psychology. 4th ed. Wrightsman. (Psychology Ser.). 1975. pap., student ed. 6.25 (0-8185-0165-0) Brooks-Cole.

Psychology, 4 vols. 4th annot. ed. Douglas A. Bernstein et al. (C). 1996. text, teacher ed. 69.56 (0-395-77983-9) HM.

Psychology. 4th rev. ed. Santrock. 1994. 22.50 (0-697-22460-0) McGraw.

Psychology. 5th ed. 1996. pap. text, student ed. 24.00 (0-205-26200-7) Allyn.

Psychology. 5th ed. (C). 2000. pap. text 80.00 (0-205-31402-3) Allyn.

Psychology. 5th ed. 684p. (C). 1997. 24.00 (0-321-00429-9) P-H.

Psychology. 5th ed. (C). 1997. 67.00 (0-321-00436-1) Pearson Custom.

Psychology. 5th ed. (C). 1997. 67.00 (0-321-00433-7) Pearson Custom.

Psychology. 5th ed. Dworetzky. Date not set. pap. text, teacher ed. write for info. (0-314-03273-8); pap. text, teacher ed. write for info. (0-314-03274-6); pap. text, student ed. 20.00 (0-314-03725-X) West Pub.

Psychology. 5th ed. John P. Dworetzky. Ed. by Clyde Perlee. LC 93-41549. 650p. (C). 1994. text 60.00 (0-314-02478-6) West Pub.

Psychology. 5th ed. Gleitman & Reisberg. LC 98-29515. 848p. 1999. text 78.00 (0-393-97364-6) Norton.

Psychology. 5th ed. David G. Myers. (Illus.). (C). 1997. text 52.40 (1-57259-590-6) Worth.

Psychology. 5th ed. Santrock. LC 95-80643. 1996. (0-697-29678-4) McGrw-H Hghr Educ.

Psychology. 5th ed. John W. Santrock et al. 288p. (C). 1996. text, student ed. 19.37 (0-697-25308-2) Brown & Benchmark.

Psychology. 5th ed. Sdorow. 2000. 50.00 (0-07-235832-7) McGraw.

Psychology. 5th ed. Wortman. 320p. 1998. pap., student ed. 23.13 (0-07-303374-X) McGraw.

Psychology. 5th ed. Camille B. Wortman et al. LC 98-14650. 1998. write for info. (0-07-115869-3) McGraw.

Psychology. 5th ed. Camille B. Wortman et al. LC 98-14650. 768p. 1998. 73.75 (0-07-071931-4) McGraw.

Psychology. 5th enl. rev. ed. John M. Darley et al. 752p. (C). 1990. text 66.00 (0-13-734377-9, 670106) P-H.

***Psychology.** 6th ed. (C). 1999. text. write for info. (0-321-05956-5) Addison-Wesley.

***Psychology.** 6th ed. 448p. (C). 1999. pap. 26.67 (0-321-05957-3) Addison-Wesley.

***Psychology.** 6th ed. (C). 2000. text. write for info. (0-321-05958-1); text. write for info. (0-321-05975-1); text. write for info. (0-321-05976-X) Addison-Wesley.

***Psychology.** 6th ed. (C). 1999. write for info. (0-13-018089-0) P-H.

***Psychology.** 6th ed. (C). 2000. write for info. (0-13-018521-3); write for info. (0-13-018522-1); write for info. (0-13-018523-X); write for info. (0-13-088012-4); write for info. (0-13-028799-7); text. write for info. (0-13-026422-9) P-H.

***Psychology.** 6th ed. (C). 2000. text (0-321-05979-4) S&S Trade.

Psychology. 6th ed. Coon. Date not set. pap. text, teacher ed. write for info. (0-314-01114-5); pap. text, student ed. 17.75 (0-314-00693-1); pap. text, wbk. ed. write for info. (0-314-00691-5) West Pub.

Psychology. 6th ed. Coon. 1992. pap. text, teacher ed. write for info. (0-314-00689-3) West Pub.

***Psychology.** 6th ed. Myers. 2000. pap. text, student ed. write for info. (1-57259-958-8) Worth.

Psychology. 6th ed. Spencer A. Rathus. LC 94-79633. (C). 1995. text 77.50 (0-15-501699-7) Harcourt Coll Pubs.

Psychology. 6th ed. Santrock. LC 99-25380. 1999. pap. text 53.25 (0-07-039469-5) McGraw.

Psychology. 6th ed. John W. Santrock. 1999. pap., student ed. 21.88 (0-07-232420-1) McGraw.

***Psychology.** 6th ed. Carole Wade & Carol Tavris. LC 99-56220. 750p. (C). 1999. 78.67 (0-321-04931-4, Prentice Hall) P-H.

***Psychology.** 7th ed. (C). 1999. text. write for info. (0-205-31684-0); text. write for info. (0-205-31685-9) Allyn.

Psychology. 7th ed. Ed. by Allyn & Bacon Incorporated Staff. (C). 1999. write for info. (0-205-30737-X) Allyn.

Psychology. 7th ed. Coon. Date not set. pap. text, teacher ed. write for info. (0-314-06859-7) West Pub.

Psychology. 7th ed. Lefton. 1999. pap. text, student ed. 15.00 (0-205-29671-8) Allyn.

***Psychology.** 7th ed. Lester A. Lefton. LC 99-29523. 728p. (C). 1999. 83.00 (0-205-28529-5, Macmillan Coll) P-H.

***Psychology.** 9th ed. (C). 2000. text. write for info. (0-321-05959-X) Addison-Wesley.

Psychology. 9th ed. 1996. write for info. (0-13-959057-9) P-H.

P

An Asterisk (*) at the beginning of an entry indicates that the title is appearing for the first time.

Psychology. 9th ed. Bishop. 1996. pap. text, student ed. 21.00 (*0-13-443243-6*) P-H.
Psychology. 9th ed. Morris. 1996. text. write for info. (*0-13-443136-7*) Allyn.
Psychology. 9th ed. Morris. 1996. text. write for info. (*0-13-443144-8*) Allyn.
Psychology. 9th ed. Slife. 1996. teacher ed. 1.56 (*0-697-31397-2*, WCB McGr Hill) McGrw-H Hghr Educ.
Psychology. 10th ed. (C). 1998. write for info. (*0-13-095703-8*, Macmillan Coll) P-H.
***Psychology.** 10th ed. 752p. 1999. 53.97 (*0-13-436104-0*) P-H.
Psychology. 14th ed. (C). 1997. text 177.00 (*0-673-55811-8*, GoodYrBooks) Addson-Wesley Educ.
Psychology. 24th ed. Duffy. 1994. 12.74 (*1-56134-286-6*) McGraw.
Psychology. 25th ed. Duffy. 1995. (*1-56134-368-4*, Dshkn McG-Hill) McGrw-H Hghr Educ.
Psychology, No. 2. 3rd ed. Sdorow. 1995. 23.12 (*0-697-22879-7*, WCB McGr Hill) McGrw-H Hghr Educ.
Psychology, No. 4. Rebecca Stark. Date not set. teacher ed. 5.95 (*0-910857-38-5*, 038-5APB) Educ Impress.
Psychology, Vol. 1. 3rd ed. Sdorow. 1995. 13.75 (*0-697-15065-8*, WCB McGr Hill) McGrw-H Hghr Educ.
Psychology, Vol. 4. Rebecca Stark. Date not set. teacher ed., suppl. ed. 9.95 (*0-910857-37-7*, 037-7APT) Educ Impress.
***Psychology: A - Level Psychology.** 2000. student ed. write for info. (*0-582-31655-3*) Addison-Wesley.
Psychology: A Behavioral Overview. A. Poling et al. (Applied Clinical Psychology Ser.). (Illus.). 412p. (C). 1989. 45.00 (*0-306-43432-6*, Plenum Trade) Perseus Pubng.
Psychology: A Biopsychosocial Approach. 2nd ed. Peterson. 1997. 90.66 (*0-201-32664-7*) P-H.
***Psychology: A Biopsychosocial Approach Professional Copy.** 2nd ed. (C). 1998. write for info. (*0-321-40256-1*) Addson-Wesley Educ.
Psychology: A Concise Introduction. 2nd ed. Dunn. (C). 1995. pap. text, student ed. 276.50 (*0-03-012852-8*, Pub. by Harcourt Coll Pubs) Harcourt.
Psychology: A Concise Introduction. 3rd ed. Terry F. Pettijohn. LC 91-77531. (Illus.). 496p. (C). 1992. text 25.95 (*1-56134-063-4*, Dshkn McG-Hill) McGrw-H Hghr Educ.
Psychology: A Contemporary Introduction. Peter Scott & Christopher Spencer. LC 97-16961. (Illus.). 736p. (C). 1998. text 83.95 (*0-631-19234-4*) Blackwell Pubs.
Psychology: A Contemporary Introduction. Peter Scott & Christopher Spencer. LC 97-16961. (Illus.). 736p. (C). 1998. pap. text 41.95 (*0-631-19235-2*) Blackwell Pubs.
Psychology: A Global Perspective. Marrone. Date not set. write for info. (*1-57259-647-3*) Worth.
Psychology: A Guide to Reference & Information Sources. Pam M. Baxter. (Reference Sources in the Social Sciences Ser.). xxi, 219p. 1993. lib. bdg. 36.50 (*0-87287-708-6*) Libs Unl.
Psychology: A Multicultural Perspective Instructor's Manual. K. Huang & L. Uba. 18.00 (*0-321-40152-2*) Addson-Wesley Educ.
Psychology: A Multiculture Approach Study Wizard for Windows. Uba. (C). 1998. pap. 22.00 (*0-321-40155-7*) Addson-Wesley Educ.
***Psychology: A Student's Handbook.** Michael W. Eysenck. 1200p. 1999. student ed. 74.95 (*0-86377-474-1*, Pub. by Psychol Pr); pap., student ed. 39.95 (*0-86377-475-X*, Pub. by Psychol Pr) Taylor & Francis.
***Psychology: A Very Short Introduction.** 160p. 2000. 8.95 (*0-19-285381-3*) OUP.
Psychology: Amazing Science of Behavior. Don Jacobs. 308p. (C). 1996. text 38.40 (*0-536-59885-1*) Pearson Custom.
Psychology: An Elementary Text-Book. Hermann Ebbinghaus. Ed. & Tr. by Max Meyer. LC 73-2965. (Classics in Psychology Ser.). 1977. reprint ed. 19.95 (*0-405-05138-7*) Ayer.
Psychology: An Introduction. 5th ed. Lahey. 1994. student ed. 6.25 (*0-697-23284-0*) McGraw.
Psychology: An Introduction. 5th ed. Lahey. 1994. 86.87 (*0-697-22875-4*, WCB McGr Hill) McGrw-H Hghr Educ.
Psychology: An Introduction. 5th ed. Benjamin B. Lahey. 784p. (C). 1994. text. write for info. (*0-697-27484-5*) Brown & Benchmark.
Psychology: An Introduction. 6th ed. Lahey. 272p. 1997. pap., student ed. 22.50 (*0-697-25314-7*) McGraw.
Psychology: An Introduction. 6th ed. Benjamin B. Lahey. LC 96-78737. 752p. (C). 1997. text. write for info. (*0-697-25310-4*, WCB McGr Hill) McGrw-H Hghr Educ.
Psychology: An Introduction. 8th ed. Kagan. (C). 1994. pap. text, teacher ed. 35.00 (*0-15-502508-2*) Harcourt Coll Pubs.
Psychology: An Introduction. 8th ed. Jerome Kagan & Julius Segal. LC 94-35276. 771p. (C). 1994. pap. text 25.95 (*0-15-501476-5*) Harcourt.
Psychology: An Introduction. 9th ed. Kagan. (C). 2001. pap. text 22.50 (*0-15-508114-4*) Harcourt Coll Pubs.
Psychology: An Introduction. 10th ed. Charles G. Morris. LC 98-14514. 724p. 1998. 78.67 (*0-13-676537-8*) P-H.
Psychology: An Introduction, Language Enhancement Guide. 5th ed. Benjamin B. Lahey. 112p. (C). 1994. text. write for info. (*0-697-26250-2*) Brown & Benchmark.
Psychology: An Introduction, Study Guide. 5th ed. Benjamin B. Lahey. 400p. (C). 1994. text, student ed. 18.75 (*0-697-14521-2*) Brown & Benchmark.
Psychology: An Introduction, Study Guide. 5th ed. Benjamin B. Lahey. (C). 1995. text, student ed. 15.62 (*0-697-26753-9*) Brown & Benchmark.
Psychology: An Introduction - Student Practice Tests. 6th ed. 80p. (C). 1997. pap. 11.88 (*0-07-292603-1*) McGrw-H Hghr Educ.
Psychology: An Introduction - Test Bank. 8th ed. Kagan. (C). 1995. pap. text, teacher ed., suppl. ed. 41.50 (*0-15-502509-0*, Pub. by Harcourt Coll Pubs) Harcourt.
Psychology: An Introduction - Text Index File, No. 2. 5th ed. Lahey. 1995. 20.62 (*0-697-26612-5*, WCB McGr Hill) McGrw-H Hghr Educ.
Psychology: An Introduction S-Cart. 10th ed. Morris. 1999. 63.00 (*0-13-020663-6*) P-H.
Psychology: An Introduction with Student Practice Test. Benjamin B. Lahey. 272p. 1995. student ed. write for info. (*0-614-03036-6*); student ed. write for info. incl. audio (*0-614-03037-4*) Brown & Benchmark.
Psychology: An Introduction with Student Study Guide. 5th ed. Lahey. 1994. 59.74 (*0-697-23285-9*) McGraw.
Psychology: An Introductory Bibliography. Salem Press Editors. Ed. by Susan E. Beers. LC 95-48933. (Magill Bibliographies Ser.). 440p. 1996. 55.00 (*0-8108-3119-8*) Scarecrow.
Psychology: An Introductory Study of the Structure & Function of Human Consciousness. 4th ed. James R. Angell. LC 73-2957. (Classics in Psychology Ser.). 1979. reprint ed. 36.95 (*0-405-05131-X*) Ayer.
Psychology: An Orthodox Christian Perspective. Apostolos Makrakis. Ed. by Orthodox Christian Educational Society Staff. Tr. by Denver Cummings. (Logos & Holy Spirit in the Unity of Christian Thought Ser.: Vol. 2). 151p. 1977. reprint ed. pap. 5.00 (*0-938366-05-X*) Orthodox Chr.
Psychology: Another View. Harold F. Sorensen. LC 88-62824. 240p. (C). 1990. text 18.00 (*0-9622100-0-5*) Pawprint Pr.
Psychology: Another View, Set. Harold F. Sorensen. LC 88-62824. 240p. (C). 1990. pap. text 140.00 (*0-685-58428-3*) Pawprint Pr.
Psychology: Applied Teaching, 7 vols. Biehler. (C). 1992. pap., teacher ed. 3.96 (*0-395-63771-6*) HM.
Psychology: Applied Teaching, 7 vols. Robert F. Biehler. (C). 1992. pap. 61.56 (*0-395-61598-4*) HM.
Psychology: Behavior in Context. Lyle E. Bourne & Nancy F. Russo. LC 97-43774. 1998. text 78.50 (*0-393-97209-7*) Norton.
Psychology: Biographical Approach. Malinda Muzi. 680p. (C). 1997. text 64.00 (*0-536-00131-6*) Pearson Custom.
Psychology: Biopsychosocial Approach. 2nd ed. (C). 1997. write for info. (*0-13-087590-2*) Addison-Wesley.
Psychology: Biopsychosocial Approach. 2nd ed. (C). 1997. 24.00 (*0-673-54257-2*, GoodYrBooks); 24.00 (*0-673-54253-X*, GoodYrBooks) Addson-Wesley Educ.
Psychology: Biopsychosocial Approach. 2nd ed. (C). 1997. 52.66 (*0-673-54256-4*, GoodYrBooks); 67.00 (*0-673-54254-8*) Addson-Wesley Educ.
***Psychology: Brief Edition.** John W. Santrock. LC 99-89679. 560p. 2000. pap. 50.00 (*0-07-240372-1*) McGraw.
Psychology: Briefer Course. William James. (Works of William James). (Illus.). 512p. 1985. 50.00 (*0-674-72102-0*) HUP.
Psychology: Briefer Course. William James. (Notable American Authors Ser.). 1992. reprint ed. lib. bdg. 75.00 (*0-7812-3473-5*) Rprt Serv.
Psychology: Cirruculum Unit. Center for Learning Network Staff. (Social Studies). 268p. 1998. teacher ed., spiral bd. 37.95 (*1-56077-547-5*) Ctr Learning.
Psychology: Coast Telecourse. 3rd ed. Carole Wade & Carol Tavris. (C). 1997. pap., student ed. 14.75 (*0-06-501642-4*) Addson-Wesley Educ.
Psychology: Context & Behavior - Test Item File, Vol. 1. 2nd ed. Halonen & Santrock. 1995. 21.56 (*0-697-14922-6*) McGraw.
Psychology: Contexts & Applications. 3rd ed. Jane S. Halonen & John W. Santrock. LC 98-15014. 736p. 1998. pap. 56.56 (*0-697-37648-6*) McGraw.
Psychology: Contexts of Behavior. 2nd ed. Jane Halonen & John W. Santrock. 864p. (C). 1997. text. write for info. (*0-07-114358-0*) McGraw.
Psychology: Contexts of Behavior. 2nd ed. Halonen & Santrock. 1995. teacher ed. 17.81 (*0-697-14910-2*) McGraw.
Psychology: CUNY Panel: Rethinking the Disciplines, Vol. 8F. Angela B. Ginorio et al. (Women in the Curriculum Ser.). 53p. 1997. pap. 10.00 (*1-885303-14-9*) Towson St Univ.
Psychology Custom Edition. 5th ed. 728p. (C). 1996. text 42.00 (*0-536-59668-9*) Pearson Custom.
Psychology: Discipline Analysis, Vol. 7N. Nancy Russo. (Women in the Curriculum Ser.). 39p. (Orig.). 1997. pap. 7.00 (*1-885303-21-1*) Towson St Univ.
Psychology: Enchanced Chapters. 5th alternate ed. John W. Santrock. 640p. (C). 1996. text, suppl. ed. write for info. (*0-697-23553-X*) Brown & Benchmark.
Psychology: Explorations in Behavior & Experience. Sarnoff A. Mednick et al. LC 74-22239. 606p. reprint ed. pap. 187.90 (*0-7837-3457-3*, 205778300008) Bks Demand.
Psychology: Fifth Edition (Study Guide) 4th ed. Wade & Tavris. 1997. pap. (*0-673-98442-7*) Addison-Wesley.
Psychology: Instructor's Resource Manual. Wayne Hall & Granville Sydnor. 1997. teacher ed., ring bd. write for info. (*1-57259-194-3*); teacher ed., ring bd. write for info. (*1-57259-357-1*) Worth.
Psychology: Instructor's Resource Manual. 4th ed. Robert A. Baron. (C). 1997. text, teacher ed. write for info. (*0-205-27288-6*, T7288-8) Allyn.
Psychology: Instructor's Resources. 2nd ed. Peter Gray. 1994. teacher ed., ring bd. write for info. (*0-87901-696-5*) Worth.
Psychology: Instructor's Resources. 5th ed. Martin Bolt. 1998. teacher ed. write for info. (*1-57259-209-5*) Worth.
Psychology: Introduction. 148p. (C). 1997. write for info. (*0-321-02380-3*) Addison-Wesley.
***Psychology: Introduction.** 832p. (C). 1999. text 50.00 (*0-536-02740-4*) Pearson Custom.
Psychology: Introduction. 4th ed. Josh R. Gerow. LC 94-16489. (C). 1995. text 40.75 (*0-673-46869-0*) HarpC.
Psychology: Introduction. 5th ed. (C). 1997. write for info. (*0-13-087601-1*) Addison-Wesley.
Psychology Introduction to Psychology. 9th ed. (Prentice Hall College Titles Ser.). (C). 1996. text 10.20 (*0-13-659491-3*, Macmillan Coll) P-H.
Psychology Introduction to Psychology. 9th ed. (Prentice Hall College Titles Ser.). (C). 1996. text 9.33 (*0-13-659483-2*, Macmillan Coll) P-H.
Psychology: Learning & Behavior: Test Item File. 4th ed. Schwartz. 1995. pap. text, teacher ed. write for info. (*0-393-96662-3*) Norton.
Psychology: Lecture Guides. 5th ed. Martin Bolt. 1998. write for info. (*1-57259-548-5*) Worth.
Psychology: Lectures Lois McDermott. 226p. (C). 1994. text 34.00 (*0-536-58655-1*) Pearson Custom.
Psychology: Lectures & Study Guide. 2nd ed. Lois McDermott. 286p. (C). 1995. text 34.20 (*0-536-59077-X*) Pearson Custom.
Psychology: Mind, Brain, & Culture. 2nd ed. Drew Westen. LC 97-51291. 1024p. 1998. text 86.95 (*0-471-24049-4*) Wiley.
***Psychology: Mind, Brain, & Culture.** 2nd ed. Drew Westen. 368p. 1999. pap., student ed. 31.95 (*0-471-32201-6*) Wiley.
Psychology: Mind, Brain & Culture & Study Guide to Accompany Psychology. Drew Westen. 1216p. 1996. 80.95 (*0-471-17810-1*) Wiley.
Psychology: Mind, Brain & Culture & Writing in Psychology. Drew Westen & T. Raymond Smyth. 1110p. 1996. 101.90 (*0-471-17811-X*) Wiley.
Psychology: Mind, Brain, & Culture Study Guide. Drew Westen. 320p. 1997. pap. 14.95 (*0-471-17789-X*) Wiley.
***Psychology: Mind, Brain, & Culture, Web Access Card.** Drew Westen. 1999. pap. 14.95 (*0-471-38570-0*) Wiley.
***Psychology: Multicultural Approach.** (C). 1999. pap. text. write for info. (*0-321-04036-8*); pap. text. write for info. (*0-321-04066-X*); pap. text. write for info. (*0-321-04074-0*); pap. text. write for info. (*0-321-05213-7*); pap. text. write for info. (*0-321-05215-3*) Addison-Wesley.
***Psychology: Multicultural Approach.** (C). 1999. pap. text. write for info. (*0-321-05447-4*) Addison-Wesley.
***Psychology: Multicultural Approach.** (C). 2000. pap. text. write for info. (*0-321-04039-2*) Addison-Wesley.
***Psychology: Multicultural Approach.** (C). 1999. pap. text. write for info. (*0-321-04038-4*); pap. text. write for info. (*0-321-05214-5*) Addson-Wesley Educ.
***Psychology: Multicultural Approach.** (C). 2001. pap. text 67.00 (*0-321-04040-6*) Addson-Wesley Educ.
***Psychology: Multicultural Approach.** (C). 1998. text. write for info. (*0-321-04037-6*) Addison-Wesley.
***Psychology: Multicultural Approach.** (C). 1999. write for info. (*0-321-05216-1*) Addson-Wesley Educ.
Psychology: Natural Science. 650p. (C). 1997. pap. text 49.00 (*0-536-00150-2*) Pearson Custom.
***Psychology: Natural Science.** 392p. (C). 1998. text 22.45 (*0-536-01009-9*) Pearson Custom.
Psychology: Perspective Readings. Carol Tavis & Carole Wade. (C). 1995. text 15.00 (*0-06-502529-6*) Addson-Wesley Educ.
Psychology: Principles & Applications. 5th ed. Stephen Worchel & Wayne J. Shebilski. LC 94-31006. 715p. 1995. 86.00 (*0-13-556474-3*) P-H.
***Psychology Psychology 150 Course.** 2nd ed. Westen. 1999. pap. text 62.00 (*0-471-37361-3*) Wiley.
Psychology: Reader. Henry L. Roediger. 1996. mass mkt. 25.95 (*0-314-09382-6*) West Pub.
Psychology: Reader's Guide. 6th ed. Coon. Date not set. pap. 8.25 (*0-314-00692-3*) West Pub.
Psychology: Realizing Human Potential. 8th ed. Rene V. Dawis & Rosemary T. Fruehling. LC 94-20886. 1994. text 34.95 (*1-56118-341-5*) Paradigm MN.
Psychology: Realizing Human Potential. 8th ed. Rene V. Dawis & Rosemary T. Fruehling. LC 94-20886. 1995. text, teacher ed. 14.00 (*1-56118-343-1*); text, student ed. 12.95 (*1-56118-342-3*) Paradigm MN.
Psychology: Science & Application. Mark G. McGee & David W. Wilson. (Illus.). 666p. (C). 1984. text 60.00 (*0-314-77927-2*) West Pub.
Psychology: Science & Understanding. Barry D. Smith. LC 97-25300. 832p. (C). 1997. 73.75 (*0-07-058652-7*) McGraw.
Psychology: Science, Behavior. 3rd ed. Ettinger. (C). 1994. pap. text, student ed. 29.00 (*0-15-501359-9*, Pub. by Harcourt Coll Pubs) Harcourt.
Psychology: Science, Behavior. 3rd ed. Ettinger. (C). 1994. pap. text, teacher ed. 35.00 (*0-15-501358-0*) Harcourt Coll Pubs.
Psychology: Science, Behavior - TB. 3rd ed. Ettinger. (C). 1994. pap. text, teacher ed., suppl. ed. 41.50 (*0-15-501360-2*, Pub. by Harcourt Coll Pubs) Harcourt.
Psychology: Science, Behavior & Life. 3rd ed. Robert L. Crooks et al. (Illus.). 750p. (C). 1993. text 83.50 (*0-15-500998-2*, Pub. by Harcourt Coll Pubs) Harcourt.
Psychology: Science Mental. (C). 1930. text. write for info. (*0-06-044480-0*) S&S Trade.
Psychology: Study Guide. 5th ed. Gleitman & Reisberg. 1999. pap. text, student ed. write for info. (*0-393-97366-2*) Norton.
***Psychology: Study Guide: Canadian Edition.** 3rd ed. Baron. 2000. pap. 20.00 (*0-205-32290-5*) Allyn.
Psychology: Study Human Behavior Telecourse GD CUS. 3rd ed. Wade. (C). 1997. pap. text 30.00 (*0-321-00117-6*, Prentice Hall) P-H.
Psychology: Study of Human Nature. 266p. (C). 1997. text 19.37 (*0-536-00127-8*) Pearson Custom.
Psychology: Telecourse Faculty Guide. 6th ed. Spencer A. Rathus. (C). 1995. pap. text, teacher ed. 44.50 (*0-15-503653-X*, Pub. by Harcourt Coll Pubs) Harcourt.
Psychology: Telecourse Study Guide. 6th ed. Spencer A. Rathus. (C). 1995. pap. text, student ed. 28.50 (*0-15-503654-8*) Harcourt Coll Pubs.
Psychology: Test Bank. 2nd ed. Margaret W. Matlin. (C). 1994. pap. text 41.50 (*0-15-502109-5*, Pub. by Harcourt Coll Pubs) Harcourt.
***Psychology Test Bank.** 5th ed. Huffman. 1999. pap. text 25.00 (*0-471-35472-4*) Wiley.
***Psychology: Test Item File.** 3rd ed. 432p. 2000. write for info. (*0-13-025377-4*, Prentice Hall) P-H.
Psychology: Testbank, 4 vols. 4th ed. Douglas A. Bernstein. (C). 1996. pap. text, suppl. ed. 11.96 (*0-395-82882-1*) HM.
Psychology: Testbank. 5th ed. Dworetzky. Date not set. pap. text, suppl. ed. write for info. (*0-314-03275-4*) West Pub.
Psychology: The Adaptive Mind. James S. Nairne. 1996. pap., teacher ed. write for info. (*0-534-34373-2*) Brooks-Cole.
Psychology: The Adaptive Mind. James S. Nairne. LC 96-28954. (Psychology Ser.). 659p. (C). 1996. mass mkt. 52.50 (*0-534-20682-4*) Brooks-Cole.
Psychology: The Adaptive Mind. Narine. (Psychology Ser.). 1996. pap., student ed. 17.25 (*0-534-33853-4*) Brooks-Cole.
***Psychology: The Adaptive Mind.** 2nd ed. James S. Nairne. LC 99-16382. (Psychology Ser.). 750p. 1999. mass mkt. 79.95 (*0-534-35766-0*) Brooks-Cole.
Psychology: The Adaptive Mind. 2nd ed. Proctor. (Psychology Ser.). 1999. pap. 20.25 (*0-534-36774-7*) Brooks-Cole.
Psychology: The Basic Principles. John F. Hahn & Sanford Lopater. (Quality Paperback Ser.: No. 324). 220p. 1977. pap. 11.00 (*0-8226-0324-1*) Littlefield.
Psychology: The Brain, the Personality, the World. Stephen M. Kosslyn & Robin S. Rosenberg. (C). Date not set. 62.00 (*0-205-27465-X*, Macmillan Coll) P-H.
Psychology: The Briefer Course. William James. Ed. by Gordon W. Allport. LC 84-40821. 360p. (C). 1985. reprint ed. pap. text 15.00 (*0-268-01557-0*) U of Notre Dame Pr.
Psychology: The Cognitive Powers. James McCosh. LC 75-3263. reprint ed. 34.50 (*0-404-59249-X*) AMS Pr.
Psychology: The Contexts of Behavior. 2nd ed. Jane Holonen & John W. Santrock. LC 94-73271. 810p. (C). 1995. text 62.35 (*0-697-14908-0*); text, student ed. 21.25 (*0-697-14923-4*) Brown & Benchmark.
Psychology: The Contexts of Behavior, Microguide - IBM 3.5. 2nd ed. Jane Holonen & John W. Santrock. 800p. (C). 1995. text, student ed. 15.00 (*0-697-26986-8*) Brown & Benchmark.
***Psychology: The Core.** Rathus. (C). 1999. pap. text 22.50 (*0-15-507459-8*); pap. text 57.50 (*0-15-507452-0*) Harcourt.
Psychology: The Core. Rathus. (C). 1999. pap. text 44.50 (*0-15-507454-7*) Harcourt Coll Pubs.
***Psychology: The Core.** Spencer Rathus. (C). 1999. pap. text 22.50 (*0-15-507461-X*) Harcourt.
Psychology: The Cultivation & Development of Mind & Will by Positive & Negative Processes, the Primacy of Will Power. Frank H. Randall. 193p. 1996. reprint ed. spiral bd. 14.50 (*0-7873-0692-4*) Hlth Research.
Psychology: The Essential Science. Robert A. Baron. 630p. 1989. boxed set 48.00 (*0-205-11432-6*, H14327) Allyn.
Psychology: The Foundations of Human Behavior Student Manual. D. Bruce Carter. 100p. (C). 1994. per. 8.95 (*0-8403-8974-4*) Kendall-Hunt.
Psychology: The Hope of a Science. Gregory A. Kimble. (Illus.). 176p. 1995. 27.50 (*0-262-11204-3*, Bradford Bks) MIT Pr.
Psychology: The Motive Powers-Emotions, Conscience, Will. James McCosh. LC 75-3264. reprint ed. 36.00 (*0-404-59250-3*) AMS Pr.
Psychology: The Science of Behavior. 3rd ed. Neil R. Carlson. 800p. 1989. text 48.00 (*0-205-12166-7*, H21660); trans. 100.00 (*0-685-29842-6*, H21694) Allyn.
Psychology: The Science of Behavior. 5th ed. Neil H. Carlson & William Buskist. LC 96-3411. 683p. 1996. 84.00 (*0-205-19345-5*) Allyn.
Psychology: The Science of Behavior, Test Bank. 5th ed. Neil R. Carlson & William Buskist. (C). 1997. write for info. (*0-205-26196-5*, T6196-4) Allyn.
***Psychology: The Science of Behaviour.** 5th ed. 2000. write for info. (*0-205-26875-7*) Addison-Wesley.
***Psychology: The Science of Behaviour European Adaptation.** 2000. write for info. (*0-13-021228-8*) P-H.
Psychology: The Science of Mental Life. 3rd ed. George A. Miller. LC 98-12443. (Illus.). 388p. 1998. reprint ed. pap. text 29.95 (*0-937431-06-0*) Adams Bannister Cox.
Psychology: The Science of Mind. Johnson. (C). 1997. text 63.50 (*0-15-503004-3*) Harcourt.
Psychology: The Science of Mind & Behavior. 4th ed. John W. Santrock. (C). 1995. text. write for info. (*0-697-27782-8*) Brown & Benchmark.
Psychology: The Science of Mind & Behavior. 4th rev. ed. John W. Santrock. 326p. (C). 1995. pap. text. write for info. (*0-697-20890-7*) Brown & Benchmark.
Psychology: The Science of Mind & Behaviour. 2nd ed. Richard D. Gross. (Illus.). 1056p. 1993. pap. 29.95 (*0-340-56136-X*, B0098, Pub. by E A) Routledge.
Psychology: The Science of Mind & Behaviour: Study Guide. 2nd ed. Richard D. Gross & Paul Humphreys. (Illus.). 192p. 1993. pap. 12.95 (*0-340-58736-9*, B2218, Pub. by E A) Routldge.

P

Psychology: The Science of People. 2nd ed. Frank J. Landy. (Illus.). 672p. (C). 1987. pap. text, student ed. write for info. (*0-318-61592-4*) P-H.

Psychology: Themes & Variation Brief. 3rd ed. Wayne Weiten. (Psychology Ser.). (C). 1996. mass mkt., student ed. 17.75 (*0-534-34187-X*) Brooks-Cole.

Psychology: Themes & Variation Brief. 3rd expanded ed. Wayne Weiten. (Psychology Ser.). 1996. student ed. 17.00 (*0-534-34193-4*); student ed. 17.00 (*0-534-34195-0*) Brooks-Cole.

Psychology: Themes & Variation Brief Paper with InfoTrac. 3rd ed. Weiten. (Psychology Ser.). 1998. 43.75 incl. cd-rom (*0-534-36370-9*) Brooks-Cole.

Psychology: Themes & Variations. Weiten. (Psychology Ser.). 1989. student ed. 16.50 (*0-534-08761-2*); text, teacher ed. write for info. (*0-534-08762-0*) Brooks-Cole.

Psychology: Themes & Variations. Wayne Weiten. LC 88-26207. 697p. (C). 1989. mass mkt. 45.50 (*0-534-08760-4*) Brooks-Cole.

Psychology: Themes & Variations. 2nd ed. Richard B. Stalling & Wayne Weiten. (Psychology Ser.). 1993. mass mkt. 18.00 (*0-534-19969-0*) Brooks-Cole.

Psychology: Themes & Variations. 2nd ed. Weiten. (Psychology Ser.). 1991. pap. write for info. (*0-534-15334-8*) Brooks-Cole.

Psychology: Themes & Variations. 2nd ed. Weiten. 1993. teacher ed. write for info. (*0-534-15353-4*) Thomson Learn.

Psychology: Themes & Variations. 2nd ed. Wayne Weiten. LC 91-6752. 752p. (C). 1991. text 53.95 (*0-534-15330-5*) Brooks-Cole.

Psychology: Themes & Variations. 2nd ed. Wayne Weiten. LC 91-6752. 752p. (C). 1991. pap., student ed. 17.95 (*0-534-15331-3*) Brooks-Cole.

Psychology: Themes & Variations. 3rd ed. Wayne Weiten. (Psychology Ser.). 1994. pap., teacher ed. 18.75 (*0-534-24673-7*); text 54.50 (*0-534-24666-4*) Brooks-Cole.

Psychology: Themes & Variations. 3rd ed. Wayne Weiten. LC 96-6003. (Psychology Ser.). 564p. (C). 1996. pap. 41.00 (*0-534-33926-3*) Brooks-Cole.

Psychology: Themes & Variations. 3rd ed. Wayne Weiten. 1997. teacher ed. write for info. (*0-534-34188-8*) Brooks-Cole.

Psychology: Themes & Variations. 3rd ed. Wayne Weiten. 1996. pap. 74.95 (*0-534-34653-7*) Thomson Learn.

Psychology: Themes & Variations. 3rd ed. Wayne Weiten. text 47.00 (*0-534-33730-9*) Wadsworth Pub.

Psychology: Themes & Variations. 3rd expanded ed. Wayne Weiten & Wasden. (Psychology Ser.). 1995. student ed. 18.50 (*0-534-24670-2*) Brooks-Cole.

Psychology: Themes & Variations. 4th ed. Wayne Weiten. LC 97-26784. (Psychology Ser.). 809p. 1997. pap. 79.95 (*0-534-34014-8*); pap. 18.00 (*0-534-35066-6*) Brooks-Cole.

Psychology: Themes & Variations. 4th ed. Wayne Weiten. (Psychology Ser.). 1999. 63.95 (*0-534-36378-4*) Brooks-Cole.

Psychology: Themes & Variations. 4th ed. Wayne Weiten. (Psychology Ser.). 1999. pap. text, student ed. 20.75 (*0-534-36674-0*) Brooks-Cole.

Psychology: Themes & Variations. 5th ed. Weiten. (Psychology Ser.). (C). 2000. pap., student ed. 20.25 (*0-534-36716-X*) Brooks-Cole.

Psychology: Themes & Variations. 5th ed. Weiten. (Psychology). 2000. pap. 55.00 (*0-534-36714-3*) Thomson Learn.

Psychology: Themes & Variations Brief Paper. 4th ed. Wayne Weiten. LC 98-32260. (Psychology Ser.). 1999. 54.95 (*0-534-36379-2*) Brooks-Cole.

Psychology: Themes & Variations, Briefer Version. 2nd ed. Wayne Weiten. LC 93-19857. 1993. mass mkt. 40.25 (*0-534-19968-2*) Brooks-Cole.

Psychology: Themes & Variations, Test Items. 3rd ed. Wayne Weiten. 1996. mass mkt. write for info. (*0-534-34189-6*) Brooks-Cole.

Psychology: Themes & Variations with InfoTrac. 4th ed. Weiten. (Psychology Ser.). 1998. pap. 52.00 incl. cd-rom (*0-534-36372-5*) Brooks-Cole.

Psychology: Themes & Various brief Cases with Infotrac. 3rd ed. Wayne Weiten. (Psychology Ser.). 1998. 48.50 (*0-534-36371-7*) Brooks-Cole.

Psychology: Theoretical-Historical Perspectives. 2nd rev. ed. Ed. by Robert W. Rieber & Kurt D. Salzinger. LC 98-28447. 509p. 1998. 49.95 (*1-55798-524-3*) Am Psychol.

Psychology: Thinking & Writing Workbook. 6th ed. Spencer A. Rathus. (C). 1995. wbk. ed. 13.50 (*0-15-503220-8*) Harcourt Coll Pubs.

***Psychology: Website.** 7th ed. 1999. write for info. (*0-205-29669-6*) Allyn.

***Psychology Writing & Reading.** 2nd ed. Westen. 1999. pap. text 60.00 (*0-471-37728-7*) Wiley.

Psychology Smartbox: Introduction to Psychology. 9th ed. (Prentice Hall College Titles Ser.). (C). 1997. text 81.00 (*0-13-443516-8*, Macmillan Coll) P-H.

Psychology Smartbox: Introduction to Psychology. 9th ed. Michael Renner. (Prentice Hall College Titles Ser.). (C). 1996. text 81.00 (*0-13-443250-9*, Macmillan Coll) P-H.

***Psychology a European Text.** 720p. 2000. write for info. (*0-00-499002-1*) Collins SF.

Psychology, A-L see Comprehensive Dissertation Index: Five-Year Cumulation, 1983-1987

Psychology & Adult Learning. Mark Tennant. 224p. (C). 1988. lib. bdg. 45.00 (*0-415-00560-4*) Routledge.

Psychology & Adult Learning. Mark Tennant. 186p. (C). 1990. pap. 19.95 (*0-415-05032-4*, A4563) Routledge.

Psychology & Adult Learning. 2nd ed. Mark Tennant. LC 96-28530. 176p. (C). 1997. pap. 20.99 (*0-415-14991-6*) Routledge.

Psychology & African Americans: A Humanistic Approach. 2nd ed. Adelbert H. Jenkins. 352p. (C). 1994. pap. text 62.00 (*0-205-16488-9*, Longwood Div); pap. text 31.00 (*0-205-16489-7*) Allyn.

Psychology & AIDS. Ed. by Thomas E. Backer et al. (Special Issue, American Psychologist Ser.: Vol. 43, No. 11). 156p. 1988. pap. 16.00 (*1-55798-053-5*) Am Psychol.

Psychology & A.I.D.S. Index of Modern Information. Roth Polinski. LC 88-47613. 150p. 1990. 47.50 (*1-55914-232-4*); pap. 44.50 (*1-55914-233-2*) ABBE Pubs Assn.

Psychology & American Law. Curt R. Bartol. 373p. (C). 1983. mass mkt. 44.00 (*0-534-01217-5*) Brooks-Cole.

Psychology & Arthur Miller. Richard I. Evans. LC 81-15375. 136p. 1981. 38.50 (*0-275-90620-5*, C0620, Praeger Pubs) Greenwood.

Psychology & Child Custody Determinations: Knowledge, Roles, & Expertise. Ed. by Lois A. Weithorn. LC 86-25071. (Children & the Law Ser.). 240p. 1987. pap. 74.40 (*0-608-05117-0*, 206567600005) Bks Demand.

Psychology & Christianity: An Introduction to Controversial Issues. rev. ed. Ronald P. Philipchalk. 258p. (Orig.). (C). 1988. pap. text 22.50 (*0-8191-7124-7*) U Pr of Amer.

***Psychology & Christianity: Four Views.** Ed. by Eric L. Johnson. 220p. 2000. pap. 14.99 (*0-8308-2263-1*) InterVarsity.

Psychology & Cognitive Therapy of the Neuroses. rev. ed. Hans Lungwitz. Ed. by Reinhold Becker. Tr. by Norman Maclean from GER. LC 93-17037.Tr. of Systematik der Neurosen. (Illus.). 200p. 1993. 48.50 (*0-8176-2866-5*) Birkhauser.

Psychology & Community Change: Challenges of the Future. 2nd rev. ed. Kenneth Heller et al. 421p. (C). 1989. mass mkt. 40.00 (*0-534-10561-0*) Brooks-Cole.

Psychology & Crime: An Introduction to Criminological Psychology. Clive R. Hollin. 240p. 1989. 49.95 (*0-415-01806-4*, A3249) Routledge.

Psychology & Crime: An Introduction to Criminological Psychology. Clive R. Hollin. 288p. (C). 1989. pap. 24.99 (*0-415-01807-2*, A3253) Routledge.

***Psychology & Crime: Myths & Reality** / Peter B. Ainsworth. LC 99-36913. (Criminology Ser.). 2000. write for info. (*0-582-41424-5*) Addison-Wesley.

Psychology & Criminal Behavior. Cassel. (C). 2000. 60.00 (*0-205-28040-4*, Macmillan Coll) P-H.

Psychology & Criminal Justice: International Review of Theory & Practice. Janos Boros et al. LC 98-36246. (Publications of the European Association of Psychology & Law). 1998. 127.25 (*3-11-016329-2*) De Gruyter.

Psychology & Deterrence. Robert Jervis et al. LC 85-8060. 288p. 1989. reprint ed. pap. text 15.95 (*0-8018-3842-8*) Johns Hopkins.

Psychology & Education: Parallel & Interactive Approaches. J. M. Notterman & H. N. Drewry. LC 93-1257. (Illus.). 292p. (C). 1993. 42.50 (*0-306-44364-3*, Plenum Trade) Perseus Pubng.

Psychology & Education: The State of the Union. Ed. by Frank Farley & Neal J. Gordon. LC 80-82902. (National Society for the Study of Education Publication Ser.). 400p. (C). 1981. 40.00 (*0-8211-0506-X*) McCutchan.

Psychology & Education for Special Needs. Ed. by Ingrid Lunt. 264p. 1995. 69.95 (*1-85742-306-2*, Pub. by Arena) Ashgate Pub Co.

Psychology & Education of the Gifted. 3rd ed. Ed. by Walter B. Barbe & Joseph S. Renzulli. LC 80-11174. 544p. 1981. pap. text 22.95 (*0-8290-0234-0*) Irvington.

Psychology & Educational Practice. Ed. by Herbert J. Walberg & Geneva D. Haertel. LC 97-70793. 458p. 1997. 40.00 (*0-8211-0733-X*) McCutchan.

Psychology & Effective Behavior. Jewell. (Psychology Ser.). (C). 1989. pap. 42.50 (*0-314-27033-7*) West Pub.

Psychology & Environment. Claude Levy-Leboyer. Tr. by David Canter & Ian Griffiths. LC 81-21382. 197p. reprint ed. pap. 61.10 (*0-8357-4821-9*, 203775800009) Bks Demand.

Psychology & Family Law: A New Zealand Perspective. M. E. Pipe & Fred Seymour. LC 98-168648. 176p. 1997. pap. 39.95 (*1-877133-22-1*, Pub. by Univ Otago Pr) Intl Spec Bk.

Psychology & General Sociology Reviews: Future Prospects for Population Phenogenetics, Vol. 4. V. M. Zakharov. Ed. by E. T. Turpaev & A. V. Yaslokov. (Soviet Scientific Reviews Ser.: Vol. 4, Pt. 3). iv, 84p. 1989. text 92.00 (*3-7186-5012-6*) Gordon & Breach.

Psychology & General Sociology Reviews: Neuronal Basis of Associative Learning; Neuronal Mechanisms of Short-Term Memory, Vol. 4. V. M. Storozhuk & A. S. Batuev. Ed. by E. T. Turpaev & A. V. Yaslokov. (Soviet Scientific Reviews Ser.: Vol. 4, Pt. 4). 188p. 1990. pap. text 89.00 (*3-7186-5013-4*) Gordon & Breach.

Psychology & General Sociology Reviews: Population Biology of Phytopathogenic Fungi & Plants, Vol. 4. Y. T. D'yakov et al. Ed. by E. T. Turpaev & A. V. Yaslokov. (Soviet Scientific Reviews Ser.: Vol. 4, Pt. 2). iv, 96p. 1989. text 108.00 (*3-7186-5001-0*) Gordon & Breach.

Psychology & General Sociology Reviews: Population Problems in the Biology of Unicellular Organisms, Vol. 4. I. I. Gitel'zon et al. Ed. by E. T. Turpaev & A. V. Yaslokov. (Soviet Scientific Reviews Ser.: Vol. 4, Pt. 1). iv, 84p. 1989. text 94.00 (*3-7186-4975-6*) Gordon & Breach.

Psychology & General Sociology Reviews: The Problems of Higher Nervous Activity, Vol. 4. P. V. Simonov. Ed. by E. T. Turpaev & A. V. Yaslokov. (Soviet Scientific Reviews Ser.: Vol. 4, Pt. 5). iv, 108p. 1990. text 123.00 (*3-7186-5014-2*) Gordon & Breach.

Psychology & Gynaecological Problems. Annabel K. Broome & Louise Wallace. 320p. (Orig.). 1984. pap. 14.95 (*0-422-78590-3*, 9251, Pub. by Tavistock) Routldge.

Psychology & Health. 2nd ed. Donald A. Bakal. LC 91-5241. Orig. Title: Psychology & Medicine, 1979. 256p. (C). 1992. text 36.95 (*0-8261-7900-2*) Springer Pub.

Psychology & Health: Index of Modern Information with Bibliography. Manfred J. Robineault. LC 89-78054. 150p. 1990. 47.50 (*1-55914-228-6*); pap. 44.50 (*1-55914-229-4*) ABBE Pubs Assn.

Psychology & Health Promotion. P. Bennett. LC 97-9042. 1997. pap. 28.95 (*0-335-19765-5*) OpUniv Pr.

Psychology & Health Promotion. Paul Bennett & Simon Murphy. LC 97-9042. 1997. 96.00 (*0-335-19766-3*) OpUniv Pr.

Psychology & Historical Interpretation. Ed. by William M. Runyan. (Illus.). 320p. 1988. pap. text 22.95 (*0-19-505328-1*) OUP.

Psychology & History. Harry E. Barnes. 1971. 59.95 (*0-87700-034-4*) Revisionist Pr.

***Psychology & 'Human Nature'** Peter D. Ashworth. LC 00-33761. 2000. write for info. (*0-415-21300-2*) Taylor & Francis.

Psychology & Industrial Efficiency. Hugo Munsterberg. 333p. 90.00 (*1-85506-700-5*) Thoemmes Pr.

Psychology & Industrial Efficiency. Hugo Munsterberg. LC 73-2979. (Classics in Psychology Ser.). 1974. reprint ed. 23.95 (*0-405-05151-4*) Ayer.

Psychology & Its Allied Disciplines. Ed. by Marc H. Bornstein. (Cross Currents in Contemporary Psychology Bornstein Ser.). 992p. (C). 1984. lib. bdg. 145.00 (*0-89859-318-2*) L Erlbaum Assocs.

Psychology & Its Allied Disciplines, 3 vols., Set. Ed. by Marc H. Bornstein. (Crosscurrents in Contemporary Psychology Ser.). 1984. pap. 79.95 (*0-89859-319-0*) L Erlbaum Assocs.

Psychology & Its Allied Disciplines Vol. 1: Psychology & the Humanities. Ed. by Marc H. Bornstein. 352p. 1984. 34.50 (*0-89859-320-4*) L Erlbaum Assocs.

Psychology & Its Allied Disciplines Vol. 2: Psychology & the Social Sciences. Ed. by Marc H. Bornstein. 304p. 1984. pap. 32.50 (*0-89859-321-2*) L Erlbaum Assocs.

Psychology & Its Practice: Index of Modern Information. Althea Y. Peltier. LC 89-78057. 150p. 1990. 47.50 (*1-55914-202-2*); pap. 44.50 (*1-55914-203-0*) ABBE Pubs Assn.

Psychology & Its Role in Spirituality. Ferdinand Wulliemier. 310p. 1996. 20.00 (*0-945242-33-6*) Shri Ram Chandra.

Psychology & Kabbalah. Z'ev ben Shimon Halevi. 272p. 1992. pap. 12.50 (*0-87728-529-2*) Weiser.

Psychology & Language: An Introduction to Psycholinguistics. Herbert H. Clark & Eve V. Clark. (Illus.). 608p. (C). 1977. write for info. (*0-318-52974-2*) Harcourt Coll Pubs.

***Psychology & Law.** (C). 2000. text. write for info. (*0-321-04715-X*) Addison-Wesley.

Psychology & Law. 2nd ed. Bartol. 1994. write for info. (*0-534-16321-1*) Thomson Learn.

Psychology & Law: A Critical Introduction. Andreas Kapardis. (Illus.). 396p. (C). 1997. text 74.95 (*0-521-55321-0*); pap. text 29.95 (*0-521-55738-0*) Cambridge U Pr.

Psychology & Law: Inside & Outside the Courtroom. Ed. by Van. (C). 1998. text. write for info. (*0-321-01134-1*) Addison-Wesley Educ.

Psychology & Law: International Perspectives. Ed. by Freidrich Losel et al. LC 92-30454. xxviii, 557p. 1992. lib. bdg. 144.65 (*3-11-013725-9*) De Gruyter.

Psychology & Law: Research & Application. 2nd ed. Curt R. Bartol & Anne M. Bartol. LC 93-39459. 1993. mass mkt. 48.00 (*0-534-16320-3*) Brooks-Cole.

Psychology & Law: Topics from an International Conference. Ed. by Dave J. Muller et al. LC 83-21684. 494p. reprint ed. pap. 153.20 (*0-7837-5204-0*, 204493200005) Bks Demand.

***Psychology & Law: Truthfulness, Accuracy & Credibility.** Amina Memon et al. (C). 1998. pap., student ed. 56.56 (*0-07-709316-X*) McGrw-H Hghr Educ.

Psychology & Law for the Helping Professions. 2nd ed. Leland C. Swenson. LC 96-9241. (Counseling Ser.). 500p. (C). 1996. mass mkt. 74.95 (*0-534-34285-X*) Brooks-Cole.

Psychology & Law for the Helping Professions. 2nd ed. Leland C. Swenson. (C). 1997. text, teacher ed. write for info. (*0-534-34565-4*) Brooks-Cole.

Psychology & Learning. Barbara L. Hammonds. LC 84-73343. (Master Lecture Ser.: Vol. 4). (Illus.). 249p. (Orig.). reprint ed. pap. 77.20 (*0-608-09012-3*, 206964700005) Bks Demand.

Psychology & Life. (C). 1997. 177.00 (*0-673-97560-6*, GoodYrBooks) Addson-Wesley Educ.

Psychology & Life. Ed. by Leslie D. Weatherhead. (C). 1990. pap. 35.00 (*0-85305-267-0*, Pub. by Arthur James) St Mut.

***Psychology & Life.** 2nd ed. (C). 1998. text 25.00 (*0-321-04046-5*) Addison-Wesley.

Psychology & Life. 13th ed. Philip G. Zimbardo. (C). 1997. text 69.00 (*0-673-46838-0*) Addson-Wesley Educ.

Psychology & Life. 14th ed. (C). 1997. text 24.00 (*0-673-55806-1*, GoodYrBooks); text 67.00 (*0-673-55808-8*, GoodYrBooks); text 24.00 (*0-673-55809-6*, GoodYrBooks) Addson-Wesley Educ.

Psychology & Life. 14th ed. Philip G. Zimbardo & Richard Gerrig. (C). 1996. pap. text, student ed. 26.25 (*0-673-99385-X*) Addson-Wesley Educ.

***Psychology & Life.** 15th ed. (C). 1999. text 67.00 (*0-321-03507-0*); text 67.00 (*0-321-03511-9*); text 11.00 (*0-321-03518-6*) Addison-Wesley.

***Psychology & Life.** 15th ed. (C). 1999. text 21.00 (*0-321-03515-1*) Addison-Wesley.

Psychology & Life. 15th ed. Philip G. Zimbardo. (C). 1999. text 22.00 (*0-321-03516-X*) Addson-Wesley Educ.

***Psychology & Life.** 15th ed. Philip G. Zimbardo. 1999. 57.75 (*0-321-06049-0*) Addson-Wesley Educ.

***Psychology & Life.** 15th ed. Zimbards. 1999. student ed. write for info. (*0-201-69752-1*) Addison-Wesley.

Psychology & Life: Psychology & Study Guide Pk. Philip G. Zimbardo. (C). 1997. pap. text 89.67 (*0-321-80121-0*) Addison-Wesley.

Psychology & Life: Study Guide Pk. Philip G. Zimbardo. (C). 1997. pap. text 89.67 (*0-321-80049-4*) Addison-Wesley.

Psychology & Life: Study Guide Pk. 14th ed. Philip G. Zimbardo. (C). 1996. pap. text 72.95 (*0-673-98398-6*) Addison-Wesley.

Psychology & Life: With SuperSite & MindMatters CD-ROM. 15th ed. Philip G. Zimbardo. LC 98-34502. 848p. (C). 1998. text 84.00 incl. cd-rom (*0-321-01650-5*) Allyn.

***Psychology & Life Study Guide.** 15th ed. Philip G. Zimbardo. (C). 1999. pap. text, student ed. 22.50 (*0-321-03505-4*) Addson-Wesley Educ.

***Psychology & Life Telecourse Study Guide.** 15th ed. Philip G. Zimbardo. 352p. (C). 1998. pap. text, student ed. 26.00 (*0-321-03517-8*) Addson-Wesley Educ.

Psychology & Literature in the Eighteenth Century. Ed. by Christopher Fox. LC 86-48001. (Studies in the Eighteenth Century: No. 8). (Illus.). 1987. 42.50 (*0-404-61474-4*) AMS Pr.

Psychology & Logic, 2 vols. J. R. Kantor. 1950. 25.00 (*0-911188-36-3*) Principia Pr.

Psychology & Medical Care. 3rd ed. Kent. (C). 1996. pap. text 36.00 (*0-7020-2065-6*) Harcourt.

Psychology & Medical Research of Self Concepts: Index of New Information & Research Bible. rev. ed. Bakus G. Francis. LC 96-3123. 159p. 1996. 47.50 (*0-7883-1036-4*); pap. 44.50 (*0-7883-1037-2*) ABBE Pubs Assn.

Psychology & Medicine of Appetite Disorders: Research Subject Analysis with Reference Bibliography. rev. ed. Barbara C. Poole. LC 85-48101. 149p. 1994. 47.50 (*0-7883-0652-9*); pap. 44.50 (*0-7883-0653-7*) ABBE Pubs Assn.

Psychology & Medicine, 1979 see Psychology & Health

***Psychology & Mental Health, 2 Vols.** (Illus.). 640p. 2000. 95.00 (*0-89356-066-9*, Magills Choice) Salem Pr.

Psychology & Mental Health: A Report of the Institute on Education & Training for Psychological Contributions to Mental Health, Held at Stanford University in August, 1955. American Psychological Association Staff. Ed. by Charles R. Strother. LC 57-11124. 160p. reprint ed. pap. 49.60 (*0-7837-0488-7*, 204081200018) Bks Demand.

Psychology & Mental Health of Afro-American Women: A Selected Bibliography. Ed. by Glenell S. Young & Janet Sims-Wood. LC 83-51604. (Resources on Afro-American Women Ser.: No. 1). 102p. 1984. pap. 6.95 (*0-915549-00-X*) Afro Res Inc.

Psychology & Methodology see Twin Research: Proceedings of the International Congress on Twin Studies, 2nd

Psychology & Military Proficiency. Charles W. Bray. LC 69-13837. 242p. 1969. reprint ed. lib. bdg. 59.75 (*0-8371-1444-6*, BRMI, Greenwood Pr) Greenwood.

Psychology & Modern Problems. Ed. by James A. Hadfield. LC 72-10844. (Essay Index Reprint Ser.). 1977. reprint ed. 20.95 (*0-8369-7220-1*) Ayer.

Psychology & Myth. Ed. & Intro. by Robert A. Segal. LC 95-38826. (Theories of Myth Ser.: Vol. 1). 416p. 1995. reprint ed. text 80.00 (*0-8153-2255-0*) Garland.

Psychology & National Health Insurance: A Sourcebook. American Psychological Association Staff. Ed. by Charles A. Kiesler et al. LC 79-19251. 659p. reprint ed. pap. 200.00 (*0-7837-0489-5*, 204081300018) Bks Demand.

Psychology & Nihilism: A Genealogical Critique of the Computational Model of Mind. Fred J. Evans. LC 91-42019. (SUNY Series in the Philosophy of the Social Sciences). 303p. (C). 1992. text 19.50 (*0-7914-1249-0*) State U NY Pr.

Psychology & Pedagogy of Reading. Edmund Burke Huey. 491p. 120.00 (*1-85506-692-0*) Thoemmes Pr.

Psychology & Performing Arts. Ed. by Glenn D. Wilson. 324p. 1991. 57.00 (*90-265-1119-1*) Swets.

Psychology & Personal Growth. 3rd ed. Abe Arkoff. 1987. text 36.00 (*0-205-10533-5*, H05333) Allyn.

Psychology & Personal Growth. 3rd ed. Abe Arkoff. 1987. pap. text, wbk. ed. 34.00 (*0-205-10534-3*, H0534-1) Allyn.

Psychology & Personal Growth. 5th ed. Abe Arkoff & Nelson Goud. LC 96-40313. 375p. 1997. pap. 63.00 (*0-205-26102-7*) Allyn.

Psychology & Physiologic Findings in Psychosomatic Disorders. Marilyn H. Light. 3.00 (*0-317-05970-X*) Hypoglycemia Foun.

Psychology & Physiology of Breathing: In Behavioral Medicine, Clinical Psychology, & Psychiatry. R. Fried. LC 93-512. (Behavioral Psychophysiology & Medicine Ser.). (Illus.). 398p. (C). 1993. 54.50 (*0-306-44278-7*, Plenum Trade) Perseus Pubng.

Psychology & Policing. Ed. by Neil Brewer & Carlene Wilson. 504p. 1995. text 89.95 (*0-8058-1418-3*) L Erlbaum Assocs.

Psychology & Postmodernism. Steiner Kvale. (Inquiries in Social Construction Ser.). (Illus.). 340p. (C). 1992. 45.00 (*0-8039-8603-3*); pap. 15.99 (*0-8039-8604-1*) Sage.

Psychology & Practice. 4th ed. Andrew B. Crider et al. LC 92-30213. (C). 1997. pap. text 93.00 (*0-673-46835-6*) Addson-Wesley Educ.

P

An Asterisk (*) at the beginning of an entry indicates that the title is appearing for the first time.

Psychology & Preparation of the Teacher for the Elementary School. Clara L. Robinson. LC 71-177197. (Columbia University. Teachers College. Contributions to Education Ser.: No. 418). reprint ed. 37.50 (*0-404-55418-0*) AMS Pr.

Psychology & Productivity. Ed. by P. Whitney & R. B. Ochsman. (Illus.). 212p. 1989. 75.00 (*0-306-42937-3*, Plenum Trade) Perseus Pubng.

Psychology & Professional Practice: The Interface of Psychology & the Law. Ed. by Francis R. Fields & Rudy J. Horwitz. LC 81-19899. (Illus.). 210p. 1982. 55.00 (*0-89930-015-4*, FIH/, Quorum Bks) Greenwood.

Psychology & Promotion of Health. Ed. by Jean-Pierre Dauwalder. LC 93-46517. (Swiss Monographs in Psychology: Vol. 2). (Illus.). 250p. 1994. pap. text 36.00 (*0-88937-089-3*) Hogrefe & Huber Pubs.

Psychology & Psychiatry: Study Guide Pkg. 2nd ed. Philip G. Zimbardo. (C). 1997. pap. text, student ed. 68.00 (*0-321-80188-1*) Addison-Wesley.

Psychology & Psychiatry Serials: A Bibliographic Aid for Collection Development. Ed. by Dorothy M. Persson & Michael F. Winter. LC 90-39559. (Behavioral & Social Sciences Librarian Ser.: Vol. 9, No. 2). 121p. 1990. text 39.95 (*1-56024-048-2*) Haworth Pr.

Psychology & Psychiatry Today: A Marxist View. Joseph Nahem. LC 81-680. 264p. reprint ed. pap. 81.90 (*0-7837-0580-8*, 204092400019) Bks Demand.

Psychology & Psychological Principles, 8. James Ward. LC 77-72191. (Contributions to the History of Psychology Ser.: Vol. 8, Pt. A, Orientations). 504p. 1977. lib. bdg. 95.00 (*0-313-26932-7*, U6932, Greenwood Pr) Greenwood.

Psychology & Psychology Study Guide, 2 bks. 4th ed. Baron. 1997. text, student ed. 77.00 (*0-205-28706-9*) A&B Bks.

Psychology & Psychotherapy of Otto Rank: An Historical & Comparative Introduction. Fay B. Karpf. LC 70-90539. 132p. 1970. reprint ed. lib. bdg. 55.00 (*0-8371-3029-8*, KAOR, Greenwood Pr) Greenwood.

Psychology & Public Policy: Balancing Public Service & Professional Need. Ed. by Raymond P. Lorion et al. LC 95-26810. 417p. 1996. pap. text 19.95 (*1-55798-347-X*, 431-6700) Am Psychol.

Psychology & Religion. C. G. Jung. LC 91-38405. (Terry Lectures Ser.). 131p. 1960. pap. 12.00 (*0-300-00137-1*, Y14) Yale U Pr.

Psychology & Religion: Eight Points of View. 2nd ed. Andrew R. Fuller. 286p. 1986. pap. text 24.50 (*0-8191-5336-2*) U Pr of Amer.

Psychology & Religion: Eight Points of View. 3rd ed. Andrew R. Fuller. LC 94-20210. (Adams Quality Paperbacks Ser.). 310p. 1994. pap. 16.95 (*0-8226-3036-2*) Rowman.

***Psychology & Religion: Introduction.** Michael Argyle. LC 99-16956. 320p. 1999. pap. write for info. (*0-415-18907-1*) Routledge.

***Psychology & Religion: Introduction.** Michael Argyle. LC 99-16956. 304p. (C). 2000. text. write for info. (*0-415-18906-3*) Routledge.

Psychology & Religion at the Millennium & Beyond. J. Marvin Spiegelman. LC 98-84915. (Psychology & Religion Ser.). 186p. 1999. pap. 14.95 (*1-56184-138-2*) New Falcon Pubns.

Psychology & Religious Education. 3rd rev. ed. John L. Elias. LC 90-31999. 174p. 1990. text 21.95 (*0-89464-460-2*) Krieger.

Psychology & Scientific American Mysteries of the Mind Magazine. 5th ed. David G. Myers & Scientific American Staff. (Illus.). (C). 1997. text 52.40 (*1-57259-206-0*) Worth.

Psychology & Sexual Orientation: Coming to Terms. Janis Bohan. LC 96-2187. 256p. (C). 1996. pap. 19.99 (*0-415-91514-7*) Routledge.

Psychology & Sexual Orientation: Coming to Terms. 2nd ed. Janis Bohan. LC 96-2187. 256p. (C). 1996. 65.00 (*0-415-91513-9*) Routledge.

Psychology & Silence. Stanislaw Zielinski. Ed. by Daniel Bassuk. LC 75-7413. (Illus.). 32p. (Orig.). 1975. pap. 4.00 (*0-87574-201-7*) Pendle Hill.

Psychology & Social Change. Ed. by David Thomas & Arthur Veno. (C). 1992. pap. text 53.00 (*0-86469-146-7*) Intl Spec Bk.

Psychology & Social Issues: A Tutorial Text. Ed. by Raymond Cochrane & Douglas Carroll. (Contemporary Psychology Ser.). 224p. 1991. 79.95 (*1-85000-835-3*, Falmer Pr); pap. 29.95 (*1-85000-836-1*, Falmer Pr) Taylor & Francis.

Psychology & Social Policy. Ed. by Peter Suedfeld & Peter Tetlock. 408p. 1991. 73.95 (*1-56032-063-X*) Hemisp Pub.

Psychology & Social Responsibility: Facing Global Challenges. Ed. by Sylvia Staub & Paula Green. 432p. (C). 1992. text 65.00 (*0-8147-7931-X*); pap. text 25.00 (*0-8147-7941-7*) NYU Pr.

Psychology & Social Work Career Directory. Ed. by Bradley J. Morgan & Joseph M. Palmisano. (Career Advisor Ser.). 300p. 1993. 17.95 (*0-8103-9445-6*, 089164) Visible Ink Pr.

Psychology & Society: Radical Theory & Practice. Parker. 384p. 1996. pap. 21.95 (*0-7453-0879-1*, Pub. by Pluto GBR) Stylus Pub VA.

Psychology & Sociology of Sport, Set. Ed. by James H. Humphrey. LC 85-43473. 1986. write for info. (*0-404-63400-1*) AMS Pr.

***Psychology & the Aging Revolution: How We Adapt to Longer Life.** Sarah Honn Qualls & Norman Abeles. LC 00-36265. 2000. write for info. (*1-55798-707-6*) Am Psychol.

Psychology & the Critical Revolution. Anton G. Hardy. 145p. 1988. 18.50 (*0-9615267-0-X*) James Pubns NY.

Psychology & the Cross: A Christian Approach to Psychology. H. Newton Malony. (Illus.). 284p. (Orig.). 1996. pap. 15.00 (*0-9650740-0-5*) Fuller Theolog.

Psychology & the Developing World. Ed. by Stuart C. Carr & John F. Schumaker. LC 95-43767. 248p. 1996. 75.00 (*0-275-95245-2*, Praeger Pubs) Greenwood.

Psychology & the East. C. G. Jung. Ed. by G. Adler. Tr. by R. F. C. Hull. LC 77-92815. (Jung Extracts Ser.). (Illus.). 232p. 1978. pap. 12.95 (*0-691-01806-5*, Pub. by Princeton U Pr) Cal Prin Full Svc.

Psychology & the Human Dilemma. Rollo May. 336p. 1996. pap. 13.00 (*0-393-31455-3*, Norton Paperbks) Norton.

Psychology & the Industrial Worker. Eric G. Chambers. LC 53-5436. 199p. reprint ed. pap. 56.80 (*0-608-11142-2*, 2050766) Bks Demand.

Psychology & the Internet: Intrapersonal, Interperson, & Transpersonal Implications. Ed. by Jayne Gackenbach. (Illus.). 369p. (C). 1998. boxed set 55.00 (*0-12-271950-6*) Acad Pr.

Psychology & the Law. Ed. by C. James Scheirer & Barbara L. Hammonds. LC 83-11889. (Master Lecture Ser.: No. 2). 182p. reprint ed. pap. 56.50 (*0-7837-8830-4*, 204947700012) Bks Demand.

Psychology & the Law: The State of the Discipline. Ed. by R. Roesch et al. LC 98-45167. (Perspectives in Law & Psychology Ser.: No. 10). (Illus.). 434p. (C). 1999. write for info. (*0-306-45949-3*, Kluwer Plenum) Kluwer Academic.

Psychology & the Law: The State of the Discipline. Ed. by R. Roesch et al. LC 98-45167. (Perspectives in Law & Psychology Ser.: No. 10). (Illus.). xviii, 459p. (C). 1999. pap. write for info. (*0-306-45950-7*, Plenum Trade) Perseus Pubng.

Psychology & the Legal System. Wrightsman. (Psychology Ser.). 1986. text, teacher ed. write for info. (*0-534-06733-6*) Brooks-Cole.

Psychology & the Legal System. Lawrence S. Wrightsman. LC 86-9680. 402p. (C). 1986. mass mkt. 32.75 (*0-534-06732-8*) Brooks-Cole.

Psychology & the Legal System. 2nd ed. Lawrence S. Wrightsman. LC 90-41445. 464p. (C). 1990. mass mkt. 48.50 (*0-534-14634-1*) Brooks-Cole.

Psychology & the Legal System. 3rd ed. Lawrence S. Wrightsman et al. LC 92-46588. 1994. text 63.95 (*0-534-17514-7*) Brooks-Cole.

Psychology & the Legal System. 4th ed. Lawrence S. Wrightsman & Michael T. Nietzel. LC 97-19080. (Psychology Ser.). 1997. pap. 43.75 (*0-534-34085-7*) Brooks-Cole.

***Psychology & the Legal System.** 5th ed. Wrightsman. 2000. 51.25 (*0-534-36544-2*) Brooks-Cole.

Psychology & the Legal System with Infotrac. 4th ed. Wrightsman & Nietzel. (Psychology Ser.). 1998. pap. 46.50 (*0-534-36374-1*) Brooks-Cole.

***Psychology & the Media Vol. 2: A Second Look.** Ed. by Lita L. Schwartz. LC 99-34543. 223p. 1999. pap. 29.95 (*1-55798-578-2*, 431-625A) Am Psychol.

Psychology & the Occult. C. G. Jung. Ed. by G. Adler. Tr. by R. F. C. Hull. LC 75-34810. (Jung Extracts Ser.). (Illus.). 177p. 1976. pap. 12.95 (*0-691-01791-3*, Pub. by Princeton U Pr) Cal Prin Full Svc.

Psychology & the Older Adult: Challenges for Training in the 1980s: Proceedings of the Conference on Training Psychologists for Work in Aging, Boulder, Colorado, June 14-18, 1981. Conference on Training Psychologists for Work in A. Ed. by John F. Santos & Gary R. VandenBos. LC 81-72065. 289p. reprint ed. pap. 89.60 (*0-7837-0490-9*, 204081400018) Bks Demand.

Psychology & the Poetics of Growth: Figurative Language in Psychology, Psychotherapy, & Education. Howard R. Pollio et al. 272p. 1977. text 49.95 (*0-89859-484-7*) L Erlbaum Assocs.

Psychology & the Problems of Society. American Psychological Association Staff. Ed. by Frances F. Korten et al. LC 72-115967. 471p. reprint ed. pap. 146.10 (*0-7837-0491-7*, 204081500018) Bks Demand.

Psychology & the Soul: A Study of Origin, Conceptual Evolution, & Nature of the Soul. Otto Rank. Tr. by Gergory C. Richter & James Lieberman. LC 97-30223. 360p. 1998. text 29.95 (*0-8018-5739-2*) Johns Hopkins.

Psychology & the Teacher. 5th ed. Dennis Child. (Education Ser.). 416p. 1993. pap. 39.95 (*0-304-32649-6*) Continuum.

Psychology & the World of Work. David A. Statt. LC 94-33770. (C). 1994. text 55.00 (*0-8147-8009-1*); pap. text 19.50 (*0-8147-8010-5*) NYU Pr.

Psychology & Torture. Peter Suedfeld. 1990. 55.95 (*0-89116-976-8*) Hemisp Pub.

Psychology & Treatment of Addictive Behavior, No. 8. Ed. by Scott Dowling. (Workshop Series of the American Psychoanalytic Association: Monograph 8). 207p. 1995. 35.00 (*0-8236-5562-8*) Intl Univs Pr.

Psychology & Treatment of the Youthful Offender. David E. Brandt & S. Jack Zlotnick. (Illus.). 262p. 1988. pap. 33.95 (*0-398-06027-4*) C C Thomas.

Psychology & Treatment of the Youthful Offender. David E. Brandt & S. Jack Zlotnick. (Illus.). 262p. (C). 1988. text 45.95 (*0-398-05454-1*) C C Thomas.

Psychology & Western Religion. C. G. Jung. Ed. by G. Adler. Tr. by R. F. C. Hull. LC 84-42548. (Bollingen Ser.). (Illus.). 312p. (Orig.). 1984. pap. 12.95 (*0-691-01862-6*, Pub. by Princeton U Pr) Cal Prin Full Svc.

Psychology & Work: Productivity, Change, & Employment. Ed. by Michael S. Pallak & Robert Perloff. LC 86-7952. (Master Lectures: Vol. 5). 220p. (Orig.). 1986. pap. 24.95 (*0-912704-48-9*) Am Psychol.

Psychology & Work: Productivity, Change, & Employment. Ed. by Michael S. Pallak & Robert O. Perloff. LC 86-7952. (Master Lectures). (Illus.). 224p. (Orig.). reprint ed. pap. 69.50 (*0-608-09011-5*, 206964600005) Bks Demand.

Psychology & Work Today. 7th ed. Duane Schultz & Sydney E. Schultz. LC 97-24847. 566p. (C). 1997. 81.00 (*0-13-636465-9*) P-H.

Psychology & You. McMahon. Date not set. pap. text, teacher ed. 16.95 (*0-314-52495-9*) West Pub.

Psychology & You. McMahon. 1989. mass mkt., wbk. ed. 19.00 (*0-314-52496-7*) West Pub.

Psychology & You. Frank B. McMahon. 1989. mass mkt. 41.50 (*0-314-47357-2*) West Pub.

Psychology & You. 2nd ed. McMahon. 1994. mass mkt., teacher ed. 66.25 (*0-314-02771-8*) West Pub.

Psychology & You. 2nd ed. McMahon. (CA - Career Development Ser.). 1994. mass mkt., wbk. ed. 22.50 (*0-314-04524-4*) West Pub.

Psychology & You. 2nd ed. McMahon. (Career Development Ser.). 1996. teacher ed. 12.00 (*0-314-21636-7*) West Pub.

Psychology & You. 2nd ed. Frank B. McMahon et al. LC 93-41159. 1994. mass mkt. write for info. (*0-314-02772-6*) West Pub.

Psychology & You. 3rd ed. McMahon. (Career Development Ser.). 1999. pap. text, student ed., wbk. ed. 24.24 (*0-538-42663-2*) Thomson Learn.

Psychology & You: Worksheets. 2nd ed. McMahon. (Career Development Ser.). 1994. pap. 24.50 (*0-314-04662-3*) Thomson Learn.

Psychology Applied Teaching, 8 vols. Biehler. (C). 1996. pap., teacher ed. 11.96 (*0-395-82880-5*) HM.

Psychology Applied Teaching: Testbank, 8 vols. Biehler. (C). 1996. pap., suppl. ed. 11.96 (*0-395-82881-3*) HM.

Psychology Applied to Law. Costanzo. (Psychology Ser.). 2001. pap. 28.00 (*0-534-36629-5*) Brooks-Cole.

Psychology Applied to Life & Work. 6th ed. Harry W. Hepner. LC 78-11923. (Illus.). 1979. text 54.00 (*0-13-732461-8*) P-H.

Psychology Applied To Modern Life. 6th ed. Weiten. (Psychology Ser.). 2000. pap., student ed. 20.00 (*0-534-36666-X*) Brooks-Cole.

Psychology Applied to Modern Life: Adjustment in the 80's. 2nd ed. Wayne Weiten. LC 85-11645. (Psychology Ser.). 566p. (C). 1985. pap. 37.75 (*0-534-05412-9*) Brooks-Cole.

Psychology Applied to Modern Life: Adjustment in the 80's. 2nd ed. Wayne Weiten. LC 85-11645. (Psychology Ser.). 566p. (C). 1985. pap. 14.75 (*0-534-05413-7*) Brooks-Cole.

Psychology Applied to Modern Life: Adjustment in the 90s. 3rd ed. Margaret A. Lloyd et al. 500p. (C). 1990. pap. 46.00 (*0-534-09708-1*) Brooks-Cole.

Psychology Applied to Modern Life: Adjustment in the 90s. 3rd ed. Wayne Weiten & Sosulski. (Counseling Ser.). 1990. pap. text, student ed. 18.00 (*0-534-09709-X*) Brooks-Cole.

Psychology Applied to Modern Life: Adjustment in the 90s. 4th ed. Wayne Weiten. (Counseling Ser.). 1993. pap., student ed. 17.00 (*0-534-19892-9*) Wadsworth Pub.

Psychology Applied to Modern Life: Adjustment in the 90s. 4th ed. Wayne Weiten & Margaret A. Lloyd. LC 93-19884. (Illus.). 607p. 1993. pap. 50.00 (*0-534-19890-2*) Brooks-Cole.

Psychology Applied to Modern Life: Adjustment in the 90s. 4th ed. Wayne Weiten et al. (Counseling-Psychology Ser.). 1993. pap. text, teacher ed. write for info. (*0-534-19893-7*) Brooks-Cole.

Psychology Applied to Modern Life: Adjustment in the '90s. 5th ed. Wayne Weiten & Margaret A. Lloyd. (C). 1996. pap., teacher ed. write for info. (*0-534-34358-9*); pap., student ed. 17.00 (*0-534-34357-0*) Brooks-Cole.

Psychology Applied to Modern Life: Adjustment in the 90's. 5th ed. Wayne Weiten & Margaret A. Lloyd. LC 96-34649. (Psychology). 630p. (C). 1996. pap. 50.25 (*0-534-33938-7*) Brooks-Cole.

Psychology Applied to Modern Life: Adjustment in the 90s. 6th ed. Wayne Weiten & Margaret A. Lloyd. LC 99-24198. (Counseling Ser.). 583p. 1999. pap. 78.95 (*0-534-35553-6*) Brooks-Cole.

Psychology Applied to Modern Life: Adjustment in the 90s, Personal Explorations. 4th ed. Wayne Weiten & Margaret A. Lloyd. 1993. wbk. ed. write for info. (*0-534-19894-5*) Brooks-Cole.

Psychology Applied to Modern Life: Adjustment in the 90s, Personal Explorations Workbook. 5th ed. Wayne Weiten & Margaret A. Lloyd. 1996. pap., wbk. ed. 2.00 (*0-534-34359-7*) Brooks-Cole.

Psychology Applied to Modern Life: Adjustment in the '90s, Test Items. 5th ed. Wayne Weiten & Margaret A. Lloyd. 1996. pap. 2.56 (*0-534-34360-0*) Brooks-Cole.

Psychology Applied to Teaching. 5th ed. Robert F. Biehler & Jack Snowman. LC 85-60849. 752p. (C). 1985. 47.96 (*0-395-40820-2*); 47.96 (*0-395-40822-9*); 47.96 (*0-395-40821-0*); audio 5.00 (*0-395-40823-7*) HM.

Psychology Applied to Teaching, 6 vols. 6th ed. Robert F. Biehler & Jack Snowman. (C). 1989. pap. text 2.76 (*0-395-52634-5*); pap. text 3.16 (*0-395-52636-1*) HM.

Psychology Applied to Teaching, 6 vols. 6th ed. Robert F. Biehler & Jack Snowman. (C). 1990. 80.36 (*0-395-52906-9*) HM.

Psychology Applied to Teaching, 7 vols. 6th ed. Robert F. Biehler & Jack Snowman. (C). 1990. pap. text 9.96 (*0-395-53286-8*) HM.

Psychology Applied to Teaching, 8 vols. 8th ed. Robert F. Biehler & Jack Snowman. LC 96-76870. 672p. (C). 1996. pap. text 63.16 (*0-395-77685-6*) HM.

Psychology Applied to Teaching, 8 vols. 8th ed. Robert F. Biehler & Jack Snowman. (C). 1996. pap. text, student ed. 21.56 (*0-395-83817-7*) HM.

Psychology Applied to Work. 2nd ed. Paul M. Muchinsky. 602p. (C). 1989. mass mkt. 38.50 (*0-534-10729-X*) Brooks-Cole.

Psychology Applied to Work. 4th ed. Muchinsky. (Psychology Ser.). 1993. pap., teacher ed. write for info. (*0-534-16622-9*) Brooks-Cole.

Psychology Applied to Work. 6th ed. Muchinsky. LC 99-26100. (Psychology Ser.). 1999. pap. text 87.95 (*0-534-36252-4*) Brooks-Cole.

Psychology Applied to Work. 6th ed. Muchinsky. (Psychology Ser.). 1999. mass mkt., wbk. ed. 14.00 (*0-534-36254-0*) Brooks-Cole.

Psychology Applied to Work: An Introduction to Industrial & Organizational Psychology. 3rd ed. Paul M. Muchinsky. 650p. (C). 1990. mass mkt. 50.00 (*0-534-13032-1*) Brooks-Cole.

Psychology Applied to Work: An Introduction to Industrial & Organizational Psychology. 4th ed. Paul M. Muchinsky. 738p. (C). 1993. text 47.50 (*0-534-16620-2*) Brooks-Cole.

Psychology Applied to Work: An Introduction to Industrial & Organizational Psychology. 5th ed. Paul M. Muchinsky. 1996. mass mkt., teacher ed. write for info. (*0-534-34238-8*) Brooks-Cole.

Psychology Applied to Work: An Introduction to Industrial & Organizational Psychology. 5th ed. Paul M. Muchinsky. LC 96-20143. (Psychology Ser.). 538p. (C). 1996. pap. 53.25 (*0-534-33876-3*) Brooks-Cole.

Psychology Applied to Work: Student Exercise Book. 5th ed. Paul M. Muchinsky. (Psychology Ser.). 1996. mass mkt., wbk. ed. 18.00 (*0-534-34237-X*) Brooks-Cole.

Psychology Applied to Work: Student Workbook. 4th ed. Paul M. Muchunsky. (Psychology Ser.). 1993. pap., wbk. ed. 19.95 (*0-534-16623-7*) Brooks-Cole.

Psychology As Applied to Nursing. 8th ed. Andrew McGhie. LC 83-7753. (Illus.). 329p. 1986. pap. text 26.00 (*0-443-02836-2*) Church.

Psychology As Metaphor. John Soyland. LC 94-65555. 192p. 1994. 69.95 (*0-8039-8957-1*); pap. 26.95 (*0-8039-8958-X*) Sage.

Psychology As Religion: The Cult of Self-Worship. rev. ed. Paul C. Vitz. 176p. (C). 1994. pap. text 14.00 (*0-8028-0725-9*) Eerdmans.

Psychology Assistant. Jack Rudman. (Career Examination Ser.: C-1774). 1994. pap. 29.95 (*0-8373-1774-6*) Nat Learn.

Psychology Assistant I. Jack Rudman. (Career Examination Ser.: C-919). 1994. pap. 29.95 (*0-8373-0919-0*) Nat Learn.

Psychology Assistant III. Jack Rudman. (Career Examination Ser.: C-922). 1994. pap. 34.95 (*0-8373-0922-0*) Nat Learn.

Psychology Assistant II. Jack Rudman. (Career Examination Ser.: C-921). 1994. pap. 34.95 (*0-8373-0921-2*) Nat Learn.

Psychology at Iowa: Centennial Essays. Ed. by J. H. Cantor. 176p. (C). 1991. text 39.95 (*0-8058-0761-6*) L Erlbaum Assocs.

Psychology at Work. Lilly M. Berry & John P. Houston. 704p. (C). 1994. text. write for info. (*0-697-24613-2*) Brown & Benchmark.

Psychology at Work. Ed. by Paul S. Achilles. LC 74-156602. (Essay Index Reprint Ser.). 1977. reprint ed. 20.95 (*0-8369-2262-X*) Ayer.

Psychology at Work. 2nd ed. Berry-Houston. LC 97-13527. 592p. 1997. 64.69 (*0-697-20173-2*) McGraw.

Psychology at Work. 3rd ed. Berry-Houston. 2000. 43.00 (*0-697-36182-9*) McGraw.

Psychology at Work. 4th ed. Peter E. Warr. 1996. pap. 19.95 (*0-14-024648-7*, Pub. by Pnguin Bks Ltd) Trafalgar.

Psychology Aweigh! A History of Clinical Psychology in the United States Navy, 1900-1988. Frederick L. McGuire. LC 90-279. 249p. 1990. 19.95 (*1-55798-086-1*) Am Psychol.

Psychology Basics, 2 vols., Set. Ed. by Salem Press Editors. 704p. 1998. lib. bdg. 95.00 (*0-89356-963-1*, Magills Choice) Salem Pr.

Psychology Boundries & Froniters. William Buskist & David Gerbing. LC 93-22902. (C). 1989. reprint ed. text 83.44 (*0-673-38023-8*) Addson-Wesley Educ.

Psychology, Descriptive & Explanatory: A Treatise of the Phenomena, Laws & Development of Human Mental Life. George T. Ladd. LC 75-3226. reprint ed. 46.50 (*0-404-59224-4*) AMS Pr.

Psychology, Discourse & Social Practice: From Regulation to Resistance. Gill Aitken et al. LC 97-121064. 208p. 1996. 69.95 (*0-7484-0503-8*, Pub. by Tay Francis Ltd); pap. 24.95 (*0-7484-0504-6*, Pub. by Tay Francis Ltd) Taylor & Francis.

Psychology, Education, Gods, & Humanity. Laurence Simon. LC 98-11136. 232p. 1998. 59.95 (*0-275-96058-7*, Praeger Pubs) Greenwood.

***Psychology Encyclopedia Lasderdisc III.** Carson. 1998. 231.00 (*0-321-02092-8*) Addson-Wesley Educ.

***Psychology Essays & Practicals.** 2nd ed. 160p. 2000. student ed. write for info. (*0-582-28810-X*) Addison-Wesley.

Psychology, Ethics & Change. Ed. by Susan Fairbairn & Gavin J. Fairbairn. 288p. (C). 1988. text 45.00 (*0-7102-0558-9*, Routledge Thoemms) Routledge.

Psychology Every Day. Muzi. (C). 2000. text. write for info. (*0-15-507352-4*); pap. text, student ed. write for info. (*0-15-507354-0*) Harcourt Coll Pubs.

Psychology Experimenter. Microteac Staff. (C). 1986. 295.00 (*0-15-572674-9*, Pub. by Harcourt Coll Pubs) Harcourt.

Psychology Exposed or, the Emperor's New Clothes. Paul Kline. 208p. 1988. text 45.00 (*0-415-00643-0*); pap. text 13.95 (*0-415-00644-9*) Routledge.

***Psychology for as Level.** Michael W. Eysenck & Cara Flanagan. LC 00-25537. 2000. 29.95 (*0-86377-665-5*) Psychol Pr.

P

Psychology for Better Living. Lyle Tussing. LC 59-14126. (Illus.). 508p. reprint ed. pap. 157.50 (0-608-30614-2, 201647900004) Bks Demand.

Psychology for Educators. Sharpes. 576p. 1998. pap. 52.19 (0-697-35412-1) McGraw.

Psychology for Effective Managers: Understanding & Managing Human Behavior in the Workplace. Robert B. Burns. (Illus.). 323p. 1999. pap. 24.95 (1-875680-34-9) Woodslane.

Psychology for Health Fitness Professionals. James Gavin & Nettie Gavin. LC 94-23549. 136p. (Orig.). 1994. pap. text 17.00 (0-87322-775-1, BGAV0775) Human Kinetics.

Psychology for Kids: 40 Fun Tests That Help You Learn about Yourself. rev. ed. Jonni Kincher. Ed. by Julie S. Bach & Pamela Espeland. LC 95-5908. (Self-Help for Kids Ser.). (Illus.). 152p. (YA). (gr. 5 up). 1995. pap. 16.95 (0-915793-85-7) Free Spirit Pub.

Psychology for Kids II: 40 Fun Experiments That Help You Learn about Others, Vol. II. Jonni Kincher. Ed. by Pamela Espeland. LC 94-46251. (Illus.). 168p. (Orig.). (YA). (gr. 6 up). 1995. pap. 17.95 (0-915793-83-0) Free Spirit Pub.

Psychology for Language Teachers: A Social Constructivist Approach. Marion Williams & Bob Burden. (Cambridge Language Teaching Library). 249p. 1997. text 54.95 (0-521-49528-8); pap. text 20.95 (0-521-49880-5) Cambridge U Pr.

Psychology for Law Enforcement. Edward J. Green. LC 75-15634. 178p. (C). reprint ed. 55.20 (0-8357-9969-7, 205514300008) Bks Demand.

Psychology for Law Enforcement Officers. George J. Dudycha. (Illus.). 416p. 1982. 63.95 (0-398-00482-X); pap. 49.95 (0-398-06098-3) C C Thomas.

Psychology for Leaders: Using Motivation, Conflict, & Power to Manage More Effectively. Dean R. Tjosvold & Mary M. Tjosvold. LC 94-12760. (Portable MBS Ser.). 283p. 1995. 32.95 (0-471-59755-4) Wiley.

Psychology for Living. 4th ed. G. A. Forehand et al. 1977. text 30.96 (0-07-021520-0) McGraw.

Psychology for Living: Adjustment, Growth, & Behavior Today. 6th ed. Eastwood Atwater & Karen G. Duffy. LC 98-15321. 507p. (C). 1998. pap. text 63.00 (0-13-958778-0) P-H.

Psychology for Living: The Science of Individual Behavior. 4th rev. ed. Mark F. Sohn. 404p. 1999. 19.95 (1-883207-04-5) M F Sohn Pubns.

Psychology for Making Money in Real Estate: An Aggressive, Common Sense Approach to Buying , Renting, & Selling. James M. Hood. 100p. (Orig.). 1987. pap. 17.95 (0-9618356-0-5) Myrna Pub Co.

Psychology for Medicine. pap. text. write for info. (0-7131-4543-9, Pub. by E A) Routldge.

Psychology for Nurses & the Caring Professions. Sheila Payne & Janet Walker. LC 95-14761. (Social Science for Nurses & the Caring Professions Ser.). 192p. 1995. 98.95 (0-335-19411-7); pap. 31.95 (0-335-19410-9) OpUniv Pr.

Psychology for Parents & Teachers. 2nd ed. Mark F. Sohn. 1991. 13.00 (0-9616911-7-4) M F Sohn Pubns.

Psychology for Performing Artists: Butterflies & Bouquets. Glenn D. Wilson. 200p. 1993. pap. 29.50 (1-85302-166-0) Taylor & Francis.

Psychology for Physical Educators. Ed. by Yves Vanden Auweele et al. LC 98-39170. (Illus.). 536p. (C). 1999. text 39.00 (0-88011-761-3, BVAN0761) Human Kinetics.

***Psychology for Psychiatrists.** Deepa S. Gupta. 1999. 42.95 (1-86156-140-7) Whurr Pub.

***Psychology for Social Careers.** David J. Messer. LC 98-32273. 1999. pap. text 32.95 (1-85302-762-6) Taylor & Francis.

Psychology for Social Workers: Black Perspectives. Lena Robinson. LC 95-8131. 208p. (C). 1995. pap. 25.99 (0-415-10108-5) Routledge.

Psychology for Social Workers: Black Perspectives. Lena Robinson. LC 95-8131. 208p. (C). (gr. 13). 1995. 75.00 (0-415-10107-7) Routledge.

Psychology for Social Workers & Related Professionals. David Messer & Fiona Jones. LC 97-40758. 1998. write for info. (0-13-565417-3) P-H.

Psychology for Swimmers. Keith Bell. LC 89-49231. (Illus.). 72p. 1980. pap. 11.95 (0-945609-00-0) Keel Pubns.

Psychology for Teaching. 2nd ed. LeFrancois. (Education Ser.). 1975. pap. 9.00 (0-534-00368-0) Wadsworth Pub.

Psychology for Teaching. 7th ed. Lefrancois. (Education Ser.). 1991. mass mkt., teacher ed. write for info. (0-534-14413-6) Wadsworth Pub.

Psychology for Teaching. 9th ed. LeFrancois. (Education Ser.). 1996. student ed. 15.25 (0-534-50679-8) Wadsworth Pub.

Psychology for Teaching. 9th ed. Guy R. Lefrancois. LC 96-8707. (Education Ser.). 592p. (C). 1996. 53.25 (0-534-50678-X) Wadsworth Pub.

***Psychology for Teaching.** 10th ed. Lefrancois. (Education Ser.). (C). 1999. text 19.00 (0-534-57454-8) Wadsworth Pub.

Psychology for Teaching. 10th ed. Guy R. Lefrancois. LC 99-44849. (Education Ser.). 1999. 79.95 (0-534-57447-5) Thomson Learn.

Psychology for Teaching: A Bear Always Faces the Front. 6th ed. Guy R. Lefrancois. 411p. (C). 1987. pap. write for info. (0-534-08634-9) Wadsworth Pub.

Psychology for Teaching: A Bear Never Faces the Front. 5th ed. Guy R. Lefrancois. (C). 1984. pap. write for info. (0-534-04464-6) Wadsworth Pub.

Psychology for Teaching: A Bear Will Not Commit Himself Just Now. 7th ed. Guy R. Lefrancois. 448p. (C). 1990. pap. 45.95 (0-534-14412-8) Wadsworth Pub.

Psychology for the Lawyer. Dwight G. McCarty. (Historical Foundations of Forensic Psychiatry & Psychology Ser.). 1980. lib. bdg. 59.50 (0-306-76068-1) Da Capo.

Psychology for the MRC Psych. Munafo. LC 98-189084. 208p. 1998. pap. text 40.00 (0-7506-3403-0) Buttrwrth-Heinemann.

Psychology for Theatre. A. L. Groysman. LC 99-28897. (Russian Studies in Art, Literature, Theatre: Vol. 1). 456p. 1999. text 109.95 (0-7734-3233-7) E Mellen.

Psychology for Trainers. Alison Hardingham. 184p. 1998. pap. 42.00 (0-85292-681-2, Pub. by IPM Hse) St Mut.

***Psychology for Trainers 1998.** Alison Hardingham. 184p. 2000. pap. 44.99 (0-8464-5137-9) Beekman Pubs.

Psychology from a Christian Perspective. 2nd ed. Ronald L. Koteskey. 122p. (C). 1991. pap. text 19.00 (0-8191-8203-6) U Pr of Amer.

Psychology from a Personal Perspective. 4th ed. Stephen W. Link & Daniel Perkins. 168p. (C). 1993. text 32.00 (0-536-58445-9) Pearson Custom.

Psychology from an Empirical Standpoint. Franz Brentano. Tr. by Linda L. McAlister et al. LC 95-7729. (International Library of Philosophy). 448p. (C). 1995. pap. 27.99 (0-415-10661-3, B4322) Routledge.

Psychology Guide to Understanding & Enjoyment Human Behavior. 6th ed. Frederick Nesbit. 170p. (C). 1994. text 25.00 (0-536-58736-1) Pearson Custom.

Psychology, Human Relations & Organizations Communication. Cworetzky et al. (Adaptable Courseware Ser.). pap. 22.25 (0-314-11357-6) Brooks-Cole.

Psychology, Humanism, & Scientific Inquiry: The Selected Essays of Hadley Cantril. Ed. by Albert H. Cantril. 288p. 1987. 44.95 (0-88738-176-6) Transaction Pubs.

Psychology in a Physical World: Forty Years of Just Thinking About Science. Art Z. Orzeck. 108p. (Orig.). (C). 1995. pap. text 18.50 (0-8191-9799-8) U Pr of Amer.

Psychology in Action. Ed. by David Canter. (Dartmouth Benchmark Ser.). (Illus.). 340p. 1995. text 77.95 (1-85521-365-6, Pub. by Dartmth Pub) Ashgate Pub Co.

Psychology in Action. 4th ed. Huffman. 1996. text 54.00 (0-471-19048-9) Wiley.

Psychology in Action. 4th ed. Huffman. 1996. text 30.95 incl. mac hd (0-471-17528-5) Wiley.

***Psychology in Action.** 4th ed. Huffman. 1998. text 51.00 (0-471-32433-7, Wiley Heyden) Wiley.

Psychology in Action. 4th ed. Karen Huffman et al. 1997. cd-rom 31.95 (0-471-16773-8) Wiley.

***Psychology in Action.** 5th ed. Karen Huffman et al. LC 99-25930. 752p. 1999. text 81.95 (0-471-24932-7) Wiley.

***Psychology in Action, Chapter 17.** 5th ed. Huffman. 1999. text 1.00 (0-471-35902-5) Wiley.

Psychology in Action: ESL Handbook. 4th ed. Karen Huffman et al. 135p. 1996. pap. 14.95 (0-471-16762-2, SI05) Wiley.

Psychology in Action: Study Guide Set. 5th ed. Karen Huffman. 1999. pap. text 20.00 (0-471-35473-2) Wiley.

***Psychology in Action: Web Access Card.** 5th ed. Karen Huffman et al. 1999. pap. 14.95 (0-471-38569-7) Wiley.

Psychology in Action & Activity Kit to Accompany Psychology in Action, Textbook & Study Guide. 4th ed. Karen Huffman et al. 1056p. 1997. text 112.85 (0-471-25255-7) Wiley.

Psychology in Africa. J. Mallory Wober. LC 76-381649. 258p. reprint ed. pap. 80.00 (0-8357-3234-7, 205712800010) Bks Demand.

Psychology in & Out of Court: Critical Examination of Legal Psychology. Michael King. LC 86-91528. 1986. 65.00 (0-08-026798-X, Pub. by Pergamon Repr) Franklin.

Psychology in Childbearing. Nora Tisdall. LC 97-200218. 1997. pap. text 17.50 (1-898507-28-7) Buttrwrth-Heinemann.

Psychology in Christian Perspective: An Analysis of Key Issues. Harold W. Faw. LC 94-47067. 200p. 1995. pap. 14.99 (0-8010-2012-3) Baker Bks.

Psychology in Context. David N. Sattler. LC 96-76957. (C). 1996. pap. text 20.76 (0-395-75749-5) HM.

Psychology in Context: Behaviorism. 2nd ed. Halonen-Santrock. 1995. pap. text 86.56 (0-697-14921-8) McGraw.

Psychology in Context: Behaviorism. 2nd ed. Halonen-Santrock. 1996. text (0-697-34014-7, WCB McGr Hill) McGrw-H Hghr Educ.

Psychology in Context: Voices & Perspectives. David N. Sattler & Virginia Shabatay. (C). 1996. text, teacher ed. 11.96 (0-395-83513-5) HM.

Psychology in Counselling & Therapeutic Practice. Jill Wilkinson et al. LC 96-32463. 286p. 1997. pap. 47.95 (0-471-95562-0) Wiley.

Psychology in Economics & Business. Gerrit Antonides. 360p. 1991. lib. bdg. 145.00 (0-7923-1375-5) Kluwer Academic.

Psychology in Economics & Business: An Introduction to Economic Psychology. 2nd ed. Gerrit Antonides. LC 96-19922. 430p. 1996. lib. bdg. 172.00 (0-7923-4107-4) Kluwer Academic.

Psychology in Europe: Facts, Figures, Realities. A. Schorr & S. Saari. (Illus.). 332p. 1995. pap. 34.50 (0-88937-155-5) Hogrefe & Huber Pubs.

Psychology in Foreign Language Teaching. 2nd ed. Steven H. McDonough. (Illus.). 192p. 1987. pap. text 16.95 (0-04-418006-3) Routledge.

***Psychology in Human Context: Essays in Dissidence & Reconstruction.** Sigmund Koch. LC 98-52008. 1999. pap. text 24.00 (0-226-44931-9) U Ch Pr.

Psychology in India Vol. 1: The State-of-the-Art: Personality & Mental Process, Vol. 1. Ed. by Janak Pandey. 336p. (C). 1989. text 35.00 (0-8039-9552-0) Sage.

Psychology in India Vol. 2: The State-of-the-Art: Basic & Applied Social Psychology, Vol. 2. Ed. by Janak Pandey. 356p. (C). 1989. text 35.00 (0-8039-9553-9) Sage.

Psychology in India Vol. 3: The State-of-the-Art: Organizational Behavior & Mental Health, Vol. 3. Ed. by Janak Pandey. 342p. (C). 1989. text 35.00 (0-8039-9554-7) Sage.

***Psychology in India Revisited: Developments in the Discipline.** Janak Pandey. LC 00-22300. 2000. pap. write for info. (0-7619-9442-4) Sage.

Psychology in Industrial Organizations. 3rd ed. Laurence Siegel & Irving Lane. (C). 1974. 20.95 (0-256-01563-5, Irwn McGrw-H) McGrw-H Hghr Educ.

Psychology in Industrial Organizations, 5 vols. 5th ed. Norman R. Maier & Trudy G. Verser. LC 81-81702. (Illus.). 672p. (C). 1982. text 75.96 (0-395-31740-1) HM.

Psychology in International Perspective. Ed. by Uwe P. Gielen et al. LC 92-9057. xii, 340p. 1992. pap. 55.00 (90-265-1236-8) Swets.

***Psychology in Later Adulthood.** Susan Krauss Whitbourne. (Series on Adulthood & Aging). 352p. 2000. 65.00 (0-471-19359-3) Wiley.

Psychology in Litigation & Legislation. Ed. by Bruce D. Sales & Gary R. VandenBos. 216p. 1994. pap. text 14.95 (1-55798-247-3) Am Psychol.

Psychology in New Millennium. 7th ed. Rathus. (C). 1998. pap. text, student ed. 28.00 (0-15-508221-3) Harcourt.

Psychology in Organizations: Integrating Science & Practice. Ed. by Kevin R. Murphy & Frank E. Saal. 304p. (C). 1990. text 75.00 (0-8058-0477-3) L Erlbaum Assocs.

Psychology in Perspective. 2nd ed. (C). 1997. text 24.00 (0-673-97815-X, GoodYrBooks) Addson-Wesley Educ.

Psychology in Perspective. 2nd ed. (C). 1997. 67.00 (0-321-40778-4) Pearson Custom.

Psychology In Perspective. 2nd ed. (C). 1997. write for info. (0-13-087599-6) Addison-Wesley.

Psychology In Perspective. 2nd ed. 216p. (C). 1997. 10.00 (0-673-97811-7, GoodYrBooks) Addson-Wesley Educ.

Psychology in Perspective. 2nd ed. Carol Tavris & Carole Wade. LC 96-28865. 704p. (C). 1997. pap. text 66.00 (0-673-98314-5, GoodYrBooks) Addson-Wesley Educ.

***Psychology in Perspective.** 3rd ed. Carol Tavris & Carole Wade. LC 00-37310. 2000. write for info. (0-13-028326-6) P-H.

Psychology in Perspective: Supershell Dos. 2nd ed. Tavris & Wade. 1997. pap. 18.75 (0-673-97813-3) Addison-Wesley.

Psychology in Perspective: Supershell Mac. 2nd ed. Tavris & Wade. 1997. pap. 50.63 (0-673-97814-1) Addison-Wesley.

Psychology in Practice: Perspectives on Professional Psychology. Ed. by Sandra Canter & David Canter. LC 82-2733. (Illus.). 369p. reprint ed. pap. 114.40 (0-8357-7550-X, 203627300001) Bks Demand.

Psychology in Practice: with Young People, Families, & Schools. Ed. by Allan Sigston et al. LC 96-141650. 256p. 1996. pap. 27.95 (1-85346-390-6, Pub. by David Fulton) Taylor & Francis.

Psychology in Prisons. David J. Cooke et al. LC 92-47425. 1993. pap. write for info. (0-04-159414-2) Routledge.

Psychology in Prisons. David J. Cooke et al. 160p. (C). 1993. pap. 24.99 (0-415-09714-2, B2537) Routledge.

Psychology in Science: Towards a Universal Science of Human Progress. Kevin Shepherd. 205p. (C). 1989. 75.00 (0-9508680-0-0, Pub. by Anthropographia) St Mut.

Psychology in Sport. John M. Kremer & Deirdre M. Scully. LC 93-46607. 1994. write for info. (0-7484-0181-4, Pub. by Tay Francis Ltd); pap. 27.00 (0-7484-0182-2, Pub. by Tay Francis Ltd) Taylor & Francis.

Psychology in Teaching, Learning & Growth. 5th ed. Don E. Hamachek. LC 94-6126. 640p. 1994. pap. text 75.00 (0-205-15269-4) Allyn.

Psychology in the Classroom: Reconstructing Teachers & Learners. Phillida Salmon. (Cassell Education Ser.). 144p. 1995. 100.00 (0-304-33254-2); pap. 29.95 (0-304-33256-9) Continuum.

Psychology in the Common Cause. B. R. Bugelski. LC 88-17838. 228p. 1989. 59.95 (0-275-93034-3, C3034, Praeger Pubs) Greenwood.

Psychology in the Dental Office. Ann Ehrlich. (Illus.). 1983. 7.95 (0-940012-15-4) Colwell Syst.

Psychology in the New Millenium. 6th ed. Spencer A. Rathus. (C). 1995. pap. text, student ed. 27.00 (0-15-503218-6) Harcourt Coll Pubs.

Psychology in the New Millenium. 6th ed. Spencer A. Rathus. (C). 1995. pap. text, teacher ed. 35.00 (0-15-503217-8) Harcourt Coll Pubs.

Psychology in the New Millennium. 7th ed. Spencer A. Rathus. 832p. (C). 1998. text 77.50 (0-15-508215-9, Pub. by Harcourt Coll Pubs) Harcourt.

Psychology in the Nursery School. Nelly Wolffheim. Tr. by Charles L. Hannam. LC 77-162630. 143p. 1972. reprint ed. lib. bdg. 49.50 (0-8371-6197-5, WONS, Greenwood Pr) Greenwood.

Psychology in the U. S. S. R. An Historical Perspective. Ed. by Josef Brozek & Dan I. Slobin. LC 72-112930. 312p. reprint ed. pap. 96.80 (0-608-30672-X, 202185300023) Bks Demand.

Psychology in Utopia: Toward a Social History of Soviet Psychology. Alex Kozulin. 180p. 1984. 30.00 (0-262-11087-3) MIT Pr.

Psychology Is Social. 3rd ed. Edward Krupat. (C). 1994. text 32.81 (0-673-46918-2) Addison-Wesley Educ.

***Psychology is Social: Readings & Conversations in Social Psychology, 4/e.** 4th ed. Edward Krupat. 350p. (C). 1998. pap. text 35.40 (0-321-04035-X, Prentice Hall) P-H.

Psychology Journal. 5th ed. Cole & Semb. 1995. pap. text, student ed. 26.00 (0-13-563578-0) P-H.

Psychology Lab Manual. Plotnik et al. (Adaptable Courseware Ser.). 1996. lab manual ed. 14.00 (0-534-49746-2) Brooks-Cole.

Psychology Law. 2nd ed. Ed. by Horowitz. (C). 1997. pap. text 50.00 (0-673-46689-2) Addison-Wesley.

Psychology, Law & Criminal Justice: International Developments in Research & Practice. Ed. by Graham Davies et al. LC 95-22785. xx, 606p. 1995. lib. bdg. 152.30 (3-11-013858-1) De Gruyter.

Psychology, Law, & Eyewitness Testimony. Peter B. Ainsworth. LC 98-19886. (Psychology of Crime, Policing, & Law Ser.). 208p. 1998. 110.00 (0-471-96931-1) Wiley.

Psychology, Law, & Eyewitness Testimony. Peter B. Ainsworth. LC 98-19886. (Psychology of Crime, Policing, & Law Ser.). 208p. 1999. pap. 35.50 (0-471-98238-5) Wiley.

Psychology, M-Z see Comprehensive Dissertation Index: Five-Year Cumulation, 1983-1987

Psychology Made Easy. Chuck T. Falcon. LC 95-69949. 553p. 2000. pap. 25.00 (0-9628254-1-7) Sensible Psy Pr.

***Psychology Major: Career Options & Strategies for Success.** Stephen Davis. LC 99-35067. 160p. 2000. pap. 11.25 (0-13-083753-9) P-H.

***Psychology Majors.** 2nd ed. Julie DeGalan. (Great Jobs for ... Majors Ser.). 2000. pap. 12.95 (0-658-00452-2, VGM Career) NTC Contemp Pub Co.

Psychology Mastery. 6th ed. Coon. 1993. pap. text, student ed. 20.50 (0-314-00738-5) West Pub.

Psychology, Mental Health & Yoga. A. S. Dalal. LC 90-85067. 166p. (Orig.). 1991. pap. 9.95 (0-941524-64-7) Lotus Pr.

Psychology, Mental Health & Yoga: Essays on Sri Aurobindo's Psycholigical Thought; Implications of Yoga for Mental Health. 2nd ed. A. S. Dalal. 166p. 1996. pap. 9.95 (81-7058-231-8, Pub. by SAA) E-W Cultural Ctr.

Psychology, 1996-1997. annuals 26th ed. Karen Duffy. 288p. (C). 1995. text. write for info. (0-697-31676-9) Brown & Benchmark.

Psychology, 98-99. 28th ed. Karen G. Duffy. (Annual Ser.). (Illus.). 240p. 1998. pap. text 12.25 (0-697-39195-7, Dshkn McG-Hill) McGrw-H Hghr Educ.

Psychology Notebook. Saul M. Kassin. (C). Date not set. pap. write for info. (0-395-60271-8) HM.

Psychology of a Broken Heart: An Essay on Romantic Love. Gary Streit. (Orig.). 1987. pap. 9.95 (0-9618180-0-X) Golden Blossom Pub.

Psychology of a Fairy Tale. David Hart. Ed. by Harriett Crosby. LC 76-56563. (Orig.). 1976. pap. 4.00 (0-87574-210-6) Pendle Hill.

Psychology of a Musical Prodigy. Geza Revesz. LC 70-114890. (Select Bibliographies Reprint Ser.). 1977. 19.95 (0-8369-5294-4) Ayer.

Psychology of a Musical Prodigy. Geza Revesz. LC 78-100832. 180p. 1970. reprint ed. lib. bdg. 49.75 (0-8371-4004-8, REMP, Greenwood Pr) Greenwood.

Psychology of a Musical Prodigy. Geza Revesz. LC 77-173178. (Illus.). 1972. reprint ed. 20.95 (0-405-08879-5) Ayer.

Psychology of a Musical Prodigy. Geza Revesz. 180p. 1990. reprint ed. lib. bdg. 59.00 (0-7812-9002-3) Rprt Serv.

Psychology of a Primitive People: Study of the Australian Aborigine. Stanley D. Porteus. LC 71-37910. (Select Bibliographies Reprint Ser.). 1977. reprint ed. 41.95 (0-8369-6748-8) Ayer.

Psychology of Abnormal Behavior. Harold J. Vetter. LC 70-188883. 624p. reprint ed. pap. 193.50 (0-608-30494-8, 201242200081) Bks Demand.

Psychology of Abnormal Behavior: A Dynamic Approach. Louis P. Thorpe & Barney Katz. LC 61-9428. (Illus.). 689p. reprint ed. pap. 200.00 (0-608-11257-7, 201253100081) Bks Demand.

Psychology of Abnormality. Peterson. (C). 1995. pap. text 44.50 (0-15-503031-0) Harcourt.

Psychology of Abnormality. Peterson. (C). 1995. pap. text, teacher ed. 35.00 (0-15-503029-9); pap. text, student ed. 25.00 (0-15-503030-2, Pub. by Harcourt Coll Pubs) Harcourt.

Psychology of Abnormality. Christopher Peterson. (C). 1995. 3.5 hd 279.50 (0-15-503032-9); 5.25 hd 279.50 (0-15-503033-7) Harcourt Coll Pubs.

Psychology of Abnormality. Christopher Peterson. 656p. (C). 1995. text 82.00 (0-15-500092-6, Pub. by Harcourt Coll Pubs) Harcourt.

Psychology of Abnormality. Christopher Peterson. (C). 1996. mac hd 279.50 (0-15-503034-5) Harcourt Coll Pubs.

***Psychology of Action.** John L. Smith. LC 99-49206. 2000. text 59.95 (0-312-23066-4) St Martin.

Psychology of Action: Linking Cognition & Motivation to Behavior. Ed. by Peter M. Gollwitzer & John A. Bargh. LC 95-39728. 683p. 1995. lib. bdg. 70.00 (1-57230-032-9, 0032) Guilford Pubns.

Psychology of Adaptation to Absurdity: Tactics of Make-Believe. Seymour Fisher & Rhoda L. Fisher. 248p. 1993. text 59.95 (0-8058-1205-9) L Erlbaum Assocs.

Psychology of Addiction. Mary McMurran. LC 94-16356. (Contemporary Psychology Ser.). 1994. write for info. (0-7484-0187-3, Pub. by Tay Francis Ltd); pap. write for info. (0-7484-0188-1, Pub. by Tay Francis Ltd) Taylor & Francis.

Psychology of Adjustment. Thomas L. Creer. 374p. (C). 1996. pap. text 63.00 (0-13-254863-1) P-H.

Psychology of Adjustment. Jack Rudman. (Dantes Subject Standardized Tests Ser.: DANTES-34). 1994. pap. 23.95 (0-8373-6634-8) Nat Learn.

Psychology of Adjustment. Jack Rudman. (DANTES Ser.: No. 34). 1994. 39.95 (0-8373-6534-1) Nat Learn.

P

An Asterisk (*) at the beginning of an entry indicates that the title is appearing for the first time.

Psychology of Adjustment: Personal Experience & Development. Richard W. Coan. LC 82-13413. (Illus.). 568p. reprint ed. pap. 176.10 (*0-7837-3498-0*, 205783100008) Bks Demand.

Psychology of Adjustment & Human Relations. 3rd ed. James F. Calhoun & Joan R. Acocella. 512p. (C). 1990. 62.81 (*0-07-557738-0*) McGraw.

Psychology of Adjustment & Human Relations. 3rd ed. James F. Calhoun & Joan R. Acocella. (C). 1990. text, student ed. 22.74 (*0-07-009761-5*) McGraw.

Psychology of Adjustment & Well-Being. Stanley L. Brodsky. 480p. (C). 1988. pap. text 67.00 (*0-03-013368-8*) Harcourt Coll Pubs.

Psychology of Adolescence. 2nd ed. Marvin Powell. 678p. 1971. text 13.15 (*0-672-60782-4*, Bobbs) Macmillan.

Psychology of Adolescence: Essential Readings. Ed. by Aaron H. Esman. LC 74-21177. 425p. (Orig.). 1975. 85.00 (*0-8236-5565-2*) Intl Univs Pr.

Psychology of Adolescent Satanism: A Guide for Parents, Counselors, Clergy, & Teachers. Anthony Moriarty. LC 92-12731. 168p. 1992. 39.95 (*0-275-94307-0*, C4307, Praeger Pubs) Greenwood.

Psychology of Adoption. David M. Brodzinsky. (Illus.). 416p. 1993. pap. text 39.95 (*0-19-508273-7*) OUP.

Psychology of Adversity. Ed. by Robert S. Feldman. LC 95-46886. (Illus.). 304p. 1996. text 40.00 (*1-55849-036-1*) U of Mass Pr.

Psychology of Advertising. Walter D. Scott. 294p. 90.00 (*1-85506-694-7*) Thoemmes Pr.

Psychology of Advertising. Walter D. Scott. Ed. by Henry Assael. LC 78-305. (Century of Marketing Ser.). 1979. reprint ed. lib. bdg. 25.95 (*0-405-11171-1*) Ayer.

Psychology of African Americans. (C). 1999. pap. text 49.00 (*0-205-28192-3*, Macmillan Coll) P-H.

Psychology of Aging. Erber. (Psychology Ser.). 2002. pap. text 44.00 (*0-534-35636-2*) Brooks-Cole.

Psychology of Aging. 3rd ed. Belsky. LC 98-17981. (Psychology Ser.). 1998. pap. 75.95 (*0-534-35912-4*) Brooks-Cole.

Psychology of Aging: An Annotated Bibliography, 28. Ed. by Bert Hayslip et al. LC 95-6291. (Bibliographies & Indexes in Gerontology Ser.: No. 28). 152p. 1995. lib. bdg. 59.95 (*0-313-29376-7*, Greenwood Pr) Greenwood.

Psychology of Aging: An Introduction. 2nd ed. Ian Stuart-Hamilton. LC 93-39928. 1994. 27.00 (*1-85302-233-0*) Taylor & Francis.

***Psychology of Aging: The Essential Readings.** Ed. by William Gekowski. (Essential Readings in Developmental Psychology Ser.). 256p. 1999. 59.95 (*0-631-21750-9*); pap. 24.95 (*0-631-21751-7*) Blackwell Pubs.

Psychology of Aging: Theory, Research & Intervention. 2nd ed. Janet K. Belsky. (Psychology Ser.). 460p. (C). 1989. pap. 49.75 (*0-534-12114-4*) Brooks-Cole.

Psychology of Aging: Theory, Research & Practice. Janet K. Belsky. LC 83-20923. (Psychology Ser.). 550p. (C). 1984. mass mkt. 32.25 (*0-534-02868-3*) Brooks-Cole.

Psychology of Aid: Cassandra's Perspective. Stuart C. Carr et al. LC 97-35288. 256p. (C). 1998. 75.00 (*0-415-14207-5*) Routledge.

***Psychology of Alcohol & Other Drugs: A Research Perspective.** John Jung. LC 00-8773. 2000. pap. write for info. (*0-7619-2100-1*) Sage.

Psychology of Alcoholism. George B. Cutten. Ed. by Gerald N. Grob. LC 80-1223. (Addiction in America Ser.). 1981. reprint ed. lib. bdg. 35.95 (*0-405-13579-3*) Ayer.

Psychology of Animal Learning. N. J. Mackintosh. 1974. text 125.00 (*0-12-464650-6*) Acad Pr.

Psychology of Anomalous Experience. rev. ed. Graham Reed. LC 88-61531. 209p. 1988. pap. 24.95 (*0-87975-435-4*) Prometheus Bks.

Psychology of Anxiety. 2nd ed. Eugene E. Levitt. LC 80-107. 188p. 1980. text 29.95 (*0-89859-040-X*) L Erlbaum Assocs.

Psychology of Anxiety, Worry & Troublesome Problems: Index of New Information with Authors & Subjects. rev. ed. Frances B. Lopez. LC 94-24769. 157p. 1994. 47.50 (*0-7883-0370-8*); pap. 44.50 (*0-7883-0371-6*) ABBE Pubs Assn.

Psychology of Apashia. Dennis Tanner. 172p. 1996. pap. text 27.95 (*0-7872-1923-1*) Kendall-Hunt.

Psychology of Art Appreciation. Bjarne S. Funch. LC 98-186647. (Illus.). 312p. 1998. 97.50 (*87-7289-402-4*, Pub. by Almqvist Wiksell) Coronet Bks.

Psychology of Associative Learning. David R. Shanks. (Problems in the Behavioral Sciences Ser.: No. 13). (Illus.). 206p. (C). 1995. text 69.95 (*0-521-44515-9*); pap. text 27.95 (*0-521-44976-6*) Cambridge U Pr.

Psychology of Asthma Management. Hyland. (C). 1998. pap. text 19.95 (*0-443-05682-X*) Church.

Psychology of Astrocartography. Jim Lewis & Kenneth Irving. LC 97-223553. (Illus.). 341p. 1997. pap. 13.95 (*0-14-019512-2*) Viking Penguin.

Psychology of Attachment & Bonding: Index of Modern Information. Lottie F. Lydeen. LC 88-47600. 150p. 1988. 47.50 (*0-88164-790-X*); pap. 44.50 (*0-88164-791-8*) ABBE Pubs Assn.

Psychology of Attempted Suicide: A Medical Subject Analysis with Reference Bibliography. rev. ed. Harold P. Drummond. 163p. (Orig.). 1992. 47.50 (*1-55914-952-3*); pap. 44.50 (*1-55914-953-1*) ABBE Pubs Assn.

Psychology of Attention. Harold E. Pashler. LC 96-29300. 510p. 1997. 49.50 (*0-262-16165-6*, Bradford Bks) MIT Pr.

Psychology of Attention. Elizabeth A. Styles. 304p. 1997. pap. text 26.95 (*0-86377-465-2*) L Erlbaum Assocs.

Psychology of Attention. Harold E. Pashler. (Illus.). 512p. 1999. reprint ed. pap. 24.50 (*0-262-66156-X*, Bradford Bks) MIT Pr.

Psychology of Attention, 2 vols., 1. Ed. by Geoffrey Underwood. LC 93-28669. (International Library of Critical Writings in Business History). (C). 1994. lib. bdg. 150.00 (*0-8147-8558-1*) NYU Pr.

Psychology of Attention, 2 vols., 2. Ed. by Geoffrey Underwood. LC 93-28669. (International Library of Critical Writings in Business History). (C). 1994. lib. bdg. 150.00 (*0-8147-8559-X*) NYU Pr.

Psychology of Attention, 2 vols., Set. Ed. by Geoffrey Underwood. LC 93-28669. (International Library of Critical Writings in Business History). (C). 1994. lib. bdg. 295.00 (*0-8147-8560-3*) NYU Pr.

Psychology of Attentional Behaviour. Elizabeth C. Styles. 304p. 1997. 64.95 (*0-86377-464-4*) L Erlbaum Assocs.

Psychology of Attitude Change & Social Influence. 3rd ed. Philip G. Zimbardo & Michael R. Leippe. 288p. (C). 1991. pap. 33.13 (*0-07-072877-1*) McGraw.

Psychology of Attitudes. Alice Eagly & Shelly Chaiken. Ed. by Dawn Youngblood. (Illus.). 800p. (C). 1993. text 84.00 (*0-15-500097-7*) Harcourt Coll Pubs.

***Psychology of Awakening: Buddhism, Science & Our Day-to-Day Lives.** Ed. by Gay Watson et al. LC 99-59447. 368p. 2000. pap. 16.95 (*1-57863-172-6*) Weiser.

Psychology of Back Pain: A Clinical & Legal Handbook. Albert M. Drukteinis. (American Behavioral Science & Law Ser.). (Illus.). 208p. (C). 1996. text 41.95 (*0-398-06559-4*); pap. text 26.95 (*0-398-06560-8*) C C Thomas.

Psychology of Behaviour at Work: The Individual in the Organization. Adrian Furnham. LC 96-52978. 722p. 1997. 80.00 (*0-86377-493-8*, HF6648, Pub. by Psychol Pr) Taylor & Francis.

Psychology of Behaviour at Work: The Individual in the Organization. Adrian Furnham. 500p. 1997. 95.00 (*1-85728-668-5*, Pub. by UCL Pr Ltd); pap. 34.95 (*1-85728-278-7*, Pub. by UCL Pr Ltd) Taylor & Francis.

***Psychology of Being: Your No-Fail Guide to Lasting Self-Esteem.** Greg Korzenowski. LC 99-66514. xii, 132p. 1999. pap. write for info. (*1-930017-00-6*) Adv Therapeutics.

Psychology of Birth. Leslie Feher. 224p. 1985. reprint ed. pap. text 27.00 (*0-9612182-1-5*) Assn Birth Psych.

Psychology of Blacks. Joseph L. White & Thomas A. Parham. 1990. pap. text 29.00 (*0-13-733791-4*) P-H.

Psychology of Blacks: An African-Centered Perspective. 3rd ed. W. White. LC 99-24474. (Illus.). 194p. 1999. pap. text 25.20 (*0-13-095946-4*) P-H.

Psychology of Body, Soul & Spirit. Rudolf Steiner. Tr. by Marjorie Spock et al from GER. LC 99-11939. 320p. 1999. pap. 24.95 (*0-88010-397-3*) Anthroposophic.

Psychology of C. G. Jung. Jolande Jacobi. Tr. by Ralph Manheim. (Illus.). (C). 1973. pap. 14.00 (*0-300-01674-3*, Y75) Yale U Pr.

Psychology of C. G. Jung. Carl A. Meier. Tr. by Eugene Rolfe. LC 85-13996. (Unconscious in Its Empirical Manifestations Ser.: Vol. I). (Illus.). 236p. (C). 1985. 35.00 (*0-938434-10-1*); pap. 16.95 (*0-938434-68-3*) Sigo Pr.

Psychology of C. G. Jung: The Meaning & Significance of Dreams, Vol. II. Carl A. Meier. 163p. 1987. 40.00 (*0-938434-11-X*); pap. 16.95 (*0-938434-69-1*) Sigo Pr.

Psychology of C. G. Jung, Vol. III: Consciousness, Vol. III. Carl A. Meier. Tr. by David Roscoe from GER. (Illus.). 128p. (C). 1989. 40.00 (*0-938434-12-8*); pap. 16.95 (*0-938434-70-5*) Sigo Pr.

Psychology of Call Reluctance see Psychology of Sales Call Reluctance: Earning What You're Worth in Sales

Psychology of Call-Reluctance: How to Overcome the Fear of Self-Promotion. George W. Dudley & Shannon L. Goodson. LC 85-73334. 208p. (Orig.). 1986. reprint ed. 26.95 (*0-935907-00-9*); reprint ed. pap. 18.95 (*0-935907-01-7*) Behavioral Sci.

Psychology of Carl Jung: Essays in Application & Deconstruction. David Holt. LC 92-5417. 536p. 1992. lib. bdg. 119.95 (*0-7734-9481-2*) E Mellen.

Psychology of Character: With a Survey of Temperament. Abraham A. Roback. LC 73-2988. (Classics in Psychology Ser.). 1974. reprint ed. 37.95 (*0-405-05160-3*) Ayer.

Psychology of Chess Skill. Dennis H. Holding. 288p. (C). 1985. text 55.00 (*0-89859-575-4*) L Erlbaum Assocs.

Psychology of Childbirth. Aidan MacFarlane. (Developing Child Ser.). (Illus.). 160p. 1977. pap. text 8.95 (*0-674-72106-3*) HUP.

Psychology of Childhood. Peter Mitchell. (Contemporary Psychology Ser.). 224p. 1992. 79.95 (*1-85000-954-6*, Falmer Pr); pap. 34.95 (*1-85000-950-3*, Falmer Pr) Taylor & Francis.

Psychology of Childhood Illness. Christine Eiser. (Contributions to Psychology & Medicine Ser.). (Illus.). 210p. 1985. 79.95 (*0-387-96096-1*) Spr-Verlag.

Psychology of Choice & the Assumptions of Economics. Richard H. Thaler. (Working Papers on Risk & Rationality). 1988. 2.50 (*0-318-33320-1*, RR3) IPPP.

Psychology of Chronic Illness: The Healing Work of Patients, Therapists, & Families. Robert Shuman. LC 96-10957. 288p. 1996. 35.00 (*0-465-09534-8*, Pub. by Basic) HarpC.

Psychology of Clothes. John C. Flugel. LC 75-41097. reprint ed. 37.50 (*0-404-14721-6*) AMS Pr.

Psychology of Clothing. George Van Ness Dearborn. (Psychological Monographs General & Applied: Vol. 26). 1974. reprint ed. pap. 55.00 (*0-8115-1425-0*) Periodicals Srv.

Psychology of Cognition. 2nd ed. Gillian Cohen. 1983. pap. text 44.95 (*0-12-178762-1*) Acad Pr.

Psychology of Communication. 284p. (C). 1996. text 33.80 (*0-536-59871-1*) Pearson Custom.

Psychology of Computer Programming, Silver Anniversary Edition: Looking Forward after 25 Years. 2nd rev. ed. Gerald M. Weinberg. LC 98-38794. (Illus.). 360p. 1998. pap. 44.95 (*0-932633-42-0*) Dorset Hse Pub Co.

Psychology of Computer Use. Ed. by Thomas Green et al. (Computers & People Ser.). 1983. text 67.00 (*0-12-297420-4*) Acad Pr.

Psychology of Concentration in Sport Performers: A Cognitive Analysis. Ed. by Aidan P. Moran. 328p. 1996. 49.95 (*0-86377-443-1*) L Erlbaum Assocs.

Psychology of Confession & the Orthodox Church. Nicholas V. Gamvas. 1989. pap. 11.95 (*0-937032-65-4*) Light&Life Pub Co MN.

Psychology of Conflict & Combat. Ben Shalit. LC 87-23729. 215p. 1988. 57.95 (*0-275-92753-9*, C2753, Praeger Pubs) Greenwood.

Psychology of Consciousness. G. William Farthing, Jr. 480p. (C). 1991. text 47.20 (*0-13-728668-6*) P-H.

Psychology of Consciousness: An Intelligent Guide to Psychic Liberation. Charles Spaegel & Ruth E. Norman. (Illus.). 375p. (Orig.). (C). 1985. student ed., spiral bd. 90.00 (*0-932642-97-7*) Unarius Acad Sci.

Psychology of Consumer Behavior. Brian Mullen & Craig Johnson. 232p. 1990. 36.00 (*0-89859-857-5*) L Erlbaum Assocs.

Psychology of Consumer Behavior. Brian Mullen & Craig Johnson. 36p. 1990. teacher ed. write for info. (*0-8058-1165-6*) L Erlbaum Assocs.

Psychology of Control. Ellen J. Langer. LC 83-11224. (Illus.). 311p. reprint ed. pap. 96.50 (*0-8357-4816-2*, 203775300009) Bks Demand.

Psychology of Control & Aging. Ed. by Margret M. Baltes & Paul B. Baltes. LC 85-25363. 449p. reprint ed. pap. 139.20 (*0-7837-5184-2*, 204491700004) Bks Demand.

Psychology of Cooperation & Group Consciousness. Torkom Saraydarian. LC 89-192444. 165p. (YA). 1989. pap. 12.00 (*0-929874-11-0*) TSG Pub Found.

Psychology of Cosmetic Treatments. Jean A. Graham & Albert M. Klingman. LC 84-26651. 272p. 1985. 75.00 (*0-275-91315-5*, C1315, Praeger Pubs) Greenwood.

Psychology of Counseling. Clyde M. Narramore. 303p. 1960. 16.99 (*0-310-29930-6*, 10409) Zondervan.

***Psychology of Couples & Illness: Theory, Research & Practice.** Ed. by Karen B. Schmaling & Tamara Goldman Sher. LC 99-59782. 2000. 49.95 (*1-55798-649-5*) Am Psychol.

Psychology of Crime. David Abrahamsen. LC 59-13606. 372p. reprint ed. pap. 115.40 (*0-608-12521-0*, 202497600040) Bks Demand.

Psychology of Crime: A Social Science Textbook. Philip Feldman. (Illus.). 542p. (C). 1993. text 74.95 (*0-521-33120-X*); pap. text 22.95 (*0-521-33732-1*) Cambridge U Pr.

Psychology of Criminal Conduct. 2nd ed. D. A. Andrews & James Bonta. LC 98-6867. 423p. (C). 1998. pap. 39.95 (*0-87084-712-0*) Anderson Pub Co.

Psychology of Criminal Conduct: Theory, Research & Practice. Blackburn. 506p. 1998. pap. 79.95 (*0-471-96175-2*) Wiley.

Psychology of Culture: A Course of Lectures. Edward Sapir. Ed. by Judith T. Irvine. LC 93-38287. (Illus.). x, 266p. (C). 1993. pap. text 24.95 (*3-11-012920-5*) Mouton.

Psychology of Dance. Jim Taylor & Ceci Taylor. LC 94-40398. (Illus.). 168p. (Orig.). 1995. pap. text 22.95 (*0-87322-486-8*, BTAY0486) Human Kinetics.

Psychology of Deafness: Understanding Deaf & Hard-of-Hearing People. McCay Vernon & Jean F. Andrews. 304p. (C). 1990. text 52.33 (*0-8013-0322-2*, 78090) Longman.

Psychology of Deafness: Understanding Deaf & Hard-of-Hearing People. McCay Vernon & Jean F. Andrews. LC 89-2255. (Illus.). 311p. 1990. reprint ed. pap. 96.50 (*0-608-07818-2*, AU0049500010) Bks Demand.

Psychology of Death. 2nd rev. ed. Robert J. Kastenbaum. LC 91-33877. 280p. (C). 1992. text 36.95 (*0-8261-1922-0*) Springer Pub.

***Psychology of Death.** 3rd ed. Robert Kastenbaum. LC 99-43555. (Illus.). 288p. 1999. text 36.95 (*0-8261-1300-1*) Springer Pub.

Psychology of Decision Making: People in Organizations. Lee R. Beach. LC 96-51267. (Foundations for Organizational Science Ser.: Vol. 6). 240p. (C). 1997. 30.00 (*0-7619-0079-9*, 00799); pap. 13.99 (*0-7619-0080-2*, 00802) Sage.

Psychology of Dementia. Edgar Miller & Robin Morris. (Clinical Psychology Ser.). 216p. 1994. 165.00 (*0-471-92776-7*) Wiley.

Psychology of Dental Care. 2nd rev. ed. G. Kent & Anthony S. Blinkhorn. (Dental Handbook Ser.). (Illus.). 176p. 1991. pap. text 45.00 (*0-7236-2339-2*) Buttrwrth-Heinemann.

Psychology of Dictatorship: Based on an Examination of the Leaders of Nazi Germany. Gustave M. Gilbert. LC 79-15335. (Illus.). 327p. 1979. reprint ed. lib. bdg. 65.00 (*0-313-21975-3*, GIPD, Greenwood Pr) Greenwood.

Psychology of Difference: The American Lectures. Otto Rank. Ed. & Intro. by Robert Kramer. 416p. 1996. text 39.50 (*0-691-04470-8*, Pub. by Princeton U Pr) Cal Prin Full Svc.

Psychology of Disability. Toot. 1994. write for info. (*0-8151-8824-2*) Mosby Inc.

Psychology of Disability. Carolyn L. Vash. (Series on Rehabilitation: Vol. 1). 288p. (C). 1981. 39.95 (*0-8261-3340-1*) Springer Pub.

Psychology of Discipleship. Douglas M. Baker. (C). 1976. 26.50 (*0-906006-05-8*, Pub. by Baker Pubns) New Leaf Dist.

Psychology of Discipline: Six Approaches to Discipline. Darwin Dorr et al. LC 81-20775. xi, 253p. 1981. 40.00 (*0-8236-5581-4*) Intl Univs Pr.

***Psychology of Diversity: Perceiving & Experiencing Social America.** Bruce E. Blaine. LC 99-44172. 1999. pap. text 29.95 (*1-55934-938-7*) Mayfield Pub.

Psychology of Dreams. Paul R. Robbins. LC 87-29889. (Illus.). 184p. 1988. lib. bdg. 29.95 (*0-89950-270-9*) McFarland & Co.

Psychology of Dress: An Analysis of Fashion & Its Motive. Elizabeth B. Hurlock. LC 72-176089. (Illus.). 224p. 1972. reprint ed. 23.95 (*0-405-08644-X*, Pub. by Blom Pubns) Ayer.

Psychology of Early Childhood up to the Sixth Year of Age. William L. Stern. LC 74-21428. (Classics in Child Development Ser.). (Illus.). 566p. 1979. reprint ed. 56.95 (*0-405-06477-2*) Ayer.

Psychology of Eating & Drinking. 2nd ed. Alexandra W. Logue. (Illus.). 352p. (C). 1991. pap. 22.95 (*0-7167-2197-X*) W H Freeman.

Psychology of Economics. Walter A. Weisskopf. LC 55-9826. 272p. reprint ed. pap. 84.40 (*0-608-15113-0*, 202579400046) Bks Demand.

***Psychology of Education.** Martyn Long. LC 00-42466. 2000. write for info. (*0-415-23906-0*) Routledge.

***Psychology of Education: Major Themes, 4 vols.** Peter K. Smith & Anthony D. Pellegrini. LC 00-34476. (C). 2000. write for info. (*0-415-19306-0*) Routledge.

Psychology of Educational Technology & Instructional Media. K. Spencer. 1993. 85.00 (*1-873534-00-0*, Pub. by Manutius Pr) St Mut.

Psychology of Educational Technology & Instructional Media. Ken Spencer. 208p. (C). 1988. lib. bdg. 45.00 (*0-415-00567-1*) Routledge.

Psychology of Educational Technology & Instructional Media. Ken Spencer. LC 89-112272. (Illus.). 208p. reprint ed. pap. 64.50 (*0-608-20385-8*, 207163800002) Bks Demand.

Psychology of Embarrassment. Robert J. Edelmann. LC 86-28208. 234p. reprint ed. pap. 72.60 (*0-608-05300-7*, 206583800001) Bks Demand.

Psychology of Emotion. John G. Carlson & Elaine Hatfield. (Illus.). 519p. (C). 1992. text 74.00 (*0-03-055419-5*, Pub. by Harcourt Coll Pubs) Harcourt.

Psychology of Emotion: Theories of Emotion in Perspective. 4th ed. K. T. Strongman. LC 96-20324. 266p. 1996. pap. 69.95 (*0-471-96619-3*) Wiley.

Psychology of Emotions. C. E. Izard. (Emotions, Personality, & Psychotherapy Ser.). (Illus.). 472p. (C). 1991. 42.50 (*0-306-43865-8*, Plenum Trade) Perseus Pubng.

Psychology of Everyday Things. Donald A. Norman. LC 87-47782. (Illus.). 288p. 1930. 26.00 (*0-465-06709-3*, Pub. by Basic) HarpC.

Psychology of Evidence & Trial Procedure. Ed. by Saul M. Kassin & Lawrence S. Wrightsman. LC 85-1688. 384p. 1985. reprint ed. pap. 119.10 (*0-608-01462-1*, 205950600001) Bks Demand.

Psychology of Exceptional Children. Karl C. Garrison & Dewey G. Force. LC 65-21809. 577p. reprint ed. pap. 178.90 (*0-608-18550-7*, 205514400008) Bks Demand.

Psychology of Existence: An Integrative, Clinical Perspective. Kirk J. Schneider & Rollo May. LC 94-19497. 416p. (C). 1994. 53.44 (*0-07-041017-8*) McGraw.

Psychology of Expertise: Cognitive Research & Empirical AI. Ed. by Robert R. Hoffman. 408p. 1994. text 79.95 (*0-8058-1900-2*) L Erlbaum Assocs.

Psychology of Facial Expression. Ed. by James A. Russell & Jose-Miguel Fernandez-Dols. LC 96-36250. (Studies in Emotion & Social Interaction). (Illus.). 413p. (C). 1997. text 74.95 (*0-521-49667-5*); pap. text 29.95 (*0-521-58796-4*) Cambridge U Pr.

***Psychology of Female Violence: Crimes Against the Body.** Annabelle B. Motz. LC 00-42499. 2000. pap. write for info. (*0-415-12675-4*) Routledge.

Psychology of Finance. Lars Tvede. (Illus.). 300p. 1991. pap. 18.00 (*82-00-02772-4*) Scandnvan Univ Pr.

Psychology of Finance. Lars Tvede. LC 99-25242. 304p. 1999. 79.95 (*0-471-99677-7*) Wiley.

Psychology of Flight Training. Ross Telfer & John Biggs. LC 87-29952. (Illus.). 178p. (Orig.). 1988. 29.95 (*0-8138-1347-6*) Iowa St U Pr.

Psychology of Free Associations: Index of New Information with Authors, Subjects & References. Neil R. Ogden. 150p. 1996. 47.50 (*0-7883-1282-0*); pap. 44.50 (*0-7883-1283-9*) ABBE Pubs Assn.

Psychology of Freedom. Thomas Pink. 294p. (C). 1996. text 52.95 (*0-521-55504-3*) Cambridge U Pr.

Psychology of Freedom & Dignity: The Last Train to Survival. E. Rae Harcum. LC 93-11864. 208p. 1994. 57.95 (*0-275-94744-0*, Praeger Pubs) Greenwood.

Psychology of Funeral Service. 6th ed. Edward A. Martin. text 12.50 (*0-686-20530-8*) E A Martin.

Psychology of Gambling. Edmund Bergler. LC 84-22381. 254p. 1985. 37.50 (*0-8236-5570-9*) Intl Univs Pr.

Psychology of Gambling. Michael Walker, Jr. 272p. 1995. pap. 31.95 (*0-7506-2743-3*) Buttrwrth-Heinemann.

Psychology of Gender. (C). 2000. text 47.00 (*0-205-29770-6*, Longwood Div) Allyn.

***Psychology Of Gender.** (C). 2000. text. write for info. (*0-321-04995-0*) Addison-Wesley.

Psychology of Gender. Ed. by Anne E. Beall & Robert J. Sternberg. LC 93-11508. 278p. 1993. lib. bdg. 42.00 (*0-89862-286-7*) Guilford Pubns.

Psychology of Gender. Ed. by Anne E. Beall & Robert J. Sternberg. 278p. 1995. pap. text 21.00 (*0-89862-283-2*) Guilford Pubns.

Psychology of Gender. Smith. (C). 2000. text 39.00 (*0-15-501995-3*) Harcourt Coll Pubs.

Psychology of Gender: Advances Through the Meta-Analysis. Ed. by Janet S. Hyde & Marcia C. Linn. LC 85-19822. 304p. 1986. text 49.95 (*0-8018-2974-7*) Johns Hopkins.

***Psychology of Gender & Sexuality: An Introduction.** Wendy Stainton Rogers & Rex Stainton Rogers. LC 00-35614. 2000. write for info. (*0-335-20224-1*, Pub. by OpUniv Pr) Taylor & Francis.

Psychology of Gesture. 2nd ed. Charlotte Wolff. Tr. by Anne Tennant from FRE. LC 72-348. (Body Movement Perspectives in Research Ser.). 268p. 1973. reprint ed. 25.95 (*0-405-03147-5*) Ayer.

Psychology of Gifted Children: Perspectives on Development & Education. fac. ed. Ed. by Joan Freeman. LC 84-17340. (Wiley Series in Development Psychology). 426p. pap. 132.10 (*0-7837-7384-6*, 204718900005) Bks Demand.

Psychology of Group Influence. 2nd ed. Ed. by Paul B. Paulus. LC 88-36616. (Illus.). 460p. 1989. pap. 142.60 (*0-608-05186-1*, 206572300001) Bks Demand.

Psychology of Group Influence. 2nd ed. Paul B. Paulus. 456p. (C). 1989. pap. 36.00 (*0-8058-0545-1*); text 79.95 (*0-8058-0445-5*) L Erlbaum Assocs.

Psychology of Growing Old: Looking Forward. Robert Slater. LC 95-5368. (Rethinking Aging Ser.). 160p. 1995. 98.95 (*0-335-19319-6*); pap. text 32.95 (*0-335-19318-8*) OpUniv Pr.

Psychology of Habit According to William Ockham. Oswald Fuchs. (Philosophy Ser.). xix, 110p. 1952. pap. 8.00 (*1-57659-097-6*) Franciscan Inst.

Psychology of Handwriting. Nadya Olyanova. (Illus.). 395p. 1978. pap. 10.00 (*0-87980-128-X*) Wilshire.

Psychology of Handwriting. Robert Saudek. (Illus.). 1978. 40.00 (*0-935422-01-3*) Bks for Profs.

Psychology of Happiness. Michael Argyle. pap. 14.95 (*0-317-65255-9*) Routledge.

Psychology of Health. Salovey. (C). Date not set. text. write for info. (*0-395-79686-5*) HM.

Psychology of Health: An Introduction. 2nd ed. Marian Pitts & Keith Phillips. LC 97-40283. (Illus.). 432p. (C). 1998. 85.00 (*0-415-15023-X*); pap. 27.99 (*0-415-15024-8*) Routledge.

Psychology of Health: Application of Psychology for Health Professionals. Beth Alder. 208p. 1995. text 48.00 (*3-7186-5761-9*, Harwood Acad Pubs); pap. text 20.00 (*3-7186-5762-7*, Harwood Acad Pubs) Gordon & Breach.

***Psychology of Health: Applications of Psychology for Health Professionals.** 2nd ed. Beth Alder. 324p. 1999. text 42.00 (*90-5702-493-4*, Harwood Acad Pubs); pap. text 24.00 (*90-5702-494-2*, Harwood Acad Pubs) Gordon & Breach.

Psychology of Helping & Altruism: Problems & Puzzles. David A. Schroeder. LC 94-23437. 320p. (C). 1994. 34.69 (*0-07-055611-3*) McGraw.

Psychology of High Abilities. Michael J. A. Howe. LC 99-24049. 1999. text 37.50 (*0-8147-3612-2*) NYU Pr.

Psychology of Hope. Ezra Stotland. LC 76-75934. (Jossey-Bass Behavioral Science Ser.). 300p. reprint ed. pap. 93.00 (*0-608-30794-7*, 201377700087) Bks Demand.

Psychology of Hope: An Antidote to the Suicidal Pathology of Western Civilization. Kalman J. Kaplan & Matthew B. Schwartz. LC 92-36551. 208p. 1993. 62.95 (*0-275-94379-8*, C4379, Praeger Pubs) Greenwood.

Psychology of Hope: You Can Get There from Here. C. R. Snyder. 1994. 22.95 (*0-02-929715-X*) Free Pr.

Psychology of Human Behavior. Grams & Jamieson. (Psychology Ser.). 1994. student ed. 10.25 (*0-314-04685-2*) Brooks-Cole.

Psychology of Human Behavior. 2nd ed. Grams & Jamieson. (Adaptable Courseware Ser.). 1996. student ed. 11.25 (*0-314-20494-6*) Brooks-Cole.

Psychology of Human Behavior. 4th ed. Kalish. (Psychology Ser.). 1977. text, teacher ed. write for info. (*0-534-02105-0*); mass mkt. 20.75 (*0-8185-0206-1*); mass mkt., student ed. 8.00 (*0-8185-0221-5*) Brooks-Cole.

Psychology of Human Behavior. 5th ed. Richard A. Kalish. LC 82-12851. (Psychology Ser.). 144p. (C). 1983. pap., student ed. 17.95 (*0-534-01220-5*); text 47.95 (*0-534-01219-1*) Brooks-Cole.

Psychology of Human Behavior: Study Guide. 2nd ed. Grams & Jamieson. (Psychology). 1995. student ed. 11.25 (*0-314-07107-5*) Brooks-Cole.

Psychology of Human Communication. 2nd rev. ed. Blaine Goss. (Illus.). 186p. (C). 1995. pap. text 13.95 (*0-88133-827-3*) Waveland Pr.

Psychology of Human-Computer Interaction. Stuart K. Card et al. 488p. (C). 1983. pap. 55.00 (*0-89859-859-1*) L Erlbaum Assocs.

Psychology of Human Control: A General Theory of Purposeful Behavior. Myles I. Friedman & George H. Lackey, Jr. LC 90-43301. 264p. 1991. 59.95 (*0-275-93811-5*, C3811, Praeger Pubs) Greenwood.

Psychology of Human Development. 3rd ed. Franklin Ross Jones et al. 592p. (C). 1992. pap. text 39.95 (*0-8403-7405-4*) Kendall-Hunt.

Psychology of Human Freedom. M. R. Westcott. (Illus.). 225p. 1988. pap. 47.00 (*0-387-96809-1*) Spr-Verlag.

Psychology of Human Movement. Ed. by Mary Smyth & Alan M. Wing. (C). 1984. text 145.00 (*0-12-653020-3*); pap. text 59.95 (*0-12-653022-X*) Acad Pr.

Psychology of Human Possibility & Constraint. Jack Martin & Jeff Sugarman. LC 98-21999. (SUNY Series, Alternatives in Psychology). 192p. (C). 1999. text 59.50 (*0-7914-4123-7*); pap. text 19.95 (*0-7914-4124-5*) State U NY Pr.

Psychology of Humor: Theoretical Perspectives & Empirical Issues. Ed. by Jeffrey H. Goldstein & Paul E. McGhee. 1972. text 65.00 (*0-12-288950-9*) Acad Pr.

Psychology of Hypertension: Medical Analysis Index with Research Bibliography. rev. ed. Rosetta R. Hardine. LC 85-47583. 145p. 1994. 47.50 (*0-7883-0676-6*); pap. 44.50 (*0-7883-0677-4*) ABBE Pubs Assn.

Psychology of Illness: In Sickness & in Health. Richard G. Druss. LC 94-23688. 144p. 1995. text 23.50 (*0-88048-661-9*, 8661) Am Psychiatric.

Psychology of Illustration. Ed. by H. A. Houghton & D. M. Willows. (Instructional Issues Ser.: Vol. 2). (Illus.). 210p. 1987. 128.00 (*0-387-96453-3*) Spr-Verlag.

Psychology of Illustration Vol. 1: Basic Research. Ed. by D. M. Willows & H. A. Houghton. (Illus.). 225p. 1987. 104.00 (*0-387-96424-X*) Spr-Verlag.

Psychology of Imagination. Jean-Paul Sartre. 1980. pap. 8.95 (*0-8065-0305-X*, Citadel Pr) Carol Pub Group.

Psychology of Imagination. Jean-Paul Sartre. LC 78-6632. 282p. 1978. lib. bdg. 35.00 (*0-313-20498-5*, SAPI, Greenwood Pr) Greenwood.

Psychology of Indians of North America: Index of New Information with Authors, Subjects & Bibliographical References. Swedlo A. Sampos. 150p. 1996. 47.50 (*0-7883-0788-6*); pap. 44.50 (*0-7883-0789-4*) ABBE Pubs Assn.

Psychology of Individual Differences. 226p. (C). 1997. pap. 36.72 (*0-536-00427-7*) Pearson Custom.

Psychology of Individual Differences. 2nd ed. 336p. (C). 1999. pap. text 32.20 (*0-536-02423-5*) Pearson Custom.

***Psychology of Intelligence Analysis.** Richards J. Heuer. 210p. 1999. per. 20.00 (*0-16-059035-3*) USGPO.

Psychology of Interpersonal Behaviour. Michael Argyle. 1994. pap. 17.95 (*0-14-017274-2*, Pub. by Pnguin Bks Ltd) Trafalgar.

Psychology of Interpersonal Perception. Perry Hinton. LC 92-15272. 240p. (C). 1993. pap. 22.99 (*0-415-08452-0*, B0226) Routledge.

Psychology of Interpersonal Perception. Perry Hinton. LC 92-15272. 240p. (C). (gr. 13). 1993. 65.00 (*0-415-08451-2*, B0222) Routledge.

Psychology of Interpersonal Relations. Fritz Heider. 336p. (C). 1983. reprint ed. pap. 34.50 (*0-89859-282-8*) L Erlbaum Assocs.

Psychology of Interrogations & Confessions. Gisli H. Gudjonsson. text. write for info. (*0-471-49136-5*) Wiley.

Psychology of Interrogations, Confessions & Testimony. Gisli H. Gudjonsson. (Wiley Series in Family Psychology). 376p. 1999. pap. 65.00 (*0-471-96177-9*) Wiley.

Psychology of Interrogations, Confessions & Testimony. Gisli H. Gudjonsson. LC 91-41516. (Wiley Series in Psychology of Crime, Policing, & Law). 376p. 1992. reprint ed. pap. 116.60 (*0-608-04003-7*, 206474000011) Bks Demand.

Psychology of Interviewing. Lewis Miller. (C). 1989. 60.00 (*0-7223-2388-3*, Pub. by A H S Ltd) St Mut.

Psychology of Intimacy. Karen J. Prager. LC 95-37284. (Personal Relationships Ser.). 367p. 1995. lib. bdg. 39.95 (*1-57230-006-X*, 0006) Guilford Pubns.

Psychology of Intimacy. Karen J. Prager. LC 95-37284. (Personal Relationships Ser.). 367p. 1997. pap. text 24.00 (*1-57230-267-4*, C0267) Guilford Pubns.

Psychology of Invention in the Mathematical Field. Jacques Hadamard. 145p. 1945. pap. text 5.95 (*0-486-20107-4*) Dover.

Psychology of Investing. Lawrence E. Lifson & Richard Geist. LC 99-18529. (Investments Ser.). 208p. 1999. 34.95 (*0-471-18339-3*) Wiley.

Psychology of Jealousy & Envy. Ed. by Peter Salovey. LC 90-23329. 293p. 1991. lib. bdg. 40.00 (*0-89862-555-6*) Guilford Pubns.

Psychology of Judgement & Decision Making. Scott Plous. LC 92-38542. 352p. (C). 1993. pap. 29.69 (*0-07-050477-6*) McGraw.

Psychology of Juvenile Crime. Amy Lamson. 123p. 1982. 32.95 (*0-89885-060-6*, Kluwer Acad Hman Sci); pap. 18.95 (*0-89885-290-0*, Kluwer Acad Hman Sci) Kluwer Academic.

Psychology of Kundalini Yoga: Notes of the Seminar Given in 1932. C. G. Jung. Ed. by Sonu Shamdasani. LC 95-44198. (Jung Extracts Ser.: Vol. 99). (Illus.). 176p. 1996. text 24.95 (*0-691-02127-9*, Pub. by Princeton U Pr) Cal Prin Full Svc.

***Psychology of Kundalini Yoga: Notes of the Seminar Given in 1932 By C. G. Jung, XCI.** C. G. Jung. 1999. pap. text 14.95 (*0-691-00676-8*, Pub. by Princeton U Pr) Cal Prin Full Svc.

Psychology of Language. David W. Carroll. LC 85-22393. (Psychology Ser.). 467p. (C). 1985. mass mkt. 44.00 (*0-534-05640-7*) Brooks-Cole.

Psychology of Language. Whitney. (C). Date not set. pap. 11.96 (*0-395-75751-7*) HM.

Psychology of Language. Whitney. LC 97-72560. (C). 1997. text 56.36 (*0-395-75750-9*) HM.

Psychology of Language. 2nd ed. David W. Carroll. LC 93-26969. 1993. pap. 45.75 (*0-534-21300-6*) Brooks-Cole.

Psychology of Language. 2nd ed. David W. Carroll. 1994. mass mkt., teacher ed. write for info. (*0-534-21301-4*) Brooks-Cole.

Psychology of Language. 3rd ed. David W. Carroll. LC 98-28457. (Psychology Ser.). 24p. 1998. pap. 72.95 (*0-534-34973-0*) Brooks-Cole.

Psychology of Language: A Critical Introduction. Michael A. Forrester. LC 96-67702. 224p. (C). 1996. 42.50 (*0-8039-7990-8*); pap. 14.99 (*0-8039-7991-6*) Sage.

Psychology of Language: An Introduction to Sentence & Discourse Processes. Ed. by Murray Singer. 320p. (C). 1990. text 29.95 (*0-8058-0005-0*) L Erlbaum Assocs.

Psychology of Language: From Data to Theory. Trevor A. Harley. 512p. 1995. 39.95 (*0-86377-381-8*); pap. 22.00 (*0-86377-382-6*) L Erlbaum Assocs.

Psychology of Language & Communication. Andrew W. Ellis & Geoffrey Beattie. LC 86-14828. 374p. 1993. pap. text 23.95 (*0-89862-046-5*) Guilford Pubns.

Psychology of Language & Learning. Ed. by O. Hobart Mowrer. LC 79-17959. (Cognition & Language Ser.). 312p. 1980. reprint ed. pap. 96.80 (*0-608-05436-4*, 206590500006) Bks Demand.

Psychology of Law: Integrations & Applications. 2nd ed. (C). 1997. text 24.00 (*0-321-40008-9*) Addson-Wesley Educ.

Psychology of Law: Integrations & Applications. 2nd ed. Irwin A. Horowitz. LC 97-37879. 560p. (C). 1997. 75.00 (*0-321-00600-3*) Allyn.

Psychology of Learning. rev. ed. Edwin R. Guthrie. 1952. 16.50 (*0-8446-1213-8*) Peter Smith.

Psychology of Learning: Principles & Processes. James T. Walker. LC 95-3494. 437p. 1995. 83.00 (*0-13-720335-7*) P-H.

Psychology of Learning: Research & Theory. Laird S. Cermak. LC 74-22534. (Illus.). 410p. reprint ed. pap. 127.10 (*0-8357-9970-0*, 201247500081) Bks Demand.

Psychology of Learning & Behavior. 4th ed. Barry Schwartz. LC 94-48642. (C). 1995. text 73.75 (*0-393-96661-5*) Norton.

Psychology of Learning & Motivation, Vol. 30. Ed. by Douglas L. Madin. (Illus.). 328p. 1993. text 99.95 (*0-12-543330-1*) Acad Pr.

Psychology of Learning & Motivation, Vol. 31. Ed. by Douglas L. Medin. (Illus.). 366p. 1994. text 99.95 (*0-12-543331-X*) Acad Pr.

Psychology of Learning & Motivation, Vol. 33. Ed. by Douglas L. Medin. (Illus.). 296p. 1995. text 85.00 (*0-12-543333-6*) Acad Pr.

Psychology of Learning & Motivation, Vol. 35. Ed. by Douglas L. Medin. (Illus.). 337p. 1996. text 69.95 (*0-12-543335-2*) Acad Pr.

Psychology of Learning & Motivation, Vol. 37. Ed. by Donald L. Medin. (Illus.). 350p. 1997. text 79.95 (*0-12-543337-9*) Morgan Kaufmann.

Psychology of Learning & Motivation, Vol. 38. Ed. by Douglas L. Medin. (Illus.). 306p. (C). 1998. boxed set 89.95 (*0-12-543338-7*) Acad Pr.

***Psychology of Learning & Motivation, Vol. 39.** Douglas L. Medin. Vol. 39. 276p. 1999. 79.95 (*0-12-543339-5*) Acad Pr.

Psychology of Learning & Motivation Vol. 27: Advances in Research & Theory. Ed. by Gordon H. Bower. (Illus.). 349p. (C). 1991. text 99.95 (*0-12-543327-1*) Acad Pr.

Psychology of Learning & Motivation Vol. 28: Advances in Research & Theory. Ed. by Douglas L. Medin. (Illus.). 296p. 1992. text 99.95 (*0-12-543328-X*) Acad Pr.

Psychology of Learning & Motivation Vol. 32: Decision Making from a Cognitive Perspective. Ed. by Douglas L. Medin et al. (Illus.). 426p. 1995. text 99.95 (*0-12-543332-8*) Acad Pr.

Psychology of Learning & Motivation Vol. 34: Causal Learning. Ed. by Douglas L. Medin et al. (Illus.). 442p. 1996. text 74.95 (*0-12-543334-4*) Acad Pr.

Psychology of Learning & Motivation Vol. 36: Perceptual Learning, Vol. 36. Ed. by Robert L. Goldstone et al. (Illus.). 393p. 1997. text 75.00 (*0-12-543336-0*) Morgan Kaufmann.

Psychology of Learning & Motivation- Advances in Research & Theory: Categorization by Human & Machines, Vol. 29. Ed. by Doug L. Medin et al. (Illus.). 552p. 1993. text 99.95 (*0-12-543329-8*) Acad Pr.

Psychology of Learning & Teaching. Patricia C. Stetson et al. 1973. 42.50 (*0-8422-5113-8*) Irvington.

Psychology of Learning Mathematics. Richard R. Skemp. 232p. 1987. pap. text 27.50 (*0-8058-0058-1*) L Erlbaum Assocs.

Psychology of Learning Mathematics. Richard R. Skemp. 304p. 1994. pap. 16.95 (*0-14-013619-3*, Pub. by Pnguin Bks Ltd) Trafalgar.

Psychology of Learning Science. Ed. by Shawn M. Glynn et al. 280p. (C). 1991. text 49.95 (*0-8058-0668-7*) L Erlbaum Assocs.

Psychology of Left & Right. Michael C. Corballis & Ivan L. Beale. 240p. 1976. text 49.95 (*0-89859-114-7*) L Erlbaum Assocs.

Psychology of Left & Right. Michael C. Corballis & Ivan L. Beale. LC 76-13233. (Illus.). 239p. 1976. reprint ed. pap. 74.10 (*0-608-07972-3*, 206794400012) Bks Demand.

Psychology of Literacy. Sylvia Scribner & Michael Cole. (Illus.). 348p. 1981. pap. 16.95 (*0-674-72114-4*) HUP.

Psychology of Literacy. Sylvia Scribner & Michael Cole. LC 81-607. (Illus.). 348p. (C). 1981. 46.50 (*0-674-72115-2*) HUP.

Psychology of Love. (Quick Study Academic Ser.). 4p. pap. 3.95 (*1-57222-216-6*) Barcharts.

Psychology of Love. Robert J. Sternberg & Michael L. Barnes. 383p. (C). 1989. reprint ed. pap. 22.50 (*0-300-04589-1*) Yale U Pr.

Psychology of Love According to St. Bonaventure. Robert P. Prentice. (Philosophy Ser.). 156p. 1957. pap. 8.00 (*1-57659-096-8*) Franciscan Inst.

Psychology of Macbeth. George Sexton. LC 70-175847. reprint ed. 22.50 (*0-404-05753-5*) AMS Pr.

Psychology of Man's Possible Evolution. 2nd ed. P. D. Ouspensky. 1973. pap. 8.00 (*0-394-71943-3*) Knopf.

Psychology of Marriage: Basic Issues & Applications. Ed. by Frank D. Fincham & Thomas N. Bradbury. LC 90-3038. 432p. 1990. lib. bdg. 49.95 (*0-89862-433-9*) Guilford Pubns.

Psychology of Marxian Socialism. Henri De Man. Tr. by Eden Paul & Cedar Paul. 518p. (C). 1984. pap. 29.95 (*0-87855-992-2*) Transaction Pubs.

Psychology of Mathematical Abilities in School Children. V. A. Krutetskii. Ed. by Izaak Wirszup & Jeremy Kilpatrick. Tr. by Joan W. Teller. LC 74-33520. 1992. pap. text 15.00 (*0-226-45485-1*) U Ch Pr.

Psychology of Mathematics for Instruction. Lauren B. Resnick & Wendy W. Ford. LC 80-29106. 288p. 1981. text 59.95 (*0-89859-029-9*) L Erlbaum Assocs.

***Psychology of Mature Spirituality: Integrity, Wisdom, Transcendence.** Polly Young-Eisendrath & Melvin E. Miller. LC 00-25538. 2000. pap. write for info. (*0-415-17960-2*) Routledge.

***Psychology of Medicine & Surgery: A Guide for Psychologists, Counsellors, Nurses & Doctors.** Peter Salmon. LC 99-59484. (Series in Clinical Psychology). 2000. pap. write for info. (*0-471-85214-7*) Wiley.

Psychology of Memory. Balch. (C). Date not set. pap. text. write for info. (*0-15-507163-7*) Harcourt Coll Pubs.

Psychology of Memory, 3 vols. Ed. by Peter E. Morris & Martin E. Conway. LC 92-45221. (International Library of Critical Writings in Business History). (C). 1993. lib. bdg. 375.00 (*0-8147-5496-1*) NYU Pr.

Psychology of Memory, Vol. 1. P. E. Morris. (C). 1993. lib. bdg. 125.00 (*0-8147-5493-7*) NYU Pr.

Psychology of Memory, Vol. 2. Morris. (C). 1993. lib. bdg. 125.00 (*0-8147-5494-5*) NYU Pr.

Psychology of Memory, Vol. 3. Morris. (C). 1993. lib. bdg. 125.00 (*0-8147-5495-3*) NYU Pr.

Psychology of Men: Psychoanalytic Perspectives. Gerald I. Fogel. LC 95-62214. 310p. 1996. pap. 18.00 (*0-300-06620-1*) Yale U Pr.

Psychology of Mental Retardation. I. Biler & Manny Sternlicht. LC 77-4137. 800p. 1977. 39.95 (*0-88437-013-5*) Psych Dimensions.

Psychology of Mind-Body Healing: New Concepts of Therapeutic Hypnosis. 2nd rev. ed. Ernest L. Rossi. 304p. (C). 1993. 39.00 (*0-393-70168-9*) Norton.

Psychology of Misconduct, Vice & Crime. Bernard Hollander. (Historical Foundations of Forensic Psychiatry & Psychology Ser.). 220p. 1980. reprint ed. lib. bdg. 27.50 (*0-306-76063-0*) Da Capo.

Psychology of Missionary Adjustment. Marge Jones & E. Grant Jones. LC 94-36181. 176p. 1995. text 12.95 (*0-88243-321-0*) Gospel Pub.

Psychology of Money. Adrian Furnham & Michael Argyle. LC 97-36974. (Illus.). 344p. (C). 1998. 80.00 (*0-415-14605-4*); pap. 25.99 (*0-415-14606-2*) Routledge.

Psychology of Money. Henry C. Lindgren. 342p. (C). 1991. lib. bdg. 39.50 (*0-89464-399-1*) Krieger.

***Psychology of Money: An Investment Manager's Guide to Beating the Market.** Jim Ware. 304p. 2000. 29.95 (*0-471-39074-7*) Wiley.

Psychology of Motocross. Anthony Curcio. Ed. by Barbara Walls. (Illus.). xiv, 240p. 1999. pap. 49.00 (*0-9669578-0-6*) Two Thous Twelve.

Psychology of Motor Behavior. Ed. by Leonard Zaichkowsky & C. Zvi Fuchs. (Illus.). 300p. 1989. pap. 34.95 (*0-932392-24-5*) Mouvement Pubns.

Psychology of Motor Behavior & Sport, 1976, Vol. 1. North American Society for the Psychology of Sport. Ed. by Robert W. Christina & Daniel M. Landers. LC 78-641529. 296p. 1977. reprint ed. pap. 91.80 (*0-608-10450-7*, 202952800001) Bks Demand.

Psychology of Motor Behavior & Sport, 1976, Vol. 2. North American Society for the Psychology of Sport. Ed. by Robert W. Christina & Daniel M. Landers. LC 78-641529. 283p. 1977. reprint ed. pap. 87.80 (*0-608-10451-5*, 202952800002) Bks Demand.

Psychology of Motor Behavior & Sport, 1978. Glyn C. Roberts. Ed. by Karl M. Newell. LC 78-641529. 309p. 1979. reprint ed. pap. 95.80 (*0-608-10452-3*, 202953100061) Bks Demand.

Psychology of Motor Behavior & Sport, 1979. North American Society for the Psychology of Sport & Physical Activity Staff. Ed. by Claude H. Nadeau. LC 78-641529. 760p. 1980. reprint ed. pap. 200.00 (*0-608-10453-1*, 202953000061) Bks Demand.

Psychology of Motor Behavior & Sport, 1980. North American Society for the Psychology of Sport & Physical Activity Staff. Ed. by Glyn C. Roberts & Daniel M. Landers. LC 78-641529. 220p. 1981. reprint ed. pap. 68.20 (*0-608-10454-X*, 202953300061) Bks Demand.

Psychology of Murder: A Study in Criminal Psychology. Andreas Bjerre. Tr. by E. Classen from SWE. (Historical Foundations of Forensic Psychiatry & Psychology Ser.). 164p. 1980. reprint ed. lib. bdg. 22.50 (*0-306-76067-3*) Da Capo.

Psychology of Music. John B. Davies. LC 77-92339. 240p. 1978. 37.50 (*0-8047-0980-7*) Stanford U Pr.

Psychology of Music. Diana Deutsch. 1984. pap. text 54.00 (*0-12-213562-8*) Acad Pr.

Psychology of Music. James L. Mursell. 1991. lib. bdg. 45.00 (*0-403-01750-5*) Scholarly.

Psychology of Music. James L. Mursell. LC 77-110274. (Illus.). 389p. 1971. reprint ed. lib. bdg. 69.50 (*0-8371-4500-7*, MUPM, Greenwood Pr) Greenwood.

Psychology of Music. James L. Mursell. 1988. reprint ed. lib. bdg. 25.00 (*0-317-90101-X*) Rprt Serv.

Psychology of Music. H. P. Rao. (Illus.). 80p. 1986. reprint ed. 15.00 (*0-8364-1765-8*, Pub. by Abhinav) S Asia.

Psychology of Music. Carl E. Seashore. 408p. 1967. reprint ed. pap. 10.95 (*0-486-21851-1*) Dover.

Psychology of Music. 2nd ed. Diana Deutsch. LC 98-85210. (Illus.). 807p. (C). 1998. pap. text 69.95 (*0-12-213565-2*); boxed set 129.95 (*0-12-213564-4*) Acad Pr.

Psychology of Music: A Survey for Teacher & Musician. Max Schoen. 1988. reprint ed. lib. bdg. 49.00 (*0-7812-0241-8*) Rprt Serv.

Psychology of Music: A Survey for Teacher & Musician. Max Schoen. LC 73-181248. 258p. 1940. reprint ed. 39.00 (*0-403-01673-8*) Scholarly.

An Asterisk (*) at the beginning of an entry indicates that the title is appearing for the first time.

Psychology of Myth, Folklore & Religion. Leo Schneiderman. LC 81-9471. 232p. (C). 1981. text 36.95 (*0-88229-659-0*) Burnham Inc.

Psychology of Nationalism. Josha Searle-White. text. write for info. (*0-312-23369-8*) St Martin.

Psychology of Nuclear Conflict. Ed. by Ian Fenton. 1991. pap. 14.95 (*0-904575-40-3*) Sigo Pr.

***Psychology of Nursery Education.** Ivan Ward. 96p. 1998. pap. 14.00 (*1-85575-206-9*, Pub. by H Karnac Bks Ltd) Other Pr LLC.

Psychology of Nutrition. David Booth. LC 93-45603. 264p. 1994. pap. 27.50 (*0-7484-0159-8*, Pub. by Tay Francis Ltd) Taylor & Francis.

Psychology of Nutrition. David Booth. LC 93-45603. 264p. 1994. 85.00 (*0-7484-0158-X*) Taylor & Francis.

Psychology of Occupations. Anne Roe. Ed. by Leon Stein. LC 77-70529. (Work Ser.). (Illus.). 1977. reprint ed. lib. bdg. 35.95 (*0-405-10197-X*) Ayer.

Psychology of Officiating. Robert S. Weinberg & Peggy A. Richardson. LC 90-31893. (Illus.). 192p. 1990. pap. 15.95 (*0-87322-875-8*, PWEI0875) Human Kinetics.

Psychology of Pain. Skevington. 360p. 1995. pap. text 51.95 (*0-471-95773-9*) Wiley.

Psychology of Pain. Ed. by Richard A. Sternbach. LC 86-20413. 256p. 1986. reprint ed. pap. 79.40 (*0-608-04688-4*, 206540900004) Bks Demand.

Psychology of Peacekeeping. Ed. by Harvey J. Langholtz. LC 98-23552. 280p. 1998. 69.50 (*0-275-96232-6*, Praeger Pubs) Greenwood.

Psychology of Peoples. Gustave Le Bon. LC 73-14164. (Perspectives in Social Inquiry Ser.). 252p. 1979. reprint ed. 19.95 (*0-405-05509-9*) Ayer.

Psychology of Perception. Hamlyn. 140p. 1994. 48.95 (*0-7512-0309-2*) Ashgate Pub Co.

Psychology of Perceptions: Index of Modern Information. rev. ed. Roth Polinski. LC 88-47983. 150p. 1991. 47.50 (*1-55914-486-6*); pap. 44.50 (*1-55914-487-4*) ABBE Pubs Assn.

***Psychology of Personal Effectiveness.** 336p. (C). 1998. text 30.75 (*0-536-01447-7*) Pearson Custom.

Psychology of Personality. Bernardo J. Carducci. LC 97-25802. 1997. pap. 76.95 (*0-534-35019-4*) Brooks-Cole.

Psychology of Personality. David Funder. (C). Date not set. pap. 16.00 (*0-393-96744-1*, Norton Paperbks) Norton.

Psychology of Personality: An Epistemological Inquiry. James T. Lamiell. (Critical Assessments of Contemporary Psychology Ser.). (Illus.). 256p. 1987. text 57.50 (*0-231-06020-3*) Col U Pr.

Psychology of Personnel Selection: A Quality Approach. Ivan T. Robertson & Dominic Cooper. LC 95-7748. (Essential Business Psychology Ser.). 224p. (C). 1995. pap. 24.95 (*0-415-10326-6*) Thomson Learn.

Psychology of Personnel Selection: A Quality Approach. Ivan T. Robertson & Dominic Cooper. LC 95-7748. (Essential Business Psychology Ser.). 224p. (C). (gr. 13). 1995. pap. 43.95 (*0-415-13081-6*) Thomson Learn.

Psychology of Persuasion: How to Persuade Others to Your Way of Thinking. Kevin Hogan. LC 96-3423. (Illus.). 288p. 1996. text 22.00 (*1-56554-146-4*) Pelican.

Psychology of Physical Symptoms. James W. Pennebaker. (Illus.). 192p. 1982. 47.00 (*0-387-90730-0*) Spr-Verlag.

Psychology of Picture Perception. John Miller Kennedy. LC 72-5892. (Jossey-Bass Behavioral Science Ser.). 190p. 1974. reprint ed. pap. 58.90 (*0-608-12209-2*, 202388000034) Bks Demand.

Psychology of Play. Brian Sutton-Smith. LC 75-35082. (Studies in Play & Games). (Illus.). 1978. reprint ed. 35.95 (*0-405-07930-3*) Ayer.

Psychology of Play Activities. Harvey C. Lehman & Paul A. Witty. LC 75-35074. (Studies in Play & Games). (Illus.). 1976. reprint ed. 23.95 (*0-405-07924-9*) Ayer.

Psychology of Political Communication. Ed. by Ann N. Crigler. LC 96-10324. 280p. (C). 1996. text 49.50 (*0-472-10641-4*, 10641) U of Mich Pr.

Psychology of Political Communication. Ed. by Ann N. Crigler. 280p. 1998. pap. text 19.95 (*0-472-08579-4*, 08579) U of Mich Pr.

Psychology of Political Violence. Emma Goldman. 1972. 250.00 (*0-87968-160-8*) Gordon Pr.

Psychology of Politics. Hans J. Eysenck. LC 98-24888. 343p. 1998. pap. 29.95 (*0-7658-0430-1*) Transaction Pubs.

Psychology of Pregnancy & Childbirth. L. Sherr. (Illus.). 256p. 1995. pap. 29.95 (*0-632-03388-6*, Pub. by Blckwll Scitfc UK) Blackwell Sci.

Psychology of Prejudice. (C). 2001. text 37.00 (*0-205-29769-2*, Longwood Div) Allyn.

Psychology of Prejudice. Ed. by Mark P. Zanna & James M. Olson. LC 93-32412. (Ontario Symposia on Personality & Social Psychology Ser.: Vol. VII). 344p. 1993. pap. 36.00 (*0-8058-1355-1*); text 79.95 (*0-8058-1119-2*) L Erlbaum Assocs.

Psychology of Programming. Ed. by Jean-Michel Hoc et al. (Computers & People Ser.). 290p. 1991. text 65.00 (*0-12-350772-3*) Acad Pr.

Psychology of Proof: Deductive Reasoning in Human Thinking. Lance J. Rips. LC 93-5811. 463p. 1994. 55.00 (*0-262-18153-3*, Bradford Bks) MIT Pr.

Psychology of Questions. Ed. by Arthur C. Graesser & John B. Black. 392p. 1985. text 79.95 (*0-89859-444-8*) L Erlbaum Assocs.

Psychology of Radio. Hadley Cantril & Gordon W. Allport. LC 72-161159. (History of Broadcasting: Radio & Television Ser.). 1980. reprint ed. 27.95 (*0-405-03574-8*) Ayer.

Psychology of Reading. Eleanor J. Gibson & Harry T. Levin. 642p. 1978. pap. text 22.50 (*0-262-57052-1*) MIT Pr.

Psychology of Reading. Keith Rayner & Alexander Pollatsek. 536p. 1994. pap. 49.95 (*0-8058-1872-3*) L Erlbaum Assocs.

Psychology of Reading: An Interdisciplinary Approach. 2nd ed. Mildred C. Robeck & Randall R. Wallace. 1990. pap., teacher ed. write for info. (*0-8058-0885-X*) L Erlbaum Assocs.

Psychology of Reading: An Interdisciplinary Approach. 2nd ed. Ed. by R. R. Wallace & Mildred C. Robeck. 456p. (C). 1990. pap. 49.95 (*0-8058-0374-2*); text 99.95 (*0-8058-0373-4*) L Erlbaum Assocs.

Psychology of Reading: An Introduction. 2nd ed. Robert G. Crowder & Richard K. Wagner. (Illus.). 288p. (C). 1992. text 24.95 (*0-19-506593-X*) OUP.

Psychology of Reading & Spelling. Authur I. Gates. LC 73-176798. (Columbia University. Teachers College. Contributions to Education Ser.: No. 129). reprint ed. 37.50 (*0-404-55129-7*) AMS Pr.

Psychology of Reading & Spelling Disabilities. Anthony F. Jorm. (International Library of Psychology). 150p. 1983. pap. 14.95 (*0-7100-9344-6*, Routledge Thoemms) Routledge.

Psychology of Reasoning. Alfred Binet. 201p. 55.00 (*1-85506-674-2*) Thoemmes Pr.

Psychology of Reasoning: Structure & Content. P. C. Wason & P. N. Johnson-Laird. LC 78-189160. 272p. 1972. pap. 16.00 (*0-674-72127-6*) HUP.

Psychology of Relationship Banking: Profiting in the Psyche. James J. Lynch. 240p. 1996. 135.00 (*1-85573-244-0*, Pub. by Woodhead Pubng) Am Educ Systs.

***Psychology of Relationships.** Kieran T. Sullivan. 342p. 2000. write for info. (*1-58692-008-1*) Copyright Mgmt.

Psychology of Religion. Joseph F. Byrnes. LC 84-47854. 320p. (C). 1984. 35.00 (*0-02-903580-5*) Free Pr.

Psychology of Religion. George A. Coe. LC 75-3113. reprint ed. 49.50 (*0-404-59109-4*) AMS Pr.

***Psychology of Religion.** 6th ed. John Santrock. (Alternate Chapter Ser.). 32p. (C). 1999. pap. 3.13 (*0-07-234557-8*) McGraw-H Hghr Educ.

***Psychology of Religion: A Short Introduction.** Kate M. Loewenthal. 2000. pap. 15.95 (*1-85168-212-0*, Pub. by Onewrld Pubns) Penguin Putnam.

Psychology of Religion: An Empirical Approach. 2nd ed. Ralph W. Hood, Jr. et al. LC 96-22625. 546p. 1996. lib. bdg. 62.00 (*1-57230-116-3*) Guilford Pubns.

Psychology of Religion: Classic & Contemporary. 2nd ed. David M. Wulff. LC 96-43970. 784p. 1996. text 80.95 (*0-471-03706-0*) Wiley.

Psychology of Religion: Theoretical Approaches. Daniel N. McIntosh. Ed. by Bernard Spilka. LC 96-41128. (C). 1996. pap. text 25.00 (*0-8133-2947-7*, Pub. by Westview) HarpC.

Psychology of Religion & Coping: Theory, Research, Practice. Kenneth I. Pargament. LC 97-9599. 548p. 1997. lib. bdg. 55.00 (*1-57230-214-3*, 0214) Guilford Pubns.

Psychology of Religion for Ministry. H. Newton Malony. LC 94-41661. (Integration Bks.). 144p. 1994. pap. 12.95 (*0-8091-3483-7*) Paulist Pr.

Psychology of Religious Behaviour, Belief, & Experience. Benjamin Beit-Hallahmi & Michael Argyle. LC 97-205504. 336p. (C). 1997. 80.00 (*0-415-12330-5*); pap. 24.99 (*0-415-12331-3*) Routledge.

Psychology of Religious Belief. L. B. Brown. 1988. text 100.00 (*0-12-136355-4*) Acad Pr.

Psychology of Religious Belief. James B. Pratt. LC 75-3326. (Philosophy America Ser.). reprint ed. 54.00 (*0-404-59321-6*) AMS Pr.

Psychology of Religious Commitment & Development. Leland F. Asa. 190p. (C). 1995. pap. text 28.50 (*0-8191-9839-0*); lib. bdg. 51.50 (*0-8191-9838-2*) U Pr of Amer.

Psychology of Religious Experience in Its Personal & Institutional Dimensions. Bruce T. Riley. (American University Studies: Theology & Religion: Ser. VII, Vol. 49). XVI, 361p. (C). 1988. text 47.70 (*0-8204-0862-X*) P Lang Pubng.

Psychology of Religious Ritual. Manly P. Hall. pap. 4.95 (*0-89314-347-2*) Philos Res.

Psychology of Religious Sects. Henry C. McComas. LC 70-172763. reprint ed. 37.50 (*0-404-04107-8*) AMS Pr.

Psychology of Retirement: How to Successfully Cope with a Major Life Transition. Everyday Psychologist Staff. (Everyday Psychology Ser.: Vol. 2). 68p. 1999. 12.95 (*0-9668417-2-7*) BPRI.

Psychology of Revolution. Gustave Le Bon. LC 68-29699. 1968. reprint ed. pap. 19.00 (*0-87034-026-3*) Fraser Pub Co.

Psychology of Rigorous Humanism. Joseph F. Rychlak. LC 76-54838. (Illus.). 561p. reprint ed. pap. 174.00 (*0-608-10674-7*, 201988900015); reprint ed. pap. 159.90 (*0-608-30559-6*, 2019889) Bks Demand.

Psychology of Rigorous Humanism. Contrib. by Joseph F. Rychlak. LC 76-54838. (Illus.). 561p. reprint ed. pap. 159.90 (*0-608-30299-6*) Bks Demand.

Psychology of Risk Taking Behavior. Rudiger M. Trimpop. LC 94-10006. (Advances in Psychology Ser.: Vol. 107). 412p. 1994. 145.75 (*0-444-89961-8*, North Holland) Elsevier.

Psychology of Rollo May: Reflections & Commentary by Rollo May. Clement Reeves. LC 76-50708. (Jossey-Bass Behavioral Science Ser.). 352p. reprint ed. pap. 109.20 (*0-8357-6885-6*, 203793700009) Bks Demand.

Psychology of Safety: How to Change Behaviors & Attitudes at Work. E. Scott Geller. 412p. 1996. lib. bdg. 85.00 (*0-8019-8733-4*) NP-Chilton.

Psychology of Sales Call Reluctance: Earning What You're Worth in Sales. 4th rev. ed. George W. Dudley & Shannon L. Goodson. LC 99-60831. Orig. Title: Psychology of Call Reluctance. 424p. 1999. pap. 22.95 (*0-935907-07-6*) Behavioral Sci.

Psychology of Sales Success. Gerhard Gschwandtner. LC 97-65355. (Illus.). 203p. 1997. 19.95 (*0-939613-11-5*) Personal Selling.

Psychology of Saving: A Study on Economic Psychology. Karl-Erik Warneryd. LC 98-31080. 400p. 1999. 95.00 (*1-84064-016-2*) E Elgar.

Psychology of School Learning, 2 vols. Ed. by William M. Bart & Martin R. Wong. Incl. Vol. 1. Environmentalism. 249p. 1974. text 1974. pap. write for info. (*0-318-53724-9*) Irvington.

Psychology of Science: Contributions to Metascience. Ed. by Barry Gholson et al. (Illus.). 480p. (C). 1989. text 74.95 (*0-521-35410-2*) Cambridge U Pr.

Psychology of Second Language Learning: Papers from the Second International Congress of Applied Linguistics 2nd, Cambridge, England, Sept 8-12, 1969. International Congress of Applied Linguistics Staf. Ed. by Paul Pimsleur & Terence Quinn. LC 75-173811. 206p. reprint ed. pap. 58.80 (*0-608-13052-4*, 2024517) Bks Demand.

Psychology of Self-Affirmation with an Assertiveness Attitude: Index of New Information with Authors & Subjects. Rosetta R. Hardine. 180p. 1993. 47.50 (*1-55914-862-4*); pap. 44.50 (*1-55914-863-2*) ABBE Pubs Assn.

Psychology of Self & Other. Elizabeth R. Moberly. 112p. 1985. 18.95 (*0-422-79740-5*, 9417, Pub. by Tavistock) Routldge.

Psychology of Self-Esteem: How Our Judgments about Ourselves Affect Our Success in Love & Human Relationships. Nathaniel Branden. (Orig.). 1999. pap. 17.00 (*0-7879-4526-9*) Jossey-Bass.

Psychology of Self-Motivation see Lay Counseling Series

Psychology of Selling: How to Read Your Customer, Set. pap. 155.00 incl. audio (*0-7612-0905-0*, 80154); pap., wbk. ed. 30.00 incl. audio (*0-7612-0906-9*, 80155) AMACOM.

Psychology of Set. Dmitri N. Uznadze. LC 65-21186. (International Behavioral Sciences Ser.). 268p. reprint ed. pap. 83.10 (*0-608-13313-2*, 205580300038) Bks Demand.

Psychology of Sex Differences, 2 vols., Vol. I. Eleanor E. Maccoby & Carol N. Jacklin. LC 73-94488. xv, 634p. 1974. pap. 17.95 (*0-8047-0974-2*) Stanford U Pr.

Psychology of Sex Differences, 2 vols., Vol. II. Eleanor E. Maccoby & Carol N. Jacklin. LC 73-94488. xv, 634p. 1974. pap. 11.95 (*0-8047-0975-0*) Stanford U Pr.

Psychology of Sex Relations. Theodor Reik. LC 74-28525. 243p. 1975. reprint ed. lib. bdg. 65.00 (*0-8371-7916-5*, RESR, Greenwood Pr) Greenwood.

Psychology of Sexual Emotion: The Basis of Selective Attraction. Vernon W. Grant. LC 75-36356. 270p. 1979. reprint ed. lib. bdg. 38.50 (*0-8371-8631-5*, GRPS, Greenwood Pr) Greenwood.

Psychology of Sexual Orientation, Behavior, & Identity: A Handbook. Ed. by Louis Diamant & Richard D. McAnulty. LC 95-7512. 544p. 1995. lib. bdg. 119.50 (*0-313-28501-2*, Greenwood Pr) Greenwood.

Psychology of Sexual Victimization: A Handbook. Ed. by Michele Antoinette Paludi. LC 98-14239. 272p. 1999. lib. bdg. 69.50 (*0-313-30248-0*, Greenwood Pr) Greenwood.

Psychology of Shakespeare. John C. Bucknill. LC 72-131514. reprint ed. 39.50 (*0-404-01147-0*) AMS Pr.

Psychology of Shame: Theory & Treatment of Shame Based Syndromes. 2nd ed. Gershen Kaufman. LC 95-52777. (Illus.). 376p. 1996. 47.95 (*0-8261-6671-7*) Springer Pub.

Psychology of Skill: Three Studies. William F. Book & William L. Bryan. LC 73-3029. (Classics in Psychology Ser.). 1977. reprint ed. 24.95 (*0-405-05157-3*) Ayer.

Psychology of Smart Investing: Meeting the Six Mental Challenges. Ira Epstein & David A. Garfield. LC 92-436. 256p. 1992. 29.95 (*0-471-55071-X*) Wiley.

***Psychology of Soccer.** Massimo Cabrini. (Illus.). 137p. 1999. pap. 12.95 (*1-890946-25-7*) Reedswain.

Psychology of Social Change. Leo Schneiderman. 253p. 1988. 42.95 (*0-89885-372-9*, Kluwer Acad Hman Sci); pap. 20.95 (*0-89885-379-6*, Kluwer Acad Hman Sci) Kluwer Academic.

Psychology of Social Class. Michael Argyle. LC 93-3445. 256p. (C). 1993. pap. 25.99 (*0-415-07955-1*, A9838) Routledge.

Psychology of Social Institutions. Charles H. Judd. LC 73-14160. (Perspectives in Social Inquiry Ser.). 360p. 1974. reprint ed. 23.95 (*0-405-05506-4*) Ayer.

Psychology of Social Movements. Pryns Hopkins. 1972. 59.95 (*0-8490-0913-8*) Gordon Pr.

Psychology of Socialism. Henry Deman. LC 73-14152. (Perspectives in Social Inquiry Ser.). 514p. 1974. reprint ed. 33.95 (*0-405-05498-X*) Ayer.

Psychology of Socialism. Gustave LeBon. LC 81-1973. 415p. (C). 1982. reprint ed. pap. 24.95 (*0-87855-703-2*) Transaction Pubs.

Psychology of Speculation. Henry H. Harper. LC 66-26207. 1966. reprint ed. pap. 12.00 (*0-87034-015-8*) Fraser Pub Co.

Psychology of Spiritual Growth. Mary E. Carreiro. LC 86-20799. (Gentle Wind Ser.: Vol. 1). 160p. 1987. reprint ed. lib. bdg. 29.95 (*0-89789-123-6*) Gentle Wind Proj.

Psychology of Spiritual Growth. Mary E. Carreiro. LC 86-20799. (Gentle Wind Ser.: Vol. 1). 160p. 1988. reprint ed. pap. 12.95 (*0-89789-124-4*) Gentle Wind Proj.

Psychology of Spiritual Healing. Eugene Taylor. LC 97-18275. xx, 208p. (Orig.). 1997. pap. 14.95 (*0-87785-375-4*, Chrysalis Books) Swedenborg.

Psychology of Sport Injury. John Heil. LC 92-35854. (Illus.). 352p. 1995. reprint ed. pap. text 25.00 (*0-88011-564-5*, BHEI0564) Human Kinetics.

Psychology of Sports, Exercise, & Fitness: Social & Adjustmental Issues. Louis Diamant. 256p. 1991. 79.95 (*1-56032-170-9*) Hemisp Pub.

Psychology of Stalking. Ed. by J. Reid Meloy. LC 98-84369. (Illus.). xvii, 327p. (C). 1998. text 59.95 (*0-12-490560-9*) Acad Pr.

Psychology of Status. Herbert H. Hyman. Ed. by Harriet Zuckerman & Robert K. Merton. LC 79-9005. (Dissertations on Sociology Ser.). 1980. lib. bdg. 15.95 (*0-405-12974-2*) Ayer.

Psychology of Stress. Sarah A. Culton. 207p. (Orig.). 1991. pap. text 18.95 (*0-89420-281-2*, 345000) Natl Book.

Psychology of Stress: From Distress to Eustress. 2nd ed. Lynette Crane. 144p. 1996. ring bd. 46.95 (*0-7872-1980-0*) Kendall-Hunt.

Psychology of Stress & Distress - Mental, Emotional & Behavioral Actions & Reactions: Index of Information with Authors & Subjects. rev. ed. Howard D. Jetter. 137p. 1998. 47.50 (*0-7883-1874-8*); pap. 44.50 (*0-7883-1875-6*) ABBE Pubs Assn.

Psychology of Success: Developing Your Self-Esteem. 2nd ed. Denis E. Waitley. 256p. (C). 1993. text 18.30 (*0-256-11496-X*, Irwn McGrw-H) McGrw-H Hghr Educ.

Psychology of Success: Developing Your Self-Esteem. 3rd ed. Denis Waitley. 1997. teacher ed. 14.13 (*0-256-19478-5*, Irwn McGrw-H) McGrw-H Hghr Educ.

Psychology of Success: Developing Your Self-Esteem. 3rd ed. Denise Waitley. 288p. (C). 1996. text 18.30 (*0-256-19477-7*, Irwn McGrw-H) McGrw-H Hghr Educ.

Psychology of Sufism. Javad Nurbakhsh. 1993. 22.95 (*0-933646-49-6*) Aries Pr.

Psychology of Sufism. Javad Nurbakhsh. 142p. 1996. 22.95 (*0-614-21557-9*, 1020) Kazi Pubns.

Psychology of Sufism. Javad Nurbakhsh. 141p. 1992. 20.00 (*0-933546-49-1*) KNP.

Psychology of Suggestion: A Research into the Subconscious Nature of Man & Society. Boris Sidis. LC 73-2415. (Mental Illness & Social Policy; the American Experience Ser.). 1973. reprint ed. 25.95 (*0-405-05225-1*) Ayer.

Psychology of Suicide. Edwin S. Shneidman et al. LC 84-2818. 744p. 1983. 45.00 (*0-87668-668-4*) Aronson.

***Psychology of Survey Response.** Roger Tourangeau et al. (Illus.). 400p. (C). 2000. text 59.95 (*0-521-57246-0*); pap. text 22.95 (*0-521-57629-6*) Cambridge U Pr.

Psychology of Sympathy. L. Wispe. (Perspectives in Social Psychology Ser.). (Illus.). 224p. (C). 1991. 47.50 (*0-306-43798-8*, Plenum Trade) Perseus Pubng.

Psychology of Synergy: A Guide to Personal Power. Madeleine Singer. (Illus.). 176p. (Orig.). 1991. pap. 9.95 (*0-941404-03-X*) New Falcon Pubns.

Psychology of System Design. D. Meister. (Advances in Human Factors/Ergonomics Ser.: Vol. 17). 548p. 1991. 201.25 (*0-444-88378-9*) Elsevier.

Psychology of Tactical Communication. Ed. by Michael J. Cody & Margaret L. MacLaughlin. 350p. 1989. 99.00 (*1-85359-040-1*, Pub. by Multilingual Matters); pap. 44.95 (*1-85359-039-8*, Pub. by Multilingual Matters) Taylor & Francis.

Psychology of Teaching. rev. ed. Asahel D. Woodruff. LC 73-136091. (Illus.). 617p. 1974. reprint ed. lib. bdg. 35.00 (*0-8371-5241-0*, WOPT, Greenwood Pr) Greenwood.

***Psychology of Teaching & Learning in the Primary School.** David Whitebread. LC 00-30594. 2000. pap. write for info. (*0-415-21405-X*) Routledge.

Psychology of Teaching Foreign Languages: Teaching Method 1. B. Belyayev & R. Hingley. LC 63-11576. (American & International Library of Science Technology, Engineering & Liberal Studies). 1963. 104.00 (*0-08-009802-9*, Pub. by Pergamon Repr) Franklin.

Psychology of Technical Analysis: Profiting from Crowd Behavior & the Dynamics of Price. 2nd rev. ed. Tony Plummer. 275p. 1993. text 50.00 (*1-55738-543-2*, Irwn Prfssnl) McGraw-Hill Prof.

Psychology of Television. John Condry. 336p. (C). 1989. pap. 39.95 (*0-8058-0621-0*) L Erlbaum Assocs.

Psychology of Temperament: Index of New Information with Authors, Subjects & References. rev. ed. Lorna S. Collett. 150p. 1998. 47.50 (*0-7883-1944-2*); pap. 44.50 (*0-7883-1945-0*) ABBE Pubs Assn.

Psychology of the American Jury. Jeffrey T. Frederick. 384p. 1987. 55.00 (*0-87473-333-2*, 61960-10, MICHIE) LEXIS Pub.

Psychology of the Artist. Sheldon Cholst. LC 91-7319. 1978. pap. 9.95 (*0-931174-00-7*) Beau Rivage.

Psychology of the Artist. 2nd rev. ed. Sheldon Cholst. (Illus.). 333p. 1997. pap. 14.95 (*0-931174-05-8*) Beau Rivage.

Psychology of the Arts. Hans Kreitler & Shulamith Kreitler. LC 70-185566. (Illus.). xiv, 514p. 1972. text 45.00 (*0-8223-0269-1*); pap. text 25.95 (*0-8223-0437-6*) Duke.

Psychology of the Catholic Intellectual. Ed. by A. Van Kaam. (Synthesis Ser.). 1967. pap. 1.00 (*0-8199-0384-1*, L38669, Frnescn Herld) Franciscan Pr.

Psychology of the Child. Jean Piaget & Barbel Inhelder. Tr. by Helen Weaver. LC 73-78449. 192p. 1972. pap. 17.00 (*0-465-09500-3*, Pub. by Basic) HarpC.

Psychology of the Child in the Middle Class. Allison Davis. LC 60-15158. (Horace Mann Lectures). 80p. reprint ed. pap. 30.00 (*0-608-30575-8*, 201787500010) Bks Demand.

Psychology of the Chinese People. Ed. by Michael H. Bond. (Illus.). 366p. 1988. pap. text 24.95 (*0-19-584279-0*) OUP.

Psychology of the Consumer & Its Development: An Introduction. R. C. Webb. LC 99-15838. (Series in Adult Development & Aging). (Illus.). 375p. (C). 1999. write for info. (*0-306-46073-4*, Plenum Trade) Perseus Pubng.

P

An Asterisk (*) at the beginning of an entry indicates that the title is appearing for the first time.

Psychology of the Courtroom. Ed. by Norbert L. Kerr & Robert M. Bray. (Illus.). 370p. 1995. reprint ed. pap. text 39.95 (0-12-404921-4) Acad Pr.

Psychology of the Criminal. M. Hamblin Smith. (Historical Foundations of Forensic Psychiatry & Psychology Ser.). viii, 182p. 1983. reprint ed. lib. bdg. 22.50 (0-306-76176-9) Da Capo.

Psychology of the Criminal Act & Punishment. Gregory Zilboorg. LC 68-54445. (Illus.). 141p. 1969. reprint ed. lib. bdg. 55.00 (0-8371-0773-3, ZIPC, Greenwood Pr) Greenwood.

Psychology of the Dentist-Patient Relationship. S. Bochner. (Contributions to Psychology & Medicine Ser.). (Illus.). 200p. 1988. 112.00 (0-387-96642-0) Spr-Verlag.

Psychology of the Esoteric. 3rd ed. Osho. Ed. by Anand Prem et al. (Psychology Ser.). 184p. 1994. 12.95 (3-89338-123-6, Pub. by Rebel Hse) Oshos.

Psychology of the Family in Health, Stress & Disease: Index of New Information. Valerie N. Hullinger. 149p. 1997. 47.50 (0-7883-1538-2); pap. 44.50 (0-7883-1539-0) ABBE Pubs Assn.

Psychology of the Female Body. Jane M. Ussher. 200p. 1989. 45.00 (0-415-01556-1, A1686) Routledge.

***Psychology of the Future: Lessons from Modern Consciousness Research.** Stanislav Grof. 2000. pap. 19.95 (0-7914-4622-0) State U NY Pr.

Psychology of the Great War: The First World War & Its Origins. Gustave LeBon. LC 98-27088. 505p. 1999. pap. 29.95 (0-7658-0479-4) Transaction Pubs.

Psychology of the Grotesque in August Strindberg's The Ghost Sonata. Terry J. Converse. LC 98-50017. (Studies in Comparative Literature: Vol. 24). 268p. 1999. text 89.95 (0-7734-8207-5) E Mellen.

***Psychology of the Home.** Barrie Gunter. 2000. pap. 34.95 (1-86156-146-6) Whurr Pub.

***Psychology of the Image.** Michael A. Forrester. LC 99-59599. 2000. write for info. (0-415-16515-6) Routledge.

Psychology of the Imagination. 256p. (C). Date not set. pap. write for info. (0-415-11954-5) Routledge.

Psychology of the Internet. Patricia M. Wallace. LC 99-12696. (Illus.). 304p. 1999. 24.95 (0-521-63294-3) Cambridge U Pr.

Psychology of the Mexican: Culture & Personality. Rogelio Diaz-Guerrero. LC 74-23309. (Texas Pan American Ser.). 193p. 1975. pap. 7.95 (0-292-76430-8) U of Tex Pr.

Psychology of the Negro: An Experimental Study. George O. Ferguson. LC 74-107481. 138p. 1970. reprint ed. lib. bdg. 49.50 (0-8371-3783-7, FEP&, Greenwood Pr) Greenwood.

Psychology of the Observer. Richard Rose. (Illus.). 92p. 1979. pap. 7.00 (1-878683-06-3) TAT Found.

Psychology of the Physically Handicapped. Jon Eisenson et al. Ed. by William R. Phillips & Janet Rosenberg. LC 79-6922. (Physically Handicapped in Society Ser.). 1980. reprint ed. lib. bdg. 37.95 (0-405-13130-5) Ayer.

Psychology of the Physically Ill Patient: A Clinician's Guide. M. E. Backman. LC 88-39667. (Illus.). 252p. (C). 1989. 49.50 (0-306-43051-7, Plenum Trade) Perseus Pubng.

Psychology of the Planets. Francoise Gauquelin. 28p. (Orig.). 1982. pap. 12.95 (0-917086-32-5) ACS Pubns.

Psychology of the Poet Shelley. Edward Carpenter & George Barnefield. LC 72-1334. (English Literature Ser.: No. 33). 1972. reprint ed. lib. bdg. 75.00 (0-8383-1431-7) M S G Haskell Hse.

Psychology of the Psalms. Maralene Wesner & Miles E. Wesner. 63p. 1997. pap. 5.95 (0-936715-49-9, 127) Diversity Okla.

***Psychology of the Psychic.** David F. Marks. 305p. 2000. pap. 22.95 (1-57392-798-8) Prometheus Bks.

Psychology of the Psychic. David Marks & Richard Kammann. LC 80-7458. (Science & the Paranormal Ser.). 238p. (C). 1980. 28.95 (0-87975-121-5) Prometheus Bks.

Psychology of the Psychic. David Marks & Richard Kammann. LC 80-7458. (Science & the Paranormal Ser.). (Illus.). 238p. (C). 1980. pap. 21.95 (0-87975-122-3) Prometheus Bks.

Psychology of the Self: A Casebook. Ed. by Arnold Goldberg. 468p. 1992. reprint ed. pap. 24.95 (0-8236-8262-5) Intl Univs Pr.

Psychology of the Self & the Treatment of Narcissism. Richard D. Chessick. LC 85-15621. 366p. 1985. 45.00 (0-87668-745-1) Aronson.

Psychology of the Self & the Treatment of Narcissism. Richard D. Chessick. LC 85-15621. 384p. 1993. reprint ed. pap. 50.00 (0-87668-171-2) Aronson.

Psychology of the Social. Ed. by Uwe Flick. LC 97-42130. 304p. (C). 1998. text 59.95 (0-521-58159-1); pap. text 22.95 (0-521-58851-0) Cambridge U Pr.

Psychology of the Social Self. Ed. by Tom R. Tyler et al. (Applied Social Research Ser.). 300p. 1998. write for info. (0-8058-2849-4) L Erlbaum Assocs.

Psychology of the Social Self. Ed. by Tom R. Tyler et al. (Applied Social Research Ser.). vi, 280 p. 1999. pap. write for info. (0-8058-2850-8) L Erlbaum Assocs.

Psychology of the Stock Market. G. C. Selden. LC 65-20560. 1965. reprint ed. pap. 11.00 (0-87034-016-6) Fraser Pub Co.

Psychology of the Transference. C. G. Jung. Ed. by G. Adler. Tr. by R. F. C. Hull. LC 74-171958. (Bollingen Ser.: Vol. 20). (Illus.). 222p. 1969. pap. 12.95 (0-691-01752-2, 158, Pub. by Princeton U Pr) Cal Prin Full Svc.

Psychology of the Unconscious: A Study of the Transformations & Symbolisms of the Libido: A Contribution to the History of the Evolution of Thought. C. G. Jung. Tr. by Beatrice M. Hinkle. LC 91-17591. (Bollingen Series: Supplementary to the Collected Works of C. G. Jung: Vol. XX: B). (Illus.). 420p. 1992. text 49.50 (0-691-09973-1, Pub. by Princeton U Pr) Cal Prin Full Svc.

Psychology of the Unconscious: Mesmer, Janet, Freud, Jung, & Current Issues. William L. Kelly. LC 89-48954. 210p. (C). 1991. 33.95 (0-87975-590-3) Prometheus Bks.

Psychology of the Youthful Offender. 3rd ed. Robert N. Walker. LC 95-16135. 130p. (C). 1995. text 40.95 (0-398-06529-2); pap. text 26.95 (0-398-06530-6) C C Thomas.

Psychology of Time & Death. Steve Chaplin. 300p. 1999. 25.00 (0-9669878-0-2) Sonnet.

Psychology of Today's Woman. Ed. by Toni Bernay & Dorothy W. Cantor. LC 89-31197. 400p. 1989. pap. text 15.95 (0-674-72109-8) HUP.

Psychology of Today's Woman: New Psychoanalytic Visions. Ed. by Toni Bernay & Dorothy W. Cantor. 377p. (C). 1986. text 45.00 (0-88163-036-5) Analytic Pr.

Psychology of Touch. Ed. by Morton Heller & William Schiff. 408p. (C). 1991. pap. 45.00 (0-8058-0751-9) L Erlbaum Assocs.

Psychology of Touch: A Special Issue of Journal of Nonverbal Behavior. Ed. by Stephen Thayer. LC 80-649435. 80p. 1986. pap. 16.95 (0-89885-321-4, Kluwer Acad Hman Sci) Kluwer Academic.

Psychology of Tourism. Ross. 212p. 1999. pap. text 34.95 (0-7506-3459-6) Buttrwrth-Heinemann.

Psychology of Trading Success: Optimizing Trader Performance by Controlling Stress, Superstitious Behavior, Imagery & Personal Style. Clifford Sherry. 225p. 1995. 34.95 (1-55738-856-3, Irwn Prfssnl) McGraw-Hill Prof.

Psychology of Transcendence. Andrew Neher. 384p. 1990. pap. 12.95 (0-486-26167-0) Dover.

Psychology of Treasure Dowsing. Bill Cox. (Illus.). 96p. 1989. pap. 12.75 (0-88234-010-7) Life Understanding.

Psychology of Twins: A Practical Handbook for Parents of Multiples. 3rd rev. ed. Herbert L. Collier. LC 96-79634. (Orig.). 1996. pap. 13.95 (0-9655442-0-6) Busn Word.

Psychology of Twinship. Ricardo C. Ainslie. LC 96-46672. 288p. 1997. pap. 40.00 (1-56821-664-5) Aronson.

Psychology of Ultimate Concerns: Motivation & Spirituality in Personality. Robert A. Emmons. LC 99-26409. 230p. 1999. 32.00 (1-57230-456-1) Guilford Pubns.

Psychology of Underachievement: Differential Diagnosis & Differential Treatment. Harvey P. Mandel & Sander I. Marcus. LC 87-37127. (Personality Processes Ser.). 397p. 1988. 165.00 (0-471-84855-7) Wiley.

Psychology of Values: The Ontario Symposium, Vol. 8. Ed. by Clive Seligman et al. LC 96-35299. (Ontario Symposia on Personality & Social Psychology Ser.). (Illus.). 350p. 1996. 69.95 (0-8058-1574-0) L Erlbaum Assocs.

Psychology of Vandalism. Arnold P. Goldstein. LC 95-44578. (Social/Clinical Psychology Ser.). (Illus.). 308p. (C). 1996. 42.50 (0-306-45140-9, Plenum Trade) Perseus Pubng.

Psychology of Violence. (C). 2000. pap. 32.00 (0-205-31662-X) Allyn.

Psychology of Violent Women. Joyce L. Carbonell. 200p. 1996. lib. bdg. 39.95 (1-57444-051-9, SL0519) St Lucie Pr.

Psychology of Visual Illusion. unabridged ed. J. O. Robinson. LC 98-24691. (Illus.). 288p. 1998. pap. 9.95 (0-486-40449-8) Dover.

Psychology of Voice Disorders. Deborah C. Rosen & Robert T. Sataloff. LC 96-50038. (Illus.). 302p. (Orig.). 1997. pap. 76.95 (1-56593-839-9, 1638) Thomson Learn.

Psychology of War: Comprehending Its Mystique & Its Madness. Lawrence LeShan. LC 92-50438. 163p. 1992. 16.95 (1-879360-20-9) Noble Pr.

Psychology of War & Peace: The Image of the Enemy. R. W. Rieber. (Illus.). 302p. (C). 1990. 52.50 (0-306-43543-8, Plenum Trade) Perseus Pubng.

Psychology of Well Being. William M. Miley. LC 98-44533. 280p. 1999. 65.00 (0-275-96275-X, Praeger Pubs) Greenwood.

Psychology of Winning. Denis E. Waitley. 160p. 1986. mass mkt. 5.99 (0-425-09999-7) Berkley Pub.

Psychology of Winning Baseball. Rick Wolff. 1990. pap. 9.95 (0-13-734138-5) P-H.

Psychology of Winning for Women: What Every Woman Needs to Know; What Every Man Needs to Underst. Denis Waitley. 1999. 21.95 (1-890009-13-X) Exec Excell.

Psychology of Women, 2 vols. Helene Deutsch. Incl. Vol. I. Girlhood. LC 44-5287. 413p. 1944. text 72.00 (0-8089-0115-X, 791031, W B Saunders Co); Vol. II. Motherhood. LC 44-5287. 505p. 1945. text 60.00 (0-8089-0116-8, 791032, W B Saunders Co); LC 44-5287. write for info. (0-318-52863-0, Grune & Strat) Harcrt Hlth Sci Grp.

Psychology of Women. Etaugh. 464p. (C). 2000. pap. 46.67 (0-205-28596-1, Macmillan Coll) P-H.

Psychology of Women. Forden & Hunter. LC 98-21669. 383p. 1998. pap. text 36.00 (0-205-26510-3) P-H.

Psychology of Women. Michele A. Paludi. 416p. (C). 1992. text. write for info. (0-697-11499-6) Brown & Benchmark.

Psychology of Women. Michele A. Paludi. LC 97-41464. 406p. (C). 1998. pap. text 42.00 (0-13-955840-3) P-H.

Psychology of Women. Karen S. Pfost. (C). 1995. 33.33 (0-205-15270-8, Macmillan Coll) P-H.

Psychology of Women. Mary R. Walsh. LC 87-6167. 480p. 1987. pap. 19.00 (0-300-03966-2) Yale U Pr.

Psychology of Women. 3rd ed. Matlin. (C). 1996. pap. text, teacher ed. 42.00 (0-15-503301-8) Harcourt Coll Pubs.

Psychology of Women. 3rd ed. Margaret W. Matlin. LC 95-79405. (C). 1996. text 46.00 (0-15-503008-6, Pub. by Harcourt Coll Pubs) Harcourt.

Psychology of Women. 4th ed. Matlin. (C). Date not set. pap. write for info. (0-15-507896-8) Harcourt Coll Pubs.

Psychology of Women: A Handbook of Issues & Theories. Ed. by Florence L. Denmark & Michele A. Paludi. LC 92-8642. 784p. 1993. lib. bdg. 135.00 (0-313-26295-0, DEH/, Greenwood Pr) Greenwood.

Psychology of Women: A Partially Annotated Bibliography. Joyce J. Walstedt. 76p. 1973. pap. 2.50 (0-912786-23-X) Know Inc.

Psychology of Women: Behavior in a Biosocial Context. 3rd ed. Juanita H. Williams. LC 86-231655. 470p. (C). 1987. pap. text 37.50 (0-393-95567-2) Norton.

Psychology of Women: Future Directions in Research. J. A. Sherman & F. L. Denmark. LC 78-31824. 800p. 1979. 59.95 (0-88437-009-7) Psych Dimensions.

Psychology of Women: Index of Modern Information. rev. ed. Sherry A. Walker. LC 88-47971. 159p. 1994. 47.50 (0-7883-0234-5); pap. 44.50 (0-7883-0235-3) ABBE Pubs Assn.

Psychology of Women: Psychoanalytic Perpectives. Ed. by Arnold Richards & Phyllis Tyson. LC 97-784. 580p. 2000. 69.95 (0-8236-5588-1, No. 05588) Intl Univs Pr.

Psychology of Women: Psychoanalytic Perspectives. Ed. by Arnold Richards & Phyllis Tyson. 555p. 1997. pap. 45.00 (0-8236-5587-3) Intl Univs Pr.

Psychology of Women: Selected Readings. Karen W. Bauer. 172p. 1993. spiral bd. 26.95 (0-8403-8409-2) Kendall-Hunt.

Psychology of Women: Selected Readings. 2nd ed. Ed. by Juanita H. Williams. (C). 1985. pap. text 33.50 (0-393-95379-3) Norton.

Psychology of Women's Health: Progress & Challenges in Research & Application. Ed. by Annette L. Stanton & Sheryle J. Gallant. LC 95-10460. 651p. 1995. text 24.95 (1-55798-296-1, 431-7530) Am Psychol.

Psychology of Word Meanings. Ed. by Paula Schwanenflugel. 320p. 1991. text 69.95 (0-8058-0661-X) L Erlbaum Assocs.

***Psychology Of Work.** 4th ed. (C). 2000. text. write for info. (0-321-04714-1) Addison-Wesley.

***Psychology of Work & Human Performance.** 3rd ed. 304p. (C). 1998. 24.00 (0-321-00590-2) P-H.

Psychology of Work & Human Performance. 3rd ed. Ed. by Robert D. Smither. LC 97-27497. 600p. (C). 1998. 82.00 (0-321-01256-9, Prentice Hall) P-H.

Psychology of Work & Unemployment. Gordon E. O'Brien. LC 85-29604. (Wiley Series in Psychology & Productivity at Work). 329p. 1986. pap. 102.00 (0-7837-8492-9, 204929900010) Bks Demand.

Psychology of Work Behavior. 3rd ed. Landy. (Psychology Ser.). Date not set. mass mkt., student ed. 10.50 (0-534-10664-1) Brooks-Cole.

Psychology of Work Behavior. 3rd ed. Frank J. Landy. 1985. mass mkt. 39.25 (0-534-10663-3) Brooks-Cole.

Psychology of Writing. Ronald T. Kellogg. (Illus.). 264p. 1994. text 55.00 (0-19-508139-0) OUP.

***Psychology of Writing.** Ronald T. Kellogg. LC 93-44667. (Illus.). 264p. 1999. pap. 19.95 (0-19-512908-3) OUP.

Psychology of Writing: The Affective Experience, 13. Alice G. Brand. LC 88-25090. (Contributions in Psychology Ser.: No. 13). 281p. 1989. 59.95 (0-313-26382-5, BPH/, Greenwood Pr) Greenwood.

Psychology of Written Composition. Ed. by Carl Bereiter & Marlene Scardamalia. 389p. (C). 1987. text 89.95 (0-89859-647-5) L Erlbaum Assocs.

Psychology of Written Composition. Ed. by Carl Bereiter & Marlene Scardamalia. 389p. (C). 1987. pap. text 45.00 (0-8058-0038-7) L Erlbaum Assocs.

Psychology of Written Language: Developmental & Educational Perspectives. Ed. by Margaret Martlew. LC 82-21933. (Wiley Series in Developmental Psychology & Its Applications). (Illus.). 442p. reprint ed. pap. 137.10 (0-8357-7544-5, 203626600001) Bks Demand.

Psychology Office Manual. Donald J. Weinstein. (Office Manual Ser.). 155p. 1994. 89.00 (1-890018-06-6) Anadem Pubng.

Psychology On-Line 1999. 2nd ed. Wallace. 144p. 1998. pap. 13.75 (0-07-232023-0) McGraw.

Psychology on the Internet. Stull. (C). 1996. pap. 10.20 (0-13-266602-2, Macmillan Coll) P-H.

***Psychology on the Internet: 1999-2000.** Ed. by Prentice-Hall Staff. (C). 1999. text. write for info. (0-13-022074-4) P-H.

Psychology on the Internet 1997-1998. Stull. 96p. (C). 1997. write for info. (0-13-646159-X, Macmillan Coll) P-H.

Psychology on the Streets: Mental Health Practice With Homeless Persons. Thomas L. Kuhlman. (Personality Processes Ser.). 223p. 1994. 85.00 (0-471-55243-7) Wiley.

Psychology I: A Tour Guide. 3rd ed. James Thomas. 128p. 1996. pap. text 13.95 (0-7872-1964-9) Kendall-Hunt.

Psychology 1: A Tour Guide. 4th ed. Thomas-Davis. 98p. (C). 1998. per. 16.95 (0-7872-5400-2) Kendall-Hunt.

Psychology 1A6 Student Handbook. 5th ed. Richard Day. 212p. (C). 1996. pap. text, spiral bd. 19.95 (0-7872-2792-7, 41279201) Kendall-Hunt.

***Psychology 101.** Ed. by Maas. 346p. 1999. pap. text 30.00 (0-536-02647-5) P-H.

Psychology 101. Maas. 368p. 1998. pap. text 29.75 (0-536-01389-6) Pearson Custom.

Psychology 101 Supplement: Getting Familiar with the Study of Behavior. Bruce B. Svore. 100p. (C). 1998. pap. text 26.00 (0-9666323-1-1, 100-2) Bordalice.

Psychology 122. Sockloff. (C). 1998. pap. text, wbk. ed. 10.00 (0-471-32528-7) Wiley.

Psychology: or A View of the Human Soul, Including Anthropology. Friedrich Rauch. LC 74-22335. (History of Psychology Ser.). 416p. 1975. 60.00 (0-8201-1142-2) Schol Facsimiles.

Psychology, Pain & Anaesthesia. Ed. by Hamilton B. Gibson. LC 93-32615. 220p. 1993. 54.25 (1-56593-129-7, 0441) Thomson Learn.

Psychology, Parapsychology & Clairvoyance: Index of New Information & Research. rev. ed. Angella M. Calvine. LC 94-24770. 125p. 1995. 47.50 (0-7883-0460-7); pap. 44.50 (0-7883-0461-5) ABBE Pubs Assn.

Psychology Personnel Selection. Robertson, Jr. & Cooper. 1995. pap. write for info. (1-86152-612-1, Pub. by ITBP) Thomson Learn.

Psychology, Phenomenology, & Chinese Philosophy: Chinese Philosophical Studies VI. Vincent Shen et al. LC 94-7728. (Cultural Heritage & Contemporary Change Series III: Vol. 6). 185p. 1994. 45.00 (1-56518-044-5); pap. 17.50 (1-56518-045-3) Coun Res Values.

Psychology Pied Piper of New Age. Louise S. Idomir. LC 96-222525. 180p. (C). 1994. pap. 10.95 (1-879366-90-8) Hearthstone OK.

***Psychology Place.** (C). 1999. pap. text 0.00 (0-201-64927-6) HEPC Inc.

***Psychology Place Sticker One.** 1999. write for info. (0-321-06042-3) Addison-Wesley.

***Psychology Plus for Instructors.** 5th ed. Myers. 1998. 4.95 (1-57259-748-8) Worth.

Psychology Pract. Test. 6th ed. Lahey. 1997. 44.25 (0-07-561122-8) McGraw.

Psychology Problem Solver. rev. ed. Research & Education Association Staff. LC 80-53174. (Illus.). 1056p. (C). 1999. pap. text 23.95 (0-87891-523-0) Res & Educ.

Psychology, Psychiatry, & the Law: A Clinical & Forensic Handbook. Charles P. Ewing. LC 85-60449. 576p. (C). 1985. pap. 39.45 (0-943158-11-7, PPL-BBP) Pro Resource.

Psychology Quick Review. Theo Sonderegger. LC 98-230651. (Cliffs Quick Reviews Ser.). (Illus.). 201p. (C). 1998. pap. text, student ed. 7.95 (0-8220-5327-6, Cliff) IDG Bks.

Psychology Readings Catalogue of the North East London Polytechnic, London, England, 2 vols, Set. North East London Polytechnic, London, England Sta. 1976. 180.00 (0-8161-1179-0, G K Hall & Co) Mac Lib Ref.

Psychology Research & Public Policy. Richard A. Kasschau. LC 85-3600. 1985. 49.95 (0-275-90126-2, C0126, Praeger Pubs) Greenwood.

Psychology Research Handbook: A Primer for Graduate Students & Research Assistants. Ed. by Frederick T. Leong & James T. Austin. LC 96-10017. 408p. 1996. 36.00 (0-8039-7048-X); pap. 16.99 (0-8039-7049-8) Sage.

***Psychology Resources on the World Wide Web.** Kardas. (Psychology Ser.). 1998. pap. 13.95 (0-534-35941-8) Brooks-Cole.

***Psychology Seducation.** William K. Kirkpatrick. 240p. 2000. reprint ed. pap. 19.95 (0-9661325-0-5) R A McCaffrey.

Psychology, Sin, & Society: An Essay on the Triumvirate of Psychology, Religion, & Democracy. M. Munawar Butt. 268p. (C). 1992. lib. bdg. 52.00 (0-8191-8606-6) U Pr of Amer.

Psychology Smartbox: Introduction to Psychology. 5th ed. Kalat. (Psychology). 1999. text 57.25 (0-534-36818-2) Brooks-Cole.

Psychology, Society & Subjectivity: An Introduction to German Critical Psychology. Charles W. Tolman. LC 94-3934. (Critical Psychology Ser.). 184p. (C). 1994. pap. 25.99 (0-415-08976-X, B3200); text 62.95 (0-415-08975-1, B3196) Routledge.

Psychology, Spelling, & Education. Ed. by Chris M. Sterling & Cliff Robson. LC 92-15153. 1992. 99.00 (1-85359-166-1, Pub. by Multilingual Matters); pap. 39.95 (1-85359-165-3, Pub. by Multilingual Matters) Taylor & Francis.

Psychology Student Writer's Manual. Koch & Scott. LC 98-21462. 221p. 1998. pap. text, student ed. 25.00 (0-13-633041-X) P-H.

Psychology Study Guide. Richard Saudargas. 1999. text 1150.00 (0-324-01872-X) Thomson Learn.

Psychology Study Guide. 3rd ed. Philip G. Zimbardo. (C). 2000. pap., student ed. 21.00 (0-321-06051-2) Addison-Wesley.

Psychology The Search For Understanding. Janet Simons et al. (Psychology). (Illus.). 716p. (C). 1987. mass mkt. 50.75 (0-314-26213-X) West Pub.

Psychology, Theology, & Spirituality in Christian Counseling. Mark M. McMinn. LC 96-12604. (AACC Counseling Library Prof. Ser.). 327p. 1996. 24.99 (0-8423-5252-X) Tyndale Hse.

Psychology Through the Eyes of Faith. David Myers & Malcolm Jeeves. 240p. 1987. pap. 14.00 (0-06-065557-7, Pub. by Harper SF) HarpC.

Psychology Today. 7th ed. Richard R. Bootzin et al. 728p. (C). 1991. 79.06 (0-07-006539-X); pap., student ed. 23.75 (0-07-006541-1) McGraw.

Psychology Today. 7th ed. Garrison. 1991. student ed. 47.81 (0-07-006542-X) McGraw.

Psychology Today Reader. Epstein-Sussex Publishers Staff. 488p. 1999. per. 19.95 (0-7872-5617-X, 41561701) Kendall-Hunt.

***Psychology 2.** 2nd ed. Stephen F. Davis. 1999. 55.00 (0-13-025787-7) P-H.

Psychology II: Optimum Psycho-Social Life Skills. Darrell Franken. 631p. 1995. pap. (0-934957-67-3) Wellness Pubns.

P

An Asterisk (*) at the beginning of an entry indicates that the title is appearing for the first time.

Psychology Versus Metapsychology: Psychoanalytic Essays in Memory of George S. Klein. Ed. by Merton M. Gill & Philip S. Holzman. LC 75-23354. (Psychological Issues Monographs: No. 36, Vol. 9, No. 4). 376p. 1975. 55.00 (*0-8236-5586-5*) Intl Univs Pr.

Psychology with Machiavellianism: Index of New Information for Reference & Research. Lois A. Hutton. 150p. 1997. 47.50 (*0-7883-1240-5*); pap. text 44.50 (*0-7883-1241-3*) ABBE Pubs Assn.

Psychology with Psychplace. 2nd ed. Philip G. Zimbardo. (C). 1999. pap. text 56.00 (*0-321-04939-X*) Addison-Wesley.

***Psychology with Psychplace.** 5th ed. Wade. (C). 1998. text 77.00 (*0-321-04937-3*) Addison-Wesley.

***Psychology with Study Guide.** Lyle E. Bourne, Jr. & Russo. 1998. pap. text 56.50 (*0-393-97309-3*) Norton.

***Psychology with Supersite Pin Code.** 5th ed. Robert A. Baron. 768p. 2000. 80.00 (*0-205-32404-5*) Allyn.

***Psychology with the Instant Psychology.** Lyle E. Bourne, Jr. 1998. text 60.50 (*0-393-97389-1*) Norton.

Psychology, 1995. 4th ed. David G. Myers. 1994. text 50.80 (*0-87901-644-2*) Worth.

Psychology, 1995. 4th ed. David G. Myers. 1994. pap. text, student ed. 12.40 (*0-87901-645-0*) Worth.

Psychology 1996/97. 26th annot. ed. Duffy. 1996. teacher ed. (*0-697-31677-7*, WCB McGr Hill) McGrw-H Hghr Educ.

***Psychology 1999 & Psychology 1999 & Psychobabble 1996.** 5th ed. Wade. 1998. student ed. 99.00 (*0-201-39427-8*) Addisn-Wesley Iberoamer.

Psychology 2000. Wallace. 1999. 21.50 (*0-07-234762-7*) McGraw.

Psychology 2000. Wallace. 2000. 21.50 (*0-07-233589-0*) McGraw.

***Psychology 2000 Catalog.** (C). 1999. write for info. (*0-205-31943-2*) Allyn.

***Psychology 2000-2001.** 30th ed. Karen Duffy. (Annual Editions Ser.). 240p. (J). 1999. pap. 16.56 (*0-07-236396-7*) McGrw-H Hghr Educ.

Psychology's Crisis of Disunity: Philosophy & Method for a Unified Science. Arthur W. Staats. LC 83-2154. 401p. 1983. 65.00 (*0-275-91082-2*, C1082, Praeger Pubs) Greenwood.

Psychology's Myths & Misconceptions. Dawes. 19.95 (*0-465-06700-X*, Pub. by Basic) HarpC.

Psychology's Second Century: Enduring Issues, Vol. 2. Richard A. Kasschau & Charles N. Cofer. LC 81-11882. 303p. 1981. 55.00 (*0-275-90659-0*, C06592, Praeger Pubs) Greenwood.

Psycholsocial Treatment of Chronic Mental Patients: Milieu Versus Social-Learning Programs. Gordon L. Paul & Robert J. Lentz. LC 77-10868. 528p. 1977. reprint ed. pap. 163.70 (*0-7837-4174-X*, 205902300012) Bks Demand.

Psycholytic & Psychedelic Therapy Research, 1931-1995: A Complete International Bibliography Torsten Passie. LC 97-195979. (Kleine Bibliographische Reihe Ser.). 102p. 1997. write for info. (*0-393-61483-2*) Norton.

Psychoma (Soul-Sleep) 1908. Helen Rhodes. 150p. 1998. reprint ed. pap. 19.95 (*0-7661-0411-7*) Kessinger Pub.

Psychomancy & Crystal Gazing. William W. Atkinson. reprint ed. pap. 3.00 (*0-911662-41-3*) Yoga.

Psychomathematics: The Key to the Universe. (Nikola Tesla Ser.). 1991. lib. bdg. 79.95 (*0-8490-4324-7*) Gordon Pr.

Psychomech. Brian Lumley. 448p. (Orig.). 1992. mass mkt. 5.99 (*0-8125-2023-8*, Pub. by Tor Bks) St Martin.

Psychomental Complex of the Tungus. Sergei M. Shirokogorov. LC 76-44788. 488p. reprint ed. 120.00 (*0-404-15879-X*) AMS Pr.

Psychometric Foundations & Behavioral Assessment. Fernando Silva. (Illus.). 160p. (C). 1993. text 42.00 (*0-8039-5266-X*); pap. text 18.95 (*0-8039-5267-8*) Sage.

Psychometric Foundations & Behavioral Assessment. Fernando Silva. LC 93-7506. 175p. reprint ed. pap. 54.30 (*0-608-09799-3*, 206996800007) Bks Demand.

Psychometric Methodology: Proceedings of the 7th European Meeting of the Psychometric Society in Trier. Ed. by Rolf Steyer et al. LC 93-18266. (Illus.). 620p. (Orig.). 1993. pap. 90.00 (*1-56081-371-7*, Pub. by Gustav Fischer) Balogh.

***Psychometric Methods: Item Response Theory for Psychologists.** Susan E. Embretson & Steve Reise. LC 99-48454. (Multivariate Applications Ser.). 2000. write for info. (*0-8058-2819-2*) L Erlbaum Assocs.

***Psychometric Primer.** Paul Kline. 160p. 2000. 40.00 (*1-85343-488-4*, Pub. by Free Assoc Bks); pap. 22.50 (*1-85343-489-2*, Pub. by Free Assoc Bks) Intl Spec Bk.

Psychometric Properties of Fourteen Latent Constructs from the Oregon Youth Society. D. Capaldi & G. R. Patterson. (Recent Research in Psychology Ser.). (Illus.). 440p. 1988. 78.95 (*0-387-96845-8*) Spr-Verlag.

***Psychometric Scaling: A Toolkit for Imaging systems Development.** Peter G. Engeldrum. (Illus.). 200p. (C). 2000. 94.95 (*0-9678706-0-7*) Imcotek Pr.

Psychometric Theory. 3rd ed. Jim C. Nunnally & Ira H. Bernstein. LC 93-22756. (Series in Social Psychology). 736p. (C). 1994. 101.88 (*0-07-047849-X*) McGraw.

Psychometrician. Jack Rudman. (Career Examination Ser.: C-1830). 1994. pap. 39.95 (*0-8373-1830-0*) Nat Learn.

Psychometrics for Educational Debates. International Symposium on Educational Testing (3d. Ed. by Leo J. Van der Kamp et al. LC 79-4308. 347p. reprint ed. pap. 107.60 (*0-608-18846-8*, 203044200069) Bks Demand.

Psychometry: Reading by Vibration. Alexander Verner & Swami Brahma. reprint ed. pap. 2.00 (*0-911662-15-4*) Yoga.

Psychometry: The Science of Touch. Beverly C. Jaegers. (Illus.). 125p. 1985. pap. text 6.00 (*0-317-20489-0*) Aries Prod.

Psychomotor Domain: Movement Behaviors. Ed. by Robert N. Singer. LC 72-79355. (Illus.). 429p. (C). reprint ed. pap. 133.00 (*0-8357-9417-2*, 201458200093) Bks Demand.

Psychomotor Domain & the Seriously Handicapped. 3rd ed. Ed. by Paul Jansma. (Illus.). 520p. 1989. pap. text 42.00 (*0-8191-7240-5*) U Pr of Amer.

Psychomotor Domain Training & Serious Disabilities. 4th ed. Paul Jansma. LC 93-19856. (Illus.). 408p. (Orig.). (C). 1993. pap. text 39.50 (*0-8191-9163-9*); lib. bdg. 69.50 (*0-8191-9170-1*) U Pr of Amer.

***Psychomotor Domain Training & Serious Disabilities.** 5th ed. Ed. by Paul Jansma. LC 99-33749. 528p. (Orig.). 1999. pap. 52.50 (*0-7618-1469-8*) U Pr of Amer.

Psychomotor Performances: Medical & Psychological Subject Index with Bibliography. Katie L. Holt. LC 88-47606. 150p. 1988. 44.50 (*0-88164-740-3*); pap. 39.50 (*0-88164-741-1*) ABBE Pubs Assn.

Psychonavigation see Psiconavegacion: Tecnicas Para Viajar Ma's All a Del Tiempo

Psychonavigation: Techniques for Travel Beyond Time. expanded rev. ed. John Perkins. (Orig.). 1999. pap. 12.95 (*0-89281-800-X*) Inner Tradit.

Psychonephrology Vol. 1: Psychological Factors in Hemodialysis & Transplantation. Ed. by Norman B. Levy. LC 80-20681. 306p. 1981. 75.00 (*0-306-40586-5*, Plenum Trade) Perseus Pubng.

Psychonephrology Vol. 2: Psychological Problems in Kidney Failure & Their Treatment. Ed. by Norman B. Levy. LC 83-8015. 312p. 1983. 85.00 (*0-306-41154-7*, Plenum Trade) Perseus Pubng.

***Psychoneural Reduction: The New Wave.** John Bickle. LC 97-28252. (Illus.). 372p. 1998. 35.00 (*0-262-02432-2*, Bradford Bks) MIT Pr.

Psychoneuroendocrine Dysfunction. Ed. by Nandkumar S. Shah & Alexander G. Donald. LC 83-19202. 660p. 1984. 140.00 (*0-306-41320-5*, Plenum Trade) Perseus Pubng.

Psychoneuroendocrinology. Ed. by C. S. Holmes. (Illus.). xiii, 359p. 1989. 112.00 (*0-387-97112-2*) Spr-Verlag.

Psychoneuroendocrinology: Proceedings. Conference of the International Society for Psycho. Ed. by Noboru Hatotani. (Illus.). 450p. 1974. 116.75 (*3-8055-1711-4*) S Karger.

Psychoneuroendocrinology & Abnormal Behavior. Ed. by Julien Mendlewicz. (Advances in Biological Psychiatry Ser.: Vol. 5). (Illus.). vi, 130p. 1980. pap. 50.50 (*3-8055-0599-X*) S Karger.

Psychoneuroendocrinology of Aging. Ed. by G. Valenti. (FIDIA Research Ser.: Vol. 16). 175p. 1989. 70.00 (*0-387-96943-8*) Spr-Verlag.

Psychoneuroimmunology. 2nd ed. Ed. by Robert Ader et al. 1218p. 1990. text 210.00 (*0-12-043782-1*) Acad Pr.

***Psychoneuroimmunology: An Interdisciplinary Introduction.** Manfred Schedlowski & Uwe Tewes. LC 99-38184. 535p. 1999. pap. write for info. (*0-306-45976-0*, Kluwer Plenum) Kluwer Academic.

***Psychoneuroimmunology: An Interdisciplinary Introduction.** Manfred Schedlowski & Uwe Tewes. LC 99-38184. 1999. pap. write for info. (*0-306-45975-2*, Kluwer Plenum) Kluwer Academic.

Psychoneuroimmunology: Interactions Between Brain, Nervous System, Behavior, Endocrine & Immune System. Ed. by H. J. Schmoll et al. LC 91-35385. (Illus.). 276p. 1992. text 34.00 (*0-88937-066-4*) Hogrefe & Huber Pubs.

Psychoneuroimmunology: Stress, Mental Disorders, & Health. Ed. by Karl Goodkin & Adriaan P. Visser. LC 98-51393. (Progress in Psychiatry Ser.: No. 59). 1999. 55.00 (*0-88048-171-4*, 8171) Am Psychiatric.

Psychoneuroimmunology, Stress, & Infection. Ed. by Herman Friedman et al. 304p. 1995. boxed set 179.95 (*0-8493-7638-6*, 7638) CRC Pr.

Psychoneuroses & Their Treatment by Psychotherapy. Joseph J. Dejerine & E. Gauckler. Tr. by Smith E. Jelliffe. LC 75-16697. (Classics in Psychiatry Ser.). 1976. reprint ed. 34.95 (*0-405-07425-5*) Ayer.

Psychoneurosis, Organic Brain Disease, Psychopharmacology see Teaching Program in Psychiatry

Psychopath in Film. Wayne Wilson. LC 98-49824. 328p. 1999. 49.00 (*0-7618-1316-0*); pap. 34.50 (*0-7618-1317-9*) U Pr of Amer.

Psychopathia Sexualis. Von Krafft & Richard Ebing. LC 98-13156. 464p. 1998. pap. 19.45 (*1-55970-425-X*, Pub. by Arcade Pub Inc) Time Warner.

Psychopathia Sexualis. John P. Shanley. LC 98-158142. 1998. pap. 5.25 (*0-8222-1615-9*) Dramatists Play.

Psychopathia Sexualis. Richard Von Krafft-Ebbing. Ed. & Tr. by Jack D. Hunter from GER. (Velvet Ser.). 256p. 1997. pap. 14.95 (*1-871592-55-0*) Creation Books.

Psychopathia Sexualis. Richard Von Krafft-Ebing. Tr. by Franklin S. Klaf from GER. LC 98-13156. 464p. 1998. pap. 40.00 (*1-55970-426-8*, Pub. by Arcade Pub Inc) Time Warner.

Psychopathia Sexualis: A Clinical-Forensic Study. unabridged ed. Richard Von Krafft-Ebing. Ed. by Brian King. 712p. 1998. pap. 16.50 (*0-9650324-1-8*) Bloat.

Psychopathic Behaviour: Approaches to Research. Ed. by Robert D. Hare & D. Schalling. LC 77-22873. 406p. reprint ed. pap. 125.90 (*0-608-17647-8*, 203050500069) Bks Demand.

Psychopathic God: Adolf Hitler. Robert G. Waite. LC 92-36790. (Illus.). 512p. 1993. reprint ed. pap. 15.95 (*0-306-80514-6*) Da Capo.

Psychopathic Mind: Origins, Dynamics, & Treatment. J. Reid Meloy. LC 88-3454. 496p. 1988. 60.00 (*0-87668-922-5*) Aronson.

Psychopathic Personality Commitment Law: A Study of Its Implementation in Minnesota. Marlys McPherson. (Illus.). 48p. 1997. reprint ed. pap. text 25.00 (*0-7881-4707-2*) DIANE Pub.

Psychopathic Racial Personality: And Other Essays. Bobby E. Wright. LC 97-2889. 40p. (Orig.). 1985. pap. 6.95 (*0-88378-071-2*) Third World.

Psychopathological & Neurological Dysfunctions Following Open-Heart Surgery, Milwaukee 1980: Proceedings. Ed. by R. Becker et al. (Illus.). 384p. 1983. 103.00 (*0-387-11621-4*) Spr-Verlag.

Psychopathological Art, 1948-1950. Karel Appel. (Illus.). 1998. 120.00 (*3-906127-52-4*, Pub. by Gachnang & Springer) Dist Art Pubs.

Psychopathological Disorders of Childhood. 3rd ed. Ed. by Herbert C. Quay & John S. Werry. LC 86-11105. 704p. 1986. text 89.95 (*0-471-88974-1*) Wiley.

Psychopathological Notebook: Drawings & Gouaches 1948-1950. Karel Appel. 200p. 1999. pap. text 65.00 (*3-906127-57-5*) Gachnang & Springer.

Psychopathologie de la Vie Quotidienne. Sigmund Freud. (FRE.). 1989. pap. 24.95 (*0-7859-3039-6*) Fr & Eur.

Psychopathologies & Treatments. (C). 1991. 35.20 (*0-536-57918-0*) Pearson Custom.

***Psychopathology.** John D. Stirling. LC 98-33124. (Modular Psychology Ser.). 1999. 40.00 (*0-415-19270-6*); pap. 12.99 (*0-415-19271-4*) Routledge.

Psychopathology. L. Willerman & D. B. Cohen. (C). 1989. pap. text 21.87 (*0-07-070312-4*) McGraw.

Psychopathology. L. Willerman & D. B. Cohen. 350p. (C). 1989. 56.56 (*0-07-070311-6*) McGraw.

Psychopathology. Edward J. Kempf. LC 75-16711. (Classics in Psychiatry Ser.). (Illus.). 1976. reprint ed. 65.95 (*0-405-07440-9*) Ayer.

Psychopathology: A Case Book. Robert L. Spitzer. (Illus.). 352p. (C). 1983. 54.06 (*0-07-060350-2*) McGraw.

Psychopathology: A Competency Based Model for Social Work. Zide. (Social Work Ser.). 2000. pap. 40.00 (*0-534-36766-6*) Brooks-Cole.

Psychopathology: A Source Book. Ed. by Charles F. Reed et al. LC 58-10405. (Illus.). 815p. 1958. 77.50 (*0-674-72200-0*) HUP.

Psychopathology: Contemporary Jungian Perspectives. Ed. by Andrew Samuels. LC 91-12646. 355p. 1991. reprint ed. lib. bdg. 42.00 (*0-89862-765-6*) Guilford Pubns.

Psychopathology: Contemporary Jungian Perspectives. Ed. by Andrew Samuels. LC 91-12646. 355p. 1992. reprint ed. pap. text 26.00 (*0-89862-473-8*) Guilford Pubns.

Psychopathology: Its Causes & Symptoms. rev. ed. Frederick K. Taylor. LC 78-31648. 372p. reprint ed. pap. 115.40 (*0-608-16419-4*, 202670400051) Bks Demand.

Psychopathology: The Evolving Sciences of Mental Disorder. Ed. by Steven Matthysse et al. (Illus.). 647p. (C). 1996. text 69.95 (*0-521-44469-1*) Cambridge U Pr.

Psychopathology among Mentally Retarded Children & Adolescents. Johnny L. Matson & Cynthia L. Frame. LC 85-14388. (Developmental Clinical Psychology & Psychiatry Ser.: No. 6). 119p. (Orig.). 1986. reprint ed. pap. 36.90 (*0-608-01463-X*, 205950700001) Bks Demand.

Psychopathology & Adaptation in Infancy & Early Childhood. Stanley I. Greenspan. LC 81-19282. (Clinical Infant Reports: No. 1). 263p. 1983. 42.00 (*0-8236-5660-8*) Intl Univs Pr.

Psychopathology & Addictive Disorders. Ed. by Roger E. Meyer. LC 85-30547. 384p. 1986. lib. bdg. 47.50 (*0-89862-680-3*) Guilford Pubns.

Psychopathology & Cognition. Ed. by Keith Dobson & Philip C. Kendall. LC 93-19571. (Personality, Psychopathology & Psychotherapy Ser.). (Illus.). 492p. 1993. text 65.00 (*0-12-404175-2*) Acad Pr.

Psychopathology & Differential Diagnosis: A Primer, 2 vols., Set. Henry Kellerman & Anthony Burry. (Personality, Psychopathology & Psychotherapy: Theoretical & Clinical Perspectives Ser.). 1989. text 87.50 (*0-231-06702-X*) Col U Pr.

Psychopathology & Differential Diagnosis - A Primer Vol. 2: Diagnosis. Henry Kellerman & Anthony Burry. (Personality, Psychopathology & Psychotherapy: Theoretical & Clinical Perspectives Ser.). 250p. 1989. text 52.50 (*0-231-06704-6*) Col U Pr.

Psychopathology & Education of the Brain-Injured Child. Lehtinen Straus. Incl. Vol. I. Fundamentals & Treatment. (Illus.). 206p. 1953. text 42.00 (*0-8089-0487-6*, 794391, W B Saunders Co); 1953. write for info. (*0-318-52864-9*, Grune & Strat) Harcrt Hlth Sci Grp.

Psychopathology & Function. 2nd ed. Bette Bonder. (Illus.). 304p. 1995. pap. 30.00 (*1-55642-270-9*, 32709) SLACK Inc.

Psychopathology & Nosology. Ed. by E. Gabriel & H. G. Zapotoczky. (Journal: Psychopathology: Vol. 8, No. 2-3, 1985). 124p. 1985. pap. 65.25 (*3-8055-4218-6*) S Karger.

Psychopathology & Pictorial Expression, Vol. IV. Ed. by Sandoz. (Series 19-22, & 25). (Illus.). 1978. boxed set 104.50 (*3-8055-2929-5*) S Karger.

Psychopathology & Political Leadership. Ed. by Robert S. Robins. LC 77-85747. (Tulane Studies in Political Science: Vol. 16). 212p. 1977. reprint ed. pap. 65.80 (*0-608-00824-9*, 206161300010) Bks Demand.

Psychopathology & Political Leadership, Vol. 16. R. S. Robins et al. LC 77-85747. 1977. pap. text 11.00 (*0-930598-16-4*) Tulane Stud Pol.

Psychopathology & Politics. Harold D. Lasswell. xxvi, 368p. 1986. pap. text 23.00 (*0-226-46919-0*) U Ch Pr.

Psychopathology & Psychiatry. Anna Pavlova. LC 93-5454. 550p. (C). 1993. pap. text 29.95 (*1-56000-707-9*) Transaction Pubs.

Psychopathology & Psychopharmacology: Proceedings of the Sixty-Second Annual Meeting. American Psychopathological Association Staff. Ed. by Jonathan O. Cole et al. LC 72-12347. 312p. reprint ed. pap. 96.80 (*0-608-14755-9*, 202309100032) Bks Demand.

Psychopathology & Psychotherapy in Homosexuality. Ed. by Michael Ross. LC 87-29894. (Journal of Homosexuality: Vol. 15, Nos. 1-2). 222p. 1988. text 49.95 (*0-86656-499-3*) Haworth Pr.

Psychopathology & the Brain. Ed. by Bernard J. Carroll & James E. Barrett. (American Psychopathological Association Ser.). 312p. 1991. text 138.50 (*0-88167-802-3*) Lppncott W & W.

Psychopathology & the Brain. Ed. by Bernard J. Carroll & James E. Barrett. LC 91-14227. (American Psychopathological Association Ser.). (Illus.). 315p. reprint ed. pap. 97.70 (*0-608-09744-6*, 206991300007) Bks Demand.

Psychopathology & Violent Crime. Ed. by Andrew E. Skodol. LC 97-51790. (Review Ser.). 156p. 1998. pap. text 27.00 (*0-88048-834-4*, 8834) Am Psychiatric.

Psychopathology in Adulthood. 2nd ed. Ed. by Michel Hersen & Alan S. Bellack. LC 99-25834. 481p. (C). 1999. 56.95 (*0-205-20027-3*) Allyn.

Psychopathology in Persons with Mental Retardation: Clinical Guidelines for Assessment & Treatment. Christine M. Nezu et al. LC 92-61116. 342p. (Orig.). 1992. pap. text 24.95 (*0-87822-328-2*, 4625) Res Press.

Psychopathology in the Mentally Retarded. Ed. by Johnny L. Matson. 312p. (C). 1991. write for info. (*0-205-13463-7*) Allyn.

Psychopathology of Childhood: A Clinical-Experimental Approach. 3rd ed. Schwartz. (C). 2000. 42.95 (*0-205-17523-6*, Macmillan Coll) P-H.

Psychopathology of Childhood & Adolescence. (C). 1997. text 24.00 (*0-673-55842-8*, GoodYrBooks) Addson-Wesley Educ.

Psychopathology of Crime: Criminal Behavior As a Clinical Disorder. Adrian Raine. LC 93-911. (Illus.). 377p. 1993. text 69.95 (*0-12-576160-0*) Acad Pr.

Psychopathology of Crime: Criminal Behavior As a Clinical Disorder. Adrian Raine. (Illus.). 377p. 1997. reprint ed. pap. text 44.95 (*0-12-576155-4*) Morgan Kaufmann.

Psychopathology of Everyday Racism & Sexism. Ed. by Lenora Fulani. LC 88-6159. (Women & Therapy Ser.: Vol. 6, No. 4). 120p. 1994. text 9.95 (*0-918393-51-5*, Harrington Park) Haworth Pr.

Psychopathology of Language & Cognition. Harold J. Vetter & R. W. Rieber. LC 94-44347. (Cognition & Language Ser.). (Illus.). 212p. (C). 1995. 49.50 (*0-306-44757-6*, Plenum Trade) Perseus Pubng.

Psychopathology of Perception: Proceedings of the Third Leeds Psychopathology Symposium, September 1988 - Psychopathology Journal, Vol. 24, No. 6. Ed. by A. M. Mortimer & K. J. Rix. (Illus.). 36p. 1991. pap. 55.00 (*3-8055-5536-9*) S Karger.

Psychopathology of Serial Murder: A Theory of Violence. Stephen J. Giannangelo. LC 96-10437. (Criminology & Crime Control Policy Ser.). 136p. 1996. 55.00 (*0-275-95434-X*, Praeger Pubs) Greenwood.

Psychopathology Today: The Current Status of Abnormal Psychology. 3rd ed. Ed. by William S. Sahakian et al. LC 84-61421. 595p. reprint ed. pap. 184.50 (*0-7837-1432-7*, 204180900023) Bks Demand.

Psychopath's Bible. Christopher S. Hyatt. LC 94-69287. 112p. 1999. pap. 12.95 (*1-56184-122-6*) New Falcon Pubns.

Psychopathy: A History of the Concepts. Henry Werlinder. 218p. 1978. pap. text 37.50 (*91-554-0782-X*) Coronet Bks.

Psychopathy: Antisocial, Criminal & Violent Behavior. Ed. by Theodore Millon et al. LC 98-6845. 476p. 1998. lib. bdg. 60.00 (*1-57230-344-1*, C0344) Guilford Pubns.

Psychopathy: Theory, Research & Implications for Society. Cooke. 1998. pap. text 97.50 (*0-7923-4920-2*) Kluwer Academic.

Psychopathy: Theory, Research & Implications for Society, Alvor, Portugal, November 29-December 7, 1995. Ed. by David J. Cooke et al. LC 97-49859. (NATO ASI Ser., Series D, Behavioural & Social Sciences). 428p. 1998. 194.00 (*0-7923-4919-9*) Kluwer Academic.

Psychopharmaco-Endocrinology & Depression Research. G. Laakmann. (Illus.). xii, 219p. 1990. 79.95 (*0-387-52075-9*) Spr-Verlag.

Psychopharmacological Agents, 3 vols. Ed. by Maxwell Gordon. Incl. Vol. 1. 1964. 90.00 (*0-12-290550-4*); Vol. 2. 1967. 80.00 (*0-12-290556-3*); Vol. 3. 1974. 80.00 (*0-12-290558-X*); (Medicinal Chemistry Ser.). write for info. (*0-318-50351-4*) Acad Pr.

Psychopharmacologic Treatment: Theory & Practice: Proceedings of a Symposium on Psychopharmacologic Treatment in Psychiatry, University of Florida, College of Medicine, Departments of Psychiatry & Pharmacology, Gainesville, Florida. Symposium on Psychopharmacologic Treatment in Psyc. Ed. by Herman C. Denber. LC 74-78968. (Modern Pharmacology-Toxicology Ser.: No. 2). (Illus.). 313p. reprint ed. pap. 97.10 (*0-7837-0778-9*, 204109200019) Bks Demand.

Psychopharmacologists, Vol. 2. David Healy. 672p. 1998. pap. text 78.50 (*1-86036-010-6*, Pub. by E A) OUP.

Psychopharmacology. Ed. by Alan A. Boulton et al. LC 88-32813. (Neuromethods Ser.: Vol. 13). (Illus.). 836p. 1989. 129.50 (*0-89603-129-2*) Humana.

Psychopharmacology. Ed. by Geroge. (C). 1999. text. write for info. (*0-321-01394-8*) Addson-Wesley Educ.

Psychopharmacology: An Introduction. 3rd ed. Rene Spiegel. Tr. by Terry Watson from GER. LC 95-32202. (Medical Publications).Tr. of Einfuhrung in die Psychopharmakologie. 312p. 1996. 159.95 (*0-471-95729-1*) Wiley.

Psychopharmacology: Basic Mechanisms & Applied Interventions. Ed. by John Grabowski & Gary R. VandenBos. 207p. (Orig.). 1992. pap. 24.95 (*1-55798-158-2*) Am Psychol.

P

An Asterisk (*) at the beginning of an entry indicates that the title is appearing for the first time.

Psychopharmacology: Basics for Counselors. Gregory L. Little. (Illus.). 279p. (C). 1996. pap. text 24.95 (*0-9655392-0-2*) Advanced Trnging.

Psychopharmacology: The Fourth Generation of Progress. 4th ed. Ed. by David J. Kupfer & Floyd E. Bloom. LC 94-7409. 2048p. 1994. text 186.00 (*0-7817-0166-X*) Lppncott W & W.

Psychopharmacology: The Third Generation of Progress in Association with the American College of Neuropsychopharmacology. Ed. by Herbert Y. Meltzer et al. LC 85-43136. 1824p. 1987. reprint ed. pap. 200.00 (*0-608-03430-4*, 206413100008) Bks Demand.

Psychopharmacology & Drug Treatment of Schizophrenia. Ed. by Philip B. Bradley & S. R. Hirsch. (British Association for Psychopharmacology Monographs). (Illus.). 475p. 1986. 95.00 (*0-19-261260-3*) OUP.

Psychopharmacology & Psychobiology of Ethnicity. Ed. by Keh-Ming Lin et al. LC 92-49996. (Progress in Psychiatry Ser.: No. 39). 276p. 1993. text 29.95 (*0-88048-471-3*, 8471) Am Psychiatric.

Psychopharmacology & Psychotherapy: A Collaborative Approach. Ed. by Michelle B. Riba & Richard Balon. 1999. 36.45 (*0-88048-913-8*, 8913) Am Psychiatric.

Psychopharmacology & Psychotherapy: Strategies for Maximizing Treatment Outcomes. Len Sperry. LC 95-21881. (Mental Health Practice under Managed Care Ser.: No. 1). 208p. 1995. text 22.95 (*0-87630-787-X*) Brunner-Mazel.

Psychopharmacology & Psychotherapy: Synthesis or Antithesis? Ed. by Norman Rosenzweig & Hilda Griscon. LC 78-4088. 256p. 1978. 35.95 (*0-87705-354-5*, Kluwer Acad Hman Sci) Kluwer Academic.

Psychopharmacology & Women: Sex, Gender, & Hormones. Ed. by Margaret F. Jensvold et al. 615p. 1996. text 69.95 (*0-88048-545-0*, 8545) Am Psychiatric.

Psychopharmacology Consultation. Ed. by David C. Jimerson & John P. Docherty. LC 86-14136. (Clinical Insights Ser.). 141p. reprint ed. pap. 43.80 (*0-8357-2810-2*, 203623500011) Bks Demand.

***Psychopharmacology Desktop Reference.** Ed. by Stephen Saklad. 1999. pap. 149.00 (*1-884937-61-6*) Manisses Communs.

Psychopharmacology for Everyday Practice. T. A. Ban & M. H. Hollender. x, 198p. 1981. pap. 32.75 (*3-8055-2241-X*) S Karger.

Psychopharmacology for Psychotherapists & Counselors. Brems. (Counseling Ser.). 2001. 25.00 (*0-534-53065-6*) Wadsworth Pub.

Psychopharmacology for the Aged. Ed. by T. H. Ban. xii, 216p. 1980. pap. 34.00 (*3-8055-1204-X*) S Karger.

Psychopharmacology from a Feminist Perspective. Ed. by Jean A. Hamilton et al. LC 95-14408. 137p. 1995. 39.95 (*1-56024-684-7*); pap. 14.95 (*1-56023-059-2*, Harrington Park) Haworth Pr.

Psychopharmacology of Addiction. Ed. by Malcolm H. Lader. (British Association for Psychopharmacology Monographs: No. 10). (Illus.). 192p. 1988. 55.00 (*0-19-261626-9*) OUP.

Psychopharmacology of Aggression. Ed. by F. A. Freyhan et al. (Modern Problems of Pharmacopsychiatry Ser.: Vol. 13). (Illus.). 1978. 68.00 (*3-8055-2751-9*) S Karger.

Psychopharmacology of Aggression. Ed. by Merton Sandler. LC 79-62973. (Illus.). 247p. 1979. reprint ed. pap. 76.60 (*0-7837-9525-4*, 206027400005) Bks Demand.

Psychopharmacology of Aging. Carl Eisdorfer. Ed. by W. E. Fann. (Illus.). 327p. 1980. text 55.00 (*0-88331-190-9*) R B Luce.

Psychopharmacology of Animal Behavior Disorders. Nicholas H. Dodman & Louis Shuster. LC 97-27824. (Illus.). 1998. 78.95 (*0-632-04358-X*) Blackwell Sci.

***Psychopharmacology of Antipsychotics.** Stephen M. Stahl. 148p. 1999. 24.95 (*1-85317-601-X*) Martin Dunitz.

Psychopharmacology of Anxiolytics & Antidepressants. Ed. by Sandra E. File. (International Encyclopedia of Pharmacology & Therapeutics Ser.: 136). (Illus.). 284p. 1991. 128.00 (*0-08-040698-X*, Pub. by PPI) Elsevier.

Psychopharmacology of Childhood. Ed. by D. Siva Sankar. LC 74-27253. 1976. 49.95 (*0-915340-00-3*) PJD Pubns.

Psychopharmacology of Cognitive & Psychiatric Disorders in the Elderly. 2nd ed. LC 97-69680. (Illus.). 240p. 1997. text 55.00 (*0-412-82470-1*, Pub. by E A) OUP.

Psychopharmacology of Depression. Ed. by Stuart A. Montgomery & Tim H. Corn. LC 93-44896. (British Association for Psychopharmacology Monographs: No. 13). 272p. (C). 1994. 98.50 (*0-19-262278-1*) OUP.

Psychopharmacology of Panic. Ed. by Stuart A. Montgomery. LC 92-16486. (British Association for Psychopharmacology Monographs: No. 12). (Illus.). 160p. 1993. text 47.50 (*0-19-262087-8*) OUP.

***Psychopharmacology of Schizophrenia.** Ed. by Michael A. Reveley & J. F. William Deakin. (An Arnold Publication). 2000. 55.00 (*0-340-75912-7*, Pub. by E A) OUP.

Psychopharmacology of Sleep. Ed. by David Wheatley. LC 81-17926. 256p. 1981. reprint ed. pap. 79.40 (*0-608-00422-7*, 206113700007) Bks Demand.

Psychopharmacology of the Developmental Disabilities. Ed. by Michael G. Aman & N. N. Singh. (Disorders of Human Learning, Behavior, & Communication Ser.). (Illus.). 235p. 1988. 96.95 (*0-387-96679-X*) Spr-Verlag.

Psychopharmacology of the Limbic System. Ed. by Michael R. Trimble & E. Zarifian. (Illus.). 280p. 1985. pap. 29.95 (*0-19-261575-0*) OUP.

***Psychopharmacology Sourcebook.** Mark Zetin. 272p. 2000. pap. 17.95 (*0-7373-0266-6*, 02666W) NTC Contemp Pub Co.

Psychophysical & Physiological Advances in Hearing: Proceedings of the 11th International Symposium on Hearing, Grantham, U. K., 1-6th August, 1997. International Symposium on Hearing Staff. Ed. by A. R. Palmer. LC 98-150714. iii, 614 p. 1998. write for info. (*1-86156-069-9*) Whurr Pub.

Psychophysical Approaches to Cognition. Ed. by Daniel Algom. LC 92-19503. (Advances in Psychology Ser.: Vol. 92). 628p. 1992. 192.00 (*0-444-88978-7*, North Holland) Elsevier.

Psychophysical Elements in Parapsychological Traditions. A. Tanagras. LC 67-19168. (Parapsychological Monographs: No. 7). 1967. pap. 6.00 (*0-912328-10-X*) Parapsych Foun.

Psychophysical Explorations of Mental Structures: Selected Papers of the Centennial Symposium in Honor of Gustav Theodor Fechner. Ed. by Hans-Georg Geissler et al. LC 90-4265. (Illus.). 560p. 1990. text 79.00 (*0-88937-031-1*) Hogrefe & Huber Pubs.

Psychophysical Physiological & Behavioral Studies in Hearing: Proceedings of the International Symposium on Hearing, 5th, Noordwijkerhout, the Netherlands, April 8-12, 1980. International Symposium on Hearing Staff. Ed. by G. Van Den Brink & F. A. Bilsen. 480p. 1980. lib. bdg. 132.00 (*90-286-0780-3*) Kluwer Academic.

Psychophysics: Introduction to Its Perceptual, Neural, & Social Prospects. S. S. Stevens. 335p. 1986. reprint ed. pap. text 24.95 (*0-88738-643-1*) Transaction Pubs.

Psychophysics: Introduction to Its Perceptual, Neural, & Social Prospects. Stanley S. Stevens. Ed. by Geraldine Stevens. LC 74-13473. 336p. reprint ed. pap. 104.20 (*0-608-13395-7*, 202249300027) Bks Demand.

Psychophysics: Method, Theory, & Application. 2nd ed. George A. Gescheider. 304p. (C). 1984. text 49.95 (*0-89859-375-1*) L Erlbaum Assocs.

Psychophysics: The Fundamentals. 3rd ed. George A. Gescheider. LC 96-41791. 424p. 1997. 49.95 (*0-8058-2281-X*) L Erlbaum Assocs.

Psychophysics in Action. Ed. by G. Ljunggren & S. Dornic. (Illus.). 170p. 1989. 77.95 (*0-387-50686-1*) Spr-Verlag.

Psychophysics, Physiology & Models of Hearing: Oldenburg, Germany 31 August - 4 September 1998. Dau Torsten. 1999. 101.00 (*981-02-3741-3*) World Scientific Pub.

Psychophysiological Aspects of Reading & Learning. Victor Rentel et al. (Monographs in Psychobiology). xx, 352p. 1985. text 174.00 (*2-88124-000-3*); pap. text 83.00 (*2-88124-025-9*) Gordon & Breach.

Psychophysiological Disorders: Research & Clinical Applications. Ed. by Robert J. Gatchel & Edward B. Blanchard. (Application & Practice in Health Psychology Ser.). (Illus.). 483p. 1993. pap. 29.95 (*1-55798-523-5*) Am Psychol.

Psychophysiological Measurement of Covert Behavior: A Guide for the Laboratory. Frank J. McGuigan. LC 79-18482. (Illus.). 143p. reprint ed. pap. 44.40 (*0-8357-4208-3*, 203698500003) Bks Demand.

***Psychophysiological Recording.** 2nd ed. LC 99-49560. 272p. 2000. text 50.00 (*0-19-511358-6*); pap. text 24.95 (*0-19-511359-4*) OUP.

Psychophysiology: Human Behavior & Physiological Response. 2nd ed. John L. Andreassi. 488p. 1989. pap. 34.50 (*0-8058-0180-4*) L Erlbaum Assocs.

Psychophysiology: Human Behavior & Physiological Response. 3rd ed. John L. Andreassi. 400p. 1995. pap. 55.00 (*0-8058-1104-4*); text 99.95 (*0-8058-1103-6*) L Erlbaum Assocs.

Psychophysiology: Human Behavior & Physiological Response. 4th ed. John L. Andreassi. LC 99-41207. 450p. 2000. pap. text. write for info. (*0-8058-2833-8*) L Erlbaum Assocs.

***Psychophysiology: Human Behavior & Physiological Response.** 4th ed. John L. Andreassi. LC 99-41207. 450p. 2000. write for info. (*0-8058-2832-X*) L Erlbaum Assocs.

Psychophysiology: The Mind-Body Perspective. Kenneth Hugdahl. (Perspectives in Cognitive Neuroscience Ser.). (Illus.). 448p. (C). 1996. 56.00 (*0-674-72207-8*) HUP.

Psychophysiology & the Electronic Workplace. Ed. by Anthony Gale & Bruce Christie. LC 87-2148. (Illus.). 361p. 1987. reprint ed. pap. 112.00 (*0-608-05273-6*, 206581100001) Bks Demand.

Psychophysiology for Clinical Psychologists. Walter W. Surwillo. Ed. by Glenn R. Caddy. LC 90-37389. (Developments in Clinical Psychology Ser.). 192p. (C). 1990. text 73.25 (*0-89391-679-X*) Ablx Pub.

Psychophysiology of Low Back Pain. Adams. 1997. text 36.95 (*0-443-05259-X*, W B Saunders Co) Harcrt Hlth Sci Grp.

Psychophysiology of Mental Imagery: Theory, Research, & Application. Ed. by Robert G. Kunzendorf & Anees A. Sheikh. (Imagery & Human Development Ser.). 236p. 1990. text 35.95 (*0-89503-063-2*); pap. text 26.97 (*0-89503-062-4*) Baywood Pub.

Psychophysiology of the Gastrointestinal Tract: Experimental & Clinical Applications. Ed. by Rupert Holzl & William E. Whitehead. 390p. 1983. 85.00 (*0-306-41089-3*, Plenum Trade) Perseus Pubng.

Psychophysiology of Visual Masking: The Fine Structure of Conscious Experience, Horizons in Psychology. T. Bachmann. LC 93-19895. 191p. (C). 1994. pap. text 125.00 (*1-56072-066-2*) Nova Sci Pubs.

Psychophysiology Today & Tomorrow. N. P. Bechtereva. 1981. 126.00 (*0-08-025930-8*, Pub. by Pergamon Repr) Franklin.

Psychopup: Ant Other Stories. Janice Knapp. 1999. pap. 13.95 (*0-88739-181-8*) Creat Arts Bk.

Psychos, Sickos, & Sequels: Horror Films of the 1980s. John Stell. LC 97-76026. (Illus.). 320p. 1998. pap. 20.00 (*1-887664-16-5*) Midnght Marquee Pr.

Psychosemantics: The Problem of Meaning in the Philosophy of Mind. Jerry A. Fodor. (Explorations in Cognitive Science Ser.: Vol. 2). 192p. 1989. reprint ed. pap. text 12.50 (*0-262-56052-6*, Bradford Bks) MIT Pr.

Psychoses. Jacques Lacan. Date not set. 24.95 (*0-393-01925-X*) Norton.

Psychoses & Pervasive Developmental Disorders in Childhood & Adolescence. Ed. by Fred R. Volkmar. 368p. 1996. text 48.50 (*1-882103-01-7*, 0301) Am Psychiatric.

Psychoses of Epilepsy. Michael R. Trimble. 224p. 1991. text 76.00 (*0-88167-739-6*, 2215) Lppncott W & W.

Psychoses of Power: African Personal Dictatorships. 2nd rev. ed. Samuel Decalo. LC 97-75225. (African Studies Ser.: Vol. 3). 320p. 1998. 49.95 (*1-890357-02-2*, SAN 299-3643) Fla Acad Pr.

Psychoses of the Schizophrenic Spectrum in Twins: A Discussion on the Nature-Nurture Debate in the Etiology of "Endogenous" Psychoses. Ernest Franzek & H. Beckmann. LC 99-25477. 200p. 1999. pap. 49.95 (*3-211-83298-X*) Spr-Verlag.

Psychosexual Imperatives: Their Role in Identity Formation. Ed. by Marie C. Nelson & Jean Ikenberry. LC 78-17739. (Self-in-Process Ser.: Vol. 2). 397p. 1979. 45.95 (*0-87705-302-2*, Kluwer Acad Hman Sci) Kluwer Academic.

Psychosexual Medicine: A Study of Underlying Themes. Lincoln. 230p. 1992. pap. 47.75 (*1-56593-049-5*, 0297) Thomson Learn.

Psychosexual Therapy: A Cognitive Behavioural Approach. S. H. Spence. (Illus.). 224p. 1991. mass mkt. 39.95 (*0-412-35450-0*, A6300) Chapman & Hall.

Psychosexual Training & the Doctor/Patient Relationship: Edited Transcripts of Leaders Workshops. R. L. Skrine. (Illus.). 390p. (Orig.). 1995. pap. 34.95 (*1-56593-785-6*, 1532) Singular Publishing.

Psychosis: Ship of Fools. Charles Ryan & John Fletcher. (Illus.). 170p. (Orig.). 1995. pap. 15.00 (*0-9628748-9-2*) Chameleon Eclectic.

Psychosis: Understanding & Treatment. Ed. by Jane Ellwood. 224p. 1994. pap. 34.95 (*1-85302-265-9*) Taylor & Francis.

Psychosis & Civilization. Herbert Goldhamer & Andrew W. Marshall. Ed. by Gerald N. Grob. LC 78-22560. (Historical Issues in Mental Health Ser.). (Illus.). 1980. reprint ed. lib. bdg. 17.95 (*0-405-11914-3*) Ayer.

Psychosis & Near Psychosis: Ego Function, Symbol Structure & Treatment. Eric R. Marcus. xviii, 308p. 2000. pap. 29.95 (*0-8236-8264-1*) Intl Univs Pr.

Psychosis & Near Psychosis: Ego Function, Symbol Structure & Treatment. Eric R. Marcus. 328p. 1993. 100.00 (*0-387-97765-1*) Spr-Verlag.

Psychosis & Power: Threats to Democracy in the Self & the Group. James M. Glass. LC 94-35314. (Illus.). 230p. 1995. text 32.50 (*0-8014-3037-2*) Cornell U Pr.

Psychosis & Sexual Identity: Toward a Post-Analytic View of the Schreber Case. Ed. by David B. Allison et al. LC 87-10077. (SUNY Series, Intersections: Philosophy & Critical Theory). (Illus.). 343p. 1988. pap. text 24.95 (*0-88706-617-8*) State U NY Pr.

***Psychosis God, Pt. 1.** Allan Picardy. 1999. pap. write for info. (*1-57553-997-7*) Watermrk Pr.

***Psychosis God, Pt. 2.** Allan Picardy. 1999. pap. write for info. (*1-57553-998-5*) Watermrk Pr.

Psychosis in the Inner City: The Camberwell First Episode Study. David J. Castle. LC 99-159356. (Maudsley Monographs Ser.). 1998. 44.95 (*0-86377-516-0*, Pub. by Psychol Pr) Taylor & Francis.

Psychosocial Adaptation in Pregnancy: Assessment of Seven Dimensions of Maternal Development. 2nd rev. ed. Regina P. Lederman. (Illus.). 1996. 49.95 (*0-8261-6710-1*) Springer Pub.

Psychosocial Adaptation to Chronic Illness & Disability. Hanoch Livneh & Richard F. Antonak. LC 97-14138. 576p. 1997. 49.00 (*0-8342-0967-5*) Aspen Pub.

***Psychosocial & Biomedical Interactions in HIV Infection.** Kenneth H. Nott & Kav Vedhara. (Biobehavioural Perspectives on Health & Disease Prevention Ser.: Vol. 2). 288p. 2000. 58.00 (*90-5823-037-6*, Harwood Acad Pubs) Gordon & Breach.

Psychosocial & Public Health Impacts of New HIV Therapies. Ed. by D. G. Ostrow & S. C. Kalichman. LC 98-56536. (AIDS Prevention & Mental Health Ser.). (Illus.). 240p. (C). 1999. text 75.00 (*0-306-45973-6*, Kluwer Plenum) Kluwer Academic.

Psychosocial Approach to Alcoholism. Noble. (Substance & Alcohol Actions & Misuse). 1984. pap. 20.00 (*0-08-031611-5*, Pergamon Pr) Elsevier.

Psychosocial Approaches to Deeply Disturbed Persons. Ed. by Peter R. Breggin & E. Mark Stern. LC 96-12677. 231p. (C). 1996. 39.95 (*1-56024-841-6*) Haworth Pr.

Psychosocial Aspects of AIDS. 1997. lib. bdg. 250.95 (*0-8490-6078-8*) Gordon Pr.

Psychosocial Aspects of AIDS: A Bibliography & Sourcebook. 1996. lib. bdg. 252.75 (*0-8490-5985-2*) Gordon Pr.

Psychosocial Aspects of Aids: Current Bibliographies in Medicine, (Jan. '92-May '94) Peggie S. Tillman & Edward R. Turner. 52p. 1997. reprint ed. pap. text 20.00 (*0-7881-3286-5*) DIANE Pub.

Psychosocial Aspects of Cancer. Ed. by Jerome Cohen et al. LC 80-5057. Orig. Title: Research Issues in Psychological Dimensions of Cancer. 336p. 1982. reprint ed. pap. 104.20 (*0-608-03397-9*, 206409400008) Bks Demand.

Psychosocial Aspects of Cardiovascular Disease. Ed. by James Reiffel et al. LC 79-27765. 365p. 1980. 12.50 (*0-930194-32-2*) Ctr Thanatology.

Psychosocial Aspects of Chemotherapy in Cancer Care: The Patient, Family, & Staff. Ed. by Robert DeBellis et al. LC 86-33623. (Loss, Grief & Care Ser.: Vol. 1, No. 3 & 4). 136p. 1987. text 39.95 (*0-86656-627-9*) Haworth Pr.

Psychosocial Aspects of Chronic Illness & Disability among African Americans. Faye Z. Belgrave. LC 98-9635. 176p. 1998. 59.95 (*0-86569-242-4*, Auburn Hse) Greenwood.

Psychosocial Aspects of Cystic Fibrosis: A Model for Chronic Lung Disease. Ed. by Paul Patterson et al. LC 72-9893. 234p. 1973. 12.50 (*0-930194-33-0*) Ctr Thanatology.

Psychosocial Aspects of Cystic Fibrosis: A Model for Chronic Lung Disease. Ed. by Paul R. Patterson et al. LC 72-9893. 246p. reprint ed. pap. 76.30 (*0-8357-4573-2*, 203748200008) Bks Demand.

Psychosocial Aspects of Death & Dying. John Canine. 320p. (C). 1996. pap. 44.95 (*0-8385-8098-X*, A8098-4, Apple Lange Med) McGraw.

Psychosocial Aspects of Depression. Ed. by Joseph Becker & Arthur Kleinman. 272p. (C). 1990. text 89.95 (*0-8058-0079-4*) L Erlbaum Assocs.

Psychosocial Aspects of Depression: No Way Out? Lars Freden. LC 81-16444. 214p. reprint ed. pap. 66.40 (*0-8357-4614-3*, 203754600008) Bks Demand.

Psychosocial Aspects of Disability. 2nd ed. George Henderson & Willie V. Bryan. LC 96-34655. 342p. 1997. text 64.95 (*0-398-06678-7*); pap. text 49.95 (*0-398-06679-5*) C C Thomas.

Psychosocial Aspects of Disaster. Gist. LC 88-33898. (Personality Processes Ser.). 357p. 1989. 175.00 (*0-471-84894-8*) Wiley.

Psychosocial Aspects of End-Stage Renal Disease: Issues of Our Times. Mark A. Hardy et al. (Loss, Grief & Care Ser.: Vol. 5 Nos. 1 & 2). (Illus.). 216p. 1991. text 49.95 (*1-56024-149-7*) Haworth Pr.

Psychosocial Aspects of Genetics Counseling. Gerry Evers-Kieboorns et al. (Birth Defects: Original Article Ser.). 222p. 1992. 285.00 (*0-471-56185-1*, Wiley-Interscience) Wiley.

Psychosocial Aspects of HIV & AIDS & the Evaluation of Preventive Strategies: Report on a WHO Meeting. (WHO Regional Publications, European Ser.: No. 36). 45p. 1991. pap. text 10.00 (*92-890-1127-0*) World Health.

Psychosocial Aspects of Narcolepsy. Ed. by Meeta Goswami et al. LC 92-1525. (Loss, Grief & Care Ser.: Vol. 5, Nos. 3-4). 203p. 1992. 49.95 (*1-56024-222-1*) Haworth Pr.

Psychosocial Aspects of Narcolepsy. Ed. by Meeta Goswami et al. LC 92-1525. (Loss, Grief & Care Ser.: Vol. 5, Nos. 3-4). 203p. 1996. reprint ed. pap. 19.95 (*0-7890-6047-7*) Haworth Pr.

Psychosocial Aspects of Nonresponse to Antidepressant Drugs. Ed. by Uriel Halbreich & S. Shalom Feinberg. LC 86-10859. 121p. reprint ed. pap. 37.60 (*0-8357-7849-5*, 203622600002) Bks Demand.

Psychosocial Aspects of Nuclear Developments: Report. American Psychiatric Association Staff, Task Force. LC 82-71902. (American Psychiatric Association Tasl Fprce Report Ser.: No. 20). 105p. reprint ed. pap. 32.60 (*0-8357-7802-9*, 203617100002) Bks Demand.

Psychosocial Aspects of Pediatrics. Dane G. Prugh. LC 81-8289. 700p. reprint ed. pap. 200.00 (*0-7837-2741-0*, 204312100006) Bks Demand.

Psychosocial Aspects of Sickle Cell Disease: Past, Present, & Future Directions of Research. Ed. by Kermit B. Nash. LC 94-12367. (Journal of Health & Social Policy: Vol. 5, Nos. 3 & 4). (Illus.). 282p. 1994. 49.95 (*1-56024-578-6*) Haworth Pr.

***Psychosocial Aspects of the Health Care Process.** Robert J. Edelmann. LC 99-33761. 1999. pap. text. write for info. (*0-582-35724-1*) Addison-Wesley.

Psychosocial Assessment in Terminal Care. David M. Dush et al. LC 86-22801. (Hospice Journal: Vol. 2, No. 3). 150p. 1987. text 39.95 (*0-86656-461-6*) Haworth Pr.

Psychosocial Components of Occupational Therapy. Anne C. Mosey. 624p. 1986. text 53.00 (*0-89004-334-5*) Lppncott W & W.

Psychosocial Constructs of Alcoholism & Substance Abuse. Ed. by Barry Stimmel. LC 83-12615. (Advances in Alcohol & Substance Abuse Ser.: Vol. 2, No. 4). 110p. 1983. text 39.95 (*0-86656-244-3*) Haworth Pr.

Psychosocial Costs of Police Corruption. Charles Bahn. (Criminal Justice Center Monographs). 1979. pap. text 3.00 (*0-318-37483-8*) John Jay Pr.

Psychosocial Development During Adolescence: Progress in Developmental Contextualism. Gerald R. Adams et al. (Advances in Adolescent Development Ser.: Vol. 8). 346p. 1996. 37.00 (*0-7619-0532-4*) Sage.

Psychosocial Development During Adolescence: Progress in Developmental Contextualism. Gerald R. Adams et al. (Advances in Adolescent Development Ser.: Vol. 8). 346p. 1996. pap. 16.99 (*0-7619-0533-2*) Sage.

Psychosocial Development of Puerto Rican Women. Ed. by Cynthia G. Coll & Marie D. Mattei. LC 88-26047. (Illus.). 290p. 1989. 55.00 (*0-275-92345-2*, C2345, Praeger Pubs) Greenwood.

Psychosocial Dimensions of Cancer. Susan L. Groenwald. 1991. pap. 19.95 (*0-86720-303-X*) Jones & Bartlett.

Psychosocial Dimensions of Oncology Nursing Care. Ed. by Catherine Burke. LC 98-68085. 218p. 1998. pap. text 18.00 (*1-890504-06-8*) Oncology Nursing.

Psychosocial Disorders in Young People: Time Trends & Their Causes. Ed. by Michael E. Rutter & David J. Smith. LC 95-1906. (Series in Clinical Psychology). 864p. 1995. 255.00 (*0-471-95054-8*) Wiley.

Psychosocial Disturbances in Young People: Challenges for Prevention. Ed. by Michael Rutter. (Illus.). 583p. (C). 1995. text 47.95 (*0-521-46187-1*) Cambridge U Pr.

An Asterisk (*) at the beginning of an entry indicates that the title is appearing for the first time.

Psychosocial Education of Nurses: The Interpersonal Dimension. Josephine Gregory. (Nursing Ser.). 320p. 1996. 72.95 (*1-85972-345-4*, Pub. by Avebry) Ashgate Pub Co.

Psychosocial Effects of Screening for Disease Prevention & Detection. Robert T. Croyle. (Illus.). 232p. 1995. text 45.00 (*0-19-507556-0*) OUP.

Psychosocial Factors Affecting Health. Mack Lipkin, Jr. LC 82-11249. 374p. 1982. 75.00 (*0-275-91371-6*, C1371, Praeger Pubs) Greenwood.

Psychosocial Factors & Metabolic Control in Insulin-Dependent Diabetes Mellitus. Ulf Stenstrom. (Studia Psychologica et Paedagogica: No. 126). 102p. 1997. pap. 45.00 (*91-22-01739-9*, Pub. by Almqvist Wiksell) Coronet Bks.

Psychosocial Factors at Work & Their Relation to Health. C. L. Cooper. Ed. by R. Kalimo et al. 254p. 1987. pap. text 39.00 (*92-4-156102-5*, 1150264) World Health.

Psychosocial Factors in Pain: Critical Perspectives. Ed. by Robert J. Gatchel & Dennis C. Turk. LC 98-50870. 510p. 1999. lib. bdg. 62.00 (*1-57230-285-2*) Guilford Pubns.

Psychosocial Interior of the Family. 4th ed. Ed. by Gerald Handel & Gail G. Whitchurch. 704p. 1994. pap. text 38.95 (*0-202-30494-9*); lib. bdg. 66.95 (*0-202-30493-0*) Aldine de Gruyter.

Psychosocial Intervention in HIV Illness: A Stage Focused & Culture Specific Approach. Baruch Fishman & Isiah Crawford. LC 96-14097. (Cognitive-Behavioral Therapy Ser.). 1995. 40.00 (*1-56821-825-7*) Aronson.

Psychosocial Intervention in Long-Term Care: An Advanced Guide. Gary W. Hartz & D. Michael Splain. LC 96-48819. (Illus.). 219p. 1997. pap. 22.95 (*0-7890-0189-6*) Haworth Pr.

Psychosocial Intervention in Long-Term Care: An Advanced Guide. Gary W. Hartz & D. Michael Splain. LC 96-48819. (Illus.). 219p. 1997. 49.95 (*0-7890-0114-4*) Haworth Pr.

***Psychosocial Intervention with Aged African Americans--A Primer.** James H. Carter. LC 99-93821. 2000. pap. 10.95 (*0-533-13157-X*) Vantage.

Psychosocial Interventions for Cardiopulmonary Patients. Wayne M. Sotile. LC 95-35146. (Illus.). 424p. 1996. text 36.00 (*0-87322-766-2*, BSOT0766) Human Kinetics.

Psychosocial Interventions in Patients with Cancer & Coronary Heart Disease: Examples of Field Studies & Methodological Considerations. Ed. by C. L. Mulder & E. J. De Bruin. LC 93-19354. 96p. 1993. pap. 22.00 (*90-265-1349-6*) Swets.

Psychosocial Interventions in the Criminal Justice System: Proceedings (Reports Presented to the 20th Criminological Research Conference, 1993) (Collected Studies in Criminological Research: Vol. XXXI). 1995. 21.00 (*92-871-2749-2*, Pub. by Council of Europe) Manhattan Pub Co.

Psychosocial Interventions with Physically Disabled Persons. Ed. by Bruce W. Heller et al. 246p. 1992. write for info. (*1-85302-050-8*, Pub. by Jessica Kingsley); pap. write for info. (*1-85302-051-6*, Pub. by Jessica Kingsley) Taylor & Francis.

Psychosocial Interventions with Physically Disabled Persons. Ed. by Bruce W. Heller et al. (Mind & Medicine Ser.). 336p. (C). 1989. text 38.00 (*0-8135-1423-1*); pap. text 17.00 (*0-8135-1424-X*) Rutgers U Pr.

Psychosocial Issues for Children & Families in Disasters: A Guide for the Primary Care Physician. Stanford B. Friedman. (Illus.). 40p. 1996. reprint ed. pap. text 20.00 (*0-7881-3123-0*) DIANE Pub.

Psychosocial Issues in Day Care. Ed. by Shahla S. Chehrazi. LC 90-561. 292p. 1990. text 14.95 (*0-88048-310-5*, 8310) Am Psychiatric.

Psychosocial Issues in Health. Ramsden. (C). 1999. text 31.00 (*0-7020-2230-6*, Pub. by W B Saunders) Saunders.

Psychosocial Issues in Malignant Disease: Proceedings of the First Annual Conference of the British Psychosocial Oncology Group, London, 7-8 November, 1984. Ed. by M. Watson & S. Greer. LC 85-26043. 100p. 1986. 53.00 (*0-08-032010-4*, Pub. by Pergamon Repr) Franklin.

Psychosocial Issues in the Treatment of Alcoholism. Ed. by David Cook et al. LC 84-28966. (Alcoholism Treatment Quarterly Ser.: Vol. 2, No. 1). 134p. 1985. text 39.95 (*0-86656-363-6*) Haworth Pr.

Psychosocial Issues in the Treatment of Alcoholism. Ed. by David Cook et al. LC 84-28966. (Alcoholism Treatment Quarterly Ser.: Vol. 2, No. 1). 134p. 1985. pap. text 14.95 (*0-86656-401-2*) Haworth Pr.

Psychosocial Methods of Pain Management: An Interdisciplinary Team Approach. Linda C. Davisson. (Illus.). 134p. 1996. 26.50 (*1-877735-40-X*, 2302PP) Prof Prnting & Pub.

Psychosocial Nursing: Care of Physically Ill Patients & Their Families. 3rd ed. Patricia D. Barry. LC 95-40125. 624p. 1996. pap. text 31.95 (*0-397-55146-0*) Lppncott W & W.

Psychosocial Nursing Care along the Cancer Continuum. Ed. by Rose Mary Carroll-Johnson et al. LC 98-65615. (Illus.). 502p. 1998. pap. text 29.95 (*1-890504-04-1*) Oncology Nursing.

Psychosocial Nursing Handbook for the Nonpsychiatric Nurse. Linda Gorman et al. 304p. 1989. pap. text 26.00 (*0-683-03666-1*) Lppncott W & W.

***Psychosocial Occupational Therapy.** 2nd ed. Stein. 2001. pap. 48.50 (*0-7693-0032-4*) Thomson Learn.

Psychosocial Occupational Therapy: A Clinical Practice. Cara MacRae. LC 97-46388. (Teaching Methods Ser.). 704p. (C). 1997. pap. 37.95 (*0-8273-6283-8*) Delmar.

Psychosocial Occupational Therapy: A Holistic Approach. Franklin Stein & Susan K. Cutler. LC 97-51710. (Illus.). 600p. 1998. pap. 58.95 (*1-56593-925-5*, 1832) Thomson Learn.

Psychosocial Occupational Therapy: Frames of Reference for Intervention. 2nd ed. Mary A. Bruce & Barbara Borg. LC 91-52849. (Illus.). 450p. (C). 1993. pap. 37.00 (*1-55642-203-2*) SLACK Inc.

***Psychosocial Occupational Therapy: Frames of Reference Intervention.** Mary Ann Bruce & Barbara Borg. (C). 2001. pap. text 37.00 (*1-55642-494-9*) SLACK Inc.

Psychosocial Occupational Therapy: Proactive Approaches. Rita P. Cottrell. 600p. (C). 1993. pap. text 60.00 (*0-910317-96-8*) Am Occup Therapy.

Psychosocial Oncology. Houldin. 320p. write for info. (*0-7817-2020-6*) Lppncott W & W.

***Psychosocial Oncology & Palliative Care in Hong Kong: The First Decade.** Ed. by Richard Fielding & Cecilia Lai-wan Chan. 298p. 2000. pap. 32.50 (*962-209-503-8*, Pub. by HK Univ Pr) Coronet Bks.

Psychosocial Origins of Mental Retardation. Harold E. Simmons. 1980. pap. 10.00 (*0-87312-011-6*) Psychogenic Disease.

Psychosocial Perspectives on AIDS: Etiology, Prevention & Treatment. Ed. by Lydia Temoshok & Andrew Baum. 336p. 1990. 89.95 (*0-8058-0207-X*) L Erlbaum Assocs.

Psychosocial Perspectives on Donor Insemination: International Social Science Perspectives. Ed. by Ken Daniels & Erica Haimes. LC 97-40984. 192p. (C). 1998. text 59.95 (*0-521-49709-4*); pap. text 18.95 (*0-521-49783-3*) Cambridge U Pr.

Psychosocial Perspectives on Health: Implications for Research & Developing Services. Ed. by David A. Hamburg & Norman Sartorius. (Illus.). 240p. (C). 1989. text 80.00 (*0-521-36352-7*) Cambridge U Pr.

Psychosocial Processes & Health: A Reader. Ed. by Andrew Steptoe & Jane Wardle. (Illus.). 537p. (C). 1995. text 125.00 (*0-521-41610-8*); pap. text 44.95 (*0-521-42618-9*) Cambridge U Pr.

Psychosocial Research on American Indian & Alaska Native Youth: An Indexed Guide to Recent Dissertations, 1. Ed. by Spero M. Manson et al. LC 84-6583. (Bibliographies & Indexes in Psychology Ser.: No. 1). (Illus.). 228p. 1984. lib. bdg. 65.00 (*0-313-23991-6*, MPY/) Greenwood.

Psychosocial Research on Pediatric Hospitalization & Health Care: A Review of the Literature. Richard H. Thompson. (Illus.). 364p. 1985. pap. 37.95 (*0-398-06457-1*) C C Thomas.

Psychosocial Research on Pediatric Hospitalization & Health Care: A Review of the Literature. Richard H. Thompson. (Illus.). 364p. (C). 1985. 56.95 (*0-398-05070-8*) C C Thomas.

Psychosocial Resource Variables in Cancer Studies: Conceptual & Measurement Issues. Ed. by Barbara Curlow & Mark R. Somerfield. LC 95-23013. (Journal of Psychosocial Oncology: Vol. 13, No. 1-2). 216p. 1995. pap. 39.95 (*1-56024-758-4*, Hawrth Medical) Haworth Pr.

Psychosocial Spaces: Verbal-Visual Readings of British Culture, 1750-1820. Steven J. Gores. LC 99-41382. 1999. text 39.95 (*0-8143-2663-3*, Great Lks Bks) Wayne St U Pr.

Psychosocial Stress. A. Vingerhoets. xiv, 146p. 1985. pap. 24.25 (*90-265-0629-5*) Swets.

Psychosocial Stress: Perspectives on Structure, Theory, Life-Course, & Methods. Ed. by Howard B. Kaplan. LC 95-41461. (Illus.). 428p. 1996. text 59.95 (*0-12-397565-4*) Acad Pr.

Psychosocial Stress & Cancer. Ed. by Carey L. Cooper. LC 84-5264. 280p. 1985. 340.00 (*0-471-90477-5*) Wiley.

Psychosocial Studies. Ed. by Phyllis Caroff & Mary Gottesfeld. LC 86-22806. 185p. 1987. text 32.50 (*0-89876-100-X*) Gardner Pr.

Psychosocial Theories of the Self. Benjamin Lee. (PATH in Psychology Ser.). 230p. 1982. 55.00 (*0-306-41117-2*, Plenum Trade) Perseus Pubng.

Psychosocial Treatments. Ed. by David Reiss. 104p. 1994. pap. text 14.95 (*0-89862-298-0*, 2298) Guilford Pubns.

Psychosocial Treatments for Child & Adolescent Disorders: Empirically Based Strategies for Clinical Practice. Ed. by Euthymia D. Hibbs & Peter S. Jensen. LC 96-1003. 761p. 1996. 59.95 (*1-55798-330-5*) Am Psychol.

***Psychosocial Wellness of Refugees: Issues in Qualitative & Quantitative Research.** Frederick L. Ahearn, Jr. LC RC451.4.R43P77 1999. (Studies in Forced Migration). 2000. pap. 19.95 (*1-57181-205-9*); pap. 59.95 (*1-57181-204-0*) Berghahn Bks.

Psychosocial Work Environment: Work, Organization, Democatization & Health. Ed. by Gunn Johansson & Jeffrey Johnson. (Policy, Politics, Health & Medicine Ser.). 335p. 1991. text 43.00 (*0-89503-078-0*); pap. text 29.14 (*0-89503-077-2*) Baywood Pub.

Psychosocial Worlds of the Adolescent: Public & Private. Vivian C. Seltzer. LC 89-5710. 336p. 1989. 135.00 (*0-471-63258-9*) Wiley.

Psychosoical Scenarios for Pediatrics. Paul V. Trad. 265p. 1987. 86.95 (*0-387-96586-6*) Spr-Verlag.

Psychosomatic Approach to Prevention of Disease: Proceedings of the 20th Annual Conference for Psychosomatic Research, London, Nov. 15-16, 1976. Annual Conference for Psychosomatic Research Staff. Ed. by M. Carruthers & R. Priest. 1978. pap. 26.00 (*0-08-022253-6*, Pergamon Pr) Elsevier.

Psychosomatic Classics: Selected Papers from Psychosomatic Medicine, 1939-1958. Psychosomatic Medicine, Editorial Committee. 1971. pap. 31.00 (*3-8055-1232-5*) S Karger.

Psychosomatic Concepts. Roy R. Grinker. LC 84-451254. 228p. 1983. 40.00 (*0-87668-698-6*) Aronson.

Psychosomatic Delusion: Why the Mind Is Not the Source of All Our Ills. Robert Dantzer. 247p. 1993. 24.95 (*0-02-906937-8*) Free Pr.

Psychosomatic Disorders. (Technical Report Ser.: No. 275). 27p. 1964. pap. text 3.00 (*92-4-120275-0*) World Health.

Psychosomatic Disorders. B. B. Wolman. LC 88-22555. (Illus.). 326p. (C). 1988. text 57.50 (*0-306-42945-4*, Kluwer Plenum) Kluwer Academic.

Psychosomatic Disorders: A Psychological Approach to Etiology & Treatment. Ed. by Stephen N. Haynes et al. LC 81-10754. 546p. 1981. 52.95 (*0-275-90640-X*, C0640, Praeger Pubs) Greenwood.

Psychosomatic Disorders: Theoretical & Clinical Aspects, No. 7. Ghazi Asaad. (Basic Principles into Practice Ser.: Vol.67). 147p. 1996. pap. text 21.95 (*0-87630-803-5*) Brunner-Mazel.

Psychosomatic Disorders in Childhood. Melitta Sperling. LC 76-22870. 1978. 35.00 (*0-87668-274-3*) Aronson.

Psychosomatic Disorders in General Practice. 3rd enl. rev. ed. Fred Kroger et al. Tr. by G. Blythe from GER. (Illus.). 296p. 1992. 64.95 (*0-387-54556-5*) Spr-Verlag.

Psychosomatic Families: Anorexia Nervosa in Context. Salvador Minuchin et al. 351p. 1978. 38.50 (*0-674-72220-5*) HUP.

Psychosomatic Illnesses. Brian Broom. 1997. 55.00 (*1-85343-379-9*, Pub. by Free Assoc Bks); pap. 21.50 (*1-85343-381-0*, Pub. by Free Assoc Bks) NYU Pr.

Psychosomatic Medicine: A Core Approach to Clinical Medicine. Ed. by Y. Ikemi & H. Ishikawa. (Illus.). 1979. pap. 113.25 (*3-8055-3022-6*) S Karger.

Psychosomatic Medicine: Past & Future. Ed. by G. N. Christodoulou. LC 87-29075. (Illus.). 396p. 1988. 95.00 (*0-306-42780-X*, Plenum Trade) Perseus Pubng.

Psychosomatic Medicine: Theory, Physiology, & Practice. Ed. by Stanley Cheren. (Stress & Health Ser.: No. 1-2). 1000p. 1989. 62.50 (*0-8236-5725-6*, BN#05725); 75.00 (*0-8236-5726-4*, BN#05726) Intl Univs Pr.

Psychosomatic Medicine & Contemporary Psychoanalysis. Graeme J. Taylor. LC 86-27698. (Stress & Health Ser.: No. 3). 1987. 60.00 (*0-8236-5723-X*, BN#05723) Intl Univs Pr.

Psychosomatic Medicine & Liaison Psychiatry: Selected Papers. Zbigniew J. Lipowski. LC 85-12474. (Illus.). 470p. (C). 1985. text 108.00 (*0-306-42038-4*, Kluwer Plenum) Kluwer Academic.

Psychosomatic Medicine & Logotherapy. Hiroshi Takashima. (Illus.). 91p. (Orig.). 1977. pap. 6.95 (*0-917867-03-3*) V Frankl Inst.

Psychosomatic Medicine in a Changing World: Theoretical, Clinical & Transcultural Aspects. Ed. by Adam J. Krakowski & C. P. Kimball. (Journal: Psychotherapy & Psychosomatics: Vol. 38, No. 1-4). (Illus.). 310p. 1982. pap. 115.00 (*3-8055-3544-9*) S Karger.

Psychosomatic Medicine in Obstetrics & Gynecology: Proceedings of the International Congress, 3rd, London, 1971. International Congress of Psychosomatic Obstetrics. Ed. by Norman Morris. (Illus.). 1972. 130.50 (*3-8055-1314-3*) S Karger.

Psychosomatic Medicine: New Facts & Old Controversies: Proceedings of the World Congress of the International College of Psychosomatic Medicine Held in Sydney-Australia, 9th, August-September, 1987, Pt. I. Ed. by D. G. Byrne et al. (Journal: Psychotherapy & Psychosomatics: Vol. 47, No. 3-4, 1987). (Illus.). iv, 108p. 1988. pap. 99.25 (*3-8055-4845-1*) S Karger.

Psychosomatic Medicine: New Facts & Old Controversies: Proceedings of the World Congress of the International College of Psychosomatic Medicine Held in Sydney-Australia, 9th, August-September, 1987, Pt. II. Adam J. Krakowski. (Journal: Psychotherapy & Psychosomatics: Vol. 48, No. 1-4, 1987). (Illus.). 3p. 1988. pap. 124.50 (*3-8055-4847-8*) S Karger.

Psychosomatic Obstetrics & Gynecology. Ed. by Miriam B. Rosenthal & D. H. Smith. (Advances in Psychosomatic Medicine Ser.: Vol. 12). (Illus.). vi, 190p. 1985. 71.50 (*3-8055-3967-3*) S Karger.

Psychosomatic Research: Proceedings of the European Conference on Psychosomatic Research, 12th, Bodo, July 1978. European Conference on Psychosomatic Research Staf. Ed. by H. Freyberger. (Psychotherapy & Psychosomatics Ser.: Vol. 32, No. 1-4). (Illus.). 1980. 113.25 (*3-8055-3044-7*) S Karger.

Psychosomatic Symptoms: Psychodynamic Treatment of The Underlying Personality Disorder. Ed. by C. Philip Wilson & Ira L. Mintz. LC 88-19470. 460p. 1989. 65.00 (*0-87668-877-6*) Aronson.

Psychosomatic Syndromes & Somatic Symptoms. Robert Kellner. LC 91-4867. 260p. 1991. text 14.95 (*0-88048-110-2*, 8110) Am Psychiatric.

Psychosomatics, Bk. 1. Oluremilekun A. Oke. LC 92-96858. 200p. 1996. 15.00 (*0-533-10441-6*) Vantage.

Psychosomatics - A Challenge to Health Care: Journal: Psychotherapy & Psychosomatics, Pt. 1. Ed. by P. Tienari & G. A. Fava. (Illus.). iv, 152p. 1991. pap. 121.75 (*3-8055-5412-5*) S Karger.

Psychosomatics - A Challenge to Health Care: Journal: Psychotherapy & Psychosomatics, Pt. 2. Ed. by P. Tienari & G. A. Fava. (Illus.). 112p. 1991. pap. 81.00 (*3-8055-5415-X*) S Karger.

Psychosomatics & Pleasure: Proceedings of the Twenty-Third Annual Conference of the Society for Psychosomatic Research Held at the Royal College of Physicians, London, 19-20 November 1979. Ed. by C. Aitken. 88p. 1981. pap. 24.00 (*0-08-026797-1*, Pergamon Pr) Elsevier.

Psychosomatics in War & Peace: Proceedings of the Society for Psychosomatic Research, 22nd, Royal College of Physicians, London, Nov. 27-28, 1978. Society for Psychosomatic Research Staff. Ed. by P. Williams. 112p. 1980. pap. 26.00 (*0-08-026064-0*, Pergamon Pr) Elsevier.

Psychosomatics, Psychoanalysis, & Inflammatory Disease of the Colon. Charles C. Hogan. (Stress & Health Ser.: Monograph 5). 312p. 1995. 46.50 (*0-8236-5732-9*) Intl Univs Pr.

Psychosomatik der Bewegungsorgane - Motivation der Patienten - Differentielle Therapieindikation: 5. Fachtagung der Stiftung Psychosomatik der Wirbelsaule, Bad Pyrmont. Sicco Henk van der Mei & Jorg K. Merholz. (Illus.). 351p. 1998. 28.95 (*3-631-33010-3*) P Lang Pubng.

Psychosomatische Medizin: Grundlagen und Anwendungsgebiete. 4th rev. ed. Franz Alexander. (GER., Illus.). xvi, 244p. 1985. pap. text 44.65 (*3-11-010192-0*) De Gruyter.

Psychosomatische Rehabilitation und Sozialmedizin. Ed. by Dieter Olbrich & Reinhard Plassmann. (Illus.). 210p. 1997. pap. 37.95 (*3-631-31866-9*) P Lang Pubng.

Psychosoziale Aspekte in der Betreuung von Kindern und Jugendlichen mit Diabetes. Ed. by Roswitha Roth & H. M. Borkenstein. (Illus.). x, 202p. 1991. 35.00 (*3-8055-5414-1*) S Karger.

Psychosphere. Brian Lumley. 448p. (Orig.). 1992. mass mkt. 5.99 (*0-8125-2030-0*, Pub. by Tor Bks) St Martin.

PsychoSpiritual Power. A. Lee Henderson. (Illus.). 225p. (Orig.). 1988. pap. 7.95 (*0-929386-01-9*) AMEC Sunday Schl Union.

***Psychostrategies of Avant-Garde Art.** Donald B. Kuspit. LC 99-49985. (Illus.). 304p. 2000. text. write for info. (*0-521-45277-5*) Cambridge U Pr.

Psychosynthesis Counselling in Action. Diana Whitmore. (Counselling in Action Ser.). 160p. 1991. text 49.95 (*0-8039-8278-X*); pap. text 21.50 (*0-8039-8279-8*) Sage.

Psychosynthesis for the Next Century: 1996 Psychosynthesis World Conference Proceedings. Willis Harman et al. LC 97-223347. (Illus.). x, 231p. 1997. spiral bd. 29.00 (*0-940111-04-7*) Triangle.

***Psychotechnology of Brainwashing: Crucifying Willie Lynch.** 2nd ed. Kwabena Faheem Ashanti. (Illus.). 230p. 2000. pap. 24.95 (*0-911325-14-X*) Tone Bks Inc.

Psychotechnology of Brainwashing: How to Reprogram Your Mind. 181p. (Orig.). 1991. pap. 34.95 (*0-685-48730-X*) Tone Bks Inc.

Psychotherapeutic Action of the Physician: Proceedings of the International Congress of Psychosomatic Medicine, 4th, Paris, Sept., 1970, Vol. 21, Nos. 1-6. International Congress of Psychosomatic Obstetrics. Ed. by Leon Chertok & M. Sapir. (Illus.). 1973. reprint ed. 75.00 (*3-8055-1482-4*) S Karger.

***Psychotherapeutic & Pharmacological Treatment of Depression & Sleep Disorders.** Karl Doghramji. (LEA/DLN Mental Health Professionals Video Reference Library). 1999. VHS 129.95 (*0-8058-3304-8*) L Erlbaum Assocs.

Psychotherapeutic Conspiracy. Robert J. Langs. 1995. pap. text 50.00 (*1-56821-731-5*) Aronson.

Psychotherapeutic Drugs, 2 pts., Pt. 1. Ed. by Earl Usdin & Irene S. Forrest. LC 75-32389. (Illus.). 718p. reprint ed. pap. 200.00 (*0-7837-0708-8*, 204104000001) Bks Demand.

Psychotherapeutic Drugs, 2 pts., Pt. 2. Ed. by Earl Usdin & Irene S. Forrest. LC 75-32389. (Illus.). 927p. reprint ed. pap. 200.00 (*0-7837-0709-6*, 204104000002) Bks Demand.

Psychotherapeutic Instrument. Stanley L. Olinick. LC 80-620. 216p. 1980. 40.00 (*0-87668-403-7*) Aronson.

Psychotherapeutic Intervention in Hysterical Disorders. William J. Mueller & Albert S. Aniskiewicz. LC 85-15. 300p. 1986. 50.00 (*0-87668-913-6*) Aronson.

Psychotherapeutic Intervention in Schizophrenia. Lewis B. Hill. LC 94-71837. 224p. 1994. pap. 40.00 (*1-56821-313-1*) Aronson.

Psychotherapeutic Interventions for Adults with Brain Injury or Stroke A C: A Clinician's Treatment Resource. Ed. by Karen G. Langer et al. LC 99-24556. 250p. 1999. 35.00 (*1-887841-23-7*, 65433, Psychosocial) Intl Univs Pr.

Psychotherapeutic Interventions in Life-Threatening Illness. Ed. by H. Freyberger. (Advances in Psychosomatic Medicine Ser.: Vol. 10). (Illus.). xviii, 206p. 1980. 82.75 (*3-8055-3066-8*) S Karger.

Psychotherapeutic Metaphors: A Guide to Theory & Practice. Philip Barker. LC 95-20643. (Basic Principles into Practice Ser.: Vol. 5). 176p. 1996. pap. text 21.95 (*0-87630-776-4*) Brunner-Mazel.

Psychotherapeutic Process: A Research Handbook. Ed. by Leslie S. Greenberg & William M. Pinsof. LC 85-30596. 734p. 1986. lib. bdg. 85.00 (*0-89862-651-X*) Guilford Pubns.

Psychotherapeutic Process: Proceedings of the International Congress of Psychotherapy, 10th, Paris, July, 1976. International Congress of Psychotherapy Staff. Ed. by J. C. Benoit et al. (Psychotherapy & Psychosomatics Ser.: Vol. 29, Nos. 1-4). 1978. 123.50 (*3-8055-2762-4*) S Karger.

Psychotherapeutic Strategies in Late Latency Through Early Adolescence. Charles A. Sarnoff. LC 87-19474. 275p. 1987. 40.00 (*0-87668-937-3*) Aronson.

Psychotherapeutic Strategies in the Latency Years. Charles A. Sarnoff. LC 87-24194. 550p. 1987. 50.00 (*0-87668-936-5*) Aronson.

Psychotherapeutic Techniques of Richard A. Gardner. Richard A. Gardner. LC 86-11531. 893p. 1992. 45.00 (*0-933812-14-0*) Creative Therapeutics.

Psychotherapeutic Treatment of Cancer Patients. Intro. by Jane Goldberg. 396p. 1990. pap. 24.95 (*0-88738-829-9*) Transaction Pubs.

P

An Asterisk (*) at the beginning of an entry indicates that the title is appearing for the first time.

Psychotherapeutics: A Symposium. Morton Prince et al. LC 75-16728. (Classics in Psychiatry Ser.). 1976. reprint ed. 18.95 (*0-405-07451-4*) Ayer.

Psychotherapeutische Aspekte in der Philosophie Platons. Johannes Thome. (Altertumswissenschaftliche Texte und Studien: Bd. 29). (GER.). xii, 288p. 1995. write for info. (*3-487-09988-8*) G Olms Pubs.

Psychotheraphy & Culture Conflict in Community Mental Health. Georgene H. Seward. LC 74-190213. 238p. reprint ed. pap. 67.90 (*0-608-30292-9*, 2012537) Bks Demand.

Psychotheraphy & Multiple Personality: Selected Essays. Morton Prince. Ed. by Nathan G. Hale, Jr. LC 74-82574. 336p. 1975. 41.50 (*0-674-72225-6*) HUP.

***Psychotheraphy for Borderline Personality.** John F. Clarkin et al. LC 98-28270. 390p. 1998. 55.00 (*0-471-17042-9*) Wiley.

Psychotherapie - Heilkunst Oder Heilslehre? Reprint from Journal: Daseinsanalyse, Vol. 9, No. 2-3, 1992. Ed. by G. Condrau. (Illus.). 212p. 1992. reprint ed. pap. 47.00 (*3-8055-5681-0*) S Karger.

Psychotherapies, Dictionnaire, Critique, Concepts. N. Sinelnikoff. (FRE.). 1998. 95.00 (*0-320-00289-6*) Fr & Eur.

Psychotherapies with Children & Adolescents: Adapting the Psychodynamic Process. Ed. by John D. O'Brien et al. 346p. 1992. text 49.50 (*0-88048-406-3*, 8406) Am Psychiatric.

Psychotherapist: Use & Abuse of Psychological Influence. Gordon Warme. 1996. pap. 40.00 (*1-56821-736-6*) Aronson.

Psychotherapist & Managed Care: A Traumatic Bond. Ed. by Karen Weisgerber. LC 98-23700. 1998. 40.00 (*0-7657-0180-4*) Aronson.

Psychotherapist's Book Guide. Ed. by Aronson, Jason, Inc. Staff. 208p. 1994. pap. 3.95 (*1-56821-277-1*) Aronson.

Psychotherapist's Guide to Cost Containment: How to Survive & Thrive in an Age of Managed Care. Bernard D. Beitman. LC 97-33921. 1998. write for info. (*0-8039-7381-0*) Sage.

Psychotherapist's Guide to Human Memory. Janet Jones. 288p. 1999. 40.00 (*0-465-08517-2*, Pub. by Basic) HarpC.

Psychotherapists' Guide to Managed Care in the 21st Century: Surviving Big Brother. Sondra Tuckfelt et al. LC 96-40915. Orig. Title: How to Get Along with Big Brother. 416p. 1997. text 50.00 (*0-7657-0002-6*) Aronson.

Psychotherapist's Guide to Neuropsychiatry: Diagnostic & Treatment Issues. Ed. by James M. Ellison et al. 684p. 1994. text 82.95 (*0-88048-566-3*, 8566) Am Psychiatric.

Psychotherapist's Guide to Psychopharmacology. Michael J. Gitlin. 432p. 1990. 40.00 (*0-02-911781-X*) Free Pr.

Psychotherapist's Guide to Psychopharmacology. 2nd ed. Gitlin. 1996. 39.95 (*0-02-874050-5*) Free Pr.

Psychotherapist's Guide to Psychopharmacology. 2nd ed. Michael J. Gitlin. 560p. 1996. 39.95 (*0-684-82737-9*) Free Pr.

Psychotherapist's Handbook of Essential Forms & Marketing Strategies. 83p. 1999. spiral bd. 30.00 (*0-9670502-0-0*, 00001) Mark Vellucci.

Psychotherapist's Interventions: Integrating Psychodynamic Perspectives in Clinical Practice. T. Byram Karasu. LC 97-42382. 360p. 1998. 45.00 (*1-56821-689-0*) Aronson.

Psychotherapist's Resource on Psychiatric Medications. 2nd ed. Hebert Buelow. LC 99-33331. 183p. 1999. 43.95 (*0-534-35703-2*) Thomson Learn.

Psychotherapists' Sexual Involvement with Clients: Intervention & Prevention. Gary R. Schoener et al. (Illus.). 850p. (C). 1989. lib. bdg. 69.95 (*0-9624337-0-5*) Walk-In Counseling.

Psychotherapists' Sexual Involvement with Clients - Intervention & Prevention. Gary R. Schoener et al. (Illus.). 800p. (C). 1989. 49.95 (*0-685-28848-X*) Walk-In Counseling.

Psychotherapy. Simon & Schuster Staff. LC 94-1141. 248p. 1994. 65.00 (*0-275-94690-8*, Praeger Pubs) Greenwood.

Psychotherapy. Marie-Louise Von Franz. LC 92-56454. (C. G. Jung Foundation Bks.). 312p. (Orig.). 1993. pap. 20.00 (*0-87773-879-3*, Pub. by Shambhala Pubns) Random.

Psychotherapy. 2nd ed. Maxwell. 168p. 1991. pap. 43.95 (*1-56593-574-8*, 0304) Singular Publishing.

Psychotherapy: A Basic Text. Robert J. Langs. LC 81-17663. 800p. 1982. 70.00 (*0-87668-466-5*) Aronson.

Psychotherapy: An Eclectic-Integrative Approach. 2nd ed. Sol L. Garfield. LC 94-38838. (Series on Personality Processes). 290p. 1995. 39.95 (*0-471-59556-X*) Wiley.

Psychotherapy: Impact on Psychoanalytic Training. Ed. by Edward D. Joseph & Robert S. Wallerstein. LC 82-12719. (Influence of the Practice & Theory of Psychotherapy on Education in Psychoanalysis International Psycho-Analytical Association Monograph: No. 1). xvi, 174p. 1983. 40.00 (*0-8236-5405-2*) Intl Univs Pr.

Psychotherapy: Portraits in Fiction. Jesse Geller & Paul E. Spector. LC 87-17528. 302p. 1987. 55.00 (*0-87668-935-7*) Aronson.

Psychotherapy: Practice, Research, Policy. Ed. by Gary R. VandenBos. LC 80-23098. (Sage Studies in Community Mental Health: No. 1). (Illus.). 288p. reprint ed. pap. 89.30 (*0-8357-4861-8*, 203779300009) Bks Demand.

Psychotherapy: Processes & Techniques. Christiane Brems. LC 98-13438. 352p. 1998. 63.00 (*0-205-27532-X*) Allyn.

Psychotherapy: The Analytic Approach. Ed. by Morton J. Aronson & Melvin A. Scharfman. LC 92-10540. 400p. 1992. 60.00 (*0-87668-508-4*) Aronson.

Psychotherapy: The Art of Wooing Nature. Sheldon Roth. LC 86-28753. 304p. 1987. 50.00 (*0-87668-945-4*) Aronson.

Psychotherapy: The Mystery Solved. Charles W. Patterson. LC 84-61941. 118p. (Orig.). 1984. pap. 8.00 (*0-9614334-1-8*) Passages.

Psychotherapy: The Mystery Solved. 2nd ed. Charles W. Patterson. LC 95-68732. 187p. (Orig.). 1995. pap. text 17.95 (*0-9614334-3-4*) Passages.

Psychotherapy: The Purchase of Friendship. William Schofield. 212p. 1986. reprint ed. pap. 24.95 (*0-88738-659-8*) Transaction Pubs.

***Psycho'therapy' Theory, Practice, Modern & Postmodern Influences.** Laurence Simon. 2000. pap. write for info. (*0-275-97100-7*, Praeger Trade) Greenwood.

Psychotherapy Abbreviation: A Practical Guide. Gene Pekarik. LC 95-42382. (Illus.). 191p. 1996. 39.95 (*1-56024-934-X*) Haworth Pr.

Psychotherapy, Adolescents, & Self-Psychology. Gustavo A. Lage & Harvey K. Nathan. LC 90-4924. 500p. 1991. 67.50 (*0-8236-5403-6*) Intl Univs Pr.

Psychotherapy after Kohut: A Textbook of Self Psychology. Ronald R. Lee & J. Colby Martin. 352p. 1991. 45.00 (*0-88163-129-9*) Analytic Pr.

Psychotherapy, an Erotic Relationship: Transference & Countertransference Passions. David Mann. LC 96-27225. 224p. (C). 1997. 80.00 (*0-415-14851-0*); pap. 25.99 (*0-415-14852-9*) Routledge.

Psychotherapy & a Christian View of Man. David E. Roberts. LC 88-21391. 162p. 1990. reprint ed. lib. bdg. 55.00 (*0-313-25326-9*, RPSY, Greenwood Pr) Greenwood.

Psychotherapy & AIDS: The Human Dimension. Lucy A. Wicks. LC 97-1721. 1997. write for info. (*1-56032-617-4*); pap. write for info. (*1-56032-618-2*) Hemisp Pub.

Psychotherapy & Buddhism: Toward an Integration. Jeffrey B. Rubin. (Issues in the Practice of Psychology Ser.). (Illus.). 197p. (C). 1996. 47.00 (*0-306-45441-6*, Plenum Trade) Perseus Pubng.

Psychotherapy & Character Structure: How to Recognize & Treat Particular Character Types. Mary Ahern & Abraham J. Malerstein. 260p. (C). 1993. text 22.50 (*0-9644089-2-9*) Cole Valley Pr.

Psychotherapy & Confidentiality: Testimonial Privileged Communication, Breach of Confidentiality, & Reporting Duties. Ralph Slovenko. LC 97-39505. (Illus.). 660p. 1998. text 79.95 (*0-398-06827-5*) C C Thomas.

Psychotherapy & Counseling in the Treatment of Drug Abuse. 1992. lib. bdg. 75.00 (*0-8490-8820-8*) Gordon Pr.

Psychotherapy & Counseling in the Treatment of Drug Abuse. 1993. lib. bdg. 254.95 (*0-8490-8500-4*) Gordon Pr.

Psychotherapy & Culture Conflict in Community Mental Health. 2nd ed. Georgene H. Seward. LC 74-190213. 238p. 1972. reprint ed. pap. 73.80 (*0-608-10455-8*, 201253700081) Bks Demand.

Psychotherapy & Human Science see Proceedings

Psychotherapy & Its Discontents. Ed. by Wendy Dryden & Colin Feltham. 256p. 1992. 123.00 (*0-335-09678-6*); pap. 38.95 (*0-335-09677-8*) OpUniv Pr.

***Psychotherapy & Managed Care: Reconciling Research & Reality.** Catherine H. Chambliss. LC 98-56528. 368p. (C). 1999. 34.50 (*0-205-27950-3*) Allyn.

Psychotherapy & Mandated Reporting of Child Maltreatment. Murray Levine & Howard J. Doueck. LC 95-18434. (Practice Ser.). 169p. (C). 1995. 45.00 (*0-8039-5472-7*); pap. 18.95 (*0-8039-5473-5*) Sage.

Psychotherapy & Medication: A Dynamic Integration. Ed. by Meri Schachter. LC 92-49162. 352p. 1993. 65.00 (*0-87668-296-4*) Aronson.

Psychotherapy & Mental Handicap. Alexis Waitman. Ed. by Suzanne Conboy-Hill. 224p. (C). 1992. text 49.95 (*0-8039-8372-7*); pap. text 19.95 (*0-8039-8373-5*) Sage.

Psychotherapy & Process: The Fundamentals of an Existential-Humanistic Approach. James F. Bugental. 163p. (C). 1978. pap. text 28.25 (*0-07-554827-5*) McGraw.

Psychotherapy & Psychoanalysis: Theory, Practice, Research. Robert S. Wallerstein. LC 73-16854. 400p. (C). 1975. 70.00 (*0-8236-5410-9*) Intl Univs Pr.

Psychotherapy & Religion. Josef Rudin. Tr. by Elisabeth Reinecke & Paul C. Bailey. LC 68-12291. 258p. 1968. reprint ed. pap. 80.00 (*0-608-00880-X*, 206167400010) Bks Demand.

Psychotherapy & Society. David Pilgrim. 170p. 1997. 69.95 (*0-8039-7504-X*); pap. 23.95 (*0-8039-7505-8*) Sage.

Psychotherapy & Spirit: Theory & Practice in Transpersonal Psychotherapy. Brant Cortright. LC 96-46518. (SUNY Series in the Philosophy of Psychology). (Illus.). 257p. (C). 1997. text 54.50 (*0-7914-3465-6*); pap. text 19.95 (*0-7914-3466-4*) State U NY Pr.

Psychotherapy & Substance Abuse: A Practitioner's Handbook. Ed. by Arnold M. Washton. LC 95-183. 500p. 1995. lib. bdg. 46.95 (*0-89862-838-5*) Guilford Pubns.

Psychotherapy & Substance Abuse: A Practitioner's Handbook. Ed. by Arnold M. Washton. LC 95-183. 500p. 1996. lib. bdg. 26.00 (*1-57230-202-X*) Guilford Pubns.

Psychotherapy & the Abrasive Patient. Ed. by E. Mark Stern. LC 84-6644. (Psychotherapy Patient Ser.: Vol. 1, No. 1). 140p. 1984. text 4.95 (*0-86656-325-3*) Haworth Pr.

Psychotherapy & the Bored Patient. Ed. by E. Mark Stern. LC 87-31085. (Psychotherapy Patient Ser.: Vol. 3, Nos. 3-4). (Illus.). 164p. 1988. text 39.95 (*0-86656-641-4*) Haworth Pr.

Psychotherapy & the Confrontation Problem-Solving Technique. Harry H. Garner. LC 74-110426. 362p. 1971. 18.50 (*0-87527-011-5*) Green.

Psychotherapy & the Creative Patient. Ed. by E. Mark Stern. LC 88-2694. (Psychotherapy Patient Ser.: Vol. 4, No. 1). (Illus.). 174p. 1988. text 39.95 (*0-86656-642-2*); pap. text 19.95 (*0-86656-831-X*) Haworth Pr.

Psychotherapy & the Dangerous Patient. Ed. by E. Mark Stern & Jerome A. Travers. LC 94-44247. (Psychotherapy Patient Ser.). (Illus.). 219p. 1995. 39.95 (*1-56024-719-3*) Haworth Pr.

Psychotherapy & the Dual Research Tradition. Group for the Advancement of Psychiatry Staff. LC 62-2872. (Group for the Advancement of Psychiatry, Symposium Ser.: Vol. 7, No. 73). 67p. reprint ed. pap. 30.00 (*0-7837-2117-X*, 204239700004) Bks Demand.

Psychotherapy & the Grandiose Patient. Frwd. by E. Mark Stern. LC 89-24438. (Psychotherapy Patient Ser.: Vol. 5, Nos. 3-4). (Illus.). 205p. 1989. text 6.95 (*0-86656-946-4*) Haworth Pr.

Psychotherapy & the Grieving Patient. Ed. by E. Mark Stern. LC 85-17618. (Psychotherapy Patient Ser.: Vol. 2, No. 1). 138p. 1986. text 4.95 (*0-86656-514-0*) Haworth Pr.

Psychotherapy & the Grieving Patient. Ed. by E. Mark Stern. LC 85-17619. (Psychotherapy Patient Ser.: Vol. 2, No. 1). 138p. 1986. reprint ed. pap. text 29.95 (*0-918393-24-8*, Harrington Park) Haworth Pr.

Psychotherapy & the Interminable Patient. Ed. by Jerome A. Travers & E. Mark Stern. 144p. 1986. 4.95 (*0-86656-635-X*) Haworth Pr.

Psychotherapy & the Lonely Patient. Ed. by Samuel M. Natale. LC 86-12108. (Psychotherapy Patient Ser.: Vol. 2, No. 3). 120p. (C). 1986. text 3.95 (*0-86656-517-5*) Haworth Pr.

Psychotherapy & the Lonely Patient. Ed. by Samuel M. Natale. LC 86-12101. (Psychotherapy Patient Ser.: Vol. 2, No. 3). 120p. 1986. reprint ed. pap. 29.95 (*0-918393-26-4*, Harrington Park) Haworth Pr.

Psychotherapy & the Memorable Patient. Ed. by William Kir-Stimon & Mark Stern. LC 86-25648. (Psychotherapy Patient Ser.: Vol. 2, No. 4). 152p. 1986. text 4.95 (*0-86656-516-7*) Haworth Pr.

Psychotherapy & the Memorable Patient. William Kir-Stimon. LC 86-22852. (Psychotherapy Patient Ser.: Vol. 2, No. 4). 152p. (C). 1986. reprint ed. pap. 29.95 (*0-918393-25-6*, Harrington Park) Haworth Pr.

Psychotherapy & the Obsessed Patient. Ed. by E. Mark Stern. 158p. 1987. 4.95 (*0-86656-636-8*) Haworth Pr.

Psychotherapy & the Paranoid Process. William W. Meissner. LC 85-15614. 432p. 1994. 60.00 (*0-87668-752-4*) Aronson.

Psychotherapy & the Poverty Patient. Intro. by E. Mark Stern. (Psychotherapy Patient Ser.). 198p. 1991. text 39.95 (*1-56024-066-0*) Haworth Pr.

Psychotherapy & the Promiscuous Patient. Intro. by E. Mark Stern. LC 92-49176. (Psychotherapy Patient Ser.: Vol. 8, Nos. 1-2). (Illus.). 192p. 1992. lib. bdg. 39.95 (*1-56024-316-3*) Haworth Pr.

Psychotherapy & the Promiscuous Patient. Intro. by E. Mark Stern. LC 92-49176. (Psychotherapy Patient Ser.: Vol. 8, Nos. 1-2). (Illus.). 192p. 1993. pap. text 14.95 (*1-56024-317-1*) Haworth Pr.

Psychotherapy & the Religiously Committed Patient. Ed. by E. Mark Stern. LC 84-25276. (Psychotherapy Patient Ser.: Vol. 1, No. 3). 158p. 1985. text 4.95 (*0-86656-394-6*); pap. text 19.95 (*0-86656-396-2*) Haworth Pr.

Psychotherapy & the Remorseful Patient. Ed. by E. Mark Stern. 330p. 1989. 49.95 (*0-86656-755-0*) Haworth Pr.

Psychotherapy & the Remote Patient. Intro. by Jerome A. Travers. LC 89-26686. (Psychotherapy Patient Ser.: Vol. 6, Nos. 1-2). (Illus.). 280p. 1990. text 39.95 (*0-86656-971-5*) Haworth Pr.

Psychotherapy & the Sacred: Religious Experience & Religious Resources in Psychotherapy. C. Michael Smith. LC 92-74688. (Studies in Religion, Society & Personality). 201p. 1995. text 32.95 (*0-913348-28-7*) Ctr Sci Study.

Psychotherapy & the Self-Contained Patient. Ed. by E. Mark Stern. LC 88-37929. (Psychotherapy Patient Ser.: Vol. 4, Nos. 3-4). (Illus.). 360p. 1989. text 6.95 (*0-86656-754-2*) Haworth Pr.

Psychotherapy & the Self-Less Patient. Ed. by Jerome A. Travers. LC 85-24817. (Psychotherapy Patient Ser.: Vol. 2, No. 2). 109p. 1986. text 3.95 (*0-86656-515-9*) Haworth Pr.

Psychotherapy & the Self-Righteous Patient. Ed. by E. Mark Stern & Jerome A. Travers. LC 91-17950. (Psychotherapy Patient Ser.). 168p. 1991. lib. bdg. 5.95 (*1-56024-169-1*) Haworth Pr.

Psychotherapy & the Selfless. Jerome A. Travers. 1986. pap. 14.95 (*0-918393-27-2*, Harrington Park) Haworth Pr.

Psychotherapy & the Somatizing Patient. Ed. by E. Mark Stern & Virginia F. Stern. LC 88-16476. (Psychotherapy Patient Ser.: Vol. 4, No. 2). 208p. 1989. text 6.95 (*0-86656-753-4*) Haworth Pr.

Psychotherapy & the Terrorized Patient. Ed. by E. Mark Stern. LC 85-8468. (Psychotherapy Patient Ser.: Vol. 1, No. 4). 116p. 1985. text 3.95 (*0-86656-442-X*) Haworth Pr.

Psychotherapy & the Uncommitted Patient. Ed. by Jerome A. Travers & E. Mark Stern. LC 84-19754. (Psychotherapy Patient Ser.: Vol. 1, No. 2). 105p. 1985. text 3.95 (*0-86656-371-7*) Haworth Pr.

Psychotherapy & the Widowed Patient. E. Mark Stern. LC 90-4502. (Psychotherapy Patient Ser.: Vol. 6, Nos. 3-4). 257p. 1990. text 39.95 (*1-56024-016-4*) Haworth Pr.

Psychotherapy As a Mutual Process. J. Marvin Spiegelman. 208p. 1996. pap. 14.95 (*1-56184-063-7*) New Falcon Pubns.

Psychotherapy As a Personal Relationship. Valerian J. Derlega et al. LC 90-3997. 227p. 1991. lib. bdg. 31.50 (*0-89862-554-8*) Guilford Pubns.

Psychotherapy As If Life Really Mattered. Christopher A. Anderson. LC 95-76211. (Illus.). 147p. (Orig.). 1995. pap. 12.00 (*0-931353-39-4*) Andersons Pubns.

Psychotherapy Based on Human Longing. Robert Murphy, Jr. LC 60-14173. (Orig.). 1960. pap. 4.00 (*0-87574-111-8*) Pendle Hill.

Psychotherapy by Reciprocal Inhibition. Joseph Wolpe. xiv, 239p. 1958. 32.50 (*0-8047-0509-7*) Stanford U Pr.

Psychotherapy by Reciprocal Inhibition. Joseph Wolpe. LC 58-6709. (Illus.). 253p. 1958. reprint ed. pap. 30.00 (*0-7837-3947-8*, 204377600011) Bks Demand.

Psychotherapy by Structured Learning Theory. Raymond B. Cattell. (Illus.). 192p. 1987. 37.95 (*0-8261-5080-2*) Springer Pub.

Psychotherapy, Counselling & Primary Mental Health Care: Assessment for Brief or Longer-Term Treatment. Mary Burton. LC 98-13952. 270p. 1998. 91.50 (*0-471-97657-1*) Wiley.

***Psychotherapy, Counselling & Primary Mental Health Care: Assessment for Brief or Longer-Term Treatment.** Mary Burton. LC 98-13952. 270p. 1998. pap. 48.50 (*0-471-98228-8*) Wiley.

Psychotherapy Documentation Primer. Donald E. Wiger. LC 98-18229. (Practice Planners Ser.). 224p. 1998. pap. 45.00 (*0-471-28990-6*) Wiley.

Psychotherapy East & West: A Unifying Paradigm. Swami Ajaya. LC 83-22608. 340p. 1984. pap. 15.95 (*0-89389-087-1*) Himalayan Inst.

Psychotherapy Education & Training: An Integrative Perspective. Malcolm H. Robertson. LC 95-6412. 181p. 1995. 27.50 (*0-8236-5402-8*) Intl Univs Pr.

***Psychotherapy for Children & Adolescents: Directions for Research & Practice.** 2nd ed. Alan E. Kazdin. LC 99-17112. (Illus.). 320p. 2000. text 39.95 (*0-19-512618-1*) OUP.

Psychotherapy for Depression. Byram Karasu. LC 90-1103. 200p. 1990. 40.00 (*0-87668-691-9*) Aronson.

Psychotherapy for Women: Treatment Toward Equality. Edna I. Rawlings & Dianne K. Carter. (Illus.). 500p. 1977. pap. 59.95 (*0-398-06338-9*); text 74.95 (*0-398-03584-9*) C C Thomas.

Psychotherapy Grounded in the Feminine Principle. Barbara S. Sullivan. LC 89-9713. (Illus.). 224p. (Orig.). 1989. pap. 24.95 (*0-933029-43-8*) Chiron Pubns.

Psychotherapy in a New Key: A Guide to Time-Limited Dynamic Psychotherapy. Hans H. Strupp & Jeffrey L. Binder. LC 83-46075. 352p. 1985. pap. 45.00 (*0-465-06747-6*, Pub. by Basic) HarpC.

Psychotherapy in a Religious Framework: Spirituality in the Emotional Healing Process. Rebecca L. Propst. LC 86-27582. 209p. 1987. 38.95 (*0-89885-350-8*, Kluwer Acad Hman Sci) Kluwer Academic.

Psychotherapy in Chemical Dependence Treatment: A Practical & Integrative Approach. Sidne Buelow & George Buelow. LC 97-23147. (Counseling Ser.). 200p. 1997. mass mkt. 23.95 (*0-534-26118-3*) Brooks-Cole.

Psychotherapy in Independent Practice: Current Issues for Clinicians. Ed. by Robert D. Weitz. LC 92-1537. (Psychotherapy in Private Practice Ser.). (Illus.). 207p. 1992. text 39.95 (*1-56024-232-9*) Haworth Pr.

Psychotherapy in Managed Health Care: The Optimal Use of Time & Resources. Ed. by Carol S. Austad & William H. Berman. 285p. 1991. pap. text 19.95 (*1-55798-314-3*) Am Psychol.

Psychotherapy in Practice: Past Reflections. Jennifer Stein & Samuel Stein. LC 99-22362. 358p. 1999. pap. text 50.00 (*0-7506-3002-7*) Buttrwrth-Heinemann.

Psychotherapy in the Age of Accountability. Lynn D. Johnson. 240p. 1995. 29.00 (*0-393-70209-X*) Norton.

Psychotherapy in the Community: A Psychoanalytically Based Guide to the Treatment of the Adult. Eric Lager & Isreal Zwerling. Ed. by Alvin F. Gardner. (Allied Health Professions Monograph). 208p. (C). 1983. 22.50 (*0-87527-315-7*) Green.

Psychotherapy in the Third Reich. 2nd expanded rev. ed. Geoffrey Cocks. LC 96-34060. 283p. (Orig.). 1996. pap. text 29.95 (*1-56000-904-7*) Transaction Pubs.

Psychotherapy Indications & Outcomes. Ed. by David S. Janowsky. LC 98-43413. (American Psychopathological Association Ser.). 1999. 51.95 (*0-88048-761-5*, 8761) Am Psychiatric.

Psychotherapy Insight & Style: The Existential Moment. Len Bergantino. LC 86-71119. 288p. 1986. 45.00 (*0-87668-906-3*) Aronson.

Psychotherapy Isn't What You Think: Bringing the Psychotherapeutic Engagement into the Living Moment. James F. Bugental. LC 98-41823. 1999. 38.95 (*1-891944-13-4*) Zeig Tucker.

Psychotherapy Maze: A Consumer's Guide to Getting in & Out of Therapy. rev. ed. Otto Ehrenberg & Miriam Ehrenberg. LC 86-28748. 240p. 1986. 30.00 (*0-87668-959-4*) Aronson.

Psychotherapy Maze: A Consumers Guide to Getting In & Out of Therapy. rev. ed. Otto Ehrenberg & Miriam Ehrenberg. LC 94-70252. 240p. 1994. pap. 40.00 (*1-56821-245-3*) Aronson.

Psychotherapy of Abused & Neglected Children. John W. Pearce & Terry D. Pezzot-Pearce. LC 96-43650. 368p. 1997. lib. bdg. 40.00 (*1-57230-163-5*) Guilford Pubns.

Psychotherapy of Addicted Persons. Edward Kaufman. LC 94-8644. 232p. 1994. lib. bdg. 32.00 (*0-89862-116-X*, C2116) Guilford Pubns.

Psychotherapy of Antisocial Behavior & Depression in Adolescence. Richard A. Gardner. LC RJ506.C65G373 1999. 9176p. 1999. pap. 22.00 (*0-7657-0208-8*) Aronson.

Psychotherapy of Carl Rogers: Cases & Commentary. Ed. by Barry A. Farber et al. 383p. 1998. pap. text 23.00 (*1-57230-377-8*) Guilford Pubns.

An Asterisk (*) at the beginning of an entry indicates that the title is appearing for the first time.

Psychotherapy of Cocaine Addiction: Entering the Interpersonal World of the Cocaine Addict. David Mark & Jeffrey Faude. LC 97-6518. 288p. 1997. 50.00 (*0-7657-0072-7*) Aronson.

Psychotherapy of Everyday Life. Peter Lomas. LC 92-456. 168p. (C). 1992. pap. 21.95 (*1-56000-629-3*) Transaction Pubs.

Psychotherapy of Neurotic Character. David Shapiro. LC 65-23044. 256p. 1999. pap. 22.00 (*0-465-09563-1*, Pub. by Basic) HarpC.

*__Psychotherapy of Personality Disorders.__ John G. Gunderson & Glen O. Gabbard. LC 00-24853. (Review of Psychiatry Ser.). 2000. write for info. (*0-88048-273-7*) Am Psychiatric.

Psychotherapy of Preoedipal Conditions. Hyman Spotnitz. LC 75-37489. 448p. 1987. 65.00 (*0-87668-242-5*) Aronson.

Psychotherapy of Preoedipal Conditions: Schizophrenia & Severe Character Disorders. Hyman Spotnitz M.D. LC 75-37489. 400p. 1995. pap. 50.00 (*1-56821-633-5*) Aronson.

Psychotherapy of Schizophrenia. Gaetano Benedetti. 274p. 1996. pap. 50.00 (*1-56821-756-0*) Aronson.

Psychotherapy of Schizophrenia. Ed. by John S. Strauss et al. LC 93-73984. 320p. 1994. pap. 50.00 (*1-56821-165-1*) Aronson.

Psychotherapy of Schizophrenia: Effective Clinical Approaches - Controversies, Critiques & Recommendations. Ed. by Gaetano Benedetti & Pier Furlan. (Illus.). 429p. 1993. text 39.90 (*0-88937-077-X*) Hogrefe & Huber Pubs.

Psychotherapy of Sexually Abused Children & Their Families. William N. Friedrich. 1990. 34.95 (*0-393-70079-8*) Norton.

Psychotherapy of the Adolescent: At Different Levels of Psychiatric Practice with Special Emphasis on the Role of the School. Ed. by Benjamin H. Balser. LC 57-9326. 270p. (Orig.). 1959. reprint ed. pap. 24.95 (*0-8236-8249-8*, 225400) Intl Univs Pr.

Psychotherapy of the Borderline Adult: A Developmental Approach. James F. Masterson. LC 76-16564. 377p. 1988. text 38.95 (*0-87630-127-8*) Brunner-Mazel.

Psychotherapy of the Brain-Injured Patient: Reclaiming the Shattered Self. Laurence Miller. 256p. (C). 1993. 29.95 (*0-393-70158-1*) Norton.

Psychotherapy of the Disorders of the Self: The Masterson Approach. Ed. by James F. Masterson & Ralph Klein. LC 88-19341. 480p. 1988. text 45.95 (*0-87630-533-8*) Brunner-Mazel.

Psychotherapy of the Elderly Self. Hyman L. Muslin. LC 91-43419. 240p. 1992. text 31.95 (*0-87630-657-1*) Brunner-Mazel.

Psychotherapy of the Personality Disorders: A MOMI-III-Based Approach. Ed. by Paul D. Retzlaff. 288p. (C). 1995. 49.00 (*0-205-15932-X*, Longwood Div) Allyn.

Psychotherapy of the Religious Patient. Ed. by Moshe H. Spero. LC 96-10343. 1996. pap. 50.00 (*1-56821-811-7*) Aronson.

Psychotherapy of the Submerged Personality. Ed. by Alexander Wolf & Irwin L. Kutash. LC 90-1234. 304p. 1991. 50.00 (*0-87668-644-7*) Aronson.

Psychotherapy Process Research: Paradigmatic & Narrative Approaches. Shake G. Toukmanian & David L. Rennie. (Focus Editions Ser.: Vol. 143). 320p. (C). 1992. text 59.95 (*0-8039-4354-7*) Sage.

Psychotherapy, Psychological Treatments & the Addictions. Ed. by Griffith Edwards & Christopher Dare. (Illus.). 284p. (C). 1996. text 100.00 (*0-521-55357-1*) Cambridge U Pr.

Psychotherapy, Psychological Treatments & the Addictions. Ed. by Griffith Edwards & Christopher Dare. (Illus.). 84p. (C). 1996. pap. text 42.95 (*0-521-55675-9*) Cambridge U Pr.

Psychotherapy Relationship Theory, Research, & Practice. Charles J. Gelso & Jeffrey A. Hayes. LC 98-10212. 304p. 1998. 55.00 (*0-471-12720-5*) Wiley.

Psychotherapy, Religion & the Teilhardian Visions. John Ryan. (Teilhard Studies: No. 34). 1997. pap. write for info. (*0-89012-076-5*) Am Teilhard.

Psychotherapy Research: An International Review of Programmatic Studies. Ed. by Larry E. Beutler & Marjorie Crago. 334p. 1991. pap. 19.95 (*1-55798-090-X*) Am Psychol.

Psychotherapy Research: Methodological & Efficacy Issues. American Psychiatric Association, Commission on Ps. LC 82-8763. 277p. reprint ed. pap. 85.90 (*0-8357-7796-0*, 203615800002) Bks Demand.

Psychotherapy Research & Behavior Change. Ed. by John H. Harvey & Marjorie M. Parks. LC 82-1668. (Master Lecture Ser.: No. 1). 197p. reprint ed. pap. 61.10 (*0-7837-8829-0*, 204947600012) Bks Demand.

Psychotherapy Revised: New Frontiers in Research & Practice. E. Lakin Phillips. 264p. (C). 1985. text 49.95 (*0-89859-571-1*) L Erlbaum Assocs.

*__Psychotherapy Supervision: An Integrative Rational Approach to Psychotherapy Supervision.__ Maria Gilbert & Kenneth Evans. LC 00-35623. 2000. pap. write for info. (*0-335-20139-3*, Pub. by OpUniv Pr) Taylor & Francis.

Psychotherapy Through Imagery. Joseph E. Shorr. LC 82-51144. 476p. 1994. pap. 35.00 (*1-56474-121-4*) Fithian Pr.

Psychotherapy to Go: 14 Mind-Expanding Comedies & Dramas. LC 97-173140. 1997. pap. 15.99 (*0-8341-9602-6*) Lillenas.

Psychotherapy Today. Ved P. Varma. LC 74-180779. 351p. 1974. reprint ed. pap. 108.90 (*0-608-10456-6*, 205126600093) Bks Demand.

Psychotherapy Tradecraft: The Technique & Style of Doing Therapy. Theodore H. Blau. LC 87-21786. 328p. 1988. text 38.95 (*0-87630-479-X*) Brunner-Mazel.

Psychotherapy Training: Contextual & Developmental Influences in Settings, Stages & Mind Sets. Thomas H. Peake & John D. Ball. (Clinical Supervisor Ser.). (Illus.). 230p. 1991. text 6.95 (*1-56024-133-0*); pap. text 19.95 (*1-56024-134-9*) Haworth Pr.

Psychotherapy Versus Iatrogeny: A Confrontation for Physicians. Nikola Schipkovenski. LC 76-49515. 508p. reprint ed. pap. 157.50 (*0-8357-7000-1*, 205674800085) Bks Demand.

Psychotherapy vs. Behavior Therapy. R. Bruce Sloane et al. LC 75-778. 284p. reprint ed. pap. 88.10 (*0-7837-4191-X*, 205904100012) Bks Demand.

Psychotherapy with Adolescent Girls. Doris Lamb. LC 78-62560. (Jossey-Bass Social & Behavioral Science Ser.). 224p. reprint ed. pap. 69.50 (*0-8357-4900-2*, 203783000009) Bks Demand.

Psychotherapy with Adolescent Girls. 2nd ed. D. Lamb. LC 86-12211. (Illus.). 278p. (C). 1986. 54.50 (*0-306-42242-5*, Plenum Trade) Perseus Pubng.

Psychotherapy with Adolescents. Richard A. Gardner. LC 88-20280. xxvi, 806p. 1988. 45.00 (*0-933812-18-3*) Creative Therapeutics.

*__Psychotherapy with African American Women: Innovations in Psychodynamic Perspectives & Practice.__ Ed. by Leslie C. Sharpe & Beverly Greene. 298p. 2000. lib. bdg. 35.00 (*1-57230-585-1*) Guilford Pubns.

Psychotherapy with Children. Richard Gardner. LC 93-708. 360p. 1993. reprint ed. pap. 40.00 (*1-56821-030-2*) Aronson.

Psychotherapy with College Students. Group for the Advancement of Psychiatry Staff. LC 90-2345. (Group for the Advancement of Psychiatry, Symposium Ser.: Vol. 130). 153p. 1990. reprint ed. pap. 47.50 (*0-608-02015-X*, 206267100003) Bks Demand.

Psychotherapy with Couples: Theory & Practice at the Tavistock Institute of Marital Studies. Ed. by Stanley Ruszczynski. 256p. 1993. pap. text 30.00 (*1-85575-045-7*, Pub. by H Karnac Bks Ltd) Other Pr LLC.

Psychotherapy with Deaf & Hard of Hearing Persons: A Systemic Model. Michael A. Harvey. 288p. 1989. 59.95 (*0-8058-0204-5*) L Erlbaum Assocs.

Psychotherapy with Deaf Clients from Diverse Groups. Ed. by Irene W. Leigh. LC 99-40434. 290p. 1999. 65.00 (*1-56368-083-1*) Gallaudet Univ Pr.

Psychotherapy with High-Risk Clients: Legal & Professional Standards. Richard L. Bednar et al. 226p. (C). 1991. text 45.95 (*0-534-15408-5*) Brooks-Cole.

Psychotherapy with Homosexual Men & Women: Integrated Identity Approaches for Clinical Practice. Ed. by Eli Coleman. 343p. 1987. 49.95 (*0-86656-638-4*) Haworth Pr.

Psychotherapy with Impossible Cases: The Efficient Treatment of Therapy Veterans. Barry L. Duncan et al. LC 96-35581. 256p. (C). 1997. 35.00 (*0-393-70246-4*) Norton.

Psychotherapy with Lesbian Clients: Theory into Practice. Kristine L. Falco. LC 90-15083. 208p. 1991. text 30.95 (*0-87630-622-9*) Brunner-Mazel.

Psychotherapy with Older Adults. Bob G. Knight. 240p. 1985. 20.95 (*0-8039-3534-X*); 46.00 (*0-8039-2633-2*) Sage.

Psychotherapy with Older Adults. Bob G. Knight. (Illus.). 192p. 1996. 48.00 (*0-8039-5401-8*) Sage.

Psychotherapy with Older Adults. 2nd ed. Bob G. Knight. (Illus.). 192p. 1996. pap. 21.00 (*0-8039-5402-6*) Sage.

*__Psychotherapy with People Who Engage in Self-Inflicted Violence.__ 2001. 45.00 (*0-7657-0264-9*) Aronson.

Psychotherapy with Priests, Protestant Clergy & Catholic Religious: A Practical Guide. Joseph W. Ciarrocchi & Robert J. Wicks. 250p. 2000. 40.00 (*1-887841-22-9*, 65430, Psychosocial) Intl Univs Pr.

Psychotherapy with Psychotherapists. Ed. by Florence W. Kaslow. LC 94-72278. 218p. 1994. pap. 45.00 (*1-56821-326-3*) Aronson.

Psychotherapy with Psychotherapists. Florence W. Kaslow. LC 83-18655. 202p. 1984. text 39.95 (*0-86656-207-9*) Haworth Pr.

Psychotherapy with Schizophrenics. Ed. by Eugene B. Brody & Frederick C. Redlich. (Monograph Series on Schizophrenia: No. 3). 246p. (Orig.). 1964. 35.00 (*0-8236-5420-6*) Intl Univs Pr.

Psychotherapy with Severely Deprived Children. Ed. by Mary Boston & Rolene Szur. 176p. 1983. pap. 11.95 (*0-7100-9536-8*, Routledge Thoemms) Routledge.

Psychotherapy with Severely Deprived Children. Ed. by Mary Boston & Rolene Szur. 168p. 1990. reprint ed. pap. text 26.50 (*0-946439-97-4*, Pub. by H Karnac Bks Ltd) Other Pr LLC.

Psychotherapy with Sex-Abuse Victims: True, False, & Hysterical. Richard A. Gardner. LC 95-47817. (Dr. Richard A. Gardner's Books on Psychology & Psychiatry). xxiii, 512p. 1996. pap. 40.00 (*0-933812-41-8*) Creative Therapeutics.

Psychotherapy with Sexually Abused Boys: An Integrated Approach, Vol. IV. William N. Friedrich. LC 95-3736. (Interpersonal Violence: the Practice Ser.: Vol. 12). (Illus.). 249p. 1995. 48.00 (*0-8039-5694-0*) Sage.

Psychotherapy with the Arab Patient. Kutaiba S. Chaleby & John C. Racy. LC 98-89893. 1999. pap. 25.00 (*0-9669830-0-9*) Q S O V.

Psychotherapy with the Elderly: Becoming Methuselah's Echo. George Bouklas. LC 96-46668. 392p. 1997. 60.00 (*0-7657-0051-4*) Aronson.

Psychotherapy with the Orthodox Jew. Herbert S. Strean. LC 94-2461. 200p. 1994. 40.00 (*1-56821-230-5*) Aronson.

Psychotherapy with Women: Feminist Perspectives. Marilyn Lawrence et al. LC 98-38228. 1999. pap. 24.99 (*0-415-92265-8*) Routledge.

Psychotherapy Workbook: A Home-Study Guide for Growth & Change. Kathleen Cairns. 255p. 1997. pap. 19.95 (*1-891409-00-X*) Life Goes On.

Psychothereapy for Mothers & Infants: Interventions for Dyads at Risk. Eva R. G. Gochman. LC 94-24215. 160p. 1995. 59.95 (*0-275-94927-3*, Praeger Pubs) Greenwood.

Psychotic: Aspects of the Personality. David Rosenfeld. 336p. 1991. pap. text 37.50 (*0-946439-96-6*, Pub. by H Karnac Bks Ltd) Other Pr LLC.

Psychotic Conflict & Reality. Edith Jacobson. LC 67-29736. (New York Psychoanalytic Institute Freud Anniversary Lecture Ser.). 80p. 1967. 27.50 (*0-8236-5680-2*) Intl Univs Pr.

Psychotic Core. Michael Eigen. LC 85-3956. 387p. 1986. 50.00 (*0-87668-895-4*) Aronson.

*__Psychotic Disorders in Children & Adolescents.__ Robert L. Findling. LC 00-9512. (Developmental Clinical Psychology & Psychiatry Ser.). 2000. pap. write for info. (*0-7619-2237-7*) Sage Pub.

Psychotic Metaphysics. Eric Rhode. 344p. 1994. pap. text 25.00 (*1-85575-074-0*, Pub. by H Karnac Bks Ltd) Other Pr LLC.

Psychotic Patient: Medication & Psychotherapy. David Greenfield. LC 94-72516. 206p. 1994. pap. text 40.00 (*1-56821-343-3*) Aronson.

Psychotic Process. John Frosch. LC 82-21392. xiii, 521p. 1983. 77.50 (*0-8236-5690-X*) Intl Univs Pr.

Psychotic Reactions & Carburetor Dung: An Anthology. Lester Bangs. Ed. by Greil Marcus. 1988. reprint ed. pap. 16.00 (*0-679-72045-6*) Vin Bks.

Psychotic States in Children. Margaret Rustin. LC 97-50306. (Tavistock Clinic Ser.). 304p. (C). 1998. pap. 25.00 (*0-415-92083-3*) Routledge.

Psychotic States in Children. Margaret Rustin. LC 97-50306. (Tavistock Clinic Ser.). 304p. (C). 1998. 75.00 (*0-415-92082-5*) Routledge.

Psychotix & Drunkenkwix Meet Texus Separatus: A Psychotix & Drunkenkwix Adventure. Griswold. (Illus.). 120p. (C). 1999. pap. 14.95 (*0-9662984-0-3*) Landwaster Bks.

*__Psychotix the Gaul in Dullus International.__ Griswold. (Illus.). 150p. 1999. pap. 14.95 (*0-9662984-8-9*) Landwaster Bks.

*__Psychotix the Gaul in Tiberius' Palace.__ Griswold. (Illus.). 140p. 1999. pap. 14.95 (*0-9662984-1-1*) Landwaster Bks.

Psychotrauma. Ed. by W. S. De Loos & W. Op den Velde. (Psychotherapy & Psychosomatics Ser.: Vol. 57, No. 4, 1992). (Illus.). iv, 72p. 1992. pap. 22.75 (*3-8055-5662-4*) S Karger.

Psychotraumatology: Key Papers & Core Concepts in Post-Traumatic Stress. Ed. by George S. Everly, Jr. & J. M. Lating. (The Plenum Series on Stress & Coping). (Illus.). 440p. (C). 1994. pap. text 65.00 (*0-306-44783-5*, Kluwer Plenum) Kluwer Academic.

Psychotraumatology: Key Papers & Core Concepts in Post-Traumatic Stress. Ed. by George S. Everly, Jr. & J. M. Lating. (The Plenum Series on Stress & Coping). (Illus.). 440p. (C). 1994. 65.00 (*0-306-44782-7*, Plenum Trade) Perseus Pubng.

Psychotrends: What Sort of People Are We Becoming? Shervert Frazier. 272p. 1994. 23.00 (*0-671-75159-X*) S&S Trade.

Psychotronic Encyclopedia of Film. Michael J. Weldon. 832p. 1987. pap. 20.00 (*0-345-34345-X*) Ballantine Pub Grp.

Psychotronics: A Primer on Instruments Using Variable Capacity Tuning. rev. ed. Ed. & Intro. by Peter J. Kelly. 106p. 1986. pap. text 15.00 (*0-943975-01-8*) Interdimens Sci.

Psychotrope. Lisa Smedman. (Shadowrun Ser.). 1998. mass mkt. 5.99 (*0-451-45708-0*, ROC) NAL.

Psychotropic Agents: Anxiolytics, Gerontopsychopharmacological Agents, & Psychomotor Stimulants. Ed. by F. Hoffmeister & G. Stille. (Handbook of Experimental Pharmacology Ser.: Pt. II). (Illus.). 830p. 1981. 312.00 (*0-387-10300-7*) Spr-Verlag.

Psychotropic Agents: Part I, Antipsychotics & Antidepressants. Ed. by G. Stille & F. Hoffmeister. (Handbook of Experimental Pharmacology Ser.: Vol. 55, Pt. 1). (Illus.). 800p. 1980. 256.00 (*0-387-09858-5*) Spr-Verlag.

Psychotropic Drug Development: Social, Economic & Pharmacological Aspects. D. Healy. (Illus.). 128p. 1995. text 59.00 (*0-412-71220-2*, Pub. by E A) OUP.

Psychotropic Drug Handbook. 6th ed. Paul J. Perry et al. LC 90-71835. (Illus.). vi, 358p. 1991. pap. text 4.00 (*0-929375-06-8*) H W Bks.

Psychotropic Drug Handbook. 7th ed. Paul J. Perry et al. 757p. 1997. spiral bd. 44.50 (*0-88048-851-4*, 8851) Am Psychiatric.

Psychotropic Drug Use in the Medically Ill. Ed. by P. Silver. (Advances in Psychosomatic Medicine Ser.: Vol. 21). (Illus.). viii, 170p. 1994. 107.00 (*3-8055-5969-0*) S Karger.

Psychotropic Drugs. 2nd ed. Norman L. Keltner & David G. Folks. LC 96-10647. (Illus.). 624p. (C). (gr. 13). 1996. pap. text 32.95 (*0-8151-4968-9*, 28187) Mosby Inc.

Psychotropic Drugs. 3rd ed. Keltner. 2000. pap. text 32.95 (*0-323-01003-2*) Mosby Inc.

Psychotropic Drugs. 3rd ed. Maxmen. 480p. 1999. 45.00 (*0-393-70301-0*) Norton.

Psychotropic Drugs: Fast Facts. 2nd ed. Jerrold S. Maxmen & Nicholas G. Ward. 421p. 1995. pap. 35.00 (*0-393-70181-6*) Norton.

Psychotropic Drugs: Plasma Concentration & Clinical Response. Ed. by Graham D. Burrows & Trevor R. Norman. LC 80-25685. (Experimental & Clinical Psychiatry Ser.: No. 4). (Illus.). 544p. reprint ed. pap. 168.70 (*0-7837-0659-6*, 204099500019) Bks Demand.

Psychotropic Drugs: Understanding Adverse Reactions. F. Gary Mears. 352p. 1999. 42.00 (*0-393-70284-7*) Norton.

Psychotropic Drugs & Nursing Intervention. Patricia Irons. (Illus.). 1978. text 20.95 (*0-07-032052-7*) McGraw.

Psychotropic Drugs & the Human EEG. Ed. by M. Itil Turan et al. (Modern Problems of Pharmacopsychiatry Ser.: Vol. 8). (Illus.). 300p. 1974. 130.50 (*3-8055-1419-0*) S Karger.

Psychotropic Drugs in Psychiatry. Michael Shepherd. LC 77-17731. 288p. 1979. 30.00 (*0-87668-273-5*) Aronson.

Psychotropic Drugs of Abuse. D. J. K. Balfour. (International Encyclopedia of Pharmacology & Therapeutics Ser.). (Illus.). 384p. 1990. 193.00 (*0-08-036851-4*, Pergamon Pr) Elsevier.

Psychotropic Medication Compliance by Elders. David A. Smith. (Geriatric Psychopathology Ser.). (Orig.). 1995. pap. text 29.95 (*1-884937-30-6*) Manisses Communs.

Psychotropic Medications Pt. II: A Desktop Reference for Mental Health Practitioners. 2nd ed. Ed. by John J. Sramek et al. 400p. 1997. ring bd. 149.00 (*1-884937-45-4*) Manisses Communs.

Psychotropic Medications & Developmental Disabilities Vol. 1: The International Consensus Handbook. Ed. by Steven Reiss & Michael G. Aman. 300p. 1998. text 80.00 (*0-9658966-0-9*) OSU Nisonger.

Psychotropic Substances: Assessments of Medical & Scientific Requirements for Substances in Schedules II, III & IV. Requirement of Import Authorization for Substances in Schedules III & IV. 240p. 40.00 (*92-1-048059-7*, T.95.XI.2); 42.00 (*92-1-048064-3*) UN.

Psychotropic Substances: Assessments of Medical & Scientific Requirements for Substances in Schedules II, III & IV. Requirement of Import Authorization for Substances in Schedules III & IV. International Narcotics Board Staff. 252p. 40.00 (*92-1-048062-7*) UN.

Psychotropic Substances: Statistics for 1996; Assessments of Medical & Scientific Requirements for Substances in Schedules II, III, & IV. International Narcotics Control Board, Vienna Staff. 258p. 1998. pap. 42.00 (*92-1-048067-8*) UN.

*__Psychotropic Substances: Statistics for 1997: Assessments of Medical & Scientific Requirements for Substances in Schedules II, III, & IV.__ International Narcotics Control Board Staff. 266p. 1999. pap. (*92-1-048069-4*) UN.

Psychotropic Substances in Europe: Trends in Licit Use. 76p. 1990. 12.00 (*92-1-148081-7*, 90.XI.2) UN.

Psychovenereology: Personality & Lifestyle Factors in Sexually Transmitted Diseases in Homosexual Men, 3. Michael W. Ross. LC 85-25683. (Sexual Medicine Ser.). 258p. 1986. 55.00 (*0-275-92122-0*, C2122, Praeger Pubs) Greenwood.

Psychovisuals: Handbook of Theory & Visual Analysis. 3rd ed. John Grady. 126p. (C). 1995. text 38.80 (*0-536-58772-8*) Pearson Custom.

Psychozone: Kidzilla & Other Stories. David Lubar. 1997. pap. 4.99 (*0-8125-5880-4*, Pub. by Tor Bks) St Martin.

Psychozone: The Witches' Monkey & Other Stories. David Lubar. 1997. mass mkt. 4.99 (*0-8125-5881-2*, Pub. by Tor Bks) St Martin.

Psychrometrics: Theory & Practice. Ed. by Mildred Geshwiler. (Illus.). 228p. 1996. pap. text 79.00 (*1-883413-39-7*) Am Heat Ref & Air Eng.

Psychrometrics Manual P: Theory & Applications. Hank Rutkowski. (Illus.). 55p. Date not set. pap. 38.00 (*1-892765-08-X*) Air Conditioning Cont.

Psychrotrophic Microorganisms in Spoilage & Pathogenicity. Ed. by Terence A. Roberts et al. LC 81-67902. 552p. 1982. text 157.00 (*0-12-589720-0*) Acad Pr.

Psychrotropic Bacteria in Foods: Disease & Spoilage. Allen A. Kraft. LC 91-47887. 274p. 1992. lib. bdg. 189.00 (*0-8493-4872-2*, QR115) CRC Pr.

PsychState MAX 2.2. Tobey K. Koop. LC 93-92566. 136p. 1994. 59.95 incl. disk (*0-9631763-1-5*) PsychStat.

PschState MAX 2.1: Psychometric - Statistical Programs. Tobey K. Koop. LC 91-91488. 116p. 1992. student ed. 59.95 incl. disk (*0-9631763-0-7*) PsychStat.

Psychware Sourcebook. 4th ed. Samuel Krug. 1993. 37.00 (*0-9635895-0-4*) MetriTech.

PsycINFO User Manual. American Psychological Association Staff. (Illus.). 351p. 1992. ring bd. 45.00 (*1-55798-164-7*) Am Psychol.

Psycles: Using Your Circadian Rhythms to Control Accidents, Illness, & Psychological Problems. Dwight H. Bulkley. LC 80-692. 224p. 1981. 10.95 (*0-672-52651-4*, Bobbs) Macmillan.

Psycology. 3rd ed. Matlin. (C). 1998. pap. text, student ed. 25.00 (*0-15-508400-3*, Pub. by Harcourt Coll Pubs) Harcourt.

Psycology & Sociology Applied to Medicine. M. Porter. LC 98-44803. (Illustrated Colour Text Ser.). 1998. write for info. (*0-443-04971-8*) Church.

Psycotherapy of Carl Rogers: Cases & Commentary. Ed. by Barry A. Farber et al. LC 96-38553. 383p. 1996. lib. bdg. 39.95 (*1-57230-064-7*, 0064) Guilford Pubns.

*__Psyduck's Tongue Twisters, Vol. 5.__ Hajime Yume. (Pokemon Tales Ser.: 5). (Illus.). 18p. 1999. bds. 4.95 (*1-56931-418-7*) Viz Commns Inc.

Psyearth Quest: A Prophetic Novel. Charles Bensinger. LC 98-13071. 240p. 1998. pap. 15.00 (*1-879181-53-3*) Bear & Co.

Psykosis. Wilhelmina Baird. 416p. (Orig.). 1995. mass mkt. 5.99 (*0-441-00238-2*) Ace Bks.

Psyllium Production in India. V. K. Gupta et al. (C). 1989. 22.00 (*81-204-0466-1*) S Asia.

Psylloidea (Homoptera) of Fennoscandia & Demark. F. Ossiannilsson. LC 92-16949. (Fauna Entomologica Scandinavica Ser.: Vol. 26). (Illus.). 348p. 1992. lib. bdg. 142.00 (*90-04-09610-8*) Brill Academic Pubs.

P

An Asterisk (*) at the beginning of an entry indicates that the title is appearing for the first time.

PSYOP (Psychological Operations Warfare) Waging Warfare for the Mind. (Illus.). 54p. (Orig.). (C). 1995. pap. text 15.00 (*0-7881-2548-6*) DIANE Pub.

Psywar: Psychological Warfare in Korea, 1950-53. Stephen E. Pease. LC 92-21511. (Illus.). 192p. 1992. 12.95 (*0-8117-2592-8*) Stackpole.

Psywar on Cuba: The Declassified History of U. S. Anti-Castro Propaganda. John Elliston. LC 98-65907. 300p. 1998. pap. 21.95 (*1-876175-09-5*) Ocean Pr NJ.

Pszichologiai Ertelmezo Szotar: Explanatory Psychological Dictionary. B. Lajos. (HUN.). 1981. 24.95 (*0-8288-2220-4*, M172) Fr & Eur.

PT Activities for Pediatric Groups. Karen L. Kane. 1998. pap. text 39.00 (*0-12-784595-X*) Acad Pr.

PT Assistant in the Schools. Laurie L Gombash. 1999. pap. text 39.00 (*0-12-784597-6*) Acad Pr.

PT Boats. Michael Green. LC 98-15239. (Land & Sea Ser.). (J). 1998. 19.00 (*0-7368-0042-5*, Cpstone High Low) Capstone Pr.

PT Boats. Michael Green. (J). 1998. 19.00 (*0-516-21454-3*) Childrens.

PT Boats at War: World War II to Vietnam. Norman Polmar & Samuel L. Morison. LC 99-13550. (Illus.). 160p. 1999. pap. 19.95 (*0-7603-0499-8*) MBI Pubg.

PT Boats in Action. T. Garth Connelly. LC 94-213847. (Warships in Action Ser.). (Illus.). 50p. 1994. pap. 9.95 (*0-89747-312-4*) Squad Sig Pubns.

PT Exam Review: The Essential Guide for the Foreign-Trained Physical Therapist. Iwona Korzeniowska et al. 128p. 1995. pap. 33.00 (*1-55642-296-2*, 42962) SLACK Inc.

PT 105. Dick Keresey. LC 96-13062. (Illus.). 232p. 1996. 29.95 (*1-55750-460-1*) Naval Inst Pr.

PT-109: WWII Patrol Torpedo Simulation. 1987. disk 14.95 Spectrum Holo.

***PT Primer.** Kathleen Curtis. 300p. 2000. pap. text 35.00 (*1-55642-411-6*) SLACK Inc.

Pt. Reyes, Marin Peninsula, Lake Tahoe Area Mountain Bike. 1995. 6.99 (*0-925873-94-2*) Trails Illustrated.

Design & Installation. William Culross & Son Ltd. Staff. (C). 1991. 90.00 (*0-900323-86-8*, Pub. by W Culross & Son Ltd) St Mut.

Pt. 6 see Advances in Research & Technology of Seeds

Pt. 7 see Advances in Research & Technology of Seeds

Pt. 8 see Advances in Research & Technology of Seeds

Pt. 9 see Advances in Research & Technology of Seeds

***PTA Primer.** Kathleen Curtis. 300p. (C). 2000. pap. text 35.00 (*1-55642-413-2*) SLACK Inc.

PTA Story: A Century of Commitment to Children. National PTA Staff. 200p. 1997. 34.95 (*0-88109-001-8*) Natl PTA.

***Ptam Comm.** Germaine Copeland. 1999. 24.99 (*1-57794-121-7*) Harrison Hse.

PTC 19.5-1972 Application of Fluid Meters Pt. 2: Interim Supplement on Instruments & Apparatus. 1972. pap. text 14.00 (*0-685-30666-6*, G00018) ASME.

PTC '91 Proceedings: Accessing the Global Network: Weaving Technology & Trade in the Pacific. Ed. by Dan J. Wedemeyer & Mark D. Lofstrom. (PTC '91 Proceedings Ser.). 915p. 1991. pap. text 55.00 (*1-880672-02-2*) Pac Telecom.

PTC 31-1973. 1974: Ion Exchange Equipment. 1979. pap. text 8.00 (*0-685-41933-9*, C00016) ASME.

PTC 20.1-1977: Speed & Load Governing Systems for Steam Turbine-Generator Units. 1977. pap. text 12.00 (*0-685-81975-2*, C00019) ASME.

PTCA - An Investigational Tool & a Non-Operative Treatment of Acute Ischemia. Ed. by Patrick W. Serruys et al. (Developments in Cardiovascular Medicine Ser.). (C). 1990. text 257.50 (*0-7923-0346-6*) Kluwer Academic.

PTC'95 Proceedings: Convergence: Closing the Gap. Ed. by Richard L. Nickelson & Dan J. Wedemeyer. (Orig.). 1994. cd-rom 50.00 (*1-880672-09-X*) Pac Telecom.

PTC'95 Proceedings: Convergence: Closing the Gap. Ed. by Richard L. Nickelson & Dan J. Wedemeyer. (Illus.). 740p. (Orig.). 1994. pap. 130.00 (*1-880672-06-5*) Pac Telecom.

PTC'96 Proceedings: The Information Infrastructure: Users, Resources & Strategies. Ed. by Richard L. Nickelson & Dan J. Wedemeyer. (Orig.). 1995. cd-rom 50.00 (*1-880672-08-1*) Pac Telecom.

PTC'96 Proceedings: The Information Infrastructure: Users, Resources & Strategies. Ed. by Richard L. Nickelson & Dan J. Wedemeyer. (Illus.). 750p. (Orig.). 1995. pap. 130.00 (*1-880672-07-3*) Pac Telecom.

Pteranodon. (Microfaxc Ser.). (J). 1997. pap. text 0.99 (*0-7894-2127-5*) DK Pub Inc.

***Pteranodon.** Daniel Cohen. (Discovering Dinosaurs Ser.). 24p. (J). (ps-3). 2000. lib. bdg. 15.93 (*0-7368-0617-2*, Bridgestone Bks) Capstone Pr.

***Pteranodon.** Contrib. by K. S. Rodriguez. LC 99-54469. (Prehistoric Creatures Then & Now Ser.). 32p. (J). 2000. 22.03 (*0-7398-0101-5*) Raintree Steck-V.

Pteranodon: The Flying Reptile. Elizabeth Sandell. Ed. by Marjorie Oelerich & Howard Schroeder. LC 88-953. (Dinosaur Discovery Era Ser.). (Illus.). 32p. (J). (gr. k-5). 1988. pap. 5.95 (*0-944280-11-0*); lib. bdg. 12.95 (*0-944280-05-6*) Bancroft-Sage.

Pteridology in Perspective. xx, 700p. 1996. 120.00 (*1-900347-09-1*, Pub. by Royal Botnic Grdns) Balogh.

Pteridophyta. E. A. Schelpe & N. C. Anthony. (Flora of Southern Africa Ser.). (Illus.). 292p. 1986. 30.00 (*0-621-08877-3*, Pub. by Natl Botanical Inst) Balogh.

Pteridophyte Flora of Fiji. G. Brownlie. (Beiheft zur Nova Hedwigia Ser.: No. 55). 1977. lib. bdg. 170.00 (*3-7682-5455-0*) Lubrecht & Cramer.

Pteridophyte Flora of Oaxaca, Mexico. J. T. Mickel & J. M. Beitel. LC 88-12474. (Memoirs Ser.: Vol. 46). (Illus.). 558p. (C). 1988. text 45.00 (*0-89327-323-6*) NY Botanical.

Pteridophytes. Alan R. Smith. Ed. by Dennis E. Breedlove. (Flora of Chiapas Ser.: Pt. 2). (Illus.). 370p. (Orig.). 1981. pap. 30.00 (*0-940228-01-7*) Calif Acad Sci.

Pteridophytes: Some Aspects of Their Structure & Morphology. S. S. Bir. (Aspects of Plant Sciences Ser.: Vol. III). 170p. 1980. 15.00 (*0-88065-064-8*) Scholarly Pubns.

Pteridophytes: Some Aspects of Their Structure Morphology. S. S. Bir. (C). 1988. 40.00 (*0-7855-3259-5*, Pub. by Scientific) St Mut.

Pteridophytes: Their Morphology, Cytology, Taxonomy & Phylogeny. S. S. Bir. (C). 1988. 60.00 (*0-7855-3260-9*, Pub. by Scientific) St Mut.

Pteridophytes: Their Morphology, Cytology, Taxonomy & Phytogeny. S. S. Bir. (Aspects of Plant Sciences Ser.: Vol. 6). vii, 253p. 1983. 19.00 (*1-55528-012-9*, Pub. by Today Tomorrow) Scholarly Pubns.

Pteridophytes of Kansas, Nebraska, South Dakota & North Dakota, U. S. A. Nova Hedwigia Beiheft, No. 61. A. J. Petrik-Ott. 1979. lib. bdg. 80.00 (*3-7682-5461-5*) Lubrecht & Cramer.

Pteridophytes of the Society Islands. E. B. Copeland. (BMB Ser.). 1974. reprint ed. 25.00 (*0-527-02199-7*) Periodicals Srv.

Pteridophytes of Tropical East Africa: A Preliminary Check-List of the Species. R. J. Johns. 131p. 1991. pap. 20.00 (*0-947643-33-8*, Pub. by Royal Botnic Grdns) Balogh.

Pterocarpus (Leguminosae-Papilionaceae) Revised for the World. J. P. Rojo. 1971. 36.00 (*3-7682-0726-9*) Lubrecht & Cramer.

Pterodactyl & Other Short Stories. Tushar K. Ghosh. (C). 1991. 4.50 (*81-7018-691-9*, Pub. by BR Pub) S Asia.

Pterodactyl in the Wilderness. Chuck Oliveros. 56p. (Orig.). 1983. pap. 3.00 (*0-911757-00-7*) Dead Angel.

Pterodactyl Rose: Poems of Ecology. William Heyen. LC 90-72138. 61p. 1991. 18.95 (*1-877770-24-8*); pap. 12.50 (*1-877770-25-6*); audio 12.95 (*1-877770-27-2*) Time Being Bks.

Pterodactyl Tunnel: Amusement Park Math see I Love Math Series

Pterodactyls. Elaine Landau. 1999. lib. bdg. 6.95 (*0-516-26500-8*) Childrens.

Pterodactyls. Elaine Landau. LC 98-8280. (Dinosaurs Ser.). (J). 1999. 21.50 (*0-516-20447-5*) Childrens.

Pterodactyls. Nicky Silver. 1994. pap. 5.25 (*0-8222-1375-3*) Dramatists Play.

Pterodactylus: A Dinosaur from the Jurassic Period see New Dinosaur Collection

PteroDARKtyl II: Layouts for a Modern Palazzo. Artemis Smith, pseud. (Pterodactyl Ser.). 2001. pap. 200.00 (*1-878998-19-6*) Savant Garde.

PteroDARKtyl II: Vol. II: Layouts for a Modern Palazzo. deluxe limited ed. Artemis Smith, pseud. (Skeets Ser.). 2001. cd-rom 25.00 (*1-878998-09-9*) Savant Garde.

Pteronodon. Stuart A. Kallen. Ed. by Julie Berg. LC 94-4534. (If the Dinosaurs Could Talk Ser.). (J). 1994. 14.98 (*1-56239-283-2*) ABDO Pub Co.

Pterosauria. P. Wellnhofer. (Handbook of Paleoherpatology: Pt. 19). (Illus.). 82p. 1978. pap. text 67.50 (*3-437-30269-8*) Lubrecht & Cramer.

Pterosaurs: The Flying Reptiles. S. Christopher Bennett. LC 93-29845. (Prehistoric Life Ser.). (Illus.). 64p. (J). (gr. 5-7). 1995. lib. bdg. 24.00 (*0-531-11181-4*) Watts.

PTFE Seals in Reciprocating Compressors: Manual of Material Selection, Design & Operating Practices. American Society of Mechanical Engineers Staff. LC 74-32657. 90p. reprint ed. pap. 30.00 (*0-608-11747-1*, 201682400005) Bks Demand.

P38 Automatic Pistol. Gene Gangaroea. 1993. pap. 16.95 (*0-88317-170-8*) Stoeger Pub Co.

Pthreads Programming: A Posix Standard for Better Understanding. Bradford Nichols et al. Ed. by Andy Oram. (Illus.). 284p. 1996. reprint ed. pap. 34.95 (*1-56592-115-1*) Thomson Learn.

P'tit Gars de Georgie. Erskine Caldwell. (FRE.). 182p. 1978. pap. 10.95 (*0-7859-1881-7*, 2070370593) Fr & Eur.

Ptolemaei, Claudii Vol. III, Fascicule 2: Peri Kriteriu Kai Hegemoniku. Ed. by Lammert & Boer. (GRE.). 1961. 22.95 (*3-322-00908-4*, T1966, Pub. by B G Teubner) U of Mich Pr.

Ptolemaic Alexandria, 3 vols. P. M. Fraser. 2,102p. 1985. reprint ed. text 225.00 (*0-19-814278-1*) OUP.

Ptolemaic Lexikon, No. Ola 78. E. Peters. LC 98-218348. 1998. 171.95 (*90-6831-933-7*, Pub. by Peeters Pub) Bks Intl VA.

Ptolemaios und Porphyrios Uber die Musik. Ingemar During. 293p. 1987. reprint ed. write for info. (*3-487-07932-1*) G Olms Pubs.

Ptolemais: City of the Libyan Pentapolis. Carl H. Kraeling. LC 62-9742. 288p. 1963. lib. bdg. 48.00 (*0-226-62193-6*, OIP90) U Ch Pr.

Ptolemais Cyrenaica. Oriental Institute Staff & David Nasgowitz. LC 80-26769. (Illus.). 84p. 1981. lib. bdg. 60.00 incl. fiche (*0-226-69474-7*) U Ch Pr.

Ptolemaischen Munz-und Rechnugswerte. F. Hultsch. (GER.). 66p. 1980. 15.00 (*0-916710-81-5*) Obol Intl.

***Ptolemy & the Foundations of Ancient Mathematical Optics Pt. 3: A Guided Study.** A. Mark Smith. LC 99-15221. (Transactions of the American Philosophical Society Ser.: Vol. 89). 1999. 20.00 (*0-87169-893-5*) Am Philos.

Ptolemy's Almagest. G. J. Toomer. LC 98-33565. 693p. 1998. pap. text 39.50 (*0-691-00260-6*, Pub. by Princeton U Pr) Cal Prin Full Svc.

Ptolemy's First Commentator. Alexander Jones. LC 90-83199. (Transactions Ser.: Vol. 80, Pt. 7). (Illus.). 61p. (C). 1990. pap. 15.00 (*0-87169-807-2*, T807-JOA) Am Philos.

***Ptolemy's Geography: An Annotated Translation of the Theoretical Chapters.** J. Lennart Berggren. (Illus.). 232p. 2000. 39.50 (*0-691-01042-0*) Princeton U Pr.

Ptolemy's Handy Tables: The Astronomical Tables of Codex Vaticanus Graecus 1291. Tr. & Intro. by William D. Stahlman. (Sources & Studies in the History & Philosophy of Classical Science: Vol. 3). 230p. 43.00 (*0-8153-0216-9*) Garland.

Ptolemy's Pyre. Kurt A. Weischedel. 87p. (Orig.). 1995. pap. write for info. (*0-9623780-6-2*) Ars Obscura.

Ptolemy's Tetrabiblos or Quadripartite Being Four Books of the Influence of the Stars. J. M. Ashmand. 190p. 1993. reprint ed. pap. 13.95 (*1-56459-407-6*) Kessinger Pub.

Ptolemy's Tetrabiblos, Quadripartite: Being Four Books of the Influence of the Stars. J. M. Ashmand. 240p. 1996. reprint ed. pap. 15.50 (*0-7873-0042-X*) Hlth Research.

Ptolemy's Theory of Visual Perception: An English Translation of the Optics with Introduction & Commentary. A. Mark Smith. LC 94-78521. (Transactions Ser.: Vol. 86, Pt. 2). (Illus.). 300p. (Orig.). 1996. pap. 15.00 (*0-87169-862-5*, T862-sma) Am Philos.

PTSD-Borderlines in Therapy: Finding the Balance. Jerome Kroll. 240p. (C). 1993. 35.00 (*0-393-70157-3*) Norton.

P2 Nucleotide Receptors. Ed. by John T. Turner et al. LC 97-39694. (Receptors Ser.). (Illus.). 456p. 1997. 139.00 (*0-89603-425-9*) Humana.

P2 Purinoceptors: Localization, Function, & Transduction Mechanisms. Ed. by Derek J. Chadwick & Jamie A. Goode. LC 96-1089. (Ciba Foundation Symposium Ser.: No. 198). 346p. 1996. 128.00 (*0-471-96125-6*) Wiley.

***Pu Der Bar.** A. A. Milne, pseud. 1999. pap. text 12.95 (*3-423-70395-4*) Distribks Inc.

***PU-239 & Other Russian Fantasies.** Ken Kalfus. 320p. 2000. reprint ed. 13.95 (*0-7434-0075-5*, WSP) PB.

Pu-239: And Other Russian Fantasies. Ken Kalfus. LC 99-18183. 272p. 1999. 22.00 (*1-57131-029-0*) Milkweed Ed.

PU Vulpeculae Light Curves, 1979-1995. Compiled by Janet A. Mattei et al. (AAVSO Monographs: No. 11). (Illus.). 25p. 1997. pap. text 10.00 (*1-878174-22-3*) Am Assn Var Star.

Pua Nani: Hawaii Is a Garden. Jeri Bostwick. (Illus.). 136p. 1987. boxed set 19.95 (*0-935180-60-5*) Mutual Pub HI.

Puav Paab Tau Ntau Yaam (Hmong) Arthur Morton. Tr. by Yer J. Thao. (J). (gr. k-3). 1994. 12.50 (*1-57842-047-4*) Delmas Creat.

Pub & English Social Change. Daniel E. Vasey. LC 89-31180. (Studies in Anthropology: No. 4). 1990. 52.50 (*0-404-62604-1*) AMS Pr.

Pub, Club & Grub Guide to Washington, D. C. 3rd rev. ed. Zena L. Polin & Stephen G. Gatward. LC 95-69592. (Illus.). 173p. 1997. pap. 9.95 (*0-9647062-2-9*) Patmos Pr DC.

Pub Crawler's Guide to Montana's Small Town Taverns: A Field Guide to 365 Taverns in Montana's Smallest Communities. Doug Ardary. LC 96-93006. (Illus.). x, 392p. (Orig.). 1997. pap. 14.95 (*0-9655981-0-1*, 0101) Pub Crawler.

Pub Games of England. Patrick T. Finn. (Games & Pastimes Ser.: Vol. 5). (Illus.). 156p. 1981. reprint ed. 18.95 (*0-900891-66-1*) Oleander Pr.

Pub Trivia Quiz. rev. ed. Lagoon Bks Staff. (Illus.). 96p. 1996. 6.95 (*1-899712-50-X*, Pub. by Lagoon Bks) Midpt Trade.

Pub Walks Around Portsmouth & the South Downs. John Price. (C). 1989. 39.00 (*1-85455-070-5*, Pub. by Ensign Pubns & Print) St Mut.

Pub Walks in the New Forest. Diana Smith. (C). 1989. 39.00 (*0-7855-6615-5*, Pub. by Ensign Pubns & Print) St Mut.

Pubelo Potter: A Study of Creative Imagination in Primitive Art. Ruth L. Bunzel. LC 73-82257. (Columbia Univ. Contributions to Anthropology Ser.: Vol. 8). (Illus.). reprint ed. 55.00 (*0-404-50558-9*) AMS Pr.

Pubertal Maturation in Female Development. Ed. by Haken Stattin & David Magnusson. (Paths Through Life Ser.). 408p. 1990. 99.95 (*0-8058-0595-8*) L Erlbaum Assocs.

Puberty. Jacqueline A. Ball. (Looking Good Ser.: Set II). 32p. (J). 1989. lib. bdg. 19.93 (*0-86625-283-5*) Rourke Pubns.

***Puberty.** Alvin Silverstein et al. LC 99-45289. (Watts Library). 2000. 24.00 (*0-531-11750-2*) Watts.

Puberty: An Illustrated Manual for Parents & Daughters. Angela Hynes. (Illus.). 147p. (YA). (gr. 6-10). 1999. reprint ed. text 13.00 (*0-7881-6361-2*) DIANE Pub.

Puberty: The Game Show. Greg Atkins. 31p. 1998. pap. 4.00 (*0-87440-064-3*) Bakers Plays.

***Puberty & Growing Up.** Pete Sanders & Steve Myers. LC 99-45552. (What Do You Know About...Ser.). 32p. (J). (gr. 4-6). 2000. lib. bdg. 21.90 (*0-7613-1151-3*, Copper Beech Bks) Millbrook Pr.

Puberty & Reproduction. Catherine S. Golliher. (Comprehensive Health for Middle Grades Ser.). (J). (gr. 6-9). 1996. 24.00 (*1-56071-462-X*, H564) ETR Assocs.

Puberty Game: A Guide to Help Parents Get Ready to Play. John Court. 224p. 1998. pap. 13.95 (*0-7322-5786-7*) HarpC.

Puberty, Sexuality & the Self: Girls & Boys at Adolescence. Karin A. Martin. 176p. (C). 1996. 70.00 (*0-415-91424-8*); pap. 17.99 (*0-415-91425-6*) Routledge.

Puberty Tree: New & Selected Poems. D. M. Thomas et al. 192p. 1993. pap. 19.95 (*1-85224-200-0*, Pub. by Bloodaxe Bks) Dufour.

***Pubis Angelical.** Manuel Puig. 2000. pap. write for info. (*0-8166-3681-8*) U of Minn Pr.

Public: Art: Space. Mel Gooding. LC 98-165807. (Illus.). 112p. 1998. pap. 35.00 (*1-85894-048-6*, Pub. by Merrell Holberton) U of Wash Pr.

Public - Private Interplay in Social Protection. Ed. by martin Rein & Lee Rainwater. LC 86-11911. (Comparative Public Policy Analysis Ser.). 256p. (gr. 13). 1986. pap. text 42.95 (*0-87332-498-6*) M E Sharpe.

Public Accepts: Stories Behind Famous Trade-Marks, Names, & Slogans. Isaac E. Lambert. LC 75-39256. (Getting & Spending: The Consumer's Dilemma Ser.). (Illus.). 1976. reprint ed. 20.95 (*0-405-08029-8*) Ayer.

Public Access: Literary Theory & American Cultural Politics. Michael Berube. LC 94-11163. 256p. (C). 1994. pap. 20.00 (*0-86091-678-2*, Pub. by Verso) Norton.

Public Access - Public Interest. 1975. 2.00 (*0-686-09559-6*) Network Project.

Public Access Microcomputers. 2nd ed. Patrick R. Dewey. (Professional Librarian Ser.). 300p. (C). 1990. 40.00 (*0-8161-1896-5*, Hall Reference); 30.00 (*0-8161-1897-3*, Hall Reference) Macmillan.

Public Access Microcomputers in Academic Libraries: The Mann Library Model at Cornell University. fac. ed. Ed. by Howard Curtis. LC 86-22315. 231p. 1987. pap. 71.70 (*0-7837-7319-6*, 204724600007) Bks Demand.

Public Access Television: America's Electronic Soapbox. Laura R. Linder. LC 98-56631. (Illus.). 192p. 1999. 55.00 (*0-275-96487-6*, C6487, Praeger Pubs); pap. 19.95 (*0-275-96488-4*, C6487, Praeger Pubs) Greenwood.

Public Access Terminals: Determining Quantity Requirements. John E. Tolle. LC 84-164540. (Library, Information, & Computer Science Ser.: No. 3). (Illus.). 182p. (Orig.). 1983. pap. 14.50 (*0-933418-51-5*) OCLC Online Comp.

Public Access to Art in Paris: A Documentary History from the Middle Ages to 1800. Robert W. Berger. LC 97-48464. 1362p. 1999. 75.00 (*0-271-01749-X*) Pa St U Pr.

Public Access to Government Information. 1984. pap. 49.50 (*0-89391-252-2*) Ablx Pub.

Public Access to Government Information. Peter Hernon & Charles R. McClure. LC 83-25797. (Libraries & Information Science). 472p. 1984. text 89.50 (*0-89391-100-3*) Ablx Pub.

Public Access to Government Information: Trends, Strategies. 2nd rev. ed. Peter Hernon & Charles R. McClure. LC 88-19249. (Information Management, Policies & Services Ser.). 560p. (C). 1994. text 89.50 (*0-89391-522-X*); pap. text 49.50 (*0-89391-523-8*) Ablx Pub.

Public Access to Government Information in the 21st Century: Hearings Before the Committee on Rules & Administrations, U. S. Senate. (Illus.). 526p. (C). 1998. pap. text 50.00 (*0-7881-4979-2*) DIANE Pub.

Public Access to Information. Ed. by Andrew C. Gordon & John P. Heinz. LC 78-63009. 400p. 1979. reprint ed. 44.95 (*0-87855-278-2*) Transaction Pubs.

Public Access to Library Automation: Proceedings of the Clinic on Library Applications of Data Processing,1980. Ed. by J. L. Divilbiss. LC 81-11685. 128p. 1981. 15.00 (*0-87845-065-3*) U of Ill Grad Sch.

Public Access to the Internet. Ed. by Brian Kahin & James Keller. LC 95-8808. 390p. 1995. pap. text 22.50 (*0-262-61118-X*) MIT Pr.

Public Accomodations under the American with Disabilities Act: Compliance & Litigation Manual. Jason E. Searns et al. LC 96-22768. 288p. 1996. text. write for info. (*0-314-09632-9*) West Pub.

Public Accountability: Evaluating Technology-Based Institutions. Albert N. Link. 5p. 1998. 95.00 (*0-7923-8312-5*) Kluwer Academic.

Public Accountability for Student Success: Standards for Education Accountability Systems. NASBE Study Group on Education Accountability Staff. 55p. 1998. pap. 12.00 (*1-58434-038-X*) NASBE.

Public Accountability of State Enterprise in India. Satish K. Batra. 1992. text 25.00 (*81-7045-050-0*, Pub. by Assoc Pub Hse) Advent Bks Div.

Public Accounting Deskbook, 1994. Ed. by Mark Carr. 72p. (Orig.). 1994. pap. text 39.00 (*0-9616858-6-7*) Strafford Pubns.

Public Accounting Deskbook, 1995. Ed. by Suzanne Verity. (Illus.). 91p. (Orig.). 1995. pap. 39.00 (*1-887986-00-6*) Strafford Pubns.

Public Accounting Deskbook, 1996. Ed. by Suzanne Verity & Michael Hunter. (Illus.). 150p. (Orig.). 1996. pap. write for info. (*1-887986-03-0*) Strafford Pubns.

Public Accounting Practice Manual. Allan B. Afterman. 1993. pap. 130.00 (*0-685-69599-9*, CRP) Warren Gorham & Lamont.

Public Address in the Twentieth Century South: The Evolution of a Region. W. Stuart Towns. LC 98-23036. 256p. 1999. 59.95 (*0-275-96224-5*, Praeger Pubs) Greenwood.

***Public Address in the Twentieth-Century South: The Evolution of a Region.** W. Stuart Towns. LC 98-23036. 256p. 2000. pap. 24.95 (*0-275-96970-3*, Praeger Pubs) Greenwood.

Public Administration. M. P. Barber. 245p. (C). 1984. 120.00 (*0-7855-5652-4*, Pub. by Inst Pur & Supply) St Mut.

***Public Administration.** Greene. 2001. pap. 42.00 (*0-534-55343-5*) Thomson Learn.

Public Administration. Hyde. (C). 1996. pap. text, teacher ed. 40.00 (*0-15-502207-5*) Harcourt Coll Pubs.

Public Administration. Laura Lemay. (Political Science). 2001. pap. text 37.00 (*0-534-57663-X*) Wadsworth Pub.

Public Administration. Herbert A. Simon et al. 600p. (C). 1991. pap. 29.95 (*0-88738-895-7*) Transaction Pubs.

P

An Asterisk (*) at the beginning of an entry indicates that the title is appearing for the first time.

Public Administration. 2nd ed. Jeffrey D. Straussman. 422p. (C). 1990. teacher ed. write for info. (*0-8013-0180-7*, 75838) Longman.

Public Administration: A Bibliographic Guide to the Literature. McCurdy. (Public Administration & Public Policy Ser.: Vol. 29). (Illus.). 328p. 1986. text 95.00 (*0-8247-7518-X*) Dekker.

Public Administration: An Action Orientation. 2nd ed. Robert B. Denhardt. 450p. (C). 1981. text 62.00 (*0-534-24738-5*) Harcourt.

Public Administration: An Action Orientation. 3rd ed. Bob Denhardt. LC 98-71721. 320p. (C). 1998. text 69.50 (*0-15-505524-0*) Harcourt Coll Pubs.

Public Administration: An Introduction. Khan. 192p. (C). 1997. per. 53.95 (*0-7872-4298-5*, 41429801) Kendall-Hunt.

Public Administration: Balancing Power & Accountability. 2nd ed. Jerome B. McKinney & Lawrence C. Howard. LC 96-47619. 520p. 1998. 75.00 (*0-275-95564-8*, Praeger Pubs); pap. 29.95 (*0-275-95565-6*, Praeger Pubs) Greenwood.

Public Administration: Comparative Perspective. 5th ed. Ferrel Heady. LC 95-21421. (Public Administration & Public Policy Ser.: Vol. 59). (Illus.). 520p. 1995. text 69.75 (*0-8247-9657-8*) Dekker.

Public Administration: Design & Problem Solving. Jong S. Jun. LC 94-71218. 350p. 1994. reprint ed. 41.95 (*0-9639874-2-9*) Chatelaine.

Public Administration: History & Theory in Contemporary Perspective. Ed. by Joseph A. Uveges. (Annuals of Public Administration Ser.: Vol. 1). (Illus.). 144p. 1982. text 99.75 (*0-8247-1557-8*) Dekker.

Public Administration: Policy, Politics & Practice. 2nd ed. William C. Johnson. (Illus.). 460p. (C). 1995. text 38.95 (*1-56134-425-7*, Dshkn McGill-Hill) McGrw-H Hghr Educ.

Public Administration: Scenarios in Public Management. Allan W. Lerner & John Wanat. LC 92-16366. 192p. (C). 1993. pap. text 23.60 (*0-13-739046-7*) P-H.

Public Administration: The Execution & Formulation of Public Policy. David Bresnick. 240p. (C). 1991. 40.00 (*0-9610834-5-X*) Human Serv Pr.

Public Administration: The Grassroot Concerns. Amita Singh. LC 99-932825. 183p. 1998. 25.00 (*81-7099-657-0*, Pub. by Mittal Pubs Dist) Nataraj Bks.

Public Administration: Understanding Management, Politics, & Law in the Public Sector. 2nd ed. David H. Rosenbloom & Deborah D. Goldman. (Illus.). 576p. (C). 1989. text. write for info. (*0-318-62942-9*) Random.

Public Administration: Understanding Management, Politics & Law in the Public Sector. 4th ed. David H. Rosenbloom & Deborah D. Goldman. LC 96-53404. 600p. (C). 1997. 63.44 (*0-07-053972-3*) McGraw.

***Public Administration & Civil Service in Developing Asia.** Asian Development Bank Staff. 350p. 2000. 15.00 (*971-561-244-X*, Pub. by Asian Devel Bank) Paul & Co Pubs.

Public Administration & Decision-Aiding Software: Improving Procedure & Substance, 23. Ed. by Stuart S. Nagel. LC 90-36737. (New Directions in Information Management Ser.: No. 23). 280p. 1990. 65.00 (*0-313-27518-1*, NPA, Greenwood Pr) Greenwood.

Public Administration & Development: Improving Accountability, Responsiveness & Legal Framework. Ed. by Ilias. LC 98-70647. (International Institute of Administrative Sciences Monographs: No. 5). 129p. 1998. pap. 50.00 (*90-5199-383-8*, Pub. by IOS Pr) IOS Press.

Public Administration & Government. Cooper. LC 97-72037. (C). 1997. text 53.00 (*0-15-500481-6*, Pub. by Harcourt Coll Pubs) Harcourt.

Public Administration & Law. 2nd ed. Ed. by David H. Rosenbloom & Rosemary O'Leary. LC 96-31378. (Public Administration & Public Policy Ser.: Vol. 61). (Illus.). 368p. 1996. text 150.00 (*0-8247-9769-8*) Dekker.

Public Administration & Public Affairs. 2nd ed. Nicholas L. Henry. LC 79-15414. 1980. 23.95 (*0-13-737296-5*) P-H.

Public Administration & Public Affairs. 7th ed. Nicholas Henry. LC 98-21617. 500p. (C). 1998. 58.00 (*0-13-639089-7*) P-H.

***Public Administration & Public Affairs.** 8th ed. Nicholas Henry. LC 99-86554. 504p. 2000. pap. 53.33 (*0-13-027271-X*) P-H.

Public Administration & Public Opinion in Bengal (1854-1885) Anuradha Chanda. 187p. 1986. 17.50 (*0-8364-2002-0*, Pub. by KP Bagchi) S Asia.

Public Administration & the Crisis of the State. Richard Bates. 117p. (C). 1985. 48.00 (*0-7300-0212-8*, Pub. by Deakin Univ) St Mut.

Public Administration & the Department of Agriculture. John M. Gaus & Leon O. Wolcott. LC 75-8788. (FDR & the Era of the New Deal Ser.). 1975. reprint ed. lib. bdg. 65.00 (*0-306-70704-7*) Da Capo.

Public Administration & the Korean Transformation: Concepts, Policies, & Value Conflicts. Chung-Hyun Ro. LC 93-3592. (Library of Management for Development). (Illus.). 224p. 1993. 34.95 (*1-56549-023-1*); pap. 18.95 (*1-56549-022-3*) Kumarian Pr.

Public Administration as a Developing Discipline: Organization Development As One of a Future Family of Miniparadigms, Pt. 2. Robert T. Golembiewski. (Illus.). 232p. 1977. text 85.00 (*0-8247-6566-4*) Dekker.

Public Administration As a Developing Discipline: Perspectives on Past & Present, Pt. 1. Robert T. Golembiewski. (Political Science Ser.: Vol. 1). (Illus.). 264p. 1977. text 85.00 (*0-8247-6565-6*) Dekker.

Public Administration Desk Book. James R. Coleman & Robert E. Dugan. 175p. (Orig.). 1990. pap. text 35.00 (*0-931684-12-9*) Gov Res Pubns.

Public Administration Dictionary. William Fox & Ivan H. Meyer. 1995. pap. 23.00 (*0-7021-3219-5*, Pub. by Juta & Co) Intl Spec Bk.

Public Administration Dictionary. 2nd ed. Ralph C. Chandler & Jack C. Plano. LC 87-32045. (Clio Dictionaries in Political Science Ser.). 430p. 1988. pap. text 24.75 (*0-87436-499-X*) ABC-CLIO.

Public Administration Dictionary. 2nd ed. Ralph C. Chandler & Jack C. Plano. LC 87-32045. (Clio Dictionaries in Political Science Ser.). 430p. 1988. lib. bdg. 51.50 (*0-87436-498-1*) ABC-CLIO.

Public Administration Illuminated & Inspired by the Arts. Ed. by Charles T. Goodsell & Nancy Murray. LC 94-36666. 240p. 1995. 59.95 (*0-275-94806-4*, Praeger Pubs) Greenwood.

***Public Administration in a New Era: Postmodern & Critical Perspectives.** Ed. by Mario A. Rivera & Gary M. Woller. LC 99-50927. (Illus.). xii, 210p. (C). 2000. pap. 24.95 (*1-57420-071-2*, JF1351.P8) Chatelaine.

Public Administration in Action: Readings, Profiles & Cases. Robert B. Denhardt & Barry R. Hammond. LC 91-25592. 413p. (C). 1980. pap. text 43.00 (*0-534-15960-5*) Harcourt.

Public Administration in Africa: Main Issues & Selected Country Studies. Ed. by Oladipupo Adamolekun. LC 99-10544. 440p. 1999. 70.00 (*0-8133-3653-8*, Pub. by Westview) HarpC.

Public Administration in America. Mark Huddleston. (C). 1999. text. write for info. (*0-8013-1886-6*) Longman.

Public Administration in America. 5th ed. Michael E. Milakovich. 1995. pap. text, teacher ed. 5.00 (*0-312-11992-5*) St Martin.

Public Administration in America. 6th ed. Gordon Staff. LC 97-65179. 560p. 1997. pap. 60.95 (*0-312-15275-2*) St Martin.

Public Administration in an Information Age: A Handbook. Ed. by Wim Van Der Donk & Ignace Snellen. (Information Development & the Public Sector Ser.: No. 6). 1998. 95.00 (*90-5199-395-1*, Pub. by IOS Pr) IOS Press.

Public Administration in Britain. D. J. Wilson. (Illus.). 1987. pap. text 14.95 (*0-04-352110-X*) Routledge.

Public Administration in China, 323. Ed. by Miriam K. Mills & Stuart S. Nagel. LC 92-42675. (Contributions in Political Science Ser.: No. 323). 184p. 1993. 55.00 (*0-313-28847-X*, GM8847, Greenwood Pr) Greenwood.

Public Administration in Developed Democracies: A Comparative Study. Donald C. Rowat. (Public Administration & Public Policy Ser.: Vol. 32). (Illus.). 528p. 1987. text 145.00 (*0-8247-7807-3*) Dekker.

Public Administration in Hong Kong. Charles H. Collins. LC 70-179180. reprint ed. 37.50 (*0-404-54810-5*) AMS Pr.

Public Administration in India. V. Bhaskara Rao. (C). 1989. 31.00 (*81-202-0233-3*, Pub. by Ajanta) S Asia.

Public Administration in India. Krishna K. Tummala. LC 95-948483. 1994. pap. 28.50 (*981-210-051-2*, Pub. by Times Academic) Intl Spec Bk.

Public Administration in Latin America: A Bibliography. Ed. by Jorge Grossman. 1976. lib. bdg. 59.95 (*0-8490-2488-9*) Gordon Pr.

Public Administration in Massachusetts: The Relation of Central to Local Activity. Robert H. Whitten. LC 73-82249. (Columbia University. Studies in the Social Sciences: No. 22). reprint ed. 29.50 (*0-404-51022-1*) AMS Pr.

Public Administration in Nigeria. N. Akpan. 1982. pap. text. write for info. (*0-582-64398-8*, Pub. by Addison-Wesley) Longman.

Public Administration in Nigeria. R. O. Ola. 220p. 1984. pap. 24.50 (*0-7103-0044-1*) Routledge.

Public Administration in Siam. W. D. Reeve. LC 74-179236. reprint ed. 24.50 (*0-404-54863-6*) AMS Pr.

Public Administration in Small & Island States. Ed. by Randall Baker. LC 91-44015. (Library of Management for Development, New Direction). (Illus.). xv, 310p. 1992. 35.00 (*1-56549-001-0*); pap. 12.95 (*1-56549-000-2*) Kumarian Pr.

Public Administration in the Federal Republic of Germany. Ed. by K. Konig et al. 350p. 1983. pap. 20.00 (*90-6544-126-3*) Kluwer Academic.

Public Administration in the Global Village. Ed. by Jean-Claude Garcia-Zamor & Renu Khator. LC 93-23489. 208p. 1994. 57.95 (*0-275-94671-1*, Praeger Pubs) Greenwood.

Public Administration in the NICs: Challenges & Accomplishments. Ed. by Ahmed S. Huque et al. LC 96-11843. 192p. 1996. text 65.00 (*0-312-16110-7*) St Martin.

Public Administration in the Third World: An International Handbook. Ed. by V. Subramanian. LC 88-7706. 456p. 1990. lib. bdg. 105.00 (*0-313-24730-7*, SUP/, Greenwood Pr) Greenwood.

Public Administration in the United States. 2nd ed. David F. Schuman & Dick W. Olufs, III. 528p. (C). 1993. text 57.16 (*0-669-29411-X*); teacher ed. 2.66 (*0-669-29412-8*) HM Trade Div.

***Public Administration in the United States: A Reader.** John C. Koritansky. 320p. (C). 2000. pap. text 22.95 (*1-58510-001-3*) Focus Pub-R Pullins.

Public Administration in Theory & Practice. Raymond W. Cox, III et al. LC 93-5592. 281p. (C). 1993. 48.00 (*0-13-739384-9*) P-H.

Public Administration in World Perspective. Ed. by O. P. Dwivedi & Keith Henderson. LC 90-10712. (Illus.). 428p. 1990. text 49.95 (*0-8138-0154-0*) Iowa St U Pr.

Public Administration Intern. Jack Rudman. (Career Examination Ser.: C-628). 1994. pap. 23.95 (*0-8373-0628-0*) Nat Learn.

Public Administration, 1999-2000. 6th ed. Howad R. Balanoff. (Annual Ser.). (Illus.). 240p. 1998. pap. text 12.25 (*0-07-039227-7*, Dshkn McG-Hill) McGrw-H Hghr Educ.

Public Administration, Politics & the People: Selected Readings for Administrators, Employees & Citizens. Dean L. Yarwood. LC 86-10381. (Illus.). 421p. 1986. pap. text 19.96 (*0-582-29024-4*, 71723) Longman.

Public Administration Workbook. Mark W. Huddleston. (Illus.). 241p. 1987. pap. text 18.95 (*0-582-29028-7*, 71727) Longman.

Public Administration Workbook. 2nd ed. Mark W. Huddleston. 272p. (C). 1992. teacher ed. write for info. (*0-8013-0499-7*, 78352) Longman.

Public Administration Workbook. 3rd ed. Mark W. Huddleston. 35p. (C). 1995. pap. text 36.56 (*0-8013-1621-9*) Longman.

Public Administration Workbook. 4th ed. Mark Huddleston. 323p. (C). 1999. pap., wbk. ed. 46.00 (*0-8013-3268-0*) Longman.

Public Administrator. Jack Rudman. (Career Examination Ser.: C-1440). 1994. pap. 29.95 (*0-8373-1440-2*) Nat Learn.

Public Administrtn For Twenty First Century. Whicker. 1999. pap. text. write for info. (*0-13-466335-7*) P-H.

Public Affair. Margie Walker. 256p. 1998. pap. 4.99 (*0-7860-0501-7*, Pinncle Kensgtn) Kensgtn Pub Corp.

***Public Affair: Bill Clinton's Allies & Enemies & the Price They Paid.** Roger Simon. 352p. 2001. 25.00 (*0-8129-3204-8*, Times Bks) Crown Pub Group.

Public Affairs: The Military & the Media, 1962-1968. W. M. Hammond. 1989. lib. bdg. 300.00 (*0-87700-879-5*) Revisionist Pr.

Public Affairs: The Military & the Media, 1962-1968. William M. Hammond. LC 88-931. (Center for Military History Publication German Report Series, DA Pam: No. 91-13). (Illus.). 429p. 1996. pap. 26.00 (*0-16-001673-8*, 008-020-01123-1) USGPO.

Public Affairs: The Military & the Media, 1968-1973, 2 vols. 1997. lib. bdg. 600.95 (*0-8490-6074-5*) Gordon Pr.

Public Affairs 1968-1973-(Clothbound) The Military & the Media. William M. Hammond. 679p. 1996. text 45.00 (*0-16-048542-8*) USGPO.

Public Affairs 1968-1973(Paperbound) The Military & the Media. William M. Hammond. 679p. 1996. per. 35.00 (*0-16-048696-3*) USGPO.

Public Affairs Handbook. Ed. by Joseph S. Nagelschmidt. LC 82-6710. 319p. reprint ed. pap. 98.90 (*0-608-12449-4*, 205575000036) Bks Demand.

Public Affairs Information Service: Cumulative Author Index, 1965-1969. Ed. by C. Edward Wall. LC 70-143248. (Cumulative Author Index Ser.: No. 3). 1973. 110.00 (*0-87650-014-9*) Pierian.

Public Affairs Internships: Theory & Practice. Ed. by Alan P. Balutis & Joseph C. Honan. 297p. 1984. 22.95 (*0-87073-727-9*); pap. 16.95 (*0-87073-728-7*) Schenkman Bks Inc.

Public Affairs Reporting: The Citizens' News. 2nd ed. Ralph S. Izard & Marilyn S. Greenwald. 400p. (C). 1991. text. write for info. (*0-697-08615-1*) Brown & Benchmark.

Public Affairs Research Methods: A Quantitative Introduction. Scott Bennett. LC 96-26631. 392p. 1996. text 99.95 (*0-7734-8770-0*) E Mellen.

Public Agency Officials' Complete Source Book. abr. ed. Wayne K. Lemieux. 851p. 1998. lib. bdg. write for info. (*0-327-00883-0*, 8097411) LEXIS Pub.

Public Agency Officials' Complete Source Book. 4th ed. Wayne K. Lemieux. 1998. disk. write for info. (*0-327-00903-9*) LEXIS Pub.

Public Agenda. Lawrence G. Brewster. LC 97-65178. 341p. 1997. pap. text 21.95 (*0-312-15394-5*) St Martin.

Public Alternative Education: Options & Choice for Today's Schools. Timothy W. Young. 160p. (C). 1990. pap. text 16.95 (*0-8077-3023-8*) Tchrs Coll.

Public & Academic History: Philosophy & Pardism. Phyllis K. Leffler & Joseph Brent, III. LC 89-2628. 108p. (Orig.). (C). 1990. 16.00 (*0-89464-298-7*) Krieger.

Public & Academic History: Philosophy & Pardism. Phyllis K. Leffler & Joseph Brent, III. LC 89-2628. 108p. (Orig.). (C). 1990. pap. 12.50 (*0-89464-299-5*) Krieger.

Public & Academic Library Electronic Access to Information Survey. Elizabeth A. Breedlove. (Illus.). 80p. (Orig.). 1997. pap. text 30.00 (*0-7881-3884-7*) DIANE Pub.

Public & Atlantic Defense. Ed. by Gregory Flynn & Hans Rattinger. LC 84-15894. (Atlantic Institute for International Affairs Research Ser.). (Illus.). 416p. (C). 1985. 75.50 (*0-8476-7365-0*) Rowman.

Public & Community Health Nurse's Consultant: A Health Promotion Guide. Marcia Stanhope & Ruth N. Knollmueller. LC 96-219771. (Illus.). 800p. (C). (gr. 13). 1996. pap. text 32.95 (*0-8151-9003-4*, 29089) Mosby Inc.

Public & Confidential. Duncan Forbes. 49p. 1989. reprint ed. pap. 11.95 (*1-870612-45-0*, Pub. by Enitha Pr) Dufour.

Public & Its Problems. John Dewey. LC 76-178242. 236p. 1954. pap. text 11.95 (*0-8040-0254-1*) Swallow.

***Public & Media Relations for the Fire Service.** Tim Birr. LC 98-48123. 156p. 1998. pap. 32.50 (*0-912212-79-9*) Fire Eng.

Public & Nonprofit Marketing: Readings & Cases. Christopher H. Lovelock & Charles B. Weinberg. 380p. (C). 1990. pap. text 37.50 (*0-89426-148-7*) Course Tech.

Public & Parliamentary Speeches, 2 vols. John Stuart Mill. Ed. by John M. Robson & Bruce L. Kinzer. (Collected Works of John Stuart Mill: Nos. XXVIII-XXIX). 760p. 1988. text 135.00 (*0-8020-2693-1*) U of Toronto Pr.

Public & Performance in the Greek Theatre. Peter D. Arnott. 224p. 1989. 45.00 (*0-415-02914-7*, A3036) Routledge.

Public & Performance in the Greek Theatre. Peter D. Arnott. 224p. (C). 1991. pap. 24.99 (*0-415-06299-3*, A5383) Routledge.

Public & Play Without a Title: Two Posthumous Plays. Federico Garcia Lorca. Tr. by Carlos Bauer from SPA. LC 83-12117. 96p. 1983. 8.95 (*0-8112-0880-X*, Pub. by New Directions) Norton.

Public & Private: Feminist Legal Debates. Ed. by Margaret Thornton. 336p. 1996. pap. text 42.00 (*0-19-553662-2*) OUP.

Public & Private: Gender, Class & the British Novel (1764-1878) Patricia McKee. LC 96-35350. 1997. pap. 19.95 (*0-8166-2935-8*); text 49.95 (*0-8166-2934-X*) U of Minn Pr.

***Public & Private: Legal, Political & Philosophical Perspectives.** Maurizio Passerin d'Entraeves & Ursula Vogel. LC 00-28413. 2000. pap. write for info. (*0-415-16684-5*) Routledge.

Public & Private Agricultural Extension: Beyond Traditional Frontiers. Dina L. Umali & Lisa A. Schwartz. LC 94-8509. (World Bank Discussion Papers: Vol. 236). 98p. 1994. pap. 22.00 (*0-8213-2803-4*, 12803) World Bank.

Public & Private Doctrine: Essays in British History Presented to Maurice Cowling. Ed. by Michael Bentley. LC 92-32135. 369p. (C). 1993. text 69.95 (*0-521-40013-9*) Cambridge U Pr.

***Public & Private Economic Advisor: Paul W. McCracken.** Sidney L. Jones. 464p. 2000. pap. 44.50 (*0-7618-1699-2*) U Pr of Amer.

Public & Private Economy, 3 vols. in 1. Theodore Sedgwick. LC 68-27855. (Reprints of Economic Classics Ser.). 1974. reprint ed. 65.00 (*0-678-01258-X*) Kelley.

Public & Private Economy, Pt. 1. Theodore Sedgwick. LC 77-137187. (Poverty U. S. A. Historical Record Ser.). 1978. reprint ed. 26.95 (*0-405-03125-4*) Ayer.

Public & Private English-German Schools of Baltimore, 1836 to 1904. Dimitri Katsareas. LC 96-22186. (New German-American Studies: Vol. 13). 1997. pap. write for info. (*0-8204-3386-1*) P Lang Pubng.

Public & Private Enterprise. John Jewkes. LC 66-12709. (Lindsay Memorial Lectures: 1964). 100p. reprint ed. pap. 31.00 (*0-608-12123-1*, 202411800035) Bks Demand.

Public & Private Enterprise & the Energy Future. Ed. by Gregory Daneke. 192p. (Orig.). 1985. pap. 15.00 (*0-918592-78-X*) Pol Studies.

Public & Private Families. 2nd ed. Cherlin. 416p. 2000. pap. 31.25 (*0-07-231992-5*) McGraw.

Public & Private Families: A Reader. Andrew J. Cherlin. LC 97-1314. 384p. 1997. pap. 33.13 (*0-07-011929-5*) McGraw.

Public & Private Families: An Introduction. Andrew J. Cherlin. LC 95-8973. 530p. (C). 1995. 57.19 (*0-07-010632-0*) McGraw.

Public & Private Families: An Introduction. 2nd ed. Andrew J. Cherlin. LC 98-18511. 1998. 56.38 (*0-07-011987-2*) McGraw.

Public & Private Financing of Higher Education: Shaping Public Policy for the Future. Ed. by Patrick M. Callan & Joni E. Finney. LC 97-29457. (Ace/Oryx Series on Higher Education). 264p. (C). 1997. boxed set 39.95 (*1-57356-116-9*) Oryx Pr.

Public & Private Hearth. Patricia Wilcox. 1978. pap. 12.95 (*0-685-11941-6*) Bellevue Pr.

Public & Private Humanitarian Aid: Legal & Ethical Issues. Tom Barry. 21p. 1988. 5.95 (*0-911213-17-1*) Interhemisp Res Ctr.

***Public & Private in Dutch Culture of the Golden Age.** Arthur K. Wheelock & Adele F. Seeff. LC 97-53081. (Illus.). 280p. 2000. 65.00 (*0-87413-640-7*) U Delaware Pr.

Public & Private in Thought & Practice: Perspectives on a Grand Dichotomy. Ed. by Jeff Weintraub & Krishan Kumar. LC 96-8506. 344p. 1996. pap. text 19.95 (*0-226-88624-7*) U Ch Pr.

Public & Private in Thought & Practice: Perspectives on a Grand Dichotomy. Ed. by Jeff Weintraub & Krishan Kumar. LC 96-8506. 344p. 1997. lib. bdg. 60.00 (*0-226-88623-9*) U Ch Pr.

Public & Private in Vergil's "Aeneid" Susan F. Wiltshire. LC 88-14702. 192p. (C). 1989. lib. bdg. 30.00 (*0-87023-650-4*) U of Mass Pr.

Public & Private Interplay in Social Protection. Ed. by Martin Rein & Lee Rainwater. LC 86-11911. (Comparative Public Policy Analysis Ser.). 256p. (gr. 13). 1986. text 85.95 (*0-87332-383-1*) M E Sharpe.

Public & Private Life of the Soviet People: Changing Values in Post-Stalin Russia. Vladimir Shlapentokh. 296p. 1989. text 55.00 (*0-19-504266-2*) OUP.

Public & Private Lives of Psychotherapists. William E. Henry et al. LC 73-49. (Jossey-Bass Behavioral Science Ser.). (Illus.). 288p. reprint ed. pap. 89.30 (*0-8357-4699-2*, 205235400008) Bks Demand.

Public & Private Operation of Railways in Brazil. Julian S. Duncan. (Columbia University. Studies in the Social Sciences: No. 367). reprint ed. 29.50 (*0-404-51367-0*) AMS Pr.

Public & Private Ownership in Britain, 1820-1990. James Foreman-Peck & Robert E. Millward. LC 93-30848. 408p. 1994. 69.00 (*0-19-820359-4*, Clarendon Pr) OUP.

Public & Private Partnerships for Financing Highway Improvements. (National Cooperative Highway Research Program Report Ser.: No. 307). 83p. 1988. 11.00 (*0-309-04604-1*, NR307) Transport Res Bd.

P

Public & Private Pensions in Canada: An Economic Analysis. James E. Pesando & Samuel A. Rea. LC 77-376564. (Ontario Economic Council Research Studies: No. 9). 193p. reprint ed. pap. 59.90 (*0-8357-4001-3*, 203670200005) Bks Demand.

Public & Private Responsibilities in Long-Term Care: Finding the Balance. Leslie C. Walker et al. LC 98-3335. 348p. 1998. 42.00 (*0-8018-5901-8*) Johns Hopkins.

Public & Private Roles in Maintaining Military Equipment at the Depot Level. (Illus.). 54p. (Orig.). (C). 1995. pap. text 30.00 (*0-7881-2446-3*) DIANE Pub.

***Public & Private School Choices in the District of Columbia: Congressional Hearing.** Ed. by Frank D. Riggs. 165p. (C). 2000. reprint ed. pap. text 30.00 (*0-7881-8762-7*) DIANE Pub.

Public & Private School Principals in the United States: A Statistical Profile, 1987-88 to 1993-94. Thomas A. Fiore. LC 97-191896. 202p. 1997. pap. 15.00 (*0-16-049084-7*) USGPO.

Public & Private Schools: How Do They Differ? Susan P. Choy & National Center for Education Statistics Staff. LC 98-179013. (Findings from the Condition of Education Ser.). 39 p. 1997. write for info. (*0-16-049221-1*) USGPO.

Public & Private Science: The King George III Collection. Alan Q. Morton & Jane A. Wess. (Illus.). 720p. 1993. 125.00 (*0-19-856392-2*) OUP.

Public & Private Secondary Education in Developing Countries: A Comparative Study. Emmanuel Jimenez & Marlaine E. Lockheed. (World Bank Discussion Papers: Vol. 309). 143p. 1996. pap. 22.00 (*0-8213-3479-4*) World Bank.

Public & Private Worlds of Elizabeth I. Photos by Mark Fiennes. LC 98-60339. (Illus.). 208p. 1998. 40.00 (*0-500-01869-3*, Pub. by Thames Hudson) Norton.

***Public & Professional Speaking: A Confident Approach for Women.** Barbara Berckhan et al. 180p. 1999. pap. 22.50 (*1-85343-473-6*, Pub. by Free Assoc Bks) Intl Spec Bk.

Public & Republic. Alfred De Grazia. LC 84-22449. 271p. 1985. reprint ed. lib. bdg. 65.00 (*0-313-24679-3*, DEPR, Greenwood Pr) Greenwood.

Public & Social Policy: Subject Analysis with Reference Bibliography. rev. ed. Pamela N. Paonessa. LC 94-3138. 1994. 47.50 (*0-7883-0346-5*) ABBE Pubs Assn.

Public & Social Policy: Subject Analysis with Reference Bibliography. rev. ed. Pamella N. Paonessa. LC 94-31238. 1994. pap. 44.50 (*0-7883-0347-3*) ABBE Pubs Assn.

Public & the Motion Picture Industry. William M. Seabury. LC 75-160247. (Moving Pictures Ser.). xiv, 340p. 1971. reprint ed. lib. bdg. 41.95 (*0-89198-048-2*) Ozer.

Public & the National Agenda: How People Learn about Important Issues. Wayne Wanta. LC 97-3347. 200p. 1997. write for info. (*0-8058-2460-X*); pap. write for info. (*0-8058-2461-8*) L Erlbaum Assocs.

Public & the Private in Aristotle's Political Philosophy. Judith A. Swanson. LC 91-55528. 264p. 1992. 39.95 (*0-8014-2319-8*) Cornell U Pr.

Public & the Private in Aristotle's Political Philosophy. Judith A. Swanson. LC 91-55528. 264p. 1994. pap. text 16.95 (*0-8014-8233-X*) Cornell U Pr.

Public Archaeology in Annapolis: A Critical Approach to History in Maryland's "Ancient City" Parker B. Potter, Jr. LC 93-20779. (Illus.). 288p. (C). 1994. pap. text 19.95 (*1-56098-410-4*) Smithsonian.

Public Argument. Robert O. Weiss. LC 95-3478. 198p. (Orig.). (C). 1995. pap. text 25.00 (*0-8191-9900-1*) U Pr of Amer.

Public Art. Francoise Yohalem. Ed. by Drew Steis. (Art Calendar Guide Ser.). 1999. pap. 9.95 (*0-945388-09-8*) Art Calendar.

Public Art in Ann Arbor & Washtenaw County. Martha R. Keller & Michael J. Curtis. Ed. by John Hilton & Paula Shanks. (Illus.). 136p. (Orig.). 1993. pap. 14.95 (*0-9635786-0-X*) Citizens Pub Art.

***Public Art in Lower Austria, Vol. 5 5.** Katharina Blaas-Pratscher. (Illus.). 240p. 2000. 45.00 (*3-211-83416-8*) Spr-Verlag.

Public Art in Philadelphia. Penny B. Bach. LC 92-11735. (Illus.). 288p. (C). 1992. 29.95 (*0-87722-822-1*) Temple U Pr.

Public Art in the Bronx. Sally Webster & Susan S. Hoeltzel. (Illus.). 60p. (Orig.). 1993. 12.00 (*1-884352-00-6*) Lehman Coll.

Public Art in the City. Malcolm Miles. LC 96-48742. (Illus.). 280p. (C). 1997. pap. 27.99 (*0-415-13943-0*) Routledge.

Public Art in the City. Malcolm Miles. LC 96-48742. (Illus.). 280p. (C). 1997. 85.00 (*0-415-13942-2*) Routledge.

Public Art, Public Controversy: The Tilted Arc on Trial. LC 87-18741. 208p. (Orig.). (C). 1987. pap. 14.95 (*0-915400-57-X*, ACA Bks) Am for the Arts.

Public Art Works: The Arizona Models. Phoenix Arts Commission. LC 93-6893. 1992. spiral bd. 20.00 (*0-9611710-7-3*) Western States.

Public Arts. Gilbert Seldes. LC 94-395. 313p. (C). 1994. pap. 24.95 (*1-56000-748-6*) Transaction Pubs.

Public Assembly Facilities: Planning & Management. 2nd ed. Don Jewell. LC 83-14905. 158p. 1992. text 48.50 (*0-89464-406-8*) Krieger.

Public Assistance & Your Client: A Handbook. Louise Skolnik. 1982. ring bd. 15.00 (*0-686-47708-1*) Adelphi Univ.

Public Attitude Monitor, 1995. Insurance Research Council, Inc. Staff. 96p. 1995. pap. text 10.00 (*1-56594-006-7*) Ins Res Coun.

Public Attitude Monitor, 1996. Insurance Research Council, Inc. Staff. 75p. 1996. pap. 10.00 (*1-56594-012-1*) Ins Res Coun.

***Public Attitude Monitor, 1998: Insurance Regulation Choice in Auto Insurance, No. 2.** Insurance Research Council Staff. 23p. 1998. pap. 10.00 (*1-56594-020-2*) Ins Res Coun.

Public Attitude Monitor, 1997: Issue Five: Drinking & Driving, Speeding. Insurance Research Council Staff. (Illus.). 18p. 1997. pap. text 10.00 (*1-56594-018-0*) Ins Res Coun.

Public Attitude Monitor, 1997: Issue Four: Aggressive Driving, No-Fault Insurance, Uninsured Motorist Fraud. Insurance Research Council Staff. (Illus.). 20p. 1997. pap. text 10.00 (*1-56594-017-2*) Ins Res Coun.

Public Attitude Monitor, 1998: Issue One - Insurer Profitability. Insurance Research Council Staff. (Illus.). 18p. 1998. pap. text 10.00 (*1-56594-019-9*) Ins Res Coun.

Public Attitude Monitor, 1997: Issue One: Domestic Violence. Insurance Research Council Staff. (Illus.). 19p. 1997. pap. text 10.00 (*1-56594-014-8*) Ins Res Coun.

Public Attitude Monitor, 1997: Issue Three: Cellular Phones, Truck Safety, Insurance Rating Factors. Insurance Research Council Staff. (Illus.). 16p. 1997. pap. text 10.00 (*1-56594-016-4*) Ins Res Coun.

Public Attitude Monitor, 1997: Issue Two: Air Bags. Insurance Research Council Staff. (Illus.). 16p. 1997. pap. text 10.00 (*1-56594-015-6*) Ins Res Coun.

***Public Attitude Monitor 1999 - Issue 3: Vehicle Theft - Reducing Accidents among the Youngest & Oldest Drivers.** Insurance Research Council Staff. 31p. 1999. pap. 10.00 (*1-56594-051-2*) Ins Res Coun.

***Public Attitude Monitor, 1999: Worker's Compensation Fraud, Year 2000 Computer Problems.** Insurance Research Council Staff. 23p. 1999. pap. 10.00 (*1-56594-024-5*) Ins Res Coun.

Public Attitude Monitor, 1999 Issue 1: Perceptions of the Risk of Natural Disaster, No. 1. Insurance Research Council Staff. 23p. (Orig.). 1999. pap. 10.00 (*1-56594-023-7*) Ins Res Coun.

***Public Attitude Monitor 1999 Issue No. 4: Vehicle Safety Issues.** Insurance Research Council Staff. 31p. 1999. pap. 10.00 (*1-56594-052-0*) Ins Res Coun.

Public Attitudes & International Development Co-operation. Ed. by Tony German et al. LC 99-177174. 172p. 1998. pap. 27.00 (*92-64-16195-3*, 4198141P, Pub. by Org for Econ) OECD.

Public Attitudes to Genetic Engineering: Some European Perspectives. Louis Lemkow. (Illus.). 44p. (Orig.). (C). 1995. pap. text 25.00 (*0-7881-1883-8*) DIANE Pub.

Public Attitudes to State Provision for Widows & Widowers: A Study Carried Out on Behalf of the Department of Social Security Andrew Thomas. LC 99-160834. (In-House Report Ser.). 45 p. 1998. write for info. (*1-85197-860-7*) Dept of Social Security.

Public Attitudes Toward Church & State. Ted G. Jelen & Clyde Wilcox. LC 95-17896. (American Political Institutions & Public Policy Ser.). (Illus.). 208p. (gr. 13). 1995. pap. text 32.95 (*1-56324-149-8*) M E Sharpe.

Public Attitudes Toward Church & State. Clyde Wilcox & Ted G. Jelen. LC 95-17896. (American Political Institutions & Public Policy Ser.). (Illus.). 208p. (gr. 13). 1995. text 69.95 (*1-56324-148-X*) M E Sharpe.

***Public Attitudes toward Immigration in the United States, France, & Germany.** Joel S. Fetzer. LC 99-59173. (Illus.). 256p. 2000. write for info. (*0-521-78149-3*); pap. write for info. (*0-521-78679-7*) Cambridge U Pr.

Public Authorities & Public Policy. Ed. by Jerry Mitchell. (Orig.). 1990. pap. 15.00 (*0-944285-15-5*) Pol Studies.

Public Authorities & Public Policy: The Business of Government. Ed. by Jerry Mitchell. LC 91-47088. (Contributions in Political Science Ser.: No. 301). 216p. 1992. pap. 21.95 (*0-275-94321-6*, B4321, Praeger Pubs) Greenwood.

Public Authorities & Public Policy: The Business of Government, 301. Ed. by Jerry Mitchell. LC 91-47972. (Contributions in Political Science Ser.: No. 301). 216p. 1992. 65.00 (*0-313-28503-9*, MBT, Greenwood Pr) Greenwood.

Public Awareness of the Nebraska Regional Poison Control Center. Michael A. Montwill et al. 14p. (Orig.). 1979. pap. 1.50 (*1-55719-023-2*) U NE CPAR.

Public Benefits Law. 9.00 (*0-317-03735-8*, 37,357PB) NCLS Inc.

Public Benefits Manual. 505p. 1987. 40.00 (*0-685-30202-4*, 43,300) NCLS Inc.

Public Bodies - Private States: New Views on Women & Representation. Ed. by Jane Brett & Sally Rice. (Photography: Critical Views Ser.). (Illus.). 156p. 1994. text 36.00 (*0-7190-4121-X*, Pub. by Manchester Univ Pr) St Martin.

***Public Bodies 1998.** 91p. 1998. pap. 55.00 (*0-11-430154-9*, HMO1549) Statnry Office.

Public Body. Raymond Flynn. 320p. 1997. pap. 10.95 (*0-340-64975-5*, Pub. by Hodder & Stought Ltd) Trafalgar.

Public Broadcasters: Accountability & Efficiency. Robin Foster. 96p. 1993. pap. 19.50 (*0-7486-0410-3*, Pub. by Edinburgh U Pr) Col U Pr.

Public Broadcasting & the Public Trust. Ed. by David Horowitz & Laurence Jarvick. LC 95-235835. 1995. pap. 9.95 (*1-886442-03-7*, Sec Thght Bks) Ctr Study Popular.

Public Broadcasting Coverage in the United States. 1991. lib. bdg. 88.95 (*0-8490-5069-3*) Gordon Pr.

Public Broadcasting Coverage in the United States. 1995. lib. bdg. 602.95 (*0-8490-6750-2*) Gordon Pr.

Public Broadcasting 21st Century. Lutton Staff. LC 96-206805. 1997. pap. 49.95 (*1-86020-006-0*, Pub. by U of Luton Pr) Bks Intl VA.

Public Budgeting: A Managerial Perspective. K. Thai. (Public Administration & Public Policy Ser.). Date not set. write for info. (*0-8247-9018-9*) Dekker.

Public Budgeting: Program Planning & Implementation. 4th ed. Fremont J. Lyden & Ernest G. Miller. (Illus.). 384p. (C). 1982. pap. text 16.95 (*0-13-737403-8*) P-H.

Public Budgeting & Finance. 4th expanded rev. ed. Ed. by Robert T. Golembiewski & Jack Rabin. LC 97-13943. (Public Administration & Public Policy Ser.: Vol. 64). (Illus.). 1024p. 1997. text 215.00 (*0-8247-9389-7*) Dekker.

Public Budgeting in America. 4th ed. Thomas D. Lynch. LC 94-519. 400p. 1994. 56.00 (*0-13-735846-6*) P-H.

Public Budgeting in the United States: The Cultural & Ideological Setting. Steven G. Koven. LC 99-18208. (Text & Teaching Politics, Policy, Administration Ser.). 192p. 1999. 55.00 (*0-87840-738-3*); pap. 19.95 (*0-87840-752-9*) Georgetown U Pr.

Public Budgeting Politics Institutions & Processes. Robert W. Kweit. (C). 1995. pap. text. write for info. (*0-8013-1482-8*) Addison-Wesley.

Public Budgeting Systems. 6th ed. Robert D. Lee & Ronald W. Johnson. LC 97-47672. 540p. 1998. 49.00 (*0-8342-1044-4*) Aspen Pub.

Public Budgeting Using One-Two-Three. Keith Baker. 1988. 49.95 incl. disk (*1-55828-143-6*, MIS Pr) IDG Bks.

Public Budgets Lab: Student Workbook. Jack Rabin et al. LC 97-171602. (Public Budgeting Laboratory Ser.). 118p. 1996. pap., student ed. 12.95 (*0-89854-183-2*) U of GA Inst Govt.

Public Buildings: Architecture Under the Public Works Administration 1933-1939, Vol. 1. Intro. by Richard G. Wilson. (Quality Paperbacks Ser.). (Illus.). 398p. 1986. pap. 24.50 (*0-306-80265-1*) Da Capo.

Public Buildings & Structures: Snip 2.08.02-89. 2nd rev. ed. Russia's Gosstroy Staff. Ed. & Tr. by Snip Register Inc. Staff from RUS. (Building Codes of Russia Ser.). (Illus.). iv, 78p. 1998. ring bd. write for info. (*1-57937-052-7*, Snip Bldg) Snip Register.

Public Buildings Manager. Jack Rudman. (Career Examination Ser.: C-2719). 1994. pap. 29.95 (*0-8373-2719-9*) Nat Learn.

Public Bureaucracies Between Reform & Resistance: Legacies, Trends & Effects in China, the U. S. S. R., Poland & Yugoslavia. Ed. by Jaroslaw Piekalkiewicz & Christopher Hamilton. LC 90-20250. 256p. 1991. 19.50 (*0-85496-295-6*) Berg Pubs.

Public Burning. Robert Coover. LC 97-28954. 560p. 1998. pap. 14.00 (*0-8021-3527-7*, Grove) Grove-Atltic.

Public Capital: Revitalizing America's Communities. David P. Rosen. 150p. 1987. 14.95 (*0-89788-102-8*) CPA Washington.

Public Capital Expenditure in OECD Countries: The Causes & Impact of the Decline in Public Capital Spending. Jan-Egbert Sturm. LC 97-47519. 208p. 1998. 80.00 (*1-85898-827-6*) E Elgar.

Public Career of John Archdale (1642-1717) Henry G. Hood, Jr. 48p. 1976. pap. 2.00 (*0-614-04680-7*) NC Frnds Hist Soc.

Public Career of Sir James Graham. Arvel B. Erickson. LC 74-382. 433p. (C). 1974. reprint ed. lib. bdg. 75.00 (*0-8371-7383-3*, ERJG, Greenwood Pr) Greenwood.

Public Career of Sir Thomas More. John A. Guy. LC 80-16259. 232p. reprint ed. pap. 72.00 (*0-7837-2789-5*, 204318100006) Bks Demand.

Public Career of William M. Evarts. Brainerd Dyer. (Publications of the University of California Humanities Research Institute: Vol. 2). 1933. pap. 30.00 (*0-686-17390-2*) R S Barnes.

Public Career of William M. Evarts. Brainerd Dyer. LC 72-87565. (American Scene Ser.). 279p. 1969. reprint ed. lib. bdg. 35.00 (*0-686-42966-4*) Da Capo.

Public Cemeteries of Sumter County, Alabama, 1834-1972: A Geneaological Listing. Ed. by Jud K. Arrington. LC 98-66417. (Regional History Ser.: Vol. 4). 480p. 1998. 27.00 (*0-942979-48-6*) Livingston AL.

Public Choice: An Introduction to the New Political Economy. David B. Johnson. LC 90-46311. 372p. (C). 1992. pap. text 51.95 (*1-55934-022-3*, 1022) Mayfield Pub.

Public Choice Analysis in Historical Perspective. Ed. by Alan Peacock. (Raffaele Mattioli Lectures on the History of Economic Thought). 246p. 1997. pap. text 19.95 (*0-521-59976-8*) Cambridge U Pr.

Public Choice Analysis of Economic Policy. K. Alec Chrystal et al. LC 98-55205. 240p. 1999. text 69.95 (*0-312-22137-1*) St Martin.

Public Choice & Constitutional Economics. Ed. by James D. Gwartney et al. LC 88-1915. (Political Economy & Public Policy Ser.: Vol. 6). 422p. 1988. 78.50 (*0-89232-935-1*) Jai Pr.

Public Choice & Environmental Regulation: Tradable Permit Systems in the United States & CO2 Taxation in Europe. Gert T. Svendsen. LC 98-24873. (New Horizons in Environmental Economics Ser.). 240p. 1998. 80.00 (*1-85898-628-1*) E Elgar.

Public Choice & Public Law: Readings & Commentary. Ed. by Maxwell L. Stearns. 1080p. (C). 1997. 59.95 (*0-87084-806-2*) Anderson Pub Co.

Public Choice & Rural Development. Ed. by Clifford S. Russell & Norman K. Nicholson. LC 80-8775. (Resources for the Future Research Paper: R-21). (Illus.). 312p. 1981. pap. text 15.00 (*0-8018-2600-4*) Johns Hopkins.

Public Choice Approach to Politics. Dennis C. Mueller. (Economists of the Twentieth Century Ser.). 552p. 1993. 110.00 (*1-85278-805-4*) E Elgar.

***Public Choice Essays in Honor of a Maverick Scholar: Gordon Tullock.** Gordon Tullock et al. LC 99-48299. 1999. write for info. (*0-7923-7715-X*) Kluwer Academic.

Public Choice II. rev. ed. Dennis C. Mueller. (Illus.). 544p. (C). 1989. pap. text 27.95 (*0-521-37952-0*) Cambridge U Pr.

Public Choice II. rev. ed. Dennis C. Mueller. (Illus.). 544p. (C). 1989. text 85.00 (*0-521-37083-3*) Cambridge U Pr.

***Public Choice Interpretations of American Economic History.** Jac C. Heckelman et al. LC 99-48310. 1999. write for info. (*0-7923-7721-4*) Kluwer Academic.

Public Choice Theory, 3 vols., Set. Ed. by Charles K. Rowley. (International Library of Critical Writings in Economics: Vol. 24). 1616p. 1993. 560.00 (*1-85278-160-2*) E Elgar.

Public Choices & Policy Change: The Political Economy of Reform in Developing Countries. Merilee S. Grindle & John W. Thomas. LC 90-19212. (Illus.). 256p. 1991. text 40.00 (*0-8018-4155-0*); pap. text 16.95 (*0-8018-4156-9*) Johns Hopkins.

Public Citizen's Action Manual. Donald Ross. 238p. pap. 1.95 (*0-686-36537-2*) Ctr Responsive Law.

Public City: The Political Construction of Urban Life in San Francisco, 1850-1900. Philip J. Ethington. (Illus.). 480p. (C). 1994. text 64.95 (*0-521-41565-9*) Cambridge U Pr.

Public Clash of Private Values: The Politics of Morality Policy. Ed. by Christopher Z. Mooney. LC 99-50743. (Illus.). 312p. 2000. pap. text 29.95 (*1-889119-40-7*, Chatham House Pub) Seven Bridges.

Public College & University Development. Ed. by Michael J. Worth. 164p. 1985. pap. 17.00 (*0-89964-232-2*, 29101) Coun Adv & Supp Ed.

Public Colleges & Universities, 9. John F. Ohles & Shirley M. Ohles. LC 85-17725. (Encyclopedia of American Institutions Ser.: No. 9). 1024p. 1986. lib. bdg. 115.00 (*0-313-23257-1*, OHC/, Greenwood Pr) Greenwood.

Public Communication. 2nd ed. Roderick P. Hart et al. 362p. (C). 1987. reprint ed. pap. text 29.50 (*0-8191-6429-1*) U Pr of Amer.

Public Communication: Rhetoric & Leadership. Neher et al. 352p. (C). 1998. per. 54.95 (*0-7872-5267-0*) Kendall-Hunt.

Public Communication & Behavior Series, Vol. 3. Comstock. 1997. write for info. (*0-12-543203-8*) Acad Pr.

Public Communication Campaigns. Ed. by Ronald E. Rice & William J. Paisley. LC 81-2706. 328p. reprint ed. pap. 101.70 (*0-8357-4848-0*, 203777900009) Bks Demand.

Public Communication Campaigns. 2nd ed. Ed. by Ronald E. Rice & Charles K. Atkin. 416p. (C). 1989. text 58.00 (*0-8039-3262-6*); pap. text 24.50 (*0-8039-3263-4*) Sage.

Public Communication: The New Imperatives: Future Directions for Media Research. Ed. by Marjorie Ferguson. (CIS Ser.: Vol. 4). 256p. (C). 1989. text 45.00 (*0-8039-8267-4*); pap. text 18.95 (*0-8039-8268-2*) Sage.

***Public Companies & Their Equity Securities: Principles of Regulation under Hong Kong.** Betty M. Ho. LC 99-210254. (Studies in Comparative Corporate & Financial Law: Vol. 2). 1208p. 1998. 270.00 (*90-411-9648-X*) Kluwer Law Intl.

Public Company Auditor Changes & Big Eight Firms: Disagreements & Other Issues. Donald K. McConnell, Jr. Ed. by Richard Farmer. LC 83-5953. (Research for Business Decisions Ser.: No. 62). 330p. reprint ed. pap. 102.30 (*0-8357-1425-X*, 207040600088) Bks Demand.

Public Concept of Land Ownership: Reports & Discussions of a German-Korean Symposium Held in Seoul on October 7-9, 1996. Ed. by Bernd Von Hoffmann & Myong-Chan Hwang. (Comparative & International Law Studies: Vol. 43). (Illus.). VIII, 229p. 1997. pap. 51.95 (*0-8204-3516-3*) P Lang Pubng.

Public Concerns: Philosophical Studies of Social Science. Nicholas Rescher. 208p. (Orig.). (C). 1995. pap. text 21.95 (*0-8476-8126-2*); lib. bdg. 52.50 (*0-8476-8125-4*) Rowman.

Public Concerns, Community Initiatives: The Successful Management of Nursing Home Consumer Information Programs. United Hospital Fund Staff. Ed. by Carol Ewig & John Griggs. 268p. 1985. 25.00 (*0-934459-25-8*) United Hosp Fund.

Public Contract Code of the State of California: Adopted September 21, 1981, with Amendments through the 1984 Session of the 1983-1984 Legislature. write for info. (*0-318-60797-2*) West Group.

Public Contract Law Journal, 1967-1995/96, 26 vols., Set. 1964. 1000.00 (*0-8377-9132-4*, Rothman) W S Hein.

Public Control of Business. Ed. by Alfred Lief. LC 96-77572. xx, 324p. 1996. reprint ed. 65.00 (*1-57588-121-7*, 310680) W S Hein.

Public Control of Business: A Study of Antitrust Law Enforcement, Public Interest Regulation, & Government Participation in Business. Dexter M. Keezer & Stacy May. LC 73-2515. (Big Business; Economic Power in a Free Society Ser.). 1973. reprint ed. 19.95 (*0-405-05095-X*) Ayer.

***Public Conversations: Building Skills & Confidence.** 4th ed. Helen Sands. (C). 1999. pap. 31.25 (*0-07-240066-8*) McGrw-H Hghr Educ.

Public Corporations of Nepal: A Study of Financial Ratios. Radhe S. Pradhan. 1986. 19.00 (*0-8364-1943-X*, Pub. by Natl Bk Orgn) S Asia.

Public Culture: An Argument with the Future. 2nd ed. Horne. (C). 66.50 (*0-7453-0908-9*); pap. 19.95 (*0-7453-0907-0*, Pub. by Pluto GBR) Stylus Pub VA.

Public Culture in the Early Republic: Peale's Museum & Its Audience. David R. Brigham. LC 94-7705. (Illus.). 240p. 1995. text 45.00 (*1-56098-416-3*) Smithsonian.

Public Data Networks: From Separate PDNs to the ISDN. J. Puzman & B. Kubin. (Illus.). x, 241p. 1991. 116.95 (*0-387-19580-7*) Spr-Verlag.

An Asterisk (*) at the beginning of an entry indicates that the title is appearing for the first time.

Public Debt: Breaking the Habit of Deficit Spending. abr. ed. National Issues Forum Institute Staff. 32p. 1988. 3.25 (*0-8403-4794-4*) Kendall-Hunt.

Public Debt & Economic Development in India. D. K. Mishra. 552p. (C). 1984. 225.00 (*81-85009-07-4*, Pub. by Print Hse) St Mut.

Public Debt & Future Generations. James M. Ferguson. LC 82-2966. 234p. 1982. reprint ed. lib. bdg. 59.50 (*0-313-23537-6*, FEPU, Greenwood Pr) Greenwood.

Public Debt, External Competitiveness, & Fiscal Discipline in Developing Countries. Helmut Reisen. LC 89-24746. (Studies in International Finance: No. 66). 30p. 1989. pap. text 13.50 (*0-88165-238-5*) Princeton U Int Finan Econ.

Public Debt Management: Theory & History. Ed. by Rudiger Dornbusch & Mario Draghi. (Illus.). 376p. (C). 1990. text 64.95 (*0-521-39266-7*) Cambridge U Pr.

***Public Debt Management: Theory & History.** Alessandro Missale. LC 99-17544. 320p. 2000. text 70.00 (*0-19-829085-3*) OUP.

Public Debt of the United States: An Historical Perspective, 1775-1990. Donald R. Stabile & Jeffrey A. Cantor. LC 90-37780. 264p. 1991. 57.95 (*0-275-93664-3*, C3664, Praeger Pubs) Greenwood.

Public Debts: An Essay in the Science of Finance. Henry C. Adams. LC 75-2619. (Wall Street & the Security Market Ser.). 1975. reprint ed. 35.95 (*0-405-06946-4*) Ayer.

Public Debts in China. Huang Feng-Hua. LC 72-77997. (Columbia University. Studies in the Social Sciences: No. 197). reprint ed. 32.50 (*0-404-51197-X*) AMS Pr.

Public Defender: A Necessary Factor in the Administration of Justice. Mayer C. Goldman. LC 74-3826. (Criminal Justice in America Ser.). 1974. reprint ed. 18.95 (*0-405-06146-3*) Ayer.

Public Defender: The Practice of Law in the Shadows of Repute. Lisa J. McIntyre. LC 87-5070. (Studies in Crime & Justice). (Illus.). 1995. 24.95 (*0-226-55961-0*) U Ch Pr.

Public Defender Experience: A Student Career Guide into the Heads & Hearts of America's "Real Lawyers" Bradley M. Bittan. 1997. 30.00 (*0-938609-11-4*) Graduate Group.

***Public Deficits: A Comparative Study of Their Economic & Political Consequences in Britain, Canada, Germany & the United States.** Roland Sturm. LC 98-56530. (Perspectives in Comparative Politics Ser.). 152p. (C). 1999. pap. text 26.95 (*0-582-25343-8*) Addison-Wesley.

Public Deliberation: Pluralism, Complexity, & Democracy. James Bohman. LC 96-599. (Studies in Contemporary German Social Thought). (Illus.). 320p. (C). 1996. 35.50 (*0-262-02410-1*) MIT Pr.

***Public Deliberation: Pluralism, Complexity & Democracy.** James Bohman. LC 96-599. (Studies in Contemporary German Social Thought). (Illus.). 320p. 2000. reprint ed. pap. 17.00 (*0-262-52278-0*) MIT Pr.

Public Dimension of Foreign Policy. David D. Newsom. LC 95-20450. 304p. 1996. 35.00 (*0-253-32960-4*); pap. 16.95 (*0-253-21024-0*) Ind U Pr.

Public Diplomacy: U. S. A. vs. U. S. S. R. Ed. by Richard F. Staar. (Publication Ser.: No. 345). 350p. 1986. 9.58 (*0-8179-8451-8*) Hoover Inst Pr.

Public Diplomacy & International Politics: The Symolic Constructs of Summits & International Radio News. Robert S. Fortner. LC 93-37879. (Series in Political Communication). 216p. 1994. 59.95 (*0-275-93594-9*, Praeger Pubs) Greenwood.

Public Diplomacy & Political Change: Four Case Studies: Okinawa, Peru, Czechoslovakia, Guinea. Gregory Henderson et al. LC 72-14204. (Special Studies in International Politics & Government). 1973. 42.50 (*0-275-28710-6*) Irvington.

Public Disputation, Power, & Social Order in Late Antiquity. Richard Lim. LC 93-43761. (Transformation of the Classical Heritage Ser.: No. 23). 1995. 55.00 (*0-520-08577-9*, Pub. by U CA Pr) Cal Prin Full Svc.

Public Documents from Sinnar. Jay Spaulding. Ed. by Muhammad I. Salim. LC 89-12896. (African Historical Sources Ser.: No. 1). 426p. (C). 1989. text 34.95 (*0-87013-280-6*) Mich St U Pr.

Public Dollars for Private Schools: The Case of Tuition Tax Credits. Ed. by Thomas James & Henry M. Levin. 285p. 1985. pap. 14.95 (*0-87722-386-6*) Temple U Pr.

Public Domain. Gil Ott. 84p. (Orig.). 1989. pap. 8.50 (*0-937013-29-3*) Potes Poets.

Public Domain & Democracy. Robert T. Hill. (Columbia University. Studies in the Social Sciences: No. 100). 1968. reprint ed. 27.50 (*0-404-51100-7*) AMS Pr.

Public Drinking & Popular Culture in Eighteenth-Century Paris. Thomas E. Brennan. LC 87-29122. 348p. 1988. reprint ed. pap. 107.90 (*0-608-04654-X*, 206534000003) Bks Demand.

Public Duties: The Moral Obligations of Government Officials. Ed. by Mark H. Moore et al. LC 81-6253. 328p. reprint ed. pap. 101.70 (*0-7837-3835-8*, 204365600010) Bks Demand.

Public Duties & Public Law. Andrew J. Harding. 340p. 1989. 95.00 (*0-19-825607-8*) OUP.

Public Duties in Islam: The Institution of the Hisba. Ibn Taymiya. Tr. by Muhtar Holland. 160p. (Orig.). 1996. 14.95 (*0-614-21523-4*, 1021) Kazi Pubns.

Public Duties in Islam: The Institution of the Hisba. Ibn Taymiya. Tr. by Muhtar Holland from ARA. 159p. (Orig.). 1982. pap. 6.95 (*0-86037-113-1*) New Era Publns MI.

Public Duty & Private Conscience in Seventeenth-Century England: Essays Presented to G. E. Aylmer. Ed. by John Morrill et al. LC 92-32519. (Illus.). 362p. 1993. text 59.00 (*0-19-820229-6*, Clarendon Pr) OUP.

Public Eating: Proceedings of the Oxford Symposium on Food & Cookery, 1991. Ed. by Harlan Walker. (Proceedings of the Oxford Symposium on Food Ser.). (Illus.). 323p. (Orig.). 1992. pap. 56.00 (*0-907325-47-5*, Pub. by Prospect) Food Words.

***Public Economics.** 1999. teacher ed. write for info. (*0-321-40426-2*) Addison-Wesley.

Public Economics. Gareth D. Myles. LC 94-44774. 560p. (C). 1995. pap. text 26.95 (*0-521-49769-8*) Cambridge U Pr.

Public Economics. Ed. by Peter Sinclair & Martin Slater. (Oxford Economic Papers Special Issue). (Illus.). 328p. 1991. pap. 39.95 (*0-19-828729-1*) OUP.

Public Economics: Selected Papers. Ed. by Richard Arnott & William Vickrey. (Illus.). 570p. 1997. pap. text 29.95 (*0-521-59763-3*) Cambridge U Pr.

Public Economics & the Environment in an Imperfect World. Ed. by Lans Bovenberg & Sijbren Cnossen. (Natural Resource Management & Policy Ser.). 388p. (C). 1995. lib. bdg. 163.50 (*0-7923-9618-9*) Kluwer Academic.

Public Economics & the Quality of Life. Lowdon Wingo & Alan W. Evans. LC 76-47393. (Resources for the Future Ser.). (Illus.). 352p. 1978. text 23.50 (*0-8018-1941-5*) Johns Hopkins.

Public Economics & the Quality of Life. Ed. by Lowdon Wingo & Alan Evans. LC 76-47393. 343p. reprint ed. pap. 106.40 (*0-7837-3041-1*, 204288500006) Bks Demand.

Public Economics in Action: The Basic Income - Flat Tax Proposal. Anthony B. Atkinson. (Lindahl Lectures on Monetary & Fiscal Policy). (Illus.). 184p. 1997. reprint ed. pap. text 17.95 (*0-19-829216-3*) OUP.

Public Economy for the United States. 2nd ed. Calvin Colton. LC 68-30517. (Reprints of Economic Classics Ser.). xvi, 536p. 1969. reprint ed. 57.50 (*0-678-00513-3*) Kelley.

Public Economy of Athens: To Which Is Added a Dissertation on the Silver Mines of Laurion. 2nd rev. ed. Augustus Boeckh. Tr. by George C. Lewis. LC 75-13364. (History of Ideas in Ancient Greece Ser.). (ENG.). 1976. reprint ed. 61.95 (*0-405-07299-6*) Ayer.

Public Economy of Urban Communities: Papers Presented at the 2nd Conference on Urban Public Expenditures, Feb. 21-22, 1964. Ed. by Julius Margolis. LC 77-86404. (Resources for the Future, Inc. Publications). 288p. reprint ed. 55.00 (*0-404-60339-4*) AMS Pr.

Public Education. Alan Gartner. (Task Force on the Eighties Ser.). 28p. 1981. pap. 2.50 (*0-87495-037-6*) Am Jewish Comm.

Public Education. Gerald Leinwand. (American Issues Ser.). 144p. (YA). (gr. 7-12). 1992. lib. bdg. 17.95 (*0-8160-2100-7*) Facts on File.

Public Education: An Autopsy. Myron Lieberman. LC 92-46732. 400p. 1993. text 27.95 (*0-674-72232-9*) HUP.

Public Education: An Autopsy. Myron Lieberman. 400p. 1995. pap. 14.95 (*0-674-72234-5*, LIEPUX) HUP.

Public Education: Who's in Charge? Fred G. Burke. LC 89-38008. 205p. 1990. 55.00 (*0-275-93402-0*, C3402, Greenwood Pr) Greenwood.

Public Education & Day Care: One District's Story. Carol M. Hoffman. LC 84-52676. 123p. 1985. pap. 9.95 (*0-87762-389-9*) Scarecrow.

Public Education & Indoctrination. Intro. by Hans F. Sennholz. (Freeman Classics Ser.). 207p. (Orig.). 1993. pap. 12.95 (*0-910614-86-5*) Foun Econ Ed.

Public Education & State Politics: The South Dakota Perspective. Frederick W. Zuercher. 1971. 1.00 (*1-55614-098-3*) U of SD Gov Res Bur.

Public Education & the Future of Puerto Rico: Survey, 1948-1949. Institute of Field Studies, Columbia University St. LC 74-14237. (Puerto Rican Experience Ser.). (Illus.). 636p. 1975. reprint ed. 53.95 (*0-405-06225-7*) Ayer.

Public Education Finances. 1994. lib. bdg. 250.00 (*0-8490-8587-X*) Gordon Pr.

Public Education for Children with Brain Dysfunction. Sheldon R. Rappaport. LC 69-17693. (Illus.). 257p. reprint ed. pap. 79.70 (*0-8357-3983-X*, 203668100005) Bks Demand.

Public Education in a Multicultural Society: Policy, Theory, Critique. Robert K. Fullinwider. (Cambridge Studies in Philosophy & Public Policy). 301p. (C). 1996. text 64.95 (*0-521-49624-1*); pap. text 23.95 (*0-521-49958-5*) Cambridge U Pr.

Public Education in America: A New Interpretation of Purpose & Practice. Ed. by George Z. Bereday & Luigi Volpicelli. LC 77-23510. 212p. 1977. reprint ed. lib. bdg. 59.50 (*0-8371-9702-3*, BEPU, Greenwood Pr) Greenwood.

Public Education in California: Its Origin & Development with Personal Reminiscences of Half a Century. John Swett. LC 74-89242. (American Education: Its Men, Institutions, & Ideas. Series 1). 1970. reprint ed. 16.95 (*0-405-01479-1*) Ayer.

Public Education in Detroit. Arthur B. Moehlman. LC 73-11930. (Metropolitan America Ser.). (Illus.). 268p. 1974. reprint ed. 23.95 (*0-405-05404-1*) Ayer.

Public Education in Hungary. Jozsef Bencedy. 44p. 1982. 50.00 (*0-7855-1240-3*) St Mut.

***Public Education, Law & Religion in America: A Comprehensive History.** Frank C. Nelsen. 397p. 2000. pap. text 40.00 (*1-55605-302-9*) Wyndham Hall.

Public Education Series. Alan C. Walter. Ed. by Beverly Miles. 56p. (Orig.). 1995. pap. text 17.77 (*1-57569-009-8*) Wisdom Pubng.

Public Education, the First Amendment, & the Influence of New Religious Movements: A Policy Analysis. Francis J. Beckwith. 22p. 1993. 10.00 (*1-886306-07-9*) Nevada Policy.

Public Education under Criticism. Ed. by Cecil W. Scott & Clyde M. Hill. LC 72-167416. (Essay Index Reprint Ser.). 1977. reprint ed. 29.95 (*0-8369-2520-3*) Ayer.

Public Educational Work in Baltimore. Herbert B. Adams. (Principle Works of Herbert Baxter Adams). 1989. reprint ed. lib. bdg. 79.00 (*0-7812-1481-5*) Rprt Serv.

***Public Elementary & Secondary Education Statistics: School Year 1997-98.** Lena M. McDowell. 17p. 1998. pap. 2.00 (*0-16-049487-7*) USGPO.

Public Employee Compensation & Its Role in Public Sector Strategic Management. Gilbert B. Siegel. LC 91-27718. 208p. 1992. 59.95 (*0-89930-592-X*, SGK/, Quorum Bks) Greenwood.

Public Employee Discharge & Discipline, 3 vols., Vol. 3. 2nd ed. Isadore Silver. LC 95-7660. (Employment Law Library). 1600p. 1997. boxed set 365.00 (*0-471-04318-4*) Wiley.

Public Employee Labor Relations in Japan: Three Aspects. Alice H. Cook et al. LC 71-634401. (Comparative Studies in Public Employment Labor Relations Ser.). 1971. 10.00 (*0-87736-019-7*); pap. 5.00 (*0-87736-020-0*) U of Mich Inst Labor.

Public Employee Organizing & the Law. Michael T. Leibig & Wendy L. Kahn. LC 87-18398. 258p. reprint ed. pap. 80.00 (*0-7837-4604-0*, 204432300002) Bks Demand.

Public Employee Privacy: A Legal & Practical Guide to Issues Affecting the Workplace. LC 94-74278. 240p. 1995. pap. 74.95 (*1-57073-140-3*, 533-0057, ABA Urban) Amer Bar Assn.

Public Employee Relations in West Germany. William H. McPherson. LC 77-634396. (Comparative Studies in Public Employment Labor Relations Ser.). 1971. 10.95 (*0-87736-009-X*); pap. 5.95 (*0-87736-010-3*) U of Mich Inst Labor.

Public Employee Reporter for California. LRP Publications Staff. text. write for info. (*0-934753-01-6*) LRP Pubns.

Public Employee Reporter for California, Vol. 10. Ed. by LRP Publications Staff. 1987. text. write for info. (*0-934753-18-0*) LRP Pubns.

Public Employee Retirement Administration. MFOA Committee Staff. 134p. 1977. 15.00 (*0-686-84367-3*) Municipal.

Public Employee Retirement Plans in South Dakota. W. H. Cape. 1956. 5.00 (*1-55614-099-1*) U of SD Gov Res Bur.

Public Employee Retirement Systems: The Structure & Politics of Teacher Pensions. Suzanne S. Taylor. LC 86-2993. 200p. (Orig.). 1986. text 32.50 (*0-87546-123-9*, ILR Press); pap. text 14.95 (*0-87546-124-7*, ILR Press) Cornell U Pr.

Public Employee Trade Unionism in the United Kingdom: The Legal Framework. B. A. Hepple & Paul O'Higgins. LC 70-634397. (Comparative Studies in Public Employment Labor Relations Ser.). 1971. 10.00 (*0-87736-011-1*); pap. 5.00 (*0-87736-012-X*) U of Mich Inst Labor.

Public Employee Turnover in State Government: Costs & Benefits. Kenneth Meyer et al. 1978. 1.00 (*1-55614-100-9*) U of SD Gov Res Bur.

Public Employee Unionism: Structure, Growth, Policy. Jack Stieber. LC 73-1591. (Studies of Unionism in Government). 256p. 1973. pap. 9.95 (*0-8157-8159-8*) Brookings.

Public Employee Unionism in Belgium. Roger Blanpain. LC 76-634393. (Comparative Studies in Public Employment Labor Relations Ser.). 1971. 10.00 (*0-87736-003-0*); pap. 5.00 (*0-87736-004-9*) U of Mich Inst Labor.

Public Employee Unionism in Israel. Jerome Lefkowitz. LC 78-634400. (Comparative Studies in Public Employment Labor Relations Ser.). 1971. 10.00 (*0-87736-017-0*); pap. 5.00 (*0-87736-018-9*) U of Mich Inst Labor.

Public Employees Conference, Dec. 7-10, 1980, Monterey, CA: Proceedings. Ed. by Mary E. Brennan. Incl. Public Employees Conference Proceedings, Nov. 11-14, 1981, Williamsburg. 119p. (Orig.). 1982. pap. 10.00 (*0-89154-173-X*); 114p. (Orig.). 1981. Set pap. 10.00 (*0-89154-151-9*) Intl Found Employ.

Public Employees Conference Proceedings, Nov. 11-14, 1981, Williamsburg see Public Employees Conference, Dec. 7-10, 1980, Monterey, CA: Proceedings

Public Employees in Georgia: How Many Is Too Many? Lawrence R. Hepburn. LC 93-42928. 32p. 1994. pap. 5.00 (*0-89854-171-9*) U of GA Inst Govt.

Public Employees, Unions, & the Erosion of Civic Trust: A Study of San Francisco in the 1970s. Randolph H. Boehm & Dan C. Heldman. LC 82-51294. 265p. 1982. pap. 24.95 (*0-313-27094-5*, P7094); lib. bdg. 59.95 (*0-313-27070-8*, U7070) Greenwood.

Public Employer's Compliance Audit. Lee T. Paterson. Ed. by Margaret L. Johnson. 156p. 1990. pap. 79.50 (*0-932823-07-6*) Am Somerset.

Public Employer's Compliance Review. 2nd ed. Lee T. Paterson. 182p. 1993. pap. 39.50 (*1-55943-200-4*, MICHIE) LEXIS Pub.

Public Employer's Wage Manual. Lee T. Paterson. 400p. 1991. pap. 39.50 (*1-55943-066-4*, MICHIE) LEXIS Pub.

Public Employment & Economic Flexibility. Mathew Forstater. (Public Policy Briefs Highlights Ser.: Vol. 50A). 6p. 1999. pap. write for info. (*0-941276-67-8*) J Levy.

Public Employment & Economic Flexibility: The Job Opportunity Approach to Full Employment. Mathew Forstater. (Public Policy Brief Ser.: Vol. 50). 24p. 1999. pap. write for info. (*0-941276-65-1*) J Levy.

Public Employment Compulsory Arbitration in Australia. Gerald E. Caiden. LC 79-634392. (Comparative Studies in Public Employment Labor Relations Ser.). 1971. 10.00 (*0-87736-001-4*); pap. 5.00 (*0-87736-002-2*) U of Mich Inst Labor.

Public Employment Labor Relations: An Overview of Eleven Nations. Ed. by Charles M. Rehmus. LC 74-22858. (Comparative Studies in Public Employment Labor Relations Ser.). 1974. 10.00 (*0-87736-025-1*); pap. 5.00 (*0-87736-026-X*) U of Mich Inst Labor.

Public Employment Law: The Role of the Contract of Employment in Australia & Britain. Graham F. Smith. 208p. 1987. pap. 46.00 (*0-409-49256-6*, AT, MICHIE) LEXIS Pub.

Public Employment Relations Law (PERC) Esther R. Strassman et al. (School Board Library Ser.: Vol. 6). 163p. 1991. 29.90 (*0-912337-09-5*) NJ Schl Bds.

Public Employment Service: Belgium. OECD Staff. LC 97-120045. 140p. 1997. pap. 20.00 (*92-64-15496-5*, 81-97-01-1, Pub. by Org for Econ) OECD.

Public Employment Service: Denmark, Finland, Italy. OECD Staff. LC 96-181857. 218p. (Orig.). 1996. pap. 50.00 (*92-64-14777-2*, Pub. by Org for Econ) OECD.

Public Employment Service: Greece, Ireland, Portugal. OECD Staff. LC 99-204589. 264p. 1998. pap. 36.00 (*92-64-16133-3*, 8198091P) OECD.

Public Employment Service: Organization in Change. Frank H. Cassell. LC 68-27448. (Orig.). (C). 1968. pap. 5.00 (*0-87736-310-2*) U of Mich Inst Labor.

***Public Employment Service in a Changing Labour Market.** International Labour Office. 256p. 2000. pap. 19.95 (*92-2-111388-4*, Pub. by ILO) ILO Pubns Ctr.

Public Employment Service in Austria, Germany, & Sweden. OECD Staff. LC 97-120045. 126p. (Orig.). 1996. pap. 18.00 (*92-64-14930-9*, 81-96-09-1) OECD.

Public Employment Service in the United States. Raymond C. Atkinson et al. LC 72-69. (Select Bibliographies Reprint Ser.). 1977. reprint ed. 24.95 (*0-8369-9950-9*) Ayer.

***Public Employment Service in the United States with Special Reference to Connecticut & Wisconsin.** Robert Fay & Douglas Lippoldt. LC 99-225189. 232p. (Orig.). 1999. pap. 36.00 (*92-64-17011-1*, 81 1999 02 1 P, Pub. by Org for Econ) OECD.

Public Employment Services & Their Role in Employment Policy. 1995. 12.00 (*92-871-2728-X*, Pub. by Council of Europe) Manhattan Pub Co.

Public Encounter: Where State & Citizen Meet. Ed. by Charles T. Goodsell. LC 81-47007. (Illus.). 280p. (C). 1981. 27.50 (*0-253-15363-8*) Ind U Pr.

Public Enemies. Leo Regan. (Illus.). 114p. 1994. pap. 19.95 (*0-233-98830-0*, Pub. by Andre Deutsch) Trafalgar.

Public Enemies: America's Criminal Past, 1919 to 1940. William J. Helmer & Rick Mattix. LC 98-5032. (Illus.). 320p. 1998. 35.00 (*0-8160-3160-6*); pap. 17.95 (*0-8160-3161-4*) Facts on File.

Public Enemies: PJ's Irreverent Hit List of Institutions, Individuals, Assorted Morons. P. J. O'Rourke. 1995. pap. 8.95 (*0-9629072-1-9*) Amer Spectator.

Public Enemies, Public Heroes: Screening the Gangster from Little Caesar to Touch of Evil. Jonathan Munby. LC 98-22151. (Illus.). 249p. 1999. pap. 16.00 (*0-226-55033-8*); lib. bdg. 45.00 (*0-226-55031-1*) U Ch Pr.

Public Enemy see Ghosts & Other Plays

Public Enemy. Ed. by Henry Cohen. LC 80-52292. (Warner Bros. Screenplay Ser.). (Illus.). 190p. (Orig.). 1981. pap. 9.95 (*0-299-08464-7*) U of Wis Pr.

Public Enemy. V. Lawrence. 1996. pap., mass mkt. 5.99 (*0-671-89561-3*) PB.

Public Enemy. Rillo. 48p. (Orig.). 1997. pap. 9.00 (*1-880516-21-7*) Left Hand Bks.

Public Enemy #1. T. Lee Wiggins. (Illus.). v, 100p. (Orig.). 1997. mass mkt. 7.00 (*0-9659108-0-6*) New Aeion Minist.

***Public Enemy Number One: A Research Study of Rap Music, Culture & Black Nationalism in America.** David L. Shabazz. LC 98-74808. 116p. 1999. pap. 15.00 (*1-893680-01-0*) Awesome.

Public Enquiry. Picton Publishing Staff. (C). 1987. 25.00 (*0-7855-2180-1*, Pub. by Picton) St Mut.

Public Entrepreneurs: Agents for Change in American Government. Mark Schneider & Paul Teske. LC 94-21311. 264p. 1995. text 42.50 (*0-691-03725-6*, Pub. by Princeton U Pr) Cal Prin Full Svc.

Public Enterprise: An International Bibliography. Compiled by Alfred H. Saulniers. LC 85-14601. (Special Publications). xxv, 469p. (Orig.). 1985. 27.50 (*0-86728-014-X*); pap. 14.95 (*0-86728-013-1*) U TX Inst Lat Am Stud.

Public Enterprise: An International Bibliography, a Supplement. Compiled by Alfred H. Saulniers. LC 86-15290. (Special Publications). xxiii, 208p. 1986. 15.95 (*0-86728-017-4*); pap. 8.95 (*0-86728-018-2*) U TX Inst Lat Am Stud.

Public Enterprise: Economics & Transport Problems. Tillo E. Kuhn. LC 76-5904. (Illus.). 243p. 1976. reprint ed. lib. bdg. 75.00 (*0-8371-8798-2*, KUPE, Greenwood Pr) Greenwood.

***Public Enterprise & Privatization.** N. P. Manandhar. 1998. pap. 25.00 (*0-7855-7627-4*) St Mut.

Public Enterprise Economics. D. Bos. 1996. write for info. (*0-614-17901-7*, North Holland) Elsevier.

Public Enterprise Economics: Theory & Applications. Dieter Bos. (Advanced Textbooks in Economics Ser.: Vol. 23). vi,472p. 1989. 88.00 (*0-444-87899-8*, North Holland) Elsevier.

Public Enterprise in Kenya: What Works, What Doesn't, & Why. Barbara Grosh. LC 91-20375. 223p. 1991. lib. bdg. 45.00 (*1-55587-209-3*) L Rienner.

Public Enterprise in Mixed Economies: Some Macroeconomic Aspects. Robert H. Floyd et al. LC HD3845.6. 214p. reprint ed. pap. 66.40 (*0-608-12349-8*, 202427000036) Bks Demand.

Public Enterprise in Mixed Economies: Some Macroeconomic Aspects. Robert H. Floyd et al. xiv, 196p. 1984. pap. 12.00 (*0-939934-30-2*) Intl Monetary.

P

Public Enterprise in Monopolistic & Oligopolistic Industries, Vol. 36. Ingo Vogelsang. Ed. by Jacques Lesourne & Hugo Sonnenschein. (Fundamentals of Pure & Applied Economics Ser.: 36). viii, 120p. 1990. pap. text 71.00 (*3-7186-4973-X*) Gordon & Breach.

Public Enterprise in Transition: Industrial Relations in State & Privatized Corporations. Ed. by Andrew Pendleton & Jonathon Winterton. LC 92-44127. 288p. (C). (gr. 13). 1993. pap. 74.95 (*0-415-07572-6*) Thomson Learn.

Public Enterprise Management: International Case Studies, 370. Ed. by Ali Farazmand. LC 95-46135. (Contribution in Political Science Ser.: Vol. 370). 312p. 1996. 75.00 (*0-313-28025-8*, Greenwood Pr) Greenwood.

Public Enterprises: Restructuring & Privatization. Ed. by Jack L. Upper & George B. Baldwin. 370p. 1995. pap. 90.00 (*90-411-0993-5*) Kluwer Law Intl.

Public Enterprises: Restructuring & Privatization. Ed. by Jack L. Upper & George B. Baldwin. (International Development & Negotiation Sourcebooks for Policy & Practice Ser.). 370p. 1997. reprint ed. pap. 69.00 (*0-935328-80-7*) Intl Law Inst.

Public Entrepreneurship: Toward a Theory of Bureaucratic Political Power. Eugene Lewis. LC 79-2451. 286p. reprint ed. pap. 88.70 (*0-8357-3953-8*, 205704900004) Bks Demand.

Public Environments. Ed. by Joan Harvey & Don Henning. 1987. 36.00 (*0-939922-10-X*) EDRA.

Public Environments: An International Forum on Environmental Design Research. Ed. by Joan Harvey & Don Henning. 1987. 38.00 (*0-317-58653-X*) EDRA.

Public Ethics & Staff Training. (Congress of Local & Regional Authorities of Europe Ser.: No. 32). 1993. 15.00 (*92-871-2339-X*, Pub. by Council of Europe) Manhattan Pub Co.

Public Ethics for a Pluralistic Society: Contrasting Visions of America's Religious & Moral Foundations. Ronald P. Hesselgrave. LC 97-35588. 286p. 1998. 74.95 (*1-57309-113-8*); pap. 54.95 (*1-57309-112-X*) Intl Scholars.

Public Executive's Complete Guide to Employment Agreements. 2nd ed. Ron Holifield. Ed. by Madeleine Havlick. 129p. (Orig.). 1996. pap. 34.95 (*0-87326-107-0*) Intl City-Cnty Mgt.

Public Expectations of Health Care Quality: Role of the Agency for Health Care Policy & Research: Hearing Before the Subcommittee on Public Health & Safety of the Committee on Labor & Human Resources, United States Senate, One Hundred Fifth Congress, Second Session on Examining Proposed Legislation Authorizing Funds for the Agency Contribution to Assessment & Health Care Quality Improvement, April 30, 1998. USGPO Staff. LC 98-207567. (S. Hrg. Ser.). iii, 85 p. 1998. write for info. (*0-16-057236-3*) USGPO.

Public Expectations of the Final Stage of Compulsory Education. LC 95-231723. (ENG & FRE.). 147p. (Orig.). 1995. pap. 25.00 (*92-64-04356-X*, Pub. by Org for Econ) OECD.

Public Expenditure. Corry. 1998. pap. 19.99 (*1-86152-428-5*) Thomson Learn.

Public Expenditure: Allocation Between Competing Ends. Ed. by Michael Posner. LC 76-53522. 278p. reprint ed. pap. 79.30 (*0-608-15766-X*, 2031712) Bks Demand.

Public Expenditure: Statistical Analysis, 1998-99. (Command Papers: No. 3901). 1998. 30.00 (*0-10-139012-2*, HM90122, Pub. by Statnry Office) Bernan Associates.

Public Expenditure & Economic Development. Sibani Dutta. 395p. 1986. 42.00 (*81-7024-020-4*, Pub. by Ashish Pub Hse) S Asia.

Public Expenditure & Select Committees of the Commons. Wilma Flegmann. 160p. 1986. text 69.95 (*0-566-05013-7*, Pub. by Dartmth Pub) Ashgate Pub Co.

Public Expenditure Decision Making: The Indian Experience. Anuradha Basu. 244p. 1995. 32.00 (*0-8039-9250-5*) Sage.

Public Expenditure Decisions Vol. 5: Behavior, Institutions, Procedures & Performance. Earl R. Brubaker. Ed. by William Breit & Kenneth G. Elzinga. LC 89-1891. (Political Economy & Public Policy Ser.: Vol. 5). 179p. 1989. 78.50 (*0-89232-835-5*) Jai Pr.

Public Expenditure Decisions in the Urban Community: Papers Presented at a Conference, May 14-15, 1962, under the Sponsorship of the Committee on Urban Economics of Resources for the Future, Inc. Conference on Public Expenditure Decisions in the. Ed. by Howard G. Schaller. LC 63-22774. 208p. reprint ed. pap. 64.50 (*0-7837-3045-4*, 204287800006) Bks Demand.

Public Expenditure in Nepal: Growth, Patterns & Impact. Dilli R. Khanal. 176p. (C). 1988. 225.00 (*0-89771-056-8*, Pub. by Ratna Pustak Bhandar) St Mut.

Public Expenditure in Nepal: Growth Patterns & Impact. Dilli R. Khanal. 1988. 57.00 (*0-7855-0251-3*, Pub. by Ratna Pustak Bhandar) St Mut.

Public Expenditure, Inflation & Growth: A Macro-Econometric Analysis for India. B. B. Bhattacharya. (Illus.). 250p. (C). 1985. text 21.00 (*0-19-561713-4*) OUP.

Public Expenditure Management. A. Premchand. LC 92-44308. x, 282p. 1993. pap. 20.00 (*1-55775-323-7*) Intl Monetary.

Public Expenditure on Higher Education: A Comparative Study in the Member States of the European Community. Frans Kaiser et al. Ed. by Raymond Florax. 250p. 1992. 59.95 (*1-85302-532-1*) Taylor & Francis.

Public Expenditure Reform under Adjustment Lending: Lessons from World Bank Experiences. Jeff Huther et al. LC 97-46144. (Discussion Paper Ser.: No. 382). 68p. 1997. pap. 22.00 (*0-8213-4160-X*, 14160) World Bank.

***Public Expenditures & the Poor in Indonesia, Vol. 397.** Nicholas M. Prescott. LC 98-53681. (World Bank Discussion Papers Ser.). 1998. write for info. (*0-8213-4315-7*) World Bank.

Public Expenditures in Communist & Capitalist Nations. Frederic L. Pryor. LC 68-14872. 550p. reprint ed. pap. 170.50 (*0-8357-8292-1*, 203386200087) Bks Demand.

Public Expenditures in the United States, 1952-1993. John E. Dawson & Peter J. Stan. LC 95-8386. 132p. 1995. pap. text 15.00 (*0-8330-1634-2*, MR-555-RC) Rand Corp.

Public Eye: Television & the Politics of Canadian Broadcasting, 1952-68. Frank W. Peers. LC 79-311230. 475p. reprint ed. pap. 147.30 (*0-8357-6400-1*, 203575800096) Bks Demand.

Public Face of Architecture: Civic Culture & Public Spaces. Ed. by Nathan Glazer & Mark Lilla. 512p. 1987. 40.00 (*0-02-911811-5*) Free Pr.

***Public Face of Modernism: Little Magazines, Audiences & Reception, 1905-1920.** Mark Morrisson. LC 00-8425. (Illus.). 2000. write for info. (*0-299-16924-3*) U of Wis Pr.

Public Face of the Gospel: New Testament Ideas of the Church. J. L. Houlden. 1997. pap. 15.00 (*0-334-02666-0*) TPI PA.

Public Faces, Private Voices: Community & Individuality in South India. Mattison Mines. LC 93-35609. 1994. 50.00 (*0-520-08478-0*, Pub. by U CA Pr); pap. 19.95 (*0-520-08479-9*, Pub. by U CA Pr) Cal Prin Full Svc.

***Public Faith.** Charles Drew. 2000. pap. 8.00 (*1-57683-215-5*) NavPress.

Public Faith: Reflections on the Political Role of American Churches. Ed. by W. Clark Gilpin. 112p. (Orig.). 1990. pap. 9.99 (*0-8272-2942-9*) Chalice Pr.

Public Family: The Ideas That Shaped Your Child's School. Don Johnson. 111p. 1997. pap. 8.95 (*0-9654828-2-0*) Charlotte Mus.

***Public Finance.** Alan J. Auerbach. LC 99-45658. (Series in Outstanding Contributions). 1999. write for info. (*1-57259-927-8*) Worth.

***Public Finance.** Neil Bruce. (C). 1998. text. write for info. (*0-321-01771-4*) Addison-Wesley.

***Public Finance.** Hines. 2002. pap. 60.00 (*0-324-05592-7*) Sth-Wstrn College.

Public Finance. Randall G. Holcombe. Date not set. pap. text, teacher ed. write for info. (*0-314-07898-3*) West Pub.

Public Finance. Elisabeth Marlow. (C). 1994. pap. text, teacher ed. 49.75 (*0-03-007856-3*) Harcourt Coll Pubs.

Public Finance. Michael Marlow. 272p. (C). 1995. pap. text, student ed. 34.00 (*0-03-007861-X*) Harcourt Coll Pubs.

Public Finance. Carl S. Shoup. LC 69-11227. 652p. (C). 1969. text 39.50 (*0-932400-02-7*) Intervale Pub Co.

Public Finance. 4th ed. Harvey Rosen. 1994. write for info. (*0-318-72960-1*, Irwn McGrw-H) McGrw-H Hghr Educ.

Public Finance. 4th ed. Harvey Rosen. 623p. (C). 1994. text 69.75 (*0-256-16019-8*, Irwn McGrw-H) McGrw-H Hghr Educ.

Public Finance. 5th ed. Hyman. (C). 1995. pap. text, teacher ed., suppl. ed. 45.00 (*0-03-011318-0*); pap. text, student ed. 32.00 (*0-03-011319-9*) Harcourt Coll Pubs.

Public Finance. 5th ed. Harvey S. Rosen. LC 98-13616. 1998. 85.93 (*0-256-17329-X*, Irwn Prfssnl) McGraw-Hill Prof.

***Public Finance.** 6th ed. Hyman. LC 98-71610. (C). 1998. text 88.50 (*0-03-021308-8*, Pub. by Harcourt Coll Pubs) Harcourt.

Public Finance. 6th ed. Hyman. (C). 1998. pap. text, student ed. 30.50 (*0-03-021309-6*, Pub. by Harcourt Coll Pubs) Harcourt.

Public Finance. 6th ed. Rosen. 2001. 67.51 (*0-07-237405-5*) McGraw.

Public Finance: Policy Issues for India. Ed. by Sidipto Mundle. LC 97-914023. (Oxford India Readings Ser.). 320p. (C). 1998. 29.95 (*0-19-563771-2*) OUP.

Public Finance: "Readings, Issues, & Problems" 4th ed. Harvey S. Rosen & Eleanor Brown. 296p. (C). 1995. text 25.00 (*0-256-16174-7*, Irwn McGrw-H) McGrw-H Hghr Educ.

Public Finance Administration. 2nd ed. B. J. Reed & John W. Swain. LC 96-25311. 496p. 1996. 49.95 (*0-8039-7405-1*) Sage.

Public Finance & Development Strategy. Dirk J. Wolfson. LC 78-23240. 278p. reprint ed. pap. 86.20 (*0-608-06096-8*, 206642800008) Bks Demand.

Public Finance & Economic Development of Natal, 1893-1910. Zbigniew A. Konczacki. LC 67-23301. 242p. reprint ed. pap. 75.10 (*0-608-15276-5*, 205221000060) Bks Demand.

Public Finance & Economic Growth: Finances Publiques et Croissance Economique: Proceedings of the 37th Congress of the International Institute of Public Finance, Tokyo, 1981. International Institute of Public Finance Congress. Ed. by Dieter Biehl et al. LC 83-12447. (ENG & FRE., Illus.). 448p. reprint ed. pap. 138.90 (*0-7837-3589-8*, 204345300009) Bks Demand.

Public Finance & Performance of Enterprises: Proceedings of the 43rd Congress of the International Institute of Public Finance, Paris, 1987. Ed. by Manfred J. Neumann & Karl W. Roskamp. LC 89-5521. 512p. (C). 1989. 49.95 (*0-8143-2269-7*) Wayne St U Pr.

Public Finance & Performance of Enterprises (Finances Publiques et Performance des Entreprises) Proceedings of the 43rd Congress of the International Institute of Public Finance, Paris, 1987. International Institute of Public Finance Congress. Ed. by Manfred Neumann & Karl W. Roskamp. LC 89-5521. (ENG & FRE.). 457p. reprint ed. pap. 141.70 (*0-608-10592-9*, 207121300009) Bks Demand.

Public Finance & Public Choice. 2nd ed. John Cullis & Philip Jones. (Illus.). 448p. 1998. text 78.00 (*0-19-877580-6*); pap. text 39.95 (*0-19-877579-2*) OUP.

Public Finance & Public Choice: Two Contrasting Visions of the State. James M. Buchanan & Richard A. Musgrave. LC 99-15446. (Illus.). 264p. 1999. 27.50 (*0-262-02462-4*) MIT Pr.

Public Finance & Public Employment: An Analysis of Public Sector Retrenchment Programs in Ghana & Guinea. Bradford Mills et al. (Working Papers: No. 52). 44p. Date not set. pap. 7.00 (*1-56401-152-6*) Cornell Food.

***Public Finance & the American Economy.** 1998. text. write for info. (*0-673-99825-8*, GoodYrBooks) Addson-Wesley Educ.

Public Finance & the American Economy. Neil Bruce. LC 97-30044. 691p. (C). 1997. 98.00 (*0-321-01167-8*) Addson-Wesley Educ.

Public Finance & the American Economy. Neil Bruce. 160p. (C). 1997. text 24.00 (*0-321-01770-6*) Addson-Wesley Educ.

Public Finance & the Political Process. Randall G. Holcombe. LC 82-10803. (Political & Social Economy Ser.). 224p. 1983. 26.95 (*0-8093-1082-1*) S Ill U Pr.

Public Finance & the Price System. 4th ed. 1994. teacher ed. 7.00 (*0-02-315672-4*, Macmillan Coll) P-H.

Public Finance & the Price System. 4th ed. Edgar K. Browning & Jacquelene M. Browning. LC 93-34339. (Illus.). 566p. (C). 1994. 101.27 (*0-02-315671-6*, Macmillan Coll) P-H.

Public Finance During the Korean Modernization Process. Roy W. Bahl et al. (East Asian Monographs: No. 107). 1986. 30.00 (*0-674-72233-7*) HUP.

***Public Finance in a Democratic Society Vol. III: The Foundations of Taxation & Expenditure.** Richard A. Musgrave. 528p. 2000. 120.00 (*1-84064-113-4*) E Elgar.

Public Finance in Democratic Process: Fiscal Institutions & Individual Choice. James M. Buchanan. LC 98-43535. (Collected Works of James M. Buchanan : Vol. 4). 1999. 12.00 (*0-86597-220-6*) Liberty Fund.

***Public Finance in Democratic Process: Fiscal Institutions & Individual Choice.** James M. Buchanan. LC 98-43535. (Collected Works of James M. Buchanan : Vol. 4). 1999. 20.00 (*0-86597-219-2*) Liberty Fund.

Public Finance in Developing Countries: Theory & Practice. Vito Tanzi. 272p. 1990. text 100.00 (*1-85278-374-5*) E Elgar.

Public Finance in Islam. S. A. Siddiqui. 1991. 12.50 (*1-56744-198-X*) Kazi Pubns.

Public Finance in Japan. Ed. by Tokue Shibata. 195p. 1986. pap. 26.00 (*0-86008-387-X*, Pub. by U of Tokyo) Col U Pr.

Public Finance in Small Open Economies: The Caribbean Experience. Michael C. Howard. LC 92-9805. 208p. 1992. 55.00 (*0-275-94205-8*, C4205, Praeger Pubs) Greenwood.

***Public Finance in Theory & Practice.** Hewitt & Ulbrich. 2001. pap. 65.00 (*0-324-01660-3*) Thomson Learn.

Public Finance, International. 3rd ed. Harvey Rosen. (C). 1991. text, student ed. 32.50 (*0-256-11393-9*, Irwn McGrw-H) McGrw-H Hghr Educ.

Public-Finance, Officers, Works, Records see Rhode Island General Laws, 1998 Cumulative Supplement

Public Finance, Planning & Economic Development: Essays in Honor of Ursula Hicks. Ed. by Wilfred L. David. LC 73-77734. (Illus.). 349p. 1973. 42.50 (*0-8290-0201-4*) Irvington.

Public Finance Reform During the Transition: The Expeirence of Hungary. Ed. by Lajos Bokros & Jean-Jacques Dethier. 596p. 1998. pap. 60.00 (*0-8213-4252-5*, 14252) World Bank.

Public Finance Restructuring for Sustainable Development in Emerging Market Economies. Ed. by Theresa Bradley. LC 98-87590. 64p. 1998. pap. 20.00 (*1-56973-274-4*) World Resources Inst.

Public Finance, Trade & Development (Finances Publiques, Commerce et Development) Proceedings of the 44th Congress of the International Institute of Public Finance, Istanbul, Turkey, 1988. International Institute of Public Finance Congress. Ed. by Vito Tanzi. LC 90-34412. (ENG & FRE.). 378p. reprint ed. pap. 117.20 (*0-608-10602-X*, 207122300009) Bks Demand.

Public Financee. Cebula. (Miscellaneous/Catalogs Ser.). 2002. mass mkt. 55.95 (*0-538-86948-8*) S-W Pub.

Public Finances: Needs, Sources, & Utilization. Universities-National Bureau Staff. (Conference Ser.: No. 12). 526p. 1961. reprint ed. 136.80 (*0-87014-303-4*) Natl Bur Econ Res.

Public Finances in Latin America in the 1980s. (Cuadernos de la CEPAL: No. 69). 96p. pap. 12.00 (*92-1-121179-4*) UN.

Public Finances, Stabilization & Structural Reform in Latin America see Finanzas Publicas, Estabilizacion y Reforma Estructural en America Latina

Public Finances, Stabilization & Structural Reform in Latin America. Guillermo Perry & Ana M. Herrera. (Inter-American Development Bank Ser.). 140p. 1994. 12.50 (*0-940602-92-X*) IADB.

Public Financial Disclosure: A Reviewers Reference. 1995. lib. bdg. 275.95 (*0-8490-7441-X*) Gordon Pr.

Public Financial Disclosure: A Reviewers Reference, 2 vols. 1997. lib. bdg. 600.95 (*0-8490-6261-6*) Gordon Pr.

***Public Financial Disclosure: A Reviewer's Reference.** rev. ed. Ed. by Stephen D. Potts. (Illus.). 500p. 2000. pap. text 45.00 (*0-7881-8485-7*) DIANE Pub.

Public Financial Disclosure: Reviewer's Reference. 404p. 1996. ring bd. 30.00 (*0-16-062663-3*) USGPO.

Public Fire Education. IFSTA Committee. Ed. by FPP Staff et al. LC 79-89165. (Illus.). 169p. (Orig.). 1979. pap. 16.50 (*0-87939-034-4*) IFSTA.

Public Footpath. Herbert Lomas. Date not set. pap. 14.95 (*0-85646-062-1*, Pub. by Anvil Press) Dufour.

Public Freehold. Lawrence Weiner & Ulrich Ruckheim. (Illus.). 96p. (Orig.). 1991. pap. 14.95 (*3-89322-253-7*, Pub. by Edition Cantz) Dist Art Pubs.

***Public Garden, Boston.** rev. ed. Henry Lee et al. Ed. by Barbara W. Moore & Gail Weesner. (Illus.). 88p. 2000. 25.00 (*0-9676835-0-5*); pap. 15.00 (*0-9676835-1-3*) Friends of Garden.

Public General Acts - All (Not Including Scotland or NI) (Changed to Group No. 810.22.282) Income & Corporation Taxes Act 1988, Chapter 1. 1037p. 1988. 90.00 (*0-10-540188-9*, HM3133, Pub. by Statnry Office) Bernan Associates.

Public General Acts & General Synod Measures, 1996: Tables & Index. (Public General Acts & General Synod Measures & Tables Ser.: Vol. 81022281). 1998. 130.00 (*0-11-840361-3*, HM03613, Pub. by Statnry Office) Bernan Associates.

Public General Acts & Measures Bound Volumes, 1996. 1998. 850.00 (*0-11-840360-5*, HM03605, Pub. by Statnry Office) Bernan Associates.

Public Golf in Orange County California. Oliver Cathey et al. 80p. 1994. pap. text. write for info. (*0-9641557-0-2*) R Limmers Golf.

Public Good. Ed. by Stuart Hall et al. (Soundings Ser.). (C). 1996. pap. 19.95 (*0-85315-836-3*) Humanities.

Public Good. Thomas Paine. 41p. 1989. reprint ed. 5.00 (*0-935680-24-1*) Kentucke Imprints.

Public Good. Thomas Paine. (Notable American Authors Ser.). 1999. reprint ed. lib. bdg. 125.00 (*0-7812-4720-9*) Rprt Serv.

***Public Goods.** Anton. 416p. 2000. 68.00 (*0-8133-6617-8*, Pub. by Westview) HarpC.

***Public Goods.** Anton et al. 416p. 2000. pap. 25.00 (*0-8133-6618-6*, Pub. by Westview) HarpC.

Public Goods & Market Failures: A Critical Examination. Ed. by Tyler Cowen. 384p. (C). 1999. pap. text 24.95 (*1-56000-570-X*) Transaction Pubs.

Public Goods & Private Communities: The Market Provision of Social Services. Ed. by Fred E. Foldvary. (John Locke Ser.). 276p. 1994. 95.00 (*1-85278-951-4*) E Elgar.

Public Goods & Public Policy. Ed. by William Loehr & Todd Sandler. LC 77-17865. (Comparative Political Economy & Public Policy Ser.: Vol. 3). 240p. reprint ed. pap. 74.40 (*0-608-10136-2*, 202192300026) Bks Demand.

Public Goods, Mixed Goods, & Monopolistic Competition. Stephen Shmanske. LC 90-41465. (Economics Ser.: No. 12). 240p. 1991. 45.00 (*0-89096-464-5*) Tex A&M Univ Pr.

Public Health. (Illus.). 80p. (YA). (gr. 6-12). 1996. pap. 2.40 (*0-614-25727-1*, 33233) BSA.

Public Health. 1991. 58.95 (*0-387-53185-8*) Spr-Verlag.

Public Health. 2nd ed. George E. Pickett & Terry W. Pickett. (Opportunities In . . . Ser.). (Illus.). 160p. pap. 11.95 (*0-8442-4416-3*, 44163, VGM Career) NTC Contemp Pub Co.

Public Health: Index of New Information of Advances, Practices, Problems, Risks, & Research Development. Henrick H. Hoffstaetter. LC 95-18252. 1995. 47.50 (*0-7883-0242-6*); pap. 44.50 (*0-7883-0243-4*) ABBE Pubs Assn.

Public Health: Its Promise for the Future. Wilson G. Smillie. LC 75-22841. (America in Two Centuries Ser.). (Illus.). 1976. reprint ed. 41.95 (*0-405-07712-2*) Ayer.

Public Health: Myth, Mysticism & Reality. U. Ko Ko. (SEARO Regional Health Papers: No. 14). 72p. 1986. pap. text 12.00 (*92-9022-183-6*, 1580014) World Health.

***Public Health: Policy & Politics.** Rob Baggott. LC 00-33319. 2000. write for info. (*0-312-23814-2*) St Martin.

Public Health: What It Is & How It Works. Bernard J. Turnock. LC 96-39565. 300p. pap. 39.00 (*0-8342-0898-9*, 20898) Aspen Pub.

***Public Health: What It Is & How It Works.** 2nd ed. Bernard J. Turnock. 2000. 49.00 (*0-8342-1811-9*) Aspen Pub.

Public Health Action in Emergencies Caused by Epidemics: A Practical Guide. P. Bres. 299p. 1986. pap. text 49.00 (*92-4-154207-1*, 1150253) World Health.

***Public Health Administration.** Novick et al. 2000. 79.00 (*0-8342-1751-1*) Aspen Pub.

Public Health Administrator. Jack Rudman. (Career Examination Ser.: C-2082). 1994. reprint ed. pap. 39.95 (*0-8373-2082-8*) Nat Learn.

Public Health Adviser. Jack Rudman. (Career Examination Ser.: C-3093). 1994. pap. 27.95 (*0-8373-3093-9*) Nat Learn.

Public Health Advocacy: Creating Community Change to Improve Health. David G. Altman et al. (Illus.). 150p. (Orig.). 1994. pap. 24.00 (*1-879552-12-4*) SCRDP.

Public Health Aide. Jack Rudman. (Career Examination Ser.: C-1441). 1994. pap. 23.95 (*0-8373-1441-0*) Nat Learn.

Public Health Aide I. Jack Rudman. (Career Examination Ser.: C-2334). 1994. pap. 27.95 (*0-8373-2334-7*) Nat Learn.

Public Health Aide II. Jack Rudman. (Career Examination Ser.: C-1812). 1994. pap. 29.95 (*0-8373-1812-2*) Nat Learn.

Public Health & Aging. Ed. by Tom Hickey et al. LC 96-2928. 324p. 1997. text 60.00 (*0-8018-5558-6*); pap. text 24.95 (*0-8018-5559-4*) Johns Hopkins.

Public Health & Human Ecology. 2nd ed. John M. Last. LC 97-7896. 464p. (C). 1998. pap. 42.50 (*0-8385-8080-7*, A-8080-2, Apple Lange Med) McGraw.

An Asterisk (*) at the beginning of an entry indicates that the title is appearing for the first time.

Public Health & Insurance. Arthur Newsholme. LC 78-19270. 1979. 28.95 (*0-405-10617-3*) Ayer.

Public Health & Preventive Medicine. 14th ed. Robert B. Wallace. LC 97-53116. 1200p. (C). 1998. 135.00 (*0-8385-6185-3*, Apple Lange Med) McGraw.

Public Health & Public Health Services. Dona Schneider et al. LC 91-47919. (Rutgers Regional Report). 242p. 1992. pap. 1.00 (*0-88285-136-5*) Ctr Urban Pol Res.

Public Health & Social Justice in the Age of Chadwick: Britain, 1800-1854. Christopher Hamlin. LC 97-20658. (Studies in the History of Medicine). (Illus.). 368p. (C). 1998. text 64.95 (*0-521-58363-2*) Cambridge U Pr.

Public Health & the Medical Profession in the Renaissance. Carlo M. Cipolla. LC 75-22984. 144p. reprint ed. pap. 41.10 (*0-608-15704-X*, 2031631) Bks Demand.

Public Health & the Medical Use of Ionizing Radiation. (Technical Report Ser.: No. 306). 41p. 1965. pap. text 5.00 (*92-4-120306-4*) World Health.

Public Health & the State: Changing Views in Massachusetts, 1842-1936. Barbara G. Rosenkrantz. LC 70-172321. (Illus.). 271p. 1972. 35.95 (*0-674-72235-3*) HUP.

Public Health & the State: Changing Views in Massachusetts, 1842-1936. Barbara G. Rosenkrantz. LC 70-172321. (Illus.). 271p. 1972. pap. 17.95 (*0-674-72236-1*) HUP.

Public Health & Urban Development: The Plague in Surat. Ghanshyam Shah. LC 97-14483. (Illus.). 316p. 1997. 36.00 (*0-8039-9386-2*) Sage.

Public Health Approaches to Violence Prevention. Mary Haug. (Illus.). 64p. 1999. reprint ed. pap. text 25.00 (*0-7881-7530-0*) DIANE Pub.

Public Health Aspects of Criminal Prosecution of Workplace-Related Deaths, Injury, & Disease. Ed. by Eula Bingham et al. (International Journal of Occupational Medicine, Immunology, & Toxicology Ser.: Vol. 3, No. 4). (Illus.). 1994. pap. text 50.00 (*0-911131-79-5*) Specialist Journals.

Public Health Aspects of Low Birth Weight. (Technical Report Ser.: No. 217). 16p. 1961. pap. text 3.00 (*92-4-120217-3*) World Health.

Public Health Aspects of the Use of Antibiotics in Food & Feedstuffs. (Technical Report Ser.: No. 260). 30p. 1963. pap. text 3.00 (*92-4-120260-2*) World Health.

Public Health Assistant. Jack Rudman. (Career Examination Ser.: C-629). 1994. pap. 23.95 (*0-8373-0629-9*) Nat Learn.

Public Health at the Crossroads: Achievements & Prospects. Robert Beaglehole & Ruth Bonita. (Illus.). 260p. (C). 1997. text 74.95 (*0-521-58373-X*); pap. text 32.95 (*0-521-58665-8*) Cambridge U Pr.

Public Health Australia: An Introduction. James S. Lawson. (Illus.). 225p. 1991. pap. text 24.00 (*0-07-452913-7*) McGraw-Hill HPD.

Public Health Concerns of Environmental Radiation: Chernobyl: Oregon's Response. (Illus.). 43p. (Orig.). (C). 1996. pap. text 20.00 (*0-7881-2663-6*) DIANE Pub.

Public Health Consequences of Disasters. 1990. lib. bdg. 74.00 (*0-8490-4013-2*) Gordon Pr.

Public Health Consequences of Disasters. Ed. by Eric K. Noji. (Illus.). 488p. 1996. text 59.95 (*0-19-509570-7*) OUP.

Public Health Consultant. Jack Rudman. (Career Examination Ser.: C-312). 1994. pap. 34.95 (*0-8373-0312-5*) Nat Learn.

***Public Health Data: Our Silent Partner.** 134p. 2000. ring bd., wbk. ed. 20.00 (*0-16-059052-3*) USGPO.

Public Health Director. Jack Rudman. (Career Examination Ser.: C-2240). 1994. pap. 39.95 (*0-8373-2240-5*) Nat Learn.

Public Health Education Trainee. Jack Rudman. (Career Examination Ser.: C-983). 1994. pap. 27.95 (*0-8373-0983-2*) Nat Learn.

Public Health Educator. Jack Rudman. (Career Examination Ser.: C-630). 1994. pap. 29.95 (*0-8373-0630-2*) Nat Learn.

Public Health Educator 1. Jack Rudman. (Career Examination Ser.: C-2354). 1994. pap. 34.95 (*0-8373-2354-1*) Nat Learn.

Public Health Engineer. Jack Rudman. (Career Examination Ser.: C-1979). 1994. pap. 29.95 (*0-8373-1979-X*) Nat Learn.

Public Health Engineer Trainee. Jack Rudman. (Career Examination Ser.: C-1881). 1994. pap. 27.95 (*0-8373-1881-5*) Nat Learn.

Public Health Epidemiologist. Jack Rudman. (Career Examination Ser.: C-2246). 1994. pap. 34.95 (*0-8373-2246-4*) Nat Learn.

Public Health Impact of Mental Disorders. Ed. by David Goldberg & Digby Tantam. LC 90-4355. (Illus.). 250p. 1990. text 48.00 (*0-920887-65-1*) Hogrefe & Huber Pubs.

Public Health Impact of Pesticides Used in Agriculture. (ENG, FRE, RUS & SPA.). 128p. 1990. pap. text 21.00 (*92-4-156139-4*, 1150348) World Health.

Public Health Implications of Alcohol Production & Trade. B. Walsh & M. Grant. (WHO Offset Publications: No. 88). 55p. 1985. 8.00 (*92-4-170088-2*) World Health.

Public Health Implications of Medical Waste. 1995. lib. bdg. 252.75 (*0-8490-7545-9*) Gordon Pr.

Public Health Implications of Medical Waste: A Report to Congress. (Illus.). 225p. (Orig.). (C). 1993. pap. text 40.00 (*0-7881-0161-7*) DIANE Pub.

Public Health Implications of Radioactive Waste Releases. C. W. Straub. 61p. 1970. pap. text 9.00 (*92-4-156006-1*, 1150129) World Health.

Public Health in America, 46 bks. Ed. by Barbara G. Rosenkrantz. (Public Health in America Ser.). 1977. reprint ed. lib. bdg. 1242.50 (*0-405-09804-9*) Ayer.

Public Health in British India: Anglo-Indian Preventive Medicine, 1859-1914. Mark Harrison. (Cambridge History of Medicine Ser.). (Illus.). 344p. (C). 1994. pap. text 30.95 (*0-521-46688-1*) Cambridge U Pr.

Public Health in British India: Anglo-Indian Preventive Medicine, 1859-1914. Mark Harrison. (Cambridge History of Medicine Ser.). (Illus.). 344p. (C). 1994. text 74.95 (*0-521-44127-7*) Cambridge U Pr.

Public Health in Europe. European Commission. LC 98-125524. (Employment & Social Affairs Ser.). 193 p. 1997. write for info. (*92-828-0390-2*) Comm Europ Commun.

Public Health in Europe. McKee & Dickens. 56.95 (*1-85972-634-8*) Ashgate Pub Co.

***Public Health in the Market: Facing Managed Care, Lean Government & Health Disparities.** Nancy Milio. LC 99-50720. 432p. 2000. text 42.50 (*0-472-11136-1*, 11136) U of Mich Pr.

Public Health in the Town of Boston, 1630-1822. John B. Blake. LC 59-10314. (Historical Studies: No. 72). (Illus.). 288p. 1959. 20.00 (*0-674-72250-7*) HUP.

Public Health Informatics: Current Bibliographies in Medicine: January 1980 Through December 1995. Catherine Selden et al. 21p. (Orig.). 1996. pap. text 15.00 (*0-7881-3346-2*) DIANE Pub.

Public Health Inspector. Jack Rudman. (Career Examination Ser.: C-1753). 1994. pap. 29.95 (*0-8373-1753-3*) Nat Learn.

Public Health Laboratory Service. (Technical Report Ser.: No 128). 49p. 1957. pap. text 3.00 (*92-4-120128-2*) World Health.

***Public Health Law: Power, Duty, Restraint.** Larry O. Gostin. LC 00-37773. (California/Milbank Series on Health & the Public : Vol. 3). (Illus.). 518p. 2001. pap. 24.95 (*0-520-22648-8*, Pub. by U CA Pr) Cal Prin Full Svc.

***Public Health Law: Power, Duty, Restraint.** Lawrence O. Gostin. (California/Milbank Series on Health & the Public). (Illus.). 518p. 2001. 60.00 (*0-520-22646-1*) U CA Pr.

Public Health Law in Australia. Christopher Reynolds. 290p. 1995. pap. 39.00 (*1-86287-158-2*, Pub. by Federation Pr) Gaunt.

Public Health Law Manual. 2nd ed. Frank P. Grad. 337p. 1990. 45.00 (*0-87553-167-9*); pap. 35.00 (*0-685-38973-1*) Am Pub Health.

Public Health Leaders Tell Their Stories. Lloyd F. Novick et al. LC 97-15629. 168p. 1997. 35.00 (*0-8342-0961-6*) Aspen Pub.

Public Health Leadership for the 21st Century. Louis Rowitz. 275p. 2000. 50.00 (*0-8342-0738-9*) Aspen Pub.

Public Health Nurse. Jack Rudman. (Career Examination Ser.: C-631). 1994. pap. 27.95 (*0-8373-0631-0*) Nat Learn.

Public Health Nursing. Mary S. Gardner. Ed. by Barbara G. Rosenkrantz. LC 76-25664. (Public Health in America Ser.). 1977. reprint ed. lib. bdg. 26.95 (*0-405-09819-7*) Ayer.

Public Health Nutritionist. Jack Rudman. (Career Examination Ser.: C-632). 1994. pap. 27.95 (*0-8373-0632-9*) Nat Learn.

Public Health, Occupational Safety & Environmental Concerns in Municipal Solid Waste Recycling Operations. (Illus.). 250p. (C). 1996. reprint ed. pap. text 35.00 (*0-7881-3190-7*) DIANE Pub.

Public Health Policies & Social Inequality. Charles F. Andrain. LC 97-48835. 292p. 1998. text 50.00 (*0-8147-0676-2*) NYU Pr.

***Public Health Policies in the European Union.** Ed. by Walter Holland et al. LC 99-43342. 388p. 1999. text 87.95 (*0-7546-2072-7*, Pub. by Ashgate Pub) Ashgate Pub Co.

***Public Health Policy & Administration.** Ed. by Brij M. Mathur. 1998. 38.00 (*81-7169-510-8*, Pub. by Commonwealth) S Asia.

Public Health, Preventive Medicine & Social Services. 6th ed. Davies. LC 96-218055. write for info. (*0-340-61373-4*, Pub. by E A) Routldge.

Public Health, Preventive Medicine & Social Services. 6th ed. Brian M. Davies. 368p. 1995. pap. text 29.95 (*1-56593-503-9*, 1164) Singular Publishing.

Public Health Primer. Jo Fairbanks & William Wiese. LC 97-21134. 1997. pap. 21.95 (*0-7619-0653-3*) Sage.

Public Health Primer. Jo Fairbanks & William H. Wiese. LC 97-21134. 167p. 1997. 48.00 (*0-7619-0652-5*) Sage.

Public Health Progress. John A. R. Miles. 1984. lib. bdg. 107.50 (*90-277-9085-X*) Kluwer Academic.

Public Health Reports: Journal of the United States Public Health Service. per. 13.00 (*0-16-010562-5*) USGPO.

Public Health Reports Vol. 113, Suppl., 1, 1998: HIV Prevention with Drug-Using Populations - Current Status & Future Prospects. Anthony Robbins. (DHHS Publication Ser.: Vol. 98-50193). (Illus.). 206p. 1998. pap. 17.00 (*0-16-049601-2*) USGPO.

Public Health Representative. Jack Rudman. (Career Examination Ser.: C-2369). 1994. pap. 27.95 (*0-8373-2369-X*) Nat Learn.

Public Health Representative I. Jack Rudman. (Career Examination Ser.: C-2972). 1994. pap. 27.95 (*0-8373-2972-8*) Nat Learn.

Public Health Representative II. Jack Rudman. (Career Examination Ser.: C-2973). 1994. pap. 29.95 (*0-8373-2973-6*) Nat Learn.

Public Health Researcher: A Methodological Guide. Jeanne Daly et al. LC 98-148134. 232p. 1998. pap. text 34.50 (*0-19-554075-1*) OUP.

Public Health Responsibilities in Radiation Protection. (Technical Report Ser.: No. 254). 23p. 1963. pap. text 3.00 (*92-4-120254-8*) World Health.

Public Health, Safety & Highways. Peter J. Loughlin. (New Hampshire Municipal Practice Ser.: Vol. 3). 590p. 1991. ring bd. 70.00 (*0-88063-705-6*, MICHIE) LEXIS Pub.

Public Health Sanitarian. Jack Rudman. (Career Examination Ser.: C-633). 1994. pap. 27.95 (*0-8373-0633-7*) Nat Learn.

Public Health Sanitarian Trainee. Jack Rudman. (Career Examination Ser.: C-984). 1994. pap. 23.95 (*0-8373-0984-0*) Nat Learn.

Public Health Scientist. Jack Rudman. (Career Examination Ser.: C-634). 1994. pap. 34.95 (*0-8373-0634-5*) Nat Learn.

Public Health Service: Its History, Activities & Organization. Laurence F. Schmeckebier. LC 72-3023. (Brookings Institution. Institute for Government Research. Service Monographs of the U. S. Government: No. 10). reprint ed. 49.50 (*0-404-57110-7*) AMS Pr.

Public Health Services for All: Revitalizing a Shattered Plan. Colin Erickson & Harold M. Erickson, Sr. (Illus.). 275p. (Orig.). 1993. pap. 8.95 (*0-9640626-0-7*) H M Erickson.

Public Health Social Work Assistant. Jack Rudman. (Career Examination Ser.: C-1442). 1994. pap. 27.95 (*0-8373-1442-9*) Nat Learn.

Public Health Sourcebook. Ed. by Wendy Wilcox. LC 98-15705. (Health Reference Ser.). 700p. 1998. lib. bdg. 78.00 (*0-7808-0220-9*) Omnigraphics Inc.

Public Health Surveillance. Ed. by William Halperin et al. 238p. 1992. 43.95 (*0-471-28432-7*, VNR) Wiley.

Public Health Surveillance. Ed. by William Halperin & Edward L. Baker. (Illus.). 272p. 1992. pap. 34.95 (*0-442-00762-0*, VNR) Wiley.

Public Health System in Texas. Barbara N. Samuels. (Working Paper Ser.: No. 66). 127p. 1992. pap. 5.50 (*0-89940-548-7*) LBJ Sch Pub Aff.

***Public Health Systems & Emerging Infections: Assessing the Capabilities of the Public & Private Sectors.** Johnathan R. Davis et al. 128p. 2000. pap. 23.00 (*0-309-06829-0*) Natl Acad Pr.

Public Health Technician. Jack Rudman. (Career Examination Ser.: C-2226). 1994. pap. 27.95 (*0-8373-2226-X*) Nat Learn.

***Public Health 2000.** LC 98-212832. iii, 90 p. 1998. write for info. (*0-16-057234-7*) USGPO.

Public Heroes, Private Felons: Athletes & Crimes Against Women. Jeff Benedict. LC 97-6528. 224p. 1997. text 32.50 (*1-55553-316-7*) NE U Pr.

Public Heroes, Private Felons: Athletes & Crimes Against Women. Jeff Benedict. 1999. pap. text 12.95 (*1-55553-382-5*) NE U Pr.

Public History: An Introduction. Ed. by Barbara J. Howe & Emory L. Kemp. LC 85-23665. 516p. 1986. text 38.50 (*0-89874-881-X*) Krieger.

Public History: Essays from the Field. Ed. by James B. Gardner & Peter S. LaPaglia. LC 98-34148. 438p. 1999. 48.50 (*1-57524-017-3*) Krieger.

***Public History: Essays from the Field.** Ed. by James B. Gardner & Peter S. LaPaglia. LC 98-34148. xv, 422p. 1999. pap. 39.50 (*1-57524-021-1*) Krieger.

Public History & the Environment. Ed. by Martin V. Melosi & Philip Scarpino. 2000. write for info. (*1-57524-071-8*) Krieger.

Public History, Private Stories: Italian Women's Autobiography. Graziella Parati. LC 95-39547. 1996. pap. 17.95 (*0-8166-2607-3*); text 44.95 (*0-8166-2606-5*) U of Minn Pr.

Public History Readings: A Book of Readings. Phyllis K. Leffler & Joseph Brent, III. 552p. (C). 1992. 31.50 (*0-89464-433-5*) Krieger.

Public Holidays in Latin America. Andres D. Puello. (International Business Reports). 45p. 1993. spiral bd. 14.95 (*0-9631210-1-4*) DPA Intl.

Public Hospital Systems in New York & Paris. Ed. by Victor G. Rodwin et al. 320p. (C). 1992. text 50.00 (*0-8147-7422-9*) NYU Pr.

Public Hospitals in Developing Countries: Resource Use, Cost, Financing. Howard Barnum & Joseph Kutzin. 352p. 1993. 35.95 (*0-8018-4532-7*, 44532) Johns Hopkins.

Public Hospitals in Developing Countries: Resource Use, Cost, Financing. Howard Barnum & Joseph Kutzin. LC 92-49341. 345p. reprint ed. pap. 107.00 (*0-608-08811-0*, 206945000004) Bks Demand.

***Public House & Beverage Management: Key Principles & Issues.** Andrew Roberts et al. 224p. 2000. pap. 36.95 (*0-7506-4678-0*) Buttrwrth-Heinemann.

***Public Housing: HUD Has Several Opportunities to Promote Private Management.** Ed. by Judy A. England-Joseph & Eric Marts. (Illus.). 67p. (C). 1999. pap. text 20.00 (*0-7881-8460-1*) DIANE Pub.

Public Housing: HUD Should Improve the Usefulness & Accuracy of Its Management Assessment Program. Lawrence J. Dyckman et al. (Illus.). 61p. 1998. reprint ed. pap. text 20.00 (*0-7881-4331-X*) DIANE Pub.

Public Housing: Index of New Information with Authors, Subjects & Bibliography. Lester W. Wakefield. 180p. 1993. 47.50 (*1-55914-830-6*); pap. 44.50 (*1-55914-831-4*) ABBE Pubs Assn.

Public Housing Advocacy. pap. 3.00 (*0-317-02648-8*, 37,357PH) NCLS Inc.

Public Housing & Selected Housing Issues. 275p. 1985. 18.00 (*0-685-30169-9*, 43,830) NCLS Inc.

Public Housing Drug Elimination Program Resource Document: Case Studies. Theodore M. Hammett et al. (Illus.). 564p. (C). 1997. reprint ed. pap. text 50.00 (*0-7881-4523-1*) DIANE Pub.

Public Housing Drug Elimination Program Resource Document: Final Report. Theodore M. Hammett et al. (Illus.). 276p. (C). 1997. reprint ed. pap. text 40.00 (*0-7881-4522-3*) DIANE Pub.

Public Housing Energy Efficiency Through Private Financing. 57p. 1982. 10.00 (*0-318-17333-6*, DG82-302) Pub Tech Inc.

Public Housing in a Competitive Market: An Example of How It Would Fare. Marty Abrauanel. (Illus.). 38p. (Orig.). (C). 1997. pap. text 30.00 (*0-7881-3764-6*) DIANE Pub.

Public Housing Reform & Responsibility Act of 1997--S. 462: Hearing Before the Subcommittee on Housing Opportunity & Community Development of the Committee on Banking, Housing & Urban Affairs, United States Senate, 105th Congress, 1st Session, on S. 462... April 9, 1997. USGPO Staff. LC 98-176025. v, 571 p. 1998. pap. write for info. (*0-16-056413-1*) USGPO.

Public Hug: New & Selected Poems. fac. ed. Robert Hershon. LC 79-9446. 99p. 1980. reprint ed. pap. 30.70 (*0-7837-7739-6*, 204749500007) Bks Demand.

Public Hygiene in America. Henry I. Bowditch. LC 70-180557. (Medicine & Society in America Ser.). (Illus.). 415p. 1972. reprint ed. 29.95 (*0-405-03937-9*) Ayer.

Public Image. Muriel Spark. LC 92-46593. (New Directions Classics Ser.). 160p. 1993. pap. 9.95 (*0-8112-1246-7*, NDP767, Pub. by New Directions) Norton.

Public Image of Big Business in America, 1880-1940: A Quantitative Study in Social Change. Louis P. Galambos & Barbara B. Spence. LC 75-11347. (Illus.). 336p. reprint ed. pap. 104.20 (*0-8357-4331-4*, 203713100007) Bks Demand.

Public Image of Courts, 1977: General Publics Data. U. S. Department of Justice, Bureau of Justice Sta. LC 79-91248. 384p. 1980. write for info. (*0-89138-962-8*) ICPSR.

Public Image of Courts, 1977: Special Publics Data. U. S. Department of Justice, Bureau of Justice Sta. LC 79-91248. 292p. 1980. write for info. (*0-89138-961-X*) ICPSR.

Public Image of Henry Ford: An American Folk Hero & His Company. David Lewis. LC 76-807. (Great Lakes Bks.). (Illus.). 600p. 1987. pap. 24.95 (*0-8143-1892-4*) Wayne St U Pr.

Public Images of Western Security. Gregory F. Treverton et al. (Atlantic Papers: 54-55). 92p. (C). 1985. pap. 22.00 (*0-8476-7491-6*) Rowman.

Public in Your Woods. J. A. Irving. 148p. (C). 1991. pap. text 90.00 (*0-906527-19-8*, Pub. by Surrey Beatty & Sons) St Mut.

Public Information: Desire, Disaster, Document. Gary Garrels et al. LC 94-29415. (Illus.). 188p. 1995. pap. 34.95 (*1-881616-45-2*) Dist Art Pubs.

Public Information about Osteoporosis: What's Available, What's Needed? (Illus.). 62p. (Orig.). 1995. pap. text 25.00 (*0-7881-2499-4*) DIANE Pub.

Public Information & Media Relations in State Legislatures. Mary Renstrom. (State Legislative Reports: Vol. 17, No. 22). 29p. 1992. pap. text 15.00 (*1-55516-295-9*, 7302-1722) Natl Conf State Legis.

Public Information Assistant. Jack Rudman. (Career Examination Ser.: C-2956). 1994. pap. 27.95 (*0-8373-2956-6*) Nat Learn.

Public Information Circular for Shipments of Irradiated Reactor Fuel. 31p. 1997. pap. 3.50 (*0-16-062711-7*) USGPO.

***Public Information Circular for Shipments of Irradiated Reactor Fuel.** 33p. 1998. pap. 3.00 (*0-16-062773-7*) USGPO.

Public Information, Education & Relations in Emergency Medical Services. Brenda Sullivan. 120p. 1997. ring bd. 17.00 (*0-16-048912-1*) USGPO.

***Public Information Officer.** Michelle Charlesworth. (Illus.). 112p. (C). 1999. pap. write for info. (*0-87939-170-7*) IFSTA.

Public Information Officer. Jack Rudman. (Career Examination Ser.: C-2950). 1994. pap. 29.95 (*0-8373-2950-7*) Nat Learn.

Public Information Specialist. Jack Rudman. (Career Examination Ser.: C-2111). 1994. pap. 29.95 (*0-8373-2111-5*) Nat Learn.

***Public Infrastructure Performance in Developing Countries.** Abdul Ghafoor. 248p. 2000. text 69.95 (*1-84014-925-6*, Pub. by Ashgate Pub) Ashgate Pub Co.

Public Infrastructure Planning & Management. Ed. by Jay M. Stein. (Urban Affairs Annual Review Ser.: Vol. 33). 270p. (C). 1988. text 62.00 (*0-8039-2690-1*); pap. text 26.00 (*0-8039-2691-X*) Sage.

Public Institutions see Collected Works of Count Rumford

Public Institutions for Personal Learning: Establishing a Research Agenda. Ed. by John H. Falk & Lynn D. Dierking. (Illus.). 143p. (Orig.). 1995. pap. 43.00 (*0-931201-24-1*) Am Assn Mus.

Public Integrity. J. Patrick Dobel. LC 99-21569. 288p. 1999. 38.00 (*0-8018-5930-1*) Johns Hopkins.

Public Integrity, Vol. 1, No. 2. James Bowman. 1999. pap. text. write for info. (*0-8133-6833-2*) Westview.

Public Integrity: Inaugural Issue. Jim Bowman & Jonathan West. 118p. 1998. pap. text. write for info. (*0-8133-6678-X*) Westview.

Public Interest: A Critique of the Theory of a Political Concept. Glendon A. Schubert. LC 82-15509. 244p. 1982. reprint ed. lib. bdg. 35.00 (*0-313-22364-5*, SCPU, Greenwood Pr) Greenwood.

Public Interest & the Business of Broadcasting: The Broadcast Industry Looks at Itself. Ed. by Jon T. Powell & Wally Gair. LC 88-3098. 203p. 1988. 65.00 (*0-89930-198-3*, PLI/, Quorum Bks) Greenwood.

Public Interest in a Private Economy. Ed. by Albert T. Sommers. LC 96-116315. (Report: No. 1082-94-RR). (Illus.). 55p. 1994. pap. text 100.00 (*0-8237-0529-3*) Conference Bd.

Public Interest in Conversions of Nonprofit Health Charities. Judith E. Bell et al. LC 98-124762. 60p. 1997. pap. write for info. (*1-887748-15-6*) Milbank Memorial.

Public Interest in the Use of Private Lands: Environmental Regeneration. Ed. by Benjamin C. Dysart, III & Marion Clawson. LC 89-3913. 200p. 1989. 57.95 (*0-275-92991-4*, C2991, Praeger Pubs) Greenwood.

Public Interest Law: An Annotated Bibliography & Research Guide. Lee Epstein et al. Ed. by Joseph F. Kobylka. LC 91-45119. (Organizations & Interest Groups Ser.: Vol. 4). 232p. 1992. text 10.00 (*0-8240-7636-2*, SS#693) Garland.

Public Interest Law Groups: Institutional Profiles. Karen O'Connor & Lee Epstein. LC 88-37382. 278p. 1989. lib. bdg. 75.00 (*0-313-24787-0*, OPI, Greenwood Pr) Greenwood.

Public Interest Liberalism, & the Crisis of Affluence. Robert D. Holsworth. 320p. 1981. text 11.95 (*0-87073-061-4*) Schenkman Bks Inc.

Public Interest on Education. Ed. by Nathan Glazer. (Illus.). 280p. 1984. reprint ed. pap. text 24.00 (*0-8191-4141-0*); reprint ed. lib. bdg. 58.50 (*0-8191-4140-2*) U Pr of Amer.

Public Interest Profiles, 1996-1997. LC 86-645195. 890p. 1996. 215.00 (*1-56802-220-4*) Congr Quarterly.

Public Interest Profiles, 1998-1999. Ed. by Foundation for Public Affairs Staff. 900p. 1998. 215.00 (*1-56802-424-X*) Congr Quarterly.

Public International Law. Ray August. LC 94-40810. 624p. 1995. 69.80 (*0-13-299892-0*) P-H.

Public International Law. Kalyan Chaudhuri. (C). 1989. 25.00 (*0-89771-459-8*, Pub. by Current Dist) St Mut.

Public International Law. Omer Y. Elagab. (Q & A Ser.). 300p. 1996. pap. write for info. (*1-874241-37-6*, Pub. by Cavendish Pubng) Gaunt.

Public International Law. Timothy Hillier. (Lecture Notes Ser.). 398p. 1995. pap. 27.00 (*1-874241-81-3*, Pub. by Cavendish Pubng) Gaunt.

Public International Law. Branimir M. Jankovic. LC 83-9155. 450p. (C). 1984. lib. bdg. 55.00 (*0-941320-16-2*) Transnatl Pubs.

Public International Law. Ed. by Robert M. MacLean. 316p. (C). 1990. pap. 40.00 (*1-85352-752-1*, Pub. by HLT Pubns) St Mut.

Public International Law. Ed. by Robert M. MacLean. 325p. (C). 1991. 90.00 (*1-85352-398-4*, Pub. by HLT Pubns) St Mut.

Public International Law. Ed. by Robert M. MacLean. 430p. 1996. pap. 110.00 (*0-7510-0699-8*, Pub. by HLT Pubns) St Mut.

Public International Law: A Selective Bibliography. 56p. pap. 15.00 (*92-1-133488-8*) UN.

Public International Law: An Australian Perspective. Sam Blay et al. LC 98-158255. 1997. write for info. (*0-19-550690-1*) OUP.

Public International Law: An Australian Perspective. Ed. by Sam Blay et al. LC 98-158255. (Illus.). 476p. 1998. pap. text 55.00 (*0-19-553993-1*) OUP.

Public International Law & the Future World Order: Liber Amicorum in Honor of A. J. Thomas, Jr. Ed. by Joseph J. Norton. LC 87-4688. (Illus.). xxxii, 583p. 1987. 65.00 (*0-8377-2510-0*, Rothman) W S Hein.

Public International Law Cases. Robert M. MacLean. 276p. 1996. pap. 110.00 (*0-7510-0665-3*, Pub. by HLT Pubns) St Mut.

Public International Law in a Nutshell. 2nd ed. Thomas Buergenthal & Harold G. Maier. (Nutshell Ser.). 275p. (C). 1989. reprint ed. pap. 21.00 (*0-314-66371-1*) West Pub.

Public International Law in the Airspace of the High Seas. Nicholas Grief. LC 94-35260. (Utrecht Studies in Air & Space Law: Vol. 14). 336p. (C). 1994. lib. bdg. 117.00 (*0-7923-2725-X*) Kluwer Academic.

Public International Law of Taxation: Text, Cases & Materials. Ed. by Asif H. Qureshi. LC 93-33344. 640p. (C). 1994. lib. bdg. 221.00 (*1-85333-950-4*, Pub. by Graham & Trotman) Kluwer Academic.

Public Intimacies: Talk Show Participants & Tell All TV. Patricia J. Priest. Ed. by Brenda Dervin. LC 95-3929. (Communication Series). 192p. 1995. pap. text 21.95 (*1-57273-003-X*) Hampton Pr NJ.

Public Intimacies: Talk Show Participants & Tell All TV. Patricia J. Priest. Ed. by Brenda Dervin. LC 95-3929. (Communication Series). 192p. (C). 1995. text 49.50 (*1-57273-002-1*) Hampton Pr NJ.

Public Investment & Full Employment. (I.L.O. Studies & Reports New Ser.: No. 3). 1974. reprint ed. 51.00 (*0-8115-3329-8*) Periodicals Srv.

Public Investment & Private Sector Growth: The Economic Benefits of Reducing America's "Third Deficit" David A. Ashhauer. (Illus.). 36p. (Orig.). 1991. pap. text 12.00 (*0-944826-38-5*) Economic Policy Inst.

Public Investment Planning in Civilian Nuclear Power. John M. Vernon. LC 78-132029. 181p. reprint ed. pap. 56.20 (*0-608-12827-9*, 202346400033) Bks Demand.

Public Investment, the Rate of Return, & Optimal Fiscal Policy. Kenneth Joseph Arrow & Mordecai Kurz. LC 73-108380. 248p. reprint ed. pap. 76.90 (*0-608-16182-9*, 202562700045) Bks Demand.

Public Involvement As an Organizational Development Process: A Proactive Theory for Environmental Planning Program Management. Daniel S. Iacofano. LC 90-24496. (Environment: Problems & Solutions Ser.). 224p. 1991. text 20.00 (*0-8240-9784-X*) Garland.

Public Involvement in Environmental Decision-Making: An Annotated Bibliography. B. Jaffray. (CPL Bibliographies Ser.: No. 61). 57p. 1981. 10.00 (*0-86602-061-6*, Sage Prdcls Pr) Sage.

***Public Involvement in the Nuclear Regulatory Process.** 12p. 1998. pap. 1.00 (*0-16-062998-5*) USGPO.

Public Involvement Strategies: A Manager's Handbook. (Illus.). 96p. 1995. pap. 45.00 (*0-89867-819-6*, 90694) Am Water Wks Assn.

Public Inwardness, Intimate Scripts, Vol. 28. Ed. by Julie Chandler Hayes & Timothy Erwin. (Studies in Eighteenth-Century Culture). (Illus.). 397p. 1999. 40.00 (*0-8018-6247-7*) Johns Hopkins.

Public Is Invited to Dance: Representation, the Body, & Dialogue in Gertrude Stein. Harriet S. Chessman. 264p. 1989. 35.00 (*0-8047-1484-3*) Stanford U Pr.

Public Issues Handbook: A Guide for the Concerned Citizen. Robert A. Rosenbaum. LC 82-15812. (Illus.). 409p. 1983. lib. bdg. 75.00 (*0-313-23504-X*, RPI/, Greenwood Pr) Greenwood.

Public Issues, Private Tensions: Contemporary American Drama. Ed. by M. C. Roudane. LC 91-58147. (Georgia State Literary Studies: No. 9). 1993. 55.00 (*0-404-63209-2*) AMS Pr.

Public Joint Ventures in Developing Countries: Organization, Management & Critical Issues. 144p. pap. 17.00 (*92-1-123110-8*, E.89.II.H.1) UN.

***Public Journalism & Political Knowledge.** Ed. by Anthony J. Eksterowicz & Robert N. Roberts. 224p. 2000. 65.00 (*0-8476-9539-5*); pap. 22.95 (*0-8476-9540-9*) Rowman.

Public Journalism & Public Life. 2nd ed. Davis B. Merritt. LC 97-15069. 216p. 1997. text. write for info. (*0-8058-2707-2*); pap. text. write for info. (*0-8058-2708-0*) L Erlbaum Assocs.

Public Journalism Movement in America: Evangelists in the Newsroom. Don H. Corrigan. LC 98-50240. 256p. 1999. 59.95 (*0-275-95781-0*, Praeger Pubs) Greenwood.

Public (K-12) Education's Hot Jalapenos: Topics Picantes in Special Education. Ed. by Carlos A. Bonilla & Joyce L. Goss. LC 96-79027. (Illus.). 58p. (Orig.). 1997. pap. 19.95 (*1-879774-03-8*) ICA Pub Co.

Public-Key Cryptography. 1993. lib. bdg. 253.95 (*0-8490-8932-8*) Gordon Pr.

Public-Key Cryptography. 1990. 52.95 (*0-387-52831-8*) Spr-Verlag.

Public-Key Cryptography. 2nd enl. ed. Arto Salomaa. LC 96-31537. (Texts in Theoretical Computer Science Ser.). x, 270p. 1996. 49.95 (*3-540-61356-0*) Spr-Verlag.

Public Key Cryptography: First International Workshop on Practice on Theory in Public Key Cryptography, PKC '98, Pacifico Yokohama, Japan, February 5-6, 1998, Proceedings. Ed. by Hideki Imai et al. LC 98-26204. (Lecture Notes in Computer Science Ser.: Vol. 1431). xi, 263p. 1998. pap. 49.00 (*3-540-64693-0*) Spr-Verlag.

***Public Key Cryptography: Proceedings of the 3rd International Workshop on Practice & Theory in Public Key Cryptosystems, PKC 2000, Melbourne, Victoria, Australia, January 18-20, 2000.** Hideki Imai & Yuliang Zheng. LC 99-89214. (Lecture Notes in Computer Science Ser.: Vol. 1751). xi, 485p. 2000. pap. 73.00 (*3-540-66967-1*) Spr-Verlag.

***Public Key Cryptography: Second International Workshop on Practice & Theory in Public Key Cryptography, PKC'99, Kamakura, Japan, March 1-3, 1999: Proceedings.** International Workshop on Practice and Theory in Public Key Cryptography. Ed. by H. Imai & Y. Zheng. LC 99-19968. (Lecture Notes in Computer Science Ser.). ix, 327p. 1999. 56.00 (*3-540-65644-8*) Spr-Verlag.

Public-Key Cryptography: State of the Art & Future Directions. Ed. by T. Beth et al. (Lecture Notes in Computer Science Ser.: Vol. 578). xi, 97p. 1992. 31.95 (*0-387-55215-4*) Spr-Verlag.

Public Key Infrastructure. CommerceNet PKI Task Force Staff. 1997. pap. 39.95 (*0-614-28496-1*) McGraw-Hill Prof.

***Public Key Infrastructure (PKI) & Federal Contracting.** 203p. 1999. ring bd. 10.00 (*1-56986-053-X*, GVC-99-203) Federal Bar.

Public Knowledge & Christian Education. Theodore Plantinga. LC 87-35552. (Studies in Religious Education: Vol. 1). 136p. 1988. 69.95 (*0-88946-477-4*) E Mellen.

Public Knowledge, Private Ignorance: Toward a Library & Information Policy, 10. Patrick Wilson. LC 76-52327. (Contributions in Librarianship & Information Science Ser.: No. 10). 156p. 1977. 55.00 (*0-8371-9485-7*, WPN/, Greenwood Pr) Greenwood.

Public Land Law II. (Mineral Law Ser.). 500p. 1997. wbk. ed. 125.00 (*0-929047-72-9*) Rocky Mtn Mineral Law Found.

Public Land Laws. Henry N. Copp. Ed. by Stuart Bruchey. LC 78-53559. (Development of Public Land Law in the U. S. Ser.). 1979. reprint ed. lib. bdg. 69.95 (*0-405-11372-2*) Ayer.

Public Land Policies: An Original Anthology. Ed. by Paul W. Gates & Stuart Bruchey. LC 78-56714. (Management of Public Lands in the U. S. Ser.). 1979. lib. bdg. 44.95 (*0-405-11360-9*) Ayer.

Public Land Surveys. Lowell O. Stewart. Ed. by Stuart Bruchey. LC 78-53567. (Development of Public Land Law in the U. S. Ser.). 1979. reprint ed. lib. bdg. 19.95 (*0-405-11386-2*) Ayer.

Public Land System of Texas, 1823-1910. Reuben McKitrick. Ed. by Stuart Bruchey. LC 78-56659. (Management of Public Lands in the U. S. Ser.). (Illus.). 1979. reprint ed. lib. bdg. 17.95 (*0-405-11342-0*) Ayer.

Public Landing Revisited. Robert Phillips. 208p. 1992. 19.95 (*0-934257-78-7*) Story Line.

***Public Lands: Forests.** Holly Lippke Fretwell. Ed. by Linda E. Platts. (Illus.). 32p. 1999. pap. 5.00i (*0-9668243-3-4*) Pol Econo Res.

Public Lands: Studies in the History of the Public Domain. Ed. by Vernon Carstensen. LC 62-21554. (Illus.). 538p. reprint ed. pap. 166.80 (*0-608-09848-5*, 206923600003) Bks Demand.

Public Lands & Pioneer Farmers, Gage County, Nebraska, 1850-1900. Yasue Okada. Ed. by Stuart Bruchey. LC 78-56687. (Management of Public Lands in the U. S. Ser.). (Illus.). 1979. reprint ed. lib. bdg. 18.95 (*0-405-11348-X*) Ayer.

Public Lands & Private Rights: The Failure of Scientific Management. Robert H. Nelson. 400p. (C). 1995. lib. bdg. 73.00 (*0-8476-8008-8*) Rowman.

Public Lands Conflict & Resolution: Managing National Forest Disputes. J. M. Wondolleck. LC 88-13991. (Environment, Development, & Public Policy: Public Policy & Social Services Ser.). (Illus.). 280p. (C). 1988. 57.50 (*0-306-42861-X*, Plenum Trade) Perseus Pubng.

***Public Lands Management Improvement Act of 1997: Hearings Before the Subcommittee on Forests & Public Land Management of the Committee on Energy & Natural Resources, United States Senate, 105th Congress, 1st Session, on S. 1253, to Provide to the Federal Land Management Agencies the Authority & Capability to Manage the Federal Lands in Accordance with the Principles of Multiple Use & Sustained Yield, Oct. 30, 1997, Dec. 15, 1997, Feb. 3, 1998.** USGPO Staff. LC 98-155975. iv, 195p. 1998. pap. write for info. (*0-16-056310-0*) USGPO.

Public Lands Management in the West: Citizens, Interest Groups, & Values. Brent Steel. LC 96-26878. 224p. 1997. 55.00 (*0-275-95695-4*) Greenwood.

Public Lands Politics: Interest Group Influence on the Forest Service & the Bureau of Land Management. Paul J. Culhane. LC 80-8776. 416p. reprint ed. pap. 129.00 (*0-8357-4680-1*, 203762700008) Bks Demand.

Public Lands vs. the United States: Docket # Pending. O. Charles Horne. LC 99-188397. 50p. 1998. pap. 10.95 (*1-888106-98-0*) Agreka Bks.

Public Landscape of the New Deal. Phoebe Cutler. LC 85-2437. 200p. 1986. 35.00 (*0-300-03256-0*) Yale U Pr.

Public Law. Peter Wallington & Bob Lee. (C). 1990. 110.00 (*1-85431-020-8*, Pub. by Blackstone Pr) St Mut.

Public Law & Democracy in the United Kingdom & the United States of America. Paul Craig. (Clarendon Law Ser.). 454p. 1991. text 95.00 (*0-19-825637-X*) OUP.

Public Law & Health Service Accountability. Diane Longley. LC 92-13011. (State of Health Ser.). 1993. 123.00 (*0-335-09686-7*); pap. 35.95 (*0-335-09685-9*) OpUniv Pr.

Public Law & Political Theory. Martin Loughlin. LC 92-5647. 304p. 1992. pap. text 27.00 (*0-19-876268-2*) OUP.

***Public Law in Germany, 1800-1914.** Michael Stolleis. LC KK4413.S858 2000. 500p. 2000. 90.00 (*1-57181-057-9*) Berghahn Bks.

Public Law in Israel. Ed. by Itzhak Zamir & Allen Zysblat. 460p. (C). 1997. text 120.00 (*0-19-825853-4*) OUP.

Public Law in New Zealand: 25 Years of Change. A. Ladley & P. Rishworth. 350p. 1995. pap. write for info. (*0-409-78898-8*, MICHIE) LEXIS Pub.

Public Law, 1956-1995, 41 vols., Set. 1956. 3936.00 (*0-8377-9133-2*, Rothman) W S Hein.

Public Law 99-457 & the Basics of the Family-Centered Intervention: A Module for Training Early Intervention Special Education Personnel. Infant Hearing Resource Staff. (Early Intervention Series II). 40p. (C). 1994. pap. text 89.00 incl. VHS (*1-883204-05-4*) Hearing & Speech.

Public Law 99-457 & the Basics of Family-Centered Intervention: A Module for Training Personnel Serving Families of Deaf & Hard of Hearing Infants & Young Children. Ed. by Valerie Schuyler. (Early Intervention Ser.). 40p. (C). 1993. 89.00 incl. VHS (*0-9618297-0-2*) Hearing & Speech.

Public Law 101-336: Americans with Disabilities Act of 1990. large type ed. United States Congress Staff. 1990. 14.00 (*0-614-08368-0*, J-60000-00) Am Printing Hse.

Public Lettering: Script, Power, & Culture. Armando Petrucci. Tr. by Linda Lappin. (Illus.). 256p. 1993. 37.50 (*0-226-66386-8*) U Ch Pr.

Public Librarian. Jack Rudman. (Career Examination Ser.: C-989). 1994. pap. 27.95 (*0-8373-0989-1*) Nat Learn.

Public Librarian As Adult Learners' Advisor: An Innovation in Human Services, 38. Jane A. Reilly. LC 80-27307. (Contributions in Librarianship & Information Science Ser.: No. 38). (Illus.). 152p. 1981. 45.00 (*0-313-22134-0*, REP/) Greenwood.

Public Librarian's Human Resources Handbook: Employer Rights & Responsibilities. David A. Baldwin. LC 98-15020. 185p. 1998. pap. 30.00 (*1-56308-618-2*) Libs Unl.

Public Librarianship: An Issues - Oriented Approach, 63. Verna L. Pungitore. LC 89-2189. (Contributions in Librarianship & Information Science Ser.: No. 63). 240p. 1989. 55.00 (*0-313-26072-9*, PPB/, Greenwood Pr) Greenwood.

Public Libraries: An Economic View. Malcolm Getz. LC 80-10651. 228p. reprint ed. pap. 70.70 (*0-7837-2191-9*, 204252900004) Bks Demand.

Public Libraries: Travel Treasures of the West. Marty Rabkin & Anna Rabkin. LC 93-34680. (Illus.). 352p. 1993. pap. 19.95 (*1-55591-915-4*) Fulcrum Pub.

Public Libraries & Nontraditional Clienteles: The Politics of Special Services. Marcia J. Nauratil. LC 84-19342. (New Directions in Librarianship Ser.: No. 8). 180p. 1985. 47.95 (*0-313-23819-7*, NAP/, Greenwood Pr) Greenwood.

Public Libraries & Private Fundraising: Opportunities & Issues. Thomas Jeavons. 1994. pap. 8.00 (*1-885251-00-9*) Urban Libraries.

Public Libraries & Public Education. Herbert B. Adams. (Principle Works of Herbert Baxter Adams). 1989. reprint ed. lib. bdg. 79.00 (*0-7812-1482-3*) Rprt Serv.

Public Libraries & the Information Society EUR 17648. 1997. 60.00 (*92-828-0505-0*, CD-NA-17648-ENC, Pub. by Comm Europ Commun) Bernan Associates.

Public Libraries & the Internet. 1996. lib. bdg. 250.95 (*0-8490-5923-2*) Gordon Pr.

Public Libraries & the Internet: Study Results, Poicy Issues, & Recommendations. Charles R. McClure et al. (Illus.). 62p. (Orig.). (C). 1994. pap. text 20.00 (*0-7881-1391-7*) DIANE Pub.

Public Libraries As Agents of Communication: A Semiotic Analysis. Gulten S. Wagner. LC 92-29073. (Illus.). 277p. 1992. 40.00 (*0-8108-2604-6*) Scarecrow.

Public Libraries in India: Development & Finance. V. K. Thomas & Raja Rammohun Roy Library Foundation Staff. LC 97-905305. xii, 260 p. 1997. 27.50 (*81-259-0394-1*, Pub. by Vikas) S Asia.

Public Libraries in Nazi Germany. Margaret F. Stieg. LC 90-46771. 368p. (C). 1992. text 59.95 (*0-8173-0556-4*) U of Ala Pr.

Public Libraries in Nazi Germany. Margaret F. Stieg. LC 90-46771. (Illus.). 368p. reprint ed. pap. 114.10 (*0-608-09247-9*, 205275100005) Bks Demand.

Public Libraries in the United States. 1994. lib. bdg. 255.95 (*0-8490-9038-5*) Gordon Pr.

Public Libraries in the United States. 1995. lib. bdg. 251.95 (*0-8490-6703-0*) Gordon Pr.

Public Libraries in the United States. 125p. 1995. pap. 8.50 (*0-16-048308-5*) USGPO.

Public Libraries in the United States: Fy 1994. Adrienne Chute. 127p. 1997. pap. 11.00 (*0-16-049059-6*) USGPO.

***Public Libraries in the United States: FY 1995.** Adrienne Chute. 140p. 1998. per. 14.00 (*0-16-063669-8*) USGPO.

Public Libraries since 1945: The Impact of the McColvin Report. Philip Whiteman. LC 86-222446. 231p. reprint ed. pap. 71.70 (*0-608-08885-4*, 206952200004) Bks Demand.

Public Library. Ed. by Asheim. LC 76-106680. 1970. reprint ed. lib. bdg. 65.00 (*0-8371-3351-3*, ASPL, Greenwood Pr) Greenwood.

Public Library: Circumstances & Prospects: Proceedings of the Thirty-Ninth Conference of the Graduate Library School, April 10-11, 1978. Chicago University, Graduate Library School Staff. Ed. by W. Boyd Rayward. LC 78-19604. 168p. reprint ed. pap. 52.10 (*0-608-16501-8*, 202673900051) Bks Demand.

Public Library: Its Origins, Purpose, & Significance. 3rd ed. William J. Murison. LC 88-19335. 261p. reprint ed. pap. 81.00 (*0-608-08886-2*, 206952300004) Bks Demand.

Public Library Administration. Royston Brown. LC Z 0678.B828. (Outlines of Modern Librarianship Ser.: Vol. 9). 95p. reprint ed. pap. 30.00 (*0-608-08887-0*, 206952400004) Bks Demand.

Public Library Administrator's Planning Guide to Automation. Donald J. Sager. (Library, Information, & Computer Science Ser.: No. 2). 144p. (Orig.). 1983. pap. 12.50 (*0-933418-43-4*) OCLC Online Comp.

Public Library & Federal Policy. Ed. by J. B. Wellisch et al. LC 73-20302. 349p. 1974. 65.00 (*0-8371-7334-5*, PLF/, Greenwood Pr) Greenwood.

Public Library As Public Knowledge. Bob Usherwood. LC 88-47729. 160p. 1989. reprint ed. pap. 49.60 (*0-7837-9274-3*, 206001200004) Bks Demand.

Public Library Budget & Materials Expenditure Report. James Moses & Peter Park. 150p. 1991. ring bd. 95.00 (*0-9626749-3-1*) Primary Research.

Public Library Catalog: Guide to Reference Books & Adult Nonfiction. 10th ed. Ed. by Juliette Yaakov. LC 94-15986. 1325p. 1994. lib. bdg. 230.00 (*0-8242-0859-5*) Wilson.

***Public Library Catalog: Guide to Reference Books & Adult Nonfiction. 11th rev. ed. Juliette Yaakov. LC 99-27574. (Standard Catalog Ser.). 1456p. 1999. 299.00 (0-8242-0981-8) Wilson.**

The 11th edition features revised & updated coverage of health, personal finance, & science; expanded coverage of cooking & gardening, & more. Here you'll find annotated entries for more than 8,000 books; 2,000 analytical entries for composite works; & information on CD-ROM versions of print titles, accessible via a single-alphabet author, title, subject, & analytical index. Free annual paperbound supplements, published 2000 through 2003, deliver information on some 1,200 new titles. As with previous editions, titles were elected by experienced librarians representing 18 public libraries across the United States. In libraries for more than 60 years, Public Library Catalog provides librarians help with resource selection & purchasing, readers advisory & reference, and collection maintenance & information verification. To Order: H.W. WILSON -- 1-800-367-6770 (1-718-588-8400 outside U.S. & Canada), or visit www.hwwilson.com. *Publisher Paid Annotation.*

Public Library Collection Development in the Information Age. Ed. by Annabel K. Stephens. LC 98-7845. 211p. 1998. 49.95 (*0-7890-0528-X*) Haworth Pr.

Public Library Data, 1995. American Library Association Staff. 1996. 60.00 (*0-8389-7784-7*) ALA.

Public Library Development Program: Manual for Trainers. Peggy O'Donnell. LC Z 0670.O366. (Illus.). 154p. reprint ed. pap. 47.80 (*0-7837-5908-8*, 204570600007) Bks Demand.

Public Library Effectiveness: A Study. 1990. lib. bdg. 75.00 (*0-8490-4023-X*) Gordon Pr.

An Asterisk (*) at the beginning of an entry indicates that the title is appearing for the first time.

Public Library Effectiveness Study: A Complete Report. Nancy A. Van House & Thomas A. Childers. LC 93-18970. (Illus.). 110p. 1993. pap. text 28.00 (*0-8389-0619-2*) ALA.

Public Library in Non-Traditional Education. Jean S. Brooks & David L. Reich. LC 73-21903. (Illus.). 256p. 1974. 24.95 (*0-88280-008-6*) ETC Pubns.

Public Library in the Bibliographic Network. Ed. by Betty J. Turock. LC 86-14915. (Resource Sharing & Information Networks Ser.: Vol. 3, No. 2). 89p. 1986. text 29.95 (*0-86656-595-7*) Haworth Pr.

Public Library Movement in the United States. Samuel S. Greene. 1972. 59.95 (*0-8490-0914-6*) Gordon Pr.

Public Library Networking & Interlibrary Co-Operation. Ed. by Ann E. Prentice & Debra Shaw. (Public Library Quarterly: Vol. 2, Nos. 3-4). 113p. 1982. pap. text 24.95 (*0-86656-116-1*) Haworth Pr.

Public Library of New South Wales Dictionary Catalog of Printed Books. Mitch. 1982. 4710.00 (*0-8161-1362-9*, G K Hall & Co) Mac Lib Ref.

Public Library of New South Wales Dictionary Catalog of Printed Books, Supplement 1. Mitch. 1981. suppl. ed. 180.00 (*0-8161-1323-8*, G K Hall & Co) Mac Lib Ref.

Public Library Operations & Services. C. G. Viswanathan. 232p. (C). 1985. 180.00 (*81-85009-09-0*, Pub. by Print Hse) St Mut.

Public Library Planning: Case Studies for Management. Brett Sutton. LC 94-24579. (Greenwood Library Management Collection). 328p. 1995. lib. bdg. 72.95 (*0-313-28776-7*, Greenwood Pr) Greenwood.

Public Library Politics: The Role of the Elected Member. Bob Usherwood. 272p. 1993. 65.00 (*1-85604-059-3*, LAP0593, Pub. by Library Association) Bernan Associates.

Public Library Purpose: A Reader. Ed. by Barry Totterdell. LC 77-20129. 159p. 1978. reprint ed. pap. 49.30 (*0-608-07774-7*, 206786200010) Bks Demand.

Public Library Service for Ethnic Minorities in Great Britain. Ed. by Eric Clough & Jacqueline Quarmby. LC 78-13622. (Illus.). 369p. 1978. 69.50 (*0-313-21201-5*, CPL, Greenwood Pr) Greenwood.

Public Library Services for Immigrant Populations in California. Amado M. Padilla. (Partnerships for Change Ser.: No. 4). 48p. 1992. pap. text 8.50 (*0-929722-49-3*) CA State Library Fndtn.

***Public Library Services for Youth with Special Needs: A Plan for Wisconsin.** Frances De Usabel & Coral S. Swanson. (Illus.). 60p. 2000. pap. text 20.00 (*0-7567-0032-9*) DIANE Pub.

Public Library Services to Business. Rosemarie Riechel. LC 94-7018. 131p. 1994. pap. 45.00 (*1-55570-168-X*) Neal-Schuman.

Public Library Trade Directory: A Directory of the Largest Public Libraries of the U. S. Ed. by Florencio O. Garcia. 117p. (Orig.). 1993. 15.00 (*0-929928-18-0*) Fog Pubns.

Public Library User Fees: The Use & Finance of Public Libraries, 43. Nancy A. Van House. LC 82-11741. (Contributions in Librarianship & Information Science Ser.: No. 43). (Illus.). 140p. 1983. 47.95 (*0-313-22753-5*, DPU/, Greenwood Pr) Greenwood.

Public Library Users & Uses: A Market Research Handbook. Choong H. Kim & Robert D. Little. LC 87-13126. 384p. 1987. 38.00 (*0-8108-2021-8*) Scarecrow.

Public Library Youth Services: A Public Policy Approach. Holly G. Willett. LC 94-15773. 304p. 1995. pap. 39.50 (*1-56750-123-0*); text 73.25 (*1-56750-122-2*) Ablx Pub.

Public Lies & Private Truths: An Introduction to PR. Bill Mallinson. (Illus.). 176p. 1997. 79.50 (*0-304-33832-X*); pap. 32.50 (*0-304-33833-8*) Continuum.

Public Life & Propertied Englishmen, 1689-1798. Paul Langford. (Ford Lectures 1990). (Illus.). 622p. 1994. reprint ed. pap. text 32.00 (*0-19-820534-1*) OUP.

Public Life & Propertied Englishmen, 1689-1798: The Ford Lectures Delivered in the University of Oxford, 1990. Paul Langford. (Ford Lectures 1990). (Illus.). 622p. 1991. text 95.00 (*0-19-820149-4*) OUP.

Public Life in Industrial America, 1877-1917. 2nd expanded rev. ed. Richard L. McCormick. (New American History Ser.). 26p. (C). 1997. reprint ed. pap. 5.00 (*0-87229-091-3*) Am Hist Assn.

Public Life in Renaissance Florence. Richard C. Trexler. LC 91-55259. 620p. 1991. text 59.95 (*0-8014-2694-4*); pap. text 19.95 (*0-8014-9979-8*) Cornell U Pr.

Public Life in Toulouse, 1463-1789: From Municipal Republic to Cosmopolitan City. Robert A. Schneider. LC 89-42880. (Illus.). 416p. 1989. text 57.50 (*0-8014-2191-8*) Cornell U Pr.

Public Life in Urban Places. Suzanne H. Crowhurst-Lennard & Henry L. Lennard. LC 83-83342. 80p. (Orig.). 1984. pap. 8.95 (*0-935824-03-0*) Gondolier.

Public Life of Captain John Brown. James Redpath. LC 79-126251. (Select Bibliographies Reprint Ser.). 1977. 34.95 (*0-8369-5478-5*) Ayer.

Public Life of Eugene Semple: Promoter & Politician of the Pacific Northwest. Alan Hynding. LC 73-9903. 220p. 1973. 30.00 (*0-295-95288-1*) U of Wash Pr.

Public Life of Henry Dearborn. Richard A. Erney. Ed. by Richard H. Kohn. LC 78-22419. (American Military Experience Ser.). 1980. lib. bdg. 30.95 (*0-405-11893-7*) Ayer.

***Public Life of the Arts in America.** Ed. by Joni Maya Cherbo & Margaret Jane Wyszomirski. LC 99-42390. (Public Life of the Arts Ser.). 288p. 2000. text 55.00 (*0-8135-2767-8*) Rutgers U Pr.

***Public Life of the Arts in America.** Ed. by Joni Maya Cherbo & Margaret Jane Wyszomirski. LC 99-42390. (Public Life of the Arts Ser.). (Illus.). 288p. (C). 2000. pap. text 27.00 (*0-8135-2768-6*) Rutgers U Pr.

Public Life of Thomas Cooper, 1783-1839. Dumas Malone. LC 75-3122. reprint ed. 46.00 (*0-404-59117-5*) AMS Pr.

Public Like a Frog: Entering the Lives of Three Great Americans. Jean Houston. LC 93-14025. 1993. pap. 14.00 (*0-8356-0694-5*, Quest) Theos Pub Hse.

Public Linkage, Dialogue & Education Task Force Report: From Classroom to Community & Beyond, Educating for a Sustainable Future. 135p. 1997. per. 14.00 (*0-16-063422-9*) USGPO.

Public Literacy. 112p. (C). 2000. pap. text 14.80 (*0-321-06498-4*) Addison-Wesley.

Public Lives of Rural Older Americans. Steven A. Peterson & Robert J. Maiden. LC 93-13840. 166p. (Orig.). (C). 1993. pap. text 24.00 (*0-8191-9189-2*); lib. bdg. 49.50 (*0-8191-9188-4*) U Pr of Amer.

***Public Lives, Private Virtues: Images of American Revolutionary War Heroes, 1782-1832.** Christopher Harris. LC 99-43611. (Studies in American Popular History & Culture). (Illus.). 1999. write for info. (*0-8153-3482-6*) Garland.

Public Loans to Private Business. John D. Glover. Ed. by Stuart Bruchey & Vincent P. Carosso. LC 78-18961. (Small Business Enterprise in America Ser.). (Illus.). 1979. lib. bdg. 40.95 (*0-405-11465-6*) Ayer.

Public Love. Talmage Cooley & Andy Spade. LC 98-42891. (Illus.). 96p. 1999. 14.95 (*0-8118-2153-6*) Chronicle Bks.

Public Man, Private Woman: Women in Social & Political Thought. 2nd ed. Jean B. Elshtain. LC 92-29726. 408p. 1993. reprint ed. pap. 126.50 (*0-7837-9499-1*, 206024300004) Bks Demand.

***Public Management: As Art, Science & Profession.** 2nd ed. Lawrence Lynn. 2001. pap. text 27.95 (*1-889119-45-8*, Chatham House Pub) Seven Bridges.

Public Management: Its Grassroots. D. F. Du Toit et al. 310p. 1996. 38.95 (*0-7021-3833-9*, Pub. by Juta & Co) Intl Spec Bk.

Public Management: OECD Country Profiles. OECD Staff. 470p. (Orig.). 1993. pap. 80.00 (*92-64-13809-9*) OECD.

Public Management: Technocracy, Democracy, & Organizational Reform. James Parkin. 153p. (C). 1993. text 61.95 (*1-85628-685-1*, Pub. by Avebry) Ashgate Pub Co.

Public Management: The New Zealand Model. Jonathan Boston et al. LC 97-189281. 416p. 1996. pap. text 65.00 (*0-19-558325-6*) OUP.

Public Management: The State of the Art. Ed. by Barry Bozeman. LC 93-4025. (Public Administration Ser.). 450p. 1993. 48.95 (*1-55542-546-1*) Jossey-Bass.

Public Management & Administration: An Introduction. 2nd ed. Hughes. LC 98-21078. 288p. 1998. text 69.95 (*0-312-21688-2*) St Martin.

Public Management & Administration for Effective Governance. J. Cheminais et al. 1998. pap. 39.95 (*0-7021-4421-5*) Intl Spec Bk.

***Public Management & Administrative Reform in Western Europe.** Ed. by Walter J. Kickert. LC 96-35155. 304p. 1998. 85.00 (*1-85898-553-6*) E Elgar.

Public Management As Art, Science, & Profession. Laurence E. Lynn, Jr. LC 95-41793. (Illus.). 208p. (C). 1996. pap. text 22.95 (*1-56643-034-8*, Chatham House Pub) Seven Bridges.

Public Management in an Interconnected World: Essays in the Minnowbrook Tradition, 293. Ed. by Mary T. Bailey & Richard T. Mayer. LC 91-34160. (Contributions in Political Science Ser.: No. 293). 216p. 1992. 57.95 (*0-313-27457-6*, BYD/, Greenwood Pr) Greenwood.

Public Management in Britain. Farnham Horton. LC 99-28095. 304p. 1999. text 55.00 (*0-312-22634-9*) St Martin.

Public Management in Lean Years: Operating in a Cutback Management Environment. James L. Mercer. LC 92-15782. 288p. 1992. 62.95 (*0-89930-357-9*, MEB, Quorum Bks) Greenwood.

Public Management in the States: A Comparative Study of Administrative Performance & Politics. Richard C. Elling. LC 92-15784. 304p. 1992. 65.00 (*0-275-93432-2*, C3432, Praeger Pubs) Greenwood.

***Public Management Reform: A Comparative Analysis.** Christopher Pollitt & Geert Bouckaert. LC 99-37269. (Illus.). 328p. 2000. text 74.00 (*0-19-829596-0*); pap. text 35.00 (*0-19-829722-X*) OUP.

Public Management Reform & Innovation: Research, Theory, & Application. H. George Frederickson. LC 98-58024. 1999. 59.95 (*0-8173-0964-0*) U of Ala Pr.

Public Management Reform & Innovation: Research, Theory & Application. H. George Frederickson & Jocelyn M. Johnston. LC 98-58024. 1999. 29.95 (*0-8173-0971-3*) U of Ala Pr.

Public Management Research in the U. S. G. David Garson & E. Samuel Overman. LC 83-2400. 194p. 1983. 55.00 (*0-275-90984-0*, C0984, Praeger Pubs) Greenwood.

Public Management Strategies: Guidelines for Managerial Effectiveness. Barry Bozeman & Jeffrey D. Straussman. LC 89-77574. (Public Administration Ser.). 264p. 1990. 34.95 (*1-55542-237-3*) Jossey-Bass.

Public Management Systems: Monitoring & Managing Government Performance. James Swiss. 368p. 1990. pap. text 41.20 (*0-13-737545-X*) P-H.

Public Markets Community Revitalization. Theodore M. Spitzer & Hilary S. Baum. LC 94-61232. 128p. 1994. pap. text 27.95 (*0-87420-764-9*, P91) Urban Land.

Public MCH Program Functions Framework: Essential Public Health Services to Promote Maternal & Child Health. Holly A. Grason & Bernard Guyer. 40p. 1995. pap. write for info. (*1-893692-00-0*, Pub. by Wom & Child Hlth) Ntl Maternal.

Public Men: A Novel. Allen Drury. LC 98-6729. 384p. 1999. 26.00 (*0-684-80703-3*) S&S Trade.

Public Men & Events, 2 vols. Nathan Sargent. LC 79-106496. (American Public Figures Ser.). 1970. reprint ed. lib. bdg. 85.00 (*0-306-71873-1*) Da Capo.

Public Men & Virtuous Women: The Gendered Languages of Religion & Politics in Upper Canada, 1791-1850. Cecilia Morgan. (Studies in Gender & History). 280p. 1997. text 55.00 (*0-8020-0725-2*); pap. text 18.95 (*0-8020-7671-8*) U of Toronto Pr.

Public Mental Health: A Changing System in an Era of Managed Care. American Psychiatric Assocation Staff. LC 97-11029. 74p. 1997. pap. text 26.00 (*0-89042-452-7*, 2452) Am Psychiatric.

Public Mental Health Marketing: Developing a Consumer Attitude. Ed. by Donald R. Self. LC 91-41001. (Journal of Nonprofit & Public Sector Marketing). 212p. 1993. lib. bdg. 49.95 (*1-56024-189-6*) Haworth Pr.

Public Middle Schools: New York City's Best. Clara Hemphill. LC 99-36305. 1999. pap. 24.00 (*1-56947-170-3*) Soho Press.

Public Mind: Les Levine's Media Sculpture & Mass Ad Campaigns. Dominique Nahas & John Perreault. Ed. by Thomas E. Piche. LC 90-84035. (Illus.). 128p. (Orig.). 1990. text. write for info. (*0-914407-14-7*) Everson Mus.

Public Mirror. Richard Katrovas. LC 89-36080. (Wesleyan Poetry Ser.). 63p. 1990. pap. 12.95 (*0-8195-1170-6*, Wesleyan Univ Pr) U Pr of New Eng.

Public Mirror: Moliere & the Social Commerce of Depiction. Larry F. Norman. LC 99-32926. 216p. 1999. pap. text 16.00 (*0-226-59152-2*) U Ch Pr.

Public Mirror: Moliere & the Social Commerce of Depiction. Larry F. Norman. LC 99-32926. 216p. 1999. lib. bdg. 40.00 (*0-226-59151-4*) U Ch Pr.

Public Money & the Muse. Stephen Benedict. 288p. (C). 1991. pap. text 12.50 (*0-393-96135-4*, Norton Paperbks) Norton.

Public Money & the Muse: Essays on Government Funding for the Arts. Stephen Benedict. 1991. 22.95 (*0-393-03015-6*) Norton.

Public Monuments: Art in Political Bondage, 1870-1997. Sergiusz Michalski. (Essays in Art & Culture Ser.). (Illus.). 256p. 1998. pap. 24.95 (*1-86189-025-7*, Pub. by Reaktion Bks) Consort Bk Sales.

Public Moralists: Political Thought & Intellectual Life in Britain, 1850-1930. Stefan Collini. -90p. 1993. reprint ed. pap. text 35.00 (*0-19-820422-1*) OUP.

Public Morality & Liberal Society: Essays on Decency, Law, & Pornography. Harry M. Clor. LC 95-50808. 272p. (C). 1996. pap. text 17.00 (*0-268-03823-6*) U of Notre Dame Pr.

***Public Morality, Civic Virtue & the Problem of Modern Liberalism.** Ed. by T. William Boxx & Gary M. Qinlivan. LC 99-88895. 231p. 2000. pap. 18.00 (*0-8028-4754-4*) Eerdmans.

Public Morals & Private Interests: Ethics in Government & Public Service. John J. Stuhr. (Autzen Lectures in Humanities & Professions). 1989. pap. 4.00 (*0-87114-225-2*) U of Oreg Bks.

Public Murders. 1999. mass mkt. 3.95 (*0-446-73749-6*, Pub. by Warner Bks) Little.

Public Murders. Bill Granger. 1987. mass mkt. 4.95 (*0-446-34406-0*, Pub. by Warner Bks) Little.

Public Natural Resources Law, 2 vols. George C. Coggins. LC 89-27186. (Environmental Law Ser.). 1990. ring bd. 250.00 (*0-87632-689-0*) West Group.

Public Nature of Meaning. Fredrik Stjernberg. (Stockholm Studies in Philosophy: No. 10). 173p. (Orig.). 1991. pap. 43.00 (*91-22-01447-0*) Coronet Bks.

Public Nature of Private Violence. Ed. by Martha A. Fineman. LC 94-4591. 416p. (C). 1994. pap. 23.99 (*0-415-90845-0*) Routledge.

Public Network Telephone System in Brazil: A Strategic Entry Report, 1998. Compiled by Icon Group International Staff. (Country Industry Report). (Illus.). 160p. 1999. ring bd. 1600.00 incl. audio compact disk (*0-7418-0363-1*) Icon Grp.

Public of Herondas. Giuseppe Mastromarco. (London Studies of Classical Philology: Vol. 11). 136p. 1984. text 40.00 (*90-70265-94-X*, Pub. by Gieben) J Benjamins Pubng Co.

Public of the Music Theatre--Louis Riel: A Case Study. R. Murray Schafer. 1972. pap. 15.00 (*0-685-93739-9*, UE26702) Eur-Am Music.

Public Office in Early Rome: Ritual Procedure & Political Practice. Roberta Stewart. LC 98-19709. 272p. 1998. text 47.50 (*0-472-10785-2*, 10785) U of Mich Pr.

***Public Office, Private Interest: Bureaucracy & Corruption in India.** S. K. Das. (Illus.). 320p. 2000. text 24.95 (*0-19-565382-3*) OUP.

Public Officers & Employees see Tennessee Code Annotated 1999 Supplement

Public Official Associations & State & Local Government: A Bridge Across One Hundred Years. David S. Arnold & Jeremy F. Plant. (C). 1993. lib. bdg. 45.00 (*0-913969-65-6*) Univ Pub Assocs.

Public Opinion. Walter Lippman. LC 97-5340. 1997. per. 13.00 (*0-684-83327-1*) S&S Trade.

Public Opinion. Walter Lippmann. LC 97-28875. 463p. 1997. pap. text 24.95 (*1-56000-999-3*) Transaction Pubs.

Public Opinion. Vincent Price. (Communication Concepts Ser.: Vol. 4). 112p. (C). 1992. text 28.00 (*0-8039-4022-X*); pap. text 11.95 (*0-8039-4023-8*) Sage.

Public Opinion. Wilcox. 2000. pap. text 32.95 (*0-312-15350-3*) St Martin.

Public Opinion. 2nd ed. Harry Holloway & John George. LC 83-61602. 286p. (C). 1985. teacher ed. write for info. (*0-312-65486-3*) St Martin.

Public Opinion: Developments & Controversies in the 20th Century. Slavko Splichal. LC 99-17452. (Critical Media Studies). 392p. 1999. 69.00 (*0-8476-9162-4*); pap. 27.95 (*0-8476-9163-2*) Rowman.

Public Opinion: Measuring the American Mind. B. Bardes. LC 99-16353. (Political Science Ser.). 1999. pap. 40.95 (*0-534-56043-1*) Brooks-Cole.

Public Opinion: Politics, Communication & Social Process. Carroll J. Glynn et al. LC 98-27824. 496p. (C). 1998. text 75.00 (*0-8133-2916-7*, Pub. by Westview); pap. text 35.00 (*0-8133-2917-5*, Pub. by Westview) HarpC.

Public Opinion: The Visible Politics. 3rd ed. Jerry L. Yeric & John R. Todd. LC 95-69691. 280p. (C). 1995. pap. text 29.50 (*0-87581-396-8*, PUB3) F E Peacock Pubs.

***Public Opinion about Abortion.** Everett Carll Ladd & Karlyn H. Bowman. 56p. 1999. pap. 9.95 (*0-8447-7126-0*, Pub. by Am Enterprise) Pub Resources Inc.

Public Opinion about Charitable Solicitation & the Law. John Doble et al. 60p. (Orig.). 1990. pap. 15.00 (*1-889483-41-9*) Public Agenda.

Public Opinion & American Foreign Policy. Ole R. Holsti. LC 96-10151. (Orig.). 1996. pap. 20.95 (*0-472-06619-6*, Pub. by Amsterdam U Pr) U of Mich Pr.

Public Opinion & Collective Action: The Boston School Desegregation Conflict. D. Garth Taylor. LC 86-4359. 320p. 1995. 34.95 (*0-226-79155-6*) U Ch Pr.

Public Opinion & Congressional Elections. Ed. by William N. McPhee & William A. Glaser. LC 80-29534. (Illus.). 326p. 1981. reprint ed. lib. bdg. 65.00 (*0-313-22779-9*, MCOP, Greenwood Pr) Greenwood.

Public Opinion & Foreign Policy. Lester Markel. (History - United States Ser.). 227p. 1993. reprint ed. lib. bdg. 79.00 (*0-7812-4814-0*) Rprt Serv.

Public Opinion & Foreign Policy. Lester Markel et al. LC 78-167404. (Essay Index Reprint Ser.). 1977. reprint ed. 21.95 (*0-8369-7242-2*) Ayer.

Public Opinion & Foreign Policy: America's China Policy, 1949-1979, 114. Leonard A. Kusnitz. LC 83-26508. (Contributions in Political Science Ser.: No. 114). (Illus.). 191p. 1984. 55.00 (*0-313-24264-X*, KPO/, Greenwood Pr) Greenwood.

Public Opinion & Historians: Interdisciplinary Perspectives. Ed. by Melvin Small. LC 71-97244. 200p. reprint ed. pap. 62.00 (*0-7837-3817-X*, 204363700010) Bks Demand.

Public Opinion & International Governance, Vol. 2. Ed. by Oskar Niedermayer & Richard Sinnott. (Beliefs in Government Ser.: No. 2). (Illus.). 512p. 1996. text 69.00 (*0-19-827958-2*) OUP.

Public Opinion & Internationalized Governance, Vol. 2. Ed. by Oskar Niedermayer & Richard Sinnott. (Beliefs in Government Ser.). (Illus.). 508p. 1998. reprint ed. pap. text 35.00 (*0-19-829476-X*) OUP.

Public Opinion & National Security in Western Europe. Richard C. Eichenberg. LC 88-47751. (Cornell Studies in Security Affairs). 296p. 1989. text 42.50 (*0-8014-2237-X*) Cornell U Pr.

Public Opinion & Political Development in Pakistan, 1947-1958. Inamur Rehman. 298p. (Orig.). 1983. pap. text 26.00 (*0-19-577268-7*) OUP.

Public Opinion & Public Policy in Canada. Richard Johnston. (Collected Research Studies of the Royal Commission on the Economic Union & Development Prospects for Canada: Vol. 35). 262p. 1986. pap. text 21.95 (*0-8020-7279-8*) U of Toronto Pr.

Public Opinion & Relations to the Jews in Nazi Europe see Nazi Holocaust

Public Opinion & the Communication of Consent. Theodore L. Glasser. Ed. by Charles T. Salmon. (Communication Ser.). 475p. 1995. pap. text 27.00 (*0-89862-499-1*) Guilford Pubns.

Public Opinion & the Communication of Consent. Ed. by Theodore L. Glasser & Charles T. Salmon. (Communication Ser.). 475p. 1995. lib. bdg. 49.95 (*0-89862-405-3*, 2405) Guilford Pubns.

Public Opinion & the Political Future of the Nation's Capital. Edward M. Meyers. LC 96-11860. 288p. 1996. 60.00 (*0-87840-622-0*); pap. 23.95 (*0-87840-623-9*) Georgetown U Pr.

Public Opinion & the Supreme Court. Thomas R. Marshall. 256p. 1988. text 39.95 (*0-04-497046-3*); pap. text 14.95 (*0-04-497047-1*) Routledge.

Public Opinion & the War in Vietnam Study, 1966. Sidney Verba et al. 1975. reprint ed. write for info. (*0-89138-053-1*) ICPSR.

Public Opinion & World-Politics. Ed. by Quincy Wright. LC 72-4687. (International Propaganda & Communications Ser.). 251p. 1972. reprint ed. 18.95 (*0-405-04771-1*) Ayer.

***Public Opinion, Crime & Criminal Justice.** Julian V. Roberts & Loretta J. Stalans. (Crime & Society Ser.). 352p. 1999. pap. 30.00 (*0-8133-6793-X*) Westview.

Public Opinion in America: Moods, Cycles & Swings. 2nd ed. James A. Stimson. LC 98-36784. 192p. 1998. pap. 28.00 (*0-8133-6890-1*, Pub. by Westview); text 49.00 (*0-8133-6679-8*, Pub. by Westview) HarpC.

***Public Opinion in American Foreign Policy: From Vietnam to the Nineties.** Richard Sobel. 272p. (C). 2001. pap. 24.95 (*0-19-510528-1*); text 49.95 (*0-19-510527-3*) OUP.

***Public Opinion in Belarus, 1999.** Larissa Titarenko. ii, 118p. 1999. pap. 14.00 (*1-879720-62-0*) Intl Fndt Elect.

Public Opinion in Ghana, 1997. Christopher McCarty. ii, 128p. 1997. pap. 15.00 (*1-879720-80-9*) Intl Fndt Elect.

Public Opinion in Kazakhstan: 1996. Craig Charney. LC 96-41936. (Illus.). ii, 134p. 1997. pap. text 15.00 (*1-879720-20-5*) Intl Fndt Elect.

Public Opinion in Kyrgyzstan: 1996. Hugh W. Olds, Jr. (Illus.). iv, 116p. 1997. pap. text 13.00 (*1-879720-21-3*) Intl Fndt Elect.

Public Opinion in Occupied Germany: The OMGUS Surveys, 1945. Ed. by Anna J. Merritt & Richard L. Merritt. LC 74-94397. (Illus.). 350p. reprint ed. pap. 108.50 (*0-608-30423-9*, 202022300016) Bks Demand.

P

An Asterisk (*) at the beginning of an entry indicates that the title is appearing for the first time.

Public Opinion in Postcommunist Russia. Matthew Wyman. (Studies in Russian & East European History & Society). 256p. 1997. text 65.00 (*0-312-15943-9*) St Martin.

Public Opinion in Soviet Russia: A Study in Mass Persuasion. 2nd ed. Alex Inkeles. LC 58-4768. (Russian Research Center Studies: No. 1). 313p. 1958. 34.50 (*0-674-72350-3*) HUP.

Public Opinion in Tajikistan: 1996. Steven Wagner. (Illus.). ii, 116p. 1997. pap. text 13.00 (*1-879720-58-2*) Intl Fndt Elect.

Public Opinion in U. S. Foreign Policy: The Controversy over Contra Aid. Ed. by Richard Sobel. 328p. (C). 1993. text 71.50 (*0-8476-7871-7*) Rowman.

***Public Opinion in Ukraine: 1998.** Gary Ferguson. ii, 186p. 1998. pap. text 20.00 (*1-879720-37-X*) Intl Fndt Elect.

***Public Opinion in Ukraine, 1999.** Gary A. Ferguson. ii, 114p. 1999. 13.00 (*1-879720-60-4*) Intl Fndt Elect.

Public Opinion in Uzbekistan: 1996. Steven Wagner. (Illus.). ii, 118p. 1997. pap. text 14.00 (*1-879720-22-1*) Intl Fndt Elect.

Public Opinion in War & Peace. Abbott L. Lowell. LC 73-14167. (Perspectives in Social Inquiry Ser.). 320p. 1974. reprint ed. 21.95 (*0-405-05512-9*) Ayer.

Public Opinion Polling & Politics in Britain. David Broughton. LC 95-10435. (Contemporary Political Studies). 216p. (C). 1995. pap. text 29.00 (*0-13-433921-5*) P-H.

Public Opinion Polling in Czechoslovakia, 1968-1969: Results & Analysis of Surveys Conducted During the Dubcek Era. Jaroslaw Piekalkiewicz & Barry Bede. LC 70-176398. (Special Studies in International Politics & Government). 1972. 32.50 (*0-275-28631-2*) Irvington.

Public Opinion Polls & Survey Research: A Selective Annotated Bibliography of U. S. Guides & Studies from the 1980s. Graham R. Walden. LC 89-25956. (Public Affairs & Administration Ser.: Vol. 24). 338p. 1990. text 15.00 (*0-8240-5732-5*, SS575) Garland.

Public Opinion Process: How the People Speaks. Irving Crespi. LC 97-1381. 1997. 49.95 (*0-8058-2664-5*); pap. 22.50 (*0-8058-2665-3*) L Erlbaum Assocs.

Public Opinion, Propaganda & Politics in Eighteenth Century England: A Study of the Jew Bill of 1753. Thomas W. Perry. LC 62-17222. (Historical Monographs: No. 51). (Illus.). 215p. 1962. 20.00 (*0-674-72400-3*) HUP.

Public Opinion, the First Ladyship, & Hillary Rodham Clinton. Barbara C. Burrell. Ed. by Barbara Bardes. LC 96-29385. (Women in American Politics Ser.: Vol. 1). (Illus.). 172p. 1997. text 39.00 (*0-8153-2142-2*) Garland.

Public Opinion, the Press & Public Policy. Ed. by David J. Kennamer. LC 92-8400. 216p. 1992. 55.00 (*0-275-93743-7*, C3743, Praeger Pubs) Greenwood.

Public Opinion, the Press & Public Policy. David J. Kennamer. LC 92-8400. 208p. 1994. pap. 19.95 (*0-275-95097-2*, Praeger Pubs) Greenwood.

Public Order: A Guide to the 1986 Public Order Act. John Marston. 189p. 1987. 105.00 (*1-85190-024-1*, Pub. by Fourmat Pub) St Mut.

Public Order - the New Law. Richard Card. 170p. 1987. reprint ed. pap. 30.00 (*0-406-50440-7*, U.K., MICHIE) LEXIS Pub.

Public Order & Law Enforcement: The Local Administration of Criminal Justice, 1294-1350. Anthony Musson. LC 96-6124. (Illus.). 331p. (C). 1996. 90.00 (*0-85115-635-5*) Boydell & Brewer.

Public Order Campaign Badges: Protest: While You Still Can in Red & Black. NCCL Staff. 1988. 30.00 (*0-7855-1466-X*, Pub. by NCCL) St Mut.

Public Order in Ancient Rome. Wilfried Nippel. (Key Themes in Ancient History Ser.). 173p. (C). 1995. text 59.95 (*0-521-38327-7*) Cambridge U Pr.

Public Order in Ancient Rome. Wilfried Nippel. (Key Themes in Ancient History Ser.). 173p. (C). 1995. pap. text 18.95 (*0-521-38749-3*) Cambridge U Pr.

Public Order Law. Peter Thornton. 242p. 1987. pap. 32.00 (*1-85185-040-6*, Pub. by Blackstone Pr) Gaunt.

Public Order Law: Including the Public Order Act, 1986. Peter Thornton. (C). 1988. 75.00 (*0-7855-4420-8*, Pub. by NCCL) St Mut.

Public Order of the Oceans: A Contemporary International Law of the Sea. Myres S. McDougal & William T. Burke. LC 86-14171. (New Haven Studies in International Law & World Public Order: No. 5). 1987. lib. bdg. 316.50 (*0-89838-901-1*) Kluwer Academic.

Public Organization in Ancient Greece. Nicholas F. Jones. LC 86-72885. (Memoirs Ser.: Vol. 176). (Illus.). (C). 1987. 35.00 (*0-87169-176-0*, M176-JON) Am Philos.

Public Organization Management: The Development of Theory & Process. Jamil Jreisat. 264p. 1999. pap. 24.95 (*0-275-96767-0*, Praeger Pubs) Greenwood.

Public Organization Management: The Development of Theory & Process. Jamil E. Jreisat. LC 97-8853. 264p. 1997. 59.95 (*1-56720-121-0*, Quorum Bks) Greenwood.

Public Organizations & Policy: An Experiential Approach to Public Policy & Its Execution. David Bresnick. LC 81-14471. 256p. reprint ed. pap. 79.40 (*0-7837-3012-8*, 204292800006) Bks Demand.

Public Orphanage. Eric Buehrer. 1995. pap. 14.99 (*0-8499-3532-6*) Word Pub.

Public Outreach Handbook for Departments of Transportation. Frank Wilson & Associates Staff & National Research Council (U. S.) Staff. LC 94-60890. (National Cooperative Highway Research Program Report Ser.). 37p. 1994. 24.00 (*0-309-05363-3*, NR364) Natl Acad Pr.

Public Oversight of Managed Health Care Entities: Issues for State Policymakers. Patricia A. Butler. 31p. 1996. pap. 33.00 (*1-55877-254-5*) Natl Governor.

Public Papers. Louis Sullivan. Ed. by Robert C. Twombly. (Illus.). xxii, 280p. 1988. 35.95 (*0-226-77996-3*) U Ch Pr.

Public Papers of Chief Justice Earl Warren. Earl Warren. Ed. by Henry M. Christman. LC 74-10019. 237p. 1974. reprint ed. lib. bdg. 38.50 (*0-8371-7654-9*, WAPP, Greenwood Pr) Greenwood.

Public Papers of Governor Keen Johnson, Nineteen, 1939-1943. Keen Johnson. Ed. by Frederic D. Ogden. LC 79-57562. (Public Papers of the Governors of Kentucky). 618p. 1982. 45.00 (*0-8131-0605-2*) U Pr of Ky.

Public Papers of Governor Lawrence W. Wetherby, 1950-1955. Lawrence W. Wetherby. Ed. by John E. Kleber. LC 82-40182. (Public Papers of the Governors of Kentucky). 344p. 1983. 40.00 (*0-8131-0606-0*) U Pr of Ky.

Public Papers of Governor Simeon Willis, 1943-1947. Simeon G. Willis. Ed. by James C. Klotter. LC 87-24085. (Public Papers of the Governors of Kentucky). (Illus.). 424p. 1988. 45.00 (*0-8131-0607-9*) U Pr of Ky.

Public Papers of Governor Wendell H. Ford, 1971-1974. Wendell H. Ford. Ed. by W. Landis Jones. LC 77-73702. (Public Papers of the Governors of Kentucky). 722p. 1978. 45.00 (*0-8131-0602-8*) U Pr of Ky.

Public Papers of President William Clinton, 6 vols. William J. Clinton. 1997. lib. bdg. write for info. (*0-8490-6369-8*) Gordon Pr.

***Public Papers of the Presidents of the United States, Gerald Ford, 1976-77 Book 1: Containing the Public Messages, Speeches & Statements of the President, January 1 To April 9, 1976.** 1186p. 1999. boxed set 78.00 (*0-16-058870-7*) USGPO.

***Public Papers of the Presidents of the United States, Herbert Hoover, 1931: Containing the Public Messages, Speeches & Statements of the President, January 1 To December 31, 1931.** 914p. 1999. boxed set 62.00 (*0-16-058840-5*) USGPO.

Public Papers of the Presidents of the United States, William J. Clinton, 1995, January 1 To June 30, 1995 Book 1. 1092p. 1996. boxed set 60.00 (*0-16-063686-8*) USGPO.

Public Papers of the Presidents of the United States, William J. Clinton, 1995, July 1 to December 31, 1995 Book 2. 998p. 1997. boxed set 65.00 (*0-16-063688-4*) USGPO.

***Public Papers of the Presidents of the United States, William J. Clinton, 1996, July 1 to December 31, 1996 Book 2.** 1281p. 1998. boxed set 72.00 (*0-16-063689-2*) USGPO.

***Public Papers of the Presidents of the United States, William J. Clinton, 1998, January 1 to June 30, 1998 Book 1.** 1206p. 2000. boxed set 74.00 (*0-16-050132-6*) USGPO.

Public Papers of the Secretaries-General of the United Nations Vol. 1: Trygve Lie, 1946-1953. Ed. by Andrew W. Cordier & Wilder Foote. LC 68-8873. 535p. 1978. text 81.00 (*0-231-03137-8*) Col U Pr.

Public Papers of the Secretaries-General of the United Nations Vol. 4: Dag Hammarskjold, 1958-1960, Vol. 4. Ed. by Andrew W. Cordier & Wilder Foote. LC 68-8873. 659p. 1978. text 81.00 (*0-231-03810-0*) Col U Pr.

Public Papers of the Secretaries-General of the United Nations, Vol. 2: Dag Hammarskjold, 1953-1956. Ed. by Andrew W. Cordier & Wilder Foote. LC 68-8873. 115p. 1978. text 81.00 (*0-231-03633-7*) Col U Pr.

Public Papers of the Secretaries-General of the United Nations, Vol. 3: Dag Hammarskjold, 1956-1957. Ed. by Andrew W. Cordier & Wilder Foote. LC 68-88873. 729p. 1978. text 81.00 (*0-231-03735-X*) Col U Pr.

Public Papers of the Secretaries-General of the United Nations, Vol. 5: Dag Hammarskjold, 1960-1961. Ed. by Andrew W. Cordier & Wilder Foote. LC 68-8873. 592p. 1978. text 81.00 (*0-231-03897-6*) Col U Pr.

Public Papers of the Secretaries-General of the United Nations, Vol. 6: U Thant, 1961-1964. Ed. by Andrew W. Cordier & Max Harrelson. LC 68-8873. 708p. 1978. text 81.00 (*0-231-03966-2*) Col U Pr.

Public Papers of the Secretaries-General of the United Nations, Vol. 7: U Thant, 1965-1967. Ed. by Andrew W. Cordier & Max Harrelson. LC 68-8873. 633p. 1978. text 81.00 (*0-231-04098-9*) Col U Pr.

Public Papers of Woodrow Wilson, 6 vols., Set. Woodrow Wilson. (History - United States Ser.). 1992. reprint ed. lib. bdg. 450.00 (*0-7812-6225-9*) Rprt Serv.

Public Parks. Hazel Conway. (Garden History Ser.: No. 9). (Illus.). 96p. 1996. pap. 12.50 (*0-7478-0332-3*, Pub. by Shire Pubns) Parkwest Pubns.

Public Parks & the Enlargement of Towns. Frederick L. Olmsted, Jr. LC 76-112564. (Rise of Urban America Ser.). 1973. reprint ed. 15.95 (*0-405-02469-X*) Ayer.

Public Parks & the Enlargement of Towns. Frederick L. Olmsted. (Notable American Authors Ser.). 1999. reprint ed. lib. bdg. 125.00 (*0-7812-4675-X*) Rprt Serv.

Public Participation in Development & Health Programs: Lessons from Rural Bangladesh. Wasim A. Zaman. 312p. (Orig.). 1984. pap. text 25.50 (*0-8191-3875-4*); lib. bdg. 52.00 (*0-8191-3874-6*) U Pr of Amer.

Public Participation in Environmental Decision Making. LC 94-78327. 45p. 1994. pap. 15.00 (*0-89707-945-0*, 359-0022, ABA Environ) Amer Bar Assn.

***Public Participation in Environmental Decisions: Recent Developments in Hungary.** Ed. by Anna Vari & Joanne Caddy. 192p. 1999. pap. 48.00 (*963-05-7613-9*, Pub. by Akade Kiado) Intl Spec Bk.

Public Participation in Local Services. Noel Boaden et al. LC 81-14269. 200p. reprint ed. pap. 62.00 (*0-7837-1605-2*, 204189700024) Bks Demand.

Public Participation in Planning. Ed. by W. Derrick Sewell & J. T. Coppock. LC 76-56800. 231p. reprint ed. pap. 71.70 (*0-608-14538-6*, 202480400038) Bks Demand.

Public Participation in Public Decisions: New Skills & Strategies for Public Managers. John C. Thomas. LC 95-13425. (Public Administration Ser.). 235p. 1995. 28.95 (*0-7879-0129-6*) Jossey-Bass.

Public Participation in Quasi-Judicial Administrative Hearings: A Training Manual. Nancy E. Stroud. 53p. 1985. 10.00 (*0-317-01545-1*) Fla Atlantic.

Public Participation in Urban Development: The European Experience. James Barlow. LC 95-212298. 86p. (C). 1995. pap. 17.95 (*0-85374-644-3*, Pub. by Pol Studies Inst) Brookings.

Public Peace Process. Saunders. LC 98-48410. 6p. 1999. text 45.00 (*0-312-21939-3*) St Martin.

Public Pension Administration. Archibald L. Patterson. 116p. (Orig.). 1982. pap. 9.50 (*0-89854-082-8*) U of GA Inst Govt.

Public Pension Economics. Ed. by Bernhard Felderer. LC 93-15468. (Journal of Economics: Suppl. 2). 1996. 92.00 (*0-387-82432-4*) Spr-Verlag.

Public Pension Funds' Investment Practices. Roland K. Snell & Susan Wolfe. (Legislative Finance Papers: No. 72). 36p. 1990. pap. 15.00 (*1-55516-072-7*, 5101-72) Natl Conf State Legis.

Public Pension Plans: Evaluation of Economically Targeted Investment Programs. (Illus.). 66p. (Orig.). (C). 1995. pap. text 20.00 (*0-7881-1801-3*) DIANE Pub.

Public Pension Plans: The State Regulatory Framework. Sarah C. Reilly. 115p. write for info. (*0-318-60967-3*) Natl Coun Teach.

Public Pensions: A Legislator's Guide. NCSL Fiscal Dept. & Oversight & Intergovrmtl. Affa. 50p. 1995. 10.00 (*1-55516-085-9*, 5327) Natl Conf State Legis.

Public Pensions: Summary of Federal Pension Plan Data. 232p. (Orig.). (C). 1996. pap. text 40.00 (*0-7881-2880-9*) DIANE Pub.

Public People, Private People: Portraits of Some Japanese. Donald Richie. 212p. 1997. reprint ed. pap. 12.00 (*4-7700-2104-6*) Kodansha.

Public Perceptions: The Bishops Lobby. rev. ed. Denise Shannon & Maggie Hume. (Powerful Conceptions Ser.). (Illus.). 8p. 1994. pap. text 3.00 (*0-915365-28-6*) Cath Free Choice.

Public Perceptions of Child Abuse & Neglect in Singapore. Tong Chee Kiong et al. LC 97-945726. (Research Monograph). 1996. write for info. (*981-00-8317-3*) Miscell Pubs.

Public Perceptions of the Police in Texas. Raymond H. Teske. 28p. 1982. 2.00 (*0-318-02512-4*) S Houston Employ.

Public Personnel Administration. Ronald D. Sylvia. 318p. (C). 1966. text 63.50 (*0-534-15504-9*) Harcourt.

Public Personnel Administration: Policies & Practices for Personnel. ring bd. write for info. (*0-318-57376-8*) P-H.

Public Personnel Administration: Problems & Prospects. 3rd ed. Ed. by Steven W. Hays & Richard C. Kearney. LC 94-34628. 384p. 1994. pap. text 52.00 (*0-13-037714-7*) P-H.

Public Personnel Administration & Constitutional Values. Yong S. Lee. LC 92-8404. 184p. 1992. 55.00 (*0-89930-610-1*, LCS, Quorum Bks) Greenwood.

Public Personnel Administration in the U. S. 2nd ed. N. Joseph Cayer. LC 85-61242. 175p. (C). 1986. pap. text 25.00 (*0-312-65521-5*) St Martin.

Public Personnel Administration in the U. S. 3rd ed. N. Joseph Cayer. 214p. 1995. pap. 36.95 (*0-312-11611-X*) St Martin.

Public Personnel Management. 2nd ed. Carolyn Ban. LC 96-25492. 275p. (C). 1996. pap. text 52.00 (*0-8013-1699-5*) Addison-Wesley.

Public Personnel Management: Contexts & Strategies. 4th ed. Donald E. Klingner & John Nalbandian. LC 97-9746. 408p. 1997. 56.00 (*0-13-624818-7*) P-H.

Public Personnel Management: Current Concerns, Future Challenges. Carolyn Ban & Norma M. Riccucci. 256p. (Orig.). (C). 1991. pap. text 40.95 (*0-8013-0508-X*, 78402) Longman.

Public Personnel Management: Structure, Process & Practice. Marvin J. Levine. 1983. 22.95 (*0-913878-27-8*) T Horton & Dghts.

Public Personnel Management & Public Policy. 3rd ed. Dennis Dresang. LC 98-38626. 352p. (C). 1998. 65.00 (*0-8013-1694-4*) Addison-Wesley.

***Public Personnel Management Public Policy.** 3rd ed. 22p. (C). 1998. text 25.20 (*0-321-04189-5*) Addson-Wesley Educ.

Public Personnel Managemnt: Current Concern. 2nd ed. 352p. (C). 1996. text. write for info. (*0-8013-2012-7*) Longman.

Public Personnel Mangement & Public Policy. 3rd ed. Dennis Dresang. (C). 1996. text. write for info. (*0-8013-1693-6*) Addison-Wesley.

Public Personnel Policy in a Political Environment: A Symposium. Ed. by David Rosenbloom. (Orig.). 1982. pap. 15.00 (*0-918592-59-3*) Pol Studies.

Public Personnel Systems. 3rd ed. Robert D. Lee, Jr. 448p. 1993. 57.00 (*0-8342-0392-8*, 20392) Aspen Pub.

Public Personnel Update. Ed. by Michael Cohen & Robert T. Golembiewski. LC 84-19892. (Public Administration & Public Policy Ser.: No. 27). 277p. 1984. reprint ed. pap. 85.90 (*0-608-01362-5*, 206210100002) Bks Demand.

Public Persons. Walter Lippmann. Ed. by Gilbert A. Harrison. 189p. 1976. 7.95 (*0-87140-620-9*, Pub. by Liveright) Norton.

Public Philosophy. Walter Lippmann. 209p. 1989. pap. 24.95 (*0-88738-791-8*) Transaction Pubs.

***Public Place: Citizen Participation in the Neighbourhood & the City.** Dimitrios I. Roussopoulos. 2000. 48.99 (*1-55164-157-7*) Black Rose.

Public Place: Citizen Participation in the Neighbourhood & the City. Dimitrios J. Roussopoulos. 200p. 2000. pap. 19.99 (*1-55164-156-9*) Consort Bk Sales.

Public Places: Exploring Their History. Gerald A. Danzer. LC 97-541. (American Association for State & Local History Book Ser.). (Illus.). 152p. 1987. pap. 17.95 (*0-7619-8931-5*) AltaMira Pr.

Public Places: Lighting Solutions for Exhibitions, Museums & Historic Spaces. Janet Turner. (Designing with Light Ser.). (Illus.). 160p. 1999. 39.50 (*2-88046-333-5*, Rotovision) Watsn-Guptill.

Public Places & Spaces. I. Altman & E. H. Zube. (Human Behavior & Environment Ser.: Vol. 10). (Illus.). 334p. (C). 1989. 60.00 (*0-306-43079-7*, Plenum Trade) Perseus Pubng.

Public Places Urban Spaces. Carmona. 129p. 1999. pap. text 49.95 (*0-7506-3632-7*) Buttrwrth-Heinemann.

Public Poet: Five Lectures on the Art & Craft of Poetry. Lewis Turco. (Writers-in-Residence Ser.). 96p. (Orig.). 1991. pap. 7.00 (*0-912592-30-3*) Ashland Poetry.

Public Policies Affecting Lignite Development in Texas. Stephen H. Spurr. (Policy Research Project Report Ser.: No. 20). 240p. 1977. pap. 3.00 (*0-89940-613-0*) LBJ Sch Pub Aff.

Public Policies & Household Saving. Ed. by James M. Poterba. LC 93-42088. (National Bureau of Economic Research Project Report Ser.). 212p. 1994. 36.00 (*0-226-67618-8*) U Ch Pr.

Public Policies & Political Development in Canada. Ronald A. Manzer. 256p. 1985. pap. text 19.95 (*0-8020-6559-7*) U of Toronto Pr.

Public Policies & Political Development in Canada. Ronald A. Manzer. LC 86-110537. (Illus.). 250p. reprint ed. pap. 77.50 (*0-7837-0527-1*, 204085300019) Bks Demand.

Public Policies & the Japanese Economy: Savings, Investments, Unemployment, Equality. Toshiaki Tachibanaki. LC 96-34778. (Studies in the Modern Japanese Economy). 224p. 1996. text 69.95 (*0-312-16430-0*) St Martin.

Public Policies for Communities in Economic Crisis. F. Stevens Redburn & Terry Buss. 1981. pap. 15.00 (*0-918592-54-2*) Pol Studies.

Public Policies for Environmental Protection. Ed. by Paul R. Portney. LC 89-24363. 308p. 1990. pap. 12.95 (*0-915707-53-5*) Resources Future.

***Public Policies for Environmental Protection.** 2nd ed. Ed. by Paul R. Portney. (Illus.). 308p. (C). 2000. write for info. (*1-891853-03-1*, Pub. by Resources Future) Johns Hopkins.

Public Policies for Women in India. Ed. by Susheela Kaushik. (C). 1993. 30.00 (*0-7069-5958-2*, Pub. by Vikas) S Asia.

Public Policies in East Asian Development: Facing New Challenges. Ed. by F. Gerard Adams & William E. James. LC 98-56628. 272p. 1999. 65.00 (*0-275-96444-2*, Praeger Pubs) Greenwood.

Public Policies in Singapore: Changes in the 1980s & Future Signposts. Ed. by Linda Low & Toh M. Heng. 392p. 1992. pap. 25.00 (*981-210-022-9*, Pub. by Times Academic) Intl Spec Bk.

Public Policies Toward Business. 8th ed. William G. Shepherd. (C). 1990. text 57.95 (*0-256-08464-5*, Irwn McGrw-H) McGrw-H Hghr Educ.

Public Policy. Richardson & Lyons. (Political Science). 2000. mass mkt. 35.00 (*0-534-54882-2*) Wadsworth Pub.

Public Policy. Peter Woll. LC 81-40886. 27p. 1982. reprint ed. pap. text 23.50 (*0-8191-2098-7*) U Pr of Amer.

Public Policy. 2nd ed. Cochran. LC 98-42232. 480p. 1998. pap. 49.69 (*0-07-290896-3*) McGraw.

Public Policy: A Critical Approach. Mark Considine. 350p. 1995. 64.95 (*0-7329-1297-0*, Pub. by Macmill Educ); pap. 32.95 (*0-7329-1296-2*, Pub. by Macmill Educ) Paul & Co Pubs.

Public Policy: An Evolutionary Approach. James P. Lester & Joseph Stewart, Jr. 350p. (C). 1996. 36.75 (*0-314-06750-7*) West Pub.

***Public Policy: An Evolutionary Approach.** 2nd ed. Lester. LC 99-462500. (Political Science Ser.). 1999. pap. 57.95 (*0-534-55008-8*) Wadsworth Pub.

Public Policy: An Introduction to the Theory & Practice of Policy Analysis. Wayne Parsons. LC 95-10756. 704p. 1996. 100.00 (*1-85278-553-5*); pap. text 35.00 (*1-85278-554-3*) E Elgar.

Public Policy: Goals, Means & Methods. Stuart S. Nagel. 546p. (C). 1983. teacher ed. write for info. (*0-318-57732-1*) St Martin.

Public Policy: Goals, Means & Methods. Stuart S. Nagel. 480p. (C). 1990. reprint ed. pap. text 39.00 (*0-8191-7912-4*) U Pr of Amer.

Public Policy: Issues, Analysis, & Ideology. Ed. by Ellen F. Paul & Philip A. Russo. LC 81-10027. (Chatham House Series on Change in American Politics). 333p. reprint ed. pap. 103.30 (*0-7837-2600-7*, 204276400006) Bks Demand.

Public Policy: Perspectives & Choices. Charles L. Cochran & Eloise F. Malone. LC 94-33885. 457p. (C). 1994. 51.56 (*0-07-011528-1*) McGraw.

Public Policy: The Essential Readings. Ed. by Stella Z. Theodoulou & Matthew A. Cahn. LC 94-6817. 464p. (C). 1994. pap. text 37.00 (*0-13-059255-2*) P-H.

***Public Policy , Crime & Criminal Justice.** 2nd ed. Barry W. Hancock. LC 99-30362. 448p. 1999. pap. 51.00 (*0-13-020615-6*) P-H.

Public Policy Across Nations, Vol. 8. Ed. by Alexander J. Groth et al. LC 85-23146. (Public Policy Ser.). 279p. 1987. 73.25 (*0-89232-373-6*) Jai Pr.

Public Policy Across States & Communities. Ed. by Dennis R. Judd & Stuart S. Nagel. LC 85-18102. (Public Policy Ser.: Vol. 7). 250p. 1985. 73.25 (*0-89232-513-5*) Jai Pr.

Public Policy Analysis: An Introduction. 2nd ed. William N. Dunn. 480p. (C). 1993. 56.00 (*0-13-738550-1*) P-H.

Public Policy & Aboriginal Peoples Series, 1965-1992 Vol. 1: Soliloquy & Dialogue: Overview of Major Trends in Public Policy Relating to Aboriginal Peoples. 2nd

An Asterisk (*) at the beginning of an entry indicates that the title is appearing for the first time.

ed. Ed. by Royal Commission on Aboriginal Peoples Staff. 353p. 1996. pap. 39.95 (*0-660-16644-5*, Pub. by Canadian Govt Pub) Accents Pubns.

Public Policy & Administration. Ed. by M. Kistaiah. 257p. 1986. 29.95 (*0-318-36599-5*) Asia Bk Corp.

Public Policy & Administrative Reform. Ed. by Gerald Caiden. (Orig.). (C). 1981. pap. 15.00 (*0-918592-47-X*) Pol Studies.

Public Policy & Administrative Renewal: Canada & the U. S. Ed. by Wayne Petrozzi. 250p. (Orig.). 1996. pap. 21.95 (*0-88962-617-0*) Mosaic.

Public Policy & Collective Bargaining, 27. Ed. by Joseph Shister et al. LC 81-20181. (Industrial Relations Research Association Publication Ser.: No. 27). 248p. 1982. reprint ed. lib. bdg. 65.00 (*0-313-23455-8*, SHPA, Greenwood Pr) Greenwood.

Public Policy & College Management: Title III of the Higher Education Act. Edward P. St. John. LC 81-5204. 278p. 1981. 55.00 (*0-275-90723-6*, C0723, Praeger Pubs) Greenwood.

Public Policy & Community: Activism & Governance in Texas. Robert H. Wilson. LC 96-33338. (Illus.). 328p. 1997. 40.00 (*0-292-79104-6*); pap. 18.95 (*0-292-79105-4*) U of Tex Pr.

Public Policy & Economic Development: Essays in Honor of Ian Little. Ed. by Maurice F. Scott & Deepak Lal. (Illus.). 414p. 1990. text 79.00 (*0-19-828582-5*) OUP.

Public Policy & Economic Institutions, Vol. 10. Ed. by Mel Dubnick et al. LC 90-41571. (Public Policy Ser.). 408p. 1991. 73.25 (*0-89232-376-0*) Jai Pr.

Public Policy & Economic Theory. Ed. by Torben M. Andersen & Karl O. Moene. LC 98-29798. 275p. 1998. pap. 32.95 (*0-631-20943-3*) Blackwell Pubs.

***Public Policy & Electoral Reform: The Case of Israel.** Gideon Doron & Michael Harris. 144p. 2000. 45.00 (*0-7391-0134-X*) Lxngtn Bks.

Public Policy & Federalism: Issues in State & Local Politics. Jeffrey R. Henig. LC 84-51680. 400p. (C). 1985. pap. text 15.50 (*0-312-65560-6*) St Martin.

Public Policy & Global Technological Integration. Ed. by Frederick M. Abbott & David J. Gerber. LC 98-116502. 1997. 225.00 (*90-411-0655-3*) Kluwer Law Intl.

Public Policy & Higher Education. Ed. by Lester F. Goodchild et al. (ASHE Reader Ser.). 704p. (C). 1997. pap. text 52.00 (*0-536-00292-4*) Pearson Custom.

Public Policy & Land Use in Georgia: A Concise Reference Book. Forster O. Ndubisi. LC 96-11689. 1996. pap. write for info. (*0-911847-09-X*) U GA Inst Community.

***Public Policy & Local Governance: Institutions in Postmodern Society.** Peter Bogason. LC 99-45191. (New Horizons in Public Policy Ser.). 208p. 2000. text 75.00 (*1-84064-349-8*) E Elgar.

Public Policy & Markets for Recycled Materials. 4th ed. Laura H. Nelson et al. 1996. pap. 5.00 (*1-55516-509-5*, 4655) Natl Conf State Legis.

Public Policy & Mental Illness: Four Investigations, 1915-1939, an Original Anthology. Ed. by Gerald N. Grob. LC 78-22585. (Historical Issues in Mental Health Ser.). (Illus.). 1980. lib. bdg. 55.95 (*0-405-11936-4*) Ayer.

***Public Policy & Political Ideas.** Ed. by Dietmar Braun & Andreas Busch. LC 99-41927. 240p. 2000. 80.00 (*1-84064-182-7*) E Elgar.

***Public Policy & Political Institutions: The Role of Culture in Traffic Policy.** Frank Hendriks. LC 99-39497. (New Horizons in Public Policy Ser.). 304p. 2000. 100.00 (*1-84064-062-6*) E Elgar.

Public Policy & Political Institutions Vol. 5: United States Defense & Foreign Policy - Policy Coordination & Integration. Ed. by Duncan L. Clarke & Stuart S. Nagel. LC 85-12705. (Public Policy Ser.: Vol. 5). 414p. 1985. 73.25 (*0-89232-374-4*) Jai Pr.

Public Policy & Private Higher Education. Ed. by David W. Breneman & Chester E. Finn. LC 77-91798. (Studies in Higher Education Policy). 468p. 1978. 29.95 (*0-8157-1066-6*) Brookings.

Public Policy & Program Evaluation. Evert Vedung. LC 96-52816. 240p. 1997. text 34.95 (*1-56000-299-9*) Transaction Pubs.

***Public Policy & Program Evaluation.** Evert Vedung. 368p. 2000. pap. 29.95 (*0-7658-0687-8*) Transaction Pubs.

Public Policy & Social Institutions: A Multi-Volume Treatise. Ed. by Harrell R. Rogers, Jr. & Stuart S. Nagel. LC 84-9680. (Public Policy Studies: Vol. 1). 375p. 1984. 73.25 (*0-89232-377-9*) Jai Pr.

***Public Policy & Statistics: Case Studies from RAND.** Ed. by S. Morton & J. Rolph. LC 00-20827. (Illus.). 304p. 2000. 49.95 (*0-387-98777-0*) Spr-Verlag.

Public Policy & the Aesthetic Interest: Critical Essays on Defining Cultural & Educational Relations. Ed. by Ralph A. Smith & Ronald Berman. 296p. (C). 1992. text 39.95 (*0-252-01899-0*); pap. text 16.95 (*0-252-06244-2*) U of Ill Pr.

Public Policy & the Arts: A Comparative Study of Great Britain & Ireland. Ruth-Blandina M. Quinn. LC 97-78099. (Illus.). 352p. 1998. text 72.95 (*1-84014-174-3*, Pub. by Ashgate Pub) Ashgate Pub Co.

Public Policy & the Black Hospital: From Slavery to Segregation to Integration, 165. Mitchell F. Rice & Woodrow Jones, Jr. LC 93-4851. (Contributions in Afro-American & African Studies: No. 165). 176p. 1994. 55.00 (*0-313-26309-4*, RBP/, Greenwood Pr) Greenwood.

Public Policy & the Economy since 1900. Jim Tomlinson. (Illus.). 392p. 1990. text 85.00 (*0-19-828658-9*) OUP.

Public Policy & the Economy since 1900. Jim Tomlinson. (Illus.). 392p. 1993. reprint ed. pap. text 19.95 (*0-19-828774-7*) OUP.

Public Policy & the Impact of the New Right: The Impact of Ideology. Ed. by Grant Jordan & Nigel Ashford. (Themes in Right-Wing Ideology & Politics Ser.). 288p. 1993. 95.00 (*1-85567-002-X*) Bks Intl VA.

***Public Policy & the Internet: Privacy, Taxes & Contract.** Ed. by Nicholas Imparato. LC 00-26125. (Publication Ser: Vol. 481). 156p. 2000. pap. 17.95 (*0-8179-9892-6*) Hoover Inst Pr.

Public Policy & the Misuse of Forest Resources. Ed. by Robert C. Repetto & Malcolm Gillis. 448p. 1988. pap. text 42.95 (*0-521-33574-4*) Cambridge U Pr.

Public Policy & the Natural Environment, Vol. 4. Ed. by Helen Ingram et al. LC 85-14743. (Public Policy Ser.). 342p. 1985. 73.25 (*0-89232-452-X*) Jai Pr.

Public Policy & the Old Age Revolution in Japan. Ed. by Scott A. Bass et al. LC 96-38930. (Journal of Aging & Social Policy: Vol. 8, Nos. 2/3). 203p. (C). 1996. 34.95 (*0-7890-0012-1*) Haworth Pr.

Public Policy & the Practice & the Problems of Accounting. Ahmed R. Belkaoui. LC 85-3568. (Illus.). 204p. 1985. 62.95 (*0-89930-105-3*, BIF/, Quorum Bks) Greenwood.

Public Policy & the Problem of Addiction: Four Studies, 1914 to 1924, an Original Anthology. Ed. by Gerald N. Grob. LC 70-1208. (Addiction in America Ser.). 1981. lib. bdg. 18.95 (*0-405-13564-5*) Ayer.

Public Policy & the Public Good, 276. Ed. by Ethan Fishman. LC 90-22397. (Contributions in Political Science Ser.: No. 276). 200p. 1991. 52.95 (*0-313-27224-7*, FPG, Greenwood Pr) Greenwood.

Public Policy & the Quality of Life: Market Incentives Versus Government Planning, 161. Randall G. Holcombe. LC 94-25060. (Contributions in Economics & Economic History Ser.: Vol. 161). 208p. 1995. 59.95 (*0-313-29358-9*, Greenwood Pr) Greenwood.

Public Policy & the Regulatory Environment. Kenneth M. Parzych. LC 92-42156. 1993. 57.50 (*0-8191-9024-1*); pap. 32.00 (*0-8191-9025-X*) U Pr of Amer.

Public Policy & the Supply of Coal to London, 1700-1770. William J. Hausman. Ed. by Stuart Bruchey. LC 80-2809. (Dissertations in European Economic History Ser.). (Illus.). 1981. lib. bdg. 34.95 (*0-405-13993-4*) Ayer.

Public Policy & the Two States of Kansas. Ed. by H. George Fredrickson. LC 93-41338. 216p. (Orig.). 1994. pap. 17.95 (*0-7006-0665-3*) U Pr of KS.

Public Policy & Transit System Management, 245. Ed. by George M. Guess. LC 89-11873. (Contributions in Political Science Ser.: No. 245). 265p. 1990. 65.00 (*0-313-26372-8*, GPU/, Greenwood Pr) Greenwood.

Public Policy & World Food Sufficiency. Ed. by Don F. Hadwiger & William Browne. (Orig.). 1984. pap. 15.00 (*0-918592-73-9*) Pol Studies.

Public Policy Applications of Life-Cycle Assessment: Proceedings from the Pellson Workshop on Application of Life-Cycle Assessment to Public Policy, 14-19 August 1995, Wintergreen, Virginia, U. S. A. Setac Organization Staff & Setac Foundation for Environmental Education Staff. Ed. by David T. Allen et al. LC 97-29289. (Setac Technical Publications). (Illus.). 1997. pap. 22.00 (*1-880611-18-X*, SETAC Pr) SETAC.

Public Policy, Canada, & the United States. Ed. by Martin Lubin. 164p. (Orig.). 1986. pap. 15.00 (*0-918592-89-5*) Pol Studies.

Public Policy Dialogues. Donald H. Roy. 240p. (Orig.). (C). 1994. pap. text 28.50 (*0-8191-9336-4*); lib. bdg. 49.50 (*0-8191-9335-6*) U Pr of Amer.

Public Policy Dictionary. Earl R. Kruschke & Byron M. Jackson. (Clio Dictionaries in Political Science Ser.: No. 15). 159p. 1987. lib. bdg. 49.00 (*0-87436-443-4*) ABC-CLIO.

Public Policy Disasters in Western Europe. Pat Gray & Paul T. Hart. LC 97-47004. 240p. (C). 1998. 90.00 (*0-415-17070-2*) Routledge.

Public Policy Evaluation. Ed. by Kenneth M. Dolbeare & John A. Gardiner. LC 75-14631. (Sage Yearbooks in Politics & Public Policy Ser.: No. 2). 286p. 1975. reprint ed. pap. 88.70 (*0-608-01464-8*, 205950800001) Bks Demand.

Public Policy Evaluation: Making Super-Optimum Decisions. Stuart S. Nagel. LC 97-27227. (Policy Studies Organization). (Illus.). 361p. 1997. text 89.95 (*1-84014-017-8*, Pub. by Ashgate Pub) Ashgate Pub Co.

Public Policy for Democracy. Ed. by Helen Ingram & Steven R. Smith. 274p. (C). 1993. 38.95 (*0-8157-4152-9*); pap. 16.95 (*0-8157-4153-7*) Brookings.

Public Policy for Developing Market Economies. Manuel V. Montes. 119p. 1969. pap. 2.50 (*0-8477-2425-5*) U of PR Pr.

Public Policy for Local Government. J. A. Chandler. 224p. 1988. 65.00 (*0-7099-3455-6*, Pub. by C Helm) Routldge.

Public Policy for the Humanities in Texas. Susan Hadden. (Policy Research Project Report Ser.: No. 74). 185p. 1986. pap. 10.00 (*0-89940-676-9*) LBJ Sch Pub Aff.

Public Policy for the Promotion of Family Farms in Italy: The Experience of the Fund for the Promotion of Peasant Property, 262. Eric B. Shearer. LC 94-33267. (World Bank Discussion Papers). 80p. 1994. pap. 22.00 (*0-8213-3026-8*) World Bank.

Public Policy Formation. Ed. by Robert Eyestone & Stuart S. Nagel. LC 84-23352. (Public Policy Studies: Vol. 2). 363p. 1985. 73.25 (*0-89232-372-8*) Jai Pr.

Public Policy Implementation. Ed. by George C. Edward & Stuart S. Nagel. LC 84-25056. (Public Policy Studies: Vol. 3). 272p. 1985. 73.25 (*0-89232-453-8*) Jai Pr.

Public Policy in a Divided Society: Schooling, Culture & Identity in Northern Ireland. Alex McEwen. LC LC93.G7M336 1999. 160p. (C). 1999. text 56.95 (*1-84014-316-9*, Pub. by Ashgate Pub) Ashgate Pub Co.

Public Policy in a New Key. Amitai Etzioni. LC 92-20089. 210p. (C). 1992. 39.95 (*1-56000-075-9*) Transaction Pubs.

Public Policy in America. 2nd ed. Dennis J. Palumbo. LC 94-75332. (C). 1994. text 56.00 (*0-15-500383-6*, Pub. by Harcourt Coll Pubs) Harcourt.

Public Policy in Britain. Ed. by Stephen P. Savage et al. LC 94-24880. 1994. text 55.00 (*0-312-12267-5*) St Martin.

Public Policy in Canada: An Introduction. 3rd ed. Stephen Brooks. LC 99-182452. (Illus.). 312p. 1998. pap. text 29.95 (*0-19-541272-9*) OUP.

Public Policy in China, 318. Ed. by Stuart S. Nagel & Miriam K. Mills. LC 92-37519. (Contributions in Political Science Ser.: No. 318). 176p. 1993. 62.95 (*0-313-28848-8*, GM8848) Greenwood.

Public Policy in Industrial Growth: The Case of the Early Ruhr Mining Region, 1766-1865. Manfred Jankowski. Ed. by Stuart Bruchey. LC 77-77175. (Dissertations in European Economic History Ser.). (Illus.). 1978. lib. bdg. 40.95 (*0-405-10788-9*) Ayer.

Public Policy in Temporal Perspective. Ed. by William Michelson. 1978. pap. text 28.50 (*90-279-7824-7*) Mouton.

Public Policy in the New Europe: Eurogovernance in Theory & Practice. Fergus Carr & Andrew Massey. LC 99-30949. (New Horizons in Public Policy Ser.). 304p. 1999. 90.00 (*1-85898-982-5*) E Elgar.

Public Policy in the United States: Toward the 21st Century. 2nd ed. Mark E. Rushefsky. LC 95-45292. (Political Science Ser.). 400p. (C). 1996. pap. text 62.00 (*0-534-24996-5*) Harcourt.

Public Policy in Transnational Relationships. M. Rubino-Sammartano & C. G. Morse. 1990. ring bd. 97.00 (*90-6544-955-8*) Kluwer Law Intl.

***Public Policy Instruments: Evaluating the Tools of Public Administration.** Ed. by B. Guy Peters & Frans K. Van Nispen. LC 97-47513. (New Horizons in Public Policy Ser.). 264p. 1998. 85.00 (*1-85898-744-X*) E Elgar.

Public Policy Issues & Latin American Library Resources. Ed. by Pamela Howard. (Papers of the Seminar on the Acquisition of Latin American Library Materials: No. 27). 234p. 1984. pap. 45.00 (*0-917617-01-0*) SALALM.

Public Policy Issues for Management. Rogene A. Buchholz. (Illus.). 400p. (C). 1988. pap. text 14.25 (*0-13-738840-3*) P-H.

Public Policy Issues for Management. 2nd ed. Rogene A. Buchholz. 352p. (C). 1991. pap. text 31.60 (*0-13-678087-3*, 140703) P-H.

Public Policy Issues in Wildlife Management, 286. Ed. by William R. Mangun. LC 91-20774. (Contributions in Political Science Ser.: No. 286). 208p. 1991. 57.95 (*0-313-28010-X*, MIW, Greenwood Pr) Greenwood.

Public Policy Making: Process & Principles. Larry N. Gerston. LC 96-29823. 176p. (C). (gr. 13). 1997. text 60.95 (*0-7656-0079-X*); pap. text 20.95 (*0-7656-0080-3*) M E Sharpe.

Public Policy Making in a Federal System. Ed. by Robert D. Jones. (Organization Ser.). 288p. 1976. pap. 15.00 (*0-317-35634-8*) Pol Studies.

Public Policy on Reproductive Choice: A Community Action Guide. League of Women Voters Education Fund Staff. 1992. 5.00 (*0-89959-379-8*, 953) LWVUS.

Public Policy Opinion & the Elderly, 1952-1978: A Kaleidoscope of Culture, 6. John E. Tropman. LC 86-27150. (Contributions to the Study of Aging Ser.: No. 6). (Illus.). 265p. 1987. 59.95 (*0-313-25432-X*, TPO/, Greenwood Pr) Greenwood.

***Public Policy Praxis - Theory & Pragmatism: A Case Approach.** Randall Clemons & Mark McBeth. 352p. 2000. pap. 40.00 (*0-13-025882-2*, Prentice Hall) P-H.

Public Policy Primer. Edwin S. Davis. 74p. (C). 1992. pap. text 18.60 (*0-536-58314-5*) Pearson Custom.

***Public Policy Problems.** 192p. (C). 2000. 21.00 (*0-536-60787-7*) Pearson Custom.

Public Policy Reader. Derek Shearer & Lee Webb. 658p. 1976. pap. text 17.95 (*0-87855-627-3*) Transaction Pubs.

Public Policy, Science, & Environmental Risk. Ed. by Sandra Panem. LC 83-73029. 65p. 1983. pap. 10.95 (*0-8157-6901-6*) Brookings.

Public Policy Skills. 3rd rev. ed. William D. Coplin & Michael K. O'Leary. (Illus.). 206p. 1998. text 38.00 (*0-936826-42-8*) PS Assocs Croton.

Public Policy Studies: Basic Concepts & Methods, 10 vols. Ed. by Stuart S. Nagel. 1986. 732.50 (*0-89232-370-1*) Jai Pr.

Public Policy Toward Corporate Takeovers. Ed. by Murray Weidenbaum & Kenneth Chilton. 192p. 1987. 32.95 (*0-88738-166-9*) Transaction Pubs.

Public Policy Toward Corporations. Ed. by Arnold A. Haggestad. LC 87-21324. 214p. 1988. 49.95 (*0-8130-0880-8*) U Press Fla.

Public Policy Toward Pensions. Ed. by Sylvester Schieber & John Shoven. LC 97-34285. (Illus.). 350p. 1997. 40.00 (*0-262-19387-6*) MIT Pr.

Public Policy Towards Cable Television Vol. 1: The Economics of Rate Control. Thomas W. Hazlett & Matthew L. Spitzer. LC 97-20440. (AEI Ser.). (Illus.). 190p. (C). 1997. 32.50 (*0-262-08253-5*) MIT Pr.

Public Policy Towards Risk. Ed. by Susan Hadden. (Orig.). (C). 1982. pap. 15.00 (*0-918592-53-4*) Pol Studies.

Public Policymaking, 2 vols. 2nd ed. James Anderson. LC 93-78691. (C). 1993. pap. text 41.56 (*0-395-67529-4*) HM.

Public Policymaking: An Introduction, 3 vols. 3rd ed. James Anderson. 352p. (C). 1996. pap. text 42.76 (*0-395-75396-1*) HM.

Public Policymaking in the American States. Jack M. Treadway. LC 85-6498. 206p. 1985. 45.00 (*0-275-90175-0*, C0175, Praeger Pubs) Greenwood.

Public Policymaking Reexamined. Yehezkel Dror. LC 83-351. 415p. 1995. pap. text 24.95 (*0-87855-928-0*) Transaction Pubs.

Public PolicyTheories, Models & Concepts: An Anthology. Ed. by Daniel C. McCool. LC 94-22744. 352p. 1994. pap. text 51.00 (*0-13-737867-X*) P-H.

Public Politics in an Authoritarian State: Making Foreign Policy During the Brezhnev Years. Richard D. Anderson, Jr. LC 93-15240. 288p. 1993. text 45.00 (*0-8014-2900-5*) Cornell U Pr.

Public Poor Relief in America, 1790-1860: Doctoral Dissertation, Columbia University, 1951, 2 vols. Benjamin J. Klebaner. LC 75-17228. (Social Problems & Social Policy Ser.). 1976. reprint ed. 52.95 (*0-405-07498-0*) Ayer.

Public Poor Relief in North Carolina. Roy M. Brown. LC 75-17208. (Social Problems & Social Policy Ser.). (Illus.). 1976. reprint ed. 19.95 (*0-405-07480-8*) Ayer.

Public Ports for Indiana: A History of the Indiana Port Commission. Ralph D. Gray. LC 98-173988. (Indiana Historical Collections: Vol. 55). (Illus.). xvi, 167p. (Orig.). 1997. pap. 14.95 (*1-885323-54-9*, 4031) IN Hist Bureau.

Public Power During the Truman Administration. John R. Waltrip. Ed. by Stuart Bruchey. LC 78-22711. (Energy in the American Economy Ser.). 1979. lib. bdg. 17.95 (*0-405-12021-4*) Ayer.

Public Power, Politics & Technology in the Eisenhower & Kennedy Years: The Hanford Dual-Purpose Reactor Controversy, 1956-1962. Bonnie B. Pendergrass. Ed. by Stuart Bruchey. LC 78-22705. (Energy in the American Economy Ser.). 1979. lib. bdg. 19.95 (*0-405-12007-9*) Ayer.

Public Prayer & the Constitution: A Case Study in Constitutional Interpretation. Rodney K. Smith. LC 86-28020. 305p. 1987. 45.00 (*0-8420-2260-0*) Scholarly Res Inc.

Public Prayers. Arthur C. McGiffert, Jr. LC 83-83269. (Studies in Ministry & Parish Life). 44p. 1984. pap. 4.50 (*0-913552-24-0*) Exploration Pr.

Public Preference in Hydro Power Relicensing: The Consumer Interest in Competition. 120p. 1984. 60.00 (*0-318-03354-2*) Consumer Energy Coun.

Public Preferences for Life Saving. Maureen L. Cropper et al. (Illus.). 78p. (Orig.). (C). 1993. pap. text 20.00 (*1-56806-370-9*) DIANE Pub.

Public Pricing of Nursing Home Care. Howard Birnbaum et al. (Illus.). 222p. 1984. reprint ed. lib. bdg. 52.00 (*0-8191-4065-1*) U Pr of Amer.

Public Primary School System in France, with Special Reference to the Training of Teachers. Frederic E. Farrington. LC 70-176765. (Columbia University. Teachers College. Contributions to Education Ser.: No. 7). reprint ed. 37.50 (*0-404-55007-X*) AMS Pr.

***Public Principles of Public Debt.** James M. Buchanan. LC 98-45533. (Collected Works of James M. Buchanan : Vol. 2). 1999. 20.00 (*0-86597-215-X*); pap. 12.00 (*0-86597-216-8*) Liberty Fund.

Public Priority Setting: Rules & Costs. P. B. Boorsma et al. LC 97-38233. 350p. 1997. lib. bdg. 164.00 (*0-7923-4823-0*, D Reidel) Kluwer Academic.

Public-Private Collaboration in Agricultural Research: New Institutional Arrangements & Economic Implication. Ed. by Keith O. Fuglie & David E. Schimmelpfennig. LC 99-47027. (Illus.). 352p. 1999. 84.95 (*0-8138-2789-2*) Iowa St U Pr.

Public-Private Collaboration in Health Information Policy. Frwd. by John M. Colmers et al. 32p. 1999. pap. write for info. (*1-887748-29-6*) Milbank Memorial.

***Public/Private Divide.** Dawn Oliver. 256p. 1999. pap. 39.95 (*0-406-98303-8*, Pub. by Buttrwrth Co Ltd) Northwestern U Pr.

Public-Private Mix in Social Services: Health Care & Education in Chile, Costa Rica & Venezuela. Ed. by Elaine Zuckerman & Emanuel De Kadt. 187p. 1997. pap. text 10.00 (*1-886938-17-2*) IADB.

Public-private Partnership: A New Concept for Infrastructure Development. 24p. 20.00 (*92-1-100780-1*) UN.

Public-Private Partnership: An Opportunity for Urban Communities. LC 82-1504. (CED Statement on National Policy Ser.). 106p. 1982. pap. 7.50 (*0-87186-074-0*); lib. bdg. 9.50 (*0-87186-774-5*) Comm Econ Dev.

Public-Private Partnership: New Opportunities for Meeting Social Needs. Ed. by Harvey Brooks et al. LC 83-27564. (American Academy of Arts & Sciences Ser.). 392p. 1984. text 34.95 (*0-88410-482-6*, HarpBusn) HarpInfo.

Public-Private Partnership Case Studies: Profiles of Success in Providing Environmental Services. (Illus.). 118p. (Orig.). (C). 1995. pap. text 30.00 (*0-7881-2383-1*) DIANE Pub.

Public-Private Partnerships. (Proceedings of the Academy of Political Science Ser.: Vol. 36, No. 2). 1986. pap. 12.95 (*0-614-04170-8*) Acad Poli Sci.

***Public Private Partnerships: Theory & Practice in International Perspective.** Stephen P. Osborne. LC 00-38248. (Studies in the Management of Voluntary & Non-Profit Organizations). 2000. pap. write for info. (*0-415-21268-5*) Routledge.

Public-Private Partnerships for Child Care: A Feasibility Study of New York State. Dana E. Friedman & Margaret King. 98p. 1991. pap. 20.00 (*1-888324-06-6*, C91-01) Families & Work.

Public Private Partnerships for Environmental Facilities: A Self-Help Guide for Local Governments. (Illus.). 39p. 1996. reprint ed. pap. text 20.00 (*0-7881-3199-0*) DIANE Pub.

Public-Private Partnerships for Local Economic Development. Ed. by Norman D. Walzer & Brian Jacobs. LC 97-27923. 264p. 1998. 65.00 (*0-275-96153-2*, Praeger Pubs) Greenwood.

P

An Asterisk (*) at the beginning of an entry indicates that the title is appearing for the first time.

***Public-Private Policy Partnerships.** Ed. by Pauline Vaillancourt Rosenau. LC 99-89689. (Illus.). 225p. 2000. 45.00 (*0-262-18198-3*); pap. 19.95 (*0-262-68114-5*) MIT Pr.

Public Privates: Performing Gynecology from Both Ends of the Speculum. Terri Kapsalis. LC 92-29409. (Illus.). 272p. 1997. pap. 16.95 (*0-8223-1921-7*); lib. bdg. 49.95 (*0-8223-1928-4*) Duke.

Public Procurement, Vol. III-2. Shane Rimmer. (Single Market Review Ser.). 1998. 90.00 (*0-7494-2325-0*) Kogan Page Ltd.

Public Procurement: A Harmonization of the National Judicial Review Of The Application of European Community Law. Dorthe Dahlgaard Dingel. LC 99-18786. (European Monographs). 1999. 99.00 (*90-411-1161-1*) Kluwer Law Intl.

Public Procurement: Global Revolution. Sue Arrowsmith & Arwel Davies. LC 98-29820. (International Economic Development Law Ser.). 1998. 91.00 (*90-411-9662-5*) Kluwer Law Intl.

Public Procurement in European Community Law. Friedl Weiss. LC 92-21078. (European Community Law Ser.: Vol. 4). 240p. (C). 1993. text 85.00 (*0-485-70002-6*, Pub. by Athlone Pr) Humanities.

Public Procurement Law in the EC. Christopher Bovis. LC 96-47753. (European Law Ser.). x, 133p. 1997. pap. 28.00 (*0-582-29439-8*, 15714) Gaunt.

Public Productivity Handbook. Mark Holzer. (Public Administration & Public Policy Ser.: Vol. 45). 720p. 1991. text 220.00 (*0-8247-8562-2*) Dekker.

Public Productivity Through Quality & Strategic Management. Ed. by G. Bouckaert & Arie Halanchini. LC 94-7847. (YA). (gr. 12). 1995. 120.00 (*90-5199-189-4*) IOS Press.

Public Programs for Private Forestry: A Reader on Programs & Options. R. Neil Sampson & Lester A. DeCoster. LC 98-153231. (Illus.). 100p. (C). 1997. pap. 20.00 (*0-935050-07-8*) Am Forests.

Public Property & Private Power: The Corporation of the City of New York in American Law, 1730-1870. Hendrik Hartog. LC 88-43304. (Illus.). 274p. 1989. pap. text 17.95 (*0-8014-9560-1*) Cornell U Pr.

Public Property & Private Power: The Corporation of the City of New York in American Law, 1730-1870. Hendrik Hartog. LC 82-24724. (Studies in Legal History). (Illus.). xi, 274p. (C). 1983. 49.95 (*0-8078-1562-4*) U of NC Pr.

Public Prosecutor. Georgi Dzhagarov. Tr. by Marguerite Alexieva from BUL. 112p. 1969. 16.95 (*0-910278-16-4*) Boulevard.

Public Prosecutor of the Terror: Antoine Quentin Fouquier-Tinville. Alphonse Dunoyer. 1977. lib. bdg. 59.95 (*0-8490-2489-7*) Gordon Pr.

Public Prosecutors & Discretion: A Comparative Study. Julia Fionda. (Oxford Monographs on Criminal Law & Justice). 286p. 1995. text 49.95 (*0-19-825915-8*) OUP.

Public Protest in Indonesia. Ann R. Willner. LC 75-631234. (Papers in International Studies: No. 2). 23p. reprint ed. pap. 30.00 (*0-608-30702-5*, 200744100062) Bks Demand.

Public Purpose. Tom Kent. 464p. (C). 1988. 55.00 (*0-7735-0649-7*, Pub. by McG-Queens Univ Pr) CUP Services.

Public Purpose of Education & Schooling. John I. Goodlad & Timothy J. McMannon. LC 96-45875. 1997. 29.95 (*0-7879-0934-3*) Jossey-Bass.

Public Purse, Public Purpose: Autonomy & Accountability in the Groves of Academe. Ed. by James Cutt & Rodney Dobell. 300p. 1992. pap. text 19.95 (*0-88645-129-9*, Pub. by Inst Res Pub) Ashgate Pub Co.

Public Radiation Exposure from Nuclear Power Generation in the United States. LC 87-24696. (Report Ser.: No. 92). 204p. (Orig.). 1987. pap. text 45.00 (*0-913392-90-1*) NCRP Pubns.

Public Radio & Television in America: A Political History. Ralph Engelman. LC 95-50232. 400p. (C). 1996. 52.00 (*0-8039-5406-9*); pap. 24.95 (*0-8039-5407-7*) Sage.

Public Reactions to Nuclear Waste: Citizens' Views of Repository Siting. Ed. by Riley E. Dunlap et al. LC 93-6980. (Illus.). 384p. (C). 1993. text 54.95 (*0-8223-1355-3*); pap. text 24.95 (*0-8223-1373-1*) Duke.

Public Reading & the Reading Public in Late Medieval England & France. Joyce Coleman. LC 95-37984. (Studies in Medieval Literature: No. 26). (Illus.). 264p. (C). 1996. text 69.95 (*0-521-55391-1*) Cambridge U Pr.

P

***Public Realm: Exploring the City's Quintessential Social Territory.** Lyn H. Lofland. LC 97-42290. (Communication & Social Order Ser.). 324p. 1998. pap. text 26.95 (*0-202-30608-9*) Aldine de Gruyter.

Public Realm: Exploring the City's Quintessential Social Territory. Lyn H. Lofland. LC 97-42290. (Communication & Social Order Ser.). 324p. 1998. lib. bdg. 54.95 (*0-202-30607-0*) Aldine de Gruyter.

Public Realm & the Public Self: The Political Theory of Hannah Arendt. Shiraz Dossa. LC 88-94398. xiv, 154p. (C). 1989. text 29.95 (*0-88920-967-7*) W Laurier U Pr.

Public Reason. Ed. by Fred D'Agostino & Gerald F. Gaus. LC 97-37026. (International Research Library of Philosophy). 470p. 1998. text 153.95 (*1-85521-954-9*, Pub. by Ashgate Pub) Ashgate Pub Co.

Public Reason: Mediated Authority in the Liberal State Fred M. Frohock. LC 99-29687. 1999. 35.00 (*0-8014-3677-X*) Cornell U Pr.

Public Receipts in the United States, 1952-1994. John E. Dawson & Peter J. Stan. LC 96-21963. 1996. pap. text 15.00 (*0-8330-2409-4*, MR-589-RC) Rand Corp.

Public Record Office, 1838-1958. John D. Cantwell. x, 631p. 1991. 115.00 (*0-11-440224-8*, Pub. by Statnry Office) Balogh.

Public Record Research System, 3 vols. Ed. by Michael L. Sankey et al. Incl. Vol. II. 812p. 1999. ring bd. Not sold separately (*1-879792-53-2*); Vol. I. 808p. 1999. ring bd. Not sold separately (*1-879792-52-4*); Vol. III. 792p. 1999. ring bd. Not sold separately (*1-879792-54-0*); 2412p. 1999. Set ring bd. 169.00 (*1-879792-51-6*) BRB Pubns.

Public Records & Archives in Classical Athens. James P. Sickinger. LC 98-30098. (Studies in the History of Greece & Rome). 274p. (C). 1999. 49.95 (*0-8078-2469-0*) U of NC Pr.

Public Records Law for North Carolina Local Government: 1997-1998 Supplement. David M. Lawrence. 1999. pap. text, suppl. ed. 10.00 (*1-56011-343-X*, 97.02A) Institute Government.

Public Records Law for North Carolina Local Governments. David M. Lawrence. LC 97-151573. 207p. 1997. pap. text 34.00 (*1-56011-299-9*) Institute Government.

Public Records of the Colony of Connecticut, from 1665 to 1678, with the Journal of the Council of War, 1675 to 1678. J. Hammond Trumbull. 610p. 1995. reprint ed. lib. bdg. 59.00 (*0-8328-4457-8*) Higginson Bk Co.

Public Records of the Colony of Connecticut, 1636-1776, 15 vols. Ed. by J. Hammond Trumbull & Charles J. Hoadley. LC 74-18353. 1890. 1215.00 (*0-404-06630-5*) AMS Pr.

Public Records of the State of Connecticut: From May, 1780 to October 1781, Vol. 3. Ed. by Charles J. Hoadly. 624p. 1922. 20.00 (*0-940748-36-3*) Conn Hist Soc.

Public Records Officer. (Career Examination Ser.: C-3416). 1994. pap. 29.95 (*0-8373-3416-0*) Nat Learn.

Public Records on Internet. Ed. by David Vine. 220p. 1998. ring bd. 44.95 (*0-9653174-5-5*) D Vine Assocs.

Public Records Online: The National Guide to Private & Government Online Sources of Public Records. 2nd ed. Carl R. Ernst & Michael Sankey. 416p. 1999. pap. 19.95 (*1-889150-10-X*, Pub. by Facts on Demand) Natl Bk Netwk.

***Public Records Online: The National Guide to Private & Government Online Sources of Public Records.** 3rd rev. ed. Ed. by Michael L. Sankey & James R. Flowers, Jr. 480p. 2000. pap. 20.95 (*1-889150-21-5*, Pub. by Facts on Demand) Natl Bk Netwk.

Public Recreation: Study of Parks Playgrounds & Other Recreation Facilities, Vol. 7. 1974. 25.95 (*0-405-05420-3*) Ayer.

Public Regulation of Dangerous Products. Marshall S. Shapo. LC 80-13733. (University Casebook Ser.). 393p. 1980. pap. text 14.00 (*0-88277-003-9*) Foundation Pr.

Public Regulation of Site Selection for Nuclear Power Plants: Present Procedures & Reform Proposals--An Annotated Bibliography. Ernest D. Klema & Robert L. West. LC 77-71670. (Resources for the Future, RFF Research Paper Ser.: R-2). 151p. reprint ed. pap. 46.90 (*0-608-13493-7*, 201994800015) Bks Demand.

Public Relations. Heath. 2000. pap. text. write for info. (*0-312-15440-2*) St Martin.

Public Relations. 3rd ed. Baskin & Aronoff. 1992. 13.75 (*0-697-08631-3*, WCB McGr Hill) McGrw-H Hghr Educ.

Public Relations. 4th ed. Baskin. 1996. 20.00 (*0-697-20123-6*, WCB McGr Hill) McGrw-H Hghr Educ.

Public Relations. 4th ed. Doug Newsom. (Mass Communication Ser.). 1995. pap., suppl. ed. 19.95 (*0-534-25501-9*) Wadsworth Pub.

Public Relations. 5th ed. Baskin. 2000. 50.74 (*0-07-231456-7*) McGraw.

Public Relations. 5th ed. Frank Jefkins. 352p. 1997. pap. 42.50 (*0-273-63432-1*, Pub. by Pitman Pub) Trans-Atl Phila.

Public Relations: A Managerial. 2nd ed. Grunig. (C). 1999. text 42.50 (*0-03-046429-3*) Harcourt Coll Pubs.

Public Relations: An Introduction. Shirley Harrison. LC 95-3535. 224p. (C). 1995. pap. 26.95 (*0-415-10320-7*) Thomson Learn.

Public Relations: An Introduction. Shirley Harrison. LC 95-3535. 208p. (C). (gr. 13). 1995. pap. 69.95 (*0-415-10319-3*) Thomson Learn.

***Public Relations: An Introduction.** 2nd ed. Shirley Harrison. 2000. pap. 26.95 (*1-86152-547-8*) Thomson Learn.

Public Relations: Communication. Gayle Pohl. 176p. (C). 1995. pap. text, per. 24.95 (*0-7872-0432-3*) Kendall-Hunt.

Public Relations: Ghostwriting fur Medien? Eine Linguistische Analyse der Journalistischen Leistung Bei Der Adaption Von Pressemitteilungen. Cornelia Bachmann. (Zurcher Germanistische Studien Ser.: No. 49). 252p. 1997. 40.95 (*3-906757-87-0*, Pub. by P Lang) P Lang Pubng.

Public Relations: Management by Objectives. Norman R. Nager & T. Harrell Allen. (Illus.). 416p. (C). 1991. reprint ed. pap. text 26.50 (*0-8191-8330-X*) U Pr of Amer.

Public Relations: New British Photography. Florian Muller. 1998. 29.95 (*3-89322-338-X*, Pub. by Edition Cantz) Dist Art Pubs.

Public Relations: Principles & Practice. Philip J. Kitchen. LC 97-5338. 325p. 1997. pap. 24.99 (*1-86152-091-3*) Thomson Learn.

***Public Relations: Strategies & Tactics.** 5th ed. (C). 1998. text. write for info. (*0-321-00408-6*); text. write for info. (*0-321-00410-8*); text. write for info. (*0-321-00411-6*) Addison-Wesley Educ.

***Public Relations: Strategies & Tactics.** 6th ed. (C). 2000. cd-rom 71.00 (*0-321-07528-5*) Addison-Wesley.

Public Relations: Strategies & Tactics. 6th ed. Wilcox. LC 99-34544. 584p. (C). 1999. 88.00 (*0-321-05555-1*) Addison-Wesley Educ.

***Public Relations: Strategies & Tactics.** 6th ed. Dennis L. Wilcox et al. 608p. 1999. 80.00 (*0-321-03103-2*) Longman.

***Public Relations: Strategies Tactics.** 6th ed. (C). 1999. write for info. (*0-321-06344-9*) Addison-Wesley.

***Public Relations: Strategies Tactics.** 6th ed. (C). 2000. write for info. (*0-321-06349-X*) Addison-Wesley.

***Public Relations: Strategies Tactics.** 6th ed. (C). 2000. cd-rom 67.00 (*0-321-06345-7*) Addison-Wesley.

***Public Relations: Strategies, Tactics.** 6th ed. (C). 2000. text. write for info. (*0-321-06346-5*) Addson-Wesley Educ.

Public Relations: The Necessary Art. David A. Haberman & Harry A. Dolphin. LC 87-17139. (Illus.). 436p. 1988. text 32.95 (*0-8138-1457-X*) Iowa St U Pr.

Public Relations: The Profession & the Practice. 4th ed. Otis W. Baskin & Craig Aronoff. 528p. (C). 1997. text, student ed. write for info. (*0-07-114032-8*) Brown & Benchmark.

Public Relations: The Profession & the Practice. 4th ed. Otis W. Baskin et al. LC 96-83186. 528p. (C). 1996. text. write for info. (*0-697-20122-8*) Brown & Benchmark.

***Public Relations: Theory & Practice.** Ed. by Jane Johnston & Clara Zawawi. (Illus.). 368p. 2000. pap. 39.00 (*1-86508-360-7*, Pub. by Allen & Unwin Pty) Paul & Co Pubs.

Public Relations: What Research Tells Us. John V. Pavlik. (CommText Ser.: Vol. 16). (C). 1987. text 42.00 (*0-8039-2950-1*); pap. text 18.95 (*0-8039-2951-X*) Sage.

Public Relations: What Research Tells Us. John V. Pavlik. LC 87-13200. (Sage Commtext Ser.: No. 16). 152p. reprint ed. pap. 47.20 (*0-608-09626-1*, 205278400007) Bks Demand.

Public Relations: Writing, Media & Techniques. 3rd ed. (C). 1992. text. write for info. (*0-06-501000-0*) HarpC.

Public Relations Activities of German Companies in the United States. Daniel Mahler. (ENG & GER.). 1996. 25.00 (*0-86640-056-7*) German Am Chamber.

Public Relations & Communication for Natural Resource Managers. 2nd ed. James R. Fazio & Douglas Gilbert. 416p. (C). 1995. boxed set 32.95 (*0-8403-3882-1*) Kendall-Hunt.

Public Relations & Community: A Reconstructed Theory. Dean Kruckeberg & Kenneth Starck. LC 87-30536. 155p. 1988. 49.95 (*0-275-92911-6*, C2911, Praeger Pubs) Greenwood.

Public Relations & Ethics: A Reference Guide. John P. Ferre & Shirley C. Willihnganz. LC 91-3781. 110p. (C). 1991. 35.00 (*0-8161-7255-2*, Hall Reference) Macmillan.

Public Relations & Merchandising: A Handbook for College & University Food Services. Paul Fairbrook. LC 84-71563. (Illus.). 1984. pap. 22.00 (*0-9602456-1-8*) Colman Pubs.

Public Relations & Organizational Decision Making. Christopher Spicer. LC 96-23822. (Communication Ser.). 372p. (C). 1996. text 79.95 (*0-8058-1837-5*) L Erlbaum Assocs.

Public Relations & the Law. Frank E. Walsh. LC KF0390.5.P8.. 144p. reprint ed. pap. 44.70 (*0-7837-0078-4*, 204033000016) Bks Demand.

Public Relations Are an Asset for Archives & Museums. rev. ed. Kenneth R. Lawrence. Ed. by Virginia Joyner. 32p. (Orig.). (C). 1996. pap. 8.95 (*0-910653-26-7*, 8004L) Archival Servs.

Public Relations As Communication Management. Richard E. Crable & Steven L. Vibbert. (Illus.). 436p. (C). 1986. text. write for info. (*0-8087-4878-5*) Pearson Custom.

Public Relations As Relationship Management: A Relational Approach to the Study & Practice of Public Relations. Ed. by John A. Ledingham & Stephen D. Bruning. LC 99-13642. (LEA's Communication Ser.). 240p. 1999. write for info. (*0-8058-3050-2*) L Erlbaum Assocs.

Public Relations As Rhetorical Criticism: Case Studies of Corporate Discourse & Social Influence. Ed. by William N. Elwood. LC 94-42837. (Political Communication Ser.). 352p. 1995. pap. 32.95 (*0-275-95150-2*, Praeger Pubs) Greenwood.

Public Relations Assistant. Jack Rudman. (Career Examination Ser.: C-635). 1994. pap. 27.95 (*0-8373-0635-3*) Nat Learn.

Public Relations Bibliography. 2nd ed. Scott M. Cutlip. LC 65-16360. 319p. 1965. pap. 98.90 (*0-608-01903-8*, 206255500003) Bks Demand.

Public Relations Bibliography Nineteen Eighty-Six to Nineteen Eighty-Seven. Albert Walker. Ed. by Michael Shermis. 1990. pap. 12.00 (*0-927516-11-X*) ERIC-REC.

Public Relations Campaign Strategies. 3rd ed. Kendall. (C). 1999. text. write for info. (*0-321-01838-9*) Addison-Wesley.

Public Relations Campaign Strategy. E. Kendall. (C). 1930. text, teacher ed. 11.00 (*0-06-363609-3*) HarpC.

Public Relations Campaigns. (C). 1999. pap. text. write for info. (*0-205-31539-9*) Allyn.

Public Relations Campaigns. Frances R. Matera & Ray J. Artigue. LC 99-48412. 280p. (C). 1999. pap. text 49.00 (*0-205-15815-3*, Macmillan Coll) P-H.

Public Relations Career Directory: A Practical One-Stop Guide to Getting a Job in Public Relations. 5th ed. Bradley J. Morgan. Ed. by Diane Dupuis. (Career Advisor Ser.). 1993. 17.95 (*0-8103-9439-1*, 089141) Visible Ink Pr.

***Public Relations Casebook.** (C). 2000. text. write for info. (*0-321-03104-0*) Addison-Wesley Educ.

Public Relations Cases. Jerry A. Hendrix. 447p. (C). 1987. pap. write for info. (*0-534-08647-0*) Wadsworth Pub.

Public Relations Cases. 2nd ed. Hendrix. (Mass Communication Ser.). 1991. pap., teacher ed. write for info. (*0-534-16483-8*) Wadsworth Pub.

Public Relations Cases. 2nd ed. Jerry A. Hendrix. 484p. (C). 1991. pap. 30.95 (*0-534-16482-X*) Wadsworth Pub.

Public Relations Cases. 3rd ed. Jerry A. Hendrix. LC 94-13772. 477p. 1994. mass mkt. 38.95 (*0-534-24840-3*) Wadsworth Pub.

Public Relations Cases. 4th ed. Jerry A. Hendrix. LC 97-19270. (Mass Communication Ser.). (C). 1997. pap. 52.95 (*0-534-52236-X*) Wadsworth Pub.

Public Relations Cases. 5th ed. Hendrix. (Mass Communication Ser.). 2000. mass mkt. 52.95 (*0-534-51432-4*) Wadsworth Pub.

Public Relations Director. Jack Rudman. (Career Examination Ser.: C-1901). 1994. pap. 34.95 (*0-8373-1901-3*) Nat Learn.

Public Relations Ethics. P. Seib. LC 94-77555. (C). 1994. pap. text 31.00 (*0-15-501943-0*, Pub. by Harcourt Coll Pubs) Harcourt.

Public Relations for Building Service Success. Barbara Darraugh & Donald Tepper. vi, 79p. 1997. pap. 50.00 (*1-892725-12-6*, RP147) Building Serv.

Public Relations for Healthcare Facilities. Lisa Gardner. 143p. 26.50 (*0-929442-60-1*) Prof Prnting & Pub.

Public Relations for Hospitality Managers: Communicating for Greater Profits. Albert E. Kudrle & Melvin Sandler. LC 94-45408. 264p. 1995. 49.95 (*0-471-03977-2*) Wiley.

Public Relations for Libraries: Essays in Communications Techniques, 5. Ed. by Allan Angoff. LC 72-776. (Contributions in Librarianship & Information Science Ser.: No. 5). 246p. 1973. 49.95 (*0-8371-6060-X*, ANP/, Greenwood Pr) Greenwood.

Public Relations for Local Government. Dick Fedorcio et al. LC 92-145155. vii, 106 p. 1991. pap. write for info. (*0-582-08191-2*) Longman.

***Public Relations for Pharmacists.** Tina L. Pugliese. 150p. 2000. pap. 28.00 (*1-58212-011-0*) Am Pharm Assn.

Public Relations for Public Schools. Doyle M. Bortner. LC 79-183947. 425p. 1983. pap. 18.95 (*0-87073-509-8*) Schenkman Bks Inc.

Public Relations for School Library Media Programs: 500 Ways to Influence People & Win Friends for Your School Library Media Center. Helen F. Flowers. LC 98-11470. 150p. 1998. pap. 38.50 (*1-55570-320-8*) Neal-Schuman.

Public Relations For Schools. Adolph Unruh & Robert Willier. LC 73-91798. v, 169 p. 1974. write for info. (*0-8224-5750-4*) Globe Fearon.

Public Relations for Small Business: What It Is & Why You Need It. Ruth Hammond & W. Forbes LeClair. LC 80-463213. (Canadian Small Business Ser.). x, 112p. 1979. write for info. (*0-7705-1647-5*) CN Pub Corp.

Public Relations for the Franchisee: How to Create Your Own Publicity. Ed. by Lisa I. Bernfeld. 144p. 1990. pap. text 17.00 (*0-9636466-0-5*) LIBooks.

Public Relations for the Local Church: A Practical Guide for Ministry Leaders. Joel B. Curry. Ed. by Cindy G. Spear. 130p. (C). 1991. student ed., ring bd. 89.95 incl. audio (*0-941005-36-4*) Chrch Grwth VA.

Public Relations for the Smaller Library. James C. Dance. 1979. pap. 8.00 (*0-8389-5547-9*) ALA.

Public Relations History: From the 17th to the 20th Century. Scott M. Cutlip. (LEA's Communication Ser.). 320p. 1995. pap. 32.50 (*0-8058-1780-8*); text 59.95 (*0-8058-1779-4*) L Erlbaum Assocs.

Public Relations in Action. Robert T. Reilly. 1981. 34.00 (*0-13-738526-9*) P-H.

***Public Relations in Educational Organizations.** 2nd ed. Ed. by Theodore J. Kowalski. LC 98-33122. (Illus.). 390p. (C). 1999. 67.00 (*0-13-974411-8*) P-H.

Public Relations in Health & Welfare. Ed. by Frances Schmidt et al. LC 75-31550. 161p. reprint ed. pap. 50.00 (*0-608-08669-X*, 206919200003) Bks Demand.

Public Relations in Health Care: A Guide for Professionals. 2nd ed. Ed. by Kathleen L. Lewton. 284p. (Orig.). 1995. pap. 69.00 (*1-55648-143-8*, 166123) AHPI.

Public Relations in Local Governments: Strategic Approaches to Better Communications. David Walker. LC 97-157336. (Managing Local Governments Ser.). 146p. (Orig.). 1997. pap. 62.50 (*0-273-62522-5*, Pub. by Pitman Pub) Trans-Atl Phila.

Public Relations in Museums. Alfonz Lengyel. 1990. pap. 15.00 (*0-9626500-0-5*) Fudan Mus Fndtn.

Public Relations in Practice: A Casebook. Ed. by Danny Moss. 240p. (C). (gr. 13). 1990. pap. 65.00 (*0-415-05528-8*, A4893) Thomson Learn.

Public Relations in the Emergency Department. Cyril T. Cameron. LC 80-15894. 126p. 1980. text 18.95 (*0-87619-746-2*) P-H.

Public Relations in the Marketing Mix. Jordan Goldman. LC 83-71076. (Illus.). 200p. 1994. pap. 17.95 (*0-8442-3084-7*, NTC Business Bks) NTC Contemp Pub Co.

Public Relations Inquiry As Rhetorical Criticism: Case Studies of Corporate Discourse & Social Influence. Ed. by William N. Elwood. LC 94-42837. (Political Communication Ser.). 352p. 1995. 75.00 (*0-275-94971-0*, Praeger Pubs) Greenwood.

Public Relations Intro. Harrison. (ITBP Textbks). 1998. pap. 24.95 (*1-86152-397-1*) Thomson Learn.

***Public Relations Kit for Dummies.** Eric Yaverbaum. (For Dummies Ser.). 384p. 2001. pap. 24.99 incl. cd-rom (*0-7645-5277-5*) IDG Bks.

Public Relations Libraries. Harrison. (C). 1977. text 15.00 (*0-233-95657-3*) Westview.

Public Relations Manual for Future Homemakers of America Inc. 48p. 1988. 7.00 (*0-318-35388-1*) Future Home.

Public Relations Marketing: Making a Splash Without Much Cash. Stephanie Seacord. LC 99-18207. 145p. 1999. pap. 19.95 (*1-55571-459-5*, BPRMP, Oasis Pr) PSI Resch.

An Asterisk (*) at the beginning of an entry indicates that the title is appearing for the first time.

Public Relations of the Motion Picture Industry: A Report by the Department of Research & Education. Federal Council of the Churches of Christ in Ameri. LC 76-160231. (Moving Pictures Ser.). 156p. 1971. reprint ed. lib. bdg. 24.95 (*0-89198-032-6*) Ozer.

Public Relations on the Net: Winning Strategies to Inform & Influence the Media, the Investment Community, the Government, the Public, & More! Shel Holtz. LC 98-8580. 368p. 1998. pap. 35.95 (*0-8144-7987-1*) AMACOM.

Public Relations Practices. 6th ed. E. Center. 2000. text 46.67 (*0-13-613803-9*) P-H.

Public Relations Practices: Managerial Case Studies & Problems. 5th ed. Allen H. Center. 574p. (C). 1995. pap. text 59.00 (*0-13-098153-2*) P-H.

Public Relations Program. Brad Hainsworth & Laurie Wilson. 112p. (C). 1995. pap. text, per. 35.95 (*0-7872-1843-X*) Kendall-Hunt.

Public Relations Programming & Production. E. W. Brody. LC 87-24626. 328p. 1988. 59.95 (*0-275-92677-X*, C2677, Praeger Pubs); pap. 24.95 (*0-275-92682-6*, B2682, Praeger Pubs) Greenwood.

Public Relations Publications. Morton. (Communications Ser.). 1919. pap. 30.00 (*0-534-52209-2*) Brooks-Cole.

Public Relations Research. E. W. Brody & Gerald C. Stone. LC 88-29270. 295p. 1989. 55.00 (*0-275-92870-5*, C2870, Praeger Pubs); pap. 18.95 (*0-275-92871-3*, B2871, Praeger Pubs) Greenwood.

Public Relations Research: An International Perspective. Danny Moss & Toby McManus. 256p. 1997. pap. 74.95 (*0-415-10995-7*) Thomson Learn.

Public Relations Research Annual, Vol. 1. Ed. by James E. Grunig & Larissa A. Grunig. 240p. 1989. 49.95 (*0-8058-0312-2*) L Erlbaum Assocs.

Public Relations Research Annual, Vol. 2. Ed. by James E. Grunig & Larissa A. Grunig. 280p. (C). 1990. text 49.95 (*0-8058-0678-4*) L Erlbaum Assocs.

Public Relations Research Annual, Vol. 3. Ed. by Larissa A. Grunig. 240p. (C). 1991. text 49.95 (*0-8058-0930-9*) L Erlbaum Assocs.

Public Relations Skills see Productive Supervisor: A Program of Practical Managerial Skills

Public Relations Specialist. Jack Rudman. (Career Examination Ser.: C-2934). 1994. pap. 29.95 (*0-8373-2934-5*) Nat Learn.

Public Relations Starter Pacs Book. (Illus.). 150p. 1996. ring bd. 49.95 (*0-914607-43-X*, 1718) Master Tchr.

Public Relations Techniques. Hunt. (C). 1994. pap. text, teacher ed. 5.75 (*0-03-001868-4*) Harcourt Coll Pubs.

Public Relations Techniques. Todd Hunt. LC 93-77649. (C). 1994. pap. text 51.50 (*0-03-046433-1*, Pub. by Harcourt Coll Pubs) Harcourt.

Public Relations Techniques. 2nd ed. Hunt. (C). 1999. pap. text. write for info. (*0-15-508054-7*) Harcourt Coll Pubs.

Public Relations Theory. Ed. by Jennings Bryant et al. 368p. 1989. pap. 39.95 (*0-8058-0692-X*) L Erlbaum Assocs.

***Public Relations Values in the New Millennium.** Elizabeth L. Toth. 136p. 1999. pap. 24.95 (*0-8058-9773-9*) L Erlbaum Assocs.

Public Relations Workbook: Writing & Techniques. Raymond Simon & Joseph M. Zappala. LC 98-50717. (Illus.). 165p. (C). 1995. pap., wbk. ed. 24.95 (*0-8442-3667-5*, NTC Business Bks) NTC Contemp Pub Co.

Public Relations Writer's Handbook. Merry Aronson & Don Spetner. LC 98-7627. 1998. 20.95 (*0-7879-4570-6*) Jossey-Bass.

***Public Relations Writing.** 112p. 1999. text, teacher ed. write for info. (*0-205-31084-2*) Allyn.

Public Relations Writing. E. W. Brody. LC 89-22983. 288p. 1990. 65.00 (*0-275-92895-0*, C2895, Greenwood Pr); pap. 22.95 (*0-275-92896-9*, B2896, Greenwood Pr) Greenwood.

Public Relations Writing. 3rd ed. Newsom. (Mass Communication Ser.). 1990. mass mkt., teacher ed. write for info. (*0-534-14390-3*) Wadsworth Pub.

***Public Relations Writing.** 6th ed. Newsom & Carrell. (Mass Communication Ser.). (C). 2000. text, wbk. ed. 19.25 (*0-534-55640-X*) Wadsworth Pub.

Public Relations Writing: An Issue Driven Behavioral Approach. 3rd ed. Kerry Tucker et al. LC 96-46216. 358p. (C). 1996. 69.00 (*0-13-256488-2*, Prentice Hall) P-H.

Public Relations Writing: Form & Style. 2nd ed. Doug Newsom & Bob Carrell. 442p. (C). 1986. pap. write for info. (*0-534-06096-X*) Wadsworth Pub.

Public Relations Writing: Form & Style. 3rd ed. Doug Newsom & Bob Carrell. 458p. (C). 1990. pap. 26.95 (*0-534-14388-1*) Wadsworth Pub.

Public Relations Writing: Form & Style. 4th ed. Doug Newsom & Bob Carrell. LC 94-33763. 504p. 1994. mass mkt. 37.95 (*0-534-25500-0*) Wadsworth Pub.

Public Relations Writing: Form & Style. 5th ed. Doug Newsom & Bob Carrell. LC 97-20092. (Mass Communication Ser.). (C). 1997. 50.95 (*0-534-52290-4*) Wadsworth Pub.

Public Relations Writing: Form & Style. 6th ed. Carrell Newsom. 2000. pap. text 50.95 (*0-534-55639-6*) Thomson Learn.

Public Relations Writing: Principles in Practice. Treadwell & Treadwell Staff. 518p. 1999. pap. text 47.00 (*0-205-30015-4*) Allyn.

***Public Relations Writing: The Essentials of Style & Format.** 4th ed. Thomas H. Bivins. LC 98-45630. 1998. pap. write for info. (*0-8442-0352-1*) NTC Contemp Pub Co.

***Public Relations Writing: The Essentials of Style & Format.** 4th ed. Thomas H. Bivins. LC 98-45630. 1999. pap. text 29.95 (*0-8442-0351-3*) NTC Contemp Pub Co.

***Public Relations Writing: Workbook.** 192p. 1999. pap. 25.00 (*0-205-31083-4*) Allyn.

Public Relations Writing & Media Techniques. 3rd ed. Dennis L. Wilcox & Lawrence W. Nolte. LC 96-26402. 494p. (C). 1997. pap. text 57.00 (*0-673-98083-9*) Longman.

Public Relations Writing Exercises. 3rd ed. Newsom. (Mass Communication Ser.). 1992. pap., wbk. ed. 8.75 (*0-534-14389-X*) Wadsworth Pub.

***Public Relations Writing Media Techniques: Instruction Manual & Test Bank.** 4th ed. (C). 2000. 26.00 (*0-321-08707-0*) Addson-Wesley Educ.

Public Relief & Private Charity. Josephine S. Lowell. LC 76-137176. (Poverty U. S. A. Historical Record Ser.). 1975. reprint ed. 16.95 (*0-405-03115-7*) Ayer.

Public Relief in New York State. Elsie Bond. 64p. 1993. reprint ed. lib. bdg. 69.00 (*0-7812-5244-X*) Rprt Serv.

***Public Religion & Urban Transformation.** Lowell W. Livezey. LC 99-50622. 280p. 1999. pap. text 18.50 (*0-8147-5158-X*) NYU Pr.

***Public Religion & Urban Transformation.** Ed. by Lowell W. Livezey. LC 99-50622. (Religion, Race, & Ethnicity Ser.). 280p. 1999. text 65.00 (*0-8147-5157-1*) NYU Pr.

Public Religions in the Modern World. Jose Casanova. LC 93-37485. 330p. 1994. pap. text 18.00 (*0-226-09535-5*); lib. bdg. 49.95 (*0-226-09534-7*) U Ch Pr.

Public Report of Basic Education in India. Anuradha De. LC 99-932760. (Illus.). 168p. 1999. pap. text 8.95 (*0-19-564870-6*) OUP.

Public Report of the White House Security Review. David L. Douglass. (Illus.). 106p. (C). 1998. reprint ed. pap. text 25.00 (*0-7881-4654-8*) DIANE Pub.

Public Report of the White House Security Review, May 1995. Government Printing Office Staff. 119p. 1995. per. 8.00 (*0-16-048388-3*) USGPO.

Public Resource Allocation & Agricultural Performance in Nepal. G. B. Thapa. 1994. pap. 25.00 (*0-7855-0475-3*, Pub. by Ratna Pustak Bhandar) St Mut.

Public Resource Management. E. Schwella et al. LC 98-138568. 368p. 1996. pap. 59.95 (*0-7021-3802-9*, Pub. by Juta & Co) Intl Spec Bk.

Public Rights in Shoreline Recreation Areas: A Selectively Annotated Bibliography, No. 894. David W. Owens. 1975. 5.00 (*0-686-20369-0*, Sage Prdcls Pr) Sage.

Public Rights, Public Rules: Constituting Citizens in the World Polity & National Policy. Connie L. McNeely. LC 98-35377. (States & Societies Ser.: No. 1). 424p. 1998. text 75.00 (*0-8153-2126-0*) Garland.

Public Roads. Government Printing Office Staff. pap. 17.00 (*0-16-011832-8*) USGPO.

Public Safety see Alaska Administrative Code--Register 150 Supplement (July 1999)

Public Safety see Alaska Administrative Code--Register 151 Supplement (October 1999)

Public Safety, Binder 6, TITLE 13. write for info. (*0-327-06377-7*) LEXIS Pub.

Public Safety see Alaska Administrative Code 4/99 Supplement

Public Safety Aide. Jack Rudman. (Career Examination Ser.: C-3740). 1994. pap. 23.95 (*0-8373-3740-2*) Nat Learn.

Public Safety & Security Administration. P. J. Ortmeier. LC 98-21489. 1998. pap. 29.95 (*0-7506-7079-7*) Buttrwrth-Heinemann.

Public Safety & Security Administration. P. J. Ortmeier. 171p. (C). 1997. pap. text 19.95 (*0-9644304-2-8*) Vanderblumen.

Public Safety & Underground Nuclear Detonations. AEC Technical Information Center Staff & Samuel Glasstone. 286p. 1971. 36.50 (*0-87079-315-2*, TID-25708) DOE.

Public Safety Background Investigation Sourcebook. Designs in Modern Learning Staff. (Public Safety Educational Technology Ser.). 196p. 1994. student ed. 35.00 (*1-885602-00-6*) Designs in Modern.

Public Safety Background Investigation Sourcebook. 2nd ed. Sid Smith. (Public Safety Educational Technology Ser.). 222p. (C). 45.00 (*1-885602-02-2*) Designs in Modern.

Public Safety Dispatcher I. Jack Rudman. (Career Examination Ser.: C-116). 1994. pap. 23.95 (*0-8373-0116-5*) Nat Learn.

Public Safety Dispatcher II. Jack Rudman. (Career Examination Ser.: C-117). 1994. pap. 27.95 (*0-8373-0117-3*) Nat Learn.

Public Safety Diver Manual. Don Freeman. 212p. 1994. pap. text. write for info. (*1-880229-19-6*) Concept Sys.

Public Safety Diver Workbook. Don Freeman. 22p. 1994. pap. text. write for info. (*1-880229-20-X*) Concept Sys.

***Public Safety Diving.** Walt Hendrick et al. LC 00-25798. (Illus.). 2000. pap. write for info. (*0-912212-94-2*) Fire Eng.

Public Safety in the Nineties: The Attorney General's Summit on Law Enforcement Responses to Violent Crime. (Illus.). 90p. (Orig.). (C). 1992. pap. text 20.00 (*0-941375-72-2*) DIANE Pub.

Public Safety Officer IV. Jack Rudman. (Career Examination Ser.: C-3053). 1994. pap. 29.95 (*0-8373-3053-X*) Nat Learn.

Public Safety Officer I. Jack Rudman. (Career Examination Ser.: C-2895). 1994. pap. 23.95 (*0-8373-2895-0*) Nat Learn.

Public Safety Officer III. Jack Rudman. (Career Examination Ser.: C-2897). 1994. pap. 29.95 (*0-8373-2897-7*) Nat Learn.

Public Safety Officer II. Jack Rudman. (Career Examination Ser.: C-2896). 1994. pap. 27.95 (*0-8373-2896-9*) Nat Learn.

Public Sale of Securities in the United States: A Guide for Foreign Bankers. Peat, Marwick, Mitchell & Co. Staff. iv, 133p. write for info. (*0-318-57034-3*) Peat Marwick.

Public Sammy: A Cat Friendship. Teddy Milne. 24p. 1998. pap. 4.50 (*0-938875-41-8*) Pittenbruach Pr.

Public Scandal see Escandalo Publico: A Very Public Affair

Public Scandals: Sexual Orientation & Criminal Law in Romania. Human Right Watch/Helsinki Staff. LC 98-84053. 104p. 1998. pap. 10.00 (*1-56432-178-9*) Hum Rts Watch.

Public School: History of Common School Education in New York. Charles Fitch. 124p. 1993. reprint ed. lib. bdg. 69.00 (*0-7812-5320-9*) Rprt Serv.

Public School Districts in the United States: A Statistical Profile, 1987-88 to 1993-94. Roger E. Levine et al. LC 98-176202. (Statistical Analysis Report National Center for Education Statistics Reports). 1998. write for info. (*0-16-049420-6*) USGPO.

Public School Education of Second-Generation Japanese in California. Reginald Bell. Ed. by Roger Daniels. LC 78-54808. (Asian Experience in North America Ser.). 1979. reprint ed. lib. bdg. 15.95 (*0-405-11264-5*) Ayer.

Public School Finance in the U.S. Kern Alexander & Richard G. Salmon. LC 94-35294. 416p. 1995. 85.00 (*0-205-16631-8*) Allyn.

Public School in the New Society: The Social Foundations of Education. Grace Graham. LC 69-11113. 416p. reprint ed. pap. 129.00 (*0-8357-9149-1*, 201322900083) Bks Demand.

Public School Law. 2nd ed. McCarthy & Nelda H. Cambron-McCabe. 1987. text 40.95 (*0-205-10489-4*, H04898) Allyn.

Public School Law. 4th ed. Martha M. McCarthy et al. LC 96-53463. 514p. 1997. 84.00 (*0-205-16676-8*) Allyn.

***Public School Laws of Missouri: 1999-2000 Edition.** 616p. 2000. pap. 30.00 (*0-327-10430-9*, 2760510) LEXIS Pub.

***Public School Laws of North Carolina: 2000 Edition.** 556p. 2000. write for info. (*0-327-10457-0*, 3049115) LEXIS Pub.

***Public School Morass: Problems, Analysis & Solutions.** ix, 106p. 2000. pap. 14.75 (*0-615-11381-8*) W Korvin.

Public School of Your Own: Your Guide to Creating & Running a Charter School. Catherine Blakemore. LC 97-77067. xiii, 256p. 1998. pap. 22.95 (*0-9661009-1-3*) Adams-Pomeroy.

Public School Plumbing Equipment. Minor W. Thomas. LC 75-177715. (Columbia University. Teachers College. Contributions to Education Ser.: No. 282). reprint ed. 37.50 (*0-404-55282-X*) AMS Pr.

Public School Reform in Puerto Rico: Sustaining Colonial Models of Development, 60. Jose Solis. LC 93-15841. 184p. 1994. 55.00 (*0-313-28978-6*, Greenwood Pr) Greenwood.

Public School Restructuring: A Selected Bibliography. Jeannette R. Olson et al. LC 95-23157. (Educational Technology Selected Bibliography Ser.). 50p. 1996. pap. 24.95 (*0-87778-291-1*) Educ Tech Pubns.

Public School System: A Voice to Revitalize. Rishel L. Whitham. LC 82-81315. 176p. (Orig.). 1982. pap. 7.95 (*0-88100-008-6*) Natl Writ Pr.

Public School System of the United States. J. M. Rice. LC 77-89224. (American Education: Its Men, Institutions, & Ideas. Series 1). 1975. reprint ed. 26.95 (*0-405-01461-9*) Ayer.

Public School Tax Management in Texas. Eugene G. Wilkins. LC 78-177642. (Columbia University. Teachers College. Contributions to Education Ser.: No. 703). reprint ed. 37.50 (*0-404-55703-1*) AMS Pr.

Public School Volunteers: Law & Liability in North Carolina. Ingrid M. Johansen. 1999. pap. 16.00 (*1-56011-358-8*) Institute Government.

Public Schooling & the Education of Democratic Citizens. Richard M. Battistoni. LC 85-9133. 200p. 1985. text 35.00 (*0-87805-280-1*) U Pr of Miss.

Public Schooling in America. Richard D. Van Scotter. LC 91-28497. (Contemporary World Issues Ser.). 238p. 1991. lib. bdg. 39.50 (*0-87436-595-3*) ABC-CLIO.

Public Schools: A Law Treatise on the Rights, Powers, Duties & Liabilities of School Boards, Officers & Teachers. Irwin Taylor. 411p. 1980. reprint ed. 43.00 (*0-8377-1204-1*, Rothman) W S Hein.

Public Schools: Issues in Budgeting & Financial Management. Ed. by John Augenblick. 204p. (Orig.). 1985. pap. text 21.95 (*0-88738-626-1*) Transaction Pubs.

Public Schools & British Opinion since 1860: The Relationship Between Contemporary Ideas & the Evolution of an English Institution. Edward C. Mack. LC 75-109777. 511p. 1971. reprint ed. lib. bdg. 75.00 (*0-8371-4267-9*, MAPS, Greenwood Pr) Greenwood.

Public Schools by Choice: Expanding Opportunities for Parents, Students & Teachers. Ed. by Joe Nathan. LC 89-80266. 266p. (Orig.). 1989. pap. 9.00 (*0-9622302-0-0*) Inst Learn Teach.

Public Schools California: A Statistical Sourcebook. 389p. (Orig.). 1996. pap. 49.00 (*1-884925-07-3*) Toucan Valley.

***Public Schools I: Is There a Way to Fix Them?** NIF Staff. 28p. 1999. pap. text 3.60 (*0-7872-6394-X*) Kendall-Hunt.

Public Schools I: Is There a Way to Fix Them? abr. ed. NIF Staff. 28p. pap. text. write for info. (*0-7872-6516-0*) Kendall-Hunt.

Public Schools in Hard Times: The Great Depression & Recent Years. David B. Tyack et al. (Illus.). 288p. 1984. pap. 15.50 (*0-674-73801-2*) HUP.

Public Schools in Hard Times: The Great Depression & Recent Years. David B. Tyack et al. LC 83-22679. (Illus.). 288p. 1984. 32.00 (*0-674-73800-4*) HUP.

Public Schools in Renaissance France. George Huppert. LC 83-1333. 184p. 1984. text 24.95 (*0-252-01053-1*) U of Ill Pr.

Public Schools of Choice: Key to Colorado Education Reform. Richard Kraft. (Issue Papers: No. 14-87). 10p. 1987. pap. text 8.00 (*1-57655-015-X*) Independ Inst.

Public Schools of Colonial Boston. Robert F. Seybolt. LC 73-89231. (American Education: Its Men, Institutions, & Ideas. Series 1). 1975. reprint ed. 15.95 (*0-405-01469-4*) Ayer.

Public Schools, Private Prospects: Lessons from English School Reform. 2nd ed. Carla Claycomb. 24p. 1998. pap. 9.00 (*1-58434-025-8*) NASBE.

Public Schools That Work: Creating Community. Ed. by Gregory A. Smith. (Critical Social Thought Ser.). 256p. (C). (gr. 13). 1993. 31.99 (*0-415-90577-X*, A7172) Routledge.

Public Schools U. S. A. A Comparative Guide to School Districts. 2nd ed. Charles Harrison. LC 91-30607. 496p. (Orig.). 1991. 44.95 (*1-56079-081-4*) Petersons.

Public Schools vs. American Political Liberty: Restoring Freedom of Education in a Nation Imperiled by Public Schools. George L. Bate. LC 87-82986. 91p. (Orig.). 1987. pap. 7.00 (*0-944776-00-0*) Freesponse Pr.

Public Schools/Private Enterprise: What You Should Know & Do about Privatization. Samuel Flam & William Keane. LC 97-60458. 190p. 1997. text 44.95 (*1-56676-535-8*) Scarecrow.

Public Science & Public Policy in Victorian England. Roy M. MacLeod. (Collected Studies: Vol. CS509). 352p. 1996. 106.95 (*0-86078-535-1*, Pub. by Variorum) Ashgate Pub Co.

Public Scrutiny of Protection. Olivier Long. 114p. 1989. text 22.95 (*0-566-05780-8*, Pub. by Avebry) Ashgate Pub Co.

Public Sculptor: Lorado Taft & the Beautification of Chicago. Timothy J. Garvey. LC 87-24481. (Illus.). 240p. 1988. text 24.95 (*0-252-01501-0*) U of Ill Pr.

Public Sculpture: America's Legacy. 64p. 1994. 85.00 incl. VHS, sl. (*1-56290-104-4*, 6048) Crystal.

Public Sculpture & the Civic Ideal in New York City, 1890-1930. Michele H. Bogart. LC 97-839. 406p. 1997. pap. text 27.50 (*1-56098-766-9*) Smithsonian.

Public Sculpture & the Civic Ideal in New York City, 1890-1930. Michele H. Bogart. LC 88-21815. (Illus.). 408p. 1997. 48.00 (*0-226-06309-7*) U Ch Pr.

***Public Sculpture in New Jersey: Monuments to Collective Identity.** Meredith Arms Bzdak. LC 98-55319. 220p. 1999. pap. 22.00 (*0-8135-2700-7*) Rutgers U Pr.

***Public Sculpture in New Jersey: Monuments to Collective Identiy.** Meredith A. Bzdak. LC 98-55319. (Illus.). 220p. 1999. 55.00 (*0-8135-2699-X*) Rutgers U Pr.

***Public Sculpture in Wisconsin: An Atlas of Outdoor Monuments, Memorials & Masterpieces in the Badger State.** Anton Rajer & Christine Style. (Illus.). 160p. (Orig.). 1999. pap. text 27.95 (*0-9664180-2-6*) U of Wis Pr.

Public Sculpture of Birmingham. George Noszlopy. Ed. by Jeremy Beach. (Public Sculpture of Britain Ser.: Vol. 2). (Illus.). 256p. 1998. 58.95 (*0-85323-682-8*, Pub. by Liverpool Univ Pr); pap. 25.95 (*0-85323-692-5*, Pub. by Liverpool Univ Pr) Intl Spec Bk.

Public Sculpture of Liverpool. Terry Cavanagh. LC 96-225806. (Public Sculpture of Britain Ser.: Vol. 1). 58.95 (*0-85323-701-8*, Pub. by Liverpool Univ Pr) Intl Spec Bk.

Public Sculpture of Liverpool. Terry Cavanagh. LC 96-225806. (Public Sculpture of Britain Ser.: Vol. 1). (Illus.). 1998. pap. 25.95 (*0-85323-711-5*, Pub. by Liverpool Univ Pr) Intl Spec Bk.

***Public Sculpture of North-East England.** Paul Usherwood et al. (Illus.). 368p. 2000. 76.95 (*0-85323-625-9*, Pub. by Liverpool Univ Pr); pap. 32.00 (*0-85323-635-6*, Pub. by Liverpool Univ Pr) Intl Spec Bk.

Public Secondary Education in Canada. Walter F. Dyde. LC 72-176736. (Columbia University. Teachers College. Contributions to Education Ser.: No. 345). reprint ed. 37.50 (*0-404-55345-1*) AMS Pr.

Public Secrets. Nora Roberts. 512p. 1998. mass mkt. 7.50 (*0-553-28578-5*) Bantam.

Public Secrets: Collected Skirmishes of Ken Knabb (1970-1997) Ken Knabb. LC 96-95067. 408p. (Orig.). 1997. pap. 15.00 (*0-939682-03-6*, SAN 216-2261) Bur Public Secrets.

***Public Secrets, Public Spaces: Cinema & Civility in China.** Stephanie Donald. LC 99-44346. 240p. 2000. pap. 24.95 (*0-8476-9877-7*); text 64.00 (*0-8476-9876-9*) Rowman.

Public Sector: Challenge for Coordination & Learning. rev. ed. Ed. by Franz-Xaver Kaufmann. (Studies in Organization: No. 31). xii, 533p. (C). 1991. pap. text 39.95 (*3-11-012380-0*, 174-91) De Gruyter.

Public Sector: Concepts, Models & Approaches. Jan-Erik Lane. (Illus.). 240p. (C). 1993. text 65.00 (*0-8039-8818-4*); pap. text 21.95 (*0-8039-8819-2*) Sage.

Public Sector: Concepts, Models & Approaches. Jan-Erik Lane. 288p. 1995. pap. 21.95 (*0-8039-7652-6*) Sage.

Public Sector: Concepts, Models & Approaches. 2nd ed. Jan-Erik Lane. 288p. 1995. 69.95 (*0-8039-7651-8*) Sage.

Public Sector Accounting. Michael Rogers. 318p. (C). 1999. pap. 64.50 (*0-7487-1908-3*, Pub. by S Thornes Pubs) Trans-Atl Phila.

Public Sector Accounting. 4th ed. Rowan Jones & Maurice Pendlebury. 320p. (Orig.). 1996. pap. 57.50 (*0-273-61415-0*, Pub. by Pitman Pub) Trans-Atl Phila.

Public Sector Accounting & Accountability in Australia. Warwick Funnell & Kathie Cooper. 320p. (C). 1998. pap. 49.95 (*0-86840-768-2*, Pub. by New South Wales Univ Pr) Intl Spec Bk.

Public Sector Accounting & Financial Control. 3rd ed. D. Henley et al. 288p. 1990. pap. 34.50 (*0-412-02751-8*, A4474, Chapman & Hall NY) Chapman & Hall.

Public Sector Accounting & Financial Control. 4th ed. D. Henley et al. LC 92-25125. (Accounting & Finance Ser.). 1992. mass mkt. 37.95 (*0-412-46380-6*) Chapman & Hall.

P

Public Sector & the Latin America Crisis. 351p. 1991. pap. 19.95 (*1-55815-118-4*); 6.95 (*1-55815-125-7*) ICS Pr.

Public Sector Auditing: Practical Techniques for an Integrated approach. P. Jones & Jonathan B. Bates. 300p. 1991. mass mkt. 81.95 (*0-412-36260-0*, A5100) Chapman & Hall.

Public Sector Auditing: Practical Techniques for an Integrated Approach. 2nd ed. P. C. Jones & J. Bates. (Illus.). 416p. 1991. mass mkt. 89.95 (*0-412-56500-5*, Chap & Hall NY) Chapman & Hall.

Public-Sector Aviation Issues: Graduate Research Award Papers, 1990-1991. LC 92-15610. 1992. write for info. (*0-309-05171-1*) Transport Res Bd.

Public-Sector Aviation Issues: Graduate Research Award Papers 1992-1993 (TRR 1428) Ed. by Norman Solomon. (Transportation Research Record Ser.). (Illus.). 44p. 1994. pap. text 19.00 (*0-309-05506-7*, R1428) Transport Res Bd.

Public-Sector Aviation Issues: Graduation Research Award Papers 1988-1989. (Transportation Research Record Ser.: No. 1257). 57p. 1990. 12.00 (*0-309-05012-X*) Transport Res Bd.

Public Sector Banks in India & the Productivity Question. K. Srinivasa Rao. (C). 1989. 34.00 (*81-7024-252-5*, Pub. by Ashish Pub Hse) S Asia.

Public Sector Bargaining in the 1980's. John Sheldrake & Rene Saran. 104p. 1988. text 72.95 (*0-566-05597-X*, Pub. by Dartmth Pub) Ashgate Pub Co.

Public Sector Budgets: A Comparative Study. Ed. by Attiat F. Ott. (Illus.). 304p. 1993. 95.00 (*1-85278-618-3*) E Elgar.

Public Sector Communication: How Organizations Manage Information. Doris Graber. LC 91-40338. 424p. 1992. text 43.95 (*0-87187-685-X*) Congr Quarterly.

Public Sector Communication: How Organizations Manage Information. Doris Graber. LC 91-40338. 424p. (YA). 1992. pap. text 27.95 (*0-87187-560-8*) Congr Quarterly.

Public Sector Compensation: An Overview of Present Practices & Emerging Trends. Howard W. Risher. LC 98-116487. 1998. 34.65 (*1-57963-051-0*) Am Compensation.

***Public Sector Corruption: An International Survey of Prevention Measures.** Alexandra Mills. 120p. 1999. pap. 31.00 (*92-64-17071-5*, 42 1999 04 1 P, Pub. by Org for Econ) OECD.

Public Sector Decentralization: Economic Policy & Sector Investment Programs. rev. ed. Jerry M. Silverman. LC 92-35725. (Technical Paper, Africa Technical Department Ser.: No. 188). 123p. 1992. pap. 22.00 (*0-8213-2279-6*, 12279) World Bank.

Public Sector Decision-Making. D. Pearce. 1980. pap. 24.00 (*0-08-025832-8*, Pergamon Pr) Elsevier.

Public Sector Decision Making: Legal Fringe Benefits & Union Parameters. Ed. by Paul A. Weinstein. LC 78-70342. (Public Sector Labor Relations Conference Board Ser.: No. 3). 1978. pap. 7.50 (*0-913400-02-5*) Pub Sect Lab Rel.

Public Sector Designs. Clint Page & Penelope Cuff. LC 83-82147. (Illus.). 64p. (Orig.). 1984. pap. 12.00 (*0-941182-12-6*) Partners Livable.

Public Sector Economics. British Association for the Advancement of Science. Ed. by A. R. Prest. LC 68-6526. vii, 206p. 1968. 37.50 (*0-678-06765-1*) Kelley.

Public Sector Economics. Robert E. Millward et al. LC 82-4609. (Surveys in Economics Ser.). 293p. reprint ed. pap. 90.90 (*0-7837-1590-0*, 204188200024) Bks Demand.

Public Sector Economics. 4th ed. C. V. Brown & P. M. Jackson. (Illus.). 500p. (C). 1992. pap. text 37.95 (*0-631-16208-9*) Blackwell Pubs.

Public Sector Economics: Papers Presented at the 1967 Section F Meeting of the British Association for the Advancement of Science. British Association for the Advancement of Science Staff & A. R. Prest. LC 79-406507. vii, 206p. 1968. write for info. (*0-7190-0330-X*) Manchester Univ Pr.

Public Sector Efficiency Measurement: Applications of Data Envelopment Analysis. J. A. Ganley & J. S. Cubbin. LC 92-27224. xiv,180p. 1992. 125.50 (*0-444-89047-5*) Elsevier.

Public Sector Employment in a Time of Transition. Ed. by Dale Belman et al. LC 97-171707. (ILR Press Book - IRRA Research Volume Ser.). 1996. pap. 24.95 (*0-913447-67-6*) Indus Relations Res.

Public Sector Ethics: Finding & Implementing Values. Ed. by Charles Samford & Noel Preston. (Studies in Public Sector Management: No. 1). 232p. (C). 1998. 85.00 (*0-415-19481-4*, D6278) Routledge.

Public Sector Financial Control & Accounting. 2nd ed. John Glynn. LC 92-29621. 1993. pap. 43.95 (*0-631-18862-2*) Blackwell Pubs.

Public Sector Financial Management. H. Coombs & E. Jenkins. (Series in Accounting & Finance). 288p. (C). 1991. mass mkt. 52.95 (*0-412-38550-3*, A5664) Chapman & Hall.

Public Sector Financial Management. Bernard Jones. LC 96-15745. 1996. write for info. (*0-07-707888-8*) McGraw.

Public Sector Financial Management. 2nd ed. H. M. Coombs. 1994. pap. 31.95 (*0-412-56560-9*) Chapman & Hall.

Public Sector Financial Management. 2nd ed. Coombs & Jenkins. (ITBP Textbooks Ser.). 1994. pap. 34.95 (*1-86152-206-1*) Thomson Learn.

Public Sector Financial Management: Teachers' Manual. 2nd ed. H. M. Coombs. 88p. (Orig.). 1994. pap. text 52.00 (*0-412-57130-7*, Chap & Hall NY) Chapman & Hall.

Public Sector Housing Law. 2nd ed. David J. Hughes. 392p. 1987. pap. 46.00 (*0-406-60062-7*, UK, MICHIE) LEXIS Pub.

***Public Sector in Canada: Programs, Finance & Policy.** John C. Strick. 288p. 1999. pap. 23.95 (*1-55077-101-9*) Thompson Educ.

Public Sector in Latin America. Ed. by Alfred H. Saulniers. LC 83-3646. (Special Publications). x, 235p. (Orig.). 1984. pap. 9.95 (*0-86728-009-3*) U TX Inst Lat Am Stud.

Public Sector Jobs. Michael Rinzler. 1992. pap. write for info. (*0-201-52230-6*) Addison-Wesley.

Public Sector Labor & Employment Law. Jerome Lefkowitz. LC 87-62965. 1100p. 1987. text 90.00 (*0-942954-18-1*) NYS Bar.

Public Sector Labor & Employment Law: 1995 Supplement. New York Bar Association Staff. Ed. by Rosemary A. Townley. 440p. 1995. pap. text 45.00 (*0-942954-77-7*) NYS Bar.

Public Sector Labor Law: Counseling Clients, Negotiating Contracts & Making Law in the Nineties. 189p. 1993. pap. 30.00 (*0-614-26705-6*, 19356); pap. 92.00 incl. audio (*0-614-26706-4*, 29356); pap. 175.00 incl. VHS (*0-614-26707-2*, 39356) NYS Bar.

Public Sector Labor Relations. 3rd ed. David Lewin et al. LC 82-64038. 648p. (C). 1988. pap. 29.95 (*0-669-12893-7*) Lxngtn Bks.

Public Sector Labor Relations in Maryland: Issues & Prospects. Ed. by Donald W. O'Connell. LC 72-92069. (PSLRCB Publication Ser.: No. 1). (Illus.). (Orig.). 1972. pap. 7.50 (*0-913400-00-9*) Pub Sect Lab Rel.

Public Sector Labor Relations in Wisconsin. Charles C. Mulcahy et al. 620p. 1988. ring bd. 75.00 (*0-945574-03-7*) State Bar WI.

Public Sector Management. Ed. by Marcia L. Whicker & Todd W. Areson. LC 89-36913. 290p. 1990. 62.95 (*0-275-93381-4*, C3381, Praeger Pubs) Greenwood.

Public Sector Management. 3rd ed. Norman Flynn. LC 96-35065. 1997. pap. write for info. (*0-13-269259-7*) P-H.

Public Sector Management, 2 vols., Set. Ed. by John Bourn. LC 95-7413. (International Library of Management). 784p. 1995. 346.95 (*1-85521-517-9*, Pub. by Dartmth Pub) Ashgate Pub Co.

Public Sector Management: Theory, Critique & Practice. Ed. by David McKevitt & Alan Lawton. 320p. 1994. 75.00 (*0-8039-7712-3*); pap. 32.00 (*0-8039-7713-1*) Sage.

***Public Sector Management in Australia: New Challenges, New Directions.** Ciaran O'Faircheallaigh et al. 327p. 2000. 37.95 (*0-7329-4073-7*, Pub. by Macmill Educ) Paul & Co Pubs.

Public Sector Management, Systems, & Ethics. Louis C. Gawthrop. LC 83-48176. (Illus.). 183p. reprint ed. pap. 56.80 (*0-8357-3954-6*, 205705000004) Bks Demand.

Public Sector Managerial Effectiveness: Theory & Practice in the NHS. Hugh Flanagan & Peter Spurgeon. LC 95-15674. 160p. 1995. 108.95 (*0-335-15777-7*); pap. 33.95 (*0-335-15776-9*) OpUniv Pr.

Public Sector Mediation. Arnold M. Zack. LC 85-7702. 215p. 1985. reprint ed. pap. 66.70 (*0-608-00704-8*, 206147600009) Bks Demand.

Public Sector Pay & Adjustment: Lessons from Five Countries. Chrisopher Colclough. LC 96-22701. 176p. (C). 1997. 80.00 (*0-415-15338-7*) Routledge.

***Public Sector Pay Determination in The European Union.** R F Elliott. LC 99-11253. 1999. text 69.95 (*0-312-22320-X*) St Martin.

Public Sector Payrolls. Ed. by David A. Wise. LC 86-24962. (National Bureau of Economic Research Project Report Ser.). x, 336p. (C). 1987. lib. bdg. 48.00 (*0-226-90291-9*) U Ch Pr.

Public Sector Performance: A Turning Point. Trudi C. Miller. LC 83-23895. 288p. 1984. pap. 15.95 (*0-8018-3147-4*) Johns Hopkins.

***Public Sector Performance: Management, Motivation & Measurement.** Richard C. Kearney & Evan M. Berman. LC 99-10751. 340p. 1999. 69.00 (*0-8133-6827-8*, Pub. by Westview); pap. 29.00 (*0-8133-6828-6*, Pub. by Westview) HarpC.

Public Sector Privatization: Alternative Approaches to Service Delivery. Ed. by Lawrence K. Finley. LC 88-36486. 198p. 1989. 57.95 (*0-89930-330-7*, FPC/, Quorum Bks) Greenwood.

Public Sector Productivity Programs: Background & Analysis with Special Reference to State Governments. Richard L. Schott. (Policy Research Project Report Ser.: No. 19). 44p. 1977. pap. 3.00 (*0-89940-612-2*) LBJ Sch Pub Aff.

Public Sector Reform: Rationale, Trends & Problems. Ed. by Jan-Erik Lane. 320p. 1997. 85.00 (*0-7619-5366-3*); pap. 29.95 (*0-7619-5367-1*) Sage.

Public Sector Reform & the Citizen's Charter. Ed. by Chris Willett. (Law in Its Social Setting Ser.). 126p. 1996. pap. 44.00 (*1-85431-601-X*, Pub. by Blackstone Pr) Gaunt.

Public Sector Reform in Hong Kong: Key Concepts, Progress-to-Date & Future Directions. Ed. by Jane C. Lee & Anthony B. Cheung. LC 96-118897. 338p. (C). 1997. pap. text 27.50 (*962-201-655-3*, Pub. by Chinese Univ) U of Mich Pr.

***Public Sector Risk Management.** Martin Fone. 384p. 2000. 145.00 (*0-7506-5161-X*) Buttrwrth-Heinemann.

***Public Sector Road Transport Corporation: A Comparative Study with Private Sector** G. J. Gunaseelan. LC 98-901887. xvi, 176 p. 1998. write for info. (*81-7629-081-5*) S Asia.

Public Sector Transformation: Rethinking Markets & Hierarchies in Government. Frieder Naschold & Casten Von Otter. LC 96-291. (Dialogues on Work & Innovation Ser.: Vol. 1). vi, 176p. 1996. pap. 47.95 (*1-55619-825-6*) J Benjamins Pubng Co.

Public Self & Private Self. Ed. by Roy F. Baumeister. (Social Psychology Ser.). (Illus.). 270p. 1986. 63.00 (*0-387-96303-0*) Spr-Verlag.

Public Selves & Political Stages. Leigh Woods & Agusta Gunnarsdottir. (Contemporary Theatre Studies). 304p. 1997. text 65.00 (*3-7186-5873-9*, Harwood Acad Pubs); pap. text 22.00 (*3-7186-5883-6*, Harwood Acad Pubs) Gordon & Breach.

Public Service. Holzer. LC 99-49305. 2000. pap. text 29.00 (*0-8133-6826-X*) Westview.

Public Service: Callings, Commitments & Contributions. Marc Holzer. LC 99-49305. 340p. 1999. 70.00 (*0-8133-6825-1*) Westview.

Public Service: Issues Confronting the Federal Civilian Workforce. 61p. (Orig.). (C). 1993. pap. text 25.00 (*1-56806-921-9*) DIANE Pub.

Public Service Accountability: A Comparative Perspective. fac. ed. Ed. by Joseph G. Jabbra & O. P. Dwivedi. LC 88-13220. (Illus.). 287p. 1989. pap. 89.00 (*0-7837-7581-4*, 204733400007) Bks Demand.

Public Service Alliance of Canada: A Look at a Union in the Public Sector. Maurice Lemelin. (Monograph & Research Ser.: No. 21). 1978. 6.50 (*0-89215-085-8*) U Cal LA Indus Rel.

***Public Service & Democracy: Ethical Imperatives for the 21st Century.** Louis C. Gawthrop. LC 98-25377. (Ethical Imperatives for the 21st Century Ser.). (Illus.). 184p. (C). 1998. pap. text 21.95 (*1-56643-070-4*, Chatham House Pub) Seven Bridges.

Public Service & Democracy: The Ethical Imperatives for the 21st Century. Louis C. Gawthrop. LC 98-25377. (Illus.). 184p. 1998. 35.00 (*1-56643-075-5*, Chatham House Pub) Seven Bridges.

Public Service Careers, 5 vols., Set. 89.00 (*0-685-23047-3*, CG369) Ready Ref Pr.

Public Service Commission Law of Maryland: 1998 Edition. ii, 407p. 1998. write for info. (*0-327-06293-2*, 26349-11) LEXIS Pub.

Public Service Commission Law of Maryland, 1998 Edition. LC 99-180256. 338p. 1998. write for info. (*0-327-06363-7*, 2634911) LEXIS Pub.

Public Service Commission Law of West Virginia: 1998 Edition. Ed. by Gail D. Haskins. LC 99-170047. 233p. 1998. 22.00 (*0-327-05787-4*, 36501-12) LEXIS Pub.

Public Service Employment: A Field Evaluation. Richard P. Nathan et al. LC 81-4596. 121p. 1981. pap. 12.95 (*0-8157-5987-8*) Brookings.

Public Service Employment: An Analysis of Its History, Problems & Prospects. Ed. by Alan Gartner et al. LC 72-93186. (Special Studies in U. S. Economic, Social & Political Issues). 1973. 59.50 (*0-275-06630-4*) Irvington.

Public Service Employment: The Experience of a Decade. Robert F. Cook et al. LC 85-22495. 131p. 1985. text 22.00 (*0-88099-030-9*); pap. text 12.00 (*0-88099-031-7*) W E Upjohn.

***Public Service Employment Relations in Europe: Transformation, Modernization or Inertia?** Ed. by Stephen Bach et al. LC 99-10532. 288p. (C). 1999. text write for info. (*0-415-20342-2*) Routledge.

Public Service Employment Relations in Europe: Transformation, Modernization or Inertia? Stephen E. Bach. LC 99-10532. (Routledge in Employment Relations Studies). 1999. pap. write for info. (*0-415-20343-0*) Routledge.

Public Service, Ethics, & Constitutional Practice. John A. Rohr. LC 98-28445. (Studies in Government & Public Policy). 208p. 1999. 29.95 (*0-7006-0925-3*) U Pr of KS.

Public Service, Ethics & Constitutional Practice. John A. Rohr. LC 98-28445. (Studies in Government & Public Policy). 208p. 1999. pap. 15.95 (*0-7006-0926-1*) U Pr of KS.

Public Service in Higher Education: Practices & Priorities. Patricia H. Crosson. Ed. & Frwd. by Jonathan D. Fife. LC 84-166237. (ASHE-ERIC Higher Education Reports: No. 83-7). 138p. (Orig.). 1983. pap. 24.00 (*0-913317-06-3*) GWU Grad Schl E&HD.

Public Service in the New States: A Study in Some Trained Manpower Problems. Kenneth G. Younger. LC 87-8684. 121p. 1987. reprint ed. lib. bdg. 57.50 (*0-313-25959-3*, YOPS, Greenwood Pr) Greenwood.

Public Service Labour Relations: Recent Trends & Future Prospects. Tiziano Treu et al. xiii, 287p. (Orig.). 1987. pap. 29.25 (*92-2-106049-7*) Intl Labour Office.

Public Service Liberalism: Telecommunications & Transitions in Public Policy. Alan Stone. LC 90-22302. 310p. 1991. reprint ed. pap. 96.10 (*0-608-02555-0*, 206320000004) Bks Demand.

Public Service Reforms Issues of Accountability & Public Law: Towards Efficiency & Empowerment. Dawn H. Oliver & Gavin Drewry. LC 96-529. (Constitutional Reform Ser.). 192p. (C). 1996. text 99.00 (*1-85567-391-6*) Bks Intl VA.

Public Service Responsibility of Broadcast Licensees. Federal Communications Commission. LC 74-5225. (Telecommunications Ser.). 64p. 1980. reprint ed. 20.95 (*0-405-06064-5*) Ayer.

Public Service Trade Unionism & Radical Politics. Chris Miller. LC 95-39634. (Illus.). 312p. 1996. 79.95 (*1-85521-641-8*, Pub. by Dartmth Pub) Ashgate Pub Co.

Public Service Trolley Lines in New Jersey. expanded rev. ed. Edward Hamm, Jr. Ed. by Marion Harris. LC 97-2949. (Illus.). 400p. 1997. text 63.00 (*0-933449-29-1*) Transport Trails.

Public Services & Citizenship in European Law: Public & Labour Law Perspectives. Mark Freedland. 224p. 1999. text 72.00 (*0-19-826575-1*) OUP.

Public Services & Market Mechanisms. Kieron Walsh. LC 94-43979. 1995. text 59.95 (*0-312-12553-4*) St Martin.

Public Services Broadcasting in Four English-Speaking Countries: A Special Issue of the "Journal of Media Economics", Vol. 9, No. 1, 1996. Brown. 1996. pap. 20.00 (*0-8058-9914-6*) L Erlbaum Assocs.

Public Services in Older Cities. 56p. 1968. 7.00 (*0-318-16378-0*, 109) Regional Plan Assn.

Public Services Management. Aidan Rose & Alan Lawton. 448p. 1998. pap. 54.50 (*0-273-62524-1*, Pub. by Pitman Pub) Trans-Atl Phila.

Public Services Officer. Jack Rudman. (Career Examination Ser.: C-636). 1994. pap. 29.95 (*0-8373-0636-1*) Nat Learn.

Public Sewage Disposal Systems & Structures: Snip 2.04.03-85. Russia's Gosstroy Staff. Ed. & Tr. by Snip Register, Inc. Staff from RUS. (Building Codes of Russia Ser.). (Illus.). iv, 120p. 1998. ring bd. 599.95 (*1-57937-062-4*, S4000385) Snip Register.

***Public Sex: The Culture of Radical Sex.** 2nd rev. ed. Pat Califia. 250p. 2000. pap. 16.95 (*1-57344-096-5*, Pub. by Cleis Pr) Publishers Group.

***Public Sex in a Latin Society: Little Pink Riding Hood & the Big Bad Wolf.** Ed. by Jacobo Schifter. LC 99-16945. 215p. (C). 1999. pap. 19.95 (*1-56023-986-7*, Harrington Park); text 39.95 (*1-56023-985-9*, Harrington Park) Haworth Pr.

***Public Sex/Gay Space.** William L. Leap. LC 98-26490. (Between Men - Between Women Ser.). 304p. 1998. 49.50 (*0-231-10690-4*) Col U Pr.

Public Sex/Gay Space. William L. Leap. LC 98-26490. (Illus.). 304p. 1999. pap. 17.50 (*0-231-10691-2*) Col U Pr.

***Public Sociology: From Social Facts to Literary Acts.** Ben Agger. (New Social Formations Ser.). 272p. 2000. pap. text 19.95 (*0-8476-9841-6*) Rowman.

***Public Sociology: From Social Facts to Literary Acts.** Ben Agger. (New Social Formations Ser.). 272p. 2000. text 65.00 (*0-8476-9840-8*) Rowman.

Public Sorrows & Private Pleasures. William Earle. LC 75-28911. (Indiana University Studies in Phenomenology & Existential Philosophy). 191p. reprint ed. pap. 59.30 (*0-608-13186-5*, 205603300044) Bks Demand.

Public Space. Stephen Carr et al. (Cambridge Series in Environment & Behavior). (Illus.). 416p. (C). 1993. text 85.00 (*0-521-35148-0*); pap. text 30.95 (*0-521-35960-0*) Cambridge U Pr.

Public Space: Design, Use & Management. Ed. by Chua B. Huat. 240p. (Orig.). 1992. pap. 38.50 (*9971-69-164-7*, Pub. by Sngapore Univ Pr) Coronet Bks.

Public Space Design in Museums. David A. Robillard. (Publications in Architecture & Urban Planning: No. R84-7). (Illus.). iv, 73p. 1984. 12.50 (*0-938744-36-4*) U of Wis Ctr Arch-Urban.

Public Speaker's Bible: How to Capitolize on Your Personal Style- Avoid the 9 Myths. Loren D. Crane. LC 98-87547. (Illus.). 192p. 2000. pap. 20.00 (*0-9667330-0-2*) Brain Research.

***Public Speaker's Joke Book.** 2nd ed. Kevin Goldstein-Jackson. (Illus.). 192p. 2001. pap. 8.95 (*0-7160-2071-8*, Pub. by Elliot RW Bks) Midpt Trade.

Public Speaker/The Public Listener. 2nd rev. ed. Andrew D. Wolvin et al. LC 98-21409. (Illus.). 330p. (C). 1999. pap. text. write for info. (*1-891487-12-4*) Roxbury Pub Co.

Public Speaking. (Quick Study Academic Ser.). 4p. pap. 2.95 (*1-57222-133-X*) Barcharts.

***Public Speaking.** (C). 2001. write for info. (*0-8013-3339-3*) Longman.

Public Speaking. Boy Scouts of America. (Illus.). 44p. (YA). (gr. 6-12). 1969. pap. 2.90 (*0-8395-3373-X*, 33373) BSA.

Public Speaking. Candy Center & Jean-Pau Nadeau. 176p. (C). 1995. per. 25.95 (*0-7872-1254-7*, 41125401) Kendall-Hunt.

Public Speaking. Larry Clifton. 96p. (C). 1994. pap. text, per. 17.95 (*0-8403-9972-3*) Kendall-Hunt.

Public Speaking. Thomas Farrell & Maureen M. Farrell. 192p. (C). 1996. text 24.95 (*0-256-18701-0*, Irwn McGrw-H) McGrw-H Hghr Educ.

Public Speaking. Fraleigh. 2000. pap. text. write for info. (*0-312-17072-6*) St Martin.

Public Speaking. Clella I. Jaffe. (Speech & Theater Ser.). 1994. pap., student ed. 13.95 (*0-534-23065-2*) Wadsworth Pub.

Public Speaking. Joffe. (Adaptable Courseware-Softside Ser.). Date not set. pap. 24.00 (*0-534-16071-9*) Wadsworth Pub.

Public Speaking. O'Hair. Date not set. pap. text. write for info. (*0-312-19219-3*) St Martin.

Public Speaking. Stewart O'Hair. LC 97-65197. 1998. pap. text 44.95 (*0-312-13722-2*) St Martin.

Public Speaking. Stewart O'Hair. 1999. pap. text, lab manual ed. 10.00 (*0-312-13721-4*) St Martin.

Public Speaking. Brian Schriner. 384p. (C). 1996. text, student ed., wbk. ed. 36.80 (*0-536-59380-9*) Pearson Custom.

Public Speaking. Ulloth. (Speech & Theater Ser.). 1997. mass mkt., wbk. ed. 12.50 (*0-314-20856-9*) West Pub.

Public Speaking. Andrew D. Wolvin. (C). 1992. pap., teacher ed. 3.96 (*0-395-65558-7*); pap. text 37.16 (*0-395-54011-9*) HM.

Public Speaking. Zimmerman. Date not set. pap. text, teacher ed. 11.00 (*0-314-45148-X*) West Pub.

Public Speaking. 2nd ed. Laurie E. Rozakis. (Complete Idiot's Guides (Lifestyle) Ser.). (Illus.). 358p. 1999. pap. 16.95 (*0-02-863383-0*, Pub. by Macmillan Gen Ref) S&S Trade.

Public Speaking. 3rd ed. Beebe. 1997. text 53.27 (*0-205-28003-X*, Longwood Div) Allyn.

Public Speaking, 3 vols. 3rd ed. Osborn. LC 93-78696. (C). 1993. pap. text 39.96 (*0-395-67578-2*) HM.

Public Speaking. 4th ed. King. 1998. wbk. ed. 16.24 (*0-07-154045-8*) McGraw.

Public Speaking, 4 vols. 4th ed. Micheal Osborn. LC 96-76943. (C). 1996. pap. text 39.16 (*0-395-80882-0*) HM.

P

An Asterisk (*) at the beginning of an entry indicates that the title is appearing for the first time.

Public Speaking, 4 vols. 4th annot. ed. Michael Osborn & Suzanne Osborn. (C). 1996. text, teacher ed. 41.16 (*0-395-80883-9*) HM.

***Public Speaking.** 5th ed. Osborn. 1999. pap. text, teacher ed. 8.97 (*0-395-96048-7*) HM.

***Public Speaking.** 5th ed. Michael Osborn & Suzanne Osborn. 1999. pap. text 34.17 (*0-395-96046-0*) HM.

Public Speaking: A Cultural Perspective. Clella I. Jaffe. LC 94-29028. 446p. 1994. pap. 36.95 (*0-534-23064-4*) Wadsworth Pub.

Public Speaking: A Handbook for Christians. 2nd ed. Duane Litfin. LC 91-42786. 368p. 1992. pap. 24.99 (*0-8010-5675-6*) Baker Bks.

***Public Speaking: An Audience-Centered Approach.** 4th ed. Beebe. LC 99-14266. 454p. 1999. pap. text 50.00 (*0-205-29559-2*) Allyn.

Public Speaking: An Experiential Approach. Dana R. Ulloth & Richard Alderfer. LC 96-31872. (C). 1997. 50.95 (*0-314-20571-3*) West Pub.

Public Speaking: An Experiential Approach. 2nd ed. Ulloth. (Speech & Theater Ser.). Date not set. 31.25 (*0-534-52930-5*) Wadsworth Pub.

Public Speaking: Analysis & Application. Allan M. Winkler. 192p. 1993. spiral bd. 21.95 (*0-8403-7927-7*) Kendall-Hunt.

***Public Speaking: Audience Centered Approach.** 4th ed. 528p. 1999. write for info. (*0-205-30485-0*) S&S Trade.

Public Speaking: Concepts & Skills for a Diverse Society. 2nd ed. Clella Jaffe. LC 97-20144. (Speech & Theater Ser.). (C). 1997. pap. 50.95 (*0-534-52920-8*) Wadsworth Pub.

Public Speaking: Concepts & Skills for a Diverse Society. 3rd ed. Jaffe. (Speech & Theater Ser.). 2000. 31.25 (*0-534-52992-5*) Wadsworth Pub.

***Public Speaking: Concepts & Skills for a Diverse Society.** 3rd ed. Clella Iles Jaffe. LC 00-32497. 2000. write for info. (*0-534-52994-1*) Wadsworth Pub.

***Public Speaking: Concepts, Skills for a Diverse Society.** 3rd ed. Jaffe. (Speech & Theater Ser.). (C). 2000. text 16.75 (*0-534-52998-4*) Wadsworth Pub.

***Public Speaking: Connecting You & Your Audience.** Patricia Andrews et al. LC 98-71976. 1999. write for info. (*0-395-84603-X*) HM.

Public Speaking: Content & Communication. 6th ed. Charles Mudd & Malcolm O. Sillars. (Illus.). 424p. (C). 1991. pap. text 24.95 (*0-88133-587-8*) Waveland Pr.

Public Speaking: Developmental Guide. 3rd ed. (C). 1995. write for info. (*0-8087-1483-X*) Pearson Custom.

***Public Speaking: From Ideas to Action.** David Cheshier et al. 190p. (C). 1998. spiral bd. 33.95 (*0-7872-4696-4*) Kendall-Hunt.

Public Speaking: Guide To Better Presentations. 128p. (C). 1999. pap. text 18.00 (*0-536-02457-X*) Pearson Custom.

Public Speaking: Planning, Patterning & Presenting. Daniel J. O'Neill. 164p. (Orig.). (C). 1992. pap. text 16.95 (*0-89641-205-9*) American Pr.

Public Speaking: Process & Product. 2nd ed. Harold R. Ross & Bill Hill. 240p. 1995. per. 29.95 (*0-8403-8843-8*) Kendall-Hunt.

***Public Speaking: Proven Techniques for Giving Successful Talks Every Time.** Steven Frank. LC 99-46083. (Adams Ser.). 256p. 1999. pap. 9.95 (*1-58062-184-8*) Adams Media.

Public Speaking: Skills for Success. Thomas J. Farrell. 1997. pap. text 16.00 (*0-256-23169-9*) McGraw.

***Public Speaking: Speech Organizing.** O'Hair & Stewart. 2000. pap. text, wbk. ed. 2.95 (*0-312-25054-1*) St Martin.

Public Speaking: Strategic Choices. 3rd ed. Michael R. Schliessmann & Laurie L. Haleta. 200p. 1995. per. 24.76 (*0-7872-0538-9*) Kendall-Hunt.

Public Speaking: Strategies for Success. 2nd ed. (C). 1999. text. write for info. (*0-205-29734-X*, Longwood Div) Allyn.

***Public Speaking: Strategies For Success.** 2nd ed. 1999. 48.00 (*0-205-30789-2*) Allyn.

Public Speaking: Strategies for Success. 2nd ed. Zarefsky. 452p. 1998. pap. text 50.00 (*0-205-28651-8*, Longwood Div) Allyn.

Public Speaking: Testbank, 4 vols. Osborn. (C). 1996. pap., teacher ed. 11.96 (*0-395-80884-7*) HM.

Public Speaking: Theory & Practice. 2nd ed. John J. Makay. (C). 1995. pap. text, teacher ed. 47.75 (*0-15-503062-0*) Harcourt Coll Pubs.

Public Speaking: Theory into Practice. 3rd ed. John Makay. 500p. 1997. 36.95 (*0-7872-3247-5*) Kendall-Hunt.

Public Speaking: Theory into Practice, a Coursebook. Leigh Makay. 256p. (C). 1995. pap. text, per. 33.95 (*0-7872-1780-8*) Kendall-Hunt.

Public Speaking: Traditional Approach in Modern World. 2nd ed. Brian Schriner. 268p. (C). 1996. text 43.00 (*0-536-59017-6*) Pearson Custom.

Public Speaking & Argumentation. 366p. (C). 1996. text 52.00 (*0-536-59112-1*) Pearson Custom.

***Public Speaking & Argumentation.** 2nd ed. 360p. (C). 1998. text 30.00 (*0-536-01546-5*) Pearson Custom.

Public Speaking & the Multicultural Environment. 2nd ed. Lieberman. 59p. 1996. pap. text 3.00 (*0-205-26511-1*) Allyn.

***Public Speaking & Writing Skills for Engineering Students.** P. Aarne Vesilind. (Illus.). 98p. (C). 1999. pap. 8.00 (*0-9650539-2-X*) Lakeshore Pr.

Public Speaking Anxiety: How to Face the Fear. L. Todd Thomas. 48p. (C). 1996. pap. text 7.50 (*0-03-018243-3*, Pub. by Harcourt Coll Pubs) Harcourt.

Public Speaking: Choices & Challenges Powerpoint Presentation. O'Hair & Stewart. pap. text. write for info. (*0-312-20179-6*); pap. text. write for info. (*0-312-20180-X*) St Martin.

Public Speaking College. Gregory. 1993. 55.00 (*0-07-074565-X*) McGraw.

Public Speaking for Analysis. John J. Makay. (C). 1995. pap. text 30.00 (*0-15-503304-2*) Harcourt Coll Pubs.

Public Speaking for College & Career. 4th ed. Hamilton Gregory. LC 95-34114. (C). 1995. pap. text 35.50 (*0-07-024754-4*) McGraw.

Public Speaking for College & Career. 4th ed. Gregory Hamilton. 1995. pap. text, suppl. ed. 9.00 (*0-07-024758-7*) McGraw.

Public Speaking for College & Career. 5th ed. Hamilton Gregory. LC 98-16221. 1998. 44.69 (*0-07-290575-1*) McGraw.

Public Speaking for Dummies. Malcolm Kushner. (For Dummies Ser.). 400p. 1999. pap. 16.99 (*0-7645-5159-0*, Dummies Trade Pr) IDG Bks.

***Public Speaking for Dummies: Kushner,&Malcolm.** Malcolm Kushner. 1998. audio 12.00 (*0-694-51918-9*, CPN10146) HarperAudio.

Public Speaking for Personal Success. Michael S. Hanna & James W. Gibson. 480p. (C). 1995. pap. text. write for info. (*0-697-26122-0*) Brown & Benchmark.

Public Speaking for Personal Success. 4th ed. Michael S. Hanna & James W. Gibson. 480p. (C). 1994. text. write for info. (*0-697-20144-9*) Brown & Benchmark.

Public Speaking for Personal Success. 4th ed. Michael S. Hanna & James W. Gibson. (C). 1995. audio. write for info. (*0-697-24958-1*) Brown & Benchmark.

Public Speaking for Personal Success. 4th ed. Michael S. Hanna & James W. Gibson. 480p. (C). 1995. text. write for info. (*0-697-24959-X*) Brown & Benchmark.

Public Speaking for Personal Success. 5th rev. ed. Michael S. Hanna & James W. Gibson. (Illus.). 480p. (C). 1999. pap. text 28.00 (*0-536-02336-0*) Pearson Custom.

Public Speaking, Grades 2-12. rev. ed. Lois F. Roets. 44p. (J). (gr. k-12). 1989. pap., teacher ed. 9.00 (*0-911943-17-X*) Leadership Pub.

Public Speaking Handbook. Susan Benjamin. 136p. (Orig.). 1995. pap., teacher ed. 7.95 (*0-673-36159-4*, GoodYrBooks) Addson-Wesley Educ.

Public Speaking Handbook: A Liberal Arts Approach. Harry C. Hazel & John Caputo. 80p. (C). 1995. pap., per. 11.95 (*0-8403-9690-2*) Kendall-Hunt.

Public Speaking Handbook: A Liberal Arts Approach. 2nd ed. Hazel & Caputo. 80p. (C). 1998. per. 12.95 (*0-7872-4842-8*) Kendall-Hunt.

***Public Speaking in a Diverse Society.** Patricia Kearney & Timothy G. Plax. (Illus.). 481p. 2000. pap. text 25.00 (*0-7881-9031-8*) DIANE Pub.

Public Speaking in a Diverse Society. 2nd ed. Patricia Kearney & Timothy G. Plax. LC 98-22069. xxiv, 438p. 1999. pap. text 42.95 (*0-7674-0287-1*) Mayfield Pub.

Public Speaking in a Diverse Society: Instructor's Manual & Test Bank. 2nd rev. ed. Patricia Kearney & Timothy G. Plax. 1999. pap. text, teacher ed. write for info. (*0-7674-0983-3*) Mayfield Pub.

Public Speaking in a Free Society. Tedford. 1990. teacher ed. 15.31 (*0-07-063389-4*) McGraw.

Public Speaking in a Free Society. Thomas L. Tedford. (C). 1991. text 29.74 (*0-07-063388-6*) McGraw.

Public Speaking in the Age of Diversity. (C). 1998. text. write for info. (*0-205-29465-0*, Longwood Div) Allyn.

***Public Speaking in the Age of Diversity.** (C). 2000. 44.50 (*0-536-61275-7*) Pearson Custom.

Public Speaking in the Age of Diversity. 2nd ed. (C). 1998. text. write for info. (*0-205-29502-9*, Longwood Div) Allyn.

***Public Speaking in the Age of Diversity.** 2nd ed. Teri K. Gamble & Michael Gamble. LC 97-25533. 456p. 1998. pap. text 50.00 (*0-205-27559-1*) Allyn.

Public Speaking in the Reshaping of Great Britain. Robert T. Oliver. LC 86-40355. (Illus.). 248p. 1987. 40.00 (*0-87413-315-7*) U Delaware Pr.

Public Speaking Made Easy. Pam Chambers & Ron Martin. 1997. 27.95 (*0-9650527-3-7*) Success Dynamic.

Public Speaking Made Easy. Thomas Montalbo. 1994. pap. 10.00 (*0-87980-434-3*) Wilshire.

Public Speaking Made Easy. Darlene Ortiz. (Four-H Ser.). (Illus.). 12p. (J). (gr. 6-8). 1991. pap. 2.25 (*1-57753-210-4*, 105M-1-4) Corn Coop Ext.

Public Speaking Made Simple. Curt Simmons. 208p. 1996. pap. 12.00 (*0-385-48185-3*, Made) Doubleday.

Public Speaking Plus. Thomas J. Farrell & Robert E. Burns. 304p. (C). 1984. pap. text 26.95 (*0-89702-044-8*, Irwn McGrw-H) McGrw-H Hghr Educ.

Public Speaking Speech Preparation 2nd ed. (C). 1994. text, wbk. ed. 9.00 (*0-13-559569-X*, Macmillan Coll) P-H.

Public Speaking Today. Diana Prentice. 512p. 1989. 30.60 (*0-8442-5515-7*) NTC Contemp Pub Co.

Public Speaking Today! 2nd ed. LC 93-86239. 480p. 1995. 39.92 (*0-8442-5630-7*) NTC Contemp Pub Co.

Public Speaking Today. 3rd ed. Diana B. Carlin & James Payne. LC 98-14372. 1998. 49.94 (*0-8442-0369-6*) NTC Contemp Pub Co.

Public Speaking Transcripts, 2 vols. 2nd ed. Osborn. (C). 1991. 25.96 (*0-395-57299-1*) HM.

Public Speaking Video Guide, 3 vols. Osborn. (C). 1993. pap. 9.96 (*0-395-67580-4*) HM.

Public Speaking Workbook. Charlene Berquist. 224p. (C). 1995. spiral bd. 21.95 (*0-7872-1351-9*, 41135101) Kendall-Hunt.

Public Speaking Workbook. King. 1999. pap., wbk. ed. 18.75 (*0-07-236820-9*) McGraw.

Public Speaking Workbook. Wendy Papa. 252p. (C). 1996. pap. text, per. 26.95 (*0-7872-2353-0*) Kendall-Hunt.

Public Speaking Workbook: Communication 111. 2nd ed. Nancy Wendt. 90p. (C). 1998. spiral bd., wbk. ed. 14.95 (*0-7872-4983-1*, 41498301) Kendall-Hunt.

***Public Speaking Workbook: Communication 111.** 3rd ed. Nancy Wendt. 90p. (C). 1999. spiral bd. 15.95 (*0-7872-6331-1*, 41633101) Kendall-Hunt.

Public Speeches for Analysis I. 2nd ed. John J. Makay. (C). 1995. 139.00 (*0-15-502117-6*) Harcourt Coll Pubs.

Public Spending & the Poor: Theory & Evidence. Ed. by Dominique Van De Walle & Kimberly Nead. LC 95-43787. (World Bank Ser.). 619p. (C). 1996. text 69.95 (*0-8018-5255-2*) Johns Hopkins.

***Public Spending in the 20th Century: A Global Perspective.** Vito Tanzi & Ludger Schuknecht. (Illus.). 296p. (C). 2000. text 54.95 (*0-521-66291-5*); pap. text 19.95 (*0-521-66410-1*) Cambridge U Pr.

Public Sphere & Experience: Analysis of the Bourgeois & Proletarian Public Sphere. Oskar Negt & Alexander Kluge. Tr. by Peter Labanyi et al. LC 93-610. (Theory & History of Literature Ser.: Vol. 85). 327p. (C). 1993. 44.95 (*0-8166-2031-8*) U of Minn Pr.

***Public Spheres & Collective Identities.** Shmuel N. Eisenstadt. 2000. pap. 29.95 (*0-7658-0714-9*) Transaction Pubs.

Public Spheres, Public Mores & Democracy: Hamburg & Stockholm, 1870-1914. Madeleine Hurd. 350p. 1999. text 49.50 (*0-472-11067-5*, 11067) U of Mich Pr.

Public Spirit in the Thrift Tragedy. Mark C. Rom. LC 95-48261. (Policy & Institutional Studies). 325p. (C). 1996. pap. 22.95 (*0-8229-5600-4*); text 49.95 (*0-8229-3943-6*) U of Pittsburgh Pr.

Public Stake in Revisionism. Harry E. Barnes. 1971. 250.00 (*0-87700-282-7*) Revisionist Pr.

Public Stake in Union Power. Philip D. Bradley. LC 59-11490. 392p. reprint ed. pap. 121.60 (*0-8357-2706-8*, 203981900013) Bks Demand.

Public Storage. unabridged ed. Joel Dailey. (Modern Poetry in English Ser.: No. 46). (Illus.). 28p. 1995. pap. 5.00 (*1-879457-49-0*) Norton Coker Pr.

Public Street Illumination in Washington, D. C. An Illustrated History, Vol. M2. Sarah P. Noreen. 1975. 5.00 (*1-888028-01-7*) GWU Ctr WAS.

Public Streets for Public Use. Ed. by Anne Vernez Moudon. (Illus.). 352p. 1991. pap. text 38.50 (*0-231-07599-5*) Col U Pr.

Public Style: A Study of the Community Participation of Protestant Ministers. Walter M. Stuhr, Jr. LC 72-89687. (Studies in Religion & Society). 134p. 1972. 16.95 (*0-913348-12-0*); pap. 12.95 (*0-913348-02-3*) Ctr Sci Study.

Public Subsidies to Private Corporations: Stop Violating the Colorado Constitution. Dale F. Rubin. (Issue Paper #7-96 Ser.). 11p. 1996. pap. text 8.00 (*1-57655-151-2*) Independ Inst.

***Public Support for Food Security: The Public Distribution System in India.** N. Krishnaji & T. N. Krishnan. LC 99-89149. (Strategies for Human Development in India Ser.). 2000. pap. write for info. (*0-7619-9398-3*) Sage.

***Public Support for Higher Education.** James Harvey & John Immerwahr. 113p. (C). 2000. reprint ed. pap. text 25.00 (*0-7881-8860-7*) DIANE Pub.

Public Support for International Development. LC 97-102596. 186p. 1996. 37.00 (*92-64-14865-5*, 41-96-04-1, Pub. by Org for Econ) OECD.

Public Support for Private Residential Care. Jonathan Bradshaw & Ian Gibbs. 187p. 1988. text 72.95 (*0-566-05661-5*, Pub. by Avebry) Ashgate Pub Co.

Public Swimming Pools: Recommended Regulations for Design & Construction, Operation & Maintenance. Ed. by Eric W. Mood. LC 81-68843. 72p. 1981. 6.00 (*0-87553-096-6*, 055) Am Pub Health.

Public Technology: Key to Improved Government Productivity. James L. Mercer & Ronald J. Philips. LC 80-69693. 287p. reprint ed. pap. 89.00 (*0-608-12907-0*, 202353800033) Bks Demand.

***Public Technology Procurement & Innovation.** Charles Edquist et al. LC 99-46682. (Economics of Science, Technology & Innovation Ser.). 1999. write for info. (*0-7923-8685-X*) Kluwer Academic.

Public Television: America's First Station. William Hawes. LC 96-14798. (Illus.). 160p. 1996. 24.95 (*0-86534-245-8*) Sunstone Pr.

Public Television: Panacea, Pork Barrel, or Public Trust?, 33. Marilyn E. Lashley. LC 91-34482. (Contributions to the Study of Mass Media & Communications Ser.: No. 33). 176p. 1992. 42.95 (*0-313-27964-0*, LPT/, Greenwood Pr) Greenwood.

Public Television: Politics & the Battle over Documentary Film. B. J. Bullert. LC 97-17633. (Communications, Media, & Culture Ser.). (Illus.). 224p. 1997. pap. text 20.00 (*0-8135-2470-9*); lib. bdg. 49.00 (*0-8135-2469-5*) Rutgers U Pr.

Public Theology & Political Economy: Christian Stewardship in Modern Society. David Tracy. 1999. write for info. (*0-8245-1807-1*) Crossroad NY.

Public Theology & Political Economy: Christian Stewardship in Modern Society. Max L. Stackhouse. 192p. (Orig.). (C). 1991. reprint ed. pap. text 21.00 (*0-8191-8301-6*) U Pr of Amer.

Public, Trade Union & Cooperative Enterprise in Germany. Walter Hesselbach. 158p. 1976. 32.50 (*0-7146-2978-2*, Pub. by F Cass Pubs) Intl Spec Bk.

Public Transit: Bus, Paratransit, & Ridesharing. LC 92-21588. (Transportation Research Record Ser.: No. 1338). 101p. 1992. 22.00 (*0-309-05200-9*) Transport Res Bd.

Public Transit: Current Research in Planning, Marketing, Operations, & Technology (TRR 1402) Ed. by Susan Taylor Brown. (Transportation Research Record Ser.). (Illus.). 116p. 1993. pap. text 28.00 (*0-309-05473-7*) Transport Res Bd.

Public Transit: Management, Operations Planning, & Development. LC 92-26084. (Transportation Research Record Ser.: No. 1349). 154p. 1992. 26.00 (*0-309-05212-2*) Transport Res Bd.

Public Transit Economics & Deregulation Policy. Joseph Berechman. LC 92-41258. (Studies in Regional Science & Urban Economics: Vol. 23). (Illus.). 360p. 1993. 133.50 (*0-444-89275-3*, North Holland) Elsevier.

Public Transit, 1993: Bus, Paratransit, & Ridesharing: a Peer-Reviewed Publication of the Transportation Research Board. LC 93-29884. (Transportation Research Record Ser.: No. 1390). 1993. write for info. (*0-309-05461-3*) Transport Res Bd.

Public Transport: Its Planning, Management & Operation. 3rd ed. White. LC 94-47431. 192p. 1994. pap. 27.50 (*1-85728-159-4*, Pub. by UCL Pr Ltd) Taylor & Francis.

Public Transport Planning in Shire Counties: An Evaluation of the Public Transport Plan As an Aid to Transport Policy Making. Ed. by John P. Rigby. (C). 1980. 35.00 (*0-7855-3870-4*, Pub. by Oxford Polytechnic) St Mut.

Public Transportation: Bus, Rail, Ridesharing, Paratransit Services, & Transit Security (TRR 1433) Ed. by Susan Taylor Brown. (Transportation Research Record Ser.). (Illus.). 220p. 1994. pap. text 43.00 (*0-309-05510-5*, R1433) Transport Res Bd.

Public Transportation Alternative Fuels, 2 vols., Set. 1995. lib. bdg. 600.95 (*0-8490-8356-7*) Gordon Pr.

Public Treasury of the Muslims: Monthly Budgets of the Mahdist State in the Sudan, 1897. Ahmad I. Shouk & Anders Bjorkelo. (Ottoman Empire & Its Heritage: No. 5). xliv, 371p. 1995. 134.00 (*90-04-10358-9*) Brill Academic Pubs.

Public Trust. Sarah Gregory. 1997. mass mkt. 5.99 (*0-451-19076-9*) NAL.

Public Trust & the First Americans. Ed. by Ruthann Knudson & Bennie C. Keel. LC 95-17555. 212p. 1995. pap. text 24.95 (*0-87071-025-7*) Oreg St U Pr.

Public Trust Doctrine & the Management of America's Coasts. Jack H. Archer et al. LC 93-48759. 208p. 1994. lib. bdg. 35.00 (*0-87023-898-1*) U of Mass Pr.

Public Trusts & Taxation. V. K. Varadachari. (C). 1987. 145.00 (*0-7855-3496-2*) St Mut.

Public Tuition & State Expenditures for Higher Education, 1984-1988. (Legislative Finance Papers: No. 77). 24p. 1991. 15.00 (*1-55516-077-8*, 5101-77) Natl Conf State Legis.

Public Understanding of Economic Policies: The Tax Cuts of 1962 & 1964. Michael A. MacDowell. LC 77-14765. (Dissertations in American Economic History Ser.). 1978. 33.95 (*0-405-11048-0*) Ayer.

Public Use of the Forest Preserve. C. R. Pettis. 17p. 1993. reprint ed. lib. bdg. 69.00 (*0-7812-5262-8*) Rprt Serv.

Public Utilities: An Annotated Guide to Information Sources. Anne C. Roess. LC 91-22954. 406p. 1991. 50.00 (*0-8108-2443-4*) Scarecrow.

Public Utilities & Carriers Property see Tennessee Code Annotated 1999 Supplement

Public Utilities & the National Power Policies. James C. Bonbright. LC 73-172007. (FDR & the Era of the New Deal Ser.). 1972. reprint ed. lib. bdg. 19.50 (*0-306-70424-2*) Da Capo.

Public Utilities & the Poor: Rights & Responsibilities. David C. Sweet & Kathryn W. Hexter. LC 87-6979. 197p. 1987. 57.95 (*0-275-92572-2*, C2572, Praeger Pubs) Greenwood.

Public Utilities; Human Services; Mental Health; Sports see Rhode Island General Laws, 1998 Cumulative Supplement

***Public Utilities in Japan: Past, Present & Future.** Ed. by Japan Society of Public Utilities Staff. (Public Utilities Papers). viii, 243p. 2000. 34.95 (*0-87744-183-9*) MSU Inst Pub.

Public Utilities Law Anthology, No. XVIII, Pt. II, Jul-Dec. 95. Ed. by Allison P. Zabriskie. 1000p. 1996. 154.95 (*1-57024-027-2*) Intl Lib.

Public Utilities Law Anthology, Set, XVII(II)-XVIII(II) (1994-1995) Ed. by Allison P. Zabriskie. (National Law Anthology Ser.). 3000p. 1994. text 299.95 (*0-914250-41-8*) Intl Lib.

Public Utilities Law Anthology: 1974-1995, Set, Vols. I-XVII (II) (National Law Anthology Ser.). 1996. 1550.00 (*1-57024-040-X*) Intl Lib.

Public Utilities Law Anthology Vol. XVIII, Pt. I: Jan.-June 1995. Ed. by Allison P. Zabriskie. (National Law Anthology Ser.). 1995. 154.95 (*1-57024-021-3*) Intl Lib.

Public Utilities Law Anthology Vol. XIX, Pt. I: Jan.-June 1996. Ed. by Allison P. Zabriskie. (National Law Anthology Ser.). 1000p. (C). 1996. 154.95 (*1-57024-033-7*) Intl Lib.

Public Utilities Law Anthology Vol. XIX, Pt. II: July-Dec. 1996. Ed. by Allison P. Zabriskie. (National Law Anthology Ser.). 1000p. (C). 1997. 154.95 (*1-57024-039-6*) Intl Lib.

Public Utilities Reports Fourth Series: Containing Decisions of the Regulatory Commissions & of State & Federal Courts. Vols. 1 to 74, 1974-1986. Public Utilities Reports Staff. LC KF2085.A2P84. 604p. pap. 187.30 (*0-608-16093-8*, 202959800001) Bks Demand.

Public Utility Accounting: Theory & Application. James E. Suelflow. LC 72-619568. (MSU Public Utilities Papers: No. 1973). 343p. reprint ed. pap. 106.40 (*0-8357-2593-6*, 205237300013) Bks Demand.

Public Utility Depreciation Practices. 446p. 1968. pap. 17.00 (*0-317-03336-0*) NARUC.

Public Utility Economics. Paul Garfield & W. Lovejoy. (Illus.). 1963. text 26.95 (*0-13-739367-9*) P-H.

Public Utility Holding Company Act of 1935: 1935-1992. (Illus.). 82p. (Orig.). (C). 1994. pap. text 25.00 (*0-7881-0499-3*) DIANE Pub.

Public Utility Regulation. Ed. by Kenneth Nowotny & David B. Smith. (C). 1989. lib. bdg. 100.50 (*0-7923-9019-9*) Kluwer Academic.

Public Utility Regulation & the So-Called Sliding Scale: A Study of the Sliding Scale As a Means of Encouraging & Rewarding Efficiency in the Management of Regulated Monopolies. Irvin Bussing. LC 68-58552. (Columbia University. Studies in the Social Sciences: No. 415). reprint ed. 20.00 (*0-404-51415-4*) AMS Pr.

Public Utility Regulation in an Environment of Change: Proceedings of the Institute of Public Utilities Seventeenth Annual Conference, Williamsburg, VA, 1985. Michigan State University, Institute of Public Utilities Staff. Ed. by Patrick C. Mann & Harry M. Trebing. LC 87-81826. (MSU Public Utilities Papers: Vol. 1987). 605p. reprint ed. pap. 187.60 (*0-608-20500-1*, 207175200002) Bks Demand.

Public Values, & Private Power in American Politics. Ed. by J. David Greenstone. LC 81-16416. (C). 1993. pap. text 10.00 (*0-226-30717-4*) U Ch Pr.

Public Values & Private Power in American Politics. Ed. by J. David Greenstone. LC 81-16416. (Illus.). 306p. reprint ed. pap. 94.90 (*0-608-09318-1*, 205419200004) Bks Demand.

Public Values in Constitutional Law. Ed. by Stephen E. Gottlieb. 296p. (C). 1993. text 54.50 (*0-472-10434-9*, 10434) U of Mich Pr.

Public Values, Private Lands: Farmland Preservation Policy. Tim Lehman. LC 94-19636. 240p. 1995. pap. text 19.95 (*0-8078-4491-8*); lib. bdg. 49.95 (*0-8078-2177-2*) U of NC Pr.

Public Versus Private Power During the Truman Administration: A Study of Fair Deal Liberalism. Phyllis K. De Luna. (Modern American History Ser.: Vol. 1). XII, 253p. (C). 1998. text 49.95 (*0-8204-3144-3*) P Lang Pubng.

Public Video Surveillance: Is It an Effective Crime Prevention Tool? Marcus Nieto. 1997. write for info. (*1-58703-062-4*) CA St Libry.

Public Violence in Canada, 1867-1982. Judy Torrance. 282p. 1988. pap. 27.95 (*0-7735-0666-7*, Pub. by McG-Queens Univ Pr) CUP Services.

Public Voice in a Democracy at Risk. Ed. by Michael M. Salvador & Patricia Sias. LC 97-22809. 216p. 1998. 55.00 (*0-275-96013-7*, Praeger Pubs) Greenwood.

Public Voices: Catholics in the American Context. Ed. by Steven M. Avella & Elizabeth McKeown. LC 99-48732. (American Catholic Identities Ser.). 256p. 1999. 50.00 (*1-57075-267-2*); pap. 25.00 (*1-57075-266-4*) Orbis Bks.

Public Voices, Private Interests: Australia's Media Policy. Jennifer Craik et al. 296p. 1996. pap. 29.95 (*1-86373-628-X*, Pub. by Allen & Unwin Pty) Paul & Co Pubs.

Public Voucher for Purchases & Services Other Than Personal, Standard Form 1034. 1p. 1988. pap. 11.00 (*0-16-003249-0*) USGPO.

***Public Vows: A History of Marriage & the Nation.** Nancy F. Cott. 288p. 2001. 27.95 (*0-674-00320-9*) HUP.

Public vs. Private Free Zones. Ed. by Richard L. Bolin. 84p. 1993. pap. 40.00 (*0-945951-09-4*) Flagstaff Inst.

Public Water Supply: Models, Data & Operational Management. P. Lonsdale. LC 98-231834. (Illus.). 480p. (C). 1998. 110.00 (*0-419-23220-6*, E & FN Spon) Routledge.

Public Water Supply Systems & Structures: Snip 2.04.02-84. Russia's Gosstroy Staff. Ed. & Tr. by Snip Register, Inc. Staff from RUS. (Building Codes of Russia Ser.). (Illus.). iv, 120p. 1998. ring bd. 599.95 (*1-57937-061-6*, S4000284) Snip Register.

Public Weighmaster Law of Virginia: 1997 Edition. 1998. pap. write for info. (*0-327-05003-9*, 34457-10) LEXIS Pub.

Public Welfare see Burns Indiana Statutes Annotated 1999 Cumulative Supplement Set: Pocket Part

Public Welfare: Notes from Underground. Michael Greenblatt & Steven Richmond. 132p. 1979. boxed set 32.95 (*0-87073-767-8*) Transaction Pubs.

Public Welfare Administration in Canada. Margaret K. Strong. LC 69-16248. (Criminology, Law Enforcement, & Social Problems Ser.: No. 94). 1969. reprint ed. 24.00 (*0-87585-094-4*) Patterson Smith.

Public Welfare Administration in Louisiana. Elizabeth Wisner. LC 75-17253. (Social Problems & Social Policy Ser.). 1976. reprint ed. 21.95 (*0-405-07527-8*) Ayer.

Public Welfare Directory Vol. 58: A Resource Guide to the Human Services. Ed. by Amy J. Plotnick. LC 41-4981. xx, 568p. (Orig.). 1997. pap. 80.00 (*0-910106-27-4*) Am Human Servs.

Public Will: Its Connection to Public Policy & Philanthropy. Sarah E. Jones & Margaret A. Siegel. 172p. (Orig.). 1993. pap. 15.00 (*1-886949-10-7*) Union Inst.

***Public Women & the Confederacy.** Catherine Clinton. LC 99-6915. (Frank L. Klement Lecture Ser.). 1999. write for info. (*0-87462-332-4*) Marquette.

Public Women, Public Words: A Documentary History of American Feminism: The Twentieth Century, 2 vols. Ed. by Dawn Keetley & John Pettegrew. (Illus.). 464p. 2000. pap. write for info. (*0-945612-65-6*) Madison Hse.

Public Women, Public Words: A Documentary History of American Feminism: the Twentieth Century, No. 2, No. 2. Ed. by Dawn Keetley & John Pettegrew. 464p. 2000. 39.95 (*0-945612-64-8*) Madison Hse.

Public Women, Public Words Vol. I: A Documentary History of American Feminism, Beginnings to 1900. Ed. by Dawn Keetley & John Pettegrew. LC 97-3580. 350p. 1997. pap. 19.95 (*0-945612-45-1*); text 37.95 (*0-945612-44-3*) Madison Hse.

Public Work Wage Investigator. Jack Rudman. (Career Examination Ser.: C-990). 1994. pap. 29.95 (*0-8373-0990-5*) Nat Learn.

Public Workers & Public Unions. Ed. by Sam Zagoria. LC 75-38793. 1972. 5.95 (*0-13-739359-8*) Am Assembly.

Public Workers & Public Unions. American Assembly Staff. Ed. by Sam Zagoria. LC 75-38793. (Spectrum Bks.). 192p. reprint ed. pap. 59.60 (*0-608-16968-4*, 205625700056) Bks Demand.

***Public Works: Alternative Service Delivery Choices, 1997.** Gwen Hall & International City/County Management Association Staff. LC 99-185366. (Special Data Issue Ser.). 85 p. 1998. write for info. (*0-87326-814-8*) Intl City-Cnty Mgt.

Public Works: Engineering in Local Government. R. H. Clarke. LC 96-175407. 214p. 1996. 67.00 (*0-7277-2093-7*, 2093, Pub. by T Telford) RCH.

Public Works Administration: Current Public Policy Perspectives. Ed. by Lucy Brewer. LC 96-10038. 544p. 1996. 48.95 (*0-8039-7178-8*) Sage.

Public Works & Poverty Alleviation in Rural China. Zhu Ling & Jiang Zhongyi. 237p. (C). 1996. lib. bdg. 95.00 (*1-56072-395-5*) Nova Sci Pubs.

Public Works & the Patterns of Urban Real Estate Growth in Manhattan, 1835-1849. Eugene P. Moehring. 28.00 (*0-317-19169-1*, 19819) Ayer.

Public Works & the Patterns of Urban Real Estate Growth in Manhattan, 1835-1894. Eugene P. Moehring. xi, 452p. 1981. 30.95 (*0-405-13948-9*) Arno Press.

Public Works & Urban Real Estate Growth. Eugene P. Moehring. 1981. write for info. (*0-318-50874-5*) Ayer.

Public Works Communication Manual. 196p. 1984. 25.00 (*0-917084-48-9*) Am Public Works.

Public Works Communication Manual. American Public Works Association Staff. 128p. (Orig.). 1984. pap. text 35.00 (*0-917084-04-7*) Am Public Works.

Public Works, Government Spending & Job Creation: The Job Opportunities Program. Robert Jerrett & Thomas A. Barocci. LC 79-15972. (Praeger Special Studies). 320p. 1979. 69.50 (*0-275-90370-2*, C0370, Praeger Pubs) Greenwood.

Public Works Guide to Automated Mapping & Facilities Management. Frwd. by Phil Parent. (Special Reports: No. 64). (Illus.). 167p. (Orig.). 1992. pap. text 75.00 (*0-917084-40-3*) Am Public Works.

Public Works in Prosperity & Depression. Arthur D. Gayer. (General Ser.: No. 29). 482p. 1935. reprint ed. 125.40 (*0-87014-028-0*) Natl Bur Econ Res.

Public Works Inspector's Manual. 5th ed. Silas B. Birch, Jr. 1996. pap. 49.95 (*1-55701-169-9*) BNI Pubns.

Public Works Management Practices. Hilary Green et al. (Special Reports: No. 59). 126p. (Orig.). 1991. pap. text 50.00 (*0-917084-12-8*) Am Public Works.

Public Works Today: A Profile of Local Service Organizations & Managers. American Public Works Association Staff. (Special Reports: No. 57). 86p. (Orig.). 1990. pap. text 65.00 (*0-917084-16-0*) Am Public Works.

Public Works Wage Rate & Some of Its Economic Effects. Viola Wyckoff. LC 72-76650. (Columbia University. Studies in the Social Sciences: No. 521). reprint ed. 31.50 (*0-404-51521-5*) AMS Pr.

Public World: Syntactically Impermanence. Leslie Scalapino. LC 99-18712. 158p. 1999. pap. 17.95 (*0-8195-6379-X*, Wesleyan Univ Pr); text 45.00 (*0-8195-6378-1*, Wesleyan Univ Pr) U Pr of New Eng.

Public Worship of God: A Source Book. Henry S. Coffin. 1977. 18.95 (*0-8369-7272-4*, 8071) Ayer.

Public Worship, Private Faith: Sacred Harp & American Folksong. John Bealle. LC 97-19852. 320p. 1997. 50.00 (*0-8203-1921-X*); pap. 20.00 (*0-8203-1988-0*) U of Ga Pr.

Public Years. Bernard Baruch. 1993. reprint ed. lib. bdg. 24.95 (*1-56849-096-8*) Buccaneer Bks.

Public Years of Sarah & Angelina Grimke. Larry Ceplair. 400p. 1991. pap. text 22.00 (*0-231-06801-8*) Col U Pr.

Publica Carmina: Ovid's Books from Exile. Harry B. Evans. LC 82-10899. 214p. reprint ed. pap. 66.40 (*0-8357-3799-3*, 203652700003) Bks Demand.

Publicans & Sinners: Private Enterprise in the Service of the Roman Republic, with a Critical Bibliography. E. Badian. 176p. (Orig.). 1983. pap. text 12.95 (*0-8014-9241-6*) Cornell U Pr.

Publicaren met Pagemaker. Henkes. (C). 1993. pap. text. write for info. (*0-201-58093-4*) Addison-Wesley.

Publication Design. Roy Paul Nelson. LC 78-176306. 232 p. 1972. write for info. (*0-697-04323-1*) Brown & Benchmark.

Publication Design. 5th ed. Roy P. Nelson. 336p. (C). 1990. text. write for info. (*0-697-08620-8*) Brown & Benchmark.

Publication Editing. Don Ranly. 300p. (C). 1998. pap. 48.95 (*0-7872-5606-4*, 41560601) Kendall-Hunt.

Publication Index, 1977-1982. (Transportation Research Board Publication: No. 77). 373p. 1983. 16.00 (*0-685-38581-7*) Transport Res Bd.

Publication Index, 1973-1976. (Transportation Research Board Publication: No. 73). 248p. 1978. 10.00 (*0-685-38580-9*) Transport Res Bd.

Publication Indexing, a Writer's Guide to Inventory. Janet Leih. 12p. 1989. pap. 1.00 (*0-937953-14-8*) Tesseract SD.

Publication Manual of the American Psychological Association. 4th ed. American Psychological Association Staff. LC 94-11498. 368p. 1994. text 31.95 (*1-55798-243-0*, 420-0041); pap. text 21.95 (*1-55798-241-4*, 4200040) Am Psychol.

Publication of Guiana's Plantation. LC 72-7836. (English Experience Ser.: No. 525). 24p. 1972. reprint ed. 10.00 (*90-221-0525-3*) Walter J Johnson.

Publication Opportunities for Law Librarians: An Author's Guide. Compiled by Dennis C. Benamati & Evelina E. Lemelin. LC 95-25605. (AALL Publications Ser.: No. 49). xxiv, 318p. 1996. ring bd. 65.00 (*0-8377-9309-2*, Rothman) W S Hein.

Publication Opportunities for Tax Researchers. J. Burns et al. 241p. 1988. 3.00 (*0-685-17962-1*) Am Accounting.

Publication Peer Review: An Annotated Bibliography, 7. Compiled by Bruce W. Speck. LC 92-42695. (Bibliographies & Indexes in Mass Media & Communications Ser.: No. 7). 320p. 1993. lib. bdg. 69.50 (*0-313-28892-5*, GR8892, Greenwood Pr) Greenwood.

Publication Production. Anthony H. Firman. 141p. 1993. per. 30.00 (*0-914548-74-3*, 150-93) Soc Tech Comm.

Publications. Compiled by Rockport Publishers Editors. (Design Library). (Illus.). 80p. 1998. pap. write for info. (*1-56496-543-0*) Rockport Pubs.

Publications, Set. Shelley Society, London Staff. LC 74-2680. reprint ed. 673.00 (*0-404-11500-4*) AMS Pr.

Publications, Set, Nos. 1-14. Shakespeare Society of New York Staff. reprint ed. write for info. (*0-404-54200-X*) AMS Pr.

Publications Based on Project TALENT: An Annotated Bibliography. Emily A. Campbell. 1979. pap. 10.00 (*0-89785-628-7*) Am Inst Res.

Publications Clearing House Bulletin, Vols. 1-10. LC 90-83829. 770p. 1990. reprint ed. 75.00 (*0-89941-749-3*, 306740) W S Hein.

Publications Editor. Jack Rudman. (Career Examination Ser.: C-3146). 1994. pap. 29.95 (*0-8373-3146-3*) Nat Learn.

Publications Handbook & Style Manual. 92p. 1988. pap. 5.00 (*0-89118-096-6*) Am Soc Agron.

Publications in Chinese, 1644-1969 see Modern Chinese Society: An Analytical Bibliography

Publications in Continuing Education. Alexander N. Charters. (MS Ser.: No. 12). 1980. 4.50 (*0-686-64687-8*, MSS 12) Syracuse U Cont Ed.

Publications in Continuing Education. Ed. by Alexander N. Charters. 1983. 8.00 (*0-87060-038-9*, MSS 26) Syracuse U Cont Ed.

Publications in Japanese, 1644-1971 see Modern Chinese Society: An Analytical Bibliography

Publications in Southern California Art 1, 2, & 3, 3 vols. in 1. rev. ed. Nancy D. Moure. Incl. Vol. 1. Index to the California Watercolor Society Exhibitions 1921-1954. 1984. (*0-9614622-1-3*); Vol. 2. Index to Artists Clubs & Exhibitions in Los Angeles Before 1930. 1984. (*0-9614622-2-1*); Vol. 3. Dictionary of Art & Artists in Southern California Before 1930. 1984. (*0-9614622-3-X*); 525p. 1984. 80.00 (*0-9614622-0-5*) Dustin Pubns.

Publications in Southern California Art 4, 5, 6. Nancy D. Moure et al. 546p. 1999. pap. write for info. (*0-9614622-6-4*) Dustin Pubns.

Publications in Western Languages, 1644-1972 see Modern Chinese Society: An Analytical Bibliography

Publications Index of the Society of Actuaries, 1992-93. 1994. pap. 10.00 (*0-938959-34-4*) Soc Actuaries.

***Publications, Libraries & Other Information Resources, 2.** 11th ed. Gale Group Staff. (Medical & Health Information Directory Ser.). 4200p. 1999. 255.00 (*0-7876-3483-2*) Gale.

Publications Management: Essays for Professional Communicators. Ed. by O. Jane Allen & Lynn H. Deming. LC 94-14936. (Baywood's Technical Communications Ser.). 258p. 1994. pap. 29.22 (*0-89503-164-7*); text 38.95 (*0-89503-163-9*) Baywood Pub.

Publications of James Edward Oglethorpe. Ed. by Rodney M. Baine. LC 92-38271. 528p. 1994. 65.00 (*0-8203-1546-X*) U of Ga Pr.

Publications of 1975 see Annual Bibliography of the History of the Printed Book & Libraries

Publications of 1974 see Annual Bibliography of the History of the Printed Book & Libraries

Publications of 1973 see Annual Bibliography of the History of the Printed Book & Libraries

Publications of Resources for the Future, Inc., 12 vols., Set. Resources for the Future, Inc. Staff. reprint ed. write for info. (*0-404-60325-4*) AMS Pr.

Publications of the American Association for Netherlandic Studies: Papers from the Third Interdisciplinary Conference on Netherlandic Studies. Ed. by Ton J. Broos. 342p. (C). 1988. lib. bdg. 52.00 (*0-8191-7056-9*) U Pr of Amer.

Publications of the American Ethnological Society, Vols. 1-22. American Ethnological Society Staff. write for info. (*0-404-58150-1*) AMS Pr.

Publications of the Ballad Society, 14 vols., Set, Nos. 1-38. Ballad Society. (Ballad Society Ser.: Nos. 1-38). reprint ed. 1315.00 (*0-404-50820-0*) AMS Pr.

Publications of the Bannatyne Club, Set, Nos. 1-120 & 8 Extra Vols. Bannatyne Club Staff. reprint ed. write for info. (*0-404-52700-0*) AMS Pr.

Publications of the IRS, 3 vols. (Information Services Ser.). 1987. 252.00 (*0-685-07437-4*); 225.00 (*0-685-07438-2*) P-H.

Publications of the Maitland Club, Nos. 1-75. Maitland Club Staff. reprint ed. write for info. (*0-404-52920-8*) AMS Pr.

Publications of the Metropolitan Museum of Art on Microfiche, 1870 to the Present. Metropolitan Museum of Art Staff. (Monographs). 1800p. 1990. 5665.00 (*0-8161-1747-0*, G K Hall & Co) Mac Lib Ref.

Publications of the World Health Organization, 1963-1967: A Bibliography. (ENG & FRE.). 152p. 1969. pap. text 16.20 (*92-4-152002-7*, 1150010) World Health.

Publications of the World Health Organization, 1968-1972: A Bibliography. 1974. pap. text 18.00 (*92-4-152004-3*, 1150009) World Health.

***Publicidad.** O'Guinn et al. (C). 1999. pap. 87.95 (*968-7529-59-8*) Thomson Learn.

Publicidad. Samson. (C). 1997. 11.00 (*0-673-19238-5*) Addison-Wesley.

Publicidad en Puerto Rico: Como Fue, Como es, Como se Hace. Rafael H. Benitez. LC 85-1017. (SPA., Illus.). 275p. 1985. 9.00 (*0-8477-2908-7*) U of PR Pr.

Publicidad, Modernidad, Hegemonia. Eliseo Colon. (SPA.). 1996. pap. 9.95 (*0-8477-0235-9*) U of PR Pr.

Publicistes Modernes. Henri J. Baudrillart. Ed. by J. P. Mayer. LC 78-67330. (European Political Thought Ser.). 1979. reprint ed. lib. bdg. 42.95 (*0-405-11676-4*) Ayer.

Publicity: The Fine Points of Promoting Your Event. 3rd rev. ed. George M. D. Frink. (Illus.). 52p. 1997. pap. 7.95 (*0-9679882-0-9*, CB9001) Carol Pr.

Publicity Advice & How-To Handbook. rev. ed. Rolf Gompertz. LC 88-50026. (Illus.). 148p. (Orig.). 1992. pap. 21.95 (*0-918248-07-8*) Word Doctor.

Publicity & Communications Bilingual Dictionary. Fabienne Duvillier. 464p. 1990. lib. bdg. 150.00 (*0-8288-2609-9*, F83360) Fr & Eur.

Publicity & Customer Relations in Transport Management. David W. Wragg. LC 82-145491. (Gower Pegasus Transport Library). xiii, 144p. 1981. write for info. (*0-566-00516-6*) Ashgate Pub Co.

Publicity & Media Relations Checklist. David R. Yale. Ed. by Anne Knudsen. (Illus.). 376p. 1995. pap. 22.95 (*0-8442-3218-1*, NTC Business Bks) NTC Contemp Pub Co.

Publicity & Public Relations. deluxe ed. Dorothy I. Doty. (Barron's Business Library). 320p. 1990. pap. 18.95 (*0-8120-4413-4*) Barron.

***Publicity & Public Relations.** 2nd rev. ed. Dorothy I. Doty & Marilyn Pincus. LC 00-33727. (Business Library). 2001. write for info. (*0-7641-1401-8*) Barron.

Publicity for Books & Authors: A Do-It-Yourself Handbook for Small Publishing Firms & Enterprising Authors. Peggy Glenn. LC 84-28288. (Illus.). 180p. 1985. 16.95 (*0-936930-92-6*); pap. 12.95 (*0-936930-91-8*) Aames-Allen.

Publicity for Mental Health Clinicians: Using TV, Radio, & Print Media to Enhance Your Public. Douglas H. Rueben. LC 95-6249. 238p. 1997. pap. text 22.95 (*0-7890-0411-9*) Haworth Pr.

Publicity for Mental Health Clinicians: Using TV, Radio, & Print Media to Enhance Your Public Image. Douglas H. Ruben. LC 95-6249. 222p. (C). 1995. lib. bdg. 39.95 (*1-56024-953-6*) Haworth Pr.

Publicity for Volunteers: A Handbook. Virginia Bortin. LC 81-50233. 128p. 1981. 10.95 (*0-8027-0685-1*); pap. 6.95 (*0-8027-7176-9*) Walker & Co.

Publicity Guide for Nutrition Education. 21p. 1985. pap. 8.00 (*0-910869-22-7*) Soc Nutrition Ed.

Publicity Handbook: How to Maximize Publicity for Products, Services & Organizations. David R. Yale. (Illus.). 376p. 1994. pap. 19.95 (*0-8442-3286-6*, NTC Business Bks) NTC Contemp Pub Co.

Publicity Handbook for Churches & Christian Organizations. Jim A. Vitti. 160p. (Orig.). 1987. pap. 7.99 (*0-310-37601-7*, 12089P) Zondervan.

Publicity Kit, Options: Expanding Educational Services for Adults. National Center for Research in Vocational Educati. 1987. 29.95 (*0-317-03912-1*, SP500C) Ctr Educ Trng Employ.

Publicity Manual. Kate Kelly. LC 79-55946. 184p. 1988. 29.95 (*0-9603740-1-9*) Visibility Ent.

Publicity Manual for Law Enforcement Agencies. Edwin M. Field & Selma G. Field. LC 94-77847. 1994. pap. text 29.95 (*0-9636092-1-1*) Knowledge Ntwk.

Publicity Manual for Librarians: A Professional Guide to Communicating with the Community. Edwin Field. 150p. 1999. reprint ed. pap. 20.00 (*0-7351-0143-4*) Replica Bks.

Publicity Manual for Libraries. Edwin M. Field & Selma G. Field. LC 93-77311. (Illus.). (Orig.). 1993. pap. text 19.95 (*0-9636092-0-3*) Knowledge Ntwk.

Publicity on the Internet: Creating Successful PublicityCampaigns on the internet & the Commercial online Services. Steve O'Keefe. LC 96-32539. (Illus.). 416p. 1996. pap. 29.95 (*0-471-16175-6*) Wiley.

Publicity Power: A Practical Guide to Effective Promotion. Charles Mallory. Ed. by Michael G. Crisp. LC 88-92737. (Fifty-Minute Ser.). (Illus.). 70p. (Orig.). 1989. pap. 10.95 (*0-931961-82-3*) Crisp Pubns.

Publicity Process. 3rd rev. ed. Ed. by Christine F. Goff. LC 88-13618. (Illus.). 320p. (C). 1989. pap. text 29.95 (*0-8138-1316-6*) Iowa St U Pr.

Publicity! Secrets of Getting It for People, Products & Businesses: Getting & Using Publicity As Free Advertising to Promote Yourself, Your Product, or Your Business. Dennis Stricker. Ed. by Joan Villa. LC 92-91209. (Illus.). 192p. 1993. pap. 19.95 (*1-882661-21-4*) Mktg Mgmt Mot.

Publicity Writing for Television & Film: "A How-To Handbook" Rolf Gompertz. LC 92-80079. 222p. (Orig.). 1992. pap. 26.95 (*0-918248-08-6*) Word Doctor.

Publick Employment & the Active Life Prefer'd to Solitude. John Evelyn. Ed. by Brian Vickers. LC 86-137650. (Public & Private Life in the Seventeenth Century Ser.). 324p. 1986. 50.00 (*0-8201-1417-0*) Schol Facsimiles.

Publick Spanking. Drew Pisarra. (Illus.). 75p. (Orig.). 1996. pap. 8.95 (*1-882550-16-1*) Quiet Lion Pr.

Publicly Traded Corporation Governance, Operation & Regulation, 1 vol. John H. Matheson. (Corporate Law Ser.). 1993. 110.00 (*0-685-68838-0*) West Group.

An Asterisk (*) at the beginning of an entry indicates that the title is appearing for the first time.

Publicly Traded Corporations: Governance, Operation & Regulation. John H. Matheson. 1993. 130.00 (*0-318-72145-7*) West Group.

***Public/Private Finance & Development: Methodology/Deal Structuring/Development Solicitation.** John Stainback. LC 99-88951. 352p. 2000. text 89.00 (*0-471-33367-0*) Wiley.

***Public/Private Partnerships: Implications for Innovation in Transportation.** Ed. by Barry Leonard. 52p. (C). 2000. reprint ed. pap. text 20.00 (*0-7881-8692-2*) DIANE Pub.

***Public/Private Partnerships in the Wine Industry (in California)** Ed. by Mike Thompson. 90p. 2000. pap. text 25.00 (*0-7881-8653-1*) DIANE Pub.

Public's Business: The Politics & Practices of Government Corporations. Annmarie H. Walsh. LC 77-15595. (Twentieth Century Fund Bk.). 456p. 1978. 37.50 (*0-262-23086-0*) MIT Pr.

Public's Business: The Politics & Practices of Government Corporations. Annmarie H. Walsh. LC 77-15595. (Twentieth Century Fund Bk.). 456p. 1980. pap. text 18.00 (*0-262-73055-3*) MIT Pr.

Public's Capacity for Deliberation. Steve Farkas et al. 26p. (Orig.). 1995. pap. 7.50 (*1-889483-38-9*) Public Agenda.

Public's First Right to Federally Generated Power: An Analysis of the Preference Clause. American Public Power Association Staff et al. LC 85-243014. 38p. 1985. 10.00 (*0-317-01241-X*) APPA.

Public's Perspective on Social Welfare Reform. 52p. (Orig.). 1988. pap. 10.50 (*1-889483-03-6*) Public Agenda.

Public's Right to Know: The Supreme Court & the First Amendment. David M. O'Brien. LC 81-988. 205p. 1981. 55.00 (*0-275-90694-9*, C0694, Praeger Pubs) Greenwood.

Public's Role in Science Issues: A Series of Informal Conversations with Science Leaders & Observers. Ed. by Richard Harwood. 36p. (Orig.). 1989. pap. 6.00 (*1-889483-37-0*) Public Agenda.

Public's View of the Outdoor Environment As Interpreted by Magazine Ad-Makers. Robert E. Coughlin & Karen A. Goldstein. (Discussion Papers: No. 25). 1968. pap. 10.00 (*1-55869-102-2*) Regional Sci Res Inst.

Publii Ovidii Nasonis Epistularum Ex Ponto, Liber IV: A Commentary on Poems 1 to 7 & 16. Martin Helzle. (Spudasmata Ser.: Vol. XLIII). (GER.). 211p. 1989. 25.87 (*3-487-09141-0*) G Olms Pubs.

Publikation Aelterer Praktischer und Theoretischer Musikwerke, 29 vols. in 27. Ed. by Robert Eitner. (Illus.). 5176p. 1966. reprint ed. lib. bdg. 1750.00 (*0-8450-1700-4*) Broude.

Publikumsbeschimpfung und Andere Sprechstucke. Handke. (GER.). (C). 1966. 12.00 (*0-8442-2896-6*, X2896-6) NTC Contemp Pub Co.

Publish-a-Book, 4 vols. (Publish-a-Book Ser.). pap. 23.80 (*0-7398-0223-2*) Raintree Steck-V.

Publish & Be Murdered. Ruth Dudley Edwards. LC 99-60079. 217p. 1999. pap. 12.95 (*1-890208-13-2*) Poisoned Pen.

***Publish & Be Murdered.** large type unabridged ed. Ruth Dudley Edwards. 2000. 25.95 (*0-7531-5975-9*, 159759, Pub. by ISIS Lrg Prnt) ISIS Pub.

Publish & Flourish: A Guide for Writing in Education. Council for Exceptional Children Staff. Ed. by Bob Algozzine et al. LC 98-44123. 1998. pap. text 24.95 (*0-86586-319-9*, P5273) Coun Exc Child.

Publish & Perish. Sally S. Wright. 1999. mass mkt. 5.99 (*0-345-42588-X*) Ballantine Pub Grp.

Publish & Perish. Sally S. Wright. LC 96-37551. (Ben Reese Mystery Ser.: Vol. 1). 300p. 1997. pap. 9.99 (*1-57673-067-0*, Multnomah Bks) Multnomah Pubs.

Publish & Perish. large type ed. Sally S. Wright. LC 98-27445. (Ben Reese Mystery Ser.). 1998. 22.95 (*0-7862-1566-6*) Thorndike Pr.

Publish & Perish: Three Tales of Tenure & Terror. James Hynes. LC 96-53532. 3834p. 1997. text 24.00 (*0-312-15628-6*) St Martin.

Publish & Perish: Three Tales of Tenure & Terror. James Hynes. 352p. 1998. pap. 14.00 (*0-312-18696-7*) St Martin.

Publish & Perish Vol. 8: The Organizational Ecology of Newspaper Industries. Glenn R. Carroll. Ed. by Samuel B. Bacharach. LC 87-3267. (Monographs in Organizational Behavior & Industrial Relations: Vol. 8). 291p. 1987. 78.50 (*0-89232-440-6*) Jai Pr.

Publish, Don't Perish: The Scholars Guide to Academic Writing & Publishing. Joseph M. Moxley. LC 92-22639. 208p. 1992. pap. 18.95 (*0-275-94453-0*, B4453, Praeger Pubs); lib. bdg. 52.95 (*0-313-27735-4*, MUD, Praeger Pubs) Greenwood.

Publish It Now Vol. 1: Your Complete Guide to Self-Publishing Success & Small Business Expansion. Pamela K. Costa. (Illus.). 90p. (Orig.). 1997. pap. 14.95 (*0-9643002-1-4*) Costa Pubng.

Publish It on the Web! Macintosh. 2nd ed. Bryan Pfaffenberger. LC 97-40600. (Illus.). 568p. 1997. pap., pap. text 37.95 incl. cd-rom (*0-12-553162-1*) Morgan Kaufmann.

Publish It on the Web! Windows. 2nd ed. B. Pfaffenberger. LC 97-18404. (Illus.). 587p. 1997. pap., pap. text 37.95 incl. cd-rom (*0-12-553160-5*) Morgan Kaufmann.

Publish It Yourself: Understanding Self-Publishing & Its Effects on the Industry. F. P. Shum. 1999. 14.95 (*1-55212-230-1*) Trafford Pub.

Publish-It-Yourself Handbook: Literary Tradition & How-To. 2nd rev. ed. Ed. by Bill Henderson. 1987. pap. 11.95 (*0-916366-44-8*, Pub. by Pushcart Pr) Norton.

Publish It Yourself Handbook: Literary Tradition & How-To. 4th ed. Bill Henderson. 350p. 2000. pap., wbk. ed. 18.00 (*1-888889-03-9*, Pub. by Pushcart Pr) Norton.

Publish Now! large type ed. Herb Marlow. (Illus.). 233p. 1999. spiral bd. 24.95 (*0-9666858-3-0*, PN-1) Four Seasons Bks.

Publish or Perish. Ed. by Philip Hills. 186p. 1990. 80.00 (*1-870167-01-5*, Pub. by P Francis) St Mut.

Publish or Perish: The Wrong Issue. Leslie H. Cochran. 180p. 1992. 22.50 (*0-9631438-1-6*) Step Up Inc.

Publish to Win: Smart Strategies to Sell More Books. Jerrold R. Jenkins & Anne M. Stanton. LC 97-65078. 320p. (Orig.). 1997. pap. 20.00 (*0-9649401-2-4*) Rhodes & Easton.

Publish Without Perishing. Peter Benjaminson. 144p. 1992. pap. 16.95 (*0-8106-1544-4*) NEA.

Publish Your Book in Six Months: A Handbook. Garbo. 42p. 1991. student ed. 9.95 (*1-881152-00-6*) Big Breakfast.

Publish Your Book Yourself with Your Computer: A How-To Manual. William G. White. 50p. 1995. pap. write for info. (*1-888296-01-1*) Jen Comp.

Publish Your Own Novel: Get Your Book into Print & into the Stores Now. Connie Shelton. Ed. by Lee Ellison. LC 96-85198. (Illus.). 272p. 1996. pap. 18.95 (*0-9643161-6-1*) Intrigue Press.

***Published Essays, 1940-1952 Vol. 10: The Collected Works of Eric Voegelin.** Ed. by Ellis Sandoz. 288p. 2000. 34.95 (*0-8262-1304-9*) U of Mo Pr.

Published Pottery of Palestine. Larry G. Herr & Warren C. Trenchard. LC 96-2091. (ASOR Bks.: Vol. 1). 310p. (C). 1996. pap. text 21.00 (*0-7885-0280-8*, 85 03 01, Pub. by Am Sch Orient Res) David Brown.

Published Screenplays: A Checklist. Clifford McCarty. LC 73-138656. (Serif Series: Bibliographies & Checklists: No. 18). 141p. reprint ed. pap. 43.80 (*0-8357-5574-6*, 203520100093) Bks Demand.

Published Works. Howard Prescott. Ed. by Judy Knop et al. LC 98-88102. 1998. pap. 9.95 (*1-892109-01-8*) Founders Hill.

***Published Writings of Wilbur & Orville Wright.** Wilbur Wright & Orville Wright. Ed. by Peter L. Jakab & Rick Young. LC 99-39653. (History of Aviation Ser.). (Illus.). 352p. 2000. 49.95 (*1-56098-938-6*) Smithsonian.

Publisher & His Circle: The Life & Work of John Taylor, Keats's Publisher. Tim Chilcott. LC 72-194396. xi, 247p. 1972. write for info. (*0-7100-7198-1*, Routledge Thoemms) Routledge.

Publisher & His Friends, 2 vols. Samuel Smiles. LC 77-148304. reprint ed. 125.00 (*0-404-07492-8*) AMS Pr.

***Publisher Essentials.** 160p. (C). 2001. spiral bd. 16.00 (*0-13-026198-X*) S&S Trade.

Publisher 98 Fast & Easy. Paul Marchesseault. LC 97-76321. 400p. 1998. per. 19.99 (*0-7615-1513-5*) Prima Pub.

Publisher-Public Official: Real or Imagined Conflict of Interest? Don Sneed & Daniel Riffe. LC 91-4203. 144p. 1991. 55.00 (*0-275-94087-X*, C4087, Praeger Pubs) Greenwood.

***Publisher to the Decadents: Leonard Smithers in the Careers of Beardsley, Wilde & Dowson.** James G. Nelson. 2000. 35.00 (*0-271-01974-3*) Pa St U Pr.

***Publisher 2000.** (Illus.). (YA). 1999. pap. write for info. (*0-7423-0354-3*, PUBL2K001LG) ComputerPREP.

***Publisher 2000 for Windows: Visual QuickStart Guide.** Gillian Hall. LC 00-503128. (Illus.). 368p. (C). 1999. pap. text 17.99 (*0-201-35462-4*) Peachpit Pr.

***Publisher 2000 Professional Results.** Roger C. Parker. (Illus.). 448p. 2000. pap. 29.99 (*0-07-212298-6*) McGrw-H Intl.

***Publisher 2000 Fast & Easy.** Paul Marchesseault. LC 99-70008. (Fast & Easy Ser.). (Illus.). 407p. 1999. pap. 16.99 (*0-7615-2033-3*) Random.

Publishers & Librarians: A Foundation for Dialogue Proceedings of the 42nd Conference of the Graduate Library School, May 13-15, 1983. Ed. by Mary Biggs. LC 83-18124. (University of Chicago Studies in Library Science Ser.). 106p. Date not set. reprint ed. pap. 32.90 (*0-608-21016-1*, 205454400003) Bks Demand.

Publishers & Librarians: A Foundation for Dialogue: Proceedings of the 42nd Annual Conference of the Graduate Library School. Ed. by Mary Biggs. LC 83-18124. (Studies in Library Science). 112p. 1984. pap. text 7.50 (*0-226-04847-0*) U Ch Pr.

Publishers Association, 1896-1946: With an Epilogue. Reginald J. Kingsford. LC 74-101445. 238p. reprint ed. pap. 67.90 (*0-608-12065-0*, 2024483) Bks Demand.

Publisher's Direct Mail Handbook. Nat G. Bodian. LC 86-27471. 288p. 1987. 42.50 (*0-89495-079-7*) Oryx Pr.

***Publishers Directory.** 21st ed. Gale Group Staff. 2000p. 1999. 370.00 (*0-7876-3472-7*) Gale.

***Publishers Directory.** 22nd ed. 2000p. 2000. 385.00 (*0-7876-3473-5*, UXL) Gale.

Publishers, Distributors & Wholesalers of the United States 1998-1999, 2 vols., Set. 20th ed. Ed. by Bowker Staff. 4000p. 1998. 215.00 (*0-8352-4049-5*) Bowker.

***Publishers, Distributors & Wholesalers of the United States 1999-2000, 2 vols.** Ed. by Bowker Staff. 4000p. 1999. 229.00 (*0-8352-4261-7*) Bowker.

***Publishers Distributors & Wholesalers of the United States 2000-2001, 2 vols., Set. 21st ed. Ed. by Bowker Staff. 5,300p. 2000. 249.00 (0-8352-4302-8) Bowker. "An asset to all library order departments." -Booklist "Easy to use with information accessible in a variety of ways ...Highly recommended." -AMERICAN REFERENCE BOOKS ANNUAL Save time and effort locating any of more than 100,000 U.S. publishers, wholesalers, distributors, software firms, audiocassette producers, museum and association imprints, and trade publishers who have gone out of business! This two-volume time-saver lets you track down firms and organizations by name...by imprints, subsidiaries, and division...by state...by firms with toll-free and fax numbers...by ISBN prefix...and by publishers who have gone out of business! This two-volume time-saver lets you track down firms and organizations by name...by imprints, subsidiaries, and division...by state...by ISBN prefix...and by publisher's field of activity. Discount schedules and return policies are provided. And a separate index lists inactive and out-of-business publishers.**
Publisher Paid Annotation.

Publisher's Guide to Binding & Finishing. Geoff Potter. (Illus.). 192p. 1991. 41.95 (*0-948905-18-2*) Chapman & Hall.

Publisher's Guide to Distribution. Roger Woodham. (Illus.). 176p. 1991. mass mkt. 62.95 (*0-948905-30-1*) Chapman & Hall.

Publisher's Guide to Litho Printing. Ian Faux. (Illus.). 200p. 1991. 41.95 (*0-948905-03-4*) Chapman & Hall.

Publisher's Guide to Successful Multinational Mailings. Alfred M. Goodloe. (Illus.). 117p. 1986. write for info. (*0-9616409-0-1*) Direct Intl.

Publishers International ISBN Directory, 1996/97, 3 vols. 23rd ed. Ed. by International ISBN Agency, Berlin Staff. 1996. 375.00 (*3-598-21605-X*) K G Saur Verlag.

Publisher's International ISBN Directory, 1998-99, 3 vols. 25th ed. Ed. by International ISBN Agency-Berlin Staff. 4436p. 1998. 410.00 (*3-598-21607-6*) K G Saur Verlag.

Publishers' International ISBN Directory, 1999-2000, 3 vols., Set. 26th ed. 3380p. 1999. 410.00 (*3-598-21608-4*) K G Saur Verlag.

***Publishers' International ISBN Directory 2000-2001, 3 vols., set.** 27th ed. Ed. & Compiled by International ISBN Agency, Berlin Staff. 5500p. 2000. 425.00 (*3-598-21609-2*, Pub. by K G Saur Verlag) Bowker.

Publishers Office Manual: How to Do Your Paperwork in the Music Publishing Industry. Walter E. Hurst & William S. Hale. LC 66-19600. (Entertainment Industry Ser.: Vol. 3). 1966. pap. 10.00 (*0-911370-57-9*) Seven Arts.

Publishers Office Manual: How to Do Your Paperwork in the Music Publishing Industry. 2nd rev. ed. Walter E. Hurst & William S. Hale. LC 66-19600. (Entertainment Industry Ser.: Vol. 3). 1986. 25.00 (*0-911370-58-7*) Seven Arts.

Publisher's Portraits: Publishing in Central & Eastern Europe. Ed. by Vera Ebels Dolanova'. 125p. 1997. pap. text 16.95 (*0-9664654-1-5*) Index Intl.

Publisher's Practical Dictionary in Twenty Languages. Imre Mora. 417p. 1984. 75.00 (*963-05-3151-8*, Pub. by Akade Kiado) St Mut.

Publisher's Practical Dictionary in 20 Languages. 3rd rev. ed. Imre Mora. 418p. 1984. 250.00 (*0-8288-3399-0*, M6933) Fr & Eur.

Publisher's Trade List Annual Index, 1903-1963. Ed. by Anthony Abbott. 150p. 1980. lib. bdg. 60.00 (*0-930466-25-X*) Mecklermedia.

Publishers' Trade List Annual Index, 1964-1980. Ed. by Anthony Abbott. 175p. 1984. lib. bdg. 75.00 (*0-88736-015-7*) Mecklermedia.

***Publishers Trade List Annual 2000.** Ed. by Bowker Staff. 2000. 335.00 (*0-8352-4316-8*) Bowker.

Publishers Trade List Annual 1998. Ed. by Bowker Staff. 1998. 335.00 (*0-8352-4150-5*) Bowker.

Publishers Trade List Annual 1999: A Buying & Reference Guide to Books & Related Products. Ed. by Bowker Staff. 1999. 265.95 (*0-8352-4212-9*) Bowker.

Publishing: The Creative Business. Harald Bohne & Harry VanIerssel. LC 72-96455. 100p. reprint ed. pap. 31.00 (*0-608-18596-5*, 202045600018) Bks Demand.

Publishing: The Future. Ed. & Intro. by Peter Owen. LC 88-61919. 128p. 1988. pap. 14.95 (*0-7206-0721-3*) Dufour.

Publishing: The Future. Ed. & Intro. by Peter Owen. LC 88-61919. 128p. 1988. 21.00 (*0-7206-0720-5*, Pub. by P Owen Ltd) Dufour.

Publishing a Book: How to Publish Your Own Work & Make a Profit. 3rd ed. Robert Spicer. 144p. 1998. pap. 19.95 (*1-85703-262-4*, Pub. by How To Bks) Trans-Atl Phila.

Publishing a Newspaper. Belshaw. (J). (gr. 3-8). 1996. pap. text, wbk. ed. 11.95 (*1-55734-209-1*) Tchr Create Mat.

Publishing Agreements: A Book of Precedents. 3rd ed. Charles Clark. 1990. text 44.95 (*0-04-440237-6*) Routledge.

Publishing Agreements: A Book of Precedents. 3rd rev. ed. Charles Clark. 238p. (C). 1989. 30.00 (*0-941533-56-5*, NAB) I R Dee.

Publishing Agreements: A Book of Precedents. 4th ed. Charles Clark. 270p. 1993. boxed set 75.00 (*0-406-02094-9*, U.K., MICHIE) LEXIS Pub.

Publishing & Book Culture in Russia & the New States: Challenges for the West. 134p. (Orig.). (C). 1995. pap. text 40.00 (*0-7881-1915-X*) DIANE Pub.

Publishing & Book Development in Sub-Saharan Africa, 1960-1994: An Annotated Bibliography. Ed. by Hans M. Zell & Cecile Lomer. 410p. 1996. 100.00 (*1-873836-46-5*) Bowker-Saur.

Publishing & Cultural Politics in Revolutionary Paris, 1789-1810. Carla Hesse. LC 90-26493. (Studies on the History of Society & Culture: No. 12). (Illus.). 256p. 1991. 40.00 (*0-520-07443-2*, Pub. by U CA Pr) Cal Prin Full Svc.

Publishing & Development: A Book of Readings. Philip G. Altbach & Damtew Teferra. LC 97-43609. (Studies in Publishing). 1997. 20.00 (*0-09-640784-0*) Bellagio Pub.

Publishing & Development in the Third World. Ed. by Philip G. Altbach. 442p. 1992. 90.00 (*1-873836-40-6*, Pub. by H Zell Pubs) Seven Hills Bk.

***Publishing & Licensing Your Art: An Art Calendar Guide.** Drew Steis. Ed. by Sally Steis. 27p. 1999. pap. 9.95 (*0-945388-29-2*) Art Calendar.

Publishing & Presenting Clinical Research. Warren S. Browner. LC 98-36024. 206p. 1998. pap. 34.95 (*0-683-30745-2*) Lppncott W & W.

Publishing & Publication Bias in Health Sciences: Index of New Information & Research Reference Book. Thomas Q. Sheltze. 150p. 1996. 47.50 (*0-7883-1164-6*); pap. 44.50 (*0-7883-1165-4*) ABBE Pubs Assn.

Publishing & Readership in Revolutionary France & America: A Symposium at the Library of Congress, Sponsored by the Center for the Book & the European Division, 4. Carol Armbruster. LC 92-38070. (Beta Phi Mu Monograph: No. 4). 240p. 1993. 52.95 (*0-313-28793-7*, GM8793) Greenwood.

Publishing & Review of Reference Sources. Ed. by Bill Katz & Robin Kinder. LC 86-22910. (Reference Librarian Ser.: No. 15). 336p. (C). 1987. text 49.95 (*0-86656-571-X*) Haworth Pr.

Publishing Books. Ed. by Graig LaMay et al. LC 96-30691. 190p. (Orig.). 1997. pap. text 19.95 (*1-56000-905-5*) Transaction Pubs.

Publishing by Microcomputer: Its Potential & Its Problems. Ed. by Tom Carney. 184p. 1990. 75.00 (*1-870167-04-X*, Pub. by P Francis) St Mut.

***Publishing Careers.** rev. ed. Robert A. Carter. (Opportunities in . . . Ser.). 2000. 14.95 (*0-658-00483-2*, VGM Career) NTC Contemp Pub Co.

Publishing Careers, 5 vols., Set. 89.00 (*0-685-23045-7*, CG368) Ready Ref Pr.

Publishing Child-Oriented Articles in Psychology: A Compendium of Publication Outlets. Ed. by Michael C. Roberts et al. LC 82-45067. 178p. (Orig.). (C). 1982. pap. text 20.50 (*0-8191-2661-6*); lib. bdg. 52.50 (*0-8191-2660-8*) U Pr of Amer.

Publishing Digital Video. 2nd ed. Jan Ozer. LC 97-10922. (Illus.). 557p. 1997. pap., pap. text 34.95 incl. cd-rom (*0-12-531942-8*) Morgan Kaufmann.

***Publishing Economics: Analyses of the Academic Journal Market in Economics.** Ed. by Joshua Gans. LC 99-89245. 320p. 2000. 95.00 (*1-84064-283-1*) E Elgar.

Publishing for Fun & Profit. large type ed. (For Fun & Profit Ser.). (Illus.). 350p. (Orig.). Date not set. pap. 24.95 (*1-56559-929-2*) HGI-Over Fifty.

Publishing for Library Markets, 1999. LC 98-105334. (Illus.). 172p. 1999. 1995.00 (*0-88709-146-6*) Simba Info Inc.

Publishing for Professional Markets: 99-2000 Review, Trends & Forecast. Matthew Bechard et al. Ed. by Linda Kopp. 282p. 1999. 1995.00 (*0-88709-109-1*) Simba Info Inc.

Publishing for Professional Markets: 99-2003 Review, Trends & Forcast. 3rd rev. ed. Matthew Bechard. Ed. by Kathleen Martucci & Victor Robell. (Illus.). 282p. 1999. 1995.00 (*0-88709-155-5*) Simba Info Inc.

Publishing for Profit: Successful Bottom-Line Management for Book Publishers. Thomas Woll. LC 98-23962. 304p. 1998. pap. 24.95 (*1-55561-170-2*) Fisher Bks.

***Publishing for Small Press Runs: How to Print & Market from 20 to 200 Copies of Your Book.** Gary Michael Smith. 188p. 1999. pap. 19.95 (*0-9658380-3-X*, Chatgris Pr) G M Smith.

Publishing for Tenure & Beyond. Franklin H. Silverman. LC 99-13526. 184p. 1999. 65.00 (*0-275-96390-X*, Praeger Pubs); pap. 18.95 (*0-275-96391-8*, Greenwood Pr) Greenwood.

Publishing for the College Market: Review, Trends & Forecast. 3rd ed. 1996. 1795.00 (*0-614-25713-1*) Simba Info.

Publishing for the People: The Firm Posrednik, 1885-1905. Robert C. Otto. LC 87-240. (Modern European History Ser.). 264p. 1987. text 15.00 (*0-8240-8060-2*) Garland.

Publishing from a Full Text Data Base. 1986. lib. bdg. 79.95 (*0-8490-3541-4*) Gordon Pr.

Publishing Glad Tidings: Essays on Christmas Music. William E. Studwell & Dorothy E. Jones. LC 97-46983. 115p. 1998. pap. 24.95 (*0-7890-0398-8*) Haworth Pr.

Publishing Guide for Engineering Sciences. Haluk Beliroglu & Kip Becker. (Topics in Operations Research Ser.). xxv, 506p. 1986. pap. 10.00 (*1-877640-13-1*) INFORMS.

Publishing in African Languages: Challenges & Prospects. Philip G. Altbach & Damtew Teferra. LC 99-10511. (Bellagio Studies in Publishing ; 10 Ser.). 1999. write for info. (*0-9646078-5-9*) Bellagio Pub.

Publishing in Journals on the Family: A Survey & Guide for Scholars, Practitioners, & Students. Ed. by Roma S. Hanks et al. LC 92-11452. (Marriage & Family Review Ser.: Vol. 17, Nos. 3-4). Orig. Title: Marriage & Family Review. 280p. 1992. text 49.95 (*1-56024-256-6*) Haworth Pr.

Publishing in Journals on the Family: Essays on Publishing. Ed. by Linda Matocha & Marvin B. Sussman. LC 93-9424. (Marriage & Family Review Ser.: Vol. 18, Nos. 1-2). (Illus.). 272p. 1993. lib. bdg. 49.95 (*1-56024-341-4*) Haworth Pr.

Publishing in Rhetoric & Composition. Ed. by Gary A. Olson & Todd W. Taylor. LC 96-36302. 247p. (C). 1997. text 59.50 (*0-7914-3395-1*); pap. text 19.95 (*0-7914-3396-X*) State U NY Pr.

Publishing in the Digital Age. Gareth Ward. LC 99-182022. 160p. 1998. pap. 24.95 (*0-906097-94-0*, Pub. by Bowerdean Pub) Capital VA.

P

Publishing in the Information Age: A New Management Framework for the Digital Era. Douglas M. Eisenhart. LC 93-5581. 312p. 1994. 65.00 (*0-89930-847-3*, Quorum Bks) Greenwood.

Publishing in the Information Age: A New Management Framework for the Digital Era. Douglas M. Eisenhart. LC 93-5581. 320p. 1996. pap. 27.95 (*0-275-95696-2*, Praeger Pubs) Greenwood.

Publishing in the Life Sciences: Index of Modern Authors & Subjects with Guide for Rapid Research. Science & Life Consultants Association Staff. LC 90-56272. 200p. 1991. 47.50 (*1-55914-318-5*); pap. 44.50 (*1-55914-319-3*) ABBE Pubs Assn.

Publishing in the Organizational Sciences. 2nd ed. L. L. Cummings & Peter J. Frost. (Foundations for Organizational Ser.: 1). 320p. 1995. text 58.00 (*0-8039-7144-3*) Sage.

Publishing in the Third World: Knowledge & Development. Ed. by Philip G. Altbach et al. LC 84-27920. 240p. (C). 1985. text 35.00 (*0-435-08006-7*, 08006) Heinemann.

Publishing in the Third World: Trend Report & Bibliography. Philip G. Altbach & Eva-Maria Rathgeber. LC 80-20146. 186p. 1980. 55.00 (*0-275-90446-6*, C0446, Praeger Pubs) Greenwood.

Publishing in the U. S. S. R. Boris I. Gorokhoff. LC 59-63390. (Indiana University, Indiana University Publications, Social Science: No. 19). 323p. reprint ed. pap. 100.20 (*0-608-11217-8*, 205522500011) Bks Demand.

Publishing Intellectual Capital: Getting Your Business into Print. Cortada. LC 98-51906. 228p. 1999. 41.00 (*0-13-021438-8*, Pub. by P-H) S&S Trade.

Publishing Internet Documents with Office 97: Module 1. Ed. by Victoria Fodale & Stephanie Savage. (Illus.). 141p. (C). 1997. pap. write for info. (*0-7423-0008-0*) ComputerPREP.

Publishing Law. Hugh Jones. LC 96-24665. 312p. (C). 1996. 100.00 (*0-415-15110-4*); pap. 32.99 (*0-415-15466-9*) Routledge.

Publishing Law Handbook, 2 vols. 2nd ed. E. Gabriel Perie & John T. Williams. 1675p. ring bd. 285.00 (*0-13-739525-6*, 44225) Aspen Law.

Publishing Law Handbook, 2 vols. 2nd ed. E. Gabriel Perle & John T. Williams. 1675p. 1993. 285.00 (*0-13-109364-9*) Aspen Law.

Publishing List: The Self-Publishers' Book of Essential Information. A. S. Brown. 256p. 1999. pap. 14.95 (*0-9665306-1-6*) New Park Pr.

Publishing Lives: Interviews with Independent Book Publishers in the Pacific Northwest & British Columbia. Jerome Gold. (Illus.). 584p. 1995. pap. 22.95 (*0-930773-41-1*); lib. bdg. 31.95 (*0-930773-40-3*) Black Heron Pr.

Publishing Newsletters. 3rd rev. ed. Howard P. Hudson. LC 97-76810. (Illus.). 251p. (C). 1998. pap. text 39.95 (*0-9617642-9-5*) H Penn Hudson.

Publishing Now. 2nd ed. Peter Owen. LC 97-180158. 176p. 1997. pap. 26.00 (*0-7206-1009-5*, Pub. by P Owen Ltd) Dufour.

Publishing on Command: How to Publish & Print 1-1,000 Books at a Time! Carole Marsh. (ProPub Ser.). 1994. 29.95 (*1-55609-960-6*); pap. 19.95 (*1-55609-959-2*); lib. bdg. 29.95 (*1-55609-958-4*); disk 29.95 (*1-55609-961-4*) Gallopade Intl.

Publishing on the Internet. Richard Mackie. 96p. (Orig.). 1997. pap. 9.85 (*1-885372-05-1*) Solution CA.

Publishing on the Web: Featuring Netscape Navigator Gold 3 Software - Illustrated Brief Edition. 10th ed. Donald I. Barker & Chia-Ling H. Barker. (Illustrated Ser.). (Illus.). 96p. (C). 1996. pap. write for info. (*0-7600-4650-6*) Course Tech.

Publishing on the World Wide Web for Macintosh: Part of the Don Crabb Library. Greg Holden. (Illus.). 400p. (Orig.). 1995. 30.00 (*1-56830-228-2*) Hayden.

Publishing on Web. Gottleber. 1998. pap., student ed. 45.31 (*0-07-913675-3*) McGraw.

Publishing Opportunities for Energy Research: A Descriptive Guide to Selective Serials in the Social & Technical Sciences, 1. Compiled by Roberta A. Scull. LC 86-14975. (Bibliographies & Indexes in Science & Technology Ser.: No. 1). 416p. 1986. lib. bdg. 79.50 (*0-313-25160-6*, SPG/) Greenwood.

Publishing, Piracy, & Politics: An Historical Study of Copyright in Britain. John Feather. LC 94-7320. 1995. 90.00 (*0-7201-2135-3*) Continuum.

Publishing, Printing, & the Origins of Intellectual Life in Russia, 1700-1800. Gary Marker. LC 84-42893. 316p. reprint ed. pap. 98.00 (*0-608-06329-0*, 206669000008) Bks Demand.

Publishing, Promoting & Selling Your Book for Self-Publishers & Impatient Writers. John C. Bartone. LC 88-47598. (Illus.). 150p. 1988. 39.50 (*0-88164-624-5*); pap. 34.50 (*0-88164-643-1*) ABBE Pubs Assn.

Publishing Standards in the Life Sciences: Index of Activities, Research & Reports. Science & Life Consultants Association Staff. LC 90-56274. 160p. 1991. 47.50 (*1-55914-330-4*); pap. 44.50 (*1-55914-331-2*) ABBE Pubs Assn.

Publishing the Literary Magazine. Ann E. Klaiman. 176p. 1994. pap. 19.95 (*0-8442-5646-3*, Natl Textbk Co) NTC Contemp Pub Co.

***Publishing Timeline 2000: A Chronology of Publishing & Graphic Arts Events.** unabridged ed. Richard Sasso. (Illus.). 400p. (C). 2000. text 80.00 incl. cd-rom (*0-9679051-0-9*); pap. text 65.00 incl. cd-rom (*0-9679051-1-7*) QBC Pubng.

Publishing to Niche Markets. rev. ed. Gordon Burgett. (Illus.). 200p. (Orig.). 1995. pap. 14.95 (*0-910167-27-3*) Comm Unltd CA.

***Publishing with Indesign.** David Bergsland. (Student Material TV Ser.). 352p. (C). 2000. pap. 39.95 (*0-7668-2001-7*) Thomson Learn.

***Publishing with Students.** Chris Weber. 2001. pap. text. write for info. (*0-325-00283-5*) Heinemann.

Publishing Your Art As Cards, Posters & Calendars. 2nd ed. Harold Davis. Ed. by Susan P. Levy. 160p. 1993. pap. 19.95 (*0-913069-42-6*) Consultant Pr.

Publishing Your Medical Research Paper: What They Don't Teach in Medical School. Daniel W. Byrne. LC 97-29896. 298p. 1997. pap. 23.95 (*0-683-30074-1*) Lppncott W & W.

Publishing Your Own Book. Arthur F. Ide. LC 98-14146. viii, 80p. 1998. pap. 10.00 (*0-86663-236-0*) Ide Hse.

Publishments, Marriages, Births & Deaths from the Earlier Records of Gorham, Maine. Ed. by Russell S. Bickford. LC 91-60228. 192p. 1991. 29.50 (*0-929539-83-4*, 1183) Picton Pr.

Publit. Ferdinand Kriwet. (Illus.). 96p. (Orig.). 1971. pap. 4.50 (*0-89366-018-3*) Ultramarine Pub.

Publius: Annual Review of American Federalism: 1981. Ed. by Stephen L. Schechter & Daniel J. Elazar. LC 83-5960. 228p. (Orig.). (C). 1983. lib. bdg. 49.50 (*0-8191-3170-9*) U Pr of Amer.

***Publizist Karl Philipp Moritz.** Susanne Knoche. 382p. 1999. 56.95 (*3-631-33345-5*) P Lang Pubng.

Publizitatsverhalten Mittelgrober Kapitalgesellschaften. Ralf Hager. (GER., Illus.). XXII, 231p. 1993. 46.80 (*3-631-46038-4*) P Lang Pubng.

Pubs & Clubs: Bar Excellence. Pbc International Staff. 1999. 45.00 (*0-688-16055-7*, Wm Morrow) Morrow Avon.

Pubs, Ploughs & "Peculiar People" Towns, Farms & Social Life. Maurice French. (History of the Darling Downs Ser.: Vol. 3). (Illus.). xvi, 327p. (Orig.). 1992. pap. 24.95 (*0-949414-66-2*, Pub. by U Sthrn Queenslnd) Accents Pubns.

PUC Sections 1-20409, Vol. 147. 61p. 1999. write for info. (*0-327-06996-1*, 57774-12) LEXIS Pub.

PUC Sections 20410-End, Vol. 148. 13p. 1999. write for info. (*0-327-06997-X*, 57775-12) LEXIS Pub.

Pucci: A Renaissance in Fashion. Shirley Kennedy. (Illus.). 216p. 1991. 75.00 (*1-55859-057-9*) Abbeville Pr.

Puccini. (Portraits of Greatness Ser.). (ENG & ITA.). 1984. 17.50 (*0-918367-06-9*) Elite.

Puccini: A Critical Biography. 3rd rev. ed. Mosco Carner. (Illus.). 566p. 1992. 59.95 (*0-8419-1326-9*) Holmes & Meier.

Puccini: His International Art. Michele Girardi. LC 99-45342. 1997. 65.00 (*0-226-29757-8*) U Ch Pr.

***Puccini & His Operas.** Stanley Sadie. (Illus.). 256p. 2000. text 24.95 (*0-312-24418-5*) St Martin.

***Puccini Companion.** William Weaver. (Illus.). 352p. 2000. pap. 19.95 (*0-393-32052-9*) Norton.

Pucciniosireae: Uredinales, Pucciniaceae. P. Buritica & J. F. Hennen. LC 79-27151. (Flora Neotropica Monographs: No. 24). (Illus.). 50p. 1980. pap. 7.75 (*0-89327-219-1*) NY Botanical.

Puccini's La Boheme. Giacomo Puccini. (Music (General) Ser.). 96p. 1984. pap. 2.95 (*0-486-24607-8*) Dover.

Puccini's Madama Butterfly. Giacomo Puccini. (Opera Libretto Ser.). 79p. (Orig.). 1983. pap. 2.95 (*0-486-24465-2*) Dover.

Puchasing & Supply Management: Future Directions & Trends. Joseph R. Carter & Ram Narasimhan. LC 95-71340. 128p. (Orig.). 1996. pap. text 20.00 (*0-945968-24-8*) Ctr Advanced Purchasing.

Puck! Kirby Puckett: Baseball's Last Warrior. Chuck Carlson. Ed. by Steve Cameron. LC 97-13818. 224p. 1997. 22.95 (*1-886110-14-X*, Pub. by Addax Pubng) Midpt Trade.

Puck of Pook's Hill. Rudyard Kipling. 1976. 22.95 (*0-8488-0173-3*) Amereon Ltd.

Puck of Pook's Hill, Set. unabridged ed. Rudyard Kipling. (YA). 1997. pap. 67.20 incl. audio (*0-7887-1719-7*, 40587) Recorded Bks.

Puck of Pook's Hill; &, Rewards & Fairies. Rudyard Kipling. Ed. by Donald Mackenzie. LC 92-14450. (World's Classics Ser.). 496p. (J). (gr. 4 up). 1993. pap. 7.95 (*0-19-282575-5*) OUP.

Puck of Pool's Hill. Burnett. (Children's Library). 1998. pap. 3.95 (*1-85326-138-6*, 1386WW, Pub. by Wrdsworth Edits) NTC Contemp Pub Co.

Puck Power. Evan Skolnick. (Disney's Action Club Ser.). 1997. pap. text 4.50 (*1-57840-069-4*, Pub. by Acclaim Bks) Penguin Putnam.

Puck Starts Here. Garth Vaughan. (Illus.). 210p. 1997. pap. 19.95 (*0-86492-212-4*, Pub. by Goose Ln Edits) Genl Dist Srvs.

***Puck-Stoppin' Trivia: Great Goalies Galore!** Don Weekes. (J). 1999. pap. text 6.95 (*1-55054-710-0*, Greystone) DGL.

Puck'em All: We've Got the Magick. Rachel L. Manning & Al G. Manning. 150p. (Orig.). 1985. pap. 7.95 (*0-941698-10-6*) Pan Ishtar.

***Pucker up, Buttercup.** A. J. Wood. (Books for Valentine's Day). (Illus.). 14p. (J). 2000. 12.95 (*0-7613-1286-2*, Copper Beech Bks) Millbrook Pr.

Puckerbrush: The Writings of Edward Sprague. Edward Sprague. (Illus.). 124p. (Orig.). 1995. pap. 13.50 (*1-883957-03-6*) R Hood Little.

Puck's Nightly Pranks, 1870. Charles T. Brooks. (Illus.). 20p. 1998. reprint ed. pap. 25.00 (*0-87556-860-2*) Saifer.

PUD P. R. O. S. E. A. Vol. V: (Timber Trees) Major Commercial Timbers. Ed. by I. Soerianegara & F. N. Soerianegara. 300p. (C). 1991. text 600.00 (*0-89771-638-8*, Pub. by Intl Bk Distr) St Mut.

Puddephatt's Primers. Puddephatt. 110p. 1976. pap. 2.95 (*0-85032-136-0*, Pub. by C W Daniel) Natl Bk Netwk.

Puddin Hill Cookbook: Recollections & Recipes. Mary L. Kearns. LC 88-90762. (Illus.). 299p. 1988. text 19.95 (*0-9621248-0-X*) Mary Puddin Hill.

Pudding & Pie. Vince Cross & Nick Sharratt. (Illus.). 48p. (J). 1994. (*0-19-279988-6*) OUP.

Pudding Book: Authentic American & English Pudding Recipes from 1782-1882 with Instructions for the Modern Kitchen. Robert G. Stone & David M. Hinkley. (Illus.). 67p. (Orig.). 1996. pap. 9.95 (*0-9647895-1-5*) FLPB Pr.

Pudding Is Nice. Dorothy Kunhardt. LC 75-19948. (Illus.). 64p. (J). (gr. 1 up). 1975. 15.00 (*0-912846-18-6*); pap. 10.00 (*0-912846-12-7*) Bookstore Pr.

Puddings: Classical Essential. Koenemann Inc. Staff. (Illus.). 64p. 1999. pap. 1.95 (*3-8290-3015-0*) Konemann.

***Puddings A to Z: Sweet & Savory Puddings, Custards, Flans & Mousses.** Marie Simmons. LC 99-32150. (Illus.). 96p. 1999. 17.00 (*0-395-90990-2*) HM.

***Puddings & Cobblers.** (Cordon Bleu Home Collection). 2000. 12.00 (*962-593-822-2*, Pub. by Periplus) Tuttle Pubng.

Puddings & Pies: Traditional Desserts for a New Generation. Barbara Grunes. 208p. (Orig.). 1990. pap. 14.95 (*0-89909-329-9*, 80-152-3) Yankee Bks.

Puddings from A to Z, Vol. 2. Fred Brengelman & Russ Leavenworth. LC 96-104409. 62p. 1995. spiral bd. 14.95 (*0-938911-09-0*) Indiv Ed - Poppy Ln.

***Puddle.** David McPhail. (Illus.). 32p. (J). (ps-k). 2000. pap. 4.95 (*0-374-46030-2*) FS&G.

Puddle. David M. McPhail. LC 97-10872. 32p. (J). (ps-k). 1998. 15.00 (*0-374-36148-7*) FS&G.

***Puddle Duck Identification.** Creative Publishing International Staff. (Hunter's Pocket Guides Ser.). (Illus.). 2000. pap. 4.99 (*0-86573-484-4*) Creat Pub Intl.

Puddle Jumpers: Fun Weather Projects for Kids. Jennifer S. Gillis. (Illus.). 64p. (Orig.). (J). (ps-5). 1996. pap. 9.95 (*0-88266-938-9*) Storey Bks.

Puddle Pail. Elisa Kleven. LC 96-45291. (Illus.). 32p. (J). 1997. 15.99 (*0-525-45803-4*, Dutton Child) Peng Put Young Read.

***Puddle Pail.** Elisa Kleven. (Illus.). (J). 2000. pap. 5.99 (*0-14-056521-3*, PuffinBks) Peng Put Young Read.

Puddle Pail. Elisa Kleven. (J). 1999. pap. 14.99 (*0-525-45741-0*, Dutton Child) Peng Put Young Read.

Puddle Pals & Butterfly Buddies. Annie J. Lang. (Illus.). 50p. 1998. pap. 10.95 (*1-57377-040-X*) Easl Pubns.

Puddleman. Ted Staunton. (Illus.). 32p. (J). (ps-4). 1999. pap. 5.95 (*0-88995-190-X*, Pub. by Red Deer) Genl Dist Srvs.

Puddles. Jonathan London. (Illus.). (J). (ps-1). 1999. 5.99 (*0-14-056175-7*, PuffinBks) Peng Put Young Read.

Puddles. Jonathan London. LC 96-52794. (Illus.). 32p. (J). (ps-1). 1997. 15.99 (*0-670-87218-0*) Viking Penguin.

Puddles & Poop: The Handbook for All Dog Lovers. Rebecca Harvin. (Illus.). 157p. 1999. pap. 7.95 (*0-9641477-4-2*) Rebecca Entpses.

Puddles & Wings & Grapevine Swings: Things to Make & Do with Nature's Treasures for Kids & Their Grown-Up Friends. Imogene Forte & Marge Frank. LC 81-85014. (Illus.). 304p. (J). (gr. k-6). 1982. pap. text 18.95 (*0-86530-004-6*, IP-046) Incentive Pubns.

Puddles on the Prairie. Gloria Bauske. 108p. 1999. pap. 12.95 (*1-57579-146-3*) Pine Hill Pr.

Puddlestamp Records Acoustic Venue Directory, Vol. 1. Garth Cormier. 418p. 1997. pap. 39.95 (*0-9661375-0-7*); lib. bdg. 69.95 (*0-9661375-1-5*) Puddlestomp.

Pudd'nhead Wilson. Mark Twain, pseud. (Classics Illustrated Notes Ser.). (Illus.). 1997. pap. text 4.99 (*1-57840-065-1*, Pub. by Acclaim Bks) Penguin Putnam.

Pudd'nhead Wilson. Mark Twain, pseud. (Airmont Classics Ser.). (Illus.). (YA). (gr. 8 up). 1966. mass mkt. 2.50 (*0-8049-0124-4*, CL-124) Airmont.

Pudd'nhead Wilson. Mark Twain, pseud. 20.95 (*0-89190-348-8*) Amereon Ltd.

Pudd'nhead Wilson. Mark Twain, pseud. LC 99-25710. (Thrift Editions Ser.). 96p. 1999. pap. text 1.50 (*0-486-40885-X*) Dover.

Pudd'nhead Wilson. Mark Twain, pseud. 1964. mass mkt. 3.95 (*0-451-52374-1*, Sig Classics) NAL.

Pudd'nhead Wilson. Mark Twain, pseud. LC 96-41220. 141p. 1998. 21.50 (*0-684-81908-2*) S&S Trade.

Pudd'nhead Wilson. Mark Twain, pseud. Ed. by Malcolm Bradbury. (English Library). 320p. 1969. pap. 8.95 (*0-14-043040-7*, Penguin Classics) Viking Penguin.

Pudd'nhead Wilson. Mark Twain, pseud. (Classics Library). pap. 3.95 (*1-85326-572-1*, 5721WW, Pub. by Wrdsworth Edits) NTC Contemp Pub Co.

Pudd'nhead Wilson. Mark Twain, pseud. 172p. 1987. reprint ed. lib. bdg. 19.95 (*0-89966-577-2*) Buccaneer Bks.

Pudd'nhead Wilson. Mark Twain, pseud. (Works of Samuel Clemens). 1989. reprint ed. lib. bdg. 79.00 (*0-7812-1119-0*) Rprt Serv.

Pudd'nhead Wilson, Vol. 1. Mark Twain, pseud. 160p. 1984. mass mkt. 4.95 (*0-553-21158-7*, Bantam Classics) Bantam.

Pudd'nhead Wilson & Other Tales: Those Extraordinary Twins, The Man that Corrupted Hadleyburg. Mark Twain, pseud. Ed. by R. D. Gooder. (Oxford World's Classics Ser.). 320p. 1999. pap. 7.95 (*0-19-283730-3*) OUP.

Pudd'nhead Wilson & Those Extraordinary Twins. Mark Twain, pseud. Ed. by Sidney E. Berger. LC 79-23679. (Critical Editions Ser.). (Illus.). 384p. (C). 1981. pap. text 12.50 (*0-393-95027-1*) Norton.

Pudgie Pies: Recipes for Camping Pie Irons & Electric Snack Makers. Heidi Kulibert. 52p. 1998. pap. 4.95 (*1-879432-27-7*) Explorers Guide Pub.

Pudgy Book of Babies. Illus. by Kathy Wilburn. (Pudgy Board Bks.). 18p. (J). (ps up). 1984. bds. 3.99 (*0-448-10207-2*, G & D) Peng Put Young Read.

Pudgy Book of Farm Animals. Illus. by Julie Durrell. (Pudgy Board Bks.). 18p. (J). (ps). 1984. bds. 3.99 (*0-448-10211-0*, G & D) Peng Put Young Read.

Pudgy Book of Mother Goose. Illus. by Richard Walz. (Pudgy Board Bks.). 18p. (J). (ps up). 1984. bds. 3.99 (*0-448-10212-9*, G & D) Peng Put Young Read.

Pudgy Merry Christmas Book. Illus. by Mary Morgan. (Pudgy Board Bks.). 18p. (J). (ps-3). 1989. bds. 3.50 (*0-448-02262-1*, G & D) Peng Put Young Read.

Pudgy Pat-a-Cake. Illus. by Terri Super. (Pudgy Board Bks.). 18p. (J). (ps). 1983. bds. 3.99 (*0-448-10204-8*, G & D) Peng Put Young Read.

Pudgy Peek-a-Boo Book. Illus. by Amye Rosenberg. (Pudgy Board Bks.). 18p. (J). (ps). 1983. bds. 3.95 (*0-448-10205-6*, G & D) Peng Put Young Read.

Pudgy Pooch, Picky Pooch. Cheryl S. Smith. LC 98-2868. (Illus.). 144p. 1998. pap. 9.95 (*0-7641-0289-3*, 835899Q) Barron.

Pudgy Where Is Your Nose? Book. Illus. by Laura Rader. (Pudgy Board Bks.). 18p. (J). (ps). 1989. bds. 3.99 (*0-448-02258-3*, G & D) Peng Put Young Read.

Pudlo: Thirty Years of Drawing. Marie Routledge & Marion E. Jackson. (Illus.). 176p. 1995. pap. 24.95 (*0-88884-603-7*) U Ch Pr.

Pudmuddles. Carol B. York. LC 91-23596. (Illus.). 48p. (J). (gr. 2-5). 1993. lib. bdg. 13.89 (*0-06-020437-0*) HarpC Child Bks.

Pudovkin's Films & Film Theory. Peter Dart. LC 74-986. (Dissertations on Film Ser.). 1974. 18.95 (*0-405-04874-2*) Ayer.

Pud's in Practice. Colleen G. Moore. LC 85-51488. 94p. 1985. pap. 36.95 (*0-87420-644-8*, P36) Urban Land.

Puebla & Beyond: Documentation & Commentary. Ed. by John Eagleson & Philip J. Scharper. Tr. by John Drury. LC 79-24098. 384p. reprint ed. pap. 119.10 (*0-8357-4070-6*, 203676000005) Bks Demand.

Puebla de las Mujeres - Genio Alegre. Alvarez G. Quintero. (SPA.). 142p. 1979. 5.95 (*0-8288-7101-9*) Fr & Eur.

Pueblo see Pueblo

Pueblo. Raymond Bial. LC 98-48299. (Lifeways Ser.). (Illus.). 128p. (YA). (gr. 4-7). 1999. lib. bdg. 32.79 (*0-7614-0861-4*) Marshall Cavendish.

Pueblo. Mary D'Apice. (Native American People Ser.). (Illus.). 32p. (J). (gr. 5-8). 1990. lib. bdg. 11.95 (*0-685-36390-2*) Rourke Corp.

Pueblo. Mary D'Apice. (Native American People Ser.: Set II). (Illus.). 32p. (J). (gr. 4-8). 1990. lib. bdg. 22.60 (*0-86625-385-8*) Rourke Pubns.

Pueblo. Rita D'Apice & Mary D'Apice. (Pueblos Americanos Nativos Ser.).Tr. of Pueblo. (SPA.). 32p. (J). (gr. 5-8). 1990. lib. bdg. 21.27 (*0-86625-453-6*) Rourke Pubns.

Pueblo. Charlotte Yue. 128p. (J). (gr. 4-7). 1990. pap. 6.95 (*0-395-54961-2*) HM.

Pueblo: Mountain, Village, Dance. 2nd ed. Vincent Scully. LC 88-29747. (Illus.). 430p. 1989. pap. 35.00 (*0-226-74393-4*) U Ch Pr.

Pueblo: Mountain, Village, Dance. 2nd ed. Vincent Scully. LC 88-29747. (Illus.). 440p. 1989. lib. bdg. 72.00 (*0-226-74392-6*) U Ch Pr.

Pueblo: Plays, Players, Playhouses in the Gilded Age, 1865-1900. Alice Eikenberry. (Illus.). 52p. (Orig.). 1985. pap. 3.75 (*0-915617-08-0*) Pueblo Co Hist Soc.

Pueblo & Mission: Cultural Roots of the Southwest. Susan Lamb. LC 96-39593. (Illus.). 160p. 1997. pap. 19.95 (*0-87358-653-0*) Northland AZ.

***Pueblo & Navajo Contemporary Pottery & Directory of Artists.** Guy Berger & Nancy N. Schiffer. LC 99-88913. (Illus.). 192p. 1999. pap. 29.95 (*0-7643-1024-0*) Schiffer.

Pueblo & Navajo Indian Life Today: A Look at Indian Life in New Mexico. Kris Hotvedt. LC 93-14236. (Illus.). 96p. (Orig.). 1993. pap. 8.95 (*0-86534-204-0*) Sunstone Pr.

Pueblo Architecture & Modern Adobes: The Residential Designs of William Lumpkins. Joseph Traugott & William T. Lumpkins. LC 98-4201. 1998. pap. 19.95 (*0-89013-367-0*) Museum NM Pr.

Pueblo Artists: Portraits. Toba Tucker. LC 98-4203. 1998. 55.00 (*0-89013-363-8*) Museum NM Pr.

Pueblo Bonito. George H. Pepper. 398p. 1996. 45.00 (*0-8263-1735-9*); pap. 19.95 (*0-8263-1736-7*) U of NM Pr.

***Pueblo Boy: Growing up in Two Worlds.** Marcia Keegan. (Illus.). 48p. 2000. reprint ed. 14.95 (*1-57416-059-1*) Clear Light.

Pueblo Boy, Growing up in Two Wolrds. Marcia Keegan. LC 90-45187. (J). 1997. 11.19 (*0-606-11768-7*, Pub. by Turtleback) Demco.

Pueblo Children of the Earth Mother, Vol. 2. Thomas Mails. LC 98-27441. (Illus.). 544p. 1998. reprint ed. pap. 27.50 (*1-56924-669-6*) Marlowe & Co.

Pueblo Crafts. Ruth M. Underhill. (Wild & Woolly West Ser.: No. 36). (Illus.). 143p. 1979. pap. 12.00 (*0-910584-51-6*) Filter.

Pueblo Crafts. Ruth M. Underhill. Ed. by Willard W. Beatty. LC 76-43880. (U. S. Office of Indian Affairs Indian Handcrafts Ser.: 7). reprint ed. 55.00 (*0-404-15737-8*) AMS Pr.

Pueblo Crafts. Ruth M. Underhill. (Illus.). 147p. 1984. reprint ed. pap. 7.95 (*0-936984-07-4*) Schneider Pubs.

Pueblo Cultures. B. Wright. (Iconography of Religions Ser.: No. X-4). (Illus.). xii, 29p. 1986. pap. 51.00 (*90-04-07106-7*) Brill Academic Pubs.

Pueblo de la Promesa, Vol. I. S. G. De Graaf. (SPA.). 415p. pap. 16.00 (*1-55883-065-0*, 6700-2510C) Libros Desafio.

Pueblo de la Promesa, Vol. II. S. G. De Graaf. (SPA.). 419p. pap. 16.00 (*1-55883-066-9*, 6700-2520C) Libros Desafio.

Pueblo de la Promesa, Vol. III. S. G. De Graaf. (SPA.). 413p. pap. 16.00 (*1-55883-067-7*, 6700-2530C) Libros Desafio.

Pueblo de la Promesa, Vol. IV. S. G. De Graaf. (SPA.). 248p. pap. 12.00 (*1-55883-068-5*, 6700-2540C) Libros Desafio.

P

An Asterisk (*) at the beginning of an entry indicates that the title is appearing for the first time.

Pueblo de Mexico. Laura Conlon. (Al Sur de Nuestra Frontera Ser.).Tr. of People of Mexico. 24p. (J). (gr. k-4). 1994. lib. bdg. 17.27 (*1-55916-073-X*) Rourke Bk Co.

Pueblo del Cargador del Ano. Oliver La Farge & Douglas Byers. Tr. by Victor Montejo & Oscar Velazquez. (SPA., Illus.). 377p. (Orig.). 1997. pap. 24.95 (*1-886502-16-1*) Yax Te Found.

Pueblo del Espiritu. Jack W. Hayford. (SVP Ser.). Date not set. pap. text 7.99 (*0-89922-513-6*) Caribe Betania.

Pueblo del Sol (The People of the Sun) Alfonso Caso. (SPA., Illus.). 154p. 1983. pap. 5.99 (*968-16-2901-9*, Pub. by Fondo) Continental Bk.

Pueblo Designs: One Hundred Seventy-Six Illustrations of the Rain Bird. Harry P. Mera. (Illus.). 113p. 1970. reprint ed. pap. 8.95 (*0-486-22073-7*) Dover.

Pueblo en la Cruz see Tragedy of Bolivia: A People Crucified

Pueblo en Vilo (An Undecided People) Luis Gonzalez. (SPA., Illus.). 349p. 1984. pap. 12.99 (*968-16-1737-1*, Pub. by Fondo) Continental Bk.

Pueblo Girls: Growing up in Two Worlds. Marcia Keegan. (Illus.). 48p. (J). (gr. 4-10). 1999. 14.95 (*1-57416-020-6*) Clear Light.

Pueblo God & Myths. Hamilton A. Tyler. LC 64-11317. (Civilization of the American Indian Ser.: Vol. 71). (Illus.). 336p. 1984. pap. 15.95 (*0-8061-1112-7*) U of Okla Pr.

Pueblo Indian. Steven Cory. LC 95-3739. (American Pastfinder Ser.). (Illus.). 48p. (J). (gr. 4-7). 1996. lib. bdg. 21.27 (*0-8225-2976-9*, Lerner Publctns) Lerner Pub.

Pueblo Indian. Joe S. Sando. 1976. pap. 12.25 (*0-685-65151-7*) Indian Hist Pr.

Pueblo Indian Cookbook. rev. ed. Phyllis Hughes. LC 77-76238. (Illus.). 64p. 1977. pap. 11.95 (*0-89013-094-9*) Museum NM Pr.

Pueblo Indian Embroidery. Harry P. Mera. LC 94-34722. (Illus.). 80p. 1995. pap. text 6.95 (*0-486-28418-2*) Dover.

Pueblo Indian Folk-Stories. Charles F. Lummis. LC 91-40614. (Illus.). xxx, 257p. 1992. reprint ed. pap. 15.00 (*0-8032-7938-8*, Bison Books) U of Nebr Pr.

Pueblo Indian Land Grants of the "Rio Abajo", New Mexico. Herbert O. Brayer. Ed. by Stuart Bruchey. LC 78-56700. (Management of Public Lands in the U. S. Ser.). 1979. reprint ed. lib. bdg. 15.95 (*0-405-11320-X*) Ayer.

Pueblo Indian Painting: Tradition & Modernism in New Mexico, 1900-1930. J. J. Brody. LC 96-50100. (Illus.). 238p. 1997. 60.00 (*0-933452-45-4*); pap. 30.00 (*0-933452-46-2*) Schol Am Res.

***Pueblo Indian Pottery: 750 Artist Biographies.** Gregory Schaaf. (American Indian Art Ser.: Vol. 2). (Illus.). 304p. 2000. 55.00 (*0-9666948-1-3*) CIAC Pr.

Pueblo Indian Religion, Vol. 1. Elsie C. Parsons. LC 95-47046. (Illus.). xl, 577p. 1996. pap. 25.00 (*0-8032-8735-6*, Bison Books) U of Nebr Pr.

Pueblo Indian Religion, Vol. 2. Elsie C. Parsons. LC 95-47046. (Illus.). xix, 760p. 1996. pap. 25.00 (*0-8032-8736-4*, Bison Books) U of Nebr Pr.

Pueblo Indian Revolt of Sixteen Ninety-Six & the Franciscan Missions in New Mexico: Letters of the Missionaries & Related Documents. Tr. & Intro. by J. Manuel Espinosa. LC 88-10022. (Illus.). 336p. 1991. reprint ed. pap. 21.95 (*0-8061-2365-6*) U of Okla Pr.

Pueblo Indian Vocational Rehabilitation Services Study: Final Report. W. E. Martin & J. C. O'Connell. 85p. 1986. pap. text. write for info. (*1-888557-11-7*, 100109) No Ariz Univ.

Pueblo Indian Water Rights: Struggle for a Precious Resource. Ed. by Charles T. DuMars et al. LC 84-2490. 183p. 1984. 29.50 (*0-8165-0832-1*) U of Ariz Pr.

***Pueblo Indian Wisdom: Native American Legends & Mythology.** Teresa Pijoan. (Illus.). 117p. 2000. pap. 10.95 (*0-86534-319-5*) Sunstone Pr.

Pueblo Indian World. Edgar L. Hewett & Bertha P. Dutton. Ed. by John P. Harrington. LC 76-43737. reprint ed. 37.50 (*0-404-15578-2*) AMS Pr.

Pueblo Indians see Junior Library of American Indians

Pueblo Indians. Liza N. Burby. (Junior Library of American Indians). (J). 1994. 13.15 (*0-606-08044-9*) Turtleback.

Pueblo Indians. Pamela Ross. LC 98-7244. (Native Peoples Ser.). (J). 1998. 14.00 (*0-7368-0079-4*, Bridgestone Bks) Capstone Pr.

Pueblo Indians. Pamela Ross. (Native Peoples Ser.). (J). 1998. 14.00 (*0-516-21357-1*) Childrens.

Pueblo Indians of New Mexico: Their Land, Economy & Civil Organization. S. B. De Aberle. LC 49-2640. (American Anthropological Association Memoirs Ser.: No. 70). 1974. reprint ed. 25.00 (*0-527-00569-X*) Periodicals Srv.

Pueblo Indians of North America. Edward P. Dozier. (Illus.). 224p. 1983. reprint ed. pap. text 12.50 (*0-88133-059-0*) Waveland Pr.

Pueblo Indians of San Ildefonso. William Whitman. LC 73-82352. (Columbia Univ. Contributions to Anthropology Ser.: Vol. 34). reprint ed. 31.50 (*0-404-50584-8*) AMS Pr.

Pueblo Indians of the Southwest. Mira Bartok & Christine Ronan. (Big World Read Along Ser.). (Illus.). 20p. (J). (gr. k-2). 1995. bds. 4.95 (*0-673-36258-2*, GoodYrBooks) Addson-Wesley Educ.

Pueblo Indians of the Southwest: Stencils. Mira Bartok & Christine Ronan. (Ancient & Living Cultures Ser.). (Illus.). 32p. (J). (gr. 3 up). 1993. pap. 9.95 (*0-673-36102-0*, GoodYrBooks) Addson-Wesley Educ.

Pueblo Life Postcards. (Postcard Archive Ser.). (Illus.). 64p. (Orig.). 1994. pap. 9.95 (*0-89013-263-1*) Museum NM Pr.

Pueblo Lindo: Users Manual. Syracuse Language Systems. (J). 1998. pap. 10.00 (*0-8384-6105-0*) Heinle & Heinle.

Pueblo Mothers & Children: Essays by Elsie Clews Parsons, 1915-1924. Elsie C. Parsons. Ed. by Barbara Babcock. LC 89-82082. (Illus.). 140p. 1991. 29.95 (*0-941270-66-1*); pap. 17.95 (*0-941270-65-3*) Ancient City Pr.

Pueblo Nations: Eight Centuries of Pueblo Indian History. Joe S. Sando. LC 91-72483. (Illus.). 296p. (C). 1992. 24.95 (*0-940666-17-0*); pap. 14.95 (*0-940666-07-3*) Clear Light.

Pueblo of Jemez. Elsie W. Parsons. LC 76-43805. (Phillips Academy: No. 3). reprint ed. 67.50 (*0-404-15661-4*) AMS Pr.

Pueblo of San Felipe. Leslie Alvin White. LC 32-30651. (American Anthropological Association Memoirs Ser.: No. 38). 1932. 25.00 (*0-527-00537-1*) Periodicals Srv.

Pueblo of Santa Ana, New Mexico. Leslie Alvin White. LC 43-10004. (American Anthropological Association Memoirs Ser.: No. 60). 1942. 35.00 (*0-527-00559-2*) Periodicals Srv.

Pueblo of Sia, New Mexico. Leslie Alvin White. (Bureau of American Ethnology Bulletins Ser.). 358p. 1995. lib. bdg. write for info. (*0-7812-4184-7*) Rprt Serv.

Pueblo People: Ancient Traditions, Modern Lives. Marcia Keegan & Claude M. Saks. LC 98-30832. (Illus.). 264p. 1999. 39.95 (*1-57416-000-1*) Clear Light.

Pueblo Population & Society: The Arroyo Hondo Skeletal & Mortuary Remains. Ann M. Palkovich. LC 80-51310. (Arroyo Hondo Archaeological Ser.: Vol. 3). (Illus.). 194p. 1981. pap. 14.95 (*0-933452-03-9*) Schol Am Res.

Pueblo Potter: A Study of Creative Imagination in Primitive Art. Ruth L. Bunzel. (Illus.). 134p. 1972. reprint ed. pap. 7.95 (*0-486-22875-4*) Dover.

Pueblo Pottery Designs. Kenneth M. Chapman. LC 94-41764. (Pictorial Archive Ser.). 208p. 1995. 9.95 (*0-486-28476-X*) Dover.

Pueblo Pottery Families: Acoma, Cochiti, Hopi, Isleta, Jemez, Laguna, Nambe, Picuris, Pojoaque, San Ildefonso, San Juan, Santa Clara, Santo Domingo, Taos, Tesuque, Zia, Zuni. Lillian Peaster. LC 97-3643. 160p. 1997. pap. 19.95 (*0-7643-0233-7*) Schiffer.

***Pueblo Pottery Making: A Study at the Village of San Idelfonso.** limited ed. Carl E. Guthe. (Illus.). 131p. 2000. 120.00 (*1-57898-248-0*) Martino Pubng.

Pueblo Pottery Making: A Study of the Village of San Ildefonso. Carl E. Guthe. LC 76-43718. reprint ed. 44.50 (*0-404-15554-5*) AMS Pr.

Pueblo Pottery of the New Mexico Indians. Betty Toulouse. LC 77-71898. (Guidebooks Ser.). (Illus.). 96p. 1977. pap. 12.95 (*0-89013-091-4*) Museum NM Pr.

Pueblo Profiles: Cultural Identity Through Centuries of Change. Joe S. Sando. LC 94-17268. (Illus.). 324p. 1997. 24.95 (*0-940666-39-1*); pap. 14.95 (*0-940666-40-5*) Clear Light.

Pueblo Que Testifica de Cristo. Darrell W. Robinson.Tr. of People Sharing Jesus. (SPA.). 272p. 1996. student ed. 10.99 (*0-89922-339-7*, C001-3397) Caribe Betania.

Pueblo Que Testifica de Cristo. Darrell W. Robinson.Tr. of People Sharing Jesus. (SPA.). 1996. teacher ed. 10.99 (*0-89922-310-9*, C001-3109) Caribe Betania.

Pueblo Revolt. Robert Silverberg. LC 93-44801. (Illus.). xi, 216p. 1994. pap. 10.95 (*0-8032-9227-9*, Bison Books) U of Nebr Pr.

Pueblo Revolt. Weber. LC 98-87544. 132p. 1999. pap. text 12.95 (*0-312-19174-X*) St Martin.

Pueblo Revolt of 1680: Conquest & Resistance in Seventeenth-Century New Mexico. Andrew L. Knaut. LC 94-23666. (Illus.). 272p. 1997. pap. 14.95 (*0-8061-2992-1*) U of Okla Pr.

Pueblo Shields from the Fred Harvey Fine Arts Collection. Barton Wright. LC 75-43343. (Illus.). 96p. 1976. 9.50 (*0-87358-146-6*) Heard Mus.

***Pueblo Steel Town Trollies.** Morris Cafkey & John A. Haney. LC 99-73843. (Illus.). 144p. 1999. pap. 29.95 (*0-918654-57-2*) CO RR Mus.

Pueblo Stories & Storytellers. 2nd rev. ed. Mark Bahti. LC 96-61115. (Illus.). 56p. 1996. pap. 12.95 (*1-887896-01-5*, Rio Nuevo) Treas Chest Bks.

Pueblo Storyteller. Diane Hoyt-Goldsmith. (Illus.). (J). (gr. 4-6). 1991. pap. 6.95 (*0-8234-1080-3*); lib. bdg. 16.95 (*0-8234-0864-7*) Holiday.

Pueblo Storyteller. 93rd ed. Ed. by Harcourt Brace Staff. 1993. pap. text 12.20 (*0-15-300343-X*, Harcourt Child Bks) Harcourt.

Pueblo Storyteller: Development of a Figurative Ceramic Tradition. Barbara A. Babcock et al. LC 86-4279. (Illus.). 201p. 1990. reprint ed. pap. 25.95 (*0-8165-1193-4*) U of Ariz Pr.

Pueblo Village Sticker Picture Book. Steven James Petruccio. (Illus.). (J). 1995. pap. 4.50 (*0-486-28689-4*) Dover.

Pueblos. Alice K. Flanagan. Ed. by Brendan January. (True Bks.). (Illus.). 48p. (J). 1998. pap. 6.95 (*0-516-26383-8*) Childrens.

Pueblos. Suzanne Powell. LC 93-18368. (First Bks.). (Illus.). 64p. (J). (gr. 4-6). 1993. lib. bdg. 22.00 (*0-531-20068-X*) Watts.

Pueblos. large type ed. Suzanne Powell. (First Bks.). (Illus.). 64p. (J). (gr. 5-8). 1994. pap. 6.95 (*0-531-15703-2*) Watts.

Pueblos: A True Book. Alice Flanagan. LC 97-12683. (True Bks.). 48p. (J). (gr. 2-4). 1998. 21.00 (*0-516-20626-5*) Childrens.

Pueblos: Prehistoric Indian Cultures of the Southwest. Sylvio Acatos & Maximilien Bruggman. Tr. by Barbara Fritzemeier. (Illus.). 240p. 1990. 45.00 (*0-8160-2437-5*) Facts on File.

Pueblos de Puerto Rico en Poesia. Joaquin Hernandez. (SPA.). 190p. 1997. pap. write for info. (*1-881713-05-9*) Pubns Puertorriquenas.

Pueblos del Pasado. Claire Forbes. (Bibiloteca de Descubrimientos Ser.).Tr. of Ancient Peoples. (SPA., Illus.). (J). (gr. 3-6). 1997. 11.95 (*0-915741-89-X*, SY7076) C D Stampley Ent.

Pueblos Enfermos: The Discourse of Illness in the Turn-of-the-Century Spanish & Latin American Essay. Michael Aronna. LC 99-42034. No. 262. 160p. 1999. pap. 27.50 (*0-8078-9266-1*) U of NC Pr.

Pueblos Villages Forts & Trails: A Guide to New Mexico's Past. David Grant Noble. LC 93-42192. (Coyote Bks.). 346p. (C). 1994. pap. 13.95 (*0-8263-1485-6*) U of NM Pr.

Pueblos y Lugares de Espana. C. Flores. (SPA., Illus.). 390p. 1993. 295.00 (*84-239-5289-4*) Elliots Bks.

Puede el Hombre Vivir Sin Dios. Tr. of Can Man Live Without God. (ENG & SPA.). 1995. pap. text 10.99 (*0-89922-571-3*) Caribe Betania.

Pueden Salir a Jugar los Santos see Can the Saints Come Out to Play! - A Saint Story for Every Day, Vol. 5, January Saints

***Puedo Intentario?** Karen M. Rogers. Tr. by Ana M. Alvarado. (Think-Kids Book Collection).Tr. of Can I Try?. (SPA., Illus.). 16p. (J). (gr. 1-4). 2000. pap. 2.95 (*1-58237-039-7*) Creat Think.

Puedo Leer, Vol. 4066. Rozanne L. Williams. Ed. by Christine Hood. Tr. by Rancho Park Publishing Staff. (Fun & Fantasy Spanish Learn to Read Ser.).Tr. of I Can Read. (Illus.). 8p. (J). (ps-2). 1996. pap. 1.75 (*1-57471-148-2*, 4066) Creat Teach Pr.

***Puedo Ver: La Historia Del Hombre Que Nacio Ciego.** Marilyn Lashbrook. (Libros Yo Tambien! Ser.).Tr. of Now I See. (SPA., Illus.). 32p. (J). (ps-2). 2000. 5.95 (*1-58170-038-5*) Rainbow Studies.

***Puente - The Bridge.** Ito Romo. LC 00-8197. 2000. 18.95 (*0-8263-2252-2*) U of NM Pr.

Puente en la Selva (Bridge on the Jungle) B. Traven. (SPA., Illus.). 260p. (YA). 1992. reprint ed. pap. 6.99 (*968-16-3662-7*, Pub. by Fondo) Continental Bk.

Puente Hasta Terabithia. Katherine Paterson. 1996. 15.05 (*0-606-10524-7*, Pub. by Turtleback) Demco.

Puentes. Jason Cooper. (Maravillas de la Humanidad Ser.: Set VI).Tr. of Bridges. (SPA.). 24p. (J). (gr. k-4). 1991. lib. bdg. 14.60 (*0-86592-934-3*) Rourke Enter.

Puentes. Patti J. Marinelli. (College Spanish Ser.). (SPA.). (C). 1994. student ed., suppl. ed. 53.95 incl. audio (*0-8384-5409-7*) Heinle & Heinle.

Puentes. Patti J. Marinelli. (College Spanish Ser.). (SPA.). (C). 1994. mass mkt., suppl. ed. 31.95 (*0-8384-5411-9*) Heinle & Heinle.

Puentes. Patti J. Marinelli. (College Spanish Ser.). (SPA.). (C). 1995. 53.95 incl. cd-rom (*0-8384-5410-0*) Heinle & Heinle.

Puentes. annot. ed. Marinelli. 1994. text, teacher ed. 49.25 (*0-8384-4296-X*) Thomson Learn.

Puentes. 2nd ed. Marinelli. (College Spanish Ser.). (C). 1997. pap., wbk. ed. 24.00 (*0-8384-7870-0*) Heinle & Heinle.

Puentes. 2nd ed. Patti J. Marinelli. (College Spanish Ser.). (C). 1997. pap., teacher ed. 50.95 (*0-8384-7861-1*) Heinle & Heinle.

Puentes. 2nd ed. Patti J. Marinelli. LC 97-36718. (College Spanish Ser.). (C). 1997. pap. 50.95 (*0-8384-7834-4*) Wadsworth Pub.

Puentes: Spanish for Intensive & High-Beginner Courses. Patti J. Marinelli & Lizette M. Laughlin. LC 93-38316. (C). 1994. mass mkt. 53.95 (*0-8384-2163-6*) Heinle & Heinle.

Puentes Text. 2nd ed. Patti J. Marinelli. 1997. pap. 60.95 incl. audio (*0-8384-7825-5*) Heinle & Heinle.

Puentes y Fronteras. Gina Valdes. Tr. by Katherine King from SPA. LC 96-35468. (SPA.). 88p. (Orig.). 1996. pap. 9.00 (*0-927534-62-2*) Biling Rev-Pr.

Puer Aeternus. 2nd ed. Marie-Louise Von Franz. LC 80-28090. (Illus.). 292p. 1981. 32.50 (*0-938434-03-9*); pap. 17.95 (*0-938434-01-2*) Sigo Pr.

Puerco Raro Vol. 1: Pasitos Spanish Language Development Books. Darlyne F. Schott. (Pasitos Hacia la Lectura Ser.). 16p. (J). (gr. k-1). 1990. pap. text 11.50 (*1-56537-050-3*) D F Schott Educ.

***Puerta: A Doorway into the Academy.** 2nd ed. U of New Mexico Staff. LC 99-64590. 298p. (C). 1999. per. 24.95 (*0-7872-5955-1*) Kendall-Hunt.

Puerta de la Esperanza. Juan A. Vallejo-Nagera. 1998. pap. text 8.95 (*84-239-7340-9*, Pub. by Espasa Calpe) Continental Bk.

Puerta De Oro (Golden Door) T. Amaya. (SPA.). 0.75 (*0-685-74976-2*, 540640) Editorial Unilit.

Puerta Llamada Divorcio. David Hormachea. (SPA.). 1997. pap. text 9.99 (*0-88113-496-1*) Caribe Betania.

Puertas a la Comunicacion: An Activities Manual. 3rd ed. John G. Copeland et al. (C). 1990. pap. text 32.25 (*0-07-540846-5*) McGraw.

Puertas a la Lengua Espanola: An Introductory Course. John G. Copeland et al. 1990. teacher ed., student ed. write for info. incl. audio (*0-318-67200-6*) McGraw.

Puertas a la Lengua Espanola: An Introductory Course. 3rd ed. John G. Copeland et al. 1988. pap. text. write for info. (*0-07-540855-4*) McGraw.

Puertas a la Lengua Espanola: An Introductory Course. 3rd ed. John G. Copeland et al. 479p. (C). 1990. pap. 65.63 (*0-07-540845-7*) McGraw.

Puertas a la Lengua Espanola: An Introductory Course. 3rd ed. John G. Copeland et al. (C). 1990. teacher ed. 22.18 (*0-07-540851-1*); pap. text 20.62 (*0-07-540852-X*) McGraw.

Puertas a la Lengua Espanola: An Introductory Course. 3rd ed. John G. Copeland et al. 1990. write for info. (*0-07-909484-8*) McGraw.

Puertas a la Lengua Espanola: An Introductory Course. 3rd ed. John G. Copeland et al. (C). 1990. pap., wbk. ed. 27.50 (*0-07-540848-1*); pap., lab manual ed. 28.13 (*0-07-540849-X*) McGraw.

Puertas a la Lengua Espanola: An Introductory Course. 3rd ed. John G. Copeland et al. (C). 1990. audio 52.19 (*0-07-540850-3*) McGraw.

Puertas Abiertas see Open Doors

Puertas al Mundo Hispanico: A Cultural Reader. 3rd ed. John G. Copeland et al. (C). 1990. pap. text 27.25 (*0-07-540847-3*) McGraw.

Puertas de Sion. Bodie Thoene.Tr. of Gates of Zion. (SPA.). 357p. 1986. pap. 7.99 (*1-56063-371-9*, 494580) Editorial Unilit.

Puerto Mochima to Morro del Barcelona. Wilson Ltd. Staff & Imray L. Norie. (C). 1989. 53.00 (*0-7855-5911-6*, Pub. by Laurie Norie & Wilson Ltd) St Mut.

***Puerto Plata, Sosua.** 2000. pap. 9.95 (*2-89464-308-X*, Pub. by Ulysses Travel) Globe Pequot.

Puerto Plata, Sosua, Cabarete: Ulysses Due South Guide. Pascale Couture. (Illus.). 80p. 1994. pap. 5.95 (*2-921444-91-7*) Ulysses Travel.

Puerto Real: The Archaeology of a Sixteenth-Century Spanish Town in Hispaniola. Ed. by Kathleen Deagan. (Ripley P. Bullen & Columbus Quincentennary Ser.). (Illus.). 560p. 1995. 49.95 (*0-8130-1334-8*) U Press Fla.

Puerto Rican: Born in the USA. Clara E. Rodriguez. 256p. 1989. 44.95 (*0-04-497041-2*); pap. 14.95 (*0-04-497042-0*) Routledge.

Puerto Rican & Caribbean Cookbook. Ed. by Raoul Gordon. (Puerto Rico Ser.). 1982. lib. bdg. 72.95 (*0-8490-3228-8*) Gordon Pr.

Puerto Rican & Cuban Catholics in the U. S., 1900-1965. Ed. by Jay P. Dolan & Jaime R. Vidal. LC 94-15463. (Notre Dame History of Hispanic Catholics in the U.S. Ser.: Vol. 2). (C). 1994. text 29.00 (*0-268-03805-8*) U of Notre Dame Pr.

Puerto Rican Communication Studies. Ed. & Intro. by Joan M. Fayer. 188p. (C). 1993. pap. text 14.95 (*0-9627257-5-7*) Aye-Aye Arts.

Puerto Rican Community & Its Children on the Mainland: A Source Book for Teachers, Social Workers & Other Professionals. 3rd rev. ed. Francesco Cordasco & Eugene Bucchioni. LC 81-21250. 469p. 1982. 34.50 (*0-8108-1506-0*) Scarecrow.

Puerto Rican Community Development Project. Puerto Rican Forum Staff. LC 74-14243. (Puerto Rican Experience Ser.). (Illus.). 162p. 1975. reprint ed. 13.95 (*0-405-06230-3*) Ayer.

Puerto Rican Community Participation in East Harlem Bilingual Programs. Alicia Pousada. 66p. 1987. lib. bdg. 5.00 (*1-878483-14-5*) Hunter Coll CEP.

Puerto Rican Cookery. 8th ed. Carmen Aboy Valldejuli. LC 83-2149. (Illus.). 408p. 1983. reprint ed. 21.95 (*0-88289-411-0*) Pelican.

Puerto Rican Cuisine in America: Nuyorican & Bodega Recipes. Oswald Rivera. LC 92-41478. (Illus.). 294p. (Orig.). 1993. pap. 16.95 (*0-941423-84-0*) FWEW.

***Puerto Rican Cultural Identity & the Work of Luis Rafael Sanchez (RLS #268)** John Dimitri Perivolaris. (North Carolina Studies in the Romance Languages). 224p. 2001. pap. text 32.50 (*0-8078-9272-6*) U of NC Pr.

Puerto Rican Culture: An Introduction. Ed. by Raoul Gordon. (Puerto Rico Ser.). 1982. lib. bdg. 59.95 (*0-8490-3226-1*) Gordon Pr.

Puerto Rican Danza, with an Essay on la Borinquena. Ernesto J. Fonfrias. (Puerto Rico Ser.). 1979. lib. bdg. 59.95 (*0-8490-2988-0*) Gordon Pr.

Puerto Rican Discourse: A Sociolinguistic Study. Lourdes M. Torres. LC 96-46361. (Everyday Communication Ser.). 168p. 1997. text 32.50 (*0-8058-1930-4*) L Erlbaum Assocs.

Puerto Rican Discourse: A Sociolinguistic Study. Lourdes M. Torres. LC 96-46361. (Everyday Communication Ser.). 168p. 1997. pap. text 16.95 (*0-8058-1931-2*) L Erlbaum Assocs.

Puerto Rican Dishes. 3rd ed. Berta Cabanillas. 151p. 1971. 21.50 (*0-8477-2780-7*) Adlers Foreign Bks.

Puerto Rican Drama. Ed. by Raoul Gordon. 1976. lib. bdg. 59.95 (*0-8490-0916-2*) Gordon Pr.

Puerto Rican Equation: Puerto Rican Artists Ponder 100 Years since the 1898 Invasion. Juan Sanchez. (Illus.). 47p. 1998. pap. 10.00 (*1-885998-13-9*) Hunter College.

Puerto Rican Experience. Ed. by Francesco Cordasco. (Illus.). 10610p. 1975. 827.50 (*0-405-06210-9*) Ayer.

Puerto Rican Folk-Tales. Ed. by Raoul Gordon. (Puerto Rico Ser.). 1982. lib. bdg. 59.95 (*0-8490-3229-6*) Gordon Pr.

Puerto Rican Folklore. J. Alden Mason. Ed. by Aurelio M. Espinosa. (Puerto Rico Ser.). 1979. lib. bdg. 59.95 (*0-8490-2989-9*) Gordon Pr.

***Puerto Rican Government & Politics: A Comprehensive Bibliography.** Edgardo Melendez. LC 00-24784. 350p. 2000. lib. bdg. 75.00 (*1-55587-894-6*) L Rienner.

Puerto Rican Historiography. Ed. by Raoul Gordon. 1976. lib. bdg. 250.00 (*0-8490-0917-0*) Gordon Pr.

Puerto Rican Historiography. Allen L. Woll. (Studies in Puerto Rican History, Literature & Culture). 1979. lib. bdg. 250.00 (*0-8490-1393-3*) Gordon Pr.

Puerto Rican Houses in Sociohistorical Perspective. Carol F. Jopling. LC 87-6025. 300p. 1992. pap. 18.00 (*0-87049-763-4*) U of Tenn Pr.

Puerto Rican in New York & Other Sketches. Jesus Colon. LC 74-14229. (Puerto Rican Experience Ser.). 206p. 1979. reprint ed. 20.95 (*0-405-06218-4*) Ayer.

Puerto Rican in New York & Other Sketches. Jesus Colon. LC 82-6100. (Illus.). 204p. 1992. reprint ed. pap. 6.95 (*0-7178-0589-1*) Intl Pubs Co.

Puerto Rican Jam: Rethinking Colonialism & Nationalism. Ed. by Frances Negron-Muntaner & Ramon Grosfoguel. LC 97-9569. 256p. (C). 1997. pap. 19.95 (*0-8166-2849-1*); text 49.95 (*0-8166-2848-3*) U of Minn Pr.

P

Puerto Rican Literature: A Bibliography of Secondary Sources. David W. Foster. LC 82-6198. 232p. 1982. lib. bdg. 49.95 (0-313-23419-1, FPR/, Greenwood Pr) Greenwood.

Puerto Rican Migrants of New York City. Manual Alers-Montalvo. LC 83-45349. (Immigrant Communities & Ethnic Minorities in the U. S. & Canada Ser.: No. 8). 1985. 37.50 (0-404-19400-1) AMS Pr.

Puerto Rican Movement: Voices from the Diaspora. Ed. by Andres Torres & Jose E. Velazquez. LC 97-45189. (Puerto Rican Studies). (Illus.). 432p. (C). 1998. text 69.95 (1-56639-617-4); pap. text 24.95 (1-56639-618-2) Temple U Pr.

Puerto Rican Music. Ed. by Raoul Gordon. 1976. lib. bdg. 59.95 (0-8490-0918-9) Gordon Pr.

Puerto Rican Neighbor. Roy Schuckman. (C). 1954. pap. 4.00 (0-87574-075-8) Pendle Hill.

***Puerto Rican Newspaper Coverage of the Puerto Rican Independence Party: A Content Analysis of Three Elections.** Maria Cristina Santana. LC 00-26426. (Latino Communities Ser.). (Illus.). 2000. write for info. (0-8153-3520-2) Garland.

Puerto Rican Perspectives. Ed. by Edward Mapp. LC 73-20175. 179p. 1974. 21.00 (0-8108-0691-6) Scarecrow.

Puerto Rican Politics in Urban America, 107. Ed. by James Jennings & Monte Rivera. LC 83-10739. (Contributions in Political Science Ser.: No. 107). (Illus.). 166p. 1984. 39.95 (0-313-23801-4, JER/, Greenwood Pr) Greenwood.

Puerto Rican Population: A Study of Human Biology. Frederick P. Thieme. (Anthropological Papers Ser.: No. 13). (Illus.). 1959. pap. 1.00 (0-932206-19-0) U Mich Mus Anthro.

Puerto Rican Population of New York City. Ed. by Jaffe Abram. LC 74-14328. (Puerto Rican Experience Ser.). 65p. 1975. reprint ed. 13.95 (0-405-06226-5) Ayer.

Puerto Rican Poverty & Migration: We Just Had to Try Elsewhere. Julio Morales, Jr. LC 85-19439. 271p. 1986. 59.95 (0-275-92020-8, C2020, Praeger Pubs) Greenwood.

Puerto Rican Presence in the History of Cuba. Joaquin Freire. (Puerto Rico Ser.). 1979. lib. bdg. 59.95 (0-8490-2990-2) Gordon Pr.

Puerto Rican Press Reaction to the United States, 1888-1898. Paul N. Chiles. LC 74-14225. (Puerto Rican Experience Ser.). 124p. 1975. reprint ed. 13.95 (0-405-06215-X) Ayer.

Puerto Rican Public Papers of R. G. Tugwell, Governor. Rexford G. Tugwell. LC 74-14251. (Puerto Rican Experience Ser.). 1975. reprint ed. 31.95 (0-405-06237-0) Ayer.

Puerto Rican Question. Jorge Heine & Juan M. Garcia-Passalacqua. LC 84-80499. (Headline Ser.: No. 266). 1983. pap. 5.95 (0-87124-088-2, HS 266) Foreign Policy.

***Puerto Rican Students in U. S. Schools.** Sonia Nieto. LC 99-47154. 2000. write for info. (0-8058-2765-X) L Erlbaum Assocs.

Puerto Rican Study, 1953-1957. 267p. 1972. 35.00 (0-88211-024-1) St Aedans Pr & Bk.

Puerto Rican Study, 1953-1957. J. Cayce Morrison. Ed. by Carlos E. Cortes. LC 79-6217. (Hispanics in the United States Ser.). (Illus.). 1981. reprint ed. lib. bdg. 31.95 (0-405-13165-8) Ayer.

Puerto Rican Tales: Legends of Spanish Colonial Times. 4th ed. Cayetano Coll Y Toste. Tr. by Jose Ramirez-Rivera. LC 78-108190. (Illus.). 111p. 1977. reprint ed. pap. 9.95 (0-9601700-3-0) Editl Libero.

Puerto Rican Tourist Industry. Ed. by Raoul Gordon. 1976. lib. bdg. 250.00 (0-8490-0920-0) Gordon Pr.

Puerto Rican Voices in English: Interviews with Writers. Carmen D. Hernandez. LC 96-53924. 264p. 1997. 62.95 (0-275-95809-4, Praeger Pubs); pap. 22.95 (0-275-95810-8, Praeger Pubs) Greenwood.

Puerto Rican Woman. Edna Acosta-Belen & Eli H. Christensen. LC 79-17638. 186p. 1979. 31.95 (0-275-90325-7, C0325, Praeger Pubs) Greenwood.

Puerto Rican Woman: Perspectives on Culture, History & Society. 2nd ed. Ed. by Edna Acosta-Belen. LC 86-91521. 224p. 1986. pap. 15.95 (0-275-92134-4, B2134, Praeger Pubs) Greenwood.

Puerto Rican Women & Children: Issues in Health, Growth & Development. Ed. by G. Lamberty & C. G. Coll. (Topics in Social Psychiatry Ser.). (Illus.). 306p. (C). 1994. text 47.50 (0-306-44615-4, Kluwer Plenum) Kluwer Academic.

Puerto Rican Women & Work: Bridges in Transnational Labor. Ed. by Altagracia Ortiz. LC 95-43822. (Puerto Rican Studies). 272p. (C). 1996. pap. 22.95 (1-56639-451-1) Temple U Pr.

Puerto Rican Women & Work: Bridges in Transnational Labor. Ed. by Altagracia Ortiz. LC 95-43822. (Puerto Rican Studies). 272p. (C). 1996. 69.95 (1-56639-450-3) Temple U Pr.

Puerto Rican Women's History: New Perspectives. Ed. by Felix V. Matos-Rodriguez & Linda C. Delgado. LC 98-10750. (Perspectives on Latin America & the Caribbean Ser.). 272p. (C). (gr. 13). 1998. pap. text 27.95 (0-7656-0246-6) M E Sharpe.

Puerto Rican Women's History: New Perspectives. Ed. by Felix V. Matos-Rodriguez & Linda C. Delgado. LC 98-10750. (Perspectives on Latin America & the Caribbean Ser.). 272p. (C). (gr. 13). 1998. text 66.95 (0-7656-0245-8) M E Sharpe.

Puerto Rican Workers & the Socialist Party, 1932-1940 see Trabajadores Puertoriquenos y el Partido Socialista, 1932 a 1940

Puerto Rican Writers at Home in the U. S. A. An Anthology. Intro. by Faythe Turner. (Illus.). 352p. (C). 1991. pap. 19.95 (0-940880-31-8) Open Hand.

Puerto Ricans. 2nd ed. Jerome J. Aliotta. LC 95-10125. (Immigrant Experience Ser.). 120p. (YA). (gr. 5 up). 1995. lib. bdg. 19.95 (0-7910-3360-0) Chelsea Hse.

Puerto Ricans: A Documentary History. Ed. by Kal Wagenheim & Olga Jimenez de Wagenheim. LC 93-20849. 355p. 1994. pap. 18.95 (1-55876-077-6) Wiener Pubs Inc.

Puerto Ricans: Culture Change & Language Deviance. Ruby R. Rohrlich. LC 73-90914. (Viking Fund Publications in Anthropology: No. 51). 278p. 1974. pap. 86.20 (0-608-05653-7, 206610700006) Bks Demand.

Puerto Ricans: Migration & General Bibliography. Francesco Cordasco. LC 74-14245. (Puerto Rican Experience Ser.). (Illus.). 1979. reprint ed. 39.95 (0-405-06232-X) Ayer.

Puerto Ricans: Their History, Culture & Society. Ed. by Adalberto Lopez. 490p. 1981. pap. text 24.95 (0-87073-845-3) Schenkman Bks Inc.

Puerto Ricans & Educational Opportunity: An Orginal Anthology. Francesco Cordasco. LC 74-14246. (Puerto Rican Experience Ser.). (Illus.). 1979. reprint ed. 23.95 (0-405-06231-1) Ayer.

Puerto Ricans & Higher Education Policies: Issues of Scholarship, Fiscal Policies & Admissions. Ed. by Camille Rodriguez & Ramon B. Perez. 68p. 1994. pap. 10.00 (1-878483-52-8) Hunter Coll CEP.

Puerto Ricans in New York City. Welfare Council, New York City Staff. LC 74-14230. (Puerto Rican Experience Ser.). (Illus.). 64p. 1975. reprint ed. 11.95 (0-405-06219-2) Ayer.

Puerto Ricans in Philadelphia. Arthur Siegel et al. LC 74-14250. (Puerto Rican Experience Ser.). (Illus.). 150p. 1975. reprint ed. 12.95 (0-405-06236-2) Ayer.

***Puerto Ricans in the United States.** Perez y Gonzalez, Maria. LC 99-55207. 2000. write for info. (0-313-29748-7) Greenwood.

Puerto Rico see Cultures of the World - Group 9

Puerto Rico see Festivals of the World

Puerto Rico see Fiesta 2!

Puerto Rico. Capstone Press Editors. LC 98-44035. (One Nation Ser.). (Illus.). 48p. (J). (gr. 3-7). 1999. 19.00 (0-7368-0118-9, Cpstone High Low) Capstone Pr.

Puerto Rico. Elena E. Cevallos. (World Bibliographical Ser.: No. 52). 193p. 1985. lib. bdg. 45.00 (0-903450-89-5) ABC-CLIO.

***Puerto Rico** Lucile Davis. LC 99-26988. (J). 2000. 32.00 (0-516-21042-4) Childrens.

Puerto Rico. Pamela S. Falk. (Profiles of Latin America Ser.). 1996. text 28.00 (0-86531-629-5) Westview.

***Puerto Rico.** Leila Merrell Foster. LC 00-29531. (Illus.). (YA). 2000. lib. bdg. write for info. (1-57572-381-6) Heinemann Lib.

Puerto Rico. Dennis B. Fradin. (From Sea to Shining Sea Ser.). (J). 1998. pap. text 7.95 (0-516-26282-3) Childrens.

Puerto Rico. Dennis B. Fradin & Judith B. Fradin. LC 95-16892. (Illus.). 64p. (J). (gr. 3-5). 1995. lib. bdg. 26.00 (0-516-03856-7) Childrens.

Puerto Rico. Gousha, H. M., Editors. 1995. 2.95 (0-671-55122-1, H M Gousha) Prntice Hall Bks.

Puerto Rico. Harlan. 1996. write for info. (0-8050-5279-8) H Holt & Co.

Puerto Rico. Joyce Johnston. LC 93-36950. (Hello U. S. A. Ser.). (Illus.). 72p. (J). (gr. 3-6). 1994. lib. bdg. 19.95 (0-8225-2752-9, Lerner Publctns) Lerner Pub.

Puerto Rico. Joyce Johnston. (Hello U. S. A. Ser.). (SPA., Illus.). 72p. (J). (gr. 3-6). 1994. lib. bdg. 19.95 (0-8225-2753-7, Lerner Publctns) Lerner Pub.

Puerto Rico. Elaine Landau. LC 98-45092. (Geography Ser.). (J). 1999. 21.50 (0-516-20986-8) Childrens.

***Puerto Rico.** Elaine Landau. (True Bks.). (J). 2000. pap. text 6.95 (0-516-26770-1) Childrens.

***Puerto Rico.** Joann Milivojevic. LC 99-39109. (Ticket to Ser.). (Illus.). 48p. (J). 2000. lib. bdg. 22.60 (1-57505-144-3, Carolrhoda) Lerner Pub.

Puerto Rico. Joann Milivojevic. LC 98-54648. (Globe-Trotters Club Ser.). (Illus.). 48p. (J). (gr. 3-5). 2000. lib. bdg. 22.60 (1-57505-119-2, Carolrhoda) Lerner Pub.

Puerto Rico. Patricia M. Moritz. LC 98-15473. (Dropping in on Ser.). (J). 1998. 19.93 (0-86593-492-4) Rourke Corp.

***Puerto Rico.** Randall Peffer. (Illus.). 304p. 1999. pap. 15.95 (0-86442-552-X) Lonely Planet.

Puerto Rico. Don Philpott. (Caribbean Sunseekers Ser.). (Illus.). 256p. 1996. pap. 14.95 (0-8442-4940-8, Passprt Bks) NTC Contemp Pub Co.

***Puerto Rico.** Martin Schwebacher. (Celebrate the States Ser.). (Illus.). (J). 2001. 35.64 (0-7614-1070-8, Benchmark NY) Marshall Cavendish.

Puerto Rico. Kathleen Thompson. LC 95-38247. (Portrait of America Library). 48p. (J). (gr. 4-8). 1996. pap. 5.95 (0-8114-7465-8) Raintree Steck-V.

Puerto Rico. Kathleen Thompson. LC 95-38247. (Portrait of America Library). (Illus.). 48p. (YA). (gr. 3-6). 1996. lib. bdg. 22.83 (0-8114-7384-8) Raintree Steck-V.

Puerto Rico. Anne Welsbacher. LC 97-40658. (United States Ser.). (Illus.). 32p. (J). 1998. lib. bdg. 19.93 (1-56239-897-0, Checkerboard Library) ABDO Pub Co.

Puerto Rico. Wilson Ltd. Staff & Imray L. Norie. (C). 1988. 60.00 (0-7855-5946-9, Pub. by Laurie Norie & Wilson Ltd) St Mut.

Puerto Rico. rev. ed. Deborah Kent. LC 91-543. (America the Beautiful Ser.). (Illus.). 144p. (J). (gr. 4 up). 1992. lib. bdg. 28.00 (0-516-00498-0) Childrens.

Puerto Rico. 2nd ed. Insight Guides Staff. (Insight Guides). 1998. pap. text 22.95 (0-88729-745-5); pap. text 12.95 (0-88729-929-6) Langenscheidt.

Puerto Rico. 3rd ed. (Insight Guides Ser.). (Illus.). 1999. pap. 22.95 (0-88729-178-3) Langenscheidt.

***Puerto Rico, 36.** Capstone Press Geography Department Staff. 1999. 19.93 (0-516-21796-8) Capstone Pr.

Puerto Rico!, Vol. 1. Rick Graetz et al. (Illus.). (Orig.). 1995. pap. 13.95 (1-56037-081-5) Am Wrld Geog.

Puerto Rico: A Guide to the Island of Boriguen. Ed. by Gordon Raoul. 1976. lib. bdg. 250.00 (0-8490-1375-5) Gordon Pr.

Puerto Rico: A Guide to the Island of Boriquen. Writers Program, Puerto Rico Staff. LC 73-3650. (American Guide Ser.). 1940. reprint ed. 23.50 (0-404-57950-7) AMS Pr.

Puerto Rico: A Political & Cultural History. Arturo M. Carrion. (Illus.). 400p. (C). 1984. reprint ed. pap. text 18.25 (0-393-30193-1) Norton.

Puerto Rico: An Interpretive History from Precolumbian Times to 1900. Olga Jimenez De Wagenheim. LC 97-36076. (Illus.). 320p. (C). 1998. text 39.95 (1-55876-121-7); pap. text 18.95 (1-55876-122-5) Wiener Pubs Inc.

Puerto Rico: An Introduction. Ed. by Raoul Gordon. (Pureto Rico Ser.). 1982. lib. bdg. 69.95 (0-8490-3227-X) Gordon Pr.

Puerto Rico: Cien Anos de Lucha Politica, 5 vols. Reece B. Bothwell. LC 77-10904. 1980. 100.00 (0-8477-2444-1) U of PR Pr.

Puerto Rico: Classroom Resources for Secondary Schools. Ed. by Deborah Menkart & Catherine A. Sunshine. LC 90-62779. (Caribbean Connections Ser.). (Illus.). 106p. (Orig.). 1990. pap. 12.00 (1-878554-04-2) Netwrk of Educ.

Puerto Rico: Culture & History. Rochester N.Y. Staff. LC 98-178668. (The Peoples' Voice Ser.). ix, 117p. 1993. 26.00 (1-56256-095-6) Peoples Pub Grp.

Puerto Rico: Culture, Politics, & Identity. Nancy Morris. LC 95-14416. (Illus.). 224p. 1995. 57.95 (0-275-95228-2, Praeger Pubs); pap. 19.95 (0-275-95452-8, Praeger Pubs) Greenwood.

Puerto Rico: Cuna y Forja (Historia de la Isla Desde su Descubriiento en 1493 Hasta el Ultimo Periedo de Munoz en 1965) Edilberto Marban. LC 86-81158. (Coleccion Textos). (SPA., Illus.). 298p. (Orig.). 1987. pap. 19.00 (0-89729-405-X) Ediciones.

Puerto Rico: Equality & Freedom at Issue. J. Garcia. LC 83-27239. (Politics in Latin America Ser.). 1984. 29.95 (0-275-91161-6, C1161, Praeger Pubs) Greenwood.

Puerto Rico: Freedom & Power in the Caribbean. Gordon K. Lewis. LC 63-20065. 638p. 1963. reprint ed. pap. 197.80 (0-7837-9607-2, 206036400005) Bks Demand.

Puerto Rico: Hello U. S. A. Joyce Johnston. (Illus.). 72p. (J). (gr. 3-6). 1996. pap. text 5.95 (0-8225-9721-7, First Ave Edns) Lerner Pub.

Puerto Rico: Independence Is a Necessity. Rafael C. Miranda. 3.00 (0-87348-896-2) Pathfinder NY.

***Puerto Rico: Independence Is A Necessity: Rafael Cancel Miranda on the Fight Against U. S. Colonial Rule.** Rafaheal C. Myranda. LC 99-187953. 36p. 1998. pap. 3.00 (0-87348-895-4) Pathfinder NY.

Puerto Rico: Its History, Products & Possibilities see Cuba: Its Past, Present & Future

Puerto Rico: Major World Nations. Zachery Winslow. LC 98-4336. (Major World Nations Ser.). (Illus.). 144p. (YA). (gr. 5 up). 1999. lib. bdg. 19.95 (0-7910-4991-4) Chelsea Hse.

Puerto Rico: Off the Beaten Path: A Guide to Unique Places. John Marino. LC 99-41721. (Off the Beaten Path Ser.). (Illus.). 256p. 1999. pap. 12.95 (0-7627-0275-3) Globe Pequot.

Puerto Rico: The Foundations of Colonialism & Nationhood. Francisco A. Scarano. (Latin American Histories Ser.). (Illus.). 384p. (C). Date not set. text 19.95 (0-19-504626-9) OUP.

Puerto Rico: The Four Storied Country. Jose L. Gonzalez. LC 92-45619. 164p. 1993. reprint ed. pap. text 16.95 (1-55876-072-5) Wiener Pubs Inc.

Puerto Rico: The Trials of the Oldest Colony in the World. Jose T. Monge. LC 97-8965. (Illus.). 288p. 1997. 35.00 (0-300-07110-8) Yale U Pr.

Puerto Rico: The/Trials of the Oldest Colony in the World. Jose Trias Monge. LC 97-8965. (Illus.). 288p. 1997. pap. text 16.95 (0-300-07618-5) Yale U Pr.

Puerto Rico: Trasfondo de su Economia. Sol L. Descartes. LC 73-84204. (SPA.). 50p. 1973. pap. 1.95 (0-913480-14-2) Inter Am U Pr.

Puerto Rico: U. S. Colony in the Caribbean. Jose G. Perez. 23p. 1976. reprint ed. pap. 2.50 (0-87348-380-4) Pathfinder NY.

Puerto Rico: UNA ISLA que Cristobal Colon Descubrio Hace 500 Anos. Louise Cripps. (SPA., Illus.). 1989. 3.50 (0-942423-01-1) Borinquen Bks.

Puerto Rico: 500 Years of Change & Continuity. Ed. by Institute for Puerto Rican Affairs Staff.Tr. of Quinientos Anos de Cambio y Continuidad. (Illus.). 128p. (Orig.). 1991. pap. text 6.95 (0-9631236-0-2) Inst PR Affairs.

Puerto Rico - Deciding Its Future see Single Titles Series

Puerto Rico - Magnifico! A Celebration of an Enchanted Island. Roger LaBrucherie. Tr. by Maria D. Trelles. (ENG & SPA., Illus.). 176p. Date not set. 45.00 (0-939302-34-9) Imagenes.

Puerto Rico - Magnifico! A Celebration of an Enchanted Island. deluxe ed. Roger LaBrucherie. Tr. by Maria D. Trelles. (ENG & SPA., Illus.). 192p. Date not set. 55.00 (0-939302-35-7) Imagenes.

Puerto Rico Advanced Legislative Service (Avanzadas del Servicio Legislativo), No. 98-1. 435p. 1998. pap. write for info. (0-327-06837-X, 4751613) LEXIS Pub.

Puerto Rico & Its People. Trumbull White. LC 74-14258. (Puerto Rican Experience Ser.). (Illus.). 434p. 1975. 35.95 (0-405-06243-5) Ayer.

Puerto Rico & Its Problems. Victor S. Clark et al. LC 74-14226. (Puerto Rican Experience Ser.). (Illus.). 748p. 1975. reprint ed. 62.95 (0-405-06216-8) Ayer.

Puerto Rico & the Non-Hispanic Caribbean: A Study in the Decline of Spanish Exclusivism. Arturo M. Carrion. 160p. (C). 1974. pap. 2.50 (0-8477-0835-7) U of PR Pr.

Puerto Rico & the Sea. Ed. by William S. Beller. Tr. by Irma Balzac. (Illus.). 129p. 1974. pap. 5.00 (0-8477-2301-1) U of PR Pr.

Puerto Rico & the Section 936 Tax Credit: U. S. Operations in Puerto Rico & Its Tax Implications. (Illus.). 66p. (Orig.). (C). 1994. pap. text 35.00 (0-7881-0211-7) DIANE Pub.

Puerto Rico & the United States in the Revolutionary Period of Europe & America. Arturo F. Santana. (Puerto Rico Ser.). 1979. lib. bdg. 69.95 (0-8490-2991-0) Gordon Pr.

Puerto Rico & the United States, 1917-1933. Truman R. Clark. LC 74-26019. (Pitt Latin American Ser.). 254p. reprint ed. pap. 78.80 (0-608-12633-0, 202543300043) Bks Demand.

***Puerto Rico & Virgin Islands Wildlife Viewing Guide.** David W. Nellis. LC 99-26752. (Watchable Wildlife Ser.). (Illus.). 93p. 1999. pap. text 8.95 (1-56044-836-9) Falcon Pub Inc.

Puerto Rico, Borinquen Querida: A Loving Portrait of an Island. Roger A. LaBrucherie. (Illus.). 156p. 1995. 35.00 (0-939302-26-8) Imagenes.

***Puerto Rico Civil Code: 1999 Edition.** 1082p. 1999. pap. 45.00 (0-327-09104-5, 3180113) LEXIS Pub.

Puerto Rico desde Sus Origenes Hasta el Cese de la Dominacion e Panola. Luis M. Diaz Soler. 1995. pap. 12.95 (0-8477-0177-8) U of PR Pr.

Puerto Rico en America Latina. Ed. by Aline F. Buxeda. (SPA., Illus.). 400p. 1994. 25.00 (0-9623590-5-X) Libros-Ediciones.

Puerto Rico en la Economia Politica del Caribe. Ed. by Angel R. Ortiz & Idsa A. Ortega. LC 90-80515. 204p. 1990. pap. 12.50 (0-929157-06-0) Ediciones Huracan.

Puerto Rico en la Lucha por la Hegemonia del Caribe: Siglos XVI-XVIII. Arturo Morales Carrion. (SPA.). 272p. 1995. 14.95 (0-8477-0251-0) U of PR Pr.

Puerto Rico en las Relaciones Internacionales del Caribe. Ed. by Angel R. Ortiz & Idsa A. Ortega. LC 90-80514. 197p. 1990. pap. 12.50 (0-929157-05-2) Ediciones Huracan.

Puerto Rico English Tables No. II: Replacement Volume. 670p. 1998. write for info. (0-327-07237-7, 4756911) LEXIS Pub.

Puerto Rico Environmental Law Handbook. 2nd ed. Fiddler, Gonzales & Rodrigues Staff. LC 96-179491. 499p. 1996. pap. text 95.00 (0-86587-442-5) Gov Insts.

***Puerto Rico Facts & Symbols.** Kathy Feeney. LC 00-23946. (States & Their Symbols Ser.). (Illus.). 24p. (J). (ps-3). 2000. lib. bdg. 15.93 (0-7368-0644-X, Hlltop Bks) Capstone Pr.

***Puerto Rico, Hurricane Georges, September 1998: The President's Long-Term Recovery Action Plan.** Frwd. by William Clinton & Pedro Rossello. (Illus.). 73p. (C). 2000. pap. text 25.00 (0-7881-8647-7) DIANE Pub.

Puerto Rico in Pictures. Lerner Publications, Department of Geography Staff. (Visual Geography Ser.). (Illus.). 64p. (YA). (gr. 5 up). 1989. lib. bdg. 19.95 (0-8225-1821-X, Lerner Publctns) Lerner Pub.

Puerto Rico in Pictures & Poetry. Cynthia P. Maus. 1976. lib. bdg. 250.00 (0-8490-1385-2) Gordon Pr.

***Puerto Rico Insurance Laws & Related Laws.** Puerto Rico. LC 98-66240. 1999. write for info. (0-89246-500-X) NILS Pub.

Puerto Rico Land of Longevity. Raoul Gordon. (Studies in Puerto Rican History, Literature & Culture). 1980. lib. bdg. 250.00 (0-8490-3070-6) Gordon Pr.

Puerto Rico Land of Longevity: Living a Long Life in Puerto Rico. Raoul Gordon. 1978. lib. bdg. 250.00 (0-8490-2490-0) Gordon Pr.

Puerto Rico, Middle Road to Freedom. Carl J. Freidrich. LC 74-14234. (Puerto Rican Experience Ser.). 100p. 1979. reprint ed. 16.95 (0-405-06223-0) Ayer.

Puerto Rico Mio, Four Decades of Change, in Photographs by Jack Delano: Puerto Rico Mio, Cuatro Decadas de Cambio, en Fotografias de Jack Delano. Jack Delane. LC 89-600274. (Illus.). 242p. (Orig.). 1990. pap. 34.95 (0-87474-389-3) Smithsonian.

Puerto Rico Nineteen Hundred: Turn-of-the-Century Architecture in the Hispanic Caribbean 1890-1930. Jorge Rigau. LC 91-11264. (Illus.). 232p. 1992. 50.00 (0-8478-1400-9, Pub. by Rizzoli Intl); pap. 35.00 (0-8478-1430-0, Pub. by Rizzoli Intl) St Martin.

Puerto Rico 1999 Replacement Index. (SPA.). 1225p. 1999. write for info. (0-327-08446-4, 47508-15) LEXIS Pub.

Puerto Rico Past & Present: An Encyclopedia. Ronald M. Fernandez et al. LC 97-1689. (Illus.). 408p. 1998. 59.95 (0-313-29822-X, Greenwood Pr) Greenwood.

Puerto Rico Past & Present & Santo Domingo of Today. A. Hyatt Verrill. 1978. lib. bdg. 59.95 (0-8490-2491-9) Gordon Pr.

Puerto Rico Plan: Environmental Protection Through Development Rights Transfer. John J. Costonis & Robert S. DeVoy. LC 75-15460. 64p. reprint ed. pap. 30.00 (0-608-12219-X, 202388300034) Bks Demand.

***Puerto Rico Pocket Guide.** Berlitz Publishing Staff. (Berlitz Pocket Guide Ser.). (SPA.). 144p. 1999. pap. 8.95 (2-8315-7277-0) Berlitz.

***Puerto Rico Pocket Guide.** Berlitz Publishing Staff. (Berlitz Pocket Guide Ser.). 144p. 1999. pap. 8.95 (2-8315-7225-8) Berlitz.

Puerto Rico Regulations: Containing Regulations, Selected Circular Letters, & Selected Rulings of the Office of the Commissioner of Insurance. Puerto Rico. Office of the Commissioner of Insurance. LC 97-69921. (Illus.). 1997. write for info. (0-89246-484-4) NILS Pub.

An Asterisk (*) at the beginning of an entry indicates that the title is appearing for the first time.

Puerto Rico Restaurant Guide & Recipe Book. unabridged ed. Charles H. Eanes & Susan E. Eanes. LC 94-62028. (Illus.). 96p. (Orig.). 1994. pap. 14.95 (*1-890494-02-X*) Espichel Enterp.
Puerto Rico Seguros, 1998 Edition, 2 vols. Lexis Pub Editorial Staff. pap. 75.00 (*0-327-06221-5*) LEXIS Pub.
Puerto Rico Sessions Laws: English Edition of Leyes de Puerto Rico. Ed. by Butterworths Staff. 1990. boxed set 70.00 (*0-88063-447-2*, MICHIE) LEXIS Pub.
Puerto Rico Sings. 48p. 1984. pap. 6.95 (*0-7935-2626-4*, 8635) H Leonard.
Puerto Rico Spanish Tables No. II: Replacement Volume. 700p. 1998. write for info. (*0-327-07238-5*, 4749811) LEXIS Pub.
Puerto Rico Status: Workshop Before the Committee on Energy & Natural Resources, United States Senate, One Hundred Fifth Congress, Second Session, to Provide the Committee with An Overview of the Political Status Discussion in Puerto Rico. United States. LC 98-194337. 1998. write for info. (*0-16-057361-0*) USGPO.
Puerto Rico Taxes. Ralph J. Sierra, Jr. ring bd. write for info. (*0-318-57390-3*) P-H.
Puerto Rico Teachers' Association & It's Relationship to Teacher Personnel Administration. Irma G. De Serrano. 427p. 1971. 5.00 (*0-8477-2202-3*); pap. 4.00 (*0-8477-2203-1*) U of PR Pr.
Puerto Rico the Island Christopher Columbus Discovered 500 Years. Louise Cripps. 103p. 1987. pap. 3.65 (*0-942423-00-3*) Borinquen Bks.
Puerto Rico, Tierra Adentro y Mar Afuera: Historia y Cultura de los Puertorriquenos. Fernando Pico & Carmen R. Izcoa. LC 91-71358. (SPA.). 304p. (J). (gr. 7). 1991. text 24.95 (*0-929157-12-5*) Ediciones Huracan.
Puerto Rico to Anguilla. Wilson Ltd. Staff & Imray L. Norie. (C). 1990. 60.00 (*0-7855-5940-X*, Pub. by Laurie Norie & Wilson Ltd) St Mut.
Puerto Rico Tres Caminos Hacia un Futuro. Efrain Rivera Perez. (SPA.). 170p. 1991. pap. write for info. (*0-929441-18-4*) Pubns Puertorriquenas.
Puerto Rico Turistico. Hector Sanchez. (SPA.). 197p. 1993. pap. write for info. (*0-929441-44-3*) Pubns Puertorriquenas.
Puerto Rico y el Mar: Un Programa de Accion Sobre Asuntos Marinos. Administracion de Fomento Economico Staff. 129p. 1974. pap. 5.00 (*0-8477-2300-3*) U of PR Pr.
Puerto Rico y la Lucha por la Hegemonia en el Caribe. Arturo Morales Carrion. (Caribbean Collection). (SPA.). 272p. 1995. pap. 12.95 (*0-8477-0196-4*) U of PR Pr.
***Puerto Rico y las Americas.** (C). 1998. 36.33 (*0-06-633118-8*) P-H Intl.
Puerto Rico y los Estados Unidos: El Proceso de Consulta y Negociacion de 1989, Vol. 1. Juan M. Garcia Passalacqua & Carlos Rivera Lugo. (SPA.). 162p. 1991. pap. 7.75 (*0-8477-0891-8*) U of PR Pr.
Puerto Rico y los Estados Unidos Tomo II: El Proceso de Consulta y Negociacion de 1990. Juan Garcia Passalacqua & Carlos Rivera Lugo. (SPA.). 1992. pap. 12.95 (*0-8477-0895-0*) U of PR Pr.
Puerto Rico y Occidente. 6th ed. Ramon Mellado. (UPREX, Ensayo Ser.: No. 31). 189p. (C). 1973. pap. 1.50 (*0-8477-0031-3*) U of PR Pr.
Puerto Rico's Economic Future: A Study in Planned Development. Harvey S. Perloff. LC 74-14240. (Puerto Rican Experience Ser.). (Illus.). 484p. 1975. reprint ed. 52.95 (*0-405-06228-1*) Ayer.
Puerto Rico's Revolt for Independence: El Grito de Lares. Olga J. De Wagenheim. LC 93-15391. (Illus.). 186p. (C). 1993. reprint ed. pap. text 14.95 (*1-55876-071-7*) Wiener Pubs Inc.
Puerto Rico's Statehood Movement, 220. Edgardo Melendez. LC 88-10249. (Contributions in Political Science Ser.: No. 220). 212p. 1988. 52.95 (*0-313-26131-8*, MPH/, Greenwood Pr) Greenwood.
Puerto Rico's Winter League: A History of Major League Baseball's Launching Pad. Thomas E. Van Hyning. LC 95-5914. (Illus.). 304p. 1995. lib. bdg. 29.95 (*0-7864-0128-1*) McFarland & Co.
***Puerto Vallarta & Acapulco.** Ed. by Berlitz Publishing Staff. (Pocket Guides Ser.). (Illus.). 2000. pap. 8.95 (*2-8315-6984-2*) Berlitz.
Puerto Vallarta Square. Robert James Waller. 226p. 1998. reprint ed. 29.95 (*0-7351-0062-4*) Replica Bks.
Puerto Vallarta Squeeze. Robert James Waller. 256p. 1996. mass mkt. 5.99 (*0-446-60360-0*, Pub. by Warner Bks) Little.
Puerto Vallarta Squeeze. large type ed. Robert James Waller. LC 95-33517. 1996. pap. 21.95 (*0-7862-0559-8*) Thorndike Pr.
***Puertorriquednos: Mentalidad Y Actitudes, Siglo XVIII.** Angel Lbopez Cantos. LC 99-25123. 1999. write for info. (*0-8477-0375-4*) U of PR Pr.
Puertorriquenos: Album de la Sagrada Familia Puertorriguena a Partir de 1898. Edgardo Rodriguez-Julia. (Biblioteca de Autores de Puerto Rico Ser.). (SPA., Illus.). 176p. (Orig.). 1992. reprint ed. pap. 6.00 (*1-56328-025-6*) Edit Plaza Mayor.
Puertorriquenos en Nueva York. Amelia A. De Del Rio. (SPA.). 1970. pap. 5.50 (*0-86515-015-X*) Edit Mensaje.
Puertorriquenos en Nueva York: Un Analisis de su Participacion Laboral y Experiencia Migratoria, 1970. Mary G. Powers & John J. Macisco, Jr. vi, 201p. 1982. pap. 5.00 (*0-8477-2468-9*) U of PR Pr.
Puertorriquenos Que Regresaron: Un Analisis de su Participacion Laboral. Luz M. Torruellas & Jose L. Vazquez. Tr. by Nancy Lopez. xiii, 232p. 1984. pap. 5.00 (*0-8477-2469-7*) U of PR Pr.
Puff Daddy. Ariel. 1999. 4.95 (*0-8362-8183-7*) Andrews & McMeel.
***Puff Daddy & the Family: No Way Out.** 64p. 1999. otabind 14.95 (*0-7935-9461-8*) H Leonard.
Puff of Smoke. Ray Lincoln. (Illus.). 88p. (J). (gr. 2-6). 1989. pap., per. 10.00 (*0-9659447-0-0*) Three Friends.
Puffa at the Zoo. (Toddlers' First Stories Ser.: No. 9202). (Illus.). 12p. (J). (ps). 1999. bds. write for info. (*1-85854-673-7*) Brimax Bks.
Puffa on the Farm. (Toddlers' First Stories Ser.: No. 9201). (Illus.). 12p. (J). (ps). 1999. bds. write for info. (*1-85854-672-9*) Brimax Bks.
Puffed Corn Natural Snack or Breakfast Pack Recipe Workbook. Cookbook Consortium Staff. 1993. ring bd. 21.95 (*0-318-04317-3*) Prosperity & Profits.
Puffed Millet Rhyming Natural Snack or Breakfast Pack Recipe Workbook. Cookbook Consortium Staff. 1993. ring bd. 21.95 (*0-318-04318-1*) Prosperity & Profits.
Puffenberger. Descendants of George Puffenberger. Rachel S. Tefft. 38p. 1997. pap. 8.00 (*0-8328-9495-8*); lib. bdg. 18.00 (*0-8328-9494-X*) Higginson Bk Co.
Puffer Ahoy! G. W. Burrows. (C). 1987. 104.00 (*0-85174-419-2*) St Mut.
Puffin. 1994. pap. 7.95 (*0-9635083-4-2*) Misty Mtn.
Puffin: A Journey Home. Jim Tilly. (Illus.). 32p. (J). 1993. 14.95 (*0-9635083-3-4*) Misty Mtn.
Puffin: With Plush Animal. Betsy Girard. (Alphabet Zoop Ser.). 1997. 12.95 (*1-888170-08-5*) Advent Quest.
Puffin Ashore. Delia Huddy. (Illus.). 32p. (J). (ps-1). 1993. 13.95 (*1-85681-171-9*, Pub. by Julia MacRae) Trafalgar.
Puffin at Sea. Delia Huddy. (Illus.). 32p. (J). (ps-1). 1993. 13.95 (*1-85681-161-1*, Pub. by Julia MacRae) Trafalgar.
***Puffin Book of Classic Children's Stories.** (Illus.). 416p. (J). 1998. pap. 13.95 (*0-14-036815-9*, Pub. by Pnguin Bks Ltd) Trafalgar.
***Puffin Book of Classic Verse.** (Illus.). 384p. (J). 1998. pap. 13.95 (*0-14-036816-7*, Pub. by Pnguin Bks Ltd) Trafalgar.
***Puffin Book of Nonsense Stories.** Selected by Quentin Blake. (Illus.). 288p. (YA). (gr. 2 up). 2000. pap. 10.95 (*0-14-038213-5*, Pub. by Pnguin Bks Ltd) Trafalgar.
Puffin Book of Nursery Rhymes. Nick Butterworth. (J). 1995. 10.19 (*0-606-08045-7*, Pub. by Turtleback) Demco.
Puffin Book of School Stories. Bernard Ashley. (Illus.). (J). 1993. pap. 9.95 (*0-14-034675-9*, Pub. by Pnguin Bks Ltd) Trafalgar.
Puffin Book of Stories for Eight Year Olds. Wendy Cooling. (Illus.). 128p. (J). (gr. 3). pap. 8.95 (*0-14-038052-3*, Pub. by Pnguin Bks Ltd) Trafalgar.
Puffin Book of Stories for Seven Year Olds. Wendy Cooling. (Illus.). 176p. (J). 1996. pap. 8.95 (*0-14-037460-4*, Pub. by Pnguin Bks Ltd) Trafalgar.
Puffin Cove: A Queen Charlotte Islands Odyssey. Neil G. Carey. 178p. 1984. pap. 11.95 (*0-88839-216-8*) Hancock House.
Puffin First Picture Dictionary. Brian Thompson. (Illus.). 38p. (J). (ps-3). 1989. pap. 4.99 (*0-14-050777-9*, PuffinBks) Peng Put Young Read.
Puffins. Deborah Allen. LC 98-17172. (Let's Investigate Ser.). (Illus.). 32p. (YA). (gr. 2 up). 1999. lib. bdg. 19.95 (*0-88682-610-1*, Creat Educ) Creative Co.
Puffins. Roy Dennis. (Illus.). 48p. (Orig.). 1994. pap. 11.95 (*0-948661-16-X*, Pub. by Colin Baxter Ltd) Voyageur Pr.
Puffins. Ronald M. Lockley. 15.00 (*0-8159-6511-7*) Devin.
Puffins. Susan E. Quinlan. LC 97-38983. (Illus.). (J). (gr. 2-6). 1998. 19.93 (*1-57505-090-0*, Carolrhoda) Lerner Pub.
Puffins. Lynn M. Stone. (Unusual Animals Discovery Library). 24p. (J). (gr. k-4). 1993. lib. bdg. 10.95 (*0-86593-281-6*) Rourke Corp.
Puffins. Kenny Taylor. LC 98-51771. (WorldLife Library). (Illus.). 72p. (YA). (gr. 6 up). 1999. pap. 16.95 (*0-89658-419-4*) Voyageur Pr.
Puffins. Kenny Taylor. (Illus.). 128p. text 19.95 (*1-873580-06-1*, Pub. by Whittet Bks) Diamond Farm Bk.
Puffin's Advice. Simon Drew. 48p. 1988. 12.50 (*1-85149-102-3*) Antique Collect.
Puffins & Pine Trees: Maine Designs for Machine Knitters. Catherine R. Costa. LC 91-117128. (Illus.). 142p. 1990. spiral bd. 14.95 (*0-89272-277-0*) Down East.
Puffins Are Back! Gail Gibbons. LC 90-30525. (Illus.). 32p. (J). (gr. 4-7). 1991. 15.95 (*0-06-021603-4*) HarpC Child Bks.
Puffins Climb, Penguins Rhyme. Bruce McMillan. LC 94-27225. (Illus.). 32p. (J). (ps-1). 1995. 14.00 (*0-15-200362-2*, Gulliver Bks) Harcourt.
Puffin's Homecoming: The Story of an Atlantic Puffin. Darice Bailer. (Smithsonian Wild Heritage Collection). (Illus.). 32p. (J). (gr. k-3). 1995. pap. 4.95 (*1-56899-141-X*) Soundprints.
Puffin's Homecoming: The Story of an Atlantic Puffin, Incl. 8" toy. Darice Bailer. (Smithsonian Wild Heritage Collection). (Illus.). 32p. (J). (gr. k-3). 1995. pap. 15.95 (*1-56899-147-9*) Soundprints.
Puffin's Homecoming: The Story of an Atlantic Puffin, Incl. Sm. & Lg. Plush Toy. Darice Bailer. (Smithsonian Wild Heritage Collection). (Illus.). 32p. (J). (gr. k-3). 1993. 43.95 incl. audio (*1-56899-647-0*) Soundprints.
Puffin's Homecoming, the Story of an Atlantic Puffin. Darice Bailer. (Smithsonian Wild Heritage Collection). 1993. 10.15 (*0-606-08046-5*, Pub. by Turtleback) Demco.
Puffling in a Pickle. Margaret Ryan. pap. 7.95 (*0-14-037062-5*, Pub. by Pnguin Bks Ltd) Trafalgar.
***Puffy, Xena, Quentin, Uma & 10,000 Other Names for Your New Millenium Baby.** Joal Ryan. LC 98-50403. 432p. 1999. pap. 13.95 (*0-452-28091-5*, Plume) Dutton Plume.
Pufkins. Ed. by Collectors' Publishing Company, Inc. Staff. (Illus.). (Orig.). Date not set. pap. 7.95 (*1-888914-45-9*) CheckerBee.
Pufnstuf & Other Stuff: The Weird & Wonderful World of Sid & Marty Krofft. David Martindale. LC 97-51752. (Illus.). 288p. 1998. pap. 16.95 (*1-58063-007-3*) Renaissance.
Pug. Ian Dunbar. LC 98-46322. 96p. 1999. pap. 7.95 (*1-58245-025-0*) Howell Bks.
Pug: An Owner's Guide to a Happy, Healthy Pet. Edward Patterson. (Illus.). 1996. 12.95 (*0-87605-496-3*) Howell Bks.
Pug Bread Recipe Book: A Guide to Making Homemade Cereal Bars & Granola. rev. ed. Tony T. (Illus.). 63p. 1998. ring bd. 16.95 (*0-9668481-1-X*) Red Hawk Publ.
Pug Champions, 1987-1994. Camino E. E. & Bk. Co. Staff. (Illus.). 120p. 1998. pap. 32.95 (*1-55893-046-9*) Camino E E & Bk.
Pug Champions, 1983-1986. Camino E. E. & Bk. Co. Staff. (Illus.). 115p. 1989. pap. 28.95 (*1-55893-021-3*) Camino E E & Bk.
Pug Champions, 1952-1982. Jan L. Freund & Dorothy L. Johnson. (Illus.). 274p. 1987. pap. 36.95 (*0-940808-33-1*) Camino E E & Bk.
Pug Shots. Jim Dratfield. (Illus.). 96p. 1999. 19.95 (*0-670-88726-9*) Studio Bks.
Pug, Slug, & Doug the Thug. Carol Saller. LC 92-44340. (Illus.). (J). (ps-3). 1994. lib. bdg. 14.95 (*0-87614-803-8*, Carolrhoda) Lerner Pub.
Pugad Baboy Three. Pol Medina, Jr. (TAG., Illus.). 80p. (Orig.). 1992. pap. text 7.50 (*971-10-0518-2*, Pub. by New Day Pub) Cellar.
Pugdog. Andrea Uren. text (*0-374-36149-5*) FS&G.
Puget Sound. Elwood Evans. (Shorey Historical Ser.). 16p. reprint ed. pap. 10.00 (*0-8466-0051-X*, S51) Shoreys Bkstore.
***Puget Sound: Sea Between the Mountains.** Photos by Tim Thompson. LC 99-58711. (Illus.). 112p. 2000. 34.95 (*1-55868-407-7*) Gr Arts Ctr Pub.
Puget Sound Arts Directory. Ed. by Beckey Vedovatti. 146p. (Orig.). 1993. pap. 13.00 (*0-9636400-0-3*) Busn Vol Arts.
Puget Sound Catechism: A Convenient Compendium of Useful Information Respecting the State of Washington. Llewellyn & Co. Staff. (Shorey Historical Ser.). 33p. 1990. reprint ed. pap. 10.00 (*0-8466-0078-1*, S78) Shoreys Bkstore.
Puget Sound Current Guide: North Sound, South Sound. 1997. 21.95 (*0-918439-22-1*) Island Canoe.
Puget Sound Region: A Portfolio of Computer Maps. Mairs & Hoerauf. (Occasional Papers: No. 3). 1986. pap. 2.95 (*0-318-23323-1*) WWU CPNS.
Puget Sounds: A Nostalgic Review of Radio & TV in the Great Northwest. David Richardson. LC 80-26557. (Illus.). 192p. 1981. 14.95 (*0-87564-636-0*) Orcas Pub.
Pugets. Gordon Morse. 1995. pap. text 11.95 (*1-885129-05-X*) My Island.
Puget's Sound: A Narrative of Early Tacoma & the Southern Sound. M. Morgan. LC 79-4844. (Illus.). 370p. 1981. pap. 17.50 (*0-295-95842-1*) U of Wash Pr.
Puggala-Pannatti. Ed. by Richard Morris. LC 78-70109. reprint ed. 42.50 (*0-404-17359-4*) AMS Pr.
Pughis Total Design: Integrated Methods for Successful Product. 2nd ed. Bill Low. 320p. (C). 2000. pap. 59.95 (*0-201-17783-8*) Addison-Wesley.
Pugh's Dictionary of Acronyms & Abbreviations: Abbreviations in Management, Technology, & Information Science. 5th ed. Eric Pugh. LC 86-17352. 372p. 1987. reprint ed. pap. 115.40 (*0-608-02474-0*, 206311800004) Bks Demand.
Pughs of Bayou Lafourche. R. Dana Russell. 100p. 1985. 10.00 (*0-911051-25-2*) Plain View.
Pugilist at Rest: Stories. Thom Jones. 230p. 1994. pap. 11.95 (*0-316-47304-9*) Little.
***Pugilist at Rest: Stories.** Thom Jones. 1998. 11.95 (*0-316-19005-5*, Back Bay) Little.
Pugin: A Gothic Passion. Paul Atterbury. Ed. by Clive Wainwright. LC 94-15209. 310p. 1995. pap. 35.00 (*0-300-06014-9*) Yale U Pr.
Pugin's Builder: The Life & Work of George Myers. Patricia Spencer-Silver. (Illus.). 350p. 1993. text 29.95 (*0-85958-611-1*, Pub. by Univ of Hull Pr) Paul & Co Pubs.
Pugin's Gothic Ornament: The Classic Sourcebook of Decorative Motifs-with 100 Plates. Augustus C. Pugin. (Pictorial Archive Ser.). (Illus.). 112p. 1987. reprint ed. pap. 8.95 (*0-486-25500-X*) Dover.
Pugnax the Gladiator. Paul L. Anderson. LC 61-1111. (Illus.). (J). (gr. 7-11). 1939. pap. 18.00 (*0-8196-0104-7*) Biblo.
Pugnose Has Two Special Families. Karis Kruzel. (Illus.). 16p. (J). 1996. pap. 7.95 (*0-9641035-5-9*) R-Squared Pr.
Pugs. Filomena Doherty. (Illus.). 1997. pap. 9.95 (*0-7938-2391-9*, KW-104S) TFH Pubns.
***Pugs.** Bob Temple. LC 00-36190. (Illus.). 2000. write for info. (*1-57765-422-6*) ABDO Pub Co.
Pugs. Matthew M. Vriends. (Barron's Pet Owner's Manuals Ser.). (Illus.). 96p. (Orig.). 1994. pap. 6.95 (*0-8120-1824-9*) Barron.
***Pugs: Everything about Purchase, Care, Nutrition, Breeding, Behavior & Training.** 2nd ed. Phil Maggitti. LC 99-40285. (Complete Pet Owner's Manual Ser.). (Illus.). 64-104p. 2000. 6.95 (*0-7641-1045-4*) Barron.
Pug's Hugs, No. 2905. Margaret Allen. Ed. by Joel Kupperstein. (Dr. Maggie's Phonics Readers Ser.). (Illus.). 16p. (J). (ps-1). 1999. pap. 2.99 (*1-57471-565-8*) Creat Teach Pr.
***Pugs in Public.** Kendall Farr. LC 99-32418. (Illus.). 80p. 1999. 15.95 (*1-55670-939-0*) Stewart Tabori & Chang.
PugSpotting: A True History of How Pugs Saved Civilization. Susanne McCaffery-Saville. (Illus.). 2000. pap. 26.99 (*0-9671399-0-2*) Cliocopia Pr.
Pugwash Aloft. John Ryan. (Illus.). 32p. (J). (gr. k-2). 1994. 19.95 (*0-370-00692-5*, Pub. by Bodley Head) Trafalgar.
Pugwash the Smuggler. John Ryan. (Illus.). 32p. (J). (gr. k-2). 1994. 19.95 (*0-370-10786-1*, Pub. by Bodley Head) Trafalgar.
Puhpohwee for the People: A Narrative Account of Some Uses of Fungi among the Ahnishinaabeg. Keewaydinoquay Peschel. LC 96-9321. (Illus.). 70p. 1998. pap. 24.95 (*1-879528-18-5*) Ed Studies Pr.
Pius XXII & the Holocaust: A Reader. Robert A. Graham & Joseph L. Lichten. Ed. by John C. Pantuso & Virgil C. Blum. 168p. 1988. 4.95 (*0-945775-01-6*) Cath League Rts.
Puissance du Rationnel see Powers of the Rational: Science, Technology, & the Future of Thought
Puits aux Images. Marcel Ayme. (FRE.). 254p. 1932. pap. 13.95 (*0-7859-1102-2*, 2070203883) Fr & Eur.
Puja: Darsan Dena, Darsan Lena. Marilyn Turkovich. (Passages to India Ser.). (C). 1989. spiral bd. 20.00 (*1-56709-008-7*) Indep Broadcast.
Puk-Wud-Jies of Indiana. Paul Startzman. (Illus.). 72p. 1998. pap. 9.00 (*0-8059-4475-3*) Dorrance.
Puking Horse. John M. Bennett. 1980. pap. 5.00 (*0-935350-04-7*) Luna Bisonte.
Puking Horse. deluxe limited ed. John M. Bennett. 1980. pap. 10.00 (*0-935350-86-1*) Luna Bisonte.
Pul Eliya, A Village in Ceylon: A Study of Land Tenure & Kinship. Edmund Leach. LC 61-1517. 375p. reprint ed. pap. 106.90 (*0-608-12064-2*, 2024486) Bks Demand.
Pulaar-English - English-Pulaar Standard Dictionary. Niang. LC 97-24082. 450p. (Orig.). 1997. pap. 24.95 (*0-7818-0479-5*) Hippocrene Bks.
***Pulaski County: Arkansas.** Paulette Walter & Alan Paulson. (Images of America Ser.). (Illus.). 128p. 1999. pap. 18.99 (*0-7385-0006-2*) Arcadia Publng.
***Pulaski County, Arkansas, Marriage Record Index, 1820-1901.** Intro. by Emily Tucker. 408p. 2000. pap. 48.00 (*1-56546-166-5*) Arkansas Res.
Pulaski County Illinois, 1819-1987. Pulaski County Board of Commissioners. LC 87-71197. 408p. 1988. 55.00 (*0-938021-21-4*) Turner Pub KY.
Pulaski County, Virginia Marriages, 1839-1857. John Vogt & T. William Kethley, Jr. 48p. 1984. pap. 5.00 (*0-935931-13-9*) Iberian Pub.
Pulci's Morgante & Medici Politics. Constance Jordan. LC 85-45572. 216p. 1987. 39.50 (*0-918016-89-4*) Folger Bks.
Pulga y el Piojo (The Flea & the Louse) Illus. by Victor Perez. (SPA.). 24p. (J). (ps-1). pap. 6.95 (*980-257-106-7*, Pub. by Ediciones Ekare) Kane-Miller Bk.
Pulgada a Pulgada. Leo Lionni. (SPA., Illus.). (J). (gr. k-1). 1961. 15.95 (*0-8392-3030-3*) Astor-Honor.
Pulham Pigs. Gordon Kinsey. 176p. 1990. 50.00 (*0-86138-050-9*, Pub. by T Dalton) St Mut.
Puli: A Complete & Reliable Handbook. Leslie Benis. (Illus.). 96p. 1999. 19.95 (*0-7938-0779-4*, RX-129) TFH Pubns.
Puligny-Montrachet. Simon Loftus. 1995. pap. write for info. (*0-8050-3175-8*) H Holt & Co.
Pulik Champions, 1952-1990. Camino E. E. & Bk. Co. Staff. 175p. 1993. pap. 28.95 (*0-940808-94-3*) Camino E E & Bk.
***Pulitzer.** Brian. 400p. 2000. 30.00 (*0-471-33200-3*) Wiley.
Pulitzer Diaries: Inside America's Greatest Prize. John Hohenberg. LC 96-3412. 350p. 1997. 39.95 (*0-8156-0392-4*, HOPD) Syracuse U Pr.
Pulitzer Prize: The Inside Story of America's Most Prestigious Award. Douglas Bates. 1991. 19.95 (*1-55972-070-0*, Birch Ln Pr) Carol Pub Group.
***Pulitzer Prize: The Inside Story of America's Most Prestigious Award.** J. Douglas Bates. (Illus.). 291p. 2000. reprint ed. text 20.00 (*0-7881-9053-9*) DIANE Pub.
Pulitzer Prize Archive: A History & Anthology of Award-Winning Materials in Journalism Part C: Nonfiction Literature Volume 7. Ed. by Heinz-Dietrich Fischer & Erika J. Fischer. LC 94-159042. (Pulitzer Prize Archive Ser.). 436p. 1993. 90.00 (*3-598-30177-4*) K G Saur Verlag.
Pulitzer Prize Archive: A History & Anthology of Award-Winning Materials in Journalism Part D: Delles Lettres Volume 10: Novel/Fiction. Ed. by Heinz-Dietrich Fischer & Erika J. Fischer. LC 97-105818. (Pulitzer Prize Archive Ser.). 400p. 1996. 100.00 (*3-598-30180-4*) K G Saur Verlag.
Pulitzer Prize Archive Pt. C, Vol. 9: General Nonfiction Awards, 1962-1993. Ed. by Heinz-Dietrich Fischer. LC 96-119466. (Pulitzer Prize Archive Ser.). 400p. 1995. 100.00 (*3-598-30179-0*) K G Saur Verlag.
Pulitzer Prize Archive Pt. D: Belles-Lettres, Vol. 11: Poetry - Verse Awards, 1918-1995. Ed. & Intro. by Heinz-Dietrich Fischer. LC 97-228580. lxxxii, 310p. 1997. write for info. (*3-598-30181-2*) K G Saur Verlag.
Pulitzer Prize Archives: A History & Anthology of Award-Winning Materials in Journalism Part C: Nonfiction Literature Volume 8: Biography/ Autobiography Awards 1917-1992. Ed. by Heinz-Dietrich Fischer & Erika J. Fischer. LC 95-115890. (Pulitzer Prize Archive Ser.). 406p. 1994. 100.00 (*3-598-30178-2*) K G Saur Verlag.
Pulitzer Prize Feature Stories. David Garlock. LC 97-44251. 224p. 1998. pap. text 29.95 (*0-8138-2389-7*) Iowa St U Pr.
Pulitzer Prize Story II: Award-Winning News Stories, Columns, Editorials, Cartoons, & News Pictures, 1959-1980. John Hohenberg. LC 80-16880. (Illus.). 375p. 1980. text 62.00 (*0-231-04978-1*) Col U Pr.
Pulitzer Prize-Winning Editorials: America's Best Editorial Writing, 1917-1993. 2nd ed. Ed. by Laird B. Anderson. LC 93-45742. 292p. (C). 1994. pap. text 24.95 (*0-8138-1491-X*) Iowa St U Pr.
Pulitzer Prizes in Journalism, 1917-1985: A Guide to the Microfilm Edition. Ed. by Mary E. Morrison. 187p. 1986. 70.00 (*0-8357-0709-1*) Univ Microfilms.

P

An Asterisk (*) at the beginning of an entry indicates that the title is appearing for the first time.

Pulitzer Prizes, 1990. Kendall J. Wills. 1990. 9.95 (*0-671-72583-1*) S&S Trade.

Pulitzer Prizewinning Playwrights. Tom Dunn. 280p. 1995. 24.95 (*0-435-08688-X*, 08688) Heinemann.

Pulitzer's Prize Editor: A Biography of John A. Cockerill, 1845-1896. LC 64-7798. 364p. reprint ed. pap. 112.90 (*0-608-12754-X*, 202340900033) Bks Demand.

Pull & Be Damned. Brad Reynolds. (Orig.). 1997. mass mkt. 5.50 (*0-614-27710-8*, Avon Bks) Morrow Avon.

Pull Down a Horseman & Gale Day. Eugene McCabe. 70p. 1979. pap. 12.95 (*0-902996-96-7*) Dufour.

Pull No More Bines: Hop Picking-Memories of a Vanished Way of Life. Gilda O'Neill. pap. 17.95 (*0-7043-4229-4*, Pub. by Womens Press) Trafalgar.

Pull No More Bines: Memoirs of a Vanished Way of Life. large type ed. Gilda O'Neill. (Reminiscence Ser.). 22.95 (*1-85695-079-4*, Pub. by ISIS Lrg Prnt) Transaction Pubs.

Pull of Moving Water. Alice Koskela. LC 99-14948. (Illus.). 128p. 1999. pap. 13.95 (*0-87422-180-3*) Wash St U Pr.

Pull of the Moon. Elizabeth Berg. 271p. 1997. mass mkt. 6.50 (*0-515-12089-8*, Jove) Berkley Pub.

***Pull of the Moon.** Elizabeth Berg. 2000. pap. 12.95 (*0-425-17648-7*) Berkley Pub.

Pull of the Moon. large type ed. Elizabeth Berg. 1996. 22.95 (*0-7862-0816-3*) Thorndike Pr.

Pull of the Moon: Nine Months Later, 838. Darlene Graham. (Harlequin Super Romance Ser.). 1999. per. 4.25 (*0-373-70838-6*) Harlequin Bks.

Pull-over Rouge. Charles Perrault. (FRE.). 1980. pap. 12.95 (*0-7859-3104-X*, 2253025437) Fr & Eur.

Pull-Tab & Pop-Up Fun: If You're Happy & You Know It; This Is the Way We Make a Face, 2 bks. Jo Lodge. (Illus.). 12p. (J). 1996. boxed set 11.95 (*0-8120-8496-9*) Barron.

Pull the Cord: Discover Who You Really Are. 3 Simple Steps. Francine Poelstra. Ed. by Nancy Mitchell. LC 98-96420. (Illus.). 144p. 1998. 9.95 (*0-9666228-0-4*) Dynamic Poss.

***Pull the Other One: String Games & Stories Book 1.** Michael Taylor. (Illus.). 128p. (J). 2000. pap. 79.99 (*1-869890-49-3*, Pub. by Hawthorn Press) Anthroposophic.

Pull Yourself Together. David Seabury. 104p. 1967. pap. 5.95 (*0-911336-14-1*) Sci of Mind.

Pulled Thread Embroidery. Moyra McNeill. (Illus.). 208p. 1994. reprint ed. pap. text 7.95 (*0-486-27857-3*) Dover.

Pullers. Tom Graves. 186p. 1998. 21.00 (*0-8038-9424-4*) Hastings.

Pullet on the Midden. large type ed. Rachel Knappett. 1998. 24.95 (*0-7531-5045-X*, Pub. by ISIS Lrg Prnt) T T Beeler.

Pulley. Patricia Armentrout. LC 97-15148. (Simple Machines Ser.). (J). 1997. lib. bdg. 17.27 (*1-57103-178-2*) Rourke Pr.

Pulley Activities. rev. ed. Graham Peacock & Robin Smith. Ed. by Connie Doyle. (Design & Make Ser.). (Illus.). 33p. (J). (gr. 3-6). 1994. reprint ed. 6.99 (*1-884461-08-5*) NES Arnold.

Pulleys see Simple Machines Series

***Pulleys.** Anne Welsbacher. (Understanding Simple Machines Ser.). 24p. (J). (ps-3). 2000. lib. bdg. 15.93 (*0-7368-0612-1*, Bridgestone Bks) Capstone Pr.

Pulleys & Gears. David Glover. LC 96-15815. (Simple Machines Ser.). (J). 1998. (*1-57572-084-1*) Heinemann Lib.

***Pulleys & Gears.** Angela Royston. LC 00-29593. (Machines in Action Ser.). (Illus.). 2000. lib. bdg. write for info. (*1-57572-320-4*) Heinemann Lib.

Pulling. Jennifer G. Welch. 1981. pap. 5.00 (*0-944754-65-1*) Pudding Hse Pubns.

***Pulling Apart: A State-by-state Analysis of Income Trends.** 62p. 2000. pap. text 20.00 (*0-7881-8962-X*) DIANE Pub.

Pulling Back from the Nuclear Brink: Reducing & Countering Nuclear Threat. Ed. by William L. Dowdy & Barry R. Schneider. LC 97-53200. 328p. 1998. 52.50 (*0-7146-4856-6*, Pub. by F Cass Pubs); pap. 19.50 (*0-7146-4412-9*, Pub. by F Cass Pubs) Intl Spec Bk.

Pulling Back the Curtain, Vol. I. Ed Okonowicz. (Spirits Between the Bays Ser.). (Illus.). 64p. (Orig.). 1994. pap. 8.95 (*0-9643244-0-7*) Myst & Lace.

Pulling down Strongholds see Destruyendo Fortalezas

Pulling down Strongholds. John Osteen. 40p. 1972. mass mkt. 1.50 (*0-912631-07-4*) J O Pubns.

Pulling Leather: Being the Early Recollections of a Cowboy on the Wyoming Range, 1884-1889. Reuben B. Mullins. Ed. by Lawrence Clayton. LC 88-16491. (Illus.). 219p. (Orig.). 1988. pap. 11.95 (*0-931271-10-X*) Hi Plains Pr.

Pulling My Leg. Jo Carson. LC 89-70978. (Illus.). 32p. (J). (ps-2). 1990. 15.95 (*0-531-05817-4*) Orchard Bks Watts.

Pulling My Leg. Jo Carson. LC 89-70978. (Illus.). 32p. (J). (ps-2). 1994. pap. 5.95 (*0-531-07046-8*) Orchard Bks Watts.

Pulling Myself Together: An Anglesey Childhood. Arthur H. Haley. 1990. 50.00 (*0-9511427-0-4*, Pub. by Bullfinch Pubns) St Mut.

Pulling Our Own Strings: Feminist Humor & Satire. Ed. by Gloria Kaufman & Mary Kay Blakely. LC 79-3382. (Midland Bks.: No. 251). (Illus.). 192p. 1994. pap. 14.95 (*0-253-20251-5*) Ind U Pr.

Pulling Our Own Strings: Feminist Humor & Satire. Gloria J. Kaufman. Ed. by Mary Kay Blakely. LC 79-3382. (Illus.). 192p. Date not set. reprint ed. pap. 59.60 (*0-608-20552-4*, 205446600002) Bks Demand.

Pulling Power. Cheryl Mildenhall. 256p. (Orig.). 1997. mass mkt. 5.95 (*0-352-33139-9*, Pub. by BLA4) London Bridge.

Pulling Punches. large type ed. Paul Heiney. 23.95 (*1-85695-068-9*, Pub. by ISIS Lrg Prnt) Transaction Pubs.

***Pulling Taffy.** (J). (gr. 7). 2000. per. 17.00 (*0-689-82994-9*) S&S Childrens.

Pulling the Lion's Tail. Jane Kurtz. LC 93-22836. (Illus.). (J). 1995. pap. 14.00 (*0-671-88183-3*) S&S Bks Yung.

Pulling the Lion's Tail. Jane Kurtz. LC 93-22836. (Illus.). 32p. (J). (ps-3). 1995. pap. 15.00 (*0-689-80324-9*) S&S Bks Yung.

Pulling the Siamese Dragon: Performance As a Theological Agenda for Christian Ritual Praxis. Timothy D. Hoare. LC 96-22739. (Illus.). 192p. 1996. lib. bdg. 36.50 (*0-7618-0415-3*) U Pr of Amer.

Pulling the Temple Down: The Fire-Eaters & the Destruction of the Union. David S. Heidler. (Illus.). 262p. 1999. text 23.00 (*0-7881-5911-9*) DIANE Pub.

Pulling Together. Dawn L. Watkins. Ed. by Carolyn Cooper. (Illus.). 136p. (J). (gr. 1-2). 1992. pap. 6.49 (*0-89084-609-X*, 057596) Bob Jones Univ.

Pulling Together: A Planning & Development Consensus-Building Manual. Urban Land Institute Staff. LC 94-60413. 145p. 1994. ring bd. 32.95 (*0-87420-758-4*, P90) Urban Land.

Pulling Together: Teamwork in Practice. Ed. by Alison Hardingham & Jenny Royal. 200p. (C). 1994. pap. 30.00 (*0-85292-558-1*, Pub. by IPM Hse) St Mut.

Pulling Together: The International Monetary Fund in a Multipolar World. Catherine Gwin et al. Ed. by Valeriana Kallab. (U. S. Third World Policy Perspectives Ser.: Vol. 13). 174p. 1990. 32.95 (*0-88738-313-0*); pap. 17.95 (*0-88738-819-1*) Transaction Pubs.

Pulling Together: The Power of Teamwork. John J. Murphy. LC 93-61170. 200p. (Orig.). 1993. pap. 12.00 (*0-9639013-0-3*) Venture Mgmt.

Pulling Together: The Power of Teamwork. John J. Murphy. LC 96-49713. 192p. (Orig.). 1997. pap. 14.99 (*0-922066-92-2*) Wynwood.

Pulling Together for Cooperative Learning: Cooperative Learning Activities & Projects for Middle Grades. Imogene Forte & Joy MacKenzie. (Illus.). 96p. (Orig.). (J). (gr. 5-8). 1991. pap. text 10.95 (*0-86530-182-4*, IP 193-9) Incentive Pubns.

Pulling Together for Productivity: A Union-Management Initiative at U. S. West, Inc. (Illus.). 92p. (Orig.). (C). 1994. pap. text 20.00 (*0-7881-0443-8*) DIANE Pub.

Pulling up the Ladder: The Metaphysical Roots of Wittgenstein's 'Tractatus' Richard D. Brockhaus. 352p. (C). 1991. pap. 19.95 (*0-8126-9126-1*) Open Court.

Pulling Weeds. Les Morgan. LC 88-93031. 124p. (Orig.). (J). (ps up). 1989. pap. 6.99 (*0-87509-414-7*) Chr Pubns.

Pulling Your Own Strings. Wayne W. Dyer. 320p. 1994. mass mkt. 6.50 (*0-06-109224-X*, Harp PBks) HarpC.

Pulling Your Own Strings. Wayne W. Dyer. 1979. mass mkt. 4.95 (*0-380-44388-0*, Avon Bks) Morrow Avon.

Pulling Your Own Strings: Dyer,&Wayne W. abr. ed. Wayne W. Dyer. 1991. audio 18.00 (*1-55994-433-1*, CPN 1888) HarperAudio.

Pulling Your Own Strings: Dynamic Techniques for Dealing with Other People & Living Life as You Choose. Wayne W. Dyer. LC 77-23368. 288p. 1993. reprint ed. pap. 13.00 (*0-06-091975-2*, Perennial) HarperTrade.

Pulling Your Tail: A Primer on the Art of Motorcycle Trailering. William A. Brobst. LC 82-90072. (Illus.). 64p. 1982. pap. 5.65 (*0-9608112-0-6*) Transport Env.

Pullman: An Experiment in Industrial Order & Community Planning, 1880-1930. Stanley Buder. (Urban Life in America Ser.). (Illus.). 282p. 1970. pap. text 20.95 (*0-19-500838-3*) OUP.

Pullman: The Songbook from Aboard the Train. Paul Hunter. LC 75-8864. (Illus.). 80p. 1976. 15.00 (*0-295-95427-2*) U of Wash Pr.

Pullman Cars on the Southern, 1875-1972. R. W. Kidner. 64p. (C). 1985. 39.00 (*0-85361-356-7*) St Mut.

Pullman Case: The Clash of Labor & Capital in Industrial American. David R. Papke. LC 98-50880. (Landmark Law Cases & American Society Ser.). 152p. 1999. 25.00 (*0-7006-0953-9*); pap. 12.95 (*0-7006-0954-7*) U Pr of KS.

Pullman-Standard Color Guide to Freight Equipment. James Kinkaid. 1995. 49.95 (*1-878887-42-4*) Morning NJ.

Pullman Strike. Almont Lindsey. LC 64-32413. 1994. pap. text 12.00 (*0-226-48383-5*, P165) U Ch Pr.

Pullman Strike. Ed. by Leon Stein & Philip Taft. LC 78-89759. (American Labor, from Conspiracy to Collective Bargaining Ser., No. 1). 254p. 1974. reprint ed. 18.95 (*0-405-02150-X*) Ayer.

Pullman Strike. 2nd ed. William H. Carwardine. 160p. 1994. pap. 14.00 (*0-88286-224-3*) C H Kerr.

Pullman Strike: Mini-Play. (Labor Studies). (J). (gr. 5 up). 1978. 6.50 (*0-89550-322-0*) Stevens & Shea.

Pullman Strike & the Crisis of the 1890s: Essays on Labor & Politics. Richard Schneirov et al. LC 98-25404. 288p. 1999. pap. 18.95 (*0-252-06755-X*) U of Ill Pr.

Pullman Strike & the Crisis of the 1890s: Essays on Labor & Politics. Richard Schneirov et al. LC 98-25404. 288p. 1999. 49.95 (*0-252-02447-8*) U of Ill Pr.

Pullman Strike of 1894: American Labor Comes of Age. Rosemary Laughlin. LC 99-25695. (Great Events Ser.). 112p. (YA). (gr. 5 up). 1999. lib. bdg. 18.95 (*1-883846-28-5*) M Reynolds.

Pullman Strike of 1894: Turning Point for American Labor. Linda J. Altman. (Spotlight on American History Ser.). (Illus.). 64p. (J). (gr. 4-6). 1994. lib. bdg. 21.90 (*1-56294-346-4*) Millbrook Pr.

Pullout Switches, UL 1429. 3rd ed. (C). 1994. pap. text 135.00 (*1-55989-695-7*) Underwrtrs Labs.

Pulltrouser Swamp: Ancient Maya Habitat, Agriculture, & Settlement in Northern Belize. Ed. by B. L. Turner, II & Peter D. Harrison. (Texas Pan American Ser.). (Illus.), 310p. 1983. text 27.50 (*0-292-75067-6*) U of Tex Pr.

***Pulltrouser Swamp - The Settlement Maps: A Lowland Maya Community Cluster in Northern Belize.** Peter D. Harrison & Robert E. Fry. (Illus.). 52p. 2000. text 55.00 (*0-87480-651-8*) U of Utah Pr.

Pulmonale Aspekte der Cystischen Fibrose. Ed. by E. Bern Rossi. (Paediatrische Fortbildungskurse fuer die Praxis Ser.: Vol. 48). (Illus.). 1979. pap. 42.75 (*3-8055-2944-9*) S Karger.

Pulmonar Metastas Order. Weiss. 1979. lib. bdg. 126.50 (*90-247-2157-1*, Pub. by M Nijhoff) Kluwer Academic.

Pulmonary Actions of the Endothelins. R. G. Goldie & Douglas W. Hay. LC 99-11900. (Respiratory Pharmacology & Pharmacotherapy Ser.). 350p. 1999. (*3-7643-5859-9*) Birkhauser.

Pulmonary & Bronchial Circulations in Congenital Heart Disease. Colin M. Bloor & Averill A. Liebow. LC 79-25988. (Topics in Cardiovascular Disease Ser.). (Illus.). 296p. 1980. reprint ed. pap. 91.80 (*0-608-05448-8*, 206591700006) Bks Demand.

Pulmonary & Cardiac Imaging. Caroline Chiles & Charles E. Putman. LC 97-722. (Lung Biology in Health & Disease Ser.: Vol. 103). (Illus.). 680p. 1997, text 215.00 (*0-8247-9743-4*) Dekker.

Pulmonary & Critical Care Medicine: Update 5. 5th ed. Roger C. Bone. (Illus.). 950p. (C). (gr. 13). 1997. text 128.00 (*0-8151-1371-4*, 29725) Mosby Inc.

Pulmonary & Critical Care Medicine on CD-ROM, 1999. rev. ed. Roger C. Bone. (C). (gr. 13). 1998. spiral bd. 125.00 (*0-8151-2083-4*) Mosby Inc.

Pulmonary & Critical Care Pharmacology & Therapeutics. Ed. by Alan R. Leff. (Illus.). 1200p. 1996. text 149.00 (*0-07-037096-6*) McGraw-Hill HPD.

***Pulmonary & Peripheral Gas Exchange in Health & Disease.** Josep Roca et al. LC 00-31585. (Lung Biology in Health & Disease Ser.). 2000. write for info. (*0-8247-0335-9*) Dekker.

***Pulmonary & Respiratory Aid Equipment in Egypt: A Strategic Entry Report, 1999.** Compiled by Icon Group International. (Illus.). 158p. 1999. ring bd. 1580.00 incl. audio compact disk (*0-7418-1850-7*) Icon Grp.

Pulmonary Artery Catheter in Critical Care: A Concise Handbook. 2nd ed. Claude Perret et al. (Illus.). 360p. 1997. 125.00 (*0-632-04212-5*) Blackwell Sci.

Pulmonary Blood Vessels in Lung Disease. Ed. by J. Widimsky. (Progress in Respiratory Research Ser.: Vol. 26). (Illus.). viii, 150p. 1990. 117.50 (*3-8055-5155-X*) S Karger.

Pulmonary Blood Volume in Health & Disease. Paul N. Yu. LC 68-18860. 328p. reprint ed. pap. 101.70 (*0-608-14011-2*, 205545000022) Bks Demand.

Pulmonary Circulation. Ed. by M. Morpurgo et al. (Current Topics in Rehabilitation Ser.). 192p. 1990. 69.95 (*0-387-19542-4*) Spr-Verlag.

Pulmonary Circulation: A Handbook for Clinicians. A. J. Peacock. (Illus.). 528p. 1999. text 99.00 (*0-412-56870-5*, Pub. by E A) OUP.

Pulmonary Circulation: Moving from Passive to Active Control. Ed. by Michael R. Pinsky et al. (Illus.). 275p. 1996. text 78.95 (*0-7020-2201-2*, Pub. by W B Saunders) Saunders.

Pulmonary Circulation: Normal & Abnormal: Mechanisms, Management, & the National Registry. Ed. by Alfred P. Fishman. LC 89-40403. (Illus.). 578p. (C). 1990. text 99.95 (*0-8122-8110-1*) U of Pa Pr.

Pulmonary Circulation: Proceedings of the Symposium, Prague, 1969. Pulmonary Circulation Symposium Staff. Ed. by J. Widimsky et al. (Progress in Respiratory Research Ser.: Vol. 5). 1971. 125.25 (*3-8055-1152-3*) S Karger.

Pulmonary Circulation & Gas Exchange. Ed. by Wiltz W. Wagner, Jr. & E. Kenneth Weir. LC 93-38017. (Illus.). 440p. 1994. 75.00 (*0-87993-572-3*) Futura Pub.

Pulmonary Circulation in Chronic Lung Diseases. Ed. by J. Widimsky et al. (Progress in Respiratory Research Ser.: Vol. 20). (Illus.). viii, 192p. 1985. 120.00 (*3-8055-3961-4*) S Karger.

Pulmonary Complications of Systemic Disease. Ed. by John F. Murray. LC 92-18424. (Lung Biology in Health & Disease Ser.: Vol. 59). (Illus.). 708p. 1992. text 250.00 (*0-8247-8707-2*) Dekker.

Pulmonary Defences. Robert A. Stockley. LC 96-35098. 364p. 1997. 184.95 (*0-471-97000-X*) Wiley.

Pulmonary Disease Diagnosis & Therapy: A Practical Approach. M. Gabriel Kahn & Joseph P. Lynch, III. LC 96-43620. (Illus.). 680p. 1997. pap. 49.00 (*0-683-04613-6*) Lppncott W & W.

Pulmonary Disease in the Elderly Patient. Ed. by Donald A. Mahler. LC 92-49321. (Lung Biology in Health & Disease Ser.: Vol. 63). (Illus.). 528p. 1992. text 210.00 (*0-8247-8752-8*) Dekker.

Pulmonary Disease 2000. Jett. (Illus.). 450p. 2000. text 87.00 (*0-8151-2735-9*, 31318) Mosby Inc.

Pulmonary Diseases. Ed. by F. B. Askin et al. (Perspectives in Pediatric Pathology Ser.: Vol. 18). (Illus.). x, 234p. 1995. 248.75 (*3-8055-6049-4*) S Karger.

Pulmonary Diseases. Ed. by Carlo Grassi et al. (Clinical Medicine Ser.). (Illus.). 650p. 1999. pap. text 75.00 (*0-07-709521-9*) McGraw-Hill HPD.

Pulmonary Diseases: Mechanisms of Altered Structure & Function. Adam Wanner & Marvin A. Sackner. 282p. (C). 1983. 36.95 (*0-316-92150-5*, Little Brwn Med Div) Lppncott W & W.

Pulmonary Diseases & Disorders: Companion Handbook. 2nd ed. Ed. by Alfred P. Fishman. (Companion Handbook Ser.). (Illus.). 368p. 1993. pap., suppl. ed. 32.00 (*0-07-021157-4*) McGraw-Hill HPD.

Pulmonary Disorders. Anthony A. Gal & Michael N. Koss. LC 96-40066. (Differential Diagnosis in Pathology Ser.). (Illus.). 192p. 1997. write for info. (*0-89640-329-7*) Igaku-Shoin.

Pulmonary Disorders. Anthony A. Gal & Michael N. Koss. LC 96-40066. (Differential Diagnosis in Pathology Ser.). 151p. 1997. 59.00 (*0-683-30301-5*) Lppncott W & W.

Pulmonary Edema. Michael A. Matthay & David H. Ingbar. LC 98-3647. (Lung Biology in Health & Disease Ser.). (Illus.). 688p. 1998. text 195.00 (*0-8247-0150-X*) Dekker.

Pulmonary Edema. E. Kenneth Weir & John T. Reeven. LC 97-34820. (American Heart Association Monograph Ser.). (Illus.). 432p. 1998. 98.00 (*0-87993-689-4*) Futura Pub.

Pulmonary Edema in Man & Animals. Aldo A. Luisada. LC 71-96988. (Illus.). 168p. 1970. 15.00 (*0-87527-050-6*) Green.

Pulmonary Embolism. Mario Morpurgo. LC 93-46951. (Lung Biology in Health & Disease Ser.: Vol. 75). (Illus.). 360p. 1994. text 180.00 (*0-8247-9178-9*) Dekker.

Pulmonary Embolism. T. Nakano & Samuel Z. Goldhaber. LC 99-24991. viii, 192p. 1999. 132.00 (*4-431-70238-5*) Spr-Verlag.

Pulmonary Embolism. Ed. by J. Widimsky. (Progress in Respiratory Research Ser.: Vol. 13). (Illus.). viii, 192p. 1980. 126.25 (*3-8055-0487-X*) S Karger.

Pulmonary Embolism. Frank D. Gray. LC 66-20435. 321p. reprint ed. pap. 99.60 (*0-608-09194-4*, 205269800002) Bks Demand.

***Pulmonary Embolism: Epidemiology, Diagnosis & Treatment.** Matthijs Oudkerk. (Illus.). 430p. 1998. 160.00 (*0-632-04223-0*) Blackwell Sci.

Pulmonary Embolism & Deep Venous Thrombosis. Contrib. by Samuel Z. Goldhaber. (Illus.). 295p. 1985. text 105.00 (*0-7216-4151-2*, W B Saunders Co) Harcrt Hlth Sci Grp.

Pulmonary Emergencies. Ed. by Steven A. Sahn. LC 82-12963. (Illus.). 429p. reprint ed. pap. 133.00 (*0-7837-2566-3*, 204272500006) Bks Demand.

Pulmonary Emphysema: Proceedings. International Symposium on Pathophysiology Staff. Ed. by G. L. Scarpa. (Progress in Respiratory Research Ser.: Vol. 10). 1976. 85.25 (*3-8055-2273-8*) S Karger.

Pulmonary Endothelium in Health & Disease. Ed. by Una S. Ryan. (Lung Biology in Health & Disease Ser.: Vol. 32). (Illus.). 520p. 1987. text 255.00 (*0-8247-7758-1*) Dekker.

Pulmonary Eosinophilia. F. E. Udwadia. Ed. by H. Herzog. (Progress in Respiratory Research Ser.: Vol. 7). (Illus.). xi, 286p. 1975. 121.75 (*3-8055-1739-4*) S Karger.

Pulmonary Fibroblast Heterogeneity. Richard P. Phipps. 352p. 1992. 194.00 (*0-8493-6038-2*, RC776, CRC Reprint) Franklin.

Pulmonary Fibrosis. Ed. by Sem H. Phan & Roger S. Thrall. LC 94-43568. (Lung Biology in Health & Disease Ser.: Vol. 80). (Illus.). 1008p. 1995. text 275.00 (*0-8247-8851-6*) Dekker.

Pulmonary Fibrosis. Ed. by Tamotsu Takishima. 544p. 1994. lib. bdg. 129.00 (*0-8493-8927-5*, RC776) CRC Pr.

Pulmonary Function: A Guide for Clinicians. Gabriel Laszlo. (Illus.). 259p. (C). 1994. text 110.00 (*0-521-43050-X*); pap. text 42.95 (*0-521-44679-1*) Cambridge U Pr.

Pulmonary Function in Healthy, Exercising & Diseased Animals. Pierre Lekeux. (Illus.). 402p. 1993. 44.00 (*90-74070-02-7*) Vet Lrn Syst.

Pulmonary Function Indices in Critical Care Patients. J. Brunner & G. Wolff. 180p. 1988. 77.95 (*0-387-18432-5*) Spr-Verlag.

Pulmonary Function Testing. Costa. 1995. write for info. (*0-8493-8859-7*) CRC Pr.

Pulmonary Function Testing. 2nd ed. Reuben M. Cherniack. 1992. pap. text 34.50 (*0-7216-4014-1*, W B Saunders Co) Harcrt Hlth Sci Grp.

Pulmonary Function Testing, Vol. 3. Karen Milikowski. (Respiratory Care Workbook Ser.). 24p. (gr. 13). 1994. text 8.95 (*0-8151-6306-1*, 26024) Mosby Inc.

Pulmonary Function Testing: A Practical Approach. Jack Wanger. 248p. 1992. 29.00 (*0-683-08607-3*) Lppncott W & W.

Pulmonary Function Testing: A Practical Approach. 2nd ed. Jack Wanger. (Illus.). 302p. 1996. pap. 79.00 incl. disk (*0-683-17834-2*) Lppncott W & W.

Pulmonary Function Testing: Principles & Practice. Ed. by Stephen A. Conrad et al. (Illus.). 378p. 1984. pap. text 44.95 (*0-443-08182-4*) Church.

Pulmonary Function Testing & Cardiopulmonary Stress Testing. 2nd ed. Vince Madama. LC 97-37682. 528p. (C). 1997. mass mkt. 45.95 (*0-8273-8410-6*) Delmar.

Pulmonary Function Testing & Cardiopulmonary Stress Testing - IML. 2nd ed. Madama. 76p. 1997. teacher ed. 14.95 (*0-8273-8411-4*) Delmar.

Pulmonary Function Testing & Cardiopulmonary Stress Testing Transparency Masters. Vincent C. Madama. 126p. 1990. pap. 26.25 (*0-8273-3864-3*) Delmar.

Pulmonary Function Testing & Cardiovascular Stress Testing. Vincent C. Madama. LC 92-18604. 590p. (C). 1993. mass mkt. 33.00 (*0-8273-3863-5*) Delmar.

Pulmonary Function Tests: A Practical Guide. Robert E. Hyatt & Paul D. Scanlon. LC 97-2778. (Illus.). 192p. 1997. pap. text 39.95 (*0-316-26261-7*, Little Brwn Med Div) Lppncott W & W.

Pulmonary Gas Exchange. Ed. by M. Meyer & J. Piiper. (Progress in Respiratory Research Ser.: Vol. 21). (Illus.). xiv, 274p. 1986. 216.75 (*3-8055-4330-1*) S Karger.

Pulmonary Health - Rehab & Exercise Testing. Jody Heggestad. 435p. 1999. per. 150.00 (*1-879575-05-1*) Acad Med Sys.

Pulmonary Heart Disease. Ed. by Lewis J. Rubin. 1984. text 200.00 (*0-89838-632-2*) Kluwer Academic.

P

An Asterisk (*) at the beginning of an entry indicates that the title is appearing for the first time.

Pulmonary Hypertension: Proceedings of the International Symposium on Pulmonary Circulation, 2nd, Prague, June, 1974. International Symposium on Pulmonary Circulation S. Ed. by J. Widimsky. (Progress in Respiratory Research Ser.: Vol. 9). (Illus.). 320p. 1975. 155.00 (*3-8055-2171-5*) S Karger.

Pulmonary Infections & Immunity. H. Chmel et al. (Infectious Agents & Pathogenesis Ser.). (Illus.). 378p. (C). 1994. text 95.00 (*0-306-44609-X*, Kluwer Plenum) Kluwer Academic.

Pulmonary Lesions Induced by Bleomycin. J. O. Gebbers & A. Burkhardt. (Lectures in Toxicology: No. 13). (Illus.). 12p. 73.00 (*0-317-66864-1*, Pergamon Pr) Elsevier.

Pulmonary Macrophage & Epithelial Cells: Proceedings. Ed. by Charles L. Sanders & Richard P. Schneider. LC 77-12024. (ERDA Symposium Ser.). 629p. 1977. pap. 23.75 (*0-87079-204-0*, CONF-760927); fiche 9.00 (*0-87079-316-0*, CONF-760927) DOE.

Pulmonary Management in Physical Therapy. Ed. by Cynthia C. Zadai. (Clinics in Physical Therapy Ser.). (Illus.). 234p. 1992. text 61.00 (*0-443-08741-5*) Church.

Pulmonary Nuclear Medicine: Techniques in Diagnosis of Lung Disease. Harold L. Atkins. (Lung Biology in Health & Disease Ser.: Vol. 23). (Illus.). 386p. 1984. text 175.00 (*0-8247-7233-4*) Dekker.

Pulmonary Nursing Care. Patricia Dettenmeier. (Illus.). 465p. (C). (gr. 13). 1991. pap. text 31.95 (*0-8016-5876-4*, 05876) Mosby Inc.

Pulmonary Pathology. Ed. by D. H. Dail & Samuel P. Hammar. (Illus.). 1190p. 1987. 267.00 (*0-387-96491-6*) Spr-Verlag.

Pulmonary Pathology. 2nd ed. Dail. LC 92-2383. (Illus.). 1640p. 1993. 330.00 (*0-387-97897-6*) Spr-Verlag.

Pulmonary Pathology. 2nd ed. David H. Dail et al. LC 94-17331. (Illus.). 1608p. 1995. 165.00 (*0-387-94315-3*) Spr-Verlag.

Pulmonary Pathology: Proceedings of the 46th Annual Anatomic Pathology Slide Seminar. Merle A. Legg & Lynne M. Reid. LC 86-7992. 156p. 1986. pap. text 35.00 (*0-89189-178-1*) Am Soc Clinical.

Pulmonary Pathophysiology. Juzar Ali et al. LC 98-7634. (Illus.). 347p. 1999. pap. text 43.50 (*0-07-062170-5*) McGraw-Hill HPD.

Pulmonary Pathophysiology. G. Criner & G. D'Alonzo. (Pathophysiology Ser.). 1998. pap. text 24.95 (*1-889325-05-8*) Fence Crk Pubng.

Pulmonary Pathophysiology: A Problem-Oriented Approach. Michael A. Grippi. (Illus.). 275p. 1995. pap. text 24.95 (*0-397-51329-1*) Lppncott W & W.

Pulmonary Pathophysiology: The Essentials. 4th ed. John B. West. 229p. 1991. 26.00 (*0-683-08936-6*) Lppncott W & W.

Pulmonary Pathophysiology: The Essentials. 5th ed. John B. West. LC 97-26212. 250p. 1997. pap. 29.00 (*0-683-30225-6*) Lppncott W & W.

Pulmonary Pearls. Ed. by Steven A. Sahn & John E. Heffner. LC 88-81283. (Illus.). 242p. 1988. pap. text 34.00 (*0-932883-16-8*) Hanley & Belfus.

Pulmonary Pearls of Wisdom. Richard Lenhardt. (Pearls of Wisdom Ser.). 1998. pap. 88.00 (*1-890369-17-9*) Boston Medical.

Pulmonary Pearls II, Vol. II. 2nd ed. Ed. by John Heffner & Steven A. Sahn. LC 94-23207. (Pearls Ser.). (Illus.). 320p. (Orig.). 1994. pap. text 41.00 (*1-56053-121-5*) Hanley & Belfus.

Pulmonary Physiology. 5th ed. Michael G. Levitsky. (Illus.). 320p. 1999. pap. text 29.95 (*0-07-134543-4*) McGraw-Hill HPD.

Pulmonary Physiology Fetus, Newborn, Child, Adolescent. 2nd ed. Ed. by Emile M. Scarpelli. LC 89-2361. (Illus.). 500p. 1989. text 98.00 (*0-8121-1225-3*) Lppncott W & W.

Pulmonary Physiology of the Fetus, Newborn & Child. Ed. by Emile M. Scarpelli & Peter A. Auld. LC 75-26531. 383p. reprint ed. pap. 118.80 (*0-608-15300-1*, 205632600059) Bks Demand.

Pulmonary Radiology. Manuel Cardoso Ramon. LC 98-52914. 400p. 1998. text 80.00 (*0-7817-1449-4*) Lppncott W & W.

Pulmonary Radiology: By Members of the Fleischner Society. Ed. by James Potchen et al. LC 93-3835. 600p. 1993. text 91.00 (*0-7216-4821-5*, W B Saunders Co) Harcrt Hlth Sci Grp.

Pulmonary Rehab & Exercise Testing. Jody C. Heggestad. 252p. 1995. spiral bd. 120.00 (*1-879575-54-X*) Acad Med Sys.

Pulmonary Rehabilitation. Ed. by John R. Bach. 450p. 1995. text 71.95 (*1-56053-109-6*) Hanley & Belfus.

Pulmonary Rehabilitation. Alfred P. Fishman. (Lung Biology in Health & Disease Ser.: Vol. 91). (Illus.). 864p. 1996. text 275.00 (*0-8247-9673-X*) Dekker.

Pulmonary Rehabilitation. Ed. by J. F. Muir et al. 261p. 1996. pap. text 43.00 (*0-7279-1022-1*, Pub. by BMJ Pub) Login Brothers Bk Co.

Pulmonary Rehabilitation: Guidelines to Success. 2nd ed. Ed. by John E. Hodgkin et al. LC 92-15490. (Illus.). 500p. 1992. text 50.00 (*0-397-51065-9*) Lppncott W & W.

Pulmonary Rehabilitation: Guidelines to Success. 3rd ed. John E. Hodgkin et al. 640p. text 56.50 (*0-7817-1989-5*) Lppncott W & W.

Pulmonary Rehabilitation Program Administration & Patient Education Manual. Kathleen V. Morris & John E. Hodgkin. LC 96-3798. 432p. 1996. 135.00 (*0-8342-0754-0*) Aspen Pub.

Pulmonary Restriction & Obstruction: A Programmed Text. Patricia R. Hercules et al. LC 79-11479. (Illus.). 372p. reprint ed. pap. 115.40 (*0-8357-7620-4*, 205694300096) Bks Demand.

Pulmonary Science & Medicine: A Review of Fundamental Principles. Michael A. Grippi et al. 256p. pap. text 15.95 (*0-7817-1650-0*) Lppncott W & W.

Pulmonary Surfactant: Biochemical, Functional, Regulatory, & Clinical Concepts. Jacques R. Bourbon. (Illus.). 448p. 1991. boxed set 271.95 (*0-8493-6924-X*, QP752) CRC Pr.

Pulmonary Surfactant: From Molecular Biology to Clinical Practice. Ed. by Bengt D. Robertson et al. LC 92-48791. 754p. 1992. 337.25 (*0-444-89475-6*) Elsevier.

Pulmonary Therapy & Rehabilitation. 2nd ed. Francois Haas & Kenneth Axen. (Illus.). 424p. 1991. 68.00 (*0-683-03887-7*) Lppncott W & W.

Pulmonary Toxicology of Respirable Particles: Proceedings. Ed. by Charles L. Sanders et al. (DOE Symposium Ser.). 687p. 1980. pap. 25.25 (*0-87079-121-4*, CONF-791002); fiche 9.00 (*0-87079-404-3*, CONF-791002) DOE.

Pulmonary Vascular Diseases. K. Moser. (Lung Biology in Health & Disease Ser.: Vol. 14). (Illus.). 728p. 1979. text 250.00 (*0-8247-6609-1*) Dekker.

Pulmonary Vascular Physiology & Pathophysiology. Kenneth E. Weir. Ed. by John T. Reeves. (Lung Biology in Health & Disease Ser.: Vol. 38). (Illus.). 784p. 1988. text 215.00 (*0-8247-7972-X*) Dekker.

Pulmonary Vascular Remodelling. Ed. by J. E. Bishop et al. (Portland Press Research Monographs: Vol. 7). 288p. (C). 1995. 136.00 (*1-85578-041-0*, Pub. by Portland Pr Ltd) Ashgate Pub Co.

Pulmonary/Respiratory Therapy Secrets. Ed. by Polly E. Parsons & John E. Heffner. LC 96-47624. (Secrets Ser.). (Illus.). 350p. (Orig.). 1996. pap. text 38.00 (*1-56053-163-0*) Hanley & Belfus.

Pulp. Charles Bukowski. LC 94-4352. 202p. 1998. reprint ed. 25.00 (*0-87685-927-9*); reprint ed. pap. 14.00 (*0-87685-926-0*) Black Sparrow.

Pulp: An Illustrated Biography. Linda Holorny. (Illus.). 48p. (Orig.). pap. 11.95 (*0-7119-5818-1*, OP47843) Omnibus NY.

Pulp: Reading Popular Fiction. McCracken. LC 98-221676. 256p. 1998. text 22.95 (*0-7190-4759-5*, Pub. by Manchester Univ Pr) St Martin.

Pulp: Reading Popular Fiction. McCracken. LC 98-221676. 256p. 1998. text 69.95 (*0-7190-4758-7*, Pub. by Manchester Univ Pr) St Martin.

Pulp: The Illustrated Story. Paul Lester. (Illus.). 80p. 1996. pap. text 14.95 (*0-7935-6439-5*, 00330227) H Leonard.

Pulp Adventures (Genre Book) E. Dewey et al. (Rolemaster Standard System Ser.). (Illus.). 144p. 1997. pap. 16.00 (*1-55806-311-0*, 5701) Iron Crown Ent Inc.

Pulp & Other Plays by Tasha Fairbanks. Ed. by Gabriele Griffin & Elaine Aston. (Contemporary Theatre Studies: Vol. 15). 50p. 1996. text 43.00 (*3-7186-5744-9*, ECU55, Harwood Acad Pubs); pap. text 24.00 (*3-7186-5745-7*, ECU18, Harwood Acad Pubs) Gordon & Breach.

Pulp & Other Plays by Tasha Fairbanks: Curfew. Ed. by Gabriele Griffin & Elaine Aston. (Contemporary Theatre Studies). 50p. 1996. pap. text 6.00 (*3-7186-5939-5*, Harwood Acad Pubs) Gordon & Breach.

Pulp & Other Plays by Tasha Fairbanks: Now Wash Your Hands. Ed. by Gabriele Griffin & Elaine Aston. (Contemporary Theatre Studies). 50p. 1996. pap. text 6.00 (*3-7186-5940-9*, Harwood Acad Pubs) Gordon & Breach.

Pulp & Other Plays by Tasha Fairbanks: Pulp. Ed. by Gabriele Griffin & Eliane Aston. (Contemporary Theatre Studies). 50p. 1996. pap. text 6.00 (*3-7186-5941-7*, Harwood Acad Pubs) Gordon & Breach.

Pulp & Paper. Boy Scouts of America. (Illus.). 48p. (YA). (gr. 6-12). 1974. pap. 2.90 (*0-8395-3343-8*, 33343) BSA.

Pulp & Paper: Chemistry & Chemical Technology, 4 vols. 3rd ed. Ed. by James P. Casey. 2649p. 1983. 975.00 (*0-471-88186-4*) Wiley.

Pulp & Paper Vol. 1: Chemistry & Chemical Technology, 4 vols., Vol. 1. 3rd ed. Ed. by James P. Casey. LC 79-13435. 820p. 1980. 310.00 (*0-471-03175-5*) Wiley.

Pulp & Paper Vol. 2: Chemistry & Chemical Technology, 4 vols., Vol. 2. 3rd ed. Ed. by James P. Casey. LC 79-13435. 576p. 1980. 298.00 (*0-471-03176-3*) Wiley.

Pulp & Paper Vol. 3: Chemistry & Chemical Technology, 4 vols., Vol. 3. 3rd ed. Ed. by James P. Casey. LC 79-13435. 592p. 1981. 275.00 (*0-471-03177-1*) Wiley.

Pulp & Paper Vol. 4: Chemistry & Chemical Technology, 4 vols., Vol. 4. 3rd ed. Ed. by James P. Casey. 640p. 1983. 275.00 (*0-471-03178-X*) Wiley.

Pulp & Paper Agitation: The History, Mechanics, & Process. D. Carl Yackel. LC 90-21443. 128p. reprint ed. pap. 39.70 (*0-7837-0249-3*, 2040559) Bks Demand.

Pulp & Paper Agitation: The History, Mechanics, & Process. D. Carl Yackel. LC 90-21443. (Illus.). 128p. 1990. reprint ed. pap. 39.70 (*0-608-07571-X*, 204055900017) Bks Demand.

*__Pulp & Paper Capacities: Survey 1998-2003.__ Food & Agriculture Organization Staff. 200p. 1999. pap. 27.00 (*92-5-004273-6*, Pub. by FAO) Bernan Associates.

Pulp & Paper Capacities - Survey, 1995-2000. F. A. O. Staff. 237p. 1996. pap. 27.00 (*92-5-003852-6*, F38526, Pub. by FAO) Bernan Associates.

Pulp & Paper Capacities - Survey, 1997-2002. FAO Staff. 200p. 1998. pap. 27.00 (*92-5-004130-6*, F41306, Pub. by FAO) Bernan Associates.

Pulp & Paper Capacities - Survey 1996-2001. annuals FAO Staff. LC 98-126795. 198p. 1997. pap. 27.00 (*92-5-003998-0*, F39980, Pub. by FAO) Bernan Associates.

Pulp & Paper Capacities, 1993-1998. FAO Staff. 237p. 1994. pap. 27.00 (*92-5-003509-8*, F35098, Pub. by FAO) Bernan Associates.

Pulp & Paper Chemicals: Highlighting Environmental Considerations. 172p. 1992. 2450.00 (*0-89336-872-5*, C-149) BCC.

Pulp & Paper Dictionary. John R. Lavigne. 480p. 1986. 75.00 (*0-8288-1428-7*, M15398) Fr & Eur.

Pulp & Paper Dictionary. 2nd ed. John R. Lavigne. 370p. 1993. 65.00 (*0-87930-303-4*) Miller Freeman.

*__Pulp & Paper Dictionary.__ 3rd ed. John R. Lavigne. 452p. 1999. 69.00 (*0-87930-579-7*) Miller Freeman.

*__Pulp & Paper Equipment in Indonesia: A Strategic Entry Report, 1997.__ Compiled by Icon Group International Staff. (Illus.). 164p. 1999. ring bd. 1640.00 incl. audio compact disk (*0-7418-1076-X*) Icon Grp.

Pulp & Paper Fleet. Al Sykes & Skip Gillham. (Great Lakes Marine History Ser.). (Illus.). 96p. pap. 12.95 (*0-919549-15-2*, Pub. by RivT) Partners Pubs Grp.

Pulp & Paper in China, Hong Kong & Taiwan. James R. Glasse. 143p. 1997. pap. 760.00 (*1-85802-135-9*, Pub. by Pira Internatl) Bks Intl VA.

Pulp & Paper in Eastern Europe. Cristian Stoian. 214p. 1996. pap. 760.00 (*1-85802-134-0*, Pub. by Pira Internatl) Bks Intl VA.

Pulp & Paper Industry Corrosion Problems, Vol. 4. Swedish Corrosion Inst. Staff. (Illus.). 282p. 1984. pap. 48.00 (*0-614-02627-X*) NACE Intl.

Pulp & Paper Machinery in Chile: A Strategic Entry Report, 1997. Compiled by Icon Group International Staff. (Country Industry Report). (Illus.). 111p. 1999. ring bd. 1110.00 incl. audio compact disk (*0-7418-0325-9*) Icon Grp.

*__Pulp & Paper Machinery in Thailand: A Strategic Entry Report, 1997.__ Compiled by Icon Group International Staff. (Illus.). 144p. 1999. ring bd. 1440.00 incl. audio compact disk (*0-7418-1077-8*) Icon Grp.

Pulp & Paper Manufacture Vol. 1: Pulping of Wood. 2nd ed. Pulp & Paper Manufacture Staff. 1969. text 97.15 (*0-07-050924-7*) Glencoe.

Pulp & Paper Manufacture Vol. 2: Control, Secondary Fiber, Structural Board, Coating. 2nd ed. Pulp & Paper Manufacture Staff. 1969. text 119.92 (*0-07-050925-5*) McGraw.

*__Pulp & Paper Mill Pollution Control in India: A Strategic Entry Report, 2000.__ Compiled by Icon Group International. (Illus.). 199p. 1999. ring bd. 1990.00 incl. audio compact disk (*0-7418-2194-X*) Icon Grp.

Pulp & Paper Primer see Abecedario de Pulpa y Papel

Pulp & Paper Primer. David Saltman. 50p. 1983. pap. 20.00 (*0-89852-410-5*, 0101R110) TAPPI.

Pulp & Paper Primer. David Saltman. LC 83-50324. 52p. 1983. reprint ed. pap. 30.00 (*0-608-10457-4*, 202283000030) Bks Demand.

Pulp & Wood Densitometric Properties of Pinus Caribaea from Fiji. J. Burley & E. R. Palmer. 1979. 50.00 (*0-85074-046-0*) St Mut.

Pulp Bleaching: Principles & Practice. Ed. by Carlton W. Dence & Douglas W. Reeve. LC 96-4084. 868p. 1996. 150.00 (*0-89852-063-0*, 0102B061) TAPPI.

Pulp Culture: Hardboiled Fiction & the Cold War. Woody Haut. (Illus.). 240p. 1996. pap. 15.99 (*1-85242-319-6*) Serpents Tail.

Pulp Demons: International Dimensions of the Postwar Anti-Comics Campaign. John A. Lent. LC 98-30640. 1999. 49.50 (*0-8386-3784-1*) Fairleigh Dickinson.

*__Pulp Fiction.__ Dana Polan. 2000. pap. 12.95 (*0-85170-808-0*, Pub. by British Film Inst) Ind U Pr.

Pulp Fiction. Quentin Tarantino. 198p. (J). 1994. pap. 10.45 (*0-7868-8104-6*, Pub. by Hyperion) Time Warner.

Pulp for Papermaking: Fibre & Surface Properties & Other Aspects of Cellulose Technology. Ed. by J. F. Kennedy et al. 450p. 2000. boxed set 270.00 (*1-85573-421-4*) Am Educ Systs.

Pulp Man's Odyssey: The Hugh B. Cave Story. Audrey Parente. LC 87-26706. (Starmont Popular Culture Studies: Vol. 6). xiv, 146p. 1988. pap. 19.00 (*1-55742-038-6*) Millefleurs.

*__Pulp Surrealism: Insolent Popular Culture in Early 20th Century France__ Robin Walz. LC 99-34874. 215p. 2000. 35.00 (*0-520-21619-9*) U CA Pr.

Pulp Technology & Treatment for Paper. 2nd ed. James d'A. Clark. LC 85-62603. (Illus.). 872p. 1985. 97.00 (*0-87930-164-3*) Miller Freeman.

Pulp Voices: Interviews with Pulp Magazine Writers & Editors. Jeffrey M. Elliot. LC 81-21632. (Milford Ser.: Popular Writers of Today: Vol. 37). (Illus.). 64p. 1983. pap. 13.00 (*0-89370-257-9*) Millefleurs.

Pulp Washing Calculation Manual. A. Tomiak. 57p. 1994. pap. 17.00 (*1-895288-68-1*) Pulp & Paper.

Pulp Western: A Popular History of the Western Fiction Magazine in America. John A. Dinan. LC 81-21697. (I. O. Evans Studies in the Philosophy & Criticism of Literature: Vol. 2). (Illus.). 128p. 1983. pap. 17.00 (*0-89370-261-7*) Millefleurs.

Pulping Conference Bk. 1: Proceedings of the Technical Association of the Pulp & Paper Industry, Hyatt Regency, San Francisco, CA, November 12-14, 1984. Technical Association of the Pulp & Paper Industry. LC 86-640707. 173p. 1984. reprint ed. pap. 53.70 (*0-608-10458-2*, 202478600001) Bks Demand.

Pulping Conference Bk. 2: Proceedings of the Technical Association of the Pulp & Paper Industry, Hyatt Regency, San Francisco, CA, November 12-14, 1984. Technical Association of the Pulp & Paper Industry. LC 86-640707. 300p. 1984. reprint ed. pap. 93.00 (*0-608-10459-0*, 202478600002) Bks Demand.

Pulping Conference Bk. 3: Proceedings of the Technical Association of the Pulp & Paper Industry, Hyatt Regency, San Francisco, CA, November 12-14, 1984. Technical Association of the Pulp & Paper Industry. LC 86-640707. 180p. 1984. reprint ed. pap. 55.80 (*0-608-10460-4*, 202478600003) Bks Demand.

Pulping Conference, 1986 Bk. 1: Sheraton Center, Toronto, Ontario, October 26-30. Technical Association of the Pulp & Paper Industry. LC 86-640707. (TAPPI Proceedings Ser.). (Illus.). 223p. 1986. reprint ed. pap. 69.20 (*0-608-10461-2*, 202969000001) Bks Demand.

Pulping Conference, 1986 Bk. 3: Sheraton Center, Toronto, Ontario, October 26-30. Technical Association of the Pulp & Paper Industry. LC 86-640707. (TAPPI Proceedings Ser.). (Illus.). 215p. 1986. reprint ed. pap. 66.70 (*0-608-10463-9*, 202969000003) Bks Demand.

Pulping Conference, 1995: Sheraton Chicago, Chicago, IL, October 1-5, Bk. 1. Technical Association of the Pulp & Paper Industry. LC 86-640707. (TAPPI Proceedings Ser.). (Illus.). 491p. reprint ed. pap. 152.30 (*0-608-09151-0*, 208249500001) Bks Demand.

Pulping Conference, 1995: Sheraton Chicago, Chicago, IL, October 1-5, Bk. 2. Technical Association of the Pulp & Paper Industry. LC 86-640707. (TAPPI Proceedings Ser.). (Illus.). 501p. reprint ed. pap. 155.40 (*0-608-09152-9*, 208249500002) Bks Demand.

Pulping Conference, 1994: Sheraton Harbor Island, San Diego, CA, November 6-10, Bk. 1. Technical Association of the Pulp & Paper Industry. LC 86-640707. (TAPPI Proceedings Ser.). 453p. 1994. pap. 140.50 (*0-608-05383-X*, 208244600001) Bks Demand.

Pulping Conference, 1994: Sheraton Harbor Island, San Diego, CA, November 6-10, Bk. 2. Technical Association of the Pulp & Paper Industry. LC 86-640707. (TAPPI Proceedings Ser.). 468p. 1994. pap. 145.10 (*0-608-05384-8*, 208244600002) Bks Demand.

Pulping Conference, 1994: Sheraton Harbor Island, San Diego, CA, November 6-10, Bk. 3. Technical Association of the Pulp & Paper Industry. LC 86-640707. (TAPPI Proceedings Ser.). 469p. 1994. pap. 145.40 (*0-608-05385-6*, 208244600003) Bks Demand.

Pulping Conference 1991: Stouffer Orlando Hotel, Orlando, FL, November 3-7, Bk. 1. Technical Association of the Pulp & Paper Industry. LC 86-640707. (TAPPI Proceedings Ser.). (Illus.). 532p. reprint ed. pap. 165.00 (*0-7837-1201-4*, 204173400001) Bks Demand.

Pulping Conference 1991: Stouffer Orlando Hotel, Orlando, FL, November 3-7, Bk. 2. Technical Association of the Pulp & Paper Industry. LC 86-640707. (TAPPI Proceedings Ser.). (Illus.). 571p. reprint ed. pap. 177.10 (*0-7837-1202-2*, 204173400002) Bks Demand.

Pulping Conference, Washington, D. C., November 1-5, 1987, Bk. 1. Technical Association of the Pulp & Paper Industry. LC 86-640707. (TAPPI Proceedings Ser.). (Illus.). 223p. reprint ed. pap. 69.20 (*0-608-10464-7*, 203226600001) Bks Demand.

Pulping Conference, Washington, D. C., November 1-5, 1987, Bk. 2. Technical Association of the Pulp & Paper Industry. LC 86-640707. (TAPPI Proceedings Ser.). 234p. reprint ed. pap. 72.60 (*0-608-10465-5*, 203226600002) Bks Demand.

Pulping Conference, Washington, D. C., November 1-5, 1987, Bk. 3. Technical Association of the Pulp & Paper Industry. LC 86-640707. (TAPPI Proceedings Ser.). 310p. reprint ed. pap. 96.10 (*0-608-10466-3*, 203226600003) Bks Demand.

Pulping Conference, 1986: Sheraton Center, Toronto, Ontario, October 26-30, Bk. 2. Technical Association of the Pulp & Paper Industry. (TAPPI Proceedings Ser.). (Illus.). 287p. pap. 89.00 (*0-608-15506-3*) Bks Demand.

Pulping Conference, 1986 Bk. 2: Sheraton Center, Toronto, Ontario, October 26-30. Technical Association of the Pulp & Paper Industry. LC 86-640707. (TAPPI Proceedings Ser.). (Illus.). 287p. 1986. reprint ed. pap. 89.00 (*0-608-10462-0*, 202969000002) Bks Demand.

Pulping Conference, 1989: Westin Seattle, Seattle, WA, Oct. 22-25, Bk. 1. Technical Association of the Pulp & Paper Industry. LC 86-640707. (TAPPI Proceedings Ser.). (Illus.). 414p. reprint ed. pap. 128.40 (*0-8357-7901-7*, 203632900001) Bks Demand.

Pulping Conference, 1989: Westin Seattle, Seattle, WA, Oct. 22-25, Bk. 2. Technical Association of the Pulp & Paper Industry. LC TS1171.T43. (TAPPI Proceedings Ser.). (Illus.). 434p. reprint ed. pap. 134.60 (*0-8357-7902-5*, 203632900002) Bks Demand.

Pulping Conference, 1990: Sheraton Centre, Toronto, Ontario, October 14-17, Bk. 1. Technical Association of the Pulp & Paper Industry. LC 86-640707. (TAPPI Proceedings Ser.). 524p. reprint ed. pap. 162.50 (*0-8357-3005-0*, 203927300001) Bks Demand.

Pulping Conference, 1990: Sheraton Centre, Toronto, Ontario, October 14-17, Bk. 2. Technical Association of the Pulp & Paper Industry. LC 86-640707. (TAPPI Proceedings Ser.). 487p. reprint ed. pap. 151.00 (*0-8357-3006-9*, 203927300002) Bks Demand.

Pulping Conference, 1992: Marriott Copley Place Hotel, Boston, MA, November 1-5, Bk. 1. Technical Association of the Pulp & Paper Industry. LC 86-640707. (TAPPI Proceedings Ser.). (Illus.). 438p. reprint ed. pap. 135.80 (*0-7837-4223-1*, 204391200001) Bks Demand.

Pulping Conference, 1992: Marriott Copley Place Hotel, Boston, MA, November 1-5, Bk. 2. Technical Association of the Pulp & Paper Industry. LC 86-640707. (TAPPI Proceedings Ser.). (Illus.). 437p. reprint ed. pap. 135.50 (*0-7837-4224-X*, 204391200002) Bks Demand.

Pulping Conference, 1992: Marriott Copley Place Hotel, Boston, MA, November 1-5, Bk. 3. Technical Association of the Pulp & Paper Industry. LC 86-640707. (TAPPI Proceedings Ser.). (Illus.). 473p. reprint ed. pap. 146.70 (*0-7837-4225-8*, 204391200003) Bks Demand.

Pulping Fictions: Consuming Culture Across the Literature-Media Divide. Deborah Cartmell. 168p. 1996. pap. 15.95 (*0-7453-1070-2*, Pub. by Pluto GBR) Stylus Pub VA.

Pulping Fictions: Consuming Culture Across the Literature-Media Divide. Ed. by Deborah Cartmell et al. LC 95-52785. (Film - Fiction Ser.: Vol. 1). 168p. 1996. 49.95 (*0-7453-1071-0*) Pluto GBR.

Pulping the South: Third World Tree Plantations in the Global Paper Economy. Ricardo Carrere & Larry Lohmann. 256p. 1996. pap. 25.00 (*1-85649-438-1*, Pub. by Zed Books); text 65.00 (*1-85649-437-3*, Pub. by Zed Books) St Martin.

Pulpit & Press. Mary Baker Eddy. reprint ed. pap. 10.00 (*0-87952-046-9*) Writings of Mary Baker.

Pulpit Bible see Santa Biblia Para Pulpito RVA

Pulpit Bible. 1464p. 1997. 500.00 (*0-19-107014-9*) OUP.

***Pulpit Bible.** 1998. 306.00 (*0-529-10988-3*); 299.00 (*0-529-10987-5*) World Publng.

Pulpit Commentary, 23 vols., Set. Ed. by H. D. Spence & Joseph S. Exell. 26612p. 1985. 795.00 (*0-917006-32-1*) Hendrickson MA.

Pulpit Confessions: Exposing the Black Church. N. Moore. 93p. 1997. 16.00 (*0-9658299-2-8*, Exodus Bks) AOP Bks.

Pulpit Echoes. Joe A. Patterson. 181p. 1988. 12.00 (*0-9641696-0-6*) Heritage TX.

Pulpit Humor. James F. Colaianni. 320p. (Orig.). pap. 14.95 (*0-941685-05-5*) Voicings Pubns.

Pulpit in the American Revolution: Political Sermons of the Period of 1776. Ed. by John W. Thornton. LC 71-109611. (Era of the American Revolution Ser.). 1970. reprint ed. lib. bdg. 49.50 (*0-306-71907-X*) Da Capo.

Pulpit Incendiary. Nathaniel Ward. (Notable American Authors Ser.). 1999. reprint ed. lib. bdg. 125.00 (*0-7812-9885-7*) Rprt Serv.

Pulpit Is Waiting: A Guide for Pastoral Preaching. Joe H. Cothen. LC 97-53291. 304p. 1998. 22.50 (*1-56554-301-7*) Pelican.

Pulpit Politics: Faces of American Protestant Nationalism in the Twentieth Century. Warren L. Vinz. LC 96-10703. 224p. (C). 1996. text 54.50 (*0-7914-3175-4*) State U NY Pr.

Pulpit Politics: Faces of American Protestant Nationalism in the Twentieth Century. Warren L. Vinz. LC 96-10703. 224p. (C). 1997. pap. text 19.95 (*0-7914-3176-2*) State U NY Pr.

***Pulpit Psycho.** Donald F. Black. 220p. 1999. pap. 14.95 (*1-885631-43-X*, 43-X, Family Of Man Pr) G F Hutchison.

Pulpit Publications, 1660-1782, 6 vols. Ed. by John G. Spaulding. Incl. Vol. 1. 1996. lib. bdg. Not sold separately (*0-88354-126-2*); Vol. 2. 1996. lib. bdg. Not sold separately (*0-88354-127-0*); Vol. 3. 1996. lib. bdg. Not sold separately (*0-88354-128-9*); Vol. 4. 1996. lib. bdg. Not sold separately (*0-88354-129-7*); Vol. 5. 1996. lib. bdg. Not sold separately (*0-88354-130-0*); Vol. 6. 1996. lib. bdg. Not sold separately (*0-88354-131-9*); 450.00 (*0-88354-149-1*) N Ross.

Pulpit, Table, & Song: Essays in Celebration of Howard G. Hageman. Ed. by Heather M. Elkins & Edward C. Zaragoza. LC 95-35830. (Drew Studies in Liturgy: No. 1). (Illus.). 290p. 1996. 39.50 (*0-8108-3068-X*) Scarecrow.

Pulpit under the Sky: A Life of Hans Nielson Hauge. Joseph M. Shaw. LC 78-12391. 250p. 1979. reprint ed. lib. bdg. 59.50 (*0-313-21123-X*, SHPU, Greenwood Pr) Greenwood.

Pulpit Words Translated for Pew People. Charles W. Turner. pap. 5.99 (*0-88469-046-6*) BMH Bks.

Pulpmaster: The Theodore Roscoe Story. Audrey Parente. LC 93-202524. (Starmont Popular Culture Studies: No. 13). xvi, 173p. 1992. pap. 21.00 (*1-55742-169-2*) Millefleurs.

Pulptime. P. H. Cannon. LC 84-50724. (Illus.). 96p. 1985. reprint ed. 15.00 (*0-932445-07-1*) Necronomicon.

Pulpwood Editor. Harold B. Hersey. LC 74-4841. 301p. 1974. reprint ed. lib. bdg. 59.50 (*0-8371-7490-2*, HEPE, Greenwood Pr) Greenwood.

Pulsar Astronomy. 2nd rev. ed. Andrew G. Lyne & Francis Graham-Smith. LC 97-16354. (Cambridge Astrophysics Ser.: No. 31). (Illus.). 276p. (C). 1998. text 80.00 (*0-521-59413-8*) Cambridge U Pr.

Pulsar Mission. Arthur Ries. 228p. 1988. pap. 8.95 (*0-89697-306-9*) Intl Univ Pr.

Pulsars. Ed. by W. Sieber & W. R. Wielebinski. xvi, 474p. 1981. lib. bdg. 135.00 (*90-277-1280-8*) Kluwer Academic.

Pulsars: Proceedings of the Lebedev Physics Institute. Ed. by A. D. Kuzmin. 158p. (C). 1992. pap. text 175.00 (*1-56072-051-4*) Nova Sci Pubs.

Pulsars as Astrophysical Laboratories for Nuclear & Particle Physics. F. Weber. LC 99-25434. (Studies in High Energy Physics, Cosmology & Gravitation). (Illus.). 680p. 1999. 180.00 (*0-7503-0332-8*) IOP Pub.

Pulsars As Physics Laboratories. Ed. by Roger D. Blandford et al. LC 92-42239. (Illus.). 202p. 1994. text 55.00 (*0-19-853983-5*) OUP.

Pulsars: Problems & Progress Vol. 105: Iau Colloquium 160. Ed. by S. Johnston et al. (ASP Conference Series Proceedings). 592p. 1996. 34.00 (*1-886733-25-2*) Astron Soc Pacific.

Pulsatile Drug Delivery/Current Applications, Future Trends. Robert Gurny & Junginger. 1993. 63.00 (*3-8047-1257-6*) CRC Pr.

Pulsatile Flow Velocity of the Central Arterial Blood. D. Scheu. (Bibliotheca Cardiologica Ser.: No. 28). (Illus.). vi, 74p. 1972. pap. 22.75 (*3-8055-1259-7*) S Karger.

Pulsatility in Neuroendocrine Systems. Ed. by Gareth Leng. 272p. 1988. 155.00 (*0-8493-4944-3*, QP356, CRC Reprint) Franklin.

Pulsation & Mass Loss in Stars. Ed. by R. Stalio & L. A. Willson. (C). 1988. text 185.00 (*90-277-2770-8*) Kluwer Academic.

***Pulsation of Love.** 2nd ed. Gurumayi Chidvilasananda. 2001. pap. write for info. (*0-911307-88-5*, Pub. by SYDA Found) Words Distrib.

Pulsation, Rotation & Mass Loss in Early-Type Stars: Proceedings of the 162nd Symposium of the International Astronomical Union Held in Antibes-Juan-Les-Pins, France, October 5-8, 1993. Ed. by Luis A. Balona. 572p. (C). 1994. pap. text 95.00 (*0-7923-3045-5*); lib. bdg. 186.50 (*0-7923-3044-7*) Kluwer Academic.

Pulse. Edna R. Buchanan. LC 97-32292. 336p. 1999. mass mkt. 6.99 (*0-380-72833-8*, Avon Bks) Morrow Avon.

Pulse. Joe Cardillo. 1999. pap. 4.99 (*0-14-038177-5*) Viking Penguin.

Pulse. William R. Dantz. 288p. 1990. pap. 3.95 (*0-380-75714-1*, Avon Bks) Morrow Avon.

Pulse. large type ed. Edna R. Buchanan. LC 98-27979. 1998. 26.95 (*0-7862-1622-0*) Thorndike Pr.

Pulse: A History of Music. Lena McLin. LC 77-75478. (Illus.). (YA). (gr. 6-12). 1977. pap. 10.95 (*0-8497-5600-6*, WE 3) Kjos.

Pulse: A Novel. Edna R. Buchanan. LC 97-32292. 336p. 1998. mass mkt. 23.00 (*0-380-97331-6*, Avon Bks) Morrow Avon.

Pulse & Other Poems. William Burns. 30p. (Orig.). 1991. 8.00 (*0-685-48466-1*) Talisman Research.

Pulse & Repulse: Troop Carrier & Airborne Teams in Europe During World War II. H. Rex Shama. LC 94-26711. 244p. 1995. 29.95 (*0-89015-991-2*) Sunbelt Media.

Pulse Check: National Trends in Drug Abuse. (Illus.). 62p. 1997. pap. text 25.00 (*1-57979-257-X*) DIANE Pub.

Pulse Check: National Trends in Drug Abuse. Lee P. Brown. (Illus.). 36p. (Orig.). (C). 1995. pap. text 20.00 (*0-7881-1842-0*) DIANE Pub.

***Pulse Check: National Trends in Drug Abuse, Summer 1998.** 59p. 1998. pap. 5.50 (*0-16-061884-3*) USGPO.

Pulse Check: National Trends in Drug Abuse: Summer 1998. Barry M. McCaffrey. (Illus.). 55p. 1999. text 20.00 (*0-7881-7942-X*) DIANE Pub.

***Pulse Check: National Trends in Drug Abuse, Winter 1997.** 49p. 1998. pap. 4.25 (*0-16-061879-7*) USGPO.

Pulse Check: National Trends in Drug Abuse (1997) Dana Hunt. Ed. by Sumona Guha. 60p. (C). 1999. pap. text 20.00 (*0-7881-7716-8*) DIANE Pub.

Pulse Classic: A Translation of the Mai Jing. Wang Shu-He. Ed. by Bob Flaws. Tr. by Yang Shou-Zhong from CHI. LC 96-86688. (Great Masters Ser.).Tr. of Mai Jing. 400p. 1997. 54.95 (*0-936185-75-9*) Blue Poppy Pr.

Pulse Code Formats for Fiber Optical Data Communication. David J. Morris. (Optical Engineering Ser.: Vol. 5). (Illus.). 224p. 1983. text 135.00 (*0-8247-7067-6*) Dekker.

Pulse Code Modulation Systems Design Notebook. William N. Waggener. LC 98-41590. 322p. 1998. 99.00 (*0-89006-776-7*) Artech Hse.

Pulse Compression. David K. Barton. LC 74-82597. (Radars Ser.: Vol. 3). 237p. 1975. reprint ed. pap. 73.50 (*0-608-10467-1*, 202506000041) Bks Demand.

Pulse Diagnosis. R. B. Amber & A. M. Brooke. 1993. pap. 14.95 (*0-943358-41-8*) Aurora Press.

Pulse Diagnosis. Li Shi Zhen. Ed. by Garry Seifert. Tr. by Hoc Ku Huynh from CHI. 128p. (Orig.). 1993. pap. text 14.00 (*0-912111-06-2*) Paradigm Publns.

Pulse Gas-Discharge Atomic & Molecular Lasers. Ed. by N. G. Basov. Tr. by Albin Tybulewicz from RUS. LC 76-57191. (Proceedings of the P. N. Lebedev Physics Institute Ser.: No. 81). (Illus.). 196p. 1976. reprint ed. pap. 60.80 (*0-608-05540-9*, 206600800006) Bks Demand.

Pulse Methods in 1D & 2D Liquid Phase NMR. Ed. by Wallace S. Brey. 561p. 1988. text 146.00 (*0-12-133155-5*) Acad Pr.

Pulse of Creation: God & the Transformation of the World. Paul Sponheim. LC 99-16998. 1999. pap. 22.00 (*0-8006-3188-9*, Fortress Pr) Augsburg Fortress.

Pulse of Democracy: The Public-Opinion Poll & How It Works. George H. Gallup & Saul F. Rae. LC 68-55631. (Illus.). 335p. 1968. reprint ed. lib. bdg. 35.00 (*0-8371-0439-4*, GAPD, Greenwood Pr) Greenwood.

Pulse of Enterprise: Time Frame: A.D. 1800-1850 see TimeFrame Series

Pulse of Enterprise: Time Frame: AD 1800-1850. Time-Life Books Editors. (Time Frame Ser.). (Illus.). 176p. 1990. lib. bdg. write for info. (*0-8094-6463-2*) Time-Life.

Pulse of Life: Explorations & Discoveries in Macrobiotics. Edward Esko. LC 95-100655. (Illus.). 96p. (Orig.). 1994. pap. text 7.95 (*1-882984-05-6*) One Peaceful World.

Pulse of Life: The Circulatory System. Jenny Bryan. LC 92-36410. (Body Talk Ser.). (Illus.). 48p. (J). (gr. 5 up). 1993. lib. bdg. 13.95 (*0-87518-566-5*, Dillon Silver Burdett) Silver Burdett Pr.

Pulse of Politics: Electing Presidents in the Media Age. James D. Barber. 345p. (C). 1992. pap. 24.95 (*1-56000-589-0*) Transaction Pubs.

Pulse of Praise: Form as a Second Self in the Poetry of George Herbert. Julia C. Guernsey. LC 99-18962. 272p. 1999. 46.50 (*0-87413-679-2*) U Delaware Pr.

Pulse of the Forest. James P. Jackson. LC 80-68354. 1980. 14.00 (*0-935050-01-9*) Am Forests.

Pulse of the Heartland. large type unabridged ed. (Harlequin Ser.). 1990. lib. bdg. 18.95 (*0-263-12371-5*) Mac Lib Ref.

Pulse of the Sky: Poems. Carol J. Horn. 36p. 1997. 7.00 (*0-9659180-4-1*, 97-5) C J Ink.

Pulse of the Vineyards. Martha Kranzthor-Osvat. 76p. (Orig.). 1997. pap. write for info. (*1-57502-442-X*, PO1336) Morris Pubng.

Pulse of Wisdom: Philosophy of India,China & Japan. 2nd ed. Brannigan. LC 99-54805. (Philosophy). 1999. mass mkt. 43.95 (*0-534-55127-0*) Wadsworth Pub.

Pulse of Wisdom: The Philosophies of India, China & Japan. Michael C. Brannigan. LC 94-28443. 399p. 1994. 24.50 (*0-534-24384-3*) Wadsworth Pub.

Pulse Oximetry. Ed. by J. P. Payne & J. W. Severinghaus. (Illus.). 225p. 1986. 69.95 (*0-387-16857-5*) Spr-Verlag.

Pulse Oxlmetry: Principles & Practice Series. rev. ed. Ed. by John T. B. Moyle et al. (Illus.). 140p. 1998. pap. text 31.95 (*0-7279-1235-6*) Login Brothers Bk Co.

Pulse Radiolysis. Yoneho Tabata. 512p. 1991. lib. bdg. 395.00 (*0-8493-4881-1*, QD643) CRC Pr.

Pulse Radiolysis of Water & Aqueous Solutions. Aleksefi K. Pikaev. Ed. by Edwin J. Hart. LC 66-14343. (Illus.). 311p. reprint ed. pap. 96.50 (*0-608-30102-7*, 205522600011) Bks Demand.

Pulse Test. Arthur F. Coca. LC 93-19656. 192p. 1993. pap. 12.00 (*0-942637-94-1*) Barricade Bks.

Pulse Test. Arthur F. Coca. 1996. mass mkt. 4.99 (*0-312-95699-1*, Pub. by Tor Bks) St Martin.

Pulse-to-Tone Conversion Technology: Promises & Pitfalls. Marc Robins. 40p. (Orig.). 1996. pap. 85.00 (*0-9624360-7-0*) Robins Pr.

PULSE Two: A Report on a Phenomenon. Phyllis Plous et al. (Illus.). 160p. (Orig.). 1990. pap. 20.00 (*0-295-97036-7*) U of Wash Pr.

Pulse 2: Report on a Phenomenon. Phyllis Plous et al. (Illus.). 72p. 1990. pap. 20.00 (*0-942006-20-8*) U of CA Art.

Pulse Width Modulated (PWM) Power Supplies. Valter Querciolo. LC 93-7123. (Studies in Electrical & Electronic Engineering). 324p. 1993. 190.75 (*0-444-89790-9*) Elsevier.

Pulsed & Self Regulated Drug Delivery. Hans-Peter Kost. 232p. 1990. lib. bdg. 195.00 (*0-8493-4546-4*, RS199) CRC Pr.

Pulsed Arc Welding: An Introduction. Euring J. A. Street. 1990. 108.00 (*1-85573-027-8*, Pub. by Woodhead Pubng) Am Educ Systs.

Pulsed Electrical Discharge in Vacuum. G. A. Mesyats & D. I. Proskurovsky. (Atoms & Plasmas Ser.: Vol. 5). (Illus.). 310p. 1989. 106.95 (*0-387-50725-6*) Spr-Verlag.

Pulsed Electrochemical Detection in High Performance Liquid Chromatography. William R. Lacourse. LC 97-548. (Techniques in Analytical Chemistry Ser.). 352p. 1997. 79.95 (*0-471-11914-8*) Wiley.

Pulsed Field Gel Electrophoresis: A Practical Approach. Ed. by A. P. Monaco. (The Practical Approach Ser.: No. 158). (Illus.). 216p. 1995. text 95.00 (*0-19-963536-6*); pap. text 45.00 (*0-19-963535-8*) OUP.

Pulsed Field Gel Electrophoresis: A Practical Guide. Bruce W. Birren & Eric Lai. (Illus.). 272p. 1993. pap. 34.00 (*0-12-101290-5*) Acad Pr.

Pulsed-Field Gel Electrophoresis: Protocols, Methods & Theories. Ed. by Margit Burmeister & Levy Ulanovsky. LC 92-1475. (Methods in Molecular Biology Ser.: Vol. 12). (Illus.). 488p. 1992. 99.50 (*0-89603-229-9*) Humana.

Pulsed Gas Lasers. Gennadii A. Mesiats et al. LC 94-23266. Orig. Title: Impulsnye Gazovye Lazery. (ENG & RUS.). 1994. 85.00 (*0-8194-1709-2*, PM17) SPIE.

Pulsed High Magnetic Fields, 1. H. Knoepfel. 300p. 1999. pap. 59.00 (*0-444-10035-0*) Elsevier.

Pulsed Laser Deposition of Thin Films. Ed. by Graham K. Hubler & Douglas B. Chrisey. 648p. 1994. 138.00 (*0-471-59218-8*) Wiley.

Pulsed Magnetic Resonance: NMR, ESR, & Optics. Ed. by D. M. Bagguley. (Illus.). 566p. 1992. text 140.00 (*0-19-853962-2*) OUP.

Pulsed Metal Vapour Lasers: Proceedings of the NATO Advanced Research Workshop on Pulsed Metal Vappur Lasers-Physics & Emerging Applications. Ed. by Chris E. Little & Nikola V. Sabotinov. (NATO ASI Ser.: Vol. 5). 496p. (C). 1996. text 247.00 (*0-7923-4002-7*) Kluwer Academic.

Pulsed MIG Spot Welding of Copper-Nickel to Steel for Ship's Hulls. 67p. 1983. write for info. (*0-318-60075-7*) Intl Copper.

Pulsed MIG Spot Welding of Copper-Nickel to Steel for Ship's Hulls. Franklin Research Institute Labs. Staff. 21p. 1984. write for info. (*0-318-60407-8*) Intl Copper.

Pulsed Neural Networks. Ed. by Wolfgang Maass & Christopher M. Bishop. LC 98-38511. (Illus.). 400p. 1999. 45.00 (*0-262-13350-4*, Bradford Bks) MIT Pr.

Pulsed Neutron Research. Ed. by N. G. Basov. LC 78-12997. (Proceedings of the P. N. Lebedev Physics Institute Ser.: No. 94). (Illus.). 112p. 1979. reprint ed. pap. 34.80 (*0-608-05551-4*, 206601900006) Bks Demand.

Pulsed RF Sources for Linear Colliders, Vol. CP 337. Richard C. Fernow. (AIP Conference Proceedings Ser.). (Illus.). 425p. 1995. boxed set 125.00 (*1-56396-408-2*) Am Inst Physics.

Pulses. Ed. by L. J. Van Der Maesen & Somaatmadja Sadikin. (PROSEA Ser.: No. 1). (Illus.). 105p. 1989. 67.00 (*90-220-0984-X*, Pub. by Backhuys Pubs); pap. 25.00 (*979-8316-01-0*, Pub. by Backhuys Pubs) Balogh.

Pulses & Other Wave Processes in Fluids: An Asymptotical Approach to Initial Problems. Mark Kelbert & Igor Sazonov. LC 95-48401. (Modern Approaches Ser.: Vol. 13). 236p. (C). 1996. lib. bdg. 115.00 (*0-7923-3928-2*) Kluwer Academic.

Pulses by L. J. G. Van der Maesen (Prosea No. 1) PUDOC Staff. 108p. 1993. pap. 125.00 (*81-7089-150-7*, Pub. by Intl Bk Distr) St Mut.

Pulses in India. V. S. Satyapriya. (C). 1989. 18.50 (*81-204-0429-7*, Pub. by Oxford IBH) S Asia.

Pultrusion for Engineers. Ed. by T. Starr. 208p. 2000. boxed set 170.00 (*1-85573-425-7*) Am Educ Systs.

***Pultrusion for Engineers.** Trevor F. Starr. LC 00-30422. 2000. write for info. (*0-8493-0843-7*) CRC Pr.

Pulu Did It! How a Wild Partridge Became a Family Pet. Edna H. Hong. LC 88-34149. (Illus.). 96p. (Orig.). 1989. pap. 8.95 (*0-89579-233-8*) A-R Eds.

Pulverized Coal Combustion & Gasification: Theory & Applications for Continuous Flow Processes. Ed. by L. Douglas Smoot & D. T. Pratt. LC 78-12564. 352p. 1978. 89.50 (*0-306-40084-7*, Plenum Trade) Perseus Pubng.

Pulvinus: Motor Organ for Leaf Movement. Ed. by Ruth L Satter et al. LC 90-801102. (Current Topics in Plant Physiology: an American Society of Plant Physiologists Ser.: Vol. III). (Illus.). 280p. (Orig.). (C). 1990. pap. 25.00 (*0-943088-17-8*) Am Soc of Plan.

Puma & Other German Heavy Reconnaissance Vehicles. Horst Scheibert. (Illus.). 48p. pap. 9.95 (*0-88740-680-7*) Schiffer.

Puma Range. Michael C. Armour. (Smithsonian Wild Heritage Collection). (Illus.). 32p. (J). (ps-3). 1995. pap. 4.95 (*1-56899-202-5*) Soundprints.

Puma Range. Michael C. Armour. (Smithsonian Wild Heritage Collection). 1994. 10.15 (*0-606-08047-3*, Pub. by Turtleback) Demco.

Puma Range, Incl. 6" toy. Michael C. Armour. (Smithsonian Wild Heritage Collection). (Illus.). 32p. (J). (gr. k-3). 1995. pap. 15.95 (*1-56899-208-4*) Soundprints.

***Pumas.** Jon Middleton. LC 97-49016. (Big Cats Ser.). 24p. (J). (gr. k-4). 1999. 17.27 (*0-8239-5211-8*, PowerKids) Rosen Group.

Pumas. Anne Welsbacher. LC 98-16644. (Wild Cats Ser.). (Illus.). 24p. (J). 2000. lib. bdg. 18.60 (*1-57765-091-3*, Checkerboard Library) ABDO Pub Co.

***Pume et Leurs Reves.** G. Orobitg Canal. (FRE.). 192p. 1998. pap. text 50.00 (*90-5709-008-2*) Craftsman House.

Pummeled Heart: Finding Peace Through Pain. Antoinette Bosco. LC 93-61500. 140p. 1994. pap. 9.95 (*0-89622-584-4*) Twenty-Third.

Pump & Circumstance: The Glory Days of the Gas Station. John Margolies. LC 93-12966. (Illus.). 127p. 1993. 29.95 (*0-8212-1995-2*, Pub. by Bulfinch Pr) Little.

Pump Application Desk Book. 3rd ed. Paul N. Garay. LC 96-25944. 701p. 1996. 88.00 (*0-88173-231-1*) Fairmont Pr.

Pump Application Desk Book. 3rd ed. Paul N. Garay. 712p. (C). 1996. 82.00 (*0-13-607771-4*) P-H.

Pump Applications Desk Book. Paul N. Garay. LC 87-45343. 300p. 1989. text 67.00 (*0-88173-043-2*) Fairmont Pr.

Pump Applications Desk Book. 2nd ed. Paul N. Garay. LC 92-18512. 1992. 69.00 (*0-88173-158-7*) Fairmont Pr.

Pump Characteristics & Applications. Michael Volk. LC 95-49096. (Mechanical Engineering Ser.: No. 103). (Illus.). 352p. 1996. text 75.00 (*0-8247-9580-6*) Dekker.

Pump Handbook. 2nd ed. Igor J. Karassik & William C. Krutzch. 1344p. 1986. 125.00 (*0-07-033302-5*) McGraw.

***Pump Handbook.** 3rd ed. Igor J. Karassik. (Illus.). 1280p. 2000. 125.00 (*0-07-034032-3*) McGraw-Hill Prof.

Pump House Gang. Tom Wolfe. 304p. 1999. pap. 14.95 (*0-553-38061-3*) Bantam.

Pump House Gang. Tom Wolfe. LC 67-10922. (Illus.). 320p. 1987. 18.95 (*0-374-23864-2*) FS&G.

Pump Maintenance Handbook for Water & Water Waste Treatment Plants. John F. Newell. Date not set. 55.00 (*1-56670-099-X*, L1099) Lewis Pubs.

Pump Manufacturers. Ed. by ICC Information Group Staff. 1987. 695.00 (*1-85319-043-8*, Pub. by ICC Info Group Ltd) St Mut.

Pump Operation & Maintenance. Tyler Gregory Hicks. LC 81-20890. 324p. 1983. reprint ed. 39.50 (*0-89874-409-1*) Krieger.

Pump Operations. Kidd-Czajkowski & First Due Engine Company. 66p. (gr. 13). 1995. teacher ed. 37.00 (*0-8151-5118-7*) Mosby Inc.

Pump Station Operator. Jack Rudman. (Career Examination Ser.: C-2442). 1994. pap. 27.95 (*0-8373-2442-4*) Nat Learn.

Pump Technology New Challenges - Where Next. Ed. by B. Glanfield. 300p. 1989. 158.95 (*0-387-51208-X*) Spr-Verlag.

Pump Turbine Schemes: Planning, Design, & Operation. Ed. by D. Webb & C. M. Papadakis. 196p. 1979. 8.00 (*0-317-33601-0*, G00144) ASME.

Pump up Your Profits: 52 Cost-Saving Ideas to Build Your Bottom Line. Pencom International Staff. (Illus.). 132p. 1996. pap. 19.95 (*1-879239-08-6*) Pencom.

Pump User's Handbook. 4th ed. 428p. 1995. 167.00 (*1-85617-216-3*, R103) Elsevier.

***Pumped: Straight Facts for Athletes about Drugs, Supplements & Training.** Cynthia Kuhn et al. 192p. 2000. pap. 14.95 (*0-393-32129-0*) Norton.

Pumped Gravel. C. Mehrl & John M. Bennett. 1980. pap. 2.00 (*0-935350-87-X*) Luna Bisonte.

Pumped Gravel. deluxe limited ed. C. Mehrl & John M. Bennett. 1980. pap. 5.00 (*0-935350-88-8*) Luna Bisonte.

Pumped Storage. Ed. by T. H. Douglas. 449p. 1990. 16.00 (*0-7277-1586-0*) Am Soc Civil Eng.

Pumped-up Pizza Problem. Franklin W. Dixon. (Hardy Boys Are: The Clues Brothers Ser.: No. 9). (Illus.). 80p. (J). (gr. 2-4). 1998. pap. 3.99 (*0-671-02142-7*, Minstrel Bks) PB.

***Pumpernickel Tickle & Mean Green Cheese.** Nancy Patz. (Illus.). 40p. 2000. reprint ed. 16.95 (*1-893116-17-4*) Baltimore Sun.

***Pumpers: Workhorse Fire Engines.** Motorbooks Staff & Larry Shapiro. LC 99-37654. (Illus.). 128p. 1999. pap. text 21.95 (*0-7603-0672-9*, 128966AP, Pub. by MBI Pubg) Motorbooks Intl.

***Pumping Apparatus Driver - Operator Curriculum Package.** Ed. by Susan S. Walker. 1954p. 2000. 299.00 (*0-87939-173-1*) IFSTA.

***Pumping Apparatus Driver - Operator Instructor's Packet.** Ed. by Susan S. Walker. 1128p. 2000. 199.00 (*0-87939-174-X*) IFSTA.

P

An Asterisk (*) at the beginning of an entry indicates that the title is appearing for the first time.

***Pumping Apparatus Driver - Operator Student Applications.** Ed. by Susan S. Walker. 826p. 2000. 112.00 (*0-87939-175-8*) IFSTA.

Pumping Granite: And Other Portraits of People at Play. Mike D'Orso. (Illus.). 288p. 1994. 25.00 (*0-89672-338-0*) Tex Tech Univ Pr.

***Pumping Images.** Thomas Ward. 101p. 2000. 19.95 (*0-7541-1170-9*) Minerva Pr.

***Pumping Insulin: Everything You Need for success with An Insulin Pumb. 3rd rev. ed. John T. Walsh & Ruth E. Roberts. Ed. by Barb Schreiner et al. LC 00-190817. 288p. 2000. 23.95 (*1-884804-84-5*) Torrey PP.**
"Pumping Insulin explains how to make my pump do what I want it to do. I use the precise tables for getting basals & boluses without doing tedious math. It's like having my own personal consultant or trainer." "Wonderful! Detailed suggested doses using Humalog insulin." "My advice to anyone thinking about pumping or getting ready to go on a pump...Get This Book! It's so logical &U easy to follow it gave me confidence to start on my own pump. Now I use it as a resource. I'm still learning from it." These are a few of the enthusiastic reviews for Pumping Insulin. This book teaches pumpers & health care providers how to achieve excellent blood sugar control, adjust insulin doses to carbs & exercise, correct pump problems, prevent & treat blood sugar highs & lows, lessen risks for complications & chart blood sugars. One author has worn a pump for 18 years & provided clinical care for over 400 patients on pumps. Contact Torrey Pines Press, 1030 W. Upas Street, San Diego, CA 92103.http://www.diabetesnet.com (800) 988-4772 for discount pricing (30-40) ***Publisher Paid Annotation.***

Pumping Ions. Tom Wujec. 1988. pap. 15.95 (*0-385-25113-0*) Doubleday.

Pumping Iron: The Art & Sport of Bodybuilding. rev. ed. Charles Gaines & George Butler. 1982. pap. 12.00 (*0-671-42688-5*) S&S Trade.

***Pumping Irony: Working Out the Angst of a Lifetime.** Tony Kornheiser. 299p. 1999. text 20.00 (*0-7881-6773-1*) DIANE Pub.

Pumping Ivory. Robert Dumm. 220p. (YA). pap. 16.95 (*0-943748-36-4*, PF0606) Ekay Music.

Pumping Machinery, 1993. Ed. by P. Cooper. LC 89-84349. (FED Ser.: Vol. 154). 395p. 1993. pap. 60.00 (*0-7918-0962-5*, H00794) ASME.

Pumping Mad. (Mad Ser.: No. 56). (Illus.). 192p. (Orig.). 1984. mass mkt. 2.25 (*0-446-32334-9*, Pub. by Warner Bks) Little.

Pumping Manual. 5th ed. Institute for Power System Staff. 800p. 1979. 150.00 (*0-85461-063-4*) St Mut.

Pumping Manual. 9th ed. Christopher Dickenson. LC 95-127127. 1995. 190.25 (*1-85617-215-5*, R101, Pub. by Elsvr Adv Tech) Elsevier.

Pumping Nylon. Scott Tennant. 1995. pap. 11.95 (*0-88284-721-X*) Alfred Pub.

Pumping Nylon: Easy to Early Intermediate Repertoire. Scott Tennant. (National Guitar Workshop Arts Ser.). 64p. 1998. pap. 8.50 (*0-88284-919-0*, 18408); pap. 18.50 incl. audio compact disk (*0-88284-920-4*, 18409) Alfred Pub.

Pumping Nylon in TAB. Scott Tennant. 1995. pap. 14.95 (*0-88284-835-6*) Alfred Pub.

Pumping Nylon: Intermediate to Advance Repertoire. Scott Tennant. 64p. 1999. pap. 8.50 (*0-7390-0073-X*, 18489) Alfred Pub.

Pumping Nylon: Intermediate to Advanced Repertoire. Scott Tennant. 64p. 1999. pap. 18.50 incl. audio compact disk (*0-7390-0074-8*, 18490) Alfred Pub.

Pumping Paper: The Student Athlete's Guide to Winning the Academic Game. unabridged ed. Richard M. Fenker, Jr. & Judith Lambiotte. LC 90-38324. (Illus.). 131p. (Orig.). 1990. pap. text 11.95 (*0-940352-01-X*) Mesa Hse.

Pumping Station Design. 2nd ed. Robert L. Sanks. LC 97-15436. 976p. 1998. 205.00 (*0-7506-9483-1*) Buttrwrth-Heinemann.

Pumping System Analysis see Technical Engineering Training Series

Pumpkin - A Young Woman's Struggle with Lupus. Patricia M. Fagan. Ed. by Adolfo Caso. 190p. 1994. text 12.95 (*0-8283-1961-8*) Branden Bks.

Pumpkin Art. Philip Macht. (Illus.). 48p. (Orig.). 1991. pap. 20.00 (*0-930339-02-9*) Maxrom Pr.

Pumpkin Blanket. Deborah T. Zagwyn. (Illus.). 32p. (J). (ps-5). 1995. 15.95 (*0-89087-637-1*) Celestial Arts.

Pumpkin Blanket. Deborah T. Zagwyn. (Illus.). 32p. (J). (gr. k-3). 1997. 14.95 (*1-883672-63-5*); pap. 6.95 (*1-883672-59-7*) Tricycle Pr.

***Pumpkin Book.** Gail Gibbons. LC 98-45267. (Illus.). 32p. (J). (ps-3). 1999. 19.95 (*0-8234-1465-5*) Holiday.

***Pumpkin Book.** Gail Gibbons. (Illus.). (gr. 4-7). 2000. 6.95 (*0-8234-1636-4*) Holiday.

Pumpkin Book. 4th ed. Susan O. Higgins. Ed. by V. I. Wexner. (Holiday Ser.). (Illus.). 66p. (J). (gr. k-3). 1983. reprint ed. pap. 5.95 (*0-939973-00-6*) Pumpkin Pr Pub Hse.

Pumpkin Carving. Edward Palmer. 1995. 24.95 (*0-8069-1387-8*) Sterling.

Pumpkin Carving. Edward Palmer. LC 95-11549. (Illus.). 96p. 1996. pap. 10.95 (*0-8069-1388-6*, Chapelle) Sterling.

Pumpkin Carving Book: How to Create Glowing Lanterns & Seasonal Displays. Deborah Schneebeli-Morrell. (Illus.). 64p. 1996. 9.95 (*1-85967-305-8*, Lorenz Bks) Anness Pub.

Pumpkin Carving Book & Kit. (Illus.). 1996. 19.95 (*0-8069-1391-6*) Sterling.

Pumpkin Circle: The Story of a Garden. George Levenson. LC 99-20081. (Illus.). 40p. (J). (gr. k-3). 1999. 14.95 (*1-58246-004-3*) Tricycle Pr.

Pumpkin Companion. E. Brabb. Ed. by J. Colby. LC 95-80493. (Traditional Country Life Recipe Ser.). (Illus.). 96p. (Orig.). 1996. pap. 9.95 (*1-883283-08-6*) Brick Tower.

Pumpkin Corner. Estelle K. Abernathy. (Illus.). 160p. 1979. reprint ed. pap. 12.95 (*0-9608428-2-9*) Straw Patchwork.

Pumpkin Cut-Ups: Super Stencils for Perfect Pumpkins. Emily Widmann. 32p. (J). (gr. 4-6). 1992. pap. 1.95 (*0-590-46204-0*) Scholastic Inc.

***Pumpkin Day, Pumpkin Night.** Anne F. Rockwell. LC 98-48370. (Illus.). 32p. (J). (gr. k-2). 1999. 15.95 (*0-8027-8696-0*) Walker & Co.

***Pumpkin Day, Pumpkin Night.** Anne F. Rockwell. LC 98-48370. (Illus.). 32p. (J). (ps-2). 1999. lib. bdg. 16.85 (*0-8027-8697-9*) Walker & Co.

Pumpkin Decorating. Vicki Rhodes. LC 97-1936. (Illus.). 96p. 1997. 10.95 (*0-8069-9574-2*) Sterling.

Pumpkin-Eaters. Lois Braun. 1997. pap. 10.95 (*0-88801-148-2*, Pub. by Turnstone Pr) Genl Dist Srvs.

Pumpkin Faces: A Glowing Book You Can Read in the Dark. Emma Rose. (Illus.). 24p. (J). (ps). 1997. 6.95 (*0-590-13454-X*) Scholastic Inc.

Pumpkin Fair. Eve Bunting. LC 96-20626. (Illus.). 32p. (J). (ps-1). 1999. 15.00 (*0-395-70060-4*, Clarion Bks) HM.

Pumpkin Fever. Created by Francine Pascal. (Sweet Valley Twins Ser.: No. 110). 144p. (Orig.). (J). (gr. 3-7). 1997. pap. 3.50 (*0-553-48441-9*) BDD Bks Young Read.

Pumpkin Fiesta. Caryn Yacowitz. LC 96-48580. (Illus.). 32p. (J). (ps-1). 1998. 15.95 (*0-06-027658-4*) HarpC.

Pumpkin Happy. Erik Knud-Hansen. 64p. 2.50 (*0-318-14333-X*) Hudson Clearwater.

***Pumpkin Heads!** Wendell Minor. LC 99-86364. (Illus.). 32p. (J). (ps-2). 2000. 15.95 (*0-590-52105-5*, Blue Sky Press) Scholastic Inc.

***Pumpkin Jack.** William Hubbell. LC 00-8282. (Illus.). 32p. (J). (gr. k-3). 2000. lib. bdg. 15.95 (*0-8075-6665-9*) A Whitman.

Pumpkin Light. David Ray. LC 92-25118. (Illus.). 32p. (J). (ps-3). 1993. 15.95 (*0-399-22028-3*, Philomel) Peng Put Young Read.

Pumpkin Light. David Ray. LC 92-25118. (Illus.). 32p. (J). (ps-3). 1996. pap. 5.99 (*0-698-11397-7*, PapStar) Peng Put Young Read.

Pumpkin Light. David Ray. 1996. 11.15 (*0-606-09769-4*, Pub. by Turtleback) Demco.

Pumpkin Lovers Cookbook. 3rd ed. Ed. by Betty B. Gabbert. 128p. 1995. ring bd. 6.95 (*1-885590-11-3*) Golden West Pub.

Pumpkin Magic. Marcia Leonard. (J). 1996. pap. 2.95 (*0-8167-1888-1*) Troll Communs.

Pumpkin Man. Judith Moffatt. LC 98-21324. (Hello Reader! Ser.). (Illus.). 32p. (J). (gr. k-2). 1998. 3.99 (*0-590-63865-3*) Scholastic Inc.

Pumpkin Man from Piney Creek. Darleen B. Beard. LC 94-34696. (Illus.). 32p. (J). (gr. k-3). 1995. 15.00 (*0-689-80315-X*) S&S Bks Yung.

Pumpkin Moonshine. Tasha Tudor. (Illus.). 46p. (J). 1998. 6.95 (*0-446-91246-8*) Warner Bks.

Pumpkin Painting. Jordan McKinney. LC 96-15594. (Illus.). 96p. 1996. pap. 10.95 (*0-8069-4858-2*) Sterling.

Pumpkin Painting Book & Kit. (Illus.). 1996. pap. 19.95 (*0-8069-9539-4*) Sterling.

Pumpkin Patch. Walter Elias Disney. LC 97-209626. (Illus.). 10p. (J). 1997. 5.98 (*1-57082-631-5*, Pub. by Mouse Works) Time Warner.

Pumpkin Patch. Elizabeth King. (Picture Puffin Ser.). (J). 1996. 11.19 (*0-606-11769-5*, Pub. by Turtleback) Demco.

Pumpkin Patch. Elizabeth King. (Illus.). 40p. (J). 1996. pap. 5.99 (*0-14-055968-X*) Viking Penguin.

Pumpkin Patch Cats. Frank Fiorello. LC 96-96485. (Illus.). 40p. (Orig.). (J). (ps-6). 1996. pap. 7.95 (*0-9646300-1-X*) Fiorellos Pumpkin Patch.

Pumpkin Patch Parable. Liz C. Higgs. (Illus.). 36p. (J). (ps-2). 1995. 7.99 (*0-7852-7722-6*) Tommy Nelson.

Pumpkin Patch Party. (Illus.). 35p. 1987. pap. 8.00 (*1-58302-064-0*, BRE-32) One Way St.

Pumpkin Patch Party. Sesame Street Staff. (J). 1997. 3.99 (*0-679-88699-0*, Pub. by Random Bks Yng Read) Random.

Pumpkin Patch Scarecrows. Frank Fiorello. (Illus.). 40p. (J). (ps-1). 1998. pap. 7.95 (*0-9646300-3-6*) Fiorellos Pumpkin Patch.

***Pumpkin Pie.** Harriet Ziefert. (Illus.). (J). 2000. pap. 15.00 (*0-618-04883-9*) HM.

Pumpkin Pumpkin. Jeanne Titherington. LC 84-25334. (Illus.). 24p. (J). (ps-3). 1986. 16.89 (*0-688-05696-2*, Grenwillow Bks) HarpC Child Bks.

Pumpkin Pumpkin. Jeanne Titherington. LC 84-25334. (Illus.). 24p. (J). (ps-3). 1990. mass mkt. 4.95 (*0-688-09930-0*, Wm Morrow) Morrow Avon.

Pumpkin, Pumpkin. Jeanne Titherington. LC 84-25334.Tr. of Citrouille, Ma Citrouille. (Illus.). 24p. (J). (ps-3). 1986. 16.95 (*0-688-05695-4*, Grenwillow Bks) HarpC Child Bks.

Pumpkin, Pumpkin. Jeanne Titherington.Tr. of Citrouille, Ma Citrouille. (J). 1986. 9.15 (*0-606-04779-4*, Pub. by Turtleback) Demco.

Pumpkin Pumpkin. large type ed. Jeanne Titherington. (J). 1999. pap. 19.95 (*0-590-72452-5*) Scholastic Inc.

Pumpkin, Pumpkin! Lore, History, Outlandish Facts & Good Eating. Anne C. MacCallum. LC 84-81831. (Illus.). 200p. (Orig.). 1986. pap. 8.95 (*0-9600300-9-3*) Heather Foun.

***Pumpkin Recipes.** Rose Stauffer. 36p. 1999. pap. 3.95 (*1-930354-04-5*) Bean Burner.

Pumpkin Rollers. Elmer Kelton. LC 95-33652. 320p. 1996. 22.95 (*0-312-86076-5*, Pub. by Forge NYC) St Martin.

Pumpkin Rollers. Elmer Kelton. 1997. mass mkt. 5.99 (*0-8125-4399-8*, Pub. by Tor Bks) St Martin.

Pumpkin Runner. Marsha D. Arnold. LC 97-26666. (Illus.). (J). 1998. 15.89 (*0-8037-2125-0*, Dial Yng Read) Peng Put Young Read.

Pumpkin Seed Massacre: The First Ben Pecos Mystery. Susan Slater. Ed. by Lee Ellison. LC 99-16433. 240p. 1999. 22.95 (*1-890768-17-0*) Intrigue Press.

Pumpkin Seed Point: Being Within the Hopi. Frank Waters. LC 76-75741. 175p. 1973. pap. 11.95 (*0-8040-0635-0*) Swallow.

Pumpkin-Shell Wife. Susanna H. McShea. (Hometown Heroes Ser.). 352p. 1993. mass mkt. 4.99 (*0-380-71980-0*, Avon Bks) Morrow Avon.

Pumpkin Soup. Helen Cooper. LC 98-18677. 32p. (J). (ps-3). 1999. 15.00 (*0-374-36164-9*) FS&G.

Pumpkin Soup. Lori Gardner. (Illus.). 40p. 1998. 8.99 (*1-58050-026-9*, 40-6155) Provo Craft.

Pumpkin Story see Sopa de Calabaza

Pumpkin Story. Mariko Shinju. LC 98-71912. (Illus.). 32p. (J). (ps-4). 1998. 16.95 (*1-880851-36-9*) Greene Bark Pr.

Pumpkin Time. Jan Andrews. (Illus.). 32p. (J). (ps-3). 1991. text 12.95 (*0-88899-112-6*) Publishers Group.

Pumpkined Heart. Brett Rutherford. 40p. 1973. 5.00 (*0-318-64162-3*) Poets Pr.

Pumpkins see Foods Series

Pumpkins. Ann L. Burckhardt. (Early-Reader Science Foods Ser.). (Illus.). 24p. (J). (gr. k-3). 1996. 13.25 (*0-516-20276-6*) Childrens.

Pumpkins. M. L. Ray. Ed. by Barry Root. LC 90-47305. (Gulliver Green Book Ser.). (Illus.). 32p. (J). (ps-3). 1992. 15.00 (*0-15-252252-2*, Gulliver Bks) Harcourt.

***Pumpkins!** School Zone Publishing Staff. (Illus.). (J). 2000. mass mkt. 4.99 (*0-88743-607-2*) Sch Zone Pub Co.

Pumpkins. Intro. by Rynn Williams. LC 98-230237. (Illus.). 72p. 1998. 15.00 (*1-56799-694-9*, Friedman-Fairfax) M Friedman Pub Grp Inc.

***Pumpkins.** Rynn Williams. (Illus.). 72p. 2000. 6.98 (*1-58663-065-2*) M Friedman Pub Grp Inc.

Pumpkins: A Story for a Field. Mary L. Ray. LC 90-47305. (Illus.). 32p. 1996. pap. 6.00 (*0-15-201358-X*) Harcourt.

***Pumpkins: The Hands-On Way to Build Reading Skills, 2 vols.** Scholastic, Inc. Staff. 1999. pap. text 7.95 (*0-439-05142-8*) Scholastic Inc.

Pumpkins, a Story for a Field. Mary Lyn Ray. 1996. 11.20 (*0-606-11770-9*, Pub. by Turtleback) Demco.

Pumpkins & Squashes. Caroline Boisset. LC 97-4070. (Illus.). 120p. 1997. 19.95 (*0-89577-957-9*, Pub. by RD Assn) Penguin Putnam.

Pumpkins Are Orange. Jack D. Breckenridge. 280p. (Orig.). 1997. pap. 12.95 (*0-9656993-0-7*) J D Breckenridge.

***Pumpkins from the Sky! A Cobtown Story: From the Diaries of Lucky Hart.** Julia Van Nutt. LC 98-39601. (Illus.). 32p. (J). 1999. 15.95 (*0-385-32568-1*, DD Bks Yng Read) BDD Bks Young Read.

Pumpkins Gone Crazy. (Guides Ser.). (Illus.). (YA). (gr. 4-7). 1999. 4.95 (*1-57054-360-7*) Klutz.

Pumpkins of Time. Mel Gilden. LC 94-16894. 192p. (YA). (gr. 6 up). 1994. 10.95 (*0-15-276603-0*); pap. 4.95 (*0-15-200889-6*) Harcourt.

Pumpkins! Pumpkins! Pumpkins! M. Mosley. (Illus.). 176p. 1997. spiral bd. 5.95 (*1-57166-087-9*) Hearts N Tummies.

Pumpkinville Mystery. Bruce Cole. LC 87-2533. (Illus.). 32p. (J). (ps-3). 1991. pap. 3.95 (*0-671-74199-3*) Litle Simon.

Pumpkinville Mystery. Bruce Cole & James Warhola. (Illus.). 32p. (J). (gr. 1-4). 1988. pap. 6.95 incl. audio (*0-671-67147-2*) S&S Trade.

Pumpkinville Mystery. Illus. by James Warhola. LC 87-2533. 32p. (J). (gr. 1-4). 1987. pap. 5.95 (*0-671-66906-0*); lib. bdg. 10.95 (*0-671-66905-2*) S&S Trade.

Pumps. Multimedia Development Services Staff. (Plant Fundamentals Ser.). (Illus.). 54p. (Orig.). 1995. student ed. 30.00 (*1-57431-012-7*) Tech Trng Systs.

Pumps, Vol. IV, Module I. Multimedia Development Services Staff. (Illus.). (Orig.). 1995. teacher ed. 49.95 (*1-57431-052-6*) Tech Trng Systs.

Pumps: Pumps - Polymer Materials Selection. (Illus.). 12p. 1997. pap. 30.00 (*1-880952-23-8*, S123) Hydraulic Inst.

Pumps: The Developing Needs. 1982. 135.00 (*0-7855-7320-8*) St Mut.

Pumps, a Workbook for Engineers: Presented at the Energy-Sources Technology Conference & Exibition, Houston, Texas, January 19-21, 1981. Ed. by J. Kovacik. LC 81-111446. 100p. reprint ed. pap. 31.00 (*0-608-11530-4*, 201573100098) Bks Demand.

Pumps & Pump Systems. (Illus.). 230p. 1983. 12.00 (*0-318-18067-7*) Am Soc Plumb Eng.

Pumps As Turbines: A User's Guide. Arthur Williams. 60p. (Orig.). 1995. pap. 12.00 (*1-85339-285-5*, Pub. by Intermed Tech) Stylus Pub VA.

Pumps-Compressors-Fans Pocket Handbook. Nicholas P. Cheremisinoff & Paul N. Cheremisinoff. LC 88-51422. 160p. 1988. 19.95 (*0-87762-623-5*) Technomic.

Pumps for Chemical Processing. J. T. McGuire. (Illus.). 304p. 1990. text 145.00 (*0-8247-8324-7*) Dekker.

Pumps for Fire-Protection Service, UL 448. 8th ed. (C). 1994. pap. text 135.00 (*1-55989-636-1*) Underwrtrs Labs.

Pumps for Oil-Burning Appliances, UL 343. 8th ed. 1997. pap. 195.00 (*1-55989-300-1*) Underwrtrs Labs.

***Pumps in Hong Kong: A Strategic Entry Report, 1998.** Compiled by Icon Group International Staff. (Country Industry Report). (Illus.). 103p. 1999. ring bd. 1030.00 incl. audio compact disk (*0-7418-0552-9*) Icon Grp.

***Pumps in Japan: A Strategic Entry Report, 1995.** Compiled by Icon Group International Staff. (Illus.). 157p. 1999. ring bd. 1570.00 incl. audio compact disk (*0-7418-1657-1*) Icon Grp.

Pumps in Mexico: A Strategic Entry Report, 1996. Compiled by Icon Group International Staff. (Illus.). 142p. 1999. ring bd. 1420.00 incl. audio compact disk (*0-7418-1423-4*) Icon Grp.

Pumps in Municipal Water & Wastewater Applications. Richard K. Miller et al. (Market Research Survey Ser.: No. 281). 50p. 1996. 200.00 (*1-55865-299-X*) Future Tech Surveys.

Pumps Pre-Prints. Saito & Igarashi. 1990. pap. 35.00 (*0-08-040194-5*, Pergamon Pr) Elsevier.

Pumps, Valves & Compressors in Egypt: A Strategic Entry Report, 1996. Compiled by Icon Group International Staff. (Illus.). 154p. 1999. ring bd. 1540.00 incl. audio compact disk (*0-7418-1424-2*) Icon Grp.

***Pumps, Valves & Compressors in Israel: A Strategic Entry Report, 1999.** Compiled by Icon Group International. (Illus.). 117p. 1999. ring bd. 1170.00 incl. audio compact disk (*0-7418-1741-1*) Icon Grp.

Pumps, Valves & Compressors in Peru: A Strategic Entry Report, 1997. Compiled by Icon Group International Staff. (Illus.). 139p. 1999. ring bd. 1390.00 incl. audio compact disk (*0-7418-0904-4*) Icon Grp.

***Pumps, Valves & Compressors in Singapore: A Strategic Entry Report, 1997.** Compiled by Icon Group International Staff. (Illus.). 115p. 1999. ring bd. 1150.00 incl. audio compact disk (*0-7418-1078-6*) Icon Grp.

Pumps, Valves, Pipes & Pipeline, Filtration & Water Treatment Technologies. 212p. 1994. text 36.00 (*981-3049-01-4*) World Scientific Pub.

Pumsy in Pursuit of Excellence: Self-Esteem for the Elementary School Child. Jill Anderson. (Illus.). 270p. 1990. teacher ed. 80.00 (*0-9608284-3-5*) Timberline Pr.

Pumsy Storybook. Jill Anderson. (Illus.). 40p. (Orig.). (J). (gr. 2-5). 1990. pap. text 4.95 (*0-9608284-2-7*) Timberline Pr.

Pun & Games: Jokes, Riddles, Rhymes, Daffynitions, Tairy Fales, & More Wordplay for Kids. Richard Lederer. LC 96-11609. (Illus.). 112p. (Orig.). (YA). (gr. 5 up). 1996. pap. 9.95 (*1-55652-264-9*) Chicago Review.

***Pun in Cheek: A Collection of Punny Limericks.** William J. Middleton. LC 99-61132. (Illus.). 76p. 1999. pap. 6.00 (*1-886467-47-1*) WJM Press.

Pun My Word: A Humorously Enlightened Path to English Usage. Robert O. Shipman. 288p. (C). 1991. pap. text 14.95 (*0-8226-3011-7*) Rowman.

Pun with the Professor: Punology 101. Allen P. Schantz. 100p. 1992. pap. 8.95 (*0-9635275-0-9*) A P Schantz.

Puna Kahuna: A Ben McMillen Hawaiian Mystery. Mark Brown. LC 93-24262. 1993. 19.95 (*1-881987-02-7*) Ox Bow.

Punahou Story. Norris W. Potter. LC 68-31288. (Illus.). 224p. 1969. 18.95 (*0-87015-176-2*) Pacific Bks.

Punaluu to Manuka Field Site Guide for Teachers. Faith M. Roelofs. (Exploring the Islands Ser.). 1994. teacher ed. write for info. (*1-882163-36-2*) Moanalua Grdns Fnd.

Punch: The Lively Youth of a British Institution, 1841-1851. Richard D. Altick. LC 96-32091. (Studies in Victorian Life & Literature). 1997. text 62.50 (*0-8142-0710-3*) Ohio St U Pr.

Punch & Cookies Forever: And Other Stories for LDS Youth. Jack Weyland. LC 80-84566. 150p. (YA). 1981. 10.98 (*0-88290-173-7*) Horizon Utah.

Punch & His Friends. Coby Hol. (J). pap. 14.95 (*0-86315-206-6*, 1823, Pub. by Floris Bks) Anthroposophic.

Punch & Judy. Ed. by Lisl Beer. (Silver Series of Puppet Plays). 1997. pap. 3.95 (*0-8283-1244-3*) Branden Bks.

Punch & Judy. Ed. by William-Alan Landes. LC 95-37906. (Illus.). 24p. 1995. pap. 7.00 (*0-88734-290-6*) Players Pr.

Punch & Judy. Bill Svanoe. 1996. pap. 5.25 (*0-8222-1504-7*) Dramatists Play.

Punch & Judy. Illus. by George Cruikshank. LC 70-174866. 1972. reprint ed. 26.95 (*0-405-09123-0*, Pub. by Blom Pubns) Ayer.

Punch & Judy: Musical. Aurand Harris. 47p. (J). 1970. 6.00 (*0-87602-183-6*) Anchorage.

Punch & Judy & Other Essays. Maurice Baring. LC 68-16904. (Essay Index Reprint Ser.). 1977. reprint ed. 23.95 (*0-8369-0172-X*) Ayer.

Punch, Brothers, Punch! Samuel L. Clemens. 141p. 1998. reprint ed. lib. bdg. 75.00 (*0-7812-4781-0*) Rprt Serv.

Punch Brothers Punch & Other Sketches. Mark Twain, pseud. (Works of Samuel Clemens). 1989. reprint ed. lib. bdg. 79.00 (*0-685-28376-3*) Rprt Serv.

Punch-Drunk in America: Reviving the American Revolutionary Movement. Joe Duval. 120p. (Orig.). 1987. pap. 10.00 (*0-9618680-0-7*) Rights Pr.

Punch Happy: Punch Art Secrets for Scrapbooks & Gifts. Tracey L. Isidro. LC 98-22876. 1998. pap. 14.95 (*0-9663318-1-8*) Living Vision.

***Punch in the Stomach: Taking Back Your Life after Job Loss.** Celeste A. Turner. 64p. 1999. pap. 8.00 (*0-8059-4652-7*) Dorrance.

Punch Line Rhyme. Jack Nussbaum. LC 92-96976. (Illus.). 102p. 1992. 13.50 (*0-9636110-0-3*); pap. 9.50 (*0-9636110-1-1*) Nut Tree Ent.

Punch Lines. McRobbie. 1987. pap. text. write for info. (*0-582-66799-2*, Pub. by Addison-Wesley) Longman.

Punch Lines: Berger on Boxing. Phil Berger. LC 92-38537. (Illus.). 328p. 1993. 24.95 (*0-941423-93-X*) FWEW.

P

Punch Out! The Illustrated Guide to the World's Ejection Seats. David H. Klaus. (KLAUSguide Ser.: No. 2). (Illus.). 1991. pap. write for info. (0-9629146-1-4) Meteor Prod Inc.

Punch with Care. Phoebe Atwood Taylor. 21.95 (0-8488-1202-6) Amereon Ltd.

Punch with Care. Phoebe Atwood Taylor. (Asey Mayo Cape Cod Mystery Ser.). 224p. 1992. pap. 7.95 (0-88150-229-4, Foul Play) Norton.

Punch with Judy. Avi. 1997. mass mkt. 4.50 (0-380-72980-6, Avon Bks) Morrow Avon.

Punch with Judy. Avi. LC 92-27157. 1993. 9.09 (0-606-06684-5, Pub. by Turtleback) Demco.

Punch with Judy. Avi. 1997. 9.60 (0-606-11771-7, Pub. by Turtleback) Demco.

Punch Your Art Out. Satellite Press Staff. 1999. pap. text 12.50 (1-892127-00-8) Satellite Publ.

Punch Your Art Out, 2 vols., Vol. II. Satellite Press Staff. (Illus.). 52p. 1999. pap. text 12.50 (1-892127-01-6) Satellite Publ.

Punchdrunk Man Reader. Chester Mack. LC 87-51416. (Illus.). 140p. 1988. 14.95 (0-9605630-1-6) Thistlerose.

Punched Card Methods in Scientific Computation. W. J. Eckert & J. C. McPherson. 165p. 1984. 27.50 (0-262-05030-7) MIT Pr.

Puncher Pie & Cowboy Lies. Steve Sederwall. LC 99-17306. 1999. pap. text 16.95 (1-55622-683-7) Wordware Pub.

***Punching.** Geoff Thompson. (Real Summersdale Ser.). 1999. pap. 16.95 (1-84024-088-1) Seven Hills Bk.

Punching-Ball & la Vache a Lait: La Critique Universitaire Nord-Americaine Face au Surrealisme. Guy Ducornet. LC 97-48645. (FRE.). 174p. 1994. pap. 30.00 (0-941194-30-2) Black Swan Pr.

Punching Out. Jim Daniels. LC 89-16662. 94p. (C). 1990. pap. 11.95 (0-8143-2191-7) Wayne St U Pr.

Punching Out. Jim Daniels. LC 89-16662. 93p. reprint ed. pap. 30.00 (0-608-10522-8, 2054433) Bks Demand.

Punching the Clock: Funny Action Idioms. Marvin Terban. (Illus.). 64p. (J). (gr. 3-7). 1990. pap. 6.95 (0-89919-865-1) HM.

Punching the Clock: Funny Action Idioms. Marvin Terban. (J). 1990. 12.15 (0-606-04519-8, Pub. by Turtleback) Demco.

Punchline. Jacqueline Diamond. 1997. per. 3.50 (0-373-44011-1, 1-44011-4) Silhouette.

Punchlines. David Goines. (Illus.). 74p. 1994. pap. 5.95 (0-89815-652-1) Ten Speed Pr.

Punch's Companion to the Classics. H. A. White. 68p. (C). 1982. pap. text 65.00 (0-900269-00-6, Pub. by Old Vicarage) St Mut.

Punctual Hilbert Schemes. Anthony A. Iarrobino. LC 77-3947. (Memoirs Ser.: No. 10/188). 112p. 1977. pap. 21.00 (0-8218-2188-1, MEMO/10/188) Am Math.

Punctuate It Right! Punctuate It Right. Harry Shaw. 224p. 1996. mass mkt. 4.99 (0-06-100813-3) HarpC.

Punctuate It Right: Second Edition. 2nd ed. Harry Shaw. LC 92-8352. 224p. 1993. pap. 13.00 (0-06-461045-4, Harper Ref) HarpC.

Punctuation. Lindell Bruce. 60p. (C). 1994. pap. text 13.95 (0-8403-9697-X, 40969701) Kendall-Hunt.

Punctuation. Humberg. (YA - Adult Education Ser.). 1993. pap. 5.95 (0-538-70774-7) S-W Pub.

Punctuation. Nancy O'Rourke. 1997. pap., wbk. ed. 2.25 (1-56293-916-5, McClanahan Book) Learn Horizon.

Punctuation. 2nd ed. (Illus.). 80p. (J). (gr. 1-3). 1997. pap., teacher ed. 7.95 (1-55799-030-1, 141) Evan-Moor Edu Pubs.

Punctuation: A Simplified Approach. 3rd ed. Perkins. (EC - HS Communication/English Ser.). 1989. mass mkt. 15.95 (0-538-60122-1) S-W Pub.

Punctuation: Syllabus. 2nd ed. Carl W. Salser & C. Theodore Yerian. 1972. pap. text 8.95 (0-89420-020-8, 357498); audio 56.20 (0-89420-178-6, 357500) Natl Book.

Punctuation - Parts of a Sentence: Sing & Learn. John Carratello. 1994. pap. 9.95 incl. audio (0-7604-0019-9, JPC001) Wrner Bros.

Punctuation & Capitalization Flipper. Jack L. Cushman. (Illus.). 49p. (J). (gr. 5 up). 1989. reprint ed. 6.95 (1-878383-00-0) C Lee Pubns.

Punctuation & Grammar. NCPTA Staff. (Illus.). (J). 1996. mass mkt. 6.95 (0-340-65106-7, Pub. by Hodder & Stought Ltd) Trafalgar.

Punctuation & Grammar Guide. Roberta M. Humble. 79p. 1997. pap. text 12.95 (0-940139-45-6) Consortium RI.

Punctuation & Its Dramatic Value in Shakespearean Drama. Anthony Graham-White. LC 94-33129. 191 p. 1995. 36.50 (0-87413-542-7) U Delaware Pr.

Punctuation & Spelling. Diana Bonet. 128p. 1997. pap. 12.95 (1-56052-360-3) Crisp Pubns.

Punctuation Capitalization. Renae B. Humburg. 1992. pap. text. write for info. (0-7854-1375-8) Am Guidance.

Punctuation, Capitalization & Handwriting for Job & Personal Use. Humberg. (YA - Adult Education Ser.). 1992. pap. 9.95 (0-538-70518-3) S-W Pub.

Punctuation Drills & Exercises. 2nd ed. LeRoy A. Brendel & Doris Near. (gr. 9-12). 1978. text 13.24 (0-07-007479-8) McGraw.

Punctuation for Court Reporters. 2nd ed. Nathaniel Weiss. 100p. 1994. spiral bd. 18.95 (1-881859-05-3) Natl Ct Report.

Punctuation for Review & Reference: A Style Manual with Exercises. Edward Voeller. LC 97-38204. (Illus.). 80p. 1997. pap. 10.95 (0-8442-0817-5, 08175) NTC Contemp Pub Co.

Punctuation Handbook. Joan I. Miller & Bruce J. Taylor. 96p. (Orig.). 1989. pap. 4.95 (0-937473-14-6) Alcove Pub Co OR.

Punctuation Made Easy. Jeanette Adkins. 112p. (C). 1997. pap. text 25.95 (1-56226-353-6) CAT Pub.

Punctuation Marks. Martha C. Hodrick. (J). (gr. 6-9). 1998. pap. 14.95 (0-533-12761-0) Vantage.

Punctuation Marks. Roslyn Snow. 24p. 1978. pap. 5.00 (0-9679093-7-6) Easy Guides.

Punctuation Marks: The Rhymes of My Life in Poetry. Edna M. Hermann. 170p. 1998. pap. 14.95 (1-57502-898-0, PO2464) Morris Pubng.

***Punctuation 1999c: Globe Fearon English.** 45p. 1998. write for info. (0-13-023257-2) S&S Trade.

***Punctuation Pals.** Hope. Ed. by Tim Anders. LC 99-63177. (Life Lessons Ser.). (Illus.). 38p. (J). (gr. k-4). 2000. 16.95 (1-885624-56-5) Alpine Pubng.

Punctuation Plain & Simple. Edgar C. Alward & Jean A. Alward. LC 96-51152. (In Plain English Ser.). 192p. (Orig.). 1997. pap. 11.99 (1-56414-274-4) Career Pr Inc.

Punctuation Plus see Learning Writing & Grammar Quickly

Punctuation Pockets: A Student Folder. Patrick Sebranek & Verne Meyer. (Illus.). (YA). (gr. 7-12). 1984. pap. text 2.60 (0-669-38557-3) Great Source.

Punctuation Power. Marvin Terban. LC 99-19179. (Scholastic Guides Ser.). Date not set. pap. write for info. (0-590-38674-3) Scholastic Inc.

***Punctuation Power: Punctuation & How to Use It.** Marvin Terban. LC 99-19179. (Guides Ser.). (Illus.). 96p. (J). (gr. 3-9). 2000. 12.95 (0-590-38673-5, Scholastic Ref) Scholastic Inc.

Punctuation Puzzles. J. Tyler & R. Gee. (English Skills Ser.). (Illus.). 32p. (J). (gr. 2-6). 1993. pap. 6.95 (0-7460-1054-0) EDC.

Punctuation Repair Kit. W. Vandyck. 1996. mass mkt. 8.95 (0-340-63618-1, Pub. by Hodder & Stought Ltd) Trafalgar.

Punctuation Thesaurus of the English Language. Howard Lauther. 360p. 1991. 19.95 (0-8283-1945-6) Branden Bks.

Punctuation Tips: External & Internal Punctuation Rules. 2nd ed. Maryhelen H. Hoffman & Lanny L. Hoffman. 115p. 1999. pap. text 49.95 incl. cd-rom (1-928592-07-4) MHP Commns.

***Punctuation Tips Workbook: External & Internal Punctuation Rules.** Maryhelen H. Hoffman & Lanny L. Hoffman. 109p. 2000. pap., wbk. ed. 49.95 (1-928592-16-3) MHP Commns.

***Puncturing Our Illusions: Developing Your Critical Thinking.** 2nd ed. 210p. (C). 2000. 24.00 (0-536-60871-7) Pearson Custom.

Pundemonium: Puns Are Everywhere! Harvey C. Gordon. LC 83-61419. (Illus.). 108p. (Orig.). 1983. pap. 3.95 (0-9601402-2-0) Punsters Pr.

Pundits: British Exploration of Tibet & Central Asia. Derek Waller. LC 90-32802. (Illus.). 344p. 1990. 38.00 (0-8131-1666-X) U Pr of Ky.

Pundits & Patriots Lessons from the Gulf War. Philip Towle. (C). 1990. 60.00 (0-907967-24-8, Pub. by Inst Euro Def & Strat) St Mut.

Pundit's Folly. Sinclair B. Ferguson. 88p. (Orig.). 1995. pap. 3.99 (0-85151-676-9) Banner of Truth.

Pundits Scribes Pupils. Patrick F. Durgin. 44p. 1998. 7.00 (0-937013-88-9, Pub. by Potes Poets) SPD-Small Pr Dist.

Punga: The Goddess of Ugly. Deborah N. Lattimore. LC 92-23191. (Illus.). 32p. (J). (ps-3). 1993. 14.95 (0-15-292862-6) Harcourt.

***Pungenee: Poems from Hollywood.** Mark Dunster. 11p. 1999. pap. 5.00 (0-89642-733-1) Linden Pubs.

Pungent Sounds: Constructing Identity with Popular Music in Austria. Edward Larkey. LC 93-20113. (Austrian Culture Ser.: Vol. 9). (Illus.). XXII, 342p. (Orig.). (C). 1993. pap. text 35.95 (0-8204-2170-7) P Lang Pubng.

Punia & the King of Sharks: A Hawaiian Folktale. Adapted by Lee Wardlaw. LC 93-43955. (Illus.). 32p. (J). 1997. 15.99 (0-8037-1682-6, Dial Yng Read) Peng Put Young Read.

Punic Wars. Don Nardo. LC 95-11713. (World History Ser.). (Illus.). 112p. (YA). (gr. 7 up). 1996. lib. bdg. 22.45 (1-56006-417-X) Lucent Bks.

Punica, 2 vols. Silius Italicus. No. 277-278. write for info. (0-318-53171-2) HUP.

Punica, 2 Vols, 1. Silius Italicus. (Loeb Classical Library: No. 277-278). 462p. 1934. 18.95 (0-674-99305-5) HUP.

Punica, 2 Vols, 2. Silius Italicus. (Loeb Classical Library: No. 277-278). 506p. 1934. 18.95 (0-674-99306-3) HUP.

Puniddles, 001. Bruce McMillan & Brett McMillan. (Illus.). 32p. (J). (gr. 2 up). 1982. pap. 6.95 (0-395-32076-3) HM.

Punish & Critique: Towrds a Feminist Analysis of Penality. Adrian Howe. LC 93-36845. (Sociology of Law & Crime Ser.). 256p. (C). (gr. 13). 1994. pap. 27.99 (0-415-05191-6, A7803) Routledge.

Punish the Sinners. John Saul. 416p. 1990. mass mkt. 7.50 (0-440-17084-2) Dell.

***Punished by Rewards: The Trouble with Gold Stars, Incentive Plans.** Alfie Kohn. 416p. 1999. 29.95 (0-7351-0138-8) Replica Bks.

Punished by Rewards: The Trouble with Gold Stars, Incentive Plans, A's, Praise, & Other Bribes. Alfie Kohn. 398p. 1995. pap. 13.95 (0-395-71090-1) HM.

***Punished by Rewards: The Trouble with Gold Stars, Incentive Plans, A's, Praise & Other Bribes.** Alfie Kohn. 416p. 1999. pap. 14.00 (0-618-00181-6) HM.

Punished Peoples of the Soviet Union: The Continuing Legacy of Stalin's Deportations. Ed. by Human Rights Watch Staff. 84p. (Orig.). 1991. pap. 7.00 (1-56432-039-1) Hum Rts Watch.

Punisher. Patricia Bernard. 1999. pap. 7.95 (0-7322-5775-1) Colns.

Punisher: Assassin's Guild. Jo Duffy & Jorge Zaffino. 64p. 1988. 9.95 (0-87135-460-8) Marvel Entrprs.

Punishing a Nation: Israeli Human Rights Violations During the Palestinian Uprising. Law in the Service of Man, Al Haq Staff. 300p. (Orig.). (C). 1990. 40.00 (0-89608-379-9); pap. 16.00 (0-89608-378-0) South End Pr.

Punishing Criminals: Concerning a Very Old & Painful Question. Ernest Van den Haag. 308p. (C). 1991. reprint ed. pap. text 29.50 (0-8191-8172-2) U Pr of Amer.

Punishing Criminals: Developing Community-Based Intermediate Sanctions, 41. Malcolm Davies. LC 93-9315. (Contributions in Criminology & Penology Ser.: No. 41). 192p. 1993. 55.00 (0-313-28033-9, DPY/, Greenwood Pr) Greenwood.

Punishing Criminals: Pennsylvanians Consider the Options. Steve Farkas & Ethan Gutmann. 32p. (Orig.). 1992. pap. write for info. (1-889483-29-X) Public Agenda.

Punishing Criminals: The People of Delaware Consider the Options. John Doble et al. 111p. (Orig.). 1991. pap. write for info. (1-889483-30-3) Public Agenda.

Punishing Criminals: The Public's View, an Alabama Study. John Doble & Josh Klein. 74p. (Orig.). 1989. pap. write for info. (1-889483-31-1) Public Agenda.

Punishing Hate: Bias Crimes under American Law. Frederick M. Lawrence. LC 98-49780. 1999. 39.95 (0-674-73845-4) HUP.

Punishing International Terrorists: The Legal Framework for Policy Initiatives. John F. Murphy. LC 85-15845. 152p. 1985. 45.50 (0-8476-7449-5) Rowman.

Punishing the Poor. Ed. by Laurie Udesky. (Illus.). 64p. (Orig.). 1991. pap. 5.00 (0-943810-49-3) Inst Southern Studies.

Punishing Violence. Antonia Cretney & Gwynn Davis. LC 95-8208. (Illus.). 248p. (C). (gr. 13). 1995. 85.00 (0-415-09839-4, C0341) Routledge.

Punishing Violence. Gwynn Davis & Antonia Cretney. (Illus.). 248p. (C). 1995. pap. 27.99 (0-415-09840-8, C0342) Routledge.

***Punishment.** Bedau. 2000. 65.00 (0-8133-6604-6, Pub. by Westview); pap. 19.00 (0-8133-6605-4, Pub. by Westview) HarpC.

Punishment. Ed. by Antony Duff. (International Research Library of Philosophy). 526p. 1993. 173.95 (1-85521-312-5, Pub. by Dartmth Pub) Ashgate Pub Co.

Punishment: A Philosophy & Public Safety Affairs Reader. Ed. by A. John Simmons. LC 94-19058. 360p. 1994. text 52.50 (0-691-02956-3, Pub. by Princeton U Pr); pap. text 15.95 (0-691-02955-5, Pub. by Princeton U Pr) Cal Prin Full Svc.

Punishment: Issues & Experiments. Ed. by Erling E. Boe & Russell M. Church. LC 68-23894. (Century Psychology Ser.). (Illus.). (Orig.). (C). 1968. pap. text 13.95 (0-89197-367-2) Irvington.

Punishment: Its Origin, Purpose, & Psychology. Hans Von Hentig. LC 74-172566. (Criminology, Law Enforcement, & Social Problems Ser.: No. 147). 270p. 1973. reprint ed. 26.00 (0-87585-147-9) Patterson Smith.

Punishment: Rhetoric, Rule, & Practice. Christopher S. Harding & Richard W. Ireland. 256p. 1989. 49.95 (0-415-02340-8, A3250) Routledge.

Punishment: Social Control & Coercion. Ed. by Christine Sistare. (Critic of Institutions Ser.: Vol. 7). X, 230p. (C). 1996. text 47.95 (0-8204-2803-5) P Lang Pubng.

Punishment: Theory & Practice. Mark Tunick. (C). 1992. 45.00 (0-520-07737-7, Pub. by U CA Pr) Cal Prin Full Svc.

Punishment - Forms, Functions, Attitudes, Behaviors, Trials, Reasonings & Theories: Index of New Information Including Attempts of Cures, Control & Prevention of Crimes. Sidney A. Hadlow. 160p. 1995. 47.50 (0-7883-0476-3); pap. 44.50 (0-7883-0477-1) ABBE Pubs Assn.

***Punishment & Democracy: Three Strikes & You're Out in California.** Franklin E. Zimring et al. (Studies in Crime & Public Policy). (Illus.). 288p. 2000. 30.00 (0-19-513686-1) OUP.

Punishment & Desert. S. Kleinig. 170p. 1974. pap. text 65.00 (90-247-1592-X, Pub. by M Nijhoff) Kluwer Academic.

Punishment & Human Rights. Milton Goldinger. 164p. 1974. pap. text 11.95 (0-87073-527-6) Schenkman Bks Inc.

Punishment & Modern Society: A Study in Social Theory. David Garland. LC 90-6987. (Studies in Crime & Justice). viii, 320p. (C). 1993. pap. text 18.00 (0-226-28382-8) U Ch Pr.

Punishment & Penal Discipline: Essays on the Prison & the Prisoner's Movement. 2nd ed. Ed. by Tony Platt & Paul Takagi. LC 79-90275. (Illus.). (Orig.). 1982. pap. 10.95 (0-935206-00-0) Soc Justice.

Punishment & Political Theory. Ed. by Matt Matravers. 224p. 1998. 50.00 (1-901362-88-4, Pub. by Hart Pub) Intl Spec Bk.

Punishment & Politics: The Maximum Security Prison in New Zealand. Greg Newbold. 304p. 1989. 45.00 (0-19-558179-2) OUP.

Punishment & Privilege. Graeme Newman. Ed. by W. Byron Groves. LC 86-83030. (Illus.). 180p. 1987. pap. text 22.50 (0-911577-10-6, Criminal Justice) Willow Tree NY.

Punishment & Reformation. Frederick H. Wines. (Historical Foundations of Forensic Psychiatry & Psychology Ser.). xi, 481p. 1983. reprint ed. lib. bdg. 45.00 (0-306-76184-X) Da Capo.

Punishment & Reformation: A Study of the Penitentiary System. enl. rev. ed. Frederick H. Wines. LC 73-38676. (Foundations of Criminal Justice Ser.). reprint ed. 64.50 (0-404-09192-X) AMS Pr.

Punishment & Rehabilitation. 2nd ed. Ed. by Jeffrie G. Murphy. 233p. (C). 1985. pap. 18.95 (0-534-04614-2) Wadsworth Pub.

Punishment & Rehabilitation. 3rd ed. Jeffrie G. Murphy. LC 94-11228. 313p. 1994. 36.95 (0-534-24600-1) Wadsworth Pub.

Punishment & Rehabilitation. 4th ed. Murphy. (Philosophy Ser.). 2001. pap. 26.50 (0-534-52070-7) Wadsworth Pub.

Punishment & Responsibility: Essays in the Philosophy of Law. Herbert L. Hart. 284p. (Orig.). (C). 1978. pap. text 26.95 (0-19-825181-5) OUP.

Punishment & Restitution: A Restitutionary Approach to Crime & the Criminal, 5. Charles F. Abel & Frank H. Marsh. LC 83-22837. (Contributions in Criminology & Penology Ser.: No. 5). (Illus.). 214p. 1984. 62.95 (0-313-23717-4, ABP/) Greenwood.

Punishment & Restorative Crime-handling. Fatic. 304p. 1995. 77.95 (1-85972-023-4) Ashgate Pub Co.

Punishment & Social Control. Ed. by Thomas G. Blomberg & Stanley Cohen. (Social Institutions & Social Change Ser.). 328p. 1995. lib. bdg. 49.95 (0-202-30497-3) Aldine de Gruyter.

Punishment & the Death Penalty: The Current Debate. Ed. by Robert M. Baird & Stuart E. Rosenbaum. LC 94-47521. (Contemporary Issues Ser.). 258p. 1995. pap. 16.95 (0-87975-946-1) Prometheus Bks.

Punishment & Welfare: A History of Penal Strategies. David Garland. 291p. 1985. text 63.95 (0-566-00855-6, Pub. by Avebry) Ashgate Pub Co.

Punishment & Welfare: A History of Penal Strategies. David Garland. 297p. 1987. pap. text 34.95 (0-566-05431-0, Pub. by Avebry) Ashgate Pub Co.

Punishment As Societal Defense. Phillip Montague. (Studies in Social & Political Philosophy). 224p. (C). 1995. pap. text 22.95 (0-8476-8072-X); lib. bdg. 56.50 (0-8476-8071-1) Rowman.

Punishment by Death: Its Authority & Expediency. George B. Cheever. (Capital Punishment Ser.). reprint ed. 37.50 (0-404-62409-X) AMS Pr.

***Punishment, Communication, & Community.** Antony Duff. LC 99-49374. 288p. 2000. 45.00 (0-19-510429-3) OUP.

Punishment, Crime & Market Forces. Leslie Wilkins. 220p. 1991. text 78.95 (1-85521-228-5, Pub. by Dartmth Pub) Ashgate Pub Co.

Punishment, Danger & Stigma: The Morality of Criminal Justice. Nigel Walker. LC 81-112572. 206p. 1980. 53.00 (0-389-20129-4, N6905) B&N Imports.

Punishment, Excuses & Moral Development. Ed. by Henry Tam. (Series in Philosophy). 203p. 1996. text 67.95 (1-85972-260-1, Pub. by Avebry) Ashgate Pub Co.

Punishment for Profit: Private Prisons - Public Concerns. David Shichor. 288p. 1995. text 48.00 (0-8039-7154-0); pap. text 21.95 (0-8039-7155-9) Sage.

Punishment for the Crime. Tammy J. Eckhart. (Orig.). 1996. mass mkt. 6.95 (1-56333-427-5, Rhinoceros) Masquerade.

***Punishment in America: Social Control & the Ironies of Imprisonment.** Michael Welch. LC 99-6164. 319p. 1999. 74.95 (0-7619-1083-2) Sage.

Punishment in America: Social Control & the Ironies of Imprisonment. Michael Welch. LC 99-6164. 1999. write for info. (0-7619-1084-0) Sage.

Punishment in Australian Society. Mark Finnane. (Australian Retrospectives Ser.). (Illus.). 200p. 1998. pap. text 24.00 (0-19-553732-7) OUP.

***Punishment in Botany Bay.** B. Amber. 1998. mass mkt. 6.95 (0-7472-5670-5, Pub. by Headline Bk Pub) Trafalgar.

Punishment in Islamic Law. M. S. El Awa. 162p. 1985. pap. 5.00 (0-89259-015-7) Am Trust Pubns.

Punishment in Modern Society: A Study in Social Theory. David Garland. LC 90-6987. (Studies in Crime & Justice). 320p. 1998. 35.00 (0-226-28380-1) U Ch Pr.

Punishment in Search of a Crime: Americans Speak Out Against the Death Sentence. Ian Gray & Moira Stanley. 400p. (Orig.). 1989. pap. 8.95 (0-380-75923-3, Avon Bks) Morrow Avon.

Punishment in the Community: The Future of Criminal Justice. Abbe Worrall. LC 97-13487. 1997. pap. text. write for info. (0-582-29305-7) Longman.

Punishment of Crimes in Colonial New York: The Dutch Experience in Albany During the Seventeenth Century. Dennis Sullivan. (American University Studies: Vol. 186, No. 9). VIII, 356p. (C). 1998. text 54.95 (0-8204-3764-6) P Lang Pubng.

Punishment of the Stingy & Other Indian Stories. George B. Grinnell. LC 81-21922. (Illus.). xx, 265p. 1982. reprint ed. pap. 9.95 (0-8032-7008-9, Bison Books) U of Nebr Pr.

Punishment Response. 2nd ed. Pref. by Graeme Newman. LC 85-80304. 340p. 1985. reprint ed. pap. text 27.50 (0-911577-02-5, Criminal Justice) Willow Tree NY.

***Punishment, Responsibility & Justice: A Relational Critique.** Alan Norrie. (Oxford Monographs on Criminal Law & Justice). 256p. 2000. text 65.00 (0-19-825956-5) OUP.

Punishment Season: Human Rights in China after Martial Law. Asia Watch Staff. 174p. 1990. pap. 10.00 (0-929692-51-9, Asia Watch) Hum Rts Watch.

Punishment to Fit the Crime? Alison Cooper. LC 96-2138. (Viewpoints Ser.). (J). 1997. lib. bdg. 22.00 (0-531-14411-9) Watts.

Punishment under Pressure: The Probation Service in the Inner City. R. A. Broad. 200p. 1991. 39.95 (1-85302-090-7) Taylor & Francis.

Punishment Without Crime: Administrative Detention. 1991. pap. 6.00 (0-939994-69-0) Amnesty Intl USA.

Punishment Without Walls: Community Service Sentences in New York City. Douglas C. McDonald. 278p. 1989. pap. text 16.95 (0-8135-1469-X) Rutgers U Pr.

Punishments for North Carolina Crimes & Motor Vehicle Offenses. John Rubin & Ben F. Loeb, Jr. 1999. pap. 15.00 (1-56011-359-6) Institute Government.

P

An Asterisk (*) at the beginning of an entry indicates that the title is appearing for the first time.

Punishments Imposed on Federal Offenders, 2 vols., Set. A. Partridge et al. LC 86-81506. v, 1336p. 1986. reprint ed. lib. bdg. 150.00 (*0-89941-469-9*, 304270) W S Hein.

Punishments in the Olden Time: Being an Historical Account of the Dunking Stool, Brand, Pillory, Stocks, Drunkard's Cloak, Whipping Post, Riding the Stang, Etc. William Andrews. viii, 76p. 1993. reprint ed. 24.00 (*0-8377-1909-7*, Rothman) W S Hein.

Punitive Damages, 2 vols. Linda L. Schlueter & Kenneth R. Redden. Incl. 3rd ed. 1995. 180.00 (*1-55834-248-6*, MICHIE); 3rd ed. LC 95-79909. 1995. Not sold separately (*1-55834-268-0*, MICHIE); 180.00 (*0-614-25311-X*, 66471-11, MICHIE) LEXIS Pub.

Punitive Damages, 2 Vols. 3rd ed. Linda L. Schlueter & Kenneth R. Redden. 180.00 (*0-327-12334-6*) LEXIS Pub.

Punitive Damages: Tort Reform & FDA Defenses: Hearings Before the Committee on the Judiciary, U. S. Senate. Ed. by Orrin G. Hatch. 191p. (C). 1998. pap. text 30.00 (*0-7881-7279-4*) DIANE Pub.

Punitive Damages: 1990 Supplement. 2nd ed. Schlueter & Redden. 1990. write for info. (*0-87473-723-0*, 66472-10, MICHIE) LEXIS Pub.

Punitive Damages & Business Torts: A Practitioner's Handbook. Thomas J. Collins & American Bar Association Staff. LC 98-87811. (Antitrust Practice Guide Ser.). xi, 206p. 1998. 89.00 (*1-57073-617-0*) Amer Bar Assn.

Punitive Damages in Financial Injury Cases, the Rand Report: Hearing Before the Committee on the Judiciary, United States Senate, one Hundred Fifth Congress, First Session ... June 24, 1997. LC 98-106842. (S. Hrg. Ser.). iv, 111p. 1997. write for info. (*0-16-055477-2*) USGPO.

Punitive Damages in Financial Injury Jury Verdicts. Erik Moller et al. LC 97-196864. (Illus.). 84p. 1997. pap. 9.00 (*0-8330-2536-8*, MR-888-ICJ) Rand Corp.

Punitive Damages in Financial Injury Jury Verdicts: An Executive Summary. Erik Moller et al. LC 97-196893. (Illus.). 41p. 1997. pap. 9.00 (*0-8330-2534-1*, MR-889-ICJ) Rand Corp.

Punitive Damages in Tort Law, 1 vol. Gerald W. Boston. LC 92-76065. 1993. ring bd. 135.00 (*0-685-68854-2*) West Group.

Punitive Damages, 1981-1989, 2 vols. James Ghiardi & John Kircher. LC 81-10088. 240.00 (*0-685-09245-3*) West Group.

Punitive Damages, 1998 Cumulative Supplement, Vols. 1 & 2. 3rd ed. Kenneth Redden & Linda Schlueter. 340p. 1998. suppl. ed. write for info. (*0-327-00360-X*, 6647712) LEXIS Pub.

Punitive Expedition: Pershing's Pursuit of "Chasing Villa", 1916-1917. Ed. by Donald Smythe & Clarence C. Clendenen. 1985. 31.95 (*0-8488-0022-2*, J M C & Co) Amereon Ltd.

Punitive Measures. Don Pendleton. (Stony Man Ser.: No. 33). 1998. per. 5.99 (*0-373-61917-0*, 1-61917-0, Wrldwide Lib) Harlequin Bks.

Punjab, Vol. 180. Darshan S. Tatla & Ian Talbot. LC 96-192648. (World Bibliographical Ser.). 376p. 1995. lib. bdg. 88.00 (*1-85109-232-3*) ABC-CLIO.

Punjab: Imperial Gazetteer of India, 1908. 1985. reprint ed. 75.00 (*0-8364-1318-0*, Pub. by Usha) S Asia.

Punjab: Past, Present & Future. Ed. by Gopal Singh. (C). 1994. 44.00 (*81-202-0406-9*, Pub. by Ajanta) S Asia.

Punjab: The Nomads & the Renegades. 180p. write for info. (*81-7010-304-5*) Hemkunt Pr.

Punjab - Dead Silence: The Legacy of Abuses in Punjab. Human Rights Watch Asia Staff & Physicians for Human Rights Staff. LC 94-75428. 112p. (Orig.). 1994. pap. 10.00 (*1-56432-130-4*) Hum Rts Watch.

Punjab Accord & Elections Retrospect & Prospect. A. S. Narang. 1986. pap. 8.50 (*0-8364-1796-8*, Pub. by Minerva) S Asia.

Punjab & the Freedom Struggle. Parm B. Singh et al. LC 98-915174. xii, 341p. 1998. write for info. (*81-7380-492-3*) Pubn Bureau.

Punjab & the Nationality Question in India. Ramesh K. Chauhan. LC 95-905851. (C). 1995. 26.00 (*81-7100-717-1*, Pub. by Deep & Deep Pubns) S Asia.

Punjab Campaign: Casualty Roll, 1849. Picton Publishing Staff. 76p. (C). 1987. 105.00 (*0-7855-2227-1*, Pub. by Picton) St Mut.

Punjab Castes. Denzil Ibbetson. (C). 1993. reprint ed. 12.50 (*81-85557-55-1*, Pub. by Low Price) S Asia.

Punjab Crisis. A. C. Kapur. 316p. 1986. 34.95 (*0-318-36615-0*) Asia Bk Corp.

Punjab Crisis: Challenge & Response. Ed. by Abida Samiuddin. xxviii, 714p. 1985. 44.00 (*0-318-18470-2*, Pub. by Mittal Pubs Dist) Nataraj Bks.

Punjab Crisis: The Political Perceptions of Rural Voters. Jitinder Kaur. (C). 1988. 21.00 (*81-202-0218-X*, Pub. by Ajanta) S Asia.

Punjab in Crisis: Human Rights in India. Asia Watch. Ed. by Human Rights Watch Staff. LC 91-73230. 224p. (Orig.). 1991. pap. 15.00 (*0-685-70037-2*) Hum Rts Watch.

Punjab in Indian Politics: Issues & Trends. Ed. by Amrik Singh. xvi, 479p. 1985. 25.00 (*81-202-1485-4*) Nataraj Bks.

Punjab in Peace & War. S. S. Thorburn. 1987. 36.00 (*0-8364-2021-7*, Pub. by Usha) S Asia.

Punjab in Peace & War. S. S. Thorburn. LC 73-137301. reprint ed. 49.50 (*0-404-06424-8*) AMS Pr.

Punjab Local Acts, Unified & Regional Laws, 1825-1982. (C). 1982. 110.00 (*0-7855-4759-2*) St Mut.

Punjab Mail Murder: The Story of an Indian Army Officer. 2nd enl. ed. Ed. by Roger Perkins. 91p. (C). 1979. 45.00 (*0-948251-09-3*, Pub. by Picton) St Mut.

Punjab Peasant in Prosperity & Debt. rev. ed. Malcolm L. Darling. Ed. by Clive Dewey. 1978. 14.00 (*0-8364-0070-4*) S Asia.

Punjab Plants. J. L. Stewart. 375p. (C). 1977. text 250.00 (*0-89771-659-0*, Pub. by Intl Bk Distr) St Mut.

Punjab Plants. J. L. Stewart. 375p. (C). 1977. reprint ed. 160.00 (*0-7855-3088-6*, Pub. by Intl Bk Distr) St Mut.

Punjab Story. Ed. by A. Kaur et al. 199p. 1984. 19.95 (*0-318-36622-3*) Asia Bk Corp.

Punjab Story: Decade of Turmoil. D. P. Sharma. LC 95-906504. xi, 366p. (C). 1996. 39.00 (*81-7024-721-7*, Pub. by Ashish Pub Hse) Nataraj Bks.

Punjab under Imperialism, 1885-1947. Imran Ali. LC 87-34466. 276p. 1988. reprint ed. pap. 85.60 (*0-608-02943-2*, 206400900008) Bks Demand.

Punjabi - English Mini-Books Set with Audio, 11 bks. Claudia Schwalm. (ENG & PAN., Illus.). (Orig.). (J). (gr. k-6). 1997. pap. 21.95 incl. audio (*0-614-24737-3*) Cultural Cnnect.

Punjabi & Dalit Images in Indian Literature. Chaman Lal. 1998. 35.00 (*81-7488-917-5*) Anmol.

Punjabi Century, 1857-1947. Prakash Tandon. 1968. pap. 16.95 (*0-520-01253-4*, Pub. by U CA Pr) Cal Prin Full Svc.

Punjabi Cooking. Premjit T. Gill. (C). 1993. write for info. (*81-207-0179-8*) Sterling Pubs.

Punjabi Dictionary: Roman-Punjabi-English. Compiled by Bhai M. Singh. 1221p. 1992. 28.95 (*1-881338-23-1*) Nataraj Bks.

Punjabi-English Dictionary. 575p. 1992. 10.50 (*81-7205-070-4*, Pub. by Singh Brothers) IBD Ltd.

Punjabi English Dictionary. Gurcharan Singh. 1992. reprint ed. 29.95 (*0-8288-8482-X*) Fr & Eur.

Punjabi English, English Punjabi Dictionary. W. P. Hares. 424p. 1999. 24.95 (*0-7818-0716-6*) Hippocrene Bks.

Punjabi Identity Continuity & Change. Ed. by Gurharpal Singh & Ian Talbot. (C). 1996. 32.00 (*81-7304-117-2*, Pub. by Manohar) S Asia.

Punjabi Identity in a Global Context. Ed. by Pritam Singh & Shinder S. Thandi. 430p. 2000. text 29.95 (*0-19-564864-1*) OUP.

Punjabi Manual & Grammar. 1986. reprint ed. 22.50 (*0-8364-1688-0*, Pub. by Chanakya) S Asia.

Punjabi Reader in the Arabic Script. Mumtaz Ahmad. LC 90-80441. iv, 232p. 1992. 43.00 (*0-931745-65-9*) Dunwoody Pr.

Punjabi Reader in the Arabic Script. Contrib. by Mumtaz Ahmad. 1992. audio 19.00 (*0-931745-89-6*) Dunwoody Pr.

Punjabis in Canada: A Study of an Ethnic Community. Paramjit S. Judge. (C). 1993. 14.00 (*81-7001-099-3*, Pub. by Chanakya) S Asia.

Punjabis, War & Women: The Short Stories of Gulzar Singh Sandhu. Marcus Franda. 1983. 17.00 (*0-8364-0936-1*, Pub. by Heritage IA) S Asia.

Punjat's Ruby. Marian J. Jackson. (Miss Danforth Mystery Ser.: No. 1). 1990. mass mkt. 3.50 (*1-55817-338-2*, Pinncle Kensgtn) Kensgtn Pub Corp.

***Punk.** Collectors' Guide Publishers Staff. (20th Century Rock & Roll Ser.). 2000. pap. 13.95 (*1-896522-27-0*) CN06.

Punk: The Original. Punk Magazine Editors. LC 97-104585. (Illus.). 128p. 1996. pap. text 19.95 (*0-9647858-5-4*) Trans-High Corp.

Pun(K) Deconstruction: Experifigural Writings in Art & Art Education. Jan Jagodzinski. LC 97-22452. (Illus.). xviii, 244p. 1997. 95.00 (*0-8058-2606-8*); pap. write for info. (*0-8058-2607-6*) L Erlbaum Assocs.

Punk Diary, 1970-1979. George Gimarc. (Illus.). 256p. (Orig.). 1994. pap. 21.95 (*0-312-11048-0*) St Martin.

Punk Guitar Method. 40p. 1996. pap. 17.95 (*0-7935-5165-X*, 00695035) H Leonard.

***Punk Planet: The Collected Interviews.** Dan Sinker. 2001. pap. 14.95 (*1-888451-14-9*) Akashic Bks.

Punk Rock: So What? Roger Sabin. LC 98-37416. 247p. 1999. pap. 22.99 (*0-415-17030-3*) Routledge.

Punk Rock: So What?; The Cultural Legacy of Punk Rock. Roger Sabin. LC 98-37416. 1999. 75.00 (*0-415-17029-X*) Routledge.

***Punk Rock Guitar Styles.** Tobias Hurwitz. 1999. 14.95 incl. audio compact disk (*0-7390-0228-7*, 18509) Alfred Pub.

Punk Rotten & Nasty: The Saga of the Pacific Railway & Navigation Co. Paul M. Clock. LC 98-93979. (Illus.). 112p. 1998. pap. write for info. (*0-9668987-0-2*) Corbett Pr.

***Punk '77: An Inside Look at the San Francisco Rock n' Roll Scene, 1977.** James Stark. (Illus.). 98p. 1999. reprint ed. pap. 13.99 (*1-889307-07-6*, Pub. by RE Search) Subterranean Co.

***Punk Strips.** Simon Gane. (Illus.). 2000. pap. 12.00 (*1-899866-35-3*) Slab-O-Concrete Pubns.

Punkin Center Stories. limited ed. Cal Stewart. (Illus.). 192p. 1986. pap. 25.00 (*0-940152-04-5*) Hamilton Hobby.

Punkin in the Frost. Fred J. Fisher. LC 91-66980. (Illus.). 96p. 1992. 14.95 (*1-880807-12-2*) Cammium Phate.

Punkin's Night Out. Edith Castleberry. LC 96-27279. (Illus.). (J). 1997. write for info. (*1-56763-247-5*); pap. write for info. (*1-56763-248-3*) Ozark Pub.

Punks: Street Revolution. Stuart Coles. (Illus.). 128p. 1999. pap. 15.95 (*0-85965-251-3*) Publishers Group.

Punktown. Jeffrey Thomas. 128p. 1999. pap. 11.99 (*1-890464-04-X*) Ministry of Whimsy.

Punky Spends the Day. Sally G. Ward. 1999. pap. write for info. (*0-14-055288-X*) NAL.

Punny Papers. Bob Smalling. (Illus.). 108p. (Orig.). 1993. pap. 6.95 (*0-9636870-0-X*) Wrd Mouth Pr.

***Puns & Pundits: Word Play in the Hebrew Bible & Ancient Near Eastern Literature.** Scott B. Noegel. LC 99-53810. 350p. 2000. 50.00 (*1-883053-49-8*) CDL Pr.

***Puns upon a Rhyme: A Collection of Punny Limericks.** William J. Middleton. LC 00-100113. (Illus.). 71p. 2000. pap. 6.00 (*1-886467-56-0*) WJM Press.

Punt, Pass & Point! Bonnie-Alise Leggat. Ed. by Nancy R. Thatch. LC 92-17598. (Books for Students by Students). (Illus.). 26p. (J). (gr. 3-5). 1992. lib. bdg. 15.95 (*0-933849-39-7*) Landmark Edns.

Punta Gorda. D. C. Kip. (Illus.). 111p. (Orig.). 1984. pap. 5.00 (*0-9614549-0-3*) Maedon.

Punta Rassa. Ann O. Rust. (Floridians Ser.). 275p. (Orig.). 1988. pap. 12.95 (*0-9620556-0-3*) Amaro Bks.

Punta Rassa. Ann O. Rust. LC 88-70994. (Floridians Ser.). 275p. (Orig.). 1991. pap. text 17.50 (*0-9620556-7-0*) Amaro Bks.

Puntas de Vista Conversacion. Koike & Biron. (SPA.). 1994. text 34.25 incl. audio (*0-8384-4667-1*) Heinle & Heinle.

Puntigam or the Art of Forgetting. Gerald Szyszkowitz. Tr. by Adrian Del Caro. (Studies in Austrian Literature, Culture, & Thought. Translation Ser.). 280p. 1990. 24.50 (*0-929497-20-1*); pap. 18.50 (*0-929497-24-4*) Ariadne CA.

Punto Critico. Michael Crichton. 1998. pap. text 6.95 (*84-01-46683-0*) Lectorum Pubns.

Punto y Aparte: Spanish in Review, Moving Towards Fluency. Sharon W. Foerster et al. LC 98-35765. (ENG & SPA.). 288p. 1998. pap. 45.00 (*0-07-021661-4*) McGraw.

Puntos Claves Sobre las Reuniones en Casa. Witness Lee.Tr. of KEY POINTS ON THE HOME MEETINGS. (SPA.). 91p. 1986. per. 5.50 (*0-87083-250-6*, 12-009-002) Living Stream Ministry.

Puntos de Partida. 5th ed. Knorre. (SPA.). 1996. pap., wbk. ed. 21.88 (*0-07-038228-X*); pap., lab manual ed. 21.88 (*0-07-038229-8*) McGraw.

Puntos de Partida. 5th ed. Knorre. 1997. audio 15.31 (*0-07-038237-9*) McGraw.

Puntos de Partida. 5th ed. Knorre. 1997. student ed. 23.00 (*0-07-847833-2*) McGraw.

Puntos de Partida: An Invitation to Spanish. 4th ed. Marty Knorre et al. LC 92-41173. (ENG & SPA.). (C). 1993. text 52.25 (*0-07-035892-3*) McGraw.

Puntos de Partida: An Invitation to Spanish. 4th ed. Marty Knorre et al. LC 92-41173. (ENG & SPA.). 1993. pap. text, student ed. 16.50 (*0-07-035894-X*) McGraw.

Puntos de Partida: An Invitation to Spanish. 4th ed. Marty Knorre et al. LC 92-41173. (ENG & SPA.). 1993. pap. text, student ed. 16.50 (*0-07-035895-8*) McGraw.

Puntos de Partida: An Invitation to Spanish. 5th ed. Marty Knorre et al. 608p. (C). 1997. 66.88 (*0-07-913134-4*) McGraw.

Puntos de Partida/Points of Departure. Garcia D. Toro et al. (ENG & SPA., Illus.). 328p. (C). 1997. pap. text 16.95 (*1-56328-066-3*) Edit Plaza Mayor.

Puntos de Vista. Jill Welch. (College Spanish Ser.). (C). 1993. mass mkt., teacher ed. 21.95 (*0-8384-4663-9*) Heinle & Heinle.

Puntos de Vista: Narrativa Moderna Espanola. Sandra N. Harper. (SPA.). 300p. (C). 1994. pap. text 29.16 (*0-669-21787-5*) HM Trade Div.

Puntos de Vista: Voces de Espana e Hispanoamerica. 2nd ed. Solomon Tilles. 236p. (C). 1986. reprint ed. pap. text 22.00 (*0-8191-5383-4*) U Pr of Amer.

Puntos de Vista en la Conversacion. Koike & Makara. (Bridging the Gap Ser.). (C). 1993. text 31.75 (*0-8384-4658-2*) Heinle & Heinle.

Puntos de Vista en la Conversacion. Koike & Makara. (Bridging the Gap Ser.). (C). 1996. 11.95 (*0-8384-4660-4*) Heinle & Heinle.

Puntos de Vista en la Lectura. Susan Polansky. (Bridging the Gap Ser.). (C). 1993. mass mkt., student ed. 24.95 (*0-8384-4665-5*) Heinle & Heinle.

Puntos de Vista en la Redaccion. Jill Welch. (Bridging the Gap Ser.). (C). 1993. mass mkt., student ed. 37.95 (*0-8384-4662-0*) Heinle & Heinle.

Puntos Practicos en Cuanto a la Compenetracion. Witness Lee.Tr. of PRACTICAL POINTS CONCERNING THE BLENDING. (SPA.). 48p. 1994. pap. 4.25 (*0-87083-786-9*, 08-040-002) Living Stream Ministry.

Puntos Supp. Materials. 4th ed. Forester. 1997. pap. 12.80 (*0-07-021954-0*) McGraw.

Puntos y Aparte. Foerster. (SPA.). 152p. 1998. pap. 26.25 (*0-07-021662-2*) McGraw.

Punxsutawney Phil: Preview Kit. Judy Stoehr. (Illus.). (Orig.). (J). 1995. pap. text, teacher ed. write for info. (*0-89724-963-1*, BMR06012P); pap. text, teacher ed. write for info. (*0-89724-964-X*, BMR06012) Wrner Bros.

Punxsutawney Phil: Singer's Pack. Judy Stoehr. Ed. by Debbie Cavalier. (Illus.). (Orig.). (J). 1995. pap. text 12.95 (*1-57623-375-8*, BMR06012SP); audio 34.95 (*1-57623-377-4*, BM06012AT); audio compact disk 34.95 (*1-57623-376-6*, BMR06012CD) Wrner Bros.

Punzie, ICQ! Geoff Havel & Owen Bell. (J). 1999. pap. 12.95 (*1-86368-198-1*) Fremantle Arts.

Pup Grew Up! Samuel Marshak. Tr. by Richard Pevear from RUS. LC 88-28428. (Illus.). 32p. (J). (ps-2). 1995. 13.95 (*0-8050-0952-3*, Bks Young Read) H Holt & Co.

Pup in King Arthur's Court. Joanne Barkan & Brad Strickland. LC 97-81263. (Adventures of Wishbone Ser.: Vol. 14). (Illus.). 164p. (J). (gr. 3-7). 1998. pap. 3.99 (*1-57064-325-3*) Lyrick Pub.

Pup in King Arthur's Court see Adventures of Wishbone

***Pup Just for Me - A Boy Just for Me.** Doreatha Seebert. LC 98-45702. (Illus.). 48p. (J). (ps-3). 2000. 16.99 (*0-399-23403-9*, Philomel) Peng Put Young Read.

Pup Pup & Murray Find a New Home. Jean C. Stoneback. (Illus.). 45p. (Orig.). (J). (ps). 1984. pap. 5.00 (*0-931440-09-2*) Stoneback Pub.

Pup to Grizzly Bear. Oliver S. Owen. LC 95-3317. (Lifewatch Ser.). 32p. (J). (gr. 2-8). 1995. lib. bdg. 14.98 (*1-56239-486-X*) ABDO Pub Co.

Pup to Timber Wolf. Oliver S. Owen. LC 95-1172. (Lifewatch Ser.). 32p. (J). (gr. 2-8). 1995. lib. bdg. 14.98 (*1-56239-487-8*) ABDO Pub Co.

Pupa Digging. Joseph Greene. 1984. 30.00 (*0-7855-0671-3*) St Mut.

Pupil. E. Alexandridis. Tr. by Terry C. Telger from GER. (Illus.). 115p. 1985. 105.00 (*0-387-96109-7*) Spr-Verlag.

Pupil see Works of Henry James Jr.: Collected Works

Pupil: A Memory of Love. Monk Gibbon. 9.95 (*0-905473-68-X*, Pub. by Wolfhound Press) Irish Amer Bk.

Pupil: Anatomy, Physiology & Clinical Applications. Irene E. Loewenfeld & Otto Lowenstein. LC 98-53982. 2312p. 1999. text 250.00 (*0-7506-7143-2*) Buttrwrth-Heinemann.

Pupil as Scientist? Ed. by Rosalind Driver. 128p. 1983. pap. 38.95 (*0-335-10178-X*) OpUniv Pr.

Pupil Behavior & Teacher Culture. Andy Miller. (Introduction to Education Ser.). (Illus.). 176p. 1997. pap. 33.95 (*0-304-33683-1*); text 90.00 (*0-304-33684-X*) Continuum.

Pupil Issues, Vol. 13. Ed. by Fred Hartmeister. 44p. 1992. pap. 30.00 (*1-56534-051-5*) Ed Law Assn.

Pupil of the Eye: African Americans in the World Order of Baha'u'llah. Bonnie J. Taylor. 194p. 1995. 12.00 (*1-890101-00-1*) Palabra Pubns.

Pupil Profiles. Roger C. Reeds. (Sunday School Workers Training Course Ser.: No. 3). (C). 1973. pap. 6.95 (*0-89265-010-9*) Randall Hse.

Pupil Services: A Resource & Planning Guide. Sean Mulhern. LC 95-621571. 115p. (C). 1995. pap. text 21.00 (*1-57337-016-9*) WI Dept Pub Instruct.

Pupil Transportation & the Law. 2nd ed. Ralph D. Mawdsley. 100p. (C). 1996. text 27.00 (*1-56534-091-4*) Ed Law Assn.

Pupil Transportation Management: School Bus Operations, Personnel Management for Transportation Managers & Supervisors. Anthony R. Miller. LC 88-61377. 210p. (Orig.). (C). 1988. pap. text 15.75 (*0-929298-00-4*) Ramsburg & Roth Pubs.

Pupil's Concerto No. 2 In G: Opus 13 Violin. F. Seitz. 16p. 1986. pap. 5.95 (*0-7935-3912-9*) H Leonard.

Pupil's Concerto No. 4 in D: Opus 15 Violin & Piano. F. Seitz. 16p. 1986. pap. 5.95 (*0-7935-5238-9*) H Leonard.

Pupils in Transition. Gill Nichols & John Gardner. LC 98-25926. 128p. (C). (gr. 13). 1999. pap. 24.99 (*0-415-17467-8*, D6051) Routledge.

Pupils in Transition: Moving Between Key Stages. Gill Nichols & John Gardner. LC 98-25926. 128p. (C). (gr. 13). 1999. 75.00 (*0-415-17466-X*, D6047) Routledge.

Pupils of Low Mentality in High School. Lillian G. Portenier. LC 76-177158. (Columbia University. Teachers College. Contributions to Education Ser.: No. 568). reprint ed. 37.50 (*0-404-55568-3*) AMS Pr.

Pupils' Perceptions of Europe. Anne Convery. LC 97-179435. (Illus.). 1997. 89.50 (*0-304-33637-8*) Continuum.

Pupils with Attention Deficit. Paul Cooper. 1999. pap. text 29.95 (*1-86156-108-3*) Whurr Pub.

Pupils with Severe Learning Disabilities Who Present Challenging Behaviours: A Whole School Approach to Assessment & Intervention. John Harris et al. LC 95-49670. 1996. write for info. (*1-873791-86-0*, Pub. by Brit Inst Lrning); pap. 29.95 (*1-873791-18-6*, Pub. by Brit Inst Lrning) Taylor & Francis.

Puppen restaurieren. Jacintha Smulders. Tr. by Marlene Palmen-Goemans from DUT. (GER., Illus.). 128p. (C). 1996. 51.00 (*3-8170-1021-4*, Pub. by Knstvrlag Weingrtn) Intl Bk Import.

***Puppet: A Chicano Novella.** Margarita Cota-Cardenas. LC 00-8469. 2000. pap. write for info. (*0-8263-2229-8*) U of NM Pr.

Puppet Aprons - Just for Fun. Teri Felts & Mary Locke. 134p. (Orig.). 1995. pap. 19.95 (*0-9648196-1-9*) Pr for Tomorrow.

Puppet Book: How to Make & Operate Puppets. Claire Buchwald. LC 90-38080. (Illus.). 134p. (Orig.). (YA). 1990. pap. 13.95 (*0-8238-0293-0*) Kalmbach.

Puppet Booth. Henry B. Fuller. (Collected Works of Henry B. Fuller). 1988. reprint ed. lib. bdg. 59.00 (*0-7812-1202-2*) Rprt Serv.

Puppet Director's Notebook. 2nd rev. ed. Dale VonSeggen & Jim Scott. (Illus.). 61p. 1998. pap. 20.00 (*1-58302-065-9*, BPR-24) One Way St.

Puppet Director's Survival Kit. David Cole & Elaine Cole. (Illus.). 36p. 1994. 14.00 (*1-883426-04-9*) Chldrns Outrch.

Puppet in the Big Black Box. Steve Chaney. (Illus.). 32p. (J). (gr. k-3). 1989. write for info. (*0-318-65294-3*) Stiff Lip.

Puppet King. TSR Inc. Staff. (DragonLance Chaos War Ser.). 1999. pap. 5.99 (*0-7869-1324-X*, Pub. by TSR Inc) Random.

Puppet Making. Book Sales Staff. 1998. 8.99 (*0-7858-1007-2*) Bk Sales Inc.

Puppet Making. Deborah Schneebeli-Morrell. (Start a Craft Ser.). 1994. 7.98 (*0-7858-0058-1*) Bk Sales Inc.

Puppet Master. Barry T. Hawkins. 352p. 1993. mass mkt. 4.50 (*0-8217-4098-9*, Zebra Kensgtn) Kensgtn Pub Corp.

Puppet Masters. Robert A. Heinlein. 352p. 1986. mass mkt. 5.99 (*0-345-33014-5*, Del Rey) Ballantine Pub Grp.

Puppet Masters. Robert A. Heinlein. 1999. lib. bdg. 20.95 (*1-56723-156-X*) Yestermorrow.

Puppet Ministry. James Christy. 80p. 1978. pap. 7.99 (*0-8341-0532-2*) Beacon Hill.

Puppet of Desire: The Psychology of Hysteria, Possession & Hypnosis. Jean-Michel Oughourlian. Tr. by Eugene Webb from FRE. LC 90-42448. 289p. 1991. 37.50 (*0-8047-1823-7*) Stanford U Pr.

Puppet on a Chain. Alistair MacLean. reprint ed. lib. bdg. 21.95 (*0-89190-175-2*, Riverciry Pr) Amereon Ltd.

P

An Asterisk (*) at the beginning of an entry indicates that the title is appearing for the first time.

Puppet Parade: Easy-to-Make Imaginative Puppets from Readily- Found Materials. Imogene Forte. 80p. (Orig.). (J). (gr. 1-6). 1992. pap. text 9.95 (0-86530-152-2, 195-1) Incentive Pubns.

Puppet Patterns: Integrate Easy-to-Make Puppets with Thematic Activities Across the Curriculum. Linda Milliken. (Illus.). 40p. 1995. pap., wbk. ed. 5.95 (1-56472-060-8) Edupress Inc.

Puppet Patterns for Farm Folk. Jill Hierstein-Morris. (Illus.). 56p. (J). 1995. lib. bdg. 20.00 (1-877588-05-9) Creatively Yours.

Puppet Plays for All Seasons. 3rd rev. ed. Dale VonSeggen & Liz VonSeggen. 38p. 1996. pap. 10.00 (1-58302-069-1, BPS-03) One Way St.

Puppet Plays Plus: Hand Puppet Plays for Two Puppeteers. Phyllis N. Pflomm. LC 94-4875. (Illus.). 253p. 1994. 31.00 (0-8108-2738-7) Scarecrow.

Puppet Power. Nancy M. Laughlin. (Illus.). 128p. 1998. pap. 10.95 (0-673-36389-9, GoodYrBooks) Addson-Wesley Educ.

Puppet Programs, No. 1. Vann Trapp. 56p. 1980. 6.99 (0-8341-9631-X, MP-609) Lillenas.

Puppet Programs, No. 2. Marilyn Millikan. 52p. 1980. pap. 6.99 (0-8341-9242-X, MP-610) Lillenas.

Puppet Programs, No. 3. Donna F. Crow. 55p. 1985. 6.99 (0-8341-9309-4, MP-631) Lillenas.

Puppet Programs, No. 5. Doug Smee. 70p. 1987. 6.99 (0-8341-9005-2, MP-646) Lillenas.

Puppet Programs, No. 6. Doug Smee. 74p. 1990. 6.99 (0-8341-9048-6, MP-660) Lillenas.

Puppet Programs, No. 9. Davidene Humphreys. 1995. 6.99 (0-8341-9274-8, MP-757) Lillenas.

Puppet Programs No. 7: The Further Adventures of Penelope & Wilbur. Davidene Humphreys. 43p. 1991. pap. 6.99 (0-8341-9728-6, MP-668) Nazarene.

Puppet Programs No. 8: Puppet Parables for School & Church. Arranged by Doug Smee. 73p. 1994. pap. 6.99 (0-8341-9054-0, MP-698) Lillenas.

Puppet Projects for Scripture Stories. Phyllis Wezeman. 106p. 1995. pap. 10.95 (1-877871-85-0, 5185) Ed Ministries.

Puppet Scripts by the Situation. Margaret Cheasebro. LC 88-7537. (Orig.). 1989. pap. 6.99 (0-8054-7527-3, 4275-27) Broadman.

Puppet Scripts for Use, Set. Everette Robertson. 1979. pap. 12.99 incl. audio (0-8054-7925-2) Broadman.

Puppet Scripts for Use at Church. Ed. by Everett Robertson. LC 78-72843. 96p. 1978. pap. 7.99 (0-8054-7516-8, 4275-16) Broadman.

Puppet Scripts for Use at Church, No. 2. Ed. by Everett Robertson. LC 78-72843. 96p. (J). (gr. k up). 1980. pap. 7.99 (0-8054-7519-2, 4275-19) Broadman.

***Puppet Scripts-Genesis Comes to Life.** large type ed. (Bible Comes to Life Ser.: Bk. 1). 107p. 1999. reprint ed. spiral bd. 9.99 (0-9658103-0-5) SonLife Pub.

Puppet Scripts on Missions. 16p. 1992. pap. 8.00 (1-58302-070-5, BPS-06) One Way St.

Puppet Scrits: For Use with Cassette. 1997. pap. text 27.99 (0-8054-7919-8) Broadman.

Puppet Show. Sharon Peters. (Illus.). 32p. (J). (gr. k-2). 1997. pap. 2.50 (0-89375-286-X) Troll Communs.

***Puppet Show.** Josie Stewart & Lynn Salem. (Illus.). 8p. (J). (gr. k-2). 1999. pap. 3.75 (1-58323-004-1) Seedling Pubns.

Puppet Show. Martin D. Armstrong. LC 71-163020. (Short Story Index Reprint Ser.). 1977. reprint ed. 16.95 (0-8369-3934-4) Ayer.

Puppet Shows Made Easy! Nancy Renfro. Ed. by Celeste Cromack. (Puppetry in Education Ser.). (Illus.). 96p. (Orig.). (J). (gr. 2-12). 1995. spiral bd. 16.95 (0-931044-13-8) Renfro Studios.

Puppet Tales. Valerie Marsh. LC 97-35074. (Alleyside Press Storytelling Ser.). (Illus.). 80p. (J). 1998. pap. 14.95 (0-917846-92-3, Alleyside) Highsmith Pr.

***Puppeteer.** rev. ed. Ivan Bulloch. (I Want to Be Ser.). (Illus.). (J). 2000. 9.95 (1-58728-085-X); pap. 5.95 (1-58728-091-4) Two Can Pub.

Puppeteer. 11th ed. R. Kroetsch. 1993. 11.00 (0-394-22364-0) Random.

Puppeteer Training Manual. David Cole & Elaine Cole. (Illus.). 32p. (J). (gr. 4-12). 1994. pap. 4.00 (1-883426-03-0) Chldrns Outrch.

Puppeteers: Studies of Obsessive Control. Gerald Alper. LC 94-33056. 224p. 1994. 19.95 (0-88064-160-6) Fromm Intl Pub.

Puppeteers: Studies of Obsessive Control. Gerald Alper. LC 98-24869. 228p. 1998. pap. 19.95 (1-57309-316-5) Intl Scholars.

Puppeteer's Library Guide Vol. II: The Bibliographic Index to the Literature of the World Puppet Theatre: The Puppet As an Educator. J. Frances Crothers. LC 71-149991. 366p. 1983. 50.00 (0-8108-1611-3) Scarecrow.

Puppetmasters: The Political Use of Terrorism in Italy. Philip Willan. LC 92-154080. 375p. 1991. write for info. (0-09-470590-9) Constable & Co.

Puppetools: Introductory Guide. Jeffrey L. Peyton. LC 85-19176. Orig. Title: Puppetry: A Tool for Teaching Puppetry & Creative Learning Techniques. (Illus.). 200p. 1986. pap. text 24.95 (0-9609506-1-3) Prescott Durrell & Co.

Puppetry: A Packet of Designs, Drawings & Ideas for & about Hand Puppets. Vern Adix. (Encore Theatre Book Ser.). 93p. 1985. pap. 9.95 (1-57514-010-1, 5001) Encore Perform Pub.

Puppetry: A Tool for Teaching Puppetry & Creative Learning Techniques see Puppetools: Introductory Guide

Puppetry & Other Folk Dramas for Non-Formal Education. Anupama Shah & Uma Joshi. 144p. (C). 1992. 27.50 (81-207-1406-7) Apt Bks.

Puppetry ClipArt. (Illus.). 31p. 1995. pap. 13.00 (1-58302-071-3, BCA-01) One Way St.

Puppetry in Early Childhood Education. Tamara Hunt & Nancy Renfro. Ed. by Ann W. Schwalb. (Puppetry in Education Ser.). (Illus.). 264p. (Orig.). (J). (ps-3). 1981. pap. 20.95 (0-931044-04-9) Renfro Studios.

Puppetry Language & the Special Child: Discovering Alternate Languages. Nancy Renfro. Ed. by Celeste Cromack. (Puppetry in Education Ser.). (Illus.). 160p. (Orig.). (J). (ps-6). 1984. spiral bd. 17.95 (0-931044-12-X) Renfro Studios.

Puppetry Library: An Annotated Bibliography Based on the Batchelder-McPharlin Collection at the University of New Mexico. Compiled by George B. Miller, Jr. et al. LC 80-23474. 171p. 1981. lib. bdg. 47.95 (0-313-21359-3, HPL/, Greenwood Pr) Greenwood.

Puppetry Stages. rev. ed. Dale VonSeggen. (Illus.). 17p. 1991. pap. 6.00 (1-58302-072-1, BPR-06) One Way St.

Puppetry Yearbook, Vol. 2. Ed. by James Fisher. (Illus.). 204p. 1996. text 89.95 (0-7734-8799-9) E Mellen.

Puppetry Yearbook, Vol. 3. James Fisher. (Illus.). 260p. 1997. text 89.95 (0-7734-8646-1) E Mellen.

Puppets see Titeres

Puppets. (Kids Krafts Ser.). (J). 1989. 2.95 (0-934593-04-3) Wicklow Ltd.

***Puppets.** Kelly Burkholder. LC 00-25372. (Artistic Adventures Ser.). (Illus.). (J). 2000. write for info. (1-57103-355-6) Rourke Bk Co.

Puppets. Meryl Doney. LC 95-11433. (World Crafts Ser.). (Illus.). 32p. (J). (gr. 4-7). 1996. lib. bdg. 21.00 (0-531-14399-6) Watts.

Puppets. Meryl Doney. (World Crafts Ser.). (J). (gr. 4). 1997. pap. text 6.95 (0-531-15872-1) Watts.

Puppets. Susan Hodges. (Play & Learn Ser.). (Illus.). 48p. (J). (ps-k). 1998. pap. 3.95 (1-57029-231-0, W02310) Totline Pubns.

Puppets. Helen McNiven & Peter McNiven. (First Arts & Crafts Ser.). (Illus.). 32p. (J). 1994. lib. bdg. 21.40 (1-56847-215-3) Raintree Steck-V.

Puppets: Methods & Materials. Cedric Flower & Alan Fortney. LC 82-74004. (Illus.). 144p. (YA). (gr. 9-12). 1983. 20.75 (0-87192-142-1) Davis Mass.

Puppets: Ministry Magic. Dale VonSeggen & Liz VonSeggen. 156p. (Orig.). 1990. pap. 14.99 (0-931529-65-4) Group Pub.

Puppets Year II: For 2 & 3. 1991. 17.99 (1-55513-261-8, 72553) Cook.

Puppets Year II: For 4 & 5. 1991. 17.99 (1-55513-215-4, 72223) Cook.

Puppets & Marionettes. Jan Lindenberger. (Schiffer Book for Collectors Ser.). (Illus.). 176p. 1997. pap. 19.95 (0-7643-0279-5) Schiffer.

Puppets & Masks: Stagecraft & Storytelling. Nan Rump. LC 94-73962. (Illus.). 192p. (J). (gr. k-6). 1995. spiral bd. 20.75 (0-87192-298-3) Davis Mass.

Puppets & "Popular" Culture. Scott C. Shershow. (Illus.). 256p. 1995. text 37.50 (0-8014-3094-1) Cornell U Pr.

***Puppets & Puppet Theatre.** David Currell. (Illus.). 176p. 1999. 40.00 (1-86126-135-7, Pub. by Cro1wood) Trafalgar.

Puppets & Puppetry. Peter Fraser. 1996. pap. 14.95 (0-8128-6201-5, Scrbrough Hse) Madison Bks UPA.

Puppets & Puppets. Bernadine Boyd. (Illus.). 72p. (J). 1998. pap. 14.00 (0-8059-4394-3) Dorrance.

Puppets & Shadows: A Selective Bibliography to 1930. Compiled by Grace G. Ransome. LC 97-26981. (Studies in Puppetry: No. 1). 68p. 1997. text 29.95 (0-7734-8573-2) E Mellen.

Puppets & the Theater. Carla Clason et al. (Technical Notes Ser.: No. 12). 29p. (Orig.). 1975. pap. 2.00 (0-932288-26-X); pap. 2.00 (0-932288-27-8) Ctr Intl Ed U of MA.

***Puppets Can Be Storytelling Partners.** Suzie Shaeffer. (Illus.). 108p. 1999. spiral bd. 18.95 (0-9671999-1-3) StoryHat.

Puppets for Dreaming & Scheming. J. Sims. (Holiday & Art Ser.). (J). (gr. 1-6). 1988. 15.95 (0-88160-167-5, LW 277) Learning Wks.

Puppets for Peace. James McGinnis et al. LC 85-159843. (Illus.). 44p. 1984. pap. text 5.00 (0-912765-13-5) Inst Peace.

Puppets Go to Church. Earl Perry & Wilma Perry. 88p. 1975. pap. 6.99 (0-8341-0385-0) Beacon Hill.

Puppets, Jumping Jacks & Other Paper People. unabridged ed. Michael Grater. LC 94-9546. (Illus.). 208p. (J). 1994. pap. text 6.95 (0-486-28175-2) Dover.

***Puppets, Masks & Performing Objects.** Ed. by John Bell. (TDR Book Ser.). (Illus.). 190p. (C). 2000. reprint ed. pap. 19.95 (0-262-52293-4) MIT Pr.

Puppets of Nostalgia: The Life, Death, & Rebirth of the Japanese Awaji Ningyo Tradition. Jane M. Law. LC 96-33487. 321p. 1997. text 35.00 (0-691-02894-X, Pub. by Princeton U Pr) Cal Prin Full Svc.

Puppets, Poems, & Songs. Catherine Shelton. (J). (ps-3). 1993. pap. 21.99 (0-8224-5152-2) Fearon Teacher Aids.

Puppets' Tale. Manik Bandyopadyaya. Tr. by Sachindralal Ghosh. (C). 1995. reprint ed. 8.00 (81-7201-655-7, Pub. by Indian Pubs) S Asia.

Puppets U. S. A. - Texas: Exploring Folklore, Music & Crafts with Puppets. Nancy Renfro & Debbie Sullivan. Ed. by Ann W. Schwalb & Craig A. Marion. (Puppetry in Education Ser.). (Illus.). 96p. (Orig.). (J). (gr. 1-6). 1985. pap., spiral bd. 17.95 (0-931044-11-1) Renfro Studios.

Puppets with Purpose. Rita Jamieson. (Illus.). 67p. (Orig.). (C). 1992. 10.00 (0-9622329-3-9) R Jamieson.

Puppies see Books for Young Explorers

Puppies see Preschool Puppet Board Books

***Puppies!** John E. Barrett. (Sesame Street Elmo's World Ser.). (Illus.). 12p. (J). (ps). 2000. bds. 4.99 (0-375-80575-3, Pub. by Random Bks Yng Read) Random.

***Puppies.** Barron's Educational Editors. (Animal Babies Ser.). (Illus.). 32p. (J). (gr. k-2). 2000. pap. 5.95 (0-7641-1482-4) Barron.

Puppies. Lisa Bonforte. (Illus.). 32p. (J). 1998. pap. 1.00 (0-486-40350-5) Dover.

Puppies. Brigitte Bulard-Cordeau. LC 97-8732. (Illus.). 240p. 1997. 24.95 (0-8120-6631-6) Barron.

Puppies. DK Publishing Staff. LC 97-15459. 40p. (J). (gr. k-5). 1997. 12.95 (0-7894-2133-X) DK Pub Inc.

Puppies. Kelly Doudna. LC 98-21704. (Baby Animals Ser.). (Illus.). 24p. (J). 2000. lib. bdg. 18.50 (1-57765-181-2, SndCastle) ABDO Pub Co.

Puppies! Ed. by Helen Exley. (Mini Square Giftbooks). (Illus.). 64p. 1998. 6.00 (1-86187-021-3) Exley Pubns Ltd.

Puppies. Gabrielle Forbush. (Illus.). 96p. 1989. 9.95 (0-86622-707-5, KW-023) TFH Pubns.

Puppies. Contrib. by David Lewis. LC 97-29293. (Junior Pet Care Ser.). (Illus.). 48p. (J). (gr. 2 up). 1999. 16.95 (0-7910-4905-1) Chelsea Hse.

Puppies. Lorenz Books Staff. (First Picture Bks.). (Illus.). 24p. (J). 1996. 4.95 (1-85967-124-1, Lorenz Bks) Anness Pub.

***Puppies.** Lorenz Books Staff. (My Very First Picture Book Ser.). (Illus.). (J). 2000. 4.95 (0-7548-0384-8, Lorenz Bks) Anness Pub.

Puppies. Kate Petty. (Baby Animals Ser.). 1992. 9.15 (0-606-01610-4, Pub. by Turtleback) Demco.

***Puppies.** Marcus H. Schneck. 1998. pap. 10.98 (1-880908-32-8) Todtri Prods.

Puppies. VALERIE SHAFF. 15.00 (0-06-093279-1) HarpC.

Puppies. Eileen Spinelli. (Childrens' Nature Library). (Illus.). 64p. (J). (gr. k-4). 1992. lib. bdg. 14.95 (1-878363-87-5, HTS Bks) Forest Hse.

Puppies. John Valentine. 1997. per. 12.95 (0-85449-094-9, Pub. by Gay Mens Pr) LPC InBook.

Puppies. Zuza Vrbova. (Junior Pet Care Ser.). (Illus.). 48p. (J). (gr. 2 up). 1990. 9.95 (0-86622-552-8, J-002) TFH Pubns.

***Puppies.** William Wegman. LC 96-54626. (Illus.). 96p. (ps-3). 1999. pap. text 14.99 (0-7868-1402-0, Pub. by Hyprn Child) Time Warner.

Puppies. 2nd ed. John Valentine. 173p. 1997. reprint ed. pap. 12.95 (0-85449-258-5, Pub. by Gay Mens Pr) LPC InBook.

Puppies: A Very First Picture Book see Pictures & Words

Puppies: Shaped Coloring Book. Golden Books Staff. 32p. (J). 1998. pap. text 1.79 (0-307-17158-2, 17158, Goldn Books) Gldn Bks Pub Co.

Puppies: Your Guide to Successful Ownership. Angela White. 1999. 29.95 (1-85279-023-7) TFH Pubns.

***Puppies & Dogs: Stickers.** Lorenz Books Staff. 1999. 4.95 (1-85967-987-0, Lorenz Bks) Anness Pub.

Puppies & Kittens. DK Publishing Staff. 1997. 6.99 (0-7894-2366-9) DK Pub Inc.

Puppies & Kittens, Miniature. Dubin. (Itty Bitties Ser.). (Illus.). 20p. (J). (ps). 1991. bds. 2.50 (0-8120-6265-5) Barron.

Puppies & Kittens - God's Furry Friends: Coloring Book. (Coloring Bks.). 16p. (J). (gr. k-5). 1996. pap. 1.49 (0-7847-0512-7) Standard Pub.

***Puppies are for Life.** Linda Phillips. 408p. 2000. 31.99 (0-7089-4233-4) Ulverscroft.

Puppies Are Here! 101 Dalmations. Marc Tetro. LC 96-83675. (Illus.). 24p. (J). (ps-1). 1996. 12.95 (0-7868-3120-0, Pub. by Disney Pr) Time Warner.

Puppies Are Like That see Big Red Box of Books: Five Picture-Book Favorites

Puppies Are Like That. Jan Pfloog. LC 74-2542. (Pictureback Ser.). (Illus.). 32p. (J). (ps-3). 1975. pap. 3.25 (0-394-82923-9, Pub. by Random Bks Yng Read) Random.

Puppies Are Like That. Jan Pfloog. (Random House Pictureback Ser.). 1975. 8.45 (0-606-06145-2, Pub. by Turtleback) Demco.

Puppies As a New Pet. James B. Michaelson. 64p. 1991. pap. 6.95 (0-86622-616-8, TU-008) TFH Pubns.

Puppies at Play: A 101 Dalmations Word Book. Samantha Walker. LC 94-71800. (Illus.). 24p. (J). (ps-k). 1995. 10.95 (0-7868-3040-9, Pub. by Disney Pr) Little.

Puppies Die Every Day. Murry Steinbeck. LC 97-90248. 185p. 1997. 17.95 (0-533-12343-7) Vantage.

Puppies, Dogs, & Blue Northers: Reflections on Being Raised by a Pack of Sled Dogs. Gary Paulsen. LC 95-18981. (Illus.). 81p. (J). 1996. 16.00 (0-15-292881-2) Harcourt.

Puppies, Dogs, & Blue Northers: Reflections on Being Raised by a Pack of Sled Dogs. Gary Paulsen. 1998. 14.15 (0-606-13019-5, Pub. by Turtleback) Demco.

Puppies, Dogs, & Blue Northers: Reflections on Being Raised by a Pack of Sled Dogs. Gary Paulsen. (Illus.). 96p. (YA). (gr. 7 up). 1998. reprint ed. pap. 9.95 (0-385-32585-1, Delacorte Pr Bks) BDD Bks Young Read.

***Puppies for Dummies.** Sarah Hodgson. (For Dummies Ser.). 384p. 2000. pap. 19.95 (0-7645-5255-4) IDG Bks.

***Puppies for Sale.** Dan Clark. 1999. (1-57759-262-X) Dalmatian Pr.

Puppies for Sale & Other Inspirational Tales: A "Litter" of Stories & Anecdotes That Hug the Heart & Snuggle the Soul. Dan Clark. LC 97-36047. 365p. 1997. 24.00 (1-55874-469-X); pap. 12.95 (1-55874-452-5) Health Comm.

Puppies for Those Who Care. Dennis Kelsey-Wood. (Illus.). 32p. 1994. 4.95 (0-7938-1381-6, B107) TFH Pubns.

Puppies in the Pantry. Ben M. Baglio. (Animal Ark Ser.: No. 3). (Illus.). 133p. (J). (gr. 3-5). 1998. pap. 3.99 (0-590-18751-1) Scholastic Inc.

***Puppies in the Pantry.** Lucy Daniels. (Animal Ark Ser.: No. 3). (J). (gr. 3-5). 1999. 16.95 (0-7540-6058-6) Chivers N Amer.

***Puppies in the Pantry.** Illus. by Shelagh McNicholas. (Animal Ark Ser.: No. 3). (J). (gr. 3-5). 1998. 9.09 (0-606-13131-0, Pub. by Turtleback) Demco.

Puppies in the Snow. Helen E. Simcox. Ed. by Jane Weinberger. LC 97-62239. (Illus.). 48p. (J). (ps-3). 1997. pap. 8.95 (1-883650-43-7) Windswept Hse.

Puppies in Your Life. Bardi McLennan & Critter Press. LC 97-38184. 1997. write for info. (0-87605-437-8) Howell Bks.

Puppies Love. Lisa McCue. 24p. (J). 1999. 1.99 (0-679-89470-5) Random.

Puppies Love. Lisa McCue. (J). 1999. lib. bdg. 7.99 (0-679-99470-X, Pub. by Random Bks Yng Read) Random.

Puppies 'n Pooches: Charted for Counted Thread, Embroidery & Applique. Jean D. Crowther. 1988. 5.98 (0-88290-325-X) Horizon Utah.

Puppies Need Love Too. Suzanne Taylor-Moore. 48p. 1980. pap. 3.50 (0-938758-08-X) MTM Pub Co.

Puppies or Poppies? ESL Bingo. Elizabeth K. Romijn. (Illus.). viii, 184p. 1998. pap. 19.95 (0-929724-42-9) Command Performance.

Puppies, Pussycats & Other Friends. Gyo Fujikawa. (Illus.). 16p. (J). (ps). 1989. reprint ed. bds. 6.95 (1-55987-000-1, Sunny Bks) J B Comns.

***Puppy.** DK Publishing Staff. LC 99-185569. (Touch & Feel Ser.). (Illus.). 10p. (ps-k). 1999. 6.95 (0-7894-3991-3) DK Pub Inc.

***Puppy.** DK Publishing Staff. (Illus.). 16p. (ps-k). 2000. 4.95 (0-7894-6656-2) DK Pub Inc.

Puppy. Mark Evans. LC 92-52828. (ASPCA Pet Care Guides for Kids Ser.). (Illus.). 40p. (J). (gr. 2 up). 1992. 10.95 (1-56458-127-6) DK Pub Inc.

***Puppy.** Honor Head. (My Pet Ser.). (Illus.). (J). 2000. pap. 8.95 (0-7398-3012-0) Raintree Steck-V.

***Puppy.** Honor Head & Jane Burton. LC 00-27051. (Illus.). (J). 2000. pap. 25.69 (0-7398-2885-1) Raintree Steck-V.

Puppy. Angela Laroyster. (See How They Grow Ser.). (Illus.). (J). 10.95 (0-590-73805-4) Scholastic Inc.

***Puppy.** Steve Shott. 12p. (J). 2000. 6.95 (0-7894-5402-5) DK Pub Inc.

***Puppy.** Bradley Viner. (All about Your Pet Ser.). (Illus.). 32p. 1999. pap. 3.50 (0-7641-1006-3) Barron.

***Puppy.** large type ed. Julia Hunter et al. (Illus.). 8p. (J). (gr. k-3). 2000. pap. text 6.00 (1-58084-206-2) Lower Kuskokwim.

***Puppy Baby Book.** Dawn Greenfield Ireland. Ed. by M. A. S. Stautberg. (Illus.). 80p. 2000. 21.95 (0-9701137-0-6) Artistic Origins.

Puppy Book. Camilla Jessel. LC 91-71825. (Illus.). 32p. (J). (ps up). 1994. pap. 4.99 (1-56402-279-X) Candlewick Pr.

Puppy Book. Jan Pfloog. (Super Shape Bks.). (Illus.). 24p. (J). (ps-k). 1968. pap. 3.29 (0-307-10078-2, 10078) Gldn Bks Pub Co.

Puppy Book, My Dog's Tail: A Complete Journal. Judi M. Lowrance. (Illus.). 50p. 1995. 19.95 (0-9651391-1-5) SCT Retrievers.

Puppy Care. DK Publishing Staff. (101 Essential Tips Ser.: Vol. 29). 72p. (J). 1997. pap. 4.95 (0-7894-1463-5) DK Pub Inc.

Puppy Care & Critters, Too! Judy Petersen-Fleming & Bill Fleming. LC 93-23129. (Illus.). 40p. (J). 1994. 15.00 (0-688-12563-8, Wm Morrow); lib. bdg. 14.93 (0-688-12564-6, Wm Morrow) Morrow Avon.

***Puppy Care & Training.** Bardi McLennan. 64p. 2000. 12.95 (0-7938-3040-0) TFH Pubns.

Puppy Care & Training: An Owner's Guide to a Happy Healthy Pet. Bardi McLennan. (Owner's Guide to a Happy Healthy Pet Ser.). (Illus.). 160p. 1996. 12.95 (0-87605-391-6) Howell Bks.

Puppy Counts. (J). 1994. 12.98 (0-7853-0671-4) Pubns Intl Ltd.

***Puppy (Cup'ik)** large type ed. Julia Hunter et al. (ESK., Illus.). 8p. (J). (gr. k-3). 2000. pap. text 6.00 (1-58084-208-9) Lower Kuskokwim.

Puppy Dog's Special Friends. Lynn Derraugh. LC 98-224241. (Touch & Squeak Bks.). (Illus.). 14p. (J). (gr. k-3). 1998. bds. 7.99 (1-57584-092-8) Rdrs Digest.

Puppy Fat. Morris Gleitzman. 144p. (J). (gr. 3-7). 1996. pap. 5.00 (0-15-200052-6) Harcourt.

Puppy Fat. Morris Gleitzman. LC 95-30930. 144p. (J). (gr. 1-7). 1996. 11.00 (0-15-200047-X) Harcourt.

Puppy Fat. Morris Gleitzman. 1995. 10.10 (0-606-09771-6, Pub. by Turtleback) Demco.

***Puppy Finds a Friend.** Mary Risk. (I Can Read Bks.). (Illus.). 2000. 6.95 (0-7641-5283-1) Barron.

***Puppy Finds a Friend.** Mary Risk. (I Can Read Bks.). (Illus.). (J). (ps-3). 2000. 6.95 (0-7641-5285-8) Barron.

Puppy Lost. Cyndy Szekeres. LC 85-81147. (Naptime Tales Bks.). (Illus.). 16p. (J). (ps-3). 1986. 3.99 (0-307-12287-5, 12287, Goldn Books) Gldn Bks Pub Co.

Puppy Love. Ariel Books Staff. LC 96-85921. 80p. 1997. 4.95 (0-8362-2651-8, Arie Bks) Andrews & McMeel.

Puppy Love. Jeanne Betancourt. 96p. (J). (gr. 4-8). 1986. pap. 2.50 (0-380-89958-2, Avon Bks) Morrow Avon.

Puppy Love. Ginger Chambers. (Hometown Reunion Ser.). 1997. per. 4.50 (0-373-82558-7, 1-82558-7) Harlequin Bks.

Puppy Love. Betsy Duffey. (Pet Patrol Ser.: No. 1). (Illus.). 80p. (J). (gr. 2-6). 1994. pap. 4.99 (0-14-034997-9) Peng Put Young Read.

Puppy Love. Betsy Duffey. (J). 1995. 9.19 (0-606-08007-4, Pub. by Turtleback) Demco.

An Asterisk (*) at the beginning of an entry indicates that the title is appearing for the first time.

Puppy Love. Linsey Fann. Ed. by David Abdulai. (Illus.). 32p. (J). (gr. 4-6). Date not set. pap. 19.95 (*0-9647012-6-X*, Dawn of a New Day) Konkori Intl.
Puppy Love. Glen W. Gonder. Ed. by Sharon J. Gonder. LC 96-67294. (Adventures of Willy Whacker Ser.: Vol. 3). (Illus.). (J). (gr. 3-4). 1996. lib. bdg. 8.95 (*0-9626245-5-1*) Osage Bend Pub.
Puppy Love. Dick King-Smith. LC 96-47423. (Read & Wonder Bks.). (Illus.). 32p. (J). (ps-3). 1997. 15.99 (*0-7636-0116-0*) Candlewick Pr.
***Puppy Love.** Dick King-Smith. LC 96-47423. (Illus.). 32p. (J). (ps-3). 1999. pap. 5.99 (*0-7636-0698-7*, Pub. by Candlewick Pr) Penguin Putnam.
Puppy Love. Mouse Works Staff. LC 97-120424. 5p. (J). 1997. 5.98 (*1-57082-554-8*, Pub. by Mouse Works) Time Warner.
Puppy Love. Christine Simpson. LC 98-13306. 32p. (J). (ps-2). 1998. pap. text 7.95 (*0-8091-6652-6*) Paulist Pr.
Puppy Love. Voyageur Press Editors. LC 97-37828. (Illus.). 112p. 1998. 12.95 (*0-89658-369-4*) Voyageur Pr.
Puppy Love: True Life Stories of Animal Friends. Kate Tym. 128p. 1999. pap. 4.95 (*1-901881-34-2*, Pub. by Element MA) Penguin Putnam.
Puppy on the Farm. Illus. by Jenny Tulip. 12p. (J). (ps). 1996. bds. 4.98 (*1-85854-494-7*) Brimax Bks.
Puppy on the Go. (J). 1994. write for info. (*0-7853-0672-2*) Pubns Intl Ltd.
Puppy Parade, Level 2. Cecilia Venn. LC 97-80108. (Disney First Reader Ser.: No. 11). 32p. (J). (gr. 1-3). 1998. pap. 2.95 (*0-7868-4170-2*, Pub. by Disney Pr) Time Warner.
Puppy Parenting. Gail I. Clark. LC 98-34718. 292p. 1999. pap. 16.95 (*1-57779-012-X*) Alpine Pubns.
***Puppy Parenting.** Jan Greye. 208p. 2000. 20.00 (*0-06-039315-7*, ReganBks) HarperTrade.
***Puppy Patrol: Teachers Pet.** large type ed. Jenny Dale. (Illus.). (J). 1999. pap. write for info. (*0-7540-6086-1*) Chivers N Amer.
Puppy Prayers. Illus. by Tessa Richardson-Jones. (Paws for Thought Ser.). 5p. (J). (ps). 1998. bds. 4.95 (*1-901881-81-4*, Pub. by Element MA) Penguin Putnam.
Puppy Preschool: Raising Your Puppy Right-Right from the Start. 3rd ed. John Ross & Barbara McKinney. LC 95-41346. 224p. 1996. text 22.95 (*0-312-14029-0*) St Martin.
Puppy Problem. Carolyn Keene. (Nancy Drew Notebooks: No. 12). 80p. (J). (gr. 2-4). 1996. pap. 3.99 (*0-671-53551-X*, Minstrel Bks) PB.
Puppy Problem. Carolyn Keene. (Nancy Drew Notebooks: No. 12). (J). (gr. 2-4). 1996. 8.60 (*0-606-09675-2*, Pub. by Turtleback) Demco.
Puppy Puppy . . . What Are You Doing Now? Jennie Lawrence. 180p. 1996. pap. 12.95 (*0-9646463-2-3*) Heritage Concepts.
Puppy Puppy, Peekaboo: Includes Miniature Blanket. Frances Coe. LC 98-44265. (Little Blanket Bks.). (Illus.). 10p. (J). 1999. bds. 3.95 (*0-7641-5179-7*) Barron.
Puppy Puzzle. Lucy Daniels. (Animal Ark Pets Ser.: No. 1). (Illus.). 107p. (J). (gr. 1-4). 1999. mass mkt. 3.50 (*0-439-05158-4*) Scholastic Inc.
***Puppy Riddles.** Katy Hall. (Illus.). 48p. (J). (gr. 1-4). 2000. pap. 3.99 (*0-14-130575-4*, PuffinBks) Peng Put Young Read.
Puppy Riddles. Katy Hall & Lisa Eisenberg. LC 97-6375. (Illus.). 48p. (J). 1998. 13.99 (*0-8037-2126-9*, Dial Yng Read) Peng Put Young Read.
Puppy Round & Square. Illus. by Norman Gorbaty. (Pet Parade Bks.). 12p. (J). (ps). 1991. pap. 3.95 (*0-671-74436-4*) Litle Simon.
Puppy Sister. S. E. Hinton. (J). 1995. mass mkt. 20.95 (*0-385-31009-9*) BDD Bks Young Read.
Puppy Sister. S. E. Hinton. (Illus.). 128p. (J). (gr. 2-6). 1997. pap. 4.50 (*0-440-41384-2*) Dell.
Puppy Sister. S. E. Hinton. 1997. 9.09 (*0-606-11772-5*, Pub. by Turtleback) Demco.
Puppy Stickers. Christopher Santoro. (Illus.). (J). (gr. k-3). 1994. pap. 1.00 (*0-486-27996-0*) Dover.
Puppy Stuff. Jodi Alessandrini & Kathy Kinser. (Illus.). 144p. 1997. 24.95 (*0-9647465-6-5*) Pallachip Pubng.
***Puppy Tales.** 80p. (J). 2000. 9.98 (*0-7651-0964-6*) Smithmark.
Puppy Tales. Ed. by Penguin Books Staff. (Two Minute Tales Ser.). 48p. (J). 1996. 2.99 (*0-7214-5445-3*, Ladybrd) Penguin Putnam.
Puppy to Love: A Child's Guide to Dog Care. F. F. Kotes. LC 91-67328. 40p. (Orig.). (J). (gr. 3-8). 1991. pap. 9.95 (*1-878500-00-7*, Valley Hse Bks) Martin Mgmt.
Puppy Training & Critters, Too! Judy Petersen-Fleming & Bill Fleming. LC 95-23031. (Illus.). 39p. (J). (ps-2). 1996. lib. bdg. 15.93 (*0-688-13385-1*, Wm Morrow) Morrow Avon.
Puppy Who Wanted a Boy. Jane Thayer. LC 85-15465. (Illus.). 32p. (J). (ps up). 1988. mass mkt. 5.95 (*0-688-08293-9*, Wm Morrow) Morrow Avon.
Puppy Who Wanted a Boy. Jane Thayer. (J). 1958. 10.15 (*0-606-04304-7*, Pub. by Turtleback) Demco.
***Puppy Who Went to School.** Gail Herman. (Illus.). 32p. (J). (ps-3). 2000. reprint ed. pap. write for info. (*0-448-42163-1*, G & D) Peng Put Young Read.
Puppy with a Waggly Tail. (Illus.). 24p. (J). 1998. write for info. (*1-85854-721-0*) Brimax Bks.
Puppys Colors. (J). 1994. write for info. (*0-7853-0670-6*) Pubns Intl Ltd.
Puppy's Day. Dick McCue & Lisa McCue. (Animal Shape Board Bks.). (J). (ps). 1984. pap. 2.95 (*0-671-50945-4*) Little Simon.
Puppy's First Book. Ellen Sinaiko & Ernestine Sinaiko. (Illus.). 1996. 12.95 (*0-533-11743-7*) Vantage.
Puppy's First Year: A Guide to Veterinary Care for Your Puppy. Race Foster & Marty Smith. LC 98-52387. (Illus.). 256p. 1999. 19.95 (*1-58245-052-8*) Howell Bks.
Puppy's Games. Kate Spohn. LC 96-72457. (Illus.). 12p. (J). (ps-4). 1998. 4.99 (*0-679-88678-8*, Pub. by Random Bks Yng Read) Random.
***Puppy's Memory Book.** Charlotte King. (Illus.). 26p. 1999. pap. write for info. (*1-882194-53-5*) TN Valley Pub.
Puppys Pals. (J). 1994. write for info. (*0-7853-0669-2*) Pubns Intl Ltd.
Puppy's Tail. Florence C. Chang. LC 81-82176. (Chinese Can Be Fun Bks.: Level 1). (Illus.). 72p. (Orig.). (J). (gr. 1-2). 1981. pap. 4.50 (*0-936620-06-4*) Ginkgo Hut.
Pup's Supper see Cena del Cachorro
Pup's Supper. Victoria Miles. LC 98-30062. (Illus.). (J). 1998. bds. 5.95 (*1-878244-22-1*) Monterey Bay Aquarium.
Pupster Pizza: And Other Classics from the K-9 Kitchen. S. S. Genova. 1992. pap. 9.95 (*0-9632892-0-9*) Shifting Sand.
Pupus: An Island Tradition. Sachi Fukuda. 180p. (Orig.). 1995. pap. 12.95 (*1-57306-019-4*) Bess Pr.
Pupus...Again. Sachi Fukuda. 123p. (Orig.). 1989. pap. 5.95 (*0-9624774-0-0*) Fukuda Pub.
***PUR Directory of Electric & Gas Utility Executives.** 200p. 1999. pap. 199.00 (*0-910325-78-2*) Public Util.
Pur et l'Impur. Sidonie-Gabrielle Colette. (FRE.). 191p. 1971. pap. 11.95 (*0-8288-9149-4*, F97400) Fr & Eur.
Pur et l'Impur dans la Pensee des Grecs d'Homere a Aristote. Louis Moulinier. LC 75-10642. (Ancient Religion & Mythology Ser.). (FRE.). 1976. reprint ed. 47.95 (*0-405-07260-0*) Ayer.
PUR Sections 1-4000, Vol. 149. 81p. 1999. write for info. (*0-327-06998-8*, 57777-12) LEXIS Pub.
PUR Sections 21190-30999, Vol. 153. 20p. 1999. write for info. (*0-327-07002-1*, 57781-12) LEXIS Pub.
PUR Sections 31000-End, Vol. 154. 84p. 1999. write for info. (*0-327-07003-X*, 57782-12) LEXIS Pub.
PUR Sections 4001-5399, Vol. 150. 68p. 1999. write for info. (*0-327-06999-6*, 57778-12) LEXIS Pub.
PUR Sections 5400-7500, Vol. 151. 47p. 1999. write for info. (*0-327-07000-5*, 57779-12) LEXIS Pub.
PUR Sections 7501-21189, Vol. 152. 43p. 1999. write for info. (*0-327-07001-3*, 57780-12) LEXIS Pub.
Pura Belpre Papers. Ed. by Evelina L. Antonetty. (Finding Aid Ser.). 23p. 1992. reprint ed. pap. text 5.00 (*1-878483-19-6*) Hunter Coll CEP.
Pura Vida. J. Maria Mendiluce. LC 99-168490. (Autores Espanoles E Iberoamericanos Ser.). 1999. 22.95 (*84-08-02848-0*) Planeta.
Pura Vida - Waterfalls & Hot Springs of Costa Rica. Sam Mitchell. (Illus.). 96p. 1995. pap. 9.95 (*0-89732-172-3*) Menasha Ridge.
Purana Index. A. B. Awasthi. (C). 1992. 42.00 (*81-7013-074-3*, Pub. by Navarang) S Asia.
Purana Index, 3 vols., Set. V. R. Dikshitar. (C). 1995. reprint ed. 110.00 (*0-614-13270-3*, Pub. by Motilal Bnarsidass) S Asia.
Purana Perennis: Reciprocity & Transformation in Hindu & Jaina Texts. Ed. by Wendy Doniger. LC 92-25322. 352p. (C). 1993. pap. text 21.95 (*0-7914-1382-9*) State U NY Pr.
Purana Perennis: Reciprocity & Transformation in Hindu & Jaina Texts. Ed. by Wendy Doniger. LC 92-25322. 352p. (C). 1993. text 64.50 (*0-7914-1381-0*) State U NY Pr.
Puranas: Skanda Purana, Vamana Purana, Kurma Purana, Matsya Purana, Garuda Purana, Brahmanda Purana, Vayu Purana, Set. Bibek Debroy & Dipvali Debroy. (C). 1994. 94.00 (*81-7018-806-7*, Pub. by BR Pub) S Asia.
Puranic Encyclopaedia: A Comprehensive Work with Special Reference to the Epic & Puranic Literature. Vettam Mani. 992p. (C). 1996. reprint ed. 68.00 (*81-208-0597-6*, Pub. by Motilal Bnarsidass) S Asia.
Puranic Myth & Culture. Sadashiv Ambadas Dange. (C). 1987. 21.00 (*81-202-0192-2*, Pub. by Ajanta) S Asia.
Purbeck Shop: A Stoneworker's Story of Stone. Eric Benfield. (C). 1989. 39.00 (*1-85455-035-7*, Pub. by Ensign Pubns & Print) St Mut.
Purcell. Maureen Duffy. (Illus.). 306p. 1996. pap. 15.95 (*1-85702-368-4*, Pub. by Fourth Estate) Trafalgar.
***Purcell.** J. A. Westrup. (Master Musicians Ser.). (Illus.). 340p. 2000. pap. 18.95 (*0-19-816546-3*) OUP.
Purcell. William H. Cummings. LC 68-25285. (Studies in Drama: No. 39). 1969. reprint ed. lib. bdg. 75.00 (*0-8383-0285-8*) M S G Haskell Hse.
Purcell. William H. Cummings. 124p. 1990. reprint ed. lib. bdg. 59.00 (*0-7812-9080-5*) Rprt Serv.
Purcell. Henri Dupre. LC 74-24071. reprint ed. 21.50 (*0-404-12899-8*) AMS Pr.
Purcell: A Biography. Jonathan Keates. (Illus.). 316p. 1996. text 40.00 (*1-55553-287-X*) NE U Pr.
Purcell: Music Book Index. Jack A. Westrup. 323p. 1993. reprint ed. lib. bdg. 89.00 (*0-7812-9614-5*) Rprt Serv.
Purcell Anthology: Eleven Anthems for Mixed Choir, with Or Without Organ. Ed. by Bruce Wood. 112p. 1995. pap. 19.50 (*0-19-353351-0*) OUP.
Purcell, Crenshaw & Letcher Artillery. Peter L. Carmichael. (Virginia Regimental Histories Ser.). (Illus.). 234p. 1990. 19.95 (*0-930919-93-9*) H E Howard.
***Purcell Manuscripts: The Principal Musical Sources.** Robert Shay & Robert Thompson. (Illus.). 375p. (C). 2000. text 79.95 (*0-521-58094-3*) Cambridge U Pr.
Purcell Papers. Joseph Sheridan Le Fanu. LC 75-2524. 1975. 12.95 (*0-87054-072-6*) Arkham.
Purcell Papers, 3 vols. Joseph Sheridan Le Fanu. LC 71-148813. reprint ed. 145.00 (*0-404-08880-5*) AMS Pr.
Purcell Papers: With a Memoir by Alfred Perceval Graves, 3 vols., Set. Joseph Sheridan Le Fanu. LC 76-5274. (Collected Works). 1977. reprint ed. 76.95 (*0-405-09225-3*) Ayer.
Purcell Papers: With a Memoir by Alfred Perceval Graves, 3 vols., Vol. 1. Joseph Sheridan Le Fanu. Ed. by Devendra P. Varma. LC 76-5274. (Collected Works). 1977. reprint ed. 25.95 (*0-405-09226-1*) Ayer.
Purcell Papers: With a Memoir by Alfred Perceval Graves, 3 vols., Vol. 2. Joseph Sheridan Le Fanu. Ed. by Devendra P. Varma. LC 76-5274. (Collected Works). 1977. reprint ed. 25.95 (*0-405-09227-X*) Ayer.
Purcell Papers: With a Memoir by Alfred Perceval Graves, 3 vols., Vol. 3. Joseph Sheridan Le Fanu. Ed. by Devendra P. Varma. LC 76-5274. (Collected Works). 1977. reprint ed. 25.95 (*0-405-09228-8*) Ayer.
Purcell Studies. Ed. by Curtis Price. (Illus.). 317p. (C). 1995. text 69.95 (*0-521-44174-9*) Cambridge U Pr.
Purcell's Thesaurus of Knowledge. Royal Purcell. (Illus.). 301p. 1993. ring bd. 19.95 (*0-933189-04-4*) Purcell Pub.
Purchase Inspector. Jack Rudman. (Career Examination Ser.: C-637). 1994. pap. 27.95 (*0-8373-0637-X*) Nat Learn.
Purchase Inspector (Shop Steel) Jack Rudman. (Career Examination Ser.: C-2258). 1994. reprint ed. pap. 29.95 (*0-8373-2258-8*) Nat Learn.
Purchase Knob: Essays from a Mountain Notebook. Kathryn K. McNeil. LC 98-33508. (Illus.). 80p. 1999. pap. 8.00 (*1-56474-279-2*) Fithian Pr.
Purchase of Alaska. Victor J. Farrar. 1971. reprint ed. 59.00 (*0-403-00590-6*) Scholarly.
Purchase of Medical Care Through Fixed Periodic Payment. Pierce Williams. LC 75-17251. (National Bureau of Economic Research Ser.). 1976. reprint ed. 26.95 (*0-405-07525-1*) Ayer.
Purchase of Medical Care Through Fixed Periodic Payment. Pierce Williams & Isabel C. Chamberlain. (General Ser.). 328p. 1932. reprint ed. 85.30 (*0-87014-019-1*) Natl Bur Econ Res.
Purchase of Order. Gail G. Adams. LC 88-4724. (Flannery O'Connor Award for Short Fiction Ser.). 160p. 1995. pap. 12.95 (*0-8203-1734-9*) U of Ga Pr.
Purchase of Paradise: Gift Giving & the Aristocracy, 1307-1485. Joel Thomas Rosenthal. LC 72-194728. (Studies in Social History). xiv, 169 p. 1972. write for info. (*0-7100-7262-7*, Routledge Thoemms) Routledge.
Purchase of Service Contracting. Peter M. Kettner & Lawrence L. Martin. (Human Services Guides Ser.: Vol. 44). 174p. (Orig.). (C). 1987. pap. 18.95 (*0-8039-2630-8*) Sage.
Purchase of Small Secrets. David L. Harrison. LC 97-77903. (Illus.). 48p. (J). (gr. 2-5). 1998. 9.95 (*1-56397-054-6*) Boyds Mills Pr.
Purchase of the Danish West Indies. Charles C. Tansill. LC 68-23332. 548p. 1968. reprint ed. lib. bdg. 35.00 (*0-8371-0245-6*, TADI, Greenwood Pr) Greenwood.
Purchase of the North Pole. Jules Verne. lib. bdg. 22.95 (*0-8488-2072-X*) Amereon Ltd.
Purchase Specifications Assistant. Jack Rudman. (Career Examination Ser.: C-2542). 1994. pap. 23.95 (*0-8373-2542-0*) Nat Learn.
Purchase Supply Management. 11th ed. Leenders. 1997. teacher ed. 36.25 (*0-256-24628-9*) McGraw.
Purchaser's Formbook of Contracts & Agreements, 3 vols., Set, No. 18. 900p. 1985. ring bd. 195.00 (*0-929576-05-5*) Busn Laws Inc.
Purchasing. William K. Carter & Robert M. Monczka. LC 97-17872. (SB - Marketing Education Ser.). (C). 1997. mass mkt. 92.95 (*0-538-81495-0*) S-W Pub.
Purchasing. deluxe ed. Michael Harding & Mary L. Harding. (Barron's Business Library). 320p. 1991. pap. 18.95 (*0-8120-4552-1*) Barron.
***Purchasing.** 2nd ed. Michael Harding & Mary L. Harding. LC 00-40348. (Business Library). 2001. write for info. (*0-7641-1164-7*) Barron.
Purchasing. 4th ed. Kenneth Lysons. 320p. 2000. pap. 39.50 (*0-273-63422-4*) F T P H.
Purchasing: Continued Improvement Through Integration. Joseph R. Carter. 270p. 1992. 45.00 (*1-55623-535-6*, Irwn Prfssnl) McGraw-Hill Prof.
Purchasing: Principles & Applications. 6th ed. Stuart F. Heinritz & Paul V. Farrell. (Illus.). 448p. 1981. text 29.95 (*0-13-742163-X*) P-H.
Purchasing: Selection & Procurement for the Hospitality Industry. 4th ed. John M. Stefanelli. LC 96-46444. 672p. 1997. 60.00 (*0-471-13583-6*) Wiley.
Purchasing Agent. Jack Rudman. (Career Examination Ser.: C-638). 1994. pap. 23.95 (*0-8373-0638-8*) Nat Learn.
Purchasing Agent (Food) Jack Rudman. (Career Examination Ser.: C-2731). 1994. pap. 27.95 (*0-8373-2731-8*) Nat Learn.
Purchasing Agent (Lumber) Jack Rudman. (Career Examination Ser.: C-2732). 1994. pap. 27.95 (*0-8373-2732-6*) Nat Learn.
Purchasing Agent (Medical) Jack Rudman. (Career Examination Ser.: C-2733). 1994. pap. 27.95 (*0-8373-2733-4*) Nat Learn.
Purchasing Agent (Printing) Jack Rudman. (Career Examination Ser.: C-2734). 1994. pap. 27.95 (*0-8373-2734-2*) Nat Learn.
Purchasing an Encyclopedia: 12 Points to Consider. 5th ed. Ed. by Sandy Whiteley. 48p. 1996. pap. 7.95 (*0-8389-7823-1*, 7823-1-2045) ALA.
Purchasing & Evaluating Airplanes. Brian M. Jacobson. LC 97-66659. (Illus.). 200p. 1997. pap. 29.95 (*0-9653640-8-9*) Odyssey Aviation.
Purchasing & Handling Fresh Flowers & Foliage. Redbook Florist Services Educational Advisory Comm. LC 91-66386. (Encycloflora Ser.). (Illus.). 332p. (Orig.). 1992. pap. text 34.95 (*1-56963-013-5*) Redbk Florist.
Purchasing & Inventory: 25 Keys to Profitable Success. David V. Pavesic. LC 98-39302. (Restaurant Manager's Pocket Handbook Ser.). 96p. 1999. pap. 12.95 (*0-86730-756-0*, Pub. by Lebhar Friedman) Natl Bk Netwk.
Purchasing & Inventory Control, 1990. 224p. 1990. ring bd. 63.00 (*0-930530-97-7*, P308) Am Soc Hlth-Syst.
Purchasing & Inventory Management for Owners see Compras E Inventarios
Purchasing & Materials Management see Purchasing & Supply Management: Text & Cases
Purchasing & Materials Management. L. Lee et al. Ed. by B. Burt. 796p. (C). 1984. 540.00 (*0-7855-5759-8*, Pub. by Inst Pur & Supply); student ed. 170.00 (*0-7855-5760-1*, Pub. by Inst Pur & Supply) St Mut.
Purchasing & Materials Management. 6th ed. Wilbur B. England & Michael R. Leenders. (C). 1975. 18.95 (*0-256-01635-6*, Irwn McGrw-H) McGrw-H Hghr Educ.
Purchasing & Materials Management. 9th ed. Michael R. Leenders et al. 672p. (C). 1989. text 61.95 (*0-256-06984-0*, Irwn McGrw-H) McGrw-H Hghr Educ.
Purchasing & Materials Management. 10th ed. Michael R. Leenders & Harold E. Fearon. LC 92-20079. 704p. (C). 1992. text 71.75 (*0-256-10334-8*, Irwn McGrw-H) McGrw-H Hghr Educ.
Purchasing & Materials Management. 11th ed. Michael R. Leenders & Harold Fearon. 736p. (C). 1996. text 71.75 (*0-256-14144-4*, Irwn Prfssnl) McGraw-Hill Prof.
Purchasing & Materials Management: Integrative Strategies. Joseph L. Cavinato. (Illus.). 475p. (C). 1984. pap. text, teacher ed. write for info. (*0-314-77870-5*) West Pub.
Purchasing & Materials Management's Role in Total Quality Management & Customer Satisfaction. Joseph R. Carter & Ram Narasimhan. Ed. by Carol L. Ketchum. LC 93-70434. 87p. (Orig.). (C). 1993. pap. text 20.00 (*0-945968-12-4*) Ctr Advanced Purchasing.
Purchasing & Provide Costs. Drummond. (C). 1994. pap. text 33.50 (*0-443-04946-7*, W B Saunders Co) Harcrt Hlth Sci Grp.
Purchasing & Sourcing Strategy: Trends & Implications. Robert M. Monczka & Robert J. Trent. LC 94-68975. 77p. (C). 1995. pap. text 20.00 (*0-945968-19-1*) Ctr Advanced Purchasing.
Purchasing & Supplier Involvement: New Product Development & Production/Operations Process Development & Improvement. Michael A. McGinnis & Rafeekh Mele Vallopra. LC 98-198504. 1998. write for info. (*0-945968-31-0*) Ctr Advanced Purchasing.
Purchasing & Supply Chain Management. 2nd ed. Robert M. Monczka et al. (SWC-General Business Ser.). 2000. pap. 60.75 (*0-324-02315-4*) Thomson Learn.
***Purchasing & Supply Chain Management: Analysis, Plan & Practice.** 2nd ed. Arjan Van Weele. (ITBP Textbooks Ser.). 2000. pap. 24.99 (*1-86152-512-5*) Thomson Learn.
Purchasing & Supply Management. P. J. Baily. 296p. (C). 1989. 150.00 (*0-7855-6111-0*, Pub. by Inst Pur & Supply) St Mut.
Purchasing & Supply Management. 5th ed. P. J. Baily. 304p. 1987. mass mkt. 34.95 (*0-412-28940-7*) Chapman & Hall.
Purchasing & Supply Management. 7th ed. Burt. 2002. 68.00 (*0-07-229070-6*) McGraw.
Purchasing & Supply Management: Text & Cases. 6th rev. ed. Donald W. Dobler et al. LC 95-36200. (Management Ser.). Orig. Title: Purchasing & Materials Management. 864p. (C). 1995. 86.88 (*0-07-037089-3*) McGraw.
***Purchasing & Supply Yearbook.** National Association of Purchasing Management. LC 99-57984. (Illus.). 540p. 2000. 89.95 (*0-07-135860-9*, McGrw-H College) McGrw-H Hghr Educ.
Purchasing & the Management of Materials. 7th ed. Gary J. Zenz. Ed. by George H. Thompson. LC 93-5911. 752p. 1993. text 92.95 (*0-471-54983-5*) Wiley.
Purchasing Capital Equipment. Wayne Douchkoff. LC 97-30475. (Orig.). 1998. pap. 14.95 (*0-945456-29-8*) PT Pubns.
Purchasing Casebook: 25 Critical Purchasing Law Issues. Rene Sacasas. LC 99-164680. 55p. 1998. write for info. (*0-87622-757-4*) Aspen Pub.
Purchasing Clerk see Gregg Office Job Training Program, Classroom Installation
Purchasing Computer Software Products. C. Dilloway. 126p. (C). 1985. 335.00 (*0-7855-5749-0*, Pub. by Inst Pur & Supply) St Mut.
Purchasing Consortiums: Horizontal Alliances among Firms Buying Common Goods & Services. What? Who? Why? How? Harold E. Fearon & William A. Bales. LC 98-197717. 1998. write for info. (*0-945968-27-2*) Ctr Advanced Purchasing.
Purchasing Consortiums: Horizontal Alliances among Firms Buying Common Goods & Services What? Who? Why? How? Thomas E. Hendrick et al. LC 98-198503. 76 p. 1996. write for info. (*0-945968-29-9*) Ctr Advanced Purchasing.
Purchasing Contract Law. Mark Grieco. LC 97-37853. 1998. pap. 14.95 (*0-945456-30-1*) PT Pubns.
Purchasing, Costing & Control. Peter Odgers. 272p. 1999. pap. 70.00 (*0-7487-0324-1*, Pub. by S Thornes Pubs) Trans-Atl Phila.
Purchasing Education & Training: Requirements & Resources. Michael G. Kolchin et al. LC 93-70757. 108p. (Orig.). (C). 1993. pap. text 20.00 (*0-945968-13-2*) Ctr Advanced Purchasing.
Purchasing Ethical Practices. Robert L. Janson. Ed. by Carol L. Ketchum. LC 88-71748. 32p. (Orig.). (C). 1988. 20.00 (*0-945968-01-9*) Ctr Advanced Purchasing.
Purchasing Ethics. Peter L. Grieco, Jr. LC 97-30938. 1998. pap. 14.95 (*0-945456-28-X*) PT Pubns.
Purchasing Excellence Achieved. (C). 1992. text 24.95 (*0-13-742602-X*, Macmillan Coll) P-H.

P

An Asterisk (*) at the beginning of an entry indicates that the title is appearing for the first time.

Purchasing for Bottom Line Impact: Improving the Organization Through Strategic Procurement. Laura M. Birou & Lisa M. Ellram. 240p. 1995. pap. 45.00 (*0-7863-0217-8*, Irwn Prfssnl) McGraw-Hill Prof.

Purchasing for Food Service: Self-Instruction. Lynne N. Ross. LC 84-81612. (Illus.). 165p. 1985. reprint ed. pap. 51.20 (*0-608-00070-1*, 206083600006) Bks Demand.

Purchasing for Food Service Managers. 3rd ed. M. C. Warfel & Marion Cremer. LC 96-75425. 498p. 1995. text 44.00 (*0-8211-2272-X*) McCutchan.

Purchasing for Foodservice. 2nd ed. Lynne N. Robertson. LC 94-5798. (Illus.). 160p. 1994. pap. text 21.95 (*0-8138-1463-4*) Iowa St U Pr.

Purchasing for Foodservice Managers: Student Manual. Educational Foundation of the National Restaurant. 96p. (Orig.). 1991. pap. write for info. (*0-915452-70-7*) Educ Found.

Purchasing for Health: A Multidisciplinary Introduction to the Theory & Practice of Health Purchasing. John Vretveit. LC 94-27592. 224p. (Orig.). 1994. text 123.00 (*0-335-19333-1*) OpUniv Pr.

Purchasing for Health: A Multidisciplinary Introduction to the Theory & Practice of Health Purchasing. John Vretveit. LC 94-27592. 224p. (Orig.). 1994. pap. text 38.95 (*0-335-19332-3*) Taylor & Francis.

Purchasing for Hospitality Operations. William B. Virts. LC 86-29196. (Illus.). 385p. 1996. text. write for info. (*0-86612-114-5*) Educ Inst Am Hotel.

Purchasing for Manufacturing. Harry E. Hough. LC 95-25848. 208p. 1996. 39.95 (*0-8311-3066-0*) Indus Pr.

Purchasing from Minority Business Enterprises: Best Practices. Richard J. Auskalnis et al. 79p. (C). 1995. pap. text 20.00 (*0-945968-23-X*) Ctr Advanced Purchasing.

Purchasing from Small Minority-Owned Firms: Corporate Problems. Marc J. Dollinger & Catherine M. Daily. Ed. by Carol L. Ketchum. LC 89-60726. 72p. (Orig.). (C). 1989. pap. text 20.00 (*0-945968-03-5*) Ctr Advanced Purchasing.

Purchasing from Small Women-Owned Suppliers. Carol L. Ketchum. 38p. (Orig.). (C). 1990. pap. text 20.00 (*0-945968-05-1*) Ctr Advanced Purchasing.

Purchasing Fundamentals for Today's Buyer. Harry Hough. LC 98-47965. (Illus.). 416p. 1999. 59.95 (*0-13-246356-3*) P-H.

Purchasing Group Users' Handbook. Ed. by Karen Cutts. 410p. (C). 1999. ring bd. 540.00 (*1-891025-03-1*) Insure Commns.

Purchasing Handbook. C. K. Lysons. 211p. (C). 1989. 130.00 (*0-7855-5757-1*, Pub. by Inst Pur & Supply) St Mut.

Purchasing Handbook. 3rd ed. George W. Aljian. 1152p. 1973. 59.95 (*0-07-001068-4*) McGraw.

Purchasing Handbook. 5th ed. Harold E. Fearon et al. 752p. 1991. 84.95 (*0-07-045918-5*) McGraw.

Purchasing Handbook. 6th ed. Kauffman. LC 99-28707. 1082p. 1999. 99.95 (*0-07-134526-4*) McGraw.

Purchasing in the Industrial, Institutional, Governmental, & Retail Sectors: A Comparative Study. Michael G. Kolchin. Ed. by Carol L. Ketchum. LC 90-61278. 80p. (Orig.). (C). 1990. pap. text 20.00 (*0-945968-06-X*) Ctr Advanced Purchasing.

Purchasing in the 21st Century: A Guide to State-of-the-Art Techniques. John E. Schorr. LC 92-60538. 275p. 1993. 120.00 (*0-939246-22-8*, TM7586) Wiley.

***Purchasing in the 21st Century: A Guide to State-of-the-Art Techniques & Strategies.** 2nd ed. John E. Schorr. LC 97-49412. 272p. 1998. 59.95 (*0-471-24094-X*) Wiley.

***Purchasing Injection Molds: A Buyer's Guide.** Clare Goldsberry. LC 00-40770. (Illus.). 2000. write for info. (*1-893677-07-9*) Abby Communs.

Purchasing Law Deskbook. 750p. 1993. 125.00 (*1-56789-000-8*, 124) Busn Laws Inc.

Purchasing Managed Care Services for Alcohol & Other Drug Treatment: Essential Elements & Policy Issues. Stephen Moss & Jeffrey N. Kushner. (Illus.). 58p. (C). 1997. reprint ed. pap. text 30.00 (*0-7881-4035-3*) DIANE Pub.

P

Purchasing Management. Eberhard E. Scheuing. 480p. 1989. boxed set 48.00 (*0-13-742040-4*) P-H.

Purchasing Management: Analysis, Planning & Practice. Arjan Van Weele. 304p. 1994. pap. 39.95 (*1-86152-237-1*) Thomson Learn.

Purchasing Management Guide to Selecting Suppliers. William O. Ford. LC 93-29644. (Illus.). 296p. (C). 1995. 69.95 (*0-13-742594-5*) P-H.

Purchasing Manager's Desk Book of Purchasing Law, 1999 Cumulative Supplement. 3rd ed. James J. Ritterskamp, Jr. & Donald King. 272p. 1998. pap. 39.95 (*0-13-959669-0*) P-H.

Purchasing Manager's Deskbook of Purchasing Law. 2nd ed. Donald B. King & James J. Ritterskamp, Jr. LC 97-30492. 688p. (C). 1997. text 79.95 (*0-13-671462-5*) P-H.

Purchasing Manager's Deskbook of Purchasing Law Supplement. James J. Ritterskamp. 210p. 1990. pap. text 35.00 (*0-13-739210-9*) P-H.

Purchasing Manager's Guide to Strategic Proactive Procurement. David N. Burt & Richard L. Pinkerton. LC 95-44558. 240p. 1996. 55.00 (*0-8144-0288-7*) AMACOM.

Purchasing of Nontraditional Goods & Services. Harold E. Fearon & William A. Bales. LC 95-68085. 73p. (C). 1995. pap. text 20.00 (*0-945968-21-3*) Ctr Advanced Purchasing.

Purchasing Oil & Gas. Terry Robinson. 99p. (C). 1989. 210.00 (*0-7855-4613-8*, Pub. by Inst Pur & Supply) St Mut.

Purchasing Organizational Relationships. Harold E. Fearon. Ed. by Carol L. Ketchum. LC 88-148548. 58p. (Orig.). (C). 1988. pap. text 20.00 (*0-945968-00-0*) Ctr Advanced Purchasing.

Purchasing People in Major Corporations. 65p. 1997. 31.00 (*1-885786-08-5*) Try Us Res.

Purchasing Performance Measurements: A Roadmap for Excellence. Mel Pilachowski. LC 95-49424. (Illus.). 100p. (Orig.). 1996. pap. text 14.95 (*0-945456-21-2*) PT Pubns.

Purchasing Policies, 2 vols., Set, No. 60. Ed. by George A. Harris. 1400p. 1988. ring bd. 195.00 (*0-929576-02-0*) Busn Laws Inc.

Purchasing Population Health: Paying for Results. David A. Kindig. LC 97-29010. 216p. (C). 1997. text 24.95 (*0-472-10893-X*, 10893) U of Mich Pr.

Purchasing Power. 248p. 1997. pap. 36.00 (*0-13-442625-8*) P-H.

Purchasing Power: Consumer Organizing, Gender, & the Seattle Labor Movement, 1919-1929. Dana Frank. LC 93-567. (Illus.). 363p. (C). 1994. pap. text 19.95 (*0-521-46714-4*) Cambridge U Pr.

Purchasing Power: Consumer Organizing, Gender, & the Seattle Labor Movement, 1919-1929. Dana Frank. LC 93-567. (Illus.). 363p. (C). 1994. text 74.95 (*0-521-38367-6*) Cambridge U Pr.

Purchasing Power in Health: Business, the State, & Health Care Politics. Linda A. Bergthold. LC 89-37778. 264p. (C). 1990. text 40.00 (*0-8135-1487-8*) Rutgers U Pr.

Purchasing Power of the Consumer: A Statistical Index. William A. Berridge et al. LC 75-39232. (Getting & Spending: The Consumer's Dilemma Ser.). (Illus.). 1976. reprint ed. 29.95 (*0-405-08009-3*) Ayer.

Purchasing Power Parities: Volume & Price Level Comparisons for the Middle East 1993-Results of the International Comparison Programme (ICP) for the ESCWA) 92p. 20.00 (*92-1-128182-2*) UN.

Purchasing Power Parities & Real Expenditures EKS Results, 1993 Vol. 1. OECD Staff. (ENG & FRE.). 72p. (Orig.). 1995. pap. 29.00 (*92-64-04491-4*, Pub. by Org for Econ) OECD.

Purchasing Power Parities & Real Expenditures for Nordic Countries 1993. (ENG & FRE.). 78p. (Orig.). 1995. pap. 21.00 (*92-64-04446-9*, Pub. by Org for Econ) OECD.

Purchasing Power Parity. Moon H. Lee. LC 76-22815. (Business Economics & Finance Ser.: No. 9). 144p. reprint ed. pap. 44.70 (*0-7837-0965-X*, 204127000019) Bks Demand.

Purchasing Power Parity & Exchange Rates: Theory, Evidence & Relevance. Lawrence H. Officer. LC 80-82479. (Contemporary Studies in Economic & Financial Analysis: Vol. 35). 384p. 1982. 78.50 (*0-89232-229-2*) Jai Pr.

Purchasing Power Parity & the International Transmission of Price Disturbances under Alternative Exchange Regimes: The Swiss Experience. Georg Junge. 251p. 1984. pap. 19.95 (*3-87895-263-5*) Transaction Pubs.

***Purchasing Power Parties & Real Expenditures: 1996 Results (1999 Edition)** OECD Staff. 168p. 2000. pap. 42.00 (*92-64-05823-0*, 30 1999 06 3 P, Pub. by Org for Econ) OECD.

Purchasing Power Parities & Real Expenditures Vol. II: GK Results 1993. OECD Staff. (ENG & FRE.). 92p. (Orig.). 1996. pap. 32.00 (*92-64-04761-1*, Pub. by Org for Econ) OECD.

Purchasing Practices of Large Foodservice Firms. R. Dan Reid & Carl D. Riegel. Ed. by Carol L. Ketchum. LC 89-60232. 76p. (Orig.). (C). 1989. pap. text 20.00 (*0-945968-02-7*) Ctr Advanced Purchasing.

Purchasing Principles & Management. Ed. by B. Baily & D. Farmer. 324p. (Orig.). (C). 1990. 165.00 (*0-7855-5758-X*, Pub. by Inst Pur & Supply) St Mut.

Purchasing Principles & Management. 8th ed. Peter Baily et al. LC 99-220508. 352p. 2000. pap. write for info. (*0-273-62381-8*) F T P H.

Purchasing Role: A View from the Top. Charles F. Carpenter. LC 77-6349. (AMA Management Briefing Ser.). 31p. reprint ed. pap. 30.00 (*0-608-14414-2*, 205169800002) Bks Demand.

Purchasing Strategies for Total Quality: A Guide to Achieving Continuous Improvement. Gregory B. Hutchins. (APICS Series in Production Management). 200p. 1991. 47.50 (*1-55623-380-9*, Irwn Prfssnl) McGraw-Hill Prof.

Purchasing Supervisor. Jack Rudman. (Career Examination Ser.: C-2720). 1994. pap. 29.95 (*0-8373-2720-2*) Nat Learn.

Purchasing Systems & Records. 3rd ed. Peter Baily. 150p. 1991. text 49.95 (*0-566-09061-9*, Pub. by Gower) Ashgate Pub Co.

Purchasing Technician. Jack Rudman. (Career Examination Ser.: C-913). 1994. pap. 23.95 (*0-8373-0913-1*) Nat Learn.

Purchasing Transportation. Charles L. Perry. LC 96-30411. (Illus.). 100p. (Orig.). 1998. pap. 14.95 (*0-945456-45-X*) PT Pubns.

Purchasing's Contributions to Time-Based Strategies. Thomas E. Hendrick. LC 94-68758. 97p. (C). 1994. pap. text 20.00 (*0-945968-18-3*) Ctr Advanced Purchasing.

Purchasing's Involvement in Transportation Decision Making. Julie J. Gentry. Ed. by Carol L. Ketchum. LC 91-73552. 40p. (Orig.). (C). 1991. pap. text 20.00 (*0-945968-07-8*) Ctr Advanced Purchasing.

Purchasing's Organizational Roles & Responsibilities. Harold E. Fearon & Michiel R. Leenders. 70p. (Orig.). 1995. pap. text 20.00 (*0-945968-25-6*) Ctr Advanced Purchasing.

Purdah: The Status of Indian Women. S. Das. 287p. 1979. 19.95 (*0-318-37070-0*) Asia Bk Corp.

Purdah & the Status of Women in Islam. S. Abul Ala Maududi. 1991. 12.00 (*0-934905-00-2*, Library of Islam); pap. 7.50 (*1-56744-200-5*) Kazi Pubns.

Purdey's, the Guns & the Family. Richard Beaumont. (Illus.). 248p. 1984. 32.50 (*0-940143-41-0*) Safari Pr.

Purdue Academic Rating Scale. John Feldhusen et al. 1990. pap. 15.00 (*0-89824-501-X*) Trillium Pr.

Purdue Industrial Waste Conference, 41st: Proceedings. Ed. by John Bell. (Illus.). 831p. 1987. boxed set 159.00 (*0-87371-094-0*, L094) Lewis Pubs.

Purdue Pharmacy: The First Century. Robert B. Eckles. LC 78-58099. (Illus.). 114p. 1979. 10.00 (*0-931682-01-0*) Purdue U Pubns.

Purdue University. 1991. 4.95 (*0-942618-32-7*) Penrod-Hiawatha.

Purdue Vocational Talent Scale. John Feldhusen et al. 1990. pap. 15.00 (*0-89824-502-8*) Trillium Pr.

Purdy: Allied Families of Purdy, Fauconnier (Falconer), Archer & Perrin. A. F. Perrin & M. F. Meeker. 114p. 1991. reprint ed. pap. 16.50 (*0-8328-1759-7*) Higginson Bk Co.

Purdy's Instrument Handbook. 2nd ed. Ralph G. Dewey. (Illus.). 104p. 1996. pap. 9.95 (*1-880215-26-8*, Glen Enterp) Deweys GNB.

Pure. Carol Frost. LC 93-43889. 64p. (C). 1994. 26.95 (*0-8101-5029-8*, TriQuart); pap. 10.95 (*0-8101-5004-2*, TriQuart) Northwestern U Pr.

***Pure.** Rebecca Gay. 416p. 2000. pap. 13.50 (*0-8021-3700-8*, Pub. by Grove-Atltic) Publishers Group.

Pure Alexia (Letter-by-Letter Reading) Ed. by Max Coltheart. LC 99-168807. 240p. 1998. 59.95 (*0-86377-999-9*) Minerals Metals.

***Pure & Applied.** Gig Ryan. 92p. 1999. pap. text 11.95 (*0-9586482-6-3*, Paper Bark) Gordon & Breach.

Pure & Applied Geophysics **see Source Mechanism & Seismotectonics**

Pure & Applied Science Books, 1876-1982, 6 vols., Set. 7784p. 1982. 345.00 (*0-8352-1437-0*) Bowker.

Pure & Powerful: Studies in Contemporary Muslim Society. Nadia Abu-Zahra. LC 97-146859. 1998. 45.00 (*0-86372-179-6*, Pub. by Garnet-Ithaca) LPC InBook.

Pure & Simple. Peggy Nicholson. (Romance Ser.). 1993. per. 2.89 (*0-373-03250-1*, 1-03250-7) Harlequin Bks.

Pure & Simple. large type ed. Peggy Nicholson. LC 93-13219. 1993. pap. 13.95 (*1-56054-758-8*) Thorndike Pr.

Pure & Simple: An Incircle Cookbook. Neiman Marcus InCirlce Staff. (Illus.). 320p. 1993. 19.95 (*0-15-175122-6*) Harcourt.

Pure & Simple: An Incircle Cookbook. Neiman Marcus Staff. 1991. 19.95 (*0-9629473-0-X*) Neiman-InCircle.

Pure & Simple Natural Weight Control. rev. ed. Norman W. Walker. LC 81-11080. 132p. 1995. pap. 6.95 (*0-89019-078-X*) Norwalk Pr.

Pure & Simple Politics: The American Federation of Labor & Political Activism, 1881-1917. Julie Greene. LC 97-25547. (Illus.). 350p. (C). 1998. 54.95 (*0-521-43398-3*) Cambridge U Pr.

***Pure & the Impure.** Sidonie-Gabrielle Colette. (Classics Ser.). 200p. 2000. pap. 12.95 (*0-940322-48-X*, Pub. by NY Rev Bks) Midpt Trade.

***Pure & the Powerful: Studies in Contemporary Muslim Society.** Nadia Abu-Zahra. 340p. 2000. pap. 21.00 (*0-86372-269-5*) Garnet-Ithaca.

***Pure & Untouched.** large type ed. Barbara Cartland. 304p. 1999. 31.99 (*0-7505-1420-5*, Pub. by Mgna Lrg Print) Ulverscroft.

Pure & Wholesome. LC 81-70989. 181p. 1982. pap. 5.00 (*0-87262-290-8*) Am Soc Civil Eng.

Pure As the Lily. Catherine Cookson. 320p. 1988. mass mkt. 4.50 (*0-552-09596-6*) Bantam.

Pure As the Lily. Catherine Cookson. 1998. mass mkt. 7.99 (*0-552-14073-2*) Bantam.

Pure at Heart. Stuff Smith & Timme Rosenkrantz. Ed. by Eva Ugager. (Illus.). 64p. (Orig.). 1991. pap. 9.95 (*0-907954-15-4*, Pub. by Allardyce Barnett) Paul & Co Pubs.

Pure-Bred Arabian Horse. Carlo Guarmani. Ed. by Angelo Pesce. 112p. (C). 1995. 100.00 (*0-907151-26-4*, Pub. by IMMEL Pubng) St Mut.

Pure Breed Poultry Raising. Rick Kemp. (Illus.). 80p. (Orig.). 1994. pap. 12.95 (*0-86417-058-0*, Pub. by Kangaroo Pr) Seven Hills Bk.

Pure Bull, Well Organized. Bob Schild. LC 98-113418. (Illus.). 112p. (Orig.). 1996. pap. 11.95 (*0-9616569-1-3*) B-B Leather.

***Pure C++** Ed. by Eric Gufford. (Sams Unleashed Series). 600p. 2000. pap. 24.99 (*0-672-31511-4*) Sams.

Pure C Programming. Amir Afzal. LC 98-10224. 515p. 1998. pap. text 86.00 (*0-13-840703-7*) P-H.

Pure Classical Guitar Solos. 14.95 (*1-56922-168-5*, 07-4079) Creat Cncpts.

***Pure Clear Light.** Madeleine St. John. 240p. 2000. 22.00 (*0-7867-0756-9*, Pub. by Carroll & Graf) Publishers Group.

Pure Clear Light. Madeleine St. John. LC 96-175166. 233p. 1996. write for info. (*1-85702-387-0*) Fourth Estate.

Pure Clear Word: Essays on the Poetry of James Wright. Ed. by Dave Smith. LC 81-2976. 288p. 1982. 29.95 (*0-252-00876-6*) U of Ill Pr.

Pure Cold Light. Gregory Frost. 256p. (Orig.). 1993. mass mkt. 4.99 (*0-380-76774-0*, Avon Bks) Morrow Avon.

Pure Color. Maria Schindler. pap. 29.95 (*0-85440-916-5*, 1487, Pub. by R Steiner Pr) Anthroposophic.

Pure Com Plus. 608p. 1920. 34.99 (*0-672-31874-1*) Sams.

Pure Concept of Diplomacy, 214. Jose Calvet De Magalhaes. Tr. by Bernardo F. Pereira. LC 88-3109. (Contributions in Political Science Ser.: No. 214). 150p. 1988. 49.95 (*0-313-26259-4*, CPT/, Greenwood Pr) Greenwood.

Pure Corba Three. 608p. 1900. 34.99 (*0-672-31812-1*) Sams.

Pure Cure for Arthritis & Other Auto-Immune & Inflammatory Diseases. Bob L. Owen & Thomas Johnson. LC 97-93664. (Illus.). 112p. (Orig.). 1997. pap. 14.00 (*1-882657-14-4*) Health Digest.

Pure Deck-Adence. Tina Skinner. LC 97-35940. 160p. 1998. 29.95 (*0-7643-0445-3*) Schiffer.

Pure Delights. Stella Cameron. 432p. 1995. mass mkt. 5.99 (*0-8217-4798-3*, Zebra Kensgtn) Kensgtn Pub Corp.

Pure Delights. large type ed. Stella Cameron. LC 97-34967. (ROMC-Hall Ser.). 488p. 1997. lib. bdg. 24.95 (*0-7838-8325-0*, G K Hall Lrg Type) Mac Lib Ref.

Pure Drivel. Steve Martin. LC 98-28739. 128p. 1998. 19.95 (*0-7868-6467-2*, Pub. by Hyperion); 19.95 (*0-7868-7915-7*) Hyperion.

***Pure Drivel.** large type ed. Steve Martin. LC 98-45064. 206p. 1999. 28.95 (*0-7838-0419-9*, G K Hall & Co) Mac Lib Ref.

***Pure Drivel.** Steve Martin. LC 98-28739. 128p. 1999. reprint ed. pap. text 9.95 (*0-7868-8505-X*, Pub. by Hyperion) Time Warner.

Pure Drop: A Book of Irish Drinking. Ed. by John Killen. LC 87-18332. 185p. 1996. pap. 16.95 (*0-85640-385-7*, Pub. by Blackstaff Pr) Dufour.

Pure Economics. Maffeo Pantaleoni. iii, 315p. 1957. reprint ed. 39.50 (*0-678-00674-1*) Kelley.

***Pure Ejb Enterprise Javabeans.** 850p. 2000. 29.99 (*0-672-31865-2*) Sams.

Pure English of the Soil **see Fate of French-E in English: The Plural of Nouns Ending in-th**

Pure Evil. Franklin W. Dixon. Ed. by Anne Greenberg. (Hardy Boys Casefiles Ser.: No. 97). 160p. (YA). (gr. 7 up). 1995. mass mkt. 3.99 (*0-671-88208-2*, Archway) PB.

Pure Evil. Franklin W. Dixon. (Hardy Boys Casefiles Ser.: No. 97). (YA). (gr. 6 up). 1995. 9.09 (*0-606-07619-0*, Pub. by Turtleback) Demco.

Pure Excitement. Joe White. LC 96-41465. 1996. pap. 8.99 (*1-56179-483-X*) Focus Family.

Pure Experience: The Response to William James. Ed. by Eugene Taylor & Robert H. Wozniak. (Key Issues Ser.: No. 8). 300p. 1996. 72.00 (*1-85506-413-8*); pap. 24.00 (*1-85506-412-X*) Bks Intl VA.

Pure Food: Securing the Federal Food & Drugs Act of 1906. James H. Young. LC 89-30355. 334p. 1989. reprint ed. pap. 103.60 (*0-608-04652-3*, 206533800003) Bks Demand.

***Pure Food, Drink & Drug Crusaders, 1879-1914.** Lorine Swainston Goodwin. LC 99-28286. 359p. 1999. lib. bdg. 45.00 (*0-7864-0618-6*) McFarland & Co.

Pure Fuel. Fuel Staff. (Illus.). 208p. 1997. 50.00 (*0-688-15229-5*) Watsn-Guptill.

Pure Geography. Johannes G. Grano. Ed. by Olavi Grano & Annsi Paasi. Tr. by Malcolm Hicks from FIN. LC 97-7649. (Illus.). 248p. 1997. text 49.95 (*0-8018-5591-8*) Johns Hopkins.

Pure Gesture: Macrodimensional Glimpses of Other Realities--Art of E. J. Gold. Text by Linda Corriveau. LC 89-23642. 128p. 1990. 35.00 (*0-89556-062-3*) Gateways Bks & Tapes.

Pure Gold. Bud Allen & Diana Bosta. 87p. 1981. vinyl bd. 8.95 (*0-9605226-7-0*) Rae John.

Pure Gold. Beverly B. Kelly. LC 90-92019. 265p. (Orig.). 1990. pap. 7.95 (*0-9627838-0-3*) B B Kelly.

Pure Gold - Colorado Treasures: Recipes from Bed & Breakfast Innkeepers of Colorado. Tracy Winters & Phyllis Winters. LC 92-93907. (Illus.). 96p. (Orig.). 1992. pap. 9.95 (*0-9625329-3-2*) Winters IN.

Pure Gold Rock & Roll Trivia Questions: The Game Book. Ron Foster. 1995. pap. 14.95 (*1-881825-04-3*) Hist Pubns TX.

Pure, Golden Light of Love: A Scientist's New & Startling Report on the Discovery of God's Great Plan for Life on Earth. H. King. LC 93-84329. 278p. (Orig.). 1993. pap. 16.00 (*0-9636849-2-2*) Spirit Hse Pr.

Pure Goldie: The Life & Career of Goldie Hawn. Marc Shapiro. LC 98-3268. (Illus.). 224p. 1998. 21.95 (*1-55972-467-6*, Birch Ln Pr) Carol Pub Group.

Pure Heart: Gourmet Cooking from Japan. Yutaka Kawamura. LC 89-84890. (Illus.). 240p. 1990. 14.95 (*0-923891-16-1*, M4) Ishi Pr Intl.

Pure Heart: The Window to God. Anne Hummel. (Beatitudes Ser.). 48p. 1993. 5.99 (*0-310-59643-2*) Zondervan.

Pure Heart, Clear Conscience: Living a Catholic Moral Life. James Keating. LC 98-67815. 120p. 1999. pap. 7.95 (*0-87973-572-4*) Our Sunday Visitor.

Pure Heart, Enlightened Mind: The Zen Journal & Letters of Maura "Shoshin" O'Halloran. Maura S. O'Halloran. LC 95-22765. (Illus.). 320p. 1995. pap. 14.00 (*1-57322-503-7*, Riverhd Trade) Berkley Pub.

Pure Heart, Enlightened Mind: The Zen Journal & Letters of Maura Soshin O'Halloran. Maura S. O'Halloran. (Illus.). 192p. (Orig.). 1994. pap. 18.00 (*0-8048-1977-7*) Tuttle Pubng.

***Pure Hearts.** Shaykh Nazim Al-Naqshbandi. 64p. (C). 2000. pap. 12.00 (*1-898863-19-9*, Pub. by Zero Prods) Kazi Pubns.

Pure in Heart. Dallin H. Oaks. 1988. 14.95 (*0-88494-650-9*) Bookcraft Inc.

Pure in Heart. William E. Sangster. pap. 9.99 (*0-88019-160-0*) Schmul Pub Co.

Pure in Heart. Jimmy E. Seow. 86p. 1992. pap. 6.50 (*0-909991-41-3*) Bahai.

Pure Instinct. Robert W. Walker. 416p. (Orig.). 1995. pap. 6.99 (*0-515-11755-2*, Jove) Berkley Pub.

***Pure Java 2.** Kenneth Litwak. 700p. 1999. 24.99 (*0-672-31654-4*) Sams.

Pure JavaScript. Ed. by Eric Gufford. 1448p. pap. 34.99 (*0-672-31547-5*) Sams.

An Asterisk (*) at the beginning of an entry indicates that the title is appearing for the first time.

***Pure JFC Swing: The Swing Toolkit.** Satyaraj Pantham. LC 98-87276. (Illus.). 806p. 1999. pap. 19.99 (*0-672-31423-1*) Sams.

***Pure JFC 2D Graphics & Imaging.** Satyaraj Pantham. (Pure... Ser.). 1999. pap. 24.99 (*0-672-31669-2*) Sams.

Pure Jini. 512p. 1920. 34.99 (*0-672-31912-8*) Sams.

Pure Joy. Sondra Ray. LC 86-26911. 216p. 1995. pap. 9.95 (*0-89087-491-3*) Celestial Arts.

Pure Joy: Searching for Our Most Powerful Emotion. Rush W. Dozier, Jr. 256p. 2000. text 24.95 (*0-7167-3557-1*, Sci Am Lib) W H Freeman.

***Pure JSP JAVA Server Pages.** James Goodwill. 336p. 2000. pap. 34.99 (*0-672-31902-0*) Sams.

Pure Justice. Suzann Ledbetter. 1997. mass mkt. 5.99 (*0-451-19194-3*, Sig) NAL.

Pure Ketchup: A History of America's National Condiment, with Recipes. Andrew F. Smith. LC 96-25196. (Illus.). 240p. 1996. 24.95 (*1-57003-139-8*) U of SC Pr.

Pure Kingdom: Jesus' Vision of God. Bruce D. Chilton. (Studying the Historical Jesus Ser.). 188p. (Orig.). 1996. pap. 15.00 (*0-8028-4187-2*) Eerdmans.

Pure Land Tradition: History & Development. Ed. by James Foard et al. (Berkeley Buddhist Studies). x, 548p. 1996. 45.00 (*0-87725-313-7*) U of Cal IAS.

Pure Light. Leonard Slade, Jr. 96p. (C). 1996. pap., student ed. 14.38 (*0-07-057963-6*) McGraw.

Pure Lives: The Early Biographers. Reed Whittemore. LC 87-16822. 176p. 1988. text 19.95 (*0-8018-3548-8*) Johns Hopkins.

Pure Logic & Other Minor Works. W. Stanley Jevons. 1986. reprint ed. pap. 27.95 (*0-935005-49-8*); reprint ed. lib. bdg. 44.95 (*1-57171-027-2*) Lincoln-Rembrandt.

Pure Logic of Choice. Richard D. Fuerle. 221p. 1986. 16.95 (*0-533-06401-5*) Spooner Pr.

Pure Love: Readings on Enduring Virtues. Marilyn Arnold. LC 97-23499. xxii, 519p. 1997. 24.95 (*1-57345-239-4*) Deseret Bk.

Pure Lust: Elemental Feminist Philosophy. Mary Daly. 470p. 1998. pap. 11.95 (*0-7043-3935-8*, Pub. by Womens Press) Trafalgar.

Pure Mathematics. School Mathematics Project Staff. (School Mathematics Project 16-19 Ser.). 816p. (C). 1998. pap. text 29.95 (*0-521-56617-7*) Cambridge U Pr.

Pure Mathematics. Ann Whitehouse. 604p. (C). 1990. pap. 75.00 (*1-85352-525-1*, Pub. by HLT Pubns) St Mut.

Pure Mathematics: Algebra. Anthony Nicolaides. (C). 1990. pap. 39.95 (*1-872684-01-7*, Pub. by P A S S Pubns) St Mut.

Pure Mathematics: Cartesianand Polar Curve Sketching. Anthony Nicolaides. (C). 1990. pap. 50.00 (*1-872684-06-8*, Pub. by P A S S Pubns) St Mut.

Pure Mathematics: Complete Advanced Level Mathematics. Andy Martin et al. (Illus.). 736p. (YA). (gr. 11 up). 1999. pap. 43.50 (*0-7487-3558-5*, Pub. by S Thornes Pubs) Trans-Atl Phila.

Pure Mathematics: Complex Numbers. Anthony Nicolaides. (C). 1990. pap. 50.00 (*1-872684-00-9*, Pub. by P A S S Pubns) St Mut.

Pure Mathematics: Differential Calculus & Applications. Anthony Nicolaides. (C). 1990. pap. 45.00 (*1-872684-08-4*, Pub. by P A S S Pubns) St Mut.

Pure Mathematics: Trigonometry. Anthony Nicolaides. (C). 1990. pap. 39.95 (*1-872684-02-5*, Pub. by P A S S Pubns) St Mut.

***Pure Mathematics Bk. 1, Pt. 1: The Core Syllabus for A Level.** Joyce S. Batty. 1999. pap. 39.95 (*0-7217-2356-X*, Pub. by Schofield) St Mut.

Pure Mathematics 1. L. Bostock & S. Chandler. 768p. 1994. pap. 38.50 (*0-85950-092-6*, Pub. by S Thornes Pubs) Trans-Atl Phila.

Pure Mathematics 2. L. Bostock & S. Chandler. 656p. 1994. pap. 39.00 (*0-85950-097-7*) St Mut.

***Pure Metals Properties: A Scientific & Technical Handbook.** A. Buch. 306p. 1999. 85.00 (*0-87170-637-7*, 06815G) ASM.

Pure No More. 480p. 1997. mass mkt. 6.95 (*0-7867-0498-5*) Carroll & Graf.

Pure Passion. Marion Duckworth. LC 93-45044. (Tapestry Collection). 96p. (Orig.). 1994. pap. 6.50 (*1-56476-222-X*, 6-3222, Victor Bks) Chariot Victor.

***Pure Patsy: A Lighthearted Look at Life.** Perpetual. 1998. pap. 9.99 (*0-8423-8821-4*) Tyndale Hse.

Pure Pleasure: Making Your Marriage a Great Affair. Bill Farrell et al. LC 94-18635. 204p. (Orig.). 1994. pap. 10.99 (*0-8308-1637-2*, 1637, Saltshaker Bk) InterVarsity.

Pure Poetry. Binnie Kirshenbaum. LC 99-45323. 208p. 2000. 21.50 (*0-684-86471-1*) S&S Trade.

Pure Politics & Impure Science: The Swine Flu Affair. Arthur M. Silverstein. LC 81-47590. (Illus.). 192p. reprint ed. pap. 59.60 (*0-608-06146-8*, 206647900008) Bks Demand.

Pure Practice for ECG's. Louise Smith. 452p. 1995. pap. text 27.95 (*0-8151-7923-5*, 25711) Mosby Inc.

Pure Practice for ECGs Instructor's Kit. Louise Smith & Frank Fish. (Illus.). 290p. 1995. teacher ed. write for info. (*0-8151-7873-5*, 25726) Mosby Inc.

Pure Practice in 12-Lead ECG's. Robin B. Purdie & Sam L. Earnest. (Illus.). 576p. 1997. pap. text 34.95 (*0-8151-4669-8*) Mosby Inc.

Pure Practice in 12-Lead ECGS Instructor's Kit. Robin B. Purdie & Sam L. Earnest. (Illus.). 576p. (C). 1997. text, teacher ed. write for info. (*0-8151-4670-1*) Mosby Inc.

Pure Pragmatics & Possible Worlds: The Early Essays of Wilfrid Sellars. Wilfrid Sellars. Ed. by Jeffrey Sicha. LC 78-65271. (Orig.). (C). 1980. pap. text 15.00 (*0-917930-06-1*); lib. bdg. 32.00 (*0-917930-26-6*) Ridgeview.

Pure Prairie: Farm Fresh & Wildly Delicious Foods from the Prairie. Judith Fertig. 160p. (Orig.). 1995. pap. 15.95 (*1-878686-16-X*) Pig Out Pubns.

Pure Product. John Kessel. LC 97-23554. 384p. 1997. text 24.95 (*0-312-86117-6*) St Martin.

Pure Product. John Kessel. 1999. pap. 14.95 (*0-312-86680-1*, Pub. by Tor Bks) St Martin.

***Pure Profit: The Financial Implications of Environmental Performance.** Robert Repetto & Duncan Austin. 80p. 2000. pap. 20.00 (*1-56973-442-9*) World Resources Inst.

Pure Pulp. Ed. by Ed Gorman et al. 572p. 1999. pap. text 13.95 (*0-7867-0700-3*) Carroll & Graf.

Pure Red Cell Aplasia. Emmanuel N. Dessypris. LC 87-27378. (Johns Hopkins Series in Contemporary Medicine & Public Health). (Illus.). 176p. 1988. reprint ed. pap. 54.60 (*0-608-05949-8*, 206628600008) Bks Demand.

***Pure Resistance: Queer Virginity in Early Modern English Drama.** Theodora A. Jankowski. LC 99-89833. 2000. 46.50 (*0-8122-3552-5*) U of Pa Pr.

Pure Scents for Relaxation. Joannah Metcalfe. LC 99-21362. (Illus.). 1999. pap. 12.95 (*0-8069-4845-0*) Sterling.

Pure Scents for Romance. Joannah Metcalfe. LC 99-14534. (Illus.). 1999. pap. 12.95 (*0-8069-4824-8*) Sterling.

***Pure Scents for Vitality.** Joannah Metcalfe. 80p. 1999. pap. text 12.95 (*0-8069-4815-9*) Sterling.

Pure Scents for Well Being. Joannah Metcalfe. LC 99-33942. 1999. pap. text 12.95 (*0-8069-4813-2*) Sterling.

Pure Sex see Sexo Puro

Pure Sex. Ed Young. LC 97-33614. 1997. 18.99 (*1-57673-200-2*, Multnomah Bks) Multnomah Pubs.

Pure Silver: The Second Best of Everything. David Reid & John Jerald. 1987. 14.95 (*0-15-179950-4*, Harvest Bks); pap. 6.95 (*0-685-19152-4*, Harvest Bks) Harcourt.

Pure Silver: The Second Best of Everything. David Reid & Jonathan Jerald. 320p. 1988. pap. 10.95 (*0-15-679960-X*) Harcourt.

Pure Sin. Susan Johnson. 400p. 1994. mass mkt. 5.99 (*0-553-29956-5*) Bantam.

Pure Slaughter Value. Robert Bingham. 208p. 1998. pap. 11.00 (*0-385-48867-X*) Doubleday.

***Pure Sociology.** Lester F. Ward. (Notable American Authors Ser.). 1999. reprint ed. lib. bdg. 125.00 (*0-7812-9877-6*) Rprt Serv.

Pure Sociology: A Treatise on the Origin & Spontaneous Development of Society. 2nd ed. Lester F. Ward. LC 74-117916. xiv, 607p. 1970. reprint ed. 49.50 (*0-678-00653-9*) Kelley.

Pure Spring: Craft & Craftsmen of the U. S. S. R. A. Milovskii. 256p. (C). 1987. text 110.00 (*0-7855-5871-3*, Pub. by Collets) St Mut.

***Pure State of Nature: Sacred Cows, Destructive Myths & the Environment.** David Horton. 208p. 2000. pap. 19.95 (*1-86508-107-8*, Pub. by Allen & Unwin Pty) Paul & Co Pubs.

Pure Style: Accessible New Ideas for Every Room in Your Home. Jane Cumberbatch. LC 96-68265. (Illus.). 160p. 1996. 27.50 (*1-55670-489-5*) Stewart Tabori & Chang.

Pure Style Outdoors. Jane Cumberbatch. LC 97-41167. 160p. 1998. 27.50 (*1-55670-599-9*) Stewart Tabori & Chang.

Pure Talk about Sexual Purity Lesson Plans. Catherine E. Wood. (Illus.). 98p. Date not set. teacher ed., ring bd. 139.90 incl. trans. (*0-9642092-1-7*) Treas Values.

Pure Temptation. Connie Mason. 400p. 2000. mass mkt. 5.99 (*0-8439-4041-2*, Leisure Bks) Dorchester Pub Co.

Pure Temptation. Vicki Lewis Thompson. 1999. per. 3.75 (*0-373-25844-5*, 1-25844-1) Harlequin Bks.

Pure Temptation. large type ed. Sara Wood. 1994. 27.99 (*0-7505-0740-3*, Pub. by Mgna Lrg Print) Ulverscroft.

Pure Theory of Capital. Friedrich A. Hayek. LC 41-2440. (Midway Reprint Ser.). xxxii, 454p. 1992. reprint ed. pap. text 27.00 (*0-226-32081-2*) U Ch Pr.

Pure Theory of Foreign Trade & the Pure Theory of Domestic Values. Alfred Marshall. LC 73-22013. (Reprints of Economic Classics Ser.). (Illus.). 65p. 1975. reprint ed. lib. bdg. 17.50 (*0-678-01194-X*) Kelley.

Pure Theory of Law. Hans Kelsen. 1990. 23.75 (*0-8446-6364-6*) Peter Smith.

Pure Theory of Law. William Ebenstein. xii, 211p. 1969. reprint ed. 27.50 (*0-8377-2100-8*, Rothman) W S Hein.

***Pure Theory of Politics.** Bertrand De Jouvenel. LC 00-20493. 2000. pap. write for info. (*0-86597-265-6*) Liberty Fund.

***Pure Unlimited Love.** John M. Templeton. LC 00-29881. 64p. 2000. pap. write for info. (*1-890151-41-6*, Pub. by Templeton Fnd) U Ch Pr.

Pure Vegetarian Indian Cookery. Pritam Uberoi. 167p. 1996. pap. 12.95 (*0-940500-61-2*, Pub. by Sterling) Asia Bk Corp.

Pure War. Paul Virilio. 180p. Date not set. 7.00 (*0-936756-03-9*) Autonomedia.

Pure War. Paul Virilio & Sylvere Lotringer. 186p. 1998. pap. 8.00 (*1-57027-078-3*) Autonomedia.

Pure Wisdom: Insights for Those Seeking Happiness & Peace of Mind. Shantanand Saraswati. Ed. by Naomi Steinfeld-Rose. LC 91-77864. 312p. (Orig.). 1992. pap. 10.95 (*1-880741-24-5*) Dickens Pr.

Pure XML. George M. Doss. (Illus.). 600p. (Orig.). 2000. pap. text 24.99 (*0-672-31601-3*) Sams.

Pure Yoga: A Translation from the Sanskrit into English of the Tantric Work, the Gherandasamhita, with a Guiding Commentary. Yogi Pranavananda. (C). 1992. text 20.00 (*81-208-0922-X*, Pub. by Motilal Bnarsidass) S Asia.

Purebred. Bonnie Bryant. (Saddle Club Ser.: No. 39). (J). (gr. 4-6). 1994. 9.09 (*0-606-08111-9*) Turtleback.

Pureed Foods with Substance & Style. J. William Richman. LC 93-43913. 242p. 1994. 56.00 (*0-8342-0554-8*) Aspen Pub.

Purely for Pleasure. E. A. Elders. 278p. (C). 1989. text 49.00 (*0-946270-64-3*, Pub. by Pentland Pr) St Mut.

***Purely Fun: The Humor Book: Techniques for Adding Life to Your Years & Years to Your Life.** Mike Purinton. LC 99-91527. (Illus.). 128p. 1999. 10.00 (*0-9674996-0-7*) Lakeside Pubng.

Purely Functional Data Structures. Chris Okasaki. LC 98-15367. 232p. (C). 1998. text 39.95 (*0-521-63124-6*) Cambridge U Pr.

***Purely Functional Data Structures.** Chris Okasaki. 230p. (C). 1999. pap. 24.95 (*0-521-66350-4*) Cambridge U Pr.

Purely Original Verse. limited ed. J. Gordon Coogler. (Illus.). 1974. reprint ed. 6.00 (*0-686-09908-7*) C H Neuffer.

Purely Poliquin: A Collection of 100 Writings. Bud Poliquin. LC 94-21816. 1994. write for info. (*0-9629159-8-X*) Pine Tree NY.

Purely Rosie Pearl. Patricia Cochrane. 144p. (J). (gr. 4-7). 1997. pap. 3.99 (*0-440-41344-3*) Dell.

Purely Rosie Pearl. Patricia A. Cochrane. (J). 1997. 9.09 (*0-606-11773-3*, Pub. by Turtleback) Demco.

Purer Taste: The Reading & Writing of Fiction in English in Nineteenth-Century Canada. Carole Gerson. (Illus.). 224p. 1989. text 35.00 (*0-8020-5820-5*); pap. text 16.95 (*0-8020-6733-6*) U of Toronto Pr.

Purer Than Diamond see Mas Puro Que el Diamante

***Purest of Bastards: Works of Mourning, Art & Affirmation in the Thought of Jacques Derrida.** David F. Krell. LC 99-32685. (American & European Philosophy Ser.). 240p. 2000. 18.00 (*0-271-01992-1*) Pa St U Pr.

Pureza Bajo Presion. N. Anderson.Tr. of Purity under Pressure. (SPA.). 242p. 1996. 8.99 (*0-7899-0219-2*, 497391) Editorial Unilit.

Purgatorio. Dante Alighieri. 1999. pap. text 14.95 (*88-17-15233-1*) CE27.

***Purgatorio.** Dante Alighieri. 2000. pap. write for info. (*0-375-70839-1*) Knopf.

***Purgatorio: A New Verse Translation.** Dante Alighieri. Tr. by W. S. Merwin from ITA. LC 99-40708. 368p. 2000. 30.00 (*0-375-40921-1*) Knopf.

Purgatorio by Dante. Tr. by John Ciardi. 1961. mass mkt. 7.99 (*0-451-62714-8*, Ment) NAL.

Purgatorio, 1970-1977. Raul Zurita. Ed. by Yvette E. Miller. Tr. by Jeremy Jacobson. LC 85-8058. (Discoveries Ser.). (ENG & SPA.). 105p. 1985. pap. 11.95 (*0-935480-21-8*) Lat Am Lit Rev Pr.

Purgatory see Eleven Plays of William Butler Yeats

Purgatory. Mike Resnick. 320p. 1994. mass mkt. 4.99 (*0-8125-3535-9*) Tor Bks.

Purgatory. Michael J. Taylor. 112p. 1998. pap. 5.95 (*0-87973-955-X*) Our Sunday Visitor.

Purgatory. Tim Wilson. 384p. 1995. pap. 9.95 (*0-7472-4404-9*, Pub. by Headline Bk Pub) Trafalgar.

Purgatory. William Butler Yeats. Ed. by Sandra F. Siegel. LC 84-45799. (Cornell Yeats Ser.). (Illus.). 240p. (C). 1985. text 57.50 (*0-8014-1802-X*) Cornell U Pr.

Purgatory, Vol. 1. 100p. 1998. pap. 19.95 (*0-9653570-3-1*) N J Cipriani.

Purgatory: Explained by the Lives & Legends of the Saints. F. X. Schouppe. LC 79-112489. 1991. reprint ed. pap. 13.50 (*0-89555-042-3*) TAN Bks Pubs.

Purgatory--Explained by the Lives & Legends of the Saints. F. X. Schouppe. LC 86-50579. 427p. (Orig.). 1983. reprint ed. pap. 9.00 (*0-89555-301-5*) TAN Bks Pubs.

Purgatory & Heaven. J. P. Arendzen. (Canterbury Ser.). 1990. reprint ed. pap. 5.00 (*0-89555-045-8*) TAN Bks Pubs.

Purgatory & Paradise of Aubrey Beardsley: An Essay & a Narrative Confession in Verse. Derek Stanford. (Illus.). 76p. 1999. 45.00 (*0-930126-57-2*) Typographeum.

Purgatory & Utopia: A Maxahua Indian Village of Mexico. Alicja Iwanska. 214p. 1971. text 39.95 (*0-685-54932-1*); pap. text 24.95 (*0-685-54933-X*) Transaction Pubs.

Purgatory & Utopia: A Mazahua Indian Village of Mexico. Alicja Iwanska. (Illus.). 214p. 1971. 18.95 (*0-87073-762-7*); pap. 11.95 (*0-87073-763-5*) Schenkman Bks Inc.

Purgatory Manuscript - Le Manuscrit du Purgatoire: The Relations of a Nun with a Soul in Purgatory. Tr. by Alun I. Jones from FRE. LC 90-39429. (Studies in Women & Religion: Vol. 29). 148p. 1990. lib. bdg. 69.95 (*0-88946-067-1*) E Mellen.

Purgatory Prayers. Stephen F. Wilcox. (Thumbprint Mysteries Ser.). 128p. 1999. pap. 5.95 (*0-8092-0604-8*, 060480) NTC Contemp Pub Co.

Purgatory Quizzes to a Street Preacher. Charles M. Carty & Leslie Rumble. (Radio Replies Quizzes to a Street Preacher Ser.). 32p. 1992. reprint ed. pap. 1.50 (*0-89555-108-X*) TAN Bks Pubs.

Purgatory Road. large type ed. Bob Reiss. LC 96-35542. 1996. pap. 22.95 (*1-56895-384-4*, Compass) Wheeler Pub.

Purge of Japanese Leaders under the Occupation, Vol. 8--8. Hans H. Baerwald. LC 77-22428. (University of California Publications in Social Welfare: No. 8). 111p. 1977. reprint ed. lib. bdg. 35.00 (*0-8371-9088-6*, BAPJ, Greenwood Pr) Greenwood.

Purged see My Experience with Clinical Depression

Purged by Fire. Jerry Savelle. (Mini-Bks.). 32p. 1993. pap. 1.00 (*0-89274-642-4*, HH-642) Harrison Hse.

Purges from the Lower Anatomy. 32p. (Orig.). 1999. pap. 12.00 (*0-9652538-2-1*, Pub. by L S Shevshenko) Moon Dog.

Purging of an Evil. Roger L. Brewer. LC 91-91951. 143p. 1991. 16.95 (*0-9628797-0-3*) R L Brewer.

Purging of the Civil Service. NCCL Staff. 95p. 1988. 30.00 (*0-946088-17-9*, Pub. by NCCL) St Mut.

Purging Principles & Practice. 2nd ed. 180p. 1975. pap. 7.00 (*0-318-12687-7*, XK0775) Am Gas Assn.

Puri: A Gazetteer. 1985. reprint ed. 34.00 (*0-8364-1341-5*, Pub. by Usha) S Asia.

Puri: Heritage of an Ancient Land. Somanath Khuntia. (Illus.). 217p. (YA). 1997. 24.95 (*0-89213-995-1*) Bhaktivedanta.

Purification: An Illustrated Answer to Drugs. Contrib. by L. Ron Hubbard. (Illus.). 104p. 1990. pap. 17.50 (*0-88404-567-6*) Bridge Pubns Inc.

Purification & Analysis of Recombinant Proteins. Ed. by Ramnath Seetharam & Satish K. Sharma. (Bioprocess Technology Ser.: Vol. 12). (Illus.). 344p. 1991. text 155.00 (*0-8247-8277-1*) Dekker.

Purification & Characterization of the Glycogen-Bound Protein Phosphatase from Rat Liver. S. Wera. No. 50. 126p. (Orig.). 1991. pap. 32.50 (*90-6186-484-4*, Pub. by Leuven Univ) Coronet Bks.

Purification Ceremony. Mark T. Sullivan. LC 96-44565. 1997. mass mkt. 24.00 (*0-380-97428-2*, Avon Bks) Morrow Avon.

Purification Ceremony. Mark T. Sullivan. 352p. 1998. mass mkt. 6.99 (*0-380-79042-4*, Avon Bks) Morrow Avon.

Purification of a Yogi: A Complete Panchakarma Program. Brahm. LC 99-189809. 70p. 1998. pap. 95.00 (*0-9665617-0-8*) Vedic Arts.

Purification of Fermentation Products: Applications to Large-Scale Processes. Ed. by Derek LeRoith et al. LC 84-24316. (ACS Symposium Ser.: No. 271). 198p. 1985. lib. bdg. 49.95 (*0-8412-0890-5*) Am Chemical.

Purification of Fermentation Products: Applications to Large-Scale Processes - Based on a Symposium Sponsored by the Division of Microbial & Biochemical Technology. Ed. by Derek LeRoith et al. LC 84-24316. (ACS Symposium Ser.: No. 271). 208p. reprint ed. pap. 64.50 (*0-7837-1966-3*, 205244400001) Bks Demand.

Purification of Inorganic & Organic Materials: Techniques of Fractional Solidification. Ed. by Morris Zief. LC 79-80748. 338p. reprint ed. pap. 104.80 (*0-7837-2639-2*, 204299200006) Bks Demand.

Purification of Laboratory Chemicals. 2nd ed. D. D. Perrin et al. LC 79-41708. 580p. 1980. 110.00 (*0-08-022961-1*, Pergamon Pr) Elsevier.

Purification of Laboratory Chemicals. 4th ed. W. L. Armarego & D. D. Perrin. 512p. 2000. reprint ed. pap. text 74.95 (*0-7506-3761-7*, TD1050) Buttrwrth-Heinemann.

***Purification of Wilderness Waters: A Practical Guide.** David O. Cooney. LC 99-75562. (Illus.). 80p. 1999. pap. 12.95 (*0-9675854-1-4*) Balsam Bks.

Purification Offering in the Priestly Literature: Its Meaning & Function. N. Kiuchi. (Journal for the Study of the Old Testament Supplement Ser.: Vol. 56). 204p. 1988. pap. 23.75 (*1-85075-102-1*, Pub. by Sheffield Acad) CUP Services.

Purification Problem for Constrained Games with Incomplete Information. H Meister. (Lecture Notes in Economics & Mathematical Systems Ser.: Vol. 295). 140p. 1987. 23.95 (*0-387-18429-5*) Spr-Verlag.

Purification Tools for Monoclonal Antibodies. Peter S. Gagnon. LC 96-90448. (Illus.). 254p. (Orig.). 1996. pap. 89.00 (*0-9653515-9-9*) Validated Biosysts.

***Purified by Fire: A History of Cremation in America.** Stephen Prothero. (Illus.). 279p. 2001. 27.50 (*0-520-20816-1*) U CA Pr.

Purify Your System for Health & Beauty. Illus. by Margot Helmiss & Falk Scheithauer. LC 99-160211. 96p. 1998. pap. 10.95 (*0-8069-4219-3*) Sterling.

Purifying Acetanilide by Recrystallization. Carl Wigal. Ed. by J. Jeffers. (Modular Laboratory Program in Chemistry Ser.). 12p. (C). 1997. pap. text 1.75 (*0-87540-703-X*) Chem Educ Res.

Purifying America: Women, Cultural Reform & Pro-Censorship. 304p. Date not set. text 42.50 (*0-252-02330-7*) U of Ill Pr.

Purifying America: Women, Cultural Reform & Pro-Censorship Activism, 1873-1933. Alison M. Parker. LC 96-45897. 304p. 1997. pap. text 16.95 (*0-252-06625-1*) U of Ill Pr.

Purifying India. Steger. 1999. text. write for info. (*0-312-22177-0*) St Martin.

Purifying Power of Gethsemane & the Seven Deadly Heresies. Bruce R. McConkie. LC 97-78185. (Classic Talk Ser.). 51 p. 1998. write for info. (*0-87579-883-7*) Deseret Bk.

Purifying the Earthly Body of God: Religion & Ecology in Hindu India. Ed. by Lance E. Nelson. LC 97-50608. (Series in Religious Studies). 352p. (C). 1998. text 73.50 (*0-7914-3923-2*); pap. text 24.95 (*0-7914-3924-0*) State U NY Pr.

Purifying the Heart: Buddhist Meditation for Christians. Kevin Culligan et al. 176p. (Orig.). 1994. pap. 14.95 (*0-8245-1420-3*) Crossroad NY.

Purim. Molly Cone. LC 67-10071. (Harper Holiday Ser.). (Illus.). (J). (gr. k-3). 1967. lib. bdg. 10.89 (*0-690-65922-9*) HarpC Child Bks.

Purim. Yaffa Ganz. (ArtScroll Youth Holiday Ser.). (YA). 1991. 8.99 (*0-89906-980-0*) Mesorah Pubns.

Purim. A. Gold. (Holiday Ser.). 1991. 17.99 (*0-89906-607-0*); pap. 14.99 (*0-89906-608-9*) Mesorah Pubns.

Purim! Camile Kress. (Illus.). 10p. (J). (ps-k). 1999. bds. 5.95 (*0-8074-0654-6*, 102555) UAHC.

Purim. Miriam Nerlove. Ed. by Abby Levine. LC 91-19516. (Illus.). 24p. (J). (ps-1). 1992. lib. bdg. 13.95 (*0-8075-6682-9*) A Whitman.

Purim. Miriam Nerlove. LC 91-19516. (Albert Whitman Prairie Bks.). (Illus.). 24p. (J). (ps-1). 1994. pap. 4.95 (*0-8075-6683-7*) A Whitman.

***Purim: Esther.** Lin Johnson. 1999. pap. write for info. (*1-880226-44-8*) M J Pubs.

Purim: Season of Miracles. Z. Fendel. 1997. pap. 7.95 (*1-58330-117-8*) Feldheim.

P

Purim Anthology. Philip Goodman. (Holiday Anthologies Ser.). (Illus.). 526p. 1988. reprint ed. pap. 19.95 (*0-8276-0319-3*) JPS Phila.

Purim Party. Norma Simon. (Festival Series of Picture Storybooks). (Illus.). (J). (ps). 1959. spiral bd. 4.50 (*0-8381-0707-9*) USCJE.

Purim Play. Roni Schotter. LC 95-52364. (Illus.). 32p. (J). (gr. k-3). 1998. 15.95 (*0-316-77518-5*) Little.

Purim Programming see Kadima Hagim Series

Purim Story. Linda Davis. (Illus.). (J). (ps-3). 1988. 9.95 (*0-87306-454-2*) Feldheim.

Purina Encyclopedia of Cat Care. Amy Shojai. LC 97-36133. 480p. 1998. 25.00 (*0-345-41287-7*) Ballantine Pub Grp.

***Purina Encyclopedia of Cat Care: An Authoritative A to Z Guide, from Cat Care & Behavior to Breed Characteristics!** Amy D. Shojai. (Illus.). 480p. 2000. pap. 15.00 (*0-345-43498-6*) Ballantine Pub Grp.

Purina Encyclopedia of Dog Care. Amy D. Shojai. LC 99-10800. 1998. 25.00 (*0-345-41286-9*) Ballantine Pub Grp.

Purine & Pyrimidine Metabolism. CIBA Foundation Staff. LC 76-52420. (CIBA Foundation Symposium: New Ser.: No. 48). 381p. reprint ed. pap. 118.20 (*0-608-14311-1*, 202217400024) Bks Demand.

Purine & Pyrimidine Metabolism in Man: Second Europeon Symposium, Chiemsee, Sept. 1989. Ed. by N. Zoellner et al. (Journal: Annals of Nutrition & Metabolism: Vol. 33, No. 4 1989). (Illus.). 48p. 1989. pap. 35.00 (*3-8055-5072-3*) S Karger.

Purine & Pyrimidine Metabolism in Man Vol. 7B: Structural Biochemistry, Pathogenesis & Metabolism. R. A. Harkness et al. (Advances in Experimental Medicine & Biology Ser.: Vol. 309B). (Illus.). 416p. (C). 1991. text 125.00 (*0-306-44093-8*, Kluwer Plenum) Kluwer Academic.

Purine & Pyrimidine Metabolism in Man Vol. 7A: Chemotherapy, ATP Depletion & Gout. R. A. Harkness et al. (Advances in Experimental Medicine & Biology Ser.: Vol. 309A). (Illus.). 496p. (C). 1991. text 140.00 (*0-306-44092-X*, Kluwer Plenum) Kluwer Academic.

Purine & Pyrimidine Metabolism in Man V, 2 Vols., Set. Ed. by W. L. Nyhan et al. LC 85-32557. (Advances in Experimental Medicine & Biology Ser.: Vol. 195). 1986. 195.00 (*0-685-13929-8*, Plenum Trade) Perseus Pubng.

Purine & Pyrimidine Metabolism in Man V, 2 vols., Vol. 1. Ed. by W. L. Nyhan et al. LC 85-32557. (Advances in Experimental Medicine & Biology Ser.: Vol. 195). 634p. 1986. 120.00 (*0-306-42230-1*, Plenum Trade) Perseus Pubng.

Purine & Pyrimidine Metabolism in Man V, 2 vols., Vol. 2. Ed. by W. L. Nyhan et al. LC 85-32557. (Advances in Experimental Medicine & Biology Ser.: Vol. 195). 720p. 1986. 125.00 (*0-306-42231-X*, Plenum Trade) Perseus Pubng.

Purine & Pyrimidine Metabolism in Man VI, 2 pts., Pt. A. Ed. by K. Mikanagi et al. (Illus.). 574p. 1989. 120.00 (*0-306-43233-1*, Plenum Trade) Perseus Pubng.

Purine & Pyrimidine Metabolism in Man VI, 2 pts., Pt. B. Ed. by K. Mikanagi et al. (Illus.). 566p. 1989. 120.00 (*0-306-43234-X*, Plenum Trade) Perseus Pubng.

Purine & Pyrimidine Metabolism in Man VI, 2 pts., Set. Ed. by K. Mikanagi et al. (Illus.). 1989. 210.00 (*0-685-44617-4*, Plenum Trade) Perseus Pubng.

Purine & Pyrimidine Metabolism in Man VIII: Proceedings of the Eighth International Symposium Held in Bloomington, Indiana, May 22-27, 1994. Ed. by Amerik Sahota & Milton W. Taylor. (Advances in Experimental Medicine & Biology Ser.: Vol. 370). (Illus.). 858p. (C). 1995. text 169.50 (*0-306-44997-8*, Kluwer Plenum) Kluwer Academic.

Purine & Pyrimidine Metabolism in Man 11. Ed. by Andrea Griesmacher et al. LC 97-52565. (Advances in Experimental Medicine & Biology Ser.: No. 431). (Illus.). 892p. (C). 1998. text 185.00 (*0-306-45778-4*, Kluwer Plenum) Kluwer Academic.

Purine & Pyrimidine Nucleotide Metabolism see Methods in Enzymology

P

Purinergic Approaches in Experimental Therapeutics. Kennethalan Jacobson & Michael F. Jarvis. LC 96-38941. 581p. 1997. 155.00 (*0-471-14071-6*) Wiley.

Purines, Vol. 54. John H. Lister. LC 95-45002. 465p. 1996. suppl. ed. 289.00 (*0-471-08094-2*) Wiley.

Purines: Basic & Clinical Aspects. Trevor W. Stone. 264p. 1991. text 174.50 (*0-7923-8925-5*) Kluwer Academic.

Purines & Myocardial Protection. Ed. by Anwar-Saad A. Abd-Elfattah & Andrew S. Wechsler. (Developments in Cardiovascular Medicine Ser.: Vol. 161). 592p. (C). 1995. text 272.50 (*0-7923-3831-6*) Kluwer Academic.

Purines in Cellular Signaling: Targets for New Drugs. Ed. by K. A. Jacobson et al. (Illus.). xv, 448p. 1990. 102.95 (*0-387-97244-7*) Spr-Verlag.

Purines Pyrimidines & Nucleotides & Chemical Nucleic. T. Ulbricht & R. Robinson. LC 64-8554. (Course in Organic Chemistry, Advanced Section Ser.: Vol. 25). 1964. reprint ed. 40.00 (*0-08-010930-6*, Pub. by Pergamon Repr) Franklin.

Purinton Pottery. Jamie Bero-Johnson & Jamie Johnson. LC 97-66896. (Schiffer Book for Collectors Ser.). (Illus.). 224p. 1997. pap. 29.95 (*0-7643-0290-6*) Schiffer.

Purisima Sex Addict, No. II. Ivan Arguelles & Jake Berry. 23p. 1997. pap. 7.00 (*0-935350-64-0*) Luna Bisonte.

Purisimeno Chumash Prehistory. Michael A. Glassow. LC 95-80318. (C). 1995. pap. text 23.50 (*0-15-503084-1*) Harcourt Coll Pubs.

Purism & Language. Paul N. Wexler. LC 61-9706. (Language Science Monographs: Vol. 11). 462p. (Orig.). 1973. pap. text 30.00 (*0-87750-175-0*) Res Inst Inner Asian Studies.

Puritan, 2 vols. Harry A. Poole. 1185p. 1995. 45.00 (*1-887189-00-9*); pap. text 30.00 (*1-887189-01-7*) Symi Pub.

Puritan & Anglican: Studies in Literature. Edward Dowden. LC 67-23208. (Essay Index Reprint Ser.). 1977. 23.95 (*0-8369-0386-2*) Ayer.

Puritan & Anglican: Studies in Literature. Edward Dowden. (BCL1-PR English Literature Ser.). 341p. 1992. reprint ed. lib. bdg. 89.00 (*0-7812-7039-1*) Rprt Serv.

Puritan & His Daughter. James K. Paulding. (Notable American Authors Ser.). 1999. reprint ed. lib. bdg. 125.00 (*0-7812-8708-1*) Rprt Serv.

Puritan & His Daughter, 2 vols., Vols. 1 - 2. James K. Paulding. LC 78-64087. reprint ed. 75.00 (*0-404-17350-0*) AMS Pr.

Puritan As a Colonist & Reformer. Ezra H. Byington. LC 75-31115. reprint ed. 34.50 (*0-404-13601-X*) AMS Pr.

Puritan Boston & Quaker Philadelphia. E. Digby Baltzell. LC 79-7581. (Illus.). 1980. 45.00 (*0-02-901320-8*) Free Pr.

Puritan Boston & Quaker Philadelphia. Intro. by E. Digby Baltzell. 608p. (C). 1996. pap. text 24.95 (*1-56000-830-X*) Transaction Pubs.

Puritan Colonies see English in America

Puritan Colony in Maryland. Daniel R. Randall. LC 78-63763. (Johns Hopkins University. Studies in the Social Sciences. Thirtieth Ser. 1912: 6). reprint ed. 29.50 (*0-404-61031-5*) AMS Pr.

Puritan Commonwealth. Peter Oliver. LC 75-31127. reprint ed. 41.50 (*0-404-13606-0*) AMS Pr.

Puritan Conscience & Modern Sexuality. Edmund Leites. (C). 1995. pap. 13.00 (*0-300-06549-3*) Yale U Pr.

Puritan Daily Devotional Chronicles. Hearthstone Publishing Staff & I. D. Thomas. LC 96-228185. 381p. 1995. pap. 15.95 (*1-879366-99-1*) Hearthstone OK.

Puritan Dilemma: The Story of John Winthrop. 2nd ed. Morgan. 244p. 1998. pap. text 21.20 (*0-321-04369-3*) Addison-Wesley.

Puritan Doctrine of the Last Judgment see Millennium in America: From the Puritan Migration to the Civil War

Puritan Economic Experiments. Gary North. 65p. (Orig.). 1989. pap. 5.95 (*0-930464-14-1*) Inst Christian.

Puritan Ethic & Woman Suffrage. Alan P. Grimes. LC 80-21799. 159p. 1980. reprint ed. lib. bdg. 49.75 (*0-313-22689-X*, GRPE, Greenwood Pr) Greenwood.

***Puritan Evangelism/A Biblical Approach.** Joel R. Beere. 52p. (Orig.). 1999. pap. 2.50 (*1-892777-16-9*) Reform Heritage Bks.

Puritan Experiment: New England Society from Bradford to Edwards. Francis J. Bremer. LC 95-18209. (Illus.). 283p. 1995. pap. 19.95 (*0-87451-728-1*) U Pr of New Eng.

Puritan Family. rev. ed. Ed. by Edmund S. Morgan. 208p. 1942. pap. 13.50 (*0-06-131227-4*, TB1227, Torch) HarpC.

Puritan Family: Religion & Domestic Relations in Seventeenth-Century New England. Edmund S. Morgan. LC 80-18819. 196p. 1980. reprint ed. lib. bdg. 57.50 (*0-313-22703-9*, MOPFA, Greenwood Pr) Greenwood.

***Puritan Family Life: The Diary of Samuel Sewall.** Judith S. Graham. LC 99-57962. (Illus.). 272p. 2000. text 40.00 (*1-55553-445-7*) NE U Pr.

Puritan Frontier: Town Planning in New England Colonial Development, 1630-60. William Haller, Jr. (Columbia University. Studies in the Social Sciences: No. 568). reprint ed. 20.00 (*0-404-51568-1*) AMS Pr.

Puritan Heritage. George M. Stephenson. LC 78-10512. 282p. 1979. reprint ed. lib. bdg. 59.75 (*0-313-20733-X*, STPU, Greenwood Pr) Greenwood.

Puritan Hope. Iain H. Murray. 1975. pap. 9.99 (*0-85151-247-X*) Banner of Truth.

Puritan in Babylon: The Story of Calvin Coolidge. William A. White. (History - United States Ser.). 460p. 1993. reprint ed. lib. bdg. 99.00 (*0-7812-4925-2*) Rprt Serv.

Puritan in the Wilderness: A Biography of the Rev. James Fitch. John T. Fitch. LC 93-85354. 352p. 1993. 39.50 (*0-89725-131-8*, 1444) Picton Pr.

Puritan Influences in American Literature. Emory Elliott. LC 79-12270. (Illinois Studies in Language & Literature: No. 65). 232p. reprint ed. pap. 72.00 (*0-608-13868-1*, 202023200016) Bks Demand.

Puritan Interpretation of Scripture see Millennium in America: From the Puritan Migration to the Civil War

Puritan Justice & the Indian: White Man's Law in Massachusetts, 1630-1763. Yasuhide Kawashima. LC 85-8879. 350p. 1986. reprint ed. pap. 108.50 (*0-608-02302-7*, 206294300004) Bks Demand.

Puritan Legacies: Paradise Lost & the New England Tradition, 1630-1890. Keith W. Stavely. LC 87-47551. 312p. (C). 1987. 39.95 (*0-8014-2016-4*) Cornell U Pr.

Puritan Legacies: Paradise Lost & the New England Tradition, 1630-1890. Keith W. Stavely. LC 87-47551. 312p. 1990. pap. text 16.95 (*0-8014-9777-9*) Cornell U Pr.

Puritan London: A Study of Religion & Society in the City Parishes. Tai Liu. LC 85-40534. 256p. 1986. 45.00 (*0-87413-283-5*) U Delaware Pr.

***Puritan Millenium: Literature & Theology, 1550-1682.** Crawford Gribben. 320p. 2000. 55.00 (*1-85182-577-0*, Pub. by Four Cts Pr) Intl Spec Bk.

Puritan Moment: The Coming of Revolution in an English County. William Hunt. (Historical Studies: No. 102). (Illus.). 376p. 1984. pap. 14.95 (*0-674-73904-3*) HUP.

Puritan, or, The Widow of Watling Street. Ed. by Tudor Facsimile Texts Editing Staff. LC 78-133724. (Tudor Facsimile Texts. Old English Plays Ser.: No. 120). reprint ed. 49.50 (*0-404-53420-1*) AMS Pr.

Puritan Ordeal. Andrew Delbanco. LC 88-11218. 306p. 1989. 42.00 (*0-674-74055-6*) HUP.

Puritan Ordeal. Andrew Delbanco. 320p. 1991. pap. 18.95 (*0-674-74056-4*, DELPUX) HUP.

***Puritan Origins of American Sex: Religion, Sexuality & National Identity in American Literature.** Tracy Fessenden. 2000. 85.00 (*0-415-92639-4*); pap. write for info. (*0-415-92640-8*) Routledge.

Puritan Origins of the American Self. Sacvan Bercovitch. LC 74-29713. 260p. 1977. write for info. (*0-300-01754-5*); pap. 18.00 (*0-300-02117-8*) Yale U Pr.

Puritan Origins of the American Self. Sacvan Bercovitch. LC 74-29713. 260p. reprint ed. pap. 80.60 (*0-8357-8753-2*, 203366900087) Bks Demand.

***Puritan Papers: 1956-1959.** Ed. by D. Martyn Lloyd-Jones. 332p. 2000. pap. 14.99 (*0-87552-466-4*) P & R Pubng.

Puritan Personal Writings: Autobiographies & Other Writings see Library of American Puritan Writings: The Seventeenth Century

Puritan Personal Writings: Diaries see Library of American Puritan Writings: The Seventeenth Century

Puritan Poets & Poetics: Seventeenth-Century American Poetry in Theory & Practice. Ed. by Peter White. LC 85-6366. xvii, 343p. 1985. text 40.00 (*0-271-00413-4*) Pa St U Pr.

Puritan Political Ideas, 1558-1794. Ed. by Edmund S. Morgan. LC 65-22347. (Orig.). 1965. pap. 7.35 (*0-672-60042-0*, AHS33, Bobbs) Macmillan.

Puritan Profiles: 54 Influential Puritans When the Westminster Confession of Faith Was Written. unabridged ed. William Barker. 320p. 1996. 23.99 (*1-85792-191-7*, Pub. by Christian Focus) Spring Arbor Dist.

Puritan Promenade. Martha S. Bacon. LC 81-1913. (Illus.). 160p. 1981. reprint ed. lib. bdg. 55.00 (*0-313-22954-6*, BAPUP, Greenwood Pr) Greenwood.

Puritan Protagonist: President Thomas Clap of Yale College. Louis L. Tucker. LC 62-16069. (Illus.). 307p. reprint ed. pap. 95.20 (*0-8357-3913-9*, 203664700004) Bks Demand.

Puritan-Provincial Vision: Scottish & American Literature in the Nineteenth Century. Susan A. Manning. (Cambridge Studies in American Literature & Culture: No. 41). 253p. (C). 1990. text 69.95 (*0-521-37237-2*) Cambridge U Pr.

Puritan Revolution: A Documentary History. Stuart E. Prall. 1990. 16.50 (*0-8446-2756-9*) Peter Smith.

Puritan Revolution & the English Civil War. Stuart E. Prall. (Orig.). Date not set. pap. write for info. (*0-89464-889-6*) Krieger.

Puritan Sensibility in T. S. Eliot's Poetry, Vol. 165. Dal-Yong Kim. LC 92-35646. (American University Studies: English Language & Literature: Ser. IV, Vol. 165). XII, 202p. (C). 1994. text 41.95 (*0-8204-2095-6*) P Lang Pubng.

Puritan Sermon in America, 1630-1750, 4 vols. Ed. by Ronald A. Bosco. LC 78-114749. (Sermon in America Ser.). 1840p. 1978. reprint ed. 200.00 (*0-8201-1320-4*) Schol Facsimiles.

Puritan Sermons, Sixteen Fifty-Nine To Sixteen Eighty-Nine Being the Morning Exercises at Cripplegate, St. Giles in the Fields & in Southwark: By 75 Ministers of the Gospel in or Near London, with Notes & Translations by James Nichols, 6 vols., Set. Samuel Annesley. Ed. by James Nichols. 4200p. (C). 1981. reprint ed. lib. bdg. 150.00 (*0-940033-19-4*) R O Roberts.

Puritan Smile: A Look Toward Moral Reflection. Robert C. Neville. LC 86-30162. 248p. 1987. text 19.50 (*0-88706-542-2*) State U NY Pr.

Puritan Tradition in America, 1620-1730. rev. ed. Ed. by Alden T. Vaughan. LC 97-23558. 384p. 1997. pap. text 19.95 (*0-87451-852-0*) U Pr of New Eng.

Puritan Tradition in Revolutionary, Federalist, & Whig Political Theory: A Rhetoric of Origins, Vol. 13. Dean Hammer. LC 97-11669. (Major Concepts in Politics & Political Theory Ser.). XXIII, 218p. (C). 1998. pap. text 32.95 (*0-8204-3821-9*) P Lang Pubng.

Puritan Treasury of Quotations. 1977. pap. 11.50 (*0-85151-249-6*) Banner of Truth.

Puritan Village: The Formation of a New England Town. Sumner C. Powell. LC 63-8862. (Illus.). 235p. 1970. pap. 17.95 (*0-8195-6014-6*, Wesleyan Univ Pr) U Pr of New Eng.

Puritan Village Evolves: A History of Wayland, Massachusetts. Helen F. Emery. LC 81-5185. (Illus.). 384p. 1981. 15.00 (*0-914016-78-4*) Phoenix Pub.

Puritan Vision of New Jerusalem see Millennium in America: From the Puritan Migration to the Civil War

Puritan Way of Death: A Study in Religion, Culture & Social Change. David E. Stannard. (Illus.). 236p. 1997. 11.95 (*0-930194-16-0*) Ctr Thanatology.

Puritan Way of Death: A Study in Religion, Culture & Social Change. David E. Stannard. LC 76-42647. (Illus.). 250p. 1979. pap. text 12.95 (*0-19-502521-0*) OUP.

Puritanism: Transatlantic Perspectives on a Seventeenth-Century Anglo-American Faith. Ed. by Francis J. Bremer. LC 93-14428. (Studies in American History & Culture: No. 3). 1993. 45.00 (*0-934909-34-2*, Pub. by Mass Hist Soc); pap. 15.95 (*0-934909-38-5*, Pub. by Mass Hist Soc) NE U Pr.

Puritanism & Democracy. Ralph B. Perry. 1980. 24.50 (*0-8149-0180-8*) Random.

Puritanism & Historical Controversy. William Lamont. (McGill-Queen's Studies in the History of Religion Ser.). 256p. 1996. 60.00 (*0-7735-1445-7*, Pub. by McG-Queens Univ Pr); pap. text 22.95 (*0-7735-1446-5*, DA375, Pub. by McG-Queens Univ Pr) CUP Services.

Puritanism & Liberty. Ed. & Intro. by A. S. Woodhouse. 544p. 1986. pap. 12.95 (*0-460-87206-0*, Everyman's Classic Lib) Tuttle Pubng.

Puritanism & Revolution: Studies in Interpretation of the English Revolution of the Seventeenth Century. Christopher Hill. LC 97-32015. 384p. 1997. pap. 18.95 (*0-312-17434-9*); text 49.95 (*0-312-17433-0*) St Martin.

Puritanism & the English Revolution, 3 vols. William Lamont. (Modern Revivals in History Ser.). 810p. 1992. 177.95 (*0-7512-0004-2*, Pub. by Gregg Revivals) Ashgate Pub Co.

Puritanism & the English Revolution, Vol. 2. Lamont. 1992. 56.95 (*0-7512-0002-6*) Ashgate Pub Co.

Puritanism & the English Revolution, Vol.1. Lamont. 1992. 56.95 (*0-7512-0001-8*) Ashgate Pub Co.

Puritanism & the English Revolution, Vol.3. Lamont. 1992. 63.95 (*0-7512-0003-4*) Ashgate Pub Co.

Puritanism & the Rise of Modern Science: The Merton Thesis. Ed. by I. Bernard Cohen. 360p. (Orig.). (C). 1990. text 45.00 (*0-8135-1529-7*); pap. text 19.00 (*0-8135-1530-0*) Rutgers U Pr.

Puritanism As a Revolutionary Ideology. Michael Walzer. (Reprint Series in Sociology). (C). 1993. reprint ed. pap. text 2.30 (*0-8290-2697-5*, S-770) Irvington.

Puritanism in Old & New England. Alan Simpson. LC 55-13637. (Walgreen Foundation Lectures). 1994. pap. text 8.95 (*0-226-75929-6*, P66) U Ch Pr.

Puritanism, Pietism, & Science. Robert K. Merton. (Reprint Series in Social Sciences). (C). 1993. reprint ed. pap. text 2.30 (*0-8290-2664-9*, S-192) Irvington.

Puritans. Arlo Bates. LC 68-20005. (Americans in Fiction Ser.). 424p. reprint ed. pap. text 5.95 (*0-89197-911-5*); reprint ed. lib. bdg. 29.00 (*0-8398-0155-6*) Irvington.

Puritans: An American Family Portrait. Jack Cavanaugh. 432p. 1994. pap. text 11.99 (*1-56476-440-0*, Victor Bks) Chariot Victor.

Puritans: Religion & Politics in Seventeenth-century England & America. John E. Adair. LC 98-230233. x, 302 p. 1998. write for info. (*0-7509-2117-X*) Sutton Pub Ltd.

Puritans: Religion & Politics in 17th Century England & America. John Eric Adair. LC 98-230233. 320p. 1998. pap. 24.95 (*0-7509-1950-7*, Pub. by Sutton Pub Ltd) Intl Pubs Mktg.

Puritans: Their Origins & Successors. D. Martyn Lloyd-Jones. 436p. (C). 1987. 35.99 (*0-85151-496-0*) Banner of Truth.

Puritans, Algonkians & Roger Williams. (YA). (gr. 5-8). 13.50 (*0-382-44447-7*) Cobblestone Pub Co.

Puritans among the Indians: Accounts of Captivity & Redemption 1676-1724. Ed. by Alden T. Vaughan & Edward W. Clark. (John Harvard Library). (Illus.). 285p. (C). 1981. 39.50 (*0-674-73901-9*) HUP.

Puritans among the Indians: Accounts of Captivity & Redemption, 1676-1724. Ed. by Alden T. Vaughan & Edward W. Clark. (John Harvard Library). 285p. 1986. pap. 16.50 (*0-674-73899-3*) Belknap Pr.

Puritans & Adventurers: Change & Persistence in Early America. T. H. Breen. 288p. 1982. pap. text 20.95 (*0-19-503207-1*) OUP.

Puritans & Pragmatists: Eight Eminent American Thinkers. Paul K. Conkin. LC 75-34730. 505p. reprint ed. pap. 156.60 (*0-8357-6689-6*, 205686900094) Bks Demand.

Puritans & Predestination: Grace in English Protestant Theology, 1525-1695. Dewey D. Wallace. LC 81-11563. (Studies in Religion). 304p. reprint ed. pap. 94.30 (*0-8357-3904-X*, 203663800004) Bks Demand.

Puritans & Prigs. Marilynne Robinson. 1999. 22.50 (*0-8050-4919-3*) H Holt & Co.

Puritans & Radicals in North England: Essays on the English Revolution. Roger Howell, Jr. LC 84-10411. 226p. (Orig.). 1984. lib. bdg. 48.00 (*0-8191-4013-9*) U Pr of Amer.

Puritans Beseiged: The Legacies of King Philip's War in the Massachusetts Bay Colony. Michael J. Puglisi. 256p. (Orig.). 1991. pap. text 28.00 (*0-8191-8291-5*); lib. bdg. 51.50 (*0-8191-8278-8*) U Pr of Amer.

Puritans in America: A Narrative Anthology. Ed. by Alan Heimert & Nicholas Delbanco. 456p. 1985. 35.00 (*0-674-74065-3*); pap. 18.95 (*0-674-74066-1*) HUP.

Puritans in Babylon: The Ancient Near East & American Intellectual Life, 1880-1930. Bruce Kuklick. 240p. 1996. text 32.50 (*0-691-02582-7*, Pub. by Princeton U Pr) Cal Prin Full Svc.

Puritans on Conversion. Samuel Bolton et al. Ed. by Don Kistler. 211p. 1990. 16.95 (*1-877611-11-5*) Soli Deo Gloria.

Puritans on Loving One Another. Ralph Venning et al. Ed. by Don Kistler. LC 97-169874. 130p. 1997. 16.95 (*1-57358-049-X*) Soli Deo Gloria.

Puritans on Prayer. John Preston et al. Ed. by Don Kistler. 293p. 1995. 24.95 (*1-877611-77-8*) Soli Deo Gloria.

Puritans on the Lord's Supper. Richard Vines et al. Ed. by Don Kistler. LC 97-222198. 196p. 1997. 19.95 (*1-57358-041-4*) Soli Deo Gloria.

Puritans, Pilgrims & Merchants: Founders of the Northeastern Colonies. Kieran Doherty. LC 98-10957. (Shaping America Ser.: Vol. 1). (Illus.). 176p. (YA). (gr. 7 up). 1999. lib. bdg. 21.95 (*1-881508-50-1*) Oliver Pr MN.

Puritans, Pioneers & Planters: Ingraham-Abbott-Wardwell-Culver-Burbank Genealogy. Norma Q. Hare. LC 95-68359. 325p. 1995. 38.95 (*0-9646342-0-1*) N L Enter.

Purity. Ignatius Brianchaninov. 1994. pap. 0.75 (*0-89981-155-8*) Eastern Orthodox.

An Asterisk (*) at the beginning of an entry indicates that the title is appearing for the first time.

***Purity: A Love Story.** Marguerite Calais. LC 99-90814. 124p. 1999. 25.00 (*0-7388-0520-3*); pap. 18.00 (*0-7388-0521-1*) Xlibris Corp.

Purity: The Mystery of Christian Sexuality. Dietrich Von Hildebrand. 142p. 1989. pap. 12.95 (*0-940535-26-2*, UP126) Franciscan U Pr.

Purity & Danger: An Analysis of the Concepts of Pollution & Taboo. Mary Douglas. 208p. (C). 1984. pap. 21.99 (*0-415-06608-5*) Routledge.

Purity & Exile: Violence, Memory, & National Cosmology Among Hutu Refugees in Tanzania. Liisa H. Malkki. LC 94-37099. 374p. 1995. pap. text 21.50 (*0-226-50272-4*) U Ch Pr.

Purity & Exile: Violence, Memory, & National Cosmology Among Hutu Refugees in Tanzania. Liisa H. Malkki. LC 94-37099. 374p. 1995. lib. bdg. 60.00 (*0-226-50271-6*) U Ch Pr.

***Purity & Holiness** Marcel Poorthuis & Joshua Schwartz. LC 99-34025. (Jewish & Christian Perspectives Ser.). 1999. write for info. (*90-04-11418-1*) Brill Academic Pubs.

Purity & Monotheism: Clean & Unclean Animals in Biblical Law. Walter Houston. (Journal for the Study of the Old Testament Supplement Ser.: Vol. 140). 314p. 1993. 85.00 (*1-85075-368-7*, Pub. by Sheffield Acad) CUP Services.

Purity & Peace of Mind. Michael D. Evans. 169p. 1995. pap. 8.00 (*0-935199-05-5*) Bedfrd Books.

Purity & Pollution: Gender, Embodiment & Victorian Medicine. Bashford. LC 97-28323. 250p. 1998. text 59.95 (*0-312-21038-8*) St Martin.

Purity Crusade: Sexual Morality & Social Control, 1868-1900, 23. David J. Pivar. LC 70-179650. (Contributions in American History Ser.: No. 23). 308p. 1973. 38.50 (*0-8371-6319-6*, PPC/, Greenwood Pr) Greenwood.

Purity Determinations by Thermal Methods - STP 838. Ed. by R. L. Blaine & C. K. Schoff. LC 83-72815. 150p. 1984. text 24.00 (*0-8031-0222-4*, STP838) ASTM.

Purity in the Christian Home. Paul Landis. 29p. 1978. pap. 1.65 (*0-7399-0213-X*, 2365); pap. 1.35 (*0-7399-0214-8*, 2365.1) Rod & Staff.

Purity in the Christian Home. Paul Landis. (GER.). tpp. 1980. 1.50 (*0-7399-0234-2*, 2365.2) Rod & Staff.

Purity of a Pig. Carles Casajuana. Tr. by Jennifer Denhard from SPA. (Catalan Studies: Vol. 19). 72p. (C). 1996. pap. text 24.95 (*0-8204-2793-4*) P Lang Pubng.

Purity of Diction in English Verse & Articulate Energy. Donald Davie. 380p. 1995. pap. 9.95 (*1-85754-121-9*, Pub. by Carcanet Pr) Paul & Co Pubs.

Purity of Heart. Soren Kierkegaard. Tr. by Douglas V. Steere. LC 48-9399. 224p. 1956. pap. 14.50 (*0-06-130004-7*, TB4, Torch) HarpC.

Purity of Heart in Early Ascetic & Monastic Literature: Essays in Honor of Juana Raasch, O. S. B. Ed. by Harriet Luckman & Linda Kulzer. LC 98-37386. 252p. 1999. pap. 21.95 (*0-8146-2485-5*) Liturgical Pr.

Purity of Kingship: An Edition of Cht 569 & Related Hittite Oracle Inquiries of Tuthaliya Iv. Theo P. Van Den Hout. LC 98-22430. (Documenta et Monumenta Orientis Antiqui Ser.). xxii, 372p. 1998. 86.00 (*90-04-10986-2*) Brill Academic Pubs.

Purity or Prison: One Man's Pilgrimage Through Prison - Finding Grace . . . Bruce Hunter. LC 99-217131. 174p. 1998. pap. 14.95 (*1-57502-988-X*, PO2693) Morris Pubng.

Purity under Pressure see Pureza Bajo Presion

Purity under Pressure: Making Decisions You Can Live With, Friendships, Dating & Relationships That Last. Neil T. Anderson & Dave Park. LC 95-14443. (Orig.). (J). 1995. pap. 8.99 (*1-56507-292-8*) Harvest Hse.

Purlie Victorious: A Commemorative. Ossie Davis. Ed. by Nora D. Day. LC 94-94236. 124p. 1993. write for info. (*0-9638416-0-2*); pap. write for info. (*0-9638416-1-0*) Emmalyn Ent.

***Purlieus: Poems from Hollywood.** Mark Dunster. 11p. 1999. pap. 5.00 (*0-89642-921-0*) Linden Pubs.

Purloined Clinic: Selected Writings. Janet Malcolm. LC 93-7859. 382p. 1993. reprint ed. pap. 13.00 (*0-679-74810-5*) Vin Bks.

Purloined Corn Popper. E. W. Hildick. LC 96-51195. (Felicity Snell Mystery Ser.). (Illus.). 160p. (J). (gr. 3-7). 1997. 14.95 (*0-7614-5010-6*) Marshall Cavendish.

Purloined Image. Christopher R. Young. LC 93-70652. (Illus.). 100p. (Orig.). 1993. pap. 30.00 (*0-939896-03-6*) Flint Inst Arts.

Purloined Letters: Originality & Repetition in American Literature. Joseph N. Riddel. Ed. by Mark Bauerlain. LC 94-30483. (Horizons in Theory & American Culture Ser.). 232p. (C). 1995. text 32.50 (*0-8071-1872-9*) La State U Pr.

Purloined Paperweight. P. G. Wodehouse & Mary Sievert. LC 86-71036. 188p. 1986. reprint ed. 19.95 (*0-933756-09-7*) Paperwght Pr.

Purloined Poe: Lacan, Derrida, & Psychoanalytic Reading. Ed. by John P. Muller & William J. Richardson. LC 87-2760. 424p. 1988. pap. text 17.95 (*0-8018-3293-4*) Johns Hopkins.

Purloined Punch Line: Freud's Comic Theory & the Postmodern Text. Jerry A. Flieger. LC 90-4513. (Illus.). 309p. 1991. reprint ed. pap. 95.80 (*0-608-06719-9*, 206691600009) Bks Demand.

Purloined Self: Interpersonal Perspective in Psychoanalysis. Edgar A. Levenson. 266p. 1991. 30.95 (*0-9629993-0-X*); pap. 24.95 (*0-9629993-1-8*) Contemp Psycho.

Purls of Wisdom: 94 Three-Minute Moments of Unconventional Views to Fill Life's Short Breaks. Don Hansler. LC 95-60178. 200p. (Orig.). 1995. pap. 7.95 (*1-886839-12-3*) Fun Ed Prods.

Purmort Genealogy, Consisting of Nineteen Generations, Nine in England, Ten in America. Charles H. Purmort. (Illus.). 148p. 1995. reprint ed. pap. 21.00 (*0-8328-4886-7*); reprint ed. lib. bdg. 31.00 (*0-8328-4885-9*) Higginson Bk Co.

Purnima. Ahmad Nawaz. LC 98-70829. (BEN.). xiv, 69p. 1998. pap. 10.00 (*1-58225-147-9*) Ananta Prakashani.

***Puro Conjunto! An Album in Words & Pictures.** Ed. by Juan Tejeda & Avelardo Valdez. (CMAS Coleccion Cultura Ser.). (Illus.). 328p. 2000. 35.00 (*0-292-78174-1*); pap. 19.95 (*0-292-78172-5*) U of Tex Pr.

***Puro Teatro, a Latina Anthology: A Latina Anthology.** Ed. by Alberto Sandoval-Sanchez & Nancy S. Sternbach. LC 99-6567. (Illus.). 416p. 1999. lib. bdg. 40.00 (*0-8165-1826-2*) U of Ariz Pr.

***Puro Teatro, a Latina Anthology: A Latina Anthology.** Ed. by Alberto Sandoval-Sanchez & Nancy S. Sternbach. (Illus.). 416p. 2000. pap. 19.95 (*0-8165-1827-0*) U of Ariz Pr.

Purpaleanie & Other Permutations. Sietze Buning. LC 78-61207. 1978. pap. 5.95 (*0-931940-00-1*) Middleburg Pr.

Purple. Mary E. Salzmann. LC 98-26684. (What Color Is It? Ser.). (Illus.). 24p. (J). (ps). 2000. lib. bdg. 18.50 (*1-57765-160-X*, SndCastle) ABDO Pub Co.

***Purple, No. 1.** Belle Heleine Association Staff. 1998. pap. text 14.00 (*2-912684-06-4*, Pub. by Assn Belle) Dist Art Pubs.

***Purple, No. 2.** Belle Heleine Association Staff. (Illus.). 1998. pap. text 14.00 (*2-912684-07-2*, Pub. by Assn Belle) Dist Art Pubs.

Purple, No. 3. 300p. 1999. pap. 14.00 (*2-912684-10-2*, 910242, Pub. by Assn Belle) Dist Art Pubs.

Purple America. Rick Moody. 1998. pap. 13.95 (*0-316-19006-3*, Back Bay) Little.

Purple America: A Novel. Rick Moody. LC 96-48781. 304p. (gr. 8). 1997. 23.95 (*0-316-57925-4*) Little.

Purple America: A Novel. Rick Moody. 304p. 1998. pap. 13.95 (*0-316-55977-6*) Little.

Purple & Fine Women. Edgar E. Saltus. LC 79-182714. reprint ed. 37.50 (*0-404-05549-4*) AMS Pr.

Purple & Fine Women. Edgar E. Saltus. (BCL1-PS American Literature Ser.). 191p. 1992. reprint ed. lib. bdg. 69.00 (*0-7812-6851-6*) Rprt Serv.

Purple & Green: Poems by Thirty-Three Women Poets. Illus. by Vikki Slowe. 196p. (C). 1988. 50.00 (*0-947612-15-7*, Pub. by Rivelin Grapheme Pr); pap. 45.00 (*0-947612-16-5*, Pub. by Rivelin Grapheme Pr) St Mut.

Purple Book see Miquon Math Lab Series: Complete Home School

Purple Book. Laumer. 1987. mass mkt. write for info. (*0-8125-3768-8*) Tor Bks.

***Purple Book: Learning Language Arts Through Literature.** 2nd ed. Debbie Strayer & Susan S. Simpson. (Learning Language Arts Through Literature Ser.). 284p. (J). (gr. 5). 1998. pap., teacher ed. 25.00 (*1-880892-85-5*) Com Sense FL.

***Purple Cane Road: A Novel.** James Lee Burke. LC 99-54080. 330p. 2000. 24.95 (*0-385-48844-0*) Doubleday.

***Purple Cane Road: A Novel.** large type ed. James Lee Burke. LC 00-21643. 528p. 2000. 24.95 (*0-375-43055-5*) Random Hse Lrg Prnt.

Purple Car. Robert Holland. (Books Boys Want to Read Ser.). 163p. (YA). (gr. 6-12). 1998. pap. 10.95 (*0-9658523-3-4*) Frost Hollow.

Purple Climbing Days. Patricia Reilly Giff. (Kids of the Polk Street School Ser.: No. 9). (Illus.). 80p. (J). (gr. 5 up). 1985. pap. 3.99 (*0-440-47309-8*, YB BDD) BDD Bks Young Read.

Purple Climbing Days. Patricia Reilly Giff. 70p. pap. 3.99 (*0-8072-1258-X*) Listening Lib.

Purple Climbing Days. Patricia Reilly Giff. (J). 1991. 8.94 (*0-606-00973-6*, Pub. by Turtleback) Demco.

***Purple Cloud.** M. P. Shiel. (Bison Frontiers of Imagination Ser.). 304p. 2000. pap. 13.95 (*0-8032-9279-1*, Bison Books) U of Nebr Pr.

Purple Cloud. M. P. Shiel. 365p. 1998. reprint ed. lib. bdg. 24.00 (*1-58287-010-1*) North Bks.

Purple Coat. Amy Hest. (Reading Rainbow Bks.). (J). 1992. 10.15 (*0-606-02001-2*, Pub. by Turtleback) Demco.

Purple Coat. Amy Hest. LC 91-38499. (Illus.). 32p. (J). (gr. k-3). 1992. reprint ed. mass mkt. 4.95 (*0-689-71634-6*) Aladdin.

Purple Connection. Philip H. Warren. (Illus.). 140p. 1987. pap. 10.95 (*0-915081-01-6*) Williams Coll.

***Purple Cow.** Betsy Blizzard Lee. (Illus.). (J). (ps-4). 2000. pap. write for info. (*0-9658853-4-8*) Learning Abil.

Purple Cow--Handset Type. Gelett Burgess. 1987. pap. 7.95 (*0-89979-039-9*) British Am Bks.

Purple Cow & Its Parodies. Gelett Burgess & Carolyn Wells. 1987. pap. 4.95 (*0-89979-038-0*) British Am Bks.

Purple Cows & Potato Chips: Multi-Sensory Language Acquisition Activities. Mary A. Christison & Sharron Bassano. (Illus.). viii, 104p. 1995. pap. text 16.95 (*1-882483-31-6*) Alta Bk Ctr.

***Purple Coyote.** Cornette. LC 98-36425. (Illus.). 40p. (J). 1999. 12.95 (*0-385-32664-5*) Doubleday.

Purple Decades: A Reader. Tom Wolfe. (Illus.). 396p. 1982. 17.50 (*0-374-23927-4*) FS&G.

Purple Decades: A Reader. limited ed. Tom Wolfe. (Illus.). 396p. 1982. 60.00 (*0-374-23928-2*) FS&G.

Purple Delicious Blackberry Jam. Lisa W. Peters. (Illus.). 32p. (J). (ps-3). 1992. 14.45 (*1-55970-167-6*, Pub. by Arcade Pub Inc) Time Warner.

Purple Dots. large type ed. Jim Lehrer. 1999. 27.95 (*0-7862-1809-6*) Mac Lib Ref.

Purple Dots: A Novel. Jim Lehrer. LC 98-12962. 262p. 1998. 23.95 (*0-679-45237-0*) McKay.

Purple Dust. Sean O'Casey. 1957. pap. 5.25 (*0-8222-0922-5*) Dramatists Play.

Purple Fables Quartet. Ingo Swann. LC 95-137322. 98p. 1994. pap. 9.95 (*1-57174-009-0*) Hampton Roads Pub Co.

Purple Flat Top: In Pursuit of a Place. Jack Nisbet. 196p. (Orig.). 1996. pap. 12.95 (*1-57061-058-4*) Sasquatch Bks.

Purple Gang. Paul R. Kavieff. 2000. 24.95 (*1-56980-147-9*) Barricade Bks.

Purple Gorilla. Richard D. Lansing, Jr. (Illus.). 48p. (J). (ps-4). 1997. mass mkt. 6.00 (*0-9661844-0-8*) Purple Gorilla.

Purple, Green & Yellow see Verde, Violeta y Amarillo

Purple, Green & Yellow. Robert Munsch. (Illus.). 32p. (J). (ps-2). 1992. pap. 5.95 (*1-55037-256-4*, Pub. by Annick); lib. bdg. 15.95 (*1-55037-255-6*, Pub. by Annick) Firefly Bks Ltd.

Purple, Green & Yellow. Robert Munsch. 1992. 11.15 (*0-606-02285-6*, Pub. by Turtleback) Demco.

Purple Hair? I Don't Care! Dianne Young. (Illus.). 32p. (Orig.). (J). (ps-3). 1995. pap. 6.95 (*0-916291-55-3*) Kane-Miller Bk.

Purple Hat. Tracey C. Pearson. LC 96-3116. 32p. (J). (ps-1). 1997. 16.00 (*0-374-36153-3*) FS&G.

***Purple Haze: The Puzzle of Consciousness.** Joseph Levine. LC 99-87912. (Philosophy of Mind Ser.). 224p. 2000. 29.95 (*0-19-513235-1*) OUP.

Purple Heart. Marc Talbert. LC 91-23084. (Willa Perlman Bks.). 144p. (J). (gr. 4-8). 1992. 14.95 (*0-06-020428-1*) HarpC Child Bks.

Purple Heart. Marc Talbert. 128p. (J). (gr. 6). 1993. pap. 3.50 (*0-380-71985-1*, Avon Bks) Morrow Avon.

***Purple Hearts & Golden Memories: 35 Years with the Minnesota Vikings.** Jim Klobuchar. (Illus.). 1999. pap. 32.00 (*1-885758-15-4*) Quality Sports.

Purple Heaven. John M. Culler. 200p. 1997. 21.95 (*1-887269-01-0*) J Culler & Sons.

Purple Heaven. John M. Culler. 1997. pap. text 21.95 (*1-887269-30-4*) J Culler & Sons.

Purple Hills. Cynthia Parsons. 200p. (Orig.). 1990. pap. 5.00 (*0-9617872-6-0*) VT Schoolhse Pr.

Purple Irises: A Woman in Transition Discovers Passion & Unforseen Encounters. Dorothy K. Portnoy. 336p. 1998. pap. 15.95 (*1-58151-000-4*) BookPartners.

***Purple is Best.** Dana Meachen Rau. (Rookie Readers Ser.). (J). 2000. pap. text 4.95 (*0-516-27001-X*) Childrens.

Purple Is Best. Dana Meachen Rau. LC 98-53053. (Rookie Readers Ser.). (Illus.). 32p. (J). (gr. 1-2). 1999. 17.50 (*0-516-21638-4*) Childrens.

Purple Is My Game, Morgan Is My Name. Judi Miller. 119p. (J). (gr. 4-7). 1998. per. 3.99 (*0-671-00280-5*) PB.

Purple Is Part of the Rainbow. Carolyn Kowalczyk. LC 85-11693. (Rookie Readers Ser.). (Illus.). 32p. (J). (ps-2). 1985. pap. 4.95 (*0-516-42068-2*); lib. bdg. 17.00 (*0-516-02068-4*) Childrens.

Purple Island. Phineas Fletcher. LC 72-196. (English Experience Ser.: No. 313). 132p. 1971. reprint ed. 75.00 (*90-221-0313-7*) Walter J Johnson.

Purple Kiss. Mercer Mayer. LC 93-80651. (LC & the Critter Kids Mini-Novels Ser.). (Illus.). 72p. (J). (ps-3). 1994. 4.69 (*0-307-15980-9*, 15980, Goldn Books) Gldn Bks Pub Co.

Purple Land. William Henry Hudson. reprint ed. 35.00 (*0-404-03391-1*) AMS Pr.

Purple Martin. R. B. Layton. LC 71-92883. (Illus.). 192p. 1969. reprint ed. pap. 9.95 (*0-912542-01-2*) Nature Bks Pubs.

Purple Martin Book: A Complete Guide to Attracting & Housing Purple Martins. Donald Stokes et al. 1998. 12.00 (*0-316-18889-1*) Little.

Purple Moonlight. Balwant Gargi. (C). 1993. 18.50 (*81-85674-06-X*, Pub. by UBS Pubs Dist) S Asia.

Purple Moose: A Children's Story in Verse with Pictures to be Colored. Vonnie Van. (Illus.). 28p. (gr. 2 up). 1998. pap. 4.95 (*1-891232-08-8*) R Crane Pub.

***Purple Mop Story.** Linda Garvel. (Illus.). 24p. (J). (ps-3). 2000. pap. write for info. (*0-9679979-0-9*) Readers Wrtes.

***Purple #05.** Belle Haleine Association Staff. 496p. 2000. pap. 14.00 (*2-912684-14-5*) Assn Belle.

Purple Palace. Chris Malami. LC 95-5817. 76p. 1995. 11.95 (*1-883911-05-2*) Brandylane.

Purple Parrots Eating Carrots: A Rebus Reader see Time-Life Early Learning Program Series

Purple Parrots Eating Carrots: A Rebus Reader. Time-Life Books Editors. Ed. by Neil Kagan. (Early Learning Program Ser.). 64p. (J). (ps-2). 1991. lib. bdg. write for info. (*0-8094-9263-6*) Time-Life.

Purple Patches. Betty K. Schultz. LC 94-69004. (Illus.). 32p. (J). (gr. k-3). 1995. lib. bdg. 11.95 (*0-929568-01-X*) Raspberry IL.

Purple Patches & Other Praises. unabridged ed. Alice H. Wise. (Illus.). 61p. 1998. pap. 11.95 (*1-892651-15-7*) Columbia Pubns.

Purple Pen. Gladys C. Minteer. 18p. (Orig.). 1995. pap. 5.00 (*1-884226-04-3*) Dark River.

Purple Pickle Juice. Erica Farber. LC 94-43913. (Step into Reading Ser.: A Step 2 Book). (Illus.). 13p. (J). (ps-3). 1996. lib. bdg. 11.99 (*0-679-97366-4*) McKay.

Purple Pickle Juice. Erica Farber. (Step into Reading Ser.: A Step 2 Book). (J). (gr. 1-3). 1996. pap. 3.99 (*0-679-87366-X*) Random.

Purple Pickle Juice. Erica Farber. (Step into Reading Ser.: A Step 2 Book). (J). (gr. 1-3). 1996. 9.19 (*0-606-09772-4*, Pub. by Turtleback) Demco.

Purple Place for Dying. John D. MacDonald. 1995. mass mkt. 5.99 (*0-449-22438-4*) Fawcett.

Purple Pussycat. M. Hillert. 1985. 4.95 (*0-87895-665-4*) Modern Curr.

Purple Pussycat. Margaret Hillert. (Illus.). (J). (ps). 1981. pap. 5.10 (*0-8136-5572-2*, TK2358); lib. bdg. 7.95 (*0-8136-5072-0*, TK2357) Modern Curr.

Purple Reign: The Artist Formerly Known as Prince. Liz Jones. LC 97-51915. (Illus.). 284p. 1998. 19.95 (*1-55972-448-X*, Birch Ln Pr) Carol Pub Group.

Purple Reign: The Artist Formerly Known as Prince. Liz Jones. (Illus.). 304p. 1999. pap. 14.95 (*0-8065-2065-5*, Citadel Pr) Carol Pub Group.

Purple Ring. Auner Gold. (Ruach Ami Ser.). (Illus.). 191p. (YA). (gr. 9-12). 1986. 15.95 (*0-935063-16-1*); pap. 11.95 (*0-935063-15-3*) CIS Comm.

Purple Rose Within: A Woman's Basic Guide for Developing a Business Plan. Millicent G. Lownes. Ed. by Lynne Deming. 70p. (Orig.). 1989. pap. 9.95 (*0-943267-14-5*) Busn Your Own.

Purple Roses: Northwestern's Glorious March to Pasadena. Tim Cronin. (Illus.). 200p. (Orig.). 1996. pap. 19.95 (*1-57167-072-6*) Sports Pub.

Purple Sage & Other Pleasures. Ed. by Junior League of Tucson Staff. (Illus.). 256p. 18.95 (*0-9616403-0-8*) Jr League Tucson.

Purple Sea: More Splashes of Chinese Color. Frank F. Owen. Ed. by R. Reginald & Douglas Melville. LC 77-84262. (Lost Race & Adult Fantasy Ser.). 153 p. 1978. reprint ed. lib. bdg. 19.95 (*0-405-11003-0*) Ayer.

Purple Sea Horse & Other Stories. Loretta M. King. LC 79-56712. (Illus.). (Orig.). (J). (gr. k-3). 1979. pap. 4.95 (*0-934104-02-6*) Woodland.

***Purple Sexe, No. 3.** Belle Heleine Association Staff. 1999. pap. text 12.00 (*2-912684-08-0*, Pub. by Assn Belle) Dist Art Pubs.

Purple Sexe, No. 4. 96p. 1999. pap. 10.00 (*2-912684-11-0*, 910243, Pub. by Assn Belle) Dist Art Pubs.

***Purple Sexe #06.** Belle Haleine Association Staff. 2000. pap. 14.00 (*2-912684-15-3*) Assn Belle.

Purple Sexe #05. Belle Haleine Association. 1999. pap. text 10.00 (*2-912684-13-7*) Assn Belle.

***Purple Snerd.** Rozanne Lanczak Williams. LC 99-50810. (Illus.). 20p. (ps-3). 2000. 10.95 (*0-15-202654-1*, Harcourt Child Bks); 3.95 (*0-15-202661-4*, Harcourt Child Bks) Harcourt.

Purple Springs. 2nd ed. Nellie L. McClung. (Illus.). 400p. 1992. text 40.00 (*0-8020-5924-4*); pap. text 19.95 (*0-8020-6864-2*) U of Toronto Pr.

***Purple Student Activity Book: Learning Language Arts Through Literature.** 2nd rev. ed. Debbie Strayer & Susan S. Simpson. (Learning Language Arts Through Literature Ser.). 312p. (J). 1998. pap. 20.00 (*1-880892-20-0*) Com Sense FL.

Purple Thoughts 'n Purple Dreams: A Book about Magical-Mystical Stuff. Sylvia J. Hollenbeck. 60p. (Orig.). 1995. pap. 14.95 (*0-9651584-1-1*) Wise Astro.

Purple Turtles Mystery: The Legend of Lost Boy. Kathi Belford. LC 97-169128. (Illus.). 90p. (J). (ps-5). 1996. 14.95 (*0-9646803-2-7*) Plant Speak Prods.

Purple Turtles Say No, No to Drugs. Gilson Henry. Ed. & Illus. by Ronnie Hansen. LC 87-62124. 24p. (J). (ps-4). 1987. pap. 3.95 (*0-943925-00-2*) Purple Turtle Bks.

Purple Vineyard. Courage Books Staff. 160p. 1997. 5.98 (*0-7624-0221-0*, Courage) Running Pr.

Purple #04. Belle Haleine Association. 1999. pap. text 14.00 (*2-912684-12-9*) Assn Belle.

Purples. John North. 120p. 1999. pap. 7.95 (*1-891929-16-X*) Four Seasons.

***Purpose.** Iyanla Vanzant. (Inner Visions Practicing the Principles Ser.). 2000. pap. 14.95 (*0-684-87267-6*, Fireside) S&S Trade Pap.

Purpose: A Little Gift in the Adventure of Life. Buddy Sears. 169p. (Orig.). 1986. pap. 6.95 (*0-87418-023-6*, 160) Coleman Pub.

***Purpose: Achieving the Greatness for Which You Were Created.** Ned Frey. LC 99-91590. 1999. 25.00 (*0-7388-0916-0*); pap. 18.00 (*0-7388-0917-9*) Xlibris Corp.

***Purpose: Focusing on What Matters Most.** 2000. 10.95 (*1-929494-11-4*) Franklin Covey.

Purpose: For a Life Here & Herafter. Dorothy Svenning. Ed. by Glenn Svenning. 212p. 1999. pap. write for info. (*0-7392-0277-4*, PO3367) Morris Pubng.

***Purpose! The Forgotten Principle.** Raymond M. Wikstrom. LC 99-67998. 208p. 2000. pap. 13.95 (*0-9668231-2-5*, Pub. by DeWitt Bks) Quality Bks IL.

Purpose & Cause in Pauline Exegesis: Romans 1.16-4.25 & a New Approach to the Letters. Wendy Dabourne. LC 98-20490. (Society for New Testament Studies Monograph Ser.: No. 104). 272p. (C). 1999. text 59.95 (*0-521-64003-2*) Cambridge U Pr.

Purpose & Necessity in Social Theory. Maurice Mandelbaum. LC 86-46283. 208p. 1987. reprint ed. pap. 64.50 (*0-608-06711-3*, 206690800009) Bks Demand.

Purpose & Pattern: A Handbook For Writers Of English. Anne Thompson. (Illus.). 320p. (C). 1994. pap. text 21.95 (*0-19-541026-2*) OUP.

Purpose & Process. Sandra Mayfield. 650p. (C). 1994. text 37.20 (*0-536-58629-2*) Pearson Custom.

Purpose & Process. 3rd ed. Ed. by Stephen Reid. 572p. 1996. pap. text 39.60 (*0-13-237389-0*) P-H.

Purpose & Process: A Reader for Writers. 4th ed. Ed. by Stephen Reid. 592p. (C). 2000. pap. 30.00 (*0-13-021026-9*) P-H.

Purpose & Thought: The Meaning of Pragmatism. John E. Smith. LC 83-18136. 236p. 1992. pap. 8.95 (*0-226-76383-8*) U Ch Pr.

Purpose at Sunset. Ed. by R. M. Davis & P.D. Buford. 160p. 1987. reprint ed. pap. 4.99 (*1-56722-057-6*) Word Aflame.

Purpose Clauses: Syntax, Thematics, & Semantics of English Purpose Constructions. Charles Jones. 276p. (C). 1991. text 120.50 (*0-7923-1400-X*) Kluwer Academic.

Purpose Driven Church see Zhi Ben Biao Gan

P

Purpose-Driven Church. 256p. 1995. 19.99 (*0-310-20106-3*) Zondervan.

Purpose-Driven Church. R. Warren. pap. 14.99 (*0-310-21924-8*) Zondervan.

Purpose Driven Church. rev. ed. Rick Warren. 1996. pap. 10.99 (*0-310-20813-0*) Zondervan.

Purpose Driven Life. Rick Warren. pap. 11.99 (*0-310-21074-7*) Zondervan.

Purpose-Driven Life: 7 Steps for Discovering & Fulfilling Your Life Mission. Rick Warren. 240p. 1997. 18.99 (*0-310-20571-9*) Zondervan.

***Purpose Driven Youth Ministry.** Doug Fields. 176p. 2000. pap. 19.99 (*0-310-23108-6*) Zondervan.

***Purpose Driven Youth Ministry: Participants Guide.** Doug Fields. 112p. 2000. pap. 5.99 (*0-310-23109-4*) Zondervan.

Purpose-Driven Youth Ministry: 9 Essential Foundations for Healthy Growth. Doug Fields. LC 97-40916. 256p. 1998. 17.99 (*0-310-21253-7*) Zondervan.

Purpose, Financing & Governance of Museums: Three Conferences on Present & Future Issues. June B. Arey. 1978. pap. text 2.50 (*0-932676-01-4*) Spring Hill.

Purpose in Prayer. E. M. Bounds. 189p. 1997. mass mkt. 5.99 (*0-88368-438-1*) Whitaker Hse.

Purpose Lies Within. Kimberly Phillips. 240p. 1998. pap. 15.95 (*0-9667913-0-4*) Messenger.

***Purpose Lies Within: A Motivational Book for the Heart & Soul.** Kimberly S. Phillips. 80p. 2000. pap. 9.95 (*0-9667913-1-2*, 500) Messenger Publ.

Purpose Made Joinery. 2nd ed. E. V. Foad. LC 89-39588. (Illus.). 320p. 1990. pap. 14.95 (*0-941936-17-1*) Linden Pub Fresno.

Purpose, Meaning, & Grace: The Essential Wisdom of Seth. Janet Mills. 168p. 1999. pap. 12.95 (*1-878424-32-7*) Amber-Allen Pub.

Purpose Movement Color: A Strategy for Effective Presentations. Tom Mucciolo & Rich Mucciolo. (Illus.). 80p. (Orig.). 1994. pap. 24.95 (*0-9647428-0-2*) MediaNet.

Purpose of American Politics. Hans J. Morgenthau. LC 82-20057. 382p. (C). 1983. reprint ed. pap. text 27.00 (*0-8191-2847-3*) U Pr of Amer.

Purpose of Higher Education. Johann G. Fichte. Tr. by Jorn K. Bramann from GER. LC 87-63358. 75p. (C). 1988. pap. text 8.00 (*0-945073-04-6*) Nightsun MD.

Purpose of Islam. M. Yameen Zubairi. LC 84-90999. 100p. (Orig.). (C). 1984. pap. text. write for info. (*0-930895-02-9*) Byron Daven Pubs.

Purpose of Life. Torkom Saraydarian. LC 90-90141. 224p. 1991. pap. 10.95 (*0-929874-03-X*) TSG Pub Found.

Purpose of Life: Experience Your True Calling. Gary R. Blair. 48p. 1998. pap. 6.95 (*1-889770-20-5*, POL) GoalsGuy.

Purpose of Man: The Purpose of God. John N. Darouse. LC 98-92646. 190p. 1998. pap. 17.77 (*1-57502-771-2*, PO2126) Morris Pubng.

Purpose of Physical Reality: The Kingdom of Names. rev. ed. John Hatcher. 159p. 1987. pap. 10.95 (*0-87743-208-2*) Bahai.

Purpose of Playing: Shakespeare & the Cultural Politics of the Elizabethan Theatre. Louis A. Montrose. 248p. 1996. pap. text 16.00 (*0-226-53483-9*) U Ch Pr.

Purpose of Playing: Shakespeare & the Cultural Politics of the Elizabethan Theatre. Louis A. Montrose. 248p. 1998. lib. bdg. 45.00 (*0-226-53482-0*) U Ch Pr.

Purpose of Romans: A Comparative Letter Structure Investigation. L. Ann Jervis. (JSNT Supplement Ser.: Vol. 55). 187p. 1991. 57.50 (*1-85075-304-0*, Pub. by Sheffield Acad) CUP Services.

***Purpose of Suffering.** Bob Davis. 19p. 1999. pap. 1.95 (*0-9671507-2-8*) Apply Within.

Purpose of Temptation. Bob Mumford. 1997. pap. 8.99 (*0-88270-674-8*) Bridge-Logos.

Purpose of Tragedy. Hugh Shearman. 1992. pap. 4.25 (*81-7059-193-7*, 7175, Quest) Theos Pub Hse.

Purpose of Yoga. Gopi Krishna. (C). 1993. pap. 7.00 (*81-85674-97-3*, Pub. by UBS Pubs Dist) S Asia.

Purpose of Your Life: Finding Your Place in the World Using Synchronicity, Intuition, & Uncommon Sense. Carol Adrienne. 320p. 1999. pap. 13.00 (*0-688-16625-3*, Wm Morrow) Morrow Avon.

Purpose of Your Life: Finding Your Place In The World Using Synchronicity, Intuition, And Uncommon Sense. Carol Adrienne. LC 97-36912. 224p. 1998. 22.00 (*0-688-15512-X*, Wm Morrow) Morrow Avon.

Purpose of Your Life: Finding Your Place in the World Using Synchronicity, Intuition & Uncommon Sense, abr. ed. Carol Adrienne. 1998. 16.95 incl. audio (*1-55927-512-X*) Audio Renaissance.

***Purpose of Your Life Experiential Guide.** Carol Adrienne. 2001. pap. 13.00 (*0-688-17802-2*) Morrow Avon.

Purpose of Your Life Experiential Guide: Proven Exercises to Help You Find Your Way in the World. Carol Adrienne. LC 99-12818. 320p. 1999. 22.00 (*0-688-16714-4*, Wm Morrow) Morrow Avon.

Purpose of Your Life on Planet Earth, Vol. 11. James Carroll. (Illus.). 294p. 1994. pap. 14.92 (*1-891897-05-5*) Mission Evangelism.

***Purpose, Passion, Positive, Push: Are You Following the Desires of Your Heart?** 72p. 2000. write for info. (*0-9679990-0-6*) P R Clements.

Purpose, Pattern & Process. 4th ed. Lennis R. Polnac. LC 97-220153. 334p. (C). 1997. per. 33.95 (*0-7872-3799-X*) Kendall-Hunt.

Purpose Perspective. Joanne S. Hayden. (C). 1989. pap. write for info. (*0-9619427-3-8*) J S Hayden.

Purposeful Jettison of Petroleum Cargo. National Research Council, Committee on Vision Sta. 216p. (Orig.). (C). 1994. pap. text 33.00 (*0-309-05081-2*) Natl Acad Pr.

Purposeful Prayer. Ken Parker. 20p. 1980. 0.50 (*0-89814-051-X*) Grace Publns.

Purposeful Reading & Writing: Strategies in Context. Karen K. Allan & Margery S. Miller. 170p. (C). 1994. pap. text 50.00 (*0-15-501164-2*) Harcourt.

Purposeful Restructuring: Creating a Culture for Learning & Achievement in Elementary Schools. Janet H. Chrispeels. 224p. 1992. 85.00 (*0-7507-0022-X*, Falmer Pr) Taylor & Francis.

Purposeful Writer: A Rhetoric with Readings. Donna Gorrell. 550p. 1990. pap. text 30.00 (*0-205-12659-6*, H26594) Allyn.

Purposes & Conditions Affecting the Nature & Extent of Participation of Adults in Courses in the Home Study Department of Columbia University, 1925-1932. George B. Smith. LC 78-177772. (Columbia University. Teachers College. Contributions to Education Ser.: No. 663). reprint ed. 37.50 (*0-404-55663-9*) AMS Pr.

***Purposes & Procedures of the NAIC Securities Valuation Office.** Robert Carcano. 160p. 2000. pap. 65.00 (*0-89382-664-2*) Nat Assn Insurance.

Purposes & Procedures of the NAIC Securities Valuation Office. rev. ed. Ed. by Robert Carcano. 160p. 1998. ring bd. 65.00i (*0-89382-519-0*, SVO-PP97-2) Nat Assn Insurance.

***Purposes & Procedures of the NAIC Securities Valuation Office.** rev. ed. Robert Carcano. 160p. 1998. pap. 65.00 (*0-89382-567-0*) Nat Assn Insurance.

Purposes & Procedures of the Securities Valuation Office. rev. ed. 132p. (C). 1997. ring bd. 65.00 (*0-89382-455-0*, SVO-PP) Nat Assn Insurance.

Purposes in Education. F. D. Rushworth et al. 38p. 1974. pap. 6.00 (*0-904674-01-0*, Pub. by Octagon Pr) ISHK.

Purposes of American Power: An Essay on National Security. Robert W. Tucker. LC 81-8675. 190p. 1981. 38.50 (*0-275-91704-5*, C1704, Praeger Pubs) Greenwood.

Purposes of Art. 4th ed. Albert E. Elsen. (C). 1997. pap. text 59.00 (*0-15-504545-8*) Harcourt Coll Pubs.

Purposes of Art: An Introduction to the History & Appreciation of Art. 4th ed. Albert E. Elsen. 453p. (C). 1981. pap. text 41.25 (*0-03-049766-3*) Harcourt Coll Pubs.

Purposes of Groups & Organizations. Alvin F. Zander. LC 85-45068. (Joint Publication in the Jossey-Bass Management Series & the Jossey-Bass Social & Behavioral Science Ser.). 207p. reprint ed. pap. 64.20 (*0-7837-2539-6*, 204269800006) Bks Demand.

Purposes of Luke-Acts. Robert Maddox. 228p. pap. text 27.95 (*0-567-29270-3*, Pub. by T & T Clark) Bks Intl VA.

Purposes of Pentecost. (ENG & IND.). 1992. pap. write for info. (*0-934920-35-4*, B-13IN) Derek Prince.

Purposes of Pleasure. Richard A. Hawley. (gr. 9-12). 1983. pap. text 8.95 (*0-88334-171-9*) Longman.

Purposes, Principles, & Standards for School Art Programs: NAEA Position Statement. rev. ed. 33p. 1994. pap. 14.00 (*0-937652-83-0*, 409) Natl Art Ed.

Purposive Behaviour & Teleological Explanations. Ed. by Frank George & Les Johnson. (Studies in Cybernetics: Vol. 8). xxii, 310p. 1985. text 137.00 (*2-88124-110-7*) Gordon & Breach.

Purposive Biology. Li Kung Shaw. LC 81-90747. (Illus.). 359p. (C). 1982. text 20.00 (*0-9607806-0-2*); pap. text 15.00 (*0-9607806-1-0*) Li Kung Shaw.

Purposive Diversification & Economic Performance. John T. Scott. (Illus.). 282p. (C). 1993. text 52.95 (*0-521-43015-1*) Cambridge U Pr.

Purposive Explanation in Psychology. Margaret A. Boden. LC 73-169858. 422p. reprint ed. pap. 130.90 (*0-7837-3843-9*, 204366500010) Bks Demand.

Purpur Koshenill Krapp see Red Dyes: Cochineal, Madder & Murex Purple

Purr... Children's Book Illustrators Brag About Their Cats. Ed. by Michael J. Rosen. LC 95-17622. (Illus.). 42p. (J). (gr. 2 up). 1996. 18.00 (*0-15-200837-3*) Harcourt.

Purr-Ceptions. Joanne Gallo. 1998. pap. write for info. (*1-57553-993-4*) Watermrk Pr.

Purr Diem: A Daily Calendar of Cats. Randy Mertens. (Illus.). 366p. 1994. spiral bd. 7.50 (*1-882835-26-3*) STA-Kris.

Purr-fect Crime. Ed. by Isaac Asimov et al. 272p. 1996. 6.98 (*1-56731-084-2*, MJF Bks) Fine Comms.

Purr-Fect Little Book of Cats. Andrews & McMeel Staff. (Little Bks.). 1998. 4.95 (*0-8362-3604-1*) Andrews & McMeel.

Purr-fect Places to Stay: Bed & Breakfasts, Country Inns, & Hotels with Resident Cats. Susan Bard Hall. LC 98-92073. (Illus.). 172p. 1999. pap. 19.95 (*0-9666989-0-8*) Letters Etc.

Purr-fect Shiatsu: Tender Touches for the 90s Cat. Hirotoshi Narikawa & Teruko Takimoto. (Illus.). 96p. (Orig.). 1993. pap. 9.95 (*1-881267-07-5*) Intercultural.

Purrables: Words of Wisdom from the World of a Cat. Alma Barkman. LC 93-84309. 160p. 1993. pap. 6.95 (*0-914984-53-5*) Starburst.

Purrceptive Detective. Alan Robbins. (YA). (gr. 7 up). 1994. 20.00 (*0-922242-71-2*) Bepuzzled.

Purrfect 4 String Bass Method. Brian Emmel. (Illus.). 56p. (Orig.). 1996. pap. 9.95 (*1-57424-036-6*) Centerstream Pub.

***Purrfect Parenting.** Beverly Guhl & Don H. Fontenelle. (Illus.). 160p. (Orig.). 2000. pap. 12.95 (*1-55561-248-2*) Fisher Bks.

Purrfect Romance. large type ed. Jennifer Blake et al. LC 95-46652. (Large Print Bks.). 1996. pap. 22.95 (*1-56895-284-8*) Wheeler Pub.

Purrfectly Purrfect: Life at the Acatemy. Patricia Lauber. (J). Date not set. pap. write for info. (*0-380-73308-0*) Morrow Avon.

Purrfectly Purrfect: Life at the Acatemy. Patricia Lauber. 1924. lib. bdg. write for info. (*0-688-17300-4*, Wm Morrow) Morrow Avon.

***Purrfectly Purrfect: Life at the Acatemy.** Patricia Lauber. (Illus.). 80p. (J). (gr. 3-7). 2000. 15.89 (*0-06-029209-1*); 15.95 (*0-688-17299-7*, Wm Morrow) Morrow Avon.

Purro & the Prattleberries. Suzanne Newton. LC 74-127657. 144p. (J). (gr. 2-6). 1998. pap. 5.00 (*0-9664376-4-0*) Green Ridge Bks.

Purrrfection: The Cat. J. L. Lynnlee. LC 90-61743. (Illus.). 96p. (Orig.). 1990. pap. 16.95 (*0-88740-269-0*) Schiffer.

Purrrrr. Pat Cummings. (Chapter Book Charmers Ser.). (Illus.). 14p. (J). (ps up). 1999. 5.95 (*0-694-01056-1*) HarpC.

***Purs of My Thumb: Poems from Hollywood.** Mark Dunster. 11p. 2000. pap. 5.00 (*0-89642-990-3*) Linden Pubs.

***Purse.** 1999. spiral bd. 9.00 (*1-57977-956-5*) Havoc Pub.

Purse. Kathy Caple. 32p. (J). (gr. k-3). 1992. pap. 6.95 (*0-395-62981-0*, Sandpiper) HM.

Purse Seining Manual. M. Ben-Yami. (Illus.). 336p. 1994. 115.00 (*0-85238-193-X*) Blackwell Sci.

***Purse Shaped.** Havoc Publishing Staff. 1999. 18.00 (*1-57977-884-4*) Havoc Pub.

***Pursemonger of Fugu: A Bathroom Mystery.** Greg Kramer. LC 95-206190. (Illus.). 424p. 1998. pap. text 18.99 (*1-896332-00-5*) Rvrbank Pr.

Purser's Handbook. William E. Armstrong. LC 65-21748. 288p. 1966. reprint ed. pap. 89.30 (*0-7837-9069-4*, 204981800003) Bks Demand.

PURST LIB VOL 2 AMER PK, Vol. 2. 3rd ed. Wilson. (C). 1997. 45.00 (*0-201-34984-1*) Addison-Wesley.

Pursue & Destroy. Leonard C. Carson. (Illus.). 1978. text 19.95 (*0-913194-05-0*) Sentry.

Pursue Your Goals. Eric Lindros. LC 99-54410. 1999. 14.95 (*0-87833-167-0*) Taylor Pub.

Pursued. Patricia H. Rushford. LC 93-74536. (Jennie McGrady Ser.: Vol. 3). 176p. (YA). (gr. 7-10). 1994. mass mkt. 4.99 (*1-55661-333-4*) Bethany Hse.

Pursued. J. Vera Schlamm & Bob Friedman. LC 72-77800. 212 p. (YA). 1972. write for info. (*0-8307-0153-2*, Dial Yng Read) Peng Put Young Read.

Pursued. rev. ed. J. Vera Schlamm & Bob Friedman. LC 86-600. 189p. 1986. pap. 3.95 (*0-8307-1146-5*, 5018631, Regal Bks) Gospel Lght.

Pursued by Furies. Gordon Bowker. 1997. pap. 19.95 (*0-312-16356-8*) St Martin.

Pursued by Grace: A Newspaperman's Own Story of Spiritual Recovery. Jim Klobuchar. LC 98-28754. 128p. 1998. pap. 12.99 (*0-8066-3649-1*, 9-3649) Augsburg Fortress.

Pursued by Love Everlasting. Focus on the Family Staff. (Focus on the Family Ser.). (Illus.). 80p. 1999. 16.99 (*0-7369-0043-8*) Harvest Hse.

Pursued by Shadows. Medora Sale. (Inspector John Sanders - Harriet Jeffries Mystery Ser.). 256p. 1992. text 20.00 (*0-684-19505-4*) S&S Trade.

Pursuing a Deeper Faith. Charles Stanley. (In Touch Study Ser.). 120p. 1999. pap. 7.99 (*0-7852-7290-9*) Nelson.

Pursuing a Just & Durable Peace: John Foster Dulles & International Organization, 212. Anthony C. Arend. LC 87-37552. (Contributions in Political Science Ser.: No. 212). 253p. 1988. 59.95 (*0-313-25637-3*, ADJ/, Greenwood Pr) Greenwood.

Pursuing Amy. Marilyn Kaye. (Replica Ser.: No. 2). 176p. (J). (gr. 3-7). 1998. pap. 3.99 (*0-553-49239-X*) Bantam.

***Pursuing Amy.** Marilyn Kaye. (Replica Ser.: No. 2). (J). (gr. 4-7). 1999. 9.34 (*0-606-15934-7*, Pub. by Turtleback) Demco.

Pursuing Diversity: Recruiting College Minority Students. Barbara Astone & Elsa Nunez-Wormack. Ed. by Jonathan D. Fife. LC 91-60268. (ASHE-ERIC Higher Education Reports: No. 90-7). 123p. 1990. pap. 24.00 (*1-878380-04-4*) GWU Grad Schl E&HD.

Pursuing Excellence: A Study f U. S. Eighth-Grade Mathematics & Science Teaching, Learning, Curriculum & Achievement in International Context. Lois Peak & Third International Mathematics & Science Study Staff. LC 97-156299. 80p. 1996. write for info. (*0-16-048936-9*) USGPO.

Pursuing Excellence: United States Fourth-Grade Mathematics & Science Achievement in International Context. Mary Frase. 68p. 1997. pap. 5.50 (*0-16-063624-8*) USGPO.

***Pursuing Excellence: United States Twelfth-Grade Mathematics &Science Achievement in International Context.** Sayuri Takahira. 150p. 1998. pap. 14.00 (*0-16-063670-1*) USGPO.

Pursuing Excellence in a Time of Declining Resources - The Role of Automated Information Systems: Proceedings, Ninth Annual MSIS National Users Group Conference. Ed. by Joan DiBlasi et al. (Orig.). 1986. pap. 20.00 (*0-936934-05-0*) N S Kline Inst.

Pursuing God's Purpose: Defining & Determining Direction for Your Life. David P. Bertch. Ed. by Terry Martin & Dyna Martin. (Minding Your Own Business Ser.). (Illus.). 227p. (Orig.). 1994. pap., student ed. 16.95 (*0-9634472-2-X*) Good Works Pr.

Pursuing Happiness: American Consumers in the Twentieth Century. Stanley Lebergott. LC 92-40491. 208p. 1993. text 42.50 (*0-691-04322-1*, Pub. by Princeton U Pr); pap. text 15.95 (*0-691-02599-1*, Pub. by Princeton U Pr) Cal Prin Full Svc.

Pursuing Happiness: American Consumers in the Twentieth Century. Stanley Lebergott. (C). 1996. pap. 14.95 (*0-614-12621-5*) Princeton U Pr.

Pursuing History: Middle English Manuscripts & Their Texts. Ralph Hanna. LC 95-22805. (Figurae Ser.). 336p. 1996. 39.50 (*0-8047-2613-2*) Stanford U Pr.

Pursuing Justice: Lee Pressman, the New Deal, & the CIO. Gilbert J. Gall. LC 98-20002. (SUNY Series in American Labor History). (Illus.). 320p. (C). 1999. text 65.50 (*0-7914-4103-2*); pap. text 21.95 (*0-7914-4104-0*) State U NY Pr.

Pursuing Justice for the Child. Ed. by Margaret K. Rosenheim. LC 75-43238. (Studies in Crime & Justice). (Illus.). 1978. pap. text 6.50 (*0-226-72788-2*) U Ch Pr.

Pursuing Justice for the Child. Ed. by Margaret K. Rosenheim. LC 75-43238. (Studies in Crime & Justice). (Illus.). 1992. lib. bdg. 22.50 (*0-226-72789-0*) U Ch Pr.

Pursuing Majorities: Congressional Campaign Committees in American Politics. Robin Kolodny. LC 98-9412. (Congressional Studies Ser.: No. 1). (Illus.). 320p. 1998. 29.95 (*0-8061-3069-5*); pap. 18.95 (*0-8061-3070-9*) U of Okla Pr.

Pursuing Melville, 1940-1980. Merton M. Sealts, Jr. LC 81-70014. 432p. 1982. 35.00 (*0-299-08870-7*) U of Wis Pr.

Pursuing Military Justice, Vol. 2, The History of the United States Court of Appeals for the Armed Forces, 1951-1980 see Arming/Pursuing Military Justice

Pursuing Peace: An American Strategy for the Arab-Israeli Peace Process: Strategic Study Group Final Report. Strategic Study Group Staff. LC 92-26631. 75p. 1992. pap. 5.00 (*0-944029-20-5*) Wash Inst NEP.

Pursuing Perfection: People, Groups & Society. Leonard W. Doob. LC 98-33610. 232p. 1999. 59.95 (*0-275-96448-5*, Praeger Pubs) Greenwood.

Pursuing Postdependency Politics: South-South Relations in the Caribbean. H. Michael Erisman. LC 92-19097. 164p. 1992. lib. bdg. 36.00 (*1-55587-078-3*) L Rienner.

Pursuing Power: Latinos & the Political System. Ed. by F. Chris Garcia. LC 96-26440. 480p. (C). 1996. text 50.00 (*0-268-01312-8*); pap. text 25.00 (*0-268-01313-6*) U of Notre Dame Pr.

***Pursuing Professional Development.** Bailey. (C). 2000. pap. 21.95 (*0-8384-1130-4*) Heinle & Heinle.

Pursuing Sexual Wholeness. Andrew Comiskey. LC 89-80824. 1989. pap. 10.99 (*0-88419-259-8*) Creation House.

Pursuing the Dream: From the Selma-Montgomery March to the Formation of PUSH (1965-1971) Robert Jakoubek. (Milestones in Black American History Ser.). (Illus.). 128p. (YA). (gr. 5 up). 1994. pap. 8.95 (*0-7910-2680-9*); lib. bdg. 19.95 (*0-7910-2254-4*) Chelsea Hse.

Pursuing the Dream: What Helps Children & Their Families Succeed. Kathy G. Wolf et al. LC 97-70516. (Illus.). 160p. 1997. 60.00 (*0-89381-728-7*) Aperture.

Pursuing the Higher Criticism: New Testament Scholarship & Library Collections at the University of Chicago. Maria Freeman. LC 93-14240. (Illus.). 34p. 1993. pap. 10.00 (*0-943056-20-9*) Univ Chi Lib.

Pursuing the Just Cause of Their People: A Study of Contemporary Armenian Terrorism, 152. Michael M. Gunter. LC 85-27295. (Contributions in Political Science Ser.: No. 152). 190p. 1986. 49.95 (*0-313-25247-5*, GUA/, Greenwood Pr) Greenwood.

Pursuing the Muses: Female Education & Nonconformist Culture. Marjorie Reeves. LC 96-51474. 192p. 1997. 65.00 (*0-7185-0105-5*) Bks Intl VA.

Pursuing the Past. E. Provenzo. 1984. text, teacher ed., student ed. 16.95 (*0-201-20124-0*) Addison-Wesley.

Pursuing the Pearl: A Comprehensive Resource for Multi-Asian Ministry. Kenneth U. Fong. LC 99-35734. 192p. 1999. pap. 18.00 (*0-8170-1304-0*) Judson.

Pursuing the Permanent: Meeting the Part of You That Lives Forever. Jayne Reizner. LC 96-61106. 184p. 1997. pap. 9.99 (*1-56384-126-6*, Vital Issue Pr) Huntington Hse.

Pursuing the Ten Million Dollar Dream, 3 vols., Set. Paul Oman. 1991. pap. text 30.00 (*1-879317-05-2*) Success Info Mktg.

Pursuing the Ten Million Dollar Dream: A Field Guide for All Entrepreneurs. Paul Oman. (Illus.). 156p. (Orig.). 1990. pap. 21.95 (*1-879317-00-1*) Success Info Mktg.

Pursuing the Ten Million Dollar Dream No. 1: The Lifestyle. Paul Oman. 114p. (Orig.). 1991. pap. text 10.00 (*1-879317-02-8*) Success Info Mktg.

Pursuing the Ten Million Dollar Dream No. 2: Tips & Tricks. Ed. by Paul Oman. 119p. (Orig.). 1991. pap. text 10.00 (*1-879317-03-6*) Success Info Mktg.

Pursuing the Ten Million Dollar Dream No. 3: How to - How Come. Ed. by Paul Oman. 118p. 1991. pap. text 10.00 (*1-879317-04-4*) Success Info Mktg.

Pursuing the Text: Studies in Honor of Ben Zion Wacholder on the Occasion of His 70th Birthday. Ed. by John C. Reeves & John Kampen. (JSOT Supplement Ser.: No. 184). 434p. 1994. 90.00 (*1-85075-501-9*, Pub. by Sheffield Acad) CUP Services.

Pursuing the Will of God: Reflections & Meditations on the Life of Abraham. Jack W. Hayford. LC 97-28693. 400p. 1997. 18.99 (*1-57673-079-4*, Multnomah Bks) Multnomah Pubs.

Pursuing Total Quality: One Hundred One Logical Ways to Improve Quality for Your Customers (Without Hiring a Guru, Attending Countless Meetings or Spending Thousands of Dollars!) Dick Schaaf & Margaret Kaeter. 124p. 1992. 14.95 (*0-943210-22-4*) Lakewood Pubns.

Pursuing Wellness, Finding Spirituality. Richard J. Gilmartin. LC 95-61489. 208p. (Orig.). 1996. pap. 12.95 (*0-89622-674-3*) Twenty-Third.

Pursuing Wild Bamboo: Portraits of Asian American Artists. Zand Gee et al. 1992. pap. 15.00 (*0-9609630-6-5*) Kearny St Wkshop.

Pursuing Wild Trout: A Journey in Wilderness Values. unabridged ed. Bob Madgic. LC 97-92758. (Illus.). 192p. 1998. pap. 14.95 (*0-9660743-1-9*) River Bend Bks.

Pursuing Wisdom: A Biblical Approach from Proverbs. Kenneth Boa & Gail Burnett. 128p. 1999. pap. 8.00 (*1-57683-121-3*) NavPress.

P

An Asterisk (*) at the beginning of an entry indicates that the title is appearing for the first time.

Pursuit. Jerry Ahern. (Survivalist Ser.: No. 13). 240p. 1986. mass mkt. 2.50 (*0-8217-1877-0*, Zebra Kensgtn) Kensgtn Pub Corp.

Pursuit! Alice Leonhardt. 2001. pap. 4.99 (*0-679-89367-9*) Random.

***Pursuit.** Nancy Rue. LC 99-55398. (Christian Heritage Ser.: Vol. 4). 192p. (J). (gr. 3-7). 2000. pap. 5.99 (*1-56179-856-8*) Bethany Hse.

Pursuit. Ward M. Tanneberg. LC 96-20289. 500p. 1996. pap. 11.99 (*1-56476-584-9*, Victor Bks) Chariot Victor.

Pursuit: A Real Live Look at Disciples. (Bring 'Em Back Alive Ser.). 10.99 (*0-7814-5320-8*, 22038) Cook.

Pursuit: Western Stories. Verne Athanas. Ed. by Jon Tuska. LC 99-41701. 1999. 19.95 (*0-7862-1842-8*) Mac Lib Ref.

***Pursuit: Western Stories.** Verne Athanas & Jon Tuska. LC 00-40779. 2000. write for info. (*0-7838-9134-2*, G K Hall & Co) Mac Lib Ref.

Pursuit - Evasion Differential Games. Ed. by Y. Yavin & M. Pachter. (International Series in Modern Applied Mathematics & Computer Science: No. 14). 250p. 1987. 98.00 (*0-08-034862-9*, Pergamon Pr) Elsevier.

Pursuit Absolute Integrity. Anechiarico. 1998. pap. text 15.00 (*0-226-02052-5*) U Ch Pr.

***Pursuit & Persuasion.** Sally S. Wright. LC 99-50894. (Ben Reese Mystery Ser.: Vol. 3). 350p. 2000. pap. 10.99 (*1-57673-416-1*, Pub. by Multnomah Pubs) GL Services.

***Pursuit & Pursuasion.** Sally Wright. 2000. mass mkt. 6.50 (*0-345-42590-1*, Ballantine) Ballantine Pub Grp.

Pursuit History. 2nd ed. John Tosh. 264p. (C). 1991. pap. text 32.81 (*0-582-02634-2*, 78927) Longman.

Pursuit into Darkness. Daniel Pollock. 1995. mass mkt. 5.99 (*0-671-70576-8*) PB.

PURSUIT LIB V1&PURSUI PK, Vol. 1. 3rd ed. Wilson. (C). 1997. 55.60 (*0-673-79116-5*) Addison-Wesley.

PURSUIT LIB V2&PURSUI PK, Vol. 2. 3rd ed. Wilson. (C). 1997. 55.60 (*0-673-79117-3*) Addison-Wesley.

Pursuit Liberty , Vol. 1. 3rd ed. (C). 1997. text 139.00 (*0-673-55766-9*) S&S Trade.

PURSUIT LIBERTY VOL 2. 3rd ed. R. Jackson Wilson et al. 595p. (C). 1997. pap. text 56.00 (*0-673-46921-2*) Addson-Wesley Educ.

Pursuit of a Dream. Janet S. Hermann. LC 98-41462. 303p. 1999. reprint ed. pap. 17.00 (*1-57806-129-6*) U Pr of Miss.

Pursuit of a Woman on the Hinge of History. Hans Koning. LC 97-2550. 220p. (Orig.). 1997. pap. 15.95 (*1-57129-045-1*, Lumen Eds) Brookline Bks.

***Pursuit of a Wound.** Sydney Lea. LC 99-6987. 2000. pap. 14.95 (*0-252-06817-3*) U of Ill Pr.

Pursuit of Absolute Integrity: How Corruption Control Makes Government Ineffective. Frank Anechiarico & James B. Jacobs. LC 96-15863. (Studies in Crime & Justice). 248p. 1996. 24.95 (*0-226-02051-7*) U Ch Pr.

Pursuit of Acting: Working Actors Share Their Experience & Advice. Starra Andrews. LC 98-10919. 192p. 1998. 49.95 (*0-275-95692-X*, Praeger Pubs); pap. 16.95 (*0-275-96281-4*, Praeger Pubs) Greenwood.

Pursuit of Arms. large type ed. Gerald Hammond. (Linford Mystery Library). 352p. 1998. pap. 17.99 (*0-7089-5215-1*, Linford) Ulverscroft.

***Pursuit of Attention: Power & Ego in Everyday Life.** 2nd ed. Charles Derber. LC 99-56755. 160p. 2000. 25.00 (*0-19-513550-4*); 10.95 (*0-19-513549-0*) OUP.

Pursuit of Attention: Power & Individualism in Everyday Life. Charles Derber. 110p. 1979. pap. 21.95 (*0-87073-885-2*) Transaction Pubs.

Pursuit of Beauty: Finding True Beauty That Will Last Forever. Katie Luce. LC 97-75890. 160p. 1998. pap. 10.99 (*0-89221-373-6*) New Leaf.

Pursuit of Certainty. Hume et al. 408p. 1993. 79.95 (*0-7512-0284-3*) Ashgate Pub Co.

Pursuit of Certainty: David Hume, Jeremy Bentham, John Stuart Mill, Beatrice Webb. Shirley R. Letwin. LC 97-47485. 1998. 18.50 (*0-86597-194-3*); pap. 9.50 (*0-86597-195-1*) Liberty Fund.

Pursuit of Certainty: Religious & Cultural Formulations. Ed. by Wendy James. LC 94-45143. 256p. (C). 1995. pap. 27.99 (*0-415-10791-1*) Routledge.

Pursuit of Certainty: Religious & Cultural Formulations. Ed. by Wendy James. LC 94-45143. (ASA Decennial Ser.). (Illus.). 304p. (C). (gr. 13). 1995. 85.00 (*0-415-10790-3*) Routledge.

Pursuit of Competence in Social Work. Ed. by Frank W. Clark et al. LC 79-83570. (Jossey-Bass Social & Behavioral Science Ser.). 352p. reprint ed. pap. 109.20 (*0-8357-4973-8*, 203790600009) Bks Demand.

Pursuit of Continuous Improvement in Educational Organizations. Michael D. Richardson et al. LC 97-30107. 280p. (C). 1997. 56.00 (*0-7618-0878-7*); pap. 34.50 (*0-7618-0879-5*) U Pr of Amer.

Pursuit of Crime: Art & Ideology in Detective Fiction. Dennis Porter. LC 81-3399. 277p. reprint ed. pap. 85.90 (*0-8357-3756-X*, 203648200003) Bks Demand.

Pursuit of Criminal Justice: Essays from the Chicago Center. Ed. by Gordon J. Hawkins & Franklin E. Zimring. LC 84-12. (Studies in Crime & Justice). x, 358p. 1995. pap. text 24.00 (*0-226-32002-2*, Midway Reprint) U Ch Pr.

Pursuit of Criminal Justice: Essays from the Chicago Center. Ed. by Gordon J. Hawkins & Franklin E. Zimring. LC 84-12. (Studies in Crime & Justice). x, 358p. 2000. lib. bdg. 24.95 (*0-226-32001-4*, Midway Reprint) U Ch Pr.

Pursuit of Curriculum: Schooling & the Public Interest. William A. Reid. LC 93-46339. 198p. 1994. pap. 39.50 (*1-56750-051-X*); text 73.25 (*0-89391-980-2*) Ablx Pub.

Pursuit of Death: A Study of Shelley's Poetry. Benjamin P. Kurtz. 1971. reprint ed. 9.00 (*0-403-00766-6*) Scholarly.

***Pursuit of Destiny: A History of Prediction.** Paul Halpern. 256p. 2000. text 25.00 (*0-7382-0095-6*, Pub. by Perseus Pubng) HarpC.

Pursuit of Division: Race, Gender & Preferential Hiring in Canada. Martin Loney. 360p. 1998. pap. 22.95 (*0-7735-1769-3*, Pub. by McG-Queens Univ Pr); text 65.00 (*0-7735-1744-8*, Pub. by McG-Queens Univ Pr) CUP Services.

Pursuit of Ecstasy: The MDMA Experience. Jerome Beck & Marsha Rosenbaum. LC 93-3371. (SUNY Series in New Social Studies on Alcohol & Drugs). 239p. (C). 1994. pap. text 19.95 (*0-7914-1818-9*) State U NY Pr.

Pursuit of Equality in American History. 2nd enl. rev. ed. J. R. Pole. LC 92-12928. 1993. 40.00 (*0-520-07987-6*, Pub. by U CA Pr) Cal Prin Full Svc.

Pursuit of Excellence see Busca da Excelencia

Pursuit of Excellence see Alas de Aquilas

Pursuit of Excellence. Ted W. Engstrom. 112p. (Orig.). 1982. mass mkt. 7.99 (*0-310-24241-X*, 9576P) Zondervan.

Pursuit of Excellence. Ted W. Engstrom. 128p. (Orig.). 1982. 9.95 (*0-310-24240-1*, 9576) Zondervan.

Pursuit of Excellence. Ted W. Engstrom. (Orig.). 1994. 4.99 (*0-310-96276-5*) Zondervan.

Pursuit of Excellence. John Hohenberg. (Illus.). 312p. 1995. 49.95 (*0-8130-1339-9*) U Press Fla.

Pursuit of God. large type ed. A. W. Tozer. 1997. pap. 10.99 (*0-87509-712-X*) Chr Pubns.

Pursuit of God. A. W. Tozer. LC 96-37158. 128p. 1993. reprint ed. pap. 9.99 (*0-87509-366-3*) Chr Pubns.

Pursuit of God: A 31 Day Experience. A. W. Tozer. LC 95-71543. (Illus.). 216p. (Orig.). 1995. pap. 11.99 (*0-87509-615-8*, 0016158) Chr Pubns.

Pursuit of God: Gift Edition. A. W. Tozer. 119p. 1993. 13.99 (*0-87509-522-4*) Chr Pubns.

Pursuit of God: With Study Guide. A. W. Tozer. 1998. pap., student ed. 11.99 (*0-87509-773-1*) Chr Pubns.

Pursuit of God Study Guide. Jonathan L. Graf. 64p. (Orig.). 1992. pap. 6.99 (*0-87509-504-6*) Chr Pubns.

***Pursuit of Godliness: Sanctification in Christological Perspective.** Donald L. Alexander. LC 99-34636. 240p. 1999. 52.00 (*0-7618-1451-5*); pap. 31.50 (*0-7618-1452-3*) U Pr of Amer.

***Pursuit of God/the Pursuit of Man: Classic Collector's Edition.** A. W. Tozer. 350p. 1999. 19.99 (*0-87509-866-5*) Chr Pubns.

Pursuit of Happiness. Anne Peters. 1993. per. 2.69 (*0-373-08927-9*, 5-08927-1) Silhouette.

Pursuit of Happiness. Anne Roiphe. 579p. 1992. mass mkt. 5.99 (*0-446-36334-0*, Pub. by Warner Bks) Little.

Pursuit of Happiness. large type ed. Anne Peters. LC 93-30342. 227p. 1993. lib. bdg. 13.95 (*0-7862-0058-8*) Thorndike Pr.

Pursuit of Happiness: Evolving a Soul. William J. O'Malley. LC 98-122580. 320p. (C). 1998. 18.95 (*0-88347-333-X*) T More.

Pursuit of Happiness: Government & Politics in America. 5th ed. John A. Moore, Jr. 448p. (C). 1991. pap. text 67.00 (*0-02-383190-1*, Macmillan Coll) P-H.

Pursuit of Happiness - God's Way: Living the Beatitudes. Servais Pinckaers. Tr. by Mary T. Noble from FRE. LC 97-19086. Orig. Title: La Quete du Bonheur. 216p. (Orig.). 1998. mass mkt. 5.95 (*0-8189-0797-5*) Alba.

Pursuit of Happiness Co. David G. Myers. 336p. 1993. reprint ed. pap. 13.50 (*0-380-71522-8*, Avon Bks) Morrow Avon.

Pursuit of Happy Results, Barry Spann. (Illus.). 116p. 1991. 40.00 (*0-87923-905-0*) Godine.

Pursuit of His Presence. Kenneth Copeland. 1998. 19.99 (*1-57794-137-3*) Harrison Hse.

Pursuit of His Presence Daily Devotional. Kenneth Copeland. 1998. 12.99 (*1-57794-139-X*) Harrison Hse.

Pursuit of History. 3rd ed. John Tosh. LC 99-34340. 228p. (C). 1999. pap. 29.06 (*0-582-30471-7*) Addison-Wesley.

Pursuit of Holiness see En Pos de la Santidad

Pursuit of Holiness. Jerry Bridges. (NavClassics Ser.). 1996. pap. 8.00 (*0-89109-940-9*) NavPress.

Pursuit of Holiness. large type ed. Jerry Bridges. 172p. 1985. pap. 13.95 (*0-8027-2507-4*) Walker & Co.

Pursuit of Holiness: Bible Study. Jerry Bridges. 64p. 1996. pap. 5.00 (*0-89109-025-8*) NavPress.

Pursuit of Inquiry. Jay Schulkin. LC 91-33859. 207p. (C). 1992. pap. text 19.95 (*0-7914-1120-6*) State U NY Pr.

Pursuit of Justice. Mimi Latt. 1999. per. 6.99 (*0-671-03411-1*, Pocket Star Bks) PB.

Pursuit of Justice. Mimi Latt. LC 97-29855. 384p. 1998. 22.50 (*0-684-81184-7*) S&S Trade.

Pursuit of Justice. Mimi Latt. LC 98-47823. (Large Print Bks). 1998. 23.95 (*1-56895-589-8*) Wheeler Pub.

Pursuit of Justice & Jewish Law: Halakhic Perspectives on the Legal Profession. Michael J. Broyde. LC 96-22594. 1996. 29.50 (*0-88125-559-9*) Ktav.

***Pursuit of Justices.** David A. Yalof. 1998. pap. text 16.00 (*0-226-94546-4*) U Ch Pr.

Pursuit of Justices: Presidential Politics & the Selection of Supreme Court Nominees. David A. Yalof. LC 99-27979. 240p. 1999. 27.50 (*0-226-94545-6*) U Ch Pr.

Pursuit of Knowledge in the Early American Republic: American Scientific & Learned Societies from Colonial Times to the Civil War. Ed. by Alexandra Oleson & Sanborn C. Brown. LC 75-36941. 400p. reprint ed. pap. 124.00 (*0-8357-8294-8*, 203411700088) Bks Demand.

Pursuit of Knowledge under Difficulties: From Self-Improvement to Adult Education in America. 1730-1900. Joseph F. Kett. LC 93-41885. 600p. (Orig.). 1996. pap. 24.95 (*0-8047-2680-9*) Stanford U Pr.

Pursuit of Knowledge under Difficulties: From Self-Improvement to Adult Education in America, 1750-1990. Joseph F. Kett. LC 03-41885. 592p. 1994. 69.50 (*0-8047-2297-8*) Stanford U Pr.

Pursuit of Leisure: Victorian Depictions of Pastimes. Joanne Wright. 1998. pap. text 30.00 (*0-85331-761-5*, Pub. by Lund Humphries) Antique Collect.

Pursuit of Liberty. 3rd ed. Raymond Jackson Wilson et al. 1996. teacher ed. write for info. (*0-673-55763-4*) Addson-Wesley Educ.

Pursuit of Liberty Vol. 2: A History of the American People. 3rd ed. R. Jackson Wilson et al. 595p. (C). 1997. pap. text 56.00 (*0-673-46922-0*) Addson-Wesley Educ.

Pursuit of Life. Chiu-Nan Lai. 90p. 1993. pap. 12.95 (*0-9638477-0-8*) Chiu-Nan Lai.

Pursuit of Local History: Readings on Theory & Practice. Ed. by Carol Kammen. LC 96-9947. (American Association for State & Local History Book Ser.). 240p. 1996. pap. 24.95 (*0-7619-9169-7*) AltaMira Pr.

Pursuit of Loneliness: America's Discontent & the Search for a New Democratic Ideal. 3rd anniversary ed. Philip Slater. LC 75-36045. 256p. 1976. pap. 14.00 (*0-8070-4201-3*, BP535) Beacon Pr.

Pursuit of Love. Irving Singer. LC 93-34176. (C). 1994. 35.00 (*0-8018-4792-3*) Johns Hopkins.

Pursuit of Love & Love in a Cold Climate. 19th ed. Nancy Mitford. LC 93-43632. 672p. 1994. 18.50 (*0-679-60090-6*) Random.

Pursuit of Man. A. W. Tozer. 1997. pap. 9.99 (*0-87509-704-9*) Chr Pubns.

Pursuit of Meaning: The Road to Self-Esteem & Social Conscience. Ed. by Margaret D. Finck. 181p. (Orig.). 1989. pap. 12.95 (*0-917867-11-4*) V Frankl Inst.

Pursuit of Meaning: Viktor Frankl, Logotherapy, & Life. rev. ed. Joseph B. Fabry. 197p. 1987. pap. 11.95 (*0-917867-04-1*) V Frankl Inst.

Pursuit of Miracles: Eight Stories. George Turner. 209p. (Orig.). 1990. pap. 10.00 (*1-875346-00-7*, Pub. by Aphelion) Firebird Dist.

Pursuit of Nationalized Property. Ed. by M. Sornarajah. 1986. lib. bdg. 146.00 (*90-247-3130-5*) Kluwer Academic.

Pursuit of Organizational Intelligence: Decisions & Learning in Organizations. James G. March. LC 98-36982. 400p. 1999. 69.95 (*0-631-21101-2*); pap. 34.95 (*0-631-21102-0*) Blackwell Pubs.

Pursuit of Painting. Stephen McKenna. 1997. pap. text 39.50 (*0-85331-706-2*, Pub. by Lund Humphries) Antique Collect.

Pursuit of Peace. Leonard W. Doob. LC 80-1201. 335p. 1981. 55.00 (*0-313-22630-X*, DPO/, Greenwood Pr) Greenwood.

***Pursuit of Pleasure.** rev. ed. Lionel Tiger. LC 00-23401. 340p. 2000. pap. 24.95 (*0-7658-0696-7*) Transaction Pubs.

Pursuit of Power: Studies in the Vocabulary of Puritanism. Ellwood Johnson. LC 94-13423. (American University Studies: Vol. 180). IX, 282p. (C). 1995. text 49.95 (*0-8204-2533-8*) P Lang Pubng.

Pursuit of Power: Technology, Armed Force & Society since A. D. 1000. William H. McNeill. LC 81-24095. (Illus.). x, 416p. 1984. pap. text 16.00 (*0-226-56158-5*) U Ch Pr.

***Pursuit of Power in Modern Japan; 1825-1995.** Chushichi Tsuzuki. (Illus.). 560p. 2000. text 105.00 (*0-19-820589-9*) OUP.

Pursuit of Prime: Maximize Your Company's Success with "The Adizes" Method. Ichak Adizes. 304p. 1997. 22.95 (*1-888232-22-6*) Knowldge Exchange.

Pursuit of Public Power: Political Culture in Ohio, 1787-1861. Ed. by Jeffrey P. Brown & Andrew R. Cayton. LC 94-6142. 272p. 1994. pap. 22.00 (*0-87338-496-2*) Kent St U Pr.

Pursuit of Quality in Higher Education: Case Studies in Total Quality Management. Ed. by Deborah J. Teeter & G. Gregory Lozier. LC 85-645339. (New Directions for Institutional Research Ser.: No. IR 78). 143p. (Orig.). 1993. pap. 22.00 (*1-55542-693-X*) Jossey-Bass.

Pursuit of Race & Gender Equity in American Academe. Stephanie L. Witt. LC 90-7014. 104p. 1990. 45.00 (*0-275-93553-1*, C3553, Praeger Pubs) Greenwood.

Pursuit of Reason. Edwards. 1995. 49.95 (*0-07-103623-7*) McGraw.

Pursuit of Reason: The Economist, 1843-1993. Ruth D. Edwards. LC 94-34596. 1040p. 1995. 49.95 (*0-87584-608-4*) Harvard Busn.

Pursuit of Revival see En Busca del Avivamiento

Pursuit of Revival. Stephen Hill. LC 97-68350. 1997. pap. 10.99 (*0-88419-506-6*) Creation House.

Pursuit of Salvation: A Critical Guide to the Novels of Graham Greene. George M. A. Gaston. LC 84-50635. vi, 164p. 1984. 40.00 (*0-87875-289-7*) Whitston Pub.

Pursuit of Serenity: Havelock Ellis & the New Politics. Chris Nottingham. 1999. pap. 29.95 (*90-5356-386-5*, Pub. by Amsterdam U Pr) U of Mich Pr.

***Pursuit of Significance: Strategies for Managerial Success in Public Organizations.** Robert B. Denhardt. 300p. (C). 2000. pap. 19.95 (*1-57766-114-1*) Waveland Pr.

Pursuit of Signs: Semiotics, Literature, Deconstruction. Jonathan Culler. LC 80-70539. 256p. (C). 1981. pap. text 14.95 (*0-8014-9224-6*) Cornell U Pr.

Pursuit of Sodomy: Male Homosexuality in Renaissance & Enlightenment Europe. Kent Gerard & Gert Hekma. LC 88-38811. (Journal of Homosexuality Ser.: Vol. 16, Nos. 1 & 2). (Illus.). 553p. 1989. pap. text 19.95 (*0-918393-49-3*, Harrington Park) Haworth Pr.

Pursuit of Sodomy: Male Homosexuality in Renaissance & Enlightenment Europe. Kent Gerard & Gert Hekma. LC 88-32231. (Journal of Homosexuality: Vol. 16, Nos. 1-2). (Illus.). 553p. 1989. text 17.95 (*0-86656-491-8*) Haworth Pr.

***Pursuit of Spiritual Wisdom: The Thought & Art of Vincent Van Gogh & Paul Gauguin.** Naomi Maurer et al. LC 98-16272. (Illus.). 330p. 1998. 65.00 (*0-8386-3749-3*) Fairleigh Dickinson.

Pursuit of the Enemy. Copeland, Kenneth Ministries Staff. (Superkids Novels Ser.). 1999. pap. text 6.99 (*1-57794-152-7*) Harrison Hse.

Pursuit of the House-Boat. John K. Bangs. (BCL1-PS American Literature Ser.). 204p. 1992. reprint ed. lib. bdg. 69.00 (*0-7812-6672-6*) Rprt Serv.

Pursuit of the Houseboat. Bangs. 1995. per. 8.00 (*1-57283-002-6*) S&S Trade.

Pursuit of the Houseboat. John K. Bangs. 1897. 5.00 (*0-403-00474-8*) Scholarly.

Pursuit of the Houseboat. John K. Bangs. LC 79-89550. (Illus.). reprint ed. 34.50 (*0-404-00497-0*) AMS Pr.

Pursuit of the Houseboat. John K. Bangs. reprint ed. lib. bdg. 20.95 (*0-89190-626-6*, Rivercity Pr) Amereon Ltd.

Pursuit of the Ideal: Jewish Writings of Steven Schwarzschild. Ed. by Menachem M. Kellner. LC 89-4441. (SUNY Series in Jewish Philosophy). 394p. (C). 1990. text 64.50 (*0-7914-0219-3*); pap. text 21.95 (*0-7914-0220-7*) State U NY Pr.

Pursuit of the Millennium. rev. ed. Norman Cohn. (Illus.). 412p. 1970. pap. text 16.95 (*0-19-500456-6*) OUP.

Pursuit of the Mountain Man. William W. Johnstone. 1991. mass mkt. 3.50 (*0-8217-3515-2*, Zebra Kensgtn) Kensgtn Pub Corp.

Pursuit of the Mountain Man. William W. Johnstone. 256p. 1996. mass mkt. 4.99 (*0-8217-5246-4*, Zebra Kensgtn) Kensgtn Pub Corp.

Pursuit of the Mountain Man. William W. Johnstone. 256p. 1998. mass mkt. 4.99 (*0-8217-6011-4*, Zebra Kensgtn) Kensgtn Pub Corp.

Pursuit of the Presidency: 'Ninety-Two & Beyond. Christine M. Black. LC 93-37593. (Illus.). 216p. 1993. pap. 24.50 (*0-89774-845-X*) Oryx Pr.

Pursuit of the Seawolf. William P. Mack. LC 91-22050. (Destroyer Ser.). 419p. 1991. 22.95 (*1-877853-12-7*) Nautical & Aviation.

Pursuit of the Shield: The U. S. Quest for Limited Ballistic Missile Defense. K. Scott McMahon. LC 96-52030. 408p. 1997. 62.50 (*0-7618-0686-5*); pap. 39.50 (*0-7618-0687-3*) U Pr of Amer.

Pursuit of the Well-Beloved & the Well-Beloved. Thomas Hardy. Ed. by Patricia Ingham. LC 98-147248. xxxvii, 374p. 1998. pap. 9.95 (*0-14-043519-0*, Penguin Classics) Viking Penguin.

Pursuit of the White House: A Handbook of Presidential Election Statistics & History. G. Scott Thomas. LC 87-11968. 501p. 1987. lib. bdg. 79.50 (*0-313-25795-7*, TPT/, Greenwood Pr) Greenwood.

Pursuit of True Strength see True Strength: Hercules & Amazon: Africa's Native Heroes, Yesterday, Today & Tomorrow

Pursuit of Truth. Willard V. Quine. 128p. 1990. 24.95 (*0-674-73950-7*) HUP.

Pursuit of Truth. rev. ed. Willard V. Quine. LC 92-5606. 128p. (C). 1992. pap. text 14.50 (*0-674-73951-5*) HUP.

Pursuit of Urdu Literature: A Select History. Ralph Russell. LC 92-12331. 320p. (C). 1993. text 65.00 (*1-85649-028-9*, Pub. by Zed Books) St Martin.

Pursuit of Victory: From Napoleon to Saddam Hussein. Brian Bond. (Illus.). 272p. (C). 1996. 29.95 (*0-19-820497-3*) OUP.

Pursuit of Victory: From Napoleon to Saddam Hussein. Brian Bond. (Illus.). 250p. 1998. reprint ed. pap. text 19.95 (*0-19-820735-2*) OUP.

Pursuit of Virtue: A Study of Order in "la Nouvelle Heloise" Jeanne T. Fuchs. LC 91-31073. (Reading Plus Ser.: Vol. 10). XII, 208p. (C). 1994. text 41.95 (*0-8204-1715-7*) P Lang Pubng.

Pursuit of Wealth: The Incredible Story of Money Throughout the Ages. Robert Sobel. LC 99-23274. 347p. 1999. 27.95 (*0-07-059613-1*) McGraw.

Pursuit of William Rounseville Alger: An Experiment in Biography. Gary Scharnhorst. LC 89-12788. (Studies in New England Thought & Literature: Vol. 2). 272p. 1990. lib. bdg. 89.95 (*0-88946-576-2*) E Mellen.

Pursuit of Wisdom & Other Works. Ed. & Tr. by James Walsh. (Classics of Western Spirituality Ser.: Vol. 58). 384p. 1988. pap. 22.95 (*0-8091-2972-8*) Paulist Pr.

Pursuit of Wow! Every Person's Guide to Topsy-Turvy Times. Tom Peters. 349p. 1995. pap. 15.00 (*0-679-75555-1*) Vin Bks.

Pursuit to Appomattox: The Last Battles see Civil War Series

Pursuit to Appomattox: The Last Battles. Jerry Korn & Time-Life Books Editors. Ed. by Thomas Flaherty. (Civil War Ser.). 176p. 1989. lib. bdg. write for info. (*0-8094-4789-4*) Time-Life.

Pursuits. Carla S. Harvey. 244p. 1997. pap. 13.99 (*1-889210-02-1*) A Writ Pl.

Pursuits Amateur & Academic: The Selected Prose of E. J. Pratt. E. J. Pratt. (Collected Works of E. J. Pratt). 373p. 1995. text 50.00 (*0-8020-2907-8*) U of Toronto Pr.

Pursuits of Happiness: The Hollywood Comedy of Remarriages. Stanley Cavell. (Harvard Film Studies). 296p. 1984. pap. text 16.95 (*0-674-73906-X*) HUP.

Pursuits of Happiness: The Social Development of Early Modern British Colonies & the Formation of American Culture. Jack P. Greene. LC 88-5908. xvii, 284p. (C). 1988. pap. 18.95 (*0-8078-4227-3*) U of NC Pr.

Pursuits of Leisure & Other Essays. Ian Z. Malcolm. LC 68-20317. (Essay Index Reprint Ser.). 1977. reprint ed. 17.95 (*0-8369-0671-3*) Ayer.

Pursuits of Quality: A Guide for Lawyers. Andrew Lockley. 150p. 1993. 80.00 (*0-85459-751-4*, Pub. by Tolley Pubng) St Mut.

Pursuits of Reason: Essays in Honor of Stanley Cavel. Ed. by Ted Cohen et al. (Philosophical Inquiries Ser.: No. 2). 412p. (C). 1992. text 45.00 (*0-89672-266-X*) Tex Tech Univ Pr.

PURSUT LIBRTY V1 AMER PK. 3rd ed. Wilson. (C). 1996. 49.00 (*0-321-80163-6*) Addison-Wesley.

Purt' Near One Hundred Uses for a Texas Cow Chip. Ralph Sweet. (Illus.). 80p. 1982. pap. 4.95 (*0-9618888-1-4*) Anglo-Am TX.

Purushartha-Siddhyupaya (Jaina-Pravachana-Rahasya-Kosha) Ed. by Swami Amristaswarupananda & Ajit Prasada. LC 73-3838. (Sacred Books of the Jainas: No. 4). reprint ed. 34.50 (*0-404-57704-0*) AMS Pr.

Purusottamadeva as Grammarian. Narendra K. Dash. (C). 1991. 22.00 (*0-685-56362-6*, Pub. by Agam) S Asia.

Purva-Mimamsa-Sutras of Jaimini. Jaimini. Tr. & Comment by Ganganath Jha. LC 73-3797. (Sacred Books of the Hindus: No. 10). reprint ed. 55.00 (*0-404-57810-1*) AMS Pr.

Purveyor of Enchantment. Marika Cobbold. LC 97-32201. 240p. 1997. text 22.95 (*0-312-18160-4*) St Martin.

***Purveyor of Enchantment.** Marika Cobbold. 2000. 27.95 (*0-593-04076-7*, Pub. by Transworld Publishers Ltd); pap. 12.95 (*0-552-99687-4*, Pub. by Transworld Publishers Ltd) Trafalgar.

Purveyor of Enchantment. large type ed. Marika Cobbold. LC 98-12007. 277p. 1998. 25.95 (*0-7838-0122-X*, G K Hall & Co) Mac Lib Ref.

***Purview Of Wesley's Theology.** Howard Alexander Slaatte. LC 00-41180. 2000. write for info. (*0-7618-1770-0*) U Pr of Amer.

***Purviews: Poems from Hollywood.** Mark Dunster. 11p. 1999. pap. 5.00 (*0-89642-927-X*) Linden Pubs.

Pusan & Sarasvati. J. Gonda. (Verhandelingen der Koninklijke Nederlandse Akademie van Wetenschappen, Afd. Letterkunde, Nieuwe Reeks Ser.: No. 127). 176p. 1985. pap. 68.75 (*0-444-85610-2*) Elsevier.

Pusan Perimeter, Korea, 1950: An Annotated Bibliography, 11. Paul M. Edwards, Jr. LC 93-2586. (Bibliographies of Battles & Leaders Ser.: No. 11). 160p. 1993. lib. bdg. 65.00 (*0-313-28740-6*, Greenwood Pr) Greenwood.

Push. Sapphire. 179p. 1996. 20.00 (*0-679-44626-5*) Random.

Push. Sapphire. 1997. pap. 11.00 (*0-679-76675-8*) Vin Bks.

Push a Button, Pull a String. John W. Prehn. iv, 96p. (Orig.). 1996. pap. 12.00 (*0-9652983-0-2*) J W Prehn.

Push & Pull. Susan Canizares. LC 98-53316. (Science Emergent Readers Ser.). 1999. pap. 10.01 (*0-439-08119-X*) Scholastic Inc.

Push & Pull. Maria Gordon. (Simple Science Ser.). (Illus.). 32p. (J). (ps-4). 1995. lib. bdg. 19.97 (*1-56847-458-X*) Raintree Steck-V.

Push & Pull. Brenda Parkes. Ed. by Jennifer Mooney. (Newbridge Links Ser.). 8p. (J). (gr. k up). 1997. pap. 2.75 (*1-56784-904-0*) Newbridge Educ.

***Push & Pull.** Lola M. Schaefer. 1999. 13.25 (*0-516-21923-5*) Capstone Pr.

Push & Pull. Lola M. Schaefer. LC 99-19416. (Way Things Move Ser.). 24p. (J). 2000. 13.25 (*0-7368-0396-3*, Pebble Bks) Capstone Pr.

Push & Pull: Photo Card Set. Marcia S. Freeman. Ed. by Susan Evento. (Early Science Ser.). (Illus.). (J). (ps-2). 1997. pap. text 14.95 (*1-56784-389-1*) Newbridge Educ.

Push & Pull: Theme Pack. Ed. by Susan Evento. (Early Science Ser.). (Illus.). (J). (ps-2). 1997. pap. text 49.95 (*1-56784-394-8*) Newbridge Educ.

Push & Pull of Standards-Based Reform: How Does It Affect Local School Districts & Students with Disabilities? 2nd ed. Suzanne Raber & Virginia Roach. 48p. 1998. pap. 12.00 (*1-58434-036-3*) NASBE.

Push & Shove: Bully & Victim Activity Book. Jim Boulden et al. Ed. by Evelyn M. Ward. (Illus.). 32p. (Orig.). (J). (gr. 2-6). 1994. pap. 5.95 (*1-878076-37-X*) Boulden Pub.

***Push Back the Darkness: The Story of Don Stamps & the Full Life Study Bible.** 2nd ed. Bob Burke & David A. Womack. (Illus.). 261p. 2000. reprint ed. pap. write for info. (*0-7361-0168-3*) Life Pubs Intl.

Push Back the Night: A Clergyman-Columnist's Views on the Relevance of Religion in the Nineties. Milton H. Keene. LC 92-20659. 191p. 1993. 16.75 (*0-930950-39-9*); pap. 10.75 (*0-930950-40-2*) Nopoly Pr.

Push Cart War. Jan Merrill. (J). 1996. pap. 5.99 (*0-440-91157-5*) BDD Bks Young Read.

Push-Hands: The Handbook for Tai Chi Practice with a Partner. Herman Kauz. LC 96-30615. (Illus.). 176p. 1997. 24.95 (*0-87951-754-9*, Pub. by Overlook Pr) Penguin Putnam.

Push It! Young Adults Engage the Bible. Ed. by Sidney D. Fowler. 160p. 1999. pap. 9.95 (*0-8298-1342-X*) Pilgrim OH.

Push Me, Pull Me. Sandra Chick. (Livewire Ser.). 128p. (J). (gr. 6-9). pap. 5.95 (*0-7043-4901-9*, Pub. by Womens Press) Trafalgar.

Push or Pull: Big Book. Ed. by Susan Evento. (Early Science Ser.). 16p. (J). (ps-2). 1997. pap. 16.95 (*1-56784-318-2*) Newbridge Educ.

Push or Pull: Mini Book. Ed. by Susan Evento. (Early Science Ser.). 16p. (J). (ps-2). 1997. pap. 16.95 (*1-56784-343-3*) Newbridge Educ.

Push ups & Razor Blades. Blacky Hix. 50p. (Orig.). 1988. pap. 8.00 (*1-885466-02-1*) Smoke The Soul.

Pushbutton Fantasies: Critical Perspectives on Videotex & Information Technology. Vincent Mosco. Ed. by Melvin J. Voigt. LC 82-11601. (Communication & Information Science Ser.). 240p. (C). 1982. pap. 39.50 (*0-89391-132-1*); text 73.25 (*0-89391-125-9*) Ablx Pub.

Pushcart Book of Essays. Anthony Brandt. 30.00 (*1-888889-24-1*, Pub. by Pushcart Pr) Norton.

Pushcart Book of Short Stories. Bill Henderson. 30.00 (*1-888889-23-3*, Pub. by Pushcart Pr) Norton.

Pushcart Peddlers - The Flatulist & Other Plays. Murray Schisgal. 1979. pap. 5.25 (*0-8222-0923-3*) Dramatists Play.

***Pushcart Prize Vol. XXIV: The Best of the Small Presses.** Bill Henderson. 2000. pap. 15.00 (*1-888889-21-7*, Pub. by Pushcart Pr) Norton.

Pushcart Prize XVIII: Best of the Small Presses, 1993-94 Edition. Bill Henderson. 1993. 29.00 (*0-916366-89-8*, Pub. by Pushcart Pr) Norton.

Pushcart Prize XI: Best of the Small Presses, 1986-87 Edition. Ed. by Bill Henderson. LC 76-58675. 550p. 1986. 26.00 (*0-916366-39-1*, Pub. by Pushcart Pr) Norton.

Pushcart Prize XV: Best of the Small Presses, 1990-91 Edition. Ed. by Bill Henderson. LC 76-58675. 580p. 1990. 27.95 (*0-916366-65-0*, Pub. by Pushcart Pr) Norton.

Pushcart Prize XIV: Best of the Small Presses, 1989-90. Ed. by Bill Henderson. LC 76-58675. 520p. 1989. 28.00 (*0-916366-58-8*, Pub. by Pushcart Pr) Norton.

Pushcart Prize, No. XVI: Best of the Small Presses (1991-92 Edition) Ed. by Bill Henderson. LC 76-58675. 1991. 28.50 (*0-916366-71-5*, Pub. by Pushcart Pr) Norton.

Pushcart Prize X: Best of the Small Presses. Ed. by Bill Henderson. LC 76-58675. 635p. 1996. 29.50 (*0-614-15981-4*) Pushcart Pr.

Pushcart Prize X: Best of the Small Presses, 1985-86 Edition. Ed. by Bill Henderson. LC 76-58675. 500p. 1985. 25.00 (*0-916366-37-5*, Pub. by Pushcart Pr) Norton.

Pushcart Prize Vol. XXI: Best of the Small Presses, 1996. 21st ed. Ed. by Bill Henderson. 600p. 1995. pap. 15.00 (*1-888889-00-4*, Pub. by Pushcart Pr) Norton.

Purshcart Prize Vol. XXII: Best of the Small Presses, 1997. Ed. by Bill Henderson. LC 76-58675. 675p. 1996. 29.50 (*1-888889-01-2*, Pub. by Pushcart Pr); pap. 15.00 (*1-888889-07-1*, Pub. by Pushcart Pr) Norton.

Pushcart Prize XIII: Best of the Small Presses, 1988-1989 Edition. Ed. by Bill Henderson. LC 76-58675. 500p. 1988. 27.95 (*0-916366-52-9*, Pub. by Pushcart Pr) Norton.

Pushcart Prize XII: Best of the Small Presses, 1987-88 Edition. Ed. by Bill Henderson. LC 76-58675. 500p. 1987. 28.00 (*0-916366-45-6*, Pub. by Pushcart Pr) Norton.

Pushcart Prize XX: Best of the Small Presses. Ed. by Bill Henderson & Pushcart Prize Editors. 570p. 1995. 29.50 (*0-916366-99-5*, Pub. by Pushcart Pr) Norton.

Pushcart Prize XX Vol. 20: Best of the Small Presses. Bill Henderson. Ed. by Pushcart Prize Editors et al. 570p. 1996. pap. 16.00 (*0-916366-63-4*, Pub. by Pushcart Pr) Norton.

Pushcart Prize XXI: Best of the Small Presses. Ed. by Bill Henderson. 600p. 1995. 29.50 (*0-916366-96-0*, Pub. by Pushcart Pr) Norton.

Pushcart Prize XXIII: Best of the Small Presses. Ed. by Bill Henderson & Pushcart Prize Editors. LC 76-58675. 600p. 1998. 29.50 (*1-888889-09-8*, Pub. by Pushcart Pr) Norton.

***Pushcart Prize: Best of the Small Presses, 1999, Vol. 99.** 23rd ed. Bill Henderson. 606p. 1999. pap. 15.00 (*1-888889-13-6*, Pub. by Pushcart Pr) Norton.

***Pushcart Prize 2000: Best of the Small Presses.** Bill Henderson. 620p. 1999. text 29.50 (*1-888889-19-5*, Pub. by Pushcart Pr) Norton.

Pushcart Prize XIX: Best of the Small Presses, 1994-95 Edition. Bill Henderson. 1994. 29.50 (*0-916366-92-8*, Pub. by Pushcart Pr) Norton.

Pushcart Prize XIX: Best of the Small Presses, 1994-95 Edition. Ed. by Pushcart Prize Staff & Bill Henderson. 580p. 1995. pap. 15.00 (*0-916366-98-7*, Pub. by Pushcart Pr) Norton.

Pushcart Prize XVII: Best of the Small Presses (1992-93 Edition) Ed. by Bill Henderson. LC 76-58675. 600p. 1992. 29.50 (*0-916366-77-4*, Pub. by Pushcart Pr) Norton.

Pushcart War. Gregory A. Falls. (J). (gr. 4 up). 1985. pap. 6.00 (*0-87602-248-4*) Anchorage.

Pushcart War. Jean Merrill. 224p. (J). 1978. pap. 4.99 (*0-440-47147-8*, YB BDD) BDD Bks Young Read.

Pushcart War. Jean Merrill. (J). 1964. 10.09 (*0-606-01278-8*, Pub. by Turtleback) Demco.

Pushcart War: A Study Guide. Norma Marsh. (Novel-Ties Ser.). (J). (gr. 5-7). 1988. pap. text, teacher ed., student ed. 15.95 (*0-88122-095-7*) Lrn Links.

Pushcart War Activity Book. Bronson & Sims. 160p. 1997. spiral bd. 22.95 (*0-7872-3570-9*) Kendall-Hunt.

***Pushcarts & Stalls: The Soulard Market History Cookbook.** Suzanne Corbett. (Illus.). 235p. 1999. pap. 16.95 (*0-911921-38-9*, 1-300-04) Palmerston & Reed.

Pushcart's Complete Rotten Reviews & Rejections: A History of Insult, a Solace to Writers. Ed. by Bill Henderson & Andre Bernard. 300p. (C). 1998. pap. 15.00 (*1-888889-04-7*, Pub. by Pushcart Pr) Norton.

Pushed Back to Strength. Gloria Wade-Gayles. 288p. 1995. pap. 11.00 (*0-380-72426-X*, Avon Bks) Morrow Avon.

Pushed to the Limit. Patricia Rosemoor. (Intrigue Ser.: No. 161). 1991. per. 2.75 (*0-373-22161-4*) Harlequin Bks.

***Pusher & the Sufferer: An Unsentimental Reading of Moby Dick.** Suzanne K. Steinmetz. LC 00-44236. (Studies in Major Literary Authors Ser.). 2000. write for info. (*0-8153-3959-3*) Garland.

Pushes & Pulls. Terry Jennings. (Find Out About Bks.). (Illus.). (J). 8.95 (*0-563-37467-5*, BBC-Parkwest) Parkwest Pubns.

Pushing & Pulling. Gary Gibson. (Science for Fun Ser.). (Illus.). 32p. (J). (gr. 2-4). 1995. lib. bdg. 20.90 (*1-56294-630-7*, Copper Beech Bks) Millbrook Pr.

Pushing & Pulling. Gary Gibson. (Science for Fun Ser.). (Illus.). 32p. (J). (gr. 2-4). 1996. pap. 4.95 (*0-7613-0461-4*, Copper Beech Bks) Millbrook Pr.

Pushing & Pulling. Gary Gibson. (Science for Fun Ser.). 1995. 10.15 (*0-606-09830-5*, Pub. by Turtleback) Demco.

Pushing Back The Boundaries: The European Union & Central & Eastern Europe. Ed. by Mike Mannin. 352p. 1999. 69.95 (*0-7190-5214-9*, Pub. by Manchester Univ Pr) St Martin.

Pushing Back The Boundaries: The European Union & Central & Eastern Europe. Mike Mannin. (Illus.). 352p. 1999. pap. text 29.95 (*0-7190-5215-7*, Pub. by Manchester Univ Pr) St Martin.

Pushing Boundaries: Language & Culture in a Mexicano Community. Olga A. Vasquez et al. (Illus.). 237p. (C). 1994. text 49.95 (*0-521-41935-2*) Cambridge U Pr.

Pushing Electrons. 3rd ed. Weeks. LC 97-68076. 205p. 1997. pap. text 20.00 (*0-03-020693-6*, Pub. by SCP) Harcourt.

Pushing Fifty is Exercise Enough. Lewis Grizzard. 1993. 18.00 (*0-679-40686-7*) Villard Books.

Pushing Forty: A for Better or for Worse Collection. Lynn Johnston. (Illus.). 128p. (Orig.). 1988. pap. 8.95 (*0-8362-1807-8*) Andrews & McMeel.

Pushing Murder. large type ed. Eleanor Boylan. LC 93-33652. 221p. 1994. lib. bdg. 20.95 (*0-7862-0105-3*) Thorndike Pr.

Pushing Sexual Limits. Bakos. 1995. mass mkt. write for info. (*0-312-95424-7*) St Martin.

Pushing the Bear. 2nd ed. Diane Glancy. (C). 1998. pap. 12.00 (*0-15-600544-1*) Harcourt.

Pushing the Envelope: Airplanes of the Jet Age. Harold Rabinowitz. LC 98-4132. 1998. 24.98 (*1-56799-596-9*, MetroBooks) M Friedman Pub Grp Inc.

Pushing the Envelope: All the Way to the Top. Harvey Mackay. LC 98-45526. 418p. 1999. 24.95 (*0-345-43295-9*) Ballantine Pub Grp.

***Pushing the Envelope: All the Way to the Top.** Harvey Mackay. 368p. 2000. pap. 16.00 (*0-449-00669-7*, Ballantine) Ballantine Pub Grp.

Pushing the Envelope: The American Aircraft Industry. Donald M. Pattillo. LC 97-45390. (Illus.). 484p. (C). 1998. text 49.50 (*0-472-10869-7*, 10869) U of Mich Pr.

***Pushing the Envelope: The American Aircraft Industry.** Donald M. Pattillo. (Illus.). 484p. 2000. pap. text 27.95 (*0-472-08671-5*, 08671) U of Mich Pr.

Pushing the Envelope: What I've Learned in 40 Years of Business. Harvey Mackay. 1999. 24.95 (*0-449-00445-7*) Fawcett.

Pushing the Envelope Vol. 1: New Trends in Direct Marketing. Jerry Danzig. 1994. 45.00 (*0-86636-326-2*) PBC Intl Inc.

Pushing the Horizon: Seventy-Five Years of High Stakes Science & Technology at the Naval Research Laboratory. Ivan Amato. (Illus.). 417p. 1998. boxed set 35.00 (*0-16-049579-2*) USGPO.

Pushing the Limits. Walter Boyne. 27.50 (*0-06-019455-3*); 15.00 (*0-06-093254-6*) HarpC.

***Pushing the Limits.** Melanie Stewart. 128p. 1999. mass mkt. 3.99 (*0-307-23452-5*, Goldn Books) Gldn Bks Pub Co.

***Pushing the Limits: A Nordic Skiing Saga.** Marcus Nash & Scott B. Loomis. (Illus.). 142p. 1999. pap. 14.95 (*0-914339-89-3*) P E Randall Pub.

Pushing the Limits: American Women 1940-1961, Vol. 9. Elaine T. May. (Young Oxford History of Women in the United States Ser.). (Illus.). 144p. (J). 1998. reprint ed. pap. 10.95 (*0-19-512407-3*) OUP.

Pushing the Limits: Disabled Dykes Produce Culture. Ed. by Shelley Tremain. 240p. 1996. pap. 13.95 (*0-88961-218-8*, Pub. by Womens Pr) LPC InBook.

Pushing the Limits: The Female Administrative Aspirant. Sakre K. Edson. LC 87-1893. (SUNY Series, Educational Leadership). 299p. (C). 1988. pap. text 24.95 (*0-88706-557-0*) State U NY Pr.

Pushing the Limits: The Female Administrative Aspirant. Sakre K. Edson. LC 87-1893. (SUNY Series, Educational Leadership). 299p. (C). 1988. text 74.50 (*0-88706-556-2*) State U NY Pr.

Pushing the Limits, Vol. 9, American Women 1940-1961 see Young Oxford History of Women in the United States

Pushing the Numbers in Marketing: A Real-World Guide to Essential Financial Analysis. David L. Rados. LC 91-47643. 200p. 1992. 49.95 (*0-89930-736-1*, RPH, Quorum Bks) Greenwood.

Pushing to the Front. Orison S. Marden. 1995. reprint ed. lib. bdg. 39.95 (*1-56849-620-6*) Buccaneer Bks.

Pushing to the Front, 2 vols., Set. Orison S. Marden. 873p. 1997. pap. 65.00 (*0-89540-333-1*, SB-333) Sun Pub.

Pushing to the Front, Vol. I. Orison S. Marden. 432p. 1997. pap. 40.00 (*0-89540-331-5*, SB-331) Sun Pub.

Pushing to the Front, Vol. II. Orison S. Marden. 441p. 1997. pap. 40.00 (*0-89540-332-3*, SB-332) Sun Pub.

Pushing up the Sky: Elevating Your Thinking, Learning & Communicating. Lee Donaldson & Jonathan Rand. 186p. 1997. pap. 12.95 (*0-9658105-1-8*) Candlewick Press.

Pushing up the Sky: Seven Native American Plays for Children. Joseph Bruchac. LC 98-20483. (Illus.). 96p. (J). (gr. 1-5). 2000. 17.99 (*0-8037-2168-4*, Dial Yng Read) Peng Put Young Read.

Pushkin. T. J. Binyon. 1999. pap. 11.95 (*0-14-011152-2*, Viking); pap. 23.00 (*0-670-82278-7*) Viking Penguin.

Pushkin. Dimitry S. Mirsky. LC 74-34587. (Studies in Russian Literature & Life: No. 100). 1974. lib. bdg. 75.00 (*0-8383-1998-X*) M S G Haskell Hse.

Pushkin. Martha W. Beckwith et al. LC 75-168509. (Black Heritage Library Collection). 1977. reprint ed. 27.95 (*0-8369-8862-0*) Ayer.

Pushkin. U. S. S. R. Society for Cultural Relations with Fo. LC 72-173612. (Black Heritage Library Collection). 1977. reprint ed. 32.95 (*0-8369-8904-X*) Ayer.

Pushkin: A Biography. Elaine Feinstein. LC 98-38981. (Illus.). 336p. 1998. 29.95 (*0-88001-674-4*) HarpC.

***Pushkin: A Biography.** Elaine Feinstein. LC 00-23262. 336p. 2000. pap. 14.00 (*0-06-095655-0*, Ecco Press) HarperTrade.

Pushkin: A Concordance to the Poetry, 2 vols., Set. J. Thomas Shaw. x, 1300p. 1985. 99.95 (*0-89357-130-X*) Slavica.

Pushkin: Boris Godunov. Ed. by Victor Terras. (Russian Texts Ser.). (RUS.). 1995. pap. 20.95 (*1-85399-467-7*, Pub. by Brist Class Pr) Focus Pub-R Pullins.

Pushkin: Eugene Onegin (Eugenii Onegin) Aleksandr Pushkin. (Bristol Russian Texts Ser.). (RUS.). 282p. (C). 1993. reprint ed. pap. 20.95 (*1-85399-396-4*, Pub. by Brist Class Pr) Focus Pub-R Pullins.

Pushkin: Literature & Social Ideas. Sam N. Driver. 192p. 1989. text 44.00 (*0-231-06848-4*) Col U Pr.

Pushkin: Little Tragedies (Malen'kie Tragedii) Ed. by V. Terras. (Bristol Russian Texts Ser.). (RUS.). 142p. 1991. pap. 18.95 (*1-85399-269-0*, Pub. by Brist Class Pr) Focus Pub-R Pullins.

Pushkin: Queen of Spades (Pikovaya Dama) Ed. by J. Forsyth. (Bristol Russian Texts Ser.). (RUS.). 132p. 1992. pap. 16.95 (*1-85399-313-1*, Pub. by Brist Class Pr) Focus Pub-R Pullins.

Pushkin: Tales of the Late Ivan Petrovich Belkin (Povesti Pokoinogo Ivana Petrovicha Belkina) Ed. by A. D. Briggs & Boris O. Unbegaun. (Russian Texts Ser.). (RUS.). 167p. 1994. pap. 20.95 (*1-85399-402-2*, Pub. by Brist Class Pr) Focus Pub-R Pullins.

Pushkin: The Bronze Horseman. Ed. by T. E. Little. (Bristol Russian Texts Ser.). (RUS.). 80p. (C). 1991. reprint ed. pap. 16.95 (*1-85399-245-3*, Pub. by Brist Class Pr) Focus Pub-R Pullins.

Pushkin - Eugene Onegin. Aleksandr Pushkin. Tr. & Intro. by Walter Arndt. 224p. 1993. reprint ed. pap. 12.95 (*0-87501-106-3*) Ardis Pubs.

Pushkin - Eugene Onegin. unabridged ed. Aleksandr Pushkin. (World Classic Literature Ser.). (RUS.). pap. 6.95 (*2-87714-256-6*, Pub. by Bookking Intl) Distribks Inc.

Pushkin & Romantic Fashion: Fragment, Elegy, Orient & Irony. Monika Greenleaf. LC 94-15593. xiii , 412p. 1995. 55.00 (*0-8047-2287-0*) Stanford U Pr.

Pushkin & Romantic Fashion: Fragment, Elegy, Orient & Irony. Monkia Greenleaf. 1996. pap. 17.95 (*0-8047-2799-6*) Stanford U Pr.

Pushkin & the Creative Process. Brett Cooke. LC 97-32899. 192p. 1998. 49.95 (*0-8130-1561-8*) U Press Fla.

Pushkin Centennial Meeting, February 11, 1937: Addresses & Translations of Songs. Alexander Petrunkevitch et al. (Connecticut Academy of Arts & Sciences Ser., Trans.: Vol. 33). 1937. pap. 49.50 (*0-685-22915-7*) Elliots Bks.

Pushkin House. Andrei Bitov. Tr. by Susan Brownsberger from RUS. (Contemporary Russian Prose Ser.). 414p. 1990. pap. 13.95 (*0-679-73009-5*) Vin Bks.

Pushkin House. Andrei Bitov. Tr. by Susan Brownsberger from RUS. LC 98-23360. 371p. 1998. reprint ed. pap. 13.95 (*1-56478-200-X*) Dalkey Arch.

***Pushkin I Poety Ego Vremeni.** Vladislav Khodasevich. Ed. by Robert Hughes. (Modern Russian Literature & Culture: Vol. 42). (RUS., Illus.). 489p. 1999. pap. 45.00 (*1-57201-055-X*) Berkeley Slavic.

Pushkin Meets the Bundle. Harriet Ziefert. LC 96-37748. (Illus.). 40p. (J). (gr. k-2). 1998. 16.00 (*0-689-81413-5*) Atheneum Yung Read.

***Pushkin Minds the Bundle.** Harriet Ziefert. LC 99-27578. (Illus.). 32p. (J). 2000. 16.00 (*0-689-83216-8*, Anne Schwartz) Atheneum Yung Read.

Pushkin Museum of Fine Arts, Moscow: Painting. Irina Antonova. (Illus.). 184p. (C). 1988. text 90.00 (*0-569-09109-8*, Pub. by Collets) St Mut.

Pushkin on Literature. Aleksandr Pushkin. Ed. & Tr. by Tatiana Wolff. LC 98-16799. (Studies in Russian Literature & Theory). 592p. 1998. pap. text 24.95 (*0-8101-1615-4*) Northwestern U Pr.

Pushkin, Palaces & Parks. Vera Lemus. (Illus.). 170p. (C). 1984. 250.00 (*0-7855-6499-3*, Pub. by Collets) St Mut.

Pushkin State Museum of Fine Arts. Irina Antonova. (FRE & RUS.). 1981. 116.00 (*0-7855-1655-7*) St Mut.

Pushkin Threefold: Narrative, Lyric, Polemic & Ribald Verse, the Originals with Linear & Metric Translations. 2nd ed. Aleksandr Pushkin. Tr. & Intro. by Walter Arndt. 455p. 1993. reprint ed. pap. 18.95 (*0-87501-107-1*) Ardis Pubs.

Pushkin's Bronze Horseman: The Story of a Masterpiece, Vol. 1--1. Waclaw Lednicki. LC 78-5547. (Univ. of California Publications Slavis Studies: Vol. 1). 163p. 1978. lib. bdg. 35.00 (*0-313-20482-9*, LEPB, Greenwood Pr) Greenwood.

Pushkin's Button. Serena Vitale. Tr. by Ann Goldstein & John Rothschild from ITA. LC 97-39082. 352p. 1999. 30.00 (*0-374-23935-5*) FS&G.

Pushkin's Drawings: Risunki Pushkina. 446p. 1983. 55.00 (*0-7855-1661-1*) St Mut.

Pushkin's Historical Imagination. Svetlana Evdokimova. LC 98-9228. (Russian Literature & Thought Ser.). 1998. 35.00 (*0-300-07023-3*) Yale U Pr.

Pushkin's I. P. Belkin. Andrej Kodjak. 112p. 1979. pap. 14.95 (*0-89357-057-5*) Slavica.

Pushkin's Poetics of the Unexpected: The Nonrhymed Lines in the Rhymed Poetry & the Rhymed Lines in the Nonrhymed Poetry. J. Thomas Shaw. 369p. 1994. 24.95 (*0-89357-245-4*) Slavica.

Pushkin's Prose. Abram Lezhnev. Orig. Title: Proza Pushkina. 300p. 27.95 (*0-88233-627-4*) Ardis Pubs.

Pushkin's Prose. Abram Lezhnev. Orig. Title: Proza Pushkina. 225p. 1983. pap. 9.95 (*0-88233-628-2*) Ardis Pubs.

Pushkin's Prose. Abram Lezhnev. Tr. by Roberta Reeder. Orig. Title: Proza Pushkina. 225p. 1986. pap. 45.00 (*0-7855-0906-2*) St Mut.

P

An Asterisk (*) at the beginning of an entry indicates that the title is appearing for the first time.

Pushkin's Tatiana. Olga Peters Hasty. LC 99-6271. (Publications of the Center for Pushkin Studies). 296p. 1999. pap. text 19.95 (*0-299-16404-7*) U of Wis Pr.

***Pushkin's Tatiana.** Olga Peters Hasty. LC 99-6271. (Wisconsin Center for Pushkin Studies Ser.). 296p. 1999. text 45.00 (*0-299-16400-4*) U of Wis Pr.

Pushkin's the Queen of Spades: Critical Study. N. Cornwell. (Critical Studies in Russian Literature Ser.). 100p. 1993. pap. 14.95 (*1-85399-342-5*, Pub. by Brist Class Pr) Focus Pub-R Pullins.

Puskas on Puskas: The Life & Times of a Footballing Legend. Ed. by Rogan Taylor & Klara Jamrich. (Illus.). 242p. 1997. 29.95 (*1-86105-083-6*, Robson-Parkwest) Parkwest Pubns.

Puskin & His Sculptural Myth. Roman Jakobson. Ed. & Tr. by John Burbank from CZE. (De Proprietatibus Litterarum, Ser. Practica: No. 116). (Illus.). 88p. (Orig.). 1975. pap. text 45.40 (*90-279-3426-6*) Mouton.

Puskin Today. Ed. by David M. Bethea. LC 92-7861. 276p. 1993. 31.50 (*0-253-31161-6*) Ind U Pr.

Puss in Books. Ed. by Maria Polushkin Robbins. LC 97-22656. 1998. 19.00 (*0-88001-588-8*) HarpC.

Puss in Boots see Gato con Botas

Puss in Boots. (ARA., Illus.). 52p. (J). (gr. 2-6). 1987. 4.95 (*0-86685-220-4*) Intl Bk Ctr.

Puss in Boots. (J). 1999. per. 10.95 (*0-689-80682-5*, Rabbit Ears) Litle Simon.

Puss in Boots. (Fun-to-Read Fairy Tales Series III). (Illus.). 24p. (J). (gr. k-3). 1993. pap. 2.50 (*1-56144-297-6*, Honey Bear Bks) Modern Pub NYC.

Puss in Boots. Nicola Baxter. (Favorite Tales Ser.). (Illus.). 28p. (J). 1994. 2.99 (*0-7214-5455-0*, Ladybrd) Penguin Putnam.

Puss in Boots. Alix Berenzy. (J). 1995. 14.95 (*0-8050-1284-2*) H Holt & Co.

Puss in Boots. Moira Butterfield. LC 97-27966. (Playtales Ser.). (J). 1998. 19.92 (*1-57572-649-1*) Heinemann Lib.

Puss in Boots. Lorinda B. Cauley. LC 86-7629. (Illus.). 32p. (J). (ps-3). 1988. pap. 3.95 (*0-15-264228-5*, Harcourt Child Bks) Harcourt.

Puss in Boots. Illus. by Debbie Dieneman. 32p. (J). (ps-3). 1992. 6.95 (*0-8362-4932-1*) Andrews & McMeel.

Puss in Boots. Paul Galdone. LC 75-25505. 32p. (J). (gr. k-3). 1983. pap. 6.95 (*0-89919-192-4*, Clarion Bks) HM.

Puss in Boots. Paul Galdone. LC 75-25505. (Carry-Along Book & Cassette Favorites Ser.). (J). (ps-3). 1987. 9.95 incl. audio (*0-89919-682-9*, 111505) Ticknor & Flds Bks Yng Read.

Puss in Boots. J. Sainsbury's Pure Tea Staff. (Illus.). 12p. (Orig.). (J). 1993. pap. text 1.00 (*0-486-27800-X*) Dover.

Puss in Boots. Lincoln Kirstein. LC 91-19352. 1992. 12.15 (*0-606-06685-3*, Pub. by Turtleback) Demco.

Puss in Boots. Ed McBain, pseud. 1988. mass mkt. 4.95 (*0-445-40621-6*, Pub. by Warner Bks) Little.

Puss in Boots. Ed McBain, pseud. 224p. 1994. mass mkt. 5.99 (*0-446-60135-7*, Pub. by Warner Bks) Little.

Puss in Boots. Eric Metaxas. LC 92-7789. (We All Have Tales Ser.). (Illus.). 36p. (J). (gr. k-3). 1992. 19.95 incl. audio (*0-88708-286-6*, Rabbit Ears) Litle Simon.

Puss in Boots. Eric Metaxas. LC 92-7789. (We All Have Tales Ser.). (Illus.). 40p. (J). (ps-3). 1992. 14.95 (*0-88708-285-8*, Rabbit Ears) Litle Simon.

***Puss in Boots.** Charles Perrault. Tr. by Anthea Bell from GER. LC 99-17366. (Illus.). 32p. (J). (gr. k-3). 1999. lib. bdg. 15.88 (*0-7358-1159-8*, Pub. by North-South Bks NYC) Chronicle Bks.

Puss in Boots. Charles Perrault. Tr. by Malcolm Arthur. (Illus.). 32p. (J). 1990. 16.00 (*0-374-36160-6*) FS&G.

Puss in Boots. Charles Perrault. (Illus.). 32p. (J). (ps up). 1998. pap. 8.95 (*0-374-46034-5*) FS&G.

Puss in Boots. Charles Perrault. Tr. by Anthea Bell. LC 96-15963. (Illus.). 48p. (J). (gr. k-3). 1996. lib. bdg. 15.88 (*1-55858-643-1*, Pub. by North-South Bks NYC) Chronicle Bks.

***Puss in Boots.** Charles Perrault. Tr. by Anthea Bell from FRE. LC 99-17366. (Illus.). 32p. (J). (gr. k-3). 1999. 15.95 (*0-7358-1158-X*, Pub. by North-South Bks NYC) Chronicle Bks.

Puss in Boots. Charles Perrault. LC 78-18061. (Illus.). 32p. (J). (gr. k-3). 1997. pap. 3.95 (*0-89375-108-1*) Troll Communs.

Puss in Boots. Maria P. Robbins. (J). 1999. pap. 9.95 (*0-452-27538-5*, Plume) Dutton Plume.

Puss In Boots. Illus. by Alain Vaes. 32p. (J). (gr. k-3). 1994. pap. 7.95 (*0-316-89501-6*) Little.

Puss in Boots: A Fairy Tale by Perrault. Charles Perrault. LC 97-23047. (Little Pebbles Ser.). (Illus.). 32p. (J). (ps-1). 1999. 6.95 (*0-7892-0422-3*, Abbeville Kids) Abbeville Pr.

Puss in Boots: A One-Act Play. Sally Netzel. (Illus.). 32p. (J). (gr. k up). 1979. pap. 3.50 (*0-88680-157-5*) I E Clark.

Puss in Boots: (A Participation Play) Moses Goldberg. (J). 1992. pap. 6.00 (*0-87602-299-9*) Anchorage.

Puss in Boots: Miniature Play. Madge Miller. 37p. (J). 1954. 6.00 (*0-87602-184-4*) Anchorage.

Puss in Boots, Toads & Diamonds, The Donkey, the Table, & the Stick, The Three Wishes. Sarah Hayes. LC 86-8878. (Read Me a Story Ser.). (Illus.). Date not set. write for info. (*0-517-61552-5*) Derrydale.

***Puss in Cowboy Boots.** Jan Huling & Phil Huling. LC 99-14498. (J). 2000. write for info. (*0-689-83119-6*) S&S Childrens.

Puss 'n' Boots see Chat Botte

Puss 'n Boots. (FRE.). (J). (gr. k-3). 9.95 (*0-685-28440-9*) Fr & Eur.

***Puss-N-Boots.** (Penguin Young Reader Ser.). (C). 2000. 8.00 (*0-582-42847-5*) Pearson Educ.

Puss-n-Boots. Claire Jones & Bob Varga. 42p. (J). (gr. k-5). 1995. mass mkt. 4.00 (*1-58193-173-5*) Brown Bag Prods.

***Puss 'n' Boots.** Illus. by Annabel Malak. (Pocketaudio Ser.). 2000. 9.95 incl. audio (*2-921997-85-1*, Pub. by Coffragants) Penton Overseas.

Puss 'n Boots. Illus. by Carme Peris. 32p. (J). (ps-3). 1999. 8.95 (*0-7641-5156-8*) Barron.

Pussey! Daniel Clowes. 64p. 1995. pap. 8.95 (*1-56097-183-5*) Fantagraph Bks.

Pussey! Daniel Clowes. 64p. 1995. 29.95 (*1-56097-186-X*) Fantagraph Bks.

Pussy-Cat & Queen. S & J Products Int., Inc. Staff. (Mother Goose & Then Some Ser.). (Illus.). 16p. (Orig.). (J). (ps). 1995. pap. 5.45 incl. audio (*1-884851-18-5*) S&J Prods.

Pussy Game: The Journey to Pleasure & Power. 54p. (Orig.). 1997. pap. 11.95 (*0-9656006-0-2*, 0606) World View Pub.

Pussy, King of the Pirates. Kathy Acker. 288p. 1997. reprint ed. pap. 12.00 (*0-8021-3484-X*, Grove) Grove-Atltic.

Pussycat Fever. Kathy Acker. (Illus.). 76p. (Orig.). 1995. pap. 7.00 (*1-873176-63-5*) AK Pr Dist.

Pussycat, Pussycat. Annalisa McMorrow. (Illus.). 80p. (J). (ps-k). 1997. pap. 9.95 (*1-57612-008-2*, MM2036) Monday Morning Bks.

Pussycat, Pussycat & Other Rhymes. Ed. by Iona Opie. LC 97-65082. (My Very First Mother Goose Board Bks.). (Illus.). 16p. (J). (ps). 1997. bds. 6.99 (*0-7636-0355-4*) Candlewick Pr.

Pussycat's Christmas. Margaret Wise Brown. LC 93-4424. (Illus.). 32p. (J). (gr. k-4). 1998. pap. 5.95 (*0-06-443466-4*) HarpC.

Pussycat's Christmas. Margaret Wise Brown. LC 93-4424. (Illus.). 32p. (J). (ps-3). 1994. 15.95 (*0-06-023532-2*) HarpC Child Bks.

***Pussycats Everywhere!** Sheila McGraw. (Illus.). 32p. (J). (gr. k-3). 2000. pap. 6.95 (*1-55209-348-4*); lib. bdg. 19.95 (*1-55209-346-8*) Firefly Bks Ltd.

Pussyfoot. Carole Nelson Douglas. (Midnight Louie Mystery Ser.). 304p. 1994. mass mkt. 4.99 (*0-8125-1683-4*, Pub. by Tor Bks) St Martin.

Pussyfooting: Essential Dance Procedures for Cats. Viv Quillin. (Illus.). 96p. 1995. 10.00 (*1-56836-078-9*) Kodansha.

***Pussy's Bow.** Neal Drinnan. 272p. 2000. text 23.95 (*0-312-25255-2*) St Martin.

Put . . . Shoes on His Feet. Arthur B. Chestnut. 240p. 1989. pap. 6.95 (*0-88144-137-6*) Christian Pub.

Put a Book in Their Hands: Whole Language Projects for Beginning Readers. Mary L. Blansett. (Illus.). 128p. (Orig.). (J). (ps). 1992. pap. text 12.95 (*0-86530-151-4*, 197-0) Incentive Pubns.

Put a Fan in Your Hat! Inventions, Contraptions, & Gadgets Kids Can Build. Robert Carrow. LC 96-41247. (Illus.). 160p. (YA). (gr. 5 up). 1996. pap. 14.95 (*0-07-011658-X*, Lrng Triangle) McGraw-Hill Prof.

Put a Frog in Your Pocket: Educational Art Activities for Young Children. Mary L. Blansett & Lorraine Schimminger. (Illus.). 112p. (J). (gr. k-6). 1985. pap. text, student ed. 10.95 (*0-86530-085-2*, IP 85-2) Incentive Pubns.

Put a Smile on Your Face: It's Time to Be Happy. Dee Frances. Date not set. pap. 29.95 (*1-885519-69-9*) DDDD Pubns.

Put a Stop to Auto Theft. Ed. by Jean O'Neil. 12p. 1991. pap. 7.95 (*0-934513-46-5*, R10A) Natl Crime DC.

Put 'Em down, Take 'Em Out: Knife Fighting Techniques from Folsom Prison. Don Pentecost. (Illus.). 64p. 1988. pap. 14.00 (*0-87364-484-0*) Paladin Pr.

Put English to Work. 1997. pap. 49.95 (*0-8092-0793-1*) NTC Contemp Pub Co.

Put English to Work. Contemp Bks Staff. 100p. (J). (gr. 1). 1996. pap., teacher ed. 4.50 (*0-8092-3352-5*) NTC Contemp Pub Co.

Put English to Work. Contemp Bks Staff. 100p. (J). (gr. 2). 1996. pap., teacher ed. 4.50 (*0-8092-3279-0*) NTC Contemp Pub Co.

Put English to Work. Contemp Bks Staff. 100p. (J). (gr. 3). 1996. pap., teacher ed. 4.50 (*0-8092-3295-2*) NTC Contemp Pub Co.

Put English to Work. Contemp Bks Staff. 100p. (J). (gr. 4). 1996. pap., teacher ed. 4.50 (*0-8092-3296-0*) NTC Contemp Pub Co.

Put English to Work. Contemp Bks Staff. 100p. (J). (gr. 5). 1996. pap., teacher ed. 4.50 (*0-8092-3293-6*) NTC Contemp Pub Co.

Put English to Work. Contemp Bks Staff. 100p. (J). (gr. 6). 1996. pap., teacher ed. 4.50 (*0-8092-3294-4*) NTC Contemp Pub Co.

Put English to Work, Bk. 3. Contemp Bks Staff. 100p. 1996. pap. 11.93 (*0-8092-3357-6*) NTC Contemp Pub Co.

Put English to Work, Vol. 1. Contemp Bks Staff. 100p. 1996. pap. 11.93 (*0-8092-3359-2*) NTC Contemp Pub Co.

Put English to Work, Vol. 2. Contemp Bks Staff. 100p. 1996. pap. 11.93 (*0-8092-3358-4*) NTC Contemp Pub Co.

Put English to Work: Literacy Level. 100p. 11.93 (*0-8092-0919-5*); teacher ed. 4.50 (*0-8092-0927-6*) NTC Contemp Pub Co.

Put Hemorrhoids & Constipation Behind You Vol. 1: A Natural Healing Guide for Easy, Quick & Lasting Relief. Ken Yasny. LC 96-70945. (Illus.). 208p. (Orig.). 1997. pap. 14.95 (*1-884820-22-0*) SAFE GOODS.

Put It in Perspective. Marsha Weiser. (Illus.). 54p. Date not set. pap. 10.95 (*1-57377-056-6*, 01988402256) Easl Pubns.

***Put It in the History Book.** Selmer Sam Hatlestad. LC 99-94218. 164p. 1999. pap. write for info. (*1-57579-152-8*) Pine Hill Pr.

Put It in Writing. Albert M. Joseph. LC 97-52954. 280p. 1998. pap. 12.95 (*0-07-039308-7*) McGraw.

Put It in Writing. 4th ed. Albert M. Joseph. LC 86-81013. 114p. 1986. write for info. (*0-911481-02-8*) Intl Writing Inst.

Put It in Writing, Bk. 1. Brian Schenk. (Writing Ser.). (Orig.). 1988. pap. text 5.50 (*0-8428-9717-8*); pap. text, student ed. 3.50 (*0-8428-9720-8*) Cambridge Bk.

Put It in Writing, Bk. 2. Brian Schenk & Laura Daly. (Put It in Writing Ser.). 128p. (Orig.). 1988. pap. text 5.50 (*0-8428-9718-6*) Cambridge Bk.

Put It in Writing, Bk. 3. Ed. by Laura Daly. (Writing Ser.). 1988. student ed. 1.95 (*0-8428-9722-4*) Cambridge Bk.

Put It in Writing: A Way of Life for Three Generations of a New Hampshire Family, Books, Journals & Letters, 1892-1996. Alvah W. Sulloway. LC 98-24213. (Illus.). 666p. 1999. 35.00 (*0-914659-83-9*) Phoenix Pub.

Put It in Writing: Engineering & Scientific Edition. Albert M. Joseph. LC 86-81013. 116p. 1989. write for info. (*0-911481-03-6*) Intl Writing Inst.

Put It in Writing: One-Day Workshop. Albert M. Joseph. 117p. 1989. write for info. (*0-911481-08-7*) Intl Writing Inst.

Put It in Writing: Self-Study Edition. Albert M. Joseph. 164p. 1989. write for info. (*0-911481-05-2*) Intl Writing Inst.

Put It in Writing: Writing Activities for Students of ESL. David Blot & David Davidson. (Illus.). 104p. (Orig.). (C). 1981. mass mkt. 8.50 (*0-8384-2782-0*, Newbury) Heinle & Heinle.

Put It in Writing Guide for Populore Narratives. Melinda J. St. Louis. LC 96-68847. (Illus.). 229p. 1996. pap., wbk. ed. 16.00 (*0-9652699-0-6*) Populore Pub.

Put It Together. (Sesame Street Ser.: No. 11). (J). 1989. 1.49 (*0-553-18392-3*) Bantam.

Put Me in the Alphabet. Judith Conaway. (J). 1997. pap., wbk. ed. 3.99 (*0-679-88164-6*) McKay.

Put Me in the Zoo. Robert Lopshire. LC 60-13494. (Beginner Books Ser.). (Illus.). 61p. (J). (ps-3). 1960. 7.99 (*0-394-80017-6*) Beginner.

Put Me in the Zoo. Robert Lopshire. LC 60-13494. (Illus.). 72p. (J). (gr. 1-2). 1966. lib. bdg. 11.99 (*0-394-90017-0*) Beginner.

***Put Me in Zoo Puzzle Book.** Robert Lopshire. 1999. 7.99 (*0-375-80254-1*, Pub. by Random Bks Yng Read) Random.

Put Money in Your Pockets: How to Retire Your Mortgage on Your Own Terms at a Fraction of the Cost. Josh Bruno. LC 94-94531. (Illus.). 384p. 1995. write for info. (*0-9641964-1-7*) Capital Search.

Put Money in Your Pockets: How to Retire Your Mortgage on Your Own Terms at a Fraction of the Cost. Josh Bruno. LC 94-84531. (Illus.). 384p. 1995. pap. 29.95 (*0-9641964-2-5*) Capital Search.

The book shows how the total cost of a mortgage can actually reach OVER THREE TIMES the original amount during the course of the term. It exposes five dire consequences that may occur when a buyer allows the cost build-up. The author reveals in clear, step-by-step illustrated details how a homeowner can: * Reduce the massive interest cost on a mortgage & produce substantial money savings * Tap six little known sources of extra cash to help pay off the mortgage early * Correctly & easily apply a POWERFUL KEY technique that will eliminate ALL debts at a DAZZLING pace * Use four different techniques alone or in combination to prepay the mortgage & eliminate a big burden before retirement * Determine exactly when the mortgage will be paid off & how much interest cost will be eliminated for any fixed prepayment amount * Determine exactly how much to prepay in order to eliminate the mortgage within a precise number of years * Activate, automatically & virtually COST-FREE, two forms of bi-weekly mortgage payment handling to disintegrate YEARS off the term & painlessly SAVE a major portion of the interest cost * Determine when it's better to invest available money rather than use it for prepayments. To order contact: Capital Search Systems, 84 Surrey Lane, Hempstead, NY 11550. *Publisher Paid Annotation.*

Put on a Circus. Kathy Christensen & Barbara Li. (Illus.). 96p. (Orig.). 1991. 9.95 (*1-878079-02-6*) Arts Pubns.

Put on a Happy Face. Debbie Wiersma. (Little Golden Storybks.). (J). 1997. 3.99 (*0-307-16166-8*, 16166, Goldn Books) Gldn Bks Pub Co.

Put on by Cunning. Ruth Rendell. 1982. pap. 3.75 (*0-09-927730-1*) Arrow Bks.

Put on Some Antlers & Walk Like a Moose: How Scientists Find, Follow, & Study Wild Animals. April P. Sayre. LC 97-8072. (Science Titles on Target Ser.). 80p. (YA). (gr. 5 up). 1997. 20.40 (*0-8050-5182-1*) TFC Bks NY.

Put on the Armour of God: The Divine Warrior from Isaiah to Ephesians. Thomas R. Yoder Neufeld. LC 97-199077. (JSNTS Ser.: Vol. 140). 182p. 1997. 57.50 (*1-85075-655-4*, Pub. by Sheffield Acad) CUP Services.

Put on Thy Beautiful Garments see Everyday Dress of Rural America, 1783-1800: With Instructions & Patterns

Put on Your Dancing Shoes. Nancy Telfel. Ed. by Frances Clark & Louise Goss. 12p. 1985. pap. text 3.50 (*0-913277-16-9*) New Schl Mus Study.

Put on Your Green Shoes - Various Artists. pap. 17.95 (*0-89524-784-4*) Cherry Lane.

Put on Your Thinking Cap in Following Directions-Understanding Sentences. Jean G. DeGaetano. 80p. 1986. pap. text 27.95 (*1-886143-23-4*) Grt Ideas Tching.

Put' Otrecheniya. Mark Altshuller & Elena Dryzhakova. LC 85-24728. (RUS.). 350p. 1985. pap. 16.50 (*0-938920-53-7*) Hermitage Pubs.

Put Out the Fires. Maureen Lee. 416p. 1996. 27.00 (*1-85797-624-X*, Pub. by Orion Pubng Grp) Trafalgar.

Put Out the Light. Ann Quinton. 224p. 26.00 (*0-7278-5523-9*) Severn Hse.

Put Out the Light. Sara Woods. 240p. 1987. pap. 3.50 (*0-380-70476-5*, Avon Bks) Morrow Avon.

Put Power in Your Personality: Match Your Potential with America's Leaders. Florence Littauer. LC 95-6912. 288p. (YA). (gr. 10). 1995. pap. 9.99 (*0-8007-5563-4*) Revell.

Put Prevention into Practice: Child Health Guide. 40p. 1997. pap. 26.00 (*0-16-061409-0*) USGPO.

Put Prevention Into Practice: Clinician's Handbook of Preventive Services. LC 98-121900. 571p. 1998. per. 29.00 (*0-16-049227-0*) USGPO.

Put Prevention into Practice: Clinician's Handbook of Preventive Services. 419p. 1994. per. 23.00 (*0-16-043115-8*) USGPO.

Put Prevention into Practice: Personal Health Guide. 32p. 1997. pap. 24.00 (*0-16-061408-2*) USGPO.

Put Prevention into Practice: Prevention Prescription Pads. 1994. pap. 28.00 (*0-16-061390-6*) USGPO.

Put San Francisco on Your Tongue. Jane Sixty-Nine Staff. 10p. 1993. pap. 1.00 (*1-884047-50-5*) Mass Extinct.

Put the Vermonters Ahead: The First Vermont Brigade in the Civil War. George W. Parsons. LC 96-2060. (Illus.). 216p. 1996. 24.95 (*0-942597-97-4*) White Mane Pub.

***Put the Vermonters Ahead: The First Vermont Brigade in the Civil War.** George W. Parsons. 228p. 2000. pap. 12.95 (*1-57249-193-0*, Burd St Pr) White Mane Pub.

Put to Work: Relief Programs in the Great Depression. Nancy E. Rose. (Illus.). 144p. 26.00 (*0-85345-870-7*, Pub. by Monthly Rev) NYU Pr.

Put to Work: Relief Programs in the Great Depression. Nancy E. Rose. LC 93-26617. (J). (ps-12). 1993. pap. 13.00 (*0-85345-871-5*, Pub. by Monthly Rev) NYU Pr.

Put up or Give Way: States, Economic Competitiveness, & Poverty. John Sidor. 250p. 1991. pap. write for info. (*1-880942-00-3*) CSC Dev Agcies.

Put Work in Its Place: How to Redesign Your Job to Fit Your Life. 2nd rev. ed. Bruce O'Hara. (Illus.). 298p. 1994. pap. 12.00 (*0-921586-40-X*, Pub. by New Star Bks) Genl Dist Srvs.

***Put Your Best Foot Forward: Make a Great Impression by Taking Control of How Others See You.** Jo-Ellan Dimitrius & Mark Mazzarella. LC 99-59604. 304p. 2000. 24.00 (*0-684-86406-1*) S&S Trade.

***Put Your Best Foot Forward: More Little Lessons for a Happier World.** Allison Stoutland. 2000. 14.95 (*0-9670941-1-9*) Inch By Inch.

Put Your Best Foot Forward - Asia: A Fearless Guide to International Communication & Behavior. Mary M. Bosrock. Ed. by Terry Wolkerstorfer. LC 93-79394. (Put Your Best Foot Forward Ser.). (Illus.). 552p. (C). 1994. pap. 19.95 (*0-9637530-4-5*) Int Educ Systs.

Put Your Best Foot Forward - Asia: A Fearless Guide to International Communication & Behavior. 2nd ed. Mary M. Bosrock. LC 93-79394. (Put Your Best Foot Forward Ser.: Vol. 2). (Illus.). 572p. 1997. reprint ed. pap. 22.95 (*0-9637530-7-X*) Int Educ Systs.

Put Your Best Foot Forward - Europe: A Fearless Guide to International Communication & Behavior. Mary M. Bosrock. (Put Your Best Foot Forward Ser.). (Illus.). 504p. 1995. pap. 22.95 (*0-9637530-3-7*) Int Educ Systs.

Put Your Best Foot Forward - Mexico-Canada: A Fearless Guide to Communication & Behavior - NAFTA. Mary M. Bosrock. (Put Your Best Foot Forward Ser.: Bk. 3). (Illus.). (Orig.). 1995. pap. 14.95 (*0-9637530-5-3*) Int Educ Systs.

Put Your Best Foot Forward - Russia: A Fearless Guide to International Communication & Behavior. Mary M. Bosrock. (Put Your Best Foot Forward Ser.: Bk. 4). (Illus.). (Orig.). 1995. pap. 11.95 (*0-9637530-6-1*) Int Educ Systs.

Put Your Best Foot Forward - South America: A Fearless Guide to International Communication & Behavior. Mary M. Bosrock. LC 97-71673. (Put Your Best Foot Forward Ser.: Vol. 5). (Illus.). 400p. (Orig.). 1997. pap. 22.95 (*0-9637530-8-8*) Int Educ Systs.

Put Your Best Foot Forward - U. S. A. Vol. VI: A Fearless Guide to Understanding the United States of America. Mary Murray Bosrock. Ed. by Catherine A. Walker. LC 98-75164. (Put Your Best Foot Forward Ser.: Bk. 6). (Illus.). 475p. 1999. pap. 22.95 (*0-9637530-9-6*) Int Educ Systs.

Put Your Butt-Out Forever: How to Live Through a Nicotine Fit. Sharon Woloz. (Illus.). 96p. (Orig.). 1988. pap. 6.95 (*0-9621447-0-3*) Little Sam.

***Put Your Dreams Away: A Frank Sinatra Discography, 84.** Compiled by Luiz Carlos do Nascimento Silva. LC 99-87684. (Discographies Ser.: Vol. 84). 640p. 2000. lib. bdg. 99.50 (*0-313-31055-6*, Greenwood Pr) Greenwood.

Put Your English to Work. David Prince & Julia Gage. (Illus.). 160p. (C). 1986. pap. text 9.95 (*0-13-744350-1*) P-H.

Put Your Heart on Paper: Writing to Connect in a Loose-Ends World. Henriette A. Klauser. LC 95-8739. 336p. 1995. pap. 13.95 (*0-553-37446-X*) Bantam.

Put Your Money Where Your Heart Is: An Easy-to-Understand Guide to Investments. Sherman S. Smith. 208p. 1996. 18.99 (*0-9643136-1-8*) Meister Pr.

Put Your Mother on the Ceiling. Richard Demille. 1976. pap. 8.95 (*0-14-004379-9*, Penguin Bks) Viking Penguin.

P

Put Your Mother on the Ceiling. rev. ed. Richard De Mille. LC 99-222012. 160p. 1997. 20.00 (*0-939266-28-8*) Gestalt Journal.

Put Your Mouth Where the Money Is: Get Your Voice on Radio & TV Commercials. Sunny Quinn. LC 97-94503. 176p. 1998. pap. 49.95 (*0-9660531-0-9*) Airwave Pub.

Put Your Oxygen Mask on First: And Other Strategies for Succeeding in Teaching! Mary C. Clement. (Illus.). 118p. write for info. (*1-888793-04-X*) Tchrs Little Secrets.

Put Yourself in Their Shoes: Understanding How Your Child Sees the World. Barbara Meltz. LC 98-38609. 432p. 1999. pap. 12.95 (*0-440-50823-1*, Dell Trade Pbks) Dell.

Put Yourself in Their Shoes: Understanding Teenagers with Attention-Deficit Hyperactivity Disorder. Harvey C. Parker & Alan Goodstat. LC 98-43908. 249p. 1999. pap. 19.00 (*1-886941-19-X*, 0950) Spec Pr FL.

Put Yourself on Paper! The Warmth, Power & Influence of Handwritten Expression. Barry Packer & Boyd C. Matheson. 96p. 1995. pap. text 12.95 (*1-882441-12-5*) InANutshell Bks.

Put Yourself on the Fast Track: A Guide for Supervisors & Managers Who Want to Get Promoted. Doug Mealy. LC 84-28648. (Illus.). 104p. 1986. pap. 12.95 (*0-88280-110-4*) ETC Pubns.

Putain. Guy Verville. (FRE.). 48p. 1991. pap. write for info. (*2-89135-039-1*) Guernica Editions.

Putain Respectueuse. Incl. Morts Sans Sepulture. write for info. (*0-318-63582-8*) Fr & Eur.

Putain Respectueuse. Jean-Paul Sartre. (Folio Ser.: No. 868). pap. 6.95 (*0-685-35916-6*) Schoenhof.

Putain Respectueuse: Morts Sans Sepulture. Jean-Paul Sartre. (FRE.). 1976. pap. 10.95 (*0-8288-3778-3*, F125470) Fr & Eur.

Putative Melatonin Receptors in Peripheral Tissues. Ed. by S. F. Pang et al. (Journal: Biological Signals: Vol. 2, No. 4, 1993). (Illus.). 64p. 1994. pap. 28.75 (*3-8055-5947-X*) S Karger.

Putera Reports No. 51: Problems in Indonesian-Japanese Wartime Co-Operation. Tr. by Mohammad Hatta & William H. Frederick. (Modern Indonesia Project Ser.). 114p. 1971. pap. 4.00 (*0-87763-009-7*) Cornell Mod Indo.

Putevoditel' Po Nauchnym Obshchestvam Rossii, 5 vols. Compiled by Irina I. Komarova.Tr. of Guide to the Learned Societies of the Russian Empire. (RUS.). 300p. 1999. lib. bdg. 500.00 (*0-88354-380-X*) N Ross.

Puti Izgnaniia. Zinaida Zhemchuzhnaia. LC 87-8905. (RUS., Illus.). 302p. 1987. pap. 14.00 (*0-938920-88-X*) Hermitage Pubs.

Putman's Digital Electronics: Lac Manual. James W. Nice. (Illus.). 144p. 1986. pap. text 25.00 (*0-13-212549-8*) P-H.

Putnam Aeronautical Review, Vol. I. Ed. by John Motum. LC 89-61978. (Illus.). 256p. 1990. 47.95 (*0-87021-610-4*) Naval Inst Pr.

Putnam Aeronautical Review, Vol. II. Ed. by John Motum. (Illus.). 256p. 1991. 47.95 (*1-55750-676-0*) Naval Inst Pr.

Putnam & Marshall Counties Records of the Olden Time: Or Fifty Years on the Prairies, Embracing Sketches of the Discovery, Exploration & Settlement of the Country & the Organization of the Counties of Putnam & Marshall, Biographies of Citizens, Etc. Spencer Ellsworth. (Illus.). 772p. 1997. reprint ed. lib. bdg. 79.50 (*0-8328-5785-8*) Higginson Bk Co.

***Putnam & Pennyroyal.** Patrick Jennings. LC 98-54218. (Illus.). 192p. (J). (gr. 2-5). 1999. 15.95 (*0-439-07965-9*, Pub. by Scholastic Inc) Penguin Putnam.

Putnam Anniversary Volume: Anthropological Essays Presented to Frederic Ward Putnam, in Honor of His Seventieth Birthday, April 16, 1909, by His Friends & Associates. Ed. by Stephen Williams. LC 72-5222. (Illus.). reprint ed. 97.50 (*0-404-10626-9*) AMS Pr.

Putnam County, Indiana. Jessie W. Weik. (Illus.). 78p. reprint ed. lib. bdg. 78.50 (*0-8328-2566-2*) Higginson Bk Co.

Putnam's Geology. 5th rev. ed. Peter W. Birkeland & Edwin E. Larson. (Illus.). 656p. (C). 1989. pap. text 49.95 (*0-19-505517-9*) OUP.

Putonghua: A Practical Course in Spoken Chinese. Mabel Lee & Zhang Wu-Ai. 110p. 1991. pap. text 14.00 (*0-9590735-0-7*, Pub. by Wild Peony Pty) UH Pr.

Puts & Calls. W. D. Gann. 30p. 1976. pap. 20.00 (*0-939093-15-4*) Lambert Gann Pub.

Putsch: The Diary: Thre Days That Collapsed the Empire. Ed. by Alexander Avelichev. (Illus.). 155p. 1998. pap. text 22.00 (*0-7881-5833-3*) DIANE Pub.

Putsch: The Diary: Three Days That Collapsed the Empire. Intro. by Boris Yeltsin. (Illus.). 180p. 1992. 19.95 (*0-88962-509-3*) Mosaic.

***Putt at the End of the World.** Lee K. Abbott et al. Ed. by Les Standiford. LC 99-89030. 256p. 2000. 23.95 (*0-446-52600-2*, Pub. by Warner Bks) Little.

Putt Like a Champion. Horton Smith & Dawson Taylor. (Illus.). 164p. 1997. pap. 12.95 (*1-887269-08-8*) J Culler & Sons.

Putt Like the Pros: Dave Pelz's Scientific Way to Improve Your Stroke Reading the Greens, & Lowering Your Score. Dave Pelz & Nick Mastroni. LC 86-46095. (Illus.). 240p. 1991. reprint ed. pap. 15.00 (*0-06-092078-5*, Perennial) HarperTrade.

***Putt Putt.** Linda Dowdy. (Illus.). 112p. (J). (ps-2). 2000. pap. 2.99 (*1-57064-943-X*, 73110, Humongous Bks) Lyrick Pub.

***Putt-Putt Lost in Time!** Nancy Parent. LC 00-105017. (Humongous Ser.). (Illus.). 24p. (J). (ps-1). 2001. 3.99 (*1-58668-060-9*) Lyrick Studios.

***Putt-Putt the Great Pet Chase.** Jo Arnold. LC 00-100698. (Illus.). 24p. (J). (ps-2). 2000. pap. 3.99 (*1-57064-944-8*, 73111, Humongous Bks) Lyrick Pub.

Putter Principle: Golfs Greatest Legends. Criswell Freeman. 1997. pap. text 6.95 (*1-887655-39-5*) Walnut Gr Pr.

Puttering about in a Small Land. Philip K. Dick. 290p. 1985. reprint ed. pap. 11.95 (*0-89733-384-5*) Academy Chi Pubs.

Puttermesser Papers. Cynthia Ozick. LC 96-39155. 236p. 1997. 23.00 (*0-679-45476-4*) Knopf.

Puttermesser Papers. Cynthia Ozick. 256p. 1998. pap. 12.00 (*0-679-77739-3*) Vin Bks.

Putters Pocket Compa. Jim McLean & Fran Pirozzolo. LC 94-18734. 128p. 1994. 10.00 (*0-06-017189-8*) HarperTrade.

Putties: Poems from Hollywood - A Play by Mark Dunster. Mark Dunster. 32p. 1996. pap. 5.00 (*0-89642-433-2*) Linden Pubs.

Puttin' on the Peachtree. Junior League of DeKalb County Staff. 344p. 1999. 16.95 (*0-9618508-2-5*) Wimmer Bks.

Puttin' on the Peachtree. Compiled by Junior League of Dekalb County Staff. 352p. 1979. 16.95 (*0-918544-69-6*) Jr Lgue Dekalb Cty.

Putting a Lid on Legal Fees: How to Deal Effectively with Lawyers. Raymond M. Klein. LC 86-82987. (Illus.). 192p. 1987. 22.50 (*0-9617950-7-7*); pap. 12.95 (*0-9617950-8-5*) Interlink Pr.

Putting a Message Together. 2nd ed. Glen E. Mills. LC 78-179367. Orig. Title: Message Preparation: Analysis & Structure. 1972. pap. 3.95 (*0-672-61299-2*, SC8, Bobbs) Macmillan.

Putting a New Spin on Groups: The Science of Chaos. Bud A. McClure. LC 98-13600. 300p. 1998. 59.95 (*0-8058-2904-0*); pap. write for info. (*0-8058-2905-9*) L Erlbaum Assocs.

Putting ACUNS Together. Gene M. Lyons. LC 99-219053. (ACUNS Reports & Papers). 56p. 1999. pap. text 5.00 (*1-880660-18-0*) Acad Coun UN Syst.

Putting Amazing Back into Grace. Michael S. Horton. LC 94-5566. (Illus.). 320p. 1994. pap. 14.99 (*0-8010-4391-3*) Baker Bks.

Putting America's House in Order: The Nation As a Family. David M. Abshire & Brock Brower. LC 95-40577. 208p. 1996. 19.95 (*0-275-95431-5*, Praeger Pubs) Greenwood.

Putting an End to Worship Wars. Elmer L. Towns. LC 96-27811. 208p. 1997. pap. 17.99 (*0-8054-3017-2*, 4230-17) Broadman.

***Putting Anger in its Place: A Woman's Guide to Getting Emotions Under Control.** Annie Chapman. 176p. 2000. pap. 8.99 (*0-7369-0442-5*) Harvest Hse.

Putting Anger to Work for You! Joel Schroeder & Ruth Schroeder. Ed. by Kelly Scanlon. LC 95-69000. (Illus.). 74p. 1995. 12.95 (*1-878542-86-9*, 12-0025) SkillPath Pubns.

Putting Away Childish Things. David Seamands. (Personal Growth Bookshelf). 64p. 1993. pap., teacher ed. 6.50 (*1-56476-206-8*, 6-3206, Victor Bks) Chariot Victor.

Putting Away Childish Things. David Seamands. (Personal Growth Bookshelf Ser.). 144p. 1993. pap. 9.99 (*1-56476-103-7*, 6-3103, Victor Bks) Chariot Victor.

Putting Away Childish Things. David A. Seamands. 144p. 1982. pap. 7.99 (*0-88207-308-7*, Victor Bks) Chariot Victor.

***Putting Away Childish Things: Reaching for Spiritual & Emotional Maturity in Christ.** David A. Seamands. 141p. 1999. reprint ed. pap. 10.99 (*0-89367-244-0*) Light & Life Comm.

Putting Biotechnology to Work: Bioprocess Engineering. National Research Council Staff. LC 92-61717. 132p. (Orig.). (C). 1992. pap. text 24.00 (*0-309-04785-4*) Natl Acad Pr.

Putting Body & Soul Together: Essays in Honor of Robin Scroggs. Ed. by Graydon F. Snyder et al. LC 97-227. 384p. (Orig.). 1997. 30.00 (*1-56338-209-1*); pap. 20.00 (*1-56338-206-7*) TPI PA.

Putting Buddhism to Work: A New Approach to Management & Business. Shinichi Inoue. Tr. by Duncan R. Williams. LC 97-41338. 1997. 22.00 (*4-7700-2124-0*, Pub. by Kodansha Int) OUP.

Putting Building Materials Containing Recycled Content to Work in Wisconsin. Gary Edelman. Ed. by Atiya Mahmood. 69p. 1995. pap. 10.00 (*1-886437-01-7*) U of Wis Ctr Arch-Urban.

Putting Chance to Work...A Life in Statistics: A Biography of C. R. Rao. Nalini Krishnankutty. LC 96-71951. (Illus.). iv, 178p. (Orig.). 1996. pap. 15.00 (*0-9655797-6-X*) Dialogue PA.

Putting Childish Things. 1993. pap. write for info. (*1-56476-194-0*, Victor Bks) Chariot Victor.

Putting Children & Families First: A Challenge for Our Church, Nation, & World. United States Catholic Conference Staff. 24p. (Orig.). (C). 1992. pap. 1.95 (*1-55586-469-4*) US Catholic.

Putting Children First: A Guide for Parents Breaking Up. Hanna McDonough & Christina Bartha. 192p. 1999. pap. 15.95 (*0-8020-8064-2*); text 45.00 (*0-8020-4217-1*) U of Toronto Pr.

Putting Children First: A Report on the Effectiveness of U. S. Agency for International Development Child Survival Programs in Fiscal Year 1991. Ed. by Marc J. Cohen et al. (Hunger Policy Occasional Papers: No. 3). (C). 1995. pap. text 5.00 (*1-884361-00-5*) Bread for the World.

Putting Children First: Making Pesticide Levels in Food Safer for Infants & Children. David Wallinga. 73p. 1998. pap. write for info. (*1-893340-09-0*) Natl Resources Defense Coun.

Putting Children First: State-Level Collaboration Between Education & Health. National Health & Education Consortium Staff. 50p. 1995. 10.00 (*0-937846-43-0*) Inst Educ Lead.

Putting Children First: Visions for a Brighter Future for Young Children & Their Families. Ed. by Elizabeth J. Erwin. LC 96-11846. 336p. (Orig.). 1996. pap. text 39.95 (*1-55766-244-4*, 2444) P H Brookes.

Putting Children in the Electoral Arena. 40p. 1994. write for info. (*92-806-3103-9*) U N I C E.

Putting Children in Their Place. Stuart C. Aitken. Ed. by Robert Cromley & Ellen Cromley. LC 94-7839. (Resource Publications in Geography). (C). 1994. pap. text 15.00 (*0-89291-216-2*) Assn Am Geographers.

Putting Choice Before Democracy: A Critique of Rational Choice Theory. Emily Hauptmann. LC 95-37347. (SUNY Series in Political Theory). 138p. (C). 1996. text 44.50 (*0-7914-3027-8*); pap. text 14.95 (*0-7914-3028-6*) State U NY Pr.

Putting Christ First: A Woman's Workshop on Colossians. Margaret Fromer & Paul Fromer. Ed. by Janet Kobobel. (Woman's Workshop Ser.). 128p. 1986. pap. 5.99 (*0-310-44801-8*, 11313P) Zondervan.

Putting Citizens First: The Portuguese Experience in Administrative Reform. Atila Alpoge & Liz Dacier. (Public Management Occasional Papers: No. 13). 164p. (Orig.). 1996. pap. 24.00 (*92-64-15332-2*, 42-96-63-1) OECD.

Putting Class in Its Place: Worker Identities in East Asia. Ed. by Elizabeth J. Perry. LC 95-50860. (China Research Monographs: Vol. 48). 1996. pap. 18.50 (*1-55729-050-4*) IEAS.

Putting Computer Power in School: A Step-by-Step Approach. Jerry L. Patterson & Janice H. Patterson. 1984. 17.95 (*0-317-38248-9*, Parker Publishing Co); pap. 12.95 (*0-317-38249-7*, Parker Publishing Co) P-H.

Putting Computer Power in Schools: A Step-by-Step Approach. Jerry L. Patterson & Janice H. Patterson. LC 83-8017. 227p. 1983. 17.95 (*0-13-744474-5*, Busn); pap. 12.95 (*0-13-744467-2*, Busn) P-H.

Putting Customers First: Standards for Serving the American People. Report of the National Performance Review. Bill Clinton & Al Gore, Jr. 160p. (Orig.). (C). 1995. pap. text 30.00 (*0-7881-2174-X*) DIANE Pub.

Putting Dell on the Map: A History of the Dell Paperbacks, 5. William H. Lyles. LC 83-1641. (Contributions to the Study of Popular Culture Ser.: No. 5). 178p. 1983. 49.95 (*0-313-23667-4*, LPD/, Greenwood Pr) Greenwood.

Putting Democracy to Work: A Practical Guide for Starting & Managing Worker-Owned Businesses. Frank T. Adams & Gary B. Hansen. LC 92-28434. (Illus.). 352p. (Orig.). 1993. pap. 19.95 (*1-881052-09-5*) Berrett-Koehler.

Putting Democracy to Work: A Practical Guide to Starting & Managing Worker-Owned Businesses. 2nd rev. ed. Frank T. Adams & Gary B. Hansen. 324p. 1992. pap. 19.95 (*0-938493-19-1*) Hulogosi Inc.

Putting Difference to Work. Steve De Shazer. 1991. 22.95 (*0-393-70110-7*) Norton.

***Putting down Roots.** Susan Davis Price. LC 99-38320. 2000. pap. write for info. (*0-8166-3306-1*) U of Minn Pr.

***Putting down Roots: A Delightful Blend of Gardening Wisdom, Wit & Whimsy.** LC 99-94239. x, 166p. 1999. pap. 12.00 (*0-9670927-0-1*) C Johnson Mrktg.

Putting down Stones: A Faithful Response to Urban Violence. Sojourners Editors. (Illus.). 50p. 1995. pap. 4.50 (*0-9641109-3-8*) Sojrners.

Putting Emotional Intelligence to Work, Successful Leadership Is More Than IQ: The New Ethic of Self-Management. David Ryback. LC 97-15319. 224p. 1997. pap. text 17.95 (*0-7506-9956-6*) Buttrwrth-Heinemann.

***Putting Empowerment into Practice: Stories & Strategies for Diabetes Educators.** Robert M. Anderson & Martha Mitchell Funnell. LC 00-28898. 2000. pap. write for info. (*1-58040-010-8*) Am Diabetes.

***Putting Energy into Profits, Energy Star Small Business Guide.** Government Printing Office Staff. 112p. 1998. per. 12.00 (*0-16-049393-5*) USGPO.

Putting Faith to Work: Lessons of Help & Hope for Women. F. Jean Meppelink. 118p. 1992. ring bd. 15.00 (*0-9657979-3-7*) Growing Life.

Putting Families First. Linda McCart & Anne Heller. Ed. by Karen Glass. 56p. (Orig.). 1993. pap. text 15.00 (*1-55877-211-1*) Natl Governor.

Putting Families First: America's Family Support Movement & the Challenge of Change. Ed. by Sharon L. Kagan & Bernice Weissbourd. LC 94-9713. (Education Ser.). 558p. 1994. text 45.00 (*1-55542-667-0*) Jossey-Bass.

Putting Families First: An Experiment in Family Preservation. John R. Schuerman et al. LC 94-30535. (Modern Applications of Social Work Ser.). 326p. 1994. pap. text 28.95 (*0-202-36092-X*); lib. bdg. 51.95 (*0-202-36091-1*) Aldine de Gruyter.

Putting Fiction in Its Place: The West Country As a Literary Invention. Simon D. Trezise. (Illus.). 240p. 1999. 70.00 (*0-85989-537-8*, Pub. by Univ Exeter Pr); pap. 26.95 (*0-85989-538-6*, Pub. by Univ Exeter Pr) Northwestern U Pr.

Putting Folklore to Use. Ed. by Michael O. Jones. LC 93-2101. 280p. (C). 1994. text 33.00 (*0-8131-1825-5*); pap. text 18.00 (*0-8131-0818-7*) U Pr of Ky.

Putting Food By. Janet Greene et al. 420p. 1992. pap. 15.95 (*0-452-26899-0*, Plume) Dutton Plume.

Putting Freelance Graphics to Work. Gralla. 1995. pap. text 24.95 (*1-56276-317-2*, Ziff-Davis Pr) Que.

***Putting God First.** Alistair Begg. 2000. 19.99 (*0-8024-1716-7*) Moody.

Putting God First. Sandra S. Neal. 1998. pap. 6.95 (*0-9641845-6-7*) Wingspan Christian.

Putting God First: The Tithe. Norma Wimberly. LC 88-71011. 56p. (Orig.). 1988. pap. 5.95 (*0-88177-058-2*, DR058) Discipleship Res.

Putting God on the Guest List: How to Reclaim the Spiritual Meaning of Your Child's Bar or Bat Mitzvah. 2nd rev. ed. Jeffrey K. Salkin. 224p. 1996. 24.95 (*1-879045-58-3*); pap. 16.95 (*1-879045-59-1*) Jewish Lights.

Putting Health Care on the National Agenda. Arnold Birenbaum. LC 95-3861. 256p. 1995. 65.00 (*0-275-95163-4*, Praeger Pubs) Greenwood.

Putting Health Care on the National Agenda. rev. ed. Arnold Birenbaum. LC 95-3861. 256p. 1995. pap. 20.95 (*0-275-95164-2*, Praeger Pubs) Greenwood.

Putting Health into Place: Landscape, Identity, & Well-Being. Robin A. Kearns & Wilbert M. Gesler. LC 97-36239. (Space, Place, & Society Ser.). 1998. 49.95 (*0-8156-2767-X*) Syracuse U Pr.

Putting Health into Place: Landscape, Identity, & Well-Being. Robin A. Kearns & Wilbert N. Gesler. LC 97-36239. (Space, Place, & Society Ser.). 1998. pap. 24.95 (*0-8156-2768-8*) Syracuse U Pr.

***Putting Healthcare Promises into Practice.** Robbins. 2000. 29.95 (*0-7668-1972-8*) Delmar.

***Putting History to the Question: Power, Politics & Society in English Renaissance Drama.** Michael Neill. LC 99-29886. 464p. 1999. 37.50 (*0-231-11332-3*) Col U Pr.

Putting Humpty Back Together. John A. Caticchio. Ed. by Eileen Goren. 152p. 1990. pap. 9.95 (*0-9625876-0-5*) Vivere Pub.

Putting Impotence to Bed: What Every Man & Woman Should Know. Joseph L. Godat. LC 99-6711. 272p. 1999. 22.95 (*1-56530-302-4*, Pub. by Summit TX) BookWorld.

Putting Institutional Economics to Work: From Participation to Governance. Robert Picciotto. LC 95-40233. (Discussion Paper Ser.: No. 304). 30p. 1995. pap. 22.00 (*0-8213-3458-1*) World Bank.

Putting Islam to Work: Education, Politics & the Transformation of Faith. Gregory Starrett. LC 96-50454. (Comparative Studies on Muslim Societies). 370p. 1997. 55.00 (*0-520-20926-5*, Pub. by U CA Pr); pap. 22.00 (*0-520-20927-3*, Pub. by U CA Pr) Cal Prin Full Svc.

Putting It All Together. Sunal. (C). 1999. pap. text 43.50 (*0-15-503953-9*, Pub. by Harcourt Coll Pubs) Harcourt.

Putting It All Together: Readings for Students of English As a Second Language. George M. Jacobs & Michael A. Power. (Illus.). 110p. (C). 1991. pap. text 12.95 (*0-472-08158-6*, 08158) U of Mich Pr.

Putting It All Together: Seven Patterns for Relating Science & the Christian Faith. Richard H. Bube. 224p. (Orig.). (C). 1995. lib. bdg. 49.00 (*0-8191-9755-6*) U Pr of Amer.

Putting It All Together: The New Orthomolecular Nutrition. rev. ed. Abram Hoffer & Morton Walker. Ed. by Don R. Bensen. 224p. 1996. pap. 17.95 (*0-87983-633-4*, 36334K, Keats Publng) NTC Contemp Pub Co.

Putting It All Together: World Conquest, Global Genocide & African Liberation. Terrance Jackson. 136p. (Orig.). 1994. pap. 8.95 (*1-56411-090-7*) Untd Bros & Sis.

Putting It in Writing. Steven Otfinoski. 144p. (YA). (gr. 7-12). 1994. pap. 4.95 (*0-590-49459-7*) Scholastic Inc.

Putting It Together. Jeanne Altstatt & Judith Handy. 170p. (C). 1996. text 28.20 (*0-536-59681-6*) Pearson Custom.

Putting It Together. 2nd ed. Altstatt & Ferrand. 200p. (C). 1998. spiral bd. 24.80 (*0-536-01192-3*) S&S Trade.

Putting it Together: A Conversation Management Text. Kevin McClure. 240p. (C). 1995. pap. text 26.27 (*0-13-128174-7*) P-H.

Putting It Together: Middle School Math in Transition. Gary Tsuruda. LC 93-46755. 111p. 1994. pap. 18.00 (*0-435-08355-4*, 08355) Heinemann.

Putting It Together: Positive Strategies for Student Success. Kathleen M. Fad & James E. Gilliam. (Illus.). 200p. 1996. pap. text 24.50 (*1-57035-070-1*, C90PASS) Sopris.

Putting It up with Honey: A Natural Foods Canning & Preserving Cookbooks. Susann Geiskopf-Hadler. LC 78-59871. (Illus.). 224p. 1979. pap. 10.95 (*0-930356-13-6*) Quicksilver Prod.

Putting Kids First: Walking Away from a Marriage Without Walking over the Kids. Michael L. Oddenina. LC 96-231499. (Illus.). 151p. 1995. 16.95 (*1-884862-03-9*) Fmly Connect.

Putting Knowledge to Use: Facilitating the Diffusion of Knowledge & the Implementation of Planned Change. Edward M. Glaser et al. LC 83-11281. 656p. reprint ed. pap. 200.00 (*0-7837-6526-6*, 204563800007) Bks Demand.

Putting Learning First: Governing & Managing the School for High Performance. LC 94-22399. 1994. 17.50 (*0-87186-100-3*) Comm Econ Dev.

Putting Library Instruction in Its Place: In the Library & in the Library School. Ed. by Carolyn B. Kirkendall. LC 78-53996. (Library Orientation Ser.: No. 8). 112p. 1978. 25.00 (*0-87650-092-0*) Pierian.

Putting Life Back Together. Marion R. Brown. LC 85-51548. 106p. 1986. pap. 1.98 (*0-87159-132-4*) Unity Bks.

Putting "Loafing Streams" to Work: The Building of Lay, Mitchell, Martin & Jordan Dams, 1910-1929. Harvey Jackson, III. LC 96-48810. 280p. 1997. pap. 24.95 (*0-8173-0889-X*) U of Ala Pr.

P

An Asterisk (*) at the beginning of an entry indicates that the title is appearing for the first time.

Putting Markets to Work: The Design & Use of Marketable Permits & Obligations. OECD Staff. LC 98-144605. (Public Management Occasional Papers: No. 19). 52p. 1998. pap. 7.00 (*92-64-15615-1*, 42-97-69-1, Pub. by Org for Econ) OECD.

Putting Mathematics to Use. Cathy Brady. (Middle School Ser.). 1996. wbk. ed. 9.99 (*1-884461-20-4*) NES Arnold.

Putting Metaclasses to Work: A NEW DIMENTION IN OBJECT-ORIENTED PROGRAMMING. Ira R. Forman. LC 98-38783. 320p. (C). 1998. pap. text 39.95 (*0-201-43305-2*) Addison-Wesley.

Putting Microsoft Works to Work in Your Classroom. John F. Beaver. LC 97-146940. (Illus.). 496p. (Orig.). (C). 1997. pap. text 39.95 (*0-943025-95-8*) Cummngs & Hath.

Putting Money in Its Place. Ken Rouse. 164p. 1993. per. 14.95 (*0-8403-9115-3*) Kendall-Hunt.

Putting My Foot in It. Rene Crevel. Tr. by Thomas Buckley from FRE. LC 92-504. 200p. 1993. reprint ed. pap. 9.95 (*1-56478-017-1*) Dalkey Arch.

Putting Myself in the Picture. 2nd ed. Jo Spence. LC 88-42844. (Illus.). 224p. 1988. reprint ed. 25.95 (*0-941104-38-9*); reprint ed. pap. 17.95 (*0-941104-35-4*) Real Comet.

Putting Nature in Order. David W. Chambers. 60p. (C). 1992. pap. 45.00 (*0-7300-0155-5*, HUS204, Pub. by Deakin Univ) St Mut.

***Putting Off Anger: A Biblical Study of What Anger Is & What to Do about It.** John Coblentz. 109p. 1999. 5.95 (*0-87813-579-0*) Christian Light.

Putting on a Concert: The Television News. Roger Hall. LC 93-24527. (Voyages Ser.). (Illus.). (J). (gr. 4 up). 1994. 4.25 (*0-383-03770-0*) SRA McGraw.

***Putting on a Gentle & Quiet Spirit: 1 Peter.** Elizabeth George. 160p. 2000. pap. 6.99 (*0-7369-0290-2*) Harvest Hse.

Putting on a Play. Michael Legat. LC 84-13242. 208p. 1984. 12.95 (*0-685-08886-3*) St Martin.

Putting on a Play: The Young Playwright's Guide to Scripting, Directing, & Performing. Nancy Bentley & Donna Guthrie. LC 95-47543. (Illus.). 64p. (J). (gr. 2-4). 1996. lib. bdg. 22.40 (*0-7613-0011-2*) Millbrook Pr.

Putting on Appearances: Gender & Advertising. Diane Barthel. (Women in the Political Economy Ser.). 232p. 1989. pap. 19.95 (*0-87722-661-X*) Temple U Pr.

Putting on the Armor of God. Steven A. Cramer. pap. 14.98 (*1-55517-283-0*) CFI Dist.

"Putting on the Brakes" Activity Book for Young People with ADHD. Patricia O. Quinn & Judith M. Stern. (Illus.). 88p. (J). (gr. 3-8). pap. 14.95 (*0-945354-57-6*) Am Psychol.

Putting on the Dog with Little Effort. Ed. by Emily C. Dockery. 73p. (Orig.). 1985. pap. text. write for info. (*0-9616053-0-8*) Grand Strand.

***Putting on the Mind of Christ: The Inner Work of Christian Spirituality.** Jim Marion. 2000. 21.95 (*1-57174-173-9*) Hampton Roads Pub Co.

Putting on the Polish: A Guide to Image Enhancement for Men & Women. Decima Malet-Veale. (Illus.). 488p. 1993. pap. 21.95 (*1-55059-074-X*) Temeron Bks.

Putting on the Ritz. Joe Keenan. 336p. 1992. reprint ed. pap. 13.95 (*0-14-014989-9*, Penguin Bks); reprint ed. audio. write for info. (*0-318-69298-8*, Penguin Bks) Viking Penguin.

Putting Out: The Essential Publishing Resource Guide for Gay & Lesbian Writers. 4th rev. ed. Ed. by Edisol W. Dotson. LC 94-77798. 200p. 1998. pap. 14.95 (*1-57344-033-7*) Cleis Pr.

Putting Out of Your Mind. Robert J. Rotella. 1996. audio 12.00 (*0-671-56796-9*, 647403) S&S Audio.

***Putting Out the Fire of Addiction: A Holistic Guide to Recovery.** Barry Sultanoff. 256p. 2000. pap. 16.95 (*0-658-00281-3*, 002813, Keats Publng) NTC Contemp Pub Co.

Putting Pascal to Work. Don Etling. (Illus.). 380p. 1986. pap. 16.95 (*0-8306-2691-3*, 2691P) McGraw-Hill Prof.

***Putting Patients First: Resolving Allocations of Transplant Organs: Congressional Hearings.** Ed. by Michael Bilirakis. 240p. (C). 1999. reprint ed. pap. text 40.00 (*0-7881-8452-0*) DIANE Pub.

Putting People First: Sociological Variables in Rural Development. 2nd enl. rev. ed. Ed. by Michael M. Cernea. (World Bank Publications). (Illus.). 600p. 1991. pap. text 24.95 (*0-19-520827-7*, 60827) OUP.

***Putting People Last: Tribal Displacement & Rehabilitation** H. S. Saksena & Chandranath Sen. LC 99-933238. (Tribal Studies of India). 320p. 1999. write for info. (*81-210-0390-3*) Inter-India Pubns.

Putting Plant Physiology on the Map: Genetical Analysis of Developmental & Adaptive Traits. Ed. by H. Thomas & J. F. Farrar. (New Phytologist Symposium: No. 2). (Illus.). 188p. (C). 1998. pap. text 34.95 (*0-521-64654-5*) Cambridge U Pr.

Putting Popular Music in Its Place. Charles Hamm. (Illus.). 402p. (C). 1995. text 69.95 (*0-521-47198-2*) Cambridge U Pr.

Putting Prevention into Practice: Problem Solving in Clinical Prevention. Richard K. Riegelman & Gail J. Povar. 432p. 1988. 32.95 (*0-316-74519-7*, Little Brwn Med Div) Lppncott W & W.

Putting Process into Practice. Deborah Pickering. 241p. (C). 1991. pap. text 35.40 (*0-673-38066-1*) Addson-Wesley Educ.

Putting Profit into Ranching: The Livestock Owner's Guide to Success! S. D. Parsons. Ed. by H. E. Parsons. (Illus.). 150p. (Orig.). 1988. pap. write for info. (*0-318-63364-7*) Ranch Pubns.

Putting Psychology in Its Place: An Introduction from a Critical Historical Perspective. Graham Richards. 208p. (C). 1996. 70.00 (*0-415-12862-5*); pap. 24.99 (*0-415-12863-3*) Routledge.

Putting Quality into Practice. Les Walklin. 284p. (C). 1999. pap. 115.00 (*0-7487-1360-3*, Pub. by S Thornes Pubs) Trans-Atl Phila.

Putting 'Reality' Together: BBC News. rev. ed. Philip Schlesinger. 336p. 1988. pap. 17.95 (*0-416-90190-5*) Routledge.

***Putting Research into Practice in Primary Teaching & Learning.** Suzi Clipson-Boyles. 2000. pap. 26.95 (*1-85346-642-5*) David Fulton.

Putting Research to Work in Your School. (C). 1999. pap. text 30.95 (*0-205-29409-X*, Longwood Div) Allyn.

Putting Research to Work in Your School. David C. Berliner & Ursula Casanova. LC 96-76991. 246p. (Orig.). 1996. pap. 32.95 (*1-57517-064-7*, 1448) SkyLght.

Putting Risk in Perspective. Renee White. LC 98-28145. 232p. 1998. pap. 17.95 (*0-8476-8587-X*) Rowman.

Putting Risk in Perspective: Black Teenage Lives in the Era of AIDS. Renee White. LC 98-28145. 232p. 1998. text 65.00 (*0-8476-8586-1*) Rowman.

Putting Secrets: Weekend Golfer. 2nd ed. Steve Page. LC 96-36558. (Illus.). 144p. 1997. pap. 11.95 (*0-312-15197-7*) St Martin.

Putting Sense into Consensus: Solving the Puzzle of Making Team Decisions. Judy Ness & Connie Hoffman. (Illus.). 127p. 1998. pap. text 26.50 (*0-9665529-0-3*) Vista Assocs.

Putting "Service" into Library Staff Training: A Patron-Centered Guide. Joanne M. Bessler. Ed. by Phil Tramdack. LC 93-31055. (Occasional Papers - Library Administration & Management Association). 72p. (Orig.). 1994. pap. 20.00 (*0-8389-3437-4*) ALA.

Putting Sheep on the Mountain: The Foundation for North American Wild Sheep, Twenty-Five Years Dedicated to Wild Sheep, 1974 to 1999. Ed. by Roy A. Schultz et al. (Illus.). 720p. 49.95 (*1-888223-13-8*) Sigler Print.

***Putting Skeptics in Their Place: The Nature of Skeptical Arguments & Their Role in Philosophical Inquiry.** John Greco. (Cambridge Studies in Philosophy). 296p. (C). 2000. text 54.95 (*0-521-77263-X*) Cambridge U Pr.

Putting the Amazing Back in Grace. Ann Weems. LC 99-23197. 212p. 1999. 16.95 (*0-664-22150-5*) Westminster John Knox.

Putting the Brakes on Crime: A Modest Proposal. Intro. by Roy Demouchette. 144p. Date not set. pap. 19.95 (*0-89896-404-0*, Better Life Bks) Larksdale.

Putting the Charter to Work: Designing a Constitutional Labour Code. David M. Beatty. 264p. 1987. 65.00 (*0-7735-0600-4*, Pub. by McG-Queens Univ Pr); pap. 24.95 (*0-7735-0601-2*, Pub. by McG-Queens Univ Pr) CUP Services.

Putting the Earth First: Alternatives to Nuclear Security in Pacific Island States. Ronni Alexander. LC 94-22585. 1994. 10.00 (*1-880309-09-2*) S M Matsunaga.

Putting the Estate Agents Act 1979 & Its Order & Regulations into Practice. RICS Staff. (C). 1991. pap. text 90.00 (*0-85406-503-2*, Pub. by R-I-C-S Bks) St Mut.

Putting the Estate Agents Act 1979 & the Property Misdescriptions Act 1991 into Practice. Guidance for Estate Agents Staff. 1993. 80.00 (*0-85406-575-X*, Pub. by R-I-C-S Bks) St Mut.

Putting the Family First: Identities, Decisions, & Citizenship. Jordan et al. LC 94-8866. 1994. 60.00 (*1-85728-165-9*, Pub. by UCL Pr Ltd); pap. 24.95 (*1-85728-166-7*, Pub. by UCL Pr Ltd) Taylor & Francis.

Putting the Giants to Sleep: Stories & Exercises for Awakening Self Worth. David Sheinkin. 1991. pap. 11.95 (*0-8356-0673-2*, Quest) Theos Pub Hse.

Putting the Heart Back into Teaching: A Manual for Junior Primary Teachers. Stanford Miller & Yvonne Bleach. pap. 22.95 (*0-9583885-5-5*, 2009, Pub. by Novalis Trust) Anthroposophic.

Putting the Information Infrastructure to Work. (Illus.). 109p. (Orig.). (C). 1994. pap. text 35.00 (*0-7881-1217-1*) DIANE Pub.

Putting the Information Superstructure to Work. 1997. lib. bdg. 250.75 (*0-8490-7751-6*) Gordon Pr.

Putting the One-Minute Manager to Work. Kenneth Blanchard. (Illus.). 110p. 1988. pap. 11.95 (*0-425-10425-7*) Berkley Pub.

Putting the Patient First: Up Front with Advocacy & Community Service. Bob Richards & Jeanan Yasiri. 149p. (Orig.). 1997. pap. 90.00 (*1-56829-082-9*, 5001) Med Group Mgmt.

Putting the Pieces Together: A Status Report on Integrated Child & Family Services. Lynn R. De Lapp. 62p. (Orig.). (C). 1994. pap. text 20.00 (*0-7881-0688-0*) DIANE Pub.

Putting the Pieces Together: Comprehensive School-Linked Strategies for Children & Families. Government Printing Office Staff. 104p. 1996. pap. 8.50 (*0-16-048779-X*) USGPO.

Putting the Pieces Together: Comprehensive School-Linked Strategies for Children & Families. rev. ed. Leila Fiester. 98p. (C). 1998. pap. text 25.00 (*0-7881-7145-3*) DIANE Pub.

Putting the Pieces Together: Controlling Lead Hazards in the Nation's Housing. Cushing N. Dolbeare. (Illus.). 205p. 1997. reprint ed. pap. text 30.00 (*0-7881-4717-X*) DIANE Pub.

Putting the Pieces Together: Survey of State Systems for Children in Crisis. 40p. 1990. 10.00 (*1-55516-630-X*, 6120) Natl Conf State Legis.

Putting the Pieces Together Vol. 4: A Linguistically Based Cognitive Retraining Manual. Kathryn Kilpatrick. (Illus.). 389p. 1985. student ed. 37.00 (*1-880504-04-9*) Visit Nurse.

Putting the Pieces Together Again. rev. ed. Frederic F. Flach. LC 95-50894. 212p. 1995. pap. 8.95 (*1-886330-03-4*, Pub. by Hatherleigh) Norton.

Putting the Positive Thinker to Work. Alice Potter. 1998. mass mkt. 5.99 (*0-425-16376-8*) Berkley Pub.

***Putting the Power of Public Engagement to Work for Your Schools & Community.** William G. O'Callaghan. 110p. 1999. ring bd. 49.95 (*0-914607-68-5*, 1748) Master Tchr.

Putting the Record Straight: World Helicopter Speed Record. Picton Publishing (Chippenham) Ltd. Staff. (C). 1987. 22.00 (*0-948251-38-7*, Pub. by Picton) St Mut.

Putting the "T" in Health Care TQM Application Report: A Model for Integrated TQM: Clinical Care & Operations. 165p. 1992. pap. write for info. (*1-879364-26-3*) GOAL-QPC.

Putting the Thanks Back in Thanksgiving. Dennis Rainey & Barbara Rainey. 16p. (Orig.). 1.95 (*1-57229-007-2*) FamilyLife.

Putting the Web to Work. David D. Thornburg. (Illus.). 201p. 1996. pap. 24.95 (*0-942207-12-2*) Starsong CA.

Putting the Work Ethic to Work. Daniel Yankelovich & John Immerwahr. 45p. (Orig.). 1983. pap. 20.00 (*1-889483-33-8*) Public Agenda.

Putting the World in a Nutshell: The Art of the Formula Tale. Sheila Dailey. LC 94-829. 126p. 1994. 35.00 (*0-8242-0860-9*) Wilson.

Putting Together a Staff Development Program for Early Education. 1975. 2.00 (*0-939418-36-3*) Ferguson-Florissant.

Putting Together & Taking Apart: Addition & Subtraction. Karen Economopoulos & Susan J. Russell. Ed. by Catherine Anderson et al. (Investigations in Number, Data, & Space Ser.). (Illus.). 195p. (Orig.). (J). (gr. 2). 1996. pap., teacher ed. 22.95 (*1-57232-218-7*, DS21649) Seymour Pubns.

Putting Together & Taking Apart: Addition & Subtraction. rev. ed. Karen Economopoulos & Susan J. Russell. Ed. by Catherine Anderson et al. (Investigations in Number, Data, & Space Ser.). (Illus.). 202p. (Orig.). (J). (gr. 2 up). 1997. pap. text 22.95 (*1-57232-657-3*, 43804) Seymour Pubns.

Putting Total Quality Management to Work: What TQM Means, How to Use It & How to Sustain It over the Long Run. Marshall Sashkin & Kenneth J. Kiser. LC 92-31296. (Illus.). 216p. 1993. pap. 19.95 (*1-881052-24-9*) Berrett-Koehler.

Putting Transfer of Development Rights to Work in California. Rick Pruetz. 232p. (Orig.). 1993. pap. text 25.00 (*0-923956-29-8*) Solano Pr.

***Putting Trust in the U. S. Budget: Federal Trust Funds & the Politics of Commitment.** Eric M. Patashnik. LC 99-57404. (Theories of Institutional Design Ser.). (Illus.). 280p. 2000. write for info. (*0-521-77174-9*); pap. write for info. (*0-521-77748-8*) Cambridge U Pr.

Putting up Roots. Charles Sheffield. LC 97-16926. 256p. 1997. text 21.95 (*0-312-86241-5*) St Martin.

Putting up Roots. Charles Sheffield. (Tor Science Fiction Ser.). 1998. mass mkt. 5.99 (*0-8125-3892-7*, Pub. by Tor Bks) St Martin.

Putting up Roots. Charles Sheffield. (Jupiter Ser.: 3). 1998. mass mkt. 5.99 (*0-8125-5392-6*, Pub. by Tor Bks) St Martin.

Putting up with Mr. Right. Len D. McMillan & Marvin Wray. LC 96-135963. 158p. 1996. pap. 10.99 (*0-8280-0967-8*) Review & Herald.

Putting You in Creative Aerobic Dance: The Fun & Fitness of a Lifetime Sport Through Movement to Music. Colleen Kirby & Laura Roberts. Ed. by David Fritze. LC 80-84937. (Illus.). 130p. (Orig.). 1981. pap. 5.95 (*0-9605744-0-9*) Korakas-Roberts-Kirby.

Putting Your Angels to Work. Norvel Hayes. 64p. (Orig.). 1989. pap. 5.99 (*0-89274-571-1*, HH571) Harrison Hse.

Putting Your Best Foot Forward: How to Advertise & Promote Your Business. Steven F. Diggs. LC 89-85880. (Illus.). 1990. 17.95 (*0-9624293-0-9*) Boyd & Franklin.

Putting Your Daughters on the Stage: British Lesbian Theatre from the 1960s to the Present. Sandra Freeman. (Sexual Politics Ser.). (Illus.). 256p. 1996. pap. 16.95 (*0-304-33309-3*) Continuum.

Putting Your Heart Online. Nancy Capulet & Nancy Blachman. (Illus.). xvi, 244p. 1998. pap. 14.95 (*0-9663774-0-0*) Variable Symbols.

Putting Your Heart Online: Matchmaker Edition. Nancy Capulet & Nancy Blachman. (Illus.). xvi, 237p. 1998. pap. 14.95 (*0-9663774-1-9*) Variable Symbols.

Putting Your Money Where Your Heart Is. Jack B. Scott. 1985. pap. 4.95 (*0-934688-14-1*) Great Comm Pubns.

Putting Your Past Behind You: Finding Hope for Life's Deepest Hurts. expanded rev. ed. Erwin Lutzer. 168p. 1997. pap. 11.99 (*0-8024-5644-8*, 12) Moody.

***Putting Your Small Business on the Web.** Maria Langer. 352p. 2000. pap. text 24.99 (*0-201-71713-1*) Peachpit Pr.

Putting Your Talent to Work: Identifying, Cultivating & Marketing Your Natural Talents. Lucia Capacchione & Peggy Van Pelt. 200p. (Orig.). 1996. pap. 12.95 (*1-55874-406-1*, 4061) Health Comm.

Putty. Keith Abbott. (Illus.). 1971. 29.95 (*0-912652-31-4*) Blue Wind.

Putty: Poems from Hollywood. Mark Dunster. 11p. 1998. pap. 5.00 (*0-89642-608-4*) Linden Pubs.

Putu Wijaya in Performance: A Script & Study of Indonesian Literature. Ed. by Ellen Rafferty. LC 89-52201. (Monographs: No. 5). 163p. (C). lib. bdg. 24.95 (*0-614-24178-2*) U Wisc Ctr SE Asian.

PUU Sections 1-2500, Vol. 155. 234p. 1999. write for info. (*0-327-07004-8*, 57784-12) LEXIS Pub.

PUU Sections 10001-21600, Vol. 157. 30p. 1999. write for info. (*0-327-07006-4*, 57786-12) LEXIS Pub.

PUU Sections 101000-End, Vol. 160. 159p. 1999. write for info. (*0-327-07009-9*, 57789-12) LEXIS Pub.

PUU Sections 21601-39999, Vol. 158. 60p. 1999. write for info. (*0-327-07007-2*, 57787-12) LEXIS Pub.

PUU Sections 2501-10000, Vol. 156. 161p. 1999. write for info. (*0-327-07005-6*, 57785-12) LEXIS Pub.

PUU Sections 40000-100999, Vol. 159. 114p. 1999. write for info. (*0-327-07008-0*, 57788-12) LEXIS Pub.

Puuhonua o Honaunau: A Place of Refuge. 2nd ed. Richard W. Hazlett. (Illus.). 74p. (J). (gr. 3-8). 1998. reprint ed. pap. 3.95 (*0-940295-17-2*) HI Natural Hist.

Puvis de Chavannes. Brian Petrie. Ed. by Simon Lee. LC 97-74710. (Illus.). 192p. 1997. text 86.95 (*1-85928-451-5*, Pub. by Ashgate Pub) Ashgate Pub Co.

Puyallup-Nisqually. Marian W. Smith. LC 73-82360. (Columbia Univ. Contributions to Anthropology Ser.: Vol. 32). 1969. reprint ed. 34.50 (*0-404-50582-1*) AMS Pr.

Puzzle. Juliet Martin. LC 93-18051. (Illus.). (J). 1994. write for info. (*0-383-03710-7*) SRA McGraw.

Puzzle. Jessica Pierce. (Spider's Child Ser.: No. 5). 144p. 1999. mass mkt. 3.50 (*0-8217-4985-4*, Pinncle Kensgtn) Kensgtn Pub Corp.

***Puzzle.** Norita J. Sieffert. (Illus.). 258p. 1999. pap. 9.99 (*0-9672999-0-X*) Wandering Star Bks.

Puzzle: Linking Life's Pieces. Solaya Schero & Jewel Smith-Lane. pap. 12.95 (*1-56167-555-5*) Am Literary Pr.

Puzzle Adventure Kit: The Message in the Mirror. Sarah Dixon. (Illus.). (J). (gr. 4 up). 1997. pap. 8.95 (*0-7460-2829-6*, Usborne) EDC.

Puzzle Adventures. Gaby Waters et al. (Illus.). 144p. (J). (gr. 4-7). 1988. pap. 9.95 (*0-7460-0155-X*) EDC.

Puzzle Arcade: For People Who Like Lots of Hints. Jerry Slocum. (Illus.). 48p. (YA). (gr. 7 up). 1996. spiral bd. 19.95 (*1-57054-056-X*) Klutz.

Puzzle Castle. S. Leigh. (Young Puzzles Ser.). (Illus.). 32p. (J). (ps up). 1993. text 5.95 (*0-7460-1284-5*); lib. bdg. 13.95 (*0-88110-624-0*) EDC.

Puzzle Castle Book. E D C Publishing Staff. 1997. pap. text 39.95 incl. cd-rom (*0-88110-920-7*) EDC.

Puzzle Cloth Book. Willabel L. Tong. (Baby Einstein's Brainy Baby Ser.). (Illus.). (J). Date not set. 15.95 (*1-58117-090-4*, Piggy Toes Pr) Intervisual Bks.

Puzzle Club Activity Book. Dandi Daley Mackall. (Puzzle Club Mystery Ser.). 1997. pap. text 0.99 (*0-570-05025-1*, 56-1849) Concordia.

Puzzle Club Christmas Mystery. Mark Young. 76p. (J). (gr. 3-5). 1997. pap. text 4.99 (*0-570-05026-X*, 56-1850) Concordia.

Puzzle Club Picture Book. Dandi Daley Mackall. LC 97-215582. 1997. pap. text 6.99 (*0-570-05024-3*, 56-1848) Concordia.

Puzzle Dungeon. S. Leigh. (Young Puzzles Ser.). (Illus.). 32p. (J). (ps up). 1995. pap. 5.95 (*0-7460-1679-4*, Usborne); lib. bdg. 13.95 (*0-88110-753-0*, Usborne) EDC.

Puzzle Farm. S. Leigh. (Young Puzzles Ser.). (Illus.). 32p. (J). (ps up). 1992. pap. 5.95 (*0-7460-0712-4*, Usborne); lib. bdg. 13.95 (*0-88110-555-4*, Usborne) EDC.

Puzzle for Players. Patrick Quentin. 250p. 1989. reprint ed. pap. 5.95 (*1-55882-008-6*, Lib Crime Classics) Intl Polygonics.

Puzzle for Puppets. Patrick Quentin. LC 89-85719. 206p. 1989. pap. 7.95 (*1-55882-020-5*, Lib Crime Classics) Intl Polygonics.

Puzzle for Wantons. Patrick Quentin. LC 90-80764. 229p. 1990. reprint ed. pap. 7.95 (*1-55882-063-9*) Intl Polygonics.

***Puzzle from the Past: Multimedia Edition.** Janet Golio & Mike Golio. (Illus.). 150p. (J). 2000. cd-rom 10.95 (*1-883573-03-3*, Little Blue) Pride & Imprints.

Puzzle Holiday. Susannah Leigh. (Illus.). 32p. (J). (ps up). 1998. pap. 5.95 (*0-7460-2680-3*, Usborne); lib. bdg. 13.95 (*0-88110-970-3*, Usborne) EDC.

Puzzle in the Pond. Margaret Sutton. Date not set. lib. bdg. 19.95 (*0-8488-2130-0*) Amereon Ltd.

Puzzle in the Portrait. Eleanor F. Rosellini. LC 99-71651. (Illus.). 115p. (gr. 3-6). 1999. 16.95 (*1-57860-026-X*) Guild Pr IN.

Puzzle Island. Paul Adshead. (ITA.). (J). 1991. 13.99 (*0-85953-558-4*) Childs Play.

Puzzle Island. Paul Adshead. LC 91-33416. (Illus.). 24p. (J). (gr. k-7). 1991. 13.99 (*0-85953-402-2*); pap. 7.99 (*0-85953-403-0*) Childs Play.

Puzzle Island. Paul Adshead. (J). 1996. lib. bdg. 16.95 (*0-85953-885-0*) Childs Play.

Puzzle Island. S. Leigh. (Young Puzzles Ser.). (Illus.). 32p. (J). (ps up). 1991. lib. bdg. 13.95 (*0-88110-558-9*, Usborne) EDC.

Puzzle Island. S. Leigh. (Young Puzzles Ser.). (Illus.). 32p. (J). (ps up). 1991. pap. 5.95 (*0-7460-0596-2*, Usborne) EDC.

Puzzle Journey Around the World. Lesley Sims. (Puzzle Journey Ser.). (Illus.). 32p. (J). (gr. 3-7). 1998. pap. 5.95 (*0-7460-2682-X*, Usborne) EDC.

Puzzle Journey Around the World. Lesley Sims. (Puzzle Journey Ser.). (Illus.). 32p. (YA). (gr. 3 up). 1998. lib. bdg. 13.95 (*0-88110-975-4*, Usborne) EDC.

Puzzle Journey into Space. Rebecca Heddle. (Puzzle Journey Ser.). (Illus.). 32p. (J). (gr. 3 up). 1996. lib. bdg. 13.95 (*0-88110-825-1*, Usborne) EDC.

Puzzle Journey into Space. Lesley Sims. (Puzzle Journey Ser.). (Illus.). 32p. (J). (gr. 3 up). 1996. pap. 5.95 (*0-7460-1715-4*, Usborne) EDC.

Puzzle Journey Through Time. Rebecca Heddle & A. Spenceley. (Puzzle Journey Ser.). (Illus.). 32p. (J). (gr. 3 up). 1995. pap. 5.95 (*0-7460-1656-5*, Usborne); lib. bdg. 13.95 (*0-88110-723-9*, Usborne) EDC.

Puzzle Journey under the Sea. Ed. by Lesley Sims. (Puzzle Journey Ser.). (Illus.). 32p. (YA). (gr. 3 up). 1999. pap. 6.95 (*0-7460-2685-4*); lib. bdg. 14.95 (*1-58086-133-4*) EDC.

Puzzle Jungle. Susannah Leigh. (Young Puzzles Ser.). (Illus.). 32p. (J). (ps up). 1995. text 5.95 (*0-7460-1707-3*, Usborne); lib. bdg. 13.95 (*0-88110-767-0*, Usborne) EDC.

P

Puzzle King: Sam Loyd's Chess Problems & Selected Mathematical Puzzles. Ed. by Sid Pickard. 240p. 1996. pap. 22.95 (*1-886846-05-7*) Pickard & Son.

Puzzle Maps U. S. A. Nancy L. Clouse. (J). (gr. 2-6). 1995. pap. 5.95 (*0-8050-3597-4*) H Holt & Co.

Puzzle Maps U. S. A. Spanish Edition. Nancy Clouse. (J). (gr. 2-6). 1995. pap. 5.95 (*0-8050-3598-2*) H Holt & Co.

Puzzle Maps Usa Spanish. Clouse. 1993. pap., teacher ed. 4.95 (*0-8050-1846-8*) St Martin.

Puzzle Master. (Understanding Computers Ser.). (Illus.). 128p. 1988. lib. bdg. 25.93 (*0-8094-5742-3*) Time-Life.

Puzzle Master. (Understanding Computers Ser.). (Illus.). 128p. (gr. 7). 1999. 16.95 (*0-8094-5741-5*) Time-Life.

Puzzle Mountain. Susannah Leigh & Brenda Haw. (Young Puzzles Ser.). (Illus.). 32p. (J). (ps up). 1994. pap. 5.95 (*0-7460-1288-8*, Usborne); lib. bdg. 13.95 (*0-88110-665-8*, Usborne) EDC.

Puzzle Ocean. Susannah Leigh. (Young Puzzles Ser.). (Illus.). 32p. (J). (ps up). 1996. text 5.95 (*0-7460-2333-2*, Usborne); lib. bdg. 13.95 (*0-88110-846-4*, Usborne) EDC.

Puzzle of Ethics. Peter Vardy & Paul Grosch. LC 95-23005. 240p. 1996. pap. 12.95 (*1-55778-746-8*) M E Sharpe.

Puzzle of Ethics. Peter Vardy & Paul Grosch. LC 97-2913. 238p. (C). (gr. 13). 1997. text 74.95 (*0-7656-0163-X*); pap. text 24.95 (*0-7656-0164-8*) M E Sharpe.

Puzzle of Evil. Peter Vardy. LC 97-2910. 206p. (C). (gr. 13). 1997. text 70.95 (*0-7656-0167-2*); pap. text 23.95 (*0-7656-0168-0*) M E Sharpe.

Puzzle of Evil. Peter Vardy. LC 95-23004. 208p. 1997. pap. 10.95 (*1-55778-747-6*) M E Sharpe.

Puzzle of Experience. J. J. Valberg. LC 92-13570. 234p. 1992. text 58.00 (*0-19-824291-3*, Clarendon Pr) OUP.

Puzzle of God. Peter Vardy. LC 97-2912. 240p. (C). (gr. 13). 1997. text 74.95 (*0-7656-0169-9*); pap. text 24.95 (*0-7656-0170-2*) M E Sharpe.

Puzzle of Heart Failure - Putting the Pieces Together: For Heart Failure Patients. Susan D. Allen et al. (Illus.). 64p. 1991. pap. text 3.25 (*0-916999-09-2*) HERC Inc.

Puzzle of Integration. Ed. by CYRCE - Circle for Youth Research Cooperation in E. (European Yearbook on Youth Policy & Research Ser.: Vol. 1). xv, 339p. (C). 1995. lib. bdg. 101.55 (*3-11-014565-0*) De Gruyter.

Puzzle of Judicial Behavior. Lawrence Baum. LC 97-4870. (Analytical Perspectives on Politics Ser.). 232p. (C). 1997. text 44.50 (*0-472-10670-8*, 10670); pap. text 19.95 (*0-472-08335-X*, 08335) U of Mich Pr.

Puzzle of Latin American Economic Development. Patrice Franko. LC 99-23761. 552p. 1999. pap. 29.95 (*0-8476-9525-5*); text 79.00 (*0-8476-9524-7*) Rowman.

Puzzle of Pain. Genevieve Levy. (Illus.). 176p. 1994. text 43.00 (*976-8097-89-2*) Gordon & Breach.

Puzzle of Sex. Peter Vardy. LC 97-29752. 256p. (C). (gr. 13). 1998. text 72.95 (*0-7656-0171-0*); pap. text 24.95 (*0-7656-0172-9*) M E Sharpe.

Puzzle of Strikes: Class & State Strategies in Postwar Italy. Roberto Franzosi. LC 93-51254. (Cambridge Studies in Comparative Politics). (Illus.). 528p. (C). 1995. text 69.95 (*0-521-45287-2*) Cambridge U Pr.

Puzzle of the Cross. Elmer E. Burrall. 1991. pap. 5.25 (*1-55673-278-3*, 9111) CSS OH.

Puzzle of the Dinosaur-Birds: The Story of Archaeopteryx. Miriam Schlein. LC 95-44586. (Illus.). 40p. (J). (gr. 1-4). 1996. pap. 15.89 (*0-8037-1283-9*, NewStar Pr) NewStar Media.

Puzzle of the Gospels. Peter Vardy & Mary Mills. LC 97-2911. 256p. (C). (gr. 13). 1997. text 76.95 (*0-7656-0165-6*) M E Sharpe.

Puzzle of the Gospels. Peter Vardy & Mary E. Mills. LC 97-2911. 256p. (C). (gr. 13). 1997. pap. text 27.95 (*0-7656-0166-4*) M E Sharpe.

Puzzle of the 613 Commandments & Why Bother. Philip J. Caplan. LC 96-6422. 272p. 1996. 40.00 (*1-56821-893-1*) Aronson.

Puzzle of the Tacoma Narrows Bridge Collapse. Robert G. Fuller et al. Ep. 1982. 195.00 (*0-471-87320-9*) Wiley.

Puzzle of the Week Teaching Plan Book: For Grades 5-6. 146p. 1993. 24.95 (*1-56892-002-4*) CSL Assocs.

Puzzle Palace: A Report on America's Most Secret Agency. James Bamford. 656p. 1983. pap. 15.95 (*0-14-006748-5*, Penguin Bks) Viking Penguin.

Puzzle Palace: Inside the National Security Agency, America's Most Secret Intelligence Organization. rev. ed. James Bamford. 656p. 1999. pap. 13.95 (*0-14-023116-1*, Penguin Bks) Viking Penguin.

Puzzle Pals. Ed. by Scholastic, Inc. Staff. (J). 1993. pap. 7.95 (*0-590-49034-6*) Scholastic Inc.

Puzzle People. Helen Oxenbury. LC 94-68898. (Illus.). 18p. (J). (ps up). 1995. pap. 4.99 (*1-56402-572-1*) Candlewick Pr.

Puzzle People: Memoirs of a Transplant Surgeon. Thomas E. Starzl. LC 92-455. (Illus.). 400p. (C). 1992. text 24.95 (*0-8229-3714-X*) U of Pittsburgh Pr.

Puzzle Pieces. unabridged ed. Ken Otis. (Illus.). 160p. 1998. pap. 12.95 (*0-9666106-0-1*) K Otis.

Puzzle Place. Illus. by Diaz, Jamie, Studios Staff. (Look & Find Ser.). 24p. (J). 1996. lib. bdg. 14.95 (*1-56674-210-2*, HTS Bks) Forest Hse.

Puzzle Planet. Susannah Leigh. (Young Puzzles Ser.). (Illus.). 32p. (J). (ps up). 1993. pap. 5.95 (*0-7460-1286-1*, Usborne); lib. bdg. 13.95 (*0-88110-646-1*, Usborne) EDC.

Puzzle Playground. Ed. by Highlights for Children Staff. (Illus.). 32p. (J). (ps-2). 1995. pap. 3.95 (*1-56397-453-3*) Boyds Mills Pr.

Puzzle Poems: Poems of Form & Substance - An Exercise in Experimentation, a Work in Progress. Roberta Mendel. (Chameleon Ser.). 1997. pap. 10.00 (*0-936424-16-8*, 015) Pin Prick.

Puzzle School. Susannah Leigh. Ed. by Michelle Bates. (Young Puzzles Ser.). (Illus.). 32p. (Orig.). (J). (ps up). 1997. pap. 5.95 (*0-7460-2678-1*, Usborne); lib. bdg. 13.95 (*0-88110-940-1*, Usborne) EDC.

Puzzle Tables. Thomas C. O'Bries. 64p. (J). (gr. 3-8). 1980. pap. text 9.50 (*0-914040-83-9*) Cuisenaire.

Puzzle Tables: Number Problems with Computational Skills. Thomas C. O'Brien. (J). (gr. 4-7). 1995. pap. 8.95 (*0-201-48011-5*) Addison-Wesley.

Puzzle Town. S. Leigh. (Young Puzzles Ser.). (Illus.). 32p. (J). (ps up). 1991. pap. 5.95 (*0-7460-0681-0*, Usborne); lib. bdg. 13.95 (*0-88110-554-6*, Usborne) EDC.

Puzzle Train. Susanna Leigh. (Young Puzzles Ser.). (Illus.). 32p. (J). (ps up). 1996. pap. 5.95 (*0-7460-2331-6*, Usborne); lib. bdg. 13.95 (*0-88110-798-0*, Usborne) EDC.

Puzzle Trains in Chinatown & Ancient Rome. A. Rayment. Date not set. 4.99 (*1-871676-92-4*, Pub. by Christian Focus) Spring Arbor Dist.

Puzzle with Four Pieces: The Betrayal, Death & Resurrection of Jesus Christ. Michael C. Nichols. (Illus.). vi, 136p. 1997. 19.95 (*0-9662051-0-3*) DayStar Pubns.

Puzzle World (B - U) S. Leigh. (Young Puzzles Ser.). (Illus.). 96p. (J). (ps up). 1992. pap. 9.95 (*0-7460-0731-0*) EDC.

Puzzled about God? Word Search Puzzles. Theresa Hayes. Ed. by Pat Fittro. 48p. (Orig.). 1997. pap. 3.99 (*0-7847-0639-5*, 02687) Standard Pub.

Puzzled America. Sherwood Anderson. (History - United States Ser.). 287p. 1993. reprint ed. lib. bdg. 79.00 (*0-7812-4916-3*) Rprt Serv.

Puzzled America (1935) Sherwood Anderson. 287p. 1970. reprint ed. 15.00 (*0-911858-07-5*) Appel.

Puzzled Heart. Amanda Cross. 1999. mass mkt. 5.99 (*0-345-41884-0*) Ballantine Pub Grp.

Puzzled Heart. large type ed. D. Y. Cameron. 320p. 1988. 27.99 (*0-7089-1909-X*) Ulverscroft.

Puzzled Penguin. Keith Faulkner. LC 98-56275. (Illus.). 16p. (J). (gr. k-2). 1999. 11.95 (*0-7613-1042-8*, Copper Beech Bks) Millbrook Pr.

Puzzled Penguins. Patrick Merrell. LC 99-175238. (Illus.). 32p. (J). (ps-1). 1998. pap. 3.50 (*0-8167-4937-X*) Troll Communs.

Puzzled Prodigy. Jeffrey A. Nesbit. (Capital Crew Ser.). (Orig.). (J). (gr. 3-6). 1992. pap. 1.00 (*0-89693-075-0*, Victor Bks) Chariot Victor.

Puzzled Which to Choose: Conflicting Socio-Political Views in the Works of Captain Frederick Marryat. Louis J. Parascandola. LC 95-49576. (American University Studies IV: Vol. 182). 142p. (C). 1997. text 33.95 (*0-8204-3077-3*) P Lang Pubng.

Puzzled Which To Choose: Conflicting Socio-Political Views in the Works of Captain Frederick Marryat. Louis J. Parascandola. 152p. 1997. 33.95 (*0-614-30264-1*) P Lang Pubng.

Puzzlegrams: A Colorful Challenging Collection of 178 Classic Puzzles. Compiled by Pentagram Partnership Staff. 192p. 1989. per. 18.00 (*0-671-68740-9*, Fireside) S&S Trade Pap.

Puzzlemania. Jonathon J. Thompson, Jr. (Illus.). 100p. 1992. write for info. (*0-933479-36-0*) Thompson.

***Puzzlemania Superchallenge, Bk. 1.** Ed. by Jeff O'Hare. (Illus.). 48p. (YA). (gr. 5 up). 1999. pap. 6.95 (*1-56397-789-3*) Boyds Mills Pr.

Puzzlemania Superchallenge, Bk. 2. Ed. by Jeff O'Hare. (Illus.). 48p. (YA). (gr. 5 up). 1999. pap. 6.95 (*1-56397-790-7*) Boyds Mills Pr.

Puzzlemania Superchallenge, Bk. 3. Ed. by Jeff O'Hare. (Illus.). 48p. (YA). (gr. 5 up). 1999. pap. 6.95 (*1-56397-791-5*) Boyds Mills Pr.

Puzzlemania Superchallenge Book 4. Highlights Staff. Ed. by Jeff O'Hare. Vol. 4. (Illus.). 48p. (YA). (gr. 4-7). 1999. pap. 6.95 (*1-56397-792-3*) Boyds Mills Pr.

Puzzlemaster Presents: 200 Mind-Bending Challenges. Will Shortz. LC 96-203342. 192p. 1996. pap. 12.00 (*0-8129-6386-5*, Times Bks) Crown Pub Group.

Puzzlers. Nancy Krulik. LC 98-88309. (My Very First Winnie the Pooh Ser.). (Illus.). 64p. (J). (ps-1). 1999. pap. 4.99 (*0-7868-4344-6*, Pub. by Disney Pr) Time Warner.

Puzzlers, Vol. 1. Beckie Karras. 51p. (Orig.). 1992. pap. 7.95 (*1-879633-10-8*) Eldersong.

Puzzler's Almanac. Sole. 1998. pap. write for info. (*0-8069-6327-1*) Sterling.

Puzzles. Sally Hewitt. (Take Off With Ser.). (Illus.). 32p. 1996. lib. bdg. 21.40 (*0-8172-4115-9*) Raintree Steck-V.

Puzzles. Durby Peterson. (Play & Learn Ser.). (Illus.). 48p. (J). (ps-k). 1998. pap. 3.95 (*1-57029-232-9*, W02311) Totline Pubns.

Puzzles. Dava J. Walker. LC 95-39033. (Illus.). (J). 1996. pap. 6.95 (*0-914996-29-0*) Lollipop Power.

Puzzles about Art. 2nd ed. Battin. 2001. pap. text. write for info. (*0-312-15759-2*) St Martin.

Puzzles about Art: An Aesthetics Casebook. Margaret P. Battin et al. LC 87-60519. 226p. (Orig.). 1989. pap. text 26.95 (*0-312-00307-2*) St Martin.

Puzzles & Games. (Home Workbooks Ser.). (Illus.). 64p. (Orig.). (J). (gr. 2-3). 1997. pap., wbk. ed. 2.49 (*0-88724-374-6*, CD-6871) Carson-Dellos.

Puzzles & Games. Peter Lerangis. Ed. by Jane Sovndal. (Thinking Skills Library). (Illus.). 106p. (Orig.). (J). (gr. 2-5). 1997. pap., teacher ed. 9.95 (*1-56784-712-9*) Newbridge Educ.

Puzzles & Games. Virginia Satkowski. Ed. by Susan Evento. (Macmillan Early Skills Program - Conversion Ser.). 64p. (J). (ps-2). 1995. pap. 9.95 (*1-56784-510-X*) Newbridge Educ.

Puzzles & Games. Illus. by Pam Thayer. (Home Workbooks Ser.). 64p. (Orig.). (J). (gr. k-1). 1997. pap., wbk. ed. 2.49 (*0-88724-373-8*, CD-6870) Carson-Dellos.

Puzzles & Games for Critical & Creative Thinking. June Bailey. (Gifted & Talented Ser.). (Illus.). 80p. (J). (ps-1). 1994. pap. 4.95 (*1-56565-129-4*, 01294W, Pub. by Lowell Hse) NTC Contemp Pub Co.

Puzzles & Games for Critical & Creative Thinking. Martha Cheney. (Gifted & Talented Ser.). (Illus.). 80p. (J). (gr. 1-3). 1994. pap. 4.95 (*1-56565-139-1*, 01391W, Pub. by Lowell Hse) NTC Contemp Pub Co.

Puzzles & Games for Reading & Math, Bk. 2. Martha C. Cheney. (Gifted & Talented Ser.: Vol. 2). (Illus.). 64p. (Orig.). (J). (ps-3). 1996. pap. text, wbk. ed. 4.95 (*1-56565-374-2*, 03742W, Pub. by Lowell Hse Juvenile) NTC Contemp Pub Co.

Puzzles & Games in Logic & Reasoning. Terry M. Badger. LC 94-36774. 1995. pap. 4.95 (*0-486-28583-9*) Dover.

Puzzles & Games to Reinforce Basic Skills. Dona H. Rice. (Illus.). 334p. (J). 1998. pap., teacher ed. 24.95 (*1-57690-208-0*, TCM2208) Tchr Create Mat.

Puzzles & Games Workbook. Oksana Hlodan. (Monster Math Ser.). (Illus.). 64p. (J). (ps-1). 1998. pap., wbk. ed. 4.95 (*1-56565-845-0*, 08450W, Pub. by Lowell Hse Juvenile) NTC Contemp Pub Co.

Puzzles & Games Workbook, Bk. 2. Oksana Hlodan. (Monster Math Ser.). (Illus.). 64p. (J). (ps-1). 1999. pap., wbk. ed. 4.95 (*0-7373-0212-7*, 02127W) NTC Contemp Pub Co.

Puzzles & Paradoxes in Economics. Mark Skousen & Kenna C. Taylor. LC 96-42202. 232p. 1997. 70.00 (*1-85898-378-9*) E Elgar.

Puzzles & Paradoxes in Economics. Mark Skousen & Kenna C. Taylor. LC 96-42202. 232p. (C). 1998. pap. 25.00 (*1-84064-049-9*) E Elgar.

***Puzzles & Prayers.** Margaret Shauers. 2000. pap. 5.99 (*0-570-07032-5*) Concordia.

Puzzles & Purses. Alan M. Hofmeister et al. (Reading for All Learners Ser.). (Illus.). (J). pap. write for info. (*1-56861-177-3*) Swift Lrn Res.

Puzzles & Puzzlers, Mini-Bk. Owl Magazine Editors. (Illus.). 96p. (J). (gr. 3 up). 1992. pap. 4.95 (*0-920775-67-5*, Pub. by Owl Bks) Firefly Bks Ltd.

Puzzles & Revolutions. Fred Jevons. 70p. (C). 1979. 40.00 (*0-86828-368-1*, Pub. by Deakin Univ) St Mut.

Puzzles & Thinking Games. Penny Holland & Carole Kubota. (BrainBooster Ser.). (Illus.). 32p. (J). (gr. 3 up). 1986. 6.95 (*0-88679-459-5*) Educ Insights.

Puzzles, Boxes & Toys: Creative Scroll Saw Patterns. Percy W. Blandford. (Illus.). 200p. 1991. 19.95 (*0-8306-6706-7*, 3706); pap. 12.95 (*0-8306-8706-8*) McGraw-Hill Prof.

PUZZLES ENGLISH BOOK1, PEP 1. Keith Methold et al. (English As a Second Language Bk.). 1978. pap. text 3.50 (*0-582-55260-5*) Longman.

Puzzles for Pleasure. Barry R. Clarke. (Illus.). 128p. (C). 1994. pap. 11.95 (*0-521-46634-2*) Cambridge U Pr.

Puzzles for the High IQ. Lloyd King. Ed. by Philip J. Cart. LC 96-27357. (Illus.). 195p. (Orig.). 1996. pap. 5.95 (*0-8069-4381-5*) Sterling.

Puzzles for the Mind. Tom Werneck. Tr. by Annette Englander. LC 98-14802. 80p. 1998. 5.95 (*0-8069-9971-3*) Sterling.

Puzzles for the Will. Jordan H. Sobel. (Toronto Studies in Philosophy). (Illus.). 256p. 1998. text 55.00 (*0-8020-4326-7*) U of Toronto Pr.

Puzzles from Catel's Cabinet & Bestelmeier's Magazine 1785 to 1823. Jerry Slocum & Dieter Gebhardt. (History of Puzzles Ser.). (Illus.). 59p. 1997. pap. 10.00 (*1-890980-02-1*) Slocum Puzzle.

Puzzles in Math & Logic: One Hundred New Recreations. Aaron J. Friedland. (Orig.). 1971. pap. 3.95 (*0-486-22256-X*) Dover.

***Puzzles in Paper: Concepts in Historical Watermarks: Essays from the International Conference on Watermarks in Roanoke, Virginia.** International Conference on Watermarks Staff et al. LC 00-32649. 2000. write for info. (*1-58456-029-0*) Oak Knoll.

Puzzles in Space. David Stonerod. (Illus.). 1982. pap. text 7.95 (*0-914534-03-3*) Stokes.

Puzzles in Wood. E. M. Wyatt. LC 79-67740. (Illus.). 64p. 1981. reprint ed. pap. 6.50 (*0-918036-09-7*) Woodcraft Supply.

Puzzles, Mazes & Numbers. Charles Snape & Heather Scott. (Illus.). 128p. (C). 1995. 21.95 (*0-521-46500-1*) Cambridge U Pr.

Puzzles of Amish Life. Donald B. Kraybill. LC 90-71119. (People's Place Book Ser.: No. 10). (Illus.). 112p. 1997. pap. 7.95 (*1-56148-001-0*) Good Bks PA.

***Puzzles of Finance: Six Practical Problems & Their Remarkable Solutions.** Mark P. Kritzman. LC 99-55828. (Investments Ser.). 256p. 2000. 29.95 (*0-471-24657-3*) Wiley.

Puzzles of Power. Michael Howlett. (C). 1994. pap. text 35.95 (*0-7730-4914-2*) Addison-Wesley.

Puzzles of Power: An Introduction to Political Science. 2nd ed. David H. Laycock & Michael Howlett. LC 99-176185. 440p. 1998. pap. text 35.00 (*0-19-541377-6*) OUP.

Puzzles of Productivity in Public Organizations. Ed. by Norman Uphoff. LC 93-47560. 1994. pap. 19.95 (*1-55815-291-1*) ICS Pr.

Puzzles of the Body: The Labyrinth in Kafka's Prozess, Hesse's Steppenwolf, & Mann's Zauberberg. David Kenosian. LC 93-44803. (Studies on Themes & Motifs in Literature: Vol. 10). 156p. (C). 1995. 34.95 (*0-8204-2426-9*) P Lang Pubng.

Puzzles on the Electroweak Scale: Proceedings of the Fourteenth International Warsaw Meeting on Elementary Particle Physics, Warsaw, Poland, 27-31 May 1991. Ed. by Z. Ajduk et al. 500p. 1992. text 130.00 (*981-02-0852-9*) World Scientific Pub.

Puzzles, Paradoxes & Brain Teasers. Stan Gibilisco. (Illus.). 140p. 1988. 14.95 (*0-8306-7895-6*, 2895); pap. 8.95 (*0-8306-2895-9*) McGraw-Hill Prof.

Puzzles Paradoxes & Problems. 2nd ed. French & Brown. pap. text. write for info. (*0-312-03653-1*) St Martin.

***Puzzles, Patterns & Problem Solving: Creative Connections to Critical Thinking.** Ruth Toor & Hilda K. Weisburg. (Illus.). 176p. 1999. 28.95 (*0-931315-10-7*) Lib Learn Res.

Puzzles Plus, 1. 48p. 1993. 3.00 (*0-88336-330-5*) New Readers.

Puzzles Plus, 2. 48p. 1993. 3.00 (*0-88336-329-1*) New Readers.

Puzzles Plus, 3. 48p. 1993. 3.00 (*0-88336-327-5*) New Readers.

Puzzles, Riddles & Muddles. (J). (gr. 4-7). 1992. pap. 3.95 (*0-8167-2698-1*) Troll Communs.

Puzzles, the Bible Has the Answers. Agnes Maddy. (Illus.). 48p. (Orig.). 1993. pap. 3.25 (*0-915374-75-7*, 75-7) Rapids Christian.

Puzzling about South Dakota. Gerry Burdick & Julie Burdick. (Illus.). 61p. (Orig.). (J). (gr. 8 up). 1992. pap. 4.95 (*0-9632844-0-1*, 050111557) Dakota Desktop.

Puzzling Adventures of Dr. Ecco. Dennis Shasha. LC 97-43592. (Illus.). 192p. 1998. reprint ed. pap. text 7.95 (*0-486-29615-6*) Dover.

***Puzzling Auditing Puzzles.** J. P. Russell & Janice Russell. LC 00-21479. 2000. write for info. (*0-87389-478-2*) ASQ Qual Pr.

Puzzling Book. Katherine Paterson. Date not set. pap. 1.75 (*0-906731-81-X*, Pub. by Christian Focus) Spring Arbor Dist.

Puzzling Child: From Recognition to Treatment. Ed. by Mary Frank. LC 82-11692. (Journal of Children in Contemporary Society: Vol. 14, No. 4). 109p. 1982. text 39.95 (*0-86656-119-6*) Haworth Pr.

Puzzling Day at Castle MacPelican: A Search & Solve Gamebook. Scoular Anderson. LC 94-14835. (Candlewick Gamebks.). (Illus.). 32p. (J). (gr. 1-5). 1996. reprint ed. pap. 7.99 (*1-56402-852-6*) Candlewick Pr.

Puzzling Day in the Land of the Pharaohs. Scoular Anderson. LC 95-43949. (Illus.). 32p. (J). (gr. 4-7). 1996. 14.99 (*1-56402-877-1*) Candlewick Pr.

Puzzling Day in the Land of the Pharaohs. Scoubar Anderson. LC 95-41016. (Candlewick Gamebook Ser.). (Illus.). 32p. (J). (gr. 2-5). 1997. reprint ed. pap. write for info. (*0-7636-0139-X*) Candlewick Pr.

Puzzling Day in the Land of the Pharaohs Level 2: A Search-&-Solve Gamebook. Scoular Anderson. LC 95-43949. (J). (gr. 2-5). 1997. pap. text 7.99 (*0-7636-0138-1*) Candlewick Pr.

Puzzling Mazes. Lee D. Quinn. (Illus.). (J). (gr. k-3). 1994. pap. 1.00 (*0-486-27980-4*) Dover.

Puzzling Optical Illusions. Thomas Crawford. LC 99-42487. 1999. pap. text 1.00 (*0-486-40151-0*) Dover.

Puzzling Quality Puzzles. J. P. Russell & Janice Russell. (Illus.). 200p. 1998. pap. 10.00 (*0-87389-425-1*, H0993) ASQ Qual Pr.

Puzzling Questions about the Solar System. enl. rev. ed. Martin Gardner. LC 97-1063. (Illus.). 96p. 1997. reprint ed. pap. text 4.95 (*0-486-29440-4*) Dover.

Puzzling Reflections: Test Your Thinking Powers with Mirror-Cubes. Ivan Moscovich. (J). 1991. pap. 6.95 (*0-906212-72-3*, Pub. by Tarquin Pubns) Parkwest Pubns.

Puzzling Through Mark. C. Mackenzie. Date not set. pap. 4.99 (*1-85792-056-2*, Pub. by Christian Focus) Spring Arbor Dist.

Puzzling Through the Bible. C. Stone. Date not set. 2.99 (*1-871676-46-0*, Pub. by Christian Focus) Spring Arbor Dist.

Puzzling Through the News. Pat Rushin. 130p. 1991. pap. 11.95 (*0-913123-33-1*) Galileo.

Puzzling Your Way into Algebra. Pat Stallings. (Illus.). 64p. (YA). (gr. 7-10). 1978. pap. text 8.50 (*0-918932-58-0*, A-1575) Activity Resources.

Puzzling Your Way into Geometry. Pat Stallings. (Illus.). 64p. (YA). (gr. 7-12). 1978. pap. text 8.50 (*0-918932-52-1*, A-1397) Activity Resources.

Puzzlooney: Really Ridiculous Math Puzzles. Russell M. Ginns. (J). (gr. 4-7). 1994. pap. 4.00 (*0-7167-2576-2*) W H Freeman.

PV-Generator Hybrid System for Your PV Home. New England Solar Electric, Inc. Staff. (PV Home Series Booklets). (Illus.). 25p. (Orig.). 1991. pap. text 8.00 (*1-879523-03-5*) Nw England Solar.

PVC: Formulation, Compounding & Processing. rev. ed. Ed. by C. Brewer & G. Epstein. 230p. 1991. reprint ed. pap. 48.00 (*0-938648-19-5*, 1508) T-C Pr CA.

PVC: Production, Properties & Uses. G. Matthews. 512p. 1997. 90.00 (*0-901716-59-6*, Pub. by Inst Materials) Ashgate Pub Co.

PVC & the Environment: Resin Replacement Opportunities. 128p. 1992. 2350.00 (*0-89336-905-5*, P-133) BCC.

PVC Blends, Alloys, & Graft Polymers: October 10-12, 1989, Hyatt Regency Ravinia, Atlanta, GA. Society of Plastics Engineers Staff. LC TP1180.V48. (Illus.). 284p. reprint ed. pap. 88.10 (*0-8357-3623-7*, 203632400003) Bks Demand.

PVC Building Opportunities: Technical Papers, Vinyl RETEC '94, September 28-29, 1994, Sheraton Inn at Station Square, Pittsburgh, PA. Society of Plastics Engineers Staff. LC TP1105.S733. (Illus.). 242p. 1994. reprint ed. pap. 75.10 (*0-7837-9715-X*, 206044600005) Bks Demand.

PVC Furniture. Edward A. Baldwin. (Weekend Woodworker Ser.). 144p. 1992. 24.95 (*0-8306-4077-0*, 4202); pap. 12.95 (*0-8306-4076-2*, 4202) McGraw-Hill Prof.

PVC Pipe, No. M23: Design & Installation. (AWWA Manual of Water Supply Practices Ser.: No. M23). 96p. 1990. pap. 45.00 (*0-89867-241-4*, 30023) Am Water Wks Assn.

P

An Asterisk (*) at the beginning of an entry indicates that the title is appearing for the first time.

***PVC Projects for the Outdoorsman: Building Shelters, Camping Gear, Weapons, & More Out of Plastic Pipe.** Tom Forbes. 96p. 1999. pap. 12.00 (*1-58160-021-6*) Paladin Pr.

PVM--Parallel Virtual Machine: A User's Guide & Tutorial for Network Parallel Computing. Al Geist et al. LC 94-23404. (Scientific & Engineering Computation Ser.). 1994. pap. text 27.50 (*0-262-57108-0*) MIT Pr.

PVP: A Critical Review of the Kinetics & Toxicology of Polyvinylpyrrolidone (Povidone) B. V. Robinson et al. (Illus.). 232p. 1990. lib. bdg. 159.00 (*0-87371-288-9*, L288) Lewis Pubs.

PVRC-MPC Task Group on Fracture Toughness Properties for Nuclear Components: Final Report. 1977. 35.00 (*0-318-18634-9*) Welding Res Coun.

PVT & Phase Behaviour of Petroleum Reservoir Fluids. Ali Danesh. LC 98-18286. (Developments in Petroleum Science Ser.: 47). 1998. 158.00 (*0-444-82196-1*) Elsevier.

Pvt. Wars (Full-Length) James McLure. 1980. pap. 5.25 (*0-8222-0925-X*) Dramatists Play.

Pvt. Wars (One-Act) James McLure. 1980. pap. 3.25 (*0-8222-0924-1*) Dramatists Play.

PWBK COMPN W/3 5 MAC DSK. 2nd ed. Richard Wolfson & Sharon Z. Aker. LC 93-17703. 416p. 1993. pap. text 24.95 (*0-201-62621-7*) Addison-Wesley.

PWCs (Personal Watercraft) Owner's Manual. TAL Marketing Services Staff. LC 97-127418. (Illus.). 87p. (Orig.). 1996. pap. 6.95 (*1-887960-06-6*, 596-207E) TotalConcepts.

Pwease Wuv Me! More 'Art' of Mitch O'Connell. Mitch O'Connell. (Illus.). 84p. 1998. pap. 17.95 (*0-9639762-1-4*) Good Taste.

PWR Nuclear Power Plant Technology. Ed. by Robert W. Deutsch & J. W. Whitney. (Academic Program for Nuclear Power Plant Personnel Ser., BWR Version: Vol. III-CPWR Version). (Illus.). 404p. 1972. teacher ed., ring bd. 195.00 (*0-87683-156-0*); teacher ed., ring bd. 25.00 (*0-87683-163-3*); teacher ed., ring bd. 35.00 (*0-87683-170-6*); ring bd. 39.50 (*0-87683-149-8*, A 377747) GP Courseware.

PWR Passive Secondary Condensing System. Frank A. Elia, Jr. et al. (ICONE 4 - Technical Papers). 1996. write for info. (*0-614-16719-1*, 96-NE-7) ASME.

Pwrpt Slide Mgrl Acc S99. 3rd ed. Schneider. 146p. 1999. pap. text 19.00 (*0-536-02301-8*) Pearson Custom.

Pwrpt Stud Notes T/a Fin Acctg. 2nd ed. Porter. (C). 1998. pap. text 9.00 (*0-03-021339-8*) Harcourt Coll Pubs.

Pwyll, Peer of Dyfed: Being the First Part of the Old Welsh Mabinogion. Tr. by Peter D. Hays from WEL. 117p. (Orig.). (J). 1996. pap. 5.95 (*1-885554-03-6*) P D Hays.

PX: A Computational Logic. Susumu Hayashi & Hiroshi Nakano. (Foundations of Computing Ser.). 216p. 1988. 30.00 (*0-262-08174-1*) MIT Pr.

Pyaments, Clearance, & Settlement: A Guide to the Systems, Risks, & Issues. Nolani T. Traylor et al. (Illus.). 189p. (C). 1998. pap. text 35.00 (*0-7881-4842-7*) DIANE Pub.

Pycckuii Tpuniux see Russian Triptych

Pychic Mafia. M. Lamar Keene. LC 97-25291. (Illus.). 195p. 1997. pap. 16.95 (*1-57392-161-0*) Prometheus Bks.

Pycnogenol. Rita Elkins. 1995. pap. text 3.95 (*1-885670-09-5*) Woodland UT.

Pycnogenol: Miracle Antioxidant. 1996. lib. bdg. 250.95 (*0-8490-5908-9*) Gordon Pr.

Pycnogenol: The Super "Protector" Nutrient. Richard A. Passwater & Chithan Kandaswami. 112p. (Orig.). 1994. pap. 4.95 (*0-87983-648-2*, 36482K, Keats Publng) NTC Contemp Pub Co.

Pycnogonida from Waters Adjacent to Japan. Koichiro Nakamura & C. Allan Child. LC 91-1984. (Smithsonian Contributions to Zoology Ser.: No. 512). 80p. reprint ed. pap. 30.00 (*0-7837-0268-X*, 204057700017) Bks Demand.

Pycnogonida of the Western Pacific Islands Vol. 10: Collections from the Aleutians & Other Bering Sea Islands, Alaska. C. Allan Child. LC 94-28013. (Smithsonian Contributions to Zoology Ser.: Vol. 569). 34p. 1995. reprint ed. pap. 30.00 (*0-608-00506-1*, 206132600008) Bks Demand.

Pyelonephritis. F. Renyi-Vamos & F. Balogh. 190p. (C). 1979. 55.00 (*963-05-1724-8*, Pub. by Akade Kiado) St Mut.

Pyers Plowmans Exhortation unto the Lordes, Knights, Etc. LC 76-57405. (English Experience Ser.: No. 821). 1977. reprint ed. lib. bdg. 15.00 (*90-221-0821-X*) Walter J Johnson.

***Pygmalion.** 2000. 11.95 (*1-56137-928-X*) Novel Units.

Pygmalion. Charles A. Berst. (Twayne's Masterwork Studies). 1995. 29.00 (*0-8057-9447-6*, Twyne); pap. 18.00 (*0-8057-4538-6*, Twyne) Mac Lib Ref.

Pygmalion. George Bernard Shaw. 1991. pap. text. write for info. (*0-582-06015-X*, Pub. by Addison-Wesley) Longman.

Pygmalion. George Bernard Shaw. 19.95 (*0-88411-452-X*) Amereon Ltd.

Pygmalion. George Bernard Shaw. Ed. by Harry Shefter. (Enriched Classics Edition Ser.). 176p. 1989. per. 5.50 (*0-671-70496-6*, WSP) PB.

Pygmalion. George Bernard Shaw. 1916. 10.60 (*0-606-03039-5*, Pub. by Turtleback) Demco.

Pygmalion. George Bernard Shaw. 128p. 1988. pap. 7.95 (*0-14-045022-X*) Viking Penguin.

Pygmalion. Claudia Weiser. (Europaische Hochschulschriften Ser.: Reihe 1, Bd. 1673). 230p. 1998. pap. 39.95 (*3-631-33311-0*) P Lang Pubng.

Pygmalion. Thomas Woolner. LC 72-148335. reprint ed. 37.50 (*0-404-07032-9*) AMS Pr.

Pygmalion. unabridged ed. George Bernard Shaw. 96p. 1994. pap. text 1.00 (*0-486-28222-8*) Dover.

Pygmalion: A Unit Plan. Mary B. Collins. 140p. 1994. teacher ed., ring bd. 26.95 (*1-58337-107-9*) Teachers Pet Pubns.

Pygmalion: Curriculum Unit. Center for Learning Network Staff & George Bernard Shaw. (Drama Ser.). 100p. (YA). (gr. 9-12). 1990. spiral bd. 18.95 (*1-56077-115-1*) Ctr Learning.

Pygmalion: Reproducible Teaching Unit. rev. ed. James Scott. 27p. (YA). (gr. 7-12). 1996. teacher ed., ring bd. 29.50 (*1-58049-030-1*, TU63/U) Prestwick Hse.

Pygmalion & Major Barbara. George Bernard Shaw. 288p. 1992. mass mkt. 5.95 (*0-553-21408-X*, Bantam Classics) Bantam.

Pygmalion & My Fair Lady. George Bernard Shaw. 1975. mass mkt. 5.95 (*0-451-52476-4*) NAL.

Pygmalion & My Fair Lady. George Bernard Shaw. 1975. 11.05 (*0-606-02368-2*, Pub. by Turtleback) Demco.

Pygmalion in the Classroom. Robert Rosenthal. 1996. 39.50 (*0-8290-3153-7*) Irvington.

Pygmalion in the Classroom: Teacher Expectation & Pupils' Intellectual Development. enl. ed. Robert Rosenthal & Lenore Jacobson. 265p. 1989. text 39.50 (*0-8290-1768-2*); pap. text 14.95 (*0-8290-1265-6*) Irvington.

Pygmalion in the Gym: Causes & Effects of Expectations in Teaching & Coaching. Thomas J. Martinek et al. LC 81-81634. (Illus.). 160p. 1982. reprint ed. pap. 49.60 (*0-608-07103-X*, 206733000009) Bks Demand.

Pygmalion, les Surprises de l'Amour see Oeuvres Completes de Jean-Philippe Rameau

Pygmalion Project Vol. I: The Artisans. Stephen E. Montgomery. 178p. (Orig.). 1989. pap. 9.95 (*0-9606954-2-7*) Prometheus Nemesis.

Pygmalion Project Vol. II: The Guardian. Stephen E. Montgomery. (Love & Coercion among the Types Ser.). 255p. (Orig.). (C). 1990. pap. 9.95 (*0-9606954-5-1*) Prometheus Nemesis.

Pygmalion Project Vol. III: The Idealist, Vol. 3. Stephen E. Montgomery. 297p. (Orig.). (C). 1993. pap. 9.95 (*0-9606954-9-4*) Prometheus Nemesis.

Pygmalion's Figure: Reading Old French Romance. Jean M. Dornbush. LC 89-81169. (Edward C. Armstrong Monographs on Medieval Literature: No. 5). 153p. (Orig.). 1990. pap. 14.95 (*0-917058-75-5*) French Forum.

Pygmalion's Wordplay: The Postmodern Shaw. Jean Reynolds. LC 99-10186. 1999. 49.95 (*0-8130-1681-9*) U Press Fla.

Pygmies & Papuans: The Stone Age To-Day in Dutch New Guinea. Alexander F. Wollaston. LC 75-34889. reprint ed. 45.00 (*0-404-14451-9*) AMS Pr.

Pygmies & Pyramids. Richard Moore. LC 97-41900. 80p. 1998. pap. 12.95 (*0-914061-71-2*) Orchises Pr.

Pygmies of Central Africa, Reading Level 5. Schuyler Jones. (Original People Ser.: Set II). (Illus.). 48p. (J). (gr. 4-8). 1989. lib. bdg. 16.67 (*0-86625-268-1*) Rourke Pubns.

Pygmies, Poems & Pyramids: The Dot Program. (Illus.). xi, 60p, 1997. reprint ed. pap. write for info. (*1-891544-00-4*) Pygmie Pubns.

Pygmy Chimpanzee: Evolutionary Biology & Behavior. R. L. Susman. LC 84-13236. (Illus.). 464p. (C). 1984. text 120.00 (*0-306-41595-X*, Kluwer Plenum) Kluwer Academic.

Pygmy Forest. Robert E. Sholars. (Illus.). 50p. (Orig.). 1982. pap. 6.95 (*0-9611178-0-X*) Sholars.

Pygmy (Goat) in America. rev. ed. Alice G. Hall. (Illus.). 100p. (Orig.). 1982. pap. 9.50 (*0-932218-13-X*) Hall Pr.

Pygmy Goats: Management & Veterinary Care. Lorrie Boldrick & Lydia Hale. LC 96-85589. (Illus.). 238p. (Orig.). 1996. pap. 19.95 (*0-9624531-3-7*) All Pub.

Pygmy Hedgehogs - The Perfect Pet. Sharon Massena & Bryan Smith. LC 97-164947. (Illus.). 80p. (Orig.). (J). 1996. pap. 19.50 (*0-9655629-1-3*) Bear Tree.

Pyjama. Pierre Daninos. (FRE.). 1972. 15.95 (*0-8288-9173-7*, FA880) Fr & Eur.

Pyke Koch: Paintings & Drawings. P. F. Koch et al. (DUT & ENG., Illus.). 288p. 1996. pap. 45.00 (*90-6918-143-6*, Pub. by Boymans Mus) U of Wash Pr.

Pyles War. Tobin. 24.00 (*0-02-932681-8*) Macmillan.

Pylgremage of the Sowle. Guillaume De Deguileville. Tr. by J. Lydgate. LC 74-28845. (English Experience Ser.: No. 726). 1975. reprint ed. 10.00 (*90-221-0726-4*) Walter J Johnson.

Pylgrymage of Sir Richard Guylforde to the Holy Land, A. D. 1506. Ed. by Henry Ellis. LC 75-166023. (Camden Society, London. Publications, First Ser.: No. 51). reprint ed. 28.50 (*0-404-50151-6*) AMS Pr.

Pylon. William Faulkner. Ed. by Noel Polk. LC 86-40166. (Illus.). 336p. 1987. pap. 9.00 (*0-394-74741-0*) Vin Bks.

Pylon: A Concordance to the Novel. William Faulkner. Ed. by Noel Polk & John D. Hart. LC 89-37165. 692p. reprint ed. lib. bdg. 200.00 (*0-8357-0880-2*, 207061900007) Bks Demand.

Pylon, (1935) William Faulkner. Ed. by Noel Polk. (William Faulkner Manuscripts). 360p. 1987. text 50.00 (*0-8240-6816-5*) Garland.

Pylone. William Faulkner. (FRE.). 1984. pap. 12.95 (*0-7859-2486-8*, 2070375315) Fr & Eur.

Pyloric Sphincteric Cylinder in Health & Disease. A. D. Keet. LC 92-48803. 1993. 217.00 (*0-387-55814-4*) Spr-Verlag.

Pylos: Palmprints & Palmleaves. Karl-Erik Sjoquist & Paul Astrom. (Studies in Mediterranean Archaeology & Literature: No. 31). (Illus.). 105p. (Orig.). 1985. pap. 43.50 (*91-86098-22-5*, Pub. by P Astroms) Coronet Bks.

Pylos Comes Alive: Industry & Administration in the Mycenaean Palace. 107p. 1984. 10.00 (*0-318-17842-7*) Archaeological Inst.

Pynchon: The Voice of Ambiguity. Thomas H. Schaub. LC 80-11944. 176p. 1981. 19.95 (*0-252-00816-2*) U of Ill Pr.

***Pynchon & Mason & Dixon.** Brooke Horvath & Irving Malin. LC 00-29926. 2000. write for info. (*0-87413-720-9*) U Delaware Pr.

Pynchon Papers, Vol. 1. John Pynchon. Ed. by Carl Bridenbaugh. LC 81-70057. (Publications of the Colonial Society of Massachusetts: No. 60-61). 378p. reprint ed. pap. 117.20 (*0-7837-3741-6*, 204342300001) Bks Demand.

Pynchon Papers, Vol. 2. John Pynchon. Ed. by Carl Bridenbaugh. LC 81-70057. (Publications of the Colonial Society of Massachusetts: No. 60-61). 539p. reprint ed. pap. 167.10 (*0-7837-3742-4*, 204342300002) Bks Demand.

Pynchon's Mythography: An Approach to Gravity's Rainbow. Kathryn Hume. LC 86-25970. (Crosscurrents-Modern Critiques, Third Ser.). 276p. 1987. text 31.95 (*0-8093-1357-X*) S Ill U Pr.

Pynchon's Poetics: Interfacing Theory & Text. Hanjo Berressem. 288p. (C). 1993. text 37.50 (*0-252-01919-9*); pap. text 15.95 (*0-252-06248-5*) U of Ill Pr.

Pyne U. S. History 97-98. Bellesiles. (C). Date not set. pap. text 29.16 (*0-395-88682-1*) HM.

Pyngyp. Peter Hassinger. (J). Date not set. write for info. (*0-06-028469-2*); lib. bdg. write for info. (*0-06-028470-6*) HarpC Child Bks.

Pynn. Paul Witcover. pap. 14.00 (*0-06-105364-3*, HarperPrism) HarpC.

Pyongyang Conference: Primary Health Care in Action. (SEARO Regional Health Papers: No. 6). 352p. 1985. pap. text 20.00 (*92-9022-175-5*, 1580006) World Health.

Pyralidae & Microlepidoptera of the Marquesas Archipelago. John F. Clarke. LC 85-600124. (Smithsonian Contributions to Zoology Ser.: No. 416). 489p. reprint ed. pap. 151.60 (*0-608-15427-X*, 202935700060) Bks Demand.

Pyramid. Houghton Mifflin Company Staff. (Literature Experience 1993 Ser.). (J). (gr. 6). 1992. pap. 11.04 (*0-395-61836-3*) HM.

Pyramid. Ismail Kadare. Tr. by Jusuf Vrioni & David Bellos from FRE. LC 95-17859. 176p. 1996. 21.45 (*1-55970-314-8*, Pub. by Arcade Pub Inc) Time Warner.

Pyramid. Ismail Kadare. Tr. by David Bellos from FRE. LC 97-53239. 1998. pap. 11.00 (*0-375-70095-1*) Vin Bks.

Pyramid. Loretta H. Kurban. (Orig.). 1993. pap. text 3.00 (*0-938863-59-2*) HCI Pr.

Pyramid, 001. David Macaulay. (Illus.). 80p. (J). (gr. 7 up). 1975. 18.00 (*0-395-21407-6*) HM.

Pyramid. David Macaulay. 1975. 13.15 (*0-606-00557-9*, Pub. by Turtleback) Demco.

Pyramid. Henrietta McCall. LC 99-27869. (Fast Forward Ser.). 1999. 26.00 (*0-531-14584-0*) Watts.

***Pyramid.** James Putnam. (Eyewitness Books). (Illus.). (J). (gr. 4-7). 2000. 19.99 (*0-7894-6602-3*) DK Pub Inc.

***Pyramid.** James Putnam. (Eyewitness Books). (J). (gr. 4-7). 2000. 15.95 (*0-7894-5898-5*) DK Pub Inc.

Pyramid. James Putnam. LC 94-8804. (Eyewitness Books). (Illus.). 64p. (YA). (gr. 5 up). 1994. lib. bdg. 20.99 (*0-679-96170-4*, Pub. by Knopf Bks Yng Read) Random.

Pyramid: An Interactive Guide to the Pyramids of Ancient Egypt. Michele Claiborne. (DK Action Packs Ser.). (Illus.). (J). (gr. 3-7). 1994. pap. 19.95 (*1-56458-684-7*) DK Pub Inc.

Pyramid: Four One-Act Plays for Three Virtuosos. Artemis Smith, pseud. 1992. boxed set 150.00 (*1-878998-04-8*) Savant Garde.

Pyramid: Special Reading Exercises. 3rd large type ed. Dolores Hiskes. LC LB1573.H57 1997. (Illus.). 80p. (Orig.). (J). (gr. 1-12). 1997. reprint ed. pap. text 17.95 (*1-884580-30-0*) Dorbooks.

Pyramid & the Urn: The Life in Letters of a Restoration Squire: William Lawrence of Shurdington. William Lawrence. LC 95-148922. 1998. 30.95 (*0-7509-0765-7*, Pub. by Sutton Pub Ltd) Intl Pubs Mktg.

Pyramid Approach to Education. Ed. & Illus. by Andrew Bondy. 80p. 1996. ring bd. 25.00 (*1-928598-00-5*) Pyramid Educ.

Pyramid Builders. Carter Smith. (Turning Points in World History Ser.). (Illus.). 64p. (YA). (gr. 7 up). 1991. pap. 7.95 (*0-382-24137-1*); lib. bdg. 14.95 (*0-382-24131-2*) Silver Burdett Pr.

Pyramid Builders of Ancient Egypt: A Modern Investigation of Pharaoh's Workforce. Rosalie David. 304p. (C). 1997. pap. 25.99 (*0-415-15292-5*) Routledge.

***Pyramid Building & Its Consequences.** Ed. by Robert H. Dreisbach. 48p. 2000. pap. text 5.00 (*0-942153-12-X*, 27388X) Entropy Conserv.

Pyramid Cafe. Jane Jarrell & Deborah Saathoff. 1998. pap. 6.99 (*0-8054-0361-2*) Broadman.

***Pyramid Complex of Senwosret III at Dahshur Architectural Studies.** Dieter Arnold. LC 00-35505. 2000. write for info. (*0-87099-956-7*) Metro Mus Art.

Pyramid Cookbook. Pat Baird. 1995. pap. 14.95 (*0-8050-3262-2*) H Holt & Co.

Pyramid Cookbook: Pleasure of the Food Guide Pyramid. Pat Baird. 272p. 1995. 24.00 (*0-8050-2648-7*) H Holt & Co.

Pyramid Framework for Early Vision. Jean-Michel Jolion. LC 93-37464. 232p. (C). 1993. text 127.00 (*0-7923-9402-X*) Kluwer Academic.

***Pyramid Handbook.** rev. ed. Moustafa Gadalla. LC 00-130200. Orig. Title: Pyramid Illusions: A Journey to the Truth. (Illus.). 192p. 2000. pap. 11.95 (*0-9652509-4-6*) Tehuti Res Foun.

Pyramid Illusions: A Journey to the Truth see Pyramid Handbook

Pyramid Lake Indian War Guidebook. Jamison Station Press Staff. (Desert Rat Guidebook Ser.: No. 1). (Illus.). 21p. 1984. 1.95 (*0-317-01482-X*) Jamison Stn.

Pyramid Odyssey. William Fix. LC 78-14540. (Illus.). 291p. 1984. reprint ed. pap. 19.95 (*0-932487-00-9*) Mercury Media.

Pyramid of Bone. Thylias Moss. Ed. by Charles H. Rowell. LC 88-25855. (Callaloo Poetry Ser.). ix, 56p. 1989. pap. 10.95 (*0-8139-1202-4*) U Pr of Va.

Pyramid of Dreams. Marilyn Campbell. 368p. 1994. pap. text 4.99 (*0-505-51993-3*, Love Spell) Dorchester Pub Co.

Pyramid of Ice. F. Sanders. 1982. pap. 1.50 (*0-937816-30-2*) Tech Data.

Pyramid of Snacks. Patricia F. Thonney. 76p. (J). (gr. 4-7). 1998. pap. 7.75 (*1-57753-287-2*, 399LM19) Corn Coop Ext.

Pyramid PA, 001. David Macaulay. (Illus.). 80p. (J). (gr. 5 up). 1982. pap. 8.95 (*0-395-32121-2*) HM.

Pyramid Piano Tutor. Kenneth Murdoch. 48p. 1996. pap. 9.95 (*1-85756-275-5*, Pub. by Janus Pubng) Paul & Co Pubs.

Pyramid Plot. J. Somper. (Puzzle Adventures Ser.). (Illus.). 48p. (J). (gr. 3-8). 1993. pap. 5.95 (*0-7460-0506-7*) EDC.

Pyramid Plot. J. Somper. (Puzzle Adventures Ser.). (Illus.). 48p. (J). (gr. 3-8). 1999. lib. bdg. 13.95 (*0-88110-403-5*) EDC.

Pyramid Portal. 200p. 2000. lib. bdg. 21.95 (*0-9650204-3-6*) Neurotechtonics.

Pyramid Power. Toth Nielsen. 1977. mass mkt. 2.25 (*0-446-82569-7*, Pub. by Warner Bks) Little.

Pyramid Power. Max Toth et al. (Illus.). 207p. 1985. reprint ed. pap. 9.95 (*0-89281-106-4*, Destiny Bks) Inner Tradit.

Pyramid Power: The Millennium Science. G. P. Flanagan. 1997. pap. text 14.95 (*0-9648812-6-8*) Earthpulse Pr.

Pyramid Principle: The Logic in Writing & Thinking. rev. ed. Barbara Minto. 250p. 1995. write for info. (*0-273-61710-9*) F T P H.

Pyramid Prophecies. Max Toth. (Illus.). 382p. 1988. pap. 10.95 (*0-89281-203-6*, Destiny Bks) Inner Tradit.

Pyramid Truth Gateway Universe: The Purpose, Intent & Overview of Extraterrestrial Visitations. Reg T. Miller. (Illus.). 380p. 1998. pap. 24.95 (*0-9651546-4-5*) Med Bear.

Pyramid Wisdom: The World's Most Mysterious Monuments Interpreted by Modern-Day Descendants of the Pharaohs. Tarek Atai & Youssef Khalil. (Illus.). 64p. 1999. mass mkt. 6.99 (*0-9671359-0-7*) Dragonfly Books.

Pyramidal Architectures for Computer Vision. V. Cantoni & M. Ferretti. LC 93-29212. (Advances in Computer Vision & Machine Intelligence Ser.). (Illus.). 356p. (C). 1994. 85.00 (*0-306-44453-4*, Kluwer Plenum) Kluwer Academic.

Pyramidal Neural Networks. Horst Bischof. 216p. 1995. text 39.95 (*0-8058-1913-4*); pap. text 24.50 (*0-8058-1914-2*) L Erlbaum Assocs.

Pyramide see Pyramids

Pyramide. (Meyers Klein Kinderbibliothek Ser.). (GER.). 24p. (J). 1995. 13.25 (*3-411-08731-5*) Langenscheidt.

Pyramids see Young Scientist Concepts & Projects

Pyramids. Harriette S. Abels. LC 87-15455. (Mystery of...Ser.). (Illus.). 48p. (J). (gr. 5-6). 1987. lib. bdg. 12.95 (*0-89686-345-X*, Crstwood Hse) Silver Burdett Pr.

Pyramids. Phillip Biard & Claude Delafosse. LC 94-49424. (First Discovery Book).Tr. of Pyramide. (ENG & FRE., Illus.). 24p. (J). (ps-3). 1995. 11.95 (*0-590-42786-5*, Cartwheel) Scholastic Inc.

***Pyramids.** Ron Bonewitz. (Guides for Beginners Ser.). (Illus.). 96p. 2000. pap. 11.95 (*0-340-75383-8*, Pub. by Headway) Trafalgar.

Pyramids. Book Sales Staff. 1998. pap. text 6.99 (*0-7858-1000-5*) Bk Sales Inc.

Pyramids. Brughton. (C). 1999. teacher ed. write for info. (*0-321-40643-5*) Addison-Wesley.

Pyramids. Flora Simmons Clancy. LC 94-18949. (Exploring the Ancient World Ser.). (Illus.). 176p. 1995. text 24.95 (*0-89599-039-3*) Smithsonian.

Pyramids. Henrietta McCall.Tr. of Pyramide. 1999. pap. text 9.95 (*0-531-15435-1*) Watts.

Pyramids. Anne Millard. LC 95-39660. (Story Library). (Illus.). 64p. (J). (gr. 3-7). 1996. 16.95 (*1-85697-674-2*) LKC.

Pyramids. Anne Millard. LC 95-13269. (Mysteries Of-- Ser.). (J). 1995. 12.15 (*0-606-09659-0*, Pub. by Turtleback) Demco.

Pyramids. Ed. by Scholastic, Inc. Staff. (Discovery Box Ser.). (Illus.). 32p. (gr. 3-5). 1999. 12.95 (*0-590-92688-8*) Scholastic Inc.

Pyramids. John Weeks. (Cambridge Introduction to World History Topic Bks.). (Illus.). 48p. (YA). (gr. 7 up). 1971. pap. 12.95 (*0-521-07240-9*) Cambridge U Pr.

Pyramids. 2nd ed. Ahmed Fakhry. LC 61-8645. (Illus.). 284p. reprint ed. pap. 88.10 (*0-608-09294-0*, 205416800004) Bks Demand.

Pyramids. 2nd ed. Ahmed Fakhry. LC 61-8645. 272p. 1974. reprint ed. pap. 14.95 (*0-226-23473-8*, P571) U Ch Pr.

Pyramids: Opposing Viewpoints. Michael O'Neal. (Opposing Viewpoints Juniors Ser.). (Illus.). 96p. (J). (gr. 5-12). 1995. lib. bdg. 22.45 (*1-56510-216-9*, 2169) Greenhaven.

Pyramids: Structurally Based Tasks for E. S. L. Learners. Carolyn G. Madden & Susan M. Reinhart. (English As a Second Language Ser.). (Illus.). 120p. (C). 1987. pap. text 12.95 (*0-472-08073-3*, 08073); pap. text, teacher ed. 12.95 (*0-472-08072-5*, 08072) U of Mich Pr.

Pyramids: The Latest Secrets Revealed in the Light of Recent Scientific Discoveries. Anne Millard. (Mysteries of...Ser.). (Illus.). 40p. (J). (gr. 4-6). 1995. pap. 6.95 (*1-56294-194-1*, Copper Beech Bks) Millbrook Pr.

Pyramids: Tombs for Eternity. Mildred M. Pace. LC 97-46032. (Illus.). 192p. (J). 1998. pap. 10.95 (*0-87226-548-X*, 6548XB, P Bedrick Books) NTC Contemp Pub Co.

P

Pyramids! 50 Hands-On Activities to Experience Ancient Egypt. Avery Hart & Paul Mantell. Ed. by Susan Williamson. LC 96-40033. (Kaleidoscope Kids Ser.). (Illus.). 96p. (J). (gr. 1-7). 1997. pap. 10.95 (*1-885593-10-4*) Williamson Pub Co.

Pyramids & Palaces, Monsters & Masks: The Golden Age of Maya Architecture, 3 vols. George F. Andrews. LC 93-77664. (Illus.). 1090p. (C). 1999. text 150.00 (*0-911437-82-7*) Labyrinthos.

Pyramids & Palaces, Monsters & Masks Vol. II: The Golden Age of Maya Architecture. George F. Andrews. LC 93-77664. (Illus.). 332p. (C). 1997. text 65.00 (*0-911437-81-9*) Labyrinthos.

Pyramids & Puns Vol. 1: The First Book of Egyptian Humor. Everett A. Blackman. (Illus.). 112p. (Orig.). (C). 1988. pap. 2.95 (*0-9622469-9-9*) Norcor Enterprises.

Pyramids & Stonehenge. A. P. Sinnett. 1994. pap. 6.95 (*1-55818-271-3*, Sure Fire) Holmes Pub.

Pyramids & Temples. Jane Parker. LC 96-4769. (Superstructures Ser.). (Illus.). 48p. (J). (gr. 4-8). 1997. lib. bdg. 24.26 (*0-8172-4330-5*) Raintree Steck-V.

***Pyramids & Temples of Gizeh.** W. M. Flinders Petrie. 260p. 2000. text 212.50 (*0-7103-0709-8*) Col U Pr.

Pyramids at the Louvre: Music, Culture, & Collage from Stravinsky to the Postmodernists. Glenn Watkins. LC 93-31703. (Illus.). 608p. 1994. text 29.95 (*0-674-74083-1*) HUP.

***Pyramids Ii, I/M.** 1999. text. write for info. (*0-321-02671-3*) P-H.

Pyramids of Ancient Egypt. Zahi A. Hawass. LC 89-85827. (Illus.). 60p. (Orig.). (C). 1990. pap. text 7.95 (*0-911239-21-9*) Carnegie Mus.

Pyramids of Ancient Egypt. abr. ed. Ed. by John D. Clare. LC 91-11735. (Living History Ser.). (Illus.). 64p. (J). (gr. 2-7). 1992. 16.95 (*0-15-200509-9*, Gulliver Bks) Harcourt.

Pyramids of Egypt. I. E. Edwards. 1991. pap. 14.95 (*0-14-013634-7*) Viking Penguin.

Pyramids of Giza. Tim McNeese. LC 96-45622. (Building History Ser.). (Illus.). (YA). (gr. 4-12). 1997. lib. bdg. 22.45 (*1-56006-426-9*) Lucent Bks.

Pyramids of Glass: Short Fiction from Modern Mexico. Ed. by David Bowen & Juan A. Ascencio. Tr. by E. Grossman et al from SPA. LC 94-71404. xxii, 244p. (C). 1994. 22.95 (*0-931722-99-3*); pap. 12.95 (*0-931722-83-7*) Corona Pub.

***Pyramids of Life: Patterns of Life & Death in the Ecosystem.** rev. ed. Harvey Croze. (Illus.). 2000. pap. 32.00 (*1-86046-613-3*) Harvill Press.

Pyramids of Montauk No. 3: Explorations in Consciousness. Preston B. Nichols & Peter Moon. LC 94-69941. (Illus.). 266p. 1995. pap. 19.95 (*0-9631889-2-5*) Sky Bks NY.

***Pyramids of Teotihuacan.** Charles William Johnson. (Science in Ancient Artwork Ser.). (Illus.). 95p. 1999. pap. 30.00 (*1-58616-187-3*, 187-3) Earth Matrix.

Pyramids, People, & Piccadilly. Ramses Sidrak. 112p. 1996. pap. 11.95 (*1-899151-01-X*, Pub. by Poetry Salzburg) Intl Spec Bk.

Pyramids to Pueblos: 15 Pop-Up Models for Students to Make. Helen H. Moore. 1996. pap. text 9.95 (*0-590-67481-1*) Scholastic Inc.

Pyramus & Thisbe: A Dramatization Arranged from Shakespeare's "A Midsummer Night's Dream" rev. ed. William Shakespeare. Ed. by William-Alan Landes. LC 96-3102. 55p. (Orig.). (J). (gr. 4-12). 1996. pap. 5.00 (*0-88734-103-9*) Players Pr.

Pyramus & Thisby: A Cutting of a Midsummer Nights Dream. Paul Caywood & William Shakespeare. (Half Hour Classics Ser.). (YA). 1997. pap. 2.50 (*1-57514-300-3*, 3099) Encore Perform Pub.

Pyrenean Festivals: Calendar Customs, Music & Magic, Drama & Dance. Violet Alford. LC 77-87730. 1977. reprint ed. 47.50 (*0-404-16577-X*) AMS Pr.

Pyrenean Prehistory. P. Bahn. pap. 85.00 (*0-85668-260-8*, Pub. by Aris & Phillips) David Brown.

Pyrenees. 3rd ed. Marc Dubin. (Rough Guides Ser.). 1998. pap. 17.95 (*1-85828-308-6*, Penguin Bks) Viking Penguin.

Pyrenees-Aquitaine Green Guide. 3rd ed. Michelin Staff. (FRE.). 1992. pap. 18.95 (*0-7859-9156-5*) Fr & Eur.

Pyrenees-Aquitaine Green Guide: France (Guides Regionaux) Michelin Staff. (FRE., Illus.). 1997. per. 20.00 (*2-06-036705-0*, 367) Michelin.

Pyrenees-Aquitaine Green Guide French Edition. Michelin Staff. (FRE.). pap. 17.95 (*0-7859-7237-4*, 2067003674) Fr & Eur.

Pyrenees-Roussillon Green Guide. 3rd ed. Michelin Staff. (FRE.). 1992. pap. 18.95 (*0-7859-9157-3*) Fr & Eur.

Pyrenees-Roussillon Green Guide: France (Guides Regionaux) 5th ed. (FRE.). 1997. per. 20.00 (*2-06-036805-7*, 368) Michelin.

Pyrenees-Roussillon Green Guide French Edition. Michelin Staff. (FRE.). pap. 17.95 (*0-7859-7238-2*, 2067003682) Fr & Eur.

Pyrenomycetes Described by J. B. Ellis. Margaret E. Barr et al. LC 96-47492. (Memoirs of the New York Botanical Garden Ser.: No. 79). 136p. 1996. text 25.00 (*0-89327-415-1*, MEM 79) NY Botanical.

Pyrenomycetous Fungi. Lewis E. Wehmeyer. (Mycologia Memoirs Ser.: No. 6). 1975. text 64.00 (*3-7682-0967-9*) Lubrecht & Cramer.

Pyrethroid Residues, Immunoassays for Low Molecular Weight Compounds. (Chemistry of Plant Protection Ser.: Vol. 3). (Illus.). x, 230p. 1989. 69.95 (*0-387-51312-4*) Spr-Verlag.

Pyrethrum Flowers: Production, Chemistry, Toxicology & Uses. Ed. by John E. Casida. (Illus.). 384p. 1995. text 70.00 (*0-19-508210-9*) OUP.

Pyretics & Antipyretics. Ed. by A. S. Milton. (Handbook of Experimental Pharmacology Ser.: Vol. 60). 715p. 1982. 392.00 (*0-387-11511-0*) Spr-Verlag.

Pyrex by Corning: A Collector's Guide. Susan T. Rogove & Marcia B. Steinhauer. (Illus.). 140p. 1993. pap. 24.95 (*0-915410-94-X*, 4044) Antique Pubns.

Pyrex by Corning: A Supplement & 1997-98 Price Guide. Susan T. Rogove. (Illus.). 32p. 1996. pap. 9.95 (*1-57080-029-4*, 4105) Antique Pubns.

***Pyrex, the Unauthorized Collector's Guide.** Barbara Mauzy. (Illus.). 160p. 2000. pap. 29.95 (*0-7643-1069-0*) Schiffer.

Pyrexia. Michel Mery. 192p. (Orig.). 1997. pap. 10.00 (*1-886625-02-6*) III Pub.

Pyrheliometry. A. A. Kmito. 1987. 116.00 (*90-6191-497-3*) Ashgate Pub Co.

Pyrheliometry. A. A. Kmito & Yua Sklyarov. (C). 1987. 36.00 (*81-7087-003-8*, Pub. by Oxford IBH) S Asia.

***Pyridazines.** D. J. Brown. LC 99-28985. (Chemistry of Heterocyclic Compounds, a Series of Monographs). 672p. 2000. text 450.00 (*0-471-25137-2*, Wiley-Interscience) Wiley.

Pyridine & Its Derivatives, Vol. 14, Pt. 5. Ed. by George R. Newkome et al. LC 59-103038. (Chemistry of Heterocyclic Compounds, a Series of Monographs: Vol. 14, Pt. 5). 714p. 1984. 635.00 (*0-471-05072-5*, 1-079) Wiley.

Pyridine-Metal Compounds, Vol. 14, Pt. 6, 3 Vol. Set. Piotr Tomasik & Zbigniew Ratajewicz. LC 84-26939. (Chemistry of Heterocyclic Compounds, a Series of Monographs: Vol. 14, Pts. 6A-C). 2246p. 1985. 1925.00 (*0-471-05073-3*) Wiley.

Pyrimidines, Vol. 52. D. J. Brown et al. LC 92-35909. (Chemistry of Heterocyclic Compounds, a Series of Monographs: vOL. 52). 1509p. 1994. 599.00 (*0-471-50656-7*) Wiley.

Pyrite Oxidation & Its Control: Solution Chemistry, Surface Chemistry, Acid Mine Drainage (AMD), Molecular Oxidation Mechanisms, Microbial Role, Kinetics, Control, Ameliorates & Limitations, Microencapsulation. V. P. Evangelou. LC 95-7044. 304p. 1995. boxed set 189.95 (*0-8493-4732-7*, 4732) CRC Pr.

Pyroclastic Geology of Oahu. C. K. Wentworth. (BMB Ser.). 1974. reprint ed. 25.00 (*0-527-02133-4*) Periodicals Srv.

Pyroclastic Rocks. R. V. Fisher & H. U. Schmincke. (Illus.). 350p. 1991. 54.00 (*0-387-12756-9*); 115.95 (*0-387-51341-8*) Spr-Verlag.

Pyroclastic Volcanism & Deposits of Cenozoic Intermediate to Felsic Volcanic Islands with Implications for Precambrian Greenstone-Belt Volcanoes. Ed. by L. D. Ayres. LC QE0522.P97. (Geological Association of Canada. Short Course Notes Ser.: Vol. 2). 369p. reprint ed. pap. 114.40 (*0-608-17194-8*, 202784700056) Bks Demand.

Pyrocysteen der Plankton-Expedition der Humboldt-Stiftung. C. Apstein. 1971. reprint ed. 15.00 (*3-7682-0807-9*) Lubrecht & Cramer.

Pyrogens: Endotoxins & LAL Testing & Depyrogenation. F. C. Pearson. (Advances in Parenteral Science Ser.: Vol. 2). (Illus.). 288p. 1985. text 135.00 (*0-8247-7436-1*) Dekker.

Pyrogens: Endotoxins, LAL Testing & Depyrogenation. 2nd expanded rev. ed. F. C. Pearson. (Advances in Parenteral Science Ser.). (Illus.). Date not set. write for info. (*0-8247-9362-5*, 9362-5) Dekker.

Pyrography: Burning Images on Wood, Paper & Leather. Al Chapman & Learning the Art of Pyrography. LC 94-43169. (Books for Woodworkers). (Illus.). 64p. (Orig.). 1995. pap. 12.95 (*0-88740-729-3*) Schiffer.

Pyrography Designs. Norma Gregory. (Illus.). 112p. 1999. pap. 12.95 (*1-86108-116-2*, Pub. by Guild Master) Sterling.

Pyrography Handbook. Stephen Poole. LC 98-145970. (Illus.). 136p. 1998. 14.95 (*1-86108-061-1*, Pub. by Guild Master) Sterling.

Pyrolysis: Theory & Industrial Practice. Lyle Albright et al. 446p. 1983. text 152.00 (*0-12-048880-9*) Acad Pr.

Pyrolysis & GC in Polymer Analysis. S. A. Liebman & E. J. Levy. (Chromatographic Science Ser.: Vol. 29). (Illus.). 576p. 1984. text 250.00 (*0-8247-7187-7*) Dekker.

Pyrolysis Oils from Biomass: Producing, Analyzing & Upgrading. Ed. by Ed J. Soltes & Thomas A. Milne. LC 88-24172. (ACS Symposium Ser.: No. 376). (Illus.). xii, 354p. 1988. 74.95 (*0-8412-1536-7*, Pub. by Am Chemical) OUP.

Pyrolysis Oils from Biomass: Producing, Analyzing & Upgrading. Ed. by Ed J. Soltes & Thomas A. Milne. LC 88-24172. (ACS Symposium Ser.: No. 376). (Illus.). 368p. 1988. reprint ed. pap. 114.10 (*0-608-03278-6*, 206379600007) Bks Demand.

Pyromancer. Don Callander. 1992. mass mkt. 5.50 (*0-441-69222-2*) Ace Bks.

Pyrometallurgical Processes in Nonferrous Metallurgy. Ed. by J. N. Anderson & P. E. Queneau. LC 67-26570. (Metallurgical Society Conference Ser.: Vol. 39). 529p. reprint ed. pap. 164.00 (*0-608-11342-5*, 200152800079) Bks Demand.

Pyrometallurgy. Fathi Habashi. (Principles of Extractive Metallurgy Ser.: Vol. 3). xiv, 480p. 1986. text 318.00 (*2-88124-041-0*) Gordon & Breach.

Pyrometallurgy for Complex Materials & Wastes: International Conference Staged by the G. K. Williams Cooperative Research Centre of the Department of Chemical Engineering, University of Melbourne, Held at the University of Melbourne, Victoria, Australia, June 6-8, 1994. Ed. by Madhu Nilmani et al. LC 94-76293. 403p. 1994. reprint ed. pap. 125.00 (*0-608-03829-6*, 206279100004) Bks Demand.

Pyrophoric Behavior & Combustion of Reactive Metals, Pub. No. 32. D. McIntyre. LC 88-61124. (MTI Publication: No. 32). (Illus.). 21p. 1988. pap. 16.00 (*0-915567-35-0*) NACE Intl.

***Pyrotechnic Insanitarium: American Culture on the Brink of the Millennium.** Mark Dery. LC 98-40837. (Illus.). 304p. 1999. 25.00 (*0-8021-1640-X*, Grove) Grove-Atltic.

***Pyrotechnic Insanitarium: American Culture on the Brink of the Millennium.** Mark Dery. 304p. 2000. pap. 14.00 (*0-8021-3670-2*, Grove) Grove-Atltic.

Pyrotechnic Literature Series, Set. (Monographic Ser.). (Illus.). 1996. pap. write for info. (*1-889526-04-5*) Jrnl of Pyrotechnics.

Pyrotechnic Reference Series: Monographic Series, Set. (Monographic Ser.). (Illus.). 1995. pap. write for info. (*1-889526-00-2*) Jrnl of Pyrotechnics.

Pyrotechnic Signals: Operator's Manual. 1995. lib. bdg. 250.95 (*0-8490-6572-0*) Gordon Pr.

Pyrotechnics. George W. Weingart. (Illus.). 1968. reprint ed. 55.00 (*0-8206-0112-8*) Chem Pub.

Pyrrhichios. Regina Pagoulatou. Tr. by Apostolos N. Athanassakis from GRE. LC 78-62044.Tr. of Pyrrichios. (ENG & GRE., Illus.). 111p. 1978. pap. text 5.00 (*0-918618-15-0*) Pella Pub.

***Pyrrho, His Antecedents & His Legacy.** Richard Bett. 300p. 2000. text 55.00 (*0-19-825065-7*) OUP.

Pyrrhonian Reflections on Knowledge & Justification. Robert J. Fogelin. LC 93-40068. (Illus.). 256p. 1994. text 60.00 (*0-19-508987-1*) OUP.

Pyrrichios see Pyrrhichios

Pyrroles: The Synthesis, Reactivity, & Physical Properties of Substituted Pyrroles, Vol. 48. Ed. by R. Alan Jones. (Chemistry of Heterocyclic Compounds, a Series of Monographs: Vol. 48, Pt. 2). 640p. 1992. 499.00 (*0-471-51306-7*) Wiley.

Pyrroles, Vol. 48, Pt. 1, The Synthesis & the Physical & Chemical Aspects of the Pyrrole Ring, Vol. 48, Pt. 1, The Synthesis and the Physical and. Ed. by R. Alan Jones. LC 89-16553. (Chemistry of Heterocyclic Compounds, a Series of Monographs: Vol. 48, Pt. 1). 742p. 1990. 650.00 (*0-471-62753-4*) Wiley.

Pyrrolizidine Alkaloids. WHO Staff. (Environmental Health Criteria Ser.: No. 60). 345p. 1988. 54.00 (*92-4-154280-2*) World Health.

Pyrrolizidine Alkaloids Health & Safety Guide. WHO Staff. (Health & Safety Guide: No. 26). 17p. 1989. 5.00 (*92-4-154347-7*) World Health.

Pyrsos Hymnon: Festliche Gegenwart und Mythisch-Rituelle Tradition als Voraussetzung einer Pindarinterpretation (Isthmie 4, Pythie 5, Olympie 1 und 3) Eveline Krummen. (Untersuchungen zur Antiken Literatur und Geschichte Ser.: Vol. 35). x, 291p. (C). 1990. lib. bdg. 121.55 (*3-11-012231-6*) De Gruyter.

Pyruvate. Remi Cooper. 1999. pap. 3.95 (*1-885670-80-X*) Woodland UT.

Pyruvate Carboxylase. John C. Wallace & D. Bruce Keech. 280p. 1985. 155.00 (*0-8493-6552-X*, QP619, CRC Reprint) Franklin.

Pyruvate Phenomenon: Discovering the Remarkable Strength, Stamina & Weight-Loss Supplement. Pax Beale. 1997. pap. text 12.00 (*1-885670-79-6*) Woodland UT.

Pysics & Chemistry of Photochromic Glasses. A. V. Dotsenko et al. LC 97-20870. (Laser & Optical Science & Technology Ser.). 208p. 1997. boxed set 104.95 (*0-8493-3780-1*) CRC Pr.

Pythagoraen Sodality of Crotona. Alberto Gianola. 28p. 1997. pap. 8.00 (*0-9651315-2-1*) Spirit of the Sun.

Pythagoras: His Life & Teachings. Thomas Stanley. 19.95 (*0-89314-408-8*) Philos Res.

Pythagoras & Early Pythagoreanism. James A. Philip. LC 66-9226. (Phoenix Supplementary Ser.: Supplementary Vol. 7). 232p. reprint ed. pap. 72.00 (*0-608-09952-X*, 201434000095) Bks Demand.

***Pythagoras & Hermes.** Albert Pike. (Illus.). 1999. pap. 6.95 (*1-55818-466-X*) Holmes Pub.

Pythagoras & the Delphic Mysteries. Edouard Schure. Tr. by F. Rothwell. 180p. 1995. reprint ed. pap. 12.95 (*1-56459-515-3*) Kessinger Pub.

Pythagoras & the Delphic Mysteries. Tr. by Edouard Schure & F. Rothwell. 180p. 1996. reprint ed. spiral bd. 14.00 (*0-7873-0745-9*) Hlth Research.

Pythagoras & the Quantum World. limited ed. Ben Iverson. (Illus.). vi, 112p. 1982. boxed set 225.00 (*0-8062-1935-1*) ITAM.

Pythagoras & the Quantum World, Vol. 1. 2nd rev. ed. Ben Iverson. (Illus.). iv, 219p. Date not set. pap. 25.00 (*1-883401-00-3*) ITAM.

Pythagoras & the Quantum World, Vol. 2. Ben Iverson. (Illus.). xii, 220p. Date not set. pap. 25.00 (*1-883401-02-X*) ITAM.

Pythagoras & the Quantum World, 3 vols., Vol. 3. Ben Iverson & Carl Elkin. (Illus.). 300p. Date not set. 25.00 (*1-883401-03-8*, 9) ITAM.

***Pythagora's Bow Tie: Pre-Algebra Investigations Using the 121-Pin Geoboard.** Ronald E. Ritchart. (Illus.). 1999. pap. 18.95 (*1-57452-256-6*) Cuisenaire.

***Pythagoras' College Football Book: The World's Greatest Mathematicians Rank the College Football Teams.** Mike Goodman. LC 99-178983. 293 p. 1998. write for info. (*1-889534-26-9*) Jay St Pubs.

***Pythagoras' 1999 College Football Book: The World's Greatest Mathematicians Rank the College Football Teams.** Michael K. Goodman. (Illus.). 278p. 1999. pap. 19.95 (*0-9669694-0-5*) Pythagoras.

Pythagoras on the Fine Arts As Therapy: A Lecture Delivered in 1993 at Wellesley College. Constantine Cavarnos. LC 94-75725. (Illus.). 80p. 1994. pap. 6.00 (*1-884729-00-2*) Inst Byzantine.

Pythagoras Revived: Mathematics & Philosophy in Late Antiquity. Dominic J. O'Meara. 264p. 1991. reprint ed. pap. text 29.95 (*0-19-823913-0*) OUP.

Pythagoras, the Immortal Sage. Raymond W. Bernard. 69p. 1958. reprint ed. spiral bd. 11.00 (*0-7873-0101-9*) Hlth Research.

Pythagoras' Trousers: God, Physics, & the Gender War. Margaret Wertheim. 288p. 1997. pap. 13.95 (*0-393-31724-2*) Norton.

Pythagorean Brotherhood. R. Christopher Abel. Ed. by J. D. Holmes. (Orig.). 1997. pap. 4.95 (*1-55818-375-2*, Alexandrian) Holmes Pub.

Pythagorean Golden Verses: With Introduction & Commentary. Johan C. Thom. LC 94-35319. (Religions in the Graeco-Roman World Ser.: Vol. 123). xv, 277p. 1994. 97.00 (*90-04-10105-5*) Brill Academic Pubs.

Pythagorean Intertext in Ovid's Metamorphoses: A New Interpretation. Maria M. Colavito. LC 89-13155. (Studies in Comparative Literature: Vol. 5). 168p. 1989. lib. bdg. 79.95 (*0-88946-398-0*) E Mellen.

Pythagorean Plato: Prelude to the Song Itself. Ernest G. McClain. LC 77-13355. (Illus.). 192p. (Orig.). 1984. pap. 8.95 (*0-89254-010-9*) Nicolas-Hays.

Pythagorean Precepts. Thomas Taylor. 1983. reprint ed. pap. 9.95 (*0-916411-00-1*) Holmes Pub.

Pythagorean Relations. Joseph A. Uphoff, Jr. LC 88-28752. 40p. 1988. pap. text 2.00 (*0-943123-09-7*) Arjuna Lib Pr.

Pythagorean Sourcebook & Library: An Anthology of Ancient Writings Which Relate to Pythagoras & Pythagorean Philosophy. Kenneth S. Guthrie et al. LC 87-60459. (Illus.). 391p. 1987. pap. 20.00 (*0-933999-51-8*) Phanes Pr.

Pythagorean Triangle: The Science of Numbers. George R. Oliver. 260p. 1993. reprint ed. pap. 17.95 (*1-56459-372-X*) Kessinger Pub.

Pythagoreans & Eleatics. J. E. Raven. 196p. 1981. 20.00 (*0-89005-367-7*) Ares.

Pytheas: Europe & the Greek Explorers. C. F. Hawkes. 7.00 (*0-903563-07-X*) David Brown.

Pytheas of Massalia: On the Ocean. Christina H. Roseman. (Illus.). 190p. (Orig.). 1994. pap. 15.00 (*0-89005-545-9*) Ares.

Pythia on Ellis Island: Rethinking the Greco-Roman Legacy in America. Nancy Kassell. LC 97-35637. 280p. (C). 1997. text 49.00 (*0-7618-0942-2*) U Pr of Amer.

Pythia's Drunken Song. Jerry A. Dibble. (International Archives of the History of Ideas Ser.: No. 19). 87p. 1978. pap. text 57.00 (*90-247-2011-7*, Pub. by M Nijhoff) Kluwer Academic.

Pythien, Nemeen und Isthmien Aus Den Schriftund Bildwerken Des Altertums Dargestellt. Johann H. Krause. xxx, 257p. 1975. reprint ed. write for info. (*3-487-05420-5*) G Olms Pubs.

Python. Joseph Fontenrose. 1959. 36.00 (*0-8196-0285-X*) Biblo.

Python: Picture Roo Book. Pauline Reilly. (Illus.). 32p. (Orig.). (J). (gr. 3-7). 1995. pap. 6.95 (*0-86417-698-8*, Pub. by Kangaroo Pr) Seven Hills Bk.

Python & Tkinter Programming. John E. Grayson. (Illus.). 688p. 2000. pap. 49.95 (*1-884777-81-3*, Pub. by Manning Pubns) IPG Chicago.

***Python Annotated Archives.** Martin C. Brown. 722p. 1999. pap. 49.99 (*0-07-212104-1*) Osborne.

Python Caught the Eagle. David Drew. LC 92-31134. (Voyages Ser.). (Illus.). (J). 1993. 2.50 (*0-383-03648-8*) SRA McGraw.

Python Developer's Handbook. 600p. 1900. 39.99 (*0-672-31994-2*) Sams.

Python Essential Reference. 304p. 1999. pap. 34.95 (*0-7357-0901-7*) New Riders Pub.

***Python in 24 Hours.** Ivan Laningham. LC 99-65588. (Illus.). 528p. 2000. pap. 24.99 (*0-672-31735-4*) Sams.

Python Killer: Stories of Nzema Life. Vinigi L. Grottanelli. (Illus.). xii, 236p. 1988. 29.95 (*0-226-31005-1*) U Ch Pr.

***Python Play & Other Recipes for Fun.** Robert Heidbreder & Karen Patkau. (Illus.). 48p. (J). (ps-2). 2000. 14.95 (*0-7737-3213-6*, Stoddart Kids) Stoddart Publ.

Python Pocket Reference. Mark Lutz. Ed. by Gigi Estabrook. (Illus.). 80p. 1998. reprint ed. pap. 8.95 (*1-56592-500-9*) OReilly & Assocs.

Python Programming on Win32. Andrew Robinson & Mark Hammond. Ed. by Robert Denn. (Illus.). 450p. 1999. pap. 34.95 (*1-56592-621-8*) OReilly & Assocs.

Pythons see Animals & the Environment

Pythons. Sherie Bargar & L. Johnson. (J). 1997. pap. 2.50 (*0-8167-1449-5*) Troll Communs.

Pythons. James E. Gerholdt. LC 95-4731. (Snakes Ser.). (Illus.). 24p. (J). (ps-4). 1995. lib. bdg. 13.98 (*1-56239-517-3*) ABDO Pub Co.

Pythons. Mary A. McDonald. (Illus.). 48p. (J). (gr. 3-7). 1995. lib. bdg. 19.00 (*0-516-35296-2*) Childrens.

Pythons. Don Patton. LC 95-7388. (Nature Books Ser.). (Illus.). 32p. (J). (gr. 2-6). 1995. lib. bdg. 22.79 (*1-56766-180-7*) Childs World.

Pythons. R. Pinney. LC 97-38570. (Complete Pet Owner's Manual Ser.). (Illus.). 120p. 1997. pap. 6.95 (*0-8120-9365-8*) Barron.

***Pythons.** Doug Wechsler. LC 00-23747. (Really Wild Life of Snakes Ser.). (Illus.). (J). 2000. write for info. (*0-8239-5604-0*) Rosen Group.

Pythons, Set II. Sherie Bargar & Linda Johnson. (Snake Discovery Library). (Illus.). 24p. (J). (gr. k-4). 1987. lib. bdg. 14.60 (*0-86592-244-6*) Rourke Enter.

Pythons & Boas. Gloria G. Schlaepfer & Mary L. Samuelson. LC 97-47127. (Dillon Remarkable Animals Book Ser.). (J). 1999. pap. 5.95 (*0-382-39753-3*, Dillon Silver Burdett); lib. bdg. 13.95 (*0-382-39752-5*, Dillon Silver Burdett) Silver Burdett Pr.

Pythons & Boas. Peter J. Stafford. (Illus.). 192p. 1986. 26.95 (*0-86622-084-4*, PS-846) TFH Pubns.

An Asterisk (*) at the beginning of an entry indicates that the title is appearing for the first time.

Pythons & Book Reports. Sandra Klaus. (Illus.). 51p. (J). (gr. k-6). 1987. pap. 7.75 (*1-55976-178-4*) CEF Press.

***Python's Back: Pathways of Comparison Between Indonesia & Melanesia.** Andrew J. Strathern & Pamela Stewart. LC 99-56452. 208p. 2000. 55.00 (*0-89789-707-2*, Bergin & Garvey) Greenwood.

Pythons of the World, Australia. David Barker & Tracy Barker. 171p. 1994. 59.95 (*1-882770-34-X*); pap. 39.95 (*1-882770-27-7*) Adv Vivarium.

Python's Party. Brian Wildsmith. (Illus.). 32p. (J). (ps up). 1991. pap. 9.95 (*0-19-272229-8*, 12355) OUP.

Pyxis: Among Lost Children & Grizzled Dogs. Anthony Panzardi. LC 93-13585. 64p. 1993. pap. 14.95 (*0-7734-2774-0*, Mellen Poetry Pr) E Mellen.

Pyzdek's Guide to SPC Vol. 1: Fundamentals. Thomas Pyzdek. (Pyzdek's Guide to SPC Ser.). (Illus.). 154p. (Orig.). 1989. pap. 29.95 (*0-930011-03-1*, H0595) ASQ Qual Pr.

Pyzdek's Guide to SPC Vol. 1: Fundamentals. Thomas Pyzdek. (Pyzdek's Guide to SPC Ser.). (Illus.). 58p. (Orig.). 1989. student ed. 14.35 (*0-930011-06-6*) Quality Am.

Pyzdek's Guide to SPC Vol. 1: Fundamentals, Workbook for Services. (Illus.). 82p. 1991. pap. 16.35 (*0-930011-08-2*) Quality Am.

Pyzdeks Guide to SPC Vol. II: Applications & Special Topics. Thomas Pyzdek. (Illus.). 250p. (C). 1991. pap. 34.75 (*0-930011-04-X*) Quality Am.

PzKpffw IV in Action. (Armor in Action Ser.). (Illus.). 1984. pap. 9.95 (*0-89747-045-1*, 2012) Squad Sig Pubns.

PzKpfw V Panther. Bryan Perrett. (Vanguard Ser.: No. 21). (Illus.). 48p. pap. 10.95 (*0-85045-397-6*, 9310, Pub. by Ospry) Stackpole.

PzKpfw IV. Bryan Parrett. (New Vanguard Ser.: Vol. 28). (Illus.). 48p. 1999. pap. 12.95 (*1-85532-843-7*, Pub. by Ospry) Stackpole.

PzKpfw III. Bryan Perrett. (New Vanguard Ser.: Vol. 27). (Illus.). 48p. 1999. pap. text 12.95 (*1-85532-845-3*, Pub. by Ospry) Stackpole.

PZL Fighters: P.1 Through P.8. Warren A. Eberspacher & Jan P. Koniarek. LC 96-142306. (International Squadron Ser.: Vol. 2). (Illus.). 48p. (Orig.). 1995. pap. 12.95 (*1-883809-12-6*, 4028) Specialty Pr.

Q

Q: Passing Through Q. C. Brian Kelly. (Illus.). 64p. (Orig.). 1991. pap. 5.95 (*0-9624875-2-X*) Montpelier Pub.

***Q: The Autobiography of Quincy Jones.** Quincy Jones & James McBride. 352p. 2001. 25.00 (*0-385-48896-3*) Doubleday.

Q - Systems: Two Quintessential Kiss Methods for Bidding Bridge Hands. Arthur L. Henderson. LC 98-92657. 116p. 1998. pap. write for info. (*1-57502-769-0*, P02118) Morris Pubng.

***Q @ccess: Q Series Web OPAC Module.** EOS International Staff. (Illus.). 98p. 2000. 40.00 incl. disk (*0-929795-72-5*) EOS Intl.

Q & A: Employee Drug Screening. 12p. (Orig.). 1987. pap. text 2.95 (*0-9610026-9-7*) Perf Resource Pr.

Q & A: Queer in Asian America. Ed. by David L. Eng & Alice Y. Hom. LC 98-14990. (Asian American History & Culture Ser.). (Illus.). 432p. 1998. text 69.95 (*1-56639-639-5*); pap. text 27.95 (*1-56639-640-9*) Temple U Pr.

Q & A: Wills Probate & Administration. Robert M. Abbey. 226p. 1997. pap. 16.00 (*1-85431-607-9*, Pub. by Blackstone Pr) Gaunt.

***Q & A No. 2: Life Curriculum.** Harvey A. Smit. 32p. 1998. pap. 1.50 (*1-56212-006-9*) CRC Pubns.

Q & A a Level Law. Timothy Blakemore & Brendan Greene. 240p. 1998. pap. 22.00 (*1-85431-534-X*, Pub. by Blackstone Pr) Gaunt.

Q & A about the Silva Method. 3.95 (*0-913343-45-5*) Inst Psych Inc.

Q & A Constitutional & Administrative Law. Richard Clements & Jane Kay. 209p. 1997. pap. 22.00 (*1-85431-539-0*, Pub. by Blackstone Pr) Gaunt.

Q & A Conveyancing. Robert M. Abbey & Mark B. Richards. (Q & A Ser.). 272p. 1995. pap. 20.00 (*1-85431-407-6*, Pub. by Blackstone Pr) Gaunt.

***Q & A Dating Book.** Sherry Amatenstein. 240p. 2000. pap. 10.95 (*1-58062-274-7*) Adams Media.

Q & A EC Law. Nigel Foster. 1995. 8.95 (*1-85431-324-X*, Pub. by Blackstone Pr) Gaunt.

Q & A EC Law. 2nd ed. Nigel Foster. 227p. 1998. pap. 24.00 (*1-85431-811-X*, Pub. by Blackstone Pr) Gaunt.

Q & A English Legal System. Susan McKenzie & S. Kunalen. 218p. 1996. pap. 22.00 (*1-85431-533-1*, Pub. by Blackstone Pr) Gaunt.

Q & A Equity & Trusts. Margaret Wilkie et al. (Q & A Ser.). 215p. 1994. pap. 20.00 (*1-85431-305-3*, Pub. by Blackstone Pr) Gaunt.

Q & A Family Law. Chris Barton et al. 1994. 8.95 (*1-85431-307-X*, Pub. by Blackstone Pr) Gaunt.

Q & A Family Law. 2nd ed. Chris Barton & Mary Hibbs. 251p. 1998. pap. 24.00 (*1-85431-809-8*, Pub. by Blackstone Pr) Gaunt.

Q & A for Windows Instructor Guide. xvii, 232p. 1993. teacher ed., spiral bd., wbk. ed. 29.00 (*0-7402-0398-3*, SYQWW101IG) Accelerated Comput Train.

Q & A 4.0 Day 2 Instructor Guide. (Illus.). xvii, 150p. 1991. teacher ed., spiral bd., wbk. ed. 29.00 (*0-7402-0397-5*, SYQAD402IG) Accelerated Comput Train.

Q & A from the Heart. John-Roger. 102p. 1991. pap. 5.00 (*0-914829-28-9*) Mandeville LA.

Q & A Land Law. Margaret Wilkie et al. (Q & A Ser.). 238p. 1995. pap. 22.00 (*1-85431-372-X*, Pub. by Blackstone Pr) Gaunt.

Q & A Land Law. 2nd ed. Margaret Wilkie et al. 255p. 1998. pap. 24.00 (*1-85431-808-X*, Pub. by Blackstone Pr) Gaunt.

Q & A Landlord & Tenant. Mark Pawlowski & James Brown. (Q & A Ser.). 230p. 1995. pap. 20.00 (*1-85431-398-3*, Pub. by Blackstone Pr) Gaunt.

Q & A Law of Contract. Ian Brown & Adrian Chandler. (Q & A Ser.). 287p. 1994. pap. 20.00 (*1-85431-306-1*, Pub. by Blackstone Pr) Gaunt.

Q & A Law of Evidence: Blackstone's Law Questions & Answers. C. Chang et al. 208p. 1996. pap. 22.00 (*1-85431-496-3*, Pub. by Blackstone Pr) Gaunt.

Q & A Manual for State Boiler License Exam. Duane Keller. 84p. 1997. pap. 39.95 (*0-9673928-0-2*) D Keller.

Q & A on Drug Education. Jack Rudman. (General Aptitude & Abilities Ser.: CS-24). 1994. pap. 29.95 (*0-8373-6724-7*) Nat Learn.

Q & A on PKD, Vol. 3. rev. ed. PKR Foundation Scientific Advisors Staff. Ed. by Jared J. Grantham et al. 96p. (C). 1995. pap. 15.00 (*0-9614567-2-8*) PKR Foundation.

Q & A on Reporting Periodontal Services. American Academy of Periodontology Staff. 32p. 1992. pap. 25.00 (*0-9624699-4-7*) Amer Acad Periodontology.

***Q & A on the Basic Beliefs.** Jim Starr. (Illus.). 133p. 2000. pap. 1.50i (*1-930264-04-6*) True Jesus.

Q & A on the Real Estate License Examinations (RE) Jack Rudman. (Admission Test Ser.: ATS-6). 1994. pap. 23.95 (*0-8373-5006-9*) Nat Learn.

Q. & A. on the Real Estate License Examinations (RE) Jack Rudman. (Admission Test Ser.: Vol. 6). 43.95 (*0-8373-5106-5*) Nat Learn.

Q & A Popcorn Dictation, 180 WPM. Monette Benoit. (Q & A Popcorn Ser.: Vol. III). 1997. pap. 22.95 (*1-881149-15-3*) CRRB.

Q & A Popcorn Dictation, 225 WPM. Monette Benoit. (Q & A Popcorn Ser.). (Orig.). 1993. pap. 22.95 (*1-881149-03-X*) CRRB.

Q & A Popcorn Dictation, 200 WPM. Monette Benoit. (Q & A Popcorn Ser.: Vol. II). (Orig.). 1996. pap. 22.95 (*1-881149-09-9*) CRRB.

Q & A Write for Windows Day 1 Student Guide. (Illus.). ii, 116p. 1993. student ed., spiral bd., wbk. ed. 15.95 (*0-7402-0373-8*, SYQWW101WB) Accelerated Comput Train.

Q & the History of Early Christianity. Christopher Tuckett. 492p. 1996. 29.95 (*1-56563-246-X*) Hendrickson MA.

Q. B. L.: or The Bride's Reception. Frater Achad. 150p. 1992. reprint ed. pap. 17.95 (*1-56459-139-5*) Kessinger Pub.

Q Basic. Mandell Baumann. (Computer Programming Ser.). 1996. spiral bd. 48.25 incl. disk (*0-314-00822-5*, Pub. by West Pub) Thomson Learn.

Q-Basic: A Short Course. Martin. (C). 1995. lab manual ed. write for info. (*0-15-555519-7*) Harcourt Coll Pubs.

Q-Basic: A Short Course. Martin. (C). 1995. pap. text 20.50 (*0-15-504304-8*) Harcourt Coll Pubs.

Q Basic: Test Bank. Susan K. Baumann. Date not set. pap. text, teacher ed. 15.95 (*0-314-00884-5*) West Pub.

Q-Bear's Book of Rhymes & Songs - Grade One. Carol Apacki et al. (Illus.). 32p. (J). (gr. 1-2). 1993. pap. text 12.95 (*1-56095-095-1*) Quest Intl.

Q-Bear's Book of Rhymes & Songs - Kindergarten. Carol Apacki et al. (Illus.). 32p. (J). (gr. k-1). 1993. pap. text 12.95 (*1-56095-094-3*) Quest Intl.

Q Book. Rinvolucri. Date not set. pap. text. write for info. (*0-582-79606-7*, Pub. by Addison-Wesley) Longman.

Q Book: The Physics of Radiotherapy X-Rays: Problems & Solutions. Peter Metcalfe et al. (Illus.). 100p. (C). 1998. pap. text, wbk. ed. 33.95 (*0-944838-86-3*) Med Physics Pub.

Q Chronicles, Vol. 1. Gene Roddenberry. LC 99-212213. (Star Trek: The Next Generation Ser.: Vol. 1). 752p. 1998. pap. 18.00 (*0-671-03446-4*) PB.

Q-Continuum No. 1: Q-Space. Greg Cox. (Star Trek: The Next Generation Ser.: No. 47). 271p. 1998. per. 6.50 (*0-671-01915-5*, Star Trek) PB.

Q Continuum No. 2: Q-Zone. Greg Cox. (Star Trek: The Next Generation Ser.: No. 48). 270p. 1998. per. 6.50 (*0-671-01921-X*, Star Trek) PB.

Q Continuum No. 3: Q-Strike. Greg Cox. (Star Trek: The Next Generation Ser.: Vol. 49). 272p. 1998. per. 6.50 (*0-671-01922-8*, Star Trek) PB.

Q. C.'s Diary. Gordon Stott. 304p. 1997. 64.00 (*1-873644-71-X*, Pub. by Mercat Pr Bks) St Mut.

Q 11:2B-4 The Lord's Prayer=Q. E. Peters. LC 96-207580. 1998. 25.00 (*90-6831-788-1*, Pub. by Peeters Pub) Bks Intl VA.

Q Factor. Darko Kajfez. LC 93-91069. (Illus.). 174p. (C). 1994. 69.00 (*0-930071-06-9*) Vector Forum.

Q Factor: The Road to Excellence in Sales & Management. Frank M. Munson. LC 97-74260. (Illus.). iii, 214p. 1997. pap. 13.95 (*1-891156-00-4*) HSR Pub.

Q Fever: The Biology of Coxiella Burnetii. Jim C. Williams & Herbert A. Thompson. (Illus.). 360p. 1991. lib. bdg. 189.95 (*0-8493-5983-X*, QR201) CRC Pr.

Q Fever Vol. 1: The Disease, Vol. 1. Ed. by Thomas J. Marrie. LC 96-3686. (Illus.). 545p. 1990. lib. bdg. 179.00 (*0-8493-5984-8*, RC182) CRC Pr.

Q. Horatius Flaccus: His Art of Poetry: Englished by Ben Johnson, with Other Works of the Author Never Printed Before. Horace. Tr. by Ben Jonson. LC 74-80190. (English Experience Ser.: No. 670). 166p. 1974. reprint ed. 45.00 (*90-221-0670-5*) Walter J Johnson.

Q-in-Law. Peter David. Ed. by Dave Stern. (Star Trek Ser.: No. 18). 272p. 1991. mass mkt. 5.99 (*0-671-73389-3*, Star Trek) PB.

Q Is for Duck, 001. Mary Elting & Michael Folsom. LC 80-13854. (Illus.). 64p. (J). (ps-3). 1980. pap. 6.95 (*0-395-30062-2*, Clarion Bks) HM.

Q Is for Quantum: An Encyclopedia of Particle Physics. John Gribbin. 560p. 2000. per. 20.00 (*0-684-86315-4*) S&S Trade.

Q is for Quantum: An Encyclopedia of Particle Physics. John Gribbin et al. LC 98-9918. (Illus.). 560p. 1999. 35.00 (*0-684-85578-X*) Free Pr.

"Q" Kids: A Disaster Safety Workbook for Children of All Ages. Mattie Simms. 64p. (J). (gr. 1-6). 1998. pap. 7.00 (*0-8059-4307-2*) Dorrance.

Q Letters: True Stories of Sado-Masochism. Sir John. LC 92-42171. 198p. (C). 1993. 27.95 (*0-87975-821-X*) Prometheus Bks.

***Q Logic.** Jonathan A. Abbott. LC 99-97026. 2000. pap. 10.95 (*0-533-13370-X*) Vantage.

Q. M. E. D. - Advanced Machine Shop. V. J. Gianelloni, III. Ed. by Richard A. Block. (QMED Ser.). 68p. (Orig.). 1993. pap. 17.50 (*1-879778-14-9*, BK-0068-4) Marine Educ.

Q. M. E. D. - Boilers. V. J. Gianelloni, III. Ed. by Richard A. Block. (QMED Ser.). 58p. (Orig.). 1993. pap. 17.50 (*1-879778-12-2*, BK-0068-2) Marine Educ.

Q. M. E. D. - Electricity. V. J. Gianelloni, III. Ed. by Richard A. Block. (QMED Ser.). 52p. (Orig.). 1993. pap. 17.50 (*1-879778-13-0*, BK-0068-3) Marine Educ.

Q. M. E. D. General. rev. ed. V. J. Gianelloni, III. Ed. by Richard A. Block. (QMED Ser.). (Illus.). 118p. 1997. pap. 24.95 (*1-879778-51-3*, BK-0068) Marine Educ.

Q. M. E. D. Oiler - Including O. S. V. rev. ed. V. J. Gianelloni, III. Ed. by Richard A. Block. (QMED Ser.). 82p. 1996. pap. 24.95 (*1-879778-50-5*) Marine Educ.

Q Methodology. Bruce McKeown & Dan Thomas. (Quantitative Applications in the Social Sciences Ser.: Vol. 66). 93p. (C). 1988. pap. text 10.95 (*0-8039-2753-3*) Sage.

Q of the Earth: Global, Regional & Laboratory Studies. Ed. by Brian J. Mitchell & Barbara A. Romanowicz. LC 99-17774. (Pageoph Topical Volumes Ser.). 500p. 1999. (*3-7643-6049-6*) Birkhauser.

Q Parallels: Synopsis, Critical Notes & Concordance. John S. Kloppenborg. LC 87-62921. (Foundations & Facets: Reference Ser.). (Illus.). 288p. (C). 1988. pap. 19.95 (*0-944344-01-1*) Polebridge Pr.

q-Schur Algebra. Stephen Donkin. (London Mathematical Society Lecture Note Ser.: No. 253). 235p. (C). 1999. pap. text 39.95 (*0-521-64558-1*) Cambridge U Pr.

***Q Series: Acquisitions.** EOS International Staff. (Illus.). 328p. 2000. 40.00 incl. disk (*0-929795-68-7*) EOS Intl.

***Q Series: Cataloging.** EOS International Staff. (Illus.). 308p. 2000. 40.00 incl. disk (*0-929795-65-2*) EOS Intl.

***Q Series: Circulation.** EOS International Staff. (Illus.). 290p. 2000. 40.00 incl. disk (*0-929795-66-0*) EOS Intl.

***Q Series: OPAC.** EOS International Staff. (Illus.). 90p. 1999. 40.00 incl. disk (*0-929795-71-7*) EOS Intl.

Q Series: Power Search. EOS International Staff. (Illus.). 98p. 1999. 40.00 (*0-929795-70-9*) EOS Intl.

***Q Series: Report Writer.** EOS International Staff. Orig. Title: Q Series: Database Structure. (Illus.). 339p. 1999. 40.00 incl. disk (*0-929795-69-5*) EOS Intl.

***Q Series: Serials.** EOS International Staff. (Illus.). 280p. 2000. 40.00 incl. disk (*0-929795-67-9*) EOS Intl.

***Q Series: Setup & Utilities.** EOS International Staff. (Illus.). 338p. 2000. 40.00 incl. disk (*0-929795-64-4*) EOS Intl.

Q-Series: Their Development & Application in Analysis, Number Theory, Combinatorics, Physics & Computer Algebra. G. Andrews. LC 86-14061. (CBMS Regional Conference Series in Mathematics: No. 66). 130p. 1986. pap. 18.00 (*0-8218-0716-1*, CBMS/66) Am Math.

Q-Series & Partitions. Ed. by D. W. Stanton. (IMA Volumes in Mathematics & Its Applications Ser.: Vol. 18). (Illus.). xi, 212p. 1989. 47.95 (*0-387-97086-X*) Spr-Verlag.

Q Series: Database Structure see Q Series: Report Writer

***Q-Series from a Contemporary Perspective: Ams-Ims-Siam Joint Summer Research Conference on Q-Series, Combinatorics & Computer Algebra, June 21-25, 1998, Mount Holyoke College, South Hadley, Massachusetts.** Mourad E. H. Ismail & Dennis W. Stanton. LC 99-87057. (Contemporary Mathematics Ser.). 440p. 2000. 93.00 (*0-8218-1150-9*) Am Math.

***Q-Ship Versus U-Boats: America's Secret Project.** Keeneth M. Beyer. LC 98-53195. 1999. 32.95 (*1-55750-044-4*) Naval Inst Pr.

Q-Ships: Britain's Secret Weapon Against the U-Boats, 1914-1918. Carson I. Ritchie. 236p. 1990. 48.00 (*0-86138-011-8*, Pub. by T Dalton) St Mut.

Q-Ships & Their Story. E. Keble Chatterton. LC 79-6105. (Navies & Men Ser.). (Illus.). 1980. reprint ed. lib. bdg. 31.95 (*0-405-13034-1*) Ayer.

***Q Ships, Commerce Raiders & Convoys.** P. E. D. Stearns. 256p. 2000. 80.00 (*1-873376-84-7*, Pub. by Spellmnt Pubs) St Mut.

Q-Sort As a Needs Assessment Technique. Sean Tate. (Technical Notes Ser.: No. 21). 20p. (Orig.). (C). 1982. pap. 2.00 (*0-932288-92-8*) Ctr Intl Ed U of MA.

Q-Squared. Peter David. (Star Trek Ser.: No. 37). 448p. 1995. per. 6.50 (*0-671-89151-0*, Star Trek) PB.

Q. T., MIS & Data Processing, Vol. I. S. K. Chakabarty. (C). 1989. 100.00 (*0-89771-439-3*, Pub. by Current Dist) St Mut.

Q. T., MIS & Data Processing, Vol. II. S. K. Chakabarty. (C). 1989. 125.00 (*0-89771-440-7*, Pub. by Current Dist) St Mut.

Q That Lost Its Tail. Betsy Brown. (Illus.). 14p. (Orig.). (J). (gr. 1-2). 1996. pap. write for info. (*1-888479-05-1*) Tarpley Pubng.

Q-Thomas Reader: The Gospels Before the Gospels. John S. Kloppenborg et al. LC 90-30774. (Illus.). 176p. (C). 1990. pap. 14.95 (*0-944344-11-9*) Polebridge Pr.

Q12:8-12 Confessing. E. Peters. 1998. 87.95 (*90-6831-990-6*, Pub. by Peeters Pub) Bks Intl VA.

Q 12:49-59 Children vs. Parents. E. Peters. 1998. 56.95 (*90-6831-931-0*, Pub. by Peeters Pub) Bks Intl VA.

***Q 2000: QVC Desk Diary.** (Illus.). 128p. 1999. write for info. (*1-928998-31-3*) Q V C Pubg.

Q-Values & Excitation Functions of Nuclear Reactions: Q-Values see Nuclear Particles & Physics: Group I

Q-Values & Excitation Functions of Nuclear Reactions, Vol. 5, Pt. B, Excitation Functions for Charged-Particle Induced Nuclear Reactions see Nuclear Particles & Physics: Group I

Q Working Guide for Carbon Steel Equipment in Wet H2S Service. EEMUA Staff. 1990. pap. 125.00 (*0-85931-085-X*, Pub. by EEMUA) St Mut.

QA-CQI Manual for Clinical Lab. M. Cronin. 208p. (C). 1994. 99.95 (*0-933195-67-2*); write for info. (*0-933195-70-2*) CA College Health Sci.

QA-CQI Manual for Home Care. rev. ed. M. Cronin. 122p. (C). 1994. ring bd. 99.95 (*0-933195-39-7*) CA College Health Sci.

QA-CQI Manual for Physical Therapy. rev. ed. M. Cronin. 110p. (C). 1994. ring bd. 99.95 (*0-933195-38-9*) CA College Health Sci.

QA-CQI Manual for Respiratory Care. rev. ed. M. Cronin. 208p. (C). 1994. ring bd. 99.95 (*0-933195-32-X*) CA College Health Sci.

QA Issues in Clinical Toxicology. Ed. by Shirley Welch. 70p. 1996. pap. 24.00 (*0-915274-86-8*, 202687) Am Assn Clinical Chem.

QA-1, (Natural Arithmetic) No. 1: The Ancient Mathematics. 2nd ed. Ben Iverson. (Illus.). xvi, 96p. (YA). (gr. 5 up). Date not set. pap. 15.00 (*1-883401-06-2*) ITAM.

QA-3, (Natural Aritmetic), Vol. 3. Ben Iverson. (Illus.). vi, 120p. (Orig.). (YA). (gr. 11 up). Date not set. pap. 15.00 (*1-883401-08-9*) ITAM.

QA-2, (Natural Arithmetic) Natural Arithmetic, No. 2. Ben Iverson. (Illus.). xii, 133p. (Orig.). (YA). (gr. 9 up). 1993. pap. 15.00 (*1-883401-07-0*) ITAM.

Qaav Taub Luj Tuaj Os Qaav Taub (Hmong) Carlleen Spencer. Tr. by Yer J. Thao. (J). (gr. k-3). 1994. 12.50 (*1-57842-042-3*) Delmas Creat.

***Qabalah: A Beginner's Guide.** Kate Rheeders. (Headway Guides for Beginners Ser.). (Illus.). 96p. 2000. pap. 11.95 (*0-340-74262-3*, Pub. by Headway) Trafalgar.

Qabalah: A Beginner's Guide. Kate Rheeders. (Beginners Ser.). (Illus.). 96p. 1996. pap. 11.95 (*0-340-67339-7*, Pub. by Hodder & Stought Ltd) Trafalgar.

***Qabalah: Secret Tradition of the West.** Papus, pseud. (Illus.). 384p. 2000. pap. (*1-57863-936-0*); pap. 19.95 (*0-87728-936-0*) Weiser.

Qabalah, Tarot & the Western Mystery Tradition: The 22 Connecting Paths on the Tree of Life. Ed. & Compiled by Clifford Bias. Orig. Title: The Way Back. (Illus.). 158p. 1998. pap. 12.95 (*1-57281-106-4*, BK177) US Games Syst.

Qabalah, Tarot & the Western Mystery Tradition: The 22 Connecting Paths on the Tree of Life. rev. ed. Clifford Bias. LC 97-29495. Orig. Title: The Way Back. (Illus.). 160p. 1997. pap. 12.95 (*1-57863-031-2*) Weiser.

Qabalism. Henry B. Pullen-Burry. 167p. 1972. reprint ed. 15.00 (*0-911662-45-6*) Yoga.

Qabalistic Concepts: Living the Tree. William G. Gray. LC 96-47895. (Illus.). 400p. 1997. pap. 16.95 (*1-57863-000-2*) Weiser.

Qabalistic Tarot: A Textbook of Mystical Philosophy. Robert Wang. LC 82-61871. (Illus.). 304p. 1983. reprint ed. pap. 22.95 (*0-87728-672-8*) Weiser.

Qabbalah: The Philosophical Writings of Solomon Ben Yehudah Ibn Gabirol. Isaac Myer. 1975. 250.00 (*0-8490-0922-7*) Gordon Pr.

QA/CQI Strategies in Health Care Quality. 2nd ed. Christopher R. Wilson. 388p. 1993. pap. text 38.00 (*0-920513-12-3*, Pub. by Saulnders) Saunders.

Qaddafi: His Ideology in Theory & Practice. Mohamed El-khawas. (Illus.). 200p. (Orig.). (C). 1986. 18.95 (*0-915597-24-1*) Amana Bks.

Qaddafi: His Ideology in Theory & Practice. Mohamed El-Khawas. (Illus.). 200p. (Orig.). (C). 1986. pap. 9.95 (*0-915597-23-3*) Amana Bks.

Qaddafi: The Man & His Policies. Janice Monti-Belkaoui & Ahmed Riahi-Belkaoui. 107p. 1996. text 61.95 (*1-85972-385-3*, Pub. by Avebry) Ashgate Pub Co.

Qaddafi & the United State since 1969. P. Edward Haley. LC 83-26993. 364p. 1984. 69.50 (*0-275-91181-0*, C1181, Praeger Pubs) Greenwood.

Qaddafi, Terrorism, & the Origins of the U. S. Attack on Libya. Brian L. Davis. LC 89-16095. 213p. 1990. 45.00 (*0-275-93302-4*, C3302, Praeger Pubs) Greenwood.

Qadesh, 1300 BC. Mark Healy. (Campaign Ser.: No. 22). (Illus.). 96p. pap. 14.95 (*1-85532-300-1*, 9521, Pub. by Ospry) Stackpole.

Qadhafi's Libya, 1969-1994. Dirk Vandewalle. LC 95-9835. 304p. 1995. text 55.00 (*0-312-12587-9*) St Martin.

Qadi & the Fortune Teller. Nabil Saleh. LC 97-134283. 256p. 1997. pap. 12.95 (*0-7043-8019-6*, Pub. by Quartet) Interlink Pub.

Qadiyat al Manhajiyah fi al Fikr al Islami: (The Issue of Methodology in Islamic Thought) AbdulHamid AbuSulayman. (Rasa'il Islamiyat al Ma'rifah Ser.: No. 4). (ARA.). 42p. (Orig.). 1989. pap. 2.00 (*1-56564-163-9*) IIIT VA.

Qaids, Captains, & Colons: French Military Administration in the Colonial Maghrib 1844-1934. Kenneth J. Perkins. LC 80-13114. 278p. (C). 1981. 45.00 (*0-8419-0564-9*, Africana) Holmes & Meier.

Qaidu & the Rise of the Independent Mongol State in Central Asia. Michal Biran. LC 98-170584. 288p. 1997. 75.00 (*0-7007-0631-3*, Pub. by Curzon Pr Ltd) Paul & Co Pubs.

Q

Qa'imah Mukhtarah Hawla al Ma'rifah wa al Fikr wa al Manhaj wa al Thaqafah wa al Hadarah: (A Select Bibliography on Knowledge, Thought, Method, Culture, & Civilization) Muhyialdin Atiyah. LC 92-20080. (Silsilat al Maraji' wa al Adillah Wa'l Kashshafat Ser.: No. 4). (ARA.). 111p. (Orig.). 1992. pap. 6.00 (*1-56564-038-1*) IIIT VA.

Qajar Iran: Political, Social & Cultural Changes, 1800-1925. Ed. by C. E. Bosworth & Carole Hillenbrand. (Illus.). 462p. (C). 1992. reprint ed. pap. text 25.00 (*0-939214-98-9*) Mazda Pubs.

Qajar Iran & the Rise of Reza Khan, 1796-1925. Nikki R. Keddie. LC 99-12715. (Illus.). 138p. 1999. pap. text 16.95 (*1-56859-084-9*) Mazda Pubs.

Qala'at al Bahrain Vol. 1: The Northern City Wall & the Islamic Fortress. Ed. by Flemming Hojlund et al. LC 96-160098. (Carlsberg Foundation's Gulf Project Ser.: No. 30, Pt. 1). (Illus.). 511p. (C). 1994. text 60.00 (*87-7288-574-2*, Pub. by Aarhus Univ Pr) David Brown.

Qala'at Al-Bahrain Vol. 2: The Central Monumental Buildings. Flemming Hojlund & H. Hellmuth Andersen. (Jutland Archaeological Society Publications: Vol. XXX: 2). (Illus.). 288p. 1997. 45.00 (*87-7288-590-4*, Pub. by Aarhus Univ Pr) David Brown.

Qal'at Ja'bar Pottery: A Study of a Syrian Fortified Site of the Late 11th-14th Centuries. Cristina Tonghini. (British Academy Monographs in Archaeology: No. 11). (Illus.). 440p. 1999. text 130.00 (*0-19-727010-7*) OUP.

Qaltayak Aquiyaryugyaaquq. Magdalena McDalton.Tr. of Qaltayak Wants to Play Outside. (ESK., Illus.). 8p. (J). (gr. k-3). 1998. pap. text 6.00 (*1-58084-037-X*) Lower Kuskokwim.

Qaltayak Wants to Play Outside see Qaltayak Aquiyaryugyaaquq

Qanemcikarluni Tekitnarqelartuq: One Must Arrive with a Story to Tell: Traditional Narratives by the Elders of Tununak, Alaska. Ed. by Eliza C. Orr & Ben Orr. LC 95-2303. (ESK.). xxx, 377p. 1995. pap. 19.00 (*1-55500-052-5*) Alaska Native.

Q'anil: El Hombre Rayo. Victor D. Montejo. (MYN & SPA.). 165p. 1998. pap. 12.95 (*1-886502-22-6*) Yax Te Found.

***Q'anil, Man of Lightning: A Legend of Jacaltenango, Guatemala, in English, Spanish & Popb'al Ti'** Victor Montejo et al. LC 00-9431. (Sun Tracks Ser.). (ENG & SPA.). 2001. write for info. (*0-8165-2082-8*) U of Ariz Pr.

Qanum-i Madani see Civil Code of Iran

Qanuq Itqanaiyarnagpat Qalut. large type ed. Alice Andrew et al.Tr. of How to Prepare Fishs. (ESK., Illus.). 8p. (J). (gr. k-3). 1999. pap. text 6.00 (*1-58084-139-2*) Lower Kuskokwim.

Qanuqitipit. large type ed. Veronica Michael & Frances Caole.Tr. of My Feelings. (ESK., Illus.). 8p. (J). (gr. k-3). 1999. pap. text 6.00 (*1-58084-123-6*) Lower Kuskokwim.

Qanuqitpit. large type ed. Veronica Michael & Frances Caole.Tr. of My Feelings. (ESK., Illus.). 8p. (J). (gr. k-3). 1999. pap. text 6.00 (*1-58084-138-4*) Lower Kuskokwim.

Qashqa'i of Iran. Lois Beck. LC 85-23404. (Illus.). 422p. reprint ed. pap. 130.90 (*0-7837-2498-5*, 208029200004) Bks Demand.

Qasida Poetry in Islamic Asia & Africa: Classical Tradition & Modern Meanings, 2 vols., Set. Ed. by Stefan Sperl & Christopher Shackle. (Studies in Arabic Literature: No. 20). 1055p. 1996. 291.50 (*90-04-10452-6*) Brill Academic Pubs.

Qatar see Commercial Laws of the Middle East

Qatar see Enchantment of the World Series

Qatar. Bernard Reich & Steven Dorr. (Profiles of the Middle East Ser.). 1996. text 36.00 (*0-8133-0344-3*) Westview.

Qatar. Stacey International Staff. (Illus.). 1984. 49.95 (*0-86685-531-9*, STA3431, Pub. by Stacey Intl) Intl Bk Ctr.

***Qatar: A Country Study Guide.** Global Investment & Business Center, Inc. Staff. (World Country Study Guides Library: Vol. 139). (Illus.). 350p. 2000. pap. 59.00 (*0-7397-2437-1*) Intl Business Pubns.

Qatar: Energy & Development. Ragaei E. Mallakh. LC 84-29317. (Illus.). 184p. 1985. 21.00 (*0-7099-0955-1*, Pub. by C Helm) Routldge.

Qatar - A Country Study Guide: Basic Information for Research & Pleasure. Global Investment Center, USA Staff. (World Country Study Guide Library: Vol. 139). (Illus.). 350p. 1999. pap. 59.00 (*0-7397-1536-4*) Intl Business Pubns.

Qatar Business & Investment Opportunities Yearbook, 1998: Business, Investment, Export-Import. Russian Information & Business Center, Inc. Staff. (Business & Investment Opportunities Library, '98). (Illus.). 1998. pap. 99.00 (*1-57751-996-5*) Intl Business Pubns.

***Qatar Business Intelligence Report, 190 vols.** Global Investment & Business Center, Inc. Staff. (World Business Intelligence Library: Vol. 139). (Illus.). 350p. 2000. pap. 99.95 (*0-7397-2637-4*) Intl Business Pubns.

***Qatar Business Law Handbook.** Global Investment & Business Center, Inc. Staff. (Global Business Law Handbooks Library: Vol. 139). (Illus.). 2000. pap. 99.95 (*0-7397-2037-6*) Intl Business Pubns.

***Qatar Business Opportunity Yearbook.** Global Investment & Business Center, Inc. Staff. (Global Business Opportunity Yearbooks Library: Vol. 139). (Illus.). 2000. pap. 99.95 (*0-7397-2237-9*) Intl Business Pubns.

***Qatar Business Opportunity Yearbook: Export-Import, Investment & Business Opportunities.** International Business Publications, U. S. A. Staff & Global Investment Center, U. S. A. Staff. (Global Business Opportunity Yearbooks Library: Vol. 139). (Illus.). 350p. 1999. pap. 99.95 (*0-7397-1337-X*) Intl Business Pubns.

***Qatar Country Review 2000.** Robert C. Kelly et al. (Illus.). 60p. 1999. pap. 39.95 (*1-58310-563-8*) CountryWatch.

***Qatar Foreign Policy & Government Guide.** Contrib. by Global Investment & Business Center, Inc. Staff. (World Foreign Policy & Government Library: Vol. 133). (Illus.). 350p. 1999. pap. 99.00 (*0-7397-3631-0*) Intl Business Pubns.

***Qatar Foreign Policy & Government Guide.** Global Investment & Business Center, Inc. Staff. (World Foreign Policy & Government Library: Vol. 133). (Illus.). 350p. 2000. 99.95 (*0-7397-3837-2*) Intl Business Pubns.

***Qatar Investment & Business Guide.** Global Investment & Business Center, Inc. Staff. (Global Investment & Business Guide Library: Vol. 139). (Illus.). 2000. pap. 99.95 (*0-7397-1837-1*) Intl Business Pubns.

Qatar Investment & Business Guide: Economy, Export-Import, Business & Investment Climate, Business Contacts. Contrib. by Russian Information & Business Center, Inc. Staff. (Russia, NIS & Emerging Markets Investment & Business Library-98). (Illus.). 350p. 1998. pap. 99.00 (*1-57751-918-3*) Intl Business Pubns.

***Qatar Investment & Business Guide: Export-Import, Investment & Business Opportunities.** International Business Publications, USA Staff & Global Investment Center, USA Staff. (World Investment & Business Guide Library-99: Vol. 139). (Illus.). 350p. 1999. pap. 99.95 (*0-7397-0334-X*) Intl Business Pubns.

Qatari Women: Past & Present. Abeer Abu Saud. (Illus.). 184p. (C). 1984. text 32.95 (*0-582-78372-0*) Longman.

Qateperewaaghmeng Aatkaqelghii (The Man Dressed in White) G. Slwooko. (ESK.). 30p. 1977. pap. 3.00 (*0-933769-78-4*) Alaska Native.

Qawiaraq Inupiaq Literacy Manual. Lawrence D. Kaplan. 50p. (C). 1987. pap. 6.00 (*1-55500-028-2*) Alaska Native.

***Qayaq: Kayaks of Siberia & Alaska.** David W. Zimmerly. LC 00-27096. (Illus.). 2000. write for info. (*1-889963-10-0*) U of Alaska Pr.

Qazaqs in the People's Republic of China: The Local Processes of History. Nathan Light. Ed. by Victoria J. Cuffel. LC 93-655022. (MacArthur Scholar Series, Occasional Paper: No. 22). (Illus.). 107p. (Orig.). 1994. pap. 4.00 (*1-881157-24-5*) In Ctr Global.

QB VII. Leon Uris & Jill Uris. 432p. 1982. mass mkt. 7.99 (*0-553-27094-X*) Bantam.

QB VII. Leon Uris & Jill Uris. 1982. 13.09 (*0-606-12492-6*, Pub. by Turtleback) Demco.

QB VII. Leon Uris & Jill Uris. 1994. reprint ed. lib. bdg. 29.95 (*1-56849-563-3*) Buccaneer Bks.

Qbase Surgery No. 1: Mcq Companion to 'Fundamentals of Surgical Practice' T. Diamond et al. 208p. 2000. pap. text 47.50 (*1-84110-005-6*) OUP.

Qbasic. Susan K. Baumann. (DG - Computer Programming Ser.). (C). 1992. mass mkt. 39.00 (*0-314-00071-2*) West Pub.

Qbasic. Susan K. Baumann & Steven L. Mandell. Ed. by Clyde Perlee. 450p. (YA). 1992. mass mkt. 43.50 (*0-314-78351-2*) West Pub.

Qbasic. Beekman. (C). 1996. text 76.00 (*0-8053-5149-3*) Benjamin-Cummings.

Qbasic. H. L. Capron. (C). 1995. pap. text 50.66 (*0-8053-1428-8*) Addison-Wesley.

Qbasic. Don Cassel. (Source 1 Ser.). (C). 1994. pap. text 9.40 (*0-13-834326-8*) P-H.

Qbasic. Schneider & Norton. 1991. pap. 5.00 incl. 3.5 hd (*0-13-747494-6*) Macmillan USA.

Qbasic. 2nd ed. Mandell Baumann. (Computer Applications). (C). 1997. text 30.25 (*0-314-22026-7*) West Pub.

Qbasic. 2nd ed. Susan K. Baumann. LC 97-123321. (DF - Computer Applications Ser.). (C). 1996. mass mkt. 61.95 (*0-314-20547-0*) West Pub.

Qbasic. 2nd ed. Susan K. Baumann & Steven L. Mandell. 550p. (C). 1996. mass mkt. 36.75 (*0-314-20659-0*) West Pub.

Qbasic: A Brief Introduction. Antoine Wennington. 224p. 1996. pap. write for info. (*1-880634-34-1*) Access Pubs.

Qbasic: A Short Course in Structured Programming. Gary W. Martin. 195p. (C). 1994. pap. text 15.00 (*0-03-098845-4*) Dryden Pr.

Qbasic: An Introduction. Gary B. Shelly & T. Cashman. (Shelly-Cashman Ser.). 464p. 1996. mass mkt. 58.95 (*0-7895-0384-0*) Course Tech.

Qbasic: An Introduction to Programming. Gary B. Shelly et al. (Shelly Cashman Ser.). 464p. 1996. mass mkt. 50.00 incl. cd-rom (*0-7895-1318-8*) Course Tech.

***Qbasic: Intro to Programming W/visio Cd.** Shelly et al. (C). 1998. pap. 89.00 (*0-7895-4631-0*) Course Tech.

QBASIC Beginning to Advanced. Seth M. Hochwald et al. 535p. (C). 1994. pap. text. write for info. (*1-880634-02-3*) Access Pubs.

QBASIC by Example. 1994. teacher ed. 39.99 (*1-56529-477-7*) Que.

QBASIC by Example: Special Edition. Greg M. Perry. (Illus.). 620p. (Orig.). 1993. 29.99 (*1-56529-439-4*) Que.

QBASIC by Example Academic Edition. Greg M. Perry. LC 93-86968. 620p. 1994. 46.99 (*1-56529-454-8*) Que.

QBASIC for Business Problem Solving. John Forsmark. 384p. (C). 1995. pap. write for info. (*0-697-26668-0*) Bus & Educ Tech.

QBASIC For Business Problem Solving. John Forsmark. LC 95-36328. 512p. (C). 1996. text 28.95 (*0-256-20434-9*, Irwn McGrw-H) McGrw-H Hghr Educ.

QBASIC for Rookies. 1993. 19.95 incl. disk (*1-56529-392-4*) Macmillan USA.

QBASIC for Rookies - International. 1993. 16.95 (*1-56529-393-2*) Que.

QBASIC for Students. Michael Trombetta. 736p. (C). 1993. pap. 50.31 (*0-07-065261-9*) McGraw.

QBASIC Fundamentals & Style with an Introduction to Microsoft Visual Basic for Windows. James Quasney et al. (Shelly Cashman Ser.). 608p. (C). 1995. pap. 40.00 incl. disk (*0-87709-896-4*) Course Tech.

QBASIC Fundamentals & Style with an Introduction to Microsoft Visual Basic for Windows, Incl. instr. manual. James S. Quasney et al. 608p. (C). 1995. text 57.95 incl. 3.5 ld (*0-7895-0021-3*) Course Tech.

***Qbasic, Fundamentals & Style with introduction to MS Visual Basic.** 2nd ed. James Quasney. (Programming Ser.). (C). 2000. pap. 42.50 (*0-619-01625-6*) Course Tech.

Qbasic Using Subprograms. 2nd ed. Quasney. (Programming Ser.). (C). 1997. pap. 56.95 (*0-7600-5099-6*) Course Tech.

QBASIC with an Introduction to Visual BASIC: For Engineering, Mathematis & Sciences. 2nd ed. David I. Schneider. Orig. Title: Microsoft QuickBASIC. 676p. (C). 1994. pap. 61.00 (*0-02-407611-2*, Macmillan Coll) P-H.

QBASIC with an Introduction to Visual Basic 5.0. 4th ed. David I. Schneider. LC 98-27509. 644p. 1998. pap. 59.33 (*0-13-973876-2*) P-H.

QC Laboratory Chemist: Plain & Simple. Clifford L. Nilsen. (Illus.). 275p. 1997. ring bd. 159.00 (*1-57491-053-1*) Interpharm.

QC Problem-Solving Approach: Solving Workplace Problems the Japanese Way. Katsuya Hosotani. 190p. 1992. pap. text 29.50 (*4-906224-91-1*, Pub. by Three A) Qual Resc.

QC Sources. Charles Bastien. 420p. (Orig.). (C). 1984. 17.95 (*0-916429-00-8*) IAQC Pr.

QC to SPC: A Workbook. William J. Tobin. 135p. 1991. student ed. 25.00 (*0-936994-06-1*) W J T Assocs.

***QCD: Perturbative or Nonperturbative?** Ed. by Lidia S. Ferreira et al. 500p. 2000. 98.00 (*981-02-4316-2*) World Scientific Pub.

QCD - 20 Years Later, 2 vols. 892p. 1993. 34.00 (*981-02-1086-8*) World Scientific Pub.

QCD - 20 Years Later, 2 vols., Set. P. M. Zerwas & H. A. Kastrup. 892p. 1993. text 95.00 (*981-02-1085-X*) World Scientific Pub.

QCD & Beyond: Proceedings of the TASI, 1995. LC 97-102563. 600p. 1996. text 97.00 (*981-02-2521-0*) World Scientific Pub.

QCD & Collider Physics. R. K. Ellis et al. (Cambridge Monographs on Particle Physics, Nuclear Physics & Cosmology: No. 7). 450p. 1996. text 57.95 (*0-521-58189-3*) Cambridge U Pr.

***QCD & Multiparticle Production.** Ed. by Chung-I Tan & Ina Sarcevic. 550p. 2000. 108.00 (*981-02-4294-8*) World Scientific Pub.

Qcd At Hera: The Hadronic Final State in Deep Inelastic Scattering, 150. Michael Kulhen. LC 98-46731. 1998. 109.95 (*3-540-65118-7*) Spr-Verlag.

QCD at 200 TeV. Ed. by L. Cifarelli & Y. Dokshitzer. (Ettore Majorana International Science Ser., Life Sciences: Vol. 60). (Illus.). 304p. (C). 1992. text 126.00 (*0-306-44222-1*, Kluwer Plenum) Kluwer Academic.

QCD Corrections & New Physics: Proceedings of the International Symposium Hiroshima, Japan 27-29 October, 1997. Ed. by Jiro Kodaira et al. 300p. 1998. 76.00 (*981-02-3466-X*) World Scientific Pub.

QCD Hard Hadronic Processes. Ed. by B. Cox. (NATO ASI Series B, Physics: Vol. 197). (Illus.). 566p. 1988. 140.00 (*0-306-43204-8*, Plenum Trade) Perseus Pubng.

QCD, Lightcone Physics & Hadron Phenomenology: Proceedings of the 10th Symposium on Nuclear Physics Seoul, Korea 23-28 June, 1997. Ed. by Cheung-Ryong Ji & Dong-Phil Min. 300p. 1998. 78.00 (*981-02-3385-X*) World Scientific Pub.

QCD Spectral Sum Rules. S. Narison. (Lecture Notes in Physics Ser.: Vol. 26). 544p. 1990. text 48.00 (*9971-5-0653-X*) World Scientific Pub.

QCD Vacuum, Hadrons & Superdense Matter. E. V. Shuryak. 416p. 1988. text 90.00 (*9971-978-32-6*); pap. text 41.00 (*9971-978-33-4*) World Scientific Pub.

QCD Vacuum Structure: Proceedings of the Workshop on QCD Vacuum Structure & Its Applications. 388p. 1993. text 49.00 (*981-02-1352-2*) World Scientific Pub.

QCD Vacuum Structure: Proceedings of the Workshop on QCD Vacuum Structure & Its Applications. B. Muller & H. M. Fried. 388p. 1993. text 95.00 (*981-02-1280-1*) World Scientific Pub.

QC's & Unions: Together QC's & Unions. spiral bd. 8.95 (*0-317-69751-X*) IAQC Pr.

QDROs: A Guide for Plan Administration. 2nd ed. Julie L. Bloss. Ed. by Mary Jo Brzezinski. LC 97-70271. 132p. 1997. pap. 38.00 (*0-89154-511-5*) Intl Found Employ.

QDT, 1997: Quintessence of Dental Technology, Vol. 20. Ed. by John Sorensen. (Illus.). 190p. 1997. pap. text 56.00 (*0-86715-322-9*) Quint Pub Co.

QDT, 1993. Ed. by Robert Renner. (Illus.). 188p. (Orig.). 1993. pap. text 54.00 (*0-86715-186-2*) Quint Pub Co.

QDT 2000. Ed. by Avishai Sadan. (Illus.). 200p. pap. 60.00 (*0-86715-378-4*) Quint Pub Co.

QED: A Proof of Renormalization. J. S. Feldman et al. (Lecture Notes in Physics Ser.: Vol. 312). vii, 176p. 1988. 34.95 (*0-387-50213-0*) Spr-Verlag.

QED: The Strange Theory of Light & Matter. Richard Phillips Feynman. LC 85-42685. (Alix G. Mautner Memorial Lectures). (Illus.). 152p. 1985. pap. 10.95 (*0-691-02417-0*, Pub. by Princeton U Pr); text 39.50 (*0-691-08388-6*, Pub. by Princeton U Pr) Cal Prin Full Svc.

QED & the Men Who Made It: Dyson, Feynman, Schwinger, & Tomonaga. S. S. Schweber. LC 93-33550. (Princeton Series in Physics). 784p. 1994. text 135.00 (*0-691-03685-3*, Pub. by Princeton U Pr) Cal Prin Full Svc.

QED & the Men Who Made It: Dyson, Feynman, Schwinger, & Tomonaga. Silvan S. Schweber. LC 93-33550. (Physics Ser.). 784p. 1994. pap. text 39.50 (*0-691-03327-7*, Pub. by Princeton U Pr) Cal Prin Full Svc.

QED Report on Venture Capital Financial Analysis. James L. Plummer. 217p. 1987. 295.00 (*0-9620093-0-X*) QED Research.

QED Structure Functions: AIP Conference Proceedings, No. 201. Ed. by Giovanni Bonvicini. LC 90-80229. (Particles & Fields Ser.: No. 39). (Illus.). 456p. 1990. lib. bdg. 85.00 (*0-88318-671-3*) Am Inst Physics.

QED 3.04. Oehler. (C). 1991. text 40.00 (*0-7167-2253-4*) W H Freeman.

QED Tutorial 3.04. Hollerbach. (C). 1991. text 20.00 (*0-7167-2255-0*) W H Freeman.

QED's Guide to U. S. School Districts, 1987-88. Quality Education Data Staff. (School Trend Ser.). 400p. 1988. pap. 79.95 (*0-88747-295-8*, 2958Q) Quality Ed Data.

QED's State School Guides. 13th ed. (Orig.). 1995. write for info. (*0-614-16050-2*) Quality Ed Data.

QE8 - 8th National Quantum Electronics Conference: Special Issue - Journal of Modern Optics, Vol. 35 No. 3. A. Maitland & W. Sibbett. 320p. 1988. pap. 66.00 (*0-85066-899-9*) Taylor & Francis.

Qemant: A Pagan-Hebraic Peasantry of Ethiopia. Frederick C. Gamst. (Illus.). 128p. (C). 1984. reprint ed. pap. text 10.50 (*0-88133-047-7*) Waveland Pr.

Qermez Dere: The Excavation of an Acermaic Neolithic Settlement Near Tell Afar, N. Iraq, 1987. T. F. Watkins & D. Baird. (Illus.). 14p. 1987. pap. 5.98 (*0-614-21841-1*) David Brown.

Qermez Dere, Interim, Vol. 3. T. F. Watkins. 1995. pap. 18.00 (*0-614-21849-7*) David Brown.

Qermez Dere, Tell Afar: Interim 2, Vol. 2. T. F. Watkins et al. 62p. 1991. pap. 7.50 (*0-614-21848-9*) David Brown.

QE7, Vol. 33, No. 4. Ed. by E. Jakeman. (Journal of Modern Optics Ser.). 1986. 55.00 (*0-85066-974-X*) Taylor & Francis.

Qetun'am Ellallugmi Aquilla. Frank Nicholai.Tr. of Oscar Plays Out in the Rain. (ESK., Illus.). 12p. (J). (gr. k-3). 1998. pap. text 6.00 (*1-58084-028-0*) Lower Kuskokwim.

QE2: The Cunard Line Flagship, Queen Elizabeth 2. 3rd ed. Ronald W. Warwick. LC 98-46901. (Illus.). 224p. 1999. text 40.00 (*0-393-04772-5*) Norton.

QE2 Is Missing. Harry Harrison. 352p. 1993. mass mkt. 4.99 (*0-8125-3424-7*) Tor Bks.

QFD: The Customer-Driven Approach to Quality Planning & Deployment. Ed. by Shigeru Mizuno & Yoji Akao. LC 95-169834. (Illus.). 365p. 1994. text 59.95 (*92-833-1121-3*) Productivity Inc.

QFD: The Customer-Driven Approach to Quality Planning & Deployment. Ed. by Shigeru Mizuno & Yoji Akao. (Illus.). 365p. 1994. pap. text 49.95 (*92-833-1122-1*) Productivity Inc.

QFD Handbook. Jack B. ReVelle et al. LC 97-6508. 432p. 1998. text 99.00 incl. disk (*0-471-17381-9*) Wiley.

QFD Institute Forum Hardcopy, 1993-1994. (Illus.). 337p. (Orig.). 1994. pap. 100.00 (*1-889477-50-8*, QFDHC 1994) QFD Inst.

QFD Institute Forum Hardcopy, 1995. (Illus.). 281p. (Orig.). 1995. pap. 100.00 (*1-889477-51-6*, QFDHC 1995) QFD Inst.

QFD Overview Handbook. Council for Continuous Improvement Staff. (Illus.). 29p. 1994. pap. text 11.95 (*0-527-76235-0*, 762350) Productivity Inc.

QI Analyst 3.0. SPSS Inc. Staff. LC 96-72186. xiv, 260 p. 1997. write for info. (*1-56827-163-8*) SPSS Inc.

QI Coloring Book Instructor Guide: Quantum Improvements Made Easy. Lowell J. Arthur. (QI Coloring Bks.). (Illus.). 188p. 1997. student ed., ring bd. 39.95 (*1-884180-06-X*) LifeStar.

QI Coloring Book Macros for Excel: Graphing Made Easy. Lowell J. Arthur. (Illus.). 32p. 1999. pap. 59.95 (*1-884180-09-4*) LifeStar.

***Qi Gong: The Energy of Harmony & Healing.** Ariel. 272p. 1999. 5.95 (*0-7407-0101-0*) Andrews & McMeel.

Qi Gong-Der Chinesische Weg fur ein Gesundes Langes Leben see Chinese Fitness - A Mind/Body Approach: Qigong for Healthy Joyful Living

Qi Gong for Health & Longevity: The Ancient Chinese Art of Relaxation-Meditation-Physical Fitness. Simon Wang & Julius L. Liu. LC 94-32135. 285p. (Orig.). 1994. 29.98 (*0-9641605-0-1*); pap. 24.98 (*0-9641605-2-8*) East Hlth Dev.

Qi Gong Therapy: The Chinese Art of Healing with Energy. Tsu Kuo Shih. (Illus.). 160p. 1992. pap. 15.95 (*0-88268-138-9*) Station Hill Pr.

***Qi Healing: The Way to a New Mind & Body.** Toshihiko Yayama. LC 98-52760. (Illus.). 140p. 1999. pap. 19.95 (*4-7700-2382-0*, Pub. by Kodansha Intl) Kodansha.

Qi Lai: Mobilizing One Billion Chinese: The Chinese Communication System. Robert L. Bishop. LC 87-36153. (Illus.). 208p. 1989. reprint ed. pap. 64.50 (*0-608-00153-8*, 206093400006) Bks Demand.

Qi, the Treasure & Power of Your Body. Yanling L. Johnson. (Illus.). 168p. pap. 14.95 (*0-9652792-1-9*) Qigong Assn.

Qian Jiaju's Reading Notes on History. 228p. 1992. pap. text 9.00 (*1-879771-02-0*) Global Pub NJ.

***Qiaoxiang Ties: Interdisciplinary Approaches to 'Cultural Capitalism' in South China.** Ed. by Leo Douw et al. 240p. 1999. 110.00 (*0-7103-0653-9*, Pub. by Kegan Paul Intl) Col U Pr.

Qigone for Arthritis see Arthritis: The Chinese Way of Healing & Prevention

Qigong: Chinese Medicine or Pseudoscience? Lin Zixin et al. LC 99-36666. 148p. 2000. 24.95 (*1-57392-232-3*) Prometheus Bks.

Qigong: Chinese Movement & Meditation for Health. Danny Connor & Michael Tse. LC 92-1762. (Illus.). 96p. 1992. pap. 12.95 (*0-87728-758-9*) Weiser.

Qigong: Essence of the Healing Dance. H. Wallin & Garri Garripoli. LC 99-22682. (Illus.). 320p. 1999. pap. 8.95 (*1-55874-674-9*) Health Comm.

Q

An Asterisk (*) at the beginning of an entry indicates that the title is appearing for the first time.

Qigong - a Legacy in Chinese Healing: The Eight Treasures. Dean Y. Deng & Enid Ballin. LC 97-67808. (Illus.). 160p. 1997. pap. 18.50 (*0-9657560-8-4*) Qigong Intl.

Qigong Empowerment: A Guide to Medical, Taoist, Buddhist, Wushu Energy Cultivation. Shou-Yu Liang & Wen-Ching Wu. Ed. & Photos by Denise Breiter-Wu. LC 96-61197. (Illus.). 348p. 1996. pap. 34.95 (*1-889659-02-9*) Way of Dragon.

Qigong for Health & Martial Arts: Exercises & Meditation. 2nd ed. Jwing-Ming Yang. Ed. by Andrew Murray. LC 97-62516. (Qigong - Health & Healing Ser.). Orig. Title: Chi Kung: Health & Martial Arts. (Illus.). 176p. 1998. pap. 16.95 (*1-886969-57-4*, B005R/574) YMAA Pubn.

Qigong for Health & Vitality. Michael Tse. 144p. 1996. pap. 12.95 (*0-312-14128-9*, St Martin Griffin) St Martin.

Qigong for Health & Well-Being. H. Wallin & Mark V. Wiley. LC 98-47042. (Illus.). 1999. pap. 14.95 (*1-885203-79-9*) Tuttle Pubng.

Qigong for Life. Gao Yun. 170p. 1990. pap. 12.50 (*0-9629484-0-3*) Gao Yun Qigong.

Qigong for Life. 2nd ed. 134p. 1990. 12.50 (*0-614-28375-2*) Gao Yun Qigong.

***Qigong for Treating Common Ailments: The Essential Guide to Self Healing.** Xu Xiancai. (Practical TCM Ser.). (Illus.). 128p. 2000. pap. 15.95 (*1-886969-70-1*, Pub. by YMAA Pubn) Natl Bk Netwk.

Qigong of the Center, the Essence of Taijiquan: The Teachings of Grandmaster Cai Song Fang, 3 vols. Jan Diepersloot. LC 95-96121. (Warriors of Stillness - Meditative Traditions in the Chinese Martial Arts Ser.: Vol. 1). (Illus.). 278p. (Orig.). 1996. pap. 24.95 (*0-9649976-0-6*) CCCFH & TA.

***Qigong, the Secret of Youth: Da Mo's Muscle/Tendon & Marrow/Brain Washing Classics.** 2nd rev. ed. Yang Jwing-Ming. (Qigong Ser.). Orig. Title: Muscle/Tendon & Marrow/Brain Washing Chi Kung. (Illus.). 304p. 2000. pap. 24.95 (*1-886969-84-1*, Pub. by YMAA Pubn) Natl Bk Netwk.

Qigong Therapy & How to Use It. Linhai. Date not set. pap. 14.95 (*0-8488-1821-0*) Amereon Ltd.

***Qimugkauyar'** large type ed. Julia Hunter et al.Tr. of A Puppy. (ESK., Illus.). 8p. (J). (gr. k-3). 2000. pap. text 6.00 (*1-58084-207-0*) Lower Kuskokwim.

Qin Bowei Anthology. Qin Bowei. Ed. by Robert L. Felt, Jr. Tr. by Charles Chace. LC 97-4783. 220p. (Orig.). (C). 1997. pap. text 35.00 (*0-912111-41-0*) Paradigm Publns.

Qin Terracotta Army: A Guide to Lintong. Zhang Wenli. (National Museums & Monuments of Ancient China Ser.). (Illus.). 96p. 1996. 30.00 (*0-85667-450-8*) Scala Books.

Qin Terracotta Army: Treasures of Lintong. Zhang Wenli. 1997. 35.00 (*0-614-27845-7*, Pub. by P Wilson) Antique Collect.

Qin Yuan-Yue. Ed. by Fonda Shen. (Illus.). 80p. 1990. pap. 39.95 (*0-9663884-1-0*) Q Studio.

Qing Imperial Porcelain of the Kangxi, Yongzheng & Qianlong Reigns. Ed. by Peter Y. K. Lam. 270p. 1995. 165.00 (*962-7101-31-1*, Pub. by Chinese Univ of Hong Kong) St Mut.

Qira'ah fi "Kitab al-Hubb wa-al-Mu'jizat" Adnan Al-Subayi & Bashshar Al-Bitar. 168p. 1995. pap. 4.95 (*1-57547-207-4*) Dar Al-Fikr.

Qiu's Baccarat Winning Strategy. Jun Qiu. (CHI., Illus.). 200p. (Orig.). 1996. pap. 3.88 (*0-9651663-6-8*) Gldn Autumn Pubng.

QLM - Quality Leading & Managing: A Practical Guide for Improving Schools. Jack G. Blendinger. 108p. (C). 1996. spiral bd. 25.95 (*0-7872-2883-4*, 41288301) Kendall-Hunt.

QM for Windows. Howard J. Weiss. 1996. pap. text 22.20 incl. disk (*0-13-569740-9*) P-H.

***Qm for Windows Version 2.** Howard J. Weiss. 1999. cd-rom 25.20 (*0-13-025612-9*) P-H.

Qmail. John R. Levine & Russell Nelson. Ed. by Tim O'Reilly. (Illus.). 400p. 1999. pap. 29.95 (*1-56592-628-5*) OReilly & Assocs.

Introduction to Statistical Methods. Kim Tamura. 266p. (C). 1998. spiral bd. 26.95 (*0-7872-4896-7*, 41489601) Kendall-Hunt.

QMF Quick Reference Guide. Gabriel F. Gargiulo. 48p. 1993. pap. 9.95 (*0-471-56158-4*) Wiley.

QNVQ Advanced Leisure & Tourism. 2nd ed. John Ward et al. 208p. 1999. pap. 43.50 (*0-7487-2789-2*, Pub. by S Thornes Pubs) Trans-Atl Phila.

***Qoheleth.** Stephen Garfunkel. (Berit Olam (The Everlasting Covenant) Ser.). 2000. 0.00 (*0-8146-5066-X*) Liturgical Pr.

Qoheleth. Graham Ogden. (Readings Ser.). 236p. 1987. 47.50 (*1-85075-071-8*, Pub. by Sheffield Acad) CUP Services.

Qoheleth & Its Pessimistic Theology: Hermeneutical Struggles in Wisdom Literature. William H. Anderson. LC 97-12632. (Mellen Biblical Press Ser.: No. 54). 294p. 1997. text 89.95 (*0-7734-2429-6*) E Mellen.

***QOS & Traffic Management in IP & ATM Networks.** David McDysan. LC 99-53277. 480p. 1999. pap. 55.00 (*0-07-134959-6*) McGraw-Hill Prof.

QR-Quicken 4 for Windows for Dummies. Steven L. Nelson. 224p. 1994. spiral bd. 9.95 (*1-56884-950-8*) IDG Bks.

QR/Access 2 for Dummies. Stuart J. Stuple. LC 94-75723. (For Dummies Ser.). 176p. 1994. spiral bd. 8.95 (*1-56884-167-1*) IDG Bks.

***Q'Raj Void Protectorate: Silent Death House Book.** Sheldon Greaves. Ed. by Donald G. Dennis. (Silent Death - The Next Millennium Ser.). (Illus.). 112p. (YA). (gr. 7 up). 1999. pap. 18.00 (*1-55806-381-1*, 7224) Iron Crown Ent Inc.

***QR/C++ for Dummies.** 2nd ed. Namir C. Shammas. LC 98-85677. (For Dummies Ser.). 240p. 1998. spiral bd. 14.99 (*0-7645-0390-1*) IDG Bks.

QR/Data Database 5 for DOS for Dummies. Barrie Sosinsky & Stuart J. Stuple. LC 94-79608. (For Dummies Ser.). 224p. 1994. spiral bd. 9.99 (*1-56884-954-0*) IDG Bks.

QR/Database 5 for Windows for Dummies. Stuart J. Stuple. LC 94-79603. (For Dummies Ser.). 176p. 1994. spiral bd. 9.99 (*1-56884-953-2*) IDG Bks.

QR/DOS for Dummies. Greg Harvey. (For Dummies Ser.). (Illus.). 175p. 1993. spiral bd. 8.95 (*1-56884-007-1*) IDG Bks.

QR/Excel for Windows for Dummies. 2nd ed. John Walkenbach. LC 94-75048. (Quick Reference Ser.). (Illus.). 175p. 1994. spiral bd. 8.95 (*1-56884-096-9*) IDG Bks.

QR/Harvard Graphics for Windows for Dummies. Michael Partington & Raymond E. Werner. LC 94-79836. 224p. 1994. spiral bd. 9.99 (*1-56884-962-1*) IDG Bks.

QR/HTML for Dummies. Richard Ray. 224p. 1996. spiral bd. 12.99 (*1-56884-990-7*) IDG Bks.

QR/Internet Explorer 4 for Windows for Dummies. Greg Harvey. 224p. 1997. spiral bd. 12.99 (*0-7645-0188-7*) IDG Bks.

QR/Internet for Dummies. John Levine. LC 94-75909. 176p. 1994. spiral bd. 8.95 (*1-56884-168-X*) IDG Bks.

QR/Internet for Macs for Dummies. Charles Seiter. 192p. 1993. spiral bd. 9.99 (*1-56884-967-2*) IDG Bks.

QRL Poetry Book Series, Vol. 36. Warren Carrier et al. 1997. 20.00 (*1-888545-02-X*) Quarterly Rev.

QRL Poetry Book Series, Vol. 36. Carrier et al. 1997. pap. 12.00 (*1-888545-03-8*) Quarterly Rev.

QRL Poetry Book Series: Last Day & the 1st. Theodore Weiss. 1968. 15.00 (*0-317-05326-4*) Macmillan.

QRL Poetry Book Series Vol. XX: Swann, Burrows, Gibbons, Slotznick, & Galler. 304p. 1978. 20.00 (*1-888545-04-6*) Quarterly Rev.

QRL Poetry Book Series, Vol. XXI: Flanders, Hill, Morgan, Hebert, & Sulkin. 316p. 1980. 20.00 (*1-888545-05-4*) Quarterly Rev.

QRL Poetry Book Series, Vol. XXII: Barton, MacInnes, Thompson, Nejar, & So Chongju. 360p. 1981. 20.00 (*1-888545-06-2*) Quarterly Rev.

QRL Poetry Book Series, Vol. XXIII: Szymborska, Hirshfield, Bouvard, Bursk, & Gustafsson. 344p. 1982. 20.00 (*1-888545-07-0*) Quarterly Rev.

QRL Retrospective Anthologies: Criticism Retrospective. Ed. by R. Weiss & T. R. Weiss. 350p. 1977. 20.00 (*1-888545-09-7*) Quarterly Rev.

QRL Retrospective Anthologies: Poetry Retrospective. Ed. by T. Weiss & R. Weiss. 500p. 1974. 35.00 (*0-691-01324-1*) Quarterly Rev.

QRL Retrospective Anthologies: Prose Retrospective. T. Weiss. Ed. by T. R. Weiss. 600p. 1975. 20.00 (*1-888545-08-9*) Quarterly Rev.

QRL Retrospective Anthologies: Special Issues Retrospective. Ed. by R. Weiss & T. R. Weiss. 550p. 1976. 20.00 (*1-888545-10-0*) Quarterly Rev.

QR/MacIntosh System 7.5 for Dummies. Stuart J. Stuple. 224p. 1994. spiral bd. 9.99 (*1-56884-956-7*) IDG Bks.

QR/Memory Management for Dummies: Quick Reference. Doug Lowe. 240p. 1995. spiral bd. 9.99 (*1-56884-362-3*) IDG Bks.

QRP Power. 1996. pap. 12.00 (*0-87259-561-7*) Am Radio.

"QRP Projects from Down Under" Radio Projects for the Amateur. 2nd ed. Drew C. Diamond. (Illus.). 136p. 1998. reprint ed. pap. 19.95 (*1-891237-22-5*, MFJ-3510) MFJ Ent.

QR/Painting & Decorating for Dummies. Housenet, Inc. Staff. 1999. pap. 12.99 (*0-7645-5007-1*) IDG Bks.

QR/Paradox 5 for Windows for Dummies. John Kaufeld. LC 94-79832. 224p. 1994. spiral bd. 9.99 (*1-56884-960-5*) IDG Bks.

QRPD: The Guidebook to Quality Rapid Product Development. Orion Kopelman. (Illus.). 139p. pap. write for info. (*1-885261-01-2*) Global Brain.

QR/Photoshop 3 for Macs for Dummies. Deke McClelland. 224p. 1995. spiral bd. 9.99 (*1-56884-968-0*) IDG Bks.

QR/Plumbing & Electricity for Dummies. Housenet, Inc. Staff. 1999. pap. 12.99 (*0-7645-5008-X*) IDG Bks.

QR/UNIX for Dummies. Margaret L. Young & John Levine. LC 93-81199. (For Dummies). (Illus.). 375p. 1994. spiral bd. 8.95 (*1-56884-094-2*) IDG Bks.

QR/Windows 95 for Dummies. Greg Harvey. 224p. 1995. spiral bd. 9.99 (*1-56884-964-8*) IDG Bks.

QR/Windows 3.1 for Dummies. 2nd ed. Greg Harvey. LC 94-77187. 176p. 1994. spiral bd. 8.95 (*1-56884-951-6*) IDG Bks.

QR/Word for Windows for Dummies. George Lynch. (Illus.). 175p. 1993. spiral bd. 8.95 (*1-56884-029-2*) IDG Bks.

QR/WordPerfect for DOS Dummies. Greg Harvey. (Illus.). 350p. 1993. spiral bd. 8.95 (*1-56884-009-8*) IDG Bks.

Q's Baccarat: The System. John Qiu. (Q's Baccarat Winning Strategies Ser.: No. 2). 1997. pap. text 26.99 (*0-9651663-0-9*) Gldn Autumn Pubng.

Q's Guide to the Continuum. Michael Friedman & Robert Greenberger. LC 98-220793. (Illus.). 176p. 1998. pap. 16.00 (*0-671-01948-1*) PB.

Q's Legacy. Helene Hanff. LC 85-29767. 252 p. 1985. write for info. (*0-89621-689-6*) Mac Lib Ref.

Q's Legacy. Helene Hanff. 1986. pap. 12.95 (*0-14-008936-5*, Penguin Bks) Viking Penguin.

QS-9000: Automotive Quality Standard Explained. Ed. by David N. Middleton. 1997. 19.95 (*1-891578-02-2*) INFORM VA.

QS-9000 Answer Book: What You Need to Know to Survive an Audit. 2nd rev. ed. Radley M. Smith. LC 97-28846. 152p. (Orig.). 1997. pap. 24.95 (*0-9650445-2-1*) Paton Pr.

QS-9000 Answer Book: 101 Questions & Answers about the Automotive Quality System Standard. Rob Kantner. LC 96-17931. 304p. 1996. 39.95 (*0-471-15700-7*) Wiley.

QS-9000 Book: The Fast Track to Compliance. John T. Rabbitt & Peter A. Bergh. (Illus.). 240p. 1997. 32.95 (*0-527-76334-9*, 763349) Productivity Inc.

QS-9000 Handbook: A Guide to Registration & Audit. Jayanata K. Bandyoapadhyay. 256p. 1996. boxed set 74.95 (*1-57444-011-X*) St Lucie Pr.

QS-9000 Miniguide. John T. Rabbit & Peter A. Bergh. 88p. 1997. pap. 4.50 (*0-527-76323-3*) Productivity Inc.

***QS-9000 Miniguide.** John T. Rabbitt. 1999. pap. 5.25 (*0-527-76356-X*) Productivity Inc.

QS 9000 Pioneers: Registered Companies Share Their Strategies for Success. Subir Chowdhury & Ken Zimmer. LC 96-10433. (Illus.). 288p. 1996. text 50.00 (*0-7863-0865-6*, H0947) ASQ Qual Pr.

QS 9000 Quality System Manual for the Automotive Industry: (Includes PC-Diskette Word for Windows 7.0) Includes 48 Control Forms & Step by Step Instruction Guide: How to Implement Your System. Gunther Gumpp. Ed. by Brisitte Gumpp. 165p. (C). 1998. text, lab manual ed. 450.00 incl. disk (*1-881006-50-6*) Qual Cont Systs Srvs.

QS-9000 Quality Systems Handbook. David Hoyle. 512p. 1997. pap. text 44.95 (*0-7506-9861-6*) Buttrwrth-Heinemann.

QS-9000 Registration & Implementation. Gurmeet Naroola. LC 96-32729. (Quality & Reliability Ser.: Vol. 49). (Illus.). 288p. 1996. text 49.75 (*0-8247-9808-2*) Dekker.

QS-9000 Requirements: 107 Requirements Checklist & Compliance Guide. Jack Kanholm. 178p. 1995. 59.00 (*1-882711-09-2*, P619) AQA.

QS-2000 the Future Role of the Chartered Quantity Surveyor. RICS Staff. (C). 1991. pap. text 90.00 (*0-85406-495-8*, Pub. by R-I-C-S Bks) St Mut.

Q's Who in Pay-per-View. Dantia Quirk. 80p. 1988. 24.95 (*0-910767-17-3*) QV Pub.

Q's Who in Television Sports. Dantia Quirk. 130p. 1987. 19.95 (*0-910767-20-3*) QV Pub.

QS-9000 Book: The Fast Track to Compliance. John T. Rabbit & Peter A. Bergh. LC 97-27673. 224p. 1998. 32.95 (*0-8144-7982-0*) AMACOM.

QS-9000 Essentials. Rod Carpenter. LC 97-37955. 1997. 49.95 (*1-56990-240-2*) Hanser-Gardner.

QSAR: Hansch Analysis & Related Approaches, Vol. 1. H. Kubinyi. (Methods & Principles in Medicinal Chemistry Ser.). 240p. 1993. 215.00 (*3-527-30035-X*) Wiley.

QSAR & Drug Design: New Developments & Applications. Ed. by Toshio Fujita & H. Timmerman. LC 95-45138. (Pharmacochemistry Library: No. 23). 508p. 1995. 238.00 (*0-444-88615-X*) Elsevier.

QSAR, Quantitative Structure-Activity Relationships in Drug Design: Proceedings of the 7th European Symposium on QSAR Held in Interlaken, Switzerland, September 5-9, 1988. European Symposium on QSAR Staff. Ed. by J. L. Fauchere. LC 88-38355. (Progress in Clinical & Biological Research Ser.: Vol. 291). 471p. reprint ed. pap. 146.10 (*0-7837-2394-6*, 204007900006) Bks Demand.

QSB II Plus: Quantitative Business Systems. Yih-Long Chang. 240p. (C). 1988. write for info. (*0-318-63665-4*) P-H.

QSFX2. Lars Eighner & Clay Caldwell. (Orig.). 1995. mass mkt. 5.95 (*1-56333-278-7*, Badboy) Masquerade.

QSO Absorption Lines: Proceedings of the ESO Workshop Held at Garching, Germany, 21-24 November 1994, Vol. XXIII. Ed. by G. Meylan & P. Crane. (ESO Astrophysics Symposia, European Southern Observatory Ser.). 471p. 1995. 39.95 (*3-540-60152-X*) Spr-Verlag.

QSQR in Environmental Toxicology - II. Ed. by Klaus L. Kaiser. (C). 1987. text 247.50 (*90-277-2555-1*) Kluwer Academic.

***QT: The Official Documentation.** Troll Tech Inc., Staff. (Circle Ser.). 1000p. 1999. 74.95 (*1-57870-209-7*) New Riders Pub.

***QT Dispersion.** Marek Malik & Velislav Batchvarov. (Clinical Approaches to Tachyarrhythmias Ser.: Vol. 12). (Illus.). 160p. 2000. pap. 24.50 (*0-87993-456-5*) Futura Pub.

***Qt 2.1 Programming for Linux & Windows 2000.** Patrick Ward. 300p. 2000. pap. 39.99 (*0-13-027001-6*) P-H.

QTC: I Have a Message for You. Ray Redwood. Ed. by Tom Noe. LC 88-90627. (Illus.). 376p. (Orig.). 1989. 15.00 (*0-945845-00-6*); pap. 9.95 (*0-945845-01-4*) Sequoia Pr TX.

Qu-Est-Ce Qu-une Promesse? Per A. Brandt & Annie Prassoloff. 148p. 1996. pap. 18.95 (*87-7288-398-7*, Pub. by Aarhus Univ Pr) David Brown.

Qu-Est-Ce Que le Couddhisme. Alicia Jurado. (FRE.). 122p. 1979. pap. 10.95 (*0-7859-2256-3*, 2070354040) Fr & Eur.

Quaaludes. Maryann Ziemer. LC 96-13597. (Drug Library Ser.). (Illus.). 112p. (YA). (gr. 6 up). 1997. lib. bdg. 20.95 (*0-89490-847-2*) Enslow Pubs.

Quabbin: The Accidental Wilderness. rev. ed. Thomas Conuel. LC 90-11048. (Illus.). 120p. 1990. reprint ed. pap. 13.95 (*0-87023-730-6*) U of Mass Pr.

Quabbin! The Lost Valley. Donald W. Howe. Ed. by Roger N. Lincold. (Illus.). 631p. 1992. reprint ed. lib. bdg. 65.00 (*0-8328-2616-2*) Higginson Bk Co.

***Quack: Tales of Medical Fraud from the Museum of Questionable Medical Devices.** Bob McCoy. LC 99-59928. (Illus.). 240p. 2000. pap. 19.95 (*1-891661-10-8*, Pub. by Snta Monica) IPG Chicago.

***Quack! The Sound of Q.** Cynthia Klingel. LC 99-15891. (Wonder Books Ser.). (Illus.). 24p. (J). (ps-2). 1999. lib. bdg. 21.41 (*1-56766-724-4*) Childs World.

Quack - A Tale of Diabetics, Rheumatics, Olives. Eli Davis. 344p. 1986. pap. 18.00 (*965-09-0115-9*, 73825, Pub. by R Mass Ltd) Lambda Pubs.

Quack & Count! Keith Baker. LC 98-7924. 24p. (J). 1999. 14.00 (*0-15-292858-8*, Harcourt Child Bks) Harcourt.

Quack & Honk. Allan Fowler. LC 92-35056. (Rookie Read-About Science Ser.). (Illus.). 32p. (J). (ps-3). 1993. lib. bdg. 18.50 (*0-516-06012-0*) Childrens.

Quack Corps. Arthur W. Wells. LC 92-24624. 336p. 1992. pap. 14.95 (*0-9633631-1-5*) Dolart Pub.

Quack Quack. Sian Tucker. 6p. (J). (ps up). 1994. 5.50 (*0-671-89116-2*) Litle Simon.

Quack! Said the Billy-Goat. Charles Causley. LC 85-23856. (Illus.). 24p. (J). (ps-2). 1986. lib. bdg. 11.89 (*0-397-32192-9*) HarpC Child Bks.

"Quack!" Said the Billy-Goat. Charles Causley & Barbara Firth. LC 98-21932. (Illus.). 24p. (J). (ps-k). 1999. pap. 5.99 (*0-7636-0692-8*, Pub. by Candlewick Pr) Penguin Putnam.

***Quackenbush Guns.** John C. Groenewold. (Illus.). 1999. pap. write for info. (*0-9674667-0-9*) J Groenewold.

Quacker Meets Canadian Goose: Tales from a Duck Named Quacker. Ricky Van Shelton. (Illus.). 40p. (Orig.). (J). 1994. pap. 7.00 (*0-9634257-2-2*) RVS Bks.

Quacker Meets His Dad the Squirrel: Tales from a Duck Named Quacker. Ricky V. Shelton. (Illus.). (J). (ps-1). Date not set. pap. 7.00 (*0-9634257-3-0*) RVS Bks.

Quacker Meets Mrs. Moo: In Tales from a Duck Named Quacker. Ricky Van Shelton. (Illus.). 32p. (Orig.). (J). 1993. pap. 7.00 (*0-9634257-1-4*) RVS Bks.

Quackers, an Idea Book for Preschool Teachers. rev. ed. Susan Majors. 288p. 1986. pap. text 24.95 (*0-937104-03-5*) Programs Comm.

Quackery & You. William T. Jarvis. (Illus.). (Orig.). 1983. pap. 1.49 (*0-8280-0148-0*) Review & Herald.

Quackless see Take Along Stories

***Quacks: Fakers & Charlatans in English Medicine.** Roy Porter. (Illus.). 224p. 2000. 39.99 (*0-7524-1776-2*, Pub. by Tempus Pubng) Arcadia Publng.

Quacky Quack-Quack! 2nd ed. Ian Whybrow. LC 97-29776. (Illus.). 32p. (J). (ps-k). 1998. pap. 5.99 (*0-7636-0510-7*) Candlewick Pr.

Quad Cities: An American Mosaic. Roald Tweet. (Illus.). 120p. (Orig.). 1996. pap. 10.00 (*1-878326-05-8*) East Hall Pr.

Quad-Cities & the People. Jim Renkes. LC 94-24648. (Illus.). 112p. (Orig.). 1994. pap. 9.95 (*1-56037-067-X*) Am Wrld Geog.

Quad Cities Guide, 1988. Basil Williams & Blake Lewis. (Guides U. S. A. Ser.). (Illus.). 72p. (Orig.). 1987. pap. text 4.95 (*0-938185-01-2*) Wms & Assocs IA.

Quad Cities U. S. A. Book. Basil Williams & Blake Lewis. (Illus.). 48p. (Orig.). 1986. pap. text 6.95 (*0-938185-00-4*) Wms & Assocs IA.

Quad City Guide. Basil Williams & Blake Lewis. (Illus.). 84p. 1990. pap. text 4.95 (*0-938185-03-9*) Wms & Assocs IA.

Quad City Guide, 1989. rev. ed. Ed. & Tr. by Basil Williams. (Illus.). 1989. pap. text 4.95 (*0-317-93059-1*) Wms & Assocs IA.

Quaderns 217: Land Architecture. 70p. 1998. pap. 25.00 (*84-89698-63-5*, Pub. by Actar) Dist Art Pubs.

Quaderns 218: Mobility. 70p. 1998. pap. 25.00 (*84-89698-64-3*, Pub. by Actar) Dist Art Pubs.

Quaderns #219 Reactive Architecture. 1999. pap. text 25.00 (*84-89698-83-X*) Actar.

***Quadice.** rev. ed. Elizabeth Stage et al. Ed. by Lincoln Bergman & Kay Fairwell. (Great Explorations in Math & Science (GEMS) Ser.). (Illus.). 64p. (J). (gr. 4-8). 1999. pap., teacher ed. 10.50 (*0-924886-29-3*, GEMS) Lawrence Science.

Quadpack: A Subroutine Package for Automatic Integration. R. Piessens et al. (Computational Mathematics Ser.: Vol. 1). (Illus.). 301p. 1983. 79.95 (*0-387-12553-1*) Spr-Verlag.

Quadralingual Economics Dictionary. De Jong. 150.00 (*0-8288-9437-X*) Fr & Eur.

Quadralingual Legal Dictionary. Edgard Le Docte. (ENG, FRE, GER & SPA.). 822p. 1992. 295.00 (*0-8288-9433-7*) Fr & Eur.

Quadratic Algebras, Clifford Algebras, & Arithmetic Forms. Alexander J. Hahn. LC 93-5139. (Universitext Ser.). (Illus.). xi, 286p. (C). 1993. 39.95 (*0-387-94110-X*) Spr-Verlag.

Quadratic & Hermitian Forms. W. Scharlau. (Grundlehren der Mathematischen Wissenschaften Ser.: Vol. 270). 430p. 1984. 173.95 (*0-387-13724-6*) Spr-Verlag.

Quadratic & Hermitian Forms. Ed. by I. Hambleton & C. R. Riehm. LC 84-18561. (Conference Proceedings, Canadian Mathematical Society Ser.: Vol. 4). 338p. 1984. reprint ed. 50.00 (*0-8218-6008-9*, CMSAMS/4C) Am Math.

Quadratic & Hermitian Forms over Rings. M. A. Knus. (Grundlehren der Mathematischen Wissenschaften Ser.: Vol. 294). 524p. 1991. 158.95 (*0-387-52117-8*) Spr-Verlag.

Quadratic Assignment & Related Problems. Ed. by Panos M. Pardalos & Henry Wolkowicz. LC 94-20393. (DIMACS Series in Discrete Mathematics & Theoretical Computer Science: Vol. 16). 364p. 1994. 73.00 (*0-8218-6607-9*, DIMACS/16C) Am Math.

Quadratic Assignment Problem: Theory & Algorithms. Eranda Cela. LC 97-43113. (Combinatorial Optimization Ser.). 287p. 1998. text 147.00 (*0-7923-4878-8*) Kluwer Academic.

Quadratic Differentials. K. Strebel. (Ergebnisse der Mathematik und Ihrer Grenzgebiete Ser.: Vol. 5). (Illus.). 200p. 1984. 115.95 (*0-387-13035-7*) Spr-Verlag.

Q

An Asterisk (*) at the beginning of an entry indicates that the title is appearing for the first time.

Quadratic Forms & Hecke Operators. A. N. Andrianov. (Grundlehren der Mathematischen Wissenschaften Ser.: Band 286). (Illus.). 400p. 1987. 182.95 (*0-387-15294-6*) Spr-Verlag.

Quadratic Forms in Random Variables: Theory & Applications. A. M. Mathai & S. B. Provost. (Statistics Ser.: Vol. 126). (Illus.). 424p. 1992. text 175.00 (*0-8247-8691-2*) Dekker.

Quadratic Forms over Q & Galois Extensions of Commutative Rings. F. DeMeyer et al. LC 88-8167. (Memoirs Ser.: No. 77/394). 63p. 1989. pap. 16.00 (*0-8218-2457-0*, MEMO/77/394) Am Math.

Quadratic Forms with Applications to Algebraic Geometry & Topology. Albrecht Pfister. (London Mathematical Society Lecture Note Ser.: No. 217). 187p. (C). 1995. pap. text 39.95 (*0-521-46755-1*) Cambridge U Pr.

Quadratic Models. Spode Group Staff. 1991. pap. 13.95 (*1-871315-20-4*) Ashgate Pub Co.

Quadratic Programming Models Applied to Agricultural Policies. Anton D. Meister et al. LC 77-25931. (Illus.). 120p. 1978. reprint ed. pap. 37.20 (*0-608-00023-X*, 206078900006) Bks Demand.

Quadratics. Richard A. Mollin. Ed. by Kenneth Rosen. (Discrete Mathematics Ser.). 416p. 1995. boxed set 99.95 (*0-8493-3983-9*, 3983) CRC Pr.

***Quadrennial Defense Review & the Impact of Its Recommendations on National Security & on the Future Years Defense Program.** Ed. by Strom Thurmond. (Illus.). 200p. (C). 1999. reprint ed. pap. text 30.00 (*0-7881-8217-X*) DIANE Pub.

Quadrennial Defense Review (QDR) Analysis: A Retrospective Look at Joint Staff Participation. John Y. Schrader et al. LC 99-184244. (Illus.). 119p. 1999. pap. 6.00 (*0-8330-2694-1*, DB-236-JS) Rand Corp.

Quadrilaterals see Let's Investigate - Group 1

Quadrilingual Dictionary of the Press & Media (Dictionnaire Quadrilingue de la Presse et des Medias) CILF Staff. (FRE, ITA, POR & SPA.). 304p. 1990. 95.00 (*0-7859-4580-6*, 2853192210) Fr & Eur.

Quadrilingual Economics Dictionary. Ed. by Frits J. De Jong et al. 1981. lib. bdg. 234.00 (*90-247-2243-8*) Kluwer Academic.

Quadrille. Illus. by Cynthia Kintzer. 48p. 1982. reprint ed. 24.00 (*0-88014-037-2*) Mosaic Pr OH.

Quadrille of Gender: Casanova's 'Memoirs' Francois Roustang. Tr. by Anne C. Vila from FRE. LC 87-27807. 184p. 1988. 32.50 (*0-8047-1456-8*) Stanford U Pr.

Quadrillen see Werke fur Pianoforte

Quadrillen, Marsche & Andere Werkes. Joseph Lanner. (Samtliche Werke fur Klavier Ser.: Vol. 8). (Illus.). 1973. reprint ed. pap. 65.00 (*0-8450-1018-2*) Broude.

Quadrilog: Tradition & the Future of Ecumenism. Ed. by Kenneth Hagen. 432p. (Orig.). 1994. pap. text 28.95 (*0-8146-5838-5*, M Glazier) Liturgical Pr.

Quadroon: Or, Adventures in the Far West. Thomas M. Reid. LC 67-29278. (Americans in Fiction Ser.). (Illus.). 447p. reprint ed. pap. text 6.95 (*0-89197-912-3*); reprint ed. lib. bdg. 39.00 (*0-8398-1751-7*) Irvington.

Quadrupeds of North America, 3 vols., Set. John James Audubon & John Bachman. LC 73-17796. (Natural Sciences of America Ser.). (Illus.). 1406p. 1975. reprint ed. 108.95 (*0-405-05706-7*) Ayer.

Quadrupeds of North America, 3 vols., Vol. 1. John James Audubon & John Bachman. LC 73-17796. (Natural Sciences of America Ser.). (Illus.). 1406p. 1974. reprint ed. 36.95 (*0-405-05707-5*) Ayer.

Quadrupeds of North America, 3 vols., Vol. 2. John James Audubon & John Bachman. LC 73-17796. (Natural Sciences of America Ser.). (Illus.). 1406p. 1974. reprint ed. 36.95 (*0-405-05708-3*) Ayer.

Quadrupeds of North America, 3 vols., Vol. 3. John James Audubon & John Bachman. LC 73-17796. (Natural Sciences of America Ser.). (Illus.). 1406p. 1974. reprint ed. 36.95 (*0-405-05709-1*) Ayer.

Quadruplet Studies. 1996. 8.00 (*1-881986-22-5*) Demibach Eds.

Quadruplets & Higher Multiple Births. Marie M. Clay. (Clinics in Developmental Medicine Ser.: No. 107). (Illus.). 186p. (C). 1991. text 49.95 (*0-521-41223-4*, Pub. by Mc Keith Pr) Cambridge U Pr.

Quadrupole Mass Spectrometry: And Its Applications. Ed. & Intro. by Peter H. Dawson. LC 95-21857. (AIP-AVS Classics Ser.). (Illus.). 373p. (C). 1994. reprint ed. pap. text 69.95 (*1-56396-455-4*, AIP Pr) Spr-Verlag.

Quadrupole Optics. 1966. 22.95 (*0-387-03671-7*) Spr-Verlag.

Quadrupole Storage Mass Spectrometry. Richard Hughes & Raymond E. March. LC 88-20672. (Chemical Analysis Ser.). 496p. 1989. 175.00 (*0-471-85794-7*) Wiley.

Quad's Odds. Charles B. Lewis. (Notable American Authors Ser.). 1999. reprint ed. lib. bdg. 125.00 (*0-7812-3789-0*) Rprt Serv.

***Quads, Shoeboxes & Sunken Living Rooms: A History of Los Alamos Housing.** Craig Martin. (Los Alamos Story Ser.: Vol. 4). 2000. 10.00 (*0-941232-24-7*) Los Alamos Hist Soc.

Quae Exstant Omnia, Vol. I. Dio Prusaensis. Ed. by Hans F. Von Arnim. xl, 338p. 1962. write for info. (*3-296-12301-6*) G Olms Pubs.

Quae Exstant Omnia, Vol. II. Dio Prusaensis. Ed. by Hans F. Von Arnim. xiv, 380p. 1962. write for info. (*3-296-12302-4*) G Olms Pubs.

Quae Supersunt Omnia, 2 vols., Set. P. Aelius Aristides. Ed. by Bruno Keil. xlii, 472p. 1958. 130.00 (*3-296-10200-0*) G Olms Pubs.

***Quaestio de Potestate Papae - Rex Pacificus: An Enquiry into the Power of the Pope: A Critical Edition & Translation.** R. W. Dyson. LC 99-43563. (Texts & Studies in Religion : Vol. 83). 104p. 1999. text 59.95 (*0-7734-7955-4*) E Mellen.

Quaestio Disputata de Virtutibus in Communi & Quaestio Disputata de Virtutibus Cardinalibus see Disputed Questions on Virtue

Quaestiones Alberti de Modis Significandi: A Critical Edition. Pseudo-Albertus Magnus. (Studies in the History of Language Sciences: No. 15). xxxvii, 191p. 1977. 59.00 (*90-272-4510-X*) J Benjamins Pubng Co.

Quaestiones Disputatae de Veritate see Truth

Quaestiones Epicae. Karl Lehrs. viii, 339p. 1977. reprint ed. write for info. (*3-487-06235-6*) G Olms Pubs.

Quaestiones Epicae. Wilhelm Schulze. vi, 575p. 1967. reprint ed. write for info. (*0-318-71025-0*) G Olms Pubs.

Quaestiones 1.1 - 2.15. Alexander of Aphrodisias. Tr. by R. W. Sharples. LC 91-21146. (Ancient Commentators on Aristotle Ser.). 192p. 1992. text 52.50 (*0-8014-2714-2*) Cornell U Pr.

Quaestiones Physicas et Epistolas. Simocattes Theophylactus. (GER.). 1997. reprint ed. 94.00 (*3-487-05870-7*) G Olms Pubs.

Quaestiones Propertianae. Hans C. Gunther. LC 97-3868. (Mnemosyne, Supplements Ser.: Vol. 169). 190p. 1997. 84.50 (*90-04-10793-2*) Brill Academic Pubs.

Quaestiones Super Libro Elenchorum. Simon of Faversham. Ed. by Sten Ebbesen. (FRE.). pap. 38.86 (*0-88844-060-X*) Brill Academic Pubs.

Quaestiones Theologicae. Kurt Niederwimmer. 360p. 1997. text 105.00 (*3-11-015711-X*) De Gruyter.

Quaestiones 2.16 - 3.15. Alexander of Aphrodisias. Tr. by R. W. Sharples. (Ancient Commentators on Aristotle Ser.). 1994. text 45.00 (*0-8014-3088-7*) Cornell U Pr.

Quaestionum et Responsionum Christianarum Libellus see Little Book of Christian Questions & Responses in Which the Principal Headings of the Christian Religion Are Briefly Set Forth

Quaestionum Juris Publici Libri Duo. Cornelius Van Bynkershoek. LC 95-77094. (Classics in International Law Reprint Ser.: No. 14, Vol. 1). 1995. reprint ed. 125.00 (*1-57588-515-8*) W S Hein.

Quaestonum Juris Publici Libri Duo, Vol. 1. Cornelius Von Bynkershoek. LC 95-77094. (Classics in International Law Reprint Ser.: No.14, Vol.2). (LAT.). 1995. reprint ed. 100.00 (*0-89941-957-7*, 310270) W S Hein.

Quagga see Extinct Species Collection

Quaglino's, the Cookbook. Richard Whittington & Martin Webb. LC 96-88. 1996. 29.95 (*0-87951-678-X*, Pub. by Overlook Pr) Penguin Putnam.

Quagmire: America in the Middle East. Leon T. Hadar. LC 92-13488. 240p. 1992. 24.95 (*0-932790-94-1*); pap. 14.95 (*0-932790-93-3*) Cato Inst.

Quahog State of Mind. Don Bousquet. (Illus.). 128p. (Orig.). 1996. pap. 10.95 (*0-924771-62-3*, Covered Brdge Pr) Douglas Charles Ltd.

Quahog Stops Here. Don Bousquet. (Illus.). 128p. 1992. pap. 8.95 (*0-924771-38-0*, Covered Brdge Pr) Douglas Charles Ltd.

Quahogs Are a Girl's Best Friend. Don Bousquet. (Illus.). 128p. 1994. pap. 9.95 (*0-924771-50-X*, Covered Brdge Pr) Douglas Charles Ltd.

Quai des Brumes. Pierre MacOrlan. (FRE.). 1972. pap. 8.95 (*0-7859-3985-7*) Fr & Eur.

Quai des Grand-Augustins. Jean Rhys. (FRE.). 1981. pap. 10.95 (*0-7859-4156-8*) Fr & Eur.

Quai Malaquais: A Novel. John Guenther. 200p. 1984. pap. 10.00 (*0-938266-02-0*) Purchase Pr.

Quaid-I-Azam Jinnah: A Chronology. Riaz Ahmad. 169p. 1989. 12.50 (*1-56744-362-1*) Kazi Pubns.

Quaid-I-Azam Jinnah: Studies in Interpretation. Sharif Al-Mujahid. 810p. 1989. 39.95 (*1-56744-363-X*) Kazi Pubns.

Quaid-I-Azam Jinnah: Studies in Interpretation. Sharif A. Mujahid. (C). 1993. 22.00 (*81-85557-04-7*, Pub. by Low Price) S Asia.

Quaid-I-Azam Jinnah: The Story of a Nation. G. Allana. 550p. 1989. 39.00 (*1-56744-361-3*) Kazi Pubns.

Quaid-I-Azam Mohammad Ali Jinnah: An Annotated Bibliography. Anis Khurshid. 402p. 1989. 29.00 (*1-56744-364-8*) Kazi Pubns.

Quaid-i-Azam Mohammad Ali Jinnah: His Personality & His Politics. S. M. Burke & Salim A. Quraishi. LC 98-107916. (The Jubilee Ser.). 428p. 1997. 39.95 (*0-19-577783-2*) OUP.

Quaid-I-Azam Mohammad Ali Jinnah Papers: On the Threshold of Pakistan, July 1-July 25, 1947, Vol. III. Ed. by Z. H. Zaidi. (Illus.). 1120p. 1997. 160.00 (*969-8156-07-0*) OUP.

Quaid-I-Azam Mohammad Ali Jinnah Papers: Prelude to Pakistan, 2 Vols., Vol. I, Pt. I & II. Ed. by Zafar H. Zaidi. (Illus.). 1936p. 1994. 295.00 (*969-8156-03-8*) OUP.

Quail Hunting in America. Tom Huggler. LC 86-14590. (Illus.). 288p. 1987. 22.95 (*0-8117-1277-X*) Stackpole.

Quail in My Bed. Burley Packwood. LC 89-92060. (Illus.). 195p. (Orig.). 1989. pap. 6.95 (*0-9624358-0-5*) Quantum Pr AZ.

Quail Plantations of South Georgia & North Florida. Photos by Hank Margeson. LC 91-3054. (Illus.). 120p. 1991. 34.95 (*0-8203-1386-6*) U of Ga Pr.

Quail Production Systems: A Review. 153p. 1994. 20.00 (*92-5-103384-6*, F33846, Pub. by FAO) Bernan Associates.

Quail Southwest. Larry Ketron. 1977. pap. 5.25 (*0-8222-0926-8*) Dramatists Play.

Quail III: National Quail Symposium. Kevin E. Church & Thomas V. Dailey. (Illus.). 217p. (Orig.). 1993. pap. 12.00 (*0-9639902-0-9*) KS Dept Wldlife.

***Quaille's Practical Chinese Students' Dictionary.** Ed. by Yu Yaosheng. 936p. 1999. 24.95 (*962-7160-14-8*) Asia.

Quail's Egg. Joanna Troughton. (Illus.). 32p. (J). pap. 11.95 (*0-14-038417-0*, Pub. by Pnguin Bks Ltd) Trafalgar.

Quails, Partridges, & Francolins of the World. Paul A. Johnsgard. (Illus.). 288p. 1988. text 115.00 (*0-19-857193-3*) OUP.

Quaint & Historic Forts of North America. John M. Hammond. LC 98-162624. (Illus.). 309p. 1998. pap. 30.00 (*0-7884-0834-8*, H056) Heritage Bk.

***Quaint Birdhouses You Can Paint & Decorate.** Dorothy Egan. LC 99-36672. (Illus.). 128p. 2000. pap. 23.99 (*0-89134-986-3*, North Lght Bks) F & W Pubns Inc.

Quaint Corners of Ancient Empires: Southern India, Burma & Manila. Michael M. Shoemaker. LC 72-4582. (Essay Index Reprint Ser.). 1977. reprint ed. 36.95 (*0-8369-2978-0*) Ayer.

Quaint Furniture. Ed. by Stephen Gray. (Mission Furniture Catalogues Ser.: No. 1). 80p. 1981. pap. 7.95 (*0-940326-01-9*) Turn of Cent.

***Quaint Furniture Catalog, No. 42.** Don Marek. Ed. by Peter A. Copeland & Janet H. Copeland. (Illus.). 128p. 1999. pap. 25.00 (*0-9638771-2-7*) Parchment NJ.

Quaint Furniture in Arts & Crafts. Ed. by Stephen Gray. (Mission Furniture Catalogues Ser.: No. 9). 144p. 1988. pap. 16.50 (*0-940326-11-6*) Turn of Cent.

***Quaint Sermons.** Samuel Rutherford. 384p. 1999. 27.95 (*1-57358-101-1*) Soli Deo Gloria.

***Quaint Signs of Olde Inns.** G. J. Monson-Fitzjohn. (Illus.). 157p. 2000. reprint ed. pap. text 20.00 (*0-7881-9222-1*) DIANE Pub.

Quaint Whimsier. L. E. Tigard. 120p. (C). 1988. pap. 7.95 (*0-9620451-0-1*) Asilomar Pub.

***Quaintnesses: Poems from Hollywood.** Mark Dunster. 11p. 1999. pap. 5.00 (*0-89642-885-0*) Linden Pubs.

Quake! Joe Cottonwood. LC 94-18193. (J). 1995. 13.95 (*0-614-32018-6*) Scholastic Inc.

Quake. Catherine McMorrow. 2000. lib. bdg. 11.99 (*0-679-96945-4*) Random.

***Quake.** Catherine McMorrow. 1999. pap. 3.99 (*0-679-86945-X*, Pub. by Random Bks Yng Read) Random.

***Quake.** Rudy Wurlitzer. 158p. 2000. pap. 10.99 (*1-56649-116-9*) Welcome Rain.

Quake. 2nd ed. Rudolph Wurlitzer. (Midnight Classics Ser.). 158p. 1995. pap. 10.99 (*1-85242-409-5*) Serpents Tail.

Quake! A Novel. Joe Cottonwood. LC 94-18193. (J). (gr. 5 up). 1996. pap. 3.50 (*0-590-22233-3*) Scholastic Inc.

Quake! A Novel. Joe Cottonwood. 1995. 8.60 (*0-606-09773-2*, Pub. by Turtleback) Demco.

Quake: Stories by Nance Van Winckel. Nance Van Winckel. LC 96-52710. 168p. 1997. pap. 17.95 (*0-8262-1091-0*) U of Mo Pr.

Quake: The Offering for Linux. 1999. 39.95 (*1-57595-271-8*) S&S Trade.

Quake Authorized Strategy Guide. Bradygames Staff. 162p. 1996. 19.99 (*1-56686-494-1*) Brady Pub.

Quake City. John B. Spencer. LC 97-130000. 158p. 1997. pap. 12.95 (*1-899344-02-0*) Dufour.

Quake Construction Guide, with CD-ROM. Bradygames Staff. 700p. 1997. 13.00 incl. cd-rom (*1-56686-504-2*) Brady Pub.

Quake Game Secrets Unauthorized Guide to Shareware Levels. Mike Van Mantgem. LC 95-74912. 112p. 1996. pap., per. 9.99 (*0-7615-0908-9*) Prima Pub.

Quake II: Authorized Strategy Guide. John K. Waters & Michael Koch. LC 97-81437. 1997. pap. 7.95 incl. cd-rom (*1-56893-959-0*) GT Interactive Software.

Quake II: Colossus for Linux. 1999. 49.95 (*1-57595-272-6*) S&S Trade.

***Quake II: Official Strategy Guide.** Steve Honeywell. LC 99-62820. (Illus.). 112p. 1999. pap. 12.99 (*0-7615-2201-8*) Prima Pub.

***Quake II: Official Strategy Guide.** Prima Development Staff. LC 99-62819. (Illus.). 81p. 1999. pap. 12.99 (*0-7615-2200-X*) Prima Pub.

Quake II: The Reckoning: Official Strategies & Secrets. Jonathan Mendoza. 1998. pap. 14.99 (*0-7821-2300-7*) Sybex.

Quake Level Design Strategies & Secrets. 1997. pap. 29.99 incl. cd-rom (*0-7821-2046-6*) Sybex.

Quake 64: The Official Strategy Guide. Prima Publishing Staff & Vince Mathews. LC 97-69347. 112p. 1998. per. 12.99 (*0-7615-1216-0*) Prima Pub.

Quake 64 Official Strategy Guide. Brady Games Staff. 1998. 11.99 (*1-56686-783-5*) Brady Pub.

Quake Strategy Guide: Unauthorized. Kip Ward. LC 96-67196. 240p. 1996. pap. text 19.99 (*0-7615-0532-6*) Prima Pub.

Quake Stress: Preparation for the Psychological Effects of a Major Disaster. Marianne L. McManus. LC 88-71569. 44p. (Orig.). 1988. pap. 6.95 (*0-922248-02-8*); text 12.95 (*0-922248-08-7*); audio 7.95 (*0-922248-06-0*) Calif Psychol Pubs.

***Quake III Arena.** Steve Honeywell. (Official Strategy Guides Ser.). 200p. 1999. pap. 19.99 (*0-7615-2588-2*) Prima Pub.

Quake 2: Prima's Strategy Guide. Ward Kip. LC 96-69794. 208p. 1998. per. 16.99 (*0-7615-1306-X*) Prima Pub.

Quake! Unauthorized Map Guide. I.D. Software Staff. LC 95-73070. 160p. 1996. pap. text 14.99 (*0-7615-0513-X*) Prima Pub.

Quake 64, Authorized Strategy Guide. Brady Games Staff. (Illus.). 112p. (J). 1998. 11.99 (*1-56686-729-0*) Brady Pub.

Quaker: A Study in Costume. Amelia M. Gummere. LC 68-56494. (Illus.). 232p. 1972. reprint ed. 23.95 (*0-405-08585-0*, Pub. by Blom Pubns) Ayer.

Quaker Adventures: Three Hundred Years in Carolina. Mary E. Hinshaw. (Illus.). 74p. (Orig.). (J). (gr. 5-7). 1971. pap. 1.50 (*0-942727-01-0*) NC Yrly Pubns Bd.

Quaker Anecdotes. Irvin C. Poley & Ruth V. Poley. (C). 1983. pap. 4.00 (*0-87574-033-2*) Pendle Hill.

Quaker Approach to Contemporary Problems. Ed. by John Kavanaugh. LC 70-110047. 243p. 1970. reprint ed. lib. bdg. 59.50 (*0-8371-4432-9*, KAGA, Greenwood Pr) Greenwood.

Quaker Arrivals at Philadelphia, 1682-1750: Being a List of Certificates of Removal Received at Philadelphia Monthly Meeting of Friends. Albert C. Myers. LC 70-77321. 131p. 1999. reprint ed. pap. 16.50 (*0-8063-0253-4*) Clearfield Co.

***Quaker Book of Wisdom: Life Lessons in Simplicity, Service & Common Sense.** Robert L. Smith. LC 98-16294. 144p. 1998. 19.95 (*0-688-15653-3*, Wm Morrow) Morrow Avon.

Quaker Book of Wisdom: Life Lessons In Simplicity, Service, And Common Sense. Robert L. Smith. 208p. 1999. pap. 10.00 (*0-688-17233-4*, Wm Morrow) Morrow Avon.

Quaker Census of 1828: Members of the NY Yearly Meeting, the Religious Society of Friends (in New York, Ontario, Vermont, Conn., Mass, & Quebec) at the Time of the Separation of 1828. Loren V. Fay. LC 89-80271. 239p. 1989. lib. bdg. 20.00 (*1-56012-100-9*, 93) Kinship Rhinebeck.

Quaker City: or The Monks of Monk Hall: A Romance of Philadelphia Life, Mystery, & Crime. George Lippard. Ed. & Intro. by David S. Reynolds. LC 94-44599. 632p. 1995. pap. 22.95 (*0-87023-971-6*) U of Mass Pr.

Quaker Colonies: A Chronicle of the Proprietors of the Delaware. Sydney G. Fisher. (BCL1 - U. S. History Ser.). 244p. 1991. reprint ed. lib. bdg. 79.00 (*0-7812-9088-0*) Rprt Serv.

Quaker Couple in Nazi Germany. Brenda Bailey. 300p. 1999. pap. 32.00 (*1-85072-131-9*, Pub. by W Sessions) St Mut.

Quaker Crosscurrents: 300 Years of New York Yearly Meetings. Ed. by Hugh Barbour et al. LC 94-48761. (Illus.). 432p. 1995. 59.95 (*0-8156-2651-7*); pap. 19.95 (*0-8156-2664-9*) Syracuse U Pr.

Quaker Doctrine of Inward Peace. Howard H. Brinton. LC 64-23230. (Orig.). 1948. pap. 4.00 (*0-87574-044-8*) Pendle Hill.

Quaker Education in the Colony & State of New Jersey. Thomas Woody. LC 76-89256. (American Education: Its Men, Institutions, & Ideas. Series 1). 1975. reprint ed. 35.95 (*0-405-01494-5*) Ayer.

Quaker Encounters Vol. I: Friends & Relief. John Ormerod Greenwood. 1999. pap. 21.00 (*0-900657-29-4*, Pub. by W Sessions) St Mut.

Quaker Encounters Vol. II: Vines on the Mountains. John Ormerod Greenwood. 1999. pap. 21.00 (*0-900657-41-3*, Pub. by W Sessions) St Mut.

Quaker Encounters Vol. III: Whispers of Truth. John Ormerod Greenwood. 1999. pap. 21.00 (*0-900657-42-1*, Pub. by W Sessions) St Mut.

Quaker Experiement in Education & Community. Eleanore P. Mather & Charles Price. LC 79-93378. 128p. 1993. 7.00 (*0-87574-954-2*, 1064) Pendle Hill.

Quaker Experiences in International Conciliation. C. H. Yarrow. LC 78-7415. 308p. 1978. 45.00 (*0-300-02260-3*) Yale U Pr.

Quaker Family Through Six Generations - The Passmores in America. Robert H. Smith. LC 92-18928. 336p. 1992. text 99.95 (*0-7734-9565-7*) E Mellen.

Quaker Funeral. rev. ed. 32p. (Orig.). 1986. pap. 1.50 (*0-942727-12-6*) NC Yrly Pubns Bd.

Quaker Idyls. Sarah M. Gardner. LC 70-110193. (Short Story Index Reprint Ser.). 1977. 19.95 (*0-8369-3344-3*) Ayer.

Quaker Indictment, Vol. 4. Allen. (Quaker Mystery Ser.: 4). Date not set. mass mkt. 5.99 (*0-312-96684-9*, Pub. by Tor Bks) St Martin.

Quaker Indictment: An Elizabeth Elliot Mystery. Irene Allen. LC 97-31615. 256p. 1997. text 21.95 (*0-312-16970-1*) St Martin.

Quaker Influence in American Literature. Howard W. Hintz. LC 74-104238. 96p. 1970. reprint ed. lib. bdg. 45.00 (*0-8371-3945-7*, HIGA, Greenwood Pr) Greenwood.

Quaker Influence on American Ideals. Seth B. Hinshaw. (Orig.). 1986. pap. 1.50 (*0-942727-03-7*) NC Yrly Pubns Bd.

Quaker Invasion of Massachusetts. Richard P. Hallowell. 1977. 16.95 (*0-8369-7139-6*, 7972) Ayer.

Quaker Journals: Varieties of Religious Experiences among Friends. Howard H. Brinton. LC 78-188399. 130p. 1993. pap. 9.00 (*0-87574-908-9*, 1065) Pendle Hill.

Quaker Looks at Yoga. Dorothy Ackerman. LC 76-23909. (Orig.). 1976. pap. 4.00 (*0-87574-207-6*) Pendle Hill.

Quaker Meeting. Howard E. Collier. (C). 1944. pap. 4.00 (*0-87574-026-X*) Pendle Hill.

Quaker Meeting: A Risky Business. Eric W. Johnson. (Illus.). 120p. 1991. pap. 11.00 (*0-8059-3197-X*) Dorrance.

Quaker Memoirs: Recollections of Meetings at Hastings, Bedford, Allonby (Cumbria) & High Flatts (Yorkshire) Lilian Carroll. 1995. pap. 45.00 (*1-85072-154-8*, Pub. by W Sessions) St Mut.

Quaker Message. Sidney Lucas. (C). 1948. pap. 4.00 (*0-87574-040-5*) Pendle Hill.

Quaker Message: A Personal Affirmation. Hugh L. Doncaster. LC 79-182982. (C). 1972. pap. 4.00 (*0-87574-181-9*) Pendle Hill.

Quaker Money. S. Francis Nicholson. 290p. (Orig.). 1990. pap. 4.00 (*0-87574-290-4*) Pendle Hill.

Quaker Mutation. Gerald Heard. (C). 1939. pap. 4.00 (*0-87574-007-3*) Pendle Hill.

Quaker Nantucket. Robert Leach & Peter Gow. LC 97-70901. (Illus.). 224p. 1998. 29.95 (*0-9638910-7-3*) Mill Hill Pr.

Quaker Necrology. Haver. 1982. 295.00 (*0-8161-1343-2*, G K Hall & Co) Mac Lib Ref.

Quaker Oats Company: A Report on the Company's Environmental Policies & Practices. (Illus.). 36p. (C). 1994. reprint ed. pap. text 40.00 (*0-7881-0945-6*, Coun on Econ) DIANE Pub.

Q

An Asterisk (*) at the beginning of an entry indicates that the title is appearing for the first time.

Quaker Oats Favorite Recipe Collection. Ed. by Time-Life Books Editors. LC 96-32916. (Illus.). 96p. (J). (gr. 11). 1999. 14.95 (0-7835-4863-X) Time-Life.

Quaker Parrot: An Owner's Guide to a Happy, Healthy Pet. Pamela L. Higdon. LC 97-41806. (Illus.). 128p. 1998. 12.95 (0-87605-448-3) Howell Bks.

Quaker Partisans: A Story of the Revolution. Edward Williamson. 1993. reprint ed. lib. bdg. 89.00 (0-7812-5857-X) Rprt Serv.

Quaker Peace Testimony, 1660-1914. Peter Brock. 400p. 1991. text 40.00 (1-85072-074-6, Pub. by Ebor Pr) Syracuse U Pr.

Quaker Peace Testimony, 1660-1914. Peter Brock. 400p. 1999. pap. 45.00 (1-85072-065-7, Pub. by W Sessions) St Mut.

Quaker Peacemakers: A Saga of Fruitgrowing & Christian Service. unabridged ed. Smauel R. Levering. (Illus.). 81p. 1993. pap. 7.50 (0-9656330-3-9) Orchard Gap Pr.

Quaker Poets Past & Present. Mary H. Jones. LC 75-7414. 32p. (Orig.). 1975. pap. 1.00 (0-87574-202-5) Pendle Hill.

Quaker Profiles. Jewell C. Edgerton. Ed. by William Edgerton. LC 95-67546. 200p. (Orig.). 1995. pap. 13.95 (0-923687-34-3) Celo Valley Bks.

Quaker Profiles & Practices. William C. Kashatus. LC 96-71916. 105p. 1997. pap. 9.50 (0-938875-36-1) Pittenbruach Pr.

Quaker Promise Kept: Philadelphia Friends' Work with the Allegany Senecas, 1795-1965. Lois Barton. (Illus.). 128p. (Orig.). 1990. pap. 14.95 (0-9609420-3-3) S Butte Pr.

Quaker Quimericks. Seth B. Hinshaw. (Illus.). 50p. (Orig.). 1992. pap. 3.00 (0-942727-20-7) NC Yrly Pubns Bd.

Quaker Reader. Ed. by Jessamyn West. LC 92-24943. 540p. 1993. pap. 18.00 (0-87574-916-X, 1066) Pendle Hill.

***Quaker Records of the Hudson Monthly Meeting: Columbia County, NY, 1793+** Ed. by Arthur C. M. Kelly. 130p. 1999. lib. bdg. 28.00 (1-56012-156-4, 160) Kinship Rhinebeck.

Quaker Relief During the Siege of Boston. Henry J. Cadbury. (C). 1983. pap. 4.00 (0-686-43965-1, 004) Pendle Hill.

Quaker Sailors: University of Pennsylvania & the U. S. Navy. Robert B. Hamilton, Jr. LC 95-94809. 250p. 1995. 20.00 (0-9648802-0-2) Hamilton Bks.

Quaker Service at the Crossroads. Ed. by Charles E. Fager. 200p. (Orig.). 1987. pap. 9.95 (0-945177-02-X) Kimo Pr.

Quaker Singer's Recollections. David Bispham. Ed. by Andrew Farkas. LC 76-29927. (Opera Biographies Ser.). (Illus.). 1977. reprint ed. lib. bdg. 30.95 (0-405-09669-0) Ayer.

Quaker Social History: Sixteen Sixty-Nine to Seventeen Thirty-Eight. Arnold Lloyd. LC 79-4398. 207p. 1979. reprint ed. lib. bdg. 59.50 (0-313-20943-X, LLQU, Greenwood Pr) Greenwood.

Quaker Spirituality: Selected Writings. Ed. by Douglas V. Steere. (Classics of Western Spirituality Ser.). 384p. 1984. pap. 19.95 (0-8091-2510-2) Paulist Pr.

Quaker Strongholds. Caroline Stephen. Ed. by Mary G. Ogilvie. LC 51-4625. 32p. (Orig.). 1951. pap. 4.00 (0-87574-059-6) Pendle Hill.

Quaker Testimonies & Economic Alternatives. Severyn Bruyn. LC 80-80915. 35p. 1980. pap. 1.00 (0-87574-231-9) Pendle Hill.

Quaker Testimony, Vol. 1. Irene Allen. (Elizabeth Elliot Mystery Ser.). 1998. mass mkt. 5.99 (0-312-96424-2) St Martin.

Quaker Testimony of Integrity. Wilmer Cooper. LC 91-60175. 32p. (Orig.). 1991. pap. 4.00 (0-87574-296-3) Pendle Hill.

Quaker Way. rev. ed. FGC Religious Education Committee. (Illus.). 100p. (J). (gr. 4-9). 1998. pap. 7.50 (1-888305-06-1) Friends Genl Conf.

***Quaker Witness.** Allen. 2000. mass mkt. write for info. (0-312-97285-7) St Martin.

Quaker Women of Carolina. Seth B. Hinshaw & Mary E. Hinshaw. LC 94-66862. (Illus.). 72p. (Orig.). 1994. pap. text 8.00 (0-942727-24-X) NC Yrly Pubns Bd.

Quaker Women Passing: Deathbed As Pulpit: The Memoirs of Susanna Lightfoot (1720-1781) & Martha Thomas (1805-1836) Susanna Lightfoot & Martha Thomas. Ed. by Anne Rutherford. LC 98-68490. 60p. (Orig.). 1999. reprint ed. pap. 10.95 (1-889298-33-6) Rhwymbooks.

Quaker Work in Southwest France. Stanley Johnson. 1999. pap. 21.00 (1-85072-070-3, Pub. by W Sessions) St Mut.

Quaker World Wide. Herbert M. Hadley. (C). 1989. 49.00 (0-7855-6534-5, Pub. by W Sessions) St Mut.

Quaker Worship & Techniques of Meditation. Scott Crom. LC 74-82795. (C). 1974. pap. 4.00 (0-87574-195-9) Pendle Hill.

Quakerism & Christianity. Edwin B. Bronner. LC 67-18689. (Orig.). 1967. pap. 4.00 (0-87574-152-5) Pendle Hill.

Quakerism & Other Religions. Howard H. Brinton. LC 57-10748. (C). 1957. pap. 4.00 (0-87574-093-6) Pendle Hill.

Quakerism in India. Horace Alexander. (C). 1945. pap. 4.00 (0-87574-031-6) Pendle Hill.

Quakerism of the Future: Mystical, Prophetic & Evangelical. John R. Yungblut. LC 74-81830. (Orig.). 1974. pap. 4.00 (0-87574-194-0) Pendle Hill.

Quakers. Jean K. Williams. LC 97-35133. (American Religious Experience Ser.). (Illus.). 110p. (YA). (gr. 6-9). 1998. lib. bdg. 21.50 (0-531-11377-9) Watts.

Quakers, 3. Hugh Barbour & J. William Frost. LC 88-10240. (Denominations in America Ser.). (Illus.). 421p. 1988. reprint ed. lib. bdg. 75.00 (0-313-22816-7, BSF/) Greenwood.

***Quakers: Money & Morals.** James Walvin. 1999. pap. 29.95 (0-7195-5768-2) John Murray.

Quakers: Their Story & Message. A. Neave Brayshaw. 1999. pap. 23.00 (0-900657-64-2, Pub. by W Sessions) St Mut.

Quakers & Baptists in Colonial Massachusetts. Carla G. Pestana. 211p. (C). 1991. text 64.95 (0-521-41111-4) Cambridge U Pr.

Quakers & Nazis: Inner Light in Outer Darkness. Hans A. Schmitt. LC 97-18914. (Illus.). 312p. 1997. 29.95 (0-8262-1134-8) U of Mo Pr.

Quakers & Politics: Pennsylvania, 1681-1726. rev. ed. Gary B. Nash. 384p. 1993. pap. text 18.95 (1-55553-166-0) NE U Pr.

Quakers & Railways. Edward H. Milligan. 1999. pap. 21.00 (1-85072-099-1, Pub. by W Sessions) St Mut.

Quakers & the American Family: British Quakers in the Delaware Valley, 1650-1765. Barry Levy. (Illus.). 368p. 1992. reprint ed. pap. text 19.95 (0-19-504976-4) OUP.

Quakers & the American Revolution. Arthur Mekeel. 432p. 1999. pap. 41.00 (1-85072-176-9, Pub. by W Sessions) St Mut.

***Quakers & the Arts: Plain & Fancy.** David Sox. (Illus.). 125p. 2000. pap. 18.50 (0-944350-52-6) Friends United.

Quakers & the Salvationists. John D. Waldron. 1991. pap. 3.95 (0-86544-063-8) Salv Army Suppl South.

Quakers & the Use of Power. Paul A. Lacey. LC 81-85558. 32p. (Orig.). 1982. pap. 4.00 (0-87574-241-6) Pendle Hill.

Quakers As Pioneers in Social Work. Auguste Jorns. Tr. by Thomas K. Brown. LC 69-14934. (Criminology, Law Enforcement, & Social Problems Ser.: No. 27). 1969. reprint ed. 8.50 (0-87585-027-8) Patterson Smith.

Quakers in Conflict: The Hicksite Reformation. H. Larry Ingle. 310p. 1998. pap. 10.00 (0-87574-926-7, 1977) Pendle Hill.

Quakers in Conflict: The Hicksite Reformation. Homer L. Ingle. LC 86-1528. 326p. reprint ed. pap. 101.10 (0-7837-7079-0, 204689100004) Bks Demand.

***Quakers in English Society, 1655-1725.** Adrian Davies. LC 99-45356. (Oxford Historical Monographs). 280p. 2000. 65.00 (0-19-820820-0) OUP.

Quakers in Fiction: Annotated Bibliography, Indexed. Anna B. Caulfield. 170p. 1993. pap. 13.95 (0-938875-29-9) Pittenbruach Pr.

Quakers in Nazi Germany. Michael Seadle. (Studies in Quakerism: No. 5). 44p. (Orig.). 1978. pap. 2.00 (0-89670-006-2) Progresiv Pub.

Quakers in Peace & War: An Account of Their Peace Principles & Practice. Margaret E. Hirst. LC 73-137545. (Peace Movement in America Ser.). 560p. 1972. reprint ed. lib. bdg. 60.95 (0-89198-073-3) Ozer.

Quakers in Pennsylvania. Albert C. Applegarth. LC 78-63813. (Johns Hopkins University. Studies in the Social Sciences. Thirtieth Ser. 1912: 8-9). reprint ed. 27.50 (0-404-61076-5) AMS Pr.

***Quakers in Science & Industry.** Arthur Raistrick. 1999. pap. 30.00 (1-85072-106-8, Pub. by W Sessions) St Mut.

Quakers in South Carolina, Wateree & Bush River, Cane Creek, Piney Grove & Charleston Meetings. Ed. by S. E. Lucas, Jr. (Illus.). 150p. 1991. reprint ed. pap. 25.00 (0-89308-450-6, SC 90) Southern Hist Pr.

Quakers in the Colonial Northeast. Arthur J. Worrall. LC 79-63086. 248p. 1980. reprint ed. pap. 76.90 (0-608-02313-2, 206295400004) Bks Demand.

Quakers Observed in Prose & Verse. Mollie Grubb. 1999. pap. 24.00 (1-85072-122-X, Pub. by W Sessions) St Mut.

Quakers on the Move: A Storybook of Quaker History. Religious Education Committee. (Illus.). 128p. (J). (gr. 2-5). 1996. pap. 9.00 (1-888305-03-7) Friends Genl Conf.

Quakers World Wide. Herbert M. Hadley. (C). 1988. 65.00 (1-85072-111-4, Pub. by W Sessions) St Mut.

Quakers Worldwide. Herbert M. Hadley. 1999. pap. 21.00 (1-85072-078-9, Pub. by W Sessions) St Mut.

Quakes, Eruptions & Other Geologic Cataclysms. Jon Erickson. (Changing Earth Ser.). (Illus.). 208p. 1994. 26.95 (0-8160-2949-0) Facts on File.

Quakes Split The Ground Open: And Other Amazing Facts about Earthquakes. Clare Oliver. LC 98-54110. (I Didn't Know That... Ser.). (Illus.). 32p. (J). 1999. 8.95 (0-7613-0795-8, Copper Beech Bks) Millbrook Pr.

***Quakes Split the Ground Open: And Other Amazing Facts about Earthquakes.** Clare Oliver. LC 98-54110. (I Didn't Know That... Ser.). (Illus.). 32p. (J). 1999. lib. bdg. 21.90 (0-7613-0912-8, Copper Beech Bks) Millbrook Pr.

Quakey Bear's Amazing Earthquake Adventure. Kathleen A. Sage. 24p. (J). (ps-3). 1992. pap. write for info. (0-9630089-5-1) Quakey Bear.

Quakey Bear's Earthquake Lessons: A Gentle Earthquake Journey for Children. Kathleen A. Sage. (J). (ps-3). 1991. pap. write for info. (0-9630089-0-0) Quakey Bear.

Quaking Aspen. Bonnie Holmes. LC 98-31909. (Illus.). 48p. (J). (gr. 3-6). 1999. 22.60 (1-57505-351-9, Carolrhoda) Lerner Pub.

Quaking Aspen Grove. Phyllis Walsh. (Haiku Ser.: No. 18). 16p. 1985. pap. 5.00 (1-55780-087-1) Juniper Pr ME.

***Quaking Houses: Art, Science & the Community: A Collaborative Approach to Water Pollution.** Penny Kemp & John Griffiths. (Illus.). 144p. 2000. pap. 19.95 (1-897766-57-2, Pub. by Jon Carpenter) Paul & Co Pubs.

QUAL ANL/PROP IONS AQU SOL 2E+ 2nd ed. Emil J. Slowinski & William L. Masterton. 208p. (C). 1990. pap. text 26.50 (0-03-031234-5) SCP.

Qualification for Computer-Integrated Manufacturing. Ed. by Felix Rauner. 240p. 1995. pap. 59.95 (3-540-19971-3) Spr-Verlag.

Qualification of Computer Networks. (Illus.). Date not set. 39.50 (1-930114-23-0) Serentec Pr.

Qualification of Inspection Procedures: Proceedings of an Advanced Seminar on Non-Destructive Testing Techniques for the Inspection of Industrial Structural Components, Joint Research Centre, Ispra, Italy, 25-29 October 1993. Ed. by E. Borloo et al. LC 94-39302. (Eurocourses: Mechanical & Materials Science Ser.: Vol. 2). 1995. text 272.50 (0-7923-3257-1) Kluwer Academic.

***Qualification of SCADA Systems.** (Illus.). 28p. 2000. 39.50 (1-930114-04-4) Serentec Pr.

Qualifications & Certification of Instrumentation & Control Technicians in Nuclear Facilities: S67.14. ANSI/ISA Staff. 1994. pap. 40.00 (1-55617-524-8, S67.14) ISA.

Qualifications & Certification of Instrumentation & Control Technicians in Nuclear Power Plants. Instrument Society of America Staff. LC TK0173.. (Standard Ser.: No. ISA-S67.14, 1983). 16p. reprint ed. pap. 30.00 (0-7837-8770-7, 204951500012) Bks Demand.

Qualifications Division Five of the Organization Executive Course see Organization Executive Course

Qualifications for a Director of Music Ministries: A Statement & Bibliography. Sheila Browne & John Miller. 21p. 1995. reprint ed. pap. text 3.50 (1-888360-00-3) NPM Pubns.

Qualifications for the Priesthood in the Liberal Catholic Church. rev. ed. William H. Pitkin & Lawrence J. Smith. 13p. 1994. pap. 2.25 (0-918980-15-1) St Alban Pr.

Qualifications of the Public School Teacher Workforce, 1988 & 1991. Sharon A. Bobbitt et al. LC 95-137286. (Statistical Analysis Report National Center for Education Statistics Reports). ii, 31 p. 1994. write for info. (0-16-045436-0) USGPO.

Qualifications, Startups & Tryouts of Injection Molds: How to Start up New Tooling, How to Keep Tools Optimized, How to Qualify New Tooling. William J. Tobin & WJT Associates Staff. (Illus.). 115p. (Orig.). (C). 1992. pap. 15.00 (0-936994-07-X) W J T Assocs.

Qualified Deferred Compensation Plans: Forms. Neil Mancoff & Allen T. Steinberg. LC 83-23222. 798p. 1990. 135.00 (0-317-11358-5) West Group.

Qualified Deferred Compensation Plans: Treatise, 2 vols., Set. Gary Boren & Norman P. Stein. LC 83-23912. 1446p. 1990. 240.00 (0-317-11357-7) West Group.

Qualified Domestic Relations Order: Forms & Worksheets 2nd ed. Mark W. Dundee. LC 98-193442. (Panel Answer Bks). 1998. write for info. (0-7355-0120-3) Panel Pubs.

Qualified Domestic Relations Order Answer Book. Victor B. Meyen & Mark Dundee. 608p. boxed set 118.00 (1-56706-358-6, S294) Panel Pubs.

Qualified Domestic Relations Order Answer Book. annuals Victor B. Meyen & Mark Dundee. 616p. 1996. 116.00 (1-56706-175-3) Panel Pubs.

Qualified Domestic Relations Order Answer Book. annuals 2nd ed. Victor B. Meyen & Mark Dundee. LC 98-129925. 608p. 1996. boxed set 118.00 (1-56706-433-7, 64337) Panel Pubs.

Qualified Domestic Relations Order Answer Book: Forms & Worksheets. annuals Mark W. Dundee. LC 97-200589. 1560p. 1997. pap. 96.00 (1-56706-381-0, 63810) Panel Pubs.

***Qualified Domestic Relations Order Handbook, Second Edition.** Gary A. Shulman. 864p. 1998. boxed set 145.00 (0-7355-0065-5) Panel Pubs.

Qualified Domestic Relations Orders, 1 vol. Michael B. Snyder. LC 93-22588. (Family Law Ser.). 1993. 135.00 (0-685-68062-2); 110.00 (0-685-68842-9) West Group.

Qualified Pension & Profit-Sharing Plans. 2nd ed. Pamela D. Perdue & Michelle Wilson. LC 98-86484. 1998. write for info. (0-7913-3544-5) Warren Gorham & Lamont.

Qualified Plan Administrator's Manual. Ronald A. Kladder & Paul J. Routh. ring bd. 187.00 (0-685-69674-X, QUAL) Warren Gorham & Lamont.

Qualified Products List & Sources, 1999 Edition. Global Engineering Documents Staff. 886p. 1999. per. 125.00 (1-57053-084-X) Global Eng Doc.

Qualified Products List Set, 10 vols., Set. 1993. ring bd. 695.00 (1-57053-068-8) Global Eng Doc.

Qualified Products Lists (QPL) Index, Issue 99-1. Global Engineering Documents Staff. Ed. by Global Staff. 240p. 1999. pap. text 35.00 (1-57053-086-6) Global Eng Doc.

Qualified Retirement & Other Employee Benefit Plans. Michael J. Canan. 1223p. 1991. pap. text. write for info. (0-314-83467-2) West Pub.

Qualified Retirement & Other Employee Benefit Plans. 1992nd ed. Michael J. Canan. 1218p. 1992. pap. text. write for info. (0-314-00413-0) West Pub.

Qualified Retirement & Other Employee Benefit Plans, 1990. Michael J. Canan. (Lawyers Practice Ser.). 1989. pap. text. write for info. (0-314-69557-5) West Pub.

Qualified Retirement & Other Employee Benefit Plans, 1993. Michael J. Canan. 1450p. 1993. pap. text. write for info. (0-314-01726-7) West Pub.

Qualified Retirement & Other Employee Benefit Plans, 1995: Practitioner Edition - Text Table. Michael Cunan. (West's Employment Law Ser.). 1250p. (C). 1995. pap. text. write for info. (0-314-06034-0) West Pub.

Qualified Retirement & Other Employee Benefit Plans, 1996: Student Edition. Michael J. Canan. 1405p. (C). 1996. pap. text. write for info. (0-314-09883-6) West Pub.

Qualified Retirement & Other Employee Benefit Plans, 1996 Practitioner Edition, Vol. 1. Michael J. Canan. (West's Employment Law Ser.). 1300p. 1996. pap. text. write for info. (0-314-20330-3) West Pub.

Qualified Retirement & Other Employee Benefit Plans, 1996 Practitioner Edition, Vol. 2. Michael J. Canan. (West's Employment Law Ser.). 550p. 1996. pap. text. write for info. (0-314-20331-1) West Pub.

Qualified Retirement & Other Employee Benefit Plans, 1997. 7th ed. Michael J. Canan. 1500p. (C). 1997. pap. text, student ed. write for info. (0-314-22312-6) West Pub.

***Qualified Teachers for All California Students: Current Issues in Recruitment, Retention, Preparation, & Professional Development.** Chloe Bullard. 67p. 1998. pap. write for info. (1-58703-091-8, CRB-98-012) CA St Libry.

Qualified Types: Theory & Practice. Mark P. Jones. (Distinguished Dissertations in Computer Science Ser.: No. 9). 169p. (C). 1995. text 49.95 (0-521-47253-9) Cambridge U Pr.

***Qualifikationsanforderungen in den Kaufmannischen Berufen: Regionale Arbeitskraftebedarfsanalyse.** Maria Deuling. (Arbeit - Technik - Organisation - Soziales Ser.). 306p. 1999. 48.95 (3-631-32738-2) P Lang Pubng.

Qualifinish Conference Proceedings, 1993. Products Finishing Staff. 405p. 1993. pap. 45.00 (1-56990-078-7) Hanser-Gardner.

QUALIFLEX Version 2.3: A Software Package for Multi-Criteria Analysis. Jan Van Der Linden. 32p. (C). 1995. pap. text 1287.50 (0-7923-3428-0) Kluwer Academic.

Qualify! A Guide to Successful Handling in AKC Pointing Breed Hunting Tests. Mark Powell. LC 95-78078. (Illus.). 210p. 1995. pap. 16.95 (0-9647671-4-7) Attwater Pub.

Qualifying Adjective in Spanish. Ernesto Zierer. LC 72-94516. (Janua Linguarum, Ser. Practica: No. 192). 54p. 1974. pap. text 47.70 (90-279-2722-7) Mouton.

Qualifying & Attacking Expert Witnesses. Robert C. Clifford. 1998. ring bd. 89.98 (0-938065-39-4) James Pub Santa Ana.

Qualifying As a Nonprofit Tax-Exempt Organization: A Guide for Attorneys, Accountants, & Executive Management. Robert N. Sughrue & Michelle L. Kopnski. LC 90-42965. 232p. 1991. 55.00 (0-89930-483-4, SQN/, Quorum Bks) Greenwood.

Qualifying Examination/Management Service. Jack Rudman. (General Aptitude & Abilities Ser.: CS-39). 1994. pap. 29.95 (0-8373-6739-5) Nat Learn.

Qualifying for Admission to the Service Academies: A Student's Guide. rev. ed. Robert F. Collins. Ed. by Ruth C. Rosen. (Military Opportunities Ser.). (Illus.). 154p. (YA). (gr. 7-12). 1990. lib. bdg. 15.95 (0-8239-1187-X) Rosen Group.

***Qualifying Paper for use on the AGFA Chromapress.** Vincent Lasceve. (Research & Technology Reports Ser.: Vol. 20). (Illus.). 64p. (C). 2000. pap. 50.00 (0-88362-304-8) GATFPress.

Qualifying Resources Recovery Operator (QRO) (Career Examination Ser.: C-3646). pap. 39.95 (0-8373-3646-5) Nat Learn.

Qualitative Analysis: A Guide to Best Practice. W. A. Hardcastle. viii, 24p. 1998. pap. 19.50 (0-85404-462-0, Pub. by Royal Soc Chem) Spr-Verlag.

Qualitative Analysis for Social Scientists. Anselm L. Strauss. LC 86-21608. (Illus.). 336p. 1987. pap. text 22.95 (0-521-33806-9) Cambridge U Pr.

Qualitative Analysis of Behavior, Vol. 11: Neural Network Models of Conditioning & Action, Vol. 11. Michael L. Commons et al. 376p. 1991. 79.95 (0-8058-0842-6); pap. 39.95 (0-8058-0843-4) L Erlbaum Assocs.

Qualitative Analysis of Human Movement. Duane Knudson & Craig Morrison. LC 96-48347. (Illus.). 216p. (Orig.). 1997. text 32.00 (0-88011-523-8, BKNU0523) Human Kinetics.

***Qualitative Analysis of Some Common Anions.** 5th ed. James M. Postma et al. 2000. pap. text, lab manual ed. 1.95 (0-7167-9445-4) W H Freeman.

Qualitative Analysis of the Anistropic Kepler Problem. Josefina Casasayas & Jaume Llibre. LC 84-18521. (Memoirs of the American Mathematical Society Ser.: No. 52/312). 115p. 1984. pap. 21.00 (0-8218-2309-4, MEMO/52/312) Am Math.

***Qualitative Analysis of the Jehovah's Witnesses: The Rhetoric, Reality & Religion in the Watchtower Society.** Daniel Cronn-Mills. LC 99-41403. (Studies in American Religion: Vol. 70). 224p. 1999. text 89.95 (0-7734-7943-0) E Mellen.

Qualitative Analysis of the Periodically Forced Relaxation Oscillations. Mark Levi. LC 81-3642. (Memoirs of the American Mathematical Society Ser.: No. 32/224). 147p. 1981. pap. 17.00 (0-8218-2244-6, MEMO/32/244) Am Math.

***Qualitative Analysis of Unlabeled Solutions.** 5th ed. James M. Postma et al. 2000. pap. text, lab manual ed. 1.95 (0-7167-9446-2) W H Freeman.

Qualitative & Action Research: A Practitioner Handbook. Michael P. Grady. LC 98-68069. 61p. 1998. pap. 12.00 (0-87367-808-7) Phi Delta Kappa.

Qualitative & Instrumental Analysis of Environmental Significant Elements. Ed. by Thomas G. Chasteen. 140p. 1993. pap. 50.95 (0-471-58649-8) Wiley.

Qualitative & Quantitative Analyses of Plankton Diatoms. Matthew H. Hohn. (Bulletin New Ser.: Vol. 3, No. 1). 1969. pap. text 6.00 (0-86727-057-8) Ohio Bio Survey.

Qualitative & Quantitative & Calibration Levels of Human Consciousness. David R. Hawkins. 200p. 1998. pap. 29.95 (0-9643261-8-3) Veritas AZ.

Qualitative & Quantitative Behavior of Planetary Systems: Proceedings of the Third Alexander von Humboldt Colloquium on Celestial Mechanics. Ed. by Rudolf Dvorak & Jacques Henrard. LC 93-17750. 406p. (C). 1993. text 196.50 (0-7923-2339-4) Kluwer Academic.

Q

Qualitative & Quantitative Mathematical Economics. J. H. Paelinck. 1982. lib. bdg. 112.50 (*90-247-2623-9*) Kluwer Academic.

Qualitative & Quantitative Methods in Evaluation Research. Thomas D. Cook. Ed. by Charles S. Reichardt. LC 79-20962. (Sage Research Progress Series in Evaluation: Vol. 1). 160p. 1979. reprint ed. pap. 49.60 (*0-608-03379-0*, 205964300008) Bks Demand.

Qualitative & Quantitative Practical Reasoning: First International Joint Conference on Qualitative & Quantitative Practical Reasoning, ECSQARU-FAPR'97, Bad Honnef, Germany, June 9-12, 1997, Proceedings. Ed. by D. M. Gabbay et al. LC 97-20662. (Lecture Notes in Artificial Intelligence Ser.: No. 1244). x, 621p. 1997. pap. 91.00 (*3-540-63095-3*) Spr-Verlag.

Qualitative & Quantitative Social Research: Papers in Honor of Paul F. Lazarsfeld. Ed. by Robert K. Merton et al. LC 78-24752. 1979. 29.95 (*0-02-920930-7*) Free Pr.

Qualitative Approaches to Evaluation in Education: The Silent Scientific Revolution. Ed. by David M. Fetterman. LC 88-2746. (Illus.). 312p. 1988. 69.50 (*0-275-92917-5*, C2917, Praeger Pubs) Greenwood.

Qualitative Aspects & Applications of Nonlinear Evolution Equations: Proceedings of the Workshop. LC 95-106359. 228p. 1994. text 86.00 (*981-02-1708-0*) World Scientific Pub.

Qualitative Assessment of Text Difficulty: A Practical Guide for Teachers & Writers. Jeanne S. Chall. LC 96-24405. 112p. 1996. pap. 19.95 (*1-57129-023-0*) Brookline Bks.

Qualitative Choice Analysis: Theory, Econometrics, & an Application to Automobile Demand. Kenneth E. Train. (Transportation Studies). 224p. (C). 1985. 38.00 (*0-262-20055-4*) MIT Pr.

Qualitative Communications Research Methods. Thomas R. Lindlof. (Current Communication: An Advanced Text Ser.: Vol. 3). 364p. 1994. 58.00 (*0-8039-3517-X*); pap. 26.95 (*0-8039-3518-8*) Sage.

Qualitative Computing: Using Software for Qualitative Data Analysis. Mike Fisher. (Cardiff Papers in Qualitative Research). 160p. 1997. text 69.95 (*1-85972-561-9*, Pub. by Avebry) Ashgate Pub Co.

Qualitative Credit Control. William E. Dunkman. (Columbia University. Studies in the Social Sciences: No. 395). reprint ed. 32.50 (*0-404-51395-6*) AMS Pr.

Qualitative Data Analysis: A User-Friendly Guide. Ian Dey. LC 92-26082. (Illus.). 304p. (C). 1993. pap. 24.99 (*0-415-05852-X*, B0240) Routledge.

Qualitative Data Analysis: An Expanded Sourcebook. 2nd ed. Matthew B. Miles & A. Michael Huberman. 352p. (C). 1994. text 75.00 (*0-8039-4653-8*); pap. text 34.00 (*0-8039-5540-5*) Sage.

Qualitative Dissertation: A Guide for Students & Faculty. Maria Piantanida & Noreen Garman. LC 98-58139. (One-Off Ser.). (Illus.). 368p. 1999. 74.95 (*0-8039-6688-1*) Corwin Pr.

Qualitative Dissertation: A Guide for Students & Faculty. Maria Piantanida et al. LC 98-58139. (1-Off Ser.). (Illus.). 368p. 1999. pap. 34.95 (*0-8039-6689-X*) Corwin Pr.

Qualitative Educational Research in Developing Countries: Current Perspectives. Ed. by Michael Crossley et al. LC 96-16786. (Reference Books in International Education: Vol. 35). (Illus.). 328p. 1996. text 65.00 (*0-8153-1494-9*, SS927) Garland.

Qualitative Enquiry for Rural Development: A Review. Jon Moris & James Copestake. 118p. (Orig.). 1993. pap. 15.95 (*1-85339-215-4*, Pub. by Intermed Tech) Stylus Pub VA.

Qualitative Estimates for Partial Differential Equations: An Introduction. M. N. Flavin & S. Rionero. 300p. 1995. lib. bdg. 94.95 (*0-8493-8512-1*, 8512) CRC Pr.

Qualitative Evaluation & Research Methods. 2nd ed. Michael Q. Patton. (Illus.). 536p. (C). 1990. text 49.95 (*0-8039-3779-2*) Sage.

Qualitative Evaluation Concepts & Cases in Curriculum Criticism. Ed. by George Willis. LC 77-23647. (Education Ser.). 579p. 1978. 41.00 (*0-8211-2257-6*) McCutchan.

Qualitative Evaluation Methods for Reference Services: An Introductory Manual. Lynn Westbrook. 25p. 1989. pap. 20.00 (*0-918006-59-7*, SS04) ARL.

Qualitative Gerontology. Ed. by Shulamit Reinharz & Graham D. Rowles. 336p. (C). 1987. 36.95 (*0-8261-5230-9*) Springer Pub.

Qualitative Health Research. Ed. by Janice M. Morse. (Illus.). 272p. (C). 1992. 58.00 (*0-8039-4774-7*) Sage.

Qualitative Hydrologie - Wasserbeschaffenheit und Stoff-Flusse. Hubert Hellmann. (Lehrbuch der Hydrologie Ser.: Band 2).Tr. of Qualitative Hydrology - Water Composition & Material Fluxes. (GER., Illus.). xix, 468p. 1999. 99.00 (*3-443-30003-0*, Pub. by Gebruder Borntraeger) Balogh.

Qualitative Hydrology - Water Composition & Material Fluxes see Qualitative Hydrologie - Wasserbeschaffenheit und Stoff-Flusse

Qualitative Inquiry: A Dictionary of Terms. Thomas A. Schwandt. LC 97-4587. 192p. (C). 1997. 46.00 (*0-7619-0253-8*, 02538); pap. 19.95 (*0-7619-0254-6*, 02546) Sage.

Qualitative Inquiry & Research Design: Choosing among 5 Traditions. John W. Creswell. LC 97-4820. 430p. 1997. text 62.00 (*0-7619-0143-4*); pap. text 28.95 (*0-7619-0144-2*) Sage.

Qualitative Inquiry in Education: The Continuing Debate. Ed. by Elliot W. Eisner & Alan Peshkin. 400p. (C). 1990. text 43.00 (*0-8077-3017-3*); pap. text 22.95 (*0-8077-3016-5*) Tchrs Coll.

Qualitative Interviewing: The Art of Hearing Data. Irene B. Rubin & Herbert J. Rubin. 302p. (C). 1995. 52.00 (*0-8039-5095-0*); pap. 24.00 (*0-8039-5096-9*) Sage.

Qualitative Investigations into Schools & Schooling see Readings on Equal Education, Vol. 10, Critical Issues for a New Administration & Congress

Qualitative Market Research. Wendy Gordon & Roy Langmaid. 280p. 1988. text 86.95 (*0-566-05115-X*, Pub. by Gower) Ashgate Pub Co.

Qualitative Media Analysis. David L. Altheide. LC 95-41796. (Qualitative Research Methods Ser.: Vol. 38). 112p. 1996. 24.00 (*0-7619-0198-1*); pap. 10.50 (*0-7619-0199-X*) Sage.

***Qualitative Method Interpretations in Communication Skills.** James A. Schnell. 208p. 2000. 65.00 (*0-7391-0147-1*) Lxngtn Bks.

Qualitative Methodology. Ed. by John Van Maanen. 272p. 1983. pap. 19.50 (*0-8039-2117-9*) Sage.

Qualitative Methodology & Sociology: Describing the Social World. David Silver. 220p. 1985. pap. text 64.95 (*0-566-00884-X*, Pub. by Dartmth Pub) Ashgate Pub Co.

Qualitative Methods for Reasoning under Uncertainty. Simon Parsons. LC 96-44044. (A. I. Ser.). (Illus.). 404p. Date not set. 45.00 (*0-262-16168-0*) MIT Pr.

Qualitative Methods in Aging Research. Ed. by Jaber F. Gubrium & Andrea Sankar. LC 93-21401. (Focus Editions Ser.: Vol. 168). (C). 1993. text 59.95 (*0-8039-4943-X*); pap. text 26.00 (*0-8039-4944-8*) Sage.

Qualitative Methods in Continuum Mechanics. R. V. Goldstein. 1994. ring bd. 100.00 (*0-582-08372-9*, Pub. by Addison-Wesley) Longman.

Qualitative Methods in Family Research. Jane F. Gilgun. 320p. (C). 1992. text 45.00 (*0-8039-4462-4*); pap. text 21.00 (*0-8039-4463-2*) Sage.

Qualitative Methods in Management Research. Evert Gummesson. (Illus.). 200p. 1991. text 48.00 (*0-8039-4203-6*) Sage.

Qualitative Methods in Management Research. rev. ed. Evert Gummesson. (Illus.). 200p. 1991. pap. text 22.95 (*0-8039-4204-4*) Sage.

Qualitative Methods in Mathematical Analysis. L. E. El'sgol'c. LC 64-16170. (Translations of Mathematical Monographs: Vol. 12). 250p. 1964. reprint ed. pap. 50.00 (*0-8218-1562-8*, MMONO/12) Am Math.

Qualitative Methods in Physical Kinetics & Hydrodynamics. Vladimir P. Krainov. 224p. 1992. 79.95 (*0-88318-953-4*) Spr-Verlag.

Qualitative Methods in Psychology: A Research Guide. Peter Banister et al. LC 94-25724. 160p. 1994. pap. 30.95 (*0-335-19181-9*) OpUniv Pr.

***Qualitative Methods in Quantum Theory.** A. B. Migdal. (Illus.). 256p. 2000. pap. text 39.00 (*0-7382-0302-5*) Perseus Pubng.

Qualitative Methods in Quantum Theory. Arkadii B. Migdal. Tr. by Anthony J. Leggett. (Advanced Book Classics Ser.). 1977. 29.95 (*0-8053-7064-1*) Addison-Wesley.

Qualitative Methods in Social Work Research: Challenges & Rewards. Deborah Padgett. LC 97-33908. (Sage Sourcebooks for the Human Services Ser.). 1998. write for info. (*0-7619-0200-7*); pap. write for info. (*0-7619-0201-5*) Sage.

***Qualitative Methods in Sociolinguistics.** Barbara Johnstone. LC 99-33400. 176p. (C). 1999. pap. text 19.95 (*0-19-513397-8*) OUP.

Qualitative Modeling of Complex Systems: An Introduction to Loop Analysis & Time Averaging. Charles J. Puccia & Richard Levins. (Illus.). 256p. 1986. 54.00 (*0-674-74110-2*) HUP.

Qualitative Motion Planning. Wilhelm Burger & Bir Bhanu. LC 92-13870. (International Series in Engineering & Computer Science, VLSI, Computer Architecture, & Digital Screen Processing: Vol. 184). 224p. (C). 1992. text 139.50 (*0-7923-9251-5*) Kluwer Academic.

Qualitative Music Therapy Research: Beginning Dialogues. Ed. by Mechtild Langenberg et al. 276p. (C). 1996. pap. text 25.00 (*0-9624080-4-2*) Barcelona Pubs.

Qualitative Nursing Research: A Contemporary Dialogue. rev. ed. Ed. by Janice M. Morse. (Illus.). 360p. (C). 1990. text 52.00 (*0-8039-4078-5*); pap. text 24.50 (*0-8039-4079-3*) Sage.

Qualitative Problems for Differential Equations & Control Theory. C. Corduneanu. 320p. 1995. text 85.00 (*981-02-2257-2*) World Scientific Pub.

Qualitative-Quantitative Debate: New Perspectives. Ed. by Charles S. Reichardt & Sharon F. Rallis. LC 85-644749. (New Directions for Evaluation Ser.: No. PE 61). 98p. (Orig.). 1994. pap. 20.00 (*0-7879-9967-9*) Jossey-Bass.

Qualitative-Quantitative Research Methodology: Exploring the Interactive Continuum. Isadore Newman & Carolyn R. Benz. LC 97-23117. (Illus.). 176p. (Orig.). 1998. pap. 14.95 (*0-8093-2150-5*) S Ill U Pr.

Qualitative Reading Inventory. Lauren Leslie & JoAnne Caldwell. 278p. (C). 1997. pap. text 41.40 (*0-673-18791-8*) Addson-Wesley Educ.

***Qualitative Reading Inventory, 3.** Lauren Leslie & JoAnne Caldwell. LC 00-30498. 2001. write for info. (*0-321-03786-3*) Longman.

Qualitative Reading Inventory, II. 2nd rev. ed. Lauren Leslie & JoAnne Caldwell. LC 94-18636. 277p. (C). 1997. pap. text 40.75 (*0-673-99086-9*) Addson-Wesley Educ.

***Qualitative Reaseach Methods: A Health Focus.** Pranee Liamputtong Rice & Douglas Ezzy. 240p. 2000. pap. text 29.95 (*0-19-550610-3*) OUP.

Qualitative Reasoning: An Approach to Modeling & Behavior Generation. Hannes Werthner. LC 94-12105. 1994. 35.95 (*0-387-82579-7*) Spr-Verlag.

Qualitative Reasoning: Modeling & Simulation with Incomplete Knowledge. Benjamin Kuipers. (Artificial Intelligence Ser.). (Illus.). 452p. 1994. 55.00 (*0-262-11190-X*) MIT Pr.

Qualitative Reasoning: The Twelfth International Workshop: Papers from the 1998 Workshop. Ed. by Feng Zhao & Kenneth Yip. (Technical Reports: No. WS-98-01). 182p. 1998. pap. text 25.00 (*1-57735-054-5*) AAAI Pr.

Qualitative Reasoning about Physical Sciences. Ed. by Daniel G. Bobrow. 504p. 1985. 35.00 (*0-262-02218-4*, Bradford Bks) MIT Pr.

Qualitative Representation of Spatial Knowledge. Daniel Hernandez. LC 94-16025. (Lecture Notes in Artificial Intelligence Ser.: Vol. 804). 1994. 39.95 (*0-387-58058-1*) Spr-Verlag.

Qualitative Research. R. Tesch. 1990. pap. 32.95 (*1-85000-609-1*, Falmer Pr) Taylor & Francis.

Qualitative Research: Applications in Organizational Communication. Sandra Herndon & Gary L. Kreps. LC 92-38373. (Speech Communication Association Applied Communication Ser.). 208p. (C). 1993. text 39.50 (*1-881303-38-1*); pap. text 22.95 (*1-881303-39-X*) Hampton Pr NJ.

Qualitative Research: The Emotional Dimension. Ed. by Sarah Delamont & Keith Carter. LC 96-83716. (Cardiff Papers in Qualitative Research). 160p. 1996. 68.95 (*1-85972-263-6*, Pub. by Avebry) Ashgate Pub Co.

Qualitative Research: Theory, Method & Practice. Ed. by David Silverman. LC 97-66133. 288p. (C). 1997. 69.95 (*0-8039-7665-8*, 76658); pap. 21.95 (*0-8039-7666-6*, 76666) Sage.

Qualitative Research & Case Study Applications in Education. Sharan B. Merriam. LC 97-7167. (Joint Publication of the Jossey-Bass Education Series & the Jossey-Bass Higher & Adult Education Ser.). 1997. 21.95 (*0-7879-1009-0*) Jossey-Bass.

Qualitative Research & Evaluation in Group Care. Ed. by Rivka A. Eisikovits & Yitzhak Kashti. LC 86-14848. (Child & Youth Services Ser.: Vol. 8, Nos. 3 & 4). 132p. 1987. text 4.95 (*0-86656-608-2*) Haworth Pr.

Qualitative Research Design: An Interactive Approach. Joseph A. Maxwell. LC 95-50209. (Applied Social Research Methods Ser.: Vol. 41). 204p. (C). 1996. 42.00 (*0-8039-7328-4*); pap. 18.95 (*0-8039-7329-2*) Sage.

Qualitative Research for Education. 3rd ed. Robert C. Bogdan & Sari K. Biklen. LC 97-30859. 276p. 1997. 77.00 (*0-205-27564-8*) P-H.

Qualitative Research for Education: An Introduction to Theory & Methods. Robert C. Bogdan & Sari K. Biklen. 350p. (C). 1981. text 41.00 (*0-205-07695-5*, H76953) Allyn.

Qualitative Research for Nurses. Immy Holloway & Stephanie Wheeler. LC 95-26498. 1996. pap. 29.95 (*0-632-03765-2*) Blackwell Sci.

Qualitative Research for the Information Profession: A Practical Handbook. G. E. Gorman & Peter Clayton. 296p. 1997. 75.00 (*1-85604-178-6*, LAP1786, Pub. by Library Association) Bernan Associates.

Qualitative Research in Creativity. Cecilia Yau. 1995. pap. 14.95 (*0-930222-95-4*) Creat Educ Found.

Qualitative Research in Criminology. Ed. by Fiona Brookman & Emma Wincup. LC 98-74933. (Cardiff Papers in Qualitative Research). 190p. 1999. 59.95 (*1-84014-571-4*, Pub. by Ashgate Pub) Ashgate Pub Co.

Qualitative Research in Early Childhood Settings. Ed. by J. Amos Hatch. LC 94-32916. 272p. 1995. 75.00 (*0-275-94921-4*, Praeger Pubs); pap. 27.95 (*0-275-95151-0*, Praeger Pubs) Greenwood.

Qualitative Research in Education: A Guide to Study Design & Proposal Preparation. Nancy F. Dana & Thomas N. Dana. Ed. by Joe Kincheloe & Shirley R. Steinberg. (Critical Education Practice Ser.). 200p. 1997. text 30.00 (*0-8153-2198-8*) Garland.

Qualitative Research in Education: An Introduction to the Major Traditions. David F. Lancy. LC 92-20128. 352p. (C). 1993. text 46.95 (*0-8013-0309-5*, 78014) Longman.

Qualitative Research in Education: Focus & Methods. Robert R. Sherman & Rodman B. Webb. 275p. 1988. pap. 32.95 (*1-85000-381-5*, Falmer Pr) Taylor & Francis.

Qualitative Research in Higher Education: Experiencing Alternative Perspectives & Approaches. Ed. by Clifton F. Conrad et al. (ASHE Reader Ser.). 706p. (C). 1993. pap. text 54.00 (*0-536-58417-6*) Pearson Custom.

***Qualitative Research in Intelligence & Marketing: The New Strategic Convergence.** Alf H. Walle. LC 00-25250. 288p. 2000. 67.00 (*1-56720-366-3*, Q366, Quorum Bks) Greenwood.

Qualitative Research in Marketing. Danny N. Bellenger et al. LC 76-3765. (American Marketing Association Monograph: No. 3). 86p. reprint ed. pap. 30.00 (*0-608-13400-7*, 202248200027) Bks Demand.

Qualitative Research in Nursing: Advancing the Humanistic Imperative. Helen J. Streubert & Dona R. Carpenter. LC 94-13709. 352p. 1994. pap. text 36.95 (*0-397-55091-X*) Lppncott W & W.

Qualitative Research in Nursing: Advancing the Humanistic Imperative. 2nd ed. Helen J. Streubert & Dona R. Carpenter. 1999. 36.95 (*0-7817-1628-4*) Lppncott W & W.

***Qualitative Research in Nursing: Methods in Context.** J. Lawler. 176p. 1998. pap. write for info. (*0-443-05207-7*) Church.

***Qualitative Research in Occupational Therapy.** Cook. 2001. pap. 35.25 (*0-7693-0079-0*) Thomson Learn.

Qualitative Research in Pharmacy Practice. Ed. by Sheila Phillips et al. (Cardiff Papers in Qualitative Research). 224p. 1996. 72.95 (*1-85972-211-3*, Pub. by Avebry) Ashgate Pub Co.

Qualitative Research in Psychology. Ed. by P. Ashworth et al. LC 85-27415. 384p. (C). 1986. text 24.95 (*0-8207-0187-4*) Duquesne.

Qualitative Research in Social Work. Ed. by Edmund Sherman & William J. Reid. LC 93-23421. 1994. 77.50 (*0-231-08032-8*); pap. 39.00 (*0-231-08033-6*) Col U Pr.

Qualitative Research Methodology in Nursing & Health Care. Open Learning Foundation Staff. 120p. 1997. pap. write for info. (*0-443-05738-9*) Church.

Qualitative Research Methods. 2nd ed. Janice M. Morse & Peggy A. Field. (Illus.). 304p. 1995. pap. 26.00 (*0-8039-7327-6*) Sage.

Qualitative Research Methods: Social Epistemology & Practical Inquiry. Steven I. Miller & Marcel Fredericks. LC 96-177811. 160p. (C). 1996. pap. 32.95 (*0-8204-3458-2*) P Lang Pubng.

Qualitative Research Methods for Health Professionals. 2nd ed. Janice M. Morse & Peggy A. Field. LC 95-11488. (Illus.). 254p. 1995. 54.00 (*0-8039-7326-8*) Sage.

Qualitative Research Methods for the Social Sciences. 3rd ed. Bruce L. Berg. LC 96-49934. 290p. 1997. pap. 40.00 (*0-205-26475-1*) Allyn.

***Qualitative Research Methods for the Social Sciences.** 4th ed. Bruce Lawrence Berg. LC 00-23770. 336p. 2000. pap. 40.00 (*0-205-31847-9*) Allyn.

***Qualitative Research Methods in Human Geography.** Ed. by Jain Hay. (Meridian). (Illus.). 176p. 2000. pap. 24.95 (*0-19-550787-8*) OUP.

Qualitative Research Methods in Mathematics Education. Ed. by Anne R. Teppo. LC 98-36575. (Journal for Research in Mathematics Education Monograph Ser.: No. 9). 180p. 1998. pap. 12.50 (*0-87353-459-X*) NCTM.

Qualitative Research Methods in Nursing. Ed. by Madeleine M. Leininger. 384p. 1985. text 64.00 (*0-8089-1676-9*, 792508, Grune & Strat) Harcrt Hlth Sci Grp.

Qualitative Research Methods in Organizational Psychology: A Practical Guide. Ed. by Cathy Cassell & Gillian Symon. LC 94-66701. 272p. 1994. 69.95 (*0-8039-8769-2*); pap. 26.95 (*0-8039-8770-6*) Sage.

Qualitative Research Proposals & Reports: A Guide. Patricia L. Munhall. 40p. 1994. 12.95 (*0-88737-606-1*, 19-2609, NLN Pr) Natl League Nurse.

***Qualitative Research Proposals & Reports: A Guide.** 2nd ed. Patricia L. Munhall & NLN Staff. (Illus.). 64p. (C). 1999. pap. text 18.75 (*0-7637-1171-3*) JB Pubns.

Qualitative Researching. Jennifer Mason. 208p. 1996. 69.95 (*0-8039-8985-7*); pap. 21.95 (*0-8039-8986-5*) Sage.

Qualitative Simulation Modeling & Analysis. Ed. by Paul A. Fishwick et al. (Advances in Simulation Ser.: Vol. 5). (Illus.). 360p. 1991. 79.95 (*0-387-97400-8*) Spr-Verlag.

***Qualitative Sociology As Everyday Life.** Barry Glassner. LC 98-40243. 1998. pap. 24.95 (*0-7619-1369-6*) Sage.

***Qualitative Sociology As Everyday Life.** Ed. by Barry Glassner & Rosanna Hertz. LC 98-40243. 280p. 1999. 65.00 (*0-7619-1368-8*) Sage.

Qualitative Studies in Education. Ed. by Jane Salisbury & Sara Delamont. 224p. 1995. 72.95 (*1-85628-582-0*, Pub. by Avebry) Ashgate Pub Co.

Qualitative Studies in Health & Medicine. Ed. by Michael Bloor & Patricia Taraborrelli. (Cardiff Papers in Qualitative Research). 139p. 1994. 66.95 (*1-85628-579-0*, Pub. by Avebry) Ashgate Pub Co.

Qualitative Studies in Social Work Research. Ed. by Catherine K. Riessman. (Illus.). 256p. (C). 1993. text 52.00 (*0-8039-5451-4*); pap. text 24.00 (*0-8039-5452-2*) Sage.

Qualitative Studies of Organizations. John Van Maanen. LC 98-25344. (Administrative Science Quarterly Series in Organizational Theory & Behavior). 360p. 1998. 65.00 (*0-7619-1694-6*); pap. 29.95 (*0-7619-1695-4*) Sage.

Qualitative Study of the Co-Construction of Therapeutic Reality: A Process & Outcome Model. Jon L. Winek. LC 98-30820. (Studies in Sociology: Vol. 20). 143p. 1998. text 79.95 (*0-7734-8236-9*) E Mellen.

Qualitative Study of the Co-construction of Therapeutic Reality: A Process & Outcome Model Jon L. Winek. LC 98-30820. (Mellen Studies In Sociology Ser.). viii, 143 p. 1998. write for info. (*0-08-894663-0*) Elsevier.

Qualitative Testing for Carbohydrates. James O. Schreck & William M. Loffredo. Ed. by H. Anthony Neidig. (Modular Laboratory Program in Chemistry Ser.). 12p. (C). 1994. pap. text 1.50 (*0-87540-446-4*, REAC 446-4) Chem Educ Res.

Qualitative Testing for Lipids. Frank R. Milio & William M. Loffredo. Ed. by H. Anthony Neidig. (Modular Laboratory Program in Chemistry Ser.). 16p. (C). 1994. pap. text 1.50 (*0-87540-447-2*, REAC 447-2) Chem Educ Res.

Qualitative Tests for Alkenes. Robert Silberman. Ed. by Conrad L. Stanitski. (Modular Laboratory Program in Chemistry Ser.). 12p. (C). 1996. pap. text 1.50 (*0-87540-472-3*, REAC 472-3) Chem Educ Res.

Qualitative Tests for Amino Acids & Proteins. William M. Loffredo & Frank R. Milio. (Modular Laboratory Program in Chemistry Ser.). 12p. (C). 1995. pap. text 1.50 (*0-87540-448-0*, REAC 448-0) Chem Educ Res.

Qualitative Tests for the OH Group in Organic Compounds. James O. Schreck & Robert Silberman. Ed. by Conrad L. Stanitski. (Modular Laboratory Program in Chemistry Ser.). 12p. (C). 1995. pap. text 1.50 (*0-87540-469-3*, REAC 469-3) Chem Educ Res.

Qualitative Theory for Dynamical Systems. Anthony N. Michel & Kaining Wang. LC 94-35418. (Pure & Applied Mathematics Ser.: Vol. 186). (Illus.). 472p. 1994. text 175.00 (*0-8247-9420-6*) Dekker.

Qualitative Theory of Control Systems. A. A. Davydov. LC 94-30834. (Translations of Mathematical Monographs: Vol. 141). 147p. 1994. text 75.00 (*0-8218-4590-X*, MMONO/141) Am Math.

Qualitative Theory of Differential Equations. Tong-Ren Dong et al. LC 91-23961. (Translations of Mathematical Monographs). 461p. 1992. text 288.00 (*0-8218-4551-9*, MMONO/101) Am Math.

An Asterisk (*) at the beginning of an entry indicates that the title is appearing for the first time.

Qualitative Theory of Differential Equations. V. V. Nemytskii & V. V. Stepanov. 523p. 1989. pap. 14.95 (0-486-65954-2) Dover.

*__Qualitative Theory of Hybrid Dynamical Systems.__ A. Matveev & A. Savkin. (Control Engineering Ser.). 352p. 2000. 69.95 (0-8176-4141-6, Pub. by Birkhauser) Spr-Verlag.

Qualitative Theory of Ordinary Differential Equations. Fred Brauer & John A. Nohel. 320p. 1994. pap. 8.95 (0-486-65846-5) Dover.

Qualitative Theory of Parabolic Equations, Vol. 1. T. I. Zelenyak et al. (Illus.). 424p. 1997. 205.00 (90-6764-236-3, Pub. by VSP) Coronet Bks.

Qualitative Topics in Integer Linear Programming. V. N. Shevchenko. Tr. by H. H. McFaden. LC 96-32702. (Translations of Mathematical Monographs: Vol. 156). 146p. 1996. 69.00 (0-8218-0535-5, MMONO/156) Am Math.

Qualitative Utilitarianism. Daniel Holbrook. 146p. (Orig.). (C). 1988. pap. text 17.50 (0-8191-6989-7); lib. bdg. 38.00 (0-8191-6988-9) U Pr of Amer.

Qualitatssicherung in der Gerontopsychiatrischen Tagesklinik: Ergebnisse Einer Begleitstudie Mit Einer Einleitung von Holger K. Schneider, Direktor des Bezirkskrankenhauses Erlangen. Krista Stosberg & Harald J. Losch. (GER.). xi, 187p. 1997. 42.95 (3-631-49869-1) P Lang Pubng.

Qualitatssicherung in der Stationaren Altenhilfe: Eine an HeimbewohnerInnen Orientierte Empirische Studie zum Qualitatssicherungselement "Einrichtungsziele" Gerhard Tepe. (Europaische Hochschulschriften Ser.: Reihe 23, Bd. 594). (GER., Illus.). 310p. 1997. 57.95 (3-631-31175-3) P Lang Pubng.

Qualities Associated with Leadership in the Extra-Curricular Activities of the High School. George C. Bellingrath. LC 74-176549. (Columbia University. Teachers College. Contributions to Education Ser.: No. 399). reprint ed. 37.50 (0-404-55399-0) AMS Pr.

Qualities of Community Life. Roger G. Barker & Phil Schoggen. LC 72-13601. (Jossey-Bass Behavioral Science Ser.). (Illus.). 576p. reprint ed. pap. 178.60 (0-8357-4696-8, 205235100008) Bks Demand.

Qualities of Experience & Educational Philosophy. Ed. by John P. Wynne. (Orig.). 1960. pap. 16.95 (0-8084-0257-9) NCUP.

Qualities of Greatness: From the World's Religions. Illus. by David S. Ruhe. 96p. 1998. pap. 16.95 (0-9659945-4-6) Global Classrm.

Qualities of Love. large type ed. I. M. Fresson. (Romance Ser.). 1994. pap. 16.99 (0-7089-7603-4, Linford) Ulverscroft.

Qualities of Mercy: Justice, Punishment, & Discretion. Ed. by Carolyn Strange. LC 97-151117. 192p. 1996. 65.00 (0-7748-0584-6) U of Wash Pr.

Qualities of Mercy: Justice, Punishment, & Discretion. Ed. by Carolyn Strange. LC 96-910493. 192p. 1997. pap. 25.95 (0-7748-0585-4) U of Wash Pr.

Quality. Ledolter. 192p. (C). 1998. pap. text, teacher ed. 17.50 (0-471-09278-9) Wiley.

*__Quality.__ 2nd ed. Donna C. S. Summers. LC 98-51773. (Illus.). 653p. (C). 1999. 88.00 incl. cd-rom (0-13-099924-5) P-H.

Quality: A Critical Introduction. John Beckford. LC 97-51904. 352p. (C). 1998. 100.00 (0-415-18163-1); pap. 34.99 (0-415-18164-X) Routledge.

Quality: ASTD Trainer's Sourcebook. J. Smith. 1997. pap. text 39.95 (0-07-053434-9) McGraw.

Quality: From Customer Needs to Customer Satisfaction. Bo Bergman & Bengt Klefsjo. LC 94-7346. 478p. (C). 1994. pap. 44.69 (0-07-709016-0) McGraw.

Quality: Home Plans. 115p. 1998. pap. 4.95 (0-934039-51-8) Hme Dsgn Altntves.

Quality: People Management Matters. IPM Reseaarch Staff. 156p. (C). 1993. pap. text 150.00 (0-85292-516-6, Pub. by IPM Hse) St Mut.

Quality: Systems, Concepts, Strategies & Tools. William J. Kolarik. LC 94-31883. (C). 1995. text 64.25 (0-07-035217-8) McGraw.

Quality: The (MCS) Material Control System for Nonconforming Material & Corrective Actions. Robert E. Schomberg. 72p. 1991. 895.00 incl. disk (1-880354-01-2) Qual-Tech.

Quality: The Reference Book for a Structured Programming System. Robert E. Schomberg. 525p. (C). 1991. lib. bdg. 89.95 (1-880354-02-0) Qual-Tech.

Quality: Transforming Postsecondary Education. Ellen E. Chaffee & Lawrence A. Sherr. Ed. by Jonathan D. Fife. LC 92-62286. (ASHE-ERIC Higher Education Reports: No. 92-3). 114p. (Orig.). 1993. pap. text 24.00 (1-878380-16-8) GWU Grad Schl E&HD.

Quality - A Challenge for Tourism. LC 99-172213. iii, 183p. 1997. 20.00 (92-844-0217-4, WTO0217, Pub. by Wrld Tourism Org) Bernan Associates.

Quality Acceleration in Hygiene & Operative. Michael J. Segerdal. (Illus.). 52p. 1995. write for info. incl. VHS (1-883558-04-2) PIBL.

Quality Achievements in Spiral Bevel Gears by the HPG-Method. H. Trapp. (Technical Papers: Vol. P239.16). (Illus.). 20p. 1981. pap. text 30.00 (1-55589-312-0) AGMA.

Quality Advantage: A Strategic Guide for Health Care Leaders. Julianne M. Morath. LC 98-36020. 248p. 1998. 36.00 (1-55648-256-6) Aha Pub.

Quality Alternatives to Government Schools in Greater Denver. Damon M. Zinn. 50p. 1992. pap. text 8.00 (1-57655-102-4) Independ Inst.

*__Quality Analects of Mr. Funny Guy.__ Timothy Rogers. 168p. 1999. pap. 10.00 (0-9672452-0-6) Entropy Enter.

Quality & Accessibility of Food-Related Data. Ed. by Heather Greenfield. LC 95-76836. 310p. 1995. pap. 53.00 (0-935584-56-0) AOAC Intl.

Quality & Availability of Family Planning Services & Contraceptive Use in Tanzania. Kathleen Beegle. LC 95-13435. (LSMS Working Papers: No. 114). 66p. 1995. pap. 22.00 (0-8213-3198-1, 13198) World Bank.

Quality & Control: An Accounting Perspective. Ahmed Riahi-Belkaoui. LC 92-34942. 240p. 1993. 67.95 (0-89930-767-1, BQC, Quorum Bks) Greenwood.

Quality & Cost-Containment in Care of the Elderly: Health Services Research Perspectives. Ed. by James C. Romeis & Rodney Coe. LC 90-10439. 248p. 1990. 42.95 (0-8261-7170-2) Springer Pub.

Quality & Cost in Health Care Choice in Developing Countries. Victor Lavy & Jean-Marc Germain. LC 94-12590. (LSMS Working Papers: No. 105). 48p. 1994. pap. 22.00 (0-8213-2854-9, 12854) World Bank.

Quality & Diversity in Early Learning: A Framework for Early Childhood Practitioners. Early Childhood Education Forum Staff. LC 99-203331. 114p. 1998. pap., spiral bd. 24.00 (1-900990-30-X, Pub. by Natl Childrens Bur) Paul & Co Pubs.

Quality & Economic Significance of Anticipations Data. Universities-National Bureau Staff. (Conference Ser.: No. 10). 480p. 1960. reprint ed. 124.80 (0-87014-301-8) Natl Bur Econ Res.

Quality & Education. Christopher Winch. 164p. (Orig.). 1996. pap. text 30.95 (0-631-20085-1) Blackwell Pubs.

Quality & Equality: Promoting Opportunities in Schools. Kathryn Riley. Ed. by John Sayer. (Educational Management Ser.). (Illus.). 160p. 1994. 95.00 (0-304-32687-9) Continuum.

Quality & Excellence in Human Services. Paul Dickens. LC 93-36190. (Clinical Psychology Ser.). 220p. 1994. pap. 89.95 (0-471-94054-2) Wiley.

Quality & Experiment: The Prints of John Piper (1903-92) Orde Levinson. (Illus.). 192p. 1996. 99.00 (0-85331-690-2, Pub. by Lund Humphries) Antique Collect.

Quality & GMP Auditing: Clear & Simple. James L. Vesper. LC 97-22012. (Illus.). 150p. 1997. 115.00 (1-57491-055-8) Interpharm.

Quality & Grading of Carcasses of Meat Animals. S. D. Jones. LC 97-15223. 240p. 1995. boxed set 224.95 (0-8493-5023-9, 5023) CRC Pr.

*__Quality & Inequality: A Primer on America's Schools.__ Ed. by Williamson Evers & Terry Moe. 2000. 18.95 (0-8179-9942-6) Hoover Inst Pr.

*__Quality & Internationalisation in Higher Education.__ OECD Staff. 272p. 1999. pap. 40.00 (92-64-17049-9, 89 1999 10 1 P, Pub. by Org for Econ) OECD.

Quality & Me: Lessons from an Evolving Life. Philip B. Crosby. LC 98-58073. (Illus.). 272p. 1999. 30.00 (0-7879-4702-4) Jossey-Bass.

Quality & Preservation of Fruits. N. A. Eskin. (Illus.). 176p. 1990. lib. bdg. 159.00 (0-8493-5561-3, TX612) CRC Pr.

Quality & Preservation of Vegetables. Ed. by N. A. Eskin. LC 96-6549. (Illus.). 328p. 1989. lib. bdg. 259.00 (0-8493-5560-5, SB324) CRC Pr.

Quality & Productivity for Bankers & Financial Managers. William Latzko. (Qualtiy & Reliability Ser.: Vol. 10). (Illus.). 224p. 1986. text 75.00 (0-8247-7682-8) Dekker.

Quality & Productivity in the Graphic Arts. Miles F. Southworth & Donna Southworth. LC 88-83955. 544p. 1989. 34.95 (0-933600-05-4) Graph Arts Pub.

Quality & Quality Changes in Fresh Fish. Hans H. Huss. (Fisheries Technical Papers: Vol. 348). 200p. 1995. pap. 30.00 (92-5-103507-5) Food & Agri Org UN.

Quality & Quantity: The Quest for Biological Regeneration in Twentieth Century France. William H. Schneider. (History of Medicine Ser.). (Illus.). 402p. (C). 1990. text 69.95 (0-521-37498-7) Cambridge U Pr.

*__Quality & Reliability in Analytical Chemistry.__ Hassan Y. Aboul-Enein. 2000. 79.95 (0-8493-2376-2) CRC Pr.

Quality & Reliability Methods for Primary Batteries. P. Bro & S. C. Levy. (Electrochemical Society Ser.). 302p. 1990. 179.00 (0-471-52427-1) Wiley.

Quality & Reliability of Technical Systems see Reliability Engineering: Theory & Practice

Quality & Reliability of Technical Systems: Theory, Practice & Management. A. Birolini. Tr. by C. Podaras from GER. xiii, 524p. 1994. 135.95 (0-387-50603-9) Spr-Verlag.

Quality & Reliability of Technical Systems: Theory, Practice & Management. A. Birolini. LC 94-7744. 1994. write for info. (0-387-57569-3) Spr-Verlag.

Quality & Reliability of Technical Systems: Theory, Practice & Management. 2nd ed. Alessandro Birolini. LC 97-27839. (Illus.). xiii, 502p. 1997. 129.00 (3-540-63310-3) Spr-Verlag.

Quality & Reliability of Telecommunications Infrastructure. Ed. by William Lehr. (Telecommunications Ser.). 256p. 1995. text 49.95 (0-8058-1610-0) L Erlbaum Assocs.

Quality & Statistics: Total Quality Management. Ed. by Milton J. Kowalewski, Jr. LC 94-29563. (Special Technical Pubns.: Vol. 1209). 1994. pap. 39.00 (0-8031-1872-4, STP1209) ASTM.

Quality & Treatment of Drinking Water II. Ed. by J. Hrubec & O. Hutzinger. (Handbook of Environmental Chemistry Ser.: Vol. 5, Pt. C). (Illus.). 165p. 1998. 129.00 (3-540-62574-7) Spr-Verlag.

Quality Angles & the "Tantalus" Complex: Unique Perspectives on Balance & Performance. Rick Griggs et al. 200p. (C). 1993. 24.95 (0-922530-01-7) Tantalus Bks.

Quality Around the World. LC 97-52055. x, 92p. 1997. pap. write for info. (1-56395-091-X) Am Assn Blood.

Quality Art Education: An Interpretation. 41p. 1986. pap. 4.00 (0-937652-45-8) Natl Art Ed.

Quality As a Determinant of Vegetable Prices. Frederick V. Waugh. LC 68-58635. (Columbia University. Studies in the Social Sciences: No. 312). reprint ed. 21.50 (0-404-51312-3) AMS Pr.

Quality Assessment & Assurance in Long-Term Care Facilities. Charlotte K. Eliopoulos. 97p. 1992. pap. 25.00 (1-882515-01-3) Hlth Educ Netwk.

Quality Assessment & Improvement in Long Term Care: A Continuous Process. Barbara A. Vitale & Stella M. Vengroski. LC 92-48816. (Illus.). 346p. (C). 1993. pap. text 90.00 (0-8036-8960-8) Davis Co.

Quality Assessment & Improvement in Obstetrics & Gynecology. American College of Obstetricians & Gynecologists Staff. LC 94-1230. 113p. 1994. 40.00 (0-915473-19-4) Am Coll Obstetric.

Quality Assessment, Assurance, Forms & Worksheets: Forms & Worksheets. Marguerite A. Bouvette. 94p. 1995. 23.50 (1-877735-39-6, 2223PP) Prof Prnting & Pub.

Quality Assessment for Healthcare: A Baldrige-Based Handbook. Ned Barber. LC 95-41103. 204p. 1995. pap. 29.95 (0-527-76305-5) Productivity Inc.

Quality Assessment for Primary Care Centers. 3rd rev. ed. Dale S. Benson & Jane A. Miller. (Quality Primary Care Ser.). 1993. pap. 28.00 (0-9603164-9-3) Clarian Hlth.

Quality Assessment of Television. Sakae Isikawa. LC 96-145012. 1997. 40.00 (1-86020-507-0, Pub. by U of Luton Pr) Bks Intl VA.

Quality Assessment of Textiles. K. Mahall. 1993. 107.00 (0-614-20937-4) Spr-Verlag.

Quality Assessment of Textiles: Damage Detection by Microscopy. Karl Mahall. LC 93-42572. (Illus.). 322p. 1993. 141.95 (0-387-57390-9) Spr-Verlag.

Quality Assurance. (National Cooperative Highway Research Program Report Ser.: No. 65). 42p. 1979. 5.60 (0-309-03007-2) Transport Res Bd.

Quality Assurance. Richard C. Vaughn. LC 90-33582. (Illus.). 403p. 1990. reprint ed. pap. 125.00 (0-608-00172-4, 206095400006) Bks Demand.

Quality Assurance. 2nd ed. Ed. by Fred Owen & Derek Maidment. 64p. 1996. pap. 30.00 (0-85295-372-0, 53720) Gulf Pub.

Quality Assurance: A Framework to Build On. 2nd ed. Terry Hughes & Trefor Williams. LC 95-22026. 200p. 1995. 65.00 (0-632-03904-3) Blackwell Sci.

Quality Assurance: A National Commitment: Proceedings of the Conference, Minneapolis, Minnesota, October 5-8, 1997. American Society of Civil Engineers Staff. Ed. by Rao Niyargikar & Debra Reinhart. LC 97-36203. (Illus.). 280p. 1997. pap. text 29.00 (0-7844-0292-2, 40292-2) Am Soc Civil Eng.

Quality Assurance: A Primer for Hospice Programs. National Hospice Organization, Standards & Accredi. 38p. 1989. 10.50 (0-931207-17-7) Natl Hospice.

*__Quality Assurance: ISO 9000 as A Management Tool.__ Lee Davis. LC 98-132811. 1999. 24.00 (87-16-13361-7) Mksgaard.

Quality Assurance: Its Management & Techniques. Technical Association of the Pulp & Paper Industry. LC TS0156.6.Q83. (Illus.). 599p. reprint ed. pap. 185.70 (0-8357-6341-2, 203561300096) Bks Demand.

Quality Assurance: Its Management & Techniques: a Review of 1989. Technical Association of the Pulp & Paper Industry. LC 90-10865. 750p. reprint ed. pap. 200.00 (0-8357-4228-8, 203701500002) Bks Demand.

Quality Assurance: Methods, Management, & Motivation. Ed. by Hans J. Bajaria. LC 81-50392. 260p. reprint ed. pap. 80.60 (0-608-13127-X, 202417500035) Bks Demand.

Quality Assurance: Philosophies, Methods, & Technologies. Keneth L. Arnold & Michael Holler. 1995. teacher ed. 12.21 (0-02-802334-X) Glencoe.

Quality Assurance: Philosophies, Methods & Technologies. Kenneth L. Arnold & Michael Holler. LC 94-20426. 1994. 69.12 (0-02-802333-1) Glencoe.

Quality Assurance: The Route to Efficiency & Competitiveness. 2nd ed. Lionel Stebbing. 1989. text 44.95 (0-470-21405-8) P-H.

Quality Assurance Activities for Stat Laboratories. Rita R. Miller & Joseph R. Bailey. 220p. 1996. ring bd. 60.00 (0-915274-81-7, 202671) Am Assn Clinical Chem.

Quality Assurance & Assessment in Primary Health Care. M. Roemer & C. Montoya-Aguilar. (WHO Offset Publications: No. 105). 82p. 1988. 15.00 (92-4-170105-6) World Health.

Quality Assurance & Control in the Manufacture of Metal-Clad UO2 Reactor Fuels. IAEA Staff. (Technical Reports: No. 173). (Illus.). 66p. 1976. pap. 25.00 (92-0-155076-6, IDC173, Pub. by IAEA) Bernan Associates.

Quality Assurance & Image Artifacts in Magnetic Resonance Imaging. James R. Knowles & John A. Markisz. (Illus.). 160p. 1987. 36.95 (0-316-49974-9, Little Brwn Med Div) Lppncott W & W.

Quality Assurance & NVQ. IPM Staff. (Assessment of NVQs & SVQs Ser.: No. 8). (C). 1994. 62.25 (0-08-042123-7, Pub. by IPM Hse) St Mut.

Quality Assurance & Quality Control for Waste Containment Facilities. David E. Daniel & Robert M. Koerner. (Illus.). 305p. (Orig.). (C). 1995. pap. text 95.00 (0-7881-1605-3) DIANE Pub.

*__Quality Assurance & the Law.__ Elaine Pritchard & Richard Reeves. 224p. 2000. pap. text 54.95 (0-7506-4176-2, Newnes) Buttrwrth-Heinemann.

Quality Assurance & Tolerances. G. Kirschling. (Illus.). 368p. 1991. 118.95 (0-387-53258-7) Spr-Verlag.

Quality Assurance & TQM for Analytical Laboratories. Ed. by M. Parkany. 288p. 1995. 76.00 (0-85404-760-3) CRC Pr.

Quality Assurance Compliance: Procedures for Pharmaceutical & Biotechnology Manufacturers. Ira Peine. 279p. 1994. ring bd. 199.00 (0-935184-51-1) Interpharm.

Quality Assurance Coordinator. (Career Examination Ser.: C-3741). pap. 34.95 (0-8373-3741-0) Nat Learn.

Quality Assurance Criteria Sets for Pediatric Nutrition Conditions: A Model. LC 88-72200. 1988. ring bd. 24.00 (0-88091-039-9, 0109) Am Dietetic Assn.

Quality Assurance for Activity Programs. 2nd rev. ed. Richelle N. Cunninghis & Elizabeth Best-Martini. Ed. by Joan Burlingame. (Illus.). 110p. 1996. pap. 12.00 (1-882883-23-3, 185) Idyll Arbor.

Quality Assurance for Biopharmaceuticals. Jean F. Huxsoll. 206p. 1994. 89.95 (0-471-03656-0) Wiley.

Quality Assurance for Building Design. Malcolm B. Taylor & Harry H. Hosker. LC 92-27174. (C). 1996. pap. text 116.95 (0-582-07246-8) Longman.

Quality Assurance for Clinical Radiotherapy Treatment Planning: Report of the AAPM Radiation Therapy Committee TG#53. Benedick A. Fraass et al. (Report Ser.: No. 62). 57p. 1998. 10.00 (1-888340-18-5, TG#53) AAPM.

Quality Assurance for Commercially Prepared Microbiological Culture Media: Approved Standard (1996) 2nd ed. 1996. 100.00 (1-56238-316-7, M22-A2) NCCLS.

Quality Assurance for Diagnostic Imaging. LC 88-25435. (Report Ser.: No. 99). 252p. (C). 1988. pap. text 50.00 (0-929600-00-2) NCRP Pubns.

Quality Assurance for Environmental Analysis: Method Evaluation Within the Measurements & Testing Programme (BCR) Ed. by B. Griepink et al. LC 94-40004. (Techniques & Instrumental in Analytical Chemistry Ser.: Vol. 17). 670p. 1995. 311.25 (0-444-89955-3) Elsevier.

Quality Assurance for Environmental Measurements - STP 867. Ed. by John K. Taylor & Thomas W. Stanley. LC 85-6074. (Illus.). 440p. 1985. text 50.00 (0-8031-0224-0, STP867) ASTM.

Quality Assurance for Food Processors. 474p. 1980. pap. 25.00 (0-318-22938-2) Am Inst Baking.

Quality Assurance for Home Health Care. Claire G. Meisenheimer. 288p. 1989. 77.00 (0-8342-0026-0, 20026) Aspen Pub.

Quality Assurance for Information Systems: Methods, Tools & Techniques. William E. Perry. 848p. 1993. 84.99 (0-471-58804-0, GD3470) Wiley.

Quality Assurance for Long-Term Care: Guidelines & Procedres for Monitoring Practices. Tari Vinz Miller & Marilyn Rantz. 1996. 110.00 (0-8342-0223-9) Aspen Pub.

Quality Assurance for Long-Term Care Providers: Nursing Home Management in the 1990s. William Ammentorp et al. (Human Services Guides Ser.: Vol. 64). (Illus.). 192p. (C). 1990. pap. text 18.95 (0-8039-4024-6) Sage.

Quality Assurance for Nurses. Robertson. 1992. pap. text. write for info. (0-582-20904-8, Pub. by Addison-Wesley) Longman.

Quality Assurance for Nurses. Robertson. 1994. pap. text. write for info. (0-582-22977-4, Pub. by Addison-Wesley) Longman.

Quality Assurance for Pharmacy-Prepared Sterile Products Workbook: A Multi-Media Self-Instructional Program. Ed. by Gergory A. Snyder et al. 112p. (Orig.). 1994. pap. 15.00 (1-879907-46-1) Am Soc Hlth-Syst.

Quality Assurance for Psychiatric Nursing. Anita W. Finkelman. LC 90-711. 300p. 127.00 (0-8342-0166-6, S32) Aspen Pub.

Quality Assurance for Radioactive Waste Packages. I.A.E.A. Staff. LC 96-117316. (Technical Reports: Vol. 376). 68p. 1995. pap. text 35.00 (92-0-100695-0, STI/DOC/376, Pub. by IAEA) Bernan Associates.

Quality Assurance for Textile Products. Sara J. Kadolph. 106p. 1998. teacher ed. write for info. (1-56367-149-2) Fairchild.

Quality Assurance for Textile Products. Sara J. Kadolph. LC 97-78089. (Illus.). 581p. (C). 1998. 60.00 (1-56367-144-1) Fairchild.

Quality Assurance for the Chemical & Process Industries: A Manual of Good Practices. ASQ Chemical & Process Industries Division, Chemic. 56p. (Orig.). 1987. pap. 22.00 (0-87389-035-3, T184) ASQ Qual Pr.

Quality Assurance for the Indirect Immunofluorescence Test for Autoantibodies to Nuclear Antigen (IF-ANA) Approved Guideline (1996) 1996. 75.00 (1-56238-311-6, I/LA2-A) NCCLS.

Quality Assurance for the Indirect Immunofluorescence Test for Autoantibodies to Nuclear Antigen (IF-ANA) Tentative Guideline (1993) Contrib. by Robert M. Nakamura. 1993. 75.00 (1-56238-187-3, I/LA2-T) NCCLS.

Quality Assurance for University Teaching. Ed. by Roger Ellis. LC 92-31746. 176p. (C). 1993. pap. 41.95 (0-335-19025-1) OpUniv Pr.

Quality Assurance Guidelines for Research & Development. ASQ Energy & Environmental Division Staff et al. LC 94-8907. (ASQC Briefing Ser.). 38p. 1994. 13.00 (0-87389-302-6, MB104) ASQ Qual Pr.

*__Quality Assurance Handbook for Veterinary Laboratories.__ James E. C. Bellamy & Dennis W. Olexson. (Illus.). 106p. 2000. pap. 32.95 (0-8138-0276-8) Iowa St U Pr.

Quality Assurance in Adhesive Technology. A. W. Espie et al. 120p. 1997. pap. 159.95 incl. disk (1-85573-259-9) Technomic.

Quality Assurance in Blood Banking & Its Clinical Impact. Ed. by C. T. Sibinga & P. C. Das. (Developments in Hematology & Immunology Ser.). 268p. 1984. text 78.50 (*0-89838-618-7*) Kluwer Academic.

Quality Assurance in Building Services: A One-Day Conference. BSRIA Staff. (C). 1989. 175.00 (*0-7855-4405-4*, Pub. by Build Servs Info Assn) St Mut.

Quality Assurance in Concrete Construction. 98p. 1992. 51.95 (*0-685-62958-9*, C-16BOW6) ACI.

Quality Assurance in Construction. Ed. by Institution of Civil Engineers Staff. 92p. 1990. text 42.00 (*0-7277-1536-4*, Pub. by T Telford) RCH.

Quality Assurance in Construction. 2nd ed. Brian Thorpe et al. 250p. 1996. 74.95 (*0-566-07758-2*, Pub. by Gower) Ashgate Pub Co.

Quality Assurance in Diagnostic Radiology. (Nonserial Publication). 65p. 1982. pap. text 11.00 (*92-4-154164-4*, 1150204) World Health.

Quality Assurance in Diagnostic Radiology. Joy M. McLemore. LC 80-27154. (Illus.). 237p. reprint ed. pap. 73.50 (*0-608-18271-0*, 203300200082) Bks Demand.

Quality Assurance in Dialysis. Ed. by Lee W. Henderson & Richard S. Thuma. LC 94-970. (Developments in Nephrology Ser.: Vol. 36). 272p. (C). 1994. text 161.50 (*0-7923-2723-3*) Kluwer Academic.

Quality Assurance in Dialysis. 2nd ed. L. W. Henderson & Richard S. Thuma. LC 98-39426. (Developments in Nephrology Ser.). 1998. 146.00 (*0-7923-5281-5*) Kluwer Academic.

Quality Assurance in Environmental Monitoring: Instrumental Methods. Ed. by G. Subramanian. LC 95-20634. 335p. 1995. 179.95 (*3-527-28682-9*, Wiley-VCH) Wiley.

Quality Assurance in Environmental Monitoring: Sampling & Sample Pretreatment, 2 vols. Ed. by Philippe H. Quevauviller. (Illus.). 306p. 1995. 178.00 (*3-527-28724-8*, Wiley-VCH) Wiley.

Quality Assurance in Health Care. write for info. (*0-340-55273-5*, Pub. by E A) Routldge.

Quality Assurance in Health Care: A Handbook. Ellis. 286p. 1993. pap. 59.80 (*1-56593-566-7*, 0536) Singular Publishing.

Quality Assurance in Higher Education. Ed. by Alma Craft. 238p. 1992. 79.95 (*0-7507-0070-X*, Falmer Pr) Taylor & Francis.

Quality Assurance in In-House Continuing Training: Case Studies from Europe. 220p. 1996. pap. 50.00 (*92-827-7131-8*, C295-96-528-ENC, Pub. by Comm Europ Commun) Bernan Associates.

Quality Assurance in Long-Term Care: Managing the Process. James E. Rohrer. (Learning the Continuum: AUPHA Modules for Management Education Ser.). (Illus.). 48p. (Orig.). (C). 1989. pap. text 20.00 (*0-910591-21-0*) AUPHA Pr.

Quality Assurance in Marketing: Setting Action Standards for Better Results. Keith Sparling. LC 94-4258. (McGraw-Hill Marketing for Professionals Ser.). 1994. write for info. (*0-07-707876-4*) McGraw.

Quality Assurance in Microbiology & Biotechnology Research. Cross & Smiecinsk. 128p. 1994. boxed set 73.95 (*0-8493-8693-4*) CRC Pr.

Quality Assurance in Nuclear Medicine. (Nonserial Publication). 72p. 1982. pap. text 11.00 (*92-4-154165-2*, 1150203) World Health.

Quality Assurance in Nuclear Power Plants, Vol. 6. Ron Matfield. (Ispra Courses on Nuclear Engineering & Technology Ser.). xiv, 306p. 1984. text 184.00 (*3-7186-0151-6*) Gordon & Breach.

Quality Assurance in Pavement Construction, Vol. STP 709. 44p. 1980. pap. 9.00 (*0-8031-0769-2*, STP709) ASTM.

Quality Assurance in Prehospital Care. National Association of EMS Physicians Staff. Ed. by Robert A. Swor et al. LC 92-49237. (Illus.). 272p. (gr. 13). 1992. pap. text 19.95 (*0-8016-6579-5*, 06579) Mosby Inc.

Quality Assurance in Radiotherapy. WHO Staff. 52p. 1988. 11.00 (*92-4-154224-1*) World Health.

Quality Assurance in Radiotherapy Physics: Proceedings of an American College of Medical Physics Symposium, May 1991. Ed. by George Starkschall & John Horton. (Illus.). 387p. (Orig.). (C). 1991. pap. text 28.95 (*0-944838-21-9*) Med Physics Pub.

Quality Assurance in Rehabilitation Nursing: A Practical Guide. Adrianne E. Avillion & Barbara B. Mirgon. 206p. (C). 1989. 59.00 (*0-8342-0053-8*, 20053) Aspen Pub.

Quality Assurance in Research & Development. George Roberts. (Industrial Engineering Ser.: Vol. 8). (Illus.). 152p. 1983. text 75.00 (*0-8247-7071-4*) Dekker.

Quality Assurance in Social Work: A Handbook. write for info. (*0-340-62508-2*, Pub. by E A) Routldge.

Quality Assurance in Social Work: An Introductory Workbook. write for info. (*0-340-62509-0*, Pub. by E A) Routldge.

Quality Assurance in Social Work: Handbook/Workbook Pack. write for info. (*0-340-67669-8*, Pub. by E A) Routldge.

Quality Assurance in the Fish Industry: Proceedings of an International Conference, Copenhagen, Denmark, 26-30 August 1991. Ed. by Hans H. Huss et al. LC 92-24363. 588p. 1992. 254.50 (*0-444-89077-7*) Elsevier.

Quality Assurance in the Hospitality Industry. Stephen S. Hall. 304p. 1990. text 32.95 (*0-527-91653-6*, 916536) Productivity Inc.

***Quality Assurance in the Knitting Industry.** J. M. Kelly. 224p. 2000. text 135.00 (*1-85573-452-4*, Pub. by Woodhead Pubng) Am Educ Systs.

Quality Assurance in Transfusion Medicine, Vol. I. M. J. Seghatchian. 544p. 1992. 295.00 (*0-8493-4938-9*, RM171, CRC Reprint) Franklin.

Quality Assurance in Transfusion Medicine: Methodological Advances & Clinical Aspects, Vol. 2. M. J. Seghatchian & Gail A. Rock. LC 92-9276. 528p. 1993. 288.00 (*0-8493-4939-7*, RM171) Franklin.

Quality Assurance in Tropical Fruit Processing. Ahmed Omar Askar. LC 93-9518. (Laboratory Ser.). 1993. 114.95 (*0-387-55766-0*) Spr-Verlag.

Quality Assurance in Water Quality Monitoring. James E. Gaskin. (Illus.). 325p. (Orig.). 1993. pap. 97.45 (*0-660-15183-9*, Pub. by Canadian Govt Pub) Accents Pubns.

Quality Assurance Integrated Training Packages: A Manual. (Technical Reports: No. 340). 121p. 1992. pap. 50.00 (*92-0-103692-2*, STI/DOC/340, Pub. by IAEA) Bernan Associates.

Quality Assurance Management. Michael J. Fox. LC 92-40417. 1993. mass mkt. 75.00 (*0-412-46790-9*) Chapman & Hall.

Quality Assurance Management. 2nd ed. M. J. Fox. (Illus.). 408p. 1995. pap. 70.00 (*0-412-63660-3*) Thomson Learn.

Quality Assurance Manual for Industrial Hygiene Chemistry. American Industrial Hygiene Association Staff. 74p. 1988. 40.00 (*0-932627-32-3*) Am Indus Hygiene.

Quality Assurance Nurse. Jack Rudman. (Career Examination Ser.: C-3742). 1994. pap. 29.95 (*0-8373-3742-9*) Nat Learn.

Quality Assurance of Chemical Measurements. John K. Taylor. 352p. 1987. lib. bdg. 79.95 (*0-87371-097-5*, L097) Lewis Pubs.

Quality Assurance of Food. John E. Stauffer. 304p. 1988. 57.00 (*0-917678-23-0*) Food & Nut Pr.

Quality Assurance of Pharmaceuticals: A Compendium of Guidelines & Related Materials, Vol. 1. WHO Staff. LC 98-130399. 1997. write for info. (*92-4-154504-6*) World Health.

Quality Assurance of Polymeric Materials & Products - STP 846. Ed. by Francis T. Greene et al. LC 83-73514. (Illus.). 145p. 1985. pap. text 24.00 (*0-8031-0408-1*, STP846) ASTM.

Quality Assurance of Welded Construction. 2nd ed. N. T. Burgess. 214p. 1989. mass mkt. 87.50 (*1-85166-274-X*) Elsevier.

Quality Assurance Policies & Procedures for Ambulatory Health Care. Judith M. Bulau. 368p. 1990. 150.00 (*0-8342-0138-0*, 20138) Aspen Pub.

Quality Assurance Practices, Course 31. (Illus.). 272p. 1979. ring bd. 95.00 (*0-87683-131-5*) GP Courseware.

Quality Assurance Principles for Analytical Laboratories. F. M. Garfield. (JPN.). 188p. 1997. pap. 150.00 (*0-935584-63-3*) AOAC Intl.

Quality Assurance Principles for Analytical Laboratories. 2nd ed. F. M. Garfield. (SPA.). 193p. 1993. pap. 102.00 (*0-935584-50-1*) AOAC Intl.

Quality Assurance Principles for Analytical Laboratories. 2nd ed. Frederick M. Garfield. LC 91-22409. (Illus.). 192p. (Orig.). 1991. pap. 65.00 (*0-935584-46-3*) AOAC Intl.

Quality Assurance Program on Stereotactic Radiosurgery: Report From a Quality Assurance Task Group. Gunther H. Hartmann et al. LC 95-32580. 96p. 1995. 44.95 (*3-540-59199-0*) Spr-Verlag.

Quality Assurance, Quality Control & Inspection Handbook. 5th ed. C. L. Carter, Jr. LC 78-78394. (Illus.). 212p. 1991. pap. 16.50 (*1-879519-09-7*) C L Carter.

Quality Assurance Resource Manual for Nuclear Medicine. Ed. by Susan Gilbert et al. LC 89-21640. 132p. 1990. student ed. 18.00 (*0-932004-35-0*) Soc Nuclear Med.

Quality Assurance SOPs for GLP Compliance. Robert DeWoskin. 1994. ring bd. 247.00 (*0-935184-63-5*) Interpharm.

Quality Assurance Specialist Trainee. (Career Examination Ser.: C-3421). 1994. pap. 29.95 (*0-8373-3421-7*) Nat Learn.

Quality Assurance System Development Reviews. William E. Perry. (Illus.). 1981. pap. 24.95 (*0-318-20493-2*) Quality Assurance.

***Quality Assurance Through Credentialing Vol. 1: Global Perspectives.** Ed. by Ann H. Cary & Chris Wharton. 79p. 1999. write for info. (*1-55810-146-2*) Am Nurses Pub.

***Quality Assurance Through Credentialing Vol. 2: Concepts, Issues, & Trends.** Ed. by Ann H. Cary & Chris Wharton. 85p. 1999. write for info. (*1-55810-147-0*) Am Nurses Pub.

Quality Assurance Through Integration of Manufacturing Processes & Systems. Ed. by A. R. Thangaraj et al. (PED Ser.: Vol. 56). 196p. 1992. 52.50 (*0-7918-1059-3*, G00703) ASME.

Quality Assurance with Care Planning. Mattie Locke. 290p. (C). 1992. 42.00 (*1-877735-36-1*, 2185PP) Prof Prnting & Pub.

Quality at Risk: Are Employee Participation Programs in Jeopardy? Edward E. Potter. 72p. 1991. pap. 10.00 (*0-614-06154-7*, 2034-PP-4040) EPF.

Quality at Work: A Personal Guide to Professional Standards. Diane Bone & Rick Griggs. LC 88-72252. (Fifty-Minute Ser.). (Illus.). 88p. (Orig.). 1989. pap. 10.95 (*0-931961-72-6*) Crisp Pubns.

Quality at Work in Research & Development. George J. Kidd. 160p. 1992. text 29.95 (*0-527-91655-2*, 916552) Productivity Inc.

Quality Attributes & Their Measurement in Meat, Poultry & Fish Products: Advances in Meat Research, Vol. 9. T. R. Dutson & A. M. Pearson. 505p. 1995. 239.00 (*0-8342-1305-2*) Aspen Pub.

Quality Attributes of Muscle Foods. Youling L. Xiong et al. LC 99-20233. (C). 1999. text. write for info. (*0-306-46116-1*, Kluwer Plenum) Kluwer Academic.

***Quality Audit for ISO 9001: 2000: A Practical Guide.** David Wealleans. LC 99-40394. 2000. 86.95 (*0-566-08245-4*, Pub. by Gower) Ashgate Pub Co.

Quality Audit Handbook. Ed. by J. P. Russell. LC 96-47516. 218p. 1997. 45.00 (*0-87389-374-3*, H0939) ASQ Qual Pr.

***Quality Audit Handbook.** 2nd ed. ASQ Quality Audit Divison Staff. LC 99-44972. 320p. 2000. 60.00 (*0-87389-460-X*) ASQ Qual Pr.

Quality Audit Systems for Primary Care Centers. 3rd rev. ed. Dale S. Benson & William R. Van Osdol. (Quality Primary Care Ser.). x, 451p. 1993. pap. 85.00 (*1-884742-01-7*) Clarian Hlth.

Quality Auditors Handbook. Don L. Freeman. LC 97-13448. 256p. (C). 1997. 55.00 (*0-13-268202-8*) P-H.

Quality Audits for Improved Performance. 2nd ed. Dennis R. Arter. LC 93-46980. 119p. 1994. 32.00 (*0-87389-263-1*, H0844) ASQ Qual Pr.

Quality Based Safety Process. Thomas R. Krause. 304p. 1995. text 76.95 (*0-442-01671-9*, VNR) Wiley.

Quality Begins with Me Johnson A. Edosomwan. LC 99-163982. 211p. 1998. write for info. (*1-891034-12-X*) Contin Improve.

Quality Business: Quality Issues & Smaller Firms. Ed. by Julian North & Robert Blackburn. LC 98-133987. 224p. (C). 1998. 90.00 (*0-415-14608-9*) Routledge.

Quality by Experimental Design. 2nd expanded rev. ed. Thomas B. Barker. LC 94-18956. (Quality & Reliability Ser.: Vol. 43). (Illus.). 504p. 1994. text 65.00 (*0-8247-8910-5*) Dekker.

Quality Care: Prescription for Injecting Quality into Health Care Systems. Marlene Caroselli. LC 97-163014. (Illus.). 304p. 1997. boxed set 69.95 (*1-57444-043-8*) St Lucie Pr.

Quality Care: Prescription for Injecting Quality into Healthcare Systems. Marlene Caroselli & Linda Edison. 1998. lib. bdg., teacher ed. 39.95 (*1-57444-138-8*, SL1388) St Lucie Pr.

Quality Care for Elderly People. Ed. by Peter P. Mayer et al. LC 97-65432. (Illus.). 256p. 1997. text 55.00 (*0-412-61830-3*, Pub. by E A) OUP.

Quality Care for Tough Kids: Studies of the Maintenance of Subsidized Foster Placements in the Casey Family Program. James A. Walsh & Roberta A. Walsh. 133p. 1990. pap. 9.50 (*0-87868-372-0*) Child Welfare.

Quality Care in Geriatric Settings. Ed. by Paul R. Katz et al. (Series on Advances in Long-Term Care). 288p. 1995. 46.95 (*0-8261-6832-9*) Springer Pub.

Quality Care in Mental Health: Assuring the Best Clinical Services. Robert H. Woody. LC 90-15607. (Social & Behavioral Sciences Ser.). 208p. 1991. 37.95 (*1-55542-319-1*) Jossey-Bass.

Quality Care in the Nursing Home. John Morris et al. LC 96-17375. 900p. (gr. 13). 1996. text 54.95 (*0-8151-4222-6*, 26266) Mosby Inc.

***Quality Care Management of the Elderly: A Cost Effective Approach.** Ed. by Center for Applied Gerontology Staff. 97p. 2000. pap. text 29.95 (*0-9677434-1-9*) Ctr for Applied Gerontology.

Quality, Careers & Training in Educational & Social Research. Caroline H. Persell. LC 76-9294. (Illus.). 321p. 1976. pap. text 22.95 (*0-930390-31-8*) Gen Hall.

Quality-Centered Strategic Planning: A Step-by-Step Guide. John R. Dew. LC 97-505. 222p. 1997. 42.50 (*0-527-76308-X*) Productivity Inc.

Quality Centered/Team-Focused Management. John Hodge-Williams et al. LC 97-52053. 150p. 1998. pap. 18.95 (*0-87868-636-3*, 6363) Child Welfare.

Quality Checklist for Education Consumers: Thirty Tools to Improve Colorado Schools Without New Laws or New Money. John K. Andrews, Jr. (Issue Papers: No. 2-90). 9p. 1990. pap. text 8.00 (*1-57655-035-4*) Independ Inst.

Quality Circle Management: The Human Side of Quality. Harry Katzan, Jr. (Illus.). 168p. 1989. 19.95 (*0-8306-3386-3*) McGraw-Hill Prof.

Quality Circle Management: The Human Side of Quality. Harry Katzan, Jr. (Illus.). 180p. 1988. 24.95 (*0-89433-326-7*, 8260) Petrocelli.

***Quality Circle Time in the Secondary School: A Handbook of Good Practice.** Jenny Mosley. (Illus.). 160p. 1999. pap. 29.95 (*1-85346-616-6*) David Fulton.

Quality Circles. (Open Learning for Supervisory Management Ser.). 1986. pap. text 19.50 (*0-08-034170-5*, Pergamon Pr) Elsevier.

Quality Circles. (Open Learning for Supervisory Management Ser.). 1986. pap. text 19.50 (*0-08-070049-7*, Pergamon Pr) Elsevier.

Quality Circles: A Practical Guide. 2nd ed. Mike Robson. 256p. 1988. text 69.95 (*0-566-02748-8*, Pub. by Gower) Ashgate Pub Co.

Quality Circles: An Approach to Productivity Improvement. Price Gibson. (Studies in Productivity: Highlights of the Literature Ser.: Vol. 26). 79p. 1982. pap. 55.00 (*0-08-029507-X*) Work in Amer.

Quality Circles: Applications in Vocational Education. Russell F. Lloyd & Virgil R. Rehg. 47p. 1983. 4.95 (*0-318-22183-7*, IN249) Ctr Educ Trng Employ.

Quality Circles: Changing Images of People at Work. William L. Mohr & Harriet Mohr. LC 83-5970. (Illus.). 256p. 1983. write for info. (*0-201-05207-5*) Addison-Wesley.

Quality Circles: One Approach to Productivity Improvement. Price Gibson. (Work in America Institute Studies in Productivity). 1982. pap. 35.00 (*0-685-06117-5*, Pergamon Pr) Elsevier.

Quality Circles Data Bank. Cathy Kramer. 44.95 (*0-317-07128-9*) IAQC Pr.

Quality Circles in Action. Mike Robson. LC 84-4095. 176p. 1984. text 65.95 (*0-566-02433-0*, Pub. by Gower) Ashgate Pub Co.

Quality Circles in Health Care Facilities. Alvin Goldberg & C. Carl Pegels. 193p. 1984. 75.00 (*0-89443-570-1*) Aspen Pub.

Quality Circles Members. Robson. 1982. student ed. 13.95 (*0-566-02344-X*) Ashgate Pub Co.

Quality Classroom Manager. Bob Norton. LC 95-22715. 138p. 1995. 28.95 (*0-89503-131-0*) Baywood Pub.

Quality Clip Art Collection. 1993. ring bd. 59.00 (*0-929321-08-1*) WEKA Pub.

***Quality Concealed.** Betty Briggs. (Illus.). 203p. 1999. pap. 9.95 (*0-9656307-1-4*, Pub. by Sunrise Selections) Evans Bk Dist.

Quality Concepts, 1991: A National Forum on Total Quality Management. Ed. by A. Hamood. (Illus.). 562p. 1991. 50.00 (*1-56378-002-X*) ESD.

Quality Concrete. rev. ed. Thomas A. Hoerner & W. Forrest Bear. (Illus.). 36p. 1971. pap. text 4.45 (*0-913163-00-7*, 164) Hobar Pubns.

Quality Conformance & Qualification of Microelectronic Packages & Interconnects. Michael G. Pecht. Ed. by John Evans et al. LC 93-9709. 461p. 1994. pap. 110.00 (*0-471-59436-9*) Wiley.

Quality Conspiracy. David Straker. LC 97-28409. 65p. 1997. 43.95 (*0-566-07957-7*, Pub. by Gower) Ashgate Pub Co.

Quality Control. (Open Learning for Supervisory Management Ser.). 1986. pap. text 19.50 (*0-08-034167-5*, Pergamon Pr) Elsevier.

Quality Control. (Open Learning for Supervisory Management Ser.). 1987. pap. text 19.50 (*0-08-070040-3*, Pergamon Pr) Elsevier.

Quality Control. 5th ed. Dale H. Besterfield. LC 97-9443. 519p. (C). 1997. pap. 88.00 (*0-13-632571-8*) P-H.

Quality Control. 6th ed. 480p. (C). 2000. 78.67 incl. cd-rom (*0-13-022668-4*) P-H.

***Quality Control.** 6th ed. (C). 2000. write for info. (*0-13-026484-9*) P-H.

Quality Control: A System Approach. Webb & Sorbrowski. 1997. text 52.95 (*0-8273-6443-1*) Delmar.

Quality Control: An Annotated Bibliography Through 1988. Carol Krismann. 500p. 1990. lib. bdg. 85.00 (*0-527-91659-5*, 916595) Productivity Inc.

Quality Control: Principles & Practice in the Microbiology Laboratory. Ed. by J. J. Snell et al. (Public Health Laboratory Service Publication). (Illus.). 172p. (C). 1992. pap. text 27.95 (*0-521-43983-3*) Cambridge U Pr.

Quality Control Advisor & GC Advisor. Lawrence H. Keith. 20p. 1991. lib. bdg. 125.00 (*0-87371-347-8*, L347) Lewis Pubs.

Quality Control & Acceptance of Superpave-Designed Hot Mix Asphalt. Ronald J. Cominsky et al. LC 98-60936. (NCHRP Report Ser.). 209p. 1998. 51.00 (*0-309-06269-1*, NR409) Natl Acad Pr.

Quality Control & Assurance in Advanced Surface Engineering. Ed. by K. N. Stafford & C. Subramanian. (Illus.). 232p. 1997. 90.00 (*1-86125-037-1*, Pub. by Inst Materials) Ashgate Pub Co.

Quality Control & Design of Experiments. Towers. (Mechanical Technology Ser.). 1997. text 46.95 (*0-8273-6064-9*) Delmar.

Quality Control & Industrial Statistics. 5th ed. Acheson J. Duncan. 1125p. (C). 1986. text 61.00 (*0-256-03535-0*, Irwn McGrw-H) McGrw-H Hghr Educ.

Quality Control & Quality Assurance for Seafood: A Conference: May 16-18, 1993 Newport, Oregon. Ed. by Gilbert Sylvia et al. 1994. pap. 15.00 (*1-881826-08-2*) OR Sea Grant.

Quality Control & Reliability: Handbook of Statistics. Ed. by P. R. Krishnaiah & C. R. Rao. 504p. 1988. 190.00 (*0-444-70290-3*, North Holland) Elsevier.

Quality Control & Reliability: Proceedings IASTED Symposium, Los Angeles, U. S. A., June 1-3, 1987. Ed. by M. H. Hamza. 108p. 1987. 45.00 (*0-88986-114-5*, 117) Acta Pr.

Quality Control Audit: A Management Evaluation Tool. Charles E. Mills. 309p. 1989. 57.00 (*0-07-042428-4*) McGraw.

Quality Control Chart. Jack Prins. LC 92-37808. (Six Sigma Research Institute Ser.). 1993. 295.95 (*0-201-63403-1*) Addison-Wesley.

Quality Control Circles at Work: Cases from Japan's Manufacturing & Service Sectors. Intro. by Kaoru Ishikawa. (Illus.). 200p. 1984. text 27.00 (*92-833-1073-X*, 310730); pap. text 22.00 (*92-833-1074-8*) Productivity Inc.

Quality Control for Food & Agricultural Products see Analysis & Control Methods for Food & Agricultural Products

Quality Control for Foods & Agricultural Products: General Principles & Legal Aspects. Ed. by J. L. Multon. LC 94-39865. (Analysis & Control Methods for Foods & Agricultural Products Ser.). (Illus.). 300p. 1995. 125.00 (*1-56081-698-8*, Wiley-VCH) Wiley.

Quality Control for Management. Kenneth Kivenko. LC 83-26928. 324p. 1984. 59.95 (*0-13-745217-9*, Busn) P-H.

Quality Control for Operators & Foremen. K. S. Krishnamoorthi. (Statistical Quality Control Ser.). (Illus.). 100p. 1989. pap. 27.00 (*0-87389-048-5*, H0560) ASQ Qual Pr.

Quality Control for Plastics: How to Set up & Run a Quality Program in a Plastics Processing Facility. rev. ed. William J. Tobin et al. 150p. 1992. reprint ed. pap. 55.00 (*0-938648-26-8*) T-C Pr CA.

Quality Control for Profit. 3rd expanded rev. ed. Ed. by Ronald H. Lester et al. (Illus.). 592p. 1992. text 115.00 (*0-8247-8658-0*) Dekker.

Quality Control in Analytical Chemistry. 2nd ed. G. Kateman & Lutgarde M. Buydens. LC 93-12519. (Chemical Analysis Ser.: Vol. 60). 336p. 1993. 79.95 (*0-471-55777-3*) Wiley.

An Asterisk (*) at the beginning of an entry indicates that the title is appearing for the first time.

Quality Control in Diagnostic Imaging: A Quality Control Cookbook. Joel E. Gray et al. 249p. 1983. 84.00 (*0-8391-1681-0*) Aspen Pub.

Quality Control in Japan. Ed. by Kageyu Noro. (Ergonomics Special Issue Ser.: Vol. 27, No. 7). 102p. 1984. pap. 20.00 (*0-85066-992-8*) Taylor & Francis.

Quality Control in Mortgage Lending Correspondence Course. rev. ed. 210p. 1998. pap. 270.00 (*1-57599-040-7*) Mortgage Bankers.

Quality Control in Pharmaceutical Analysis: Separation Methods. Ed. by Z. Deyl. 252p. 1997. 187.00 (*0-444-82876-1*) Elsevier.

Quality Control in Remedial Site Investigation: Hazardous & Industrial Solid Waste Testing, Vol. 5. Ed. by Cary L. Perket. LC 86-25873. (Special Technical Publication Ser.: No. 925). (Illus.). 227p. 1986. text 29.00 (*0-8031-0451-0*, STP925) ASTM.

Quality Control in the Food Industry, 4 vols., Vol. 3. 2nd ed. S. M. Herschdoerfer. (Food Science & Technology Ser.). 1987. text 157.00 (*0-12-343003-8*) Acad Pr.

Quality Control in the Food Industry, 4 vols., Vol. 4. 2nd ed. S. M. Herschdoerfer. (Food Science & Technology Ser.). 512p. 1988. text 157.00 (*0-12-343004-6*) Acad Pr.

Quality Control in the Soviet Food-Processing Industry. Alexander Kruglikov. Ed. by Erika D. Nobel. Tr. by Linda Morris from RUS. (Illus.). 83p. (Orig.). 1988. pap. text 75.00 (*1-55831-087-8*) Delphic Associates.

Quality Control Inspector (U. S. P. S.) Jack Rudman. (Career Examination Ser.: C-2458). 1994. pap. 39.95 (*0-8373-2458-0*) Nat Learn.

Quality Control Investigator. Jack Rudman. (Career Examination Ser.: C-2137). 1994. pap. 34.95 (*0-8373-2137-9*) Nat Learn.

Quality Control Manual for Citrus Processing Plants, Vol. 1. Ed. by James E. Redd & Charles M. Hendrix. 250p. 1986. 58.00 (*0-614-25176-1*) AgScience.

Quality Control Manual for Citrus Processing Plants: Flavor, Vol. 111. unabridged ed. James B. Redd et al. (Illus.). 338p. 1996. text 78.00 (*0-9631397-4-6*) AgScience.

Quality Control Manual for Citrus Processing Plants: Processing & Operating Procedures, Blending Techniques, Formulating, Citrus Mathematics & Costs, Vol. 2. James B. Redd et al. LC 91-42295. 290p. (C). 1992. text 68.00 (*0-9631397-0-3*) AgScience.

Quality Control Manual for Injection Molding. William J. Tobin. 85p. 1990. reprint ed. pap. 42.00 (*0-938648-13-6*, 0909) T-C Pr CA.

Quality Control Manual for Local CPA Firms. Robert D. Goldstein et al. 471p. 1990. text 99.00 (*1-878375-13-X*) Panel Pubs.

Quality Control Manual for Local CPA Firms: 1991 Update. Robert D. Goldstein et al. 250p. 1991. 79.00 (*1-878375-71-7*) Panel Pubs.

Quality Control of Cloth Dimensions & the Shrinkage of Yarns & Fabrics. Ed. by Bruce Wira. 1977. 40.00 (*0-7855-7313-5*) St Mut.

Quality Control of Concrete On-Site - Users Manual. David Whiting et al. (SHRP Ser.: C-414). (Illus.). 51p. (C). 1994. pap. text 55.00 (*0-309-05818-X*, PC414) Natl Res Coun.

Quality Control of Concrete Structures: Proceedings of the Second International Rilem/Ceb Symposium. Ed. by L. Taerwe & H. Lambotte. (Rilem Proceedings Ser.). (Illus.). 592p. (C). 1991. 145.00 (*0-419-15800-6*, E & FN Spon) Routledge.

Quality Control of Concrete Structures: Proceedings of the Second International Symposium. L. Taerwe & H. Lambotte. 592p. 1991. 99.95 (*0-412-43220-X*) Chapman & Hall.

Quality Control of Diabetes Care & Chronic Compications in Young People after St. Vincent & Kos: 4th International Workshop "Diabetic Angiopathy in Children (DAC)", Berlin, September 4 - 6, 1997. Ed. by Thomas Danne & Bruno Weber. (Hormone Research Ser.: Vol. 50, Suppl. 1). (Illus.). vi, 108p. 1998. pap. 48.75 (*3-8055-6720-0*) S Karger.

Quality Control of Electronic Images. Don M. Avedon. 70p. 1997. per. 79.00 (*0-89258-309-6*, C137) Assn Inform & Image Mgmt.

***Quality Control of Home Schooling in Pennsylvania.** Steven A. Melnick. Ed. by Diane E. Shoop. 32p. 1999. pap. 20.00 (*1-58036-137-4*) Penn State Data Ctr.

Quality Control of Pharmaceutical Preparations. (Technical Report Ser.: No. 249). 35p. 1962. pap. text 3.00 (*92-4-120249-1*) World Health.

Quality Control of Wastewater for Irrigated Crop Production. (Water Reports: No. 10). 86p. 1997. pap. 10.00 (*92-5-103994-1*, F39941, Pub. by FAO) Bernan Associates.

Quality Control Plan for Loan Origination Operations, Vol. 1. California MBA Staff. (C). 1997. ring bd. 100.00 (*1-57599-018-0*, Real Est Fin Pr) Mortgage Bankers.

Quality Control Plan for Loan Servicing Operations, Vol. 2. California MBA Staff. 1997. ring bd. 100.00 (*1-57599-017-2*, Real Est Fin Pr) Mortgage Bankers.

Quality Control, Quality Assurance: Manual for Food & Nutrition Services. Kathleen Ruf. LC 88-22662. 418p. 1989. 220.00 (*0-87189-793-8*) Aspen Pub.

Quality Control, Reliability, & Engineering Design. Dhillon. (Industrial Engineering Ser.: Vol. 10). (Illus.). 312p. 1985. text 135.00 (*0-8247-7278-4*) Dekker.

Quality Control Specialist. Jack Rudman. (Career Examination Ser.: C-1618). 1994. pap. 34.95 (*0-8373-1618-9*) Nat Learn.

Quality Control Technician-Inspector Training Manual. 235p. 1988. 35.00 (*0-318-35227-3*, TM-101) P-PCI.

Quality Control Testing of Contagious Bovine Pleuropneumonia Live Attenuated Vaccine. J. Litamoi et al. LC 97-204943. (Animal Production & Health Papers: No. 128). 53p. 1996. pap. 11.00 (*92-5-103796-5*, F37965, Pub. by FAO) Bernan Associates.

Quality Control Testing of Rinderpest Cell Culture Vaccine - Standard Operating Procedure. M. Rweyemamu et al. LC 95-131051. (Animal Production & Health Papers: No. 118). 112p. 1994. pap. 15.00 (*92-5-103444-3*, F34443, Pub. by FAO) Bernan Associates.

Quality Cooking: Cookbook. 1988. pap. 13.25 (*0-89137-448-5*) Quality Pubns.

Quality Costing. B. G. Dale & J. J. Plunkett. (Illus.). 192p. 1991. pap. 54.95 (*0-442-31369-1*) Chapman & Hall.

***Quality Costing.** 3rd ed. B. G. Dale & James J. Plunkett. LC 99-34483. 1999. 87.95 (*0-566-08260-8*, Pub. by Gower) Ashgate Pub Co.

Quality Costs: Ideas & Applications, Vol. I. 2nd ed. ASQ Quality Costs Committee. Ed. by Andrew F. Grimm. 592p. 1987. pap. 54.00 (*0-87389-046-9*, H0565) ASQ Qual Pr.

Quality Costs: Ideas & Applications, Vol. 2. ASQ Quality Costs Committee. Ed. by Jack Campanella. (Illus.). 495p. 1989. 54.00 (*0-87389-047-7*, H0569) ASQ Qual Pr.

Quality Counts: Managing for Better Standards in Social & Community Care. Des Kelly & Bridget Warr. 224p. 1992. pap. text 19.95 (*1-871177-21-9*, Pub. by Whiting & Birch) Paul & Co Pubs.

Quality Criteria for Water Reuse. National Research Council (U. S.), Panel on Altern. LC 82-61430. (Illus.). 153p. reprint ed. pap. 47.50 (*0-8357-6815-5*, 203549800095) Bks Demand.

Quality Customer Service: A Positive Guide to Superior Service. 3rd rev. ed. William Martin. Ed. by Michael Crisp. LC 92-82933. (Fifty-Minute Ser.). 89p. (Orig.). 1993. pap. 10.95 (*1-56052-203-8*) Crisp Pubns.

Quality Czech Mushroom Recipes. Ed. by Melinda Bradnan. (Illus.). 160p. 1999. spiral bd. 6.95 (*1-57216-070-5*) Penfield.

Quality Depends on You: 7 Simple Things You Can Do for Your Company & Your Career. Ed. by Dartnell Corp. Staff. LC 96-83847. (Illus.). 269p. 1996. pap. 18.95 (*0-85013-251-7*) Dartnell Corp.

Quality Determinants of Mammography. 1995. lib. bdg. 251.95 (*0-8490-6845-2*) Gordon Pr.

Quality Determinants of Mammography: Clinical Practice Guideline. Lawrence W. Bassett & R. Edward Hendrick. (Illus.). 170p. (Orig.). (C). 1995. pap. text 45.00 (*0-7881-0782-8*) DIANE Pub.

Quality Determinants of Mammography, Clinical Practice Guideline, No. 13. Lawrence W. Bassett. 184p. 1994. per. 7.00 (*0-16-045303-8*) USGPO.

Quality Documentation for Long-Term Care: A Nursing Diagnosis Approach. Marilyn Rantz & Tari V. Miller. 250p. ring bd. 120.00 (*0-8342-0384-7*, S75) Aspen Pub.

Quality-Driven Designs: Thirty-Six Activities to Reinforce TQM Concepts. Marlene Caroselli. LC 92-60880. 120p. 1992. ring bd. 89.95 (*0-88390-061-0*, Pfffr & Co) Jossey-Bass.

***Quality Dumpling Recipes.** Melinda Bradnan. Ed. by Dorothy Crum. 120p. 2000. spiral bd. 6.95 (*1-57216-071-3*) Penfield.

Quality Education. Gray Rinehart. (Illus.). 329p. 1993. text 21.95 (*0-87389-184-8*, Irwn Prfssnl) McGraw-Hill Prof.

Quality Education at No Extra Cost. Gene Koskey. LC 97-93990. 250p. 1997. pap. 14.95 (*0-9656757-1-8*) Genteel Pubs.

Quality Education Challenge. Carolyn J. Downey et al. LC 94-5964. (Total Quality Education for the World's Best Schools Ser.: Vol. 1). 152p. 1994. pap. 21.95 (*0-8039-6129-4*) Corwin Pr.

Quality Education for All: Community-Oriented Approaches. H. Dean Nielsen & William K. Cummings. Ed. by Edward Beauchamp. LC 97-1995. (Reference Books in International Education, Vol. 3B, Reference Library of Social Science: Vol. 38). (Illus.). 288p. 1997. text 72.00 (*0-8153-2378-6*, SS1105) Garland.

Quality Education for Less Money. Louis R. Meeth. LC 73-18502. (Jossey-Bass Higher Education Ser.). 224p. reprint ed. pap. 69.50 (*0-608-14791-5*, 202566300045) Bks Demand.

Quality Education in the Early Years. Lesley Abbott & Rosemary Rodger. LC 94-16355. 224p. 1994. 98.95 (*0-335-19231-9*); pap. 22.95 (*0-335-19230-0*) OpUniv Pr.

Quality Electric Lamps. 2nd rev. ed. (Illus.). 188p. 1996. 39.95 (*0-89538-009-9*) L-W Inc.

***Quality Electronic Design: Proceedings International Symposium, 2000, San Jose, California.** LC 00-69220. 524p. 2000. 110.00 (*0-7695-0525-2*) IEEE Comp Soc.

***Quality Engineering Handbook.** Thomas Pyzdek. LC 99-52010. (Quality & Reliability Ser.). 1999. write for info. (*0-8247-0365-0*) Dekker.

Quality Engineering Handbook. Ed. by Thomas Pyzdek & Roger W. Berger. (Quality & Reliability Ser.: Vol. 29). (Illus.). 640p. 1991. text 99.75 (*0-8247-8132-5*, H0603) Dekker.

Quality Engineering in Production Systems. Genichi Taguchi et al. (Industrial Engineering & Management Science Ser.). 192p. (C). 1988. 86.25 (*0-07-062830-0*) McGraw.

Quality Engineering Statistics. Robert A. Dovich. 111p. 1992. 25.00 (*0-87389-141-4*, H0679) ASQ Qual Pr.

Quality Engineering Using Robust Design. Madhav S. Phadke. 250p. 1995. 77.00 (*0-13-745167-9*) P-H.

Quality Environments: Developmentally Appropriate Experiences for Young Children. Ed. by Mac H. Brown. 109p. (Orig.). (C). 1988. pap. text 6.80 (*0-87563-321-8*) Stipes.

***Quality ESL Programs: An Administrator's Guide.** Judith Simons & Mark Connelly. (Illus.). 256p. 2000. 29.95 (*0-8108-3757-9*) Scarecrow.

Quality Evaluation of Dental Restorations. Ed. by Kenneth J. Anusavice. (Illus.). 424p. 1989. text 106.00 (*0-86715-202-8*) Quint Pub Co.

Quality, Evidence, & Effectiveness in Health Promotion. John K. Davies & Gordon MacDonald. LC 98-22995. 240p. (C). 1998. pap. 24.99 (*0-415-17967-X*) Routledge.

Quality, Evidence, & Effectiveness in Health Promotion. John K. Davies & Gordon MacDonald. LC 98-22995. (Illus.). 248p. (C). 1998. 85.00 (*0-415-17966-1*) Routledge.

Quality Excellence Achieved: Quality Assurance. (C). 1992. 24.95 (*0-13-749805-5*, Macmillan Coll) P-H.

Quality Exchange: A Practical Guide for Improving Work Relationships. John D. Ingalls & Karyn E. Ingalls. (Illus.). (Orig.). 1991. pap. 16.95 (*0-9630318-0-5*) CDI Bks.

Quality Facility Management: A Marketing & Customer Service Approach. Stormy Friday & David G. Cotts. 240p. 1994. 64.95 (*0-471-02322-1*) Wiley.

Quality Factor in Radiation Protection. Ed. by International Commission on Radiation Units & Meas. LC 86-181. (ICRU Reports: No. 40). 30p. 1986. 40.00 (*0-913394-34-3*) Intl Comm Rad Meas.

Quality Factors of Fruits & Vegetables: Chemistry & Technology. Ed. by Joseph J. Jen. (ACS Symposium Ser.: No. 405). 393p. 1989. text 98.00 (*0-8412-1663-0*, Pub. by Am Chemical) OUP.

Quality Fat: Quality Gems Within You. Ida Benjamin. 1994. pap. 22.50 (*0-9640649-0-1*) Ida B Enter.

Quality First: Better Health Care for All Americans : Final Report to the President of the United States. United States. LC 98-144253. xi, 225p. 1997. write for info. (*0-16-049533-4*) USGPO.

Quality First: Better Health Care for All Americans: Final Report to the President of the United States. Ed. by Janet Corrigan. 315p. (C). 1999. pap. text 35.00 (*0-7881-7796-6*) DIANE Pub.

Quality Food in Quantity: Management & Science. Marion L. Cremer. LC 97-84186. (Illus.). 370p. 1998. 60.00 (*0-8211-0232-X*) McCutchan.

Quality Foundation: 50 Activities for Organizational Change. Mardy Wheeler & Betsy Kendall. 350p. 1995. ring bd. 99.95 (*0-87425-273-3*) HRD Press.

Quality Friendship. Gary Inrig. 192p. pap. 10.99 (*0-8024-2891-6*, 260) Moody.

Quality from the Top. James Orlikoff. 1990. 39.95 (*0-944496-15-6*) Precept Pr.

Quality Function Deployment: A Practitioner's Approach. James L. Bossert. 127p. 1990. 34.00 (*0-87389-089-2*, H0607) ASQ Qual Pr.

Quality Function Deployment: How to Make It Work. Louis Cohen. 368p. (C). 1995. 52.00 (*0-201-63330-2*) Addison-Wesley.

Quality Function Deployment: Integrating Customer Requirements into Product Design. Ed. by Yoji Akao. LC 89-43209. (Illus.). 387p. 1990. 85.00 (*0-915299-41-0*) Productivity Inc.

Quality Function Deployment: Linking a Company with Its Customers. Ronald G. Day. LC 93-4479. 245p. 1993. 48.00 (*0-87389-202-X*, H0749) ASQ Qual Pr.

Quality Function Deployment: The Practitioner's Approach. Bossert. (Quality & Reliability Ser.: Vol. 21). (Illus.). 152p. 1990. text 45.00 (*0-8247-8378-6*) Dekker.

Quality Function Deployment Research Report: Advanced QFD Application Articles. 50p. 1990. pap. write for info. (*1-879364-23-9*) GOAL-QPC.

Quality Fusion: Turning Total Quality Management into Classroom Practice. Margaret Byrnes & Robert Cornesky. 290p. 1994. pap. text, teacher ed. 22.50 (*1-881807-05-3*) Cornesky & Assocs.

Quality Games for Trainers: 101 Playful Lessons in Quality & Continuous Improvements. Marlene Caroselli. LC 95-40601. (Illus.). 304p. 1995. 79.95 (*0-07-011502-8*); pap. 34.95 (*0-07-011503-6*) McGraw.

Quality Goes to School: Readings in Total Quality Management in Education. American Association of School Administrators Staf. 1993. pap. 24.95 (*0-87652-204-5*, 21-00425) Am Assn Sch Admin.

Quality Government: Designing, Developing & Implementing TQM. Jerry W. Koehler. 296p. 1996. boxed set 54.95 (*1-57444-013-6*) St Lucie Pr.

Quality Hand Soldering & Circuit Board Design. 2nd ed. H. Smith. LC 96-37427. (C). 1997. mass mkt. 21.95 (*0-8273-7886-6*) Delmar.

Quality Hand Soldering & Circuit Board Repair. H. Ted Smith. LC 93-32832. 104p. 1994. pap. 16.00 (*0-8273-6347-8*) Delmar.

Quality Handbook for Small Business. David J. Ames et al. Ed. by Larry N. Stoiaken. (Illus.). 1994. write for info. (*0-9643779-0-X*) Small Business.

Quality Handbook for Small Business. 2nd rev. ed. David J. Ames et al. Ed. by Larry N. Stoiaken. (Illus.). 1996. pap. 29.95 (*0-9652338-0-4*) Small Business.

Quality Handbook for the Architectural, Engineering, & Construction Community. Roger D. Hart. LC 93-49745. 530p. 1994. 90.00 (*0-87389-245-3*, H0798) ASQ Qual Pr.

Quality Happens Through People: Why Quality Initiatives Succeed - Or Don't. Susan Annitto. (AT&T Quality Library). (Illus.). 110p. (Orig.). 1994. pap. 19.95 (*0-932764-47-9*) AT&T Customer Info.

Quality Health Care for the Elderly: A Manual for Instructors for Nurses & Other Health Workers. (Western Pacific Education in Action Ser.: No. 6). 256p. (C). 1995. pap. text 22.00 (*92-9061-136-7*, 1500006) World Health.

Quality Hill. Donald Berger. (Lost Roads Ser.: No. 39). 64p. (Orig.). 1993. pap. 9.95 (*0-918786-44-4*) Lost Roads.

Quality Home Designs. Ed. by National Plan Service Staff. (Illus.). 32p. reprint ed. 4.95 (*0-934039-34-8*, A103) Hme Dsgn Altntves.

***Quality Human Resources Leadership: A Principal's Handbook.** L. David Weller & Sylvia J. Weller. 300p. 2000. text 45.00 (*1-56676-850-0*) Scarecrow.

Quality Impact of Home Care for the Elderly. Ed. by Francis G. Caro & Arthur E. Blank. LC 88-11292. (Home Health Care Services Quarterly Ser.: Vol. 9, Nos. 2 & 3). (Illus.). 204p. 1989. text 39.95 (*0-86656-820-4*) Haworth Pr.

***Quality Imperative: Measurement & Mangement of Quality in Healthcare.** John R. Kimberly. 1999. 44.00 (*1-86094-173-7*, Pub. by Imperial College) World Scientific Pub.

Quality Improvement: A Systems Perspective. William F. Roth. LC 98-38861. 288p. 1998. boxed set 49.95 (*1-57444-236-8*) St Lucie Pr.

Quality Improvement: Teamwork Solutions from the U. K. & U. S. A. Lesley Munro-Faure et al. LC 99-178262. 224p. 1998. pap. 27.95 (*0-304-70311-7*) Continuum.

Quality Improvement: Tools & Techniques. Peter Mears. LC 94-34752. 1995. text 49.95 incl. disk (*0-07-041229-4*) McGraw.

Quality Improvement & Evaluation in Child & Family Services: Managing into the Next Century. Ed. by Peter J. Pecora et al. LC 96-15333. 315p. (Orig.). 1997. pap. 26.95 (*0-87868-606-1*, CWLA Pr) Child Welfare.

Quality Improvement & Management: HSM 535 Course. Michael Cronin. 192p. (C). 1993. spiral bd. write for info. (*0-933195-22-2*) CA College Health Sci.

Quality Improvement Book of Bows & Arrows: Quality Planning Made Easy. Lowell J. Arthur. (QI Coloring Bks.). 48p. 1999. pap., student ed. 9.95 (*1-884180-03-5*) LifeStar.

Quality Improvement by Peer Review. Ed. by Richard Grol & Martin Lawrence. (Oxford General Practice Ser.: No. 32). (Illus.). 184p. 1995. pap. text 59.95 (*0-19-262521-7*) OUP.

Quality Improvement Coloring Book: Problem Solving Made Easy. Lowell J. Arthur. (QI Coloring Bks.). 48p. 1999. student ed. 9.95 (*1-884180-01-9*) LifeStar.

Quality Improvement Connect-the-Dots Book: SPC Made Easy. Lowell J. Arthur. (QI Coloring Bks.). 48p. 1999. pap., student ed. 9.95 (*1-884180-02-7*) LifeStar.

Quality Improvement Handbook: Team Guide to Tools & Techniques. Roger C. Swanson. LC 94-46625. 288p. 1995. boxed set 54.95 (*1-884015-59-X*) St Lucie Pr.

Quality Improvement in Continuing Higher Education & Service Organizations. Ed. by Paul F. Fendt & G. Michael Vavrek. LC 92-40882. 176p. 1993. text 79.95 (*0-7734-9220-8*) E Mellen.

Quality Improvement in Education: Case Studies in Schools, Colleges & Universities. Ed. by Carl Parsons. 160p. 1994. pap. 27.00 (*1-85346-327-2*, Pub. by David Fulton) Taylor & Francis.

Quality Improvement in European Public Services: Concepts, Cases, & Commentary. Christopher Pollitt & Geert Bouckaert. 256p. 1995. 75.00 (*0-8039-7464-7*); pap. 29.95 (*0-8039-7465-5*) Sage.

Quality Improvement in Health Care: Putting Evidence into Practice. 2nd ed. Karen Parsley & Philomena Corrigan. (Illus.). 448p. 1999. pap. 37.50 (*0-7487-3355-8*) Standard Pub.

Quality Improvement Practices in Local Government. William W. Farris et al. Ed. by Madeleine Havlick. (Illus.). 228p. 1994. 34.95 (*1-882403-17-7*) The Innovation Grps.

Quality Improvement Projects in Health Care: Problem Solving in the Workplace. Eleanor G. Gilpatrick. LC 98-25380. 1998. 69.00 (*0-7619-1166-9*); pap. 34.95 (*0-7619-1167-7*) Sage.

Quality Improvement Series. 1994. pap. text 109.95 (*1-883553-24-5*) R Chang Assocs.

Quality Improvement Team Handbook. Al Jaehn & Technical Association of the Pulp and Paper Industry. LC 97-120984. (Illus.). 1997. write for info. (*0-89852-329-X*) TAPPI.

Quality Improvement Team Helper. 2nd rev. ed. Kevin Wigenton. Ed. by Susan Annitto. (AT&T Quality Library). (Illus.). 39p. (Orig.). 1990. pap. 12.50 (*0-932764-34-7*, 500-444) AT&T Customer Info.

Quality Improvement Team Trainer's Kit: Mastering J. M. Juran's 6-Step Quality Improvement Process. Juran Institute Staff. (Illus.). 300p. 1997. pap. 149.95 (*0-07-065343-7*) McGraw.

Quality Improvement Techniques for Hospital Safety. Hugh Greeley & Jennifer I. Cofer. (Health Care Quality Improvement Ser.). 246p. 1993. pap. text 57.00 (*1-885829-08-6*) Opus Communs.

Quality Improvement Techniques for Long-Term Care *see* **Continuous Quality Improvement for Long-Term Care**

Quality Improvement Techniques for Medical Records. Jennifer I. Cofer & Hugh Greeley. (Health Care Quality Improvement Ser.). 217p. 1996. pap. text 47.00 (*1-885829-04-3*) Opus Communs.

Quality Improvement Techniques for Radiology. Jennifer I. Cofer & Hugh Greeley. (Health Care Quality Improvement Ser.). 230p. 1994. pap. text 47.00 (*1-885829-06-X*) Opus Communs.

Quality Improvement Techniques for Respiratory Care. Jennifer L. Cofer & Hugh Greeley. (Health Care Quality Improvement Ser.). 220p. 1993. pap. text 42.00 (*1-885829-05-1*) Opus Communs.

Quality Improvement Techniques in Construction. Steven McCabe. (C). 1998. pap. text 54.95 (*0-582-30776-7*) Addison-Wesley.

Quality Improvement Through Planned Experimentation. 2nd ed. Ronald D. Moen et al. (Illus.). 480p. 1998. 64.95 (*0-07-043952-4*) McGraw.

Quality Improvement Through Planned Experimentation. 2nd ed. Ronald D. Moen et al. LC 98-8290. 464p. 1998. 69.95 (*0-07-913781-4*) McGraw.

Quality Improvement Through Standards. 2nd expanded rev. ed. Barrie Dale & John Oakland. LC 94-187536. 338p. (C). 1999. pap. 142.50 (*0-7487-1699-8*, Pub. by S Thornes Pubs) Trans-Atl Phila.

Q

An Asterisk (*) at the beginning of an entry indicates that the title is appearing for the first time.

Quality Improvement Through Statistical Methods. Ed. by B. Abraham. LC 97-51995. (Statistics for Industry & Technology Ser.). 450p. 1998. text 79.95 (*0-8176-4052-5*) Birkhauser.

Quality Improvement Through Statistical Methods. Bovas Abraham & Nair N. Unnikrishnan. LC 97-51995. (Statistics for Industry & Technology Ser.). 1998. write for info. (*3-7643-4052-5*) Birkhauser.

Quality Improvement Tools & Techniques. Peter Mears. LC 94-34752. 326p. 1994. 32.95 (*0-07-041219-7*) McGraw.

Quality Improvement Tools & Techniques. Peter Mears. LC 94-34752. 1995. disk 19.95 (*0-07-852726-0*) McGraw.

Quality in Action. Ed. by Judy B. Duckett et al. (Illus.). 90p. 1996. pap. text 55.00 (*1-56395-063-4*, PC97-960016) Am Assn Blood.

Quality in Action: 93 Lessons in Leadership, Participation & Measurement. Patrick L. Townsend & Joan E. Gebhardt. LC 91-25776. 262p. 1992. 27.95 (*0-471-55206-2*) Wiley.

Quality in Action: 93 Lessons in Leadership, Participation & Measurement. Patrick L. Townsend & Joan E. Gebhardt. LC 91-25776. 262p. 1997. pap. 16.95 (*0-471-16136-5*) Wiley.

Quality in America: How to Implement a Competitive Quality Program. Daniel Hunt. 1995. text 16.95 (*0-7863-0529-0*, Irwn Prfssnl) McGraw-Hill Prof.

*__Quality in Chemical Measurement: Current Concepts in Training & Teaching.__ Bernd Neidhart. 150p. 2000. 79.95 (*3-540-65994-3*) Spr-Verlag.

Quality in Child Care: What Does Research Tell Us? Ed. by Deborah A. Phillips. LC 87-62195. 130p. 1987. pap. text 6.00 (*0-935989-08-0*, NAEYC #140) Natl Assn Child Ed.

Quality in Education. Ed. by Keith Watson et al. LC 97-181158. (International Debates Ser.). 440p. 1996. text 130.00 (*0-304-32890-1*) Continuum.

Quality in Education: An Implementation Handbook. Jerry Arcaro. LC 94-46378. 192p. 1995. boxed set 49.95 (*1-884015-58-1*) St Lucie Pr.

Quality in Family Child Care & Relative Care. Susan Kontos et al. (Early Childhood Education Ser.). 240p. (C). 1994. text 34.00 (*0-8077-3409-8*) Tchrs Coll.

Quality in Frozen Food. Ed. by Marilyn C. Erickson & Yen-Con Hung. LC 97-10083. (Illus.). 484p. 1997. 89.00 (*0-412-07041-3*) Chapman & Hall.

Quality in Health Care: Theory, Application & Evolution. 3rd ed. Nancy D. Graham. 384p. 1995. 55.00 (*0-8342-0625-0*, 20625) Aspen Pub.

Quality in Higher Education. Ed. by Brent D. Ruben. 300p. (C). 1994. 39.95 (*1-56000-190-9*); pap. 24.95 (*1-56000-795-8*) Transaction Pubs.

Quality in Instructional Television. Ed. by Wilbur L. Schramm. LC 72-90004. (East-West Center Bk.). 231p. reprint ed. pap. 71.70 (*0-7837-3982-6*, 204381200011) Bks Demand.

Quality in Nursing Services. Beyers. 1997. text. write for info. (*0-7216-4255-1*, W B Saunders Co) Harcrt Hlth Sci Grp.

*__Quality in Photography: How to Take, Process, & Print Excellent Photographs.__ Roger Hicks & Frances Schultz. (Illus.). 192p. 2000. pap. 29.95 (*0-8174-5634-1*) Watsn-Guptill.

Quality in Primary Education. Hawes. Date not set. pap. text. write for info. (*0-582-05200-9*, Pub. by Addison-Wesley) Longman.

Quality in Quantity. Clara L. Gerwick. (Illus.). 1993. ring bd. 49.95 (*0-915187-06-X*) Nutrition Ed.

Quality in Reggae Music: Q. R. M. - Guidelines to Pure Reggae Music. Ricardo A. Scott. (Illus.). 50p. 1994. 19.95 (*1-883427-15-0*) Crnerstone GA.

Quality in Resistance Welding: An Analysis of the Process & Its Control. J. O. Zwolsman. 96p. 1991. pap. 125.00 (*1-85573-033-2*, Pub. by Woodhead Pubng) Am Educ Systs.

Quality in Student Financial Aid Programs: A New Approach. Ed. by Ronald S. Fesco. 264p. (Orig.). (C). 1993. pap. text 35.00 (*0-309-04877-X*) Natl Acad Pr.

Quality in Teaching. OECD Staff. 130p. (Orig.). 1994. pap. 23.00 (*92-64-14242-8*) OECD.

Quality in Teaching: Arguments for a Reflective Profession. Wilfred Carr. 230p. 1989. 75.00 (*1-85000-546-X*, Falmer Pr); pap. 34.95 (*1-85000-547-8*, Falmer Pr) Taylor & Francis.

Quality in the Analytical Chemistry Laboratory: Analytical Chemistry by Open Learning. F. Elizabeth Prichard. (Analytical Chemistry by Open Learning Ser.). 334p. 1995. pap. 69.95 (*0-471-95470-5*) Wiley.

Quality in the Constructed Project: A Guide for Owners, Designers & Constructors. LC 90-14408. (ASCE Manual & Report on Engineering Practice: No. 73). 144p. 1990. pap. text 30.00 (*0-87262-781-0*) Am Soc Civil Eng.

Q

*__Quality in the Food Analysis Laboratory.__ R. Wood et al. (RSC Food Analysis Monographs). 322p. 1999. 99.00 (*0-85404-566-X*) Spr-Verlag.

Quality Index: Self-Assessment for Golf & Country Clubs. Andrew Cornesky & Robert Cornesky. (Illus.). 18p. (Orig.). 1995. pap. text 19.00 (*1-881807-12-6*) Cornesky & Assocs.

*__Quality Indicator Resource Manual: Of the Kansas Association of Homes & Services for the Aging.__ 2nd ed. Diane P. Atchinson & Debra Zehr. 441p. 2000. write for info. (*1-929162-04-9*) DPA Assocs.

Quality Indicators. 1994. write for info. (*1-880678-76-4*) HCIA.

Quality Indicators for Residential Programs: A Survey Instrument. Gary O. Carman & Brian J. Farragher. 1994. pap. 16.95 (*0-87868-590-1*) Child Welfare.

Quality Indices: Self-Assessment Rating Instrument for Educational Institutions. Robert Cornesky. (Illus.). 44p. (C). 1995. pap. text 14.00 (*1-881807-10-X*) Cornesky & Assocs.

Quality Information & Knowledge. Huang & Wang. 1999. text 28.50 (*0-13-030063-2*) P-H.

Quality Information Systems. 10th ed. Fatemeh Zahedi. 432p. (C). 1997. write for info. (*0-7600-4944-0*) Course Tech.

Quality Initiative Law Offices. Sally S. Brashear & Eric. W. Herman. 192p. 1995. pap. text, per. 59.95 (*0-7872-0061-1*) Kendall-Hunt.

Quality Innovation: An Economic Analysis of Rapid Improvements in Microelectronic Components. G. M. Swann. LC 86-454. 189p. 1986. 55.00 (*0-89930-193-2*, SQI/, Quorum Bks) Greenwood.

Quality Interviewing: A Step-by-Step Action Plan for Success. 3rd rev. ed. Robert B. Maddux. Ed. by Michael Crisp. LC 93-7049. (Fifty-Minute Ser.). (Illus.). 72p. 1994. pap. 10.95 (*1-56052-262-3*) Crisp Pubns.

Quality Interviews with Adult Students & Trainees: A Communication Course in Student Personnel & In-Service Training. Margery A. Neely. (Illus.). 384p. 1992. pap. 49.95 (*0-398-06302-8*) C C Thomas.

Quality Interviews with Adult Students & Trainees: A Communication Course in Student Personnel & In-Service Training. Margery A. Neely. (Illus.). 384p. (C). 1992. text 75.95 (*0-398-05813-X*) C C Thomas.

*__Quality Is Everybody's Business.__ Patrick L. Townsend & Joan E. Gebhardt. LC 99-59249. 379p. 1999. boxed set 39.95 (*1-57444-284-8*) CRC Pr.

Quality Is Free: The Art of Making Quality Certain. Philip B. Crosby. 1980. mass mkt. 6.99 (*0-451-62585-4*, Ment) NAL.

Quality Is Free: The Art of Making Quality Free. Philip B. Crosby. 352p. 1979. 34.95 (*0-07-014512-1*) McGraw.

Quality Is Personal: A Foundation for Total Quality Management. Harry V. Roberts & Bernard F. Sergesketter. LC 93-21723. 192p. 1993. 29.95 (*0-02-926626-2*); per. 22.95 (*0-02-926625-4*) Free Pr.

*__Quality Is Still Free.__ Crosby. 1999. write for info. (*0-07-134880-8*) McGraw.

Quality Is Still Free: Making Quality Certain in Uncertain Times. Philip B. Crosby. LC 95-32400. (Illus.). 288p. 1995. 24.95 (*0-07-014532-6*) McGraw.

Quality Is the Key: Stories from Huntington Woods School. Sally A. Ludwig & Kaye W. Mentley. LC 97-92693. 200p. 1997. pap. 14.00 (*0-9660916-0-4*) KWM Educ.

*__Quality Issue.__ William Kozlowski. LC 00-190751. 374p. 2000. 25.00 (*0-7388-1975-1*); pap. 18.00 (*0-7388-1976-X*) Xlibris Corp.

*__Quality Issues in Heritage Vistor Attractions.__ Yeoman. 2000. 66.95 (*0-7506-4675-6*) Buttrwrth-Heinemann.

Quality Leadership & Management in the Hospitality Industry. Robert H. Woods & Judy Z. King. LC 95-49728. (Illus.). 438p. 1995. pap. write for info. (*0-86612-069-6*) Educ Inst Am Hotel.

*__Quality Leadership Skills: Standards of Leadership Behavior.__ 2nd rev. ed. Dick Leatherman. 466p. 2000. pap. 29.95 (*0-9674325-1-0*) Intl Training.

Quality Learning for Student Teachers: University Tutors' Educational Practices. Della Fish. 176p. 1995. pap. 24.95 (*1-85346-352-3*, Pub. by David Fulton) Taylor & Francis.

Quality Lesson Plans for Secondary Physical Education. Dorothy B. Zakrajsek et al. LC 93-42162. (Illus.). 448p. 1994. pap. text 36.00 (*0-87322-671-2*, BZAK0671) Human Kinetics.

Quality Living on a Tight Budget. large type ed. Richard Calendar. (Illus.). 300p. Date not set. pap. 24.95 (*1-56559-915-2*) HGI-Over Fifty.

Quality Longevity, Vol. 10. rev. ed. Mark Lovendale. LC 94-73781. (Illus.). 260p. (Orig.). 1998. pap. 28.00 (*0-945196-22-9*) Advanced CA.

*__Quality Lumber Drying in the Pacific Northwest: The Team Approach to Improving Your Bottom Line.__ 122p. 1998. pap. 40.00 (*1-892529-01-7*, 7271) Forest Prod.

Quality Maid. large type ed. Mira Stables. (Ulverscroft Large Print Ser.). 320p. 1997. 27.99 (*0-7089-3872-8*) Ulverscroft.

Quality Maintenance: Zero Defects Through Equipment Management. Seiji Tsuchiya. 1997. pap. text 30.00 (*1-56327-137-0*) Productivity Inc.

Quality Management: A Guide for Health Care Managers. Marylane Wade Koch. (Illus.). 352p. 1991. 36.95 (*0-8016-2731-1*) Mosby Inc.

Quality Management: Applications for Therapeutic Recreation. Ed. by Bob Riley. LC 91-66102. 242p. (C). 1991. text 23.95 (*0-910251-47-9*) Venture Pub PA.

Quality Management: Best Practices for Home Builders. Edward Caldeira & NAHB Research Center, Inc. Staff. LC 96-46804. (National Housing Quality Best Practices Ser.: Vol. 1). 64p. (Orig.). 1997. pap. 20.63 (*0-86718-426-4*) Home Builder.

Quality Management: Implementing the Best Ideas of the Masters. Bruce Brocka & M. Suzanne Brocka. 300p. 1992. text 44.95 (*1-55623-540-2*, Irwn Prfssnl) McGraw-Hill Prof.

Quality Management: Survey of Federal Organizations. (Illus.). 67p. (Orig.). (C). 1993. pap. text 20.00 (*1-56806-676-7*) DIANE Pub.

Quality Management: Tools & Methods for Improvement. 2nd ed. Howard S. Gitlow et al. LC 94-15814. (Series in Statistics). 503p. (C). 1994. text 71.00 (*0-256-10665-7*, Irwn McGrw-H) McGrw-H Hghr Educ.

Quality Management & Benchmarking in the Information Sector. J. Brockman. LC 97-171520. (British Library Research). 1997. 60.00 (*1-85739-189-6*) Bowker-Saur.

Quality Management & Institutional Investing. 1994. 30.00 (*1-879087-36-7*) Assn I M&R.

*__Quality Management & Qualification Needs 2: Towards Quality Capability of Companies & Employees in Europe.__ Ed. by J. Koper & H. J. Zaremba. xii, 377p. 2000. pap. (*3-7908-1262-5*) Spr-Verlag.

Quality Management & the Small Business. Lionel Stebbing. 144p. (C). 1994. 24.00 (*0-13-123340-8*) P-H.

Quality Management Benchmark Assessment. 2nd ed. J. P. Russell. 171p. 1995. spiral bd. 24.00 (*0-87389-332-8*, H0890) ASQ Qual Pr.

Quality Management Benchmark Assessment. 2nd rev. ed. J. P. Russell. 192p. 1995. spiral bd. 24.00 (*0-527-76295-4*) Productivity Inc.

Quality Management Concepts. Donna C. Summers. (C). 2002. 66.67 (*0-13-262643-8*, Macmillan Coll) P-H.

Quality Management for Building Design. Tim Cornick. 200p. 1991. text 61.95 (*0-7506-1225-8*) Buttrwrth-Heinemann.

Quality Management for Building Design. Tim Cornick. LC 90-47836. (Butterworth Architecture Management Guides Ser.). (Illus.). 234p. 1990. reprint ed. pap. 72.60 (*0-608-04417-2*, 206519800001) Bks Demand.

Quality Management for Chemical Safety Testing. (Environmental Health Criteria Ser.: No. 141). (ENG, FRE & SPA.). 112p. 1992. pap. text 26.00 (*92-4-157141-1*, 1160141) World Health.

Quality Management for Government: A Guide to Federal, State & Local Implementation. V. Daniel Hunt. LC 93-6397. 384p. 1993. text 35.00 (*0-87389-239-9*, H0788) ASQ Qual Pr.

Quality Management for Information & Library Managers. Peter Brophy & Kate Coulling. 206p. 1996. 74.95 (*0-566-07725-6*, Pub. by Gower) Ashgate Pub Co.

Quality Management for Projects & Programs. Lewis R. Ireland. LC 91-26905. 128p. 1992. pap. 32.95 (*1-880410-11-7*) Proj Mgmt Inst.

Quality Management for the Construction Professional: What a Mess! Barrett. 1995. pap. 24.00 (*0-85406-677-2*, Pub. by R-I-C-S Bks) St Mut.

*__Quality Management for the Technology Sector.__ Joe Berk & Susan Berk. LC 00-22363. 208p. 2000. pap. 34.95 (*0-7506-7316-8*) Buttrwrth-Heinemann.

Quality Management Handbook. 2nd rev. ed. Raymond J. Kimber et al. LC 97-22485. (Quality And Reliability ;). (Illus.). 848p. 1997. text 145.00 (*0-8247-9356-0*) Dekker.

Quality Management Implementation Guidelines, July 1997. 75p. 1997. pap. 9.00 (*0-16-063435-0*) USGPO.

Quality Management in Education: Sustaining the Vision Through Action Research. Ed. by Pamela Lomax. 176p. (C). 1996. pap. 22.99 (*0-415-15253-4*) Routledge.

Quality Management in Hospitality: Best Practice in Action. Michael B. Lockwood & Andrew Ghillyer. (Illus.). 224p. 1997. pap. 31.95 (*0-304-33485-5*); text 80.00 (*0-304-33486-3*) Continuum.

Quality Management in Nursing & Health Care. June Schmele. 640p. (C). 1995. pap. 82.95 (*0-8273-6056-8*) Delmar.

*__Quality Management in the Imaging Sciences.__ Jeffrey Papp. (Illus.). 320p. 1998. teacher ed. write for info. (*1-55664-474-4*) Mosby Inc.

Quality Management in Urban Tourism. Ed. by Peter E. Murphy. LC 96-48035. 312p. 1997. 110.00 (*0-471-97099-9*) Wiley.

Quality Management Integration in Long-Term Care: Guidelines for Excellence. Maryjane G. Bradley & Nancy R. Thompson. LC 99-27315. 174p. 1999. 31.95 (*1-878812-61-0*) Hlth Prof Pr.

Quality Management Manual: How to Write & Develop a Successful Manual for Quality Management Systems. Jenny Waller et al. (Illus.). 256p. (Orig.). 1993. pap. 49.95 (*0-89397-388-2*) Nichols Pub.

Quality Management of Hot Mix Asphalt. 2nd ed. ASTM Committee D-4 on Road & Paving Materials. Ed. by Dale S. Decker. LC 96-37099. (STP 1299 Ser.). (Illus.). 141p. 1996. pap. text 29.00 (*0-8031-2024-9*) ASTM.

Quality Management of Safety & Risk Analysis. Ed. by Jouko Suokas & Veikko Rouhiainen. LC 92-37777. (Industrial Safety Ser.: No. 3). 296p. 1993. 205.00 (*0-444-89864-6*) Elsevier.

Quality Management Plus: The Continuous Improvement of Education. Roger Kaufman & Douglas Zahn. LC 92-42929. 208p. 1993. 45.95 (*0-8039-6062-X*) Corwin Pr.

Quality Management Policy & Procedures. Olga Cotera. 1993. 90.00 (*0-685-66663-8*) Acad Med Sys.

Quality Management Resources on the Internet. James R. Clauson. LC 99-36247. 140p. 1999. pap. 49.00 (*0-86587-665-7*) Gov Insts.

Quality Management Review. Dowd. (Radiographic Technology Ser.). (C). 2000. pap. 24.95 (*0-7668-1258-8*) Delmar.

Quality Management Sourcebook. Christine Avery & Diane Zable. LC 96-8911. 336p. (C). 1996. 125.00 (*0-415-10831-4*) Routledge.

Quality Management System: A Planning & Auditing Guide. Walter O. Willborn. (Illus.). 240p. 1989. 26.95 (*0-8311-3013-X*) Indus Pr.

Quality Management System Audit. David Hoyle. 224p. Date not set. pap. 49.95 (*0-7506-5001-X*) Buttrwrth-Heinemann.

*__Quality Management Systems.__ Howard S. Gitlow. LC 99-43472. 1999. write for info. (*1-57444-261-9*) St Lucie Pr.

Quality Management Systems: Assessment to ISO 9000, 1994 Series. Ed. by T. E. Lim & Bock C. Niew. LC 95-35169. 420p. (C). 1997. pap. 48.00 (*0-13-240714-0*) P-H.

Quality Management Systems for the Food Industry. Bolton. (Food Science & Technology Ser.). 1996. text 64.95 (*0-7514-4030-2*) Chapman & Hall.

Quality Management Systems for the Food Industry: A Guide To Iso 9001/2. Andrew Bolton. 193p. 1997. 95.00 (*0-8342-1333-8*) Aspen Pub.

Quality Management Today: What Local Governments Need to Know. Ed. by Jonathan P. West. LC 95-11543. (Practical Management Ser.). 1995. 23.95 (*0-87326-100-3*) Intl City-Cnty Mgt.

Quality Management, 2000: Preparing the Quality Improvement Professional for the Future. Deborah K. Wall & Mitchell M. Proyect. LC 97-23808. (Illus.). 192p. 1997. pap. 40.00 (*0-944496-51-2*) Precept Pr.

Quality Management/Return Quality. 2nd ed. Gitlow-Rust. 1996. 75.50 (*0-256-26489-9*) McGraw.

Quality Manager's Complete Guide to ISO 9000. Richard B. Clements. 368p. (C). 1993. text 79.95 (*0-13-017534-X*) P-H.

Quality Manager's Complete Guide to ISO 9000: 2000 Edition. Richard B. Clements. (C). 1999. pap. text, suppl. ed. 39.95 (*0-13-021242-3*) P-H.

Quality Manager's Handbook. 2nd rev. ed. Brian Leary & John MacDorman. Ed. by Patti Carlisle. (AT&T Quality Library). (Illus.). 146p. (Orig.). 1992. reprint ed. pap. 24.95 (*0-932764-35-5*, 500-462) AT&T Customer Info.

Quality Managment in the Imaging Sciences. Papp. LC 97-46903. (Illus.). 320p. (gr. 13). 1998. text 38.00 (*0-8151-2968-8*, 31848) Mosby Inc.

Quality Managment in the Imaging Sciences. 3rd ed. David L. Goetsch. LC 98-51539. (Illus.). 778p. (C). 1999. 93.00 (*0-13-011638-6*) P-H.

Quality Matters: Excellence in Early Childhood Programs. Gillian Doherty. 202p. 1995. pap. text 23.96 (*0-201-76614-0*) Addison-Wesley.

Quality Means Survival: Caveat Vendidor, Let the Seller Beware. Rene T. Domingo. LC 96-30052. (C). 1997. pap. text 24.95 (*0-13-626780-7*) P-H.

Quality Measurement in Economics: New Perspectives on the Evolution of Goods & Services. Steven Payson. 256p. 1994. 95.00 (*1-85278-926-3*) E Elgar.

Quality Measures & the Design of Telecommunications Systems. John H. Fennick. LC 88-6318. 412p. reprint ed. pap. 127.80 (*0-7837-3259-7*, 204327800007) Bks Demand.

Quality Measuring Instruments in On-Line Process Analysis. D. J. Huskins. 455p. 1982. text 149.00 (*0-470-27521-9*) P-H.

*__Quality Mentoring for Novice Teachers.__ Sandra J. Odell & Leslie Huling-Austin. LC 00-20424. 2000. write for info. (*0-912099-37-2*) Kappa Delta Pi.

Quality Middle School Leadership: Eleven Central Skill Areas. L. David Weller. LC 98-86722. 480p. 1998. text 49.95 (*1-56676-681-8*) Scarecrow.

Quality Middle Schools: Open & Healthy. Wayne K. Hoy et al. LC 97-4883. 216p. 1997. 61.95 (*0-8039-6420-X*); pap. 27.95 (*0-8039-6421-8*) Corwin Pr.

Quality Mind, Quality Life. Paul Lisnek. LC 95-76817. 220p. 1995. 19.95 (*0-916990-35-4*) META Pubns.

Quality Movement: What Total Quality Management Is Really All About. Helga Drummond. 128p. (C). 1992. pap. 14.95 (*0-89397-383-1*) Nichols Pub.

Quality Multimedia Systems. Carpenter. (Multimedia Ser.). 1997. mass mkt. 43.95 (*0-534-23364-3*) Wadsworth Pub.

Quality Networking in Europe. Ed. by Paul Kunst et al. LC 96-83717. (Perspectives on Europe Ser.). 232p. 1996. 68.95 (*1-85972-364-0*, Pub. by Avebry) Ashgate Pub Co.

Quality of American Jewish Life: Two Views. Steven M. Cohen & Charles S. Liebman. LC 87-72930. (Jewish Sociology Papers). 55p. (Orig.). 1987. pap. 3.50 (*0-87495-095-3*) Am Jewish Comm.

Quality of American Life: Perceptions, Evaluations & Satisfactions. Angus Campbell et al. LC 75-7176. 600p. 1976. 55.00 (*0-87154-194-7*) Russell Sage.

Quality of American Life, 1978. Angus Campbell & Phillip E. Converse. LC 80-84081. 1980. write for info. (*0-89138-951-2*) ICPSR.

Quality of Bank Loans: A Study of Bank Examination Records. Albert M. Wojnilower. (Occasional Papers: No. 82). 90p. 1962. reprint ed. 23.40 (*0-87014-396-4*) Natl Bur Econ Res.

Quality of Care: Do Contemporary Nursing Approaches Make a Difference? Alan Pearson & Helen Baker. (Research Monographs: No. 5). 1995. pap. 20.00 (*0-7300-1497-5*, Pub. by Deakin Univ) St Mut.

Quality of Care: Selections from the New England Journal of Medicine. Ed. by Jerome P. Kassirer & Marcia Angell. LC 97-71084. 77p. 1997. pap. 15.00 (*0-910133-40-9*) Mass Med Pub Div.

Quality of Communication-Based Systems: Proceedings of an International Workshop Held at the TU, Berlin, Germany, September 1994. Ed. by G. Unter Hommel. LC 94-39301. (1994: TU Berlin, Germany). 195p. 1995. text 144.00 (*0-7923-3259-8*) Kluwer Academic.

Quality of Consumer Instalment Credit. Geoffrey H. Moore & Philip A. Klein. (Financial Research Program II: Studies in Consumer Installment Financing: No. 13). 282p. 1967. reprint ed. 73.40 (*0-87014-484-7*) Natl Bur Econ Res.

Quality of Courage: Heroes in & Out of Baseball. Mickey Mantle & Robert W. Creamer. LC 98-31558. 185p. 1999. pap. 9.95 (*0-8032-8259-1*, Bison Books) U of Nebr Pr.

*__Quality of Death Rates by Race & Hispanic-Origin.__ Harry M. Rosenberg & National Center for Health Statistics Staff. LC 99-41288. (Vital & Health Statistics Ser.). 1999. pap. write for info. (*0-8406-0559-5*) Natl Ctr Health Stats.

*__Quality of Deaths by Race & Hispanic Origin: A Summary of Current Research, 1999.__ Harry M. Rosenberg. 17p. 1999. pap. 2.25 (*0-16-050138-5*) USGPO.

Quality of Earnings: The Investor's Guide to How Much Money a Company Is Really Making. Thornton O'Glove. 200p. 1987. 35.00 (*0-02-922630-9*) Free Pr.

An Asterisk (*) at the beginning of an entry indicates that the title is appearing for the first time.

Quality of Education in Developing Countries. Clarence E. Beeby. LC 66-14438. 149p. 1966. 22.00 (*0-674-74050-5*) HUP.

Quality of Effort: Integrity in Sport & Life for Student-Athletes, Parents, & Coaches. Reggie Marra. LC 90-84335. 113p. (Orig.). 1991. pap. 11.50 (*0-9627828-0-7*) From Heart Pr.

Quality of Federal Policymaking: Programmed Failure in Public Housing. Eugene J. Meehan. LC 78-27663. 256p. reprint ed. pap. 79.40 (*0-7837-3200-7*, AU0042800007) Bks Demand.

Quality of Fertilizers in West Africa, 1995. Cinty Visker et al. LC 96-3062. (Miscellaneous Fertilizer Studies: No. 13). 1996. write for info. (*0-88090-113-6*) Intl Fertilizer.

Quality of Frozen Food. Jul Mogens. 1984. text 94.00 (*0-12-391980-0*) Acad Pr.

Quality of Ground Water: Guidelines for Selection & Application of Frequently Used Models - A Report on the State-of-the-Art. ASCE, Environmental Engineering Division, Committe. LC 96-21049. (ASCE Manual & Report of Engineering Practice: No. 85). 160p. 1996. pap. 48.00 (*0-7844-0137-3*) Am Soc Civil Eng.

***Quality of Growth.** Vinod Thomas et al. (World Bank Publications). 200p. 2000. 35.00 (*0-19-521593-1*, 61593) OUP.

Quality of Health Care: Research Reference Analysis with Bibliography. Roy R. Zimmerman. LC 84-45988. 150p. 1987. 47.50 (*0-88164-298-3*); pap. 44.50 (*0-88164-299-1*) ABBE Pubs Assn.

Quality of Hurt: The Autobiography of Chester Himes - The Early Years. 2nd ed. Chester B. Himes. LC 98-164302. (Illus.). 360p. 1995. reprint ed. pap. 13.95 (*1-56025-093-3*, Thunders Mouth) Avalon NY.

Quality of Inspectors: In Search of Excellence. Ed. by Robert H. Welsh. (Sessions Proceedings Ser.). 80p. 1986. 3.00 (*0-87262-565-6*) Am Soc Civil Eng.

Quality of Life. Cynthia King. LC 98-14252. (Nursing Ser.). 390p. 1998. 50.00 (*0-7637-0628-0*) Jones & Bartlett.

Quality of Life. Ed. by Martha C. Nussbaum & Amartya K. Sen. (WIDER Studies in Development Economics). (Illus.). 480p. 1993. pap. text 29.95 (*0-19-828797-6*) OUP.

***Quality of Life.** Shauna Ries. 2000. pap. write for info. (*0-688-17804-9*, Wm Morrow) Morrow Avon.

Quality of Life. Philip Seed & Greg Lloyd. LC 97-196480. 200p. 1997. pap. write for info. (*1-85302-413-9*, Pub. by Jessica Kingsley) Taylor & Francis.

Quality of Life. James A. Michener. 1994. reprint ed. lib. bdg. 24.95 (*1-56849-311-8*) Buccaneer Bks.

Quality of Life: Achieving Balance in an Unbalanced World. H. Stanley Jones. LC 94-96087. 182p. 1994. 22.95 (*1-885161-07-7*) Kauai Pr.

***Quality of Life: Assessment, Analysis & Interpertation.** Peter M. Fayers. 448p. 2000. text 59.95 (*0-471-96861-7*) Wiley.

Quality of Life: Assessment & Application. Ed. by S. R. Walker. (CMR Workshop Ser.). 350p. (C). 1988. text 208.50 (*0-7462-0042-0*) Kluwer Academic.

Quality of Life: How To Get It, How To Keep It. Genna Murphy & Ries Shauna. LC 98-49836. 204p. 2000. 22.00 (*0-688-16744-6*, Wm Morrow) Morrow Avon.

Quality of Life: Perspectives & Policies. Ed. by Sally Baldwin et al. LC 93-25921. 272p. (C). 1993. pap. 27.99 (*0-415-09581-6*) Routledge.

Quality of Life: The New Medical Dilemma. Thomas A. Shannon. Ed. by James J. Walter. 368p. 1991. pap. 14.95 (*0-8091-3191-9*) Paulist Pr.

Quality of Life: Valuation in Social Research. Ramkrishna Mukherjee. 240p. (C). 1989. text 24.00 (*0-8039-9587-3*) Sage.

Quality of Life Vol. 1: Conceptualization & Measurement. Ed. & Pref. by Robert L. Schalock. LC 95-50087. (Illus.). 139p. 1996. pap. 35.00 (*0-940898-38-1*) Am Assn Mental.

Quality of Life Vol. II: Application to Persons with Disabilities, 2 vols. Ed. by Robert L. Schalock. LC 95-50087. (Illus.). 267p. (Orig.). 1997. pap. 35.00 (*0-940898-41-1*) Am Assn Mental.

Quality of Life & Health. I. Guggenmoos-Holzman et al. (Illus.). 200p. (Orig.). (C). 1996. pap. text 75.00 (*0-86542-668-6*) Blackwell Sci.

Quality of Life & Mental Health Care. Stefan Priebe et al. LC 99-12782. 1999. 75.00 (*1-871816-40-8*) Taylor & Francis.

Quality of Life & Mental Health Services. J. P. Oliver. LC 96-44152. (Illus.). 256p. (C). 1997. pap. 27.99 (*0-415-16151-7*) Routledge.

Quality of Life & Pharmacoeconomics in Clinical Trials. 2nd abr. ed. Joyce Cramer. LC 97-37999. 190p. 1997. pap. text 45.00 (*0-397-51845-5*) Lppncott W & W.

Quality of Life & Pharmacoeconomics in Clinical Trials. 2nd rev. ed. Ed. by Bert Spilker. LC 95-17690. (Illus.). 1259p. 1995. text 162.00 (*0-7817-0332-8*) Lppncott W & W.

***Quality of Life & Psychosomatics: In Mechanical Circulation in Heart Transplantation.** Ed. by W. Albert et al. x, 118p. 1998. 38.00 (*3-7985-0991-3*) Spr-Verlag.

Quality of Life & Technology Assessment. Institute of Medicine Staff. 132p. 1989. pap. text 18.00 (*0-309-04098-1*) Natl Acad Pr.

Quality of Life Assessment - International Perspectives: Proceedings of the Joint Meeting Organized by the World Health Organization & the Foundation IPSEN in Paris, July 2-3,1993. Ed. by J. Orley & W. Kuyken. LC 94-26934. 1994. 96.95 (*0-387-58205-3*) Spr-Verlag.

Quality of Life Assessment in Clinical Trials: Methods & Practice. Ed. by Maurice J. Staquet et al. (Illus.). 370p. 1998. text 47.50 (*0-19-262785-6*) OUP.

Quality of Life Following Renal Failure: Psychosocial Challenges Accompanying High Technology Medicine. Hannah McGee. 1994. pap. write for info. (*3-7186-5522-5*) Gordon & Breach.

Quality of Life Following Renal Failure: Psychosocial Challenges Accompanying High Technology Medicine. Ed. by Hannah M. McGee & Clare Bradley. 312p. 1994. text 59.00 (*3-7186-5501-2*) Gordon & Breach.

Quality of Life for Handicapped People. Ed. by Roy I. Brown. (Rehabilitation Education Ser.: Vol. 3). 300p. 1988. lib. bdg. 59.50 (*0-7099-3992-2*, Pub. by C Helm) Routldge.

Quality of Life for People with Disabilities. 2nd ed. R. I. Brown. (Illus.). 384p. 1997. pap. 85.00 (*1-56593-780-5*, 1522) Singular Publishing.

Quality of Life for Persons with Disabilities: International Perspectives & Issues. Ed. by David A. Goode. LC 94-12011. 334p. 1994. pap. text 35.00 (*0-914797-92-1*) Brookline Bks.

Quality of Life, Health & Happiness. Lennart Nordenfelt. 186p. 1993. 61.95 (*1-85628-553-7*, Pub. by Avebry) Ashgate Pub Co.

Quality of Life in Behavioral Medicine Research. Ed. by Joel E. Dimsdale & Andrew S. Baum. (Perspectives on Behavioral Medicine Ser.). 304p. 1995. text 59.95 (*0-8058-1653-4*) L Erlbaum Assocs.

Quality of Life in Cities: An Overview & Guide to the Literature. Lesley Grayson & Ken Young. (Keynote Ser.). 160p. 1994. pap. 69.95 (*0-7123-0801-6*, Pub. by SRIS) L Erlbaum Assocs.

Quality of Life in Clinical Cancer Trials: Workshop Held at the National Institutes of Health, Bethesda, Maryland, March 1-2, 1995. 124p. 1996. per. 8.00 (*0-16-061573-9*) USGPO.

Quality of Life in Health Care. Ed. by Gary L. Albrecht & Ray Fitzpatrick. (Advances in Medical Sociology Ser.: Vol. 5). 311p. 1994. 78.50 (*1-55938-838-2*) Jai Pr.

Quality of Life in Health Promotion & Rehabilitation: Conceptual Approaches, Issues, & Applications. Rebecca Renwick et al. LC 95-41770. (Illus.). 320p. 1996. 58.00 (*0-8039-5913-3*); pap. 26.95 (*0-8039-5914-1*) Sage.

Quality of Life in London. Roger Jowell et al. LC 95-1651. 1995. 72.95 (*1-85521-676-0*, Pub. by Dartmth Pub) Ashgate Pub Co.

Quality of Life in Long-Term Care. Dorothy H. Coons et al. LC 96-356. (Illus.). 160p. 1996. lib. bdg. 39.95 (*0-7890-6039-6*) Haworth Pr.

Quality of Life in Mental Disorders. Heinz Katschnig et al. LC 97-23241. 402p. 1997. 150.95 (*0-471-96643-6*) Wiley.

***Quality of Life in Rural Asia.** David Bloom. (A Study of Rural Asia: Vol. 4). 496p. 2000. pap. 29.95 (*0-19-592454-1*); text 55.00 (*0-19-592453-3*) OUP.

Quality of Life in South Africa. Ed. by Valerie Moller. LC 97-225175. 300p. 1997. 130.50 (*0-7923-4797-8*) Kluwer Academic.

Quality of Life in the ESCAP Region. 176p. 35.00 (*92-1-127037-5*, E.95.II.F.94) UN.

Quality of Life in the German Democratic Republic: Changes & Developments in a State Socialist Society. Ed. by Marilyn Rueschemeyer & Christiane Lemke. LC 88-4089. 256p. (C). (gr. 13). 1989. text 85.95 (*0-87332-484-6*) M E Sharpe.

Quality of Life Measurement among Persons with Chronic Mental Illness: A Critique of Measures & Methods. Mark J. Atkinson & Sharon Zibin. iv, 65p. 1996. write for info. (*0-662-25002-8*) Intl Spec Bk.

Quality of Life of Lone Parents. McKendrick. 55.95 (*1-85972-190-7*) Ashgate Pub Co.

Quality of Light. Richard Wagamese. LC 97-174485. 288p. 1997. mass mkt. 18.95 (*0-385-25606-X*) Doubleday.

Quality of Light: Modern Italian Short Stories. Ann Caesar. (Modern European Short Stories Ser.). 212p. 1994. pap. 13.99 (*1-85242-188-6*) Serpents Tail.

Quality of Living: Environmental Viewpoints. Ed. by Adamantia Pollis. (Make up Your Own Mind, Ser.: Bk. 3). 1973. 2.50 (*0-910092-03-6*) Am Inst Disc.

***Quality of Meat & Fat in Pigs as Affected by Genetics & Nutrition.** Caspar Wenk. (Illus.). 250p. 2000. pap. 59.00 (*90-74134-74-2*) Wageningen Pers.

Quality of Medical Care: Evaluation & Improvement. Beverly C. Payne. LC 75-27157. 1976. 10.00 (*0-87914-029-1*, 669153) Hosp Res & Educ.

Quality of Mercy. Gerald Grey. 1998. mass mkt. 6.95 (*1-56333-650-2*) Masquerade.

Quality of Mercy. William Dean Howells. LC 78-20655. (Selected Edition of W. D. Howells Ser.). (Illus.). 472p. 1979. 31.50 (*0-253-35789-6*) Ind U Pr.

Quality of Mercy. William Dean Howells. LC 07-5766. 24.00 (*0-403-00067-X*) Scholarly.

Quality of Mercy. Faye Kellerman. 544p. 1990. mass mkt. 6.99 (*0-449-21892-9*, Crest) Fawcett.

Quality of Mercy. Louis S. Means. LC 97-101664. 320p. (Orig.). 1996. pap. write for info. (*0-9652561-1-1*) Pelican Pr CA.

Quality of Mercy. Gilbert Morris. LC 93-32432. (Danielle Ross Mystery Ser.). 312p. (gr. 10). 1993. pap. 9.99 (*0-8007-5474-3*) Revell.

Quality of Mercy. William Dean Howells. (Notable American Authors Ser.). 1992. reprint ed. lib. bdg. 75.00 (*0-7812-3245-7*) Rprt Serv.

Quality of Mercy: A Fresh Look at the Sacrament of Reconciliation. John Arnold. 128p. (C). 1996. pap. 39.95 (*0-85439-433-8*, Pub. by St Paul Pubns) St Mut.

Quality of Mercy: Homelessness in Santa Cruz 1985-1992. Paul A. Lee. 141p. 1992. pap. 7.95 (*0-937011-50-9*) Platonic Acad Pr.

Quality of Mercy: Southern Baptists & Social Christianity, 1890-1920. Keith Harper. (Illus.). 184p. (Orig.). 1996. pap. text 21.95 (*0-8173-0814-8*) U of Ala Pr.

Quality of Nonmetropolitan Living: Evaluations, Behaviors, & Expectations of Northern Michigan Residents. Robert W. Marans & John D. Wellman. LC 78-69913. 279p. reprint ed. pap. 86.50 (*0-7837-5692-5*, 204498300005) Bks Demand.

***Quality of Our Nation's Waters: Nutrients & Pesticides.** Gregory J. Fuhrer. (Illus.). 82p. 2000. pap. text 25.00 (*0-7881-8785-6*) DIANE Pub.

Quality of Pig Meat: Progress of Food & Nutrition Science, Vol. 4, No. 6. Mogens Jul & Peter Zeuthen. 80p. 1981. pap. 24.00 (*0-08-026831-5*, Pergamon Pr) Elsevier.

Quality of Police Education. Lawrence W. Sherman. LC 78-62575. (Jossey-Bass Higher Education Ser.). 289p. reprint ed. pap. 89.60 (*0-608-16906-4*, 202776800056) Bks Demand.

Quality of Primary Schools in Different Development Contexts. Gabriel Carron & Ta N. Chau. 306p. 1992. pap. 35.00 (*0-614-31163-2*, U4591, Pub. by UNESCO) Bernan Associates.

Quality of Prisoner Self-Reports: Arrest & Conviction Response Errors. Kent H. Marquis & Patricia A. Ebener. LC 81-168320. 176p. 1981. pap. 15.00 (*0-8330-0300-3*, R-2637-DOJ) Rand Corp.

Quality of Pupil Learning Experiences. Neville S. Bennett et al. 272p. (C). 1984. 59.95 (*0-86377-010-X*) L Erlbaum Assocs.

Quality of Selected Fruits & Vegetables of North America. Ed. by Roy Teranishi & Heriberto Barrera-Benitez. LC 81-14853. (ACS Symposium Ser.: No. 170). 1981. 32.95 (*0-8412-0662-7*) Am Chemical.

Quality of Selected Fruits & Vegetables of North America. Ed. by Roy Teranishi & Heriberto Barrera-Benitez. LC 81-14853. (ACS Symposium Ser.: No. 170). (Illus.). 251p. 1981. reprint ed. pap. 77.90 (*0-608-03249-2*, 206376800007) Bks Demand.

***Quality of Service: Delivering QoS on the Internet & in Corporate Networks.** Paul Ferguson & Geoff Huston. LC 97-41656. 288p. 1998. pap. 39.99 (*0-471-24358-2*) Wiley.

***Quality of Service in ATM Networks: State-of-the-Art Traffic Management.** Natale Giroux. LC 98-40883. 400p. 1998. 67.00 (*0-13-095387-3*) P-H.

***Quality of Service in IP Networks.** 300p. 2000. 50.00 (*1-57870-189-9*) Macmillan Tech.

Quality of Service in Telecommunications. A. P. Oodan et al. (Telecommunications Ser.: No. 39). 400p. 1998. 95.00 (*0-85296-919-8*, TE039) INSPEC Inc.

***Quality of Service Networking with Microsoft Windows Nt.** Bernet Yoram. (gr. 8). 1999. pap. 39.99 (*0-7356-0681-1*) Microsoft.

Quality of Social Relations: Some Aspects of Self-Conception of a Group of Elderly People. Satya M. Klason. (Studia Psychologica & Paedagogica: No. CXIV). 310p. (Orig.). 1994. pap. 65.00 (*91-22-01624-4*) Coronet Bks.

Quality of Surface Fresh Water Common Procedure for the Exchange of Information: 1990-92 Synthesis Report. 300p. 1997. pap. 80.00 (*92-827-8952-7*, CR-99-96-811ENC, Pub. by Comm Europ Commun) Bernan Associates.

Quality of Surface Freshwater: Common Procedure for the Exchange of Information. European Communities Staff. 280p. 1995. pap. text 55.00 (*92-826-9396-1*, CR-86-94-836-EN, Pub. by Comm Europ Commun) Bernan Associates.

Quality of the Educational Process in the United States & Europe. William S. Learned. LC 75-165740. (American Education Ser., No. 2). 1972. reprint ed. 13.95 (*0-405-03610-8*) Ayer.

Quality of the Environment. James L. McCamy. LC 72-80576. 1972. 19.95 (*0-02-920480-1*) Free Pr.

Quality of the Environment: An Economic Approach to Some Problems in Using Land, Water & Air. Orris C. Herfindahl & Allen V. Kneese. (Resources for the Future Ser.). 104p. (Orig.). 1965. pap. 9.95 (*0-8018-0268-7*) Johns Hopkins.

Quality of the Indoor Environment: Scientific & Regulatory Aspects. Ed. by D. F. Weetman. (Journal: Indoor Environment: Vol. 2, No. 4, 1993). (Illus.). 64p. 1993. pap. 35.00 (*3-8055-5917-8*) S Karger.

Quality of the Light. Teresa Kao. 432p. 1992. pap. 10.95 (*0-9631499-0-3*) Gangor Pr.

Quality of the Urban Environment: Essays on "New Resources" in an Urban Age. Ed. by Harvey S. Perloff. LC 69-16858. 332p. 1969. pap. 14.95 (*0-8018-1028-0*) Resources Future.

Quality of Trade Credit. Martin H. Seiden. (Occasional Papers: No. 87). 151p. 1964. reprint ed. 39.30 (*0-87014-401-4*) Natl Bur Econ Res.

Quality of U. S. Agricultural Products. Task Force of Scientists Staff. LC 95-20910. (Task Force Reports: No. 125). (Illus.). 288p. (Orig.). 1996. pap. 40.00 (*1-887383-04-2*) CAST.

Quality of U. S. Agricultural Products: Summary & Conclusions. Task Force of Scientists Staff. (Illus.). 21p. (Orig.). 1996. pap. 10.00 (*1-887383-05-0*) CAST.

Quality of Urban Life. Fakhruddin. (C). 1991. 18.00 (*0-685-59785-7*, Pub. by Rawat Pubns) S Asia.

Quality of Urban Life. Ed. by Henry J. Schmandt & Warner Bloomberg, Jr. LC 69-18752. (Urban Affairs Annual Reviews Ser.: Vol. 3). 590p. reprint ed. pap. 168.20 (*0-608-09941-4*, 2021955) Bks Demand.

Quality of Urban Life: Social, Psychological & Physical Conditions. Ed. by Dieter Frick. (Illus.). x, 262p. 1986. lib. bdg. 95.75 (*3-11-010577-2*) De Gruyter.

Quality of Work Life: Perspectives for Business & the Public Sector. American Society for Training & Development (ASTD). Ed. by Daniel J. Skrovan. 208p. 1983. text. write for info. (*0-201-07755-8*) Addison-Wesley.

Quality of Work Life Assessment: A Survey-Based Approach. James L. Bowditch & Anthony F. Buono. LC 82-3945. 188p. 1982. 49.95 (*0-86569-067-7*, Auburn Hse) Greenwood.

Quality of Work Life in Japan. Japan Productivity Center Staff. Ed. & Tr. by Asian Productivity Organization Staff. (Monograph Ser.: No. 10). 77p. 1991. pap. text 7.50 (*92-833-1810-2*, 318102) Productivity Inc.

Quality of Working Life in Western & Eastern Europe, 25. Ed. by Cary L. Cooper & Enid Mumford. LC 78-27692. (Contributions in Economics & Economic History Ser.: No. 25). 348p. 1979. 75.00 (*0-313-20957-X*, CWL/, Greenwood Pr) Greenwood.

Quality of Working Life of Women Construction Workers. R. N. Mathur. 1989. 26.50 (*81-7169-000-9*, Pub. by Commonwealth) S Asia.

Quality of Worklife & the Supervisor. Leonard A. Schlesinger. LC 82-11291. 208p. 1982. 57.95 (*0-275-91711-8*, C1711, Praeger Pubs) Greenwood.

Quality of Writing. Andrew Wilkinson. LC 85-29774. (English, Language & Education Ser.). 176p. 1986. 33.95 (*0-335-15229-5*) OpUniv Pr.

Quality on Trial: Bringing Bottom-Line Accountability to the Quality Effort. 2nd ed. Roger J. Howe et al. 163p. 1994. 24.95 (*0-07-030583-8*) McGraw.

Quality on Trial: Is Your Quality Initiative Paying Off? Roger J. Howe et al. (Illus.). 150p. (Orig.). 1992. write for info. (*0-9632939-0-7*); pap. write for info. (*0-9632939-3-1*) Quality Inst Intl.

Quality or Else: The Revolution in World Business. Lloyd Dobyns & Clare Crawford-Mason. 320p. 1993. pap. 11.95 (*0-395-63749-X*) HM.

***Quality-Oriented Design of Business Processes** K. Mertins & R. Jochem. LC 99-29500. 1999. write for info. (*0-7923-8484-9*) Kluwer Academic.

Quality Pasture: How to Create It, Manage It & Profit from It. Allan Nation. (Illus.). (C). 1995. pap. 32.50 (*0-9632460-3-8*) Green Park.

Quality Perceptions of Parboiled Rice Marketed in Sri Lanka. P. A. Clarke et al. 1997. pap. 60.00 (*0-85954-479-6*, Pub. by Nat Res Inst) St Mut.

Quality Performance: How to Implement: Quality Awareness; Statistical Process Control; Task Teams; & Statistical Quality Control for Continuous Improvement in Your Organization. Nancy S. Mitchell. LC 90-91657. (Illus.). 184p. 1991. 39.95 (*0-9626692-5-3*) QP Pub PA.

Quality Performance in Human Services: Leadership, Values & Vision. James F. Gardner et al. LC 98-30589. 371p. 1998. 38.00 (*1-55766-360-2*) P H Brookes.

Quality Plan: Practical Advice to Keep Claims Clients Coming Back. Kevin M. Quinley. 204p. 1992. 19.95 (*0-9634957-0-4*) Insuranceweek.

Quality Planning & Analysis. 3rd ed. Juran. 1993. teacher ed. 27.50 (*0-07-033184-7*) McGraw.

Quality Planning & Analysis. 3rd ed. Joseph M. Juran. 672p. (C). 1993. 90.63 (*0-07-033183-9*) McGraw.

Quality Planning, Control & Improvement in Research & Development. Ed. by George W. Roberts. LC 94-39690. (Quality & Reliability Ser.: Vol. 44). (Illus.). 384p. 1994. text 125.00 (*0-8247-9585-7*) Dekker.

***Quality Point of Care Testing: A Joint Commission Handbook.** Joint Commission on Accreditation of Healthcare Organizations. (Illus.). 142p. 1999. pap. 47.00 (*0-86688-604-4*, POC-100) Joint Comm Hlthcare.

Quality Policing: The Madison Experience. David C. Couper. LC 90-61772. 100p. (C). 1991. pap. 11.00 (*1-878734-22-9*) Police Exec Res.

Quality Practice Management: A Manual for Law Firms. Ed. by Ronald J. Waicukauski & Richard B. Allen. LC 95-77969. 252p. 1995. pap. 95.00 (*0-9621989-6-X*) IADC IL.

Quality Practices & the Law. Harold L. Federow. LC 96-41907. 234p. 1996. pap. 34.95 (*0-527-76307-1*) Productivity Inc.

Quality Principles. Multimedia Development Services Staff. (Plant Fundamentals Ser.: Vol. XII, Module I). (Illus.). 1995. teacher ed. 49.95 (*1-57431-077-1*); student ed. 30.00 (*1-57431-037-2*) Tech Trng Systs.

Quality Principles & Practices in Higher Education: Different Questions for Different Times. Jann E. Freed & Marie Klugman. LC 97-33706. (American Council on Education/Oryx Press Series on Higher Education). 264p. (C). 1997. boxed set 34.95 (*1-57356-052-9*) Oryx Pr.

Quality Problem Solving. Gerald F. Smith. LC 97-44035. (Illus.). 332p. 1998. 33.00 (*0-87389-394-8*, H0983) ASQ Qual Pr.

Quality Professor: Implementing TQM in the Classroom. Robert Comesky. 209p. 1993. pap. text 22.95 (*1-891859-15-3*) Atwood Pub LLC.

Quality Professor: Implementing TQM in the Classroom. Robert A. Cornesky. Ed. by Jennifer Lind et al. LC 93-43859. 209p. 1993. 22.95 (*0-912150-29-7*) Atwood Pub LLC.

Quality Program: Quality Plan Manual. Ed. by Jenni L. Robbins. LC 94-27478. (Illus.). (C). 1994. ring bd. 175.00 (*1-56395-040-5*) Am Assn Blood.

Quality Program: Self-Assessment Manual. Ed. by Jenni L. Robbins. LC 94-27478. (Illus.). (C). 1994. ring bd. 175.00 (*1-56395-039-1*) Am Assn Blood.

Quality Promise. Ed. by Lester Wollschlaeger. (Quality & Reliability Ser.: Vol. 22). (Illus.). 216p. 1990. text 99.75 (*0-8247-8389-1*) Dekker.

Quality Promotion in Europe. Brendan Barker. 300p. 1994. 113.95 (*0-566-07512-1*, Pub. by Gower) Ashgate Pub Co.

Quality Protein Maize. Ed. by Edwin T. Mertz. LC 92-71401. (Illus.). 294p. (Orig.). 1992. pap. 76.00 (*0-913250-75-9*) Am Assn Cereal Chem.

Quality Pursuit: Assuring Standards in the Practice of Law. LC 89-84877. 275p. 1989. pap. 84.95 (*0-89707-477-7*, 511-0268) Amer Bar Assn.

Quality Quilting Quarters. Elizabeth Chandler & Joanne Donahue. (Illus.). 240p. (Orig.). 1995. pap. 9.95 (*0-9636371-3-4*) Lizanne Pub.

Quality Quotes. Helio Gomes. LC 96-8141. 249p. 1996. text 24.25 (*0-87389-407-3*, H0909) ASQ Qual Pr.

Quality Reengineering in Healthcare: A Case Study from the Clinical Laboratory of the University of Wisconsin Hospital & Clinics. Russel H. Tomar et al. LC 98-7848. 1998. 35.00 (*0-89189-435-7*) Am Soc Clinical.

Quality, Reliability & Process Improvement. 8th ed. Norbert L Enrick. (Illus.). 396p. 1985. 26.95 (*0-8311-1125-9*) Indus Pr.

Quality Requirements of Super-Duty Steels. Ed. by R. W. Lindsay. LC 59-14904. (Metallurgical Society Conference Ser.: Vol. 3). 319p. reprint ed. pap. 98.90 (*0-608-11551-7*, 200066600038) Bks Demand.

Quality Resource Packet for Trustees. American Hospital Association Staff. 78p. (Orig.). 1992. pap. 100.00 (*0-87258-629-4*, 196300) Am Hospital.

Quality Resource Planning: How to Integrate & Automate Your Quality Management System. unabridged ed. Jack Blazejak. LC 98-92986. (Illus.). 219p. 1998. pap. 27.95 (*0-9664918-0-7*) Elemental Pubns.

Quality Restaurant Service Guaranteed: A Training Outline. Nancy L. Scanlon. LC 98-4730. 224p. 1998. 44.95 (*0-471-02852-5*) Wiley.

Quality Review Schemes for Auditors: Their Potential for Sub-Saharan Africa. Sonia R. Johnson. LC 95-1367. (Technical Papers: Vol. 276). 104p. 1995. pap. 22.00 (*0-8213-3168-X*, 13168) World Bank.

Quality Roadmap: How to Get on the Quality Track & Keep It There. Ray Svenson et al. 196p. 1993. 24.95 (*0-8144-5117-9*) AMACOM.

Quality, Safety, & Environment: Synergy in the 21st Century. Pascal Dennis. LC 96-39878. 213p. 1997. 38.00 (*0-87389-379-4*, H0959) ASQ Qual Pr.

Quality Sampling & Reliability: New Uses for the Poisson Distribution. John J. Heldt. LC 98-29939. 1998. 49.95 (*1-57444-241-4*) St Lucie Pr.

Quality Sanitation Management. Ronald F. Cichy. LC 94-16272. (Illus.). 448p. 1994. write for info. (*0-86612-084-X*) Educ Inst Am Hotel.

Quality School. 2nd ed. William Glasser. LC 92-52634. 336p. 1992. pap. 13.00 (*0-06-096955-5*, Perennial) HarperTrade.

Quality School RI. 3rd rev. ed. William Glasser. LC 98-12112. 192p. 1998. pap. 12.00 (*0-06-095286-5*, Perennial) HarperTrade.

Quality School Teacher. William Glasser. LC 92-56268. 176p. (Orig.). 1993. pap. 12.00 (*0-06-095019-6*, Perennial) HarperTrade.

Quality School Teacher RI. rev. ed. William Glasser. LC 92-56268. 144p. 1998. pap. 12.00 (*0-06-095285-7*) HarpC.

Quality Secret: The Right Way to Manage. 1992. write for info. (*0-9631464-0-8*) Conway Qual.

Quality Secretary: Success Secrets from TOM Support Staff. Marlene Caroselli. 150p. (Orig.). 1992. pap. 9.95 (*0-922411-02-6*) CPD NY.

Quality Service: The Restaurant Manager's Bible. William B. Martin. 1986. 9.95 (*0-937056-05-7*, FB5) Cornell U Sch Hotel.

Quality Service - The Restaurant Manager's Bible. 176p. 1988. 11.95 (*0-318-33265-5*, 118) Am Bartenders.

Quality Service Pays: Six Keys to Success. Henry L. Lefevre. (Illus.). 375p. 1989. 32.95 (*0-527-91629-3*, 916293) Productivity Inc.

Quality Service Teamwork: The Foundations of Excellence. Compiled by Successories, Inc. Editors. (Power of One Ser.). 48p. 1998. pap. 5.95 (*1-880461-46-3*) Successories Inc.

Quality Services: A Progress Report 1996. LC 98-228646. ii, 55p. 1997. write for info. (*0-662-62837-3*) Can7 Govern Pub.

Quality Shipping: Market Mechanisms for Safer Shipping & Cleaner Oceans. Ed. by H. E. Haralambides. (Illus.). 468p. 1998. 140.00 (*90-5235-128-7*) Erasmus Pub.

Quality Software Applications for C++ Duffy. (C). 2000. pap. 40.00 (*0-13-261157-0*) P-H.

Quality Software Applications for C++ Daniel J. Duffy. (Advances in Object Technology Ser.: Vol. 13). (Orig.). 1996. pap. 40.00 (*1-884842-35-6*, 2356) SIGS Bks & Multimedia.

Quality Software Management, Vol. 1: Systems Thinking. Gerald M. Weinberg. LC 91-18061. (Illus.). 336p. 1992. 41.95 (*0-932633-22-6*) Dorset Hse Pub Co.

Quality Software Management, Vol. 2: First-Order Measurement. Gerald M. Weinberg. LC 91-18061. (Illus.). 360p. (C). 1993. 43.95 (*0-932633-24-2*) Dorset Hse Pub Co.

Quality Software Management, Vol. 3: Congruent Action. Gerald M. Weinberg. LC 91-18061. (Illus.). 328p. 1994. 39.95 (*0-932633-28-5*) Dorset Hse Pub Co.

Quality Software Management Vol. 4: Anticipating Change. Gerald M. Weinberg. LC 91-18061. (Illus.). 480p. 1996. 44.95 (*0-932633-32-3*) Dorset Hse Pub Co.

Quality Specification for the UPC Printed Symbol. 1994. 30.00 (*0-614-15092-2*) Uniform Code.

Quality Standard for Instrument Air. William E. Lewis. LC 98-45186. 448p. 1998. ring bd. 285.00 (*0-8493-9980-7*) CRC Pr.

Quality Standard for Instrument Air: S7.0.01. ANSI/ISA Staff. (Pneumatics & Instrument Air Ser.). 1996. 80.00 (*1-55617-606-6*, S7.0.01) ISA.

***Quality Standards for Evaluating Multimedia & Online Training.** Lynette Gillis. 240p. 2000. 99.95 (*0-07-086385-7*, Schaums Outlne) McGraw-Hill Prof.

Quality Standards for the Professional Remodeler. rev. ed. National Association of Home Builders, Remodelors. LC 90-24100. 81p. 1991. reprint ed. 18.00 (*0-86718-359-4*) Home Builder.

Quality Supervision: Theory & Practice. Best. (C). 1996. text 51.00 (*0-7020-2121-0*) Harcourt.

QUALITY SUPPL-CONTEMP BUS 7E,8. 7th ed. Alice Fugate. 47p. (C). 1993. pap. text 13.50 (*0-03-097686-3*) Dryden Pr.

Quality System: A Sourcebook for Managers & Engineers. 2nd ed. Frank Caplan. LC 89-42860. 352p. 1990. lib. bdg. 49.95 (*0-8019-7975-7*) NP-Chilton.

Quality System Compendium: GMP Requirements & Industry Practice. Susan S. Reilly et al. (Orig.). 1996. pap. 295.00 (*1-57020-076-9*, GMPS-209) Assn Adv Med Instrn.

Quality System in Construction. Compiled by American Society of Civil Engineers Staff. 210p. 1974. pap. 3.00 (*0-87262-073-5*) Am Soc Civil Eng.

Quality Systems & GMP Regulations for Device Manufacturers: A Practical Guide to U. S., European, & ISO Requirements. Steven S. Kuwahara. LC 98-10632. 256p. 1998. 50.00 (*0-87389-426-X*, H0994) ASQ Qual Pr.

Quality Systems for Medical Laboratories: Guidelines for Implementation & Monitoring. (WHO Regional Publications, Eastern Mediterranean Ser.: No. 14). 105p. (Orig.). 1995. pap. text 18.00 (*0-614-17672-7*, 1440014) World Health.

Quality Systems for Medical Laboratories: Guidelines for Implementation & Monitoring. M. M. El-Nageh et al. LC 96-190901. (Regional Publications, Eastern Mediterranean Ser.: Vol. 14). 105p. 1995. pap. 20.00 (*92-9021-203-9*, 1440014) World Health.

Quality Systems in the Blood Bank & Laboratory Environment. David E. Nevalainen & Marjana F. Callery. (Illus.). (C). 1994. pap. text 89.00 (*1-56395-038-3*) Am Assn Blood.

Quality Systems in the Blood Bank Environment. 2nd ed. Ed. by Leane Ziebel & Kathy Keuemeir. LC 99-182220. 1999. text. write for info. (*1-56395-098-7*) Am Assn Blood.

Quality Systems in the Nuclear Industry - STP 616. Ed. by B. W. Marguglio. 700p. 1977. 37.75 (*0-8031-0197-X*, STP616) ASTM.

Quality Systems Manual: The Definitive Guide to ISO 9000 Family & TickIT. 2nd ed. Terence J. Hall. 406p. 1995. pap. 225.00 (*0-471-95588-4*, TS156) Wiley.

Quality Teaching: A Sample of Cases. Edgar Stones. LC 94-17231. 352p. (C). 1994. pap. 22.99 (*0-415-11987-1*, B4878) Routledge.

Quality Teaching in Higher Education: Reflections of Award-Winning Missouri Professors. Ed. by Betty J. Bush. 137p. (C). 1994. pap. 19.95 (*0-9633819-7-0*) Prescott Pub.

Quality Teaching Through Professional Development. Allan A. Glatthorn & Linda E. Fox. Ed. by John T. Greer & Donn W. Gresso. LC 95-21332. (Principals Taking Action (PTA) Ser.). (Illus.). 160p. 1995. pap. 22.95 (*0-8039-6274-6*) Corwin Pr.

Quality Teaching Through Professional Development. Allan A. Glatthorn & Linda E. Fox. Ed. by John T. Greer & Donn W. Gresso. LC 95-21332. (Principals Taking Action (PTA) Ser.). (Illus.). 160p. 1995. 51.95 (*0-8039-6273-8*) Corwin Pr.

Quality Team Learning for Schools: A Principal's Perspective. James E. Abbott. LC 97-49869. 170p. 1998. 25.00 (*0-87389-384-0*, H0973) ASQ Qual Pr.

Quality Team Workbook. Barbara Katz. 112p. 1999. ring bd. 9.95 (*0-9640405-2-2*, Pub. by Hlth Interact) BookMasters.

Quality Teams. Multimedia Development Services Staff. (Plant Fundamentals Ser.: Vol. XII, Module III). (Illus.). 1995. teacher ed. 49.95 (*1-57431-079-8*); student ed. 30.00 (*1-57431-039-9*) Tech Trng Systs.

Quality Technicians Handbook. 4th ed. Griffith. LC 99-32127. 577p. 1999. 81.00 (*0-13-674250-5*) P-H.

Quality Tests for Florida Citrus. W. F. Wardowski et al. LC 95-48875. 1995. write for info. (*0-916287-16-5*) Univ Fla Food.

Quality Through Design: Experimental Design, Off-line Quality Control, & Taguchi's Contributions. Nicholas Logothetis & H. P. Wynn. (Oxford Series on Advanced Manufacturing: No. 7). (Illus.). 476p. 1995. pap. text 60.00 (*0-19-859395-3*) OUP.

Quality Through Design: Experimental Design, Off-Line Quality Control, & Taguchi's Contributions. Nicholas Logothetis & H. P. Wynn. (Oxford Series on Advanced Manufacturing: No. 7). (Illus.). 476p. 1990. text 120.00 (*0-19-851993-1*) OUP.

Quality Time. Dennis O'Driscoll. LC 97-201170. 96p. 1997. pap. 17.95 (*0-85646-290-X*, Pub. by Anvil Press) Dufour.

Quality Time: Parenting, Progeny & Pets. Edward Koren. 1995. 15.00 (*0-679-74835-0*) Villard Books.

Quality Time: The Report of the Twentieth Century Fund Task Force on the Future of Public Television: With Background Paper "A System in Crisis" Richard Somerset-Ward. LC 93-17145. 188p. (Orig.). 1993. pap. 9.95 (*0-87078-354-8*) Century Foundation.

Quality Time: The Thoughts & Observations of an Ex-Con. Arthur Rayford. 144p. (Orig.). 1995. pap. text 15.95 (*1-885066-03-1*) Four-G Pubs.

Quality Time Easy Readers, 5 vols., Set. (Illus.). 160p. (J). (gr. k-3). 1990. lib. bdg. 64.75 (*1-56674-925-5*) Forest Hse.

Quality Time for Quality Kids. Glenn Smith & Kathy Tomberlin. LC 92-50331. (Illus.). 183p. (J). (gr. k-5). 1992. reprint ed. pap. 25.00 (*0-944337-09-0*, 090) New View Pubns.

Quality Time on Highway 1. Garry B. Trudeau. LC 92-75355. (Doonesbury Bks.). (Illus.). 96p. 1993. pap. 7.95 (*0-8362-1712-8*) Andrews & McMeel.

Quality Toolbox. Nancy R. Tague. LC 94-33049. 298p. 1995. pap. 37.00 (*0-87389-314-X*, H0861) ASQ Qual Pr.

Quality Tools. Multimedia Development Services Staff. (Plant Fundamentals Ser.: Vol. XII, Module II). (Illus.). 1995. teacher ed. 49.95 (*1-57431-078-X*); student ed. 30.00 (*1-57431-038-0*) Tech Trng Systs.

Quality, TQC, TQM: A Meta Literature Study. Robert E. Kemper. LC 97-20971. 1997. 59.50 (*0-8108-3346-8*) Scarecrow.

Quality up, Costs Down: A Manager's Guide to Taguchi Methods & QFD. William E. Eureka & Nancy Ryan. LC 94-14951. 240p. 1994. text 25.00 (*0-7863-0218-6*, Irwn Prfssnl) McGraw-Hill Prof.

Quality Upstream: Quality Concepts Conference & Exposition, 1992. Pref. by Jim Paulsen. (Illus.). 1992. 50.00 (*1-56378-009-7*) ESD.

***Quality Use of Medicines.** Mant. (Illus.). 160p. 1999. 34.95 (*0-07-470769-8*, McGrw-H College) McGrw-H Hghr Educ.

Quality Venison: Homemade Recipes & Homespun Deer Tales. Steve Loder & Gale Loder. LC 98-140318. (Illus.). 176p. 1998. 14.95 (*0-9662284-0-5*) Loders Game.

***Quality Venison Vol. II: All New Recipes & Deer Tales Too.** Steve Loder & Gale Loder. (Illus.). 192p. 1999. 14.95 (*0-9662284-1-3*) Loders Game.

Quality Verification of Recollection. Beverly Sheridan. (C). 1991. text 9.95 (*0-913412-63-5*) Brandon Hse.

Quality, Warranty, & Preventive Maintenance. Izzet Sahin & Hakan Polatoglu. LC 98-38749. (International Series in Operations Research & Management Science). 1998. 135.00 (*0-7923-8292-7*) Kluwer Academic.

Quality Wars. Main. 1994. text 29.95 (*0-13-440744-X*) S&S Trade.

Quality Wars: The Triumphs & Defeats of American Business. Jeremy Main. LC 93-41905. 256p. 1994. 32.95 (*0-02-916684-5*) Free Pr.

Quality Whitetails: The Why & How of Quality Deer Management. R. Larry Marchinton & Karl V. Miller. LC 95-18450. (Illus.). 320p. 1995. 29.95 (*0-8117-1387-3*) Stackpole.

Quality Without Tears. Philip B. Crosby. 1985. pap. 12.00 (*0-452-26398-0*, Plume) Dutton Plume.

Quality Without Tears: The Art of Hassle-Free Management. Philip B. Crosby. 205p. 1984. 29.95 (*0-07-014530-X*) McGraw.

Quality Without Tears: The Art of Hassle-Free Management. Philip B. Crosby. 205p. 1995. pap. 11.95 (*0-07-014511-3*) McGraw.

Quality Work. Jim Joyner. 1993. write for info. (*0-931117-14-3*) Univ Pub.

***Quality Work: A People-Centered Agenda.** Graham S. Lowe. (Illus.). 200p. 2000. pap. text 19.95 (*0-19-541479-9*) OUP.

Quality Yearbook, 1998. James W. Cortada & John A. Woods. 800p. 1997. 89.95 (*0-07-071853-9*) McGraw.

Quality Yearbook, 1999. James W. Cortada & John A. Woods. (ASQ Ser.). (Illus.). 800p. 1999. 128.95 (*0-07-071874-1*) McGraw-Hill Prof.

Quality Yearbook, 1997. James W. Cortada & John A. Woods. 787p. 1996. 89.95 (*0-07-913281-2*) McGraw.

***Quality Yearbook 2001.** James W. Cortada. 2001. 89.95 (*0-07-136506-0*) McGraw.

***Quality Yearbook 2000.** 2nd ed. James W. Cortada. 784p. 1999. 89.95 (*0-07-135247-3*) Datapro Res.

Qualitysense: Organizational Approaches to Improving Product Quality & Service. Martin R. Smith. LC 79-18139. 208p. reprint ed. pap. 64.50 (*0-608-12447-8*, 205575100036) Bks Demand.

Qualla: Home of the Middle Cherokee Settlement. T. Walter Middleton. LC 98-37861. (Illus.). 287p. 1998. pap. 16.95 (*1-56664-136-5*) WorldComm.

Qualla Cherokee Surviving in Two Worlds. Laurence A. French. LC 98-8628. (Native American Studies: Vol. 5). 252p. 1998. text 89.95 (*0-7734-8308-X*) E Mellen.

***Qualms Before the Storm.** David P. Hammond. LC 99-96962. 275p. 1999. pap. 12.95 (*0-9676042-0-6*) D P Hammond.

QualServe Guidance for Peer Review. Glenn Nestel et al. LC 97-184383. (Illus.). 184p. 1997. pap. 195.00 (*0-89867-908-7*, 90730) Am Water Wks Assn.

Qualtitative Analysis & Ionic Equilibrium, 3 vols. 3rd ed. George H. Schenk. (C). 1995. pap. text 21.96 (*0-395-77079-3*) HM.

Qualtiy Assurance in Analytical Chemistry. Werner Funk et al. Tr. by Ann Gray. LC 95-30345. 238p. 1995. 115.00 (*3-527-28668-3*, Wiley-VCH) Wiley.

"Quam Pulchra Es", for a Cappella SATB Chorus: After Dunstable. Brian Banks. (University Choral Ser.: No. 3). 6p. 1992. pap. text 2.00 (*1-56571-065-7*, UC003) PRB Prods.

Quanah: Pictorial History of the Last Comanche Chief. unabridged ed. Pauline Durrett Robertson & R. L. Robertson. (Illus.). 230p. 2000. 39.95 (*0-942376-08-0*) Paramount TX.

Quanah Parker. Bill Dugan. (War Chiefs Ser.: No. 4). 320p. 2000. mass mkt. 5.50 (*0-06-100449-9*, Harp PBks) HarpC.

Quanah Parker: Comanche Chief. Rosemary K. Kissinger. LC 90-23036. (Illus.). 136p. (gr. 4-7). 1991. pap. 13.95 (*1-56554-557-5*) Pelican.

Quanah Parker: Warrior for Freedom, Ambassador for Peace. Len Hilts. LC 87-8488. (Great Episodes Ser.). (Illus.). 96p. (J). (gr. 3-7). 1987. 12.95 (*0-15-200565-X*, Gulliver Bks) Harcourt.

Quanah Parker: Warrior for Freedom, Ambassador for Peace. Len Hilts. LC 87-8488. (Great Episodes Ser.). (Illus.). 96p. (J). (gr. 3-7). 1992. pap. 4.95 (*0-15-264447-4*, Gulliver Bks) Harcourt.

Quanah Parker Comanche Chief. William T. Hagan. LC 92-31563. (Oklahoma Western Biographies Ser.: Vol. 6). (Illus.). 160p. 1995. pap. 9.95 (*0-8061-2772-4*) U of Okla Pr.

Quanah Parker's Strange Encounters: A Biography. Mary R. Dees. LC 97-93449. (Illus.). 252p. (Orig.). 1997. pap. 14.95 (*0-9630600-4-X*, 0-9630600) Marmor.

Quanah Route: A History of the Quanah, Acme & Pacific Railway. Don L. Hofsommer. LC 90-35219. (Illus.). 232p. 1991. 42.50 (*0-89096-437-8*) Tex A&M Univ Pr.

Quanative Analysis & Statistics for Management, 1998 (C). 1997. pap. 38.89 (*0-536-00954-6*) Pearson Custom.

Quand Elle Etait Gentille. Philip Roth. (FRE.). 1985. pap. 19.95 (*0-7859-4233-5*) Fr & Eur.

Quand Gesu Sorrise see When Jesus Smiled

Quand J'etais Photographie. Gaspard F. Nadar. Ed. by Robert A. Sobieszek & Peter C. Bunnell. LC 76-24657. (Sources of Modern Photography Ser.). (FRE.). 1979. reprint ed. lib. bdg. 18.95 (*0-405-09636-4*) Ayer.

Quand la Ville Dort. William R. Burnett. (FRE.). 310p. 1989. pap. 11.95 (*0-7859-2133-8*, 2070382087) Fr & Eur.

Quand les Petites Filles s'Appelaient Sarah. Remo Forlani. (FRE.). 285p. 1989. pap. 11.95 (*0-7859-2567-8*, 2070381277) Fr & Eur.

Quand Prime le Spirituel. Simone de Beauvoir. (FRE.). 250p. 1980. 29.95 (*0-8288-9681-X*, 2070286223) Fr & Eur.

Quand Tu Vas Chez les Femmes. Christiane Rochefort. (FRE.). 1983. pap. 4.95 (*0-7859-3112-0*) Fr & Eur.

Quandary 2000: The How to Guide for Developing & Implementing a Plan to Address the Y2K Computer Issues. 2nd rev. ed. William H. Dudley. Ed. by Miguel Fuentes & Bev Dudley. vi, 43p. 1998. 29.95 (*0-9669857-0-2*) JC Cnsltng.

Quanderno Di Quattro Anni see It Depends: A Poet's Notebook

Quando a Corde Se Rompe. Stephen Brown.Tr. of When Your Rope Breaks. (POR & SPA.). 156p. 1991. pap. 7.95 (*0-8297-1642-4*) Vida Pubs.

Quando il Papa Chiede Perdono see When a Pope Asks Forgiveness: The Mea Culpa's of John Paul II

Quandt'sche Gebuhrentabellen: Fur Rechtsanwaete und Notare, Gerichtsvollzieher und Rechtsbestande, Ordentliche Gerichte und Arbeitsgerichte, Gerichte der Verwaltungs, Sozial und Finanzgerichtsbarkeit, Freiwillige Gerichtsbarkeit und Strafsachen. Begrundet Von Gottfried Quandt. (GER.). 72p. 1985. pap. 16.95 (*3-11-010335-4*) De Gruyter.

Quang Tri Cadence: Memoir of a Rifle Platoon Leader in the Mountains of Vietnam. Jon Oplinger. LC 92-56676. (Illus.). 220p. 1993. pap. 17.95 (*0-89950-873-1*) McFarland & Co.

Quangle Wangle's Hat. Edward Lear. LC 87-29616. (Illus.). 32p. (J). (ps-3). 1988. 12.95 (*0-15-264450-4*) Harcourt.

Quangle Wangle's Hat. Edward Lear. LC 87-29616. (Illus.). 32p. (J). 1997. pap. 6.00 (*0-15-201478-0*) Harcourt.

Quangle Wangle's Hat. Edward Lear. (J). 1997. 11.20 (*0-606-11774-1*, Pub. by Turtleback) Demco.

Quangos, Accountability & Reform: The Politics of Quasi-Government. Flinders. LC 98-28244. 256p. 1998. text 65.00 (*0-312-21644-0*) St Martin.

QUANGOs & Local Government: A Changing World. Ed. by Howard Davis. 220p. 1996. pap. 22.00 (*0-7146-4324-6*, Pub. by F Cass Pubs); text 35.00 (*0-7146-4735-7*, Pub. by F Cass Pubs) Intl Spec Bk.

Quant a la Femme. Francis Iles. (FRE.). 247p. 1986. pap. 11.95 (*0-7859-2523-6*, 2070377857) Fr & Eur.

Quant a Moi. Bragger. (College French Ser.). (FRE.). (C). 1996. mass mkt., teacher ed. 41.95 (*0-8384-6346-0*) Heinle & Heinle.

Quant a Moi. Bragger. (College French Ser.). (FRE.). (C). 1996. text, suppl. ed. 6.95 (*0-8384-6348-7*) Heinle & Heinle.

Quant a Moi. Bragger. (College French Ser.). (FRE.). (C). 1996. mass mkt., suppl. ed. 36.95 (*0-8384-6349-5*) Heinle & Heinle.

Quant a Moi. Bragger & Rice. (FRE.). 1996. text, wbk. ed. 33.00 incl. audio (*0-8384-5599-9*) Thomson Learn.

Quant a Moi. 2nd ed. Bragger. (College French Ser.). (FRE.). (C). 1996. suppl. ed. 14.95 incl. audio (*0-8384-6347-9*) Heinle & Heinle.

***Quant a Moi.** 2nd ed. Bragger & Rice. (C). 2000. text 46.95 (*0-8384-0585-1*) Heinle & Heinle.

Quant a Moi . . . Manuel de Preparation. 2nd ed. Jeannette D. Bragger & Donald Rice. (FRE.). (C). 1996. pap. 36.95 (*0-8384-6345-2*) Heinle & Heinle.

Quant a Moi... Temoignages de France et Du Monde Francophone: Manuel de Classe. Jeanette D. Bragger & Donald Rice. LC 95-40418. (FRE.). (C). 1996. mass mkt., student ed. 61.95 (*0-8384-6344-4*) Heinle & Heinle.

Quant Method For Business 5e. 5th ed. David R. Anderson et al. Ed. by Schiller. (SWC-Finance). 851p. (C). 1991. mass mkt. 64.75 (*0-314-90781-5*) West Pub.

Quanta: A Handbook of Concepts. 2nd ed. P. W. Atkins. (Illus.). 440p. 1991. pap. text 55.00 (*0-19-855573-3*) OUP.

Quanta: Essays in Theoretical Physics Dedicated to Gregory Wentzel. Ed. by Peter G. Freund & C. J. Goebel. LC 70-108268. 430p. reprint ed. pap. 133.30 (*0-608-30624-X*, 201996600015) Bks Demand.

***Quanta Cura & the Syllabus of Errors Condemning Current Errors.** Piux IX. 28p. 1998. reprint ed. pap. 3.45 (*0-935952-63-2*) Angelus Pr.

Q

An Asterisk (*) at the beginning of an entry indicates that the title is appearing for the first time.

Quanta, Relativity, Gravitation: Proceedings of the XVIII Workshop on High Energy Physics & Field Theory June, 1995, Held at State Research Center of Russia in Protyino. Ed. by A. P. Samokhin et al. (Illus.). 348p. (C). 1996. pap. text 70.00 (*1-57485-024-5*) Hadronic Pr Inc.

Quantales & Applications. Kimmo I. Rosenthal. 1990. pap. 43.00 (*0-582-06423-6*, Pub. by Addison-Wesley) Longman.

Quantales & Their Applications. Kimmo I. Rosenthal. LC 90-30122. (Pitman Research Notes in Mathematics Ser.: No. 234). 182p. 1990. pap. 56.50 (*0-608-05238-8*, 206577500001) Bks Demand.

Quantam Leap: Foreknowledge. Christopher Defilippis. 1998. mass mkt. 6.99 (*0-425-16487-X*) Berkley Pub.

***Quantam Theory of Magmetism.** Norberto Majlis. 2000. pap. 41.00 (*981-02-4018-X*) World Scientific Pub.

***Quantative Analysis: Grauimetric, Volumetric & Instrumental Analysis.** 4th ed. Charles M. Earnest & Larry Wilson. 2000. 40.00 (*0-923231-39-0*) Mohican Pub.

Quantative Environmental Science. Davis. 2001. 69.25 (*0-07-235053-9*) McGraw.

Quantative Investigation of Indian Mounds: With Special Reference to the Relation of the Physical Components to the Probable Material Culture. fac. ed. S. F. Cook & Adam E. Treganza. Ed. by Edward W. Gifford et al. (University of California Publications in American Archaeology & Ethnology: No. 40:5). 43p. (C). 1950. reprint ed. pap. 4.69 (*1-55567-315-5*) Coyote Press.

Quantative Methods. 6th ed. Lapin. (C). 1994. pap. text 33.50 (*0-03-097816-5*) Harcourt Coll Pubs.

***Quantative Methods for Business Decisions.** 5th ed. Curwin & Slater. 2001. pap. 39.95 (*1-86152-531-1*) Thomson Learn.

Quantative Methods in Marketing. Hussey Hooley. (ITBP Acquisitions Ser.). 1994. 24.95 (*1-86152-443-9*) Thomson Learn.

Quantative Methods in Marketing. 2nd ed. Hooley. (ITBP Acquisitions Ser.). 1999. pap. 28.99 (*1-86152-417-X*) Thomson Learn.

Quantenmechanik see Quantum Mechanics: Symmetries

Quantenmechanik 1 + 2, Vol. 1. Claude Cohen-Tannoudji et al. 756p. 1997. text 61.00 (*3-11-013592-2*) De Gruyter.

Quantenmechanik 1 + 2, Vol. 2. Claude Cohen-Tannoudji et al. 676p. 1997. text 61.00 (*3-11-015859-0*) De Gruyter.

Quantics: Rudiments. Jean-Marc Levy-Leblond & F. Balibar. Tr. by S. T. Ali. xx, 540p. 1990. 177.25 (*0-444-87424-0*) Elsevier.

Quantics: Rudiments. Jean-Marc Levy-Leblond & F. Balibar. Tr. by S. T. Ali. xx, 540p. 1990. pap. 72.25 (*0-444-88120-4*) Elsevier.

Quantification: A History of the Meaning of Measurement in the Natural & Social Sciences. Ed. by Harry Woolf. 1961. reprint ed. text 42.50 (*0-672-60844-8*) Irvington.

Quantification & Modelling of Heterogeneous Systems. I. Saxl et al. 110p. 1995. pap. 70.00 (*1-898326-04-5*, Pub. by CISP) Balogh.

Quantification & Prediction of Hydrocarbon Resources: Proceedings of the Norwegian Petroleum Society Conference, Stavanger, Norway, 6-8 December 1993. Ed. by A. G. Dore & R. Sinding-Larsen. LC 97-125849. (Norwegian Petroleum Society (NPF), Special Publication Ser.: Vol. 6). 362p. 1996. 230.00 (*0-444-82496-0*) Elsevier.

Quantification & the Quest for Medical Certainty. J. Rosser Matthews. LC 94-24091. 200p. 1995. text 39.50 (*0-691-03794-9*, Pub. by Princeton U Pr) Cal Prin Full Svc.

Quantification-Assessment of Mutagens & Carcinogens in Humans. F. J. Koschier. 60p. 1987. text 85.00 (*2-88124-417-3*) Gordon & Breach.

Quantification in Natural Languages, Vol. I. Ed. by Emma Bach et al. (Studies in Linguistics & Philosophy: No. 54). 1994. lib. bdg. write for info. (*0-7923-3128-1*, Pub. by Kluwer Academic) Kluwer Academic.

Quantification in Natural Languages, Vol. II. Ed. by Emmon Bach et al. (Studies in Linguistics & Philosophy: No. 54). 1995. lib. bdg. write for info. (*0-7923-3351-9*, Pub. by Kluwer Academic) Kluwer Academic.

Quantification in Natural Languages, Vols. I & II. Ed. by Emmon Bach et al. (Studies in Linguistics & Philosophy: Vol. 54). 740p. 1995. lib. bdg. 261.00 (*0-7923-3352-7*, Pub. by Kluwer Academic) Kluwer Academic.

Quantification in Science. Michele G. Melaragno. (Illus.). 336p. (C). (gr. 13). 1991. ring bd. 83.95 (*0-442-00641-1*, Chap & Hall CRC) CRC Pr.

Quantification in the History of Political Thought: Toward a Qualitative Approach, 55. Robert Schware. LC 80-1704. (Contributions in Political Science Ser.: No. 55). 168p. 1981. 55.00 (*0-313-22228-2*, SPT/, Greenwood Pr) Greenwood.

Quantification in the Theory of Grammar. Taisuke Nishigauchi. (C). 1990. pap. text 64.50 (*0-7923-0644-9*); lib. bdg. 98.00 (*0-7923-0643-0*) Kluwer Academic.

Quantification of Brain Function: Tracer Kinetics & Image Analysis in Brain PET. Ed. by K. Uemura et al. LC 93-6089. (International Congress Ser.: No. 1030). 720p. 1993. 289.00 (*0-444-89859-X*, Excerpta Medica) Elsevier.

Quantification of Circulating Proteins. W. T. Hermens. 1982. text 141.50 (*90-247-2755-3*) Kluwer Academic.

Quantification of Human Defense Mechanisms. Ed. by M. Olff et al. (Recent Research in Psychology Ser.). (Illus.). vi, 327p. 1991. 70.95 (*0-387-53821-6*) Spr-Verlag.

Quantification of Literary Images. Maria Joyner. (Orig.). 1990. pap. text 12.12 (*0-913412-34-1*) Brandon Hse.

Quantification of Neurologic Deficit. Theodore L. Munsat. (Illus.). 372p. 1989. text 89.95 (*0-409-90152-0*) Buttrwrth-Heinemann.

Quantification of Occupational Cancer. Ed. by Richard Peto & Marvin Schneiderman. LC 81-10218. (Banbury Reports: Vol. 9). 756p. (C). 1981. 99.00 (*0-87969-208-1*) Cold Spring Harbor.

Quantification of Road User Savings. Jan De Weille. LC 66-28028. (World Bank Staff Occasional Papers: Vol. 2). (Illus.). 103p. reprint ed. pap. 32.00 (*0-608-18339-3*, 203301600082) Bks Demand.

Quantification of the Effects of Air Pollution on Health in the United Kingdom. 1998. 40.00 (*0-11-322102-9*, HM221029, Pub. by Statnry Office) Bernan Associates.

Quantification of Uncertainty in Computational Fluid Dynamics. Ed. by I. Celik et al. LC 93-71641. (FED Ser.: Vol. 158). 121p. 1993. pap. 35.00 (*0-7918-0966-8*, H00798) ASME.

Quantification of Uncertainty in Computational Fluid Dynamics, 1995 Vol. 213: Quantification of Uncertainty in Computational Fluid Dynamics - 1995. Ed. by R. W. Johnson & D. Hughes. LC 93-71641. (1995 ASME/JSME Fluids Engineering Conference Ser.: FED-Vol. 213). 64p. 1995. 56.00 (*0-7918-1468-8*, G00963) ASME.

Quantified Societal Risk & Policy Making. Ed. by R. E. Jorissen & P. J. Stallen. LC 97-51621. (Technology, Risk, & Society Ser.). 252p. 1998. 100.00 (*0-7923-4955-5*) Kluwer Academic.

Quantifier Elimination & Cylindrical Algebraic Decomposition. Bob F. Caviness & J. R. Johnson. LC 96-43590. (Texts & Monographs in Symbolic Computation Ser.). 430p. 1996. 79.95 (*3-211-82794-3*) Spr-Verlag.

Quantifiers: Logics, Models, & Computation, 2 vols. Ed. by Michal Krynicki. Incl. Quantifiers Vol. 1: Logics, Models & Computation: Surveys. Marcin Mostowski & Leslaw W. Szczerba. LC 95-8252. 428p. (C). 1995. lib. bdg. 135.00 (*0-7923-3448-5*, Pub. by Kluwer Academic); Quantifiers Vol. 2: Logics, Models & Computation: Contributions. 280p. (C). 1995. lib. bdg. 114.00 (*0-7923-3449-3*, Pub. by Kluwer Academic); LC 95-8252. (Synthese Library: Vol. 248). 1995. Set lib. bdg. 212.00 (*0-7923-3450-7*, Pub. by Kluwer Academic) Kluwer Academic.

Quantifiers, Vol. 1, Logics, Models & Computation: Surveys see Quantifiers: Logics, Models, & Computation

Quantifiers, Vol. 2, Logics, Models & Computation: Contributions see Quantifiers: Logics, Models, & Computation

Quantifiers, Deduction & Context. Ed. by Makoto Kanazawa et al. (CSLI Lecture Notes Ser.). 200p. 1996. 49.95 (*1-57586-005-9*); pap. 22.95 (*1-57586-004-X*) CSLI.

Quantifiers, Deduction, & Context. Ed. by Makoto Kanazawa. (CSLI Lecture Notes Ser.). 1996. 64.95 (*0-521-86005-9*); pap. 22.95 (*0-521-86004-0*) Cambridge U Pr.

Quantifiers, Logic, & Language. 2nd ed. Ed. by Jaap Van Der Does et al. 432p. 1996. 69.95 (*1-57586-001-5*) Cambridge U Pr.

Quantifiers, Logic, & Language. 2nd ed. Ed. by Jaap Van Der Does & Jan Van Eijck. 432p. 1996. pap. text 28.95 (*1-57586-000-7*) Cambridge U Pr.

Quantifizierung Quartaerer Subtropischer Verwitterung auf Kalk. Dieter Burger. (Relief, Boden, Palaeoklima Ser.: Band 7). (GER., Illus.). xiv, 132p. 1992. pap. 40.00 (*3-443-09007-9*, Pub. by Gebruder Borntraeger) Balogh.

Quantifying Archaeology. Stephen Shennan. 364p. (C). 1988. text 64.95 (*0-12-639860-7*) Acad Pr.

Quantifying Archaeology. Stephen Shennan. LC 97-60561. 224p. 1996. pap. 23.00 (*0-7486-0791-9*, Pub. by Edinburgh U Pr) Col U Pr.

Quantifying Archaeology. 2nd rev. ed. Stephen Shennan. LC 97-60561. (Illus.). 432p. 1997. pap. text 32.95 (*0-87745-598-8*) U of Iowa Pr.

Quantifying Consciousness: An Empirical Approach. R. J. Pekala. (Illus.). 448p. (C). 1990. 59.50 (*0-306-43750-3*, Plenum Trade) Perseus Pubng.

Quantifying Impacts (QI) Handbook: A Comprehensive Guide to Quantifying Bottom-Line Impacts of Public & Government Affairs Activities. Nick L. Laird & Rita K. Roosevelt. (Illus.). 82p. (Orig.). (C). 1994. pap. text 29.95 (*0-9644865-0-4*) Laird & Assoc.

Quantifying Language: A Researcher's & Teacher's Guide to Gathering Language Data & Reducing It to Figures. Phil Scholfield. LC 94-30330. 1994. 34.95 (*1-85359-253-6*) Taylor & Francis.

Quantifying Language: A Researcher's & Teacher's Guide to Gathering Language Data & Reducing It to Figures. Phil Scholfield. LC 94-30330. 1995. pap. text 89.95 (*1-85359-254-4*) Taylor & Francis.

Quantifying Marketability Discounts: Developing & Supporting Marketability Discounts in the Appraisal of Closely Held Business Interests. Z. Christopher Mercer. 525p. 1997. 115.00 (*0-9658358-0-4*) Peabody Pub LP.

Quantifying Music. H. F. Cohen. 328p. 1984. lib. bdg. 203.00 (*90-277-1637-4*, D Reidel) Kluwer Academic.

Quantifying Quality in Policing. Ed. by Larry T. Hoover. LC 95-71869. 286p. (Orig.). 1995. pap. text 22.00 (*1-878734-40-7*) Police Exec Res.

Quantifying Secondary Gas Resources in Fluvial-Deltaic Reservoirs: A Case History from Stratton Field, South Texas. R. A. Levey et al. (Reports of Investigations: No. RI 221). (Illus.). 38p. 1994. pap. 4.00 (*0-614-01870-6*) Bur Econ Geology.

Quantifying Sedimentary Geochemical Processes: Royal Society Discussion Meeting. Ed. by M. L. Coleman et al. (Illus.). 194p. 1994. text 70.00 (*0-19-854831-1*) OUP.

Quantifying Spirit in the Eighteenth Century. Ed. by Tore Frangsmyr et al. 1990. 55.00 (*0-520-07022-4*, Pub. by U CA Pr) Cal Prin Full Svc.

***Quantifying Sustainable Development: The Future of Tropical Economies.** 3rd ed. Charles A. Hall. 676p. (C). 1999. 110.00 (*0-12-318860-1*) Acad Pr.

Quantifying the Battlefield: Rand Research at the National Training Center. Martin Goldsmith et al. LC 93-16050. xi, 26p. 1993. pap. text 6.00 (*0-8330-1389-0*, MR-105) Rand Corp.

Quantifying Weldability. Ed. by R. J. Pargeter. (Illus.). 80p. (Orig.). (C). 1988. pap. 49.95 (*0-85300-222-3*, Pub. by Woodhead Pubng) Am Educ Systs.

Quantifying Your Preferences for Qualitatively Different Outcomes. Hans Bleiker & Annemarie Bleiker. 1988. ring bd. write for info. (*0-925368-02-4*) IPMP.

Quantile Processes with Statistical Applications. Miklos Csorgo. LC 83-60222. (CBMS-NSF Regional Conference Series in Applied Mathematics: No. 42). xiii, 156p. 1983. pap. text 33.00 (*0-89871-185-1*) Soc Indus-Appl Math.

Quantiques Symmetries/Symmetries Quantiques. Alain Connes et al. LC 97-49073. (Les Houches Summer School Proceedings Ser.: 64). 1032p. 1998. 296.00 (*0-444-82867-2*) Elsevier.

Quantitation of MRNA by Polymerase Chain Reaction: Nonradioactive PCR Methods. T. Kohler et al. LC 95-35772. (Illus.). 186p. 1995. student ed. 53.95 (*3-540-59192-3*) Spr-Verlag.

Quantitative Anaesthesia. Ed. by K. Van Ackern et al. (Anaesthesiologie & Intensivmedizin - Anaesthesiol: Vol. 204). (Illus.). 170p. 1989. 38.95 (*0-387-50436-2*) Spr-Verlag.

Quantitative Analyses of Law: A Comparative Empirical Study. Attila J. Racz et al. (Sources of Law in Eastern & Western Europe Ser.). (Illus.). 404p. (C). 1990. 120.00 (*963-05-5673-1*, Pub. by Akade Kiado) St Mut.

***Quantitative Analysis.** Vladimir Alexeyev. 496p. 2000. pap. 37.50 (*0-89875-034-2*) U Pr Pacific.

Quantitative Analysis. 6th ed. R. A. Day, Jr. & Arthur L. Underwood, Jr. 768p. 1991. 72.80 (*0-13-747155-6*, 520104) P-H.

Quantitative Analysis. 6th ed. Day & Underwood. 1991. pap. text, lab manual ed. 38.00 (*0-13-747403-2*) P-H.

Quantitative Analysis: An Introduction. Roy M. Chiulli. (Automation & Production Systems Ser.: Vol. 3). 592p. 1998. text 60.00 (*90-5699-629-0*, ECU86, Harwood Acad Pubs) Gordon & Breach.

Quantitative Analysis: Gravimetric, Volumetric & Instrumental Analysis. 3rd ed. Larry Wilson. 391p. (C). 2000. pap. 30.00 (*0-923231-21-8*) Mohican Pub.

Quantitative Analysis: Solutions to Problems. 5th ed. R. A. Day, Jr. & Arthur L. Underwood, Jr. 180p. (C). 1986. pap. text 12.95 (*0-317-40029-0*) P-H.

Quantitative Analysis by Gas Chromatography. 2nd ed. Josef P. Novak. (Chromatographic Science Ser.: Vol. 41). (Illus.). 360p. 1987. text 175.00 (*0-8247-7818-9*) Dekker.

Quantitative Analysis for Business. Andrew J. Vazsonyi & Herbert F. Spirer. (Illus.). 1072p. (C). 1984. text 47.95 (*0-13-746578-5*) P-H.

Quantitative Analysis for Business. Ed. by Veranelli. (C). 1998. text. write for info. (*0-321-01419-7*) Addson-Wesley Educ.

Quantitative Analysis for Health Services Administration. Charles J. Austin & Stuart B. Boxerman. 333p. 1995. 60.00 (*1-56793-032-8*, 0964) Health Admin Pr.

Quantitative Analysis for Investment Management. Robert A. Taggart. 306p. (C). 1996. pap. text 23.80 (*0-13-319690-9*) P-H.

Quantitative Analysis for Management. 7th ed. Barry Render. LC 99-21605. 766p. 1999. text 97.33 incl. audio compact disk (*0-13-021538-4*) P-H.

Quantitative Analysis in Confocal Image Cytometry. K. C. Strasters. 188p. 1994. pap. 57.50 (*90-407-1038-4*, Pub. by Delft U Pr) Coronet Bks.

Quantitative Analysis in Financial Markets: Collected Papers of the New York University Mathematics. Jeffery D. Phillips. LC 99-44136. 367p. 1999. 86.00 (*981-02-3788-X*); pap. text 48.00 (*981-02-3789-8*) World Scientific Pub.

Quantitative Analysis in Marketing Management. Luiz Moutinho et al. LC 97-49694. 1998. text 93.00 (*0-471-96339-9*) Wiley.

Quantitative Analysis in Marketing Management. Luiz Moutinho et al. LC 97-49694. 342p. 2000. pap. 47.00 (*0-471-96430-1*) Wiley.

Quantitative Analysis in Sobolev Imbedding Theorems & Applications to Spectral Theory. M. S. Birman & M. Z. Solomjak. LC 79-27339. (Translations Ser. 2: Vol. 114). 132p. 1980. text 47.00 (*0-8218-3064-3*, TRANS2/114) Am Math.

***Quantitative Analysis Laboratories F/multi-component System.** Draves et al. 2001. pap. 6.25 (*0-534-37868-4*) Thomson Learn.

Quantitative Analysis of Biospecific Interactions. Ed. by Lundahl. (Illus.). 248p. 1998. text 120.00 (*90-5702-378-4*, Harwood Acad Pubs) Gordon & Breach.

Quantitative Analysis of Computer Systems. Clement H. Leung. LC 87-2046. 184p. 1988. reprint ed. pap. 57.10 (*0-608-04601-9*, 206537100003) Bks Demand.

Quantitative Analysis of Mineral & Energy Resources. Ed. by C. F. Chung et al. (C). 1987. text 326.50 (*90-277-2635-3*) Kluwer Academic.

Quantitative Analysis of Movement: Measuring & Modeling Population Redistribution in Animals & Plants. Peter Turchin. LC 98-4838. 396p. (C). 1998. pap. text 39.95 (*0-87893-847-8*) Sinauer Assocs.

Quantitative Analysis of Organic Mixtures: General Principles, Pt. 1. Tsu-Sheng Ma. LC 78-23202. 384p. reprint ed. pap. 119.10 (*0-608-10031-5*, 205560100029) Bks Demand.

***Quantitative Analysis of Shipping Markets.** Albert Willem Veenstra. (TRAIL Thesis Series). (Illus.). 286p. 1999. pap. 57.50 (*90-407-1876-8*, Pub. by Delft U Pr) Coronet Bks.

Quantitative Analysis of Social Represenations. Willem Doise & Alain Clemence. 176p. 1994. pap. text 56.00 (*0-13-302142-4*) P-H.

Quantitative Analysis of the Growth & Diffusion of Steam Power in Manufacturing in the U. S., 1919-1938. Allen H. Fenichel. Ed. by Stuart Bruchey. LC 78-22679. (Energy in the American Economy Ser.). (Illus.). 1979. lib. bdg. 21.95 (*0-405-11982-8*) Ayer.

***Quantitative Analysis 1.** 333p. (C). 2000. text 42.00 (*0-536-60565-3*) Pearson Custom.

Quantitative Analysis, Rutgers Fall 99 (C). 1999. text 17.52 (*0-536-02503-7*) Pearson Custom.

***Quantitative Analysis, Trading Strategies & Risk Management for Fixed-Income Markets.** Bingren Li et al. 300p. 2000. 46.00 (*981-02-4079-1*) World Scientific Pub.

***Quantitative Analysis 2: Quickprint.** 371p. (C). 2000. text 42.00 (*0-536-60562-9*) Pearson Custom.

Quantitative Analyst. Jack Rudman. (Career Examination Ser.: C-1714). 1994. pap. 29.95 (*0-8373-1714-2*) Nat Learn.

Quantitative Analytic Studies in Epilepsy. fac. ed. Ed. by Peter Kellaway & Ingemar S. Petersen. LC 76-22912. (Illus.). 588p. pap. 182.30 (*0-7837-7521-0*, 204698400005) Bks Demand.

Quantitative Analytical Chemistry. 5th ed. James S. Fritz & George H. Schenk. 1987. teacher ed. write for info. (*0-318-61501-0*, H04815) P-H.

Quantitative & Analytical Studies in East-West Economic Relations. Ed. by Josef C. Brada. LC 76-10986. (Studies in East European & Soviet Planning, Development, & Trade: No. 24). (Illus.). 1976. pap. text 6.00 (*0-89249-015-2*) Intl Development.

Quantitative & Dynamic Thermal Imaging in Medical Diagnosis. Michael Anbar. 288p. 1994. lib. bdg. 110.00 (*0-8493-4409-3*) CRC Pr.

Quantitative & Ecological Aspects of Plant Breeding. John Hill et al. (Plant Breeding Ser.). 352p. 1997. write for info. (*0-412-75390-1*) Kluwer Academic.

Quantitative & Numerical Methods in Soil Classification & Survey. R. K. Webster. (Monographs on Soil Survey: No. 2). (Illus.). 280p. 1978. text 70.00 (*0-19-854512-6*) OUP.

***Quantitative & Qualitative Reasoning Skills.** James Burkhart. 188p. (C). 1999. per. 20.95 (*0-7872-6378-8*, 41637801) Kendall-Hunt.

Quantitative & Qualitative Techniques in Human Geography. Guy M. Robinson. LC 97-43766. 572p. 1998. 175.00 (*0-471-96231-7*); pap. 54.95 (*0-471-96232-5*) Wiley.

Quantitative & Theoretical Geography. Ed. by A. Kilchenman. 100p. (C). 1975. pap. 23.00 (*0-08-019680-2*, Pergamon Pr) Elsevier.

Quantitative Approach in Political Science: An Introduction. Scott Bennett. 376p. 1986. lib. bdg. 99.95 (*0-88946-205-4*) E Mellen.

Quantitative Approach to Software Management: The AMI PRO Handbook. Kevin Pulford et al. Ed. by A. Ware & Katherine Harutunian. LC 95-37088. 200p. (C). 1996. pap. 44.95 (*0-201-87746-5*) Addison-Wesley.

Quantitative Approach to the Relation Between Population & Settlement Size, No. 64. S. F. Cook & R. F. Heiger. (University of California Archaeological Research Facility Ser.). 105p. 1965. pap. text 11.56 (*1-55567-815-7*) Coyote Press.

Quantitative Approaches in Business Studies. 4th ed. Clare Morris. 480p. (Orig.). 1996. pap. 57.50 (*0-273-61697-8*, Pub. by Pitman Pub) Trans-Atl Phila.

***Quantitative Approaches in Business Studies.** 5th ed. Clare Morris. 512p. (Orig.). 1999. pap. 57.50 (*0-273-63828-9*, Pub. by F T P-H) Trans-Atl Phila.

Quantitative Approaches to Management. 8th ed. Richard I. Levin et al. (C). 1992. pap., student ed. 26.88 (*0-07-037579-8*) McGraw.

Quantitative Approaches to Metabolism: The Role of Tracers & Models in Clinical Medicine. Ed. by D. G. Cramp. LC 81-21992. 402p. reprint ed. pap. 124.70 (*0-608-15666-3*, 203193600077) Bks Demand.

Quantitative Approaches to Phytogeography. Ed. by P. L. Nimis & T. J. Crovello. (Tasks for Vegetation Science Ser.). (C). 1990. text 285.00 (*0-7923-0795-X*) Kluwer Academic.

***Quantitative Approximations.** George A. Anastassiou. LC 00-34615. 2000. write for info. (*1-58488-221-2*, Chap & Hall CRC) CRC Pr.

Quantitative Aspects of Polymer Stabilizers. Ed. by G. E. Zaikov. LC 95-24687. 217p. 1995. 175.00 (*1-56072-253-3*) Nova Sci Pubs.

Quantitative Aspects of Post-War European Economic Growth. Bart Van Ark & Nicholas Crafts. LC 96-16149. (Illus.). 464p. (C). 1997. text 69.95 (*0-521-49628-4*) Cambridge U Pr.

Quantitative Aspects of Ruminant Digestion & Metabolism. Ed. by J. M. Forbes & J. France. (Illus.). 528p. 1993. text 140.00 (*0-85198-831-8*) OUP.

Quantitative Aspects of the Evolution of Concepts. Clark L. Hull. (Psychology Monographs General & Applied: Vol. 28). 1974. reprint ed. pap. 55.00 (*0-8115-1427-7*) Periodicals Srv.

Quantitative Assessment in Epilepsy Care. H. Meinardi et al. LC 93-26823. (NATO ASI Series A, Life Sciences: Series A, Vol. 255). (Illus.). 222p. (C). 1993. text 85.00 (*0-306-44620-0*) Plenum.

Q

Quantitative Auriculotherapy. Meyer R. Rosen. LC 94-76974. 52p. 1994. pap. 35.00 (*0-9641617-1-0*) Interact Cnslting.

Quantitative Bacteriology: Its Role in the Armamentarium of the Surgeon. John P. Heggers & Martin C. Robson. (Illus.). 136p. 1990. lib. bdg. 119.00 (*0-8493-5129-4*, RD98) CRC Pr.

Quantitative Bases for Developing an Index of Harm: ICRP Publicatino Number 45. Ed. by M. C. Thorne. 90p. 1986. pap. 32.75 (*0-08-033665-5*, Pub. by PPL) Elsevier.

Quantitative Biology of the Pig. I. Kyriazakis. LC 98-22769. (Illus.). 408p. 1999. text 110.00 (*0-85199-273-0*) OUP.

Quantitative Business Analysis. William M. Bassin. LC 80-21090. 256p. (YA). (gr. 11-12). 1981. teacher ed. write for info. (*0-672-97697-8*); text. write for info. (*0-672-97696-X*) Macmillan.

Quantitative Business Analysis. David Johnson. 256p. 1986. pap. 36.00 (*0-406-50381-8*, UK, MICHIE) LEXIS Pub.

Quantitative Business Analysis. Meredith & Turban. 1999. 45.00 (*0-324-01600-X*) Sth-Wstrn College.

Quantitative Business Analysis: Text & Cases. Samuel Bodily et al. LC 97-24214. 672p. (C). 1997. text 57.50 (*0-256-14713-2*, Irwn McGrw-H) McGrw-H Hghr Educ.

Quantitative Business Methods Using Excel. David Whigham. (Illus.). 476p. 1998. pap. text 39.95 (*0-19-877545-8*) OUP.

***Quantitative Business Valuation: A Mathematical Approach for Today's Professionals.** Jay B. Abrams. (Illus.). 2000. 95.00 (*0-07-000215-0*) McGraw.

Quantitative Calculations in Pharmaceutical Practice & Research. Ed. by T. P. Hadjiioannou. 461p. 1993. pap. 89.95 (*0-471-18898-0*, Wiley-VCH) Wiley.

Quantitative Calculations in Pharmaceutical Practice & Research. Themistocles P. Hadjioannou et al. LC 93-3446. (Analytical Techniques in Clinical Chemistry & Laboratory Medicine Ser.). 1993. pap. 59.95 (*1-56081-654-6*, Wiley-VCH); boxed set 120.00 (*0-89573-282-3*, Wiley-VCH) Wiley.

Quantitative Cellular Biology: An Approach to the Quantitative Analysis of Life Processes. Ferdinand Heinmets. LC 70-84774. (Quantitative Approach to Life Science Ser.). 341p. reprint ed. pap. 105.80 (*0-608-17013-5*, 202711300054) Bks Demand.

Quantitative Cerebral Blood Flow Measurements Using Stable Xenon/CT: Clinical Applications. Ed. by Masamichi Tomonaga et al. LC 94-42191. (Illus.). 368p. 1995. 75.00 (*0-87993-609-6*) Futura Pub.

Quantitative Characterization & Performance of Porous Implants for Hard Tissue Applications. Ed. by Jack E. Lemons. LC 87-33430. (Special Technical Publication Ser.: No. 953). 420p. 1988. text 75.00 (*0-8031-0965-2*, STP953) ASTM.

Quantitative Characterization of Ligand Binding. Donald J. Winzor & William H. Sawyer. LC 95-31858. 168p. 1995. 129.95 (*0-471-05957-9*); pap. 65.00 (*0-471-05958-7*) Wiley.

Quantitative Chemical Analysis. Harris. LC 97-48837. 1998. pap. text 90.95 (*0-7167-2881-8*) W H Freeman.

Quantitative Chemical Analysis. 3rd ed. Daniel C. Harris. LC 90-38694. (Illus.). 880p. (C). 1991. text 52.80 (*0-7167-2170-8*); write for info. (*0-7167-2190-2*) W H Freeman.

Quantitative Chemical Analysis. 3rd ed. Daniel C. Harris. LC 90-38694. (Illus.). 880p. (C). 1991. teacher ed. 11.20 (*0-7167-2191-0*) W H Freeman.

Quantitative Chemical Analysis. 5th ed. Harris. 1998. pap. text 24.95 (*0-7167-3272-6*) W H Freeman.

Quantitative Clinical Pathology. P. Hamilton & D. C. Allen. (Illus.). 352p. 1995. 135.00 (*0-632-03286-3*, Pub. by Blckwll Scitfc UK) Blackwell Sci.

Quantitative Concepts for Management. 3rd ed. Gary D. Eppen et al. 800p. (C). 1989. text 95.00 (*0-13-746777-X*) P-H.

Quantitative Content Analysis. Daniel Riffe et al. LC 97-47384. (LEA Communication Ser.). 150p. 1998. write for info. (*0-8058-2018-3*); pap. write for info. (*0-8058-2019-1*) L Erlbaum Assocs.

Quantitative Coronary Angiography in Clinical Practice. Ed. by Patrick W. Serruys et al. LC 93-22792. (Developments in Cardiovascular Medicine Ser.: Vol. 145). 1994. text 402.50 (*0-7923-2368-8*) Kluwer Academic.

Quantitative Coronary Arteriography. Ed. by Johan H. Reiber & Patrick W. Serruys. (Developments in Cardiovascular Medicine Ser.). (C). 1991. text 272.50 (*0-7923-0913-8*) Kluwer Academic.

Quantitative Data Analysis with Minitab: A Guide to Social Scientists. Alan Bryman & Duncan Cramer. LC 95-44812. (Illus.). 304p. (C). 1996. 80.00 (*0-415-12323-2*); pap. 25.99 (*0-415-12324-0*) Routledge.

Quantitative Data Analysis with SPSS for Windows: A Guide for Social Scientists. Alan Bryman & Duncan Cramer. LC 96-7866. (Illus.). 332p. (C). 1997. 85.00 (*0-415-14719-0*); pap. 27.99 (*0-415-14720-4*) Routledge.

Quantitative Data Analysis with SPSS Release 8 for Windows: For Social Scientists. Alan Bryman. LC 98-44332. 1999. 90.00 (*0-415-20696-0*) Routledge.

Quantitative Data Analysis with SPSS Release 8 for Windows: For Social Scientists. Alan Bryman & Duncan Cramer. LC 98-44332. 303p. 1999. pap. 27.99 (*0-415-20697-9*) Routledge.

Quantitative Decision Making: Student Book. Powell. 1991. pap. text, student ed. write for info. (*0-582-06791-X*, Pub. by Addison-Wesley) Longman.

Quantitative Decision Making for Business. 422p. (C). 1995. text 58.00 (*0-536-59052-4*) Pearson Custom.

Quantitative Decision Making for Business. 2nd ed. 204p. (C). 1997. text 21.00 (*0-536-00809-4*) Pearson Custom.

Quantitative Description & Analysis of the Growth of the Pennsylvania Anthracite Coal Industry, 1820-1865. Donald F. Schaefer. Ed. by Stuart Bruchey. LC 76-45113. (Nineteen Seventy-Seven Dissertations Ser.). (Illus.). 1977. lib. bdg. 26.95 (*0-405-09924-X*) Ayer.

Quantitative Description of the Microstructure of Materials. Krzysztof J. Kurzydlowski & Brian Ralph. 432p. 1995. boxed set 124.95 (*0-8493-8921-6*, 8921) CRC Pr.

Quantitative Development Policy Analysis. Elisabeth Sadoulet & Alain De Janvry. 359p. (Orig.). 1995. pap. text 35.00 (*0-8018-4782-6*) Johns Hopkins.

Quantitative Development Policy Analysis: Instructor's Manual. Elisabeth Sadoulet & Alain De Janvry. 57p. (Orig.). 1995. pap. text 25.95 (*0-8018-4783-4*) Johns Hopkins.

Quantitative Diagenesis: Recent Developments & Applications to Reservoir Geology. Ed. by Andrew Parker & Bruce W. Sellwood. LC 94-39299. (NATO ASI Series, Series C, Mathematical & Physical Sciences: Vol. 453). 1995. text 132.50 (*0-7923-3261-X*) Kluwer Academic.

Quantitative Ecology: Spatial & Temporal Scaling. David Schneider. (Illus.). 395p. 1994. text 53.00 (*0-12-627860-1*) Acad Pr.

Quantitative Ecological Theory: An Introduction to Basic Models. Ed. by Routledge, Chapman, Hall Ltd Staff. (C). text 95.50 (*0-7099-2289-2*) C Helm.

Quantitative Ecological Theory: An Introduction to Basic Models. Michael R. Rose. LC 87-4106. (Illus.). 215p. reprint ed. pap. 66.70 (*0-608-06135-2*, 206646800008) Bks Demand.

Quantitative Ecology & Marine Biology. Gerald J. Bakus. (Illus.). 165p. (C). 1991. text 60.00 (*90-6191-917-7*, Pub. by A A Balkema) Ashgate Pub Co.

Quantitative Ecology & the Brown Trout. J. M. Elliott. (Oxford Series in Ecology & Evolution). (Illus.). 298p. 1994. text 65.00 (*0-19-854678-5*); pap. text 35.00 (*0-19-854090-6*) OUP.

Quantitative Economic History. Ed. by N. F. Crafts et al. (Oxford Economic Papers Special Issue). (Illus.). 280p. 1991. pap. 24.95 (*0-19-828310-5*) OUP.

Quantitative Economics of Socialism: Input-Output Approaches. Masaaki Kuboniwa. (Hitotsubashi University Economic Research Ser.: No. 27). 292p. 1989. 69.00 (*4-314-10014-1*) OUP.

Quantitative Electron Microscopy. Ed. by J. N. Chapman & A. J. Craven. (Scottish Universities Summer School in Physics, a NATO Advanced Study Institute Ser.: No. 25). (Illus.). 446p. 1983. 189.00 (*0-905945-08-5*) IOP Pub.

Quantitative Electron-Probe Microanalysis. Ed. by V. D. Scott & G. Love. LC 83-18366. 343p. 1984. text 83.95 (*0-470-27510-3*) P-H.

Quantitative Electron-Probe Microanalysis. 2nd ed. C. Love & V. D. Scott. 384p. (C). 1995. pap. text 77.00 (*0-13-104050-2*) P-H.

Quantitative Evaluation & Prediction of Donor-Acceptor Interactions see Coordinative Interactions

Quantitative Evaluation of Computing & Communication Systems: 8th International Conference on Modeling Techniques & Tools for Computer Performance Evaluation, Heidelberg, Germany, September 20-22, 1995, Proceedings, Vol. X. Ed. by Heinz Beilner et al. (Lecture Notes in Computer Science Ser.: Vol. 977). 415p. 1995. 68.00 (*3-540-60300-X*) Spr-Verlag.

Quantitative Evaluation of Predicted Reserves of Oil & Gas (Authorized Translation from the Russian) N. I. Buialov et al. LC 64-7759. 73p. reprint ed. pap. 30.00 (*0-608-11386-7*, 200335900021) Bks Demand.

Quantitative Examination of Neurologic Functions, 2 vols., Vol. I. Ed. by Alfred R. Potvin & Wallace W. Tourtellotte. 272p. 1985. 147.00 (*0-8493-5926-0*, RC348, CRC Reprint) Franklin.

Quantitative Examination of Neurologic Functions, 2 vols., Vol. II. Ed. by Alfred R. Potvin & Wallace W. Tourtellotte. 224p. 1985. 125.00 (*0-8493-5927-9*, CRC Reprint) Franklin.

Quantitative Explorations in Drug Abuse Policy. Ed. by Irving Leveson. LC 79-21399. 183p. 1980. 45.00 (*0-88331-192-5*) R B Luce.

Quantitative Feedback Design of Linear & Nonlinear Control Systems. Oded Yaniv. LC 99-27956. (International Series in Engineering & Computer Science). 1999. write for info. (*0-7923-8529-2*) Kluwer Academic.

Quantitative Feedback Design Theory (QFT), Vol. 1. Isaac M. Horowitz. LC 93-92596. 512p. 1993. 63.00 (*0-9635760-0-3*) QFT Pubns.

***Quantitative Feedback Theory: Fundamentals & Applications.** Constantine S. Houpis & Steven J. Rasmussen. LC 99-26669. (Control Engineering Ser.: Vol. 3). (Illus.). 408p. 1999. text 150.00 (*0-8247-7872-3*) Dekker.

Quantitative Financial Economics: Stocks, Bonds & Foreign Exchange. Keith Cuthbertson. LC 95-48355. (Financial Economics & Quantitative Analysis Ser.). 492p. 1996. pap. 85.00 (*0-471-95360-1*) Wiley.

Quantitative Fish Dynamics. Terrance J. Quinn & Richard B. Deriso. LC 97-35538. (Biological Resource Management Ser.). (Illus.). 560p. 1999. text 95.00 (*0-19-507631-1*) OUP.

Quantitative Fluorescence Microscopy. F. W. Rost. (Illus.). 250p. (C). 1991. text 80.00 (*0-521-39422-8*) Cambridge U Pr.

Quantitative Foundations of Counseling Psychology Research. Ed. by Bruce E. Wampold. (Special Issue, Journal of Counseling Psychology Ser.: Vol. 34, No. 4). 133p. 1987. pap. 16.00 (*1-55798-007-1*) Am Psychol.

Quantitative Functional Brain Imaging with Positron Tomography. Ed. by Richard E. Carson et al. LC 98-85439. (Illus.). 504p. (C). 1998. boxed set 139.95 (*0-12-161340-2*) Acad Pr.

Quantitative Gas Chromatography for Laboratory Analyses & On-Line Process Control. G. Guichon & C. L. Guillemin. (Journal of Chromatography Library: Vol. 42). 798p. 1988. 281.00 (*0-444-42857-7*) Elsevier.

Quantitative Genetic Studies of Behavioral Evolution. Ed. by Christine R. B. Boake. LC 93-33824. 400p. 1994. pap. text 24.95 (*0-226-06216-3*); lib. bdg. 66.00 (*0-226-06215-5*) U Ch Pr.

Quantitative Genetics: The Selection, Pt. II. Hill. 52.95 (*0-317-64262-6*) Chapman & Hall.

Quantitative Genetics & Selection in Plant Breeding. Gunter Wricke & Eberhard Weber. (Illus.). xii, 405p. 1986. 152.35 (*3-11-007561-X*) De Gruyter.

Quantitative Genetics with Special Reference to Plant & Animal Breeding. Ralph E. Comstock. LC 94-48902. 436p. 1996. text 114.95 (*0-8138-2011-1*) Iowa St U Pr.

Quantitative Geometry of Thrust & Fold Belt Structures. Peter B. Jones. LC QE0601.2.J6. (Methods in Exploration Ser.: No. 6). (Illus.). 32p. reprint ed. pap. 30.00 (*0-7837-1651-6*, 204194900024) Bks Demand.

***Quantitative Geophysics & Geology.** Luis Lliboutry. LC 99-34589. (Praxis Series in Geophysics). 415p. 1999. pap. 59.95 (*1-85233-115-1*, Pub. by Spr-Verlag) Spr-Verlag.

Quantitative Hydrogeology. Ghislain De Marsily. 1986. pap. text 63.00 (*0-12-208916-2*) Acad Pr.

Quantitative Imaging: Neuroreceptors, Neurotransmitters, & Enzymes. Ed. by J. James Frost & Henry N. Wagner, Jr. LC 90-8354. 212p. 1990. reprint ed. pap. 65.80 (*0-608-04675-2*, 206539600004) Bks Demand.

Quantitative Indicators in World Politics: Timely Assurance & Early Warning. Ed. by David J. Singer. LC 83-17792. 221p. 1984. 55.00 (*0-275-91269-8*, C1269, Praeger Pubs) Greenwood.

Quantitative Infrared Thermography QIRT 94. Ed. by D. Balageas et al. (Proceedings of the Eurotherm Seminar Ser.: No. 42). 370p. 169.00 (*2-85933-042-9*) Elsevier.

Quantitative International Investing: A Handbook of Analytical & Modeling Techniques &... Brian R. Bruce. (Guide to World Markets Ser.). 1990. 69.95 (*1-55738-121-6*, Irwn Prfssnl) McGraw-Hill Prof.

***Quantitative Investigations in the Biosciences Using Minitab.** J. C. Eddison. 1999. 29.95 (*0-8493-0305-2*) CRC Pr.

***Quantitative Investigations in the Biosciences Using MINITAB.** John Eddison. LC 99-43693. 472p. 1999. per. 49.95 (*1-58488-033-3*, Chap & Hall CRC) CRC Pr.

Quantitative Investing for the Global Markets: Strategies, Tactics & Advanced Analytical Techniques. Ed. by Peter Carman. 400p. 1997. 65.00 (*1-888998-03-2*) Glenlake Pub.

Quantitative Investment for the Global Markets: Strategies, Tactics, & Advanced Analytical Techniques. Peter Carman. (Glenlake Business Monographs). 400p. 1998. 65.00 (*1-884964-71-0*) Fitzroy Dearborn.

Quantitative Management. Guisseppi A. Forgionne. (Business Statistics). 912p. 1990. pap. 58.75 (*0-534-51120-1*) Wadsworth Pub.

Quantitative Marketing. 1983. 29.95 (*0-387-12840-9*) Spr-Verlag.

Quantitative Marxism. Ed. by Paul Dunne. 220p. (C). 1990. 61.95 (*0-7456-0647-4*) Blackwell Pubs.

Quantitative Mathematical Models in Radiation Biology. Ed. by J. C. Kiefer. (Illus.). 200p. 1988. 56.95 (*0-387-50453-2*) Spr-Verlag.

Quantitative Measurement of Fetal Hemoglobin by the Alkali Denaturation Method: Approved Guideline, Vol. 6. National Committee for Clinical Laboratory Standar. 1989. 75.00 (*1-56238-043-5*, H13-A) NCCLS.

Quantitative Measures & Chemical Equations. Swift. (C). 1972. pap. text. write for info. (*0-7167-1557-0*) W H Freeman.

Quantitative Method for Deriving Cultural Chronology. James A. Ford. LC 75-24231. (Museum Briefs Ser.: No. 9). (Illus.). vi, 62p. 1972. reprint ed. pap. 3.25 (*0-913134-08-2*) Mus Anthro MO.

Quantitative Methods. (C). 1995. pap. 67.16 (*0-395-77582-5*) HM.

Quantitative Methods. Douglas Downing. 1988. pap. 12.95 (*0-8120-3947-5*) Barron.

Quantitative Methods. Graham Hackett & David Caunt. (Illus.). 512p. (Orig.). (C). 1994. pap. 47.95 (*0-631-19537-8*) Blackwell Pubs.

Quantitative Methods. Graham James. (C). 1990. pap. 60.00 (*0-948691-94-8*, Pub. by Witherby & Co) St Mut.

Quantitative Methods. 2nd ed. Verret. 344p. (C). 1999. pap. text 33.00 (*0-536-01171-0*) Pearson Custom.

Quantitative Methods. 3rd ed. Verret. 272p. 1998. pap. text 33.00 (*0-536-01718-2*) Pearson Custom.

Quantitative Methods. 3rd ed. Welch. (C). Date not set. pap. text. write for info. (*0-15-507863-1*) Harcourt Coll Pubs.

Quantitative Methods. 3rd rev. ed. Verreth. 272p. 1999. pap. text 33.00 (*0-536-02391-3*) Pearson Custom.

***Quantitative Methods.** 4th ed. 262p. (C). 2000. pap. text 38.00 (*0-536-60350-2*) Pearson Custom.

Quantitative Methods. 6th ed. Lapin. 1995. 191.00 (*0-534-51052-3*) Brooks-Cole.

Quantitative Methods. 6th ed. Lapin. 1995. teacher ed. 9.25 (*0-534-51055-8*) Brooks-Cole.

***Quantitative Methods: A Business Perspective.** Diana Bedward. 281p. 1999. pap. text 39.95 (*0-7506-4093-6*) Buttrwrth-Heinemann.

Quantitative Methods: Applications to Managerial Decision Making. 99th ed. Robert E. Markland & James R. Sweigart. LC 87-2025. 560p. 1987. text 73.95 (*0-471-87885-5*) Wiley.

***Quantitative Methods: Custom Edition.** (C). 1998. pap. 43.00 (*0-536-01039-0*) Pearson Custom.

Quantitative Methods: Data, Models & Decision. Dimitris Bertsimas. (MI - Management Science Ser.). 2000. mass mkt. 85.95 (*0-538-85906-7*) S-W Pub.

Quantitative Methods & Statistics: A Guide to Social Research. Sonia Rosenbaum. LC 79-12570. 171p. 1979. reprint ed. pap. 53.10 (*0-608-01465-6*, 205950900001) Bks Demand.

Quantitative Methods for Accounting & Business Studies. 3rd ed. Gordon Bancroft & George O'Sullivan. LC 93-10243. 1993. 15.95 (*0-07-707731-8*) McGraw.

Quantitative Methods for Business. 7th ed. Rob Anderson & Sweeney. LC 97-16589. (QM - Quantitative Methods Ser.). 1997. mass mkt. 85.95 (*0-538-87601-8*); mass mkt. 18.95 (*0-538-87605-0*); mass mkt., student ed. 18.95 (*0-538-87602-6*) S-W Pub.

Quantitative Methods for Business & Economics. Glyn Burton et al. LC 98-27625. (Longman Modular Texts in Business & Economics Ser.). 1998. pap. text. write for info. (*0-582-31165-9*) Longman.

Quantitative Methods for Business & Economics. Adil H. Mouhammed. LC 99-28683. (Illus.). 392p. 1999. text 48.95 (*0-7656-0458-2*) M E Sharpe.

Quantitative Methods for Business Decisions. 3rd ed. J. Curwin & Roger Slater. 300p. 1991. mass mkt. 62.95 (*0-412-40240-8*, A6301) Chapman & Hall.

Quantitative Methods for Business Decisions. 4th ed. Jon Curwin & Roger Slater. 480p. 1996. mass mkt. 31.95 (*0-412-74940-8*) Chapman & Hall.

Quantitative Methods for Business Decisions. 4th rev. ed. Jon Curwin & Roger Slater. (Illus.). 480p. 1996. pap. 24.99 (*1-86152-027-1*) Thomson Learn.

Quantitative Methods for Business Decisions, Lecturers' Resource Manual. 4th ed. Jon Curwin & Roger Slater. 150p. 1997. pap., student ed. 34.95 (*1-86152-028-X*, Pub. by ITBP) Thomson Learn.

Quantitative Methods for Business Decisions: With Cases. 6th ed. Lawrence L. Lapin. (Illus.). 1250p. (C). 1995. pap. 75.95 (*0-534-51051-5*) Wadsworth Pub.

Quantitative Methods for Business Studies. Richard Thomas. 496p. 1997. pap. 68.00 (*0-13-231119-4*, Prentice Hall) P-H.

Quantitative Methods For Business 6e. 6th ed. David R. Anderson et al. LC 94-30130. (SWC-Finance). 938p. (C). 1994. pap. 68.00 (*0-314-04436-1*) West Pub.

***Quantitative Methods for Conservation Biology.** S. Ferson & Mark A. Burgman. LC 99-36218. (Illus.). 360p. 2000. 59.95 (*0-387-94322-6*) Spr-Verlag.

Quantitative Methods for Decision Makers. 2nd ed. Mik Wisniewski. 1997. pap. 67.50 incl. disk (*0-273-62404-0*, Pub. by Pitman Pub) Trans-Atl Phila.

Quantitative Methods for Executive Decisions: Principles & Critical Issues. Richard R. Sylvester. 260p. 1997. text 99.00 (*0-932010-77-6*) PhD Pub.

Quantitative Methods for Historians: A Guide to Research, Data, & Statistics. Konrad H. Jarausch & Kenneth A. Hardy. LC 90-40746. (Illus.). xviii, 248p. (C). 1991. pap. 18.95 (*0-8078-4309-1*) U of NC Pr.

Quantitative Methods for Lawyers. Steven M. Crafton & Margaret F. Brinig. LC 94-72118. 1192p. (C). 1994. pap. 65.00 (*0-89089-604-6*) Carolina Acad Pr.

Quantitative Methods for Life Safety Analysis: Proceedings of the 1986 Symposium. Harold E. Nelson et al. 1988. 35.30 (*0-318-24020-3*) Society Fire Protect.

Quantitative Methods for Management. 9th ed. Harold Bierman et al. 768p. (C). 1997. text 71.95 (*0-256-14021-9*, Irwn McGrw-H) McGrw-H Hghr Educ.

Quantitative Methods for Managerial Decision Making. 2nd ed. A. Redelinghuis et al. 479p. 1989. pap. 49.95 (*0-409-10961-4*) Buttrwrth-Heinemann.

Quantitative Methods for Managerial Decisions. C. M. Paik. LC 72-7093. xiii, 403p. 1973. write for info. (*0-07-048086-9*) McGraw.

Quantitative Methods for Managers. Albright. LC 98-48547. (Business Statistics Ser.). 996p. 1999. pap. 93.95 (*0-534-26124-8*) Wadsworth Pub.

Quantitative Methods for Market Oriented Economic Analysis over Space & Time. Ed. by Walter C. Labys. (Illus.). 337p. 1989. text 91.95 (*0-566-07024-3*, Pub. by Avebry) Ashgate Pub Co.

Quantitative Methods for Portfolio Analysis: MTV Model Approach. Takeaki Kariya. (Theory & Decision Library, Series B). 320p. (C). 1993. lib. bdg. 156.00 (*0-7923-2254-1*) Kluwer Academic.

Quantitative Methods for Public Administration: Techniques & Applications. 2nd ed. Susan Welch & John Comer. 380p. (C). 1989. pap. text 46.00 (*0-534-10888-1*) Harcourt.

Quantitative Methods for Public Administration in Developing Countries. fac. ed. Scott C. Iverson. LC 85-6381. (Wiley Series on Public Administration in Developing Countries). 177p. pap. 54.90 (*0-7837-7363-3*, 204717200005) Bks Demand.

Quantitative Methods for Tax Planning & Decision Making. K. Posel. 265p. 1991. pap. 74.00 (*0-409-10962-2*, SA, MICHIE) LEXIS Pub.

***Quantitative Methods for Valuation of Financial Assets: 100 Questions & Answers.** A. S. Ramasastri. LC 99-51499. 2000. pap. write for info. (*0-7619-9408-4*) Sage.

Quantitative Methods in Aquatic Ecotoxicology. Micheal C. Newman. 448p. 1994. lib. bdg. 95.00 (*0-87371-622-1*, L622) Lewis Pubs.

Quantitative Methods in Biological & Medical Sciences: A Historical Essay. H. O. Lancaster. LC 94-8063. 297p. 1994. 89.95 (*0-387-94279-3*) Spr-Verlag.

Quantitative Methods in Bone Densitometry. Alan Huddleston. (C). 1988. text 179.50 (*0-89838-362-5*) Kluwer Academic.

An Asterisk (*) at the beginning of an entry indicates that the title is appearing for the first time.

Quantitative Methods in Business. Audrey Curnock. 448p. 1999. pap. 49.50 (*0-7487-2083-9*, Pub. by S Thornes Pubs) Trans-Atl Phila.

Quantitative Methods in Education Research: A Cast Study. Richard F. Gunstone & Gilah C. Leder. 1992. pap. 48.00 (*0-7300-1486-X*, EED402, Pub. by Deakin Univ) St Mut.

Quantitative Methods in Finance. Terry J. Watsham & Keith Parramore. 393p. 1997. pap. 29.99 (*1-86152-367-X*) Thomson Learn.

Quantitative Methods in Fractography, STP 1085. Ed. by Bernard M. Strauss & Susil K. Putatunda. LC 90-35242. (Special Technical Publication (STP) Ser.). (Illus.). 165p. 1990. text 49.00 (*0-8031-1387-0*, STP1085) ASTM.

Quantitative Methods in Landscape Ecology: The Analysis & Interpretation of Landscape Heterogeneity. Ed. by Hermann Remmert et al. (Ecological Studies: Vol. 82). (Illus.). 520p. 1992. 130.95 (*0-387-97326-5*) Spr-Verlag.

Quantitative Methods in Landscape Ecology: The Analysis & Interpretation of Landscape Heterogeneity. Ed. by M. G. Turner & R. H. Gardner. (Ecological Studies: Vol. 82). (Illus.). 552p. 1996. 42.95 (*0-387-94241-6*) Spr-Verlag.

Quantitative Methods in Librarianship: Standards, Research, & Management, 4. Ed. by Irene B. Hoadley & Alice S. Clark. LC 73-149962. (Contributions in Librarianship & Information Science Ser.: No. 4). 270p. 1972. 35.00 (*0-8371-6061-8*, HOQ/) Greenwood.

Quantitative Methods in Management. Leslie Jarvis. LC 96-24602. 304p. 1997. pap. text 34.00 (*0-7618-0441-2*) U Pr of Amer.

Quantitative Methods in Management: Text & Cases. Paul A. Vatter et al. (C). 1978. text 66.95 (*0-256-02006-X*, Irwn McGrw-H) McGrw-H Hghr Educ.

*__Quantitative Methods in Mathmatics: Quantitative Methods in Mathmatics.__ 3rd ed. Joseph Sukta & Charlotte Sukta. 350p. (C). 1999. per. 34.95 (*0-7872-6107-6*, 41610701) Kendall-Hunt.

Quantitative Methods in Quality Management: A Guide for Practitioners. Ed. by Daniel R. Longo & Deborah Bohr. LC 90-14398. 150p. 1991. pap. 46.95 (*1-55648-060-1*, 169102) AHPI.

Quantitative Methods in Social Work: State of the Art. Ed. by David F. Gillespie & Charles Glisson. LC 92-29647. (Journal of Social Service Research: Vol. 16, Nos. 1-2). (Illus.). 296p. 1993. pap. text 19.95 (*1-56024-275-2*); lib. bdg. 49.95 (*1-56024-274-4*) Haworth Pr.

Quantitative Methods in Soil Mineralogy. Ed. by Lucian W. Zelazny & R. J. Luxmoore. LC 93-48098. 462p. 1994. pap. 39.00 (*0-89118-806-1*) Soil Sci Soc Am.

Quantitative Microbeam Analysis. Ed. by A. G. Fitzgerald et al. (Scottish Universities Summer School in Physics, a NATO Advanced Study Institute Ser.: No. 40). 496p. 1993. 189.00 (*0-7503-0256-9*) IOP Pub.

Quantitative Microbial Risk Assessment. Charles N. Haas et al. LC 98-45800. (Illus.). 464p. 1999. 90.00 (*0-471-18397-0*) Wiley.

Quantitative Microscopy. Robert T. DeHoff & Frederick N. Rhines. (Illus.). 432p. (C). 1991. reprint ed. 104.00 (*1-878907-31-X*) TechBooks.

Quantitative Microscopy & Image Analysis: ASM 1993 Charleston, SC International Conference Proceedings. Ed. by David J. Diaz. 135p. 1994. 49.00 (*0-87170-511-7*, 6399) ASM.

*__Quantitative Modeling of Derivative Securities: From Theory to Practice.__ Marco Avellaneda & P. Laurence. LC 99-47242. 336p. 1999. boxed set 59.95 (*1-58488-031-7*, Chap & Hall CRC) CRC Pr.

Quantitative Modeling of Human Performance in Complex, Dynamic Systems. National Research Council, U. S. Staff. Ed. by Sheldon Baron et al. LC 89-63540. 108p. reprint ed. pap. 33.50 (*0-7837-1298-7*, 204143900020) Bks Demand.

Quantitative Modeling of Soil Forming Process. Ed. by R. B. Bryant et al. LC 94-31647. (Special Publications: Vol. 39). 185p. 1994. pap. 24.00 (*0-89118-814-2*) Soil Sci Soc Am.

Quantitative Modelling for Management & Business, w/disk. Mike Carter & David Williamson. 320p. (Orig.). 1995. pap. 64.50 incl. disk (*0-273-60510-0*, Pub. by Pitman Pub) Trans-Atl Phila.

Quantitative Models for Project Planning. Adedeji B. Badiru. LC 92-34377. 376p. 1993. 69.50 (*0-89930-730-2*, BQT, Quorum Bks) Greenwood.

Quantitative Models for Supply Chain Management. Sridhar R. Tayur et al. LC 98-37476. 8p. 1998. 250.00 (*0-7923-8344-3*) Kluwer Academic.

Quantitative Models in Accounting: A Procedural Guide for Professionals. Ahmed R. Belkaoui. LC 86-16993. 373p. 1987. 85.00 (*0-89930-186-X*, BQU/, Quorum Bks) Greenwood.

Quantitative Models in Parallel Systems, Vol. XVIII. Ed. by Francois L. Baccelli et al. LC 95-37495. (ESPRIT Basic Research Ser.). 298p. 1995. 62.00 (*3-540-60125-2*) Spr-Verlag.

Quantitative Models of Trophic Interactions in Caribbean Coral Reefs. S. Opitz. (ICLARM Technical Reports: No. 43). 350p. 1996. pap. 27.00 (*971-8709-60-6*, Pub. by ICLARM) Intl Spec Bk.

*__Quantitative Molecular Pharmacology & Informatics in Drug Discovery.__ Michael W. Lutz. LC 99-29628. (Illus.). 428p. 1999. 140.00 (*0-471-98861-8*) Wiley.

Quantitative NDE in the Nuclear Industry: Proceedings of the Fifth International Conference on Nondestructive Evaluation in the Nuclear Industry, San Diego, CA, 10-13 May 1982--Sponsored by the American Society for Metals. Ed. by Roger B. Clough. LC 82-74019. 487p. reprint ed. pap. 151.00 (*0-608-16512-3*, 202704300053) Bks Demand.

Quantitative Neuroanatomy in Transmitter Research. Ed. by Luigi F. Agnati & Kjell Fuxe. (Wenner-Gren International Symposia Ser.: Vol. 42). 432p. 1986. 95.00 (*0-306-42160-7*, Plenum Trade) Perseus Pubng.

Quantitative Nuclear Cardiology. Ed. by Richard N. Pierson. LC 74-20990. (Illus.). 299p. reprint ed. pap. 92.70 (*0-608-30260-0*, 201258200082) Bks Demand.

Quantitative Nursing Research. Thomas R. Knapp. LC 97-45338. 287p. 1998. 57.95 (*0-7619-1362-9*); pap. write for info. (*0-7619-1363-7*) Sage Pubng.

Quantitative Pareto Analysis by Cone Separation Technique. Ignacy Kaliszewski. LC 94-22525. 1994. lib. bdg. 127.00 (*0-7923-9492-5*) Kluwer Academic.

Quantitative Particle Physics: Cargese 1992. M. Levy et al. (NATO ASI Ser.: Vol. 311). (Illus.). 444p. (C). 1993. text 129.50 (*0-306-44560-3*, Kluwer Plenum) Kluwer Academic.

Quantitative PCR Protocols. Bernd Kochanowski & Udo Reischl. LC 99-10332. (Methods in Molecular Medicine Ser.: Vol. 26). 320p. 1999. 79.50 (*0-89603-518-2*) Humana.

Quantitative Population Dynamics. Ed. by D. G. Chapman & V. F. Gallucci. (Statistical Ecology Ser.). 290p. 1981. 30.00 (*0-89974-010-3*) Intl Co-Op.

Quantitative Practice of Anesthesia: Use of Closed Circuit. Harry J. Lowe & Edward A. Ernst. LC 80-21803. (Illus.). 249p. reprint ed. pap. 77.20 (*0-608-15558-6*, 205638600063) Bks Demand.

Quantitative Problem Solving in Maternal, Child, & Adolescent Health. Ed. by Jeffrey B. Gould. (Illus.). 222p. (Orig.). 1994. pap. 19.95 (*0-89914-042-4*) Third Party Pub.

Quantitative Problems in Physical & Chemical Biology. D. Siva Sankar. write for info. (*0-685-77285-3*) PJD Pubns.

*__Quantitative Production Analysis.__ Rita Sloan Berndt. 1999. pap. text. write for info. (*0-86377-769-4*) L Erlbaum Assocs.

Quantitative Psychology. J. Drosler. LC 89-7457. (Illus.). 200p. (C). 1989. text 38.00 (*0-88937-028-1*) Hogrefe & Huber Pubs.

*__Quantitative-Qualitative Friction Ridge Analysis: An Introduction to Basic & Advanced Ridgeology.__ David R. Ashbaugh. LC 99-33096. (Practical Aspects of Criminal & Forensic Investigation Ser.). 248p. 1999. boxed set 69.95 (*0-8493-7007-8*) CRC Pr.

*__Quantitative Reasoning.__ 372p. (C). 2000. text 29.35 (*0-536-60528-9*) Pearson Custom.

Quantitative Reasoning: Mathematics for Citizens in the 21St Century. Bennett. 128p. (C). 1996. pap. text 26.00 (*0-201-80958-3*) Addison-Wesley.

Quantitative Reasoning Preliminary Edition: Mathematics for Citizens in the 21st Century. Bennett. 1996. teacher ed. 24.00 (*0-201-80959-1*) Addison-Wesley.

Quantitative Reasoning for College Graduates: A Complement to the Standards. Ed. by Linda Sons. (MAA Reports). 56p. 1998. pap. 18.00 (*0-88385-800-2*) Math Assn.

Quantitative Research for the Behavioral Sciences. Celia C. Reaves. LC 91-39997. 400p. (C). 1991. text 81.95 (*0-471-61683-4*) Wiley.

Quantitative Research in Archaeology: Progress & Prospects. Ed. by Mark S. Aldenderfer. LC 86-15564. (Illus.). 312p. reprint ed. pap. 96.80 (*0-7837-4576-1*, 204410500003) Bks Demand.

Quantitative Research Methods in the Social Sciences. Paul S. Maxim. LC 98-18953. (Illus.). 416p. (C). 1999. text 55.00 (*0-19-511465-5*) OUP.

Quantitative Risk Analysis 2nd ed. Vose. LC 99-52968. 1978. text 100.00 (*0-471-99765-X*) Wiley.

Quantitative Risk Assessment. Ed. by Robert F. Almeder & James M. Humber. LC 84-640015. (Biomedical Ethics Reviews Ser.: No. 1986). 278p. 1987. 49.50 (*0-89603-056-3*) Humana.

Quantitative Risk Assessment for Environmental & Occupational Health. Bill Hallenbeck. (Illus.). 216p. 1986. lib. bdg. 68.00 (*0-87371-055-X*, L055) Lewis Pubs.

Quantitative Risk Assessment for Environmental & Occupational Health. 2nd ed. William H. Hallenbeck. 240p. 1993. lib. bdg. 75.00 (*0-87371-801-1*, L801) Lewis Pubs.

Quantitative Risk Assessment in Regulation. Ed. by Lester B. Lave. LC 82-22603. (Studies in the Regulation of Economic Activity). 264p. 1983. 34.95 (*0-8157-5164-8*); pap. 14.95 (*0-8157-5163-X*) Brookings.

Quantitative Risk Assessment of Hazardous Materials Transport Systems: Rail, Road, Pipelines & Ship. Michel Nicolet-Monnier & Adrian V. Gheorge. LC 95-49989. (Topics in Safety, Risk, Reliability & Quality Ser.). xviii, 343p. 1996. text 184.00 (*0-7923-3923-1*) Kluwer Academic.

Quantitative Seismology: Theory & Methods, Vol. I. Keiiti Aki & Paul G. Richards. LC 79-17434. (Geology Ser.). (Illus.). 573p. (C). 1980. text 43.20 (*0-7167-1058-7*) W H Freeman.

Quantitative Skill Assessment for Coastal Ocean Models. Ed. by Daniel R. Lynch & Alan M. Davies. LC 95-9943. (Coastal & Estuarine Studies: Vol. 49). 510p. 1995. 70.00 (*0-87590-261-8*) Am Geophysical.

Quantitative Social Science Research on Latin America. Ed. by Robert S. Byars & Joseph L. Love. LC 72-95001. (University of Illinois at Urbana-Champaign. Occasional Papers: No. 1). 280p. reprint ed. pap. 86.80 (*0-608-13890-8*, 202024500016) Bks Demand.

Quantitative Sociodynamics: Stochastic Methods & Models of Social Interaction Processes. Dirk Helbing. (Theory & Decision Library, Series B: Vol. 31). 356p. (C). 1995. text 147.00 (*0-7923-3192-3*) Kluwer Academic.

Quantitative Solutions in Hydrogeology & Groundwater Modeling. Neven Kresic. LC 96-54297. 461p. 1997. lib. bdg. 75.00 (*1-56670-219-4*) Lewis Pubs.

Quantitative Stratigraphic Correlation. Ed. by J. M. Cubitt & Richard A. Reyment. LC 81-21926. (International Geological Correlation Programme Ser.: No. 148). 321p. reprint ed. pap. 99.60 (*0-7837-3228-7*, 204324600007) Bks Demand.

Quantitative Stratigraphic Correlation: Proceedings of the 6th Geochautauqua, Syracuse University, October 1977. Ed. by Daniel F. Merriam. (Illus.). 112p. 1979. pap. 50.00 (*0-08-023979-X*, Pergamon Pr) Elsevier.

Quantitative Stratigraphy. F. M. Gradstein et al. LC 85-18331. 1985. text 285.50 (*90-277-2116-5*) Kluwer Academic.

Quantitative Structure: Chromatographic Retention Relationships. Roman Kaliszan. LC 87-14802. (Chemical Analysis Ser.). 303p. 1987. 185.00 (*0-471-85983-4*) Wiley.

Quantitative Structure - Activity Relationships in Environmental Sciences Vol. VII: Proceedings of QSAR 96, 24-28 June 1996, Elsinore, Denmark. Ed. by Fei Chen & Gerrit Schuurmann. LC 97-30982. (SETAC Technical Publications Ser.). (Illus.). 1997. 98.00 (*1-880611-23-6*, SETAC Pr) SETAC.

Quantitative Structure-Activity Relations in Environmental Toxicology. Klaus L. Kaiser. 1984. text 185.50 (*90-277-1776-1*) Kluwer Academic.

Quantitative Studies in Agrarian History. Ed. by Morton Rothstein & Daniel Field. LC 93-24729. (Illus.). 288p. 1993. text 59.95 (*0-8138-1673-4*) Iowa St U Pr.

Quantitative Studies in the Geological Sciences: A Memoir in Honor of William C. Krumbein. Ed. by E. H. Whitten. LC 74-15932. (Geological Society of America, Memoir Ser.: No. 142). 424p. reprint ed. pap. 131.50 (*0-608-13946-7*, 202373300033) Bks Demand.

Quantitative Study of Islamic Literature. Mohamed Taher. 183p. (C). 1998. pap. 100.00 (*81-85880-11-5*, Pub. by Print Hse) St Mut.

Quantitative Study of Rotatoria in Terwilliger's Pond, Put-In Bay, Ohio. Elbert H. Ahlstrom. (Bulletin Ser.: No. 30). 1934. pap. text 2.00 (*0-86727-029-2*) Ohio Bio Survey.

Quantitative Surface Analysis for Materials Science. Graham Smith. 173p. 1991. text 60.00 (*0-901462-79-9*, Pub. by Inst Materials) Ashgate Pub Co.

Quantitative Surface Analysis of Materials - STP 643. 217p. 1986. 21.50 (*0-8031-0543-6*, STP643) ASTM.

Quantitative Systemic Analysis & Control. Ralph F. Breyer. Ed. by Henry Assael. LC 78-250. (Century of Marketing Ser.). 1979. reprint ed. lib. bdg. 33.95 (*0-405-11164-9*) Ayer.

Quantitative Techniques in a Business Context. G. Ascroft & Roger Slater. (Business in Context Ser.). 416p. 1995. pap. 29.95 (*0-412-37570-2*) Chapman & Hall.

Quantitative Techniques in a Business Context. P. G. Ashcroft & Roger Slater. (Business in Context Ser.). 416p. 1990. pap. text 34.50 (*0-412-02641-4*, A4433, Chap & Hall NY) Chapman & Hall.

Quantitative Techniques in Geography. 2nd ed. R. Hammond & P. S. McCullagh. (Illus.). 384p. 1978. pap. text 24.95 (*0-19-874067-0*) OUP.

Quantitative Techniques in Landscape Planning. J. Eugenio Falero & Santiago G. Alonso. LC 95-2602. 288p. 1995. lib. bdg. 85.00 (*1-56670-157-0*, L1157) Lewis Pubs.

Quantitative Theory of Foliations. H. Blaine Lawson. LC 76-51339. (Regional Conference Series in Mathematics: Vol. 27). (Illus.). 78p. 1977. reprint ed. pap. 30.00 (*0-7837-8856-8*, 204956600001) Bks Demand.

Quantitative Theory of Foliations. H. Blaine Lawson, Jr. LC 76-51339. (CBMS Regional Conference Series in Mathematics: No. 27). 65p. 1977. reprint ed. pap. 22.00 (*0-8218-1677-2*, CBMS/27) Am Math.

Quantitative TLC & Its Industrial Applications. Laszlo Treiber. (Chromatographic Science Ser.: Vol. 36). (Illus.). 376p. 1986. text 190.00 (*0-8247-7597-X*) Dekker.

Quantitative Tools for Decision Support Using IFPS-Optimum. Donald R. Plane & Roy E. Crummer. LC 84-24368. 400p. (C). 1986. pap. text 45.25 (*0-201-05844-8*) Addison-Wesley.

Quantitative Trading & Money Management: A Guide to Risk Analysis & Trading, Revised Edition. 5th rev. ed. Fred Gehn. 340p. 1995. text 55.00 (*1-55738-585-8*, Irwn Prfssnl) McGraw-Hill Prof.

Quantitative Treatments of Solute Solvent Interactions. Ed. by P. Politzer & J. S. Murray. LC 94-31159. (Theoretical & Computational Chemistry Ser.: 1). 380p. 1994. 261.75 (*0-444-82054-X*) Elsevier.

*__Quantitative Ultrasound: Assessment of Osteoporosis & Bone Status.__ Ed. by Christopher F. Njeh. 420p. 1999. 125.00 (*1-85317-679-6*, Pub. by Martin Dunitz) Blackwell Sci.

Quantitative X-Ray Diffractometry. L. S. Zevin & Giora Kimmel. Ed. by Inez Mureinik. LC 95-19428. (Illus.). 300p. 1995. 59.95 (*0-387-94541-5*) Spr-Verlag.

Quantitative X-Ray Fluorescence Analysis: Theory & Application. Gerald R. Lachance et al. LC 94-10486. 424p. 1995. 285.00 (*0-471-95167-6*) Wiley.

Quantitative X-ray Spectrometry. 2nd ed. Ed. by Ron Jenkins Jenkins et al. (Practical Spectroscopy Ser.: Vol. 20). (Illus.). 504p. 1995. text 165.00 (*0-8247-9554-7*) Dekker.

Quantitative Zooarchaeology: Topics in the Analysis of Archaeological Faunas. Donald K. Grayson. Ed. by Geoffrey W. Dimbleby. (Studies in Archaeology Science). 1984. text 59.95 (*0-12-297280-5*) Acad Pr.

Quantitatively Determining the Acid Content of Fruit Juices. Andrew W. Zanella. Ed. by H. Anthony Neidig. (Modular Laboratory Program in Chemistry Ser.). 11p. (C). 1993. pap. text 1.50 (*0-87540-427-8*, ANAL 427-8) Chem Educ Res.

Quantitive Analysis of Social Representations. Willem Doise et al. Tr. by Julian Kabeko. (European Monographs in Social Psychology Ser.). 170p. 1996. pap. text 27.95 (*0-7450-1348-1*) Taylor & Francis.

Quantities - Damages: Early Poems. Richard Howard. LC 83-23304. (Wesleyan Poetry Ser.). 151p. reprint ed. pap. 46.90 (*0-7837-0215-9*, 204052300017) Bks Demand.

Quantities & Units In Radiation Protection Dosimetry. ICRU Staff. Ed. by W. Roger Ney. (ICRU Reports: No. 51). 19p. 1993. pap. 30.00 (*0-913394-50-5*) Intl Comm Rad Meas.

Quantities & Units of Measurement. J. V. Drazil. (ENG, FRE & GER.). 314p. 1983. 110.00 (*0-8288-0009-X*, M6719) Fr & Eur.

Quantities May Be Limited: Strategies For Balancing Work & Family. Brenda Jernigan. 1999. pap. 4.95 (*0-9658659-8-3*) Kaleidoscope.

Quantities, Symbols, Units & Abbreviations in the Life Sciences: A Guide for Authors & Editors. Arnost Kotyk. 152p. 1999. 39.50 (*0-89603-616-2*); pap. 19.50 (*0-89603-649-9*) Humana.

Quantities, Units, & Symbols in Physical Chemistry. 2nd ed. Ian Mills et al. LC 92-40104. 176p. 1993. pap. 21.00 (*0-632-03583-8*) Blackwell Sci.

Quantitive Approach Management. 8th ed. Stinson. 1992. text, teacher ed. 51.56 (*0-07-037558-5*) McGraw.

Quantitive Description of Ionospheric Storm Effects & Irregularities: Proceedings of the C4.2 Symposium of COSPAR Scientific Commission C Which Was Held During the 31st COSPAR Scientific Assembly, Birmingham, UK, 14-21 July 1996. Ed. by K. Rawer & D. Bilitza. 162p. 1997. pap. 100.50 (*0-08-043306-5*, Pergamon Pr) Elsevier.

Quantitive Estimation & Prediction of Human Cancer Risks. Ed. by H. Moller et al. (IARC Scientific Publications Ser.: No. 131). 440p. 1999. pap. text 69.00 (*92-832-2131-1*) OUP.

Quantitive Expression of Cultural Relationships. fac. ed. H. E. Driver & A. L. Kroeber. (University of California Publications in American Archaeology & Ethnology: Vol. 31: 4). (Illus.). 49p. (C). 1932. reprint ed. pap. text 5.31 (*1-55567-284-1*) Coyote Press.

Quantitive Methods for Management with Decisions Support Software (DSS) Textbook/Workbook with 2.6 Version Disk. rev. ed. Pinney et al. LC 97-67112. 1998. wbk. ed. 97.95 incl. disk (*0-87393-691-4*) Dame Pubns.

Quantity Adjustment: Vowel Lengthening & Shortening in Early Middle English. Nikolaus Ritt. (Studies in Linguistics: Supplementary Volumes). (Illus.). 216p. (C). 1995. text 52.95 (*0-521-46232-0*) Cambridge U Pr.

Quantity & Quality in Economic Research, Vol. 2. Ed. by Roy C. Brown. LC 85-26360. 212p. (Orig.). (C). 1988. pap. text 23.00 (*0-8191-6702-9*) U Pr of Amer.

Quantity & Quality in Economic Research: Studies in Applied Business Research, Vol. IV. Ed. by Theologos H. Bonitsis & Chamberlain Brown. 272p. 1997. text 59.95 (*1-85972-682-8*, Pub. by Avebry) Ashgate Pub Co.

Quantity & Quality in Higher Education. John Radford. LC 96-36549. (Higher Education Policy Ser.). 1996. pap. write for info. (*1-85302-433-3*, Pub. by Jessica Kingsley) Taylor & Francis.

Quantity & Quality in Social Research. Alan Bryman. 208p. (C). 1988. pap. 22.99 (*0-415-07898-9*) Routledge.

Quantity & Quality of Breast Milk: Report on the WHO Collaborative Study on Breast-Feeding. WHO Staff. 148p. 1985. 17.00 (*92-4-154201-2*) World Health.

Quantity Cookery. 4th rev. ed. Nola Treat & Lenore Richards. 1967. 24.95 (*0-316-85251-1*) Little.

Quantity Food Preparation. Jack Rudman. (Occupational Competency Examination (OCE) Ser.: Vol. 30). 47.95 (*0-8373-5780-2*) Nat Learn.

Quantity Food Preparation. Jack Rudman. (Occupational Competency Examination Ser.: OCE-30). 1994. pap. 27.95 (*0-8373-5730-6*) Nat Learn.

Quantity Food Preparation: Standardizing Recipes & Controlling Ingredients. 3rd ed. Polly W. Buchanan. LC 93-6122. 1993. write for info. (*0-88091-150-6*) Am Dietetic Assn.

Quantity Food Production. Noel Cullen & Linda Cullen. 516p. (C). 2001. 65.33 (*0-13-242165-8*, Macmillan Coll) P-H.

Quantity Food Production, Planning, & Management. 2nd ed. John B. Knight & Lendal H. Kotschevar. 445p. 1988. 59.95 (*0-471-28927-2*, VNR) Wiley.

Quantity Food Production, Planning, & Management. 2nd ed. John B. Knight & Lendal H. Kotschevar. (Illus.). 640p. (C). 1989. text 55.95 (*0-442-24016-3*, VNR) Wiley.

*__Quantity Food Production, Planning & Management.__ 3rd ed. John B. Knight & Lendal H. Kotschevar. 512p. (C). 2000. 59.95 (*0-471-33347-6*) Wiley.

Quantity Food Production Skillbook. Educational Foundation of the National Restaurant. (Management Skills Program Ser.). 68p. (Orig.). 1993. pap. 10.95 (*0-915452-07-3*) Educ Found.

Quantity Food Purchasing. 5th ed. Lendal H. Kotschevar. LC 98-18805. 665p. (C). 1998. 76.00 (*0-13-095881-6*, Pub. by P-H) S&S Trade.

Quantity Food Sanitation. 5th ed. Karla Longree et al. LC 95-36504. (Illus.). 480p. 1996. 69.95 (*0-471-59660-4*) Wiley.

Quantity in the Skolt (Lappish) Saami Language: An Acoustic Analysis. Zita McRobbie-Utasi. LC 99-70017. (Uralic & Altaic Ser.: Vol. 165). 255p. 1999. 35.00 (*0-933070-45-4*) Ind U Res Inst.

Quantity Recipes. 3rd rev. ed. Marion A. Wood et al. (Illus.). 233p. 1983. pap. 7.50 (*1-57753-017-9*, 399QR) Corn Coop Ext.

Quantity Surveying Techniques: New Directions. P. S. Brandon. (Illus.). 288p. 1992. pap. 49.95 (*0-632-03297-9*) Blackwell Sci.

Quantity Takeoff for Contractors: How to Get Accurate Material Counts. Paul J. Cook. Orig. Title: Quantity Takeoff for the General Contractor. (Illus.). 250p. 1991. pap. 35.95 (*0-87629-268-6*, 67262) R S Means.

Quantity Takeoff for the General Contractor see Quantity Takeoff for Contractors: How to Get Accurate Material Counts

Quantity Theory of Insanity: Together with Five Supporting Propositions. Will Self. LC 95-45867. 1996. pap. 13.00 (*0-679-75094-0*) Vin Bks.

Quantity Theory of Money: From Locke to Keynes & Friedman. Mark Blaug et al. 160p. 1995. 80.00 (*1-85898-177-8*) E Elgar.

Quantity Time: Moving Beyond the Quality Time Myth. rev. ed. Steffen T. Kraehmer. LC 94-21343.Tr. of Time Well Spent. 224p. 1994. reprint ed. pap. 11.95 (*0-925190-30-6*) Fairview Press.

Quantization & Coherent States Methods - Proceedings of XI Workshop on Geometric Methods in Physics. S. T. Ali et al. 256p. 1993. text 121.00 (*981-02-1447-2*) World Scientific Pub.

Quantization & Infinite-Dimensional Systems. J. P. Antoine et al. LC 94-44822. (Lecture Notes in Physics: Vol. 248). (Illus.). 300p. (C). 1995. text 95.00 (*0-306-44834-3*, Kluwer Plenum) Kluwer Academic.

Quantization & Phase. D. A. Dubin et al. 350p. 1999. 60.00 (*981-02-3919-X*) World Scientific Pub.

Quantization, Coherent States, & Complex Structures: Proceedings of the Thirteenth Workshop on Geometric Methods in Physics Held in Bialowieza, Poland, July 9-15, 1994. J. P. Antoine et al. (Illus.). 312p. (C). 1996. text 110.00 (*0-306-45214-6*, Kluwer Plenum) Kluwer Academic.

Quantization, Gravitation & Group Methods in Physics. Ed. by A. A. Komar. (Proceedings of the Lebedev Physics Institute Ser.: Vol. 176 Suppl. Vol. 1). 317p. 1988. text 185.00 (*0-941743-17-9*) Nova Sci Pubs.

Quantization, Nonlinear Partial Differential Equations, & Operator Algebra: 1994 John von Neumann Symposium on Quantization & Nonlinear Wave Equations June 7-11, 1994, Massachusetts Institute of Technology, Cambridge, Massachusetts. Ed. by Thomas Branson et al. LC 96-5187. (Proceedings of Symposia in Pure Mathematics Ser.: Vol. 59). 224p. 1996. text 54.00 (*0-8218-0381-6*, PSPUM/59) Am Math.

Quantization of Fields with Constraints. D. M. Gitman & I. V. Tyutin. Ed. by E. F. Hefter et al. (Series in Nuclear & Particle Physics). 312p. 1990. 96.00 (*0-387-51679-4*) Spr-Verlag.

Quantization of Gauge Systems. M. Henneaux & C. Teitelboim. 552p. 1993. pap. text 39.50 (*0-691-03769-8*, Pub. by Princeton U Pr) Cal Prin Full Svc.

Quantization of Gauge Systems. Marc Henneaux & Claudio Teitelboim. (Illus.). 628p. 1993. text 95.00 (*0-691-08775-X*, Pub. by Princeton U Pr) Cal Prin Full Svc.

***Quantization, the Segal-Bargmann Transform & Semiclassical Analysis: First Summer School in Analysis & Mathematical Physics, Cuernavaca Morelos, Mexico, June 8-18, 1998.** Salvador Perez-Esteva & Carlos Villegas-Blas. LC 00-34991. 2000. write for info. (*0-8218-2115-6*) Am Math.

Quantized Hall Resistance: RISP-3. unabridged ed. Intrinsic-Derived Standards Committee. (RISP Ser.: No. 3). (Illus.). 64p. 1997. 15.00 (*1-58464-008-1*) Natl Conf Stds Labs.

Quantized Vortices in Helium, No. II. Russell J. Donnelly. (Studies in Low Temperature Physics: No. 3). (Illus.). 364p. (C). 1991. text 115.00 (*0-521-32400-9*) Cambridge U Pr.

Quanto-Geometrie Vol. 1: Nouvelle Philosophie Mathematique Permettant l'Interpretation Globale De la Manifestation De la Matiere Dans l'Univers. Joseph J. Jean-Claude. Ed. by Bertrand J. Jean-Claude. (Illus.). 257p. (Orig.). 1995. pap. 38.80 (*0-9647466-1-1*) Quantometrix.

Quantrell's Raiders. Frank Gruber. 1981. mass mkt. 1.95 (*0-451-09735-1*, J9735, Sig) NAL.

Quantrell's Raiders. Frank Gruber. 352p. 1984. mass mkt. 3.50 (*0-451-12777-3*, Sig) NAL.

Quantrell's Raiders. large type ed. Frank Gruber. (Linford Western Library). 368p. 1994. pap. 16.99 (*0-7089-7578-X*, Linford) Ulverscroft.

Quantrigue. Stephan M. Sechi & Tony Herring. (Talislanta Ser.). (Illus.). 64p. (Orig.). 1993. pap. 9.95 (*1-880992-11-6*) Wizards Coast.

Quantrill: The Wildest Killer of the Civil War & Other Stories. Paul Ditzel. (True Adventure Stories from the Civil War Ser.). (Illus.). 112p. (Orig.). 1991. pap. 9.95 (*0-925165-06-9*) Fire Buff Hse.

Quantrill & the Border Wars. William E. Connelley. (Illus.). 542p. (C). 1992. pap. 22.95 (*1-878882-04-X*) KS Heritage Pr.

Quantrill's Scattered Bones Buried at Last. rev. ed. Sybil Montana. (Illus.). 72p. 1994. pap. 7.00 (*1-892035-04-9*) Sybil Montana.

Quantrill's War: The Life & Times of William Clarke Quantrill, 1837-1865. Duane Schultz. LC 96-23709. 368p. 1996. 24.95 (*0-312-14710-4*) St Martin.

Quantrill's War: The Life & Times of William Clarke Quantrill, 1837-1865. Duane Schultz. (Illus.). 352p. 1997. pap. 14.95 (*0-312-16972-8*) St Martin.

Quantulumcumque. Jonathan Williams. 36p. 1991. pap. 15.00 (*0-9622572-9-X*) French Broad.

Quantulumcumque. deluxe limited ed. Jonathan Williams. 36p. 1991. pap. 60.00 (*0-685-48487-4*) French Broad.

***Quantum.** Tom Grace. LC 99-87230. 384p. 2000. 24.95 (*0-446-52410-7*, Pub. by Warner Bks) Little.

Quantum: The Quantum Theory of Particles, Fields & Cosmology. E. Elbaz. Ed. by W. Beiglbsck et al. LC 97-33659. (Texts & Monographs in Physics). (Illus.). 350p. 1997. 89.00 (*3-540-62093-1*) Spr-Verlag.

Quantum & Classical Many-Body Theory in Condensed Matter Physics: Proceedings of the Symposium. G. Vignale & G. F. Giuliani. 1994. text 75.00 (*981-02-1105-8*) World Scientific Pub.

Quantum & Fermion Differential Geometry, Pt. A. Robert Hermann. (Interdisciplinary Mathematics Ser.: No. 16). 196p. 1977. 35.00 (*0-915692-22-8*, 991600339) Math Sci Pr.

Quantum & Non-Commutative Analysis: Past, Present, & Future Perspectives. Ed. by Huzihiro Araki et al. LC 93-31537. (Mathematical Physics Studies: Vol. 16). 468p. (C). 1993. text 264.50 (*0-7923-2532-X*) Kluwer Academic.

Quantum & Statistical Field Theory. Michel Le Bellac. Tr. by Gabriel Barton. (Illus.). 608p. 1992. pap. text 55.00 (*0-19-853964-9*) OUP.

Quantum Aspects of Beam Physics. Pisin Chen. 1998. 84.00 (*981-02-3551-8*) World Scientific Pub.

Quantum Aspects of Catoinic Polymerization of Olffins. V. A. Babkin et al. LC 98-106172. (Illus.). 247p. 1997. lib. bdg. 115.00 (*1-56072-501-X*) Nova Sci Pubs.

***Quantum Aspects of Gauge Theories, Supersymmetry & Unification: Proceedings of the 2nd International Conference Held in Corfu, Greece, September 20-26, 1998.** Ed. by A. Cersole et al. LC 99-36318. (Lecture Notes in Physics Ser.: Vol. 525). xx, 511p. 1999. 94.00 (*3-540-66005-4*) Spr-Verlag.

Quantum Aspects of Optical Communications: Proceedings of a Workshop Held at the CNRS Paris, France, 26-28 November 1990. Ed. by Cherif Bendjaballah et al. 389p. 1991. 56.95 (*0-387-53862-3*) Spr-Verlag.

Quantum-Based Electronic Devices & Systems. Dutta Mitra. 1999. 41.00 (*981-02-3700-6*) World Scientific Pub.

Quantum Beat: The Physical Principles of Atomic Clocks. Fouad G. Major. LC 97-24027. (Illus.). 336p. (C). 1998. 49.95 (*0-387-98301-5*) Spr-Verlag.

Quantum Biology & Quantum Pharmacology - Quantum Biology Symposium Proceedings, 17. 17th ed. Ed. by Per-Olov Lowdin. 248p. 1991. pap. 183.95 (*0-471-54598-8*) Wiley.

Quantum Biophysics. Date not set. pap. write for info. (*1-893637-13-1*) Hlth & Hap.

Quantum Brain. Jeffrey Satinover. 288p. (C). 2001. 24.95 (*0-471-33326-3*) Wiley.

Quantum Brain: Theory & Implications. August Stern. LC 94-2209. 222p. 1994. 108.00 (*0-444-81864-2*, North Holland) Elsevier.

Quantum Brain Dynamics & Consciousness: An Introduction. Mari Jibu & Kunio Yasue. LC 95-35756. (Advances in Consciousness Research Ser.: Vol. 3). xvi, 244p. 1995. 34.95 (*1-55619-183-9*) J Benjamins Pubng Co.

Quantum Breeze: Meditations in Postmodern Time. JaneAnne Narrin. Ed. by John Boylan. (Illus.). 102p. 2000. 14.95 (*0-9658545-0-7*, Pub. by Little Whte Buffalo) New Leaf Dist.

Quantum Challenge: Modern Research on the Foundations of Quantum Mechanics. George Greenstein & Arthur Zajonc. LC 96-36637. (Physics Ser.). 240p. 1997. 38.75 (*0-7637-0467-9*) Jones & Bartlett.

Quantum Challenge: Modern Research on the Foundations of Quantum Mechanics. George Greenstein & Arthur G. Zajonc. LC 96-36637. (Physics Ser.). 240p. 1997. pap. 33.75 (*0-7637-0216-1*) Jones & Bartlett.

Quantum Chance & Nonlocality: Probability & Nonlocality in the Interpretations of Quantum Mechanics. W. Michael Dickson. LC 97-8813. (Illus.). 264p. (C). 1998. text 69.95 (*0-521-58127-3*) Cambridge U Pr.

Quantum Chaos. Ed. by Hilda A. Cerdeira. 480p. (C). 1991. text 128.00 (*981-02-0621-6*) World Scientific Pub.

Quantum Chaos: An Introduction. H. J. Stockmann. LC 98-45454. (Illus.). 350p. (C). 1999. 85.00 (*0-521-59284-4*) Cambridge U Pr.

Quantum Chaos: Between Order & Disorder. Ed. by Giulio Casati & Boris Chirikov. LC 93-37135. (Illus.). 699p. (C). 1995. text 115.00 (*0-521-43291-X*) Cambridge U Pr.

Quantum Chaos: Proceedings of the International School of Physics "Enrico Fermi," Course CXIX, 23 July-2 August, 1991. Ed. by G. Casati et al. (Enrico Fermi International School of Physics Ser.: Vol. 119). 432p. 1993. 210.00 (*0-444-81588-0*, North Holland) Elsevier.

Quantum Chaos & Mesoscopic Systemsmathematical Methods in the Quantum Signatures of Chaos. Norman E. Hurt. LC 97-3669. 1997. text 174.00 (*0-7923-4459-6*) Kluwer Academic.

Quantum Chaos & Statistical Nuclear Physics. Ed. by T. H. Seligman & H. Nishioka. (Lecture Notes in Physics Ser.: Vol. 263). ix, 382p. 1986. 53.95 (*0-387-17171-1*) Spr-Verlag.

Quantum Chaos-Quantum Measurement. Ed. by P. Cvitanovic et al. (C). 1992. text 202.50 (*0-7923-1599-5*) Kluwer Academic.

Quantum Chemical & Statistical Theory of Solutions: A Computational Approach. B. J. Simkin & I. I. Sheykhet. 350p. (C). 1995. 92.00 (*0-13-747460-1*) P-H.

Quantum Chemistry. Donald A. McQuarrie. LC 82-51234. (Physical Chemistry Ser.). (Illus.). 517p. (C). 1983. text 61.50 (*0-935702-13-X*) Univ Sci Bks.

Quantum Chemistry. Raymond Daudel et al. LC 82-23688. (Illus.). 574p. reprint ed. pap. 178.00 (*0-8357-4319-5*, 203711800007) Bks Demand.

Quantum Chemistry. 2nd ed. John P. Lowe. (Illus.). 711p. 1993. text 71.00 (*0-12-457555-2*) Acad Pr.

Quantum Chemistry. 3rd ed. Melvin W. Hanna. 320p. (C). 1981. text 30.25 (*0-8053-3708-3*) Benjamin-Cummings.

***Quantum Chemistry.** 5th ed. Ira N. Levine. LC 99-28558. 1999. write for info. (*0-13-685511-3*) P-H.

***Quantum Chemistry.** 5th ed. Ira N. Levine. LC 99-28558. 739p. (C). 1999. 96.00 (*0-13-685512-1*) P-H.

***Quantum Chemistry: Fundamental Theories & Applications.** Tamas Veszpremi & Miklos Feher. LC 99-42895. 1999. write for info. (*0-306-46164-1*, Kluwer Plenum) Kluwer Academic.

Quantum Chemistry: The Challenge of Transition Metals & Coordination Chemistry. Ed. by Alain Veillard. 1986. text 248.00 (*90-277-2237-4*) Kluwer Academic.

Quantum Chemistry Aided Design of Organic Polymers for Molecular Electronics: An Introduction to the Quantum Chemistry of Polymers & Its Applications. Ed. by J. M. Andre et al. 392p. (C). 1991. text 74.00 (*981-02-0004-8*) World Scientific Pub.

Quantum Chemistry Approaches to Chemisorption & Heterogeneous Catalysis. Ed. by F. Ruette. (C). 1992. text 185.00 (*0-7923-1543-X*) Kluwer Academic.

Quantum Chemistry, Classic Scientific Papers. 500p. 1998. lib. bdg. 55.00 (*981-02-2771-X*) World Scientific Pub.

Quantum Chemistry of Organic Compounds: Mechanisms of Reactions. V. I. Minkin et al. (Illus.). xvi, 270p. 1990. 130.95 (*0-387-52530-0*) Spr-Verlag.

Quantum Chemistry of Polymers: Solid State Aspects. Ed. by Janos J. Ladik & Jean-Marie Andre. LC 84-3367. 1984. text 200.00 (*90-277-1741-9*) Kluwer Academic.

Quantum Chemistry Solutions Manual. Donald A. McQuarrie. (Physical Chemistry Ser.). 241p. (C). 1985. student ed. 22.00 (*0-935702-16-4*) Univ Sci Bks.

Quantum Chemistry Workbook: Basic Concepts & Procedures in the Theory of the Electronic Structure of Matter. Jean-Louis Calais. 216p. 1994. pap. 49.95 (*0-471-59435-0*) Wiley.

Quantum Chromodynamics. Ed. by William Frazer & Frank Henyey. LC 79-54969. (AIP Conference Ser.; Particles & Fields Sub-Ser.: No. 55; No. 18). (Illus.). 1979. lib. bdg. 20.50 (*0-88318-154-1*) Am Inst Physics.

Quantum Chromodynamics. W. Greiner & A. Schafer. 464p. 1994. 89.00 (*0-387-57102-7*) Spr-Verlag.

Quantum Chromodynamics. Francisco J. Ynduraín. LC 92-27021. (Texts & Monographs in Physics). 1993. 97.95 (*0-387-55803-9*) Spr-Verlag.

Quantum Chromodynamics. W. Greiner & A. Schafer. (Illus.). 414p. 1994. reprint ed. 59.95 (*0-387-57103-5*) Spr-Verlag.

***Quantum Chromodynamics.** 2nd ed. Walter Greiner. (Illus.). 2000. pap. text 59.95 (*3-540-66610-9*) Spr-Verlag.

Quantum Chromodynamics: An Introduction to the Theory of Quarks & Gluons. Francisco J. Ynduraín. (Texts & Monographs in Physics). (Illus.). 227p. 1983. 81.00 (*0-387-11752-0*) Spr-Verlag.

Quantum Chromodynamics: Collisions, Confinement & Chaos. LC 97-172262. 500p. 1997. 66.00 (*981-02-3028-1*) World Scientific Pub.

Quantum Chromodynamics: Proceedings of the IV Workshop American University of Paris, France 1-6. H. M. Fried. 500p. 1999. 88.00 (*981-02-3866-5*) World Scientific Pub.

***Quantum Chromodynamics: Proceedings of the 13th Lake Louise Winter Institute Lake Louise, Alberta, Canada 15 - 21 February 1998.** Ed. by A. Astbury et al. 600p. 1999. 128.00 (*981-02-3747-2*) World Scientific Pub.

Quantum Chromodynamics & the Pomeron. J. R. Forshaw & D. A. Ross. (Lecture Notes in Physics Ser.: Vol. 9). (Illus.). 263p. (C). 1997. pap. text 34.95 (*0-521-56880-3*) Cambridge U Pr.

Quantum Chromodynamics, Theory & Experiment: Proceedings of the Third Lake Louise Winter Institute, Chateau Lake Louis, Canada, Maryc 6-12, 1988. Ed. by B. A. Campbell et al. 656p. 1988. text 125.00 (*9971-5-0657-2*) World Scientific Pub.

***Quantum City.** Arida. (Illus.). 160p. 2001. pap. 37.95 (*0-7506-5012-5*, Architectural Pr) Buttrwrth-Heinemann.

Quantum Classical Correspondence: The 4th Drexel Symposium on Quantum Nonintegrability. Ed. by H. Feng & B. L. Hu. LC 98-216054. (Illus.). 512p. 1998. 42.00 (*1-57146-099-3*) Intl Pr Boston.

Quantum Coherence & Decoherence: Proceedings of the 5th International Symposium (ISQM - Tokyo '95) Advanced Research Laboratory, Hitachi, Ltd., Hatoyama, Saitama, Japan, August 21-24, 1995. Ed. by K. Fujikawa & Yoshimasa A. Ono. LC 96-33968. (North-Holland Delta Ser.). 386p. 1996. 123.50 (*0-444-82219-4*, North Holland) Elsevier.

***Quantum Coherence & Decoherence: Proceedings of the 6th International Symposium of Quantum Mechanics in the Light of New Technology, Tokyo, 1998.** International Symposium Foundations of Quantum Mechanics in the Light of New Technology Staff et al. LC 99-56387. (North-Holland Delta Ser.). 380p. 2000. 107.50 (*0-444-50091-X*) Elsevier.

Quantum Coherence & Reality - In Celebration of the 60th Birthday of Yakir Aharonov. Jeeva S. Anandan & John L. Safko. 384p. 1995. text 99.00 (*981-02-2117-7*) World Scientific Pub.

Quantum Coherence Conference: Proceedings of the Conference on Fundamental Aspects of Quantum Theory. Jeeva S. Anandan. 404p. (C). 1991. pap. 38.00 (*981-02-0257-1*); text 118.00 (*981-02-0256-3*) World Scientific Pub.

Quantum Coherence in Mesoscopic Systems. B. Kramer. (NATO ASI Ser.: Vol. 254). (Illus.). 648p. (C). 1991. text 165.00 (*0-306-43889-5*, Kluwer Plenum) Kluwer Academic.

Quantum Communication. (C). 1996. write for info. (*0-8087-1490-2*) Pearson Custom.

Quantum Communication, Computing & Measurement: Proceedings of the Third International Conference Held in Shizuoka, Japan, September 25-30, 1996. O. Hirota et al. LC 97-17030. 558p. (C). 1997. text 139.50 (*0-306-45685-0*, Kluwer Plenum) Kluwer Academic.

***Quantum Communication, Computing & Measurement 2.** Prem Kumar et al. Ed. by International Conference on Quantum Communication Staff. LC 99-86155. 2000. write for info. (*0-306-46307-5*, Kluwer Plenum) Kluwer Academic.

Quantum Communications & Measurement: Proceedings of an International Workshop Held in Nottingham, England, July 11-16, 1994. V. P. Belavkin et al. LC 95-32969. (Illus.). 544p. (C). 1995. text 162.00 (*0-306-45128-X*, Kluwer Plenum) Kluwer Academic.

Quantum Companies: One Hundred Companies That Will Change the Face of Tomorrow's Business. A. David Silver. LC 94-33198. 348p. 1995. 24.95 (*1-56079-373-2*, Petersons Pacesetter) Petersons.

Quantum Companies II: 100 More Cutting-Edge, High-Growth Companies to Track into the 21st Century, No. 2. A. David Silver. (Pacesetter Bks.). 416p. 1996. text 26.95 (*1-56079-594-8*, Petersons Pacesetter) Petersons.

***Quantum Computation & Information.** Isaac I. Chuang & M. A. Nielsen. (Illus.). 700p. 2000. write for info. (*0-521-63235-8*); pap. write for info. (*0-521-63503-9*) Cambridge U Pr.

***Quantum Computation & Quantum Information Theory.** Ed. by C. Macchiavello et al. 450p. 1999. 84.00 (*981-02-4117-8*) World Scientific Pub.

***Quantum Computing.** Mika Hirvensalo. (Illus.). 2000. 59.95 (*3-540-66783-0*) Spr-Verlag.

Quantum Computing: Where Do We Want To Go Tomorrow? Ed. by Pierre Braunstein. 306p. 1999. 160.00 (*3-527-40284-5*) Wiley.

Quantum Computing & Communications. Michael Brooks. LC 99-19975. (Illus.). 152p. 1999. pap. 44.95 (*1-85233-091-0*) Spr-Verlag.

***Quantum Computing & Quantum Communications: 1st NASA International Conference, QCQC '98, Palm Springs, California, U. S. A., February 17-20, 1998, Selected Papers.** Ed. by Colin P. Williams. LC 99-34195. (Lecture Notes in Computer Science Ser.: Vol. 1509). x, 480p. 1999. pap. 73.00 (*3-540-65514-X*) Spr-Verlag.

Quantum Confinement: Nanoscale Materials, Devices & Systems: 4th International Symposium. Ed. by J. P. Leburton et al. LC 97-229055. (Proceedings Ser.: Vol. 97-11). 494p. 1997. 75.00 (*1-56677-138-2*) Electrochem Soc.

Quantum Confinement: Quantum Confinement & Dots: 3rd International Symposium. Ed. by S. Bandyopadhyay et al. (Proceedings Ser.: Vol. 95-17). (Illus.). 367p. 1996. 78.00 (*1-56677-112-9*) Electrochem Soc.

Quantum Consciousness: A Guide to Experiencing Quantum Psychology. Stephen Wolinsky. LC 93-24895. (Illus.). 266p. (Orig.). 1993. pap. 14.95 (*0-9626184-8-9*, Bramble Bks) Bramble Co.

Quantum Consciousness: A Philosophy of the Self's Potential Through Quantum Cosmology. Lily Splane. 104p. (Orig.). 1993. pap. 12.95 (*0-945962-05-3*) Anaphase II.

Quantum Cosmology. Ed. by Fang Lizhi & Remo Ruffini. (Advanced Series in Astrophysics & Cosmology: Vol. 3). 340p. (C). 1987. text 98.00 (*9971-5-0293-3*); pap. text 47.00 (*9971-5-0312-3*) World Scientific Pub.

Quantum Cosmology & Baby Universes: Proceedings of the Seventh Jerusalem Winter School. Ed. by Sidney Coleman et al. 300p. (C). 1991. text 68.00 (*981-02-0345-4*); pap. text 40.00 (*981-02-0346-2*) World Scientific Pub.

Quantum Cosmology & the Laws of Nature: Scientific Perspectives on Divine Action. Ed. by Robert J. Russell et al. (C). 1994. pap. text 21.95 (*0-268-03976-3*) U of Notre Dame Pr.

Quantum Creativity: Nine Principles for a Life of Possibility. Pamela Meyer. LC 97-91009. x, 175p. 1997. pap. 19.95 (*0-9660114-0-6*, Yezand Pr) Meyer Creativity.

***Quantum Creativity: Nine Principles to Transform the Way You Work.** Pamela Meyer. LC 99-57946. 224p. 2000. pap. 16.95 (*0-8092-2439-9*, 243990, Contemporary Bks) NTC Contemp Pub Co.

Quantum Creativity: Waking up to Our Creative Potential. Amit Goswami. (Perspectives on Creativity Ser.). (Illus.). 336p. (C). 1998. text 69.50 (*1-57273-226-1*) Hampton Pr NJ.

Quantum Creativity: Waking up to Our Creative Potential. Amit Goswami. (Perspectives on Creativity Ser.). (Illus.). xvi, 320 p. (C). 1999. pap. text 27.50 (*1-57273-227-X*) Hampton Pr NJ.

***Quantum Cybernetics: Towards a Unification of Relativity & Quantum Theory via Circularly Casual Modeling.** Gerhard Grossing. LC 99-53571. (Illus.). 168p. 2000. 49.95 (*0-387-98960-9*) Spr-Verlag.

Quantum Description of High-Resolution NMR in Liquids. Maurice Goldman. (International Series of Monographs on Chemistry: No. 15). (Illus.). 280p. 1991. reprint ed. pap. text 49.95 (*0-19-855652-7*, 986) OUP.

Quantum Devices & Circuits: Proceedings of the International Conference, 4-7 June, 1996, Alexandria, Egypt. Ed. by K. Ismail et al. LC 97-143641. 316p. 1996. 78.00 (*1-86094-032-3*) World Scientific Pub.

An Asterisk (*) at the beginning of an entry indicates that the title is appearing for the first time.

Quantum Dialogue: The Making of a Revolution. Mara Beller. LC 99-35499. (Science & Its Conceptual Foundations Ser.). 328p. 1999. 35.00 (*0-226-04181-6*) U Ch Pr.

Quantum Dice. Ed. by L. I. Ponomarev. (Illus.). 256p. 1993. 137.00 (*0-7503-0251-8*); pap. 40.00 (*0-7503-0241-0*) IOP Pub.

Quantum Dice: An Introduction to Stochastic Electrodynamics. Luis De La Pena & Ana M. Cetto. LC 95-40168. (Fundamental Theories of Physics Ser.: Vol. 75). 528p. (C). 1996. text 235.50 (*0-7923-3818-9*) Kluwer Academic.

Quantum Dissipative Systems. Ulrich Weiss. (Series in Modern Condensed Matter Physics: Vol. 2). 252p. (C). 1993. text 61.00 (*981-02-0754-9*); pap. text 36.00 (*981-02-0755-7*) World Scientific Pub.

***Quantum Dissipative Systems.** 2nd ed. Ulrich Weiss. (Series in Modern Condensed Matter Physics: Vol. 10). 460p. 1999. 68.00 (*981-02-4091-0*) World Scientific Pub.

***Quantum Dissipative Systems, Vol. 10.** 2nd ed. Ulrich Weiss. 460p. 1999. pap. 38.00 (*981-02-4092-9*) World Scientific Pub.

Quantum Dot: A Journey into the Future of Microelectronics. Richard Turton. (Illus.). 211p. (C). 1998. text 30.00 (*0-7881-5638-1*) DIANE Pub.

Quantum Dot: A Journey into the Future of Microelectronics. Richard Turton. (Illus.). 224p. 1996. reprint ed. pap. 15.95 (*0-19-510959-7*) OUP.

***Quantum Dot Heterostructures.** Dieter Bimberg et al. LC 98-7734. 338p. 1999. 205.00 (*0-471-97388-2*) Wiley.

Quantum Dots. Lucjan Jacak et al. LC 97-32688. (Illus.). viii, 177p. 1998. 44.95 (*3-540-63653-6*) Spr-Verlag.

Quantum Dynamical Semigroups & Applications. R. Alicki & K. Lendi. (Lecture Notes in Physics Ser.: Vol. 286). viii, 196p. 1987. 34.95 (*0-387-18276-4*) Spr-Verlag.

Quantum Dynamics of Chaotic Systems: Proceedings of the Third Drexel Symposium on Quantum Nonintegrability, Philadelphia, Pennsylvania. Ed. by Jian-Min Yuan et al. LC 93-3093. 392p. 1993. pap. text 74.00 (*2-88124-595-1*) Gordon & Breach.

Quantum Dynamics of Simple Systems: Proceedings of the Scottish Universities Summer School in Physics, 1994, Stirling, Scotland. 44th ed. Ed. by G. L. Oppo. 373p. 1996. pap. 53.00 (*0-7503-0490-1*) IOP Pub.

Quantum Dynamics of Simple Systems: Proceedings of the 44th Scottish Universities Summer School in Physics, University of Stirling, 15-26 August, 1994. G. L. Oppo et al. (Scottish Universities Summer School in Physics, a NATO Advanced Study Institute Ser.: Vol. 44). (Illus.). 300p. 1996. 180.00 (*0-7503-0351-4*) IOP Pub.

Quantum Dynamics of Submicron Structures: Proceedings of the NATO Advanced Research Workshop on Submicron Quantum Dynamics. Trieste, Italy, June 13 - July 1, 1994. Ed. by Bernard J. Kramer et al. LC 95-10624. (NATO Advanced Science Institutes Series C: Vol. 291). 760p. (C). 1995. text 375.00 (*0-7923-3469-8*) Kluwer Academic.

Quantum Effect Physics, Electronics & Applications: Proceedings of the International Workshop, Luxor, Egypt, 5-9 January 1992. Ed. by K. Ismail et al. (Institute of Physics Conference Ser.: No. 127). (Illus.). 282p. 1992. 139.00 (*0-7503-0225-9*) IOP Pub.

***Quantum Effects in Semiconductor Materials & Devices.** T. P. Pearsall. LC 99-89632. (Electronic Materials Ser.). 2000. write for info. (*0-7923-7748-6*) Kluwer Academic.

Quantum Effects in the Minimal Supersymmetric Standard Model: 1st Conference Proceedings Held in Barcelona, Spain 9-13 September 1997. Ed. by Joan Sola. 400p. 1998. 82.00 (*981-02-3450-3*) World Scientific Pub.

Quantum Electrodynamics. (C). 1994. text. write for info. (*0-201-42027-9*) Addison-Wesley.

Quantum Electrodynamics. Richard Phillips Feynman. LC 61-18179. (Frontiers in Physics Ser.: No. 3). (Illus.). (C). 1962. pap. 39.95 (*0-8053-2501-8*) Addison-Wesley.

Quantum Electrodynamics. Richard Phillips Feynman. LC 98-2759. 1998. pap. 35.00 (*0-201-36075-6*) Addison-Wesley.

Quantum Electrodynamics. Walter Greiner & Joachim Reinhardt. Vol. 4. (Illus.). 336p. 1992. write for info. (*0-318-69559-6*); pap. write for info. (*3-540-52078-3*); pap. write for info. (*0-387-52078-3*) Spr-Verlag.

Quantum Electrodynamics. Walter Greiner & Joachim Reinhardt. LC 92-25371. (Theoretical Physics - Text & Exercise Bks.: Vol. 4). (Illus.). 336p. 1994. pap. 59.00 (*0-387-55802-0*) Spr-Verlag.

Quantum Electrodynamics. S. N. Gupta. xii, 226p. 1977. text 274.00 (*0-677-04240-X*) Gordon & Breach.

Quantum Electrodynamics. T. Kinoshita. (Directions in High Energy Physics Ser.: Vol. 7). 1020p. (C). 1990. pap. 46.00 (*981-02-0214-8*); text 150.00 (*981-02-0213-X*) World Scientific Pub.

QED Coherence in Matter. Giuliano Preparata. LC 95-13463. 300p. 1995. text 67.00 (*981-02-2249-1*) World Scientific Pub.

Quantum Electrodynamics. 2nd ed. W. Greiner & J. Reinhardt. 400p. 1996. 69.95 (*0-387-58092-1*) Spr-Verlag.

Quantum Electrodynamics 2nd ed. Walter Greiner & J. Reinhardt. LC 95-119144. xvi, 405p. 1994. write for info. (*3-540-58092-1*) Spr-Verlag.

Quantum Electrodynamics, Vol. 4. 2nd ed. V. B. Berestetskii & L. D. Landau. 667p. 1982. pap. text 66.95 (*0-7506-3371-9*) Buttrwrth-Heinemann.

***Quantum Electrodynamics: Gribov Lectures on Theoretical Physics.** V. D. Gribov & J. Nyiri. LC 99-57211. (Cambridge Monographs on Particle Physics, Nuclear Physics & Cosmology). (Illus.). 240p. 2000. write for info. (*0-521-66228-1*) Cambridge U Pr.

Quantum Electrodynamics at High Energies. P. S. Isaev. Tr. by David Parsons. (AIP Translation Ser.). 268p. 1989. 69.95 (*0-88318-602-0*) Spr-Verlag.

Quantum Electrodynamics at High Energies. P. S. Isaev. Tr. by David Parsons. (Illus.). 224p. 1989. 50.00 (*0-88318-572-5*) Spr-Verlag.

Quantum Electrodynamics of Strong Fields. Walter Greiner et al. (Texts & Monographs in Physics). (Illus.). 610p. 1985. 117.95 (*0-387-13404-2*) Spr-Verlag.

Quantum Electrodynamics with Unstable Vacuum. E. S. Fradkin et al. (Series in Nuclear & Particle Physics). (Illus.). 304p. 1991. 123.95 (*0-387-52935-7*) Spr-Verlag.

Quantum Electrodynamics with Unstable Vacuum. Ed. by Vitaly L. Ginzburg. LC 94-43741. (Proceedings of the Lebedev Physics Institute Ser.: Vol. 220). 275p. (C). 1994. lib. bdg. 165.00 (*1-56072-205-3*) Nova Sci Pubs.

Quantum Electron Liquids & High-TC Superconductivity. J. Gonzalez et al. LC 95-45944. (Lecture Notes in Physics Ser.: Vol. 38). 303p. 1995. 59.95 (*3-540-60503-7*) Spr-Verlag.

***Quantum Electronics.** Ed. by Peter A. Atanasov & Dimitar V. Stoyanov. 420p. 1999. pap. text 92.00 (*0-8194-3034-X*) SPIE.

Quantum Electronics. 3rd ed. Amnon Yariv. LC 88-719. 704p. 1989. text 114.95 (*0-471-60997-8*) Wiley.

Quantum Electronics: Lasers - Physics & Applications. Ed. by Peter Atanasov. LC 96-72057. 426p. 1997. pap. 89.00 (*0-8194-2466-8*) SPIE.

Quantum Electronics & Electo-Optics: Proceedings of the Fifth National Quantum Electronics Conference, Hull University, Hull, September 1981. National Quantum Electronics Conference (4th: 1979. Ed. by Peter Knight. LC 82-24778. (Illus.). 477p. reprint ed. pap. 147.90 (*0-8357-4315-2*, 203711400007) Bks Demand.

Quantum Electronics & Laser Science. LC 92-80624. (Nineteen Ninety-Two Technical Digest Ser.: Vol. 13). (Illus.). 350p. (Orig.). 1992. pap. 92.00 (*1-55752-240-5*); pap. 60.00 (*1-55752-239-1*) Optical Soc.

Quantum Electronics & Laser Science Conference. LC 95-727766. (Nineteen Ninety-Six Technical Digest Ser.: No. 10). 272p. 1996. pap. 92.00 (*1-55752-445-9*) Optical Soc.

Quantum Electronics & Laser Science Conference (QELS) (Nineteen Ninety-Nine OSA Technical Digest Ser.). 400p. (C). 1999. pap. 92.00 (*1-55752-596-X*) Optical Soc.

Quantum Electronics & Laser Science Conference (QES) LC 97-65509. (Nineteen Ninety-Seven Technical Digest Ser.: Vol. 12). (Illus.). 250p. 1997. pap. 92.00 (*1-55752-502-1*, CH36111) Optical Soc.

Quantum Engineering: From Elections to Your Compact Disc. Fredy Zypman. (Illus.). 65p. 1999. pap. write for info. (*0-7392-0280-4*, PO3376) Morris Pubng.

Quantum Enigma: Finding the Hidden Key. Wolfgang Smith. (Illus.). 143p. (Orig.). 1995. pap. 14.95 (*0-89385-042-X*) Sugden.

Quantum Entropy & Its Use. Masanori Ohya & Denes Petz. LC 92-29580. (Texts & Monographs in Physics). 1993. 107.95 (*0-387-54881-5*) Spr-Verlag.

***Quantum Evolution: An Introduction to Time-Dependent Quantum Mechanics.** James E. Bayfield. LC 98-53673. 386p. 1999. 99.95 (*0-471-18174-9*) Wiley.

***Quantum Evolution: The New Science of Life.** John Joe McFadden. (Illus.). 352p. 2000. 27.95 (*0-393-05041-6*) Norton.

Quantum Field Theoretical Methods in Statistical Physics, Vol. 4. A. A. Abrikosov et al. 1965. 166.00 (*0-08-013470-X*, Pub. by Pergamon Repr) Franklin.

Quantum Field Theory. Lowell S. Brown. (Illus.). 556p. (C). 1994. pap. text 49.95 (*0-521-46946-5*) Cambridge U Pr.

Quantum Field Theory. Kerson Huang. LC 98-13437. 448p. 1998. 84.95 (*0-471-14120-8*) Wiley.

Quantum Field Theory. Claude Itzykson & J. B. Zuber. (C). 1980. text 90.25 (*0-07-032071-3*) McGraw.

Quantum Field Theory. Michio Kaku. 808p. 1994. 33.95 (*0-19-509158-2*) OUP.

Quantum Field Theory. Albert S. Schwarz. LC 93-32530. (Grundlehren der Mathematischen Wissenschaften Ser.: Vol. 307).Tr. of Kvantovaia Teoriia Polia i Topologiia. (Illus.). viii, 272p. 1993. 111.95 (*0-387-54753-3*) Spr-Verlag.

Quantum Field Theory. rev. ed. G. Shaw & Franz Mandl. 372p. 1993. pap. 98.00 (*0-471-94186-7*) Wiley.

Quantum Field Theory. 2nd ed. Lewis H. Ryder. (Illus.). 505p. (C). 1996. text 125.00 (*0-521-47242-3*); pap. text 42.95 (*0-521-47814-6*) Cambridge U Pr.

Quantum Field Theory: A Modern Introduction. Michio Kaku. LC 92-27704. (Illus.). 808p. 1993. text 62.95 (*0-19-507652-4*) OUP.

Quantum Field Theory: Perspective & Prospective. Cecile DeWitt-Morette et al. LC 99-13269. (NATO ASI Series, Series C., Mathematical & Physical Sciences). 14p. 1999. write for info. (*0-7923-5672-1*) Kluwer Academic.

Quantum Field Theory & Condensed Matter Physics: Proceedings of the 4th Trieste Conference on Quantum Field. S. Randjbar-Daemi & Yu Lu. 148p. 1994. text 53.00 (*981-02-1622-X*) World Scientific Pub.

Quantum Field Theory & Critical Phenomena. 3rd ed. J. Zinn-Justin. (International Series of Monographs on Physics). (Illus.). 1,030p. 1996. text 90.00 (*0-19-851882-X*) OUP.

Quantum Field Theory & Parastatistics. Y. Ohnuki & S. Kamefuchi. (Illus.). 489p. 1982. 120.00 (*0-387-11643-5*) Spr-Verlag.

Quantum Field Theory & String Theory. L. Baulieu et al. (NATO ASI Ser.: 328). (Illus.). 430p. (C). 1995. text 144.00 (*0-306-44886-6*, Kluwer Plenum) Kluwer Academic.

Quantum Field Theory & the Many-Body Problem. Theodore D. Schultz. (Many-Body Problem: Current Research & Reviews Ser.). viii, 150p. 1964. text 171.00 (*0-677-01130-X*) Gordon & Breach.

Quantum Field Theory for Mathematicians. Robin Ticciati. LC 98-39473. (Encyclopedia of Mathematics & Its Applications Ser.: No. 72). 750p. (C). 1999. text 110.00 (*0-521-63265-X*) Cambridge U Pr.

***Quantum Field Theory in Condensed Matter Physics.** N. Nagaosa. Tr. by S. Heusler from JPN. LC 99-35358. (Texts & Monographs in Physics). (Illus.). x, 208p. 1999. 54.00 (*3-540-65537-9*) Spr-Verlag.

Quantum Field Theory in Condensed Matter Physics. Alexei M. Tsvelik. (Illus.). 348p. (C). 1995. text 90.00 (*0-521-45467-0*) Cambridge U Pr.

Quantum Field Theory in Condensed Matter Physics. Alexei M. Tsvelik. 348p. 1996. pap. text 32.95 (*0-521-58989-4*) Cambridge U Pr.

Quantum Field Theory in Curved Spacetime, Vol. 1. B. L. Hu. 500p. (C). 1997. text 106.00 (*9971-5-0443-X*); pap. text 61.00 (*9971-5-0444-8*) World Scientific Pub.

Quantum Field Theory in Curved Spacetime & Black Hole Thermodynamics. Robert M. Wald. (Chicago Lectures in Physics Ser.). (Illus.). 220p. 1994. pap. text 16.95 (*0-226-87027-8*); lib. bdg. 50.00 (*0-226-87025-1*) U Ch Pr.

***Quantum Field Theory in Strongly Correlated Electronic Systems.** N. Nagaosa. Tr. by S. Heusler from JPN. LC 99-16714. (Texts & Monographs in Physics). (Illus.). x, 170p. 1999. 59.95 (*3-540-65981-1*) Spr-Verlag.

Quantum Field Theory of Point Particles & Strings. Brian Hatfield. (Frontiers in Physics Ser.: Vol. 75). 750p. (C). 1992. 54.95 (*0-201-11982-X*) Addison-Wesley.

Quantum Field Theory of Point Particles & Strings. Brian Hatfield. 1998. pap. 45.00 (*0-201-36079-9*) Addison-Wesley.

Quantum Field Theory, Quantum Mechanics & Quantum Optics: Symmetries & Algebraic Structures In Physics, Pt. 1. Ed. by V. V. Dodonov & V. I. Man'ko. (Proceedings of the Lebedev Physics Institute Ser.: Vol. 187). 271p. 1991. pap. text 175.00 (*1-56072-037-9*) Nova Sci Pubs.

Quantum Field Theory, Statistical Mechanics, Quantum Groups & Topology: NATO Advanced Research Workshop. T. Cartright et al. 400p. 1992. text 109.00 (*981-02-0959-2*) World Scientific Pub.

Quantum Field Theory, Statistical Mechanics, Quantum Groups & Topology: Proceedings of the NATO Advanced Research Workshop, University of Miami, 7-12 January 1991. Ed. by Thomas Curtright et al. LC 92-30893. 364p. 1992. pap. write for info. (*981-02-0960-6*) World Scientific Pub.

Quantum Fields: Algebras, Processes. Ed. by Ludwig Streit. (Illus.). 144p. 1980. 52.95 (*0-387-81607-0*) Spr-Verlag.

Quantum Fields & Quantum Space Time: Proceedings of a NATO ASI Held in Cargese, France, July 22-August 3, 1996. Ed. by Gerard T'Hooft et al. LC 97-38053. (NATO ASI Ser.: Vol. 364). 382p. (C). 1997. text 125.00 (*0-306-45697-4*, Kluwer Plenum) Kluwer Academic.

Quantum Fields & Strings: A Course for Mathematicians. Pierre Deligne. LC 99-20755. 1999. write for info. (*0-8218-1988-7*) Am Math.

Quantum Fields on a Lattice. Istvan Monvay & Gernot Munster. 505p. 1997. pap. text 47.95 (*0-521-59917-2*) Cambridge U Pr.

Quantum Fields on the Computer. M. Creutz. (Advanced Series on "Directions in High Energy Physics": No. 11). 444p. 1992. text 121.00 (*981-02-0939-8*) World Scientific Pub.

Quantum Fields on the Computer. Ed. by M. Creutz. (Advanced Series on Directions in High Energy Physics": Vol. 11). 444p. 1992. pap. 67.00 (*981-02-0940-1*) World Scientific Pub.

Quantum Fluctuations. Edward Nelson. LC 84-26449. (Physics Ser.). 155p. 1985. pap. text 29.95 (*0-691-08379-7*, Pub. by Princeton U Pr) Cal Prin Full Svc.

Quantum Fluctuations: Proceedings of the Les Houces Summer School, Session LXIII, 27 June-28 July 1995. Jean Zinn-Justin. Ed. by S. Reynaud et al. LC 97-7628. (Les Houches Summer School Proceedings Ser.: No. 63). 640p. 1997. 250.00 (*0-444-82593-2*) Elsevier.

Quantum Fluctuations in Mesoscopic & Macroscopic Systems. Ed. by Hilda A. Cerdeira et al. 300p. (C). 1991. text 89.00 (*981-02-0629-1*) World Scientific Pub.

Quantum Fluids. Ed. by N. Wiser & Daniel J. Amit. 624p. 1970. text 621.00 (*0-677-13700-1*) Gordon & Breach.

Quantum Fluids & Solids, 1989. Ed. by Gary G. Ihas & Yasumasa Takano. LC 89-81079. (AIP Conference Proceedings Ser.: No. 194). 456p. 1989. lib. bdg. 75.00 (*0-88318-395-1*) Am Inst Physics.

Quantum Fluids & Solids, 1983: AIP Conference Proceedings No. 103, Sanibel Island, Florida. Ed. by E. D. Adams & Gary G. Ihas. LC 83-72240. 512p. 1983. lib. bdg. 39.75 (*0-88318-202-5*) Am Inst Physics.

Quantum Flux Parametron. W. Hioe & E. Goto. (Series in Josephson Supercomputers: Vol. 2). 264p. 1991. text 48.00 (*981-02-0459-0*) World Scientific Pub.

Quantum Focus: A Quick, Mind-Powered Total Program for Self-Development, Healing & Happiness. Michael Ellner & Richard Jamison. LC 97-5115. (Illus.). 400p. 1997. 38.00 (*0-941683-35-4*) Instant Improve.

Quantum Future: From Volta & Como to Present & Beyond. Ed. by P. Blanchard et al. LC 99-12347. (Lecture Notes in Physics Ser.: Vol. 517). x, 257p. 1999. 73.00 (*3-540-65218-3*) Spr-Verlag.

Quantum Gate: A Novel. Jane E. Hawkins. 288p. 1996. mass mkt. 5.99 (*0-7615-0198-3*) Prima Pub.

Quantum Generation: Highlights & Tragedies of the Golden Age of Physics. M. Ryotova Kemoklidze. Tr. by J. Hine. (Illus.). 368p. 1995. 39.95 (*0-387-53298-6*) Spr-Verlag.

Quantum Generations: A History of Physics in the Twentieth Century. Helge Kragh. LC 99-17903. 480p. 1999. 29.95 (*0-691-01206-7*, Pub. by Princeton U Pr) Cal Prin Full Svc.

Quantum Genesis & Other Poems. Philip Fried. LC 96-61807. 72p. (Orig.). 1997. pap. 12.00 (*0-9655200-0-5*) Zohar Pr.

Quantum Geometry: A Framework for Quantum General Relativity. Eduard Prugovecki. (Fundamental Theories of Physics Ser.). 544p. (C). 1992. text 247.50 (*0-7923-1640-1*) Kluwer Academic.

Quantum Geometry: A Statistical Field Theory Approach. Jan Ambjorn et al. (Cambridge Monographs on Mathematical Physics). 377p. 1997. text 105.00 (*0-521-46167-7*) Cambridge U Pr.

Quantum Golf: The Path to Golf Mastery. Kjell Enhager. 144p. 1992. reprint ed. mass mkt. 10.95 (*0-446-39196-4*, Pub. by Warner Bks) Little.

Quantum Gravity. 633p. 1997. text 78.00 (*981-02-3087-7*) World Scientific Pub.

Quantum Gravity. M. A. Markov. Ed. by V. Beresin & V. P. Frolov. 960p. (C). 1988. text 181.00 (*9971-5-0409-X*) World Scientific Pub.

Quantum Gravity: Proceedings of the Seventh Nishinomiya-Yuk. M. Ninomiya & K. Kikkawa. 216p. 1993. text 67.00 (*981-02-1460-X*) World Scientific Pub.

Quantum Gravity: Proceedings of the Third Seminar, Moscow, 1984. Ed. by M. A. Markov et al. 716p. 1985. 130.00 (*9971-978-90-3*) World Scientific Pub.

Quantum Gravity: Proceedings of the 5th Seminar. M. A. Markov et al. 716p. 1991. text 130.00 (*981-02-0440-X*) World Scientific Pub.

Quantum Gravity & Beyond: Essays in Honor of Louis Witten on His Retirement. F. Mansouri & J. J. Scanio. 392p. 1993. text 116.00 (*981-02-1290-9*) World Scientific Pub.

Quantum Gravity & Cosmology: Proceedings of the Twenty-Second Gift International Seminar on Theoretical Physics, Sant Feliu de Guixols, Spain 3-8 June 1991. Ed. by Emilio Elizalde et al. 300p. 1992. text 98.00 (*981-02-0851-0*) World Scientific Pub.

Quantum Gravity & Cosmology: Proceedings of the 8th Summer Kyoto Institute (KSI'85) Kyoto, Japan, May 1985. Ed. by H. Sato & Inami. 420p. 1986. pap. 64.00 (*9971-5-0047-7*); text 137.00 (*9971-5-0043-4*) World Scientific Pub.

Quantum Gravity in 2 + 1 Dimensions. Steven Carlup. LC 97-42893. (Monographs on Mathematical Physics). (Illus.). 287p. (C). 1998. 80.00 (*0-521-56408-5*) Cambridge U Pr.

Quantum Gravity, Proceedings of 14th Course of International School of Cosmology & Gravitation. LC 97-109054. 464p. 1996. lib. bdg. 76.00 (*981-02-2786-8*) World Scientific Pub.

Quantum Gravity, Quantum Cosmology, & Lorentzian Geometries. Giampiero Esposito. LC 92-27337. (Lecture Notes in Physics, New Series, Monographs: Vol. 12). xvi, 326p. reprint ed. 50.00 (*0-387-55836-5*); reprint ed. write for info. (*3-540-55836-5*) Spr-Verlag.

Quantum Gravity, Quantum Cosmology, & Lorentzian Geometries. 2nd rev. ed. Giampiero Esposito. LC 93-41254. (Lecture Notes in Pure & Applied Mathematics Ser.: M12). xviii, 349p. 1994. 69.95 (*0-387-57521-9*) Spr-Verlag.

Quantum Group & Quantum Integrable Systems: Nankai Lectures on Mathematical Physics, Nankai Institution of Mathematics, April 1991. Ed. by M. L. Ge. 200p. (C). 1992. pap. 20.00 (*981-02-0746-8*); text 67.00 (*981-02-0745-X*) World Scientific Pub.

Quantum Group Symetry & Q-Tensor Algebras. L. C. Biedenharn. 270p. 1995. text 64.00 (*981-02-2331-5*) World Scientific Pub.

Quantum Group Symposium at Group 21: Proceedings of the Quantum Group Symposium at the XXI International Colloquium on Group Theoretical Methods on Physics Goslar, 1996. Ed. by H. D. Doebner & V. K. Dobrev. 408p. 1997. 94.95 (*954-580-027-5*, Pub. by Heron Pr) Intl Scholars.

Quantum Groups. Walter Griener. LC 94-31760. (Graduate Texts in Mathematics Ser.: Vol. 155). 1995. write for info. (*3-540-94370-6*) Spr-Verlag.

Quantum Groups. Christian Kassel. LC 94-31760. (Graduate Texts in Mathematics Ser.: Vol. 155). (Illus.). 531p. 1994. 59.95 (*0-387-94370-6*) Spr-Verlag.

Quantum Groups. Ed. by P. P. Kulish et al. (Lecture Notes in Mathematics Ser.: Vol. 1510). 398p. 1992. 75.95 (*0-387-55305-3*) Spr-Verlag.

Quantum Groups: From Coalgebras to Drinfeld Algebras. Steven Shnider & Schlomo Sternberg. (Series in Mathematical Physics). 496p. (C). 1994. text 42.00 (*1-57146-000-4*) Intl Pr Boston.

Quantum Groups: Spring Workshop on Quantum Groups, Argonne Laboratory, April 16 to May 11, 1990. Ed. by Thomas Curtright. 344p. 1991. text 81.00 (*981-02-0381-0*) World Scientific Pub.

Quantum Groups & Their Applications in Physics. Ed. by L. Castellani & J. Wess. LC 95-8172. (International School of Physics Enrico Fermi Ser.: Vol. 127). 629p. (YA). (gr. 12). 1996. pap. 176.00 (*90-5199-247-5*, 247-5) IOS Press.

Quantum Groups & Their Primitive Ideals. Anthony Joseph. LC 94-21758. 1994. 149.95 (*0-387-57057-8*) Spr-Verlag.

Quantum Groups & Their Representations. A. U. Klimyk & Konrad Schmudgen. LC 97-45870. (Texts & Monographs in Physics). x, 530p. (C). 1998. 79.95 (*3-540-63452-5*) Spr-Verlag.

Q

An Asterisk (*) at the beginning of an entry indicates that the title is appearing for the first time.

Quantum Groups in Two-Dimensional Physics. Cesar Gomez et al. (Cambridge Monographs on Mathematical Physics). (Illus.). 475p. (C). 1996. text 115.00 (*0-521-46065-4*) Cambridge U Pr.

Quantum Groups, Integrable Models & Statistical Systems. J. Letrouneux & Luc Vinet. 300p. 1993. text 95.00 (*981-02-1555-X*) World Scientific Pub.

Quantum Groups, Integrable Statistical Models & Knot: Nankai Lectures on Mathematical Physics Ser. H. J. De Vega & M. L. Ge. 352p. 1993. text 100.00 (*981-02-1474-X*) World Scientific Pub.

***Quantum Groups, Noncommutative Geometry & Fundamental Physical Interactions.** Daniel Kastler. (Horizons in World Physics Ser.: Vol. 226). 461p. 1999. 165.00 (*1-56072-651-2*) Nova Sci Pubs.

Quantum Groups, Quantum Categories, & Quantum Field Theory. Jurg Frohlich & Thomas Kerler. LC 93-15378. (Lecture Notes in Mathematics Ser.: Vol. 1542). 1995. 82.95 (*0-387-56623-6*) Spr-Verlag.

Quantum Hall Effect. Ed. by A. H. MacDonald. (C). 1990. pap. text 96.00 (*0-7923-0538-8*); lib. bdg. 163.00 (*0-7923-0537-X*) Kluwer Academic.

Quantum Hall Effect. Ed. by R. E. Prange & S. M. Girvin. (Graduate Texts in Contemporary Physics Ser.). (Illus.). 440p. 1986. 32.00 (*0-387-96286-7*) Spr-Verlag.

Quantum Hall Effect. M. Stone. 400p. 1992. text 86.00 (*981-02-0883-9*); pap. text 48.00 (*981-02-0884-7*) World Scientific Pub.

Quantum Hall Effect. 2nd ed. Ed. by R. E. Prange & S. M. Girvin. (Graduate Texts in Contemporary Physics Ser.). (Illus.). 488p. 1989. 59.95 (*0-387-97177-7*) Spr-Verlag.

Quantum Hall Effects. 2nd ed. Tapash Chakraborty & P. Pietilainen. (Illus.). 300p. 1995. 48.95 (*3-540-58515-X*) Spr-Verlag.

Quantum Healing: Exploring the Frontiers of Body, Mind, Medicine. Deepak Chopra. 272p. 1990. pap. 14.95 (*0-553-34869-8*) Bantam.

Quantum Heterostructures: Microelectronics & Optoelectronics. Vladimir V. Mitin et al. LC 98-40658. (Illus.). 664p. (C). 1999. text 120.00 (*0-521-63177-7*); pap. text 49.95 (*0-521-63635-3*) Cambridge U Pr.

Quantum Hydrodynamics. Eric Varoquaux. (C). 1998. write for info. (*0-201-54665-5*) Addison-Wesley.

Quantum Implications: Essays in Honour of David Bohm. Ed. by Basil Hiley & F. David Peat. (Illus.). 464p. (C). 1991. pap. 25.99 (*0-415-06960-2*, A6303) Routledge.

Quantum Implications: Essays in Honour of David Bohn. Ed. by Basil Hiley & F. David Peat. 384p. 1987. 49.95 (*0-7102-0806-5*, 08065, Routledge Thoemms) Routledge.

Quantum Information: Proceedings of the First International Conference. 4th ed. Takeyuki Hida. LC 99-34733. 250p. 1999. 75.00 (*981-02-3934-3*) World Scientific Pub.

***Quantum Information II.** Ed. by K. Saito & T. Hida. 250p. 2000. 78.00 (*981-02-4317-0*) World Scientific Pub.

Quantum Infrared Physics. H. M. Fried & B. Muller. 552p. 1995. text 124.00 (*981-02-2173-8*) World Scientific Pub.

Quantum Infrared Physics: Proceedings of the Workshop. H. M. Fried & B. Muller. 425p. 1995. text 98.00 (*981-02-2020-0*) World Scientific Pub.

Quantum Interferometry. Francesco De Martini et al. 320p. 1994. text 121.00 (*981-02-1517-7*) World Scientific Pub.

Quantum Invariants of Knots & 3-Manifolds. V. G. Turaev. LC 94-21249. (Studies in Mathematics: Vol. 18). 588p. 1994. 129.95 (*3-11-013704-6*) De Gruyter.

Quantum Inverse Scattering Method & Correlation Functions. V. E. Korepin et al. (Illus.). 574p. (C). 1993. text 125.00 (*0-521-37320-4*) Cambridge U Pr.

Quantum Inverse Scattering Method & Correlation Functions. V. E. Korepin et al. 574p. 1997. pap. text 49.95 (*0-521-58646-1*) Cambridge U Pr.

Quantum Inversion Theory & Applications: Proceedings of the 109th W. E. Heraeus Seminar Held at Bad Honnef, Germany, May 17-19, 1993. Ed. by H. V. Von Geramb. LC 93-40611. (Lecture Notes in Physics Ser.: Vol. 427). 481p. 1994. 104.95 (*0-387-57576-6*) Spr-Verlag.

Quantum Ising Phases & Transitions in Traverse Ising Models. B. K. Chakrabarti et al. LC 96-4092. (Lecture Notes in Physics Ser.: Vol. 41). 204p. 1996. 49.00 (*3-540-61033-2*) Spr-Verlag.

Quantum Jump: A Survival Guide for the Next Renaissance. W. R. Clement. LC 99-175362. 528p. 1999. pap. 19.99 (*1-895837-45-6*) Insomniac.

Quantum Kenpo: Pulling the Pieces Together. Lee Bachman. 92p. (C). 1997. pap. 10.95 (*0-9652672-3-7*) Bachman Pub.

***Quantum Kinematics & Dynamics.** Julia Schwinger. (Illus.). 304p. 2000. pap. text 39.00 (*0-7382-0303-3*) Perseus Pubng.

Quantum Kinematics & Dynamics. Julian Seymour Schwinger. (Advanced Book Program Ser.). (Illus.). 400p. (C). 1991. text 29.75 (*0-685-50038-1*) Addison-Wesley.

Quantum Kinetics in Transport & Optics of Semiconductors. Hartmut Haug & Antti-Pekka Jauho. LC 96-3405. (Solid-State Sciences Ser.: Vol. 123). (Illus.). 320p. 1996. 79.95 (*3-540-61602-0*) Spr-Verlag.

Quantum Labyrinth. Dick J. Hoekzema. LC 92-38478. (Fundamental Theories of Physics Ser.: Vol. 51). 296p. (C). 1992. lib. bdg. 185.00 (*0-7923-2066-2*, Pub. by Kluwer Academic) Kluwer Academic.

Quantum Leap: A to Z. Julie Barrett. 288p. (Orig.). 1995. mass mkt. 5.99 (*1-57297-044-8*) Blvd Books.

Quantum Leap: Double or Nothing, No. IX. C. J. Henderson. 240p. (Orig.). 1995. mass mkt. 5.99 (*1-57297-055-3*) Blvd Books.

Quantum Leap: Heat Wave. Melanie Kent. (Quantum Leap Ser.: No. XV). 240p. 1997. mass mkt. 5.99 (*1-57297-312-9*) Blvd Books.

Quantum Leap: In Speed to Market. John R. Costanza. 352p. 1996. 45.00 (*0-9628182-1-6*, Irwn Prfssnl) McGraw-Hill Prof.

Quantum Leap: Prelude. Ashley McConnell. 1994. mass mkt. 5.99 (*1-57297-134-7*) Blvd Books.

Quantum Leap: Pulitzer, No. VIII. L. Elizabeth Storm. 352p. (Orig.). 1995. mass mkt. 5.99 (*1-57297-022-7*) Blvd Books.

Quantum Leap: Search & Rescue, No. 5. Melissa Crandall. 240p. (Orig.). 1994. pap. text 4.99 (*0-441-00122-X*) Ace Bks.

Quantum Leap: Song & Dance. Mindy Peterman. 256p. 1998. pap. 6.99 (*0-425-16577-9*) Berkley Pub.

Quantum Leap: The Novel. Ashley McConnell. 1992. mass mkt. 5.99 (*1-57297-094-4*) Blvd Books.

Quantum Leap: The Wall. Ashley McConnell. 256p. 1994. mass mkt. 4.99 (*0-441-00015-0*) Ace Bks.

Quantum Leap: The Wall. Ashley McConnell. 1994. mass mkt. 5.99 (*1-57297-216-5*) Blvd Books.

Quantum Leap: Too Close for Comfort. Ashley McConnell. 272p. (Orig.). 1993. mass mkt. 4.99 (*0-441-69323-7*) Ace Bks.

Quantum Leap . . . In Speed to Market. John R. Costanza. (Illus.). 336p. 1990. 64.95 (*0-9628182-0-8*) J I T Inst.

Quantum Leap Book: The Official Publication of the Television Series. Louis Chunovic. (Illus.). 160p. 1992. pap. 16.95 (*0-8065-1374-8*, Citadel Pr) Carol Pub Group.

Quantum Leap Foreknowledge. Christopher Defilippis. (Quantum Leap Ser.). 1998. mass mkt. 5.99 (*1-57297-343-9*) Blvd Books.

Quantum Leap Strategy. Price Pritchett. 90p. (Orig.). 1991. pap. 5.95 (*0-944002-08-0*) Pritchett Assocs.

Quantum Leap to Collegiate Athletics: A Guidebook for High School Athletes, Parents & Coaches. Kei Gilbert. (Illus.). 252p. (Orig.). 1996. reprint ed. pap. 22.00 (*0-9650386-0-2*) Soras.

Quantum Leap to Collegiate Athletics: A Guidebook for High School Athletes, Parents & Coaches. 2nd rev. ed. Kei Gilbert. (Illus.). 1998. pap. 24.99 (*0-9650386-2-9*) Soras.

Quantum Leaps: Skills for Workplace Re-Creation. Charlotte Shelton. LC 98-35607. 240p. 1998. text 24.95 (*0-7506-7077-0*) Buttrwrth-Heinemann.

Quantum Learning: Unleashing the Genius in You. Bobbi Deporter & Mike Hernacki. 368p. 1992. pap. 13.95 (*0-440-50427-9*, Dell Trade Pbks) Dell.

***Quantum Legacy: Seminal Papers of Julian Schwinger.** Kimball A. Milton. 2000. 99.00 (*981-02-4006-6*) World Scientific Pub.

Quantum-Like Models & Coherent Effects: Erice, Italy 13 - 20 June, 1994. Ed. by R. Fedele & P. K. Shukla. (Science & Culture Ser.). 500p. 1995. text 128.00 (*981-02-2412-5*, Phm-P2890) World Scientific Pub.

Quantum Linear Groups. rev. ed. J. Wang. LC 90-19310. (Memoirs Ser.: Vol. 89/439). 157p. 1993. reprint ed. pap. 24.00 (*0-8218-2501-1*, MEMO/89/439) Am Math.

Quantum Logic. Peter Mittelstaedt. (Synthese Library: 126). 157p. 1978. text 106.00 (*90-277-0925-4*) Kluwer Academic.

Quantum Logic in Algebraic Approach. Miklos Redel. LC 97-46597. (Fundamental Theories of Physics Ser.). 238p. 1998. 129.00 (*0-7923-4903-2*) Kluwer Academic.

Quantum Many-Body Systems in One Dimension. Zachary Ha. LC 97-102565. (Series on Advances in Statistical Mechanics: Vol. 12). 200p. 1996. text 28.00 (*981-02-2275-0*) World Scientific Pub.

Quantum Many-Particle Systems. John W. Negele & Henri Orland. (Frontiers in Physics Ser.). (Illus.). 500p. (C). 1988. 54.95 (*0-201-12593-5*) Addison-Wesley.

Quantum Many-Particle Systems. John W. Negele & Henri Orlando. LC 98-88186. (Advanced Book Classics Ser.). 480p. 1998. pap. text 39.00 (*0-7382-0052-2*) Perseus Pubng.

Quantum Mass Theory Compatible with Quantum Field Theory. Petar K. Anastasovski & Trevor M. Benson. (Illus.). 212p. (C). 1994. lib. bdg. 125.00 (*1-56072-157-X*) Nova Sci Pubs.

Quantum Measurement. Vladimir B. Braginsky & F. Y. Khalili. (Illus.). 212p. (C). 1992. text 69.95 (*0-521-41928-X*) Cambridge U Pr.

Quantum Measurement: Beyond Paradox. Richard H. Hellman. 232p. 1998. 39.95 (*0-8166-3065-8*) U of Minn Pr.

Quantum Measurement & Chaos. Ed. by E. R. Pike & S. Sarker. LC 87-18934. (NATO ASI Series B, Physics: Vol. 161). (Illus.). 304p. 1987. 79.50 (*0-306-42669-2*, Plenum Trade) Perseus Pubng.

Quantum Measurement Approach to Tunnelling: Tunnelling by Quantum Measurement. Dilip K. Roy. 200p. 1993. text 48.00 (*981-02-1223-2*) World Scientific Pub.

Quantum Measurement Problem. LC 97-41555. 200p. 1997. text 33.00 (*981-02-3077-X*) World Scientific Pub.

***Quantum Measurements & Decoherence: Models & Phenomenology.** M. B. Menskifi. LC 00-28408. (Fundamental Theories of Physics Ser.). 2000. write for info. (*0-7923-6227-6*) Kluwer Academic.

Quantum Measurements in Optics. P. Tombesi & D. F. Walls. (NATO ASI Series B, Physics: Vol. 282). (Illus.). 446p. (C). 1992. 135.00 (*0-306-44101-2*, Plenum Trade) Perseus Pubng.

Quantum Measures & Spaces. Gudrun Kalmbach. LC 98-30761. (Mathematics & Its Applications Ser.). 1998. write for info. (*0-7923-5288-2*) Kluwer Academic.

Quantum Mechanic. Sara M. McMurry. 346p. (C). 1993. text, pap. text 70.00 incl. disk (*0-201-54439-3*) Addison-Wesley.

Quantum-Mechanical Ab-Initio Calculation of the Properties of Crystalline Materials: Proceedings of the IV School of Computational Chemistry of the Italian Chemical Society, Vol. 67. C. Pisani. LC 96-36109. 336p. 1996. 71.00 (*3-540-61645-4*) Spr-Verlag.

Quantum Mechanical Cluster Calculations in Solid State Studies. Ed. by C. R. Catlow et al. 450p. (C). 1992. text 114.00 (*981-02-0750-6*) World Scientific Pub.

Quantum Mechanical Electronic Structure Calculations with Chemical Accuracy. Ed. by Stephen R. Langhoff. LC 94-39289. (Understanding Chemical Reactivity Ser.: Vol. 13). 1995. text 239.50 (*0-7923-3264-4*) Kluwer Academic.

Quantum Mechanical Simulation Methods for Studying Biological Systems: Les Houches Workshops, 2-7 May, 1995. Ed. by D. Bicout et al. xvii, 314p. 1996. pap. 98.50 (*3-540-60869-9*) Spr-Verlag.

Quantum Mechanical Tunnelling & Its Applications. Dilip K. Roy. 400p. 1986. text 77.00 (*9971-5-0024-8*) World Scientific Pub.

Quantum Mechanics. Anderson. (C). 1912. text 65.00 (*0-03-005647-0*) Harcourt Coll Pubs.

Quantum Mechanics. D. I. Blokhintsev. Tr. by J. B. Sykes & M. J. Kearsley from RUS. 535p. 1964. text 137.50 (*90-277-0104-0*) Kluwer Academic.

Quantum Mechanics. P. C. Davies. (Student Physics Ser.). 12800p. (Orig.). (C). 1984. pap. text 13.95 (*0-7100-9962-2*, Routledge Thoemms) Routledge.

Quantum Mechanics. Moshe Flato. 1975. text 173.50 (*90-277-0623-9*) Kluwer Academic.

Quantum Mechanics. Goswami. 1991. student ed. 14.06 (*0-697-11812-6*) McGraw.

Quantum Mechanics. Hendrik F. Hameka. LC 81-3430. 340p. 1981. 42.95 (*0-471-09223-1*) Krieger.

***Quantum Mechanics.** K. T. Hecht. Ed. by J. L. Birman et al. LC 99-42830. (Graduate Texts in Contemporary Physics Ser.). (Illus.). 661p. 1999. 89.95 (*0-387-98919-6*) Spr-Verlag.

Quantum Mechanics. L. D. Landau & E. M. Lifshitz. LC 74-167927. (Shorter Course Theoretical Physics Ser.: Vol. 2). 1974. 166.00 (*0-08-017801-4*, Pub. by Pergamon Repr) Franklin.

Quantum Mechanics. Franz Mandl. LC 91-24255. (Manchester Physics Ser.: No. 1173). 314p. 1992. pap. 85.00 (*0-471-93155-1*) Wiley.

Quantum Mechanics. Sara M. McMurray. LC 93-43852. 374p. 1994. pap. 53.75 (*0-685-71176-5*) Addison-Wesley.

Quantum Mechanics. Sara M. McMurry. LC 93-43852. 1993. 26.00 (*0-685-70937-X*) Addison-Wesley.

Quantum Mechanics. Albert Messiah. LC 99-55362. 1152p. 2000. pap. 29.95 (*0-486-40924-4*) Dover.

Quantum Mechanics. P. J. Peebles. 408p. 1992. text 45.00 (*0-691-08755-5*, Pub. by Princeton U Pr) Cal Prin Full Svc.

Quantum Mechanics. John L. Powell & Bernd Crasemann. (Illus.). 1961. write for info. (*0-201-05920-7*) Addison-Wesley.

Quantum Mechanics. Fayyazuddin Riazuddin. 504p. (C). 1990. text 61.00 (*9971-5-0752-8*) World Scientific Pub.

Quantum Mechanics. F. Schwabl. Tr. by Robert W. Kates from GER. (Illus.). xiii, 407p. 1992. 44.50 (*0-387-54217-5*) Spr-Verlag.

Quantum Mechanics. Theodore Y. Wu. 436p. 1986. text 48.00 (*9971-978-47-4*) World Scientific Pub.

Quantum Mechanics. Zettili. text. write for info. (*0-471-48943-3*); pap. text. write for info. (*0-471-48944-1*) Wiley.

Quantum Mechanics. fac. ed. Franz Mandl. LC 91-24255. (The Manchester Physics Ser.). 314p. 1992. reprint ed. pap. 97.40 (*0-7837-8284-5*, 204906600009) Bks Demand.

***Quantum Mechanics.** 2nd ed. B. H. Bransden & C. J. Joachain. LC 99-55742. 2000. write for info. (*0-582-35691-1*) Addison-Wesley.

Quantum Mechanics. 2nd ed. Amit Goswami. L. LC 96-83911. 560p. (C). 1996. text. write for info. (*0-697-15797-0*, WCB McGr Hill) McGrw-H Hghr Educ.

Quantum Mechanics. 2nd ed. Amit Goswami. 576p. (C). 1996. text. write for info. (*0-07-114833-7*, WCB McGr Hill) McGrw-H Hghr Educ.

Quantum Mechanics. 2nd ed. Eugen Merzbacher. 640p. (C). 1969. text 95.95 (*0-471-59670-1*) Wiley.

Quantum Mechanics. 2nd ed. F. Schwabl. LC 95-22048. (Illus.). 407p. 1995. 44.95 (*3-540-59187-7*) Spr-Verlag.

Quantum Mechanics. 2nd enl. ed. Arno Bohm. LC 85-4710. (Texts & Monographs in Physics). (Illus.). 550p. 1986. pap. 75.50 (*0-387-13985-0*) Spr-Verlag.

Quantum Mechanics. 3rd ed. Eugen Merzbacher. LC 97-20756. 672p. 1997. text 103.95 (*0-471-88702-1*) Wiley.

Quantum Mechanics. 3rd ed. Alastair I. Rae. (Illus.). 280p. 1992. pap. 30.00 (*0-7503-0217-8*) IOP Pub.

Quantum Mechanics. 3rd ed. Leonard I. Schiff. LC 68-25665. (International Series in Pure & Applied Physics). (Illus.). (C). 1968. text 59.00 (*0-07-055287-8*) McGraw.

Quantum Mechanics, 2 vols., 2 Vol. Claude Cohen-Tannoudji et al. 1524p. 1992. pap. 175.00 (*0-471-56952-6*) Wiley.

Quantum Mechanics, 2 vols., Vol. 1. Claude Cohen-Tannoudji et al. Vol. 1. 898p. 1978. pap. 98.50 (*0-471-16433-X*) Wiley.

Quantum Mechanics, Vol. I. Albert Messiah. 504p. 1961. pap. 61.75 (*0-7204-0044-9*, North Holland) Elsevier.

Quantum Mechanics, 2 vols., Vol. 2. Claude Cohen-Tannoudji et al. LC 76-5874. 626p. 1978. pap. 98.50 (*0-471-16435-6*) Wiley.

Quantum Mechanics, Vol. 2. A. Messiah. xvi, 632p. 1961. pap. 29.75 (*0-7204-0045-7*, North Holland) Elsevier.

Quantum Mechanics, Vol. 3. 3rd ed. L. D. Landau. 689p. 2000. pap. text 49.95 (*0-7506-3539-8*) Buttrwrth-Heinemann.

Quantum Mechanics: A Modern Development. 2nd ed. LC 98-12768. 658p. 1997. lib. bdg. 41.00 (*981-02-2707-8*) World Scientific Pub.

Quantum Mechanics: A Modern Introduction. Ashok Das & Adrian C. Melissinos. xviii, 640p. 1986. text 132.00 (*2-88124-053-4*); pap. text 59.00 (*2-88124-052-6*) Gordon & Breach.

Quantum Mechanics: A Physical World Picture. Antal Muller. LC 73-18062. 1974. 55.00 (*0-08-017936-3*, Pub. by Pergamon Repr) Franklin.

Quantum Mechanics: An Empiricist View. Bas C. Van Fraassen. (Illus.). 558p. 1991. pap. text 35.00 (*0-19-823980-7*) OUP.

Quantum Mechanics: An Introduction. 3rd ed. Walter Greiner. LC 94-3433. (Illus.). 445p. 1994. 49.50 (*0-387-58079-4*) Spr-Verlag.

Quantum Mechanics: An Introduction for Device Physicists & Electrical Engineers. David K. Ferry. (Illus.). 300p. 1995. 132.00 (*0-7503-0327-1*); pap. 54.00 (*0-7503-0328-X*) IOP Pub.

Quantum Mechanics: Classical Results, Modern Systems & Visualized Examples. Richard W. Robinett. (Illus.). 600p. (C). 1996. text 74.95 (*0-19-509202-3*) OUP.

Quantum Mechanics: Concepts & Applications. John D. McGervey. (Illus.). 408p. 1995. text 58.00 (*0-12-483545-7*) Acad Pr.

Quantum Mechanics: For Engineering, Materials Science, & Applied Physics. Herbert Kroemer. LC 93-34286. (Alan R. Apt Book Ser.). 639p. (C). 1994. 71.00 (*0-13-747098-3*) P-H.

Quantum Mechanics: Foundations & Applications. 3rd enl. rev. ed. Arno Bohm. LC 92-44947. (Texts & Monographs in Physics). (Illus.). 688p. 1994. 69.95 (*0-387-97944-1*) Spr-Verlag.

Quantum Mechanics: Fundamentals. Kurt Gottfried. 494p. 1966. text 49.50 (*0-8053-3332-0*) Addison-Wesley.

Quantum Mechanics: Fundamentals & Applications to Technology. Jasprit Singh. LC 96-28540. 505p. 1996. 84.95 (*0-471-15758-9*) Wiley.

Quantum Mechanics: Historical Contingency & the Copenhagen Hegemony. James T. Cushing. LC 94-8427. (Science & Its Conceptual Foundations Ser.). 328p. 1994. pap. text 27.00 (*0-226-13204-8*) U Ch Pr.

Quantum Mechanics: Historical Contingency & the Copenhagen Hegemony. James T. Cushing. LC 94-8427. (Science & Its Conceptual Foundations Ser.). 328p. 1994. lib. bdg. 65.00 (*0-226-13202-1*) U Ch Pr.

Quantum Mechanics: New Approaches to Selected Topics. H. J. Lipkin. LC 72-79733. (North-Holland Personal Library). xvi, 466p. 1992. reprint ed. pap. 71.00 (*0-444-87010-5*, North Holland) Elsevier.

Quantum Mechanics: New Subtitle, 1. rev. ed. Gottfried. write for info. (*0-7382-0175-8*, Pub. by Perseus Pubng) HarpC.

Quantum Mechanics: New Subtitle, 2. rev. ed. Gottfried. write for info. (*0-7382-0198-7*, Pub. by Perseus Pubng) HarpC.

Quantum Mechanics: Selected Topics. Askold M. Perelomov & Yakov B. Zel ' dovich. (Selected Topics Ser.). 350p. 1999. 48.00 (*981-02-3550-X*) World Scientific Pub.

Quantum Mechanics: Special Chapters. Walter Greiner. LC 97-24126. (Illus.). xiv, 376p. (C). 1998. pap. 59.95 (*3-540-60073-6*) Spr-Verlag.

Quantum Mechanics: Symmetries. 2nd ed. Walter Greiner & Berndt Muller. LC 94-28230. (Theoretical Physics Ser.: Vol. 2). Orig. Title: Quantenmechanik. (ENG.). 1994. 49.95 (*0-387-58080-8*) Spr-Verlag.

Quantum Mechanics Vol. 1: Fundamentals. Kurt Gottfried. LC 89-30696. (C). 1993. pap. 40.00 (*0-201-40633-0*) Addison-Wesley.

Quantum Mechanics, a Half Century Later. Ed. by Jose L. Lopes & Michel Paty. (Episteme Ser.: No. 5). 320p. 1977. text 155.50 (*90-277-0784-7*, D Reidel) Kluwer Academic.

Quantum Mechanics, Algebras & Distributions. D. A. Dubin & M. A. Hennings. LC 90-42157. (Pitman Research Notes in Mathematics Ser.: No. 238). 252p. 1990. pap. 78.20 (*0-608-05237-X*, 206577400001) Bks Demand.

Quantum Mechanics & Experience. David Z. Albert. (Illus.). 232p. 1993. 37.95 (*0-674-74112-9*) HUP.

Quantum Mechanics & Experience. David Z. Albert. (Illus.). 224p. (C). 1994. pap. 17.00 (*0-674-74113-7*) HUP.

Quantum Mechanics & Nonlinear Waves: Physics, Vol. 1. Philip B. Burt. (Monographs & Tracts Ser.). xii, 332p. (C). 1981. text 355.00 (*3-7186-0072-2*) Gordon & Breach.

Quantum Mechanics & Path Integrals. P. Feyman & A. R. Hibbs. (International Series in Earth & Planetary Sciences). 365p. (C). 1965. 102.81 (*0-07-020650-3*) McGraw.

Quantum Mechanics & Statistical Methods. Ed. by M. M. Sushchinskiy. (Proceedings of the Lebedev Physics Institute Ser.: Vol. 173). 337p. (C). 1988. text 165.00 (*0-941743-08-X*) Nova Sci Pubs.

Quantum Mechanics, Diffusion & Chaotic Fractals. Ed. by M. S. El Naschie et al. 320p. 1995. 53.25 (*0-08-042027-3*, Pergamon Pr) Elsevier.

Quantum Mechanics for Applied Physics & Engineering. Albert T. Fromhold. 448p. 1991. pap. 12.95 (*0-486-66741-3*) Dover.

Quantum Mechanics from General Relativity. Mendel Sachs. 1986. text 176.50 (*90-277-2247-1*) Kluwer Academic.

An Asterisk (*) at the beginning of an entry indicates that the title is appearing for the first time.

Quantum Mechanics, High Energy Physics & Accelerators: Selected Papers of John S. Bell. M. Bell et al. (Series on 20th Century Physics). 1000p. 1995. text 109.00 (*981-02-2115-0*) World Scientific Pub.

Quantum Mechanics in Chemistry. Jack Simons & Jeff Nichols. (Topics in Physical Chemistry Ser.). (Illus.). 640p. (C). 1997. text 79.00 (*0-19-508200-1*) OUP.

Quantum Mechanics in Chemistry. 3rd ed. Melvin W. Hanna. 320p. (C). 1981. pap. text 33.75 (*0-8053-3705-9*) Benjamin-Cummings.

Quantum Mechanics in Curved Space-Time. Ed. by J. Audretsch & Venzo De Sabbata. LC 90-14188. (NATO ASI Ser.: Vol. 230). (Illus.). 566p. (C). 1990. text 168.00 (*0-306-43661-2*, Kluwer Plenum) Kluwer Academic.

Quantum Mechanics of Fundamental Systems, Vol. 1. C. Teitelboim. (Centro de Estudios Cientificos de Santiago Ser.). (Illus.). 248p. (C). 1988. text 89.50 (*0-306-42759-1*, Kluwer Plenum) Kluwer Academic.

Quantum Mechanics of Fundamental Systems, Vol. 2. C. Teitelboim & J. Zanelli. (Centro de Estudios Cientificos de Santiago Ser.). (Illus.). 328p. (C). 1989. text 107.00 (*0-306-43167-X*, Kluwer Plenum) Kluwer Academic.

Quantum Mechanics of Fundamental Systems, Vol. 3. C. Teitelboim & J. Zanelli. (Centro de Estudios Cientificos de Santiago Ser.). (Illus.). 256p. (C). 1992. text 89.50 (*0-306-44066-0*, Kluwer Plenum) Kluwer Academic.

Quantum Mechanics of Many Degrees of Freedom. Daniel S. Koltun & Judah M. Eisenberg. LC 87-28579. 313p. 1988. 175.00 (*0-471-88842-7*) Wiley.

***Quantum Mechanics of Minds & Worlds.** Jeffrey A. Barrett. LC 99-28680. 288p. 2000. text 45.00 (*0-19-823838-X*) OUP.

Quantum Mechanics of Molecular Conformations. Ed. by Bernard Pullman. LC 75-43927. (Perspectives in Quantum Chemistry & Biochemistry Ser.). 422p. reprint ed. pap. 130.90 (*0-7837-0195-0*, 204049100017) Bks Demand.

Quantum Mechanics of Molecular Rate Processes. unabridged ed. Raphael D. Levine. LC 99-21051. 335p. 1999. pap. text 12.95 (*0-486-40692-X*) Dover.

Quantum Mechanics of One- & Two-Electron Atoms. H. A. Bethe & E. E. Salpeter. LC 76-30829. (Illus.). 382p. (C). 1977. text 37.50 (*0-306-20022-8*, Kluwer Plenum) Kluwer Academic.

Quantum Mechanics on Phase Space. Franklin E. Schroeck, Jr. (Fundamental Theories of Physics Ser.: Vol. 74). 688p. (C). 1995. text 323.50 (*0-7923-3794-8*) Kluwer Academic.

Quantum Mechanics on the Macintosh. S. Brandt & H. D. Dahmen. (Illus.). x, 306p. 1992. 49.95 incl. disk (*0-387-97627-2*) Spr-Verlag.

Quantum Mechanics on the Macintosh. 2nd ed. Siegmund Brandt & Hans D. Dahmen. LC 94-19963. (Illus.). x, 305p. 1997. 49.95 (*0-387-94272-6*) Spr-Verlag.

Quantum Mechanics on the PC: Macintosh Supplement. S. Brandt & H. D. Dahmen. (Illus.). 16p. 1991. pap. 19.95 incl. disk (*0-387-14105-7*) Spr-Verlag.

Quantum Mechanics on the Personal Computer. S. Brandt & H. D. Dahmen. (Illus.). x, 267p. 1991. 49.50 (*0-387-51541-0*) Spr-Verlag.

Quantum Mechanics on the Personal Computer. 2nd ed. S. Brandt & H. D. Dahmen. LC 92-25960. (Illus.). xxi, 267p. 1992. write for info. (*3-540-55722-9*); 59.00 incl. disk (*0-387-55722-9*) Spr-Verlag.

Quantum Mechanics on the Personal Computer. 3rd ed. S. Brandt & H. D. Dahmen. LC 93-49418. (Illus.). 327p. 1995. 59.00 incl. disk (*0-387-57470-0*) Spr-Verlag.

Quantum Mechanics One. A. Galindo. Ed. by W. Beiglbock et al. Tr. by J. D. Garcia from SPA. (Texts & Monographs in Physics). 448p. 1990. 69.95 (*0-387-51406-6*) Spr-Verlag.

Quantum Mechanics I: An Introduction. 1989. pap. 39.50 (*0-387-18755-3*) Spr-Verlag.

Quantum Mechanics 1: Foundations. N. J. Green. LC 97-29103. (Oxford Chemistry Primers Ser.: No. 48). (Illus.). 96p. (C). 1997. pap. text 12.95 (*0-19-855761-2*) OUP.

Quantum Mechanics Simulations: The Consortium for Upper-Level Physics Software. John R. Hiller et al. LC 94-38847. 240p. 1995. pap. 46.95 incl. disk (*0-471-54884-7*) Wiley.

***Quantum Mechanics Solver: How to Apply Quantum Theory to Modern Physics.** Jean-Louis Basdevant & J. Dalibard. LC 99-58086. (Advanced Texts in Physics Ser.). (Illus.). xii, 239p. 1999. pap. 48.00 (*3-540-63409-6*) Spr-Verlag.

Quantum Mechanics 2. A. Galindo & P. Pascual. Tr. by L. Alvarez-Gaume from SPA. (Texts & Monographs in Physics). (Illus.). 384p. 1991. 69.95 (*0-387-52309-X*) Spr-Verlag.

Quantum Mechanics II: A Second Couse in Quantum Theory. 2nd ed. Rubin H. Landau. LC 95-17502. 520p. 1995. pap. 69.95 (*0-471-11608-4*, Wiley-Interscience) Wiley.

Quantum Mechanics II: Symmetries. 1991. pap. 49.50 (*0-387-19201-8*) Spr-Verlag.

***Quantum Mechanics 2: The Toolkit.** N. J. Green. (Oxford Chemistry Primers Ser.). (Illus.). 96p. 1998. pap. text 12.95 (*0-19-850227-3*) OUP.

Quantum Mechanics Using Computer Algebra. Willi-Hans Steeb. 200p. 1994. text 37.00 (*981-02-1770-6*) World Scientific Pub.

Quantum Mechanics Using Maple. Marko Horbatsch. (Illus.). 331p. 1995. 49.00 incl. disk (*3-540-58875-2*) Spr-Verlag.

Quantum Mechanics Versus Local Realism: The Einstein-Podolosky-Rosen Paradox. F. Selleri. LC 88-15124. (Physics of Atoms & Molecules Ser.). (Illus.). 480p. (C). 1988. text 135.00 (*0-306-42739-7*, Kluwer Plenum) Kluwer Academic.

Quantum Mechanics with Mathematica. James M. Feagin. 482p. 1994. 59.95 (*0-387-97973-5*) Spr-Verlag.

Quantum Mechanicsn, Vol. 1. 4th rev. ed. Kurt Gottried. 1998. write for info. (*0-201-15696-2*) Addison-Wesley.

***Quantum Mind: The Edge Between Physics & Psychology.** Arnold Mindell. LC 99-66088. (Illus.). 632p. 2000. pap. 26.95 (*1-887078-64-9*) Lao Tse Pr.

Quantum Monte Carlo Methods. Ed. by M. Suzuki. (Solid-State Sciences Ser.: Vol. 74). (Illus.). x, 241p. 1987. 78.95 (*0-387-18061-3*) Spr-Verlag.

Quantum Monte Carlo Methods in Condensed Matter. Masuo Suzuki. 376p. 1993. text 109.00 (*981-02-1659-9*) World Scientific Pub.

Quantum Monte Carlo Methods in Physics & Chemistry. Ed. by M. P. Nightingale & Cyrus J. Umrigar. LC 98-51578. (NATO ASI Series C). 14p. 1999. write for info. (*0-7923-5551-2*) Kluwer Academic.

Quantum Moon. Denise Vitola. 288p. 1996. mass mkt. 5.99 (*0-441-00357-5*) Ace Bks.

Quantum Murder. Peter F. Hamilton. 1996. mass mkt. write for info. (*0-614-08674-4*) Tor Bks.

Quantum Murder. Peter F. Hamilton. 1998. mass mkt. 6.99 (*0-8125-5524-4*, Pub. by Tor Bks) St Martin.

Quantum Networks. G. Mahler. (Illus.). 390p. 1995. 79.95 (*3-540-58850-7*) Spr-Verlag.

Quantum Networks: Dynamics of Open Nanostructures. 2nd enl. rev. ed. Gunter Mahler & V. A. Weberrub. LC 98-12039. (Illus.). xviii, 411p. 1998. 59.95 (*3-540-63668-4*) Spr-Verlag.

Quantum Noise. C. W. Gardiner. Ed. by H. Haken. (Synergetics Ser.: Vol. 56). (Illus.). xviii, 367p. 1991. 73.00 (*0-387-53608-6*) Spr-Verlag.

***Quantum Noise: A Handbook of Markovian & Non-Markovian Quantum Stochastic Methods with Applications to Quantum Optics.** 2nd ed. C. W. Gardiner & P. Zoller. LC 99-52147. (Series in Synergetics: Vol. 56). (Illus.). xxi, 438p. (C). 2000. 89.95 (*3-540-66571-4*) Spr-Verlag.

Quantum Non-Integrability. Ed. by Da-Hsuan Feng et al. LC 92-24407. (Directions in Chaos Ser.: Vol. 4). 560p. (C). 1992. text 130.00 (*981-02-0622-4*) World Scientific Pub.

Quantum of Damages. R. K. Nathan. 455p. 1991. boxed set 160.00 (*0-409-99598-3*, SI, MICHIE) LEXIS Pub.

Quantum I - F Noise & Other Low Frequency Fluctuations in Electronic. Ed. by Peter H. Handel & Alma L. Chung. (AIP Conference Proceedings Ser.: No. 282). (Illus.). 208p. 1993. text 90.00 (*1-56396-252-7*, AIP Pr) Spr-Verlag.

***Quantum 1/f Noise & Other Low Frequency Fluctuations in Electronic Devices: Seventh Symposium.** Ed. by Peter H. Handel & Alma L. Chung. LC 99-60815. (AIP Conference Proceedings Ser.: Vol. 466). (Illus.). 18p. 1999. 90.00 (*1-56396-854-1*) Am Inst Physics.

***Quantum Optics.** Ed. by Anatoli V. Andreev et al. 452p. 1999. pap. text 92.00 (*0-8194-3210-5*) SPIE.

Quantum Optics. Ed. by A. Kujawski & M. Lewenstein. 1986. text 184.00 (*90-277-2281-1*) Kluwer Academic.

***Quantum Optics.** M. Orszag. LC 99-33296. (Illus.). 400p. 1999. 79.95 (*3-540-65008-3*) Spr-Verlag.

Quantum Optics. Wolfgang P. Schleich et al. 282p. 1996. pap. 70.00 (*3-527-29435-X*, Wiley-VCH) Wiley.

Quantum Optics. Marlan O. Scully & M. Suhail Zubairy. LC 94-42949. (Illus.). 652p. (C). 1997. pap. text 49.95 (*0-521-43595-1*) Cambridge U Pr.

Quantum Optics. D. F. Walls & G. J. Milburn. LC 93-44955. (Illus.). 351p. 1994. 59.95 (*0-387-57179-5*) Spr-Verlag.

Quantum Optics. D. F. Walls & G. J. Milburn. LC 94-48500. 1995. write for info. (*0-387-58831-0*) Spr-Verlag.

Quantum Optics. 2nd ed. D. F. Walls & G. J. Milburn. LC 94-48500. (Illus.). 351p. (C). 1995. 44.50 (*3-540-58831-0*) Spr-Verlag.

Quantum Optics see Optics

Quantum Optics: Proceedings of the Summer School on Quantum Optics, Sept. 2-8, 1985, Gdansk, Poland. Ed. by J. Mizerski & J. Fiutak. 410p. 1986. pap. 64.00 (*9971-5-0098-1*); text 159.00 (*9971-5-0097-3*) World Scientific Pub.

Quantum Optics & Fundamentals of Physics. Jan Perina. (Fundamental Theories of Physics Ser.). 352p. (C). 1994. text 186.50 (*0-7923-3000-5*) Kluwer Academic.

Quantum Optics & Spectroscopy. Ed. by J. Mizerski et al. 172p. 1993. text 145.00 (*1-56072-110-3*) Nova Sci Pubs.

Quantum Optics & the Spectroscopy of Solids: Concepts & Advances. Ed. by T. Hakioglu & A. S. Shumovsky. LC 96-51042. (Fundamental Theories of Physics Ser.). 266p. (C). 1997. text 130.50 (*0-7923-4414-6*) Kluwer Academic.

Quantum Optics, Experimental Gravitation, & Measurement Theory. Ed. by Pierre Meystre & Marian O. Scully. LC 83-4159. (NATO ASI Series B, Physics: Vol. 94). (Illus.). 712p. 1983. 145.00 (*0-306-41354-X*, Plenum Trade) Perseus Pubng.

Quantum Optics V. Ed. by J. D. Harvey & D. F. Walls. (Proceedings in Physics Ser.: Vol. 41). (Illus.). ix, 261p. 1989. 66.00 (*0-387-51456-2*) Spr-Verlag.

Quantum Optics in Phase Space. Wolfgang P. Schleich. LC 99-202756. 710p. 1999. 285.00 (*3-527-29436-8*, Wiley-VCH) Wiley.

Quantum Optics of Confined Systems: Proceedings of the NATO Advanced Study Institute, Les Houches, France, May 23-June 2, 1995. Ed. by Martial Ducloy & Daniel Bloch. LC 96-244. (NATO Advanced Science Institutes Ser.: Vol. 314, Pt. E). 416p. (C). 1996. text 217.50 (*0-7923-3974-6*) Kluwer Academic.

Quantum Optoelectronics. LC 92-62841. (Nineteen Ninety-Three Technical Digest Ser.: Vol. 8). 350p. 1993. pap. 75.00 (*1-55752-292-8*) Optical Soc.

Quantum Optoelectronics. LC 92-62841. (Technical Digest Ser.: Vol. 8, 1993). 350p. 1993. pap. text 48.00 (*1-55752-291-X*) Optical Soc.

Quantum Optoelectronics. LC 95-67798. (1995 Technical Digest Ser.: Vol. 13). 224p. 1995. pap. 75.00 (*1-55752-396-7*) Optical Soc.

***Quantum Optoelectronics.** (Nineteen Ninety-Nine OSA Technical Digest Ser.). 200p. (C). 1999. pap. 75.00 (*1-55752-600-1*) Optical Soc.

Quantum Optoelectronics. Compiled by Optical Society of America Staff. LC 97-65500. (Nineteen Ninety-Seven Technical Digest Ser.: Vol. 9). (Illus.). 152p. 1997. pap. 75.00 (*1-55752-493-9*) Optical Soc.

Quantum Origins of Cosmic Structure: Probability Density Function of Quantity-Mass-Ratio Logarithm. E. H. VanMarcke. (Illus.). 250p. (C). 1997. pap. 35.00 (*90-5410-687-5*, Pub. by A A Balkema) Ashgate Pub Co.

Quantum Origins of Cosmic Structure: Probability Density Function of Quantity-Mass-Ratio Logarithm. Erik VanMarcke. (Illus.). 240p. (C). 1997. text 81.00 (*90-5410-674-3*, Pub. by A A Balkema) Ashgate Pub Co.

Quantum Paradoxes & Physical Reality. Franco Selleri. Ed. by Alwyn Van der Merwe. (C). 1990. text 255.50 (*0-7923-0253-2*) Kluwer Academic.

***Quantum Phase Transitions.** Subir Sachdev. LC 99-12280. (Illus.). 408p. (C). 2000. 85.00 (*0-521-58254-7*) Cambridge U Pr.

Quantum Phenomena in Networks of Josephson Junctions. W. J. Elion. 124p. 1995. pap. 57.50 (*90-407-1106-2*, Pub. by Delft U Pr) Coronet Bks.

Quantum Philosophy: Understanding & Interpreting Contemporary Science. Roland Omnaes. LC 98-42445. 1999. text 29.95 (*0-691-02787-0*, Pub. by Princeton U Pr) Cal Prin Full Svc.

***Quantum Physics.** M. S. Rogalski & S. B. Palmer. 488p. 1999. text 70.00 (*90-5699-184-1*, G & B Science); pap. text 35.00 (*90-5699-185-X*, G & B Science) Gordon & Breach.

Quantum Physics. 2nd ed. Stephen Gasiorowicz. LC 95-20414. 480p. 1995. text 100.95 (*0-471-85737-8*) Wiley.

Quantum Physics. 2nd ed. Rolf G. Winter. (Textbooks in Science & Mathematics Ser.). (Illus.). 413p. (C). 1993. reprint ed. pap. text 33.00 (*1-880930-01-3*) IPI Pr.

Quantum Physics see Berkeley Physics Course

Quantum Physics: A Functional Integral Point of View. 2nd ed. J. Glimm & A. Jaffe. (Illus.). 560p. 1996. reprint ed. pap. 53.95 (*0-387-96477-0*) Spr-Verlag.

Quantum Physics: A Functional Integral Point of View. 2nd ed. J. Glimm & Arthur Jaffe. (Illus.). xxii, 535p. 1987. reprint ed. 98.95 (*0-387-96476-2*) Spr-Verlag.

Quantum Physics: Illusion or Reality? Alastair Rae. (Canto Book Ser.). (Illus.). 135p. (C). 1994. pap. 10.95 (*0-521-46716-0*) Cambridge U Pr.

Quantum Physics: Of Atoms, Molecules, Solids, Nuclei & Particles. 2nd ed. Robert M. Eisberg & Robert E. Resnick. LC 84-10444. 864p. 1985. text 103.95 (*0-471-87373-X*) Wiley.

Quantum Physics & Observed Reality: A Critical Interpretation of Quantum Mechanics. Hermann Wimmel. LC 92-10265. 150p. 1992. text 43.00 (*981-02-1010-8*) World Scientific Pub.

Quantum Physics & Parapsychology: Proceedings of the International Conference, August 26-27, 1974. International Conference, Geneva Staff. Ed. by Laura Oteri. LC 75-14867. 1975. 17.00 (*0-912328-26-6*) Parapsych Foun.

Quantum Physics, Chaos Theory & Cosmology. Mikio Namiki. LC 96-31759. 1996. 65.00 (*1-56396-544-5*) Spr-Verlag.

Quantum Physics in America: Nineteen Hundred Twenty to Nineteen Hundred Thirty-Five. Katherinne Sopka. Ed. by I. Bernard Cohen. LC 79-7997. 1980. lib. bdg. 53.95 (*0-405-12585-2*) Ayer.

Quantum Physics in America: The Years Through 1935. Katherine R. Sopka. (History of Modern Physics & Astronomy Ser.). (Illus.). 410p. 1988. 79.95 (*0-88318-553-9*) Spr-Verlag.

Quantum Physics, Logic & Spacetime: Variations on Finkelstein's Quantum Relativity. Steve Selesnick. LC 98-15361. 320p. 1998. 48.00 (*981-02-3255-1*) World Scientific Pub.

Quantum Physics of Atomic Frequency Standards, 2 vols., 1. Jacques Vanier & C. Audoin. 1176p. 1989. 330.00 (*0-85274-432-3*) Taylor & Francis.

Quantum Physics of Atomic Frequency Standards, 2 vols., 2. Jacques Vanier & C. Audoin. 1176p. 1989. 330.00 (*0-85274-433-1*) Taylor & Francis.

Quantum Physics of Atomic Frequency Standards, 2 vols., Set. Ed. by Jacques Vanier & C. Audoin. (Illus.). 1588p. 1989. 893.00 (*0-85274-434-X*) IOP Pub.

Quantum Poetics: Yeats, Pound, Eliot & the Science of Modernism. Daniel Albright. (Illus.). 317p. (C). 1997. text 64.95 (*0-521-57305-X*) Cambridge U Pr.

Quantum Practicle Internet. Stephen R. Petersen. 1997. pap. 7.95 (*1-890711-18-7*) Empyrean Quest.

Quantum Principle. Jagdish Mehra. LC 74-77965. 150p. 1974. text 88.00 (*90-277-0469-4*) Kluwer Academic.

Quantum Probability. Stanley P. Gudder. (Probability & Mathematical Statistics Ser.). 316p. 1988. text 94.00 (*0-12-305340-4*) Acad Pr.

Quantum Probability - Quantum Logic. Ed. by I. Pitowsky. (Lecture Notes in Physics Ser.: Vol. 321). ix, 209p. 1989. 36.95 (*0-387-50679-9*) Spr-Verlag.

Quantum Probability & Applications, IV. Ed. by L. Accardi & W. Von Waldenfels. (Lecture Notes in Mathematics Ser.: Vol. 1396). vi, 355p. 1989. 50.95 (*0-387-51613-1*) Spr-Verlag.

Quantum Probability & Applications III. Ed. by L. Accardi & W. Von Waldenfels. (Lecture Notes in Mathematics Ser.: Vol. 1303). vi, 373p. 1988. 54.95 (*0-387-18919-X*) Spr-Verlag.

Quantum Probability & Applications to the Quantum Theory of Irreversible Processes: Proceedings of the International Workshop Held at Villa Mondragone, Italy, Sept. 6-11, 1982. Ed. by L. Accardi et al. (Lecture Notes in Mathematics Ser.: Vol. 1055). vi, 411p. 1984. 49.95 (*0-387-12915-4*) Spr-Verlag.

Quantum Probability & Applications II. Ed. by L. Accardi & W. V. Waldenfels. (Lecture Notes in Mathematics Ser.: Vol. 1136). vi, 534p. 1985. 64.95 (*0-387-15661-5*) Spr-Verlag.

Quantum Probability & Applications, V: Proceedings of the Fourth Workshop, Held in Heidelberg, FRG, Sept. 26-30, 1988. Ed. by L. Accardi et al. (Lecture Notes in Mathematics Ser.: Vol. 1442). vi, 413p. 1990. 63.95 (*0-387-53026-6*) Spr-Verlag.

Quantum Probability & Related Topics. Ed. by L. Accardi. 500p. (C). 1991. pap. 48.00 (*981-02-0716-6*); text 113.00 (*981-02-0680-1*) World Scientific Pub.

Quantum Probability & Related Topics, Vol. 7. Ed. by L. Accardi. LC 92-24406. 388p. 1992. pap. write for info. (*981-02-1979-2*) World Scientific Pub.

Quantum Probability & Related Topics, Vol. 8. 350p. 1993. text 43.00 (*981-02-1141-4*) World Scientific Pub.

Quantum Probability & Related Topics, Vol. 8. L. Accardi. 350p. 1993. text 100.00 (*981-02-1140-6*) World Scientific Pub.

Quantum Probability & Related Topics, Vol. IX. L. Accardi. 420p. 1994. text 106.00 (*981-02-2047-2*) World Scientific Pub.

Quantum Probability & Related Topics: QP-PQ, Vol. 7. L. Accardi. 350p. 1992. text 95.00 (*981-02-1011-6*) World Scientific Pub.

Quantum Probability Communications, Vol. X. R. L. Hudson. 1998. 78.00 (*981-02-3541-0*) World Scientific Pub.

Quantum Probability for Probabilists. P. A. Meyer. Ed. by A. Dold et al. (Lecture Notes in Mathematics Ser.: Vol. 1538). 297p. 1993. pap. 43.00 (*0-387-56476-4*) Spr-Verlag.

Quantum Probability for Probabilists, Vol. X. 2nd ed. Paul A. Meyer. Ed. by A. Dold et al. LC 95-37123. (Lecture Notes in Mathematics Ser.: Vol. 1538). 312p. 1995. 62.95 (*3-540-60270-4*) Spr-Verlag.

Quantum Processes in Semiconductors. 4th ed. Brian K. Ridley. LC 99-16185. (Illus.). 464p. 2000. text 110.00 (*0-19-850580-9*); pap. text 50.00 (*0-19-850579-5*) OUP.

Quantum Profiles. Jeremy Bernstein. 166p. (C). 1991. text 29.95 (*0-691-08725-3*, Pub. by Princeton U Pr) Cal Prin Full Svc.

Quantum Psychology: How Brain Software Programs You & Your World. 2nd ed. Robert A. Wilson. LC 92-63046. 256p. (Orig.). 1993. pap. 14.95 (*1-56184-071-8*) New Falcon Pubns.

Quantum Psychology: Steps to a Postmodern Ecology of Being. Stephen T. DeBerry. LC 92-28474. 224p. 1993. 55.00 (*0-275-94171-X*, C4171, Praeger Pubs) Greenwood.

Quantum Quality: Quality Improvement Through Innovation, Learning, & Creativity. William C. Miller. LC 93-12408. 208p. 1993. pap. 19.95 (*0-527-91719-2*) Productivity Inc.

Quantum Quandaries. Ed. by Timothy Weber. (Illus.). 64p. 1996. pap. text 7.95 (*0-87355-136-2*, PB123X) Natl Sci Tchrs.

Quantum Questions: Mystical Writings of the World's Great Physicists. Ed. by Ken Wilber. LC 83-20332. 210p. 1984. pap. 18.00 (*0-394-72338-4*, Pub. by Shambhala Pubns) Random.

Quantum Questions, Mystical Writings of the World's Great Physicists. Ken Wilber. 1986. pap. 18.00 (*0-87773-266-3*, Pub. by Shambhala Pubns) Random.

Quantum Reality. Nick Herbert. (Illus.). 288p. 1987. pap. 12.95 (*0-385-23569-0*, Anchor NY) Doubleday.

Quantum Reality: A New Philosophical Perspective. David Kreiter. 160p. 1994. pap. 14.29 (*0-944266-17-7*) Maecenas Pr.

***Quantum Reflections.** Ed. by John Ellis & Daniele Amati. LC QC174.12. E45 2000. (Illus.). 200p. (C). 2000. text 49.95 (*0-521-63008-8*) Cambridge U Pr.

Quantum Relativity: A Synthesis of the Ideas of Einstein & Heisenberg. Ed. by W. Beiglbock et al. (Texts & Monographs in Physics). (Illus.). 600p. 1996. 89.00 (*3-540-57084-5*) Spr-Verlag.

Quantum Relativity: A Synthesis of the Ideas of Einstein & Heisenberg. D. Finkelstein. (Texts & Monographs in Physics). 496p. 1997. 89.00 (*0-387-57084-5*) Spr-Verlag.

Quantum Relativity: An Introductory Monograph. W. Cordell Scotten. LC 96-90006. 71p. 1996. text 46.40 (*0-9650714-0-5*); pap. text 18.90 (*0-9650714-1-3*) Theoretical.

Quantum Reprogramming: Ensembles & Single Systems: A Two-Tier Approach to Quantum Mechanics. Evert J. Post. LC 95-17463. (Boston Studies in the Philosophy of Science: Vol. 181). 332p. 1995. lib. bdg. 137.00 (*0-7923-3565-1*, Pub. by Kluwer Academic) Kluwer Academic.

Quantum Retirement: Waltzing in Cosmic Babylon. Daniel McDonald. (Illus.). 150p. 1997. pap. write for info. (*0-9659311-0-2*) Gulf Coast AL.

***Quantum Rose.** Catherine Asaro. 2000. text 25.95 (*0-312-89062-1*) St Martin.

Quantum Scattering & Spectral Theory. Ed. by D. B. Pearson. (Techniques of Physics Ser.). 519p. 1988. text 160.00 (*0-12-548260-4*) Acad Pr.

Quantum Scattering Theory: Selected Papers. Marc Ross. LC 63-16622. 313p. reprint ed. pap. 97.10 (*0-608-30602-9*, 205522700011) Bks Demand.

Quantum Scattering Theory for Several Particle Systems. L. D. Fadeev & S. P. Merkuriev. LC 93-11377. (Mathematical Physics & Applied Mathematics Ser: Vol. 11). 1993. text 264.50 (*0-7923-2414-5*) Kluwer Academic.

Q

Quantum Self: Human Nature & Consciousness Defined by the New Physics. Danah Zohar. LC 89-13194. (Illus.). 272p. 1991. reprint ed. pap. 11.00 (*0-688-10736-2*, Quil) HarperTrade.

Quantum Selling: Using Virtual Reality to Tap Your Limitless Sales Potential. Howard Wallin. 126p. 1994. 14.95 (*0-9641950-0-3*) Catalyst Bks.

Quantum Semiconductor Structures: Fundamentals & Applications. Claude Weisbuch & Borge Vinter. (Illus.). 252p. 1991. pap. text 48.00 (*0-12-742680-9*) Acad Pr.

Quantum Signatures of Chaos. 2nd ed. F. Haake. (Synergetics Ser.: Vol. 54). (Illus.). 242p. 1992. reprint ed. 64.95 (*0-387-53144-0*) Spr-Verlag.

Quantum Simulations of Condensed Matter Phenomena. Ed. by J. E. Gubernatis & J. D. Doll. 454p. (C). 1989. text 151.00 (*981-02-0047-1*) World Scientific Pub.

Quantum Society. Danah Zohar & Ian Marshall. LC 93-34348. 1995. pap. 15.00 (*0-688-14230-3*, Quil) HarperTrade.

Quantum Solid-State Physics. S. V. Vonsovsky & M. I. Katsnelson. (Solid-State Sciences Ser.: Vol. 73). (Illus.). 535p. 1989. 165.95 (*0-387-19103-8*) Spr-Verlag.

Quantum Soup: Fortune Cookies in Crises. Chungliang A. Huang. (Illus.). 144p. (Orig.). 1995. pap. 18.95 (*0-89087-606-1*) Celestial Arts.

***Quantum Squeezing.** Peter D. Drummond. 360p. 1999. 79.95 (*3-540-65989-7*) Spr-Verlag.

Quantum State Diffusion. Ian Percival. LC 98-7168. (Illus.). 160p. (C). 1999. 49.95 (*0-521-62007-4*) Cambridge U Pr.

Quantum Statistical Mechanics. Leo P. Kadanoff. (C). 1994. pap. 45.00 (*0-201-41046-X*) Addison-Wesley.

Quantum Statistical Mechanics. Leo P. Kadanoff & Gordon Baym. (Classics Ser.). (Illus.). 224p. (C). 1989. 39.95 (*0-201-09422-3*) Addison-Wesley.

Quantum Statistical Mechanics, Vol. 7. Ed. by P. H. Meijer. (Documents on Modern Physics Ser.). x, 172p. (Orig.). 1966. text 235.00 (*0-677-01310-8*) Gordon & Breach.

Quantum Statistical Mechanics & Lie Group Harmonic Analysis, Pt. A. Norman Hurt & R. Hermann. LC 80-13949. (Lie Groups; History, Frontiers & Applications Ser.: Vol. 10). 250p. 1980. text 50.00 (*0-915692-30-9*, 991600118) Math Sci Pr.

***Quantum Statistical Methods in Quantum Optics.** Howard Carmichael. LC 98-40873. (Texts & Monographs in Physics Ser.). 1999. 64.95 (*3-540-54882-3*) Spr-Verlag.

Quantum Statistical Properties of Radiation. William H. Louisell. (Classics Library). 544p. 1990. pap. 84.95 (*0-471-52365-8*) Wiley.

Quantum Statistical Theory of Superconductivity. S. Fujita & S. Godoy. LC 96-22326. (Selected Topics in Superconductivity Ser.). (Illus.). 357p. (C). 1996. text 71.00 (*0-306-45363-0*, Kluwer Plenum) Kluwer Academic.

Quantum Statistics & Cooperative Phenomena, Vol. 1. John G. Kirkwood. Ed. by F. Stillinger. (Documents on Modern Physics Ser.). x, 182p. 1965. text 172.00 (*0-677-00370-6*) Gordon & Breach.

Quantum Statistics of Charged Particle Systems. W. D. Kraeft et al. (Illus.). 308p. (C). 1986. text 114.00 (*0-306-42190-9*, Kluwer Plenum) Kluwer Academic.

Quantum Statistics of Dynamic Processes. enl. ed. E. Fick & G. Sauermann. Ed. by M. Cardona et al. (Solid-State Sciences Ser.: Vol. 86). 408p. 1990. 108.95 (*0-387-50824-4*) Spr-Verlag.

Quantum Statistics of Linear & Nonlinear Optical Phenomena. Jan Perina. 1984. text 185.50 (*90-277-1512-2*) Kluwer Academic.

Quantum Statistics of Linear & Nonlinear Optical Phenomena. 2nd rev. ed. Jan Perina. (C). 1991. text 272.50 (*0-7923-1171-X*) Kluwer Academic.

Quantum Stochastic Calculus & Representations for Lie Superalgebras, Vol. 169. Timothy M. Eyre. LC 98-38721. (Lecture Notes in Mathematics Ser.). 1998. pap. 27.00 (*3-540-64897-6*) Spr-Verlag.

Quantum Strength & Power Training: (Gaining the Winning Edge) Pat O'Shea. (Illus.). Date not set. write for info. (*0-9648698-0-2*) Patricks Bks.

Quantum String Theory. Ed. by N. Kawanoto & T. Kugo. (Proceedings in Physics Ser.: Vol. 31). (Illus.). ix, 147p. 1988. 71.95 (*0-387-50313-7*) Spr-Verlag.

***Quantum Structures & the Nature of Reality: The Indigo Book of 'Einstein Meets Magritte'** Diederik Aerts & Jaroslaw Pykacz. LC 99-27066. (Einstein Meets Magritte Ser.). 260p. 1999. 126.00 (*0-7923-5763-9*) Kluwer Academic.

Quantum Symmetries. H. D. Doebner. 392p. 1993. text 121.00 (*981-02-1475-8*) World Scientific Pub.

Quantum Symmetries on Operator Algebras. David E. Evans & Yasuyuki Kawahigashi. (Oxford Mathematical Monographs). (Illus.). 846p. 1998. text 200.00 (*0-19-851175-2*) OUP.

Quantum Systems: New Trends & Methods. LC 97-172256. 380p. 1997. text 61.00 (*981-02-3049-4*) World Scientific Pub.

Quantum Systems: New Trends & Methods. Asim O. Barut et al. 420p. 1995. text 122.00 (*981-02-2099-5*) World Scientific Pub.

***Quantum Systems: Proceedings of the 3rd International Workshop.** Ed. by L. M. Tomilchik et al. 300p. 2000. 68.00 (*981-02-4144-5*) World Scientific Pub.

***Quantum Systems in Chemistry & Physics: Granada, Spain, (1997) (i.e. 1998)** Alfonso Hernandez-Laguna. LC 99-45982. 416p. 2000. write for info. (*0-7923-5971-2*) Kluwer Academic.

***Quantum Systems in Chemistry & Physics: Granada, Spain, 1997-1998, 2 vols.** Alfonso Hernandez-Laguna. LC 99-45982. (Progress in Theoretical Chemistry & Physics Ser.). 1999. write for info. (*0-7923-5970-4*) Kluwer Academic.

Quantum Systems in Chemistry & Physics: Trends in Methods & Applications. Ed. by Roy McWeeny et al. LC 98-136403. (Topics in Molecular Organization & Engineering Ser.: No. 16). 300p. 1997. 137.00 (*0-7923-4699-8*) Kluwer Academic.

Quantum Teaching: Orchestrating Student Success. Bobbi Deporter. LC 98-186080. 230p. 1998. pap. text 27.95 (*0-205-28664-X*) P-H.

Quantum Theology. Diarmuid O'Murchu. LC 96-49656. 1997. pap. text 19.95 (*0-8245-1630-3*) Crossroad NY.

Quantum Theories & Geometry. Ed. by M. Cahen & Moshe Flato. (C). 1988. text 140.50 (*90-277-2803-8*) Kluwer Academic.

Quantum Theory. David Bohm. 655p. 1998. pap. 14.95 (*0-486-65969-0*) Dover.

Quantum Theory: Concepts & Methods. Asher Peres. LC 93-32994. (Fundamental Theories of Physics Ser.). 460p. (C). 1993. lib. bdg. 155.00 (*0-7923-2549-4*, Pub. by Kluwer Academic) Kluwer Academic.

Quantum Theory: Concepts & Methods, Vol. 72. Asher Peres. LC 95-34044. (Fundamental Theories of Physics Ser.). 1995. pap. text 73.00 (*0-7923-3632-1*, Pub. by Kluwer Academic) Kluwer Academic.

Quantum Theory & Applications of Chemical Reaction Dynamics. John Z. Zhang. LC 98-38058. 450p. 1998. 64.00 (*981-02-3388-4*) World Scientific Pub.

Quantum Theory & Measurement. John A. Wheeler. LC 82-47620. (Princeton Series in Physics). (Illus.). 839p. reprint ed. pap. 200.00 (*0-608-09582-6*, 205438400006) Bks Demand.

Quantum Theory & Pictures of Reality. Ed. by W. Schommers. (Illus.). 360p. 1989. 75.95 (*0-387-50152-5*) Spr-Verlag.

***Quantum Theory & Symmetries: Proceedings of the International Symposium: Goslar, Germany, 18-22 July 1999.** H. D. Doebner & Arnold-Sommerfeld-Institut FHUR Mathematische Physik Staff. LC 00-35185. 2000. write for info. (*981-02-4237-9*) World Scientific Pub.

***Quantum Theory & the Flight from Realism: Philosophical Responses to Quantum Mechanics.** Christopher Norris. LC 99-38146. (Critical Realism--Interventions Ser.). 280p. 1999. pap. 25.99 (*0-415-22322-9*) Routledge.

***Quantum Theory & the Flight from Realism: Philosophical Responses to Quantum Mechanics.** Christopher Norris. LC 99-38146. 280p. (C). 2000. text 85.00 (*0-415-22321-0*) Routledge.

Quantum Theory & the Schism in Physics. Karl R. Popper. LC 92-23685. (Postscript to the Logic of Scientific Discovery Ser.). 256p. (C). 1992. pap. 27.99 (*0-415-09112-8*) Routledge.

Quantum Theory & the Schism in Physics. Karl R. Popper. Ed. by W. W. Bartley, III. LC 81-8706. (Postscript to the Logic of Scientific Discovery Ser.). 250p. 1984. pap. 23.00 (*0-8476-7389-8*) Rowman.

Quantum Theory, Black Holes & Inflation. I. G. Moss. 174p. 1996. 98.00 (*0-471-95736-4*) Wiley.

Quantum Theory, Groups, Fields & Particles. Ed. by Asim O. Barut. 1983. text 180.50 (*90-277-1552-1*) Kluwer Academic.

Quantum Theory of Angular Momentum. D. A. Varshalovich et al. 528p. 1988. text 97.00 (*9971-5-0107-4*); pap. text 36.00 (*9971-5-0996-2*) World Scientific Pub.

Quantum Theory of Angular Momentum: Selected Topics. K. S. Rao & V. Rasjeswari. xxiii, 315p. 1993. 69.00 (*0-387-56308-3*) Spr-Verlag.

Quantum Theory of Chemical Reactions. Ed. by Raymond Daudel et al. 1982. lib. bdg. 88.00 (*90-277-1467-3*) Kluwer Academic.

Quantum Theory of Chemical Reactions: Collision Theory, Reaction Path, Static Indices, Vol. 1. Ed. by Raymond Daudel et al. 1979. text 155.00 (*90-277-1047-3*) Kluwer Academic.

Quantum Theory of Chemical Reactions: Solvent Effect, Reaction Mechanisms, Photochemical Processes, Vol. 11. Ed. by Raymond Daudel et al. 340p. 1980. lib. bdg. 112.00 (*90-277-1182-8*) Kluwer Academic.

Quantum Theory of Chemical Reactivity. Raymond Daudel. LC 73-75762. 1973. pap. text 88.00 (*90-277-0420-1*) Kluwer Academic.

Quantum Theory of Collective Phenomena. G. L. Sewell. (Monographs on the Physics & Chemistry of Materials). (Illus.). 248p. 1990. reprint ed. pap. 35.00 (*0-19-851386-0*) OUP.

Quantum Theory of Fields, Set, Vols. I & II. Steven Weinberg. (C). 1996. text 110.00 (*0-521-58555-4*) Cambridge U Pr.

Quantum Theory of Fields Vol. I: Foundations. Steven Weinberg. (Illus.). 635p. (C). 1995. text 57.95 (*0-521-55001-7*) Cambridge U Pr.

Quantum Theory of Fields Vol. II: Modern Applications, Vol. II. Steven Weinberg. (Illus.). 500p. (C). 1996. text 49.95 (*0-521-55002-5*) Cambridge U Pr.

Quantum Theory of Fields Vol. 3: Supersymmetry. Steven Weinberg. (Illus.). 500p. (C). 2000. 49.95 (*0-521-66000-9*) Cambridge U Pr.

Quantum Theory of Finite Systems. Jean-Paul Blaizot & Georges Ripka. (Illus.). 680p. (C). 1985. 70.00 (*0-262-02214-1*) MIT Pr.

Quantum Theory of Josephson Radiation see Progress in Quantum Electronics

Quantum Theory of Light. 2nd ed. Rodney Loudon. (Illus.). 410p. 1983. pap. text 44.95 (*0-19-851155-8*) OUP.

Quantum Theory of Many - Body Systems: Techniques & Applications. Alexandre M. Zagoskin. LC 98-12964. (Graduate Texts in Contemporary Physics Ser.). (Illus.). 229p. Date not set. write for info. (*0-387-98384-8*) Spr-Verlag.

Quantum Theory of Many Particle Systems. J. Dirk Walecka & Alexander L. Fetter. Ed. by Bradford Banes & Marge Eakens. (International Series in Pure & Applied Physics). (Illus.). 576p. (C). 1971. 125.94 (*0-07-020653-8*) McGraw.

Quantum Theory of Many Variable Systems & Fields. B. Sakita. (Lecture Notes in Physics Ser.: Vol. 1). 228p. 1985. text 47.00 (*9971-978-55-5*); pap. text 28.00 (*9971-978-57-1*) World Scientific Pub.

Quantum Theory of Matter: A Novel Introduction. A. Modinos. LC 95-49410. 368p. 1996. 155.00 (*0-471-96363-1*); pap. 64.95 (*0-471-96364-X*) Wiley.

Quantum Theory of Measurement. P. Mittelstaedt et al. Ed. by W. Beiglbock et al. (Lecture Notes in Physics Ser.: Vol. M2). xiii, 165p. 1991. 29.00 (*0-387-54334-1*) Spr-Verlag.

Quantum Theory of Measurement. 2nd ed. Paul Busch et al. LC 96-26743. (Lecture Notes in Physics Ser.). 181p. 1996. 46.00 (*3-540-61355-2*) Spr-Verlag.

***Quantum Theory of Measurement of a Single System.** Orly Alter & Yoshihisa Yamamoto. LC 99-59408. 160p. 2000. text 74.95 (*0-471-28308-8*) Wiley.

Quantum Theory of Motion: An Account of the de Broglie-Bohm Causal Interpretation of Quantum Mechanics. Peter R. Holland. LC 92-20205. (Illus.). 618p. (C). 1995. pap. text 47.95 (*0-521-48543-6*) Cambridge U Pr.

Quantum Theory of Optical & Electronic Properties of Semiconductors. 3rd ed. Hartmut Haug & Stephan W. Koch. 492p. 1994. pap. text 48.00 (*981-02-1864-8*) World Scientific Pub.

Quantum Theory of Particles & Fields: Birthday Volume Dedicated to Jan Lopuszanski. Ed. by B. Jancewicz & J. Lukierski. 292p. (C). 1983. 52.00 (*9971-950-77-4*) World Scientific Pub.

Quantum Theory of Polymers. Ed. by J. Andre et al. (NATO Advanced Study Institute Ser.). 1978. text 141.50 (*90-277-0870-3*) Kluwer Academic.

Quantum Theory of Polymers As Solids. Janos Ladik. LC 87-29159. (Illus.). 431p. reprint ed. pap. 133.70 (*0-608-08572-3*, 206909500002) Bks Demand.

Quantum Theory of Radiation. E. R. Pike & Sarben Sarkar. (International Series of Monographs on Physics: No. 86). (Illus.). 354p. 1996. text 105.00 (*0-19-852032-8*) OUP.

Quantum Theory of Radiation. W. Heitler. (Physics Ser.). 430p. 1984. reprint ed. pap. 11.95 (*0-486-64558-4*) Dover.

Quantum Theory of Real Materials. Ed. by James R. Chelikowsky & Steven G. Louie. LC 95-45353. (International Series in Engineering & Computer Science, Natural Language Processing & Machine Translation: No. 348). 568p. (C). 1996. text 236.00 (*0-7923-9666-9*) Kluwer Academic.

Quantum Theory of Solids. 2nd rev. ed. Charles Kittel. LC 86-32478. 528p. 1987. pap. 58.95 (*0-471-62412-8*) Wiley.

Quantum Theory of the Laser see Progress in Quantum Electronics

Quantum Theory of the Optical & Electronic Properties of Semiconductors. Ed. by Stephan W. Koch & Hartmut Haug. 408p. (C). 1990. text 86.00 (*981-02-0024-2*); pap. text 40.00 (*981-02-0249-0*) World Scientific Pub.

Quantum Theory of the Optical & Electronic Properties of Semiconductors. 2nd ed. Hartmut Haug & Stephan W. Koch. 492p. 1993. text 97.00 (*981-02-1341-7*); pap. text 48.00 (*981-02-1347-6*) World Scientific Pub.

Quantum Theory of the Optical & Electronic Properties of Semiconductors. 3rd ed. Hartmut Haug & Stephan W. Koch. 492p. 1994. text 97.00 (*981-02-2002-2*) World Scientific Pub.

Quantum Theory of the Solid State. 2nd ed. Joseph Callaway. 954p. (C). 1991. text 82.00 (*0-12-155203-9*) Acad Pr.

Quantum Theory Without Reduction. Ed. by M. Cini & Jean-Marc Levy-Leblond. (Illus.). 180p. 1990. 66.00 (*0-7503-0031-0*) IOP Pub.

***Quantum Thory of Fields, 3 vols.** Steven Weinberg. 2000. 155.00 (*0-521-78082-9*) Cambridge U Pr.

Quantum Topology. 392p. 1993. 26.00 (*981-02-2575-X*) World Scientific Pub.

Quantum Topology. Louis H. Kauffman & Randy A. Baadhio. 350p. 1993. text 68.00 (*981-02-1544-4*) World Scientific Pub.

Quantum Topology: Proceedings of the Conferece. D. N. Yetter. 388p. 1994. text 99.00 (*981-02-1727-7*) World Scientific Pub.

Quantum Topology & Global Anomalies, Advanced Series in Mathematical Physics. LC 97-106820. (Advanced Series in Mathematical Physics). 284p. 1996. lib. bdg. 34.00 (*981-02-2726-4*); lib. bdg. 25.00 (*981-02-2727-2*) World Scientific Pub.

Quantum Touch: The Power to Heal. Richard Gordon. LC 99-30631. (Illus.). 200p. 1999. pap. 18.95 (*1-55643-320-4*) North Atlantic.

Quantum Transport & Dissipation. Bernhard J. Kramer et al. LC 98-131557. 382p. 1998. 95.00 (*3-527-29261-6*, Wiley-VCH) Wiley.

Quantum Transport in Semiconductor Submicron Structures: Proceedings of the NATO Advanced Study Institute, Bad Lauterberg, Germany, Aug. 20-31, 1995. Ed. by Bernhard J. Kramer. LC 96-31598. (NATO ASI Series E: Applied Sciences). 400p. (C). 1996. text 202.50 (*0-7923-4190-2*) Kluwer Academic.

Quantum Transport in Semiconductors. D. K. Ferry & C. Jacoboni. (Physics of Solids & Liquids Ser.). (Illus.). 320p. (C). 1991. text 89.50 (*0-306-43853-4*, Kluwer Plenum) Kluwer Academic.

Quantum Transport in Ultrasmall Devices. D. K. Ferry et al. LC 95-17275. (NATO ASI Series B: Vol. 342). (Illus.). 554p. (C). 1995. text 167.00 (*0-306-44999-4*) Plenum.

Quantum Transport Theory. Rammer. (C). 1998. write for info. (*0-201-48320-3*) Addison-Wesley.

Quantum Transport Theory. Jorgen Rammer. LC 98-86414. (Frontiers in Physics Ser.). 528p. 1998. text 55.00 (*0-7382-0048-4*) Perseus Pubng.

Quantum Tunneling of Magnetization - QTM '94: Proceedings of the NATO Advanced Research Workshop, Grenoble & Chichilianne, France, June 27-July 2, 1994. Ed. by Leon Gunther & Bernard Barbara. LC 95-38838. (NATO Advanced Science Institutes Ser.: Series E). 520p. (C). 1995. text 257.50 (*0-7923-3775-1*) Kluwer Academic.

Quantum Tunnelling in Condensed Media. Ed. by Yu A. Kagan & Anthony J. Leggett. LC 92-18968. (Modern Problems in Condensed Matter Sciences Ser.: Vol. 34). xx, 496p. 1992. 310.00 (*0-444-88041-0*, North Holland) Elsevier.

Quantum Uncertainties: Recent & Future Experiments & Interpretations. Ed. by W. M. Honig et al. LC 87-20223. (NATO ASI Series B, Physics: Vol. 162). (Illus.). 496p. 1987. 120.00 (*0-306-42670-6*, Plenum Trade) Perseus Pubng.

Quantum Universe. A. J. Hey & Patrick Walters. (Illus.). 190p. 1987. pap. 34.95 (*0-521-31845-9*) Cambridge U Pr.

Quantum Vacuum: An Introduction to Quantum Electrodynamics. Peter W. Milonni. (Illus.). 522p. 1993. text 88.00 (*0-12-498080-5*) Acad Pr.

Quantum Velocity of Light: The Unification of Quantum & Classical Physics. John A. Mayes. LC 83-61674. (C). 1984. text 35.00 (*0-9611548-0-2*) Quantum Pubns.

Quantum Versus Chaos: Questions Emerging from Mesoscopic Cosmos. Katsuhiro Nakamura. LC 97-13936. (Fundamental Theories of Physics Ser.). 1997. text 107.00 (*0-7923-4557-6*) Kluwer Academic.

Quantum Vortices & Quantum Interference Effects in Circuits of Small Tunnel Junctions. Alexander Van Oudenaarden. (Illus.). 122p. 1998. pap. 39.50 (*90-407-1622-6*, Pub. by Delft U Pr) Coronet Bks.

Quantum Well Detectors. LC 97-15121. 350p. 1997. lib. bdg. 49.00 (*981-02-2872-4*) World Scientific Pub.

Quantum Well Intersubband Transition Physics & Devices: Proceedings of the NATO Advanced Research Workshop, Whistler, Canada, September 7-10, 1993. Ed. by H. C. Liu et al. LC 94-12285. (NATO ASI Series E: Applied Sciences: Vol. 270). 588p. (C). 1994. text 336.00 (*0-7923-2877-9*) Kluwer Academic.

Quantum Well Lasers. Ed. by Peter S. Zory, Jr. (Quantum Electronics Ser.). (Illus.). 504p. 1993. text 94.00 (*0-12-781890-1*) Acad Pr.

Quantum Wells: Physics & Electronics of Two-Dimensional Systems. A. Shik. LC 97-42055. 100p. 1997. pap. 16.00 (*981-02-3279-9*) World Scientific Pub.

***Quantum Wells, Wires & Dots.** Harrison. LC 99-38881. 104p. 2000. text 180.00 (*0-471-98495-7*) Wiley.

Quantum World. J. C. Polkinghorne. LC 84-42953. 112p. 1985. pap. 10.95 (*0-691-02388-3*, Pub. by Princeton U Pr) Cal Prin Full Svc.

Quantum World Unveiled by Electron Waves. 200p. 1998. 26.00 (*981-02-2510-5*); pap. 12.00 (*981-02-2615-2*) World Scientific Pub.

Quantz & His Versuch: Three Studies. Edward R. Reilly. (Studies & Documents: Vol. 5). 180p. 1971. pap. 10.00 (*1-878528-07-6*) Am Musicological.

Quaqtaq: Modernity & Identity in an Inuit Community. Louis-Jacques Dorais. LC 97-160570. (Illus.). 132p. 1997. text 45.00 (*0-8020-4105-1*, E99) U of Toronto Pr.

Quaranic Commentary & Tradition: Studies in Arabic Literary Papyri, Vol. 2. Nabia Abbott. LC 56-5027. (Oriental Institute Publications: No. 76). 1996. lib. bdg. 42.00 (*0-226-62177-4*, OIP76) U Ch Pr.

Quar'anic Concepts of Human Psyche. Ed. by Zafar A. Ansari. (Islamization of Knowledge Ser.: No. 11). 118p. (Orig.). 1992. 12.00 (*969-462-004-X*); pap. 7.00 (*969-462-003-1*) IIIT VA.

Quarante-Cinq. Alexandre Dumas. 12.50 (*0-686-55830-8*) Fr & Eur.

Quarantine. Patricia L. Barnes-Svarney. (Star Trek: No. 3). (YA). 1997. per. 3.99 (*0-671-00733-5*, Star Trek) PB.

Quarantine. Patricia L. Barnes-Svarney. (Star Trek Voyager Starfleet Academy Ser.). 1997. 9.09 (*0-606-13803-X*, Pub. by Turtleback) Demco.

Quarantine. Jim Crace. LC 97-61489. 256p. 1998. 23.00 (*0-374-23962-2*) FS&G.

Quarantine. Jim Crace. LC 98-51205. 256p. 1999. pap. 13.00 (*0-312-19951-1*, Picador USA) St Martin.

Quarantine. Greg Egan. 288p. 1995. mass mkt. 5.99 (*0-06-105423-2*, HarperPrism) HarpC.

Quarantine. Juan Goytisolo. Tr. by Peter Bush. LC 93-29198. (SPA.). 122p. 1994. 19.95 (*1-56478-044-9*) Dalkey Arch.

Quarantine. Josh Webster. 384p. 1988. per. 3.95 (*0-373-97063-3*) Harlequin Bks.

Quarantine. large type ed. Jim Crace. LC 98-12779. (Core Ser.). 308p. 1998. 28.95 (*0-7838-0113-0*, G K Hall & Co) Mac Lib Ref.

***Quarantine, Bk. 4.** J. Oldfield. (J). 1998. mass mkt. 7.95 (*0-340-68172-1*, Pub. by Hodder & Stought Ltd) Trafalgar.

Quarantine! East European Jewish Immigrants & the New York City Epidemics of 1892. Howard Markel. LC 96-43095. (Illus.). 296p. 1997. 29.95 (*0-8018-5512-8*) Johns Hopkins.

Quarantine: The Story of Typhoid Mary. Mercedes Graf. LC 97-90902. 135p. 1998. pap. 11.95 (*0-533-12512-X*) Vantage.

An Asterisk (*) at the beginning of an entry indicates that the title is appearing for the first time.

***Quarantine No. 4: Double Helix.** John Vornholt. (Star Trek: The Next Generation Ser.: Vol. 4). 259p. 1999. per. 6.50 (*0-671-03477-4*, Star Trek) PB.

Quarantine for Seed. 308p. 1993. 25.00 (*92-5-103324-2*, F33242, Pub. by FAO) Bernan Associates.

Quarantine Pests for Europe: Quarentine Pests for Europe & Illustrations of Quarentine Pests, 2 vols. 2nd ed. M. J. Pearce et al. (Illus.). 1660p. 1998. text 265.00 (*0-85199-206-4*) OUP.

Quarantine Pests of Europe. 2nd ed. Ed. by I. M. Smith et al. LC 97-165817. (CAB International Publication). 1432p. 1997. text 225.00 (*0-85199-154-8*) OUP.

Quarantine Reader's Guide. J. Crace. 1997. text. write for info. (*0-374-95783-5*) FS&G.

Quarantine World. Murray Leinster. 272p. 1992. mass mkt. 4.50 (*0-88184-844-1*) Carroll & Graf.

Quarantined. Gerald McCathern. 200p. 1998. 24.95 (*0-9656946-1-5*) Outlaw Bks TX.

Quarantined Culture: Australian Reactions to Modernism, 1913-1939. John Williams. (Studies in Australian History). (Illus.). 296p. (C). 1996. text 64.95 (*0-521-47139-7*) Cambridge U Pr.

Quare Fellow see **Complete Plays**

Quare Fremeurunt Gentes, Notus in Judaea Deus, Exaudiat Te Dominus. Jean-Baptiste Lully. (Collected Works: Vol. 4/5). 1997. lib. bdg. 200.00 (*0-8450-7851-8*) Broude.

Quare Joyce. Ed. by Joseph Valente. (Illus.). 312p. (C). pap. text 19.95 (*0-472-08689-8*, 08689) U of Mich Pr.

Quare Joyce. Ed. by Joseph Valente. LC 97-45415. 312p. (C). 1998. text 44.50 (*0-472-10898-0*, 10898) U of Mich Pr.

Quare Women's Journals: May Stone & Katherine Pettit's Summers in the Kentucky Mountains & the Founding of the Hindman Settlement School. Ed. by Jess Stoddart. LC 97-25374. 1997. 34.95 (*0-945084-67-6*) J Stuart Found.

Quark & Creative Writing. Maureen Gibbons et al. (C). 1990. 25.00 (*0-7316-5784-5*, Pub. by Pascoe Pub) St Mut.

Quark Cluster Dynamics: Proceedings of the 99th WE-Heraeus Seminar, Held at the Physikzentrum Bad Honnef, Germany, 29 June-1 July 1992. Ed. by K. Goeke et al. LC 92-46172. (Lecture Notes in Physics Ser.: Vol. 417). 1993. write for info. (*3-540-56437-3*); 80.95 (*0-387-56437-3*) Spr-Verlag.

Quark Confinement & Liberation: Numerical Results & Theory: Proceedings of the Conference Held at Berkeley, California, May, 1985. Ed. by M. B. Halpern & F. R. Klinkhamer. 260p. 1985. 91.00 (*9971-5-0000-0*) World Scientific Pub.

Quark Confinement & the Hadron Spectrum: Proceeding of the International Conference. G. M. Prosperi & N. Brambilla. 396p. 1995. text 112.00 (*981-02-2085-5*) World Scientific Pub.

Quark Confinement & the Hadron Spectrum II. 400p. 1997. lib. bdg. 68.00 (*981-02-2865-1*) World Scientific Pub.

Quark Confinement Model of Hadrons. G. V. Efimov & M. A. Ivanov. (Illus.). 179p. 1993. 134.00 (*0-7503-0240-2*) IOP Pub.

Quark Design: A Step-by-Step Approach to Page Layout Software. Nancy McCarthy. (Illus.). 144p. (C). 1995. pap. text 34.95 (*0-201-88376-7*) Peachpit Pr.

Quark Gluon Plasma. Ed. by R. C. Hwa. (Advanced Series on Directions in High Energy Physics: Vol. 6). 724p. 1990. text 109.00 (*9971-5-0900-8*); pap. text 61.00 (*9971-5-0901-6*) World Scientific Pub.

Quark-Gluon Plasma: Lectures. Ed. by S. Raha et al. (Research Reports in Physics). (Illus.). 384p. 1991. 53.95 (*0-387-51984-X*) Spr-Verlag.

Quark-Gluon Plasma 2. Ed. by R. C. Hwa. LC 95-37190. 800p. 1995. text 85.00 (*981-02-2399-4*) World Scientific Pub.

Quark Machines: How Europe Fought the Particle Physics War. Gordon Fraser. LC 97-14853. (Illus.). 200p. 1997. pap. 21.00 (*0-7503-0447-2*) IOP Pub.

Quark Matter Formation & Heavy Ion Collisions: Proceedings of the Bielefeld Workshop, May 10-14, 1982. Ed. by M. Jacob & H. Satz. 591p. 1982. 98.00 (*9971-950-46-4*); pap. 41.00 (*9971-950-47-2*) World Scientific Pub.

Quark Model & High Energy Collisions. V. V. Anisovich et al. 450p. 1985. text 51.00 (*9971-966-68-9*) World Scientific Pub.

Quark Prepress: Desktop Production for Graphics Professionals. Robert Virkus. 473p. 1993. pap. 32.95 (*0-471-58635-8*) Wiley.

Quark Structure of Matter. Ed. by Maurice Jacob. 400p. 1992. text 74.00 (*981-02-0962-2*) World Scientific Pub.

Quark Structure of Matter: Proceedings of the Strasbourg-Karlsruhe Conference, September 26-October 1, 1985. Ed. by M. Jacob & K. Winter. 800p. 1986. pap. 60.00 (*9971-5-0076-0*); text 150.00 (*9971-5-0075-2*) World Scientific Pub.

Quark Structure of Matter: Proceedings of the Yukon Advanced Study Institute, Canada, August 1984. Ed. by N. Isgur et al. 372p. 1985. 68.00 (*9971-978-30-X*) World Scientific Pub.

Quark 3.3 Macintosh Goodies Disk. 1994. pap. 10.00 incl. disk (*0-201-48584-2*) Peachpit Pr.

Quark 3.3 Windows Goodies Disk. 1995. pap. 6.00 incl. disk (*0-201-48585-0*) Peachpit Pr.

Quark Victory: The 52nd Street Project, Musical. Willie Reale & Robert Reale. 1995. spiral bd. 25.00 (*0-8222-1447-4*) Dramatists Play.

Quark XPress 4.0: A Step-by-Step Approach. Joanne R. Saliger. 3p. 1999. spiral bd. 29.95 (*0-89582-511-2*) Morton Pub.

Quark XPress in a Nutshell. Donnie O'Quinn. (Illus.). 546p. 1998. pap. 24.95 (*1-56592-399-5*) OReilly & Assocs.

Quarks: A Source Guide. 1991. lib. bdg. 76.00 (*0-8490-4866-4*) Gordon Pr.

Quarks: Frontiers in Elementary Particle Physics. Y. Nambu. 240p. 1985. text 47.00 (*9971-966-65-4*); pap. text 14.00 (*9971-966-66-2*) World Scientific Pub.

Quarks & Colliders: Tenth Lake Louise Winter Institute. LC 96-222485. 552p. 1996. lib. bdg. 69.00 (*981-02-2708-6*) World Scientific Pub.

Quarks & Gluons: A Century of Particle Charges M. Y. Han. LC 98-53246. 250p. 1999. write for info. (*981-02-3745-6*) World Scientific Pub.

***Quarks & Gluons: A Century of Particle Charges.** M Y Han. LC 98-53246. 250p. 1999. 38.00 (*981-02-3704-9*) World Scientific Pub.

Quarks & Leptons. Ed. by C. A. Engelbrecht. (Lecture Notes in Physics Ser.: Vol. 248). x, 417p. 1986. pap. 45.00 (*0-387-16457-X*) Spr-Verlag.

Quarks & Leptons Clo: An Introductory Course in Modern Particle Physics. Francis Halzen & Alan D. Martin. LC 83-16449. 416p. 1984. text 92.95 (*0-471-88741-2*) Wiley.

Quarks & Nuclear Forces. Ed. by D. E. Fries & B. Zeitnitz. (Tracts in Modern Physics Ser.: Vol. 100). (Illus.). 223p. 1982. 53.00 (*0-387-11717-2*) Spr-Verlag.

Quarks & Nuclei. Wolfram Weise. (International Review of Nuclear Physics Ser.: Vol. 1). 716p. 1985. text 98.00 (*9971-966-61-1*); pap. text 52.00 (*9971-966-62-X*) World Scientific Pub.

Quarks & Sparks: The Story of Nuclear Power. J. S. Kidd & Renee A. Kidd. LC 98-44389. (Science & Society Ser.). (Illus.). 144p. (YA). (gr. 7-12). 1999. 19.95 (*0-8160-3587-3*) Facts on File.

Quarks Bound by Chiral Fields: The Quark Structure of the Vacuum & of Light Mesons & Baryons. Georges Ripka. LC 97-15622. (Oxford Studies in Nuclear Physics: No. 21). (Illus.). 222p. 1997. text 105.00 (*0-19-851784-X*) OUP.

Quarks, Chaos, & Christianity: Questions to Science & Religion. John Polkinghorne. LC 95-30120. 120p. 1995. pap. 12.95 (*0-8245-1521-8*) Crossroad NY.

Quarks '88. Ed. by A. N. Tavkhelidze et al. 816p. (C). 1989. text 138.00 (*9971-5-0779-X*) World Scientific Pub.

Quarks, '86: Proceedings of the U. S. S. R. Seminar. Ed. by A. N. Tavkhelidze et al. 526p. 1987. lib. bdg. 150.00 (*90-6764-097-2*, Pub. by VSP) Coronet Bks.

Quarks, Gluons & Hadronic Matter: Proceedings of the International Workshop on Quarks, Gluons & Hadronic Matter. Ed. by R. Viollier. 484p. (C). 1987. text 137.00 (*9971-5-0415-4*) World Scientific Pub.

Quarks, Gluons & Lattices. Michael Creutz. LC 83-2089. (Cambridge Monographs on Mathematical Physics). 176p. 1985. pap. text 29.95 (*0-521-31535-2*) Cambridge U Pr.

Quarks, Lepton & Gauge Fields. K. S. Huang. 292p. 1981. text 51.00 (*9971-950-03-0*) World Scientific Pub.

Quarks, Lepton & Gauge Fields. 2nd ed. K. S. Huang. 400p. (C). 1992. text 78.00 (*981-02-0659-3*); pap. text 44.00 (*981-02-0660-7*) World Scientific Pub.

Quarks, Leptons & the Big Bang. J. Allday. LC 97-49110. 1997. 98.00 (*0-7503-0461-8*) IOP Pub.

Quarks, Leptons & the Big Bang. Jonathan Allday. LC 97-49110. (Illus.). 315p. 1997. pap. 29.50 (*0-7503-0462-6*) IOP Pub.

Quarks, Leptons, & Their Constituents. Ed. by Antonio L. Zichichi. LC 86-22672. (Subnuclear Ser.: Vol. 22). (Illus.). 614p. 1988. 130.00 (*0-306-42401-0*, Plenum Trade) Perseus Pubng.

Quarks, Mesons & Isobars in Nuclei: Proceedings of the Fifth Topical School Motril, Granada, Spain, Sept. 6-11, 1982. Ed. by R. Guardiola & A. Polls. 334p. 1983. 66.00 (*9971-950-49-9*) World Scientific Pub.

Quarks '90: Proceedings of the International Seminar. V. R. Rubakov et al. 572p. 1991. text 151.00 (*981-02-0441-8*) World Scientific Pub.

Quarks '94. D. Yu Grigoriev et al. 700p. 1995. text 124.00 (*981-02-2055-3*) World Scientific Pub.

Quarks '92: Proceedings of the 7th International Seminar. D. Yu Grigoriev et al. 480p. 1993. text 121.00 (*981-02-1425-1*) World Scientific Pub.

Quarks, Quasars, & Quandaries. Ed. by Gordon Aubrecht. (Occasional Publications). 358p. (C). 1987. per. 22.00 (*0-917853-26-1*, OP-56) Am Assn Physics.

Quarks, Strings, Dark Matter & All the Rest: Proceedings of the Vanderbilt High Energy Physics Conference, 7th, Nashville, Tennessee, May 15-17, 1987. Ed. by R. S. Panvini & T. Weiler. 344p. 1987. pap. 40.00 (*9971-5-0278-X*); text 110.00 (*9971-5-0272-0*) World Scientific Pub.

Quarks, Symmetries & Strings. Ed. by Michio Kaku et al. 436p. (C). 1991. pap. 44.00 (*981-02-0527-9*); text 118.00 (*981-02-0526-0*) World Scientific Pub.

QuarkXPress Book for Windows. 2nd ed. David Blatner & Bob Weibel. (Illus.). 708p. (C). 1995. pap. text 29.95 (*1-56609-135-7*) Peachpit Pr.

QuarkXPress for Graphic Designers: Version 3.2/3.3. Suzanne S. Thomas. LC 93-43643. 320p. (C). 1994. mass mkt. 31.00 (*0-8273-6673-6*) Delmar.

QuarkXPress for the Macintosh. Danny Goodman. LC 94-8358. 1994. write for info. (*0-02-801054-X*) Glencoe.

QuarkXPress for Windows Handbook. Barbara Assadi. 600p. 1992. pap. 29.95 (*1-878058-45-2*) IDG Bks.

QuarkXPress for Windows Handbook. Suzanne S. Thomas. LC 93-33975. 294p. (C). 1993. mass mkt. 31.00 (*0-8273-6447-4*) Delmar.

QuarkXpress 4. Bill Harrell. LC 98-34105. 609p. 1998. pap. 49.99 (*1-57610-273-4*) Coriolis Grp.

***Quarkxpress Four: Advanced Electronic Mechanics.** 346p. 1999. spiral bd. 33.33 (*0-13-022966-0*) P-H.

QuarkXPress 4 Book. David Blatner. Ed. by Nancy Davis. LC 98-228953. 964p. (C). 1998. pap. 34.95 (*0-201-69695-9*, Pub. by Peachpit Pr) Addison-Wesley.

QuarkXPress 4 Complete. Kelly Anton & Rochelle Barnhart. 900p. 1999. 45.00 (*1-56830-412-9*) Hayden.

***QuarkXPress 4 for Macintosh: Visual QuickStart Guide.** Elaine Weinmann. LC 98-159578. (Illus.). 376p. (C). 1998. pap. 18.95 (*0-201-69623-1*, Pub. by Peachpit Pr) Addison-Wesley.

QuarkXPress 4 for Windows: Visual QuickStart Guide. Elaine Weinmann. Ed. by Corbin Collins. LC 98-184967. (Illus.). 368p. (C). 1998. pap. text 18.95 (*0-201-69699-1*, Pub. by Peachpit Pr) Addison-Wesley.

QuarkXPress 4 One Step at a Time. Sharyn Venit. (New Tutorial Ser.). (Illus.). 352p. 1999. pap. 29.99 (*0-7645-8034-5*) IDG Bks.

***QuarkXPress 4 Only.** Eike Lumma & Frank J. Romano. LC 98-37889. 1999. pap. 34.99 (*0-13-099770-6*) P-H.

QuarkXPress 4.O for Dummies. Galen Gruman. LC 97-81227. 408p. 1998. pap. 19.99 (*0-7645-0242-5*) IDG Bks.

QuarkXPress 4.04 Made Easy. Nancy Mueller. LC 99-13250. 314p. 1999. 34.95 incl. cd-rom (*1-881795-16-0*) Bellwether-Cross.

***Quarkxpress 4.0: Module 1.** Niit. (CT Course Instructor Training Ser.). 2000. 8.00 (*0-619-02300-7*) Course Tech.

QuarkXPress Production Techniques. Gary Poyssick. (Illus.). 300p. (Orig.). 1997. 35.00 (*1-56830-134-0*) Hayden.

QuarkXpress Studio Skills. Kathryn Binder. 350p. 1997. 35.00 (*1-56830-391-2*) Hayden.

QuarkXPress 3.3: Training on CD. Quay2 Multimedia Staff. 1995. pap. 99.95 incl. cd-rom (*0-201-88408-9*) Peachpit Pr.

QuarkXPress 3.3 by Example. Cynthia Williams. LC 94-34888. 89p. 1994. pap. 26.95 incl. disk (*1-55851-423-6*, M&T Bks) IDG Bks.

QuarkXPress 3.3 for Macintosh: Visual QuickStart Guide. 2nd ed. Elaine Weinmann. (Illus.). 248p. (C). 1995. pap. text 15.95 (*1-56609-128-4*) Peachpit Pr.

QuarkXPress 3.3 Training Combo for Macintosh. Elaine Weinmann. (C). 1996. pap. 69.95 incl. cd-rom (*0-201-88683-9*) Peachpit Pr.

QuarkXPress Tips & Tricks. 2nd ed. David Blatner et al. (Illus.). 456p. 1995. pap. 34.95 incl. cd-rom (*1-56609-137-3*) Peachpit Pr.

QuarkXPress, Version 4. Christopher Lumgair. (Teach Yourself Ser.). 208p. 1999. pap. 10.95 (*0-8442-2628-9*) NTC Contemp Pub Co.

***Quarkxpress 4: Advanced Electronic Mechanicals, Revised Edi.** Against the Clock, Inc. Staff. 346p. 1999. pap. text 33.33 (*0-13-025609-9*, Prentice Hall) P-H.

***Quarrel & Quandary.** Cynthia Ozick. 288p. 2000. 25.00 (*0-375-41061-9*) Knopf.

Quarrel Between Philosophy & Poetry: Studies in Ancient Thought. Stanley Rosen. 256p. 1988. text 29.95 (*0-415-00184-6*) Routledge.

Quarrel Between Philosophy & Poetry: Studies in Ancient Thought. Stanley Rosen. 256p. (C). 1993. pap. 19.99 (*0-415-90745-4*, B0257) Routledge.

Quarrel of Apophis & Seqenenre. Hans Goedicke. (Orig.). 1986. pap. 18.50 (*0-933175-06-X*) Van Siclen Bks.

***Quarrel of Macaulay & Croker: Politics & History in the Age of Reform.** William Thomas. (Illus.). 280p. 2000. text 70.00 (*0-19-820864-2*) OUP.

Quarrel of Reason with Itself: Essays on Hamann, Nietzsche, Lessing, & Michaelis. James C. O'Flaherty. LC 87-70862. (GERM Ser.: Vol. 35). (Illus.). xviii, 260p. 1991. 35.00 (*0-938100-56-4*) Camden Hse.

Quarrel over Future Contingents (Louvain, 1465-1475) Leon Baudry. 468p. (C). 1989. lib. bdg. 245.00 (*0-7923-0454-3*, Pub. by Kluwer Academic) Kluwer Academic.

Quarreling. Gail Hudson. LC 98-220779. (Child's Magazine Guide To... Ser.). 1997. per. 5.99 (*0-671-88040-3*) PB.

Quarreling Book. Charlotte Zolotow. LC 63-14445. (Charlotte Zolotow Bk.). (Illus.). 32p. (J). (gr. k-3). 1963. 13.00 (*0-06-026975-8*) HarpC Child Bks.

Quarreling Book. Charlotte Zolotow. LC 63-14445. (Trophy Picture Bk.). (Illus.). 32p. (J). (ps-3). 1982. pap. 5.95 (*0-06-443034-0*, HarpTrophy) HarpC Child Bks.

Quarrell: Law of Pension Fund Investment. John J. Quarrell. 230p. 1990. boxed set 134.00 (*0-406-67819-7*, MICHIE) LEXIS Pub.

Quarrels That Have S. John A. Garraty. 400p. 1989. pap. 16.00 (*0-06-132084-6*, Perennial) HarperTrade.

Quarries & Quarrying. P. H. Stanier. (Album Ser.). (Illus.). 32p. 1985. pap. text 5.85 (*0-85263-728-4*, Pub. by Shire Pubns) Lubrecht & Cramer.

Quarry. Charles Waddell Chesnutt & Dean McWilliams. LC 98-26422. 1998. 35.00 (*0-691-05995-0*, Pub. by Princeton U Pr) Cal Prin Full Svc.

Quarry. Charles Waddell Chesnutt & Dean McWilliams. LC 98-26422. 1999. pap. 14.95 (*0-691-05996-9*, Pub. by Princeton U Pr) Cal Prin Full Svc.

***Quarry.** Daniel Huws. LC 99-487874. 80p. 1999. pap. 12.00 (*0-571-19711-6*) Faber & Faber.

***Quarry.** Laurie Loveman. LC 99-91220. (Firehouse Family Ser.: Bk. 2). 476p. 1998. 25.00 (*0-7388-0676-5*); pap. 18.00 (*0-7388-0677-3*) Xlibris Corp.

Quarry. Jeffery D. Phillips. 1998. 24.95 (*1-891128-54-X*) Chapel & Croft.

Quarry. Joanna Rawson. LC 98-25468. (Pitt Poetry Ser.). 48p. 1998. pap. 12.95 (*0-8229-5681-0*); text 25.00 (*0-8229-4081-7*) U of Pittsburgh Pr.

Quarry. Mildred Walker. LC 95-16578. xiii, 341p. 1995. pap. 14.00 (*0-8032-9779-3*, Bison Books) U of Nebr Pr.

***Quarry.** Don W. Whipple. 157p. 1999. pap. 9.95 (*1-891929-27-5*) Four Seasons.

Quarry: A Collection in Lieu of Memoirs by Lincoln Kirstein. Lincoln Kirstein. (Illus.). 112p. 1986. 45.00 (*0-942642-27-9*) Twelvetrees Pr.

Quarry: Closing in on the Missing Link. Noel T. Boaz. 268p. 1993. 24.95 (*0-02-904501-0*) Free Pr.

Quarry: Stories by Harvey Grossinger. Harvey Grossinger. LC 96-30803. 1997. 24.95 (*0-8203-1896-5*) U of Ga Pr.

Quarry Farm: A Study of the "Picturesque" Lorraine W. Lanmon. (Quarry Farm Papers: No. 3). 36p. 1991. pap. 5.00 (*1-880817-03-9*) EC Ctr Mark T Stu.

Quarry Wood. Nan Shepherd. (Classics Ser.). 213p. 1996. pap. 9.95 (*0-86241-141-6*, Pub. by Canongate Books) Interlink Pub.

Quarry's Contract. large type ed. Robin Hunter. 483p. 1989. 11.50 (*0-7089-1976-6*) Ulverscroft.

Quart Livre. Francois Rabelais. (FRE.). 256p. 1990. pap. 10.95 (*0-7859-1425-0*, 2080702408) Fr & Eur.

Quart Livre. Ed. by Albert Seay. (Transcriptions Ser.: No. 6). v, 48p. 1981. 4.00 (*0-933894-09-0*) Colo Coll Music.

Quart Livre: Des Faicts et Dicts Heroiques du Bon Pantagruel. Francois Rabelais. Ed. by Michael J. Heath. (FRE.). 309p. 1990. pap. 6.95 (*1-870725-06-9*, PR2, Pub. by Runnymede) Pegasus Pr.

Quartaer Deutschlands: Hrsg. im Auftrag der Deutschen Quartaervereinigung von L. Benda. Und den Geologischen Diensten der Bundesrepublik Deutschland zum 14. Kongress der Internationalen Quartaervereinigung (INQUA), Berlin 1995. xxii, 408p. 1995. 47.00 (*3-443-01031-8*, Pub. by Gebruder Borntraeger) Balogh.

Quartenary Science Reviews, Vol. 3. Ed. by D. Q. Bowen. (Illus.). 328p. 1985. pap. 105.00 (*0-08-032760-5*, Pub. by PPL) Elsevier.

Quarter-Acre of Heartache. Claude C. Smith. LC 85-28097. (Illus.). 186p. 1985. 12.95 (*0-936015-01-2*); pap. 8.95 (*0-936015-00-4*) Pocahontas Pr.

Quarter Century in Lawrence County, Indiana, 1917-1941. James M. Guthrie. (Author's Second History of Lawrence County Ser.). (Illus.). 430p. 1984. text 40.00 (*0-685-48509-9*) J M Guthrie.

Quarter Century in Lawrence County, Indiana, 1917-1941. James M. Guthrie. LC 84-8009. (Illus.). 432p. 1984. 40.00 (*0-318-03788-2*) J M Guthrie.

Quarter Century of Fuzzy Systems. G. J. Klir. 208p. 1990. text 358.00 (*2-88124-452-1*) Gordon & Breach.

Quarter Century of Learning, 1904-1929. Columbia University Staff. LC 68-58780. (Essay Index Reprint Ser.). 1977. 23.95 (*0-8369-1028-1*) Ayer.

Quarter-Century of Social Work Education. Ed. by Miriam Dinerman & Ludwig L. Geismar. LC 84-6951. 272p. reprint ed. pap. 84.40 (*0-7837-6540-1*, 204567700007) Bks Demand.

Quarter Century of the Black Experience in Elementary & Secondary Education, 1950-1975. J. Rupert Picott. (YA). 1990. 9.95 (*0-87498-087-9*) Assoc Pubs DC.

Quarter Century of UNIX. Peter H. Salus. (Illus.). 272p. (C). 1994. pap. text 29.95 (*0-201-54777-5*) Addison-Wesley.

Quarter Century of Visiting Fellowships at the American Antiquarian Society, 1972-97. Ellen S. Dunlap et al. (Illus.). 56p. 1998. pap. 9.50 (*0-944026-89-3*) Am Antiquarian.

Quarter from the Tooth Fairy. Caren Holtzman. LC 95-13232. (Hello Math Reader Ser.: Level 3). (Illus.). 32p. (J). (ps-3). 1995. pap. 2.95 (*0-590-26598-9*, Cartwheel) Scholastic Inc.

Quarter from the Tooth Fairy. Caren Holtzman. (Hello Math Reader Ser.). (J). 1995. 8.15 (*0-606-08048-1*, Pub. by Turtleback) Demco.

Quarter Horse see **Learning about Horses Series**

Quarter Horse. (Learning about Horses Ser.). (Illus.). 48p. (J). (gr. 3-7). 1995. lib. bdg. 19.00 (*0-516-35242-3*) Childrens.

Quarter Horse. Bonnie Bryant. (Saddle Club Ser.: No. 82). 144p. (J). (gr. 4-7). 1998. pap. 3.99 (*0-553-48632-2*, Skylark BDD) BDD Bks Young Read.

Quarter Horse. Ann Hyland. 140p. 1990. 52.00 (*0-85131-505-4*, Pub. by J A Allen) Trafalgar.

Quarter Horse Spirit. Betsy S. Siino. LC 97-32169. (Spirit of the Horse Ser.). (Illus.). 64p. 1998. pap. 16.95 (*1-889540-17-X*) Bowtie Press.

Quarter Horses see **Great American Horses**

Quarter Horses. Lynn Stone. LC 98-25097. (Horses Ser.). (J). 1998. 55.01 (*0-86593-514-9*) Rourke Corp.

Quarter Horses: A Story of Two Centuries. Robert M. Denhardt. LC 67-15580. (Illus.). 1991. pap. 15.95 (*0-8061-2285-4*) U of Okla Pr.

Quarter-Mile Link: History & Reflection of Shady Oaks & the Rock Valley Community. Illus. by Helen Degner. vii, 120p. (Orig.). 1996. pap. 20.00 (*0-9652976-0-8*) M Gift.

Quarter Notes: Improvisations & Interviews. Charles Wright. LC 95-19281. 192p. (C). 1995. pap. 13.95 (*0-472-06604-8*, 06604) U of Mich Pr.

Quarter Notes: Improvisations & Interviews. Charles Wright. LC 95-19281. 192p. (C). 1995. text 39.50 (*0-472-09604-4*, 09604) U of Mich Pr.

Quarter of a Millennium: The Library Company of Philadelphia, 1731-1981. Ed. by Edwin Wolf & Marie E. Korey. LC 81-80392. (Illus.). viii, 355p. (Orig.). 1981. pap. 25.00 (*0-914076-81-7*) Lib Co Phila.

Quarter-Pie Window. Marianne Brandis. 204p. 1985. pap. write for info. (*0-88984-085-7*) Porcup Quill.

Quarter Race in Kentucky & Other Sketches Illustrative of Scenes, Characters & Incidents Throughout the Universal Yankee Nation. Ed. by William T. Porter. LC 78-174281. reprint ed. 32.50 (*0-404-05088-3*) AMS Pr.

Quarter Sessions Records for Family Historians. (C). 1987. 45.00 (*0-7855-2053-8*, Pub. by Birmingham Midland Soc) St Mut.

Quarter Sessions Records for Family Historians: A Select List. 4th ed. J. S. W. Gibson. 40p. 1995. pap. 7.50 (*0-8063-1568-7*) Genealog Pub.

Quarter Story see **Math Set A**

Quarter Turn. Debra Nystrom. LC 90-26317. 65p. 1991. text 14.95 (*1-878818-02-3*, Pub. by Sheep Meadow); pap. text 12.95 (*1-878818-00-7*, Pub. by Sheep Meadow) U Pr of New Eng.

Quarterback. Edward M. Eveland. Ed. by Gwen Costa. LC 91-15104. 190p. 1992. 13.95 (*0-87949-339-9*) Ashley Bks.

Quarterback. Terry Shea. (Illus.). 88p. (Orig.). 1980. pap. 12.95 (*0-89279-060-1*) Championship Bks & Vid Prodns.

Quarterback Exchange: I Was John Elway. Gordon Korman. LC 97-71801. (Monday Night Football Club Ser.: No. 1). 96p. (J). (gr. 3-7). 1997. pap. 3.95 (*0-7868-1236-2*, Pub. by Hyprn Ppbks) Little.

Quarterback Sneak. S. S. Gorman. Ed. by Pat MacDonald. (High-Fives Ser.). 144p. (J). (gr. 4-6). 1991. per. 2.99 (*0-671-70383-8*, Minstrel Bks) PB.

Quarterback Walk-On. Thomas J. Dygard. 1989. 10.09 (*0-606-02293-7*, Pub. by Turtleback) Demco.

Quarterback Who Almost Wasn't. Jorge Prieto. LC 93-29314. 128p. 1994. pap. 9.95 (*1-55885-109-7*) Arte Publico.

***Quarterback Your Investment Plan: The Basics for Beginners.** Eamonn A. Nohilly. 300p. 2001. pap. 19.95 (*0-9676249-9-1*) Personal Finance.

***Quarterbacks! 18 of Football's Greatest.** Sullivan. LC 97-34167. 60p. (YA). (gr. 5 up). 1998. 18.00 (*0-689-81334-1*) S&S Childrens.

(Quarter)backs-to-(Running)backs: The NFL's Finest Passers & Rushers. Richard Deitsch. Ed. by Cathrine Wolf. 32p. (J). (gr. 4-6). 1998. pap. 3.95 (*1-886749-45-0*) SI For Kids.

Quarterblack: Shattering the NFL Myth. Doug Williams & Bruce Hunter. (Illus.). 209p. 1990. 18.95 (*0-929387-47-3*) Bonus Books.

Quarterdeck & Bridge: Two Centuries of American Naval Leaders. Ed. by James C. Bradford. LC 96-43106. (Illus.). 480p. 1996. 22.95 (*1-55750-073-8*) Naval Inst Pr.

Quarterdeck & Bridge: Two Centuries of American Naval Leaders. Ed. by James C. Bradford. LC 96-43106. (Illus.). 480p. 1996. pap. 22.95 (*1-55750-096-7*) Naval Inst Pr.

Quarterdecks & Spanish Grants. Raymond C. Clar. (Illus.). 156p. 1984. pap. 30.00 (*0-910845-23-9*, 909) Landmark Ent.

Quartered in Hell: The Story of the American North Russia Expeditionary Force 1918-1919. Dennis Gordon. LC 81-71127. (Illus.). 320p. (Orig.). (C). 1982. pap. 19.50 (*0-942258-00-2*) Gos Inc.

Quartered Sea. Tanya Huff. 416p. 1999. mass mkt. 6.99 (*0-88677-839-5*, Pub. by DAW Bks) Penguin Putnam.

***Quartering Deer.** Creative Publishing International Staff. (Hunter's Pocket Guides Ser.). (Illus.). 2000. pap. 4.99 (*0-86573-477-1*) Creat Pub Intl.

QuarterKeeper Map. write for info. (*0-9677571-0-X*) GUPI.

Quarterly, No. 32. Gutter Press Staff. 1996. pap. text 10.00 (*1-896356-04-4*, Pub. by Gutter Pr) Dist Art Pubs.

Quarterly, No. 33. Gutter Press Staff. 1996. pap. text 10.00 (*1-896356-08-7*, Pub. by Gutter Pr) Dist Art Pubs.

Quarterly Coal Report. Government Printing Office Staff. pap. text 28.00 (*0-16-012608-8*) USGPO.

Quarterly Concerns: Human Behavior & Education. CBS Staff. (C). 1995. 84.00 (*0-15-503120-1*, Pub. by Harcourt Coll Pubs) Harcourt.

Quarterly Financial Report for Manufacturing, Mining & Trade Corporations. Government Printing Office Staff. per. 34.00 (*0-16-010054-2*) USGPO.

Quarterly Musical Magazine & Review, 1818-1828, 2 vols., Vols. 1 & 2. Ed. by H. Robert Cohen. (Repertoire International de la Presse Musicale Ser.). 1989. 240.00 (*0-8357-0807-1*) Univ Microfilms.

Quarterly National Accounts: Sources & Methods. 178p. 1996. 54.00 (*92-64-14899-X*, 90-96-05-1, Pub. by Org for Econ) OECD.

Quarterly Preview of Literature Poetry Book Series: 50th Anniversary Anthology, Vols. XXXVII-XXXVIII. Philip Dacey et al. 1999. 40.00 (*1-888545-43-7*) Quarterly Rev.

Quarterly Review of Literature: Poetry Books, 5 vols. in 1. Lynne Knight et al. (Contemporary Poetry Ser.: Vol. XXXV). (Illus.). 344p. Date not set. 20.00 (*1-888545-00-3*) Quarterly Rev.

Quarterly Review of Literature: The 1940s, Poetry. Austin et al. (Poetry Ser.: Vol. III, No. 2). 1940. pap. 15.00 (*1-888545-18-6*) Quarterly Rev.

Quarterly Review of Literature: The 1940s, Special Issue. Paul Valery. (Poetry Ser.: Vol. III, No. 3). 1940. pap. 10.00 (*1-888545-17-8*) Quarterly Rev.

Quarterly Review of Literature: The 1940s, Special Issue, Vol. IV, No. 2. M. Moore. 1940. pap. 50.00 (*1-888545-19-4*) Quarterly Rev.

Quarterly Review of Literature: The 1940s, Special Issue, Vol. V, No. 2. Ezra Pound. 1940. pap. 10.00 (*1-888545-20-8*) Quarterly Rev.

Quarterly Review of Literature: The 1950s, Homestead Called Damascus, Vol. IX, No. 2. Kenneth Rexroth. 1950. pap. 10.00 (*1-888545-23-2*) Quarterly Rev.

Quarterly Review of Literature: The 1950s, Poetry, Vol. IX, No. 4. Char et al. 1950. pap. 10.00 (*1-888545-24-0*) Quarterly Rev.

Quarterly Review of Literature: The 1950s, Special British Writers Issue, Vol. VI, No. 2. 1950. pap. 15.00 (*1-888545-21-6*) Quarterly Rev.

Quarterly Review of Literature: The 1950s, Special Issue, Vol. VIII, No. 1. Giacomo Leopardi. 1950. pap. 10.00 (*1-888545-22-4*) Quarterly Rev.

Quarterly Review of Literature: The 1960s, Essay of Indirect Criticism, Vol. XII, No. 4. Jean Cocteau. 1960. pap. 5.00 (*1-888545-29-1*) Quarterly Rev.

Quarterly Review of Literature: The 1960s, Poetry, Vol. XV, Nos. 1-2. Brock et al. 1960. pap. 15.00 (*1-888545-32-1*) Quarterly Rev.

Quarterly Review of Literature: The 1960s, Poetry, 20th Anniversary Double Issue, Vol. Vol. XIII, Nos. 1-2. Walt Whitman et al. 1960. pap. 15.00 (*1-888545-30-5*) Quarterly Rev.

Quarterly Review of Literature: The 1960s, Prose, Vol. XIV, Nos. 3-4. Peter Weiss et al. 1960. pap. 10.00 (*1-888545-31-3*) Quarterly Rev.

Quarterly Review of Literature: The 1960s, Prose, Vol. XV, Nos. 3-4. Jorge Luis Borges et al. 1960. pap. 10.00 (*1-888545-33-X*) Quarterly Rev.

Quarterly Review of Literature: The 1960s, Prose (Including Play by D. Finkel), Vol. XII, Nos. 1-2, 3. D. Finkel et al. 1960. pap. 30.00 (*1-888545-28-3*) Quarterly Rev.

Quarterly Review of Literature: The 1960s, Special Issue, Vol. X, Nos. 1-2. Friedrich Holderlin. 1980. pap. 10.00 (*1-888545-25-9*) Quarterly Rev.

Quarterly Review of Literature: The 1960s, Special Issue, Vol. XI, No. 4. Osip Mandelshtam. 1960. pap. 35.00 (*1-888545-26-7*) Quarterly Rev.

Quarterly Review of Literature: The 1970s, Poetry, Vol. XVI, Nos. 1-2. Yehuda Amichai et al. 1970. pap. 35.00 (*1-888545-11-9*) Quarterly Rev.

Quarterly Review of Literature: The 1970s, Poetry, Vol. XVII, Nos. 1-2. Carl Rakosi et al. 1970. pap. 15.00 (*1-888545-13-5*) Quarterly Rev.

Quarterly Review of Literature: The 1970s Poetry, Vol. XVIII, Nos. 1-2. C. P. Cavafy et al. 1970. pap. 10.00 (*1-888545-15-1*) Quarterly Rev.

Quarterly Review of Literature: The 1970s, Prose, Vol. XVI, Nos. 3-4. Walt Whitman et al. 1970. pap. 10.00 (*1-888545-12-7*) Quarterly Rev.

Quarterly Review of Literature: The 1970s, Prose, Vol. XVII, Nos. 3-4. Erle Stanley Gardner et al. 1970. pap. 10.00 (*1-888545-14-3*) Quarterly Rev.

Quarterly Review of Literature: The 1970s, Prose, Vol. XVIII, Nos. 3-4. Osip Mandelshtam et al. 1970. pap. 15.00 (*1-888545-16-X*) Quarterly Rev.

Quarterly Review of Literature Vol. I, No. 4: The 1940s, Poetry & Prose - Stefan George, O. Williams, Gurrigue, J. G. Fletcher, Brock, Heilman, & Weiss. 1949. pap. 15.00 (*1-888545-34-8*) Quarterly Rev.

Quarterly Review of Literature Vol. II, No. 4: The 1940s, Poetry & Prose - Cummings, Taggard, Moore, J. T. Farrel, Kazin, Williams, Mizenes, & Snell. 1940. pap. 10.00 (*1-888545-35-6*) Quarterly Rev.

Quarterly Review of Literature Vol. IV, Nos. 3 & 4: The 1940s, Poetry & Prose - Cummings, Sitwell, Kock, Putchen, Austin, Flaubert, & Rexroth. 1940. pap. 20.00 (*1-888545-36-4*) Quarterly Rev.

Quarterly Review of Literature Vol. V, Nos. 1, 3 & 4: The 1940s, Poetry & Prose - Watkins, Simon, Cavalcanti, Eberhart, Gongora, Merrill, Shapiro, Villa, Wilbur, Bellit, Goodman, W. C. Williams, & Zukofsky. 1940. pap. 30.00 (*1-888545-37-2*) Quarterly Rev.

Quarterly Review of Literature Vol. VI, Nos. 1, 3 & 4: The 1950s, Poetry & Prose - Carruth, Duncan, Gregor, Herbert, Lattimore, Lorca, Merwin, Martial, Schubert, Triem, Fiedler, Garrigue, Lizen, & Orlovitz. 1950. pap. 30.00 (*1-888545-38-0*) Quarterly Rev.

Quarterly Review of Literature Vol. VII, Nos. 1, 2 & 4: The 1950s, Poetry & Prose - Cassanueva, Cummings, Ford, Golffing, Heath-Stubbs, Holmes, Mayhall, Norse, Olson, Seferis, Elliott, Humphrey, & Nakajimn. 1950. pap. 30.00 (*1-888545-39-9*) Quarterly Rev.

Quarterly Review of Literature Vol. VIII, No. 2: The 1950s, Poetry & Prose - Ashbery, Lattimore, Hughes, Kessler, Fitts, Levin, Wright, Zukofsky, Garrique, Summers, & J. Merrill (Play) 1950. pap. 10.00 (*1-888545-40-2*) Quarterly Rev.

Quarterly Review of Literature Vol. X, Nos. 3 & 4: The 1960s, Poetry & Prose - Cummings, Nathan, Dickey, Merrill, Seferis, Rudnik, Snodgrass, Sonnars, Daniels, Ellison, & Klabund. 1960. pap. 20.00 (*1-888545-41-0*) Quarterly Rev.

Quarterly Review of Literature Vol. XI, Nos. 1, 2-3: The 1960s, Poetry (Including Gregory's "Ovid" & Jarrell's "Faust") - Andrade, Fargue, Gregory, Hugo, Levertov, Jarrell, Vliet, Wright, Beye, Muvil, Goodman Play - Holly Beye Plays. 1960. pap. 40.00 (*1-888545-27-5*) Quarterly Rev.

Quarterly Review of Literature Vol. XIII, Nos. 3 & 4: The 1960s, Fiction, (Includes Lattimore's "Homer"), 20th Anniversary Double Issue - H. D., Ellison, Humphrey, Brooke-Rose, Eich, Gardien, Leviant, Oates, & Lattimore - Holly Beye Play. 1960. pap. 10.00 (*1-888545-42-9*) Quarterly Rev.

Quarterly Review of Literature Poetry Book Series Vol. XXXVII-XXXVIII. James Richardson et al. 287p. 1999. 20.00 (*1-888545-44-5*) Quarterly Rev.

Quartermaster Books of George Rogers Clark's Fort Jefferson, 1780-81: An Inventory of Quartermaster Activities in the Western Department in Support of George Rogers Clark's Illinois Battalion. Ed. by Kenneth C. Carstens. LC 91-57966. (Studies in Social History: No. 12). 1993. 49.50 (*0-404-61612-7*) AMS Pr.

Quartermaster Professional Bulletin. Government Printing Office Staff. 1991. pap. 12.00 (*0-16-033578-7*) USGPO.

Quartermaster Rangers. L. J. Bolar. 1992. 13.95 (*0-533-08931-X*) Vantage.

Quaternary Borocarbide Superconductors & Hg-Based High Tc Superconductors Vol. 26: Studies of High Temperature Superconductors. Ed. by Anant Narlikar. (Advances in Research & Applications Ser.). 279p. 1998. 97.00 (*1-56072-628-8*) Nova Sci Pubs.

Quaternary Coastlines & Marine Archaeology: Towards the Prehistory of Land Bridges & Continental Shelves. P. M. Masters. Ed. by N. C. Fleming. LC 82-45021. 1983. text 139.95 (*0-12-479250-2*) Acad Pr.

Quarternary Coasts of the United States: Marine & Lacustrine Systems. Ed. by Charles H. Fletcher, III & John Wehmiller. (Special Publications: Vol. 48). (Illus.). 460p. 1992. 106.00 (*0-918985-98-6*) SEPM.

Quarternary Environment in Hungary: Contribution of the Hungarian National Committee to the XIIIth Inqua Congress, Beijing, China, August 1991. F. Schweitzer & Marton Pecsi. 103p. (C). 1991. 55.00 (*963-05-6080-1*, Pub. by Akade Kiado) St Mut.

Quarternary History of the Sangamon River Drainage System, Central Illinois. James A. Miller. (Reports of Investigations: No.27). (Illus.). 36p. 1973. pap. 2.00 (*0-89792-051-1*) Ill St Museum.

Quarternary Shells Collected by the Fifth Thule Expedition, 1921-24. Dan Laursen. LC 76-21342. (Thule Expedition, 5th, 1921-1924 Ser.: Vol. 1, No. 7). (Illus.). reprint ed. 37.50 (*0-404-58307-5*) AMS Pr.

Quarters & Dimes & Nickels & Pennies. Baila Olidort. LC 98-20559. (Illus.). 24p. (J). 1993. reprint ed. 12.00 (*0-8266-0358-0*, Merkos LInyonei Chinuch) Kehot Pubn Soc.

***Quarters of Iowa.** Louis Thomas Jones. 1999. reprint ed. pap. 27.50 (*0-7884-1283-3*, J559) Heritage Bk.

Quarter's Worth of Blessings. J. Brendonly Cunningham. 160p. (Orig.). 1994. pap. write for info. (*0-9628295-3-6*) Blue Hse NY.

Quartet. 1994. 35.97 (*1-57251-026-9*) TWI.

Quartet. Angela Ball. LC 94-70464. (Poetry Ser.). 72p. 1995. pap. 11.95 (*0-88748-189-2*) Carnegie-Mellon.

Quartet. Hobart Bell. (C). 1988. pap. 6.00 (*0-9620060-0-9*) Atelier Pr.

Quartet. Jean Rhys. 192p. 1997. pap. 11.00 (*0-393-31546-0*) Norton.

Quartet. Rubindranath Tagore. (Asian Writers Ser.). 96p. 1994. pap. 9.95 (*0-435-95086-X*, 95086) Heinemann.

Quartet in Autumn. Barbara Pym. 1992. pap. 12.95 (*0-452-26934-2*, Plume) Dutton Plume.

***Quartet in Autumn.** Barbara Pym. LC 99-87259. 218p. 2000. pap. 11.95 (*1-55921-278-0*) Moyer Bell.

Quartet in Heaven. Sheila Kaye-Smith. LC 75-136649. (Biography Index Reprint Ser.). 1977. 20.95 (*0-8369-8044-1*) Ayer.

Quartet of Joy. Muhammad A. Matar. Tr. by Ferial J. Ghazoul & John Verlenden from ARA. LC 97-26841. 1998. pap. 10.00 (*1-55728-488-1*) U of Ark Pr.

Quartet of Joy. Muhammad A. Matar et al. Tr. by Ferial J. Ghazoul & John Verlenden from ARA. LC 97-26841. 1998. 16.00 (*1-55728-487-3*) U of Ark Pr.

Quartet of Poems. Walker . 1993. pap. text. write for info. (*0-582-08299-4*, Pub. by Addison-Wesley) Longman.

Quartet of Stories. Maya Angelou. 1993. pap. text. write for info. (*0-582-08298-6*, Pub. by Addison-Wesley) Longman.

Quartet Recorder, 2 bks., Bk. 1. Gerald Burakoff & Willy Strickland. 1975. 4.00 (*0-913334-21-9*, CM1025) Consort Music.

Quartet Recorder, 2 bks., Bk. 2. Gerald Burakoff & Willy Strickland. 1976. 4.00 (*0-913334-33-2*, CM1031) Consort Music.

Quartet Recorder, 2 bks., Bks. 1-2. Gerald Burakoff & Willy Strickland. 1975. 4.00 (*0-685-74377-2*) Consort Music.

Quartets. Toby Lurie. LC 90-32741. (Poetry Ser.: Vol. 8). 84p. 1990. lib. bdg. 24.95 (*0-88946-883-4*) E Mellen.

Quartettsatz. Ned Condini. LC 96-418808. (VIA Folios Ser.: Vol. 7). 51p. (C). 1996. pap. 7.00 (*1-884419-06-2*) Bordighera.

Quartic Surfaces with Singular Points. Charles M. Jessop. LC 17-11584. 236p. reprint ed. pap. 67.30 (*0-608-11669-6*, 2051691) Bks Demand.

Quartier Perdu. Patrick Modiano. (FRE.). 1988. pap. 10.95 (*0-7859-2916-9*) Fr & Eur.

Quartier Perdu. Patrick Modiano. (Folio Ser.: No. 1942). (FRE.). pap. 8.95 (*2-07-037942-6*) Schoenhof.

Quartz & Mica. Yolande Villemaire. 52p. 1987. pap. 5.00 (*0-919349-92-7*) Guernica Editions.

***Quartz Cementation in Sandstones.** R. Worden & S. Morad. LC 99-32636. (International Association of Sedimentologists Special Publication Ser.: No. 29). (Illus.). 2000. pap. 110.00 (*0-632-05482-4*) Blackwell Sci.

Quartz Crystals: Gems of Poetry. 1969. 13.50 (*0-912314-04-4*) Academy Santa Clara.

Quartzite Building Stone Industry of the Raft River & Grouse Creek Mountains, Box Elder County, Utah. Bryce T. Tripp. LC TN24.U8A315. (Special Study of the Utah Geological Survey Ser.: Vol. 84). (Illus.). 19p. 1994. pap. 5.00 (*1-55791-203-3*, SS-84) Utah Geological Survey.

Quasar Absorption Lines: Probing The Universe. Ed. by C. Blades et al. (Space Telescope Science Institute Symposium Ser.). 360p. 1988. text 69.95 (*0-521-34561-8*) Cambridge U Pr.

Quasar Astronomy. Daniel W. Weedman. (Cambridge Astrophysics Ser.: No. 9). 232p. 1988. pap. text 27.95 (*0-521-35674-1*) Cambridge U Pr.

Quasar Hosts: Proceedings of the ESO-IAC Conference Held in Tenerife, Spain, 24-27 September 1996. Ed. by David L. Clements & Ismael Perez-Fournon. LC 97-39144. (ESO Astrophysics Symposia, European Southern Observatory Ser.). xvii, 336p. 1997. 29.95 (*3-540-63793-1*) Spr-Verlag.

Quasars. Ed. by G. Swarup & V. K. Kapahi. 1986. lib. bdg. 212.00 (*90-277-2297-8*) Kluwer Academic.

Quasars & Active Galactic Nuclei: An Introduction. Ajit K. Kembhavi & Jayant V. Narlikar. LC 97-28655. (Illus.). 480p. (C). 1998. text 80.00 (*0-521-47477-9*); pap. text 34.95 (*0-521-47989-4*) Cambridge U Pr.

***Quasars & Cosmology, Vol. 162.** Ed. by Gary Ferland & Jack Baldwin. (Conference Series Proceedings: Vol. 162). 490p. (C). 1999. text 52.00 (*1-886733-83-X*) Astron Soc Pacific.

Quasars, Redshifts & Controversies. Halton C. Arp. LC 87-80290. (Illus.). 208p. 1987. 19.95 (*0-941325-00-8*) Interstellar Media.

Quasi-Conservative Systems: Cycles, Resonances & Chaos. LC 98-3919. (Nonlinear Science Ser.). 300p. 1997. lib. bdg. 49.00 (*981-02-2810-4*) World Scientific Pub.

Quasi-Eigenkapital Im Kapitalmarkt- und Unternehmensrecht: Ein Deutsch-Amerikanischer Vergleich und Beitrag Zum Internationalen Wirtschaftsrecht. Harald Herrmann. 330p. 1996. write for info. (*3-11-015205-3*) De Gruyter.

Quasi Erotic Poems. Owen Hill. Ed. by Edward Mycue. (Took Modern Poetry in English Ser.: No. 7). (Illus.). 28p. (Orig.). 1993. pap. 3.00 (*0-9625855-9-9*) Norton Coker Pr.

Quasi-Exactly Solvable Models in Quantum Mechanics. A. G. Ushveridze. (Illus.). 480p. 1994. 227.00 (*0-7503-0266-6*) IOP Pub.

Quasi-Experimental Approaches: Testing Theory & Evaluating Policy. Ed. by James A. Caporaso & Leslie L. Roos, Jr. LC 72-96703. 388p. (C). reprint ed. 120.30 (*0-8357-9467-9*, 201146800078) Bks Demand.

Quasi-Experimentation, 2 vols. Cook. (C). Date not set. pap. write for info. (*0-395-61556-9*) HM.

Quasi-Experimentation, 001. Thomas H. Cook & Donald T. Campbell. (C). 1979. pap. 58.76 (*0-395-30790-2*) HM.

Quasi-Fiscal Operations of Public Financial Institutions, Vol. 144. LC 96-36350. (Occasional Paper Ser.: No. 142). 1996. pap. 15.00 (*1-55775-583-3*) Intl Monetary.

Quasi-Ideals in Rings & Semigroups. O. Steinfeld. (Disquisitiones Mathematicae Hungaricae Ser.: No. 10). 154p. (C). 1978. 44.00 (*963-05-1696-9*, Pub. by Akade Kiado) St Mut.

Quasi-Likelihood & Its Application: A General Approach to Optimal Parameter Estimation. C. C. Heyde. LC 97-11168. (Springer Series in Statistics). 240p. 1997. 54.95 (*0-387-98225-6*) Spr-Verlag.

Quasi-Morticide: Self-Destructive Behavior: Reversing the Cycle in the African-American Community. Catherine Smallwood & Gayle Shields. 64p. 1997. pap. 18.00 (*0-8059-4119-3*) Dorrance.

Quasi-Periodic Motions in Families of Dynamical Systems: Order Amidst Chaos, Vol. XI. H. W. Broer et al. LC 96-39689. (Lecture Notes in Mathematics Ser.: Vol. 1645). 195p. 1996. pap. 43.00 (*3-540-62025-7*) Spr-Verlag.

Quasi-Projective Moduli for Polarized Manifolds. 3rd ed. Eckart Viehweg. LC 95-15903. (Ergebnisse der Mathematik und Ihrer Greuzgebiete: Bd. 30). 325p. 1995. 129.95 (*3-540-59255-5*) Spr-Verlag.

Quasi-Rational Economics. Richard Thaler. LC 91-9797. (Illus.). 416p. 1991. 49.95 (*0-87154-846-1*) Russell Sage.

Quasi Rational Economics. Richard H. Thaler. (Illus.). 416p. 1994. reprint ed. pap. 19.95 (*0-87154-847-X*) Russell Sage.

Quasi-Reorganizations: A Survey of Quasi-Reorganizations Disclosed in Corporate Annual Reports to Shareholders. fac. ed. Hal G. Clark & Leonard Lorensen. LC 89-17656. (Financial Report Survey Ser.: No. 39). 179p. 1989. pap. 55.50 (*0-7837-8229-2*, 204798900009) Bks Demand.

Quasi-Symmetric Designs. Mohan S. Shrikhande & Sharad S. Sane. (London Mathematical Society Lecture Note Ser.: No. 164). (Illus.). 241p. (C). 1991. pap. text 34.95 (*0-521-41407-5*) Cambridge U Pr.

Quasi una Fantasia: Essays on Modern Music. 2nd ed. Theodor W. Adorno. 1998. pap. 20.00 (*1-85984-159-7*, Pub. by Verso) Norton.

Quasi-Uniform Spaces. Peter Fletcher. (Lecture Notes in Pure & Applied Mathematics Ser.: Vol. 77). (Illus.). 232p. 1982. pap. text 135.00 (*0-8247-1839-9*) Dekker.

Quasiclassical Methods. Ed. by J. Rauch et al. LC 97-26430. (IMA Volumes in Mathematics & Its Applications Ser.: No. 95). (Illus.). 243p. 1997. 54.95 (*0-387-98310-4*) Spr-Verlag.

Quasiconformal Mappings & Analysis: A Collection of Papers Honoring F. W. Gehring. Frederick W. Gehring & Peter L. Duren. LC 97-26432. 392p. 1997. write for info. (*0-387-98299-X*) Spr-Verlag.

Quasiconformal Mappings & Sobolev Spaces. V. M. Gol'dshtein & Reshetnyak. (C). 1990. text 268.50 (*0-7923-0543-4*) Kluwer Academic.

Quasiconformal Space Mappings: A Collection of Surveys, 1960-1990. Ed. by Matti Vuorinen. LC 92-12192. (Lecture Notes in Mathematics Ser.: Vol. 1508). ix, 148p. 1992. 37.95 (*0-387-55418-1*) Spr-Verlag.

***Quasiconformal Teichmuller Theory.** Frederick P. Gardiner & Nikola Lakic. LC 99-45788. (Mathematical Surveys & Monographs: Vol. 76). 372p. 2000. 89.00 (*0-8218-1983-6*) Am Math.

Quasiconvex Optimization & Location Theory. Joaquim Gromicho. LC 97-31691. (Applied Optimization Ser.: No. 9). 240p. 1997. 109.00 (*0-7923-4694-7*, D Reidel) Kluwer Academic.

Quasicrystalline Materials: Proceedings of the Ill - Codest Workshop. Christian Janot. 448p. 1988. text 108.00 (*9971-5-0631-9*) World Scientific Pub.

***Quasicrystals.** Ed. by Esther Belin-Ferre et al. 600p. 2000. 118.00 (*981-02-4281-6*) World Scientific Pub.

Quasicrystals. Ed. by M. V. Jaric & S. Lunqvist. 480p. (C). 1990. text 130.00 (*981-02-0054-4*) World Scientific Pub.

Quasicrystals. Ed. by K. H. Kuo. (Materials Science Forum Ser.: Vols 22/24). 660p. 1987. text 203.00 (*0-87849-559-2*, Pub. by Trans T Pub) Enfield Pubs NH.

An Asterisk (*) at the beginning of an entry indicates that the title is appearing for the first time.

***Quasicrystals, Vol. 553.** Ed. by Jean M. DuBois et al. LC 99-13855. (Symposium Proceedings Ser.). 524p. 1999. 88.00 (*1-55899-459-9*) Materials Res.

Quasicrystals: A Primer. 2nd ed. C. Janot. (Monographs on the Physics & Chemistry of Materials: No. 50). (Illus.). 426p. 1997. pap. text 55.00 (*0-19-856551-8*) OUP.

Quasicrystals: A Primer. 2nd ed. Christian Janot. (Monographs on the Physics & Chemistry of Materials: No. 50). (Illus.). 432p. 1995. text 95.00 (*0-19-851778-5*) OUP.

Quasicrystals: An Introduction to Structure, Physical Properties, & Application of Quasicrysta. J. B. Suck. 1998. 69.95 (*3-540-64224-2*) Spr-Verlag.

Quasicrystals: China-Japan Seminars on, Tokyo, Japan, 29 October-1 November 1989, Beijing, China, 6-9 November 1990. Ed. by K. H. Kuo & T. Ninomiya. 432p. (C). 1991. text 118.00 (*981-02-0646-1*) World Scientific Pub.

Quasicrystals: Microscopic Models of Nonperiodic Structures. Jacek Miekisz. (Notes in Mathematical & Theoretical Physics, Series A: Vol. 5). 106p. (Orig.). 1993. pap. 36.50 (*90-6186-573-5*, Pub. by Leuven Univ) Coronet Bks.

Quasicrystals: Proceedings of the 12th Taniguchi Symposium, Shima, Mie Prefecture, Japan, November 14-19, 1989. Ed. by T. Fujiwara et al. (Solid-State Sciences Ser.: Vol. 93). (Illus.). 256p. 1990. 64.95 (*0-387-52900-4*) Spr-Verlag.

Quasicrystals: Proceedings of the 5th International Conference, Avignon, France 22- 26 May 1995. Ed. by Christian Janot. LC 96-137365. 1000p. 1995. text 162.00 (*981-02-2418-4*, PdCPcS-P2894) World Scientific Pub.

Quasicrystals: Proceedings of the 6th International Conference (Yamada Conference XLVII) Tokyo, Japan 26-30 May, 1997. Ed. by Takeo Fujiwara & Shin Takeuchi. 720p. 1998. 48.00 (*981-02-3343-4*) World Scientific Pub.

Quasicrystals: The State of the Art. Ed. by P. Steinhardt & D. Di Vincenzo. (Series on Directions in Condensed Matter Physics: Vol. 11). 300p. (C). 1991. pap. 28.00 (*981-02-0523-6*); text 89.00 (*981-02-0522-8*) World Scientific Pub.

***Quasicrystals: The State of the Art.** 2nd ed. Paul J. Steinhardt. (Directions in Condensed Matter Ser.). 2001. pap. 55.00 (*981-02-4156-9*) World Scientific Pub.

Quasicrystals & Discrete Geometry. Ed. by Jiri Patera. LC 98-4530. (Fields Institute Monographs: Vol. 10). 289p. 1998. 79.00 (*0-8218-0682-3*, FIM/10) Am Math.

Quasicrystals & Geometry. Marjorie Senechal. (Illus.). 302p. (C). 1995. text 74.95 (*0-521-37259-3*) Cambridge U Pr.

Quasicrystals & Geometry. Marjorie Senechal. 302p. 1996. pap. text 30.95 (*0-521-57541-9*) Cambridge U Pr.

Quasicrystals & Imperfectly Ordered Crystals. Ed. by K. H. Kuo & S. Takeuchi. (Materials Science Forum Ser.: Vols. 150-1). (Illus.). 510p. (C). 1994. text 183.00 (*0-87849-673-4*, Pub. by Trans T Pub) Enfield Pubs NH.

Quasicrystals & Incommensurate Structures in Condensed Matter: Third International Quasicrystal Conference. E. Gomes et al. 592p. 1990. text 151.00 (*981-02-0001-3*) World Scientific Pub.

Quasicrystals, Networks & Molecules of Fivefold Symmetry. Ed. by Istvan Hargittai. 314p. 1990. 149.00 (*0-471-18738-0*) Wiley.

Quasicrystals, Networks & Molecules of Fivefold Symmetry. Ed. by Istvan Hargittai. 314p. 1990. 90.00 (*0-89573-723-X*, Wiley-VCH) Wiley.

Quasidifferentiability & Nonsmooth Modelling in Mechanics, Engineering & Economics. V. F. Demianov. LC 96-21725. 1996. lib. bdg. 169.00 (*0-7923-4093-0*, D Reidel) Kluwer Academic.

***Quasidifferentiability & Related Topics.** V. F. Dem'kilanov & Aleksandr Moiseevich Rubinov. LC 00-38938. (Nonconvex Optimization & Its Applications Ser.). 2000. write for info. (*0-7923-6284-5*, Kluwer Plenum) Kluwer Academic.

Quasidifferential Calculus. V. F. Dem'yanov & A. M. Rubinov. Ed. by A. V. Balakrishnan. LC 86-5422. (Translations Series in Mathematics & Engineering). 301p. (Orig.). 1986. text 92.00 (*0-911575-35-9*) Optimization Soft.

Quasielastic Neutron Scattering: Principles & Applications in Solid State Chemistry, Biology & Materials Science. Marc J. Bee. (Illus.). 452p. 1988. 229.00 (*0-85274-371-8*) IOP Pub.

Quasielastic Neutron Scattering: Proceeding of the Conference. J. Colmenero. 324p. 1994. text 121.00 (*981-02-1604-1*) World Scientific Pub.

***Quasielastic Neutron Scattering & Solid State Diffusion.** Rolf Hempelmann. (Oxford Series on Neutron Scattering in Condensed Matter: 13). (Illus.). 384p. 2000. text 160.00 (*0-19-851743-2*) OUP.

Quasilinear Degenerate & Nonuniformly Elliptic & Parabolic Equations of Second Order. A. Ivanov. LC 84-12386. (Proceedings of the Steklov Institute of Mathematics Ser.: Vol. 160). 288p. 1984. pap. 102.00 (*0-8218-3080-5*, STEKLO/160) Am Math.

Quasilinear Elliptic Equations with Degenerations & Singularities. Pavel Drabek et al. LC 97-17293. (Series in Nonlinear Analysis & Applications). 219p. 1997. text 98.95 (*3-11-015490-0*) De Gruyter.

Quasilinear Hyperbolic Systems & Dissipation Mechanism. L. Hsiao. LC 97-28760. 230p. 1997. text 36.00 (*981-02-3205-5*) World Scientific Pub.

Quasilinearization & the Identification Problem. Richard Ernest Bellman & R. S. Roth. (Series in Modern Applied Mathematics: Vol. 2). 260p. 1983. text 48.00 (*9971-950-44-8*); pap. text 26.00 (*9971-950-45-6*) World Scientific Pub.

Quasimolecular Modelling. Donald Greenspan. 250p. (C). 1991. text 40.00 (*981-02-0719-0*) World Scientific Pub.

Quasioptical Systems. Chapman & Hall Staff. text 124.00 (*0-412-83940-7*) Chapman & Hall.

Quasioptical Systems: Gaussian Beam Quasioptical Propagation & Applications. Paul F. Goldsmith & IEEE Microwave Theory & Techniques Society Staff. LC 97-39614. 432p. 1997. 99.95 (*0-7803-3439-6*, PC 3079) Inst Electrical.

Quasiparticle Theory of Defects in Solids. Ed. by D. I. Pushkarov. 200p. (C). 1991. text 36.00 (*981-02-0180-X*) World Scientific Pub.

Quasiregular Mappings. Seppo Rickman. LC 93-4824. (Ergebnisse der Mathematik und Ihrer Grenzgebiete Ser.: Vol. 3). 1993. 118.95 (*0-387-56648-1*) Spr-Verlag.

***Quasispecies & RNA Virus Evolution: Principles & Consequences.** Esteban Domingo & John J. Holland. (Molecular Biology Intelligence Unit Ser.). 233p. 2000. 99.00 (*1-58706-010-8*, Pub. by Eurekah) Landes Bioscience.

Quatations from Women on Life Book/Journal Set. (C). 1998. pap. 12.48 (*0-13-095255-9*) P-H.

Quaternary & Environmental Research on East African Mountains. Ed. by W. C. Mahaney. 400p. (C). 1989. text 136.00 (*90-6191-794-8*, Pub. by A A Balkema) Ashgate Pub Co.

Quaternary Climates, Environments & Magnetism. Ed. by Barbara Maher & Roy Thompson. LC 99-11967. (Illus.). 335p. (C). 1999. 115.00 (*0-521-62417-7*) Cambridge U Pr.

Quaternary Codes. Z. X. Wan. LC 97-29178. (Series on Applied Mathematics). 256p. 1997. 42.00 (*981-02-3274-8*) World Scientific Pub.

Quaternary Deserts & Climatic Change: Proceedings of an International Conference, Al Ain, 9-11 December 1995. Ed. by A. S. Alsharhan et al. LC 99-496401. (Illus.). 636p. (C). 1998. text 104.00 (*90-5410-597-6*, Pub. by A A Balkema) Ashgate Pub Co.

Quaternary Environmental Chang. Robert L. Metcalf. pap. text 65.00 (*0-471-98551-1*) Wiley.

Quaternary Environments. M. A. Williams et al. (Illus.). 352p. 1994. pap. text 29.95 (*0-7131-6590-1*, A6118, Pub. by E A) Routldge.

Quaternary Environments. 2nd ed. Martin Williams et al. LC 98-28792. (Illus.). 352p. (Orig.). 1998. pap. text 45.00 (*0-340-69151-4*, Pub. by E A) OUP.

Quaternary Environments: The Eastern Canadian Arctic, Baffin Bay & West Greenland. J. T. Andrews. (Illus.). 750p. (C). 1985. text 115.00 (*0-04-551094-6*) Routledge.

Quaternary Evolution & Biogeography of the Large South American Canidae (Mammalia, Carnivora) Annalisa Berta. LC 88-23378. (University of California Publications in Geological Sciences: No. 132). 174p. 1988. pap. 54.00 (*0-7837-7472-9*, 204919400010) Bks Demand.

Quaternary Evolution of Playa Lakes on the Southern High Plains: A Case Study from the Amarillo Area, Texas. S. D. Hovorka. (Reports of Investigations: No. 236). (Illus.). 52p. (Orig.). 1996. pap. 7.50 (*0-614-11614-7*) Bur Econ Geology.

Quaternary Extinctions: A Prehistoric Revolution. Ed. by Paul S. Martin & Richard G. Klein. LC 83-18053. 892p. 1989. reprint ed. pap. text 44.00 (*0-8165-1100-4*) U of Ariz Pr.

Quaternary Faults, Folds & Selected Volcanic Features in the Cedar City 1x2-Degree Quadrangle, Utah. Gary E. Christenson. (Miscellaneous Publication Ser.: Vol. 89-6). (Illus.). 29p. 1989. pap. 5.00 (*1-55791-306-4*, MP-89-6) Utah Geological Survey.

Quaternary Geologic Map of the Old River Bed & Vicinity, Millard, Juab, & Tooele Counties, Utah. Charles G. Oviatt et al. (Map of the Utah Geological Survey Ser.: Vol. 161). (Illus.). 24p. 1994. pap. 6.00 (*1-55791-563-6*, M-161) Utah Geological Survey.

Quaternary Geology see Proceedings of the 30th International Geological Congress

Quaternary Geology & Environment in China. Ed. by Liu Tungsheng. 504p. 1996. 30.00 (*7-03-002538-5*, Pub. by Sci Pr) Lubrecht & Cramer.

Quaternary Geology & Geomorphology: Proceedings of the 27th International Geological Congress, Vol. 3. International Geological Congress Staff. 262p. 1984. lib. bdg. 92.50 (*90-6764-012-3*, Pub. by VSP) Coronet Bks.

Quaternary Geology & Geomorphology of South America. C. M. Clapperton. LC 93-5243. 796p. 1993. 241.00 (*0-444-88247-2*) Elsevier.

Quaternary Geology & Neotectonics of the West Flank of the Northern Sangre de Cristo Mountains, South-Central Colorado. James P. McCalpin. Ed. by Jon W. Raese & J. H. Goldberg. LC 82-17899. (Colorado School of Mines Quarterly Ser.: Vol. 77, No. 3). 97p. 1983. pap. text 12.00 (*0-686-82132-7*) Colo Sch Mines.

Quaternary Geology & Permafrost along the Richardson & Glenn Highways Between Fairbanks & Anchorage, Alaska. Ed. by Pewe. (IGC Field Trip Guidebooks Ser.). 64p. 1989. 21.00 (*0-87590-603-6*, T102) Am Geophysical.

Quaternary Geology for Scientists & Engineers. John A. Catt. 312p. 1988. text 73.95 (*0-470-21135-0*) P-H.

Quaternary Geology of Canada & Greenland, Vol. 1. Ed. by R. J. Fulton. (Geology of Canada Ser.: No. 1). (Illus.). 850p. 1990. pap. 91.00 (*0-660-13114-5*, GNC-K1, Pub. by Canadian Govt Pub) Accents Pubns.

Quaternary Geology of Fish Springs Flat, Juab County, Utah. Charles G. Oviatt. LC TN24.U8 A322. (Special Study Ser.: Vol. 77). (Illus.). 16p. 1991. pap. 6.00 (*1-55791-196-7*, SS-77) Utah Geological Survey.

Quaternary Geology of Lake Zurich: An Interdisciplinary Investigation by Deep-Lake Drilling. Ed. by K. J. Hsue & K. R. Kelts. (Contributions to Sedimentology Ser.: No. 13). (Illus.). v, 210p. 1984. pap. 50.00 (*3-510-57013-8*, Pub. by E Schweizerbartsche) Balogh.

Quaternary Geology of Part of the Sevier Desert, Millard County, Utah. Charles G. Oviatt. LC TN24.U8A322. (Special Study Ser.: Vol. 70). (Illus.). 41p. 1989. pap. 7.50 (*1-55791-189-4*, SS-70) Utah Geological Survey.

Quaternary Geology of the Black Rock Desert, Millard County, Utah. Charles G. Oviatt. LC TN24.U8 A322. (Special Study Ser.: Vol. 73). (Illus.). 23p. 1991. pap. 6.00 (*1-55791-192-4*, SS-73) Utah Geological Survey.

Quaternary Geology of the Great Basin. Ed. by Smith. (IGC Field Trip Guidebooks Ser.). 80p. 1989. 21.00 (*0-87590-651-6*, T117) Am Geophysical.

Quaternary Geology of the Lower Mississippi Valley. Roger T. Saucier. (Illus.). 28p. 1974. pap. 6.50 (*1-56349-007-2*, RS06) AR Archaeol.

Quaternary Geology of the Scipio Valley Area, Millard & Juab Counties, Utah. Charles G. Oviatt. LC TN24.U8 A322. (Special Study Ser.: Vol. 79). (Illus.). 16p. 1992. pap. 6.00 (*1-55791-198-3*, SS-79) Utah Geological Survey.

Quaternary Glaciations in the Northern Hemisphere: IGCP Project 24. Ed. by V. Sibrava et al. (Quaternary Science Reviews Ser.: No. 5). (Illus.). 522p. 1987. 142.00 (*0-08-034299-X*, Pergamon Pr) Elsevier.

Quaternary History of Ireland. Ed. by Kevin J. Edwards & William P. Warren. 1985. text 149.00 (*0-12-232730-6*) Acad Pr.

Quaternary History of Scandinavia. Joakim Donner. (World & Regional Geology Ser.: No. 7). (Illus.). 210p. (C). 1995. text 115.00 (*0-521-41730-9*) Cambridge U Pr.

Quaternary History of the Irish Sea. Ed. by Clarence Kidson. LC 78-309177. (Geological Journal Special Issues Ser.: No. 7). 368p. reprint ed. pap. 114.10 (*0-608-14536-X*, 202480200038) Bks Demand.

Quaternary Insects & Their Environments. Scott A. Elias. LC 93-18570. (Illus.). 256p. (C). 1994. text 45.00 (*1-56098-303-5*) Smithsonian.

Quaternary Landscapes. Ed. by Linda C. Shane & Edward J. Cushing. (Illus.). 272p. (C). 1991. text 32.95 (*0-8166-1943-3*) U of Minn Pr.

Quaternary Nonglacial Geology: Conterminous U. S. Ed. by R. B. Morrison. (DNAG, Geology of North America Ser.: Vol. K2). 670p. 1991. 42.50 (*0-8137-5215-9*) Geol Soc.

Quaternary of Scotland. J. M. Gray & C. K. Ballantyne. (Quaternary Science Reviews Ser.: Vol. 3). 181p. 1985. 31.50 (*0-08-032718-4*, Pergamon Pr) Elsevier.

Quaternary of South America & Antarctic Peninsula. Ed. by Jorge Rabassa & Monica Salemme. (Illus.). 332p. (C). 1997. text 76.00 (*90-5410-664-6*, Pub. by A A Balkema) Ashgate Pub Co.

Quaternary of South America & Antarctic Peninsula, Vol. 1. Ed. by Jorge Rabassa. 166p. (C). 1982. text 76.00 (*90-6191-513-9*, Pub. by A A Balkema) Ashgate Pub Co.

Quaternary of South America & Antarctic Peninsula, Vol. 2. Ed. by Jorge Rabassa. 224p. 1984. text 91.00 (*90-6191-542-2*, Pub. by A A Balkema) Ashgate Pub Co.

Quaternary of South America & Antarctic Peninsula, Vol. 6. Ed. by Jorge Rabassa. 318p. (C). 1990. text 76.00 (*90-6191-995-9*, Pub. by A A Balkema) Ashgate Pub Co.

Quaternary of South America & Antarctic Peninsula, Vol. 7. Ed. by Jorge Rabassa. 384p. (C). 1990. text 76.00 (*90-6191-784-0*, Pub. by A A Balkema) Ashgate Pub Co.

Quaternary of South America & Antarctic Peninsula, Vol. 9. Ed. by Jorge Rabassa. (Illus.). 225p. (C). 1995. text 70.00 (*90-5410-615-8*, Pub. by A A Balkema) Ashgate Pub Co.

Quaternary of South America & Antarctic Peninsula, Vol. 11. Ed. by Jorge Rabassa & Monica Salemme. 328p. (C). 1998. text 76.00 (*90-5410-453-8*, Pub. by A A Balkema) Ashgate Pub Co.

Quaternary of South America & Antarctic Peninsula: With Selected Papers of the International Symposium on Late Quaternary Sea-Level Changes & Coastal Evolution, Mar del Plata, 30 Sept. - 3 October 1984, Vol. 3. Ed. by Jorge Rabassa. 232p. (C). 1986. text 76.00 (*90-6191-591-0*, Pub. by A A Balkema) Ashgate Pub Co.

Quaternary of South America & Antarctic Peninsula: With Selected Papers of the International Symposium on Sea-Level Changes Quaternary Shorelines, Sao Paulo, 7-14 July 1986, Vol. 4. Ed. by Jorge Rabassa. 344p. 1987. text 76.00 (*90-6191-732-8*, Pub. by A A Balkema) Ashgate Pub Co.

Quaternary of South America & Antarctic Peninsula: With Selected Papers of the XIIth INQUA Congress, Ottawa, 1987 on the Quaternary of South America, Vol. 5. Ed. by Jorge Rabassa. 250p. (C). 1987. text 76.00 (*90-6191-733-6*, Pub. by A A Balkema) Ashgate Pub Co.

Quaternary of South America & Antarctic Peninsula Vol. 8: With Selected Papers of the International Symposium on Quarterrary Climates of South America, International Geological Correlation Program UNESCO, Project 281, Medellin, Colombia, 3-6 May 1990. Ed. by Jorge Rabassa & Monica Salemme. (Illus.). 224p. 1993. text 76.00 (*90-5410-140-7*, Pub. by A A Balkema) Ashgate Pub Co.

***Quaternary of South America & Antarctic Peninsula, 1996-1997 Vol. 12: Special Volume: Quaternary Vertebrate Palaeontology in Southern South America.** Ed. by Jorge Rabassa & Monica Salemme. (Illus.). 320p. 1999. text 76.00 (*90-5410-479-1*) A A Balkema.

Quaternary of South-West England. S. Campbell & Joint Nature Conservation Committee (Great Britain) Staff. LC 97-78418. (The Geological Conservation Review Ser.). 1998. write for info. (*0-412-83220-8*, Chap & Hall NY) Chapman & Hall.

Quaternary of the Karakoram & Himalya. Ed. by Edward D. Derbyshire & L. A. Owen. (Annals of Geomorphology Ser.: Suppl. 76). (Illus.). 255p. 1989. pap. text 107.50 (*3-443-21076-7*, Pub. by Gebruder Borntraeger) Balogh.

Quaternary Paleoclimatology: Methods of Paleoclimatic Reconstruction. Raymond S. Bradley. (Illus.). (C). 1985. text 90.00 (*0-04-551067-9*); pap. text 39.95 (*0-04-551068-7*) Routledge.

Quaternary Period in Saudi Arabia, Sedimentological, Hydrogeological, Hydrochemical, Geochronological, & Climatological Investigations in Western Saudi Arabia, Vol. 2. Ed. by A. R. Jado & J. G. Zotl. (Illus.). 420p. 1984. 126.95 (*0-387-81749-2*) Spr-Verlag.

Quaternary Period in Saudi Arabia One. Ed. by S. S. Al-Sayari & J. G. Zoetl. (Illus.). 1978. 75.00 (*0-387-81448-5*) Spr-Verlag.

Quaternary Quadratic Forms: Computer Generated Tables. G. L. Nipp. vii, 155p. 1991. 79.95 (*0-387-97601-9*) Spr-Verlag.

Quaternary Science Reviews, Vol. 1. Ed. by D. Q. Bowen. (Illus.). 340p. 1984. 92.00 (*0-08-031491-0*, Pergamon Pr) Elsevier.

Quaternary Science Reviews, Vol. 2. Ed. by D. Q. Bowen. (Illus.). 328p. 1984. 105.00 (*0-08-031736-7*, Pergamon Pr) Elsevier.

Quaternary Sedimentation in South Florida. Paul Enos & Ronald D. Perkins. LC 76-44123. (Geological Society of America Ser.: Vol. 147). (Illus.). 334p. 1977. reprint ed. pap. 103.60 (*0-608-07704-6*, 206779400010) Bks Demand.

Quaternary Sediments: Petrographic Methods for the Study of Unlithified Rocks. Stephen J. Gale & Peter G. Hoare. LC 91-11477. 332p. 1993. 150.00 (*0-471-94605-2*) Wiley.

Quaternary Sediments Patrographic Methods for the Study of Unlithified Rocks. S. J. Gale. 323p. 1992. pap. 325.00 (*81-7089-160-4*, Pub. by Intl Bk Distr) St Mut.

Quaternary Stratigraphy of Asia & the Pacific IGCP 296: China, Malaysia, Indonesia, Sri Lanka, Thailand, Republic of Korea, Australia & New Zealand. (Mineral Resources Development Ser.: No. 60). 114p. 35.00 (*92-1-119583-7*, E.91.II.F.16) UN.

Quaternary Stratigraphy of Asia & the Pacific IGCP 296 (ESCAP Atlas of Stratigraphy XII) (Mineral Resources Development Ser.: No. 62). 104p. 35.00 (*92-1-119620-5*, E.93.II.F.15) UN.

Quaternary Stratigraphy of Asia & the Pacific IGCP 296 (1990) China, Hong Kong, Lao PDR, Malaysia, Indonesia, Thailand, Viet Nam & Australia. (Mineral Resources Developement Ser.: No. 61). 64p. 25.00 (*92-1-119586-1*, E.91.II.F.17) UN.

Quaternary Tectonics of Utah with Emphasis on Earthquake-Hazard Characterization. Suzanne Hecker. (Bulletin of the Utah Geological Survey Ser.: No. 127). (Illus.). 157p. (Orig.). 1993. pap. 16.00 (*1-55791-094-4*, B-127) Utah Geological Survey.

Quaternary Type Sections: Imagination or Reality?: Proceedings of the INQUA-Subcommission on European Quaternary Stratigraphy Symposium, Zurich, 14-15 October 1985. Ed. by J. Rose & C. Schluchter. 216p. 1989. 110.00 (*90-6191-734-4*, Pub. by A A Balkema) Ashgate Pub Co.

Quaternionic Analysis & Elliptic Boundary Value Problem. K. Gurlebeck & W. Sprassig. (International Series of Numerical Mathematics: No. 89). 256p. 1990. 83.00 (*0-8176-2382-5*) Birkhauser.

Quaternionic & Clifford Calculus for Physicists & Engineers. 2nd ed. Gurlebeck. LC 98-169958. 384p. 1998. 74.95 (*0-471-96200-7*) Wiley.

Quaternionic Quantum Mechanics & Quantum Fields. Stephen L. Adler. (International Series of Monographs on Physics). 608p. 1995. text 95.00 (*0-19-506643-X*) OUP.

Quaternions & Cayley Numbers: Algebra & Applications. LC 97-8144. 237p. 1997. text 130.50 (*0-7923-4513-4*) Kluwer Academic.

Quaternions & Rotation Sequences. J. B. Kuipers. LC 98-35389. 384p. 1998. text 49.50 (*0-691-05872-5*, Pub. by Princeton U Pr) Cal Prin Full Svc.

Quatrain. Karen Tellefsen. LC 97-211732. (Illus.). 32p. (Orig.). 1997. pap. 3.00 (*1-888431-12-1*) ASGP.

Quatrains. Exantus. (Illus.). 144p. 1997. pap. 12.50 (*0-9660521-0-2*) Green Leaf Pub.

***Quatrains.** Moranwali. 2000. 12.50 (*81-202-0542-1*, Pub. by Ajanta Pubns) S Asia.

***Quatrains: Poems from Hollywood.** Mark Dunster. 11p. 1999. pap. 5.00 (*0-89642-984-9*) Linden Pubs.

Quatrains of Khalilullah Khalili. Khalilullah Khalili & Alauddin H. Aljubouri. 86p. 1981. 30.00 (*0-900860-84-7*, Pub. by Octagon Pr) ISHK.

Quatrains of Nesimi Fourteenth-Century Turkic Hurufi. Kathleen R. Burrill. (Publications in Near & Middle East Studies: Ser. A, No. 14). 1972. 138.50 (*90-279-2328-0*) Mouton.

Quatre Contes. Denis Diderot. 212p. 1964. 8.95 (*0-686-56026-4*) Fr & Eur.

Quatre Etudes Anglaises. Andre Maurois. pap. 17.95 (*0-685-36956-0*) Fr & Eur.

Quatre Evangiles, 3 pts. Emile Zola. Incl. Fecondite. 7.50 Travail. 7.50 Verite. 7.50 write for info. (*0-318-52234-9*) Fr & Eur.

Quatre Filles du Docteur March. Louisa May Alcott. (Folio - Junior Ser.: No. 413). (FRE., Illus.). (J). (gr. 5-10). 1993. 10.95 (*2-07-033413-9*) Schoenhof.

Quatre Jours de Liberte. Sylvie Desrosiers. (Novels in the Roman Plus Ser.). (FRE., Illus.). 160p. (YA). (gr. 8 up). 1989. pap. 7.95 (*2-89021-108-8*, Pub. by La Courte Ech) Firefly Bks Ltd.

Quatre Lettres au Sujet de Nietzsche. Paul Valery. 6.95 (*0-685-36623-5*) Fr & Eur.

Q

An Asterisk (*) at the beginning of an entry indicates that the title is appearing for the first time.

Quatre Saisons. Pierre De Ronsard. (Poesie Ser.). (FRE.). 320p. 1985. pap. 11.95 (*2-07-032308-0*) Schoenhof.
Quatre Saisons de Ronsard. Pierre De Ronsard. (FRE.). 1985. pap. 16.95 (*0-7859-2797-2*) Fr & Eur.
Quatre-Vingt-Treize. Victor Hugo. (Coll. GF). pap. 4.50 (*0-685-34920-9*) Fr & Eur.
Quatre-Vingt-Treize. Victor Hugo. Ed. by Boudout. 1965. write for info. (*0-318-63584-4*) Fr & Eur.
Quatre-Vingt-Treize. Victor Hugo. Ed. by Boudout. (Folio Ser.: No. 1093). 1965. pap. 12.95 (*2-07-037093-3*) Schoenhof.
Quatre Vingt-Treize. unabridged ed. Hugo. (FRE.). pap. 7.95 (*2-87714-131-4*, Pub. by Bookking Intl) Distribks Inc.
Quatrefoil of Love. (EETS, OS Ser.: No. 195). 1935. reprint ed. pap. 30.00 (*0-527-00195-3*) Periodicals Srv.
Quatremere de Quincy & the Invention of a Modern Language of Architecture. Sylvia Lavin. (Illus.). 352p. 1992. 55.00 (*0-262-12166-2*) MIT Pr.
***Quatremere de Quincy's Historical Dictionary of Architecture.** Samir Younes. 256p. 1999. 55.00 (*1-901092-17-8*) Andreas Papadakis.
Quatres Verites. Marcel Ayme. 1954. pap. 14.95 (*0-7859-0370-4*, F84040) Fr & Eur.
Quatrevingt-Treize. Victor Hugo. 1999. pap. 12.95 (*2-266-08306-6*) Midwest European Pubns.
Quatrieme Siecle. Edouard Glissant. (Imaginaire Ser.). (FRE.). 296p. 1990. pap. 17.95 (*2-07-071962-6*) Schoenhof.
Quat'Saisons. Antoine Blondin. (FRE.). 212p. 1977. pap. 10.95 (*0-7859-1860-4*, 2070369730) Fr & Eur.
Quattlebaum Family History. M. M. Quattlebaum. 280p. 1994. reprint ed. pap. 48.50 (*0-8328-4079-3*); reprint ed. lib. bdg. 58.50 (*0-8328-4078-5*) Higginson Bk Co.
Quattro. Don Cassel. 122p. (C). 1993. pap. 9.33 (*0-13-013665-4*) P-H.
Quattro: A Ready Reference Manual. Catherine Garrison & Mercedes McGowen. (Illus.). 128p. (C). 1989. pap. text 12.95 (*0-201-19712-X*) Addison-Wesley.
Quattro: Quality Approach in Tendering Urban Public Transport Operations. European Commission. LC 98-234490. 229p. 1998. write for info. (*92-828-5009-9*) Comm Europ Commun.
Quattro Antichi Conservatorii Musicali di Napoli, 2 vols., Nos. MDXLIII-MDCCC. Salvatore Di Giacomo. (Illus.). 616p. reprint ed. write for info. (*0-318-71585-6*) G Olms Pubs.
Quattro 5 Wind. Told to Smith. Date not set. pap. text, teacher ed. write for info. (*0-314-04937-1*) West Pub.
Quattro for the Professional. Elna R. Tymes. (Illus.). 256p. 1988. 28.95 (*0-8306-1078-2*, 3078); pap. 19.95 (*0-8306-9378-5*) McGraw-Hill Prof.
Quattro Pro. Don Cassel. 122p. (C). 1993. pap. 9.33 (*0-13-013673-5*) P-H.
Quattro Pro. James E. Potter. Ed. by Alfred J. Garrotto. (FasTrak Jr. Ser.). 21p. 1993. spiral bd. 6.00 (*0-9632069-7-4*) Bridge Lrn Systs.
Quattro Pro: A Software Tool for Engineers. Dolores M. Etter. LC 93-6522. (C). 1993. pap. text 22.95 incl. disk (*0-8053-1780-5*) Benjamin-Cummings.
Quattro Pro: Concepts & Applications. Craig. (C). 1992. 35.25 (*0-538-70723-2*); 35.25 (*0-538-70724-0*) Thomson Learn.
Quattro Pro: Concepts & Applications. Dale Craig. LC 92-29442. (C). 1992. mass mkt. 27.95 (*0-538-70720-8*) S-W Pub.
Quattro Pro: Everything You Need to Know: A Friendly, Easy-to-Follow Guide from Basic Spreadsheet Design to Intermediate Techniques. Michael Hyde. LC 92-8453. (Illus.). 240p. (Orig.). 1992. pap. 19.95 (*1-55958-208-1*) Prima Pub.
Quattro Pro 5 for Windows. DDC Publishing Staff. 1993. spiral bd. 12.00 (*1-56243-137-4*, OQPW5) DDC Pub.
Quattro Pro 5 for Windows. Gary B. Shelly et al. LC 94-30617. (Shelly Cashman Ser.). (Illus.). 208p. (C). 1994. mass mkt. 22.95 (*0-87709-384-9*) Course Tech.
Quattro Pro 5 Made Easy. Deborah Craig. 512p. 1993. pap. 24.95 (*0-07-881963-6*) McGraw.
Quattro Pro 5.O. Shelly Cashman. (C). 1994. text. write for info. (*0-318-70363-7*) S-W Pub.
Quattro Pro 5.O for DOS. Timothy J. O'Leary & Linda I. O'Leary. (C). 1994. pap. text 11.50 (*0-07-049047-3*) McGraw.
Quattro Pro 5.O for Windows. Sarah E. Hutchinson et al. 184p. (C). 1994. text 12.50 (*0-256-16470-3*, Irwn McGrw-H) McGrw-H Hghr Educ.
Quattro Pro 5.O for Windows. Rick Sullivan. (Computer Training Ser.). 144p. (C). pap. 17.95 (*0-538-64153-3*) S-W Pub.
Quattro Pro 5.O for Windows at a Glance. Eugene W. Teglovic. (At a Glance Ser.). 128p. (Orig.). 1994. pap. 15.95 (*1-55622-413-3*) Wordware Pub.
Quattro Pro 5.0 for Engineers: Toolkit. Delores M. Etter. (Illus.). 128p. 1995. pap. text 21.33 (*0-8053-6521-4*) Benjamin-Cummings.
Quattro Pro for DOS for Dummies. John Walkenbach. (Illus.). 350p. 1993. pap. 16.95 (*1-56884-023-3*) IDG Bks.
Quattro Pro for Windows. Steven Cobb. 1993. pap. 27.95 (*0-07-881964-4*) McGraw.
Quattro Pro for Windows. Fritz H. Grupe. 128p. (C). 1992. text 13.77 (*0-697-20983-0*, Irwn McGrw-H) McGrw-H Hghr Educ.
Quattro Pro for Windows Inside & Out. Stephen Cobb. 832p. 1992. pap. 27.95 (*0-07-881768-4*) Osborne-McGraw.
Quattro Pro for Windows 2.O. Shelly Cashman. (C). 1994. text. write for info. (*0-318-70364-5*) S-W Pub.
Quattro Pro 4.O. Sarah E. Hutchinson & Stacey C. Sawyer. LC 94-149942. 200p. (C). 1993. text 12.50 (*0-256-13738-2*, Irwn McGrw-H) McGrw-H Hghr Educ.
Quattro Pro 4.O: Production Software Guide, 1993. Martin. LC 93-71330. (C). 1993. pap. text 9.75 (*0-03-098359-2*) Harcourt Coll Pubs.
Quattro Pro 4.0 for DOS SmartStart: The Step by Step Approach. Linda Erickson. LC 93-86104. 268p. 1993. 25.99 (*1-56529-408-4*) Que.
Quattro Pro 1.O - 2.O Quick Ref. Microref Educational Systems Staff. 1991. pap. 19.95 (*0-913365-89-0*) Microref Educ Systs.
Quattro Pro Quick Reference Guide. Jeff Burgess. (DDC Quick Reference Guides Ser.). 1990. spiral bd. 12.00 (*1-56243-001-7*, Q-17) DDC Pub.
Quattro Pro 6 for Windows Essentials. John Preston. LC 94-69261. 195p. 1995. 22.99 (*0-7897-0107-3*) Que.
Quattro Pro 6 for Windows, Incl. instr. resource kit, test bank, transparency. Neil J. Salkind. (Illustrated Ser.). (Illus.). 192p. 1995. pap. 20.95 (*0-7600-3430-3*) Course Tech.
Quattro Pro 6 for Windows for Dummies. John Walkenbach. LC 94-78910. 416p. 1995. pap. 19.95 (*1-56884-174-4*) IDG Bks.
Quattro Pro 6.O for Windows. Timothy J. O'Leary & Linda I. O'Leary. 240p. (C). 1995. pap. 14.69 (*0-07-049065-1*) McGraw.
Quattro Pro 6.O for Windows. Sullivan. (Computer Training Ser.). (C). 1995. spiral bd. 21.95 (*0-538-64158-4*) S-W Pub.
Quattro Pro 6.O for Windows: Easy Reference Guide. Sandra Cable. (DF - Computer Applications Ser.). 144-160p. 1996. mass mkt. 9.95 (*0-538-71460-3*) S-W Pub.
Quattro Pro 6.O for Windows: Quick Course. Dill. (Quick Course Ser.). 192p. 1995. mass mkt. 15.95 (*0-538-65043-5*) S-W Pub.
Quattro Pro 6.O for Windows: Standard Course. Dill. (DF - Computer Applications Ser.). 1995. mass mkt. 34.95 (*0-538-63946-6*) S-W Pub.
Quattro Pro 6.O for Windows: Standard Course. large type ed. Raylene Dill. 1995. 108.50 (*0-614-09605-7*, L-83782-00) Am Printing Hse.
Quattro Pro 6.0 Introduction. Pamela W. Adams & Kathryn K. Baskett. Ed. by Susan D. Carnes. (Perfect Office Ser.). (Illus.). 91p. 1995. pap. text 26.03 (*1-58163-017-4*) CPI Train.
QUATTRO PRO SOFTWARE 3.5. Dolores M. Etter. LC 93-6522. (C). 1993. pap. text 22.95 (*0-8053-1778-3*) Benjamin-Cummings.
Quattro Pro 3 Quick Reference Guide. 19.95 (*1-56351-060-X*, G162) Microref Educ Systs.
Quattro Pro 5 for Windows - New Perspectives Introductory, Incl. instr. resource kit, test bank, transparency. David Auer et al. (New Perspectives Ser.). (Illus.). 304p. 1994. text. write for info. (*1-56527-162-9*) Course Tech.
Quattro Pro 6 for Windows - New Perspectives Introductory, Incl. instr. resource kit, test bank, transparency. David Auer et al. (New Perspectives Ser.). (Illus.). 320p. 1995. pap. 29.95 (*0-7600-3280-7*) Course Tech.
Quattrocento Adriatico: Fifteenth-Century Art of the Adriatic Rim. Ed. by Charles Dempsey. (Villa Spelman Colloquium Ser.: Vol. 5). 348p. (C). 1996. text 49.95 (*88-7779-052-0*) Johns Hopkins.
Quatum Confinement V: Nanostructures. Ed. by M. Cahay et al. 690p. 90.00 (*1-56677-213-3*, PV 98-19) Electrochem Soc.
Quatuor. Jean Rhys. (FRE.). 1982. pap. 10.95 (*0-7859-4166-5*) Fr & Eur.
Quavers. P. L. Cartwright. 178p. 1997. pap. 10.00 (*0-9658421-0-X*) P L Cartwright.
Quazimodo! Victor Hugo & David Koren. 1994. 3.50 (*0-87129-461-3*, Q16) Dramatic Pub.
Qubebec Focus on Jobs: Shaping an Innovative Economy : an Economic Development Strategy for Job Creation. LC 98-166148. 1998. write for info. (*2-550-32694-6*) Gvt Quebec.
Qucillgaq. large type ed. Aggie Kairaiuak & Sophie Shield. (ESK., Illus.). 16p. (J). (gr. k-3). 1997. pap. text 6.00 (*1-58084-011-6*) Lower Kuskokwim.
Que. Tim Reynolds. LC 76-155304. 1971. 25.00 (*0-912604-06-9*); pap. 3.50 (*0-912604-05-0*) Halty Ferguson.
***Que Alegria/I Rejoiced.** Composed by Jaime Cortez. 136p. 1998. pap. 8.95 (*0-915531-97-6*) OR Catholic.
Que Ayuda. Brenda. (Serie Rompecabezas en Libro - Jigsaw Puzzles in Book Ser.).Tr. of One Who Helped. (SPA.). (J). 1992. pap. 4.99 (*1-56063-308-5*, 490446) Editorial Unilit.
***Que Buena Idea!** Karen M. Rogers. Tr. by Ana M. Alvarado. (Think-Kids Book Collection).Tr. of Good Thinking. (SPA., Illus.). 16p. (J). (gr. 1-4). 2000. pap. 2.95 (*1-58237-058-3*) Creat Think.
Que Bueno Que Me Dijiste lo Que No Queria Oir. Tr. of I'm So Glad You Told Me What I Didn't Wanna Hear!. (ENG & SPA.). 1996. pap. text 9.99 (*0-88113-434-1*) Caribe Betania.
***Que Cartas Tengo en el Juego de la Vida?** Donna Vander Griend. Ed. by Alejandro Pimentel. Tr. by Luis Bernal Lumpuy. (Animo! Ser.).Tr. of Where Do I Go to Trade in My Hand?. (SPA.). 62p. 1999. 8.95 (*1-55883-114-2*) Libros Desafio.
Que Creen las Sectas? Irvine G. Robertson.Tr. of What Do the Sects Believe?. (SPA.). 1993. pap. 11.50 (*0-311-05768-3*) Casa Bautista.
Que Debe de Hacer Si Tiene un Accidente Automovilistico: 50 Preguntas y Respuestes. Jon R. Abele.Tr. of 50 Questions & Answers about Automobile Accidents. (SPA.). 32p. 1993. pap. 1.80 (*0-913875-49-X*, 6122-N) Lawyers & Judges.
Que Deberia Hacer? Cuidado de Emergencia Y Seguridad. Judith Schneider. (SPA.). 57p. 1997. pap. 10.95 (*0-944454-20-8*) CAPE Center.
Que Debo Comer? (SPA., Illus.). 1980. pap. 1.00 (*0-910869-17-0*) Soc Nutrition Ed.
Que Dice Dios Acerca del Aborto? (Serie Enfoque a la Familia - Focus on the Family Ser.).Tr. of What Does God Say about Abortion?. (SPA.). 20p. 1992. pap. 1.99 (*1-56063-335-2*, 497438) Editorial Unilit.
Que Dice el Periodico. Dionisio Canas. (Lecturas Faciles). (SPA.). 70p. 1983. pap. text 3.75 (*0-88345-522-6*, 21268); pap. text 7.00 (*0-13-748138-1*) Prentice ESL.
Que Dice Usted Despues de Decir Hola? Eric Berne. 1997. pap. text 18.98 (*968-419-610-5*) Grijalbo Edit.
Que Diria Jesus de Tu Iglesia? Richard Mayhue. 128p. 1997. pap. 7.99 (*0-8254-1473-3*, Edit Portavoz) Kregel.
Que' Es. Tr. by Anne T. Perkins & Maria Ringlstetter. (Big Books - Mini Bks.). (SPA., Illus.). 8p. (J). (ps-k). 1994. 12.00 (*1-884204-11-2*) Teach Nxt Door.
Que Es el Clasicismo. H. Peyre. (Breviarios Ser.). (SPA.). pap. 9.99 (*968-16-5019-0*, Pub. by Fondo) Continental Bk.
Que es el Hombre? Buber. (Breviarios Ser.). (SPA.). pap. 6.99 (*968-16-0246-3*, Pub. by Fondo) Continental Bk.
Que Es el Milenio? - Cuatro Enfoques Para una Respuesta. Ed. by Robert G. Clouse. Tr. by V. David Sedaca.Tr. of Meaning of the Millennium - Four Views. (SPA.). 208p. (Orig.). 1992. pap. 9.99 (*0-311-09136-9*) Casa Bautista.
Que Es el Modernismo? Nueva Encuesta, Neuvas Lecturas. Ed. by Richard A. Cardwell & Bernard McGuirk. LC 92-64364. (SPA.). 456p. 1993. pap. 60.00 (*0-89295-067-6*) Society Sp & Sp-Am.
Que es el Sol? Reeve Lindbergh. Tr. by Veronica Uribe.Tr. of What Is the Sun?. (SPA., Illus.). 32p. (J). (gr. k-2). 1998. 14.95 (*1-880507-37-4*) Lectorum Pubns.
Que Es Ese Ruido, Isabel? (Isabel's Noisy Tummy) David McKee. (SPA.). (J). (gr. k-2). 1997. pap. 7.50 (*84-480-0102-8*) Lectorum Pubns.
***Que Es Eso Mama? Que Es Eso?** Susan F. Tierno. Tr. by Ana M. Alvarado. (Think-Kids Book Collection).Tr. of What's That Mom? What's That?. (SPA., Illus.). 16p. (J). 2000. pap. 2.95 (*1-58237-048-6*) Creat Think.
Que Es in Virus? Un Libro para Ninos Sobre el SIDA. David Fassler & Kelly McQueen. Tr. by Wanda M. Quinones from ENG. LC 90-24631. (Illus.). 70p. (Orig.). (J). (ps-5). 1991. pap. 8.95 (*0-914525-17-4*); spiral bd. 12.95 (*0-685-47790-8*); write for info. (*0-914525-16-6*) Waterfront Bks.
Que Es la Agricultura Biodynamica. Koepf. 1980. pap. 3.50 (*0-938250-31-0*) Bio-Dynamic Farm.
Que Es la Doctrina Cristiana? - Su Valor, Necesidad y Base (What Is Christian Doctrine?) (Biblioteca de Doctrina Cristiana Ser.).Tr. of What Is Christian Doctrine?. (SPA.). 1985. pap. 6.75 (*0-311-09111-3*) Casa Bautista.
Que Es la Historia? E. Kahler. (Breviarios Ser.). (SPA.). pap. 7.99 (*968-16-0930-1*, Pub. by Fondo) Continental Bk.
***Que es "la Iglesia"? Identificando la Naturaleza y Diseno de la Iglesia del Nuevo Testamento.** Eddie Cloer. Orig. Title: What Is "the Church"?. 236p. 1998. pap. 2.50 (*0-945441-29-0*) Res Pubns AR.
Que Es la Metafisica. Connie Mendez. 1997. pap. text 7.98 (*980-6114-34-5*) Bienestar.
Que Es Material Castro Peligroso? (What Is Household Hazardous Material?) Ann M. Wolf & Anna H. Spitz. Tr. by Jose Valenzuela. (Environmental Ser.). (SPA., Illus.). 133p. (J). (gr. 6-8). 1998. pap. 13.50 (*1-892816-05-9*, SER-102) Sonora Environ.
Que Es Peligroso En Nuestro Hogar? (What's Hazardous in Our Home?) unabridged ed. Ann M. Wolf & Anna H. Spitz. Tr. by Jose Valenzuela. (Environmental Ser.). (SPA., Illus.). 93p. (J). (gr. 6-8). 1998. pap. 9.50 (*1-892816-06-7*, SER-202) Sonora Environ.
Que Es Que Spanish English. Reginald Bragonier & David Fisher. 1990. 40.00 (*0-8437-3324-1*) Hammond World.
Que Es Redondo? Barbara Shook-Hazen. Ed. by Don Curry. Tr. by Leyla Torres from ENG. (Spanish Discovery Links Ser.). (SPA.). 8p. (J). (gr. k). 1997. pap. text 2.75 (*1-56784-973-3*) Newbridge Educ.
Que Es Ser Catolico? MACC Team Staff.Tr. of About Being Catholic. (SPA., Illus.). 36p. 1976. write for info. (*0-614-04901-6*) Mex Am Cult.
Que Es un Cristiano? Nystrom.Tr. of What Is a Christian?. (SPA.). 29p. (J). write for info. (*0-614-27127-4*) Editorial Unilit.
Que Es un Cristiano? C. Nystrom.Tr. of What Is a Christian?. (SPA.). 29p. (J). 1995. 2.99 (*1-56063-782-X*, 490459) Editorial Unilit.
Que Es un Cristiano y Fe en Accion: John - James. Catherine Schell & Marilyn Kunz. (Serie Encuentros). (SPA.). 48p. 1989. pap. 1.50 (*0-945792-55-7*, 490453) Editorial Unilit.
Que Es un Pez. David Eastman. (SPA.). (J). 1997. pap. 3.50 (*0-8167-3260-4*) Troll Communs.
Que Es un Sintetizador? see What's a Synthesizer?
Que Es un Virus? Un Libro para Ninos Sobre Sel SIDA. David Fassler. (SPA.). (J). 1990. 14.15 (*0-606-05558-4*, Pub. by Turtleback) Demco.
Que Es y Como Se Hace el Analisis y Diagnostico de la Realidad en la CLAT. Victor M. Duran. (SPA.). 130p. (Orig.). 1987. pap. 8.00 (*0-917049-10-1*) Saeta.
Que Esconde Su Letra? Y la de Su Pareja? Malvin Kristus. (SPA., Illus.). 112p. (Orig.). 1985. pap. 2.95 (*0-939193-04-3*) Edit Concepts.
***Que Esta Arriba Cuando Tu Estas Abajo?** David F. Marx. (Rookie Espanol Ser.). (SPA., Illus.). (J). 2000. 15.00 (*0-516-22022-5*) Childrens.
Que Esta Vivo? Lisa Trumbauer. Ed. by Don Curry. Tr. by Leyla Torres from ENG. (Spanish Discovery Links Ser.). (SPA.). 8p. (J). (gr. k). 1997. pap. text 2.75 (*1-56784-992-X*) Newbridge Educ.
***Que Fait la Police, Vol. 1.** Bill Watterson. (Calvin & Hobbes Ser.). 1999. pap. 16.95 (*2-258-03642-9*) Midwest European Pubns.
Que Gitano! Gypsies of Southern Spain. Bertha B. Quintana & Lois G. Floyd. Ed. by Louise S. Spindler & George D. Spindler. (Case Studies in Cultural Anthropology). (Illus.). 137p. (C). 1983. reprint ed. pap. text 9.95 (*0-8290-0582-X*) Irvington.
Que Gitano! Gypsies of Southern Spain. Bertha B. Quintana & Lois G. Floyd. (Illus.). 126p. (C). 1986. reprint ed. pap. text 9.95 (*0-88133-217-8*) Waveland Pr.
Que Gordita! A Study of Weight among Women in a Puerto Rican Community. Emily B. Massara. LC 88-35144. (Immigrant Communities & Ethnic Minorities in the U. S. & Canada Ser.: No. 46). 1989. 57.50 (*0-404-19456-7*) AMS Pr.
Que Hacemos Con Estos Musicos? Marcos Witt.Tr. of What Shall We Do with These Musicians?. (SPA.). 187p. 1995. 9.99 (*0-88113-160-1*, B048-1601) Caribe Betania.
***Que Hacemos con Estos Musicos?, 2 Vols.** Marcos Witt. 1999. audio 10.99 (*0-88113-329-9*) Caribe Betania.
Que Hacemos Hoy?/What Shall I Do Today? Ed. by Ray Gibson. (Illus.). 96p. (J). (gr. k-6). 1999. 18.95 (*0-7460-3436-9*, Usborne) EDC.
Que Hacen los Animales para Sobrevivr. Kyle Carter. (Que Hacen los Animales?).Tr. of Animals That Survive. 24p. (J). (gr. k-4). Date not set. lib. bdg. 17.27 (*1-55916-149-3*) Rourke Bk Co.
Que Hacer Cuand No Sabes Que Hacer: Confiando en Cristo en Medio de la Confusion. Chapel of the Air Ministries, Inc. Staff. Tr. by Eduardo Ramirez & Elvira Ramirez. (Nineteen Ninety-Six 50-Day Spiritual Adventure Ser.). (ENG & SPA.). 80p. (Orig.). 1995. pap., wbk. ed. 6.00 (*1-879050-83-8*) Chapel of Air.
Que Hacer Cuando Nada Parece Dar Resultado. John Osteen.Tr. of What to Do When Nothing Seems to Work. (SPA.). 32p. 1986. mass mkt. 0.75 (*0-912631-60-0*) J O Pubns.
***Que Hacer Cuando Su Nino Se Enferme: Facil de Leer & Facil de Usar.** Gloria G. Mayer & Ann Kuklierus. (SPA., Illus.). 181p. 2000. pap. 14.95 (*0-9701245-1-1*) IHA.
Que Hacer Cuando Viene el Tentador. John Osteen.Tr. of What to Do When the Tempter Comes. (SPA.). 32p. 1996. mass mkt. 1.50 (*0-912631-65-1*) J O Pubns.
***Que Hacer para la Salud de las Personas de Edad.** Albert Barnett et al. (SPA., Illus.). 2000. pap. 14.95 (*0-9701245-5-4*) IHA.
***Que Hacer para la Salud de los Adolescentes.** Gloria G. Mayer & Ann Kuklierus. (Illus.). 2000. pap. 14.95 (*0-9701245-3-8*) IHA.
Que Hare, Senor? T. S. Nee. Orig. Title: What Shall This Man Do?. (SPA.). 272p. 1992. mass mkt. 6.99 (*0-8254-1504-7*, Edit Portavoz) Kregel.
Que Harias Tu? Linda Schwartz.Tr. of What Would You Do?. (SPA., Illus.). 184p. (J). (gr. 3-7). 1994. pap. 9.95 (*0-88160-238-8*, LW333) Learning Wks.
Que Hay Debajo del Oceano. (J). 1997. pap. 3.50 (*0-8167-3143-8*) Troll Communs.
Que Hay en la Casa de Carlitos? (What's in Danny's House?) Ann M. Wolf & Anna H. Spitz. Tr. by Jose Valenzuela. (Environmental Ser.). (SPA., Illus.). 47p. (J). (ps-k). 1998. pap. 5.50 (*1-892816-09-1*, SER-502) Sonora Environ.
Que Hay Entre las Estrellas. (SPA.). (C). 1996. 14.33 (*0-201-82192-3*) P-H Intl.
Que Hay Para Comer? Shelley Harwayne. (SPA., Illus.). (J). (ps-3). 1998. pap. 4.95 (*1-57255-498-3*) Mondo Pubng.
Que Hora Es? (SPA.). 1995. bds. 4.98 (*1-85854-311-8*) Brimax Bks.
Que Jugamos Hoy? (What Can We Play Today?) Jane Belk Moncure. LC 87-32565. (Castillo Magico Ser.). (SPA., Illus.). 32p. (J). (ps-2). 1989. lib. bdg. 21.36 (*0-89565-923-9*) Childs World.
Que la Patria Se Sienta Orgullosa: Memorias de una Lucha Sin Fin. Waldo DeCastroverde. LC 98-85504. (Coleccion Cuba y Sus Jueces Ser.). (SPA., Illus.). 495p. 1999. pap. 29.00 (*0-89729-869-1*) Ediciones.
Que le Pasa Al Bebito? see What's the Matter with the Baby?
Que Lejos Hemos Llegado los Esclavos! Sudafrica y Cuba En el Mundo de Hoy. Nelson Mandela & Fidel Castro. LC 91-66761. (SPA., Illus.). 83p. (Orig.). 1991. pap. 10.95 (*0-87348-732-X*) Pathfinder NY.
Que Los Ninos Vengan a Mi. Sally Lehman Chall.Tr. of Making God Real to Your Children. (SPA.). 176p. 1995. pap. 8.99 (*0-8297-1826-5*) Vida Pubs.
Que los Odiosos No Acaben Contigo! Paul Meier.Tr. of Don't Let the Jerks Get the Best of You. (SPA.). 1997. 10.99 (*0-88113-412-0*, B001-4120) Caribe Betania.
Que Ma Joie Demeure see Oeuvres Romanesques
Que Ma Joie Demeure. Jean Giono. (FRE.). 512p. 1959. 12.95 (*0-8288-9787-5*, F103760) Fr & Eur.
Que Ma Vie Demeure. Jean Giono. 12.95 (*0-686-53985-0*) Fr & Eur.
Que Maravilla Teacher's Activity Notebook, Level 1. (Que Maravilla! Ser.). (ENG & SPA., Illus.). 224p. 1991. pap. text 85.00 (*1-56334-030-5*) Hampton-Brown.
Que Maravilla! Classroom Set. (ENG & SPA., Illus.). (Orig.). (J). (gr. 1-3). 1991. pap., teacher ed. 393.00 (*1-56334-098-4*) Hampton-Brown.
Que Maravilla! & Wonders! Series, 12 bks., Level 2. (Illus.). (Orig.). 1992. teacher ed., spiral bd. 435.00 (*1-56334-210-3*) Hampton-Brown.
Que Maravilla! & Wonders! Series Level 1: Combo Big Books. (SPA., Illus.). (Orig.). (J). (gr. 1-3). 1991. pap., teacher ed. 435.00 (*1-56334-103-4*) Hampton-Brown.
Que Maravilla! & Wonders! Series Level 1: Combo Classroom Set, Set. (SPA., Illus.). (Orig.). (J). (gr. 1-3). 1991. pap., teacher ed. 798.00 (*1-56334-102-6*) Hampton-Brown.

An Asterisk (*) at the beginning of an entry indicates that the title is appearing for the first time.

Que Maravilla! Big Book Set, Level 2. (Que Maravilla! Ser.). (ENG & SPA., Illus.). (Orig.). 1992. ring bd. 232.00 (*1-56334-208-1*) Hampton-Brown.

Que Maravilla! Series Level 1: Big Book Set. (ENG & SPA., Illus.). (Orig.). (J). (gr. 1-3). 1991. teacher ed. 232.00 (*1-56334-152-2*) Hampton-Brown.

Que Maravilla/Wonders Dual Language Classroom Set, Level 2. (Que Maravilla & Wonders Ser.). (SPA., Illus.). (Orig.). 1992. teacher ed., ring bd. 817.00 (*1-56334-209-X*) Hampton-Brown.

Que Maruilla Teacher's Activity Notebook, Level 2. (Que Maravilla! Ser.). (ENG & SPA., Illus.). 224p. 1992. ring bd. 85.00 (*1-56334-031-3*) Hampton-Brown.

Que Marvilla! Classroom Set, Level 2. (Que Maravilla! Ser.). (ENG & SPA., Illus.). (Orig.). 1992. teacher ed., ring bd. 399.00 (*1-56334-207-3*) Hampton-Brown.

Que Me Pasa con las Matematicas? Ana H. Quintero. LC 85-24617. (Illus.). 119p. 1989. pap. 11.50 (*0-8477-2749-1*) U of PR Pr.

Que Mi Pueblo Adore: Music & Worship. Edward W. Nelson. Tr. by Salom Mussiett from ENG. (SPA.). 184p. 1986. pap. 10.99 (*0-311-17029-3*) Casa Bautista.

Que Monton de Tamales! (Too Many Tamales) Gary Soto. (SPA., Illus.). 32p. (J). (ps-3). 1996. pap. 5.99 (*0-698-11413-2*, PapStar) Peng Put Young Read.

Que Monton de Tamales! (Too Many Tamales) Gary Soto. 1996. 11.15 (*0-606-10492-5*, Pub. by Turtleback) Demco.

Que Nada Se Sabe. Francisco Sanchez. Ed. by Fernando A. Palacios. (Nueva Austral Ser.: Vol. 235). (SPA.). 1991. pap. text 24.95 (*84-239-7235-6*) Elliots Bks.

Que Nenhum Pereca: Para Que Ninguno Perezca. Edward Silvoso. (POR.). 265p. 1995. write for info. (*1-56063-849-4*) Editorial Unilit.

***Que Pasa Ahi Arriba?** Elizabeth Stiemert. 1999. 17.95 (*84-88342-19-5*) SA Kokinos.

Que Pasa Cuando Comes?/What Happens to Your Food? Ed. by Alastair Smith. (Flip Flaps Ser.). (Illus.). 16p. (J). (ps up). 1999. 9.95 (*0-7460-3424-5*, Usborne) EDC.

Que Pasa Cuando Morimos? C. Nystrom.Tr. of What Happens When We Die?. (SPA.). 29p. (J). 1995. 2.99 (*1-56063-781-1*, 490458) Editorial Unilit.

Que Pasa Despues de la Muerte? 2nd ed. H. Rossier. Ed. by Gordon H. Bennett. Tr. by Sara Bautista from ENG. (Serie Diamante).Tr. of What Happens After Death?. (SPA., Illus.). 36p. 1982. pap. 0.85 (*0-942504-07-0*) Overcomer Pr.

Que Paso? An English-Spanish Guide for Medical Personnel. 4th rev. ed. Martin P. Kantrowitz et al. LC 83-14670. 77p. 1984. pap. 6.95 (*0-8263-0725-6*) U of NM Pr.

Que Paso Hoy? Frank M. Figueroa. (SPA.). 278p. 1995. pap. 25.00 (*0-9643201-2-6*) Pillar Publns.

QUE Presents Technology Essentials. 1999. write for info. (*1-58076-145-3*) Que Educ & Trng.

Que Puede Hacer para Ayudar a Su Hijos (A) a Trivnter en la Escuelai (What You Can Do to Help Your Child Succeed in School - While Keeping Your Child Safe & Drug Free: Paquete para Los Instructores (Leader's Kit) Thomas Baker & Frank Murphy. (SPA.). 1998. ring bd. 150.00 (*1-885903-07-3*) ParentingKids.

Que Puede Ser? Stephen White. (SPA., Illus.). 32p. (J). 1997. pap. text 3.25 (*1-57064-165-X*) Lyrick Pub.

Que Puede Volar? Lisa Trumbauer. Ed. by Don Curry. Tr. by Leyla Torres from ENG. (Spanish Discovery Links Ser.). (SPA.). 8p. (J). (gr. k). 1997. pap. text 2.75 (*1-56784-990-3*) Newbridge Educ.

Que Puedes Decir Cuando un Monito Actua Asi? (What Do You Say When a Monkey Acts This Way?) Jane Belk Moncure. LC 87-11736. (Castillo Magico Ser.). (SPA., Illus.). 32p. (J). (ps-2). 1989. lib. bdg. 21.36 (*0-89565-925-5*) Childs World.

***Que Quebranta Corazones.** Lori Wick. (SPA.). 352p. 1998. pap. 9.99 (*0-8254-1856-9*, Edit Portavoz) Kregel.

Que Queda Enterrado. Gaiter. text 8.95 (*0-88436-996-X*) EMC-Paradigm.

Que Quieren los Hombres? Norman Wright.Tr. of What Men Want. (SPA.). 8.99 (*0-7899-0167-6*, 497659) Editorial Unilit.

Que Quieres Que Haga Por Ti? Luis Palau. (Serie Cruzada - Crusade Ser.).Tr. of What Do You Want Me to Do?. (SPA.). 1986. 1.99 (*0-8423-6337-8*, 498002); pap. write for info. (*0-614-27126-6*) Editorial Unilit.

Que Ruido! (What Noise!) Aliana Brodmann. Tr. by Hildegard M. Krohn from GER. (Coleccion Barril Sin Fondo Ser.). (SPA., Illus.). 26p. (J). (gr. 3 up). 1990. 13.95 (*968-6465-08-1*) Hispanic Bk Dist.

Que Sabes? Ed. by Richard Meyer. (SPA., Illus.). 87p. 1997. pap., teacher ed. 5.50 (*1-879892-59-6*, SI-886) Editorial Bautista.

Que se Puede Esperar Cuando se Esta Esperando (What to Expect When You're Expecting) Arlene Eisenberg et al. (SPA., Illus.). 576p. 1997. pap. 13.95 (*0-7611-0949-8*) Workman Pub.

Que Se Quedaron. Peter LaLonde & Paul LaLonde.Tr. of Left Behind. 1997. 8.99 (*0-88113-449-X*) Caribe Betania.

Que Semana, Luchito! Big Book. Ina Cumpiano. (Que Maravilla! Ser.). (SPA., Illus.). 24p. (Orig.). (J). (gr. 1-3). 1991. pap. text 29.95 (*1-56334-023-2*) Hampton-Brown.

Que Semana, Luchito! Small Book. Ina Cumpiano. (Que Maravilla! Ser.). (SPA., Illus.). 24p. (Orig.). (J). (gr. 1-3). 1991. pap. text 6.00 (*1-56334-037-2*) Hampton-Brown.

Que Si. Annette Grant Cash et al. (College Spanish). (SPA.). (C). 1993. pap. 38.95 (*0-8384-3546-7*) Heinle & Heinle.

Que Si! M. Victoria Garcia-Serrano. (College Spanish Ser.). (SPA.). (C). 1993. mass mkt., teacher ed. 38.95 (*0-8384-3544-0*) Heinle & Heinle.

Que Si. 2nd ed. M. Victoria Garcia-Serrano. (Secondary Spanish Ser.). (C). 1998. pap., lab manual ed. 21.00 (*0-8384-7715-1*) Heinle & Heinle.

***Que Si.** 2nd ed. M. Victoria Garcia-Serrano. (C). 1998. pap. 32.50 (*0-8384-7724-0*) Thomson Learn.

***Que Si.** 2nd ed. M. Victoria Garcia-Serrano. (C). 1998. pap. 45.95 (*0-8384-7706-2*) Thomson Learn.

Que Sigue. Mendez, Jr. LC 94-61480. (Coleccion Humor: No. 1). (SPA., Illus.). 86p. (Orig.). 1994. pap. 9.95 (*0-89729-659-1*) Ediciones.

Que Son las Necesidades Humanas. Vincent W. Kafka. 12p. 1988. pap. 3.95 (*0-913261-18-1*) Effect Learn Sys.

Que Son los Cientificos. Rita G. Gelman. (SPA.). 32p. (J). (ps-3). 1995. 3.95 (*0-590-46941-X*) Scholastic Inc.

Que Sorpresa de Cumpleanos. Loretta Lopez. LC 97-6668.Tr. of Birthday Swap. (SPA., Illus.). 32p. (J). (gr. k-5). 1997. pap. 6.95 (*1-880000-56-3*) Lee & Low Bks.

Que Sorpresa de Cumpleanos. Loretta Lopez. LC 97-6668.Tr. of Birthday Swap. (SPA., Illus.). 32p. (J). (ps-3). 1997. 15.95 (*1-880000-55-5*) Lee & Low Bks.

Que Sorpresa de Cumpleanos. Loretta Lopez.Tr. of Birthday Swap. 1997. 12.15 (*0-606-12795-X*, Pub. by Turtleback) Demco.

Que Sucede Cuando Oramos por Nuestras Familias? Evelyn Christenson.Tr. of What Happens When We Pray for Our Families?. (SPA.). 216p. 1995. 7.99 (*0-7899-0013-0*, 498563) Editorial Unilit.

***Que Sucedera Despues.** Concordia Publishing House Staff. (Hear Me Read Ser.). (SPA., Illus.). 24p. (J). (ps-3). 2000. 2.95 (*0-570-09909-9*) Concordia.

Que Tal? Dorwick. 1994. 78.43 (*0-07-075123-4*) McGraw.

***Que Tal?** 5th ed. Alice A. Arana et al. 192p. (C). 1998. pap., wbk. ed. 28.75 (*0-07-013683-1*) McGrw-H Hghr Educ.

***Que Tal?** 5th ed. Alice A. Arana et al. (Illus.). 192p. (C). 1998. pap., wbk. ed., lab manual ed. 28.75 (*0-07-013684-X*) McGrw-H Hghr Educ.

***Que Tal?** 5th ed. Thalia Dorwick et al. 496p. (C). 1998. pap., student ed. 61.25 (*0-07-231140-1*); pap., student ed. 61.25 (*0-07-561954-7*) McGrw-H Hghr Educ.

Que Tal? An Intro Course. 5th ed. Dorwick. LC 98-34904. 1998. 49.95 (*0-07-013681-5*) McGraw.

Que Tal? An Introductory Course. 3rd ed. Maria J. Ruiz Morcillo. (C). 1991. pap. text 60.62 (*0-07-909968-8*) McGraw.

Que Tal? An Introductory Course. 4th ed. Thalia Dorwick et al. LC 94-39641. 1995. text, teacher ed. write for info. (*0-07-017957-3*) McGraw.

Que tal? An Introductory Course. 4th ed. Marty Knorre et al. (C). 1995. pap., lab manual ed. 26.88 (*0-07-017959-X*) McGraw.

Que tal? An Introductory Course, Listening Comprehension Manual. 3rd ed. Maria J. Morcillo. 1991. pap. text. write for info. (*0-07-017745-7*) McGraw.

Que tal? An Introductory Course. 4th ed. Alice A. Arana & Oswaldo Arana. (C). 1995. pap., wbk. ed. 29.38 (*0-07-017958-1*) McGraw.

Que tal? An Introductory Course. 4th ed. Thalia Dorwick et al. (C). 1995. 18.25 incl. audio (*0-07-911989-1*) McGraw.

Que Tan Bueno Debo Ser? Estudios Biblicos Acerca de la Gracia de Dios. Richard B. Ramsay.Tr. of Am I Good Enough? Learning to Live by God's Grace. (ENG & SPA., Illus.). 102p. 1992. pap. 4.99 (*0-87552-396-X*) P & R Pubng.

Que Te Dicen las Estrellas? Tu Horoscopo en Minutos. Grant Lewi. (SPA.). 400p. Date not set. 14.95 (*1-56718-426-X*) Llewellyn Pubns.

Que Te Gusta? Michael Grejniec. LC 94-39309. (SPA., Illus.). 32p. (J). (ps-1). 1995. pap. 6.95 (*1-55858-392-0*, Pub. by North-South Bks NYC); lib. bdg. 14.88 (*1-55858-391-2*, Pub. by North-South Bks NYC) Chronicle Bks.

Que Te Gusta? Michael Grejniec. 1995. 12.15 (*0-606-08852-0*, Pub. by Turtleback) Demco.

Que Te Parece? James F. Lee. (C). 1996. pap. text, wbk. ed. 14.06 (*0-07-038074-0*) McGraw.

Que Te Parece? James F. Lee & F. Wolf Darlene. 512p. (C). 1995. pap. 50.00 (*0-07-540891-0*) McGraw.

Que Te Parece? James F. Lee et al. (C). 1996. pap. text, suppl. ed. 26.87 (*0-07-540900-3*) McGraw.

***Que Te Parece?** 2nd ed. James F. Lee et al. 288p. (C). 1999. pap. 24.06 (*0-07-230855-9*) McGrw-H Hghr Educ.

***Que Te Parece?** 2nd ed. James F. Lee et al. 288p. (C). 2000. pap., wbk. ed. 24.06 (*0-07-230862-1*) McGrw-H Hghr Educ.

Que Te Parece?, Vol. 1. James F. Lee et al. (C). 1996. pap., wbk. ed., lab manual ed. 26.88 (*0-07-540892-9*) McGraw.

Que Te Parece?, Vol. 2. James F. Lee & F. Wolf Darlene. (C). 1996. pap., wbk. ed., lab manual ed. 26.88 (*0-07-037707-3*) McGraw.

***Que Te Parece? Intermediate Spanish.** 2nd ed. James F. Lee. LC 99-47956. 1999. write for info. (*0-07-365519-8*) McGrw-H Hghr Educ.

Que Tiempos Aquellos! Andino Acevedo Gonzales. LC 84-25639. 1989. pap. 8.50 (*0-8477-0069-0*) U of PR Pr.

Que Tiene Sed. Abelardo Castillo. (SPA.). 257p. 1985. pap. 9.00 (*0-317-46764-6*) Ediciones Norte.

Que Todas Sean Uno: Ut Unum Sint: Sobre el Empeno Ecumenico. John Paul, II, pseud. (SPA.). 114p. 1995. pap. 6.95 (*1-57455-051-9*) US Catholic.

Que Va-T-Il Arriver? Lowell Lundstrom. Ed. by Annie L. Cosson. Tr. by Valerie Chardenal from ENG.Tr. of What's Coming Next. (FRE.). 304p. 1985. mass mkt. 4.75 (*0-8297-0435-3*) Vida Pubs.

Que Veinte Anos No Es Nada. Celedonio Gonzales. LC 87-80170. (Coleccion Caniqui). (SPA.). 126p. (Orig.). 1987. pap. 9.95 (*0-89729-435-1*) Ediciones.

Que Viene en Grupos de Tres?, Vol. 4081. Marlene Beierle & Anne Sylvan. Ed. by Christine Hood. Tr. by Rancho Park Publishing Staff. (Math Spanish Learn to Read Ser.).Tr. of What Comes in Threes. (SPA., Illus.). 8p. (J). (ps-2). 1996. pap. 1.75 (*1-57471-155-5*, 4081) Creat Teach Pr.

Que Viene Primero? Lyn Swanson-Natsues. 1998. pap. text 2.95 (*1-57255-492-4*) Mondo Pubng.

Que Viva Mexico! S. M. Eisenstein. LC 70-169341. (Arno Press Cinema Program Ser.). (Illus.). 94p. 1972. reprint ed. 11.95 (*0-405-03916-6*) Ayer.

Que Vivan los Tamales! Food & the Making of Mexican Identity. Jeffrey M. Pilcher. LC 97-46508. (Dialogos Ser.). 243p. 1998. pap. 16.95 (*0-8263-1873-8*) U of NM Pr.

***Quebec.** (Canada in the Twenty First Century Ser.). (Illus.). (J). 2000. 18.95 (*0-7910-6070-5*) Chelsea Hse.

Quebec. Harry Beckett. LC 97-1422. (Journey Across Canada Ser.). 24p. (J). (gr. 3-5). 1997. lib. bdg. 18.60 (*1-55916-201-5*) Rourke Bk Co.

***Quebec.** Ed. by Alain G. Gagnon. (World Bibliographical Ser.: Vol. 211). 378p. 1998. lib. bdg. 95.00 (*1-85109-290-0*) ABC-CLIO.

***Quebec.** J. Hamilton. (Hello Canada Ser.). 1999. pap. 7.95 (*1-55041-275-2*) Fitzhenry & W Ltd.

Quebec. Janice Hamilton. LC 95-9625. (Hello Canada Ser.). (Illus.). 76p. (J). 1996. lib. bdg. 19.95 (*0-8225-2766-9*, Lerner Publctns) Lerner Pub.

Quebec. Insight Guides Staff. (Insight Guides). 1998. pap. text 12.95 (*0-88729-930-X*) Langenscheidt.

Quebec. Suzanne LeVert. (Let's Discover Canada Ser.). (Illus.). 64p. (YA). (gr. 3 up). 1991. lib. bdg. 16.95 (*0-7910-1030-9*) Chelsea Hse.

Quebec: A Chronicle, 1968-1972. Robert Chodos. Ed. by Nick Auf der Maur. 166p. 1972. mass mkt. 7.95 (*0-88862-025-X*, Pub. by J Lorimer) Formac Dist Ltd.

Quebec: A History: 1867-1929. Paul-Ande Linteau et al. 602p. 49.95 (*0-88862-605-3*, Pub. by J Lorimer) Formac Dist Ltd.

Quebec: A History: 1867-1929. Paul-Ande Linteau et al. 602p. reprint ed. pap. 29.95 (*0-88862-604-5*, Pub. by J Lorimer) Formac Dist Ltd.

Quebec: Off the Beaten Path: A Guide to Unique Places. Katharine Fletcher & Eric Fletcher. LC 99-10640. (Off the Beaten Path Ser.). (Illus.). 256p. 1999. pap. 12.95 (*0-7627-0276-1*) Globe Pequot.

Quebec: Province Divided. Peter Kizilos. LC 99-17667. (World in Conflict Ser.). 104p. (YA). (gr. 7-10). 1999. lib. bdg. 25.26 (*0-8225-3562-9*, Lerner Publctns) Lerner Pub.

Quebec: The Challenge of Independence. Anne Griffin. LC 81-72054. 260p. 1984. 35.00 (*0-8386-3135-5*) Fairleigh Dickinson.

Quebec: The Travel Notebook. Pascale Loiseau. 104p. 1997. 14.95 (*2-911141-20-2*, Pub. by Les Edtns Pascale) Assoc Pubs Grp.

Quebec: The Unfinished Revolution. Leon Dion. Tr. by Therese Romer. LC 77-352511. 232p. reprint ed. pap. 72.00 (*0-7837-1147-6*, 204167600022) Bks Demand.

Quebec: Ulysses Travel Guide. Francois Remillard. Ed. by Ulysses Travel Guide Staff. (Ulysses Travel Guide Ser.). (Illus.). 1999. 21.95 (*2-89464-202-4*) Ulysses Travel.

Quebec Act: A Study in Statesmanship. Reginald Coupland. (BCL1 - History - Canada Ser.). 224p. 1991. reprint ed. lib. bdg. 79.00 (*0-7812-6357-3*) Rprt Serv.

Quebec & Radical Social Change. Ed. by Dimitrios I. Roussopoulos. 210p. 1974. write for info. (*0-919618-52-9*); pap. write for info. (*0-919618-51-0*) Black Rose.

Quebec & the Constitution, 1960 to 1978. Edward McWhinney. LC 79-316335. 186p. reprint ed. pap. 57.70 (*0-8357-4159-1*, 203693300007) Bks Demand.

Quebec Before Duplessis: The Political Career of Louis-Alexandre Taschereau. Bernard L. Vigod. 328p. 1986. 65.00 (*0-7735-0588-1*, Pub. by McG-Queens Univ Pr) CUP Services.

***Quebec Business Directory, 2000 Edition.** rev. ed. American Business Directories Staff. 2656p. 1999. boxed set 495.00 incl. cd-rom (*0-7687-0187-2*) Am Busn Direct.

***Quebec City.** Francois Remillard & Stephane G. Marceau. 2000. pap. 12.95 (*2-89464-277-6*, Pub. by Ulysses Travel) Globe Pequot.

Quebec City Crisis see **Screech Owls Series Boxed Set: The Quebec City Crisis; The Screech Owls' Home Loss; Nightmare in Nagano**

Quebec City, 1765-1832: The Evolution of a Colonial Town. David T. Ruddel. (Mercury Ser.: History No. 41). (Illus.). 292p. 1988. pap. 24.95 (*0-660-10771-6*, Pub. by CN Mus Civilization) U of Wash Pr.

Quebec en Poesie. Jean Royer. (Folio - Junior Ser). (FRE.). pap. 9.95 (*2-07-034059-7*) Schoenhof.

Quebec Establishment: The Ruling Class & the State. Pierre Fournier. 245p. 1976. 38.99 (*0-919618-28-6*, Pub. by Black Rose); pap. 9.99 (*0-919618-27-8*, Pub. by Black Rose) Consort Bk Sales.

Quebec Green Guide French Edition. Michelin Staff. (FRE.). 1996. pap. 19.95 (*0-7859-7214-5*, 2067005723) Fr & Eur.

Quebec Inc. Un Manuel de Francais des Affaires. Steven J. Loughrin-Sacco & Robert A. Gagnon. (FRE.). (C). 1998. pap. text 29.95 (*1-891611-01-1*) SDSU Ciber Pr.

Quebec Labour. 2nd rev. ed. Intro. by Marcel Pepin. 251p. 1972. 36.99 (*0-919618-14-6*, Pub. by Black Rose); pap. 7.99 (*0-919618-15-4*, Pub. by Black Rose) Consort Bk Sales.

Quebec Nationalism in Crisis. Dominique Clift. 164p. (C). 1982. reprint ed. pap. text 24.95 (*0-7735-0383-8*, Pub. by McG-Queens Univ Pr) CUP Services.

Quebec (Province) Green Guide English Edition. Michelin Staff. 1996. pap. 19.95 (*0-7859-7181-5*, 2067015737) Fr & Eur.

Quebec, 1759. Rene Chartrand. (Order of Battle Ser.: Vol. 3). (Illus.). 96p. 1999. pap. 19.95 (*1-85532-847-X*, Pub. by Osprey) Stackpole.

Quebec since 1930. Paul-Ande Linteau et al. LC 89-94964. (FRE., Illus.). 632p. 49.95 (*1-55028-298-0*, Pub. by J Lorimer) Formac Dist Ltd.

Quebec since 1930, Vol. 2. Paul-Ande Linteau et al. 632p. pap. 29.95 (*1-55028-296-4*, Pub. by J Lorimer) Formac Dist Ltd.

Quebec Society: Critical Issues. Marcel Fournier. 1997. pap. text 45.27 (*0-13-158551-7*) P-H.

Quebec Society: Tradition, Modernity, & Nationhood. Hubert Guindon. Ed. by John McMullan. 224p. 1988. pap. 17.95 (*0-8020-6671-2*) U of Toronto Pr.

Quebec Studies in the Philosophy of Science. Ed. by Mathieu Marion & Robert S. Cohen. LC 95-17467. 336p. (C). 1995. lib. bdg. 180.00 (*0-7923-3559-7*, Pub. by Kluwer Academic) Kluwer Academic.

Quebec Studies in the Philosophy of Science, Set. Ed. by Mathieu Marion & Robert S. Cohen. LC 95-17467. (Boston Studies in the Philosophy of Science). 326p. (C). 1995. lib. bdg. 275.00 (*0-7923-3561-9*, Pub. by Kluwer Academic) Kluwer Academic.

Quebec Textile Industry in Canada. Caroline Pestieau. LC 79-302341. (Accent Quebec Ser.). 90p. 1978. reprint ed. pap. 30.00 (*0-608-01370-6*, 206211000002) Bks Demand.

***Quebec, 2000-2001.** (Illus.). 2000. pap. 21.95 (*2-89464-301-2*, Pub. by Ulysses Travel) Globe Pequot.

Quebec Women: A History. Michele Dumont et al. Tr. by Roger Gannon & Rosalind Gill. 396p. pap. 17.95 (*0-88961-101-7*, Pub. by Womens Pr) LPC InBook.

***Quebecois: The Virgin Forest.** Doris Provencher Faucher. LC 00-91765. (Illus.). viii, 264p. 2000. pap. 19.95 (*0-9679112-3-0*) Artenay Pr.

Quebec's Aboriginal Languages: History, Planning & Development, Vol. 107. Jacques Maurais. LC 96-16507. 260p. 1996. 59.00 (*1-85359-361-3*, Pub. by Multilingual Matters) Taylor & Francis.

Quebec's Jews: Vital Citizens or Eternal Strangers. Sol Littman. (Special Reports). (Illus.). 35p. (Orig.). pap. write for info. (*0-943058-11-2*) S Wiesenthal Ctr.

Quebrando la Intimidacion. John Bevere. (SPA.). 1995. pap. 9.99 (*0-88419-603-8*) Casa Creacion.

Quechua Peoples Poetry. Jesus Lara. Ed. & Tr. by Maria A. Proser & James Scully from QUE. LC 76-26704. Orig. Title: Poesia Popular Quechua. 68p. 1986. pap. 9.95 (*0-915306-09-3*) Curbstone.

Quechua Phrasebook. Ronald Wright. (QUE.). 96p. (Orig.). 1989. pap. 3.95 (*0-86442-039-0*) Lonely Planet.

Quedlinburg Treasury. Dallas Museum of Art Staff. (Illus.). 30p. (Orig.). 1991. pap. 14.95 (*0-936227-10-9*) U of Wash Pr.

Queen. Peter K. Hogan. (Complete Guides to the Music Of...Ser.). (Illus.). 136p. (Orig.). pap. 8.95 (*0-7119-3526-2*, OP 47334, Pub. by Omnibus Press) Omnibus NY.

Queen. Allen Lane. LC 78-303872. 186 p. 1977. write for info. (*0-7139-1060-7*, A Lane) Viking Penguin.

Queen: A Biography of Elizabeth II. Ben Pimlott. LC 97-21270. 672p. 1997. 30.00 (*0-471-19431-X*) Wiley.

Queen: A Biography of Elizabeth II. Ben Pimlott. 672p. 1998. pap. 18.95 (*0-471-28330-4*) Wiley.

Queen: A Night at the Opera. 104p. 1995. otabind 19.95 (*0-7935-3849-1*, 00694974) H Leonard.

Queen: A Visual Documentary. Ken Dean. (Illus.). 112p. pap. 21.95 (*0-7119-2828-2*, OP 46721) Omnibus NY.

Queen: Greatest Hits. 128p. 1996. per. 24.95 (*0-7935-3850-5*, 00694975) H Leonard.

Queen: Greatest Hits 1. 1994. 19.95 (*0-7935-4289-8*, 00306018) H Leonard.

Queen: In Their Own Words. Mick St. Michael. (In Their Own Words Ser.). (Illus.). 96p. pap. 15.95 (*0-7119-3014-7*, OP 46879) Omnibus NY.

Queen: The Bass Guitar Collection. 96p. 1996. per. 17.95 (*0-7935-4880-2*, 00690065) H Leonard.

Queen: The Early Years. Mark Hodkinson. (Illus.). 208p. (Orig.). 1997. pap. 24.95 (*0-7119-6012-7*, OP 47853) Omnibus NY.

Queen: The New Biography. large type ed. John Parker. (Charnwood Library). (Illus.). 736p. 1993. 27.99 (*0-7089-8713-3*) Ulverscroft.

Queen - These Are the Days of Our Lives: The Essential Queen Biography. Stephen Rider. (Illus.). 240p. 1993. pap. 10.00 (*0-685-72583-9*, Pub. by Castle Communs) Viking Penguin.

Queen Amidala, Vol. 1. Jude Watson. (Star Wars). (Illus.). 111p. (gr. 3-7). 1999. pap. 5.99 (*0-590-52101-2*) Scholastic Inc.

Queen Amidala Paper Dolls, 1. Ed. by Lucas Books. 1999. pap. 3.99 (*0-375-80020-4*) Random.

Queen & Country. Suzy Menkes. (Illus.). 226p. 1993. 35.00 (*0-246-13676-6*, Pub. by HarpC) HarpC.

Queen & I. Barbara J. Crane. (Crane Reading System-English Ser.). (Illus.). (gr. k-2). 1977. pap. text 4.85 (*0-89075-093-9*) Bilingual Ed Serv.

Queen & I. Sue Townsend. 96p. 1995. pap. 11.95 (*0-413-68970-0*, A0729) Heinemann.

Queen & I. Sue Townsend. LC 93-13764. 239p. 1994. pap. 12.00 (*1-56947-015-4*) Soho Press.

Queen & I: The Brian May Story. Laura Jackson. (Illus.). 216p. 1995. pap. 17.99 (*1-886894-01-9*, MBS Paperbk) Mus Bk Servs.

Queen & Lord M. large type ed. Jean Plaidy, pseud. (Shadows of the Crown Ser.). 1975. 27.99 (*0-85456-600-7*) Ulverscroft.

Queen & Lord M. Jean Plaidy, pseud. 268p. reprint ed. lib. bdg. 22.95 (*0-88411-895-9*) Amereon Ltd.

Queen & the Arts: Cultural Life in Nineteenth-Century Cincinnati. Robert C. Vitz. LC 88-30112. (Illus.). 323p. 1989. 27.50 (*0-87338-376-1*) Kent St U Pr.

Queen Ann in Oz. Karyl Carlson & Eric Gjovaag. (Illus.). 128p. (J). (gr. 2 up). 1993. 44.95 (0-929605-26-8); pap. 9.95 (0-929605-25-X) Books of Wonder.

Queen Anne & Georgian Looking Glasses: Old English & Early American. F. Lewis Hinckley. (Hinckley Furniture Ser.). (Illus.). 256p. (C). 1988. text 75.00 (0-8147-3447-2) NYU Pr.

Queen Anne Furniture. Norman Vandal. (Illus.). 256p. (C). 1990. 39.95 (0-942391-07-1) Taunton.

Queen Anne's Gate Mystery: A Novel, 2 vols. Richard Arkwright. LC 75-32733. (Literature of Mystery & Detection Ser.). 1976. reprint ed. 41.95 (0-405-07863-3) Ayer.

Queen Anne's Lace. Jerome Wexler. LC 93-29621. 32p. (J). (gr. 1-5). 1994. lib. bdg. 14.95 (0-8075-6710-8) A Whitman.

Queen Anne's Lace: Reflections. Genevieve S. Whitford. (Illus.). 53p. 1990. reprint ed. 12.95 (0-9610456-2-0) Harp Pr.

Queen Anne's Lace & Other Weeds. Mary J. Hartman. (Illus.). 160p. (Orig.). 1997. pap. 12.95 (1-57736-030-3) Providence Hse.

***Queen Anne's War.** JoAnn A. Grote. (American Adventure Ser.: No. 5). (J). (gr. 3-6). 1998. pap. 3.97 (1-57748-146-1) Barbour Pub.

Queen Anne's War. JoAnn A. Grote. LC 98-19952. (American Adventure Ser.: No. 5). 144p. (J). (gr. 4-7). 1999. lib. bdg. 15.95 (0-7910-5045-9) Chelsea Hse.

Queen Bess: Daredevil Aviator. Doris L. Rich. (Illus.). 172p. 1995. pap. 14.95 (1-56098-618-2) Smithsonian.

Queen Catalogues, 2 vols., Set. Queen, James W., & Company Staff. (Illus.). 1665p. 1993. reprint ed. 245.00 (0-930405-30-7) Norman SF.

Queen Christina. Marcia Landy & Amy Villarejo. LC 96-139030. 79p. 1996. pap. 10.95 (0-85170-523-5, Pub. by British Film Inst) Ind U Pr.

Queen Christina of Sweden & Her Circle: The Transformation of a Seventeenth-Century Philosophical Libertine. Susanna Akerman. LC 90-42995. (BSIH Ser.: No. 21). xv, 339p. 1991. 108.00 (90-04-09310-9) Brill Academic Pubs.

Queen City Jazz. Kathleen A. Goonan. 480p. 1996. mass mkt. 5.99 (0-8125-3626-6, Pub. by Tor Bks) St Martin.

Queen City of the North: Dawson City, Yukon a Pictorial History. Stan B. Cohen. 136p. 1990. pap. 9.95 (0-929521-31-5) Pictorial Hist.

Queen City Refuge. Ed. by Abraham J. Peck & Uri D. Herscher. 270p. 1989. 29.95 (0-87441-486-5) Behrman.

Queen Classic. 128p. 1995. otabind 24.95 (0-7935-3982-X, 00690003) H Leonard.

Queen Conch. Katherine S. Orr & Carl J. Berg, Jr. (Illus.). 32p. 1987. pap. 2.95 (0-89317-038-0) Windward Pub.

Queen Consorts of England: The Power Behind the Throne. Petronelle Cook. LC 93-16463. (Illus.). 320p. 1993. 35.00 (0-8160-2900-8) Facts on File.

Queen Deluxe Anthology. 144p. 1994. otabind 16.95 (0-7935-3617-0, 00308246) H Leonard.

Queen D's Fairy Recipe Book. Cindy McGonagle. Ed. by Debora Alder. (Illus.). 92p. 1994. pap. 13.25 (0-9640243-1-4) Botanic Reprod.

***Queen Eleanor: Independent Spirit of the Medieval World: A Biography of Eleanor of Aquitaine.** Polly Schoyer Brooks. 192p. (YA). (gr. 7). 1999. pap. 8.95 (0-395-98139-5) HM.

Queen Elizabeth. Edward S. Beesly. LC 74-39408. (Select Bibliographies Reprint Ser.). 1977. reprint ed. 18.95 (0-8369-9901-0) Ayer.

Queen Elizabeth & Her Subjects. Alfred L. Rowse & George B. Harrison. LC 79-76913. (Essay Index Reprint Ser.). 1977. 16.95 (0-8369-1895-9) Ayer.

Queen Elizabeth & the Making of Policy, 1572-1588. Wallace T. MacCaffrey. LC 80-8564. 540p. reprint ed. pap. 167.40 (0-608-06420-3, 206663300008) Bks Demand.

Queen Elizabeth & the Revolt of the Netherlands. Charles Wilson. LC 76-119009. (Illus.). 188p. reprint ed. pap. 58.30 (0-608-18299-0, 203155000075) Bks Demand.

Queen Elizabeth in Drama & Related Studies. Frederick S. Boas. LC 78-119954. (Select Bibliographies Reprint Ser.). 1977. 21.95 (0-8369-5397-5) Ayer.

Queen Elizabeth in Drama & Related Studies. Frederick S. Boas. (Select Bibliographies Reprint Ser.). 212p. 1982. reprint ed. lib. bdg. 14.00 (0-8290-0828-4) Irvington.

Queen Elizabeth the First. Bellerophon Books Staff. (J). (gr. 1-9). 1992. pap. 4.95 (0-88388-013-X) Bellerophon Bks.

Queen Elizabeth I. Robert Green. LC 96-51691. (First Bk.). (J). 1997. lib. bdg. 22.00 (0-531-20302-6) Watts.

***Queen Elizabeth I.** Claire Price-Groff. LC 00-9247. (Importance of Ser.). (Illus.). (J). 2001. write for info. (1-56006-700-4) Lucent Bks.

Queen Elizabeth the First. John E. Neale. 424p. (C). 1992. reprint ed. pap. 16.95 (0-89733-362-4) Academy Chi Pubs.

Queen Elizabeth II. Robert Green. LC 96-51191. (First Bk.). (J). (gr. 4-6). 1997. lib. bdg. 22.00 (0-531-20303-4) Watts.

Queen Elizabeth II: A Woman Who Is Not Amused. Nicholas Davies. LC 93-46668. 1994. 24.95 (1-55972-217-7, Birch Ln Pr) Carol Pub Group.

Queen Elizabeth II: A Woman Who Is Not Amused. rev. ed. Nicholas Davies. (Citadel Stars Ser.). (Illus.). 544p. 1996. mass mkt. 6.99 (0-8065-8001-1, Citadel Pr) Carol Pub Group.

Queen Elizabeth II: A Woman Who Is Not Amused. rev. ed. Nicholas Davies. (Illus.). 544p. 1998. mass mkt. 6.99 (0-8065-8015-1, Citadel Pr) Carol Pub Group.

Queen Elizabeth II. Susan Auerbach. LC 92-46478. (World Leaders Ser.). 112p. (YA). 1993. lib. bdg. 25.27 (0-86625-481-1) Rourke Pubns.

Queen Emma: A Woman of Vision. Miriam E. Rappolt. (Illus.). (Orig.). (YA). 1991. pap. 12.95 (0-916630-68-4) Pr Pacifica.

Queen Emma & Queen Edith: Women & Power in Eleventh-Century England. Pauline Stafford. LC 96-38246. (Illus.). xi, 371p. 1997. text 38.95 (0-631-16679-3) Blackwell Pubs.

Queen Emma & the Bishop. 2nd ed. Katherine S. Thompson. (Illus.). 1987. reprint ed. text. write for info. (0-938851-04-7) Daughters of HI.

Queen Esther. Katy K. Arnsteen. LC 96-27844. (KidScripts Ser.). (Illus.). 24p. (Orig.). (J). (gr. 2-5). 1997. pap. 3.95 (0-8198-6207-X) Pauline Bks.

Queen Esther. Myrth E. Burr. 48p. 1998. pap. text 8.95 (1-57636-055-5) SunRise Pbl.

Queen Esther. Tomie De Paola. 1985. pap. 5.95 (0-86683-702-7) Harper SF.

Queen Esther. Mable Renault. 60p. (Orig.). 1988. pap. text 6.00 (0-685-28899-4) Rivendell Hse Ltd.

Queen Esther Saves Her People see Camello y la Estrella

Queen Esther Saves Her People. Rita G. Gelman. LC 97-2568. (Illus.). 40p. (J). (gr. k-3). 1998. 15.95 (0-590-47025-6) Scholastic Inc.

Queen Esther, the Morning Star: The Story of Purim. Mordicai Gerstein. LC 97-29653. 32p. (J). 2000. 16.00 (0-689-81372-4) S&S Bks Yung.

Queen Euphoria: A Shadowrun Adventure. FASA Corp. Staff. (Illus.). 1990. pap. 8.00 (1-55560-117-0, 7304) FASA Corp.

Queen Flea: The Helen Robinson Story. Jack Kelly. Ed. by Helen Robinson. LC 97-93566. (Illus.). 175p. 1997. 20.00 (0-9657930-0-1) J Kelly.

Queen Fussy. Mister Tom. (Illus.). 48p. (J). (gr. 2-4). 1973. audio. write for info. (0-318-57347-4) Oddo.

Queen Hatshepsut: Glorifying the Past for the Present & Future. AESOP Enterprises, Inc. Staff & Gwendolyn J. Crenshaw. (Heroes & Sheroes Ser.). 14p. (J). (gr. 3-12). 1991. pap. write for info. incl. audio (1-880771-11-X) AESOP Enter.

***Queen High.** Jack Johnson. LC 00-104101. 614p. 2000. pap. 24.00 (0-9651935-4-3, Prmetheus Pr) Fisher Ent.

Queen Hynde. James Hogg. 1997. 50.00 (0-7486-0934-2, Pub. by Edinburgh U Pr) Col U Pr.

Queen in Waiting. Jean Plaidy, pseud. 26.95 (0-8488-0609-3) Amereon Ltd.

Queen Is Dead. Jane Dentinger. 288p. 1995. pap. 5.95 (0-14-015835-9, Penguin Bks) Viking Penguin.

***Queen Is Dead: A Story of Jarheads, Eggheads, Serial Killers & Bad Sex.** Mark Simpson. 2001. pap. 14.95 (1-900850-49-4) Arcadia Bks.

Queen Is Holding a Mummified Cat, Vol. 1. Mary Melfi. 88p. pap. 5.00 (0-919349-09-9) Guernica Editions.

Queen Jane's Version: The Holy Bible for Adults Only. Douglas A. Rankin. LC 98-93134. (Illus.). 1152p. 1998. 29.95 (0-9665208-6-6) Dallas Emporia.

***Queen Jeanne & the Promised Land.** David Bryson. LC 99-16388. (Studies in Intellectual History). 400p. 1999. 117.50 (90-04-11378-9) Brill Academic Pubs.

Queen Justine. Janet Quin-Harkin. LC 94-12252. (Boyfriend Club Ser.: Vol. 4). 176p. (J). (gr. 3-6). 1997. pap. 2.95 (0-8167-3417-8) Troll Communs.

Queen Katharine Parr. Anthony K. Martienssen. LC 75-329565. x, 249p. 1973. write for info. (0-436-27328-4) M Secker & Warburg.

Queen Katherine Parr. Anthony K. Martienssen. LC 73-14768. x, 249p. 1974. write for info. (0-07-040610-3) McGraw.

***Queen Latifah.** Amy Ruth. LC 99-50945. (A&E Biography Ser.). (Illus.). 128p. (YA). (gr. 4-7). 2000. lib. bdg. 25.26 (0-8225-4988-3, Lerner Publctns) Lerner Pub.

Queen Live: A Concert Documentary. Greg Brooks. (Illus.). 176p. (Orig.). (C). 1995. pap. 24.95 (0-7119-4814-3, OP 47752) Omnibus NY.

Queen Lucia. E. F. Benson. LC 97-41891. 176p. 1998. pap. 10.95 (1-55921-252-7) Moyer Bell.

***Queen Lucia, Set.** unabridged ed. E. F. Benson. (C). 1998. 41.95 incl. audio (1-55685-584-2) Audio Bk Con.

Queen Maeve & Her Lovers: A Celtic Archetype of Ecstacy, Addition & Healing. Sylvia Brinton Perera. 490p. 1999. 39.00 (0-8290-5211-9) Ardent Media.

Queen Margot. Alexandre Dumas. LC 94-7600. 542p. (J). 1994. pap. 14.45 (0-7868-8082-1, Pub. by Hyperion) Time Warner.

Queen Marinette: Spirit of Survival on the Great Lakes Frontier. Beverly H. Johnson. (Illus.). 92p. (Orig.). 1995. pap. 9.95 (0-9648524-0-3) Whte Water.

Queen Mary. James Steele. 240p. 1995. 55.00 (0-7148-2891-2, Pub. by Phaidon Press) Phaidon Pr.

Queen Mary: The Official Pictorial History. Robert O. Maguglin. LC 85-50967. (Illus.). 120p. 1988. pap. 10.95 (0-917859-21-9) Sunrise SBCA.

Queen Mary & the Cruiser: The Curacoa Disaster. David A. Thomas & Patrick Holmes. (Illus.). 208p. 1997. 32.95 (1-55750-698-1) Naval Inst Pr.

Queen Mary's Dolls' House. Mary Stewart-Wilson. (Illus.). 192p. 1988. 49.95 (0-89659-876-4) Abbeville Pr.

Queen Moo & the Egyptian Sphinx. 2nd ed. Augustus Le Plongeon. 277p. 1996. reprint ed. 32.50 (0-7873-0539-1) Hlth Research.

Queen Moo's Talisman: The Fall of the Maya Empire. Alice D. Le Plongeon. 90p. 1994. reprint ed. pap. 15.95 (1-56459-426-2) Kessinger Pub.

Queen Mother: An Alternative Portrait of Her Life & Times. Penelope Mortimer. LC 96-164692. (Illus.). 320p. 1996. pap. 16.95 (0-233-98972-2, Pub. by Andre Deutsch) Trafalgar.

***Queen Mother: Chronicle of a Remarkable Life.** Kindersley Dorling. (Illus.). 128p. 2000. 19.95 (0-7894-5844-6) DK Pub Inc.

***Queen Mother: Grandmother of a Nation.** Richard Wood & Sara Wood. LC 00-36933. 2000. write for info. (0-8172-5715-2) Raintree Steck-V.

***Queen Mother's Century.** Robert Lacey. 132p. (gr. 8). 1999. 25.95 (0-316-51154-4) Little.

Queen Must Die & Other Affairs of Bees & Men. William Longgood. (Illus.). 1988. pap. 13.95 (0-393-30528-7) Norton.

Queen Nadine. Maryann Kovalski. LC 97-81082. (Illus.). 32p. (J). (ps-2). 2000. pap. 6.95 (1-55143-095-9) Orca Bk Pubs.

Queen Named King: Henrietta of the King Ranch. Mary V. Fox. 80p. (J). (gr. 5-6). 1986. pap. 6.95 (1-57168-137-X) Sunbelt Media.

Queen Nefertiti. Bellerophon Books Staff. (J). (gr. 1-9). 1992. pap. 3.50 (0-88388-154-3) Bellerophon Bks.

Queen Number & Sociality in Insects. Ed. by Laurent Keller. (Illus.). 456p. (C). 1993. text 90.00 (0-19-854057-4, 8829) OUP.

***Queen of Aces.** Aaron Masters. 300p. 2000. pap. 14.95 (1-929976-02-X, Pub. by Top Pubns) Herveys Bklink.

Queen of America Goes to Washington City: Essays on Sex & Citizenship. Lauren G. Berlant. LC 96-35146. (Series Q). (Illus.). 336p. 1997. pap. 16.95 (0-8223-1924-1); lib. bdg. 49.95 (0-8223-1931-4) Duke.

Queen of Angels. Greg Bear. 482p. 1991. reprint ed. mass mkt. 6.99 (0-446-36130-5, Pub. by Warner Bks) Little.

Queen of Angels: Mary's Answers to Universal Questions. Janice T. Connell. LC 99-34813. 224p. 1999. 19.95 (0-87477-993-6, Tarcher Putnam) Putnam Pub Group.

Queen of Apostles Prayerbook. Compiled by Daughters of St. Paul Staff. 384p. 1991. vinyl bd. 12.95 (0-8198-6201-0) Pauline Bks.

Queen of Apostles Prayerbook. rev. ed. James Alberione. 384p. (J). 1991. pap. 9.95 (0-8198-6200-2) Pauline Bks.

Queen of Apostles Prayerbook. rev. ed. James Alberione. 384p. (J). 1991. vinyl bd. 12.95 (0-8198-6202-9) Pauline Bks.

Queen of Ashes. Deborah T. Harris. 464p. (Orig.). 1995. mass mkt. 5.99 (0-441-00118-1) Ace Bks.

Queen of Atlantis: Romance of the Caribbean Sea. Frank Aubrey. LC 74-15949. (Science Fiction Ser.). 394p. 1975. reprint ed. 33.95 (0-405-06275-3) Ayer.

***Queen of Attolia.** Megan Whalen Turner. LC 99-26916. 288p. (YA). (gr. 5 up). 2000. 15.95 (0-688-17423-X, Grenwillow Bks) HarpC Child Bks.

***Queen of Attolia Bound Galley.** (J). 2000. write for info. (0-06-029062-5) HarpC Child Bks.

***Queen of Attolia Reading Group Guide.** 2000. write for info. (0-688-18035-3) Morrow Avon.

Queen of Battle. John W. Cooley. LC 98-89880. 365p. 1999. 25.00 (0-7388-0313-8); pap. 15.00 (0-7388-0314-6) Xlibris Corp.

Queen of Bingo. Jeanne Michels & Phyllis Murphy. LC 95-186019. 1994. pap. 5.25 (0-8222-1417-2) Dramatists Play.

Queen of Bohemia: The Autobiography of Dulcie Deamer. Ed. by Peter Kirkpatrick. LC 98-226254. 1p. 1998. pap. 29.95 (0-7022-2726-9, Pub. by Univ Queensland Pr) Intl Spec Bk.

***Queen of Bohemia: The Life of Louise Bryant.** Mary V. Dearborn. (Illus.). 384p. 1999. 29.95 (0-7351-0146-9) Replica Bks.

Queen of Cherryvale. Judith Glad. 300p. Date not set. 4.50 (1-928670-87-3) Awe Struck E Bks.

Queen of Darkness. Miguel Conner. 288p. (Orig.). 1998. mass mkt. 5.99 (0-446-60506-9, Pub. by Warner Bks) Little.

Queen of Darkness. Frances M. Nordan. 168p. (Orig.). 1993. pap. 9.95 (1-880365-10-3) Prof Pr NC.

Queen of Demons. David Drake. LC 98-7132. (Lord of the Isles Ser.: Vol. 2). 480p. 1998. 25.95 (0-312-86468-X, Pub. by Tor Bks) St Martin.

Queen of Demons. David Drake. (Lord of the Isles Ser.: Vol. 2). 662p. 1999. mass mkt. 6.99 (0-8125-6493-6, Pub. by Tor Bks) St Martin.

Queen of Demonweb Pits. Gary Gygax. 1980. 5.50 (0-394-51541-2) Random.

Queen of Denial. Selina Rosen. 380p. 1999. pap. 12.00 (1-892065-06-1) Meisha Merlin.

***Queen of Diamonds: The Fabled Legacy of Evalyn Walsh McLean.** Evalyn Walsh McLean & Boyden Sparkes. LC 00-31939. 2000. write for info. (1-57736-192-X, Hillsboro Pr) Providence Hse.

Queen of Dreamland. Ingrid Tomey. 184p. (YA). (gr. 7 up). 1996. 15.00 (0-689-80458-X) S&S Bks Yung.

Queen of Glen Eyrie: Story of Mary Lincoln Mellen Palmer, Wife of General William Palmer, Founder of Colorado Springs, CO. Celeste Black. (Illus.). 128p. 1999. pap. 9.95 (0-9658535-1-9) Blck Bear Pubns.

Queen of Hearts see Reina De Corazones

Queen of Hearts. Barbara Cartland & Jove Books Publishing Staff. (Camfield Novel of Love Ser.: 119). 176p. 1993. mass mkt. 3.99 (0-515-11139-2, Jove) Berkley Pub.

Queen of Hearts. Vera Cleaver & Bill Cleaver. LC 77-18252. 160p. (YA). (gr. 6 up). 1978. 14.00 (0-397-31771-9) HarpC Child Bks.

Queen of Hearts. Heather Graham. 304p. 1997. mass mkt. 5.99 (0-8217-5746-6, Zebra Kensgtn) Kensgtn Pub Corp.

Queen of Hearts. Elizabeth Koda-Callan. LC 95-18351. (Magic Charm Bks.). (Illus.). 48p. (J). (ps-3). 1995. bds. 12.95 (0-7611-0167-5, 10167) Workman Pub.

Queen of Hearts. Michelle Martin. 1994. mass mkt. 3.99 (0-449-22203-9) Fawcett.

Queen of Hearts. Emily Maxwell. 1992. mass mkt. 3.50 (0-8217-3639-6, Zebra Kensgtn) Kensgtn Pub Corp.

Queen of Hearts. large type ed. Barbara Cartland. LC 98-14058. 176p. 1998. 24.95 (0-7862-1455-4) Thorndike Pr.

Queen of Hearts. large type ed. Heather Graham. LC 97-44873. 1998. 26.95 (0-7862-1311-6) Thorndike Pr.

Queen of Hearts. Wilkie Collins. LC 75-32740. (Literature of Mystery & Detection Ser.). 1976. reprint ed. 39.95 (0-405-07868-4) Ayer.

Queen of Hearts: Incl. the Little Novel: Mr. Lepel & the Housekeeper see Works of Wilkie Collins

***Queen of Hearts: Tales of Middle-Age Passion.** Millie Grace-Brown. LC 99-90608. 192p. 2000. 23.00 (0-9671851-7-3, Pub. by GreyCore) Allnce Hse.

Queen of Hearts: The Passionate Pilgrimage of Lola Montez. Isaac Goldberg. LC 75-91505. 308p. 1972. 20.95 (0-405-08563-X) Ayer.

***Queen of Hearts; a Transsexual Romance.** Brad Clayton. Ed. by Deni Carno. (Illus.). 200p. 1999. pap. 12.95 (0-9665900-0-7) E R Pubns.

Queen of Hearts & Other Favorite Nursery Rhymes. Illus. by Kay Widdowson. (Nursery Rhyme Fun Ser.). 12p. (J). 1995. boxed set 6.95 (1-884628-21-4, Flyng Frog) Allied Pub MD.

Queen of Hearts Journal. Illus. by Barry Moser. (Barry Moser Ser.). 160p. 1998. 9.95 (1-55156-082-8) Paperblank.

Queen of Ice, Queen of Shadows: The Unsuspected Life of Sonja Henie. Raymond Strait & Leif Henie. LC 84-40239. (Illus.). 344p. 1990. pap. 12.95 (0-8128-8518-X, Scrbrough Hse) Madison Bks UPA.

Queen of Lost Baggage. Barbara Lefcowitz. LC 85-52078. (Series Ten). 72p. (Orig.). 1986. pap. 7.00 (0-931846-29-3) Wash Writers Pub.

Queen of Mathematics: A Historically Motivated Guide to Number Theory. Jay Goldman. LC 94-20017. (Illus.). xxiv, 525 p. (C). 1997. text 59.95 (1-56881-006-7) AK Peters.

Queen of Mathematics: An Introduction to Number Theory. W. S. Anglin. LC 94-42070. (Texts in the Mathematical Sciences Ser.: No. 8). 389p. 1995. text 173.50 (0-7923-3287-3) Kluwer Academic.

Queen of My Room: A Survey of Work by Julie Speed, 1989-1999. Elizabeth Ferrer. (Illus.). 80p. 1999. 25.00 (0-9670952-0-4) Austin Mus.

Queen of Navarre, Jeanne D'Albret, 1528-1572. Nancy L. Roelker. LC 68-54024. (Illus.). 515p. 1968. 42.50 (0-674-74150-1) Belknap Pr.

Queen of October. Shelley F. Mickle. (Front Porch PB Ser.). 320p. 1992. pap. 8.95 (1-56512-003-5, 72003) Algonquin Bks.

Queen of Peace Visits Medugorie. Joseph A. Pelletier. 1998. pap. text 7.50 (5-551-70100-X) Ambasdr Bks.

Queen of Scots. Rosalind K. Marshall. (Illus.). 208p. 1986. pap. 20.00 (0-11-493122-4, Pub. by Statnry Office) Balogh.

***Queen of Sea Routes: The Merchant & Miners Transportation Company.** Edward A. Mueller. Ed. by Edwin L. Dunbaugh. LC 99-57379. (Illus.). 185p. 2000. lib. bdg. 37.50 (1-930098-00-6) Purple Mnt Pr.

Queen of Shade. Sparrow T. Laughingwand. (Orig.). 1993. pap. 3.00 (0-929730-44-5) Zeitgeist Pr.

Queen of Sheba. Thomas Bailey Aldrich. (Works of Thomas Bailey Aldrich). 1989. reprint ed. lib. bdg. 79.00 (0-7812-1673-7) Rprt Serv.

Queen of Sheba: Poetry Book Society Recommendation. Kathleen Jamie et al. 64p. (J). 1995. pap. 14.95 (1-85224-284-1) Dufour.

Queen of Sheba & Her Only Son Menyelek, Vol. I. E. A. Bode. Ed. by Al I. Obaba. (Illus.). 196p. 1922. pap. text 27.00 (0-916157-59-8) African Islam Miss Pubns.

Queen of Sheba & Her Only Son Menyelek, Vol. II. E. A. Wallis Budge. Ed. by Al I. Obaba. (Illus.). 214p. 1922. pap. text 27.00 (0-916157-60-1) African Islam Miss Pubns.

***Queen of Sheba & Her Son Menyelek: The Kebra Nagast.** Tr. by E. A. Wallis Budge. 350p. 2000. text 110.00 (0-7103-0712-8) Col U Pr.

Queen of Sicily & Gothic Stained Glass in Mussy & Tonnerre. Meredith P. Lillich. LC 98-20435. (Transactions of the American Philosophical Society Ser.: Vol. 88, Pt. 3). 1998. pap. 20.00 (0-87169-883-8) Am Philos.

Queen of Slots. H. C. Petley. 288p. (Orig.). 1990. pap. 4.95 (0-9625559-0-8) Gate Pr Pubs.

Queen of Sofa Mountain: A Cat's Fantasy. Brent Warren. LC 93-77890. (Illus.). 60p. (Orig.). 1993. pap. 12.00 (1-883350-01-8) Imagelust Stud.

Queen of Sorcery. David Eddings. (Belgariad Ser.: Bk. 2). 336p. 1986. mass mkt. 6.99 (0-345-33565-1, Del Rey) Ballantine Pub Grp.

Queen of Sorcery. David Eddings. (Belgariad Ser.). 1982. 12.09 (0-606-01240-0, Pub. by Turtleback) Demco.

Queen of Spades. Harold H. Henderson. LC 82-83127. 160p. 1985. pap. 16.00 (0-932966-58-6) Permanent Pr.

Queen of Spades. Sid Rowland. (Illus.). 86p. 1999. pap. 10.00 (0-937158-00-3) Del Valley.

Queen of Spades & Other Stories. Aleksandr Pushkin. Tr. & Intro. by Rosemary Edmonds. (Classics Ser.). 320p. 1978. pap. 12.95 (0-14-044119-0, Penguin Classics) Viking Penguin.

Queen of Spades & Other Stories. Aleksandr Pushkin. Tr. by T. Keane from RUS. 128p. 1994. reprint ed. pap. 1.50 (0-486-28054-3) Dover.

Queen of Spades & Other Stories. Aleksandr Pushkin. 128p. 1999. reprint ed. pap. 6.95 (1-57002-096-5) Univ Publng Hse.

Queen of Swords. Anne E. Crompton. LC 79-26496. 1980. 9.95 (0-416-30611-X, NO. 0165) Routledge.

Queen of Swords. Judith Tarr. LC 96-33220. 448p. 1997. 25.95 (0-312-85821-3, Pub. by Forge NYC) St Martin.

***Queen of Swords.** Judith Tarr. 464p. 2000. pap. 17.95 (0-312-86805-7) St Martin.

***Queen of Swords.** Judith Tarr. 1998. mass mkt. 6.99 (0-8125-5085-4) Tor Bks.

Queen of Terrors. Robert Kelly. 150p. 1994. 20.00 (0-929701-41-0); pap. 12.00 (0-929701-40-2) McPherson & Co.

Queen of the Air: A Study of Greek Myths. John Ruskin. 1969. pap. 22.00 (0-8196-1392-4) Biblo.

An Asterisk (*) at the beginning of an entry indicates that the title is appearing for the first time.

Queen of the Air: The Story of Katherine Stinson, 1891-1977. Mary C. Powell. Ed. by Thomas W. Petrick. (Southwesterners Ser.). (Illus.). 121p. (YA). (gr. 4 up). 1993. pap. 9.95 (*1-880384-07-8*) Coldwater Pr.

Queen of the Amazons. Kerry Millron. LC 96-14179. (Picturebacks Ser.). 23p. (ps-3). 1996. pap. 3.25 (*0-679-88296-0*) Random.

Queen of the "B" Ida Lupino Behind the Camera. Annette Kuhn. LC 95-12532. 208p. 1995. pap. 20.95 (*0-275-95332-7*, Praeger Pubs) Greenwood.

Queen of the Black Black. Megan Kelso. 1999. pap. text 12.95 (*0-9665363-0-4*) Questover Bks.

Queen of the "B"s: Ida Lupino Behind the Camera, 49. Ed. by Annette Kuhn. LC 95-12532. (Contributions to the Study of Popular Culture Ser.: Vol. 49). 208p. 1995. 65.00 (*0-313-29732-0*, Greenwood Pr) Greenwood.

Queen of the Cold-Blooded Tales. Roberta S. Brown. (American Storytelling Ser.). (Illus.). 176p. (YA). (gr. 6 up). 1995. pap. text 9.95 (*0-87483-408-2*) August Hse.

Queen of the Cosmos. Jan Connell. LC 90-61665. (Illus.). 152p. 1990. pap. 9.95 (*1-55725-018-9*, 930-009, Pub. by Paraclete MA) BookWorld.

Queen of the Damned. Anne Rice. LC 88-45311. (Vampire Chronicles: Bk. 3). 432p. 1988. 25.00 (*0-394-55823-5*) Ballantine Pub Grp.

Queen of the Damned. Anne Rice. (Vampire Chronicles: Bk. 3). 491p. 1989. mass mkt. 6.99 (*0-345-35152-5*) Ballantine Pub Grp.

Queen of the Damned. Anne Rice. (Vampire Chronicles: Bk. 3). 1997. pap. 14.00 (*0-345-41962-6*) Ballantine Pub Grp.

***Queen of the Darkness.** Anne Bishop. (Black Jewels Trilogy Ser.: Vol. 3). (J). 2000. mass mkt. 5.99 (*0-451-45673-4*, ROC) NAL.

Queen of the Dixie Drive-In. Peg Sutherland. LC 96-2336. (Superromance Ser.). 296p. 1996. per. 3.99 (*0-373-70679-0*, 1-70679-5) Harlequin Bks.

Queen of the Dump or Road to the Sky. Regina C. Rapier. 1996. reprint ed. 10.00 (*0-614-24347-5*) R C Rapier.

Queen of the Ebony Isles. Colleen J. McElroy. LC 84-7494. (Wesleyan Poetry Ser.). (Illus.). 100p. 1984. pap. 12.95 (*0-8195-6101-0*, Wesleyan Univ Pr) U Pr of New Eng.

Queen of the Elephants. large type ed. Mark Shand. (Illus.). 400p. 1997. 31.50 (*0-7089-3674-1*) Ulverscroft.

Queen of the Empire. Paul Davids. (Star Wars: No. 5). 128p. (YA). (gr. 4-7). 1993. pap. 4.50 (*0-553-15891-0*) Bantam.

Queen of the Empire. Paul Davids. (Star Wars: No. 5). (YA). (gr. 4 up). 1993. 9.09 (*0-606-02849-8*, Pub. by Turtleback) Demco.

Queen of the Empire see Star Wars

Queen of the Gargoyles. Gene Hult (Bone Chillers Ser.). 1997. 9.09 (*0-606-11151-4*, Pub. by Turtleback) Demco.

Queen of the Gypsies: The Life & Legend of Carmen Amaya. Paco Sevilla. LC 98-90943. (Illus.). 400p. 1999. pap. 26.95 (*0-9646374-1-3*) Sevilla Pr.

Queen of the Headaches. Sharon Butala. 198p. 1985. reprint ed. mass mkt. 7.95 (*0-919926-48-7*, Pub. by Coteau) Genl Dist Srvs.

Queen of the Hill. Bruce Cochran. 10p. 1995. write for info. (*1-886386-32-3*) Trisar.

Queen of the Island. Jo A. Mazoue. 280p. (Orig.). 1993. pap. 11.95 (*0-923568-30-1*) Wilderness Adventure Bks.

Queen of the Jesters & Her Strange Adventures in Old Paris. Max Pemberton. LC 76-101818. (Short Story Index Reprint Ser.). 1977. 21.95 (*0-8369-3206-4*) Ayer.

Queen of the Kings Game. Zsuzsa Polgar & Jacob Shutzman. LC 97-91528. (Illus.). 384p. (Orig.). 1997. pap. 24.95 (*0-9657059-7-8*) Compchess Consult.

Queen of the Kisses. Sheryl W. Kayne. LC 94-75985. (Illus.). 32p. (J). (ps-2). 1994. 14.95 (*1-880851-13-X*) Greene Bark Pr.

Queen of the Kisses Meets Sam under a Soup Pot. Sheryl W. Kayne. LC 95-78160. (Illus.). 32p. (J). (ps-3). 1995. 14.95 (*1-880851-18-0*) Greene Bark Pr.

Queen of the Kitchen Journal. Illus by Mary Engelbreit. 104p. 1999. spiral bd. 14.95 (*0-8362-6833-4*) Andrews & McMeel.

Queen of the Lakes. Mark L. Thompson. LC 93-34403. 224p. 1994. 34.95 (*0-8143-2393-6*, Great Lks Bks) Wayne St U Pr.

Queen of the Legal Tender Saloon. Eileen Clarke. LC 97-4031. (Montana Novel Ser.). 288p. 1997. pap. 16.95 (*0-9626663-5-1*) Greycliff Pub.

Queen of the May. Denee Cody. 416p. 1997. mass mkt. 4.99 (*0-8217-5668-0*, Zebra Kensgtn) Kensgtn Pub Corp.

Queen of the May. Steven Kroll. LC 92-16393. (Illus.). 32p. (J). (gr. k-3). 1993. lib. bdg. 15.95 (*0-8234-1004-8*) Holiday.

Queen of the May. Colleen O. McKenna. (Dr. Quinn, Medicine Woman Ser.: No. 02). 1996. pap. 3.99 (*0-590-60373-6*) Scholastic Inc.

Queen of the Methodists: The Countess of Huntingdon & the Eighteenth-Century Crisis of Faith & Society. Boyd S. Schlenther. (Illus.). xiv, 208p. 1997. 40.00 (*1-900838-08-7*) U of Wash Pr.

Queen of the Midnight Skies: The Story of America's Air Force Night Fighters. Garry R. Pape & Ronald C. Harrison. LC 92-60359. (Illus.). 320p. 1992. text 45.00 (*0-88740-415-4*) Schiffer.

***Queen of the Mist.** Joan Murray. 2000. pap. 15.00 (*0-8070-6857-8*) Beacon Pr.

Queen of the Mist: The Forgotten Heroine of Niagara. Joan Murray. LC 98-42932. 128p. 1999. 20.00 (*0-8070-6852-7*) Beacon Pr.

Queen of the Negro Leagues: Effa Manley & the Newark Eagles. James Overmyer. LC 97-49909. (Illus.). 298p. 1998. pap. 16.95 (*1-57886-001-6*) Scarecrow.

Queen of the Night see Astrological Moon: Aspects, Signs, Cycles & the Mythology of the Goddess in Your Chart

Queen of the Night. R. Ambrose. 1997. mass mkt. 6.95 (*0-7472-5719-1*, Pub. by Headline Bk Pub) Trafalgar.

Queen of the Prisons of Greece. Osman Lins. Tr. by Adria Frizzi from POR. LC 94-7326. 192p. (Orig.). 1995. pap. 12.95 (*1-56478-056-2*) Dalkey Arch.

Queen of the Reformation. Charles Ludwig. LC 86-11754. 224p. 1986. pap. 7.99 (*0-87123-652-4*) Bethany Hse.

Queen of the Shakers see We Are the Shakers

***Queen of the Silver Castle.** Claire French. (Illus.). 128p. 1999. pap. 9.95 (*0-86315-291-0*) Anthroposophic.

Queen of the Silver Dollar. Edward Hower. LC 96-27417. 1997. 24.00 (*1-877946-92-3*) Permanent Pr.

***Queen of the South: New Orleans, 1853-1862: The Journal of Thomas K. Wharton.** Thomas K. Wharton et al. LC 99-44290. 1999. 39.95 (*0-917860-43-8*) Historic New Orleans.

Queen of the Strip. L. J. Brooksby. LC 98-89794. 240p. 2000. pap. 14.95 (*0-88739-234-2*) Creat Arts Bk.

Queen of the Summer Stars. Persia Woolley. Ed. by Julie Rubenstein. 448p. 1991. reprint ed. pap. 6.50 (*0-671-62202-1*) PB.

Queen of the Sun. Janeen O'Kerry. 320p. 1998. mass mkt. 4.99 (*0-505-52269-1*, Love Spell) Dorchester Pub Co.

Queen of the Sun: A Modern Revelation. Emory J. Michael. LC 95-18437. (Illus.). (Orig.). 1995. pap. 10.00 (*0-06-251356-7*) Harper SF.

Queen of the Sun: A Modern Revelation. 2nd rev. ed. E. J. Michael. (Illus.). 250p. 1995. pap. 12.95 (*0-9642147-8-4*) Mtn Rose Pubng.

Queen of the Swamp & Other Plain Americans. Mary H. Catherwood. 1972. reprint ed. lib. bdg. 30.00 (*0-8422-8024-3*) Irvington.

Queen of the Tambourine. Jane Gardam. LC 96-4265. 240p. 1996. pap. 11.00 (*0-312-14398-2*) St Martin.

Queen of the Tambourine. large type ed. Jane Gardam. 375p. 1996. pap. 20.95 (*0-7862-0604-7*) Thorndike Pr.

Queen of the Track: The Liz McColgan Story. Adrianne Blue. (Illus.). 224p. 1994. pap. 13.95 (*0-85493-232-1*) Trafalgar.

Queen of the Track: The Liz McColgan Story. Adrianne Blue. (Illus.). 224p. 1993. 29.95 (*0-85493-223-2*, Pub. by V Gollancz) Trafalgar.

***Queen of the World.** Thomas Yezerski. LC 99-27596. (Illus.). 32p. (J). (gr. k-3). 2000. 16.00 (*0-374-36165-7*) FS&G.

Queen of Trouble. Maria Marian. Tr. by Regina Incarcaturilor from RUM. LC 98-66961.Tr. of Regina Incarcaturilor. 155p. 1998. pap. 10.99 (*0-9623183-6-1*) Moonfall Pr VA.

Queen of Ukraine. John Bird. 65p. 1992. pap. 4.00 (*1-890137-28-6*) One Hund-One Fnd.

Queen of Whale Cay. Kate Summerscale. LC 99-219882. 1999. pap. 11.95 (*0-14-027613-0*) Viking Penguin.

***Queen of Whale Cay.** large type ed. Kate Summerscale. (Illus.). 256p. 1999. 31.99 (*0-7089-9079-7*, Linford) Ulverscroft.

Queen Rat: New & Selected Poems. Lynn Crosbie. LC 99-185683. 160p. 1999. pap. 14.95 (*0-88784-628-9*) Genl Dist Srvs.

Queen Rearing & Bee Breeding. Harry H. Laidlaw, Jr. & Robert E. Page, Jr. LC 96-27881. (Illus.). 216p. 1996. text 25.00 (*1-878075-08-X*) Wicwas Pr.

Queen Sacrifice. Iakov Neishtadt. LC 90-40805. (Russian Chess Ser.). 266p. 1990. pap. 14.95 (*0-685-47231-0*, Pub. by CHES) Macmillan.

***Queen Salote of Tonga: The Story of an Era, 1900-1965.** Elizabeth Wood-Ellem. (Illus.). 472p. 1999. 49.95 (*1-86940-205-7*, Pub. by Auckland Univ) Paul & Co Pubs.

***Queen Silver: The Godless Girl.** Wendy McElroy. LC 99-45067. (Women's Studies). 300p. 1999. 28.95 (*1-57392-755-4*) Prometheus Bks.

Queen Tempest. Jane G. Austin. (Works of Jane (Goodin) Austin). 1989. reprint ed. lib. bdg. 79.00 (*0-7812-1835-7*) Rprt Serv.

Queen Titania. Hjalmar H. Boyesen. LC 77-122691. (Short Story Index Reprint Ser.). 1977. 19.95 (*0-8369-3524-1*) Ayer.

Queen Versus Billy & Other Stories. Lloyd Osbourne. LC 70-101286. (Short Story Index Reprint Ser.). 1977. 20.95 (*0-8369-3223-4*) Ayer.

Queen Victoria. Robert Green. LC 97-10990. (First Book Ser.). 64p. (J). (gr. 4-7). 1998. 22.00 (*0-531-20330-1*) Watts.

Queen Victoria. Hibbert. Date not set. pap. write for info. (*0-465-06762-X*) Basic.

Queen Victoria. Elizabeth Longford. 2000. pap. text 9.95 (*0-7509-2143-9*) Sutton Pub Ltd.

Queen Victoria. Lytton Strachey. (Chatto Pocket Library). 542p. 1994. 17.95 (*0-7011-6054-3*, Pub. by Chatto & Windus) Trafalgar.

Queen Victoria. Lytton Strachey. LC 77-92139. 434p. 1966. pap. 15.00 (*0-15-675696-X*, Harvest Bks) Harcourt.

Queen Victoria. Lytton Strachey. LC 21-9740. (Modern Classic Ser.). 1989. 15.95 (*0-15-175695-3*) Harcourt.

Queen Victoria. Lytton Strachey. LC 97-189763. 250p. 1997. reprint ed. pap. 12.95 (*0-14-018393-0*) Penguin Putnam.

Queen Victoria: A Personal History. Christopher Hibbert. (Illus.). 464p. 2000. text 35.00 (*0-465-06761-1*, Pub. by Basic) HarpC.

Queen Victoria: An Eminent Illustrated Biography. Lytton Strachey. (Illus.). 228p. 1997. 19.98 (*1-57912-002-4*) Blck Dog & Leventhal.

***Queen Victoria & Thomas Sully.** Carrie Rebora Barratt. (Illus.). 224p. 2000. 35.00 (*0-691-07034-2*) Princeton U Pr.

***Queen Victoria in Her Letters & Journals.** Ed. by Christopher Hibbert. (Illus.). 384p. 2000. pap. 16.95 (*0-7509-2349-0*) Sutton Publng.

Queen Victoria in Switzerland. Peter Arengo-Jones. (Illus.). 160p. 1999. 24.95 (*0-7090-6460-8*, Pub. by R Hale Ltd) Seven Hills Bk.

Queen Victoria's "Alice in Wonderland" 2nd ed. Continental Historical Society Staff. Orig. Title: Queen Victoria's Secret Diaries. (Illus.). 290p. 1984. pap. 9.95 (*0-9609900-1-1*) Cont Hist Soc.

Queen Victoria's "Alice in Wonderland" 2nd ed. Continental Historical Society Staff. (Queen Victoria's Secret Diaries Ser.: Vol. 1). Orig. Title: Queen Victoria's Secret Diaries. (Illus.). 476p. (C). 1990. pap. text 16.95 (*0-9609900-3-8*) Cont Hist Soc.

Queen Victoria's Baggage: The Legacy of Building Dysfunctional Organizations. Daniel A. Silverman. 200p. 1999. 27.50 (*0-7618-1282-2*); pap. 27.50 (*0-7618-1281-4*) U Pr of Amer.

***Queen Victoria's Descendants.** Marlene A. Eilers. 184p. 1998. 45.00 (*91-630-5964-9*) Intl Spec Bk.

Queen Victoria's Enemies Vol. 1: Southern Africa. Ian Knight. (Men-at-Arms Ser.: No. 212). (Illus.). 48p. pap. 11.95 (*0-85045-901-X*, 9145, Pub. by Ospry) Stackpole.

Queen Victoria's Enemies Vol. 2: Northern Africa. Ian Knight. (Men-at-Arms Ser.: No. 215). (Illus.). 48p. pap. 11.95 (*0-85045-937-0*, 9148, Pub. by Ospry) Stackpole.

Queen Victoria's Enemies Vol. 4: East Asia & Australasia. Ian Knight. (Men-at-Arms Ser.: No. 224). (Illus.). 48p. pap. 11.95 (*0-85045-951-6*, 9182, Pub. by Ospry) Stackpole.

Queen Victoria's Gene: Haemophilia & the Royal Family. D. M. Potts. 1999. pap. text 17.95 (*0-7509-1199-9*) A Sutton.

Queen Victoria's Gene: Haemophilia & the Royal Family. D. M. Potts. LC 96-143392. 1997. 33.95 (*0-7509-0868-8*, Pub. by Sutton Pub Ltd) Intl Pubs Mktg.

Queen Victoria's Little Wars. Byron Farwell. (Illus.). 432p. 1985. reprint ed. pap. 15.95 (*0-393-30235-0*) Norton.

Queen Victoria's Scottish Diaries. 2nd large type ed. John Kerr. (Illus.). 282p. 1993. 24.95 (*1-85695-155-3*, Pub. by ISIS Lrg Prnt) Transaction Pubs.

Queen Victoria's Secret Diaries see Queen Victoria's "Alice in Wonderland"

Queen Victoria's Secrets. Adrienne Munich. LC 95-43737. (Illus.). 246p. 1996. 37.00 (*0-231-10480-4*) Col U Pr.

Queen Victoria's Secrets. Adrienne Munich. (Illus.). 272p. 1998. pap. 17.50 (*0-231-10481-2*) Col U Pr.

Queen Victoria's Through the Looking Glass. Continental Historical Society Staff. (Illus.). 319p. 1986. pap. 10.95 (*0-9609900-2-X*) Cont Hist Soc.

Queen vs Louis Riel. Louis Riel. LC 73-91562. (Social History of Canada Ser.: No. 19). 419p. reprint ed. pap. 129.90 (*0-7837-0377-5*, 204069700019) Bks Demand.

Queen Who Saved Her People: Book of Esther. (Arch Bks.). 32p. (J). (gr. 3-6). 1973. pap. 1.99 (*0-570-06075-3*, 59-1194) Concordia.

***Queen Without a Country.** Rachel Bard. (Illus.). 367p. 2000. 29.95 (*0-7541-1205-5*, Pub. by Minerva Pr) Unity Dist.

Queen Zixi of Ix: The Story of the Magic Cloak. L. Frank Baum. (Illus.). 231p. (J). (gr. 1-3). 1971. reprint ed. pap. 5.95 (*0-486-22691-3*) Dover.

Queene Elizabethes Achademy: A Book of Precedence. Ed. by F. J. Furnivall. (EETS, ES Ser.: No. 8). 1974. reprint ed. 40.00 (*0-527-00222-4*) Periodicals Srv.

Queenie. 1987. mass mkt. 4.95 (*0-446-73491-8*, Pub. by Warner Bks) Little.

Queenie Hetherton. Mary J. Holmes. (Notable American Authors Ser.). 1992. reprint ed. lib. bdg. 75.00 (*0-7812-3148-5*) Rprt Serv.

Queenie, One of the Family. Bob Graham. LC 96-52757. (Illus.). 32p. (J). (gr. k-3). 1997. 15.99 (*0-7636-0359-7*) Candlewick Pr.

Queenie Peavy. Robert Burch. 160p. (J). (gr. 3-7). 1987. pap. 4.99 (*0-14-032305-8*, PuffinBks) Peng Put Young Read.

Queenie Peavy. Robert Burch. (J). 1966. 9.09 (*0-606-04394-2*, Pub. by Turtleback) Demco.

Queenie Peavy: A Study Guide. Bonnie Ferraro. Ed. by J. Friedland & R. Kessler. (Novel-Ties Ser.). (J). (gr. 4-6). 1996. pap. text 15.95 (*1-56982-638-2*) Lrn Links.

Queenie the Bantam. Bob Graham. LC 98-194699. 1997. write for info. (*0-7445-5519-1*) Walker Bks.

Queenie's Diary. L. F. Dufrechou. (Illus.). 206p. 1995. pap. 9.95 (*0-9644776-0-2*) L F Dufrechou.

***Queenie's Pond: The Barker Brothers Arrive.** Alonda Cyrkozuch. LC 99-93968. 24p. (J). (ps-12). 1999. pap. 5.95 (*1-929098-01-4*, 02) Stry Teller.

Queening of America. David Van Leer. LC 94-47059. (Illus.). 224p. (C). 1995. pap. 18.99 (*0-415-90336-X*, A4793) Routledge.

Queening of America. David Van Leer. LC 94-47059. (Illus.). 224p. (C). (gr. 13). 1995. 80.00 (*0-415-90335-1*, A4789) Routledge.

***Queenmaker: A Novel of King David's Queen.** India Edghill. LC 99-91284. 2000. 25.00 (*0-7388-0732-X*); pap. 18.00 (*0-7388-0733-8*) Xlibris Corp.

Queens. Normand Charette. Tr. by Linda Gaboriau from FRE. LC 99-176483. 1998. pap. text 10.95 (*0-88922-403-X*) Talon Pr.

Queen's Amulet. Julianne Balmain. (Illus.). 24p. 1999. 12.95 (*0-8118-2462-4*) Chronicle Bks.

Queens & Queenship in Medieval Europe: Proceedings of a Conference Held at King's College, London, April 1995. Ed. by Anne Duggan. LC 97-917. (Illus.). 384p. 1997. 90.00 (*0-85115-657-6*) Boydell & Brewer.

Queen's Bastard. Robin Maxwell. LC 98-50502. 448p. 1999. 24.95 (*1-55970-475-6*, Pub. by Arcade Pub Inc) Time Warner.

***Queen's Bastard.** Robin Maxwell. LC 00-22781. 448p. 2000. pap. 13.00 (*0-684-85760-X*, Fireside) S&S Trade Pap.

Queen's Bedfellow. Roger Bowdler. 1975. 19.95 (*0-8464-0775-2*) Beekman Pubs.

Queen's Champion: The Legend of Lancelot Retold. Cris Newport. (From the Wind Fairytale Ser.). (Illus.). 300p. 1997. pap. 11.95 (*1-886383-20-0*) Pride & Imprints.

Queen's Cloak: A Myth for Mid-Life. Joan C. Engelsman. LC 93-15576. 128p. (Orig.). 1993. pap. 14.95 (*0-933029-73-X*) Chiron Pubns.

Queens, Concubines & Dowagers: The King's Wife in the Early Middle Ages. Pauline Stafford. LC 97-52934. (Women Power & Politics Ser.). 256p. 1998. pap. 24.95 (*0-7185-0174-8*) Bks Intl VA.

***Queen's Conjurer: The Science & Magic of Dr. John Dee, Advisor to Elizabeth I.** Benjamin Woolley. 288p. 2001. text 25.00 (*0-8050-6509-1*) H Holt & Co.

***Queen's Corsair.** large type ed. Judith Saxton. 320p. 1999. pap. 20.99 (*1-85389-886-4*, Dales) Ulverscroft.

Queen's Corsair: Drake's Journey of Circumnavigation 1577-1580. Alexander McKee. 320p. (C). 1978. 16.95 (*0-285-62339-7*) Intl Spec Bk.

Queen's Counsel. large type ed. Alex Stuart. 384p. 1992. 27.99 (*0-7089-2754-8*) Ulverscroft.

Queens County Documents & Letters Intended to the Revolutionary Incidents of Queens County, with Connecting Narratives, Explanatory Notes & Additions. Ed. by Henry Onderdonk, Jr. (Illus.). 264p. 1997. reprint ed. lib. bdg. 34.50 (*0-8328-6207-X*) Higginson Bk Co.

Queen's Diadem. Carl Jonas Love Almqvist. Tr. by Yvonne Sandstroem. (SCAND Ser.). 250p. 1992. 50.00 (*1-879751-00-3*) Camden Hse.

Queens Documents & Letters Intended to Illustrate Revolutionary Incidents of Queens County, with Connecting Narratives, Explanatory Notes & Additions. Henry Onderdonk, Jr. 70p. 1997. reprint ed. pap. 14.00 (*0-8328-6206-1*) Higginson Bk Co.

Queen's Domain & Other Poems. William Winter. (Notable American Authors Ser.). 1999. reprint ed. lib. bdg. 125.00 (*0-7812-7762-0*) Rprt Serv.

Queens, Empresses, Grand Duchesses & Regents: Women Rulers of Europe, A.D. 1328-1989. Olga S. Opfell. LC 88-43484. (Illus.). 296p. 1989. lib. bdg. 39.95 (*0-89950-385-3*) McFarland & Co.

Queen's Feast - Ester. R. Woodman. Date not set. pap. 2.50 (*1-85792-089-9*, Pub. by Christian Focus) Spring Arbor Dist.

Queen's Flight. T. Lee. text 35.00 (*0-340-67247-1*, Pub. by Hodder & Stought Ltd); mass mkt. 13.95 (*0-340-67248-X*, Pub. by Hodder & Stought Ltd) Trafalgar.

Queen's Folly. Stanley J. Weyman. 14.95 (*0-8488-1508-4*) Amereon Ltd.

Queen's Folly. Elswyth Thane. 310p. 1974. reprint ed. lib. bdg. 23.95 (*0-88411-955-6*) Amereon Ltd.

Queen's Folly. Elswyth Thane. 1998. reprint ed. 31.95 (*1-56849-713-X*) Buccaneer Bks.

Queen's Folly. Stanley J. Weyman. 1977. reprint ed. lib. bdg. 13.75 (*0-89966-279-X*) Buccaneer Bks.

***Queen's Gambit.** Matthew Sadler. (Chess Bks.). (Illus.). 1999. pap. text 15.95 (*0-7134-8542-6*) B T B.

Queen's Gambit. Walter Tevis. LC 82-15058. 243p. 1983. 25.00 (*0-89366-263-1*) Ultramarine Pub.

Queen's Gambit Accepted. Iakov Neishtadt. 1997. pap. 24.95 (*1-85744-114-1*, Pub. by Cadgn Bks) Macmillan.

***Queens Gambit Accepted: A Sharp & Sound Response to 1D4.** C. Ward. (Illus.). 144p. 1999. pap. text 16.95 (*0-7134-8467-5*) B T B.

***Queen's Gambit Declined.** Matthew Sadler. 2000. pap. text 19.95 (*1-85744-256-3*) Cadgn Bks.

Queen's Gambit Declined: BG5 System. Globe Pequot Press Staff. 208p. 1999. pap. text 19.95 (*1-85744-240-7*) Cadgn Bks.

Queen's Gambit Declined Orthodox Variation. Eric Schiller. 97p. (Orig.). 1984. pap. 6.95 (*0-931462-34-7*) Chess Ent.

Queen's Gambit for the Attacking Player. Graham Burgess. 1995. pap. 19.95 (*0-8050-3581-8*, Pub. by Batsford Chess) H Holt & Co.

Queen's Gift. Inglis Fletcher. (Albemarle Ser.). 448p. reprint ed. lib. bdg. 29.95 (*0-89244-005-8*, Queens House) Amereon Ltd.

Queen's Gift. Inglis Fletcher. 1990. reprint ed. lib. bdg. 25.95 (*0-89968-506-4*) Buccaneer Bks.

Queen's Government. William I. Jennings. LC 84-12767. 158p. 1984. reprint ed. lib. bdg. 55.00 (*0-313-24571-1*, JEQG, Greenwood Pr) Greenwood.

Queen's Grace. Nigel Tranter. 256p. 1992. pap. 13.95 (*1-873631-10-3*, Pub. by B&W Pub) Firebird Dist.

Queen's Grant Inheritance. large type ed. Joanne Holden. (Linford Romance Library). 272p. 1993. pap. 16.99 (*0-7089-7413-9*) Ulverscroft.

Queens Have Died Young & Fair: A Fable of the Immediate Future. James Kirkup. 175p. 1994. 29.00 (*0-7206-0886-4*, Pub. by P Owen Ltd) Dufour.

***Queen's Head.** Edward Marston. LC 00-102398. (Missing Mystery Ser.: No. 19). 300p. 2000. pap. 14.95 (*1-890208-45-0*) Poisoned Pen.

Queen's House: A Social History of Buckingham Palace. Edna Healey. (Illus.). 448p. 1998. 27.95 (*0-7867-0565-5*) Carroll & Graf.

***Queen's House: A Social History of Buckingham Palace.** Edna Healey. (Illus.). 448p. 2000. pap. 18.95 (*0-7867-0716-X*) Carroll & Graf.

Queen's Indian Defence: Kasparov System. Mikhail Gurevich. 112p. 1995. pap. 16.95 (*0-8050-2315-1*, Pub. by Batsford Chess) H Holt & Co.

Queen's Indian Defense. Bogdan Lalic. 192p. 1996. pap. 22.95 (*1-85744-157-5*, Pub. by Cadgn Bks) Macmillan.

Queen's Jewels: The Personal Collection of Elizabeth II. Leslie Field. (Illus.). 192p. 1997. reprint ed. 17.98 (*0-8109-8172-6*, Pub. by Abrams) Time Warner.

***Queen's Knickers.** Nicholas Allan. (J). 1998. pap. 6.95 (*0-09-928161-9*, Pub. by Random) Trafalgar.

An Asterisk (*) at the beginning of an entry indicates that the title is appearing for the first time.

***Queen's Man.** Terri Brisbin. (Time Passages Romance Ser.). 2000. mass mkt. 5.99 (*0-515-12906-2*, Jove) Berkley Pub.

Queen's Man. Kay S. Penman. 288p. 1999. mass mkt. 6.99 (*0-345-42316-X*) Ballantine Pub Grp.

Queen's Man. Sharon Kay Penman. 304p. 1998. pap. 12.00 (*0-345-41718-6*) Ballantine Pub Grp.

Queen's Man: A Medieval Mystery. Sharon Kay Penman. 240p. 1995. 20.00 (*0-8050-3885-X*) H Holt & Co.

Queen's Mare. John Birkett. 240p. 1990. pap. 3.50 (*0-380-75683-8*, Avon Bks) Morrow Avon.

Queen's Men & Their Plays. Scott McMillin & Sally-Beth MacLean. LC 97-18017. (Illus.). 272p. (C). 1998. text 59.95 (*0-521-59427-8*) Cambridge U Pr.

***Queen's Mirror: Fairy Tales by German Women, 1780-1900.** Ed. by Shawn C. Jarvis & Jeannine Blackwell. (European Women Writers Ser.). (Illus.). 2001. pap. 29.95 (*0-8032-6181-0*, Bison Books); text 60.00 (*0-8032-1299-2*) U of Nebr Pr.

***Queen's Necklace.** Alexandre Dumas. 252p. 2000. pap. 9.95 (*0-594-03006-4*) Eighth Hundrd.

***Queen's Necklace, Vol. II.** Alexandre Dumas. 252p. 2000. pap. 9.95 (*0-594-03011-0*) Eighth Hundrd.

Queen's Necklace: A Swedish Folktale. Jane Langton. LC 93-34817. (Illus.). 40p. (J). (gr. k-3). 1994. 15.95 (*0-7868-0011-9*, Pub. by Hyprn Child); lib. bdg. 15.89 (*0-7868-2007-1*, Pub. by Hyprn Child) Little.

Queen's New Clothes, No. 1. Tom Dunsmuir. LC 97-40955. (J). 1998. pap. 3.25 (*0-679-89120-X*, Pub. by Random Bks Yng Read) Random.

***Queen's New Shoes.** Adwoa A. Badoe. (Illus.). 24p. (J). (gr. 3-7). 1998. pap. 6.95 (*0-88961-232-3*, Pub. by Womens Pr) LPC InBook.

Queens of American Society. Elizabeth F. Ellet. 1977. text 23.95 (*0-8369-8158-8*, 8298) Ayer.

Queens of Burlesque: Vintage Photographs from the 1940s & 1950s. Len Rothe. LC 97-80161. (Illus.). 112p. 1998. pap. 19.95 (*0-7643-0449-6*) Schiffer.

Queens of Deliria: 19977 Sci-Fi Novel - Sequel to the Time of the Hawklords. Michael Butterworth. 1995. pap. 12.95 (*1-896522-07-6*) CN06.

Queens of Egypt. Janet R. Buttles. (African Heritage Classical Research Studies). 250p. reprint ed. 35.00 (*0-938818-32-5*) ECA Assoc.

Queens of Hearts & Souls: The Story of the Miss Black Athens-Clarke County Teen Pageant, 1975-1997. Carl L. McCoy. (Illus.). 81p. 1998. lib. bdg. 10.00 (*0-9664030-1-0*) CKG Concepts.

Queens of Land & Sea, Vol. 5. John M. Roberts. 320p. (Orig.). 1994. mass mkt. 4.99 (*0-8125-2307-5*) Tor Bks.

Queens of Mobile Mardi Gras, 1893-1986. 2nd ed. Emily S. Hearin & Kathryn T. DeCelle. (Illus.). 98p. 1986. 25.00 (*0-914334-09-3*); pap. 15.00 (*0-914334-10-7*) Museum Mobile.

Queens of Pop. Ed. by Milton Okun. 104p. 1995. pap. 12.95 (*0-89524-976-6*) Cherry Lane.

Queens of Song: Being Memoirs of Some of the Most Celebrated Female Vocalists. Ellen C. Clayton. LC 77-38713. (Essay Index Reprint Ser.). 1977. reprint ed. 33.95 (*0-8369-2640-4*) Ayer.

Queens of the Shah Dynasty in Nepal: Dynasty in Nepal. Prakash Raj Adhikari. 1997. pap. 40.00 (*0-7855-7483-2*, Pub. by Ratna Pustak Bhandar) St Mut.

***Queen's Own Fool: A Novel of Mary Queen of Scots.** Jane Yolen & Robert J. Harris. LC 99-55070. (Illus.). 416p. (J). (gr. 5-9). 2000. 19.99 (*0-399-23380-6*, Philomel) Peng Put Young Read.

Queen's Own Grove. Patricia Beatty. (Illus.). 224p. (J). (gr. 4-6). 1999. pap. 8.95 (*0-96711154-5-0*) Imagine That CA.

Queen's Own Hussars: Tercentenary Edition. Ed. by Queen's Own Hussars Editors. (Illus.). 96p. 1985. pap. 16.50 (*0-08-033595-0*, P110, T120, Pergamon Pr) Elsevier.

Queen's People: A Study of Hegemony, Coercion, & Accommodation among the Okanagan of Canada. Peter Carstens. (Illus.). 416p. 1991. text 55.00 (*0-8020-5893-0*); pap. text 22.95 (*0-8020-6827-8*) U of Toronto Pr.

Queen's Play. Dorothy Dunnett. 1976. 21.95 (*0-8488-1301-4*) Amereon Ltd.

Queen's Play. Dorothy Dunnett. LC 96-46882. 1997. pap. 14.00 (*0-679-77744-X*) Vin Bks.

Queen's Play. Dorothy Dunnett. 425p. 1983. reprint ed. lib. bdg. 39.95 (*0-89966-320-6*) Buccaneer Bks.

Queen's Quair. Maurice Hewlett. 1988. reprint ed. lib. bdg. 79.00 (*0-7812-0456-9*) Rprt Serv.

Queens, Queen Mothers, Priestesses & Power Vol. 810: Case Studies in African Gender. Ed. by Flora E. Kaplan. (Women's Studies/African Studies). (Illus.). 474p. 1997. pap. 32.00 (*0-8018-6087-3*) Johns Hopkins.

Queens, Queen Mothers, Priestesses & Power Vol. 810: Case Studies in African Gender. Ed. by Flora E. Kaplan. LC 96-52006. 1997. 80.00 (*1-57331-054-9*); pap. 80.00 (*1-57331-055-7*) NY Acad Sci.

Queen's Quest: Pilgrimage for Individuation. Edith Wallace. LC 90-61333. (Illus.). 52p. (Orig.). 1990. pap. 16.00 (*0-944164-21-8*) Moon Bear Pr.

Queen's Quest & Other Tales: Stories to Live By. Joyce Marshall. (Illus.). 128p. 1994. pap. 13.50 (*0-9611552-6-4*) Realistic Living.

Queen's Quorum. Ellery Queen. Date not set. lib. bdg. 18.95 (*0-8488-2133-5*) Amereon Ltd.

Queen's Quorum. Ellery Queen. LC 68-56450. 146p. 1969. 30.00 (*0-8196-0229-9*) Biblo.

***Queen's Ransom: A Mystery at Queen Elizabeth I's Court Featuring Ursula Blanchard.** Fiona Buckley. LC 99-36455. 352p. 2000. 22.50 (*0-684-86267-0*) Scribner.

Queens, Regents & Potentates. Ed. by Theresa M. Vann. (Women of Power Ser.). 180p. (C). 1995. 60.00 (*0-85115-649-5*) Boydell & Brewer.

Queen's Regulations for the Royal Navy Changes: BR 2 Change 10. 1998. ring bd. 35.00 (*0-11-772877-2*, HM28772, Pub. by Statnry Office) Bernan Associates.

Queen's Regulations for the Royal Navy Changes: Br. 2 Change 9. 1987. pap. 40.00 (*0-11-772856-X*, HM2856X, Pub. by Statnry Office) Bernan Associates.

Queen's Silver. Wilma E. Alexander. 125p. (gr. 3-6). 1996. mass mkt. 3.95 (*0-7736-7285-0*) General Publishing Co.

Queen's Smuggler: William Tyndale. Dave Jackson & Neta Jackson. (Trailblazer Bks.). (Illus.). 128p. (J). (gr. 3-7). 1991. pap. 5.99 (*1-55661-221-4*) Bethany Hse.

Queen's Stepwell at Patan. K. Mankodi. (C). 1992. 120.00 (*81-900184-0-X*, Pub. by Franco-Indian) S Asia.

***Queen's Tiara.** C. J. L. Almovist. 2000. pap. 15.95 (*1-900850-51-6*) Arcadia Bks.

***Queen's Tragedy.** Robert Benson. 252p. 2000. pap. 9.95 (*0-594-00033-5*) Eighth Hundrd.

Queen's Travels. large type ed. Graham Fisher & Heather Fisher. (Illus.). 290p. 1989. reprint ed. 20.95 (*1-85089-222-9*, Pub. by ISIS Lrg Prnt) Transaction Pubs.

Queen's Treasure. Clifford Ashdown. 1975. 10.00 (*1-880418-12-6*) D M Grant.

Queen's Twin & Other Stories. Sarah Orne Jewett. LC 76-178443. (Short Story Index Reprint Ser.). 232p. 1977. reprint ed. 21.95 (*0-8369-4044-X*) Ayer.

Queen's Twin & Other Stories. Sarah Orne Jewett. 1972. reprint ed. lib. bdg. 16.00 (*0-685-36666-9*) Irvington.

Queen's Twin & Other Stories. Sarah Orne Jewett. (Collected Works of Sarah Orne Jewett). 1988. reprint ed. lib. bdg. 59.00 (*0-7812-1314-2*) Rprt Serv.

Queen's Twin & Other Stories. Sarah Orne Jewett. reprint ed. 59.00 (*0-403-03180-X*) Somerset Pub.

Queen's University, 1841-1914: And Not to Yield, Vol. I. Hilda Neatby et al. Ed. by Frederick W. Gibson & Roger Graham. (Illus.). 1978. 65.00 (*0-7735-0336-6*, Pub. by McG-Queens Univ Pr) CUP Services.

Queen's University, 19717-1961: To Serve & Yet Be Free. Frederick W. Gibson. 512p. 1983. 65.00 (*0-7735-0376-5*, Pub. by McG-Queens Univ Pr) CUP Services.

Queen's Wards: Wardship & Marriage under Elizabeth I. Joel Hurstfield. (Illus.). 492p. 1973. 35.00 (*0-7146-2953-7*, Pub. by F Cass Pubs) Intl Spec Bk.

Queensboro Bridge: And Other Poems. Anne Paolucci. (Petites Major Ser.). 64p. 1995. pap. 6.95 (*1-884754-27-9*) Potpourri Pubns.

Queensbury Hunt: Creativity & Industry. Susannah Walker. (Blueprint Monograph Ser.). (Illus.). 112p. 1992. 29.95 (*1-85702-011-1*) Trafalgar.

Queensbury's Heritage. Robert L. Eddy. (Illus.). 250p. 1991. 28.00 (*0-9632971-0-4*); pap. 20.00 (*0-9632971-1-2*) R L Eddy.

Queensland: Globetrotter Travel Guide. Globetrotter Staff. (Globetrotter Travel Guide Ser.). (Illus.). 128p. 1997. pap. text 10.95 (*1-85368-708-1*) Globe Pequot.

Queensland Aborigines & the Spanish Influenza Pandemic of 1918-1919. Gordon Briscoe & Australian Institute of Aboriginal & Torres Strait Islander Studies Staff. LC 97-108211. 20 p. 1996. write for info. (*0-85575-282-3*) AIB & TSIS.

***Queensland File.** Julian Jay Savarin. 1999. 26.00 (*0-7278-5445-3*, Pub. by Severn Hse) Chivers N Amer.

Queensland Legislation Cases Annotations. Drew H. Taylor. 127.00 (*0-614-05472-9*, Austral, MICHIE) LEXIS Pub.

Queenstown Patrol, 1917: The Diary of Commander Joseph Knefler Taussig, U. S. Navy. Ed. by William N. Still, Jr. LC 96-39103. (Historical Monographs: No. 12). (Illus.). 225p. (Orig.). (C). 1996. pap. 10.00 (*1-884733-07-7*) Naval War Coll.

Queensville Temptress. J. R. Roberts. (Gunsmith Ser.: No. 179). 192p. 1996. mass mkt. 4.99 (*0-515-11969-5*, Jove) Berkley Pub.

Queenswrath. (Torg Ser.). 64p. 12.00 (*0-87431-316-3*, 20555) West End Games.

Queer. William S. Burroughs. 144p. 1987. pap. 11.95 (*0-14-008389-8*, Penguin Bks) Viking Penguin.

Queer After-Life of Vaslav Nijinsky. Kevin Kopelson. LC 97-13449. 206p. 1998. 39.50 (*0-8047-2949-2*); pap. 14.95 (*0-8047-2950-6*) Stanford U Pr.

Queer Astrology: A Guide for Lesbians. Jill Dearman. LC 98-44573. 208p. 1998. pap. 13.95 (*0-312-19953-8*) St Martin.

Queer Astrology for Men: An Astrological Guide for Gay Men. 2nd ed. Jill Dearman. LC 98-37646. (Illus.). 208p. 1998. pap. 13.95 (*0-312-19952-X*) St Martin.

Queer Birds. Abraham H. Maslow. (J). 2001. mass mkt. 12.80 (*0-689-80249-8*) Aladdin.

Queer Blood: The Secret AIDS Genocide Plot. Alan Cantwell, Jr. Ed. by Sallie Fiske. 168p. (Orig.). 1993. pap. 12.95 (*0-917211-26-X*) Aries Rising.

Queer Book. James Hogg. Ed. by Peter Garside. LC 94-197354. (Collected Works of James Hogg). 272p. 1994. 60.00 (*0-7486-0506-1*, Pub. by Edinburgh U Pr) Col U Pr.

Queer Books. Edmund Pearson. (Illus.). 298p. 1990. pap. 25.00 (*0-87556-763-0*) Saifer.

Queer by Choice: Lesbians, Gay Men, & the Politics of Identity. Vera Whisman. LC 94-44781. 224p. (C). (gr. 13). 1995. 65.00 (*0-415-91014-5*, B3843); pap. 18.99 (*0-415-91015-3*, B3847) Routledge.

***Queer Chivalry: The Homoerotic Asceticism of Gerard Manley Hopkins.** Julia F. Saville. LC 99-52708. (Victorian Literature & Culture Ser.). (Illus.). 256p. 2000. 37.50 (*0-8139-1940-1*) U Pr of Va.

***Queer Corners.** Donald Olson. 1999. pap. text 15.95 (*0-9623683-6-9*) BridgeCity Bks.

Queer Destinies: Erotic Science Fiction. Gary Bowen. LC 94-219733. (Illus.). 64p. (Orig.). 1994. pap. 5.95 (*0-9633970-7-9*) Circlet Pr.

Queer Dharma Vol. 1: Voices of Gay Buddhists. Ed. by Winston Leyland. LC 97-27590. (Illus.). 416p. 1998. 50.00 (*0-940567-21-0*) Gay Sunshine.

Queer Dharma Vol. 1: Voices of Gay Buddhists. Ed. by Winston Leyland. LC 97-27590. (Illus.). 416p. 2000. pap. 19.95 (*0-940567-22-9*) Gay Sunshine.

Queer Dharma Vol. 2: Voices of Gay Buddhists. Ed. by Winston Leyland. (Illus.). 224p. 2000. 50.00 (*0-940567-24-5*); pap. 16.95 (*0-940567-23-7*) Gay Sunshine.

Queer Dog: Homo Pup Poetry, No. 2. Ed. by Gerry G. Pearlberg. LC 97-10978. 100p. (Orig.). 1997. pap. 12.95 (*1-57344-071-X*) Cleis Pr.

Queer Dutchman Castaway: Castaway on Ascencion. Peter Agnos. Ed. by C. Q. Adler. (Illus.). 144p. (Orig.). 1994. pap. 9.95 (*0-914018-03-5*) Green Eagle Pr.

Queer Edward II. Derek Jarman & Christopher Marlowe. (Illus.). 176p. 1992. pap. 22.95 (*0-85170-316-X*, Pub. by British Film Inst) Ind U Pr.

***Queer Families, Common Agendas: Gay People, Lesbians & Family Values.** Ed. by Thomas Richard Sullivan & Robert Dawidoff. LC 99-47990. (Journal of Gay & Lesbian Social Services Ser.: Vol. 10, No. 1). 120p. 1999. pap. text 18.95 (*1-56023-130-0*, Harrington Park) Haworth Pr.

***Queer Families, Common Agendas: Gay People, Lesbians & Family Values.** Ed. by Thomas Richard Sullivan & Robert Dawidoff. LC 99-47990. (Journal of Gay & Lesbian Social Services Ser.: Vol. 10, No. 1). 120p. 1999. 39.95 (*1-56023-129-7*, Harrington Park) Haworth Pr.

***Queer Family Values: Debunking the Myth of the Nuclear Family.** Valerie Lehr. LC 98-45411. (Queer Politics, Queer Theories Ser.). 224p. 1999. 59.50 (*1-56639-683-2*) Temple U Pr.

Queer Family Values: Debunking the Myth of the Nuclear Family. Valerie Lehr. LC 98-45411. (Queer Politics, Queer Theories Ser.). 224p. 1999. pap. 19.95 (*1-56639-684-0*) Temple U Pr.

Queer Fictions of the Past: History, Culture, & Difference. Scott Bravmann. (Cultural Social Studies). 190p. (C). 1997. text 54.95 (*0-521-59101-5*); pap. text 16.95 (*0-521-59907-5*) Cambridge U Pr.

Queer Forster. Robert K. Martin & George Piggford. LC 97-9960. (Worlds of Desire Ser.). 288p. 1997. pap. text 16.95 (*0-226-50802-1*); lib. bdg. 49.00 (*0-226-50801-3*) U Ch Pr.

Queer Frontiers: Millennial Geographies, Genders, & Generations. Joseph A. Boone. LC 98-48151. (Illus.). 392p. 1999. pap. text 24.95 (*0-299-16094-7*) U of Wis Pr.

Queer Frontiers: Politics, Polemics & Possibilities for the Millennium. Joseph A. Boone. LC 98-48151. 1999. 59.95 (*0-299-16090-4*) U of Wis Pr.

Queer Geography: Journeys Toward a Sexual Self. Frank Browning. LC 97-36600. 256p. 1998. pap. text 13.00 (*0-374-52542-0*, Noonday) FS&G.

***Queer German Cinema.** Alice A. Kuzniar. LC 00-20494. (Illus.). 2000. pap. write for info. (*0-8047-3995-1*) Stanford U Pr.

***Queer Iberia: Crossing Cultures, Crossing Sexualities.** Josiah H. Blackmore. LC 98-32016. (Queer Ser.). 424p. 1999. 59.95 (*0-8223-2326-5*) Duke.

Queer Iberia: Crossing Cultures, Crossing Sexualities. Josiah H. Blackmore & Gregory S. Hutcheson. LC 98-32016. (Series Q). 424p. 1999. pap. 19.95 (*0-8223-2349-4*) Duke.

Queer in Russia: A Story of Sex, Self & the Other. Laurie Essig. LC 98-42134. 260p. 1999. 49.95 (*0-8223-2312-5*) Duke.

Queer in Russia: A Story of Sex, Self & the Other. Laurie Essig. LC 98-42134. (Illus.). 244p. 1999. pap. 17.95 (*0-8223-2346-X*) Duke.

Queer Japan: Personal Stories of Japanese Lesbians, Gays, Transsexuals & Bisexuals. Ed. by Barbara Summerhawk et al. LC 98-26726. (Illus.). 200p. 1998. pap. 16.95 (*1-892281-00-7*) New Victoria Pubs.

Queer Japan: Personal Stories of Japanese Lesbians, Gays, Transsexuals & Bisexuals. Ed. by Barbara Summerhawk et al. Tr. by Cheiron McMahill et al. LC 98-26726. (Illus.). 192p. 1998. 22.95 (*0-934678-97-9*) New Victoria Pubs.

Queer Kids: The Challenges & Promise for Lesbian, Gay, & Bisexual Youth. Robert E. Owens, Jr. LC 97-39230. 355p. 1998. 49.95 (*0-7890-0439-9*, Harrington Park); pap. 24.95 (*1-56023-929-8*, Harrington Park) Haworth Pr.

Queer Kind of Death. George Baxt. LC 98-15555. 300p. 1998. pap. 10.00 (*1-55583-448-5*) Alyson Pubns.

Queer Kind of Love: A Pharoah Love Mystery. George Baxt. 288p. 1994. 20.00 (*1-883402-01-8*) S&S Trade.

Queer Kind of Umbrella: A Pharoah Love Mystery. George Baxt. 1995. 21.00 (*1-883402-35-2*) S&S Trade.

Queer Kind of Umbrella: A Pharoah Love Mystery. George Baxt. LC 95-17055. 240p. 1995. 20.50 (*0-684-81496-X*) Simon & Schuster.

Queer Looks: Perspectives on Lesbian & Gay Film & Video. Martha Gever et al. LC 93-9663. (Illus.). 416p. (C). (gr. 13). 1993. pap. 22.99 (*0-415-90742-X*, A9967) Routledge.

***Queer Nations.** Jarrod Hayes. LC 99-38490. 2000. lib. bdg. 50.00 (*0-226-32105-3*) U Ch Pr.

Queer Noises: Male & Female Homosexuality in Twentieth-Century Music. John Gill. LC 94-43922. 1995. pap. 16.95 (*0-8166-2719-3*); text 44.95 (*0-8166-2718-5*) U of Minn Pr.

Queer Papi Porn: Gay Asian Erotica. Joel Tan. LC 98-37740. 200p. 1998. pap. 14.95 (*1-57344-038-8*) Cleis Pr.

Queer People: A Novel. Carroll Graham & Garrett Graham. LC 76-3478. (Lost American Fiction Ser.). 285p. 1976. reprint ed. 16.95 (*0-8093-0784-7*) S Ill U Pr.

Queer Poetics: Five Modernist Women Writers. Mary E. Galvin. LC 97-21449. 160p. 1999. pap. 18.95 (*0-275-96106-0*, Praeger Pubs) Greenwood.

Queer Poetics: Five Modernist Women Writers, 161. Mary E. Galvin. LC 97-21449. (Contributions in Women's Studies: 161). 160p. 1999. 49.95 (*0-313-29810-6*, Greenwood Pr) Greenwood.

Queer Question: Essays on Desire & Democracy. Scott Tucker. LC 97-15786. 260p. 1997. 40.00 (*0-89608-578-3*); pap. 18.00 (*0-89608-577-5*) South End Pr.

Queer Reader: 2500 Years of Male Homosexuality. Ed. by Patrick Higgins. 384p. 1994. 25.00 (*1-56584-210-3*, Pub. by New Press NY) Norton.

Queer Reader: 2500 Years of Male Homosexuality. Ed. by Patrick Higgins. 384p. 1995. pap. 14.95 (*1-56584-211-1*, Pub. by New Press NY) Norton.

Queer Renaissance: Contemporary American Literature & the Reinvention of Lesbian & Gay Identities. Robert McRue. LC 96-51220. 1997. text 50.00 (*0-8147-5554-2*) NYU Pr.

Queer Renaissance: Contemporary American Literature & the Reinvention of Lesbian & Gay Identities. Robert McRuer. LC 96-51220. 1997. pap. text 19.00 (*0-8147-5555-0*) NYU Pr.

Queer Representations: Reading Lives, Reading Cultures. Ed. by Martin Duberman. LC 96-53042. 450p. (C). 1997. text 60.00 (*0-8147-1884-1*); pap. text 23.50 (*0-8147-1883-3*) NYU Pr.

Queer Romance: Lesbians, Gay Men, & the Popular Culture. Ed. by Paul Burston & Colin Richardson. LC 94-10783. (Illus.). 256p. (C). (gr. 13). 1995. 80.00 (*0-415-09617-0*, C0357); pap. 22.99 (*0-415-09618-9*, C0358) Routledge.

Queer Science: The Use & Abuse of Research into Homosexuality. Simon LeVay. (Illus.). 374p. (C). 1996. 32.00 (*0-262-12199-9*) MIT Pr.

Queer Science: The Use & Abuse of Research into Homosexuality. Simon Levay. (Illus.). 374p. 1997. reprint ed. pap. text 16.95 (*0-262-62119-3*) MIT Pr.

Queer Sites: Gay Urban Histories since 1600. David Higgs. LC 98-35022. 1999. 75.00 (*0-415-15897-4*); pap. 22.99 (*0-415-15898-2*) Routledge.

Queer Sixties. Patricia Juliana Smith. LC 99-13788. 1999. 70.00 (*0-415-92168-6*) Routledge.

Queer Sixties. Ed. by Patricia Juliana Smith. LC 99-13788. 288p. 1999. pap. 19.99 (*0-415-92169-4*) Routledge.

Queer Space: Architecture & Same Sex Desire. Aaron Betsky. LC 96-15992. 1997. 27.50 (*0-688-14301-6*, Wm Morrow) Morrow Avon.

Queer Spirits: A Gay Men's Myth Book. Ed. by Will Roscoe. 368p. 1996. pap. 15.00 (*0-8070-7939-1*) Beacon Pr.

Queer Street Cookbook. Donna Clark. (Sexual Politics Ser.). (Illus.). 160p. 1996. pap. 14.95 (*0-304-33812-5*) Continuum.

Queer Studies: A Lesbian, Gay, Bisexual, & Transgender Anthology. Ed. by Brett Beemyn & Mickey Eliason. LC 96-25709. (Illus.). 318p. (C). 1996. text 60.00 (*0-8147-1257-6*); pap. text 25.00 (*0-8147-1258-4*) NYU Pr.

Queer Theatre. Stefan Brecht. 178p. (Orig.). 1985. pap. 9.95 (*3-518-02489-2*, 9412) Routledge.

Queer Theory. Annamarie Jagose. 152p. pap. 29.95 (*1-877133-25-6*, Pub. by Univ Otago Pr) S Asia.

Queer Theory: A Bibliography. Ed. & Compiled by Joan Nordquist. (Social Theory: Vol. 48). 72p. (Orig.). 1997. pap. 20.00 (*0-937855-95-2*) Ref Rsch Serv.

Queer Theory: An Introduction. Annamarie Jagose. LC 96-45955. 1997. text 45.00 (*0-8147-4233-5*); pap. text 15.00 (*0-8147-4234-3*) NYU Pr.

Queer Theory/Sociology. Steven Seidman. (Twentieth Century Social Theory Ser.). (C). 1996. text 62.95 (*1-55786-739-9*) Blackwell Pubs.

Queer Theory/Sociology. Steven Seidman. (Twentieth Century Social Theory Ser.). 384p. (C). 1996. pap. text 28.95 (*1-55786-740-2*) Blackwell Pubs.

Queer Thing, Painting: Forty Years in the World of Art. Walter Pach. LC 79-156701. (Essay Index Reprint Ser.). 1977. reprint ed. 27.95 (*0-8369-2328-6*) Ayer.

Queer 13: Lesbian & Gay Writers Recall Seventh Grade. Clifford Chase. 288p. 1999. pap. 14.00 (*0-688-17161-3*, Wm Morrow) Morrow Avon.

Queer 13: Lesbian & Gay Writers Recall Seventh Grade. Ed. by Clifford Chase. LC 98-17147. 288p. 1999. 24.00 (*0-688-15811-0*, Wm Morrow) Morrow Avon.

Queer Transexions of Race, Nation & Gender: Social Text Special Issue, Vol. 15. Ed. by Anne McClintock et al. (Illus.). 425p. 1997. pap. text 19.00 (*0-8223-6452-2*) Duke.

Queer View Mirror. Ed. by James C. Johnstone & Karen X. Tulchinsky. 320p. 1996. pap. 17.95 (*1-55152-026-5*, Pub. by Arsenal Pulp) LPC InBook.

Queer View Mirror Vol. 2: Lesbian & Gay Short Short Fiction. 2nd ed. Ed. by James C. Johnstone & Karen X. Tulchinsky. LC 97-147581. 320p. (Orig.). 1997. pap. 17.95 (*1-55152-039-7*, Pub. by Arsenal Pulp) LPC InBook.

***Queer Virgins & Virgin Queens on the Early Modern Stage.** Mary Bly. 224p. 2000. text 55.00 (*0-19-818699-1*) OUP.

Queer Words, Queer Images: Communication & the Construction of Homosexuality. Ed. by R. Jeffrey Ringer. 400p. (C). 1994. text 50.00 (*0-8147-7440-7*); pap. text 18.50 (*0-8147-7441-5*) NYU Pr.

Queer World: The Center for Lesbian & Gay Studies Reader. Ed. by Martin Duberman. LC 96-53390. 600p. (C). 1997. text 65.00 (*0-8147-1874-4*); pap. text 25.00 (*0-8147-1875-2*) NYU Pr.

Queeries: Anthology of Gay Male Prose. Dennis Denisoff. 217p. 1993. per. 14.95 (*0-88978-271-7*, Pub. by Arsenal Pulp) LPC InBook.

***Queering Elementary Education: Advancing the Dialogue about Sexualities & Schooling.** Ed. by William J. Letts, IV & James T. Sears. LC 99-23762. 320p. 1999. pap. 19.95 (*0-8476-9369-4*); text 65.00 (*0-8476-9368-6*) Rowman.

Queering the Canon: Defying Sights in German Literature & Culture. Ed. by Christoph Lorey & John Plews. LC 97-32471. (Studies in German Literature & Culture). 300p. 1998. 60.00 (*1-57113-178-7*) Camden Hse.

***Queering the Color Line: Race & the Invention of Homosexuality in American Culture.** Siobhan Somerville. LC 99-33947. 240p. 2000. 49.95 (*0-8223-2407-5*) Duke.

***Queering the Color Line: Race & the Invention of Homosexuality in American Culture.** Siobhan Somerville. LC 99-33947. (Q Ser.). 240p. 2000. 17.95 (*0-8223-2443-1*) Duke.

Queering the Moderns: Poses, Portraits & Performances. Anne C. Hermann. text. write for info. (*0-312-23327-2*) St Martin.

Queering the Pitch: The New Gay & Lesbian Musicology. Ed. by Philip Brett et al. LC 93-15025. 440p. (C). (gr. 13). 1994. pap. 18.99 (*0-415-90753-5*, B0283) Routledge.

Queering the Renaissance. Ed. by Jonathan Goldberg. LC 93-28955. (Series Q). 424p. 1993. text 59.95 (*0-8223-1381-2*); pap. text 18.95 (*0-8223-1385-5*) Duke.

***Queering the Sacred: Meditations on Gay Spirituality.** Donald L. Boisvert. LC 99-54448. 160p. 2000. pap. 19.95 (*0-8298-1369-1*) Pilgrim OH.

Queerly Classed: Gay Men & Lesbians Write about Class. Ed. by Susan Raffo. LC 96-43838. 268p. 1997. 40.00 (*0-89608-562-7*); pap. 17.00 (*0-89608-561-9*) South End Pr.

Queerly Phrased: Language, Gender & Sexuality. Ed. by Anna Livia & Kira Hall. LC 97-6284. (Oxford Studies in Sociolinguistics). (Illus.). 480p. 1997. pap. 29.95 (*0-19-510471-4*); text 75.00 (*0-19-510470-6*) OUP.

Queers in Space: Communities, Public Places, Sites of Resistance. Ed. by Gordon B. Ingram et al. LC 97-11611. (Illus.). 544p. (Orig.). 1997. pap. 24.95 (*0-941920-44-5*) Bay Pr.

Queers Like Us. Clay Caldwell. (Orig.). 1995. mass mkt. 4.95 (*1-56333-262-0*, Badboy) Masquerade.

Que(e)rying Religion: A Critical Anthology. Ed. by Gary D. Comstock & Susan E. Henking. LC 78-20932. 350p. 1996. pap. 29.95 (*0-8264-0924-5*) Continuum.

Quel Petit Velo a Guidon Chrome au Fond de la Cour? Georges Perec. (FRE.). 1982. pap. 10.95 (*0-7859-2902-9*) Fr & Eur.

Quel Petit Velo a Guidon Chrome au Fond de la Cour? Georges Perec. (Folio Ser.: No. 1413). (FRE.). pap. 8.95 (*2-07-037413-0*) Schoenhof.

Quell-Finger Dialogues. J. H. Finger & E. Quell. (Language & Literature Ser.: Vol. 2). 1965. pap. 3.95 (*0-900891-01-7*) Oleander Pr.

Quelle Heure Est-Il? Marilyn Janovitz.Tr. of Is It Time?. (FRE., Illus.). (J). (ps-1). pap. 13.95 (*3-314-20859-6*, Pub. by North-South Bks NYC) Chronicle Bks.

Quelle Preposition? Maurice Grevisse. (FRE.). 88p. 1980. pap. 19.95 (*0-8288-3352-4*, 2801104310) Fr & Eur.

Quelle 1.0. James S. Noblitt & Karen C. Kossuth. (College German Ser.). (GER.). (C). 1996. mass mkt., suppl. ed. 18.95 incl. 3.5 hd, 5.25 hd, 3.5 ld (*0-8384-5458-5*) Heinle & Heinle.

Quellen der Selbstfindung in der Meditativen Kunstund Atemtherapie. Michael Schwindt. (Hildesheimer Schriftenreihe Zur Sozialpadagogik und Sozialarbeit Ser.: Vol. 5). (GER.). 236p. 1994. write for info. (*3-487-09882-2*) G Olms Pubs.

Quellen Fur eine Biographie Karl Otfried Mullers (1797-1840) Wolfhart Unte & Helmut Rohlfing. (GER., Illus.). viii, 210p. 1997. write for info. (*3-487-10497-0*) G Olms Pubs.

Quellen und Studien zur Spatbyzantinischen Geschichte. August Heisenberg. (Collected Studies: No. CS22). (Illus.). 408p. (C). 1973. reprint ed. lib. bdg. 143.95 (*0-902089-57-9*, Pub. by Variorum) Ashgate Pub Co.

Quellen und Untersuchungen zur Geschichte der Bohmischen Bruder, 2 bde. in 1. Jaroslav Goll. (GER.). vi, 236p. 1977. reprint ed. write for info. (*3-487-06433-2*) G Olms Pubs.

Quellen und Untersuchungen Zur Geschichte des Hexenwahns und der Hexenverfolgung Im Mittelalter. Joseph Hansen. (GER.). xi, 703p. 1976. write for info. (*3-487-05915-0*) G Olms Pubs.

Quellen zur Ethik Theophrasts. William Fortenbaugh. x, 380p. 1984. write for info. (*90-6032-218-5*) B R Gruner.

Quellen zur Geschichte dea Weimarar und Berliner Hofes In der Krisen- und Kriegszeit, 1865-67: Band 1 - Der Weimarer Hof; Band 2 - Der Berliner Hof, 2 vols. Wolfgang Steglich. (Illus.). 1996. 159.95 (*3-631-30447-1*) P Lang Pubng.

Quellen Zur Geschichte der Konigswahl und des Kurfurstenkollegs. Mario Krammer. (GER.). xvii, 256p. 1972. reprint ed. write for info. (*3-487-04265-7*) G Olms Pubs.

Quellen zur Geschichte des Fruhen Byzanz: (4.-9. Jahrhundert) Ed. by Friedhelm Winkelmann & Wolfram Brandes. (GER.). 399p. 1990. pap. 87.00 (*90-5063-011-1*, Pub. by Gieben) J Benjamins Pubng Co.

Quellen zur Missionsgeschichte der Herrnhuter Brudergemeine, 2 vols. David Cranz. (GER.). 1995. reprint ed. write for info. (*3-487-09992-6*) G Olms Pubs.

Quellen Zur Reform des Straf- und Strafprozebrechts. Werner Schubert et al. viii, 797p. 1996. write for info. (*3-11-015139-1*) De Gruyter.

Quellenangaben bei Herodot: Studien zur Erzaehlkunst Herodots. Detlef Fehling. (Untersuchungen zur Antiken Literatur und Geschichte Ser.: Vol. 9). 198p. (C). 1971. 52.30 (*3-11-003634-7*) De Gruyter.

Quellenkritische und Logische Untersuchungen Zur Gegensatzlehre des Aristoteles. Osvaldo N. Guariglia. (Studien und Materialien Zur Geschichte der Philosophie: Bd. 4). (GER.). 131p. 1978. write for info. (*3-487-06584-3*) G Olms Pubs.

Quellenkunde der Deutschen Reformationsgeschichte. Gustav Wolf. (GER.). xl, 1319p. 1988. reprint ed. write for info. (*3-487-01108-5*) G Olms Pubs.

Quellenschriften zu den Fruhesten Anfangen der Photographie bis zum XVIII. Ed. by Josef-Maria Eder et al. LC 76-23047. (Sources of Modern Photography Ser.). (GER & LAT., Illus.). 1979. reprint ed. lib. bdg. 18.95 (*0-405-09608-9*) Ayer.

Quellenuntersuchungen Zu Den "Maqatil At- Talibiyyin" des Abu 'l-Farag Al-Isfahani (Gest. 356-967) Sebastian Gunther. (Arabistische Texte und Studien: Vol. 4). 249p. 1991. write for info. (*3-487-09429-0*) G Olms Pubs.

Quelling the People: The Military Suppression of the Beijing Democracy Movement. Timothy Brook. LC 98-46955. 1999. pap. text 16.95 (*0-8047-3638-3*) Stanford U Pr.

Quelque Chose Beaucoup Bon Cookbook. Mercedes Vidrine. 1982. pap. 4.95 (*0-87511-127-0*) Claitors.

Quelque Chose de Deux - Arcadian Sweet Recipes. 1980. pap. 3.50 (*1-57980-089-0*) Claitors.

Quelque Chose Piquante: Arcadian Meat & Fish Recipes. Mercedes Vidrine. 1971. 3.95 (*0-87511-129-7*) Claitors.

Quelques Mots sur l'Acier, Lexique des Utilsateurs. M. Orlandi. (FRE.). 1998. 39.95 (*0-320-00154-7*) Fr & Eur.

Quelques Notions de Base pour l'Economie. L. Couffignal. (Economies et Societes Series N: No. 4). 1962. pap. 11.00 (*0-8115-0768-8*) Periodicals Srv.

Quelques Riens Pour Album. Gioachino Rossini. Ed. by Marvin Tartak. Tr. by Bruno Cagli et al from ITA. (Works of Gioachino Rossini Ser.). xxii, 346p. 1986. lib. bdg. 78.00 (*0-226-72839-0*, 728390) U Ch Pr.

Quelqu'un. Robert Pinget. (FRE.). 264p. 1965. pap. 18.95 (*0-7859-1609-1*, 270730347X) Fr & Eur.

Quem Decide? Poder, Politica e Controle Populacional. Information Project for Africa Inc., Staff. 322p. 1997. pap. text 13.00 (*1-886719-16-0*) Info Proj for Afr.

Quem Quaeritis? Whom Are You Seeking? Loretta Ross-Gotta. 29p. 1995. pap. text 8.00 (*1-888821-03-5*) Sanctuary.

Quench the Lamp. Alice Taylor. 176p. 1994. pap. 9.95 (*0-312-10528-2*) St Martin.

Quench the Lamp. large type ed. Alice Taylor. LC 92-24614. 241p. 1993. reprint ed. lib. bdg. 16.95 (*1-56054-518-6*) Thorndike Pr.

Quench the Moon. Walter Macken. LC 95-219585. 412p. 1995. pap. 11.95 (*0-86322-202-1*, Pub. by Brandon Bk Pubs) Irish Bks Media.

***Quenched.** Mary Ann Mitchell. 368p. 2000. mass mkt. 5.50 (*0-8439-4717-9*, Leisure Bks) Dorchester Pub Co.

Quenching & Carbursing: Proceedings of the Third International Seminar of the International Federation for Heat Treatment & Surface Engineering. 310p. 1993. 60.00 (*0-901716-51-0*, Pub. by Inst Materials) Ashgate Pub Co.

Quenching & Control of Distortion. Ed. by Howard E. Boyer & Philip R. Cary. LC 88-171400. 301p. reprint ed. pap. 93.40 (*0-7837-2769-0*, 204316000006) Bks Demand.

Quenching & Control of Distortion: Proceedings. Ed. by George E. Totten et al. LC 96-86539. 400p. 1996. 113.00 (*0-87170-584-2*, 6486) ASM.

Quenching & Distortion Control. Ed. by G. Totten. 341p. 1993. 99.00 (*0-87170-455-2*, 6221) ASM.

Quenching the Spirit see Apagando el Espiritu

Quenching the Spirit: Discover the Real Spirit Behind the Charismatic Controversy Spirit. rev. ed. William DeArteaga. 1996. pap. 12.99 (*0-88419-432-9*) Creation House.

***Queneau: Exercices de Style.** Teresa Bridgeman. 96p. 1999. pap. 35.00 (*0-85261-464-0*, Pub. by U of Glasgow) St Mut.

Quene's Maiesties Passage Through the Citie of London to Westminster the day before her Coronation. John Neale & James M. Osborn. 1960. 49.50 (*0-685-26707-5*) Elliots Bks.

Quennu & the Cave Bear. Marie Day. (Illus.). 32p. (J). (gr. k-5). 1999. 17.95 (*1-895688-86-8*, Pub. by Owl Bks) Firefly Bks Ltd.

Quennu & the Cave Bear. Marie Day. (Illus.). 32p. (J). (gr. 1-5). 1999. pap. 6.95 (*1-895688-87-6*, Pub. by Owl Bks) Firefly Bks Ltd.

Quentin Blake's Nursery Rhyme Book. Quentin Blake. LC 83-48171. (Illus.). 32p. (J). (gr. k-3). 1984. 7.95 (*0-06-020533-4*) HarpC Child Bks.

Quentin Corn. 2nd ed. Mary Stolz. (Illus.). 128p. (J). (gr. 3-7). 1995. pap. 12.95 (*1-56792-024-1*) Godine.

Quentin Durward see Works of Sir Walter Scott

Quentin Reynolds. Quentin Reynolds. 26.95 (*0-8488-1126-7*) Amereon Ltd.

Quentin Tarantino: Interviews. Ed. by Gerald Peary. LC 98-17837. (Conversations with Filmmakers Ser.). 256p. 1998. pap. 18.00 (*1-57806-051-6*); text 45.00 (*1-57806-050-8*) U Pr of Miss.

Quentin Tarantino: The Cinema of Cool. Jeff Dawson. LC 95-79935. (Illus.). 224p. 1995. pap. 14.95 (*1-55783-227-7*) Applause Theatre Bk Pubs.

Quentin Tarantino: The Film Creek Files. Paul A. Woods. 1999. pap. text 16.95 (*0-85965-284-X*) Plexus.

QueQueens - Easy Grilling & Simple Smoking: Menus, Recipes & Tips Galore. Karen Adler & Judith Fertig. 96p. (Orig.). 1997. pap. 9.95 (*0-925175-26-9*) Pig Out Pubns.

Quercus Ilex L. Ecosystems: Function, Dynamics, & Management. Ed. by F. Romane et al. LC 92-13699. (Advances in Vegetation Science Ser.: Vol. 13). 384p. (C). 1992. text 426.00 (*0-7923-1764-5*) Kluwer Academic.

***Quercus: Statistics for Bioscientists: A Student Guidebook.** Moya Mccloskey. 160p. 2000. pap. text 24.95 (*0-340-67768-6*) OUP.

Querelle. Jean Genet. Tr. by Anselm Hollo from FRE. LC 73-17693. 288p. 1989. pap. 12.00 (*0-8021-5157-4*, Grove) Grove-Atltic.

Querelle. Jean Genet. 1987. pap. 7.95 (*0-394-62368-1*) Random.

Querelle de Brest. Jean Genet. (FRE.). 1981. pap. 16.95 (*0-7859-2741-7*) Fr & Eur.

Querelle de Brest. Jean Genet. (Imaginaire Ser.). (FRE.). 1953. pap. 13.95 (*2-07-026329-0*) Schoenhof.

Querelle des Critiques en France a la Fin de XIXe Siecle. R. J. Berg. (American University Studies: Romance Languages & Literature: Ser. II, Vol. 151). VII, 201p. 1990. 43.95 (*0-8204-1342-9*) P Lang Pubrg.

Querelle du Cid. Armand Gaste. 495p. 1974. reprint ed. write for info. (*3-487-05249-0*) G Olms Pubs.

Querelles de Famille. Georges Duhamel. (FRE.). 224p. 1959. pap. 16.95 (*0-7859-5427-9*) Fr & Eur.

Querencia. Steve Bodio. LC 89-82474. 176p. 1990. pap. 12.95 (*0-944439-15-2*) Clark City Pr.

Querencia. 2nd ed. Steven Bodio. LC 89-82474. 176p. 1996. reprint ed. 19.95 (*0-944439-75-6*) Clark City Pr.

Querencia: Poems. Daniel J. Langton. LC 76-740443. (Devins Award Breakthrough Ser.). 64p. 1976. 7.00 (*0-8262-0192-X*) Cheltenham Pr.

Quererse... No Es Suficiente. Ricardo Homs. (SPA.). 1997. pap. text 17.98 (*968-409-911-8*) Edamex.

Queretaro Prehispanico. Ed. by Ana M. Crespo & Rosa Brambila. 206p. 1991. pap. 15.00 (*968-29-3492-3*, IN023) UPLAAP.

Querida Hermana. Kate William. Tr. by Maruja Del Pozo. (Sweet Valley High Ser.: No. 7).Tr. of Dear Sister. (YA). (gr. 7 up). 1993. 13.05 (*0-606-10469-0*, Pub. by Turtleback) Demco.

Querido Alberto: Biografia Autorizado de Juan Gabriel. Eduardo Magallanes. (SPA., Illus.). 208p. 1995. per. 12.00 (*0-684-81548-6*) S&S Trade Pap.

Querido Diego, Te Abraza Quiela. Elena Poniastowska. (SPA.). pap. 12.95 (*968-411-109-6*, Pub. by Edicnes Era) Continental Bk.

Querido Diego Te Abraza Quiela, 1. Elena Poniastowska. 1997. pap. text 15.29 (*968-411-214-9*) Edicnes Cast.

Querido Dios. (Mis Primeras Oraciones Ser.). (SPA.). 1995. bds. 2.98 (*1-85854-303-7*) Brimax Bks.

Querido Pedrin. Alma Flor Ada. 1997. 12.19 (*0-606-11775-X*, Pub. by Turtleback) Demco.

Querido Pedrin. Alma F. Ada. (SPA., Illus.). (J). (gr. k-3). 1997. reprint ed. pap. 6.99 (*0-614-29084-8*) Aladdin.

***Querido Senor Henshaw.** (SPA.). 2000. 9.95 (*1-56137-548-9*) Novel Units.

Querido Senor Henshaw. Beverly Cleary.Tr. of Dear Mr. Henshaw. (J). 1997. 11.05 (*0-606-11776-8*, Pub. by Turtleback) Demco.

Queridos Ma Ma' y Pa Pa' Marie F. Hafen.Tr. of Dear Mommy & Daddy. (ENG & SPA., Illus.). 152p. (Orig.). 1997. pap. 14.95 (*1-886990-02-6*) CareMORE.

Querini Stampalia Foundation: Venice 1961-3 Carlo Scarpa. Richard Murphy. (Architecture in Detail Ser.). (Illus.). 60p. (C). 1993. pap. 29.95 (*0-7148-2848-3*, Pub. by Phaidon Press) Phaidon Pr.

Query Letter That Never Fails. 2nd ed. Thomas A. Williams. (Illus.). 51p. 1996. ring bd. 14.95 (*1-878853-04-X*) Venture Pr FL.

Query of the Road: Selected Poems of Akhtar-ul-iman with Extensive Commentary. Ed. by Baidar Bakht. 1996. 36.00 (*81-7167-303-1*, Pub. by Rupa) S Asia.

Query Optimization by Semantic Reasoning. Jonathan J. King. LC 84-37. (Computer Science: Artificial Intelligence Ser.: No. 15). (Illus.). 136p. reprint ed. pap. 42.20 (*0-8357-1541-8*, 207035000088) Bks Demand.

Query Processing for Advanced Database Systems. Ed. by Johann C. Freytag et al. 512p. (C). 1994. text 59.95 (*1-55860-271-2*) Morgan Kaufmann.

Query Processing for Large Databases. Goetz Graefe. 1998. 54.95 (*1-55860-342-5*) Morgan Kaufmann.

Query Processing in Database Systems. Ed. by Won Kim et al. (Topics in Information Systems Ser.). (Illus.). 352p. 1985. 51.00 (*0-387-13831-5*) Spr-Verlag.

Query Processing in Parallel Relationship Database Systems. Ed. by H. Lu et al. LC 93-45665. 392p. 1994. 62.00 (*0-8186-5452-X*, 5452) IEEE Comp Soc.

Query, Quest, & Quasi: What Is It Supposed to Be? Marilyn R. Rosenberg. (Illus.). 20p. 1997. pap. 8.00 (*0-913615-15-3*) Marilyn R Rosenberg.

***Querying the Medieval: Texts & the History of Practices in South Asia.** Ronald B. Inden et al. LC 99-10675. (Illus.). 320p. 2000. text 49.95 (*0-19-512430-8*) OUP.

Que's Computer Buyer's Guide. 1991. 14.95 (*0-88022-860-1*) Que.

Que's Computer User's Dictionary. LC 92-12360. 1992. 6.95 (*0-8407-6847-8*) Nelson.

Que's Computer User's Dictionary. 4th ed. Bryan Pfaffenberger. 670p. 1993. pap. 12.95 (*1-56529-604-4*) Que.

Que's Computer Users Dictionary. 5th ed. 1994. 12.99 (*0-7897-0014-X*) Que.

Que's Computer Users Dictionary. 5th ed. Ed. by Bryan Pfaffenberger. LC 94-67366. 542p. 1994. 12.99 (*1-56529-881-0*) Que.

Que's First Look at Chicago. Que Development Group Staff. 1994. 14.99 (*0-7897-0074-3*) Que.

Que's Guide to Lotus Notes 3.O. Mark Schulman. LC 93-87386. 1994. 24.95 (*1-56529-638-9*) Que.

Que's MEGA Web Directory. 2nd ed. Robert J. Rositano et al. LC 96-70543. 1040p. 1996. 39.99 (*0-7897-0951-1*) Que.

Que's Quick Guide to Lotus Notes. Mark Schulman. (Illus.). 414p. (Orig.). 1993. 21.95 (*1-56529-182-4*) Que.

Que's Using Enable. 2nd ed. Walter Bruce & J. Schroth. (Illus.). 800p. 1993. 29.95 (*1-56529-217-0*) Que.

Quesadillas over 100 Fast, Fresh & Festive Recipes. Steve Ramsland & Katherine M. Ramsland. LC 96-15833. 192p. 1997. pap. 12.00 (*0-7615-0544-X*) Prima Pub.

Quesnay's "Tableau Economique" A Critique & Reassessment. Steven Pressman. x, 198p. 1994. lib. bdg. 37.50 (*0-678-01471-X*) Kelley.

***Quest.** Pam Binder. 2000. 19.99 (*1-891761-10-2*) Goodfellow Pr.

Quest. David Bischoff. LC 76-44815. 64 p. (J). 1977. 3.95 (*0-8172-0528-4*) Raintree Steck-V.

Quest. Tom Brown. 1991. pap. 12.95 (*0-425-12660-9*) Berkley Pub.

Quest. J. David Cooper et al. (J). (gr. 6). 1995. text 51.96 (*0-395-71958-5*) HM.

Quest. David L. Hammer & Angus MacLaren. (Illus.). 125p. 1993. 15.95 (*0-938501-19-4*) Wessex.

Quest. Helen R. Hull. LC 90-30445. 392p. 1990. pap. 11.95 (*1-55861-021-9*) Feminist Pr.

Quest. Shannah Jay. LC 97-221109. (Chronicles of Tenebrak Ser.). 436p. 1993. write for info. (*0-330-27422-8*) Pan.

Quest. Denise Linn. 288p. 1999. pap. 12.00 (*0-345-42544-8*) Ballantine Pub Grp.

Quest. Nancy Moser. LC 99-22049. (Mustard Seed Ser.: Vol. 2). 400p. 1999. pap. 11.99 (*1-57673-410-2*) Multnomah Pubs.

Quest. Christopher Nicole. 256p. 26.00 (*0-7278-5556-5*) Severn Hse.

***Quest.** David Thompson. (Wilderness Ser.: Vol. 28). 176p. 1999. mass mkt. 3.99 (*0-8439-4572-9*, Pub. by Dorchester Pub Co) CMG.

Quest, 3 vols. large type ed. J. David Cooper et al. 752p. 188.00 (*0-614-20613-8*, L-38227-00 APHB) Am Printing Hse.

***Quest.** Pam Binder. 336p. 2000. reprint ed. mass mkt. 6.50 (*0-671-77451-4*) PB.

Quest: A Guide to the Job Interview. Kathryn Barbour. 112p. (C). 1993. pap. text 18.95 (*0-8403-6984-0*) Kendall-Hunt.

***Quest: A Journal for the Teenager Whose Parent Has Cancer.** Sue P. Heiney et al. (Illus.). 24p. (YA). (gr. 6-12). 1999. pap. write for info. (*1-889863-01-7*) Palmetto Richland.

Quest: A Journey of Spiritual Rediscovery. Richard Jafolla & Mary-Alice Jafolla. LC 92-63345. 410p. 1993. pap. 13.95 (*0-87159-190-1*) Unity Bks.

Quest: A Journey Toward a New Kind of Church. Dan Dick. LC 98-88788. 96p. 1999. pap. write for info. (*0-88177-261-5*, DR261, Pub. by Discipleship Res) P B D Inc.

***Quest: A Passion for Life.** 2000. pap. 12.00 (*0-671-04771-X*) PB.

***Quest: A Passion for Life.** 2000. pap. 12.00 (*0-671-04770-1*) S&S Trade.

***Quest: A Passion for Life.** 2000. pap. 12.00 (*0-671-04772-8*) S&S Trade.

***Quest: A Passion for Life.** 2000. pap. 12.00 (*0-671-04773-6*) S&S Trade.

Quest: Academic Skills Program. Ruth Cohen et al. 293p. (C). 1973. pap. text, teacher ed. 2.50 (*0-15-574611-1*) Harcourt Coll Pubs.

Quest: Activities for the Pursuit of Empowerment. Angela D. Bottom & Mary M. Stowers. 112p. (Orig.). 1996. pap. text, spiral bd. 15.00 (*1-888406-02-X*) Phoenix Access.

Quest: An Autobiography. Leopold Infeld. LC 79-55510. viii, 361p. 1980. 19.95 (*0-8284-0309-0*) Chelsea Pub.

Quest: An Intensive American English Series for Advanced Students. Bernard Hartley & Peter Viney. 1993. write for info. (*0-19-434872-5*); student ed. write for info. (*0-19-434869-5*) OUP.

Quest: An Intensive American English Series for Advanced Students, Wkbk. A. Bernard Hartley & Peter Viney. 1993. write for info. (*0-19-434870-9*) OUP.

Quest: An Intensive American English Series for Advanced Students, Wkbk. B. Bernard Hartley & Peter Viney. 1993. write for info. (*0-19-434871-7*) OUP.

Quest: An Intensive American English Series for Intermediate Students. Bernard Hartley & Peter Viney. LC 93-27799. 1993. write for info. (*0-19-434868-7*); student ed. write for info. (*0-19-434865-2*); student ed. write for info. (*0-19-434866-0*) OUP.

Quest: History & Meaning in Religion. Mircea Eliade. LC 68-19059. (Midway Reprint Ser.). xii, 192p. 1984. reprint ed. pap. text 18.00 (*0-226-20386-7*) U Ch Pr.

***Quest: Listening & Speaking in the Academic World, Bk. 1.** Pamela Hartmann & Laurie Blass. 240p. (C). 1999. pap. 21.88 (*0-07-006249-8*) McGrw-H Hghr Educ.

***Quest: Listening & Speaking in the Academic World, Bk. 2.** Laurie Blass. 288p. (C). 1999. pap. 22.50 (*0-07-006252-8*) McGrw-H Hghr Educ.

***Quest: Listening & Speaking in the Academic World, Bk. 3.** Pamela Hartmann & Laurie Blass. 288p. (C). 1999. pap. 22.50 (*0-07-006255-2*) McGrw-H Hghr Educ.

Quest: Literacy Activity Book. J. David Cooper et al. (J). (gr. 6). 1995. student ed. 8.64 (*0-395-72487-2*) HM.

Quest: Literacy Activity Book, 2 vols. large type ed. J. David Cooper et al. 368p. (J). (gr. 6). 92.00 (*0-614-20612-X*, L-38232-00 APHB) Am Printing Hse.

***Quest: Poems from Hollywood.** Mark Dunster. 11p. 1999. pap. 5.00 (*0-89642-713-7*) Linden Pubs.

***Quest: Reading & Writing in the Academic World.** Hartmann. 192p. 1998. pap. text 21.88 (*0-07-006258-7*) McGrw-H Hghr Educ.

Q

***Quest: Reading & Writing in the Academic World.** Pamela Hartmann & Laurie Blass. 244p. (C). 1999. pap., teacher ed. 19.38 (*0-07-006259-5*) McGrw-H Hghr Educ.

Quest: Research & Inquiry in Arts Education. 2nd ed. Richard Courtney. LC 97-9478. 160p. 1997. 40.00 (*0-7618-0773-X*) U Pr of Amer.

Quest: The Search for Heroes. Lea Clark et al. Ed. by Carla Crane. (Next Level Preteen Electives Ser.). (Illus.). 128p. 1996. teacher ed. 14.99 (*0-7847-0503-8*, 42103) Standard Pub.

Quest: The Search for the Grail of Immortality. Rhuddlwm Gawr. LC 78-61716. (Illus.). (Orig.). 1985. 14.95 (*0-931760-02-X*, CP10101); pap. text 12.95 (*0-931760-01-1*) Camelot GA.

Quest: The Search for the Grail of Immortality. rev. ed. Rhuddlwm Gawr. (Illus.). 1990. 14.95 (*0-317-93327-2*); pap. 12.95 (*0-317-93328-0*) Camelot GA.

Quest: The Search for the Historical Jesus & Muhammad. F. E. Peters. (Illus.). 252p. 2000. pap. text 19.95 (*1-889119-04-0*) Seven Bridges.

Quest: The Ultimate Sourcebook for Next to Nothing Adventure Travel. Grant Shearer & Dave Hirschbain. 204p. 1995. pap. 15.95 (*0-9646854-0-X*) Atlas CA.

Quest Across Time. Andre Norton. 1999. mass mkt. 4.99 (*0-451-45262-3*, Onyx) NAL.

Quest & Other Poems. Mary De Young. 1972. pap. 10.00 (*0-936128-22-4*) De Young Pr.

Quest & Other Poems. Gertrude Johnson. Ed. by Janet Leih. (Illus.). 32p. (Orig.). 1983. pap. 3.00 (*1-877649-04-X*) Tesseract SD.

Quest Anthology. Ed. by James H. Webb, Jr. LC 75-36916. (Occult Ser.). 1976. reprint ed. 51.95 (*0-405-07971-0*) Ayer.

Quest April-May-June, 1997, Vol. 9. 82p. (J). (gr. 2-5). 1997. 20.00 (*0-913585-26-2*) Scripture U Pub.

Quest April-May-June, 1996, Vol. 8. 82p. (J). (gr. 2-5). 1996. 20.00 (*0-913585-07-6*) Scripture U Pub.

Quest Begins. Wendy Pini. (Elfquest Ser.). 1997. mass mkt. 5.99 (*0-441-00418-0*) Ace Bks.

Quest Book - Guest Book: A Biblio-Folly. Leona Rostenberg & Madeleine B. Stern. (Illus.). 124p. (Orig.). 1993. pap. 18.00 (*0-929246-04-7*) Modoc Pr.

Qu'Est-Ce Que la Litterature? Jean-Paul Sartre. (Folio Essais Ser.: No. 19). (FRE.). pap. 11.95 (*2-07-032306-4*) Schoenhof.

Qu'Est-Ce Que le Bouddhisme. Jorge Luis Borges. (FRE.). 122p. 1979. pap. 10.95 (*0-7859-1682-2*, 2070354040) Fr & Eur.

Qu'Est-Ce Que le Tiers Etat? & Sieyes, 2 vols. Emmanuel Sieyes & Charles-Augustin Sainte-Beuve. Ed. by J. P. Mayer. LC 78-67389. (European Political Thought Ser.). (FRE.). 1979. reprint ed. lib. bdg. 15.95 (*0-405-11740-X*) Ayer.

***Qu'est-ce Que "L'Eglise"? Identifier la Nature et la Dessein de l'Eglise du Nouveau Testament.** Eddie Cloer. Orig. Title: What Is "the Church"?. 232p. 1998. pap. 2.50 (*0-945441-30-4*) Res Pubns AR.

Qu'Est-Ce Qui se Passe, 3 vols. 3rd ed. Robert S. Balas & Donald Rice. (C). 1990. pap. 37.16 (*0-395-52586-1*) HM.

Qu'Est-Ce Qui se Passe, 3 vols. 3rd ed. Robert S. Balas & Donald Rice. (C). 1990. pap. 38.36 (*0-395-52626-4*) HM.

Qu'Est-Ce Qui se Passe, 3 vols. 3rd ed. Robert S. Balas & Donald Rice. (C). 1990. audio 24.36 (*0-395-52905-0*) HM.

Qu'Est-Ce Qui se Passe, 3 vols. 3rd ed. Robert S. Balas & Donald Rice. (C). 1990. pap., teacher ed. 5.96 (*0-395-52875-5*) HM.

Qu'Est-Ce Qu'On Dit? Joan H. Manley et al. LC 93-43695. (ENG & FRE.). (C). 1994. mass mkt., student ed. 56.95 (*0-8384-4487-3*) Heinle & Heinle.

Qu'Est-Ce Qu'On Dit? Joan H. Manley et al. LC 93-43695. (ENG & FRE.). (C). 1994. text, wbk. ed. 19.95 (*0-8384-4489-X*) Heinle & Heinle.

Qu'Est-Ce Qu'On Dit? Smith & Joan H. Manley. (College French Ser.). (FRE.). (C). 1994. wbk. ed. 90.95 incl. audio (*0-8384-5521-2*); pap., wbk. ed., lab manual ed. 33.95 (*0-8384-5522-0*) Heinle & Heinle.

Qu'Est-Ce Qu'On Dit? Smith & Joan H. Manley. (College French Ser.). (FRE.). (C). 1994. pap., suppl. ed., wbk. ed. 33.95 (*0-8384-5523-9*) Heinle & Heinle.

Qu'Est-Ce Qu'On Dit? Smith et al. (College French Ser.). (FRE.). (C). 1994. text, suppl. ed. 21.95 (*0-8384-4493-8*); mass mkt., suppl. ed. 36.95 (*0-8384-4496-2*) Heinle & Heinle.

Qu'Est-Ce Qu'On Dit? Smith et al. LC 93-43695. (College French Ser.). (FRE.). (C). 1994. text, lab manual ed. 19.95 (*0-8384-4499-7*); mass mkt., suppl. ed., lab manual ed. 36.95 (*0-8384-4492-X*) Heinle & Heinle.

Qu'est-ce Qu'on Dit-workbook Answer Key. Smith et al. LC 93-43695. (College French). (FRE.). (C). 1994. text, suppl. ed. 6.95 (*0-8384-5483-6*) Heinle & Heinle.

Quest for a Better Democratic Alternative. Jashwant B. Mehta. LC 94-904208. (C). 1995. 18.00 (*0-7069-8491-9*, Pub. by Vikas) S Asia.

Quest for a Child. Anna-Marie Lockard. 120p. (Orig.). 1993. pap. 6.95 (*0-89228-081-6*) Impact Christian.

Quest for a Cure: The Public Hospital in Williamsburg, Virginia, 1773-1885. Shomer S. Zwelling. LC 84-28567. (Illus.). 64p. (Orig.). 1985. pap. 5.95 (*0-87935-110-1*) Colonial Williamsburg.

Quest for a Democratic World. Maurice Rotstein. 240p. 1998. 60.00 (*0-391-04079-0*); pap. 18.50 (*0-391-04077-4*) Humanities.

***Quest for a Democratic World.** Maurice Rotstein. LC 99-51810. 288p. 2000. 54.00 (*0-7618-1568-6*); pap. 34.50 (*0-7618-1569-4*) U Pr of Amer.

Quest for a Federal Manpower Partnership. Sar A. Levitan & Joyce K. Zickler. LC 74-16541. 141p. reprint ed. pap. 43.80 (*0-7837-4140-5*, 205796300011) Bks Demand.

Quest for a Legendary Fish. T.W.F.T. Staff. 154p. (C). 1984. pap. 125.00 (*81-7089-023-3*, Pub. by Intl Bk Distr) St Mut.

Quest for a Living Wage: The History of the Federal Minimum Wage Program, 48. Willis J. Nordlund. LC 95-48354. (Contributions in Labor Studies: Vol. 48). 304p. 1997. 65.00 (*0-313-26412-0*, Greenwood Pr) Greenwood.

Quest for a Maid. Frances M. Hendry. LC 91-34333. 240p. (J). (gr. 4-7). 1992. pap. 4.95 (*0-374-46155-4*, Sunburst Bks) FS&G.

Quest for a Maid. Frances Mary Hendry. 1992. 10.05 (*0-606-02409-3*, Pub. by Turtleback) Demco.

Quest for a More Stable Economic System: Restructuring at a Time of Cyclical Adjustment. Ed. by Lawrence Robert Klein. LC 93-25699. (DIVS-Diverse Ser.). 416p. (C). 1993. lib. bdg. 156.00 (*0-7923-9389-9*) Kluwer Academic.

Quest for a Non-Violent Russia: The Partnership of Leo Tolstoy & Vladimir Chertkov. Alexander Fodor. LC 89-35598. 232p. (C). 1989. lib. bdg. 53.00 (*0-8191-7536-6*) U Pr of Amer.

Quest for a Public: French Popular Theatre Since 1945. Vera Lee. 200p. 1976. text 18.95 (*0-87073-180-7*) Schenkman Bks Inc.

Quest for a Radical Profession: Social Service Careers & Political Ideology. David Wagner. 274p. (Orig.). (C). 1990. pap. text 24.00 (*0-8191-7751-2*); lib. bdg. 45.00 (*0-8191-7750-4*) U Pr of Amer.

Quest for a Science of Accounting: An Anthology of the Research of Robert R. Sterling. Thomas A. Lee. Ed. by Peter W. Wolnizer & Richard P. Brief. LC 97-26158. (New Works in Accounting History Ser.). 854p. 1997. reprint ed. text 149.00 (*0-8153-3026-X*) Garland.

Quest for a Small Family. B. L. Raina. (C). 1991. 44.00 (*81-7169-125-0*, Pub. by Commonwealth) S Asia.

Quest for a Star: The Civil War Letters & Diaries of Colonel Francis T. Sherman of the 88th Illinois. Francis T. Sherman. Ed. by C. Knight Aldrich. LC 99-6507. (Voices of the Civil War Ser.). (Illus.). 240p. 2000. 34.00 (*1-57233-064-3*) U of Tenn Pr.

Quest for a Theology of Judaism: The Divine, the Human & the Ethical Dimensions in the Structure-of-Faith of Judaism. Manfred H. Vogel. (Studies in Judaism). 328p. (Orig.). (C). 1987. pap. text 27.00 (*0-8191-6594-8*); lib. bdg. 56.00 (*0-8191-6593-X*) U Pr of Amer.

Quest for a Tomorrow. Bruce Mecartea. 407p. (Orig.). 1995. pap. 6.95 (*0-9646744-0-8*) Dawn Pub CA.

Quest for a Unified Theory of Information: Proceedings of the Second International Conference on the Foundations of Information Science. Ed. by Wolfgang Hofkirchner. (World Futures General Evolution Studies: Vol. 13). 642p. 1999. text 98.00 (*90-5700-531-X*, ECU100, Harwood Acad Pubs) Gordon & Breach.

Quest for a United Germany. Ferenc A. Vali. LC 67-16914. 331p. reprint ed. pap. 102.70 (*0-608-15161-0*, 202587900046) Bks Demand.

***Quest for Adventure.** Chris Bonington. 2000. 35.00 (*0-7922-7953-0*) Natl Geog.

Quest for Adventure: David Horton's Conquest of the Appalachian Trail & the Trans-America Footrace. David Horton & Rebekah Trittipoe. LC 97-61968. (Illus.). 223p. 1997. pap. 14.95 (*1-890306-05-3*) Warwick Hse.

Quest for Albion: Monarchy & the Patronage of British Painting. Christopher Lloyd. LC 98-61116. (Illus.). 128p. 1999. pap. 27.50 (*0-500-97476-4*, Pub. by Thames Hudson) Norton.

Quest for Alien Planets: Exploring Worlds Outside the Solar System. Paul Halpern. LC 97-22445. (Illus.). 320p. (C). 1997. 27.95 (*0-306-45623-0*, Plenum Trade) Perseus Pubng.

Quest for an American Sociology: Robert E. Park & the Chicago School. Fred H. Matthews. LC 77-373940. 288p. reprint ed. pap. 89.30 (*0-7837-1029-1*, 204134000020) Bks Demand.

***Quest for an Ideal Legal Form for Small Businesses, 1997.** Ed. by Barry A. K. Rider & Mads Andenas. (Developments in European Company Law Ser.: Vol. 2). 192p. 1999. 87.00 (*90-411-9697-8*) Kluwer Law Intl.

Quest for an Image of Brain: Computerized Tomography in the Perspective of Past & Future Imaging Methods. William H. Oldendorf. LC 79-62971. 167p. 1980. reprint ed. pap. 51.80 (*0-608-00420-0*, 206113500007) Bks Demand.

Quest for an International Order in the Indian Ocean. K. P. Misra. 159p. 1977. 14.95 (*0-318-37255-X*) Asia Bk Corp.

Quest for an Island. Vassily Aksyonov. 250p. 1987. 17.95 (*1-55554-020-1*) PAJ Pubns.

Quest for Anastasia: Solving the Mystery of the Lost Romanovs. John Klier & Helen Mingay. LC 97-30242. (Illus.). 256p. 1997. 22.50 (*1-55972-442-0*, Birch Ln Pr) Carol Pub Group.

Quest for Anastasia: Solving the Mystery of the Lost Romanovs. John Klier & Helen Mingay. (Illus.). 256p. 1999. pap. 14.95 (*0-8065-2064-7*, Citadel Pr) Carol Pub Group.

Quest for Anonymity: The Novels of George Eliot. Henry Alley. LC 96-29628. 184p. 1997. 33.50 (*0-87413-621-0*) U Delaware Pr.

Quest for Answers: A Primer of Understanding & Treating Severe Personality Disorders. Salman Akhtar. LC 94-22794. 1995. pap. 40.00 (*1-56821-364-6*) Aronson.

Quest for Arthur's Britain. Ed. by Geoffrey Ashe. (Illus.). 252p. 1999. reprint ed. pap. 13.95 (*0-89733-287-3*) Academy Chi Pubs.

Quest for Authority & Honor in the American Professions, 1750-1900. Samuel Haber. LC 90-46752. (Illus.). 492p. 1991. 45.00 (*0-226-31173-2*) U Ch Pr.

Quest for Balance in State-Local Revenue Structures. Ed. & Intro. by Frederick D. Stocker. LC HJ4120.Q4. (Tax Policy Roundtable Property Tax Papers: TPR-16). 151p. 1987. reprint ed. pap. 46.90 (*0-608-02090-7*, 206274300004) Bks Demand.

Quest for Becket's Bones. John Butler. LC 94-30026. (Illus.). 192p. 1995. 32.50 (*0-300-06115-3*) Yale U Pr.

Quest for Becket's Bones: The Mystery of the Relics of St. Thomas Becket of Canterbury. John Butler. (Illus.). 192p. 1996. pap. 18.00 (*0-300-06895-6*) Yale U Pr.

Quest for Being. Sidney Hook. LC 91-61909. (Great Books in Philosophy). 268p. (Orig.). 1991. pap. 11.95 (*0-87975-700-0*) Prometheus Bks.

Quest for Bigfoot. Kyra P. Wayne. (Illus.). 160p. (Orig.). (J). 1996. pap. 11.95 (*0-88839-396-2*) Hancock House.

Quest for Camelot. J. J. Gardner. (J). 1998. pap. 3.98 (*0-590-12058-1*) Scholastic Inc.

Quest for Camelot. Catherine McCafferty. LC 98-171648. 1998. write for info. (*0-7853-2383-X*) Pubns Intl Ltd.

Quest for Camelot. deluxe ed. Warner Brothers Staff. LC 99-191023. 64p. (J). 1998. 5.98 (*0-590-12060-3*) Scholastic Inc.

Quest for Camelot: The Search for Excalibur. rev. ed. Bruce Weber. LC 98-171532. (J). 1979. pap. 1.25 (*0-590-12064-6*) Scholastic Inc.

Quest for Camelot Hello Reader! Warner Brothers Staff. (Quest for Camelot Ser.). (J). 1998. pap. text 3.98 (*0-590-12062-X*) Scholastic Inc.

Quest for Camelot Kayley in Camelot Jewel Sticker Book. Warner Brothers Staff. LC 99-191028. (J). 1998. pap. text 5.99 (*0-590-02436-1*) Scholastic Inc.

Quest for Certainty: A Comparative Study of Heidegger & Sankara. John A. Grimes. (Revisioning Philosophy Ser.). XXI, 239p. (C). 1989. text 43.95 (*0-8204-1029-2*) P Lang Pubng.

Quest for Certitude in E. M. Forster's Fiction. David Shusterman. LC 72-6784. (Studies in Fiction: No. 34). 1972. reprint ed. lib. bdg. 75.00 (*0-8383-1662-X*) M S G Haskell Hse.

Quest for Character. Charles R. Swindoll. LC 93-26369. 224p. 1993. pap. 11.99 (*0-310-42051-2*) Zondervan.

***Quest for Charisma: Christianity & Persuasion.** Craig R. Smith. LC 99-43103. 224p. 2000. write for info. (*0-275-96836-7*, Praeger Pubs) Greenwood.

Quest for Chilean Plants. Peter Baxter et al. (Illus.). 32p. 1998. pap. 15.00 (*1-872291-67-8*) Balogh.

Quest for Christa T. Christa Wolf. Tr. by Christopher Middleton from GER. 185p. 1979. pap. 10.00 (*0-374-51534-4*) FS&G.

Quest for Christian Purity. 2nd ed. O. Talmadge Spence. 399p. (C). 1988. 18.95 (*1-882542-03-7*); pap. 14.95 (*1-882542-04-5*) Fndtns NC.

Quest for Church Unity: From John Calvin to Isaac d'Huisseau. Richard Stauffer. LC 86-1451. (Pittsburgh Theological Monographs: No. 19). (Orig.). 1986. pap. 10.00 (*0-915138-63-8*) Pickwick.

Quest for Clues, No. II. Ed. by Shay Addams. (Illus.). 200p. (Orig.). (C). 1989. pap. 29.95 (*0-929373-01-4*) Origin Syst.

Quest for Clues, No. III. Ed. by Shay Addams. (Illus.). 198p. (Orig.). (YA). 1990. pap. 24.99 (*0-929373-02-2*) Origin Syst.

Quest for Clues: The Book of Orbs. Ed. by Shay Addams & David Ladyman. (Quest for Clues Ser.: No. 5). (Illus.). 144p. (Orig.). 1992. pap. 16.95 (*0-929373-10-3*) Origin Syst.

Quest for Clues: The Manual of Swords. Shay Addams. Ed. by David Ladyman. (Quest for Clues Ser.: No. 6). (Illus.). 144p. (Orig.). 1993. pap. 16.95 (*0-929373-11-1*) Origin Syst.

Quest for Comets: An Explosive Trail of Beauty & Danger. David H. Levy. 304p. 1995. reprint ed. pap. 12.50 (*0-380-72526-6*, Avon Bks) Morrow Avon.

Quest for Common Learning: The Aims of General Education. Ernest L. Boyer & Arthur Levine. LC 81-66307. 68p. 1981. pap. 12.00 (*0-931050-18-9*) Carnegie Fnd Advan Teach.

Quest for Community. O. H. Mowrer. LC 65-167. (Augustana College Library Occasional Papers, Wallin Lecture: No. 8). 15p. 1962. pap. 1.00 (*0-910182-38-8*) Augustana Coll.

Quest for Community: A Study in the Ethics of Order & Freedom. Robert A. Nisbet. LC 90-32568. 300p. 1990. reprint ed. pap. 21.95 (*1-55815-058-7*) ICS Pr.

Quest for Competitiveness: Lessons from America's Productivity & Quality Leaders. Ed. by Y. Krishna Shetty & Vernon M. Buehler. LC 89-49433. 448p. 1991. 69.50 (*0-89930-546-6*, SQB/, Greenwood Pr) Greenwood.

Quest for Compromise: Peacemakers in Counter-Reformation Vienna. Howard Louthan. (Studies in Early Modern History). (Illus.). 204p. (C). 1997. text 59.95 (*0-521-58082-X*) Cambridge U Pr.

Quest for Concensus. James H. Boykin. LC 97-93289. vi, 145p. 1997. pap. 16.99 (*1-880833-03-4*, Archdiocese Miami) Boykin.

Quest for Conception: Gender, Infertility, & Egyptian Medical Traditions. Marcia C. Inhorn. LC 94-10899. (Illus.). 472p. (Orig.). (C). 1994. text 49.95 (*0-8122-3221-6*); pap. text 21.95 (*0-8122-1528-1*) U of Pa Pr.

Quest for Constitutionalism in Africa: Selected Essays on Constitutionalism, the Nationality Problem, Military Rule, & Party Politics. Asmelash Beyene & Gelase Mutahabe. LC 95-106832. (Illus.). VIII, 253p. 1994. pap. 48.95 (*3-631-47110-6*) P Lang Pubng.

Quest for Context & Meaning: Studies in Biblical Intertextuality in Honor of James A. Sanders. Ed. by Craig A. Evans & Shemaryahu Talmon. LC 97-40207. (Biblical Interpretation Ser.: Vol. 28). 640p. 1997. 203.00 (*90-04-10835-1*) Brill Academic Pubs.

Quest for Control: A Critique of the Regional-Central-Rule Approach in Public Affair. Herman R. Van Gunsteren. LC 75-19228. 170p. reprint ed. pap. 52.70 (*0-608-30074-8*, 202043100017) Bks Demand.

Quest for Control: A Quarter Century of Immigration Reform in Industrial Democracies, 1964-1989. Mark J. Miller. 224p. (C). 2000. pap. 25.00 (*0-8133-1030-X*) Westview.

***Quest for Cosmic Justice.** Thomas Sowell. LC 99-31470. 224p. 1999. 24.50 (*0-684-86462-2*) Free Pr.

Quest for Cost-Effectiveness in Health Care: Achieving Clinical Excellence While Controlling Costs. Jeffrey P. Trotter. LC 94-43404. 114p. 1995. pap. 35.00 (*1-55648-130-6*, 061171) AHPI.

Quest for Courage. Stormy Rodolph. (Indian Culture Ser.). (Illus.). 102p. (Orig.). (J). (gr. 4-12). 1984. pap. 6.95 (*0-89992-092-6*) Coun India Ed.

Quest for Courage. 2nd ed. Stormy Rodolph. (Council for Indian Education Ser.). (Illus.). 112p. (Orig.). (J). (gr. 4-7). 1993. pap. 8.95 (*1-879373-57-2*) Roberts Rinehart.

***Quest for Cthulhu.** August Derleth. 448p. 2000. pap. 12.95 (*0-7867-0752-6*, Pub. by Carroll & Graf) Publishers Group.

Quest for Cure: Restoring Function after Spinal Cord Injury. Sam Maddox. LC 92-50575. (Illus.). 200p. (Orig.). 1993. pap. 22.45 (*0-929819-03-9*) Paralyzed Vets.

Quest for Dall Rams. Wayne Heimer et al. (Illus.). 224p. 1997. 34.95 (*1-885924-02-X*); pap. 19.95 (*1-885924-03-8*) Outdoor Expeditions.

Quest for Dall Sheep Vol. 1: A Historic Guide's Memories of Alaskan Hunting. Jack E. Wilson. Ed. & Photos by Tony Russ. LC 97-75887. (Illus.). 224p. 1997. pap. 19.95 (*0-9639869-2-9*, 003) Northern Pubng.

Quest for Democracy: South Africa in Transition. Frederik Van Zyl Slabbert. LC 93-163717. (Forum Ser.). vii, 107p. 1992. write for info. (*0-14-015853-7*) Penguin Books.

***Quest for Democratic Security: The Role of the Council of Europe & U. S. Foreign Policy.** Heinrich Klebes. 61p. (C). 2000. pap. text 20.00 (*0-7567-0018-3*) DIANE Pub.

Quest for Destiny. Leo H. Bradman. Ed. by Ronald C. Harshman. 200p. (Orig.). 1994. pap. write for info. (*1-883945-03-8*) UniPsych Pr.

Quest for Dr. U. H. C. Artmann. Tr. by Malcolm Green from GER. 120p. Date not set. reprint ed. pap. 14.99 (*0-947757-56-2*) Serpents Tail.

Quest for Eastern Christians: Travels & Rumor in the Age of Discovery. Francis M. Rogers. LC 62-18138. 233p. reprint ed. pap. 72.30 (*0-608-18670-8*, 205590100039) Bks Demand.

Quest for Economic Development in the Caribbean. Paul C. Clement. 150p. 1999. pap. 10.95 (*0-9670898-1-6*) Clement Inc.

Quest for Economic Empire: The European Strategies of German Big Business in the Twentieth Century. Ed. by Volker R. Berghahn. LC 95-38477. 240p. 1996. pap. 22.50 (*1-57181-931-2*) Berghahn Bks.

Quest for Economic Empire: The European Strategies of German Big Business in the Twentieth Century. rev. ed. Ed. by Volker R. Berghahn. LC 95-38477. 240p. (C). 1996. 59.95 (*1-57181-027-7*) Berghahn Bks.

Quest for El Cid. Richard Fletcher. (Illus.). 240p. 1991. pap. 13.95 (*0-19-506955-2*, 12144) OUP.

Quest for Empire: A History of the Napoleonic Wars. David Inglehart. (Illus.). 1997. 34.95 (*1-890642-11-8*) Troubadour Interact.

Quest for Empire: Spanish Settlement in the Southwest. Donald Cutter & Iris H. Engstrand. (Illus.). 360p. 1996. 27.95 (*1-55591-230-3*) Fulcrum Pub.

Quest for Empire: The Saga for Russian America. Kyra P. Wayne. (Illus.). 415p. 1986. pap. 11.95 (*0-88839-193-5*); pap. 11.95 (*0-88839-191-9*) Hancock House.

Quest for Enlightenment: Articles from Back to Godhead Magazine. A. C. Prabhupada. LC 97-41422. (Illus.). 272p. 1997. 9.95 (*0-89213-292-2*) Bhaktivedanta.

Quest for Equality: The Constitution, Congress & the Supreme Court. Robert J. Harris. LC 77-1851. 172p. 1977. reprint ed. lib. bdg. 65.00 (*0-8371-9524-1*, HAQE, Greenwood Pr) Greenwood.

Quest for Equality: Trenton's Black Community, 1890-1965. Jack Washington. LC 93-452. (Illus.). 220p. 1993. 29.95 (*0-86543-378-X*); pap. 9.95 (*0-86543-379-8*) Africa World.

Quest for Equality in Freedom. Francis M. Wilhoit. LC 78-55940. 350p. 1979. 39.95 (*0-87855-240-5*) Transaction Pubs.

Quest for Equilibrium: America & the Balance of Power on Land & Sea. George Liska. LC 77-4780. 278p. reprint ed. pap. 86.20 (*0-608-06163-8*, 206649600008) Bks Demand.

Quest for Equity & Excellence: A Staff Development Program for K-12 Teachers. Thomas J. Brown. 80p. 1999. pap., teacher ed., wbk. ed. 14.95 (*1-891404-08-3*, BA018, B&A Pr) Brown & Assocs.

Quest for Eros: Browning & Fifine. Samuel B. Southwell. LC 79-4945. 286p. reprint ed. pap. 88.70 (*0-7837-5800-6*, 204546600006) Bks Demand.

Quest for Evolutionary Socialism: Eduard Bernstein & Social Democracy. Manfred B. Steger. (Illus.). 301p. 1997. text 64.95 (*0-521-58200-8*) Cambridge U Pr.

Quest for Excellence. Marcus S. Robinson & Murray P. Kammer. 158p. (Orig.). 1993. student ed. 8.95 (*0-9639703-1-3*); pap. 12.95 (*0-9639703-0-5*); audio 8.95 (*0-9639703-2-1*) Wetware.

Q

Quest for Excellence: An Adolescent's Guide to Self-Confidence & Relationships. Deborah L. Wuerslin. 294p. (YA). (gr. 5-12). 1993. pap. 17.95 (*0-9646298-0-1*) Excellence Ga.

***Quest for Executive Effectiveness: Turning Vision Inside-Out: Charismatic-Participatory Leadership.** Ann M. O'Roark. 352p. 2000. pap. 19.95 (*1-57733-058-7*) B Dolphin Pub.

Quest for Failure: A Study of William Faulkner. Walter J. Slatoff. LC 72-4084. 275p. 1973. reprint ed. lib. bdg. 59.75 (*0-8371-6432-X*, SLQF, Greenwood Pr) Greenwood.

Quest for Faith, Quest for Freedom: Aspects of Pennsylvania's Religious Experience. Ed. by Otto Reimherr. LC 86-61790. (Illus.). 208p. 1987. 36.50 (*0-941664-26-0*) Susquehanna U Pr.

Quest for Faithfulness: The Account of a Unique Fellowship of Churches. Paul N. Tassell. LC 91-7930. 424p. (Orig.). 1991. pap. 15.99 (*0-87227-152-8*, RBP5185) Reg Baptist.

***Quest for Food: Its Role in Human Evolution & Migration.** Ivan Crowe. (History & Archaeology Ser.). (Illus.). 272p. 2000. 37.50 (*0-7524-1462-3*, Pub. by Tempus Pubng) Arcadia Publng.

***Quest for Freedom.** (In Classical Mood Ser.: Vol. 57). (Illus.). 30p. 1999. write for info. (*1-892207-10-9*) Intl Masters Pub.

***Quest for Freedom.** Loiell Dyrud. 2000. pap. write for info. (*1-58572-042-9*) Ambasdor Pubns.

Quest for Freedom: An African-American Odyssey. Mack K. Carter. LC 94-195515. 269p. (Orig.). 1993. pap. 12.00 (*0-9625423-9-3*) Four-G Pubs.

***Quest for Freedom: The Bird in the Cage & the Bird in the Forest.** Enrique Cadena. (ENG & SPA., Illus.). 222p. 1999. pap. 14.95 (*1-929342-00-4*) Olde Ridge Bk.

Quest for Freedom: The Life of a Belgian Resistance Fighter in World War Two. Yvonne Files. LC 91-17025. (Illus.). 176p. (Orig.). 1991. pap. 9.95 (*0-931832-93-4*) Fithian Pr.

Quest for Freedom: The United States & India's Independence. Kenton J. Clymer. LC 94-22120. 393p. 1995. 57.50 (*0-231-10044-2*); pap. text 22.00 (*0-231-10045-0*) Col U Pr.

***Quest for Fruition Through Ngoma: The Political Aspects of Healing in South Africa.** Ed. by Rijk Van Dijk et al. LC 99-45652. 320p. 1999. text 44.95 (*0-8214-1303-1*); pap. text 22.95 (*0-8214-1304-X*) Ohio U Pr.

***Quest for Full Assurance: Legacy of Calvin & His Successors.** Joel Beeke. 395p. 1999. pap. 14.99 (*0-85151-745-5*) Banner of Truth.

Quest for Giant Bighorns. Duncan B. Gilchrist. 1994. 34.95 (*1-885924-00-3*); pap. 19.95 (*1-885924-01-1*) Outdoor Expeditions.

Quest for Global Quality: A Manifestation of Total Quality Management by Singapore Airlines. Wee Y. Yeong et al. LC 96-15982. 1998. write for info. (*0-201-42087-2*) Addison-Wesley.

Quest for Glory: A Biography of Rear Admiral John A. Dahlgren. Robert Schneller, Jr. LC 95-20085. (Illus.). 432p. 1995. 39.95 (*1-55750-762-7*) Naval Inst Pr.

Quest for Glory: Major General Robert Howe & the American Revolution. Charles E. Bennett & Donald R. Lennon. LC 91-7825. (Illus.). x, 206p. (C). 1991. 29.95 (*0-8078-1982-4*) U of NC Pr.

Quest for Glory: Major General Robert Howe & the American Revolution. Charles E. Bennett & Donald R. Lennon. LC 91-7825. (Illus.). 219p. reprint ed. pap. 67.90 (*0-608-10493-0*, 207112200009) Bks Demand.

***Quest for Glory 5: The Official Strategy Guide.** Rick Barba. LC 97-69340. (Secrets of the Game Ser.). 240p. 1998. per. 19.99 (*0-7615-1189-X*) Prima Pub.

Quest for God: A Personal Pilgrimage. Paul Johnson. 224p. 1997. pap. 13.00 (*0-06-092823-9*) HarpC.

Quest for Godliness: The Puritan Vision of the Christian Life. J. I. Packer. LC 94-10535. 368p. 1994. pap. 17.99 (*0-89107-819-3*) Crossway Bks.

Quest for Gold: The Encyclopedia of American Olympians. Bill Mallon et al. LC 84-966. (Illus.). 496p. 1984. reprint ed. pap. 153.80 (*0-608-07084-X*, 206731300009) Bks Demand.

Quest for Goodness: An Introduction to Ethics. Keith W. Krasemann. 830p. (C). 1997. pap. text 39.00 (*0-536-00604-0*) Pearson Custom.

***Quest For Goodness: Introduction to Ethics.** 2nd ed. 850p. (C). 1999. 42.00 (*0-536-02773-0*) Pearson Custom.

Quest for Graham Greene. W. J. West. LC 97-43806. 1998. text 24.95 (*0-312-18161-2*) St Martin.

***Quest for Happiness.** Gary O'Brien. LC 99-96684. 2000. pap. 11.95 (*0-533-13313-0*) Vantage.

Quest for Harmoncy in Romen Basu Novels. G. R. Mallige. 134p. 1998. 19.95 (*0-932377-71-8*) Facet Bks.

***Quest for Harmony: Native American Spiritual Traditions.** William A. Young. 390p. 2000. pap. 24.95 (*1-889119-50-4*) Seven Bridges.

Quest for Health & Happiness: A Woman's Guide: Fitness Tips for the Body-Mind-Heart-Soul Plus Dream Planner & Daily Diary. Margo Lange. 296p. (Orig.). 1993. pap., student ed. 15.95 (*0-9635020-9-3*) M Lange Comm.

Quest for Hegemony in the Arab World: The Struggle over the Baghdad Pact. Elie Podeh. LC 95-884. (Social, Economic & Political Studies of the Middle East: Vol. 52). xii, 281p. 1995. 99.00 (*90-04-10214-0*) Brill Academic Pubs.

Quest for High Self-Esteem: Eight Great Steps to Personal Freedom. Wayne Smith. Ed. by Pamela Kirl. LC 94-67337. (Illus.). 150p. (Orig.). 1996. pap. 19.95 (*0-9642022-0-4*) S-E Pubng.

Quest for Holiness & Unity. John W. Smith. 1980. 19.95 (*0-87162-231-9*, D6250) Warner Pr.

Quest for Home: Reading Robert Southey. Christopher J. Smith. (Liverpool English Texts & Studies: No. 27). 256p. 1997. 39.95 (*0-85323-511-2*, Pub. by Liverpool Univ Pr); pap. 24.95 (*0-85323-521-X*, Pub. by Liverpool Univ Pr) Intl Spec Bk.

Quest for Human Beauty: An Illustrated History. Julian Robinson. LC 97-19491. 320p. 1998. 39.95 (*0-393-04004-6*) Norton.

Quest for Identity: The U. S. Woods. (C). 2000. pap. text 33.00 (*0-15-500999-0*, Pub. by Harcourt Coll Pubs) Harcourt.

Quest for Immortality: Science at the Frontiers of Aging. S. Jay Olshansky & Bruce A. Carnes. 176p. 2001. text 25.95 (*0-393-04836-5*) Norton.

***Quest for Inclusion: Jews & Liberalism in Modern American.** Marc J. Dollinger. LC 99-89426. (Illus.). 288p. 2000. 35.00 (*0-691-00509-5*, Pub. by Princeton U Pr) Cal Prin Full Svc.

Quest for Industrial Peace. David L. Cole. LC 77-26873. (Meyer Kestnbaum Lectures). 164p. 1978. reprint ed. lib. bdg. 55.00 (*0-313-20072-6*, COQI, Greenwood Pr) Greenwood.

Quest for Jesus & the Christian Faith. Ed. by Frederick J. Gaiser. LC 97-61607. (Word & World Supplement Ser.: Vol. 3). 214p. 1997. pap. text 16.95 (*0-9632389-2-2*) Luther Seminary.

Quest for Justice. 3rd ed. Leslie Rubin & Charles Rubin. 332p. (C). 1992. pap. text 52.00 (*0-536-58152-5*) Pearson Custom.

Quest for Justice: Aboriginal Peoples & Aboriginal Rights. Menno Boldt et al. 416p. 1985. pap. text 22.95 (*0-8020-6589-9*) U of Toronto Pr.

Quest for Justice: Aboriginal Peoples & Aboriginal Rights. Ed. by Menno Boldt & J. Anthony Long. LC 86-157870. 416p. reprint ed. pap. 129.00 (*0-7837-1227-8*, 204136300020) Bks Demand.

Quest for Justice: Essays in Honour of Michael McGregor Corbett Chief Justice of the Supreme Court of South Africa. Ellison Kahn. LC 95-229507. xx, 378p. 1995. 60.00 (*0-7021-3440-6*, Pub. by Juta & Co) Gaunt.

Quest for Justice: Systemic Discrimination in America. Garry De Young. 83p. (Orig.). 1984. 15.00 (*0-936128-05-4*) De Young Pr.

Quest for Justice on the Job: Essays & Experiments. Jerald Greenberg. LC 95-35744. 240p. 1995. 58.00 (*0-8039-5967-2*); pap. 26.95 (*0-8039-5968-0*) Sage.

Quest for Kibi & the Origins of Japan. Michael Gorman. (Illus.). 156p. 1999. pap. 34.95 (*974-8299-23-6*, Pub. by Weatherhill) Weatherhill.

Quest for Kim: In Search of Kipling's Great Game. Peter Hopkirk. LC 97-4252. (Illus.). 288p. (C). 1997. 24.95 (*0-472-10854-9*, 10854) U of Mich Pr.

***Quest for Kim: In Search of Kipling's Great Game.** Peter Hopkirk. (Illus.). 288p. 1999. pap. 16.95 (*0-472-08634-0*, 08634) U of Mich Pr.

Quest for Kwanzaa: Poems by Johnnierenee Nelson. Johnnierenee Nelson. (Illus.). 40p. (Orig.). 1988. pap. 6.00 (*0-9623205-0-1*) House Nia.

Quest for Lasting Love. Jane Peart. LC 90-40569. (Orphan Train West Ser.). 192p. (Orig.). (YA). (gr. 10 up). 1990. pap. 7.99 (*0-8007-5372-0*) Revell.

***Quest for Law.** William Seagle. xv, 439p. 1999. reprint ed. 142.50 (*1-56169-486-X*) Gaunt.

Quest for Life: An Autobiography. Ian L. McHarg. LC 95-50489. (Illus.). 448p. 1996. 34.95 (*0-471-08628-2*) Wiley.

***Quest for Life: Journey for Jesus.** James Stone. 192p. 2000. pap. 12.95 (*1-57921-284-0*, 924-177, Pub. by WinePress Pub) BookWorld.

Quest for Life in Amber. George O. Poinar & Roberta Poinar. 240p. (C). 1995. pap. 15.00 (*0-201-48928-7*) Addison-Wesley.

Quest for Links to New Physics: Proceedings of the 15th International Warsaw Meeting on Elementary Particle Physics. Z. Ajduk et al. 532p. 1993. text 121.00 (*981-02-1209-7*) World Scientific Pub.

Quest for Longitude. Ed. & Intro. by William Andrewes. (Illus.). 450p. 1996. 75.00 (*0-9644329-0-0*) Collect Hist Sci.

Quest for Lost Heroes. David Gemmell. (The Wizards of Fantasy Promotion). 1995. mass mkt. 5.99 (*0-345-37904-7*, Del Rey) Ballantine Pub Grp.

Quest for Love. Dave Erickson. (Illus.). 189p. (C). 1991. 35.00 (*2-89705-902-8*) Christian Freedom.

Quest for Love: True Stories of Passion & Purity. Elisabeth Elliot. LC 96-6791. 272p. (YA). (gr. 10). 1996. pap. 10.99 (*0-8007-5605-3*) Revell.

Quest for Loyalty: Creating Value Through Partnership. Ed. & Intro. by Frederick F. Reichheld. 252p. 1996. 29.95 (*0-87584-745-5*) Harvard Busn.

***Quest for Maleness.** Theun Mares. Ed. by Charles Mitchley. (Illus.). 232p. 1999. pap. 13.95 (*1-919792-07-4*) Lionheart Pub OH.

Quest for Meaning. L. Francis Edmunds. LC 78-20932. 320p. 1998. 27.50 (*0-8264-1070-7*) Continuum.

***Quest for Meaning: A Journey Through Philosophy, the Arts, & Creative Genius.** William Cooney. LC 99-48692. 288p. 1999. pap. 32.50 (*0-7618-1526-0*) U Pr of Amer.

Quest for Meaning: Living a Life of Purpose. Jim Rosemergy. LC 98-18423. (Continuing Quest Ser.: Vol. 1). 134p. 1998. pap. 9.95 (*0-87159-222-3*) Unity Bks.

Quest for Meekness & Quietness of Spirit. Matthew Henry. 144p. 1995. reprint ed. 18.95 (*1-57358-022-8*) Soli Deo Gloria.

Quest for Megalodon. Tom Dade. Ed. by Pete Billac. 385p. (Orig.). 1993. pap. 12.95 (*0-943629-06-3*) Swan Pub.

Quest for Mental Health in America, Eighteen Eighty to Nineteen Seventeen. Barbara Sicherman. Ed. by Gerald N. Grob. LC 78-22589. (Historical Issues in Mental Health Ser.). 1980. lib. bdg. 37.95 (*0-405-11940-2*) Ayer.

Quest for Mercy: The Forgotten Ingredient in Health Care Reform. Roger J. Bulger. 120p. 1997. pap. text 10.00 (*1-891524-01-1*) Carden Jennings.

Quest for Mind: Piaget, Levi-Strauss & the Structuralist Movement. 2nd ed. Howard Gardner. 320p. 1981. pap. text 9.00 (*0-226-28332-1*) U Ch Pr.

Quest for Modernity & the Bengal Muslims, 1921-1947. Soumitra Sinha. 1995. lib. bdg. 18.00 (*81-85195-68-4*, Pub. by Minerva) S Asia.

Quest for Monetary Stability. Marcio Ronci. Ed. by Carlos G. Langoni & James Ferrer, Jr. LC 97-139042. 248p. (Orig.). 1996. pap. text 7.50 (*0-9654065-0-4*) Inst of Brazilian.

Quest for Moral Foundations: An Introduction to Ethics. Montague Brown. LC 95-42088. 192p. (C). 1996. pap. 14.95 (*0-87840-613-1*) Georgetown U Pr.

Quest for Moral Law. Louise S. Eby. LC 78-37849. (Essay Index Reprint Ser.). 1977. reprint ed. 23.95 (*0-8369-2588-2*) Ayer.

Quest for Mount Misery & Other Studies. Keith Waldrop. (Illus.). 20p. 1983. 30.00 (*0-918824-39-7*); 150.00 (*0-918824-40-0*) Turkey Pr.

Quest for Music Divine. Suresh C. Dey. 1990. 38.00 (*81-7024-301-7*, Pub. by Ashish Pub Hse) S Asia.

Quest for Natural Forest Management in Ghana, Cote d'Ivoire & Liberia. M. P. Parren & N. R. De Graaf. (Tropenbos Technical Ser.: No. 13). (Illus.). 200p. 1995. pap. 80.00 (*90-5113-025-2*, Pub. by Backhuys Pubs) Balogh.

Quest for Nuclear Stability: John F. Kennedy & the Soviet Union, 73. Bernard J. Firestone. LC 81-13257. (Contributions in Political Science Ser.: No. 73). 176p. 1982. 52.95 (*0-313-23214-8*, FPD/, Greenwood Pr) Greenwood.

Quest for Ore. fac. ed. Russell H. Bennett. LC 63-14391. (Illus.). 422p. 1963. reprint ed. pap. 130.90 (*0-7837-7843-0*, 204760200007) Bks Demand.

Quest for Origins: The Search for the Parentage of William Dungan, Perfumer of St. Martin-in-the-Fields. Thomas P. Dungan. (Illus.). 65p. 1997. pap. 12.00 (*0-9663239-1-2*) Dungan Bks.

Quest for Paradise: Europe & the American Moral Imagination. Charles L. Sanford. LC 76-42791. reprint ed. 49.50 (*0-404-60078-6*) AMS Pr.

Quest for Peace. K. Satchidananda Murty. 1986. 17.50 (*81-202-0165-5*, Pub. by Ajanta) S Asia.

Quest for Peace. Abraham Cronbach. LC 79-137533. (Peace Movement in America Ser.). ix, 223p. 1972. reprint ed. lib. bdg. 30.95 (*0-89198-061-X*) Ozer.

Quest for Peace: Three Moral Traditions in Western Cultural History. James T. Johnson. LC 86-30568. 321p. 1987. reprint ed. pap. 99.60 (*0-608-04520-9*, 206526500001) Bks Demand.

Quest for Peace: United States-Israel Relations & the Arab-Israeli Conflict. Bernard Reich. LC 76-45940. 495p. reprint ed. pap. 153.50 (*0-608-13017-6*, 202416000035) Bks Demand.

Quest for Peace & Progress. Balkrishna Singhania. 1986. 12.00 (*81-7017-213-6*, Pub. by Patriot Pubs) S Asia.

***Quest for Peace Between Israel & the Palestinians.** Haig Khatchadourian. LC 99-46193. (Conflict & Consciousness: Vol. 8). 192p. (C). 2000. pap. text 29.95 (*0-8204-4877-X*) P Lang Pubng.

Quest for Perfection: And Why Socrates Was an Idiot. T. J. Hunt. 80p. 1997. mass mkt. 12.95 (*0-9666837-0-6*) Haystack Pubg.

Quest for Perfection: The Story of the Making of the Stained-Glass Windows in the Bryn Athyn Cathedral & Glencairn. Martin Pryke. 40p. (Orig.). 1990. pap. 2.75 (*0-910557-24-1*) Acad New Church.

Quest for Permanence: The Symbolism of Wordsworth, Shelley & Keats. David Perkins. LC 59-11515. 317p. reprint ed. pap. 98.30 (*0-7837-4175-8*, 205902400012) Bks Demand.

Quest for Personal Power: Transforming Stress into Strength. Phil Neurnberger. 304p. 1997. reprint ed. pap. 14.00 (*0-399-52346-4*, Perigee Bks) Berkley Pub.

Quest for Piety & Obedience: The Story of the Brethren in Christ. Carlton O. Wittlinger. LC 77-94894. x, 580p. 1978. 19.95 (*0-916035-05-0*) Evangel Indiana.

Quest for Political & Spiritual Liberation: A Study in the Thought of Sri Aurobindo Ghose. June O'Connor. LC 75-5249. 153p. (C). 1976. 16.50 (*0-8386-1734-4*) Fairleigh Dickinson.

Quest for Power: Darkness in the Light. Stephen Ricciardi & Thomas Gobuzas. Ed. by Douglas Schonenberg & Steven Samuels. (Quest for Power Ser.). (Illus.). 1996. boxed set 29.95 (*0-9653496-0-8*, DL1001) Infinite Imag.

Quest for Power: Hobbes, Descartes, & the Emergence of Modernity. Piotr Hoffman. LC 95-16505. 240p. (C). 1996. text 49.95 (*0-391-03924-5*) Humanities.

Quest for Power: Oppositional Movements & Post-Congress Politics in Uttar Pradesh. Zoya Hasan. LC 98-902987. (Illus.). 290p. 1998. text 24.95 (*0-19-564184-1*) OUP.

Quest for Power: The Lower Houses of Assembly in the Southern Royal Colonies 1689-1776. Jack P. Greene. LC 63-21077. 544p. reprint ed. pap. 168.70 (*0-8357-3916-3*, 203665000004) Bks Demand.

Quest for Power Games Manual: Complete Guide for Raggs. Thomas Gobuzas. Ed. by Douglas Schonenberg & Steven Samuels. (Quest for Power Ser.). (Illus.). 95p. 1996. pap. 9.95 (*0-9653496-1-6*, DL1002) Infinite Imag.

***Quest for Prayer: Coming Home to Spirit.** Mary-Alice Jafolla & Richard Jafolla. LC 99-19763. (Continuing Quest Ser.: No. 2). 140p. 1999. pap. 10.95 (*0-87159-241-X*, 82) Unity Bks.

Quest for Progress: The Way We Lived in North Carolina 1870-1920. Sydney Nathans. LC 82-20133. 120p. 1983. reprint ed. pap. 37.20 (*0-608-00293-3*, 205932100008) Bks Demand.

Quest for Purity: Dynamics of Puritan Movements. Ed. by Walter E. Van Beek. (Religion & Society Ser.: No. 26). 274p. (C). 1988. lib. bdg. 72.70 (*3-11-011382-1*) Mouton.

Quest for Q. David Catchpole. 256p. 1993. text 49.95 (*0-567-09616-5*, Pub. by T & T Clark) Bks Intl VA.

Quest for Quality: An Engineer's View on Responsibility & Liability. LC 90-10143. 64p. 1990. pap. text 9.00 (*0-87262-779-9*) Am Soc Civil Eng.

Quest for Quality: Managing the Total System. Ed. by Mehran Sepehri. 339p. 1987. pap. text 27.00 (*0-89806-088-5*, QSTQUA) Eng Mgmt Pr.

Quest for Quality: Sixteen Forms of Heresy in Higher Education. Sinclair Goodlad. LC 94-41405. 144p. 1995. pap. 34.95 (*0-335-19350-1*) OpUniv Pr.

Quest for Quality: The Challenge for Undergraduate Education in the 1990s. Lewis B. Mayhew et al. LC 90-34307. (Higher & Adult Education Ser.). 320p. 1990. text 38.45 (*1-55542-254-3*) Jossey-Bass.

Quest for Quality in Services. A. C. Rosander. (Illus.). 579p. 1989. text 37.50 (*0-527-91644-7*, 916447) Productivity Inc.

Quest for Quality in the Church: A New Paradigm . . . Korean Resource. Ezra E. Jones. (KOR.). 76p. 1996. pap. 10.95 (*0-88177-206-2*, DR206) Discipleship Res.

Quest for Quality in the Church: A New Paradigm . . . Spanish. Ezra Earl Jones. (SPA.). 84p. 1993. pap. 9.95 (*0-88177-210-0*, DR210) Discipleship Res.

Quest for Quarks. Brian McCusker. LC 83-7459. (Illus.). 164p. 1984. text 20.95 (*0-521-24850-7*) Cambridge U Pr.

Quest for Quivera: Coronado's Exploration into Southern U. S. Buford Morgan. 189p. (YA). (gr. 7 up). 1990. 6.95 (*0-89992-125-6*); 12.95 (*0-89992-325-9*) Coun India Ed.

Quest for Quivira: Spanish Explorers on the Great Plains, 1540-1821. Thomas Chavez. Ed. by Gregory McNamee et al. LC 91-67395. (Illus.). 58p. (Orig.). 1992. pap. 5.95 (*1-877856-05-3*) SW Pks Mnmts.

Quest for Reality: Subjectivism & the Metaphysics of Colour. Barry Stroud. LC 99-20505. 256p. 1999. 29.95 (*0-19-513388-9*) OUP.

Quest for Redonda. A. Reynolds Morse. (Illus.). 160p. 1986. pap. 10.00 (*0-317-39306-5*) Reynolds Morse.

Quest for Respect: A Healing Guide for Survivors of Rape. 3rd ed. Linda Braswell. Ed. by Eugene D. Wheeler. LC 89-9274. 80p. 1995. pap. 9.95 (*0-934793-44-1*, Pub. by Pathfinder CA) IPG Chicago.

Quest for Responsibility: Accountability & Citizenship in Complex Organisations. Mark Bovens. LC 97-10236. (Theories of Institutional Design Ser.). (Illus.). 264p. (C). 1998. text 59.95 (*0-521-48163-5*); pap. text 22.95 (*0-521-62898-9*) Cambridge U Pr.

Quest for Revival: Experiencing Great Revivals of the Past Empowering You for God's Move Today! Ron Meintosh. LC 99-180282. 325p. 1997. 19.99 (*1-57794-053-9*, HH2-053-9) Harrison Hse.

Quest for Saint Camber. Katherine Kurtz. (Histories of King Kelson Ser.: Vol. III). 1986. 16.95 (*0-345-31826-9*, Ballantine) Ballantine Pub Grp.

Quest for Salvation in Saul Bellow's Novels. Kyung-Ae Kim. LC 94-12791. 260p. 1994. pap. 44.95 (*3-631-47625-6*) P Lang Pubng.

Quest for Security. Alfred Martin. (Synthesis Ser.). 169p. 1979. pap. 1.00 (*0-8199-0371-X*, Frncscn Herld) Franciscan Pr.

Quest for Security. Isaac M. Rubinow. LC 75-17241. (Social Problems & Social Policy Ser.). 1976. reprint ed. 52.95 (*0-405-07512-X*) Ayer.

Quest for Security: A History of U. S. Foreign Relations. Howard Jones. 1994. text. write for info. (*0-07-033076-X*) McGraw.

Quest for Security: The Life of Samuel Parris, 1653-1720, 142. Larry Gragg. LC 90-36774. (Contributions in American History Ser.: No 142). 240p. 1990. 62.95 (*0-313-27282-4*, GQS, Greenwood Pr) Greenwood.

Quest for Security - A History of U. S. Foreign Relations Vol. I: To 1912. Howard Jones. 300p. (C). 1995. pap. 36.25 (*0-07-033077-8*) McGraw.

Quest for Security - A History of U. S. Foreign Relations Vol. II: From 1897, Vol. 2. Howard Jones. LC 95-81702. 760p. (C). 1996. pap. 42.50 (*0-07-033078-6*) McGraw.

Quest for Security in the Caribbean: Problems & Promises in Subordinate States. Ivelaw L. Griffith. LC 92-31398. 332p. (C). (gr. 13). 1994. pap. text 34.95 (*1-56324-509-4*) M E Sharpe.

Quest for Security in the Caribbean: Problems & Promises in Subordinate States. Ivelaw Lloyd Griffith. LC 92-31398. 332p. (C). (gr. 13). 1993. text 64.95 (*1-56324-089-0*) M E Sharpe.

Quest for Self: Zen in Business & Life. Takeshi Iizuka. LC 95-10488. 160p. (C). 1995. text 45.00 (*0-8147-3757-9*) NYU Pr.

Quest for Self-Expression: Painting in Moscow & Leningrad, 1965-1990. Ed. by Norma J. Roberts. LC 90-81953. (Illus.). 192p. (Orig.). 1990. pap. 29.95 (*0-918881-25-0*) Columbus Mus Art.

Quest for Self-Knowledge: An Essay in Lonergan's Philosophy. Joseph Flanagan. (Lonergan Studies). 352p. 1996. text 65.00 (*0-8020-0866-6*); pap. text 24.00 (*0-8020-7851-6*) U of Toronto Pr.

Quest for Service Quality: Rx's for Achieving Excellence. W. A. Adams et al. 320p. 1992. 24.95 (*0-9632471-2-3*) Maxcomm.

Quest for Shipwrecks: Era of New Shipwreck Discovery, 2 vols., Set, Vols. 1 & 2. 2nd ed. James A. McNutt, Jr. (Nautilus Explorer Ser.). (Illus.). 248p. 1997. pap. 22.00 (*1-884104-00-2*, QSII) Hydrodyne Marine.

Quest for Silence. John W. Clarke. 46p. 1994. pap. 6.95 (*1-877871-76-1*, 6712) Ed Ministries.

***Quest for Silence.** Harry Wilmer. 2000. pap. 18.95 (*3-85630-593-9*) Daimon Pubs.

Q

Quest for Social Justice II: The Morris Fromkin Memorial Lectures, 1981-1990. Ed. by Alan D. Corre. LC 92-81949. (Illus.). 217p. (C). 1992. 22.95 (*1-879281-05-8*) G Meir Lib.

Quest for Souls. George W. Truett. pap. 9.99 (*0-88019-101-5*) Schmul Pub Co.

Quest for Souls. 2nd rev. ed. Mike Francen. 147p. 1996. pap. 8.00 (*1-888079-10-X*, FWO Bks) Francen Wrld.

Quest for Space: A Celebration of America's Space Program. anniversary ed. Ed. by John Bailey. (Illus.). 170p. 1999. pap. 8.95 (*1-891965-01-8*) Belmont Intl.

Quest for Spiritual Hunger. Roberts Liardon. 48p. 1996. pap. 3.99 (*1-880089-77-7*, Pub. by Albury Pub) Appalach Bk Dist.

Quest for Spiritual Hunger. Roberts Liardon. 43p. 1987. pap. 2.95 (*0-88144-089-2*) Christian Pub.

***Quest for Spiritual Hunger: Quest for Spiritual Hunger/Price of Spiritual Power, No. 3.** Roberts Liardon. 2000. pap. 10.99 (*1-57778-129-5*) Albury Pub.

Quest for Spiritual Maturity. Robert G. Tuttle. 1992. pap. 8.50 (*1-55673-478-6*, 7928) CSS OH.

Quest for Stability: Problems of West European Security, 1918-1957. Ed. by R. Ahmann et al. LC 92-28439. (Studies of the German Historical Institute, London). 558p. 1993. text 85.00 (*0-19-920503-5*) OUP.

Quest for Success. Susanne Starck. 78p. (Orig.). 1994. pap. 7.95 (*1-56245-099-9*) Great Quotations.

Quest for Success Rediscovering American Business Values. Jean R. Nave. Orig. Title: Quest ...in Search of Values. 104p. 1987. pap. 9.95 (*0-930115-08-2*) Windemere Pr.

Quest for Sustainable Agriculture & Land Use. Brian Roberts. 1995. pap. 29.95 (*0-86840-374-1*, Pub. by New South Wales Univ Pr) Intl Spec Bk.

Quest for Sustainable Development in the Ganges Basin. Graham P. Chapman & Michael Thompson. (Global Development & the Environment Ser.). 192p. 1995. 95.00 (*0-7201-2191-4*) Continuum.

Quest for Sustained Growth: Southeast Asia & Southeast European Cases. Samuel F. Wells. LC 99-48678. (Woodrow Wilson Center Press Ser.). 142p. 1999. pap. 14.95 (*0-943875-94-3*) W Wilson Ctr Pr.

Quest for Symmetry: Selected Works of Bunji Sakita. Kenji Kikkawa et al. (World Scientific Series in 20th Century Physics: Vol. 22). 500p. 1998. 94.00 (*981-02-3643-3*) World Scientific Pub.

Quest for the Absolute: The Philosophical Vision of Joseph Marechal. Anthony M. Matteo. LC 91-26367. 202p. 1992. lib. bdg. 32.00 (*0-87580-165-X*) N Ill U Pr.

***Quest for the African Dinosaurs: Ancient Roots of the Modern World.** Louis L. Jacobs. LC 00-20533. (Illus.). 344p. 2000. 17.95 (*0-8018-6481-X*) Johns Hopkins.

***Quest for the Celtic Key.** Karen MacLeod-Ralls. 256p. 2000. pap. 18.95 (*0-946487-73-1*) Luath Pr Ltd.

Quest for the City of Gold. Bardwell L. Smith. 196p. (Orig.). 1992. pap. 11.95 (*1-882463-00-5*) Ben-Wal Print.

Quest for the Crystal Castle. Dan Millman. LC 92-70302. (Illus.). 32p. (J). (ps-5). 1992. 14.95 (*0-915811-41-3*, Starseed) H J Kramer Inc.

Quest for the Cup. Detroit News Staff. 1997. 24.95 (*1-57243-257-8*); pap. text 9.95 (*1-57243-258-6*) Triumph Bks.

Quest for the Dutchman's Gold. Robert Sikorsky. LC 83-11616. (Illus.). 160p. (Orig.). 1991. pap. 6.95 (*0-914846-56-6*) Golden West Pub.

Quest for the Eagle Feather. John Duncklee. Ed. by Jill Max. LC 97-8794. (Illus.). 112p. (J). (gr. 3-6). 1997. pap. 6.95 (*0-87358-657-3*, Rising Moon Bks) Northland AZ.

Quest for the Eagle Feather. John Duncklee. Ed. by Jill Max. LC 97-8794. (Illus.). 104p. (J). (gr. 3-7). 1997. lib. bdg. 12.95 (*0-87358-668-9*, Rising Moon Bks) Northland AZ.

Quest for the Eternal. J. N. Dhamija. 224p. 1998. pap. 14.95 (*1-86204-360-4*, Pub. by Element MA) Penguin Putnam.

Quest for the Eye of Light: The First Book of Mankiah. Donnie Clemons. LC 97-71118. (Mankiah Ser.: Vol. 1). (Illus.). 256p. (Orig.). 1997. pap. 12.95 (*0-9657123-2-X*) Journey Bks TN.

Quest for the Fallen Star. Piers Anthony et al. LC 98-14560. 416p. 1998. 25.95 (*0-312-86409-4*, Pub. by Tor Bks) St Martin.

Quest for the Fallen Star. Piers Anthony et al. 688p. 1999. mass mkt. 6.99 (*0-8125-6485-5*, Pub. by Tor Bks) St Martin.

Quest for the Father: A Study of the Darwin-Butler Controversy. Phyllis Greenacre. LC 63-13193. (New York Psychoanalytic Institute Freud Anniversary Lecture Ser.). 1963. 27.50 (*0-8236-5760-4*) Intl Univs Pr.

Quest for the Fine: An Inquiry into the Worth of Existence. Michael Gelven. 176p. (Orig.). (C). 1995. pap. text 22.95 (*0-8476-8124-6*); lib. bdg. 55.00 (*0-8476-8123-8*) Rowman.

Quest for the Flaming Pearl. Edward Hays. LC 94-35481. (Illus.). 239p. 1994. pap. 10.95 (*0-939516-25-X*) Forest Peace.

Quest for the Gold Plates: Thomas Stuart Ferguson's Archaeological Search for the Book of Mormon. Stan Larson. LC 94-20959. (Illus.). 320p. Date not set. reprint ed. pap. 12.95 (*0-9634732-6-3*) Signature Bks.

***Quest for the Golden Circle: The Four Corners & the Metropolitan West, 1945-1970.** Arthur R. Gomez. (Development of Western Resources Ser.). 2000. pap. 16.95 (*0-7006-1065-0*) U Pr of KS.

Quest for the Golden Circle: The Four Corners & the Metropolitan West, 1945-1970. Arthur R. Gomez. LC 94-3212. (Illus.). 252p. 1994. 18.95 (*0-8263-1540-2*) U of NM Pr.

Quest for the Golden Dove: Thoughts on Love, Human & Divine. gif. ed. Jose De Vinck. LC 93-74756. 96p. 1994. 18.75 (*0-911726-61-6*, QGD) Alleluia Pr.

Quest for the Grail. Richard Rohr. 192p. 1997. pap. 14.95 (*0-8245-1654-0*) Crossroad NY.

Quest for the Grail: Arthurian Legend in British Art 1840-1920. Poulson. LC 98-29632. (Illus.). 256p. 1999. text 79.95 (*0-7190-5379-X*) St Martin.

Quest for the Grail: Arthurian Legend in British Art, 1840-1920. Christine Poulson. LC 98-29632. (Illus.). 256p. 1999. pap. 29.95 (*0-7190-5537-7*, Pub. by St Martin) St Martin.

Quest for the Grail No. 47: Golden Blade. Andrew Wolpert & William Forward. pap. 12.95 (*0-86315-205-8*, 1870, Pub. by Floris Bks) Anthroposophic.

Quest for the Green Hills of Earth. Ned Brooks et al. (Illus.). 28p. (Orig.). 1995. pap. 5.00 (*0-9603300-4-6*) Purple Mouth.

Quest for the Historic Fremont & a Guide to the Prehistoric Pottery of Southern Idaho. B. Robert Butler. (Occasional Papers of the Idaho Museum of Natural History: No. 33). 25p. 1983. pap. 4.00 (*0-317-11776-9*) Idaho Mus Nat Hist.

***Quest for the Historical Israel.** George W. Ramsey. 208p. 1999. pap. 20.00 (*1-57910-271-9*) Wipf & Stock.

***Quest for the Historical Muhammed.** Ed. & Tr. by Ibn Warraq. LC 99-54420. 568p. 2000. 34.95 (*1-57392-787-2*) Prometheus Bks.

Quest for the Holy Grail. Ellen Cooney. LC 80-67333. 104p. (Orig.). 1981. pap. 5.95 (*0-9602912-3-7*) Duir Press.

Quest for the Holy Grail. Frederick W. Locke. LC 70-181948. (Stanford University. Stanford Studies in Language & Literature: No. 21). reprint ed. 32.50 (*0-404-51831-1*) AMS Pr.

Quest for the Holy Grill: A Guide to Fifty Crummy but Good Restaurants within Rambling Range of Washingont, D. C. Donovan Kelly. LC 99-35699. (Illus.). 128p. 2000. pap. 9.95 (*1-57427-093-1*, EPM) Howell Pr VA.

Quest for the Holy Trail. Mary M. Batson. 170p. 1999. pap. write for info. (*0-7392-0289-8*, PO3396) Morris Pubng.

Quest for the Human: An Exploration of Saul Bellow's Fiction. Eusebio L. Rodrigues. LC 80-66707. 380p. 1982. 38.50 (*0-8387-2368-3*) Bucknell U Pr.

Quest for the Jade Sea: Colonial Competition Around an East African Lake. Pascal J. Imperato. LC 98-4983. 360p. 1998. text 49.00 (*0-8133-2791-1*, Pub. by Westview) HarpC.

Quest for the Jungle City. Christopher Carrie. (Crayola Color & Activity Ser.). (Illus.). 40p. (J). (gr. k up). 1990. 1.59 (*0-86696-245-X*) Binney & Smith.

Quest for the King. John White. LC 95-10887. (Archives of Anthropos Ser.: Bk. 5). 325p. (Orig.). (J). 1995. pap. 11.99 (*0-87784-592-1*, 592) InterVarsity.

Quest for the Kingdom of God: Studies in Honor of George E. Mendenhall. Ed. by H. B. Huffmon et al. LC 83-1648. viii, 316p. 1983. text 42.50 (*0-931464-15-3*) Eisenbrauns.

Quest for the Liberated Christian. Mary Hall. (IC-Studies in the Intercultural History of Christianity: Vol. 19). 341p. 1978. pap. 57.00 (*3-261-02668-5*) P Lang Pubng.

Quest for the Lost City. Dana Lamb & Ginger Lamb. LC 84-50124. (Illus.). 352p. 1984. reprint ed. pap. 10.95 (*0-915643-00-6*) Santa Barb Pr.

Quest for the Lost Prince: Samuel Morris. Dave Jackson & Neta Jackson. (Trailblazer Bks.). 144p. (J). (gr. 3-7). 1996. pap. 5.99 (*1-55661-472-1*) Bethany Hse.

Quest for the Male Soul: In Search of Something More. Martin W. Pable. LC 96-31129. 144p. 1996. pap. 8.95 (*0-87793-580-7*) Ave Maria.

Quest for the Messiah: The History, Literature & Theology of the Johannine. John Painter. 424p. 1991. text 49.95 (*0-567-09592-4*, Pub. by T & T Clark) Bks Intl VA.

Quest for the Messiah: The History, Literature & Theology of the Johannine Community. John Painter. LC 93-31675. 466p. (C). 1994. pap. text 24.95 (*0-687-35153-7*) Abingdon.

Quest for the Messiah: The History, Literature & Theology of the Johannine Community. 2nd ed. John Painter. 512p. pap. 39.95 (*0-567-29246-0*, Pub. by T & T Clark) Bks Intl VA.

Quest for the Moon & Other Stories: Three Decades of Astronauts in Space. Anne W. Tucker. (Illus.). 60p. (Orig.). 1996. pap. 14.95 (*0-89090-065-5*) Tex A&M Univ Pr.

Quest for the Nazi Personality: A Psychological Investigation of Nazi War Criminals. Molly Harrower et al. (Personality & Clinical Psychology Ser.). 272p. 1995. text 29.95 (*0-8058-1898-7*) L Erlbaum Assocs.

Quest for the Necessary: W. H. Auden & the Dilemma of Divided Consciousness. Herbert Greenberg. LC 68-54019. 221p. reprint ed. 68.60 (*0-8357-9175-0*, 201700900006) Bks Demand.

Quest for the New Jerusalem. Trevor J. Saxby. 1987. lib. bdg. 237.50 (*90-247-3485-1*) Kluwer Academic.

Quest for the One Big Thing: A Counting Book. Steve Johnson & Lou Fancher. LC 98-13789. (Illus.). 32p. (J). (gr. k-4). 1998. 10.95 (*0-7868-3198-7*, Pub. by Disney Pr) Time Warner.

Quest for the Origin: A Source-Oriented Approach. Thomas L. Brodie. (Illus.). 208p. 1993. pap. text 24.95 (*0-19-507588-9*) OUP.

Quest for the Original Gita. Gajanan S. Khair. LC 97-913886. xv, 274p. 1997. 25.00 (*81-7039-215-2*, Pub. by Somaiya Publns) Nataraj Bks.

Quest for the Other: Ethnic Tourism in San Cristobal, Mexico. B. Van Den. LC 93-40687. 184p. 1994. pap. 24.95 (*0-295-97317-X*) U of Wash Pr.

Quest for the Past: Great Discoveries in Archaeology. 2nd rev. ed. Brian M. Fagan. LC 94-213706. (Illus.). 281p. (C). 1994. pap. text 20.95 (*0-88133-791-9*) Waveland Pr.

Quest for the Pillar of Gold: The Mines & Miners of the Grand Canyon. George H. Billingsley et al. LC 96-80426. (Monograph Ser.: Vol. 10). (Illus.). 112p. 1997. pap. 15.00 (*0-938216-56-2*) GCA.

Quest for the Presidency, 1992. Peter Goldman et al. LC 94-5403. (Illus.). 800p. 1994. 34.95 (*0-89096-644-3*) Tex A&M Univ Pr.

Quest for the Promised Land: Oppressed by British Rule, the Van der Kemps Cross a Hostile Wilderness to Find a Home. Jack Cavanaugh. (African Covenant Ser.: No. 2). 288p. 1997. pap. 10.99 (*0-8024-0863-X*, 261) Moody.

***Quest for the Queen.** Tony Abbott. (Secrets of Droon Ser.: Vol. 10). (Illus.). (J). 2000. pap. 2.99 (*0-439-20784-3*) Scholastic Inc.

Quest for the Real Samoa: The Mead-Freeman Controversy & Beyond. Lowell D. Holmes. 211p. 1986. 55.00 (*0-89789-110-4*, Bergin & Garvey) Greenwood.

Quest for The Real Samoa: The Mead-Freeman Controversy & Beyond. Lowell D. Holmes. LC 86-8317. (Illus.). 211p. (Orig.). 1988. pap. 18.95 (*0-89789-162-7*, Bergin & Garvey) Greenwood.

Quest for the Reality of Life: Theodore Dreiser's Spiritual & Esthetical Pilgrimage. Miyoko Takeda. LC 90-28309. (American University Studies: English Language & Literature: Ser. IV, Vol. 134). (Illus.). VIII, 140p. (C). 1991. text 35.95 (*0-8204-1562-6*) P Lang Pubng.

Quest for the Red Sulphur: The Life of Ibn' Arabi. Calude Addas. Tr. by Peter Kingsley from FRE. (Golden Palm Ser.). 137p. 1995. 59.95 (*0-946621-44-6*, Pub. by Islamic Texts); pap. 19.95 (*0-946621-45-4*, Pub. by Islamic Texts) Intl Spec Bk.

Quest for the Red Sulphur: The Life of Ibn Arabi. Claude Addas. 350p. 1996. pap. 19.95 (*0-614-21328-2*, 1029) Kazi Pubns.

Quest for the Rusyn Soul: The Politics of Religion & Culture in Eastern Europe & in America, World War I, 1890. Keith P. Dyrud. LC 91-77488. 160p. 1992. 29.50 (*0-944190-10-3*) Balch IES Pr.

Quest for the Second Half. Kenneth Copeland. 1999. pap. text 7.99 (*1-57794-150-0*) Harrison Hse.

Quest for the Second Half. Christopher P. Maselli. LC 98-12278. (Commander Kellie & the Superkids' Early Adventures Ser.). (J). 1998. pap. write for info. (*1-57562-216-5*) K Copeland Pubns.

Quest for the Soul: Our Search for Deeper Meaning. Robert L. Wise. 256p. 1996. pap. 14.99 (*0-7852-7554-1*) Nelson.

Quest for the Thirty-Six. Stephen Billias. 208p. 1988. mass mkt. 3.95 (*0-445-20670-5*, Pub. by Warner Bks) Little.

Quest for the West in Search of Gold. Peter Kent. LC 97-16638. (Illus.). 29p. (J). (gr. 2-4). 1997. lib. bdg. 21.40 (*0-7613-0302-2*) Millbrook Pr.

Quest for the World Record Bass. Bart Crabb. 1997. 14.95 (*1-57785-016-5*, Lghthse Pr) ProStar Pubns.

Quest for Therapy in Lower Zaire. John M. Janzen. (Comparative Studies of Health Systems & Medical Care: Vol. 1). 1978. pap. 18.95 (*0-520-04633-1*, Pub. by U CA Pr) Cal Prin Full Svc.

Quest for Total Peace: Political Thought in Roger Martin du Gard. Rafic Jouejati. 111p. 1977. 25.00 (*0-7146-3097-7*, Pub. by F Cass Pubs) Intl Spec Bk.

Quest for True Happiness. M. A. Siddiqui. 1994. pap. 2.00 (*1-56744-203-X*) Kazi Pubns.

Quest for Truth. Nathan Benjamin. 262p. (Orig.). 1990. pap. 14.95 (*0-9626412-0-0*, 001) Rose Pub FL.

Quest for Truth. Ken Johnson. LC 90-70123. 176p. 1991. pap. 7.95 (*0-914984-21-7*) Starburst.

Quest for Truth: A Journey of the Soul. Patricia L. Fry. LC 95-96132. 144p. (Orig.). 1996. pap. 10.00 (*0-9612642-1-7*) Matilija Pr.

Quest for Truth: A Study of Six Contemporary Filipino Novels in English. Lucio F. Teoxon, Jr. 164p. (Orig.). (C). 1991. pap. text 10.00 (*971-10-0398-8*, Pub. by New Day Pub) Cellar.

***Quest for Truth: Critical Reflections on Interfaith Cooperation.** Robert Traer. LC 99-40412. 196p. 1999. pap. 16.95 (*1-888570-52-0*) Davies Grp.

***Quest for Truth: Introduction to Philosophy.** 4th ed. Gustafson. 413p. (C). 1998. pap. 27.00 (*0-536-00899-X*) Pearson Custom.

Quest for Truth: The Press in Defense of Liberty. Bobby O. Wallace. LC 96-95116. 1997. 23.95 (*1-889042-24-2*) Aladdin Pub TX.

Quest for Truth: 100 Insights That Could Change Your Life. Darryl J. Anka. Ed. & Intro. by Steve Meyers. LC 96-72629. (Illus.). xiv, 258p. 1997. pap. 22.95 (*0-9656078-1-X*) Nobul Pr.

Quest for Ultimate Truth. unabridged ed. Joseph R. Barbatti. (Illus.). 192p. 1999. pap. 13.50 (*0-9671931-0-9*, 01) Barbatti.

Quest for Understanding: Arabic & Islamic Studies in Memory of Malcolm H. Kerr. Ed. by S. Seikaly & P. Dodd. (Illus.). 400p. 1991. text 29.95 (*0-8156-6083-9*) Syracuse U Pr.

Quest for Unity: Orthodox & Catholics in Dialogue - Documents of the Joint International Commission & Official Dialogues in the United States, 1965-1995. John Borelli & John H. Erickson. LC 96-23082. 1996. 11.95 (*0-88141-113-2*) St Vladimirs.

Quest for Unity: The Adventure of Physics. Etienne Klein & Marc Lachieze-Rey. Tr. by Axel Reisinger from FRE. LC 98-29622. 176p. 1999. 24.00 (*0-19-512085-X*) OUP.

***Quest for Unity, Peace & Purity in Thomas Campbell's Declaration & Address: Text & Studies.** Hans Rollmann et al. LC 00-32947. (ATLA Monographs). 2000. pap. write for info. (*0-8108-3843-5*) Scarecrow.

Quest for Utopia: Jewish Political Ideas & Institutions Through the Ages. Zvi Gitelman. LC 91-40324. 176p. (gr. 13). 1992. pap. text 34.95 (*1-56324-062-9*) M E Sharpe.

Quest for Utopia: Jewish Political Ideas & Institutions Through the Ages. Ed. by Zvi Gitelman. LC 91-40324. 176p. (gr. 13). 1992. text 65.95 (*1-56324-061-0*) M E Sharpe.

Quest for Utopia in Twentieth Century America. Timothy Miller. LC 97-48903. 254p. 1998. 34.95 (*0-8156-2775-0*) Syracuse U Pr.

Quest for Value: A Guide for Senior Managers. G. Bennett Stewart. LC 14-4. (Illus.). 781p. 1999. 50.00 (*0-88730-418-4*, HarpBusn) HarpInfo.

Quest for Vengeance. rev. ed. Jeanne Carmichael. (Regency Romance Ser.: No. 167). 1992. mass mkt. 2.99 (*0-373-31167-2*, 1-31167-9) Harlequin Bks.

Quest for Victory: The History of the Principles of War, 30. John I. Alger. LC 81-13319. (Contributions in Military History Ser.: No. 30). 318p. 1982. 45.00 (*0-313-23322-5*, AMM/, Greenwood Pr) Greenwood.

Quest for Vitality in Religion: A Theological Approach to Religious Education. rev. ed. Findley B. Edge. LC 94-17758. 220p. 1994. pap. 18.00 (*1-880837-76-5*) Smyth & Helwys.

Quest for Voice: Music, Politics & the Limits of Philosophy. Lydia Goehr. LC 98-11821. (Ernest Bloch Lectures). 224p. 1998. 45.00 (*0-520-21412-9*, Pub. by U CA Pr) Cal Prin Full Svc.

Quest for Walden: A Study of the "Country Book" in American Popular Literature, with an Annotated Bibliography, 1863-1995. Loren C. Owings. LC 97-18932. 282p. 1997. pap. 55.00 (*0-7864-0354-3*) McFarland & Co.

Quest for Water Planets. Halyard. 146p. 1996. pap. 12.95 (*0-929408-14-4*, Amer Eagle Pubns Inc.

Quest for Wholeness. Carl G. Vaught. LC 81-18365. (SUNY Series in Philosophy). 213p. (C). 1983. text 59.50 (*0-87395-593-5*); pap. text 19.95 (*0-87395-594-3*) State U NY Pr.

***Quest for Wings.** G. L. Donelly. (Illus.). 160p. 2000. 27.99 (*0-7524-2014-3*, Pub. by Tempus Pubng) Arcadia Publng.

Quest for Wisdom: Thoughts on the Bhagawadgita. Adya Rangacharya. (C). 1993. 22.00 (*81-7154-709-5*, Pub. by Popular Prakashan) S Asia.

Quest for World Order: Perspectives of a Pragmatic Idealist. Ed. by Tommy T. Koh. LC 97-945820. 416p. 1998. pap. write for info. (*981-210-108-X*, Pub. by Times Academic) Intl Spec Bk.

Quest in Modern American Poetry. Peter Revell. (Critical Studies). 246p. 1981. 44.00 (*0-389-20238-X*, 07028) B&N Imports.

Quest ...in Search of Values see Quest for Success Rediscovering American Business Values

Quest in the Sun. large type ed. Helga Moray. 1991. 27.99 (*0-7089-2396-8*) Ulverscroft.

***Quest in Time.** Frieda Wishinsky. (Illus.). 72p. (J). (gr. 3-7). 2000. pap. 12.95 (*1-894379-08-X*, Pub. by GDPB); pap. 22.95 (*1-894379-07-1*, Pub. by GDPB) Firefly Bks Ltd.

Quest January-February-March, 1997, Vol. 9. 82p. (J). (gr. 2-5). 1996. 20.00 (*0-913585-22-X*) Scripture U Pub.

Quest January-February-March, 1998, Vol. 10. 82p. (J). (gr. 2-5). 1997. 20.00 (*0-913585-41-6*) Scripture U Pub.

Quest January-March, 1996, Vol. 8. 82p. (J). (gr. 2-5). 1995. 20.00 (*0-913585-03-3*) Scripture U Pub.

Quest July-August-September, 1996, Vol. 8. 82p. (J). (gr. 2-5). 1996. 20.00 (*0-913585-11-4*) Scripture U Pub.

Quest July-August-September, 1997, Vol. 9. 82p. (J). (gr. 2-5). 1997. 20.00 (*0-913585-29-7*) Scripture U Pub.

***Quest Love Trilogy: Soul Mates, 2.** John Gray. 1998. 12.00 (*0-671-58226-7*) S&S Trade.

Quest October-November-December, 1996, Vol. 8. 82p. (J). (gr. 2-5). 1996. 20.00 (*0-913585-16-5*) Scripture U Pub.

Quest October-November-December, 1997, Vol. 9. 82p. (J). (gr. 2-5). 1997. 20.00 (*0-913585-34-3*) Scripture U Pub.

***Quest of Ajenya: A Christian Theological Appraisal of the Search for Meaning in His Three Hindi Novels.** Ed. by Roger Hardham Hooker. 262p. 1998. pap. 175.00 (*81-208-1570-X*, Pub. by Motilal Bnarsidass) St Mut.

Quest of Caroline Hunt. large type ed. Kate Howard. (Dales Large Print Ser.). 285p. 1997. pap. 18.99 (*1-85389-743-4*, Dales) Ulverscroft.

Quest of Enlightenment. Tripitaka. Tr. by E. J. Thomas from SAN. LC 35-24863. (Wisdom of the East Ser.). 95p. 1986. reprint ed. lib. bdg. 55.00 (*0-313-22185-5*, TRQE, Greenwood Pr) Greenwood.

Quest of Enlightenment: A Selection of the Buddhist Scriptures. Tr. by E. J. Thomas from SAN. LC 78-70130. reprint ed. 27.50 (*0-404-17389-6*) AMS Pr.

Quest of Excalibur. Leonard Wibberley. LC 79-192. (Illus.). 190p. 1979. reprint ed. pap. 21.00 (*0-89370-231-5*) Millefleurs.

Quest of Faith: Understanding What You Confess. Robert DeMoor. 149p. (Orig.). (YA). (gr. 9 up). 1989. pap. text 7.50 (*0-930265-74-2*) CRC Pubns.

Quest of Happiness: A Study of Victory over Lifes Troubles (1913) Newell D. Hillis. 558p. 1998. reprint ed. pap. 35.00 (*0-7661-0487-7*) Kessinger Pub.

Quest of Inquirie: Some Contexts of Tudor Literature. Howard C. Cole. LC 73-91621. 1973. 42.50 (*0-672-53583-1*) Irvington.

Quest of Jubal Kane. Doug Bowman. LC 99-21178. 304p. 1999. 22.95 (*0-312-86546-5*, Pub. by Forge NYC) St Martin.

***Quest of Jubal Kane.** Doug Bowman. 2000. mass mkt. 5.99 (*0-8125-4047-6*, Pub. by Tor Bks) St Martin.

Quest of Justice. Harold Potter. (Legal Reprint Ser.). ix, 88p. 1986. reprint ed. 25.00 (*0-421-35510-7*) W S Hein.

Quest of Lee Garrison, 1. Max Brand. 240p. 1999. mass mkt. 4.50 (*0-8439-4558-3*) Dorchester Pub Co.

Q

An Asterisk (*) at the beginning of an entry indicates that the title is appearing for the first time.

Quest of Lee Garrison. large type ed. Max Brand. LC 98-26868. 1998. 19.95 (*1-57490-145-1*, Sagebrush LP West) T T Beeler.

Quest of Noel Croucher: Hong Kong's Quiet Philanthropist. Vaudine England. 381p. 1998. 35.00 (*962-209-473-2*, Pub. by HK Univ Pr) Coronet Bks.

Quest of Self in the Collected Poems of Wallace Stevens. Michael Sexson. LC 81-16942. (Studies in Art & Religious Interpretation: Vol. 1). 216p. 1983. lib. bdg. 89.95 (*0-88946-957-1*) E Mellen.

Quest of Simon Richardson. large type ed. Dorothy Richardson. (Illus.). 384p. 1987. 27.99 (*0-7089-1714-3*) Ulverscroft.

Quest of Soul. Hua-Ching Ni. LC 89-64093. (Esoteric Teachings of the Tradition of Tao Ser.: Bk. 2). 152p. (Orig.). 1991. pap. 11.95 (*0-937064-26-2*) SevenStar Comm.

Quest of the Absolute. Honore de Balzac. 1997. pap. 11.99 (*1-873982-58-5*, Pub. by Dedalus) Subterranean Co.

Quest of the Ancients. Vince Garcia. (Illus.). 224p. (Orig.). (YA). (gr. 9-12). 1990. pap. 23.00 (*0-9628003-0-9*) Unicorn Game Pubns.

Quest of the Ballad. W. Roy MacKenzie. LC 68-815. (Studies in Poetry: No. 38). 1969. reprint ed. lib. bdg. 75.00 (*0-8383-0591-1*) M S G Haskell Hse.

Quest of the Faes. Catharine Geenen. (Illus.). 144p. 1985. pap. 7.95 (*0-9606240-6-6*) Pearl-Win.

Quest of the Folk: Antimodernism & Cultural Selection in Twentieth-Century Nova Scotia. Ian McKay. (Illus.). 392p. 1994. pap. 22.95 (*0-7735-1248-9*, Pub. by McG-Queens Univ Pr) CUP Services.

Quest of the Folk: Antimodernism & Cultural Selection in Twentieth-Century Nova Scotia. Ian McKay. (Illus.). 392p. 1994. 65.00 (*0-7735-1179-2*, Pub. by McG-Queens Univ Pr) CUP Services.

Quest of the Four. Joseph A. Altsheler. 1990. reprint ed. lib. bdg. 19.95 (*0-89968-465-3*) Buccaneer Bks.

Quest of the Four: A Story of the Comanches & Buena Vista. Joseph A. Altsheler. 386p. reprint ed. lib. bdg. 27.95 (*0-88411-939-4*) Amereon Ltd.

Quest of the Golden Boy: The Life & Letters of Richard Le Gallienne. Richard Whittington-Egan & Geoffrey Smerdon. LC 79-8087. reprint ed. 49.50 (*0-404-18395-6*) AMS Pr.

Quest of the Golden Stairs (1927) Arthur E. Waite. 180p. 1999. reprint ed. pap. 14.95 (*0-7661-0748-5*) Kessinger Pub.

Quest of the Grail. Walter Russell. 1991. 2.00 (*1-879605-02-3*) U Sci & Philos.

***Quest of the Heart.** large type ed. Janet Cookson. 208p. 1999. pap. 18.99 (*0-7089-5526-6*, Linford) Ulverscroft.

Quest of the Historical Gospel: Mark, John, & the Origins of the Gospel Genre. Lawrence Wills. LC 97-3706. 296p. (C). 1997. 80.00 (*0-415-15093-0*) Routledge.

Quest of the Historical Jesus: A Critical Study of Its Progress from Reimarus to Wrede. Albert Schweitzer. LC 97-43997. (Albert Schweitzer Library). 432p. 1998. reprint ed. pap. 18.95 (*0-8018-5934-4*) Johns Hopkins.

Quest of the Holy Grail. Tr. by P. M. Matarasso. LC 72-12898. (Classics Ser.). 304p. 1969. pap. 12.95 (*0-14-044220-0*, Penguin Classics) Viking Penguin.

Quest of the Holy Grail. Jessie L. Weston. LC 72-10823. (Arthurian Legend & Literature Ser.: No. 1). 1973. reprint ed. lib. bdg. 75.00 (*0-8383-0642-X*) M S G Haskell Hse.

Quest of the Ideal (1913) Grace Rhys. 62p. 1998. reprint ed. pap. 7.95 (*0-7661-0568-7*) Kessinger Pub.

Quest of the Individual: Roots of Western Civilization. W. Carroll et al. LC 89-13615. XVI, 364p. (C). 1990. text 67.95 (*0-8204-1156-6*) P Lang Pubng.

Quest of the Junior Blue Knights. Edward J. Jagen. (Illus.). 32p. (J). (gr. k-7). 1990. student ed. 4.95 (*0-9625641-1-7*) White Feather & Co.

Quest of the Missing Map. Carolyn Keene. LC 70-86692. (Nancy Drew Mystery Stories Ser.: No. 19). (Illus.). 180p. (J). (gr. 4-7). 1942. 5.99 (*0-448-09519-X*, G & D) Peng Put Young Read.

Quest of the One Best Way: A Sketch of the Life of Frank Bunker Gilbreth. rev. ed. Lillian M. Gilbreth. (Illus.). 88p. 1990. 20.00 (*0-9625750-0-3*) Soc Women Eng.

Quest of the One Song Hero: The Inward Journey of an Urban Shaman. Marcus S. Robinson. (Illus.). 184p. 1994. pap. 12.95 (*0-9963970-3-5*) Wetware.

Quest of the Overself. rev. ed. Paul Brunton. LC 83-159508. 240p. (Orig.). 1972. pap. 14.95 (*0-87728-594-2*) Weiser.

***Quest of the Ruby Ring.** Yvonne MacGrory. 144p. 2000. pap. 8.95 (*1-901737-15-2*, Pub. by Anvil Books Ltd) Dufour.

Quest of the Seventh Carrier. Peter Albano. 1989. mass mkt. 3.95 (*0-8217-2599-8*, Zebra Kensgtn) Kensgtn Pub Corp.

Quest of the Silver Fleece. W. E. B. Du Bois. LC 71-83922. (Black Heritage Library Collection). (Illus.). 1977. 20.95 (*0-8369-8553-2*) Ayer.

Quest of the Silver Fleece. W. E. B. Du Bois. LC 73-144599. reprint ed. 37.50 (*0-404-00154-8*) AMS Pr.

Quest of the Silver Fleece. W. E. B. Du Bois. LC 73-86658. (American Negro: His History & Literature. Series 3). 1970. reprint ed. 20.95 (*0-405-01922-X*) Ayer.

Quest of Three Abbots: The Golden Age of Celtic Christianity. Brendan Lehane. 256p. 1994. reprint ed. pap. 16.95 (*0-940262-65-7*, Lindisfarne) Anthroposophic.

Quest 64: The Official Strategy Guide. Elizabeth Hollinger. LC 97-75604. (Illus.). 125p. 1998. pap. 14.99 (*0-7615-1419-8*) Prima Pub.

Quest There Is. Elizabeth G. Vining. LC 82-83954. (C). 1982. pap. 1.00 (*0-87574-246-7*) Pendle Hill.

Quest to Define Collegiate Desegregation: Black Colleges, Title VI Compliance & Post-Adams Litigation. Ed. by M. Christopher Brown. LC 98-49934. 192p. 1999. 49.95 (*0-89789-608-4*, Bergin & Garvey) Greenwood.

Quest to Riverworld. Ed. by Philip Jose Farmer. 336p. (Orig.). 1993. mass mkt. 5.50 (*0-446-36270-0*, Pub. by Warner Bks) Little.

Quest 2000. Mary-Alice Jafolla & Richard Jafolla. 256p. 1999. 11.98 (*0-87159-236-3*, 66) Unity Bks.

***Quest 2000 French Edition: Grade 5 Extra Practice & Testing Masters.** 1998. write for info. (*0-201-38900-2*) Addison-Wesley.

***Quest 2000 French Edition: Grade 6 Extra Practice & Testing Masters.** 1998. write for info. (*0-201-38899-5*) Addison-Wesley.

Questa e Una Opera Necessaria a Tutti Li Naviganti, 1940. Alvise Ca da Mosto. LC 92-16473. (Scholars' Facsimiles & Reprints Ser.: Vol. 472). 216p. 1992. reprint ed. 75.00 (*0-8201-1472-3*) Schol Facsimiles.

***Quest/Adventures on the Quest, 2 vols.** Richard Jafolla. 2000. pap. 24.95 (*0-87159-192-8*, Unity Hse) Unity Bks.

***Quester.** Robert C. Powers. 490p. 1999. pap. 16.95 (*1-891929-41-0*) Four Seasons.

Quester: The Journey of the Brave. Patricia Beattie. LC 99-15430. (Illus.). 1999. text 24.95 (*1-86204-550-X*, Pub. by Element MA) Penguin Putnam.

Quester by the River: And Other Poems. Anniyil Tharakan. LC 96-86632. 120p. (Orig.). 1998. pap. 10.00 (*0-940121-40-9*, H310, Pub. by Cross Cultural Pubns) BookWorld.

Questfore Caper: A Jane Doe Mystery. Marilyn G. Kyd. 145p. 1997. mass mkt. 5.95 (*0-917797-01-9*) Cashmaster Busn.

Questing Fictions: Latin America's Family Romance. Djelal Kadir. LC 86-16019. (Theory & History of Literature Ser.: Vol. 32). 186p. 1986. pap. 14.95 (*0-8166-1517-9*) U of Minn Pr.

Question! Kenneth W. Brock. LC 98-90247. 1998. pap. 9.95 (*0-533-12745-9*) Vantage.

***Question.** large type ed. Jane Asher. 336p. 1999. 31.99 (*0-7089-9069-X*, Linford) Ulverscroft.

Question & Answer: Conversations with Harvard Scholars. Peter Costa. (Illus.). 304p. (C). 1991. 18.95 (*0-674-74000-9*) HUP.

Question & Answer: Forms of Dialogic Understanding. Hans R. Jauss. Tr. by Michael Hays from GER. (Theory & History of Literature Ser.: Vol. 73). 288p. (Orig.). 1989. pap. 19.95 (*0-8166-1747-3*) U of Minn Pr.

Question & Answer Bk. I: Visual & Optical Testing. (Illus.). 38p. (C). 1998. pap. 31.25 (*1-57117-065-0*, 2034) Am Soc Nondestructive.

Question & Answer Book: American Journal of Nursing. 5th ed. Ajn & Mosby Staff. 320p. (C). (gr. 13). 1996. pap. text 28.95 (*0-8151-0081-7*, 27083) Mosby Inc.

Question & Answer Book A: Radiographic Test Method, Levels I, II & III. American Society for Nondestructive Testing (ASNT). (Illus.). 74p. (Orig.). (C). 1996. pap. 31.25 (*0-931403-45-6*, 2026) Am Soc Nondestructive.

Question & Answer Book B: Magnetic Particle Method, Levels I-III. American Society for Nondestructive Testing (ASNT). (Illus.). 43p. (Orig.). 1994. pap. 31.25 (*0-931403-11-1*, 2027) Am Soc Nondestructive.

Question & Answer Book C: Ultrasonic Test Method, Levels I-III. American Society for Nondestructive Testing (ASNT). (Illus.). 55p. (Orig.). 1994. pap. 31.25 (*0-931403-46-4*, 2028) Am Soc Nondestructive.

Question & Answer Book D: Liquid Penetrant Method, Levels I, II & III. American Society for Nondestructive Testing (ASNT). 45p. (C). 1996. pap. 31.25 (*0-931403-10-3*, 2029) Am Soc Nondestructive.

Question & Answer Book E: Eddy Current Test Method, Levels I, II, III & Flux Leakage Methods, Levels I, II & III. American Society for Nondestructive Testing (ASNT). (Illus.). 56p. (C). 1995. pap. 31.25 (*0-931403-16-2*, 2030) Am Soc Nondestructive.

Question & Answer Book F: Neutron Radiographic Test Method, Level I, II, & III. American Society for Nondestructive Testing (ASNT). 40p. (Orig.). 1994. pap. 31.25 (*0-931403-14-6*, 2031) Am Soc Nondestructive.

Question & Answer Book for Ages Four to Six. Susan Amerikaner. LC 95-43319. (Gifted & Talented Ser.). 64p. (J). (ps-3). 1995. pap. 5.95 (*1-56565-349-1*, 03491W, Pub. by Lowell Hse) NTC Contemp Pub Co.

Question & Answer Book for Ages Six to Eight. Susan Amerikaner. LC 95-43318. (Gifted & Talented Ser.). 64p. (J). (ps-3). 1995. pap. 5.95 (*1-56565-351-3*, 03513W, Pub. by Lowell Hse) NTC Contemp Pub Co.

Question & Answer Book G: Acoustic Emission Testing Method. 18p. (Orig.). (C). 1995. pap. 31.25 (*1-57117-010-3*, 2032) Am Soc Nondestructive.

Question & Answer Book HH: Halogen Diode Detector Leak Testing, Levels I, II, III. American Society for Nondestructive Testing (ASNT). (Illus.). 24p. (Orig.). (C). 1995. pap. 31.25 (*0-931403-73-1*, 2033H) Am Soc Nondestructive.

Question & Answer Book HP: Pressure Change Measurement Testing. American Society for Nondestructive Testing (ASNT). (Illus.). 33p. (Orig.). 1994. pap. 31.25 (*0-931403-39-1*, 2033P) Am Soc Nondestructive.

Question & Answer Book of Money & Investing. Victor L. Harper et al. LC 95-9329. 400p. 1995. pap. 16.95 (*1-55850-438-9*) Adams Media.

Question & Answer Catholic Catechism. John A. Hardon. LC 80-2961. 336p. 1981. pap. 15.00 (*0-385-13664-1*, Image Bks) Doubleday.

Question & Answer Financial Management. CFL Staff. (C). 1984. pap. write for info. (*0-03-910497-4*) Harcourt Coll Pubs.

Question & Answer Guide to Photographic Techniques. Lee Frost. LC 98-140157. (Illus.). 128p. 1998. pap. 17.95 (*0-7153-0551-4*, Pub. by D & C Pub) Sterling.

Question & Answers Encyclopedia see Assila WA Ajwiba

Question & Answers for FHA, VA & Conventional Loans. 2nd rev. ed. Albert Santi. LC 85-63137. (Illus.). 260p. (Orig.). 1986. 15.95 (*0-9615886-2-4*); pap. 8.95 (*0-9615886-1-6*) Mortgage Tech.

***Question Answering Systems: Papers from the AAAI Fall Symposium.** Ed. by Vinay Chaudhri & Richard Fikes. (Illus.). 119p. 1999. spiral bd. 25.00 (*1-57735-104-5*) AAAI Pr.

Question Book for the Catholic Catechist's Manual: For Parents & Teachers. 2nd ed. John A. Hardon. 100p. 1995. pap. text. write for info. (*0-9625211-2-4*) Inter Mirifica.

Question Collection. Carol Eichel. (Just for Fun Ser.). (J). (gr. 4 up). 1988. pap. 7.95 (*0-88160-153-5*, LW 271) Learning Wks.

Question Concerning. Martin Heidegger. Tr. by William Lovitt. 224p. 1982. pap. 14.00 (*0-06-131969-4*, TB 1969, Torch) HarpC.

Question de l'Essence. E. Peters. 1998. 56.95 (*90-6831-894-2*, Pub. by Peeters Pub) Bks Intl VA.

Question Driven Writing. Dennis Matthies. 400p. 1996. spiral bd. 35.00 (*1-887981-05-5*) Stanford Bookstore.

Question in Baptist History: Whether the Anabaptists in England Practiced Immersion Before the Year 1641? William H. Whitsitt. Ed. by Edwin S. Gaustad. LC 79-52611. (Baptist Tradition Ser.). 1980. reprint ed. lib. bdg. 17.95 (*0-405-12476-7*) Ayer.

Question Is College: Gender, Contingent Labor & Writing Instruction. Herbert Kohl. Ed. by Susannah Sheffer. LC 97-21665. 288p. 1998. pap. 15.95 (*0-86709-434-6*, Pub. by Boynton Cook Pubs) Heinemann.

***? Poems from Hollywood.** Mark Dunster. 11p. 1999. pap. 5.00 (*0-89642-848-6*) Linden Pubs.

Question of a Reference to International Law in the United Nations Code of Conduct on Transnational Corporations. (Working Paper Ser.: No. 1). 26p. pap. 9.95 (*92-1-104178-3*, E.86.II.A.5) UN.

Question of a Reference to International Obligations in the United Nations Code of Conduct on Transnational Corporations: A Different View. (UNCTC Current Studies A: No. 2). 17p. pap. 9.95 (*92-1-104186-4*, E.86.II.A.11) UN.

Question of Access: Training Workshops on Planning Credit Projects That Take Women into Account. 180p. (Orig.). 1995. pap. 15.95 (*0-912917-36-9*) UNIFEM.

Question of AIDS. Ed. by Richard Liebmann-Smith. 89p. 1985. pap. text 6.00 (*0-89766-302-0*) NY Acad Sci.

Question of Artificial Intelligence: Philosophical & Sociological Perspectives. Ed. by Brian P. Bloomfield. 256p. 1988. lib. bdg. 59.00 (*0-7099-3957-4*, Pub. by C Helm) Routldge.

Question of Autonomy for the United States Air Arm, 1907-1945 see Autonomy of the Air Arm

Question of Balance: Artists & Writers on Motherhood. Judith P. Rosenberg. LC 95-7216. 288p. 1995. 25.00 (*0-918949-54-8*); pap. 14.00 (*0-918949-53-X*) Rosenberg.

Question of Balance: Charles Seeger's Philosophy of Music. Taylor Aitken Greer. LC 98-19450. 278p. 1998. 55.00 (*0-520-21152-9*, Pub. by U CA Pr) Cal Prin Full Svc.

Question of Balance: Labour, Management, & Society. E. A. Ramaswamy. 280p. 1997. text 23.95 (*0-19-564168-X*) OUP.

Question of Balance: Natural Resources Conflict Issues in Australia. 2nd ed. David Mercer. LC 95-139052. 350p. 1995. pap. 39.00 (*1-86287-163-9*, Pub. by Federation Pr) Gaunt.

***Question of Balance: Natural Resources Conflict Issues in Australia.** 3rd ed. David Mercer. 366p. 2000. pap. 39.95 (*1-86287-342-9*, Pub. by Federation Pr) Gaunt.

***Question of Balance: Private Rights & the Public Interest in Scientific.** National Research Council Staff. 158p. 1999. pap. 29.00 (*0-309-06825-8*) Natl Acad Pr.

Question of Balance: The President, the Congress, & Foreign Policy. Ed. by Thomas E. Mann. 265p. 1989. pap. 16.95 (*0-8157-5453-1*) Brookings.

Question of Balance: The President, the Congress, & Foreign Policy. Ed. by Thomas E. Mann. 265p. 1990. 36.95 (*0-8157-5454-X*) Brookings.

Question of Being. Martin Heidegger. (Masterworks of Literature Ser.). 1958. pap. 12.95 (*0-8084-0258-7*) NCUP.

Question of Being: A Reversal of Heidegger. Stanley Rosen. LC 92-34934. 368p. (C). 1993. 40.00 (*0-300-05356-8*) Yale U Pr.

Question of Being: A Reversal of Heidegger. Stanley Rosen. 1995. pap. 18.00 (*0-300-06315-6*) Yale U Pr.

***Question of Bruno.** Aleksandar Hemon. LC 99-57519. 240p. 2000. 22.95 (*0-385-49923-X*) Doubleday.

Question of Character: A Life of John F. Kennedy. Thomas Reeves. 528p. 1997. per. 18.00 (*0-7615-1287-X*) Prima Pub.

Question of Character: A Life of John F. Kennedy. Thomas C. Reeves. (Illus.). 528p. 1992. pap. 13.95 (*1-55958-175-1*) Prima Pub.

Question of Character: Life Lessons to Learn from Military History. Thad A. Gaebelein & Ron Simmons. LC 98-39862. 240p. 2000. 14.95 (*1-57826-019-1*, Pub. by Hatherleigh) Norton.

***Question of Character: Scientific Racism & the Genres of American Fiction, 1892-1912.** Cathy Boeckmann. LC 99-6765. (Studies in American Literary Realism & Naturalism). 256p. 2000. 39.95 (*0-8173-1021-5*) U of Ala Pr.

***Question of Chemistry: Creative Problems for Critical Thinkers.** John Garratt. 176p. 2000. pap. 21.50 (*0-582-29838-5*, Prentice Hall) P-H.

Question of Choice. Sarah Weddington. 320p. 1993. pap. 13.95 (*0-14-017798-1*, Penguin Bks) Viking Penguin.

Question of Choice: Bioethical Reflections on a Spiritual Response to the Technological Imperative. Pamela McGrath. LC 97-74821. (Series in Philosophy). 256p. 1997. text 73.95 (*1-84014-166-2*, Pub. by Ashgate Pub) Ashgate Pub Co.

Question of Christian: Philosophy Today. Ed. by Francis J. Ambrosio. (Perspectives in Continental Philosophy Ser.: Vol. 9). 300p. 1999. 35.00 (*0-8232-1981-X*, Pub. by Fordham) BookMasters.

Question of Christian: Philosophy Today. Ed. by Francis J. Ambrosio. (Perspectives in Continental Philosophy Ser.: Vol. 9). 300p. 1999. pap. 17.50 (*0-8232-1982-8*, Pub. by Fordham) BookMasters.

Question of Christian Ethics. Ralph McInerny. LC 92-25511. (Michael J. McGivney Lectures of the John Paul II Institutes for Studies on Marriage & Family: Vol. 1990). 74p. 1993. 21.95 (*0-8132-0770-3*); pap. 10.95 (*0-8132-0771-1*) Cath U Pr.

Question of Class: Capital, the State, & Uneven Development in Malaya. Jomo K. Sundaram. 400p. (Orig.). (C). 1988. pap. 18.00 (*0-85345-750-6*, Pub. by Monthly Rev) NYU Pr.

Question of Class: The Redneck Stereotype in Southern Fiction. Duane Carr. LC 96-38510. 188p. 1996. 45.95 (*0-87972-721-7*); pap. 19.95 (*0-87972-722-5*) Bowling Green Univ Popular Press.

Question of Class Struggle: Social Foundations of Popular Radicalism During the Industrial Revolution. Craig J. Calhoun. LC 81-2018. 335p. reprint ed. pap. 103.90 (*0-608-09277-0*, 205415100004) Bks Demand.

Question of Class Struggle: The Social Foundation of Popular Radicalism During the Industrial Revolution. Craig Calhoun. LC 81-2018. xiv, 322p. (C). 1994. reprint ed. pap. text 11.00 (*0-226-09091-4*) U Ch Pr.

Question of Color. Sara Smith-Beattie. 400p. mass mkt. 5.99 (*1-896329-64-0*) Picasso Publ.

Question of Compassion. Peter McWilliams. 1998. 14.95 (*83-931580-76-5*) Prelude Press.

Question of Conscience: Conscientious Objection in the Two World Wars. Felicity Goodall. (Illus.). 224p. 1997. 33.95 (*0-7509-0740-1*, Pub. by Sutton Pub Ltd) Intl Pubs Mktg.

Question of Consent: Innocence & Complicity in the Glen Ridge Rape Case. Peter Laufer. LC 93-42464. 208p. 1994. 19.95 (*1-56279-059-5*) Mercury Hse Inc.

Question of Copyright: A Summary of the Copyright Laws at Present in Force in the Chief Countries of the World. George H. Putnam. xii, 412p. 1996. reprint ed. 65.00 (*0-8377-2555-0*, Rothman) W S Hein.

Question of Copyright: Covering the 1988 Act. Eric A. Thorn. (C). 1989. 45.00 (*1-870404-05-X*, Pub. by Jay Bks) St Mut.

Question of Courage. Darke. (Longman Literature Ser.). 1995. pap. text. write for info. (*0-582-25395-0*, Pub. by Addison-Wesley) Longman.

Question of David: A Disabled Mothers Journey Through Adoption, Family, & Life. Denise S. Jacobsen. 272p. 1998. pap. 16.50 (*0-88739-201-6*) Creat Arts Bk.

Question of David: A Disabled Mother's Journey Through Adoption, Family, & Life. Denise Sherer Jacobson. 1998. 24.50 (*0-88739-145-1*) Creat Arts Bk.

Question of Dependency & Economic Development: A Quantitative Analysis. Brian R. Farmer. LC 99-20818. 160p. 1999. 45.00 (*0-7391-0025-4*) Lxngtn Bks.

Question of Doubt: The John Wayne Gacy Story. John W. Gacy. Ed. by C. Ivor McClelland. LC 91-73123. (Illus.). 225p. 1992. write for info. (*1-878865-01-3*); pap. 24.95 (*1-878865-03-X*) C Bowley Consultants.

Question of "Eclecticism" Studies in Later Greek Philosophy. Ed. by J. M. Dillon & A. A. Long. (Hellenistic Culture & Society Ser.: Vol. 3). 286p. 1996. pap. 18.95 (*0-520-20696-7*, Pub. by U CA Pr) Cal Prin Full Svc.

Question of Elementary Education in the Third Russian State Duma, 1907-1912. Phillip Santa-Maria. LC 90-20261. (Studies in Education: Vol. 16). (Illus.). 148p. 1990. lib. bdg. 69.95 (*0-88946-237-2*) E Mellen.

Question of Empire: Leopold I & the War of Spanish Succession, 1701-1705. Linda Frey & Marsha Frey. LC 83-80628. (Studies on Society in Change: No. 28). 1983. text 47.50 (*0-88033-038-4*, 146) Col U Pr.

Question of Eros: Irony in Sterne, Kierkegaard, & Barthes. John V. Smyth. LC 85-17786. (Kierkegaard & Postmodernism Ser.). 512p. (Orig.). 1986. pap. 34.95 (*0-8130-0834-4*) U Press Fla.

Question of Ethics: Nietzsche, Foucault, Heidegger. Charles E. Scott. LC 89-46341. (Studies in Continental Thought). 238p. 1990. pap. 13.95 (*0-253-20593-X*, MB-593) Ind U Pr.

Question of Faith: An Atheist & a Rabbi Debate the Existence of God. William E. Kaufman & Morton Shor. LC 93-34034. 232p. 1994. pap. 25.00 (*1-56821-089-2*) Aronson.

Question of Faith for Muslim Inmates. Frederick T. Amina McCloud. 72p. 1999. pap. 9.95 (*1-871031-91-5*) Kazi Pubns.

Question of Final Belief: John Hick's Pluralistic Theory of Salvation. Chester Gillis. LC 88-827. 256p. 1989. text 45.00 (*0-312-01863-0*) St Martin.

Question of Food Security in Cuban Socialism. Laura J. Enriquez. LC 94-9050. (Exploratory Essays Ser.: No. 1). 1994. pap. text 7.50 (*0-87725-703-5*) U of Cal IAS.

Question of Free Will: A Holistic View. Morton White. LC 93-7104. 156p. 1993. text 26.95 (*0-691-03317-X*, Pub. by Princeton U Pr) Cal Prin Full Svc.

Question of Freemasonry. Ed Decker. LC 91-78414. (Salt Ser.). 48p. 1992. pap. 3.49 (*1-56384-020-0*) Huntington Hse.

***Question of German Guilt.** Karl Jaspers. (Perspectives in Continental Philosophy Ser.). 148p. 2000. 29.95 (*0-8232-2068-0*); pap. 19.95 (*0-8232-2069-9*) Fordham.

Q

An Asterisk (*) at the beginning of an entry indicates that the title is appearing for the first time.

Question of God. Andrew Jantz. LC 98-11921. 87p. 1998. 15.95 (*0-944957-99-4*) Rivercross Pub.

Question of God in Heidegger's Phenomenology. George Kovacs. (Studies in Phenomenology & Existential Philosophy). 326p. 1990. 39.95 (*0-8101-0850-X*); pap. 19.95 (*0-8101-0851-8*) Northwestern U Pr.

Question of Greek Independence: A Study of British Policy in the Near East, 1821-1833. C. W. Crawley. LC 74-144130. 272p. 1973. reprint ed. 40.00 (*0-86527-161-5*) Fertig.

Question of Guidance. White. 188p. 1988. pap. 13.95 (*0-85207-193-0*, Pub. by C W Daniel) Natl Bk Netwk.

Question of Guidance. Ruth White. 176p. (Orig.). pap. 10.95 (*0-8464-4278-7*) Beekman Pubs.

Question of Guilt. Frances Fyfield. 288p. 1990. mass mkt. 4.50 (*0-671-67665-2*) PB.

Question of Guilt. Carolyn Keene. (Nancy Drew & Hardy Boys Super Mystery Ser.: No. 26). 224p. (YA). (gr. 6 up). 1996. per. 3.99 (*0-671-50293-X*, Archway) PB.

Question of Guilt. Carolyn Keene. (Nancy Drew & Hardy Boys Super Mystery Ser.: No. 26). (YA). (gr. 6 up). 1996. 9.09 (*0-606-09673-6*, Pub. by Turtleback) Demco.

Question of Hermeneutics: Essays in Honor of Joseph J. Kockelmans. Ed. by Timothy J. Stapleton. LC 94-18131. (Contributions to Phenomenology Ser.: Vol. 17). 508p. 1994. lib. bdg. 137.50 (*0-7923-2911-2*, Pub. by Kluwer Academic) Kluwer Academic.

Question of Hermeneutics: Essays in Honor of Joseph J. Kockelmans. Ed. by Timothy J. Stapleton. 508p. 1994. pap. text 68.50 (*0-7923-2964-3*, Pub. by Kluwer Academic) Kluwer Academic.

Question of "Home" Ed. by Angelika Bammer. (New Formations Ser.: No. 17). (Illus.). 192p. (C). 1992. pap. 19.95 (*0-85315-758-8*, Pub. by Lawrence & Wishart) NYU Pr.

Question of Honour. large type ed. Emma Drummond. (Charnwood Large Print Ser.). 656p. 1995. 27.99 (*0-7089-8834-2*, Charnwood) Ulverscroft.

Question of Honour: The Life of Lieutenant General Valentine Baker Pasha. Anne Baker. LC 97-131098. (Illus.). 191p. 1996. pap. 21.95 (*0-85052-496-2*, Pub. by Leo Cooper) Trans-Atl Phila.

Question of How: Women Writers & New Portuguese Literature, 109. Darlene J. Sadlier. LC 89-11731. (Contributions in Women's Studies: No. 109). 157p. 1989. 47.95 (*0-313-26844-4*, SOP/, Greenwood Pr) Greenwood.

Question of Hu. Jonathan D. Spence. 1989. pap. 14.00 (*0-679-72580-6*) Vin Bks.

Question of Humanism: Challenges & Possibilities. Ed. by David Goicoechea et al. LC 90-25502. 341p. (C). 1991. 39.95 (*0-87975-614-4*) Prometheus Bks.

Question of Identity. Ed. by Anne J. Kerhsen. LC 98-73761. (Studies in Migration). 316p. 1998. pap. 72.95 (*1-84014-558-7*, Pub. by Ashgate Pub) Ashgate Pub Co.

Question of Identity. large type ed. June Thomson. 372p. 1983. 27.99 (*0-7089-0994-9*) Ulverscroft.

Question of Identity: Women, Science, & Literature. Ed. by Marina Benjamin. LC 92-38796. (Illus.). 280p. (C). 1993. text 48.00 (*0-8135-1982-9*); pap. text 20.00 (*0-8135-1983-7*) Rutgers U Pr.

Question of Innocence. Brandilyn Collins. 440p. (Orig.). 1995. mass mkt. 5.99 (*0-380-77849-1*, Avon Bks) Morrow Avon.

Question of Intelligence. Seligman. 16.95 (*1-55972-131-6*) Carol Pub Group.

Question of Intelligence: The IQ Debate in America. Daniel Seligman. LC 93-45570. 1994. pap. 10.95 (*0-8065-1507-4*, Citadel Pr) Carol Pub Group.

Question of Intelligence: The IQ Debate in America. Daniel Seligman. 239p. 1998. 17.00 (*0-7881-5712-4*) DIANE Pub.

***Question of Intent: How the FDA Took on Tobacco - And Who Won.** David Kessler. 400p. 2000. 26.00 (*1-891620-80-0*, Pub. by PublicAffairs NY) HarpC.

Question of Irish Identity in the Writings of William Butler Yeats & James Joyce. Eugene O'Brien. LC 98-37620. 300p. 1998. text 89.95 (*0-7734-8237-7*) E Mellen.

Question of Journey. John Brandi. (Light a Dust Bks.). 212p. 1995. pap. 15.00 (*0-87924-067-9*) Membrane Pr.

Question of Justice. Rachel Lee. (Intimate Moments Ser.). 1995. per. 3.50 (*0-373-07613-4*, 1-07613-2) Silhouette.

Question of Labour: Indentured Immigration into Trinidad & British Guiana, 1875-1917. K. O. Lawrence. LC 94-1159. 1994. text 55.00 (*0-312-12172-5*) St Martin.

Question of Lay Analysis. Sigmund Freud. Ed. & Tr. by James Strachey. 1990. reprint ed. pap. 6.95 (*0-393-00503-8*) Norton.

Question of Leadership. Michael Gordon. (Orig.). 1993. pap. 14.95 (*0-7022-2494-4*, Pub. by Univ Queensland Pr) Intl Spec Bk.

Question of Life - Answers of Wisdom, Vol. 1. M. R. Bawa Muhaiyaddeen. 350p. 1995. pap. 15.00 (*0-914390-43-0*) Fellowship Pr PA.

Question of Life - Answers of Wisdom, Vol. 1. M. R. Muhaiyaddeen. LC 90-3822. 350p. 1991. 23.00 (*0-914390-32-5*) Fellowship Pr PA.

Question of Life, A Scribe of the Kingdom, 2 vols. Jeffery D. Phillips & A. Nichols. 1990. pap. 70.00 (*0-7220-7120-5*) St Mut.

Question of Love. Saxon Bennett. LC 97-40428. 240p. 1998. pap. 11.95 (*1-56280-205-4*) Naiad Pr.

Question of Love. large type ed. Bridget Thorn. 272p. 1992. 11.50 (*0-7089-2616-9*) Ulverscroft.

Question of Loyalty: Military Manpower Policy in Multiethnic States. Alon Peled. LC 97-51489. (Cornell Studies in Security Affairs). (Illus.). 224p. 1998. text 32.50 (*0-8014-3239-1*) Cornell U Pr.

***Question of Manhood: A Reader in U. S. Black Men's History & Masculinity Vol. 1: Manhood Rights: The Construction of Black Male History, 1750-1870.** Ed. by Darlene Clark Hine & Earnestine Jenkins. LC 99-24640. (Blacks in the Diaspora Ser.). 576p. 1999. 49.95 (*0-253-33639-2*); pap. 24.95 (*0-253-21343-6*) Ind U Pr.

Question of Mary Rose see Pregunta de Maria Rosa

Question of Max. Amanda Cross. 224p. 1987. mass mkt. 5.99 (*0-345-35489-3*) Ballantine Pub Grp.

Question of Mercy. David Rabe. LC 99-213854. 1998. pap. 5.25 (*0-8222-1643-4*) Dramatists Play.

Question of Mercy: A Play. David Rabe & Richard Selzer. LC 97-40046. 128p. 1998. pap. 12.00 (*0-8021-3549-8*, Grove) Grove-Atltic.

Question of Morality: Christian Morality & In Vitro Fertilization. Donal Murray. 1989. pap. 22.00 (*0-86217-230-6*, Pub. by Veritas Pubns) St Mut.

Question of Murder. Eric Wright. 1990. mass mkt. 3.50 (*0-373-26039-3*) Harlequin Bks.

Question of Murder. large type ed. Eric Wright. 330p. 1992. pap. 14.95 (*0-8161-5372-8*, G K Hall Lrg Type) Mac Lib Ref.

Question Of Music. Guy B. Roberts. 1999. pap. text 15.95 (*0-572-02308-1*) Foulsham UK.

Question of Namibia. Laurent C. Kaela. LC 96-16005. 256p. 1996. text 59.95 (*0-312-15991-9*) St Martin.

***Question of Nationalities & Social Democracy.** Otto Bauer. Ed. by Ephraim J. Nimni. 2000. 60.00 (*0-8166-3265-0*) U of Minn Pr.

Question of Numbers: High Migration, Low Fertility & the Politics of National Identity since 1960. Michael S. Teitelbaum & J. M. Winter. LC 97-38931. 290p. 1998. 26.00 (*0-8090-7781-7*) Hill & Wang.

Question of Offshore Oil. Ed. by Edward J. Mitchell. LC 76-16665. 171p. reprint ed. pap. 53.10 (*0-608-14345-6*, 201749200007) Bks Demand.

Question of Our Speech see Works of Henry James Jr.: Collected Works

Question of Our Speech: The Lesson of Balzac, Two Lectures. Henry James. (BCL1-PS American Literature Ser.). 115p. 1992. reprint ed. lib. bdg. 69.00 (*0-7812-6765-X*) Rprt Serv.

Question of Palestine. Edward W. Said. 1980. 12.50 (*0-8129-0832-5*, Times Bks) Crown Pub Group.

Question of Palestine. Edward W. Said. 1992. pap. 13.00 (*0-679-73988-2*) Vin Bks.

Question of Palestine: British - Jewish - Arab Relations: 1914-1918. Isaiah Friedman. 458p. (C). 1991. pap. text 29.95 (*0-88738-214-2*) Transaction Pubs.

Question of Physics: Conversations in Physics & Biology. Paul Buckley & F. David Peat. LC 78-8096. 169p. reprint ed. pap. 52.40 (*0-8357-4134-6*, 203690600006) Bks Demand.

Question of Place. 2nd ed. Eric Fischer et al. 1969. 39.50 (*0-87948-004-1*) Beatty.

Question of Pornography: Research Findings & Policy Implications. Edward Donnerstein et al. 288p. 1987. 40.00 (*0-02-907521-1*) Free Pr.

Question of Power. Bessie Head. (African Writers Ser.). 206p. (C). 1974. pap. 10.95 (*0-435-90720-4*, 90720) Heinemann.

Question of Preference: A Teal Stewart Mystery. J. Dayne Lamb. 1995. mass mkt. 4.99 (*0-8217-5099-2*, Zebra Kensgtn) Kensgtn Pub Corp.

Question of Primary Care: Legislators Get the Answers. Harry Nelson. 40p. (Orig.). 1995. pap. write for info. (*0-9629870-9-3*) Milbank Memorial.

Question of Priorities: Democratic Reform & Economic Recovery in Postwar Germany. Rebecca Boehling. LC 96-24204. (Monographs in German History Ser.: Vol. 2). (Illus.). 312p. 1996. 59.95 (*1-57181-035-8*) Berghahn Bks.

Question of Priorities: Democratic Reform & Economic Recovery in Postwar Germany. Rebecca Boehling. LC 96-24204. (Monographs in German History Ser.: Vol. 2). (Illus.). 312p. 1998. pap. 24.00 (*1-57181-159-1*) Berghahn Bks.

Question of Privacy in Public Policy: An Analysis of the Reagan-Bush Era. David Sadofsky. LC 93-6771. 216p. 1993. 57.95 (*0-275-94300-3*, C4300, Praeger Pubs) Greenwood.

Question of Quality: Popularity & Value in Modern Creative Writing. Louis Filler. 1976. 14.95 (*0-87972-077-8*); pap. 8.95 (*0-87972-078-6*) Bowling Green Univ Popular Press.

Question of Reading: National Curriculum Edition. 3rd ed. Cliff Moon & Bridie Raban. 240p. 1992. pap. 32.50 (*1-85346-146-6*, Pub. by David Fulton) Taylor & Francis.

question of reality / Kazimierz Brandys. LC 80-10793. (ENG.). 180 p. ;p. 1980. write for info. (*0-684-16599-6*) Free Pr.

Question of Rites: Friar Domingo Navarrete & the Jesuits in China. J. S. Cummins. 320p. 1992. 91.95 (*0-85967-880-6*, Pub. by Scolar Pr) Ashgate Pub Co.

Question of Saving. Harold Rose. 53p. (Orig.). 1991. pap. text 8.00 (*0-89068-106-6*, BNAC 38(NPA249)) Natl Planning.

***Question of Seeing: Poems by Donald Finkel.** Donald Finkel. LC 97-39771. 1998. 24.00 (*1-55728-501-2*); pap. 16.00 (*1-55728-502-0*) U of Ark Pr.

Question of Silence: The Sexual Economies of Modern India. Ed. by Mery John & Janaki Nair. LC 99-931904. 1998. 32.00 (*81-86706-08-9*, Pub. by Kali for Women) S Asia.

Question of Sovereignty: What Legitimate Right Did Spain Have to Its Territorial Expansion? Omaira Brunal-Perry. Tr. by Marjorie G. Driver. (Educational Ser.: No. 15). (Illus.). 52p. 1993. 3.50 (*1-878453-15-7*) Univ Guam MAR Ctr.

Question of Speech - The Lesson of Balzac: Two Lectures. Henry James. LC 72-334. (Studies of Henry James: No. 17). 1972. reprint ed. lib. bdg. 75.00 (*0-8383-1411-2*) M S G Haskell Hse.

Question of Sports. Robert Hollerman. (Illus.). 296p. 1996. pap. 8.10 (*0-7399-0226-1*, 2540) Rod & Staff.

Question of Style in Philosophy & the Arts. Ed. by Caroline Van Eck et al. (Studies in Philosophy & the Arts). (Illus.). 257p. (C). 1995. text 54.95 (*0-521-47341-1*) Cambridge U Pr.

Question of Survival. Julian F. Thompson. 320p. (J). (gr. 8 up). 1984. pap. 2.50 (*0-380-87775-9*, Avon Bks) Morrow Avon.

Question of Syllables: Essays in Nineteenth Century French Verse. Clive Scott. (Cambridge Studies in French: No. 14). 228p. 1986. text 69.95 (*0-521-32584-6*) Cambridge U Pr.

Question of the Commons: The Culture & Ecology of Communal Resources. Ed. by Bonnie J. McCay & James M. Acheson. LC 87-19833. (Arizona Studies in Human Ecology). 439p. (C). 1990. reprint ed. pap. text 21.95 (*0-8165-1205-1*) U of Ariz Pr.

Question of the Other: Essays in Contemporary Continental Philosophy. Ed. by Arleen B. Dallery & Charles E. Scott. LC 88-39152. (Selected Studies in Phenomenology & Existential Philosophy). 256p. 1989. text 19.50 (*0-7914-0032-8*) State U NY Pr.

Question of Thinking: A First Look at Students' Performance on Open-Ended Questions in Mathematics. California Department of Education Staff. (Illus.). 92p. 1989. pap. 7.00 (*0-8011-0815-2*) Calif Education.

Question of Tibet & the Rule of Law. International Commission of Jurists Staff. LC 59-3879. 221p. Date not set. reprint ed. pap. 68.60 (*0-608-20639-3*, 207207500003) Bks Demand.

Question of Time. Fred Saberhagen. 288p. 1993. mass mkt. 4.99 (*0-8125-2577-9*, Pub. by Tor Bks) St Martin.

Question of Time. large type ed. Robert Bryce. 274p. (Orig.). 1995. mass mkt. 6.99 (*1-881542-17-3*) Blue Star Prodns.

Question of Time: Essentials of Brief Dynamic Therapy. Angela Molnos. 152p. 1995. pap. text 25.00 (*1-85575-107-0*, Pub. by H Karnac Bks Ltd) Other Pr LLC.

Question of Time: J. R. R. Tolkien's Road to Faerie. Verlyn Flieger. LC 97-6777. (Illus.). 286p. 1997. 35.00 (*0-87338-574-8*) Kent St U Pr.

Question of Timing: Successful Men Talk about Having Children see Teen Pregnancy Prevention Library

Question of Trust. Marion Dane Bauer. 128p. (YA). (gr. 4 up). 1994. 14.95 (*0-590-47915-6*, Scholastic Hardcover) Scholastic Inc.

Question of Trust. Marion Dane Bauer. (YA). (gr. 4 up). 1994. 8.09 (*0-606-08591-2*, Pub. by Turtleback) Demco.

Question of Trust. Nina C. Pykare. LC 98-96611. 192p. 1998. 18.95 (*0-8034-9322-3*, Avalon Bks) Bouregy.

Question of Trust. large type ed. Maggie Kingsley. (Mills & Boon Large Print Ser.). 288p. 1996. 23.99 (*0-263-14727-4*, Pub. by Mills & Boon) Ulverscroft.

Question of Trust: The Origins of U. S.-Soviet Diplomatic Relations; The Memoirs of Loy W. Henderson. Ed. by George W. Baer. (Publication Series: Archival Documentaries: No. 333). 579p. (C). 1987. text 17.98 (*0-8179-8331-7*) Hoover Inst Pr.

Question of Upbringing see Dance to the Music of Time: First Movement

Question of Upbringing. large type unabridged ed. Anthony Powell. (Dance to Music of Time Ser.: Vol. 1). 261p. 1998. 25.95 (*0-7531-5813-2*, 158132) ISIS Pub.

Question of Value: Thinking Through Nietzsche, Heidegger, & Freud. James S. Hans. LC 88-18451. 224p. (C). 1989. 26.95 (*0-8093-1506-8*) S Ill U Pr.

Question of Values. Paul L. Errington. LC 87-16978. (Illus.). 208p. 1987. reprint ed. pap. 64.50 (*0-608-00058-2*, 206082400006) Bks Demand.

Question of Values: Johan Galtung's Peace Research. Peter Lawler. LC 94-8624. (Critical Perspectives on World Politics Ser.). 280p. 1994. lib. bdg. 52.00 (*1-55587-507-6*) L Rienner.

Question of Values: Six Ways We Make the Personal Choices that Shape Our Lives. 3rd unabridged ed. Hunter Lewis. LC 90-56471. 283p. 1990. 9.95 (*0-9661908-0-7*, 101); pap. 9.95 (*0-9661908-1-5*, 101) Axios Pr.

***Question of Values: Six Ways We Make the Personal Choices That Shape Our Lives.** 4th rev. unabridged ed. Hunter Lewis. LC 99-60982. 300p. 1999. pap. 12.95 (*0-9661908-3-1*) Axios Pr.

Question of Yams. Gloria Repp. (Light Line Ser.). (Illus.). 67p. (J). 1992. pap. 6.49 (*0-89084-614-6*, 057885) Bob Jones Univ.

***Question Presented: Model Appellate Briefs.** Maria L. Ciampi & William H. Manz. LC 99-89984. 2000. pap. text 25.00 (*0-87084-419-9*) Anderson Pub Co.

Question-Reply Argumentation, 40. LC 89-2241. (Contributions in Philosophy Ser.: No. 40). (Illus.). 424p. 1989. 79.50 (*0-313-26789-8*, WQR/, Greenwood Pr) Greenwood.

Question Review for Fleisher & Ludwig's Textbook of Pediatric Emergency Medicine. 4th ed. Sujit Sharma et al. 304p. pap. text 39.95 (*0-7817-2467-8*) Lppncott W & W.

Questionable Behavior. J. Dayne Lamb. 288p. 1993. mass mkt. 3.99 (*0-8217-4333-3*, Zebra Kensgtn) Kensgtn Pub Corp.

Questionable Remains. Beverly Connor. LC 97-24565. 288p. 1997. 20.95 (*1-888952-53-9*) Cumberland Hse.

Questionable Shapes. William Dean Howells. LC 74-86145. (Short Story Index Reprint Ser.). 1977. 19.95 (*0-8369-3049-5*) Ayer.

Questionable Shapes: Short Stories. William Dean Howells. (Notable American Authors Ser.). 1992. reprint ed. lib. bdg. 75.00 (*0-7812-3255-4*) Rprt Serv.

Questionables. Jonathan Swiller. 1995. mass mkt. 4.99 (*0-312-95584-7*, Pub. by Tor Bks) St Martin.

Questioned Document Case Studies. Luciano V. Caputo. LC 82-3563. (Illus.). 100p. 1982. text 55.95 (*0-88229-259-5*) Burnham Inc.

Questioned Document Problems: The Discovery & Proof of the Facts. Albert S. Osborn. LC 84-14716. (Criminology, Law Enforcement, & Social Problems Ser.: No. 172). (Illus.). 570p. 1991. 45.00 (*0-87585-172-X*) Patterson Smith.

***Questioned Documents.** Albert S. Osborn. xxiv, 501p. 1999. reprint ed. 158.00 (*1-56169-476-2*) Gaunt.

Questioned Documents. 2nd ed. Albert S. Osborn. LC 74-78841. (Illus.). 1072p. 1974. reprint ed. text 57.95 (*0-88229-190-4*) Burnham Inc.

Questioned Documents. 2nd rev. ed. Albert S. Osborn. LC 73-9875. (Criminology, Law Enforcement, & Social Problems Ser.: No. 207). (Illus.). 760p. 1973. lib. bdg. 27.50 (*0-87585-207-6*) Patterson Smith.

***Questioned Documents: A Lawyer's Handbook.** Jay Levinson. 260p. 2000. 69.95 (*0-12-445490-9*) Acad Pr.

Questiones Subtilissime in Libros Aristotelis de Celo et Mundo. Albertus De Saxonia. (GER.). 102p. 1986. reprint ed. write for info. (*3-487-07673-X*) G Olms Pubs.

Questioning. H. Van der Meij. (Selecta Reeks Ser.: Vol. 37). xiv, 202p. 1986. 22.00 (*90-6472-091-6*) Taylor & Francis.

Questioning: A Path to Critical Thinking. Leila Christenbury & Patricia P. Kelly. 33p. 1983. pap. 5.95 (*0-8141-3804-7*) NCTE.

Questioning & Discussion: A Multidisciplinary Study. Ed. by James T. Dillon. LC 87-33355. 352p. 1988. pap. 39.50 (*0-89391-493-2*); text 73.25 (*0-89391-442-8*) Ablx Pub.

Questioning Authority: Stories Told in School. Ed. by Linda Adler-Kassner & Susanmarie Harrington. (Illus.). 235p. (C). text 42.50 (*0-472-09759-8*, 09759); pap. text 22.95 (*0-472-06759-1*, 06759) U of Mich Pr.

Questioning Back: The Overcoming of Metaphysics in Christian Tradition. Joseph S. O'Leary. 256p. 1985. 18.95 (*0-86683-988-7*) Harper SF.

Questioning Belief. Richard Harries. 256p. 1995. pap. 14.95 (*0-687-06636-0*) Abingdon.

Questioning Chemotherapy: A Critique of the Use of Toxic Drugs in the Treatment of Cancer. Ralph W. Moss. LC 95-11440. 1995. 19.95 (*1-881025-25-X*) Equinox Pr.

Questioning Circumcision: A Jewish Perspective. Ronald Goldman. LC 97-40162. 144p. (Orig.). 1997. 11.95 (*0-9644895-6-2*) Vangrd Pub.

Questioning Consciousness: The Interplay of Imagery, Cognition, & Emotion in the Human Brain. Ralph D. Ellis. LC 95-10923. (Advances in Consciousness Research Ser.: Vol. 2). viii, 262p. 1995. pap. 34.95 (*1-55619-182-0*) J Benjamins Pubng Co.

Questioning Edmond Jabes. Warren F. Motte. LC 89-14642. 202p. 1990. reprint ed. pap. 62.70 (*0-7837-8897-5*, 204960800001) Bks Demand.

Questioning Empowerment: Working with Women in Honduras. Jo Rowlands. LC 97-222505. 208p. (C). 1997. 15.95 (*0-85598-362-0*, Pub. by Oxfam Pub) Stylus Pub VA.

Questioning Ethics: Contemporary Debates in Continental Philosophy. Ed. by Richard Kearney & Mark Dooley. LC 98-8544. 208p. 1998. pap. 18.99 (*0-415-18035-X*, D6284) Routledge.

Questioning Ethics: Contemporary Debates in Continental Philosophy. Ed. by Richard Kearney & Mark Dooley. LC 98-8544. 208p. (C). (gr. 13). 1998. 60.00 (*0-415-18034-1*, D6280) Routledge.

Questioning Foundations: Truth, Subjectivity & Culture. Ed. by Hugh J. Silverman. (Continental Philosophy Ser.: No. 5). 288p. (C). 1993. pap. 20.99 (*0-415-90624-5*, A7411) Routledge.

***Questioning Geopolitics: Political Projects in a Changing World-System.** Ed. by Georgi M. Derluguian & Scott L. Greer. LC 99-49047. 264p. 2000. pap. 22.95 (*0-275-96656-9*, Praeger Pubs) Greenwood.

***Questioning Globalization: The Culture of Capital.** Ali Mohammadi. 2000. pap. 22.50 (*0-7453-1520-8*) Pluto GBR.

Questioning History: The Postmodern Turn to the Eighteenth Century. Ed. by Greg Clingham. (Review Ser.: Vol. 41, No. 2). (Illus.). 200p. 1998. 24.00 (*0-8387-5383-3*) Bucknell U Pr.

Questioning Makes the Difference. Nancy L. Johnson. (Illus.). 80p. 1990. pap. 11.95 (*0-9623835-3-8*, CLC0072) Pieces of Lrning.

***Questioning Matters: An Introduction to Philosophical Inquiry.** Daniel Kolak. LC 99-23104. 1999. pap. text 48.95 (*0-7674-0447-5*) Mayfield Pub.

Questioning Media Ethics. Ed. by Bernard Rubin. 320p. 1978. pap., student ed. 19.95 (*0-03-046126-X*, Praeger Pubs) Greenwood.

Questioning Misfortune: The Pragmatics of Uncertainty in Eastern Uganda. Susan R. Whyte. LC 97-10235. (Studies in Medical Anthropology: No. 4). (Illus.). 272p. (C). 1998. text 64.95 (*0-521-59402-2*); pap. text 24.95 (*0-521-59558-4*) Cambridge U Pr.

Questioning Miss Quinton. Kasey Michaels. 176p. 1987. pap. 2.95 (*0-380-75296-4*, Avon Bks) Morrow Avon.

Questioning Presence: Wordsworth, Keats & the Interrogative Mode in Romantic Poetry. Susan J. Wolfson. LC 86-6407. 384p. 1986. 45.00 (*0-8014-1909-3*) Cornell U Pr.

Questioning Presence: Wordsworth, Keats & the Interrogative Mode in Romantic Poetry. Susan J. Wolfson. LC 86-6407. (Illus.). 392p. reprint ed. pap. 121.60 (*0-608-20957-0*, 207205800003) Bks Demand.

Q

An Asterisk (*) at the beginning of an entry indicates that the title is appearing for the first time.

***Questioning Ramayanas: A South Asian Tradition.** Ed. by Paula Richman. (Illus.). 400p. 2000. 50.00 (0-520-22073-0); pap. 19.95 (0-520-22074-9, Pub. by U CA Pr) Cal Prin Full Svc.

Questioning Romanticism. Ed. by John B. Beer. LC 94-49331. 328p. 1995. text 48.50 (0-8018-5052-5); pap. text 18.95 (0-8018-5053-3) Johns Hopkins.

Questioning Skills, for Teachers. 3rd ed. William W. Wilen. (What Research Says to the Teacher Ser.). 1991. pap. 3.95 (0-8106-1089-2) NEA.

Questioning Slavery. James Walvin. LC 96-14794. 216p. (C). 1996. 75.00 (0-415-15356-5); pap. 22.99 (0-415-15357-3) Routledge.

***Questioning Sovereignty.** 224p. 1999. 72.00 (0-19-826876-9) OUP.

Questioning Styles & Strategies. 2nd ed. Richard W. Strong et al. (Unity in Diversity Ser.: Vol. 3). (Illus.). 118p. 1995. pap. text 29.95 (1-58284-003-2, Thoughtful Educ) Silver Strong.

Questioning Techniques & Tactics. Jeffrey L. Kestler. LC 82-5877. (Trial Practice Ser.). 416p. 1982. text 95.00 (0-07-034285-7) Shepards.

***Questioning Technology.** Andrew Feenberg. LC 98-37421. 7p. 1999. 75.00 (0-415-19754-6) Routledge.

Questioning Technology. Andrew Feenberg. LC 98-37421. 1999. pap. 24.99 (0-415-19755-4) Routledge.

Questioning the Author: An Approach for Enhancing Student Engagement with Text. Isabel L. Beck et al. LC 96-52260. 130p. 1997. pap. 17.95 (0-87207-242-8, 242) Intl Reading.

***Questioning the Father: From Darwin to Zola, Ibsen, Strindberg & Hardy.** Ross Shideler. LC 99-39451. 1999. 45.00 (0-8047-3560-3) Stanford U Pr.

Questioning the Law in Corporate America: Agenda for Reform, 71. Gerald L. Houseman. LC 92-35554. (Contributions in Legal Studies: No. 71). 192p. 1993. 55.00 (0-313-26341-8, HQS, Greenwood Pr) Greenwood.

***Questioning the Master: Gender & Sexuality in Henry James's Writings.** Ed. by Peggy McCormack. LC 99-33518. 232p. 2000. 39.50 (0-87413-712-8) U Delaware Pr.

Questioning the Media: A Critical Introduction. 2nd ed. Ed. by John Downing et al. LC 94-48241. 1995. 59.95 (0-8039-7196-6) Sage.

Questioning the Media: A Critical Introduction. 2nd ed. John Downing et al. 400p. 1995. text 56.00 (0-8039-7199-0); pap. text 28.95 (0-8039-7197-4) Sage.

***Questioning the Millennium: A Rationalist's Guide to a Precisely Arbitrary Countdown.** Stephen Jay Gould. 1999. 17.95 (0-609-60541-0) Harmony Bks.

Questioning the Postwar Consensus Thesis: Towards an Alternative Account. James D. Marlow. 192p. 1996. text 77.95 (1-85521-826-7, Pub. by Dartmth Pub) Ashgate Pub Co.

Questioning the Solution: The Politics of Primary Health Care & Child Survival. David Werner et al. LC 96-79528. (Illus.). 206p. 1997. 25.00 (0-9655585-1-7); pap. 18.00 (0-9655585-2-5, RJ103) HealthWrights.

Questioning the Universality of Human Rights: The "African Charter on Human & People's Rights" in Botswana, Malawi & Mozambique. Lone Lindholt. LC 97-7872. (Law, Social Change & Development Ser.). 320p. 1997. text 82.95 (1-85521-828-3, Pub. by Ashgate Pub) Ashgate Pub Co.

Questioning the Validity of Masses Using the New All-English Canon. Patrick Omlor. 1997. pap. 5.00 (1-929968-05-1) Catholic Research Inst.

Questioning Tradition, Language, & Myth: The Poetry of Seamus Heaney. Michael R. Molino. LC 93-42712. 215p. 1994. pap. 19.95 (0-8132-0797-5) Cath U Pr.

Questioning Traveler & Karma. Torkom Saraydarian. 1979. pap. 2.50 (0-911794-45-X) Saraydarian Inst.

***Questionnaire: Or Prayer for a Town & a Friend.** Jiri Grusa. Tr. by Peter Kussi from CZE. LC 99-35093. 288p. 2000. reprint ed. pap. 12.95 (1-56478-227-1, Pub. by Dalkey Arch) Chicago Distribution Ctr.

Questionnaire Design, Interviewing, & Attitude Measurement. A. N. Oppenheim. LC 92-15306. 310p. 1993. pap. text 29.95 (1-85567-044-5) Bks Intl VA.

Questionnaire Design, Interviewing, & Attitude Measurement. A. N. Oppenheim. LC 92-15306. 1992. text 59.00 (1-85567-043-7) St Martin.

Questionnaire Research: A Practical Guide. Mildred L. Patten. (Illus.). 144p. (Orig.). (C). 1997. pap. text 21.95 (1-884585-07-8) Pyrczak Pub.

Questionnaires: Design & Use. 2nd ed. John F. Anderson et al. LC 86-1783. 344p. 1986. 34.50 (0-8108-1884-1) Scarecrow.

Questionnaires: Index of New Information & Scientific Research Bible. Gregory M. Fuhrman. 141p. 1997. 47.50 (0-7883-1244-8); pap. 44.50 (0-7883-1245-6) ABBE Pubs Assn.

Questionnaires & Inventories: Surveying Opinions & Assessing Personality. Lewis R. Aiken. LC 96-53659. (Illus.). 319p. 1997. 69.50 incl. disk (0-471-16871-8) Wiley.

Questionnaires from the National Health Interview Survey, 1980-84: PHS 90-1302. (Vital & Health Statistics Ser. 1: Programs & Collection Procedures: No. 24). 212p. 11.00 (0-685-61582-0, 017-022-0110-7) Natl Ctr Health Stats.

Questionnaires from the National Health Interview Survey, 1985-89. U. S. Dept. of Health & Human Services Staff et al. LC 93-854. (Vital & Health Statistics Ser. 1: Programs & Collection Procedures: No. 31). 1993. write for info. (0-8406-0480-7) Natl Ctr Health Stats.

Questions. Judy McGorray. (Illus.). 31p. (Orig.). 1996. pap. text 8.00 (1-888200-10-3) JayMac Commun.

Questions: A Sociological Perspective. 3rd ed. Joel M. Charon. LC 97-21806. (Sociology Ser.). (C). 1997. 28.95 (0-534-52569-5) Wadsworth Pub.

Questions: The Tool Most Used. Tom Contine. 45p. (C). 1995. 10.00 (1-878276-52-2) Educ Systs Assocs Inc.

Questions about Angels: Poems. Billy Collins. LC 98-45376. (Pitt Poetry Ser.). 88p. 1999. pap. 12.95 (0-8229-5698-5) U of Pittsburgh Pr.

Questions about Music. Roger Sessions. LC 72-102672. (Charles Eliot Norton Lectures: No. 1968-1969). 174p. reprint ed. pap. 54.00 (0-7837-4190-1, 205904000012) Bks Demand.

Questions about Questions: Inquiries into the Cognitive Bases of Surveys. Ed. by Judith M. Tanur. LC 91-18807. (Illus.). 352p. 1992. 42.50 (0-87154-842-9) Russell Sage.

Questions about Questions: Inquiries into the Cognitive Bases of Surveys. Ed. by Judith M. Tanur. (Illus.). 352p. 1994. reprint ed. pap. 16.95 (0-87154-841-0) Russell Sage.

Questions about Weather. M. Jean Craig. (Illus.). (J). (gr. 2-5). 1996. pap. 4.95 (0-614-15762-5) Scholastic Inc.

Questions & Admissions: Reflections on 100,000 Admissions Decisions at Stanford. Jean H. Fetter. LC 94-23098. 292p. 1995. 45.00 (0-8047-2398-2) Stanford U Pr.

Questions & Admissions: Reflections on 100,000 Admissions Decisions at Stanford. Jean H. Fetter. 292p. 1997. pap. 16.95 (0-8047-3158-6) Stanford U Pr.

Questions & Ancestors. Lorna D. Smith. 175p. 1993. pap. 9.50 (0-9632467-6-3) ApronStrings.

***Questions & Answers.** Susan Amerikaner. (Illus.). (J). 2000. pap. 9.95 (0-7373-0512-6) Lowell Hse Juvenile.

Questions & Answers. M. Claridge et al. (Quizbooks Ser.). (Illus.). 128p. (J). (gr. 4-7). 1994. pap. 12.95 (0-7460-1359-0, Usborne) EDC.

Questions & Answers. Frances Clark. 1992. 26.00 (0-317-05202-0) Instrumental.

Questions & Answers. Ed. by Ferenc Kiefer. 1983. text 126.50 (90-277-1503-3) Kluwer Academic.

Questions & Answers. John Ramsell. 128p. pap. 13.95 (0-8464-4277-9) Beekman Pubs.

Questions & Answers. John Ramsell. 110p. 1992. pap. 7.00 (0-85207-240-6, Pub. by C W Daniel) Natl Bk Netwk.

Questions & Answers. Millicent E. Selsam. 64p. (J). (gr. 2-5). 1995. pap. 4.95 (0-590-48448-6) Scholastic Inc.

Questions & Answers. Friend Stuart. 32p. 1980. pap. 3.95 (0-912132-09-4) Dominion Pr.

Questions & Answers. Jimmy Swaggart. 1985. 12.95 (0-935113-01-0) Swaggart Ministries.

Questions & Answers. 18th ed. Dearborn Financial Institute Staff. (Passtrak Ser.). 1998. pap. 35.00 (0-7931-3005-0) Dearborn.

Questions & Answers: Civil Procedure. Roy L. Brooks. (Winning in Law School Ser.: Bk. 5). 152p. (Orig.). 1988. pap. text 12.95 (0-915667-10-X) Spectra Pub Co.

Questions & Answers: Contracts. 2nd rev. ed. Jonathan Neville. (Winning in Law School Ser.). 175p. (Orig.). 1992. pap. text 12.95 (0-915667-21-5) Spectra Pub Co.

Questions & Answers: Correspondence Between Ibn Sina & Al-Biruni. Ed. by Seyyed Hossein Nasr. 156p. (C). 1997. 19.95 (1-871031-73-7) Kazi Pubns.

Questions & Answers: Criminal Law. Leslie W. Abramson & Catherine D. Edwards. (Winning in Law School Ser.: Bk. 4). 155p. (Orig.). 1989. pap. text 12.95 (0-915667-09-6) Spectra Pub Co.

Questions & Answers: Fundamentals of the Esoteric Sciences. Manly P. Hall. pap. 15.95 (0-89314-801-6) Philos Res.

Questions & Answers: Property. James H. Backman. (Winning in Law School Ser.: Bk. 8). 175p. (Orig.). 1987. pap. text 12.95 (0-915667-15-0) Spectra Pub Co.

Questions & Answers: Strategies for Using the Electronic Reference Collection. Ed. by Linda C. Smith. (C). 1989. 10.00 (0-87845-077-7) U of Ill Grad Sch.

Questions & Answers: Torts. David H. Barber & Ronald W. Eades. (Winning in Law School Ser.: Bk. 7). 236p. (Orig.). 1986. pap. text 12.95 (0-915667-12-6) Spectra Pub Co.

Questions & Answers Vol. 2: Open Forum from Freed-Hardeman College Lectures. Guy N. Woods. 1986. pap. 19.99 (0-89225-277-4) Gospel Advocate.

***Questions & Answers About Ancient Civilizations.** Kingfisher Staff. (Illus.). 40p. (YA). 2000. pap. 7.95 (0-7534-5310-X, Kingfisher) LKC.

Questions & Answers about Bees. Betty P. Reigot. (Illus.). (J). 1996. pap. 4.95 (0-590-52839-4) Scholastic Inc.

Questions & Answers about Best-Value Source Selection. Vernon J. Edwards. 45p. (Orig.). 1993. pap. 15.00 (0-935165-30-4) GWU Gov Contracts.

Questions & Answers about Bilingual Education. Alicia S. Sosa. (ENG & SPA., Illus.). 52p. (Orig.). 1993. pap. 10.00 (1-878550-48-9) Inter Dev Res Assn.

Questions & Answers about Birth Control. M. Sanger. 1992. lib. bdg. 250.00 (0-8490-5568-7) Gordon Pr.

Questions & Answers about Block Scheduling: An Implementation Guide. Donald D. Gainey & John M. Brucato. LC 98-54128. 250p. 1999. 39.95 (1-883001-68-4) Eye On Educ.

Questions & Answers about Breslov. Avraham Greenbaum. 32p. 1992. pap. 2.00 (0-930213-30-0) Breslov Res Inst.

Questions & Answers about Childhood Depression & Its Treatment. John W. Maag. 224p. 2000. pap. text 18.95 (0-914783-88-2) Charles.

***Questions & Answers about Clergy Sexual Misconduct.** Elizabeth A. Horst. 40p. 2000. pap. 3.95 (0-8146-2056-6) Liturgical Pr.

Questions & Answers about Community Associations. Jan Hickenbottom. 166p. 1991. pap. 14.95 (1-880039-00-1) Miller Pub.

Questions & Answers about Depression & Its Treatment: A Consultation with a Leading Psychiatrist. Ivan K. Goldberg. LC 93-9430. 160p. (Orig.). 1993. pap. 16.95 (0-914783-68-8) Charles.

Questions & Answers about Dinosaurs. Dougal Dixon. LC 94-31066. (Questions & Answers about Ser.). (Illus.). 40p. (J). (gr. 2-6). 1995. pap. 8.95 (1-85697-553-3) LKC.

***Questions & Answers About Dinosaurs.** Kingfisher Staff. 40p. (YA). 2000. pap. 7.95 (0-7534-5309-6, Kingfisher) LKC.

Questions & Answers about Electric & Magnetic Fields Associated with the Use of Electric Power. (Illus.). 67p. 1997. reprint ed. pap. text 30.00 (0-7881-4149-X) DIANE Pub.

Questions & Answers about Electric & Magnetic Fields (EMF) Associated with the Use of Electric Power. (Illus.). 66p. (C). 1997. reprint ed. pap. text 25.00 (0-7881-4622-X) DIANE Pub.

Questions & Answers about EMF: Electric & Magnetic Fields Associated with the Use of Electric Power. 1997. lib. bdg. 251.95 (0-8490-6124-5) Gordon Pr.

Questions & Answers About EMF: Electric & Magnetic Fields Associated with the Use of Electric Power. 68p. 1995. pap. 4.25 (0-16-063411-3) USGPO.

Questions & Answers about EMF: Electric Magnetic Fields Associated with the Use of Electric Power. 1996. lib. bdg. 252.75 (0-8490-6930-0) Gordon Pr.

Questions & Answers about Explorers. Christopher Maynard. LC 94-31067. (Questions & Answers about Ser.). (Illus.). 40p. (J). (gr. 4-7). 1995. pap. 8.95 (1-85697-555-X, Kingfisher) LKC.

Questions & Answers about Horses. Millicent Ellis Selsam. 1995. 10.15 (0-606-08049-X, Pub. by Turtleback) Demco.

***Questions & Answers About Inventions.** Kingfisher Staff. (Illus.). 40p. (YA). 2000. pap. 7.95 (0-7534-5311-8, Kingfisher) LKC.

***Questions & Answers about Life & Faith.** Mack B. Stokes. 426p. 2000. pap. 16.95 (1-885224-25-7) Bristol Hse.

Questions & Answers about Murder. David Lester. LC 91-23439. 192p. (Orig.). 1991. pap. text 16.95 (0-914783-46-7) Charles.

Questions & Answers about Pain Control: A Guide for People with Cancer & Their Families. (Illus.). 76p. (Orig.). 1994. pap. text 20.00 (0-7881-1157-4) DIANE Pub.

Questions & Answers about Seashore Animals. Michael Chinery. LC 93-29428. (Questions & Answers about Ser.). (Illus.). 40p. (J). (gr. 4-7). 1994. pap. 8.95 (1-85697-965-2) LKC.

Questions & Answers about Sex in Later Life. Margot Tallmer. LC 94-9052. 160p. (Orig.). 1996. pap. 15.95 (0-914783-75-0) Charles.

***Questions & Answers About Stars & Planets.** Kingfisher Staff. (Illus.). 40p. (YA). 2000. pap. 7.95 (0-7534-5312-6, Kingfisher) LKC.

Questions & Answers about Suicide. David Lester. LC 89-60683. 184p. (Orig.). (C). 1989. pap. text 17.95 (0-914783-31-9) Charles.

Questions & Answers About the Dinosaurs. Seymour Simon. LC 88-36226. (Illus.). 48p. (J). (gr. k up). 1990. 15.93 (0-688-08196-7, Wm Morrow) Morrow Avon.

Questions & Answers about the New Age Movement. Cathy Burns. 20p. 1989. pap. 0.50 (1-891117-04-1) Sharing.

Questions & Answers about the United Methodist Church. Tom McAnally. 24p. (Orig.). 1995. pap. 2.25 (0-687-01670-3) Abingdon.

Questions & Answers about Today's Securities Market. Nachman Bench. 216p. 1987. 17.95 (0-13-749227-8) P-H.

Questions & Answers about Weather. M. Jean Craig. (Illus.). 64p. (J). (gr. k-3). 1977. pap. 5.99 (0-590-41142-X) Scholastic Inc.

Questions & Answers about Weather. M.J. Craig. (J). 1996. 11.19 (0-606-09774-0, Pub. by Turtleback) Demco.

Questions & Answers About Whistleblower Appeals. Government Printing Office Staff. 24p. 1995. pap. 1.50 (0-16-048361-1) USGPO.

Questions & Answers Book of Science Facts. Ian Graham & Paul Sterry. LC 97-8725. (Illus.). 80p. (J). (gr. 1-6). 1997. 19.95 (0-8160-3655-1) Facts on File.

Questions & Answers for Dental Nurses. Hollins. 1997. 24.95 (0-632-04283-4) Blackwell Sci.

Questions & Answers for Electrician's Examinations. 11th ed. Rev. by Paul Rosenberg. LC 92-33277. 1993. write for info. (0-02-604962-7) Macmillan.

Questions & Answers for Medical Nurses. A. Zzizinga. 1983. pap. text. write for info. (0-582-77702-X, Pub. by Addison-Wesley) Longman.

Questions & Answers for Symptoms & Signs in Clinical Medicine. Colin Ogilvie & J. E. Earls. (Illus.). 268p. 1987. pap. text 32.50 (0-7236-0865-2) Buttrwrth-Heinemann.

Questions & Answers for the Plumbers Examination. 3rd ed. Jules Oravetz, Sr. 272p. 1991. pap. 14.95 (0-02-593510-0) Macmillan.

Questions & Answers for Young Disciples: Truth for Children Straight from Scripture. Ed. by H. Robert Cowles. 46p. 1993. pap. 1.49 (0-87509-466-X) Chr Pubns.

Questions & Answers from the Bible. Roger Carswell. 1997. pap. text 8.99 (1-898787-66-2) Emerald House Group Inc.

Questions & Answers from the Bible: Over 2,000 Q&A from the Bible. 176p. 1998. pap. 3.97 (0-916441-50-4) Barbour Pub.

Questions & Answers in Attitude Surveys: Experiments on Question Form, Wording, & Context. Howard Schuman & Stanley Presser. 1996. pap. 25.95 (0-7619-0359-3) Sage.

Questions & Answers in Lethal & Non-Lethal Violence: Proceeding of the Second Annual Workshop of the Homicide Research Working Group. Ed. by Carolyn R. Block & Richard L. Block. (Illus.). 230p. (Orig.). (C). 1994. pap. text 50.00 (0-7881-1422-0) DIANE Pub.

Questions & Answers in Lethal & Non-Lethal Violence: Proceedings of the First Annual Workshop of the Homicide Research Working Group. Ed. by Carolyn R. Block & Richard L. Block. (Illus.). 141p. 1994. reprint ed. pap. text 35.00 (0-7881-1474-3) DIANE Pub.

Questions & Answers in Marketing. L. G. Alexander. (English As a Second Language Bk.). 1977. pap. text 4.95 (0-582-55206-0) Longman.

Questions & Answers in Nuclear Medicine. Wagner et al. LC 98-22425. (Illus.). 288p. (C). 1998. text. write for info. (1-55664-428-0) Mosby Inc.

Questions & Answers in Quartz Watch Repairing. Alice B. Carpenter & Buddy Carpenter. 1989. 12.95 (0-918845-13-0) Am Watchmakers.

***Questions & Answers 1953.** 2nd ed. Mother. 417p. 1998. pap. 24.95 (81-7058-519-8, Pub. by SAA) E-W Cultural Ctr.

Questions & Answers of Rabbi Schneur Zalman of Liadi see Sha'Alois Ve'Tshuvois Admur Hazoken

***Questions & Answers of the Bible.** Richard L. Noblit. 2000. pap. 5.95 (0-9702230-0-5) R L Noblit.

Questions & Answers of the Ecological & Environmetal Issues Related to the Three Georges Project. Zhong Dalai et al. (Chinese Science Studies). 220p. 1998. pap. 69.95 (7-03-001892-3) Intl Scholars.

Questions & Answers on AIDS. Lyn Frumkin & John Leonard. 192p. (Orig.). 1987. pap. 3.95 (0-380-75467-3, Avon Bks) Morrow Avon.

Questions & Answers on AIDS. 2nd ed. Lyn Frumkin & John Leonard. (PMIC Consumer Health Ser.). 206p. (Orig.). 1995. pap. 6.99 (1-878487-86-8, ME224) Practice Mgmt Info.

Questions & Answers on AIDS. 3rd rev. ed. Lyn Frumkin & John Leonard. LC 96-78924. (Illus.). 292p. (Orig.). 1997. pap. 12.95 (1-885987-07-2, ME079, Health Info Pr) Practice Mgmt Info.

Questions & Answers on Apley's Concise System of Orthopedics. Christopher Lavy & David S. Barrett. 192p. 1991. pap. text 30.00 (0-7506-1170-7) Buttrwrth-Heinemann.

Questions & Answers on Ballroom Dancing. A. Moore. (Ballroom Dance Ser.). 1984. lib. bdg. 79.95 (0-87700-511-7) Revisionist Pr.

Questions & Answers on Bible Prophecy. George D. Hamilton. 1995. pap. text 7.00 (0-927936-67-4) Vincom Pubng Co.

Questions & Answers on Conversations with God. Neale Donald Walsch. LC 99-71610. 240p. 1999. pap. 15.95 (1-57174-140-2) Hampton Roads Pub Co.

Questions & Answers on Conversion to Judaism. Lawrence J. Epstein. LC 97-44900. 205p. 1998. pap. 30.00 (0-7657-5996-9) Aronson.

Questions & Answers on Counselling in Action. Ed. by Windy Dryden. (Counselling in Action Ser.: Vol. 16). (Illus.). 192p. (C). 1993. text 49.95 (0-8039-8858-3); pap. text 21.50 (0-8039-8859-1) Sage.

Questions & Answers on Death. Elisabeth Kubler-Ross. 192p. 1997. per. 10.00 (0-684-83937-7) S&S Trade Pap.

Questions & Answers on Executive Compensation: How to Get What You're Worth. Graef S. Crystal. LC 84-11630. 196p. 1984. 27.50 (0-13-748476-3, Busn); pap. 9.95 (0-13-748468-2, Busn) P-H.

Questions & Answers on Family Health. Jan De Vries. 320p. 1994. pap. 16.95 (1-85158-587-7, Pub. by Mainstream Pubng) Trafalgar.

Questions & Answers on Gift Substantiation & Quid Pro Quo Disclosure Statement Requirements for Private Schools. Compiled by Jefferson G. Burnett & Donna Orem. 40p. 1994. 29.95 (0-89964-308-6, 28001) Coun Adv & Supp Ed.

Questions & Answers on Healing & Deliverance. Frank Marzullo. 22p. 1995. pap. write for info. (1-892363-17-8) Christian Covenant.

Questions & Answers on Immigration in Britain. Farid R. Anthony. LC 97-112132. 192p. 1996. pap. 26.50 (0-7146-4272-X, Pub. by F Cass Pubs) Intl Spec Bk.

Questions & Answers on Immigration in Britain. Farid R. Anthony. LC 97-112132. 163p. 1996. 35.00 (0-7146-4781-0, Pub. by F Cass Pubs) Intl Spec Bk.

Questions & Answers on Practical Endgame Play. Edmar Mednis. 135p. (Orig.). 1987. pap. 7.95 (0-931462-69-X) Chess Ent.

Questions & Answers on Real Estate. 9th ed. Robert W. Semenow. LC 78-4253. 1986. 19.95 (0-13-749218-9, Busn) P-H.

Questions & Answers on Real Estate. 10th ed. Robert W. Semenow. LC 92-37995. 720p. (C). 1993. text 24.95 (0-13-747593-4) P-H.

Questions & Answers on Reincarnation & Karma. Rene Querido. 1977. pap. 5.50 (0-916786-18-8, Saint George Pubns) R Steiner Col.

Questions & Answers on Spiritual Gifts. Howard Carter. 1997. pap. text 9.99 (1-57794-065-2) Harrison Hse.

Questions & Answers on the Bible. Corinne Heline. 96p. (Orig.). 1992. pap. 14.00 (0-933963-21-1) New Age Bible.

Questions & Answers on the Federal Reserve. 1996. lib. bdg. 250.95 (0-8490-8436-9) Gordon Pr.

***Questions & Answers to Help You Pass the Real Estate Appraisal Exams.** 3rd ed. Jeffrey D. Fisher & Dennis S. Tosh. LC 00-44558. 2000. write for info. (0-7931-3656-3, Real Estate Ed) Dearborn.

Questions & Answers to Help You Pass the Real Estate Exam. 5th ed. John W. Reilly & Paige B. Vitousek. LC 96-8013. 1996. pap. 27.95 (*0-7931-1505-1*, 1970-0405, Real Estate Ed) Dearborn.

***Questions & Answers to Help You Pass the Real Estate Exam.** 6th ed. John W. Reilly & Paige Bovee Vitousek. LC 00-27969. 2000. pap. 27.95 (*0-7931-3582-6*) Dearborn.

Questions & Answers to the Six Parts of Luther's Small Catechism. 2nd ed. Wilhelm Loehe. Tr. by Edward T. Horn from GER. 198p. (YA). 1998. reprint ed. 25.00 (*1-891469-14-2*) Repristination.

Questions & Information Systems. Ed. by Thomas Lauer et al. 376p. 1992. pap. 45.00 (*0-8058-1019-6*); text 69.95 (*0-8058-1018-8*) L Erlbaum Assocs.

Questions & Politeness: Strategies in Social Interaction. Esther N. Goody. LC 77-86577. (Cambridge Papers in Social Anthropology: No. 8). 332p. reprint ed. pap. 94.70 (*0-608-12079-0*, 2024576) Bks Demand.

Questions & Problems in Auditing. F. Neumann. 484p. 1998. spiral bd. 33.80 (*0-87563-774-4*) Stipes.

Questions & Questioning. Ed. by Michel Meyer. (Foundations of Communication & Cognition Ser.). vi, 392p. (C). 1988. lib. bdg. 129.25 (*3-11-010680-9*) De Gruyter.

Questions & Stars: How to Get a Child to Read Thirty-Seven Good Books. Tom Shuford. (Illus.). 408p. (Orig.). 1989. pap. 12.95 (*0-9622339-1-9*) Questions Stars.

Questions & Their Retinue. Hatif Janabi. Tr. by Khaled Mattawa from ARA. LC 96-12896. (C). 1996. pap. 14.00 (*1-55728-432-6*) U of Ark Pr.

Questions & Their Retinue. Hatif Janabi. Tr. by Khaled Mattawa from ARA. LC 96-12896. (C). 1996. 24.00 (*1-55728-431-8*) U of Ark Pr.

Questions & Uncertainties in Prostate Cancer. Ed. by W. B. Peeling. 320p. 1996. pap. 79.95 (*0-86542-965-0*) Blackwell Sci.

Questions at Issue. Edmund W. Gosse. LC 72-3465. (Essay Index Reprint Ser.). 1977. reprint ed. 20.95 (*0-8369-2902-0*) Ayer.

Questions Behind the Answers: A Sampler in the Philosophy. Ed. by Donald R. Gregory et al. LC 80-1373. 164p. (C). 1983. pap. text 17.00 (*0-8191-2704-3*) U Pr of Amer.

Questions Book for Marriage Intimacy. Dennis Rainey & Barbara Rainey. 80p. reprint ed. 9.95 (*0-9619022-0-5*) Family Ministry.

Questions Book for Marriage Intimacy. 3rd ed. Dennis Rainey & Barbara Rainey. Ed. by Julie Denker. (Illus.). 84p. pap. text 9.95 (*1-57229-001-3*) FamilyLife.

Questions Cartesiennes. Marion. LC 98-38335. 1999. lib. bdg. 62.00 (*0-226-50542-1*) U Ch Pr.

Questions Catechists Ask: And Answers That Really Work. Carl J. Pfeifer & Janaan Manternach. 118p. (Orig.). 1993. pap. 6.95 (*1-55612-620-4*) Sheed & Ward WI.

Questions Catholics Ask. enl. rev. ed. Bill O'Shea. 344p. 1991. reprint ed. 12.95 (*0-85924-909-3*) Harper SF.

Questions Children Ask see Child Horizons

Questions Children Ask: How to Answer Them. Miriam Stoppard. LC 96-33599. 96p. 1997. pap. 14.95 (*0-7894-1471-6*) DK Pub Inc.

Questions Concerning the Law of Nature. John Locke. Ed. by Diskin Clay et al. Tr. by Jenny S. Clay. LC 89-46178. (Illus.). 256p. 1990. text 39.95 (*0-8014-2348-1*) Cornell U Pr.

Questions Couples Ask: Answers to the Top 100 Marital Questions. Leslie Parrott. 320p. 1996. pap. 12.99 (*0-310-20754-1*) Zondervan.

Questions de Litterature: Etudes Valeryennes et Autres. Hytier. 23.50 (*0-685-36629-4*) Fr & Eur.

Questions de Methode. Jean-Paul Sartre. (FRE.). pap. 3.95 (*0-685-36565-4*) Fr & Eur.

Questions de Methode. Jean-Paul Sartre. (FRE.). 1986. pap. 16.95 (*0-7859-2936-3*) Fr & Eur.

Questions de Methode. Jean-Paul Sartre. (Tel Ser.). (FRE.). 164p. 1986. pap. 13.95 (*2-07-070767-9*) Schoenhof.

Questions de Principe, Vol. 2. B. H. Levy. 1986. pap. 18.95 (*0-7859-3133-3*) Fr & Eur.

Questions de Principe Vol. 3: La Suite dans les Idees. B. H. Levy. (FRE.). 1990. pap. 18.95 (*0-7859-3156-2*, 2253054321) Fr & Eur.

Questions de Principe Vol. 4: Idees Fixes. B. H. Levy. (FRE.). 1992. pap. 22.95 (*0-7859-3172-4*, 2253061743) Fr & Eur.

Questions for Bible Contests see Esgrima Biblica

Questions for Ecclesiastes: Poems. Mark Jarman. LC 96-35008. 102p. 1997. 28.00 (*1-885266-42-1*); pap. 12.95 (*1-885266-41-3*) Story Line.

Questions for Freud: The Secret History of Psychoanalysis. Nicholas Rand. LC 97-15084. 240p. 1997. 24.95 (*0-674-74325-3*) HUP.

***Questions for Freud: The Secret History of Psychoanalysis.** Nicholas Rand. 256p. 2000. pap. 16.95 (*0-674-00421-3*) HUP.

Questions for God. LeRoy Lawson. 146p. (C). 1990. pap. 6.99 (*0-89900-414-8*) College Pr Pub.

Questions for Jehovah's Witnesses. William Cetnar. 1983. pap. 7.99 (*0-685-73959-7*) Chr Lit.

Questions for Jehovah's Witnesses. William Cetnar & Jean Cetnar. 1983. pap. 5.99 (*0-87552-162-2*) P & R Pubng.

***Questions for My Father.** Vincent Staniforth. 112p. 2000. 6.98 (*1-56731-375-2*, MJF Bks) Fine Comms.

Questions for My Father: Finding the Man Behind Your Dad. Vincent Staniforth. LC 97-49136. (Illus.). 112p. 1998. 15.00 (*1-885223-74-9*) Beyond Words Pub.

Questions for Saints to Ponder. Robert Whitelaw. pap. 1.49 (*0-87377-109-5*) GAM Pubns.

Questions for the Movie Answer Man. Roger Ebert. LC 97-5730. 288p. (Orig.). 1997. pap. 10.95 (*0-8362-2894-4*) Andrews & McMeel.

***Questions for the Soul: An Introduction to Philosophy.** Keith W. Krasemann. 660p. 2000. pap. text 35.00 (*1-58152-084-0*, Copley Custom Pub Grp) Copley Pub.

Questions for the Soul: An Introduction to Philosophy. 2nd rev. ed. Keith W. Krasemann. 570p. (C). 1997. pap. text 29.95 (*0-87411-946-4*) Copley Pub.

Questions for the Twenty-First-Century Church. Ed. by Dennis M. Campbell et al. LC 99-17834. (United Methodism & American Culture Ser.: Vol. 4). 320p. 1999. pap. 19.95 (*0-687-02146-4*) Abingdon.

Questions Frequently Asked about Vocational Education. National Center for Research in Vocational Educati. 33p. 1987. 4.75 (*0-318-23416-5*, SN 57) Ctr Educ Trng Employ.

Questions Frequently Asked Me on Prophecy. Salem Kirban. 88p. 1981. pap. 4.99 (*0-912582-01-4*) Second Comng Inc.

***Questions from Earth, Answers from Heaven: A Psychic Intuitive's Discussion of Life, Death & What Awaits Us Beyond.** Char Margolis & Victoria St. George. 320p. 2000. 6.99 (*0-312-97514-7*, St Martins Paperbacks) St Martin.

Questions from Earth, Answers from Heaven: A Psychic Intuitive's Discussion of Life, Death & What Awaits Us Beyond. 2nd ed. Char Margolis. LC 99-35896. 272p. 1999. text 23.95 (*0-312-24199-2*) St Martin.

Questions from Text of Old Testament. W. Stanley Outlaw. 1977. pap. 4.95 (*0-89265-049-4*) Randall Hse.

Questions from the City, Answers from the Forest: Simple Lessons on Living from a Western Buddhist Monk. Ajahn Sumano Bhikkhu & Jeffrey D. Phillips. LC 99-11828. 224p. 1999. pap. 16.00 (*0-8356-0774-7*, Pub. by Theos Pub Hse) Natl Bk Netwk.

Questions from the Heart: Answers to 100 Questions about Chelation Therapy, a Safe Alternative to Bypas Surgery. Terry Chappell. LC 97-111497. 136p. 1996. pap. text 10.95 (*1-57174-026-0*) Hampton Roads Pub Co.

Questions from the Shadows. Ronald Chalmers. Ed. by Kathleen Iddings. LC 92-61837. 100p. (Orig.). 1992. per. 10.00 (*0-931289-12-2*) San Diego Poet Pr.

Questions from the Text of the New Testament. W. Stanley Outlaw. 36p. 1977. pap. 4.95 (*0-89265-050-8*) Randall Hse.

Questions from Your Cosmic Dance. John Coleman. LC 96-39580. 400p. pap. 12.00 (*1-56838-143-3*) Hazelden.

Questions God Asks, Questions Satan Asks. Douglas J. Rumford. LC 98-6793. 1998. 10.99 (*0-8423-5119-1*) Tyndale Hse.

Questions I Asked My Mother. Di Brandt. 1997. pap. 7.95 (*0-88801-115-6*, Pub. by Turnstone Pr) Genl Dist Srvs.

Questions in Accounting I & II. 7th ed. T. F. Gaffney et al. 616p. 1995. pap. write for info. (*0-409-31093-X*, MICHIE) LEXIS Pub.

Questions in Aesthetic Education. H. B. Redfern. Ed. by Philip Snelders & Colin Wringe. 120p. 1986. pap. text 14.95 (*0-04-370163-9*) Routledge.

Questions in Company Accounting. 6th ed. T. F. Gaffney. 500p. 1994. pap. 55.00 (*0-409-30757-2*, NZ, MICHIE) LEXIS Pub.

Questions in Cost & Management Accounting. P. Anquetil. LC 95-167073. 288p. 1994. pap. write for info. (*0-409-30876-5*, MICHIE) LEXIS Pub.

Questions in Human Anatomy. Whitmore. 1995. mass mkt. 18.00 (*0-7234-2055-6*) Wolfe Pubng AZ.

Questions in Irish History: Ireland 500-1170. Duffy. 1992. pap. text. write for info. (*0-582-09510-7*, Pub. by Addison-Wesley) Longman.

Questions in Irish History: The Normans. Smith. 1992. pap. text. write for info. (*0-582-09509-3*, Pub. by Addison-Wesley) Longman.

Questions in Irish History: Why Remeber the Boyne? Power. 1992. pap. text. write for info. (*0-582-07320-0*, Pub. by Addison-Wesley) Longman.

Questions in Parliament. D. N. Chester & Nona Bowring. LC 74-9164. 335p. 1974. reprint ed. lib. bdg. 69.50 (*0-8371-7614-X*, CHQP, Greenwood Pr) Greenwood.

***Questions in Philsophy.** 3rd ed. Elliot Sober. LC 99-59137. 592p. 2000. 46.67 (*0-13-083537-4*, Prentice Hall) P-H.

Questions in Science & Religious Belief: The Roles of Faith & Science in Answering the Cosmological Problem. G. Tarzella-Nitti. (Philosophy in Science Library: Vol. 5). 256p. 1991. pap. 19.95 (*0-88126-730-9*) Pachart Pub Hse.

Questions Kids Ask God. LC 96-139539. 96p. 1996. 8.99 (*1-56292-069-3*, HB-069) Honor Bks OK.

Questions Kids Wish They Could Ask Their Parents. Zoe Stern & Ellen S. Stern. LC 93-6804. (Illus.). (Orig.). 1993. pap. 7.95 (*0-89087-692-4*) Celestial Arts.

Questions Most Asked about Anxiety & Phobias: A Lively, Down to Earth Guide for Overcoming Panic. J. D. Miller. 166p. (Orig.). 1996. pap. 10.50 (*0-9654873-0-X*) Pretext Pr.

Questions of Belief. T. E. Burke. 121p. (C). 1995. 61.95 (*1-85628-988-5*, Pub. by Avebry) Ashgate Pub Co.

Questions of Cinema. Stephen Heath. LC 81-47524. (Theories of Representation & Difference Ser.). (Illus.). 266p. 1982. pap. 10.95 (*0-253-15914-8*) Ind U Pr.

Questions of Communication. Anderson. LC 97-65198. 348p. 1997. pap. text 51.95 (*0-312-17086-6*) St Martin.

Questions of Competence: Culture, Classification & Intellectual Disability. Ed. by Richard Jenkins. LC 98-3022. 260p. (C). 1999. text 59.95 (*0-521-62303-0*); pap. text 22.95 (*0-521-62662-5*) Cambridge U Pr.

Questions of Conduct: Sexual Harassment, Citizenship, Government. Jeffrey B. Minson. LC 92-30625. 254p. 1993. text 39.95 (*0-312-09121-4*) St Martin.

Questions of Consciousness. Ed. by Anthony P. Cohen & Nigel Rapport. LC 95-15785. (ASA Monographs Ser.: Vol. 33). 256p. (C). 1995. pap. 27.99 (*0-415-12396-8*) Routledge.

Questions of Cultural Identity. Ed. by Stuart Hall & Paul Du Gay. 224p. (C). 1996. 69.95 (*0-8039-7882-0*); pap. 24.95 (*0-8039-7883-9*) Sage.

Questions of Destiny: Mental Retardation & Curative Education. Carlo Pietzner. (Illus.). 60p. (Orig.). 1988. pap. 6.95 (*0-88010-264-0*) Anthroposophic.

Questions of English. Ed. by Fred McDonald & Jeremy Marshall. (Illus.). 208p. 1995. 19.95 (*0-19-869230-7*) OUP.

***Questions of English: Ethics, Aesthetics, Rhetoric & the Formation of the Subject in England, Australia & the United States.** Robin Peel et al. LC 99-36308. 312p. 2000. write for info. (*0-415-19119-X*) Routledge.

Questions of Ethics: To the United States of America for 1992 & Beyond. I. M. James. Ed. by Betty Quigley & Raymond Quigley. 121p. (Orig.). 1992. pap. 5.95 (*0-9626735-5-2*) Rabeth Pub Co.

***Questions of Ethics in Counselling & Therapy.** Caroline Jones. LC 00-35627. 2000. pap. write for info. (*0-335-20611-5*, Pub. by OpUniv Pr) Taylor & Francis.

Questions of Evidence: Proof, Practice, & Persuasion Across the Disciplines. Ed. by James Chandler et al. 528p. 1994. pap. text 19.95 (*0-226-10083-9*); lib. bdg. 45.00 (*0-226-10082-0*) U Ch Pr.

***Questions of Faith: A Workbook Companion to the Catechism of the Catholic Church.** Michael Amodei. 96p. (YA). 2000. pap. 6.95 (*0-87793-689-7*) Ave Maria.

***Questions of Form.** Mickey Cleverdon. (Illus.). 36p. 1999. pap. write for info. (*0-9643940-3-0*) Slow Loris Pr.

Questions of Form & Interpretation. Noam Chomsky. v, 40p. (Orig.). (C). 1975. pap. text 11.55 (*3-11-013282-6*) Mouton.

Questions of Gender: Perspectives & Paradoxes. Dina Anselmi & Anne L. Law. LC 97-31723. 800p. 1997. pap. 36.88 (*0-07-006017-7*) McGraw.

Question of German Unification, 1806-1995. Imanuel Geiss. Tr. by Fred Bridgham. LC 96-52536. 160p. (C). 1997. pap. 16.99 (*0-415-15049-3*) Routledge.

Questions of Heaven: The Chinese Journeys of an American Buddhist. Gretel Ehrlich. (Illus.). 144p. 1998. pap. 12.00 (*0-8070-7311-3*) Beacon Pr.

Questions of Identity. large type ed. Bob Cook. 426p. 1989. 27.99 (*0-7089-1927-8*) Ulverscroft.

Questions of Interest. Yisroel Gornish. LC 92-73909. 136p. 13.95 (*1-56062-174-5*); pap. 10.95 (*1-56062-204-0*) CIS Comm.

Questions of International Law: Hungarian Perspectives, Vol. 4. H. Bokor-Szego. Tr. by Sandor Simon from HUN. 265p. (C). 1988. 78.00 (*963-05-4689-2*, Pub. by Akade Kiado) St Mut.

Questions of International Law: Hungarian Perspectives, Vol. 5. H. Bokor-Szego. 225p. (C). 1991. 100.00 (*963-05-6015-1*, Pub. by Akade Kiado) St Mut.

Questions of Jesus. W. E. McCumber. LC 98-25253. 108p. 1998. 9.99 (*0-8341-1704-5*) Nazarene.

Questions of Jesus. unabridged ed. William S. Deal. 139p. (Orig.). pap. 6.99 (*0-88019-294-1*) Schmul Pub Co.

Questions of Judgment: Determining What's Right. F. H. Low-Beer. LC 95-8726. 217p. 1995. 30.95 (*0-87975-960-7*) Prometheus Bks.

Questions of King Milinda: Abr't of Milindapanha. Ed. by N. K. Mendis. 208p. 1993. 12.00 (*955-24-0067-8*, Pub. by Buddhist Pub Soc) Vipassana Res Pubns.

Questions of Language in African Literature Today. Ed. by Eldred Durosimi et al. LC 91-64141. (African Literature Today Ser.: Vol. 17). 190p. (C). 1991. 45.00 (*0-86543-214-7*); pap. 14.95 (*0-86543-215-5*) Africa World.

Questions of Life: Diary of an Old Physician. Nikolai I. Pirogov. LC 89-24332. (Resources in Medical History Ser.). (Illus.). xxii, 480p. 1992. 29.95 (*0-88135-061-3*, Sci Hist) Watson Pub Intl.

***Questions of Love.** Sharrieff Omar. 72p. 1999. 8.00 (*1-56411-226-8*) Untd Bros & Sis.

Questions of Miracle. Ed. by Robert A. Larmer. LC 97-187330. 184p. (C). 1996. 65.00 (*0-7735-1416-3*); pap. 19.95 (*0-7735-1501-1*, Pub. by McG-Queens Univ Pr) CUP Services.

Questions of Moral Philosophy. Michael Shenefelt. LC 97-24842. 176p. 1998. 45.00 (*0-391-04067-7*); pap. 15.00 (*0-391-04068-5*) Humanities.

Questions of Moral Philosophy. Michael Shenefelt. 176p. 1999. 39.95 (*1-57392-638-8*, Humanity Bks); pap. 19.95 (*1-57392-637-X*, Humanity Bks) Prometheus Bks.

Questions of Right & Wrong: The Proceedings of the 1993 Clinical Bioethics Conference, Canadian Medical Dental Society & Regent College. Ed. by Edwin Hui. 255p. (Orig.). 1995. pap. 10.00 (*1-57383-032-1*) Regent College.

Questions of Special Urgency: The Church in the Modern World Two Decades after Vatican II. Ed. by Judith A. Dwyer. LC 86-218. 251p. (Orig.). reprint ed. pap. 77.90 (*0-7837-6319-0*, 204603400010) Bks Demand.

Questions of the Charismatics. David Gower. 28p. 1981. reprint ed. pap. 2.99 (*0-87227-088-2*, RBP5110) Reg Baptist.

Questions of the Day. John A. Ryan. LC 67-26779. (Essay Index Reprint Ser.). 1977. 23.95 (*0-8369-0846-5*) Ayer.

Questions of the Heart. Stephanie Amos. 1998. pap. 8.95 (*0-533-12767-X*) Vantage.

Questions of the Heart. Edward Chinn. (Orig.). 1987. pap. 6.75 (*0-89536-877-3*, 7863) CSS OH.

Questions of the Soul. Isaac T. Hecker. 1978. 26.95 (*0-405-10834-6*, 11840) Ayer.

Questions of Third Cinema. Ed. by Jim Pines & Paul Willemen. (Illus.). 256p. 1990. 29.95 (*0-85170-262-7*, Pub. by British Film Inst); pap. 14.95 (*0-85170-230-9*, Pub. by British Film Inst) Ind U Pr.

Questions of Time & Tense. Ed. by Robin Le Poidevin. LC 98-28486. 306p. 1998. text 65.00 (*0-19-823695-6*) OUP.

Questions of Tragedy. Arthur B. Coffin. LC 91-45037. 340p. 1992. lib. bdg. 34.95 (*0-7734-9903-2*) E Mellen.

Questions of Travel: Postmodern Discourses of Displacement. Caren Kaplan. LC 96-79. (Post-Contemporary Interventions Ser.). 256p. 1996. text 49.95 (*0-8223-1828-8*); pap. text 16.95 (*0-8223-1821-0*) Duke.

Questions of Uniqueness & Resolution in Reconstruction of 2-D & 3-D Objects from Their Projections. M. B. Katz. (Lecture Notes in Biomathematics Ser.: Vol. 26). 1978. 33.00 (*0-387-09087-8*) Spr-Verlag.

Questions of Uniqueness, Stability, & Transient Behaviour see Mathematical Theory of Diffusion & Reaction in Permeable Catalysts

***Questions of You & the Struggle of Collaborative Life.** Nicholas Paley & Janice Jipson. LC 98-30630. (Counterpoints: Vol. 104). 190p. 2000. pap. text 29.95 (*0-8204-4251-8*) P Lang Pubng.

Questions Often Asked about Focusing & Spirituality. Edwin M. McMahon & Peter A. Campbell. 12p. 1996. pap. text 1.25 (*1-55612-503-8*, LL1503) Sheed & Ward WI.

Questions on an Ethics of Divine Commands. Andrew of Neuchateau. Ed. & Tr. by Janine M. Idziak from LAT. LC 96-26435. (Texts in Medieval Culture Ser.: Vol. 3). Orig. Title: Primum Scriptum Sententiarum. 208p. (C). 1997. text 30.00 (*0-268-03977-1*) U of Notre Dame Pr.

Questions on Banking Practice. 11th ed. Ed. by Institute of Bankers Staff. 1978. 85.00 (*0-85297-045-5*, Pub. by Chartered Bank) St Mut.

Questions on Christian Faith. Constancio Amen. 1988. pap. 7.95 (*0-9618383-2-9*) GN Inc.

Questions on Dressage. Leonie Marshall. 1990. pap. 40.00 (*0-85131-474-0*, Pub. by J A Allen) St Mut.

Questions on Dressage. Leonie Marshall. 1996. pap. 40.00 (*0-85131-632-8*, Pub. by J A Allen) Trafalgar.

Questions on Financial Management in Australia. V. L. Gale. 1983. pap. 30.00 (*0-409-49127-6*, AT, MICHIE) LEXIS Pub.

Questions on International Law-Hungarian Perspectives. Ed. by Hanna Bokor-Szego. 1987. lib. bdg. 99.00 (*90-247-3293-X*) Kluwer Academic.

Questions on Management Accounting. R. Craig & M. Tippett. 1984. pap. 63.00 (*0-409-49252-3*, AT, MICHIE) LEXIS Pub.

Questions on Social Explanation: Piagetian Themes Reconsidered. Ed. by Luigia Camaioni & Claudia De Lemos. LC 85-26727. (Pragmatics & Beyond Ser.: VI-4). viii, 141p. (Orig.). 1986. pap. 49.00 (*0-915027-66-6*) J Benjamins Pubng Co.

Questions on the Christian Faith. Derek Prime. Date not set. 6.99 (*1-871676-82-7*, Pub. by Christian Focus) Spring Arbor Dist.

Questions on the De Anima of Aristotle. Adam Burley et al. (Studien und Texte zur Geistesgeschichte des Mittelalters). (ENG & LAT.). lxiv, 179p. 1996. 97.00 (*90-04-10655-3*) Brill Academic Pubs.

Questions on the Law & Practice of Company Accounting. 4th ed. R. B. Taylor & B. P. O'Shea. 1987. pap. 42.00 (*0-409-49206-X*, AT, MICHIE) LEXIS Pub.

Questions on the Metaphysics of Aristotle by John Duns Scotus. Girard Etzkorn & Allan Wolter. (Text Ser.: No. 19, Vol. 1). 586p. 1998. pap. 50.00 (*1-57659-160-3*) Franciscan Inst.

Questions on the Metaphysics of Aristotle by John Duns Scotus. Girard Etzkorn & Allan Wolter. (Text Ser.: No. 19, Vol. 2). 625p. 1998. pap. 50.00 (*1-57659-161-1*) Franciscan Inst.

Questions on the Soul. Aquinas, Thomas, Saint. Tr. by James H. Robb. LC 84-61636. (Medieval Philosophical Texts in Translation Ser.). 1984. 25.00 (*0-87462-226-3*) Marquette.

Questions on the Way: A Catechism Based on the Book of Common Prayer. 3rd rev. ed. Beverley D. Tucker & William H. Swatos, Jr. 128p. (Orig.). 1995. pap. 3.95 (*0-88028-164-2*, 887) Forward Movement.

Questions on Wittgenstein. Rudolf Haller. LC 88-4718. x, 149p. 1988. pap. text 15.00 (*0-8032-7240-5*, Bison Books) U of Nebr Pr.

Questions Parents Ask about Discipline see Preguntas Que Hacen, Padres Sobre la Disciplina

Questions Parents of Infants Ask. WFD, Inc. Staff. 32p. 1991. pap. 10.00 (*1-58373-002-8*) Ceridian Inc.

Questions Parents of Preschoolers Ask. WFD, Inc. Staff. 32p. 1991. pap. 10.00 (*1-58373-004-4*) Ceridian Inc.

Questions Parents of Preteens Ask. WFD, Inc. Staff. (Illus.). 32p. 1991. pap. 10.00 (*1-58373-006-0*) Ceridian Inc.

Questions Parents of Teenagers Ask. WFD, Inc. Staff. 64p. 1998. pap. 10.00 (*1-58373-007-9*) Ceridian Inc.

Questions Parents of Toddlers Ask. WFD, Inc. Staff. 32p. 1991. pap. 10.00 (*1-58373-003-6*) Ceridian Inc.

Questions Parents of Young School-Age Children Ask. WFD, Inc. Staff. 32p. 1991. pap. 10.00 (*1-58373-005-2*) Ceridian Inc.

Questions Pentecostals Ask. David F. Gray. LC 86-26784. 304p. (Orig.). 1986. pap. 8.99 (*0-932581-07-2*) Word Aflame.

Questions Pentecostals Ask, Vol. 2. David Gray. LC 86-26784. 350p. (Orig.). 1992. pap. 8.99 (*0-932581-96-X*) Word Aflame.

Questions Pentecostals Ask, Vol. 3. David Gray. LC 86-26784. 350p. (Orig.). 1993. pap. 8.99 (*0-932581-97-8*) Word Aflame.

Questions People & Churches Ask. rev. ed. Charles Brock. 228p. 1997. pap. 10.00 (*1-885504-43-8*) Church Gwth.

Questions Quakers Are Asking. Seth B. Hinshaw. 59p. (Orig.). 1982. pap. 1.50 (*0-942727-09-6*) NC Yrly Pubns Bd.

Questions, Queries, & Facts: A Semantics & Pragmatics for Interrogatives. Jonathan Ginzburg. (CSLI Lecture Notes Ser.). 300p. (C). 1997. text 49.95 (*1-881526-70-4*); pap. text 22.95 (*1-881526-71-2*) Cambridge U Pr.

Q

An Asterisk (*) at the beginning of an entry indicates that the title is appearing for the first time.

Questions, Questioning Techniques, & Effective Teaching. Ed. by William W. Wilen. 200p. 1987. pap. 16.95 (*0-8106-1485-5*) NEA.

Questions, Questions: A Comprehensive Listing of Frequently Asked Technical & Human Resource Questions Used by Major, National & Regional Airlines. Kit Darby. Ed. by Becky Dean & Montina L. Waymire. 96p. 1998. pap. 28.95 (*1-891726-04-8*) Aviation Info.

Questions! Questions! Questions!!! Ginger Wilson. Ed. by Cheryle Sytsma. LC 90-63620. (Illus.). 30p. (Orig.). (J). (gr. k-5). 1991. pap. write for info. (*1-879068-04-4*) Ray-Ma Natsal.

Questions, Short Poems, Water & Air. Ira B. Brukner. LC 98-65855. 78p. (Orig.). pap. 11.00 (*1-881523-08-X*) Junction CA.

Questions Teens Are Asking Today. Theodore W. Schroeder & Dean Nadasdy. 160p. 1987. pap. 7.99 (*0-570-04454-5*, 12-3062) Concordia.

Questions That Challenge the Curious Mind: A Sure-Fire Cure for Boredom. Abne M. Eisenberg. LC 94-71539. (Illus.). 80p. (Orig.). (C). 1994. pap. 13.95 (*0-9641764-0-8*) Astik Pubng.

Questions That Count: British Literature to 1750. J. David Williams. LC 82-15893. 98p. (Orig.). 1983. pap. text 8.50 (*0-8191-2743-4*) U Pr of Amer.

Questions That Demand Answers. Thomas A. Davis. 160p. (Orig.). 1988. pap. 6.95 (*0-923309-10-1*) Hartland Pubns.

Questions That Make the Sale. William Bethel. 196p. 1992. pap. 21.95 (*0-85013-196-0*, TE7608) Dartnell Corp.

Questions That Matter: An Introduction to Philosophy. 4th ed. Ed L. Miller. LC 95-35987. 624p. (C). 1995. 50.94 (*0-07-042836-0*) McGraw.

Questions That Matter: Shorte: An Introduction to Philosophy. 2nd ed. Ed L. Miller. LC 97-1299. 480p. 1997. pap. 33.13 (*0-07-042264-8*) McGraw.

Questions That Refuse to Go Away: Peace & Justice in North America. Marian Franz. Ed. by Michael A. King. LC 91-10197. (Peace & Justice Ser.: Vol. 13). 104p. (Orig.). 1991. pap. 6.99 (*0-8361-3558-X*) Herald Pr.

***Questions That Work: How to Ask Questions That Will Help You Succeed in Any Business Situation.** Andrew Finlayson. 2000. pap. 17.95 (*0-8144-7077-7*) AMACOM.

Questions This Modern Age Puts to Islam. M. Fethullah Gulen.Tr. of Asrin Getirdigi Tereddutler. 250p. 1993. pap. 8.95 (*0-9521497-1-0*) Fountain Pub.

Questions Through Pictures. Harris Winitz. (Language Through Pictures Ser.). (Illus.). 100p. (YA). (gr. 2-12). 1982. pap. 5.00 (*0-939990-33-4*) Intl Linguistics.

Questions to Ask Your Mormon Friend: Effective Ways to Challenge a Mormon's Arguments Without. Bill McKeever & E. Johnson. LC 94-16696. 192p. 1994. pap. 9.99 (*1-55661-455-1*) Bethany Hse.

Questions to the Universe: Ten Lectures on the Foundations of Physics & Cosmology. M. Heller. (Astronomy & Astrophysics Ser.: Vol. 14). 1986. pap. 38.00 (*0-88126-008-8*) Pachart Pub Hse.

Questions Women Ask in Private see Preguntas Que las Mujeres Hacen en Privado

Questions Women Ask in Private see Preguntas Mujeres Hacen en Privado

Questions You've Asked about Bible Translations. Jack P. Lewis. 423p. (Orig.). 1991. 15.95 (*0-945441-04-5*) Res Pubns AR.

Questor Tapes. D. C. Fontana. 1976. reprint ed. lib. bdg. 20.95 (*0-88411-091-5*) Amereon Ltd.

Quests. Grampa Gray. 48p. 1996. pap. 7.50 (*1-885631-21-9*, 21-9) G F Hutchison.

Quests: Journeys of Discovery. Thomas J. Tansey. LC 94-4410. 568p. 1994. 24.95 (*1-56825-015-0*) Rainbow Books.

Quests & Quandaries: A Human Development Workbook. Ed. by Carol W. Hotchkiss. (Illus.). 247p. (Orig.). 1993. pap. 27.95 (*0-9627671-4-X*) Avocus Pub.

Quests & Spells: Fairy Tales from the European Oral Tradition. Judy Sierra. LC 94-22003. 186p. (Orig.). (J). (gr. 4-12). 1994. pap. 12.95 (*0-9636089-2-4*, Q&S) Folkprint.

Quest's End, 4. Richard Pini. (Elfquest Reader's Collection: Vol. 4). 1999. pap. text 11.95 (*0-936861-58-4*, Pub. by Warp Graphics) Midpt Trade.

Quests for a Promised Land: The Works of Martin Andersen Nexo, 8. Faith Ingwersen & Niels Ingwersen. LC 84-8916. (Contributions to the Study of World Literature Ser.: No. 8). 156p. 1985. 45.00 (*0-313-24469-3*, IAT/, Greenwood Pr) Greenwood.

Quests of Difference: Reading Pope's Poems. G. Douglas Atkins. LC 85-20228. 208p. 1986. 25.00 (*0-8131-1565-5*) U Pr of Ky.

Quests of the Russian Intelligence. Jutta Scherrer. (C). 1996. text 36.00 (*0-8133-8407-9*) Westview.

Quests Old & New. G. R. Mead. 338p. 1992. reprint ed. pap. 29.95 (*0-922802-79-3*) Kessinger Pub.

Quete du Ble. Venance Dougados. Ed. by Remy Cazals. (Exeter French Texts Ser.: Vol. CI). (FRE.). 80p. 1997. pap. 21.95 (*0-85989-535-1*, Pub. by Univ Exeter Pr) Northwestern U Pr.

Quetes. Ed. by F. Caccia & A. D'Alfonso. (FRE.). 283p. 1982. pap. write for info. (*2-89135-006-5*) Guernica Editions.

Quetico Wolf. Rae Oetting. LC 71-190274. (Illus.). 48p. (J). (gr. 4 up). 1972. lib. bdg. 9.95 (*0-87783-059-2*) Oddo.

Quetico Wolf. deluxe ed. Rae Oetting. LC 71-190274. (Illus.). 48p. (J). (gr. 4 up). 1972. pap. 3.94 (*0-87783-103-3*) Oddo.

Quetzal: Sacred Bird of the Forest. Dorothy H. Patent. LC 95-14402. (Illus.). 40p. (J). 1996. 16.00 (*0-688-12662-6*, Wm Morrow); lib. bdg. 15.93 (*0-688-12663-4*, Wm Morrow) Morrow Avon.

***Quetzal & the Cool School.** Bendix Anderson. (Dragon Tales Ser.). (Illus.). 24p. (J). (ps-k). 2000. pap. 3.25 (*0-375-80634-2*, Pub. by Random Bks Yng Read) Random.

Quetzal in Flight: Guatemalan Immigrant Families in the United States. Norita Vlach. LC 91-36410. 200p. 1992. 49.95 (*0-275-93979-0*, C3979, Praeger Pubs) Greenwood.

Quetzalcoatl. Ernesto Cardenal. Tr. & Intro. by Clifton Ross. (Illus.). 59p. 1992. pap. 9.95 (*0-915117-38-X*) Freedom Voices Pubns.

Quetzalcoatl. D. H. Lawrence. Ed. & Intro. by Louis L. Martz. LC 98-14094. 358p. 1998. pap. 14.95 (*0-8112-1385-4*, NDP864, Pub. by New Directions) Norton.

Quetzalcoatl: Serpiente Emplumada (Plumed Serpent) Roman P. Chan. (SPA., Illus.). 75p. 1992. reprint ed. pap. 8.99 (*968-16-0820-8*, Pub. by Fondo) Continental Bk.

Quetzalcoatl & Guadalupe: The Formation of Mexican National Consciousness, 1531-1813. Jacques Lafaye. Tr. by Benjamin Keen from FRE. LC 75-20889. 1976. lib. bdg. 26.00 (*0-226-46794-5*) U Ch Pr.

Quetzalcoatl & Guadalupe: The Formation of Mexican National Consciousness, 1531-1813. Jacques Lafaye. Tr. by Benjamin Keen. LC 75-20889. xxx, 366p. (C). 1987. pap. text 18.00 (*0-226-46788-0*) U Ch Pr.

Quetzalcoatl & the Irony of Empire. David Carrasco. xii, 248p. 1998. pap. text 16.95 (*0-226-09490-1*) U Ch Pr.

Quetzalcoatl & the Irony of Empire: Myths & Prophecies in the Aztec Tradition. David Carrasco. LC 91-46792. (Illus.). 247p. reprint ed. pap. 76.60 (*0-608-09013-1*, 206964800005) Bks Demand.

***Quetzalcoatl & the Irony of Empire: Myths & Prophecies in the Aztec Tradition.** rev. ed. David L. Carrasco. (Illus.). 287p. 2001. pap. 24.95 (*0-87081-558-X*) U of Okla Pr.

Quetzalcoatl Legends from Mexico & Central America Set: Picture Books & Teacher's Guides, 9 bks., Set. Illus. by Lynn Castle. (ENG & SPA.). (J). (gr. k-5). 75.99 (*1-56417-771-8*, FE0059) Fearon Teacher Aids.

Quetzalcoatl Tale of Chocolate: Picture Book. Illus. by Lynn Castle. (SPA.). 48p. (J). (gr. k-5). 8.99 (*0-86653-958-1*, FE0958) Fearon Teacher Aids.

Quetzalcoatl Tale of Corn. Marilyn Parke & Sharon Panik. (SPA.). 1992. pap. 8.99 (*0-86653-964-6*) Fearon Teacher Aids.

Quetzalcoatl Tale of the Ball Game. Illus. by Lynn Castle. (SPA.). 48p. (J). (gr. k-5). 8.99 (*0-86653-961-1*, FE0961) Good Apple.

Quetzalcoatl Tale of the Ball Game - Teachers Guide. Marilyn Parke & Sharon Panik. 1992. pap. 8.99 (*0-86653-960-3*) Fearon Teacher Aids.

Quetzalcoatl y Guadalupe (Quetzalcoatl & Guadalupe) 2nd ed. Jacques Lafaye. (SPA.). 485p. 1992. pap. 14.99 (*968-16-1444-5*, Pub. by Fondo) Continental Bk.

Queueing: Basic Theory & Application. Walter C. Giffen. LC 76-44996. (Grid Industrial Engineering Ser.). 370p. (C). reprint ed. 114.70 (*0-8357-9144-0*, 201524400093) Bks Demand.

Queueing Analysis, 3 vols. H. Takagi. 442.75 (*0-444-81770-0*, North Holland) Elsevier.

Queueing Analysis: The Pseudo State Model. Donald J. Enright. LC 95-78669. (Illus.). 300p. (C). 1996. 47.00 (*0-9646716-0-3*) Tex Queueing Soft.

Queueing Analysis Vol. 1: A Foundation of Performance Evaluation: Vacation & Priority Systems, Pt. 1. Hideaki Takagi. 488p. 1991. 147.00 (*0-444-88910-8*, North Holland) Elsevier.

Queueing Analysis Vol. 2: Finite Systems. H. Takagi. 560p. 1993. 211.25 (*0-444-81614-3*, North Holland) Elsevier.

Queueing Analysis Vol. 3: Discrete-Time Systems. H. Takagi. 484p. 1993. 190.75 (*0-444-81611-9*, North Holland) Elsevier.

Queueing Methods: For Services & Manufacturing. Randolph W. Hall. 528p. (C). 1990. text 64.60 (*0-13-744756-6*) P-H.

Queueing Modelling Fundamentals. Chee H. Ng. LC 96-2146. 234p. 1997. 94.95 (*0-471-96819-6*) Wiley.

***Queueing Networks: Customers, Signals & Product form Solutions.** Xiuli Chao. LC 99-26511. 458p. 1999. 135.00 (*0-471-98309-8*) Wiley.

Queueing Networks & Markov Chains: Modeling & Performance Evaluation with Computer Science Applications. Gunter Bolch et al. LC 98-11959. 744p. 1998. 98.95 (*0-471-19366-6*) Wiley.

Queueing Studies. 2nd ed. Ed. by James King & Clifford Sloyer. (Math Text Ser.). (Illus.). 34p. 1992. text 11.00 (*1-881821-03-X*) Water St Math.

Queueing Systems, 2 vols. Incl. Vol. 1, Theory. Theory. Leonard Kleinrock. LC 44-9846. 448p. 1975. 98.95 (*0-471-49110-1*); Vol. 2, Computer Applications. Computer Applications. Ed. by Leonard Kleinrock. LC 44-9846. 576p. 1976. 125.00 (*0-471-49111-X*); LC 44-9846. 417p. 1976. write for info. (*0-318-56446-7*) Wiley.

Queueing Systems: Problems & Solutions. Leonard Kleinrock & Richard Gail. LC 95-48333. 240p. 1996. pap. 48.95 (*0-471-55568-1*) Wiley.

Queueing Systems Vol. 2: Computer Applications, Solution Manual. Leonard Kleinrock & Richard Gail. 299p. 1991. pap., suppl. ed. 58.50 (*0-471-55598-3*) Wiley.

Queues: Will This Wait Never End! Clifford Sloyer et al. (Contemporary Applied Mathematics Ser.). (Illus.). 42p. (Orig.). (YA). (gr. 9 up). 1987. pap. text 11.95 (*0-939765-08-X*, G105) Janson Pubns.

Queuing & Related Models. Ed. by Ramdas B. Bhat & Ishwarasa V. Basawa. (Oxford Statistical Science Ser.). (Illus.). 366p. 1992. text 95.00 (*0-19-852233-9*) OUP.

Queuing & Waiting: Studies in the Social Organization of Access & Delay. Barry Schwartz. LC 75-11607. (Illus.). vi, 232p. 1997. lib. bdg. 14.50 (*0-226-74210-5*) U Ch Pr.

***Queuing for Everest.** Judith Adams. (Illus.). 2000. pap. 14.95 (*1-84002-154-3*) Theatre Comm.

Queuing for Housing: A Study of Council Housing Waiting Lists. Patricia Prescott-Clarke et al. LC 88-179541. 166p. 1988. 25.00 (*0-11-752077-2*, Pub. by Statnry Office) Bernan Associates.

Queuing Networks with Blocking: Exact & Approximate Solutions. Harry G. Perros. (Illus.). 304p. 1994. text 75.00 (*0-19-508580-9*) OUP.

Queuing Theory. 3rd ed. Arnold O. Allen. 300p. 1998. write for info. (*0-12-051055-3*) Acad Pr.

Quevedo & the Grotesque, Vol. II. James Iffland. (Monagrafias A Ser.: Vol. 92). 283p. 1982. 58.00 (*0-7293-0140-0*, Pub. by Tamesis Bks Ltd) Boydell & Brewer.

Quevedo, Hombre y Escritor en Conflicto Con su Epoca. Ella R. Gomez-Quintero. LC 77-88534. 1978. pap. 10.00 (*0-89729-181-6*) Ediciones.

Quevedo in Perspective: Eleven Essays for the Quadricentennial. James Iffland. 273p. 1982. 21.75 (*0-936388-17-X*); pap. 15.75 (*0-936388-18-8*) Juan de la Cuesta.

Qui a Casse la Vase Se Soisons?, Tome I. Gaston Bonheur. (FRE.). 1976. pap. 11.95 (*0-7859-1814-0*, 2070367290) Fr & Eur.

Qui a Casse la Vasse de Soisons?, Tome II. Gaston Bonheur. (FRE.). 1976. pap. 11.95 (*0-7859-1815-9*, 2070367304) Fr & Eur.

Qui a Peur des Fantomes? Sylvie Desrosiers. (Novels in the Roman Jeunesse Ser.). (FRE.). 96p. (J). (gr. 4-7). 1988. pap. 8.95 (*2-89021-073-1*, Pub. by La Courte Ech) Firefly Bks Ltd.

Qui Dort Dine. Jim Davis. (Garfield Ser.). (FRE.). (J). 1988. 18.95 (*0-8288-4588-3*) Fr & Eur.

***Qui Est-Je? Vol. 244: L'ecriture Autobiographique des Nouveaux Romanciers.** Jeanette M. Toonder. (FRE.). vii, 244p. 1999. 37.95 (*3-906762-47-5*) P Lang Pubng.

Qui J'Ose Aimer. Herve Bazin. (FRE.). 1979. pap. 10.95 (*0-7859-3074-4*) Fr & Eur.

Qui Miscuit Utile Dulci: Fetschrift Essays for Paul Lachlan MacKendrick. Paul L. Mackendrick. Ed. by Gareth L. Schmeling & Jon D. Mikalson. LC 97-32620. xvi, 400p. 1997. pap. 50.00 (*0-86516-406-1*) Bolchazy-Carducci.

Qui Ne Souffre Pas. Rene Descartes. Tr. by Jean Sirvan from LAT. (FRE.). 152p. 1990. 13.95 (*0-7859-1215-0*, 271160182X) Fr & Eur.

Qui Parle Play & Poems. Kenneth Bernard. 160p. 1999. pap. 12.00 (*1-878580-64-7*) Asylum Arts.

***Qui Pluribus: On Faith & Religion.** Piux IX. Tr. by Padraig M. O'Cleirigh. 22p. 1998. reprint ed. pap. 3.25 (*0-935952-61-6*) Angelus Pr.

Qui Tam: Beyond Government Contracts. (Litigation & Administrative Practice Course Handbook, 1983-84 Ser.: Vol. 456). 596p. 1993. 70.00 (*0-685-65530-X*, H4-5154) PLI.

Qui Tam Litigation under the False Claims Act: Practice & Procedure. LC 95-106734. 180p. 1994. pap. 40.00 (*1-57073-041-5*, 539-0134, ABA Pub Contract) Amer Bar Assn.

Quiche Before Dying. Jill Churchill. LC 92-90438. (Jane Jeffry Mystery Ser.). 192p. 1993. mass mkt. 5.99 (*0-380-76932-8*, Avon Bks) Morrow Avon.

Quiche' Dramas & Divinatory Calendars. Tr. by Munro S. Edmonson from MYN. LC 97-18706. (Publication Ser.: No. 66). 1997. write for info. (*0-939238-96-9*) Tulane MARI.

Quiche-English Dictionary. Munro S. Edmonson. (Publications: No. 30). 168p. 1976. reprint ed. 17.50 (*0-939238-33-0*) Tulane MARI.

Quiche Quiche Quiche. Connie Newton. 36p. (Orig.). 1983. pap. 3.25 (*0-940844-15-X*) Wellspring.

Quiche Vinak: (Indigenous Legends) Anita P. Guerchoux & Manuel Vasquez-Bigi. (SPA.). 303p. 1991. pap. 9.99 (*968-16-3472-1*, Pub. by Fondo) Continental Bk.

Quiche Worlds in Creation: The Popol Vuh As a Narrative Work of Art. Jack J. Himelblau. LC 88-82907. 144p. (Orig.). 1989. pap. text 20.00 (*0-911437-27-4*) Labyrinthos.

Quiches & Flans. (Mini Cook Bks.). (Illus.). 64p. 1999. pap. 1.95 (*3-8290-1597-6*) Konemann.

Quick. Burt Cole. 304p. 1991. mass mkt. 3.99 (*0-380-71178-8*, Avon Bks) Morrow Avon.

***Quick Access: Reference For Writers.** Lynn Quitman Troyka & Cy Strom. 384p. 1999. pap. 35.93 (*0-13-021492-2*) P-H.

Quick Access: Reference for Writers. 2nd ed. Lynn Quitman Troyka. 360p. 1998. pap. text 33.40 (*0-13-096596-0*) P-H.

***Quick Access Reference for Writers.** 3rd ed. Lynn Quitman Troyka. 496p. 2000. spiral bd. 28.00 (*0-13-022562-2*) P-H.

***Quick Access Consumer Guide to Conditions, Herbs & Supplements.** Integrative Medicine Staff. 1999. pap. text 24.95 (*0-9670772-6-5*) Integratv Med Commn.

***Quick Access Patient Information: On Conditions, Herbs & Supplements.** Integrative Medicine Staff. 1999. pap. text 49.95 (*0-9670772-8-1*) Integratv Med Commn.

***Quick Access Professional Guide to Conditions, Herbs & Supplements.** Integrative Medicine Staff. 1999. 49.95 (*0-9670772-5-7*) Integratv Med Commn.

***Quick Activities to Build a Very Voluminous Vocabulary.** Leann Nickelsen. 64p. (J). 1998. pap. 9.95 (*0-590-22179-5*) Scholastic Inc.

Quick After-Work Chinese Cookbook. Kit Chan. 137p. 1999. 21.00 (*0-7499-1797-0*, Pub. by Piatkus Bks) London Brdge.

Quick After-Work Curries. Pat Chapman. LC 96-23135. (Quick After-Work Ser.). (Illus.). 128p. (Orig.). 1996. reprint ed. pap. 12.95 (*1-55561-108-7*) Fisher Bks.

Quick After-Work Dinner Parties. Hilaire Walden. 1998. pap. text 12.95 (*0-7499-1724-5*, Pub. by Piatkus Bks) London Brdge.

Quick After-Work Indian Vegetarian Cookbook. Kumud Shah. 1997. text 12.95 (*0-7499-1778-4*, Pub. by Piatkus Bks) London Brdge.

Quick After-Work Italian Cookbook. Hilaire Walden. LC 96-23901. (Quick After-Work Ser.). (Illus.). 144p. (Orig.). 1996. reprint ed. pap. 12.95 (*1-55561-109-5*) Fisher Bks.

Quick After-Work Low-Fat Cookbook. Sue Kreitzman. 1998. pap. text 12.95 (*0-7499-1806-3*, Pub. by Piatkus Bks) London Brdge.

Quick After-Work Pasta & Sauces Cookbook. Judy Ridgway. LC 96-2431. (Quick After-Work Ser.). (Illus.). 128p. 1996. pap. 12.95 (*1-55561-089-7*) Fisher Bks.

Quick After-Work Vegetarian Cookbook. Judy Ridgway. LC 96-2432. (Quick After-Work Ser.). (Illus.). 164p. 1996. pap. 12.95 (*1-55561-090-0*) Fisher Bks.

Quick After-Work Winter Vegetarian Cookbook. Judy Ridgway. 1998. pap. text 12.95 (*0-7499-1772-5*, Pub. by Piatkus Bks) London Brdge.

Quick Algebra Review: A Self-Teaching Guide. 2nd ed. Peter H. Selby & Steven L. Slavin. 240p. 1993. pap. 17.95 (*0-471-57843-6*) Wiley.

Quick Analysis, Vol. 1. Joseph Zmuda. (Illus.). 48p. (Orig.). 1986. pap. 22.00 (*0-941572-04-8*) Z Graphic Pubns.

Quick Analysis, Vol. 2. Joseph Zmuda. (Illus.). 48p. (Orig.). 1986. pap. 22.00 (*0-941572-05-6*) Z Graphic Pubns.

Quick & Accurate 12-Lead ECG Interpretation. 3rd ed. Dale Davis. 480p. text 38.00 (*0-7817-2327-2*) Lppncott W & W.

Quick & Basic Electricity: A Contractor's Easy Guide to HVAC Circuits, Controls & Wiring Diagrams. Carol Fey. LC 99-62710. (Practical Is Good (P.I.G.) Technical Training Ser.). (Illus.). 80p. (Orig.). 1999. pap. 12.95 (*0-9672564-0-2*) P I G Pr.

Quick & Cozy Afghans. Oxmoor House Staff. 128p. 1994. pap. 14.95 (*0-942237-48-X*) Leisure AR.

Quick & Delicious Bread Machine Recipes. Norman A. Garrett. LC 91-37674. (Illus.). 128p. (YA). (gr. 10-12). 1993. pap. 6.95 (*0-8069-8812-6*) Sterling.

Quick & Delicious Diabetic Desserts. Mary J. Finsand. LC 91-44523. (Illus.). 160p. 1994. pap. 10.95 (*0-8069-8304-3*) Sterling.

***Quick & Delicious Meals in Minutes.** Judith Regan. 2000. pap. 22.00 (*0-06-095659-3*) HarpC.

Quick-&-Dirty Curve Handbook. Ham Gerber. LC 91-70990. (Illus.). 48p. (Orig.). 1991. pap. 5.00 (*0-8323-0486-7*) Binford Mort.

Quick & Dirty Guide to War: Briefings on Present & Potential Wars. 3rd rev. ed. James F. Dunnigan & Austin Bay. (Illus.). 416p. 1991. pap. 15.00 (*0-688-10033-3*, Quil) HarperTrade.

Quick & Dirty Macintosh Lab Manual for CSC-115. 2nd ed. Charles H. Swim. 96p. (C). 1994. pap., per. 19.95 (*0-8403-9474-8*) Kendall-Hunt.

Quick & Easy. Connie Newton. 36p. (Orig.). 1989. pap. 3.25 (*0-940844-32-X*) Wellspring.

Quick & Easy Art of Smoking Food. Chris Dubbs. 1991. pap. 13.95 (*0-8329-0462-7*, Winchester Pr) New Win Pub.

Quick & Easy Ayurvedic Cookbook. Eileen K. Smith. LC 98-56150. (Illus.). 144p. 2000. pap. 14.95 (*1-885203-74-8*) Jrny Editions.

Quick & Easy Barbecue Inspirations. Ed. by Wendy Hobson. (Illus.). 160p. 1997. pap. 9.95 (*0-572-02259-X*, Pub. by W Foulsham) Trans-Atl Phila.

Quick & Easy Bloomin' Country Cottons: Using Quilted Muslin. Sue Penn. Ed. by Becky Johnston. LC 99-25671. (Illus.). 64p. 1999. pap. 16.95 (*1-890621-02-1*) Landauer Bks IA.

Quick & Easy Boat Maintenance: 1,001 Time-Saving Tips. Sandy Lindsey. LC 98-45846. 144p. (Orig.). 1999. pap. 15.95 (*0-07-134325-3*) McGraw.

Quick & Easy Cakes. Mary Berry. (Illus.). 136p. 1994. pap. 9.95 (*0-563-36786-5*, BBC-Parkwest) Parkwest Pubns.

Quick & Easy Cakes. Mary Ford. (Classic Step-by-Step Ser.). (Illus.). 208p. 1993. 28.50 (*0-946429-42-1*, Pub. by M OMara) Trans-Atl Phila.

Quick & Easy Calorie Counting: With Easy-to-Use Charts Plus 150 Low-Calorie Recipes. Gill MacLennan. LC 95-83718. (Illus.). 272p. 1996. pap. 7.99 (*0-563-37031-9*, BBC-Parkwest) Parkwest Pubns.

***Quick & Easy Chinese Kitchen.** 96p. 2000. pap. 12.95 (*1-85967-840-8*) Anness Pub.

Quick & Easy Chocolate. Gina Steer. (Quick & Easy Cookbook Ser.). (Illus.). 80p. 1994. 10.95 (*0-943231-74-4*) Howell Pr VA.

Quick-&-Easy Cholesterol & Calorie Counter. Compiled by Lynn Sonberg. 112p. (Orig.). 1988. mass mkt. 3.99 (*0-380-75573-4*, Avon Bks) Morrow Avon.

Quick & Easy Christmas Charted Designs. Barbara Christopher. 48p. 1990. pap. 3.50 (*0-486-26419-X*) Dover.

***Quick & Easy Christmas Crafts.** Ed. by Laura Scott. LC 99-94088. (Illus.). 176p. 1999. 19.95 (*1-882138-44-9*) Hse White Birches.

Quick & Easy Christmas Crafts, Bk. 1. (Illus.). 144p. 1996. pap. 14.95 (*0-8487-1564-0*) Oxmoor Hse.

Quick & Easy Christmas Crafts, Vol. 2. Leisure Arts Staff. (Illus.). 144p. 1997. pap. 14.95 (*0-8487-1622-1*) Oxmoor Hse.

Quick-&-Easy Christmas Crochet. Barbara Christopher. (Illus.). 32p. 1991. pap. 2.95 (*0-486-26805-5*) Dover.

Quick & Easy Container Water Gardens. Philip Swindells. LC 98-38810. (Illus.). 128p. 1999. 22.95 (*1-58017-080-3*) Storey Bks.

Q

Quick & Easy Cookbook. American Heart Association Staff. 1999. write for info. (*0-8129-2955-1*, Times Bks) Crown Pub Group.

Quick & Easy Cookbook. Robyn Supraner. LC 80-24021. (Illus.). 48p. (J). (gr. 1-5). 1981. lib. bdg. 16.65 (*0-89375-438-2*) Troll Communs.

Quick & Easy Cookies. Myra Street. (Quick & Easy Cookbook Ser.). (Illus.). 80p. 1994. 10.95 (*0-943231-73-6*) Howell Pr VA.

Quick & Easy Cooking. Cheryl T. Caviness. 112p. (Orig.). 1988. ring bd. 12.99 (*0-8280-0445-5*) Review & Herald.

Quick & Easy Cooking: A Busy Person's Guide to Simple, Nutritious Meals. Alona S. Perkes. LC 89-83432. 64p. 1991. pap. 6.98 (*0-88290-348-9*) Horizon Utah.

Quick & Easy Cooking for Diabetics. Azmina Govindji. 1998. pap. 12.00 (*0-7225-3498-1*) Thorsons PA.

***Quick & Easy Costumes & Plays.** Debra J. Housel. (Illus.). 144p. (J). 1999. pap., teacher ed. 14.95 (*1-57690-356-7*, TCM2356) Tchr Create Mat.

Quick & Easy Creative Art Lessons. Anne Martin. LC 80-17558. 254p. 1981. 18.95 (*0-13-749663-X*, Parker Publishing Co) P-H.

Quick & Easy Crochet. Mary C. Waldrep. (Illus.). 48p. 1989. pap. 2.95 (*0-486-26015-1*) Dover.

Quick & Easy Cross-Stitch Gifts. Dorothea Hall. 1999. pap. text 6.95 (*1-85391-167-4*) J B Fairfax Pr.

Quick & Easy Cross-Stitch Gifts. Leisure Arts Staff & Robert T. Teske. 144p. 1991. 24.95 (*0-8487-1069-X*) Oxmoor Hse.

Quick & Easy Curries. Pat Chapman. LC 97-74405. (Illus.). 136p. 1997. pap. 9.95 (*0-563-37119-6*, BBC-Parkwest) Parkwest Pubns.

Quick & Easy Decorating Projects. Cy DeCosse Inc., Staff. LC 94-49671. (Singer Sewing Reference Library). (Illus.). 128p. 1995. 18.95 (*0-86573-302-3*); pap. 16.95 (*0-86573-303-1*) Creat Pub Intl.

***Quick & Easy Decorative Painting.** Peggy Jessee. LC 99-86911. (Illus.). 128p. 2000. pap. 23.99 (*0-89134-990-1*, North Lght Bks) F & W Pubns Inc.

Quick & Easy Desserts & Puddings. Claire MacDonald. (Illus.). 130p. (Orig.). 1994. pap. 9.95 (*0-563-36443-2*, BBC-Parkwest) Parkwest Pubns.

Quick & Easy Diabetic Menus. Betty Wedman. 272p. 1993. pap. 14.95 (*0-8092-3853-5*, 385350, Contemporary Bks) NTC Contemp Pub Co.

Quick & Easy Diabetic Recipes for One. Kathleen Stanley & Connie Crawley. LC 97-39891. 200p. (Orig.). 1997. pap. 12.95 (*0-945448-84-8*, 00848Q, Pub. by Am Diabetes) NTC Contemp Pub Co.

Quick & Easy Dosage Calculations: Using Dimensional Analysis. Christina Nasrawi & Judith Allender. Ed. by Maura Conner et al. LC 98-24851. (Illus.). 285p. (C). 1999. pap. text 27.95 (*0-7216-7133-0*) Harcourt.

Quick & Easy Exercises for Facial Beauty. Judy Smithdeal. 1980. 2.00 (*0-87980-377-0*) Wilshire.

Quick & Easy Exercises for Figure Beauty. Judy Smithdeal. 1980. pap. 2.00 (*0-87980-381-9*) Wilshire.

Quick & Easy Fat Gram Co. Compiled by Lynn Sonberg. (Quick & Easy Ser.). 160p. 1992. mass mkt. 4.99 (*0-380-76425-3*, Avon Bks) Morrow Avon.

Quick & Easy Fish Cookery. Joanna Farrow. (Illus.). 136p. (Orig.). 1993. pap. 9.95 (*0-563-36324-X*, BBC-Parkwest) Parkwest Pubns.

Quick & Easy Flying Origami. Eiji Nakamura. (Illus.). 60p. 1993. pap. 17.00 (*0-87040-925-5*) Japan Pubns USA.

***Quick & Easy Furniture You Can Build with Dimensional Lumber.** Blair Howard. LC 99-42162. (Illus.). 128p. 2000. pap. 22.99 (*1-55870-523-6*, Popular Woodwking Bks) F & W Pubns Inc.

Quick & Easy Giant Dahlia Quilt on the Sewing Machine: Step-By-Step Instructions & Full Size Templates for Three Quilt Sizes. Susan A. Murwin & Suzzy C. Payne. (Illus.). 80p. (Orig.). 1983. pap. 5.95 (*0-486-24501-2*) Dover.

Quick & Easy Guide to Bible Prophecy. Brian R. Coffey. LC 99-22608. 1999. pap. text 5.99 (*0-8423-3842-X*) Tyndale Hse.

Quick & Easy Guide to Compass Correction. George H. Reid. LC 97-24701. (Illus.). 64p. 1997. pap. 9.95 (*1-57409-023-2*) Sheridan.

Quick & Easy Guide to Delegation: Key to Profitability & Growth. Sheryl L. Barbich. LC 95-48471. 1996. write for info. (*0-87051-173-4*) Am Inst CPA.

Quick & Easy Guide to Delegation: Key to Profitability & Growth. Sheryl L. Barbich. LC 96-6142. 1996. write for info. (*0-87051-176-9*) Am Inst CPA.

Quick & Easy Guide to Driveway Detailing. Rourke M. O'Brien & John B. Thomas. LC 89-85081. (Practice Ring Ser.). (Illus.). 80p. (Orig.). 1993. pap. 9.95 (*0-929758-05-6*) Beeman Jorgensen.

Quick & Easy Guitar Chord Chart. 2.95 (*1-56922-116-2*, 07-4068) Creat Cncpts.

Quick & Easy Guitar Writing Paper. 4.50 (*1-56922-134-0*, 07-4081) Creat Cncpts.

Quick & Easy Healthy Cookery. Beverly Piper. (Illus.). 136p. (Orig.). 1993. pap. 9.95 (*0-563-36339-8*, BBC-Parkwest) Parkwest Pubns.

Quick-&-Easy Heart Motif Quilts: Instructions & Full-Size Templates for Applique Projects. Karen O'Dowd. (Illus.). 48p. (Orig.). 1986. pap. 4.95 (*0-486-25136-5*) Dover.

Quick & Easy Holiday Activities for Early Learners: Arts & Crafts for Beginning Skills & Concepts. Lynn Brisson. (Illus.). 80p. (Orig.). (J). (ps). 1991. pap. text 8.95 (*0-86530-195-6*, 195-6) Incentive Pubns.

Quick & Easy Holiday Skits, Grades 2-6: Holidays & Celebrations. Troll Books Staff. 96p. 1999. pap. text 12.95 (*0-8167-2583-7*) Troll Communs.

Quick & Easy Ideas & Materials: To Help the Nonverbal Child "Talk" at Home. Carolyn Rouse & Katera. (Illus.). 200p. 1997. pap. 29.00 (*1-884135-33-1*, M420) Mayer-Johnson.

Quick & Easy Indian Vegetarian Cookery. Sandeep Chatterjee. (Illus.). 136p. 1993. pap. 9.95 (*0-563-36325-8*, BBC-Parkwest) Parkwest Pubns.

Quick & Easy Indoor Topiary: Crafting & Decorating with Nature. Chris Jones. LC 98-3816. (Illus.). 128p. pap. 19.95 (*1-58017-055-2*, Storey Pub) Storey Bks.

***Quick & Easy Japanese Cookbook.** Katsuyo Kobayashi. 2000. 19.95 (*4-7700-2504-1*, Pub. by Kodansha Intl) Kodansha.

Quick-&-Easy Learning Centers: Phonics. Mary B. Spann. 48p. 1997. pap. text 8.95 (*0-590-93094-X*) Scholastic Inc.

Quick-&-Easy "Little Folk" Charted Designs. Georgia L. Gorham. 32p. (Orig.). 1987. pap. 2.95 (*0-486-25342-2*) Dover.

Quick & Easy Low-Fat, Low-Cholesterol Recipes Kids Will Love. Bea Lewis. 128p. (Orig.). 1990. pap. 3.95 (*0-380-76079-7*, Avon Bks) Morrow Avon.

Quick & Easy, Low-Fat Recipes from Around the World. Annouk M. Van De Voorde. LC 96-36055. (Illus.). 192p. 1997. pap. text 14.95 (*1-882606-65-5*) Peoples Med Soc.

Quick & Easy Magic Tricks. Gyles Brandreth. (Illus.). 96p. (Orig.). (J). 1988. pap. 1.95 (*0-942025-33-4*) Kidsbks.

Quick & Easy Marketing that Works. Russell. 120p. 1996. pap. 39.95 (*0-566-07838-4*) Ashgate Pub Co.

Quick & Easy Math. M. Miller. 48p. (J). 1997. pap. 8.95 (*0-590-96374-0*) Scholastic Inc.

Quick-&-Easy Math: Quick-&-Easy Learning Centers. Patsy F. Kanter. (Illus.). (J). 1995. pap. 8.95 (*0-590-53555-2*) Scholastic Inc.

Quick & Easy Math for Grades K-2. Troll Books Staff. 96p. (J). (gr. k-2). 1999. pap. text 12.95 (*0-8167-3273-6*) Troll Communs.

Quick & Easy Math for Grades 3-6. Troll Books Staff. 96p. (J). (gr. 3-6). 1999. pap. text 12.95 (*0-8167-3272-8*) Troll Communs.

Quick & Easy Medical Terminology. 2nd ed. Peggy C. Leonard. (Illus.). 369p. 1995. pap., teacher ed., spiral bd. write for info. (*0-7216-5687-0*, W B Saunders Co) Harcrt Hlth Sci Grp.

Quick & Easy Medical Terminology. 2nd ed. Peggy C. Leonard. 352p. 1995. pap. text 30.00 (*0-7216-5686-2*, W B Saunders Co) Harcrt Hlth Sci Grp.

***Quick & Easy Menus: More Than 130 Low-Fat Recipes.** Weight Watchers Staff. (Weight Watchers Ser.). (Illus.). 2000. pap. 9.95 (*0-8487-2354-6*) Oxmoor Hse.

Quick & Easy Menus for Entertaining: Secrets of a Savvy Cook. Andy King. 1997. 9.98 (*0-89660-075-0*, Artabras) Abbeville Pr.

Quick & Easy Miniature Samplers for Cross-Stitch. Barbara Christopher. 32p. 1986. pap. 2.95 (*0-486-25209-4*) Dover.

Quick & Easy Mosaics: Innovative Project & Techniques. Mariarita Machiavelli. LC 98-3571. (Illus.). 160p. 1998. 27.95 (*0-8069-3895-1*) Sterling.

***Quick & Easy Mosaics: Innovative Projects & Techniques.** Mariarita Macchiavelli. (Illus.). 160p. 1999. pap. 14.95 (*0-8069-4475-7*) Sterling.

***Quick & Easy Muffins.** Anness Publishing Staff. 1999. pap. 12.95 (*0-7548-0268-X*, Pub. by Anness Pub) Random.

Quick & Easy Newsletters: A Step-by-Step Systems Using Software You Already Have to Create a Newsletter in an Afternoon. Elaine Floyd. (Illus.). 144p. 1998. pap. 34.99 (*0-9630222-3-7*) EFG Inc MO.

Quick & Easy Novelty Cakes: 35 Imaginative Cakes for All Occasions. Carol Deacon. (Illus.). 96p. 1996. 24.95 (*1-85368-678-6*, Pub. by New5 Holland) Sterling.

Quick & Easy Nutrition Counter for Pregnancy. Lynn Sonberg. 352p. (Orig.). 1994. mass mkt. 5.99 (*0-380-77418-6*, Avon Bks) Morrow Avon.

Quick & Easy Organic Gourmet: Quick & Delicious, Healthy Meals Without Meat, Wheat, Dairy or Sugar. Leslie Cerier. LC 95-15667. (Illus.). 352p. 1995. pap. 17.95 (*1-886449-00-7*) Barrytown Ltd.

***Quick & Easy Origami.** Toshie Takahama. (Illus.). 62p. 2000. pap. 14.95 (*4-88996-056-2*) Japan Pubn Trad.

Quick & Easy Origami. Toshie Takahoma. LC 88-80139. (Illus.). 62p. (Orig.). 1994. pap. 17.00 (*0-87040-771-6*) Kodansha.

***Quick & Easy Origami Boxes.** Tomoko Fuse. (Illus.). 62p. 2000. pap. 14.95 (*4-88996-052-X*) Japan Pubn Trad.

Quick & Easy Origami Boxes. Tomoko Fuse. (Illus.). 62p. 1994. pap. 17.00 (*0-87040-939-5*) Japan Pubns USA.

***Quick & Easy Pages.** Joanna Campbell Slan. (Illus.). (J). 2000. pap. 14.99 (*1-930500-02-5*) EFG Inc MO.

Quick & Easy Paper Planes That Really Fly. Paul Jackson. (Illus.). 32p. (J). 1997. pap. 3.99 (*1-884628-02-8*, Flyng Frog) Allied Pub MD.

***Quick & Easy Pasta.** (Illus.). 2000. pap. text 12.95 (*0-7548-0093-8*, Lorenz Bks) Anness Pub.

Quick & Easy Pasta Recipes. rev. ed. Coleen Simmons & Bob Simmons. (Illus.). 176p. 1992. pap. 8.95 (*1-55867-050-5*, Nitty Gritty Ckbks) Bristol Pub Ent CA.

Quick & Easy Pasta Sauces. Shirley Gill. (Quick & Easy Cookbook Ser.). (Illus.). 80p. 1994. 10.95 (*0-943231-66-3*) Howell Pr VA.

Quick & Easy Pasta Sauces. Carolyn Humphries. 160p. 1996. pap. text 14.95 (*0-572-02272-7*, Pub. by W Foulsham) Trans-Atl Phila.

Quick & Easy Patchwork on the Sewing Machine: Instructions & Full-Size Templates for 12 Quilts. Susan A. Murwin & Suzzy C. Payne. LC 78-74751. (Illus.). 80p. 1979. pap. 5.95 (*0-486-23770-2*) Dover.

Quick & Easy Phonics. W. Blevins. 48p. (J). (gr. 1-3). 1997. pap. 8.95 (*0-590-96380-5*) Scholastic Inc.

Quick & Easy Picture Chords for Guitar: Case Size. 4.50 (*1-56922-123-5*, 07-4076) Creat Cncpts.

Quick & Easy Picture Chords for Guitar - Full Size. 4.50 (*1-56922-122-7*, 07-4075) Creat Cncpts.

Quick & Easy Pizzas. Shirley Gill. 1999. 11.98 (*1-84038-350-X*) Hermes Hse.

Quick & Easy Plastic Canvas Projects. Illus. by Marie Thiesen. (Embroidery, Needlepoint, Charted Designs Ser.). 48p. 1984. pap. 3.95 (*0-486-24655-8*) Dover.

Quick & Easy Preserves. Simone Sekers. (Illus.). 1996. pap. 9.95 (*0-563-36946-9*, BBC-Parkwest) Parkwest Pubns.

Quick & Easy Puppets Bk. 1: Craft Pattern Book. (J). 1993. write for info. (*1-884376-00-2*) Clever Creat.

Quick & Easy Puppets - Seasonal Book. (Illus.). (J). 1993. write for info. (*1-884376-01-0*) Clever Creat.

Quick-&-Easy Quilt Patchwork with 14 Projects. Dixie Haywood. Orig. Title: The Contemporary Crazy Quilt Project Book. (Illus.). 64p. 1992. reprint ed. pap. 4.95 (*0-486-27106-4*) Dover.

Quick & Easy Recipes to Boost Your Immune System. Lori Longbotham. 112p. (Orig.). 1991. mass mkt. 3.95 (*0-380-76080-0*, Avon Bks) Morrow Avon.

Quick & Easy Recipes to Lower Your Cholesterol. Lori Longbotham & Lynn Sonberg. 112p. 1989. pap. 3.50 (*0-380-75871-7*, Avon Bks) Morrow Avon.

Quick & Easy Salads. Clare Connery. (Illus.). 136p. (Orig.). 1993. pap. 9.95 (*0-563-36253-7*, BBC-Parkwest) Parkwest Pubns.

Quick & Easy Science. M. Chang. 48p. (J). (gr. 1-3). 1997. pap. 8.95 (*0-590-96375-9*) Scholastic Inc.

Quick-&-Easy Science: Quick-&-Easy Learning Centers. Lynn Kepler. (Illus.). (J). 1995. pap. 8.95 (*0-590-53554-4*) Scholastic Inc.

Quick & Easy Scrap Quilts. Oxmoor House Staff. 160p. 1996. pap. 19.95 (*0-8487-1462-8*) Oxmoor Hse.

Quick & Easy Sewing Projects. Cy DeCosse Incorporated Staff. LC 93-25891. (Singer Sewing Reference Library). (Illus.). 128p. 1993. 18.95 (*0-86573-288-4*); pap. 16.95 (*0-86573-289-2*) Creat Pub Intl.

Quick & Easy Solutions to Marker Techniques. Yoshiharu Shimizu. (Illus.). 136p. 1995. pap. 39.95 (*4-7661-0780-2*, Pub. by Graphic-Sha) Bks Nippan.

Quick & Easy Soups. Thane Prince. (Illus.). 1996. pap. 9.95 (*0-563-36949-3*, BBC-Parkwest) Parkwest Pubns.

Quick & Easy Soups. Myra Street. (Quick & Easy Cookbook Ser.). (Illus.). 80p. 1994. 10.95 (*0-943231-67-1*) Howell Pr VA.

Quick & Easy Strip Quilting. Helen W. Rose. (Illus.). 80p. 1989. pap. 5.95 (*0-486-26018-6*) Dover.

***Quick & Easy Study Guide for the U. S. Constitution.** Sally Ramsey. 79p. 2000. 39.95 (*1-58532-092-7*) Basic Ed Materials.

Quick & Easy Suppers. Linda Fraser. (Illus.). 1996. pap. 9.95 (*0-563-36904-3*, BBC-Parkwest) Parkwest Pubns.

Quick-&-Easy Teddy Bear: With Full-Size Patterns for Clothing. Jodie Davis. (Illus.). 32p. (Orig.). 1991. pap. 2.95 (*0-486-26864-0*) Dover.

Quick & Easy Topiary & Green Sculpture: Create Traditional Effects with Fastgrowing Climbers & Wire Frames. Jenny Hendy. LC 95-22905. (Illus.). 128p. (Orig.). 1996. pap. 18.95 (*0-88266-920-6*, 920-6, Garden Way Pub) Storey Bks.

Quick & Easy Vegetable Cookery. Shaun Hill. (Illus.). 136p. (Orig.). 1994. pap. 9.95 (*0-563-36432-7*, BBC-Parkwest) Parkwest Pubns.

Quick & Easy Vegetarian Cookbook. Ruth A. Manners & William Manners. LC 93-28789. 240p. 1993. pap. 12.95 (*0-87131-738-9*) M Evans.

Quick & Easy Vegetarian Cookery. Sarah Brown. (Illus.). 136p. 1992. pap. 9.95 (*0-563-20695-0*, BBC-Parkwest) Parkwest Pubns.

Quick & Easy Vests & Jackets: Creative Fashions to Sew. Kate Mathews. LC 98-22045. (Illus.). 128p. 1999. 24.95 (*1-57990-083-6*, Pub. by Lark Books) Random.

Quick & Easy Way to Effective Speaking. Dale Carnegie. 1990. per. 7.50 (*0-671-72400-2*) PB.

Quick & Easy Way to Top Selling. unabridged ed. Robert L. Montgomery. 51p. 1985. pap. text 39.95 incl. audio (*1-55678-023-0*, 1598) Learn Inc.

Quick-&-Easy Word Play: Phonics & Spelling. Mary B. Spann. (Illus.). (J). 1996. pap. 8.95 (*0-590-53552-8*) Scholastic Inc.

Quick & Easy World Atlas. American Map Corporation. 48p. 5.95 (*0-8416-9553-9*, 695539) Am Map.

Quick-&-Easy Writing: Quick-&-Easy Learning Centers. Cynde Gregory. (Illus.). (J). 1996. pap. 8.95 (*0-590-53553-6*) Scholastic Inc.

Quick & Fun Learning Activities for Babies. Levin. 1996. pap. text, wbk. ed. 8.95 (*1-55734-553-8*) Tchr Create Mat.

Quick & Fun Learning Activities for 5-Year-Olds. Julia Jasmine. LC 97-116794. 80p. 1997. pap. 6.95 (*1-55734-558-9*) Tchr Create Mat.

Quick & Fun Learning Activities for 4-Year-Olds. Marla McGhee. LC 97-116793. 80p. 1997. pap. 6.95 (*1-55734-557-0*) Tchr Create Mat.

Quick & Fun Learning Activities for 1 Year Olds. Mcghee. (Illus.). 80p. 1996. pap. 8.95 (*1-55734-554-6*) Tchr Create Mat.

Quick & Fun Learning Activities for 3-Year-Olds. Grace Jasmine. LC 97-117441. (Quick & Fun Ser.). 80p. 1997. pap. 6.95 (*1-55734-556-2*) Tchr Create Mat.

Quick & Fun Learning Activities for 2 Years Old. Levins. (Illus.). 80p. 1996. pap. 8.95 (*1-55734-555-4*) Tchr Create Mat.

Quick & Healthy Vol. II: More Help for People Who Say They Don't Have Time to Cook Healthy Meals, 2. Brenda J. Ponichtera. LC 91-90207. (Illus.). 262p. (Orig.). 1995. pap. 16.95 (*0-9629160-1-3*) ScaleDown.

***Quick & Healthy Cooking for Dummies.** Carol Ann Rinzler. 384p. 2000. pap. 19.99 (*0-7645-5214-7*) IDG Bks.

Quick & Healthy Recipes. Fundco Staff. 160p. 1995. 5.00 (*1-885507-04-6*) Fundco Printers.

Quick & Healthy Recipes & Ideas: For People Who Say They Don't Have Time to Cook Healthy Meals. Brenda J. Ponichtera. LC 91-90207. (Illus.). 262p. (Orig.). 1991. pap. 16.95 (*0-9629160-0-5*) ScaleDown.

Quick & Hearty: Meatless Microwave Meals Everyone Will Enjoy. Pat Baird. LC 94-41784. 1995. pap. 14.95 (*0-8050-3743-8*, Owl) H Holt & Co.

Quick & Hearty Main Dishes. Frank R. Blenn. (Healthy Selects Cookbook Ser.). (Illus.). 80p. 1996. pap. 8.95 (*0-945448-46-5*, 00465Q, Pub. by Am Diabetes) NTC Contemp Pub Co.

Quick & Legal Will Book. 2nd ed. Denis Clifford. 240p. 1999. pap. 15.95 (*0-87337-309-X*) Nolo com.

***Quick & Legal Will Book.** 2nd ed. Denis Clifford. LC 98-39722. 240p. 1999. 15.95 (*0-87337-505-X*) Nolo com.

***Quick & Light Bindup.** Editors of Time-Life Books. (gr. 7). 1999. 34.95 (*0-7370-1146-7*) T-L Custom Pub.

Quick & Natural Macrobiotic Cookbook. Aveline Kushi & Wendy Esko. 320p. (Orig.). 1989. pap. 16.95 (*0-8092-4436-5*, 443650, Contemporary Bks) NTC Contemp Pub Co.

Quick & Not Dirty Guide to Business Writing. Marsh. 170p. (C). 1996. pap. text 14.50 (*0-13-777483-4*) P-H.

Quick & Short Book Reports. Randy Thorne. (Illus.). 56p. (J). (gr. 3-5). 1990. pap. 6.95 (*0-933606-86-9*, MS-690) E Sussman Educ.

Quick & Short Book Reports. Randy M. Thorne.Tr. of Critique en Herbe. (FRE.). (YA). pap. 8.99 (*0-590-74468-2*) Scholastic Inc.

Quick & Simple for Two. (Illus.). 64p. 1996. pap. 3.95 (*0-8249-3087-8*) Ideals.

Quick & Slow Animals see Animal Opposites

Quick & Tasty Christmas Gifts. Leisure Arts Staff. 128p. 1995. 19.95 (*0-942237-67-6*) Leisure AR.

Quick & the Dead. Janine Di Giovanni. 1995. mass mkt. 13.95 (*1-85799-333-0*, Pub. by Orion Pubng Grp) Trafalgar.

Quick & the Dead. Louis L'Amour. 160p. 1978. mass mkt. 4.50 (*0-553-28084-8*) Bantam.

Quick & the Dead. Wolf White Wolf Publishing Staff & Elizabeth Fischi. (Wruith Ser.). 1995. pap. 12.00 (*1-56504-613-7*, 6008(4613)) White Wolf.

***Quick & the Dead.** Joy Williams. 352p. 2000. 25.00 (*0-679-44646-X*) Knopf.

Quick & the Dead. large type ed. Sandy Dengler. LC 98-39768. 1998. 22.95 (*0-7862-1647-6*) Thorndike Pr.

***Quick & the Dead.** large type ed. Willa Marsh. LC 99-14884. 294p. 1999. 22.95 (*0-7862-1981-5*) Mac Lib Ref.

***Quick & the Dead: A Novel.** Joy Williams. 352p. 2000. 25.00 (*0-375-44646-X*) Knopf.

Quick & the Dead: A Walk Through the Deadlands. Matt Forbeck & Shane L. Hensley. (Illus.). 186p. (Orig.). 1996. pap., boxed set 30.00 (*1-889546-02-X*) Pinnacle Ent.

Quick & the Dead: Artist & Anatomy. Deanna Petherbridge. LC 99-161893. 120p. 1998. pap. 24.95 (*0-520-21738-1*, Pub. by U CA Pr) Cal Prin Full Svc.

Quick Answers to Quantitative Problems: A Pocket Primer. G. William Page & Carl V. Patton. (Illus.). 277p. (C). 1991. pap. text 39.95 (*0-12-543570-3*) Acad Pr.

Quick Arithmetic: A Self-Teaching Guide. 2nd ed. Robert A. Carman & Marilyn J. Carman. LC 83-3531. 304p. 1984. pap. 17.95 (*0-471-88966-0*, 1-581) Wiley.

Quick As a Cricket. Audrey Wood. (SPA.). (J). 1989. pap. 6.99 (*0-85953-977-6*); pap. 6.99 (*0-85953-801-X*) Childs Play.

Quick As a Cricket. Audrey Wood. (ITA.). (J). (ps-3). 1989. 13.99 (*0-85953-557-6*) Childs Play.

Quick As a Cricket. Audrey Wood. (J). 1996. lib. bdg. 15.95 (*0-85953-843-5*) Childs Play.

Quick As a Cricket. Audrey Wood. LC 92-40124. (Big Book Ser.). (Illus.). 32p. (J). 1996. pap. 26.99 (*0-85953-331-X*) Childs Play.

Quick as a Cricket. Audrey Wood. (Illus.). 24p. (J). 1998. bds. 5.99 (*0-85953-664-5*) Childs Play.

Quick as a Cricket. Audrey Wood. 1982. 12.19 (*0-606-00869-1*, Pub. by Turtleback) Demco.

Quick As a Cricket. Don Wood & Audrey Wood. 32p. (J). (ps-3). 1990. 13.99 (*0-85953-151-1*) Childs Play.

Quick As a Cricket. Don Wood & Audrey Wood. (Illus.). 31p. (J). (ps-3). 1990. pap. 6.99 (*0-85953-306-9*) Childs Play.

Quick As a Wink. Leisure Arts Staff. 144p. 1996. pap. text 19.95 (*1-57486-054-2*) Oxmoor Hse.

Quick Assembler. Monadjemi. (C). 1990. text. write for info. (*0-201-56207-3*) Addison-Wesley.

Quick Baby Knits. Bliss. 80p. 1999. pap. 18.95 (*0-312-20251-2*) St Martin.

Quick BASIC. Sarah E. Hutchinson & Stacey C. Sawyer. LC 93-247556. 96p. (C). 1993. text 12.50 (*0-256-13709-9*, Irwn McGrw-H) McGrw-H Hghr Educ.

Quick Basic for Technology Students. Kathy McClure. (C). 2001. pap. 40.00 (*0-13-610875-X*, Macmillan Coll) P-H.

Quick Books in the Classroom for Windows 5.0. (In the Classroom Ser.). (Illus.). 322p. 1997. spiral bd. 25.00 incl. disk (*1-887391-16-9*, IQBC5W) Tech Lrng Res.

***Quick Books Pro 2000: Byte by Bite.** Glenda Friesen. (Illus.). 120p. 2000. pap. 15.00 (*1-891412-22-1*) Training Solut.

Quick Bread Cook Book. Nancy Adams. 1996. ring bd. 6.95 (*1-885590-21-0*) Golden West Pub.

Quick Breads. Barry Bluestein & Kevin Morrissey. 128p. 1991. pap. 11.95 (*0-8092-3973-6*, 397360, Contemporary Bks) NTC Contemp Pub Co.

Quick Breads. Howard Early & Glenda Morris. LC 98-10591. (Specialty Cookbook Ser.). (Illus.). 128p. 1998. pap. 6.95 (*0-89594-941-5*) Crossing Pr.

Quick Bright Things. Ron Wallace. LC 99-88117. (First Ser.). 172p. 2000. pap. 14.00 (*0-922811-44-X*, Pub. by Mid-List) SPD-Small Pr Dist.

Quick Brown Fox. Susan Kelly. 256p. 1999. 25.00 (*0-7278-5404-6*, Pub. by Severn Hse) Chivers N Amer.

An Asterisk (*) at the beginning of an entry indicates that the title is appearing for the first time.

Quick Brush of Wings. Mary TallMountain. Tr. by Eliza Jones. (Illus.). 60p. (Orig.). 1991. pap. text 9.95 (*0-9625153-1-0*) Freedom Voices Pubns.

Quick Business Math: A Self-Teaching Guide. Steven L. Slavin. LC 95-32408. (Self-Teaching Guides Ser.). 272p. 1995. pap. 16.95 (*0-471-11689-0*) Wiley.

***Quick-but-Great Science Fair Projects.** Shar Levine et al. LC 99-87162. (Illus.). (J). 2000. 19.95 (*0-8069-5939-8*) Sterling Pub.

Quick Bytes: Computer Lover's Cookbook. Diane Pfeifer. LC 93-83442. (Illus.). 160p. 1993. pap. 9.95 (*0-9618306-7-0*) Strawberry GA.

Quick C for Windows 5.25. 1993. 5.00 (*0-13-749565-X*) P-H.

Quick Calculations: Medical Dosage Calculations. (C). 1994. 22.50 (*0-8053-1367-2*) Addison-Wesley.

Quick Calculus: A Self-Teaching Guide. 2nd ed. Daniel Kleppner & Norman Ramsey. LC 85-12349. 272p. 1985. pap. 17.95 (*0-471-82722-3*) Wiley.

Quick-Change Artist. Jon C. Suggs. (Illus.). 16p. (Orig.). 1971. ring bd. 1.00 (*0-685-30028-5*) Cottonwood KS.

Quick Change Displays. Paula Corbett & Leslee Huntsman. (Teacher Aid Ser.). 43p. 1985. 6.95 (*0-513-01772-0*) Denison.

Quick-Change Room. Nagle Jackson. LC 99-205947. 1997. pap. 5.25 (*0-8222-1585-3*) Dramatists Play.

Quick Changeover for Operators: The SMED System. Shigeo Shingo. LC 96-17512. 1996. pap. 25.00 (*1-56327-125-7*) Productivity Inc.

Quick Changeover for Operators Learning Package. Shigeo Shingo. (Shopfloor Ser.). (Illus.). 85p. 1996. pap. 295.00 (*1-56327-126-5*) Productivity Inc.

Quick Check: Bookkeeping with Personal Computers. 2nd ed. Chuck Atkinson. 1994. pap. text 10.00 (*0-917081-04-8*) CAP Automation.

Quick Check Food Facts. Intro. by Carolyn E. Moore. LC 98-25679. (Barron's Educational Ser.). 240p. 1999. pap. 4.95 (*0-7641-0874-3*) Barron.

Quick Chick. Julia Hoban. (Puffin Easy-To-Read. Level 1 Ser.). (J). 1995. 8.70 (*0-606-08050-3*, Pub. by Turtleback) Demco.

Quick Chick. Julia Hoban & Lillian Hoban. (Easy-to-Read Bks.). (Illus.). (J). (ps-3). 1995. pap. 3.99 (*0-14-036664-4*, PuffinBks) Peng Put Young Read.

Quick Chicken. Rose Murray. (Illus.). 192p. 1999. pap. 19.95 (*0-7788-0002-4*, Pub. by R Rose Inc) Firefly Bks Ltd.

Quick Children's Sermons: Will My Dog Be in Heaven? And 49 Other Questions Kids Ask. LC 96-48437. (J). (ps-6). 1997. pap. 14.99 (*1-55945-612-4*) Group Pub.

Quick Children's Sermons 2: Why Did God Make Mosquitos? Ed. by Jan Kershner. LC 97-49573. (Quick Children's Sermons Ser.: Vol. 2). (Illus.). 96p. (J). 1998. pap. 14.99 (*0-7644-2052-6*) Group Pub.

Quick Chills II: The Best Horror Fiction from the Specialty Press. Ed. by Robert Morrish & Peter Enfantino. (Quick Chills Ser.: Vol. II). (Illus.). 356p. 1992. 35.00 (*0-9631367-3-9*) Deadline Pr.

Quick Chocolate Fixes: 70 Fast & Easy Recipes for People Who Want Chocolate - In a Hurry! Leslie Weiner & Barbara Albright. LC 95-17390. 1995. pap. 6.95 (*0-312-13153-4*, St Martin Griffin) St Martin.

Quick Classic Quilts. Marsha R. McCloskey. 176p. 1996. pap. 19.95 (*0-8487-1465-2*) Oxmoor Hse.

Quick Clips: 120 Tips to Improve Your Technique, Performance & Equipment. John Mcullen. 1997. pap. 7.95 (*1-887216-08-1*) Elk Mtn Pr.

Quick Cognitive Inventory (QCI) Annabelle M. Markoff. 39p. (Orig.). 1990. pap. text, student ed. 20.00 (*0-87879-643-6*); student ed. 17.00 (*0-87879-644-4*) Acad Therapy.

Quick Comprehension Guide to WordPerfect 5.2 for Windows: A Professional Approach. Deborah A. Hinkle. LC 93-2712. 1993. 18.95 (*0-02-801804-4*) Glencoe.

Quick Comprehensive Guide to Word 2.O for Windows: A Professional Approach. Deborah A. Hinkle. LC 93-95. vii, 99 p. 1993. write for info. (*0-02-800383-7*) Glencoe.

Quick Consult in Critical Care. Gerald Keen. Ed. by Pamela L. Swearingen. LC 97-6318. (Illus.). 544p. (C). (gr. 13). 1997. text 49.95 (*0-8151-3178-X*, 29561) Mosby Inc.

Quick-Consult Manual of Evidence Based Medicine. Burton W. Lee et al. LC 97-3306. (Illus.). 500p. 1997. pap. text 44.95 (*0-316-51887-5*) Lppncott W & W.

Quick Consult Manual of Primary Care Medicine. Gideon Bosker & Paul Stander. LC 96-27078. 280p. 1996. spiral bd. 31.00 (*0-316-10312-8*) Lppncott W & W.

***Quick Consult to Diagnosing & Treating Ocular Disease.** Roberts. 2001. pap. 39.95 (*0-7506-7297-8*) Buttrwrth-Heinemann.

Quick Cook. Thane Prince. (Illus.). 192p. 1992. 19.95 (*0-7011-6181-7*, Pub. by Chatto & Windus) Trafalgar.

***Quick Cooking for Two.** Oxmoor House Publishing Staff. (Illus.). 240p. 2000. pap. 21.95 (*0-376-02336-8*) Sunset Books.

***Quick Cooking for Two.** Oxmoor House Staff. 2000. pap. 21.95 (*0-376-02337-6*) Sunset Books.

Quick Cooking with Pacific Flavors. Hugh Carpenter & Teri Sandison. LC 97-9785. (Illus.). 208p. 1997. 35.00 (*1-55670-645-6*) Stewart Tabori & Chang.

Quick Country Christmas Quilts. Debbie Mumm. LC 95-9830. (Illus.). 256p. 1995. text 27.95 (*0-87596-653-5*) Rodale Pr Inc.

Quick Country Christmas Quilts. Debbie Mumm. (Illus.). 1998. pap. 16.95 (*0-87596-986-0*) Rodale Pr Inc.

Quick Country Quilting: Over 80 Projects Featuring Easy, Timesaving Techniques. Debbie Mumm. (Illus.). 256p. 1995. pap. 15.95 (*0-87596-741-8*) Rodale Pr Inc.

Quick Course Access 97 Workbook Instructor's Resource Packet. Online Press Inc. Staff. (Quick Course Ser.). (Illus.). 1997. pap. text 11.95 (*1-879399-84-9*) Online Training.

Quick Course Classic American Literature. Monarch. 384p. 1995. pap. 14.95 (*0-02-860016-9*) Macmillan.

Quick Course Excel 97 Workbook Instructor's Resource Packet. Online Press Inc. Staff. (Quick Course Ser.). (Illus.). 1997. pap. text 11.95 (*1-879399-85-7*) Online Training.

Quick Course in Access 97: Education/Training Edition. Joyce K. Cox & Nathan Dudley. LC 97-66247. (Quick Course Ser.). (Illus.). 172p. 1997. pap. text 14.95 (*1-879399-73-3*) Online Training.

Quick Course in Access 7 for Windows 95: Education/Training Edition. Joyce Cox & Nathan Dudley. LC 96-70855. (Quick Course Ser.). (Illus.). 172p. (Orig.). 1996. pap. text 14.95 (*1-879399-52-0*) Online Training.

Quick Course in Access 2 for Windows: Education/ Training Edition. Joyce Cox & Mike Elison. LC 93-84869. (Quick Course Ser.). (Illus.). 172p. 1994. pap. text 14.95 (*1-879399-32-6*) Online Training.

***Quick Course in Creating a Web Site Using Microsoft FrontPage 2000: Education/Training Edition.** Joyce Cox. LC 99-70322. (Quick Course Ser.). 160p. 1999. pap. text 15.95 (*1-58278-008-0*) Online Training.

Quick Course in Excel 5 for Windows: Education/ Training Edition. Joyce Cox et al. LC 93-86431. (Quick Course Ser.). (Illus.). 164p. 1994. pap. text 14.95 (*1-879399-28-8*) Online Training.

Quick Course in Excel 97: Education/Training Edition. Joyce K. Cox et al. LC 96-72484. (Quick Course). (Illus.). 170p. (Orig.). 1997. pap. text 14.95 (*1-879399-71-7*) Online Training.

Quick Course in Excel 7 for Windows 95: Education/Training Edition. Joyce Cox et al. LC 96-67883. (Quick Course Ser.). (Illus.). 163p. (Orig.). 1996. pap. text 14.95 (*1-879399-51-2*) Online Training.

***Quick Course in Microsoft Access 97.** Online Press, Inc., Staff. 192p. 2000. pap. 9.99 (*0-7356-1072-X*) Microsoft Pr.

***Quick Course in Microsoft Access 2000.** Online Press, Inc., Staff. 2000. pap. 9.99 (*0-7356-1082-7*) Microsoft.

***Quick Course in Microsoft Access 2000: Education/Training Edition.** Joyce Cox. LC 99-70319. (Quick Course Ser.). 1999. pap. text 14.95 (*1-58278-005-6*) Online Training.

***Quick Course in Microsoft Excel 2000.** Online Press, Inc., Staff. (Quick Course Ser.). (Illus.). 2000. pap. 9.99 (*0-7356-1081-9*) Microsoft.

Quick Course in Microsoft Excel 2000: Education/ Training Edition. Joyce Cox. LC 99-70317. (Quick Course Ser.). 1999. pap. text 15.95 (*1-58278-003-X*) Online Training.

***Quick Course In Microsoft Excel 97.** Online Press, Inc., Staff. 2000. pap. 9.99 (*0-7356-1073-8*) Microsoft Pr.

***Quick Course in Microsoft FrontPage 2000.** Online Press, Inc., Staff. (Quick Course Ser.). (Illus.). 2000. pap. 9.99 (*0-7356-1086-X*) Microsoft.

Quick Course in Microsoft Internet Explorer 4. Online Press, Inc., Staff. LC 97-31807. 1997. 14.99 (*1-57231-804-X*) Microsoft.

***Quick Course in Microsoft Internet Explorer 5.** Online Press, Inc., Staff. (Quick Course Ser.). (Illus.). 2000. pap. 9.99 (*0-7356-1087-8*) Microsoft.

Quick Course in Microsoft Office for Windows Version 4.3: Education/Training Edition. Joyce Cox & Polly Urban. LC 95-68957. (Quick Course Ser.). (Illus.). 268p. 1995. pap. text 24.95 (*1-879399-39-3*) Online Training.

Quick Course in Microsoft Office for Windows 95 & Windows NT: Education/Training Edition. Joyce Cox & Polly Urban. LC 95-72653. (Quick Course Ser.). (Illus.). 284p. 1996. pap. text 24.95 (*1-879399-54-7*) Online Training.

***Quick Course in Microsoft Office 97.** Online Press, Inc., Staff. (Quick Course Ser.). (Illus.). 2000. pap. 9.99 (*0-7356-1076-2*) Microsoft.

Quick Course in Microsoft Office 97: Education/Training Edition. Joyce Cox et al. LC 96-71317. (Quick Course Ser.). (Illus.). 300p. (C). 1997. pap. text 24.95 (*1-879399-69-5*) Online Training.

***Quick Course in Microsoft Office 2000: Education/ Training Edition.** Joyce Cox et al. LC 99-70315. (Quick Course Ser.). (Illus.). 416p. 1999. pap. text 25.95 (*1-58278-001-3*) Online Training.

***Quick Course in Microsoft Office 2000.** Online Press, Inc., Staff. (Quick Course Ser.). (Illus.). 2000. pap. 9.99 (*0-7356-1083-5*) Microsoft.

Quick Course in Microsoft Outlook 98: Education/ Training Edition. Joyce Cox & Christina Dudley. LC 98-163922. (Quick Course Ser.). (Illus.). 160p. 1998. pap. text 14.95 (*1-879399-80-6*) Online Training.

***Quick Course in Microsoft Outlook 2000.** Online Press, Inc., Staff. (Quick Course Ser.). (Illus.). 2000. pap. 9.99 (*0-7356-1089-4*) Microsoft.

***Quick Course in Microsoft Outlook 2000: Education/Training Edition.** Joyce Cox. LC 99-70321. (Quick Course Ser.). 1999. pap. text 15.95 (*1-58278-006-4*) Online Training.

***Quick Course in Microsoft Outlook 98.** Online Press, Inc., Staff. 192p. 2000. pap. 9.99 (*0-7356-1080-0*) Microsoft Pr.

***Quick Course in Microsoft PowerPoint 2000.** Online Press, Inc., Staff. (Quick Course Ser.). (Illus.). 2000. pap. 9.99 (*0-7356-1084-3*) Microsoft.

***Quick Course in Microsoft PowerPoint 2000: Education/Training Edition.** Joyce Cox. LC 99-70318. (Quick Course Ser.). (Illus.). 176p. 1999. pap. text 15.95 (*1-58278-004-8*) Online Training.

***Quick Course in Microsoft PowerPoint 97.** Online Press, Inc., Staff. (Quick Course Ser.). (Illus.). 2000. pap. 9.99 (*0-7356-1074-6*) Microsoft.

***Quick Course in Microsoft Publisher 2000: Education/Training Edition.** Joyce Cox. LC 99-70320. (Quick Course Ser.). 178p. 1999. pap. text 15.95 (*1-58278-007-2*) Online Training.

***Quick Course in Microsoft Publisher 2000.** Online Press, Inc., Staff. (Quick Course Ser.). (Illus.). 2000. pap. 9.99 (*0-7356-1088-6*) Microsoft.

***Quick Course in Microsoft Windows 95.** Online Press, Inc., Staff. (Quick Course Ser.). (Illus.). 2000. pap. 9.99 (*0-7356-1077-0*) Microsoft.

Quick Course in Microsoft Windows 98: Education/ Training Edition. Joyce Cox. Ed. by Christina Dudley. (Quick Course Ser.). (Illus.). 208p. 1998. pap. text 15.95 (*1-879399-81-4*) Online Training.

***Quick Course in Microsoft Windows NT 4 Workstation.** Online Press, Inc., Staff. (Quick Course Ser.). (Illus.). 2000. pap. 9.99 (*0-7356-1079-7*) Microsoft.

Quick Course In Microsoft Windows 2000 Online Press Inc. Staff. (C). (gr. 8). 1999. pap. 16.99 (*1-57231-845-7*) Little.

***Quick Course in Microsoft Windows 98.** Online Press, Inc., Staff. (Quick Course Ser.). (Illus.). 2000. pap. 9.99 (*0-7356-1078-9*) Microsoft.

***Quick Course in Microsoft Word 2000: Education/ Training Edition.** Joyce Cox. LC 99-70316. (Quick Course Ser.). 1999. pap. text 15.95 (*1-58278-002-1*) Online Training.

Quick Course in Microsoft Word 2000. Online Press Inc. Staff. 60p. 11.95 (*1-58278-011-0*) Online Training.

***Quick Course in Microsoft Word 2000.** Online Press, Inc., Staff. (Quick Course Ser.). (Illus.). 2000. pap. 9.99 (*0-7356-1085-1*) Microsoft.

***Quick Course in Microsoft Word 97.** Online Press, Inc., Staff. (Quick Course Ser.). (Illus.). 2000. pap. 9.99 (*0-7356-1075-4*) Microsoft.

Quick Course in Microsoft Works 3 for Windows: Education/Training Edition. Joyce Cox & Ted Cox. LC 93-86356. (Quick Course Ser.). (Illus.). 170p. 1995. pap. text 14.95 (*1-879399-42-3*) Online Training.

Quick Course in PowerPoint 4 for Windows: Education/Training Edition. Joyce Cox & Polly Urban. LC 94-66495. (Quick Course Ser.). (Illus.). 164p. (Orig.). 1994. pap. text 14.95 (*1-879399-33-4*) Online Training.

Quick Course in PowerPoint 97. Online Press Inc. Staff. (Quick Course Ser.). (Illus.). 60p. 1997. pap. text, wbk. ed. 11.95 (*1-879399-79-2*) Online Training.

Quick Course in PowerPoint 97: Education/Training Edition. Joyce K. Cox & Polly Urban. LC 97-66248. (Quick Course Ser.). (Illus.). 163p. 1997. pap. text 14.95 (*1-879399-72-5*) Online Training.

Quick Course in the Internet Using Internet Explorer 4: Education/Training Edition. Joyce K. Cox et al. LC 97-69953. (Quick Course Ser.). (Illus.). 168p. 1997. pap. text 14.95 (*1-879399-68-7*) Online Training.

***Quick Course in the Internet Using Internet Explorer 5: Education/Training Edition.** Joyce Cox. LC 99-70323. (Quick Course Ser.). 1999. pap. text 15.95 (*1-879399-91-1*) Online Training.

Quick Course in the Internet Using Netscape Navigator, Versions 2 & 3: Education/Training Edition. Joyce Cox. LC 96-68408. (Quick Course Ser.). (Illus.). 138p. 1996. pap. text 14.95 (*1-879399-67-9*) Online Training.

Quick Course in Windows for Workgroups: Education/Training Edition. Joyce Cox & Patrick Kervran. LC 92-62065. (Quick Course Ser.). (Illus.). 151p. 1992. pap. text 14.95 (*1-879399-22-9*) Online Training.

Quick Course in Windows 95: Education/Training Edition. Joyce Cox. LC 95-71904. (Quick Course Ser.). (Illus.). 172p. 1995. pap. text 14.95 (*1-879399-34-2*) Online Training.

Quick Course in Windows NT Workstation 4: Education/Training Edition. Joyce Cox et al. LC 97-69952. (Quick Course Ser.). (Illus.). 204p. 1997. pap. text 16.95 (*1-879399-64-4*) Online Training.

Quick Course in Windows 3.1: Education/Training Edition. Salley Oberlin et al. LC 92-60030. (Quick Course Ser.). (Illus.). 133p. (Orig.). 1992. pap. text 14.95 (*1-879399-14-8*) Online Training.

Quick Course in Windows 2000. Online Press Inc. Staff. 224p. 15.95 (*1-58278-000-5*); wbk. ed. 12.75 (*1-58278-009-9*) Online Training.

Quick Course in Word 97: Education/Training Edition. Joyce K. Cox & Christina Dudley. LC 97-66249. (Quick Course Ser.). 164p. 1997. pap. text 14.95 (*1-879399-70-9*) Online Training.

Quick Course in Word 7 for Windows 95: Education/Training Edition. Joyce Cox & Christina/ Dudley. LC 96-67884. (Quick Course Ser.). (Illus.). 156p. 1996. pap. text 14.95 (*1-879399-50-4*) Online Training.

Quick Course in Word 6 for Windows: Education/ Training Edition. Joyce Cox & Steve Lambert. LC 93-86381. (Quick Course Ser.). (Illus.). 164p. (Orig.). 1993. pap. text 14.95 (*1-879399-27-X*) Online Training.

Quick Course in WordPerfect 6.1 for Windows: Education/Training Edition. Polly Urban & Joyce Cox. LC 93-84870. (Quick Course Ser.). (Illus.). 176p. (Orig.). 1995. pap. text 14.95 (*1-879399-49-0*) Online Training.

Quick Course Office 97: Professional Edition. Microsoft Corporation Staff. 1997. pap. text 53.99 (*1-57231-879-1*) Microsoft.

Quick Course Office 97 Workbook Instructor's Resource Packet. Online Press Inc. Staff. (Quick Course Ser.). (Illus.). 1997. pap. text 14.95 (*1-879399-83-0*) Online Training.

Quick Course PowerPoint 97 Workbook Instructor's Resource Packet. Online Press Inc. Staff. (Quick Course Ser.). (Illus.). 1997. pap. text 11.95 (*1-879399-86-5*) Online Training.

Quick Course Shakespeare. Monarch. 384p. 1995. pap. 14.95 (*0-02-860015-0*) Macmillan.

Quick Course Windows 98 Workbook Instructor's Resource Packet. Contrib. by Online Press Inc. Staff. (Quick Course). (Illus.). 1998. pap. text 12.95 (*1-879399-89-X*) Online Training.

Quick Course Word 97 Workbook Instructor's Resource Packet. Online Press Inc. Staff. (Quick Course Ser.). (Illus.). 1997. pap. text 11.95 (*1-879399-87-3*) Online Training.

Quick Cozy Flannel Quilts. Arts Leisure Staff. 64p. 1999. pap. 9.95 (*0-8487-1948-4*) Oxmoor Hse.

Quick Creative Quilting. Ed. by Sandra Hatch & Jeanne Stauffer. (Illus.). 176p. 1999. 19.95 (*1-882138-51-1*) Hse White Birches.

Quick Cricket. Houghton Mifflin Company Staff. (Literature Experience 1991 Ser.). (J). 1990. pap. 6.36 (*0-395-53876-9*) HM.

Quick Critical Care Reference. 3rd ed. Susan B. Stillwell. (Illus.). 80p. (C). (gr. 13). 1998. pap. text 8.95 (*0-8151-3694-3*, 31036) Mosby Inc.

Quick Crockery Cooking: A One Foot in the Kitchen Cookbook. Cyndi Duncan & Georgie Patrick. (Illus.). 168p. 1997. per. 14.95 (*0-9626335-5-0*) C&G Pub CO.

Quick Crowdbreakers & Games for Youth Groups: More Than 200 Fun Mixers. (Illus.). 189p. 1988. pap. 14.99 (*0-931529-46-8*) Group Pub.

Quick Cue-Rapid Review Final Exam Prep Cards. Steven Guemann. (SPA.). 194p. (C). 1994. 7.95 (*0-8403-9865-4*) Kendall-Hunt.

Quick Cuisine. Elizabeth Fraser. LC 83-82661. 144p. 1984. pap. 6.95 (*0-89709-130-2*) Liberty Pub.

Quick Cuisine: Fabulous Meals in Minutes. Dee Hobsbawn-Smith. (Illus.). 240p. 1998. pap. 14.95 (*1-55110-768-6*) Whitecap Bks.

Quick-Cut Basket Quilts. Sharon C. Ogden. LC 97-46415. (Illus.). 32p. 1998. pap., spiral bd. 3.95 (*0-486-29911-2*) Dover.

Quick Desk Reference to Mental Health Treatment Goals: Targeted Treatment Goals for Behavioral Healthcare. Howard Davol et al. 262p. 1996. ring bd. 29.99 (*0-9659932-0-5*) Behav Therapy.

Quick Die Change. David A. Smith. LC 90-62589. (Illus.). 357p. 1990. 79.00 (*0-87263-393-4*) SME.

Quick Drug Consult for Mental Health & Psychiatric Nursing. Ellen H. Janosik & Janet L. Davies. LC 95-51370. 600p. 1996. pap. text 11.95 (*0-316-17688-5*) Lppncott W & W.

Quick Drug Reference for the Optometrist. Susan W. Phillips & Jeffrey D. Phillips. 260p. 1998. spiral bd. 34.00 (*1-890018-27-9*) Anadem Pubng.

Quick Easy to Learn . . . Geography: Europe. Fred Castro. Ed. by Leah Kohlenberg & Paul Roach. LC 92-71431. (Illus.). (Orig.). 1992. pap. text 9.95 (*1-881314-03-0*) Creat Tour Mgmt Dev.

Quick Easy Way to Learn . . . Geography: Africa. Fred Castro. Ed. by Leah Kohlenberg & Paul Roach. LC 92-71431. (Illus.). (Orig.). 1992. pap. text 9.95 (*1-881314-05-7*) Creat Tour Mgmt Dev.

Quick Easy Way to Learn . . . Geography: Central & South America. Fred Castro. Ed. by Leah Kohlenberg & Paul Roach. LC 92-71431. (Illus.). (Orig.). 1992. pap. text 9.95 (*1-881314-02-2*) Creat Tour Mgmt Dev.

Quick Easy Way to Learn . . . Geography: North America & Canada. Fred Castro. Ed. by Leah Kohlenberg & Paul Roach. LC 92-71431. (Illus.). (Orig.). 1992. pap. text 9.95 (*1-881314-01-4*) Creat Tour Mgmt Dev.

Quick Easy Way to Learn . . . Geography: The Caribbean. Fred Castro. Ed. by Leah Kohlenberg & Paul Roach. LC 92-71431. (Illus.). (Orig.). 1992. pap. text 9.95 (*1-881314-06-5*) Creat Tour Mgmt Dev.

Quick Easy Way to Learn . . . Geography: The Middle East. Fred Castro. Ed. by Leah Kohlenberg & Paul Roach. LC 92-71431. (Illus.). (Orig.). 1992. pap. text 9.95 (*1-881314-07-3*) Creat Tour Mgmt Dev.

Quick Easy Way to Learn . . . World Geography. Fred Castro. Ed. by Leah Kohlenberg & Paul Roach. LC 92-71431. (Illus.). 310p. (Orig.). 1992. pap. text 24.95 (*1-881314-00-6*) Creat Tour Mgmt Dev.

Quick Easy Way to Learn Geography... The World: Asia & the Pacific. 2nd rev. ed. Fred Castro. Ed. by Paul Roach & Leah Kohlenberg. LC 92-71431. (Illus.). 264p. (Orig.). 1992. pap. text 24.95 (*1-881314-04-9*) Creat Tour Mgmt Dev.

Quick Emergency Care Reference. Gennell Lee. (Illus.). 60p. (C). (gr. 13). 1991. pap. text 8.95 (*0-8016-6584-1*, 06584) Mosby Inc.

***Quick Escapes: Philadelphia: Twenty-Four Weekend Get-a-Ways from the City of Brotherly Love.** Maria Piantanida & Marilyn Odesser-Torpey. LC 99-15495. (Quick Escapes Ser.). (Illus.). 288p. 1999. pap. text 14.95 (*0-7627-0444-6*) Globe Pequot.

Quick Escapes: San Diego. 2nd ed. Bobbi Zane. LC 99-59135. (Quick Escapes Ser.). (Illus.). 256p. 2000. pap. text 14.95 (*0-7627-0539-6*) Globe Pequot.

***Quick Escapes - Boston: 25 Weekend Getaways from the Hub.** Sandy Macdonald. (Quick Escapes Ser.). (Illus.). 320p. 2000. pap. 15.95 (*0-7627-0708-9*) Globe Pequot.

***Quick Escapes - Chicago: 26 Weekend Getaways in & Around the Windy City.** 4th ed. Bonnie Miller Rubin & Marcy Mason. LC 00-25055. (Quick Escapes Ser.). (Illus.). 320p. 2000. pap. 15.95 (*0-7627-0628-7*) Globe Pequot.

***Quick Escapes - Cleveland: 25 Weekend Getaways in & Around Northern Ohio.** Marcia Schonberg. (Quick Escapes Ser.). (Illus.). 256p. 2000. pap. 14.95 (*0-7627-0709-7*) Globe Pequot.

Q

***Quick Escapes - Dallas/Fort Worth: 37 Weekend Getaways in & Around the Lone Star State.** 3rd ed. June Naylor Rodriguez. LC 00-25056. (Quick Escapes Ser.). (Illus.). 368p. 2000. pap. 15.95 (*0-7627-0642-2*) Globe Pequot.

***Quick Escapes - Denver: 26 Weekend Getaways from the Mile High City.** 2nd ed. Sherry Spitsnaugle. LC 00-26430. (Quick Escapes Ser.). (Illus.). 240p. 2000. pap. 14.95 (*0-7627-0633-3*) Globe Pequot.

***Quick Escapes - Minneapolis/St. Paul: 25 Weekend Getaways in & Around the Twin Cities.** 2nd ed. Jane H. O'Reilly. (Quick Escapes Ser.). (Illus.). 320p. 2000. pap. 15.95 (*0-7627-0637-6*) Globe Pequot.

***Quick Escapes, Atlanta: 32 Weekend Getaways from the Gateway to the South.** 3rd ed. Carol Thalimer & Dan Thalimer. (Quick Escapes Ser.). (Illus.). 416p. 2000. pap. 14.95 (*0-7627-0641-4*) Globe Pequot.

Quick Escapes Atlanta: 38 Weekend Getaways in the Deep South. 2nd ed. Dan Thalimer & Carol Thalimer. LC 98-5707. (Quick Escapes Ser.). (Illus.). 368p. 1998. pap. 14.95 (*0-7627-0198-6*) Globe Pequot.

Quick Escapes Denver: 35 Weekend Getaways in & Around the Mile High City in Denver. Sherry Spitsnaugle. LC 97-47754. (Quick Escapes Ser.). (Illus.). 256p. 1998. pap. 14.95 (*0-7627-0197-8*) Globe Pequot.

Quick Escapes Detroit: 26 Weekend Trips from the Motor City. 2nd ed. Khristi Zimmeth. LC 98-49570. (Quick Escapes Ser.). (Illus.). 256p. 1999. pap. text 14.95 (*0-7627-0424-1*) Globe Pequot.

Quick Escapes Florida: 29 Weekend Escapes in & Around the Sunshine State. 2nd ed. W. Lynn Seldon, Jr. (Quick Escapes Ser.). (Illus.). 224p. 1999. pap. text 14.95 (*0-7627-0538-8*) Globe Pequot.

Quick Escapes from Chicago: 25 Weekend Trips from the Windy City. 3rd ed. Bonnie M. Rubin & Marcy Mason. LC 97-49972. (Quick Escapes Ser.). (Illus.). 224p. 1998. pap. 14.95 (*0-7627-0195-1*) Globe Pequot.

Quick Escapes from Dallas - Ft. Worth: 30 Weekend Getaways in & Around the Lone Star State. 2nd ed. June N. Rodriguez. LC 98-13782. (Quick Escapes Ser.). (Illus.). 240p. 1998. pap. 14.95 (*0-7627-0196-X*) Globe Pequot.

Quick Escapes from Los Angeles: 24 Weekend Getaways from the Metro Area. 3rd ed. Eleanor Harris. LC 98-41471. (Quick Escapes Ser.). (Illus.). 320p. 1999. pap. 14.95 (*0-7627-0293-1*) Globe Pequot.

Quick Escapes from Minneapolis - St. Paul: 25 Weekend Getaways from the Twin Cities. Jane O'Reilly. LC 97-47753. (Quick Escapes Ser.). (Illus.). 256p. 1998. pap. 14.95 (*0-7627-0199-4*) Globe Pequot.

Quick Escapes from New York City: 31 Weekend Trips from the Big Apple. 3rd ed. Susan Farewell. LC 98-55461. (Quick Escapes Ser.). (Illus.). 256p. 1999. pap. text 14.95 (*0-7627-0397-0*) Globe Pequot.

Quick Escapes from San Francisco: 30 Weekend Trips from the Bay Area. 3rd ed. Karen Misuraca. LC 98-41608. (Quick Escapes Ser.). (Illus.). 352p. 1999. pap. 14.95 (*0-7627-0294-X*) Globe Pequot.

***Quick Escapes from Washington, D. C. 24 Weekend Getaways from the Nation's Capital.** 3rd ed. John Fitzpatrick & Holly Burkhalter. (Quick Escapes Ser.). (Illus.). 336p. 2000. pap. 15.95 (*0-7627-0636-8*) Globe Pequot.

Quick Escapes from Washington, D. C. 25 Weekend Getaways from the Nation's Capital. 2nd ed. John Fitzpatrick & Holly Burkhalter. LC 97-46694. (Quick Escapes Ser.). (Illus.). 256p. 1998. pap. 14.95 (*0-7627-0200-1*) Globe Pequot.

Quick Escapes in the Pacific Northwest: 32 Weekend Trips from Portland, Seattle, & Vancouver, B.C. 4th ed. Marilyn McFarlane. Ed. by Christine Cunningham. LC 99-24575. (Quick Escapes Ser.). 336p. 1999. pap. text 14.95 (*0-7627-0468-3*) Globe Pequot.

***Quick Escapes Los Angeles: 23 Weekend Getaways from the Metro Area.** 4th ed. Eleanor Harris. (Illus.). 2001. pap. 15.95 (*0-7627-0834-4*) Globe Pequot.

***Quick Escapes St. Louis: 26 Weekend Getaways from the Gateway City.** Julie Gustafson. (Illus.). 2001. pap. 14.95 (*0-7627-0799-2*) Globe Pequot.

***Quick Escapes San Francisco: 26 Weekend Getaways from the Bay Area.** 4th ed. Karen Misuraca. (Quick Escapes Ser.). (Illus.). 2001. pap. 15.95 (*0-7627-0835-2*) Globe Pequot.

Quick Escapes Toronto: 26 Weekend Trips in Ontario. 2nd ed. David E. Scott. LC 99-14878. (Quick Escapes Ser.). (Illus.). 300p. 2000. pap. text 14.95 (*0-7627-0469-1*) Globe Pequot.

Quick Fasting. Nathaniel H. Bronner, Jr. (Illus.). 144p. (Orig.). 1995. pap. 9.95 (*0-9631075-1-8*) Cent Systs.

***Quick Feng Shui Cures.** Sarah Shurety. LC 99-30309. (Illus.). 144p. 2000. 25.00 (*0-688-17297-0*) Morrow Avon.

Quick, Find a Ring! Jo Leigh. 1997. per. 3.75 (*0-373-16695-8*, 1-16695-8) Harlequin Bks.

Quick Finite Element Method for Electromagnetic Waves. Giuseppe Pelosi et al. LC 98-16279. 216p. 1998. 95.00 incl. cd-rom (*0-89006-848-8*) Artech Hse.

Quick Fire & Slow Fire. Irene McKinney. 64p. 1989. pap. 7.95 (*1-55643-046-9*) North Atlantic.

Quick-Fix Home Repair. rev. ed. Richard D'Arezzo. Ed. by Christie Alexander. (Quick-Fix Ser.). (Illus.). 160p. 1987. pap. 6.95 (*0-939353-08-3*) Alexander & Alexander.

***Quick Fix Your Emotional Intelligence.** Harry Alder. 192p. 2000. pap. 9.95 (*1-85703-653-0*, Pub. by How To Bks) Midpt Trade.

Quick Fixes: 303 Ways to Help Yourself Before the Therapist Arrives. Marylou Hughes. (Illus.). 223p. 1998. pap. text 14.00 (*0-7881-5253-X*) DIANE Pub.

Quick Fixes to Change Your Life: Making Healthy Choices. Judy Walz. LC 94-48587. (Illus.). 156p. (Orig.). 1995. pap. 10.95 (*1-881915-01-8*) Creat Hlth Srvs.

***Quick-Flip Activities for Multiple Intelligences.** Constance Doti Ryan. Ed. by Kathy Rogers. 1998. 3.99 (*1-56472-490-5*) Edupress Inc.

***Quick-Flip Ideas for Writing Domains.** Constance Doti Ryan. Ed. by Kathy Rogers. 1998. 3.99 (*1-56472-491-3*) Edupress Inc.

Quick Flip Questions for Critical Thinking. 1994. pap. 3.99 (*1-56472-047-0*) Edupress Inc.

***Quick Flip Reference for Phonics.** Constance Doti Ryan. Ed. by Kathy Rogers. 1998. 3.99 (*1-56472-492-1*) Edupress Inc.

Quick Flip to Delicious Dinners. Eileen Faughey. (Illus.). 1996. spiral bd. 15.95 (*0-9650412-1-2*) Nutrition Connect.

Quick from Scratch. LC 96-42367. 1997. write for info. (*0-916103-33-1*) Am Express Food.

Quick from Scratch. LC 97-41317. 1998. write for info. (*0-916103-41-2*) Am Express Food.

Quick from Scratch. LC 98-31332. 1998. write for info. (*0-916103-51-X*) Am Express Food.

Quick from Scratch. Ed. by American Express Publisher Staff. LC 98-2721. 1998. 25.95 (*0-916103-45-5*) Am Express Food.

Quick from Scratch. Food & Wine (New York, N. Y.) Staff. LC 96-29854. 1997. write for info. (*0-916103-35-8*) Am Express Food.

Quick from Scratch. Judith Hills. LC 98-8309. 1998. 25.95 (*0-916103-49-8*) Am Express Food.

Quick from Scratch: Fish & Shellfish. LC 97-15944. (Illus.). 1997. 25.95 (*0-916103-38-2*) Am Express Food.

Quick from Scratch: One-Dish Meals. LC 97-33650. 1998. 25.95 (*0-916103-40-4*) Am Express Food.

Quick from Scratch: Real Food for Busy Weeknights. LC 96-6203. 1996. write for info. (*0-916103-31-5*) Am Express Food.

Quick from Scratch Chicken. 1998. text 25.95 (*0-312-18841-2*) St Martin.

Quick from Scratch Pasta. 1998. text 25.95 (*0-312-18842-0*) St Martin.

Quick Fun with the Autoharp. R. Yoder. 1990. 6.95 (*0-685-31450-2*, H658) Hansen Ed Mus.

Quick Fun with the Harmonica. 1990. 6.95 (*0-685-31449-9*, H723) Hansen Ed Mus.

Quick Fun with the Recorder. 1990. 6.95 (*0-685-32150-9*, H663) Hansen Ed Mus.

Quick Games for Children's Ministry: 100 Games. Ed. by Beth Rowland. LC 92-33256. 1992. 14.99 (*1-55945-157-2*) Group Pub.

Quick Gifts & Decor. Jeffery D. Phillips & Gail Brown. LC 98-65709. (Illus.). 144p. 1998. pap. 19.95 (*0-8487-1679-5*, 108603) Oxmoor Hse.

Quick Gifts of Good Taste. Leisure Arts Staff. LC 93-80810. 128p. 1994. 19.95 (*0-942237-35-8*) Leisure AR.

Quick Group Devotions for Children's Ministry: 52 Lively Activities. (Illus.). 96p. 1991. pap. 14.99 (*1-55945-004-5*) Group Pub.

Quick Guide: Attics. 2nd ed. Mark Feirer. Ed. by Dave Dchiff. LC 94-69652. (Quick Guide Ser.). (Illus.). 80p. 1998. pap. 7.95 (*1-880029-42-1*) Creative Homeowner.

Quick Guide: Basements. 2nd ed. Mark Feirer. Ed. by Patrick Quinn. LC 94-69656. (Quick Guide Ser.). (Illus.). 80p. 1998. pap. 7.95 (*1-880029-44-8*) Creative Homeowner.

Quick Guide: Ceramic Tile. Creative Homeowner Press Editors. Ed. by Jim Barrett. LC 93-71661. (Quick Guide Ser.). (Illus.). 80p. 1993. pap. 7.95 (*1-880029-21-9*) Creative Homeowner.

Quick Guide: Decks. Steve Cory. Ed. by Jeff Day et al. LC 97-75261. (Quick Guide Ser.). (Illus.). 80p. 1998. pap. 7.95 (*1-58011-000-2*) Creative Homeowner.

Quick Guide: Floors. 2nd ed. Ed. by Arnie E. Edelstein & Kimberly Kerrigone. LC 92-81621. (Quick Guide Ser.). (Illus.). 80p. 1998. pap. 7.95 (*1-880029-06-5*) Creative Homeowner.

Quick Guide: Garages & Carports. Jack P. Jones. Ed. by Timothy O. Bakke. LC 96-84691. (Quick Guide Ser.). (Illus.). 80p. (Orig.). 1997. pap. 7.95 (*1-880029-87-1*) Creative Homeowner.

Quick Guide: Gazebos. Drew Corinchock & James Russell. Ed. by David Schiff. LC 95-70916. (Quick Guide Ser.). (Illus.). 80p. (Orig.). 1995. pap. 7.95 (*1-880029-52-9*) Creative Homeowner.

Quick Guide: Insulation & Ventilation. Jerry Germer. Ed. by David Schiff & Patrick Quinn. LC 94-69657. (Quick Guide Ser.). (Illus.). 80p. 1995. pap. 7.95 (*1-880029-45-6*) Creative Homeowner.

Quick Guide: Interior & Exterior Painting. Walter Jones & Alexander Samuelson. LC 93-73999. (Quick Guide Ser.). (Illus.). 80p. 1994. pap. 7.95 (*1-880029-30-8*) Creative Homeowner.

Quick Guide: Masonry Walls. Christine Beall & Creative Homeowner Press Editors. Ed. by Alexander Samuelson. LC 97-66870. (Quick Guide Ser.). (Illus.). 80p. 1997. pap. 7.95 (*1-880029-92-8*) Creative Homeowner.

Quick Guide: Patios & Walks. Ed. by Arnie Edelstein & Kimberly Kerrigone. LC 92-81620. (Quick Guide Ser.). (Illus.). 80p. 1992. pap. 7.95 (*1-880029-07-3*) Creative Homeowner.

Quick Guide: Plumbing. 2nd ed. Ed. by Warren Ramezzana. LC 92-81624. (Quick Guide Ser.). (Illus.). 80p. 1998. pap. 7.95 (*1-880029-12-X*) Creative Homeowner.

Quick Guide: Ponds & Fountains. 2nd ed. Jim Barrett. Ed. by Laura Tringali. LC 93-73997. (Quick Guide Ser.). (Illus.). 80p. 1998. pap. 7.95 (*1-880029-29-4*) Creative Homeowner.

Quick Guide: Pool & Spa Maintenance. Alexander Samuelson. LC 94-69653. (Quick Guide Ser.). (Illus.). 80p. 1998. pap. 7.95 (*1-880029-43-X*) Creative Homeowner.

Quick Guide: Roofing. 2nd ed. Dave Toht. Ed. by Dave Schiff. LC 94-71874. (Quick Guide Ser.). (Illus.). 80p. 1997. pap. 7.95 (*1-880029-37-5*) Creative Homeowner.

Quick Guide: Shelving & Storage. Michael Presutti. Ed. by Timothy O. Bakke. LC 97-60332. (Quick Guide Ser.). (Illus.). 80p. 1997. pap. 7.95 (*1-880029-91-X*) Creative Homeowner.

Quick Guide: Siding. 2nd ed. David W. Toht. LC 94-69649. (Quick Guide Ser.). (Illus.). 80p. 1998. pap. 7.95 (*1-880029-40-5*) Creative Homeowner.

Quick Guide: Stairs & Railings. Jeff Beneke. Ed. by Timothy O. Bakke & Rich Ziegner. LC 96-84681. (Quick Guide Ser.). (Illus.). 80p. (Orig.). 1997. pap. 7.95 (*1-880029-88-X*) Creative Homeowner.

Quick Guide: Storage Sheds. Jim Barrett. LC 93-71658. (Quick Guide Ser.). (Illus.). 80p. 1996. pap. 7.95 (*1-880029-20-0*) Creative Homeowner.

Quick Guide: Trim & Molding. 2nd ed. Mark Feirer. Ed. by Creative Homeowner Press Editors. LC 93-73996. (Quick Guide Ser.). (Illus.). 80p. 1998. pap. 7.95 (*1-880029-27-8*) Creative Homeowner.

Quick Guide: Walls & Ceilings. Ed. by Kimberly Kerrigone & Arnie Edelstein. LC 92-81622. (Quick Guide Ser.). (Illus.). 80p. 1992. pap. 7.95 (*1-880029-08-1*) Creative Homeowner.

Quick Guide: Windows & Doors. Ed. by Mark Feirer. LC 93-71659. (Quick Guide Ser.). (Illus.). 80p. 1994. pap. 7.95 (*1-880029-23-5*) Creative Homeowner.

Quick Guide: Wiring. 3rd rev. ed. Ed. by Patrick Quinn & Timothy O. Bakke. LC 96-84212. (Quick Guide Ser.). (Illus.). 80p. 1998. pap. 7.95 (*1-880029-83-9*) Creative Homeowner.

***Quick Guide & Directory to Grant Money Sources.** 2nd ed. Ed. by S. David Hicks. 148p. 2000. pap. 25.00 (*1-56150-367-3*) Intl Wealth.

Quick Guide to Basic. Dill. (DF - Computer Applications Ser.). 1994. mass mkt. 19.95 (*0-538-62924-X*) S-W Pub.

Quick Guide to Decorating Your Home Yourself. Aviva Davis. (Illus.). 35p. (Orig.). 1995. pap. 12.95 (*0-9647085-0-7*) Expo Group.

Quick Guide to DOS. Dill. (DF - Computer Applications Ser.). 1992. mass mkt. 19.95 (*0-538-61778-0*) S-W Pub.

Quick Guide to Financial Formulas for 1-2-3 Users. Steve Adams. Ed. by Hunt. (Illus.). 350p. (Orig.). 1990. pap. 24.95 (*0-13-745134-2*) Brady Pub.

Quick Guide to Food Additives. 2nd ed. Robert Goodman. LC 89-63962. 62p. (Orig.). 1990. pap. 5.95 (*0-9624945-1-8*) Silvercat Pubns.

Quick Guide to Food Safety. Robert Goodman. 86p. (Orig.). 1992. pap. 6.95 (*0-9624945-3-4*) Silvercat Pubns.

Quick Guide to Solving Common Health Conditions with Commercial Herb Formulas. Steven H. Horne & Steven R. Johnson. (Illus.). 100p. 1997. pap. 9.95 (*1-890855-01-4*) Tree of Light.

Quick Guide to the Internet. Julia C. Bradley. 109p. 1995. 17.95 (*0-534-26076-4*) Wadsworth Pub.

***Quick Guide to The Internet for Psychology.** 128p. (C). 1999. pap. text 0.00 (*0-536-02827-3*) Pearson Custom.

***Quick Guide to the Verbal SAT: How to Add 100 Points or More to Your Score.** Dawn B. Sova. (Schaum's Quick Guides Ser.). (Illus.). 2000. pap. 10.95 (*0-07-135401-8*) McGraw.

Quick Guides to Inclusion: Ideas for Educating Students with Disabilities. Michael F. Giangreco. LC 97-7106. 139p. 1997. pap. text 21.95 (*1-55766-303-3*) P H Brookes.

Quick-Guides to Inclusion 2: Ideas for Educating Students with Disabilities. 2nd ed. Ed. by Michael F. Giangreco. 160p. 1998. spiral bd. 21.95 (*1-55766-335-1*, 3351) P H Brookes.

Quick Hanging. large type ed. Jerome Gardner. (Linford Western Library). 272p. 1996. pap. 16.99 (*0-7089-7813-4*, Linford) Ulverscroft.

Quick Help! Best-Ever Ideas for Youth Ministry from Group Magazine. Ed. by Debbie Gowensmith & Amy Simpson. LC 97-8355. 80p. 1997. pap. 14.99 (*0-7644-2018-6*) Group Pub.

***Quick Help with Troublesome Words & Phrases.** James E. Allison. LC 00-41357. 2001. write for info. (*0-7641-1633-9*) Barron.

***Quick History of Glenwood Springs.** Jim Nelson. 125p. 1999. pap. 7.95 (*1-928971-00-8*) Blue Chicken.

***Quick History of Grand Lake: Including Rocky Mountain National Park & the Grand Lake Lodge.** Michael M. Geary. (Illus.). 129p. 1999. pap. 9.95 (*1-890437-37-9*) Western Reflections.

***Quick History of Marble & Redstone.** Jim Nelson. 135p. 1999. pap. 7.95 (*1-928971-02-4*) Blue Chicken.

Quick Hits: Successful Strategies by Award Winning Teachers. Ed. by Eileen T. Bender et al. LC 94-3693. (Illus.). 104p. 1994. pap. text 12.95 (*0-253-20923-4*) Ind U Pr.

***Quick Home-Cooked Meals: Letting Your Microwave Work for You.** Mary Ann Zepp. LC 99-46391. 224p. 1999. pap. 13.95 (*1-56148-290-0*) Good Bks PA.

Quick Index - Banking Regulations. W. H. Heaton. 1000p. write for info. (*1-881057-15-1*) Heaton Pubns.

Quick Index - Health Administrative Laws, Regulations & Guidelines, 4 vols., Set. W. H. Heaton. 924p. 1993. 329.95 (*1-881057-09-7*) Heaton Pubns.

Quick Index - Health Administrative Laws, Regulations & Guidelines, Vol. 1. W. H. Heaton. 924p. 1993. write for info. (*1-881057-10-0*) Heaton Pubns.

Quick Index - OSHA Regulations. W. H. Heaton. 1000p. write for info. (*1-881057-08-9*) Heaton Pubns.

Quick Index - U. S. Code. W. H. Heaton. 1000p. write for info. (*1-881057-14-3*) Heaton Pubns.

Quick Index to R. O. P. Long-Term Care Facilities. W. H. Heaton. 277p. 1991. ring bd. 89.95 (*1-881057-01-1*) Heaton Pubns.

Quick Internet Guide for Careers & Labor Market Information. JIST Staff. LC 97-21862. 52p. 1997. pap. 9.95 (*1-56370-438-2*) Park Ave.

***Quick Internet Guide to Career & Education Information.** Anne Wolfinger. Ed. by Lori Cates. LC 99-39405. (Illus.). 176p. 1999. pap. 16.95 (*1-56370-622-9*) JIST Works.

***Quick Internet Guide to Career & Education Information.** Anne Wolfinger. 2000. pap. 16.95 (*1-56370-807-8*) JIST Works.

Quick Interview & Salary Negotiation Book: Dramatically Improve Your Interviewing Skills in Just a Few Hours. J. Michael Farr. (Quick Guide Ser.). 380p. (Orig.). 1995. pap. 12.95 (*1-56370-162-6*, J1626) JIST Works.

Quick IV Therapy Reference. Cynthia L. Hermey. (Illus.). 88p. (C). (gr. 13). 1994. pap. text 8.95 (*0-8151-4236-6*, 24616) Mosby Inc.

Quick Job Hunt Guide: A Sure Way to Land That Job! Robert D. Siedle. LC 90-70123. 96p. 1991. pap. 7.95 (*0-914984-33-0*) Starburst.

Quick Job Search. rev. ed. J. Michael Farr. 36p. 1989. pap. text 2.95 (*1-56370-242-8*, QJSP) JIST Works.

Quick Job Search. rev. ed. J. Michael Farr. 32p. 1995. pap. 3.80 (*1-56370-235-5*, J2355) JIST Works.

Quick Keyboard Chords. 1998. 9.95 (*1-56922-118-9*, 07-2040) Creat Cncpts.

Quick Kids' Quilts: Easy-to-Do Projects for Newborns to Older Children. Juju Vail. (Illus.). 128p. 1999. pap. 19.95 (*1-55209-350-6*) Firefly Bks Ltd.

Quick Killer. Jake McMasters. (White Apache Ser.: No. 4). 176p. (Orig.). 1994. pap. text, mass mkt. 3.99 (*0-8439-3646-0*) Dorchester Pub Co.

***Quick Killing.** James P. Bandler. LC 99-65319. 192p. 2000. pap. 11.95 (*1-56315-253-3*, Pub. by SterlingHse) Natl Bk Netwk.

Quick-Lab II for AC Circuits: Conventional-Flow Edition. Albert P. Malvino. (CGA, Hercules, EGA - VGA Graphics Ser.). (Illus.). 188p. (Orig.). (C). 1991. pap., student ed. 18.45 (*1-56048-986-3*, 982C) Malvino Inc.

Quick Learning Kits: Art & Literature. Linda Milliken. 96p. 1992. pap., teacher ed. 8.95 (*1-56472-004-7*) Edupress Inc.

Quick Learning Kits: Language & Social Studies. Linda Milliken. 96p. 1992. pap., teacher ed. 8.95 (*1-56472-005-5*) Edupress Inc.

Quick Learning Kits: Math & Science. Linda Milliken. 96p. 1992. pap., teacher ed. 8.95 (*1-56472-006-3*) Edupress Inc.

Quick Lit: Plots, Themes, Characters, & Sample Essays for the Most Assigned Books in English & Literature Courses - Written by Students for Students. Seth Godin. LC 92-52537. 304p. 1992. pap. 13.00 (*0-06-461041-1*, Harper Ref) HarpC.

Quick Little Quilts: The Complete Guide to Making Miniature & Lap Quilts. Janet Wickell & Donna Stidman. LC 97-46551. (Illus.). 192p. 1998. pap. 21.95 (*0-8442-2659-9*, Quilt Dgst Pr) NTC Contemp Pub Co.

Quick Look at Visual Basic. Trainor. 1996. 8.50 (*0-07-065321-6*) McGraw.

Quick Look Drug Book. 1991. write for info. (*0-683-07053-3*) Lppncott W & W.

Quick Look Drug Book. 600p. 1994. 24.95 (*0-683-07047-9*) Lppncott W & W.

Quick Look Drug Book, 1998. Leonard L. Lance. 1998. write for info. (*0-683-40174-2*) Lppncott W & W.

Quick Look Drug Book, 1997. Leonard L. Lance et al. 719p. 1997. pap. 34.95 (*0-683-40057-6*) Lppncott W & W.

Quick Look Drug Book, 1996. Leonard L. Lance et al. 787p. (Orig.). 1996. pap. 34.95 (*0-683-07045-2*) Lppncott W & W.

Quick Look Drug Book 1999. 750p. 34.95 (*0-683-40304-4*) Lppncott W & W.

Quick Look Drug Book 2000. 750p. pap. text 35.95 (*0-7817-2092-3*) Lppncott W & W.

Quick Look Techniques for Prospect Evaluation. Daniel J. Tearpock et al. LC 94-68541. (Illus.). 286p. 1994. 69.95 (*0-9642961-0-1*) Subsurface Conslts.

Quick Lube Guide, 1991. Chilton Automotive Editorial Staff. 304p. 1991. pap. 27.50 (*0-8019-8223-5*) Nichols Pub.

Quick Lubrication Guide, 1990. 288p. 1990. 105.00 (*0-13-130709-6*, H M Gousha) Prntice Hall Bks.

Quick Marches. John C. Moon. LC 75-19259. (Musick of the Fifes & Drums Ser.: Vol. 1). 24p. 1976. pap. 7.95 (*0-87935-031-8*) Colonial Williamsburg.

Quick Meals. Time-Life Books Editors. (Time-Life Favorite Recipes Ser.). 96p. (YA). (gr. 11). 1999. pap. 6.95 (*0-7370-1119-X*) T-L Custom Pub.

Quick Meals. Weight Watchers International Staff. LC 94-24255. (Illus.). 320p. 1995. 27.50 (*0-02-860351-6*) Macmillan.

Quick Meals for Healthly Kids & Busy Parents: Wholesome Family Recipes in 30 Minutes or Less. Sandra K. Nissenberg et al. 256p. 1995. pap. 12.95 (*1-56561-064-4*) Wiley.

Quick Meals for Healthy Kids & Busy Parents: Wholesome Family Meals in 30 Minutes or Less. Sandra K Nissenberg. (Illus.). 256p. 1995. pap. 14.95 (*0-471-34698-5*) Wiley.

Quick Medical Spanish. 2nd ed. Peter T. Rogers & Olga Ruiz-Rogers. LC 96-31450. 183p. (C). 1997. pap. text 24.95 incl. audio (*0-8385-8258-3*, A8258-4, Apple Lange Med) McGraw.

Quick Medical Terminology. 3rd ed. Genevieve L. Smith et al. LC 91-37703. (Self-Teaching Guides Ser.: No. 1581). 304p. 1992. pap. 18.95 (*0-471-54267-9*) Wiley.

An Asterisk (*) at the beginning of an entry indicates that the title is appearing for the first time.

***Quick Medication Administration Reference.** 3rd ed. Judith L. Myers. LC 99-174426. (Illus.). 80p. 1998. write for info. (*1-55664-481-7*) Mosby Inc.

Quick Memory Management Techniques. Brian Underdahl. 304p. 1994. pap. 24.95 (*0-471-05384-8*) Wiley.

Quick Method Favorite Quilts. Oxmoor House Staff. 160p. 1995. pap. 19.95 (*0-942237-61-7*) Leisure AR.

Quick Method Liberty Quilts. LC 96-76036. 160p. 1996. pap. text 19.95 (*1-57486-020-8*) Oxmoor Hse.

Quick Method Quilts, Bk. 1. Oxmoor House Staff. 160p. 1994. 19.95 (*0-942237-54-4*) Leisure AR.

Quick Method Quilts Galore. Oxmoor House Staff. LC 94-74354. 160p. 1995. pap. 19.95 (*0-942237-57-9*) Leisure AR.

Quick-Method Quilts with Style. (Quick-Method Ser.: No. 4). (Illus.). 160p. 1996. pap. text 19.95 (*1-57486-018-6*) Oxmoor Hse.

Quick Mexican Cooking: A One Foot in the Kitchen Cookbook. Cyndi Duncan & Georgie Patrick. LC 98-92651. (Illus.). 168p. 1998. 14.95 (*0-9626335-6-9*) C&G Pub CO.

Quick Mix Cakes. (Mini Cook Bks.). (Illus.). 64p. 1999. pap. 1.95 (*3-8290-1617-4*) Konemann.

Quick 'n Easy Country Cookin' Best of 1992-1993. Parkside Publication Inc. Staff. Ed. by Pam Schrag. 106p. 1994. pap. 6.95 (*0-9618379-7-7*) Parkside Pubns.

Quick-n-Easy Electronics Projects. Bob Greene. 1985. 7.95 (*0-86668-049-7*) ARCsoft.

Quick-n-Easy Mexican Recipes: Marvelous Mexican Meals, in Minutes! Susan K. Bollin. LC 93-21427. 128p. 1993. ring bd. 5.95 (*0-914846-85-X*) Golden West Pub.

Quick-n-Easy Natural Recipes. Lorrie Knutsen. LC 93-60955. 64p. 1993. per. 2.95 (*0-945383-57-6*) Teach Servs.

Quick 'n Fun Games for the IBM Personal Computer. Michael Fox. 96p. 1984. 8.95 (*0-86668-044-6*) ARCsoft.

Quick Notes & Fast Quotes for Every Occasion. 2nd ed. Jill Williams. (Lifestyles Ser.). 104p. (Orig.). (C). 1992. pap. 5.95 (*0-88908-540-4*) Self-Counsel Pr.

Quick, Now, Always. Mark Irwin. (American Poets Continuum Ser.: Vol. 36). 75p. 1996. 20.00 (*1-880238-30-6*); pap. 12.50 (*1-880238-31-4*) BOA Edns.

***Quick on the Trigger.** large type ed. Jake Douglas. 256p. 1999. pap. 18.99 (*0-7089-5516-9*, Linford) Ulverscroft.

Quick Opening Devices for Dry Pipe Valves for Fire Protection Service, UL 1486. 2nd ed. (C). 1993. pap. text 135.00 (*1-55989-442-3*) Underwrtrs Labs.

Quick Patchwork Projects. Abigail Barbier. LC 98-115177. (Illus.). 128p. 1998. 24.95 (*0-7063-7562-9*, Pub. by WrLock) Sterling.

Quick Pediatric Reference. Donna L. Wong. (Illus.). 64p. (C). (gr. 13). 1991. pap. text 8.95 (*0-8016-6362-8*, 06362) Mosby Inc.

Quick Poetry Activity. Jacqueline Sweeney. (Illus.). (J). 1994. pap. 14.95 (*0-590-49767-7*) Scholastic Inc.

Quick Printers' Ratios see 1996 PIA Ratios

Quick Psychopharmacology Reference. 2nd ed. Michele T. Laraia. (Illus.). 64p. (C). (gr. 13). 1994. pap. text 8.95 (*0-8016-8064-6*, 08064) Mosby Inc.

***Quick Python Book.** Kenneth McDonald. LC 99-38928. (Illus.). 422p. 1999. pap. 39.95 (*1-884777-74-0*) Manning Pubns.

Quick, Quack, Quick. Marsha D. Arnold. LC 94-38054. (Step into Reading Ser.: A Step 1 Book). (Illus.). 32p. (J). (ps-4). 1996. pap. 3.99 (*0-679-87243-4*) Random.

Quick, Quack, Quick. Marsha D. Arnold. (Step into Reading Ser.: A Step 1 Book). (J). (ps-1). 1996. 8.94 (*0-606-09775-9*, Pub. by Turtleback) Demco.

***Quick Question Workbook.** Nancy L. Johnson. 112p. 1999. pap. 13.95 (*1-880505-61-4*, CLC 0234) Pieces of Lrning.

Quick, Quick Said the Bird. Thor Vilhjalmsson. Tr. by John O'Kane. 206p. 1987. pap. 14.95 (*0-920806-96-1*, Pub. by Penumbra Pr) U of Toronto Pr.

Quick, Quiet & Feathered. Moira Butterfield. LC 96-30860. (What Am I? Ser.). (Illus.). 32p. (J). (ps-3). 1997. lib. bdg. 19.97 (*0-8172-4585-5*) Raintree Steck-V.

Quick, Quiet & Feathered. Moira Butterfield. (What Am I? Ser.). 1998. pap. 5.95 (*0-8172-7233-X*) Raintree Steck-V.

Quick Quilting: Rotary Cutting, Machine Piecing, Machine Applique & Machine Quilting. Kim H. Ritter. LC 97-15390. (Illus.). 128p. 1997. pap. 19.95 (*0-8442-2656-4*, Quilt Dgst Pr) NTC Contemp Pub Co.

Quick Quilts. Annette Claxton. (Needleworker's Collection). (Illus.). 112p. 10.99 (*1-57215-153-6*, JG1153) World Pubns.

Quick Quilts. Leisure Arts Staff. LC 91-61188. 160p. 1994. pap. 14.95 (*0-8487-1427-X*) Oxmoor Hse.

Quick Quilts: Patterns & Techniques. unabridged ed. Judy Florence. LC 95-15914. Orig. Title: Award-Winning Quick Quilts. 96p. 1995. reprint ed. pap. text 7.95 (*0-486-28769-6*) Dover.

Quick Quilts from the Heart. Liz Porter & Marianne Fons. 176p. 1995. pap. 19.95 (*0-8487-1442-3*) Oxmoor Hse.

Quick Quilts from Your Scrap Bag. Arts Leisure Staff. 144p. 1999. pap. 19.95 (*0-8487-1907-7*) Oxmoor Hse.

Quick Quilts to Make in a Weekend. Rosemary Wilkinson. (Illus.). 144p. 1996. pap. 16.95 (*0-8050-4683-6*, Owl) H Holt & Co.

***Quick Quips & Quotes: 532 Things I Wish I Had Said.** Daniel E. Josipovich. 100p. 1999. pap. 6.95 (*0-918767-02-4*) Blbook Clning Reconstrctn.

Quick Quizzes: 133 Ways to Measure Success. Ed. by Dartnell Corporation Editors. LC 98-72469. 168p. 1998. pap. 19.95 (*0-85013-339-4*) Dartnell Corp.

***Quick Reactions: Survival: What to Do in Most Emergencies.** (Illus.). 300p. 1999. pap. 30.00 (*0-9612018-7-8*) B RUGGED.

***Quick Recipe Cookbook.** Whitecap Books Staff. (Illus.). 2000. pap. text 19.95 (*1-55285-099-4*) Carlton Bks Ltd.

Quick Recipes. Time-Life Books Editors. Ed. by Catherine Hackett. LC 96-10641. (Great Taste - Low Fat Ser.). (Illus.). 160p. (gr. 7). 1999. spiral bd. 14.95 (*0-7835-4558-4*) Time-Life.

Quick Red Fox. John D. MacDonald. 1995. mass mkt. 5.99 (*0-449-22440-6*) Fawcett.

Quick Red Fox. John D. MacDonald. 1996. mass mkt. 5.99 (*0-449-45613-7*, Crest) Fawcett.

Quick Reference: Arithmetic with the TI-82 or TI-83. T. Patrick Burke. (Illus.). 1998. spiral bd. 15.00 (*0-9657238-4-4*) Calculator Trning.

Quick Reference: Lab & Diagnostic Tests. McFarland. (Nursing Education Ser.). 1995. 23.95 (*0-8273-6169-6*) Delmar.

Quick Reference Atlas. Rand McNally Staff. (Illus.). 1995. audio compact disk 20.36 (*0-528-52018-0*) Rand McNally.

Quick Reference Checklist: For Use in Analyzing Performance Problems, pkg. of 25. Robert F. Mager & Peter Pipe. 4p. 1996. reprint ed. 16.95 (*1-879618-12-5*) Ctr Effect Perf.

***Quick Reference Dictionary for Occupational Therapy.** 2nd ed. Ed. by Karen Jacobs. LC 99-21245. 336p. 1999. pap. text 22.00 (*1-55642-412-4*) SLACK Inc.

***Quick Reference Dictionary for Physical Therapy.** Jennifer M. Bottomley. 592p. 2000. pap. text 24.00 (*1-55642-426-4*) SLACK Inc.

Quick Reference for Advanced Cardiac Life Support. Karen Fenstemacher & Barbara D. Hudson. (Illus.). 205p. 1995. pap. text 19.95 (*0-7216-4637-9*, W B Saunders Co) Harcrt Hlth Sci Grp.

Quick Reference for Clinical Nursing. 2nd ed. June M. Thompson. (Illus.). 96p. (C). (gr. 13). 1997. pap. text 8.95 (*0-8151-3721-4*, 31299) Mosby Inc.

Quick Reference for Emergency Nursing. Beverley Tipsord-Klinkhammer & Coleen P. Andreoni. Ed. by Barbara N. Cullen. LC 96-53896. (Illus.). 230p. 1997. pap. text 29.00 (*0-7216-6889-5*, W B Saunders Co) Harcrt Hlth Sci Grp.

Quick Reference for Maternity & Gynecologic Nursing. Irene M. Bobak. 93p. (C). (gr. 13). 1992. pap. text 8.95 (*0-8016-6666-X*, 06666) Mosby Inc.

Quick Reference for Pediatric Emergency Nursing. Colleen Andreoni. LC 99-35201. (Illus.). 445p. 2000. pap. text. write for info. (*0-7216-8327-4*, W B Saunders Co) Harcrt Hlth Sci Grp.

Quick Reference for Psychiatric Nursing. Marianne W. Miles. 64p. 1994. pap. text 8.95 (*0-8151-8919-2*) Mosby Inc.

***Quick Reference for Psychopharmacology.** Elizabeth A. Rankin. LC 99-38317. 558p. 2000. 31.95 (*0-7668-0631-6*) Delmar.

Quick Reference for the Chemical Engineering PE Exam. Larry E. Wright. 52p. (Orig.). 1996. pap. 35.95 (*0-912045-96-5*, CHQR) Prof Pubns CA.

***Quick Reference for the Civil Engineering PE Exam.** 2nd ed. Michael R. Lindeburg. LC 99-38595. 65p. 1999. pap. 29.95 (*1-888577-47-9*, CEQR2) Prof Pubns CA.

Quick Reference for the Electrical Engineering PE Exam. Kenneth A. Nelson. LC 96-35106. 1996. pap. 33.95 (*1-888577-02-9*) Prof Pubns CA.

Quick Reference for the Mechanical Engineering PE Exam. 3rd ed. Michael R. Lindeburg. LC 97-7740. 72p. 1997. pap. 29.95 (*1-888577-14-2*) Prof Pubns CA.

Quick Reference Glossary of Eyecare Terminology. 2nd ed. Joseph Hoffman. LC 97-42375. (Basic Bookshelf for Eyecare Professionals Ser.). 240p. 1997. pap. text 22.00 (*1-55642-370-5*, 63705) SLACK Inc.

***Quick Reference Glossary of Eyecare Terminology.** 3rd ed. Joseph Hoffman. 200p. (C). 2000. pap. text 24.00 (*1-55642-472-8*) SLACK Inc.

Quick Reference Guide. 3rd ed. Ralph M. Holmes. LC 94-20501. 1995. write for info. (*0-02-802526-1*) Glencoe.

Quick Reference Guide. 3rd large type ed. Ralph M. Holmes. 318p. 79.50 (*0-614-20575-1*, L-32161-00 APHB) Am Printing Hse.

Quick Reference Guide: Microsoft Excel 4. 1992. spiral bd. 12.00 (*1-56243-085-8*, A18) DDC Pub.

Quick Reference Guide: Microsoft Word for Windows 2.0. 1992. pap. 12.00 (*1-56243-076-9*, WN-17) DDC Pub.

Quick Reference Guide: Quattro Pro 4. 1992. pap. 12.00 (*1-56243-084-X*, Q-18) DDC Pub.

Quick Reference Guide: UNIX. DDC Publishing Staff. 1992. pap. 12.00 (*1-56243-075-0*, U-17) DDC Pub.

Quick Reference Guide: WordPerfect 6. Marivel Salazar. 1993. spiral bd. 12.00 (*1-56243-095-5*, W-18) DDC Pub.

Quick Reference Guide Access 7 Windows 95. Maria Reidelbach. 1996. 12.00 (*1-56243-296-6*, AX95) DDC Pub.

Quick Reference Guide for Access 7 Windows 95. Maria Reidelbach. 1996. 13.00 (*1-56243-309-1*, AX95HC) DDC Pub.

Quick Reference Guide for Access 2.O for Windows. Maria Reidelbach. LC 94-224257. 1994. spiral bd. 12.00 (*1-56243-193-5*, OAX2) DDC Pub.

Quick Reference Guide for Corel Wordperfect Suite 8. D D C Publishing Staff. (Quick Reference Guides Ser.). 1997. pap. text 12.00 (*1-56243-543-4*, G32) DDC Pub.

Quick Reference Guide for Desktop Publishing Word 6 for Windows. Don Gosselin. LC 95-125664. 1994. pap. 12.00 (*1-56243-209-5*, G3) DDC Pub.

Quick Reference Guide for Desktop Publishing Wordperfect 6 for Windows. Don Gosselin. 1995. pap. 12.00 (*1-56243-207-9*, G1) DDC Pub.

Quick Reference Guide for Excel 7 Windows 95. Karl Schwartz. 1996. 15.00 (*1-56243-249-4*, XL-7); 13.00 (*1-56243-307-5*, XL7HC) DDC Pub.

Quick Reference Guide for Graphic Design for Desktop Publishing. Julie Schwartzman. LC 94-240963. 1994. pap. 12.00 (*1-56243-204-4*, GD2) DDC Pub.

Quick Reference Guide for Lotus 123 Release 4 DOS. Iris Blanc. 1995. spiral bd. 12.00 (*1-56243-229-X*, G4) DDC Pub.

Quick Reference Guide for Lotus 123 Release 5 for Windows. Iris Blanc. 1994. spiral bd. 12.00 (*1-56243-247-8*, L-19) DDC Pub.

Quick Reference Guide for Lotus Smart Suite. D D C Publishing Staff. LC 98-127516. (Quick Reference Guides Ser.). 1997. pap. text 12.00 (*1-56243-542-6*, G34) DDC Pub.

Quick Reference Guide for Microsoft Office. Rebecca Fiala. LC 95-146115. 1994. spiral bd. 12.00 (*1-56243-251-6*, MO17) DDC Pub.

Quick Reference Guide for Microsoft Office for Windows 95. Gosselin & Schwartz Staff. 1996. pap. text 12.00 (*1-56243-291-5*, MO95) DDC Pub.

Quick Reference Guide for Microsoft Office for Windows 95. Don Gosselin. 1996. 13.00 (*1-56243-311-3*, MO95HC) DDC Pub.

Quick Reference Guide for Microsoft Office 97. Rain. (Quick Reference Guide Ser.). spiral bd. 15.00 (*1-56243-469-1*, G-25HC) DDC Pub.

Quick Reference Guide for MS DOS 6.O & 6.22. Karl Schwartz. 1994. spiral bd. 12.00 (*1-56243-179-X*, ODS62) DDC Pub.

Quick Reference Guide for OS-2 Version 2.1 Warp. George Lynch. 1995. pap. 12.00 (*1-56243-273-7*, Y-19) DDC Pub.

Quick Reference Guide for Powerpoint 97. DDC Publishing Staff. (Quick Reference Guide Ser.). 15.00 (*1-56243-466-7*, Z22HC) DDC Pub.

Quick Reference Guide for PowerPoint 7 Windows 95. Pamela R. Toliver. 1996. 13.00 (*1-56243-310-5*, PPW7HC) DDC Pub.

Quick Reference Guide for PowerPoint 7 Windows 95. Pamela R. Toliver. 1996. pap. text 12.00 (*1-56243-255-9*, PPW7) DDC Pub.

Quick Reference Guide for Powerpoint 97. D D C Publishing Staff. LC 97-207321. (Quick Reference Guides Ser.). 1997. pap. text 12.00 (*1-56243-490-X*, G-31) DDC Pub.

Quick Reference Guide for Quicken 4 for Windows. Kathy M. Berkemeyer. LC 95-125665. 1995. pap. 12.00 (*1-56243-242-7*, G7) DDC Pub.

Quick Reference Guide for Windows 95. Karl Schwartz. 1995. pap. 12.00 (*1-56243-232-X*, G6) DDC Pub.

Quick Reference Guide for Windows 95. Karl Schwartz. 1996. 15.00 (*1-56243-315-6*, G-6HC) DDC Pub.

Quick Reference Guide for Word 7 Windows 95. Don Gosselin. 1996. 15.00 (*1-56243-308-3*, WDW7 HC) DDC Pub.

Quick Reference Guide for WordPerfect 6.1 for Windows. Kathy M. Berkemeyer. 1996. 15.00 (*1-56243-306-7*, W19HC); pap. 12.00 (*1-56243-257-5*, W19) DDC Pub.

Quick Reference Guide for Works 4 for Windows 95. Maria Reidelbach. 1996. 15.00 (*1-56243-314-8*, WKW4HC); pap. 12.00 (*1-56243-293-1*, WKW4) DDC Pub.

Quick Reference Guide for World Wide Web. David Gosselin. 1996. 15.00 (*1-56243-313-X*, WW17 HC) DDC Pub.

Quick Reference Guide 1996: Teacher's Manual & Key. Holmes. 1999. teacher ed. 9.14 (*0-02-802528-8*) Glencoe.

***Quick Reference Guide of Arboricultural Terms: English-Spanish & Spanish-English.** Ed. by Sharon Lilly & Iris Magaly Zayas. (SPA & ENG., Illus.). 90p. 1999. pap. 12.50 (*1-881956-24-5*, P1245) Int Soc Arboricult.

Quick Reference Guide to Astronomy Magazine: 1973-1990, Plus Update. Jack Hobart. LC 89-82074. (Quick Reference Guide Ser.). 80p. 1990. pap. 8.00 (*0-9623093-1-1*) Geoimages Pub.

Quick Reference Guide to College Physics. Vincent P. Coletta. 112p. (C). 1995. text. write for info. (*0-8151-1939-9*, WCB McGr Hill) McGrw-H Hghr Educ.

Quick Reference Guide to Harvard Graphics. Arnold Rosen & James Dolan. 96p. (C). 1992. text 10.87 (*0-697-20026-4*, Irwn McGrw-H) McGrw-H Hghr Educ.

Quick Reference Guide to Lotus 1-2-3 for Windows. Arnold Rosen & James Dolan. 80p. (C). 1993. text 10.15 (*0-697-20025-6*, Irwn McGrw-H) McGrw-H Hghr Educ.

Quick Reference Guide to Microsoft Words: Teacher's Resource Book. Jerry Funk. 1992. pap., teacher ed. 9.95 (*0-8273-4863-0*) Delmar.

Quick Reference Guide to Microsoft Works, for IBM PC's & Compatibles. Jerry A. Funk. 224p. (C). 1991. pap. 23.50 (*0-8273-4862-2*) Delmar.

Quick Reference Guide to Microsoft Works, for IBM PC's & Compatibles. Jerry A. Funk. 224p. 1992. pap. 23.50 incl. disk (*0-8273-5323-5*) Delmar.

Quick Reference Guide to National Geographic: 1955-Mid 1990, Plus Update. Jack Hobart. LC 89-84482. (Quick Reference Guide Ser.). 72p. 1990. pap. text 8.00 (*0-9623093-0-3*) Geoimages Pub.

Quick Reference Guide to PageMaker 5.O, Windows Version. Arnold Rosen & James Dolan. 112p. (C). 1994. text 11.23 (*0-697-22531-3*) Bus & Educ Tech.

Quick Reference Guide to PageMaker 4.O: IBM Version. Arnold Rosen. 80p. (C). 1992. text 10.15 (*0-697-14661-8*) Bus & Educ Tech.

Quick Reference Guide to 7 PC Quilting Programs: Computer Quilting Made Easy. Sharla R. Hicks. (Computer Quilting Made Easy Ser.). (Illus.). 76p. 1996. pap. 11.95 (*0-9653728-2-0*) Soft Expressions.

Quick Reference Guide to the Camouflage & Markings of the Focke-Wulf FW190A/F/G, Pt. 2. Thomas A. Tullis. (Cutting Edge Colortech Ser.: Vol. 5). (Illus.). 20p. 1999. pap. 9.95 (*0-9629146-6-5*) Meteor Prod Inc.

Quick Reference Guide to the Camouflage & Markings of the Focke-Wulf FW190D. Thomas A. Tullis. (Cutting Edge Colortech Ser.: Vol. 2). (Illus.). 20p. 1998. pap. 9.95 (*0-9629146-3-0*) Meteor Prod Inc.

Quick Reference Guide to the Camouflage & Markings of the Messerschmitt BF109G/K, Pt. 1. Thomas A. Tullis. (Cutting Edge Colortech Ser.: Vol. 4). (Illus.). 20p. 1998. pap. 9.95 (*0-9629146-5-7*) Meteor Prod Inc.

Quick Reference Guide to the Camouflage & Markings of the Messerschmitt ME262A/B. Thomas A. Tullis. (Cutting Edge Colortech Ser.: Vol. 3). (Illus.). 20p. 1998. pap. 9.95 (*0-9629146-4-9*) Meteor Prod Inc.

Quick Reference Guide to the Colors & Markings of the Focke-Wulf FW 190A/F/G, Pt. 1. Thomas A. Tullis. (Cutting Edge Colortech Ser.: Vol. 1). (Illus.). 20p. 1998. pap. 9.95 (*0-9629146-2-2*) Meteor Prod Inc.

Quick-Reference Guide to the U. B. C. Occupancy Requirements, 1994. 51p. 1994. pap. text 19.55 (*1-884590-59-4*, 090S94) Intl Conf Bldg Off.

Quick Reference Guide to Using Early Recollections in Treating Personality Disorders. Michael Meier. LC 87-92202. (Orig.). (C). 1988. pap. text. write for info. (*0-945628-00-5*) Diagnostic Solns.

Quick Reference Guide to Windows. Arnold Rosen & James Dolan. 96p. 1994. spiral bd. write for info. (*0-697-22284-5*) Bus & Educ Tech.

Quick Reference Guide to WordPerfect for Windows. Arnold Rosen & James Dolan. 80p. (C). 1992. text 10.15 (*0-697-20029-9*) Brown & Benchmark.

Quick Reference Guide to WordPerfect 6.O. Arnold Rosen & James Dolan. 128p. (C). 1994. text 8.70 (*0-697-24278-1*) Bus & Educ Tech.

Quick Reference Guide to WordStar. T. M. Nash & C. Robert Nash. (Opposing Viewpoints Sources Ser.). 82p. 1985. student ed. 19.95 (*0-934569-99-1*) Nash Group.

Quick Reference Guide WordPerfect 7 for Windows 95. DDC Publishing Staff. 1996. pap. text 12.00 (*1-56243-347-4*, G-12) DDC Pub.

Quick Reference Handbook of Oncology. Bay Area Hospital Staff. (Illus.). 181p. 1996. pap. text 23.00 (*0-7216-6894-1*, W B Saunders Co) Harcrt Hlth Sci Grp.

Quick Reference Health Care Guide: For Busy Families, Young Adults & Seniors: Professional Medical Advice in Clear Easy Steps. 3rd rev. ed. Health Education Resources Staff et al. LC 97-76970. Orig. Title: Health Care Recipak. (Illus.). 312p. 1997. reprint ed. pap. 15.95 (*0-9653928-4-8*, QRHCG-3) Hlth Educ Res.

Quick Reference HTML 4 for Dummies. Eric J. Ray & Deborah S. Ray. LC 97-81228. (For Dummies). (Illus.). 240p. 1998. spiral bd. 14.99 (*0-7645-0332-4*) IDG Bks.

Quick Reference Neuroscience for Rehabilitation Professionals: The Essential & Neurologic Principles Underlying Rehabilitation. Sharon A. Gutman. 150p. (C). Date not set. pap. text 36.00 (*1-55642-463-9*) SLACK Inc.

***Quick Reference of Vitamins & Minerals.** Deborah Williams. 2000. pap. 9.00 (*0-8059-4876-7*) Dorrance.

***Quick Reference System For: Basic Medication & Fluid Administration.** Jane A. Sennett. (Illus.). 7p. 1999. ring bd. 7.99 (*0-9670164-2-8*) Jalor Med.

Quick Reference Systems for Physical Assessment. rev. ed. Maria Piantanida. (Illus.). 19p. 1997. ring bd. 18.99 (*0-9670164-0-1*, Pub. by Jalor Med) Millenium Mktg.

Quick Reference Table Business Math. 4th ed. Cleaves. 1996. text. write for info. (*0-13-399361-2*) Allyn.

Quick Reference Tables. 5th ed. 80p. (C). 1998. text. write for info. (*0-13-081288-9*) P-H.

Quick Reference to Anatomy & Physiology. Patton & Gary A. Thibodeau. (Illus.). 64p. (C). (gr. 13). 1992. pap. text 9.95 (*0-8016-7530-8*, 07530) Mosby Inc.

Quick Reference to Cardiac Critical Care Nursing. Janet S. Eagan et al. LC 91-17205. (Critical Care Nursing Ser.). (Illus.). 452p. 1991. 58.00 (*0-8342-0249-2*, 20249) Aspen Pub.

Quick Reference to Cardiovascular Diseases. 2nd ed. Edward K. Chung. (Illus.). 672p. 1982. text 39.50 (*0-397-50482-9*, 65-06232, Lippnctt) Lppncott W & W.

Quick Reference to Clinical Dietetics. Ed. by Lucinda K. Lysen. LC 96-50455. 292p. 1997. pap. 34.00 (*0-8342-0629-3*) Aspen Pub.

***Quick Reference to Cobra Compliance, 1.** Joan Vigliotta & Pamela L. Sande. 504p. 1999. pap. text 125.00 (*0-7355-0499-7*) Panel Pubs.

Quick Reference to Cobra Compliance: Special Supplement, Health Insurance Portability & Accountability Act Pamela L. Sande. LC 98-215899. 1998. write for info. (*0-7355-0210-2*) Panel Pubs.

Quick Reference to Community Health Nursing. 2nd ed. Marcia Stanhope & Jeanette Lancaster. 64p. (C). (gr. 13). 1995. pap. text 8.95 (*0-8151-8335-6*, 28197) Mosby Inc.

***Quick Reference to Correctional Administration.** Richard L. Phillips & John W. Roberts. LC 99-45037. 257p. 1999. pap. 45.00 (*0-8342-1756-2*) Aspen Pub.

Quick Reference to Critical Care. Nancy H. Diepenbrock. LC 98-44543. 336p. 1999. pap. text 24.95 (*0-7817-1862-7*) Lppncott W & W.

Quick Reference to ERISA Compliance: 1998 Edition. annuals Barry M. Newman & Virginia S. Peabody. 512p. pap. 125.00 (*1-56706-380-2*, 63802) Panel Pubs.

***Quick Reference to Hipaa Compliance, 1.** Joan Vigliotta & Pamela L. Sande. 600p. 1999. pap. 125.00 (*0-7355-0500-4*) Panel Pubs.

Quick Reference to Internal Medicine. Ed. by Roger C. Bone & Robert L. Rosen. LC 93-25286. (Illus.). 1568p. 1994. 49.50 (*0-89640-229-0*) Igaku-Shoin.

Q

Quick Reference to Neurological Critical Care Nursing. Noreen M. Leahy. LC 89-18022. 224p. (C). 1990. 58.00 (*0-8342-0127-5*, 20127) Aspen Pub.

Quick Reference to Nursing Assessment. Phelps. (Nursing Education Ser.). (C). 1998. pap. text 26.95 (*0-8273-7893-9*) Delmar.

Quick Reference to Nursing Leadership. Donna Costello-Nickitas. (Professional Reference - Nursing Ser.). 240p. 1996. mass mkt. 41.95 (*0-8273-6997-2*) Delmar.

***Quick Reference to Occupational Therapy.** 2nd ed. Kathlyn L. Reed. 1024p. 2000. pap. 49.00 (*0-8342-1631-0*) Aspen Pub.

***Quick Reference to Outbreak Investigation & Control in Health Care Facilities.** Kathleen Meehan Arias. LC 99-33381. 339p. 1999. pap. 59.00 (*0-8342-1179-3*) Aspen Pub.

Quick Reference to Pediatric Emergency Nursing. Donna O. Thomas. 368p. 1991. text 60.00 (*0-8342-0199-2*) Aspen Pub.

Quick Reference to Physical Therapy. Julie A. Pauls & Kathlyn L. Reed. 688p. 1996. 45.00 (*0-8342-0654-4*, 20654) Aspen Pub.

Quick Reference to Radiology. Ed. by John C. Lipman. LC 94-33452. 447p. (C). 1995. pap. text 44.95 (*0-8385-8196-X*, A8196-6, Apple Lange Med) McGraw.

Quick Reference to Redesigning the Nursing Organization. Mary L. Fisher. LC 95-35757. (Professional Reference - Nursing Ser.). 208p. 1996. pap. 41.95 (*0-8273-6400-8*) Delmar.

Quick Reference to Respiratory Critical Care Nursing. Nancy L. Kranzley. LC 90-14526. 176p. 1991. 52.00 (*0-8342-0205-0*) Aspen Pub.

Quick Reference to Speech-Language Pathology. Sally G. Pore & Kathlyn L. Reed. LC 98-54628. 288p. 1999. pap. 41.00 (*0-8342-1278-1*) Aspen Pub.

Quick Reference to the Diagnostic Criteria from DSM-IV. APA Staff. 358p. 1994. pap. text 23.00 (*0-89042-063-7*, 2063) Am Psychiatric.

***Quick Reference to the Diagnostic Criteria from DSM-IV: Text Revision 2000.** American Psychiatric Association Staff. 496p. 2000. pap. 23.00 (*0-89042-026-2*) Am Psychiatric.

***Quick Reference to the Stock Market.** Ed. by Frank Carroll. 1999. write for info. (*0-9667136-4-8*) Alcor Pr.

Quick Reference to Triage. Valerie G. Grossman. LC 98-38546. 1999. spiral bd. 36.95 (*0-7817-1861-9*) Lppncott W & W.

Quick Reference to Veterinary Medicine. 2nd ed. William R. Fenner. (Illus.). 670p. 1991. pap. text 51.95 (*0-397-50895-6*) Lppncott W & W.

Quick Reference to Veterinary Medicine. 3rd ed. Ed. by William R. Fenner & Terence A. Olive. (Illus.). 675p. 1998. pap. text 49.95 (*0-397-51608-8*) Lppncott W & W.

***Quick Reference to Voluntary Compliance.** Boutwell. 548p. 1999. pap. text 125.00 (*0-7355-1176-4*) Panel Pubs.

Quick Reference United States Atlas. LC 93-12817. 64p. 1995. 5.95 (*0-528-83771-0*) Rand McNally.

Quick Reference Windows NT 5 for Dummies. Valda Hilley. 224p. 2000. spiral bd. 12.99 (*0-7645-0340-5*) IDG Bks.

Quick Reference Workout Diary. 4th ed. William E. Prentice. 32p. (C). 1993. text 7.50 (*0-8151-6717-2*, WCB McGr Hill) McGrw-H Hghr Educ.

Quick Reference World Atlas. European Map Graphics Staff. (Illus.). 184p. 1995. write for info. (*1-57215-093-9*) World Pubns.

Quick Reference World Atlas. Rand McNally Staff. 1p. (C). 1990. pap. text 7.93 (*0-13-749532-3*) P-H.

Quick Reference World Atlas. Rand McNally Staff. 64p. 1993. pap. 4.95 (*0-528-83622-6*) Rand McNally.

Quick Reference World Atlas. Rand McNally Staff. LC 95-675139. (Illus.). 64p. 1996. pap. 5.95 (*0-528-83733-8*) Rand McNally.

Quick Reference World Atlas with Map. Rand McNally Staff. 1995. pap. 5.95 (*0-528-83765-6*) Rand McNally.

Quick Reference World U. S. Atlas. Rand McNally Staff. 1995. pap. 7.95 (*0-528-83764-8*) Rand McNally.

***Quick Reference/DOS for Dummies.** 3rd ed. Greg Harvey. LC 98-84652. (For Dummies Ser.). 208p. 1998. spiral bd. 12.99 (*0-7645-0368-5*) IDG Bks.

Quick References to Cultural Assessment. Violet H. Barkauskas. LC 95-230936. (Illus.). 56p. 1993. pap. text 8.95 (*0-8151-0408-1*) Mosby Inc.

Quick Reference/XML for Dummies. Mariva H. Aviram. LC 98-85374. (For Dummies). 224p. 1998. spiral bd. 14.99 (*0-7645-0383-9*) IDG Bks.

***Quick Refrence Guide to Key Business Ratios Premium.** 1999. pap. 15.95 (*0-13-026851-8*) P-H.

Quick Relief for Children's Ministry Leaders. Ivy Beckwith. Ed. by Beth Wolf. LC 98-12668. (Illus.). 80p. 1998. pap. 9.99 (*0-7644-2072-0*) Group Pub.

Quick Relief for Sunday School Teachers. Ed. by Beth Wolf. LC 98-16015. (Illus.). 64p. 1998. per. 7.99 (*0-7644-2073-9*, Vital Ministry) Group Pub.

***Quick Response: Managing the Supply Chain to Meet Consumer Demand.** Alan Hunter et al. LC 99-24152. (Illus.). 281p. 1999. 60.00 (*0-471-98833-2*) Wiley.

Quick Response: Technology Guide. Kenneth D. Askelson. LC 95-30557. 1995. 19.00 (*0-87051-167-X*) Am Inst CPA.

Quick Response in Apparel Manufacturing. N. A. Hunter. 1990. pap. 45.00 (*1-870812-30-1*, Pub. by Textile Inst) St Mut.

***Quick Response in the Supply Chain.** Ed. by E. Hadjiconstantinou. LC 98-43472. (Illus.). 187p. 1998. 69.95 (*3-540-65045-8*) Spr-Verlag.

Quick Response Manufacturing: A Companywide Approach to Reducing Lead Times. Rajan Suri. LC 98-18321. 560p. 1998. 50.00 (*1-56327-201-6*) Productivity Inc.

Quick Response Therapy: A Time-Limited Treatment Approach. Judith Goldring. LC 97-16481. 144p. 1997. pap. text 30.00 (*0-7657-0092-1*) Aronson.

Quick-Response Urban Travel Estimation Techniques & Transferable Parameters: A User's Guide. (National Cooperative Highway Research Program Report Ser.: No. 187). 229p. 1978. 12.00 (*0-309-02775-6*) Transport Res Bd.

Quick Results with SAS/GRAPH Software. Arthur L. Carpenter & Charles E. Shipp. 272p. (C). 1995. pap. 32.95 (*1-55544-683-3*, BR55127) SAS Publ.

Quick Resume & Cover Letter Book: Write & Use an Effective Resume in Only One Day. J. Michael Farr. LC 94-15776. (Quick Guide Ser.). 310p. (Orig.). 1994. pap. 12.95 (*1-56370-141-3*, RCLQG) JIST Works.

Quick Resume & Cover Letter Book: Write & Use an Effective Resume in Only One Day. 2nd ed. Jist Works Staff. (Orig.). 1999. pap. text 14.95 (*1-56370-634-2*) JIST Works.

***Quick Review Family Law.** 3rd ed. Perlin. (Sum & Substance Quick Review Ser.). 1999. pap. 18.95 (*0-314-24285-6*) West Pub.

***Quick Review on Civil Procedure.** 4th ed. Blaze. (Sum & Substance Quick Review Ser.). 1999. pap. 18.95 (*0-314-24287-2*) West Pub.

***Quick Review on Civil Procedure.** 4th ed. Miller. (Sum & Substance Quick Review Ser.). 1999. pap. 19.95 (*0-314-24289-9*) West Pub.

Quick Rotary Cutter Quilts. Pam Bono. 1994. pap. 19.95 (*0-8487-1412-1*) Oxmoor Hse.

Quick Scientific Terminology: A Self-Teaching Guide. Kenneth J. Rose. LC 88-725. 267p. 1988. pap. 16.95 (*0-471-85763-7*) Wiley.

Quick Scripture Reference for Counseling. 2nd ed. John G. Kruis. 160p. 1994. spiral bd. 7.99 (*0-8010-5261-0*) Baker Bks.

Quick Seasonal Bible Studies for Any Time. Roger Sonnenberg. (Five-Minute Bible Studies). 1994. pap. 9.99 (*0-570-09523-9*, 20-2721) Concordia.

Quick Selection Guide to Chemical Protective Clothing. 2nd ed. Krister Forsberg & S. Z. Mansdorf. LC 93-11308. 99p. 1993. pap. 25.95 (*0-442-01215-2*, VNR) Wiley.

Quick Selection Guide to Chemical Protective Clothing. 3rd ed. Krister Forsberg & S. Z. Mansdorf. 124p. 1997. pap. 34.95 (*0-471-28797-0*, VNR) Wiley.

Quick Selection Guide to Chemical Protective Clothing. 3rd ed. Krister Forsberg & S. Z. Mansdorf. LC 97-3032. 128p. 1997. spiral bd. 25.95 (*0-442-02377-4*, VNR) Wiley.

Quick Series Guide Golf Log. Seven Hills Publishing Staff. 1998. pap. text 5.95 (*2-922164-16-0*) Luxart.

Quick Series Guide to a Healthy Lifestyle. Seven Hills Publishing Staff. 1998. pap. text 5.95 (*2-922164-03-9*) Seven Hills Pubs.

Quick Series Guide to Business Organizing Ideas. Seven Hills Publishing Staff. 1998. pap. text 5.95 (*2-922164-01-2*) Seven Hills Pubs.

Quick Series Guide to Casino Games. Seven Hills Publishing Staff. 1998. pap. text 5.95 (*2-9802265-6-4*) Seven Hills Pubs.

Quick Series Guide to Golf Games. Seven Hills Publishing Staff. 1998. pap. text 5.95 (*2-9802265-5-6*) Seven Hills Pubs.

Quick Series Guide to Golf Rules. Seven Hills Publishing Staff. 1998. pap. text 5.95 (*2-9802265-7-2*) Seven Hills Pubs.

Quick Series Guide to Golf Tips. Seven Hills Publishing Staff. 1998. pap. text 5.95 (*2-9802265-1-3*) Seven Hills Pubs.

***Quick Series Guide to Investment Planning.** Seven Hills Publishing Staff. 1999. pap. text 5.95 (*2-922164-22-5*) Luxart.

***Quick Series Guide to Putting.** Seven Hills Publishing Staff. 1999. pap. text 5.95 (*2-922164-14-4*) Luxart.

Quick Series Guide to Road Safety. 1999. pap. 5.95 (*2-9802265-8-0*) Serpents Tail.

***Quick Series Guide to the Internet.** Seven Hills Publishing Staff. 1998. pap. text 5.95 (*2-922164-02-0*) Seven Hills Pubs.

***Quick Series Guide to The Mental Game of Golf.** Seven Hills Publishing Staff. 1999. pap. text 5.95 (*2-922164-15-2*) Luxart.

Quick Service. P. G. Wodehouse. 20.95 (*0-8488-0679-4*) Amereon Ltd.

Quick Service That Sells! Phil Roberts & Christopher O'Donnell. (Illus.). 132p. 1997. pap. 16.95 (*1-879239-13-2*) Pencom.

Quick-Sew Fleece: Fast & Fun Fleece for All Seasons from America's Top Designers. Janet Brandt et al. LC 98-28575. (Best-Loved Designers' Collections). (Illus.). 128p. 1998. pap. 27.95 (*1-56477-231-4*, DB351, PasTimes) Martingale & Co.

Quick-Sew Quilts: Wallhangings & Coordinating Projects from America's Top Designers. Chilton Automotive Editorial Staff. LC 96-31936. (Illus.). 144p. 1996. pap. 24.95 (*0-8019-8891-8*) Krause Pubns.

Quick Sewing Projects from Placemats: Sew-Fast Gift Ideas. Susan Beck. (Illus.). 128p. 1997. pap. text 14.95 (*0-8069-9486-X*) Sterling.

Quick Sewing Projects from Placemats: Sew-Fast Gift Ideas. Susan P. Beck. LC 96-26162. (Illus.). 128p. 1996. 27.95 (*0-8069-9487-8*) Sterling.

***Quick Shots of False Hope: A Rejection Collection, Vol. 1.** Laura Kightlinger. LC 99-27581. 192p. 1999. pap. 12.50 (*0-380-81046-8*, Avon Bks) Morrow Avon.

Quick Silver. Judith Reeves-Stevens & Garfield Reeves-Stevens. LC 00-503332. 496p. 1999. 23.00 (*0-671-02853-7*, PB Hardcover) PB.

Quick Simmering Soups. Ed. by Better Homes & Gardens. LC 98-66250. (Fresh & Simple Ser.). (Illus.). 96p. 1998. pap. 15.95 (*0-696-20854-7*, Better Homes) Meredith Bks.

***Quick, Simple Access 9X: Microsoft.** (Illus.). 240p. (C). 1999. spiral bd. 16.00 (*0-13-081320-6*) P-H.

***Quick Simple Microsoft Access 2000.** 2000. teacher ed. write for info. (*0-13-020862-0*) P-H.

***Quick, Simple Microsoft Excel 2000.** Linda Ericksen. (Illus.). 240p. (C). 1999. spiral bd. 16.00 (*0-13-081333-8*) P-H.

***Quick Simple Microsoft Office 2000.** 2000. teacher ed. write for info. (*0-13-022279-8*) P-H.

Quick Simple Microsoft Office 2000. Ericksen. (Illus.). 848p. (C). 1999. spiral bd. 48.00 (*0-13-011054-X*) P-H.

***Quick, Simple Microsoft Powerpoint 2000.** Linda Ericksen. (Illus.). 240p. (C). 1999. spiral bd. 16.00 (*0-13-974460-6*) P-H.

***Quick, Simple Microsoft Windows 98.** Linda Ericksen. LC 99-175654. 240p. (C). 1998. spiral bd. 16.00 (*0-13-081328-1*) P-H.

***Quick Sketch.** Glenn V. Vilppu. (Portfolio Ser.). (Illus.). 24p. 2000. pap. 5.95 (*1-892053-05-5*) Vilppu.

Quick Skits & Discussion Starters: Skits to Involve Your Youth Group in Meaningful, Action-Packed Discussions. Chuck Bolte & Paul McCusker. (Illus.). 109p. 1989. pap. 14.99 (*0-931529-68-9*) Group Pub.

Quick Solutions to Great Layouts. Graham Davis. (Illus.). 144p. 1993. 28.99 (*0-89134-507-8*, 30529, North Lght Bks) F & W Pubns Inc.

Quick Soups 'n Salads. Cyndi Duncan & Georgie Patrick. (One Foot in the Kitchen Cookbook Ser.: No. 3). (Illus.). 168p. 1999. pap. 14.95 (*0-9626335-7-7*) C&G Pub CO.

Quick-Source: The Directory of Educational Technology Resources, 1996 Edition. (Annual Ser.). 141p. 1997. spiral bd. 37.52 (*0-9634429-4-5*) AM Educ Pub.

Quick Springs of Sense: Studies in the Eighteenth Century. Ed. by Larry S. Champion. LC 72-86783. 262p. reprint ed. pap. 81.30 (*0-608-15802-X*, 203106500073) Bks Demand.

Quick Start Guide to Blockbase: Computer Quilting Made Easy. Sharla R. Hicks. (Illus.). 40p. 1997. mass mkt. 9.95 (*0-9653728-5-5*) Soft Expressions.

Quick Start Guide to Electric Quilt 3: Computer Quilting Made Easy. Sharla R. Hicks. LC 97-164920. (Computer Quilting Made Easy Ser.). (Illus.). 38p. 1997. pap. 9.95 (*0-9653728-3-9*) Soft Expressions.

Quick Start Guide to Quilt-Pro 2: Computer Quilting Made Easy. rev. ed. Sharla R. Hicks. LC 97-164872. (Illus.). 37p. 1996. mass mkt. 9.95 (*0-9653728-0-4*) Soft Expressions.

Quick Start Guide to Quilt Pro Z for the MacIntosh: Computer Quilting Made Easy. Sharla R. Hicks. 40p. 1997. mass mkt. 9.95 (*0-9653728-4-7*) Soft Expressions.

Quick Start in JavaScript. Forest Lin. (Illus.). (C). 1998. pap. text 16.61 (*1-57676-018-9*) Scott Jones Pubng.

***Quick Start to Autocad for Interior Design.** Judith A. Trachte. 305p. 1999. pap. text 56.00 (*0-13-020853-1*, Prentice Hall) P-H.

Quick Start to Data Analysis with SAS. Frank Di Iorio & Kenneth C. Hardy. LC 95-18388. 301p. (C). 1995. mass mkt. 38.95 (*0-534-23760-6*, BR55550) PWS Pubs.

Quick STATISTICA for the Macintosh Vol. I: Statistics & Graphics. StatSoft, Inc. Staff. 518p. (C). 1993. pap. 50.00 (*1-884233-19-8*) StatSoft.

Quick Statistica for Windows Vols. I & II: Statistics & Graphics. 1000p. (C). 1993. pap. write for info. (*1-884233-34-1*) StatSoft.

Quick STATISTICA for Windows Vols. I & II: Statistics & Graphics. StatSoft, Inc. Staff. 1000p. (C). 1995. pap. 100.00 (*1-884233-14-7*) StatSoft.

Quick Success: Windows 3.1. Lisa Rosner. LC 94-33239. 1994. write for info. (*0-534-21403-7*) Course Tech.

Quick Summary & Documentation Guide: Harper Collins Concise Handbook. Adams. (C). 1997. pap. text 13.00 (*0-06-502268-8*) Addison-Wesley.

Quick Suppers, No. 10. Elizabeth Baird. 1996. pap. 12.71 (*0-345-39807-6*) Ballantine Pub Grp.

Quick Survey Course in Forms Typing. E. G. Blendon & B. H. Nalepa. 1967. text 8.96 (*0-07-005892-X*) McGraw.

Quick Survey Course in Forms Typing. fac. ed. E. G. Blendon & B. H. Nalepa. 1967. pap. text 8.96 (*0-07-005891-1*) McGraw.

Quick Takes: Short Model Essays Basic Compostion. (C). 1997. pap. text 11.00 (*0-06-501339-5*) Addison-Wesley.

Quick Takes: Short Model Essays for Composition. Elizabeth Penfield & Hill. LC 94-20373. 352p. (C). 1997. pap. text 36.93 (*0-06-501338-7*) Addson-Wesley Educ.

Quick-Takes for Teens, Family Issues Vol. 1: Easy, On-the-Spot Resources for Youth Ministry, 4 vols. Dirk DeVries. Ed. by Kathy Mulhern. (Illus.). 48p. (Orig.). 1996. pap. 5.95 (*1-889108-05-7*) Liv Good News.

Quick-Takes for Teens, Relationship Issues Vol. 4: Easy, On-the-Spot Resources for Youth Ministry, 4 vols. Dirk DeVries. Ed. by Kathy Mulhern. (Illus.). 48p. (Orig.). 1996. pap. 5.95 (*1-889108-08-1*) Liv Good News.

Quick-Takes for Teens, Tough Emotions Vol. 2: Easy, On-the-Spot Resources for Youth Ministry, 4 vols. Dirk DeVries. Ed. by Kathy Mulhern. 48p. 1996. pap. 5.95 (*1-889108-06-5*) Liv Good News.

Quick-Takes for Teens, World Problems Vol. 3: Easy, On-the-Spot Resources for Youth Ministry, 4 vols. Dirk DeVries. Ed. by Kathy Mulhern. (Illus.). 48p. (Orig.). 1996. pap. 5.95 (*1-889108-07-3*) Liv Good News.

***Quick Takes Rituals & Retreats.** Jean E. Bross et al. 120p. (Orig.). 1999. pap. text 16.95 (*1-889108-48-0*) Liv Good News.

Quick Tech Magic: Music Based Stories & Activities. Peggi McNairn et al. (Illus.). 184p. 1995. spiral bd. 29.00 (*1-884135-20-X*) Mayer-Johnson.

Quick Tech Readable, Repeatable Stories & Activities. Peggi McNairn & Cindy Shioleno. (Illus.). 223p. (Orig.). 1994. spiral bd. 24.00 (*1-884135-08-0*) Mayer-Johnson.

Quick Tests: The Life & Work of Dr. Armand J. Quick. Edith M. Ebel. (Illus.). 464p. (Orig.). 1995. 21.95 (*0-936015-60-8*); pap. 16.95 (*0-936015-57-8*) Pocahontas Pr.

Quick Thinking, Grades K-6: Critical & Creative Thinking Challenges. Beverly Cunningham. 80p. 1992. pap. text 11.95 (*0-944459-47-1*) ECS Lrn Systs.

Quick Thinking, Grades 7-12: Critical & Creative Thinking Challenges. Beverly Cunningham. 80p. 1992. pap. text 11.95 (*0-944459-48-X*) ECS Lrn Systs.

Quick Thinks Math A1. Robert Femiano. 48p. (gr. 2-5). 1998. pap. 10.95 (*0-89455-672-X*, MP4601) Crit Think Bks.

Quick Thinks Math B1. Robert Femiano. 48p. (J). (gr. 5-8). 1998. pap. 10.95 (*0-89455-673-8*, MP4602) Crit Think Bks.

Quick Tidings of Hong Kong. Austin Coates. (Illus.). 216p. 1990. text 21.00 (*0-19-584024-0*) OUP.

Quick Tips: Writing Effective Report Card Comments. Scholastic, Inc. Staff. LC 97-198017. 64p. (gr. 1-6). 1997. pap. text 8.95 (*0-590-06882-2*) Scholastic Inc.

Quick Tips Avoiding 23. P-H Editorial Staff. (C). 1997. pap. 9.95 (*0-13-268962-6*) P-H.

Quick Tips for Better Business-to-Business Marketing Communications. Bob Bly. 200p. (Orig.). 1997. pap. write for info. (*0-9656965-1-0*) Busn Mktging.

Quick Tips for Better Business Writing. Gary Blake. LC 95-3942. 186p. 1995. pap. 12.95 (*0-07-005691-9*) McGraw.

Quick Tips for Home Improvement. Patrick Caton. (Day Riser Ser.). 366p. 1995. spiral bd. 6.50 (*1-56245-220-7*) Great Quotations.

Quick Tips Survival Guide, Vol. S3. Alan Axelrod. 160p. 1997. pap. 32.85 (*0-07-913220-0*) McGraw.

Quick to Listen, Slow to Speak. Robert E. Fisher. 181p. 1990. mass mkt. 4.99 (*0-8423-5111-6*, 075111-6) Tyndale Hse.

***Quick-to-Sew One-Day Gifts.** Ed. by Beth Wheeler. (Illus.). 176p. 2000. 19.96 (*1-882138-60-0*) Hse White Birches.

Quick to Solve Brain Teasers see **Quick-to-Solve Brainteasers**

Quick-to-Solve Brainteasers. J. J. Mendoza-Fernandez. LC 98-34888.Tr. of Quick to Solve Brain Teasers. (SPA., Illus.). 96p. 1998. 6.95 (*0-8069-6151-1*) Sterling.

***Quick-to-Stitch Holiday Plastic Canvas.** Ed. by Laura Scott. (Illus.). 176p. 2000. 19.95 (*1-882138-52-X*) Hse White Birches.

Quick, Topical Studies for Any Setting. Roger Sonnenberg. (Five-Minute Bible Studies). 1994. pap. 9.99 (*0-570-09522-0*, 20-2720) Concordia.

Quick-Toss Salad Meals. Ed. by Jennifer Darling. LC 97-75844. (Fresh & Simple Ser.). 96p. 1998. pap. 15.95 (*0-696-20790-7*, Better Homes) Meredith Bks.

Quick-Trigger Country. large type ed. Clem Colt. (Linford Western Library). 272p. 1985. pap. 16.99 (*0-7089-6087-1*) Ulverscroft.

***Quick-Trigger Country.** large type ed. Nelson C. Nye. LC 99-89091. (Thorndike Western Ser.). 2000. 22.95 (*0-7862-2423-1*) Thorndike Pr.

Quick Trip Through . . . For Windows. Robert L. Stark. (For Windows Ser.). 14p. 1994. pap. text 9.95 (*0-9645571-1-8*) Stark Educ Servs.

Quick Trip Through... For DOS. Robert L. Stark. (For DOS Ser.). 7p. 1994. pap. text 3.95 (*0-9645571-0-X*) Stark Educ Servs.

Quick Trip Through... Purchasing a Computer. Robert L. Stark. 15p. 1994. pap. text 2.25 (*0-9645571-2-6*) Stark Educ Servs.

Quick Tunes & Good Times: Traditional New England Folk Music & Its Players. Newton F. Tolman. 1972. 15.00 (*0-87233-018-4*) Bauhan.

Quick-Turnaround ASIC Design in VHDL: Core-Based Behavioral Synthesis, Vol. 367. Vijay Madisetti et al. LC 96-1910. (Kluwer International Series in Engineering & Computer Science). 216p. (C). 1996. text 115.00 (*0-7923-9744-4*) Kluwer Academic.

***Quick Vegetarian Curries.** Mridula Baljekar. 224p. 1999. pap. 13.00 (*0-7225-3845-6*) Thorsons PA.

Quick Vegetarian Pleasures: Fast, Delicious, & Healthy Meatless Recipes. Jeanne Lemlin. LC 91-50515. (Illus.). 288p. 1998. pap. 17.00 (*0-06-096911-3*, Perennial) HarperTrade.

Quick Vocabulary Power: A Self-Teaching Guide. 2nd rev. ed. Jack S. Romine & Henry Ehrlich. LC 95-30999. (Self-Teaching Guides Ser.). 256p. 1995. pap. 16.95 (*0-471-05008-3*) Wiley.

Quick Watercolor Quilts: The Fuse, Fold & Stitch Method. Dina Pappas. LC 99-15970. (Illus.). 96p. 1999. pap. 26.95 (*1-56477-270-5*, B393) Martingale & Co.

Quick White Paper. Sherman N. Miller. (Illus.). 130p. (C). 1998. reprint ed. pap. 19.95 (*0-9640915-3-4*) S N M Pubng.

Quick Wholesome Foods Recipe Booklet. LeArta Moulton & Rita Bingham. 1991. pap. 2.75 (*0-935596-29-1*) LM Pubns.

Quick Wits, Worn Shoes, & a Fax Machine: A Book of Useful Quotes for Every Salesperson. Compiled by Rolf B. White. LC 94-46622. 128p. 1995. pap. 7.95 (*0-8065-1649-6*, Citadel Pr) Carol Pub Group.

Quick Workouts. (Fitness, Health & Nutrition Ser.). (Illus.). 144p. 1987. 17.27 (*0-8094-6179-X*); lib. bdg. 23.27 (*0-8094-6180-3*) Time-Life.

Quick Works: Introduction to Microsoft Window 3.0 Lawrence J. Malloy. 122p. (C). 1994. text 25.00 (0-536-58567-9) Pearson Custom.

Quick Writes; More Than 60 Short Writing Activities from the Practical to the Poetic. Pamela Marx. 1999. pap. text 14.95 (0-673-58643-X) Addson-Wesley Educ.

***Quickart Crayon Projects: 25 Instant Activities That Bring Out The Creativity in Every Child.** Robin Bernard. (Illus.). 64p. 1999. pap. 10.95 (0-590-98339-3) Scholastic Inc.

QuickBASIC & QBASIC Using Modular Structure, IBM Version. 2nd ed. Julia C. Bradley. 560p. (C). 1993. text 48.95 (0-697-12897-0) Bus & Educ Tech.

QuickBASIC & QBASIC Using Modular Structure with Visual Basic. Julia C. Bradley. LC 95-35898. 608p. (C). 1995. text 40.00 (0-256-20797-6, Irwn McGrw-H) McGrw-H Hghr Educ.

Quickbasic Fundamentals & Style. (Shelly-Cashman Ser.). 1991. pap. text 51.95 (0-87835-761-0) Course Tech.

Quickbasic Programming for Scientists & Engineers. Joseph H. Noggle. 400p. 1992. boxed set 68.95 (0-8493-4434-4, QA76) CRC Pr.

QuickBasic Using Independent Subprograms. Julia C. Bradley & Kelly Black. 528p. (C). 1991. text, pap. text 56.55 incl. disk (0-697-14580-8, Irwn McGrw-H) McGrw-H Hghr Educ.

QuickBASIC Using Modular Structure: Macintosh Version. Julia C. Bradley & Richard P. Giles. 496p. (C). 1991. pap. write for info. (0-697-12434-7) Bus & Educ Tech.

QuickBASIC 4.5. Gary Cornell. 1991. 24.95 incl. disk (0-8306-2576-3); 24.95 incl. disk (0-8306-2577-1) McGraw-Hill Prof.

Quickbasic 4.5. Lategahn. (C). 1989. text. write for info. (0-201-51469-9) Addison-Wesley.

***Quickbook 99 Quick Reference, .** Stephen J. O'Brien. 192p. 1999. 9.99 (0-7897-2029-9) Que.

QuickBooks: The Official Guide. Kathy Ivens. LC 98-212798. (Made Easy Ser.). 608p. 1998. pap. 24.99 (0-07-882574-1) Osborne-McGraw.

Quickbooks 5 for Dummies. 3rd ed. Stephen Nelson. LC 96-77701. (Illus.). 384p. 1997. pap. 19.99 (0-7645-0043-0) IDG Bks.

Quickbooks 5.0 for Accounting. Glenn Owen & Paul Solomon. LC 98-24635. 1998. write for info. (0-324-00357-9) Sth-Wstrn College.

***QuickBooks for Accountants: The Official Guide.** Kathy Ivens. (Illus.). 2000. pap. 39.99 (0-07-212695-7) Osborne-McGraw.

Quickbooks for Profit. Mary Campbell. 1993. pap. 24.95 (0-07-881934-2) Osborne-McGraw.

Quickbooks 4 for Dummies. 2nd ed. Stephen Nelson. 384p. 1993. pap. 19.99 (1-56884-947-8) IDG Bks.

***QuickBooks 99: The Official Guide.** Kathy Ivens. 515p. 1999. pap. text 24.99 (0-07-212003-7) Osborne-McGraw.

***QuickBooks 99 Bible.** Jill Gilbert. LC 99-25443. (Bible Ser.). (Illus.). 648p. 1999. pap. 34.99 (0-7645-3352-5) IDG Bks.

***QuickBooks 99 Intermediate.** (Illus.). (C). 2000. pap. write for info. (0-7423-0437-X) ComputerPREP.

***QuickBooks 99 Intermediate: Instructor Guide.** (Illus.). (C). 2000. teacher ed. write for info. (0-7423-0438-8) ComputerPREP.

***QuickBooks 99 Introduction.** (Illus.). (C). 2000. pap. write for info. (0-7423-0416-7) ComputerPREP.

***QuickBooks 99 Introduction: Instructor Guide.** (Illus.). 2000. pap., teacher ed. write for info. (0-7423-0422-1) ComputerPREP.

Quickbooks Pro 5: Byte by Bite. Glenda Friesen. (Byte by Bite Ser.). (Illus.). 1997. pap. 15.00 (1-891412-11-6) Training Solut.

QuickBooks Pro 4.0 - Introduction. Ed. by Ron Pronk. (Illus.). 180p. 1996. pap. 20.00 (1-58264-057-2, 93) ActiveEd.

***Quickbooks Pro 99: Byte by Bite.** Glenda Friesen. (Byte by Bite Ser.). 92p. 1999. pap. 15.00 (1-891412-16-7) Training Solut.

***Quickbooks Pro 99 for Accounting.** Owen. LC 99-45954. (SWC-Accounting Ser.). 1999. 55.95 (0-324-02831-8) Thomson Learn.

QuickBooks Pro 6: Byte by Bite. Glenda L. Friesen. (Byte by Byte Ser.). (Illus.). 86p. 1998. spiral bd. 15.00 (1-891412-13-2, QB6-998) Training Solut.

Quickbooks Pro 5.0 - Using. Ed. by Ron Pronk. (Illus.). 180p. 1997. pap. 20.00 (1-58264-000-9, 115) ActiveEd.

Quickbooks 6 - Using. Ed. by Ron Pronk. (Illus.). 200p. 1998. pap. 20.00 (1-58264-074-2, 174) ActiveEd.

QuickBooks 6 for Dummies. Stephen L. Nelson. (For Dummies Ser.). 384p. 1998. pap. 19.99 (0-7645-0330-8) IDG Bks.

Quickbooks 3 for Dummies. Steven L. Nelson. LC 94-79876. 384p. 1993. pap. 19.99 (1-56884-227-9) IDG Bks.

***QuickBooks 2000.** Kathy Ivens. (Official Guides Ser.). 2000. pap. 29.99 (0-07-212320-6) Osborne-McGraw.

QuickBooks "X" Bible. Jill Gilbert. LC HF5679.G49 1998. (Bible Ser.). 648p. 1998. pap. 39.99 (0-7645-4033-5) IDG Bks.

***QuickBooks X for Dummies.** Stephen L. Nelson. (For Dummies Ser.). (Illus.). 384p. 2000. pap. 19.99 (0-7645-0665-X) IDG Bks.

QuickBooks 5.0 for Accounting. 2nd ed. Glen Owen. LC 98-24635. 224p. 1999. pap. 54.95 (0-324-00402-8) Sth-Wstrn College.

***QuickBooks 99 for Dummies.** Nelson. LC HF5679.N4497 1998. 384p. 1999. pap. 19.99 (0-7645-0521-1) IDG Bks.

QuickC for Windows. Anthony DelSorbo. LC 93-39893. 1993. 49.95 (0-07-016331-6, Windcrest); pap. 34.95 (0-07-016332-4, Windcrest) TAB Bks.

QuickCalc Med Dosage Calculations. Merrilee T. McDuffie. LC 93-39298. 273p. (C). 1994. spiral bd. 37.60 (0-8053-1366-4) Benjamin-Cummings.

QuickCheck French. Francoise Mercier. LC 97-31024. (Barron's Quickcheck Language Ser.). (ENG & FRE.). 160p. 1998. pap. 8.95 (0-7641-0308-3) Barron.

QuickCheck Italian. Candida D. Tondo-Thie & Reiner Thie. LC 97-31023. (Quick Check Ser.). (ENG & ITA.). 160p. 1998. pap. 8.95 (0-7641-0309-1) Barron.

Quickcheck Placement Tests. Fowler & Coe. Date not set. spiral bd. write for info. (0-17-555563-X) Addison-Wesley.

QuickCheck Spanish. Olga J. Lazaro. Tr. by Kathleen Luft from ENG. LC 97-31024. (Barron's Quickcheck Language Ser.). (ENG & SPA.). 160p. 1998. pap. 8.95 (0-7641-0310-5) Barron.

Quicken: Self Teaching Guide. Peter G. Aitken. LC 92-782. 384p. 1992. pap. 19.95 (0-471-54889-8) Wiley.

Quicken Business User's Guide. Joseph Jacobs. LC 94-149003. ii, 60 p. 1993. write for info. (0-929804-46-5) Intuit.

Quicken 8 for DOS for Dummies. 2nd ed. Steven L. Nelson. LC 94-78901. 352p. 1994. pap. 19.95 (1-56884-210-4) IDG Bks.

Quicken 5 for MACs for Dummies. Steven L. Nelson. LC 94-78902. 360p. 1995. pap. 19.95 (1-56884-211-2) IDG Bks.

Quicken 5 for Windows for Dummies Quick Reference. 2nd ed. Steven L. Nelson. 196p. 1995. spiral bd. 9.99 (1-56884-963-X) IDG Bks.

Quicken 5 for Windows for Dummies. 3rd ed. Steven L. Nelson. 408p. 1995. pap. 19.99 (1-56884-923-0) IDG Bks.

Quicken 5, IBM PC: Quick Reference Guide. Milton Chassman. 1993. pap. 12.00 (1-56243-094-7, QB-17) DDC Pub.

Quicken 5 for Windows: The Visual Learning Guide. David Gardner. 1995. pap. 19.95 (0-7615-0339-0) Prima Pub.

Quicken for Contractors. Karen Mitchell et al. LC 97-46798. (Illus.). 240p. 1998. pap. 32.50 (1-57218-043-9) Craftsman.

Quicken for DOS for Dummies. Steven L. Nelson. (Illus.). 300p. 1994. pap. 16.95 (1-56884-006-3) IDG Bks.

Quicken for Windows. Milton Chassman. 1993. pap. 12.00 (1-56243-103-X, C-18) DDC Pub.

Quicken for Windows: The Visual Learning Guide. David C. Gardner. 336p. 1995. pap. 19.95 (1-55958-752-0) Prima Pub.

Quicken for Windows in One Hour for Lawyers. Gerald J. Robinson. LC 96-80096. 80p. 1996. pap. 29.95 (1-57073-385-6, 511-0380) Amer Bar Assn.

Quicken for Windows 3.O Quick Reference Guide. Joe Kuhr. LC 94-180912. 1994. spiral bd. 12.00 (1-56243-144-7, OQKW3) DDC Pub.

Quicken 4 for Windows for Dummies. 2nd ed. Steven L. Nelson. LC 95-128430. 352p. 1994. pap. 19.95 (1-56884-209-0) IDG Bks.

Quicken 4 for Windows Answers: Certified Tech Support. Mary Campbell & David Campbell. (Certified Tech Support Ser.). 304p. 1995. pap. text 19.95 (0-07-882129-0) Osborne-McGraw.

Quicken Guide to Personal Finance. Sindell. 1998. 19.99 (0-07-211937-3) McGraw.

Quicken in the Classroom for Windows 6.0. (In the Classroom Ser.). (Illus.). 254p. 1997. spiral bd. 25.00 incl. disk (1-887391-10-X, IQC60W) Tech Lrng Res.

Quicken 98 for Windows in the Classroom. Technical Learning Resources Inc. Staff. (In the Classroom Ser.). (Illus.). 370p. 1997. 25.00 (1-887391-24-X, 1QC98W) Tech Lrng Res.

Quicken 98 - Using. Ed. by Ron Pronk. (Illus.). 240p. 1998. pap. 20.00 (1-58264-070-X, 164) ActiveEd.

Quicken 98 Bible. Kathy Ivens. LC 97-78376. 640p. 1998. pap. text 39.99 (0-7645-3211-1) IDG Bks.

Quicken 98 for Busy People. Peter Weverka. LC 98-103130. 1997. pap. 24.99 (0-07-882440-0) Osborne-McGraw.

Quicken 98 for Macintosh: Visual QuickStart Guide. Tom Negrino. LC 99-162315. (Visual QuickStart Guide Ser.). 168p. (C). 1998. pap. text 16.99 (0-201-35401-2, Pub. by Peachpit Pr) Addison-Wesley.

Quicken 98 for the Direct Investor: An Easy to Use Guide on How to Manage Your Dividend Reinvestment & Direct Stock Purchase Plans. Richard Powers. (Illus.). 224p. 1998. pap. write for info. (0-9666997-0-X) Failte Pubg.

Quicken 98 for Windows for Dummies. 5th ed. Stephen L. Nelson. LC 97-80308. 400p. 1997. pap. 19.99 (0-7645-0243-3) IDG Bks.

Quicken 99: The Official Guide. Maria Langer. LC 99-167165. 1998. pap. text 24.99 (0-07-211889-X) Osborne-McGraw.

***Quicken 99 Bible.** Ivens. LC HG179.I939 1999. 648p. 1998. 39.99 (0-7645-3280-4) IDG Bks.

Quicken 99 Fast & Easy. Coletta Witherspoon. LC 98-67611. (Fast & Easy Ser.). 350p. 1998. per. 16.99 (0-7615-1787-1) Prima Pub.

Quicken 99 for Busy People. Peter Weverka. LC 99-174889. (For Busy People (Computers) Ser.). 304p. 1998. pap. 24.99 (0-07-211916-0) Osborne-McGraw.

Quicken 99 for Windows: Visual QuickStart Guide. Tom Negrino. LC 99-219513. (Visual QuickStart Guide Ser.). (Illus.). 256p. 1999. pap. 16.99 (0-201-35426-8, Pub. by Peachpit Pr) Addison-Wesley.

***Quicken 99 Intermediate.** (Illus.). (C). 2000. pap. write for info. (0-7423-0435-3) ComputerPREP.

***Quicken 99 Intermediate: Instructor Guide.** (Illus.). (C). 2000. pap., teacher ed. write for info. (0-7423-0436-1) ComputerPREP.

***Quicken 99 Introduction.** (Illus.). (C). 2000. pap. write for info. (0-7423-0433-7) ComputerPREP.

***Quicken 99 Introduction: Instructor Guide.** (Illus.). 2000. pap., teacher ed. write for info. (0-7423-0434-5) ComputerPREP.

Quicken 99 for Dummies. Stephen L. Nelson. LC HG179.N42658 1998. (For Dummies Ser.). 408p. 1998. pap. 19.99 (0-7645-0432-0) IDG Bks.

Quicken 7 Made Easy. David R. Campbell. 1993. pap. 19.95 (0-07-881971-7) McGraw.

Quicken 7.O Quick Reference Guide. Joe Kuhr. LC 95-114946. 1994. spiral bd. 12.00 (1-56243-143-9, 0-QK7) DDC Pub.

Quicken 6 for Macs for Dummies. 2nd ed. Steven L. Nelson. 384p. 1995. pap. 19.99 (1-56884-924-9) IDG Bks.

Quicken 6 for Windows: Visual QuickStart Guide. Steven Schwartz. LC 97-144751. (Illus.). 272p. (C). 1997. pap. text 16.95 (0-201-68860-3) Peachpit Pr.

Quicken 6 for Windows for Busy People: Learning Quicken Is a Snap with the Latest Busy People Book. Peter Weverka. LC 97-10668. (Busy People Bks.). 304p. 1996. pap. text 22.95 (0-07-882243-2) Osborne-McGraw.

Quicken 6 Made Easy. Mary Campbell & David R. Campbell. 478p. 1992. pap. 19.95 (0-07-881890-7, QA76.76) Osborne-McGraw.

Quicken 3 for Windows Made Easy. Steven L. Nelson. (Illus.). 300p. 1993. pap. 16.95 (1-56884-005-5) IDG Bks.

Quicken 3 for Windows: The Visual Learning Guide. Grace J. Beatty & David C. Gardner. LC 93-10262. 1993. pap. 19.95 (1-55958-342-8) Prima Pub.

Quicken 3 for Windows Made Easy. David R. Campbell. 1993. pap. 19.95 (0-07-881972-5) McGraw.

Quicken Tree. Bill Knott. LC 95-79361. (American Poets Continuum Ser.: No. 33). 75p. 1995. 20.00 (1-880238-24-1); pap. 12.50 (1-880238-25-X) BOA Edns.

***Quicken 2000.** Ivens et al. LC 99-49251. (Bible Ser.). (Illus.). 620p. 1999. 34.99 (0-7645-3412-2) IDG Bks.

***Quicken 2000.** Stephen J. O'Brien. (Complete Idiot's Guides (Computers) Ser.). 1999. pap. 16.99 (0-7897-2218-6) Que.

***Quicken 2000 Fast & Easy.** Colletta Witherspoon & Craig Witherspoon. 1999. pap. 16.99 (0-7615-2314-6) Prima Pub.

***Quicken 2000 for Macintosh: Visual QuickStart Guide.** 2nd ed. Tom Negrino. (Visual QuickStart Guide Ser.). 256p. (C). 1999. pap. text, student ed. 16.99 (0-201-69964-8) Peachpit Pr.

***Quicken 2000 for Windows: Visual QuickStart Guide.** 2nd ed. Tom Negrino. (Visual QuickStart Guide Ser.). 256p. (C). 1999. pap. text, teacher ed. 16.99 (0-201-69965-6) Peachpit Pr.

***Quicken 2000 Intermediate.** (Illus.). (YA). 1999. pap. write for info. (0-7423-0401-9, QUIK2K02LG) ComputerPREP.

***Quicken 2000 Intermediate: Instructor Guide.** (Illus.). (C). 2000. pap., teacher ed. write for info. (0-7423-0431-0) ComputerPREP.

***Quicken 2000 Introduction.** (Illus.). (YA). 1999. pap. write for info. (0-7423-0400-0, QUIK2K01LG) ComputerPREP.

***Quicken 2000 Introduction: Instructor Guide.** (Illus.). 232p. 1999. pap. write for info. (0-7423-0423-X) ComputerPREP.

Quicken User's Guide. Joseph Jacobs. LC 98-216777. viii, 438 p. 1993. write for info. (0-929804-45-7) Intuit.

***Quicken X for Dummies.** Stephen L. Nelson. 408p. 1999. pap. 19.99 (0-7645-0607-2) IDG Bks.

Quicken 2000: The Official Guide. Maria Langer. 1999. pap. text 24.99 (0-07-212140-8) Osborne-McGraw.

Quicken 2000 for The Mac: The Official Guide. Maria Langer. 1999. pap. text 24.99 (0-07-212141-6) Osborne-McGraw.

Quicken 6. (Quick Study Computer Ser.). 4p. pap. 3.95 (1-57222-195-X) Barcharts.

Quicken 99. (Quick Study Computer Ser.). 4p. pap. 3.95 (1-57222-298-0) Barcharts.

Quickening. Terry Griggs. 140p. 1990. pap. write for info. (0-88984-111-X) Porcup Quill.

Quickening. Stuart Wilde. 135p. 1983. pap. 9.95 (1-56170-165-3, 190) Hay House.

Quickening. Stuart Wilde. LC 88-17318. (Illus.). 135p. 1988. pap. 9.95 (0-930603-22-2) White Dove NM.

***Quickening: A Novel.** Laura Catherine Brown. LC 00-28094. 336p. 2000. 23.95 (0-375-50373-0) Random.

Quickening: Today's Trends, Tomorrow's World. Art Bell. 336p. 1997. 24.95 (1-879706-70-9) Paper Chase.

Quickening: Today's Trends, Tomorrow's World. Art Bell. 336p. 1998. pap. 15.95 (1-879706-71-7) Paper Chase.

***Quickening Begins.** P. Bradley Casey. 116p. 1999. pap. 14.95 (0-7392-0366-5, PO3570) Morris Pubng.

Quickening Heart: A Journal of Discovery for Expectant Mothers. Anne C. Buchanan & Debra K. Klingsporn. (Illus.). 160p. 1996. boxed set 18.00 (0-8358-0776-2) Upper Room Bks.

Quickening of America: Rebuilding Our Nation, Remaking Our Lives. Frances M. Lappe & Paul M. Du Bois. LC 93-35547. (Nonprofit Ser.). 353p. 1994. pap. 21.00 (1-55542-605-0) Jossey-Bass.

Quickening Spirit. Bill Panko & Margaret Panko. 150p. (Orig.). Date not set. pap. 14.95 (1-885342-08-X) Creative Ways.

Quickening Spirit of Radiance, Set. unabridged ed. Kenneth G. Mills. 1990. pap. 10.95 incl. audio (0-919842-10-0, KGOC29) Sun-Scape Ent.

Quickenings. Chris Griscom. 62p. 1992. pap. 4.00 (0-9623696-2-4) Light Inst Fndtn.

Quicker Than the Eye. Ray Bradbury. 272p. 1996. mass mkt. 22.00 (0-380-97380-4, Avon Bks) Morrow Avon.

Quicker Than the Eye. Ray Bradbury. LC 96-20481. 304p. 1997. mass mkt. 5.99 (0-380-78959-0, Avon Bks) Morrow Avon.

Quicker Than the Eye. large type ed. Ray Bradbury. LC 96-39257. (Basic Ser.). 347p. 1997. lib. bdg. 26.95 (0-7862-0945-3) Thorndike Pr.

Quickest Door, Smallest Room. Agnes McDonald. 94p. Date not set. pap. 8.95 (1-879934-04-3) St Andrews NC.

Quickest Kid Fixer-Uppers, Vol. 1. Ruth H. Wells. (Illus.). 17p. 1996. pap., teacher ed. 13.00 (1-891881-00-0) Youth Change.

Quickest Kid Fixer-Uppers, Vol. 2. Ruth H. Wells. (Illus.). 17p. 1997. pap., teacher ed. 13.00 (1-891881-01-9) Youth Change.

Quickest Kid Fixer-Uppers, Vol. 3. Ruth Herman Wells. (Illus.). 20p. 2000. pap., teacher ed. 13.00 (1-891881-13-2) Youth Change.

QuicKeys 3 Book. Steve Roth & Don Sellers. LC 94-36390. 352p. (C). 1994. pap. 22.95 (0-201-40979-8) Addison-Wesley.

Quickflip to Delicious Dinners. rev. expanded ed. Eileen Faughey. (Illus.). 1999. spiral bd. 17.95 (0-9650412-2-0) Nutrition Connect.

Quickhand. Jeremy Grossman. 152p. 1976. pap. 17.95 (0-471-32887-1) Wiley.

Quickie Comebacks. Lisa Eisenberg & Katy Hall. 96p. (YA). 1992. pap. 1.95 (0-590-44998-2) Scholastic Inc.

***Quickie Divorce Book.** Mark Warda & Edward A. Haman. (Legal Survival Guides Ser.). 272p. 2000. pap. 19.95 (1-57248-131-5, Sphinx Pubng) Sourcebks.

Quickie Wine Course. D. Ferguson. 75p. 1989. 8.95 (0-916689-19-0, 201) Am Bartenders.

Quickies: Lesbian Short-Shorts. Irene Zahava. 1992. pap. 5.00 (0-9631656-1-5) Violet Ink.

Quickies: Short Short Fiction of Gay Male Desire. Ed. by James C. Johnstone. LC 98-182131. 196p. 1998. pap. 14.95 (1-55152-052-4, Pub. by Arsenal Pulp) LPC InBook.

Quickies: 1000 Recipes, Ten Quick Ways with Everyday Foods. Monda Rosenberg. LC 98-225434. (Chatelaine Food Express Ser.). (Illus.). 224p. 1998. pap. 19.95 (0-7710-7592-8) McCland & Stewart.

***Quickies Chicken: Delicious Ideas from Bakes to Wraps.** Monda Rosenberg. (Chatelaine Food Express Ser.). (Illus.). 144p. 2000. pap. 16.95 (0-7710-7595-2) McCland & Stewart.

Quickies for Singles: Planning & Preparing Quick Meals for One. Fellowship Church, Baton Rouge, La, Members. Ed. by Gwen McKee. (Gift Cookbook Ser.: No. 4). (Illus.). 80p. 1980. ring bd. 5.95 (0-937552-03-8) Quail Ridge.

Quickies 2: Short Short Fiction on Gay Male Desire. 2nd ed. Ed. by James C. Johnstone. 220p. 1999. pap. 14.95 (1-55152-069-9) LPC InBook.

Quickies 2: Veggies & More. Monda Rosenberg. (Chatelaine Food Express Ser.). 1998. pap. text 16.95 (0-7710-7593-6) McCland & Stewart.

QUICKN PWR PK W/DSK5 25. Robert Krumm. 320p. 1992. pap. 26.95 incl. disk (0-201-58140-X) Addison-Wesley.

Quickprint Strategic Management. 1995. pap. text. write for info. (0-201-37864-7) Addison-Wesley.

***QuickPro 97.** Contexx, Inc. Staff. (Illus.). 36p. 1999. pap. text, wbk. ed. 14.99 (1-929445-00-8) Contexx.

QuickQuant Plus. Lapin. 1994. wbk. ed. 34.95 incl. disk (1-880075-05-9) Alamo Pub.

QuickQuant Plus: Version 4. Lapin. 1994. wbk. ed. 24.95 (1-880075-02-4) Alamo Pub.

QuickQuant Plus Package to Accompany QuickQuantPlus, Version 4.1 for MS-DOS PC. 1993. disk. write for info. (1-880075-06-7) Alamo Pub.

QuickQuant Plus Package to Accompany QuickQuantPlus, Version 4.1 for MS-DOS PC. Lapin. (C). 1994. wbk. ed. 34.95 incl. disk (1-880075-03-2) Alamo Pub.

QuickQuant Plus Package, Version 4.1 for MS-DOS PC. 1993. disk. write for info. (1-880075-07-5) Alamo Pub.

QuickQuant Plus Package, Version 4.1 for MS-DOS PC. Lapin. (C). 1994. wbk. ed. 34.95 incl. disk (1-880075-04-0) Alamo Pub.

Quicksand. Emmanuel Bove. Tr. by Dominic Di Bernado from FRE. LC 91-61534. 192p. 1991. 29.95 (0-910395-69-1) Marlboro Pr.

Quicksand. Emmanuel Bove. Tr. by Dominic Di Bernardi from FRE. LC 91-61534. 192p. 1993. pap. 11.95 (0-910395-70-5) Marlboro Pr.

Quicksand. Jennifer Greene. (Desire Ser.). 1993. per. 2.89 (0-373-05786-5, 5-05786-4) Silhouette.

Quicksand. Louise Hide. 243p. (C). 1990. 49.00 (0-907855-07-5, Pub. by Honeyglen Pub Ltd) St Mut.

Quicksand. Jun'ichiro Tanizaki. 1995. pap. 13.00 (0-679-76022-9) Random.

Quicksand. William P. Wood. LC 98-65135. 320p. 1998. 22.00 (1-57566-324-4, Knsington) Kensgtn Pub Corp.

Quicksand. William P. Wood. 352p. 1999. mass mkt. 5.99 (0-7860-0628-5) Kensgtn Pub Corp.

Quicksand. Nella Larsen. LC 74-75553. 312p. 1970. reprint ed. lib. bdg. 49.50 (0-8371-1127-7, LAQ&, Greenwood Pr) Greenwood.

Quicksand: Israel, the Intifada, & the Rise of Political Evil. Haim Gordon. 1995. 27.95 (0-87013-364-0) Mich St U Pr.

Quicksand (African American Lesbian Erotica Poetry) Folisade: African American Lesbian Erotic Poetry. 1992. pap. text. write for info. (0-9629532-4-5) Black Angels.

Quicksand & Cactus: A Memoir of the Southern Mormon Frontier. Juanita Brooks. LC 92-36970. (Western Experience Ser.). (Illus.). 342p. 1992. reprint ed. pap. 19.95 (0-87421-163-8) Utah St U Pr.

Q

Quicksand & Passing. Nella Larsen. Ed. by Deborah McDowell. (American Women Writers Ser.). 300p. (C). 1986. pap. text 10.00 (*0-8135-1170-4*) Rutgers U Pr.

Quicksand Book. Tomie De Paola. LC 76-28762. (Illus.). 32p. (J). (gr. k-3). 1977. lib. bdg. 15.95 (*0-8234-0291-6*) Holiday.

Quicksand Book. Tomie De Paola. LC 76-28762. (Illus.). 32p. (J). (ps-3). 1977. pap. 6.95 (*0-8234-0532-X*) Holiday.

Quicksand Book. Houghton Mifflin Company Staff. (Literature Experience 1991 Ser.). (J). (gr. 2). 1990. pap. 9.48 (*0-395-55146-3*) HM.

Quicksand Book. Houghton Mifflin Company Staff. (Literature Experience 1993 Ser.). (J). (gr. 2). 1992. pap. 9.48 (*0-395-61777-4*) HM.

Quicksand Pony. Alison Lester. LC 98-6930. 162p. (J). (gr. 4-7). 1998. 15.00 (*0-395-93749-3*) HM.

Quicksand Through the Hourglass. Dave Morice. LC 79-25714. (Illus.). 57p. (Orig.). 1979. pap. 9.00 (*0-915124-27-0*) Coffee Hse.

Quicksands: Foundational Histories in Australia & Aotearoa, New Zealand. Ed. by Nicholas Thomas et al. 288p. 1999. pap. 29.95 (*0-86840-633-3*, Pub. by New South Wales Univ Pr) Intl Spec Bk.

Quicksilver. Butler & Karl E. Rohnke. 286p. 1996. pap. text 23.50 (*0-7872-2103-1*) Kendall-Hunt.

Quicksilver. Mike Dunn. 448p. (Orig.). 1993. mass mkt. 5.50 (*0-380-77160-8*, Avon Bks) Morrow Avon.

Quicksilver. Clark Howard. 1989. pap. 4.95 (*0-317-01687-3*, Sig) NAL.

Quicksilver. Pam McCutcheon. 368p. (Orig.). 1996. mass mkt. 4.99 (*0-505-52141-5*, Love Spell) Dorchester Pub Co.

Quicksilver. Karl Rohnke. 1997. pap. text 23.50 (*0-7872-1610-0*) Kendall-Hunt.

Quicksilver. Judith Reeves-Stevens & Garfield Reeves-Stevens. 752p. 2000. reprint ed. per. 6.99 (*0-671-02854-5*, Pocket Books) PB.

Quicksilver: Adventure Games, Initiative Problems, Trust Activities & a Guide to Effective Leadership. Butler & Karl E. Rohnke. 304p. 1995. 23.50 (*0-7872-0032-8*) Kendall-Hunt.

Quicksilver: Terlingua & the Chisos Mining Company. Kenneth B. Ragsdale. LC 75-4081. (Illus.). 366p. 1995. pap. 14.95 (*0-89096-188-3*) Tex A&M Univ Pr.

Quicksilver: The Complete History of Santa Clara County's New Almaden Mine. Jimmie Schneider. Ed. by Pat Smith & Sharon Sacks. 178p. 1992. 37.00 (*0-9634577-0-5*) Z Schneider.

Quicksilver & Quills. Dana T. Moore. LC 94-60196. 272p. 1994. pap. 12.95 (*1-884570-06-2*) Research Triangle.

Quicksilver Incident: Murder at the Secret Ravine. Macey Casebeer. LC 96-84770. (Goldrush Mystery Ser.). 139p. (Orig.). 1996. pap. 14.95 (*0-9645546-2-3*) Calgold Pubns.

***Quicksilver Kid: A Gold Rush Adventure.** Steve Hailes. LC 99-91456. 2000. pap. 18.00 (*0-7388-0811-3*) Xlibris Corp.

***Quicksilver Kid: A Gold Rush Adventure.** Steve Hailes. LC 99-91456. 2000. 25.00 (*0-7388-0810-5*) Xlibris Corp.

Quicksilver Summer. D. Jean Young. 162p. (YA). (gr. 5 up). 1998. pap. 7.95 (*1-896184-36-7*) Roussan Pubs.

Quicksilver's Catch. Mary McBride. 1997. per. 4.99 (*0-373-28975-8*, 1-28975-0) Harlequin Bks.

Quicksilver's Knight. Christopher Stasheff. 288p. (Orig.). 1995. mass mkt. 5.50 (*0-441-00229-3*) Ace Bks.

Quicksolve Whodunit Puzzles. Jim Sukach. (Illus.). 96p. 1996. pap. 5.95 (*0-8069-0884-X*) Sterling.

QuickStart HTML 3.2 for the Internet & Intranets. Logical Operations Staff. LC 98-163035. 272p. 1996. 29.99 (*1-56276-493-4*, Ziff-Davis Pr) Que.

QuickStart in C++ William Jones. 124p. (C). 1995. pap. text 13.72 (*1-881991-38-5*) Scott Jones Pubng.

QuickStart in Windows: Windows. Stewart M. Venit. 146p. (C). 1994. pap. text 13.00 (*1-881991-36-9*) Scott Jones Pubng.

QuickStart in Works for Windows. Jim Payne. 152p. (C). 1995. pap. text 11.55 (*1-881991-40-7*) Scott Jones Pubng.

***Quickstart to DOS in Windows 9X.** Forest Lin. (Illus.). 154p. 1999. pap. text 23.10 (*1-57676-032-4*) Scott Jones Pubng.

Quickstart to Internet Explorer 4! Leslie Hardin & Deborah Tice. (Illus.). 120p. (C). 1998. pap. text 12.27 (*1-57676-008-1*) Scott Jones Pubng.

Quickstart to Social Dancing: An Easy to Follow Guide for Beginners-Gets You on the Dance Floor & Compliments Your Dance Lessons. 2nd rev. ed. Jeff Allen. LC 96-93013. (Quickstart Ser.: No. 1). (Illus.). 127p. 1997. pap. 19.95 (*0-9654423-1-4*) Q Q S Publns.

***Quickstart to Swing: An Easy-to-Follow Guide for Swing Dancing - Beginner Through Teaching Level.** Jeff Allen. LC 00-190078. (Quickstart to Social Dancing Program Ser.: Vol. 3). (Illus.). 216p. 2000. pap. 21.95 (*0-9654423-3-0*) Q Q S Publns.

Quickstart to Tango: An Easy-to-Follow Guide for Beginners to Passion & Drama on the Dance Floor. Jeff Allen. LC 97-91693. (Quickstart Ser.: Vol. 2). (Illus.). 130p. (Orig.). 1997. pap. 19.95 (*0-9654423-2-2*) Q Q S Publns.

Quickstep. Earl Atkinson. (Ballroom Dance Ser.). 1986. lib. bdg. 250.00 (*0-8490-3644-5*) Gordon Pr.

Quickstep Hiring: The Step-by-Step Guide to Every Manager's Most Important Responsibility. Stephen D. Bruce. 76p. 1997. 14.95 (*0-9645093-4-2*) Ransom & Benjamin.

QuickSteps to Learning: Excel 4.0 for Windows Beginners. Nancy Ziegler. (Quicksteps to Learning Ser.). 1993. spiral bd. 22.95 (*1-56951-004-0*) Sftware Trng.

QuickSteps to Learning: Excel 4.0 for Windows Intermediate. Bethany Sunny. (Quicksteps to Learning Ser.). 1993. spiral bd. 22.95 (*1-56951-014-8*) Sftware Trng.

QuickSteps to Learning: Excel 5.0 for Windows Beginning. Nancy Ziegler & Bethany Sunny. 285p. 1994. spiral bd. 22.95 (*1-56951-022-9*) Sftware Trng.

QuickSteps to Learning: Excel 7.0 for Windows Beginners. Joni Racicot. (Quicksteps to Learning Ser.). 1996. spiral bd. 22.95 (*1-56951-032-6*) Sftware Trng.

QuickSteps to Learning: Word 2.0 for Windows Advanced. Bethany Sunny. (Quicksteps to Learning Ser.). 1993. spiral bd. 22.95 (*1-56951-012-1*) Sftware Trng.

QuickSteps to Learning: Word 2.0 for Windows Beginners. James Larsen. (Quicksteps to Learning Ser.). 1993. spiral bd. 22.95 (*1-56951-003-2*) Sftware Trng.

QuickSteps to Learning: Word 2.0 for Windows Intermediate. Bethany Sunny. (Quicksteps to Learning Ser.). 1993. spiral bd. 22.95 (*1-56951-010-5*) Sftware Trng.

QuickSteps to Learning: Word 6.0 for Windows Beginning. James Larsen & Bethany Sunny. 221p. 1994. spiral bd. 22.95 (*1-56951-020-2*) Sftware Trng.

QuickSteps to Learning: Word 7.0 for Windows Beginners. Joni Racicot. (Quicksteps to Learning Ser.). (Illus.). (Orig.). 1994. spiral bd. 22.95 (*1-56951-031-8*) Sftware Trng.

Quicktime: Macintosh Multimedia. Dan P. Sydow. LC 94-197771. 1994. pap. 29.95 incl. disk (*1-55828-338-2*, MIS Pr) IDG Bks.

Quicktime: Making Movies with Your Macintosh. Robert Hone. (Illus.). 560p. (Orig.). 1995. pap. 24.95 (*1-55958-242-1*) Prima Pub.

Quicktime Vol. 1: Making Movies with Your Macintosh. 2nd ed. Robert Hone. LC 94-66732. (Illus.). 512p. 1994. pap. 24.95 (*1-55958-634-6*) Prima Pub.

QuickTime & MoviePlayer Pro 3: Visual QuickStart Guide. Judith Stern & Robert Lettieri. (Visual QuickStart Guides Ser.). 272p. (C). 1998. pap. text 17.95 (*0-201-35349-0*, Pub. by Peachpit Pr) Addison-Wesley.

***QuickTime for Java: A Developer's Reference.** John Maremaa & Bill Stewart. (QuickTime Developer Ser.). 600p. 1999. pap. 49.95 incl. cd-rom (*0-12-305440-0*) Morgan Kaufmann.

***QuickTime for the Web: A Hands-On Guide.** Steven W. Gulie. (QuickTime Developer Ser.). 350p. 1999. pap. 44.95 incl. cd-rom (*0-12-471255-X*) Acad Pr.

***QuickTime Pro 4 for Macintosh & Windows: Visual QuickStart Guide.** 2nd ed. Judith Stern & Robert A. Lettieri. 384p. 1999. pap. text 17.99 (*0-201-35469-1*) Peachpit Pr.

QuickTime VR. David Heller & Stefan Embleton. 1996. 39.95 incl. cd-rom (*0-614-14486-8*) Comp Lang.

***QuickTime VR Book: Creating Immersive Imaging on Your Desktop.** Susan Kitchens. 296p. 1998. pap. 39.95 incl. cd-rom (*0-201-69684-3*) Peachpit Pr.

Quicktorial: Pagemaker 6.0 F/wndws & Mac. Sr. Pasewark. 1996. pap. 22.95 (*0-538-71639-8*) Thomson Learn.

Quicktrigger. large type ed. Gordon D. Shirreffs. (Linford Western Library). 1990. pap. 16.99 (*0-7089-6808-2*) Ulverscroft.

***QuickVerse 6 Essentials.** Ed. by Parsons Technology Staff. (Illus.). 2000. 59.99 (*0-7630-5327-9*) Softkey Inc MA.

Quickway Crossword Dictionary. 12th ed. H. W. Hill. (Illus.). 624p. pap. 17.95 (*0-14-051401-5*, Pub. by Pnguin Bks Ltd) Trafalgar.

Quid Pro Quo: Studies in the History of Drugs. John M. Riddle. (Collected Studies: No. CS367). 320p. 1992. 111.95 (*0-86078-319-7*, Pub. by Variorum) Ashgate Pub Co.

Quiddities: An Intermittently Philosophical Dictionary. Willard V. Quine. LC 87-11974. 288p. 1987. 32.00 (*0-674-74351-2*) HUP.

Quiddities: An Intermittently Philosophical Dictionary. Willard V. Quine. 288p. 1987. reprint ed. pap. text 12.50 (*0-674-74352-0*) HUP.

Quien? Que? Donde? Cuando? Joy Evans & Jo E. Moore. Tr. by Liz Wolfe & Dora Ficklin from ENG. (SPA., Illus.). 20p. (J). (gr. 2-3). 1990. pap. text 5.95 (*1-55799-185-5*, EMC 027) Evan-Moor Edu Pubs.

Quien Ama Gilbert Grape. Peter Hedges. 1995. pap. text 12.95 (*84-01-46240-1*) Plaza.

***Quien Ayudara?** Concordia Publishing Staff. (Hear Me Read Ser.). (SPA., Illus.). 24p. (J). (ps-k). 2000. 2.95 (*0-570-09913-7*) Concordia.

***Quien Como Dios.** Eladia Gonzalaz. 1999. 24.95 (*84-239-7951-2*) Planeta.

Quien Cuenta las Estrellas? Lois Lowry. (SPA.). (J). 1998. pap. text 8.95 (*84-239-8867-8*, Pub. by Espasa Calpe) Continental Bk.

Quien Cuenta las Estrellas? Lois Lowry. 1990. 14.05 (*0-606-10493-3*, Pub. by Turtleback) Demco.

***Quien Cuenta Las Estrellas?, Vol. 20.** Lois Lowry. (SPA., Illus.). (gr. 7 up). 1999. pap. text 9.95 (*84-239-8887-2*) Espasa Calpe.

Quien de Veras Gano la Copa? (Who Won the World Cup?) Alex Ribeiro. (SPA.). 1997. 6.99 (*0-88113-495-3*, B112-4953) Caribe Betania.

Quien Dice Que la Comida Mejicana Engorda? Quite el Miedo y la Grasa de la Comida Mejicana. Julie Loera. Ed. by Robby Johnson.Tr. of Who Said That Mexican Food Is Fattening? Take the Fear & Fat Out of Mexican Food. (ENG & SPA.). 100p. 1996. pap. 9.95 (*0-9655256-1-9*) RJL Bks.

Quien Dice Que la Comida Mejicana Engorda? Quite el Miedo y la Grasa de la Comida Mejicana see Who Said That Mexican Food Is Fattening?: Take the Fear & Fat Out of Mexican Food

Quien Era Ella? Santa I. Roman. (Romance Real Ser.). (SPA.). 192p. 1981. pap. 1.50 (*0-88025-005-4*) Roca Pub.

Quien Eres Tu? Virgilio P. Elizondo. (SPA.). 133p. 1983. write for info. (*0-614-04873-7*) Mex Am Cult.

Quien es de Aqui - Who Belongs Here? Margy Burns Knight. Tr. by Clarita Kohen from ENG. (SPA., Illus.). 40p. (J). (gr. 3-8). 1995. 16.95 (*0-88448-158-1*); pap. 8.95 (*0-88448-159-X*) Tilbury Hse.

Quien Es el Espiritu Santo? Donald Hocking. (Actualidades Ser.).Tr. of Holy Spirit & You. (SPA.). 1985. 2.29 (*1-56063-160-0*, 498121); pap. write for info. (*0-614-27128-2*) Editorial Unilit.

Quien Es el Jefe. Barbara Boswell.Tr. of Who's the Boss?. (SPA.). 1998. per. 3.50 (*0-373-35219-0*) Harlequin Bks.

Quien es el Novio (The Groom, I Presume?) Annette Broadrick. (Deseo Ser.). (SPA.). 1997. per. 3.50 (*0-373-35172-0*, 1-351725) Harlequin Bks.

Quien Es Este Jesus? Michael Green.Tr. of Who Is This Jesus?. (SPA.). 134p. 1992. 8.99 (*0-89922-177-7*, C015-1777) Caribe Betania.

Quien es Jesuscristo? (Who Is Jesus Christ?) William Hendricks. Tr. by Jose L. Martinez from ENG. (Biblioteca de Doctrina Cristiana Ser.).Tr. of Who Is Jesus Christ?. (SPA.). 164p. 1986. pap. 6.75 (*0-311-09112-1*) Casa Bautista.

Quien Es la Bestia? Keith Baker. Tr. by Alma Flor Ada from ENG. LC 93-49341.Tr. of Who Is the Beast?. (SPA., Illus.). 32p. (J). (ps-3). 1994. pap. 6.00 (*0-15-200185-9*) Harcourt.

Quien Es Quien en las Lettras Espanolas (S-37344) Inle. (SPA.). 495p. 1979. 29.95 (*0-8288-4832-7*, S37344) Fr & Eur.

Quien Esta en la Biblioteca? Karen Krider. 1995. 14.95 (*84-372-2168-4*) Santillana.

Qui'en Esta en la Caja? see Homeplay: La Alegria de Aprender Entre Ninos y Adultos, Series I

Quien Ganara Esta Guerra? Luis Palau.Tr. of Say Yes! How to Renew Your Spiritual Passion. (SPA.). 142p. 1992. pap. 1.50 (*1-56063-179-1*, 498499) Editorial Unilit.

Quien Gano la Copa Mundial. Alex Dias Ribeiro. 1998. pap. 14.99 (*0-88113-523-2*) Caribe Betania.

Quien Hable por Lobo: Un Cuento de Esenanza de la Tradicion de los Nativos de America. Paula Underwood. Tr. by Felipe Barajas. Orig. Title: Who Speaks for Wolf. (SPA.). 49p. 1999. pap. 12.00 (*1-879678-13-6*) Tribe Two Pr.

Quien Jala los Hilos? Irene Sendin. (SPA., Illus.). 151p. 1985. write for info. (*0-614-04878-8*) Mex Am Cult.

Quien Jala los Hilos? Irene Sendin. Ed. by Rosa M. Icaza. (SPA., Illus.). 135p. 1985. pap. 4.95 (*0-932545-01-7*) Mex Am Cult.

Quien Manda En Cuba? Las Estructuras Del Polder. La Elite. Manuel S. Perez. LC 89-83374. (Coleccion Cuba y sus Jueces). (SPA., Illus.). 255p. 1989. 35.00 (*0-89729-551-X*) Ediciones.

Quien Mato a Palomino Molero? 13th ed. Mario Vargas Llosa. (SPA.). 189p. 1992. pap. 24.95 (*0-7859-0577-4*, S15829) Fr & Eur.

Quien Nacera Aqui? (Who's Hatching Here?), Big Book. Alma F. Ada. (Libros para Contar/Stories for the Telling Ser.). (SPA., Illus.). (J). (gr. k-1). 18.95 (*0-88272-801-6*) Santillana.

Quien Nacera Aqui? (Who's Hatching Here?), Big Book. Alma F. Ada. (Libros para Contar/Stories for the Telling Ser.). (Illus.). (J). (gr. k-1). 1989. 18.95 (*0-88272-812-1*) Santillana.

***Quien Necesita un Barco? La Historia De Moises.** Marilyn Lashbrook. (Libros Yo Tambien! Ser.).Tr. of Who Needs a Boat?. (SPA., Illus.). 32p. (J). (ps-2). 2000. 5.95 (*1-58170-037-7*) Rainbow Studies.

Quien Puede Entender a los Hombres? Transforma Tu Matrimonio y Tus Relaciones Con Otros Hombres en Tu Vida! Gloria Ricardo. (SPA.). 1998. pap. 3.00 (*1-885630-46-8*) HLM Producciones.

***Quien Puedo Aer?** Karen M. Rogers. Tr. by Ana M. Alvarado. (Think-Kids Book Collection).Tr. of Who Can I Be?. (SPA., Illus.). 16p. (J). (gr. 1-4). 2000. pap. 2.95 (*1-58237-051-6*) Creat Think.

Quien Quiere Un Rinoceronte Barato? Shel Silverstein. 1998. pap. 11.00 (*84-264-3697-8*) Lectorum Pubns.

Quien Say Cuando Nadie Me Ve? Bill Hybels.Tr. of Who You Are When No One's Looking. (SPA.). 112p. 1995. pap. 6.99 (*0-8297-1990-3*) Vida Pubs.

***Quien Se Robo Los Colores?** Alister Ramirez Marquez. (SPA., Illus.). 96p. (YA). (gr. 7-12). 2000. 8.00 (*1-877653-72-1*) Wayside Pub.

Quien Soy?/Who Am I? Spanish ed. Mike Inkpen. 1997. 14.95 (*84-480-1069-8*) Timur Publishing Inc.

Quien Tendra la Razon (Who Is Right?) L. J. Thompson. (SPA.). 6.95 (*0-685-74977-0*, 540645) Editorial Unilit.

Quien Vive en un Arbol? Lisa Trumbauer. Ed. by Don Curry. Tr. by Leyla Torres. (Spanish Discovery Links Ser.). (SPA.). 8p. (J). (gr. k). 1997. pap. text 2.75 (*1-56784-960-1*) Newbridge Educ.

Quienes Se Iran? Arrebatamiento. Yiye Avila.Tr. of Who Shall Go?: Rapture of the Church. (SPA.). 49p. 1995. 3.50 (*1-56063-996-2*, 550039) Editorial Unilit.

Quienes Somos: En Busca de las Esencia de Nuestro. Carlos Warter. (SPA.). 218p. 1998. pap. 12.95 (*0-553-06096-1*) Bantam.

***Quienes Somos las Mujeres Panzaleo.** J. Jordan & R. Cueva. (SPA.). 64p. 1999. write for info. (*92-806-3549-2*) U N I C E.

Quier Yo? Diriger el Estudio Biblico. M. Martinez.Tr. of Who Me? Direct Bible Study. (SPA.). 80p. 1995. pap. 4.99 (*0-8297-1909-1*) Vida Pubs.

***Quiere Apostar? Todo lo que Usted Siempre Quiso Saber Acerca de las Apuestas Pero Nunca Imagino Preguntor.** Adele Yorde & Elizabeth M. George. Tr. by Francisco Candemil.Tr. of Wanna Bet?. (SPA., Illus.). 24p. 1999. reprint ed. pap. 6.50 (*1-930467-11-7*, LA Zarus) MN Coun Gambling.

***Quiereme (Love Me) Love Me True.** Ann Major. (Deseo Ser.: No. 188). 1999. per. 3.50 (*0-373-35318-9*, 1-35318-4) Harlequin Bks.

Quieres un Hogar Feliz? Luis Palau. (Serie Cruzada - Crusade Ser.).Tr. of Do You Want a Happy Home?. (SPA.). 45p. 1989. pap. 1.99 (*1-56063-322-0*, 498001) Editorial Unilit.

Quiero a los Animales (I Love Animals) Flora McDonnel. (SPA.). 28p. (J). (gr. 1-3). 1996. 12.99 (*968-16-4933-8*, Pub. by Fondo) Continental Bk.

Quiero Decirte Que... Te Amo. Irene Fohri. 1997. pap. 6.98 (*968-38-0615-5*) Panorama Edit.

Quiero Decirte Que... Te Amo 2. Irene Fohri. 1997. pap. text 6.98 (*968-38-0675-9*) Panorama Edit.

Quiero Escribir Pero Me Sale Espuma. Gustavo Sainz. (SPA.). 1998. pap. 11.95 (*0-553-06084-8*) Bantam.

Quiero Ser Libre. De Castillo et al.Tr. of I Want to Be Free. (SPA.). 212p. 1994. pap. 15.00 (*968-39-0356-8*) Hazelden.

Quiero ser Lider. Rey G. Cantu. Ed. by Javier Hdalgo. (SPA.). 100p. 1998. pap. 10.00 (*0-9669489-0-4*) Nev Giv Up.

***Quiero Ser un Doctor (I Want to Be a Doctor)** Dan Liebman. LC HV7922.L53 2000. (SPA., Illus.). 24p. (J). (ps-2). 2000. pap. 5.99 (*1-55209-473-1*) Firefly Bks Ltd.

***Quiero Ser un Oficial de Policia (I Want to Be a Police Officer)** Dan Liebman. LC HV7922.L53 2000. (SPA., Illus.). 24p. (J). (ps-2). 2000. pap. 5.99 (*1-55209-475-8*) Firefly Bks Ltd.

***Quiero Ser un Veterinario (I Want to Be a Vet)** Dan Liebman. LC SF756.L53 2000. (SPA., Illus.). 24p. (J). (ps-2). 2000. pap. 5.99 (*1-55209-477-4*) Firefly Bks Ltd.

Quiescence & Passion: The Vision of Arunakiri, Tamil Mystic. Fred W. Clothey. LC 96-33520. (ISP Ser.). 178p. 1996. 64.95 (*1-57292-001-7*); pap. 69.95 (*1-57292-000-9*) Austin & Winfield.

Quiet. Patrick Billings. 256p. (Orig.). 1994. mass mkt. 4.50 (*0-8125-2131-5*, Pub. by Tor Bks) St Martin.

Quiet Adventurers in Canada. Marion G. Turk. 632p. 1993. reprint ed. pap. text 39.50 (*1-55613-832-6*) Heritage Bk.

Quiet American. Graham Greene. 21.95 (*0-88411-657-3*) Amereon Ltd.

Quiet American. Graham Greene. (Twentieth-Century Classics Ser.). 192p. 1991. pap. 11.95 (*0-14-018500-3*, Penguin Classics) Viking Penguin.

Quiet American. 19th ed. Graham Greene. LC 92-50219. 266p. 1992. 13.50 (*0-679-60014-0*) Modern Lib NY.

Quiet American: Text & Criticism. Graham Greene. Ed. by John C. Pratt. LC 95-23183. (Viking Critical Library). 400p. 1996. pap. 15.95 (*0-14-024350-X*, Penguin Bks) Viking Penguin.

Quiet American: The Secret War of Varian Fry. 2nd ed. Andy Marino. LC 99-22064. 288p. 1999. text 26.95 (*0-312-20356-X*) St Martin.

Quiet & Peaceable Life. John L. Ruth. (People's Place Book Ser.: No. 2). (Illus.). 96p. 1997. pap. 6.95 (*1-56148-232-3*) Good Bks PA.

Quiet Answer. Hugh Prather. LC 80-2979. 176p. 1982. pap. 8.95 (*0-385-17605-8*) Doubleday.

Quiet As a Mouse. Carol Roth. (Illus.). 32p. (J). (ps-3). 1991. 6.95 (*1-56288-121-3*) Checkerboard.

Quiet As a Nun. Antonia Fraser. (Jemima Shore Mysteries Ser.). 192p. 1998. pap. 10.00 (*0-393-31822-2*, Norton Paperbks) Norton.

***Quiet As It's Kept: Shame, Trauma, & Race in the Novels of Toni Morrison.** J. Brooks Bouson. LC 99-16422. (C). 1999. text 65.50 (*0-7914-4423-6*); pap. text 21.95 (*0-7914-4424-4*) State U NY Pr.

Quiet Bear, Noisy Bear. Basia Bogdanowicz. LC 98-19348. (Illus.). 12p. (J). (ps). 1998. 7.95 (*0-7613-0436-3*, Copper Beech Bks) Millbrook Pr.

Quiet Broker? A Way Out of the Irish Conflict - A Twentieth Century Fund Paper. William V. Shannon. 52p. (Orig.). 1985. pap. 7.00 (*0-87078-163-4*) Century Foundation.

***Quiet Center: A Woman's Guide to Resting in God's Presence.** Susan B. Sutton. LC 99-34888. 144p. 1999. pap. 9.99 (*0-8254-3662-1*) Kregel.

Quiet Center: Women Reflecting on Life's Passages from the Pages of Victoria Magazine. Victoria Magazine Editors. LC 96-40327. 310p. 1997. 25.00 (*0-688-15464-6*, Hearst) Hearst Commns.

Quiet Chameleon: Modern Poetry from Central Africa. Adrian Roscoe & Hangson Msika. (New Perspectives on African Literature Ser.: No. 2). 216p. 1991. lib. bdg. 85.00 (*0-905450-52-3*, Pub. by H Zell Pubs) Seven Hills Bk.

Quiet Child. Janet Collins. (Issues in Education Ser.). (Illus.). 144p. 1996. pap. 29.95 (*0-304-33473-1*); text 90.00 (*0-304-33472-3*) Continuum.

Quiet Children & the Classroom Teacher. 2nd ed. Ed. by James C. McCroskey & Virginia P. Richmond. 60p. 1991. pap. 9.50 (*0-927516-27-6*) Natl Comm Assn.

Quiet Clap: Life Lessons Appreciating God & Golf. Veronica Karaman. (Illus.). 80p. 1998. pap. 12.95 (*0-9668652-0-0*) V Karaman Minsts.

Quiet Company: A Modern History of Northwestern Mutual Life. John Gurda. LC 83-238714. (Illus.). 334p. 1983. 14.95 (*0-9612010-0-2*) NW Mutual Life.

Quiet Confidence in the Lord. Jack Hartman. 220p. (Orig.). 1996. pap. 7.95 (*0-915445-07-7*) Lamplight FL.

Quiet Contentment: The Art of Henrietta Milan. Ed. by Rob Levin. Tr. by Henrietta C. Milan. 160p. 1998. write for info. (*0-9669657-0-1*) Milan Pubg.

Quiet Corner. Ed. by John Matthew. 96p. (C). 1989. pap. 59.00 (*0-7855-6810-7*, Pub. by St Andrew) St Mut.

An Asterisk (*) at the beginning of an entry indicates that the title is appearing for the first time.

Quiet Corner. John Matthew. 96p. (C). 1991. pap. text 50.00 (86-15-30645-1, Pub. by St Andrew) St Mut.

Quiet Corner. John Matthew & Stewart Matthew. 96p. 1993. pap. 30.00 (0-7152-0645-1, Pub. by St Andrew) St Mut.

Quiet Corner in a Library. William Henry Hudson. LC 68-16940. (Essay Index Reprint Ser.). 1977. 19.95 (0-8369-0550-4) Ayer.

Quiet Courage: Kansas Congressman Clifford R. Hope. Cliff Hope, Jr. LC 98-133700. (Illus.). 415p. 1997. pap. 27.95 (0-89745-209-7) Sunflower U Pr.

Quiet Courage: Per Anger, Wallenberg's Co-Liberator of Hungarian Jews. Elizabeth Skoglund. LC 96-32993. 192p. (gr. 11). 1997. 16.99 (0-8010-1125-6) Baker Bks.

Quiet Cowboy. Jack Curtis. Ed. by Doug Grad. 192p. 1994. mass mkt. 4.99 (0-671-79317-9) PB.

Quiet Crisis in the Arts. rev. ed. Nello McDaniel & George Thorn. Ed. by Mark Rockwell & Donna McBride. 48p. (C). 1993. pap. text 6.00 (1-884345-01-8) ARTS Action.

Quiet Daily Geomagnetic Fields. Wallace H. Campbell. 234p. 1989. 27.50 (0-8176-2338-8) Birkhauser.

Quiet Days in Burgundy: A Study of Local Politics. Marc Abeles. Tr. by Annella McDermott. (Cambridge Studies in Social & Cultural Anthropology: No. 79). (Illus.). 307p. (C). 1991. text 95.00 (0-521-38302-1) Cambridge U Pr.

Quiet Days in Clichy. Henry Miller. LC 87-12377. 160p. 1987. pap. 11.00 (0-8021-3016-X, Grove) Grove-Atltic.

Quiet Desperation: The Truth about Successful Men. Jan Halper. LC 87-31585. 304p. 1989. 18.45 (0-446-51359-8); mass mkt. 4.95 (0-446-35505-4, Pub. by Warner Bks) Little.

Quiet Devotion: The Life & Work of Henry Roderick Newman. Royal W. Leith. LC 96-76318. (Illus.). 120p. (Orig.). 1996. pap. 50.00 (0-614-29361-8) V Jordan Fine Art.

Quiet Diplomat. Max M. Fisher & Peter Golden. (Illus.). 584p. 24.50 (0-8276-0434-3) JPS Phila.

Quiet Diplomat: A Biography of Max M. Fisher. Peter Golden. (Illus.). 630p. 1992. 24.50 (0-8453-4846-9, Cornwall Bks) Assoc Univ Prs.

Quiet Dreams from the Heart. Sharon McElroy. 300p. (J). 1998. pap. 12.50 (1-878431-16-1) Artist Profile Pub.

Quiet Elegance: Japan Through the Eyes of Nine American Artists. Betsy Franco & Michael Verne. LC 97-10622. 1997. 34.95 (0-8048-3126-2) Tuttle Pubng.

Quiet Enemy. Cecil Dawkins. LC 95-14566. 1995. pap. 12.95 (0-8203-1785-3) U of Ga Pr.

Quiet Evolution. 2nd ed. Ron W. Davison. v, 76p. 1997. pap. 12.95 (1-890667-01-3) Introspect Bks.

Quiet Evolution: Changing the Face of Arts Education. Brent Wilson. LC 97-8882. (Illus.). 256p. (Orig.). 1996. pap. 29.95 (0-89236-409-2, Pub. by J P Getty Trust) OUP.

Quiet Evolution: Power, Planning, & Profits in New York State. Michael K. Heiman. LC 88-5838. 337p. 1988. 69.50 (0-275-92476-9, C2476, Praeger Pubs) Greenwood.

Quiet Eye. Sylvia S. Judson. (Illus.). 74p. 1988. 10.95 (0-89526-638-5, Pub. by Regnery Pub) Natl Bk Netwk.

Quiet Fire: Asian American Poetry, 1892-1970. Ed. by Juliana Chang. LC 96-78961. 164p. 1996. pap. 19.95 (1-889876-02-X) Asian Am Writers.

Quiet Flows the Don, 2 vols., Set, Vols. 1 & 2. Mikhail Aleksandrovich Sholokhov. Tr. by Robert Daglish. 1612p. (C). 1988. 130.00 (0-569-09106-3) St Mut.

Quiet Flows the Rhine: German General Officer Casualties in World War II. French L. MacLean. 1996. 29.00 (0-921991-32-0) J J Fedorowicz.

Quiet Game. Greg Iles. LC 99-30698. 433p. 1999. 24.95 (0-525-93793-5, Dutt) Dutton Plume.

***Quiet Game.** Greg Iles. 2000. mass mkt. 6.99 (0-451-18042-9, Sig) NAL.

Quiet Gathering. David Scott. 1996. pap. 15.95 (0-906427-68-1, Pub. by Bloodaxe Bks) Dufour.

Quiet Gentleman. large type ed. Georgette Heyer. 498p. 1993. reprint ed. lib. bdg. 19.95 (1-56054-206-3) Thorndike Pr.

Quiet Gentlemen. Georgette Heyer. Date not set. 28.95 (0-8488-2318-4) Amereon Ltd.

Quiet Haven: Quakers, Moral Treatment & Asylum Reform. Charles L. Cherry. LC 88-48019. (Illus.). 240p. 1990. 38.50 (0-8386-3341-2) Fairleigh Dickinson.

Quiet, Healing Zone! Herbert L. Beierle. (C). 1980. pap. 14.95 (0-940480-10-7) UNIPress.

***Quiet Heart.** Patricia T. Holland. LC 00-40387. 2000. write for info. (1-57345-801-5) Bookcraft Inc.

Quiet Heart: Daily Devotionals for Women. June M. Bacher. LC 87-82261. 368p. (Orig.). 1988. pap. 11.99 (0-89081-624-7) Harvest Hse.

Quiet Heart Space: (Meditations & Music for Children) June McIntyre. (Illus.). (J). (ps up). 1996. pap. 11.98 incl. audio (1-889045-04-7) J McIntyre.

Quiet Hero: Figures of Temperance in Spencer, Donne, Milton, & Joyce. Richard D. Jordan. LC 88-25775. 240p. 1989. reprint ed. pap. 74.40 (0-7837-9113-5, 204991500004) Bks Demand.

Quiet Hero - A Baseball Story. Rosemary Lonborg. (Illus.). 32p. (J). (gr. 2-6). 1993. per. 7.95 (0-8283-1958-8) Branden Bks.

Quiet High Speed Gearing. W. P. Schmitter. (Technical Papers: Vol. P145). (Illus.). 44p. 1936. pap. text 30.00 (1-55589-407-0) AGMA.

Quiet Hour. Ed. by Fitzroy Carrington. LC 71-160901. (Granger Index Reprint Ser.). 1977. reprint ed. 19.95 (0-8369-6264-8) Ayer.

Quiet Hour. Ed. by FitzRoy Carrington. LC 78-74813. (Granger Poetry Library). (Illus.). 1979. reprint ed. 20.00 (0-89609-131-7) Roth Pub Inc.

Quiet I Carry with Me. Nancy P. Hastings. LC 94-66348. 66p. (Orig.). 1994. pap. 10.95 (0-9635559-2-8) Slow Tempo.

Quiet in the Grave & Other Poems. Gerald Garbarini. 1976. pap. 2.00 (0-918466-02-4) Quintessence.

Quiet in the Land. Anne Chislett. 12.95 (0-88910-270-8, Pub. by Talonbks) Genl Dist Srvs.

Quiet Indoor Revolution. Seichi Konzo & Marylee MacDonald. 400p. (C). 1992. text 29.95 (1-881016-00-5) U IL Bldg Rsch.

Quiet Invasion. Sarah Zettel. LC 99-51756. 384p. 2000. 23.95 (0-446-52489-1, Pub. by Warner Bks) Little.

Quiet Is Too Loud. Alexis Satchell. (Illus.). (Orig.). 1986. pap. 6.95 (0-931841-04-6) Satchells Pub.

Quiet Kentuckians. David B. Dick. LC 96-68559. (Illus.). 256p. 1996. 16.95 (0-9632886-4-4) Plum Lick Pub.

Quiet Land: The Diaries of Frank Debenham. Ed. by June D. Beck. 208p. 1998. pap. 135.00 (1-85297-037-5) St Mut.

Quiet Life. Ray Ashford. LC 98-44292. 1999. pap. 8.00 (0-687-03489-2) Dimen for Liv.

***Quiet Life.** Beryl Bainbridge. 208p. 1999. pap. 10.95 (0-7867-0635-X) Carroll & Graf.

Quiet Life: A Novel. Kenzaburo Oe. Tr. by Kunioki Yanagishita & William Wetherall from JPN. 256p. 1998. pap. 12.00 (0-8021-3546-3, Grove) Grove-Atltic.

Quiet Light: A Novel about St. Thomas Aquinas. Louis De Wohl. LC 96-83641. 377p. 1996. pap. text 14.95 (0-89870-595-9) Ignatius Pr.

Quiet Light: 15 Years of Photographs. John E. Sexton. (Illus.). 121p. 1990. 100.00 (0-8212-1775-5, Pub. by Bulfinch Pr) Little.

Quiet Limit of the World: A Journey to the North Pole to Investigate Global Warming. Wayne Grady. LC 98-221660. (Illus.). 280p. 1998. text 29.95 (1-55199-014-8) MW&R.

***Quiet Little Farm.** Illus. by Janet Kerr. LC 99-31769. 32p. (J). 1999. 14.95 (0-8050-5869-9) H Holt & Co.

***Quiet Little Woman: Family & Children's Edition.** Louisa May Alcott. 2000. 14.99 (1-56292-771-X) Honor Bks OK.

Quiet Little Women: A Christmas Story. Louisa May Alcott. (Illus.). 128p. 1999. 14.99 (1-56292-616-0) Honor Bks OK.

Quiet Lives. David Cope. LC 83-172. (Vox Humana Ser.). 92p. 1983. 14.95 (0-89603-048-2); pap. 11.95 (0-89603-049-0) Humana.

Quiet Magic. Sam Cook. LC 88-62599. (Illus.). 192p. 1989. 16.95 (0-938586-17-3) Pfeifer-Hamilton.

***Quiet Man.** Paula Marshall. 320p. 2000. 26.99 (0-263-16417-9, Pub. by Mills & Boon) Ulverscroft.

Quiet Man & Other Stories. Maurice Walsh. Orig. Title: Green Rushes. 240p. 1997. pap. 12.95 (1-57098-139-6) Roberts Rinehart.

Quiet Mind. White Eagle Staff. 96p. 1972. 7.95 (0-85487-104-7) White Eagle.

Quiet Mind. large type ed. White Eagle Staff. 96p. 1978. (0-85487-060-1) White Eagle.

Quiet Mind: Techniques for Transforming Stress. Ed. by John Harvey. LC 88-12055. (Illus.). 305p. 1989. pap. 15.95 (0-89389-096-0) Himalayan Inst.

Quiet Mind Companion: A Personal Journey Through White Eagle's Teaching. Jenny Dent. 158p. (Orig.). 1993. pap. (0-85487-091-1) White Eagle.

Quiet Moment in Time: A Contemporary View of Amish Society. George M. Kreps et al. (Illus.). 158p. (Orig.). 1997. pap. 8.95 (1-890050-09-1) Carlisle Press.

Quiet Moments. xiii, 59p. 1997. pap. 10.00 (0-9661309-2-8) F C Bynum.

***Quiet Moments.** Beatrice Brawley. 2000. 4.99 (1-56245-403-X) Great Quotations.

***Quiet Moments for Busy Moms.** Linda Page. 200p. 2000. pap. write for info. (1-56955-196-0) Servant.

Quiet Moments for Couples. Norman Wright. (Illus.). 1995. 10.99 (1-56507-375-4) Harvest Hse.

Quiet Moments for Homeschool Moms & Dads. Vicki Brady. LC 99-32819. 194p. 1999. pap. 10.99 (1-56955-166-9, Vine Bks) Servant.

Quiet Moments for Mothers. Norman Wright & Joyce Wright. (Illus.). 80p. 1998. 10.99 (1-56507-722-9) Harvest Hse.

***Quiet Moments for Nurses.** Sharon Fish. LC 00-28296. 2000. 10.99 (1-56955-172-3) Servant.

Quiet Moments for Teachers. Linda M. Page. LC 98-17019. 220p. 1998. pap. 9.99 (1-56955-063-8, Vine Bks) Servant.

Quiet Moments for Women: A Daily Devotional. June M. Bacher. LC 79-84722. 1979. pap. 11.99 (0-89081-187-3) Harvest Hse.

Quiet Moments for Working Women. Mary Whelchel. LC 98-40819. 268p. 1999. pap. 11.99 (1-56955-078-6) Servant.

Quiet Moments Kid's Relaxation: A Guide to the Tape Series for Parents & Teachers. Gary K. Mills. 27p. (Orig.). 1986. pap. 6.00 (0-938669-07-9) MediaHlth Pubns.

Quiet Moments Kid's Relaxation: A Guide to the Tape Series for Parents & Teachers, Set. Gary K. Mills. 27p. (Orig.). 1986. audio 20.00 (0-938669-12-5) MediaHlth Pubns.

Quiet Moments of Encouragement for Moms. Ellen B. Elwell. LC 99-35238. 112p. 1999. 10.99 (1-58134-128-8) Crossway Bks.

Quiet Moments of Faith for Moms. Ellen B. Elwell. LC 99-35237. 112p. 1999. 10.99 (1-58134-129-6) Crossway Bks.

Quiet Moments of Hope for Moms. Ellen B. Elwell. LC 99-23366. 112p. 1999. 10.99 (1-58134-127-X) Crossway Bks.

Quiet Moments of Inspiration. Compiled by Brownlow Publishing Company, Creative Department S. LC 99-237377. (Little Treasures Ser.). 64p. 1997. 5.99 (1-57051-168-3, 1683) Brownlow Pub Co.

Quiet Moments of Wisdom for Moms. Ellen B. Elwell. LC 99-27843. 112p. 1999. 10.99 (1-58134-091-5) Crossway Bks.

Quiet Moments on the Way Home. H. E. Wisloff. Ed. by David Rinden. Tr. & Intro. by A. E. Windahl. 264p. 1993. pap. 9.95 (0-943167-30-2) Faith & Fellowship Pr.

Quiet Moments Relaxation: A Guide to Deep Relaxation for Adults. Gary K. Mills. LC 86-16464. (Illus.). 72p. (Orig.). 1986. 60.00 incl. audio (0-938669-11-7); pap. 10.00 (0-938669-00-1) MediaHlth Pubns.

***Quiet Moments with Benedict Groeschel: 120 Readings.** Compiled by Evelyn Bence. 2000. 14.99 (1-56955-209-6) Servant.

Quiet Moments with Bill Bright. Bill Bright. LC 99-32268. 140p. 1999. 15.99 (1-56955-167-7, Vine Bks) Servant.

Quiet Moments with God. Emilie Barnes. 560p. 1999. 12.99 (0-88486-252-6) Galahad Bks.

Quiet Moments with God. Joseph Murphy. 1958. pap. 5.00 (0-87516-276-2) DeVorss.

***Quiet Moments with Gordon & Gail MacDonald.** Gordon MacDonald & Gail MacDonald. 2001. 14.99 (1-56955-189-8) Servant.

***Quiet Moments with Hildegard & the Women Mystics: 120 Daily Readings.** Evelyn Bence. LC 99-26263. 134p. 1999. 15.99 (1-56955-140-5, Charis) Servant.

***Quiet Moments with John Powell, S. J. 120 Readings.** Contrib. by Nancy Sabbag. 120p. 2000. 14.99 (1-56955-218-5) Servant.

***Quiet Moments with Padre Pio: 120 Daily Readings.** Patricia Treece. LC 99-12790. 1999. pap. 15.99 (1-56955-129-4) Servant.

Quiet Moments with Patrick & the Celtic Saints: 120 Daily Readings. June S. Sawyers. LC 99-38660. 134p. 1999. 15.99 (1-56955-137-5, Charis) Servant.

Quiet Mother & the Noisy Little Boy. Charlotte Zolotow. LC 88-936. (Charlotte Zolotow Bk.). (Illus.). 32p. (J). (ps-3). 1989. 13.00 (0-06-026978-2) HarpC Child Bks.

Quiet Murder. Nancy Livingston. LC 96-3735. 253p. 1995. per. 3.99 (0-373-26186-1, 1-26186-6, Wrldwide Lib) Harlequin Bks.

Quiet Musings. Rolland G. Smith. (Illus.). 96p. (Orig.). 1995. pap. 12.95 (0-919842-22-4, RGSB1) Sun-Scape Ent.

Quiet Night In. Jill Murphy. LC 93-875. (Illus.). 32p. (J). (ps-3). 1996. pap. 4.99 (1-56402-673-6) Candlewick Pr.

Quiet Night In. Jill Murphy. 1996. 10.19 (0-606-09776-7, Pub. by Turtleback) Demco.

Quiet Noise. Marjorie DeFazio. 32p. 1972. write for info. (0-318-64132-1) Poets Pr.

Quiet Odyssey: A Pioneer Korean Woman in America. Mary P. Lee. LC 89-28077. (Samuel & Althea Stroum Bks.). (Illus.). 264p. (Orig.). 1990. pap. 14.95 (0-295-96969-5) U of Wash Pr.

Quiet on the Set: Motion Picture History at the Iverson Movie Location Ranch. Robert G. Sherman. Ed. by Dean Davis. LC 83-60720. (Illus.). 150p. (Orig.). 1984. pap. 14.95 (0-912641-00-2) Sherway Pub.

Quiet One. Della R. Clark. LC 92-70830. (Illus.). 64p. (J). (ps-5). 1992. 15.00 (0-9631252-0-6) Desert Rose.

Quiet One: George Harrison. Alan Clayson. 300p. pap. 14.95 (1-86074-184-3, Pub. by Sanctuary Pubng) Music Sales.

Quiet One (The Guiness Gang) Cathryn Clare. LC 96-7311. (Intimate Moments Ser.). 248p. 1996. per. 3.99 (0-373-07701-7, 1-07701-5) Silhouette.

Quiet Operator: Special Forces Signaller Extraordinary. John Simpson & Mark Adkin. (Illus.). 168p. 1993. 27.95 (0-85052-376-1, Pub. by Leo Cooper) Trans-Atl Phila.

Quiet Passages: The Exchange of Civilians Between the United States & Japan During the Second World War. P. Scott Corbett. LC 87-2069. 235p. 1987. reprint ed. pap. 72.90 (0-608-07556-6, 205265600009) Bks Demand.

Quiet People of the Land: A Story of the North Carolina Moravians in Revolutionary Times. Hunter James. LC 75-44042. (Old Salem Ser.). (Illus.). 172p. reprint ed. pap. 53.40 (0-7837-6852-4, 204668100003) Bks Demand.

Quiet Pioneering: Robert M. Stern & His International Legacy. Ed. by Keith E. Maskus et al. LC 97-37446. 392p. (C). 1997. text 59.50 (0-472-10839-5, 10839) U of Mich Pr.

Quiet Place. Mary E. Kegel. (Orig.). 1996. pap. write for info. (1-57553-381-2) Watermrk Pr.

Quiet Place. Eddie Kennedy. 1983. 3.50 (0-87129-456-7, Q14) Dramatic Pub.

Quiet Place. Frank Murdoch. (Illus.). 128p. 1990. 45.00 (0-9625635-0-1) Sea Quest Pub.

Quiet Place. Wood. LC 98-38102. (J). 2001. 16.00 (0-689-81511-5) S&S Bks Yung.

Quiet Place. abr. ed. Peter David. (Star Trek Ser.). 1999. per. 6.50 (0-671-02079-X) PB.

Quiet Place: A Collection of Poems. Paulette H. Boothe. Ed. by Ben Booth. (Illus.). 110p. (Orig.). 1992. pap. 10.00 (1-878162-02-0) Unicorn Pr USA.

Quiet Place in a Crazy World see Lugar Tranquilo en Medio de un Mundo Loco

Quiet Place in a Crazy World. Joni Eareckson Tada. 196p. 1993. pap. 11.99 (0-88070-606-6, Multnomah Bks) Multnomah Pubs.

Quiet Place of Violence: Hunting & Ethics in the Missouri River Breaks. unabridged ed. Allen M. Jones. 160p. 1997. 25.00 (0-9653336-1-2) Sprng Creek Pub.

Quiet Place with Jesus: Meditation Themes for Kids. Anne J. Flanagan & Sheila A. Smith. LC 94-29411. (Illus.). 64p. 1996. 4.50 (0-8198-6206-1) Pauline Bks.

Quiet Places: A Woman's Guide to Personal Retreat. Jane Rubietta. LC 97-33849. 192p. 1997. pap. 9.99 (0-7642-2001-2) Bethany Hse.

Quiet Places: How to Create Peaceful Havens in Your Home, Garden & Workplace. Vinny Lee. LC 98-5092. (Simple Life Bks.). (Illus.). 160p. 1998. 15.95 (0-7621-0060-5, Pub. by RD Assn) Penguin Putnam.

Quiet Places of Massachusetts: Country Rambles, Secluded Beaches, Backroad Excursions, Romantic Retreats. Michael J. Tougias. (Quiet Places Ser.). (Illus.). 224p. (Orig.). 1996. pap. 10.95 (1-55650-729-1) Hunter NJ.

Quiet Places of the Heart in Winter: Meditations for Women. Countryman Staff. Ed. by Terry Gibbs. LC 98-109800. (Illus.). 148p. 1997. 12.99 (0-8499-1498-1) Word Pub.

***Quiet Places, Warm Thoughts.** Janette Oke. 112p. 1998. pap. 6.99 (0-934998-15-9) Bethany Hse.

Quiet Places with Jesus. Isaias Powers. LC 78-64452. 128p. (YA). (gr. 9 up). 1978. pap. 7.95 (0-89622-086-9) Twenty-Third.

Quiet Places with Mary. Isaias Powers & Andrea Star. LC 86-50123. 160p. (Orig.). (YA). (gr. 9 up). 1986. pap. 7.95 (0-89622-297-7) Twenty-Third.

Quiet Please. Phil Baron. (Teddy Ruxpin Adventure Ser.). (Illus.). 34p. (J). (ps). 1987. 9.95 incl. audio (0-934323-40-2) Alchemy Comms.

Quiet, Please. Howard Buermann. 1946. pap. 3.25 (0-8222-0927-6) Dramatists Play.

Quiet, Please. James Branch Cabell. LC 52-7061. (Illus.). 143p. reprint ed. pap. 44.40 (0-8357-4634-8, 203756300008) Bks Demand.

Quiet Poems. Gene Fowler, Jr. 70p. (Orig.). 1982. pap. 5.00 (0-932112-13-7) Carolina Wren.

Quiet Pool: Fly Fishing the Rivers & Still Waters of Washington. Daniel B. Homel. (Illus.). 116p. (Orig.). 1995. pap. 13.95 (1-879522-04-7) Forrest Pk.

Quiet Power. Helen L. Marshall. LC 92-71918. 64p. (Orig.). 1992. reprint ed. pap. 5.00 (1-881598-02-0) Marshall Ent.

Quiet Pride: Ageless Wisdom of the American West. Robert A. Clayton. Ed. & Frwd. by J. Bourge Hathaway. LC 92-15228. (Earthsong Collection). (Illus.). 128p. 1992. 39.95 (0-941831-77-9) Beyond Words Pub.

Quiet Professor. Betty A. Neels. (Romance Ser.). 1993. mass mkt. 2.99 (0-373-03279-X, 1-03279-6) Harlequin Bks.

Quiet Professor. large type ed. Betty Neals. (Harlequin Ser.). 1993. 19.95 (0-263-13358-3) Mac Lib Ref.

***Quiet Rebels: The Story of the Quakers in America.** Margaret Hope Bacon. LC 99-45119. 1999. 12.00 (0-87574-935-6) Pendle Hill.

Quiet Reflections. Carol L. Winkler. (Illus.). 77p. 1987. pap. 8.95 (0-9624694-0-8) C L Winkler.

Quiet Reflections. Carol L. Winkler. (Illus.). 1987. pap. 8.95 (0-685-29048-4) C L Winkler.

***Quiet Reflections, 1.** 44p. 2000. 12.95 (0-634-01510-9) H Leonard.

***Quiet Reflections: A Careful Thinking of Poetry.** Carol Merolla. 1999. pap. write for info. (1-58235-335-2) Watermrk Pr.

Quiet Reflections Two. Carol L. Winkler. (Illus.). 77p. 1993. pap. 8.95 (0-9624694-1-6) C L Winkler.

Quiet Reformation: Magistrates & the Emergence of Protestantism in Tudor Norwich. Muriel C. McClendon. LC 98-37996. 1999. 55.00 (0-8047-3513-1) Stanford U Pr.

Quiet Reformer: An Introduction to Edmund Schlink's Life & Ecumenical Theology. Eugene M. Skibbe. LC 99-20263. 154p. 1999. pap. 12.95 (1-886513-19-8) Kirk Hse Pubs.

Quiet Revolution. Ed. by Robin Keeley. LC BR0481.Q54. 384p. reprint ed. pap. 119.10 (0-7837-6563-0, 204612800011) Bks Demand.

***Quiet Revolution: A New Paradigm for Constitutional Government.** Mather G. Eliot. 228p. 2000. 28.95 (1-57392-768-6) Prometheus Bks.

Quiet Revolution: Hermann Kolbe & the Science of Organic Chemistry. Alan J. Rocke. LC 92-28190. (California Studies in the History of Science: No. 11). 1993. 55.00 (0-520-08110-2, Pub. by U CA Pr) Cal Prin Full Svc.

Quiet (R)evolution: Improving Student Learning in Law. Marlene Le Brun & Richard Johnstone. LC 95-102827. 412p. 1994. pap. 65.00 (0-455-21279-1, Pub. by LawBk Co) Gaunt.

Quiet Revolution: Political Development in the Republic of China. John Franklin Copper. LC 87-32930. 76p. (Orig.). (C). 1988. pap. text 12.75 (0-89633-128-8) Ethics & Public Policy.

Quiet Revolution: The Story of a Small Miracle in American Life. Sara Harris & Robert F. Allen. LC 77-17645. (C). 1990. reprint ed. 15.95 (0-941703-10-X); reprint ed. pap. 6.95 (0-941703-11-8) Healthyculture.

Quiet Revolution: The Struggle for the Democratic Party & the Shaping of Post-Reform Politics. Bryon E. Shafer. LC 83-71445. 628p. 1983. 45.00 (0-87154-765-1) Russell Sage.

Quiet Revolution: The Struggle for the Rights of Disabled Americans. James Haskins & J. M. Stifle. LC 77-27664. (Illus.). (YA). (gr. 7 up). 1979. 10.95 (0-690-03981-6) HarpC Child Bks.

Quiet Revolution: Women in Transition in Rural Bangladesh. Martha A. Chen. 256p. 1983. pap. 17.95 (0-87073-453-9) Schenkman Bks Inc.

Quiet Revolution in Welfare Economics. Robin Hahnel & Michael Albert. LC 89-10995. 454p. 1990. reprint ed. pap. 140.80 (0-608-02944-0, 206401000008) Bks Demand.

Quiet Revolutionaries: A Look at the Campaign by Agricultural Scientists to Fight Hunger... & How the Much-Neglected Cassava Could Help. David Wigg. LC 93-29189. 52p. 1993. pap. 22.00 (0-8213-2531-0, 12531) World Bank.

Quiet Revolutionary: A Biographical Sketch of James S. Sutterlin. Jean Krasno. (Reports & Papers). (Illus.). 36p. (C). 1998. pap. text 8.00 (*1-880660-16-4*) Acad Coun UN Syst.

Quiet Room: A Journey Out of the Torment of Madness. Lori Schiller & Amanda Bennett. 288p. 1996. mass mkt. 12.99 (*0-446-67133-9*, Pub. by Warner Bks) Little.

***Quiet Room: Poetry of Zen Master Jakushitsu.** Tr. by Arthur Braverman. 128p. 2000. pap. 14.94 (*0-8048-3213-7*) Tuttle Pubng.

Quiet Room in Hell. large type ed. Basil Copper. (Linford Mystery Large Print Ser.). 288p. 1998. pap. 17.99 (*0-7089-5294-1*, Linford) Ulverscroft.

Quiet Shore. Walter Havighurst. 1993. reprint ed. lib. bdg. 89.00 (*0-7812-5372-1*) Rprt Serv.

***Quiet Shouts: Stories of Lancaster Mennonite Women Leaders.** Louise Stoltzfus. LC 99-22054. 248p. 1999. pap. 12.99 (*0-8361-9116-1*) Herald Pr.

***Quiet Sickness: A Photographic Chronicle of Hazardous Work in America.** Earl Dotter & American Industrial Hygiene Association. LC 98-70894. (Illus.). 1999. write for info. (*0-932627-85-4*) Am Indus Hygiene.

Quiet Spirit: Amish Quilts from the Collection of Cindy Tietze & Stuart Hodosh. Donald B. Kraybill et al. LC 96-3079. (Illus.). 232p. 1996. 60.00 (*0-930741-52-8*); pap. 35.00 (*0-930741-53-6*) UCLA Fowler Mus.

Quiet Storm. Donna Hill. 185p. 1998. pap. 10.95 (*1-885478-29-1*, Pub. by Genesis Press) BookWorld.

Quiet Storm. Lydia Okutoro. LC 98-30346. 128p. (J). (gr. 7-12). 1999. lib. bdg. 17.49 (*0-7868-2403-4*, Pub. by Hyprn Child) Little.

Quiet Storm. Lydia Okutoro. (J). 2005. pap. write for info. (*0-7868-1320-2*) Hyprn Child.

Quiet Storm. Okuturo. LC 97-39832. (J). 1998. 16.00 (*0-689-81039-3*) S&S Childrens.

Quiet Storm. Helene Storm. LC 81-70299. 210p. 1981. pap. 7.95 (*0-9607412-0-8*) Celebrity Pr.

Quiet Storm: Voices of Young Black Poets. Lydia Okutoro. LC 98-30346. 128p. (J). (gr. 7-12). 1999. 16.99 (*0-7868-0461-0*, Pub. by Hyprn Child) Time Warner.

***Quiet Strength.** Janette Oke. LC 99-6539. No. 3. 256p. 1999. 15.99 (*0-7642-2157-4*) Bethany Hse.

***Quiet Strength.** Rosa Parks. (Illus.). 2000. pap. 9.99 (*0-310-23587-1*) Zondervan.

***Quiet Strength, 3.** Janette Oke. LC 99-6539. (Prairie Legacy Ser.). 1999. 15.99 (*0-7642-2158-2*) Bethany Hse.

***Quiet Strength, No. 3.** Janette Oke. LC 99-6539. (Prairie Legacy Ser.). 256p. 1999. pap. text 10.99 (*0-7642-2156-6*) Bethany Hse.

***Quiet Strength: A Prairie Legacy.** large type ed. Janette Oke. LC 99-46977. (G. K. Hall Inspirational Ser.). 1999. 27.95 (*0-7838-8813-9*, G K Hall Lrg Type) Mac Lib Ref.

Quiet Strength: The Susanna Ruth Krehbiel Story. Amelia Mueller. LC 92-82738. 146p. 1992. pap. 2.50 (*0-87303-201-2*) Faith & Life.

Quiet Struggle: Information & Libraries for the People of Africa. 2nd ed. R. P. Sturges & Richard Neill. LC 97-11831. 244p. 1997. 85.00 (*0-7201-2293-7*) Continuum.

Quiet Talks with Eternity see Tykhi Rozmovy z Vichnistiu

Quiet Talks with the Master. Eva B. Werber. 1936. pap. 7.95 (*0-87516-104-9*) DeVorss.

Quiet Therapies: Japanese Pathways to Personal Growth. David K. Reynolds. LC 80-17611. 144p. 1982. reprint ed. pap. 9.95 (*0-8248-0801-0*) UH Pr.

***Quiet Thoughts to Cherish.** Compiled by Garborg's Inc. Staff. 64p. 1999. 9.99 (*1-58375-413-X*) Garborgs.

Quiet Thunder. Al Lacy. LC 96-42351. (Journeys of the Stranger Ser.: Vol. 6). 248p. 1996. pap. 9.99 (*0-88070-975-8*, Multnomah Bks) Multnomah Pubs.

Quiet Time. George Duncan. 1997. pap. 10.99 (*0-907927-63-7*) Emerald House Group Inc.

Quiet Time. Inter-Varsity Staff. 30p. (Orig.). 1947. pap. 3.99 (*0-87784-250-7*, 250) InterVarsity.

Quiet Time. William Robertson Smith. Ed. by Roland Smith. 64p. (Orig.). 1991. reprint ed. pap. text 3.00 (*1-879943-00-X*) Dad Family.

***Quiet Time.** 2nd rev. ed. Ro Willoughby. LC 99-55901. 360p. 2000. pap. 14.99 (*0-8308-1189-3*) InterVarsity.

Quiet Time Companion. Ed. by Ro Willoughby. LC 88-13684. 385p. 1988. reprint ed. pap. 14.99 (*0-8308-1252-0*, 1252) InterVarsity.

Quiet Time Dynamics: What Happens When We Meet with God. Stephen D. Eyre. (PathFinder Pamphlets Ser.). 32p. (Orig.). 1989. pap. 3.99 (*0-87784-224-8*, 224) InterVarsity.

Quiet-Time Messages: Training for Believers. Jere J. McBride. Tr. by Maria Rodriguez et al. (ENG & SPA.). 375p. (Orig.). 1995. pap. 12.95 (*0-9645310-0-3*) LPC Pub.

Quiet Time Quite a Time. 1988. pap. text 1.35 (*0-8474-1012-9*) Back to Bible.

Quiet-Time Thoughts. Jim DeWitt. LC 83-90474. (Poetry for Schools Ser.). (Illus.). 64p. (Orig.). (J). (gr. 3-10). 1984. pap. text 5.95 (*0-915199-00-9*) Pen-Dec.

Quiet Times. Louise B. Scott. (Finger Plays & Rhymes Ser.). 66p. (J). (ps). 1986. 9.95 (*0-513-01785-2*) Denison.

Quiet Times. Janet Teitson. (Illus.). 64p. 1994. 8.95 (*0-8378-8809-3*) Gibson.

Quiet Times: Relaxation Activities for Young Children. Ideal Instructional Fair Staff. 1999. pap. text 7.95 (*1-56822-810-4*) Instruct Fair.

Quiet Times for Christian Growth see IVP Booklets

Quiet Times for Couples see Momentos de Quietud para Matrimonios

Quiet Times for Couples: A Daily Devotional. Norman Wright. Tr. by Ling Yang. 400p. 1995. text 17.95 (*1-885216-06-8*) Evan Formosan.

Quiet Times for Couples: A Daily Devotional. Norman Wright. 400p. 1997. 17.99 (*1-56507-698-2*) Harvest Hse.

Quiet Times for Parents. Norman Wright. LC 95-44183. 392p. 1999. pap. 11.99 (*0-7369-0126-4*) Harvest Hse.

Quiet Times for Parents: A Daily Devotional. Norman Wright. (Devotional Ser.). 1999. 17.95 (*1-885216-19-X*) Evan Formosan.

***Quiet Times for Teachers.** Zondervan Publishing House Staff. 96p. 1999. pap. 5.99 (*0-310-98008-9*) Zondervan.

Quiet Times with Catherine Marshall. 2nd ed. Catherine Marshall & Leonard LeSourd. LC 97-116484. (Catherine Marshall Library). 256p. (gr. 10). 1996. pap. 11.99 (*0-8007-9248-3*) Chosen Bks.

Quiet Times with God: 365 Daily Devotionals. Mack Thomas. (Illus.). 384p. (J). (ps-2). 1996. 15.99 (*0-88070-964-2*, Gold n Honey) Zondervan.

Quiet Times with Jesus. Mary H. Duplex et al. LC 92-20278. (J). (ps). 1992. pap. 10.99 (*0-8280-0678-4*) Review & Herald.

Quiet Times with Jesus Ronald Leinen. LC 95-172280. 366 p. 1995. write for info. (*0-939025-03-5*) Cogan Productions.

Quiet Times with the One You Love. Art Hunt. LC 98-11426. (Devotion Guide for Couples Ser.). 256p. 1998. pap. 10.99 (*1-57673-257-6*) Multnomah Pubs.

Quiet Triumphs. Mary Williams. 2000. 13.00 (*0-06-273679-5*) HarpC.

Quiet Triumphs: Celebrities Share Survival Strategies for Getting Through the Hard Times. Mary Williams. LC BF637.L53Q54 1999. (Illus.). 336p. (YA). (gr. 9-12). 1999. 24.00 (*0-06-270245-9*) HarpC.

***Quiet Undertaking.** Penny Warner. 272p. 2000. mass mkt. 5.50 (*0-553-57965-7*) Bantam.

Quiet Violence: View from a Bangladesh Village. Betsy Hartman & James K. Boyce. 284p. 1983. pap. 19.95 (*0-935028-16-1*) Inst Food & Develop.

Quiet Violence: View from a Bangladesh Village. Betsy Hartmann & James K. Boyce. (Illus.). 298p. (C). 1979. text 45.00 (*0-86232-171-9*, Pub. by Zed Books) St Martin.

Quiet Voice of Soul: How to Find Meaning in Ordinary Life. Tian Dayton. 180p. (Orig.). 1995. pap. 9.95 (*1-55874-339-1*, 3391) Health Comm.

Quiet Voices: Southern Rabbis & Black Civil Rights, 1880 to 1990. Ed. by Mark K. Bauman & Berkley Kalin. LC 97-19187. (Judaic Studies). 444p. 1997. text 34.95 (*0-8173-0892-X*) U of Ala Pr.

***Quiet Walks the Tiger.** Heather Graham. LC 00-25198. (Orig.). 2001. write for info. (*0-7862-2519-X*) Thorndike Pr.

***Quiet War of Rebecca Sheldon.** Rowntree. (J). 2000. pap. 12.95 (*0-552-99325-5*, Pub. by Transworld Publishers Ltd) Trafalgar.

Quiet Warrior. Thomas B. Buell. LC 87-15177. (Classics of Naval Literature Ser.). 544p. 1987. reprint ed. 32.95 (*0-87021-562-0*) Naval Inst Pr.

Quiet Water. Maria Piantanida. 144p. 1999. pap. 11.99 (*1-57532-129-7*) Press-Tige Pub.

Quiet Water: The Inspirational Poems of James Kavanaugh. 4th ed. James Kavanaugh. LC 91-90575. 128p. 1991. reprint ed. pap. 12.95 (*1-878995-20-0*) S J Nash Pub.

Quiet Water Canoe Guide: Maine. Alex Wilson & John Hayes. LC 94-47665. (Illus.). 336p. 1995. pap. 14.95 (*1-878239-36-8*) AMC Books.

Quiet Water Canoe Guide: Massachusetts - Connecticut - Rhode Island: Best Paddling Lakes & Ponds for All Ages. Alex Wilson. LC 93-21820. (Quiet Water Ser.). (Illus.). 240p. 1993. pap. 12.95 (*1-878239-19-8*) AMC Books.

Quiet Water Canoe Guide: New York: Best Paddling Lakes & Ponds for Canoe & Kayak. John Hayes & Alex Wilson. (Quiet Water Canoe Guide Ser.). (Illus.). 416p. 1996. pap. 15.95 (*1-878239-51-1*) AMC Books.

Quiet Waters of Inspiration: In Verse. La Dean McGonigle. 140p. (Orig.). 1997. pap. 9.95 (*1-57502-384-9*, P01219) Morris Pubng.

Quiet Way. Manly P. Hall. pap. 4.95 (*0-89314-823-7*) Philos Res.

Quiet Way Home. Bonny Becker. LC 95-6066. (Illus.). 88p. (J). (gr. k-2). 1995. 15.95 (*0-8050-3530-3*) H Holt & Co.

Quiet Whispers from God's Heart for Couples. David Arp. 128p. 1999. pap. text 12.99 (*0-8499-5484-3*) World Pubns.

Quiet Whispers from God's Heart for Men, 1. Steve Farrar. 1999. 12.99 (*0-8499-5487-8*) Word Pub.

***Quiet Whispers from God's Heart for Mom & Dad.** John Trent. 128p. 1999. 12.99 (*0-8499-5483-5*) Word Pub.

***Quiet Whispers from God's Heart for Women.** Cheri Fuller. (J. Countryman Studio Collection). 1999. 12.99 (*0-8499-5485-1*) Word Pub.

Quiet Witness. Paul Olm-Stoelting. 268p. 1998. pap. write for info. (*1-57502-718-6*, PO2018) Morris Pubng.

Quiet Woman Wakes up Shouting. Pat L. Collins. 40p. 1998. pap. 8.95 (*0-9649463-7-8*) Folly Cove.

Quiet World. Illus. by Leanne Fleming. LC 93-111. (J). 1994. write for info. (*0-383-03671-2*) SRA McGraw.

***Quiet World: Living with Hearing Loss.** David G. Myers. (Illus.). 176p. 2000. 18.50 (*0-300-08439-0*) Yale U Pr.

Quiet, Wyatt! Bill Maynard. LC 97-28183. (Illus.). 32p. (J). (ps-3). 1999. 15.95 (*0-399-23217-6*) Putnam Pub Group.

Quieter Than Sleep. Joanne Dobson. 336p. 1998. reprint ed. mass mkt. 5.99 (*0-553-57660-7*) Bantam.

Quietimes Student Prayer Journal. Becky Tirabassi. 1994. pap. text 9.99 (*0-7852-7971-7*) Nelson.

Quietist. Fanny Howe. (Illus.). 32p. 1992. pap. 8.00 (*1-882022-12-2*) O Bks.

***Quietly at Work: Township Government in America.** Monica Dwyer Abress. LC 99-86138. (Illus.). 128p. 2000. pap. 18.95 (*1-58007-032-9*, Pub. by Specialty Pr) Voyageur Pr.

Quietly Comes the Buddha: Awakening Your Inner Buddha-Nature. Elizabeth C. Prophet. 1998. pap. text 9.95 (*0-922729-40-9*) Summit Univ.

Quietly My Captain Waits. Eleanor S. Hurgronje. (Lewiston Poetry Ser.: Vol. 3). 1987. lib. bdg. 24.95 (*0-88946-045-0*) E Mellen.

Quietly Resting: Deepening Your Walk with God Through Rest. Aletha Hinthorn. LC 96-5636. (satisfied Heart Ser.). 112p. 1996. pap. 7.99 (*0-8341-1607-3*) Beacon Hill.

Quietude & Quest: Protagonists & Antagonists in the Theatre, on & off Stage, as Seen Through the Eyes of Leon Askin. Leon Askin & C. Melvin Davidson. (Studies in Austrian Literature, Culture, & Thought). (Illus.). 375p. 1989. 33.50 (*0-929497-07-4*) Ariadne CA.

Quigly's Dilemma. John Dellinger. 128p. (Orig.). 1986. pap. 6.95 (*0-937693-00-6*) Lone Wolf.

Quigmans. Buddy Hickerson. 1989. pap. 2.95 (*0-8125-7580-6*, Pub. by Tor Bks) St Martin.

Quigmans: Tunnel of Just Friends. Buddy Hickerson. LC 96-23881. (Illus.). 96p. (Orig.). 1996. pap. 9.00 (*1-56858-100-9*) FWEW.

***Quigong for Women: Low-Impact Exercises for Enhancing Energy & Toning the Body.** Dominique Ferraro. LC 99-48331. (Illus.). 176p. 2000. pap. 19.95 (*0-89281-838-7*) Inner Tradit.

Quik-Lab for AC Circuits - Electron-Flow Version: A Whole-Brain Learning System. Albert P. Malvino & Joanna M. Malvino. (IBM (MS-DOS) Ser.: No. 2). (Illus.). 224p. (C). 1989. wbk. ed. 16.45 incl. disk (*1-56048-802-6*, 802E) Malvino Inc.

Quik-Lab for Basic Electronics - Conventional-Flow Version: A Whole-Brain Learning System. Albert P. Malvino & Joanna M. Malvino. (IBM (MS-DOS) Ser.: No. 3). (Illus.). 240p. (C). 1988. wbk. ed. 16.45 incl. disk (*1-56048-813-1*, 803C) Malvino Inc.

Quik-Lab for Basic Electronics - Electron-Flow Version: A Whole-Brain Learning System. Albert P. Malvino. (IBM (MS-DOS) Ser.: No. 3). (Illus.). 240p. (C). 1988. wbk. ed. 16.45 incl. disk (*1-56048-803-4*, 803E) Malvino Inc.

Quik-Lab II for Advanced Electronics. Albert P. Malvino. (IBM PC Series, CGA, Hercules, EGA - VGA Graphics). (Illus.). 164p. (C). 1991. student ed. 18.45 (*1-56048-984-7*, 984); disk. write for info. (*0-318-68964-2*) Malvino Inc.

Quik-Lab II for Basic Electronics: Electron-Flow Edition. Albert P. Malvino. (IBM PC Series, CGA, Hercules, EGA - VGA Graphics). (Illus.). 192p. (Orig.). (C). 1991. student ed. 18.45 (*1-56048-983-9*, 983) Malvino Inc.

Quik-Lab II for AC Circuits: Electron-Flow Edition. Albert P. Malvino. (EGA - VGA - Hercules Graphics Ser.). (Illus.). 188p. (C). 1991. student ed. 18.45 (*1-56048-982-0*, 982) Malvino Inc.

Quik-Lab II for Basic Electronics: Conventional-Flow Edition. Albert P. Malvino & Joanna M. Malvino. (CGA, Hercules, EGA - VGA Graphics Ser.). (Illus.). 192p. (Orig.). (C). 1991. pap., student ed. 18.45 (*1-56048-987-1*, 983C) Malvino Inc.

Quik-Lab II for DC Circuits: Conventional-Flow Edition. Albert P. Malvino. (CGA, Hercules, EGA - VGA Graphics Ser.). (Illus.). 176p. (C). 1990. student ed. 18.45 (*1-56048-985-5*, 981C) Malvino Inc.

Quik-Lab II for DC Circuits: Electron-Flow Edition. Albert P. Malvino. (EGA - VGA - Hercules Graphics Ser.). (Illus.). 176p. (C). 1990. student ed. 18.45 (*1-56048-981-2*, 981) Malvino Inc.

Quik Notes on Christian Classics. Philip W. Comfort et al. LC 95-40488. 1999. pap. 6.99 (*0-8423-5986-9*) Tyndale Hse.

Quik Notes on the Books of the Bible. Philip W. Comfort et al. LC 95-40489. 1999. pap. 6.99 (*0-8423-5985-0*) Tyndale Hse.

Quik Notes on the Books of the New Testament. Philip W. Comfort & David P. Barrett. LC 95-40490. 1999. pap. 6.99 (*0-8423-5984-2*) Tyndale Hse.

Quik Notes on the Books of the Old Testament. James K. Hoffmeier et al. LC 95-40491. 1999. pap. 6.99 (*0-8423-5983-4*) Tyndale Hse.

Quik-Ref Business Reference Guide. Brandon Dobell. Ed. by Christopher Dobell & Charmian Dobell. 112p. (Orig.). (C). 1996. pap. 7.49 (*1-889904-00-7*) D&D Designs.

Quik-Ref Science Reference Guide. Christopher Dobell. Ed. by Brandon Dobell & Charmian Dobell. 64p. (Orig.). 1996. pap. 6.49 (*1-889904-01-5*) D&D Designs.

Quik Step Firing: Step by Step Through Management's Most Difficult Task. Stephen D. Bruce. 78p. 1998. 14.95 (*0-9645093-6-9*) Ransom & Benjamin.

Quik View Map of the United States & World. TNI Stone & Associates Staff & Petertic Design Partners Staff. (Illus.). 2p. 1998. pap. 2.95 (*1-58220-018-1*, 21213, PowerTools for Kids) Navigator.

***QuikStep Discipline: The Step-by-Step Guide to Every Manager's Least-Liked Responsibility.** Stephen D. Bruce. 74p. 1999. 14.95 (*0-9645093-8-5*) Ransom & Benjamin.

Quiktronic Records Management: Practice Set. Patton & Wolfe. (KG - FIling/Records Management Ser.). 1995. pap. 18.75 (*0-538-63089-2*) S-W Pub.

Quileute. Manuel J. Andrade. pap. 15.00 (*0-685-71707-0*) J J Augustin.

Quileute of La Push, 1775-1945. fac. ed. George A. Pettitt. Ed. by Robert H. Lowie et al. (University of California Publications: No. 14:1). 141p. (C). 1950. reprint ed. pap. 15.63 (*1-55567-134-9*) Coyote Press.

Quileute Texts. fac. ed. Manuel J. Andrade. (Columbia University Contributions to Anthropology Ser.: Vol. 12). 223p. (C). 1931. reprint ed. pap. text 23.75 (*1-55567-683-9*) Coyote Press.

Quileute Texts. Manuel J. Andrade. LC 75-82358. (Columbia Univ. Contributions to Anthropology Ser.: Vol. 12). reprint ed. 27.50 (*0-404-50562-7*) AMS Pr.

Quill & Beadwork of the Western Sioux. Carrie A. Lyford. (Illus.). 116p. 1979. reprint ed. pap. 9.95 (*0-933472-00-5*) Johnson Bks.

Quill & Beadwork of the Western Sioux. Carrie A. Lyford. LC 99-32836. (Illus.). 116p. 1984. reprint ed. pap. 9.95 (*0-936984-08-2*) Schneider Pubs.

Quill & the Scroll Stylebook. 6th ed. 1997. 2.00 (*0-318-19219-5*) Quill & Scroll.

Quill of the Wild Goose: Civil War Letters & Diaries of Private Joel Molyneux, 141st Pennsylvania Volunteers. Ed. by Kermit M. Bird. LC 96-17600. 326p. 1996. 30.00 (*1-57249-038-1*, Burd St Pr) White Mane Pub.

***Quill Pen.** Andrews & McMeel Publishing Staff. 2000. 8.95 (*0-7407-0622-5*) Andrews & McMeel.

Quill Reader. Siler. (C). 1999. pap. 37.50 (*0-15-507945-X*, Pub. by Harcourt Coll Pubs) Harcourt.

Quill Reader: Brief Edition. Siler. (C). 1999. pap. 35.50 (*0-15-507946-8*, Pub. by Harcourt Coll Pubs) Harcourt.

Quill, Solitary Apparition. Barbara Guest. 77p. (Orig.). 1996. pap. 12.95 (*0-942996-26-7*) Post Apollo Pr.

Quiller Bamboo. Adam Hall. 320p. 1992. mass mkt. 4.99 (*0-380-71161-3*, Avon Bks) Morrow Avon.

Quiller Bamboo. large type ed. Adam Hall. LC 91-24263. 495p. 1991. reprint ed. 19.95 (*1-56054-249-7*) Thorndike Pr.

Quiller Barracuda. Adam Hall. 304p. 1991. mass mkt. 4.95 (*0-380-70814-0*, Avon Bks) Morrow Avon.

Quiller Barracuda. large type ed. Adam Hall. 356p. 1992. 22.95 (*1-85089-594-5*, Pub. by ISIS Lrg Prnt) Transaction Pubs.

Quiller Book, No. 2. Adam Hall. 1995. 20.00 (*1-883402-56-5*) S&S Trade.

Quiller Memorandum. Adam Hall. 1994. lib. bdg. 24.95 (*1-56849-396-7*) Buccaneer Bks.

Quiller Meridian. Adam Hall. 288p. 1994. mass mkt. 4.99 (*0-380-71534-1*, Avon Bks) Morrow Avon.

Quiller Meridian. large type ed. Adam Hall. LC 93-26674. 445p. 1993. lib. bdg. 18.95 (*0-7862-0024-3*) Thorndike Pr.

Quiller Salamander. Adam Hall. 272p. 1994. 23.00 (*1-883402-40-9*) S&S Trade.

Quiller Salamander. large type ed. Adam Hall. LC 94-32226. 382p. 1995. 24.95 (*0-7862-0338-2*) Thorndike Pr.

Quiller Solitaire. Adam Hall. 288p. 1993. reprint ed. mass mkt. 4.99 (*0-380-71921-5*, Avon Bks) Morrow Avon.

Quillet Flammarion. 49.95 (*0-685-36079-2*) Fr & Eur.

Quilling Paper Art for Everyone. Outlet Staff. 1988. 3.99 (*0-517-19253-5*) Random Hse Value.

Quills. Doug Wright. 1996. pap. 5.25 (*0-8222-1531-4*) Dramatists Play.

Quills of the Porcupine: Asante Nationalism in an Emergent Ghana. Jean M. Allman. LC 92-45198. (Illus.). 352p. (Orig.). (C). 1993. 60.00 (*0-299-13760-0*); pap. 24.95 (*0-299-13764-3*) U of Wis Pr.

Quillwork Companion: An Illustrated Guide to Techniques of Porcupine Quill Embroidery. Jean Heinbuch. Ed. by Monte Smith. LC 90-82648. (Illus.). 94p. (Orig.). 1990. per. 12.95 (*0-943604-25-7*, BOO/17) Eagles View.

Quillworker: A Cheyenne Legend. Terri Cohlene. (Native American Legends Ser.). (Illus.). 48p. (J). (gr. 4-8). 1990. lib. bdg. 16.95 (*0-86593-004-X*); lib. bdg. 14.95 (*0-685-36334-1*) Rourke Corp.

Quillworker: A Cheyenne Legend. Terri Cohlene. (Illus.). 48p. (J). (gr. 4-7). 1996. pap. 4.95 (*0-8167-2358-3*) Troll Communs.

Quillworker: A Cheyenne Legend. Terri Cohlene. (Native American Legends Ser.). Date not set. 10.15 (*0-606-05004-3*, Pub. by Turtleback) Demco.

Quilt. T. Davis Bunn. LC 93-2413. 128p. 1993. text 11.99 (*1-55661-345-8*) Bethany Hse.

Quilt. Ann Jonas. LC 83-25385. (Illus.). 32p. (J). (ps-1). 1984. 16.00 (*0-688-03825-5*, Grenwillow Bks) HarpC Child Bks.

Quilt. Ann Jonas. (Illus.). 40p. (J). (ps-3). 1994. pap. 5.99 (*0-14-055308-8*, PuffinBks) Peng Put Young Read.

Quilt. Ann Jonas. LC 93-46684. (Picture Puffin Ser.). (J). 1994. 11.19 (*0-606-06689-6*, Pub. by Turtleback) Demco.

***Quilt.** Libby Line. 82p. 1999. pap. write for info. (*0-7392-0461-0*, PO3768) Morris Pubng.

Quilt. Ted Pong. LC 81-90056. (Illus.). 87p. (Orig.). 1981. pap. 1.95 (*0-939966-00-X*) Pong.

Quilt. 93rd ed. UK. 1993. pap. text 10.80 (*0-15-300316-2*, Harcourt Child Bks) Harcourt.

Quilt: Beauty in Fabric & Thread. Marie B. Salazar. LC 98-127840. (Illus.). 144p. 1997. 30.00 (*1-56799-474-1*, Friedman-Fairfax) M Friedman Pub Grp Inc.

Quilt: New Directions for an American Tradition. Quilt National Staff. LC 83-50843. (Illus.). 80p. 1983. pap. 10.95 (*0-916838-92-7*) Schiffer.

Quilt: Stories from the Names Project. Cindy Ruskin. (Illus.). 1988. 22.95 (*0-317-67839-6*) PB.

Quilt-a-Saurus. Toni Phillips & Juanita Simonich. (Illus.). 36p. (Orig.). 1993. 9.95 (*0-9638806-0-8*) Fabric Express.

Quilt & Other Stories. Ismat Chughtai. (C). 1996. pap. 11.00 (*81-85107-10-6*, Pub. by Kali for Women) S Asia.

Quilt & Other Stories. Ismat Chughtai. Tr. by Tahira Naqvi & Syeda S. Hameed. LC 94-19776. 175p. 1994. pap. 14.95 (*1-878818-34-1*, Pub. by Sheep Meadow) U Pr of New Eng.

Quilt & Other Stories. Tayama Katai. Tr. by Kenneth G. Henshall from JPN. 210p. 1981. 22.50 (*0-86008-279-2*, Pub. by U of Tokyo) Col U Pr.

Quilt-Block History of Pioneer Days: With Projects Kids Can Make. Mary Cobb. (Illus.). 64p. (J). (gr. 2-4). 1995. lib. bdg. 23.90 (*1-56294-485-1*) Millbrook Pr.

Q

An Asterisk (*) at the beginning of an entry indicates that the title is appearing for the first time.

Quilt-Block History of Pioneer Days: With Projects Kids Can Make. Mary Cobb. (Illus.). 64p. (J). (gr. 2-4). 1995. pap. 8.95 (1-56294-692-7) Millbrook Pr.

Quilt-Block History of Pioneer Days: With Projects Kids Can Make. Mary Cobb. 1995. 14.15 (0-606-09777-5, Pub. by Turtleback) Demco.

Quilt Challenges. Betty Boyink. 72p. (Orig.). 1991. pap. 13.50 (0-685-72806-4) B Boyink.

Quilt Culture: Tracing the Pattern. Ed. by Cheryl B. Torsney & Judy Elsley. LC 94-9388. 216p. 1994. 32.50 (0-8262-0963-7) U of Mo Pr.

Quilt Design Masters. Luanne S. Cohen. Ed. by Joan Gideon. (Illus.). 146p. (Orig.). (YA). (gr. 3-10). 1995. pap. 12.95 (0-86651-941-6, 21401) Seymour Pubns.

Quilt Designs from the Thirties. Sara A. Nephew. LC 93-41394. (Illus.). 64p. 1994. reprint ed. pap. 7.95 (0-486-28156-6) Dover.

Quilt for Elizabeth. Benette W. Tiffault. (Illus.). 32p. (Orig.). (J). (gr. 3 up). 1992. pap. 8.95 (1-56123-034-0, QFEC) Centering Corp.

Quilt for the Promised Valley. Carolyn O. Davis. Ed. by Lisa Di Donato. (Illus.). 64p. (Orig.). 1996. pap. 17.95 (0-9635092-2-5) Sanpete Pubns.

***Quilt Inspirations from Africa: A Caravan of Ideas, Patterns, Motifs & Techniques.** Kaye England & Mary Elizabeth Johnson. LC 00-21297. (Illus.). 2000. 27.95 (0-8442-4206-3, Quilt Dgst Pr) NTC Contemp Pub Co.

***Quilt It! Quilting Ideas & Inspiration for Patchwork & Applique.** Barbara Chainey. (Illus.). 192p. 1999. pap. 29.95 (1-56477-276-4, DB397) Martingale & Co.

***Quilt It for Kids: 11 Quilt Projects.** Pam Bono Designs Staff. Ed. by Liz Aneloski & Carolyn Aune. LC 99-6826. (Illus.). 112p. 2000. pap. 24.95 (1-57120-090-8, 10207, Pub. by C & T Pub) Watsn-Guptill.

Quilt Like a Pro: Complete Patchwork Quilting Course. rev. ed. Kaye Wood. (Illus.). 162p. (Orig.). 1989. reprint ed. pap. 19.95 (0-944588-04-2) K Wood.

Quilt Masterpieces, 1. Susanna Pfeffer. 1998. 14.99 (1-57866-034-3) Galahad Bks.

***Quilt of Dreams.** Mindy Dwyer. LC 00-36270. (Illus.). (J). 2000. pap. write for info. (0-88240-521-7, Alaska NW Bks) Gr Arts Ctr Pub.

***Quilt of Life: A Patchwork of Devotional Thoughts.** Mary Tatem. 288p. 2000. pap. 4.97 (1-57748-737-0) Barbour Pub.

Quilt of Many Colors: A Collage of Prose & Poetry. Grayce Confer. 116p. (Orig.). 1990. pap. 7.99 (0-8341-1358-9) Beacon Hill.

***Quilt of My Life.** Cecila Dulfano. LC 99-96753. 2000. pap. 9.95 (0-533-13337-8) Vantage.

Quilt of Sonnets. Richard Vallance. LC 98-12947. 56p. Date not set. pap. write for info. (1-896243-07-X) Providence Rd.

Quilt of Words: Women's Diaries, Letters, & Original Accounts of Life in the Southwest, 1860-1960. Sharon Niederman. LC 88-81621. (Illus.). 240p. 1988. pap. 11.95 (1-55566-047-9) Johnson Bks.

Quilt Patterns: Women of the Bible. Suzanne Schaffhausen & Judy Rehmel. 32p. (Orig.). 1991. pap. 12.50 (0-8066-2581-3, 10-25813, Augsburg) Augsburg Fortress.

Quilt Projects by Machine. Cy DeCosse Incorporated Staff. LC 92-19930. (Singer Sewing Reference Library). (Illus.). 128p. 1992. 18.95 (0-86573-278-7); pap. 16.95 (0-86573-279-5) Creat Pub Intl.

Quilt Restoration: A Practical Guide. Camille D. Cognac. LC 94-35126. (Illus.). 128p. 1994. pap. 29.95 (0-939009-83-8, EPM) Howell Pr VA.

Quilt Squares & Block Towns: 2-D & 3-D Geometry. Susan J. Russell et al. Ed. by Catherine Anderson & Beverly Cory. (Investigations in Number, Data, & Space Ser.). (Illus.). 238p. (J). (gr. 1 up). 1997. pap. text 32.95 (1-57232-469-4, 43705) Seymour Pubns.

Quilt Stories. Cecilia Macheski. LC 93-33292. 304p. 1994. 29.95 (0-8131-1849-2) U Pr of Ky.

Quilt Story. Tony Johnston. LC 84-210091. (Illus.). 27p. (J). (ps-3). 1996. pap. 5.99 (0-698-11368-3, PapStar) Peng Put Young Read.

Quilt Story. Tony Johnston. (J). 1985. 11.15 (0-606-02794-7, Pub. by Turtleback) Demco.

***Quilt Studio: Innovative Techniques for Confident & Creative Quiltmaking & Design.** Pauline Burbridge. LC 99-43585. (Illus.). 160p. 2000. pap. 29.95 (0-8442-2082-5, 20825, Quilt Dgst Pr) NTC Contemp Pub Co.

Quilt with the Best. Oxmoor House Staff. LC 91-68146. 160p. 1992. 24.99 (0-8487-1078-9, 100350) Oxmoor Hse.

Quilt with the Best. Oxmoor House Staff. LC 91-68146. 160p. 1993. pap. 14.95 (0-8487-1175-0) Oxmoor Hse.

Quilted All Day: The Prairie Journals of Ida Chambers Melugin. Carolyn O. Davis. 128p. 1993. pap. 21.95 (0-9635092-0-9) Sanpete Pubns.

Quilted Christmas. Ed. by Bonnie Browning. 112p. 1995. 18.95 (0-89145-863-8, 4542, Am Quilters Soc) Collector Bks.

Quilted for Christmas, Bk. II. Contrib. & Compiled by Christine Barnes. LC 95-13638. 1995. pap. 22.95 (1-56477-104-0, B221) Martingale & Co.

Quilted for Christmas, Bk. III. Ed. by Barbara Weiland. (Illus.). 128p. (Orig.). 1996. pap. 24.95 (1-56477-143-1, B260) Martingale & Co.

Quilted for Christmas, Bk. IV. Ed. by Janet White. (Illus.). 128p. (Orig.). 1997. pap. 24.95 (1-56477-186-5, B300) Martingale & Co.

Quilted for Christmas: A Collection of Festive Quilts for the Holidays. Des. by Country Threads Staff et al. LC 93-44135. (Illus.). 120p. 1998. reprint ed. pap. 22.95 (1-56477-054-0, B176, That Patchwrk Pl) Martingale & Co.

Quilted for Friends: Delaware Valley Signature Quilts. Jessica E. Nicoll. (Illus.). 40p. 1986. pap. 7.95 (0-912724-15-3) Winterthur.

***Quilted Garden: Design & Make Nature Inspired Quilts.** Jane A. Sassaman. Ed. by Annie Nelson & Lynn Koolish. LC 99-50954. (Illus.). 128p. 2000. pap. 25.95 (1-57120-103-3, Pub. by C & T Pub) Watsn-Guptill.

Quilted Gardens: Floral Quilts of the Nineteenth Century. Ricky Clark. LC 94-2444. (Illus.). 128p. (Orig.). 1994. pap. 19.95 (1-55853-272-2) Rutledge Hill Pr.

***Quilted Havens, City Houses, Country Homes.** Susan Purney-Mark & Daphne Greig. LC 99-59946. 128p. 1999. per. 22.95 (1-57432-731-3) Collector Bks.

Quilted Heart. R. M. Vaughan. LC 99-176096. 192p. 1998. pap. 14.99 (1-895837-39-1) Insomniac.

Quilted Landscapes: Immigrant Youth the United States. Yale Strom. LC 95-45150. (Illus.). 80p. (J). (gr. 4-9). 1996. mass mkt. 18.00 (0-689-80074-6) S&S Bks Yung.

Quilted Landscapes: Machine-Embellished Fabric Images. Joan Blalock. LC 95-48414. (Illus.). 88p. (Orig.). 1996. pap. 21.95 (1-56477-144-X, B261) Martingale & Co.

Quilted Love: A Patchwork of Thoughts & Feelings. Jimmie B. Marshall. 50p. (Orig.). 1990. pap. 5.00 (0-9625557-0-3) Excelsior Cee.

***Quilted Nursery: More Than 50 Coordinated Projects for Baby.** Leslie Beck. LC 99-44335. (Illus.). 128p. 1999. pap. 29.95 (1-56477-288-8, B410) Martingale & Co.

Quilted Projects & Garments. Cy DeCosse Incorporated Staff. LC 95-12392. (Singer Sewing Reference Library). (Illus.). 128p. 1995. 18.95 (0-86573-300-7); pap. 16.95 (0-86573-301-5) Creat Pub Intl.

Quilted Safari: A Menagerie of Patchwork & Applique. Donna Wilder. Ed. by Patty Bailey & Carter Houck. (Illus.). 40p. 1997. pap. 7.00 (0-9655270-2-6) FPC Media.

Quilted Tatting Shuttle Wall Hanging. JoAnn Stearns. 8p. 1995. pap. 4.95 (1-888837-07-1) Silver Shuttle.

Quilted Together. Joyce Ice & Linda Norris. (Illus.). 80p. 1992. pap. 9.95 (0-9622903-0-0) DCHA.

***Quilted with Love: Discovering the Patterns of Life's Grace & Beauty.** Debbie Salter Goodwin. 2000. pap. 12.99 (1-56292-781-7) Honor Bks OK.

Quilter: A Notebook. 256p. 1996. 12.95 (0-9629056-6-6) Quilters Res.

Quilters. Molly Newman & Barbara Damashek. 1986. pap. 6.00 (0-8222-0928-4) Dramatists Play.

Quilters: Women & Domestic Art : An Oral History. Patricia J. Cooper & Norma B. Allen. LC 98-41324. 1999. 17.95 (0-89672-410-7) Tex Tech Univ Pr.

Quilter's Album of Blocks & Borders. Jinny Beyer. LC 86-4262. (Illus.). 208p. 1986. pap. 19.95 (0-914440-92-6, EPM) Howell Pr VA.

Quilter's Almanac Block Party, Series No. 3. Eleanor Burns. (Illus.). 56p. 1991. 14.95 (0-922705-34-8) Quilt Day.

***Quilter's Apprentice: A Novel.** Jennifer Chiaverini. LC 99-89443. 271p. 2000. pap. 10.95 (0-452-28172-5, Plume) Dutton Plume.

Quilter's Apprentice: A Novel. Jennifer Chiaverini. LC 98-31179. 271p. 1999. 16.50 (0-684-84972-0) S&S Trade.

Quilter's Ark: More Than 50 Designs for Foundation Piecing. Margaret Rolfe. Ed. by Melissa Lowe. LC 97-23693. (Illus.). 96p. 1997. pap. 21.95 (1-56477-197-0, B311) Martingale & Co.

Quilter's Book of Design: Elements & Inspirations for Making One-of-a-Kind Quilts. Ann Johnston. LC 99-25210. 160p. 1999. pap. 27.95 (0-8442-2660-2, Contemporary Bks) NTC Contemp Pub Co.

Quilter's Christmas Cookbook. Louise Stoltzfus & Dawn J. Ranck. LC 96-36409. (Illus.). 348p. 1996. pap. 13.95 (1-56148-209-9) Good Bks PA.

Quilter's Complete Guide. Oxmoor House Staff. LC 92-60992. 256p. 1992. pap. 19.95 (0-8487-1152-1) Oxmoor Hse.

Quilter's Computer Companion: Hundreds of Easy Ways to Turn the Cyber Revolution into Your Artistic Revolution. Judy Heim & Gloria Hansen. LC 97-11527. (Illus.). 372p. 1997. pap. text 29.95 (1-886411-15-8) No Starch Pr.

***Quilters Cookbook! Who Feeds the Family When a Quilter Quilts?** Melinda Barlow. (Illus.). 184p. 1999. pap. 12.00 (0-7392-0431-9, PO3714) Morris Pubng.

Quilter's Delight, Set. Dover Staff. (Illus.). 1996. pap., boxed set 8.00 (0-486-29454-4) Dover.

Quilter's Guide to Amish Quilts. Jan Jefferson & Maggi M. Gordon. LC 98-7723. (Illus.). 128p. 1998. pap. 24.95 (0-8442-2665-3, Quilt Dgst Pr) NTC Contemp Pub Co.

Quilter's Guide to Creative Ideas for Color & Fabric. 1998. pap. 14.95 (0-87596-974-7) Rodale Pr Inc.

Quilter's Guide to Rotary Cutting. 2nd ed. Donna Poster. LC 98-87369. (Illus.). 208p. 1999. per. 19.95 (0-87341-707-0) Krause Pubns.

***Quilter's Handbook.** Rosemary Wilkinson. LC 99-44162. (Illus.). 176p. 1999. pap. 29.95 (1-56477-293-4) Martingale & Co.

Quilters Hearts with Flowing Ribbons. Betty Boyink. 68p. (Orig.). 1989. pap. 13.50 (0-925623-00-8) B Boyink.

Quilter's Index, 1985-1989, Vol. 2, No. 1. Ed. by Margaret A. Goodrich. 140p. 1992. pap. 19.95 (1-879291-01-0) Quilters Index.

Quilter's Index, 1980-1984 Vol. 1, No. 1: Patterns-Subjects-Techniques. Ed. by Margaret A. Goodrich. 69p. 1990. pap. 14.95 (1-879291-00-2) Quilters Index.

Quilter's Kitchen: Original Quilt Designs & Accompanying Recipes. Darlene Zimmerman & Joy Hoffman. (Illus.). 96p. 1993. pap. 17.95 (1-881588-04-1, 882670168) EZ Quilting.

Quilter's Notebook. 96p. 1998. pap. 6.95 (0-934672-84-9) Good Bks PA.

Quilter's Notebook Two. Illus. by Cheryl A. Benner. (Blank Notebook Ser.). 96p. (Orig.). 1990. pap. 5.95 (1-56148-005-3) Good Bks PA.

Quilters on the Go. Nancy J. Martin. LC 98-24781. (Illus.). 32p. 1998. pap. 12.95 (1-56477-236-5, B368, That Patchwrk Pl) Martingale & Co.

Quilter's Pocket Reference. Peggy Scholley. 32p. 1994. pap. 7.95 (0-9642247-0-4) P S Pubns.

Quilters' Travel Companion, 1998-2000. 5th ed. Ed. by Audrey Anderson. (Illus.). 384p. 1998. pap. 12.95 (0-9635290-7-2) Chalet CO.

***Quilters' Travel Companion, 2000-2002.** 6th ed. Ed. by Audrey Anderson. (Illus.). 2000. pap. 12.95 (0-9635290-9-9) Chalet CO.

Quilter's Ultimate Visual Guide. Ed. by Ellen Pahl. (Illus.). 288p. 1998. pap. 19.95 (0-87596-987-9) Rodale Pr Inc.

Quilter's Ultimate Visual Guide: From A to Z--Hundreds of Tips & Techniques for Successful Quiltmaking. Ellen Pahl. LC 96-27757. (Illus.). 288p. 1997. 29.95 (0-87596-710-8) Rodale Pr Inc.

Quilter's Year Block Party, Series No. 1. Eleanor Burns. (Illus.). 40p. 1988. 9.95 (0-922705-30-5) Quilt Day.

Quiltie Ladies Garden Journal. (Illus.). 128p. (Orig.). 1996. pap. 19.95 (0-9618293-2-X) Variable Star.

Quiltie Ladies Scrap Book. Variable Star Quilters Staff. (Illus.). (Orig.). 1987. pap. 12.95 (0-9618293-0-3) Variable Star.

***Quilting.** Jodi Davis & Beth Hoffman. (Quick Starts for Kids! Ser.). (Illus.). 64p. (J). (gr. 3 up). 2000. pap. 8.95 (1-885593-49-X) Williamson Pub Co.

Quilting. Laurie Swin. 128p. 1994. pap. 9.95 (1-56799-027-4, Friedman-Fairfax) M Friedman Pub Grp Inc.

Quilting: Poems, 1987-1990. Lucille Clifton. LC 91-70845. (American Poets Continuum Ser.: No. 21). 89p. 1991. pap. 10.00 (0-918526-81-7, Pub. by BOA Edns) Consort Bk Sales.

Quilting a New Canon: Stitching Women's Words. Ed. by Uma Parmeswaran. LC 97-200383. 424p. 1996. write for info. (1-896705-06-5) Sister Vis Pr.

Quilting a Thematic Unit: Easy Cross-Curricular Projects & Activities for the Classroom. Wendy Buchberg. 64p. 1997. pap. 10.95 (0-590-96558-1) Scholastic Inc.

Quilting & Applique All Around the House. Ondori Publishing Company Staff. (Illus.). 120p. 1986. 15.95 (0-87040-703-1) Japan Pubns USA.

Quilting & Applique with Southwest Indian Designs. Charlotte C. Bass. LC 98-7403. (Illus.). 48p. 1998. pap. 15.95 (0-87961-251-7) Naturegraph.

Quilting & Braiding. Shannon Schrein. LC 98-14894. 128p. 1998. pap. 11.95 (0-8146-5876-8) Liturgical Pr.

Quilting Basics. Debra R. Gillig. 1989. pap. 2.95 (0-88266-551-0, Garden Way Pub) Storey Bks.

Quilting Basics. Malone. Date not set. write for info. (0-8069-0474-7) Sterling.

Quilting Bee. Gail Gibbons. (J). 1924. write for info. (0-688-16397-1, Wm Morrow); lib. bdg. write for info. (0-688-16398-X, Wm Morrow) Morrow Avon.

Quilting Bees: Swarms of Ideas & Projects for Friends. Barbara T. Lister & Sherri B. Driver. (Illus.). 96p. 1993. pap. 19.95 (1-880972-08-5, DreamSpinners) Pssblts Denver.

Quilting Bible. LC 97-19466. (Illus.). 320p. 1997. 29.95 (0-86573-199-3) Creat Pub Intl.

Quilting Bible. LC 97-19466. (Illus.). 256p. 1998. pap. 21.95 (0-86573-200-0) Creat Pub Intl.

Quilting by Machine, Vol. 14. Cy DeCosse Incorporated Staff. LC 89-49031. (Singer Sewing Reference Library). (Illus.). 128p. 1990. 18.95 (0-86573-253-1); pap. 16.95 (0-86573-254-X) Creat Pub Intl.

Quilting Circle. Jennifer Blake. (Orig.). 1996. mass mkt. 5.99 (0-425-14980-3) Berkley Pub.

Quilting Design Sourcebook. Dorothy Osler. Ed. by Kerry Hoffman. LC 96-16464. (Illus.). 96p. (Orig.). 1996. pap., spiral bd. 19.95 (1-56477-152-0, B269) Martingale & Co.

Quilting Designs from Grandma's Attic. Elizabeth Chandler & Joanne Donahue. (Illus.). 62p. (Orig.). 1994. pap. 8.95 (0-9636371-2-6) Lizanne Pub.

Quilting for Beginners. Creative Publishing International, Inc. Staff. LC 98-28530. (Seams Sew Easy Ser.). (Illus.). 128p. 1998. spiral bd. 17.95 (0-86573-327-9) Creat Pub Intl.

***Quilting for Dummies.** Cheryl Fall. LC 99-61126. 384p. 1999. pap. 19.99 (0-7645-5118-3) IDG Bks.

Quilting for the 90's, Vol. 1. Sharlene Jorgenson et al. (Illus.). 56p. (Orig.). 1991. pap. 12.00 (0-944588-22-0, Q90) K Wood.

Quilting for the 90's, Vol. 2. Kaye Wood. 64p. 1992. pap. 13.00 (0-944588-25-5) K Wood.

***Quilting Lessons: Notes from the Scrap Bag of a Writer & Quilter.** Janet Catherine Berlo. (Illus.). 2001. 20.00 (0-8032-1318-2) U of Nebr Pr.

Quilting Made Easy. Rodale Press Staff. (Classic American Quilt Collection Ser.). (Illus.). 122p. 1997. pap. text 14.95 (0-87596-973-9) Rodale Pr Inc.

Quilting Made Easy. Mildred G. Ryan. LC 87-6854. (Illus.). 308p. 1987. 16.95 (0-87131-523-8) M Evans.

Quilting Made Easy. Ed. by Karen C. Soltys. LC 95-39659. (Classic American Quilt Collection). (Illus.). 128p. 1996. text 19.95 (0-87596-724-8) Rodale Pr Inc.

Quilting Made Easy: More Than 150 Patterns & Inspiring Ideas for Creating Beautiful Quilt Blocks. Jodie Davis & Linda H. Schiffer. LC 97-52727. (Foundation Piecing Library). 1998. 27.98 (1-56799-655-8) Kenan Bks.

Quilting Makes the Quilt. Lee Cleland. Ed. by Barbara Weiland. LC 94-29983. (Illus.). 128p. (Orig.). 1994. pap. 24.95 (1-56477-075-3, B201) Martingale & Co.

Quilting Manual. Dolores A. Hinson. (Illus.). 192p. 1980. reprint ed. pap. 5.95 (0-486-23924-1) Dover.

***Quilting Masterclass: Inspirations & Techniques from the Experts.** Katherine Guerrier. (Illus.). 160p. 2000. pap. 34.95 (1-56477-327-2) Martingale & Co.

***Quilting More Memories: More Inspiration for Designing with Image Transfer.** Sandy Bonsib. (Illus.). 80p. 2001. pap. 22.95 (1-56477-349-3) Martingale & Co.

Quilting, 1915-1983: An Annotated Bibliography. Colleen L. Makowski. LC 85-2497. (Illus.). 165p. 1985. pap. text 21.00 (0-8108-1813-2) Scarecrow.

Quilting Now & Then. Julie B. Dock & Karen B. Willing. (Illus.). 36p. (Orig.). (J). (gr. 1-5). 1994. text 12.95 (0-9641820-0-9); pap. text 8.95 (0-9641820-1-7) Now & Then.

Quilting Patch Applique. Sedgewood Press Staff. 1986. 19.95 (0-02-609020-1) Macmillan.

Quilting, Patchwork & Applique Project Book. Dorothea Hall. (Illus.). 128p. 1996. write for info. (1-57215-180-3) World Pubns.

Quilting, Patchwork & Samplers. Emma Callery. 1995. write for info. (0-7858-0248-7) Bk Sales Inc.

Quilting School. Ann Poe. LC 93-43792. (Learn-As-You-Go Guides Ser.). (Illus.). 176p. 1993. 21.00 (0-89577-471-2, Pub. by RD Assn) Penguin Putnam.

***Quilting Season.** Debbie Caffrey. (Illus.). 56p. 1999. pap. 19.00 (0-9645777-3-9) Debbies Creat.

Quilting Sourcebook: 250 Easy-to-Follow Patchwork & Quilting Patterns. Maggi M. Gordon. LC 97-60161. (Illus.). 144p. 1997. 29.95 (1-57076-096-9, Trafalgar Sq Pub) Trafalgar.

***Quilting the Journeys of Lewis & Clark: A Pattern Book for Making "Lewis & Clark in the Bitterroot"** Patricia B. Hastings. (Illus.). 32p. 1999. spiral bd. 14.95 (0-912299-91-6) Stoneydale Pr Pub.

Quilting Tile With Feathers & Otto: Activities for Learning: Shape Recognition, & Spatial Skills, 1. Learning Place Cuisenaire Staff. 1997. pap. write for info. (1-57452-126-8) Cuisenaire.

Quilting up a Storm: New Ways to Interpret a Classic Block Design. Lydia Quigley. (Illus.). 80p. 1996. pap. 19.95 (1-56477-138-5, B255) Martingale & Co.

Quilting with Anne Orr. Anne Orr. 32p. 1990. pap. 3.50 (0-486-26325-8) Dover.

***Quilting with Fons & Porter.** Liz Porter & Marianne Fons. (Illus.). 2000. pap. 24.95 (0-9676310-1-7) Fons & Porter.

***Quilting with Japanese Fabrics.** Kitty Pippen. (Illus.). 80p. 2000. pap. write for info. (1-56477-297-7, B429, Pub. by Martingale & Co) F & W Pubns Inc.

Quilting with Strips & Strings: Full with Complete Instructions for Making 12 Patchwork Quiltblocks. Helen W. Rose. (Quilting Ser.). (Illus.). 48p. (Orig.). 1983. pap. 4.95 (0-486-24357-5) Dover.

Quilting with Style: Principles for Great Pattern Design. Gwen Marston & Joe Cunningham. LC 93-7673. 1993. 24.95 (0-89145-814-X, 3470, Am Quilters Soc) Collector Bks.

***Quilting with the Muppets.** Jim Henson Company Staff & Children's Television Workshop Staff. (Illus.). 112p. 2000. pap. 25.95 (1-57120-101-7, Pub. by C & T Pub) Watsn-Guptill.

***Quilting Workshops.** Illus. by Brenda Pytlik. 32p. 2000. pap. 14.95 (1-885588-32-1) Chitra Pubns.

Quilting Your Memories: Inspirations for Designing with Image Transfers. Sandy Bonsib. LC 98-42874. (Illus.). 112p. 1999. pap. 24.95 (1-56477-251-9, B360, That Patchwrk Pl) Martingale & Co.

***Quiltmaker's Gift.** Jeff Brumbeau. LC 99-6547. (Illus.). 48p. (J). (ps-3). 1999. 17.95 (1-57025-199-1) Pfeifer-Hamilton.

Quiltmaker's Handbook. Michael James. LC 77-15592. (Creative Handcrafts Ser.). (Illus.). 1978. 16.95 (0-13-749416-5, Spectrum IN) Macmillan Gen Ref.

Quiltmaker's Handbook: A Guide to Design & Construction. Michael James. (Illus.). 160p. 1996. reprint ed. pap. text 7.95 (0-486-29281-9) Dover.

Quiltmakers of Australia: Celebrating the Traditions. Karen Fail. LC 96-1382. (Illus.). 96p. 1996. pap. 21.95 (0-8442-2607-6, Quilt Dgst Pr) NTC Contemp Pub Co.

***Quiltmaking for Beginners: Elements & Inspirations for Making One-of-a-Kind Quilts.** Ann Johnston. LC 99-25210. 160p. 1999. 19.95 (0-8442-2083-3, 20833, Quilt Dgst Pr) NTC Contemp Pub Co.

Quiltmaking in America: Beyond the Myths. Ed. by Laurel Horton et al. LC 94-22315. (Illus.). 192p. 1994. 34.95 (1-55853-319-2) Rutledge Hill Pr.

Quiltmaking Tips & Techniques: Over 1,000 Creative Ideas to Make Your Quiltmaking Quicker, Easier, & a Lot More Fun. Jane Townswick. (Illus.). 326p. 1997. pap. 16.95 (0-87596-958-5) Rodale Pr Inc.

Quilts. Christine Stevens. 51p. 1993. pap. 11.95 (0-8464-4684-7) Beekman Pubs.

Quilts. Christine Stevens. 1993. pap. 20.00 (0-86383-941-X, Pub. by Gomer Pr) St Mut.

Quilts. Susan A. Zimmerman. (Thematic Units Ser.). 80p. (J). (gr. 5-8). 1997. pap. 9.95 (1-57690-116-5) Tchr Create Mat.

Quilts: An American Heritage, 1. Maria Piantanida. 1998. 12.98 (1-57717-091-1) Todtri Prods.

Quilts: An American Legacy. Mimi Dietrich. (Illus.). 100p. 1996. reprint ed. pap. text 25.00 (0-7881-9131-4) DIANE Pub.

***Quilts: Central Extensions, Braid Actions & Finite Groups.** Timothy M. Hsu. LC 00-38828. (Lecture Notes in Mathematics Ser.). (Illus.). 2000. pap. write for info. (3-540-67397-0) Spr-Verlag.

Quilts: From Colonial to Contemporary. (Illus.). 96p. 1993. 9.98 (1-56173-299-0, 3311800) Pubns Intl Ltd.

Quilts: Identification & Price Guide. Liz Greenbacker & Kathleen Barach. (Confident Collector Ser.). (Illus.). 376p. (Orig.). 1992. pap. 14.00 (0-380-76930-1, Avon Bks) Morrow Avon.

An Asterisk (*) at the beginning of an entry indicates that the title is appearing for the first time.

***Quilts: The Fabric of Friendship.** Sharon P. Angelo et al. LC 00-9620. 2000. pap. write for info. (*0-7643-1195-6*) Schiffer.

Quilts: The Great American Art. Patricia Mainardi. xix, 57p. 1985. reprint ed. 8.95 (*0-936810-06-8*); reprint ed. pap. 3.95 (*0-936810-24-6*) M & M.

Quilts: Their Story & How to Make Them. Marie D. Webster. (Illus.). 178p. 1992. reprint ed. 48.00 (*1-55888-216-2*) Omnigraphics Inc.

Quilts: Thematic Unit. Susan Zimmerman. 1997. pap. text 11.95 (*1-55734-460-4*) Tchr Create Mat.

Quilts Vol. 2: The Permanent Collection. Museum of the American Quilter's Society Staff. (Illus.). 80p. 1998. 9.95 (*0-89145-827-1*, 3793) Collector Bks.

Quilts among the Plain People. Rachel T. Pellman & Joanne Ranck. LC 81-82209. (People's Place Book Ser.: No. 4). (Illus.). 96p. 1981. pap. 5.95 (*0-934672-03-2*) Good Bks PA.

Quilts & Quilting from Threads. Threads Editors. Ed. by Christine Timmons. LC 91-30950. (Illus.). 128p. 1992. pap. 17.95 (*1-56158-025-2*, 070166) Taunton.

***Quilts & Quilting in Claiborne County: Tradition & Change in a Rural Southern County.** David Crosby. (Illus.). 32p. 1999. pap. 8.00 (*0-9677624-0-5*) Miss Cult Cross.

Quilts & Women of the Mormon Migrations: Treasures in Transition. Mary B. Cross. LC 96-31708. 1997. pap. 24.95 (*1-55853-409-1*) Rutledge Hill Pr.

Quilts Are for Love. Lauren White. Date not set. 14.95 (*1-84072-017-4*, Pub. by Mus Quilts Pub) Sterling.

Quilts Around the Year: Classic Quilts & Projects for Every Month. Linda Seward. LC 93-49718. (Illus.). 128p. 1994. 27.95 (*0-8069-0710-X*) Sterling.

Quilts As Text(iles) Vol. 16: The Semiotics of Quilting. Judy Elsley. (Berkeley Insights in Linguistics & Semiotics Ser.). 82p. 1996. text 29.95 (*0-8204-2808-6*) P Lang Pubng.

Quilts, Coverlets, & Counterpanes: Bedcoverings from the Museum of Early Southern Decorative Arts & Old Salem Collections. Paula W. Locklair. (Old Salem Series Frank L. Horton Series, Museum for Early Southern Decorative Arts). (Illus.). 72p. (C). 1997. pap. 18.95 (*0-8078-4725-9*) U of NC Pr.

Quilts, Coverlets, & Counterpanes: Bedcoverings from the Museum of Early Southern Decorative Arts & Old Salem Collections. Paula W. Locklair et al. LC 97-18405. (Illus.). 72p. 1997. pap. 16.95 (*1-879704-04-8*) Old Salem NC.

Quilts for All Seasons. Oxmoor House Staff. LC 93-83737. 160p. 1993. pap. 19.95 (*0-8487-1176-9*) Oxmoor Hse.

Quilts for Baby: Easy as ABC. Ursula Reikes. (Illus.). 80p. 2000. pap. 19.95 (*1-56477-282-9*, B403, That Patchwrk Pl) Martingale & Co.

Quilts for Baby: Easy as ABC. Ursula G. Reikes. LC 93-28647. 1993. pap. 9.95 (*1-56477-041-9*, B168) Martingale & Co.

Quilts for Fabric Lovers. Alex Anderson. Ed. by Harold Nadel & Joyce E. Lytle. LC 94-15499. (Illus.). 64p. 1994. pap. 19.95 (*0-914881-87-6*, 10102) C & T Pub.

***Quilts for Girls & Boys.** Barbara Roberts. LC 00-24945. (Illus.). 80p. 2000. pap. write for info. (*1-56477-315-9*, B443, Pub. by Martingale & Co) F & W Pubns Inc.

***Quilts for Katie Rose.** Marsha McCloskey. (Illus.). 56p. 1999. pap. 15.95 (*0-9635422-7-3*) Feathered Star.

***Quilts for Kids.** Elaine Hammond. 2000. 24.95 (*0-7153-0773-8*, Pub. by D & C Pub) Sterling.

Quilts for Winter Days. Jan Patek. LC 93-33043. (Seasons of the Heart & Home Ser.: No. 2). 1993. 18.95 (*0-89145-824-7*, 3796, Am Quilters Soc) Collector Bks.

Quilts from Aunt Amy. Mary T. Etherington & Connie Tesene. LC 99-10296. 96p. 1999. 24.95 (*1-56477-258-6*, B375) Martingale & Co.

***Quilts from Europe: Projects & Inspiration.** Gul Laporte. Ed. by Liz Aneloski & Beate Nelleman. (Illus.). 112p. 2000. pap. 24.95 (*1-57120-095-9*, 10212) C & T Pub.

Quilts from Heaven: Finding Parables in the Patchwork of Life. gif. ed. Lucinda S. McDowell. LC 98-31315. (Illus.). 160p. 1999. 17.00 (*0-8054-1099-6*) Broadman.

Quilts from Montgomery County, New York. Maryann De Julio. (Illus.). 24p. (Orig.). 1981. pap. 3.00 (*0-9608694-0-9*) Montgomery Hist.

Quilts from Nature. Joan Colvin. Ed. by Barbara Weiland. LC 92-41488. (Illus.). 112p. (Orig.). 1993. pap. 24.95 (*1-56477-026-5*, B154, That Patchwrk Pl) Martingale & Co.

Quilts from the Civil War: Nine Projects, Historical Notes, Diary Entries. Barbara Brackman. Ed. by Liz Aneloski & Diana Roberts. LC 97-12181. (Illus.). 128p. (Orig.). 1997. pap. 25.95 (*1-57120-033-9*, 10157) C & T Pub.

***Quilts from "The Quiltmaker's Gift" 20 Traditional Patterns for a New Generation of Generous Quiltmakers.** Joanne Larsen Line & Nancy Loving Tubesing. (Illus.). 144p. 2000. pap. 26.95 (*1-57025-203-3*) Pfeifer-Hamilton.

Quilts from Two Valleys: Amish Quilts from the Big Valley, Mennonite Quilts from the Shenandoah Valley. Phyllis Pellman Good. LC 99-36723. (Illus.). 80p. 1999. pap. 18.95 (*1-56148-286-2*) Good Bks PA.

Quilts Galore! Quiltmaking Styles & Techniques. Diana McClun & Laura Nownes. LC 90-42209. (Illus.). 192p. 1990. pap. 24.95 (*0-8442-2621-1*, Quilt Dgst Pr) NTC Contemp Pub Co.

Quilts in America. Patsy Orlofsky & Myron Orlofsky. (Illus.). 368p. 1992. 65.00 (*1-55859-334-9*) Abbeville Pr.

Quilts in the Tradition of Frank Lloyd Wright. Jackie Robinson. LC 96-107155. 80p. 1994. pap. text 19.00 (*1-885156-13-8*) Animas Quilts.

Quilts of Indiana: Crossroads of Memories. Indiana Quilt Registry Project, Inc. Staff. LC 90-49157. (Illus.). 192p. 1991. 29.95 (*0-253-32925-6*) Ind U Pr.

Quilts of Provence: The Art & Craft of French Quiltmaking. Kathryn Berenson. (Illus.). 192p. 1995. 45.00 (*0-8050-4639-9*) H Holt & Co.

Quilts of Tennessee: Images of Domestic Life Prior to 1930. Bets Ramsey & Merikay Waldvogel. (Illus.). 128p. 1998. pap. 19.95 (*1-55853-613-2*) Rutledge Hill Pr.

Quilts, Patchwork & Samplers. Emma Callery. 1995. 14.98 (*0-7858-0249-5*) Bk Sales Inc.

Quilts, Quilts & More Quilts! Diana McClun & Laura Nownes. Ed. by Harold Nadel. LC 93-28345. (Illus.). 160p. (Orig.). 1995. pap. 23.95 (*0-914881-67-1*, 10081) C & T Pub.

Quilts! Quilts!! Quilts!!! The Complete Guide to Quiltmaking. Diana McClun & Laura Nownes. LC 88-18563. (Illus.). 160p. 1989. pap. 21.95 (*0-8442-2616-5*, Quilt Dgst Pr) NTC Contemp Pub Co.

Quilts! Quilts!! Quilts!!! The Complete Guide to Quiltmaking. Diana McClun & Laura Nownes. LC 98-227910. (Illus.). 64p. 1997. pap., teacher ed. 9.95 (*0-8442-2618-1*, Quilt Dgst Pr) NTC Contemp Pub Co.

Quilts! Quilts!! Quilts!!! The Complete Guide to Quiltmaking. 2nd ed. Dians McClun & Laura Nownes. LC 97-2537. (Illus.). 160p. 1997. pap. 24.95 (*0-8442-2617-3*, Quilt Dgst Pr) NTC Contemp Pub Co.

Quilts Sew Quick: Fast & Easy Quilts Using Large Print Fabrics. Nancy Smith & Lynda S. Milligan. Ed. by Sharon Holmes. (Illus.). 28p. 1992. pap. 9.95 (*1-880972-01-8*) Pssblts Denver.

Quilts to Unusual Unicorns. Christopher Carrie. (Crayola Encyclopedia of Coloring Fun Bks.). (Illus.). 40p. (Orig.). (J). (gr. k up). 1989. pap. 1.49 (*0-86696-229-8*) Binney & Smith.

Quilts to Wear. Virginia Avery. (Illus.). 168p. 1990. pap. 9.95 (*0-486-26336-3*) Dover.

Quilts with a View: A Fabric Adventure. Faye Labanaris. LC 98-43388. 96p. 1998. 16.95 (*1-57432-713-5*, Am Quilters Soc) Collector Bks.

Quiltskills: Workshops from the Quilters' Guild. Martingale & Company Staff. (Illus.). 96p. 1998. pap. text 24.95 (*1-56477-213-6*) Martingale & Co.

Quimbe: Poetics of Sound. Lasana M. Sekou. LC 91-72368. (Illus.). 129p. (Orig.). (C). 1991. pap. text 10.00 (*0-913441-14-7*) Hse of Nehesi.

Quimby Manuscripts. 2nd ed. Ed. by Horatio W. Dresser. 480p. 1984. pap. 9.95 (*0-8065-0913-9*, Citadel Pr) Carol Pub Group.

Quimby's 1998 Cruising Guide. 36th rev. ed. (Illus.). 250p. 1998. pap. 19.95 (*0-9663582-0-1*) Waterways Jour.

Quimica: Manual de Laboratorio, Curso Basico, Edicion Combinada. Vivian Torres & Jovita Rodriguez. 259p. (C). 1994. pap. text 35.95 (*1-881375-18-8*) Libreria Univ.

Quimica: Manual de Laboratorio Curso Basico Primera Parte. 5th ed. Vivian Torres & Jovita Rodriguez. 132p. (C). 1994. pap. text, student ed. 24.95 (*1-881375-03-X*) Libreria Univ.

Quimica: Manual de Laboratorio Curso Basico Segunda Parte. 4th ed. Vivian Torres & Jovita Rodriguez. 175p. (C). 1994. pap. text, student ed. 24.95 (*1-881375-04-8*) Libreria Univ.

Quimica con Nosotros. Jose A. Chamizo. (SPA.). 1994. pap. text. write for info. (*0-201-62566-0*) Addison-Wesley.

Quimica en la Sociedad. American Chemical Society Staff. (SPA.). 592p. (C). 1997. pap. text 32.00 (*0-201-62581-4*) Addison-Wesley.

Quimica General: Problemas y Ejercicios. (SPA.). 416p. (C). 1991. pap. text 19.00 (*0-201-62951-8*) Addison-Wesley.

Quimica Hacia la Conquista del Sol. Magdalena R. De Riepen. (Ciencia para Todos Ser.). (SPA.). pap. 6.99 (*968-16-2397-5*, Pub. by Fondo) Continental Bk.

Quimica Inorganica: Principios y Aplicaciones. 800p. (C). 1992. text 36.00 (*0-201-51848-1*) Addison-Wesley.

Quimica Organica: Manual de Laboratorio Escala Micro, Primera Parte. rev. ed. Maria Aponte. 141p. (C). 1992. pap. text 24.95 (*1-881375-01-3*) Libreria Univ.

Quimica Organica: Manual de Laboratorio Escala Micro Primera Parte. 2nd ed. Maria Aponte. 175p. (C). 1994. pap. text 24.95 (*1-881375-17-X*) Libreria Univ.

Quimica Organica: Manual de Laboratorio Escala Micro, Segunda Parte. rev. ed. Maria Aponte. 183p. (C). 1994. pap. text 24.95 (*1-881375-02-1*) Libreria Univ.

Quimica Organica: Manual de Laboratorio Escala Micro Segunda Parte. 2nd ed. Maria A. Aponte & Zwinda L. Rivera. (Illus.). 196p. (C). 1996. pap. text 24.95 (*1-881375-21-8*) Libreria Univ.

Quimica Terrestre. Antonio Chamizo. (Ciencia para Todos Ser.). (SPA.). pap. 6.99 (*968-16-3439-X*, Pub. by Fondo) Continental Bk.

Quimica Universitaria. 4th ed. (SPA.). 976p. (C). 1991. pap. text 30.66 (*0-201-64419-3*) Addison-Wesley.

Quimica, Universo, Tierra y Vida. Alfonso Romo. (Ciencia para Todos Ser.). (SPA.). pap. 6.99 (*968-16-2705-9*, Pub. by Fondo) Continental Bk.

Quimica y la Cocina. Jose L. Cordova Frunz. (Ciencia para Todos Ser.). (SPA.). pap. 6.99 (*968-16-3568-X*, Pub. by Fondo) Continental Bk.

Quimper City Plan. (Grafocarte Maps Ser.). 1996. 8.95 (*2-7416-0068-6*, 80068) Michelin.

Quimper Pottery: A French Folk Art Faience. Sandra V. Bondhus. (Illus.). 242p. 1995. reprint ed. 65.00 (*0-9640855-0-X*) S V Bondhus.

Quimper Pottery: A Guide to Origins, Styles, & Values. Adela Meadows. LC 97-31915. 1998. 49.95 (*0-7643-0421-6*) Schiffer.

Quimper Pottery: (Price Guide Revised, 1998) 2nd rev. ed. Anne M. O'Neill. (Illus.). 160p. 1998. pap. 19.95 (*0-7643-0466-6*) Schiffer.

Quimper S. D. #3254: Saskatchewan Potpourri. (Illus.). 348p. (Orig.). 1996. pap. 25.00 (*0-9616956-2-5*) Mary M Stensrud.

Quin. Alice H. Rice. 402p. 27.95 (*0-8488-1135-6*) Amereon Ltd.

Quinazolines Supplement I, Vol. 55. D. J. Brown. LC 96-6182. (Chemistry of Heterocyclic Compounds Ser.: Vol. 55). 756p. 1996. 385.00 (*0-471-14565-3*) Wiley.

Quincas Borba. Joaquim Maria Machado de Assis. Ed. by Celso Favaretto & David T. Haberly. Tr. by Gregory Rabassa. (Library of Latin America). 320p. 1998. 25.00 (*0-19-510681-4*) OUP.

Quincas Borba. Joaquim Maria Machado de Assis. 320p. 1999. pap. 13.95 (*0-19-510682-2*) OUP.

Quinceanera. Elizabeth King. LC 97-44539. 40p. (J). (gr. 5-10). 1998. 15.99 (*0-525-45638-4*) NAL.

Quinceaneras: A Latina's Journey to Womanhood. Mary D. Lankford. (Illus.). 48p. (J). (gr. 6-9). 1994. lib. bdg. 20.90 (*1-56294-363-4*) Millbrook Pr.

Quinceanera! The Essential Guide to Planning the Perfect Sweet Fifteen Celebration. Michele Salcedo. LC 97-11893. 208p. 1995. pap. 25.00 (*0-8050-4465-5*) H Holt & Co.

Quincentenary Year of Stockport Grammar School. Old Vicarage Publications Staff. 128p. (C). 1988. pap. text 39.00 (*0-947818-10-3*, Pub. by Old Vicarage) St Mut.

Quincentennial of Evangelization: A Time for Reflection & Action. Marina Herrera. (Illus.). 96p. (Orig.). 1992. pap. 4.00 (*1-55833-078-X*) Natl Cath Educ.

Quincunx. P. H. Colley. 258p. 1994. pap. 10.95 (*0-9643685-1-X*); lib. bdg. 15.95 (*0-9643685-0-1*) Chiron Rising.

Quincunx. Charles Palliser. 800p. 1991. reprint ed. pap. 16.00 (*0-345-37113-5*) Ballantine Pub Grp.

***Quincy.** Landrum. (Images of America Ser.). 1999. pap. 18.99 (*0-7385-0127-1*) Arcadia Publng.

Quincy: A Past Carved in Stone. Patricia Harrigan Browne. LC 96-209867. (Images of America Ser.). 128p. 1996. pap. 16.99 (*0-7524-0299-4*) Arcadia Publng.

Quincy & Adams County: History & Representative Men, 2 vols. Ed. by David F. Wilcox et al. (Illus.). 1502p. 1997. reprint ed. lib. bdg. 155.00 (*0-8328-5786-6*) Higginson Bk Co.

Quincy Blues: Stories from a River Town. Jim Andrews. LC 96-68694. (Illus.). 83p. (Orig.). 1996. pap. 10.95 (*0-9646037-5-6*) Rosehill Pr IL.

Quincy Book. Carl Andre. (Illus.). 1973. pap. write for info. (*1-879886-21-9*) Addison Gallery.

Quincy History. James Haining. LC 81-2049. (Lucky Heart Bk.). 212p. 1981. reprint ed. pap. 65.80 (*0-7837-9156-9*, 204985600003) Bks Demand.

Quincy History Sampler. James Haining. LC PS3558.A332. (Salt Lick Samplers Ser.). 12p. 1975. reprint ed. pap. 30.00 (*0-7837-9161-5*, 204986100003) Bks Demand.

***Quincy Jones.** Linda Bayer. LC 00-20605. (Black Americans of Achievement Ser.). (Illus.). 128p. (YA). (gr. 4-7). 2000. write for info. (*0-7910-5304-0*) Chelsea Hse.

***Quincy Jones.** Linda N. Bayer. (Overcoming Adversity Ser.). (Illus.). 128p. 2000. pap. text 9.95 (*0-7910-5305-9*) Chelsea Hse.

Quincy Jones. Stuart A. Kallen. (I Have a Dream Ser.). (J). 1996. lib. bdg. 15.98 (*1-56239-571-8*) ABDO Pub Co.

Quincy Jones: Musician, Composer, Producer. Lee H. Kavanaugh. LC 97-21958. (African-American Biographies Ser.). (Illus.). 128p. (YA). (gr. 6 up). 1998. lib. bdg. 20.95 (*0-89490-814-6*) Enslow Pubs.

Quincy Jones - Q's Jook Joint. Ed. by Carol Cuellar. 132p. (Orig.). (C). 1996. pap. text 24.95 (*1-57623-288-3*, PF9545) Wrner Bros.

Quincy Library Group Forest Recovery & Economic Stability Act of 1997: Hearing Before the Subcommittee on Forests & Public Land Management of the Committee on Energy & Natural Resources, United States Senate, 105th Congress, 1st Session, on S. 1028, H. R. 858... July 24, 1977 [i.e. 1997]. USGPO Staff. LC 98-139707. iii, 63 p. 1997. pap. write for info. (*0-16-055929-4*) USGPO.

***Quincy Rumpel.** Betty Waterton. (Quincy Rumpel Bks.). (Illus.). 144p. (J). 2000. pap. 3.95 (*0-88899-393-5*) Grndwd Bks.

***Quincy Rumpel.** Betty Waterton. (Quincy Rumpel Bks.). (Illus.). 144p. (J). 2000. pap. 3.95 (*0-88899-393-5*) Grndwd Bks.

Quincy Rumpel. Betty Waterton. 96p. (J). (gr. 3-5). 1991. pap. 5.95 (*0-88899-036-7*) Publishers Group.

Quincy Rumpel & the All-Day Breakfast. Betty Waterton. (Quincy Rumpel Ser.). 120p. (J). (gr. 2-5). 1996. 6.95 (*0-88899-225-4*) Publishers Group.

Quincy Rumpel & the Mystifying Experience. Betty Waterton. (Quincy Rumpel Ser.). (J). (gr. 2-5). 1996. pap. 5.95 (*0-88899-199-1*) Publishers Group.

Quincy Rumpel & the Sasquatch of Phantom Cove. Betty Waterton. (Quincy Rumpel Ser.). (J). (gr. 2-5). 1996. pap. 5.95 (*0-88899-129-0*) Publishers Group.

***Quincy Rumpel, P. I.** Betty Waterton. (Illus.). (J). 2000. pap. 3.95 (*0-88899-408-7*) Grndwd Bks.

Quincy Rumpel, P. I. Betty Waterton. (Quincy Rumpel Ser.). 116p. (J). (gr. 3-5). 1991. pap. 5.95 (*0-88899-081-2*) Publishers Group.

Quincy's Clubhouse: The Character Quest. large type ed. Paul Glenchar & Mike Fulton. (Illus.). 46p. (Orig.). (J). (gr. k-4). 1995. pap. 3.95 (*0-9647590-0-4*) Illumi Quest.

Quincy's Clubhouse: The Space Rescue. large type ed. Paul Glenchur & Mike Fulton. LC 96-94068. (Quincy's Clubhouse Ser.). (Illus.). 40p. (J). (gr. k-4). 1996. 12.95 (*0-9647590-1-2*); pap. 4.95 (*0-9647590-2-0*) Illumi Quest.

Quincy's Clubhouse: The Treasure Hunt. large type ed. Paul Glenchur & Mike Fulton. LC 97-74415. (Illus.). 40p. (J). (gr. k-4). 1998. 12.95 (*0-9647590-3-9*) Illumi Quest.

Quine. (C). 1998. 70.00 (*0-415-06398-1*) Routledge.

Quine: Language, Experience, & Reality. Christopher Hookway. LC 87-62782. (Key Contemporary Thinkers Ser.: Vol. 2). xii, 227p. 1988. 39.50 (*0-8047-1386-3*) Stanford U Pr.

Quine on Ontology, Necessity, & Experience: A Philosophical Critique. Ilham Dilman. LC 83-4815. 138p. (C). 1984. pap. text 21.95 (*0-87395-760-1*) State U NY Pr.

Quinessential Canadian Anaesthetist Wesley Bourne: A Retrospective on the Foundations of McGill Anesthesia. Joan C. Bevan & Maria A. Pacelli. LC 98-121894. 138p. 1996. 45.00 (*0-7717-0485-2*, Pub. by McG-Queens Univ Pr) CUP Services.

Quinientas Ilustraciones: 500 Illustrations. Compiled by Alfredo Lerin. (SPA.). 324p. 1966. reprint ed. pap. 12.99 (*0-311-42037-0*) Casa Bautista.

Quinientas una Ilustraciones Nuevas: 501 New Illustrations. Compiled by Adolfo Robleto. 320p. 1980. reprint ed. pap. 13.50 (*0-311-42062-1*) Casa Bautista.

Quinientos Anos de Cambio y Continuidad see Puerto Rico: 500 Years of Change & Continuity

Quinientos Anos de Historia, Sentido. . . Leopoldo Zea. (SPA.). pap. 10.99 (*968-16-3591-4*, Pub. by Fondo) Continental Bk.

***500 Sombreros de Bartolome Cubbins.** Dr. Seuss, pseud. Tr. by Eida De La Vega.Tr. of 500 Hats of Bartholomew Cubbins. (SPA., Illus.). 48p. (J). (ps-3). 1998. 14.95 (*1-880507-47-1*) Lectorum Pubns.

***Quinine & Quarantine: Missouri Medicine Through the Years.** Loren Humphrey. (Missouri Heritage Readers Ser.). 144p. 2000. pap. text 9.95 (*0-8262-1269-7*) U of Mo Pr.

Quinine's Predecessor: Francesco Torti & the Early History of Cinchona. Saul Jarcho. LC 92-49213. (Henry E. Sigerist Series in the History of Medicine). (Illus.). 400p. 1993. text 60.00 (*0-8018-4466-5*) Johns Hopkins.

Quinlan Terry. David Watkin & Robert J. Maxwell. (Academy Editions Ser.). (Illus.). 48p. 1981. pap. 19.95 (*0-312-66120-7*) St Martin.

Quinlan's Film Directors. D. Quinlan. (Illus.). 396p. 1999. 29.95 (*0-7134-7753-9*) B T B.

***Quinlan's Film Stars.** David Quinlan. 2000. 34.95 (*1-57488-318-6*) Brasseys.

Quinlan's Illustrated Registry of Film Stars. David Quinlan. (Illus.). 496p. 1995. 39.95 (*0-8050-1839-5*) H Holt & Co.

Quinn Eisley's War. Patricia G. Evans. (Intimate Moments Ser.). 1993. mass mkt. 3.39 (*0-373-07493-X*, 5-07493-5) Silhouette.

Quinn Math in Context Prelim. Quinn. Date not set. pap. text 42.27 (*0-395-88806-9*) HM.

Quinn Math in Context Ssm Prel. Quinn. Date not set. pap. text 18.57 (*0-395-88807-7*) HM.

Quinney Novel, 2. Sally Warner. 224p. (J). (gr. 3-7). 4.95 (*0-06-440763-2*) HarpC Child Bks.

Quinnie Blue. Dinah Johnson. LC 98-47830. (Illus.). 32p. (J). (ps-2). 1999. 16.95 (*0-8050-4378-0*) H Holt & Co.

Quinnipiac-Schweitzer Journal. Ed. by David Zucker. (Illus.). 64p. (Orig.). (C). 1994. pap. text 5.00 (*0-9641031-0-9*) Quinnipiac Coll.

Quinn's Book. William Kennedy. 304p. 1989. pap. 13.95 (*0-14-007737-5*, Penguin Bks) Viking Penguin.

Quinn's Dictionary & Thesaurus. Thomas Gene Quinn. LC 97-74034. xviii, 1201 p. 1997. write for info. (*1-57745-050-7*) Artex Pub.

Quinn's UCC Forms & Practice, 2 vols. Thomas M. Quinn. 1986. 210.00 (*0-88712-369-4*) Warren Gorham & Lamont.

Quinn's UCC Forms & Practice, 2 vols., 1. Thomas M. Quinn. 1986. write for info. (*0-88712-507-7*) Warren Gorham & Lamont.

Quinn's UCC Forms & Practice, 2 vols., 2. Thomas M. Quinn. 1986. write for info. (*0-88712-508-5*) Warren Gorham & Lamont.

Quinn's Uniform Commercial Code Commentary & Law Digest. Thomas M. Quinn. (Commercial Law Ser.). 2100p. 1991. suppl. ed. 175.00 (*0-7913-0889-8*, 78-50306) Warren Gorham & Lamont.

Quinoa the Supergrain. Rebecca Wood. LC 87-82908. (Illus.). 160p. (Orig.). 1989. pap. 23.00 (*0-87040-780-5*) Japan Pubns USA.

Quinolines, Pt. 1. Ed. by Gurnos Jones. LC 76-26941. (Chemistry of Heterocyclic Compounds Ser.: No. 32). 908p. reprint ed. pap. 180.00 (*0-608-17650-8*, 2030508) Bks Demand.

Quinolines, Pt. 2. Ed. by Gurnos Jones. LC 76-26941. (Chemistry of Heterocyclic Compounds Ser.: No. 32). (Illus.). 697p. reprint ed. pap. 200.00 (*0-8357-4668-2*, 203761400008) Bks Demand.

Quinolinic Acid & the Kynurenines. Ed. by T. W. Stone. 320p. 1988. 179.00 (*0-8493-6592-9*, QP563, CRC Reprint) Franklin.

Quinolone Antibacterials. D. Beermann. Ed. by J. Kuhlmann et al. LC 97-455. (Handbook of Experimental Pharmacology Ser.: No. 127). (Illus.). 480p. 1997. 359.00 (*3-540-62512-7*) Spr-Verlag.

Quinolone Antimicrobial Agents. 2nd ed. Ed. by David C. Hooper & John S. Wolfson. LC 93-10990. (Illus.). 563p. 1993. 79.00 (*1-55581-059-4*) ASM Pr.

Quinolones. 2nd ed. Ed. by Vincent T. Andriole. LC 97-80823. (Illus.). 441p. 1998. text 75.00 (*0-12-059514-1*) Acad Pr.

Quinolones in Everyday Clinical Practice. Ed. by W. Graninger. (Journal Ser.: Vol. 42, Suppl. 1, 1996). (Illus.). iv, 62p. 1996. pap. 21.75 (*3-8055-6299-3*) S Karger.

Quinolones in Pulmonary Tuberculosis Management. Len J. LaScolea, Jr. & Ramzan Rangoonwala. LC 96-13283. (Illus.). 120p. 1996. text 55.00 (*0-8247-9740-X*) Dekker.

Quinone & Similar Antibiotics see Handbook of Antibiotic Compounds

An Asterisk (*) at the beginning of an entry indicates that the title is appearing for the first time.

Quinque Claves Sapientiae. Ed. by Vidmanova & Schmidtova. (LAT.). 1969. 22.95 (3-322-00230-6, T1987, Pub. by B G Teubner) U of Mich Pr.
Quinque Sensus: The Five Senses. Kristin K. Tracy. 24p. 1991. 3.40 (0-939507-01-3, B15) Amer Classical.
Quinquennial Cumulative Personal Author Index, 1961-65 see Cumulative Personal Author Indexes for the Monthly Catalog of U. S. Government Publications, 1941-1975
Quinquennial Cumulative Personal Author Index, 1966-70 see Cumulative Personal Author Indexes for the Monthly Catalog of U. S. Government Publications, 1941-1975
Quinquennial Cumulative Personal Author Index, 1971-75 see Cumulative Personal Author Indexes for the Monthly Catalog of U. S. Government Publications, 1941-1975
Quint Etudes. Shinichi Suzuki. (Suzuki Violin School Ser.). (JPN.). 48p. (gr. k-12). 1976. pap. text 7.95 (0-87487-095-X, Suzuki Method) Summy-Birchard.
Quinta Montana. Paulo Coelho. LC 98-10477. 240p. 1998. 23.00 (0-06-017566-4) HarpC.
Quinta Montana. Paulo Coelho. 240p. 1999. pap. 13.00 (0-06-093012-8) HarpC.
Quinta Reunion de Evaluacion: Mexico y la Cumbre Mundial en Favor de la Infancia. 1994. write for info. (92-806-3034-2) U N I C E.
Quintenlieder: Music for Young Children in the Mood of the Fifth. Julius Knierim. Tr. by Peter Klaveness & Karen Klaveness from GER. (Illus.). iii, 39p. (J). 1994. pap. 14.95 (0-945803-13-3, 00174) R Steiner Col.
Quintessence. Sybil D'Ambrosi et al. Ed. by Ron Bayes. 114p. (Orig.). 1991. pap. 9.95 (0-932662-57-9) St Andrews NC.
***Quintessence.** Krauss. 2000. pap. 16.00 (0-465-03741-0, Pub. by Basic) HarpC.
***Quintessence: The Quality of Having It.** Betty Cornfield & Owen Edwards. 128p. 2000. 19.98 (1-57912-150-0) Blck Dog & Leventhal.
Quintessence: The Search for Dark Matter in the Universe. Lawrence Krauss. LC 99-47676. 356p. 1999. 26.00 (0-465-03740-2, Pub. by Basic) HarpC.
Quintessence--The Alternative Spaces Residency Program, the City Beautiful Council of Dayton, Ohio, the Wright State University, Department of Art, Vols. 2-3. City Beautiful Council of Dayton Ohio & Wright State University Staff. LC 78-64851. 1978. write for info. (0-9602550-0-1) City Beautiful Council.
***Quintessence of Dental Technology, Vol. 22.** 206p. 1999. 60.00 (0-86715-349-0) Quint Pub Co.
Quintessence of Dental Technology, 1995, Vol. 18. Ed. by John A. Sorenson. (Illus.). 217p. (Orig.). 1995. pap. text 56.00 (0-86715-289-3, B0606) Quint Pub Co.
Quintessence of Dental Technology 1998, Vol. 21. John Sorenson. 208p. 1998. pap. 60.00 (0-86715-344-X) Quint Pub Co.
Quintessence of Ibsenism. George Bernard Shaw. LC 94-5862. 112p. 1994. reprint ed. pap. 5.95 (0-486-28129-9) Dover.
Quintessence of Islamic History & Culture. S. P. Gulati. 225p. 1986. 23.00 (81-85061-44-0, Pub. by Manohar) S Asia.
Quintessence of the Animate & Imanimate: A Discourse on the Holy Dharma. Venerable L. Lodo. Ed. by Nancy Clark & Caroline Parke. LC 85-2290. (Illus.). 238p. 1985. pap. 11.95 (0-910165-01-7) KDK Pubns.
***Quintessence... Realizing the Archaic Future: A Radical Elemental Feminist Manifesto.** Mary Daly. LC 98-15286. (Illus.). 304p. 1999. pap. 18.00 (0-8070-6791-1) Beacon Pr.
Quintessence... Realizing the Archaic Future: A Radical Elemental in the Feminist Manifesto. Mary Daly. LC 98-15286. (Illus.). 304p. 1998. 24.00 (0-8070-6790-3) Beacon Pr.
Quintessence Tantras of Tibetan Medicine. Dalai Lama XIV. Tr. by Barry Clark. 260p. (Orig.). 1995. pap. 22.95 (1-55939-009-3) Snow Lion Pubns.
***Quintessences: Poems from Hollywood.** Mark Dunster. 11p. 1999. pap. 5.00 (0-89642-883-4) Linden Pubs.
Quintessential Apotheoses. Astara L. Leopold. 128p. Date not set. pap. 12.95 (1-885226-22-5) StarLineage.
Quintessential Canadian Anaesthetist, Wesley Bourne: A Retrospective on the Foundations of McGill Anesthesia. 10th ed. Joan Bevan & Maria Pacelli. (Fontanus Monographs). (Illus.). 140p. 1997. 49.95 (0-7735-1455-4, Pub. by McG-Queens Univ Pr) CUP Services.
Quintessential Cat. Robert Altman. 1996. pap. text 14.95 (0-02-861446-1) Macmillan.
Quintessential Cat: A Connoisseur's Guide to the Cat in History, Art, Literature, Legend. Roberta Altman. LC 94-14095. (Illus.). 304p. 1994. 27.50 (0-671-85008-3) Macmillan.
Quintessential Dictionary. I. Moyer Hunsburger. 448p. 1984. mass mkt. 3.95 (0-446-32443-4, Pub. by Warner Bks) Little.
Quintessential Purple Stone-Duan Inkstones through the Ages. Ed. by Mayching Kao. 166p. 1995. pap. 90.00 (962-7101-20-6, Pub. by Chinese Univ of Hong Kong) St Mut.
Quintessential Sarasota: Stories & Pictures from the 1920's-1950's. Jeff LaHurd. (Illus.). 128p. (Orig.). 1990. pap. 8.95 (1-879026-00-7) Clubhouse Pub.
Quintessential World of Darkness. Ed. by Stewart Wieck & Anna Bransicme. 1998. pap. 15.99 (1-56504-880-6, 11079, Wrld of Darkness) White Wolf.
Quintet. Robert Killoren et al. LC 81-670230. 1979. pap. 4.95 (0-933532-04-0) BkMk.
Quintet. Iliassa Sequin. 32p. 1991. pap. 4.00 (1-879645-03-3) Garlic MA.
Quintet: A Five-Play Cycle Drawn from The Children of Pride. Robert M. Myers. 256p. 1991. text 29.95 (0-252-01751-X) U of Ill Pr.
***Quintet: Five Journeys Toward Musical Fulfillment.** David Blum. LC 99-47562. 208p. 1999. 25.00 (0-8014-3731-8) Cornell U Pr.
Quintet: Five Lively Plays for Kids. Suzanne S. Art. LC 99-216315. 134p. (J). (gr. 4-6). 1998. 12.95 (0-9656557-1-7) Pemblewick Pr.
Quintet & Quartet for Piano & String. Johannes Brahms. 298p. 1985. pap. 14.95 (0-486-24900-X) Dover.
Quintet for Clarinet & String Quartet. E. Laderman. 60p. 1993. per. 45.00 (0-7935-2870-4) H Leonard.
Quintet for Piano & Strings: Score & Parts. R. Danielpour. 100p. 1994. per. 100.00 (0-7935-3037-7) H Leonard.
Quintet for Piano & Strings: Study Score. R. Danielfour. 1994. pap. 14.95 (0-7935-3040-7) H Leonard.
Quintet for Piano & Strings in A Minor, Opus 38. Arthur Foote. LC 82-17251. (Earlier American Music Ser.: No. 26). 108p. 1983. reprint ed. lib. bdg. 27.50 (0-685-42425-1) Da Capo.
Quintet for Winds. J. Harbison. 48p. 1992. pap. 40.00 (0-7935-1346-4, 50481208) H Leonard.
Quintet of Spies. Halperin. 1999. text. write for info. (0-312-16568-4) St Martin.
***Quinteto De Buenos Aires.** M Vazquez Montalban. 1999. pap. text 12.95 (84-08-02812-X) Planeta.
Quinteto de Buenos Aires. Manuel Vazquez Montalban. 1997. 27.95 (84-08-02213-X) Planeta Edit.
Quintets. Toby Lurie. LC 92-30599. (Poetry Ser.: Vol. 20). 76p. 1993. text 24.95 (0-7734-9515-0) E Mellen.
Quintets for Orchestra: Study Score. Lukas Foss. 60p. (Orig.). 1980. pap. 20.00 (0-8258-0065-X, PCB115) Fischer Inc NY.
Quinti Horatii Flacci Emblemata. Otto Van Veen. Ed. by D. Tschizewskij. (Emblematisches Cabinet Ser.). vii, 214p. 1972. reprint ed. write for info. (3-487-04333-5) G Olms Pubs.
Quinti Sereni Libri Medicinalis Concordantiae. Serenus Sammonicus. (Alpha-Omega Ser.: Vol. CXLVIII). (GER.). x, 222p. 1993. write for info. (3-487-09788-5) G Olms Pubs.
Quintiles & Tredeciles: The Geometry of the Goddess. Dusty Bunker. LC 89-51667. (Illus.). 182p. (C). 1989. pap. 12.95 (0-914918-69-9, Whitford) Schiffer.
Quintilian on the Teaching of Speaking & Writing: Translations from Books One, Two, & Ten of the Institutio Oratoria. Ed. by James J. Murphy. LC 87-4655. (Landmarks in Rhetoric & Public Address Ser.). 200p. 1987. text 21.95 (0-8093-1377-4); pap. text 14.95 (0-8093-1378-2) S Ill U Pr.
Quintiliani, M. Fabii: Declamationes Minores. Ed. by Shackleton Bailey. (LAT.). 1989. 105.00 (3-519-01753-9, T1753, Pub. by B G Teubner) U of Mich Pr.
Quintiliani, M. Fabii: Declamationes XIX Maiores, Quintiliano Falso Ascriptae. Ed. by Hakanson. (LAT.). 1982. 105.00 (3-519-01755-5, T1755, Pub. by B G Teubner) U of Mich Pr.
Quintiliani, M. Fabii Pt. I: Libri I-VI. Ed. by Radermacher & Buchheit. (LAT.). 1971. 43.50 (3-322-00146-6, T1751, Pub. by B G Teubner) U of Mich Pr.
Quintilianischen Declamationen. Constantin Ritter. xii, 275p. 1967. reprint ed. write for info. (0-318-71217-2) G Olms Pubs.
***Quinto Jinete.** Isaac Asimov. (SPA.). 1998. pap. 6.95 (84-01-49612-8, Pub. by Plaza) Lectorum Pubns.
Quinto Sol. Nicholas A. Patricca & Karen Ronstadt. (SPA.). 94p. (YA). (gr. 10 up). 1996. pap. 5.50 (0-87129-596-2, E33) Dramatic Pub.
***Quinton Brandon, the Marshal Who Tamed Zwolle.** Robert R. Gentry & Patricia Brandon Martinez. Ed. by Katherine Davis. 334p. 1999. pap. text 16.95 (1-893693-00-7) Sweet Dreams.
Quintozene. (Environmental Health Criteria Ser.: No. 41). 38p. 1984. pap. text 12.00 (92-4-154181-4, 1160041) World Health.
Quintozene Health & Safety Guide. WHO Staff. (Health & Safety Guides: No. 23). 32p. 1989. 5.00 (92-4-154335-3) World Health.
Quint's World. Samuel Fuller. 256p. 1988. per. 3.95 (0-373-97061-7) Harlequin Bks.
Quintuples. Luis Rafael Sanchez. (SPA.). 100p. 1985. pap. 9.00 (0-910061-28-9, 1310) Ediciones Norte.
Quintus Smyrnaeus - Index in Quintum Smyraneum. Ed. by Guiseppe Pompella. (Alpha-Omega, Reihe A Ser.: Bd. XLIX). v, 441p. 1982. write for info. (3-487-07134-7) G Olms Pubs.
Quinzaine for This Yule: Facsimile of the 1908 First Edition. Ezra Pound. 1973. 200.00 (0-87968-087-3) Gordon Pr.
Quinze Aventures de Mousquetaires. Alexandre Dumas et al. 256p. 1976. 9.95 (0-686-55831-6) Fr & Eur.
Quinze Chasses au Tresor. Alexandre Dumas et al. (Illus.). 224p. 1974. 9.95 (0-686-55832-4) Fr & Eur.
Quinze Contes. Guy de Maupassant. Ed. by F. C. Green. 131p. 1943. pap. text 16.95 (0-521-05693-4) Cambridge U Pr.
Quinze Minutes Learner Ptnr -users Guide. Flame. (College French). (FRE.). (C). 1997. mass mkt. 20.95 (0-8384-6388-6) Heinle & Heinle.
Quinze Recits de Noel. Victor Hugo et al. 224p. 1975. 8.95 (0-686-54037-9) Fr & Eur.
Quips & Quirks. Clyde Watson. LC 75-4678. (Illus.). 64p. (J). (gr. 3-7). 1975. 9.82 (0-690-00733-7) HarpC Child Bks.
Quips, for 3 Recorders (ATB) Stephan Chandler. (Contemporary Consort Ser.: No. 30). 15p. 1995. pap. text 7.00 (1-56571-122-X) PRB Prods.
Quirigua: A Classic Maya Center & Its Sculptures. Robert J. Sharer. LC 86-71809. (Centers of Civilization Ser.). (Illus.). 136p. 1990. lib. bdg. 45.00 (0-89089-260-1) Carolina Acad Pr.
Quirigua Reports Vol. 1: Papers 1-5. Wendy Ashmore et al. (University Museum Monographs: No. 37). (Illus.). ix, 73p. (Orig.). (C). 1979. pap. 20.00 (0-934718-26-1) U Museum Pubns.
Quirigua Reports Vol. II: Papers 6-15. Ed. by Edward Schortman & Patricia Urban. (University Museum Monographs: No. 49). (Illus.). xii, 140p. 1983. text 40.00 (0-934718-48-2) U Museum Pubns.
Quirigua Reports, III Vol. III: Archaeological Investigations in the Lower Valley, Izabel, Guatemala. Edward M. Schortman. LC 92-44440. (University Museum Monographs: Vol. 80). (Illus.). xii, 292p. 1993. 50.00 (0-924171-19-7) U Museum Pubns.
Quirk. Gordon Merrick. LC 98-20555. 400p. 1998. reprint ed. pap. 12.95 (1-55583-294-6, Alyson Bks) Alyson Pubns.
Quirks & Quillets. Karen Mac Cormack. (Illus.). 56p. (Orig.). 1990. pap. 8.00 (0-925904-04-X) Chax Pr.
Quirky Gardens. Jennifer Isaacs. (Illus.). 152p. (Orig.). 1995. pap. 24.95 (0-89815-790-0) Ten Speed Pr.
***Quirky Quiz Questions.** John Bates. (Illus.). 224p. 2001. pap. 9.95 (0-7160-2094-7, Pub. by Elliot RW Bks) Midpt Trade.
***Quirky Quotations: More Than 50 Fscinating Quotable Comments & the Stories Behind Them.** Tad Tuleja. 208p. 2000. 7.99 (1-57866-102-1) Galahad Bks.
***Quirky Tails.** large type ed. Paul Jennings. (Illus.). (J). 1999. pap. write for info. (0-7540-6088-8) Chivers N Amer.
Quiroga: A Mexican Municipio. Donald D. Brand. LC 76-44693. reprint ed. 22.50 (0-404-15853-6) AMS Pr.
Quiroga: Cuentos Escogidos. J. Franco. (SPA.). 1996. pap. 18.95 (1-85399-462-6, Pub. by Brist Class Pr) Focus Pub-R Pullins.
***Quirt & the Spur: Vanishing Shadows of the Texas Frontier.** Edgar Rye. 2000. pap. 17.95 (0-89672-441-7) Tex Tech Univ Pr.
QUI's QuarkXPress Tips & Tools. 2nd ed. Ed. by Frank Romano & Magda Knaflewska. LC 96-194110. (Illus.). 176p. 1995. pap. 27.95 (0-941845-16-8) Micro Pub Pr.
Quisling: A Study in Treachery. Hans F. Dahl. Tr. by Anne-Marie Stanton-Ife from NOR. LC 98-35102. (Illus.). 350p. (C). 1999. text 54.95 (0-521-49697-7) Cambridge U Pr.
Quisqueya: Panoramic Anthology of Dominican Verse. Ed. by Francis E. Townsend. 1976. lib. bdg. 34.95 (0-8490-2495-1) Gordon Pr.
Quisqueya la Bella: The Dominican Republic in Historical & Cultural Perspective. Alan Cambeira. LC 96-32355. (Perspectives on Latin American & the Caribbean Ser.). 286p. (C). 1996. text 74.95 (1-56324-935-9); pap. text 30.95 (1-56324-936-7) M E Sharpe.
Quit: Read This Book & Stop Smoking. rev. ed. Charles F. Wetherall. LC 88-42750. 208p. 1988. pap. 3.95 (0-89471-672-7) Running Pr.
Quit? Not Me! A Story of Dependability. 2nd ed. Raymond S. Moore et al. (Illus.). 30p. (J). (gr. 3-5). 1985. 5.95 (0-8407-6652-1) Moore Fnd.
Quit & Stay Quit: A Personal Program to Stop Smoking. Terry A. Rustin. 196p. pap. 12.95 (1-56838-109-3) Hazelden.
***Quit Claim: Pioneering in Minnesota, 1880-1940.** Roy Chaffee. Ed. by Ray Howe. (Illus.). 320p. 2000. pap. 16.95 (1-883477-44-1) Lone Oak MN.
Quit for Good. Ralph Cinque. 160p. 1994. 8.95 (1-895952-04-2, Pub. by Monrch Bks) BookWorld.
Quit for Life: The Sensational New Program for Smokers. 2nd ed. Robert S. Sobel. LC 88-90751. 164p. (Orig.). 1989. pap. 11.50 (0-929517-03-2) MDTA Pr.
Quit for Teens. Charles F. Wetherall. LC 95-75883. (Illus.). 206p. (YA). 1995. pap. 4.95 (0-8362-7031-2) Andrews & McMeel.
Quit India: American Response to the 1942 Struggle. M. S. Venkataramani. 350p. 1979. 20.95 (0-318-37262-2) Asia Bk Corp.
Quit India Movement Vol. 11: Role of Indian Big Business British Secret Documents. Ed. by P. N. Chopra. 150p. (C). 1991. 160.00 (81-85017-56-5, Pub. by Interprint) St Mut.
Quit India Movement British Secret Documents. P. N. Chopra. 440p. (C). 1990. 195.00 (81-85017-32-8, Pub. by Interprint) St Mut.
Quit It! A Teacher's Guide on Teasing & Bullying. Merle Froschl et al. LC 98-8135. 128p. 1998. pap. 19.95 (0-931629-19-5) Educ Equity Con.
Quit It! A Teacher's Guide on Teasing & Bullying for Use with Students in Grades K-3. Merle Froschl et al. LC 98-8135. 1998. 19.95 (0-8106-1881-8) NEA.
Quit Monks or Die! Maxine Kumin. LC 99-20971. 192p. 1999. 19.95 (1-885266-77-4, Pub. by Story Line) Consort Bk Sales.
***Quit Monks or Die!** Maxine Kumin. 192p. 2000. reprint ed. pap. 13.95 (1-885266-93-6, Pub. by Story Line) Consort Bk Sales.
Quit Playing with Fire. Ron Luce. LC 94-69835. 192p. 1995. pap. 8.95 (0-89221-280-2) New Leaf.
Quit-Rent System in the American Colonies. Beverley W. Bond. 1919. 16.50 (0-8446-1082-8) Peter Smith.
Quit Smart Leader Manual: Scientific Foundations & Implementation Guidelines for the Quit Smart Stop Smoking Method. Robert H. Shipley. (Illus.). 175p. 1994. ring bd. 75.00 (1-880781-95-6) Quit Smart.
***Quit Smart Leader Manual: Scientific Foundations & Implementation Guidelines for the Quit Smart Stop Smoking System.** Robert H. Shipley. 180p. 1998. ring bd. 75.00 (1-880781-96-4) Quit Smart.
Quit Smart Stop Smoking Guide: With the Quit Smart System, It's Easier Than You Think! rev. ed. Robert H. Shipley. (Illus.). 96p. 1998. pap. 8.99 (1-880781-99-9) Quit Smart.
***Quit Smart Stop Smoking Kit Stop Smoking Guide, Hypnosis Type, & Cigarette Substitute.** rev. ed. Robert H. Shipley. 1998. pap. 25.95 (1-880781-48-4) Quit Smart.
Quit Smart Stop Smoking Kit: Stop Smoking Guide, Hypnosis Type, & Cigarette Substitute. rev. ed. Robert H. Shipley & Jed Rose. 1994. pap. 24.95 (1-880781-94-8) Quit Smart.
Quit Smoking for Good: A Supportive Program for Permanent Smoking Cessation. Andrea Baer. LC 98-24697. (Personal Power Ser.). 96p. 1998. pap. 10.95 (0-89594-943-1) Crossing Pr.
Quit-Smoking Painlessly. George B. Kish. 84p. (Orig.). (C). 1988. pap. text 11.50 (0-8191-7065-8); lib. bdg. 29.50 (0-8191-7064-X) U Pr of Amer.
***Quit Smoking Using the Time Chart System.** Victoria M. St. Christopher & Koz St. Christopher. 60p. 2000. pap. 12.00 (1-930693-51-6) Creative Sol.
***Quit Smoking Using the Time Chart System.** Victoria M. St. Christopher et al. 60p. 1999. pap. 40.00 incl. VHS (0-9677405-5-X) Creative Sol.
Quit Your Day Job! Develop a Successful Career As a Freelance Writer. Robert Spiegel. pap. 14.95 (1-884956-04-1) Quill Driver.
Quit Your Job & Get Big. Gordon Miller. 112p. 1998. pap. 9.95 (0-385-49593-5) Doubleday.
Quit Your Job Often: And Get Big Raises. Gordon Miller. (Illus.). 90p. 1998. pap. 9.95 (0-9665230-5-9) Q Y J O.
Quite a Few Good Men. John A. Gunn. (Illus.). 368p. 1992. 29.95 (0-9631034-9-0) J&J Pub.
Quite a Year for Plums: A Novel. Bailey White. LC 97-41124. 224p. 1998. 22.00 (0-679-44531-5) Knopf.
Quite a Year for Plums: A Novel. Bailey White. 220p. 1999. pap. 12.00 (0-679-76492-5) Knopf.
Quite a Year for Plums: A Novel. Bailey White. 1999. pap. write for info. (0-375-70276-8) Vin Bks.
Quite a Year for Plums: A Novel. large type ed. Bailey White. LC 97-51829. 1998. pap. 22.00 (0-375-70292-X) Random.
Quite Contrary: A Biblical Reconsideration of the Apparitions of Mary. 2nd ed. Timothy F. Kauffman. LC 94-61080. 192p. 1994. pap. 7.95 (0-9637141-3-9) White Hrse.
Quite Early One Morning. Dylan Thomas. LC 54-12907. 1960. pap. 9.95 (0-8112-0208-9, NDP90, Pub. by New Directions) Norton.
Quite Remarkable Adventures of the Owl & the Pussycat. abr. ed. Eric Idle. (Illus.). (J). 1996. audio. write for info. (0-7871-1006-X, Dove Audio) NewStar Media.
Quite So. Thomas Bailey Aldrich. (Works of Thomas Bailey Aldrich). 1989. reprint ed. lib. bdg. 79.00 (0-7812-1678-8) Rprt Serv.
Quite Vacation. Maria Piantanida. 27p. 1998. 6.00 (0-937013-83-8) Potes Poets.
***Quito.** Ed. & Tr. by Peter Lowe. (SPA & ENG., Illus.). 56p. 2000. write for info. (0-9670569-1-8) P Lowe.
Quito see Monumental Cities
***Quitter.** Darrin Atkins. LC 00-100815. 198p. 1999. pap. 18.00 (0-7388-1231-5) Xlibris Corp.
***Quitter: And Other Tables of Employment.** Darrin Atkins. LC 00-100815. 198p. 1999. 25.00 (0-7388-1230-7) Xlibris Corp.
Quitters. Neal Starkman. LC 91-16797. (Illus.). 28p. (Orig.). (J). (gr. 4-6). 1991. pap. 8.00 (0-935529-26-8) Comprehen Health Educ.
Quitters Are Winners: New 30 Day Stop Smoking Plan. Yvon Morris. 51p. 1996. pap. 9.98 (1-888139-04-8) Y Morris Carib.
Quittin' Time: An Ex-Smoker's Step-by-Step Plan for Beating Your Cigarette Addiction, Vol. 1. Jenny N. Duffey. Ed. by Bonnie Welch. (Orig.). 1993. 14.95 (0-9642103-0-4, TX3-677-725) Duffey Pubng.
Quitting Cocaine. A. Washton. 1996. pap. 4.00 (0-89486-677-X) Hazelden.
Quitting Cocaine: The Struggle Against Impulse. Howard J. Shafer et al. LC 87-45977. 198p. 1990. pap. 15.95 (0-669-19690-8) Lxngtn Bks.
Quitting for Good: A Christ-Centered Approach to Nicotine Dependency. Francis L. McClain. 224p. 1995. pap. text 12.95 (0-8054-9844-3, LifeWy Press) LifeWay Christian.
Quitting in Time: How to Stop Smoking on Your Own. Jesse Lemic. (Illus.). 39p. (Orig.). 1987. write for info. (0-944566-00-6) Start Today.
Quitting Point. Michael Amico. LC 98-207120. 1998. pap. 9.99 (1-56043-307-8, Treasure Hse) Destiny Image.
***Quitting the Nairobi Trio: A Memoir.** Jim Knipfel. LC 00-21773. 304p. 2000. 23.95 (1-58542-027-1, Tarcher Putnam) Putnam Pub Group.
Quitting Time. Jack Veasey. LC 90-72085. (Illus.). 53p. (Orig.). 1991. pap. 6.95 (1-879294-00-1) Warm Spring Pr.
Quitting Time. large type ed. Robert J. Conley. LC 90-40666. 270p. 1990. reprint ed. lib. bdg. 15.95 (1-56054-040-0) Thorndike Pr.
Quitting Time. Robert J. Conley. Ed. by Doug Grad. (Michigan Bks.). 192p. 1992. reprint ed. pap. 3.50 (0-671-74364-3) PB.
Quiver: A Book of Erotic Tales. Tobsha Learner. LC 98-10972. 198p. 1998. pap. 12.95 (0-452-27984-4, Plume) Dutton Plume.
Quiver Full of Arrows. Jeffrey Archer. 224p. 1993. mass mkt. 5.50 (0-06-100715-3, Harp PBks) HarpC.
***Quiver Full of Arrows: Jeffrey Archer.** Jeffrey Archer. LC 00-42578. 2000. write for info. (0-7862-2685-4) Thorndike Pr.
Quiver of Quizzes for Quidnuncs. Nan Carpenter. 1984. pap. 6.95 (0-8158-0420-2) Chris Mass.

Quiver River. David Carkeet. LC 90-24095. (Laura Geringer Bks.). 224p. (YA). (gr. 7 up). 1991. 14.95 (*0-06-022453-3*) HarpC Child Bks.

Quivering Tree. large type ed. Sylvia Haymon. 1993. 39.95 (*0-7066-1019-9*, Pub. by Remploy Pr) St Mut.

Quiverings in the Net. Antonia P. Rabb. 100p. 1994. pap. text 10.00 (*0-9644280-0-8*) A P Rabb.

Quivey's Grove Heritage Cookbook. Margaret Guthrie. LC 94-9407. (Illus.). 208p. 1994. pap. 16.95 (*1-879483-18-1*) Prairie Oak Pr.

Quivira: Europeans in the Region of the Santa Fe Trail, 1540-1820. William Brandon. LC 90-6907. (Illus.). 352p. 1990. 34.95 (*0-8214-0950-6*) Ohio U Pr.

Quivira Society Publications, 13 vols., Set. 1967. reprint ed. 202.00 (*0-405-00071-5*) Ayer.

Quixote Cult. Genaro Gonzalez. LC 98-28334. 224p. 1998. pap. 12.95 (*1-55885-254-9*) Arte Publico.

Quixotic Desire: Psychoanalytic Perspectives on Cervantes. Ed. by Ruth A. El Saffar & Diana D. Wilson. (Illus.). 352p. 1993. text 45.00 (*0-8014-2823-8*); pap. text 17.95 (*0-8014-8081-7*) Cornell U Pr.

Quixotic Scriptures: Essays on the Textuality of Hispanic Literature. Elias L. Rivers. LC 82-49300. 164p. 1983. pap. 50.90 (*0-608-05040-7*, 205970100004) Bks Demand.

***Quixtar Revolution: Discover the New High-Tech, High Touch World of Marketing.** Coy Barefoot. LC 99-49380. 2000. pap. 15.95 (*0-7615-2338-3*) Prima Pub.

***Quixtar.com Click-by-Click.** Denise A. Reynolds & Douglas Reynolds. LC 00-190292. (Illus.). 177p. 2000. pap. 19.95 (*0-9679347-0-2*) click-by-click.

Quiz & Puzzle Book. Bernard Magee. 1998. pap. 9.95 (*0-572-02392-8*, Pub. by W Foulsham) Trans-Atl Phila.

Quiz Book. (C). pap. write for info. (*0-09-178101-9*) OUP.

***Quiz Book: Clues to You & Your Friends, Too!** Illus. by Laura Allen & Debbie Tilley. LC 99-17482. 1999. pap. text 6.95 (*1-56247-750-1*) Pleasant Co.

Quiz Book: Interesting Facts That Inform & Entertain Bill Adler, Jr. & Edward Malsberg. LC 77-78965. (Elephant Books Ser.). 94p. 1977. write for info. (*0-448-14294-5*, Tuffy) Putnam Pub Group.

Quiz Book: 1729 Academic Questions to Challenge the Mind. Gail S. Mullen & Richard Bothmer. 104p. 1990. pap. 14.95 (*0-936386-55-X*) Creative Learning.

Quiz Bowl Crash Course. Carole Marsh. (J). (gr. 5 up). 1994. 29.95 (*1-55609-288-1*); pap. 19.95 (*1-55609-195-8*); disk 29.95 (*1-55609-289-X*) Gallopade Intl.

Quiz Craze: America's Infatuation with the Radio & Television Game Shows. Thomas A. DeLong. LC 91-10573. 328p. 1991. 35.00 (*0-275-94042-X*, C4042, Praeger Pubs) Greenwood.

***Quiz Guide of Wales.** Eileen T. Jones. LC 99-202637. 128p. 1999. pap. 9.95 (*0-7083-1505-4*, Pub. by Univ Wales Pr) Paul & Co Pubs.

Quiz Kid's Book. 1985. reprint ed. 30.00 (*0-89609-039-6*) Roth Pub Inc.

***Quiz Me on Drugs.** Springhouse Corporation Staff. 1999. pap. 24.95 (*0-87434-981-8*) Springhouse Corp.

Quiz Me! Query Me! A. J. Barrett. 39p. (YA). (gr. 3-6). 1997. pap. 5.00 (*0-89824-350-5*, 3505) Trillium Pr.

Quiz of Enchantment. Michael McDonald. Ed. by Arnold Vigil. LC 91-67865. (Illus.). 136p. (Orig.). 1992. pap. 3.95 (*0-937206-23-7*) New Mexico Mag.

***Quiz of the Century.** 2000. pap. 12.95 (*1-85868-925-2*, Pub. by Carlton Bks Ltd) Natl Bk Netwk.

***Quiz of the Century.** Roy Preston. 320p. 2000. pap. 12.95 (*1-85868-858-2*) Carlton Bks Ltd.

***Quiz-Setter's Quiz Book.** Don Wilson. (Illus.). 192p. 2001. pap. 8.95 (*0-7160-2058-0*, Pub. by Elliot RW Bks) Midpt Trade.

Quiza No Lo Haga. Judy Blume. 1992. 16.05 (*0-606-10494-1*, Pub. by Turtleback) Demco.

Quizbank Structure Fortran77. 3rd ed. Dolores M. Etter. 520p. 1990. pap. text 10.75 (*0-8053-0053-8*) Benjamin-Cummings.

***Quizm Message: Trash Landing.** Gretchen Philips et al. (Illus.). 36p. (J). (gr. k-2). 1999. 11.99 (*0-9671611-0-X*) KRW Intl.

***Quizm Message: Trash Landing, 1, 1.** Gretchen Philips et al. (Illus.). 36p. (J). (gr. k-2). 1999. pap. 7.99 (*0-9671611-1-8*) KRW Intl.

***Quizmaster's Quiz Book.** Don Wilson. (Illus.). 192p. 2001. pap. 8.95 (*0-7160-2096-3*, Pub. by Elliot RW Bks) Midpt Trade.

Quizmaster's Scottish Quiz Book. Compiled by David Albury. 128p. 1996. pap. 8.95 (*0-7486-6217-0*, Pub. by Polygon) Subterranean Co.

Quizzes for 220 Great Children's Books: The Quest Motivational Reading Program. rev. ed. Polly J. Wickstrom. ix, 307p. 1996. pap. text 24.50 (*1-56308-383-3*) Teacher Ideas Pr.

Quizzes in Pathology. Heller & Klein. 647p. 1998. pap. text 95.00 (*0-7506-9584-6*) Buttrwrth-Heinemann.

Quizzes to a Street Preacher, Set. Charles M. Carty & Leslie Rumble. (Radio Replies Quizzes to a Street Preacher Ser.). 32p. 1992. reprint ed. pap. 12.00 (*0-89555-356-2*) TAN Bks Pubs.

Quizzical Look at the Rock Era. Rick Roeder. Ed. by Diane McLean. (Illus.). 136p. (Orig.). 1987. pap. 9.95 (*0-9619648-0-4*) Big Bop Bks.

Quizzles. Wayne Williams. 64p. 1997. pap. text 10.95 (*0-86651-102-4*) Seymour Pubns.

Quizzles: New Testament 1. 1993. pap. 3.00 (*1-895877-91-1*) Novar Cottage.

Quizzles: New Testament 2. 1993. pap. 3.00 (*1-895877-92-X*) Novar Cottage.

Quizzles: Old Testament 1. 1993. pap. 3.00 (*1-895877-93-8*) Novar Cottage.

Quizzles: Old Testament 2. 1993. pap. 3.00 (*1-895877-94-6*) Novar Cottage.

Quliaqtuat Mumiaksrat: Ilisaqtuanun Savaaksriat. Edna A. MacLean. (ESK., Illus.). 35p. (Orig.). (C). 1986. pap. 4.50 (*1-55500-027-4*) Alaska Native.

Qumran & Apocalyptic: Studies on the Aramaic Texts from Qumran. Florentino G. Martinez. LC 91-46425. (Studies on the Texts of the Desert of Judah: Vol. 9). xvi, 233p. 1994. 94.00 (*90-04-09586-1*) Brill Academic Pubs.

Qumran & the Essenes: A Re-Evaluation of the Evidence. Lena Cansdale. LC 97-214178. (Texte und Studien Zum Antiken Judentum Ser.: Vol. 60). 230p. 1997. 119.50 (*3-16-146719-1*, Pub. by JCB Mohr) Coronet Bks.

Qumran & the History of the Biblical Text. Ed. by Frank M. Cross & Shemaryahu Talmon. LC 75-12529. 413p. 1975. pap. 15.95 (*0-674-74362-8*) HUP.

Qumran Between the Old & New Testaments. Ed. by Frederick H. Cryer & Thomas L. Thompson. (JSOTS Ser.: Vol. 290). 398p. 1998. 85.00 (*1-85075-905-7*, Pub. by Sheffield Acad) CUP Services.

Qumran Cave 11: 11Q2-18 & 11Q20-22, Vol. II. Ed. by Florentino G. Martinez. (Discoveries in the Judaean Desert Ser.: No. XXIII). (Illus.). 560p. 1998. text 175.00 (*0-19-826959-5*) OUP.

Qumran Cave 4: IX: Deuteronomy, Joshua, Judges, Kings, Vol. 9. Ed. by Eugene Ulrich. (Discoveries in the Judaean Desert Ser.: Vol. XIV). (Illus.). 204p. 1996. text 115.00 (*0-19-826366-X*) OUP.

***Qumran Cave 4: Poetical & Liturgical Texts, Vol. XI, Pt. 1.** Ed. by Esther Eshel et al. (Discoveried in the Judean Desert Ser.: Vol. XI). (Illus.). 482p. 1998. text 150.00 (*0-19-826380-5*) OUP.

Qumran Cave 4 No. I. J. M. Allegro. (Discoveries in the Judaean Desert Ser.: No. V). (Illus.). 160p. 1997. text 90.00 (*0-19-826314-7*) OUP.

Qumran Cave 4 Pt. 1: The Sapiential Texts, Pt. 1, Vol. XV. Torleif Elgvin et al. (Discoveries in the Judaean Desert Ser.: No. XX). (Illus.). 280p. 1997. text 120.00 (*0-19-826938-2*) OUP.

Qumran Cave 4 Pt. 3: Parabiblical Texts, Pt. 3. Geroge Brooke et al. (Discoveries in the Judaean Desert Ser.: No. XXII). (Illus.). 362p. 1997. text 150.00 (*0-19-826936-6*) OUP.

Qumran Cave 4 Vol. 4: Miqsat Ma'ase Ha-Torah HQ 394-399. Ed. by Elisha Qimron & John Strugnell. (ENG & HEB., Illus.). 252p. 1994. text 85.00 (*0-19-826344-9*) OUP.

Qumran Cave 4 Vol. 4: Paleo-Hebrew & Greek Biblical Manuscripts. Eugene Ulrich et al. Vol. 9. (Illus.). 264p. 1993. text 135.00 (*0-19-826328-7*, 12029) OUP.

Qumran Cave 4 Vol. VII: Genesis to Numbers. Ed. by Eugene Ulrich & Frank M. Cross. (Discoveries in the Judaean Desert Ser.: No. XII). (Illus.). 288p. 1995. text 125.00 (*0-19-826365-1*) OUP.

Qumran Cave 4 Vol. VIII: Parabiblical Texts, Pt. 1. Ed. by Emanual Tov. (Discoveries in the Judaean Desert Ser.: No. XIII). (Illus.). 480p. 1995. text 135.00 (*0-19-826760-6*) OUP.

Qumran Cave 4 Vol. X: The Prophets. Eugene et al. (Discoveries in the Judaean Desert Ser.: No. XV). (Illus.). 340p. 1997. text 150.00 (*0-19-826937-4*) OUP.

Qumran Cave 4 Vol. XIII: The Damascus Document. Ed. by Joseph M. Baumgarten. (Discoveries in the Judaean Desert Ser.: No. XVIII). (Illus.). 256p. 1997. text 140.00 (*0-19-826396-1*) OUP.

Qumran Cave 4 Vol. XIV, Pt. 2: Parabiblical Texts, Vol. 14. Ed. by Emanuel Tov. (Discoveries in the Judaean Desert Ser.: Vol. XIX). (Illus.). 280p. 1996. text 130.00 (*0-19-826389-9*) OUP.

Qumran Cave 4 Vol. XIX: Serekh Ha-Yahad & Related Texts, 26. Ed. by Philip Alexander & Geza Vermes. (Discoveries in the Judaean Desert Ser.: Vol. XXVI). (Illus.). 272p. 1998. text 120.00 (*0-19-826981-1*) OUP.

***Qumran Cave 4 Vol. XXIV: Sapiential Texts, Part 2.** Ed. by John Strugnell et al. (Discoveries in the Judaean Desert Ser.: No. XXXIV). (Illus.). 632p. 2000. text 165.00 (*0-19-826982-X*) OUP.

***Qumran Cave 4 XVI: To Chronicles.** Ed. by Eugene Ulrich. (Discoveries in the Judaean Desert Ser.: Xvi). (Illus.). 302p. 2000. text 105.00 (*0-19-826943-9*) OUP.

Qumran Cave 4 XX: Poetical & Liturgical Texts, Part 2. Ed. by Bilhah Nitzan et al. (Discoveries in the Judaean Desert Ser.: XXIX). (Illus.). 496p. 2000. 150.00 (*0-19-827005-4*) OUP.

Qumran Cave 4 XXXV: Halakhic Texts. Ed. by Joseph M. Baumgarten et al. (Discoveries in the Judaean Desert Ser.: Xxxv). (Illus.). 192p. 2000. 85.00 (*0-19-827006-2*) OUP.

Qumran Cave 1. Ed. by Jozef T. Milik & D. Barthelemy. (Discoveries in the Judaean Desert Ser.: No. I). (Illus.). 176p. 1997. text 95.00 (*0-19-826301-5*) OUP.

Qumran Community: Its History & Scrolls. Charles T. Fritsch. 1973. reprint ed. 30.00 (*0-8196-0279-5*) Biblo.

Qumran Grotte Four, No. III. Ed. by Maurice Baillet. (Discoveries in the Judaean Desert Ser.: Vol. 7). (Illus.). 320p. 1982. text 195.00 (*0-19-826321-X*) OUP.

Qumran Grotte 4: Textes Hebreux (4Q521-4Q578), 25. Ed. by Mile Puech. (Discoveries in the Judaean Desert Ser.: Vol. XXV). (Illus.). 264p. 1998. text 105.00 (*0-19-826948-X*) OUP.

***Qumran-Messianism: Studies on the Messianic Expectations in the Dead Sea Scrolls.** Ed. by James H. Charlesworth et al. 248p. 1998. 152.50 (*3-16-146968-2*, Pub. by JCB Mohr) Coronet Bks.

Qumran Prayer & Poetry. Bilhah Nitzan. (Biblical Encyclopaedia Library: No. XIV). 453p. 1996. pap. text 50.00 (*965-342-669-9*, Pub. by Bialik) Eisenbrauns.

Qumran Prayer & Religious Poetry. Jonathan Chipman. LC 93-41774. (Studies on the Texts of the Desert of Judah: Vol. 12). xxi, 415p. 1994. 125.50 (*90-04-09658-2*) Brill Academic Pubs.

Qumran Questions. James H. Charlesworth. LC 96-156600. (Biblical Seminar Ser.: No. 36). 210p. 1995. pap. 23.75 (*1-85075-770-4*, Pub. by Sheffield Acad) CUP Services.

Qumran Studies, No. 2--2. Chaim Rabin. LC 76-40116. (Scripta Judaica Ser.: No. 2). 135p. 1977. reprint ed. lib. bdg. 35.00 (*0-8371-9060-6*, RAQS, Greenwood Pr) Greenwood.

Qumran und Jesus see Truth under Lock & Key: Jesus & the Dead Sea Scrolls

***Quo Graviora: Condemnation of Freemasonry.** Leo XIII, pseud. 33p. 1998. pap. 3.45 (*0-935952-60-8*) Angelus Pr.

Quo Vadimus? Geophysics for the Next Generation. Ed. by G. D. Garland & John R. Apel. (Geophysical Monograph Ser.: Vol. 60). 118p. 1990. 30.00 (*0-87590-455-6*, GM0604556) Am Geophysical.

Quo Vadimus: or: The Case for the Bicycle. E. B. White. LC 74-167438. (Essay Index Reprint Ser.). 1977. reprint ed. 19.95 (*0-8369-2678-1*) Ayer.

Quo Vadis. Henrik Sienkiewicz. Tr. by W. S. Kuniczak. 589p. 1999. 29.95 (*0-7818-0763-8*) Hippocrene Bks.

Quo Vadis. Henryk Sienkiewicz. 384p. 1998. pap. 14.95 (*0-89526-345-9*, Pub. by Regnery Pub) Natl Bk Netwk.

***Quo Vadis.** Henryk Sienkiewicz. (Christian Classics). 496p. 2000. pap. 4.97 (*1-57748-777-X*) Barbour Pub.

Quo Vadis? Henryk Sienkiewicz. Tr. by W. S. Kuniczak. LC 97-2694. 589p. 1997. reprint ed. pap. 19.95 (*0-7818-0550-3*) Hippocrene Bks.

Quo Vadis. Henryk Sienkiewicz. reprint ed. lib. bdg. 29.95 (*0-89190-484-0*, Rivercity Pr) Amereon Ltd.

Quo Vadis. Henryk Sienkiewicz. 1990. reprint ed. lib. bdg. 25.95 (*0-89966-694-9*) Buccaneer Bks.

***Quo Vadis: A Story of Faith in the Last Days of the Roman Empire.** Henry K. Sienkiewicz. (Focus on the Family Ser.). 2000. pap. text 15.99 (*1-56179-795-2*) Focus Family.

Quo Vadis? A Just Censure of Travell As It Is Commonly Undertaken by the Gentlemen of Our Nation. Joseph Hall. LC 74-28860. (English Experience Ser.: No. 740). 1975. reprint ed. 30.00 (*90-221-0740-X*) Walter J Johnson.

Quo Vadis, America? Phil E. Gafford. LC 76-57068. 112p. (C). 1977. 6.95 (*0-918354-01-3*) Huntleigh.

***Quo Vadis Arbitration? Sixty Years of Arbitration Practice.** Pieter Sanders. LC 99-34296. (Comparative Study Ser.). 1999. 141.00 (*90-411-1235-9*) Kluwer Law Intl.

Quo Vadis, Europe? Ed. by Horst Siebert. LC 98-105918. 352p. (C). 1997. text 105.00 (*3-16-146710-8*, 10877) U of Mich Pr.

Quo Vadis, Graph Theory? A Source Book for Challenges & Directions. Ed. by John W. Gimbel et al. LC 93-9334. (Annals of Discrete Mathematics Ser.: vol. 55). viii,398p. 1993. 149.50 (*0-444-89441-1*, North Holland) Elsevier.

Quo Vadis, Petre? Special Edition to the Collection: Eli, Eli, Lamma Sabachtani. unabridged ed. Ed. by Marion T. Horrat. 110p. (C). 1999. pap. 7.50 (*0-9672166-0-5*) Trad in Action.

Quo Warranto. Henry Goodacre. 257p. 1996. reprint ed. spiral bd. 18.50 (*0-7873-1286-X*) Hlth Research.

Quoat-Quoat. Jacques Audiberti. 9.95 (*0-686-54501-X*, FA790) Fr & Eur.

Quod Scripsi (Compiled Sword & Shield Issues) Herman Eutic. 200p. 1994. pap. 22.00 (*1-881123-02-2*) The Catacombs.

Quodlibet. John P. Kennedy. LC 75-104502. 350p. reprint ed. lib. bdg. 32.00 (*0-8398-1052-0*) Irvington.

Quodlibet. John P. Kennedy. 350p. 1986. reprint ed. pap. text 9.95 (*0-8290-1919-7*) Irvington.

Quodlibetal Questions 1 & 2. Aquinas, Thomas, Saint. Tr. & Intro. by Sandra Edwards. viii, 128p. pap. 12.00 (*0-88844-276-9*) Brill Academic Pubs.

Quoi? L'Eternite. Marguerite Yourcenar. (Folio Ser.: No. 2161). (FRE.). pap. 9.95 (*2-07-038251-6*) Schoenhof.

Quoi? L'Eternite, Vol. 3. Marguerite Yourcenar. (FRE.). 1990. pap. 11.95 (*0-8288-3808-9*, F133520) Fr & Eur.

Quoi de Neuf? Language in Action: A Beginning Course. June K. Phillips et al. (C). 1988. pap. text, lab manual ed. 19.00 (*0-07-553810-5*) McGraw.

***Quoi Qu'il en Soil Ecrit par Georges Francois Schaefier.** George Schaefer. (FRE., Illus.). 44p. 1999. pap. 4.00 (*1-930160-02-X*) Across The Universe.

***Quoit Brooch Style & Anglo-Saxon Settlement: A Casting & Recasting of Cultural Identity Symbols.** Seiichi Suzuki. LC 99-44204. (Illus.). 224p. 2000. 90.00 (*0-85115-749-1*, Suffolk Records Soc) Boydell & Brewer.

Quomodo Invidiosulus Nomine Grinchus Christi Natalem Abrogaverit: How the Grinch Stole Christmas. Dr. Seuss, pseud. Tr. by Jennifer Morrish Tunberg & Terence O. Tunberg. (Illus.). 1998. pap. 16.95 (*0-86516-420-7*); boxed set 22.50 (*0-86516-419-3*) Bolchazy-Carducci.

QR/1-2-3 for Dummies. John Walkenbach. (For Dummies Ser.). (Illus.). 175p. 1993. spiral bd. 8.95 (*1-56884-027-6*) IDG Bks.

***Quoniam.** (Book of Kells Unlined Ser.). 160p. 1998. 14.95 (*1-55156-073-9*, Pub. by Paperblank) Andrews & McMeel.

Quonset Huts on the River Styx: The Bomb Shelter Design Book. Contrib. by Architects, Designers & Planners for Social Respon. 72p. 1988. pap. 12.95 (*1-55643-027-2*) North Atlantic.

Quonset Point Naval Air Station. Sean Paul Milligan. LC 96-217641. (Images of America Ser.). 128p. 1996. pap. 16.99 (*0-7524-0274-9*) Arcadia Publng.

Quonset Point Naval Air Station II. Sean Paul Milligan. (Images of America Ser.). 1998. pap. write for info. (*0-7385-0037-2*) Arcadia Publng.

Quoof. Paul Muldoon. LC 83-50028. 64p. 1983. pap. 6.95 (*0-916390-19-5*) Wake Forest.

Quorndon Hounds. Henry W. Herbert. (Notable American Authors Ser.). 1992. reprint ed. lib. bdg. 75.00 (*0-7812-3099-3*) Rprt Serv.

Quorum. 1998. 230.00 (*0-671-71852-5*) S&S Trade.

Quorum. Kim Newman. 368p. 1995. mass mkt. 5.95 (*0-7867-0283-4*) Carroll & Graf.

Quota by Any Other Name: The Cost of Affirmative Action Programs in the Construction of Denver International Airport. Barry Poulson. (Issue Paper #6-94 Ser.). 32p. 1994. pap. text 8.00 (*1-57655-134-2*) Independ Inst.

Quota by Any Other Name: The Cost of Affirmative Action Programs in the Construction of Denver International Airport. Barry Poulson. (Issue Papers: No. 6-94). 9p. 1994. pap. text 8.00 (*1-57655-059-1*) Independ Inst.

Quota Restriction & Goldbricking in a Machine Shop. Donald Roy. (Reprint Series in Social Sciences). (C). 1993. reprint ed. pap. text 5.00 (*0-8290-2670-3*, S-244) Irvington.

Quotable Angel: A Treasury of Inspiring Quotations Spanning the Ages. Ed. by Lee A. Chearney. LC 95-31931. 240p. 1995. 14.95 (*0-471-13148-2*) Wiley.

***Quotable Athlete: Words of Wisdom from Mark McGwire, Michael Jordan, Mia Hamm, Bonnie Blair.** Michael H. McGovern. (Illus.). 2000. 14.95 (*0-07-136062-X*) McGraw.

***Quotable Baseball Fanatic.** Ed. by Louis Decimus Rubin, Jr. LC 99-45877. 2000. 20.00 (*1-58574-012-8*) Lyons Pr.

Quotable Bertrand Russell. Ed. by Lee Eisler. LC 93-20291. 336p. (Orig.). (C). 1993. pap. 19.95 (*0-87975-728-0*) Prometheus Bks.

***Quotable Birder.** Bill Adler. 2000. 20.00 (*1-58574-003-9*) Lyons Pr.

Quotable Bob Dole: Witty, Wise, & Otherwise. Jon Margolis. LC 95-42230. 224p. (Orig.). 1996. pap. 7.50 (*0-380-78585-4*, Avon Bks) Morrow Avon.

Quotable Book Lover: A Comprehensive Collection of the Best Words on Words. Ed. by Ben Jacobs & Helena Hjalmarsson. LC 99-21694. 272p. 1999. 20.00 (*1-55821-882-3*) Lyons Pr.

Quotable Bresee. Compiled by Harold I. Smith. 224p. (Orig.). 1983. pap. 12.99 (*0-8341-0835-6*) Beacon Hill.

Quotable Business. 2nd ed. Louis Boone. LC 98-36528. 1998. pap. 17.95 (*0-375-70308-X*) Random Ref & Info.

Quotable Casanova. Giacomo Casanova. Ed. & Intro. by Tom Vitelli. LC 97-77714. (Illus.). 280p. 1998. pap. 8.95 (*1-883696-04-6*) EveryWare Bks.

Quotable Cat. Jane Chambers. 9.95 (*1-85479-728-X*, Pub. by M OMara) Trafalgar.

***Quotable Cat.** C. E. Crimmins. 2000. pap. 8.95 (*1-887166-73-4*, Hysteria Pubns) Sourcebks.

Quotable Cat. Lisa A. Rogak. 144p. 1992. 11.00 (*0-8092-3941-8*, 394180, Contemporary Bks) NTC Contemp Pub Co.

***Quotable Cat Lover.** Ed. by Charles Elliott. (Illus.). 256p. 2000. 20.00 (*1-55821-996-X*) Lyons Pr.

Quotable Cats. Jane Chambers. 100p. 1995. 4.98 (*0-7858-0427-7*) Bk Sales Inc.

Quotable Chicago. Ed. by Richard C. Lindberg. 231p. (Orig.). 1996. pap. 9.95 (*0-8294-0927-0*, Wild Onion) Loyola Pr.

Quotable Christian: Favorite Quotes from Notable Christians. Helen K. Hosier. LC 99-161903. 1998. pap. text 4.97 (*1-57748-173-9*) Barbour Pub.

Quotable Climber: Literary, Humorous, Inspirational & Fearful Moments in Climbing. Ed. by Jonathan Waterman. LC 98-17992. (Illus.). 253p. 1998. 20.00 (*1-55821-718-5*) Lyons Pr.

Quotable Clinton Almanac 1994: More than 800 Amusing Quotes from the Pals, Pundits & Quipsters Who Shaped a New Presidency. Brad Zweck. 280p. 1994. pap. 12.99 (*0-9640337-0-4*) Politico Pr.

Quotable Conservative. Rod L. Evans & Irwin Berent. LC 98-8593. 288p. 1998. pap. text 12.00 (*1-58062-056-6*) Adams Media.

Quotable Conservative: The Wit & Insight of Freedom's Most Passionate Advocates. Compiled by Bill Adler, Jr. (Illus.). 288p. 1995. 9.95 (*1-55972-291-6*, Birch Ln Pr) Carol Pub Group.

***Quotable Cook.** Ed. by Kate Rowinski. (Illus.). 256p. 2000. 20.00 (*1-58574-164-7*) Lyons Pr.

Quotable Cuomo: The Mario Years. Brian Meyer. (Illus.). 120p. 1991. pap. 5.95 (*1-879201-03-8*) WNY Wares.

Quotable Cyclist: Great Moments of Bicycling Wisdom, Inspiration & Humor. Ed. by Bill Strickland. (Illus.). 360p. 1997. 20.00 (*1-55821-563-8*, Pub. by Breakaway Bks) Consort Bk Sales.

Quotable Dog: A Dog Lover's Treasury of Observations on Our Canine Companions. Compiled by Greg Snider. 144p. 1994. 12.95 (*0-8092-3529-3*) NTC Contemp Pub Co.

***Quotable Dog Lover.** Ed. by Patricia M. Sherwood. 256p. 2000. 20.00 (*1-58574-165-5*) Lyons Pr.

Quotable Einstein. Ed. & Compiled by Alice Calaprice. LC 96-3543. 310p. 1996. 16.95 (*0-691-02696-3*, Pub. by Princeton U Pr) Cal Prin Full Svc.

Quotable ESPN. Ed. by Shelly Youngblut. (Illus.). 192p. (J). 1998. pap. 9.70 (*0-7868-8291-3*, Pub. by Hyperion) Time Warner.

***Quotable Evans.** Richard Paul Evans. 122p. (Orig.). 2000. pap. 4.95 (*1-56684-580-7*) Evans Bk Dist.

Quotable Executive. Ed. by John Woods. 224p. 2000. 14.95 (*0-07-135734-3*) McGraw.

***Quotable Feline.** Jim Dratfield & Pam Coughlin. 2000. pap. 12.00 (*0-375-70214-8*) Knopf.

Quotable Feline. Jim Dratfield & Paul Coughlin. (Illus.). 1996. 20.00 (*0-614-15945-8*) Knopf.

Quotable Feline. Jim Dratfield & Paul Coughlin. LC 96-77836. 96p. 1996. 20.00 (*0-679-44699-0*) Random.

Quotable Feline. Petography. write for info. (*0-679-76585-9*) Fodors Travel.

Quotable Fisherman. Ed. by Nick Lyons. LC 98-3424. (Illus.). 176p. 1998. 20.00 (*1-55821-717-7*) Lyons Pr.

Quotable Gambler. Ed. by Paul Lyons. LC 99-48169. 1999. 20.00 (*1-55821-949-8*) Lyons Pr.

***Quotable Gardener.** Compiled by Charles Elliott. LC 99-14183. 288p. 1999. 20.00 (*1-55821-884-X*) Lyons Pr.

***Quotable Gardener: Words of Wisdom from Walt Whitman, Jane Austin, Robert Frost, Martha Stewart.** Kathy Ishizuka. (Illus.). 2000. 14.95 (*0-07-136061-1*) McGraw.

Quotable George Washington: The Wisdom Of An American Patriot. Ed. by Stephen E. Lucas. LC 99-27478. 128p. 1999. 17.95 (*0-945612-66-4*) Madison Hse.

***Quotable Golfer.** Ed. by Robert McCord. (Illus.). 256p. 2000. 20.00 (*1-55821-998-6*) Lyons Pr.

Quotable Golfer: The Greatest Things Ever Said about the Greatest @*!!?#! Game Ever Played. Robert Windeler. LC 97-66820. (Illus.). 256p. 1998. 12.95 (*0-7624-0269-5*) Running Pr.

Quotable Historian. Ed. by Alex Axelrod. 224p. 2000. 14.95 (*0-07-135733-5*) McGraw.

Quotable Horse Lover. Ed. by Steven D. Price. LC 99-16537. (Illus.). 320p. 1999. 20.00 (*1-55821-950-1*) Lyons Pr.

Quotable Hunter. Ed. by Jay Cassell & Peter Fiduccia. LC 99-34850. 1999. 20.00 (*1-55821-955-2*) Lyons Pr.

***Quotable Joe.** L. Budd Thalman. 2000. 14.95 (*0-9668774-4-6*) TowleHse Pubg.

Quotable Johnson: A Topical Conversation of His Wit & Moral Wisdom. Samuel Johnson. LC 92-71942. 148p. 1992. pap. 8.95 (*0-89870-415-4*) Ignatius Pr.

Quotable Kids - Fun in the Family Tree: Sibling Rivalry & Parent Pick-Me-Ups. Grace W. Housholder. (Illus.). 144p. 2000. pap. 8.95 (*0-9663006-1-0*, Pub. by Funny Kids) Quality Bks IL.

Quotable King: Hopes, Aspirations, & Memories. Elizabeth McKeon & Linda Everett. LC 97-6517. 192p. (Orig.). 1997. pap. 8.95 (*1-888952-44-X*) Cumberland Hse.

Quotable Knox: A Topical Compendium of the Wit & Wisdom of Ronald Knox. Ronald Knox. Ed. by George Marlin et al. LC 92-70555. 226p. 1996. pap. text 12.95 (*0-89870-407-3*) Ignatius Pr.

Quotable Kofi Annan: Selections from Speeches & Statements by the Secretary-General. 2nd ed. 146p. Price not set. (*92-1-100819-0*) UN.

Quotable Lawyer. Elizabeth Frost-Knappman et al. LC 98-2522. 1998. 34.95 (*0-8160-3753-1*) Facts on File.

Quotable Lawyer. Ed. by David Shrager & Elizabeth Frost. 384p. 1989. pap. 18.95 (*0-8160-2058-2*) Facts on File.

Quotable Lawyer. Ed. by David S. Shrager & Elizabeth Frost. 384p. 1986. 29.95 (*0-8160-1184-2*) Facts on File.

Quotable Lawyer. rev. ed. Elizabeth Frost-Knappman et al. LC 98-2522. 1998. pap. write for info. (*0-8160-3778-7*) Facts on File.

Quotable Lewis. C. S. Lewis. Ed. by Wayne Martindale & Jerry Root. (Illus.). 651p. 1990. 19.99 (*0-8423-5115-9*) Tyndale Hse.

Quotable Lincoln: A Selection from the Writings & Speeches of Abraham Lincoln. Edward Steers, Jr. (Illus.). 80p. (Orig.). 1996. pap. 6.95 (*1-57747-000-1*); pap. 6.95 (*1-57747-001-X*) Thomas Publications.

***Quotable Lover: Words of Wisdom from Shakespeare, Emily Dickinson, John Keats, Frank Sinatra.** Carol Turkington. (Illus.). 224p. 2000. 14.95 (*0-07-136064-6*) McGraw.

Quotable Mark Twain. Ed. by Kent R. Rasmussen. LC 97-43653. (Illus.). 416p. 1997. 25.00 (*0-8092-3088-7*, 308870, Contemporary Bks) NTC Contemp Pub Co.

Quotable Mark Twain. Ed. by Kent R. Rasmussen. LC 97-43653. (Illus.). 416p. 1998. pap. 16.95 (*0-8092-2987-0*, 298700, Contemporary Bks) NTC Contemp Pub Co.

Quotable Men of the Twentieth Century. Jessica Allen. LC 99-36934. 272p. 1999. 20.00 (*0-688-16285-1*, Wm Morrow) Morrow Avon.

Quotable Moose: A Contemporary Maine Reader. Ed. by Wesley McNair. LC 93-38324. 269p. 1994. pap. 17.95 (*0-87451-673-0*) U Pr of New Eng.

Quotable Nature Lover. Ed. by John A. Murray. LC 99-29832. (Nature Conservancy Book Ser.). 1999. 20.00 (*1-55821-942-0*) Lyons Pr.

Quotable New York: A Literary Companion. Ed. by William E. Cole. LC 92-44784. (Illus.). 96p. 1993. pap. 9.95 (*0-14-017631-4*, Penguin Bks) Viking Penguin.

***Quotable Oscar Wilde.** Sheridan Morley. (Illus.). 2000. 4.95 (*0-7624-0573-2*) Running Pr.

Quotable Play Therapist: 238 of the All-Time Best Quotes on Play & Play Therapy. Ed. by Charles E. Schaefer & Heidi G. Kaduson. LC 94-371. 272p. 1994. pap. 30.00 (*1-56821-229-1*) Aronson.

Quotable Politicians. Carole McKenzie. 208p. 1996. 14.95 (*1-85158-652-0*, Pub. by Mainstream Pubng) Trafalgar.

***Quotable Quips Queries & Quandaries.** Ed. by Sharon J. Gonder. LC 98-92209. (Illus.). 54p. 1999. lib. bdg. 6.95 (*1-58389-005-X*) Osage Bend Pub.

Quotable Quote Book. Ed. by Shauna Sorenson. 1990. 16.95 (*0-8065-1210-5*, Citadel Pr) Carol Pub Group.

Quotable Ronald Reagan. Peter Hannaford. LC 98-43972. 180p. 1999. 19.95 (*0-89526-323-8*, Pub. by Regnery Pub) Natl Bk Netwk.

Quotable Royalty. Carole McKenzie. 208p. 1996. 14.95 (*1-85158-575-3*, Pub. by Mainstream Pubng) Trafalgar.

Quotable Runner. Ed. by Mark Will-Weber. (Illus.). 360p. 1995. 20.00 (*1-55821-420-8*, Pub. by Breakaway Bks) Consort Bk Sales.

Quotable Runner Training Log: A Weekly Logbook & Source of Running Inspiration. Mark Will-Weber. (Illus.). 192p. 1998. spiral bd. 12.95 (*1-55821-613-8*, Pub. by Breakaway Bks) Consort Bk Sales.

***Quotable Scientist: Words of Wisdom from Charles Darwin, Albert Einstein, Richard Feyman.** Leslie A. Horvitz. (Illus.). 224p. 2000. 14.95 (*0-07-136063-8*) McGraw.

Quotable Scots. Carole McKenzie. 160p. 1996. 14.95 (*1-85158-576-1*, Pub. by Mainstream Pubng) Trafalgar.

Quotable Sex, Vol. 1. Carole Mckenzie. 1994. mass mkt. 4.99 (*0-312-95405-0*) St Martin.

Quotable Shakespeare: A Topical Dictionary. Charles Deloach. LC 87-46384. 568p. 1998. pap. 25.00 (*0-7864-0571-6*) McFarland & Co.

***Quotable Sherlock Holmes.** Arthur Conan Doyle & Gerard Van Der Leun. LC 00-40108. 2000. write for info. (*0-446-67727-2*) Mysterious Pr.

***Quotable Soldier.** Lamar Underwood. (Illus.). 2000. 20.00 (*1-58574-027-6*) Lyons Pr.

Quotable Spirit: A Treasury of Religious & Spiritual Quotations from Ancient Times to the Twentieth Century. Compiled by Peter Lorie & Manuela D. Mascetti. 448p. 1996. 25.00 (*0-02-861206-X*) Macmillan Info.

***Quotable Spirit: A Treasury of Religious & Spiritual Quotations from Ancient Times to the 20th Century.** Ed. by Peter Lorie & Manuela Dunn Masceti. 367p. 1999. reprint ed. text 25.00 (*0-7881-6737-5*) DIANE Pub.

***Quotable Spirit: A Treasury Religious & Spiritual Quotations, from Ancient Times for the 20th Century.** Peter Lorie. 2000. 9.99 (*0-7858-1167-2*) Bk Sales Inc.

Quotable Spurgeon. Charles H. Spurgeon. 444p. 1990. pap. 12.99 (*0-87788-710-1*, H Shaw Pubs) Waterbrook Pr.

Quotable Star Trek. Jill Sherwin. 320p. 1999. pap. 16.00 (*0-671-02457-4*, Star Trek) PB.

Quotable Star Wars: I'd Just as Soon Kiss a Wookiee! Compiled by Stephen J. Sansweet. LC 96-96528. 128p. 1996. pap. 6.00 (*0-345-40760-1*) Ballantine Pub Grp.

Quotable Tozer, Bk. 1. A. W. Tozer. 1994. pap. 9.99 (*0-87509-546-1*) Chr Pubns.

Quotable Tozer II: More Wise Words with a Prophetic Edge. A. W. Tozer. LC 96-84234. 223p. 1997. pap. 9.99 (*0-87509-638-7*) Chr Pubns.

Quotable Ustinov. Peter Ustinov. LC 95-21226. (Illus.). 203p. 1995. 24.95 (*1-57392-025-8*) Prometheus Bks.

Quotable Ustinov. large type ed. Peter Ustinov. LC 97-29497. (Paperback Ser.). 126p. 1997. pap. 21.95 (*0-7838-8280-7*, G K Hall Lrg Type) Mac Lib Ref.

Quotable Vampire. David Proctor. LC 97-222005. 96p. 1997. pap. 7.00 (*1-57566-218-3*, Knsington) Kensgtn Pub Corp.

Quotable Vices. Carole McKenzie. 208p. 1996. 14.95 (*1-85158-636-9*, Pub. by Mainstream Pubng) Trafalgar.

***Quotable Walker.** Walking Magazine Editors. 2000. 20.00 (*1-58574-167-1*) Lyons Pr.

***Quotable Walker: Great Moments of Wisdom & Inspirations for Walkers & Hikers.** Roger Gilbert. 256p. 2000. 22.00 (*1-891369-22-9*) Breakaway Bks.

***Quotable Wine Lover.** Ed. by Kate Fiduccia. 256p. 2000. 20.00 (*1-58574-168-X*) Lyons Pr.

Quotable Woman. Ed. by Carol Turkington. 224p. 2000. 14.95 (*0-07-135732-7*) McGraw.

Quotable Woman: From Eve to 1799. Ed. by Elaine Partnow & Claudia B. Alexander. LC 82-15511. 549p. 1985. reprint ed. pap. 170.20 (*0-608-02842-8*, 206390900007) Bks Demand.

***Quotable Woman: The 1st 4,000 Years.** Elaine Partnow. LC 00-37660. 736p. 2001. pap. 55.00 (*0-8160-4012-5*) Facts on File.

Quotable Woman: Witty, Poignant & Insightful Observations from Notable Women. Ed. by Running Press Staff. LC 91-52546. 92p. 1991. 12.95 (*1-56138-015-6*) Running Pr.

Quotable Women. Carole McKenzie. 208p. 1996. 14.95 (*1-85158-494-3*, Pub. by Mainstream Pubng) Trafalgar.

***Quotable Women: A Celebration.** Running Press Staff. 2000. 19.98 (*0-7624-0876-6*) Running Pr.

Quotable Women of the Twentieth Century. Ed. by Tracy Quinn. LC 99-211200. 288p. 1999. 20.00 (*0-688-15991-5*, Wm Morrow) Morrow Avon.

Quotable Writer. Ed. by William A. Gordon. LC 99-47303. 186p. 2000. 14.95 (*0-07-135576-6*) McGraw.

Quotas & Affirmative Action. Ed. by Lester A. Sobel et al. LC 79-26722. 199p. reprint ed. pap. 61.70 (*0-608-12280-7*, 202516000042) Bks Demand.

Quotas in International Environmental Agreements. Amanda Wolf. LC 98-159324. (Law & Sustainable Development Ser.). 224p. 1997. pap. 40.00 (*1-85383-400-9*, Pub. by Escan Pubns) Island Pr.

Quotation & Modern American Poetry: Imaginary Gardens with Real Toads. Elizabeth Gregory. 256p. (C). 1996. pap. 16.95 (*0-89263-347-6*) Tex A&M Univ Pr.

Quotation & Modern American Poetry: Imaginary Gardens with Real Toads. Elizabeth Gregory. LC 95-32708. (Illus.). 256p. (C). 1996. text 37.50 (*0-89263-341-7*) Tex A&M Univ Pr.

***Quotation Index to Children's Literature.** Melanie Axel-Lute. 300p. 2001. 40.00 (*1-56308-809-6*) Libs Unl.

***Quotation Marks: Teaching the Basics about Quotation Marks.** Susan Collins. (Teaching the Boring Stuff Ser.). (Illus.). 47p. (YA). (gr. 5-9). 1999. pap. 12.95 (*1-877673-37-4*) Cottonwood Pr.

Quotation Marks, Underlining. rev. ed. Contrib. by Beth Bridgman. (Horizons Grammar Ser.). (Illus.). 24p. (J). (gr. 4-9). 1998. pap. 5.95 (*1-58086-060-5*, Usborne) EDC.

***Quotation Overture: A History of Ideas Through the Best Quotations.** Carl H. Middleton. LC 99-32055. 1999. 34.00 (*1-56072-697-0*, Nova Kroshka Bks) Nova Sci Pubs.

***Quotationary.** Leonard Roy Frank. 2000. 12.00 (*0-375-40888-6*) Random.

Quotationary. F. Leonard. LC 98-30433. (Random House Business Division Ser.). 800p. 1998. 45.00 (*0-679-44850-0*) Random Ref & Info.

***Quotations.** (Collins Gem Ser.). (Illus.). 256p. 2000. pap. 7.95 (*0-00-472287-6*, Pub. by HarpC) Trafalgar.

Quotations. Harper Collins Staff. 1995. 10.00 (*0-00-470855-5*) Collins.

Quotations. Harper Collins Staff. 1997. pap. 8.00 (*0-00-472002-4*) Collins.

Quotations for a Man's Soul. Michael Maggio. LC 98-25270. 208p. 1998. text 14.95 (*0-7352-0054-8*) PH Pr.

***Quotations for All Occasions.** Compiled by Catherine M. Frank. LC 00-24048. 2000. 24.95 (*0-231-11290-4*) Col U Pr.

Quotations for Early Childhood Educators. Leah Adams & Patricia Kostell. LC 98-35907. 1998. 9.00 (*0-87173-146-0*) ACEI.

Quotations for Kids. J. A. Senn. LC 98-40310. (In the Footsteps of... Ser.). 256p. (J). (gr. 4-8). 1999. 37.90 (*0-7613-0267-0*, Copper Beech Bks) Millbrook Pr.

***Quotations for Kids.** J. A. Senn. (J). (gr. 3). 1999. 124.75 (*0-7613-1119-X*) Millbrook Pr.

***Quotations for Kids.** J. A. Senn. (Illus.). 256p. (J). 1999. 24.95 (*0-7613-1296-X*, Copper Beech Bks) Millbrook Pr.

Quotations for Occasions. Katherine B. Wood. 1996. reprint ed. lib. bdg. 38.00 (*0-7808-0162-8*) Omnigraphics Inc.

***Quotations for Public Speakers: A Historical, Literary & Political Anthology.** Ed. by Robert G. Torricelli. LC 00-39030. 336p. (C). 2000. 27.00 (*0-8135-2889-5*) Rutgers U Pr.

Quotations for Speeches. John Daintith & Anne Stibbs. 198p. 1998. pap. text 14.00 (*0-7881-5406-0*) DIANE Pub.

Quotations for Successful Living: How to Live Life. 2nd rev. ed. H. A. Levin. 128p. (Orig.). 1997. reprint ed. mass mkt. 7.95 (*0-9636211-6-5*) A Lincoln Pr.

Quotations for the Soul. Rosalie Maggio. LC 97-35714. 192p. (C). 1997. text 13.95 (*0-13-769159-9*) P-H.

Quotations for the Soul Book/Journal Set. (C). 1998. pap. 12.48 (*0-13-095253-2*) P-H.

Quotations from Abraham Lincoln. Ralph Y. McGinnis. LC 77-24595. (Illus.). 144p. 1978. text 41.95 (*0-88229-316-8*) Burnham Inc.

Quotations from African Americans. Great Quotations Staff. 78p. (Orig.). 1994. pap. 7.95 (*1-56245-102-2*) Great Quotations.

Quotations from Baker Street. Compiled by Christopher Redmond. 48p. (Orig.). 1994. pap. 8.00 (*1-896032-16-8*) Battered Silicon.

Quotations from Chairman Calvin. David R. Anderson. (Illus.). 38p. 1984. pap. 2.95 (*0-933467-00-1*) Brick Alley Books Press.

Quotations from Chairman Falwell. Paul R. Johnson. (Illus.). 34p. (Orig.). 1983. pap. 3.95 (*0-910097-01-1*) Paul R Johnson.

Quotations from Chairman Mao. Mao Tse-Tung. 312p. (C). 1990. 9.95 (*0-8351-2388-X*) China Bks.

***Quotations from G. I. Gurdjieff's Teaching.** Med Thring. 416p. 1999. 29.00 (*1-898942-13-7*) Weatherhill.

Quotations from Henry James. Henry James. LC 84-10428. 183p. reprint ed. pap. 56.80 (*0-7837-1770-9*, 204196700001) Bks Demand.

Quotations from the Poems & Songs of Robert Burns. Robert Bennett. 42p. 1986. 25.00 (*0-7855-2033-3*, Pub. by Saltire Soc) St Mut.

Quotations from the Wayside. Ed. by Brenda Wong. LC 99-193155. 136p. 1998. pap. 15.00 (*1-55896-373-1*, 5499, Skinner Hse Bks) Unitarian Univ.

Quotations from Women about Life. Rosalie Maggio. LC 97-35713. 192p. (C). 1997. text 13.95 (*0-13-671489-7*) P-H.

Quotations in Nudes. Wilhelm W. Reinke. (Illus.). 96p. 1996. 65.00 (*3-908182-46-7*, Pub. by Edit Stemmle) Dist Art Pubs.

Quotations of a Body. Evelyn Schlag & Claire Tomalin. Tr. by Willy Riemer from GER. LC 97-6990. (Studies in Austrian Literature, Culture & Thought; Translation Ser.). 211p. 1998. pap. 19.95 (*1-57241-050-7*) Ariadne CA.

***Quotations of Chairman Greenspan: Words from the Man Who Can Shake the World.** Larry Kahaner. 240p. 2000. 16.95 (*1-58062-420-0*) Adams Media.

***Quotations of Chairman Jesse.** Ed. by Myron Rupp. 136p. 2000. pap. 9.00 (*1-886913-39-0*, Pub. by Ruminator Bks) Consort Bk Sales.

Quotations of Dr. Deming: The Little Blue Book. W. Edwards Deming. 72p. 1996. 10.00 (*1-57074-237-5*) Greyden Pr.

Quotations of Wit & Wisdom. John W. Gardner & Francesca G. Reese. 256p. 1996. pap. 12.00 (*0-393-31446-4*, Norton Paperbks) Norton.

Quotations on Design & Material Culture. Compiled by Paul Greenhalgh. LC 93-26017. (Studies in Design & Material Culture). 1994. text 79.95 (*0-7190-3964-9*, Pub. by Manchester Univ Pr); text 29.95 (*0-7190-3965-7*, Pub. by Manchester Univ Pr) St Martin.

Quotations on Design & Material Culture. Paul Greenhalgh. (Studies in Design & Material Culture). 240p. 1994. pap. 19.95 (*0-7190-3956-8*, Pub. by Manchester Univ Pr) St Martin.

***Quotations on Education.** Maggio. 1998. text 13.95 (*0-13-973355-8*) P-H.

Quotations on Education. Rosalie Maggio. 192p. (C). 1997. text 13.95 (*0-13-769134-3*) P-H.

Quotations on Education. Rosalie Maggio. 192p. (C). 1999. pap. text 7.95 (*0-13-025780-X*) S&S Trade.

Quotations on India. S. P. Ruhela. 106p. 1997. pap. 100.00 (*81-7533-030-9*, Pub. by Print Hse) St Mut.

***Quotations on Love.** Maggio. 1998. 13.95 (*0-13-973363-9*) P-H.

***Quotations on Love.** Ed. by Rosalie Maggio. 180p. 1999. pap. text 14.00 (*0-7881-6397-3*) DIANE Pub.

Quotations on Love. Rosalie Maggio. LC 97-35711. 192p. (C). 1997. 13.95 (*0-13-769142-4*) P-H.

Quotations on the Great One: The Little Book of Wayne Gretzky. Allan Safarik & Reimer. 96p. 1993. per. 4.95 (*0-88978-258-X*, Pub. by Arsenal Pulp) LPC InBook.

Quotations on the Jays. Reimer & Safarik. 96p. 1994. per. 4.95 (*0-88978-273-3*, Pub. by Arsenal Pulp) LPC InBook.

Quotations to Cheer You up When the World Is Getting You Down. Compiled by Allen Klein. LC 93-29512. (Illus.). 208p. 1994. 8.99 (*0-517-10014-2*) Random Hse Value.

Quotations with an Attitude: A Wickedly Funny Source Book. Roy L. Stewart. LC 94-45601. (Illus.). 160p. 1995. pap. 6.95 (*0-8069-0966-8*) Sterling.

***Quote Acrostic, Vol. 1.** Charles Preston. 2000. pap. 9.95 (*0-399-52633-1*, Perigee Bks) Berkley Pub.

Quote Book: Gems from the Pen of Ellen White. Ellen Gould Harmon White. LC 94-27763. 1994. pap. 5.99 (*0-8280-0863-9*) Review & Herald.

Quote Book II: Gems from the Pen of Ellen G. White. Ellen Gould Harmon White. LC 95-44381. 1995. pap. 5.99 (*0-8280-1034-X*) Review & Herald.

Quote It! A Dictionary of Memorable Legal Quotations from Legal & Literary Sources. Ed. by Eugene C. Gerhart. LC 78-83771. xviii, 553p. 1988. reprint ed. 48.50 (*0-89941-576-8*, 305300) W S Hein.

Quote It! Memorable Legal Quotations. Eugene C. Gerhart. LC 78-83771. xii, 766p. 1987. reprint ed. lib. bdg. 47.50 (*0-89941-569-5*, 305220) W S Hein.

Quote It Completely: World Reference Guide to over 5500 Memorable Quotations from Law & Literature. Ed. by Eugene C. Gerhart. LC 98-12592. xl, 1362p. 1998. 95.00 incl. cd-rom (*1-57588-400-3*, 311470) W S Hein.

Quote Markers: Presidential & Famous People Quote Markers. Jodi Jill. Ed. by Carol Hawdz. (Illus.). 24p. (Orig.). 1997. pap. 8.95 (*1-883438-07-1*) J J Features.

Quote Quest: Something Different...for the Puzzle Buff. Teddy Milne. 43p. 1990. pap. 3.50 (*0-938875-25-6*) Pittenbruach Pr.

Quote Sleuth: A Manual for the Tracer of Lost Quotations. Anthony Shipps. 208p. 1990. text 24.95 (*0-252-01695-5*) U of Ill Pr.

***Quote Unquote: Poetry Journal.** Katharine Gardner. (Illus.). 26p. (C). 1999. pap. 12.95 (*0-9643002-3-0*) Costa Pubng.

Quotes. Harvey Jackins. 1993. pap. 6.00 (*0-913937-75-4*) Rational Isl.

Quotes & Idea Starters for Preaching & Teaching: From Leadership Journal. Ed. by Edward K. Rowell. LC 96-7147. 208p. (gr. 11). 1996. 16.99 (*0-8010-9024-5*) Baker Bks.

***Quotes & Idea Starters for Preachings & Teaching.** Edward K. Rowell. 208p. 1999. pap. 12.99 (*0-8010-9100-4*) Baker Bks.

Quotes & Quips. Covey Leadership Center, Inc Staff. pap. 8.95 (*1-883219-12-4*) Franklin Covey.

Quotes & Quips: Insights on Living the 7 Habits. Stephen R. Covey. 1998. 12.95 (*1-883219-93-0*) Franklin Covey.

Quotes Are Tremendous. Ed. by Charles E. Jones. 193p. (Orig.). 1995. pap. 10.00 (*0-937539-12-0*) Executive Bks.

Quotes for a Changing Workplace. Tom Payne. LC 97-69849. 136p. (Orig.). 1998. pap. 9.95 (*0-9627085-7-7*) Perf Pr Albuquerque.

Quotes for All Occasions. Vaneckeren. 1999. pap. text 14.95 (*0-7352-0109-9*) PH Pr.

Quotes for Kids: Today's Interpretations of Timeless Quotes Designed to Nurture the Young Spirit. Lisa Meyer. LC 97-69588. (Illus.). 160p. (J). 1998. 13.95 (*0-9660148-0-4*) Reach Pr.

Quotes for Sales Success. Gerhard Gschwandtner. LC 86-82539. (Illus.). 80p. 1986. pap. 9.00 (*0-939613-01-8*) Personal Selling.

***Quotes for the Journey, Wisdom for the Way.** Gordon S. Jackson. LC 99-49533. 2000. 12.00 (*1-57683-152-3*) NavPress.

Quotes from Great Women. Great Quotation Staff. 366p. (Orig.). 1994. pap., spiral bd. 8.95 (*1-56245-169-3*) Great Quotations.

Quotes Galore. Compiled by Lisa Talbert. Date not set. per. 8.99 (*0-927935-10-4*) Valley Pr IN.

Quotes of Rotar Storch. Rotar Storch. Ed. by Miekal And. (Illus.). 50p. (Orig.). 1989. pap. 8.00 (*0-926935-23-2*) Runaway Spoon.

Quotes to Remember: A Guide to Wisdom. 3rd rev. ed. Compiled by Michael B. Kitson & Jeffrey L. Benjamin. 40p. 1993. pap. 4.95 (*0-9646800-0-9*) On-Call Pub.

QuoteUnquote: The Game of Humorous & Revealing Quotes. Paul R. Winslow. 130p. 1994. 25.95 (*0-9642920-0-9*) Winslow Games.

Quoth the Raven. large type ed. Bruno Fischer. (Mystery Ser.). 416p. 1993. 11.50 (*0-7089-2952-4*) Ulverscroft.

***Quotian Dilemma.** Juanita L Batson. 2000. mass mkt. 7.95 (*1-55279-000-2*) Picasso Publ.

Quotidian, No. II. Ed. by Gudrun M. Cable. 250p. (C). 1989. write for info. (*0-318-65563-2*) Rimsky Copy Hse.

Quotidian Mysteries: Laundry, Liturgy & "Women's Work" Kathleen Norris. LC 98-9949. 104p. 1998. pap. 5.95 (*0-8091-3801-8*) Paulist Pr.

Quotidian Two. Gudrun M. Cable. LC 89-62678. (Illus.). 256p. 1989. write for info. (*0-9624011-0-2*) Rimsky Copy Hse.

***Quotidiana: The Continuity of the Everyday in 20th Century Art.** David Ross. (Illus.). 2000. pap. 50.00 (*88-8158-261-9*) Charta.

Quotients of Coexter Complexes & P-Partitions. V. Reiner. LC 91-36297. (Memoirs Ser.: No. 460). 134p. 1992. pap. 27.00 (0-8218-2525-9, MEMO/95/460) Am Math.

Quoting Caravaggio. Bal. LC 98-46907. (Illus.). 328p. 1999. 45.00 (0-226-03556-5) U Ch Pr.

***Quoting Shakespeare: Form & Culture in Early Modern Drama.** Douglas Bruster. LC 00-24202. 288p. 2000. text 50.00 (0-8032-1303-4) U of Nebr Pr.

Quozl. Alan Dean Foster. 1989. pap. 4.95 (0-441-69454-3) Ace Bks.

Qur'an. LC 90-71714. (ARA.). 848p. 1990. 14.00 (1-879402-00-9, 44A) Tahrike Tarsile Quran.

***Quran.** (ARA.). 34p. 2000. pap. 25.00 (1-879402-74-2) Tahrike Tarsile Quran.

Qur'an. Tr. by Thomas B. Irving. 400p. 1991. pap. 14.50 (0-915597-81-0) Amana Bks.

Quran. Tr. by Muhammad Z. Khan. (ARA & ENG.). 736p. 29.95 (0-7007-0148-6, Pub. by Curzon Pr Ltd) Paul & Co Pubs.

Quran. Muhammad Z. Khan. 736p. 1997. pap. text 19.95 (1-56656-255-4) Interlink Pub.

Qur'an. Ahmad A. Mir. Tr. by S. V. Mir Ahmed Ali. 520p. 1991. pap. 5.95 (0-9630687-0-9) Quran Soc.

Quran. Mahomodali H. Shakir. (ARA & ENG.). 1990. 39.95 (1-56744-204-8) Kazi Pubns.

Quran, Pt. 30. Mahmoud A. Qazi. 32p. 1996. pap. 3.50 (0-614-21040-2, 1031) Kazi Pubns.

Qur'an, 30 vols., Pts. 1-30. LC 90-71712. (ARA.). 848p. 1990. 25.00 (1-879402-02-5, 78) Tahrike Tarsile Quran.

Quran: A New Interpretation: In English with Arabic Text. Muhammad B. Behbudi & Colin Turner. (ARA & ENG.). 688p. 1998. 85.00 (0-7007-0407-8, Pub. by Curzon Pr Ltd) Paul & Co Pubs.

***Qur'an: An Introduction to Its Message.** Mohammad Abu-Hamdiyyah. LC 99-47371. (Illus.). 144p. 2000. pap. 17.99 (0-415-22509-4) Routledge.

Quran: An Introductory Essay. Theodor Noldeke. Ed. by N. A. Newman. 40p. 1992. pap. 5.95 (0-944788-93-9) IBRI.

Quran: Basic Teachings. Thomas B. Irving. 100p. (Orig.). 1989. pap. 16.95 (1-56744-366-4) Kazi Pubns.

Quran: Basic Teachings. Thomas B. Irving et al. 278p. (Orig.). 1979. pap. 10.00 (0-86037-021-6) New Era Publns MI.

***Qur'an: Formative Interpretation.** Ed. by Andrew Rippin. (Formation of the Classical Islamic World Ser.: 25). 420p. 1999. text 129.95 (0-86078-701-X, Pub. by Ashgate Pub) Ashgate Pub Co.

Quran: Selected Commentaries. Tr. by Muhammad Al-Akili. 238p. 1996. pap. 11.95 (0-614-21065-8, 1041) Pearl Pub Hse.

***Quran: Style & Contents.** Rippin. LC 99-58416. 2000. 117.95 (0-86078-700-1) Ashgate Pub Co.

Quran: The Final Testament. rev. ed. Tr. by Rashad Khalifa from ARA. (ENG.). 540p. 1992. pap. 7.95 (0-9623622-2-0) Kennerk Pub.

Qur'an: The First American Version. Tr. by Thomas B. Irving. LC 84-72242. 500p. (Orig.). 1985. pap. 14.50 (0-915597-08-X) Amana Bks.

Quran: The Fundamental Law of Human Life, 5 vols. Syed A. Ali. 1992. write for info. (1-56744-459-8) Kazi Pubns.

Quran: The Fundamental Law of Human Life, Vol. 1. Syed A. Ali. 385p. 1992. 29.95 (1-56744-454-7) Kazi Pubns.

Quran: The Fundamental Law of Human Life, Vol. 2. Syed A. Ali. 475p. 1992. 29.95 (1-56744-455-5) Kazi Pubns.

Quran: The Fundamental Law of Human Life, Vol. 3. Syed A. Ali. 522p. 1992. 29.95 (1-56744-456-3) Kazi Pubns.

Quran: The Fundamental Law of Human Life, Vol. 4. Syed A. Ali. 526p. 1992. 29.95 (1-56744-457-1) Kazi Pubns.

Quran: The Fundamental Law of Human Life, Vol. 5. Syed A. Ali. 505p. 1992. 29.95 (1-56744-458-X) Kazi Pubns.

Quran: The Noble Reading. Tr. by Thomas B. Irving. 600p. 1996. pap. 14.95 (0-614-21066-6, 1044) Kazi Pubns.

Quran: The Ultimate Miracle. Ahmed Deedat. 75p. 1996. pap. 3.50 (0-614-21067-4, 1046) Kazi Pubns.

Qur'an: Translation & Commentary. Tr. & Intro. by Thomas B. Irving. (Bilingual Ser.). 1304p. (C). 1992. 29.95 (0-915597-51-9) Amana Bks.

Quran: Translation & Transliteration, Pt. 30. Mahmoud A. Qazi. 1987. pap. 3.95 (0-934905-07-X, Library of Islam) Kazi Pubns.

Quran - Fundamental Law of Human Life Vol. 1: Introduction. Syed A. Ali. 386p. 1995. 29.95 (1-56744-520-9) Kazi Pubns.

Quran - Fundamental Law of Human Life Vol. 2: Surah Fatiha - Surah Baqarah: 176. Syed A. Ali. 348p. 1995. 29.95 (1-56744-521-7) Kazi Pubns.

Quran - Fundamental Law of Human Life Vol. 3: Surah Baqarah: 177-273. Syed A. Ali. 542p. 1995. 29.95 (1-56744-522-5) Kazi Pubns.

Quran - Fundamental Law of Human Life Vol. 4: Surah Baqara: 274-Surah Nisa: 14. Syed A. Ali. 548p. 1995. 29.95 (1-56744-523-3) Kazi Pubns.

Quran - Fundamental Law of Human Life Vol. 5: Surah Nisa: 15-Surah Anam: 50. Syed A. Ali. 526p. 1995. 29.95 (1-56744-524-1) Kazi Pubns.

Quran - Fundamental Law of Human Life Vol. 6: Surah Anam: Si-Surah Ta Ubah: 129. Syed A. Ali. 678p. 1995. 29.95 (1-56744-525-X) Kazi Pubns.

Quran - Fundamental Law of Human Life Vol. 7: Surah Yunus-Surah Ibrahim. Syed A. Ali. 446p. 1995. 29.95 (1-56744-526-8) Kazi Pubns.

Quran - Fundamental Law of Human Life Vol. 8: Surah Hijr-Surah Hahf. Syed A. Ali. 438p. 1995. 29.95 (1-56744-527-6) Kazi Pubns.

Quran - Fundamental Law of Human Life Vol. 9: Surah Maryam-Surah Muminun. Syed A. Ali. 497p. 1995. 29.95 (1-56744-528-4) Kazi Pubns.

***Qur'an - Introduction: An Introduction to Its Message.** Mohammad Abu-Hamdiyyah. LC 99-47371. 152p. (C). 2000. text 60.00 (0-415-22508-6) Routledge.

Qur'an Al-Karim. 25.00 (0-685-66746-4) Tahrike Tarsile Quran.

Quran, an Introduction. A. R. Doi. 1992. pap. 8.50 (0-933511-25-6) Kazi Pubns.

Qur'an & Its Exegesis: Selected Texts with Classical & Modern Muslim Interpretations. Helmut Gatje. 328p. (Orig.). 1996. pap. 23.95 (1-85168-118-3, Pub. by Onewrld Pubns) Penguin Putnam.

Qur'an & Its Interpreters: Surah Baqarah, Vol. 1. Mahmoud M. Ayoub. LC 82-21713. 450p. 1984. text 29.50 (0-87395-727-X) State U NY Pr.

Qur'an & Its Interpreters, Vol. II: The House of 'Imran. Mahmoud M. Ayoub. LC 82-21713. 444p. (C). 1992. text 64.50 (0-7914-0993-7); pap. text 21.95 (0-7914-0994-5) State U NY Pr.

Qur'an & Modern Science: Correlation Studies. Keith L. Moore et al. (Illus.). 62p. (Orig.). (C). 1991. pap. text 5.95 (0-9627236-0-6) Islamic Academy Sci Res.

Qur'an & the Bible in the Light of History & Science. William F. Campbell. ix, 343p. 1986. pap. 12.00 (1-881085-00-7, 5007, Pub. by Middle E Res) Chr Lit.

Quran & Woman. Amina Wadud-Muhsin. 118p. 1996. pap. 8.50 (0-614-21064-X, 1036); pap. 11.95 (0-614-21394-0, 1036) Kazi Pubns.

Qur'an & Woman: Re-Reading the Sacred Text from a Woman's Perspective. Amina Wadud. LC 98-49460. 144p. 1999. pap. 11.95 (0-19-512836-2) OUP.

Qur'an As Scripture. Arthur Jeffery. LC 79-52555. (Islam Ser.). 1980. lib. bdg. 17.95 (0-8369-9263-6) Ayer.

Qur'an As Scripture. Arthur Jeffery. LC 80-1924. reprint ed. 27.50 (0-404-18970-9) AMS Pr.

Qur'an As Text. Ed. & Tr. by Stefan Wild. LC 95-30502. (Islamic Philosophy, Theology & Science Studies & Texts Ser.: Vol. 27). 296p. 1996. 93.00 (90-04-10344-9) Brill Academic Pubs.

Qur'an-E-Hakeem Learning Aid. Amjad A. Khan. 320p. 1992. pap. 49.95 incl. audio (0-9634496-0-5) Islamic Sci Res.

Qur'an-E-Hakeem Learning Aid, Set. Islamic Science Research Institute Staff. 88p. 49.95 incl. audio (0-86685-765-6) Intl Bk Ctr.

Quran for Children. A. Rauf. Ed. by Laleh Bakhtiar. 1989. pap. 10.50 (0-935782-08-7) Kazi Pubns.

Qu'ran in Sixteenth-Century Spain: Six Morisco Versions of Sura. Consuelo Lopez-Morillas. (Monagrafias A Ser.: Vol. LXXXII). (Illus.). 102p. (C). 1982. 69.00 (0-7293-0121-4, Pub. by Tamesis Bks Ltd) Boydell & Brewer.

Quran in the Classroom. Haj A. Ajijola. 330p. (Orig.). 1989. pap. 5.50 (1-56744-367-2) Kazi Pubns.

Quran Large in Arabic. (ARA.). 1976. 125.00 (0-86685-134-8) Intl Bk Ctr.

Qur'an, Liberation & Pluralism: An Islamic Perspective of Interreligious Solidarity Against Oppression. Farid Esack. 280p. 1997. pap. 22.95 (1-85168-121-3, Pub. by Onewrld Pubns) Penguin Putnam.

Qur'an Made Easy. rev. ed. Raza H. Rizwani. 130p. 1983. reprint ed. pap. 6.00 (0-941724-09-3) Islamic Seminary.

Quran Made Easy (Yassar nal Quran) S. A. Behlim. 1987. pap. 7.50 (0-933511-01-9) Kazi Pubns.

Qur'An on Woman, Marriage, Birth Control & Divorce. Arthur Frederick Ide. LC 96-24775. (Women in History Ser.: Vol. 24). 1996. pap. 10.00 (0-934667-11-X) Tangelwuld.

Qur'an Selected Commentaries. Muhammad Al-Akili. LC 93-92766. 240p. (Orig.). 1993. pap. 11.95 (1-879405-09-1) Pearl Pub Hse.

Quran, Sh. Tabarsi's Commentary. M. A. Abdul. 1991. 15.95 (0-933511-27-2) Kazi Pubns.

***Quran, the Final Testament.** 2nd rev. ed. Rashad Khalifa. LC 99-54806. (Illus.). 800p. 2000. lib. bdg. 21.00 (1-881893-03-0) Universal Unity.

Quran with Transliteration. Tr. by Mohammed M. Pickthall. (ARA & ENG.). 608p. 1997. 25.00 (1-879402-52-1) Tahrike Tarsile Quran.

Qur'an with Transliteration. Tr. by Abdullah Yusufali. (ARA & ENG.). 610p. 1997. 25.00 (1-879402-53-X) Tahrike Tarsile Quran.

Quranic Advices - Arabic Text with Translation. M. M. Picthal. 154p. 1989. 8.95 (81-7151-024-8) Asia Bk Corp.

Quranic Arabic: An Elementary Course in Arabic for Non-Arabs. Omar Farrukh. (ARA.). 92p. (Orig.). 1992. pap. 5.50 (1-56744-461-X) Kazi Pubns.

Qur'anic Christians: An Analysis of Classical & Modern Exegesis. Jane D. McAuliffe. 352p. (C). 1991. text 69.95 (0-521-36470-1) Cambridge U Pr.

Quranic Concept of History. Muhammad M. Siddiqi. 1992. pap. 19.00 (0-933511-28-0) Kazi Pubns.

Quranic Concept of War. S. K. Malik. 195p. (C). 1986. 110.00 (81-7002-020-4, Pub. by Himalayan Bks) St Mut.

Quranic Ethics. B. A. Dar. 1994. pap. 5.50 (0-933511-29-9) Kazi Pubns.

Quranic Foundations & Structure of Muslim Society, Set, Vols. I & II. Muhammad Fazl ur-Rahman Ansari. 890p. 1993. text 85.00 (0-614-16644-6) Kazi Pubns.

Quranic Foundations & Structure of Muslim Society, Vol. I. Muhammad Fazl ur-Rahman Ansari. 445p. 1993. text. write for info. (1-56744-485-7) Kazi Pubns.

Quranic Foundations & Structure of Muslim Society, Vol. II. Muhammad Fazl ur-Rahman Ansari. 445p. 1993. text. write for info. (1-56744-486-5) Kazi Pubns.

Quranic Laws. M. N. Merchant. 1991. pap. 10.50 (0-933511-30-2) Kazi Pubns.

Qur'anic Phenomena. Malek Bennabi. 1988. 9.95 (0-933511-31-0) Kazi Pubns.

Quranic Phenomenon. Malek Bennabi. 290p. 1996. pap. 10.50 (0-614-21068-2, 1051) Kazi Pubns.

Quranic Phenomenon. Malik B. Nabi. Tr. by Abu B. Kirkari from FRE. LC 82-70460. (Illus.). 187p. (Orig.). 1982. pap. 7.00 (0-89259-023-8) Am Trust Pubns.

Quranic Selections, 4 vols. A. S. Hashim. Date not set. pap. 5.95 (1-56744-558-6) Kazi Pubns.

Quranic Sufism. Mir Valiuddin. (C). 1987. reprint ed. 14.00 (81-208-0320-5, Pub. by Motilal Bnarsidass) S Asia.

Quranic Sufism. 2nd rev. ed. Mir Valiuddin. 1977. 14.50 (0-89684-300-9, Pub. by Motilal Bnarsidass) S Asia.

Quranic Text: Toward A Retrieval System. Hani M. Atiyyah. LC 94-24729. 1994. write for info. (1-56564-212-0); pap. write for info. (1-56564-213-9) IIIT VA.

Quranic Way of Life. Taslim Ahmad. LC 97-90616. 121p. 1998. pap. 11.95 (0-533-12446-8) Vantage.

Qur'anwissenschaften, Hadit, Geschichte, Fiqh, Dogmatik, Mystik Bis ca. 430 H. Fuat Sezgin. (Geschichte des Arabischen Schrifttums Ser.: Vol. I). (GER.). xv, 936p. 1996. 353.00 (90-04-02007-1) Brill Academic Pubs.

Qurbono: The Book of Offering. Tr. by Hector Y. Doueihi from ARA. (Season of Epiphany Ser.). 161p. (Orig.). 1993. pap. 10.95 (0-9628727-8-4); 2.50 (0-9628727-9-2) St Maron Pubns.

Qurbono: the Book of Offering: Season of the Birth of the Lord. Tr. by Hector Y. Doueihi from ARA. 190p. (Orig.). (C). 1993. 4.50 (0-9628727-6-8); pap. text 19.95 (0-9628727-7-6) St Maron Pubns.

Quseir Al-Qadim, 1978: Preliminary Report. J. H. Johnson & Donald D. Whitcomb. (Illus.). x, 352p. 1979. pap. 15.00 (0-317-16193-8) Orientl Inst Pr.

Quseir Al-Qadim, 1978: Preliminary Report. Donald S. Whitcomb & Janet H. Johnson. (American Research Center in Egypt, Reports: Vol. 1). (Illus.). 352p. 1979. pap. 17.50 (0-936770-01-5, Pub. by Amer Res Ctr Egypt) Eisenbrauns.

Quseir al-Qadim, 1980: Preliminary Report. Donald D. Whitcomb & Janet H. Johnson. LC 81-72088. (American Research Center in Egypt, Reports: Vol. 7). (Illus.). 418p. (Orig.). 1982. 36.50 (0-89003-113-4, Pub. by Amer Res Ctr Egypt); pap. text 26.50 (0-89003-112-6, Pub. by Amer Res Ctr Egypt) Eisenbrauns.

Quseir el-Amarna: ACE Report, No. 1. Khouli & Kanawati. (Mascquarie University to Egypt Ser.). 1989. pap. 75.00 (0-85668-508-9, Pub. by Aris & Phillips) David Brown.

Qusta Ibn Luqa's Medical Regime for the Pilgrims to Mecca: The Risala Fi Tadbir Safar Al-Hajj. Ed. by Gerrit Bos. LC 91-29098. (Islamic Philosophy, Theology & Science, Studies & Texts Ser.: Vol. 11). vi, 186p. 1992. 70.50 (90-04-09541-1) Brill Academic Pubs.

Quuneq. Denise Riley.Tr. of Calm Weather. (ESK., Illus.). 12p. (J). (gr. k-3). 1998. pap. text 6.00 (1-58084-029-9) Lower Kuskokwim.

Quyurciyaraq Neqnek. large type ed. Margaret Nickerson.Tr. of Gathering Food. (ESK., Illus.). 8p. (J). (gr. k-3). 1999. pap. text 14.50 (1-58084-061-2) Lower Kuskokwim.

Qvod Temptabam. J. H. Lambert. (C). 1982. pap. text 39.00 (0-900269-08-1, Pub. by Old Vicarage) St Mut.

Qwert & the Wedding Gown: A Novel. Matias M. Huidobro. Tr. by John Mitchell & Ruth M. De Aguilar from SPA. LC 92-6005. 163p. 1992. 18.95 (0-917635-12-4) Plover Pr.

Qwert & the Wedding Gown: A Novel. Matias M. Huidobro. Tr. by John Mitchell & Ruth M. de Aguilar from SPA. LC 92-6005. 163p. 1992. pap. 9.95 (0-917635-13-2) Plover Pr.

Qwerty Keystroking & Drills: A Simple, Easy-to-Use Touch Typing Course. 2nd ed. Maryhelen H. Hoffman & Lanny L. Hoffman. 70p. 1999. pap. 25.00 incl. disk (1-928592-09-0) MHP Commns.

Qwik-Sane: Topological Puzzle. James O'Neil. 1970. 3.00 (0-911624-10-4) Wffn Proof.

QwikFile Users Manual. Silent Partners, Inc. Staff. (Illus.). 211p. 1991. ring bd. write for info. (1-878353-15-2) Silent Partners.

Qwized-Spreadsheet, Student Activities. Qwizinc. Staff. (DF - Computer Applications Ser.). 1995. mass mkt. 8.50 (0-538-65635-2) S-W Pub.

Qwized Word Processing, Student Activities. Qwizinc. Staff. (DF - Computer Applications Ser.). 1995. mass mkt., wbk. ed. 8.50 (0-538-65632-8) S-W Pub.

Qyacucho Para Cristo. W. T. Whalin & Chris Woehr.Tr. of One Bright & Shining Path. (SPA.). 224p. 1997. pap. 9.99 (0-8297-1970-9) Vida Pubs.

Qyrotrons Three, Vol. 57, No. 6. Ed. by M. Q. Tran. (International Journal of Electronics Ser.). 1984. 36.00 (0-85066-991-X) Taylor & Francis.

An Asterisk (*) at the beginning of an entry indicates that the title is appearing for the first time.